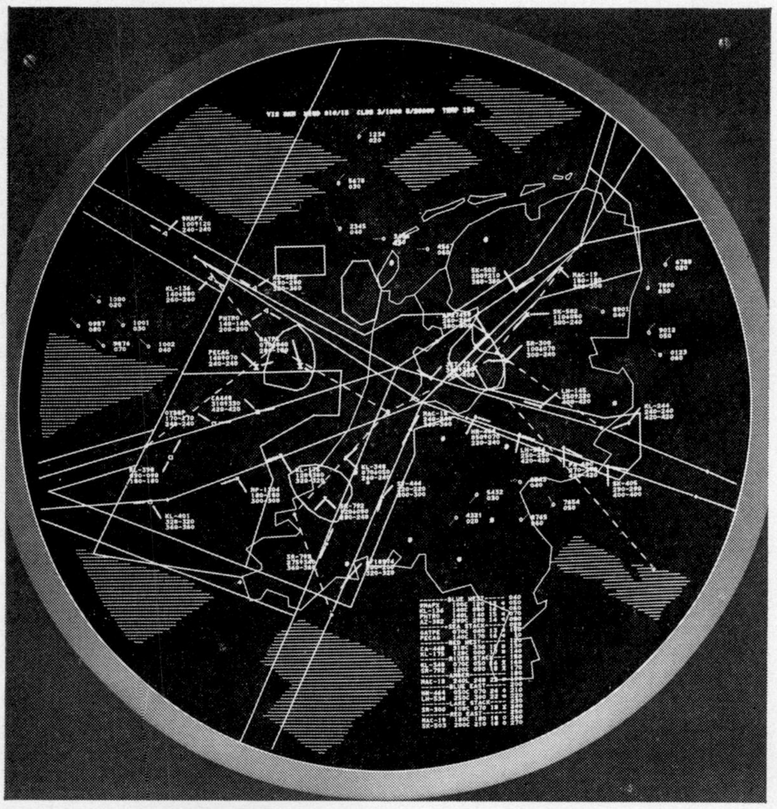

G222

JANE'S ALL THE WORLD'S AIRCRAFT

Edited by **John W. R. Taylor**
FRHistS, AFRAeS, FSLAET

Order of Contents

World Sales Distribution

Jane's Yearbooks,
St. Giles House, 49/50 Poland Street,
London, W1A 2LG, England

All the World
except

United States of America and Canada:
Franklin Watts Inc.,
730 Fifth Avenue
New York, NY 10019.

Editorial communication to:

The Editor, Jane's All The World's Aircraft
Jane's Yearbooks, St. Giles House, 49/50 Poland Street,
London W1A 2LG, England
Telephone 01-437 9844

Advertisement communication to:

Jane's Advertising Department,
Jane's Yearbooks, St. Giles House, 49/50 Poland Street,
London W1A 2LG, England
Telephone 01-437 9844

***Classified List of Advertisers**

The various products available from the advertisers in this edition are listed alphabetically in about 350 different headings.

AVIAEXPORT, Moscow,

CAN OFFER

A COMPLETE RANGE OF MODERN COMMERCIAL

AIRCRAFT FOR EVERY PURPOSE

TUPOLEV TU-154 – the medium range airliner. Up to 164 passengers can be carried at cruising speed of 850–950 kmh. Range – up 4500 km. Payload is 18000 kg. The Tu-154 can operate out of high altitude and high ambient temperature airfields. Engines – 3 turbofan NK-8-2U with thrust 10500 kg each.

IL-62M – long range commercial airliner. Brings speed and comfort to the longest air routes. Up to 198 passengers can be carried at cruising speed of 900 kmh. Range 8000 km with payload 23000 kg. Engines – 4 turbofan D-30KU.

KAMOV KA-26–light utility helicopter is being offered in the following versions: transport, agricultural, cargo-carrying, ship-landing (for surveying fish from ship bases), forest-guard and flying crane. Max. payload 900 kg. Max. level-flight speed 160 km.

MI-8 – general purpose helicopter is being offered in the following versions: transport, passenger (accommodating up to 28 passengers), executive (for 9 or 11 persons) and ambulance versions. Payload is 4000 kg. Max. speed 250 km. Helicopter is equipped with two turboshaft engines TV 2 – 117A take-off power of 1500 e.h.p. each.

For more details please apply to:

V/O "AVIAEXPORT"

MOSCOW, 121200, USSR

Telephone: 244-26-86.

Telex: Moscow 7257, 7635

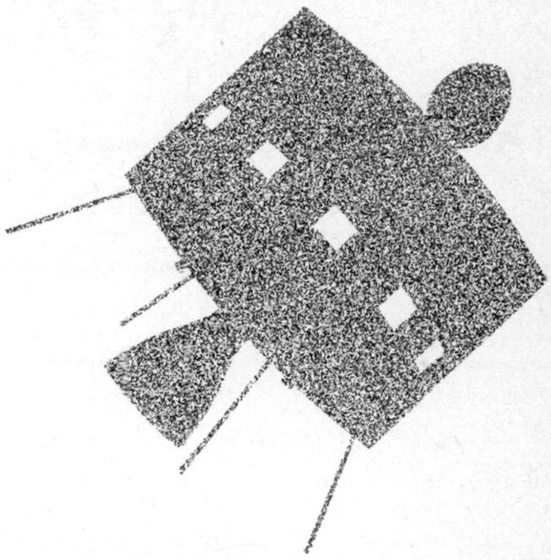

Jane's Pocket Books

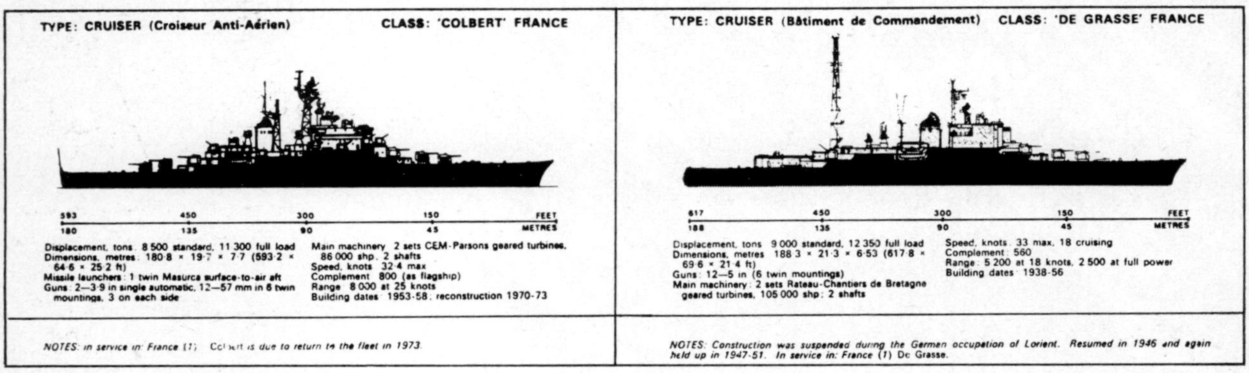
TYPE: CRUISER (Croiseur Anti-Aérien) CLASS: 'COLBERT' FRANCE

593 450 300 150 FEET
180 135 90 45 METRES

Displacement, tons 8 500 standard, 11 300 full load
Dimensions, metres: 180·8 × 19·7 × 7·7 (593·2 × 64·6 × 25·2 ft)
Missile launchers: 1 twin Masurca surface-to-air aft
Guns: 2—3·9 in single automatic, 12—57 mm in 6 twin mountings, 3 on each side
Main machinery 2 sets CEM-Parsons geared turbines, 86 000 shp, 2 shafts
Speed, knots 32·4 max
Complement 800 (as flagship)
Range 8 000 at 25 knots
Building dates 1953-58; reconstruction 1970-73

NOTES: in service in: France (1) Colbert is due to return to the fleet in 1973.

TYPE: CRUISER (Bâtiment de Commandement) CLASS: 'DE GRASSE' FRANCE

617 450 300 150 FEET
188 135 90 45 METRES

Displacement, tons 9 000 standard, 12 350 full load
Dimensions, metres 188·3 × 21·3 × 6·53 (617·8 × 69·6 × 21·4 ft)
Guns: 12—5 in (6 twin mountings)
Main machinery: 2 sets Rateau-Chantiers de Bretagne geared turbines, 105 000 shp; 2 shafts
Speed, knots: 33 max, 18 cruising
Complement: 560
Range: 5 200 at 18 knots, 2 500 at full power
Building dates 1938-56

NOTES: Construction was suspended during the German occupation of Lorient. Resumed in 1946 and again held up in 1947-51. In service in: France (1) De Grasse.

All Pocket Books are 4¼″ × 7″

Jane's Pocket Book of Major Combat Aircraft
J. W. R. Taylor

The first of a series of aircraft Pocket Books by the team responsible for *Jane's All the World's Aircraft*. They are intended as easy-to-handle working aids for people whose job or delight it is to recognise aircraft, and the information given for each type is that which will best assist in identifying it. The books will be illustrated by the finest available photographs, reproduced as large and as clearly as possible, backed up by high-quality three-view line drawings.

356 04372 X £1.50 (PVC) 264pp
356 04371 1 £1.95 (cloth)

Jane's Pocket Book of Commercial Transport Aircraft
J. W. R. Taylor

The second book in the series of aircraft Pocket Books describes and illustrates all major types of airliners and business aircraft seen throughout the world.

356 04376 2 £1.50 (PVC) 264pp
356 04375 4 £1.95 (cloth)

Jane's Pocket Book of Military Transport and Training Aircraft
J. W. R. Taylor

This book, which is complementary to the *Pocket Book of Major Combat Aircraft*, describes aircraft used for carrying military cargo.
356 04374 6 £1.75 (PVC) 264pp
356 04373 8 £2.50 (cloth)

The author of the above titles in the series is also the editor of **Jane's All the World's Aircraft.**

Jane's Pocket Book of Modern Tanks and Armoured Fighting Vehicles
Christopher Foss

Gives full particulars of post-war tanks and AFVs, including armament, dimensions, speed, range and type of engine. Each is illustrated by a full-page photograph. By the author of *Armoured Fighting Vehicles of the World.*

356 04654 0 £1.75 (PVC) 200pp
356 04653 2 £2.50 (cloth)

Jane's Pocket Book of Airship Development
Lord Ventry and Eugene M. Kolesnik

A detailed, illustrated guide to all classes of airship ever produced, ranging from Captain Renard's pioneering attempts in 1884 to the lighter-than-air craft of today. There are illustrations of every model, some of them never before published. Lord Ventry is the world's leading expert on airships, and his co-author is also an authority in this field.

356 04656 7 £1.75 (PVC) 264pp
356 04655 9 £2.50 (cloth)

Jane's Pocket Book of Major Warships
Captain John E. Moore

Will be indispensable to all those concerned with ship recognition. All major classes of warships are described and illustrated. The editor is a former Deputy Director of Naval Intelligence and the present editor of **Jane's Fighting Ships.**

356 04238 3 £1.50 (PVC) 280pp
356 04241 3 £1.95 (cloth)

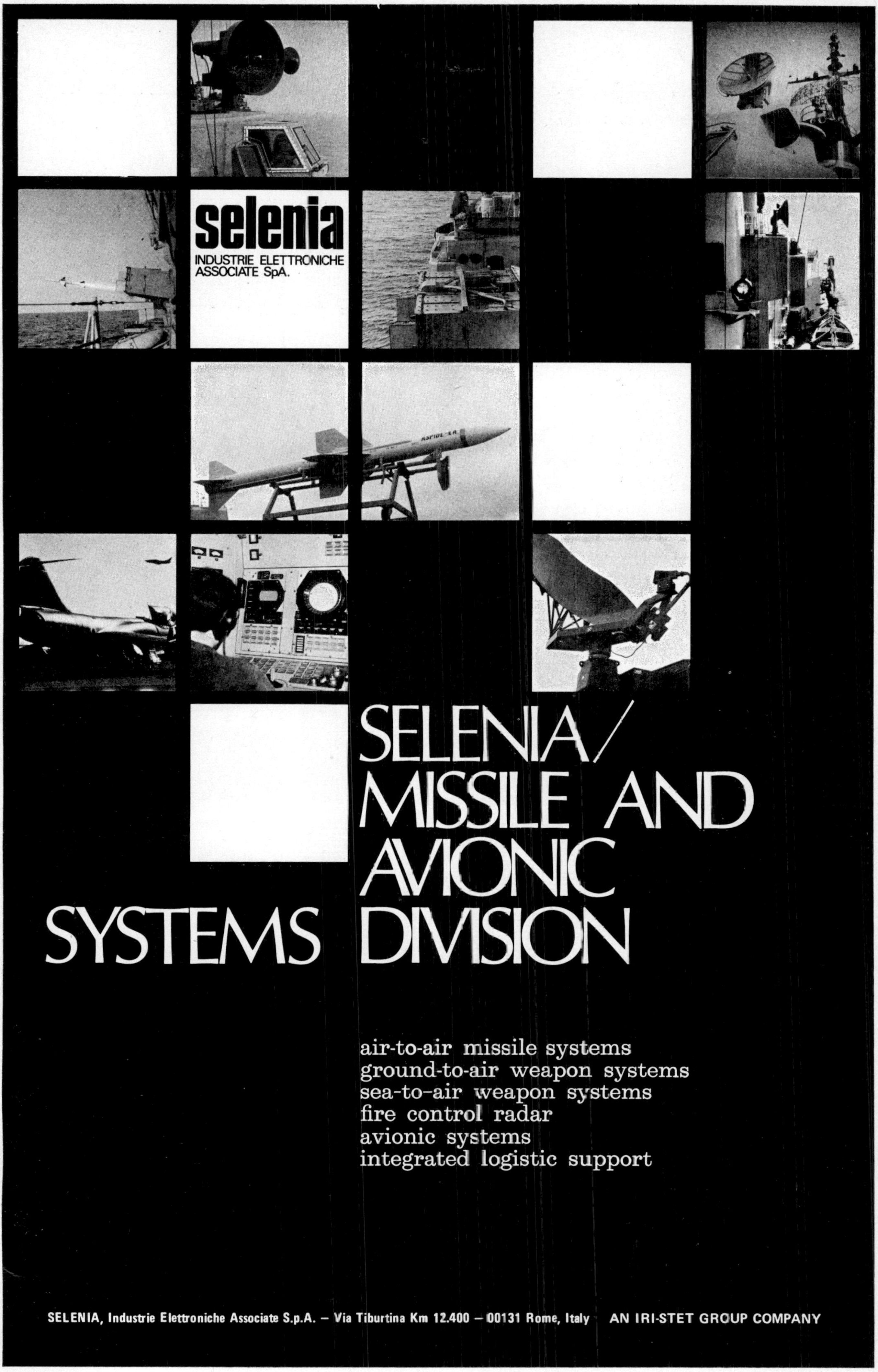
selenia
INDUSTRIE ELETTRONICHE
ASSOCIATE SpA.
SELENIA/
MISSILE AND
AVIONIC
SYSTEMS DIVISION
air-to-air missile systems
ground-to-air weapon systems
sea-to-air weapon systems
fire control radar
avionic systems
integrated logistic support
SELENIA, Industrie Elettroniche Associate S.p.A. – Via Tiburtina Km 12.400 – 00131 Rome, Italy
AN IRI-STET GROUP COMPANY

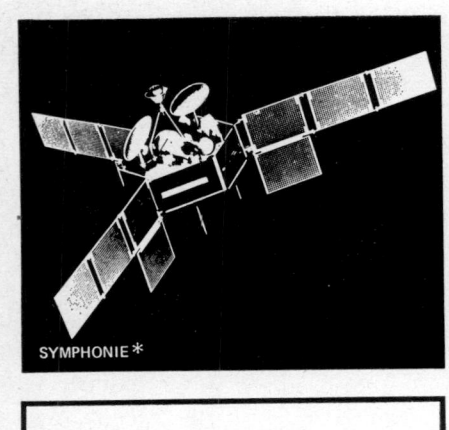

ALPHABETICAL LIST OF ADVERTISERS.

1974/75 EDITION.

ALPHABETICAL LIST OF ADVERTISERS—*continued.*

CLASSIFIED LIST OF ADVERTISERS

The companies advertising in this publication have informed us that they are involved in the fields of manufacture indicated below:

A1. ACCELEROMETERS
Aeritalia S.p.A.
Aviaexport V/O
Ferranti Limited
Marvin Tomkins Limited
S.F.E.N.A.

A2. ACCESSORIES
Aviaexport V/O
Garrett International, s.a.

A3. AC MOTORS
Aviaexport V/O
Ferranti Limited
Garrett International, s.a.
Marvin Tomkins Limited

A4. ACCUMULATORS, CADMIUM-NICKEL
Aviaexport V/O
S.A.F.T.

A5. ACTUATORS, ELECTRIC
Aeritalia S.p.A.
Aircraft Equipment (International) Ltd.
Aviaexport V/O
Garrett International, s.a.
Marvin Tomkins Limited
S.F.E.N.A.

A6. AERIAL SURVEY INSTRUMENTS
Aerospatiale (S.N.I.A.S.)
Marvin Tomkins Limited

A7. AERIALS, AIRCRAFT
British Aircraft Corporation
Dornier AG
Marvin Tomkins Limited
Messerschmitt Bölkow-Blohm GmbH

A8. AERO AUXILIARY EQUIPMENT
Aeritalia S.p.A.
Garrett Corporation
Marvin Tomkins Limited

A9. AERO-ENGINE TEST PLANT
John Curran Limited
Marvin Tomkins Limited
S.N.E.C.M.A.

A10. AERO-ENGINES
Avco Lycoming Div. of Avco Corp.
Aviaexport V/O
Garrett International, s.a.
Hamilton Aircraft Company Inc.
Marvin Tomkins Limited
Motoren- und Turbinen-Union München GmbH
S.N.E.C.M.A.

A11. AERONAUTICAL ENGINEERS AND CONSULTANTS
Aviaexport V/O
British Aircraft Corporation
Hamilton Aircraft Company Inc.

A12. AEROSYSTEMS
Boeing Company, The
British Aircraft Corporation

A13. AIR COMPRESSORS
Aircraft Equipment International Ltd
Garrett International, s.a.
Marvin Tomkins Limited

A14. AIR COMPRESSORS, CABIN
Aircraft Equipment International Ltd.
Garrett International, s.a.

A15. AIR COMPRESSORS FOR ENGINE STARTING
Aircraft Equipment International Ltd.
Garrett International, s.a.

A16. AIR CONDITIONING EQUIPMENT
Aviaexport V/O
Garrett International, s.a.
M. L. Aviation Company Ltd
Marvin Tomkins Limited

A17. AIR CONDITIONING SYSTEMS
Aviaexport V/O
Garrett International, s.a.

A18. AIR CONTROL EQUIPMENT FOR CABINS
Aeritalia S.p.A.
Aviaexport V/O
Garrett International, s.a.

A19. AIR DATA COMPUTER SYSTEMS
Aviaexport V/O
Ferranti Limited
Garrett International, s.a.

A20. AIR TRAFFIC CONTROL EQUIPMENT
Ferranti Limited
Hollandse Signaalapparaten B.V.
Selenia

A21. AIRCRAFT—AGRICULTURAL (Dusters and Sprayers)
Aerospatiale (S.N.I.A.S.)
Aviaexport V/O
Dornier AG
Hamilton Aircraft Company Inc.
Hawker Siddeley Aviation Ltd

A22. AIRCRAFT—AMBULANCE
Aerospatiale (S.N.I.A.S.)
Aviaexport V/O
Dornier AG
Fokker-VFW International N.V.
Hamilton Aircraft Company Inc.
Hawker Siddeley Aviation Ltd
Israel Aircraft Industries

A23. AIRCRAFT—COMMERCIAL
Aeritalia S.p.A.
Aerospatiale (S.N.I.A.S.)
Aviaexport V/O
British Aircraft Corporation
Dornier AG
Fokker VFW International n.v.
Hamilton Aircraft Company, Inc.
Hawker Siddeley Aviation Ltd
Israel Aircraft Industries
Marvin Tomkins Limited
Messerschmitt Bölkow-Blohm GmbH
Omnipol Foreign Trade Corp.
Templewood Aviation Limited

A24. AIRCRAFT—EXECUTIVE
Aerospatiale (S.N.I.A.S.)
Aviaexport V/O
British Aircraft Corporation
Dornier AG
Fokker VFW International n.v.
Garrett International, s.a.
Hamilton Aircraft Company Inc.
Hawker Siddeley Aviation Ltd.
Israel Aircraft Industries
Marvin Tomkins Limited
Messerschmitt Bölkow-Blohm GmbH
Siai Marchetti S.p.A.

A25. AIRCRAFT INTEGRATED DATA SYSTEMS
Ferranti Limited
Garrett International, s.a.

A26. AIRCRAFT—MILITARY
Aeritalia S.p.A.
Aeronautica Macchi S.p.A.
Aerospatiale (S.N.I.A.S.)
Aircraft Equipment (International) Ltd.
British Aircraft Corporation
Dornier AG
Fokker VFW International N.V.
Hamilton Aircraft Company, Inc.
Hawker Siddeley Aviation Ltd
Marvin Tomkins Limited
Messerschmitt Bölkow-Blohm GmbH
Siai Marchetti S.p.A.
Vought Aeronautics

A27. AIRCRAFT—NAVAL
Aerospatiale (S.N.I.A.S.)
Fokker VFW International N.V.
Hamilton Aircraft Company, Inc.
Marvin Tomkins Limited

A28. AIRCRAFT—PRIVATE
Aerospatiale (S.N.I.A.S.)
Dornier AG
Hamilton Aircraft Company, Inc.
Hawker Siddeley Aviation Ltd
Marvin Tomkins Limited
Messerschmitt Bölkow-Blohm GmbH
Omnipol Foreign Trade Corp.
Siai Marchetti S.p.A.

A29. AIRCRAFT—RADIO CONTROLLED
British Aircraft Corporation

A30. AIRCRAFT—SUPERSONIC
Aeritalia S.p.A.
Aerospatiale (S.N.I.A.S.)
British Aircraft Corporation

A31. AIRCRAFT—TRAINING
Aeritalia S.p.A.
Aeronautica Macchi S.p.A.
Aerospatiale (S.N.I.A.S.)
British Aircraft Corporation
Dornier AG
Fokker VFW International n.v.
Hawker Siddeley Aviation Ltd
Marvin Tomkins Limited
Omnipol Foreign Trade Corp.
Siai-Marchetti S.p.A.

KL543 ARR 1400
<- APRON
T-VASIS

A32. AIRCRAFT—TRANSPORT
Aeritalia S.p.A.
Aerospatiale (S.N.I.A.S.)
Aviaexport V/O
British Aircraft Corporation
Dornier AG
Fokker VFW International N.V.
Hamilton Aircraft Company, Inc.
Hawker Siddeley Aviation Ltd
Israel Aircraft Industries
Marvin Tomkins Limited

A33. AIRCRAFT—V/STOL
Aeritalia S.p.A.
Aerospatiale (S.N.I.A.S.)
Aviaexport V/O
Boeing Company, The
British Aircraft Corporation
Dornier AG
Fokker VFW International n.v.
Hamilton Aircraft Company, Inc.
Hawker Siddeley Aviation Ltd
Messerschmitt Bölkow-Blohm GmbH
Siai-Marchetti S.p.A.

A34. AIRCRAFT ARRESTING GEAR
S.N.E.C.M.A.

A35. AIRCRAFT CANOPIES
Aeronautica Macchi S.p.A.
Marvin Tomkins Limited

A36. AIRCRAFT ESCAPE SYSTEMS
Garrett International s.a.

A37. AIRCRAFT FIELD OPERATIONS AND SUPPORT
Boeing Company, The

A38. AIRCRAFT FLOATS
Dornier AG
Garrett International s.a.

A39. AIRCRAFT FREIGHT HANDLING EQUIPMENT
Aviaexport V/O
Dornier AG
Fokker VFW International N.V.
Goodyear Tyre and Rubber Company Aviation Division

A40. AIRCRAFT MECHANICAL HANDLERS
Aviaexport V/O
Dornier AG
M.L. Aviation Company Ltd.

A41. AIRCRAFT MODIFICATIONS
Aeritalia S.p.A.
Aerospatiale (S.N.I.A.S.)
Garrett International. s.a.
Hamilton Aircraft Company, Inc.
Israel Aircraft Industries
Siai-Marchetti S.p.A.

A42. AIRCRAFT PISTON ENGINE CYLINDERS
Marvin Tomkins Limited

A43. AIRCRAFT PROPELLER GOVERNERS
Aviaexport V/O
Marvin Tomkins Limited
Woodward Governor Company

A44. AIRCRAFT PROPELLERS
Aviaexport V/O
Marvin Tomkins Limited

A45. AIRCRAFT SEATS
Aviaexport V/O
Hawker Siddeley Aviation Ltd.
Messerschmitt Bölkow-Blohm GmbH

A46. AIRCRAFT TRAINING SYSTEMS
Boeing Company, The

A47. AIRCRAFT WIRE & CABLE
Standard Wire & Cable Company

A48. AIR CYCLE REFRIGERATION PACKAGES
Aviaexport V/O
Garrett International. s.a.

A49. AIRFIELD LIGHTING
Aviaexport V/O

A50. AIRLINE TECHNICAL ASSISTANCE
Boeing Company, The

A51. AIRCRAFT DEVELOPMENT
Boeing Company, The
Hawker Siddeley Aviation Ltd.

A52. AIRPORT MAINTENANCE EQUIPMENT
GIAT
Israel Aircraft Industries
M.L. Aviation Company Ltd.

A53. AIRSPEED INDICATORS
Aeritalia S.p.A.
Aircraft Equipment (International) Ltd.
Aviaexport V/O
Dornier AG
Marvin Tomkins Limited

A54. ALTERNATORS
Aviaexport V/O
Garrett International. s.a.
Marvin Tomkins Limited

A55. ALTITUDE CONTROL SYSTEMS
Aeritalia S.p.A.
Aviaexport V/O
Marvin Tomkins Limited
S.F.E.N.A.

A56. ALTIMETERS ENCODING
Marvin Tomkins Limited

A57. AMMUNITION BOOSTERS
Snia Viscosa

A58. ANTI-SKID SYSTEMS
Aviaexport V/O
Goodyear Tyre & Rubber Company Aviation Division
S.N.E.C.M.A.

A59. ARMAMENTS FOR AIRCRAFT
Aircraft Equipment (International) Ltd.
G.I.A.T.
Hamilton Aircraft Company, Inc.
Marvin Tomkins Limited
M.L. Aviation Company Ltd.
S.A.M.M.

A60. ASTRO-INERTIAL NAVIGATION SYSTEMS
Aerospatiale (S.N.I.A.S.)
British Aircraft Corporation
Ferranti Limited

A61. AUTOMATIC CHECKOUT SYSTEMS
Aerospatiale (S.N.I.A.S.)
Aviaexport V/O
British Aircraft Corporation

A62. AUTOMATIC PARACHUTE OPENERS
Aviaexport V/O

A63. AUTOMATIC PILOTS
Aviaexport V/O
Hamilton Aircraft Company Inc.,
Marvin Tomkins Limited
S.F.E.N.A.

A64. AUTOMATIC VOLTAGE AND CURRENT REGULATORS
Aviaexport V/O
Ferranti Limited
Marvin Tomkins Limited

A65. AUXILIARY POWER PLANT
Aerospatiale (S.N.I.A.S.)
Aviaexport V/O
Garrett International. s.a.

A66. AGRICULTURAL AIRCRAFT SPRAY AND DUST SYSTEMS AND COMPONENTS
Aviaexport V/O
Dornier AG

B1. BARS—STAINLESS AND HEAT-RESISTING STEEL
Aviaexport V/O

B2. BATTERIES
Aerospatiale (S.N.I.A.S.)
Aviaexport V/O
Marvin Tomkins Limited
S.A.F.T.

B3. BATTERIES, AVIATION
Aviaexport V/O
Marvin Tomkins Limited
S.A.F.T.

B4. BATTERY CHARGERS
Aviaexport V/O
Ferranti Limited
Marvin Tomkins Limited
S.A.F.T.

B5. BATTERY TESTING EQUIPMENT
M.L. Aviation Company Ltd
Marvin Tomkins Limited
S.A.F.T.

B6. BELTS, SAFETY
Aviaexport V/O

B7. BINOCULARS
Aeritalia S.p.A.
Aircraft Equipment International Ltd.
Barr & Stroud Limited
GIAT

B8. BLADES, GAS TURBINE
Aviaexport V/O
Marvin Tomkins Limited
S.N.E.C.M.A.

B9. BOMB CARRIERS
Marvin Tomkins Limited
M.L. Aviation Company Ltd.

B10. BOMBSIGHTS
Aircraft Equipment (International) Ltd.
Hamilton Aircraft Company, Inc.
Marvin Tomkins Limited
Saab Scania AB

B11. BOOKS—AVIATION AND SPACE
Profile Publications Ltd

B12. BRAKE LININGS
Goodyear Tyre & Rubber Company, Aviation Division

B13. BRAKES FOR AIRCRAFT
Aviaexport V/O
Goodyear Tyre & Rubber Company, Aviation Division
Israel Aircraft Industries
Marvin Tomkins Limited
S.N.E.C.M.A.

C1. CABIN COOLING (TROPICAL AIRFIELD EQUIPMENT)
Aviaexport V/O
Garrett International, s.a.
M.L. Aviation & Company Ltd

C2. CABIN PRESSURE CONTROL SYSTEMS
Aviaexport V/O
Garrett International, s.a.
Marvin Tomkins Limited
Saab-Scania AB

C3. CABIN PRESSURE CONTROLS
Aeritalia S.p.A.
Aviaexport V/O
Garrett International, s.a.
Marvin Tomkins Limited

C4. CABIN PRESSURISING TEST EQUIPMENT
Aviaexport V/O
Garrett International, s.a.

C5. CABLES, ELECTRIC
Aviaexport V/O
M.L. Aviation Company Ltd
Rist's Wires & Cables Ltd
Standard Wire & Cable Company

C6. CABLES, R.F.
Rist's Wires & Cables Ltd
Standard Wire & Cable Company

C7. CENTRAL AIR DATA COMPUTERS
Ferranti Limited
Garrett International, s.a.
Saab-Scania

C8. COATINGS, EROSION RESISTANT
Aerospatiale (S.N.I.A.S.)
Goodyear Tyre & Rubber Company, Aviation Division
Israel Aircraft Industries

C9. COMPONENTS
Aviaexport V/O
Dornier AG
Ferranti Limited
Flight Refuelling Ltd
Fokker VFW International N.V.
Garrett International, s.a.
Israel Aircraft Industries
Marvin Tomkins Limited
SAMM

C10. COMPUTERS
Aerospatiale (S.N.I.A.S.)
Dornier AG
Ferranti Limited
Garrett International, s.a.
Hollandse Signaalapparaten B.V.
Saab-Scania AB
S.F.E.N.A.

C11. COMPUTERS, AERODYNAMIC ANALOGUE AND DIGITAL
Aerospatiale (S.N.I.A.S.)
British Aircraft Corporation
Dornier AG
Ferranti Limited
Garrett International, s.a.
Israel Aircraft Industries
S.F.E.N.A.

C12. CONNECTORS
Aviaexport V/O
Ferranti Limited
Garrett International, s.a.
Marvin Tomkins Limited

C13. CONSTANT SPEED ALTERNATOR DRIVE UNITS
Garrett International, s.a.
S.F.E.N.A.

C14. CONTROL EQUIPMENT FOR AIRCRAFT
Aviaexport V/O
Dornier Systems GmbH
Ferranti Limited
Garrett International, s.a.
Marvin Tomkins Limited
Saab-Scania AB
S.F.E.N.A.

C15. CONTROLS, COCKPIT
Aeritalia S.p.A.
Aviaexport V/O
Marvin Tomkins Limited
Messerschmitt-Bolkow-Blohm GMBH
Saab-Scania AB

C16. CONTROLS, MAIN ENGINE FUEL
Aviaexport V/O
Marvin Tomkins Limited
Woodward Governor Company

C17. COOLING COMPRESSORS
Aviaexport V/O
Garrett International, s.a.

C18. COOLING TURBINES
Garrett International, s.a.

C19. CRYOGENIC TURBINES
Aerospatiale (S.N.I.A.S.)
Garrett International, s.a.
Selenia

D1. DATA PROCESSING EQUIPMENT
Dornier AG
Ferranti Limited
Garrett International s.a.
Hollandse Signaalapparaten B.V.
Saab-Scania AB
Selenia

D2. DATA PROCESSING EQUIPMENT FOR ATC
Ferranti Limited
Hollandse Signaalapparaten B.V.
Philips' Telecommunicatie Industrie N.V.
Selenia

D3. DATA TRANSMISSION EQUIPMENT
Aerospatiale (S.N.I.A.S.)
Dornier AG
Ferranti Limited
Philips' Telecommunicatie Industrie N.V.
Saab-Scania AB
Selenia

D4. DC MOTORS
Aviaexport V/O
Garrett International s.a.
Marvin Tomkins Limited

D5. DE-ICING EQUIPMENT
Flight Refuelling Ltd
Garrett International s.a.
Goodyear Tyre & Rubber Company, Aviation Division
Marvin Tomkins Limited

D6. DIRECTION FINDING EQUIPMENT (TRIANGULATION)
Aviaexport V/O
Ferranti Limited

D7. DROGUE GUNS
M.L. Aviation Company Ltd

D8. DRONES
Aerospatiale (S.N.I.A.S.)
Aircraft Equipment (International) Ltd
Dornier Systems GmbH
Hawker Siddeley Aviation Ltd

E1. EJECTION SEATS
Hawker Siddeley Aviation Ltd
M.L. Aviation Company Ltd
Saab-Scania AB
S.N.E.C.M.A.

E2. EJECTOR RELEASE UNITS
Aircraft Equipment (International) Ltd
M.L. Aviation Company Ltd

E3. ELECTRIC AUXILIARIES
Aviaexport V/O
Garrett International, s.a.
Marvin Tomkins Limited

E4. ELECTRICAL EQUIPMENT
Aviaexport V/O
Garrett International, s.a.
M.L. Aviation Company Ltd
Marvin Tomkins Limited

E5. ELECTRICAL PLUGS AND SOCKETS (WATERPROOF)
Marvin Tomkins Limited
Rist's Wires & Cables Ltd

E6. ELECTRICAL WIRING ASSEMBLIES
Aviaexport V/O
Fokker VFW International N.V.
Marvin Tomkins Limited
M.L. Aviation Company Ltd
Rist's Wires & Cables Ltd
Standard Wire & Cable Company

E.7 ELECTRICAL WIRE CABLE CORD OF ALL TYPES
Standard Wire & Cable Company

E8. ELECTRO-OPTICAL SYSTEMS
Aeritalia S.p.A.
Aerospatiale (S.N.I.A.S.)
Aircraft Equipment (International) Ltd
Barr & Stroud Ltd
Eltro GmbH
Ferranti Limited
Saab-Scania AB
Selenia

E9. ELECTRONIC EQUIPMENT
Aerospatiale (S.N.I.A.S.)
Aviaexport V/O
British Aircraft Corporation
Ferranti Limited
Garrett International, s.a.
Israel Aircraft Industries
Marvin Tomkins Limited
Messerschmitt-Bolkow-Blohm GMBH
M.L. Aviation Company Ltd
S.A.M.M.
Saab-Scania AB
Selenia
S.F.E.N.A.
SNECMA
Standard Wire & Cable Company

E10. ELECTRONIC FLOWMETERS
Marvin Tomkins Limited

E11. ELECTRONICS AND GUIDANCE
Aeritalia S.p.A.
Israel Aircraft Industries
Ferranti Limited
S.F.E.N.A.

E12. ENGINE HANDLING EQUIPMENT
John Curran Limited

E13. ENGINE COMPRESSOR CLEANING RIGS
John Curran Limited

E14. ENGINE PARTS FABRICATION
Fiat S.p.A.
Marvin Tomkins Limited
Motoren- und Turbinen-Union München

E15. ENGINE STARTING EQUIPMENT
Aviaexport V/O
Garrett International, s.a.
Marvin Tomkins Limited

E16. ENGINE TESTING EQUIPMENT
Avco Lycoming Div. of Avco Corp.
Garrett International, s.a.
John Curran Limited
Motoren-und Turbinen-Union München GmbH

E17. ENGINES—AIRCRAFT
Aviaexport V/O
Garrett International, s.a.
Hamilton Aircraft Company, Inc.
Marvin Tomkins Limited
Motoren- und Turbinen-Union München GmbH
S.N.E.C.M.A.

E18. ENGINES, AUXILIARY
Aviaexport V/O
Garrett International, s.a.
Hamilton Aircraft Company, Inc.
Motoren- und Turbinen-Union München GmbH

E19. ENGINE LIFE RECORDERS

E20. ENGINES—V/STOL
Aviaexport V/O
Garrett International, s.a.
Motoren- und Turbinen-Union München GmbH
S.N.E.C.M.A.

E21. ENVIRONMENTAL CONTROL SYSTEMS
Aerospatiale (S.N.I.A.S.)
British Aircraft Corporation
Garrett International, s.a.

E22. EXPERIMENTAL ASSEMBLIES
John Curran Limited
M.L. Aviation Company Ltd

E23. ELECTRIC TRACTORS
M.L. Aviation Company Ltd

F1. FIBRE OPTICS
Barr & Stroud Ltd
Ferranti Limited

F2. FILTERS, AIR
Aviaexport V/O

F3. FILTERS, ELECTRONIC
Aviaexport V/O
Barr & Stroud Ltd.
Ferranti Limited

F4. FILTERS, FUEL AND OIL
Aviaexport V/O
Flight Refuelling Ltd
Marvin Tomkins Limited

F5. FLIGHT INSPECTION EQUIPMENT AUTOMATIC
Eltro GmbH

F6. FLIGHT INSTRUMENT TEST SETS
Aeritalia S.p.A.
Garrett International, s.a.
Israel Aircraft Industries
S.F.E.N.A.

F7. FLOTATION GEAR
Garrett International, s.a.

F8. FLOW GAUGES
Aviaexport V/O
Marvin Tomkins Limited

F9. FLOWMETERS
Kent Meters Limited
Marvin Tomkins Limited

F10. FLYING CLOTHING
M.L. Aviation Company Ltd

F11. FORGINGS, STEEL
SNECMA

F12. FUEL FLOW PROPORTIONERS
Flight Refuelling Ltd
Garrett International, s.a.

F13. FUEL SYSTEMS PROTECTION
PRB s.a. Div. Polyurethane

F14. FUEL PUMPS
Aviaexport V/O
Garrett International, s.a.
Marvin Tomkins Limited

F15. FUEL SYSTEMS AND REFUELLING EQUIPMENT
Aviaexport V/O
Flight Refuelling Ltd
Israel Aircraft Industries
PRB s.a. Div. Polyurethane
Saab-Scania AB

F16. FUEL TANK PRESSURIZATION EQUIPMENT
Flight Refuelling Ltd
Garrett International, s.a.
Israel Aircraft Industries
Saab-Scania AB

F17. FURNISHINGS FOR AIRCRAFT CABINS
Aircraft Equipment (International) Ltd
Aviaexport V/O
Garrett International, s.a.
Hamilton Aircraft Company, Inc.

F18. FEEL SIMULATOR CONTROLS & JACKS
Garrett International, s.a.
Saab-Scania AB

G1. GAS TURBINE STARTER SYSTEMS
Avco Lycoming Div. of Avco Corp.
Aviaexport V/O
Garrett International, s.a.
Hamilton Aircraft Company, Inc.

G2. GAS TURBINES
Aviaexport V/O
Garrett International, s.a.
Hamilton Aircraft Company, Inc.
Motoren- und Turbinen Union München GmbH
S.N.E.C.M.A.

G3. GAS TURBINES, EQUIPMENT AND ACCESSORIES FOR
Avco Lycoming Div. of Avco Corp.
Aviaexport V/O
Flight Refuelling Ltd
Garrett International, s.a.
Hamilton Aircraft Company, Inc.
Marvin Tomkins Limited
Motoren-Und Turbinen Union München GmbH
S.N.E.C.M.A.
Woodward Governor Company

G4. GENERATORS
Aerospatiale (S.N.I.A.S.)
Aviaexport V/O
Garrett International, s.a.
Marvin Tomkins Limited

G5. GAUGES
Aerospatiale (S.N.I.A.S.)
Aviaexport, V./O
Marvin Tomkins Limited

G6. GROUND REFUELLING EQUIPMENT
Flight Refuelling Ltd
Israel Aircraft Industries

G7. GROUND WORKSHOP AND HANGAR EQUIPMENT
Israel Aircraft Industries
Marvin Tomkins Limited
M.L. Aviation Company Ltd

G8. GUIDED MISSILE GROUND HANDLING EQUIPMENT
Aerospatiale (S.N.I.A.S.)
Aircraft Equipment (International) Ltd
Garrett International, s.a.
Messerschmitt Bölkow-Blohm GmbH
M.L. Aviation Company Ltd
Saab-Scania AB

G9. GUIDED MISSILES
Aerospatiale (S.N.I.A.S.)
Aircraft Equipment (International) Ltd
British Aircraft Corporation
Dornier AG
GIAT
Messerschmitt Bölkow-Blohm GmbH
Saab-Scania AB
Selenia

G10. GUNNERY TRAINING APPARATUS
Aircraft Equipment (International) Ltd
G.I.A.T.
Saab-Scania AB

H1. HANGAR TEST STANDS
Avco Lycoming Div. of Avco Corp.
Garrett International, s.a.
Israel Aircraft Industries
John Curran Limited
Marvin Tomkins Limited

H2. HARNESS, SAFETY
Marvin Tomkins Limited

H3. HEADPHONES
Marvin Tomkins Limited

H4. HEAT EXCHANGERS
Garrett International, s.a.
Marvin Tomkins Limited
S.N.E.C.M.A.

H5. HEAT TRANSFER SYSTEMS
Garrett International, s.a.

H6. HEATED WINDOWS
Barr & Stroud Limited

H7. HEATED WINDSCREEN CONTROLLERS
Garrett International, s.a.

H8. HELICOPTER WINCHES Etc.
Garrett International, s.a.

H9. HELICOPTERS—COMMERCIAL
Aerospatiale (S.N.I.A.S.)
Aviaexport V/O
Bell Helicopter Company
Boeing Company, The
Dornier AG
Marvin Tomkins Limited
Messerschmitt Bölkow-Blohm GmbH

H10. HELICOPTERS—MILITARY
Aerospatiale (S.N.I.A.S.)
Bell Helicopter Company
Dornier AG
Hamiltion Arcraft Company, Inc.
Marvin Tomkins Limited

H11. HIGH ALTITUDE TESTING PLANT
Garrett International, s.a.

H12. HIGH ALTITUDE PRESSURE SUITS, HELMETS
Garrett International, s.a.
M.L. Aviation Company Ltd

H13. HIGH PRESSURE COUPLINGS
Flight Refuelling Ltd

H14. HIGH SPEED RESEARCH CAMERAS
Barr & Stroud Limited

H15. HOSE AND COUPLINGS HYDRAULIC FUEL
Marvin Tomkins Limited

H16. HOT AIR BALLOONS

H17. HYDRAULIC EQUIPMENT
Aerospatiale (S.N.I.A.S.)
Aviaexport V/O
Flight Refuelling Ltd
Garrett International, s.a.
Israel Aircraft Industries
Marvin Tomkins Limited
Saab-Scania AB
SAMM
S.N.E.C.M.A.

H18. HYDRAULIC PRESSURE PUMPS
Aerospatiale (S.N.I.A.S.)
Aviaexport V/O
Garrett International, s.a.
Marvin Tomkins Limited
SAMM

H19. HYDRAULIC TEST UNITS, MOBILE AND STATIC
Aeronautica Macchi S.p.A.
Marvin Tomkins Limited

H20. HELICOPTER PARTS AND COMPONENTS
Aviaexport V/O
Dornier AG
Hamilton Aircraft Company, Inc.
Israel Aircraft Industries
Marvin Tomkins Limited
S.F.E.N.A.
Siai Marchetti S.p.A.

H21. HELICOPTER SEARCHLIGHTS
Garrett International, s.a.

I 1. INDICATORS, FAULT ISOLATION
Marvin Tomkins Limited
Minelco

I 2. INERTIAL NAVIGATION SYSTEMS
Aerospatiale (S.N.I.A.S.)
Ferranti Limited
S.F.E.N.A.

I 3. INFLATABLE STRUCTURES
Garrett International, s.a.
M.L. Aviation Company Ltd

I 4. INFRA-RED LINESCAN
Barr & Stroud Limited

I 5. INFRA-RED MATERIALS
Barr & Stroud Limited

I 6. INFRA-RED SYSTEMS
Barr & Stroud Limited
Eltro GmbH
Garrett International, s.a.
Saab-Scania AB
Selenia

I 7. INSTRUMENT COMPONENTS (Mechanical)
Aeritalia S.p.A.
Aerospatiale (S.N.I.A.S.)
Marvin Tomkins Limited

I 8. INSTRUMENTS, AIRCRAFT
Aircraft Equipment (International) Ltd
Aviaexport V/O
Ferranti Limited
Hamilton Aircraft Company, Inc.
Israel Aircraft Industries
Marvin Tomkins Limited

I 9. INSTRUMENTS, ELECTRONIC
Aeritalia S.p.A.
Aerospatiale (S.N.I.A.S.)
Aircraft Equipment (International) Ltd
Aviaexport V/O
Barr & Stroud Limited
British Aircraft Corporation
Ferranti Limited
Hamilton Aircraft Company Inc.,
Israel Aircraft Industries
Marvin Tomkins Limited

I 10. INSTRUMENTS, NAVIGATION
Aeritalia S.p.A.
Aerospatiale (S.N.I.A.S.)
Aviaexport V/O
British Aircraft Corporation
Ferranti Limited
Hamilton Aircraft Company, Inc.
Marvin Tomkins Limited
S.F.E.N.A.

I 11. INSTRUMENTS, PRECISION
Aeritalia S.p.A.
British Aircraft Corporation
Ferranti Limited
Hamilton Aircraft Company, Inc.
Israel Aircraft Industries
Marvin Tomkins Limited

I 12. INSTRUMENTS, TEST EQUIPMENT
Aeritalia S.p.A.
Aerospatiale (S.N.I.A.S.)
Aircraft Equipment (International) Ltd
Aviaexport V/O
British Aircraft Corporation
Garrett International, s.a.
Israel Aircraft Industries
Marvin Tomkins Limited
Selenia

I 13. INTEGRATED TOTAL PNEUMATIC SYSTEMS
Aerospatiale (S.N.I.A.S.)
Garrett International, s.a.

I 14. INTERCOMMUNICATION EQUIPMENT
Aerospatiale (S.N.I.A.S.)

I 15. ILLUMINATED PLASTIC CONTROL PANELS AND KNOBS

J1. JACKS
Aircraft Equipment (International) Ltd
Marvin Tomkins Limited
Saab Scania AB
SAMM

J2. JET ENGINE TEST PLANT
Garrett International, s.a.
John Curran Limited
SNECMA

J3. JET FUEL STARTERS
Garrett International, s.a.
Marvin Tomkins Limited

J4. JET PROPULSION ENGINES
Aerospatiale (S.N.I.A.S.)
Garrett International, s.a.
Motoren- und Turbinen-Union München GmbH
S.N.E.C.M.A.
Snia Viscosa

J5. JOINTING COMPOUND
Goodyear Tyre & Rubber Company, Aviation Division

J6. JET ENGINE PARTS
Israel Aircraft Industries
Marvin Tomkins Limited
S.N.E.C.M.A.

L1. LAMPS—AIRSTRIP, OBSTRUCTION
Aviaexport V/O
Marvin Tomkins Limited

L2. LAMPS, COCKPIT
Aviaexport V/O
Marvin Tomkins Limited

L3. LAMPS FOR GROUND STATIONS
Marvin Tomkins Limited

L4. LANDING LAMPS
Aviaexport V/O
Marvin Tomkins Limited

L5. LASERS
Aerospatiale (S.N.I.A.S.)
Barr & Stroud Limited
Eltro GmbH
Ferranti Limited
Garrett International, s.a.
Selenia

L6. LASER RANGEFINDER
Aerospatiale (S.N.I.A.S.)
Barr & Stroud Limited
Eltro GmbH
Ferranti Limited
GIAT
Saab-Scania AB
Selenia

L7. LIFE SAVING EQUIPMENT
Garrett International, s.a.
Marvin Tomkins Limited
Saab-Scania AB

L8. LIGHTS, AIRCRAFT
Aviaexport V/O
Marvin Tomkins Limited

L9. LIGHTS, IDENTIFICATION
Marvin Tomkins Limited

L10. LIGHTS, LANDING
Aviaexport V/O
Marvin Tomkins Limited

L11. LIGHTS, NAVIGATION
Aviaexport V/O
Marvin Tomkins Limited

L12. LINEAR ACTUATORS
Garrett International, s.a.
Marvin Tomkins Limited

L13. LININGS, BRAKE
Goodyear Tyre & Rubber Company, Aviation Division
Marvin Tomkins Limited

M1. MACH NUMBER TRANSDUCERS
Garrett International s.a.

M2. MACHINE TOOLS
Marvin Tomkins Limited
SNECMA

M3. MARINE ENGINES
Garrett International, s.a.
Marvin Tomkins Limited

M4. MATERIALS TECHNOLOGY
Boeing Company, The

M5. METAL FITTINGS
Aviaexport V/O

M6. MICRO-WAVE TEST EQUIPMENT
Barr & Stroud Limited

M7. MICROPHONES
Aviaexport V/O

M8. MISSILE RECOVERY PARACHUTES
Aerospatiale (S.N.I.A.S.)

M9. MISSILES, GUIDED
Aerospatiale (S.N.I.A.S.)
Aircraft Equipment (International) Ltd
British Aircraft Corporation
Messerschmitt Bölkow-Blohm GmbH
Saab Scania AB
Selenia
Snia Viscosa

M10. MOTORS, ELECTRIC
Aersopatiale (S.N.I.A.S.)
Aircraft Equipment (International) Ltd
Aviaexport V/O
Ferranti Limited
Garrett International, s.a.
Marvin Tomkins Limited

M11. MOTOR GENERATORS
Aerospatiale (S.N.I.A.S.)
Aircraft Equipment (International) Ltd
Aviaexport V/O
Garrett International, s.a.
Marvin Tomkins Limited

M12. MOTORS, HYDRAULIC
Aerospatiale (S.N.I.A.S.)
Aviaexport V/O
Garrett International, s.a.
Marvin Tomkins Limited
SAMM
Volvo Flygmotor A.B.

N1. NIGHT VISION EQUIPMENT
Aeritalia S.p.A.
Aircraft Equipment (International) Ltd
Barr & Stroud Limited

N2. NON-DESTRUCTIVE INSPECT EQUIPMENT
Fokker VFW International N.V.

O1. OIL VALVES
Flight Refuelling Ltd
Garrett International, s.a.
Marvin Tomkins Limited

O2. OPTICAL EQUIPMENT
Aeritalia S.p.A.
Aerospatiale (S.N.I.A.S.)
Barr & Stroud Limited
Marvin Tomkins Limited

O3. OPTICAL GUN SIGHTS
Aeritalia S.p.A.
Aircraft Equipment (International) Ltd
Barr & Stroud Limited
Ferranti Limited
G.I.A.T.
Hamilton Aircraft Company, Inc.
Marvin Tomkins Limited
Saab-Scania AB

The most popular family in the sky.

The Little Giant

The Boeing 737 is built to take on the toughest assignments. On gravel, ice or short runways. It's the perfect aircraft for up-and-down short haul city routes. It's also great for medium range assignments, including charters. A 737 convertible model is also available.

World's most profitable airbus

The Boeing 727-200 is the lowest capital investment per seat of any commercial jetliner. With 134 to 189 passenger capacity, its operating cost per seat mile is comparable to the larger airbuses.

The Internationalist

The Boeing 707 was the world's first successful jetliner. It serves as the standard bearer for jet-age diplomacy and is the world's most widely used long-distance jetliner. The wide-body interior feel and overhead stowage are new improvements to the 707.

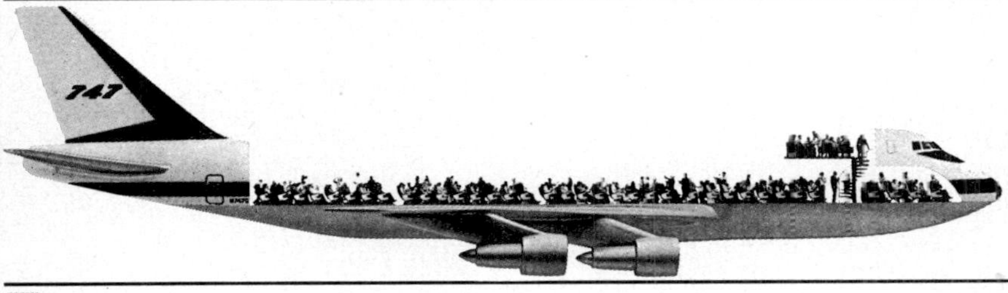

Queen of the Sky

The Boeing 747 is preferred by more passengers than any other aeroplane. With its luxurious upper deck lounge, wide-body comfort and overhead stowage for hand baggage, it has set the standard for commercial aviation comfort.

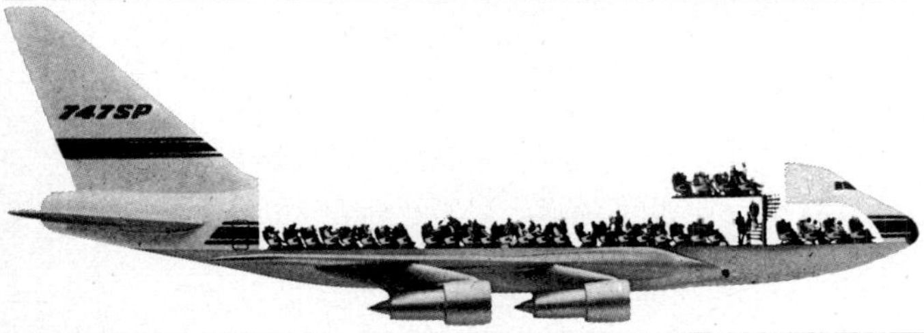

The Special Performer

The Boeing 747SP will fly faster and higher where it's usually smoother. It's shorter and lighter and costs less than the standard 747. The SP's passenger capacity and extreme long range make it possible to introduce 747 Queen of the Sky service to many new markets throughout the world.

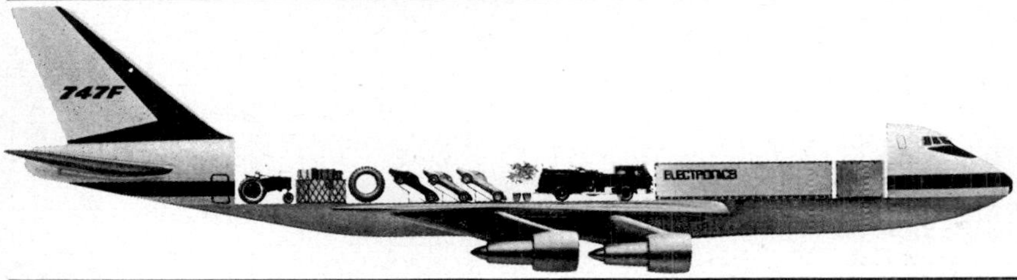

The Super Freighter

The 747F is the first commercial air freighter adaptable to intermodal containerization. It has an electrically-powered mechanized loading system that enables two men to load or off-load the 125-ton payload in less than 30 minutes.

World's most versatile jetliner

The Boeing 747 Convertible can be changed in less than 24 hours from all-passenger to all-cargo configuration. It will accommodate 500 passengers in all-economy 10-abreast seating. Or when used as a cargo ship, it handles containers 8'x8' and up to 40' in length on a powered conveyor system.

BOEING

Getting people together.

O4. OXYGEN APPARATUS
Aviaexport V/O
Marvin Tomkins Limited

O5. OXYGEN BREATHING APPARATUS
Garrett International, s.a.
Marvin Tomkins Limited
Saab-Scania AB

O6. OXYGEN BREATHING SYSTEMS
Aviaexport V/O
Garrett International, s.a.
Marvin Tomkins Limited

O7. OVERHAUL AND MODIFICATION KITS
British Aircraft Corporation
Dornier AG
Garrett International, s.a.
Hamilton Aircraft Company, Inc.
Siai-Marchetti S.p.A.

P1. PARACHUTES
Aviaexport V/O

P2. PARACHUTES—SPECIAL PURPOSE
Aviaexport V/O

P3. PARTS FOR U.S. BUILT AIRCRAFT
Garrett International, s.a.
Hamilton Aircraft Company, Inc.
Marvin Tomkins Limited
Messerschmitt Bölkow-Blohm GmbH

P4. PASSENGER BRIDGES (AVIOBRIDGE)
Fokker VFW International N.V.

P5. PERISCOPES
Aeritalia S.p.A.
Barr & Stroud Limited
Marvin Tomkins Limited

P6. PHOTOGRAPHIC EQUIPMENT
Barr & Stroud Limited
Fokker VFW International N.V.
Marvin Tomkins Limited

P7. PLASTIC EXTRUSION
Snia Viscosa

P8. PLASTIC FABRICATIONS
Aeritalia S.p.A.
Aerospatiale (S.N.I.A.S.)
Israel Aircraft Industries

P9. PLASTIC FABRICATIONS (re-inforced with fibreglass)
Aeritalia S.p.A.
Aerospatiale (S.N.I.A.S.)
Fokker VFW International N.V.
Israel Aircraft Industries
Messerschmitt Bölkow-Blohm GmbH

P10. PLASTIC MOULDINGS
Aeritalia S.p.A.
Aerospatiale (S.N.I.A.S.)
Fokker VFW International N.V.

P11. PNEUMATIC CONTROLS
Garrett International, s.a.

P12. POWER CONTROL FOR AIRCRAFT
Garrett International, s.a.
Marvin Tomkins Limited
SAMM

P13. POWERED SAILPLANES

P14. POWER—SOLCAR CELL PANELS AND ARRAYS
Aerospatiale (S.N.I.A.S.)
Messerschmitt Bölkow-Blohm GmbH
Selenia

P15. PRECISION GEARS
Barr & Stroud Limited

P16. PRECISION POTENTIOMETERS
Aerospatiale (S.N.I.A.S.)
Ferranti Limited
Marvin Tomkins Limited

P17. PRESSURE RATIO TRANSDUCERS
Aeritalia S.p.A.
Aerospatiale (S.N.I.A.S.)
Garrett International, s.a.

P18. PRESSURE CONTROL EQUIPMENT
Garrett International, s.a.

P19. PRESSURE REGULATING VALVES, FLUIDS AND GASES
Flight Refuelling Ltd
Garrett International, s.a.
Saab-Scania AB

P20. PRESSURE SWITCHES
Marvin Tomkins Limited
SAMM

P21. PRESSURE TRANSDUCERS
Aeritalia S.p.A.
Garrett International, s.a.
Marvin Tomkins Limited

P22. PROPELLER GOVERNORS
Marvin Tomkins Limited
Woodward Governor Company

P23. PROPELLER TEST STANDS
John Curran Limited

P24. PROPELLER HUBS
Marvin Tomkins Limited

P25. PROPELLERS
Marvin Tomkins Limited
Messerschmitt-Bölkow-Blohm GmbH
Snia Viscosa

P26. PROPOSALS FOR AIRCRAFT GROUND SUPPORT OPERATIONS
Aircraft Equipment (International) Ltd
Hamilton Aircraft Company, Inc.

P27. PROTECTIVE CLOTHING
Aircraft Equipment (International) Ltd
Marvin Tomkins Limited

P28. PUBLISHERS
Profile Publications Ltd

P29. PUMPS, AIR COMPRESSOR
Garrett International, s.a.
Marvin Tomkins Limited
SNECMA

P30. PUMPS, FUEL AND OIL
Aircraft Equipment (International) Ltd
Garrett International, s.a.
Israel Aircraft Industries
Marvin Tomkins Limited
SAMM

P31. PUMPS, HYDRAULIC
Aircraft Equipment (International) Ltd
Garrett International, s.a.
Israel Aircraft Industries
Marvin Tomkins Limited
Saab-Scania AB
SAMM

P32. PLATFORM TRUCKS
Fokker VFW International N.V.
M.L. Aviation Company Ltd

P33. PROVISIONING PARTS BREAKDOWN LIST
Marvin Tomkins Limited
John Curran Limited

P34. PUMPS, AGRICULTURAL SPRAY
Dornier AG

R1. ENGINE LIFE RECORDERS

R2. RADAR FOR NAVIGATION WARNING INTERCEPTION, FIRE CONTROL AND AIRFIELD SUPERVISION
Aerospatiale (S.N.I.A.S.)
Aviaexport V/O
Ferranti Limited
Israel Aircraft Industries
Hollandse Signaalapparaten B.V.
S.A.F.T.
Selenia

R3. RADAR REFLECTORS
Aerospatiale (S.N.I.A.S.)
Fokker VFW International N.V.
John Curran Limited

R4. RADAR TOWERS
John Curran Limited

R5. RADAR TURNING GEARS AND EQUIPMENT
Aerospatiale (S.N.I.A.S.)
Aviaexport V/O
John Curran Limited

R6. RADIO AIRPORT CONTROL EQUIPMENT
Philips' Telecommunicatie Industrie N.V.

R7. RADIO ALTIMETERS
Aviaexport V/O
Hamilton Aircraft Company Inc.
Marvin Tomkins Limited

R8. RADIO EQUIPMENT
Aerospatiale (S.N.I.A.S.)
Aviaexport V/O
Hamilton Aircraft Company Inc.
Israel Aircraft Industries
Marvin Tomkins Limited
Philips' Telecommunicatie Industrie N.V.

R9. RADIO NAVIGATION EQUIPMENT
Aerospatiale (S.N.I.A.S.)
Aviaexport V/O
Israel Aircraft Industries
Hamilton Aircraft Company Inc.

R10. RADIO OVERHAUL
Hamilton Aircraft Company Inc.
Marvin Tomkins Limited

R11. RAMJET PROPULSION ENGINES
Aerospatiale (S.N.I.A.S.)
Garrett International, s.a.

R12. RANGEFINDERS
Barr & Stroud Limited

R13. REFRIGERATION COMPRESSORS
Garrett International, s.a.

R14. REPAIR AND MAINTENANCE OF AIRCRAFT
Aeritalia S.p.A.
Aerospatiale (S.N.I.A.S.)
Aviaexport V/O
Dornier AG
Fokker VFW International N.V.
Garrett International, s.a.
Hamilton Aircraft Company, Inc.
Hawker Siddeley Aviation Ltd
Israel Aircraft Industries
Messerschmitt Bölkow-Blohm GmbH
Saab-Scania AB
S.F.E.N.A.
Siai Marchetti S.p.A.

R15. REPAIR AND OVERHAUL OF AERO ENGINES
Avco Lycoming Div. of Avco Corp.
Garrett International, s.a.
Hamilton Aircraft Company, Inc.
Messerschmitt Bölkow-Blohm GmbH
S.N.E.C.M.A.

R16. REPAIR OF AIRCRAFT INSTRUMENTS
Aeritalia S.p.A.
Aviaexport V/O
Fokker VFW International N.V.
Hamilton Aircraft Company, Inc.
Israel Aircraft Industries
Marvin Tomkins Limited
S.F.E.N.A.
Siai Marchetti S.p.A.

R17. ROCKET ENGINE TEST PLANT
Aerospatiale (S.N.I.A.S.)
John Curran Limited
Messerschmitt Bölkow-Blohm GmbH

R18. ROCKET PROPULSION
Aerospatiale (S.N.I.A.S.)
Snia Viscosa

R19. ROCKET, SOUNDING
Aerospatiale (S.N.I.A.S.)
British Aircraft Corporation
Dornier Systems GmbH
Saab-Scania AB
Snia Viscosa

R20. ROTARY ACTUATORS
Garrett International, s.a.
Marvin Tomkins Limited

R21. RUNWAY FRICTION MEASURING EQUIPMENT
M.L. Aviation Company Ltd.

S1. SEAT BELTS
Aviaexport V/O

S2. SERVO ACTUATORS
Garrett International, s.a.
Marvin Tomkins Limited
SAMM
S.F.E.N.A.

S3. SHAPING MACHINES
Aerospatiale (S.N.I.A.S.)

S4. SHEET METAL WORK
Aeritalia S.p.A.
Aerospatiale (S.N.I.A.S.)
Fiat S.p.A.
Fokker VFW International N.V.
Hamilton Aircraft Company, Inc.
Israel Aircraft Industries

S5. SHEET METAL WORKING MACHINES
Aerospatiale (S.N.I.A.S.)
Fokker VFW International N.V.

S6. SIMULATORS
Aerospatiale (S.N.I.A.S.)
Dornier Systems GmbH
M.L. Aviation Company Ltd
Saab-Scania AB
Siai Marchetti S.p.A.

S7. SOLENOID VALVES
Flight Refuelling Ltd
Goodyear Tyre & Rubber Company
Marvin Tomkins Limited
Saab-Scania AB

S8. SPACE HARDWARE RECOVERY SYSTEMS
Boeing Company, The
Dornier Systems GmbH

S9. SPACE SYSTEMS
Aeritalia S.p.A.
Aerospatiale (S.N.I.A.S.)
British Aircraft Corporation
Dornier Systems GmbH
Fokker VFW International N.V.
Garrett International, s.a.
MesserschmittBölkow-Blohm GmbH
Selenia

S10. SPACECRAFT
Aeritalia S.p.A.
Aerospatiale (S.N.I.A.S.)
Boeing Company, the
British Aircraft Corporation
Dornier Systems GmbH
Messerschmitt Bölkow-Blohm GmbH

S11. SPACE SATELLITES
Aeritalia S.p.A.
Aerospatiale (S.N.I.A.S.)
British Aircraft Corporation
Dornier Systems GmbH
Fokker VFW International N.V.
Messerschmitt Bölkow-Blohm GmbH
Saab-Scania AB
Selenia
Snia Viscosa

S12. SPARE PARTS FOR U.S. BUILT AIRCRAFT
Aeritalia S.p.A.
Garrett International, s.a.
Marvin Tomkins Limited

S13. STABILITY AUGMENTATION SYSTEMS
Dornier AG
Ferranti Limited
S.F.E.N.A.

S14. STALL WARNING SYSTEMS
Fokker VFW International N.V.
Saab-Scania AB

S15. STARTER PODS, AIRBORNE
Garrett International, s.a.

S16. STARTING SYSTEMS, AIRBORNE
Garrett International, s.a.
Marvin Tomkins Limited

S17. STEEL AND STEEL ALLOYS
Aerospatiale (S.N.I.A.S.)
Aviaexport V/O

S18. STORAGE TANKS
Aerospatiale (S.N.I.A.S.)
Garrett International, s.a.

S19. STRAPS, WEBBING

S20. SURVEILLANCE SYSTEMS
Aerospatiale (S.N.I.A.S.)
Selenia

S21. SURVIVAL EQUIPMENT
Garrett International, s.a.
Saab-Scania AB

S22. SWITCHGEAR
Aviaexport V/O
Marvin Tomkins Limited

S23. STEELS, STAINLESS, HEAT AND CREEP RESISTING
Aerospatiale (S.N.I.A.S.)

Throughout the history of air transportation, several airplanes warranted the description—the right plane at the right time.

Certainly the JU-52, the DC-3, the DC-4 and the Constellation. The Viscount and Caravelle. Beyond question the 707 and DC-8. And of course the 747, which ushered in the wide-body era.

Now another airplane comes along at the right time. The Airbus A300. Right to beat the crunch that rising fuel costs are creating. Right to put more profit into short and medium haul routes, just where the biggest potential lies for increased revenue passenger miles and freight, too. Right to meet new environmental standards.

The right plane? Here are ten reasons why the Airbus A300 offers so much profit potential on routes of 150 to 2600 nautical miles.

1. It has 20 percent less direct operating costs than wide-body tri-jets.

2. 15 percent less cost per seat-mile than a narrow-body tri-jet.

3. A 30 percent break-even load factor even on short stages.

4. Powered by two service-proven GE CF-6 turbofan engines. And being adapted to the RB211.

5. The A300 has a higher thrust-to-weight ratio than any other subsonic jet.

6. It's quieter, too. In fact, the A300 is considerably more quiet than even the quietest new hushed jets.

7. The A300 has a new wing section that works like a supercritical wing. For better lift, less drag, quick take-off, slow landings, more efficiency.

8. There's 4870 cubic feet in the underfloor cargo holds, room enough for 20 standard A1 (LD3) containers, without removing a single seat. A whole new source of revenue.

9. The A300 is built with proven systems and components. In fact, 25 percent of the aircraft is U.S.-built, including all "rotables," 80 percent of which are thoroughly service proven.

10. Finally, the A300 is wide-body, gives the room and convenience that the traveling public has come to appreciate and expect.

The A300. Truly, the right plane at the right time.

Airbus A300

The right plane at the right time.

FROM AIRBUS INDUSTRIE

The right plane at the right time.

S24. SWITCHES—MINIATURE ELECTRICAL
Marvin Tomkins Limited
Minelco
SAMM

T1. TACHOMETERS
Aircraft Equipment (International) Ltd
Aviaexport V/O
Marvin Tomkins Limited

T2. TARGET RELEASE AND EXCHANGER MECHANISMS
M.L. Aviation Company Ltd

T3. TARGET TOWING WINCHES
Flight Refuelling Ltd
Garrett International, s.a.
Saab-Scania AB

T4. TECHNICAL DICTIONARY
Aerospatiale (S.N.I.A.S.)

T5. TECHNICAL PUBLICATIONS
Dornier AG
Flight Refuelling Ltd.
Fokker VFW International N.V.
Israel Aircraft Industries
John Curran Limited
Profile Publications Ltd

T6. TECHNICAL PUBLICATIONS—SPECIAL STUDIES
Dornier Systems GmbH
John Curran Limited
Profile Publications Ltd.

T7. TEMPERATURE CONTROL EQUIPMENT
Garrett International, s.a.
Marvin Tomkins Limited

T8. THERMO-COUPLE CABLES
Israel Aircraft Industries
Standard Wire & Cable Company

T9. TEST EQUIPMENT
Aeronautica Macchi S.p.A.
Aircraft Equipment (International) Ltd
Aviaexport V/O
Avco Lycoming Div. of Avco Corp.
Garrett International, s.a.
Israel Aircraft Industries
John Curran Limited
Marvin Tomkins Limited
M.L. Aviation Company Ltd
Saab-Scania AB
Selenia
S.F.E.N.A.

T10. TEST EQUIPMENT, AIRBORNE RADIO
Aviaexport V/O

T11. TEST EQUIPMENT, AIRFIELD RADIO
Aviaexport V/O

T12. TEST EQUIPMENT (METAL BONDING)
Aviaexport V/O

T13. TRACTORS, ELECTRIC
M.L. Aviation Company Ltd

T14. TRAINING DEVICES
M.L. Aviation Company Ltd

T15. TRANSFORMER RECTIFIER UNITS
Israel Aircraft Industries

T16. TUBES, STAINLESS STEEL
Aviaexport V/O

T17. TURBINES—RAM AIR
Garrett International, s.a.
Hamilton Aircraft Company, Inc.

T18. TURBOFAN ENGINES
Fiat S.p.A.
Garrett International. s.a.
Hamilton Aircraft Company, Inc.
S.N.E.C.M.A.
Volvo Flygmotor AB

T19. TURBINE CONVERSIONS
Hamilton Aircraft Company, Inc.

T20. TYRES FOR AIRCRAFT
Goodyear Rubber & Tyre Company, Aviation Division

U1. UNDERCARRIAGE EQUIPMENT
Aircraft Equipment (International) Ltd
Hamilton Aircraft Company, Inc.
Marvin Tomkins Limited
SNECMA

U2. UNDERCARRIAGE GEAR RETRACTABLE
Hamilton Aircraft Company, Inc.
Siai Marchetti S.p.A.
SNECMA

V1. VALVES
Flight Refuelling Ltd
Garrett International, s.a.
Israel Aircraft Industries
Marvin Tomkins Limited
Saab-Scania AB
SAMM
Siai Marchetti S.p.A.

V2. VALVES AND MINIATURE RELAYS
Garrett International, s.a.
Marvin Tomkins Limited

V3. VALVES, CONTROL HYDRAULIC
Garrett International, s.a.
Goodyear Tyre & Rubber Company, Aviation Division
Israel Aircraft Industries
Marvin Tomkins Limited
Saab-Scania AB
SAMM

V4. VALVES, ELECTRONIC
Garrett International, s.a.
Marvin Tomkins Limited

V5. VALVES, FUSES HYDRAULIC

V6. VALVES, NON-RETURN, FUEL
Flight Refuelling Ltd
Garrett International, s.a.
Marvin Tomkins Limited
Saab-Scania AB

V7. VALVES, NON-RETURN HYDRAULIC
Flight Refuelling Ltd
Garrett International, s.a.
Marvin Tomkins Limited
Saab-Scania AB

V8. VALVES, SEQUENCE, HYDRAULIC
Marvin Tomkins Limited
Saab-Scania AB

V9. VALVES, RELIEF HYDRAULIC
Garrett International, s.a.
Marvin Tomkins Limited
Saab-Scania AB

V10. VAPOR CYCLE REFRIGERATION PACKAGES
Garrett International, s.a.

V11. VERTICAL TAKE-OFF AIRCRAFT
Aerospatiale (S.N.I.A.S.)
Boeing Company, The
Dornier AG
Messerschmitt Bölkow-Blohm GmbH

V12. VISIBILITY MEASURING EQUIPMENT
Eltro GmbH

V13. VOLTAGE AND CURRENT REGULATORS
Ferranti Limited
Garrett International, s.a.
Marvin Tomkins Limited

W1. WATER SEPARATORS
Flight Refuelling Ltd
Garrett International, s.a.
Marvin Tomkins Limited

W2. WEBBING

W3. WHEELS FOR AIRCRAFT
Aircraft Equipment (International) Ltd
Aviaexport V/O
Goodyear Tyre & Rubber Company, Aviation Division
Marvin Tomkins Limited

W4. WIND TUNNEL TESTING PLANT
Aeronautica Macchi S.p.A.
Dornier AG
John Curran Limited

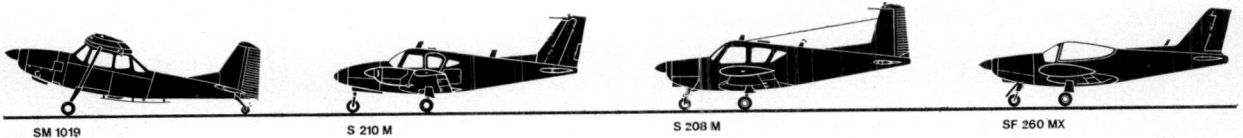

The Independent Flight Inspection System IFIS Type Frankfurt permits to calibrate ILS and VOR/TACAN facilities according to international standards up to the accuracy requirements of Category III operations. Contrary to the measuring methods conducted hitherto, the uncertainty factor of the theodolite observer which is inherent in the manual follow-up

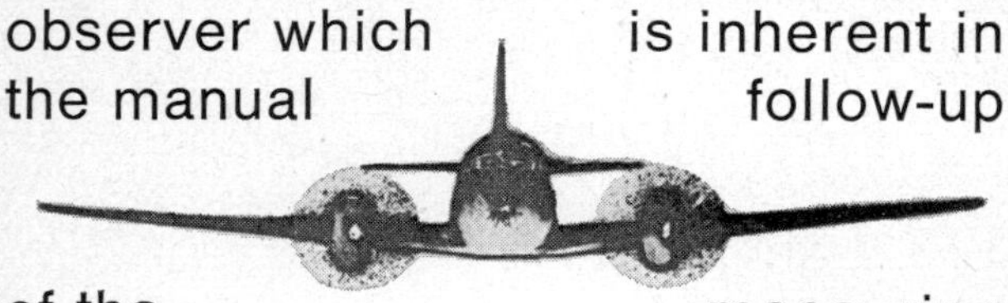

of the measuring theodolite and in no way determinable, is eliminated. The equipment produces absolutely uncomplicated written records showing the absolute error of the facilities under investigation as well as the fine structure of the antenna characteristic.

Eltro GmbH

Gesellschaft für Strahlungstechnik

69 Heidelberg 1 - Western Germany
P.O. Box 520 - Telex 04-61811

for the suppression of fuel systems explosions

be protected by

safom®

Reticulated Safety Foam

Produced to military specifications

When fitted into a fuel tank it will completely suppress the explosion which follows the ignition of a fuel/air mixture in a confined space.

Weight: 30 kg per m3.

Reduction of tank capacity: 3%.

Can be fitted during construction or retrofitted on existing aircraft fuel-system by our specialised personnel.

PRB s.a.

Division POLYURETHANE
Damstraat, 2
9200 Wetteren/BELGIUM
Tel. 191.692801
Telex : 11.363

JANE'S OCEAN TECHNOLOGY

1st Year of Issue

Edited by Robert L. Trillo

This latest addition to the JANE'S series of authoritative international reference books covers the technology of underwater exploration and engineering. JANE'S OCEAN TECHNOLOGY meets the need for a comprehensive, single source of reference on this rapidly developing science. It provides detailed coverage of research vessels, oil spill containment, and also contains Company profiles and specially commissioned reports on important areas of interest.

330pp approx/ photographs and line drawings

ISBN 0 354 00500 6/£12.50 +55p p&p U.K. – 80p Overseas

JANE'S YEARBOOKS,
Macdonald and Jane's, St Giles House, 49-50, Poland Street, London W1A 2LG

Aircraft fuel flow measurement by Kent

A range of transmitters and indicators for volume or mass fuel flow registration and totalization.

Kent also supply a summation system which enables the total amount of fuel used, or remaining to be displayed on a separate indicator. Technical literature available on request.

KENT METERS LIMITED
Aircraft Division . Luton . Bedfordshire . England
Telephone Luton 31100 Telex 825367
Cables & Telegrams Kentmeters Luton

BO 105

AIR BUS A300B

MRCA

THE WESTWIND II S.T.D.

The Latest Turbo Powered Twin from Hamilton Aircraft Company

- 840 HORSEPOWER PT6A-34 TURBINE ENGINES
- GROSS WEIGHT OF 12,499 POUNDS (5,682 KILOS APPROX.)
- USEFUL LOAD OF 6,249 POUNDS (2,841 KILOS APPROX.)
- MAXIMUM CRUISE OF 305 MPH (491 KM/H)
- SERVICE CEILING 30,000 FT. (9,144 METERS APPROX.)
- SINGLE ENGINE CEILING 18,000 FT. (5,486 METERS APPROX.)
- TO BE APPROVED UNDER S.F.A.R. 135.2 (OVER 10 PASSENGER)

HAMILTON
AIRCRAFT
COMPANY, INC.
Tucson International Airport

INQUIRIES:

MARKETING DIVISION
HAMILTON AIRCRAFT CO.
P.O. BOX 11427
TUCSON, ARIZONA 85734
U.S.A. (602) 294-3481

Rist's Cables Put Power Into Flight

NEW HORIZONS
FOR SMALL AND LARGE AIRLINES
OPEN TO-DAY *by*

YAK-40 JET

1 At present, in the United States alone, there are over 500 small towns that would like to have regular air services to nearby towns and cities, as well as to large airports within a 300 mile radius. However, the cost of airfield constructions would normally be prohibitive. Still, there is a solution to this problem — the YAK-40 JET which can operate without concrete runways. In fact any sufficiently level piece of land of limited size will do. The moderate price of the Jet and the simplicity of its operation calls for a relatively small capital investment, and as it only produces minimal noise it renders itself operable even in areas where noise level requirements are particularly strict. Come rain-or-shine, day-or-night the Jet has all the necessary radio-navigational equipment,

2 Many interesting places on our Earth are still remote from the sphere of active human life since there is no reliable communication between them and the rest of the world. Such examples are mountain regions, deserts and places which are under snow for most of the year. The YAK-40 Jet makes these places accessible for regular business, tourism, etc.

A characteristic feature of this jet is the very high thrust of its three engines which, in combination with the unswept wings provides for steep climbing and descent which cannot be overestimated in highlands and mountainous regions.

Flights in Nepal, Afghanistan, Equador, Chile, Bolivia and Peru (where the Jet landed in places that had never before seen a piston-engine plane let alone a jet liner) have proved beyond any doubt the exceptional manoeuvrability and reliability of the YAK-40. Another star feature - the extra-large low-pressure tires which let the Jet land on ground that would usually accommodate only very light planes. In short, the unique features of YAK-40 make it operable anywhere in the world, make it defy practically any flight conditions

CERTIFICATED BY REGISTRO AERONAUTICO ITALIANO AND BY LUFTFAHRT BUNDESAMT IN ACCORDANCE WITH THE REQUIREMENTS FAR-25.
Certification in England and France is under way.

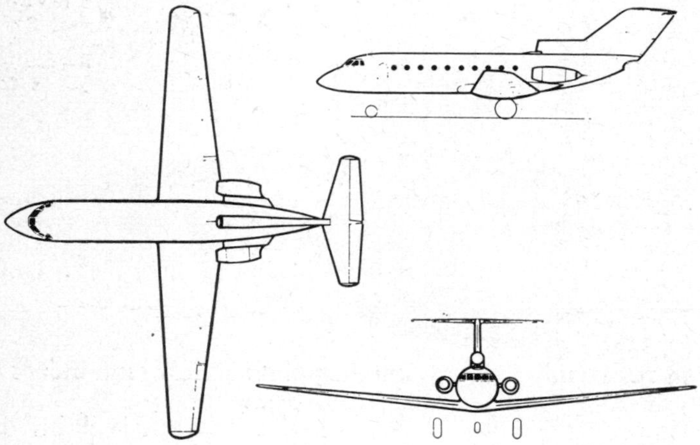

Take-off weight	16000 kg
Max. payload	2720 kg
Cruising speed	550 km/hour
Range with max. payload	1800 km
Take-off run	700 m

Passenger versions: 27 seats, 30-32 seats
Business Executive: 11, 16 or 20 seats.

For detailed information please write to:
V/O "AVIAEXPORT"
32/34 Smolenskaja-Sennaja Sq.
G-200, Moscow, 121200, USSR
Cable: Aviaexport Moscow
Telephone: 244-26-86
Telex: 7257, 7635

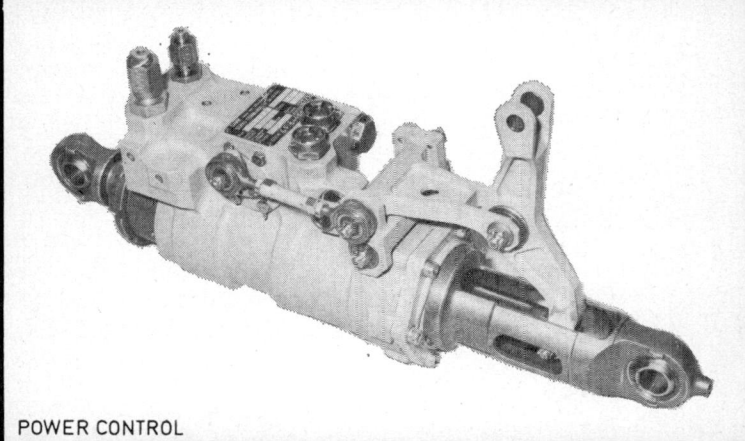

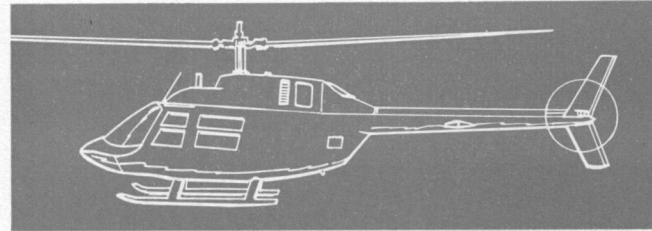

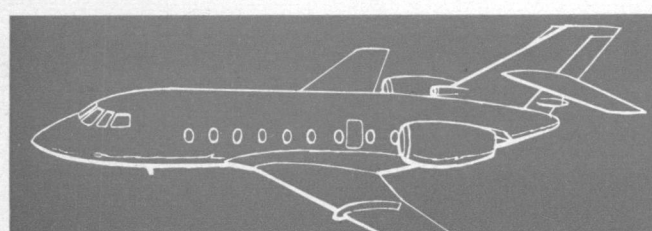

You expect Woodward to be aboard the B-1...and it will be
In order to thwart radar detection, the forthcoming B-1 Air Force bomber will hug the terrain at nearly the speed of sound. This unique capability requires advancements in virtually all components of the aircraft. Four General Electric F101 turbofan jet engines with a combined thrust of approximately 120,000 pounds, will be equipped with Woodward's type 3055 fuel control . . . destined to be the world's finest main engine control. Look to Woodward technology for the latest refinements in fuel controls and synchronizers for jet and propeller aircraft. It's your assurance of reliable, superior product performance. Contact us.
B1
WOODWARD
SERVICE
Woodward Governors for aircraft power plants and propellers; gas turbine and/or diesel prime movers for standby, peaking, and on-site power needs; hydro-electric power.
WOODWARD GOVERNOR COMPANY ROCKFORD, ILLINOIS, U.S.A., PHONE (815) 877-7441
Ft. Collins, Colorado, U.S.A.; Sydney, Australia; Tokyo, Japan • Subsidiaries: Hoofddorp, The Netherlands; Slough, England; Montreal, Canada; Lucerne, Switzerland

WHILE YOU'VE GOT RUNWAYS, DOES TH
Yes.
The V/STOL Harrier operates like any other fighter in these circumstances. It lifts up to 8,000lb (3630 kg) of weapons in short take-off, integrating perfectly with other types on your inventory.
But if your runways are out of action, then only the V/STOL Harrier can keep your base operational and capable of flying a complete range of armed missions.
Harrier is the hard-hitting conventional fighter with the V/STOL bonus – when you need it most.

Aircraft in Profile

is thirteen an unlucky number?

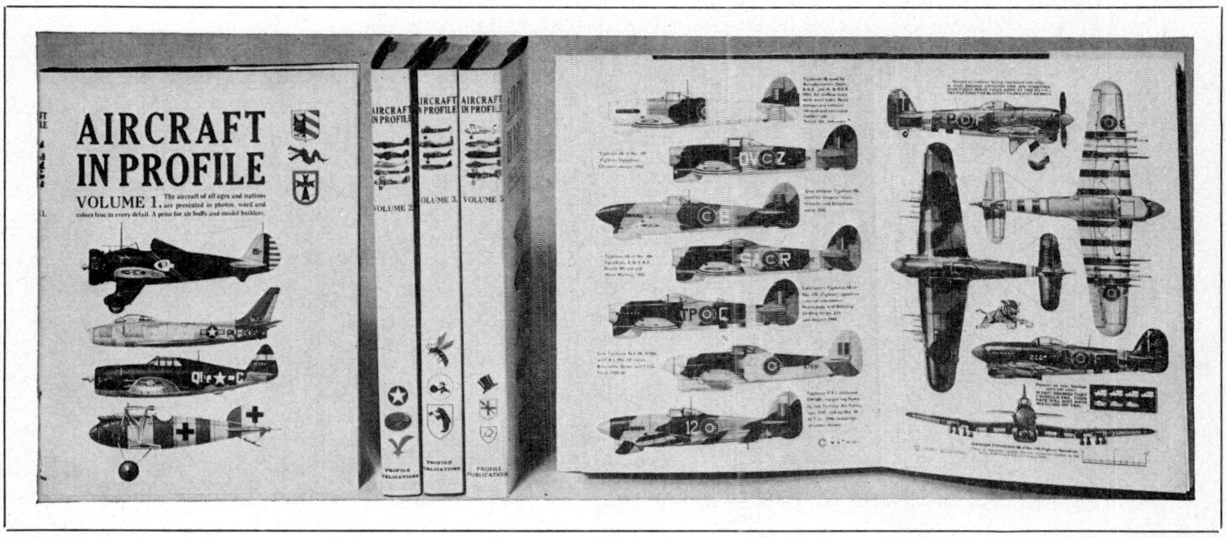

We don't think so. Thirteen volumes of Aircraft in Profile provide you with the best reference available on 246 of the World's major aircraft. All volumes are complete in themselves. Each aircraft is comprehensively covered with an authoritative text, accurate 5-view full-colour drawings and profusely illustrated with black and white photographs.

Write for full details to:

Profile Publications Limited
Coburg House, Sheet Street, Windsor,
Berks SL4 1EB

Jane's Yearbooks 1974/75

for international coverage.

Established for over three-quarters of a century, Jane's Yearbooks are internationally recognized as authoritative works of reference in their respective fields. Each of the Jane's Yearbooks is in effect an international encyclopedia of factual information on its own particular subject. The emphasis is on accurate and up-to-date facts checked and re-checked. Accuracy and comprehensiveness on a world-wide scale, give the books their reliability as works of reference. Dimensions are given in both British and metric units, and almost all the entries are illustrated with either photographs or drawings. Jane's Yearbooks are indispensible to all professional servicemen – be they naval, military or airforce – as well as to government departments.

Jane's Fighting Ships
77th Year of Issue
Edited by Captain J. E. Moore, R.N.
Unrivalled as a reference book on the world's navies, this latest edition has the usual extensive revisions, and also incorporates important changes including the re-classification of all ships. The book covers 15,000 ships in more than 110 countries. There are over 3,000 photographs, plans, silhouettes and line drawings in approximately 870 pages.

Jane's Weapon Systems
6th Edition
Edited by R. T. Pretty and D. H. R. Archer
Recognised as an important catalogue of military systems, equipment and armament, each entry is revised and updated as necessary each year. Sections with changes of particular significance in this edition include those on strategic missiles, naval missiles, drones and remotely piloted vehicles. There are over 1,000 photographs and diagrams in about 800 pages.

Jane's All The World's Aircraft
65th Year of Issue
Edited by J. W. R. Taylor
Produced with the fullest possible co-operation of the aerospace industries of the world, this volume provides all the details of every aircraft, military as well as civil, in production or development in 38 countries. The book contains about 900 pages and 1,500 photographs and 3 view drawings.

Jane's Surface Skimmers
Hovercraft and Hydrofoils. 8th Edition
Edited by Roy McLeavy
With the growing world-wide acceptance of skimmer-craft for military besides commercial use, Jane's Surface Skimmers becomes increasingly valuable for all those with interests in this field. In this young industry new developments are constantly being recorded in all areas covered by the publication. There are about 500 photographs and diagrams in approximately 450 pages.

Jane's Infantry Weapons
1st Edition
Edited by Major F. W. H. Hobart (Retd.)
This latest addition to the Jane's 'family' follows logically from the success of 'Jane's Weapon Systems' to which it is largely complimentary. The book will have four main sections i.e.: Point Target Weapons; Area Weapons; Anti-aircraft and Anti-tank Weapons, and Electronics. Each section will be sub-divided according to the nature of the subject. Each entry will be comprised of standardised and detailed descriptions and specifications data, and will be illustrated with diagrams and photographs over about 500 pages.

Typical presentation of information in Jane's Yearbooks. Top: 'Jane's Fighting Ships'; centre: 'Jane's Weapon Systems' and bottom: 'Jane's All the World's Aircraft'

JANE'S YEARBOOKS
Macdonald & Jane's
St Giles House, 49-50 Poland Street, London W1
Great Britain. Telephone 01-437 0686.
Cables Britpub London. Telex 23451

JANE'S ALL THE WORLD'S AIRCRAFT

FOUNDED IN 1909 BY FRED T. JANE

COMPILED AND EDITED BY
JOHN W. R. TAYLOR FRHistS, AFRAeS, FSLAET
ASSISTANT EDITOR
KENNETH MUNSON

1974-75

I.S.B.N. 0-531-02747-3
L. of C. Cat. Card No. 74-4787

JANE'S YEARBOOKS

FRANKLIN WATTS, INC.
NEW YORK

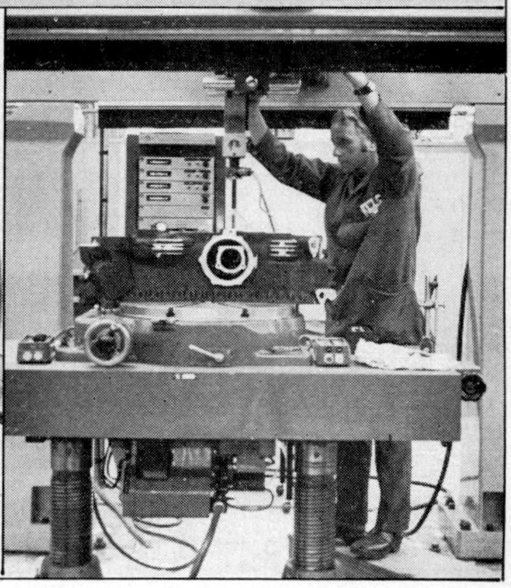

Above: The AJ 37 Viggen with the RM 8 engine. Below, left to right: Discs and shafts, Stator guide vane assembly, Inspection.

FOREWORD

In one of the most eventful years of aviation history, the star of the first truly international Farnborough air show, in England, was an aeroplane designed fifteen years ago and no longer in production. Such remarks do not disparage in any way the remarkable Lockheed SR-71A, or its achievement in flying over the Atlantic between New York and London in 1 hour 55 minutes 42 seconds as a curtain raiser to the show. They simply reflect how little the general public knows about the capabilities of the present-day aerospace industry and its products.

The SR-71A could have set up this intercontinental speed record at any time during the past decade. Yet, all the speed records in the world are insignificant by comparison with what the incredible "Blackbird" has done in its primary duty as a strategic reconnaissance aircraft, in the interests of world peace. Only when a major confrontation occurs, like the Cuban missile crisis of 1962, does public attention focus momentarily on one aspect of the work of what the newspapers call "spyplanes", of both East and West. Most of the time, most people fail to grasp the significance of such officially-issued statements as: "The UK Air Defence Region (UKADR) during recent years has received more 'trade' from Soviet long-range aircraft flying round the North Cape and down towards the British Isles than any other NATO air defence region".

These particular Soviet aircraft are engaged on electronic intelligence and reconnaissance missions, probing the NATO defences. What, one wonders, would be the public reaction to a suggestion that "flying saucers" observed over countries like West Germany and Sweden have a connection with never-mentioned Soviet RPVs? Nearly ten years have gone by since the Chinese first displayed the remains of US pilotless reconnaissance aircraft in Peking; and the Russians must appreciate the advantages of such vehicles as much as anyone else after what Teledyne Ryan RPVs achieved subsequently in Vietnam.

Peacetime reconnaissance and electronic intelligence gathering are a part of everyday life that must not be broadcast too blatantly. Often, the public is equally oblivious to aviation achievements and potential which carry no tag of secrecy and of which it should rightly be proud.

For example, on 17 June 1974, the second pre-production Concorde took off from Boston, Massachusetts, at the same time as an Air France Boeing 747 left Paris on a normal scheduled service to Boston. The SST landed at the French capital's new Charles de Gaulle Airport after a flight time of 3 hours 10 minutes. One hour and 8 minutes later, refuelled and revictualled, the Concorde took off on the return journey to Boston, recording a westbound flight time of 3 hours 8 minutes. In doing so it landed before the 747, having made the round trip in less than the normal time for a one-way crossing.

Surely this was as remarkable as the SR-71A's record dash—especially as the Concorde carried in each direction a payload of almost 26,500 lb (12,000 kg), the full entry-into-service figure promised by its makers. Yet how many people in Britain are aware of this demonstration of the aircraft's potential, and feel a glow of pride as warm as the cheers of the French schoolchildren who welcomed it in Paris with waving Tricolours, Union Jacks and Stars and Stripes? And what has been done officially to encourage more interest?

It is easy to feel, in the light of seventeen years of bitter experience, that Britain's governments continue, quite deliberately, to underrate its aerospace industry. Remembering the TSR.2, Rotodyne, HS 1154 and other cancelled programmes, there could well be truth in the suggestion that Concorde, too, would have been abandoned by the UK had not a high proportion of the British workers engaged on the project been situated in the parliamentary constituency of the Secretary of State for Industry. No government can ignore voters, and similar thoughts have been expressed in the USA, where the Texas-built F-111 and A-7 combat aircraft (though none would deny their excellence) are maintained in production at a time when the manufacturers of newer, vitally-needed combat aircraft, in other States, have to fight for every budgetary cent, not always successfully.

Those who control the purse-strings of nations are not to be envied in times of inflation, when development of the Concorde costs more than £1,000 million over twelve years, and the price of evolving a bomber like the Rockwell B-1 averages nearly $500 million (£200 million) a year. There is however another side to the coin. Concorde keeps 40,000 Europeans at work on a product of advanced technology for which even the United States can provide no competitor. As for the B-1, the mere fact that we are all alive in a nuclear age, despite wide international differences, provides the best argument for a viable East-West deterrent policy, however costly, until greed and political aspirations are replaced by finer qualities.

We are a long way from such an idyllic age. Indeed, there has never been a grimmer period for the entire worldwide aerospace industry than the present time. For the manufacturing industry and airlines, economic problems—not divorced from international political manoeuvring—are causing even the giants to falter. After the collapse and government takeover of Rolls-Royce in 1971, we have Lockheed seemingly in perpetual difficulty in America, and Pan American and TWA asking for assistance in surviving anticipated losses of $76 million and $65 million respectively in 1974. Pan American has requested a temporary subsidy of $10·2 million a month. Mergers are proposed as a possible solution to troubles in America; nationalisation is advanced as the panacea for Britain. Neither of these courses will solve the long-term problems.

However much the aerospace industry earns—and the UK industry alone reported export sales worth over £500 million in 1973—it is unlikely to attain permanent economic stability, or be able to take full advantage of the higher performance and greater safety offered by advanced technology, until some airline operations are run as a public service rather than as a profit (or loss) making venture. This does not necessarily imply state ownership; but state subsidies must become more common unless supersonic travel is to remain a dream and low-cost family holidays in the sun are to be a memory of the past.

It is unthinkable that supersonic travel will be provided only by the Soviet Union and other non-capitalist nations; and faith in the future of Concorde grows stronger with each passing month. However, some current problems are more complicated, requiring a massive expenditure of expertise as well as money. A good start has been made on tackling the environmental problems of noise and smoke pollution, but much remains to be achieved. Also, while the increased cost of aviation fuels has created much of the present financial crisis, a greater long-term problem is the depletion of the world's hydrocarbon fuel reserves.

The solution may well lay in the eventual use of liquid hydrogen fuel, now that the manned space programmes have shown that it can be manufactured, handled and used safely in very large quantities. This is no place to examine exhaustively the ways in which liquid hydrogen might replace kerosene and gasoline in aircraft. Suffice it to say that the project design teams of some of the world's leading manufacturers have worked out the basic configurations of airliners that might run on liquid hydrogen. Models tested in wind tunnels by companies like McDonnell Douglas have given results suggesting that full-scale versions might be carrying passengers in everyday service by the turn of the century. One interesting conclusion is that the new fuel not only makes possible intercontinental aircraft able to carry 500 passengers at Mach 6 to Mach 9, but would be equally suitable for 1,000-seat subsonic "Jumbos". Furthermore, liquid hydrogen is the cleanest-burning of all fuels, and might offer solutions to both airport noise and in-flight sonic boom problems, when allied to advanced design.

Any nation incapable of developing and building these enormously-expensive aircraft of the future might well earn a living from producing the liquid hydrogen fuel, which does not require the geographical good fortune of living over an oil well.

* * * * * * *

Despite a multitude of economic and political pressures, the past year has brought significant and exciting aerospace developments. The "First flights" list includes the first and second production Concordes; America's YF-16 and YF-17 lightweight fighters, promising lower-cost effectiveness through new design concepts; the Dali-esque Boeing and Teledyne Ryan Compass Cope high-altitude intelligence-gathering RPVs; Martin Marietta's X-24B dart-like wingless research aircraft; the world's first electrically-powered aeroplane (Militky MB-E1); the first production European Airbus; the long-awaited Panavia MRCA, on which the whole future of the Royal Air Force depends; and the Sikorsky YCH-53E, which has flown at an all-up weight of 70,000 lb (31,750 kg), greater than any other helicopter outside the Soviet Union.

First flight dates can seldom be attached to new Soviet aircraft, particularly combat types; but this issue of *Jane's* records much that has not hitherto been published. Dimensions quoted for the Mi-24 ("Hind") helicopter suggest that it is considerably smaller than has been reported elsewhere. There is an informative new photograph of the Tu-28P ("Fiddler"). The version of the MiG-21 known as "Fishbed-K" is shown right-way-round for the first time (pitot boom on the starboard side); and "Fishbed-L" is identified and illustrated. Much that is new can be learned about types such as the MiG-23 ("Flogger"), MiG-25 ("Foxbat"), Su-15 ("Flagon"), the latest "Bear-F" version of the Tu-95, the variable-geometry bomber known to NATO as "Backfire", and a new "Brewer-E" version of the Yak-28.

In the Addenda, among a multitude of late news items, is a brief reference to a new Soviet tandem-delta bomber. This has an all-up weight not far short of that of the B-1, and a potential that may well cause the US Department of Defense to reconsider its FY1975 budget remark that "In recognition of the reduced threat of a massive bomber attack, (all) the Nike-Hercules surface-to-air missile (SAM) batteries located in the United States, and some fighter interceptor squadrons, are being phased out".

More detailed information reveals that all Aerospace Defense Command's F-102 interceptors will have followed the Nike-Hercules SAMs into retirement by mid-1976, but that some or all of its 242 F-106s and 124 F-101s could be retained throughout the decade. Also, squadrons of F-14 and F-15 fighters and SAM-D missiles

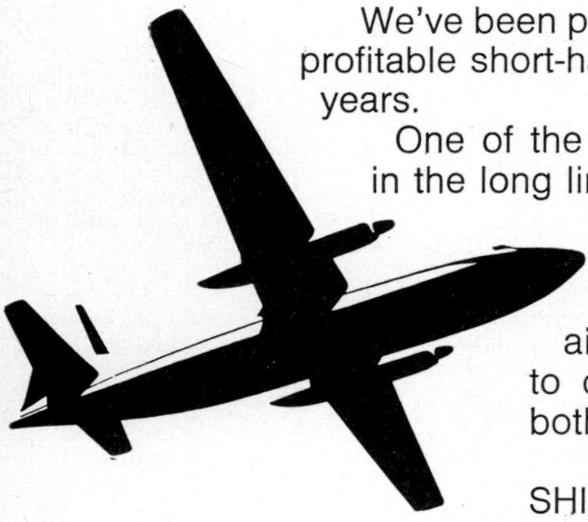

We've been providing airlines with profitable short-haul aircraft for many years.

One of the greatest successes in the long line of Fokker aircraft is of course the F27 FRIENDSHIP of which over 600 aircraft have been sold to date. We also have both feet in the jet-age. The F28 FELLOWSHIP is the quietest twin-jet in operation, seating up to 79 passengers. The VFW 614, featuring over-the-wing engines, and even quieter than the F28, carries 40 passengers in full jet comfort.

Both aircraft have all the features necessary to repeat the success of the Friendship.

Let us prove that you, too, can profit from our long experience in the economics of short-haul transport.

VFW-FOKKER
Amsterdam. Bremen. Düsseldorf.

"could augment continental US defences; but, of course, these are the same forces that frequently are deployed elsewhere in a crisis".

Clearly, there are many in high places in the Pentagon who believe that there is little point in providing a defence against Soviet bombers while the SALT agreement leaves both the USA and Soviet Union wide open to annihilation by nuclear strategic missiles. This takes into account the fact that the Red Air Force deploys only 140 intercontinental bombers at the present time and that, except for the new swing-wing "Backfires", they could be despatched on little but one-way missions against the USA.

Russia, on the other hand, needs to plan for defence against some 500 American B-52 and FB-111 intercontinental bombers, with the B-1 as a possible follow-on, unrestricted by the current SALT agreement. For this reason, it has in 1974 more than 2,500 interceptors and 9,800 SAM launchers, compared with America's year-end total of some 500 interceptors and no SAMs.

The composition of the Soviet fighter defence force is interesting. The Yak-28P ("Firebar"), Tu-28P ("Fiddler"), Su-15 ("Flagon") and MiG-25 ("Foxbat") equip 50% of the interceptor units, with the Su-9 and Su-11 ("Fishpot-B and C") accounting for 25%, and the vintage MiG-17 ("Fresco") and MiG-19 ("Farmer") still soldiering on in the other 25%.

The Arab-Israeli Yom Kippur War of October 1973 gave a false impression of the effectiveness of the Soviet SAMs, as did engagements in Vietnam. In the Suez Canal zone and around Hanoi the missile defences were massed in concentrations that could never be matched in countries as large as the Soviet Union and USA, with many widely-dispersed targets. Nor did Soviet air-to-air missiles impress the Israelis, who admitted the loss of only six aircraft in air combat in October 1973, against some 335 Arab aircraft, more than half of which were destroyed by Shafrir "dogfight" missiles.

There is no need for further explanation of why the USA is putting so much effort into improving the close-range capability of its own air-to-air missiles. It may also be significant that, in an apparent *volte-face*, the USAF is now considering the purchase of several hundred General Dynamics F-16 or Northrop F-17 lightweight fighters after prototype evaluation has been completed. With their high thrust-to-weight ratios, superb manoeuvrability and advanced features, allied to dogfight missiles, such aircraft could well fill the gap if the USAF discovered an urgent need for a successor to the once-planned last-of-the-line F-106.

The Soviet Union has no illusions concerning a continued need for interceptors. Hence a warning by the Chairman of the US Joint Chiefs of Staff in early 1974 that "By the late 1970s, the Soviet Union may have interceptors with a look-down/shoot-down radar/missile system, and may deploy a new AWACS (airborne warning and control system aircraft) with a look-down capability over land, as well as water. Such an interceptor/AWACS force could pose a formidable threat to our bombers". Preparing for that threat, the USAF is fitting new devices to its B-52 bombers to improve their survivability, and is evolving for its attack forces a complete range of new strategic cruise missiles, defence suppression missiles and other weapons, of which details can be found for the first time in *Jane's* this year.

Throughout the entire book, the emphasis is now on advanced technology, with supercritical wings, fly-by-wire control systems, boron composite structures, upper-surface and lower-surface flap-blowing, terrain-following automatic control systems, turbo-ramjet engines, and a hundred other developments that were regarded so recently as highly experimental, now appearing as features of production aeroplanes. The Spitfire could be covered in 370 words and six lines of specification data in the 1939 *Jane's*. More words are needed today to list the electronics and equipment of an aircraft like the MRCA. The entries on this aircraft and the SR-71A alone represent many days of work, as the manufacturers were not permitted to supply the raw material in such detail or even to comment officially on the end product. These are, therefore, two of the very few entries in the book—outside the Soviet and Chinese sections—that do not contain 100% officially-authenticated data.

It is a matter of considerable pride to record that no aircraft manufacturing nation in the world refuses any longer to supply information to *Jane's*. There could be no better indication of the regard in which it is held, or its value to professional readers, who would be quick to note and point out any item that was more wishful than accurate.

* * * * * *

Competition among the manufacturing nations remains particularly intense in the military field. This can lead to acrimony when a company appears to be "pushing" its own in-house product at the expense of one developed and manufactured with a foreign partner. In general, however, manufacturers throughout the world are becoming increasingly dependent on each other—not usually to take advantage of superior skills, but to smooth out the "peaks and troughs" that would otherwise have a disastrous effect on employment and the utilisation of facilities during the development/production/rundown life cycle of any product.

A glance through the introductory copy under individual company entries in this edition will give some idea of the extent of the sub-contracting. Kawasaki of Japan is found to be manufacturing doors for the Lockheed TriStar and wing flaps for the Boeing 747SP. CASA of Spain builds outer wings for the Dassault Falcon 10. The Australian Government Aircraft Factories produce rudders and elevators for the Boeing 727. More surprisingly, while Shorts are busy building wings for the Fokker-VFW Fellowship in Ireland, Fokker-VFW is responsible for producing the outer wings of Shorts' SD3-30 at Amsterdam. One might feel, wrongly, that only a computer could prove the logic of that exchange!

In terms of large subsonic transport aircraft, America's grasp of the market becomes increasingly apparent. Airlines like EgyptAir, CAAC of China and Tarom of Romania, which once operated Soviet Antonovs, Ilyushins and Tupolevs almost exclusively, now fly Boeings. CAAC is even running British Airways' European Division close second as a Trident operator. This fact and the so-far modest but promising growth of interest in the A-300 Airbus, shows that Europe can still find a place in the market for medium-size commercial transports and this, together with economic considerations, explains a development that was announced as these pages were being written.

In the words of the official statement, BAC and Hawker Siddeley of the UK, Aérospatiale of France, and Dornier, MBB and VFW-Fokker of Germany have agreed "to work together in order to meet European airline requirements of the 1980s". Officials of the various companies have stressed that discussions are at a very early stage, and no decisions have been taken on the actual type or size of the aircraft that will feature in the programme. Other European companies may eventually be brought into the group, and co-operation will be extended, as far as possible, to all European airlines.

This could prove a most significant step. The six companies involved initially have immense experience and competence, with current products that include the A-300 Airbus and Concorde. Statistics quoted in this edition indicate the success already achieved with other new European co-production aircraft like the Jaguar and Gazelle helicopter, and this is paralleled by some more-individual products.

Indeed, the second half of the 1970s promises to bring increasing prosperity to Europe's aerospace industry after several difficult years. Dassault of France is still very much in the running for important contracts to supply next-generation fighters to the Netherlands, Belgium, Denmark and Norway, although the Anglo-French Jaguar must be regarded as a strong "outsider", and the US is offering highly attractive offset contracts should these NATO nations settle for the winner of its F-16/F-17 evaluation. Both the Franco-German Alpha Jet and the British Hawker Siddeley Hawk seem assured of long production runs as dual-purpose attack/trainers, and the latter could well prove as universally popular as its illustrious predecessor, the Hunter.

Britten-Norman has passed the 650 mark with sales of its Islander family, which thus rates as the most-produced British commercial transport design of all time. Manufacture is becoming as worldwide as sales, now that assembly lines in Belgium and Romania are to be joined by a licence production line in the Philippines, where the Islander has been selected as the aeroplane on which that nation will found its aircraft industry.

In the same local-service field, Shorts continue to find customers for their utilitarian Skyvan, which has exceeded 100 sales, and had announced first orders worth nearly £3 million for their new 30-seat SD3-30 within three weeks of the prototype's first flight. As with Ireland, so too with Scotland, where the Scottish Aviation Bulldog trainer, having been selected as standard equipment for seven air forces including the RAF, is now to seek a new lease of life with retractable landing gear.

Several other nations outside the "big four" continue to produce high-quality specialised aircraft that find a ready market.

Czechoslovakia has repeated its earlier success with the L-29 Delfin by having the L-39 adopted as the standard jet trainer of all Warsaw Pact countries except Poland. This Soviet policy of encouraging its political partners to undertake responsibility for certain categories of aircraft is of benefit also to the Polish industry, which continues as sole source for the Russian-designed Mi-2 helicopter and now has prospect of very large contracts for the unique turbofan-powered M-15 agricultural aircraft, as a successor to the An-2.

Another country whose thriving modern industry owed much initially to Soviet influence is China. Its entry in *Jane's* grows only slowly in length but more rapidly in authenticity as China's contacts with the Western World become more firm and trusting. This is pleasing, because the quality of Chinese manufacture is exceptionally high, as Pakistan learned from its F-6 fighters. It will be interesting to have, eventually, further information on the new F-9 fighter and the helicopters which owe more to indigenous design and development.

The basic lesson taught by a close study of *Jane's* is that every industrial nation needs a highly-competent aircraft industry of its own if it is to be assured of meeting its precise needs. On a small scale, the Philippines will obtain the light utility transport required to improve communications between 7,000 islands by building the Islander and helping to evolve an amphibian version of it. In the military field, where else in the world could Japan have acquired a superb modern anti-submarine flying-boat like the Shin Meiwa PS-1, and where could Sweden have shopped for a fighter like the Viggen, so precisely tailored to its highly-individual defence philosophy?

The overall excellence of the Viggen is, in fact, having an influence on design thought in other countries. For proof one need only note the growing number of tandem-deltas under evaluation in the United States, and the new Soviet strategic bomber mentioned earlier.

* * * * * *

It is natural to concentrate most attention on the "Aircraft" section in the Foreword to *Jane's*, but the other parts of this 1974-75 edition are no less comprehensive, up-to-date and full of interest. The "RPVs", in particular, can be expected to grow in terms of both number of pages and importance, particularly now that a new generation of mini-RPVs is under development for the US Services. Security classification forbids the publication of many of the most fascinating facts and figures at the present time; but this promises to become one of the most eagerly-studied sections of *Jane's* in future years.

In the "Engines" section, the Rolls-Royce pages are of special interest. Four years ago, it seemed that Pratt & Whitney and General Electric were to be relieved of major European competition. As recently as the early months of 1974, a member of one of these companies was reported as saying that Rolls-Royce was "finished" and no longer to be regarded as a major developer/producer of aircraft power plants. Yet now the uprated RB.211 seems assured of the long-overdue government support it needs to become the engine for the long-range TriStar. It may also power the next batch of Boeing 747s for British Airways, and other operators, if Boeing can be convinced that the project is assured of continued UK government support.

Frequent references to "hush kits" and improved combustion systems emphasise the immense achievements of aero-engine manufacturers in reducing noise and smoke emission. The new generation of commercial power plants is cleaner and quieter than anyone would have believed possible a few years ago. This is a mixed blessing to the airlines, which—at a time of economic pressure—will be compelled to replace their older jet transports with quieter new types if they wish to continue operating into airports where stringent noise limitations apply. It means, of course, that the aircraft industry can expect orders for newer aircraft before the older types would normally have been retired or passed on to operators in less pollution-conscious parts of the world. This offers hope for good-neighbourly transports like the DH Canada Dash 7 and Dassault Mercure in a period when they might otherwise have failed to find customers, however attractive their potential.

As a change from recent years, the "Spaceflight" section seems to present no dramatic story this time. After pictures of men walking and driving on the Moon, this is understandable; but how blasé can one get? Here are satellites which often provide advance warning of hurricanes, and so prevent disasters like that which killed thousands of people in Honduras in September 1974. Here, too, is the spacecraft that journeyed to Venus and Mercury earlier this year. Is its achievement lessened because the products of scientific research fail to confirm the fantasies of science fiction?

We are on a technology plateau in the mid-1970s. The world air speed record, set by a near relative of the SR-71A, has remained unchallenged for a decade. No aeroplane flies any longer as fast or high as the X-15A flew in 1963-67. No men journey to the Moon. Nobody is building aircraft larger than the Boeing 747, and there seems little worldwide interest in carrying airline passengers at supersonic speed. The V/STOL Harrier, once portrayed as the brilliant pace-setter for a whole new breed of combat aircraft, is already valued so lightly in its homeland that the concept has been handed to America to develop—as it undoubtedly will.

This represents a sick, tired attitude in a world where too many manufacturers are now devoted to making money rather than aeroplanes. It will be a tragedy if such an attitude slows the pace of development, beyond the aircraft of today, towards the cleaner, quieter Mach 6 transports, the far higher safety standards, and all the adventure and improved living standards that aviation and spaceflight offer us before the end of our century. Do we really want to exchange the dreams and achievements of the Wright brothers, A. V. Roe, Konstantin Tsiolkowsky, Igor Sikorsky, Charles Lindbergh, Frank Whittle, "Chuck" Yeager, Wernher von Braun, Neil Armstrong and thousands of other aerospace pioneers for the transient satisfaction of a Midas touch?

ACKNOWLEDGEMENTS

So many people have contributed to this edition of *Jane's All the World's Aircraft* that to thank them all individually would be a task as formidable as compiling an aerospace "Who's Who". Correspondence arrives from many companies over the signatures of Presidents, Managing Directors and Chief Designers, who add to a wealth of facts, figures and photographs the kind of comments and suggestions that make all the effort of compiling *Jane's* seem so very worthwhile. This year, a letter from Piper, a company that has had to overcome immense difficulties during the past two years, stated that one of its senior engineers had spent many dozens of manhours checking, updating and supplementing its entries to the high standard of accuracy at which it knew we aimed. To that unnamed engineer, as representative of so many others throughout the world, known and unknown to us personally, the editorial team sends its sincere thanks.

This team is unchanged from previous years, although individual responsibilities have been switched slightly to speed production of the first 200 pages of the book, as listed on the Contents page. No editor could ask for more concentrated effort, or higher standards of compilation than Assistant Editor Kenneth Munson, David Mondey, Bill Gunston, Michael Taylor, Maurice Allward and Lord Ventry achieve in their individual sections of the work. Nor could anyone wish for better three-view drawings than those produced by Dennis Punnett of Pilot Press, Roy Grainge, Michael Badrocke and Tony Mitchell.

Jane's has a new American publisher this year—an important happening for a book that has borne the imprint of only one UK publisher, been produced by a single UK printer, and been compiled by only four Editors in its 65 years. We look forward to building up a partnership with Franklin Watts of New York as happy and mutually profitable as that we have enjoyed since 1971 with our good friends of *Air Force Magazine* (Washington), which continues to publish regular *Jane's Supplements* and features.

Once again, a complete and carefully set-out revision of the Romanian sections of the book was supplied by General Ing Stefan Ispas, Head of the Romanian Aircraft Industry, and Viorel Popescu of the Romanian Embassy Commercial Office in London. Considerable help with other sections came from Alex Reinhard (Argentina), Pierre Sparaco (Belgium), Ronaldo Olive (Brazil), Vico Rosaspina (Italy), Eiichiro Sekigawa (Japan), Dr Ulrich Haller (Switzerland), Wolfgang Wagner of *Deutscher Aerokurier* (Germany), Andrzej Glass and Andrzej Korczak of the *Biuletyn Informacyjny Instytutu Lotnictwa* (Poland), William Green and Gordon Swanborough of *Air International* (UK), Alan Hall of *Aviation News* (UK), the editorial staffs of *Flight International* (UK), *Aviation Magazine International* and *Air et Cosmos* (France), *Repules* (Hungary), *Letectvi + Kosmonautika* (Czechoslovakia) and *AiReview* (Japan), the staff of *Tass* and Aviaexport in Moscow, and Théo Pirard of Belgium, whose immaculate notes added much to the spaceflight sections of countries like India, Italy and Spain. No less, our thanks go to Howard Levy, Jean Seele, Peter M. Bowers, Gordon S. Williams, Norman Taylor, Robert Lawson, and the other photographers whose superb prints supplement those obtained from industry and official sources, and to Norman Polmar who has worked so effectively as our correspondent in Washington.

Almost every individual entry has been updated with the assistance of company engineers and publicity staff, many of whom are valued as personal friends after so many years of productive collaboration. To them all, and to the members of government departments, news and photo agencies who provided help, we express grateful thanks.

One familiar name is missing from the list this year, for Janusz Babiejczuk of Poland, who did so much to raise the standard of his country's entries, was killed in a motor accident. His ever-willing help over so many years will not be forgotten.

October 1974 JWRT

PHOTOGRAPHS

The Editor and Publishers receive many requests for prints of photographs that appear in *Jane's*. It is not possible for them to offer any form of photographic service; but photographs of a high proportion of the aircraft described in this edition, as well as of many earlier types, are available at normal trade rates from:

Air Portraits, 40 Chadcote Way, Catshill, Bromsgrove, Worcestershire

Flight International, Dorset House, Stamford Street, London SE1 9LU

Stephen Peltz, 9 Cambridge Square, London W.2

Three-view drawings are available to the press from:

Pilot Press Ltd, PO Box 16, Bromley, Kent BR2 7RB

Roy J. Grainge, 12 Bonaly Gardens, Colinton, Edinburgh EH13 0EX

JANE'S ALL THE WORLD'S AIRCRAFT 1974-75

The Editor has been assisted in the compilation of this edition as follows:

Kenneth Munson	AIRCRAFT SECTION, THE ARGENTINE TO FINLAND, GREECE TO TURKEY, THE UNITED KINGDOM (217-241); RPVS; SAILPLANES.
David Mondey	AIRCRAFT SECTION, GERMANY, THE UNITED KINGDOM (194-216), UNITED STATES OF AMERICA; INDEX
W. T. Gunston	AERO-ENGINES
Michael Taylor	METRIC CONVERSIONS
Maurice Allward	SATELLITE DATA
The Lord Ventry	AIRSHIPS

CONTENTS

SOME FIRST FLIGHTS MADE DURING THE PERIOD 1 JULY 1973 — 31 AUGUST 1974

July 1973
6 Westland/Aérospatiale Lynx, first French Navy prototype (XX904) (UK/France)
7 Mylius MY 102 Tornado (D-EMYS) (Germany)
7 McDonnell Douglas TF-15A Eagle (USA)
14 GEP TCV-03 Trucavaysse sailplane (F-CRRH) (France)
14 LAS/McDonnell Douglas A-4S Skyhawk (USA)
17 Fuji-Bell UH-1H (Japan/USA)
18 Aérospatiale Caravelle III testbed with M53 engine in starboard nacelle (France)
19 Dassault Mercure, first production (F-WTTA) (France)
21 Wotring Gyro-Falcon 201 (USA)
21 Yorkshire Sailplanes YS 53 Sovereign sailplane (UK)
25 Beets G/B Special (N711GB) (USA)
26 Sikorsky XH-59A (S-69) (USA)
28 Boeing YQM-94A B-Gull (Compass Cope B), first prototype (USA)

August 1973
1 Martin Marietta X-24B (66-13551), unpowered flight (USA)
5 Trident TR-1 Trigull-320 (CF-TRI-X) (Canada)
7 SZD-38 Jantar-1 sailplane (SP-2659) (Poland)
21 Aerosport Scamp (N8490) (USA)
22 Gates Learjet 35, first genuine prototype (USA)

September 1973
1 Kiceniuk Icarus V hang-glider (USA)
2 Coates S.A.II Swalesong (G-AYDV) (UK)
5 Neiva Lanceiro, first production (PP-ZCL) (Brazil)
6 Garrison OM-1 Melmoth (N2MU) (USA)
10 Berca JB-1 Nahuel sailplane (Argentina)
11 Neukom Super-Elfe AN-66C sailplane (Switzerland)
12 Westland Commando Mk 1 (G-17-1) (UK)
12 Grumman F-14B Tomcat (USA)
13 Kortenbach & Rauh Kora 1 sailplane (Germany)
14 Glasflügel 205 Club Libelle sailplane (D-9229) (Germany)
21 Beechcraft YT-34C Turbo Mentor (140784) (USA)
25 MBB BO 106 (D-HDCI) (Germany)
27 Fokker-VFW F.28 Fellowship Mk 6000 (PH-JHG) (Netherlands)

October 1973
3 SZD-41 Jantar Standard sailplane (SP-2685) (Poland)
8 RFB/Grumman American Fanliner (D-EJFL) (Germany)
10 PIK-20 sailplane (OH-425) (Finland)
15 SLCA-11 Topaze sailplane (France)
16 Maule M-5-210C Lunar Rocket (USA)
21 Militky MB-E1 (OE-9023) (Germany)
22 Piper PA-31T Cheyenne, first production (USA)
26 Dassault-Breguet/Dornier Alpha Jet, first prototype (International)
26 Bellanca Trainer (N9089E) (USA)
30 Nihon University NM-73 New Egret (Japan)

November 1973
9 Aérospatiale SN 601 Corvette 100, third production (F-WUQN) (France)
15 JEAA (Ito) Kirigamine K-14 sailplane (Japan)
15 Martin Marietta X-24B (66-13551), first powered flight (USA)
20 Airbus A-300, fourth (second B2) development aircraft (F-WUAA) (International)
23 AIDC XT-CH-1A (Taiwan)

December 1973
6 Aérospatiale/BAC Concorde Series 200, first production (F-WTSB) (International)
10 Saab SH 37 Viggen (Sweden)

January 1974
9 Dassault-Breguet/Dornier Alpha Jet, second prototype (D-9594) (International)
9 WSK-Mielec M-15 (SP-1974) (Poland)
20 General Dynamics YF-16, first prototype, unscheduled flight (72-01567) (USA)

February 1974
2 General Dynamics YF-16, first prototype, official first flight (72-01567) (USA)
13 Aérospatiale/BAC Concorde Series 200, second production (G-BBDG) (International)
21 HTM Skyrider (D-HHTF) (Germany)

March 1974
1 Sikorsky YCH-53E (71-59121) (USA)
4 Wilden Vo Wi 8 (D-EOWI) (Germany)
6 Robin HR 100/235 (F-WVKA) (France)
12 Fournier RF-6B (F-WPXV) (France)
13 Bell Model 214A (USA)
20 Sikorsky S-67 Blackhawk with ducted tail rotor (USA)
22 Grumman A-6E Intruder, TRAM testbed (155673) (USA)

April 1974
15 Airbus A-300, first (B2) production (F-BVGA) (International)

May 1974
6 Dassault-Breguet/Dornier Alpha Jet, third prototype (first in close-support configuration) (International)
9 General Dynamics YF-16, second prototype (72-01568) (USA)
10 Glaser-Dirks DG-100 sailplane (D-7100) (Germany)
31 AJEP (Wittman) Tailwind, second (production) prototype (G-BCBR) (UK/USA)

June 1974
6 Boeing E-4A, third aircraft (F103-GE-100 engines) (USA)
9 Northrop YF-17, first prototype (72-01569) (USA)
14 BAC One-Eleven development aircraft (G-ASYD) with Spey engine "hush kit" (UK)
14 Jacquet et Pottier J.P.15-36 Aiglon sailplane (F-WCAP) (France)
26 Aérospatiale SA 350 (France)
30 Westland Sea King Mk 50, first production (N16-098) (UK)

July 1974
2 CERVA CE 75 Silene sailplane (France)
6 Boeing E-4B (fourth E-4, first E-4B) (USA)
10 AiResearch/Lockheed 731 JetStar (TFE 731 conversion) (N731JS) (USA)

August 1974
13 Sperry (Convair/General Dynamics) PQM-102A RPV (USA)
14 Panavia MRCA (D-9591) (International)
17 Teledyne Ryan YQM-98A R-Tern (Compass Cope R) RPV (72-01872) (USA)
21 Hawker Siddeley Hawk (XX154) (UK)
21 Northrop YF-17, second prototype (72-01570) (USA)
22 Shorts SD3-30 (G-BSBH) (UK)

OFFICIAL RECORDS

Corrected to September 1974

ABSOLUTE WORLD RECORDS

Seven records are classed as Absolute World Records by the Fédération Aéronautique Internationale, as follows:

Distance in a straight line (USA)
Major Clyde P. Evely, USAF, in a Boeing B-52H Stratofortress, on 10-11 January 1962, from Okinawa to Madrid, Spain. 12,532·3 miles (20,168·78 km).

Distance in a closed circuit (USA)
Captain William M. Stevenson, USAF, in a Boeing B-52H Stratofortress, on 6-7 June 1962. Seymour Johnson AFB-Bermuda-Sondrestrom (Greenland)-Anchorage (Alaska)-March AFB-Key West-Seymour Johnson AFB. 11,337 miles (18,245·05 km).

Height (USSR)
Alexander Fedotov in an E-266 (MiG-25) on 25 July 1973. 118,898 ft (36,240 m).

Height in sustained horizontal flight (USA)
Col Robert L. Stephens and Lt Col Daniel Andre (USAF) in a Lockheed YF-12A, on 1 May 1965, over a 15/25 km course at Edwards AFB, California. 80,257·91 ft (24,462·596 m).

Height, after launch from a "mother-plane" (USA)
Major R. White, USAF, in the North American X-15A-3, on 17 July 1962, at Edwards AFB, California. 314,750 ft (95,935·99 m).

Speed in a straight line (USA)
Col Robert L. Stephens and Lt Col Daniel Andre (USAF) in a Lockheed YF-12A, on 1 May 1965, over a 15/25 km course at Edwards AFB, California. 2,070·102 mph (3,331·507 km/h).

Speed in a closed circuit (USSR)
M. Komarov in a Mikoyan E-266 (MiG-25), on 5 October 1967, at Podmoskovnœ, over a 500 km (310·7 mile) closed circuit. 1,852·61 mph (2,981·5 km/h).

WORLD RECORDS—MANNED SPACECRAFT

Greatest weight lifted to altitude (USA)
F. Borman, J. A. Lovell and W. Anders in Apollo 8, on 21-27 December 1968. 282,147 lb (127,980 kg).

Altitude (USA)
F. Borman, J. A. Lovell and W. Anders in Apollo 8, on 21-27 December 1968. 234,673 miles (377,668·9 km).

Endurance in Earth orbit (USA)
Alan L. Bean, Jack R. Lousma and Owen K. Garriott in the Skylab 3 spacecraft, from 28 July to 25 September 1973. 59 days, 11 hr 9 min 4 sec.

Awaiting confirmation is a new record of 84 days set up by Gerald Carr, Edward Gibson and William Pogue in Skylab 4, from 16 November 1973 to 9 February 1974.

Distance in Earth orbit (USA)
Alan L. Bean, Jack R. Lousma and Owen K. Garriott in Skylab 3, from 28 July to 25 September 1973. 24,425,849 miles (39,309,606 km).

Awaiting confirmation is the new record set up by Gerald Carr, Edward Gibson and William Pogue during the 84-day Skylab 4 mission.

INTERNATIONAL RECORDS

Following are details of some of the more important international records confirmed by the FAI:

CLASS C, GROUP I (Aeroplanes with piston engines)

Distance in a straight line (USA)
Cdr Thomas D. Davies, USN, and crew of three in a Lockheed P2V-1 Neptune, on 29 September-1 October 1946, from Perth, Western Australia, to Columbus, Ohio, USA. 11,235·6 miles (18,081·99 km).

Distance in a closed circuit (USA)
James R. Bede in the Bede BD-2, on 7-10 November 1969, between Columbus, Ohio, and Toledo, Ohio, USA. 8,973·3 miles (14,441·26 km).

Height (Italy)
Mario Pezzi, in a Caproni 161*bis*, on 22 October 1938. 56,046 ft (17,083 m).

Speed in a straight line (USA)
Darryl Greenamyer in a modified Grumman F8F-2 Bearcat, on 16 August 1969, at Edwards AFB, California. 482·462 mph (776·449 km/h).

CLASS C, GROUP III (Aeroplanes with jet engines)

Distance in a straight line, distance in a closed circuit, height, speed in straight line and speed in 500 km closed circuit
See "Absolute World Records" above.

Speed in a 100 km (62·14 mile) closed circuit (USSR)
Alexander Fedotov in a Mikoyan E-266 (MiG-25), on 8 April 1973. 1,618.734 mph (2,605·1 km/h).

Speed in a 1,000 km (621·4 mile) closed circuit (USSR)
P. Ostapenko in a Mikoyan E-266 (MiG-25), on 27 October 1967, at Podmoskovnœ. 1,814·81 mph (2,920·67 km/h).

CLASS C.2, ALL GROUPS (Seaplanes)

Distance in a straight line (UK)
Capt D. C. T. Bennett and First Officer I. Harvey, in the Short-Mayo Mercury, on 6-8 October 1938, from Dundee, Scotland, to the Orange River, South Africa. 5,997·5 miles (9,652 km).

Height (USSR)
Georgi Buryanov and crew of two in a Beriev M-10, on 9 September 1961, over the Sea of Azov. 49,088 ft (14,962 m).

Speed in a straight line (USSR)
Nikolai Andrievsky and crew of two in a Beriev M-10, on 7 August 1961, at Joukovski-Petrovskœ, over a 15/25 km course. 566·69 mph (912 km/h).

CLASS D, GROUP I (Single-seat sailplanes)

Distance in a straight line (Federal Germany)
Hans W. Grosse in a Schleicher AS-W12, on 25 April 1972. 907·70 miles (1,460·8 km).

Height (USA)
Paul F. Bickle, in a Schweizer SGS 1-23E, on 25 February 1961, at Mojave-Lancaster, California. 46,266 ft (14,102 m).

CLASS D, GROUP II (Two-seat sailplanes)

Distance in straight line (USSR)
J. Kuznetsov and J. Barkhamov in a Blanik, on 3 June 1967. 572·87 miles (921·954 km).

Height (USA)
L. E. Edgar and H. E. Klieforth in a Pratt-Read sailplane, on 19 March 1952, at Bishop, California. 44,256 ft (13,489 m).

CLASS E.1 (Helicopters)

Distance in a straight line (USA)
R. G. Ferry in a Hughes OH-6A, on 6-7 April 1966, 2,213 miles (3,561·55 km).

Height (France)
Jean Boulet in an Aérospatiale SA 315B Lama on 21 June 1972. 40,820 ft (12,442 m).

Speed in a straight line (USA)
Kurt Cannon in a Sikorsky S-67 Blackhawk, on 19 December 1970, over a 15/25 km course. 220·885 mph (355·485 km/h).

Speed in a 100 km closed circuit (USSR)
Boris Galitsky and crew of five in a Mil Mi-6, on 26 August 1964, at Podmoskovnœ. 211·36 mph (340·15 km/h).

CLASS E.2 (Convertiplanes)

Speed in a straight line (USSR)
D. Efremov and crew of five, in the Kamov Ka-22 Vintokryl, on 7 October 1961, at Joukovski-Petrovskœ, over a 15/25 km course. 221·4 mph (356·3 km/h).

Height (USSR)
D. Efremov and crew of two, in the Kamov Ka-22 Vintokryl, on 24 November 1961 at Bykovo. 8,491 ft (2,588 m).

Speed in a 100 km closed circuit (New Zealand)
Sqd Ldr W. R. Gellatly and J. G. P. Morton, in the Fairey Rotodyne, on 5 January 1959, White Waltham-Wickham-Radley Bottom-Kintbury-White Waltham. 190·90 mph (307·22 km/h).

THE ARGENTINE REPUBLIC

AERO BOERO
AERO TALLERES BOERO SRL

Head Office:
Boulevard H. Irigoyen 505, Morteros, Córdoba
Telephone: Morteros 409

Directors:
Cesar E. Boero
Hector A. Boero

This company is producing and developing the Aero Boero 115 BS, 180 and 210/260 series of light monoplanes, and is developing the AG.260 agricultural aircraft.

AERO BOERO 115 BS

The earlier Aero Boero 95 (1969-70 *Jane's*) and Aero Boero 95/115 (1972-73 *Jane's*) are no longer in production, manufacture of the latter version having ended in January 1973. The current production version, first flown in February 1973, is known as the Aero Boero 115 BS. This has a sweptback fin and rudder, increased wing span and greater fuel capacity than the AB 95/115, to which it is otherwise generally similar.

The description which follows applies to the AB 115 BS, of which 20 are under construction initially:

Type: Three-seat light aircraft.

Wings: Braced high-wing monoplane. Wing section NACA 23012. Dihedral 1° 45'. Incidence 3° at root, 1° at tip. Light alloy structure, Ceconite-covered. Streamline-section Vee bracing strut each side. Aluminium alloy ailerons and flaps.

Fuselage: SAE 4130 steel-tube structure, Ceconite-covered.

Tail Unit: Wire-braced welded steel-tube structure, Ceconite-covered. Sweptback vertical surfaces.

Landing Gear: Non-retractable tailwheel type. Shock-absorption by helicoidal springs inside fuselage. Main-wheel tyre size 6·00-6, pressure 24 lb/sq in (1·69 kg/cm^2). Hydraulic disc brakes. Fully-castoring steerable tailwheel.

Power Plant: One 115 hp Lycoming O-235-C2A four-cylinder horizontally-opposed aircooled engine, driving either a McCauley 1C90-7345 or a Sensenich 72CK-050 fixed-pitch propeller. Two wing fuel tanks, total capacity 28·5 Imp gallons (130 litres).

Accommodation: Normal accommodation for pilot and two passengers in enclosed cabin. Baggage compartment on port side, aft of cabin. Ambulance version can accommodate one stretcher in place of the two passengers.

Electronics and Equipment: One 40A alternator and one 12V battery. VHF radio standard. Provision for dual controls, and night or blind-flying equipment, at customer's option.

Dimensions, external:
Wing span 35 ft 2 in (10·72 m)
Wing chord (constant) 5 ft 3½ in (1·61 m)
Wing aspect ratio 7·05
Length overall 23 ft 10¼ in (7·273 m)
Height overall 6 ft 10½ in (2·10 m)
Wheel track 6 ft 8¾ in (2·05 m)
Wheelbase 16 ft 8¾ in (5·10 m)

Dimensions, internal:
Cabin: Length 6 ft 3 in (1·90 m)
Max width 2 ft 9 in (0·84 m)
Max height 3 ft 11¼ in (1·20 m)

Areas:
As for Aero Boero 180 RV and RVR

Weights and Loadings:
Weight empty, equipped 1,168 lb (530 kg)
Max T-O weight 1,697 lb (770 kg)
Max wing loading 9·65 lb/sq ft (47·1 kg/m^2)
Max power loading 14·77 lb/hp (6·7 kg/hp)

Performance (at max T-O weight, except where indicated):
Max level speed at S/L 113 knots (130 mph; 210 km/h)
Max cruising speed at S/L 102 knots (117 mph; 188 km/h)
Stalling speed, flaps down 39 knots (45 mph; 72 km/h)
Max rate of climb at S/L 1,000 ft (300 m)/min
T-O run, full load 380 ft (115 m)
T-O to 50 ft (15 m), two persons 607 ft (185 m)
Landing from 50 ft (15 m) 500 ft (150 m)
Landing run, heavy braking 150 ft (45 m)
Range with max fuel 429 nm (495 miles; 800 km)

AERO BOERO 180 RV and RVR

The original three-seat Aero Boero 180 (1972-73 *Jane's*) was designed as a light, all-purpose aircraft; the first production example was delivered in December 1969.

Production of this version was followed by that of the Aero Boero 180 RV (standard version) and 180 RVR (glider-towing version), the first of which flew for the first time in October 1972. These current versions have extended-span wings, similar to those of the AB 115 BS, increased fuel capacity, a recontoured fuselage and sweptback vertical tail surfaces.

The description which follows applies to the AB 180 RV and 180 RVR. Seven 180 RVRs had been built and five more ordered by February 1974.

Type: Three-seat light aircraft.

Wings: Strut-braced high-wing monoplane. Streamline-section Vee bracing strut each side. Wing section NACA 23012. Dihedral 1° 45'. Incidence 3° at root, 1° at tip. Light alloy structure, covered with Ceconite. Ailerons and flaps of aluminium alloy construction.

Fuselage: Welded steel-tube structure (SAE 4130), covered with Ceconite.

Tail Unit: Wire-braced welded steel-tube structure, covered with Ceconite. Sweptback vertical surfaces. Ground-adjustable tab on rudder.

Landing Gear: Non-retractable tailwheel type, with shock-absorption by helicoidal springs inside fuselage. Main wheels and tyres size 6·00-6, pressure 24 lb/sq in (1·69 kg/cm^2). Hydraulic disc brakes. Tailwheel steerable and fully castoring.

Power Plant: One 180 hp Lycoming O-360-A1A four-cylinder horizontally-opposed aircooled engine, driving (according to customer's choice) either a Hartzell constant-speed or McCauley 1A200 or Sensenich 762 fixed-pitch propeller. Two wing fuel tanks, total capacity 35 Imp gallons (160 litres).

Accommodation: Normal accommodation for pilot and two passengers in enclosed cabin. Baggage compartment on port side, aft of cabin. Transparent roof panel in 180 RVR.

Electronics and Equipment: One 40A alternator and one 12V battery. VHF radio standard. Provision for night or blind-flying instrumentation at customer's option. Towing hook in 180 RVR.

Dimensions, external:
Wing span 35 ft 2 in (10·72 m)
Wing chord (constant) 5 ft 3½ in (1·61 m)
Wing aspect ratio 7·05
Length overall 23 ft 10¼ in (7·273 m)
Height overall 6 ft 10½ in (2·10 m)
Wheel track 6 ft 8¾ in (2·05 m)
Wheelbase 16 ft 8¾ in (5·10 m)

Areas:
Wings, gross 177·3 sq ft (16·47 m^2)
Ailerons (total) 19·81 sq ft (1·84 m^2)
Flaps (total) 20·9 sq ft (1·94 m^2)
Fin 10·01 sq ft (0·93 m^2)
Rudder 4·41 sq ft (0·41 m^2)
Tailplane 15·07 sq ft (1·40 m^2)
Elevators 10·44 sq ft (0·97 m^2)

Weights and Loadings:
Weight empty, equipped 1,212 lb (550 kg)
Max T-O weight 1,860 lb (844 kg)
Max wing loading 10·7 lb/sq ft (52·0 kg/m^2)
Max power loading 10·36 lb/hp (4·7 kg/hp)

Performance (at max T-O weight, except where indicated):
Max never-exceed speed 134 knots (155 mph; 249 km/h)
Max level speed at S/L:
RV 132 knots (152 mph; 245 km/h)
RVR 122 knots (140 mph; 225 km/h)
Max cruising speed at S/L 114 knots (131 mph; 211 km/h)
Stalling speed, flaps down 41·5 knots (48 mph; 77 km/h)
Max rate of climb at S/L 1,180 ft (360 m)/min

Aero Boero 115 BS three-seat light aircraft (115 hp Lycoming O-235 engine)

Aero Boero 180 RV three-seat light aircraft (180 hp Lycoming O-360-A1A engine)

Aero Boero 180 Condor light aircraft, with ventral pack for air-droppable cargo

Time to 1,970 ft (600 m), 75% power, with Blanik two-seat sailplane 3 min 10 sec
Service ceiling 22,000 ft (6,700 m)
T-O run 330 ft (100 m)
T-O to 50 ft (15 m), two persons 615 ft (188 m)
Landing from 50 ft (15 m) 525 ft (160 m)
Landing run 195 ft (60 m)
Range with max fuel 429 nm (495 miles; 800 km)

AERO BOERO 180 CONDOR

This version of the AB 180 was evolved for high-altitude flying in the area of the Andes. It differs from the standard AB 180 in having accommodation for a pilot and one passenger only (with baggage space aft of the rear seat), modified wingtips and an optional turbocharger for the Lycoming O-360-A1A engine. Instead of a passenger, 220 lb (100 kg) of air-droppable cargo can be carried in an under-fuselage pack.

By February 1973 four Condors had been completed. None were in production in mid-1974.

WEIGHT:
Max T-O weight 1,860 lb (844 kg)

PERFORMANCE (at max T-O weight):
Max level speed 117 knots (135 mph; 217 km/h)
Max cruising speed at S/L 109 knots (125 mph; 201 km/h)
Max speed with cargo pack door open 78 knots (90 mph; 145 km/h)

AERO BOERO 210 and 260

Design of the Aero Boero 210 four-seat light aircraft was begun in 1968, and a prototype was flown for the first time on 22 April 1971. A static test airframe has also been completed.

The same prototype, re-engined with a 260 hp Lycoming O-540 engine, is now known as the Aero Boero 260. Present plans cover the testing of only this one flying prototype and one static test airframe.

The following description applies to the aircraft in its original form as the Aero Boero 210:

TYPE: Four-seat light aircraft.

WINGS: Strut-braced high-wing monoplane of mixed metal and wood construction, covered with Ceconite. Wing section NACA 23012. Dihedral 1° 45′. Incidence 2° 30′. Electrically-operated all-metal flaps and metal ailerons.

FUSELAGE: Conventional semi-monocoque structure of welded steel tube (SAE 4130), with Ceconite covering.

TAIL UNIT: Conventional single sweptback fin and rudder of welded steel tube construction, Ceconite covered. Fixed-incidence strut- and wire-braced tailplane. Trim tab in elevator.

LANDING GEAR: Non-retractable tricycle type, with coil spring shock-absorbers. Main-wheel tyre pressure 28 lb/sq in (1·97 kg/cm²). Hydraulic disc brakes on main wheels. Steerable nosewheel. Streamline fairings over all three wheels.

POWER PLANT: One 210 hp Continental IO-360 six-cylinder horizontally-opposed aircooled fuel-injection engine, driving a two-blade constant-speed propeller. Fuel in two wing tanks with total capacity of 35·2 Imp gallons (160 litres). Refuelling point on top of each wing.

ACCOMMODATION: Seats for pilot and three passengers in enclosed cabin, access to which is provided by a forward-hinged door on each side. All three passenger seats are removable.

SYSTEMS: One 25A generator and one 12V battery.

ELECTRONICS AND EQUIPMENT: Radio optional.

DIMENSIONS, EXTERNAL:
Wing span 35 ft 2 in (10·72 m)
Wing chord (constant) 5 ft 3½ in (1·61 m)
Wing aspect ratio 6·62
Length overall 24 ft 3¼ in (7·40 m)
Height overall 8 ft 10¼ in (2·70 m)
Tailplane span 10 ft 0 in (3·04 m)
Wheel track 7 ft 2⅝ in (2·20 m)
Wheelbase 6 ft 1¾ in (1·875 m)
Passenger doors (each):
Height 3 ft 0 in (0·91 m)
Width 2 ft 7 in (0·79 m)
Baggage door (port, aft):
Height 1 ft 8 in (0·51 m)
Width 1 ft 8 in (0·51 m)

DIMENSIONS, INTERNAL:
Cabin:
Max length 5 ft 8 in (1·73 m)
Max width 3 ft 1 in (0·94 m)
Max height 3 ft 11 in (1·19 m)
Floor area 12 sq ft (1·11 m²)
Volume 52 cu ft (1·50 m³)

AREAS:
Wings, gross 176·5 sq ft (16·40 m²)
Ailerons (total) 16·47 sq ft (1·53 m²)
Trailing-edge flaps (total) 19·37 sq ft (1·80 m²)

WEIGHTS AND LOADINGS:
Weight empty, equipped 1,477 lb (670 kg)
Max T-O weight 2,425 lb (1,100 kg)
Max wing loading 13·75 lb/sq ft (67 kg/m²)
Max power loading 11·57 lb/hp (5·25 kg/hp)

PERFORMANCE (estimated, at max T-O weight):
Max cruising speed at 5,900 ft (1,800 m) 122 knots (140 mph; 225 km/h)
Stalling speed, flaps down 48 knots (55 mph; 89 km/h)
Max rate of climb at S/L 1,180 ft (360 m)/min
Service ceiling 19,675 ft (6,000 m)
T-O run 558 ft (170 m)
T-O to 50 ft (15 m) 820 ft (250 m)
Landing run 427 ft (130 m)
Range with max fuel 429 nm (495 miles; 800 km)

AERO BOERO AG.260

Aero Boero began the design of this single-seat agricultural monoplane in mid-1971, at which time it was known as the AG.235/260. Construction of a prototype began in October 1971, and this aircraft flew for the first time on 23 December 1972. A static test airframe has also been completed.

TYPE: Single-seat agricultural aircraft.

WINGS: Low-wing monoplane. Wing section NACA 23012. Dihedral 5°. Structure, including trailing-edge flaps and ailerons, is of aluminium alloy, Ceconite-covered, with single Vee bracing strut on each side.

FUSELAGE: Welded SAE 4130 steel-tube structure with plastics covering.

TAIL UNIT: Wire-braced welded steel-tube structure with plastics covering.

LANDING GEAR: Non-retractable tailwheel type, with coil-spring shock-absorbers. Hydraulic disc brakes on main wheels.

POWER PLANT: One 260 hp Lycoming O-540 six-cylinder horizontally-opposed aircooled engine, driving a McCauley P235/AFA 8456 two-blade propeller. Two wing fuel tanks, total capacity 35·2 Imp gallons (160 litres).

ACCOMMODATION: Pilot only, in enclosed cabin. Door on starboard side, which can be jettisoned in an emergency. Cabin heated and ventilated by adjustable cool-air vents. Utility compartment on port side, aft of cabin.

ELECTRONICS AND EQUIPMENT: VHF radio standard. Non-corrosive glassfibre tank installed forward of cockpit, with capacity of 110 Imp gallons (500 litres) of liquid or 1,102 lb (500 kg) of dry chemical. Quick-dump valve, to jettison contents of tank in an emergency. Engine-driven pump.

DIMENSIONS, EXTERNAL:
Wing span 35 ft 9 in (10·90 m)
Wing chord (constant over most of span) 5 ft 3½ in (1·61 m)
Wing aspect ratio 6·8
Length overall (tail up) 24 ft 5¼ in (7·45 m)
Height overall (tail up) 6 ft 2¾ in (1·90 m)
Tailplane span 9 ft 11⅝ in (3·04 m)
Propeller diameter 7 ft 0 in (2·13 m)

DIMENSION, INTERNAL:
Hopper volume 17·66 cu ft (0·5 m³)

AREAS:
Wings, gross 177·28 sq ft (16·47 m²)
Ailerons (total) 19·81 sq ft (1·84 m²)
Flaps (total) 20·88 sq ft (1·94 m²)
Fin 10·01 sq ft (0·93 m²)
Rudder 4·41 sq ft (0·41 m²)
Tailplane 15·07 sq ft (1·40 m²)
Elevators 10·44 sq ft (0·97 m²)

WEIGHTS AND LOADINGS:
Weight empty 1,587 lb (720 kg)
Max T-O weight 2,976 lb (1,350 kg)
Max wing loading 15·83 lb/sq ft (77·28 kg/m²)
Max power loading 11·44 lb/hp (5·19 kg/hp)

PERFORMANCE (at max T-O weight):
Max never-exceed speed 117 knots (135 mph; 217 km/h)
Max cruising speed at S/L 109 knots (125 mph; 201 km/h)
Econ cruising speed 95·5 knots (110 mph; 177 km/h)
Stalling speed, flaps down 52·5 knots (60 mph; 97 km/h)
Max rate of climb at S/L 1,345 ft (410 m)/min
Service ceiling 21,000 ft (6,400 m)
T-O to 50 ft (15 m) 656 ft (200 m)
Landing from 50 ft (15 m) 394 ft (120 m)
Range with max fuel 377 nm (435 miles; 700 km)

Aero Boero 210 four-seat light aircraft (210 hp Continental IO-360 engine)

Aero Boero AG.260 agricultural aircraft (260 hp Lycoming O-540 engine)

AL-AIRE

TALLERES AL-AIRE SCA

ADDRESS: Aerodromo San Fernando, Provincia Buenos Aires

Talleres Al-Aire SCA undertakes overhaul and repair work, up to fuselage rebuild standard, on light aircraft.

In addition to this work, its premises are currently in use by some of the members of AVEX (which see), who have under development a new aerobatic training aircraft known as the T-11 Cacique, designed by Ing Alfredo Turbay. All known details of this aircraft follow:

TURBAY T-11 CACIQUE

A group of AVEX members, led by Ing Alfredo Turbay and including Prof Adolfo Yakstas and Sr Norberto S. Cobelo, began the development of this two-seat aerobatic and training aircraft as a potential replacement for the obsolete Piper types used by Argentine flying clubs. It is also suitable for observation and liaison duties.

The design was begun in February 1969 by Ing Turbay, and construction of a prototype began in mid-May of that year.

The following description applies to the prototype (LV-X44), which flew for the first time on 20 August 1970. No further news of this aircraft has been received during the past year.

TYPE: Two-seat training and aerobatic aircraft, stressed for $\pm 6g$.

WINGS: Cantilever high-wing monoplane, of laminar-flow profile. Wing section NACA

63_2A415 at root, NACA 63_1A212 at tip. Incidence 2° at root, 0° 30′ at tip. Dihedral 3° on outer panels. Sweepback 4° at quarter-chord. All-metal Alclad-covered structure of one main spar and one auxiliary spar. Alclad Frise-type ailerons and semi-Fowler flaps on trailing-edge. No tabs.

Fuselage: All-metal semi-monocoque Alclad structure.

Tail Unit: Cantilever two-spar Alclad metal structure, similar to wings. Sweptback fin and rudder. Variable-incidence tailplane. Trim tab in each elevator.

Landing Gear: Non-retractable tricycle type, with glassfibre cantilever one-piece leg for main units. Steerable nose unit, fitted with maintenance-free polyurethane shock-absorber. Nosewheel tyre size 5·00-4, main-wheel tyres each 6·00-6; tyre pressure (all units) 22 lb/sq in (1·55 kg/cm²). Bendix hydraulic brakes.

Power Plant: One 100 hp Continental O-200-A four-cylinder horizontally-opposed aircooled engine, driving a McCauley two-blade fixed-pitch metal propeller. Two 4·4 Imp gallon (20 litre) wing fuel tanks and two 11 Imp gallon (50 litre) wingtip tanks. Total capacity 32 Imp gallons (140 litres). Refuelling point on top of each tip-tank.

Accommodation: Seats for two persons in tandem in fully-enclosed cabin, with access via forward-opening door on starboard side. Cabin heated and ventilated.

Systems: Electrical system includes 12V battery.

Electronics and Equipment: Blind-flying instrumentation standard. Optional VHF radio and ADF.

Dimensions, external:
Wing span over tip-tanks 29 ft 6¼ in (9·00 m)
Wing span without tip-tanks 27 ft 0¼ in (8·24 m)
Wing chord at root 5 ft 1¾ in (1·573 m)
Wing chord at tip 2 ft 9½ in (0·852 m)
Wing aspect ratio 7·5
Length overall 22 ft 1 in (6·73 m)
Length of fuselage 21 ft 8⅝ in (6·62 m)
Height overall 7 ft 8¾ in (2·36 m)
Fuselage: max width over cowling 2 ft 9½ in (0·85 m)
Fuselage: max width aft of cowling 2 ft 6 in (0·76 m)
Tailplane span 8 ft 6¼ in (2·60 m)
Wheel track 5 ft 7¾ in (1·72 m)
Wheelbase 6 ft 4¾ in (1·95 m)
Propeller diameter 5 ft 8⅞ in (1·75 m)
Propeller ground clearance 11¾ in (0·30 m)
Passenger door (stbd):
Height 3 ft 5¼ in (1·05 m)
Width 3 ft 1½ in (0·95 m)

Dimensions, internal:
Cabin: Length 5 ft 11 in (1·80 m)
Max width 2 ft 4¼ in (0·72 m)
Max height 3 ft 9¼ in (1·15 m)

Areas:
Wings, gross 115·2 sq ft (10·70 m²)
Ailerons (total) 10·2 sq ft (0·95 m²)
Trailing-edge flaps (total) 16·1 sq ft (1·50 m²)
Fin 7·32 sq ft (0·68 m²)
Rudder 3·44 sq ft (0·32 m²)
Tailplane 24·5 sq ft (2·28 m²)
Elevators, incl tabs 11·2 sq ft (1·04 m²)

Prototype Turbay T-11 Cacique light aircraft (100 hp Continental O-200-A engine) (*Alex Reinhard*)

Weights and Loadings:
Weight empty 716 lb (325 kg)
Max T-O weight (aerobatic) 1,323 lb (600 kg)
Max wing loading 11·5 lb/sq ft (56 kg/m²)
Max power loading 13·23 lb/hp (6 kg/hp)

Performance (estimated, at max T-O weight):
Max never-exceed speed 194 knots (223·5 mph; 360 km/h)
Max level speed 119 knots (137 mph; 220 km/h)
Max cruising speed 108 knots (124 mph; 200 km/h)
Econ cruising speed 94 knots (108 mph; 174 km/h)
Stalling speed, flaps down 42·6 knots (49 mph; 79 km/h)
Max rate of climb at S/L 833 ft (254 m)/min
Service ceiling 17,390 ft (5,300 m)
Absolute ceiling 20,670 ft (6,300 m)
T-O run at S/L 377 ft (115 m)
T-O to 50 ft (15 m) 938 ft (286 m)
Landing from 50 ft (15 m) 476 ft (145 m)
Landing run 328 ft (100 m)
Range with max fuel 700 nm (807 miles; 1,300 km)
Range with max payload 458 nm (528 miles; 850 km)

AL-AIRE AL-2 TIJERETE

A prototype light aircraft, known as the AL-2 Tijerete (a small swallow-like bird), is under construction by Al-Aire. It is a single-seat mid-wing monoplane, of twin-boom configuration, powered by a 60 hp Franklin engine driving a pusher propeller. Construction is mainly of wood, with a balsa/plywood sandwich skin, except for the wingtip fuel tanks, which are of plastics, and the slender tailbooms, which are of duralumin. A tricycle landing gear is fitted.

Dimensions, external:
Wing span 21 ft 11¾ in (6·70 m)

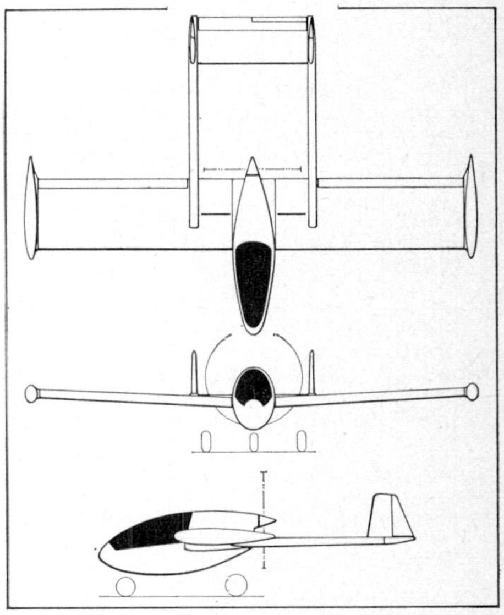

Al-Aire AL-2 Tijerete single-seat light aircraft (*Roy J. Grainge*)

Wing section Wortmann FX-168
Wing aspect ratio 5·6

Areas:
Wings, gross 86·11 sq ft (8·00 m²)
Vertical tail surfaces (total) 10·23 sq ft (0·95 m²)
Horizontal tail surfaces (total) 16·36 sq ft (1·52 m²)

Weight and Loading:
Max T-O weight 661 lb (300 kg)
Max wing loading 7·68 lb/sq ft (37·5 kg/m²)

AVEX

ASOCIACION ARGENTINA DE CONSTRUCTORES DE AVIONES EXPERIMENTALES

Address:
Accasusso 1640, Olivos-FCNGBM, Buenos Aires
Telephone: 797-1629
President: Yves Arrambide
Secretary: Norberto Marino

AVEX is an Argentine light aircraft association for amateur constructors, similar in concept to the Experimental Aircraft Association in the US. It was formed in 1968 and its members include many people well known among the Argentine aircraft industry, including specialists in most aspects of materials and construction, including the use of glassfibre and plastics.

Some of the recent AVEX activities have been described in the 1971-72 and subsequent editions of *Jane's*. Of 33 current aircraft projects by AVEX members, two have already flown and several others are nearing completion. Details of the more important of these follow:

ARRAMBIDE/MARINO ARMAR I GORRION (SPARROW)

The Gorrion single-seat ultra-light aircraft was designed in collaboration by Mr Yves Arrambide and Sr Norberto Marino in 1971. Trial flights were made with a rubber-propelled one-fortieth scale model; construction of a full-scale prototype began on 30 April 1972, and this was scheduled to make its first flight in mid-1974. Two other Gorrions are under construction.

All available details of the Gorrion follow:

Type: Single-seat ultra-light aircraft.

Wings: Parasol-wing monoplane. Centre-section braced by N strut on each side of upper fuselage, and outer panels by Vee struts from bottom of fuselage. Wing section NACA 4412 (constant). Dihedral 3° from roots. Incidence 3°. No sweepback. Two-spar wooden structure, of constant chord except for cut-out in centre of trailing-edge. Leading-edges plywood-covered; remainder fabric-covered. Frise-type fabric-covered wooden ailerons. No tabs.

Fuselage: Conventional wooden box structure. Aluminium cowling panels; remainder plywood-covered except for fabric-covered top-decking.

Tail Unit: Cantilever wooden structure; plywood-covered fin and one-piece tailplane, fabric-covered rudder and elevators. No tabs. Rudder control by cables.

Landing Gear: Non-retractable tailwheel type. Glassfibre legs provide all necessary shock absorption. Main units have scooter wheels and brakes.

Power Plant: One 39 hp Citröen 3 CV motor-car engine, with reduction gear, driving a two-blade fixed-pitch wooden propeller. Single fuel tank in fuselage, capacity 7·5 Imp gallons (35 litres). Refuelling point on top of fuselage aft of firewall. Oil capacity 0·66 Imp gallons (3 litres).

Accommodation: Single seat in open cockpit. Windscreen fitted. Headrest faired into top of fuselage.

Dimensions, external:
Wing span (excl tip fairings) 22 ft 11¾ in (7·00 m)
Wing chord (constant) 4 ft 1¼ in (1·25 m)
Wing aspect ratio 5·6
Length overall 15 ft 5¾ in (4·72 m)
Height overall (tail up) 6 ft 5¼ in (1·96 m)
Tailplane span 7 ft 2⅝ in (2·20 m)
Wheel track 4 ft 7 in (1·40 m)
Propeller diameter 5 ft 3 in (1·60 m)
Propeller ground clearance 10 in (0·25 m)

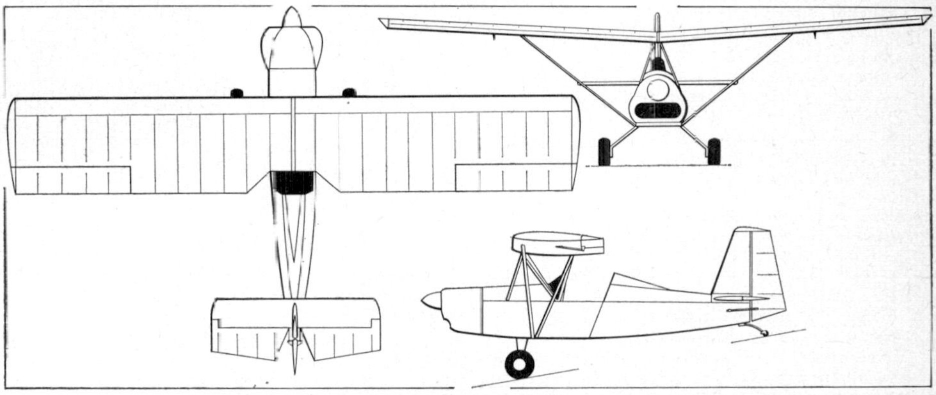

Armar I Gorrion single-seat ultra-light aircraft (*Sherwood Designs Ltd*)

Dimensions, internal:
Cabin: Length 4 ft 7 in (1·40 m)
Width (constant) 1 ft 10 in (0·56 m)

Areas:
Wings, gross 91·5 sq ft (8·50 m²)
Ailerons (total) 12·27 sq ft (1·14 m²)
Fin 3·98 sq ft (0·37 m²)
Rudder 4·74 sq ft (0·44 m²)
Tailplane 6·89 sq ft (0·64 m²)
Elevators 7·53 sq ft (0·70 m²)

Weights and Loadings:
Weight empty 366 lb (166 kg)
Max T-O weight 608 lb (276 kg)
Max wing loading 6·6 lb/sq ft (32·0 kg/m²)
Max power loading 15·43 lb/hp (7·0 kg/hp)

Performance (estimated, at max T-O weight):
Max level speed at 5,000 ft (1,500 m) 75·5 knots (87 mph; 140 km/h)
Max cruising speed at 5,000 ft (1,500 m) 65 knots (75 mph; 120 km/h)
Stalling speed 30·5 knots (35 mph; 56 km/h)
Service ceiling 9,845 ft (3,000 m)
Range with max fuel 194 nm (223 miles; 360 km)

GHINASSI HELICOPTERS

Sr Sesto Ghinassi is a specialist in, and racer of, motorcycles. He built a small single-seat helicopter, using unapproved materials and a 30 hp engine developed by himself. After being test-flown up to 3·3 ft (1 m) height, this helicopter (described and illustrated in the 1973-74 *Jane's*) was displayed at an Aeronautical Exhibition in October 1972.

This aircraft was later scrapped, but Sr Ghinassi currently has a new helicopter under construction, for which he is using aircraft quality materials. Completion of this was anticipated by the end of 1974.

Rotor System and Drive: Variable-pitch main and tail rotors, the former driven by chain drive from engine. Symmetrical-section blades, with 7% thickness/chord ratio, of wooden construction with aluminium skin. Max rpm of main rotor 400.

Fuselage: Welded steel tube structure.

Power Plant: One 30 hp 470 cc two-cylinder four-stroke turbine-cooled engine of own design; max rpm 6,300. Fuel tank capacity 4·4 Imp gallons (20 litres).

Accommodation: Single seat.

Dimensions, external:
Main rotor diameter 19 ft 8¼ in (6·00 m)
Tail rotor diameter 1 ft 11¾ in (0·60 m)
Main rotor blade chord 8¾ in (0·22 m)
Fuselage length 13 ft 1½ in (4·00 m)
Fuselage width 3 ft 3¼ in (1·00 m)
Height overall 5 ft 1 in (1·55 m)

Performance (estimated):
Range 162 nm (186 miles; 300 km)

YAKSTAS RACER

Originally begun by Prof Adolfo Yakstas as a much-modified development of the Baserga H.B.1 (see 1970-71 *Jane's*), this has now evolved into virtually a new design having only the two-cylinder Praga engine in common with its predecessor.

Work was halted in the Spring of 1973, but was restarted in the Spring of 1974. At this time the fuselage and tail unit were virtually complete, and rapid progress was being made in completing the wings.

Type: Single-seat racing monoplane.

Fuselage: Aluminium-skinned steel-tube forward section. Rear section, aft of main landing gear legs, is of wooden construction with fabric-covered upper and plywood-covered lower surfaces.

Tail Unit: Fabric-covered steel-tube structure, without sweepback.

Landing Gear: Non-retractable tailwheel type. Spring steel main gear legs.

Power Plant: One 45 hp Praga B-2 two-cylinder engine, driving a two-blade fixed-pitch propeller with spinner.

Accommodation: Single seat under two-piece moulded Plexiglas canopy.

CATA

COMPAÑIA ARGENTINA DE TRABAJOS AÉREOS

Address:
San Justo Aerodrome, Ruta 3, Km 24·7, Casanova (Buenos Aires), Aerodromo Aeroclub Argentino

CATA (FLEET) 150

This company has modified a Fleet biplane (LV-ZBZ) by installing a 150 hp Lycoming O-320 "flat-four" engine, with which the aircraft is known as the CATA (Fleet) 150. The aircraft used for the prototype conversion is a Fleet Model 5 or Model 7, and flew for the first time in its new form on 3 June 1971. A second aircraft, exhibited at Buenos Aires in late 1972, was converted from a Fleet Model 10.

The Canadian Fleet Company sold 20 Model 5 biplanes to Argentina in the 1930s, of which the majority are now believed to have been brought up to Model 10 standard with 125 hp Kinner B-5 radial piston engines. It is believed that, following successful trials with the prototype aircraft, these also are to be converted to CATA (Fleet) 150s, for use as glider-towing aircraft with Argentine flying clubs.

Second CATA-converted Fleet 150 biplane, on display in Buenos Aires (*Alex Reinhard*)

CHINCUL

CHINCUL S.A.C.A.I.F.I.

Head Office:
Mendoza S/N, Calle 6 y 7, Departamento Pocito, Casilla Correo 80, San Juan (San Juan)

Works:
25 de Mayo 489, 60 Piso, Buenos Aires

President:
José Maria Beraza

Vice-President:
Juan José Beraza

Director:
Aquiles Luis Uriarte

Sub-Directors:
Carlos Arriaga
Silvano Martin

Treasurer:
José Marina Nunez

Sub-Treasurer:
Julio Carranza Torres

This company, a wholly-owned subsidiary of La Macarena SRL, Piper's Argentine distributor, concluded an agreement with Piper Aircraft Corporation on 22 November 1971, for manufacture of a broad range of Piper products in Argentina. The proposed plan calls for a progression through five manufacturing phases of increasing complexity, designed to permit the gradual assimilation of aircraft manufacturing technology by Chincul.

The programme, officially inaugurated on 20 December 1972, schedules the completion of 1,000 single-engined and 340 twin-engined Piper aircraft by Chincul. Phase 1, following the delivery of four Seneca and 15 Cherokee kits, was carried out in 1973. Under a programme sponsored by the Comando de Regiones Aéreas, 40 Cherokees were to be built during the first two to three years for use as trainers by Argentine flying clubs.

A new assembly facility in San Juan was inaugurated on 13 December 1972. This facility, occupying a covered area of 30,623 sq ft (2,845 m²), is part of a 129,165 sq ft (12,000 m²) plant which will eventually be devoted to the assembly of all models of Piper aircraft. Finished aircraft will be test-flown and certificated by Argentine personnel.

CICARÉ

CICARÉ AERONÁUTICA SC

Address:
Ave Ibañez Frocham s/n, CC24, Saladillo, Provincia de Buenos Aires

Enquiries to:
Comodoro Antonio R. Mantel, Santa Fé 1256, Buenos Aires

Telephone: Buenos Aires 41-5260

Partners:
Augusto Ulderico Cicaré
Comodoro Ildefonso Domingo Durana
Comodoro Antonio Raúl Mantel

This company was formed in 1972 to undertake the development and construction of small aero-engines and light helicopters. Sr Cicaré, originally an engine designer, has designed and constructed two experimental helicopters, the Cicaré I and Cicaré II, brief details of which appeared in the 1970-71 and 1973-74 *Jane's*. A description follows of the more recently-designed CH-III Colibrí.

Cicaré CH-II one/three-seat experimental helicopter (180 hp Lycoming O-360-A1A engine)

CICARÉ CH-II

The Cicaré CH-II one/three-seat experimental lightweight helicopter was built primarily to test a specially-designed rotor system which can be operated as either a rigid or semi-rigid rotor. The prototype was flown for the first time on 18 May 1965. It has a free-wheel system for autorotation, but is otherwise as described in the 1973-74 *Jane's*.

CICARÉ CH-III COLIBRÍ

Design of the CH-III began in August 1973, and a prototype was under construction in 1974. This work is being done, under contract from the Argentine Air Force, to evolve a light helicopter suitable for training and agricultural duties. First flight is scheduled to take place in 1975.

Type: Two/three-seat experimental light helicopter.

Rotor System: Four-blade rigid main rotor and two-blade tail rotor. Blade section NACA 0015. All blades are of glassfibre construction. No rotor brake or blade folding.

ROTOR DRIVE: Ten Vee-belts, via a reduction gearbox, with free-wheel system for autorotation. Main rotor/engine rpm ratio 1 : 6; tail rotor/engine rpm ratio 1 : 1.

FUSELAGE: Steel-tube structure, with Aerofibra glassfibre cabin and aluminium tailboom.

TAIL UNIT: Glassfibre horizontal and vertical fixed stabilisers.

LANDING GEAR: Tubular steel skid type.

POWER PLANT: One 190 hp Lycoming HIO-360-D1A four-cylinder horizontally-opposed air-cooled engine, mounted horizontally. Single glassfibre fuel tank, capacity 29·5 Imp gallons (135 litres). Optional auxiliary tank, capacity 16·5 Imp gallons (75 litres).

ACCOMMODATION: Two or three seats side by side in enclosed cabin (instructor and pupil only in training version). Door on each side of cabin. Space for up to 100 lb (45 kg) of baggage. Cabin heated and ventilated.

ELECTRONICS AND EQUIPMENT: VHF radio standard. Mission equipment includes spraying or dusting gear and cargo sling.

DIMENSIONS, EXTERNAL:

Diameter of main rotor	24 ft 6 in (7·47 m)
Main rotor blade chord	6 in (152 mm)
Diameter of tail rotor	3 ft 7·2 in (1·10 m)
Distance between rotor centres	14 ft 0 in (4·27 m)
Length overall	28 ft 0 in (8·53 m)
Height overall	8 ft 1·2 in (2·47 m)
Skid track	6 ft 7·2 in (2·01 m)

AREAS:

Main rotor disc	471·43 sq ft (43·8 m²)
Tail rotor disc	10·18 sq ft (0·95 m²)

WEIGHTS AND LOADINGS:

Weight empty, equipped	1,034 lb (469 kg)
Max payload	500 lb (226 kg)
Max T-O weight	1,764 lb (800 kg)
Max disc loading	3·74 lb/sq ft (18·3 kg/m²)
Max power loading	9·28 lb/hp (4·21 kg/hp)

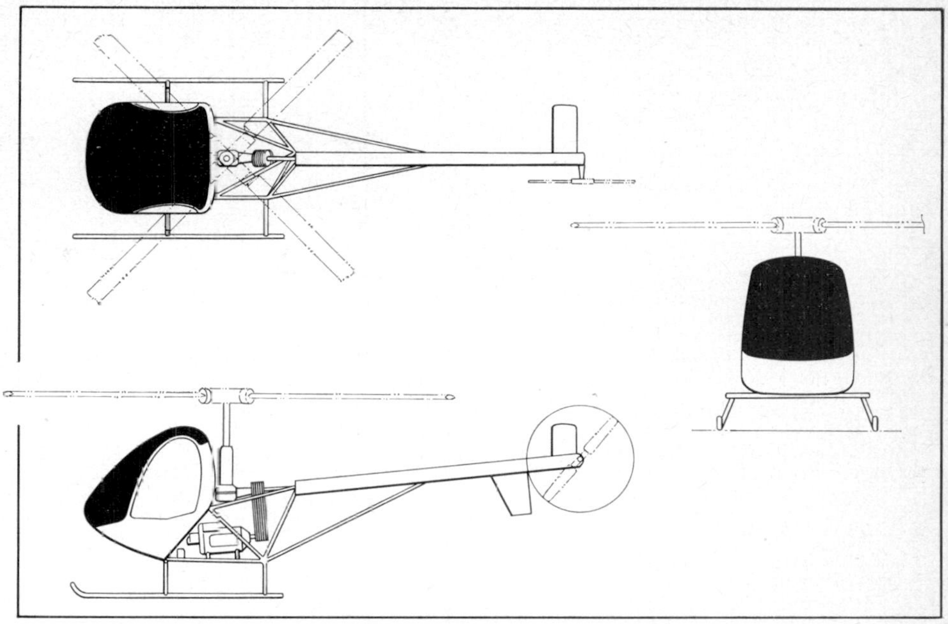

Cicaré CH-III Colibri two/three-seat experimental light helicopter (*Roy J. Grainge*)

PERFORMANCE (estimated, at max T-O weight):

Max level and cruising speed at S/L 88 knots (101 mph; 163 km/h)

Econ cruising speed 65 knots (74·5 mph; 120 km/h)

Max rate of climb at S/L 1,181 ft (360 m)/min

Service ceiling 12,800 ft (3,900 m)

Hovering ceiling out of ground effect 5,575 ft (1,700 m)

Range with internal fuel 259 nm (298 miles; 480 km)

FMA (AREA DE MATERIAL CÓRDOBA)

AGRUPACIÓN AVIONES-DEPARTAMENTO INGENIERÍA, GUARNICION AÉREA CÓRDOBA

ADDRESS:

Avenida Fuerza Aérea Argentina Km 5½, Córdoba

Telephone: 99184, 5640 and 98876

DIRECTOR:

Brigadier Enrique Zappino

CHIEF DESIGNER AND ENGINEER:

Vicecomodoro Héctor Eduardo Ruiz

The original Fábrica Militar de Aviones (Military Aircraft Factory) was founded in 1927 as a central organisation for aeronautical research and production in the Argentine. Its name was changed to Instituto Aerotécnico in 1943 and then to Industrias Aeronáuticas y Mecánicas del Estado (IAME) in 1952. In 1957 it became a State enterprise under the title of Dirección Nacional de Fabricaciones e Investigaciones Aeronáuticas (DINFIA), but reverted to its original title in 1968. It is now a component of the Area de Material Córdoba division of the Argentine Air Force.

FMA comprises two large divisions. The Instituto de Investigaciónes Aeronáuticas y Espacial (IIAE) is responsible for the design, manufacture and testing of rockets, sounding equipment and other equipment. The Fábrica Militar de Aviones itself controls the aircraft manufacturing facilities situated in Córdoba City. (Manufacture of motor vehicles in quantity by the FMA ended in 1967.) The laboratories, factories and other buildings belonging to the aeronautical divisions of FMA occupy a total covered area of 1,599,059 sq ft (148,557 m²); the Area de Material Córdoba employs 3,500 persons, of whom about 1,500 are in the FMA.

FMA's head offices are situated in Buenos Aires City. It also controls the Centro de Ensayos en Vuelo (Flight Test Centre), to which all aircraft produced in the Argentine are sent for certification tests.

The major aircraft of national design in current production are the twin-turboprop general-purpose IA 50 GII (formerly Guarani II) and the IA 58 Pucará counter-insurgency aircraft.

FMA is also producing Cessna single-engined aircraft under licence, under a renewed and extended form of the agreement announced in October 1965. First phase called for assembly of 80 aircraft from major assemblies supplied by Cessna. Phase 2 involved assembly of 100 aircraft from detail parts provided by Cessna. Phase 3 involves an estimated 320 aircraft, for which FMA is manufacturing or acquiring in the Argentine as many parts as possible. All aircraft are repurchased by Cessna for sale through its distributors and dealers in Latin America or sold directly by FMA to Argentine government agencies. Forty Cessna Model 150s have been ordered by the Comando de Regiones Aéreas for use as trainers by Argentine flying clubs.

The first A182J (Argentine 182) was completed in August 1966 from the initial batch of twelve sets of components supplied by Cessna, and was delivered to its owner on 2 September 1966. The renewed and extended agreement, announced in April 1971, provided for continued production of the Cessna 182 and, in addition, for the range to be extended to include the Model 150 trainer and the AGwagon agricultural aircraft.

By February 1974, FMA had completed 136 Cessna Model A182s, 16 Model A150 trainers, six Model A-A150 Aerobats and 16 AGwagons.

IA 50 GII

The original FA1 Guarani I twin-turboprop light transport was described in the 1962-63 *Jane's*.

From it was developed the IA 50 (formerly FA2) Guarani II, the first prototype of which (LV-X27) flew for the first time on 23 April 1963 and introduced more powerful engines, de-icing equipment, a single swept fin and rudder and a shorter rear fuselage. A second prototype (TX-01) was built, followed by a single pre-production aircraft. Production aircraft have flight deck windows of modified size and shape, to meet the US Federal Aviation Agency's CAM4B requirements, and provision for wingtip auxiliary fuel tanks.

The GII, as it is now known, is in production for the Argentine Air Force (FAA). Initial orders were for 18 standard models for communications duties, four for photographic operations with the Military Geographic Institute and one

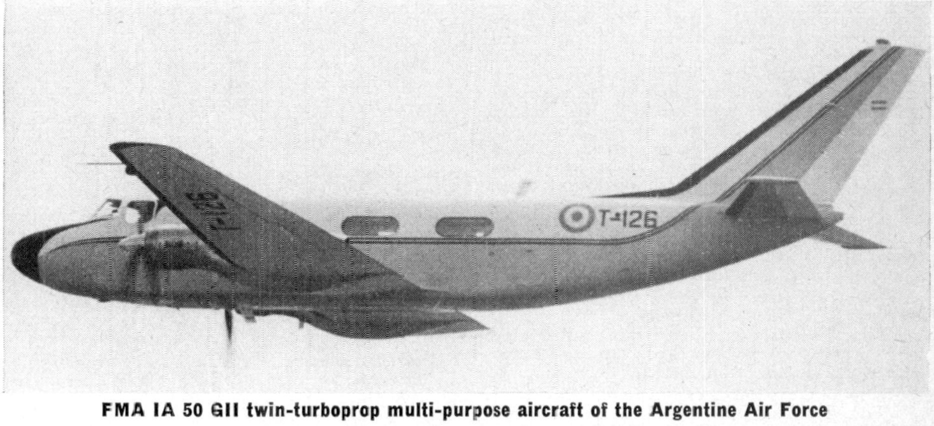

FMA IA 50 GII twin-turboprop multi-purpose aircraft of the Argentine Air Force

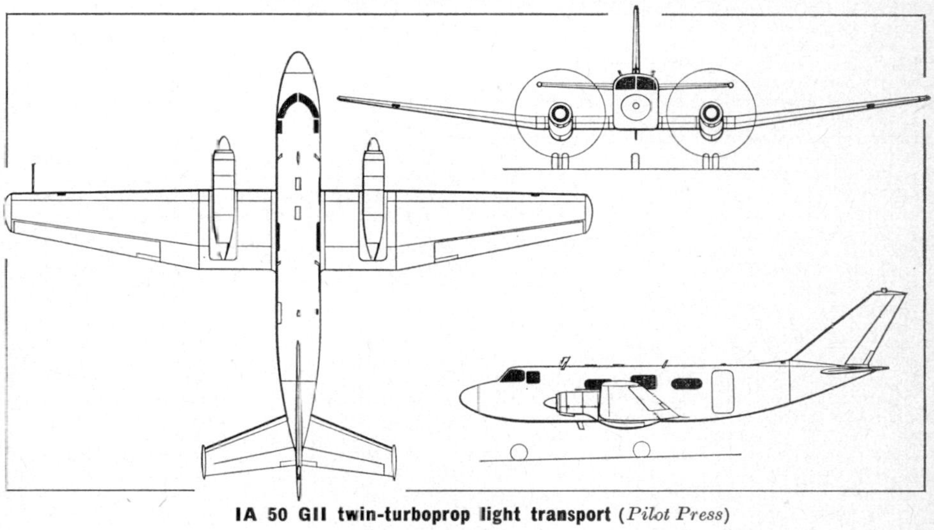

IA 50 GII twin-turboprop light transport (*Pilot Press*)

furnished as an executive transport for use by the President of Argentina. The first 18 production aircraft include one VIP transport (serial TX-110), fourteen troop transports (T-111 to T-124) and two photographic and survey aircraft (F-31 and F-32) for the Argentine Air Force; and one staff transport (5-T-30) for the Argentine Navy. The first two were in service with I Air Brigade at El Palomar by March 1967. A contract for a further 15 aircraft was placed in October 1969, and production of these was continuing in 1974. They have redesigned internal furnishings, and many of the steel structural components are replaced by components made of aluminium alloy, to reduce the aircraft's basic empty weight. Thus, with the prototypes and pre-series aircraft, a total of 41 GIIs is being produced. The 19th aircraft (T-125) was fitted with ski landing gear for use in the Antarctic.

A version of the GII with pressurised cabin and fully-automatic four-blade propellers is under consideration.

Type: Twin-engined light transport.

Wings: Cantilever low-wing monoplane. Wing section NACA 63_3218 at root, NACA 63_3212 at tip. Dihedral 7° on outer wings only. Incidence 3° at root, 1° at tip. All-metal single-spar structure. Fabric-covered metal ailerons. All-metal split flaps. Automatic trim tab in each aileron. Kléber-Colombes de-icing system optional.

Fuselage: Duralumin semi-monocoque structure.

Tail Unit: Cantilever all-metal structure with 52° 40′ sweepback on fin leading-edge and 21° 50′ on tailplane leading-edge. Variable-incidence sweptback tailplane, with streamline tip fairings. Trim tab in rudder and each elevator. Kléber-Colombes leading-edge de-icing system optional.

Landing Gear: Retractable tricycle type. Hydraulic actuation, all wheels retracting forward. Oleo-pneumatic shock-absorbers of Argentine manufacture. Each main unit fitted with two Dunlop wheels and tubeless tyres size 750 × 10. Single Dunlop nosewheel with tubeless tyre size 650 × 10. Tyre pressure 45 lb/sq in (3·16 kg/cm²). Dunlop hydraulic brakes.

Power Plant: Two Turboméca Bastan VIA turboprop engines, each rated at 930 shp plus 165 lb (75 kg) st. Ratier-Figeac FH86 three-blade variable-pitch metal propellers. Water-alcohol injection. Total internal fuel capacity 420 Imp gallons (1,910 litres) in integral tanks in wings. Provision for two wingtip fuel tanks, each with capacity of 77 Imp gallons (350 litres). Oil capacity 4·2 Imp gallons (19 litres) for each engine.

Accommodation: Crew of two side by side on flight deck. Standard seating in main cabin for 10, 12 or 15 passengers. Door with built-in steps at rear of cabin on port side. The 10-passenger executive version has a baggage compartment (port) and bar (starboard) immediately aft of flight deck; two rows of three inward-facing seats at front of main cabin and two pairs of armchair seats facing each other fore and aft with table between; toilet opposite cabin door. The utility and para-troop transport has seven inward-facing seats on the port side of the cabin and eight on the starboard side. A navigation and radar training version has six seats and comprehensive equipment in the cabin. An ambulance version carries two pairs of stretchers on the port side of the cabin and one pair on the starboard side, with two seats for attendants. All versions have a forward baggage hold and galley, and a toilet at the rear.

Systems: SEMCA Type EQ2 air-conditioning equipment. Navigation and landing lights and rotating beacon standard.

Electronics and Equipment: Radio and radar according to military role. Normally two RA-21A VHF receivers, two TA-21A VHF transmitters, one RA-21A-MNA-21B navigation system, one GSA-8A-1 glideslope receiver, one FKA-23-A marker receiver, two DFA-22A ADF installations and two ASA-31A audio panels, all manufactured by Bendix; and one Eldeco 20A HF transceiver. Full blind-flying instrumentation standard. Optional equipment includes Bendix VOR/ILS, autopilot, automatic navigation system, weather radar and oxygen equipment.

Equipment (radio calibration version): Two GIIs have been specially equipped for in-flight calibration of ground radio aids. In addition to the standard radio and navigation equipment fitted to other GIIs, these aircraft carry three Bendix RNA 26CF VOR/ILS receivers, two Bendix MKA 28CF marker receivers, one Bendix 29 ACF DME interrogator, two Bendix RTA-42A VHF transceivers, one Collins 718-5 HF transceiver, two Bendix ADF 73 automatic direction finders, two Bendix LA-17 audio amplifiers, one Bendix RDR 1 radar transceiver, one Bendix 18900-1A1 radar antenna gyro stabiliser and a complete 1942 EGET instrument panel. Electrical system includes 115V 50Hz AC supply and 27V DC stabilising supply. Much of the additional equipment listed is installed in the nose; the remainder is installed in a special console aft of the flight deck. To the rear of this console, in the main cabin, are individual seats for five equipment operators, together with an oscilloscope, radio rack, frequency counter, digital voltmeter, baggage compartment, two workbenches and a reference library. There are various underwing antennae, adjacent to the engine nacelle, for VOR, glideslope and other equipment, with appropriate reinforcement of the wing skin in these areas. An oxygen system is provided, and the aircraft are fitted with wingtip fuel tanks.

IA 58 Pucará second prototype (two 1,022 ehp Turboméca Astazou XVIG turboprops), showing under-wing stores pylons

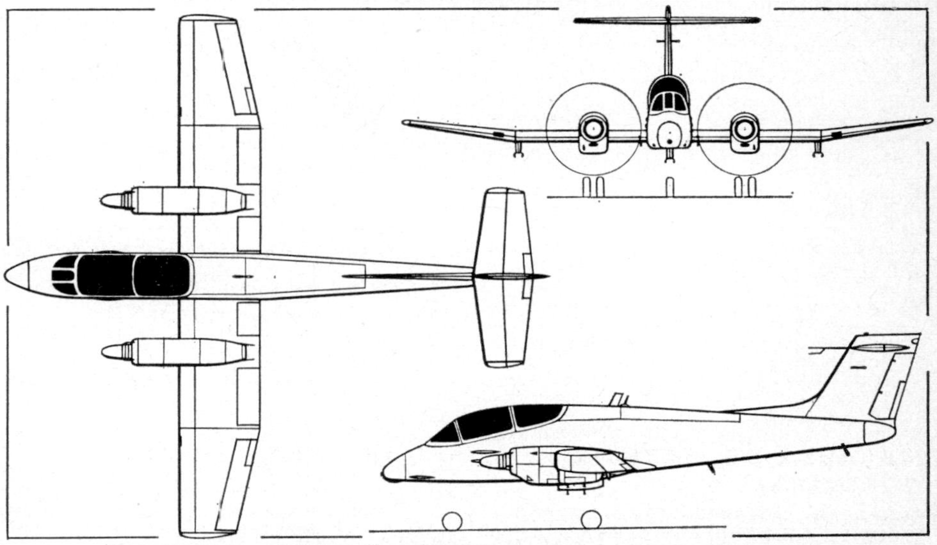

FMA IA 58 Pucará twin-turboprop counter-insurgency aircraft *(Pilot Press)*

Dimensions, external:
Wing span (without tip-tanks) 64 ft 3¼ in (19·59 m)
Wing chord (centre-section, constant) 9 ft 1 in (2·75 m)
Wing aspect ratio 9
Length overall 50 ft 2½ in (15·30 m)
Length of fuselage 46 ft 10¼ in (14·28 m)
Height over tail 18 ft 5 in (5·61 m)
Tailplane span 21 ft 4 in (6·50 m)
Fuselage: Max width 5 ft 3 in (1·60 m)
Max depth 6 ft 1¼ in (1·86 m)
Wheel track 15 ft 11¼ in (4·86 m)
Wheelbase 11 ft 1¾ in (3·40 m)
Propeller diameter 9 ft 0¼ in (2·75 m)
Passenger door:
Height 4 ft 9½ in (1·46 m)
Width 2 ft 5 in (0·74 m)

Dimensions, internal:
Cabin, excluding flight deck:
Max length 16 ft 2 in (4·93 m)
Max width 4 ft 9 in (1·45 m)
Max height 5 ft 5½ in (1·66 m)
Floor area 131·3 sq ft (12·20 m²)
Volume 618 cu ft (17·5 m³)

Areas:
Wings, gross 450 sq ft (41·81 m²)
Ailerons (total) 38·2 sq ft (3·55 m²)
Trailing-edge flaps (total) 51·73 sq ft (4·81 m²)
Vertical tail surfaces (total) 60·5 sq ft (5·62 m²)
Horizontal tail surfaces (total) 79·0 sq ft (7·34 m²)

Weights and Loadings:
Weight empty, equipped 8,650 lb (3,924 kg)
Max payload 3,307 lb (1,500 kg)
Max T-O weight:
with tip-tanks 17,085 lb (7,750 kg)
without tip-tanks 15,873 lb (7,200 kg)
Max landing weight 14,330 lb (6,500 kg)
Max wing loading:
with tip-tanks 37·9 lb/sq ft (185 kg/m²)
without tip-tanks 35·0 lb/sq ft (170·9 kg/m²)
Max power loading:
with tip-tanks 8·38 lb/ehp (3·8 kg/ehp)

Performance (at max T-O weight):
Max never-exceed speed 277 knots (320 mph; 515 km/h)
Max level speed 269 knots (310 mph; 500 km/h)
Max cruising speed 265 knots (305 mph; 491 km/h)
Econ cruising speed 243 knots (280 mph; 450 km/h)
Stalling speed 79 knots (90 mph; 145 km/h)
Max rate of climb at S/L 2,640 ft (805 m)/min
Service ceiling 41,000 ft (12,500 m)
Service ceiling, one engine out 11,000 ft (3,350 m)
T-O run 1,380 ft (420 m)
T-O to 50 ft (15 m) 2,200 ft (640 m)
Landing from 50 ft (15 m) 1,970 ft (600 m)
Landing run 820 ft (250 m)
Range with max fuel 1,389 nm (1,600 miles; 2,575 km)
Range with max payload 1,076 nm (1,240 miles; 1,995 km)

IA 58 PUCARÁ

This twin-turboprop COIN (counter-insurgency) combat aircraft was developed to meet an Argentine Air Force requirement. Originally known as the Delfin, it was later renamed Pucará. An unpowered aerodynamic prototype, with dummy engine nacelles and fixed landing gear, was first flown on 26 December 1967, and was described in the 1968-69 *Jane's*.

Detailed design work on the powered version was begun in February 1968. Construction of the first powered prototype, designated AX-01, started in September 1968, and this aircraft flew for the first time on 20 August 1969, powered by AiResearch TPE 331 engines. It was described in the 1971-72 *Jane's*.

A second prototype, designated AX-02, flew for the first time on 6 September 1970 with 1,022 ehp Turboméca Astazou XVIG turboprop engines, and the production version is powered by engines of this type. Five pre-series aircraft are being built, and work has also started on an initial production series of 100 aircraft. An order for 30 Pucarás has been placed by the Argentine Air Force, with deliveries scheduled to begin in 1974. It is anticipated that this order will later be increased to 70 aircraft. Interest in the Pucará has also been expressed by the Peruvian Air Force.

The following description applies to the production version:

Type: Twin-turboprop counter-insurgency aircraft.

Wings: Cantilever low-wing monoplane. Wing section NACA 64_2A215 at root, NACA 64_1A212 at tip. Dihedral 7° on outer wing panels. Incidence 2°. No sweepback. Conventional semi-monocoque fail-safe structure of duralumin. Frise-type fabric-covered duralumin ailerons and all-dural slotted trailing-edge flaps. No slats. Balance tab in starboard aileron, electrically-operated trim tab in port aileron. Kléber-Colombes pneumatic de-icing boots on leading-edges.

FUSELAGE: Conventional semi-monocoque fail-safe structure of duralumin. Door-type air-brakes at rear which form tailcone when closed.

TAIL UNIT: Cantilever semi-monocoque structure of duralumin. Fixed-incidence tailplane and elevators mounted near top of fin. Trim tab in rudder and each elevator. Kléber-Colombes pneumatic de-icing boots on leading-edges.

LANDING GEAR: Retractable tricycle type, all units retracting forward hydraulically. Shock-absorbers of Kronprinz Ring-Feder type, designed by Vicecomodoro Ruiz. Single wheel on nose unit, twin wheels on main units, all with Dunlop tubeless Type III tyres size 7·50-10. Tyre pressures: 41 lb/sq in (2·88 kg/cm²) on main units, 35 lb/sq in (2·46 kg/cm²) on nose unit. Dunlop hydraulic disc brakes. No anti-skid units.

POWER PLANT: Two 1,022 ehp Turboméca Astazou XVIG turboprop engines, each driving a Hamilton Standard 33LF/1015-0 three-blade metal propeller. Fuel in two fuselage tanks and one self-sealing tank in each wing, with total capacity of 313 Imp gallons (1,422 litres). Attachment point beneath each wing at junction of centre and outer panels for external weapons or jettisonable auxiliary fuel tank of 66 Imp gallons (300 litres). Oil capacity 2·6 Imp gallons (11·75 litres).

ACCOMMODATION: Crew of two in tandem on Martin-Baker Mk AP06A ejection seats beneath transparent moulded canopy. Rear seat slightly elevated. Bullet-proof windscreen.

SYSTEMS: Hydraulic system, pressure 3,000 lb/sq in (210 kg/cm²), supplied by two engine-driven pumps, actuates landing gear, flaps, wheel brakes and airbrakes. Wing and tail unit de-icing by bleed air from engines. Electrical system includes two 300A 28V starter/generators for DC power and two 500-750VA rotary inverters for 115V AC power. One 36Ah SAFT Voltabloc 4006 battery. No APU at present.

ELECTRONICS AND EQUIPMENT: Blind-flying instrumentation standard. Radio equipment includes Bendix DFA-73A-1 ADF, Bendix RTA-42A VHF communications system, Bendix RNA-2bc VHF navigation system, Northern N-420 HF 55B communications system, amplifier and audio-selector system with AS-A-31 panel. Optional equipment includes weather radar, IFF and VHF/FM tactical communications system.

ARMAMENT AND OPERATIONAL EQUIPMENT: Two 20 mm Hispano cannon and four 7·62 mm FN machine-guns in fuselage. One attachment point beneath centre of fuselage and one beneath each wing outboard of engine nacelle for a variety of external stores, including auxiliary fuel tanks. Librascope 335336 gun-sight and one AN/AWE programmer.

DIMENSIONS, EXTERNAL:
Wing span 47 ft 6¾ in (14·50 m)
Wing chord at root 7 ft 4¼ in (2·24 m)
Wing chord at tip 5 ft 3 in (1·60 m)
Wing aspect ratio 6·95
Length overall 46 ft 3 in (14·10 m)
Length of fuselage 43 ft 8¾ in (13·32 m)
Fuselage: Max width 4 ft 0¾ in (1·24 m)
Height overall 17 ft 7 in (5·36 m)
Tailplane span 15 ft 5 in (4·70 m)
Wheel track (c/l of shock struts) 13 ft 9¼ in (4·20 m)
Wheelbase 11 ft 5 in (3·48 m)
Propeller diameter 8 ft 6 in (2·59 m)

DIMENSIONS, INTERNAL:
Cabin: Floor area 31·2 sq ft (2·90 m²)
Volume 96·8 cu ft (2·74 m³)

AREAS:
Wings, gross 326·1 sq ft (30·30 m²)
Ailerons (total) 35·41 sq ft (3·29 m²)
Trailing-edge flaps (total) 38·53 sq ft (3·58 m²)
Fin 37·30 sq ft (3·465 m²)
Rudder, including tab 16·84 sq ft (1·565 m²)
Tailplane 49·51 sq ft (4·60 m²)
Elevators, including tabs 28·11 sq ft (2·612 m²)

WEIGHTS AND LOADINGS:
Weight empty 8,900 lb (4,037 kg)
Max T-O weight 14,300 lb (6,486 kg)
Max landing weight 12,800 lb (5,806 kg)
Max wing loading 44 lb/sq ft (214·8 kg/m²)
Max power loading 7 lb/ehp (3·18 kg/ehp)

PERFORMANCE (at max T-O weight, except where indicated):
Max never-exceed speed 404 knots (466 mph; 750 km/h)
Max level speed at 9,840 ft (3,000 m) 281 knots (323 mph; 520 km/h)
Max cruising speed 261 knots (301 mph; 485 km/h)
Econ cruising speed 232 knots (267 mph; 430 km/h)
Stalling speed, flaps down, at 10,580 lb (4,790 kg) AUW 77·5 knots (89 mph; 142·5 km/h)
Max rate of climb at S/L 3,543 ft (1,080 m)/min
Service ceiling at 13,668 lb (6,200 kg) AUW, 0° flap 27,165 ft (8,280 m)
Service ceiling, one engine out, at 10,934 lb (4,960 kg) AUW, 0° flap 17,533 ft (5,344 m)
T-O run 985 ft (300 m)
T-O to 50 ft (15 m) 2,313 ft (705 m)
Landing from 50 ft (15 m) at 11,243 lb (5,100 kg) AUW 1,978 ft (603 m)
Landing run at 11,243 lb (5,100 kg) AUW 656 ft (200 m)
Range with max fuel at 16,400 ft (5,000 m) 1,641 nm (1,890 miles; 3,042 km)

FMA TWIN-ENGINED TRAINER

Based on the airframe of the Pucará, Vicecomodoro Ruiz has designed a tandem two-seat training aircraft, to be powered by two Turboméca Astafan turbofan engines. As shown in the accompanying three-view drawing, these engines will be mounted in pods on the fuselage sides above the wing, with streamlined landing gear fairings replacing the turboprop engine nacelles of the standard Pucará. The following details are provisional:

DIMENSIONS, EXTERNAL: As IA 58 Pucará

WEIGHTS:
Weight empty, equipped 8,377 lb (3,800 kg)
Max T-O weight 14,330 lb (6,500 kg)

PERFORMANCE:
Max critical Mach number 0·73
Service ceiling 32,800 ft (10,000 m)

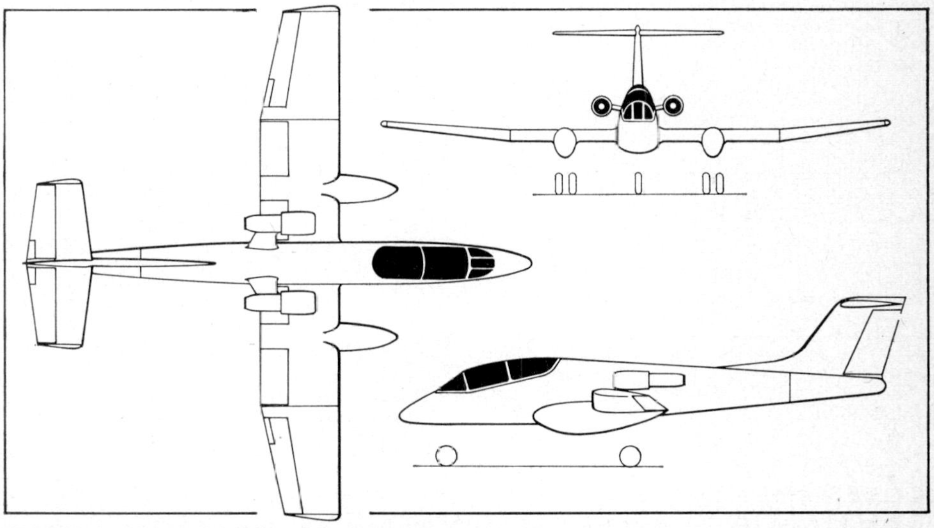

FMA tandem two-seat training aircraft (two Turboméca Astafan turbofan engines) (*Roy J. Grainge*)

RACA

REPRESENTACIONES AERO COMERCIALES ARGENTINAS SA

HEAD OFFICE:
Lavalle 715, 5° Piso, Buenos Aires
Telephone: 392-1334 and 392-9488
Telegrams: RACAVIA
Telex: 012-2844

WORKS:
Aerodromo San Fernando, Provincia Buenos Aires

DIRECTOR:
J. R. Fernandez Racca

VICE-PRESIDENT:
Luis Alberto Varisco

This company is the representative or dealer in Argentina for a number of world aerospace companies, and is the exclusive national distributor for the Concorde, BAC One-Eleven, Shorts Skyvan Srs 3, Canadair CL-215 and HFB 320 Hansa aircraft, and the MBB BO 105 and Hughes helicopters. Under a licence agreement concluded in December 1972 RACA is undertaking, with Argentine government approval (granted in mid-1973), the progressive local manufacture of Hughes Model 500 helicopters from knock-down components. These are known locally as RACA-Hughes 500s.

The total programme involves 120 helicopters of this type over the next eight years, for military and civil customers in Argentina and neighbouring countries. In anticipation of this programme, RACA expanded its workshop facilities at San Fernando aerodrome to a covered area of 49,514 sq ft (4,600 m²).

By February 1974, 25 RACA-Hughes 500s had been ordered, including six for the Prefectura Naval Argentina (National Coast Guard) and two each for the government of Santa Fé province and Yacimientos Petroliferos Fiscales; of these, five had been completed.

RRASA

RONCHETTI RAZZETTI AVIACION SA

ADDRESS: Aeropuerto International Rosario CC7, Funes, Santa Fé
Telephone: Funes 93276

DIRECTOR: Julio E. Razzetti

DIRECTOR IN CHARGE OF AVIATION DIVISION:
Ing Emilio P. Illescas

RRASA J-1 MARTIN FIERRO

This aircraft, a prototype of which was nearing completion in the Spring of 1974, is a single-seat agricultural aircraft. It is of low-wing monoplane configuration, has a non-retractable tail-wheel landing gear, and is powered by a 300 hp engine.

No other details were available at the time of closing for press.

AUSTRALIA

CAC

COMMONWEALTH AIRCRAFT CORPORATION PTY LTD

HEAD OFFICE AND WORKS:
304 Lorimer Street, Port Melbourne, Victoria 3207
Telephone: 64 0771
Telex: 30721

DIRECTORS:
Air Chief Marshal Sir Frederick Scherger, KBE, CB, DSO, AFC (Chairman)
M. L. Baillieu
Sir Ian McLennan
L. C. Bridgland
R. R. Law-Smith, CBE, AFC
A. W. Stewart
R. T. M. Rose

GENERAL MANAGER: R. L. Abbott

SECRETARY: E. W. Stodden

Commonwealth Aircraft Corporation Pty Ltd was formed in 1936 to establish an aircraft industry that would make Australia independent of outside supplies.

The Corporation has an authorised capital of $6,000,000. Shareholders include BHP Nominees Pty Ltd; North Broken Hill Ltd; B. H. South Ltd; Electrolytic Zinc Co of Australasia; Nobel (Australasia) Pty Ltd; Rolls-Royce (1971) Ltd; and P & O Australian Holdings Pty Ltd.

Under a co-production agreement between the Australian government and the Bell Helicopter Co of the USA, announced in February 1971, CAC is the prime contractor in an eight-year programme to provide 75 Bell OH-58A Kiowa helicopters for the Australian Army and 116 Bell JetRangers for the commercial market. The Australian Army received its first OH-58A in April 1973, and 20 OH-58As and 2 civil Jet-

Rangers had been delivered by mid-February 1974. Two Bell 206B-1s were delivered at about the same time to the Royal Australian Navy.

A constant overhaul programme for Atar engines used by the RAAF is maintained, together with an overhaul programme for Sabre aircraft and Avon engines operated by the air forces of Malaysia and Indonesia.

Other contracts include a variety of offset work for Boeing, Sikorsky, SNECMA and Hawker Siddeley Aviation; and manufacture of components for the Government Aircraft Factories Nomad and New Zealand Aerospace Industries CT/4 Airtrainer (which see).

Rex Aviation Ltd, Bankstown Aerodrome, New South Wales, a wholly-owned subsidiary of CAC, is the distributor of Cessna aircraft and Hughes 300 and 500 helicopters in Australia and New Guinea.

Details of the company's aero-engine activities can be found in the "Aero-engines" section.

CORBY

JOHN CORBY

ADDRESS:
86 Eton Street, Sutherland, NSW 2232

Mr Corby, a consultant aero engineer, has designed and is marketing plans for a single-seat ultra-light homebuilt aircraft known as the Starlet. Several examples are flying and under construction.

CORBY CJ-1 STARLET

By early 1974 seven Starlets had been completed and a further 31 were under construction in Australia and New Zealand.

The first Starlet (VH-ULV) was built by Mr Erle Jones (Secretary and former President of the ULAA, Latrobe Valley Aero Club, PO Box 410, Morwell, Victoria 3840) and Mr John Brown. Compared with the standard Starlet, this has the seat bulkhead inclined rearward by 3 in (7·6 cm) at the top, and uses a solid spruce landing gear beam with an ash lamination, instead of multi-laminated end-grain spruce. In its original form, with a 42 hp (approx) engine, it had a max T-O weight of 650 lb (294 kg), a max level speed of 104 knots (120 mph; 193 km/h) and a range of 260 nm (300 miles; 482 km). Now fitted with a 49 hp Ardem Mk XI engine, it averaged 100 knots (115 mph; 185 km/h) around a two-day 477 nm (550 mile; 885 km) cross-country course during the NSW air races in July 1973. Prior to this, with its original engine, it had gained second place in Grade B of the 1973 aerobatic open championships in Australia. Winner of those championships (Grade A), against the remainder of commercially-built entrants, was another Corby Starlet (VH-WDJ), fitted with a 49 hp Ardem XI engine and flown by Peter Furlong of Morwell, Victoria.

The following description applies to the standard Corby Starlet, except where indicated:

TYPE: Single-seat ultra-light homebuilt aircraft.

WINGS: Cantilever low-wing monoplane of wooden construction. Wing section NACA 43012A. Dihedral 6°. Incidence 2° 30′ at root, —1° at tip. Laminated main spar of solid spruce, sub-spars of spruce, built-up girder-type ribs and D-shaped nose section. Plywood covering from leading-edge to main spar, remainder fabric covered. Provision for dismantling into two equal halves. Ailerons, of spruce with birch plywood covering, deflect 15° up and down.

FUSELAGE: Plywood-covered spruce structure.

Corby Starlet single-seat ultra-light aircraft for amateur construction

TAIL UNIT: Cantilever type, of similar construction to wings. Fixed-incidence tailplane. Plywood-covered fixed surfaces; fabric-covered rudder and elevators. Elevators deflect 30° up, 20° down; rudder deflects 25° to left and right.

LANDING GEAR: Non-retractable two-wheel type standard. Separate spring steel leaf-type shock-absorbing main legs, attached directly to fuselage via a solid spruce/ash beam which also serves as the wing leading-edge attachment member. Wheels, tyres and brakes of customer's choice, subject to minimum main wheels of 3½ in (8·9 cm) diameter with 4·00-4 tyres and Olympic go-kart hubs. Sturmey Archer cycle drum/shoe brakes may be used. Leaf-spring tailskid, or tailwheel at customer's option. Wheel fairings optional.

POWER PLANT: Any suitable engine of up to 75 hp and 160 lb (72 kg) weight, driving a two-blade propeller. Fuel tank, capacity 8-10 Imp gallons (36-45 litres), aft of engine firewall. Oil capacity 5 lb (2·25 kg).

ACCOMMODATION: Single seat. Sliding canopy optional. Baggage locker behind seat.

DIMENSIONS, EXTERNAL:
Wing span 18 ft 6 in (5·64 m)
Wing chord at root 4 ft 4 in (1·32 m)
Length overall 14 ft 9 in (4·50 m)
Fuselage: Max width 1 ft 9⅝ in (0·55 m)
Height overall 4 ft 10 in (1·47 m)
Tailplane span 6 ft 6 in (1·98 m)
Wheel track 4 ft 6 in (1·37 m)
Propeller diameter:
standard 4 ft 9 in (1·45 m)
prototype 4 ft 4 in (1·32 m)
Propeller ground clearance 10 in (25·5 cm)

AREAS:
Wings, gross 68·50 sq ft (6·36 m²)
Horizontal tail surfaces (total) 13·75 sq ft (1·28 m²)
Vertical tail surfaces (total) 7·40 sq ft (0·69 m²)

WEIGHTS:
Weight empty 405-420 lb (183-190 kg)
Max T-O weight (semi-aerobatic) 650 lb (295 kg)

PERFORMANCE (prototype, with 49 hp engine, at 650 lb; 295 kg AUW):
Max never-exceed speed 138 knots (159 mph; 255 km/h) IAS
Max level speed 117 knots (135 mph; 217 km/h) TAS
Max cruising speed 107 knots (123 mph; 198 km/h) TAS
Stalling speed, power off: 42 knots (49 mph; 79 km/h) TAS; 30 knots (35 mph; 57 km/h) IAS
Typical rate of climb at S/L 700-850 ft (213-259 m)/min
Service ceiling 14,500 ft (4,420 m)
T-O to, and landing from, 50 ft (15 m) 1,000-1,100 ft (305-335 m)
g limits ±4·5

GOVERNMENT OF AUSTRALIA DEPARTMENT OF SUPPLY

ADDRESS:
Anzac Park West Building, Constitution Avenue, Parkes, Canberra ACT 2600
Telephone: 48 2111
Telex: 62063

SECRETARY:
N. S. Currie, OBE, BA

DEPUTY SECRETARIES:
T. F. C. Lawrence, BSc, BE, FRAeS, FIEAust (Research and Engineering)
D. J. O'Connor, BCom, DipPubAd, AASA (Senior) (Management and Supply)

DIRECTOR OF PUBLIC RELATIONS:
A. L. Witsenhuysen, BA

Government Aircraft Factories

HEADQUARTERS:
Fishermen's Bend, Private Bag No. 4, Post Office, Port Melbourne, Victoria 3207
Telephone: 64 0661

AIRFIELD AND FINAL ASSEMBLY WORKSHOPS:
Avalon Airfield, Beach Road, Lara, Victoria 3212
Telephone: Lara 82 1202

MANAGER: G. J. Churcher, BEngSc, MIEAust

The Government Aircraft Factories are units of the Defence Production facilities owned by the Government of the Commonwealth of Australia and operated by the Department of Supply. Their functions include the design, development, manufacture, assembly, maintenance and modification of aircraft and guided weapons. At Avalon airfield, subassembly of components, final assembly, modification, repair and test-flying of jet and other aircraft are undertaken.

The Factories' major recent activity was the production of Dassault Mirage III-O fighters and III-D operational trainers for the RAAF as prime contractor. Current activity includes development and production of the GAF Nomad twin-turboprop STOL transport.

The Jindivik and Turana target drones are described in the "RPVs and Targets" section of this edition.

The GAF are producing rudders and elevators for the Boeing 727 under contract to The Boeing Company; and are subcontractors to Commonwealth Aircraft Corporation in manufacturing bonded structures (main and tail rotor blades and fuselage panels) for Australian-produced examples of the Bell JetRanger series of helicopters.

GOVERNMENT AIRCRAFT FACTORIES NOMAD

This small, twin-turboprop utility aircraft is in production at the GAF. Its design was started in 1965 under the designation Project N, and the first of two Model N2 prototypes (VH-SUP) was flown for the first time on 23 July 1971; it was followed by the second aircraft (VH-SUR) on 5 December 1971.

Design certification for the Nomad is to US FAR 23 requirements administered by the Australian Dept of Civil Aviation; the Type Certificate for the N2 was issued on 11 August 1972, and certification by the FAA and CAA is being negotiated. The basic design incorporates features of common interest to military and civil operators, including quick role-change capabilities and the ability to operate from short fields and unprepared surfaces.

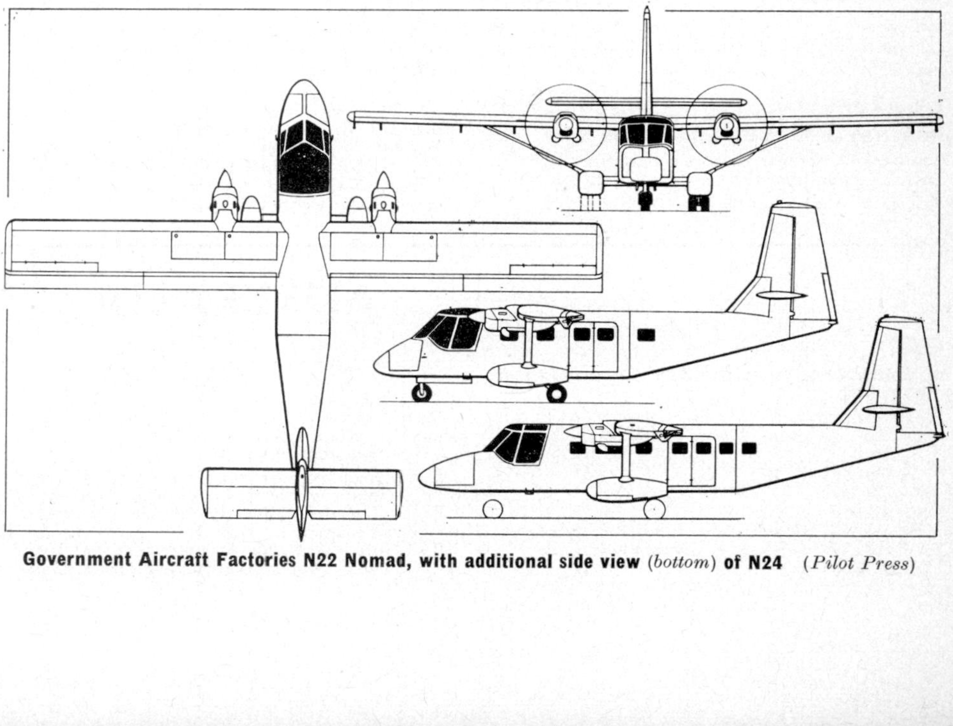

Government Aircraft Factories N22 Nomad, with additional side view *(bottom)* **of N24** *(Pilot Press)*

Prototype N22 version of the Government Aircraft Factories Nomad STOL utility aircraft

Two versions have so far been announced, as follows:

N22. Short-fuselage version, currently in production for the Australian Army Aviation Corps and commercial operators. The two prototypes were built to this standard.

N24. Higher-capacity version, with lengthened fuselage. Design includes the insertion of a 43 in (1·09 m) section in the cabin, and increased forward baggage capacity.

Production of 70 Nomads has been authorised by the Australian government. These will include an initial quantity of 11 for the Australian Army. China, the Philippines (18) and Indonesia (four) are also reported to have ordered Nomads, the last-named being intended for the Indonesian Navy. Sales of the Nomad throughout south-east Asia are handled by Hawker de Havilland.

The following description applies generally to both versions, except where a specific model is indicated:

Type: **Twin-turboprop STOL utility aircraft.**

Wings: **Braced high-wing monoplane. Basic NACA 23018 wing section, modified to incorporate increased nose radius and camber. Dihedral 1° from roots. Incidence 2°. No sweepback. Two-spar fail-safe torsion-box structure of riveted light alloy. Full-span double-slotted trailing-edge flaps. All-metal ailerons, which droop with the flaps and transfer their motion progressively to slot-lip ailerons as the flaps extend, resulting in full-span flap. Controls actuated manually by cables and pushrods. Pneumatic de-icing of leading-edges optional. Small stub wings at cabin floor level support the main landing gear fairings from which a single strut on each side braces the main wing.**

Fuselage: Conventional semi-monocoque riveted light alloy structure of stringers and frames.

Tail Unit: Cantilever all-metal structure. One-piece all-moving tailplane, with inset trim and anti-balance tab. Tailplane and rudder actuated manually by cables. Trim tab in rudder. Pneumatic de-icing of leading-edges optional.

Landing Gear: Retractable tricycle type, with electrical retraction by means of single actuator in the fuselage. GAF oleo-pneumatic shock-absorbers. Single rearward-retracting steerable nosewheel, tyre size 8·00-6, pressure 35 lb/sq in (2·46 kg/cm²). Twin wheels, tyre size 8·00-6, pressure 29 lb/sq in (2·04 kg/cm²), on each main unit. Main wheels retract forward into streamlined fairings at outer ends of stub wings. Dual hydraulically-operated single-disc brakes on main units. No anti-skid units.

Power Plant: Two 400 shp Allison 250-B17 turboprop engines, each driving a Hartzell three-blade constant-speed fully-feathering reversible-pitch metal propeller. Fuel capacity 1,794 lb (813 kg) plus 25 lb (11·3 kg) unusable in flexible bag tanks; or 1,692 lb (767 kg) plus 25 lb unusable in self-sealing bag tanks. Provision for internal auxiliary tanks for ferry purposes. Gravity refuelling via overwing point above each pair of tanks. Oil capacity 1·9 Imp gallons (8·5 litres) per engine.

Accommodation (N22): Designed for single-pilot operation, but can accommodate crew of two on side-by-side seats. Access to flight deck by forward-opening door on each side. Main cabin has individual seats for up to 12 passengers, at 31 in (78 cm) pitch, with continuous seat tracks and readily-removable seats which allow rapid rearrangement of the cabin to suit alternative loads. Access to main cabin via double doors on port side, with single emergency exit on starboard side. Baggage compartments in nose (with door on each side) and optionally in rear of fuselage (with internal access). Whole interior, including flight deck, is heated and ventilated.

Accommodation (N24): Flight deck accommodation and access as for N22. Lengthened main cabin, with similar internal provision to N22 for up to 15 passengers, and access via double port-side doors as in N22. Enlarged nose baggage compartment. Rear baggage compartment of same capacity as N22. Ventilation and heating system with individual adjustable outlets.

Systems: No air-conditioning, hydraulic or pneumatic system normally, but air-conditioning is proposed for future models and pneumatic airframe de-icing is available optionally. Electrical system comprises a 28V 150A DC starter/generator on each engine, and a 22Ah battery with AC inverters. Other optional systems include oxygen demand system for crew and continuous-flow system for passengers; electrical de-icing for propellers, cabin floor hatch and underwing pylon racks.

Electronics and Equipment: Provision is made for a wide range of nav/com equipment to meet specific customer requirements. Other optional items include full IFR instrumentation and a lightweight weather radar.

Armament and Operational Equipment (N22): The military variant has been designed to have four underwing hardpoints capable of accepting up to 500 lb (227 kg) loads, including gun and rocket pods. The nose bay can be utilised to accommodate surveillance and night vision aid equipment. Removable seat armour and self-sealing fuel tanks can be fitted for added protection.

Dimensions, external:
Wing span 54 ft 0 in (16·46 m)
Wing chord (constant) 5 ft 11¼ in (1·81 m)
Wing aspect ratio 9·11
Length overall:
N22 41 ft 2·4 in (12·56 m)
N24 46 ft 3 in (14·10 m)
Height overall 18 ft 1½ in (5·52 m)
Tailplane span 17 ft 8·4 in (5·39 m)
Wheel track 10 ft 7 in (3·23 m)
Wheelbase: N22 11 ft 11·6 in (3·65 m)
Propeller diameter 7 ft 6 in (2·29 m)
Propeller ground clearance 4 ft 0 in (1·22 m)
Distance between propeller centres 14 ft 3·6 in (4·36 m)
Crew doors (each):
Height 2 ft 10 in (0·86 m)
Width 2 ft 3 in (0·69 m)
Passenger double doors (port):
Height 4 ft 4 in (1·32 m)
Width 4 ft 0 in (1·22 m)
Height to sill 2 ft 11 in (0·89 m)
Emergency exit (stbd):
Height 1 ft 11 in (0·58 m)
Width 2 ft 1 in (0·63 m)

Dimensions, internal:
Cabin, excl flight deck and rear baggage compartment:
Length:
N22 17 ft 0 in (5·18 m)
N24 20 ft 7 in (6·27 m)
Max width 4 ft 3 in (1·30 m)
Max height 5 ft 2·4 in (1·58 m)
Floor area:
N22 70·25 sq ft (6·53 m²)
N24 87·0 sq ft (8·08 m²)
Volume:
N22 360·0 cu ft (10·19 m³)
N24 440·0 cu ft (12·46 m³)
Baggage compartment volume (nose):
N22 27 cu ft (0·76 m³)
N24 40·0 cu ft (1·13 m³)
Baggage compartment volume (optional, rear):
N22, N24 28·0 cu ft (0·79 m³)

Areas:
Wings, gross 324·0 sq ft (30·10 m²)
Ailerons (total net) 27·4 sq ft (2·55 m²)
Trailing-edge flaps (total net) 105·6 sq ft (9·81 m²)
Fin 39·1 sq ft (3·63 m²)
Rudder, incl tab 31·1 sq ft (2·89 m²)
Tailplane, incl tabs 78·0 sq ft (7·25 m²)

Weights and Loadings (N24 estimated):
Manufacturer's basic weight empty:
N22 4,451 lb (2,019 kg)
N24 4,530 lb (2,054 kg)
Typical operating weight empty:
N22 4,750 lb (2,154 kg)
Max disposable load:
N22 3,834 lb (1,739 kg)
Max T-O and landing weight:
N22, N24 8,500 lb (3,855 kg)
Max wing loading:
N22, N24 26·2 lb/sq ft (127·9 kg/m²)
Max power loading:
N22, N24 10·625 lb/shp (4·819 kg/shp)

Performance (at max T-O weight, ISA at S/L except where indicated otherwise; N24 estimated):
Normal cruising speed:
N22, N24 168 knots (193 mph; 311 km/h)
Stalling speed, power off, flaps up, at AUW of 7,500 lb (3,402 kg):
N22, N24 65 knots (75 mph; 121 km/h)
Stalling speed, power off, flaps down, at AUW of 7,500 lb (3,402 kg):
N22, N24 47 knots (54·5 mph; 88 km/h)
Max rate of climb at S/L, both engines, T-O rating for 5 min:
N22, N24 1,410 ft (430 m)/min
N22, N24 (ISA+20°C) 1,200 ft (366 m)/min
Rate of climb at S/L, one engine out, max continuous rating:
N22, N24 240 ft (73 m)/min
N22, N24 (ISA+20°C) 80 ft (24 m)/min
Service ceiling, both engines, climbing at 100 ft (30·5 m)/min, max cruise rating:
N22, N24 22,500 ft (6,860 m)
Min ground turning radius:
N22, N24 38 ft 3 in (11·66 m)
Runway LCN at max T-O weight:
N22, N24 2·3
T-O run:
N22, N24 (FAR 23) 720 ft (219 m)
N22, N24 (STOL) 580 ft (177 m)
N22, N24 (FAR 23), ISA+20°C 960 ft (293 m)
N22, N24 (STOL), ISA+20°C 820 ft (250 m)
T-O to 50 ft (15 m):
N22, N24 (FAR 23) 1,350 ft (411 m)
N22, N24 (STOL) 950 ft (290 m)
N22, N24 (FAR 23), ISA +20°C 1,790 ft (546 m)
Landing from 50 ft (15 m), AUW of 7,500 lb (3,402 kg):
N22, N24 (FAR 23) 1,295 ft (395 m)
N22, N24 (STOL) 710 ft (216 m)
N22, N24 (FAR 23), ISA +25°C 1,370 ft (418 m)
Landing run, AUW of 7,500 lb (3,402 kg):
N22, N24 (FAR 23) 620 ft (189 m)
N22, N24 (STOL) 340 ft (104 m)
N22, N24 (FAR 23), ISA + 25°C 675 ft (206 m)
Max range at 90% power, reserves for 45 min hold:
N22 at S/L 660 nm (760 miles; 1,223 km)
N22, N24 at 10,000 ft (3,050 m) 855 nm (985 miles; 1,585 km)

HAWKER DE HAVILLAND

HAWKER DE HAVILLAND AUSTRALIA PTY, LTD (Member Company of HAWKER SIDDELEY GROUP)

HEAD OFFICE:
PO Box 78, Lidcombe, NSW 2141
Telephone: 649-0111
Telex: 20214

DIRECTORS:
R. Kingsford-Smith (Chairman and Managing Director)
L. R. Jones (Deputy Managing Director)
H. B. M. Vose
B. S. Price (Commercial Director)
S. S. Schaetzel (Director and Chief Designer)
I. S. Gregg

PUBLIC RELATIONS MANAGER:
John D. S. Keatinge

This company manufactures components and equipment, and carries out repair and overhaul work, for a wide range of military and civil aircraft and aero-engines, propellers and accessories.

Details of these and other activities can be found in the 1972-73 *Jane's*.

A subsidiary of the company, Hawker Siddeley Electronics Ltd, is engaged in guided weapons and other defence contracts.

Another subsidiary, Hawker Siddeley Research Pty Ltd, is an approved research organisation and is actively engaged in a number of design and development contracts for the Australian defence authorities.

Hawker de Havilland is responsible for sales throughout south-east Asia of the GAF Nomad transport aircraft.

LOBET-DE-ROUVRAY

LOBET-DE-ROUVRAY AVIATION PTY LTD

ADDRESS:
Suite 7/506 Miller Street, Cammeray, New South Wales 2062
Telephone: 922 2599 and 922 2960

DIRECTOR:
James Lobet

The original Ganagobie was designed and built by the brothers William and James Lobet at Lille, France, and made its first flight in 1953, powered by an old Clerget engine. After modification and redesignation as Ganagobie 02 it flew for a further 30 hours before being grounded by engine failure in 1954, and later became Ganagobie 2 when fitted with a two-stroke target drone engine. Further modifications were then incorporated.

The second aircraft, Ganagobie 3, was built in Alberta, Canada, by Mr La Rue Smith; built of birch plywood, it was somewhat heavier than the first aircraft and was powered by a 72 hp McCulloch engine. A later Ganagobie 3 was fitted with a 40 hp Continental engine, and this version is also suitable for converted Volkswagen engines of 1,500 cc and above. The "ultra-light" version, known as the Ganagobie 4, is suitable for 48 hp Nelson and other small two-stroke engines. Very light okoumé mahogany, and other weight-saving features, may be used in its construction. Latest version is the Ganagobie 05.

GANAGOBIE 05

The Ganagobie 05 is a small, high-wing single-seat aircraft, designed primarily for amateur construction. Its general appearance is shown in the accompanying illustration.

Construction of the basic homebuilt aircraft is all-wooden; but production versions are under consideration, either in kit form with a fabric-covered steel-tube fuselage and wooden wings and tail, or in factory-built form with all-metal fabric-covered wing and tail control surfaces. The following description applies to the all-wood homebuilt version:

TYPE: Single-seat homebuilt light aircraft.

WINGS: Braced high-wing monoplane. Wing section NACA 23012. Constant-chord wings, with main and auxiliary spars and semi-circular tips. Centre-section integral with top of fuselage. Main panels have dihedral and can be detached for storage and transit, being carried in frames attached to the landing gear and cabane fittings on each side of the fuselage. A special frame fits over the rear of the fuselage to provide added support. Wooden spars and ribs, with non-structural plywood or aluminium leading-edge and fabric covering. Cable-operated plain ailerons. No flaps. Wings braced to fuselage by streamline-section steel-tube vee strut assembly on each side.

Ganagobie 05 ultra-light aircraft designed by James and William Lobet

FUSELAGE: Basically wooden structure, of diamond-shaped cross-section, consisting of spruce longerons, 12 bulkheads and formers, and plywood covering. Steel-tube engine mounting frame and wing-root cabane structure.

TAIL UNIT: Plywood-covered wooden fin and strut-braced tailplane; fabric-covered wooden elevators and horn-balanced rudder. Struts detachable to permit horizontal surfaces to fold upwards for storage and transit. Rudder and elevators cable-operated. Trim tab on port elevator.

LANDING GEAR: Non-retractable main wheels and tailskid or (optionally) tailwheel. Main wheels are mounted on tripod struts, the main legs of which have rubber-in-compression shock-absorption, and are of 8 in (20·3 cm) diameter with 8·00-4 tyres. Spoon-type tailskid mounted at end of a flat spring beneath rear fuselage. Front-wheel brakes are necessary if a tailwheel is fitted.

POWER PLANT: Aircraft is designed for a modified VW engine of at least 35 hp, with direct-drive two-blade propeller; a typical engine is the Sportavia Limbach SL 1700 D. Alternatively, geared-down VW engines with either vee-belt or gear reduction drive may be installed, provided that aircraft does not exceed its weight and CG range limitations. Fuel in two wing tanks between main and auxiliary spars; almost all of fuel load is usable.

ACCOMMODATION: Single seat in fully-enclosed cabin, with upward-opening door on each side. Ventilation devices in each transparent door panel. Seat belt attached to bulkhead.

DIMENSIONS, EXTERNAL:

Wing span	24 ft $3\frac{1}{4}$ in (7·40 m)
Wing chord (constant)	3 ft $11\frac{1}{4}$ in (1·20 m)
Wing aspect ratio	6·25
Length overall	16 ft $1\frac{3}{4}$ in (4·92 m)
Height overall	6 ft 0 in (1·83 m)
Tailplane span	7 ft $9\frac{3}{4}$ in (2·38 m)
Wheel track	4 ft 11 in (1·50 m)
Propeller diameter (direct drive)	4 ft 11 in (1·50 m)

AREAS:

Wings, gross	92·25 sq ft (8·57 m^2)
Ailerons (total)	11·61 sq ft (1·079 m^2)
Fin	5·02 sq ft (0·466 m^2)
Rudder	4·71 sq ft (0·438 m^2)
Tailplane	10·63 sq ft (0·988 m^2)
Elevators, incl tab	6·51 sq ft (0·605 m^2)

WEIGHTS AND LOADING:

Weight empty	630 lb (285 kg)
Max T-O weight	800 lb (362 kg)
Max wing loading	8·88 lb/sq ft (43·4 kg/m^2)

PERFORMANCE (at max T-O weight, theoretical, with SL 1700 D engine):

Max level speed	98 knots (113 mph; 182 km/h)
Max cruising speed (75% power)	87 knots (100 mph; 161 km/h)
Stalling speed	41 knots (47 mph; 76 km/h)
Service ceiling	10,000 ft (3,050 m)

MILLICER

HENRY MILLICER

ADDRESS:
c/o Royal Melbourne Institute of Technology, 124 Latrobe Street, Melbourne, Victoria

Mr Millicer, who in 1953 designed the original Airtourer light aircraft (see under "Aerospace" heading in New Zealand section), has recently designed an ultra-light aeroplane known as the Airmite.

MILLICER AIRMITE

Mr Millicer, who was for 10 years Chief Aerodynamicist of the Australian Government Aircraft Factories, is currently principal lecturer in aeronautics at the Royal Melbourne Institute of Technology. Assisted by students at the RMIT, he was building, in the Spring of 1974, the prototype of the Airmite, an all-metal single-seat ultra-light aeroplane built mainly of aluminium alloy.

It is designed for marketing in kit form, and to be capable of assembly in a normal-sized garage or workshop by homebuilders of average abilities, using standard commercially-available pop-riveting tools.

DIMENSIONS, EXTERNAL:

Wing span	19 ft 0 in (5·79 m)
Length overall	18 ft 0 in (5·49 m)

WEIGHT:

Max T-O weight	600-800 lb (272-362 kg)

PERFORMANCE (approx):

Max level speed	200 knots (230 mph; 370 km/h)
Stalling speed	42 knots (48·5 mph; 78 km/h)
Range	370 nm (425 miles; 685 km)

PHILLIPS

D. A. PHILLIPS

ADDRESS:
D. A. Phillips, VTOL Aircraft (Australia) Pty Ltd, PO Box 5195C, Newcastle West, New South Wales 2302
Telephone: 435348

PHILLIPS PHILLICOPTER Mk 1

Mr Phillips, assisted by Mr P. Gerakiteys, designed and built a prototype two-seat helicopter known as the Phillicopter Mk 1. Design work began in 1962, construction started in 1967, and the prototype flew for the first time in 1971. Certification trials were under way in early 1972. Orders for eight Phillicopters had been received by the end of February 1972.

No news of this aircraft has been received since that time.

TYPE: Two-seat light helicopter.

ROTOR SYSTEM: Two-blade main and tail rotors. Main rotor blades, of NACA 0012 section and fully-extruded hollow-section construction, are attached to hub by solid grips. Fixed tab on each trailing-edge. Tail rotor blade construction similar to main rotor blades.

ROTOR DRIVE: Via three gearboxes: one transfer box, one reduction box and one tail rotor box. Main rotor/engine rpm ratio 1 : 5·66; tail rotor/engine rpm ratio 1 : 1.

FUSELAGE: Tubular steel airframe, with aluminium and glassfibre covering.

TAIL UNIT: Tubular steel open space-frame. Tailplane incidence adjustable manually on ground.

LANDING GEAR: Tubular skid type. Shock-absorption through bending and torsion of cross-members. Ground handling wheels. Float gear available optionally.

POWER PLANT: One 145 hp Rolls-Royce Continental O-200-C four-cylinder horizontally-opposed aircooled engine. Single fuel tank, capacity 18 Imp gallons (82 litres). Oil capacity 1·25 Imp gallons (5·7 litres).

ACCOMMODATION: Side-by-side seating for pilot and one passenger. Door on each side of cabin. Accommodation ventilated.

SYSTEMS AND EQUIPMENT: Battery for electrical power. Radio fitted.

DIMENSIONS, EXTERNAL:

Main rotor diameter	25 ft 6 in (7·77 m)
Tail rotor diameter	4 ft 0 in (1·22 m)
Distance between rotor centres	13 ft 9 in (4·19 m)
Main rotor blade chord (each)	8 in (20·3 cm)
Length overall, rotors fore and aft	28 ft 10 in (8·79 m)
Length of fuselage	21 ft 10 in (6·65 m)
Height to top of rotor hub	8 ft 0 in (2·44 m)
Height overall	8 ft 4 in (2·54 m)
Skid track	6 ft 4 in (1·93 m)

DIMENSIONS, INTERNAL:

Cabin: Length	5 ft 4 in (1·63 m)
Max width	3 ft 10 in (1·17 m)
Max height	4 ft 2 in (1·27 m)

AREAS:

Main rotor blades (each)	9·56 sq ft (0·89 m²)
Tail rotor blades (each)	0·50 sq ft (0·046 m²)
Main rotor disc	510·00 sq ft (47·38 m²)
Tail rotor disc	12·56 sq ft (1·17 m²)

WEIGHTS AND LOADINGS:

Weight empty	1,050 lb (476 kg)
Max T-O and landing weight	1,650 lb (748 kg)
Max disc loading	3·24 lb/sq ft (15·82 kg/m²)
Max power loading	11·35 lb/hp (5·15 kg/hp)

PERFORMANCE (at max T-O weight):

Max level speed	78 knots (90 mph; 145 km/h)
Max cruising speed	74 knots (85 mph; 137 km/h)
Econ cruising speed	60·5 knots (70 mph; 112·5 km/h)
Max rate of climb at S/L	1,200 ft (365 m)/min
Vertical rate of climb at S/L	300 ft (91 m)/min
Service ceiling	16,000 ft (4,880 m)
Hovering ceiling in ground effect	8,000 ft (2,440 m)
Hovering ceiling out of ground effect (optimum)	6,000 ft (1,830 m)
Range with max fuel	200 nm (230 miles; 370 km)

Phillips Phillicopter Mk 1 prototype (145 hp Rolls-Royce Continental O-200-C engine) *(S. J. Cherz)*

TRANSAVIA

TRANSAVIA CORPORATION PTY, LTD

HEAD OFFICE:
Transfield House, 102-106 Arthur Street, North Sydney, NSW 2060
Telephone: 929-8600
Telex: Transho 21396

WORKS:
73 Station Road, Seven Hills, NSW 2147
Telephone: 631-0163

SERVICE DIVISION:
Hangar 120, Bankstown Aerodrome, NSW
Telephone: 70-6968

CHAIRMAN:
F. Belgiorno-Nettis

DIRECTOR:
C. Salteri

GENERAL MANAGER:
G. Forrester

Transavia Corporation was formed in 1964 as a subsidiary of Transfield Pty Ltd, one of Australia's largest construction companies.

Its first product is the multi-purpose PL-12 Airtruk.

TRANSAVIA PL-12 AIRTRUK

The Airtruk, designed by Mr Luigi Pellarini, was originally type-certificated on 10 February 1966, for spreading fertiliser and for seeding. Swath width is up to 35 yd (32 m) and of unusual uniformity. A liquid-spraying conversion, developed in 1968, is capable of covering a 33 yd (30·2 m) swath. This version has an engine-driven spray pump and a liquid chemical capacity of 180 Imp gallons (818 litres). The PL-12's unconventional layout keeps the tails clear of chemicals, and also permits rapid loading by a vehicle which approaches the aircraft between the tails.

The three-seat prototype Airtruk flew for the first time on 22 April 1965. Delivery of production Airtruks began in December 1966, and a total of 60 PL-12s had been built by June 1973, for customers in Australia, New Zealand, Thailand and Africa. These included 40 for export, of which 22 were for New Zealand and nine (including three PL-12-Us) for Thailand.

Production of the PL-12 was continuing in 1974, together with that of the **PL-12-U**, a multi-purpose cargo/passenger/ambulance/aerial survey version of which a prototype flew for the first time in December 1970. Certification of this version was granted in February 1971, by which time two production aircraft had been completed, and deliveries began later in the year.

Airtruks are being assembled by Barr Brothers in New Zealand (which see).

The following description applies to both the PL-12 and PL-12-U, except where a particular version is indicated:

TYPE: Single-engined agricultural (PL-12) or multi-purpose (PL-12-U) aircraft.

WINGS: Strut-braced sesquiplane. Wing section NACA 23012. Dihedral 1° 30′ on upper wings. Incidence (upper wings) 3° 0′. Conventional all-metal structure, covered with Alclad sheet. All-metal trailing-edge flaps and ailerons, covered with ribbed Alclad sheet, and operated manually. Small stub wings below fuselage, braced to cabin by a single strut and to upper wings by a Vee-strut each side.

FUSELAGE: Pod-shaped structure, of 4130 welded steel tube construction with 2024 Alclad covering and glassfibre tailcone.

TAIL UNIT: Twin units, each comprising a fin, rudder and separate "T" tailplane and elevator, and each carried on a cantilever tubular Alclad boom extending from the upper wings. Small bumper fairing underneath each fin. Manually-operated control surfaces. Adjustable tab in each elevator. No tabs on rudder.

LANDING GEAR: Non-retractable tricycle type, each of the three wheels being carried on a pivoted trailing leg. Shock-absorbers of Transavia patented type, of bonded rubber block moulded within four hinged plates forming a diamond shape, loaded at the long axis and deformed by loads to exchange long and short axes. All wheels and tyres same size, 8·00-6. Nosewheel tyre pressure 20 lb/sq in (1·41 kg/cm²); main-wheel tyre pressure 32 lb/sq in (2·25 kg/cm²). Cleveland brakes.

POWER PLANT: One 300 hp Continental IO-520-D six-cylinder horizontally-opposed aircooled engine, driving a McCauley D2A34C58/90AT-2 two-blade constant-speed metal propeller. Two upper-wing fuel tanks, total usable capacity 40 Imp gallons (181·5 litres). Optional long-range installation of second tank in each upper mainplane, increasing total capacity to 82 Imp gallons (373 litres). Refuelling point above each upper wing. Oil capacity 2·5 Imp gallons (11·4 litres).

ACCOMMODATION (PL-12): Single-seat cockpit, with door on starboard side. Two-seat cabin aft of chemical hopper/tank for carriage of ground crew, with door at rear of lower deck. Accommodation heated and ventilated.

ACCOMMODATION (PL-12-U): Single-seat cockpit as in PL-12. By removing the central hopper or tank, passenger cabin is enlarged to seat one passenger on upper deck (back to back with pilot's seat) and four more passengers on lower deck. Doors on upper deck (starboard side) and lower deck (port side). Lower-deck cabin is heated.

SYSTEMS: 12V electrical system standard.

ELECTRONICS AND EQUIPMENT: Optional equipment for PL-12-U includes VHF (also available optionally for PL-12), HF, ADF, artificial horizon and directional gyro.

DIMENSIONS, EXTERNAL:

Wing span	39 ft 3½ in (11·98 m)
Wing chord (constant)	5 ft 9 in (1·75 m)
Length overall	21 ft 0 in (6·40 m)
Length of fuselage	13 ft 0 in (3·96 m)

Transavia PL-12 Airtruk agricultural aircraft (300 hp Continental IO-520-D engine) *(K. Meehan)*

PL-12-U multi-purpose cargo/passenger/ambulance/survey version of the Airtruk

Height overall 9 ft 0 in (2·74 m)
Tailplane span (each) 7 ft 0 in (2·13 m)
Distance between tailplanes 11 ft 5 in (3·48 m)
Wheel track 10 ft 0 in (3·05 m)
Wheelbase 6 ft 3 in (1·91 m)
Propeller diameter 7 ft 4 in (2·23 m)
Min propeller ground clearance 1 ft 0 in (0·30 m)
Passenger door (PL-12, rear):
Height 3 ft 2 in (0·97 m)
Passenger doors (PL-12-U, stbd upper and port lower, each):
Height 3 ft 0 in (0·91 m)

DIMENSIONS, INTERNAL (PL-12):
Rear passenger cabin:
Length 6 ft 0 in (1·83 m)
Max width 3 ft 2 in (0·97 m)
Max height 6 ft 8 in (2·03 m)
Floor area 4 sq ft (0·37 m^2)
Volume 30 cu ft (0·85 m^3)

DIMENSIONS, INTERNAL (PL-12-U):
Passenger cabin:
Length 9 ft 0 in (2·74 m)
Max width 3 ft 2 in (0·97 m)
Max height 6 ft 11 in (2·11 m)
Floor area 18 sq ft (1·67 m^2)
Volume 74 cu ft (2·10 m^3)

AREAS:
Wings, gross 256 sq ft (23·8 m^2)
Ailerons, total 18·0 sq ft (1·67 m^2)
Trailing-edge flaps, total 18·0 sq ft (1·67 m^2)
Fins, total 14·0 sq ft (1·30 m^2)
Rudders, total 6·0 sq ft (0·56 m^2)
Tailplanes, total 28·0 sq ft (2·60 m^2)
Elevators, total, incl tabs 14·0 sq ft (1·30 m^2)

WEIGHTS AND LOADINGS:
Weight empty:
PL-12 1,710 lb (775 kg)
PL-12-U 1,830 lb (830 kg)
Max T-O weight:
PL-12 (normal category) 3,800 lb (1,723 kg)
PL-12 (agricultural category) 4,090 lb (1,855 kg)
PL-12-U 3,800 lb (1,723 kg)
Max landing weight (both) 3,800 lb (1,723 kg)
Max wing loading:
PL-12 16·2 lb/sq ft (79 kg/m^2)
PL-12-U 15·0 lb/sq ft (73 kg/m^2)
Max power loading:
PL-12 13·7 lb/hp (6·21 kg/hp)
PL-12-U 12·7 lb/hp (5·76 kg/hp)

PERFORMANCE (at max T-O weight except where indicated):
Max never-exceed speed
PL-12 180 knots (207 mph; 333 km/h)
PL-12-U 150 knots (172 mph; 276·5 km/h)
Max level speed at S/L, ISA:
PL-12 103 knots (119 mph; 192 km/h)
PL-12-U 112 knots (129 mph; 208 km/h)
Max cruising speed (75% power) at S/L, ISA:
PL-12 95 knots (109 mph; 175 km/h)
PL-12-U 102 knots (117 mph; 188 km/h)
Stalling speed, flaps up:
PL-12 55 knots (64 mph; 103 km/h)
PL-12-U 52 knots (60 mph; 97 km/h)
Stalling speed, flaps down:
PL-12 52 knots (60 mph; 97 km/h)
PL-12-U 50 knots (58 mph; 94 km/h)
Max rate of climb at S/L:
PL-12 600 ft (183 m)/min
PL-12-U 800 ft (244 m)/min
Service ceiling (both versions) 10,500 ft (3,200 m)
*T-O run:
PL-12 1,095 ft (334 m)
PL-12-U 900 ft (274 m)
*T-O to 50 ft (15 m):
PL-12 1,850 ft (564 m)
PL-12-U 1,500 ft (457 m)
Landing run (both versions, at max landing weight) 600 ft (183 m)
Normal range with standard fuel 286 nm (330 miles; 531 km)
Ferry range, standard fuel 330 nm (380 miles; 611 km)
*_DCA Australia technique_

YAGER
KARL YAGER

ADDRESS:
43 Victoria Street, Lewisham, New South Wales 2049
Telephone: 56-2775

Mr Yager, whose Libellula two-seat light aircraft was described briefly in the 1971-72 _Jane's_, has since advised us that this aircraft was a design study only. He built a prototype of his second design; but this was scrapped after shortcomings had been revealed during initial taxying runs and short hop-flights. Mr Yager is currently building a third design, the KY-03.

YAGER KY-03 LIBELLULA

Two examples of the KY-03 are being constructed in Australia, one by Mr Yager and the other by Mr Collin Herbert of Adelaide. The latter is intended to have a more comprehensive equipment installation. First flight, by either aircraft, is not expected until 1975.

TYPE: Four-seat homebuilt light aircraft.

WINGS: Cantilever tandem wings of 2024 light alloy box-spar construction, with PVC foam sandwiched between bonded and riveted outer skins. Eppler 531 section; thickness/chord ratio 16·8%. Front wings have 5° dihedral and an incidence of —1° 12′. Plain ailerons and Fowler trailing-edge flaps of 2024 light alloy on front wings; elevators on rear wings. Trim tabs in ailerons and elevators.

FUSELAGE: Semi-monocoque structure of 2024 light alloy, with PVC foam sandwiched between skins in cabin area.

TAIL UNIT: Twin sweptback fins and rudders, mounted at approx one-third span on rear wings. Trim tab in each rudder.

LANDING GEAR: Retractable tricycle type. Manual retraction of all units into fuselage, main units inward, nose unit rearward. Oleo shock-absorbers of Yager design. Goodyear 5·00-5 wheels and 14·25 × 5·12 tyres on all three units. Goodyear brakes.

POWER PLANT: Two 86 hp Sportavia Limbach SL 2100 D four-cylinder four-stroke engines, one in the nose and one in the tail, each driving a Hoffmann HO-V 113 three-blade automatic variable-pitch propeller. Fuel tank in outer panel of each front wing, total capacity 72 Imp gallons (327 litres).

ACCOMMODATION: Seats for four persons, in side-by-side pairs, under upward-opening framed canopy.

ELECTRONICS AND EQUIPMENT: The KY-03 being built by Mr Herbert will be equipped eventually with a full range of electronics.

DIMENSIONS, EXTERNAL:
Wing span:
front 32 ft 0 in (9·75 m)
rear 20 ft 0 in (6·10 m)
Front wing chord (constant) 4 ft 0 in (1·22 m)
Front wing aspect ratio 8
Length overall 21 ft $10\frac{3}{4}$ in (6·67 m)
Length of fuselage 17 ft $6\frac{1}{4}$ in (5·34 m)
Height overall 8 ft $9\frac{1}{2}$ in (2·68 m)
Wheel track 7 ft 6 in (2·29 m)
Wheelbase 7 ft $9\frac{1}{2}$ in (2·37 m)
Propeller ground clearance (front) 1 ft 0 in (0·305 m)

AREAS:
Wings, gross:
front 128·0 sq ft (11·90 m^2)
rear, incl elevators 69·6 sq ft (6·47 m^2)
Ailerons (total) 11·2 sq ft (1·04 m^2)
Trailing-edge flaps (front wings, total) 25·0 sq ft (2·32 m^2)
Fins (total) 10·6 sq ft (0·98 m^2)
Rudders (total, incl tabs) 5·0 sq ft (0·46 m^2)
Elevators (total, incl tabs) 9·6 sq ft (0·89 m^2)

WEIGHTS AND LOADINGS (estimated):
Weight empty 1,217 lb (552 kg)
Max T-O weight 2,200 lb (998 kg)
Max wing loading 17·2 lb/sq ft (84·0 kg/m^2)
Max power loading 12·7 lb/hp (5·76 kg/hp)

PERFORMANCE (estimated, at max T-O weight):
Max level speed at S/L 184 knots (212 mph; 341 km/h)
Max cruising speed 147 knots (169 mph; 272 km/h)
Stalling speed 36 knots (41·5 mph; 67 km/h)
Max rate of climb at S/L 1,180 ft (360 m)/min
Rate of climb at S/L, one engine out 372 ft (113 m)/min
T-O run 645 ft (197 m)
Range with max fuel 870 nm (1,000 miles; 1,610 km)

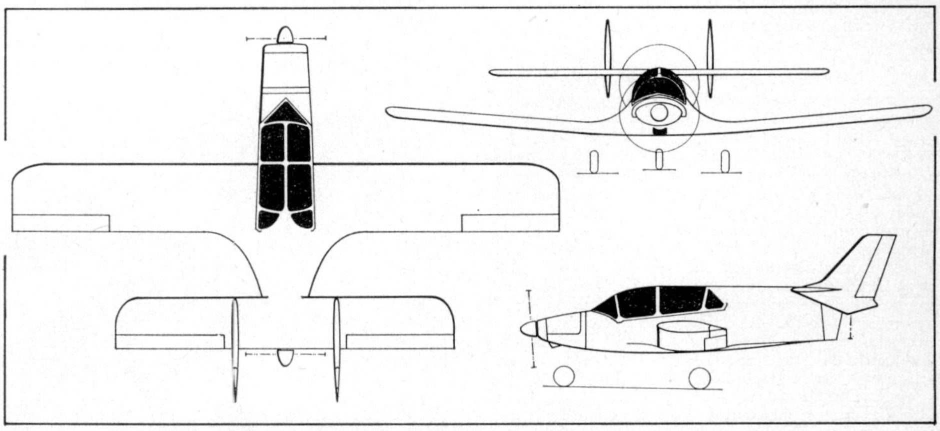

Yager KY-03 Libellula four-seat tandem-engined light aircraft (_Roy J. Grainge_)

AUSTRIA

MALLIGA
JOSEF MALLIGA

ADDRESS:
Melbensiedlung 23, 8740 Zeltweg/Lind

MALLIGA 1

Herr Josef Malliga, an officer in the Austrian Army and a flying instructor since 1962, began the design of a man-powered aircraft in August 1966. This aircraft flew for the first time in September 1967 and in 1970 was flown successfully for 492 ft (150 m). In 1971-72 Herr Malliga made major modifications to the wings, and other changes to the tail unit, airframe covering and propeller. On its first attempt to fly in 1972, with Siegfried Puch as pilot, the port wing was damaged during the take-off run, due to inaccurate rigging of the flying wires. After further modification, planned for the Summer of 1974, it was hoped to make another attempt.

All available details of the aircraft in its 1972 form were given in the 1973-74 _Jane's_.

BELGIUM

CW
CW HELICOPTER RESEARCH

ADDRESS:
Baron Ruzettelaan 267, 8200 Brugge 2
Telephone: 10575
DIRECTOR:
Willy Clybouw

CW 205

The CW 205 is a high-speed three-seat all-metal light helicopter, designed both for factory production and for marketing in kit form for amateur constructors. Design began in 1972, and construction of a prototype was started in December 1973.

TYPE: Three-seat light helicopter.

ROTOR SYSTEM: Two counter-rotating and intermeshing four-blade rigid main rotors, mounted side by side on pylons above the fuselage and canted outward from the vertical. Blades on each rotor are mounted in pairs, with included angle of only 10° instead of conventional 90°, enabling the rear blade of each pair to act as a kind of "Fowler flap" for the front one. Blades are of NACA 23015 section, constant chord, and have 5° twist. Construction is of 2024T3 aluminium alloy. The intermeshing configuration is fully controllable cyclically, and the blades of each pair are actuated collectively. Each rotor has a coning angle of 170° and is canted forward at 6°. Each rotor drive-shaft is inclined at a 12° angle. A rotor brake is fitted.

ROTOR DRIVE: Direct drive, via a centrifugal clutch and a dual rotor gearbox in the fuselage roof. Rotor rpm 400.

FUSELAGE: Streamlined semi-monocoque, of all-metal construction.

TAIL UNIT: Cantilever structure of 2024T3 aluminium alloy. Variable-incidence tailplane, with elevators. Twin sweptback endplate fins; no rudders.

LANDING GEAR: Retractable tailwheel type, with spring steel shock-absorbers. Manual or hydraulic retraction, main wheels inwards into wells in fuselage beneath cabin floor, tailwheel forward.

Power Plant: One 245 hp Lycoming O-435 six-cylinder horizontally-opposed aircooled engine, mounted at 39° from the horizontal.

Accommodation: One-piece moulded Plexiglas canopy, which slides forward to give access to three side-by-side seats in cabin. Dual controls at outer seats.

Dimensions, external:
- Rotor diameter (each) 23 ft 9 in (7·24 m)
- Rotor blade chord (constant, each) 6 in (0·15 m)
- Distance between rotor hubs 7 ft 0 in (2·13 m)
- Span over rotor tips 30 ft 9¼ in (9·38 m)
- Length overall 21 ft 4 in (6·50 m)
- Length of fuselage 20 ft 8 in (6·30 m)
- Height overall 7 ft 2¾ in (2·20 m)
- Tailplane span (c/l of vertical fins) 7 ft 3¾ in (2·23 m)
- Fuselage: Max width 5 ft 10½ in (1·79 m)
- Wheel track 5 ft 5 in (1·65 m)

Areas:
- Rotor discs (total) 882·6 sq ft (82·00 m^2)
- Rotor blades (total, 8 blades) 38·75 sq ft (3·60 m^2)

Weights and Loadings:
- Weight empty 1,631 lb (740 kg)
- Max T-O weight 2,381 lb (1,080 kg)
- Max blade loading 61·4 lb/sq ft (300 kg/m^2)
- Max power loading 9·92 lb/hp (4·5 kg/hp)

Performance (estimated, at max T-O weight):
- Max cruising speed 129 knots (149 mph; 240 km/h)
- Max rate of climb at S/L 984 ft (300 m)/min
- Max range 324 nm (373 miles; 600 km)

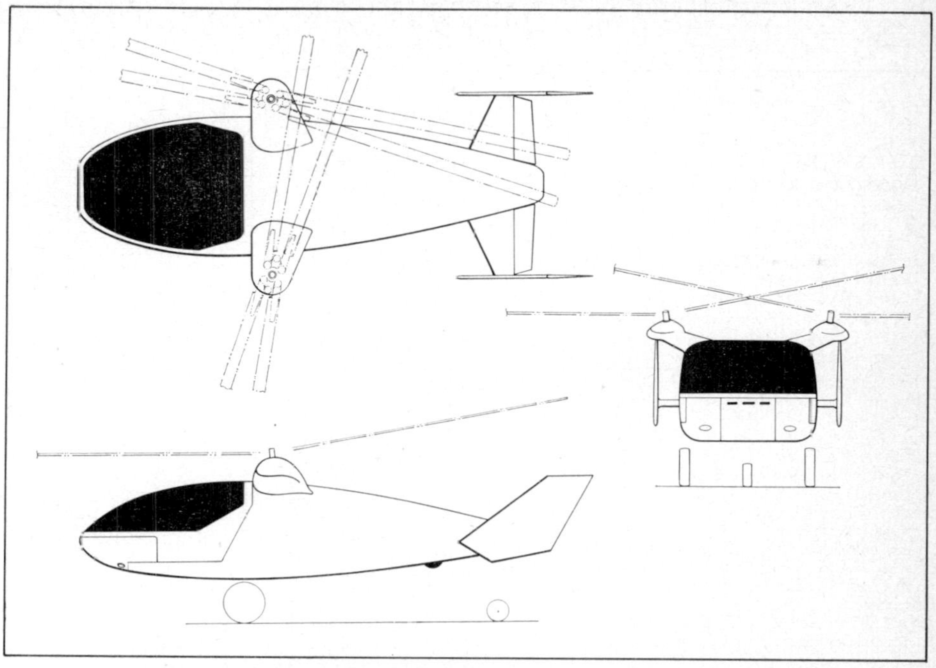

CW 205 three-seat light helicopter (245 hp Lycoming O-435 engine) (*Roy J. Grainge*)

FAIREY

FAIREY S A

Head Office, Works and Airport:
6200 Gosselies

Telephone: Charleroi (07) 35.01.90
Telex: 51/241

Chairman:
Sir Joseph Hunt

Managing Director:
A. Talbott

Directors:
R. W. Holder
A. C. Hayward
F. R. J. Britten
W. D. Norman

Production and Technical Manager:
J. Delhaye

Administrative and Financial Manager:
M. Crem

Marketing, Contracts and Sales Manager:
W. J. J. Delbecq

Personnel Manager:
A. Fogienne

Publicity and Press:
C. de Rouck

This company, known formerly as Avions Fairey SA, was formed in 1931 as a subsidiary of the English Fairey Aviation Co. Ltd, later expanding its facilities considerably to manufacture Gloster Meteor, Hawker Hunter and Lockheed F-104G fighters post-war for NATO and the Belgian Air Force.

Following completion of this work, the company contributed to the Breguet Atlantic programme. In addition, a contract was signed in 1969 whereby Fairey undertook a major share in building Mirage 5s for the Belgian Air Force. Details of this programme were given in the 1973-74 *Jane's*. The agreement also covers the manufacture of rear fuselage sections for all Mirage F1 aircraft ordered from Dassault-Breguet, no matter by whom they are ordered. Other aspects of the agreement provide for participation by Fairey in production programmes for the variable-geometry Dassault Mirage G and for other aircraft.

The company is collaborating on an international basis on many other projects, including the VFW 614 transport aircraft, the manufacture of oil tanks for J79 turbojet engines built under licence in Europe, and of special hydraulic equipment.

Overhaul and repair of military and civil aircraft constitute an important part of the company's activities. Major subcontract work currently in hand includes the manufacture of glassfibre components for Aérospatiale helicopters and the glass-reinforced plastics airframe for the MBLE Epervier (see "RPVs and Targets" section).

Since October 1972 Britten-Norman in the UK (which see) has been a member of the Fairey group of companies, as a result of which Fairey SA is now the principal constructor of the Britten-Norman Islander and Trislander light transport aircraft.

Fairey's works cover an area of some 480,825 sq ft (44,670 m^2) and employ almost 1,250 people.

SABCA

SOCIÉTÉ ANONYME BELGE DE CONSTRUCTIONS AÉRONAUTIQUES

Head Office:
Chaussée de la Hulpe 185, B-1170 Brussels
Telephone: Brussels (02) 60 00 64
Telex: SABDG 23 244

Works:
Haren-Brussels, Chaussée de Haecht 1470, B-1130 Brussels
Telephone: Brussels (02) 16 80 10
Telex: SABUSH 21 237
Aéroport de Gosselies/Charleroi, B-6200 Gosselies
Telephone: Charleroi (07) 35 01 70
Telex: SABGO 51 251

Chairman: A. Dubuisson

Director, General Manager:
P. G. Willekens

SABCA has been since 1920 the largest aircraft manufacturer in Belgium. In addition to building aircraft and aero-engines under licence pre-war for the Belgian government and the Sabena company, it also built aircraft of its own design.

Dassault-Breguet (France) and Fokker-VFW (Netherlands/Germany) have parity holdings in SABCA, through which the Belgian company now participates in various European projects.

At Haren, the company is working on components for the Dassault-Breguet/Dornier Alpha Jet; Dassault Mirage F1, Mirage III, Mirage 5 and Mercure; VFW 614; Fokker-VFW F.27 and F.28; and Aérospatiale/Westland SA 330 Puma. (Delivery of 106 Mirage 5-BA, 5-BD and 5-BR aircraft to the Belgian Air Force was completed in May 1973.) SABCA is also manufacturing hydraulic components and tanks for F-104G and TF-104G aircraft in European service.

SABCA is undertaking the maintenance of NATO Hawk surface-to-air missiles. At Haren, a specially-equipped machine shop, with clean-room, is devoted to the production of hydraulic equipment for aircraft and guided missiles.

At Gosselies, SABCA has started to maintain and overhaul Mirage 5 aircraft, and is continuing to maintain and overhaul F-104G aircraft for the Belgian Air Force. This works is also engaged on overhaul and repair of other military aeroplanes and helicopters for the Belgian and foreign armed forces.

SABCA's Electronic Division, Cobelda, is manufacturing IFF equipment for the Mirage 5, SATT electronic equipment (all-weather landing monitoring system) for the Mercure, Doppler equipment for the Atlantic and a variety of aircraft electronic ground equipment. It undertakes also work on electronic equipment under F-104G overhaul contracts, and is engaged in repair of the pulse acquisition radar of the Hawk missile. The Division is undertaking series production of a tank fire control system, which has been ordered by the Belgian Ministry of Defence to equip the Leopard tank of the Belgian Army. It is also engaged in the production of some of the equipment for this system, and of a simulator which allows the tank crews to be trained in firing. SABCA holds patents for this system in many countries.

Its work on the Belgian Mirage 5 aircraft included functional test procedures in the labora-

SABCA-built Dassault Mirage 5-BA (*right*), alongside a Lockheed F-104G overhauled by SABCA for the Belgian Air Force

tory before installation of equipment in the aircraft and checkout after such installation.

SABCA is involved in space projects, including the Ariane L 3 S space launcher and Spacelab, and for this purpose is a member of various European consortia.

In 1974 the Haren and Gosselies works occupied a total area of approx 710,420 sq ft (66,000 m²) and between them employed about 1,850 people.

BRAZIL

AEROTEC

SOCIEDADE AEROTEC LTDA

HEAD OFFICE AND WORKS:
Caixa Postal 286, São José dos Campos, São Paulo State

GENERAL AND INDUSTRIAL DIRECTOR:
Carlos Gonçalves

COMMERCIAL DIRECTOR:
Wlademir Monteiro Carneiro

ADMINISTRATIVE DIRECTOR:
Almir Medeiros

This company was formed in 1968. It designed and built the prototype Uirapuru light aircraft, which, under the military designation T-23, has been ordered by the Brazilian and Paraguayan air forces and for civil flying clubs.

Aerotec is also engaged in the manufacturing programme for the EMBRAER Ipanema agricultural aircraft (which see), being responsible for building the wings and tail unit under contract from EMBRAER; and is manufacturing, under subcontract, gun pods and Microturbo starter pods for the Xavante jet trainer and light attack aircraft.

In 1973 Aerotec employed 192 persons and its premises occupied approx 60,280 sq ft (5,600 m²) of covered space.

AEROTEC 122 UIRAPURU

Brazilian Air Force designation: T-23

The Uirapuru was designed as a private venture by Engs José Carlos de Souza Reis and Carlos Gonçalves. The prototype (PP-ZTF), with a 108 hp Lycoming O-235-C1 engine, flew for the first time on 2 June 1965 and was described and illustrated in the 1966-67 *Jane's*. It was followed by a second Uirapuru (PP-ZTT), with a 150 hp Lycoming O-320-A engine.

In early 1968, the Brazilian Air Force placed an order for 30 production aircraft, powered by 160 hp Lycoming O-320-B2B engines. Two pre-production T-23s (0940 and 0941) were completed in early 1968, making their first flights on 23 January and 11 April respectively. These differed from the production version in having 150 hp engines.

In April 1969 the number of T-23s on order by the Brazilian Air Force was increased to 70, and delivery of these has been completed. A further 20 were ordered by the Brazilian Air Force in February 1973, and Aerotec is to supply 10 additional aircraft per year to offset losses and compensate for aircraft undergoing IRAN. In addition, 20 Uirapurus were ordered by the Paraguayan Air Force. In Brazilian Air Force service the T-23 Uirapurus are employed at the Centro de Formação de Pilotos Militares (Military Pilots' Training Centre) in Natal, Rio Grande do Norte State.

Aerotec has developed a version of the Uirapuru for the civil market. This is basically similar to the military version, except for having a cockpit canopy like that of the second prototype (see 1967-68 *Jane's*). It also has outer-wing tanks, increasing the total fuel capacity to 50·5 Imp gallons (230 litres), with which maximum range and endurance are 700 nm (805 miles; 1,300 km) and 6 hr 30 min respectively. Ten civil Uirapurus had been ordered by March 1973, when the combined output of military and civil models was continuing at the rate of three aircraft per month.

The following description applies to the standard T-23 military version:

TYPE: Two-seat primary trainer.

WINGS: Cantilever low-wing monoplane. Wing section NACA 43013. Dihedral 5°. Incidence 2°. Light alloy structure of centre-section and two outer panels. All-metal ailerons and trailing-edge split flaps. Flap settings 0°, 20° and 40°; ailerons deflect 20° up and 13° down. Glassfibre wingtips.

FUSELAGE: All-metal semi-monocoque structure in 2024-T-3 aluminium, with 4130 steel for critical areas.

TAIL UNIT: Cantilever all-metal construction. Fin, rudder, tailplane and elevator tips of glassfibre. Trim tab in starboard half of elevator. Statically and aerodynamically balanced elevator. aerodynamically balanced rudder. Fixed ventral fin. Vertical and horizontal surfaces of NACA 0009 section. Sweepback 30° on fin leading-edge. Elevator deflects 30° up, 23° down; trim tab 22° up, 40° down; rudder 25° to left and right.

LANDING GEAR: Non-retractable tricycle type, with nosewheel steerable 22° to each side. Rubber-cushioned shock-absorbers on main units; oleo shock-absorber on nose unit. All wheels have Goodyear 6·00-6 tyres, pressure 26 lb/sq in (1·83 kg/cm²) on main units and 24 lb/sq in (1·69 kg/cm²) on nose unit. Independent hydraulic disc brakes on main units. Parking brake. Legs of 4130 steel, with small fairings on main-wheel legs.

POWER PLANT: One 160 hp Lycoming O-320-B2B four-cylinder horizontally-opposed aircooled engine, driving a Sensenich M-76-DM-60 two-blade fixed-pitch metal propeller. Variable-pitch propeller optional. Two integral fuel tanks in wing leading-edges, with total capacity of 31 Imp gallons (140 litres). Refuelling points above tanks. Optional 11 Imp gallon (50 litre) wingtip tanks.

ACCOMMODATION: Two fully-adjustable seats side by side under rearward-sliding transparent canopy. Two-piece windscreen. For emergency ejection, canopy separates into two pieces. Seats permit the use of either back-type or seat-type parachutes. Dual controls. Baggage compartment, capacity 66 lb (30 kg), aft of seats with access from cockpit only.

SYSTEMS: Hydraulic system for brakes. Electrical system includes 24V 50A generator, 24V 24Ah battery and electric starter.

ELECTRONICS AND EQUIPMENT: Conventional VFR equipment. Optional items include VHF transceiver, ADF, artificial horizon and directional gyro. Adjustable-angle 100W landing light in each wing leading-edge.

DIMENSIONS, EXTERNAL:	
Wing span	27 ft 10¾ in (8·50 m)
Wing chord (constant)	5 ft 0¼ in (1·53 m)
Wing aspect ratio	5·33
Length overall	21 ft 8 in (6·60 m)
Height overall	8 ft 10 in (2·70 m)
Tailplane span	9 ft 2¼ in (2·80 m)
Width of fuselage	3 ft 6½ in (1·08 m)
Wheel track	7 ft 10½ in (2·40 m)
Wheelbase	5 ft 0¼ in (1·53 m)
Propeller diameter	6 ft 1½ in (1·87 m)
Propeller ground clearance	10¾ in (0·27 m)
AREAS:	
Wings, gross	145·3 sq ft (13·50 m²)
Ailerons (total)	12·81 sq ft (1·19 m²)
Flaps (total)	10·23 sq ft (0·95 m²)
Fin	6·46 sq ft (0·60 m²)
Rudder	5·38 sq ft (0·50 m²)
Tailplane	16·15 sq ft (1·50 m²)
Elevator, incl tab	11·84 sq ft (1·10 m²)
WEIGHTS AND LOADINGS:	
Weight empty	1,191 lb (540 kg)
Max T-O weight	1,825 lb (840 kg)
Max wing loading	13·90 lb/sq ft (63·0 kg/m²)
Max power loading	12·35 lb/hp (5·60 kg/hp)
PERFORMANCE (at max T-O weight, ISA):	
Max never-exceed speed	165 knots (190 mph; 307 km/h)
Max level speed	122 knots (140 mph; 225 km/h)
Max cruising speed at 5,000 ft (1,525 m)	100 knots (115 mph; 185 km/h)
Stalling speed, flaps down	48 knots (55 mph; 88 km/h)
Max rate of climb at S/L	787 ft (240 m)/min
Service ceiling	14,760 ft (4,500 m)
T-O run (zero wind)	656 ft (200 m)
Landing run (zero wind)	590 ft (180 m)
Max range	429 nm (495 miles; 800 km)
Endurance	4 hr

Aerotec T-23 Uirapuru two-seat primary training aircraft of the Brazilian Air Force (*Ronaldo S. Olive*)

Civil version of the Aerotec 122 Uirapuru (160 hp Lycoming O-320-B2B engine) (*Ronaldo S. Olive*)

CTA

CENTRO TÉCNICO AEROESPACIAL

HEADQUARTERS:
São José dos Campos, São Paulo State

DIRECTOR OF CTA:
Major Brigadeiro Hugo de Miranda e Silva

The Centro Técnico Aeroespacial (Aerospace Technical Centre) is a Ministry of Aeronautics establishment for training aeronautical and aerospace personnel and for conducting aeronautical and aerospace research and development. It is composed of five institutes: the Instituto Tecnológico de Aeronáutica (ITA); the Instituto de Pesquisas e Desenvolvimento (IPD); the Instituto de Atividades Espaciais (IAE); the Instituto de Fomento e Coordenação Industrial (IFI); and the Instituto de Ensaios e Padrões (IEP).

The **ITA** is the college of engineering for aeronautical and aerospace personnel. It provides training for BS, MS and PhD degrees in aeronautical, electronic and mechanical engineering.

The **IPD** conducts aeronautical research and development. Its major activities are in the fields of aeronautics, electronics, energy, materials, propulsion and fuels.

The **IAE** conducts space research and development, mainly in the fields of aerospace vehicles, astrophysics, atmospheric sciences, space technology, control, guidance and navigation.

The **IFI** is a sui generis institute, acting as a liaison between the CTA and the Brazilian industry. Its main activities are devoted to increasing the development rate of aeronautical and aerospace activities, by transferring the most appropriate technology to the aerospace industry and by providing incentives for the adoption of such technology by the industrial community.

The **IEP** is devoted to the development of aeronautical and aerospace standards in Brazil.

EMBRAER

EMPRÊSA BRASILEIRA DE AERONÁUTICA SA

HEAD OFFICE AND WORKS:
Av Brig Faria Lima, Caixa Postal 343, 12200 São José dos Campos, São Paulo State
Telephone: (0123) 21-5400
Telex: 021-597 São José dos Campos

RIO OFFICE:
Av Nilo Pecanha 50, Sala 2405, 20000 Rio de Janeiro GB
Telephone: (021) 231-3652

PRESIDENT:
Aldo B. Franco

SUPERINTENDENT DIRECTOR:
Ozires Silva

PRODUCTION DIRECTOR:
Ozilio Carlos da Silva

TECHNICAL DIRECTOR:
Guido Fontegalante Pessotti

FINANCIAL DIRECTOR:
Alberto Franco Faria Marcondes

INDUSTRIAL RELATIONS DIRECTOR:
Antônio Garcia da Silveira

COMMERCIAL DIRECTOR:
Renato José da Silva

EMBRAER was created in August 1969, and came into operation on 2 January 1970 to promote the development of the Brazilian aircraft industry. It now has an authorised capital of Cr $250 million (about US $41·6 million); the Brazilian government owns 51% of the shares, the remaining 49% being held by private shareholders. EMBRAER has a work force of some 2,660 persons.

The principal current programmes of EMBRAER are the series production of the EMB-110 Bandeirante twin-turboprop transport aircraft and EMB-201 Ipanema agricultural aircraft, and licence assembly of Italian Aermacchi M.B. 326GC jet trainer/ground attack aircraft for the Brazilian Air Force.

Prototype construction has been started of a stretched and pressurised version of the Bandeirante, known as the EMB-120; and studies have begun for the construction of a 20/30-seat medium transport aircraft for the Brazilian Air Force, designated EMB-500. A jet-powered development of the Bandeirante is also being studied.

Development has been abandoned of the 400 hp EMB-210 development of the Ipanema, described briefly on page 762 of the 1973-74 *Jane's*.

EMBRAER EMB-110 BANDEIRANTE (PIONEER)

Brazilian Air Force designation: C-95

The Bandeirante twin-turboprop light transport was developed to a Ministry of Aeronautics specification calling for a general-purpose aircraft capable of carrying out missions such as transport, navigation training and aeromedical evacuation. Its Brazilian design team was, initially, under the leadership of M Max Holste, the well-known French aircraft designer.

Construction of the first YC-95 prototype, then known as the IPD/PAR-6504, was started in mid-1965. This aircraft flew for the first time on 26 October 1968, followed by the second prototype on 19 October 1969, and the basically similar third YC-95 on 26 June 1970. These prototypes were described in the 1970-71 *Jane's*. The third aircraft, registered PP-ZCN, was purchased by the Instituto Nacional de Pesquisas Espaciais (INPE), and was fitted with remote sensors for use in the space agency's Project SERE, as described briefly in the 1972-73 *Jane's*. The fourth Bandeirante, representative of the much-improved production version, was used in the static test programme at the PAR (Departamento de Aeronaves) Structures Laboratory during 1972.

The first production EMB-110 Bandeirante flew for the first time on 9 August 1972, and was test-flown until December 1972 as part of the certification programme. Following the completion of testing to FAR 23, the aircraft was granted a Type Certificate by the Aerospace Technical Centre of the Brazilian Air Ministry, and the first three Bandeirantes were delivered to the Brazilian Air Force on 9 February 1973.

By the Spring of 1974, orders for the Bandeirante had been placed by the Brazilian Air Force (80), Transbrasil Airlines (6, with a further 6 on option), VASP (8), the Servencin air taxi company (2), Furnas Centrais Eletricas (1), the Audi Group (1), and the DNOCS/Ministry of the Interior (1). Commercial services, by Transbrasil, began on 16 April 1973. By the end of March 1974, 18 Bandeirantes had been completed and production was at the rate of two aircraft per month; this rate was scheduled to increase to four per month in July 1974.

The following additional versions of the Bandeirante are also available:

EMB-110B. Aerial photographic version, with cabin floor apertures permitting the fitting of an aerial camera (Zeiss RMK A8·5/23, RMK A15/23 or RMK A30/23), a Zeiss IRU regulator, and Zeiss NT-1 navigation visors. Other equipment includes Decca 72 Doppler navigation system and Collins INS-61B inertial navigation system. Crew includes three equipment operators.

EMB-110E. Executive transport version with accommodation for seven passengers, four in individual seats and three on a sideways-mounted sofa. Other features include a galley, wardrobe, and stereo AM/FM and deck. One ordered by Spring 1974.

EMB-111. Maritime patrol version, described separately.

EMB-120. Developed version with pressurised fuselage, described separately.

The following description applies to the standard production EMB-110:

TYPE: Twin-turboprop general-purpose transport.

WINGS: Cantilever low-wing monoplane. Wing section NACA 23016 (modified) at root, NACA 23012 (modified) at tip. Sweepback 19′ 48″ at quarter-chord. Dihedral 7° at 28% chord. Incidence 3°. All-metal two-spar structure, of 2024-T3 and -T4 aluminium alloy, with detachable glassfibre wingtips. All-metal statically-balanced ailerons and double-slotted flaps. Trim tab in port aileron.

FUSELAGE: All-metal semi-monocoque structure of 2024-T3 aluminium alloy. Two upward-hinged doors, one on each side of nose, provide access to avionics equipment.

TAIL UNIT: Cantilever all-metal structure, with sweptback vertical surfaces. Trim tabs in rudder and port elevator. Tab in starboard elevator linked to flaps, to offset pitching moment during flap extension.

LANDING GEAR: Hydraulically-retractable tricycle type, of ERAM manufacture, with single wheel and oleo-pneumatic shock-absorber on each unit. Main wheels have Kléber-Colombes tyres, size 670 × 210-12, pressure 40-57 lb/sq in (2·8-4 kg/cm²). Steerable, forward-retracting nosewheel unit has Goodyear tyre, size 6·50 - 8.

POWER PLANT: Two 680 shp United Aircraft of Canada PT6A-27 turboprop engines, each driving a Hartzell HC-B3TN-3C/T10178H-8R constant-speed three-blade metal propeller with autofeathering and full reverse-pitch capability. Four integral fuel tanks in wings, with total capacity of 378 Imp gallons (1,720 litres). Gravity refuelling point on top of each wing.

ACCOMMODATION: Two seats side by side on flight deck, which is separated from main cabin by door. Cabin seats 12-15 passengers. Conversion into an ambulance for four stretcher patients takes ten minutes. Downward-hinged door on port side, aft of wing, with built-in airstairs. Cabin floor stressed for loads of up to 82 lb/sq ft (400 kg/m²). Emergency exit over wing on starboard side. Baggage compartment at rear of cabin, with total capacity of 46 cu ft (1·30 m³). Toilet/lavatory standard.

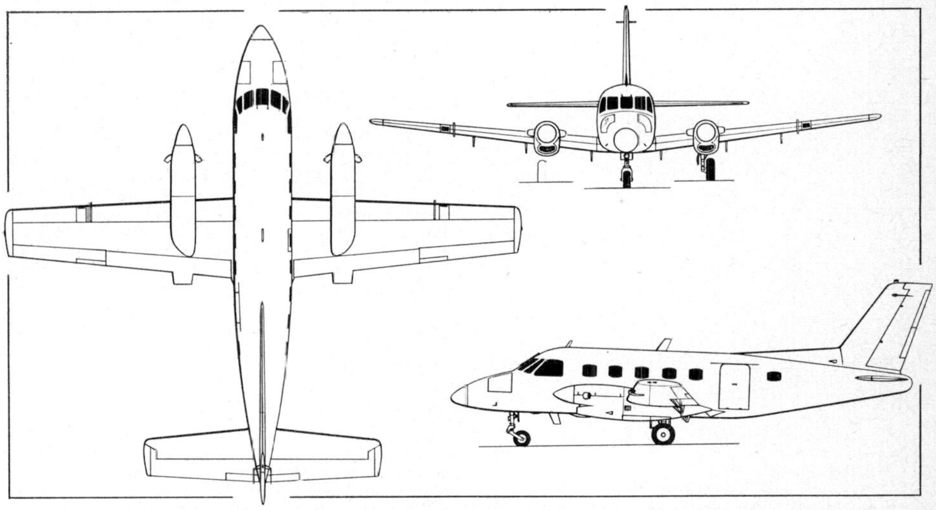

EMBRAER EMB-110 Bandeirante twin-turboprop light transport *(Pilot Press)*

Civil version of the EMBRAER EMB-110 Bandeirante twin-turboprop transport aircraft, in the insignia of Transbrasil *(Ronaldo S. Olive)*

SYSTEMS: Air-cycle-type air-conditioning system with cooling capacity of 20,000 BTU/hr and engine bleed heating. Hydraulic system, pressure 3,000 lb/sq in (210 kg/cm²), for landing gear actuation, independent braking system, nosewheel steering and parking brake. No pneumatic system. Electrical system utilises two 200A starter/generators and an MS-24498-1 24V 34Ah alkaline battery with two 250VA inverters to supply 115/26V 400Hz AC power. External power receptacle on port side of forward fuselage. Oxygen system for crew and passengers, using oxygen bottle in rear of fuselage with capacity of 115 cu ft (3·3 m³) at 1,800 lb/sq in (127 kg/cm²) pressure.

ELECTRONICS AND EQUIPMENT: Standard equipment includes one Brazilian-built Whinner CY04A03C 140-channel VHF transceiver, one Collins 618 M-2B 360-channel VHF transceiver, one HF-AM/SSB Sunair Type ASB-100 transceiver, one Collins 51 R-7A VOR/ILS receiver, two Bendix DFA-73 A1 ADF receivers, one Collins 51Z-6 marker beacon receiver and one Collins 51V-5 glideslope receiver. 450W landing light in each wing leading-edge, and 250W GE landing and taxying light on nosewheel unit. RCA AVQ-47 weather radar and Bendix M-4C autopilot optional.

DIMENSIONS, EXTERNAL:

Wing span	50 ft 3 in (15·32 m)
Wing chord at root	7 ft $7\frac{1}{2}$ in (2·32 m)
Wing chord at tip	4 ft 5 in (1·35 m)
Wing aspect ratio	8·1
Length overall	46 ft $8\frac{1}{4}$ in (14·23 m)
Length of fuselage	45 ft 1 in (13·74 m)
Height overall	13 ft $6\frac{1}{2}$ in (4·13 m)
Fuselage: Max width	5 ft 7 in (1·70 m)
Tailplane span	24 ft 9 in (7·54 m)
Propeller diameter	7 ft 9 in (2·36 m)
Distance between propeller centres	15 ft 9 in (4·80 m)
Propeller ground clearance	1 ft $1\frac{1}{2}$ in (0·345 m)
Wheel track	16 ft $2\frac{1}{2}$ in (4·94 m)
Wheelbase	14 ft $11\frac{1}{2}$ in (4·56 m)
Passenger door (rear, port):	
Height	4 ft $3\frac{1}{4}$ in (1·30 m)
Width	2 ft $9\frac{1}{2}$ in (0·85 m)
Emergency exit (stbd, over wing):	
Height	2 ft $7\frac{1}{2}$ in (0·80 m)
Width	2 ft 1 in (0·63 m)

DIMENSIONS, INTERNAL:

Cabin: Max length	28 ft $4\frac{1}{2}$ in (8·65 m)
Width	5 ft 3 in (1·60 m)
Height	5 ft 3 in (1·60 m)
Floor area	124·9 sq ft (11·60 m²)

AREAS:

Wings, gross	312 sq ft (29·00 m²)
Ailerons (total)	23·5 sq ft (2·18 m²)
Flaps (total)	54·3 sq ft (5·04 m²)
Fin, incl dorsal fin	22·3 sq ft (2·07 m²)
Rudder, incl tab	18·1 sq ft (1·68 m²)
Tailplane	58·4 sq ft (5·43 m²)
Elevators, incl tabs	47·3 sq ft (4·40 m²)

WEIGHTS AND LOADINGS:

Weight empty, equipped	7,054 lb (3,200 kg)
Max T-O weight	11,684 lb (5,300 kg)
Max landing weight	11,133 lb (5,050 kg)
Max zero-fuel weight	10,360 lb (4,699 kg)
Max wing loading	37·3 lb/sq ft (182 kg/m²)
Max power loading	8·58 lb/shp (3·89 kg/shp)

PERFORMANCE (at max T-O weight, ISA, except where indicated):

Max level speed at 10,000 ft (3,050 m), max continuous power
240 knots (277 mph; 445 km/h)

Cruising speed at 10,000 ft (3,050 m), max cruising power
232 knots (267 mph; 430 km/h)

Stalling speed, flaps and landing gear down:
at 11,133 lb (5,050 kg) AUW
73 knots (84 mph; 135 km/h) IAS
at 8,267 lb (3,750 kg) AUW
62 knots (71 mph; 113 km/h) IAS

Max rate of climb at S/L 1,890 ft (576 m)/min

Rate of climb at S/L, one engine out
480 ft (146 m)/min

Time to 8,000 ft (2,440 m) 5 min

Time to 15,000 ft (4,575 m) 11 min

Service ceiling at 11,133 lb (5,050 kg) AUW
28,400 ft (8,660 m)

Service ceiling, one engine out, at 11,133 lb (5,050 kg) AUW 10,700 ft (3,260 m)

T-O run at S/L, zero wind, at 11,684 lb (5,300 kg) AUW 1,180 ft (360 m)

T-O to 50 ft (15 m), conditions as above
1,770 ft (540 m)

Landing from 50 ft (15 m), zero wind, at 11,133 lb (5,050 kg) AUW 2,265 ft (690 m)

Landing run at S/L, conditions as above
1,130 ft (345 m)

Still-air range at 10,000 ft (3,050 m), 30 min reserves 1,119 nm (1,289 miles; 2,075 km)

EMBRAER EMB-111

This designation has been given to a shore-based patrol aircraft, based on the EMB-110 Bandeirante, which EMBRAER has designed to meet specifications issued by the Comando Costeiro, the Brazilian Air Force's Coastal Command. It is powered by two 750 shp United Aircraft of Canada PT6A-34 turboprop engines, and carries 134 Imp gallons (610 litres) of additional fuel in wingtip tanks. The main external difference in this version is the large nose radome, which houses an RCA AVQ-30X radar having a maximum range of 300 nm (345 miles; 555 km). Other electronics and equipment include a Collins INS-61B inertial navigation system, Collins VIR-30A VOR/ILS marker beacon receiver, Collins DF-301E VHF/DF, RCA AVQ-75 DME, two Bendix DFA-73-A-1 ADF, Collins ALT-50 radio altimeter, and Collins PN-101 gyro-magnetic compass. There is provision for four air-to-surface rockets to be carried. A ventrally-mounted searchlight of 10 million candlepower is fitted for night operations. For target marking, six Brazilian-built Mk 6 smoke grenades are carried, as well as a Motorola SST-121 transponder. Flares of 1 million candlepower are also available for illumination of targets at night.

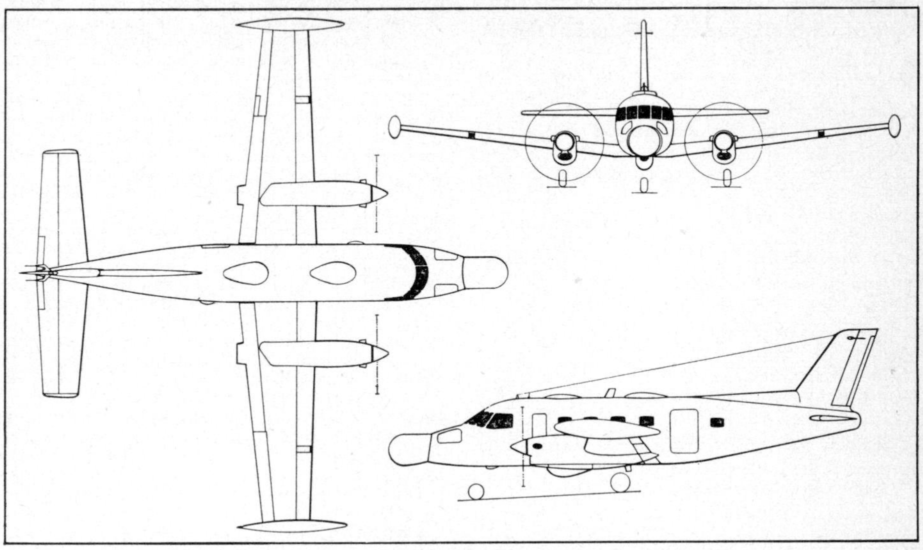

EMB-111 patrol version of the Bandeirante, developed by EMBRAER (*Roy J. Grainge*)

DIMENSIONS, EXTERNAL: As EMB-110, except:

Wing span over tip-tanks	51 ft $5\frac{3}{4}$ in (15·69 m)
Length overall	48 ft $3\frac{1}{4}$ in (14·71 m)
Length of fuselage	46 ft $7\frac{3}{4}$ in (14.22 m)
Height overall	15 ft $6\frac{1}{4}$ in (4·73 m)

WEIGHTS:

Basic operating weight with 6 crew	9,259 lb (4,200 kg)
Max T-O weight	13,558 lb (6,150 kg)
Max landing weight	11,905 lb (5,400 kg)

EMBRAER EMB-120

Design of this pressurised version of the Bandeirante began in 1972. Construction of a prototype started in January 1974 and this aircraft is scheduled to make its first flight in mid-1975. Tooling and jigs are being prepared to series production standards.

The EMB-120 will be powered by two 1,174 ehp (1,004 ehp max cruising power) UACL PT6A-45 turboprop engines, driving five-blade propellers of 8 ft $8\frac{1}{4}$ in (2·65 m) diameter with full reverse pitch. Four integral wing tanks have a total capacity of 418 Imp gallons (1,900 litres), and there is provision for an auxiliary tank in each wing leading-edge. The cabin seats a maximum of 18 passengers. There are baggage compartments in the rear of the cabin (capacity 83·34 cu ft; 2·36 m³) and in the nose (capacity 21·19 cu ft; 0·6 m³; accessible via two upward-hinged doors). Two emergency exits are each 1 ft 8 in × 3 ft $1\frac{1}{2}$ in (0·51 × 0·95 m); the airstair-type passenger door is 4 ft $8\frac{3}{4}$ in (1·44 m) high and 3 ft 0 in (0·91 m) wide. Cabin pressure differential is 6·0 lb/sq in (0·42 kg/cm²) normal, 6·17 lb/sq in (0·43 kg/cm²) maximum.

The EMB-120 is fitted with Bendix RDR-1200 weather radar, two Collins VHF-20, one Sunair ASB-100 HF, two Collins VIR-30A automatic VOR/ILS, two Collins 206 DF, two RCA AVA-310 audio control panels, two Sperry SPZ-200 flight director/autopilots, one RCA AVQ-75 DME, one Collins ALT-50 radio altimeter, one Collins TDR-90 transponder, and one Garrett Rescue 88 emergency transmitter (ELT).

PERFORMANCE (estimated, ISA conditions):

Cruising speed	281 knots (323 mph; 520 km/h)
Balanced T-O field length	4,100 ft (1,250 m)
Landing run	2,395 ft (730 m)
Range with max fuel	1,338 nm (1,541 miles; 2,480 km)

EMBRAER EMB-130

This designation has been given to a twin-turbofan light transport aircraft, a prototype of which should be flying by the end of 1975. It utilises the pressurised fuselage of the EMB-120 but has an entirely new sweptback wing and sweptback cruciform tail surfaces. Power plant will be two turbofan engines in the 4,500 lb (2,040 kg) thrust class, mounted on the rear fuselage; and an APU will be fitted as standard. New twin-wheel main landing gear units will be fitted, with the same nose-gear unit as that in the EMB-110 and EMB-120. Operating speeds will be in excess of Mach 0·8.

EMBRAER/AERMACCHI EMB-326GB XAVANTE

Brazilian Air Force designation: AT-26

In accordance with an agreement signed in May 1970, EMBRAER is assembling under licence, from Italian-built components, Aermacchi M.B. 326GC jet trainer/ground attack aircraft for the Brazilian Air Force, by whom the type is known as the AT-26 Xavante, the name of a Brazilian Indian tribe.

The initial order calls for the manufacture of 112 aircraft, at a rate of two per month. The first Brazilian-completed Xavante made its

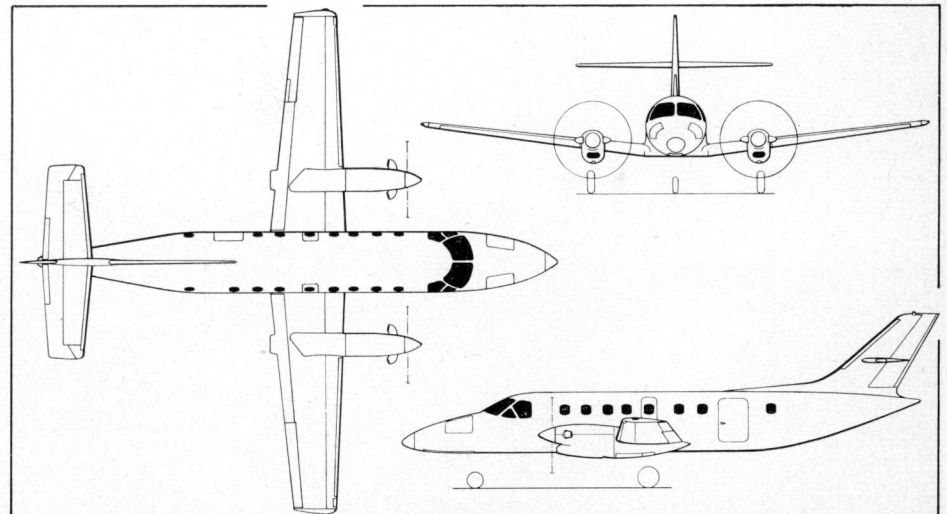

EMBRAER EMB-120 twin-turboprop pressurised transport aircraft (*Roy J. Grainge*)

first flight on 3 September 1971, and the first two aircraft were handed over to the Brazilian Air Force at an official ceremony three days later.

By the end of January 1974, 52 Xavantes had been delivered to the Brazilian Air Force. These aircraft were allocated to the 1° Grupo de Caça (1st Fighter Group) at Santa Cruz AFB, Rio de Janeiro, and to the 4° Grupo at Fortaleza, Ceará State. The Centro de Formação de Pilotos (Pilots' Training Centre) at Natal, Rio Grande do Norte State, was due to receive AT-26s at the beginning of 1974. An additional Brazilian Air Force order for Xavantes has been reported.

A full description of the standard M.B. 326GB appears in the Italian section of this edition; the version for the Brazilian Air Force is basically similar, except in the following respects:

Electronics and Equipment: Two Collins Type 618M-2B 360-channel VHF transceivers, Collins CIA-102A interphone system, Bendix DFA 73A-1 ADF, and a complete VOR/ILS system using a Collins 51V-1 VOR/LOC/glideslope receiver, Collins 51Z-4 marker beacon receiver and AN/APX-72 IFF transponder.

Armament: Six underwing pylons for bombs, gun pods or other stores. Typical loads include six 250 lb bombs; two 500 lb bombs; two 500 lb bombs and two twin 7·62 mm gun pods; four 250 lb bombs and two twin 7·62 mm gun pods; two twin 7·62 mm gun pods and two underwing drop-tanks; two twin 7·62 mm gun pods and four LM-70/7 rocket pods (each with seven SBAT 70 mm folding-fin air-to-ground projectiles); two twin 7·62 mm gun pods and two LM-37/36 rocket pods (each with thirty-six SBAT 37 mm air-to-ground rockets); six LM-70/7 rocket pods (each with seven SBAT 70 mm air-to-ground rockets); or two LM-70/19 rocket pods (each with nineteen SBAT 70 mm air-to-ground rockets); or photographic reconnaissance pods. All armament loads are designed and manufactured in Brazil.

EMBRAER EMB-200 and EMB-201 IPANEMA

This agricultural aircraft was designed and developed to specifications laid down by the Brazilian Ministry of Agriculture. Design was started in May 1969 by the PAR-Departamento de Aeronaves of the CTA, and construction of a prototype began in November 1969. Responsibility for its development was transferred to EMBRAER on 2 January 1970, and the prototype (PP-ZIP) made its first flight on 30 July 1970.

Flight and structural testing were completed successfully, and a CTA Type Certificate was granted on 14 December 1971. Series production is now under way, for which Aerotec (which see) is building the wings and tail unit under subcontract, EMBRAER being responsible for fuselage construction, complete systems installation and final assembly.

By 30 March 1974, 50 Ipanemas had been delivered. Production of the EMB-200 (260 hp Lycoming O-540-H2B5D engine, fixed-pitch propeller) and EMB-200A (same engine, variable-pitch propeller) was scheduled to end in July 1974, after the completion of 73 aircraft. These two versions were described in the 1973-74 *Jane's*. The version in current production, at a rate of six aircraft per month, is the EMB-201, to which the following description applies:

Type: Single-seat agricultural aircraft.

Wings: Cantilever low-wing monoplane. Wing section NACA 23015. Dihedral 7° from roots. Incidence 3°. All-metal single-spar structure of 2024 aluminium alloy with all-metal Frise-type ailerons outboard and all-metal slotted flaps on trailing-edge, and all-detachable leading-edges. Flap settings 0°, 8° and 30° (max); ailerons deflect 22° up, 14° down. No tabs. Variable-camber wingtips standard.

Fuselage: Rectangular-section all-metal safe-life structure, of welded 4130 steel tube with removable skin panels of 2024 aluminium alloy. Structure is specially treated against chemical corrosion.

Tail Unit: Cantilever two-spar all-metal structure of 2024 aluminium alloy. Slight sweepback on fin and rudder. Fixed-incidence tailplane. Elevators deflect 35° up, 20° down; rudder deflects 25° each side. Trim tab in starboard elevator.

Landing Gear: Non-retractable tailwheel type, with oleo shock-absorbers on main units. Tailwheel has tapered spring shock-absorber. Goodyear main wheels and tyres, size 8·50-10. Scott tailwheel, diameter 8 in (20 cm). Goodyear hydraulic disc brakes on main units.

Power Plant: One 300 hp Lycoming IO-540-K1D5 six-cylinder horizontally-opposed air-cooled engine, driving a two-blade constant-speed metal propeller. Integral fuel tank in each wing leading-edge, with total capacity of 50·6 Imp gallons (230 litres). Refuelling point on top of each tank. Oil capacity 2·6 Imp gallons (12 litres).

Accommodation: Single horizontally/vertically-adjustable seat for pilot, in fully-enclosed cabin with bottom-hinged window/door on each side. Ventilation system in cabin. Provision for inertial type shoulder harness.

EMBRAER/Aermacchi AT-26 Xavante jet trainer/ground attack aircraft of the Brazilian Air Force's 1st Fighter Group (*Ronaldo S. Olive*)

First production example of the EMBRAER EMB-201 version of the Ipanema agricultural aircraft (*Ronaldo S. Olive*)

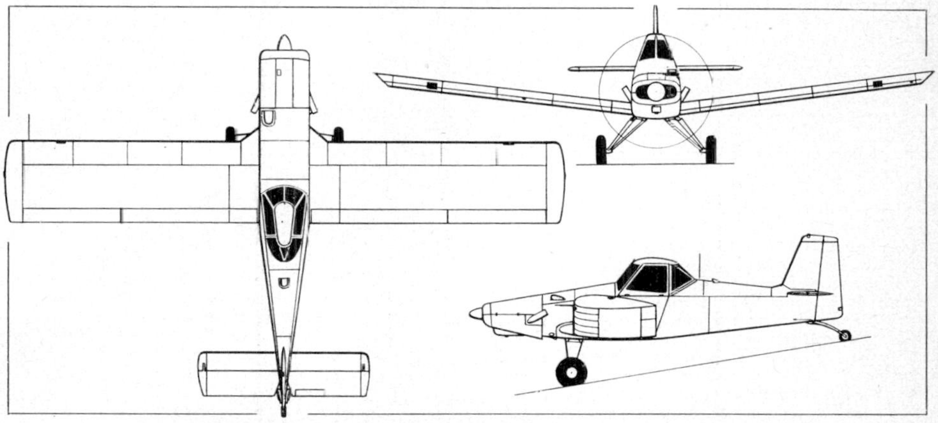

EMBRAER EMB-201 Ipanema single-seat agricultural aircraft (*Pilot Press*)

Systems: 28V DC electrical system supplied by a 24Ah AN-3151 battery and a Bosch K.1-28V-35A24 alternator. Power receptacle for external battery (AN-2552-3A type) on port side of forward fuselage.

Electronics and Equipment: Standard VFR equipment, including VHF radio transceiver (Brazilian-made 14-channel Whinner Model 601 or 360-channel Bendix RT 241A) and ADF receiver (Brazilian-made Pontes & Moraes Model ADF-101/CP-101 or Bendix Model T-12C). Hopper for agricultural chemicals has capacity of 149·5 Imp gallons (680 litres). Transland dusting system below centre of fuselage. Transland or Micronair spraybooms aft of and above wing trailing-edges.

Dimensions, external:

Wing span: 36 ft 9 in (11·20 m)
Wing chord (constant): 5 ft 3 in (1·60 m)
Wing aspect ratio: 7
Length overall: 24 ft $4\frac{1}{2}$ in (7·43 m)
Height overall (tail down): 7 ft $2\frac{1}{4}$ in (2·20 m)
Fuselage: Max width: 3 ft $0\frac{1}{2}$ in (0·93 m)
Tailplane span: 11 ft $4\frac{1}{4}$ in (3·46 m)
Wheel track: 7 ft $2\frac{1}{4}$ in (2·20 m)
Wheelbase: 17 ft $7\frac{1}{4}$ in (5·20 m)
Propeller diameter: 7 ft 0 in (2·13 m)

Dimensions, internal:

Cockpit: Max length: 3 ft $11\frac{1}{4}$ in (1·20 m)
Max width: 2 ft $9\frac{1}{2}$ in (0·85 m)
Max height: 4 ft $4\frac{3}{4}$ in (1·34 m)

Areas:

Wings, gross: 193·75 sq ft ($18·00\ m^2$)
Ailerons (total): 17·21 sq ft ($1·60\ m^2$)
Flaps (total): 24·76 sq ft ($2·30\ m^2$)
Fin: 6·24 sq ft ($0·58\ m^2$)
Rudder: 6·78 sq ft ($0·63\ m^2$)
Tailplane: 32·29 sq ft ($3·00\ m^2$)
Elevators, incl tab: 16·15 sq ft ($1·50\ m^2$)

Weights and Loadings (N: Normal; R: Restricted category):

Max payload:
N: 1,212 lb (550 kg)
R: 1,763 lb (800 kg)
Max T-O and landing weight:
N: 3,417 lb (1,550 kg)
R: 3,968 lb (1,800 kg)
Max wing loading:
N: 17·6 lb/sq ft ($86\ kg/m^2$)
R: 20·5 lb/sq ft ($100\ kg/m^2$)
Max power loading:
N: 13·14 lb/hp (5·96 kg/hp)
R: 15·21 lb/hp (6·90 kg/hp)

Performance (at max T-O weight, Normal category, "clean" configuration, ISA):

Max never-exceed speed: 165 knots (190 mph; 305 km/h) IAS
Max level speed at S/L: 128 knots (148 mph; 238 km/h)

Max cruising speed (75% power) at 6,000 ft (1,830 m) 121 knots (139 mph; 224 km/h)
Econ cruising speed (65% power) at 6,000 ft (1,830 m) 106 knots (122 mph; 196 km/h)
Stalling speed, power off:
flaps up 57 knots (65 mph; 105 km/h)
8° flap 51 knots (58 mph; 94 km/h)
30° flap 51 knots (58 mph; 94 km/h)
Max rate of climb at S/L 1,050 ft (320 m)/min
Service ceiling 17,000 ft (5,180 m)
T-O run at S/L, 8° flap, asphalt runway 660 ft (201 m)
T-O to 50 ft (15 m), conditions as above 1,125 ft (343 m)
Landing from 50 ft (15 m) at S/L, 30° flap, asphalt runway 1,310 ft (400 m)
Landing run, conditions as above 605 ft (185 m)

NEIVA

SOCIEDADE CONSTRUTORA AERONÁUTICA NEIVA LTDA

Head Office:
Rua Santa Clara 260, São José dos Campos, São Paulo State (Caixa Postal 247)
Telephone: 216333, 216267, 216467 and 216176

Works:
Estrada Velha Rio-São Paulo 2076, São José dos Campos, SP, Caixa Postal 363, Código 12200
Av Brigadeiro Faria Lima s/n, São José dos Campos, SP, Caixa Postal 363, Código 12200
Rua Nossa Senhora de Fátima 360, Botucatu, SP, Caixa Postal 10, Código 18600

Directors:
José Carlos de Barros Neiva (General Director)
Breno A. B. Junqueira

Neiva has in current production the N621 (T-25) Universal basic trainer for the Brazilian Air Force. A modified version of the Regente 420L is under development for the civil market, and a six-seat light twin-engined transport, the Ventura, is also being developed.

NEIVA REGENTE and LANCEIRO

Brazilian Air Force designations: C-42 and L-42

Design of the Regente was started in 1959 as the Neiva Model 360C, the prototype of which flew for the first time on 7 September 1961. It received its Type Certificate from the Brazilian Ministry of Aeronautics on 12 November 1963.

Three versions have appeared, as follows:

Regente 360C. Initial production version, with 180 hp Continental O-360-A1D four-cylinder engine. Total of 80 ordered as four-seat utility aircraft for Brazilian Air Force, by whom they are designated **C-42** (originally U-42). Described in 1970-71 *Jane's*.

Regente 420L. Three-seat development of Regente 360C for AOP duties with the Brazilian Air Force, by whom it is designated **L-42.** Differs from C-42 mainly in having a stepped-down rear fuselage, a 210 hp Continental IO-360-D engine, and improved controls. The YL-42 prototype flew for the first time in January 1967, and a Brazilian Type Certificate was awarded on 15 June 1971. Forty L-42s were ordered; the first of these flew in June 1969, and production ended in March 1971.

Lanceiro. Civil four-seat version of L-42, currently under development. An aerodynamic prototype (PP-ZAH) began flying in 1970; the first production aircraft (PP-ZCL) flew for the first time on 5 September 1973, and later that year was displayed at the São Paulo International Aerospace Show.

The following description applies to the L-42 and Lanceiro:

Type: Single-engined light monoplane.

Wings: Braced high-wing monoplane. Wing section NACA 4410 on L-42; NACA 4410 at root and NACA 64A410 at tip on Lanceiro. Dihedral 1° 30′. Incidence 2° 30′; Lanceiro has geometric twist of 2° 30′. All-metal single-spar structure. All-metal single-slotted semi-Fowler flaps and semi-Fowler ailerons. Taper on outer panels of Lanceiro.

Fuselage: All-metal semi-monocoque structure.

Tail Unit: Cantilever all-metal structure, with sweptback vertical surfaces. Sweepback 33° on fin leading-edge. All-moving tailplane with anti-balance tab.

Landing Gear: Non-retractable tricycle type, with steerable nosewheel. Spring steel main legs. Oleo shock-absorber in nose unit. Main-wheel tyres size 7·00-6 on L-42, size 6·00-6 on Lanceiro. Nosewheel tyre size 6·00-6 on L-42, size 5·00-6 on Lanceiro. Tyre pressures 30 lb/sq in (2·10 kg/cm²) on nose unit, 27 lb/sq in (1·90 kg/cm²) on main units. Goodyear hydraulic disc brakes on L-42, except for early production models, which have Goodrich expansion-type brakes. Lanceiro has OLDI hydraulic disc brakes.

Power Plant: One 210 hp Continental IO-360-D six-cylinder horizontally-opposed aircooled engine, driving a Hartzell BHC-C2YF-1B/7663 two-blade constant-speed metal propeller. Two aluminium fuel tanks in wing roots, with total capacity of 38 Imp gallons (172 litres). Oil capacity 1·66 Imp gallons (7·6 litres).

Accommodation: Individual front seats for pilot and co-pilot/doctor, with third seat at rear for navigator/observer (L-42) or two additional persons (Lanceiro). Forward-opening door on each side of cabin. Rear compartment for up to 40 lb (18 kg) of baggage, with external access. Cabin fully ventilated and has glassfibre soundproofing. Dual controls standard.

Systems: Hydraulic system for main-wheel braking. Battery (24V in L-42, 12V in Lanceiro) supplies electrical power.

Electronics and Equipment: L-42: complete IFR equipment standard. Provision for 140-channel Whinner VHF transceiver, HF transceiver and Bendix DFA-72 ADF transceiver. Lanceiro: complete IFR equipment optional.

Dimensions, external:
Wing span:
L-42 29 ft 11½ in (9·13 m)
Lanceiro 33 ft 0 in (10·06 m)
Wing chord (L-42, constant) 4 ft 11 in (1·50 m)
Wing chord (Lanceiro):
at root 4 ft 11 in (1·50 m)
at tip 3 ft 3¼ in (1·00 m)
Wing aspect ratio:
L-42 6·1
Lanceiro 6·87
Length overall 23 ft 7¾ in (7·21 m)
Height overall 9 ft 7¼ in (2·93 m)
Tailplane span 10 ft 3 in (3·13 m)
Wheel track 6 ft 3½ in (1·92 m)
Wheelbase 7 ft 2¼ in (2·19 m)
Propeller diameter 6 ft 4 in (1·93 m)
Propeller ground clearance 11½ in (0·29 m)
Cabin doors (each):
Height 3 ft 5¼ in (1·05 m)
Width 3 ft 2¾ in (0·98 m)
Height to sill 2 ft 1¼ in (0·64 m)
Baggage door:
Height 1 ft 6¾ in (0·48 m)
Width 1 ft 5¼ in (0·44 m)

Dimensions, internal:
Cabin: Max length 6 ft 6¾ in (2·00 m)
Max width 3 ft 3¼ in (1·00 m)
Max height 3 ft 11¼ in (1·20 m)
Floor area 19·4 sq ft (1·80 m²)
Volume 219 cu ft (6·20 m³)

Areas:
Wings, gross:
L-42 144·77 sq ft (13·45 m²)
Lanceiro 158·34 sq ft (14·71 m²)
Ailerons (total) 9·26 sq ft (0·86 m²)
Trailing-edge flaps (total) 21·31 sq ft (1·98 m²)
Fin 14·96 sq ft (1·39 m²)
Rudder 5·17 sq ft (0·48 m²)
Tailplane, incl tab 25·83 sq ft (2·40 m²)

Weights and Loadings:
Weight empty, equipped:
L-42, Lanceiro 1,642 lb (745 kg)
Max T-O and landing weight:
L-42 2,469 lb (1,120 kg)
Lanceiro 2,517 lb (1,142 kg)
Max wing loading:
L-42 17·06 lb/sq ft (83·3 kg/m²)
Lanceiro 15·90 lb/sq ft (77·6 kg/m²)
Max power loading:
L-42 11·75 lb/hp (5·33 kg/hp)
Lanceiro 11·97 lb/hp (5·43 kg/hp)

Performance (at max T-O weight):
Max never-exceed speed 150 knots (174 mph; 280 km/h)
Max level speed at S/L 132 knots (153 mph; 246 km/h)
Max cruising speed at S/L 123 knots (142 mph; 229 km/h)
Max cruising speed (75% power) at 5,000 ft (1,525 m) 116·5 knots (134 mph; 216 km/h)
Stalling speed, flaps down 43 knots (49 mph; 78 km/h)
Max rate of climb at S/L 918 ft (280 m)/min
Service ceiling 15,810 ft (4,820 m)
Min ground turning radius 18 ft 3 in (5·56 m)
T-O run 673 ft (205 m)
T-O to 50 ft (15 m) 1,296 ft (395 m)
Landing from 50 ft (15 m) 1,969 ft (600 m)
Landing run 1,102 ft (336 m)
Range with max fuel, no reserves 512 nm (590 miles; 950 km)
Range with max payload, no reserves 498 nm (574 miles; 925 km)
g limits +4·4; —2·2

NEIVA N621 UNIVERSAL

Brazilian Air Force designation: T-25

The Universal was designed by Mr Joseph Kovacs to meet a Brazilian Air Force requirement for a trainer to replace the Fokker S-11/S-12 Instructor and North American T-6 Texan.

Initial design work was started in January 1963, and construction of the prototype began in May 1965.

This aircraft (PP-ZTW), flown for the first time on 29 April 1966, had side-by-side seating to conform with Ministry of Aeronautics preference.

Neiva Lanceiro four-seat light aircraft, a civil development of the Regente 420L

Neiva T-25 Universal two/three-seat basic training aircraft of the Brazilian Air Force

The Brazilian Air Force has ordered 150 Universals under the designation T-25. Production of these is under way at the Botucatu and São José dos Campos factories, the former manufacturing the fuselage and the latter the wings, with final assembly at São José dos Campos. Wingtips, tailplanes and elevators are manufactured under subcontract by Motortec (formerly Avitec) in Rio de Janeiro. The first production T-25 was flown on 7 April 1971, and deliveries to the Brazilian Air Force began in the Autumn of 1971. Eighty T-25s had been delivered to the Brazilian Air Force by 1 February 1974.

Neiva is working on a light attack aircraft based on the Universal, as a potential replacement for the North American T-6s used by reconnaissance and attack squadrons and the aerobatic team of the Brazilian Air Force. This aircraft, to be known as the **Carajá** (a Brazilian Indian tribe), has a redesigned forward fuselage of smaller frontal area than the T-25, tandem seats, and is powered by a 400 hp Lycoming engine. Armament is to include two fixed 7·62 mm machine-guns in the wings and attachments for underwing stores.

Development of a 400 hp version of the standard Universal is also under consideration.

TYPE: Two/three-seat basic trainer.

WINGS: Cantilever low-wing monoplane. Wing section NACA 632A315 at root, NACA 631212 at tip. Dihedral 6°. Incidence 2°. Single-spar structure of riveted aluminium alloy. All-metal dynamically-balanced slotted ailerons. All-metal split flaps.

FUSELAGE: Welded steel-tube centre fuselage with aluminium skin panels. Semi-monocoque tailcone of riveted aluminium alloy.

TAIL UNIT: Cantilever all-metal structure, with electrically-actuated tab on elevator.

LANDING GEAR: Retractable tricycle type. Hydraulic retraction, main units inward, nosewheel rearward. ERAM oleo shock-absorbers. Main wheels fitted with Goodyear tyres size 6·50-8 and Goodyear or OLDI disc brakes. Nosewheel steerable and fitted with Goodyear tyre size 6·00-6. Tyre pressure 33 lb/sq in (2·33 kg/cm²) on main units, 26 lb/sq in (1·83 kg/cm²) on nose unit.

POWER PLANT: One 300 hp Lycoming IO-540-K1D5 six-cylinder horizontally-opposed air-cooled engine, driving a Hartzell HC-C2YK-4/C8475-A2 non-feathering two-blade constant-speed metal propeller. Six aluminium fuel tanks in wings, total capacity 73 Imp gallons (332 litres). Refuelling point above wing. Oil capacity 2·5 Imp gallons (11·5 litres).

ACCOMMODATION: Two seats side by side, with full dual controls, and optional third seat at rear. Large rearward-sliding transparent canopy. Baggage compartment aft of rear seat.

SYSTEMS: Electrically-actuated hydraulic system, pressure 1,500 lb/sq in (105 kg/cm²), for flaps and landing gear. Manual emergency pump. 28V electrical system.

ELECTRONICS AND EQUIPMENT: 140-channel Brazilian-made VHF radio, ADF and VOR/LOC. Complete IFR instrumentation.

DIMENSIONS, EXTERNAL:

Wing span	36 ft 1 in (11·00 m)
Wing chord at root	6 ft 6½ in (2·00 m)
Wing chord at tip	3 ft 6½ in (1·08 m)
Wing aspect ratio	7·1
Length overall	28 ft 2½ in (8·60 m)
Height overall	9 ft 9¾ in (3·00 m)
Tailplane span	12 ft 11½ in (3·95 m)
Wheel track	8 ft 8¼ in (2·65 m)
Wheelbase	7 ft 7¾ in (2·33 m)
Propeller diameter	7 ft 0 in (2·13 m)
Propeller ground clearance	1 ft 2½ in (0·37 m)

DIMENSIONS, INTERNAL:

Cabin:	
Length	7 ft 2½ in (2·20 m)
Max width	4 ft 1 in (1·25 m)
Max height	4 ft 1 in (1·25 m)
Floor area	32 sq ft (3·0 m²)
Volume	141 cu ft (4·00 m³)
Baggage compartment volume	12·5 cu ft (0·35 m³)

AREAS:

Wings, gross	185·14 sq ft (17·20 m²)
Ailerons (total)	15·82 sq ft (1·47 m²)
Trailing-edge flaps	14·42 sq ft (1·34 m²)
Fin	8·83 sq ft (0·82 m²)
Rudder	9·69 sq ft (0·90 m²)
Tailplane	18·51 sq ft (1·72 m²)
Elevator, including tab	14·53 sq ft (1·35 m²)

WEIGHTS AND LOADINGS (A: Aerobatic; U: Utility):

Weight empty, equipped:	
A, U	2,535 lb (1,150 kg)
Max T-O weight:	
A	3,306 lb (1,500 kg)
U	3,747 lb (1,700 kg)
Max wing loading:	
A	18·1 lb/sq ft (88·2 kg/m²)
U	20·5 lb/sq ft (100·0 kg/m²)
Max power loading:	
A	11·02 lb/hp (5·0 kg/hp)
U	12·57 lb/hp (5·7 kg/hp)

PERFORMANCE (at max T-O weight. A: Aerobatic; U: Utility):

Max never-exceed speed:	
A, U	269 knots (310 mph; 500 km/h)
Max level speed at S/L:	
A	162 knots (186 mph; 300 km/h)
U	160 knots (184 mph; 296 km/h)
Max cruising speed (75% power) at S/L:	
A	153 knots (177 mph; 285 km/h)
U	151 knots (174 mph; 280 km/h)
Stalling speed, flaps up:	
A	63·5 knots (73 mph; 117 km/h)
U	66 knots (76 mph; 122 km/h)
Stalling speed, flaps down:	
A	56·5 knots (65 mph; 104 km h)
U	59·5 knots (68·5 mph; 110 km/h)
Max rate of climb at S/L:	
A	1,312 ft (400 m)/min
U	1,050 ft (320 m)/min
Service ceiling:	
A	20,000 ft (6,100 m)
U	16,400 ft (5,000 m)
T-O run at S/L:	
A	1,148 ft (350 m)
U	1,493 ft (455 m)
T-O to 50 ft (15 m) at S/L:	
A	1,673 ft (510 m)
U	2,133 ft (650 m)
Landing from 50 ft (15 m) at S/L:	
A	1,970 ft (600 m)
U	2,493 ft (760 m)
Range (75% power) at 6,550 ft (2,000 m), 10% reserves:	
A	539 nm (621 miles; 1,000 km)
U	809 nm (932 miles; 1,500 km)

NEIVA VENTURA

This twin-engined, six-seat aircraft, known originally as the Bi-Universal, is developed from, and employs many components of, the T-25 Universal basic trainer.

TYPE: Six-seat cabin monoplane.

WINGS: Cantilever low-wing monoplane. Wing section NACA $63_2A(3{\cdot}5)15$ at root, NACA 63_1A212 at tip. All-metal structure, with integral tip-tanks. Conventional flaps and ailerons. No tabs.

FUSELAGE: Conventional all-metal stressed-skin structure.

LANDING GEAR: Retractable tricycle type, with single wheel on each unit. Hydraulic retraction, main units inward, nose unit rearward. Oleo shock-absorbers on all units. Main wheels fitted with size 6·50-10 tyres and disc brakes. Steerable nosewheel, fitted with size 6·00-6 tyre.

POWER PLANT: Two 300 hp Lycoming IO-540 six-cylinder horizontally-opposed aircooled engines, each driving a Hartzell three-blade fully-feathering constant-speed metal propeller. Fuel in wing main tanks and wingtip tanks, normal total capacity 132 Imp gallons (600 litres). Oil capacity 5 Imp gallons (22·7 litres).

ACCOMMODATION: Seats for pilot and up to five passengers in enclosed cabin. One forward-hinged door on starboard side, and one at rear of cabin on port side. Provision for cabin air-conditioning and individual passenger lights.

ELECTRONICS AND EQUIPMENT: Complete nav/com equipment standard. Provision for autopilot and weather radar at customer's option.

DIMENSIONS, EXTERNAL:

Wing span	39 ft 0½ in (11·90 m)
Length overall	30 ft 2¼ in (9·20 m)
Height overall	9 ft 10 in (3·00 m)
Tailplane span	16 ft 4¾ in (5·00 m)
Wheel track	9 ft 2¼ in (2·80 m)
Wheelbase	9 ft 8¼ in (2·95 m)

AREAS:

Wings, gross	206·7 sq ft (19·20 m²)
Ailerons (total)	15·50 sq ft (1·44 m²)
Trailing-edge flaps (total)	22·07 sq ft (2·05 m²)
Rudder, incl tab	7·10 sq ft (0·66 m²)
Tailplane	55·97 sq ft (5·20 m²)
Elevators (total)	21·53 sq ft (2·00 m²)

WEIGHTS AND LOADINGS (estimated):

Weight empty, equipped	3,306 lb (1,500 kg)
Max T-O weight	5,511 lb (2,500 kg)
Max wing loading	26·7 lb/sq ft (130·21 kg/m²)
Max power loading	9·19 lb/hp (4·17 kg/hp)

PERFORMANCE (estimated, at max T-O weight):

Max level speed at S/L	210 knots (242 mph; 390 km/h)
Max cruising speed (75% power)	200 knots (230 mph; 370 km/h)
Stalling speed, flaps down	59·5 knots (68·5 mph; 110 km/h)
Max rate of climb at S/L	1,673 ft (510 m)/min
Service ceiling	22,975 ft (7,000 m)
T-O to 50 ft (15 m) at S/L	1,246 ft (380 m)
Landing from 50 ft (15 m) at S/L	1,345 ft (410 m)
Max range at econ cruising speed, standard fuel, 45 min reserves	971 nm (1,118 miles; 1,800 km)

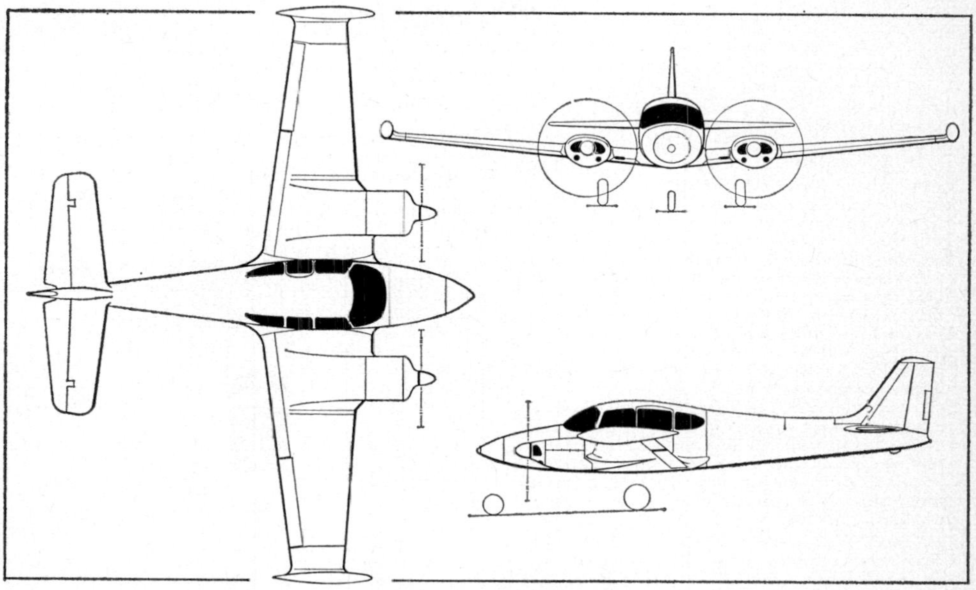

Neiva Ventura twin-engined light aircraft (*Roy J. Grainge*)

CANADA

CANADAIR

CANADAIR LIMITED (Subsidiary of General Dynamics Corporation)

HEAD OFFICE AND WORKS:
Cartierville Airport, St Laurent, Montreal, Quebec

POSTAL ADDRESS:
PO Box 6087, Station "A", Montreal, Quebec H3C 3G9

Telephone: (514) 744-1511

CHAIRMAN: Gorden E. MacDonald

PRESIDENT AND CHIEF EXECUTIVE OFFICER:
Frederick R. Kearns

VICE-PRESIDENTS:
Peter J. Aird (Finance)
Frank M. Francis (Marketing)
Harry Halton (Engineering)
Conrad Kunze (Programmes)
Jacques E. Ouellet (Industrial Relations and Materials)
Andreas Throner (Operations)
Robert A. Wohl (Administration)

Canadair Limited, the Canadian subsidiary of General Dynamics Corporation, has been engaged in the development and manufacture of commercial and military aircraft since 1944. It has also been employed in research, design, development and manufacture of missile components and systems, electronic equipment and a variety of non-aerospace products.

The company has three plants at Cartierville Airport, Montreal, comprising 2·7 million sq ft (250,840 m^2) of covered floor space, and employed about 2,700 persons in the Spring of 1974.

In current production are the CL-215 air tanker/utility amphibious aircraft and a follow-on batch of 20 CF-5Ds (see 1970-71 *Jane's*) for the Canadian Armed Forces. Production of the AN/USD-501 drone surveillance system continues for the armies of Great Britain and the Federal Republic of Germany (see "RPVs and Targets" section).

The US/UK/Canadian V/STOL Instrument Flight Test programme at the US Naval Air Test Center, Patuxent River, is continuing. The CL-84-1 was delivered to Patuxent River on 7 December 1972. During the programme an RAF pilot performed the first blind transition to hover by a V/STOL aircraft. The manoeuvre began with the wing down at 150 knots (172 mph; 278 km/h).

The manufacture of components for F-111, C-5A, F-5 and Mercure aircraft, aircraft spares, and the modification, repair and overhaul of aircraft, form a substantial part of the current work programme.

Flextrac Nodwell, a Canadair subsidiary located in Calgary, Alberta, is engaged in the design, development and production of military and commercial off-road vehicles.

CANADAIR CL-84

The CL-84 is a twin-engined tilt-wing V/STOL aircraft, the original private venture prototype of which was described in the 1967-68 *Jane's*. It was followed by three examples of the CL-84-1, ordered for evaluation by the Canadian Armed Forces (CAF designation CX-84). The first of these made its initial flight on 19 February 1970.

CAF evaluation of the CL-84-1 has been successfully completed, as described in the 1973-74 *Jane's*. The second aircraft was delivered to the US Naval Air Test Center at Patuxent River, Maryland, at the beginning of December 1972 for a tripartite V/STOL instrument flight test programme, having been specifically prepared for instrument flight evaluation by crews from the UK, US and Canada. The programme is concerned with terminal area guidance and control of V/STOL aircraft, and is investigating head-up and head-down display requirements (a Smiths' programmable HUD system is installed), and transition and steep angle approach flight profile parameter limits. In addition, the terminal area handling characteristics of the CL-84 are being investigated, together with its operating and design parameters as they might apply to shipboard operations.

In conjunction with the instrument flying the CL-84 has been undergoing evaluation by the US Navy. The latest stage of this evaluation was a 10-day exercise on board the helicopter carrier USS *Guadalcanal*, scheduled to begin on 18 March 1974. Later, the CL-84 will again go to sea, to investigate ASW applications. These evaluations are intended to assess the suitability of the CL-84 concept in the Sea Control Ship system, and are being paralleled by continuous refinement of the SCS CL-84 design (which see).

A full description of the CL-84-1 appeared in the 1973-74 *Jane's*.

TYPE: Tilt-wing V/STOL aircraft.

WINGS: Cantilever high-set tilting wing. Wing section NACA 63_3-418 (modified). No dihedral or sweep. Variable incidence, from 2° to 102°. Aluminium alloy stressed-skin structure, with full-span slotted trailing-edge flaps, each divided into two sections by engine nacelles and functioning also as ailerons. Full-span Krueger flap under leading-edge of each wing. Mechanically-controlled Krueger flap over fuselage.

FUSELAGE: Conventional rectangular-section semi-monocoque structure.

TAIL UNIT: Cantilever variable-incidence horizontal surfaces, with sweptback endplate fins. Central sweptback fin and rudder. Horizontal surfaces move with wing to angle of incidence of about 45° when wing is in STOL position, but return to horizontal if wing tilt increases further for VTOL.

LANDING GEAR: Retractable tricycle type. Nose unit retracts rearward, main units forward into fairings on sides of fuselage. Abex oleo-pneumatic shock-absorbers. Goodyear twin main wheels, size 6·50-8, and tyres, size 7·00-8 type III, pressure 62 lb/sq in (4·36 kg/cm^2). Goodyear twin nosewheels, size 6·00-6, and tyres, size 6·00-6 type III, pressure 40 lb/sq in (2·81 kg/cm^2). Goodyear independent disc brakes on each main unit.

POWER PLANT: Two 1,500 shp Lycoming T53 (LTC1K-4C) turboprop engines, each driving a Curtiss-Wright reduction gearbox and four-blade lightweight propeller. Horizontal four-blade contra-rotating Servotec tail propellers. Fuel tanks in wing spar box, with total capacity of 206 Imp gallons (936 litres). Provision for two 100 Imp gallon (455 litre) auxiliary drop-tanks beneath the fuselage. Oil capacity 5 Imp gallons (22·75 litres).

Two prototypes of the Canadair CL-84-1 tilt-wing V/STOL aircraft in Canadian Armed Forces insignia

ACCOMMODATION: Pilot and a check pilot or observer side by side on flight deck, on North American zero-zero rocket-ejection seats. Dual controls standard.

DIMENSIONS, EXTERNAL:
- Wing span: 33 ft 4 in (10·16 m)
- Wing aspect ratio: 4·76
- Max length: 47 ft 3½ in (14·41 m)
- Height overall, wing at 0°: 14 ft 2¾ in (4·34 m)
- Height overall, wing tilted 90°: 17 ft 1½ in (5·22 m)

AREA:
- Wings, gross: 233·3 sq ft (21·67 m^2)

WEIGHTS AND LOADINGS (S/L, ISA):
- Manufacturer's weight empty: 8,437 lb (3,827 kg)
- Operating weight empty (incl one pilot): 8,775 lb (3,980 kg)
- Max T-O weight:
  - VTOL: 12,600 lb (5,715 kg)
  - STOL: 14,500 lb (6,577 kg)
- Max wing loading:
  - VTOL: 54 lb/sq ft (264 kg/m^2)
  - STOL: 62 lb/sq ft (303 kg/m^2)
- Max power loading:
  - VTOL: 4·20 lb/shp (1·90 kg/shp)
  - STOL: 4·82 lb/shp (2·19 kg/shp)

PERFORMANCE (at max T-O weight, ISA, except where indicated):
- Max never-exceed speed: 360 knots (415 mph; 667 km/h)
- Max level speed at max VTO weight: 279 knots (321 mph; 517 km/h)
- Max cruising speed:
  - VTOL: 268 knots (309 mph; 497 km/h)
  - STOL: 261 knots (301 mph; 484 km/h)
- Max rate of climb at S/L:
  - VTOL: 4,200 ft (1,280 m)/min
  - STOL: 3,300 ft (1,006 m)/min
- T-O run (STOL): 140 ft (43 m)
- T-O to 50 ft (15 m) (STOL): 500 ft (153 m)
- Landing from 50 ft (15 m) (STOL) at AUW of 12,000 lb (5,440 kg): 400 ft (122 m)
- Landing run (STOL): 150 ft (46 m)
- Range with max wing fuel, allowances for 2 min at military power and 10% fuel reserve:
  - VTOL: 365 nm (421 miles; 677 km)
  - STOL: 356 nm (410 miles; 660 km)
- Range with max wing fuel and full payload, cruising at 10,000 ft (3,050 m), 10% fuel reserve:
  - VTOL: 295 nm (340 miles; 547 km)
  - STOL: 279 nm (322 miles; 519 km)

CANADAIR SCS CL-84

In terms of a potential production model of the CL-84, emphasis has shifted from the uprated CL-84-1 approach (as exemplified by the CL-84-1D, described in the 1972-73 *Jane's*) in favour of an advanced CL-84 using two T64 turboprop engines. This version, known at present as the SCS CL-84 (Sea Control Ship CL-84) has been designed to meet ship-based ASW and radar surveillance requirements, operating from a short deck where the mission profiles require operations in the STOL or VTOL modes. Emphasis has been placed on the substantial short take-off overload capability. The overall configuration, as shown in the accompanying three-view drawing, is basically that of a scaled-up CL-84-1, with provision for wing and propeller folding to facilitate shipboard stowage.

DIMENSIONS, EXTERNAL:
- Wing span: 42 ft 0 in (12·80 m)

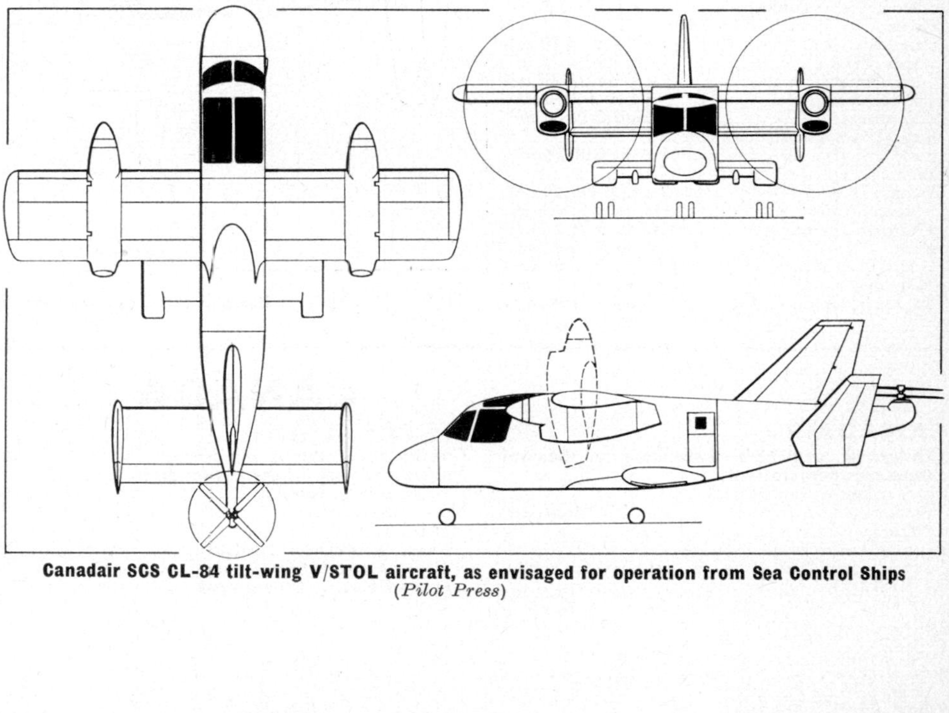

Canadair SCS CL-84 tilt-wing V/STOL aircraft, as envisaged for operation from Sea Control Ships
(*Pilot Press*)

Width, wings folded	27 ft 0 in (8·23 m)
Max length	50 ft 8 in (15·44 m)
Length of fuselage	47 ft 8 in (14·53 m)
Height overall, wing at 0°	18 ft 8 in (5·69 m)
Main propeller diameter	16 ft 6 in (5·03 m)
Tail propeller diameter	7 ft 9 in (2·36 m)

WEIGHTS (estimated):

Operating weight empty	16,500 lb (7,483 kg)
Max weight for vertical T-O at S/L:	
ISA	29,000 lb (13,154 kg)
32°C	26,500 lb (12,019 kg)
Max weight for short T-O, 250 ft (76 m) deck run, zero wind, ISA; or 20 knot (23 mph; 37 km/h) wind, 32°C	36,000 lb (16,329 kg)

PERFORMANCE (estimated):

Max level speed	375 knots (432 mph; 695 km/h)
Best-range speed	265 knots (305 mph; 491 km/h)
Best-endurance speed	220 knots (253 mph; 408 km/h)
Max rate of climb at S/L	6,500 ft (1,980 m)/min
Service ceiling	30,000 ft (9,144 m)
Range at 10,000 ft (3,050 m) with 7,000 lb (3,175 kg) payload, short T-O as above	1,400 nm (1,612 miles; 2,595 km)
Endurance at 10,000 ft (3,050 m) with 7,000 lb (3,175 kg) payload, short T-O as above	6 hr
Ferry range	2,650 nm (3,050 miles; 4,910 km)

CANADAIR CL-215

The Canadair CL-215 is a twin-engined amphibian, intended primarily for fire-fighting but adaptable to a wide variety of other duties. It is designed for simplicity of operation and maintenance, and can operate from small airstrips, lakes, ocean bays etc.

The CL-215 made its first flight on 23 October 1967, and its first water take-off on 2 May 1968.

The Protection Civile of France operates 10 aircraft, acquired between June 1969 and June 1972. They have seen considerable action fighting forest fires in southern France and Corsica.

The Province of Quebec operates 15 aircraft, mainly in a fire-fighting role. Several of these have been converted to wide-swath liquid sprayers for a massive campaign which began in Spring 1973 to protect huge tracts of valuable timberland from budworm infestation.

The Spanish government has operated two aircraft since February 1971. They are being used for general utility purposes, as well as for forest fire-fighting. Spain has ordered a further eight CL-215s, of an improved design, capable of search and rescue operations as well as other roles.

The Greek government ordered two CL-215s in 1973, thus bringing total sales of the aircraft to 37 (Quebec 15, France 10, Spain 10 and Greece 2). In addition, one CL-215 has been donated to Swaziland by the Canadian government.

The CL-215 offers fire protection agencies three methods of attacking fires in grass, brush or forest: (1) with pre-mixed long-term chemical retardants ground-loaded at a land base; (2) with short-term retardants mixed automatically during the water scooping operation; and (3) with plain water scooped from any ¾ mile (1,200 m) stretch of lake or ocean near the fire.

The CL-215 carries a maximum water or retardant load of 1,200 Imp gallons (5,455 litres). The tanks can be ground filled in 90 sec or scoop filled in 16-20 sec while the aircraft skims the water at about 60 knots (69 mph; 111 km/h). Pick-up distance in still air, from 50 ft (15 m) above the water during landing to 50 ft (15 m) on take-off, is 5,450 ft (1,660 m). A single Protection Civile CL-215 made 82 drops totalling 98,397 Imp gallons (447,310 litres) in one day during the Summer of 1970. Full loads have been scooped from the Mediterranean in wave heights of up to 6 ft (2 m).

TYPE: Twin-engined multi-purpose amphibian.

WINGS: Cantilever high-wing monoplane. No dihedral. All-metal one-piece fail-safe structure, with front and rear spars at 10% and 49% chord. Spars of conventional construction, with extruded caps and web stiffened by vertical members. Aluminium alloy skin, with riveted spanwise extruded stringers, is supported at 30 in (76 cm) pitch by interspar ribs. Leading-edge consists of aluminium alloy skin attached to pressed nose-ribs and spanwise stringers. Hydraulically-operated all-metal single-slotted flaps, supported by four external hinges on interspar ribs on each wing. Trim tab and geared tab in port aileron, rudder/aileron interconnect tab in starboard aileron. Detachable glassfibre wingtips. Provision for de-icing of leading-edges.

FUSELAGE: All-metal single-step flying-boat hull of conventional fail-safe construction.

TAIL UNIT: Cantilever all-metal fail-safe structure with horizontal surfaces mounted mid-way up fin. Structure of aluminium alloy sheet, honeycomb panels, extrusions and fittings. Elevators and rudder fitted with dynamic balance, trim tab (port elevator only) and spring tabs and geared tabs. Provision for de-icing of leading-edges.

LANDING GEAR: Hydraulically-retractable tricycle type. Fully-castoring, self-centering twin-wheel nose unit retracts rearward into hull and is fully enclosed by doors. Main gear support structures retract into wells in sides of hull. A plate mounted on each main gear assembly encloses bottom of wheel well. Main-wheel tyre pressure 77 lb/sq in (5·4 kg/cm²); nosewheel tyre pressure 95 lb/sq in (6·68 kg/cm²). Hydraulic disc brakes. Non-retractable stabilising floats are each carried on a pylon cantilevered from wing box structure, with breakaway provision.

POWER PLANT: Two 2,100 hp Pratt & Whitney R-2800-83AM2AH, -83AM12AD or -CA3 eighteen-cylinder two-row aircooled radial engines, each driving a Hamilton Standard Hydromatic constant-speed fully-feathering three-blade propeller, with 43E60 hub and type 6903 blades. First 30 aircraft have two fuel tanks, each of six flexible cells, in wing spar box, with total usable capacity of 954 Imp gallons (4,336 litres). Next 20 aircraft have two tanks each of eight flexible cells, with total usable capacity of 1,266 Imp gallons (5,755 litres). Gravity refuelling through two points above each tank. Oil in two tanks, with total capacity of 60 Imp gallons (272·75 litres), aft of engine firewalls.

ACCOMMODATION (water bomber version): Crew of two side by side on flight deck. Dual controls standard. Two 588 Imp gallon (2,673 litre) water tanks in main fuselage compartment, with retractable pick-up probe in each side of hull bottom. Water-drop door in each side of hull bottom. Doors on port side of fuselage forward and aft of wings, of sliding type on first 30 aircraft, flush type on next 20. Emergency exit on starboard side aft of wing trailing-edge. Emergency hatch above starboard cockpit. Mooring hatch on top of hull nose below flight deck windows.

ACCOMMODATION (utility versions): Basic aircraft is equipped with canvas folding seats for eight passengers. With the tank headers in situ, 15 passengers can be carried. Removing the tank headers provides space for a total of 19 passengers. In the search and rescue configuration the utility version has, in addition, a navigator's station on the starboard side, aft of the pilot's bulkhead; a flight engineer's station between the pilot and co-pilot; two observer's stations in the aft cabin, forward of the rear door; and provision for four seats or two banks of three stretchers each, one on the port side forward of the wheel well and one on the starboard side aft of the wheel well. Provision for up to 18 seats or nine stretchers in casualty evacuation/supply role, or for up to 36 passengers and/or cargo in emergency transport role.

SYSTEMS: Hydraulic system, pressure 3,000 lb/sq in (210 kg/cm²), utilises two engine-driven pumps to actuate landing gear, flaps, water-drop doors and pick-up probes, and wheel brakes. Electric pump in system provides power for emergency actuation of landing gear and brakes and closure of water doors. Electrical system includes two 250VA 115V 400Hz single-phase inverters, two 28V 200A DC generators, one 34Ah nickel-cadmium battery and one air-cooled petrol engine-driven 28V 200A generator GPU. In the SAR version, two 800 VA inverters are installed.

ELECTRONICS AND EQUIPMENT: Standard installation includes HF, VHF and FM communications equipment, VOR/ILS, glideslope receiver, ADF and marker beacon. For the SAR version, radar, radio altimeter and DME are added to the navigation equipment; other equipment for this role includes IFF/SIF, UHF intercom, and crash location communications equipment. Optional equipment includes UHF, DME and radar.

DIMENSIONS, EXTERNAL:

Wing span	93 ft 10 in (28·60 m)
Wing chord (constant)	11 ft 7½ in (3·54 m)
Wing aspect ratio	8·15
Length overall	65 ft 0¼ in (19·82 m)
Beam	8 ft 6 in (2·59 m)
Length/beam ratio	7·5
Height over tail (on land)	29 ft 5½ in (8·98 m)
Tailplane span	36 ft 0 in (10·97 m)
Wheel track	17 ft 2¾ in (5·25 m)
Wheelbase	23 ft 8½ in (7·23 m)
Propeller diameter	14 ft 3 in (4·34 m)
Forward door:	
Height	4 ft 6 in (1·37 m)
Width	3 ft 4 in (1·03 m)
Rear door:	
Height	3 ft 8 in (1·12 m)
Width	3 ft 4 in (1·03 m)
Water-drop door:	
Length	5 ft 3 in (1·60 m)
Width	2 ft 8 in (0·81 m)
Emergency exit:	
Height	3 ft 0 in (0·91 m)
Width	1 ft 8 in (0·51 m)

Canadair CL-215 amphibian (two 2,100 hp R-2800 radial piston engines) demonstrating water bombing technique

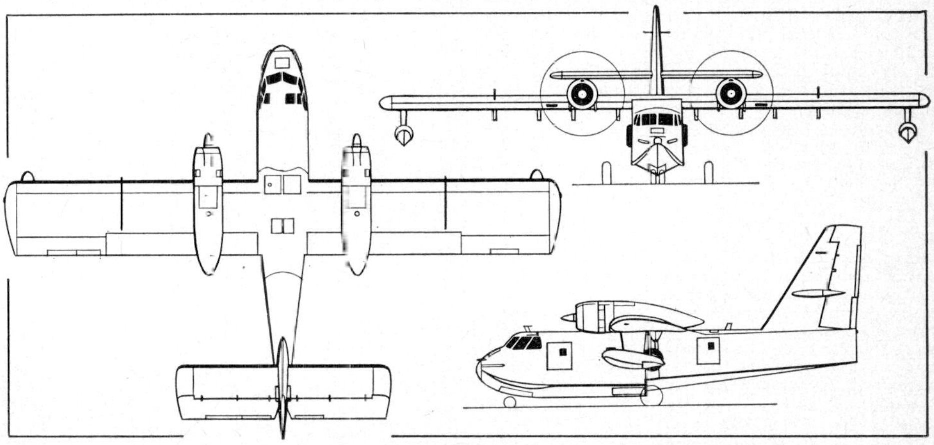

Canadair CL-215 twin-engined multi-purpose amphibian (*Pilot Press*)

DIMENSIONS, INTERNAL:
Cabin, excluding flight deck:
Length 30 ft 9½ in (9·38 m)
Max width 7 ft 10 in (2·39 m)
Max height 6 ft 3 in (1·90 m)
Floor area 212 sq ft (19·69 m^2)
Volume 1,237 cu ft (35·03 m^3)

AREAS:
Wings, gross 1,080 sq ft (100·33 m^2)
Ailerons (total) 86·6 sq ft (8·05 m^2)
Flaps (total) 241 sq ft (22·39 m^2)
Vertical tail surfaces (total) 185·5 sq ft (17·23 m^2)
Rudder, incl tabs 64·75 sq ft (6·02 m^2)
Horizontal tail surfaces (total) 306 sq ft (28·43 m^2)
Elevators, incl tabs 84·8 sq ft (7·88 m^2)

WEIGHTS AND LOADINGS (A: aircraft Nos 1-30; B: aircraft Nos 31-50):
Manufacturer's weight empty:
A 26,000 lb (11,793 kg)
B 26,600 lb (12,065 kg)
Typical operating weight empty:
A 27,000 lb (12,247 kg)
B 27,750 lb (12,587 kg)
Max payload:
Water bomber 12,000 lb (5,443 kg)
Utility version (A) 6,750 lb (3,062 kg)
Utility version (B) 6,260 lb (2,839 kg)
Max T-O weight (land) 43,500 lb (19,731 kg)
Max T-O weight (water):
all versions 37,700 lb (17,100 kg)
Max zero-fuel weight 42,500 lb (19,275 kg)
Max landing weight (land and water):
all versions 37,000 lb (16,780 kg)
Cabin floor loading 150 lb/sq ft (732 kg/m^2)
Max wing loading 40·3 lb/sq ft (196·66 kg/m^2)
Max power loading 10·36 lb/hp (4·70 kg/hp)

PERFORMANCE:
Cruising speed (max recommended power) at AUW of 41,000 lb (18,595 kg) at 10,000 ft (3,050 m) 157 knots (181 mph; 291 km/h)
Stalling speed, 15° flap, AUW of 43,500 lb (19,731 kg) 75 knots (86 mph; 139 km/h)
Stalling speed, 25° flap, AUW of 34,400 lb (15,603 kg), power off 63 knots (73 mph; 116 km/h)
Max rate of climb at S/L at AUW of 43,500 lb (19,731 kg) at max continuous power 1,000 ft (305 m)/min
Rate of climb at S/L, one engine out, at AUW of 37,700 lb (17,100 kg) at T-O power 245 ft (75 m)/min
T-O to 50 ft (15 m):
on land at AUW of 43,500 lb (19,731 kg) 2,660 ft (811 m)
on water at AUW of 37,700 lb (17,100 kg) 2,620 ft (800 m)
Landing from 50 ft (15 m):
on land at AUW of 34,400 lb (15,603 kg) 2,400 ft (732 m)
on water at AUW of 37,000 lb (16,780 kg) 2,740 ft (835 m)
Range with 3,500 lb (1,587 kg) payload:
at max cruise power 1,000 nm (1,151 miles; 1,853 km)
at long-range cruise power 1,220 nm (1,405 miles; 2,260 km)

DE HAVILLAND CANADA

THE DE HAVILLAND AIRCRAFT OF CANADA, LTD (Member Company of HAWKER SIDDELEY GROUP)

HEAD OFFICE AND WORKS:
Downsview M3K 1Y5, Ontario
Telephone: (416) 633-7310
Telex: 06-22128

CHAIRMAN: A. S. Kennedy
PRESIDENT: B. B. Bundesman
VICE-PRESIDENTS:
S. B. Kerr (Finance)
D. B. Annan (Operations)
W. T. Heaslip (Engineering)
D. L. Buchanan, DFC, BSA (Sales)
R. B. McIntyre (Director of Market Development)
CHIEF DESIGNER: F. H. Buller

The de Havilland Aircraft of Canada Ltd was established in early 1928 as a subsidiary of the de Havilland Aircraft Co Ltd, and is now a member of the Hawker Siddeley Group.

Facilities in 1974 covered a total area of 1,046,430 sq ft (97,215 m^2), comprising an 829,070 sq ft (77,022 m^2) main plant on the southern border of Downsview airport and 217,360 sq ft (20,193 m^2) of leased space on the northern boundary of the airport. The company also has a product support facility, known as de Havilland Canada Inc, at Chicago in the USA.

Until the beginning of the second World War, de Havilland Canada acted principally as a sales and servicing organisation for products of the parent company. It became a manufacturing unit during the war and has since produced several original designs.

Of these the DHC-1 Chipmunk two-seat ab initio trainer, DHC-2 Beaver STOL utility aircraft, DHC-3 Otter and DHC-4/4A Caribou have been described in previous editions of *Jane's*. In production and service are the twin-engined DHC-5 Buffalo, evolved from the Caribou, and the DHC-6 Twin Otter STOL utility transport.

DHC-4A CARIBOU

CAF designation: CC-108
USAF designation: C-7

The Caribou was developed with the co-operation of the Canadian Department of Defence Production and an order for one prototype was placed by the Royal Canadian Air Force. Construction began in 1957 and the prototype flew for the first time on 30 July 1958.

The original DHC-4 Caribou obtained US Type Approval on 23 December 1960, at a gross weight of 26,000 lb (11,793 kg). The DHC-4A was approved on 11 July 1961, at a maximum gross weight of 28,500 lb (12,928 kg).

Five YAC-1 Caribou were delivered to the US Army for evaluation in 1959. The US Army subsequently ordered a total of 159 aircraft under the designation CV-2 (originally AC-1). The 134 aircraft still in service on 1 January 1967 were transferred to the USAF. Versions of the Caribou delivered to the US Army were the CV-2A (equivalent to the DHC-4), and the C-7A (formerly CV-2B), equivalent to the DHC-4A. The change of designation of the latter version followed transfer from the US Army to the USAF.

Other orders included nine for the CAF, eight for the Republic of Ghana, four for Air Asia of Taiwan, two for the Kuwait Air Force, five for the Zambian Air Force, 20 for the Indian Air Force, 31 for the Royal Australian Air Force, six for the Kenya Air Force, 16 for the Royal Malaysian Air Force, four for the Tanzanian Air Force, 16 for the Spanish Air Force, three for the Muscat and Oman Defence Department, one for the Uganda Police Air Wing, one for Ansett-MAL for service in Papua and New Guinea, two for Guyana Airways, and others for AMOCO Equador (one), Pacific Architects (two), Global Associates (four), the Abu Dhabi Defence Force (five), the Royal Thai Police Force (three), République Fédérale du Cameroun (two) and Intermountain Aviation Inc of the USA (one).

Production of the Caribou has ended. A full description was given in the 1973-74 *Jane's*.

DHC-5 BUFFALO

CAF designation: CC-115
USAF designation: C-8A

In early May 1962, the US Army invited 25 companies to submit proposals for a new STOL tactical transport aircraft. De Havilland Canada won the competition with a developed version of the Caribou known as the Buffalo (originally Caribou II) with an enlarged fuselage and two General Electric T64 turboprop engines.

Development costs of the Buffalo were shared equally by the US Army, the Canadian government and de Havilland Canada.

Four evaluation aircraft were built initially, of which the first flew for the first time on 9 April 1964. Delivery of these aircraft to the US Army, for evaluation, began in April 1965. An order for 15 was placed by the Canadian Ministry of Defence in December 1964, deliveries of which began in 1967 and were completed at the end of 1968.

Twenty-four Buffalos were ordered in 1967 by the Brazilian government. Twelve were delivered in 1969 and the remainder in 1970. Sixteen were ordered for use by Grupo Aéreo No 8 of the Peruvian Air Force, based at Lima. The first was handed over on 16 June 1971; delivery was completed in mid-1972.

The Indian Air Force is understood to have selected the Buffalo as its next tactical transport aircraft. About 80 aircraft are involved, which it is planned will be assembled by HAL's Kanpur Division.

Differences between the US and Canadian versions are as follows:

C-8A. US model, with 2,850 ehp General Electric T64-GE-10 turboprops. Overall length 77 ft 4 in (23·57 m). Max T-O weight 38,000 lb (17,237 kg). Four evaluation aircraft only, originally designated YAC-2 by US Army; changed to YCV-7A, and later C-8A, after USAF took over the operation of US Army transport aircraft in January 1967. Described in earlier editions of *Jane's*.

One NASA-owned C-8A, modified to evaluate the "augmentor wing" concept devised by de Havilland Canada, is described under the NASA entry in the US section.

CC-115. Canadian Armed forces model (manufacturer's designation DHC-5A), with 3,055 ehp General Electric CT64-820-1 turboprops. Max T-O weight 41,000 lb (18,597 kg). Buffalos supplied to Brazil and Peru are generally similar to this model.

One CC-115, modified by de Havilland Canada, has been loaned by the Canadian Department of Defence to Bell Aerospace for tests with an air cushion landing system. This aircraft is described under the Bell Aerospace heading in the US section.

The description which follows applies to the latest DHC-5D version:

TYPE: Twin-turboprop STOL utility transport.

WINGS: Cantilever high-wing monoplane. Wing section NACA 64_2A417·5 (mod) at root, NACA 63_2A615 (mod) at tip. Dihedral 0° inboard of nacelles, 5° outboard. Incidence 2° 30′. Sweepback at quarter-chord 1° 40′. Conventional fail-safe multi-spar structure of high-strength aluminium alloys. Full-span double-slotted aluminium alloy flaps, outboard sections functioning as ailerons. Aluminium alloy slot-lip spoilers, forward of inboard flaps, are actuated by Jarry Hydraulics unit. Spoilers coupled to manually-operated ailerons for lateral control, uncoupled for symmetrical ground operation. Electrically-actuated trim tab in starboard aileron. Geared tab in each aileron. Rudder/aileron interconnect tab on port aileron. Outer wing leading-edges fitted with electrically-controlled flush pneumatic rubber de-icing boots.

FUSELAGE: Fail-safe structure of high-strength aluminium alloy. Cargo floor supported by longitudinal keel members.

TAIL UNIT: Cantilever structure of high-strength aluminium alloy, with fixed-incidence T-tailplane. Elevator aerodynamically and mass balanced. Fore and trailing serially-hinged rudders are powered by tandem jacks operated by two independent hydraulic systems manufactured by Jarry Hydraulics. Trim tab in port half of elevator, spring tab in starboard half. Electrically-controlled flush pneumatic rubber de-icing boot on tailplane leading-edge.

LANDING GEAR: Retractable tricycle type, with twin wheels on each unit. Hydraulic retraction, nose unit aft, main units forward. Jarry Hydraulics oleo-pneumatic shock-absorbers. Goodrich main wheels and tyres, size 37 × 15-12, pressure 45 lb/sq in (3·16 kg/cm^2). Goodrich nosewheels and tyres, size 8·9 × 12·5, pressure 38 lb/sq in (2·67 kg/cm^2). Goodrich multi-disc brakes.

POWER PLANT: Two General Electric CT64-820-4 turboprop engines, each rated at 3,095 shp and driving a Hamilton Standard 63E60-13 three-blade reversible-pitch propeller. Fuel in one integral tank in each inner wing, capacity 533 Imp gallons (2,423 litres), and rubber bag tanks in each outer wing, capacity 336 Imp gallons (1,527 litres). Total fuel capacity 1,738 Imp gallons (7,900 litres). Refuelling points above wings and in side of fuselage for pressure refuelling. Total oil capacity 10 Imp gallons (45·5 litres).

ACCOMMODATION: Crew of three, comprising pilot, co-pilot and crew chief. Main cabin can accommodate roll-up troop seats or folding forward-facing seats for 41 troops or 35 para-

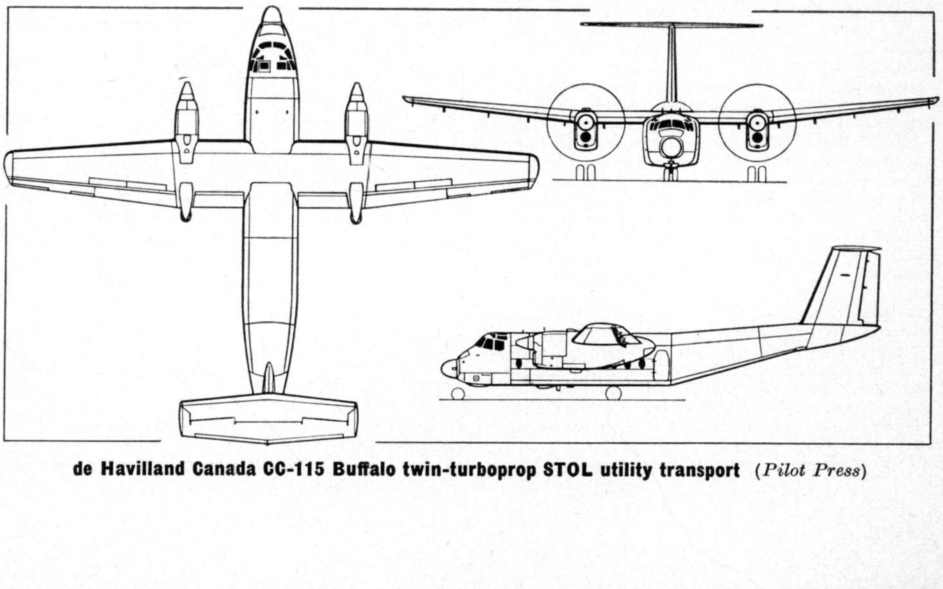

de Havilland Canada CC-115 Buffalo twin-turboprop STOL utility transport (*Pilot Press*)

de Havilland Canada DHC-5A Buffalo STOL utility transport in the insignia of the Brazilian Air Force

troops, or 24 stretchers and six seats. Provision for toilet in forward part of cabin. Door on each side at rear of cabin. Loading height with rear cargo loading door up and ramp down 9 ft 6 in (2·90 m).

SYSTEMS: AiResearch bleed air cabin heating and cooling system. Hydraulic system of 3,000 lb/sq in (210 kg/cm^2) actuates landing gear, flaps, spoilers, rudders, brakes, nosewheel steering, winch and APU starting. 50 lb/sq in (3·50 kg/cm^2) pneumatic system for engine starting, de-icing and environmental control. Two engine-driven variable-frequency 3-phase 20/30 kVA AC generators with 28V DC and 400Hz conversion subsystems. Williams Research Corpn WR9-7 APU provides electric, hydraulic and pneumatic power. Brooks & Perkins rail-type cargo handling system, with hydraulic winch and floor rollers.

ELECTRONICS AND EQUIPMENT: Radio and radar to customer's specification. Blind-flying instrumentation standard.

DIMENSIONS, EXTERNAL:
- Wing span: 96 ft 0 in (29·26 m)
- Wing chord at root: 11 ft 9¼ in (3·59 m)
- Wing chord at tip: 5 ft 11 in (1·19 m)
- Wing aspect ratio: 9·75
- Length overall: 79 ft 0 in (24·08 m)
- Height overall: 28 ft 8 in (8·73 m)
- Tailplane span: 32 ft 0 in (9·75 m)
- Wheel track: 30 ft 6 in (9·29 m)
- Wheelbase: 27 ft 11 in (8·50 m)
- Propeller diameter: 14 ft 6 in (4·42 m)
- Cabin doors (each side):
  - Height: 5 ft 6 in (1·68 m)
  - Width: 2 ft 9 in (0·84 m)
  - Height to sill: 3 ft 10 in (1·17 m)
- Emergency exits (each side, below wing leading-edge):
  - Height: 3 ft 4 in (1·02 m)
  - Width: 2 ft 2 in (0·66 m)
  - Height to sill: approx 5 ft 0 in (1·52 m)
- Rear cargo loading door and ramp:
  - Height: 20 ft 9 in (6·33 m)
  - Width: 7 ft 8 in (2·34 m)
  - Height to ramp hinge: 3 ft 10 in (1·17 m)

DIMENSIONS, INTERNAL:
- Cabin, excluding flight deck:
  - Length, cargo floor: 31 ft 5 in (9·58 m)
  - Max width: 8 ft 9 in (2·67 m)
  - Max height: 6 ft 10 in (2·08 m)
  - Floor area: 243·5 sq ft (22·63 m^2)
  - Volume: 1,715 cu ft (48·56 m^3)

AREAS:
- Wings, gross: 945 sq ft (87·8 m^2)
- Ailerons (total): 39 sq ft (3·62 m^2)
- Trailing-edge flaps (total, including ailerons): 280 sq ft (26·01 m^2)
- Spoilers (total): 25·2 sq ft (2·34 m^2)
- Fin: 92 sq ft (8·55 m^2)
- Rudder: 60 sq ft (5·57 m^2)
- Tailplane: 151·5 sq ft (14·07 m^2)
- Elevator, including tabs: 81·5 sq ft (7·57 m^2)

WEIGHTS AND LOADINGS (A: STOL assault mission from unprepared airfield; B: STOL transport mission, firm smooth airfield surface):
- Operational weight empty (incl 3 crew and 1,600 lb; 725 kg allowance for options and avionics):
  - A, B: 24,800 lb (11,249 kg)
- Max payload:
  - A: 12,200 lb (5,533 kg)
  - B: 18,000 lb (8,164 kg)
- Max normal fuel:
  - A, B: 13,696 lb (6,212 kg)
- Max unit load for air drop:
  - A, B: 6,000 lb (2,721 kg)
- Manoeuvring limit load factor:
  - A: 3·0
  - B: 2·5
- Max T-O weight:
  - A: 41,000 lb (18,597 kg)
  - B: 49,200 lb (22,316 kg)
- Max landing weight:
  - A: 39,100 lb (17,735 kg)
  - B: 46,900 lb (21,273 kg)
- Max zero-fuel weight:
  - A: 37,000 lb (16,782 kg)
  - B: 43,500 lb (19,731 kg)
- Max wing loading:
  - A: 66 lb/sq ft (322·2 kg/m^2)
  - B: 55 lb/sq ft (268·5 kg/m^2)

PERFORMANCE (at max T-O weight except where indicated. A: STOL assault mission from unprepared airfield; B: STOL transport mission from firm smooth airfield surface):
- Max cruising speed at 10,000 ft (3,050 m):
  - A: 250 knots (288 mph; 463 km/h) TAS
  - *B: 227 knots (261 mph; 420 km/h) TAS
- Stalling speed, 40° flap:
  - A at 39,000 lb (17,690 kg) AUW: 66 knots (76 mph; 122·5 km/h)
  - B at 46,900 lb (21,273 kg) AUW: 71 knots (82 mph; 132 km/h)
- Max rate of climb at S/L, normal rated power:
  - A: 2,200 ft (670 m)/min
  - B: 1,720 ft (524 m)/min
- Rate of climb at S/L, one engine out:
  - A, max power: 650 ft (198 m)/min
  - B, max power: 325 ft (99 m)/min
- Service ceiling, normal rated power:
  - A: 31,500 ft (9,600 m)
  - *B: 29,000 ft (8,840 m)
- Service ceiling, one engine out:
  - A, max power: 17,800 ft (5,425 m)
  - *B, max power: 13,200 ft (4,025 m)
- **STOL T-O run:
  - A: 780 ft (237 m)
  - B: 2,125 ft (647 m)
- **STOL T-O to 50 ft (15 m), mid-CG:
  - A: 1,000 ft (305 m)
  - B: 2,800 ft (853 m)
- **STOL landing from 50 ft (15 m):
  - A: 980 ft (299 m)
  - B: 2,550 ft (777 m)
- **STOL landing run:
  - A: 520 ft (158 m)
  - B: 1,250 ft (381 m)
- Range at 10,000 ft (3,050 m):
  - A, max payload 375 nm (431 miles; 693 km)
  - B, max payload 655 nm (754 miles, 1,213 km)
  - A, B, zero payload: 1,770 nm (2,038 miles; 3,280 km)

* at 47,000 lb (21,320 kg) AUW
**with 12,200 lb (5,533 kg) payload

DHC-5 BUFFALO AUGMENTOR WING JET STOL RESEARCH AIRCRAFT

In co-operation with the Canadian Department of Industry, Trade and Commerce, a NASA-owned C-8A Buffalo has been modified as a flying testbed for the "augmentor wing" concept devised by de Havilland Canada. A full description of the modified aircraft appears under the NASA heading in the US section of this edition.

By the end of 1973 the Buffalo augmentor wing programme had totalled 100 hours of flying, with the "proof of concept" phase essentially completed. The second phase, planned for 1974, involved an additional 300 hours of flight evaluation. This programme, called STOLAND, was to be associated with aerial navigation and terminal guidance to establish operational standards for STOL aircraft.

A second C-8A is to be acquired by NASA, for evaluation with an alternative wing lift augmentation system.

DHC-5 BUFFALO ACLS RESEARCH AIRCRAFT

Under a programme sponsored jointly by the Canadian Department of Industry, Trade and Commerce and the US Air Force Flight Dynamics Laboratory, a CAF CC-115 Buffalo was delivered to Bell Aerospace after modification by DHC to accept an air cushion landing system (ACLS). In this role the aircraft is designated XC-8A. Flight testing with the ACLS installed began in 1973.

A full description of this programme appears under the Bell Aerospace heading in the US section of this edition.

DHC-6 TWIN OTTER

CAF designation: CC-138

First announced in 1964, the Twin Otter is a STOL transport powered by two United Aircraft of Canada PT6A series turboprop engines. Design work was started in January 1964, and construction of an initial batch of five aircraft began in November of the same year. The first of these (CF-DHC-X), powered by two 579 ehp PT6A-6 engines, flew for the first time on 20 May 1965.

The fourth and subsequent aircraft of the initial Series 100 version were fitted with PT6A-20 engines, and the first delivery of a production aircraft, to the Ontario Department of Lands and Forests, was made in July 1966, shortly after the Twin Otter received FAA Type Approval. All Series are certificated to FAR 23 for Pt 135 operation.

By 1 January 1974, 410 Twin Otters had been sold, and operating hours totalled more than 2·3 million. The 400th Twin Otter was delivered on 18 December 1973, and production was continuing in 1974 at a rate of six aircraft per month.

Military operators of Twin Otters include the Argentine Air Force (five), Army (three) and Navy (one); Chilean Air Force (six); Jamaica Defence Force (one); Peruvian Air Force (eleven); Royal Norwegian Air Force (four); Uganda Police Air Wing (one); Paraguayan Air Force (one); the Panamanian Air Force (one); and the Canadian Armed Forces (eight CC-138 for SAR and utility duties).

Four versions of the Twin Otter have so far been announced, as follows:

Twin Otter Series 100. Initial production version, with 579 ehp PT6A-20 engines and

DHC-6 Twin Otter Series 300 light STOL transport in Air Mali insignia

short nose; described in 1967-68 and 1970-71 *Jane's*. Superseded by Series 200 in April 1968. Total of 115 built. Production completed.

Twin Otter Series 200. As Srs 100, but with longer nose and increased baggage volume of 126 cu ft (3·57 m³). Was also available, with short nose, as floatplane. The second 115 aircraft built were of this version, described in the 1970-71 *Jane's*. Production completed.

Twin Otter Series 300. Current production version, to which the following description applies. Deliveries began in the Spring of 1969 with the 231st Twin Otter off the line. Available with short nose, as floatplane. The eight aircraft ordered by Peru in 1970 are fitted with floats, and are operated by Grupo Aéreo No 42 of the Peruvian Air Force, based at Iquitos.

Twin Otter Series 300S. First announced at the Paris Air Show in May/June 1973, this is an improved Series 300 with added operational safety features associated with FAR Pt 25 (Transport Category) regulations and technical refinements to enhance the aircraft's STOL capability.

The improvements in the Series 300S include high-capacity brakes; anti-skid braking system; wing spoilers; electrical and hydraulic systems improvements; emergency brakes; propeller autofeather time delay; and improved power plant fire protection. The number of passenger seats has been reduced to 11, to provide an improved level of passenger comfort.

Six Twin Otters have been built to Series 300S standard, for operation by Airtransit Canada, an Air Canada subsidiary, on a government-funded experimental air service between Ottawa and Montreal. Using STOLports in the two cities, the service was due to begin in early 1974 and to run for about two years.

During the Summer of 1969, the Twin Otter was fitted for certification with a new-type external fire-bombing tank. This completely new forest fire-fighting concept, known as the Membrane Tank System, was designed and built by Field Aviation Company Ltd. A rectangular tank of two 12 ft 0 in × 1 ft 11 in (3·66 × 0·58 m) sections, capable of holding 480 US gallons (400 Imp gallons; 1,818 litres) is mounted on the underside of the aircraft. An expendable fabric membrane supports the fluid, and is jettisoned with the load. It is designed for use on the landplane Twin Otter, using chemical fire retardants. Canadian MoT type approval in the Normal category was received in September 1969.

In 1971, a 10 ft (3·05 m) long, 50 cu ft (1·4 m³) capacity ventral pod, carrying up to 600 lb (272 kg) of baggage or freight, was designed for the Twin Otter Series 300 by Field Aviation of Toronto and tested in service by Rocky Mountain Airlines of Denver.

TYPE: Twin-turboprop STOL transport.

WINGS: Strut-braced high-wing monoplane. Wing section NACA 6A series mean line; NACA 0016 (modified) thickness distribution. Dihedral 3°. No sweepback. All-metal safe-life structure, each wing being attached to the fuselage by two bolts at the front and rear spar fitting and braced by a single stream-line section strut on each side. Light alloy riveted construction is used throughout except for the upper skin panels, which have spanwise corrugated stiffeners bonded to them. All-metal double-slotted full-span trailing-edge flaps. Spoilers fitted to Series 300S aircraft only. All-metal ailerons which also droop for use as flaps. Electrically-actuated tab in port aileron; geared trim tabs in both port and starboard ailerons. Optional pneumatic-boot de-icing equipment.

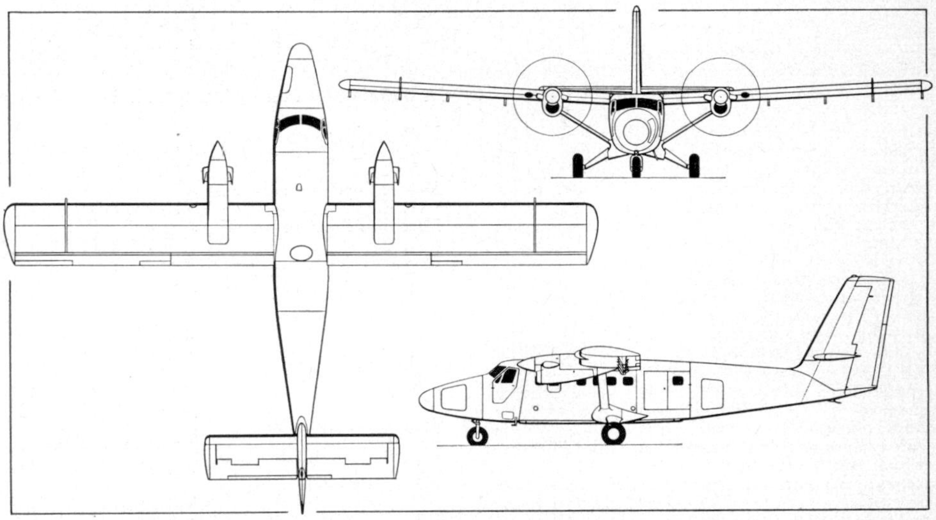

de Havilland Canada DHC-6 Twin Otter Series 300 STOL utility transport (*Pilot Press*)

FUSELAGE: Conventional semi-monocoque safe-life structure, built in three sections. Primary structure of frames, stringers and skin of aluminium alloy. Windscreen and cabin windows of acrylic plastics. Cabin floor is of low-density aluminium-faced sandwich construction and is designed to accommodate distributed loads of up to 200 lb/sq ft (976·49 kg/m²).

TAIL UNIT: Cantilever all-metal structure of high-strength aluminium alloys. Fin and fixed-incidence tailplane are bolted to rear fuselage. Manually-operated trim tabs in rudder and elevators. A geared tab is fitted to the rudder to lighten control forces, and a tab fitted to the starboard elevator is linked to the flaps to control longitudinal trim during flap retraction and extension. Optional pneumatic-boot de-icing of tailplane leading-edge.

LANDING GEAR: Non-retractable tricycle type, with single wheel on each unit. Fully-steerable nosewheel. Urethane compression-block shock-absorption on main units. Oleo-pneumatic nosewheel shock-absorber. Goodyear main-wheel tyres size 11·00-12, pressure 38 lb/sq in (2·67 kg/cm²). Goodyear nosewheel tyre size 8·90-12·50, pressure 33 lb/sq in (2·32 kg/cm²). Goodrich independent, hydraulically-operated disc brakes on main wheels. Anti-skid braking system in Series 300S. Alternatively, high-flotation wheels and tyres, for operation in soft-field conditions, are available at customer's option, size 15·0-12·0 for nose-wheel and main wheels. Provision for alternative wheel/ski landing gear. Twin-float gear available for short-nose Srs 300, with added wing fences and small auxiliary fins.

POWER PLANT: Two 652 ehp United Aircraft of Canada PT6A-27 turboprop engines, each driving a Hartzell HC-B3TN-3D three-blade reversible-pitch fully-feathering metal propeller. Two underfloor fuel tanks (eight cells), total capacity of 318 Imp gallons (1,446 litres). Refuelling point for each tank on port side of fuselage. Oil capacity 2 Imp gallons (9·1 litres) per engine. Optional electrical de-icing system for propellers and air intakes.

ACCOMMODATION: Side-by-side seats for one or two pilots on flight deck, access to which is by a forward-opening car-type door on each side or via the passenger cabin. Windscreen demisting and defrosting standard. Cabin divided by bulkhead into main passenger or freight compartment and baggage compartment. Seats for up to 20 passengers in main cabin. Standard interior is 20-seat commuter layout, with Douglas track, carpets, double windows, individual air vents and reading lights, and airstair door. Optional layouts include 18- or 19-seat commuter versions, 13/20-passenger utility version with foldaway seats and double cargo doors with ladder, and 11-passenger layout in Series 300S. Access to passenger cabin by door on each side of rear fuselage; optionally, an airstair door may be fitted on the port side. Optional double door for cargo on port side instead of passenger door. Compartments in nose and aft of main cabin, each with upward-hinged door on port side, for 300 lb (136 kg) and 500 lb (227 kg) of baggage respectively; rear baggage hold accessible from cabin in emergency. Emergency exits near front of cabin on each side. Heating of flight deck and passenger cabin by engine bleed air; ventilation via a ram-air intake on the port side of the fuselage nose. Oxygen system for crew and passengers optional. Executive, survey or ambulance interiors can be fitted at customer's option. Tie-down cargo rings are installed as standard for the freighter role.

SYSTEMS: Hydraulic system, pressure 1,500 lb / sq in (105 kg / cm²), for flaps, brakes, nosewheel steering and (where fitted) ski retraction mechanism. A hand pump in the crew compartment provides emergency pressure for standby or ground operation if the electric pump is inoperative. Accumulators smooth the system pressure pulses and provide pressure for parking and emergency braking. Optional low-pressure pneumatic system (18 lb/sq in; 1·27 kg/cm²) for operation of autopilot or wing and tail de-icing boots, if fitted. Primary electrical system is 28V DC, with one 200A starter/generator on each engine. A 22Ah nickel-cadmium battery (optionally 39Ah nickel-cadmium or 36Ah lead-acid battery) for emergency power and engine starting. Separate 3·6Ah battery supplies independent power for engine starting relays and ignition. 65VA (optionally 250VA) main and standby static inverters provide 400Hz AC power for instruments and avionics. External DC receptacle aft of port side cabin door permits operation of complete system on the ground.

ELECTRONICS AND EQUIPMENT: Navigation and communications equipment, including weather radar, to customer's specification. Dual controls and blind-flying instrumentation standard.

DIMENSIONS, EXTERNAL:
Wing span 65 ft 0 in (19·81 m)
Wing chord (constant) 6 ft 6 in (1·98 m)
Wing aspect ratio 10
Length overall 51 ft 9 in (15·77 m)
Height overall 18 ft 7 in (5·66 m)
Tailplane span 21 ft 0 in (6·40 m)
Wheel track 12 ft 6 in (3·81 m)
Wheelbase 14 ft 9 in (4·50 m)
Propeller diameter 8 ft 6 in (2·59 m)
Passenger door (port side):
Height 4 ft 2 in (1·27 m)
Width 2 ft 6 in (0·76 m)
Height to sill 3 ft 10 in (1·17 m)
Passenger door (starboard side):
Height 3 ft 9½ in (1·15 m)
Width 2 ft 6¼ in (0·77 m)
Height to sill 3 ft 10 in (1·17 m)
Baggage compartment door (nose):
Mean height 2 ft 3¼ in (0·69 m)
Width 2 ft 5¾ in (0·76 m)
Height to sill 3 ft 10 in (1·17 m)
Baggage compartment door (port, rear):
Max height 3 ft 2 in (0·97 m)
Width 2 ft 1½ in (0·65 m)
Cargo double door (port, rear):
Height 4 ft 2 in (1·27 m)
Width 4 ft 8 in (1·42 m)
Height to sill 3 ft 10 in (1·17 m)

DIMENSIONS, INTERNAL:
Cabin, excluding flight deck, galley and baggage compartment:
Length 18 ft 6 in (5·64 m)
Max width 5 ft 3¼ in (1·61 m)
Max height 4 ft 11 in (1·50 m)
Floor area 80·2 sq ft (7·45 m²)
Volume 384 cu ft (10·87 m³)
Baggage compartment (nose):
Volume 38 cu ft (1·08 m³)
Baggage compartment (rear):
Length 6 ft 2 in (1·88 m)
Volume 88 cu ft (2·49 m³)

AREAS:
Wings, gross 420 sq ft (39·02 m²)
Ailerons (total) 33·2 sq ft (3·08 m²)
Trailing-edge flaps (total) 112·2 sq ft (10·42 m²)
Fin 48·0 sq ft (4·46 m²)
Rudder, including tabs 34·0 sq ft (3·16 m²)
Tailplane 100·0 sq ft (9·29 m²)
Elevator, including tabs 35·0 sq ft (3·25 m²)

WEIGHTS:
Typical operating weight (20-seat commuter, incl 2 crew and 130 lb; 59 kg of avionics) 7,320 lb (3,320 kg)
Max payload for 100 nm (115 miles; 185 km) 4,420 lb (2,004 kg)
Max T-O weight 12,500 lb (5,670 kg)
Max landing weight:
wheels and skis 12,300 lb (5,579 kg)
floats 12,500 lb (5,670 kg)

PERFORMANCE (at max T-O weight, ISA):
Max cruising speed at 10,000 ft (3,050 m) 182 knots (210 mph; 338 km/h)
Stalling speed, flaps up 74 knots (85·5 mph; 137·5 km/h)
Stalling speed, flaps down 58 knots (67 mph; 108 km/h)
Max rate of climb at S/L 1,600 ft (488 m)/min
Rate of climb at S/L, one engine out 340 ft (104 m)/min
Service ceiling 26,700 ft (8,140 m)
Service ceiling, one engine out 11,600 ft (3,530 m)
T-O run:
STOL 700 ft (213 m)
CAR Pt 3 860 ft (262 m)
T-O to 50 ft (15 m):
STOL 1,200 ft (366 m)
CAR Pt 3 1,500 ft (457 m)
Landing from 50 ft (15 m):
STOL 1,050 ft (320 m)
CAR Pt 3 1,940 ft (591 m)
Landing run:
STOL 515 ft (157 m)
CAR Pt 3 950 ft (290 m)
Range at max cruising speed with 2,550 lb (1,156 kg) payload 690 nm (794 miles; 1,277 km)

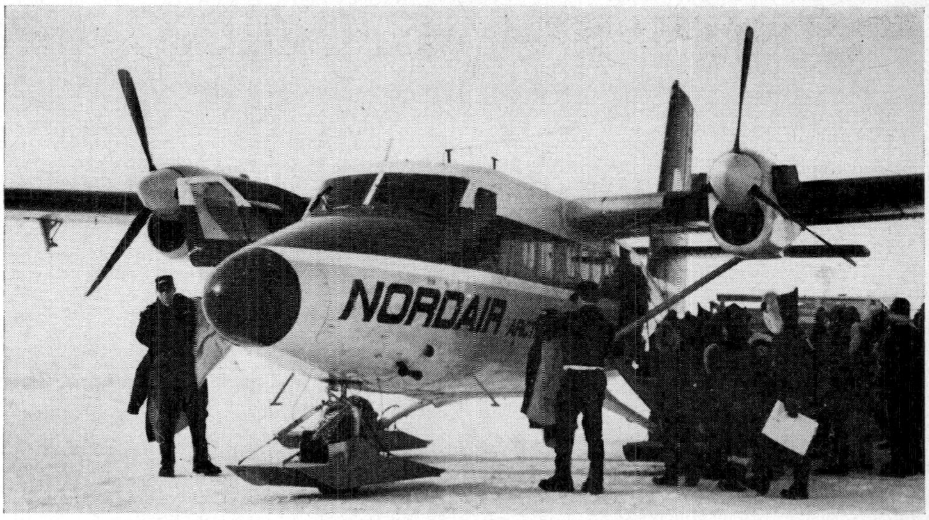

Nordair Twin Otter in the Arctic, fitted with Bristol Aerospace Ltd wheel/skis

Range at max cruising speed with 2,131 lb (966 kg) payload and wing tanks 958 nm (1,103 miles; 1,775 km)

DHC-7 DASH 7

The Dash 7 "Quiet STOL" airliner project was begun by de Havilland Canada after the company had conducted a worldwide market survey of short-haul transport requirements. The DHC-7 is designed to inaugurate Metroflight STOL service between downtown STOLports having 2,000 ft (610 m) runways. United Aircraft Corporation has participated in the development of a quiet engine/propeller combination which will limit external noise to 95 EPNdB at 500 ft (152 m) from the aircraft during take-off and landing.

A joint Canadian government/de Havilland Canada programme is now under way which includes the manufacture of two pre-production DHC-7s. The schedule for this programme provided for the beginning of final assembly in the Spring of 1974 and of flight trials in late 1974, followed by certification in 1976. The Dash 7 will be certificated by the Canadian Ministry of Transport to FAR 25; STOL performance will be approved under conventional FAR 25 and FAR 121 regulations apart from a 7·5° glideslope and 35 ft (10·7 m) landing reference height adopted by the FAA for STOL aircraft.

Widerøe's Flyveselskap of Norway has ordered two Dash 7s, for operation from early 1977, and two have been ordered by Rocky Mountain Airways of Denver, Colorado.

TYPE: Four-engined short/medium-range quiet STOL transport.

WINGS: Cantilever high-wing monoplane, with 4° 30′ dihedral from centre-section. Wing section NACA 63A418 at root, NACA 63A415 at tip. Incidence 3° at root. Conventional all-metal two-spar bonded skin/stringer structure. Double-slotted flaps, extending over approx 80% of trailing-edge, are actuated mechanically for take-off, by irreversible screwjacks, and hydraulically for landing. Two inboard ground spoilers/lift dumpers and four outboard air spoilers in each upper surface, forward of flaps. Outboard sections can be operated symmetrically, or differentially in combination with the ailerons. No tabs. Pneumatic-boot de-icing of leading-edges.

FUSELAGE: Conventional all-metal stressed-skin pressurised structure, of bonded skin/stringer construction. Basically circular cross-section, with flattened profile under floor level.

TAIL UNIT: Cantilever all-metal T-tail, with large dorsal fin. Fixed-incidence tailplane, and one-piece horn-balanced elevator. Two-piece vertically-split rudder, actuated hydraulically. Pneumatic-boot de-icing of tailplane leading-edge.

LANDING GEAR: Retractable tricycle type, with twin wheels on all units. Oleo-pneumatic shock-absorbers. Hydraulic retraction, main units into inboard engine nacelles, steerable Menasco nose unit into fuselage. Main-wheel tyres size 30 × 9-15, pressure 100 lb/sq in (7·03 kg/cm²), nosewheel tyres size 24 × 7·5-10, pressure 80 lb/sq in (5·62 kg/cm²). Larger, low-pressure tyres optional, with pressures of 70 lb/sq in (4·92 kg/cm²) on main units, 60 lb/sq in (4·22 kg/cm²) on nose unit. Anti-skid braking system for all units. Small retractable tail bumper under rear fuselage.

POWER PLANT: Four 1,120 shp UACL PT6A-50 turboprop engines, each driving a Hamilton Standard 24PF-301 fully-feathering reversible-pitch four-blade glassfibre propeller of slow-turning type (1,210 rpm) to reduce noise level. Fuel in two integral tanks in each wing, total capacity 1,573 US gallons (1,310 Imp gallons; 5,958 litres). Single pressure refuelling/defuelling point on underside of rear fuselage, aft of pressure dome. Pneumatic de-icing of engine air intakes; electrical de-icing for propellers.

ACCOMMODATION: Flight crew of two, plus one or two cabin attendants. Seats for 48 passengers at 32 in (81 cm) pitch, in pairs on each side of centre aisle, with generous provision for underseat carry-on baggage. Outward-opening airstair door at rear on port side. Emergency exits on each side at front of cabin and on starboard side at rear. Baggage compartments in nose (capacity 600 lb; 272 kg) and rear fuselage (capacity 2,200 lb; 998 kg), each with external access. Galley, coat rack and toilet at rear of cabin. Optional arrangements include movable bulkhead for mixed freight/passenger loads with forward freight door on port side. Up to five standard pallets can be accommodated in an all-cargo role. Brownline quick-change cargo handling system available optionally. Entire accommodation pressurised and air-conditioned.

SYSTEMS: Cabin pressure differential 4·26 lb/sq in (0·3 kg/cm²). Two air-cycle systems, driven by

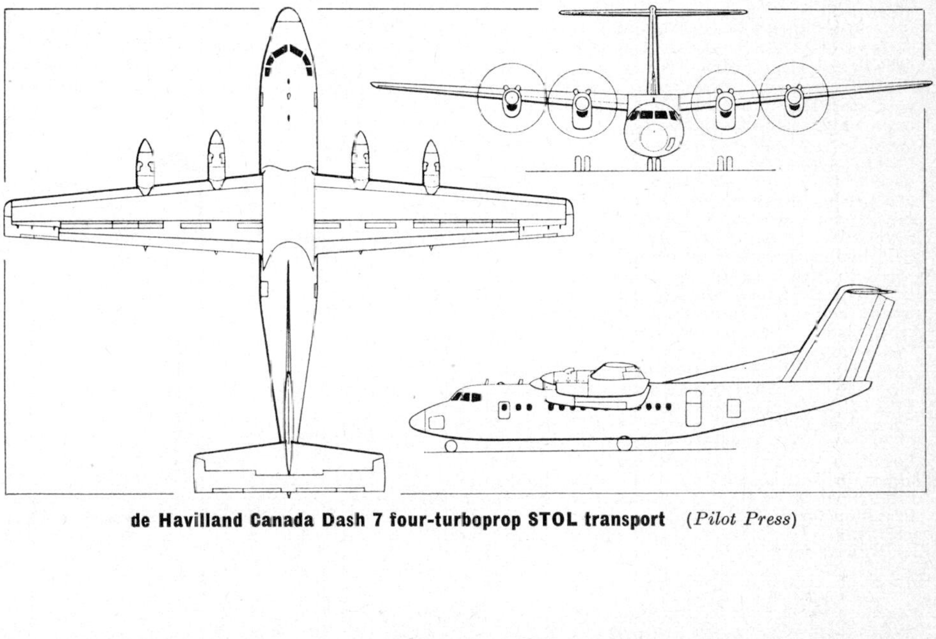

de Havilland Canada Dash 7 four-turboprop STOL transport *(Pilot Press)*

engine bleed air, for cabin air-conditioning. Two independent hydraulic systems, each of 3,000 lb/sq in (210 kg/cm²), for flap, spoiler, rudder, landing gear and brake actuation, and nosewheel steering. Primary DC power provided by four Lucas 28V 250A 7·5kW starter/generators. Variable-frequency AC power from four 10kVA Lucas brushless generators for propeller and windscreen de-icing and standby fuel pumps. Lucas static inverters supply constant-frequency 400Hz loads, including engine instrumentation and navigational systems. Nickel-cadmium batteries for engine starting.

ELECTRONICS AND EQUIPMENT: Standard avionic equipment includes compass system, flight data recorder, emergency locator transmitter, flight compartment voice recorder, crew interphone and cabin PA system. Wide range of other equipment, to customer's requirements, can include VHF/com and VHF/nav systems, HF/com system, LF/nav systems, ATC transponder, radio altimeter, area navigation system, marker beacon, DME, weather radar, collision avoidance system, microwave landing system, integrated flight director system and autopilot.

DIMENSIONS, EXTERNAL:
Wing span 93 ft 0 in (28·35 m)
Wing chord at root 12 ft 6 in (3·81 m)
Wing chord at tip 5 ft 6 in (1·68 m)
Wing mean aerodynamic chord 9 ft 9¾ in (2·99 m)
Wing aspect ratio 10
Length overall 80 ft 4 in (24·49 m)
Height overall 26 ft 2 in (7·98 m)
Tailplane span 31 ft 0 in (9·45 m)
Fuselage: Max diameter 9 ft 2 in (2·79 m)
Wheel track 23 ft 6 in (7·16 m)
Wheelbase 27 ft 6 in (8·38 m)
Propeller ground clearance (inboard engines) 5 ft 3 in (1·60 m)
Min propeller/fuselage clearance 2 ft 5·4 in (0·75 m)
Propeller diameter 11 ft 3 in (3·43 m)
Passenger door (rear, port):
Height 5 ft 10 in (1·78 m)
Width 2 ft 6 in (0·76 m)
Height to sill 3 ft 7 in (1·09 m)
Emergency exit door (rear, stbd):
Height 4 ft 5 in (1·35 m)
Width 2 ft 0 in (0·61 m)
Height to sill 3 ft 7 in (1·09 m)
Emergency exit doors (fwd, each):
Height 3 ft 0 in (0·91 m)
Width 1 ft 8 in (0·51 m)
Height to sill 5 ft 1 in (1·55 m)
Baggage hold door (rear, port):
Height 3 ft 2 in (0·97 m)
Width 2 ft 7 in (0·79 m)
Height to sill 4 ft 10 in (1·47 m)
Baggage hold door (nose, port):
Min height 1 ft 10 in (0·56 m)
Max height 2 ft 3 in (0·69 m)
Width 2 ft 6 in (0·76 m)
Height to sill 3 ft 7 in (1·09 m)
Cargo door (fwd, port, optional):
Height 5 ft 10 in (1·78 m)
Width 6 ft 2 in (1·88 m)

DIMENSIONS, INTERNAL:
Cabin, excluding flight deck:
Length 40 ft 0 in (12·19 m)
Max width 8 ft 7 in (2·62 m)
Floor width 7 ft 0 in (2·13 m)
Max height 6 ft 6 in (1·98 m)
Height under wing 6 ft 1 in (1·85 m)
Volume 1,950 cu ft (55·2 m³)
Baggage compartment (rear fuselage):
Max length 8 ft 7 in (2·62 m)
Volume 236 cu ft (6·68 m³)
Baggage compartment (nose):
Volume 50 cu ft (1·42 m³)

AREAS:
Wings, gross 860 sq ft (79·90 m²)
Vertical tail surfaces (total, excluding dorsal fin) 170 sq ft (15·79 m²)
Horizontal tail surfaces (total) 217 sq ft (20·16 m²)

WEIGHTS AND LOADING:
Basic weight empty (standard 48-passenger layout) 23,080 lb (10,465 kg)
Operating weight empty 24,440 lb (11,085 kg)
Max payload (48 passengers or cargo) 11,060 lb (5,016 kg)
Max T-O weight 41,000 lb (18,597 kg)
Max zero-fuel weight 35,500 lb (16,100 kg)
Max landing weight 39,000 lb (17,690 kg)
Max cabin floor loading 75 lb/sq ft (366·2 kg/m²)

PERFORMANCE (estimated, at 41,000 lb; 18,597 kg AUW except where indicated, FAR 25 at S/L, ISA):
Max cruising speed 239 knots (275 mph; 443 km/h)
Stalling speed, flaps down, zero thrust 65 knots (74 mph; 119 km/h)
En-route rate of climb, flaps and landing gear up:
four engines, max climb power 1,470 ft (448 m)/min
three engines, max continuous power 900 ft (274 m)/min
Service ceiling 24,000 ft (7,315 m)
Service ceiling, one engine out 15,200 ft (4,635 m)
T-O run 1,465 ft (447 m)
Accelerate/stop distance 2,200 ft (670 m)
T-O to 35 ft (10·7 m) 2,200 ft (670 m)
Landing from 35 ft (10·7 m) at max landing weight 1,230 ft (375 m)
Landing run 810 ft (247 m)
Landing field length 2,050 ft (625 m)
Min ground turning radius 34 ft 2 in (10·41 m)
Runway LCN (11·00-12 tyres) 10
Range at 15,000 ft (4,570 m) with max passenger payload, reserves for 100 nm (115 miles; 185 km) and 45 min hold 390 nm (450 miles; 724 km)
Range at 15,000 ft (4,570 m) with 6,300 lb (2,857 kg) payload, reserves as above 1,190 nm (1,370 miles; 2,204 km)

OPERATIONAL NOISE CHARACTERISTICS (estimated):
T-O noise level at 3·5 nm (4·0 miles; 6·5 km) from start of T-O run 70 EPNdB
Approach noise level at 1 nm (1·15 miles; 1·85 km) from landing threshold on 3° glideslope 91 EPNdB
Approach noise level at 1 nm (1·15 miles; 1·85 km) from landing threshold on 7° 30′ glideslope 82 EPNdB
Sideline noise level at 0·25 nm (0·29 miles; 0·46 km) from runway centre-line 81 EPNdB

DOMINION

DOMINION AIRCRAFT CORPORATION LTD

ADDRESS:
PO Box 16, International Airport, Vancouver
Telephone: (604) 273-4478

FACTORY:
1005 West Perimeter Road, Renton, Washington 98055, USA
Telephone: (206) 228-3536

PRESIDENT:
Lawrence Matanski

DOMINION SKYTRADER 800

The Skytrader 800 is a twin-engined STOL transport and general-purpose aircraft. Much of the design was carried out by former members of The Boeing Company's staff at Renton, Washington, USA, and construction of wing components and subassemblies of the prototype began at Renton in the Autumn of 1972.

The first flight of the Skytrader 800 was scheduled to take place in October 1974. Two Skytraders have been ordered by the Macmillan-Bloedel Forest Products company.

TYPE: Twin-engined STOL general-purpose transport aircraft.

WINGS: High-wing monoplane, with single bracing strut on each side. Constant-chord wings, with electrically-operated leading-edge slats. Full-span ailerons and flaps on trailing-edge. Trim tab in port aileron. Anti-icing system optional.

FUSELAGE: Conventional structure, with rectangular cabin section and upswept rear end.

TAIL UNIT: Cantilever structure, with horizontal surfaces of constant chord. Dorsal fin. Trim tabs in rudder and each elevator.

LANDING GEAR: Non-retractable tricycle type, with steel legs and rubber shock-absorbers on main units, oleo shock-absorber on nose unit. Goodyear wheels, tyres and disc brakes. Parking brake standard. Provision for alternative twin-float amphibian landing gear, oversize low-pressure tyres, or wheel/ski landing gear, at customer's option. Amphibian gear has retractable 15 in (38 cm) nosewheel and 25 in (63·5 cm) main wheel on each float.

POWER PLANT: Two 400 hp Lycoming IO-720-B1A eight-cylinder horizontally-opposed air-cooled engines in prototype, each driving a three-blade Hartzell constant-speed fully-feathering metal propeller (reversible pitch optional). Provision for fitting 475 hp Lycoming TIO-720-C engines in production aircraft. Internal fuel capacity (outer wing tanks) 160 US gallons (605 litres) normal, 240 US gallons (909 litres) with auxiliary tanks in wing roots. Provision for a further 166 US gallons (628 litres) in two underwing drop-tanks, raising total capacity to 406 US gallons (1,537 litres). Provision for JATO at customer's option.

ACCOMMODATION: Crew of two at front of cabin. Various internal layouts, including six-seat executive, 12-seat passenger transport, or all-freight. Executive layout includes toilet and wardrobe/baggage space. Passenger version has baggage space at rear but no toilet. Fold-away seats can be installed for quick-change passenger/freight conversion. Can be equipped as water-bomber, with 350 US gallon (1,324 litre) tank installed by the rear-loading doors. Cabin heated and ventilated. Access to flight deck by forward-hinged door on each side, and to main cabin via port-side double doors, starboard-side single door, and rear-loading doors in underside of fuselage. Airstair door on port side optional.

SYSTEMS AND EQUIPMENT: Electrical system includes two 70A 28V alternators. 45,000 BTU cabin heater. Optional equipment includes anti-icing system, windscreen wipers, weather radar, autopilot, oxygen equipment, engine fire extinguishers, cargo tie-downs and baggage rack, water-bombing installation and external power receptacle.

DIMENSIONS, EXTERNAL:
Wing span 55 ft 0 in (16·76 m)
Wing aspect ratio 7·9
Length overall 41 ft 0 in (12·50 m)
Height overall 18 ft 10¾ in (5·76 m)
Single passenger door (stbd):
Width 2 ft 0 in (0·61 m)
Height 4 ft 8 in (1·42 m)
Double doors (port):
Width 4 ft 0 in (1·22 m)
Height 4 ft 8 in (1·42 m)
Rear-loading cargo doors:
Width at top 3 ft 2 in (0·97 m)
Width at bottom 4 ft 2 in (1·27 m)
Length 6 ft 8 in (2·03 m)

DIMENSIONS, INTERNAL:
Cabin:
Max length, incl flight deck 17 ft 0 in (5·18 m)
Max width 4 ft 2 in (1·27 m)
Max height 5 ft 5 in (1·65 m)
Total volume 376 cu ft (10·65 m³)
Cargo volume 308 cu ft (8·72 m³)

AREA:
Wings, gross 385 sq ft (35·77 m²)
Ailerons (total) 32·96 sq ft (3·06 m²)
Trailing-edge flaps (total) 57·48 sq ft (5·34 m²)
Fin 29·33 sq ft (2·72 m²)
Rudder, incl tab 21·67 sq ft (2·01 m²)
Tailplane 100·00 sq ft (9·29 m²)
Elevators, incl tabs 46·35 sq ft (4·31 m²)

WEIGHTS AND LOADINGS:
Weight empty 4,950 lb (2,245 kg)
Max T-O weight 8,500 lb (3,855 kg)
Max wing loading 22 lb/sq ft (4·5 kg/m²)
Max power loading 10·6 lb/hp (4·8 kg/hp)

PERFORMANCE (estimated, at max T-O weight):
Max level speed 182 knots (210 mph; 338 km/h)
Max cruising speed (75% power) at 10,000 ft (3,050 m) 153 knots (177 mph; 285 km/h)
Cruising speed (55% power) at 2,500 ft (762 m) 130 knots (150 mph; 241 km/h)
Minimum control speed, one engine out 54 knots (62 mph; 100 km/h)
Stalling speed, flaps down, slats extended, power off 52 knots (60 mph; 97 km/h)
Min speed at which fully manoeuvrable, slats extended, power on 45 knots (52 mph; 84 km/h)

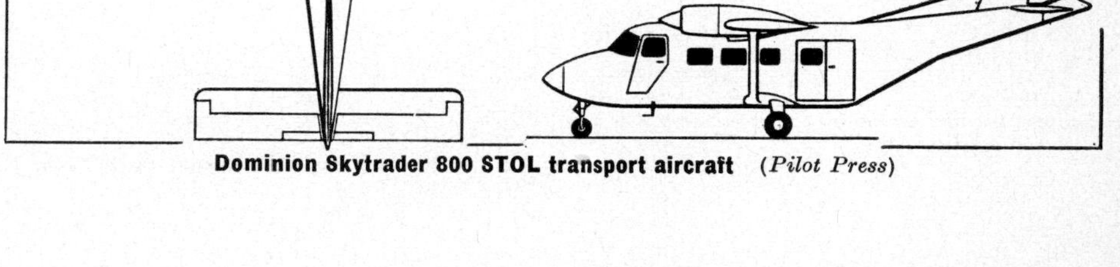

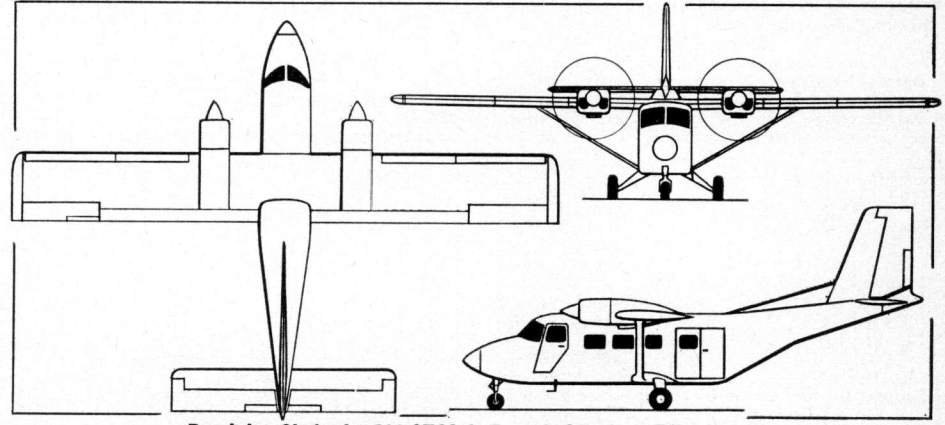

Dominion Skytrader 800 STOL transport aircraft *(Pilot Press)*

Max rate of climb at S/L 1,600 ft (487 m)/min
Rate of climb at S/L, one engine out
420 ft (128 m)/min
*Service ceiling 17,500 ft (5,335 m)
*Service ceiling, one engine out
7,000 ft (2,135 m)

T-O run 390 ft (119 m)
T-O to 50 ft (15 m) 890 ft (272 m)
Landing from 50 ft (15 m) 730 ft (223 m)
Landing run 310 ft (95 m)
Range with max internal fuel (75% power)
805 nm (930 miles; 1,495 km)

Range with max internal fuel (55% power)
1,240 nm (1,430 miles; 2,300 km)
Range with max internal and external fuel (55% power) 2,125 nm (2,450 miles; 3,940 km)
without turbocharging

HAWKER SIDDELEY

HAWKER SIDDELEY CANADA LTD (Member Company of HAWKER SIDDELEY GROUP)

HEAD OFFICE:
7 King Street East, Toronto, Ontario M5C 1A3
Telephone: (416) 362-2941
Telex: 02-2605

CHAIRMAN:
Sir Arnold Hall, FRS
PRESIDENT AND CHIEF EXECUTIVE OFFICER:
R. S. Faulkner
PUBLIC RELATIONS MANAGER:
J. F. A. Painter

Known as A. V. Roe Canada Ltd until 1962, this company controls operating units and subsidiaries in Canada employing about 8,500 people.

The company's chief aviation unit is Orenda Division (see "Aero-engines" section), which manufactures aircraft jet engines under licence and carries out repairs and overhauls.

HEINTZ

CHRISTOPHE HEINTZ

ADDRESS:
236 Richmond Street, Richmond Hill, Ontario
Telephone: (416) 884-9044

HEINTZ ZÉNITH

M Heintz is a professional aeronautical engineer. He participated in the design of several of the aircraft currently produced by Avions Pierre Robin, and is currently employed by The de Havilland Aircraft of Canada Ltd.

While in France, M Heintz designed and built the prototype of a two-seat light aircraft named the Zénith, intended for amateur construction.

Work on the Zénith began in October 1968; the prototype, registered F-WPZY (later C-FEYC), flew for the first time on 22 March 1970 and has been granted French CNRA (homebuilt experimental aircraft) certification. In October 1970 the original wing of NACA 64A315 (modified) section was replaced by one offering improved low-speed characteristics.

In June 1971, the prototype won a handicap race at Iverdon, Switzerland, at an average speed of 124 knots (143 mph; 230 km/h) from a standing start.

Sets of plans and a constructional manual for the Zénith, with engines between 85 and 160 hp, are now available to amateur builders, as follows:

France: French manual and metric measurements from D. Triques, 1b Rue Cl. Marchand, F21 Dijon.

Germany: German manual and metric measurements from K. Arens, Rollstrasse 26, D-3392 Clausthal-Zellerfeld 1.

USA and Canada: English manual and drawings to US standards, with English measurements, from Zenith Aviation, 236 Richmond Street, Richmond Hill, Ontario, Canada. Zenith Aviation also offers materials, parts and complete kits for the standard Zénith.

By early 1974 more than 100 sets of plans had been sold in all parts of the world, and five or six aircraft were flying in France.

A prototype of a three-seat version, known as the **Tri-Zénith**, is under construction in France. Zenith Aviation in Canada is building, for a first flight in 1975, the prototype of a single-seat version known as the **Mono Zénith.** This will have detachable wings and a Volkswagen engine. After satisfactory completion of flight testing, plans of this version will be made available to amateur constructors. Brief descriptions of these two versions are given separately.

The following description applies to the prototype Zénith 100 in its current form:

TYPE: Two-seat all-metal homebuilt light aircraft, with ultimate stress factor of 6*g*.

WINGS: Cantilever low-wing monoplane. Constant-chord wings, of NACA 64A515 (modified) section. Dihedral 6° from roots. Single-spar aluminium alloy structure, with aluminium alloy skin flush-riveted on leading-edge, universal-head rivets elsewhere. Hoerner wing-tips. Aluminium alloy piano-hinged ailerons and electrically-actuated plain flaps on trailing-edge. No tabs.

FUSELAGE: Conventional aluminium alloy stressed-skin structure, of basically rectangular section with rounded top-decking.

TAIL UNIT: Rectangular one-piece all-moving tailplane, with combined trim and anti-servo tabs. Rudder only, with slight sweepback. Conventional fin and rudder can be fitted if desired. Tailplane and rudder are both single-spar structures with ribs and skin of aluminium alloy.

LANDING GEAR: Non-retractable tricycle type, with rubber-block shock-absorbers. Manual locking of nosewheel. All three wheels and tyres size 380 × 150 mm. Hydraulically-actuated drum brakes on main units. Streamlined glassfibre fairings over all three wheels and legs.

POWER PLANT: One 100 hp Rolls-Royce Continental O-200-A four-cylinder horizontally-opposed aircooled engine, driving a McCauley ECM-72-50 two-blade fixed-pitch metal propeller. Design suitable for engines from 85 to 160 hp. Fuel tank in fuselage, aft of passenger seat, capacity 20 Imp gallons (90 litres). Refuelling point in port side of fuselage.

Heintz Zénith two-seat homebuilt light aircraft, built in France

ACCOMMODATION: Side-by-side seating for pilot and one passenger under sideways-opening (to starboard) Plexiglas canopy. Dual controls, with single control column located centrally between seats. Space for 77 lb (35 kg) of baggage aft of seats. Cabin heated and ventilated.

SYSTEMS: 12V battery and generator provide power for engine starting, fuel pump and flap actuation. VHF radio.

DIMENSIONS, EXTERNAL:
Wing span 22 ft 11⅝ in (7·00 m)
Wing chord (constant) 4 ft 7 in (1·40 m)
Wing aspect ratio 5
Length overall 20 ft 8 in (6·30 m)
Height overall 6 ft 0¾ in (1·85 m)
Tailplane span 7 ft 6½ in (2·30 m)
Wheel track 7 ft 4½ in (2·25 m)
Wheelbase 4 ft 8 in (1·42 m)
Min ground turning radius 13 ft 1½ in (4·00 m)
Propeller diameter 6 ft 0 in (1·83 m)
Propeller ground clearance 9⅞ in (0·25 m)

DIMENSION, INTERNAL:
Cabin: Max width 3 ft 3¾ in (1·01 m)

AREAS:
Wings, gross 105·9 sq ft (9·80 m²)
Ailerons (total) 9·26 sq ft (0·86 m²)
Trailing-edge flaps (total) 10·00 sq ft (0·93 m²)
Rudder 7·21 sq ft (0·67 m²)
Tailplane, incl tabs 19·20 sq ft (1·78 m²)

WEIGHTS AND LOADINGS:
Weight empty, equipped 881 lb (400 kg)
Normal T-O and landing weight
1,433 lb (650 kg)
Max allowable T-O weight 1,499 lb (680 kg)
Max wing loading 13·3 lb/sq ft (65 kg/m²)
Max power loading 14·33 lb/hp (6·5 kg/hp)

PERFORMANCE (at max T-O weight):
Max level speed at S/L
126 knots (145 mph; 233 km/h)
Cruising speed (75% power) at S/L
110 knots (127 mph; 205 km/h)
Cruising speed (75% power) at 9,000 ft (2,750 m)
116 knots (134 mph; 215 km/h)
Stalling speed, flaps down
46 knots (53 mph; 85 km/h)
Max rate of climb at S/L 787 ft (240 m)/min
Service ceiling 15,100 ft (4,600 m)
Range with max fuel, no reserves (75% power)
432 nm (497 miles; 800 km)

HEINTZ MONO ZÉNITH

The Mono Zénith, a prototype of which is under construction in Canada, is of generally similar all-metal construction to the two-seat Zénith, but is slightly smaller overall and is suitable for use with engines in the 50 to 100 hp range. It has no flaps, and will be available either with detachable outer wing panels, set at a dihedral angle, or in slightly simpler form with non-detachable no-dihedral outer wings. Like the two-seat Zénith, it is stressed to ±6*g* at normal max T-O weight.

DIMENSIONS, EXTERNAL:
Wing span 21 ft 11⅜ in (6·70 m)
Wing chord (constant) 4 ft 1½ in (1·26 m)
Wing aspect ratio 5·27
Width, outer wings detached
7 ft 10½ in (2·40 m)
Length overall 19 ft 8¼ in (6·00 m)
Tailplane span 7 ft 4½ in (2·25 m)
Wheel track 7 ft 0½ in (2·15 m)
Wheelbase 4 ft 2 in (1·27 m)

AREAS:
Wings, gross 91·5 sq ft (8·50 m²)
Horizontal tail surfaces (total)
16·15 sq ft (1·50 m²)
Vertical tail surfaces (total) 7·32 sq ft (0·68 m²)

WEIGHTS (estimated):
Weight empty 617-683 lb (280-310 kg)
Max T-O weight 903-970 lb (410-440 kg)

PERFORMANCE (estimated. A: 1,600 cc Volkswagen, B: 65 hp, C: 100 hp engine):
Max level speed:
A 105 knots (121 mph; 195 km/h)
B 116 knots (134 mph; 215 km/h)
C 135 knots (155 mph; 250 km/h)
Cruising speed:
A 95 knots (109 mph; 175 km/h)
B 108 knots (124 mph; 200 km/h)
C 124 knots (143 mph; 230 km/h)
Stalling speed:
A, B, C 46 knots (53 mph; 84 km/h)
Max rate of climb at S/L:
A 364 ft (111 m)/min
B 669 ft (204 m)/min
C 1,398 ft (426 m)/min
Range with 12 Imp gallons (55 litres) fuel:
A, B 334 nm (385 miles; 620 km)
C 312 nm (360 miles; 580 km)
Endurance with 12 Imp gallons (55 litres) fuel:
A, B 3 hr 30 min
C 2 hr 30 min

HEINTZ TRI-ZÉNITH

The three-seat Tri-Zénith, a prototype of which is under construction in France, is somewhat larger than the two-seat Zénith, having a greater wing span and a longer fuselage to accommodate the enlarged cabin which has a rear seat for one adult, two children or baggage, up to a weight of 209 lb (95 kg). The tailplane is also larger, and a fin and rudder vertical assembly is standard. Recommended power is in the range 125 to 160 hp, though engines of between 115 and 180 hp (max) may be installed. Limiting load factors, at max T-O weight, are +3·8*g* and −1·9*g*. Fuel is carried in two 13 Imp gallon (60 litre) tanks, one in each wing leading-edge. The wing trailing-edge is fitted with electrically-actuated slotted flaps and aerodynamically-balanced ailerons. The wings are not detachable.

DIMENSIONS, EXTERNAL:
Wing span 26 ft 6¾ in (8·10 m)
Wing chord (constant) 4 ft 10¼ in (1·48 m)
Wing aspect ratio 5·48
Length overall 22 ft 3¾ in (6·80 m)
Tailplane span 8 ft 6¼ in (2·60 m)
Wheel track 7 ft 4½ in (2·25 m)
Wheelbase 4 ft 8 in (1·42 m)

AREA:
Wings, gross 129·2 sq ft (12·00 m²)

WEIGHTS (estimated):
Weight empty 1,036-1,102 lb (470-500 kg)
Max T-O weight 1,785-1,851 lb (810-840 kg)

Performance (estimated. A: 125 hp at 1,785 lb; 810 kg AUW; B: 160 hp at 1,851 lb; 840 kg AUW):
- Max level speed:
  - A 132 knots (152 mph; 245 km/h)
  - B 140 knots (162 mph; 260 km/h)
- Max cruising speed (75% power):
  - A 119 knots (137 mph; 220 km/h)
  - B 127 knots (146 mph; 235 km/h)
- Stalling speed, flaps down:
  - A 45 knots (52 mph; 83 km/h)
  - B 46 knots (53 mph; 85 km/h)
- Max rate of climb at S/L:
  - A 827 ft (252 m)/min
  - B 1,220 ft (372 m)/min
- Range at max cruising speed:
  - A 474 nm (546 miles; 880 km)
  - B 442 nm (509 miles; 820 km)
- Endurance at max cruising speed:
  - A 4 hr 0 min
  - B 3 hr 30 min

IMP

IMP AEROSPACE LTD

Head Office and Principal Works:
Halifax International Airport

Address:
PO Box 535, Dartmouth, Nova Scotia
Telephone: (902) 861-2250
Telex: 014-423504

Chairman:
F. K. Stevens

President:
K. C. Rowe

IMP Aerospace Ltd was formed in August 1970, when a group of management personnel from the former Fairey Canada Limited (see 1970-71 *Jane's*) won a contract for continuing the aircraft work previously carried out by that company. IMP has, since its inception, been undertaking work on CL-28 Argus and CS2F-3 Tracker aircraft at its maintenance facilities at Halifax International Airport. Programmes accomplished to date include Depot Level Inspection and Repair (DLIR), Aircraft Sampling Inspection (ASI) and various modification programmes, including a major conversion on two Argus aircraft, related to the tactical navigation system (ANTAC), and modifications to CHSS-2 Sea King helicopters.

A small engineering department is maintained, primarily to support the airframe programmes but capable of a wide range of design activity when required. A small manufacturing capability supports the airframe programmes and also produces modification kits when required.

The company employs a work force of 200 persons, who were due to have processed 144 aircraft by April 1974; a further 28 aircraft are expected during 1974-75.

K & S

KAYE & STAN McLEOD

Address: 4623 Fortune Road SE, Calgary T2A-2A7, Alberta, Western Canada
Telephone: (403) 272-3658

K & S Aircraft Supply acquired from Mr Rim Kaminskas (see US section) all rights in the latter's Papoose Jungster I and Jungster II. Sets of plans of both designs are available to amateur constructors from K & S, which is carrying out continued improvement of both designs.

In addition, K & S markets plans for the SA 102 Point 5 Cavalier. Descriptions follow of all three types:

K & S JUNGSTER I

Design of this aircraft was started in the US by Mr Rim Kaminskas (which see), as the RK-1, in April 1959. The primary design requirements were to duplicate as closely as possible the performance and flight characteristics of the Bücker Jungmeister. The prototype, described in the 1972-73 *Jane's*, flew for the first time in October 1962.

More than 350 sets of plans for the Jungster I have been sold; several completed aircraft are flying, and many others are under construction.

Type: Single-seat amateur-built sporting aircraft.

Wings: Braced biplane, with two parallel interplane struts each side and N struts supporting centre-section each side. Wing section NACA 4413. Dihedral 1° 30′ on top wing, 3° 30′ on lower wings. Incidence 0° 30′ on top wing, 1° 30′ on lower wings. Sweepback 11° on outer panels at quarter-chord. All-wood two-spar structure of Sitka spruce and birch plywood, fabric-covered. Wooden Frise ailerons. No flaps or tabs.

Fuselage: Spruce truss structure, fabric-covered at rear and plywood-covered at front, except for engine cowling, which is of aluminium sheet.

Tail Unit: Braced wooden structure of spruce and birch ply. Fixed surfaces plywood-covered; rudder and elevators fabric-covered. No tabs.

Landing Gear: Non-retractable tailwheel type. Welded steel-tube main gear, with rubber cord shock absorption. Goodyear main-wheel tyres size 5·00-5, pressure 25 lb/sq in (1·76 kg/cm²). Goodyear disc brakes.

Power Plant: One horizontally-opposed air-cooled engine, driving a two-blade propeller. Wide choice of engines available, including 85/100 hp Continental C85, C90 or O-200; 125-130 hp Franklin Sport 4, 4A or 4B; 108-115 hp Lycoming O-235-C or -C1; 125-135 hp Lycoming O-290-D or -D2; 140-150 hp Lycoming O-320; or European engines in the same weight/power class. Fuel tank in fuselage aft of firewall, capacity 16·5 US gallons (62 litres); optional 7 US gallon (26 litre) tank in upper wing centre-section, increasing total capacity to 23·5 US gallons (88 litres). Oil capacity 1·5 US gallons (5·75 litres).

Accommodation: Single seat in open cockpit.

Dimensions, external:
- Wing span 16 ft 11 in (5·16 m)
- Wing chord, constant (both) 2 ft 8 in (0·81 m)
- Wing aspect ratio 6·25
- Length overall 16 ft 0 in (4·88 m)
- Tailplane span 6 ft 8 in (2·03 m)
- Propeller diameter 5 ft 8 in (1·73 m)

Area:
- Wings, gross 80 sq ft (7·43 m²)

Weights and Loadings:
- Weight empty 606 lb (275 kg)
- T-O weight, aerobatic 850 lb (385 kg)
- Max T-O weight 1,000 lb (455 kg)
- Max wing loading 10·6 lb/sq ft (51·75 kg/m²)
- Max power loading:
  - 85 hp 11·8 lb/hp (5·35 kg/hp)
  - 150 hp 6·66 lb/hp (3·02 kg/hp)

Performance (prototype, at max T-O weight, 108 hp engine):
- Max level speed at S/L 113 knots (130 mph; 209 km/h)
- Max cruising speed at S/L 109 knots (125 mph; 201 km/h)
- Stalling speed 44 knots (50 mph; 80·5 km/h)
- Max rate of climb at S/L 1,500 ft (455 m)/min
- Service ceiling 13,000 ft (3,960 m)
- T-O run 300 ft (91 m)
- Landing run 500 ft (152 m)
- Range with max fuel (incl centre-section tank) 260 nm (300 miles; 482 km)

K & S JUNGSTER II

Design of the Jungster II was started by Mr Kaminskas as the RK-2 in 1962 and this prototype flew for the first time in March 1966. At least 35 are being built by amateurs, and several others are already flying.

Type: Single-seat amateur-built sporting aircraft.

Wings: Strut-braced parasol-wing monoplane. Wing section NACA 2412. No dihedral. Incidence 1°. Sweepback at quarter-chord 15° on outer panels. All-wood spruce structure, covered with plywood and fabric. Frise ailerons. No flaps or tabs.

Fuselage: Spruce structure, covered with fabric.

Tail Unit: Wire-braced spruce structure. Fixed surfaces covered with birch plywood; control surfaces fabric-covered. Fixed-incidence tailplane. No tabs.

Landing Gear: Non-retractable tailwheel type. Rubber shock-absorbers, adapted from truck engine mountings. Main wheels size 5·00-5. Hydraulic brakes.

Power Plant (prototype): One 180 hp Lycoming O-360 six-cylinder horizontally-opposed air-cooled engine, driving a two-blade fixed-pitch propeller. Fuel tank forward of cockpit, capacity 20 US gallons (75 litres). Oil capacity 0·75 US gallons (5·5 litres). Other engines available optionally include those listed under Jungster I description, plus 160 hp Lycoming O-320 and 180 hp Lycoming O-360.

Accommodation: Single seat in open cockpit.

Dimensions, external:
- Wing span 22 ft 4 in (6·81 m)
- Wing chord at root 4 ft 2 in (1·27 m)
- Length overall (tail up) 16 ft 11 in (5·16 m)
- Height to top of wings (tail up) 6 ft 9 in (2·06 m)
- Tailplane span 7 ft 9 in (2·36 m)
- Wheel track 5 ft 0 in (1·52 m)
- Propeller diameter 5 ft 6 in (1·68 m)

Dimensions, internal:
- Cockpit: Length 4 ft 0 in (1·22 m)
  - Max width 1 ft 10 in (0·56 m)

Areas:
- Wings, gross 84 sq ft (7·80 m²)
- Ailerons (total) 10·4 sq ft (0·97 m²)
- Fin 3·15 sq ft (0·29 m²)
- Rudder 4·70 sq ft (0·44 m²)
- Tailplane 5·75 sq ft (0·53 m²)
- Elevators 7·31 sq ft (0·68 m²)

Weights and Loadings (original 180 hp version):
- Weight empty 739 lb (335 kg)
- Max T-O weight 1,139 lb (517 kg)
- Max wing loading 13·5 lb/sq ft (65·9 kg/m²)
- Max power loading 6·3 lb/hp (2·85 kg/hp)

Performance (original 180 hp version, at max T-O weight):
- Max never-exceed speed 156 knots (180 mph; 290 km/h) IAS
- Max level speed at S/L 139 knots (160 mph; 257 km/h)
- Max cruising speed up to 10,000 ft (3,050 m) 135 knots (155 mph; 249 km/h)
- Stalling speed 48 knots (55 mph; 89 km/h)
- Max rate of climb at S/L 3,500 ft (1,065 m)/min

K & S SA 102 POINT 5 CAVALIER

The SA 102 Point 5, which flew for the first time in February 1971, is a development of the SA 102 prototype described in the 1971-72 *Jane's*.

K & S Jungster I single-seat sporting biplane (140 hp Lycoming O-320 engine)

Prototype Jungster II built in the US by Mr Rim Kaminskas (180 hp Lycoming O-360 engine)

By the Spring of 1974 more than 1,200 sets of Cavalier plans had been sold, and at least 14 aircraft were flying.

Design improvements introduced in 1972 include simplified mounting brackets for all three landing gear units, and simplified main gear legs.

In its current form, the Cavalier has a 2 in (50 mm) longer forward fuselage, to give additional cockpit leg room and improve the weight and balance control. A tip fairing and streamlined strobe light have been added to the fin and rudder, to reduce drag and improve safety; tailplane incidence has been altered to 1° 30′ (±30′) for added trim and to increase cruising speeds; the power plant is now offset 2-3° to starboard and for 2-3° of downthrust, for torque correction and to increase cruising speeds; and an approx 4 in (102 mm) propeller shaft extension is fitted, reducing drag and adding some 9-13 knots (10-15 mph; 16-24 km/h) to the speed range.

SA 102 Point 5 Cavalier two/four-seat light aircraft

TYPE: Two-seat or "2+2" light aircraft.

WINGS: Cantilever low-wing monoplane. Wing section NACA 23015 at root, NACA 23012 at tip. Dihedral 6°. Incidence 3° 30′ at root, washed out to 1° at tip. No sweepback at quarter-chord. Single wooden box-spar, plywood leading-edge, and auxiliary rear spar to carry aileron and flap loads. Diagonal I-section drag spar between front and rear spar in each wing. Entire centre-section is plywood-covered and contoured to serve as cabin seat. Outer panels covered with Dacron synthetic fabric, finished with a polyurethane compound. Single-slotted Frise-type ailerons of spruce and plywood. Cable-operated split flaps of spruce and birch ply. Optional plans available for building wing in three pieces and for electrical actuation of flaps.

FUSELAGE: Truss-type structure, with four main longerons, of spruce and birch plywood construction. Cockpit canopy and doors of moulded glassfibre, rear part of top-decking fabric-covered.

TAIL UNIT: Cantilever structure, with sweptback vertical surfaces. All-wood construction, with Dacron covering. Fixed-incidence tailplane. Elevators operated by pushrods. Trim tab in starboard elevator.

LANDING GEAR: Non-retractable tricycle type. All units have spring steel legs of K & S design. Wheel size 5·00-5, tyre pressure 40 lb/sq in (2·8 kg/cm²), on all units. For rough-field operation, 6·00-6 main wheels with low-profile tyres are used optionally. Expanding-shoe brakes, operated hydraulically by dual toe-controls. Glassfibre wheel fairings. Alternative 1,500 lb (680 kg) capacity floats or ski landing gear optional.

POWER PLANT: Wide choice of four-cylinder engines available, including 85, 90 or 100 hp Continental, 125-130 hp Franklin Sport 4A, 108 or 115 hp Lycoming O-235, or 125 or 135 hp Lycoming O-290. Choice of wood or metal, fixed-pitch or variable-pitch propellers, with diameters from 5 ft 6 in (1·68 m) to 6 ft 0 in (1·83 m). Whichever engine is used, an extension shaft (3 to 5 in; 7·6 to 12·7 cm) is fitted between the propeller and the engine crankshaft, permitting the use of more streamlined cowling panels and a reduction in the compression of airflow between the propeller and engine. All fuel in permanent wingtip tanks, with choice of two sizes: 17 or 20 US gallons (64 or 75 litres) each. Oil capacity 1·5-1·8 US gallons (5·7-6·8 litres), according to engine fitted.

ACCOMMODATION: Side-by-side seating for pilot and one adult passenger, with optional rear jump-seat for two small children in what would normally be the baggage area. Without this rear seat, up to 125 lb (56·7 kg) of baggage can be carried, depending upon engine and equipment installations. Forward-opening door on each side of heated and ventilated cabin.

ELECTRONICS AND EQUIPMENT: Standard nav/com equipment, including 1 or 2 VHF sets. ADF and transponder optional.

DIMENSIONS, EXTERNAL:
Wing span, over tip-tanks 27 ft 4 in (8·33 m)
Width with outer wing panels folded 11 ft 11 in (3·63 m)
Wing chord at root 5 ft 3 in (1·60 m)
Wing chord at tip 3 ft 0 in (0·91 m)
Wing aspect ratio 6·25
Length overall 22 ft 0 in (6·71 m)
Height overall 7 ft 4 in (2·23 m)
Tailplane span 9 ft 7 in (2·92 m)
Wheelbase 4 ft 6 in (1·37 m)
Propeller diameter see under "Power Plant"

DIMENSIONS, INTERNAL:
Cabin: Max length 4 ft 2 in (1·27 m)
Max width 3 ft 1¼ in (0·95 m)
Max height (seat squab to roof) 3 ft 2 in (0·96 m)
Baggage space up to 30 cu ft (0·85 m³)

AREAS:
Wings, gross 118 sq ft (10·96 m²)
Ailerons (total) 9·2 sq ft (0·85 m²)
Trailing-edge flaps (total) 8·5 sq ft (0·79 m²)
Fin 4·5 sq ft (0·42 m²)
Rudder 5·7 sq ft (0·53 m²)
Tailplane 11·3 sq ft (1·05 m²)
Elevators (total, incl tab) 10·2 sq ft (0·95 m²)

WEIGHTS AND LOADINGS:
Basic operating weight empty 900 lb (408 kg)
Max T-O weight 1,500 lb (680 kg)
Max wing loading 12·7 lb/sq ft (2·60 kg/m²)
Max power loading (85 hp engine) 17·6 lb/hp (7·98 kg/hp)

PERFORMANCE (at max T-O weight, 125 hp Lycoming engine):
Max never-exceed speed 199 knots (230 mph; 370 km/h) TAS
Max level speed at 7,000 ft (2,135 m) 160 knots (185 mph; 297 km/h) TAS
Max cruising speed 143 knots (165 mph; 265 km/h) TAS
Econ cruising speed 134 knots (155 mph; 249 km/h) TAS
Stalling speed, flaps up 43·5 knots (50 mph; 81 km/h)
Stalling speed, flaps down 35 knots (40 mph; 65 km/h)
Max rate of climb at S/L over 1,700 ft (518 m)/min
Service ceiling 16,000 ft (4,875 m)
T-O run 350 ft (107 m)
T-O to 50 ft (15 m) 1,000 ft (305 m)
Landing from 50 ft (15 m) 1,300 ft (396 m)
Landing run 600 ft (183 m)
Max range, no reserves 720 nm (830 miles; 1,335 km)

MP

MOTO-PLANE AVIATION INC

ADDRESS:
Hangar No. 2, Aéroport St-Jean, St-Jean, Quebec
Telephone: (514) 347-0303

MOTO-PLANE

The Moto-Plane is a single-seat ultra-light homebuilt aircraft, of which plans and kits of parts (except instruments) are available from the above address.

WINGS: Braced parasol-wing monoplane.

FUSELAGE: Open-framework metal airframe (steel and aluminium) with covered nacelle for pilot at front.

TAIL UNIT: Wire-braced cruciform assembly. Fin supported between upper and lower main fuselage members.

LANDING GEAR: Non-retractable tailwheel type, with wide-track main units. Skis and floats optional.

POWER PLANT: One 55 hp 650 cc Hirth engine, driving a two-blade pusher propeller. Fuel tank capacity 8 Imp gallons (36 litres).

ACCOMMODATION: Single seat in open cockpit.

DIMENSIONS, EXTERNAL:
Wing span 20 ft 4 in (6·20 m)
Length overall 14 ft 0 in (4·27 m)
Height overall 5 ft 4 in (1·63 m)

AREA:
Wings, gross 76 sq ft (7·06 m²)

WEIGHTS AND LOADING:
Weight empty 375 lb (170 kg)
Max T-O weight approx 650 lb (295 kg)
Max wing loading 8·6 lb/sq ft (42·0 kg/m²)

PERFORMANCE:
Cruising speed 56 knots (65 mph; 104 km/h)
T-O speed 35 knots (40 mph; 64 km/h)
Stalling speed, power off 33 knots (38 mph; 61 km/h)
Stalling speed, power on 30·5 knots (35 mph; 56·5 km/h)
Max rate of climb at S/L 500 ft (152 m)/min
T-O run 400 ft (122 m)
Landing run 500 ft (152 m)

NWI

NORTHWEST INDUSTRIES LTD (Division of CAE Industries Ltd)

ADDRESS:
Industrial Airport, PO Box 517, Edmonton, Alberta
Telephone: (304) 455-3161

This company, earlier activities of which were described in the 1972-73 *Jane's*, has been awarded a contract worth some $4 million Canadian (including spares and technical support) to refurbish, for the Bolivian Air Force, 13 ex-CAF Lockheed T-33A Silver Star jet trainers.

SAL

STURGEON AIR LTD (FALCONAR AIRCRAFT DIVISION)

HEAD OFFICE AND WORKS:
36 Airport Road, Edmonton Industrial Airport, Edmonton, Alberta
Telephone: 454-7272
PRESIDENT/MANAGER:
George Chivers
SALES MANAGER:
K. Budde

SAL was formed to market plans and kits of a wide range of light aircraft and sailplanes suitable for amateur construction. These included versions of the Jodel D.9 and D.11, Druine Turbulent, Piel Emeraude, and Luton Major and Minor; and various single-, two- and three-seat aircraft designated F9, F10, F11 and F12, developed from the French Jodel D.9 and D.11 designs and offering a variety of modifications including tricycle landing gear, forward-sliding canopy and sweptback rudder.

Two other recent SAL products are the AMF-S14 and the SAL 2/3 Mustang. No news of the company's activities, if any, has been received for the past two years.

SAL AMF-S14

The AMF-S14 is a hybrid design, sharing with the Maranda Super Loisir (see 1968-69 *Jane's*) a common ancestor in the French Adam RA-14 (1956-57 *Jane's*), although the two Canadian designs are by no means identical.

Design of the first homebuilt S14 (CF-RDK) began in 1958, and this aircraft was flown in July 1961. By the Autumn of 1970 approx 25 had been built in Canada and the US, and plans had been sold for well over 300 more.

No news of this aircraft has been received since that time, and it is not known whether it is still a current SAL product. A description of the AMF-S14 appeared in the 1973-74 *Jane's*.

SAL 2/3 MUSTANG

In 1967 SAL's Falconar division began building a prototype of the Jurca M.J.7 Gnatsum two-thirds scale replica of the North American P-51D Mustang fighter of the second World War. During the course of its construction a considerable number of modifications were made to the original Jurca plans. The finished aircraft, then registered CF-XZI, was flown for the first time on 31 July 1969, and a full description can be found in the 1973-74 *Jane's*.

SAL later began marketing its own plans and construction kits for this modified version, as the SAL 2/3 Mustang. No news of the aircraft has been received since that time, and it is not known whether it continues to be available. By early 1972, 65 kits had been sold, and many purchasers of these had begun building.

SAUNDERS

SAUNDERS AIRCRAFT CORPORATION LTD

HEAD OFFICE AND WORKS:
PO Box 1230, Gimli, Manitoba
Telephone: (204) 642-5101
Telex: 07-587-850

PRESIDENT:
S. R. Kersey

VICE-PRESIDENT FINANCE:
J. A. Iverach

VICE-PRESIDENT MANUFACTURING:
G. Henshaw

VICE-PRESIDENT MARKETING:
J. Grandage

MARKETING DIRECTOR:
G. B. Smith

PRODUCT SUPPORT DIRECTOR:
F. W. Richter

Saunders Aircraft Corporation was formed in May 1968, with design, manufacturing and administrative facilities located initially in Montreal. It had more than 500 employees in February 1974. The company's principal activity is re-manufacture of the de Havilland Heron airliner, with turboprop engines and other major design changes, as the Saunders ST-27, and engineering and development of the ST-27B, a new-build aircraft very similar to the ST-27.

SAUNDERS ST-27

The Saunders ST-27 is a turboprop re-manufacture of the Hawker Siddeley (de Havilland) D.H.114 Heron Series 2 (see 1966-67 *Jane's*), for third-level and "commuter" airlines.

Modifications involve the use of two United Aircraft of Canada PT6A-34 turboprops, in place of the four Gipsy Queen piston engines which powered the original Heron, and a longer fuselage certificated to carry up to 24 persons (including a stewardess) instead of 14/17 in the original version. The wings, with a re-designed main spar, and tailplane of the standard Heron are retained, as well as the landing gear units.

The prototype ST-27 (CF-YBM-X) flew for the first time on 28 May 1969, powered by 715 ehp PT6A-27 engines, and a second (pre-production) aircraft flew in April 1970. ARB certification in the transport category was received on 16 September 1970; Canadian MoT transport category certification was received on 14 May 1971. The first production ST-27 first flew in early 1971.

Six ST-27s had been sold by February 1974: three to ACES (Aerolineas Centrales de Colombia) and one each to St Andrews Airways of Manitoba, Voyageur Airways of Ontario and Bayview Air Services of Alberta.

The details below apply to the current production ST-27:

TYPE: Twin-turboprop light transport.

WINGS: Cantilever low-wing monoplane. Thickness/chord ratio 18·3% at root, 14·5% at tip. Dihedral 6° ±10′ at chord line. Incidence 2° ±10′. Conventional two-spar light alloy structure, with light alloy sheet skin. Ailerons and three-section flaps have metal frames and fabric covering. Flaps are operated pneumatically. Trim tab in each aileron, with port tab controllable from cockpit. Pneumatic de-icing boots on leading-edge.

FUSELAGE: Conventional semi-monocoque light alloy structure. Wing centre-section spar integral with fuselage. Main cabin floor of sandwich construction, stressed for freight carrying. Compared with original Heron Srs 2, an additional 8 ft 6 in (2·59 m) section has been introduced into the centre fuselage, aft of the main spar. A longer nosecone is fitted.

TAIL UNIT: Cantilever all-metal structure, with marked dihedral on horizontal surfaces. Elevators and fixed surfaces are metal-covered, rudder fabric-covered. Trim tabs in rudder and each elevator, controlled from cockpit. Pneumatic-boot de-icing of leading-edges.

LANDING GEAR: Retractable tricycle type. Pneumatic retraction, nosewheel rearward into fuselage, main wheels outward into wings. Oleo-pneumatic shock-absorbers on all units. Nosewheel is castoring and self-centering. Single Dunlop wheel and tyre on each unit. Tyre pressure 62 lb/sq in (4·4 kg/cm²) on main units, 42 lb/sq in (2·95 kg/cm²) on nose unit. Differentially-operating pneumatic brakes.

POWER PLANT: Two 783 ehp (750 shp) UACL PT6A-34 turboprop engines, each driving a Hartzell three-blade variable-pitch constant-speed fully-feathering and reversing metal propeller with electric-boot de-icing. Fuel in cross-feeding bag-type tanks in each wing, with total capacity of 320 Imp gallons (1,455 litres). Refuelling point on top of each wing. Oil capacity 1·9 Imp gallons (8·6 litres) per engine.

ACCOMMODATION: Crew of one or two on flight deck, with dual controls. Non-pressurised main cabin can seat up to 23 persons, 20 of them on individual seats at 30 in (76 cm) pitch on each side of centre aisle, plus three on rear bulkhead tip-up seats. Alternative all-passenger layouts for 22 seats plus walk-on wardrobe facility or toilet, or 19 seats with wardrobe and toilet or wardrobe only. Walk-on wardrobe facility can be provided in 23-seat version by reducing pitch of individual seats to approx 28 in (71 cm). Alternative passenger/cargo layout available within same area or, with rear bulkhead removed, an all-cargo layout. Airstair door at front on starboard side provides access to flight deck and passenger cabin. Baggage holds in nose (capacity 240 lb; 109 kg) and aft of cabin (capacity 850 lb; 385 kg); access via upward-opening doors on port side of nose and starboard side of rear fuselage. Two emergency exits, one each side of fuselage over wing. Cabin and flight deck heated by engine bleed air. Individual fresh-air outlets. Air-conditioning optional.

SYSTEMS: Pneumatic system for flap and landing gear actuation and brakes. No hydraulic system. Electrical system includes two 200A starter/generators with primary and essential bus. Nickel-cadmium batteries (40Ah main and 23Ah emergency) are standard. Electrical de-icing of propeller blades and windscreen.

ELECTRONICS AND EQUIPMENT: To customer's specification. Dual instrumentation standard.

DIMENSIONS, EXTERNAL:	
Wing span	71 ft 6 in (21·79 m)
Wing chord at root	10 ft 6¾ in (3·22 m)
Wing chord at tip	2 ft 10 in (0·86 m)
Wing aspect ratio	10·3
Length overall	59 ft 0 in (17·98 m)
Height overall	15 ft 7 in (4·75 m)
Tailplane span	22 ft 4 in (6·81 m)
Wheel track	16 ft 8 in (5·08 m)
Wheelbase	23 ft 3 in (7·09 m)
Propeller diameter	7 ft 6 in (2·29 m)
Propeller ground clearance	1 ft 0 in (0·30 m)
Passenger door (fwd, stbd):	
Height	4 ft 7 in (1·40 m)
Width	2 ft 4 in (0·71 m)
Baggage door (rear, port):	
Height	4 ft 5 in (1·35 m)
Width	2 ft 9 in (0·84 m)
Emergency exits (each):	
Height	3 ft 0 in (0·91 m)
Width	1 ft 8 in (0·51 m)
DIMENSIONS, INTERNAL:	
Cabin (excluding flight deck):	
Max length:	
all-passenger or passenger/cargo	31 ft 6 in (9·60 m)
all-cargo	38 ft 10 in (11·84 m)
Max width	4 ft 6 in (1·37 m)
Max height	5 ft 9 in (1·75 m)
Volume:	
all-passenger or passenger/cargo	723 cu ft (20·47 m³)
all-cargo	828 cu ft (23·45 m³)
Baggage holds, volume:	
forward	14 cu ft (0·40 m³)
rear	105 cu ft (2·97 m³)

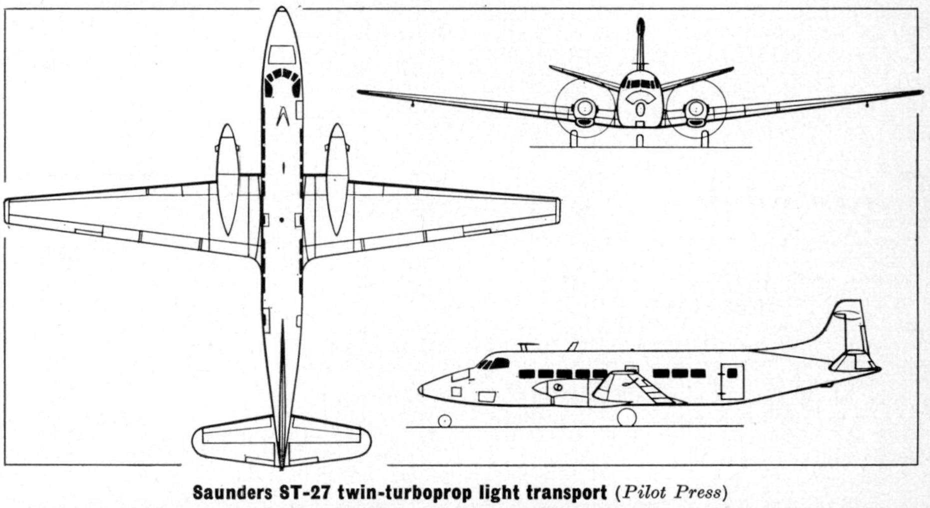

Saunders ST-27 twin-turboprop light transport (*Pilot Press*)

Saunders ST-27 twin-turboprop transport aircraft in the insignia of the Colombian operator ACES (Aerolineas Centrales de Colombia)

AREAS:
Wings, gross 499 sq ft (46·36 m²)
Ailerons (total) 34·1 sq ft (3·17 m²)
Trailing-edge flaps (total) 70·2 sq ft (6·52 m²)
Fin 30·5 sq ft (2·83 m²)
Rudder, incl tab 22·5 sq ft (2·09 m²)
Tailplane 57·6 sq ft (5·35 m²)
Elevators, incl tabs 38·0 sq ft (3·53 m²)
WEIGHTS AND LOADINGS:
Basic operating weight 7,900 lb (3,583 kg)
Max T-O weight 13,500 lb (6,124 kg)
Max zero-fuel weight 12,850 lb (5,828 kg)
Max landing weight 13,150 lb (5,965 kg)
Max wing loading 27·0 lb/sq ft (131·8 kg/m²)
Max power loading 8·69 lb/ehp (3·94 kg/ehp)
PERFORMANCE (at max T-O weight):
Max never-exceed speed
253 knots (292 mph; 470 km/h)
Max cruising speed at 7,000 ft (2,135 m)
200 knots (230 mph; 370 km/h)
Econ cruising speed at 7,000 ft (2,135 m)
182 knots (210 mph; 338 km/h)
Stalling speed, flaps up
82 knots (95 mph; 152 km/h)
Stalling speed, flaps down
71 knots (82 mph; 132 km/h)
Max rate of climb at S/L
1,600 ft (488 m)/min
Max rate of climb at S/L, one engine out
600 ft (183 m)/min
Service ceiling 25,000 ft (7,620 m)
Service ceiling, one engine out
17,000 ft (5,180 m)
T-O run, ISA + 10°C 1,650 ft (503 m)
T-O to 50 ft (15 m), ISA + 10°C
2,350 ft (716 m)
Landing from 50 ft (15 m), ISA + 10°C
1,150 ft (350 m)
Landing run, ISA + 10°C 910 ft (278 m)
Minimum ground turning radius
16 ft 8 in (5·08 m)
Range with max fuel, IFR reserves
710 nm (817 miles; 1,315 km)
Range with max payload, IFR reserves with 100 nm (115 mile; 185 km) alternate
100 nm (115 miles; 185 km)

SAUNDERS ST-27B

The ST-27B is a new-build aircraft, essentially similar to the ST-27 but with considerable internal changes and improvements. Max T-O weight is increased to 14,500 lb (6,575 kg), and partial pressurisation (cabin differential 2·5 lb/sq in; 0·175 kg/cm²) is planned.

The ST-27B will be certificated to FAR Pt 25 requirements, and is aimed at the US commuter market, operating under FAR Pt 298 regulations.

The prototype, which is designated ST-27A, was scheduled to make its first flight in mid-1974.

TRIDENT

TRIDENT AIRCRAFT LIMITED

ADDRESS:
261 Viscount Way, Richmond, British Columbia
Telephone: (604) 278-6204
PRESIDENT: D. A. Hazlewood
CHIEF ENGINEER: J. C. Galizia
MARKETING: W .T. Clark
PROJECT MANAGER: P. S. Masterton

TRIDENT TR-1 TRIGULL-320

The TR-1 incorporates a number of significant differences from earlier aircraft of its type. It is claimed that it will, compared with other similar aircraft, provide better low-speed handling (including stall) and improved general performance.

Design of the present TR-1 was restarted in Canada in July 1971, and construction began in the following month. Three prototypes are currently being built, in association with Canadian Aircraft Products Ltd, and the first of these (CF-TRI-X) flew for the first time on 5 August 1973. By February 1974, 69 flying hours had been logged. The third aircraft is being used for static testing. Production is under way, in anticipation of certification in August 1974. Trident had received deposits for the sale of 74 Trigull-320s by early 1974.

TYPE: Six-seat light amphibian.

WINGS: Cantilever high-wing monoplane. Wing section NACA 23015R-4 (modified). Dihedral 2° from roots. Incidence 2° 15′. No sweepback. Two-spar aluminium stressed-skin failsafe structure, of constant chord, with drooped leading-edges. Hydraulically-operated single-slotted aluminium Fowler flaps and Frise-type ailerons on each trailing-edge. Ailerons droop automatically with flaps. Fixed tabs.

FUSELAGE: Flying-boat type, with single-step hull and rear boom to support tail unit. Conventional aluminium stressed-skin construction.

TAIL UNIT: Cantilever type, of aluminium stressed-skin construction, with single swept-back fin and rudder. Variable-incidence tailplane, actuated by screwjack. No tabs.

LANDING GEAR: Fuselage hull and independently retractable wingtip floats for landing on water. Manually-retractable water rudder, extending from air rudder. Retractable tricycle-type wheeled gear for operation on land, with single wheel on each unit. Hydraulic retraction, both of floats and of wheeled gear. Main wheels retract outward into wings, nosewheel (which is steerable) upward to lie semi-recessed in nose to act as bumper. Oleo-pneumatic shock-absorbers and Cleveland brakes. Main wheels and tube-type tyres size 7·00-6, nosewheel 6·00-6.

POWER PLANT: One 320 hp Teledyne Continental Tiara 6-320 six-cylinder horizontally-opposed aircooled fuel-injection engine, driving a Hartzell three-blade constant-speed reversible-pitch metal pusher propeller. Fuel in single bag-type tank in lower hull, capacity 100 US gallons (378 litres). Refuelling point in hull. Oil capacity 3 US gallons (11·4 litres).

ACCOMMODATION: Seating for pilot and up to five passengers, in three pairs, in fully-enclosed, heated and ventilated cabin. Access via large forward-hinged door on each side and forward-hinged bow door on starboard side. Space for 150 lb (68 kg) of baggage in rear of cabin and below floor. Alternative layouts for use as ambulance (one stretcher and one medical attendant) or freighter.

SYSTEMS AND EQUIPMENT: Hydraulic system for landing gear, wingtip floats and flap actuation. Electrical system includes 24V 50A alternator. Basic blind-flying instrumentation standard. Radio and other equipment to customer's specification.

DIMENSIONS, EXTERNAL:
Wing span:
floats up 41 ft 9 in (12 73 m)
floats down 38 ft 6 in (11·73 m)
Wing chord (constant) 6 ft 0 in (1·83 m)
Length overall 28 ft 6 in (8·69 m)
Height overall 12 ft 0 in (3·66 m)
Wheel track 12 ft 0 in (3·66 m)
Wheelbase 11 ft 0 in (3·35 m)
Propeller diameter 6 ft 10 in (2·08 m)
Passenger doors (each):
Height 3 ft 9 in (1·14 m)
Width 3 ft 7 in (1·09 m)
Bow door (stbd):
Height 1 ft 8 in (0·51 m)
Width 1 ft 8 in (0·51 m)
DIMENSIONS, INTERNAL:
Cabin: Max length 9 ft 10 in (3·00 m)
Max width 4 ft 0 in (1·22 m)
Max height 4 ft 0 in (1·22 m)
Baggage compartments: Volume:
rear of cabin 43 cu ft (1·22 m³)
underfloor (total) 28 cu ft (0·79 m³)
AREAS:
Wings, gross:
floats up 246·0 sq ft (22·85 m²)
floats down 228·0 sq ft (21·18 m²)
Ailerons (total) 9·6 sq ft (0·89 m²)
Fin 28·0 sq ft (2·60 m²)
Rudder 12·0 sq ft (1·11 m²)
WEIGHTS AND LOADINGS:
Basic operating weight, empty
2,350 lb (1,066 kg)
Max T-O weight 3,850 lb (1,746 kg)
Max wing loading:
floats up 13·82 lb/sq ft (67·47 kg/m²)
floats down 14·92 lb/sq ft (72·85 kg/m²)
Max power loading 11·25 lb/hp (5·10 kg/hp)
PERFORMANCE (at max T-O weight):
Max never-exceed speed
183 knots (211 mph; 339 km/h)
Max level speed at S/L
154 knots (177 mph; 285 km/h)
Max cruising speed (75% power) at 6,200 ft (1,890 m) 139 knots (160 mph; 257 km/h)
Cruising speed (65% power)
135 knots (155 mph; 249 km/h)
Stalling speed at S/L, flaps and landing gear down 44 knots (50 mph; 81 km/h)
Max rate of climb at S/L 1,150 ft (351 m)/min
Service ceiling 18,000 ft (5,485 m)
T-O run at S/L, 20° flap, 15°C:
from land 520 ft (158 m)
from water 790 ft (241 m)
T-O to 50 ft (15 m), conditions as above:
from land 1,050 ft (320 m)
from water 1,400 ft (427 m)
Landing from 50 ft (15 m), conditions as above:
on land 1,300 ft (396 m)
on water 1,200 ft (366 m)
Landing run, conditions as above:
on land 570 ft (174 m)
on water 490 ft (149 m)
Optimum range, 45 min reserves:
75% power 764 nm (880 miles; 1,415 km)
65% power 934 nm (1,076 miles; 1,731 km)

Trident TR-1 Trigull-320 prototype (320 hp Teledyne Continental Tiara 6-320 engine)

WESTERN

WESTERN AIRCRAFT SUPPLIES

ADDRESS:
623 Markerville Road NE, Calgary, Alberta T2E SX1
Telephone: (403) 276 3087
DIRECTOR:
Jean J. Peters

Western Aircraft Supplies markets materials for amateur aircraft constructors, and is also selling plans for construction of the RL-3 Monsoon, a two-seat light aircraft originally designed in India.

Western is also designing another aircraft, of wooden construction, which was about 80% complete in early 1974.

RL-3 MONSOON

The RL-3 Monsoon, designed by Mr Renato Levi of Afeo (Private) Ltd, originated in India;

Indian-built example of the RL-3 Monsoon two-seat light aircraft

the prototype was described on page 105 of the 1960-61 *Jane's*, and this description was repeated under the "Western" heading in the 1972-73 edition. At least one more example of the RL-3 (see accompanying photograph) was completed in India.

Mr Jean J. Peters of Western Aircraft Supplies acquired from Mr Levi in 1969 rights to market plans of the aircraft, and up to early 1974 about 12 sets of these plans and five kits of materials had been sold. Five Monsoons are known to be under construction in Canada and the US, including one by Mr Peters himself.

The plans for the Monsoon are accepted by the EAA, and the Canadian Ministry of Transport had approved all components built up to March 1973 by Mr Peters and another Calgary constructor. It is not considered appropriate to publish a detailed description of the currently-marketed Monsoon until the Western-built prototype (which will have a Lycoming O-235 engine) is completed, and the following description is therefore of a general nature only:

Type: Two-seat homebuilt light aircraft.

Wings: Cantilever low-wing monoplane. Constant-chord single-spar wooden structure, using Canadian spruce.

Tail Unit: Cantilever wooden structure.

Landing Gear: Non-retractable tailwheel type.

Power Plant: One horizontally-opposed air-cooled engine, driving a two-blade propeller.

Accommodation: Two seats side by side in fully-enclosed cabin.

CHINA
(PEOPLE'S REPUBLIC)

STATE AIRCRAFT FACTORY

Address:
Shenyang (formerly Mukden)

Director: Professor Hsue Shen Tsien

This factory had its origin in the Mukden plant of the Manshu Aeroplane Manufacturing Company, one of several aircraft and aero-engine manufacturing facilities established in Manchukuo (Manchuria) by the Japanese invaders in 1938. After the Communist regime became responsible for the whole of mainland China in 1949 the Manchurian factories were re-established and re-equipped with Soviet assistance. Today the factories at Shenyang, Chungking and Harbin are the main centres of Chinese aircraft and aero-engine production, with design and development centres at Shenyang, Peking and Harbin.

In the middle and late 1950s the Shenyang factory produced in large numbers under licence several aircraft types, including the Soviet An-2, Yak-12 and Yak-18 and the Mi-4 helicopter, and the Czech Super Aero 45 light transport.

First combat aircraft manufactured at Shenyang, under licence, was the Soviet MiG-17 fighter, with deliveries to the Chinese Air Force beginning in 1956. Well over a thousand MiG-17s were built, under the Chinese designation F-4, plus several hundred MiG-15UTI (F-2) fighter/trainers, before production was completed in the mid-1960s. F-4s were exported to Albania (30), Cambodia and North Vietnam. These types have been followed by Chinese versions of the MiG-19 (F-6) and MiG-21 (F-8), and by the Il-28 bomber, production of which continues at a modest rate. A copy of the Tupolev Tu-16 twin-jet medium bomber is also in production in China, and a Chinese-developed twin-jet fighter designated F-9, embodying experience gained with the F-6, has been reported.

The capability of China's aircraft industry has been revealed most openly by study of the F-6 single-seat day fighters supplied to Pakistan. Generally similar to the Soviet MiG-19SF, the F-6s equipped three first-line squadrons of the Pakistan Air Force (Nos. 11, 23 and 25) at the time of the 1971 war with India. They were credited with the destruction of twelve enemy aircraft, made up of one MiG-21, eight Su-7s and three Hunters, for the loss of three F-6s.

An assessment of the F-6 by a western observer described the general standard of workmanship of the airframe as very good. At low altitudes this fighter was said to outmanoeuvre any type of combat aircraft in service in Asia except the F-86, and to outclimb the MiG-21 and F-104 Starfighter. The potential of the Pakistani F-6s has been much enhanced by supplementing their standard cannon armament with two Sidewinder missiles.

Chinese-built F-6 (MiG-19SF) fighter of the Pakistan Air Force, armed with Sidewinder missiles (*John Fricker*)

SHENYANG F-6

The F-6 is basically a MiG-19 fighter built in the Chinese State Aircraft Factory. Its original design was initiated by the Mikoyan bureau in the early 'fifties, with the aim of producing the first Soviet fighter able to exceed Mach 1 in level flight. Construction of a prototype, designated I-350 at the time, was authorised on 30 July 1951. Powered by two 4,410 lb (2,000 kg) st Mikulin AM-5 turbojets, this aircraft was flown for the first time by Major Grigori Sedov in September 1953. It achieved its maximum speed of Mach 1·1 in level flight on several occasions before being handed over for state trials in early 1954.

The initial production MiG-19 day fighter began to enter service with the Soviet air defence force in early 1955. Before long an all-moving tailplane replaced the former, ineffective elevators on the MiG-19S (S for *Stabilisator*), which also had three 30 mm guns instead of the original armament of one 37 mm and two 23 mm cannon. This version introduced an attachment under each wing for a bomb or air-to-surface rocket.

Meanwhile, Vladimir Klimov's bureau had been developing a new turbojet designated RD-9. Of similar overall dimensions to the small-diameter AM-5, it had a considerably higher rating, and was adopted as the standard power plant of the MiG-19 in 1957. Again the aircraft's designation was changed, to MiG-19SF (*Forsirovanny*; increased power). At the same time, another version with limited all-weather capability was put into production as the MiG-19PF (*Perekhvatchik*; interceptor), with a small *Izumrud* radar scanner inside its engine air intake and a ranging unit in the intake top lip. The later MiG-19PM (*Modifikatsirovanny*; modified) differed from the PF in having four first-generation radar-homing missiles (NATO "Alkali") instead of guns.

In the Soviet Union the MiG-19 was phased out of production by the end of the 'fifties, although many SFs and PMs remain in service in the Warsaw Pact countries, Cuba, Iraq and Egypt. Some had been delivered to China before the deterioration of Moscow-Peking relations and, with great skill, these were copied down to the last detail so that assembly lines of MiG-19SFs and their RD-9B turbojets could be set up at Shenyang. The designation F-6 was given to the resulting fighter, which first flew in December 1961 and from the following year became standard equipment in the Chinese air force. Many hundreds (perhaps as many as 1,500) have been built subsequently.

Immediately after the Indo-Pakistan war of September 1965, China offered F-6s to Pakistan, which had an urgent need of replacements. Forty were supplied initially and despite problems such as poor component interchangeability resulting from hand manufacture, and the fact that the spares and servicing handbooks were in Chinese, the first PAF squadron was operational within a year. Subsequent deliveries have brought to about 90 the total of F-6s acquired by Pakistan, and by the Spring of 1974 Tanzania had received sufficient F-6s for a single squadron.

The following description is based on known details of the basic MiG-19SF, modified where possible to apply specifically to the Chinese F-6:

Type: Single-seat day interceptor and air-superiority fighter.

Wings: Cantilever mid-wing monoplane of all-metal construction. Wing section TsAGI S-12S at root, SR-7S at tip. Anhedral 4° 30′. Sweepback at quarter-chord 55°. Entire trailing-edge of each wing formed by aileron (inboard) and large Fowler-type flap, both hydraulically powered. Compressed-air emergency extension system for flaps. Trim tab in port aileron. Large full-chord boundary layer fence above each wing at mid-span to enhance aileron effectiveness.

Fuselage: Conventional all-metal semi-monocoque structure of circular section, with divided air intake in nose and side-by-side twin orifices at rear. Top and bottom "pen-nib" fairings aft of nozzles. Entire rear fuselage detaches at wing trailing-edge for engine servicing. Forward-hinged door-type airbrake, operated hydraulically, on each side of fuselage aft of wing trailing-edge. Forward-hinged perforated door-type airbrake under centre-fuselage. Shallow ventral fin strake under rear fuselage. Upward-hinged pitot boom mounted on lower lip of nose intake.

Tail Unit: Conventional all-metal structure. Hydraulically-actuated one-piece horizontal surfaces, with electrical emergency actuation in the event of hydraulic failure. Anti-flutter weight projecting forward from each tailplane tip. Stick-to-tailplane gearing, via electro-mechanical linkage, reduces required stick forces during high-*g* manoeuvres. Sweepback on vertical surfaces 57° 30′. Electrically-actuated trim tab in rudder. Large dorsal fin between fin and dorsal spine enclosing actuating rods for tail control surfaces.

Landing Gear: Wide-track tricycle type, with single wheel on each unit. Hydraulic actuation, nosewheel forward, main units inward into wing-roots. Pneumatic emergency extension system. All units of levered-suspension type, with oleo-pneumatic shock-absorbers. Mainwheel tyres size 660 × 200 mm; max pressure 142 lb/sq in (10 kg/cm²). Nosewheel tyre size 500 × 180; pressure 100 lb/sq in (7 kg/cm²). Pneumatically-operated brakes on main wheels, with pneumatic emergency backup. Pneumatically-deployed brake parachute housed in bottom of rear fuselage above ventral fin strake. Small tail bumper.

Power Plant: Two Chinese-built versions of Klimov RD-9B axial-flow turbojet, each rated at 5,730 lb (2,600 kg) st dry and 7,165 lb (3,250 kg) st with afterburning. Hydraulically-actuated nozzles. Two main fuel tanks in tandem between cockpit and engines, and two smaller tanks under forward end of engine tailpipes, with total capacity of 477 Imp gallons (2,170 litres). Provision for two 176 Imp gallon (800 litre) underwing drop-tanks, raising max total fuel capacity to 829 Imp gallons (3,770 litres).

Accommodation: Pilot only, on ejection seat, under rearward-sliding blister canopy. In emergency canopy is jettisoned by an explosive charge at the lock, after which it is carried away by the slipstream. Fluid anti-icing system for windscreen.

Systems: Cockpit pressurised by air-conditioning system mounted in top of fuselage aft of cockpit, using compressor bleed air. Constant temperature maintained by adjustable electric thermostat. Two independent hydraulic systems. Main system, powered by pump on starboard engine, actuates landing gear retraction and extension, flaps, airbrakes and afterburner nozzle mechanism. System for tailplane and aileron boosters is powered by a pump on the port engine, and can also be supplied by the main system should the booster system fail. Electrical system powered by two DC starter/generators, supplemented by a battery, providing 27V DC, and 115V 400Hz and 36V 400Hz AC.

Electronics and Equipment: Standard equipment includes VHF radio, blind-flying equipment, radio compass, radio altimeter, tail-warning system, navigation lights, taxying light on nosewheel unit and landing light in bottom of front fuselage.

Armament: Installed armament of three 30 mm NR-30 guns, one in each wing root and one under starboard side of nose. Attachment under each wing for a Sidewinder air-to-air missile, outboard of drop-tank. Alternatively, an attachment inboard of each tank for a bomb weighing up to 500 lb (or 250 kg), a rocket of up to 212 mm calibre, or a pack of eight air-to-air rockets. Optical gunsight. Gun camera in top lip of air intake.

Dimensions, external:

Wing span	29 ft 6½ in (9·00 m)
Wing chord, mean	9 ft 10¾ in (3·02 m)

Wing aspect ratio 3·24
Thickness/chord ratio, mean 8·24%
Length overall:
incl nose probe 48 ft $10\frac{1}{2}$ in (14·90 m)
excl nose probe 41 ft 4 in (12·60 m)
Length of fuselage 38 ft $9\frac{1}{2}$ in (11·82 m)
Height overall 13 ft $2\frac{1}{4}$ in (4·02 m)
Tailplane span 16 ft $4\frac{3}{4}$ in (5·00 m)
Wheel track 13 ft $7\frac{1}{2}$ in (4·15 m)

Areas:
Wings, gross 269 sq ft (25·00 m^2)
Airbrakes (three, total) 16·15 sq ft (1·50 m^2)
Ventral fin 6·61 sq ft (0·614 m^2)

Weights and Loadings:
Weight empty, nominal 12,700 lb (5,760 kg)
Normal T-O weight 16,755 lb (7,600 kg)
Max T-O weight 19,180 lb (8,700 kg)
Max wing loading 71·28 lb/sq ft (348 kg/m^2)
Max power loading 1·67 lb/lb st (1·67 kg/kg st)

Performance:
Max level speed at 32,800 ft (10,000 m) 783 knots (902 mph; 1,452 km/h)
Cruising speed 512 knots (590 mph; 950 km/h)
Min flying speed, flaps up 189 knots (218 mph; 350 km/h)
Landing speed 127 knots (146 mph; 235 km/h)
Max rate of climb at S/L 22,635 ft (6,900 m)/min
Time to service ceiling 8 min 12 sec
Service ceiling 58,725 ft (17,900 m)
Absolute ceiling 65,190 ft (19,870 m)
T-O run, with afterburning 1,690 ft (515 m)
T-O run, with underwing tanks, no afterburning 2,953 ft (900 m)
T-O to 82 ft (25 m), with afterburning 5,000 ft (1,525 m)
T-O to 82 ft (25 m), with underwing tanks, no afterburning 6,170 ft (1,880 m)
Landing from 82 ft (25 m), with brake-chute 5,580 ft (1,700 m)
Landing from 82 ft (25 m), without brake-chute 6,495 ft (1,980 m)
Landing run, with brake-chute 1,970 ft (600 m)
Landing run, without brake-chute 2,920 ft (890 m)
Normal range at 46,000 ft (14,000 m) 750 nm (863 miles; 1,390 km)
Max range with external tanks 1,187 nm (1,366 miles; 2,200 km)
Combat radius with external tanks 370 nm (426 miles; 685 km)
Max endurance at 46,000 ft (14,000 m) 2 hr 38 min

SHENYANG F-8

Design of this Chinese version of the Mikoyan MiG-21 fighter was based initially on that of a number of Soviet-built aircraft of this type that had been delivered to China prior to the political break in 1960. The difficult task of copying the airframe, RD-11 afterburning turbojet and equipment was completed so quickly and efficiently that the F-8 made its first flight in December 1964 and began to enter service with the Chinese air force in 1965. The design has been updated by reference to Soviet late-model MiG-21s despatched to North Vietnam via China.

SHENYANG F-9

Few details are available of this twin-engined fighter derived from the F-6/MiG-19, which is believed to be in service with the Chinese air force. Reports suggest that it first flew in the early 'seventies, and has lateral air intakes to permit use of a pointed nose radome. The F-9 is said to be somewhat larger overall than the F-6, with a wing span of about 33 ft 5 in (10·20 m), overall length of about 50 ft 0 in (15·25 m) and T-O weight of about 22,050 lb (10,000 kg). Combat radius is thought to be up to 430 nm (500 miles; 800 km), and max level speed almost Mach 2.

SHENYANG (TUPOLEV) Tu-16

The first Chinese-built Tu-16 is believed to have been flown in the early 'seventies, and a production rate of six per month was reported in the Spring of 1972.

CZECHOSLOVAKIA

Central direction of the Czechoslovak aircraft industry is by a body known as the Generální Reditelstvi Aero—Ceskoslovenské Letecke Podniky; Trust Aero—Czechoslovak Aeronautical Works, Prague-Letnany, whose Deputy General Manager is Josef Síla. Principal factories concerned with aircraft manufacture are the Aero Vodochody National Corporation, Let National Corporation and Zlin Aircraft-Moravan National Corporation, whose current products appear under the appropriate headings in this section. Other Czechoslovak factories engaged in the production of aero-engines and sailplanes are listed in the relevant sections of this edition.

Sales of all aircraft products outside Czechoslovakia are handled by the Omnipol Foreign Trade Corporation, whose address is given below.

OMNIPOL
FOREIGN TRADE CORPORATION

Address:
Washingtonova 11, Prague 1
Telephone: 2126
Telex: 121489, 121808 and 121077

General Manager:
Tomás Marecek, GE

Sales Manager:
Frantisek Rypal, GE

Publicity Manager:
Jirí Matula

This concern handles the sales of products of the Czechoslovak aircraft industry outside Czechoslovakia and furnishes all information requested by customers with regard to export goods.

About 29,000 people are employed by the Czechoslovak aircraft industry.

AERO
AERO VODOCHODY NÁRODNÍ PODNIK (Aero Vodochody National Corporation)

Address:
Vodochody, p. Odelená Voda, near Prague

Managing Director:
Jirí Chmelícek

Vice-Directors:
Ing Milan Dibelka (Technical)
Antonín Vins (Production)
Ing Otakar Stella (Sales)
Oldrich Novák (Works Economy)

Chief Designer:
Dipl Ing Jan Vlcek

Chief Pilot:
Vlastimil David

This factory perpetuates the name of one of the three founder companies of the Czechoslovak aircraft industry, which began activities shortly after the first World War with the manufacture of Austrian Phönix fighters. Subsequent well-known products included the A 11 military general-purpose biplane and its derivatives, and licence manufacture of the French Bloch 200 twin-engined bomber. The present works was established on 1 July 1953, since when it has seven times received the Red Banner award of the Ministry of Engineering and UVOS, as well as many other awards including those of Exemplary Exporting Corporation and the Order of Labour.

AERO L-29 DELFIN
NATO Code Name: "Maya"

The L-29 was evolved by a team led by K. Tomas and the late Z. Rublic. The first prototype, the XL-29, flew for the first time on 5 April 1959, powered by a Bristol Siddeley Viper turbojet engine. The second prototype, equipped with a Czech M 701 turbojet engine, began its flight trials in July 1960. The pre-production version (third prototype) completed its tests in 1961, and the L-29 was approved for quantity production.

Manufacture is centred at the Vodochody (Aero) and Kunovice plants, which are devoted almost entirely to producing the L-29, to meet large orders from the Czechoslovak Air Force, the Soviet Union, Bulgaria, Hungary, the German Democratic Republic, Syria, Egypt, Romania, Iraq, Indonesia, Nigeria and Uganda.

The first production aircraft was completed in April 1963, a month ahead of schedule, and by the beginning of 1974 more than 3,000 had been sold, with production continuing. Of these, more than 2,000 had been supplied to the USSR for use by Soviet and other Warsaw Treaty air forces, the remainder being for the Czechoslovak Air Force or for export.

The details which follow apply to the standard L-29. A counter-insurgency version, designated L-29R, is available with nose cameras and underwing stores.

A single-seat aerobatic version, the L-29A, described in the 1973-74 *Jane's*, has not been built in quantity.

Aero L-29 Delfin two-seat jet trainer, more than 3,000 of which have been built

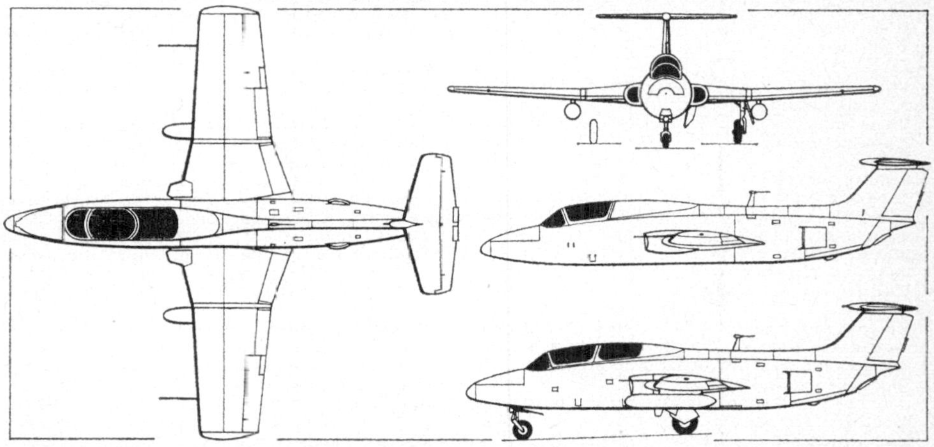

L-29 Delfin tandem two-seat jet trainer, with additional side elevation (*centre*) of single-seat L-29A aerobatic version (*Pilot Press*)

Type: Two-seat jet basic and advanced trainer.

Wings: Cantilever mid-wing monoplane. Wing section NACA 64_2A217 at root, NACA 64_2A212 at tip. Dihedral 0° on centre-section, 3° on outer wings. Incidence 1° 30'. All-metal stressed-skin structure with single main spar at 40% chord. All-metal ailerons and hydraulically-operated Fowler flaps. Trim tab in each aileron.

Fuselage: All-metal semi-monocoque structure of circular section. Front portion forms pressurised compartment for the crew, radio equipment and electronics. Centre of fuselage is integral with wing centre-section and contains main fuel tanks. Engine mounting is attached to rear bulkhead of centre-fuselage. Rear fuselage is connected to centre portion through eight attachment points, to permit quick removal for engine servicing. Zones of high stress have steel-alloy reinforcement. Hydraulically-operated sideways-opening perforated airbrake on each side of rear fuselage.

Tail Unit: All-metal T-tail with variable-incidence tailplane. Tailplane incidence is

Aero L-39 two-seat trainer in its production form (licence-built Ivchenko AI-25-TL turbofan engine)

linked with landing flaps. Trim tabs in elevator. Adjustable tab on rudder.

Landing Gear: Retractable tricycle type. Hydraulic retraction, main wheels inward into wing roots, nosewheel rearward into fuselage. Oleo-pneumatic shock-absorbers. Single wheel on each unit. Barum low-pressure tyres, size 600 × 180 on main wheels, 420 × 150 on nosewheel. Pneumatic brakes.

Power Plant: One M 701c 500 turbojet engine, rated at 1,960 lb (890 kg) st at 15,400 rpm for take-off. Two fuel tanks in fuselage, capacity 152 Imp gallons (690 litres) and 79 Imp gallons (360 litres) respectively. Total internal fuel capacity 231 Imp gallons (1,050 litres). Total usable capacity 211·5 Imp gallons (962 litres). Provision for two 33 Imp gallon (150 litre) underwing auxiliary tanks. Inverted-flying tank in rear main tank permits 15 sec of inverted flight. All tanks of aluminium alloy.

Accommodation: Crew of two in tandem on synchronised ejection seats in air-conditioned and pressurised cabin. Rear seat raised 6 in (15 cm) higher than front seat. Fittings for *g* suits. Canopy over front cockpit opens sideways, to starboard. Rearward-sliding canopy over rear cockpit.

Systems: Hydraulic system, pressure 1,565 lb/sq in (110 kg/cm²), actuates landing gear, wheel doors, flaps and airbrakes. Emergency manual system for extension of flaps and landing gear. In case of pilot error, flaps retract automatically at an air speed of 145 knots (168 mph; 270 km/h). Pneumatic system for airbrakes and canopy seals. Electrical system includes a 3kW generator on engine and a 28Ah battery which can be used for emergency engine starting.

Electronics and Equipment: Includes VHF radio, radio compass, radio altimeter and marker beacon receiver.

Armament: Provision for camera gun and gunsight, and either two bombs of up to 100 kg, eight air-to-ground rockets or two 7·62 mm machine-gun pods under the wings.

Dimensions, external:

Wing span	33 ft 9 in (10·29 m)
Wing chord at root	8 ft 10 in (2·70 m)
Wing chord at tip	4 ft 7 in (1·40 m)
Wing aspect ratio	5·36
Length overall	35 ft 5½ in (10·81 m)
Height over tail	10 ft 3 in (3·13 m)
Tailplane span	10 ft 11½ in (3·34 m)
Wheel track	11 ft 3½ in (3·44 m)
Wheelbase	12 ft 9½ in (3·90 m)

Areas:

Wings, gross	213·1 sq ft (19·80 m²)
Ailerons (total)	16·15 sq ft (1·50 m²)
Flaps (total)	30·14 sq ft (2·80 m²)
Airbrakes (total)	5·38 sq ft (0·50 m²)
Fin	14·00 sq ft (1·30 m²)
Rudder, incl tab	8·61 sq ft (0·80 m²)
Tailplane	23·68 sq ft (2·20 m²)
Elevators, incl tabs	11·84 sq ft (1·10 m²)

Weights and Loadings:

Weight empty	5,027 lb (2,280 kg)
Normal T-O weight	7,231 lb (3,280 kg)
Max permissible loaded weight with external tanks	7,804 lb (3,540 kg)
Max wing loading	36·7 lb/sq ft (179 kg/m²)
Max power loading	3·95 lb/lb st (3·95 kg/kg st)

Performance (at AUW of 7,165 lb; 3,250 kg):

Max never-exceed speed	442 knots (510 mph; 820 km/h)
Limiting Mach No	0·75
Max level speed at 16,400 ft (5,000 m)	353 knots (407 mph; 655 km/h)
Max level speed at S/L	332 knots (382 mph; 615 km/h)
Landing speed	78 knots (90 mph; 145 km/h)
Stalling speed, flaps up	87 knots (100 mph; 160 km/h)
Stalling speed, flaps down	71 knots (81 mph; 130 km/h)
Max rate of climb at S/L	2,755 ft (840 m)/min
Service ceiling	36,100 ft (11,000 m)
T-O run	1,805 ft (550 m)
Landing run	1,444 ft (440 m)
Max range on internal fuel at 16,400 ft (5,000 m)	344 nm (397 miles; 640 km)
Max range with external tanks at 16,400 ft (5,000 m)	480 nm (555 miles; 894 km)
Endurance on internal fuel at 247 knots (285 mph; 460 km/h) at 16,400 ft (5,000 m)	1 hr 47 min
Endurance with external tanks	2 hr 30 min

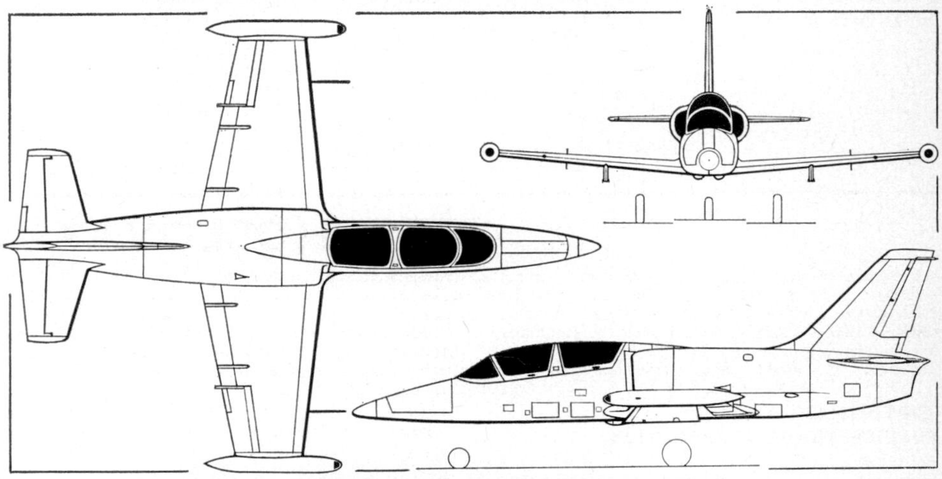

Aero L-39 two-seat basic and advanced jet trainer (*Pilot Press*)

AERO L-39

The L-39 basic and advanced jet trainer was developed in the Aero works at Vodochody by a team led by the chief designer, Dipl Ing Jan Vlcek. Two prototype airframes had been completed by 4 November 1968 when the No 02 aircraft flew for the first time. The 01 airframe was utilised for structural testing. By the end of 1970, five flying prototypes and two for ground testing had been completed. Slightly larger and longer air intake trunks were fitted after preliminary flight tests.

The fourth prototype has been flown with underwing rocket pods and air-to-air missiles, to evaluate the L-39 as a light ground attack aircraft, and this version, which is designated **L-39Z**, is reported to have been ordered by Iraq in addition to the standard L-39 trainer.

A pre-production batch of 10 aircraft began to join the flight test programme in 1971, and series production started late in 1972, following official selection of the L-39 to succeed the L-29 as the standard jet trainer of all Warsaw Treaty countries except Poland. Service acceptance trials, in Czechoslovakia and the USSR, took place in 1973, and by the Spring of 1974 the L-39 had begun to enter service with the Czech Air Force.

Type: Two-seat basic and advanced jet trainer.

Wings: Cantilever low-wing monoplane, with 2° 30′ dihedral from roots. Wing section NACA 64A012 mod. 5. Incidence 2°. One-piece all-metal stressed-skin structure, with all-metal hydraulically-operated double-slotted trailing-edge flaps. Airbrake under each leading-edge. Small fence above and below each trailing-edge between flap and aileron. Trim tab in each aileron. Non-jettisonable wingtip fuel tanks incorporating landing lights.

Fuselage: All-metal semi-monocoque structure, built in four sections. Front portion houses electrical and radio equipment and nose landing gear. Next comes the pressurised compartment for the crew. The third section contains fuel tanks and the engine bay. The rear fuselage, carrying the tail unit, can be removed quickly to provide access for engine servicing.

Tail Unit: Conventional all-metal cantilever structure, with sweepback on vertical surfaces. Variable-incidence tailplane. Trim tab in port elevator.

Landing Gear: Retractable tricycle type, with single wheel on each unit. Hydraulic retraction, main wheels inward into wings, nosewheel rearward into fuselage. Oleo-pneumatic shock-absorbers and low-pressure tyres on all units. Hydraulic disc brakes on main wheels. Pneumatic ram air system for emergency extension.

Power Plant: One 3,792 lb (1,720 kg) st Walter Titan (Motorlet-built Ivchenko AI-25-TL) turbofan engine mounted in rear fuselage, with semi-circular lateral air intake, fitted with splitter plate, on each side of fuselage above wing centre-section. Fuel in rubber bag-type main tanks aft of cockpit, capacity 1,816 lb (824 kg), and two non-jettisonable wingtip tanks with total capacity of 344 lb (156 kg).

Accommodation: Crew of two in tandem on zero-height ejection seats beneath individual transparent canopies which hinge sideways to starboard. Seats ensure safe ejection at speeds between 81 knots (94 mph; 150 km/h) and 491 knots (565 mph; 910 km/h). Dual controls standard, with rod-actuated control surfaces. Cabin air-conditioned.

Systems: High-pressure hydraulic system for landing gear retraction and control of flaps, airbrakes and wheel brakes.

Electronics: Standard equipment includes RTL-11 VHF com, RKL-41 ADF, radio altimeter, MRP-56-P/S marker beacon receiver and IFF.

Armament: Provision for bombs and rockets. ASP-3-NMU-39 gunsight and FKP-2-2 camera gun standard.

Dimensions, external:

Wing span	31 ft 0½ in (9·46 m)
Wing chord (mean)	7 ft 0½ in (2·15 m)
Wing aspect ratio	4·4
Length overall	40 ft 5 in (12·32 m)
Height overall	15 ft 5½ in (4·72 m)
Tailplane span	14 ft 5 in (4·40 m)
Wheel track	8 ft 0 in (2·44 m)
Wheelbase	14 ft 4¾ in (4·39 m)

Areas:

Wings, gross	202·4 sq ft (18·8 m²)
Ailerons (total)	13·26 sq ft (1·23 m²)
Flaps (total)	28·89 sq ft (2·68 m²)
Airbrakes (total)	5·38 sq ft (0·50 m²)
Fin	29·78 sq ft (2·77 m²)
Rudder	7·68 sq ft (0·71 m²)
Tailplane	42·30 sq ft (3·93 m²)
Elevators	12·27 sq ft (1·14 m²)

Weights and Loadings:

Weight empty	7,055 lb (3,200 kg)
Normal T-O weight	9,083 lb (4,120 kg)
Max T-O weight	9,998 lb (4,535 kg)
Max wing loading	44·65 lb/sq ft (218 kg/m²)
Max power loading	2·74 lb/lb st (2·74 kg/kg st)

Performance (at normal T-O weight):

Max limiting Mach number	0·80
Max level speed at 16,400 ft (5,000 m)	405 knots (466 mph; 750 km/h)
Cruising speed at 16,400 ft (5,000 m)	367 knots (423 mph; 680 km/h)
Stalling speed, flaps up	97 knots (112 mph; 180 km/h)
Stalling speed, flaps down	84 knots (97 mph; 155 km/h)
Max rate of climb at S/L	4,330 ft (1,320 m)/min
Service ceiling	37,075 ft (11,300 m)
T-O run	1,475 ft (450 m)
T-O to 50 ft (15 m)	2,180 ft (665 m)
Landing from 50 ft (15 m)	2,885 ft (880 m)
Landing run	2,035 ft (620 m)
Range with tip-tanks empty, 5% reserve of main fuel	491 nm (565 miles; 910 km)

LET

LET NÁRODNÍ PODNIK (Let National Corporation)

ADDRESS:
Uherské Hradiste-Kunovice
Telephone: Uherské Hradiste 5121
Telex: 060180 and 060181

MANAGING DIRECTOR:
Ing Josef Kurz

CHIEF DESIGNER:
Ing Ladislav Smrcek

CHIEF PILOT:
Vladimír Vlk

The Let plant at Kunovice was established in 1950, its early activities including licence production of the Soviet Yak-11 piston-engined trainer under the Czechoslovak designation C-11. It has also contributed to the production of the Aero 45 and L 200 Morava twin-engined air taxi aircraft, the Z-37 Cmelák agricultural aircraft, and the L 13 Blanik sailplane, and is currently responsible for development and manufacture of the L-410 twin-turboprop light transport.

The factory also produces apparatus and equipment for radar and computer technology.

LET L-410A TURBOLET

The L-410 is a twin-turboprop light transport, intended for use on local passenger and freight services. It is suitable for operation from airfields with a natural grass surface.

Design of the L-410 was started in 1966. The first prototype (OK-YKE), powered by United Aircraft of Canada PT6A-27 turboprop engines, was built by the national corporation of Let, at Kunovice, and flew for the first time on 16 April 1969. Three additional PT6A-engined prototypes were completed subsequently. Production L-410As, deliveries of which began in 1971, are also powered initially by PT6A-27 engines. The details apply primarily to this initial version, the first of which entered service with the Czechoslovak domestic operator Slov-Air in late 1971. Five L-410s underwent hot and cold weather tests, and route evaluation, in the USSR between Spring and Autumn 1973. The L-410A is under consideration for large-scale use by Aeroflot instead of the now-abandoned Beriev Be-30.

Twenty Turbolets had been sold by the end of 1973, and it was planned to introduce a version with M 601 turboprop engines in 1974.

TYPE: Twin-turboprop light passenger and freight transport.

WINGS: Cantilever high-wing monoplane. Wing section NACA 63A418 at root, NACA 63A412 at tip. Dihedral 1° 45′. Incidence +2° 0′ at root, —0° 30′ at tip. No sweepback at front spar. Conventional all-metal two-spar structure, attached to fuselage by four-point mountings. Chemically-machined skin with longitudinal reinforcement. All-metal ailerons with electrically-controlled trim tab in port aileron. No spoilers. Double-slotted metal flaps, with both slots variable. TKS hydraulic or Kléber-Colombes pneumatic de-icing of leading-edges.

FUSELAGE: Conventional all-metal semi-monocoque structure.

TAIL UNIT: Cantilever all-metal structure of conventional semi-monocoque type. Sweptback vertical surfaces, with small dorsal fin and curved ventral fin. One-piece tailplane, mounted part-way up fin. Manually-controlled trim tab in each elevator. Rudder has electrically-actuated trim tab. TKS hydraulic or Kléber-Colombes pneumatic de-icing of leading-edges.

LANDING GEAR: Retractable tricycle type with single wheel on each unit. Hydraulic retraction, nosewheel forward, main wheels inward to lie flat in fairing on each side of fuselage. Technometra Radotin oleo-pneumatic shock-absorbers. Non-braking nosewheel, with servo-assisted steering, fitted with 540 × 221 (9·00-6) tubeless tyre, pressure 39·8 lb/sq in (2·8 kg/cm^2). Main wheels fitted with 718 × 306 (12·50-10) tubeless tyres, pressure 45·5 lb/sq in (3·2 kg/cm^2). All wheels manufactured by Moravan Otrokovice, tyres by Rudy Rijen, Gottwaldov. Moravan Otrokovice hydraulic disc brakes on main wheels. No anti-skid units. Metal ski landing gear, with plastics undersurface, optional.

POWER PLANT: Two 715 ehp United Aircraft of Canada PT6A-27 turboprop engines, each driving a Hamilton Standard LF-23 Type 343 or Hartzell HC-B3TN-3D reversible-pitch fully-feathering three-blade propeller. De-icing for propeller blades (electrical) and lower intakes. Six (optionally eight) bag-type fuel tanks in wings, with total capacity (eight tanks) of 286 Imp gallons (1,300 litres). Four standard refuelling points above wings, with provision for two extra points when all eight tanks are fitted. Usable oil capacity 1·25 Imp gallons (5·6 litres) for each engine. Alternative installation, planned for introduction in 1974, of two 736 ehp M 601 turboprop engines, each driving an Avia V 508 three-blade hydraulically-adjustable and reversible-pitch constant-speed propeller. Fuel system as for PT6A-27 version. Oil capacity 2·2 Imp gallons (10 litres).

Let L-410A Turbolet light passenger transports in Slov-Air insignia

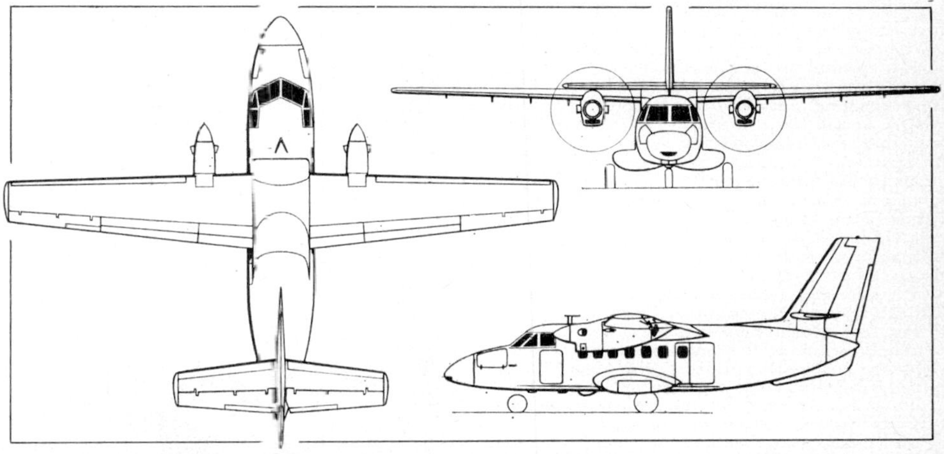

Let L-410A Turbolet twin-turboprop 15/19-passenger light transport *(Pilot Press)*

ACCOMMODATION: Crew of one or two on flight deck. Main cabin accommodates from 15 to 19 passengers, with pairs of seats on starboard side of aisle and single seats opposite, all at 30 in (76 cm) pitch. Baggage compartment in nose with two separate doors; toilet and additional baggage compartment at rear. Double upward-opening doors aft on port side, right hand door serving as passenger entrance; both doors open for cargo loading. Downward-opening crew door, forward on starboard side, serves also as emergency exit. Cargo space to rear of cabin. Cabin heated and ventilated by engine bleed air.

SYSTEMS: No air-conditioning or pressurisation systems. Isopressure duplicated hydraulic system, pressure 2,133 lb/sq in (150 kg/cm^2), for flap and landing gear actuation. Electrical system includes two 28V 6kW DC starter/generators, three 36V 400Hz rotary inverters and two 25Ah storage batteries. No APU or oxygen systems.

ELECTRONICS AND EQUIPMENT Standard equipment includes cockpit, instrument and passenger cabin lights, navigation lights, cabin-mounted fire extinguisher, three landing lights in nose, and windscreen wipers. Optional equipment includes two Mesit (LUN 3522) VKDC.1 VHF; two King KDF 800 or Collins DF 203 ADF; one Collins 51Z6 marker; two Collins 51RV2B or RCA AVN 210 VOR/ILS; anti-collision lights; wing and tail de-icing system (hydraulic or pneumatic); and windscreen de-icing.

DIMENSIONS, EXTERNAL:
Wing span 57 ft 4¼ in (17·48 m)
Wing chord at root 8 ft 3¾ in (2·534 m)
Wing chord at tip 4 ft 1¾ in (1·267 m)
Wing aspect ratio 9·3
Length overall 44 ft 7¾ in (13·61 m)
Length of fuselage 42 ft 2¾ in (12·89 m)
Height overall 18 ft 6½ in (5·65 m)
Tailplane span 22 ft 2½ in (6·77 m)
Wheel track 11 ft 11½ in (3·65 m)
Wheelbase 12 ft 0½ in (3·67 m)
Propeller diameter:
PT6A-27 8 ft 6 in (2·59 m)
M 601 8 ft 7½ in (2·63 m)
Propeller ground clearance 3 ft 8 in (1·12 m)
Distance between propeller centres 15 ft 9¾ in (4·82 m)
Passenger/cargo door (port, aft):
Height 4 ft 3¼ in (1·30 m)
Width overall 4 ft 1¼ in (1·25 m)
Width (passenger door only) 2 ft 5½ in (0·75 m)
Height to sill 2 ft 7½ in (0·80 m)
Crew door/emergency exit door (stbd, fwd):
Height 3 ft 5¼ in (1·05 m)
Width 2 ft 2 in (0·66 m)
Height to sill 2 ft 7½ in (0·80 m)
Nose baggage compartment doors (each):
Height 1 ft 5 in (0·43 m)
Width 2 ft 5 in (0·74 m)
Height to sill 4 ft 3¼ in (1·30 m)

DIMENSIONS, INTERNAL:
Cabin, excluding flight deck:
Length 20 ft 6 in (6·25 m)
Max width 6 ft 3½ in (1·92 m)
Max height 5 ft 5¼ in (1·658 m)
Floor area 104·3 sq ft (9·69 m^2)
Volume 635 cu ft (18·00 m^3)
Baggage compartment volume (nose) 38·8 cu ft (1·1 m^3)
Baggage compartment volume (rear):
15 passengers 88·3 cu ft (2·5 m^3)
19 passengers 56·5 cu ft (1·6 m^3)

AREAS:
Wings, gross 353·70 sq ft (32·86 m^2)
Ailerons (total) 24·2 sq ft (2·248 m^2)
Trailing-edge flaps (total) 63·7 sq ft (5·92 m^2)
Fin 40·26 sq ft (3·74 m^2)
Rudder, incl tab 29·92 sq ft (2·78 m^2)
Tailplane 71·04 sq ft (6·60 m^2)
Elevators, incl tabs 31·86 sq ft (2·96 m^2)

WEIGHTS AND LOADINGS:
Basic weight empty 6,834 lb (3,100 kg)
Operating weight empty (cargo version) 7,275 lb (3,300 kg)
Max payload (cargo version) 4,078 lb (1,850 kg)
Max T-O weight 12,566 lb (5,700 kg)
Max landing weight 12,125 lb (5,500 kg)
Max zero-fuel weight 11,662 lb (5,290 kg)
Max wing loading 35·53 lb/sq ft (173·46 kg/m^2)
Max power loading:
PT6A-27 8·80 lb/ehp (3·99 kg/ehp)
M 601 8·53 lb/ehp (3·87 kg/ehp)

PERFORMANCE (at max T-O weight, ISA, except where indicated):
Max never-exceed speed 278 knots (321 mph; 518 km/h) EAS
Max cruising speed at 9,845 ft (3,000 m) 202 knots (233 mph; 375 km/h) TAS
Econ cruising speed (80% power) at 9,845 ft (3,000 m) 194 knots (224 mph; 360 km/h) TAS

Stalling speed, flaps up
83 knots (95 mph; 152 km/h) EAS
Stalling speed, flaps down, at max landing weight 65 knots (74 mph; 119 km/h) EAS
Max rate of climb at S/L 1,615 ft (492 m)/min
Rate of climb at S/L, one engine out
315 ft (96 m)/min
Service ceiling 22,975 ft (7,000 m)
Service ceiling, one engine out
9,175 ft (2,800 m)
Min ground turning radius 17 ft 8¾ in (5·40 m)
T-O to 50 ft (15 m) 1,865 ft (568 m)
Landing from 50 ft (15 m) at max landing weight
1,825 ft (557 m)
Range with max fuel, 30 min reserve
701 nm (807 miles; 1,300 km)
Range with max payload (two pilots, IMC conditions) 161 nm (186 miles; 300 km)

LET Z-37-A CMELÁK (BUMBLE-BEE)

Design of the Cmelák began in August 1961, and the first XZ-37 prototype of this agricultural aircraft flew for the first time on 29 March 1963. Ten prototypes were built altogether. Certification in the Normal category, Aerial Work Class D, BCAR, was awarded on 20 June 1966. Additional applications for the production Cmelák include mail and cargo transport during the Winter season.

The improved Z-37-A version, with fixed instead of adjustable louvres, was introduced in early 1971 and is now the standard production version. It features some structural reinforcement, increased use of corrosion-resistant materials and other modifications designed to extend operational life. All main structural members are wrapped in textile material for added protection against chemical corrosion. Duralumin fittings on the hopper and wing flaps, and covering between the hopper and wing centre-section, are replaced by fittings and covering of stainless steel.

A total of 570 Cmeláks of all versions had been built by the beginning of 1974, for customers in Bulgaria, Czechoslovakia, Finland, Germany (Democratic Republic), Hungary, India, Iraq, the UK and Yugoslavia. This total includes 27 examples of the two-seat training version, which is designated **Z-237**.

The following description applies to the standard Z-37-A, which continues in production:

Type: Agricultural monoplane.

Wings: Cantilever low-wing monoplane. Wing section NACA 33015 at root, NACA 43012A at tip. Dihedral 7° on outer panels only. Incidence 3° at root, 0° at tip. All-metal single-spar fail-safe structure, with auxiliary rear spar, comprising centre-section, built integrally with fuselage, and two outer panels. Centre-section is strengthened in the vicinity of the main landing gear by comparison with original Z-37. Fabric-covered hermetically-sealed aluminium slotted ailerons. Pneumatically-operated double-slotted aluminium flaps. Leading-edge fixed slats of aluminium alloy on outer wings, in line with ailerons.

Fuselage: Welded steel-tube fail-safe structure. Engine, cockpit and underfuselage covered in dural sheet, remainder fabric-covered. Rear end of fuselage is detachable to facilitate cleaning.

Tail Unit: Cantilever aluminium alloy structure. Fin and tailplane metal-covered; rudder and elevators fabric covered and hermetically sealed. Trim tabs in elevators and rudder.

Landing Gear: Non-retractable tailwheel type. Technometra N. C. Semily oleo-pneumatic shock-absorbers. Moravan Otrokovice wheels and Rudy Rijen low-pressure tyres and tubes. Main wheel tyres size 556 × 163, pressure 32 lb/sq in (2·25 kg/cm²); anti-shimmy tailwheel, tyre size 290 × 110, pressure 40·5 lb/sq in (2·85 kg/cm²). Moravan Otrokovice hydraulic shoe-type brakes on main wheels. Chemical deflector fitted to starboard main wheel, eliminating the need for rubber protection for the shock-absorbers and undercarriage bracing struts. Provision for fitting wooden skis, with pneumatically-actuated hydraulic brakes.

Power Plant: One 315 hp M 462 RF nine-cylinder radial aircooled engine, driving an Avia V 520 two-blade constant-speed metal propeller. Aluminium alloy fuel tank in port wing centre-section is standard; provision for optional tank in starboard side of centre-section to give total capacity of 55 Imp gallons (250 litres). For carrying replenishment fuel to operating site, two externally-suspended tanks, each of 27·5 Imp gallons (125 litres) capacity, can be carried. Similar tanks can also be used to transport chemicals in concentrated form. Refuelling points above port wing centre-section. Oil capacity 2·97 Imp gallons (13·5 litres). Anti-dust filter in front of carburettor air intake. Provision for pre-heating intake air.

Accommodation: Pilot in enclosed cockpit forward of hopper. One auxiliary seat behind hopper for mechanic or loader. Cabin ventilated and heated by ram air and heat exchanger. Forward-opening door on starboard side.

Systems: Pneumatic system for engine starter, flaps, parking brake and hopper actuation. Electrical power provided by 28V 1500W generator, 24V 10Ah battery and 36V 400Hz converter.

Electronics and Equipment: ADF and Mesit LUN 3522 optional. Hopper for 143 Imp gallons (650 litres) of spray or 1,323 lb (600 kg) of dust. Spray system and distributor for dry chemicals interchangeable. Total volume available for chemical hopper or cargo 63·5 cu ft (1·8 m³). Effective swath width with the aircraft flying 16 ft (5 m) above the ground is 115 ft (35 m) for oily spray, 66 ft (20 m) for aqueous spray; at flying height of 50-65 ft (15-20 m), effective swath width is 66-82 ft (20-25 m) for granules and 130 ft (40 m) for dust.

Dimensions, external:
Wing span 40 ft 1¼ in (12·22 m)
Wing chord at root 7 ft 7¼ in (2·32 m)
Wing chord at tip 3 ft 9¾ in (1·16 m)
Wing aspect ratio 6·3
Length overall 28 ft 0½ in (8·55 m)
Height overall 9 ft 6 in (2·90 m)
Tailplane span 14 ft 10½ in (4·53 m)
Wheel track 10 ft 9¾ in (3·30 m)
Wheelbase 18 ft 0½ in (5·50 m)
Propeller diameter 8 ft 10½ in (2·70 m)
Propeller ground clearance 1 ft 1¾ in (0·35 m)

Dimensions, internal:
Pilot's cockpit:
Width at chest level 3 ft 2¼ in (0·97 m)
Height (seat to roof) 3 ft 3¾ in (1·01 m)
Height (floor to roof) 4 ft 0 in (1·22 m)
Mechanic's compartment:
Width 3 ft 0 in (0·915 m)
Height (seat to roof) 3 ft 7¾ in (1·11 m)

Areas:
Wings, gross 256·2 sq ft (23·8 m²)
Ailerons (total) 22·07 sq ft (2·05 m²)
Trailing-edge flaps (total) 47·04 sq ft (4·37 m²)
Vertical tail surfaces (total) 22·07 sq ft (2·05 m²)
Horizontal tail surfaces (total)
54·14 sq ft (5·03 m²)

Weights and Loadings:
Weight empty, standard equipment, without agricultural equipment 2,295 lb (1,043 kg)
Max chemicals 1,323 lb (600 kg)
Max T-O weight:
freight version 3,855 lb (1,750 kg)
agricultural version 4,080 lb (1,850 kg)
Max wing loading (agricultural)
15·93 lb/sq ft (77·7 kg/m²)
Max power loading (agricultural)
13·20 lb/hp (5·99 kg/hp)

Performance (at max T-O weight. A: freight version; B: agricultural version):
Max never-exceed speed
145 knots (167 mph; 270 km/h)
Max level speed (without application equipment)
113 knots (130 mph; 210 km/h)
Cruising speed at 4,920 ft (1,500 m):
A 99 knots (114 mph; 183 km/h)
B 92 knots (106 mph; 170 km/h)
Operating speed, agricultural operations:
B 65 knots (75 mph; 120 km/h)
Stalling speed, flaps up
49 knots (56 mph; 90 km/h)
Stalling speed, flaps down
45 knots (51 mph; 81 km/h)
Max rate of climb at S/L:
A 925 ft (282 m)/min
B 728 ft (222 m)/min
Service ceiling:
A 13,125 ft (4,000 m)
Min ground turning radius 18 ft 7¾ in (5·68 m)
T-O run:
A 410 ft (125 m)
B 492 ft (150 m)
Landing run:
A 328 ft (100 m)
B 400 ft (122 m)
Range, with reserves for 1 hour's flying, plus 10%:
A 345 nm (398 miles; 640 km)

Let Z-37-A Cmelák, current production version (315 hp M 462 RF engine)

Let Z-237 two-seat training version of the Z-37-A Cmelák agricultural aircraft

VZLU

VYZKUMNY A ZKUSEBNÍ LETECKY USTAV (Aeronautical Research and Test Institute)

Address:
Beranovych 130, 19905, Prague 9-Letnany

Telephone: Prague 827041 and 826541
Telex: Prague 1493

Managing Director:
Ing J. Havlicek

This Institute, whose title is self-explanatory, was founded in 1922 and undertakes a range of activities corresponding broadly to those carried out by the RAE in Britain. Details of its principal facilities appeared in the 1970-71 and 1972-73 *Jane's*. It is a member of the Czechoslovak aircraft manufacturing group, under the general management of Aero (which see).

ZLIN

MORAVAN NÁRODNÍ PODNIK (Zlin Aircraft Moravan National Corporation)

ADDRESS:
Otrokovice
Telephone: Gottwaldov 92 2041-44
Telex: Gottwaldov 067 334

MANAGING DIRECTOR:
Frantisek Klapil

VICE-DIRECTORS:
Ing Stanislav Machálka (Technical)
Jan Munclinger (Production)
Frantisek Muzny (Sales)
Ing Adolf Dolezal (Works Economy)

CHIEF DESIGNER:
Ing Jirí Navrátil

CHIEF PILOT:
Vlastimil Berg

The Moravan works, responsible for production of the famous range of Zlin aerobatic and light touring aircraft, was formed originally on 8 July 1935 as Zlinská Letecká Akciová Spolecnost (Zlin Aviation Joint Stock Co) in Zlin, although manufacture of Zlin aircraft was actually started two years earlier by the Masarykova Letecká Liga (Masaryk League of Aviation). The factory was renamed Moravan after the second World War. In 1967 it was awarded the FAI Diploma of Honour in recognition of its work in the design and manufacture of training and aerobatic aircraft. At present, in addition to production of the Zlin 42 M, Zlin 43, Zlin 526 F, Zlin 526 AFS and Zlin 726, Moravan is building fuselages for the Let Z-37-A Cmelák and items of aircraft equipment.

ZLIN 42 M

The prototype Zlin 42 was the first of a new series of small sporting and touring aircraft developed by the Moravan works at Otrokovice. Intended for basic and advanced training, aerobatic training (solo or dual), navigation training, sport, touring and glider towing, it was first flown on 17 October 1967, and in 1969 began undergoing flight trials prior to certification. Standard power plant of the initial production version, described in the 1973-74 *Jane's*, was the 180 hp M 137 A engine, with which the Z 42 conforms to FAR Pt 23 airworthiness specifications in the Aerobatic category and is suitable for service in climates with temperatures between +40° and —20°C.

The following description applies to the current **Zlin 42 M** production version, of which a prototype was first flown in November 1972, certification under FAR Pt 23 in the Aerobatic (+6*g* to —3·5*g*) and Normal categories being obtained in 1973. Production of the Z 42 M began in 1974.

TYPE: Two-seat light training and touring aircraft.

WINGS: Cantilever low-wing monoplane. Wing section NACA $63_2416\cdot5$. Dihedral 6° from roots. Sweep-forward 4° 20′ at quarter-chord. All-metal structure with single main spar. All-metal slotted ailerons and flaps all have same dimensions. Flaps and ailerons operated mechanically by control rods. Ground-adjustable tab in each aileron.

FUSELAGE: Engine cowlings of sheet metal. Centre fuselage of welded steel-tube truss construction, covered with laminated glass-fibre panels. Rear fuselage is all-metal semi-monocoque structure.

TAIL UNIT: Cantilever all-metal structure. Control surfaces have partial mass and aerodynamic balance. Trim tabs on elevator and rudder. Rudder actuated by control cables, elevator by control rods.

LANDING GEAR: Non-retractable tricycle type, with nosewheel offset to port. Oleo-pneumatic nosewheel shock-absorber. Main wheels carried on flat spring steel legs. Nosewheel steering by means of rudder pedals. Single wheel on each unit. Main wheels and Barum tyres size 420 × 150, pressure 27 lb/sq in (1·9 kg/cm²); nosewheel and Barum tyre size 350 × 135, pressure 35·6 lb/sq in (2·5 kg/cm²). Hydraulic brakes on main wheels can be operated from either seat. Wheel fairings and skis optional.

POWER PLANT: One 180 hp Avia M 137 AZ inverted six-cylinder aircooled in-line engine, with low-pressure injection pump, driving a two-blade Avia V 503 A fully-automatic constant-speed propeller. Fuel tanks in each wing leading-edge, with total capacity of 28·5 Imp gallons (130 litres). Fuel and oil systems permit inverted flying for up to 3 minutes.

ACCOMMODATION: Individual side-by-side seats for two persons, the pilot's seat being to port. Both are adjustable for height and permit the use of back-type parachutes. Baggage space aft of seats. Cabin and windscreen heating and ventilation. Forward-opening door on each side of cabin. Dual controls standard.

SYSTEMS: Electrical system includes a 600W 27V engine-driven generator and 25Ah 27V Varley battery. External power source can be used for starting the engine.

ELECTRONICS AND EQUIPMENT: VHF radio and IFR instrumentation optional.

DIMENSIONS, EXTERNAL:
Wing span 29 ft 10¾ in (9·11 m)

Zlin 42 M two-seat light training and touring aircraft (180 hp Avia M 137 AZ engine)

Zlin 43 two/four-seat light training and touring aircraft (210 hp M 337 A engine)

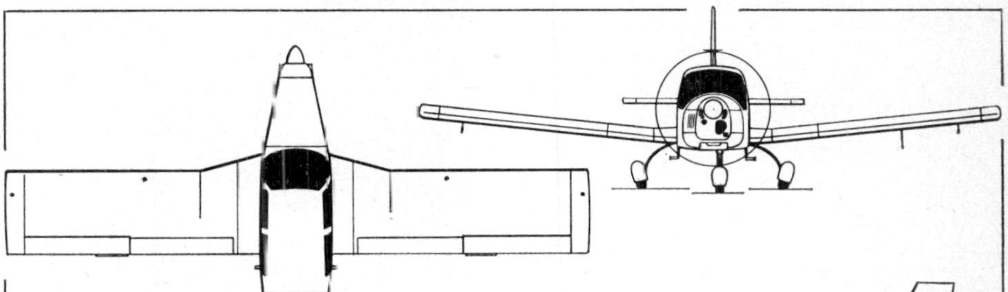

Zlin 43 two/four-seat light training and touring aircraft (*Pilot Press*)

Wing span over tip-tanks 30 ft 1¾ in (9·19 m)
Wing chord (constant) 4 ft 8 in (1·42 m)
Length overall 23 ft 2¼ in (7·07 m)
Height overall 8 ft 10 in (2·69 m)
Tailplane span 9 ft 6 in (2·90 m)
Wheel track 7 ft 7¾ in (2·33 m)
Wheelbase 5 ft 5¼ in (1·66 m)
Propeller diameter 6 ft 6¾ in (2·00 m)

DIMENSIONS, INTERNAL:
Cabin:
Length 5 ft 10⅞ in (1·80 m)
Width 3 ft 8 in (1·12 m)
Height 3 ft 11¼ in (1·20 m)
Baggage space 7·1 cu ft (0·2 m³)

AREAS:
Wings, gross 141·5 sq ft (13·15 m²)
Ailerons (total) 15·1 sq ft (1·40 m²)
Trailing-edge flaps (total) 15·1 sq ft (1·40 m²)
Fin 5·81 sq ft (0·54 m²)
Rudder, incl tab 8·72 sq ft (0·81 m²)
Tailplane 13·24 sq ft (1·23 m²)
Elevator, incl tab 14·64 sq ft (1·36 m²)

WEIGHTS AND LOADINGS:
Basic weight, empty 1,422 lb (645 kg)
Max T-O weight:
Aerobatic 2,028 lb (920 kg)
Normal 2,138 lb (970 kg)
Max wing loading:
Aerobatic 14·3 lb/sq ft (70 kg/m²)
Normal 15·2 lb/sq ft (74 kg/m²)
Max power loading:
Aerobatic 11·29 lb/hp (5·12 kg/hp)
Normal 11·90 lb/hp (5·40 kg/hp)

PERFORMANCE (at max Aerobatic T-O weight):
Max level speed at 1,975 ft (600 m), ISA
122 knots (140 mph; 226 km/h) TAS
Cruising speed at 1,975 ft (600 m), ISA
116 knots (134 mph; 215 km/h) TAS
Stalling speed, flaps down, power off
49 knots (56 mph; 89 km/h)
Max rate of climb at S/L 1,025 ft (312 m)/min
Service ceiling 13,950 ft (4,250 m)
T-O to 50 ft (15 m) 1,245 ft (380 m)
Landing from 50 ft (15 m) 1,345 ft (410 m)
Range with max standard fuel
286 nm (329 miles; 530 km)
g limits:
Aerobatic +6·0; —3·5
Normal +3·8; —1·5

ZLIN 43

The Zlin 43 was first flown in prototype form on 10 December 1968.

It is designed primarily for advanced navigation, night and all-weather flying training, but is also suitable for sports and competitive flying, touring and aerial taxi flying, basic aerobatics (solo or dual) and glider towing.

The Z 42 and Z 43 have some 80% of their structural components in common, the Z 43 differing principally in power plant and in having an enlarged centre section in the fuselage to accommodate a bigger, four-seat cabin with more comprehensive instrumentation.

Certification under FAR 23, in the Utility and Normal categories, has been obtained. Production began in 1972, and 60 Zlin 43s had been completed by the end of 1973. Production continues in 1974.

Type: Two/four-seat light training and touring aircraft.

Wings: Cantilever low-wing monoplane. Wings are of greater span and area than those of Z 42, but are otherwise similar except that they have a flat centre-section and no sweep. Tab on each aileron.

Fuselage: Similar to that of Z 42, but with additional steel-tube section inserted in centre to permit incorporation of larger cabin.

Tail Unit: Similar to Z 42, but with enlarged horizontal surfaces and dorsal fin fairing. Trim tab on starboard half of elevator and on rudder.

Landing Gear: As Z 42, but with some reinforcement of the nosewheel unit and strengthened spring steel legs on main units. Wheel and tyre sizes as Z 42; tyre pressure 35·6 lb/sq in (2·5 kg/cm²) on all units. Hydraulic brakes on main wheels. Optional streamline wheel fairings for all units.

Power Plant: One 210 hp Avia M 337A inverted six-cylinder aircooled in-line engine, with compressor for start and climb, driving an Avia V 500A two-blade constant-speed metal propeller. Fuel tanks in each wing leading-edge, with total capacity of 28·5 Imp gallons (130 litres). Standard additional tanks in each wingtip, each of 12 Imp gallons (55 litres) capacity.

Accommodation: Individual side-by-side seats for two persons in front of cabin, the pilot's seat being to port. Both are adjustable longitudinally and for height, and have tilting backs. Bench seat in rear of cabin for two additional passengers, with baggage space to rear of this seat. Forward-opening door on each side of cabin. Cabin and windscreen heating (by heat exchange system) and ventilation standard. Additional baggage compartment in rear of fuselage, with external access. Dual controls optional.

Systems: As Z 42.

Electronics and Equipment: Standard Z 43 is equipped with instrumentation for day and night flying under VMC conditions. Optional items include full radio/navigation equipment, and instrumentation for various training roles, and for flight under IFR conditions.

Dimensions, external:
Wing span 32 ft 0¼ in (9·76 m)
Wing chord (constant) 4 ft 8 in (1·42 m)
Length overall 25 ft 5 in (7·75 m)
Height overall 9 ft 6½ in (2·91 m)
Tailplane span 9 ft 10 in (3·00 m)
Wheel track 8 ft 0 in (2·44 m)
Wheelbase 5 ft 9 in (1·75 m)
Propeller diameter 6 ft 6¾ in (2·00 m)

Dimensions, internal:
Cabin:
Length 8 ft 2½ in (2·50 m)
Width 3 ft 8 in (1·12 m)
Height 3 ft 11¼ in (1·20 m)
Baggage space (inside cabin) 7·1 cu ft (0·2 m³)
Baggage compartment (rear) 8·8 cu ft (0·25 m³)

Areas:
As for Z 42, except:
Wings, gross 156·1 sq ft (14·50 m²)
Tailplane 27·88 sq ft (2·59 m²)
Elevator, incl tab 14·64 sq ft (1·36 m²)

Weights and Loadings:
Basic weight, equipped 1,609 lb (730 kg)
Max T-O weight:
Normal 2,976 lb (1,350 kg)
Utility 2,204 lb (1,000 kg)
Max wing loading:
Normal 19·1 lb/sq ft (93·2 kg/m²)
Utility 14·1 lb/sq ft (69·0 kg/m²)
Max power loading:
Normal 14·15 lb/hp (6·42 kg/hp)
Utility 10·49 lb/hp (4·76 kg/hp)

Performance (at max T-O weight):
Max level speed at S/L
127 knots (146 mph; 235 km/h)
Cruising speed 113 knots (130 mph; 210 km/h)
Stalling speed, flaps down, power off
52 knots (60 mph; 96 km/h)
Max rate of climb at S/L 689 ft (210 m)/min
Service ceiling 12,465 ft (3,800 m)
T-O to 50 ft (15 m) 2,264 ft (690 m)
Landing from 50 ft (15 m) 1,903 ft (580 m)
Max range (standard fuel)
325 nm (375 miles; 610 km)
Max range (with wingtip tanks)
590 nm (680 miles; 1,100 km)

ZLIN Z 526 F TRENER

The Z 26/126/226/326/526 series has been built at Otrokovice since 1947 and has operated in 36 countries. Sporting successes have included first place in the First, Second, Third and Fifth World Aerobatic Championships in 1960, 1962, 1964 and 1968, first place in the Lockheed Trophy aerobatic competition in Britain in 1957, 1958, 1961, 1963, 1964 and 1965, and first place in the Léon Biancotto Trophée aerobatic competition in France in 1965, 1967 and 1969.

The Z 526 F is one of the latest members of this celebrated series. Major modification, compared with the basic Z 526 (see 1968-69 *Jane's*), is the installation of an Avia M 137 A engine in place of the Walter Minor 6-III engine in the Z 526.

The prototype was flown in the Autumn of 1968 and the Z 526 F was certificated in 1969. More than 150 had been built by the beginning of 1974, with production continuing.

The Z 526 F is intended for ab initio and advanced training, aerobatic flying and training, glider towing etc. Load factors range from +6*g* to —3*g* at max Aerobatic T-O weight, and the Z 526 F is fully aerobatic whether flown dual or solo.

Type: Two-seat basic trainer.

Wings: Cantilever low-wing monoplane. Wings of combined NACA 2418 and NACA 4412 section. Dihedral 4° 30′ from roots. Sweepback 9° at quarter-chord. All-metal two-spar structure with flush-riveted light alloy stressed skin. All-metal ailerons, statically and aerodynamically balanced, are operated differentially. All-metal trailing-edge flaps. Flaps and ailerons actuated mechanically by control rods. Ground-adjustable tabs on ailerons.

Fuselage: Welded steel-tube structure. Upper and lower surfaces covered with easily-removable metal panels and remainder with fabric.

Tail Unit: Cantilever type. Removable tailplane and fin of all-metal stressed-skin construction. Elevators and rudder have metal frames with fabric covering. Trim tabs on rudder and each elevator. Rudder actuated by control cables, elevator by control rods.

Landing Gear: Tailwheel type, with retractable main units. Electrical retraction. Oleo-pneumatic shock-absorbers. Main wheels retract backward into wings. Tyres protrude in retracted position to reduce damage in event of wheels-up landing. Fully-castoring self-centering tailwheel, steerable 30° to either side of centre-line. Barum tyres, main wheels size 420 × 150, pressure 31·3 lb/sq in (2·2 kg/cm²); tailwheel size 260 × 85, pressure 35·6 lb/sq in (2·5 kg/cm²). Hydraulic brakes on main wheels, actuated from both cockpits.

Power Plant: One 180 hp Avia M 137 A inverted six-cylinder in-line aircooled engine, with low-pressure injection pump, driving an Avia V 503 fully-automatic two-blade constant-speed propeller. One fuel tank of 9·9 Imp gallons (45 litres) capacity in each wing root. Fuel and oil installation, designed for aerobatics, permits inverted flying for 3 minutes. Can be fitted with wingtip fuel tanks, with total capacity of 15 Imp gallons (68 litres).

Accommodation: Tandem seats under continuous sliding canopy which is jettisonable in an emergency. Adjustable seats and rudder

Zlin Z 526 F two-seat basic training aircraft (180 hp Avia M 137 A engine)

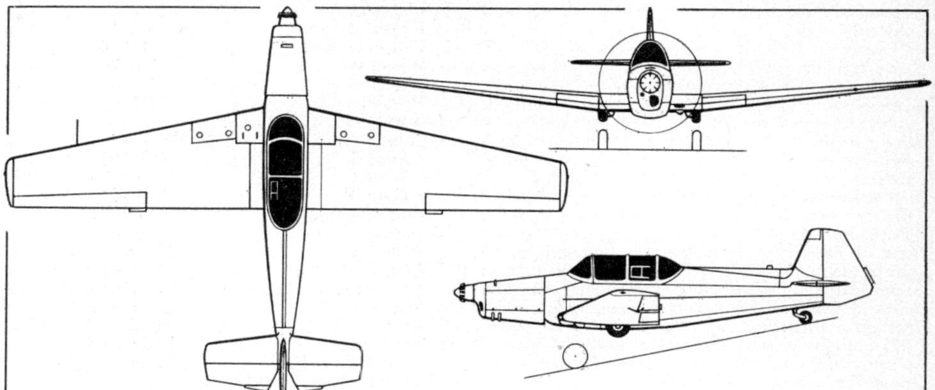

Zlin Z 526 F two-seat basic training aircraft (*Pilot Press*)

pedals in both cockpits. Seat cushions may be replaced by seat-type parachutes. Windscreen frame reinforced as crash pylon. Complete dual controls and instrumentation. Cabin ventilation.

SYSTEMS: Electrical system includes a 600W 27V engine-driven generator and 25Ah 27V Varley battery. External power source can be used for starting the engine.

ELECTRONICS AND EQUIPMENT: Optional equipment includes VKDC-1 (or alternative) radio, and glider towing gear.

DIMENSIONS, EXTERNAL:
Wing span 34 ft 9 in (10·60 m)
Wing span over tip-tanks 35 ft 11½ in (10·96 m)
Wing chord at root 5 ft 0¾ in (1·545 m)
Length overall 26 ft 3 in (8·00 m)
Height overall 6 ft 9 in (2·06 m)
Tailplane span 9 ft 10 in (3·00 m)
Wheel track 5 ft 9¼ in (1·76 m)
Propeller diameter 6 ft 6¾ in (2·00 m)

DIMENSIONS, INTERNAL:
Cabin:
Max length 7 ft 6½ in (2·30 m)
Max width 2 ft 1½ in (0·65 m)
Max height 4 ft 11 in (1·50 m)

AREA:
Wings, gross 166·3 sq ft (15·45 m^2)

WEIGHTS AND LOADINGS:
Weight empty 1,465 lb (665 kg)
Max T-O weight:
Aerobatic 2,072 lb (940 kg)
Normal 2,150 lb (975 kg)
Max wing loading:
Aerobatic 12·5 lb/sq ft (60·8 kg/m^2)
Normal 12·9 lb/sq ft (63·1 kg/m^2)
Max power loading:
Aerobatic 11·51 lb/hp (5·22 kg/hp)
Normal 11·95 lb/hp (5·42 kg/hp)

PERFORMANCE (at max Normal T-O weight, ISA):
Max level speed
131·5 knots (151·5 mph; 244 km/h)
Cruising speed 113 knots (130 mph; 210 km/h)
Stalling speed, flaps down, power off
49 knots (56 mph; 90 km/h)
Max rate of climb at S/L 1,181 ft (360 m)/min
Service ceiling 17,060 ft (5,200 m)
T-O run 722 ft (220 m)
T-O to 50 ft (15 m) 1,148 ft (350 m)
Landing from 50 ft (15 m) 1,345 ft (410 m)
Max range with standard fuel
255 nm (295 miles; 480 km)
Max range with wingtip tanks
450 nm (520 miles; 840 km)

ZLIN Z 526 AFS AKROBAT

The Z 526 AFS is a single-seat version of the Z 526 F designed exclusively for advanced aerobatics, especially those in international championships where the Aresti system of adjudication is used. A prototype was flown for the first time in October 1970; certification under FAR Part 23 in the Aerobatic (+7*g* to —4·5*g*) and Normal categories was obtained in early 1971. A total of 55 Z 526 AFS had been built by the beginning of 1974, with production continuing.

Main differences from the standard Z 526 F include a shorter fuselage, reduced wing span, the use of enlarged, differentially-operating double ailerons instead of flaps, and lower gross weight.

TYPE: Single-seat advanced aerobatic aircraft.

WINGS: Wing section, dihedral, sweepback and general construction as Z 526 F, but with reduced span. No flaps. All-metal statically and aerodynamically balanced double ailerons, capable of differential operation and each with ground-adjustable tab. Mechanical actuation by control rods.

FUSELAGE: Generally as Z 526 F, but shorter overall and with some strengthening.

TAIL UNIT: As Z 526 F.

LANDING GEAR: As for Z 526 F. Parking brake optional.

POWER PLANT: As for Z 526 F, but with wing-root fuel tanks, each of 7·7 Imp gallons (35 litres) capacity. Oil capacity 3·1 Imp gallons (14 litres).

ACCOMMODATION: Single adjustable seat, under fully-transparent rearward-sliding canopy which can be jettisoned in an emergency. Seat cushion can be replaced by seat-type parachute.

SYSTEMS AND EQUIPMENT: As Z 526 F. Radio optional.

DIMENSIONS, EXTERNAL: As Z 526 F, except:
Wing span 29 ft 0 in (8·84 m)
Length overall 25 ft 7½ in (7·81 m)
Height overall 6 ft 2¾ in (1·90 m)
Propeller diameter 6 ft 6¾ in (2·00 m)

DIMENSIONS, INTERNAL:
Cabin: Max length 5 ft 7 in (1·70 m)
Max width 2 ft 1½ in (0·65 m)
Max height 3 ft 9½ in (1·15 m)

AREAS: As Z 526 F, except:
Wings, gross 149 sq ft (13·81 m^2)
Ailerons (total) 25·0 sq ft (2·32 m^2)

WEIGHTS AND LOADINGS:
Weight empty 1,333 lb (605 kg)
Max T-O weight:
Aerobatic (+7*g*;—4·5*g*) 1,631 lb (740 kg)

Zlin Z 526 AFS Akrobat single-seat advanced aerobatic aircraft (180 hp Avia M 137 A engine)

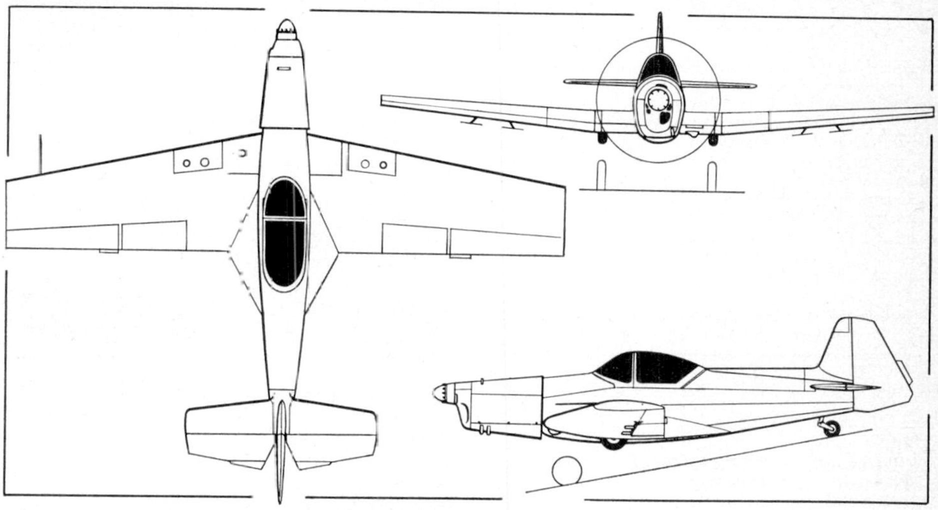

Zlin Z 526 AFS Akrobat single-seat aerobatic aircraft (*Pilot Press*)

Normal 1,851 lb (840 kg)
Max wing loading:
Aerobatic 11·0 lb/sq ft (53·6 kg/m^2)
Normal 12·5 lb/sq ft (61·0 kg/m^2)
Max power loading:
Aerobatic 9·06 lb/hp (4·11 kg/hp)
Normal 10·32 lb/hp (4·68 kg/hp)

PERFORMANCE (at max Aerobatic T-O weight, S/L, ISA):
Max never-exceed speed
164 knots (189 mph; 305 km/h) IAS
Max level speed
136 knots (157 mph; 252 km/h) IAS
Max cruising speed
116 knots (134 mph; 216 km/h) IAS
Stalling speed
54 knots (62·2 mph; 100 km/h) IAS
Max rate of climb at S/L 1,575 ft (480 m)/min
T-O to 50 ft (15 m) 1,050 ft (320 m)

ZLIN Z 726 UNIVERSAL

The Z 726, of which the first of two prototypes was flown for the first time in March 1973, is generally similar to the Z 526 F except for having a 180 hp M 137 AZ engine, shorter-span wings, and metal-covered rudder and elevators. It was certificated to FAR Pt 23 in the Aerobatic and Normal categories in February 1974, and is now in production.

TYPE: Two-seat basic trainer.

WINGS: As Z 526 F, but with reduced span.

FUSELAGE: As Z 526 F.

TAIL UNIT: As Z 526 F, except for metal-covered rudder and elevators.

LANDING GEAR: As Z 526 F.

POWER PLANT: One 180 hp Avia M 137 AZ inverted six-cylinder aircooled in-line engine, with low-pressure injection pump, driving an Avia V 503 A fully-automatic two-blade constant-speed propeller. Fuel and oil as for Z 526 F.

ACCOMMODATION: As Z 526 F. Can be flown solo from either cockpit.

ELECTRONICS AND EQUIPMENT: As Z 526 F.

DIMENSIONS, EXTERNAL: As Z 526 F, except:
Wing span 32 ft 4¾ in (9·875 m)
Wing span over tip-tanks 33 ft 11 in (10·335 m)
Length overall 26 ft 2 in (7·975 m)

DIMENSIONS, INTERNAL: As Z 526 F.

AREAS:
Wings, gross 160·3 sq ft (14·89 m^2)
Ailerons (total) 13·45 sq ft (1·25 m^2)
Trailing-edge flaps (total) 14·81 sq ft (1·376 m^2)
Fin 5·27 sq ft (0·49 m^2)
Rudder, incl tab 10·12 sq ft (0·94 m^2)
Tailplane 15·28 sq ft (1·42 m^2)
Elevators, incl tabs 11·52 sq ft (1·07 m^2)

WEIGHTS AND LOADINGS:
Weight empty:
Aerobatic 1,521 lb (690 kg)
Normal 1,543 lb (700 kg)
Max T-O weight:
Aerobatic 2,072 lb (940 kg)
Normal 2,204 lb (1,000 kg)
Max landing weight:
Normal 2,094 lb (950 kg)
Max wing loading:
Aerobatic 12·94 lb/sq ft (63·2 kg/m^2)
Normal 13·7 lb/sq ft (67·0 kg/m^2)

Zlin Z 726 Universal two-seat training aircraft (180 hp Avia M 137 AZ engine)

Max power loading:
  Aerobatic 11·51 lb/hp (5·22 kg/hp)
  Normal 12·28 lb/hp (5·57 kg/hp)
PERFORMANCE (at max Aerobatic T-O weight):
  Max never-exceed speed
    170 knots (195 mph; 315 km/h) CAS
  Max level speed at 1,525 ft (500 m), ISA
    130 knots (150 mph; 242 km/h) TAS
  Max cruising speed at 1,525 ft (500 m), ISA
    120 knots (137 mph; 221 km/h) TAS
  Stalling speed, flaps down, power off
    53 knots (61 mph; 98 km/h)
  Max rate of climb at S/L 985 ft (300 m)/min
  Service ceiling 14,775 ft (4,500 m)
  T-O run 625 ft (190 m)
  T-O to 50 ft (15 m) 1,295 ft (395 m)
  Landing from 50 ft (15 m) 1,445 ft (440 m)
  Landing run 785 ft (240 m)
  Max range with standard fuel
    237 nm (273 miles; 440 km)
  Max range with wingtip tanks
    425 nm (490 miles; 790 km)

DENMARK

SEREMET

SEREMET AERO-TEST

ADDRESS: Godsparken 50, 2670 Greve Strand
Telephone: (01) 90 29 49

Mr W. Vincent Seremet, a Danish engineer and amateur constructor, has designed and built a number of small rotating-wing aircraft, the first trials being carried out in 1962 with two aircraft designated W.S.1 and W.S.2. More recent designs include the W.S.3, W.S.4/4A, W.S.5, W.S.6 and W.S.7, described in the 1970-71 and subsequent editions of *Jane's*.

Mr Seremet's latest design, illustrated in the accompanying photograph, combines a strap-on small jet engine with an aluminium tube and nylon Rogallo-type wing. For take-off, the pilot inclines the wing 50° upward and the engine exhaust nozzles 60° downward, and runs forward for a few paces in order to acquire the necessary lift. Once in the air, the wing is realigned to a 30° angle and the exhaust nozzles to 20° for flight, and the process is reversed in order to land. Steering is by means of a grip held in each hand. The wing can be folded for portability.

Combined jet engine/parawing strap-on device designed and built by Mr Seremet

FINLAND

PIK

TEKNILLINEN KORKEAKOULU (Helsinki University of Technology)

ADDRESS:
Konelaboratorio/Kevytrakennetekniikka, SF-02150 Otaniemi

EXECUTIVES:
Stefan Nyström (Chairman and Sales Manager)
Tom Lindeman (Secretary and Public Relations)

This organisation originated in 1931 as the Polyteknikkojen Ilmailukerho (Flying Club of the Student Union at the Technical University, Helsinki). It was for many years engaged mainly in the development and construction of high-performance sailplanes (see Sailplanes section). As an extension of this work it designed and built the single-seat PIK-11, its first powered aircraft, which flew in March 1953, and followed this with a two-seat glider-towing aircraft known as the PIK-15 Hinu (see 1973-74 *Jane's*).

The University of Technology has recently built the prototype of a new two-seat glider-towing aircraft, the PIK-19.

Prototype PIK-19 Muhinu two-seat glider-towing aircraft (160 hp Lycoming O-320 engine)

PIK-19 MUHINU

A prototype of this side-by-side two-seat training and glider-towing aircraft was flown for the first time on 26 March 1972. It was designed by Tervamäki, Rantasalo, Tammi and Tervaskanto, starting in June 1969, and was built by the Aircraft Research Laboratory of the Helsinki University of Technology. Construction, which began on 1 March 1970, is largely of glassfibre-reinforced epoxy resin.

Despite extensive negotiations in 1972-73 it has not been found possible to place the PIK-19 in series production, and for this reason the intended second prototype will not be completed. Minor modifications, such as installation of horizontal tail surfaces of different materials, to withstand better the damage from stones thrown back by the propeller slipstream, were being made to the first aircraft in 1974, and Finnish certification was expected during the year.

TYPE: Two-seat glider-towing and training aircraft.

WINGS: Cantilever low-wing monoplane. Wing section NACA 63_2415. Dihedral 5°. Incidence 4°. No sweepback. One-piece glassfibre roving main spar and rear spar, passing through fuselage. Wing shell, trailing-edge flaps (which function also as airbrakes) and ailerons are all sandwich-type structures of glassfibre-reinforced epoxy resin with a honeycomb plastics core. No tabs.

FUSELAGE: Glassfibre/honeycomb sandwich structure, similar to wings.

TAIL UNIT: Cantilever shell-type structure, of similar construction to wings. Fin integral with fuselage. Fixed-incidence tailplane. Manually-operated trim tab in starboard elevator; ground-adjustable tab in rudder.

LANDING GEAR: Non-retractable tricycle type. Main-wheel legs of glassfibre roving/epoxy resin. Nosewheel is carried on oleo-pneumatic shock strut and is steerable with rudder. Main wheels size 6·00-6, tyre pressure 24 lb/sq in (1·7 kg/cm²), nosewheel size 5·00-5, tyre pressure 20 lb/sq in (1·4 kg/cm²). Goodyear hydraulic disc brakes. Streamline glassfibre/epoxy fairings on all three wheels.

POWER PLANT: One 160 hp Lycoming O-320-B2BC four-cylinder horizontally-opposed air-cooled engine, driving a McCauley two-blade fixed-pitch metal propeller, type 1A-175/GM-8241 for towing, type 1C-172/MGM-7657 for other duties. One integral fuel tank in each wing, total capacity 33 Imp gallons (150 litres). Refuelling point on top of wing. Oil capacity 1·76 Imp gallons (8 litres). Adjustable cowl flap system on engine cowling to prevent excessive engine temperature changes when on towing duties.

ACCOMMODATION: Two glassfibre seats side by side under large rearward-sliding transparent canopy. Baggage space aft of seats. Dual controls, and cockpit heating and ventilation, standard.

SYSTEMS: Electrical system only, incorporating 12V 60A alternator, engine starter and 35Ah battery.

ELECTRONICS AND EQUIPMENT: PIK-R-2 10-channel VHF radio and glider towing hook.

DIMENSIONS, EXTERNAL:
  Wing span 32 ft 9¾ in (10·00 m)
  Wing chord (constant) 4 ft 7 in (1·40 m)
  Wing aspect ratio 7·14
  Length overall 22 ft 7¾ in (6·90 m)
  Height overall 8 ft 6¼ in (2·60 m)
  Tailplane span 11 ft 0 in (3·35 m)
  Wheel track 7 ft 0½ in (2·15 m)
  Wheelbase 4 ft 9¾ in (1·47 m)
  Propeller ground clearance 11¾ in (30 cm)
DIMENSIONS, INTERNAL:
  Cockpit: Max length 6 ft 1¼ in (1·86 m)
    Max width 4 ft 0½ in (1·23 m)
    Max height 3 ft 11¼ in (1·20 m)
    Baggage space 5·3 cu ft (0·15 m³)
AREAS:
  Wings, gross 150·7 sq ft (14·00 m²)
  Ailerons (total) 14·0 sq ft (1·30 m²)
  Trailing-edge flaps (total) 12·92 sq ft (1·20 m²)
  Fin 6·78 sq ft (0·63 m²)
  Rudder, incl tab 7·21 sq ft (0·67 m²)
  Tailplane 14·64 sq ft (1·36 m²)
  Elevators, incl tab 15·5 sq ft (1·44 m²)
WEIGHTS AND LOADINGS:
  Weight empty, equipped 1,234 lb (560 kg)
  Max T-O and landing weight 1,851 lb (840 kg)
  Max wing loading 12·3 lb/sq ft (60·0 kg/m²)
  Max power loading 11·57 lb/hp (5·25 kg/hp)
PERFORMANCE (S/L, at max T-O weight):
  Max never-exceed speed
    167 knots (192 mph; 310 km/h)
  Max level speed
    129 knots (149 mph; 240 km/h)
  Max cruising speed (75% power)
    119 knots (137 mph; 220 km/h)
  Stalling speed, flaps up
    49·5 knots (57 mph; 91 km/h)
  Stalling speed, flaps down
    45 knots (52 mph; 83 km/h)
  Max rate of climb 1,378 ft (420 m)/min
  Rate of climb (75% power):
    with single-seat sailplane 656 ft (200 m)/min
    with two-seat sailplane 492 ft (150 m)/min
  T-O run 492 ft (150 m)
  T-O to 50 ft (15 m) 787 ft (240 m)
  Landing from 50 ft (15 m) 722 ft (220 m)
  Landing run 328 ft (100 m)
  Range with max fuel (65% power, no reserve)
    512 nm (590 miles; 950 km)

TERVAMÄKI

JUKKA TERVAMÄKI

ADDRESS:

Aidasmäentie 16-20E, 00650 Helsinki 65

Mr Tervamäki, who is currently Technical Manager of Wihuri-Yhtymä Oy, Lentohuolto, Finland's largest private aviation company, first became interested in autogyros in 1956. In 1959 he worked briefly for the Bensen Aircraft Corporation in the USA. He obtained a Diploma in Aeronautical Engineering at the Helsinki Institute of Technology in 1963, and later served in the helicopter section of the Finnish Air Force. He was for two years project manager and chief designer of the PIK-19 Muhinu glider-towing aircraft (which see).

Early autogyros designed by Mr Tervamäki were completed in 1958 (JT-1) and 1965 (JT-2). More recent designs are the Tervamäki-Eerola ATE-3 and Tervamäki JT-5, of which descriptions follow:

TERVAMÄKI-EEROLA ATE-3

Design of this single-seat light autogyro was begun in May 1966 by Mr Tervamäki, assisted by Mr Eerola, a former helicopter mechanic with the Finnish Air Force. Construction of a prototype began in the following September, and this aircraft (OH-XYV) flew for the first time on 11 May 1968. In November 1969 the original horizontal tail surfaces were deleted from the design, and a redesigned vertical tail was fitted. The description applies to the aircraft in this form.

The ATE-3 is available for amateur construction, and several examples were under construction in Finland in early 1974. In addition, glassfibre propellers and sets of rotor blades of the type fitted to the ATE-3 are in limited production for amateur constructors.

TYPE: Single-seat light autogyro.

ROTOR SYSTEM: Two-blade semi-rigid rotor of glassfibre-reinforced polyester or epoxy resins, with PVC or polyurethane plastics foam core. Both internally and externally balanced blades have been produced and flown. Blades, of constant chord and NACA 8-H-12 section, are each attached to hub by means of two 0·4 in (10 mm) bolts. Rotor mast comprises two co-axial, pre-loaded tubes, of which the inner tube takes the tensile loads and the outer tube the bending loads. In the event of a fatigue failure of the outer tube, the inner one would absorb both loads. Rotor head of offset-gimbal type, with provision to install centrifugal teeter stops. Tachometer transmitter is operated by a light-sensitive resistor in the rotor head, under the rotating blade roots. Rotor rpm scale is 0-600, and the same scale is used to indicate engine rpm between 0 and 6,000, the meter receiving signals from the magneto spark impulses. There is a switch on the instrument panel to select rpm reading from either rotor or engine. No rotor brake fitted.

ROTOR DRIVE: Rotor pre-rotation system consists of a Vee-belt, clutch, flexible shaft, microplanetary gearbox, chain drive and free-wheel unit. Overall reduction ratio 10. A rotor spin-up of 220-250 rpm can be achieved.

FUSELAGE: Basic structure of welded steel tubing; glassfibre cockpit, windscreen, pilot's seat and instrument panel from a Finnish Utu Standard Class sailplane.

TAIL UNIT: Fin and rudder only, of glassfibre-reinforced plastics with PVC foam ribs, attached to floor of fuselage by a single steel tube.

LANDING GEAR: Non-retractable tricycle type. Compression steel springs and oleo shock-absorbers in the main gear, compression rubber shock-absorption in nose gear. Drum brakes on main wheels; provision for additional drum brake on nosewheel. All tyres size 260 × 85. Nosewheel steering by rudder pedals.

POWER PLANT: One 75 hp Volkswagen engine, modified from a standard 1·6 litre motor car engine. Modifications include: Okrasa (West Germany) racing crankshaft, having counter-weights and 2·5 mm longer throw than standard VW and giving a final displacement of 1·7 litres; Okrasa racing cylinder heads; oversize sodium-cooled valves; thrust roller bearing behind the propeller hub; sight glass for oil level; Solex carburettors and Scintilla Vertex magneto. Two-blade pusher propeller, of glassfibre-reinforced plastics. Glassfibre fuel tank aft of cockpit, capacity 10·6 Imp gallons (48 litres).

ACCOMMODATION: Single seat in open cockpit.

EQUIPMENT: Standard equipment includes altimeter, ASI, rate of climb indicator, magnetic compass, clock, drift indicator, engine and rotor rpm indicator, cylinder head temperature gauge, combined oil pressure and temperature gauge, throttle, pre-rotation lever, brake and parking brake levers. Radio optional.

DIMENSIONS, EXTERNAL:

Rotor diameter	22 ft 11½ in (7·00 m)
Rotor blade chord (constant, each)	7·1 in (18 cm)
Length of fuselage	10 ft 6 in (3·20 m)
Height overall	6 ft 2¾ in (1·90 m)
Wheel track	5 ft 7 in (1·70 m)
Propeller diameter	3 ft 11¼ in (1·20 m)

AREAS:

Rotor blades (each)	6·78 sq ft (0·63 m²)
Rotor disc	414·4 sq ft (38·50 m²)

WEIGHTS AND LOADINGS:

Weight empty, equipped	330 lb (150 kg)
Max T-O weight	573 lb (260 kg)
Max disc loading	1·40 lb/sq ft (6·80 kg/m²)
Max power loading	7·72 lb/hp (3·50 kg/hp)

PERFORMANCE (at max T-O weight):

Max never-exceed speed	86 knots (99 mph; 160 km/h)
Max level speed at S/L	75·6 knots (87 mph; 140 km/h)
Max cruising speed at S/L	59 knots (68 mph; 110 km/h)
Econ cruising speed	54 knots (62 mph; 100 km/h)
Max rate of climb at S/L	590 ft (180 m)/min
T-O run	165 ft (50 m)
T-O to 50 ft (15 m)	495 ft (150 m)
Landing from 50 ft (15 m)	165 ft (50 m)
Landing run	16 ft (5 m)
Range with max fuel, no reserves	160 nm (185 miles; 300 km)

TERVAMÄKI JT-5

The JT-5 is a development of the ATE-3 design, the major visible differences being the use of a triple tail assembly, to improve static and dynamic stability; a fully-enclosed cockpit; improved, low-drag fuselage contours; and the extensive use of plastics materials in the basic structure and main components. Other features include an upward-directed exhaust, to reduce engine noise, and a simplified carburettor installation and heating system of Tervamäki design.

Design, development and construction of the JT-5 prototype occupied some 2,000 man-hours, spread over a three-year period. Funds to assist development were provided by the Finnish Technical Foundation, and rotor head components were built in the Wihuri-Yhtymä workshops at Lentohuolto.

The prototype JT-5 (OH-XYS) was flown for the first time on 7 January 1973. It has since been sold, together with all production rights, tools and moulds, to Sr Vittorio Magni of Italy (which see), and production of rotor blades and other parts was due to begin in 1974. In addition, Sr Magni has rights for the sale of drawings of the JT-5 to amateur constructors in French, Italian and Spanish-speaking countries. For those in other countries, drawings (with metric dimensions and English annotations) are available directly from Mr Tervamäki.

With minor modifications, glassfibre rotor blades of the type fitted to the JT-5 can be installed on other autogyros and rotor head designs, and several sets are already flying on aircraft built in Scandinavia.

TYPE: Single-seat light autogyro.

ROTOR SYSTEM: Two-blade semi-rigid rotor of glassfibre-reinforced epoxy resin, with polyurethane plastics foam core. Blades, of constant chord and NACA 8-H-12 section, are each attached to hub by means of two 0·4 in (10 mm) bolts. A 9 ft 10 in (3·0 m) long lead bar in each blade leading-edge forms the chordwise balance weight. Rotor mast of streamlined SAE 4130 steel tubing. Rotor tachometer is a German VDO automotive speed indicator, driven mechanically via a flexible shaft from the rotor head. Rotor head is of a compact offset-gimbal type with centrifugal teeter stops and rotor brake installed. There are two spiral springs for trim adjustment, which is effected via the control stick twist-grip handle. Normal rotor rpm is 400, maximum 600. Several blade sets have been tested up to 16-20 tons static tensile strength, the maximum centrifugal load being about 5 tons at 600 rpm in a 3g manoeuvre. Designed for the JT-5, but not yet fitted, is a modified Cierva-type inclined drag hinge which would allow the blades to move to zero pitch when pre-rotation torque is applied, permitting

Tervamäki-Eerola ATE-3 light autogyro

Tervamäki JT-5 single-seat autogyro (75 hp Limbach modified Volkswagen engine)

an increase of 100 rpm in pre-spin speed and, consequently, a shorter take-off.

Rotor Drive: Rotor pre-rotation system consists of a Vee-belt, clutch, 90° gearbox, sliding universal shaft and inertia-operated Bendix drive. Overall reduction ratio 8. Rotor spin-up of 300 rpm can be achieved. Pre-rotation lever is pivoted to the throttle lever for simultaneous use by the pilot's left hand.

Fuselage: Basic structure of welded 4130 steel tubing with a glassfibre/HFB honeycomb sandwich cockpit. All internal cockpit structures of glassfibre-reinforced epoxy resin. One-piece aluminium engine cowling.

Tail Unit: Central main fin and rudder, of glassfibre-reinforced epoxy resin, with rigid PVC-foam ribs and Courtauld carbon-fibre stiffeners. Horizontal tail and auxiliary end-plate fins of glassfibre sandwich construction with honeycomb core. Tail assembly attached to fuselage by a single streamlined steel tube. Small tailwheel beneath base of fin.

Landing Gear: Non-retractable tricycle type. Main gear legs consist of 1·6 × 1·6 in (4 × 4 cm) glassfibre-reinforced epoxy resin springs, encased in streamlined fairings of the same material. Cables inside these fairings to main gear drum brakes. Main-wheel tyres size 300 × 100. Compression rubber shock-absorption in nose gear. Nosewheel tyre size 260 × 80. Nosewheel steerable by rudder pedals.

Power Plant: One 75 hp (1·7 litre) Volkswagen engine, converted for autogyro use by Limbach Motorenbau. Floatless and diaphragmless Solex 35 RH carburettor. Scintilla Vertex magneto, VW fuel pump and tachometer drive. No oil cooler, generator or electric starter. Two-blade pusher propeller, of glassfibre-reinforced epoxy. Glassfibre fuel tank, integrally built into fuselage aft of pilot's seat, capacity 11 Imp gallons (50 litres).

Accommodation: Single seat under sideways-opening Plexiglas canopy. For ease of maintenance and pre-flight checks the instrument panel cover and pilot's seat back (the latter also forming a firewall to the engine compartment) open together with the canopy.

Equipment: Standard equipment includes ASI, altimeter, rate of climb indicator, magnetic compass, drift indicator, manifold pressure indicator, rotor and engine rpm indicators, cylinder head temperature gauge, combined oil pressure and temperature gauge, fuel quantity indicator. Controls include throttle, pre-rotation lever, rotor brake, wheel brake and parking brake, cockpit ventilation adjustment, carburettor heat and primer pump. A 6-channel radio is installed.

Dimensions, external:
- Rotor diameter: 22 ft 11½ in (7·00 m)
- Rotor blade chord (constant, each): 7·1 in (18 cm)
- Length of fuselage: 11 ft 5¾ in (3·50 m)
- Height overall: 6 ft 6¾ in (2·00 m)
- Wheel track: 5 ft 7 in (1·70 m)
- Propeller diameter: 3 ft 11¼ in (1·20 m)

Areas:
- Rotor blades (each): 6·78 sq ft (0·63 m²)
- Rotor disc: 414·4 sq ft (38·50 m²)

Weights and Loadings:
- Weight empty, equipped: 368 lb (167 kg)
- Max T-O weight: 639 lb (290 kg)
- Max disc loading: 1·54 lb/sq ft (7·5 kg/m²)
- Max power loading: 8·60 lb/hp (3·9 kg/hp)

Performance (at max T-O weight):
- Max never-exceed speed: 97 knots (111·5 mph; 180 km/h)
- Max level speed at S/L: 92 knots (106 mph; 170 km/h)
- Max cruising speed at S/L: 81 knots (93 mph; 150 km/h)
- Econ cruising speed: 70 knots (81 mph; 130 km/h)
- Min level speed: 19 knots (22 mph; 35 km/h)
- Max rate of climb at S/L: 590 ft (180 m)/min
- Service ceiling: 13,125 ft (4,000 m)
- T-O run: 230 ft (70 m)
- T-O to 50 ft (15 m): 394 ft (120 m)
- Landing from 50 ft (15 m): 165 ft (50 m)
- Landing run: 16 ft (5 m)
- Range with max fuel, no reserves: 189 nm (217 miles; 350 km)

VALMET

VALMET OY TAMPERE WORKS

Office and Works:
Box 387, 33101 Tampere 10
Telephone: 650622 Exchange
Telex: Tampere 22-112 Valle SF

The Valmet Oy Tampere Works is affiliated to Valmet Oy, a State-owned company consisting of several metal-working factories. The Tampere Works is a direct continuation of the former State Aircraft Factory and belongs to the factory group, Valmet Oy Tampere, which consists of the Tampere Works as the central unit and of the Instrument Works at Tampere and the Kuorevesi Works as subordinate units.

Present aviation activities are confined mainly to the Kuorevesi Works, which undertakes production of aircraft parts and components, major repairs, overhauls and test flying.

In April 1970 it was announced that Valmet Oy would be responsible for assembly of the 12 Saab 35XS Drakens ordered by Finland, the first of which (DK-201) was handed over to the Finnish Air Force on 25 April 1974.

Valmet Oy is also developing a new primary trainer, the Leko-70, for the Finnish Air Force.

On 15 September 1970, Valmet Oy and the Ministry of Commerce and Industry entered into an agreement whereby an aeronautical research and development group was established at the Tampere Works.

The Valmet Linnavuori Works at Siuro is directly subordinate to the Head Office of Valmet Oy, Helsinki, and in the aviation field is concerned primarily with aero-engine repairs and overhauls.

VALMET LEKO-70

The Leko-70 is a two/three-seat all-metal light aircraft, a prototype of which was ordered by the Finnish Air Force on 23 March 1973. A first flight date of 23 September 1974 has been set for this aircraft, and a second prototype will be built for structural testing.

The Leko-70 is designed for aerobatic flying as a two-seater; for Normal or Utility category flying it will seat two or three persons, depending upon the amount of baggage carried.

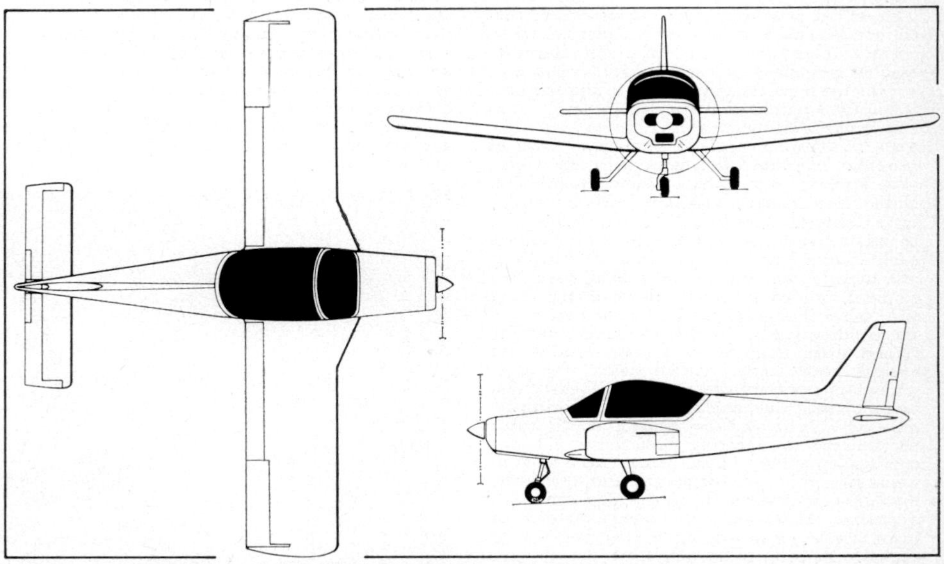

Valmet Leko-70 two/three-seat training and touring aircraft. The name is a military abbreviation of the word "Lentokone", meaning "aeroplane" (*Roy J. Grainge*)

Type: Two/three-seat training and touring light aircraft.

Wings: Cantilever low-wing monoplane. Wing section NACA 63_2A615 (modified). Dihedral 6° from roots. Constant-chord aluminium alloy wings. Leading-edges swept forward at roots. Slotted flaps and slotted ailerons, of aluminium alloy, on trailing-edge. No tabs.

Fuselage: Conventional aluminium alloy semi-monocoque structure.

Tail Unit: Cantilever aluminium alloy structure, with slight sweepback on vertical surfaces. Shallow dorsal fairing from rear of canopy to base of fin. Balanced elevators and rudder. Combined trim and balance tab in elevators; trim tab in rudder.

Landing Gear: Non-retractable tricycle type. Cantilever sprung main legs. Telescopic nose-wheel strut. Disc brakes.

Power Plant: One 200 hp Lycoming IO-360-A1B6 four-cylinder horizontally-opposed air-cooled engine, driving a two-blade constant-speed propeller. Two fuel tanks in wings, total normal capacity 33 Imp gallons (150 litres), max capacity 41·8 Imp gallons (190 litres).

Accommodation: Side-by-side seats for instructor and pupil, in trainer version, under one-piece rearward-sliding fully-transparent canopy. Third seat to rear, which can be removed to make room for additional baggage. Cabin heated and ventilated, but not pressurised.

System: 28V DC electrical system.

Electronics and Equipment: Two VHF, one ADF and VOR/ILS standard.

Dimensions, external:
- Wing span: 30 ft 6¼ in (9·30 m)
- Wing chord (constant): 5 ft 0¼ in (1·53 m)
- Wing aspect ratio: 6
- Length overall: 23 ft 11½ in (7·30 m)
- Tailplane span: 11 ft 9¾ in (3·60 m)
- Wheel track: 7 ft 6½ in (2·30 m)
- Wheelbase: 5 ft 3 in (1·60 m)

Areas:
- Wings, gross: 150·70 sq ft (14·00 m²)
- Ailerons (total): 15·07 sq ft (1·40 m²)
- Trailing-edge flaps (total): 23·68 sq ft (2·20 m²)
- Fin: 9·69 sq ft (0·90 m²)
- Rudder, incl tab: 6·46 sq ft (0·60 m²)
- Tailplane: 20·45 sq ft (1·90 m²)
- Elevators, incl tabs: 10·76 sq ft (1·00 m²)

Weights:
- Weight empty, equipped, without fuel: 1,521 lb (690 kg)
- Max T-O weight (Normal category): 2,535 lb (1,150 kg)

Performance (estimated):
- Max level speed at S/L: 129·5 knots (149 mph; 240 km/h)
- Stalling speed, flaps up: 57 knots (66 mph; 105 km/h)
- Max rate of climb at S/L: 1,180 ft (360 m)/min

FRANCE

AA

ALLIANCE AVIATION

Head Office:
1 rue de Choiseul, Paris 2e
Telephone: 742 65-96
Telex: 68232 F

Managing Director:
Michel Theoval

Alliance Aviation is the representative for France of Campbell Aircraft Ltd of the UK. It is setting up a training school for pilots of light gyroplanes, near Paris, equipped with the Campbell-Bensen Gyro-Glider and the Campbell Cricket gyroplane.

It will introduce the Campbell Cougar gyroplane into France as soon as British certification of this aircraft has been obtained, seeking French certification and, possibly, undertaking licence manufacture of the Cougar in France.

Alliance Aviation is promoting military interest in light gyroplanes as low-cost light observation, anti-tank and casualty evacuation aircraft.

AÉROSPATIALE

SOCIÉTÉ NATIONALE INDUSTRIELLE AÉROSPATIALE

Head Office:
37 boulevard de Montmorency, 75781 Paris-cédex 16
Telephone: 224-84-00
Telex: AISPA 62059F

SUPERVISORY COUNCIL

Chairman:
Général Michel Fourquet (French Air Force, ret'd)

Members:
Henri Azam, Jean Dromer, Paul Bienfait, Guy Carraz, Jean Saint-Geours, Georges Girard, Bertrand Larrera de Morel, Bernard Lathière, Jean Martre, Jacques Moreau

EXECUTIVE COUNCIL
PRESIDENT:
Charles Cristofini
MEMBERS:
André Gintrand (responsible for economic and financial affairs of the entire Group)
Ingénieur-Général Jean Soissons (responsible for Aircraft Division)
Ingénieur-Général Roger Chevalier (responsible for Tactical Missiles Division and Ballistic & Space Systems Division)
Jean Mascard (responsible for Helicopter Division and supervision of the Group's subsidiaries)

CONSULTANTS TO THE EXECUTIVE COUNCIL:
Général Jean Crépin (French Army, ret'd—Military Affairs)
Pierre Marion (Commercial Affairs)
ASSISTANTS TO THE PRESIDENT:
Michel Allier (Technical Secretariat of Executive Council)
Georges Delval (Central Commercial Service, in absence of Commercial Consultant)
DIRECTORS OF CENTRAL SERVICES:
Marc Robert (Industrial Relations and Legal Affairs)
Jean Coupain (Production)
Pierre Marion (Commercial Affairs)
Jean Calmel (Public Relations)
Michel Euvrard (Financial Affairs)
René Dor (Economic Affairs)
Jacques Dupin (Long-range Planning)
Serge Bisone (General Affairs)
GENERAL DELEGATES:
Pierre Marion (North, Central and South America)
André Thoulouze (UK and Europe)
Raymond Brohon (Africa)
C. A. Massa (Middle East)
Jean-Gabriel Demerliac (Far East)

AIRCRAFT DIVISION
Pierre Gautier (Concorde Programme Management)
Henri de Charnace (Airbus Programme Management)
Maurice Avramito (Corvette Programme Management)
Paul Duvochel (Management of other Aircraft Programmes)
Pierre Lecomte (Technical Management)
René Puydebois (Production Management)
Appointment awaited (Commercial Management; Acting Manager: Georges Barthas)
Georges Roche (Administrative and Financial Management)
André Turcat (Flight Test Management)
Edouard Debout (Quality Control Management)
WORKS AND FACILITIES:
Toulouse. MANAGEMENT: Bernard Dufour
Nantes. MANAGEMENT: Gilbert Colas
Saint-Nazaire. MANAGEMENT: René Denolly
Méaulte. MANAGEMENT: Jean Renon
Suresnes. MANAGEMENT: Séverin Golbert

HELICOPTER DIVISION
DIVISION MANAGEMENT:
François Legrand
WORKS AND FACILITIES:
Marignane. MANAGEMENT: Fernand Carayon
La Courneuve. MANAGEMENT: Lucien Fournier

TACTICAL MISSILES DIVISION
DIVISION MANAGEMENT:
Emile Stauff
WORKS AND FACILITIES:
Châtillon. MANAGEMENT: Pierre Fleuriel
Bourges-Châteauroux. MANAGEMENT: Georges Barroy

BALLISTIC AND SPACE SYSTEMS DIVISION
DIVISION MANAGEMENT:
Pierre Usunier
ASSISTANT MANAGER:
Louis Marnay
WORKS AND FACILITIES:
Aquitaine. MANAGEMENT: Robert Laurentjoye
Cannes. MANAGEMENT: Louis Marnay
Les Mureaux. MANAGEMENT: Georges Epaillard

SUBSIDIARIES
Société Girondine d'Entretien et de Réparation de Matériel Aéronautique (SOGERMA)
WORKS: Bordeaux-Mérignac Airport
PRESIDENT AND MANAGING DIRECTOR:
R. Brohon
Société de Construction d'Avions de Tourisme et d'Affaires (SOCATA)
WORKS: Tarbes-Ossun Airport
PRESIDENT AND MANAGING DIRECTOR:
H. Ziegler
Société d'Exploitation et de Constructions Aéronautiques (SECA)
WORKS: Le Bourget Airport, Paris
PRESIDENT AND MANAGING DIRECTOR:
R. Brohon
Saint-Chamond-Granat
WORKS: Courbevoie and St-Ouen-l'Aumône
PRESIDENT: A. Moynet
Electronique Aérospatiale (EAS)
WORKS: Le Bourget Airport, Paris
PRESIDENT AND MANAGING DIRECTOR:
B. de Royer
Société Charentaise d'Equipements Aéronautiques (SOCEA)
WORKS: Rochefort and Suresnes
PRESIDENT AND MANAGING DIRECTOR:
J. Goudant
European Aerospace Corporation (USA)
Vought Helicopter Corporation (USA)

The Société Nationale Industrielle Aérospatiale was formed on 1 January 1970, by decision of the French government, as a result of the merger of the former Sud-Aviation, Nord-Aviation and SEREB companies. It is a limited company and, since 1 January 1974, has been managed by an Executive Council and a Supervisory Council.

Aérospatiale is the biggest aerospace company in the Common Market countries on the Continent of Europe, with a registered capital of 427,250,000 francs, facilities covering a total area of 84,195,000 sq ft (7,822,000 m²), and a staff (including subsidiary companies) of about 41,600 persons at the beginning of 1974.

In the aircraft field, major products include the Concorde supersonic transport, developed in co-operation with BAC; the short-to-medium-range large-capacity subsonic A-300 European Airbus, in co-operation with Deutsche Airbus GmbH, Hawker Siddeley Aviation, VFW-Fokker and CASA; the N 262/Fregate twin-turboprop transport and the SN 601 Corvette twin-turbofan business and third-level transport aircraft. Production of the twin-engined Caravelle series has been completed.

Aérospatiale produces a range of light piston-engined aircraft through its subsidiary, Socata (which see).

Helicopter activities, concentrated at Marignane, include continued production of the Alouette series, and in particular the SA 315 Lama, the twin-turbine SA 330 Puma, the three-turboshaft Super Frelon and the SA 341 Gazelle light helicopter, designed to meet Anglo-French requirements; and development of the new ten-seat SA 360. Agreements have been concluded with Westland in the UK for the joint development and production of the Puma and Gazelle, and for the Westland-designed Lynx, these three types having been chosen to equip the French and British armed forces. Commercial versions of these helicopters are being produced or developed.

Tactical missiles and pilotless aircraft produced by Aérospatiale include the first-generation surface-to-surface and air-to-surface Entac, SS.11, SS.12M, AS.12, AS.20 and AS.30; target missiles; RPVs; the second-generation Harpon, Milan, Hot, Roland and Exocet anti-tank, surface-to-air and ship-to-ship missiles; and the Pluton nuclear-warhead surface-to-surface missile.

Aérospatiale also produces the SSBS (surface-to-surface) and MSBS (submarine-launched) strategic ballistic missiles; and a range of research rockets. It has made major contributions to the development and production of the Diamant, Europa II and L3S launch vehicles, and the Peole, D2-A, Eole, Symphonie, Cos-B, Meteosat, Aerosat and ECSS satellites; and is participating in the post-Apollo Spacelab programme.

AÉROSPATIALE/BAC CONCORDE

Full details of the Concorde programme can be found in the International section of this edition.

AÉROSPATIALE SE 210 CARAVELLE 12

The Caravelle twin-engined short-to-medium-range airliner was designed by the former SNCA du Sud-Est (later Sud-Aviation), and was ordered in prototype form by the Sécrétariat d'Etat à l'Air in January 1953. The first of two prototypes flew for the first time on 27 May 1955.

Production of Caravelles was undertaken by a large group of factories, with final assembly at Toulouse. It has now been completed, the final contract having covered four Caravelle 12s for the French air postal service. Altogether, 280 Caravelles were built.

Details of all versions of the Caravelle can be found in earlier editions of *Jane's*, including a full description of the Caravelle 12 in the 1972-73 issue. The following abbreviated entry applies to this final version:

TYPE: Twin-turbofan medium-range airliner.

POWER PLANT: Two Pratt & Whitney JT8D-9 turbofan engines, each rated at 14,500 lb (6,577 kg) st, mounted in nacelles on each side of the rear fuselage just ahead of tail unit. Four integral fuel tanks in wings, with total capacity of 4,180 Imp gallons (19,000 litres). Provision for additional centre tank, increasing total capacity to 4,840 Imp gallons (22,000 litres).

ACCOMMODATION: Crew compartment for two or three persons. Normally, five-abreast seating for up to 128 passengers, arranged as 12 rows at front and 9 rows in rear of cabin with seats at 32 in (81 cm) pitch; three rows in centre, in line with emergency exits; and two rows at extreme rear. An alternative tourist layout seating 118 passengers at 34 in (86 cm) pitch was available. A mixed-class layout provided for 88 tourist class passengers at the latter seat pitch and 16 first class passengers (four-abreast) at 38 in (96 cm) pitch. Max seating capacity is for 139 passengers. Entire accommodation pressurised. Main access to cabin through door under rear fuselage with hydraulically-operated integral steps. Steps serve as a tail support when lowered. Further door on port side at front of cabin. Two toilets, coat rooms and light baggage racks aft of cabin. Two galleys, one forward and one aft of cabin.

Aérospatiale SE 210 Caravelle 12 (two Pratt & Whitney JT8D-9 turbofan engines) in service with Air Inter

Aérospatiale Frégate of the Directorate of Civil Aviation, East African Community, equipped for radio aids calibration

DIMENSIONS, EXTERNAL:
Wing span 112 ft 6 in (34·30 m)
Wing aspect ratio 8·02
Length overall 118 ft 10½ in (36·24 m)
Fuselage: Max diameter 10 ft 6 in (3·20 m)
Height overall 29 ft 7 in (9·01 m)
Tailplane span 39 ft 4 in (12·00 m)
Wheel track (c/l of shock-struts) 17 ft 0 in (5·21 m)
Wheelbase 48 ft 6½ in (14·80 m)
Passenger door (fwd, port):
Height 5 ft 6½ in (1·69 m)
Width 3 ft 0 in (0·91 m)
Height to sill 7 ft 8½ in (2·35 m)
Crew door (fwd, stbd):
Height 4 ft 0 in (1·22 m)
Width 2 ft 0 in (0·61 m)
Cargo compartment doors (underfloor, stbd):
Height 3 ft 0 in (0·91 m)
Width 2 ft 6 in (0·76 m)

DIMENSIONS, INTERNAL:
Cabin, excluding flight deck:
Length:
incl toilet and rear compartments 86 ft 7 in (26·40 m)
excl toilet and rear compartments 72 ft 11 in (22·24 m)
Width at floor 8 ft 10 in (2·69 m)
Width at armrest 9 ft 9½ in (3·00 m)
Max height 6 ft 7 in (2·00 m)
Floor area 767 sq ft (71·28 m²)
Volume 5,015 cu ft (142 m³)
Freight holds (main cabin) 201 cu ft (5·70 m³)
Freight holds (underfloor):
rear 176 cu ft (5·00 m³)
fwd 406 cu ft (11·50 m³)

WEIGHTS AND LOADINGS:
Manufacturer's weight empty 65,050 lb (29,500 kg)
Basic operating weight 70,100 lb (31,800 kg)
Max payload 29,100 lb (13,200 kg)
Max T-O weight 127,870 lb (58,000 kg)
Max landing weight 109,130 lb (49,500 kg)
Max zero-fuel weight 99,200 lb (45,000 kg)
Max wing loading 81·0 lb/sq ft (395 kg/m²)
Max power loading 4·41 lb/lb st (4·41 kg/kg st)

PERFORMANCE (at AUW of 127,870 lb; 58,000 kg, except where indicated otherwise):
Max cruising speed at 25,000 ft (7,620 m) at AUW of 110,230 lb (50,000 kg) 445 knots (512 mph; 825 km/h)
Min ground turning radius 97 ft 1½ in (29·60 m)
Runway LCN at max weight:
Rigid pavement 42
Flexible pavement 43
T-O balanced field length:
ISA at S/L 8,070 ft (2,460 m)
ISA + 15°C 8,430 ft (2,570 m)
Landing distance at max landing weight 4,985 ft (1,520 m)
Range with max fuel and 24,780 lb (11,240 kg) payload:
No reserves 2,180 nm (2,510 miles; 4,040 km)
6,600 lb (3,000 kg) reserves 1,710 nm (1,970 miles; 3,170 km)
Range with 29,100 lb (13,200 kg) max payload:
No reserves 1,870 nm (2,150 miles; 3,465 km)
6,600 lb (3,000 kg) reserves 1,370 nm (1,580 miles; 2,540 km)

OPERATIONAL NOISE CHARACTERISTICS:
T-O noise level at 3·5 nm (4 miles; 6·5 km) from start of T-O roll 94 EPNdB
Approach noise level at 1·0 nm (1·15 miles; 1·85 km) from landing threshold on 3° glide-slope 104 EPNdB
Sideline noise level at 0·25 nm (0·29 miles; 0·46 km) from runway c/l 102 EPNdB

AÉROSPATIALE N 262 and FRÉGATE

Design of the N 262 began in the Spring of 1961, and the prototype (F-WKVR) flew for the first time on 24 December 1962. It was followed by three pre-production aircraft, which were built at Châtillon-sous-Bagneux and assembled at Melun-Villaroche flight test centre. Final assembly of production models is undertaken at Bourges.

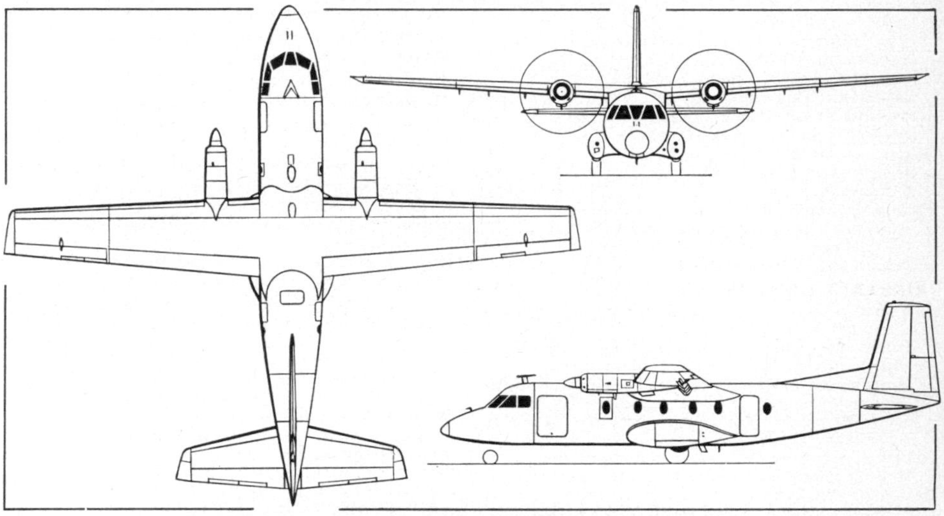

Aérospatiale Frégate twin-turboprop pressurised light transport *(Pilot Press)*

In 1969 two new versions were announced, initially designated Series C (civil) and D (military) but subsequently named Frégate. The following versions have, therefore, been produced:

N 262 Series A. Standard early production version, with 1,080 ehp Bastan VIC turboprop engines. Received FAA Type Approval on 15 March 1965. First production Series A was airframe number 9 (F-WLHX), delivered to Lake Central Airlines (now Allegheny) on 17 August 1965. Preceded by Series B, as indicated below. Production continues.

N 262 Series B. Designation of first four production aircraft only, built for Air Inter. Same power plant as Series A. First Series B (F-BLHS, airframe number 4) flown for first time on 8 June 1964. Received SGAC certification on 16 July 1964. Entered service 24 July 1964.

Frégate (formerly N 262 Series C and D). Version for both civil and military use, with more powerful Bastan VII turboprop engines, having improved single-engine ceiling, cruising speed and T-O performance at "hot and high" airfields. New power plant dispenses with water-methanol system of Series A and B and has higher initial TBO. An N 262 (airframe number 36) began flying experimentally with Bastan VIIA engines in July 1968, and was also test-flown with new wingtips (see general arrangement drawing) which bestow improved low-speed handling. The Frégate was introduced on to the production line in 1970, alongside the Series A, from the 74th aircraft. Certification granted 24 December 1970.

Orders received for the N 262 and Frégate by the early Spring of 1974 were as listed below. This list gives the original purchasers of the aircraft; resales have led to a change of operator in some cases.

Series A	
Air Ceylon	1
Air Comores	2
Air Madagascar	1
Alisarda (Italy)	2
Allegheny Airlines (USA)*	12
CEV Brétigny (France)	3
Cimber Air (Denmark)	3
Ecole Nationale Supérieure de l'Aéronautique (France)	1
Europe Aéro Service	1
Filipinas Orient Airlines	3
French Air Force	6
French Navy	15
Interregionalflug (W Germany)	2
Linjeflyg (Sweden)	4
Luftfartsdirektoratet (Denmark)	1
Rousseau Aviation (France)	3
SFA (France)	8
Tunis Air	1
Series B	
Air Inter (Rousseau Aviation)	4
Frégate	
East African Community	1
Gabon government	3
SFA (France)	1
Upper Volta government	1
French Air Force	18

**Originally purchased by Lake Central before merger with Allegheny; four sold to BC Airlines (Canada).*

TYPE: Twin-engined light transport.

WINGS: Cantilever high-wing monoplane. Wing section NACA 23016 (modified) at root, NACA 23012 (modified) at tip. Dihedral 3° from root. Incidence 3°. No sweepback. All-metal two-spar fail-safe structure in conventional light alloys. Sealed all-metal ailerons. Balance tab in starboard aileron. Electrically-controlled hydraulically-actuated all-metal three-position flaps in inner and outer sections on each trailing-edge. Kléber-Colombes (Goodrich licence) pneumatic de-icing boots on outer leading-edges.

FUSELAGE: Semi-monocoque light alloy fail-safe structure, built up from 39 circular main and secondary frames, covered with skin panels arranged circumferentially in sets of four.

TAIL UNIT: Cantilever metal structure, built as separate unit and bolted to rear fuselage frame. Fixed-incidence tailplane. Control surfaces fabric-covered. One controllable tab and one balance tab in rudder and each elevator. Kléber-Colombes (Goodrich licence) pneumatic de-icing system on leading-edges.

LANDING GEAR: Retractable tricycle type, designed and manufactured by ERAM, with single wheel on each unit. Electro-hydraulic retraction, nosewheel forward, main wheels rearward into fairings on sides of fuselage. ERAM oleo-pneumatic nitrogen-filled shock-absorbers. Main wheels have Dunlop or Kléber-Colombes tyres size 12·50-16, pressure 59 lb/sq in (4 kg/cm²). Nosewheel has Dunlop or Kléber-Colombes Type 06 tyre, size 9·00-6, pressure 47 lb/sq in (3·3 kg/cm²). Goodyear hydraulic disc brakes, with anti-skid units. Self-centering nosewheel is fitted with shimmy damper and is steerable hydraulically.

POWER PLANT (Frégate): Two 1,145 ehp Turbomèca Bastan VII turboprop engines, each driving a Ratier Forest FH 206-1 four-blade constant-speed fully-feathering metal propeller. Six bag-type flexible fuel tanks between wing spars, forming two groups of three tanks with provision for cross-feed and having a total usable capacity of 440 Imp gallons (2,000 litres). Provision for two additional optional bag tanks in wing centre-section, each of 62·5 Imp gallons (285 litres) usable capacity, giving a max usable capacity of 565 Imp gallons (2,570 litres). Refuelling point above outer wing tank on each side. Pressure refuelling point at front of starboard side main landing gear fairing. No fuel dump system. Oil capacity 5 Imp gallons (23 litres). Electrical anti-icing of engine intakes, spinners and propellers, with additional anti-icing of intakes by engine bleed air.

ACCOMMODATION: Crew of two on flight deck, with central jump-seat at rear for a third crew member if carried. Standard airline version has seating for 26 passengers at 32 in (81 cm) pitch, maximum seating for 29 at 28 in (71 cm) pitch, in three-abreast rows, with two seats on starboard side of aisle and single seat on port side. Movable forward bulkhead, to cater for variable mixed cargo (in front)/passenger (at rear) layouts. Bulkhead can be located in two intermediate positions, to provide 20 or 14 seats at 32 in pitch in rear of cabin, with 342 cu ft (9·7 m^3) or 467 cu ft (13·2 m^3) of cargo space respectively in front part of cabin. Galley, toilet and (on 27-seat version) separate coat space at rear of cabin. For quick-change passenger/cargo operation, foldaway seats can be installed which, when folded, give an available width for cargo of 5 ft 6 in (1·68 m) throughout entire cabin length. Alternative layouts include a six-person executive suite forward with 10 passengers aft; ambulance version with accommodation for 12 stretchers and two medical attendants; or aerial survey version with wide range of cameras and survey equipment and fully-equipped darkroom. Army versions can be fitted out to carry 18 paratroops or 29 troops, or as 22-seat transports. Naval versions (Series A) are capable of being fitted out for target towing, artillery and missile observation, radar calibration or crew training duties. Standard transport versions have two-section passenger door at rear on port side, the lower half of which has built-in airstairs, and a large cargo door at front on the port side. Emergency exits at front of cabin on each side, at rear on starboard side, and on port side of flight deck. Standard baggage compartments between flight deck and cabin on each side; on 27-seat version these are smaller, but additional baggage space is provided at rear of cabin on starboard side. All accommodation is pressurised, soundproofed and air-conditioned. Windscreen has electrical anti-icing.

SYSTEMS: SEMCA air-conditioning system using bleed air from engine. Max pressure differential 4·20 lb/sq in (0·29 kg/cm^2). Auxiliary ventilation via ram-air inlet at front of port main landing gear fairing. Hydraulic system, operated by two engine-driven pumps at pressure of 3,000 lb/sq in (210 kg/cm^2), actuates landing gear, nosewheel steering, flaps, brakes and gust locks. Electrically-driven (27V DC) back-up pump and 1,450 lb/sq in (100 kg/cm^2) surge accumulator. Hand pump for emergency operation of flaps, landing gear and gust locks. Pneumatic system for de-icing only. Two 24/27V 40Ah nickel-cadmium batteries, in rear fuselage, and two 9kVA engine-driven starter/generators provide 28V DC electrical supply for engine starting, feathering pumps and rotary inverters. External 28V DC power receptacle. AC system includes two engine-driven 12kVA three-phase alternators providing 115/200V 400Hz power for engine anti-icing, windscreen heating and de-icing, and heating for galley. Two single-phase 750VA rotary inverters provide continuous 115V/400Hz AC supply for flight deck instruments. System also includes four 115/26V 400Hz auto-transformers. Optional APU, in port landing gear fairing, provides power for electrical services, engine starting and cabin air-conditioning.

ELECTRONICS AND EQUIPMENT: Standard equipment includes two Collins 618 M 1 VHF, two Collins 51 RV 1 VOR/ILS, Collins 51 Z 4 marker beacon receiver, Collins DF 203 ADF, Collins 331 A6A course indicator, SFIM A 213 flight recorder, Sperry C 14 gyro compass, two Allen RMI, one Bendix OMI, interphone and public address systems. Emergency equipment includes oxygen masks and cylinders, fire extinguishers, life rafts and radio set. Optional equipment includes HF radio, autopilot, second gyro compass, second ADF, weather radar, ATC transponder, radio altimeter and DME; and alternative choice of flight director/recorder, VHF, VOR/ILS, and marker beacon receiver.

DIMENSIONS, EXTERNAL:
Wing span:
N 262 — 71 ft 10 in (21·90 m)
Frégate — 74 ft 1$\frac{3}{4}$ in (22·60 m)
Wing chord at root — 10 ft 2 in (3·10 m)
Wing chord at tip — 5 ft 11 in (1·80 m)
Wing aspect ratio:
N 262 — 8·72
Frégate — 9·10
Length overall — 63 ft 3 in (19·28 m)
Fuselage: Max diameter — 8 ft 0$\frac{1}{2}$ in (2·45 m)
Tailplane span:
N 262 — 25 ft 9 in (7·84 m)
Frégate — 28 ft 10$\frac{1}{2}$ in (8·80 m)
Wheel track — 10 ft 3 in (3·13 m)
Wheelbase — 23 ft 9 in (7·23 m)
Propeller diameter — 10 ft 6 in (3·20 m)
Distance between propeller centres — 19 ft 4$\frac{3}{4}$ in (5·91 m)
Passenger door (rear, port):
Height — 5 ft 5$\frac{1}{4}$ in (1·66 m)
Width — 2 ft 3 in (0·68 m)
Height to sill — 3 ft 6$\frac{1}{2}$ in (1·08 m)
Cargo door (forward, port):
Height — 5 ft 0$\frac{1}{4}$ in (1·53 m)
Width — 4 ft 2$\frac{1}{2}$ in (1·28 m)
Height to sill — 3 ft 6$\frac{1}{2}$ in (1·08 m)
Emergency exit doors (fwd, port and stbd):
Height — 4 ft 6$\frac{1}{4}$ in (1·38 m)
Width — 1 ft 8 in (0·51 m)
Emergency exit door (aft, stbd):
Height — 3 ft 0$\frac{1}{4}$ in (0·92 m)
Width — 1 ft 8 in (0·51 m)

DIMENSIONS, INTERNAL:
Cabin, including baggage space and toilet:
Length — 34 ft 10 in (10·61 m)
Max width — 7 ft 1 in (2·15 m)
Width at floor — 5 ft 5$\frac{1}{4}$ in (1·66 m)
Max height — 5 ft 11 in (1·80 m)
Floor area — 183 sq ft (17·0 m^2)
Volume — 1,146 cu ft (32·5 m^3)
Baggage hold (port):
26 or 29 passengers — 67 cu ft (1·9 m^3)
Baggage hold (stbd):
26 or 29 passengers — 92 cu ft (2·6 m^3)

AREAS:
Wings, gross:
N 262 — 592 sq ft (55·0 m^2)
Frégate — 601 sq ft (55·79 m^2)
Ailerons (total) — 43·8 sq ft (4·07 m^2)
Trailing-edge flaps (total) — 96·6 sq ft (8·98 m^2)
Fin — 108·7 sq ft (10·1 m^2)
Rudder, incl tabs — 40·4 sq ft (3·75 m^2)
Tailplane:
N 262 — 169·0 sq ft (15·7 m^2)
Frégate — 193·7 sq ft (18·0 m^2)
Elevators, incl tabs — 48·8 sq ft (4·54 m^2)

WEIGHTS AND LOADINGS (A: N 262, B: Frégate):
Basic weight empty:
A — 13,236 lb (6,004 kg)
B — 13,668 lb (6,200 kg)
Manufacturer's weight empty, equipped:
A — 14,909 lb (6,763 kg)
B — 15,342 lb (6,959 kg)
Basic operating weight:
A — 15,496 lb (7,029 kg)
B — 15,928 lb (7,225 kg)
Max payload:
A — 7,209 lb (3,270 kg)
B — 6,779 lb (3,075 kg)
Max T-O weight:
A — 23,370 lb (10,600 kg)
B — 23,810 lb (10,800 kg)
Max ramp weight:
A — 23,480 lb (10,650 kg)
B — 23,920 lb (10,850 kg)
Max landing weight:
A, B — 23,040 lb (10,450 kg)
Max zero-fuel weight:
A, B — 22,710 lb (10,300 kg)
Max wing loading:
A, B — 39·5 lb/sq ft (193 kg/m^2)
Max power loading:
A — 11·7 lb/ehp (5·3 kg/ehp)
B — 11·2 lb/ehp (5·09 kg/ehp)

PERFORMANCE (at max T-O weight except where indicated; A: N 262, B: Frégate):
Max level speed:
A — 208 knots (239 mph; 385 km/h)
B — 225 knots (260 mph; 418 km/h)
Max and econ cruising speed:
A — 202 knots (233 mph; 375 km/h)
B — 220 knots (254 mph; 408 km/h)
Normal operating limit speed:
A, B — 214 knots (247 mph; 397 km/h)
Max speed with landing gear extended:
A, B — 154 knots (177 mph; 285 km/h)
Max speed with 15° flap:
A, B — 143 knots (165 mph; 265 km/h)
Max speed with 35° flap:
A, B — 126 knots (146 mph; 235 km/h)
Final approach speed:
A, B — 90 knots (104 mph; 167 km/h)
Stalling speed, flaps up, at max landing weight:
A — 85·5 knots (98 mph; 157 km/h)
B — 86 knots (99 mph; 159 km/h)
Stalling speed, wheels and flaps down, at max landing weight:
A — 71·5 knots (82 mph; 132 km/h)
B — 74 knots (85 mph; 136 km/h)
Max rate of climb at S/L:
A — 1,280 ft (390 m)/min
B — 1,380 ft (420 m)/min
Service ceiling:
A — 23,500 ft (7,160 m)
B — 28,500 ft (8,690 m)
Service ceiling, one engine out, at AUW of 21,000 lb (9,525 kg):
A — 10,000 ft (3,050 m)
B — 15,000 ft (4,920 m)
Min ground turning radius — 26 ft 3 in (8·00 m)
Runway LCN at max weight — 8
T-O run:
A — 1,970 ft (600 m)
B — 1,870 ft (570 m)
T-O to 35 ft (10·7 m):
A — 3,710 ft (1,130 m)
B — 3,510 ft (1,070 m)
Landing from 50 ft (15 m):
A, B — 1,740 ft (530 m)
Range with max fuel, no reserves:
A — 1,150 nm (1,325 miles; 2,130 km)
B — 1,295 nm (1,490 miles; 2,400 km)
Range with max fuel, FAA reserves:
A — 950 nm (1,095 miles; 1,760 km)
B — 985 nm (1,135 miles; 1,825 km)
Range with 26 passengers and baggage, no reserves:
A — 750 nm (865 miles; 1,390 km)
B — 780 nm (900 miles; 1,450 km)
Range with 26 passengers and baggage, FAA reserves:
A — 525 nm (605 miles; 975 km)
B — 550 nm (633 miles; 1,020 km)

AÉROSPATIALE MOHAWK 298

Aérospatiale plans to begin deliveries of a new version of the Frégate, powered by two United Aircraft of Canada PT6A-45 turboprop engines, in 1975. It will be known in the USA as the Mohawk 298, and an engine retrofit scheme will be offered to existing operators of the type.

AÉROSPATIALE SN 601 and SN 602 CORVETTE 100

The Corvette 100 was designed to fulfil a variety of roles, including executive transport, air taxi, ambulance, freighter or training aircraft. It can be equipped for radio aids calibration or aerial photography.

Three versions have been announced, as follows:

SN 600. Prototype only (F-WRSN), with two rear-mounted United Aircraft of Canada JT15D-1 turbofan engines, each rated at 2,200 lb (1,000 kg) st. First flew on 16 July 1970, and completed more than 270 flying hours before being lost in a crash on 23 March 1971.

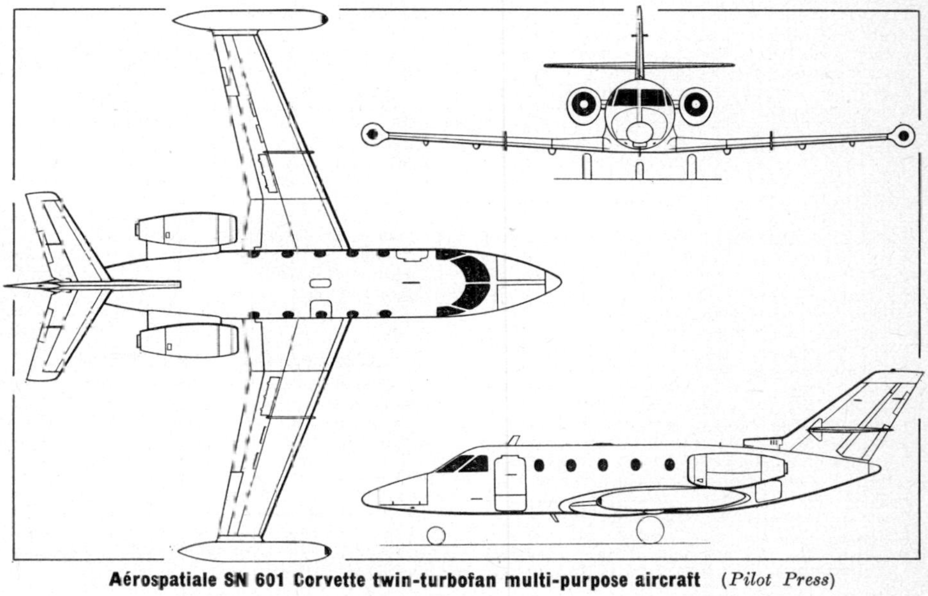

Aérospatiale SN 601 Corvette twin-turbofan multi-purpose aircraft (*Pilot Press*)

The first two production SN 601 Corvettes. Second aircraft (top) is fitted with optionally-available tip-tanks

SN 601. Initial production Corvette 100, with two 2,300 lb (1,050 kg) st United Aircraft of Canada JT15D-4 turbofan engines and a longer fuselage than the prototype. The first SN 601 (F-WUAS) was completed in 1972, together with two airframes for static and fatigue testing. It flew for the first time on 20 December 1972, and was followed by the second SN 601 (F-WRNZ) on 7 March 1973, the third (F-WUQN) on 9 November 1973 and the fourth (F-WUQP) on 12 January 1974. Type certification of this version was received on 28 May 1974. Deliveries were scheduled to begin later in the year at the rate of two aircraft per month.

SN 602. Generally similar to SN 601, but powered by two 2,755 lb (1,250 kg) st SNECMA/Turboméca Larzac 03 turbofan engines.

By May 1974 Corvette 100 orders and options totalled 87, including 70 for the USA.

The description below applies to the SN 601, except where otherwise indicated.

TYPE: Multi-purpose twin-turbofan aircraft.

WINGS: Cantilever low-wing monoplane of all-metal construction. Thickness/chord ratio 13·65% at root, 11·5% at tip. Dihedral 3° 3′ on outer panels. Sweepback 22° 32′ on leading-edge. Conventional two-spar fail-safe structure, of aluminium alloy. Manually-operated aluminium alloy ailerons and electrically-operated double-slotted long-travel trailing-edge flaps of aluminium alloy and honeycomb construction. Three-section spoiler forward of each outer flap. Hydraulically-actuated airbrakes inboard of spoilers, above and below each wing. Electrically-actuated trim tab on port aileron. TKS-type de-icing of leading-edges.

FUSELAGE: Aluminium alloy semi-monocoque fail-safe structure of circular cross-section.

TAIL UNIT: Cantilever aluminium alloy structure, with tailplane mounted on fin. Sweepback on all surfaces. Electrically-actuated variable-incidence tailplane. Manually-operated elevators and rudder. Electrically-actuated trim tab in rudder.

LANDING GEAR: Hydraulically-retractable tricycle type, with hydraulic shock-absorbers and single wheel on each unit. Main wheels retract inward, nosewheel forward, into fuselage. Low-pressure tyres of 10 in diameter on main wheels and 6 in diameter on nosewheel. Main-wheel tyre pressure 68 lb/sq in (4·8 kg/cm²); nosewheel tyre pressure 58 lb/sq in (4·1 kg/cm²). Hydraulic brakes and anti-skid units. Nosewheel steerable.

POWER PLANT: Two turbofan engines, mounted in pod on each side of rear fuselage (details under model listings). Two integral wing fuel tanks, with total capacity of 365 Imp gallons (439 US gallons; 1,660 litres). Provision for tip-tanks, of approx 154 Imp gallons (185 US gallons; 700 litres) total capacity.

ACCOMMODATION: Crew of one or two on flight deck. Normal seating for 6 to 14 passengers in single seats on each side of centre aisle. Galley, toilet and baggage compartments available to customer's requirements. Two-part door, with built-in airstairs, at front on port side; upper part of door is hinged at top, lower part is hinged at bottom of doorway.

SYSTEMS: Cabin air-conditioning and pressurisation by engine bleed air; max differential 8·5 lb/sq in (0·6 kg/cm²). Hydraulic system for actuating landing gear, nosewheel steering, wheel brakes and airbrakes. Main electrical system includes two 10·5kW 28·5V DC starter/generators, one 40Ah battery and two inverters for 400Hz AC supply.

ELECTRONICS AND EQUIPMENT: Blind-flying instrumentation standard. Radio, radar or other special equipment to customer's specification.

DIMENSIONS, EXTERNAL:
- Wing span: 42 ft 0 in (12·80 m)
- Wing aspect ratio: 7·45
- Length overall: 45 ft 4½ in (13·83 m)
- Length of fuselage: 41 ft 8¾ in (12·72 m)
- Fuselage diameter: 5 ft 7 in (1·70 m)
- Height overall: 13 ft 10½ in (4·23 m)
- Tailplane span: 16 ft 4¾ in (5·00 m)
- Wheel track: 8 ft 5¼ in (2·57 m)
- Wheelbase: 17 ft 1½ in (5·22 m)
- Passenger door:
  - Height: 4 ft 3½ in (1·31 m)
  - Width: 2 ft 4 in (0·71 m)
  - Mean height to sill: 2 ft 9½ in (0·85 m)

DIMENSIONS, INTERNAL:
- Cabin, excluding flight deck:
  - Max length: 18 ft 9½ in (5·73 m)
  - Max width: 5 ft 1½ in (1·56 m)
  - Max height: 5 ft 0 in (1·52 m)
  - Floor area: 71 sq ft (6·60 m²)
  - Volume: 351 cu ft (9·93 m³)
- Baggage compartment volume (10-passenger layout): 38·1 cu ft (1·08 m³)

AREAS:
- Wings, gross: 236·8 sq ft (22·00 m²)
- Vertical tail surfaces (total): 45·4 sq ft (4·22 m²)
- Horizontal tail surfaces (total): 58·9 sq ft (5·47 m²)

WEIGHTS:
- Weight empty, equipped: 7,698 lb (3,492 kg)
- Max ramp weight: 13,550 lb (6,150 kg)
- Max T-O weight: 13,450 lb (6,100 kg)
- Max landing and zero-fuel weight: 12,125 lb (5,500 kg)

PERFORMANCE (estimated, at max T-O weight):
- Max cruising speed at 30,000 ft (9,000 m): 430 knots (497 mph; 800 km/h)
- Econ cruising speed at 36,000 ft (11,000 m): 340 knots (391 mph; 630 km/h)
- Stalling speed, flaps down: 80 knots (92 mph; 148 km/h)
- Max rate of climb at S/L: 3,000 ft (914 m)/min
- Service ceiling: 41,000 ft (12,500 m)
- T-O run (FAR 23, ISA at S/L): 2,215 ft (675 m)
- T-O balanced field length (FAR 25): 4,085 ft (1,245 m)
- Landing distance: 2,265 ft (690 m)
- Max range with tip-tanks, 45 min reserves: 1,450 nm (1,670 miles; 2,690 km)
- Range with 12 passengers, 45 min reserves: 887 nm (1,022 miles; 1,645 km)

OPERATIONAL NOISE CHARACTERISTICS:
- T-O noise level at 3·5 nm (4 miles; 6·5 km) from start of T-O roll: 85 EPNdB
- Approach noise level at 1·0 nm (1·15 miles; 1·85 km) from landing threshold on 3° glide-slope: 93 EPNdB

AÉROSPATIALE CORVETTE 200

This developed version of the Corvette was announced at a press conference on 19 July 1973. Insertion of two additional cabin sections provides room for up to 18/19 passengers, at a seat pitch of 28 in (71 cm). Details are generally as for the Corvette 100, except as follows:

POWER PLANT: Basically as for SN 601, but tip-tanks standard.

SYSTEMS: Electrical system includes two 10kW generators, two 1,200VA static inverters and two 36Ah batteries.

DIMENSIONS, EXTERNAL:
- Wing span over tip-tanks: 45 ft 0 in (13·72 m)
- Length overall: 51 ft 10 in (15·802 m)
- Fuselage diameter: 5 ft 7 in (1·70 m)
- Height overall: 13 ft 10½ in (4·23 m)
- Tailplane span: 16 ft 4¾ in (5·00 m)
- Wheel track: 9 ft 8 in (2·944 m)
- Wheelbase: 21 ft 1¼ in (6·433 m)
- Passenger door:
  - Height: 4 ft 3¼ in (1·30 m)
  - Width: 2 ft 4 in (0·71 m)

DIMENSIONS, INTERNAL:
- Cabin, excluding flight deck:
  - Max length: 25 ft 3¼ in (7·70 m)
  - Max width: 5 ft 1½ in (1·56 m)
  - Max height: 5 ft 0 in (1·52 m)

WEIGHTS:
- Basic operating weight (18 passengers): 10,692 lb (4,850 kg)
- Max fuel: 4,133 lb (1,875 kg)
- Payload with max fuel: 3,472 lb (1,575 kg)
- Max T-O weight: 18,300 lb (8,300 kg)
- Max landing weight: 16,100 lb (7,300 kg)

PERFORMANCE (estimated, at max T-O weight):
- Max cruising speed: 430 knots (497 mph; 800 km/h)
- Max operating speed:
  - Tip-tanks empty: 340 knots (391 mph; 630 km/h) CAS, or Mach 0·77
  - Tip-tanks filled: 300 knots (348 mph; 560 km/h) CAS, or Mach 0·70
- Approach speed at max landing weight: 120 knots (137 mph; 220 km/h)
- T-O balanced field length (FAR 25): 4,925 ft (1,500 m)
- Landing field length at max landing weight (FAR 121): 4,925 ft (1,500 m)
- Range with max fuel, 661 lb (300 kg) reserves:
  - at max cruising speed at 25,000 ft (7,620 m): 728 nm (838 miles; 1,350 km)
  - at econ cruising speed at 35,000 ft (10,670 m): 1,105 nm (1,273 miles; 2,050 km)
- Range with max fuel, 1,322 lb (600 kg) reserves:
  - at max cruising speed at 25,000 ft (7,620 m): 540 nm (621 miles; 1,000 km)
  - at econ cruising speed at 35,000 ft (10,670 m): 810 nm (932 miles; 1,500 km)

AÉROSPATIALE SA 318C ALOUETTE II ASTAZOU

Developed from the SE 313B Alouette II (described fully in the 1967-68 and 1968-69 editions of *Jane's*), the prototype Alouette II Astazou flew for the first time on 31 January 1961. Extension of the Alouette II airworthiness certificate to the Alouette II Astazou was granted subsequently in France (18 February 1964) and USA (25 November 1964). A total of 1,285 Alouette IIs had been ordered by 1 January 1974, at which time helicopters of this type were being flown by 107 operators in 47 countries.

TYPE: Turbine-driven general-purpose helicopter.

ROTOR SYSTEM: Three-blade main rotor; two-blade anti-torque rotor. All-metal main rotor blades on articulated hinges, with hydraulic drag-hinge dampers. Blades may be folded towards the rear.

ROTOR DRIVE: Main rotor driven through planetary gearbox, with free-wheel for autorotation. Take-off drive for tail rotor at lower end of main gearbox, from where a torque shaft runs to a small gearbox which supports the tail rotor and houses the pitch-change mechanism. Cyclic and collective pitch controls are powered.

Fuselage: Glazed cabin has light metal frame. Centre and rear fuselage have a triangulated steel-tube framework.

Landing Gear: Skid type, with removable wheels for ground manoeuvring. Raised skid gear available for flying crane operation. Pneumatic floats for normal operation from water and emergency flotation gear, inflatable in the air, are available.

Power Plant: One 530 shp Turboméca Astazou IIA turboshaft engine, derated to 360 shp and fitted with a centrifugal clutch. Fuel tank, capacity 127·5 Imp gallons (580 litres), in centre fuselage.

Accommodation: Glazed cabin seats pilot and passenger side by side in front and three passengers behind. Can be adapted for flying crane (payload 1,322 lb; 600 kg), rescue (hoist capacity 265 lb; 120 kg), liaison, observation, training, agricultural, photographic, ambulance, and other duties. As an ambulance can accommodate two stretchers and a medical attendant internally.

Dimensions, external:
- Diameter of main rotor 33 ft 5⅝ in (10·20 m)
- Diameter of tail rotor 6 ft 3 in (1·91 m)
- Length overall, rotors turning 39 ft 8½ in (12·10 m)
- Fuselage length, tail rotor turning 31 ft 11¾ in (9·75 m)
- Width overall, blades folded 7 ft 9¾ in (2·38 m)
- Height overall 9 ft 0 in (2·75 m)
- Skid track 7 ft 9¾ in (2·38 m)

Weights:
- Weight empty 1,961 lb (890 kg)
- Max T-O weight 3,630 lb (1,650 kg)

Performance (at max T-O weight):
- Max level speed at S/L 110 knots (127 mph; 205 km/h)
- Max cruising speed at S/L 97 knots (112 mph; 180 km/h)
- Max rate of climb at S/L 1,300 ft (396 m)/min
- Service ceiling 10,800 ft (3,300 m)
- Hovering ceiling in ground effect 5,085 ft (1,550 m)
- Hovering ceiling out of ground effect 2,950 ft (900 m)
- Range with max fuel at S/L 388 nm (447 miles; 720 km)
- Range with 1,322 lb (600 kg) payload 53 nm (62 miles; 100 km)
- Range with 1,058 lb (480 kg) payload 161 nm (186 miles; 300 km)
- Max endurance at S/L 5 hr 18 min

AÉROSPATIALE SA 315B LAMA

Indian Army name: Cheetah

Design of the SA 315B Lama began in late 1968, initially to meet a requirement announced by the Indian armed forces, and a prototype was flown for the first time on 17 March 1969. French certification was granted on 30 September 1970 and FAA type approval on 25 February 1972.

Basically, the Lama combines features of the Alouette II and III, having the airframe (with some reinforcement) of the former and the dynamic components, including the Artouste power plant and rotor system, of the SA 316 Alouette III.

Aérospatiale SA 315B Lama operating as a flying crane in a mountain area

During demonstration flights in the Himalayas in 1969 a Lama, carrying a crew of two and 308 lb (140 kg) of fuel, made the highest landings and take-offs ever recorded, at a height of 24,600 ft (7,500 m).

On 21 June 1972, a Lama set up a new helicopter absolute height record of 40,820 ft (12,442 m). The pilot was Jean Boulet, holder of the previous record in an SE 3150 Alouette.

The production Lama, to which the details below apply, is capable of transporting an external load of 2,204 lb (1,000 kg) at an altitude of more than 8,200 ft (2,500 m).

A total of 108 Lamas had been ordered by 30 operators in 16 countries by 1 January 1974. In addition to manufacture by Aérospatiale, the SA 315 is produced under licence by HAL for the Indian Army under the name of Cheetah.

Type: Turbine-driven general-purpose helicopter.

Rotor System: Three-blade main and anti-torque rotors. All-metal main rotor blades, of constant chord, are on articulated hinges, with hydraulic drag-hinge dampers. Rotor brake optional.

Rotor Drive: Main rotor driven through planetary gearbox, with free-wheel for autorotation. Take-off drive for tail rotor at lower end of main gearbox, from where a torque shaft runs to a small gearbox which supports the tail rotor and houses the pitch-change mechanism. Cyclic and collective pitch controls are powered.

Fuselage: Glazed cabin has light metal frame. Centre and rear of fuselage have a triangulated steel-tube framework.

Landing Gear: Skid type, with removable wheels for ground manoeuvring. Pneumatic floats for normal operation from water, and emergency flotation gear, inflatable in the air, are available.

Power Plant: One 870 shp Turboméca Artouste IIIB turboshaft engine, derated to 550 shp. Fuel tank in fuselage centre-section, with capacity of 127·5 Imp gallons (580 litres).

Accommodation: Glazed cabin seats pilot and passenger side by side in front and three passengers behind. Provision for external sling for loads of up to 2,204 lb (1,000 kg). Can be equipped for rescue (hoist capacity 352 lb; 160 kg), liaison, observation, training, agricultural, photographic, ambulance and other duties. As an ambulance, can accommodate two stretchers and a medical attendant internally.

Dimensions, external:
- Main rotor diameter 36 ft 1¾ in (11·02 m)
- Tail rotor diameter 6 ft 3¼ in (1·91 m)
- Main rotor blade chord (constant) 13·8 in (35 cm)
- Length overall, both rotors turning 42 ft 4¾ in (12·92 m)
- Length of fuselage 33 ft 8 in (10·26 m)
- Height overall 10 ft 1¾ in (3·09 m)
- Skid track 7 ft 9¾ in (2·38 m)

Weights:
- Weight empty 2,215 lb (1,005 kg)
- Normal max T-O weight 4,300 lb (1,950 kg)
- Max T-O weight with externally-slung cargo 5,070 lb (2,300 kg)

Performance (at AUW of 4,850 lb; 2,200 kg, with slung load):
- Max cruising speed 65 knots (75 mph; 120 km/h)
- Max rate of climb at S/L 820 ft (250 m)/min
- Service ceiling 13,125 ft (4,000 m)
- Hovering ceiling in ground effect 12,300 ft (3,750 m)
- Hovering ceiling out of ground effect 9,185 ft (2,800 m)

AÉROSPATIALE SA 316B ALOUETTE III

The Alouette III helicopter is a development of the Alouette II, with larger cabin capacity, greater power, improved equipment and higher performance. It flew for the first time on 28 February 1959, and a total of 1,152 had been ordered from Aérospatiale by 1 January 1974, at which time SA 316B and SA 319B Alouette IIIs were being flown by 131 operators in 65 countries.

Those delivered up to the end of 1969 were designated **SE 3160.** The Artouste-engined **SA 316B,** described below, has strengthened main and rear rotor transmissions, higher AUW and increased payload; first deliveries were made in 1970. This version received FAA Type Approval on 25 March 1971. The **SA 319B,** with Astazou engine, is described separately.

The sale of Alouette IIIs to India, Romania and Switzerland includes a licence agreement for manufacture of the aircraft in those countries. Initial quantities of 80 are being completed in India, 50 in Romania and 60 in Switzerland.

Type: Turbine-driven general-purpose helicopter.

Rotor System: Three-blade main and anti-torque rotors. Main rotor head similar to that of Alouette II. All-metal main rotor blades, on articulated hinges, with hydraulic drag-hinge dampers. Rotor brake optional.

Rotor Drive: Main rotor driven through planetary gearbox, with free-wheel for autorotation. Take-off drive for tail rotor at lower end of main gearbox, from where a torque shaft runs to a small gearbox which supports the tail rotor and houses the pitch-change mechanism. Cyclic and collective pitch controls are powered.

Fuselage: Welded steel-tube centre-section, carrying the cabin at the front and a semi-monocoque tailboom.

Tail Unit: Cantilever all-metal fixed tailplane, with twin endplate fins, mounted on tailboom.

Landing Gear: Non-retractable tricycle type, manufactured by Messier-Hispano. Nosewheel is fully-castoring. Provision for pontoon landing gear.

Power Plant: One 870 shp Turboméca Artouste IIIB turboshaft engine, derated to 570 shp. Fuel in single tank in fuselage centre-section, with capacity of 123 Imp gallons (560 litres).

Accommodation: Normal accommodation for pilot and six persons, with three seats in front and a four-person folding seat at the rear of the cabin. Two baggage holds in centre-section, on each side of the welded structure and enclosed by the centre-section fairings. Provision for carrying two stretchers athwartships at rear of cabin, and two other persons, in addition to pilot. All passenger seats removable to enable aircraft to be used for freight-carrying. Provision for external sling for loads of up to 1,650 lb (750 kg). One forward-opening door on each side, immediately in front of two rearward-sliding doors. Dual controls and cabin heating optional.

Operational Equipment (military version): In the assault role, the military Alouette III can be equipped with a wide range of weapons. This range includes a 7·62 mm AA52 machine-gun (with 1,000 rounds of ammunition), mounted athwartships on a tripod behind the pilot's seat and firing to starboard, either through a small window in the sliding door or through the open doorway with the door locked open. The rear seat is removed to allow the gun mounting to be installed. In this configuration, max accommodation is for pilot, co-pilot, gunner and one passenger, although normally only the pilot and gunner would be carried. An alternative to this installation provides for a 20 mm MG 151/20 cannon (with 480 rounds) on an open turret-type mounting on the port side of the cabin. For this installation all seats except that of the pilot are removed, as is the port side cabin door, and the crew consists of pilot and gunner. Instead of these guns, the Alouette III can be equipped with four AS.11 or two AS.12 wire-guided missiles on external jettisonable launching rails with

Aérospatiale SA 318C Alouette II Astazou, with optionally-available pneumatic float landing gear

APX-Bézu 260 gyro-stabilised sight, or 68 mm rocket pods. Tests with Hot missiles have also been completed successfully.

Operational Equipment (naval version): The Alouette III can fulfil a variety of shipborne roles, and features common to all naval configurations include a quick-mooring harpoon to ensure instant and automatic mooring on landing and before take-off, a nosewheel locking device, and folding main rotor blades. For detecting and destroying small surface craft such as torpedo-boats, it can be equipped with a SFENA three-axis stabilisation system, OMERA ORB 31 radar, APX-Bézu 260 gyro-stabilised sight and two AS.12 wire-guided missiles. For the ASW role, it can carry two Mk 44 homing torpedoes beneath the fuselage, or one torpedo and MAD (magnetic anomaly detection) gear in a streamlined container which is towed behind the helicopter on a 150 ft (50 m) cable. The aircraft can be used for air/sea rescue when the cabin floor is protected by an anti-corrosion covering to prevent sea water from reaching vital components. Rescue hoist (capacity 500 lb; 225 kg) mounted on port side of fuselage.

Dimensions, external:
Diameter of main rotor 36 ft 1¾ in (11·02 m)
Main rotor blade chord (each) 13·8 in (35 cm)
Diameter of tail rotor 6 ft 3¼ in (1·91 m)
Length overall, rotors turning 42 ft 1½ in (12·84 m)
Length overall, blades folded 32 ft 10¾ in (10·03 m)
Width overall, blades folded 8 ft 6¼ in (2·60 m)
Height to top of rotor head 9 ft 10 in (3·00 m)
Wheel track 8 ft 6¼ in (2·60 m)

Weights:
Weight empty 2,474 lb (1,122 kg)
Max T-O weight 4,850 lb (2,200 kg)

Performance (standard version, at max T-O weight):
Max level speed at S/L 113 knots (130 mph; 210 km/h)
Max cruising speed at S/L 100 knots (115 mph; 185 km/h)
Max rate of climb at S/L 850 ft (260 m)/min
Service ceiling 10,500 ft (3,200 m)
Hovering ceiling in ground effect 9,450 ft (2,880 m)
Hovering ceiling out of ground effect 5,000 ft (1,520 m)
Range with max fuel at S/L 258 nm (298 miles; 480 km)
Range at best altitude 290 nm (335 miles; 540 km)

AÉROSPATIALE SA 319B ALOUETTE III ASTAZOU

The SA 319B Alouette III Astazou is a direct development of the SA 316B described earlier, from which it differs principally in having an Astazou XIV turboshaft engine (870 shp, derated to 600 shp) with increased thermal efficiency and a 25% reduction in fuel consumption.

A prototype SA 319 was completed in 1967. The production total to the beginning of 1974 is included in the figures given under the SA 316B entry.

Weights:
Weight empty 2,442 lb (1,108 kg)
Max T-O weight 4,960 lb (2,250 kg)

Performance (at max T-O weight):
Max level speed at S/L 118 knots (136 mph; 220 km/h)
Max cruising speed at S/L 106 knots (122 mph; 197 km/h)
Max rate of climb at S/L 885 ft (270 m)/min
Hovering ceiling in ground effect 10,170 ft (3,100 m)
Hovering ceiling out of ground effect 5,575 ft (1,700 m)
Range with 6 passengers (176 lb; 80 kg each), T-O at S/L 325 nm (375 miles; 605 km)

AÉROSPATIALE SA 321 SUPER FRELON

The Super Frelon is a three-engined multi-purpose helicopter derived from the smaller SA 3200 Frelon (see 1961-62 *Jane's*).

Aérospatiale SA 319B Alouette III Astazou (600 shp Turboméca Astazou XIV turboshaft engine)

Under a technical co-operation contract, Sikorsky Aircraft, USA, provided assistance in the development of the Super Frelon, in particular with the detail specifications, design, construction and testing of the main and tail rotor systems. Under a further agreement, the main gearcase and transmission box are produced in Italy by Fiat.

The first prototype of the Super Frelon (originally designated SA 3210-01) flew on 7 December 1962, powered by three 1,320 shp Turmo III C2 engines, and represented the troop transport version. In July 1963 this aircraft set up several international helicopter records, including a speed of 184 knots (212 mph; 341 km/h) over a 3 km course, and a speed of 189·115 knots (217·77 mph; 350·47 km/h) over a 15/25 km course.

The second prototype, flown on 28 May 1963, was representative of the naval version, with stabilising floats on the main landing gear supports. Four pre-production aircraft followed, and the French government ordered an initial production series of 17, designated SA 321G, in October 1965. By the beginning of 1974, orders totalled 78, from 10 operators in 8 countries.

Passenger and utility versions of the Super Frelon are available, and the main differences between the current versions are summarised as follows:

SA 321F. Commercial airliner version, designed to carry 34-37 passengers in a standard of comfort comparable to that of fixed-wing airliners, over 94 nm (108 mile; 175 km) stage lengths at a cruising speed of 124 knots (143 mph; 230 km/h), with 20 min reserve fuel. The prototype was designed in accordance with US FAR 29 regulations and flew for the first time on 7 April 1967. Type certification was granted by the SGAC on 27 June 1968 and by the FAA on 29 August 1968.

SA 321G. Anti-submarine version. Twenty-four ordered. First version of the SA 321 to enter production. The first SA 321G flew on 30 November 1965 and deliveries began in early 1966. In service with Flottille 32F of Aéronavale, which was commissioned at Lanvéoc-Poulmic on 5 May 1970. Duties of this squadron include patrols in support of *Redoutable* class nuclear submarines entering and leaving their base on the Ile Longue. The SA 321G can also be operated from the French helicopter carrier *Jeanne d'Arc*.

SA 321Ja. Utility and public transport version, intended to fulfil the main roles of personnel and cargo transport. It is designed to carry a maximum of 27 passengers. External loads of up to 11,023 lb (5,000 kg) can be suspended from the cargo sling and carried 27 nm (31 miles; 50 km), the aircraft returning to base without load. An internal payload of 8,818 lb (4,000 kg) can be carried over 100 nm (115 miles; 185 km) at 124 knots (143 mph; 230 km/h) with 20 min fuel reserves. The SA 321J prototype flew for the first time on 6 July 1967. A French certificate of airworthiness was granted in December 1971.

The description below applies generally to all current models of the Super Frelon, except where specific variants are indicated.

Type: Three-engined heavy-duty helicopter.

Rotors: Six-blade main rotor and five-blade anti-torque tail rotor. Main rotor head consists basically of two six-armed star-plates carrying the drag and flapping hinges for each blade. The root of each blade carries a fitting for pitch control and each blade has an individual hydraulic damper to govern movement in the drag plane. Each main blade is 28 ft 2½ in (8·60 m) long, with constant chord and NACA 0012 section. All-metal construction, with D-section main spar forming leading-edge. Tail rotor of similar construction to main rotor, with blades 5 ft 3 in (1·60 m) long. Rearward folding of all six main rotor blades of SA 321G is accomplished automatically by hydraulic jacks simultaneously with automatic folding of the tail rotor pylon.

Rotor Drive: The drive-shaft from the rear engine is geared directly to the shaft from the port forward engine. The two forward engines have a common reduction gear from which an output shaft drives the main rotor shaft through helical gearing. There are two reduction gear stages on the main rotor shaft. The tail rotor shaft is driven by gearing from the shaft linking the rear and port forward engines and incorporates two-stage reduction. The rotor can be stopped within 40 sec by a boosted disc-type rotor brake fitted to this shaft. Main rotor rpm 207 and 212. Tail rotor rpm 990.

Fuselage: Boat-hull fuselage of conventional metal semi-monocoque construction, with watertight compartments inside planing bottom. On the SA 321G, there is a small stabilising float attached to the rear landing gear support structure on each side. The tail section of the SA 321G folds for stowage. Small fixed stabiliser on starboard side of the tail rotor pylon. The SA 321F does not have stabilising floats, but large external fairings on each side of the centre fuselage serve a similar purpose and also act as baggage containers.

Landing Gear: Non-retractable tricycle type, by Messier-Hispano. Twin wheels on each unit. Oleo-pneumatic shock-absorbers can be shortened on the SA 321G to reduce height of aircraft for stowage. Magnesium alloy wheels, all of same size. Tyre pressure 100 lb/sq in (7 kg/cm²). Optionally, low-pressure (50 lb/sq in; 3·5 kg/cm²) tyres may be

Aérospatiale SA 321G Super Frelon anti-submarine helicopter of Flottille 32F, Aéronavale (*J. D. R. Rawlings*)

fitted. Hydraulic disc brakes on main wheels. Nosewheel unit is steerable and self-centering.

Power Plant: Three 1,630 shp Turboméca Turmo IIIC6-70 turboshaft engines, two mounted side by side forward of main rotor shaft and one aft of rotor shaft. Fuel in flexible tanks under floor of centre fuselage, with total capacity of 874 Imp gallons (3,975 litres). Provision for auxiliary tanks, each of 110 Imp gallons (500 litres) capacity.

Accommodation (military versions): Crew of two on flight deck, with dual controls and advanced all-weather equipment. Equipment in the SA 321G, which carries a flight crew of five, includes a tactical table and a variety of devices for anti-submarine detection and attack, towing, minesweeping and other duties. Transport version has provision for carrying 27-30 troops, 11,023 lb (5,000 kg) of internal or external cargo, or 15 stretchers and two medical attendants. Rescue hoist of 606 lb (275 kg) capacity. Main cabin is ventilated and soundproofed. Sliding door on starboard side of front fuselage. Rear loading ramp is actuated hydraulically and can be opened in flight.

Accommodation (SA 321F): Airliner-type seats for up to 37 passengers (34 if toilets are installed) in three-abreast rows with centre aisle. Alternative layouts for 8, 14 or 23 passengers, with toilets, or 11, 17 or 26 passengers without toilets, the remainder of the cabin space being blanked off by movable partitions and used for the carriage of freight; with these configurations, unused seats are folded against the cabin wall. All seats and interior furnishings are designed for quick removal when the helicopter is to be used for all-freight services. To cater for operations over marshland or water, the hull and lateral cargo compartments are sufficiently sealed to permit an occasional landing on water.

Accommodation (SA 321Ja): Seating for up to 27 passengers in the personnel transport role. As a cargo transport, external loads of up to 11,023 lb (5,000 kg) can be suspended from the cargo sling. Loading of internal cargo (up to 11,023 lb; 5,000 kg) is effected via the rear ramp-doors, with the assistance of a Tirefor hand winch.

Operational Equipment (SA 321G): This version operates normally in tactical formations of three or four aircraft, one helicopter carrying detection and tracking equipment and the others in the group carrying equipment for attack. A central navigational system, Doppler radar and a radio altimeter are common to all versions. The detection aircraft carries Sylphe panoramic radar with IFF capability and dipping sonar. Four homing torpedoes can be carried in pairs on each side of the main cabin.

Dimensions, external:
- Diameter of main rotor: 62 ft 0 in (18·90 m)
- Main rotor blade chord (each): 1 ft 9¼ in (0·54 m)
- Diameter of tail rotor: 13 ft 1½ in (4·00 m)
- Tail rotor blade chord (each): 11¾ in (0·30 m)
- Length overall, rotors turning: 75 ft 6⅝ in (23·03 m)
- Length of fuselage, incl tail rotor: 65 ft 10¾ in (20·08 m)
- Length of fuselage: 63 ft 7¾ in (19·40 m)
- Length overall (SA 321G, blades and tail folded): 56 ft 0 in (17·07 m)
- Width overall (SA 321G, blades and tail folded): 17 ft 0¾ in (5·20 m)
- Width overall, incl baggage containers (SA 321F): 16 ft 6⅜ in (5·04 m)
- Width of fuselage: 7 ft 4¼ in (2·24 m)
- Height at tail rotor (normal): 21 ft 10¼ in (6·66 m)
- Height overall (SA 321G, blades and tail folded): 16 ft 2½ in (4·94 m)
- Wheel track: 14 ft 1 in (4·30 m)
- Wheelbase: 21 ft 6¼ in (6·56 m)
- Cabin door:
  - Height: 5 ft 1 in (1·55 m)
  - Width: 3 ft 11¼ in (1·20 m)
- Rear loading ramp:
  - Length: 6 ft 2¾ in (1·90 m)
  - Width: 6 ft 2¾ in (1·90 m)

Dimensions, internal:
- Cabin:
  - Length:
    - SA 321F: 31 ft 9 in (9·67 m)
    - SA 321G and Ja: 22 ft 11½ in (7·00 m)
  - Width:
    - SA 321F: 6 ft 5 in (1·96 m)
    - SA 321G and Ja, at floor: 6 ft 2¾ in (1·90 m)
  - Height:
    - SA 321F: 5 ft 11 in (1·80 m)
    - SA 321G and Ja: 6 ft 0 in (1·83 m)
  - Usable volume:
    - SA 321G and Ja: 893 cu ft (25·3 m^3)

Weights:
- Weight empty:
  - SA 321G: 14,607 lb (6,626 kg)
- Weight empty, equipped:
  - SA 321Ja: 15,873 lb (7,200 kg)
- Max T-O weight: 28,660 lb (13,000 kg)

Performance (at max T-O weight):
- Max never-exceed speed at S/L: 148 knots (171 mph; 275 km/h)
- Cruising speed at S/L: 135 knots (155 mph; 249 km/h)
- Cruising speed at S/L, one engine out: 113 knots (130 mph; 210 km/h)
- Max rate of climb at S/L: 1,312 ft (400 m)/min
- Rate of climb at S/L, one engine out: 479 ft (146 m)/min
- Service ceiling: 10,325 ft (3,150 m)
- Service ceiling, one engine out: 3,940 ft (1,200 m)
- Hovering ceiling in ground effect: 7,120 ft (2,170 m)
- Range at S/L: 442 nm (509 miles; 820 km)
- Range at S/L, one engine out: 496 nm (572 miles; 920 km)
- Range at S/L with 7,713 lb (3,500 kg) payload: 549 nm (633 miles; 620 km)
- Ferry range at S/L with two 110 Imp gallon (500 litre) auxiliary tanks: 549 nm (633 miles; 1,020 km)
- Endurance in ASW role: 4 hr

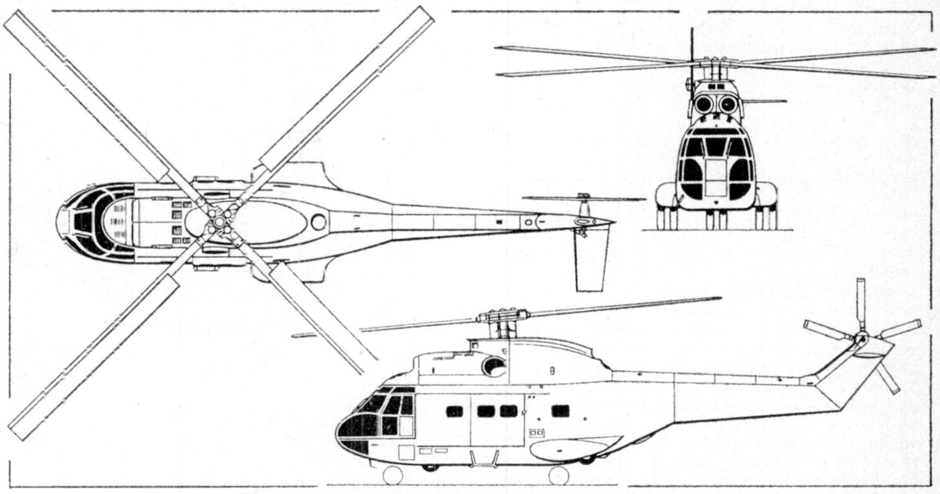

Aérospatiale/Westland SA 330 Puma transport helicopter (*Pilot Press*)

AÉROSPATIALE/WESTLAND SA 330 PUMA

The twin-engined SA 330 was developed initially to meet a French Army requirement for a medium-sized *hélicoptère de manoeuvre*, able to operate by day or night in all weathers and all climates. In 1967, the SA 330 was selected for the RAF Tactical Transport Programme, and is included in the joint production agreement between Aérospatiale and Westland in the UK. The first of two prototypes flew on 15 April 1965, and the last of six pre-production SA 330s on 30 July 1968, followed in September 1968 by the first production aircraft.

During 1971, the second prototype tested successfully the specialised electronic equipment available for search and rescue versions of the Puma (see under "Electronics and Equipment" heading).

The following versions of the Puma have been announced:

SA 330B. For French Army (ALAT) and French Air Force. First flown January 1969; deliveries began Spring 1969; became operational with the Groupe de l'Aviation Légère of the 7th French Division at Habsheim Base, Mulhouse, France, in June 1970. Turmo III C4 engines, each of 1,328 shp for T-O and 1,185 shp max continuous rating.

SA 330C/H. Military export versions. First flown September 1968. For engine details see below.

SA 330E. For Royal Air Force, by whom it is designated Puma HC Mk 1. Forty ordered, with Turmo III C4 engines. First production example (XW198) flown on 25 November 1970. First RAF squadron (No. 33) formed in 1971, followed by No. 230 in 1972. Deliveries completed.

SA 330F/G. Civil passenger or cargo versions. First flown 26 September 1969. Awarded French certification on 12 October 1970, and FAA Type Approval for IFR operation (FAR Pt 29, category A and B) on 23 June 1971. For engine details see below.

By 1 January 1974, a total of 228 Pumas had been ordered by 26 operators in 21 countries.

Type: Medium-sized transport helicopter.

Rotor System: Four-blade main rotor, with a fully-articulated hub and integral rotor brake. The blade cuffs, equipped with horns, are connected by link-rods to the swashplate, which is actuated by three hydraulic twin-cylinder servo-control units. The blades, which are of constant chord, NACA 00 series section and twisted, consist of an aluminium alloy extruded spar, milled on the outside to form the leading-edge, and a series of sheet metal pockets bot-bonded to the rear of the spar to form the trailing-edge. Attachment of the blades to their sleeve by means of two pins enables them to be folded back quickly by manual methods. The five-blade tail rotor has flapping hinges only, and is located on the starboard side of the tailboom.

Rotor Drive: Mechanical shaft and gear drive. Main gearbox, mounted on top of cabin behind engines, has two separate inputs from the engines and five reduction stages. The first stage drives, from each engine, an intermediate shaft directly driving the alternator and the ventilation fan, and indirectly driving the two hydraulic pumps. At the second stage the action of the two units becomes synchronised on a single main drive-shaft by means of free-wheeling spur gears. If one or both engines are stopped, this enables the drive gears to be rotated by the remaining turbine or the auto-rotating rotor, thus maintaining drive to the ancillary systems when the engines are stopped. Drive to the tail rotor is via shafting and an intermediate angle gearbox, terminating at a right-angle tail rotor gearbox. Turbine output 23,000 rpm, main rotor shaft 265 rpm. Tail rotor shaft 1,278 rpm. The hydraulically-controlled rotor brake, installed on the main gearbox, permits stopping of the rotor 15 seconds after engine shut-down.

Fuselage: Conventional all-metal semi-monocoque structure. Local use of titanium alloy under engine installation, which is outside the main fuselage shell. Monocoque tailboom supports the tail rotor on the starboard side and a horizontal stabiliser on the port side.

Landing Gear: Messier-Hispano semi-retractable tricycle type, with twin wheels on each unit. Main units retract upward hydraulically into fairings on sides of fuselage; self-centering nose unit retracts rearward. When landing gear is down, the nosewheel jack is extended and the main-wheel jacks are telescoped. Dual-chamber oleo-pneumatic shock-absorbers. All tyres same size (7·00-6), of Dunlop or Kléber-Colombes tubeless type, pressure 70 lb/sq in (5 kg/cm²) on all units. Hydraulic differential disc brakes, controlled by foot pedals. Lever-operated parking brake. Emergency pop-out flotation units can be mounted on rear under-carriage fairings and forward fuselage.

Power Plant: Initial civilian version has two Turboméca Turmo IV A turboshaft engines, each with max rating of 1,435 shp and equipped for air intake anti-icing. Initial military export versions have two Turmo IV B engines, each with max rating of 1,400 shp and not equipped for air intake anti-icing. From the end of 1973 SA 330G and H versions have been delivered with 1,575 shp Turmo IV C engines, with intake anti-icing. Engines are mounted side by side above cabin forward of the main rotor assembly and separated by a firewall. They are coupled to the main rotor transmission box, with shaft drive to tail rotor, and form a completely independent system from the fuel tanks up to the main gearbox inputs. Fuel in four flexible tanks and one auxiliary tank beneath cargo compartment floor, with total capacity of 341 Imp gallons (1,550 litres). Provision for additional 418 Imp gallons (1,900 litres) in four auxiliary ferry tanks installed in cabin. External auxiliary tanks (two, each 77 Imp gallons; 350 litres capacity) being designed. Each engine is supplied by a pair of interconnected tanks, the lower halves of which have self-sealing walls for protection against small-calibre projectiles. RAF version has fuel flow meters and fuel jettison system. Refuelling point on starboard side of main cabin. Oil capacity 4·8 Imp gallons (22 litres) for engines, 5·6 Imp gallons (25·5 litres) for transmission.

Accommodation: Crew of one or two side by side on anti-crash seats on flight deck, with jump-seat for third crew member if required. Pilot's door on starboard side and jettisonable door for co-pilot on port side. Internal doorway connects flight deck to cabin, with folding seat in doorway for an extra crew member or cargo supervisor. Dual controls standard.

Accommodation in main cabin for 16 individually-equipped troops, six litters and four seated patients, or equivalent freight. The number of troops can be increased to 20 in the high-density version. Strengthened floor for cargo-carrying, with lashing points. Jettisonable sliding door on each side of main cabin; or port-side door with built-in steps and starboard-side double door in VIP or airline configurations. Removable panel on underside of fuselage, aft of main cabin, permits longer loads to be accommodated and also serves as emergency exit on SA 330C and H versions. Removable door with integral steps for access to baggage racks on SA 330F and G versions. A hatch in the floor below the centre-line of the main rotor is provided for carrying loads of up to 5,511 lb (2,500 kg) on an internally-mounted cargo sling. A fixed or retractable rescue hoist (capacity 606 lb; 275 kg) can be mounted externally on the starboard side of the fuselage and is standard on the RAF version, together with an abseiling beam, cargo hook and full-width main cabin steps. The cabin can be equipped in 9/12-seat VIP, 17-seat commuter or 20-seat high-density layouts, with baggage compartment and/or toilet facilities in rear of cabin. Cabin and flight deck are heated, ventilated and soundproofed. De-misting, de-icing, washers and wipers for pilots' windscreens.

Systems: Two independent hydraulic systems, each 2,500 lb/sq in (175 kg/cm²), supplied by self-regulating pumps driven by the main gearbox. Each system supplies one set of servo unit chambers, the left-hand system supplying in addition the autopilot, landing gear, rotor brake and wheel brakes. Freewheels in main gearbox ensure that both systems remain in operation, for supplying the servo-controls, if the engines are stopped in flight. Other hydraulically-actuated systems can be operated on the ground from the main gearbox, or by external power through the ground power receptacle. There is also an independent auxiliary system, fed through a handpump, which can be used in an emergency to lower the landing gear and pressurise the accumulator for the parking brake on the ground. Three-phase 200V AC electrical power supplied by one or two 20kVA 400Hz alternators, driven by the port side intermediate shaft from the main gearbox and available on the ground under the same conditions as the hydraulic ancillary systems. 28·5V 10kW DC power provided from the AC system by two transformer-rectifiers. Main aircraft battery used for self-starting and emergency power in flight. For the latter purpose, an emergency 400VA inverter can supply the essential navigation equipment from the battery, permitting at least 20 min continued flight in the event of a main power failure. SEMCA air-conditioning system in SA 330F and G. De-icing of engines and engine air intakes by warm air bled from compressor. Anti-snow shield for Winter operations.

Electronics and Equipment: Optional communications equipment includes VHF, UHF, tactical HF and HF/SSB radio installations and intercom system. Navigational equipment includes radio compass, radio altimeter, Decca navigator and flight log, Doppler, and VOR/ILS with glidepath. Autopilot, with provision for coupling to self-contained navigation and microwave landing systems. Full IFR instrumentation available optionally. Standard equipment in the RAF version includes VHF/UHF radio, standby UHF, UHF homing, intercom, IFF/SSR, ICS, radio altimeter, and Decca navigation system with flight log. The search and rescue version has nose-mounted Bendix RDR 110 search radar, Doppler, and Decca or Crouzet self-contained navigation system, including navigation computer, polar indicator, roller-map display, hover indicator, route mileage indicator and ground speed and drift indicator. A wide range of armament can be carried, including side-firing 20 mm cannon, axial-firing 7·62 mm machine-guns and missiles.

Dimensions, external:

Diameter of main rotor	49 ft 2½ in (15·00 m)
Diameter of tail rotor	9 ft 11½ in (3·04 m)
Distance between rotor centres	30 ft 2¼ in (9·20 m)
Blade chord, main rotor	1 ft 9 in (0·54 m)
Ground clearance of tail rotor	6 ft 6¾ in (2·00 m)
Length overall	59 ft 6½ in (18·15 m)
Length of fuselage	46 ft 1½ in (14·06 m)
Length, blades folded	48 ft 6¾ in (14·80 m)
Width, blades folded	11 ft 5¾ in (3·50 m)
Height overall	16 ft 10½ in (5·14 m)
Height to top of rotor hub	14 ft 4½ in (4·38 m)
Width over wheel fairings	9 ft 10 in (3·00 m)
Wheel track	7 ft 10¾ in (2·38 m)
Wheelbase	13 ft 3 in (4·045 m)
Passenger cabin doors, each:	
Height	4 ft 5 in (1·35 m)
Width	4 ft 5 in (1·35 m)
Height to sill	3 ft 3½ in (1·00 m)
Floor hatch, rear of cabin:	
Length	3 ft 2¾ in (0·98 m)
Width	2 ft 3½ in (0·70 m)

Aérospatiale/Westland SA 330F Puma operating as a flying crane in Indonesia

Dimensions, internal:

Cabin: Length	19 ft 10½ in (6·05 m)
Max width	5 ft 11 in (1·80 m)
Max height	5 ft 1 in (1·55 m)
Floor area	84 sq ft (7·80 m²)
Usable volume	403 cu ft (11·40 m³)

Areas:

Main rotor blades (each)	43 sq ft (4·00 m²)
Tail rotor blades (each)	3·01 sq ft (0·28 m²)
Main rotor disc	1,905 sq ft (177·0 m²)
Tail rotor disc	78·6 sq ft (7·30 m²)
Horizontal stabiliser	14·4 sq ft (1·34 m²)

Weights:

Weight empty, basic aircraft	7,562 lb (3,430 kg)
Max T-O and landing weight	14,770 lb (6,700 kg)

Performance (Turmo IV C engines; at max AUW):

Max never-exceed speed at S/L	148 knots (170 mph; 274 km/h)
Max cruising speed at S/L	141 knots (162 mph; 261 km/h)
Econ cruising speed at S/L	134 knots (154 mph; 248 km/h)
Max rate of climb at S/L	1,380 ft (420 m)/min
Hovering ceiling in ground effect	6,890 ft (2,100 m)
Hovering ceiling out of ground effect	4,265 ft (1,300 m)
Max range at S/L (standard fuel), no reserves	318 nm (366 miles; 590 km)

AÉROSPATIALE/WESTLAND SA 341 GAZELLE

The SA 341 Gazelle all-purpose lightweight helicopter is a five-seat aircraft, with a Turboméca Astazou III turboshaft engine. Under an Anglo-French agreement signed in 1967, it is produced jointly with Westland Helicopters Ltd, and is also built under licence in Yugoslavia.

The first prototype (designated SA 340) made its first flight on 7 April 1967, and the second on 12 April 1968. It was followed by four pre-production SA 341 Gazelles, of which the third was equipped to British Army requirements and given the British military serial number XW276.

The first production SA 341 Gazelle, to which the description below applies, flew for the first time on 6 August 1971, with a longer cabin than its predecessors, enlarged tail unit, additional door on the starboard side at rear (optional on production aircraft) and uprated Astazou IIIA engine.

Seven production versions have been announced, as follows:

SA 341B. British Army version, with Astazou IIIN engine. Designated Gazelle AH Mk 1.

SA 341C. British Navy version. Designated Gazelle HT Mk 2.

SA 341D. Royal Air Force training version. Designated HT Mk 3.

SA 341E. Royal Air Force communications version. Designated HCC Mk 4.

SA 341F. French Army version, with Astazou IIIC engine; 166 to be procured by 1976.

SA 341G. Civil version, with Astazou IIIA engine. Certificated by SGAC on 7 June 1972 and by the FAA on 18 September 1972.

SA 341H. Military export version, with Astazou IIIB engine.

A total of 345 Gazelles had been ordered by 31 operators in 12 countries by 1 January 1974.

Three Class E1c records were set up by the SA 341-01 at Istres on 13 and 14 May 1971. These were: 167·28 knots (192·62 mph; 310·00 km/h) in a straight line over a 3 km course; 168·36 knots (193·87 mph; 312·00 km/h) in a straight line over a 15/25 km course; and 159·72 knots (183·93 mph; 296·00 km/h) over a 100 km closed circuit.

Type: Five-seat light utility helicopter.

Rotor System: Three-blade semi-articulated main rotor and 13-blade shrouded-fan anti-torque tail rotor (known as a "Fenestron" or "Fan-in-fin"). Rotor head and rotor mast form a single unit. The main rotor blades are of NACA 0012 section, attached to hub by flapping hinges. Each has a single leading-edge spar of plastics material reinforced with glassfibre, a laminated glass-fabric skin and honeycomb filler. Tail rotor blades are of die-forged light alloy, with articulation for pitch change only. Main rotor blades can be folded manually for stowage. Rotor brake optional.

Rotor Drive: Main reduction gearbox forward of engine, which is mounted above the rear part of the cabin. Intermediate gearbox beneath engine, rear gearbox supporting the tail rotor. Main rotor/engine rpm ratio 378·3 : 6,179. Tail rotor/engine rpm ratio 5,774 : 6,179.

Fuselage: Cockpit structure is based on a welded light alloy frame which carries the windows and doors. This is mounted on a conventional semi-monocoque lower structure consisting of two longitudinal box sections connected by frames and bulkheads. Central section, which encloses the baggage hold and fuel tank and supports the main reduction gearbox, is constructed of light alloy honeycomb sandwich panels. Rear section, which supports the engine and tailboom, is of similar construction. Honeycomb sandwich panels are also used for the cabin floors and transmission platform. Tailboom is of conventional sheet metal construction, as are the horizontal tail surfaces and the tail fin.

Tail Unit: Small horizontal stabiliser on tailboom, ahead of tail rotor fin.

Landing Gear: Steel-tube skid type. Wheel can be fitted at rear of each skid for ground handling. Provision for alternative float or ski landing gear.

Power Plant: One Turboméca Astazou IIIA turboshaft, installed above fuselage aft of cabin and delivering 590 shp for take-off (max continuous rating also 590 shp). Main fuel tank in fuselage, usable capacity 98 Imp gallons (445 litres). Provision for 19·8 Imp gallon (90 litre) auxiliary tank beneath baggage compartment and/or 44 Imp gallon (200 litre) ferry tank inside rear cabin. Total possible usable fuel capacity 161 Imp gallons (735 litres). Refuelling point on starboard side of cabin. Oil capacity 2·8 Imp gallons (13 litres) for engine, 0·77 Imp gallons (3·5 litres) for gearbox.

Accommodation: Crew of one or two on side-by-side seats in front of cabin, with bench seat to the rear for a further three persons. The bench seat can be folded into floor wells to leave a completely flat cargo floor. Access to baggage compartment via rear cabin bulkhead, or via optional door on starboard side. Cargo tie-down points in cabin floor. Forward-opening car-type door on each side of cabin, immediately behind which are rearward-opening auxiliary cargo-loading doors. Baggage compartment at rear of cabin. Ventilation standard. Dual controls optional.

Systems: Hydraulic system, pressure 569 lb/sq in (40 kg/cm²), serves three pitch change jacks for main rotor head and one for tail rotor. 28V DC electrical system supplied by 4kW engine-driven generator and 40Ah battery. Optional 26V AC system, supplied by 0·5kVA alternator at 115/200V 400Hz.

Electronics and Equipment: Optional communications equipment includes UHF, VHF, HF, intercom systems and homing aids. Optional navigation equipment includes radio compass, radio altimeter and VOR. Blind-flying instrumentation standard on SA 341B and F, optional on other versions. A variety of operational equipment can be fitted, according to role, including a 1,540 lb (700 kg) cargo sling, 300 lb (135 kg) rescue hoist, stretcher (internally), or photographic and survey equipment.

Armament: Military loads can include two pods of 36 mm rockets, four AS.11 or Hot wire-guided missiles or two AS.12s with APX-Bézu 334 gyro-stabilised sight, four TOW missiles with XM 26 sight, two forward-firing 7·62 mm machine-guns, reconnaissance flares or smoke markers, cabin-mounted side-firing GE Minigun or 7·62 mm machine-gun or Emerson Minitat or chin turret mounting with pantograph sight system.

Dimensions, external:

Diameter of main rotor	34 ft $5\frac{1}{2}$ in (10·50 m)
Diameter of tail rotor	2 ft $3\frac{3}{8}$ in (0·695 m)
Distance between rotor centres	19 ft $2\frac{1}{4}$ in (5·85 m)
Main rotor blade chord (constant)	11·8 in (0·30 m)
Length overall	39 ft $3\frac{5}{16}$ in (11·97 m)
Length of fuselage	31 ft $3\frac{3}{16}$ in (9·53 m)
Width, rotors folded	6 ft $7\frac{5}{16}$ in (2·015 m)
Height to top of rotor hub	8 ft $11\frac{1}{8}$ in (2·72 m)
Height overall	10 ft $2\frac{5}{8}$ in (3·15 m)
Skid track	6 ft $7\frac{5}{16}$ in (2·015 m)
Main cabin doors, each:	
Height	3 ft $4\frac{9}{16}$ in (1·05 m)
Width	3 ft $3\frac{1}{4}$ in (1·00 m)
Height to sill	2 ft $0\frac{3}{4}$ in (0·63 m)
Auxiliary cabin doors, each:	
Height	3 ft $4\frac{9}{16}$ in (1·05 m)
Width	1 ft $6\frac{3}{4}$ in (0·48 m)
Height to sill	2 ft $0\frac{3}{4}$ in (0·63 m)

Dimensions, internal:

Cabin: Length	7 ft $2\frac{9}{16}$ in (2·20 m)
Max width	4 ft 4 in (1·32 m)
Max height	3 ft $11\frac{5}{8}$ in (1·21 m)
Floor area	16·1 sq ft (1·50 m²)
Volume	63·7 cu ft (1·80 m³)
Baggage hold volume	15·9 cu ft (0·45 m³)

Areas:

Main rotor blades, each	16·9 sq ft (1·57 m²)
Tail rotor blades, each	0·075 sq ft (0·007 m²)
Main rotor disc	931 sq ft (86·5 m²)
Tail rotor disc	3·98 sq ft (0·37 m²)
Fin	4·84 sq ft (0·45 m²)
Tailplane	19·4 sq ft (1·80 m²)

Weights and Loading:

Weight empty:	
341G	2,022 lb (917 kg)
341H	2,002 lb (908 kg)
Max T-O and landing weight	3,970 lb (1,800 kg)
Max disc loading	4 lb/sq ft (19·5 kg/m²)

Performance (at max T-O weight):

Max never-exceed speed at S/L	167 knots (192·5 mph; 310 km/h)
Max cruising speed at S/L	142 knots (164 mph; 264 km/h)
Econ cruising speed at S/L	126 knots (144 mph; 233 km/h)
Max rate of climb at S/L	1,770 ft (540 m)/min
Service ceiling	16,400 ft (5,000 m)
Hovering ceiling in ground effect	9,350 ft (2,850 m)
Hovering ceiling out of ground effect	6,560 ft (2,000 m)
Range at S/L with max fuel	361 nm (416 miles; 670 km)
Range with crew of 1 and 1,102 lb (500 kg) payload	193·5 nm (223 miles; 360 km)

Aérospatiale/Westland SA 341 Gazelle (590 shp Turboméca Astazou III turboshaft engine)

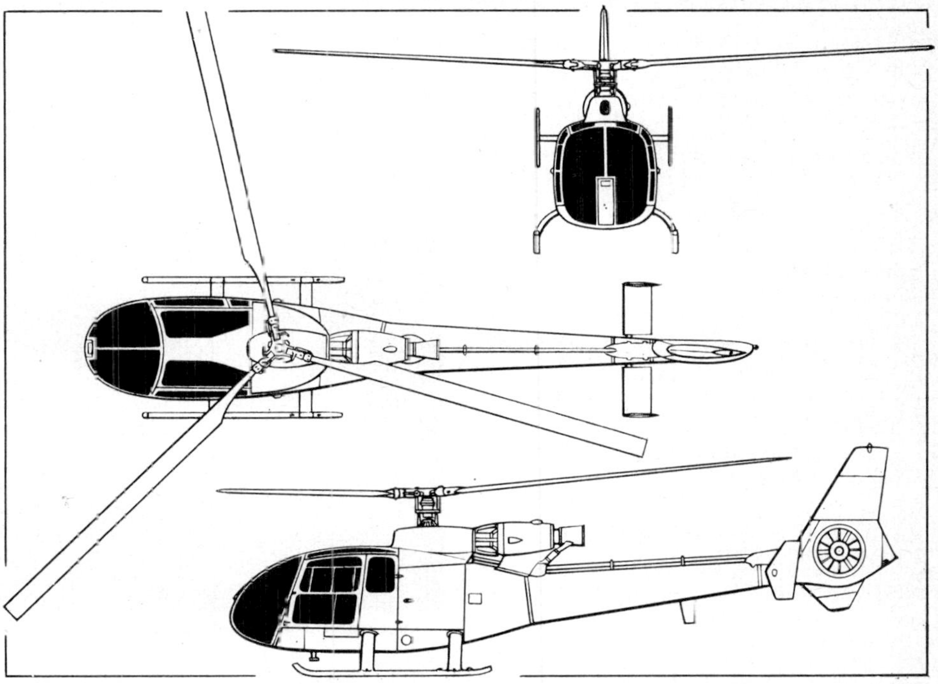

Aérospatiale/Westland SA 341 Gazelle five-seat light utility helicopter *(Pilot Press)*

AÉROSPATIALE SA 360 DAUPHIN

The first of two SA 360 prototypes (F-WSQL) flew for the first time on 2 June 1972, powered by a 980 shp Turboméca Astazou XVI turboshaft engine. After 180 flights, it was re-engined with an Astazou XVIIIA turboshaft and modified in certain respects, including the addition of small weights to the rotor blades, to eliminate ground resonance and reduce vibration to an unprecedented level, even at high speed. The aircraft flew for the first time in its modified form on 4 May 1973, having been joined by the second prototype (F-WSQX) on 29 January 1973. By the beginning of 1974, the two helicopters had logged a total of more than 400 flying hours.

Intended as a successor to the Alouette III, the SA 360 will be available to operators in about 1976. A twin-engined version, designated SA 365 (which see), is also expected to enter production at that time.

Three helicopter speed records in Class Eld (1,750 to 3,000 kg weight) were set up at Istres by the first prototype of the SA 360 on 15, 16 and 17 May 1973, piloted by Roland Coffignot. Carrying a payload equivalent to eight persons and fuel for one hour's flying, the SA 360 achieved, successively, 161·4 knots (185·8 mph; 299 km/h) over a 100 km closed circuit; 168·4 knots (193·9 mph; 312 km/h) over a 3 km course; and 163·5 knots (188·3 mph; 303 km/h) over a 15 km course.

Type: Turbine-powered general-purpose helicopter.

Rotor System: Four-blade semi-articulated main rotor and 13-blade shrouded-fan anti-torque tail rotor (known as a "Fenestron" or "Fan-in-fin"). Main rotor blades are of symmetrical NACA 0012 section, with a theoretical twist of 8° and constant chord, and are attached to the hub via a drag hinge, with damper, and flapping hinge. Each has a single leading-edge spar of polyester plastics, extending back to about 30% chord at top and bottom. The outer skin is of glassfibre, with an inner skin of carbon fibre, and the entire blade is filled with Nomex honeycomb. The leading-edge is formed by a layer of Vulkollan plastics with an outer protective shield of thin-gauge stainless steel. Tail rotor blades are of die-forged light alloy, with articulation for pitch change only. Main rotor blades can be folded manually for stowage. Rotor brake and main rotor blade de-icing optional.

Rotor Drive: Main reduction gearbox forward of engine, which is mounted above the fuselage to the rear of the cabin. Output shaft enters main transmission box above the drive-shaft to the tail rotor. Main rotor rpm: 348 normal, 393 in autorotation. Tail rotor rpm: 4,700.

Fuselage: Conventional all-metal assembly of cabin and semi-monocoque tailboom. Cabin built on a strong box structure embodying two transverse frames and the cabin floor.

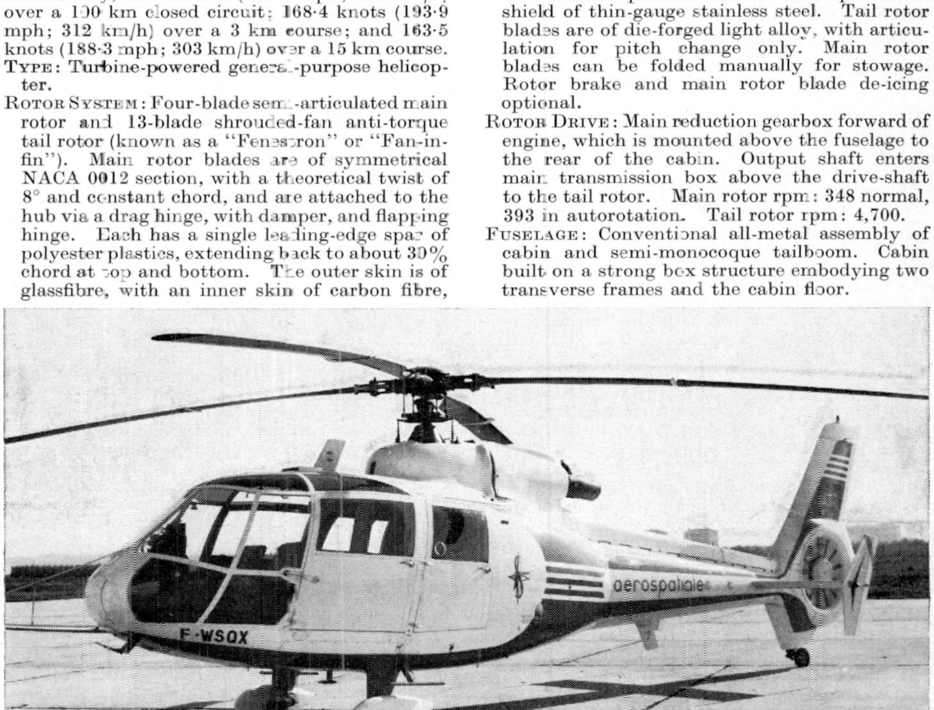

Second prototype of the Aérospatiale SA 360 Dauphin ten-seat general-purpose helicopter

TAIL UNIT: Horizontal stabiliser mid-set on tailboom, forward of shrouded tail rotor, with endplate fins. Tailboom terminates in large fin of unsymmetrical section, housing the tail rotor. The section of this fin is such that in cruising flight it counters the torque of the main rotor; the tail rotor is thus required to provide only yaw control, with minimal variation of pitch, requiring only small power intake.

LANDING GEAR: Prototypes have Eram non-retractable tailwheel-type landing gear, with single wheel on each unit. Main legs embody hydraulic shock-struts. Tailwheel carried on anti-shimmy leg which can be locked manually in central position. Dunlop main-wheel tyres size 355 × 150-4, pressure 73 lb/sq in (5·13 kg/cm²). Dunlop tailwheel tyre size 260 × 80-4, pressure 73 lb/sq in (5·13 kg/cm²). Disc brakes on main wheels. Wheel fairings standard. Two main wheels will retract forward into cabin underfloor structure on production aircraft. Provision for floats or skis.

POWER PLANT: One Turboméca Astazou XVIIIA turboshaft engine, delivering 1,044 shp for take-off. Two Kléber-Colombes bag-type fuel tanks under cabin floor, total normal capacity 104 Imp gallons (475 litres). Provision for larger tanks, capacity 145 Imp gallons (660 litres) and for two ferry tanks, one of 60·5 Imp gallons (275 litres) capacity on the cabin floor and another of 55 Imp gallons (250 litres) capacity at the back of the cabin. Tanks can be of self-sealing type in military versions.

ACCOMMODATION: Standard ten-seat version has seats for pilot (to starboard) and co-pilot or passenger in front, and two rows of four seats to the rear. Interior of the cabin is clear except for a vertical duct, housing the flying control rods, positioned centrally aft of the centre row of seats. Two large forward-hinged doors on each side. Compartment for hand baggage or coats aft of rear row of seats. Separate main baggage compartment aft of cabin, with door on starboard side. Alternative 13-seat layout has an extra row of three seats between the four-seat rows, and no space for hand baggage or coats. Ambulance version carries four stretcher patients, a medical attendant and two crew. Mixed-traffic version carries six persons at front of cabin, with 88·3 cu ft (2·50 m³) of cargo space to the rear. The floor in this area will support a loading of 122·9 lb/sq ft (600 kg/m²). Executive versions are available with VIP interiors for four or five passengers. Cabin is heated and ventilated. Provision for 2,755 lb (1,250 kg) capacity cargo sling, rescue hoist, and a wide range of other civil and military equipment.

DIMENSIONS, EXTERNAL:
Diameter of main rotor 37 ft $8\frac{3}{4}$ in (11·50 m)
Blade chord, main rotor (constant) 1 ft $1\frac{3}{4}$ in (0·35 m)
Diameter of tail rotor 2 ft $11\frac{7}{16}$ in (0·90 m)
Length overall 44 ft 0 in (13·41 m)
Length of fuselage 36 ft $3\frac{7}{8}$ in (11·07 m)
Width, rotors folded 10 ft $1\frac{5}{8}$ in (3·09 m)
Height overall 11 ft $1\frac{3}{4}$ in (3·40 m)
Wheel track 7 ft $8\frac{1}{4}$ in (2·34 m)
Wheelbase 23 ft $8\frac{3}{4}$ in (7·23 m)
Cabin doors (fwd, each):
Height 3 ft 8 in (1·12 m)
Width 3 ft $5\frac{3}{4}$ in (1·06 m)
Cabin doors (aft, each):
Height 3 ft 8 in (1·12 m)
Width 2 ft $10\frac{3}{4}$ in (0·88 m)
Freight compartment door:
Height 1 ft $6\frac{3}{4}$ in (0·48 m)
Width 2 ft $7\frac{1}{2}$ in (0·80 m)

DIMENSIONS, INTERNAL:
Cabin: Usable length 7 ft $2\frac{3}{4}$ in (2·20 m)
Width at front 6 ft $5\frac{1}{4}$ in (1·96 m)
Width at rear 5 ft 3 in (1·60 m)
Baggage compartment volume 62 cu ft (1·75 m³)

WEIGHTS:
Basic operating weight 3,087 lb (1,400 kg)
Max T-O weight 6,173 lb (2,800 kg)

PERFORMANCE:
Recommended cruising speed 140 knots (162 mph; 260 km/h)
Econ cruising speed 124 knots (143 mph; 230 km/h)
Vertical rate of climb at S/L at AUW of 5,511 lb (2,500 kg) 1,475 ft (450 m)/min
Rate of climb at 5,900 ft (1,800 m) at AUW of 3,747 lb (1,700 kg) 2,950 ft (900 m)/min
Hovering ceiling in ground effect at AUW of 5,952 lb (2,700 kg) 10,500 ft (3,200 m)
Hovering ceiling out of ground effect at AUW of 5,952 lb (2,700 kg) 9,200 ft (2,800 m)
Range with 1,653 lb (750 kg) payload at econ cruising speed 291 nm (335 miles; 540 km)
Ferry range with 145 Imp gallons (660 litres) fuel, no payload 420 nm (484 miles; 780 km)

AÉROSPATIALE SA 365/366 DAUPHIN

Announced in early 1973, the **SA 365** will be a twin-engined version of the SA 360, powered by Turboméca Arriel turboshaft engines, each rated at 690 shp. A prototype is scheduled to fly during the first months of 1975.

The **SA 366** will be similar, except for having Avco Lycoming LTS 101 engines.

BESNEUX

ALAIN BESNEUX

ADDRESS:
rue de la Sergenterie, 61-Tesse la Madeleine

M Besneux has built, to the design of Jean Pottier, a small single-seat racing aircraft designated P.70B, which was exhibited at the 1973 Paris Air Show under the auspices of the RSA. It had not flown at that time.

BESNEUX P.70B

Few details of the P.70B are available, but its general appearance is shown in the accompanying illustration. It is a conventional single-seat racing aircraft of metal construction, built in 300 hours at a cost of 3,000 francs. The power plant is a converted Volkswagen motor car engine, developing 40 hp.

DIMENSIONS, EXTERNAL:
Wing span 18 ft $0\frac{1}{2}$ in (5·50 m)
Length overall 15 ft 5 in (4·70 m)

AREA:
Wings, gross 73·4 sq ft (6·82 m²)

Besneux P.70B single-seat amateur-built aircraft (40 hp Volkswagen engine) (*J. M. G. Gradidge*)

WEIGHTS:
Weight empty 326 lb (148 kg)
Max T-O weight 580 lb (263 kg)

PERFORMANCE (estimated):
Max cruising speed 97 knots (112 mph; 180 km/h)

BRANDT

MICHEL BRANDT

ADDRESS: Résidence Biancotto, 21000-Darois

Mr Brandt, a former aeronautical student at the Swiss Federal Institute of Technology, began in 1969 the conversion of a former Swiss Army Bü 133 Jungmeister to receive a Lycoming "flat-four" engine. This aircraft, registered HB-MKM, was described briefly, and illustrated, in the 1972-73 *Jane's*.

Plans to produce further conversions of a similar type were abandoned following Mr Brandt's appointment as Chief Engineer of Avions Pierre Robin in 1972. However, he is working on a completely new design known as the Kochab. Intended initially as a competition aircraft for his own use, it is expected to be completed in time for the 1976 World Aerobatic Championships.

BRANDT KOCHAB

TYPE: Single-seat light aircraft for competitive aerobatics.

WINGS: Cantilever mid-wing monoplane of straight-tapered planform. Symmetrical wing section of 16% thickness/chord ratio. No dihedral. Semi-monocoque wood structure. Conventional slotted ailerons.

FUSELAGE: Fabric-covered steel-tube structure.

TAIL UNIT: Wire-braced steel-tube structure, fabric-covered. Horn-balanced rudder and elevators.

LANDING GEAR: Non-retractable tailwheel type. Sandow shock-absorption. Fairings over main legs and wheels.

POWER PLANT: One modified 180 hp Teledyne Continental Tiara 4-180 four-cylinder horizontally-opposed aircooled engine, driving a three-blade Hoffmann constant-speed propeller or two-blade fixed-pitch propeller.

ACCOMMODATION: Pilot only, beneath transparent "bubble" canopy.

DIMENSIONS, EXTERNAL:
Wing span 21 ft 8 in (6·60 m)
Wing aspect ratio 6
Length overall 15 ft 9 in (4·80 m)

AREA:
Wings, gross 77·5 sq ft (7·2 m²)

WEIGHT AND LOADINGS:
Max T-O weight 992 lb (450 kg)
Max wing loading 12·8 lb/sq ft (62·5 kg/m²)
Max power loading 5·5 lb/hp (2·5 kg/hp)

PERFORMANCE (estimated, at max T-O weight):
Max never-exceed speed 205 knots (236 mph; 380 km/h)
Max level speed 156 knots (180 mph; 290 km/h)
Max rate of climb at S/L 2,755 ft (840 m)/min
g limits +9; −6

C.A.A.R.P.

COOPÉRATIVE DES ATELIERS AÉRONAUTIQUES DE LA RÉGION PARISIENNE

HEAD OFFICE AND WORKS:
Aérodrome, 78650-Beynes
Telephone: 489-10-69

DIRECTOR: Auguste Mudry

This company specialised at first in aircraft modification and repair. It then began the manufacture, under subcontract, of components for sailplanes, and in 1965 took over from Scintex-Aviation production of the Super Emeraude light aircraft. It also built a prototype of the C.P. 100 side-by-side two-seat aerobatic version of the Emeraude.

C.A.A.R.P. is now associated with Avions Mudry et Cie (which see) in production of the CAP 10 and CAP 20 aerobatic aircraft, and acts as design and development centre for aircraft produced by the two companies. It is responsible for complete manufacture of the CAP 20, described below, and for fuselages for the CAP 10. Final assembly of the CAP 10 is undertaken by Mudry at Bernay.

At the design study stage in early 1974 was a new aerobatic aircraft, lighter in weight than the CAP 20 but with comparable performance. It is envisaged as a single-seater, very similar to the CAP 10 but with a 180 hp engine, driving a constant-speed propeller. Intended for flying club use, it will be no more expensive than the CAP 10.

C.A.A.R.P./MUDRY CAP 20

The CAP 20, developed in parallel with the CAP 10 (see entry under "Mudry" in this section), is essentially a single-seat derivative of the latter aircraft, although of almost completely new design. Construction of a prototype was financed by the SGAC, and this aircraft (F-WPXU) flew for the first time on 29 July 1969. It has been followed by eight more CAP 20s, of which six were delivered to the Equipe de Voltige of the Armée de l'Air (EVAA).

Under the terms of an agreement between the Armée de l'Air and the Mudry group, several significant modifications are being made and tested on two of the production aircraft, to improve the crispness of their manoeuvres, their pull-outs, rate of roll and overall performance when inverted. It was hoped that this would produce an outstanding aircraft for the French team to fly in the 1974 World Aerobatic Championships.

The progressive design changes are covered by the following designations:

CAP 20A. This is the second of six production aircraft delivered to the EVAA, as modified and flown for the first time in its new form in March 1973. Its landing gear was lightened by removal of the leg and wheel fairings, and its wings were remounted without dihedral. Subsequently, the wingtips were shortened in span (CAP 20A1); the tips were then fitted with wooden endplates (CAP 20A2); and, finally, the endplates were removed, and larger slotted ailerons were fitted in place of the former type with automatic tabs, which had required excessive balance weights (CAP 20A3). Extensive flight testing of the A3 model, including inverted flight and measurement of accelerations and vibration, showed considerable improvement by comparison with the basic CAP 20, except that the absence of dihedral made it difficult to hold precise positions in manoeuvres such as four-point or eight-point hesitation rolls.

CAP 20B. First flown in January 1974, this represents a further modification of the CAP 20A with 1° 30′ dihedral to improve rolling aerobatics; a new wing spar of spruce and glassfibre which is both stronger (+20*g*) and more rigid because of its symmetrical form; and ailerons similar to those of the CAP 20A3.

CAP 20C. This is a modification of the second prototype, which also belongs to the Armée de l'Air. It differs from the standard CAP 20 only in having a 260 hp Lycoming engine, adapted in Switzerland, with modified oil and fuel feed for inverted flight.

CAP 20D. Following satisfactory flight testing of the CAP 20B, it is expected that three EVAA aircraft will be fitted with similar new wings and landing gear, under this designation. They will retain their present 200 hp engine, and will have +9*g* and —6*g* limits.

CAP 20E. This version will be similar to the CAP 20D but with a 260 hp Lycoming engine.

The description below applies to the prototype CAP 20.

TYPE: Single-seat aerobatic light aircraft.

WINGS: Cantilever low-wing monoplane. All-wood single-spar wings, of NACA 23012 section, similar in construction and planform to those of CAP 10 but with only ailerons on trailing-edge, and hydraulically-actuated airbrakes. Dihedral 5° from roots.

FUSELAGE: Conventional all-wood structure, of basically triangular section with rounded top-decking. Wooden covering, except for laminated plastics engine cowling.

TAIL UNIT: Cantilever all-wood structure. Trim tab in rudder and each elevator.

LANDING GEAR: Non-retractable tailwheel type. Streamline fairings on main wheels and legs.

POWER PLANT: One 200 hp Lycoming AIO-360-B1B four-cylinder horizontally-opposed air-cooled engine, driving a Hartzell two-blade constant-speed metal propeller. Fuel in main fuselage tank aft of cockpit, with system modified to permit periods of inverted flight. Provision for 16·5 Imp gallon (75 litre) under-fuselage auxiliary tank for ferry purposes.

ACCOMMODATION: Single seat under transparent moulded canopy which opens sideways to starboard.

DIMENSIONS, EXTERNAL:

Wing span	26 ft 4¾ in (8·04 m)
Wing aspect ratio	5·96
Length overall	23 ft 7¾ in (7·21 m)
Propeller diameter	6 ft 0 in (1·83 m)

AREA:

Wings, gross	116·79 sq ft (10·85 m²)

WEIGHTS AND LOADING:

Weight empty	1,410 lb (640 kg)
Max T-O weight (aerobatic)	1,675 lb (760 kg)
Max wing loading	14·3 lb/sq ft (70·0 kg/m²)

PERFORMANCE (at max aerobatic T-O weight):

Max never-exceed speed	202 knots (233 mph; 376 km/h)
Max cruising speed	183 knots (211 mph; 340 km/h)
Max speed for aerobatics	146 knots (168 mph; 270 km/h)
Stalling speed	52·5 knots (60 mph; 96 km/h)
g limits	+8; —6

C.A.A.R.P./Mudry CAP 20 single-seat aerobatic aircraft (200 hp Lycoming AIO-360-B1B engine)

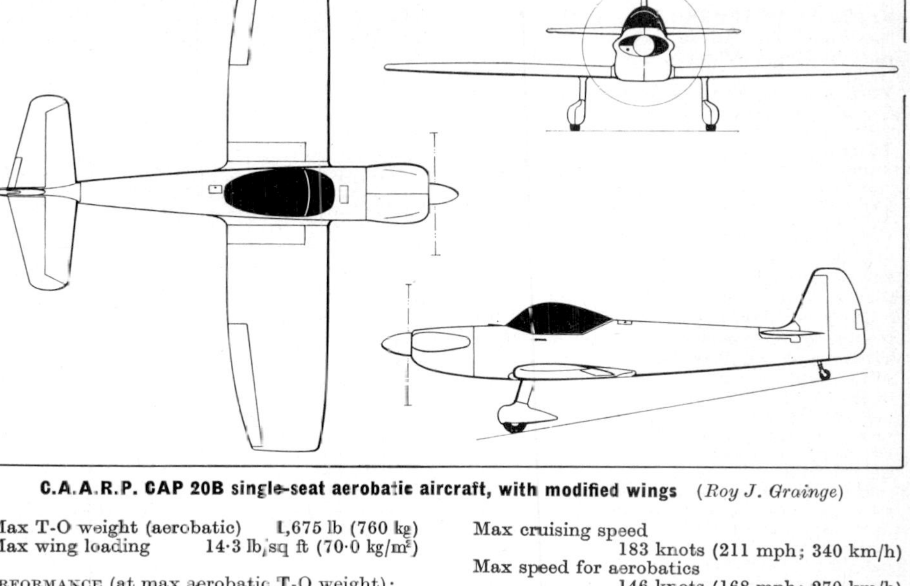

C.A.A.R.P. CAP 20B single-seat aerobatic aircraft, with modified wings (*Roy J. Grainge*)

CERVA (G.I.E.)

CONSORTIUM EUROPÉEN DE RÉALISATION ET DE VENTES D'AVIONS (GROUPEMENT D'INTÉRÊTS ÉCONOMIQUES)

ADDRESS:
13 rue Saint-Honoré, 78-Versailles
Telephone: 950-63-95

This company was formed in 1971 by Siren SA and Wassmer-Aviation SA (which see), each of which has a 50% holding, to build and market an all-metal version of the Wassmer Super 4/21, known as the CE.43 Guépard.

CERVA CE.43 GUÉPARD (CHEETAH)

The CE.43 Guépard is basically an all-metal derivative of the WA Super 4/21 (see 1972-73 *Jane's*), retaining the general features of that aircraft. The prototype (F-WSNJ) flew for the first time on 18 May 1971 and was exhibited at the Paris Air Show later that month. It was followed by a second flying prototype, which was delivered to the SFA, and a further airframe for static testing by the CEAT at Toulouse.

Following certification by the SGAC, on 1 June 1972, and a subsequent government contract for Guépards for the CEV and SFA, twelve aircraft were on the production line in early 1974. Like the prototypes, and the WA Super 4/21, these aircraft have a 250 hp Lycoming engine and are basically four-seaters. Development of the aircraft to have six seats and a more powerful engine (eg 285 hp Teledyne Continental Tiara or 290 hp Lycoming) is projected, together with a light cargo-carrying version with the rear seats removed.

The basic airframe of the Guépard is manufactured by Siren at Argenton-sur-Creuse. Equipment installation, final assembly and flight testing are performed by Wassmer at Issoire.

TYPE: Four-seat all-metal light aircraft.

WINGS: Cantilever low-wing monoplane. Wing section NACA 63-618. Dihedral 6° from roots. All-metal structure, with main spar at 33% chord, light plate front spar at 3·2% chord, and light rear spar at 65% chord to carry ailerons and flaps. Each wing contains 13 ribs, four top-surface stringers and three bottom-surface stringers, and is covered with AU4G alloy sheet. All-metal unslotted ailerons, with top hinges. Electrically-actuated slotted flaps of all-metal construction. No trim tabs. Landing and navigation lights in wingtips.

FUSELAGE: All-metal "boat-type" cabin structure of heavy frames, stringers and skin. Conventional metal semi-monocoque rear fuselage. Engine cowling and cabin door of polyester plastics.

TAIL UNIT: Cantilever metal structure, with vertical surfaces swept back at 37°. All-moving horizontal surfaces, with anti-tab at root on each side. Controllable tab on rudder.

LANDING GEAR: Retractable tricycle type, with steerable nosewheel. Main wheels retract inward into wing roots, nosewheel rearward. Electrical retraction. Oleo-pneumatic shock-absorbers. Main-wheel tyres size 420-150. Nosewheel tyre size 360-125-7. Hydraulic brakes. Small tail bumper.

POWER PLANT: One 250 hp Lycoming IO-540-C4B5 six-cylinder horizontally-opposed air-cooled engine, driving a Hartzell two-blade variable-pitch propeller. Main fuel tank in centre of each wing, aft of main spar; auxiliary tank in each wing outboard of main tank. Total capacity of main fuel tanks 48·4 Imp gallons (220 litres). Total capacity with auxiliary tanks 90·2 Imp gallons (410 litres). Refuelling point above each tank.

ACCOMMODATION: Two adjustable seats side by

CERVA CE.43 Guépard four-seat light aircraft (250 hp Lycoming IO-540-C4B5 engine)

side at front, with dual controls. Rear bench seat for two persons. Upward-hinged door on starboard side. Baggage compartment aft of cabin, with upward-hinged door on starboard side.

Electronics and Equipment: Comprehensive electronics and IFR instrumentation to customer's requirements, including dual VOR, DME, etc. Rotating beacon at tip of fin.

Dimensions, external:
Wing span 32 ft $9\frac{1}{2}$ in (10·00 m)
Wing chord (constant) 5 ft 3 in (1·60 m)
Length overall 27 ft $6\frac{1}{2}$ in (8·40 m)
Height overall 9 ft $2\frac{1}{4}$ in (2·80 m)
Tailplane span 11 ft 4 in (3·46 m)
Wheel track 10 ft 10 in (3·30 m)
Wheelbase 6 ft $10\frac{1}{2}$ in (2·10 m)

Dimension, internal:
Cabin: Max width 3 ft 7 in (1·09 m)

Area:
Wings, gross 172 sq ft (16·0 m²)

Weights and Loadings:
Weight empty 1,863 lb (845 kg)
Max T-O weight:
Utility category 3,220 lb (1,460 kg)
Normal category 3,527 lb (1,600 kg)
Wing loading:
Utility category 18·69 lb/sq ft (91·25 kg/m²)
Normal category 20·48 lb/sq ft (100 kg/m²)

Performance (at max T-O weight):
Max level speed 172 knots (198 mph; 320 km/h)
Max cruising speed 167 knots (192 mph; 310 km/h)
Econ cruising speed 140 knots (161 mph; 260 km/h)
Min flying speed 50 knots (58 mph; 93 km/h)
Max rate of climb at S/L 1,080 ft (330 m)/min
Service ceiling 17,400 ft (5,300 m)
Range with max fuel 1,565 nm (1,800 miles; 2,900 km)

CHASLE

YVES CHASLE

Address:

Le Goya, rue de Traynes, 65-Tarbes

M Chasle, a stress engineer with Aérospatiale, designed and built a light aircraft named the YC-12 Tourbillon. Its dimensions were governed by the maximum size that could be accommodated in his garage workshop. First flight was made on 9 October 1965. As a result of the flight tests leading to its restricted C of A, the height of the vertical tail surfaces was later increased slightly.

Plans are available to amateur constructors.

More recently, M Chasle designed a tandem two-seat light aircraft known as the YC-20, of which details can be found in the 1972-73 *Jane's*.

Prototype Chasle YC-12 Tourbillon single-seat light aircraft (65 hp Continental A65 engine)

CHASLE YC-12 TOURBILLON (WHIRLWIND)

The Tourbillon can be built in a variety of forms, differing only in the type of engine fitted, as follows:

YC-121. With 65 hp Continental A65 engine. Generally similar to prototype (see 1970-71 *Jane's*) except for detail changes.

YC-122. Similar to YC-121, but with 95 hp Continental C90 or 100 hp Rolls-Royce Continental O-200-A engine.

YC-123. Similar to YC-121, but with 105 hp Potez 4E-20b engine.

Construction of YC-12s has been undertaken in several countries, including France, Canada, the US, New Zealand and the UK. Marketing of the YC-12 in North America is by E. Littner, 546 83rd Avenue, Laval-Chomedey, Quebec, Canada.

Type: Single-seat amateur-built light aircraft.

Wings: Cantilever low-wing monoplane. Wing section NACA Srs 7. Dihedral 6°. Incidence 3° 30′. All-wood structure, with main box spar of spruce and okoumé, spruce plank rear spar, girder-type ribs and okoumé plywood covering. All-wood ailerons and three-position slotted flaps.

Fuselage: Conventional plywood-covered wood structure, built around four spruce longerons, four main frames, five secondary frames and stringers.

Tail Unit: Cantilever all-wood structure, with swept vertical surfaces. Fixed tailplane and conventional elevators.

Landing Gear: Non-retractable tailwheel type. Steerable tailwheel linked with rudder. Main units have ERAM oleo-pneumatic suspension. Vespa wheels, size 400-100, mounted on "L"-shape legs. Independent mechanical brakes. Tailwheel carried on leaf spring. Provision for changing to a tricycle configuration, by switching main legs port and starboard, with lower arm of "L" facing rearward, and mounting nose unit on firewall.

Power Plant: One four-cylinder horizontally-opposed aircooled engine (see introductory copy) driving an EVRA two-blade propeller. Fuel tank, capacity 13·3 Imp gallons (60·5 litres), aft of firewall. Oil capacity 0·83 Imp gallons (3·75 litres).

Accommodation: Single seat under large transparent rearward-sliding canopy. Baggage space aft of seat.

Electronics and Equipment: Optional items include Radiomaster radio, generator, starter, and night-flying equipment.

Dimensions, external:
Wing span 22 ft 0 in (6·70 m)
Wing chord at root 4 ft $7\frac{1}{4}$ in (1·40 m)
Wing chord at tip 2 ft $7\frac{1}{4}$ in (0·79 m)
Wing aspect ratio 6·0
Length overall:
YC-121 19 ft 6 in (5·95 m)
YC-122, YC-123 19 ft $2\frac{1}{4}$ in (5·85 m)
Height overall 7 ft $10\frac{1}{2}$ in (2·40 m)
Tailplane span 6 ft $6\frac{3}{4}$ in (2·00 m)
Wheel track 5 ft 3 in (1·60 m)
Wheelbase 11 ft $11\frac{3}{4}$ in (3·65 m)
Propeller diameter 5 ft 9 in (1·75 m)

Areas:
Wings, gross 80·7 sq ft (7·50 m²)
Ailerons (total) 5·94 sq ft (0·55 m²)
Flaps (total) 9·69 sq ft (0·90 m²)
Fin 5·38 sq ft (0·50 m²)
Rudder 3·77 sq ft (0·35 m²)

Weights and Loadings:
Weight empty:
YC-121 628 lb (285 kg)
YC-122, YC-123 690 lb (313 kg)
Max T-O weight, without radio:
YC-121 952 lb (432 kg)
YC-122, YC-123 1,015 lb (460 kg)
Max wing loading:
YC-121 11·77 lb/sq ft (57·5 kg/m²)
YC-122, YC-123 12·55 lb/sq ft (61·3 kg/m²)
Max power loading:
YC-121 14·64 lb/hp (6·64 kg/hp)
YC-122 10·69 lb/hp (4·85 kg/hp)
YC-123 9·63 lb/hp (4·37 kg/hp)

Performance (estimated):
Max level speed at S/L:
YC-121 127 knots (146 mph; 235 km/h)
YC-122 146 knots (168 mph; 270 km/h)
YC-123 151 knots (174 mph; 280 km/h)
Max cruising speed (70% power):
YC-121 110 knots (127 mph; 205 km/h)
YC-122 129 knots (149 mph; 240 km/h)
YC-123 135 knots (155 mph; 250 km/h)
Stalling speed:
YC-121 41 knots (47 mph; 75 km/h)
YC-122, YC-123 44 knots (50 mph; 80 km/h)
Max rate of climb at S/L:
YC-121 905 ft (276 m)/min
YC-122 1,380 ft (420 m)/min
YC-123 1,575 ft (480 m)/min
T-O run:
YC-121 855 ft (260 m)
YC-122 660 ft (200 m)
YC-123 593 ft (180 m)
Max range:
YC-121 434 nm (500 miles; 800 km)
YC-122, YC-123 377 nm (435 miles; 700 km)

COLOMBAN

MICHEL COLOMBAN

Address:

37*bis* rue Lakanal, 92500-Rueil-Malmaison
Telephone: 967-88-76

Formerly with the Morane and Potez companies, and now an aerodynamicist with Aérospatiale, M Colomban has designed and built a very small and unique twin-engined lightplane named the Cricri. Its construction required some 1,200 hours of work and cost only 5,000 francs (1971-72 prices), including the engines.

M Colomban intends to make plans of the Cricri available to amateur constructors after embodying a few design changes, mainly to the wing spar. This is considered advisable, as the aircraft's manoeuvrability is such that the spar will be redesigned for a load factor of $+10g$.

Colomban MC 10 Cricri single-seat ultra-light amateur-built aircraft (two 9 hp Rowena 6507J engines)

COLOMBAN MC 10 CRICRI (CRICKET)

Initial design studies for an aeroplane of only 20 hp, for economical operation, were completed by M Colomban in 1958. His circumstances at that time did not permit its construction, and it was not until September 1970 that manufacture of the Cricri began. In the intervening years, the design was refined to take advantage of new developments in technology and aerodynamics, often after tests carried out personally by the designer.

The prototype (F-WTXJ) is claimed to be the smallest twin-engined aeroplane currently flying, and the only one able to lift a useful load equivalent to 170 per cent of its own empty weight. Special constructional features permit assembly or disassembly in only five minutes. Its light weight and small size make it particularly easy to transport on a trailer towed by car and to store in a garage or shed.

The Cricri was flown for the first time on 19 July 1973 by Robert Buisson, a 68-year-old pilot who had already logged 12,000 flying hours. The first $5\frac{1}{2}$ hours of testing revealed generally good handling qualities, except for over-sensitive controls and engine vibration.

Flight testing was halted on 29 September to permit these shortcomings to be rectified. Modifications were made to the mountings of the engines and accessories, and the engine mounting attachments to the fuselage. The ratio of flying controls to control surface movement was increased and artificial loading was introduced to offset the earlier sensitivity.

Tests were resumed on 12 January 1974, to the complete satisfaction of the pilot. Within fifteen days the Cricri had logged a total of 13 trouble-free flying-hours, including rolls, reversements, split "S" manoeuvres and inverted flight, made possible by its Tillotson diaphragm carburettor. Flight tests by mid-February 1974 had been made at up to 119 knots (137 mph; 220 km/h) and $+4g$. They had confirmed that no special piloting skills are needed to fly this aircraft.

In particular, the Cricri handles like a single-engined design. This results from the fact that the two small engines are mounted close together, and from the carefully-conceived shape of the cockpit canopy which deflects the propeller slipstream over the tail surfaces in such a way that an engine failure produces no dangerous handling problems. If one engine is throttled back fiercely, with hands and feet off the controls, the Cricri is said to do no more than begin a gentle turn.

TYPE: Twin-engined single-seat ultra-light aircraft.

WINGS: Cantilever low-wing monoplane of constant chord. Laminar-flow aerofoil derived from a Wortmann section. Thickness/chord ratio 21·7%. Dihedral 6° from roots. No incidence or sweep. Single-spar box structure. Spar comprises a web riveted to AU4G angle-section booms. Inboard end of spar in each wing is of "forked-tongue" form, like that of many sailplanes, to permit rapid assembly and disassembly of wings. Closely-spaced Klégécel ribs are bonded fore and aft of the spar. Skin consists of a single sheet of AU4G, bonded to structure under pressure after its leading-edge has been formed. No rear spar. Wing box is closed at each end by a riveted metal rib. Entire trailing-edge is occupied by two-section external flaps of the kind fitted to many wartime Junkers aircraft, operating collectively as high-lift devices (movement —5° to +30°) and differentially as ailerons (+8° to —10°). Flaps are spar-less, consisting of a metal monocoque structure, with four metal ribs per section (at each tip and each pivot point), filled with Klégécel over the entire span and over 20% of the chord. Flaps are each actuated via a ball-joint at the root. No controls pass through the wing box, which contains only an AU4G tube as provision for any future installation of fuel tanks in wingtips.

FUSELAGE: Simple metal box structure of rectangular section. Made of AU4G sheet, riveted together at the corners without the use of angle-sections. Stiffened by Klégécel stringers, bonded in place. AU4G frames riveted in position in line with the attachments for the wings, landing gear, tail unit and engine mountings.

TAIL UNIT: Cantilever T type, with sweptback vertical surfaces and all-moving constant-chord horizontal surfaces. Construction similar to that of wings. No tabs. Tailplane actuated by control rods, rudder by cables. Tailplane provided with artificial loading by bungee cord.

LANDING GEAR: Non-retractable tricycle type. Nosewheel fitted with bungee shock-absorption and linked to rudder bar for steering. Each main wheel carried on cantilever leaf-spring. Main-wheel tyres size 210-70, pressure 14·2 lb/sq in (1·0 kg/cm²). Nosewheel tyre size 200-50, pressure 14·2 lb/sq in (1·0 kg/cm²). Colomban disc brakes. Provision for fairing on all three wheels.

POWER PLANT: Two Rowena 6507J single-cylinder two-stroke engines of 137 cc, each giving 9 hp at 7,000 rpm and weighing 14·3 lb (6·5 kg). Tillotson diaphragm carburettor to permit inverted flight. Each engine drives a Colomban MC H1 two-blade metal propeller with ground-adjustable pitch. Laminated plastics fuel tank in fuselage, with current capacity of 3·3 Imp gallons (15 litres); space for tank of 5·25 Imp gallons (24 litres) capacity. Provision for structural tank in each wingtip, total capacity 5·25 Imp gallons (24 litres). Engines not yet cowled.

ACCOMMODATION: Single seat under large transparent canopy, hinged to open sideways, to starboard. Ventilation through port in side of fuselage. No heating.

SYSTEM: Electrical system supplied by two 19W 6V and two 5W 6V batteries.

DIMENSIONS, EXTERNAL:
Wing span 16 ft 4¾ in (5·00 m)
Wing chord, incl flap (constant) 2 ft 0¾ in (0·63 m)
Wing chord, less flap (constant) 1 ft 6¾ in (0·48 m)
Wing aspect ratio 8·1
Length overall, incl nose-probe 14 ft 9¼ in (4·50 m)
Length overall, less nose-probe 12 ft 9½ in (3·90 m)
Width, wings removed 4 ft 9 in (1·45 m)
Height overall 3 ft 11¼ in (1·20 m)
Tailplane span 4 ft 9 in (1·45 m)
Wheel track 3 ft 7¼ in (1·10 m)
Wheelbase 4 ft 1¼ in (1·25 m)
Propeller diameter 2 ft 2¾ in (0·68 m)
Distance between propeller centres 2 ft 11½ in (0·90 m)

DIMENSIONS, INTERNAL:
Cabin: Length 4 ft 3¼ in (1·30 m)
Max width 1 ft 9½ in (0·55 m)
Max height 2 ft 8¼ in (0·82 m)

AREAS:
Wings, gross 33·4 sq ft (3·10 m²)
Trailing-edge flaps 6·89 sq ft (0·64 m²)
Fin 3·88 sq ft (0·36 m²)
Rudder 1·29 sq ft (0·12 m²)
Tailplane 6·46 sq ft (0·60 m²)

WEIGHTS AND LOADINGS:
Weight empty 139 lb (63 kg)
Max T-O and landing weight 375 lb (170 kg)
Max zero-fuel weight 350 lb (159 kg)
Max wing loading 11·25 lb/sq ft (55 kg/m²)
Max power loading 20·72 lb/hp (9·4 kg/hp)

PERFORMANCE (A at AUW of 330 lb; 150 kg, engines and wheels unfaired; B estimated at max AUW, engines and wheels faired):
Max never-exceed speed:
B 151 knots (174 mph; 280 km/h)
Max level speed:
A 97 knots (112 mph; 180 km/h)
B 113 knots (130 mph; 210 km/h)
Max cruising speed (75% power):
A 89 knots (103 mph; 165 km/h)
B 105 knots (121 mph; 195 km/h)
Stalling speed, flaps down:
A 38 knots (44 mph; 70 km/h)
B 41 knots (47 mph; 75 km/h)
Stalling speed, flaps up:
A 46 knots (53 mph; 85 km/h)
B 49 knots (56 mph; 90 km/h)
Max rate of climb at S/L:
A 820 ft (250 m)/min
B 835 ft (255 m)/min
Rate of climb at S/L, one engine out:
A 100 ft (30 m)/min
B 120 ft (36 m)/min
Service ceiling:
B 11,475 ft (3,500 m)
T-O run:
A 525 ft (160 m)
B 655 ft (200 m)
T-O to 50 ft (15 m):
A 1,380 ft (420 m)
B 1,640 ft (500 m)
Landing from 50 ft (15 m):
B 1,310 ft (400 m)
Landing run:
B 655 ft (200 m)
Range with max fuel:
A 166 nm (192 miles; 310 km)
B 215 nm (248 miles; 400 km)

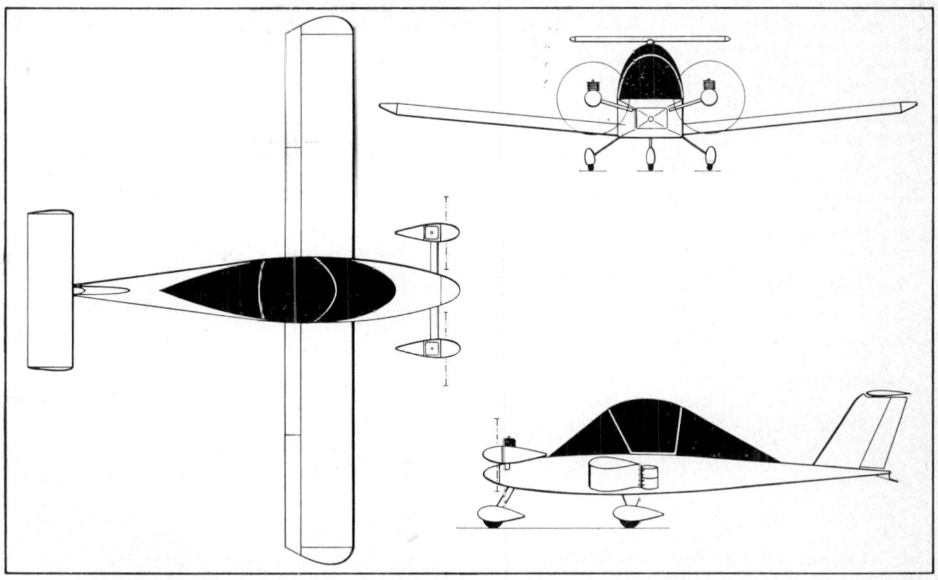

Colomban MC 10 Cricri with planned engine and wheel fairings (*Roy J. Grainge*)

CROSES

EMILIEN and ALAIN CROSES

ADDRESS:
Route de Davayé, 71-Charnay les Macon

The 1960-61 *Jane's* contained details of the Croses EC-1-02 side-by-side two-seat lightplane of the Mignet tandem-wing type. M Emilien Croses subsequently built and flew an improved version of this aircraft, known as the EC-6, and a three-seat lightplane/air ambulance development, the B-EC 7, with more powerful engine. Details of the latter design can be found in the 1970-71 *Jane's*.

M Croses also developed the EAC-3 Pouplume, an ultra-light single-seat aeroplane of the same general configuration. Brief details of the EAC-3 and EC-6 are given below.

CROSES EAC-3 POUPLUME

As in the familiar Mignet designs, the Pouplume single-seat tandem-wing biplane has a fixed rear wing and a pivoted forward wing which dispenses with the need for ailerons and elevators. A conventional rudder is fitted, with a large tail-wheel built into its lower edge.

Construction is conventional, with spruce wing structure and a square-section spruce fuselage covered with okoumé ply. The main landing gear consists of Vespa scooter wheels carried on a wooden cross-member.

The power unit in the prototype (EAC-3-01) is a 10·5 hp Moto 232 cc two-stroke motor-cycle engine, with chain reduction drive to the propeller shaft. The reduction ratio is 3·5 : 1, giving a propeller speed of 1,300 rpm. Fuel capacity is 2·2 Imp gallons (10 litres).

The EAC-3-01 Pouplume took 600 hours to build and flew for the first time in June 1961. This machine was followed, in 1967, by a second prototype (EAC-3-02), with an 8 in (20 cm) longer fuselage. M Croses is offering sets of plans to other constructors and the Pouplume shown in the accompanying illustration was built in France by an amateur constructor.

Alternative engines that may be fitted in the Pouplume include the various Volkswagen conversions.

Croses EAC-3 Pouplume light aircraft (10.5 hp Moto engine)

DIMENSIONS, EXTERNAL (EAC-3-01):
- Span of forward wing 25 ft 7 in (7·8 m)
- Span of rear wing 23 ft 0 in (7·0 m)
- Length overall 9 ft 10 in (3·0 m)
- Height overall 5 ft 11 in (1·8 m)

AREA:
- Wings, gross 172 sq ft (16·0 m²)

WEIGHTS:
- Weight empty 243-310 lb (110-140 kg)
- Max T-O weight 485-573 lb (220-260 kg)

PERFORMANCE (A: 10·5 hp engine; B: 18 hp engine):
- Max level speed:
  - A 38 knots (43·5 mph; 70 km/h)
  - B 65 knots (75 mph; 120 km/h)
- Econ cruising speed:
  - A 27 knots (31 mph; 50 km/h)
  - B 38 knots (43·5 mph; 70 km/h)
- T-O speed:
  - A 13·5 knots (15·5 mph; 25 km/h)
- Landing speed:
  - A 9·7 knots (11 mph; 18 km/h)
- T-O run:
  - A 200 ft (60 m)
  - B 131 ft (40 m)
- Landing run:
  - A 80 ft (24 m)
- Fuel consumption:
  - A 1 Imp gallon (4·5 litres)/hr

CROSES EC-6 CRIQUET (LOCUST)

This design by Emilien Croses is a development of his earlier EC-1-02 prototype and is a side-by-side two-seater based on the familiar Mignet tandem-wing formula. Construction was started in March 1964 and the EC-6-01 flew for the first time on 6 July 1965.

Plans are available to amateur constructors.

TYPE: Two-seat tandem-wing light aircraft.

WINGS: Forward wing built in one piece and pivoted on two streamlined supports, giving variable incidence between —2° and +12°. Fixed rear (lower) wing. Wing section NACA 23012 (modified). Both wings have two-spar wooden structure, with plywood leading-edge, overall fabric covering and some components of glassfibre. No ailerons.

FUSELAGE: Spruce structure, covered with plywood. Glassfibre engine cowling.

TAIL UNIT: Plywood-covered spruce fin and rudder. No tailplane or elevators.

LANDING GEAR: Non-retractable tailwheel type. Main wheels, size 420-150, carried on single cantilever arch structure made from ash wood on a forme and covered with glassfibre. Tailwheel, size 420-150, semi-enclosed in bottom of rudder.

POWER PLANT: One 90 hp Continental four-cylinder horizontally-opposed aircooled engine, driving a modified SIPA two-blade propeller. Fuel capacity originally 13 Imp gallons (60 litres); planned to be increased to 20 Imp gallons (90 litres).

ACCOMMODATION: Two seats side by side in enclosed cabin. Door on starboard side.

DIMENSIONS, EXTERNAL:
- Span of forward wing 25 ft 7 in (7·80 m)
- Span of rear wing 22 ft 11½ in (7·00 m)
- Wing chord (constant, each) 3 ft 11¼ in (1·20 m)
- Length overall 15 ft 3 in (4·65 m)

AREA:
- Wings, gross 172 sq ft (16·0 m²)

WEIGHTS:
- Weight empty 639 lb (290 kg)
- Max T-O weight 1,213 lb (550 kg)

PERFORMANCE (officially certificated, at max T-O weight):
- Max level speed at S/L 115 knots (132 mph; 213 km/h)
- Max cruising speed 92 knots (106 mph; 170 km/h)
- Econ cruising speed 86 knots (99 mph; 160 km/h)
- Min flying speed 22 knots (25 mph; 40 km/h)
- Will not stall
- T-O time (max) 6 sec
- Climb to 6,560 ft (2,000 m) 6 min 14 sec

Croses EC-6-01 Criquet two-seat light aircraft (90 hp Continental C90 engine) *(Dr Ulrich Haller)*

DALOTEL

SOCIÉTÉ DALOTEL

HEAD OFFICE:
63 rue de Varsovie, 92700-Colombes

Telephone: 242 34-85 and 242 55-70

With manufacturing assistance from the Société Poulet, M Michel Dalotel designed and flew a prototype tandem two-seat advanced training and aerobatic aircraft designated DM-165, of which details can be found under the "Poulet" heading in the 1972-73 *Jane's*.

First flight of the DM-165 (F-PPZE) was made in April 1969 and it has since logged several hundreds of flying hours. It was sent to the Centre d'Essais en Vol at Istres from 9 December 1970 to 25 March 1971 for official testing, as a result of which it was stated to meet Norme Air 2052A Category A standards as an aircraft suitable for competitive aerobatics.

Société Dalotel plans to produce and market a number of aircraft evolved from the DM-165, of which details are given below. The date envisaged for putting into production the first series of DM-160s, in both Club and Professional versions, is July 1975.

Dalotel DM-165, prototype for the DM-125 and DM-160 aerobatic aircraft *(Peter R. March)*

DALOTEL DM-125 and DM-160

Although developed from the DM-165 prototype, these projected production versions will differ from it in several important respects. They will be suited in every way for competitive aerobatics, with ultimate load factors of $\pm 14g$, but they will be designed equally for use at flying training schools and as aircraft on which pilots can perfect their aerobatic skills. Instead of the all-wood wings of the prototype, they will have wings of composite wood and metal construction. The ailerons will be fabric-covered metal structures, as will the flaps which are to replace the airbrakes of the DM-165. The capacity of the fuel tanks is to be increased to 22 Imp gallons (100 litres), and prolonged inverted flight will be practicable with all versions. Only the Professional version of the DM-160 will have a retractable main landing gear.

The three aircraft will be identified as follows:

DM-125 Club. Tandem two-seater derived directly from the DM-165 prototype. Powered by 125 hp Lycoming four-cylinder horizontally-opposed aircooled engine. Non-retractable landing gear. Optional items include modified fuel and oil systems, for prolonged inverted flight, an accelerometer and 360-channel VHF radio with VOR coupling.

DM-160 Club. Identical with DM-125 except for having a 160 hp fuel-injection Lycoming engine and fixed-pitch propeller.

DM-160 Professional. Basically similar to DM-160 Club, but with electrically-retractable (inward into wings) main landing gear, and constant-speed propeller. The following details are common to all three versions:

TYPE: Two-seat training and aerobatic light aircraft.

WINGS: Cantilever low-wing monoplane. Wing sections evolved from NACA 23015/2300. Dihedral 3°. Incidence 4° at root. Composite wood and metal structure, covered with heavy-gauge stressed skin. Each wing attached to fuselage at three points; designed for rapid replacement and for easy removal when the aircraft is to be transported by road. Fabric-covered metal ailerons, fully balanced internally and each fitted with an automatic tab. Fabric-covered trailing-edge flaps of metal construction.

FUSELAGE: Welded steel-tube structure, built in three main sections, with fabric covering.

TAIL UNIT: Conventional cantilever wooden structure, with plywood-covered fixed surfaces and fabric-covered control surfaces. Designed for easy dismantling for road transportation. Electrically-actuated trim tab in elevator.

LANDING GEAR: Non-retractable or retractable main units according to type (see above). Rubber-in-compression shock-absorbers. Mainwheel tyres size 420 × 150. Hydraulic brakes. Non-retractable Scott tailwheel, steerable with rudder.

POWER PLANT: See under individual versions above. Plastics engine cowling in two halves.

ACCOMMODATION: Tandem seating for two persons under individual jettisonable canopies. Pilot occupies rear seat.

DIMENSIONS, EXTERNAL:
- Wing span 27 ft 6¾ in (8·40 m)
- Length overall 22 ft 10 in (6·96 m)
- Height overall 5 ft 11¾ in (1·82 m)

AREA:
- Wings, gross 132·4 sq ft (12·30 m²)

PERFORMANCE (estimated, at max T-O weight. A: DM-125; B: DM-160 Club; C: DM-160 Professional):
- Max never-exceed speed:
  - A, B, C 207 knots (239 mph; 385 km/h)
- Max level speed at S/L:
  - A 127 knots (146 mph; 235 km/h)
  - C 167 knots (192 mph; 310 km/h)
- Cruising speed at S/L:
  - A 113-119 knots (130-136 mph; 210-220 km/h)
  - B 129 knots (149 mph; 240 km/h)
  - C 151 knots (174 mph; 280 km/h)
- Stalling speed, flaps up:
  - A, B 49 knots (56 mph; 90 km/h)
- Stalling speed, flaps down:
  - A, B 40·5-43·5 knots (47-50 mph; 75-80 km/h)
- Max rate of climb at S/L:
  - A 787 ft (240 m)/min
  - B 1,378 ft (420 m)/min
  - C 1,968 ft (600 m)/min

DASSAULT-BREGUET

AVIONS MARCEL DASSAULT/BREGUET AVIATION

HEAD OFFICE: 46 avenue Kléber, 75116-Paris
Telephone: 727-61-19
HEADQUARTERS: 27 Rue du Professeur Pauchet, 92420-Vaucresson
POSTAL ADDRESS:
BP 32, 92420-Vaucresson
Telephone: 970-38-50
Telex: 60755 Brevau
WORKS: 92210-Saint-Cloud, 77000-Melun Villaroche, 95100-Argenteuil, 92100-Boulogne/Seine, 78140-Vélizy-Villacoublay, 33610-Martignas, 33700-Bordeaux-Mérignac, 33400-Talence, 33630-Cazaux, 31770-Toulouse-Colomiers, 64600-Biarritz-Anglet, 64200-Biarritz-Parme, 13800-Istres, 74370-Argonay, 59113-Lille-Seclin, 86000-Poitiers
FOUNDER: Marcel Dassault
CHAIRMAN: B. C. Vallières
DEPUTY MANAGING DIRECTORS:
X. D'Iribarne (Production and Industrialisation)
A. Etesse (Civil Aircraft)
J. Barge (International Co-operation Military Aircraft)
MANAGEMENT EXECUTIVES:
P. François (General Secretary)
J. Cabrière (General Technical Manager)
H. Deplante (Technical Adviser)
M. Berjon (Technical Manager)
Y. Thiriet (Export Technical Manager)
P. E. Jaillard (Military Aircraft Manager)
F. Serralta (Military Aircraft Manager)
C. Barrière (Production Manager)
J. F. Cazaubiel (Flight Test Manager)
A. Segura (Press Information Manager)

Avions Marcel Dassault/Breguet Aviation resulted from the merger on 14 December 1971 of the Avions Marcel Dassault and Breguet Aviation companies. It is engaged in the development and production of military and civil aircraft, guided missiles and servo control equipment.

The company's principal current products are the Mirage III multi-purpose fighter; Mirage 5 ground-support aircraft; Mirage F1 fighter; Jaguar tactical support aircraft and advanced trainer (under Anglo-French collaborative programme; see "SEPECAT" in the International section of this edition); Atlantic maritime patrol aircraft (in production under a European manufacturing programme); Falcon 20 jet executive transport and its scaled-down development, the Falcon 10; and the Mercure twin-turbofan short-haul transport (in production under a multi-national programme).

Under development are the Mirage G8A air-superiority/ground attack/long-range reconnaissance aircraft; Alpha Jet basic and advanced training aircraft (under Franco-German programme); Falcon 30/Mystère 40-100 commuter transport aircraft; Breguet 941 military and civil STOL transport (described in 1973-74 *Jane's*); and a second-generation version of the Atlantic, for operational service at the end of the present decade.

The company is also engaged in the development and manufacture of equipment, notably hydraulic and electro-hydraulic powered aircraft controls with "feel" simulation. Its subsidiary, Electronique Marcel Dassault, is engaged on a variety of projects, including research and production of weapon system equipment for air-to-air, surface-to-air and surface-to-surface missiles; tracking radar for use with missiles; and equipment for supersonic jet aircraft.

Series production of Avions Marcel Dassault/Breguet Aviation aircraft is undertaken under a widespread subcontracting programme, with final assembly and flight testing being handled by the company. Its 17 separate works and facilities cover more than 7,535,000 sq ft (700,000 m^2), with a total of 15,000 employees, including 3,000 engineers.

The principal works is at Saint-Cloud, where the design office is situated and where most of the company's prototypes are built. Mérignac is the flight test centre for production aircraft. Istres is the flight test centre for all prototypes, and Cazaux the flight test centre for armament. Biarritz is devoted to production, modification and overhaul.

To cope with the important Mercure programme, Dassault-Breguet enlarged its production facilities by building five new works. Lille-Seclin is responsible for manufacturing most milled components, such as integrally-stiffened wing and fuselage panels, frames and spars; Poitiers handles assembly of the central fuselage section, centre wing section and horizontal tail surfaces; Martignas is responsible for wing assembly; Argonay manufactures servo-controls; and Istres houses the final assembly lines and flight acceptance facilities.

A factory built at Toulouse-Colomiers accommodates assembly lines for the Atlantic maritime patrol aircraft and the Jaguar tactical support/advanced training aircraft.

Avions Marcel Dassault/Breguet Aviation has established close links with the industries of other countries. The Atlantic programme associates manufacturers in Belgium, France, Germany, Italy and the Netherlands under the overall responsibility of their respective governments. In the same way the British and French governments are associated in the SEPECAT concern, formed to control the Dassault-Breguet/BAC Jaguar programme; and the German and French governments are associated in development of the Alpha Jet trainer.

Purchase of Mirage fighters by Belgium and Spain has led to Belgian and Spanish participation in Mirage III/5 and Mirage F1 production. In the Autumn of 1973, a total of 13 aircraft of these types were being produced each month at Bordeaux-Mérignac, with F1 production scheduled to reach four per month by the Spring of 1974 and five per month by the end of the year.

Dassault-Breguet has also set up a broad international collaborative programme for the Mercure. In addition to some subcontracting arrangements (wing panels are manufactured by Canadair) and to purchase of manufactured items (such as the turbofan engines and equipment), about one-third of the Mercure structure is built outside France.

DASSAULT MIRAGE III

The Mirage III was designed initially as a Mach 2 high-altitude all-weather interceptor, capable of performing ground support missions and requiring only small airstrips. Developed versions include a two-seat trainer, long-range fighter-bomber and reconnaissance aircraft, and a total of 1,170 Mirage IIIs of all types had been produced by 1 January 1974, including licence production abroad, out of a total of approx 1,300 ordered by 18 countries. The 900th Mirage III assembled in France was completed in the Spring of 1974.

The experimental prototype flew for the first time on 17 November 1956, powered by a SNECMA Atar 101G turbojet with afterburner (9,900 lb; 4,500 kg st).

Production versions of the Mirage III are as follows:

Mirage III-A. Pre-series of ten aircraft, with SNECMA Atar 9B turbojet (13,225 lb; 6,000 kg) st. First Mirage III-A flew on 12 May 1958. Last six equipped to production standard, with CSF Cyrano *Ibis* air-to-air radar.

Mirage III-B. Two-seat version of III-A, with tandem seating under one-piece canopy; radar deleted, but fitted with radio beacon equipment. Fuselage 23·6 in (60 cm) longer than that of III-A. Intended primarily as a trainer, but suitable for strike sorties, carrying same air-to-surface armament as Mirage III-C. Prototype flew for first time on 20 October 1959, and first production model on 19 July 1962. Total of 170 two-seaters ordered, including variants for 18 countries.

Mirage III-BE. Two-seat version of the III-E for French Air Force. Similar model also supplied to foreign air forces.

Mirage III-C. All-weather interceptor and day ground attack fighter. Production version of III-A with SNECMA Atar 9B turbojet engine, optional SEPR 841 rocket engine and CSF Cyrano *Ibis* air-to-air radar.

Initial series of 95 for French Air Force, of which the first flew on 9 October 1960. One supplied to Swiss Air Force. Total of 244 built, including III-CJ for Israel and III-CZ for South Africa. Full description in 1968-69 *Jane's*.

Mirage III-D. Two-seat version of the Mirage III-O, built in Australia for the RAAF. First of ten ordered for Mirage OCU was assembled in Australia and delivered in November 1966. Similar, French-built models ordered by 12 countries, including six more for Australia.

Mirage III-E. Long-range fighter-bomber/intruder version, of which 453 have been ordered for the French Air Force and for the air forces of Argentina (III-EA), Brazil (III-EBR), Lebanon (III-EL), Pakistan (III-EP), South Africa (III-EZ), Spain (III-EE) and Venezuela (III-EV).

First of three prototypes flew on 5 April 1961, and the first delivery of a production III-E was made in January 1964. Length increased by 11·8 in (30 cm) compared with III-C.

Mirage III-O. Version of the Mirage III-E manufactured under licence in Australia. Main differences compared with the standard III-E are fitment of a Sperry twin gyro platform and PHI 5CI navigation unit. First two III-Os assembled in France; first of these handed over on 9 April 1963. Further 98 built in Australia, details of which were given under entry for Commonwealth of Australia, Government Aircraft Factories, in 1969-70 *Jane's*.

Mirage III-R. Reconnaissance version of III-E for French Air Force. Set of five OMERA type 31 cameras, in place of radar in nose, can be focused in four different arrangements for very low altitude, medium altitude, high altitude and night reconnaissance missions. Self-contained navigation system and same air-to-surface armament as Mirage III-C. Two prototypes, converted from III-As, of which the first flew in November 1961. Total of 142 production models ordered, including variants for Pakistan (III-RP), South Africa (III-RZ) and Switzerland (III-RS).

Mirage III-RD. Similar to III-R but with improved Doppler navigation system in fairing under front fuselage, gyro gunsight and auto-

Dassault Mirage III-EA single-seat fighter of the Argentine Air Force

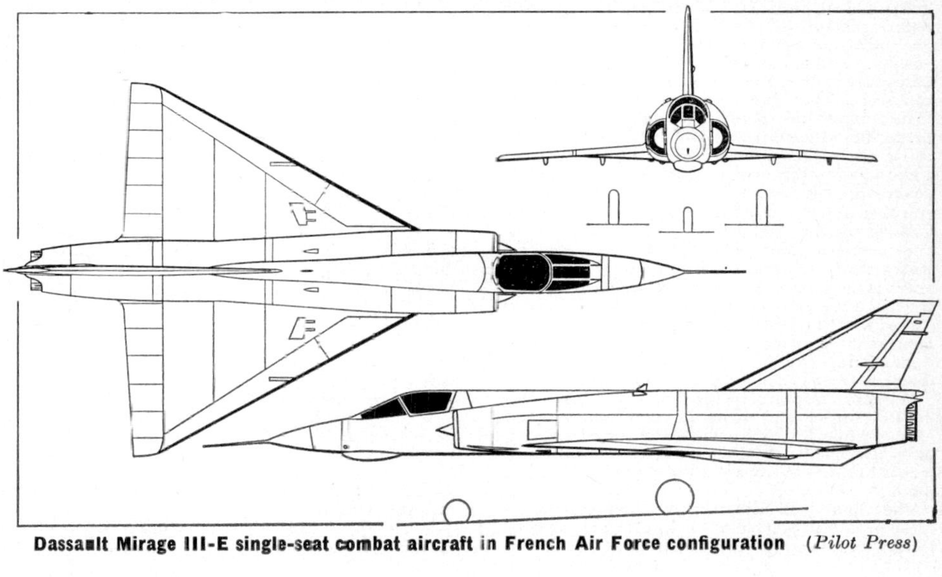

Dassault Mirage III-E single-seat combat aircraft in French Air Force configuration (*Pilot Press*)

matic cameras. Provision for carrying SAT Cyclope infra-red tracking equipment in ventral fairing, and two 374 Imp gallon (1,700 litre) underwing auxiliary fuel tanks. Twenty ordered for French Air Force.

Mirage III-S. Developed from the Mirage III-E, with a Hughes TARAN electronics fire-control system and armament of HM-55 Falcon missiles. Thirty-six supplied to Swiss Air Force, of which the first two were built in France and the remainder by the Federal Aircraft Factory in Switzerland.

The following description refers to the Mirage III-E, but is generally applicable to all versions:

TYPE: Single-seat interceptor, ground attack or reconnaissance aircraft.

WINGS: Cantilever low-wing monoplane of delta planform, with conical camber. Thickness/chord ratio 4·5% to 3·5%. Anhedral 1°. No incidence. Sweepback on leading-edge 60° 34′. All-metal torsion-box structure with stressed skin of machined panels with integral stiffeners. Elevons are hydraulically powered by Dassault twin-cylinder actuators with artificial feel. Airbrakes, comprising small panels hinged to upper and lower wing surfaces, near leading-edge.

FUSELAGE: All-metal structure, "waisted" in accordance with the area rule.

TAIL UNIT: Cantilever fin and hydraulically-actuated powered rudder only. Dassault twin-cylinder actuators with artificial feel.

LANDING GEAR: Retractable tricycle type, with single wheel on each unit. Hydraulic retraction, nosewheel rearward, main units inward. Messier-Hispano shock-absorbers and disc brakes. Main-wheel tyre pressure 85·5-142 lb/sq in (6-10 kg/cm²). Braking parachute.

POWER PLANT: One SNECMA Atar 9C turbojet engine (13,670 lb; 6,200 kg st with afterburner), fitted with an overspeed system which is engaged automatically from Mach 1·4 and permits a thrust increase of approx 8 per cent in the high supersonic speed range. Optional and jettisonable SEPR 844 single-chamber rocket motor (3,300 lb; 1,500 kg st) or interchangeable fuel tank. Movable half-cone centre-body in each air intake. Total internal fuel capacity 733 Imp gallons (3,330 litres) when rocket motor is not fitted. Provision for this to be augmented by two 132, 285 or 374 Imp gallon (600, 1,300 or 1,700 litre) underwing drop-tanks.

ACCOMMODATION: Single seat under rearward-hinged canopy. Hispano-built Martin-Baker Type RM.4 zero-altitude ejection seat.

SYSTEMS: Two separate air-conditioning systems for cockpit and electronics. Two independent hydraulic systems, pressure 3,000 lb/sq in (210 kg/cm²), for flying controls, landing gear and brakes. Power for DC electrical system from 24V 40Ah batteries and a 26·5V 9kW generator. AC electrical system power provided by one 200V 400Hz transformer and one 200V 400Hz 9kVA alternator.

ELECTRONICS AND EQUIPMENT: Duplicated UHF, TACAN, Doppler, CSF Cyrano II fire-control radar in nose, navigation computer, bombing computer, automatic gunsight.

The Mirage III-E has a normal magnetic detector mounted in the fin, and a central gyro and "black boxes" to provide accurate and stabilised heading information. The pilot's equipment determines at any instant the geographical co-ordinates of the aircraft and compares them with the co-ordinates of the target, the differences between the two being presented to the pilot as a "course to steer" and "distance to run". Associated with this facility is a rotative magazine in the cockpit in which it is possible to insert up to 12 plastics punch-cards. Each card represents the co-ordinates of a geographical position. Therefore it is possible before take-off at point A to select point B on the rotating magazine. During take-off, ie after reaching 150 knots (173 mph; 278 km/h), the computer will switch on and the heading and distance to point B will be presented to the pilot. When overhead point B (assuming a pure navigational sortie) he can either select point A or the next turning point, or if required this sequence can continue until a maximum of twelve pre-set turning points have been used. Another facility available in the computer is known as the "additional base". Assuming that between points A and B the pilot receives instructions by radio to go to point C (and that there is no punch card in the magazine for point C) the pilot can, by means of setting knobs, "wind on" the bearing and distance of point C from point B; then, when he selects the switch "additional base", the heading to steer and distance to run to point C will be indicated.

Marconi Doppler equipment provides the ground speed and drift information for the above, while TACAN is presented as a "bearing and distance" on the navigation indicator located on the starboard side of the instrument panel.

The Cyrano II installation in the aircraft's nose provides orthodox air-to-air interception radar, and has the additional mode available of control from the ground. In the latter case the pilot simply obeys his gunsight instructions, and radio silence is maintained. Cyrano II also functions in an air-to-ground role for high-level navigation, presenting a radar picture of the ground; for low-level navigation, presenting the obstacles above a preselected altitude; for blind descent, presenting obstacles that intercept the descent path; for anti-collision, presenting the obstacles that can be avoided by applying a 0·1*g* "pull-up"; and for distance measuring, by presenting in the sight the oblique aircraft-to-ground distance.

Allied to the Cyrano II installation is the CSF 97 sighting system, of illuminated points, dots, bars and figures, giving air-to-air facility for cannons and missiles, air-to-ground facility for dive-bombing or LABS, and navigation facility for horizon and heading.

ARMAMENT: Ground attack armament consists normally of two 30 mm DEFA cannon in fuselage, each with 125 rounds of ammunition, and two 1,000 lb bombs, or an AS.30 air-to-surface missile under the fuselage and 1,000 lb bombs under the wings. Alternative underwing stores include JL-100 pods, each with 18 rockets, and 55 Imp gallon (250 litre) fuel tanks. For interception duties, one Matra R.530 air-to-air missile can be carried under fuselage, with optional guns and two Sidewinder missiles.

DIMENSIONS, EXTERNAL:
- Wing span: 27 ft 0 in (8·22 m)
- Wing aspect ratio: 1·94
- Length overall:
  - III-B: 50 ft 6¼ in (15·40 m)
  - III-E: 49 ft 3½ in (15·03 m)
  - III-R: 50 ft 10¼ in (15·50 m)
- Height overall: 13 ft 11½ in (4·25 m)
- Wheel track: 10 ft 4 in (3·15 m)
- Wheelbase:
  - III-E: 16 ft 0 in (4·87 m)

AREAS:
- Wings, gross: 375 sq ft (34·85 m²)
- Vertical tail surfaces (total): 48·4 sq ft (4·5 m²)

WEIGHTS AND LOADING:
- Weight empty:
  - III-B: 13,820 lb (6,270 kg)
  - III-E: 15,540 lb (7,050 kg)
  - III-R: 14,550 lb (6,600 kg)
- Max T-O weight:
  - III-B: 26,455 lb (12,000 kg)
  - III-E, R: 29,760 lb (13,500 kg)
- Max wing loading:
  - III-E, R: 75·85 lb/sq ft (370 kg/m²)

PERFORMANCE (Mirage III-E, in "clean" condition with guns installed, except where indicated):
- Max level speed at S/L: 750 knots (863 mph; 1,390 km/h)
- Max level speed at 39,375 ft (12,000 m): 1,268 knots (1,460 mph; 2,350 km/h) (Mach 2·2)
- Cruising speed at 36,000 ft (11,000 m): Mach 0·9
- Approach speed: 183 knots (211 mph; 340 km/h)
- Landing speed: 162 knots (187 mph; 300 km/h)
- Time to 36,000 ft (11,000 m), Mach 0·9: 3 min
- Time to 49,200 ft (15,000 m), Mach 1·8: 6 min 50 sec
- Service ceiling at Mach 1·8: 55,775 ft (17,000 m)
- Ceiling, using rocket motor: 75,450 ft (23,000 m)
- T-O run, according to mission (up to max T-O weight): 2,295-5,250 ft (700-1,600 m)
- Landing run, using brake parachute: 2,295 ft (700 m)
- Combat radius, ground attack: 647 nm (745 miles; 1,200 km)

Dassault Mirage 5-V single-seat ground attack aircraft of the Venezuelan Air Force

Dassault Mirage 5-DV two-seat trainer/combat aircraft of the Venezuelan Air Force, with an Argentine Mirage III-EA (background)

DASSAULT MIRAGE 5

The Mirage 5 is a ground attack aircraft derived from the Mirage III-E, using the same airframe and engine. Basic VFR version has simplified avionics, 110 Imp gallons (500 litres) greater fuel capacity than III-E and considerably extended stores carrying capability. It combines the full Mach 2+ capability of the Mirage III, and its ability to operate from semi-prepared airfields, with simpler maintenance. In ground attack configuration, up to 8,820 lb (4,000 kg) of weapons and 220 Imp gallons (1,000 litres) of fuel can be carried externally on seven wing and fuselage attachment points. The Mirage 5 can also be flown as an interceptor, with two Sidewinder air-to-air missiles and 1,034 Imp gallons (4,700 litres) of external fuel. At customer's option, any degree of IFR/all-weather operation can be provided for, with reduced fuel or weapons load. The Mirage 5 was flown for the first time on 19 May 1967.

Up to 1 January 1974, more than 400 Mirage 5s had been ordered. The 106 aircraft for the Belgian Air Force were assembled in Belgium by SABCA (which see).

Versions announced so far are as follows:

Mirage 5-AD and 5-RAD. Ordered by Abu Dhabi in 1972.

Mirage 5-DAD. Two-seat version of Mirage 5-AD for Abu Dhabi.

Mirage 5-BA. Single-seat ground attack model, with more advanced navigation system than basic Mirage 5, for Belgian Air Force. First (Dassault-built) 5-BA flew on 6 March 1970.

Mirage 5-BD. Two-seat version of Mirage 5-BA for Belgian Air Force.

Mirage 5-BR. Single-seat reconnaissance version of 5-BA for Belgian Air Force, with five Vinten type 360 cameras installed in nose. Provision to install infra-red photographic equipment is under consideration.

Mirage 5-COA, 5-COD and 5-COR. Ordered by Colombian Air Force.

Mirage 5-D, 5-DD, 5-DE and 5-DR. Ordered by Libyan Air Force. Deliveries began January 1971.

Mirage M5-F. Former Mirage 5-J aircraft repurchased from the Israeli Air Force by the French government. In service with French Air Force tactical squadrons since mid-1973.

Mirage 5-M. Ordered by Zaïre.

Mirage 5-DM. Two-seat version of Mirage 5-M, for Zaïre.

Mirage 5-P. Ordered by Peru in April 1968. Delivery completed.

Mirage 5-DP. Two-seat version of Mirage 5-P for Peruvian Air Force.

Mirage 5-PA. Ordered by Pakistan.

Mirage 5-SDE. Ordered by Saudi Arabia.

Mirage 5-SDD. Two-seat version of Mirage 5-SDE, for Saudi Arabia.

Mirage 5-V. Ordered by Venezuela.

Mirage 5-DV. Two-seat version of Mirage 5-V, for Venezuela.

The structural description of the Mirage III-E is generally applicable to the Mirage 5, with the following exceptions:

SYSTEMS: Generally as for Mirage III-E.

ARMAMENT: Seven attachment points for external loads, with multiple launchers permitting a max load of more than 4 tons. Ground attack armament consists normally of two 30 mm DEFA cannon in fuselage, each with 125 rounds of ammunition, and two 1,000 lb bombs or an AS.30 air-to-surface missile under the fuselage and 1,000 lb bombs under the wings. Alternative underwing stores include tank/bomb carriers, each with 110 Imp gallons (500 litres) of fuel and four 500 lb or two 1,000 lb bombs, and JL-100 pods, each with eighteen 68 mm rockets and 55 Imp gallons (250 litres) of fuel. For interception duties, two Sidewinder missiles can be carried under the wings.

EQUIPMENT: Can be fitted with Aïda II radar rangefinder in nose.

DIMENSIONS, EXTERNAL:
As III-E, except:
Length overall 51 ft 0¼ in (15·55 m)

WEIGHTS AND LOADING:
As III-E, except:
Weight empty 14,550 lb (6,600 kg)

PERFORMANCE (in "clean" condition, with guns installed, except where indicated):
As III-E, plus:
Combat radius with 2,000 lb (907 kg) bomb load:
hi-lo-hi 699 nm (805 miles; 1,300 km)
lo-lo-lo 347 nm (400 miles; 650 km)
Ferry range with three external tanks
2,158 nm (2,485 miles; 4,000 km)

MIRAGE 5 "MOUSTACHES"

Developed from the Mirage III and 5 series, the Mirage 5 "Moustaches" is a ground attack aircraft capable of air-superiority operations at speeds up to Mach 2.

It offers the same variety of optional armament and same internal fuel capacity as the Mirage 5, but has a 15,800 lb (7,165 kg) st SNECMA Atar 9K-50 augmented-thrust turbojet engine, representing a 16 per cent increase in rated power by comparison with the Mirage 5.

Two small retractable foreplane surfaces, known colloquially as "moustaches", are mounted in the nose to improve take-off and landing performance. Take-off distances are reduced by more than 30 per cent, and approach speed is reduced by more than 15 per cent. Low-speed manoeuvrability, and the accuracy and ease of handling during landing are also improved greatly.

The Mirage 5 "Moustaches" is particularly suited to operations from short fields in mountainous regions, and for tight manoeuvres in hilly country or to evade anti-aircraft defences.

DASSAULT MIRAGE F1

Early in 1964 Dassault was awarded a French government contract to develop a replacement for the Mirage III, followed shortly afterwards by an order for a prototype aircraft which was designated Mirage F2. This was a two-seat fighter, powered by a SNECMA (Pratt & Whitney) TF 306 turbofan engine. It first flew on 12 June 1966 and was described and illustrated in the 1967-68 *Jane's*.

Concurrently with work on the Mirage F2 Dassault also developed, as a private venture, a much smaller single-seat aircraft, the Mirage F1, with a SNECMA Atar 9K turbojet engine. The prototype Mirage F1-01 flew for the first time on 23 December 1966, and exceeded Mach 2 during its fourth flight on 7 January 1967.

In September 1967, three pre-series F1 aircraft and a structural test airframe were ordered by the French government. The first pre-series aircraft, the Mirage F1-02, reached Mach 1·15 during its first flight on 20 March 1969, and Mach 2·03 during its third flight on 24 March. It completed the first phase of its flight test programme on 27 June 1969. This comprised 62 flights, during which the aircraft was flown at speeds of up to Mach 2·12 (1,200 knots; 1,405 mph; 2,260 km/h) at 36,000 ft (11,000 m) and up to 702 knots (808 mph; 1,300 km/h) at low level; at altitudes of more than 50,000 ft (15,250 m); and with various external military loads, including air-to-air missiles and drop-tanks.

The F1-02, during its initial flight tests, was powered by an Atar 9K-31 turbojet engine developing 14,770 lb (6,700 kg) st with afterburning. It was re-engined in 1969 with the more powerful Atar 9K-50 turbojet; this engine was also fitted in the two later pre-series aircraft, and is the standard power plant of the initial production version.

The Mirage F1-03, which flew for the first time on 18 September 1969, had its wing leading-edges extended for a greater proportion of the overall span than the preceding aircraft. It was followed by the final pre-series aircraft, the F1-04, on 17 June 1970. This had a complete avionics system and, after modification of its wing leading-edges to be similar to those of the F1-03, became representative of the initial production version.

The Mirage F1 is dimensionally similar to the Mirage III series, and its swept wing is virtually a scaled-down version of that fitted to the F2 prototype, with improved high-lift devices which help to make possible take-offs and landings within 1,600-2,600 ft (500-800 m) at average combat mission weight. Operation from semi-prepared, or even sod, runways is possible, and aircraft systems have been improved by comparison with the Mirage III, for increased efficiency and easy servicing. Compared with the Mirage III, internal fuel capacity is some 45 per cent greater, trebling the endurance of the F1 for patrol or high-altitude supersonic interception missions and doubling the possible combat radius in the attack role. Performance during flight testing met or exceeded all expectations, and included reductions of 22 per cent in approach speed and 28 per cent in take-off distance compared with the Mirage III. Manoeuvrability is claimed to have been increased by as much as 80 per cent.

The primary role of the Mirage F1 is that of all-weather interception at any altitude, and the initial **F1-C** production version, to which the description applies, utilises initially weapon systems similar to those of the Mirage III-E, with more advanced systems to follow. It is equally suitable for attack missions, carrying a variety of external loads beneath the wings and fuselage. A "utility" version, the **F1-A,** is also in production for operation only under VFR conditions, with much of the more costly electronic equipment deleted and the space so vacated occupied by an additional fuel tank. Projected further versions include the **F1-B** two-seat trainer (not yet ordered by the French Air Force).

By the Spring of 1974, a total of 170 Mirage F1s had been ordered for the French Air Force and the air forces of Kuwait, South Africa and Spain.

Production of the Atar 9K-50-engined Mirage F1s ordered initially is being undertaken by Dassault-Breguet in co-operation with the Belgian companies SABCA, in which Dassault-Breguet has a parity interest, and Fairey SA,

Dassault Mirage 5 ground attack aircraft, with Aïda II radar installed in nose

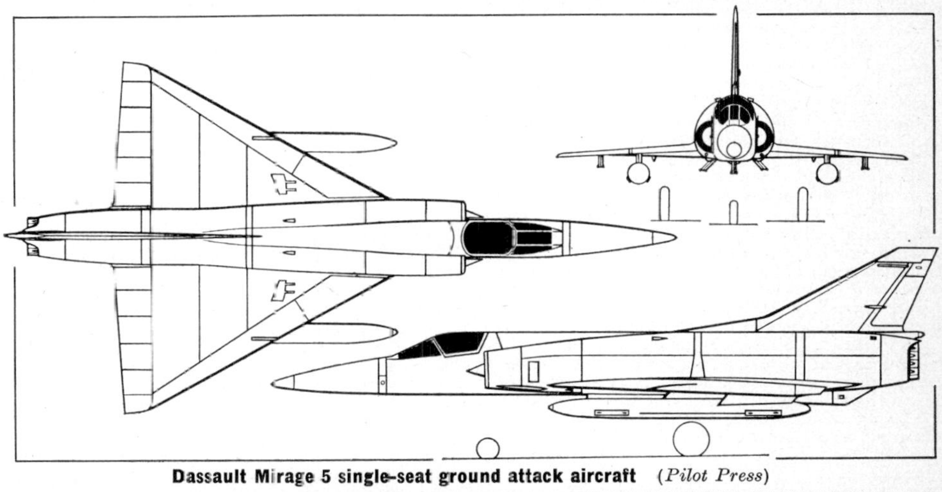

Dassault Mirage 5 single-seat ground attack aircraft (*Pilot Press*)

Dassault Mirage F1 equipped as an interceptor, with two Matra R.530 missiles underwing and two Matra 550 Magic missiles on wingtip launchers

which is building rear fuselage sections for all Mirage F1s ordered. Dassault-Breguet also has a technical and industrial co-operation agreement with the Armaments Development and Production Corporation of South Africa Ltd, whereby the latter company has rights to build the Mirage F1 under licence.

The first production Mirage F1 flew on 15 February 1973 and was delivered officially to the French Air Force on 14 March 1973. The first unit to receive the F1 was the 30e Escadre at Reims, which became operational in early 1974. It was to be followed by the 5e Escadre at Orange and the 12e Escadre at Cambrai.

By the end of 1973, pre-series and production Mirage F1s had logged a total of more than 2,500 flying hours. Twenty-six aircraft had been completed by 31 March 1974.

Meanwhile, the French government has given its go-ahead for development of a new version, the Mirage **F1-E,** powered by the SNECMA M53 turbofan engine of 12,379 lb (5,615 kg) st dry and 18,646 lb (8,458 kg) st with afterburning. With this engine, the F1-E is expected to attain a maximum level speed of Mach 2·5. It will be suitable for both interception and attack duties, and will have provision for terrain-following radar modes. Its development and production programme is expected to promote close international collaboration between the French and foreign aviation industries.

The first Mirage F1-E is scheduled to fly in late 1974, and production aircraft will be available by late 1977. It is anticipated that this version will have approximate weights of 17,120 lb (7,765 kg) empty, 24,560 lb (11,140 kg) maximum for take-off in "clean" condition, and 33,600 lb (15,200 kg) maximum for take-off with a full weapons load.

The description below applies to the F1-C initial production version for the French Air Force.

Type: Single-seat multi-mission fighter and attack aircraft.

Wings: Cantilever shoulder-wing monoplane, with anhedral from roots. Sweepback of approx 50° on leading-edges, which have extended chord (saw-tooth) on approx the outer two-thirds of each wing (prototype and first pre-series aircraft had extended chord on only approx the outer one-third of each wing). All-metal two-spar torsion-box structure, making extensive use of mechanically or chemically milled components. Trailing-edge control surfaces of honeycomb sandwich construction. Entire leading-edge can be drooped hydraulically. Two differentially-operating double-slotted flaps and one aileron on each trailing-edge, actuated hydraulically by servo controls. Ailerons are compensated by trim devices incorporated in linkage. Two spoilers on each wing, ahead of flaps.

Fuselage: Conventional all-metal semi-monocoque structure. Primary frames are milled mechanically, secondary frames and fuel tank panels chemically. Electrical spot-welding for secondary stringers and sealed panels, remainder titanium flush-riveted or bolted and sealed. Titanium alloy also used for landing gear trunnions, engine firewall and certain other major structures. High-tensile steel wing attachment points. Nose-cone over radar, and antennae fairings on fin, are of plastics. Large hydraulically-actuated door-type air-brake in forward underside of each intake trunk.

Tail Unit: Cantilever all-metal two-spar structure, with sweepback on all surfaces. All-moving tailplane mid-set on fuselage, and actuated hydraulically by electrical or manual control. Tailplane trailing-edge panels are of honeycomb sandwich construction. Auxiliary fin beneath each side of rear fuselage.

Landing Gear: Retractable tricycle type, by Messier-Hispano. Hydraulic retraction, nose unit rearward, main units outward and upward into rear of intake trunk fairings. Twin wheels on all units. Nose unit steerable and self-centering. Oleo-pneumatic shock-absorbers. Main wheel tyre pressure 128 lb/sq in (9 kg/cm^2), permitting operation from semi-prepared airfields. Messier-Hispano brakes and anti-skid units. Brake parachute in bullet fairing at base of rudder.

Power Plant (initial production version): One SNECMA Atar 9K-50 turbojet engine, rated at 15,873 lb (7,200 kg) st with afterburning. Movable semi-conical centre-body in each intake. All internal fuel in integral tanks in fuselage, on each side of intake trunks. Provision for three jettisonable auxiliary fuel tanks (each 264 Imp gallons; 1,200 litres) to be carried under fuselage and on inboard wing pylons.

Accommodation: Single SEMMB (Martin-Baker Mk 4) ejection seat for pilot, under rearward-hinged canopy. Cockpit is air-conditioned, and is heated by warm air bled from engine which also heats the radar compartment and certain equipment compartments. Intertechnique liquid oxygen system for pilot.

Systems: Two independent hydraulic systems, for landing gear retraction, flaps and flying controls, supplied by pumps similar to those fitted in Mirage III. Electrical system includes two Auxilec 15kVA variable-speed alternators, either of which can supply all functional and operational requirements. Emergency and standby power provided by SAFT Voltabloc 40Ah nickel-cadmium battery and EMD static converter. DC power provided by transformer-rectifiers operating in conjunction with battery.

Mirage F1 fighters in service with Escadron 2 "Normandie-Niemen" of the 30e Escadre de Chasse of the French Air Force, at Reims

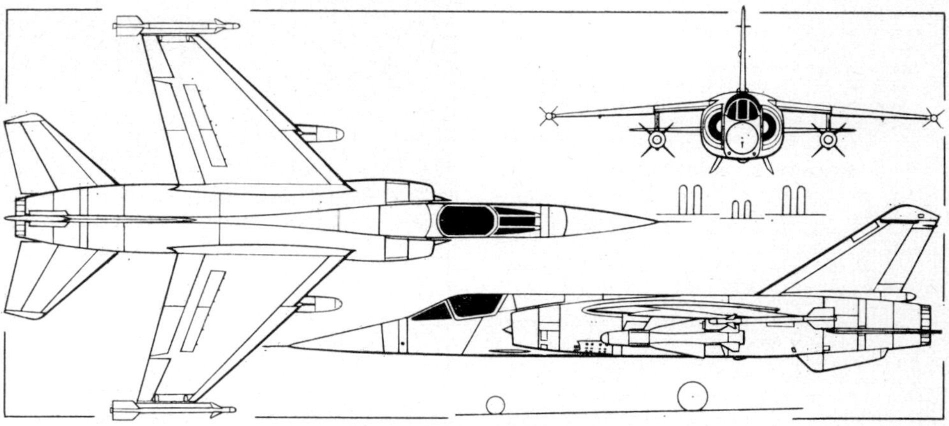

Dassault Mirage F1 single-seat multi-mission fighter and attack aircraft *(Pilot Press)*

Electronics and Equipment: Thomson-CSF Cyrano IV fire-control radar in nose. This permits all-sector interception at any altitude, and incorporates a system to eliminate "fixed" echoes when following low-flying aircraft. Two UHF transceivers (one UHF/VHF), Socrat 6200 VOR/ILS with Socrat 5600 marker, LMT TACAN, LMT NR-AI-4-A IFF, remote-setting interception system, three-axis generator, central air data computer, Bézu Sphere with ILS indicator, Crouzet Type 63 navigation indicator and SFENA 505 autopilot. CSF head-up display, with magnifying lens, provides all necessary data for flying and fire control. Equipment for attack role can include Doppler radar and bombing computer, navigation computer, position indicator, laser rangefinder and terrain-avoidance radar.

Armament and Operational Equipment: Standard fixed armament of two 30 mm DEFA 553 cannon, with 125 rounds per gun, mounted in lower front fuselage. Two Alkan universal stores attachment pylons under each wing and one under centre fuselage, plus provision for carrying one air-to-air missile at each wingtip. Max external combat load 8,820 lb (4,000 kg). Externally-mounted weapons for interception role include Matra R.530 or Super 530 radar homing or infra-red homing air-to-air missiles on underfuselage and inboard wing pylons, and/or a Sidewinder or Matra 550 Magic infra-red homing air-to-air missile at each wingtip station. For ground attack duties, typical loads may include one AS.37 Martel anti-radar missile or AS.30 air-to-surface missile, eight 450 kg bombs, four launchers each containing 18 air-to-ground rockets, or six 132 Imp gallon (600 litre) napalm tanks. Other possible external loads include three 264 Imp gallon (1,200 litre) auxiliary fuel tanks, or two photoflash containers and a reconnaissance pod incorporating an SAT Cyclope infra-red system and EMI side-looking radar.

Dimensions, external:

Wing span	27 ft $6\frac{3}{4}$ in (8·40 m)
Length overall	49 ft $2\frac{1}{4}$ in (15·00 m)
Height overall	14 ft 9 in (4·50 m)
Wheel track	8 ft $2\frac{1}{2}$ in (2·50 m)
Wheelbase	16 ft $4\frac{3}{4}$ in (5·00 m)

Area:

Wings, gross	269·1 sq ft (25·00 m^2)

Weights and loading:

Weight empty	16,314 lb (7,400 kg)
T-O weight, clean	24,030 lb (10,900 kg)
Max T-O weight	32,850 lb (14,900 kg)
Max wing loading	122·2 lb/sq ft (596 kg/m^2)

Performance:

Max level speed (high altitude)	Mach 2·2
Max level speed (low altitude)	Mach 1·2
Approach speed	141 knots (162 mph; 260 km/h)
Landing speed	124 knots (143 mph; 230 km/h)
Max rate of climb at S/L (with afterburning)	41,930 ft (12,780 m)/min
Max rate of climb at high altitude (with afterburning)	47,835 ft (14,580 m)/min
Service ceiling	65,600 ft (20,000 m)
Stabilised supersonic ceiling	60,700 ft (18,500 m)
T-O run (AUW of 25,355 lb; 11,500 kg)	1,475 ft (450 m)
Landing run (AUW of 18,740 lb; 8,500 kg)	1,640 ft (500 m)
T-O run (typical interception mission)	2,100 ft (640 m)
Landing run (typical interception mission)	2,000 ft (610 m)
Endurance	3 hr 45 min

DASSAULT MIRAGE G8

Two prototypes of the twin-engined Mirage G8 variable-geometry combat aircraft were ordered by the French government. The first of these, completed as a tandem two-seater, was flown for the first time on 8 May 1971, and reached a speed of Mach 2·03 on its fourth flight four days later. The second prototype, completed as a single-seater, flew for the first time on 13 July 1972.

The first prototype completed its test flying

The two-seat (nearest camera) and single-seat versions of the Dassault Mirage G8, with variable-geometry wings in swept and forward positions respectively

programme in mid-July 1973, after logging 221 hours in 220 flights. It explored the complete flight regime in all configurations, with sweepback of 23°, 55° and 70°. A maximum speed of Mach 2·2 was attained, at an indicated airspeed of 750 knots (864 mph; 1,390 km/h) and altitude of 65,600 ft (20,000 m).

The single-seat Mirage G8 prototype is continuing its flight testing in 1974. On 13 July 1973, piloted by Jean-Marie Saget, it attained Mach 2·34 and an altitude of 49,200 ft (15,000 m) during routine tests with reduced afterburning. Subsequent tests were to include pivot-load studies, in-flight refuelling, handling qualities at high supersonic speeds and the thermal effects of prolonged high-Mach flight.

Type: Experimental variable-geometry combat aircraft, suitable for patrol, attack and long-range reconnaissance duties.

Wings: Cantilever shoulder-wing monoplane. The wings have a sweep of 23° in the furthest-forward position and approximately 70° when fully swept. High-lift devices include leading-edge flaps (four sections each side) and double-slotted trailing-edge flaps. There are no ailerons. Roll control when the wings are swept back is provided by differential operation of the horizontal tail surfaces.

Fuselage: Conventional semi-monocoque all-metal structure, similar in design to that of the Mirage III, but making extensive use of chemical milling and spot welding.

Tail Unit: Sweptback fin and rudder; sweptback all-moving tailplane mid-mounted on rear of fuselage. The tailplane and elevators operate collectively for pitch control. Two small auxiliary fins beneath rear fuselage.

Landing Gear: Retractable tricycle type, by Messier-Hispano, with twin-wheel main and nose units. Nosewheel retracts rearward into the fuselage, the main units upward into the air intake trunks.

Power Plant: Two SNECMA Atar 9K-50 turbojet engines, mounted side by side in rear fuselage and each developing 15,873 lb (7,200 kg) st with afterburning. Intended originally to be replaced by two SNECMA M53 turbojet engines, each 18,740 lb (8,500 kg) st with afterburning, when these engines became available.

Electronics and Equipment: Provision for Cyrano IV multi-purpose radar, and low-altitude nav/attack system, including a laser rangefinder, Doppler radar and bombing computer.

Area:
Wings, gross approx 398 sq ft (37·0 m²)

Weight:
Max T-O weight approx 44,092 lb (20,000 kg)

Performance:
Max level speed at high altitude Mach 2·5

DASSAULT MIRAGE G8A/ACF

Subject of major design and development activities by Dassault-Breguet at the present time is the ACF (Avion de Combat Futur) that will be required by the French Air Force for air-superiority, ground attack, strike and long-range reconnaissance duties in the period 1980-85. An early design study was represented by a full-scale model at the 1973 Paris Air Show. Referred to as the Mirage G8A, it resembled the single-seat version of the Mirage G8, with a fixed wing of 55° sweep instead of the latter's variable-geometry wings, and powered by two SNECMA M53 turbofan engines.

On 31 January 1974, Général Claude Grigaut, Chief of Staff of the French Air Force, stated that an initial contract for a prototype of the ACF had been signed in the late Autumn of 1973, following the finalisation of its specification. Flight testing of the prototype is scheduled to begin in 1976; and the Air Force will need about 200 production models eventually.

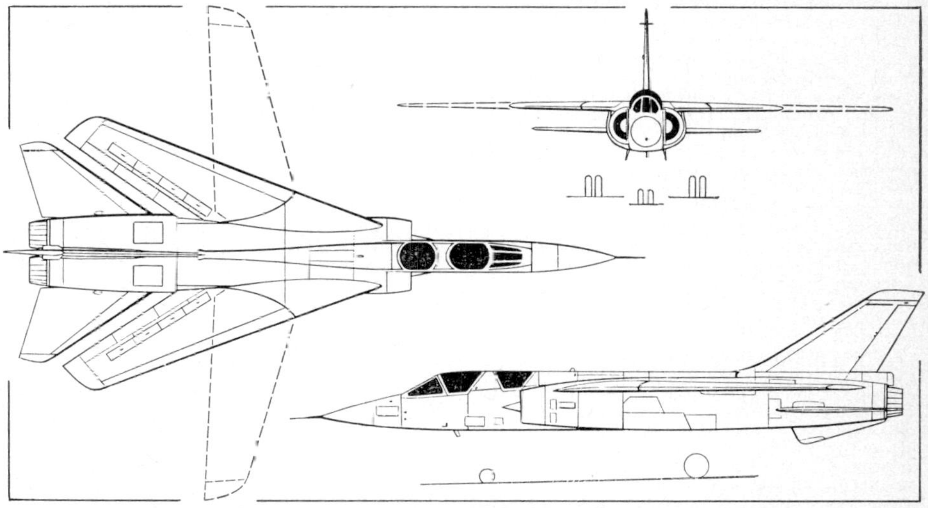

Dassault Mirage G8 two-seat variable-geometry combat aircraft (*Pilot Press*)

Model of the Mirage G8A design study for the Avion de Combat Futur

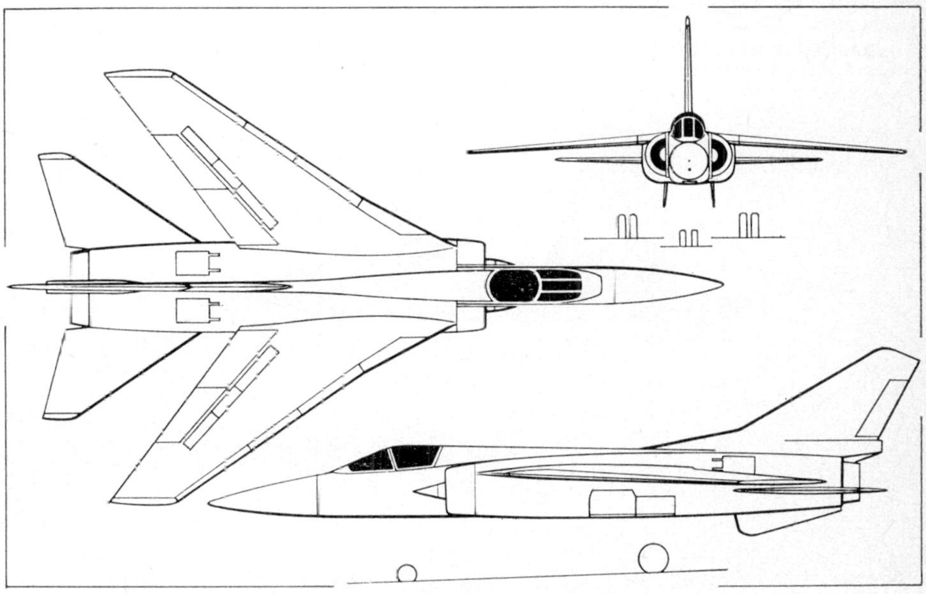

Dassault Mirage G8A design study for the Avion de Combat Futur (*Pilot Press*)

These will embody several features seen in the Mirage G8A model, including twin M53 engines and a fixed wing of 55° sweep, the angle found to be optimum during Mirage G8 flight testing. Emphasis will be placed on design simplicity, although the ACF will be capable of speeds higher than Mach 2·5.

The air-superiority version will be a single-seater with a long endurance and a thrust to weight ratio of nearly 1 : 1. Intended for head-on interception, it will have a radar antenna of around 90 cm diameter in its nose, and will be armed with Matra Super 530 infra-red homing missiles and other weapons such as 30 mm guns.

The two-seat strike version will be equipped with terrain-following radar for low-level penetration. Primary armament will comprise a nuclear-warhead air-to-surface missile with a range of at least 27 nm (31 miles; 50 km), with provision for a wide variety of conventional weapons.

Also a two-seater, the reconnaissance ACF will carry infra-red sensors, cameras and conventional weapons.

All three versions will be fitted with passive and active ECM devices, and sophisticated IFR equipment to permit operations in very low weather minima.

Model of the Dassault Super Etendard carrier-based fighter

DASSAULT SUPER ETENDARD

The Super Etendard is developed from the Dassault Etendard IV-M carrier-based fighter, which has served with operational squadrons of the French Navy since 1962. It will be a transonic single-seat strike fighter, for low and medium-altitude operations from ships of the *Clémenceau* and *Foch* class.

The general appearance of the Super Etendard is shown in the accompanying three-view drawing. It will be fitted with very comprehensive high-lift devices to suit it for shipboard use. Armament will include two 30 mm guns and a wide variety of external stores; equipment will include a highly sophisticated and accurate nav/attack integrated electronic system. Inherent long range will be increased by flight refuelling capability and, like the Etendard, the new fighter will be able to operate as a tanker for other aircraft.

The Super Etendard will be powered by a SNECMA Atar 8K-50 turbojet engine, which is a version of the Atar 9K-50 without afterburning. It has a lower specific fuel consumption than the Atar 8 of the Etendard IV-M. The thrust increase of about 10% will allow a significant increase of AUW for catapulting and, hence, make possible an increase in fuel load and range.

The prototypes of the Super Etendard are expected to be completed in 1976, with first deliveries to the French Navy in the Summer of 1977.

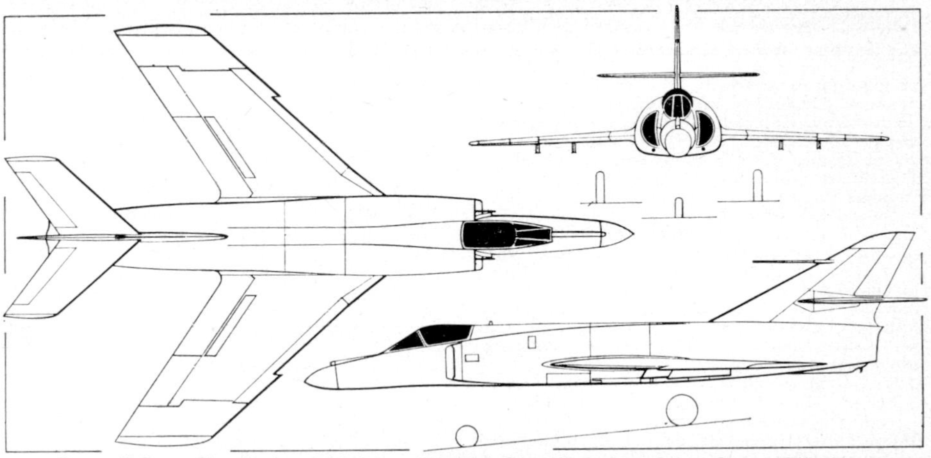

Dassault Super Etendard naval fighter (SNECMA Atar 8K-50 turbojet engine) (*Pilot Press*)

DIMENSIONS, EXTERNAL:
- Wing span: 31 ft 6 in (9·60 m)
- Length overall: 46 ft 11½ in (14·31 m)
- Height overall: 12 ft 8 in (3·85 m)

AREA:
- Wings, gross: 305·7 sq ft (28·4 m²)

WEIGHTS:
- Weight empty: 13,780 lb (6,250 kg)
- Mission T-O weight: 20,280-25,350 lb (9,200-11,500 kg)

PERFORMANCE (estimated):
- Max level speed at 36,000 ft (11,000 m): Mach 1
- Max level speed at low altitude: 650 knots (745 mph; 1,200 km/h)
- Approach speed for shipboard landing: 135 knots (155 mph; 250 km/h)
- Range, anti-ship mission with air-to-surface missile: 350 nm (403 miles; 650 km)

DASSAULT-BREGUET/DORNIER ALPHA JET

Details of the Alpha Jet programme can be found in the International section of this edition.

DASSAULT-BREGUET/BAC JAGUAR

Details of the Jaguar programme can be found under "SEPECAT" in the International section of this edition.

BREGUET 1150 ATLANTIC

Under the auspices of the NATO Armaments Committee, a specification for a maritime patrol aircraft to supersede the Lockheed P-2 Neptune was drawn up and published in 1958. Twenty-five design studies were submitted for evaluation, from aircraft manufacturers in several countries. Of these, the Breguet Type 1150 was chosen for development under the name "Atlantic", and two prototypes were ordered in December 1959, followed by an order for two pre-production aircraft.

The first prototype flew on 21 October 1961; the second flew on 23 February 1962, but was lost as the result of an accident on 19 April 1962. The first pre-production Atlantic, which flew on 25 February 1963, introduced a 3 ft 0 in (1·0 m) longer front fuselage, to provide more space in the operations control centre.

Forty production Atlantics were ordered for the French Navy, and Germany ordered 20. The first of these 60 aircraft flew on 19 July 1965, and the first delivery of an operational Atlantic was made to the French Navy on 10 December 1965. Subsequent orders were received for nine Atlantics for the Royal Netherlands Navy and 18 for the Italian Navy. The last of the 87 aircraft covered by these orders was nearing completion in early 1974.

Detail design and manufacture were undertaken on an international basis. Thus, Fokker-VFW in the Netherlands assumed responsibility for the centre wing and rear of the engine nacelles. Dornier and MBB in Germany produced the lower centre and upper rear fuselage, and the fin and tailplane. Many airframe components were supplied by the Belgian ABAP group, made up of Fairey, SABCA and Fabrique Nationale Herstal.

The outer wings were built by Aérospatiale and the landing gear by Messier-Hispano. In 1968 four Italian manufacturers, led by Aeritalia (Aerfer), joined the consortium. These companies became responsible, inter alia, for most of the wing and tail control surfaces, parts of the fuselage nose and the centre sections of the engine nacelles. Dassault-Breguet retained responsibility for the main fuselage, final assembly and development.

For the prototypes, Rolls-Royce supplied Tyne RTy.20 turboprop engines from the United Kingdom, and much of the electronic equipment came from the United States. For production aircraft, broader arrangements were made, not only for the airframe but also for engines and equipment. In particular, SNECMA built the Tyne engines under licence in France, assisted by Fabrique Nationale Herstal (Belgium), MTU (Germany) and (since 1969) Alfa Romeo and Fiat in Italy. Hawker Siddeley Dynamics (UK) and Ratier-Figeac SA (France) manufactured the propellers.

Second-generation versions of the aircraft,

Breguet 1150 Atlantic maritime patrol aircraft, retrofitted with special-purpose ECM equipment by E-Systems Inc

known as the Atlantic Mk II and Mk II-B, have been projected for operational service in the late 'seventies, with more advanced maritime reconnaissance and anti-submarine avionics. The following details apply to the basic version now in service:

Type: Twin-engined maritime patrol aircraft.

Wings: Cantilever mid-wing monoplane. Wing section NACA 64 series. Dihedral on outer wings only. All-metal three-spar fail-safe structure, with bonded light alloy honeycomb skin panels on torsion box and on main landing gear doors. Conventional all-metal ailerons actuated by SAMM twin-cylinder jacks. All-metal slotted flaps, with bonded light alloy honeycomb filling, over 75% of span. Three hinged spoilers on upper surface of each outer wing, forward of flaps. Metal airbrake above and below each wing. No trim tabs. Kléber-Colombes pneumatic de-icing boots on leading-edges.

Fuselage: All-metal "double-bubble" fail-safe structure, with bonded honeycomb sandwich skin on pressurised central section of upper fuselage, weapons bay doors and nosewheel door.

Tail Unit: Cantilever all-metal structure with bonded honeycomb sandwich skin panels on torsion boxes. Tailplane incidence fixed. Control surfaces operated through SAMM twin-cylinder jacks. No trim tabs. Kléber-Colombes pneumatic de-icing boots on leading-edges.

Landing Gear: Retractable tricycle type, supplied by Messier-Hispano, with twin wheels on each unit. Hydraulic retraction, nosewheels rearward, main units forward into engine nacelles. Kléber-Colombes dimpled tyres, size 39 × 13-16 on main wheels, 26 × 7·75-13 on nosewheels. Tyre pressures: main 138 lb/sq in (9·7 kg/cm²), nose 88 lb/sq in (6·2 kg/cm²). Messier-Hispano disc brakes with Maxaret anti-skid units.

Power Plant: Two 6,106 ehp SNECMA-built Rolls-Royce Tyne RTy.20 Mk 21 turboprop engines, each driving a Ratier-built HSD four-blade constant-speed propeller. Six integral fuel tanks with total capacity of 4,619 Imp gallons (21,000 litres). Provision for wingtip tanks to be fitted.

Accommodation: Normal flight crew of 12, comprising observer in nose; pilot and co-pilot on flight deck; a tactical co-ordinator, navigator, two sonobuoy operators, and radio, radar and ECM/MAD/Autolycus operators in tactical compartment; and two observers in beam positions. On long-range patrol missions a further 12 men can be carried as relief crew. The upper, pressurised section of the fuselage, from front to rear, comprises the nose observer's compartment, flight deck, tactical operations compartment, rest compartment for crew, and beam observers' compartment.

Systems: SEMCA air-conditioning and pressurisation system. Hydraulic system pressure 3,000 lb/sq in (210 kg/cm²). Electrical system provides 28·5V DC, 115/200V variable-frequency AC and 115/200V stabilised-frequency AC. AiResearch GTCP 85-100 APU in starboard side of front fuselage, adjacent to radar compartment, for engine starting and ground air-conditioning, and can also power one 20 kVA AC alternator and one 4kW DC generator for emergency electrical power supply.

Armament and Operational Equipment: Main weapons carried in bay in unpressurised lower fuselage. Weapons include all NATO standard bombs, 385 lb (175 kg) US or French depth charges, HVAR rockets, homing torpedoes, including types such as the Mk 44 Brush or LX.4 with acoustic heads, or four underwing air-to-surface missiles with nuclear or high-explosive warheads. Electronic equipment includes a retractable CSF radar installation, an MAD tail boom and an electronic countermeasures pod at the top of the tail-fin. Sonobuoys are carried in a compartment aft of the main weapons bay, while the whole of the upper and lower rear fuselage acts as a storage compartment for sonobuoys and marker flares. Compartment for retractable CSF radar "dustbin" forward of main weapons bay. Forward of this, the lower nose section acts as additional storage for military equipment and the APU. Weapons system includes Plotac optical tactical display, 31·5 × 31·5 in (80 × 80 cm) in size, consisting of separate tables for search display and localisation and attack display. At 1/30,000 scale, this gives coverage of an area 24,000 × 24,000 yd (21,950 × 21,950 m) to an accuracy of 1 mm (*ie*, less than 100 ft; 30·5 m at that scale). Heading references provided by duplicated gyroscopic platforms of the 3-gyro (1° of freedom) 4-gimbals type, with magnetic compasses as back-up system. Janus-type Doppler has stabilised antenna and works in the Ke band to provide direct indication of ground speed and drift. In case of failure an automatic switch is made to the air data system. The analogue-type navigation computer is accurate to 0·25%. The MAD is of the atomic resonance type and uses light-stimulation techniques. Plotac system has provision to accept additional detectors. Radar has "sea-return" circuits and stabilised antenna enabling it to detect a submarine snorkel at up to 40 nm (46 miles; 75 km) even in rough seas.

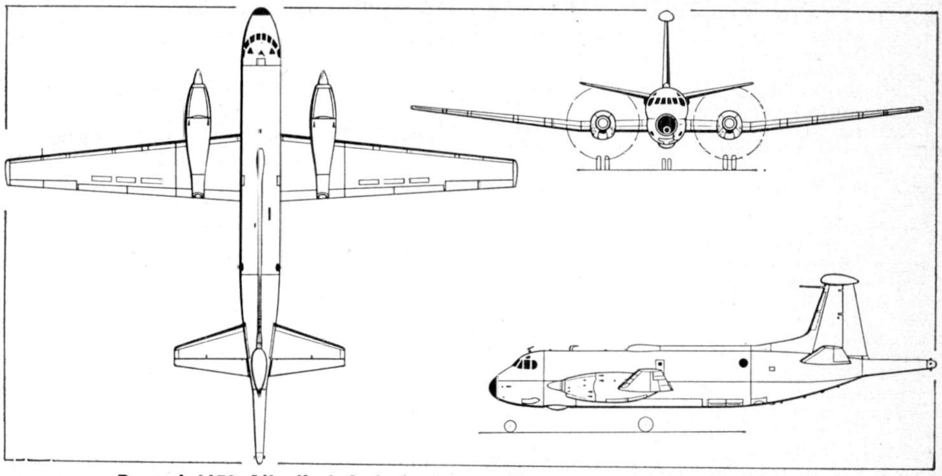

Breguet 1150 Atlantic twin-turboprop maritime patrol aircraft (*Pilot Press*)

Dimensions, external:	
Wing span	119 ft 1 in (36·30 m)
Wing aspect ratio	10·94
Length overall	104 ft 2 in (31·75 m)
Height overall	37 ft 2 in (11·33 m)
Fuselage:	
Max width	9 ft 6 in (2·90 m)
Max depth	13 ft 1½ in (4·00 m)
Tailplane span	40 ft 4½ in (12·31 m)
Wheel track	29 ft 6¼ in (9·00 m)
Wheelbase	31 ft 0 in (9·44 m)
Propeller diameter	16 ft 0 in (4·88 m)
Dimensions, internal:	
Tactical compartment:	
Length	28 ft 2½ in (8·60 m)
Height	6 ft 4 in (1·93 m)
Max width	8 ft 10½ in (2·70 m)
Rest compartment:	
Length	16 ft 8¾ in (5·10 m)
Height	6 ft 4 in (1·93 m)
Max width	8 ft 10½ in (2·70 m)
Beam observers' compartment:	
Length	3 ft 3½ in (1·00 m)
Main weapons bay:	
Length	29 ft 6¼ in (9·00 m)
Height	5 ft 1 in (1·55 m)
Height under wing	3 ft 3½ in (1·00 m)
Max width	7 ft 2½ in (2·20 m)
Areas:	
Wings, gross	1,295 sq ft (120·34 m²)
Ailerons (total)	58·0 sq ft (5·40 m²)
Trailing-edge flaps (total)	288·4 sq ft (26·80 m²)
Spoilers (total)	17·8 sq ft (1·66 m²)
Fin	179·1 sq ft (16·64 m²)
Rudder	64·1 sq ft (5·96 m²)
Tailplane	349·7 sq ft (32·5 m²)
Elevators	89·1 sq ft (8·28 m²)
Weights:	
Useful load	40,900 lb (18,551 kg)
Max zero-fuel weight	76,000 lb (34,473 kg)
Max T-O weight	95,900 lb (43,500 kg)
Performance (at max T-O weight):	
Max level speed at high altitudes	355 knots (409 mph; 658 km/h)
Cruising speed	300 knots (345 mph; 556 km/h)
Service ceiling	32,800 ft (10,000 m)
T-O to 35 ft (10·7 m), ISA	4,925 ft (1,500 m)
T-O to 35 ft (10·7 m), ISA + 17°C, 15° flap	5,575 ft (1,700 m)
Max range	4,854 nm (5,590 miles; 9,000 km)
Max endurance at patrol speed of 169 knots (195 mph; 320 km/h)	18 hr

DASSAULT MYSTÈRE 20/FALCON 20

The Dassault Mystère 20/Falcon 20 is a light twin-jet executive transport, with standard accommodation for 8-10 passengers and a crew of two. An alternative layout offers seats for 14 passengers and the aircraft can be used for a variety of alternative duties.

Its development was undertaken jointly with Aérospatiale (then Sud-Aviation) and construction of the prototype began in January 1962. The fuselage of the prototype was built by Dassault and the wings and tail unit by Sud-Aviation. Dassault was responsible for final assembly. For production aircraft, Dassault builds the wings and Aérospatiale the fuselages and tail units.

The prototype flew for the first time on 4 May 1963, with Pratt & Whitney JT12A-8 turbojets (each 3,300 lb; 1,489 kg st). It was re-engined subsequently with General Electric CF700 turbofans, which are standard on subsequent aircraft, and flew for the first time with these engines on 10 July 1964.

In August 1963 the Business Jets Division of Pan American World Airways ordered 54 production machines, with an option on 106 more. From the start, these aircraft were marketed by Pan American under the name Fan Jet Falcon, but the original name of Mystère 20 continues to be used in France. The first production machine flew on 1 January 1965.

The Mystère 20/Falcon 20 received French and US Transport Category Type Approval on 9 June 1965. On the following day, Mme Jacqueline Auriol established a Class C-1-g speed record of 463·80 knots (534·075 mph; 859·51 km/h) over a 1,000 km closed circuit in a Mystère 20/Falcon 20. On 15 June she set up a second Class C-1-g record of 442·00 knots (508·98 mph; 819·13 km/h) over a 2,000 km circuit.

By 31 January 1974, total sales of Mystère 20/Falcon 20s had reached 318, of which 109 were for customers in the areas marketed by Dassault, with options on 163 more; of these, 295 had been delivered, including 190 to the Business Jets Division of Pan American. This Division has been superseded as distributor for the western hemisphere by Falcon Jet Corporation, formed jointly by Dassault-Breguet and Pan American in 1973.

Current production versions of the Mystère 20/Falcon 20 are as follows:

Falcon Series E. As Series F (see below), but without high-lift wings.

Falcon Series F. Version with high-lift devices to improve T-O and landing performance, more powerful engines than earlier Falcons and increased wing fuel tank capacity. Prototype displayed at Paris Air Show in June 1969. Initial series of 25 being built, to meet firm orders for 20 plus options on a further 80. Deliveries began in July 1970.

The high-lift devices introduced on this version comprise a leading-edge slat inboard of each wing fence and a slotted leading-edge slat outboard of each fence.

Dassault Mystère 20 executive transport supplied to the Sultan of Oman (*P. J. Bish*)

In 1970 the Series F became the first aircraft to receive type approval under FAA FAR Pt 36 anti-noise regulations. This approval was subsequently extended to all Falcon versions.

All versions of the Mystère 20/Falcon 20 can be modified as follows for specific duties:

Calibration: Two Falcons ordered by the SGAC and one by the Spanish government are used for the calibration of radio navigation aids. The equipment includes a removable console, thus retaining the full passenger-carrying capability of the aircraft.

Airline crew training: Since 20 September 1966, several Mystère 20/Falcons have been used by Air France to train pilots for their jet airliners, with up to five aircraft being used simultaneously.

Cross-country: Similar to basic Falcon, but with low-pressure tyres for soft-field operation at the same take-off and landing weights. Described in 1968-69 *Jane's*.

Quick-change and cargo: A quick-change kit, consisting of an assembly of nets and supports, keeps the centre aisle free and allows direct access to nine freight compartments. Total usable volume of these compartments is 235 cu ft (6·65 m³), and transformation from executive configuration to cargo configuration, or vice versa, takes less than one hour. A cargo version of the Falcon is also available and is described separately. For both versions an increase of the maximum zero-fuel weight from 19,600 lb (8,900 kg) to 22,000 lb (9,980 kg) allows an increased payload of up to 6,615 lb (3,000 kg).

Aerial photography: The French Institute Géographique National has a Falcon fitted with two cameras (Zeiss RMK 610 mm focal length, and Wild RC8, RC9 or RC10) and an intervalometer. This enables the aircraft to be used for high-altitude photography and photogrammetry duties.

Systems trainer: Two Falcons fitted with Mirage III-E combat aircraft radar and navigation systems are in service with the French Air Force for training its Mirage pilots. This version, known as the **Falcon ST**, has been sold also to the Libyan Republic.

The following description applies to the Mystère 20/Falcon 20 Series F:

TYPE: Twin-turbofan executive transport.

WINGS: Cantilever low-wing monoplane. Thickness/chord ratio varies from 10·5 to 8%. Dihedral 2°. Incidence 1° 30′. Sweepback at quarter-chord 30°. All-metal (copper-bearing alloys) fail-safe torsion-box structure with machined stressed skin. Ailerons are each operated by Dassault twin-body actuators, from dual hydraulic systems, and have artificial feel. Non-slotted slats inboard of fence, and slotted slats outboard, on each wing. Hydraulically-actuated airbrakes forward of the hydraulically-actuated two-section single-slotted flaps. Leading-edges anti-iced by engine bleed air.

FUSELAGE: All-metal semi-monocoque structure of circular cross-section, built on fail-safe principles.

TAIL UNIT: Cantilever all-metal structure, with electrically-controlled variable-incidence tailplane mounted half-way up fin. Elevators and rudder each actuated by twin hydraulic servos. No trim tabs.

LANDING GEAR: Retractable tricycle type, by Messier-Hispano, with twin wheels on all three units. Hydraulic retraction, main units inward, nosewheels forward. Oleo-pneumatic shock-absorbers. Goodyear disc brakes and anti-skid units. Normal tyre pressure 133 lb/sq in (9·35 kg/cm²) on all units. Low-pressure gear (65 lb/sq in; 4·6 kg/cm²) available optionally. Steerable and self-centering nosewheels. Braking parachute standard.

POWER PLANT: Two General Electric CF700-2D-2 turbofan engines (each 4,315 lb; 1,960 kg st) mounted in pods on each side of rear fuselage. Fuel in two integral tanks in wings and two auxiliary tanks aft of rear pressure bulkhead in fuselage, with total capacity of 1,150 Imp gallons (1,385 US gallons; 5,240 litres). Separate fuel system for each engine, with provision for cross-feeding. Single-point pressure refuelling. Emergency refuelling by gravity.

ACCOMMODATION: Crew of two on flight deck, with full dual controls and airline-type instrumentation. Normal seating for eight or ten passengers in individual reclining chairs, with tables between forward pairs of seats and a central "trench" aisle, or 12-14 passengers at reduced pitch without tables. Toilet at rear. Baggage space and wardrobe on starboard side, immediately aft of flight deck opposite door, and at rear of cabin. Buffet with ice-box, food and liquid storage at front of cabin on port side. Downward-opening door has built-in steps.

SYSTEMS: Duplicated air-conditioning and pressurisation system, supplied with air bled from both engines. Pressure differential 8·3 lb/sq in (0·58 kg/cm²). Two independent hydraulic systems, pressure 3,000 lb/sq in (210 kg/cm²), with twin engine-driven pumps and emergency electric pump, actuate primary flying controls, flaps, landing gear, wheel brakes, airbrakes and nosewheel steering. 28V DC electrical system with a 9kW 28V DC starter/generator on each engine, one 1500VA and two 750VA 400Hz 118/208V inverters and two 40Ah batteries. Automatic emergency oxygen system. 9kW Microturbo Saphir II APU optional.

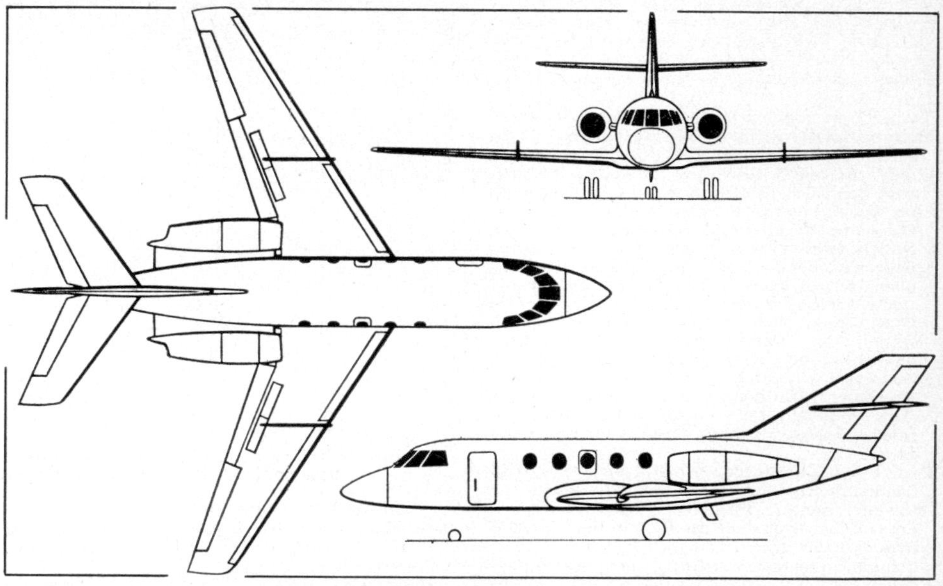

Dassault Mystère 20/Falcon 20 twin-turbofan executive transport (*Pilot Press*)

Installing the freight door on a Dassault Falcon Cargo Jet of Federal Express

ELECTRONICS AND EQUIPMENT: Standard equipment includes duplicated VHF and VOR/glideslope, single ADF and DME, marker beacon receiver, ATC transponder, cockpit audio and duplicated blind-flying instrumentation. Optional equipment includes integrated flight instrument system, weather radar, HF communications radio, autopilot, second ADF and DME, and cabin address system.

DIMENSIONS, EXTERNAL:

Wing span	53 ft 6 in (16·30 m)
Wing chord (mean)	9 ft 4 in (2·85 m)
Wing aspect ratio	6·4
Length overall	56 ft 3 in (17·15 m)
Length of fuselage	51 ft 0 in (15·55 m)
Height over tail	17 ft 5 in (5·32 m)
Tailplane span	22 ft 1 in (6·74 m)
Wheel track	12 ft 1¼ in (3·69 m)
Wheelbase	18 ft 10 in (5·74 m)
Passenger door:	
Height	5 ft 0 in (1·52 m)
Width	2 ft 7½ in (0·80 m)
Height to sill	3 ft 7 in (1·09 m)
Emergency exits (each side, over wing):	
Height	2 ft 2 in (0·66 m)
Width	1 ft 7 in (0·48 m)

DIMENSIONS, INTERNAL:

Cabin, including fwd baggage space and rear toilet:	
Length	23 ft 2¾ in (7·08 m)
Max width	6 ft 1½ in (1·87 m)
Max height	5 ft 8 in (1·73 m)
Volume	700 cu ft (20·0 m³)
Baggage compartment (fwd)	24·7 cu ft (0·70 m³)
Baggage compartment (aft)	13·1 cu ft (0·37 m³)

AREAS:

Wings, gross	440 sq ft (41·00 m²)
Horizontal tail surfaces (total)	121·6 sq ft (11·30 m²)
Vertical tail surfaces (total)	81·8 sq ft (7·60 m²)

WEIGHTS:

Weight empty, equipped	15,970 lb (7,240 kg)
Max payload	3,320 lb (1,500 kg)
Max T-O and ramp weight	28,660 lb (13,000 kg)
Max zero-fuel weight	19,600 lb (8,900 kg)
Typical landing weight	18,870 lb (8,560 kg)

PERFORMANCE:

Max never-exceed speed at S/L
350 knots (404 mph; 650 km/h) IAS

Max never-exceed speed at 23,000 ft (7,000 m)
390 knots (450 mph; 725 km/h) IAS

Max cruising speed at 25,000 ft (7,620 m) at AUW of 20,000 lb (9,071 kg)
465 knots (536 mph; 862 km/h)

Econ cruising speed at 40,000 ft (12,200 m)
405 knots (466 mph; 750 km/h)

Stalling speed 82 knots (95 mph; 152 km/h)

Absolute ceiling 42,000 ft (12,800 m)

Service ceiling, one engine out, at AUW of 18,700 lb (8,500 kg) 24,500 ft (7,480 m)

T-O to 35 ft (10·7 m) at AUW of 27,130 lb; 12,300 kg (full tanks, 8 passengers and baggage) 3,790 ft (1,155 m)

FAR 25 balanced T-O field length, AUW as above 4,750 ft (1,450 m)

FAR 121 landing field length at AUW of 18,870 lb; 8,550 kg (8 passengers, 45 min reserves)
3,230 ft (985 m)

Landing from 50 ft (15 m) 1,930 ft (590 m)

Range with max fuel and 1,600 lb (725 kg) payload at econ cruising speed, with reserves for 45 min cruise
1,930 nm (2,220 miles; 3,570 km)

DASSAULT FALCON CARGO JET

Under contract from Pan American Business Jets, Little Rock Airmotive converted a Falcon 20 into a specialised cargo aircraft. Known as the Falcon Cargo Jet, the prototype flew for the first time on 28 March 1972. By the Summer of the same year, an operator named Federal Express Corporation, of Little Rock, had three similar aircraft in service and has since expanded its fleet to a total of 33 Falcon D Cargo Jets.

The cargo conversion can be applied to any Falcon 20/Mystère 20 and is offered on the latest Series F aircraft.

Basic feature of the conversion is replacement of the standard cabin door by a hydraulically-actuated cargo door 6 ft 2 in wide by 4 ft 9 in high (1·88 × 1·44 m), forward of the wing on the port side. This door opens upward, with its sill at cabin floor level. The flooring itself is new and offers a completely flat area 23 ft long by 5 ft 4 in wide (7·01 m × 1·62 m). Made of aluminium honeycomb, it can sustain loadings of up to 100 lb/sq ft (488 kg/m²) and affords infinite tie-down points for retainer nets and pallets. Floor-mounted rollers are optional.

The Falcon Cargo Jet's Category II solid-state avionics standard includes dual com/nav, dual flight directors, autopilot and weather radar. Specifically, in the case of the Federal Express fleet, the fit comprises RCA com/nav with DME, dual Collins FD-108 flight directors, RCA AVQ-21 radar, Collins AP-105 autopilot, Teledyne angle-of-attack system, Collins ADF and RCA transponder. Also installed on these aircraft is a Fairchild integral electronic weight and balance system, which indicates as a cockpit readout whether or not cargo weight and distribution are within the legal limits. Standard safety provisions include a quick-release cargo restraint system able to withstand 9*g*.

Dimensions, weights and performance are largely unchanged by this conversion scheme. Nominal empty weight is 15,350 lb (6,963 kg) and max zero-fuel weight is increased to 22,000 lb (9,980 kg). Range varies from 1,215 nm (1,400 miles; 2,250 km) with max payload to 1,736 nm (2,000 miles; 3,215 km) with max fuel and a 4,500 lb (2,040 kg) payload. Usable cabin volume is 500 cu ft (14·15 m³).

DASSAULT FALCON 10

First announced in June 1969, the Falcon 10 is basically a scaled-down version of the Mystère 20/Falcon 20, with similar wing high-lift devices to those of the Falcon F and powered by two small turbofans in the 3,300 lb (1,500 kg) st class. Like the larger Falcons, it is designed to fail-safe principles and to comply with US FAR 25 transport category requirements.

A prototype (F-WFAL), with General Electric CJ610 turbojets, made its first flight on 1 December 1970. Flight testing was resumed on 7 May 1971 following modifications to the angles of wing incidence and dihedral and an increase in wing sweepback. The modified aircraft set up a 1,000 km closed-circuit speed record of 502·05 knots (578·13 mph; 930·4 km/h) in FAI Class C-1-f on 1 June 1971.

A second prototype (F-WTAL), with Garrett AiResearch TFE 731-2 engines, flew for the first time on 15 October 1971, followed by a third aircraft on 14 October 1972, with similar engines. This third Falcon 10 set up a 2,000 km closed-circuit speed record of 494·83 knots (569·809 mph; 917·02 km/h) in Class C-1-f on 29 May 1973.

The first production Falcon 10 with TFE 731-2 engines made its first flight on 30 April 1973. French certification of this version was granted on 11 September 1973, followed by FAA certification nine days later, allowing deliveries of production aircraft to begin on 1 November. Twelve had been delivered by 31 March 1974.

Falcon Jet Corporation, distributor for the Western hemisphere, has placed initial orders for 54, with options on a further 106. At 1 May 1974 total orders amounted to 63, plus 109 options.

The second prototype is now being used as a Larzac testbed. It resumed flying, with a Larzac 02 in its starboard nacelle, on 22 May 1973, the TFE 731-2 in its port nacelle being retained. Subsequently, the test engine was replaced by a Larzac 04 as part of the Alpha Jet development programme.

Like the Falcon 20, the Falcon 10 can be equipped for liaison, executive transport, navigation/attack system training, aerial photography, radio navigation aid calibration and ambulance duties.

TYPE: Twin-turbofan executive transport.

WINGS: Cantilever low-wing monoplane with increased sweepback on inboard leading-edges. All-metal torsion-box structure, with leading-edge slats and double-slotted trailing-edge flaps and plain ailerons. Two-section spoilers above each wing, forward of flaps.

FUSELAGE: All-metal semi-monocoque structure, designed to fail-safe principles.

TAIL UNIT: Cantilever all-metal structure, similar to that of Falcon 20.

LANDING GEAR: Retractable tricycle type, manufactured by Messier-Hispano, with twin wheels on main gear, single wheel on nose gear. Hydraulic retraction, main units inward, nosewheel forward. Oleo-pneumatic shock-absorbers. Low-pressure tyres for soft-field operation.

POWER PLANT: Two Garrett AiResearch TFE 731-2 turbofan engines (each 3,230 lb; 1,465 kg st), mounted in pod on each side of rear fuselage. Fuel in two integral tanks in wings and two feeder tanks aft of rear bulkhead, with total capacity of 735 Imp gallons (882 US gallons; 3,340 litres). Separate fuel system for each engine, with provision for cross-feeding. Pressure refuelling system.

ACCOMMODATION: Crew of two on flight deck, with dual controls and airline-type instrumentation. Provision for third crew member on a jump-seat. Normal seating for four passengers (two individual seats and a three-seat sofa) or for seven passengers, with two individual seats added. Each pair of single seats is separated by a table. Coat compartment on starboard side, immediately aft of flight deck opposite door; rear baggage compartment behind sofa. Galley on left of entrance. Optional front toilet compartment. Downward-opening door with built-in steps.

SYSTEMS: Duplicated air-conditioning and pressurisation systems supplied with air bled from both engines. Pressure differential 8·8 lb/sq in (0·615 kg/cm²). Two independent hydraulic systems, each of 3,000 lb/sq in (210 kg/cm²) pressure and with twin engine-driven pumps and emergency electric pump, to actuate primary flight controls, flaps, landing gear, wheel brakes, airbrakes, yaw damper and nosewheel steering. 28V DC electrical system with a 9kW DC starter/generator on each engine, three 750VA 400Hz 115V inverters and two 23Ah batteries. Automatic emergency oxygen system.

ELECTRONICS AND EQUIPMENT: Standard equipment includes duplicated VHF and VOR/glideslope, single ADF, marker beacon receiver, ATC transponder, autopilot, intercom systems and duplicated blind-flying instrumentation. Optional equipment includes duplicated DME and flight director, second ADF, weather radar and radio altimeter.

DIMENSIONS, EXTERNAL:
- Wing span: 42 ft 11 in (13·08 m)
- Wing chord (mean): 6 ft 8½ in (2·046 m)
- Wing aspect ratio: 7·1
- Length overall: 45 ft 5 in (13·85 m)
- Length of fuselage: 40 ft 11 in (12·47 m)
- Height overall: 15 ft 1½ in (4·61 m)
- Tailplane span: 19 ft 1 in (5·82 m)
- Wheel track: 9 ft 5 in (2·86 m)
- Wheelbase: 17 ft 8 in (5·38 m)
- Passenger door:
  - Height: 4 ft 10 in (1·47 m)
  - Width: 2 ft 7 in (0·80 m)
  - Height to sill: 2 ft 10¾ in (0·884 m)
- Emergency exit (stbd side, over wing):
  - Height: 3 ft 0 in (0·914 m)
  - Width: 1 ft 8 in (0·508 m)

DIMENSIONS, INTERNAL:
- Cabin, excluding flight deck:
  - Length: 16 ft 5 in (5·00 m)
  - Max width: 4 ft 9 in (1·46 m)
  - Max height: 4 ft 11 in (1·50 m)
  - Volume: 264·6 cu ft (7·50 m³)
- Baggage compartment volume:
  - front (wardrobe): 12·35 cu ft (0·35 m³)
  - rear: 24·7 cu ft (0·70 m³)

AREAS:
- Wings, gross: 259 sq ft (24·1 m²)
- Horizontal tail surfaces (total): 72·65 sq ft (6·75 m²)
- Vertical tail surfaces (total): 48·87 sq ft (4·54 m²)

WEIGHTS:
- Weight empty, equipped: 10,565 lb (4,792 kg)
- Max payload: 1,891 lb (858 kg)
- Max T-O weight: 18,300 lb (8,300 kg)
- Max zero-fuel weight: 12,450 lb (5,650 kg)
- Max landing weight: 17,200 lb (7,800 kg)

PERFORMANCE:
- Max never-exceed speed at S/L: 350 knots (402 mph; 648 km/h)
- Max operating Mach number: 0·87
- FAR 25 balanced T-O field length with four passengers and fuel for a 1,000 nm (1,150 mile; 1,850 km) stage, 45 min reserves: 2,900 ft (885 m)
- FAR 25 balanced T-O field length, with six passengers and max fuel: 3,900 ft (1,190 m)
- FAR 25 landing run, with six passengers and 45 min reserves: 2,020 ft (615 m)
- Range with four passengers and 45 min reserves: 1,900 nm (2,187 miles; 3,520 km)

DASSAULT FALCON 30 AND MYSTÈRE 40-100

These twin-turbofan commuter transports are variants of the same basic design. The Falcon 30 is capable of carrying 30 passengers on 820 nm (945 mile; 1,520 km) stage lengths; the Mystère 40-100 carries 40 passengers on 540 nm (620 mile;

Dassault Falcon 10 executive transport (two Garrett AiResearch TFE 731-2 turbofan engines)

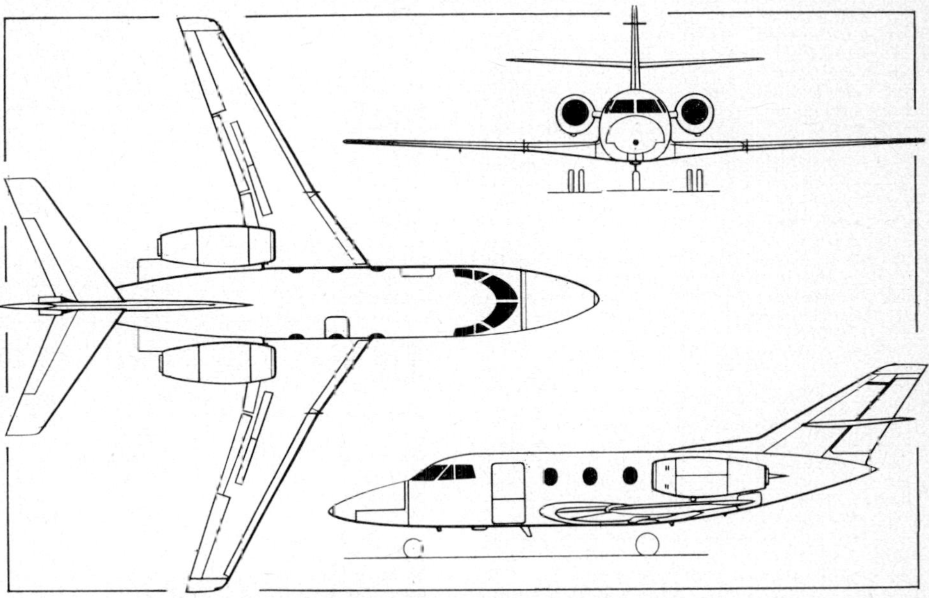

Dassault Falcon 10 four/seven-passenger executive transport (*Pilot Press*)

Prototype of the Dassault Mystère 40-100/Falcon 30 twin-turbofan commuter transport

1,000 km) stage lengths, at high speed and in a high degree of comfort.

Both aircraft are derivatives of the Mystère 20/Falcon 20, and take advantage of the improvements embodied on the latest versions of this aircraft, including the high-lift devices, and from the experience of 700,000 flying hours logged by Falcons by early 1974. The prototype flew for the first time on 11 May 1973, and had logged a total of more than 105 flying hours at the Dassault-Breguet test centre and the official Flight Test Centre at Istres by the beginning of February 1974. It differs from the production design only in having a fuselage diameter of 7 ft 9 in (2·36 m).

The French third-level operator Touraine Air Transport (TAT) has taken options on four Mystère 40-100s.

TYPE: Twin-turbofan commuter transport.

WINGS: Cantilever low-wing monoplane. All-metal fail-safe torsion-box structure, with machined stressed skin. Ailerons operated by Dassault twin-body actuators supplied by two hydraulic systems, with artificial feel units. No tabs. Hydraulically-actuated two-section single-slotted flaps. Non-slotted slats inboard of the fence on each wing, and slotted slats outboard of fence. Hydraulically-actuated airbrakes forward of flaps. Leading-edges anti-iced by engine bleed air.

FUSELAGE: All-metal semi-monocoque structure of circular cross-section, designed to fail-safe principles.

TAIL UNIT: Cantilever all-metal fail-safe structure, with shallow ventral fin. Electrically-controlled variable-incidence tailplane. Elevators and rudder each actuated by twin-body hydraulic servo controls. No tabs.

LANDING GEAR: Retractable tricycle type by Messier-Hispano, with twin wheels on all three units. Hydraulic retraction, main units inward, nosewheels forward. Oleo-pneumatic shock-absorbers. Normal tyre pressure 178 lb/sq in (12·5 kg/cm²) on main gear, 68 lb/sq in (4·8 kg/cm²) on nose gear. Steerable and self-centering nose unit. Goodyear three-disc brakes and anti-skid units.

POWER PLANT: Two Lycoming ALF 502D turbofan engines, each rated at 6,070 lb (2,753 kg) st under ISA + 10°C conditions, mounted in pods on each side of rear fuselage. Two integral wing fuel tanks, total capacity 1,165 Imp gallons (1,400 US gallons; 5,300 litres). Separate fuel system for each engine, with provision for cross-feeding. Single-point pressure refuelling. Emergency refuelling by gravity.

ACCOMMODATION: Crew of two in flight compartment, with fully-duplicated controls and airline-type instrumentation. Normal seating for 30 passengers in Falcon 30 or 40 passengers in Mystère 40-100, plus cabin crew. Toilet compartment at rear. Cargo/baggage compartment at rear, with service door. Alternative executive layout for 8-15 passengers, with galley, toilet, wardrobe compartment and larger baggage compartment. Downward-opening door at front on port side, with built-in stairs.

SYSTEMS: Duplicated air-conditioning and pressurisation systems, supplied with air bled from both engines. Pressure differential 8·5 lb/sq in (0·593 kg/cm²). Two independent hydraulic systems, each with operating pressure of 3,000 lb/sq in (210 kg/cm²), supplied by two engine-driven pumps and one electric emergency pump to actuate primary flying controls, flaps, landing gear, wheel brakes, airbrakes and nose gear steering. 28V DC electrical system, with a 9kW DC starter/generator on each engine, three 750VA inverters and two 40Ah batteries. Automatic emergency oxygen system.

ELECTRONICS AND EQUIPMENT: Standard equipment includes duplicated VOR/ILS, VHF, DME and ADF, marker beacon receiver, ATC transponder, autopilot, duplicated flight director, radio altimeter and weather radar.

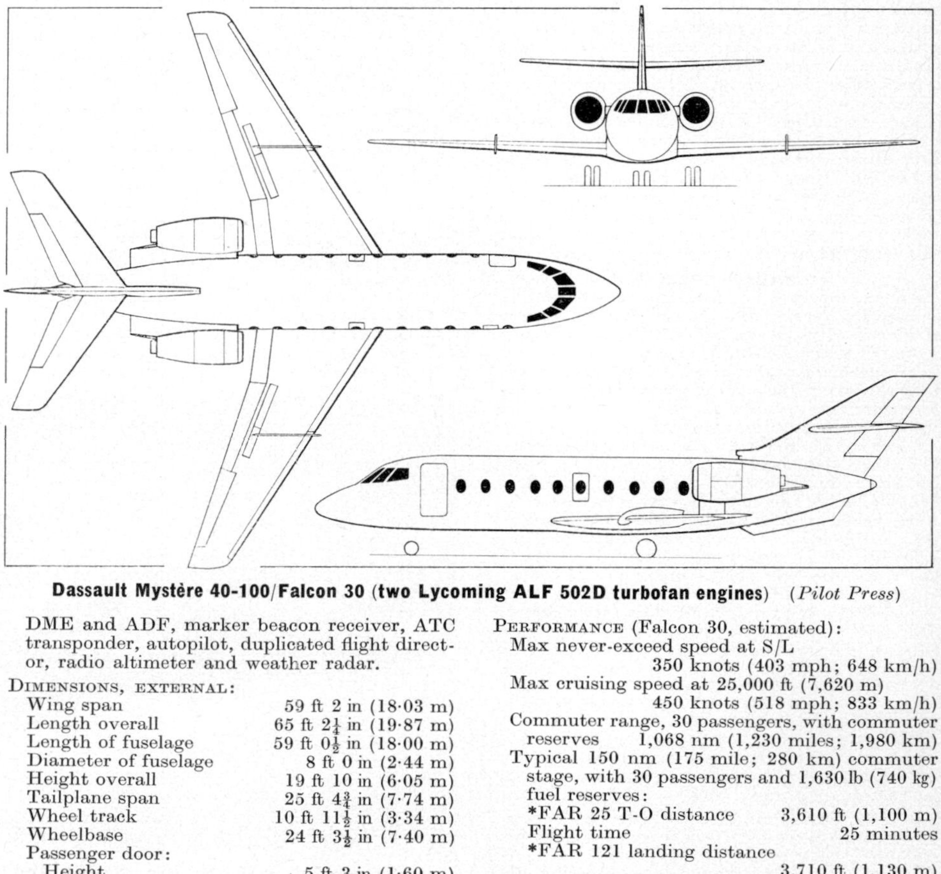

Dassault Mystère 40-100/Falcon 30 (two Lycoming ALF 502D turbofan engines) (*Pilot Press*)

DIMENSIONS, EXTERNAL:
- Wing span 59 ft 2 in (18·03 m)
- Length overall 65 ft 2¼ in (19·87 m)
- Length of fuselage 59 ft 0½ in (18·00 m)
- Diameter of fuselage 8 ft 0 in (2·44 m)
- Height overall 19 ft 10 in (6·05 m)
- Tailplane span 25 ft 4¾ in (7·74 m)
- Wheel track 10 ft 11½ in (3·34 m)
- Wheelbase 24 ft 3½ in (7·40 m)
- Passenger door:
  - Height 5 ft 3 in (1·60 m)
  - Width 2 ft 9 in (0·84 m)
  - Height to sill 4 ft 7 in (1·39 m)
- Emergency exits (each side, overwing):
  - Height 3 ft 0½ in (0·930 m)
  - Width 1 ft 8 in (0·508 m)
- Emergency exit (starboard, front):
  - Height 4 ft 0 in (1·22 m)
  - Width 1 ft 8 in (0·508 m)
- Cargo hold door:
  - Height 2 ft 7½ in (0·80 m)
  - Width 3 ft 0 in (0·915 m)
  - Height to sill 4 ft 7 in (1·39 m)

DIMENSIONS, INTERNAL:
- Cabin, excluding flight deck:
  - Length 37 ft 1 in (11·31 m)
  - Max width 7 ft 7¼ in (2·32 m)
  - Max height 6 ft 1 in (1·85 m)
  - Cargo hold volume 184 cu ft (5·20 m³)

AREAS:
- Wings, gross 527 sq ft (49·0 m²)
- Horizontal tail surfaces, total 150·8 sq ft (14·01 m²)
- Vertical tail surfaces, total 100·4 sq ft (9·33 m²)

WEIGHTS (Falcon 30):
- Operating weight, empty 22,156 lb (10,050 kg)
- Max payload 7,495 lb (3,400 kg)
- Max T-O weight 35,275 lb (16,000 kg)
- Max zero-fuel weight 29,650 lb (13,450 kg)

WEIGHTS (Mystère 40-100):
- Operating weight, empty 21,733 lb (9,858 kg)
- Max payload 9,131 lb (4,142 kg)
- Max T-O weight 35,275 lb (16,000 kg)
- Max zero-fuel weight 30,865 lb (14,000 kg)

PERFORMANCE (Falcon 30, estimated):
- Max never-exceed speed at S/L 350 knots (403 mph; 648 km/h)
- Max cruising speed at 25,000 ft (7,620 m) 450 knots (518 mph; 833 km/h)
- Commuter range, 30 passengers, with commuter reserves 1,068 nm (1,230 miles; 1,980 km)
- Typical 150 nm (175 mile; 280 km) commuter stage, with 30 passengers and 1,630 lb (740 kg) fuel reserves:
  - *FAR 25 T-O distance 3,610 ft (1,100 m)
  - Flight time 25 minutes
  - *FAR 121 landing distance 3,710 ft (1,130 m)

PERFORMANCE (Mystère 40-100, estimated):
- Speeds as for Falcon 30
- Range with 40 passengers and commuter reserves 744 nm (857 miles; 1,380 km)
- Typical 270 nm (310 mile; 500 km) stage, with 40 passengers and 1,700 lb (770 kg) fuel reserves:
  - *FAR 25 T-O distance 4,135 ft (1,260 m)
  - Flight time 42 minutes
  - *FAR 121 landing distance 3,840 ft (1,170 m)

**S/L, ISA + 10°C*

DASSAULT MERCURE

The Mercure is a 132/162-seat twin-engined short-haul transport aircraft, optimised for ranges of 100-1,000 nm (115-1,150 miles; 185-1,850 km). Development was started in 1967.

The first of two prototypes (F-WTCC), powered by 15,000 lb (6,804 kg) st Pratt & Whitney JT8D-11 turbofan engines, was flown for the first time on 28 May 1971. The second prototype (F-WTMD), which flew on 7 September 1972, has more powerful JT8D-15 engines. JT8D-15s are also fitted to production Mercures, the first of which flew for the first time on 19 July 1973.

Certification of the Mercure was received on 12 February 1974, by which date a total of 1,225 flying hours had been logged by the first three aircraft; and airline deliveries began in April 1974. Air Inter has ordered 10 Mercures, the first of which was delivered on 15 May 1974.

The Mercure is intended primarily for operation beneath the airbus level but with greater capacity than is available in the present generation of short-haul twin-jets. Cat III certification was expected by September 1974.

The launching programme for the Mercure was expected to cost 1,000m Fr (£75m), covering the construction of two prototypes, two airframes for static and fatigue testing, certification and production tooling. Of this sum, the French contribution represented 70 per cent. The remaining amount was shared principally between Aeritalia of Italy (10 per cent), which manufactures the tail unit and fuselage tailcone; CASA of Spain (10 per cent), which manufactures the first and second fuselage sections; SABCA of Belgium (6 per cent), which builds the flaps, ailerons, spoilers and airbrakes; and F+W (Emmen) of Switzerland (2 per cent), which is responsible for the engine air intakes and cowling panels.

Under an agreement signed in February 1972, Canadair Ltd of Montreal, Canada, is manufacturing wing panels, tracks for the wing leading-edges and flaps, and engine nacelle pylons for production Mercures, equivalent to 5·2% of the airframe work.

TYPE: Twin-turbofan short-range large-capacity transport.

WINGS: Cantilever low-wing monoplane. Special Dassault wing sections, having thickness/chord ratio of 12½% at root, 8% at tip. Dihedral 5°. Incidence 3° 15′ at root. Sweepback 25° at quarter-chord. Two-spar fail-safe torsion-box structure, each wing being made up of one-piece spars and eight skin panels with built-in stiffeners and cells and machined ribs. On to this torsion box is built a slotted leading-edge with a three-element slat. Two triple-slotted flaps and single plain aileron on each trailing-edge, forward of which are five additional movable surfaces: three spoilers and two airbrakes. Spoilers are for lateral control (coupled with ailerons) and lift dumping. All movable surfaces are operated hydraulically by dual actuators fed by three independent circuits. Engine bleed air for anti-icing of wing leading-edges.

FUSELAGE: Circular-section all-metal semi-monocoque structure, built in five main sections and utilising fail-safe frames, machined stress frames, integral structure panels and a chemically-machined skin stiffened by stringers and frames.

TAIL UNIT: Cantilever multi-spar structure (three-spar fin and two-spar tailplane), of basically similar construction to wings. Variable-incidence tailplane for trim and pitch emergency control. Rudder divided into two independent parts. No tabs. All control surfaces operated by hydraulic dual actuators fed by three independent circuits. No de-icing of tail surfaces.

LANDING GEAR: Retractable tricycle type, by Messier-Hispano, with twin wheels and oleo-pneumatic shock-absorbers on each unit. Hydraulic retraction, with manual back-up. Forward-retracting nosewheel unit, steerable through 70° to left or right. Main units retract inwards into wing/fuselage centre-section fairing. Messier-Hispano wheels and Kléber-Colombes tyres, size 46 × 16 on main units, 30 × 8·8 on nose unit. Tyre pressure 141 lb/sq in (9·75 kg/cm²) on main units, 123 lb/sq in (8·3 kg/cm²) on nose unit. Messier-Hispano brakes and anti-skid units.

POWER PLANT: Two 15,500 lb (7,030 kg) st Pratt & Whitney JT8D-15 turbofan engines in underwing pods, fitted with thrust reversers and Dassault-developed noise absorbers. Total fuel capacity of 4,048 Imp gallons (4,860 US gallons; 18,400 litres). Refuelling point on outer leading-edge of starboard wing. Auxiliary overwing fuelling points. Total oil capacity 9·9 Imp gallons (11·9 US gallons; 45 litres). Engine bleed air for nose cowl de-icing.

ACCOMMODATION: Crew of two side by side on flight deck, with two extra optional seats. Typical mixed-class accommodation provides 12 seats four-abreast at 38 in (96·5 cm) pitch and 120 seats six-abreast at 32 in (81·5 cm) pitch. Basic tourist class accommodation provides 140 seats at 34 in (86·5 cm) pitch. High-density layout for up to 162 seats six-abreast at 30 in (76·2 cm) pitch. Six possible locations of toilets and galleys at front and rear, according to layout. Flight deck windows can be de-iced electrically. Passenger cabin windows are polarised, to reduce glare without the need for separate screens or curtains. Two passenger doors, at front and rear on port side. Aérazur retractable integral stairway built into fuselage below forward passenger door; provision for similar stairway below rear passenger door. Individual lockable baggage compartments above seats in passenger cabin, with total volume of 247 cu ft (7·0 m³). Two service doors, at front and rear on starboard side, and two emergency exits over each wing. Cargo/baggage holds beneath cabin floor, one forward and two aft of wings. Forward hold can accommodate 7,715 lb (3,500 kg) or five standard Boeing 727 freight containers; aft hold No 1 can accommodate 6,170 lb (2,800 kg) or four Boeing 727 containers; aft hold No 2 can accommodate 3,965 lb (1,800 kg) of baggage.

SYSTEMS: Garrett air-conditioning system and Hamilton Standard pressurisation system, using engine bleed air through duplicated circuits, with automatic regulation. Max cabin differential 8·3 lb/sq in (0·6 kg/cm²). Three independent hydraulic systems, each of 3,000 lb/sq in (210 kg/cm²). Two systems powered by Abex engine-driven pumps for flying controls, flaps, slats, spoilers, tailplane, landing gear, nosewheel steering and brakes; one system powered by Vickers electrically-driven pump providing back-up for ailerons, elevators and rudder. Two 60kVA Plessey-Sundstrand engine-driven IDG alternators provide 120/208V 400Hz three-phase AC power. Additional 55kVA alternator powered by APU. 28V 150A DC power provided by two Bronzavia transformer-rectifiers and SAFT 24V 23Ah battery. Provision for third transformer-rectifier with EMD static converter. Eros/Intertechnique oxygen system for pilots and passengers. Garrett AiResearch GTCP-85-163C APU, installed in fuselage tailcone, provides emergency electrical power and air for ground conditioning and engine starting.

ELECTRONICS AND EQUIPMENT: To customer's requirements. Basic aircraft designed for all-weather (Cat III) operation.

DIMENSIONS, EXTERNAL:

Wing span	100 ft 3 in (30·55 m)
Wing chord at root	19 ft 8¼ in (6·00 m)
Wing chord at tip	5 ft 8½ in (1·74 m)
Wing aspect ratio	8
Length overall	114 ft 3½ in (34·84 m)
Length of fuselage	112 ft 11 in (34·41 m)
Height overall	37 ft 3¼ in (11·36 m)
Tailplane span	41 ft 11 in (12·77 m)
Wheel track	20 ft 4 in (6·20 m)
Wheelbase	40 ft 9 in (12·42 m)
Passenger doors (port, fwd and rear):	
Height	5 ft 11 in (1·80 m)
Width	2 ft 9½ in (0·85 m)
Height to sill (fwd)	9 ft 6 in (2·90 m)
Height to sill (rear)	9 ft 10 in (3·00 m)
Service door (stbd, fwd):	
Height	5 ft 11 in (1·80 m)
Width	2 ft 9½ in (0·85 m)
Height to sill	9 ft 6 in (2·90 m)
Service door (stbd, rear):	
Height	5 ft 5 in (1·65 m)
Width	2 ft 9½ in (0·85 m)
Height to sill	9 ft 10 in (3·00 m)
Cargo hold door (stbd, fwd):	
Height	3 ft 8 in (1·12 m)
Width	4 ft 11 in (1·50 m)
Height to sill	5 ft 2 in (1·57 m)
Cargo hold door (stbd, aft No. 1):	
Height	3 ft 8 in (1·12 m)
Width	4 ft 11 in (1·50 m)
Height to sill	5 ft 4½ in (1·64 m)
Cargo hold door (stbd, aft No. 2):	
Height	2 ft 6¾ in (0·78 m)
Width	4 ft 0 in (1·22 m)
Height to sill	5 ft 11 in (1·80 m)

DIMENSIONS, INTERNAL:

Cabin, excluding flight deck:	
Length	83 ft 7 in (25·50 m)
Max width	11 ft 11 in (3·66 m)
Max height	7 ft 2¾ in (2·20 m)
Floor area	882 sq ft (82·00 m²)
Volume	5,717 cu ft (162·0 m³)
Freight hold volume:	
forward	529 cu ft (15·0 m³)
aft No. 1	406 cu ft (11·5 m³)
aft No. 2	265 cu ft (7·5 m³)

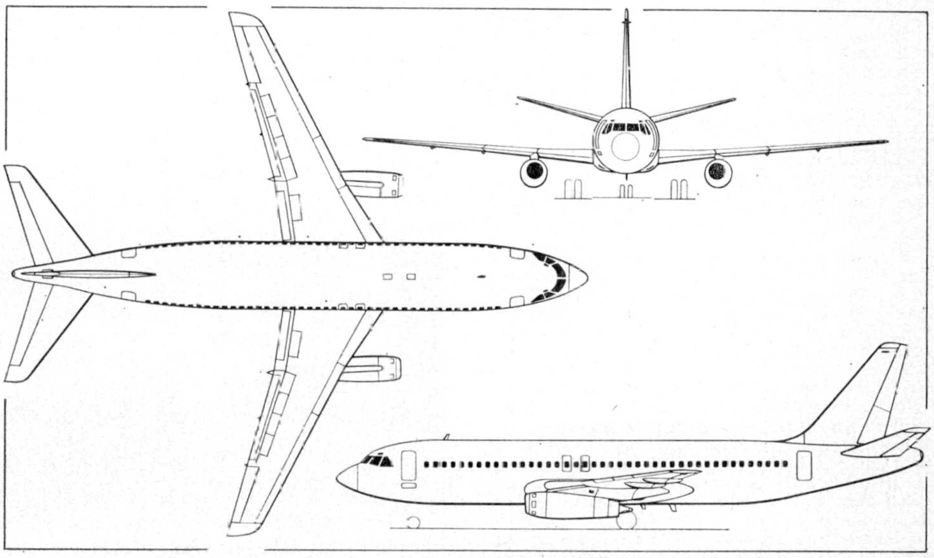

Dassault Mercure twin-turbofan short-range large-capacity transport (*Pilot Press*)

Production version of the Dassault Mercure short-haul large-capacity transport in the insignia of Air Inter (*Air & General Photographs*)

AREAS:

Wings, gross	1,250 sq ft (116·0 m²)
Ailerons (total)	45·2 sq ft (4·20 m²)
Trailing-edge flaps (total)	261·6 sq ft (24·30 m²)
Spoilers (total)	49·5 sq ft (4·60 m²)
Airbrakes (total)	36·6 sq ft (3·40 m²)
Fin	166·3 sq ft (15·45 m²)
Rudder (upper)	29·1 sq ft (2·70 m²)
Rudder (lower)	35·0 sq ft (3·25 m²)
Tailplane	257·3 sq ft (23·9 m²)
Elevators (total)	86·1 sq ft (8·0 m²)

WEIGHTS AND LOADINGS:

Operating weight, empty	68,345 lb (31,000 kg)
Max payload	33,070 lb (15,000 kg)
Max ramp weight	120,150 lb (54,500 kg)
Max T-O weight	119,050 lb (54,000 kg)
Max landing weight	109,790 lb (49,800 kg)
Max zero-fuel weight	101,410 lb (46,000 kg)
Max wing loading	95·44 lb/sq ft (466 kg/m²)
Max power loading	3·84 lb/lb st (3·84 kg/kg st)

PERFORMANCE:
Max operating speed (VMO/MMO)
380 knots (437 mph; 704 km/h) CAS up to 20,000 ft (6,100 m) and Mach 0·85 above 20,000 ft
Max cruising speed at 20,000 ft (6,100 m)
500 knots (575 mph; 926 km/h)
Max rate of climb at 7,000 ft (2,135 m) at AUW of 100,000 lb (45,360 kg)
3,300 ft (1,007 m)/min
Typical short-haul stage (500 nm; 575 miles; 925 km) with 140 passengers and 7,715 lb (3,500 kg) fuel reserves:
FAR 25 T-O distance (S/L, ISA + 14°C)
6,300 ft (1,920 m)
Flight time 1 hr 8 min
Approach speed
117 knots (135 mph; 217 km/h)
FAR 121 landing distance (S/L, ISA + 14°C)
4,630 ft (1,410 m)
Max range with 140 passengers and 8,375 lb (3,800 kg) fuel reserves
910 nm (1,047 miles; 1,680 km)

DRUINE
AVIONS ROGER DRUINE

This company was formed by the late Roger Druine, who designed, built and flew his first aircraft at the age of seventeen and died only 20 years later, in 1958. His best-known designs are the Turbulent single-seat monoplane and the Turbi, a two-seat version of the Turbulent, both of which continue to be built by amateurs throughout the world.

The Turbulent and the more refined Condor are manufactured commercially by Rollason Aircraft and Engines Ltd in the UK (which see).

DRUINE D.31 TURBULENT

Full details of this single-seat ultra-light monoplane are given under the "Rollason" heading in the UK section.

Druine D.5 Turbi, built in Vancouver, Canada, with 85 hp Continental engine (*Peter M. Bowers*)

DRUINE D.5 TURBI

The prototype Turbi had a 45 hp Beaussier 4 B02 four-cylinder inverted aircooled engine. Details of this and of the version with 62 hp Walter Mikron II engine can be found in the 1964-65 *Jane's*. The following details refer to a typical Turbi built in recent years:

TYPE: Two-seat light monoplane.

WINGS: Cantilever low-wing monoplane. NACA 23012 wing section. Wood structure, with box-spar and plywood covering. No flaps.

FUSELAGE: Rectangular four-longeron all-wood structure, plywood-covered.

TAIL UNIT: Cantilever wooden structure. Fin built integral with fuselage. Non-adjustable tailplane. All surfaces plywood-covered.

LANDING GEAR: Non-retractable tailwheel type. Spring shock-absorbers. Steerable tailwheel. Brakes.

POWER PLANT: One 85 hp Continental C85-12 four-cylinder horizontally-opposed aircooled engine, driving a two-blade fixed-pitch propeller. Glassfibre cowling. Fuel tank in fuselage in front of forward cockpit.

ACCOMMODATION: Two seats in tandem in open cockpits.

DIMENSIONS, EXTERNAL:

Wing span	28 ft 9 in (8·76 m)
Wing chord (constant)	5 ft 8 in (1·73 m)
Length overall	22 ft 0 in (6·71 m)
Height overall	5 ft 0 in (1·52 m)

AREA:

Wings, gross	139 sq ft (12·9 m²)

WEIGHTS:

Weight empty	830 lb (376 kg)
Max T-O weight	1,240 lb (562 kg)

PERFORMANCE (at max T-O weight):
Max level speed at S/L
104 knots (120 mph; 193 km/h)

Cruising speed	78 knots (90 mph; 145 km/h)
Landing speed	35 knots (40 mph; 64 km/h)
Max rate of climb at S/L	500 ft (152 m)/min
Absolute ceiling	10,000 ft (3,050 m)
T-O run	300 ft (91 m)
Landing run	700 ft (213 m)

DRUINE D.61/D.62 CONDOR

The Condor was designed primarily for factory production and incorporates many refinements in design and construction not found in the Turbulent and Turbi. A simplified version is, however, available for amateur construction.

The two standard versions are the D.61 with 65/75 hp Continental engine, and the D.62 with 90/100 hp Continental engine.

A full description of the D.62 is given under the "Rollason" heading in the UK section.

DURUBLE
ROLAND DURUBLE

ADDRESS: 40 Rue de Paradis, Les Essarts, 76530-Grand-Couronne

Telephone: 92-20-63

M Roland Duruble, with MM Guy Chaunt and Legrand, of Rouen, designed and built a two-seat all-metal light aircraft named the RD-02 Edelweiss, which flew for the first time on 7 July 1962. Full details of this aircraft can be found in the 1972-73 *Jane's*.

Plans of an enlarged and improved version, known as the RD-03 Edelweiss, are available to other constructors.

Duruble RD-02 Edelweiss amateur-built light aircraft (65 hp Walter Mikron III engine), from which the RD-03 has been evolved

DURUBLE RD-03 EDELWEISS

The RD-03 Edelweiss has been designed to AIR 2052 (CAR 3) standards, and is projected in three versions, as follows:

RD-03A. With 100 hp Continental O-200 four-cylinder horizontally-opposed aircooled engine and fuel capacity of 22 Imp gallons (100 litres) in two wing tanks. Can be fitted with 90 hp engine or 135 hp Lycoming O-320 engine. Side-by-side seats for pilot and one passenger (total weight 380 lb; 172 kg) in cabin.

RD-03B. With 135 hp Lycoming O-320 or Franklin Sport 4B engine and same fuel capacity as RD-03A. Seating as RD-03A for Utility category operation, or in "2 + 2" arrangement for pilot and three passengers (340 lb; 154 kg on front seats, 240 lb; 110 kg on rear seats) in Normal category.

RD-03C. With 150 hp Lycoming engine and additional wing tanks, increasing total fuel capacity to 33 Imp gallons (150 litres). In Utility two-seat form (as RD-03A) or with seating for four adult persons (total weight 680 lb; 308 kg) in Normal category.

Plans of the RD-03 have been available since the Autumn of 1970. Two examples were under construction in the Spring of 1974.

TYPE: Two/four-seat light aircraft.

WINGS: Cantilever low-wing monoplane. Wing section NACA 23000 series. Thickness/chord ratio 18% at root, 12% at tip. Dihedral 6° 5′ from roots. Incidence 3° at root, 0° at tip. No sweepback. All-metal two-spar duralumin structure, with metal slotted trailing-edge flaps and slotted ailerons. No trim tabs.

FUSELAGE: Conventional semi-monocoque duralumin structure.

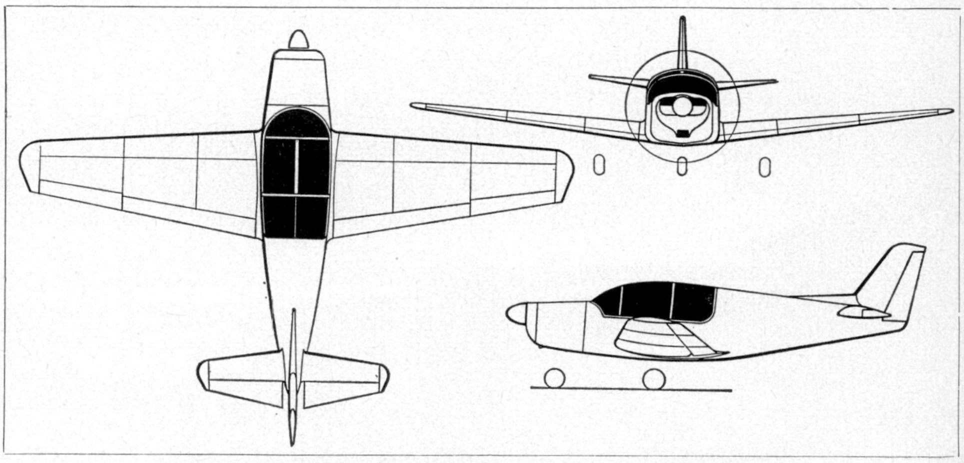

Duruble RD-03C Edelweiss two/four-seat amateur-built light aircraft

TAIL UNIT: Cantilever all-metal structure, with sweptback vertical surfaces. Fixed-incidence tailplane. Trim tab in each elevator, one actuated by flap linkage and the other manually.

LANDING GEAR: Retractable tricycle type. Hydraulic retraction, nosewheel rearward, main units inward into wings. Duruble hydro-air shock-absorbers on all three units. Main wheels and tyres size 355 × 150, nosewheel and tyre size 330 × 130. Pressure (all tyres) 18 lb/sq in (1·26 kg/cm²). Hydraulic disc brakes.

POWER PLANT: One 90, 100, 135 or 150 hp horizontally-opposed aircooled engine (see details above). Refuelling point above wing.

ACCOMMODATION: Side-by-side seats for two, three or four persons (see details above) in fully-enclosed cabin.

SYSTEMS: Hydraulic system, pressure 1,000 lb/sq in (70 kg/cm²), for flap and landing gear actuation.

ELECTRONICS AND EQUIPMENT: Radio optional. Blind-flying instrumentation not fitted.

DIMENSIONS, EXTERNAL:
Wing span 28 ft 8½ in (8·75 m)
Wing chord at root 5 ft 7 in (1·70 m)
Wing chord at tip 2 ft 10 in (0·86 m)
Wing aspect ratio 6·95
Length overall (RD-03A) 20 ft 7 in (6·27 m)
Height overall 7 ft 8½ in (2·35 m)
Tailplane span 10 ft 0 in (3·05 m)

DIMENSIONS, INTERNAL:
Cabin: Max length 8 ft 0 in (2·44 m)
Max width 3 ft 7¼ in (1·10 m)
Max height 3 ft 5¾ in (1·06 m)

AREAS:
Wings, gross 118·5 sq ft (11·04 m²)
Ailerons (total) 7·3 sq ft (0·68 m²)
Trailing-edge flaps (total) 17·5 sq ft (1·63 m²)
Fin 7·8 sq ft (0·72 m²)
Rudder 4·9 sq ft (0·46 m²)
Tailplane 12·9 sq ft (1·20 m²)
Elevators, incl tabs 10·0 sq ft (0·93 m²)

WEIGHTS AND LOADINGS (estimated. A: RD-03A; B: RD-03B; C: RD-03C):
Weight empty, equipped:
A 896 lb (406·5 kg)
B 917 lb (416 kg)
C 929 lb (421·5 kg)
Max T-O and landing weight:
A (Utility) 1,541 lb (699 kg)
B (Utility) 1,576 lb (715 kg)
B (Normal) 1,754 lb (796 kg)
C (Utility) 1,631 lb (740 kg)
C (Normal) 1,909 lb (866 kg)
Max wing loading:
A (Utility) 12·90 lb/sq ft (63·0 kg/m²)
B (Utility) 13·11 lb/sq ft (64·0 kg/m²)
B (Normal) 14·64 lb/sq ft (71·5 kg/m²)
C (Utility) 13·60 lb/sq ft (66·4 kg/m²)
C (Normal) 16·00 lb/sq ft (78·0 kg/m²)
Max power loading:
A (Utility) 14·97 lb/hp (6·79 kg/hp)
B (Utility) 11·68 lb/hp (5·30 kg/hp)
B (Normal) 13·01 lb/hp (5·90 kg/hp)
C (Utility) 10·85 lb/hp (4·92 kg/hp)
C (Normal) 12·79 lb/hp (5·80 kg/hp)

PERFORMANCE (estimated at max T-O weight):
Max never-exceed speed:
A, B, C (Utility)
170 knots (196 mph; 315 km/h)
B, C (Normal)
182 knots (210 mph; 338 km/h)
Max level speed at S/L:
A (Utility) 139 knots (160 mph; 257 km/h)
B (Utility) 143 knots (165 mph; 265 km/h)
B (Normal) 141 knots (163 mph; 262 km/h)
C (Utility) 149 knots (172 mph; 277 km/h)
C (Normal) 146 knots (168 mph; 270 km/h)
Max cruising speed at S/L:
A (Utility)
126·3 knots (145·5 mph; 234 km/h)
B (Utility) 129 knots (149 mph; 240 km/h)
B (Normal) 128 knots (148 mph; 238 km/h)
C (Utility) 136 knots (157 mph; 252 km/h)
C (Normal) 133 knots (153 mph; 246 km/h)
Econ cruising speed at S/L:
A, B (Utility) 121 knots (139 mph; 224 km/h)
B (Normal) 120 knots (138 mph; 222 km/h)
C (Utility) 128 knots (147·5 mph; 237 km/h)
C (Normal) 125 knots (144·5 mph; 233 km/h)
Stalling speed, flaps up:
A, B (Utility) 50 knots (57·5 mph; 92 km/h)
B (Normal), C (Utility)
56 knots (65 mph; 104 km/h)
C (Normal) 59 knots (68 mph; 109 km/h)
Stalling speed, flaps down:
A, B (Utility)
41 knots (47·5 mph; 76·5 km/h)
B (Normal), C (Utility)
47 knots (54 mph; 86·5 km/h)
C (Normal) 48 knots (55·5 mph; 89 km/h)
Max rate of climb at S/L:
A 650 ft (198 m)/min
B 700 ft (213 m)/min
C 800 ft (244 m)/min
Service ceiling:
A, B 15,000 ft (4,570 m)
C 16,500 ft (5,030 m)
T-O run:
A 820 ft (250 m)
B 900 ft (274 m)
C 1,000 ft (305 m)
T-O to 50 ft (15 m):
A, B, C 1,500 ft (457 m)
Landing from 50 ft (15 m):
A 610 ft (186 m)
B 800 ft (244 m)
C 940 ft (287 m)
Landing run:
A 1,000 ft (305 m)
B 1,100 ft (335 m)
C 1,400 ft (427 m)
Range with max fuel, 30 min reserve:
A 607 nm (700 miles; 1,125 km)
B 521 nm (600 miles; 965 km)
C 547 nm (630 miles; 1,010 km)

GATARD

AVIONS A. GATARD

ADDRESS:
La Devallée, 52 route de Jonzac, 17130-Montendre
Telephone: 183

M Albert Gatard has developed a control system for aeroplanes which involves the use of a variable-incidence lifting tailplane of large area, and has built or is developing a series of aircraft, including the Alouette and Poussin, incorporating his ideas. The Alouette (described in the 1959-60 *Jane's*) was purely experimental, but plans of the Poussin are available to amateur constructors.

Instead of altering the wing angle of attack to increase lift on these aircraft, the pilot lowers full-span slotted aileron/flaps and adjusts the tailplane to maintain pitching equilibrium. In consequence, the aircraft climb with the fuselage datum at no more than 4° to the horizontal, which preserves a good forward view and low body drag.

Early in 1966, M Gatard began work on a prototype of another design, the AG 04. Brief details of this are given below, together with particulars of another Gatard project, the AG 05.

Second Gatard Statoplan AG 02 Poussin in its latest form *(F. E. v. Bruggen)*

GATARD STATOPLAN AG 02 POUSSIN (CHICK)

M Gatard built two prototypes of the Poussin and the following data apply to the second of these, which introduced a number of design improvements. Flight tests revealed excellent aerobatic qualities and the power plant has been modified to permit up to 20 seconds of inverted flying.

The second prototype was extensively flight-tested at the Centre d'Essais en Vol at Istres, and the performance figures below are those obtained during these tests. As a result of recommendations by the CEV, a 36 hp Rectimo (modified Volkswagen VW 1200) engine is now suggested as the most suitable power plant for use by amateur constructors of the Poussin. The second prototype has been re-engined with a 1,200 cc Volkswagen, in a new streamlined cowling, by M Mathevet of Mollard-Chateauneuf (Loirs), on behalf of M Gatard. Installation of such an engine was expected to improve the CG position and make possible a max speed of approx 92 knots (106 mph; 170 km/h), a max cruising speed of approx 83 knots (96 mph; 155 km/h) and a rate of climb at S/L of 690 ft (210 m)/min.

Several Poussins are being built by amateur constructors, and three were nearing completion in early 1974. One of them is the work of Mr Gomès of Lubumbashi in the Zaïre Republic.

TYPE: Single-seat ultra-light monoplane.

WINGS: Cantilever low-wing monoplane. NACA 23012 wing section. Dihedral 4°. Incidence 3° 30′ at root, 2° at tip. Plywood-covered single-spar all-wood structure. Full-span slotted aileron/flaps, each in two sections which are moved together but at different angles (inboard sections up to 35°, outboard up to 20°) to give the effect of increased aerodynamic twist of the complete wing/aileron/flap assemblies. Aileron/flaps are linked with the variable-incidence tailplane.

FUSELAGE: Plywood-covered wood structure. Perforated airbrake, under fuselage, operates automatically when the main aileron/flaps are lowered at large angles, as during landing.

TAIL UNIT: Braced all-wood structure, with variable-incidence all-moving tailplane of NACA 2309 section. Endplates fitted to tailplane to increase vertical fin area and effective tailplane span. No elevators. Rudder trim tab actuated by lateral movement of control column, permitting full control by means of the control column alone in normal flight.

LANDING GEAR: Non-retractable tailwheel type. Cantilever levered-suspension main units with rubber-band shock-absorption. Modified Dunlop brakes. Steerable tailwheel.

POWER PLANT: One 24 hp modified Volkswagen four-cylinder horizontally-opposed aircooled engine, driving Gatard two-blade fixed-pitch wooden propeller. Provision for fitting any alternative engine of up to 40 hp, weighing between 110 and 132 lb (50-60 kg). Fuel tank aft of firewall, capacity 6·6 Imp gallons (30 litres). Oil capacity 0·45 Imp gallons (2 litres).

ACCOMMODATION: Single seat under large rear-ward-sliding transparent canopy. Baggage space aft of seat. Two map pockets.

DIMENSIONS, EXTERNAL:
Wing span 21 ft 0 in (6·40 m)
Wing chord (constant) 3 ft 3¼ in (1·00 m)
Length overall 14 ft 10¼ in (4·53 m)
Height overall 4 ft 11 in (1·50 m)
Wheel track 4 ft 11 in (1·50 m)
Wheelbase 10 ft 6 in (3·20 m)

AREAS:
Wings, gross 66·2 sq ft (6·15 m²)
Aileron/flaps (total) 21·5 sq ft (2·00 m²)
Fin 0·79 sq ft (0·073 m²)
Rudder 2·80 sq ft (0·26 m²)
Tailplane 18·10 sq ft (1·68 m²)

WEIGHTS:
Weight empty 375 lb (170 kg)
Max T-O weight 617 lb (280 kg)

PERFORMANCE (at max T-O weight):
Max never-exceed speed
116 knots (134 mph; 216 km/h)
Max cruising speed
77 knots (89 mph; 144 km/h)
Max speed for aerobatics
69 knots (80 mph; 130 km/h)
Stalling speed 35 knots (40·3 mph; 65 km/h)
Max rate of climb at S/L 435 ft (132 m)/min
T-O run 625 ft (190 m)
T-O to 50 ft (15 m) 1,425 ft (435 m)
Landing from 50 ft (15 m) 1,050 ft (320 m)
Landing run 655 ft (200 m)

GATARD STATOPLAN AG 04 PIGEON

The AG 04 Pigeon is a three/four-seat high-wing monoplane, powered by a Continental engine. It utilises the same type of control system as its predecessors, except that the Statoplan aileron/flaps are in three sections on each wing. As on the Poussin, they move together but through different angles (successively 45°, 30° and 20°) to give the effect of increased aerodynamic twist of the complete wing/aileron/flap assemblies.

The wings are braced by a single streamline-section strut each side and can be folded to permit the aircraft to be towed along roads behind a motor car. Overall dimensions under tow are: length 20 ft 8¼ in (6·30 m), width 7 ft 2¾ in (2·20 m) and height 9 ft 10 in (3·0 m).

A non-retractable tailwheel-type landing gear is fitted, with long-stroke rubber-ring shock-absorbers on all three units. Both manual and toe-operated brakes are specified, the former serving also as a parking brake.

The two front seats are adjustable fore and aft

and all controls are so mounted that the main cabin area is completely clear. Full control is possible in normal flight by means of the control column alone, as on the Poussin. Dual controls are provided for a second pilot, but can be disconnected easily. Entry is via a two-section door on each side; the lower section opens forward, the top section upward under the wing. The top section can be opened to a mid-position for additional ventilation while taxying. An optional door on the starboard side permits loading of a stretcher 5 ft 11 in long by 1 ft 6 in wide (1·80 m × 0·45 m) when the aircraft is used in an ambulance role. The rear seat on this side can be folded down to make room for the stretcher.

The prototype Pigeon was 80 per cent complete by the early Spring of 1974. It is expected to offer automatic stability in flight, and to take off and land at about 38 knots (44 mph; 70 km/h).

Model of Gatard Statoplan AG 04 Pigeon four-seat light aircraft

GATARD STATOPLAN AG 05 MÉSANGE (TOMTIT)

The AG 05 Mésange is essentially an enlarged development of the Poussin with side-by-side seating for two persons. It is intended primarily as a training or aerobatic aircraft, but will have provision either for seating a third occupant or for installing a supplementary fuel tank aft of the two front seats, to make the aircraft suitable for touring. The control system will be similar to that of the Poussin, but the Mésange will have larger, broader-chord wings without the rounded tips of its predecessor, and will have leading-edge fuel tanks.

Completion of the prototype will follow successful development of the AG 04 Pigeon.

TYPE: Two/three-seat light aircraft.

WINGS: Cantilever low-wing monoplane. NACA 23012 wing section. Dihedral 4°. Incidence 3° at root, —1° 30′ at tip. Plywood-covered all-wood structure. Full-span slotted aileron/flaps of similar type to those of Poussin, inboard sections movable between 35° and —20°, outboard sections between 20° and —12°. Aileron/flaps are linked with the variable-incidence tailplane.

FUSELAGE: Plywood-covered steel-tube structure. Airbrake beneath centre-section, length 4 ft 11 in (1·50 m), operates automatically in similar manner to that on Poussin.

TAIL UNIT: Plywood-covered all-wood structure. Variable-incidence all-moving tailplane.

LANDING GEAR: Non-retractable tailwheel type, with rubber-band shock-absorbers on main units. Steerable tailwheel. Main-wheel brakes and parking brake.

POWER PLANT: Installations envisaged at present are either a 1,600 cc modified Volkswagen horizontally-opposed aircooled engine or a 90/105 hp Continental flat-four engine. Fuel in two tanks in wing leading-edge, with total capacity of 15 Imp gallons (70 litres). Provision for installing 21·5 Imp gallon (100 litre) auxiliary fuel tank aft of two front seats.

ACCOMMODATION: Normal seating for pilot and one passenger on side-by-side seats in trainer version. For club or private use a third seat may be installed aft of the two front seats when no auxiliary fuselage fuel tank is fitted.

DIMENSIONS, EXTERNAL:
Wing span 28 ft 2½ in (8·60 m)
Wing chord (constant) 4 ft 5¼ in (1·35 m)
Length overall 19 ft 8¼ in (6·00 m)
Wheel track 6 ft 6¾ in (2·00 m)

AREA:
Wings, gross 121·6 sq ft (11·30 m²)

WEIGHTS:
Weight empty 793 lb (360 kg)
Max T-O weight 1,322 lb (600 kg)

PERFORMANCE (estimated, at max T-O weight):
Max cruising speed 95 knots (109 mph; 175 km/h)
Landing speed 39 knots (44·7 mph; 72 km/h)
Max rate of climb at S/L 985-1,180 ft (300-360 m)/min
Range (3-seat version) approx 807 nm (930 miles; 1,500 km)
Max endurance:
with standard fuel 3 hr 30 min
with auxiliary fuel 8 hr 30 min

GAZUIT-VALLADEAU

ÉTABLISSEMENTS GAZUIT-VALLADEAU

ADDRESS:
Aérodrome, 23-Guéret, Saint-Laurent

PRINCIPALS:
Georges Gazuit
Roger Valladeau

GAZUIT-VALLADEAU GAZELLE

The Gazelle is a two/four-seat light aircraft, designed and built by Georges Gazuit, formerly of the design department of Morane-Saulnier, and Roger Valladeau, who participated in the production of certain Wassmer aircraft as a subcontractor. Previously, Etablissements Gazuit-Valladeau's principal activities had been as a maintenance organisation for light aircraft, particularly those of Jodel or Robin (CEA) design. Its two proprietors embarked upon the design of the GV 103 (as the prototype was then known) in January 1968 in an endeavour to produce a low-cost, economical and easy-to-fly light aircraft for use by flying clubs or private pilots. One aim was to ensure that, as a two-seater, it would be suitable for elementary aerobatic training.

Construction of the original GV 103 prototype (F-WPZI) was mainly of metal, and was claimed to be extremely simple, needing no special tooling. This aircraft flew for the first time on 1 May 1969, and made its first public appearance at the Paris Air Show in June 1969. It was followed by several more prototypes, and five pre-production Gazelles were to be built next.

It was reported in the Autumn of 1972 that options had been received for about 60 production Gazelles in two basic versions, as follows:

GV 10-20. Two-seater, with aerobatic capability, powered by a 115 hp Lycoming engine.

GV 10-31. Four-seater, with 150 hp Lycoming engine. Second prototype (F-BSQE) was of this version. French and FAA FAR 23 certification received in April 1972.

A four/five-seat version, with 180 hp engine, was also said to be under development, but there has been no recent news of the Gazelle.

TYPE: Two-, three- or four-seat light aircraft.

WINGS: Cantilever low-wing monoplane. Wing section NACA 23015. Wings are of constant chord, except for leading-edge roots, which are swept forward. Dihedral on outer panels. No sweepback. Conventional two-spar structure of AU4G T4 duralumin, with ribs of laminated plastics with metal cappings, and Vascojet root attachment fittings. Skin of sheet duralumin, flush-riveted and bonded. All-metal three-position slotted trailing-edge flaps and plain ailerons of similar construction. No trim tabs.

Gazuit-Valladeau GV 10-31 Gazelle four-seat light aircraft (*Rolf H. Wild*)

FUSELAGE: All-metal structure of basically rectangular section. Basic structural member is a welded steel framework, built on the centre-section spars and providing attachments for the wings, engine mounting, nosewheel unit and seats. Envelope of fuselage consists of AU4G T4 duralumin stressed skin, flush-riveted and bonded to four main longerons.

TAIL UNIT: Cantilever structure with slight sweepback on vertical surfaces and rectangular-planform horizontal surfaces. Of similar construction to wings. No trim tabs in elevators. Trim tab on rudder.

LANDING GEAR: Non-retractable tricycle type, with oleo-pneumatic shock-absorbers. Small skid under rear fuselage. Hydraulic disc brakes. Optional streamlined wheel fairings of laminated plastics.

POWER PLANT: One 115 or 150 hp four-cylinder horizontally-opposed aircooled engine (see introductory copy), driving a two-blade metal fixed-pitch propeller. Engine cowlings of glassfibre. Two main fuel tanks in wing leading-edges, with total capacity of 19·5 Imp gallons (90 litres). Provision for auxiliary fuel tank in fuselage beneath rear passenger seat.

ACCOMMODATION: Seats for two or four persons according to version, in fully-enclosed and soundproofed cabin. Roof and doors of glassfibre. Max permissible load on rear seat of GV 10-31 is 340 lb (154 kg). Dual controls standard for training version, optional in other version. Space for 22 lb (10 kg) of baggage.

DIMENSIONS, EXTERNAL (both versions):
Wing span 28 ft 8½ in (8·75 m)
Wing aspect ratio 6·3
Length overall 21 ft 7¾ in (6·60 m)
Height overall 8 ft 3½ in (2·50 m)

AREA:
Wings, gross 130·25 sq ft (12·10 m²)

WEIGHTS AND LOADINGS:
Weight empty:
GV 10-20 1,157 lb (525 kg)
GV 10-31 1,212 lb (550 kg)
Max T-O weight:
GV 10-20 1,653 lb (750 kg)
GV 10-31 2,182 lb (990 kg)
Max wing loading:
GV 10-20 12·7 lb/sq ft (62 kg/m²)
GV 10-31 16·6 lb/sq ft (81 kg/m²)

PERFORMANCE (at max T-O weight):
Max level speed:
GV 10-20 116 knots (134 mph; 215 km/h)
GV 10-31 132 knots (152 mph; 245 km/h)
Cruising speed (75% power):
GV 10-20 102·5 knots (118 mph; 190 km/h)
GV 10-31 122 knots (140 mph; 225 km/h)
Stalling speed, flaps down:
GV 10-20 41 knots (47 mph; 75 km/h)
GV 10-31 46 knots (53 mph; 85 km/h)
Max rate of climb at S/L:
GV 10-20 590 ft (180 m)/min
GV 10-31 787 ft (240 m)/min
Service ceiling:
GV 10-20 11,480 ft (3,500 m)
GV 10-31 14,760 ft (4,500 m)
T-O run:
GV 10-20 787 ft (240 m)
GV 10-31 722 ft (220 m)
Range:
GV 10-20 404 nm (466 miles; 750 km)
GV 10-31 594 nm (683 miles; 1,100 km)

HELICOP-JET

ADDRESS:
Héliport de Paris, 4 Avenue de la Porte de Sèvres, 75015-Paris
Telephone: 642 29-61

PROPRIETOR:
Charles Déchaux

HELICOP-JET

A full-size mock-up of this "cold-jet" tip-drive light helicopter was first exhibited at the Paris Air Show in June 1969. Construction of a pre-production model was started by Établissements Charles Déchaux in 1970 and this aircraft was expected to fly in the second half of 1974.

The main rotor has four blades, containing ducts through which compressed air is channelled from a 260 hp Turboméca Palouste IV gas-turbine engine in the prototype, to exhaust at the blade tips. It is planned to install a Turboméca Astazou II turbine engine in the production version, to which the following data apply:

TYPE: Four-seat tip-driven light helicopter.

ROTOR SYSTEM: One four-blade main rotor; no anti-torque rotor. Blade section NACA 23018. Each blade is a constant-chord structure, built around a hollow extruded spar, and is attached to the hub via a laminated torsion strap of high-strength steel. Trailing-edge of each blade comprises a light alloy sheet box structure, bonded over ribs carried by a light spar. The laminated blade attachment straps permit pitch change and flapping without any need for conventional blade bearings and stops. Compressed air from engine passes through a large-diameter non-rotating steel rotor mast, via a spherical bearing to the hollow spar of each blade and thence to the blade-tip nozzle. Rotor speed 390 rpm.

FUSELAGE: Extensively-glazed light alloy cabin, with twin booms to carry the tail unit.

TAIL UNIT: Variable-incidence horizontal surface carried between tailbooms. Fixed endplate fins. Central stainless steel rudder, working in jet efflux, for particular use during hovering and slow-speed flight.

LANDING GEAR: Tubular skid type, with two small wheels for ground handling.

POWER PLANT: One 500 hp Turboméca Astazou II turbo-generator, supplying compressed air for the tip-drive nozzles at a flow rate of 4·75 lb (2·15 kg)/sec. Streamlined external fuel tanks, capacity 440 lb (200 kg), attached to rear supports for landing gear aft of the cabin.

ACCOMMODATION: Seats for four persons in side-by-side pairs. Fully-transparent forward-hinged car-type door on each side of cabin.

DIMENSIONS, EXTERNAL:
Rotor diameter 30 ft 10 in (9·40 m)
Rotor blade chord (constant, each) 9¼ in (0·235 m)

AREA:
Rotor disc 747 sq ft (69·40 m²)

WEIGHTS AND LOADING:
Weight empty 992 lb (450 kg)

Mock-up of Helicop-Jet light helicopter (Turboméca Palouste IV gas generator)

Max T-O weight 2,336 lb (1,060 kg)
Rotor disc loading 3·11 lb/sq ft (15·2 kg/m²)

PERFORMANCE (estimated, at max T-O weight):
Max level speed 108 knots (124 mph; 200 km/h)
Range with max fuel 323 nm (372 miles; 600 km)
Range with max payload 188 nm (217 miles; 350 km)

INDRAÉRO

INDRAÉRO SA

HEAD OFFICE AND WORKS:
Usine de Vavre, 36200-Argenton-sur-Creuse
Telephone: 04 07-75
Telex: 76 534 Chamco Chateauroux No. 006 1

PRESIDENT-DIRECTOR GENERAL:
M. Crepin

Indraéro SA has facilities for the design, construction and overhaul of major aircraft sub-assemblies, and for other, non-aviation products.

During the 1950s it provided assistance in the construction of a number of light aeroplanes designed by M Blanchet and M Jean Chapeau.

More recently, Indraéro assisted M Chapeau in the completion of two further prototypes known as the Aéro 20 and Aéro 30. Details and illustrations of these aircraft appeared in the 1970-71 *Jane's*.

In 1973, Indraéro began flight testing the prototype of a new all-metal two-seat light aircraft, of which details follow:

INDRAÉRO FOURNIER RF8

Designed in France by M René Fournier, the RF8 is of all-metal fail-safe construction and is, therefore, in a completely different category to that of the wooden aircraft of Fournier design produced in Germany by Sportavia (which see), although similar in outline. Indraéro has exclusive rights to manufacture the RF8, of which the prototype (F-WSOY) flew for the first time on 19 January 1973.

TYPE: Two-seat training and aerobatic light aircraft.

WINGS: Cantilever low-wing monoplane, quickly removable from short centre-section. Wing section NACA 63$_3$618. Constant dihedral from roots. All-metal fail-safe structure, consisting of a main box-spar, auxiliary rear spar, pressed ribs and sheet metal skin 0·8-1·0 mm thick, assembled with countersunk rivets to give a smooth surface finish. Statically and aerodynamically balanced ailerons and electrically-actuated unslotted flaps occupy full span of trailing-edges. Mechanically-actuated (electrically-actuated on production aircraft) retractable plate-type airbrake above and below each wing at approximately mid-span and mid-chord. All control surfaces actuated by rods which are connected automatically when the wings are fitted. No tabs.

FUSELAGE: All-metal semi-monocoque fail-safe structure in two sections. Central section embodies the wing centre-section structure,

Indraéro Fournier RF8 prototype (115 hp Lycoming engine) (*Ivan Miart*)

landing gear, engine mounting and cockpits. Rear fuselage carries the tail unit.

TAIL UNIT: Cantilever all-metal structure, with sweptback fin and rudder. All surfaces are easily removable. Rudder is cable-actuated; elevators are operated by rods. Trim tab in port elevator.

LANDING GEAR: Electrically-retractable tandem type, with retractable balancer wheels at mid-span. Messier-Hispano hydraulic shock-absorber on each unit. Twin-wheel main unit, wheel size 360 × 130, with hydraulic brake. Single steerable nosewheel, size 300 × 100.

POWER PLANT: One 115 hp (125 hp on production aircraft) Lycoming four-cylinder horizontally-opposed aircooled engine, driving a Hoffmann two-blade constant-speed propeller. Two fuel tanks, in leading-edge of each centre-section, total capacity 145 lb (66 kg).

ACCOMMODATION: Two seats in tandem, under large one-piece canopy which slides on three rails, after first lifting to clear the occupants. Dual controls. All essential flight and navigation instruments are standard on both panels.

EQUIPMENT: Provision for IFR equipment and oxygen system in production aircraft.

DIMENSIONS, EXTERNAL (production aircraft):
Wing span 40 ft 8 in (12·40 m)
Wing aspect ratio 11·6
Length overall 23 ft 7½ in (7·20 m)
Height overall 7 ft 10½ in (2·40 m)

AREA (production aircraft):
Wings, gross 142 sq ft (13·20 m²)

WEIGHTS AND LOADINGS (production aircraft):
Weight empty 1,268 lb (575 kg)
Max T-O weight:
Aerobatic 1,795 lb (814 kg)
Utility 1,918 lb (870 kg)
Max wing loading 13·3 lb/sq ft (65·0 kg/m²)
Max power loading 14·1 lb/hp (6·4 kg/hp)

PERFORMANCE (production aircraft, estimated):
Max never-exceed speed 188 knots (217 mph; 350 km/h)
Max level speed at S/L 145 knots (167 mph; 270 km/h)
Cruising speed at 5,000 ft (1,500 m) 135 knots (155 mph; 250 km/h)
Stalling speed, wheels and flaps down 43·5 knots (50 mph; 80 km/h)
Max rate of climb at S/L 1,575 ft (480 m)/min
Service ceiling 22,965 ft (7,000 m)
T-O to 50 ft (15 m) 787 ft (240 m)
Landing from 50 ft (15 m) 853 ft (260 m)
Max range 540 nm (621 miles; 1,000 km)
Best glide ratio:
Flaps up 17
Flaps down (10°) 20

JACQUET-POTTIER

SOCIÉTÉ CARMAM

ADDRESS: BP 201, 03001-Moulins
Telephone: (70) 44-36-18

MM Robert Jacquet and Jean Pottier, technical directors of the Société CARMAM (see Sailplanes section), are jointly responsible for the design of a number of light aircraft and sailplanes, including the JP-20-90 Impala, described below, and the JP-15-36 Standard Class sailplane described in the "Sailplanes" section.

The P.50 Bouvreuil and P.51R light aircraft, designed as purely amateur projects by M Pottier, are described separately under his name.

JACQUET-POTTIER JP-20-90 IMPALA

The Impala was the first racing aircraft of plastics construction built and flown in France. Its design was initiated in January 1971 and the prototype (F-WSQH) was built in the CARMAM works at Moulins. It flew for the first time on 26 July 1971, and was shown in public at the 1971 meeting of the Réseau du Sport de l'Air (RSA) at Cambrai in the following month. Work on a second Impala was started in early 1972, but had been suspended temporarily one year later to enable the designers to concentrate their efforts on the JP-15-36 sailplane.

Construction is almost entirely of plastics sandwich, consisting of two polyester skins and a Klégécel core. The major components are formed in moulds, with impregnated resin. Any engine in the 65-125 hp category can be fitted; the prototype, described below, has a 90 hp Continental with electric starter. It is designed to meet Norme Air 2052 Category A/3 requirements, with load factors of ±10g.

TYPE: Single-seat racing monoplane.

WINGS: Cantilever low-wing monoplane. Wing section NACA 65212. Slight dihedral from roots. One-piece structure, made up of single main spar, auxiliary rear spar and top and bottom skins, all of polyester/Klégécel sandwich. No ribs. Wing bolted to fuselage at four points. Statically-balanced ailerons, actuated by control rods. Manually-operated three-position flaps extend from inboard edge of ailerons to wing roots. No tabs.

FUSELAGE: Plastics monocoque structure of polyester/Klégécel, with integral tail-fin. Only three cross-members, consisting of the firewall aft of the welded steel-tube engine mounting, the bulkhead which forms the back of the pilot's seat, and the rear wall of the monocoque.

TAIL UNIT: Cantilever structure similar in construction to wings. Horn-balanced rudder, actuated by cables. One-piece horizontal surface, mass-balanced and actuated by control rods. No tabs.

LANDING GEAR: Non-retractable type. Cantilever main-wheel legs, of streamline-section plastics construction, made in one piece from wheel to wheel. Main wheels of 300 mm diameter, with mechanical brakes. Wheel fairings standard. Tailskid.

POWER PLANT: One 90 hp Continental C90-12F four-cylinder horizontally-opposed aircooled engine, driving a two-blade wooden fixed-pitch propeller, with spinner. Fuel tank in fuselage aft of firewall.

ACCOMMODATION: Pilot only, under large jettisonable transparent canopy. Crash pylon aft of seat. Cabin heated. Provision for radio.

DIMENSIONS, EXTERNAL:

Wing span	19 ft 8¼ in (6·00 m)
Wing chord at root	4 ft 7 in (1·40 m)
Wing chord at tip	2 ft 3½ in (0·70 m)
Wing aspect ratio	5·8
Length overall	16 ft 4¾ in (5·00 m)
Height overall	4 ft 7 in (1·40 m)
Tailplane span	5 ft 10¾ in (1·80 m)
Wheel track	4 ft 11 in (1·50 m)
Wheelbase	11 ft 9¾ in (3·60 m)

AREAS:

Wings, gross	66·7 sq ft (6·20 m²)
Vertical tail surfaces	6·46 sq ft (0·60 m²)
Horizontal tail surfaces	9·69 sq ft (0·90 m²)

WEIGHTS:

Max T-O weight:

Racing	820 lb (372 kg)
Touring	904 lb (410 kg)

PERFORMANCE:

Max level speed	183 knots (211 mph; 340 km/h)
Cruising speed	161 knots (186 mph; 300 km/h)
Minimum speed	46 knots (53 mph; 85 km/h)
Max rate of climb at S/L	1,475 ft (450 m)/min
Range	593 nm (683 miles; 1,100 km)

Jacquet-Pottier JP-20-90 Impala racing aircraft (90 hp Continental C90-12F engine)

JODEL

AVIONS JODEL SA

HEAD OFFICE:
36, Route de Seurre, 21-Beaune

DESIGN OFFICE:
21-Darois

PRESIDENT-DIRECTOR GENERAL:
J. Delemontez

The Société des Avions Jodel was formed in March 1946, by MM Jean Delemontez and Edouard Joly, with the former acting as business and technical manager and the latter as test pilot.

Its first activities were concerned with the repair of gliders and light aircraft of the Service d'Aviation Légère et Sportive, on behalf of the State. Simultaneously, the company designed and built the D.9 Bébé Jodel single-seat light monoplane, which made its first flight in January 1948. This aeroplane, which is certificated with various power plants, is intended for amateur construction and can be built in as little as 500 man-hours.

As the result of official tests with the D.9, the French authorities placed an order for the development and construction of two prototypes of a two-seat model, the D.11 fitted with the 45 hp Salmson, and the D.111 with the 75 hp Minié engine. Subsequent developments of the D.11 are the D.112 and D.117, which have a 65 hp and 90 hp Continental engine respectively.

These basic designs have been built in large numbers, both commercially and by amateurs.

Avions Jodel now devotes its activities mainly to designing advanced developments of its established types and to acting as a consultant to those building and developing its designs.

JODEL D.9 and D.92 BÉBÉ

The type designation of the Bébé varies according to the type of engine fitted. The original version, with 25 hp Poinsard engine, is designated D.9; the D.92 has a modified Volkswagen engine.

The following details refer to all standard versions of the D.9 Bébé:

TYPE: Single-seat light monoplane.

WINGS: Cantilever low-wing monoplane. Single-spar one-piece wing with wide-span centre-section of constant chord and thickness and two tapering outer portions set at a coarse dihedral angle (14°). Spar and ribs of spruce and plywood, with fabric covering. Ailerons similar in construction.

FUSELAGE: Rectangular spruce and plywood structure.

TAIL UNIT: Cantilever structure of spruce and plywood, with plywood covering on tailplane and fabric-covered rudder and elevators. No fin.

LANDING GEAR: Cantilever main legs with rubber-in-compression springing. Leaf-spring tailskid or tailwheel. Cable brakes.

POWER PLANT: One 25 hp Poinsard (D.9) or modified Volkswagen (D.92) flat-four aircooled engine, but other engines of from 25 to 65 hp may be fitted, including the 36 hp Aeronca JAP and Continental A40. Fuel tank in fuselage, capacity 5·5 Imp gallons (25 litres).

ACCOMMODATION: Single seat in open cockpit.

DIMENSIONS, EXTERNAL:

Wing span	22 ft 11 in (7·00 m)
Wing chord (centre-section, constant)	4 ft 7 in (1·40 m)
Wing aspect ratio	5·45
Length overall	17 ft 10½ in (5·45 m)

AREA:

Wings, gross	96·8 sq ft (9·0 m²)

WEIGHTS:

Weight empty	420 lb (190 kg)
Max T-O weight	705 lb (320 kg)

PERFORMANCE (40 hp engine, at max T-O weight):

Max level speed at S/L	87 knots (100 mph; 160 km/h)
Cruising speed	74 knots (85 mph; 137 km/h)
Stalling speed	35 knots (40 mph; 65 km/h)
Max rate of climb at S/L	590 ft (180 m)/min
T-O run	360 ft (110 m)
Landing run	330 ft (100 m)
Range with max fuel	217 nm (250 miles; 400 km)

JODEL D.11 and D.119

The D.11, with 45 hp Salmson engine, was the basic model in the series of Jodel two-seaters for amateur and commercial production.

The version for amateur construction with 90 hp Continental engine is designated D.119.

The D.11 illustrated was built over an eight-year period by Wayne Nelson, an aeronautical engineer of Bountiful, Utah, at a cost of $2,000. The wing is of wood, covered with Dacron, the fuselage and tail unit of wood covered with glassfibre. Changes from the standard design include the fitting of a fixed tail-fin forward of the rudder, and of cantilever spring main landing gear legs.

This D.11 spans 27 ft 0 in (8·23 m), has an empty weight of 750 lb (340 kg) and loaded weight of 1,240 lb (562 kg), and is powered by a 65 hp Continental A65-8 four-cylinder horizontally-opposed aircooled engine. Performance is as follows:

PERFORMANCE:

Max level speed at S/L	93 knots (108 mph; 173 km/h)
Cruising speed	86 knots (100 mph; 161 km/h)
Landing speed	35 knots (40 mph; 64·5 km/h)
Max rate of climb at S/L	500 ft (152 m)/min
Service ceiling	16,000 ft (4,875 m)
T-O run	500 ft (152 m)
Landing run	800 ft (244 m)
Range with max fuel	260 nm (300 miles; 482 km)

JODEL D.112 CLUB

The D.112 is a two-seat dual-control version of the D.9. Except for increased overall dimensions, a wider fuselage and enclosed side-by-side cockpit, the D.112 conforms in layout and structure to the D.9, but is fitted normally with a 65 hp Continental flat-four engine. Fuel capacity is 13 Imp gallons (60 litres).

DIMENSIONS, EXTERNAL:

Wing span	26 ft 10 in (8·2 m)

Jodel D.9 Bébé single-seat amateur-built light aircraft *(G. P. Jones)*

Modified Jodel D.11 built by Wayne Nelson of Bountiful, Utah *(Howard Levy)*

Length overall	20 ft 10 in (6·36 m)
Dihedral on outer wings	19°
AREA:	
Wings, gross	137 sq ft (12·72 m²)
WEIGHTS:	
Weight empty	600 lb (270 kg)
Max T-O weight	1,145 lb (520 kg)

PERFORMANCE (at max T-O weight):
Max level speed at S/L:
102 knots (118 mph; 190 km/h)
Max cruising speed
92 knots (105·5 mph; 170 km/h)
Econ cruising speed
81 knots (93 mph; 150 km/h)

Stalling speed	38 knots (43 mph; 70 km/h)
Max rate of climb at S/L	632 ft (193 m)/min
T-O run	450 ft (137 m)
Landing run	395 ft (120 m)
Range with max fuel	323 nm (373 miles; 600 km)

JURCA

MARCEL JURCA

ADDRESS:
2, Rue des Champs Philippe, 92-La Garenne-Colombes (Seine)
Telephone: 242.9633 and 551.6306
WORKS: Constructions Aéronautiques Lorraines, François et Cie, Aérodrôme de Nancy

M Marcel Jurca, an ex-military pilot and hydraulics engineer, has designed a series of high-performance light aircraft of which plans are available to amateur constructors.

A prototype of his first design, the M.J.1, was built but did not fly. To gain experience, M Jurca next built a two-seat Jodel light aircraft, with the help of members of the Aero Club of Courbevoie, and this flew for the first time in 1954.

The same team then built a prototype of M Jurca's second design, the M.J.2 Tempête single-seat light aircraft, incorporating many Jodel components. It proved so successful that sets of plans were offered to amateur constructors and many more Tempêtes are now flying or under assembly in France and overseas.

M Jurca has developed from the Tempête the two-seat M.J.5 Sirocco and the M.J.51 Sperocco. Details of these are given below, together with brief information on a series of designs produced by scaling down the basic airframes of World War II fighters to two-thirds or three-quarters of the original size.

A point of interest is that Jurca designs are considered to be suitable for the entire range of basic and advanced flying training duties. The M.J.5 Sirocco is the two-seat basic trainer, the M.J.2 Tempête the single-seat basic trainer, the M.J.51 Sperocco the two-seat advanced trainer and the M.J.7S Solo the single-seat advanced trainer.

For the North American market, Jurca plans are available from Jurca Plans Office, 581 Helen Street, Mt Morris, Michigan 48458, USA.

JURCA M.J.2 and M.J.20 TEMPÊTE

The prototype Tempête was flown for the first time, by its designer, on 27 June 1956. It obtained its certificate of airworthiness very quickly, and a total of at least 25 Tempêtes are now flying, with 20 more under construction, in France, Denmark, Luxembourg, Portugal, the UK, the United States and Canada, all amateur-built.

The type of engine fitted to a particular aircraft is indicated by a suffix letter in its designation. Suffix letters are A for the 65 hp Continental A65, B for the 75 hp Continental A75, C for the 85 hp Continental C85, D for the 90 hp Continental C90-14F, E for the 100 hp Continental O-200-A, F for the 105 hp Potez 4 E-20, G for the 115 hp Potez 4 E-30, and H for the 125 hp Lycoming.

The standard version is the M.J.2A with A65 engine. The M.J.2D, with 90 hp C90-14F, cruises at 105 knots (121 mph; 195 km/h) and climbs to 3,280 ft (1,000 m) in 3 minutes. It can also perform aerobatics without loss of height. The Tempête built in Portugal is an M.J.2D with 90 hp Continental; that under construction in Denmark is designated **M.J.20,** and has a 180 hp engine and a strengthened airframe.

The Tempête is basically a single-seat aircraft, but the 180 hp version has provision for carrying also a second person weighing not more than 154 lb (70 kg) on cross-country flights. It is intended to have an aerobatic capability adequate to compete with the American Pitts Specials in international competitions.

The following details apply generally to all basic single-seat M.J.2 models:

TYPE: Single-seat light monoplane.

WINGS: Cantilever low-wing monoplane. NACA 23012 wing section. Incidence 4° at root, 2° at tip. No dihedral. All-wood one-piece single-spar structure with fabric covering. Fabric-covered wooden ailerons.

FUSELAGE: All-wood structure of basic rectangular section, plywood-covered.

TAIL UNIT: Cantilever all-wood structure. Tailplane and fin plywood-covered, elevators and rudder fabric-covered. Trim tab on starboard elevator.

LANDING GEAR: Non-retractable tailwheel type. Jodel D.112 cantilever legs with rubber-in-compression springing. Jodel D.112 wheels and Dunlop 420 × 150 tyres. Jodel D.112 tailskid or tailwheel.

POWER PLANT: One 65 hp Continental A65 four-cylinder horizontally-opposed aircooled engine, driving Ratier two-blade wooden propeller with ground-adjustable pitch. Provision for fitting 75, 85, 90 or 100 hp Continental, 105 or 115 hp Potez or 125 hp Lycoming engine. Jodel engine mounting and cowling. Jodel fuel tank, capacity 13·2 Imp gallons (60 litres), aft of firewall in fuselage.

Registration CS-AXB indicates that this Jurca M.J.2 Tempête was Portugal's second modern homebuilt aircraft. The first was registered CS-AXA, with "X" signifying "experimental" *(Howard Levy)*

Jurca M.J.5K Sirocco homebuilt light aircraft (180 hp Lycoming engine)

ACCOMMODATION: Single seat under long rearward-sliding transparent canopy.

DIMENSIONS, EXTERNAL:	
Wing span	19 ft 8 in (6·00 m)
Wing chord (basic)	4 ft 7 in (1·40 m)
Wing aspect ratio	4·5
Length overall	19 ft 2½ in (5·855 m)
Height over tail	7 ft 10 in (2·4 m)
Tailplane span	8 ft 2 in (2·50 m)
Wheel track	7 ft 6½ in (2·30 m)
AREAS:	
Wings, gross	85·90 sq ft (7·98 m²)
Ailerons (total)	10·76 sq ft (1·00 m²)
Fin	6·94 sq ft (0·65 m²)
Rudder	5·81 sq ft (0·54 m²)
Tailplane	9·15 sq ft (0·85 m²)
Elevators	8·61 sq ft (0·80 m²)
WEIGHTS:	
Weight empty	639 lb (290 kg)
Max T-O weight	950 lb (430 kg)
PERFORMANCE (65 hp engine):	
Max level speed	104 knots (120 mph; 193 km/h)
Cruising speed	89 knots (102 mph; 165 km/h)
Landing speed	43 knots (50 mph; 80 km/h)
Max rate of climb at S/L	555 ft (170 m)/min
Service ceiling	11,500 ft (3,500 m)
T-O run	820 ft (250 m)
Endurance	3 hr 20 min

JURCA M.J.5 SIROCCO

The M.J.5 Sirocco is a tandem two-seat monoplane, developed from the M.J.2 Tempête as a potential club training and touring aircraft. It is fully aerobatic when flown as a two-seater.

The longer-span wings have an extended leading-edge inboard of the fence on each side and a completely new tip shape. A sweptback fin and rudder are standard.

The prototype M.J.5 flew for the first time on 3 August 1962, powered by a 105 hp Potez 4 E-20 engine. It was fitted originally with a non-retractable landing gear, but retractable landing gear and a more powerful engine (160 hp Lycoming O-320) were fitted in 1966. Its fuel capacity is 25·5 Imp gallons (116 litres). In its current form, it will climb to 3,280 ft (1,000 m) in 2½ min.

By mid-February 1967, five more Siroccos were flying, one of them factory-built at Nancy. This aircraft, powered by a 100 hp Continental engine, concluded tests at Istres in January 1969. The French government then concluded an agreement with Constructions Aéronautiques Lorraines, François et Cie of Nancy, who built an airframe for static tests, in March 1971. These were required in view of the fact that the Sirocco is regarded as a basic trainer suitable for amateur construction; and it was awarded subsequently a certificate of airworthiness in the Utility category. Supplementary tests were conducted at the CEV with another Sirocco, powered by a 135 hp Lycoming O-320 engine.

A full C of A, covering Aerobatic requirements and unlimited spinning, is applicable only when a power plant of 115 hp minimum rating is installed.

The version of the Sirocco for amateur construction is generally similar to the factory-built version, with optional retractable landing gear.

At least 40 Siroccos are reported to be flying or under construction by amateurs in France, Canada, Germany, Switzerland, England and the USA, with various engines.

The type of engine fitted to a particular aircraft is indicated by a suffix letter in its designation. Suffix letters are A for the 90 hp Continental C90-8 or -14F, B for the 100 hp Continental O-200-A, C for the 105 hp Potez 4 E-20, D for the Potez 4 E-30, E for the 105 hp Hirth, F for the 125 hp Lycoming, G for the 135 hp Regnier and H for the 160 hp Lycoming. Other Siroccos are flying with 150 or 180 hp engines. Addition of the numeral 1 indicates a non-retractable landing gear and the numeral 2 indicates a retractable landing gear. Thus, the designation of the original prototype in its current form is M.J.5H2. The example built at Nancy for certification has a 100 hp Continental engine and so is designated M.J.5B1.

Two examples of a new version, with a 220 hp Franklin engine, were under construction in 1974, one in the USA and one in France. These are intended for use in international aerobatic championships.

A Sirocco with 115 hp Lycoming O-235-C2B engine and 6 ft 0¾ in (1·85 m) diameter propeller has been completed by Luftsportgruppe Liebherr-Aero-Technik (LAT) in Germany. This has a modified rudder of reduced height and greater chord, and a jettisonable, sideways-hinged cockpit canopy, and is intended for certification for aerobatic flying. The details overleaf apply to this aircraft, but are generally typical of all versions.

Two developed versions, known as the M.J.50 Windy and M.J.51 Sperocco, are described separately.

DIMENSIONS, EXTERNAL:

Wing span	23 ft 0 in (7·00 m)
Wing aspect ratio	4·9
Length overall	20 ft 2 in (6·15 m)
Height overall, tail up:	
standard model	9 ft 2¼ in (2·80 m)
LAT version	8 ft 6¼ in (2·60 m)
Tailplane span	10 ft 7½ in (3·24 m)
Wheel track	9 ft 2¼ in (2·80 m)

AREA:

Wings, gross	107·64 sq ft (10·00 m^2)

WEIGHTS AND LOADINGS:

Weight empty	947 lb (430 kg)
Max T-O weight	1,499 lb (680 kg)
Max wing loading	13·9 lb/sq ft (68·0 kg/m^2)
Max power loading	13·03 lb/hp (5·91 kg/hp)

PERFORMANCE (at max T-O weight):

Max level speed	127 knots (146 mph; 235 km/h)
Cruising speed	116 knots (134 mph; 215 km/h)
Stalling speed	44 knots (50 mph; 80 km/h)
Climb to 3,280 ft (1,000 m)	4 min
Service ceiling	16,400 ft (5,000 m)
T-O run	820 ft (250 m)
Landing run	655 ft (200 m)
Endurance	4 hr 20 min

JURCA M.J.50 WINDY

The M.J.50 Windy is generally similar to the M.J.5 Sirocco, but is of all-metal construction. It embodies the retractable landing gear that is available for the M.J.5, and the M.J.7 flying control system.

A prototype was under construction by Mr Wesolowsky of Luçon in early 1974. Plans will be available to amateur constructors.

The wing section is NACA 23018 on the upper surface and NACA 23012 on the lower surface at the root, and NACA 23012 at the tip. The structure is stressed for engines in the 150-200 hp range.

DIMENSIONS, EXTERNAL:

Wing span	23 ft 11½ in (7·30 m)
Wing chord at root	5 ft 11½ in (1·814 m)
Wing chord at tip	4 ft 7 in (1·40 m)
Length overall, tail up	21 ft 10½ in (6·673 m)
Tailplane span	10 ft 8¼ in (3·26 m)
Wheel track	8 ft 5½ in (2·58 m)

JURCA M.J.51 SPEROCCO

Using knowledge gained from flight experience with the M.J.5 and the Canadian prototype M.J.7, M Jurca has, with the assistance of M J. Lecarme, evolved a new design incorporating some features of each aircraft. It is known as the M.J.51 Sperocco, the name being a contraction of "Special Sirocco", and is intended for high-performance aerobatics and competition flying. Like other Jurca designs, the M.J.51 is suitable for amateur construction.

The wings, of Habib 64-000 748 laminar-flow profile, are essentially those of the M.J.7 Gnatsum. They are without dihedral, and the angle of incidence is 1° compared with the 4° of the Sirocco. The fuselage is of completely new design, with a basically triangular cross-section, but is of similar construction to the M.J.5. The tail unit consists of M.J.7 horizontal surfaces with a shorter and wider-chord fin and rudder. Landing gear is of the M.J.5 type and is fully retractable.

Any horizontally-opposed engine of 130-240 hp may be installed. Fuel is contained in two wing tanks, each of 12 Imp gallons (55 litres) capacity, and one fuselage tank of 10 or 22 Imp gallons (45 or 100 litres) capacity.

The M.J.51 seats two persons in tandem under a one-piece sliding canopy, the rear seat being 3·9 in (10 cm) higher than the front seat.

The first M.J.51, powered by a 180 hp Lycoming AIO-360 engine, is under construction by M Serge Brillant at Melun. By early 1974, the wings, fuselage and tail unit had been completed, and the cockpit equipped. The first flight was expected to take place before the end of the year.

DIMENSIONS, EXTERNAL:

Wing span	25 ft 0 in (7·623 m)
Length overall	23 ft 9 in (7·24 m)

AREA:

Wings, gross	118 sq ft (11·00 m^2)

WEIGHT:

Max T-O weight	1,653 lb (730 kg)

PERFORMANCE (estimated, with 150 hp Lycoming engine):

Max level speed	149 knots (171 mph; 275 km/h)
Max cruising speed (75% power)	135 knots (155 mph; 250 km/h)
Stalling speed	49 knots (56 mph; 90 km/h)
Time to 3,280 ft (1,000 m)	1 min 30 sec

JURCA M.J.7 and M.J.77 GNATSUM

The Gnatsum is a scale replica, for amateur construction, of the North American P-51D Mustang single-seat fighter of World War II. Its name "Gnatsum" is "Mustang" reversed.

Initially, M Jurca designed the wings, fuselage, tail surfaces and manually-retractable landing gear. The engine installation was deliberately not designed, to permit constructors to utilise any of the suitable Lycoming, Continental, Ranger or other power plants that are available.

During construction of the M.J.7 prototype in Canada (see below), a number of modifications and improvements were made to the basic design. These were embodied in the drawings marketed by Sturgeon Air Ltd of Edmonton, Alberta, together with details of the Ranger engine installation.

Plans for two versions of the Gnatsum are available from M Jurca, as follows:

M.J.7. To two-thirds scale. Prototype (CF-XZI, now N51HR) built in the works of Falconar Aircraft Ltd on the Industrial Airport, Edmonton, Alberta, Canada, and first flown on 31 July 1969. Granted DoT type approval by early 1970. Described under the "SAL" entry in the Canadian section of the 1973-74 *Jane's*. Further examples under construction by Mr J. P. Deloyer of Torrance, California, and three others.

M.J.77. To three-quarters scale. Prototype under construction by Mr Gilbert C. McAdams of Victorville, California, and another by Mr Bob Aughton in Michigan.

Unlike previous small-scale replicas of this aircraft, the Gnatsum is scaled down precisely. Use of an in-line engine, such as the 160 hp Walter Minor 6-III or 200 hp Ranger, permits the fuselage cowling lines to follow closely those of the original. Alternative installation of a 200 hp Lycoming horizontally-opposed aircooled engine requires fairing blisters over the cylinders.

M Jurca's plans provide for alternative plywood-covered semi-monocoque fuselage construction or a square wooden box structure covered with two plastics shells.

JURCA M.J.7S SOLO

Intended as a single-seat advanced trainer, the M.J.7S Solo is basically similar to the M.J.7 Gnatsum but does not retain the under-belly scoop which the latter inherited from the original P-51 Mustang design. A prototype was under construction by M Duhamel of Strasbourg in 1974, with a 180 hp Lycoming AIO-360 four-cylinder horizontally-opposed aircooled engine. First flight was then scheduled for the Spring of 1975.

The general appearance of the M.J.7S is shown in the accompanying three-view drawing. The wing section is quoted as Habib 64-000 748-MJ7-104.

DIMENSIONS, EXTERNAL:

Wing span	24 ft 8½ in (7·523 m)
Length overall, tail up	21 ft 10 in (6·664 m)
Tailplane span	9 ft 10 in (3·00 m)

AREA:

Wings, gross	116·2 sq ft (10·8 m^2)

JURCA M.J.8 1-NINE-O

The M.J.8 is a single-seat sporting aircraft which has been designed by M Jurca by scaling down to three-quarters of the original dimensions the airframe of the Focke-Wulf Fw 190 fighter. Its general appearance is shown in the accompanying illustrations.

A prototype has been built by Mr Ronald Kitchen of Carson City, Nevada, and was being prepared for initial taxying tests in early 1974. A second example is under construction by Mr J. Kiska of Norwalk, Connecticut.

The M.J.8 prototype has a 290 hp Lycoming IO-540 engine, but the design is suitable for the **alternative use of any horizontally-opposed or radial engine in the 100-200 hp range. The landing gear is retractable.**

Jurca M.J.7 Gnatsum prototype built by Falconar in Canada

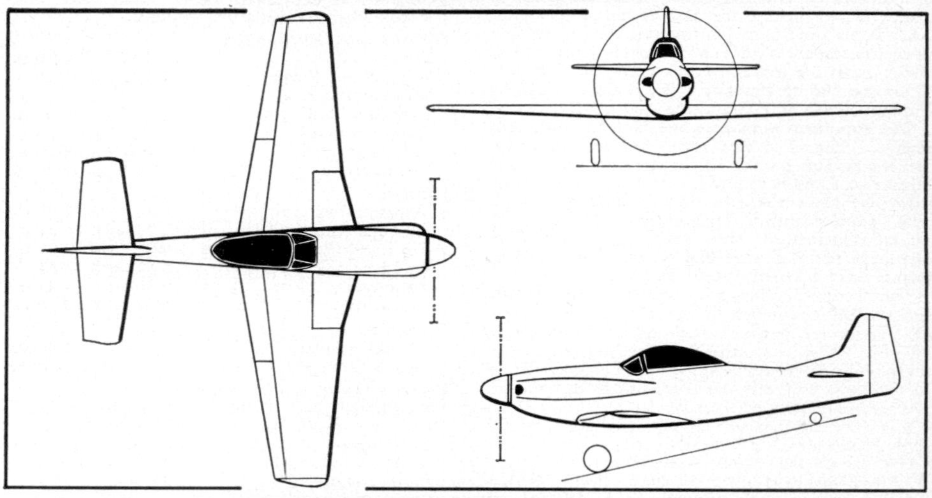

Jurca M.J.7S Solo single-seat advanced trainer (*Roy J. Grainge*)

Jurca M.J.8 1-Nine-O prototype built by Mr Ronald Kitchen of Carson City, Nevada

DIMENSIONS, EXTERNAL:

Wing span	25 ft 10 in (7·87 m)
Length overall	21 ft 9 in (6·63 m)
Wing chord at root	5 ft 7 in (1·70 m)
Wing chord at tip	2 ft 11½ in (0·90 m)
Tailplane span	9 ft 4 in (2·84 m)
AREA:	
Wings, gross	109·8 sq ft (10·2 m²)
WEIGHTS (160 hp engine):	
Weight empty	880 lb (400 kg)
Max T-O weight	1,380 lb (626 kg)
PERFORMANCE (estimated, with 160 hp engine):	
Max level speed at S/L	139 knots (160 mph; 257 km/h)
Max cruising speed	124 knots (143 mph; 230 km/h)
Stalling speed	49 knots (56 mph; 90 km/h)
Max rate of climb at S/L	1,650 ft (503 m)/min

JURCA M.J.10 SPIT

The M.J.10 is a single-seat, three-quarter scale representation of the Supermarine Spitfire which can also be modified as a two-seater. It is suitable for any horizontally-opposed or in-line engine of 120-220 hp, although some slight variations from the Spitfire's contours are necessary in the former case. Construction is entirely of wood, except for the glassfibre engine cowling and fabric covering on the control surfaces. The single-spar wing is similar in construction to that of the Sirocco. The manually-operated retractable landing gear is fitted with helicoidal spring shock-absorbers.

The basic plans adopted the Spitfire Mk IX as the standard M.J.10 version, but alternative detail plans are available for representing both Merlin- and Griffon-engined models, including the Mks VC and XIV, and for clipped, standard or extended-span wings.

A prototype is under construction by Mr Pendlebury of the Chesterfield Air Touring Group at West Bridgford, Nottingham, England, and another by Mr Ed Storo of New York, USA.

DIMENSIONS, EXTERNAL:

Wing span:	
standard	27 ft 6¾ in (8·40 m)
clipped	24 ft 5½ in (7·46 m)
Length overall	23 ft 4½ in (7·125 m)
AREA:	
Wings, gross	135·6 sq ft (12·60 m²)
WEIGHTS (160 hp engine):	
Weight empty	1,450 lb (658 kg)
Max T-O weight	2,000 lb (907 kg)
PERFORMANCE (estimated, with 160 hp engine):	
Max level speed at S/L	139 knots (160 mph; 257 km/h)
Cruising speed	124 knots (143 mph; 230 km/h)
Stalling speed	49 knots (56 mph; 90 km/h)
Max rate of climb at S/L	1,650 ft (503 m)/min
T-O run	660 ft (200 m)

JURCA M.J.12 PEE-40

The M.J.12 is a three-quarter scale representation of the Curtiss P-40 single-seat fighter of the second World War. It spans 27 ft 11½ in (8·524 m) and has an overall length (tail up) of 25 ft 0 in (7·62 m).

Two M.J.12s were under construction in the USA in early 1974.

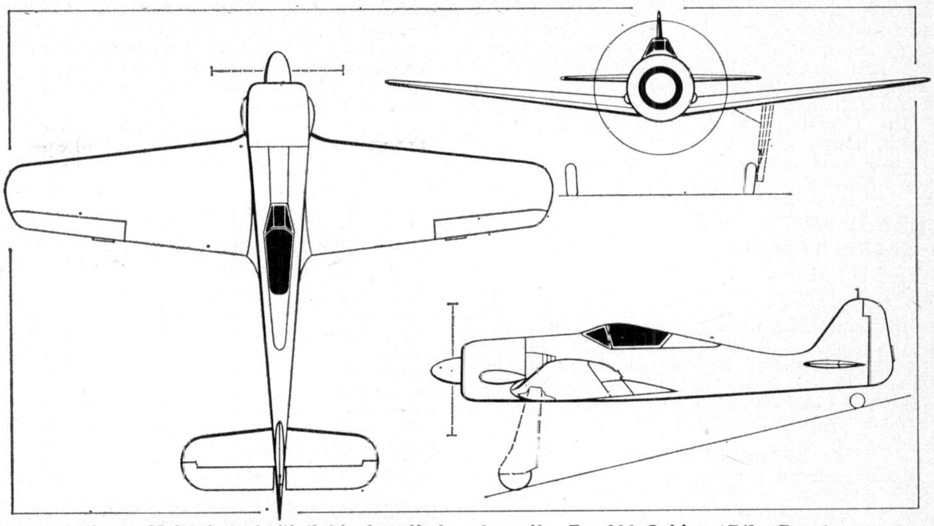

Jurca M.J.3 homebuilt light aircraft, based on the Fw 190 fighter (*Pilot Press*)

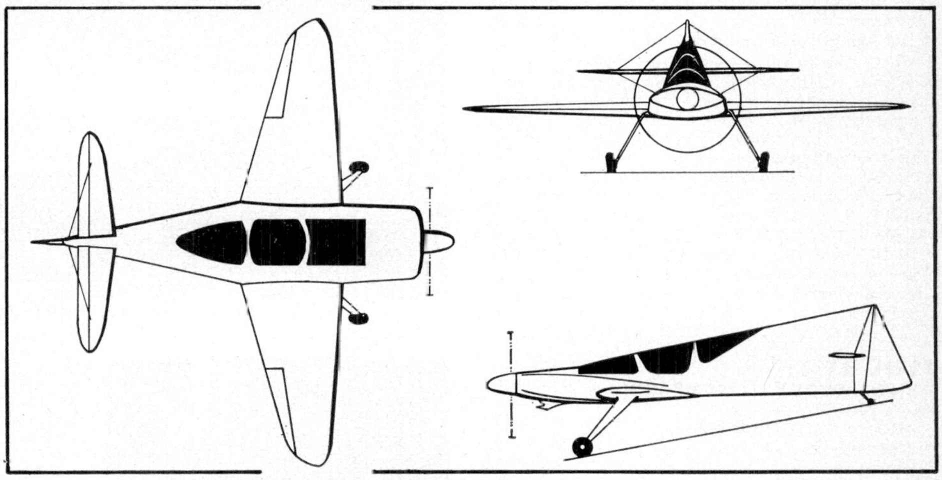

Jurca M.J.14 single-seat racing aircraft (*Roy J. Grainge*)

JURCA M.J.14 RACER

Designed in 1971, the M.J.14 will be a small single-seat racing aircraft of unorthodox configuration, with a semi-reclining seat for the pilot. Its general appearance is shown in the accompanying three-view drawing.

The standard tapered wings can be replaced by constant-chord wings of the same span if the aircraft is intended for Class III racing. Tailplane incidence is adjustable on the ground. The following data apply to the aircraft as illustrated, with a 90 hp Continental C90-8F four-cylinder horizontally-opposed aircooled engine. Fuel capacity is 15·5 Imp gallons (70 litres).

DIMENSIONS, EXTERNAL:

Wing span	19 ft 8¼ in (6·00 m)
Length overall	18 ft 7½ in (5·68 m)
Tailplane span	9 ft 9 in (2·97 m)
AREA:	
Wings, gross	65·66 sq ft (6·1 m²)
WEIGHTS:	
Weight empty	550 lb (250 kg)
Max T-O weight	925 lb (420 kg)

LEDERLIN

FRANÇOIS LEDERLIN

ADDRESS:

2 rue Charles Peguy, 38-Grenoble

M Lederlin, an architect, designed and built a two-seat light aeroplane based on the familiar Mignet "Pou-du-Ciel" formula. Although derived from the Mignet HM-380 and designated 380-L, it retains little of the original except for the wing section. First flight was made on 14 September 1965, a restricted C of A being granted in the following month.

Plans of the 380-L, annotated in English and with both English and metric measurements, are available to amateur constructors.

Lederlin 380-L two-seat light aircraft (90 hp Continental engine)

LEDERLIN 380-L

TYPE: Two-seat amateur-built light aircraft.

WINGS: Tandem-wing biplane. Wing section 3·40-13. Dihedral 3° 30′ on outer sections only (both wings). Incidence variable from 0° to 12° (forward wing). Incidence of rear wing 6°. No sweepback. Each wing is made in two parts, bolted together at the centreline. Construction is conventional, with wooden box-spar and trellis ribs, plywood leading-edge and overall fabric covering. The variable-incidence front wing is pivoted on the cabane structure by ball-joints and on the bracing struts (one each side) by cardan-joints. No ailerons or flaps. Long-span tab on trailing-edge of rear wing, controllable in flight.

FUSELAGE: Welded steel-tube structure, covered with light alloy to front of cabin and with fabric on rear fuselage, over light spruce formers.

TAIL UNIT: Fin and rudder only. Spruce and ply structure, covered with fabric. Ground-adjustable tab in rudder.

LANDING GEAR: Non-retractable tailwheel type. Cantilever main legs consist of conical spring-steel rods, inclined rearward. Fournier main wheels and tyres, size 380 × 150, with mechanical brakes. Large tailwheel, carried on telescopic leg with spring shock-absorber, can be steered by the rudder controls through a linkage engaged by the pilot.

POWER PLANT: One 90 hp Continental C90-14F four-cylinder horizontally-opposed aircooled engine, driving a McCauley two-blade metal fixed-pitch propeller. Single fuel tank, capacity 18·75 Imp gallons (85 litres). Oil capacity 1 Imp gallon (4·5 litres).

ACCOMMODATION: Two seats side by side in enclosed cabin. Forward-hinged door on each side. Controls comprise a rudder-bar for directional control and a stick, suspended from the roof of the cabin and free laterally, to control the incidence of the forward wing. A further lever, suspended from the roof, controls the tab on the rear wing. Baggage space aft of seats.

DIMENSIONS, EXTERNAL:

Wing span:	
forward	26 ft 0 in (7·92 m)
rear	19 ft 8¼ in (6·00 m)
Wing chord (constant, each)	4 ft 3¼ in (1·30 m)
Length overall	15 ft 7¾ in (4·77 m)
Height overall	6 ft 10 in (2·08 m)
Wheel track	6 ft 8¾ in (2·05 m)
Wheelbase	10 ft 2 in (3·10 m)
Propeller diameter	6 ft 0 in (1·83 m)
Doors (each): Height	2 ft 11½ in (0·90 m)
Width	2 ft 5½ in (0·75 m)
Height to sill	1 ft 7½ in (0·50 m)

DIMENSIONS, INTERNAL:

Cabin:	
Max width	3 ft 6 in (1·07 m)
Max height	3 ft 4 in (1·03 m)
Baggage space	7 cu ft (0·20 m³)

AREAS:
Wings, gross:
forward 106·8 sq ft (9·92 m²)
rear 80·0 sq ft (7·43 m²)
WEIGHTS AND LOADINGS:
Weight empty 794 lb (360 kg)
Max T-O weight 1,323 lb (600 kg)
Max wing loading 6·96 lb/sq ft (34 kg/m²)
Max power loading 14·8 lb/hp (6·7 kg/hp)
PERFORMANCE (at max T-O weight):
Max never-exceed speed
126 knots (145 mph; 233 km/h)
Max level speed at 1,000 ft (300 m)
109 knots (125 mph; 201 km/h)
Max cruising speed
97 knots (112 mph; 180 km/h)
Econ cruising speed at 2,000 ft (600 m)
87 knots (100 mph; 161 km/h)
Stalling speed, power off
26 knots (30 mph; 49 km/h)
Max rate of climb at S/L 900 ft (275 m)/min
Service ceiling over 12,000 ft (3,660 m)
T-O run 400 ft (122 m)
Landing run 500 ft (153 m)
Range at econ cruising speed
477 nm (550 miles; 885 km)

LEFEBVRE

ROBERT LEFEBVRE

ADDRESS:
CES A. Camus, rue Adeline, Rouen, 76 Seine Maritime

M Lefebvre has built and flown a small single-seat racing aircraft named the Busard, assisted by pupils of the A. Camus technical school at Rouen. Basis of the design was the MP.204 prototype racer with 75 hp Minié engine, designed by Max Plan and first flown on 5 June 1952.

LEFEBVRE BUSARD

The description below applies to the Busard as built and flown by M. Lefebvre. The airframe can be fitted with a 90 hp Continental engine, with which the gross weight is increased to 763 lb (346 kg) and max level speed at S/L to 156 knots (180 mph; 290 km/h).

TYPE: Single-seat amateur-built racing aircraft.

WINGS: Cantilever low-wing monoplane. Wing section NACA 23012. No dihedral. Conventional single-spar wood structure, covered entirely with plywood. Wooden ailerons, operated by control rods. Wooden three-position trailing-edge flaps.

FUSELAGE: Conventional wooden structure, covered with plywood. Domed plywood decking.

TAIL UNIT: Cantilever wood structure. Fixed surfaces plywood-covered; control surfaces fabric-covered. Neither rudder nor elevators are aerodynamically balanced. Flettner tab in starboard elevator. Rudder is cable-operated.

LANDING GEAR: Non-retractable tailwheel type. Cessna-type aluminium leaf-spring cantilever main legs. Steerable tailwheel. Brakes on main wheels.

POWER PLANT: One 65 hp Continental four-cylinder horizontally-opposed aircooled engine, driving a two-blade fixed-pitch propeller. Fuel tank aft of firewall in fuselage, capacity 8·8 Imp gallons (40 litres).

ACCOMMODATION: Single seat in enclosed cabin.

DIMENSIONS, EXTERNAL:
Wing span 19 ft 8¼ in (6·00 m)
Wing chord at root 4 ft 11 in (1·50 m)
Wing chord at tip 2 ft 5½ in (0·75 m)
Wing aspect ratio 6·00
Length overall 17 ft 6¾ in (5·35 m)
Height overall 4 ft 11 in (1·50 m)
AREA:
Wings, gross 64·6 sq ft (6·00 m²)
WEIGHTS AND LOADINGS:
Weight empty 474 lb (215 kg)
Max T-O weight 747 lb (339 kg)
Max wing loading 11·6 lb/sq ft (56·50 kg/m²)
Max power loading 11·46 lb/hp (5·2 kg/hp)
PERFORMANCE (estimated):
Max level speed at S/L
124 knots (143 mph; 230 km/h)
Landing speed 43 knots (50 mph; 80 km/h)
Range with max fuel
242 nm (279 miles; 450 km)

Lefebvre Busard single-seat racing aircraft (*Aviation Magazine International*)

MUDRY

AVIONS MUDRY ET COMPAGNIE

ADDRESS:
Aérodrome, 27300-Bernay
Telephone: 793
DIRECTOR:
Auguste Mudry

M Auguste Mudry, who is also Director of C.A.A.R.P. (which see), established this new company in the works of the former Société Aéronautique Normande (see 1969-70 *Jane's*) at Bernay. Between them the two companies are responsible for production of the CAP 10 and CAP 20 aerobatic light aircraft developed by C.A.A.R.P. from the Piel Emeraude.

Fuselages for the CAP 10, which is described below, are manufactured at Beynes by C.A.A.R.P., final assembly and flight testing being undertaken by Avions Mudry et Cie at Bernay. The CAP 20 is manufactured entirely by C.A.A.R.P., and is described under that company's heading in this section.

C.A.A.R.P./MUDRY CAP 10

Developed from the Piel Emeraude two-seat light aircraft (which see), via the prototype C.P. 100 aerobatic version built by C.A.A.R.P., the CAP 10 is intended for use as a training, touring or aerobatic aeroplane. The prototype was flown for the first time in August 1968, and certification of the CAP 10 was granted on 4 September 1970. Construction is to French AIR 2052 (CAR 3) Category A standards for aerobatic flying.

A total of 50 CAP 10s had been completed by early 1974, of which 30 were delivered to the French Air Force. Some are in service with the Equipe de Voltige Aérienne (EVA) at Salon-de-Provence, and others with the basic flying training school at Clermont-Ferrand-Aulnat. Two CAP 10s have been delivered to customers in Italy, one to Germany, one to Belgium and two, for demonstration and sales purposes, to Orange County Airport, near New York, USA.

TYPE: Two-seat aerobatic light aircraft.

WINGS: Cantilever low-wing monoplane. Wing section NACA 23012. Dihedral 5° from roots. Incidence 0°. No sweepback. All-spruce single-spar torsion-box structure, with trellis ribs, rear auxiliary spar and okoumé plywood covering. Inner section of each wing is rectangular in plan, outer section semi-elliptical. Wooden trailing-edge plain flaps and slotted ailerons.

FUSELAGE: Conventional spruce girder structure, built in two halves and joined by three main frames. Of basically rectangular section with rounded top-decking. Fabric covering. Forward section also has an inner plywood skin for added strength. Engine cowling panels of non-inflammable laminated plastics.

TAIL UNIT: Conventional cantilever structure. All-wood single-spar fin, integral with fuselage, and tailplane. All surfaces plywood-covered except rudder, which is covered with both plywood and fabric. Tailplane incidence adjustable on ground. Trim tab in each elevator.

CAP 10 two-seat aerobatic light aircraft (180 hp Lycoming IO-360-B2F engine)

LANDING GEAR: Non-retractable tailwheel type. Main-wheel legs of light alloy, with ERAM type 9 270 C oleo-pneumatic shock-absorbers. Single wheel on each main unit, tyre size 380 × 150. Solid tailwheel tyre, size 6 × 200. Tailwheel is steerable by rudder linkage but can be disengaged for ground manoeuvring. Hydraulically-actuated main-wheel brakes and parking brake. Streamline fairings on main wheels and legs.

POWER PLANT: One 180 hp Lycoming IO-360-B2F four-cylinder horizontally-opposed aircooled engine, with fuel injection, driving a Hoffman two-blade fixed-pitch wooden propeller. Fuel in two main tanks in fuselage, one aft of engine fireproof bulkhead and one beneath baggage compartment, with total capacity of 33 Imp gallons (150 litres). Fuel and oil systems modified to permit periods of inverted flying.

ACCOMMODATION: Side-by-side adjustable seats for two persons, with provision for back parachutes, under rearward-sliding moulded transparent canopy. Space for 44 lb (20 kg) of baggage aft of seats in training and touring models.

SYSTEMS: Electrical system includes Delco-Rémy engine-driven alternator and SAFT 12V DC battery.

ELECTRONICS AND EQUIPMENT: CSF 262 12-channel VHF radio fitted.

DIMENSIONS, EXTERNAL:
Wing span 26 ft 5¼ in (8·06 m)
Wing aspect ratio 5·96
Length overall 23 ft 11½ in (7·30 m)
Height overall 8 ft 4½ in (2·55 m)
Tailplane span 9 ft 6 in (2·90 m)
Wheel track 6 ft 9 in (2·06 m)
DIMENSION, INTERNAL:
Cabin: Max width 3 ft 5½ in (1·054 m)
AREAS:
Wings, gross 116·79 sq ft (10·85 m²)
Ailerons (total) 8·50 sq ft (0·79 m²)
Vertical tail surfaces (total) 14·25 sq ft (1·32 m²)
Horizontal tail surfaces (total)
20·0 sq ft (1·86 m²)
WEIGHTS (A: Aerobatic, U: Utility):
Weight empty, equipped:
A, U 1,168 lb (530 kg)
Fuel load:
A 119 lb (54 kg)
U 238 lb (108 kg)
Max T-O weight:
A 1,666 lb (756 kg)
U 1,829 lb (830 kg)
PERFORMANCE (at max T-O weight):
Max never-exceed speed
183 knots (211 mph; 340 km/h)
Max level speed at S/L
146 knots (168 mph; 270 km/h)
Max cruising speed (75% power)
129 knots (149 mph; 240 km/h)
Stalling speed, flaps up
52 knots (59·5 mph; 95 km/h)
Stalling speed, flaps down
44 knots (50 mph; 80 km/h)
Max rate of climb at S/L
over 1,180 ft (360 m)/min
Service ceiling over 18,050 ft (5,500 m)
Range 647 nm (745 miles; 1,200 km)

PAYEN

FLÉCHAIR SA

ADDRESS:
Aérodrome de la Ferte-Alais, Plateau de l'Ardenay, 91-Cerny

DIRECTOR: Ing N. R. Payen

ADDRESS: BP 18, 91-Montlhéry
Telephone: 901.10.00

Ing Roland Payen has been engaged in research and development of delta-wing aircraft since 1933. His Pa.49 aircraft, which flew on 22 January 1954, was the first French jet-powered delta and, with the Pa.61B Arbalette I of 1964, formed the basis for the latest Payen projects. They include the Pa.61F/H Arbalette II two/three-seat experimental aircraft, the Pa.71 single-seat racing aircraft, and the Pa.149 two-seat sporting aircraft, all of which were described and illustrated in the 1973-74 *Jane's*. There has been no news of their further development.

PIEL

AVIONS CLAUDE PIEL

ADDRESS:
104 Côte de Beulle, 78580-Maule
Telephone: 478.82.49

M Claude Piel has designed several light aircraft, including the Emeraude, Diamant and Beryl, all of which are described below. Sets of plans of these aircraft are available to amateur constructors.

In addition, M Piel has granted licence rights for their manufacture by several commercial concerns. Four French companies, listed in the 1968-69 *Jane's*, built versions of the Emeraude under licence, as did Binder Aviatik KG (in association with Schempp-Hirth KG) in Germany, Durban Aircraft Corporation in South Africa, Aeronasa in Spain and Fairtravel in the UK. Over 200 factory-built Emeraudes were completed by these manufacturers, in addition to those built by amateur constructors.

Authorised distributors of plans for amateur constructors currently include:

E. Littner, 546, 83rd Avenue, Chomedey, Quebec, Canada.

J. Lousberg, 28 C de Grootelaan, Middelkerke, Belgium.

In addition, servicing and constructional facilities for Emeraude variants are available at the works of M Choisel at Abbeville.

PIEL EMERAUDE and SUPER EMERAUDE

There have been several factory-built versions of the Emeraude and Super Emeraude, but the aircraft are no longer being produced in this form. The designs continue to be available for amateur construction, and the following amateur-built versions have flown:

C.P.301. With 90 hp Continental engine.

C.P.302. With 90 hp Salmson engine.

C.P.303. With 85 hp Salmson engine.

C.P.304. With 85 hp Continental C85-12F engine and wing flaps.

C.P.305. With 115 hp Lycoming engine.

C.P.308. With 75 hp Continental engine.

C.P.320. With Super Emeraude wings and 100 hp Continental engine. C.P.320A has sweptback fin.

C.P.321. As C.P.320, with 105 hp Potez engine.

C.P.323A. With 150 hp Lycoming engine and sweptback fin. C.P.323AB has tricycle landing gear.

The Emeraude is one of the types approved by the Popular Flying Association for amateur construction in the United Kingdom.

The Emeraude illustrated is a modified version built by Col Richard S. Robinson, a retired USAF fighter pilot of Albuquerque, New Mexico. Powered by a 160 hp Lycoming O-320 engine, driving a Hartzell constant-speed propeller, it has a military-type rearward-hinged canopy, metal wing spar, full IFR instrumentation, ARC-15 VOR and Bendix 220-260 channel radio, electrically-actuated trim tabs, and a dorsal fin to counter the torque of the larger power plant. The wing is plywood-covered; the fuselage and tail unit are Razorback-covered. Span is 27 ft 0 in (8·23 m), basic wing chord 5 ft 0 in (1·52 m), length 20 ft 0 in (6·10 m), height 5 ft 10 in (1·78 m), empty weight 1,400 lb (635 kg) and loaded weight 1,900 lb (862 kg). Performance includes a max level speed of 130 knots (150 mph; 241 km/h), landing speed of 62 knots (71 mph; 100 km/h), rate of climb of 500 ft (152 m)/min at S/L, service ceiling of 12,000 ft (3,650 m) and max range of 300 nm (345 miles; 555 km).

The following details refer to the basic C.P.301 Emeraude and C.P.320 Super Emeraude, but are generally applicable to all versions:

TYPE: **Two-seat light monoplane.**

WINGS: **Cantilever low-wing monoplane. NACA 23012 wing section. Dihedral 5° 40′. Incidence 4° 10′. Inner half of each wing is rectangular in plan, outer half elliptical. All-wood single-spar structure with fabric covering overall. Slotted ailerons and flaps.**

FUSELAGE: Conventional wood structure, covered with fabric.

TAIL UNIT: **Cantilever wood structure. Fin integral with fuselage. Single-piece all-wood tailplane. Elevators and rudder fabric-covered.** Trim tab in starboard elevator.

LANDING GEAR: Non-retractable tailwheel type. Cantilever main legs have rubber-in-compression springing. Hydraulic brakes.

POWER PLANT (C.P.301): One 90 hp Continental C90-12F four-cylinder horizontally-opposed aircooled engine. Two-blade fixed-pitch wooden propeller. Fuel tank in fuselage, behind fireproof bulkhead, capacity 17·6 Imp gallons (80 litres). Provision for auxiliary tank, capacity 8·8 Imp gallons (40 litres).

POWER PLANT (C.P.320): One 100 hp Continental O-200 "flat-four" engine and two-blade fixed-pitch wooden propeller. Fuel as for C.P.301.

ACCOMMODATION: Enclosed cockpit seating two side by side with dual controls. Sides of canopy hinge forward for access and exit. Heating and ventilation.

DIMENSIONS, EXTERNAL:
Wing span 26 ft 4½ in (8·04 m)
Wing chord at root 4 ft 11 in (1·50 m)
Wing chord at tip 1 ft 9½ in (0·55 m)
Wing aspect ratio 5·95
Length overall:
C.P.301 20 ft 8 in (6·30 m)
C.P.320 21 ft 2 in (6·45 m)
Height overall:
C.P.301 6 ft 0¾ in (1·85 m)
C.P.320 6 ft 2¾ in (1·90 m)
Wheel track 6 ft 8¾ in (2·05 m)
Propeller diameter:
C.P.301 5 ft 11 in (1·80 m)
C.P.320 5 ft 10 in (1·78 m)

AREA:
Wings, gross 116·7 sq ft (10·85 m²)

WEIGHTS AND LOADINGS:
Weight empty:
C.P.301 838 lb (380 kg)
C.P.320 903 lb (410 kg)
Max T-O weight:
C.P.301 1,433 lb (650 kg)
C.P.320 1,543 lb (700 kg)
Max wing loading:
C.P.301 12·3 lb/sq ft (60·0 kg/m²)
C.P.320 13·2 lb/sq ft (64·5 kg/m²)
Max power loading:
C.P.301 15·87 lb/hp (7·2 kg/hp)
C.P.320 15·43 lb/hp (7·0 kg/hp)

PERFORMANCE (at max T-O weight):
Max never-exceed speed:
C.P.301 118·7 knots (136·7 mph; 220 km/h)
C.P.320 149 knots (172 mph; 277 km/h)
Max level speed:
C.P.301 110 knots (127 mph; 205 km/h)
C.P.320 124 knots (143 mph; 230 km/h)
Max cruising speed (75% power) at 3,940 ft (1,200 m):
C.P.301 108 knots (124 mph; 200 km/h)
C.P.320 119 knots (137 mph; 220 km/h)
Econ cruising speed (65% power) at 3,940 ft (1,200 m):
C.P.301 101 knots (116 mph; 187 km/h)
C.P.320 110 knots (127 mph; 205 km/h)
Approach speed, flaps down:
C.P.301, C.P.320 65 knots (75 mph; 120 km/h)
Stalling speed, flaps up:
C.P.301 51 knots (58 mph; 92 km/h)
C.P.320 53 knots (61 mph; 97 km/h)
Stalling speed, flaps down:
C.P.301 46 knots (53 mph; 85 km/h)
C.P.320 49 knots (56 mph; 90 km/h)
Max rate of climb at S/L:
C.P.301 551 ft (168 m)/min
C.P.320 787 ft (240 m)/min
Service ceiling:
C.P.301 13,125 ft (4,000 m)
C.P.320 14,100 ft (4,300 m)
T-O run:
C.P.301 820 ft (250 m)
C.P.320 755 ft (230 m)
T-O to 50 ft (15 m):
C.P.301 1,443 ft (440 m)
C.P.320 1,312 ft (400 m)
Landing from 50 ft (15 m):
C.P.301 1,558 ft (475 m)
C.P.320 1,608 ft (490 m)
Landing run:
C.P.301 820 ft (250 m)
C.P.320 853 ft (260 m)
Range at econ cruising speed:
C.P.301, C.P.320 538 nm (620 miles; 1,000 km)

PIEL C.P. 1320

This new aircraft combines the general characteristics of the Super Emeraude with the Diamant's three-seat cabin and fuel tanks in the wings. It can be fitted with engines of up to 200 hp and the prototype will have a 160 hp Lycoming, driving a two-blade wooden propeller. The airframe will be of all-wood construction, with a non-retractable tailwheel-type landing gear. Slotted flaps will be standard. Fuel capacity 35 Imp gallons (160 litres).

Normal load factors will be $+5g$ and $-2·5g$. For aerobatics in two-seat form at a T-O weight of 1,585 lb (720 kg), the permissible load factors will be $+6g$ and $-3g$.

DIMENSIONS, EXTERNAL:
Wing span 26 ft 4½ in (8·04 m)
Wing aspect ratio 5·95
Wing dihedral 5° 40′
Length overall 21 ft 8 in (6·60 m)
Height overall 6 ft 2¾ in (1·90 m)
Wheel track 6 ft 8¾ in (2·05 m)
Propeller diameter 5 ft 11 in (1·80 m)

AREA:
Wings, gross 116·7 sq ft (10·85 m²)

WEIGHTS AND LOADINGS:
Weight empty 1,102 lb (500 kg)
Max T-O weight 1,852 lb (840 kg)
Max wing loading 15·87 lb/sq ft (77·5 kg/m²)
Max power loading 12·1 lb/hp (5·5 kg/hp)

PERFORMANCE (estimated, at max T-O weight):
Max never-exceed speed 183 knots (211 mph; 340 km/h)
Max level speed at S/L 145 knots (167 mph; 270 km/h)
Max cruising speed (75% power) at 3,940 ft (1,200 m) 135 knots (155 mph; 250 km/h)
Cruising speed (65% power) at 3,940 ft (1,200 m) 127 knots (146 mph; 235 km/h)
Approach speed, flaps down 70 knots (81 mph; 130 km/h)
Stalling speed, flaps up 54 knots (62 mph; 100 km/h)
Stalling speed, flaps down 51·5 knots (59 mph; 95 km/h)
Max rate of climb at S/L 1,968 ft (600 m)/min
Service ceiling 16,400 ft (5,000 m)
T-O run 657 ft (200 m)
T-O to 50 ft (15 m) 1,378 ft (420 m)
Landing from 50 ft (15 m) 1,968 ft (600 m)
Landing run 984 ft (300 m)
Range with max fuel at 65% power 593 nm (683 miles; 1,100 km)

PIEL DIAMANT and SUPER DIAMANT

The Diamant is essentially a three/four-seat version of the Emeraude. It is fully certificated

Extensively-modified Piel Emeraude built by Col Richard S. Robinson (*Howard Levy*)

for commercial production and available also in plan form for construction by amateurs. There are several versions, as follows:

C.P.60. Prototype, with 90 hp Continental engine.

C.P.601. Standard three-seat version with 100 hp Continental O-200 engine.

C.P.602. Similar to C.P.601, but with 115 hp Potez engine.

C.P.604 Super Diamant. Prototype (F-PMEC) flown in Summer of 1964, with a 145 hp Continental engine. Latest version has swept vertical tail surfaces.

C.P.605 Super Diamant. Much-modified four-seat ("2+2") version, with 150 hp Lycoming O-320-E2A engine and swept vertical tail surfaces. Fully certificated for commercial production, as well as for amateur construction.

C.P.605B Super Diamant. Version of C.P.605 with retractable tricycle landing gear.

The following description applies to the C.P.601 and C.P.605B:

TYPE: Three/four-seat light monoplane.

WINGS: Cantilever low-wing monoplane. Wing section NACA 23012. Dihedral 5° 40′. Incidence 4° 10′. All-wood single-spar structure, made in one piece, with fabric covering. Slotted ailerons and slotted flaps of wood construction, with fabric covering.

FUSELAGE: Wood structure, covered with fabric.

TAIL UNIT: Cantilever wood structure. Fixed surfaces plywood-covered. Control surfaces fabric-covered. Ground-adjustable tab on each elevator.

LANDING GEAR (C.P.601): Non-retractable tailwheel type. Main wheels size 420 × 150, pressure 24 lb/sq in (1·70 kg/cm²). Hydraulic brakes. Wheel spats. Steerable tailwheel, size 155 × 50.

LANDING GEAR (C.P.605B): Retractable tricycle type. Main wheels retract inward. All three wheels and tyres size 400 × 100.

POWER PLANT: One four-cylinder horizontally-opposed aircooled engine, driving an EVRA two-blade fixed-pitch wooden propeller. Fuel tank in fuselage, capacity 18·7 Imp gallons (85 litres). Provision for additional tankage in C.P. 605B, to give total capacity of 35 Imp gallons (160 litres). Oil capacity 0·9 Imp gallons (4 litres).

ACCOMMODATION: Three seats (four, "2+2", in Super Diamants) in enclosed cabin under large rearward-sliding transparent canopy.

DIMENSIONS, EXTERNAL:

Wing span:
C.P.601 30 ft 10 in (9·40 m)
C.P.605B 30 ft 2¼ in (9·20 m)
Wing chord at root 4 ft 11 in (1·50 m)
Wing aspect ratio:
C.P.601 6·5
C.P.605B 6·4
Length overall:
C.P.601 21 ft 9¾ in (6·65 m)
C.P.605B 22 ft 11¾ in (7·00 m)
Height overall:
C.P.601 6 ft 2¾ in (1·90 m)
C.P.605B 6 ft 6¾ in (2·00 m)
Wheel track:
C.P.601 6 ft 8¾ in (2·05 m)
C.P.605B 9 ft 10 in (3·00 m)
Propeller diameter 5 ft 11 in (1·80 m)

AREAS:

Wings, gross:
C.P.601 144·8 sq ft (13·45 m²)
C.P.605B 143·2 sq ft (13·30 m²)

WEIGHTS AND LOADINGS:

Weight empty:
C.P.601 992 lb (450 kg)
C.P.605B 1,146 lb (520 kg)
Max T-O weight:
C.P.601 1,697 lb (770 kg)
C.P.605B 1,873 lb (850 kg)
Max wing loading:
C.P.601 11·7 lb/sq ft (57·25 kg/m²)
C.P.605B 13·1 lb/sq ft (64·00 kg/m²)
Max power loading:
C.P.601 16·97 lb/hp (7·7 kg/hp)
C.P.605B 12·35 lb/hp (5·6 kg/hp)

PERFORMANCE (at max T-O weight):

Max never-exceed speed:
C.P.601, 605B 151 knots (174 mph; 280 km/h)
Max level speed:
C.P.601 116 knots (134 mph; 215 km/h)
C.P.605B 141 knots (162 mph; 260 km/h)
Max cruising speed (75% power) at 3,940 ft (1,200 m):
C.P.601 110 knots (127 mph; 205 km/h)
C.P.605B 132 knots (152 mph; 245 km/h)
Econ cruising speed (65% power) at 3,940 ft (1,200 m):
C.P.601 102 knots (118 mph; 190 km/h)
C.P.605B 124 knots (143 mph; 230 km/h)
Approach speed, flaps down:
C.P.601, 605B 68 knots (78 mph; 125 km/h)
Stalling speed, flaps up:
C.P.601, 605B 49 knots (56 mph; 90 km/h)
Stalling speed, flaps down:
C.P.601, 605B 45 knots (51 mph; 82 km/h)
Max rate of climb at S/L:
C.P.601 492 ft (150 m)/min
C.P.605B 1,082 ft (330 m)/min

Piel C.P.750 Beryl (160 hp Lycoming O-320 engine) built by Norman Taylor of Ontario, Oregon (*Howard Levy*)

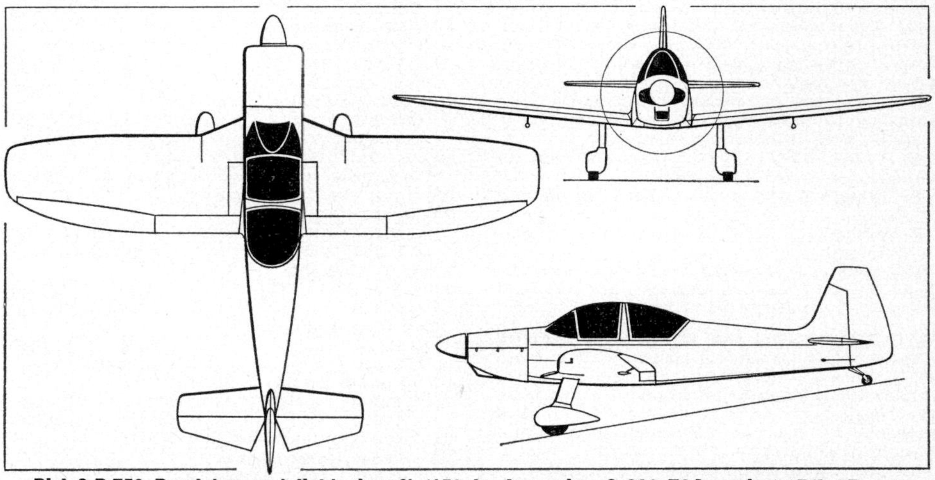

Piel C.P.750 Beryl two-seat light aircraft (150 hp Lycoming O-320-E2A engine) (*Pilot Press*)

Service ceiling:
C.P.601 11,810 ft (3,600 m)
C.P.605B 16,400 ft (5,000 m)
T-O run:
C.P.601 853 ft (260 m)
C.P.605B 525 ft (160 m)
T-O to 50 ft (15 m):
C.P.601 1,575 ft (480 m)
C.P.605B 1,247 ft (380 m)
Landing from 50 ft (15 m):
C.P.601 2,133 ft (650 m)
C.P.605B 1,969 ft (600 m)
Landing run:
C.P.601 919 ft (280 m)
C.P.605B 886 ft (270 m)
Range at econ cruising speed:
C.P.601 387 nm (446 miles; 750 km)
C.P.605B 620 nm (714 miles; 1,150 km)

PIEL C.P.70 and C.P.750 BERYL

The prototype of the **C.P.70 Beryl** tandem two-seat light aircraft was displayed publicly for the first time in August 1965. It retains the wing of the C.P.30 Emeraude virtually unchanged, combining this wing with a modified fuselage and non-retractable tricycle landing gear.

The fuselage of the Beryl is a fabric-covered wooden structure, of slimmer section than that of the Emeraude. Each main landing gear unit is articulated, with the wheel aft of the oleo-pneumatic shock-absorber. The steerable nose-wheel is carried on a conventional fork.

Intended for aerobatic flying, the **C.P.750 Beryl** is also similar in general appearance to the Emeraude but has a longer, steel-tube fuselage seating two persons in tandem, slightly reduced span, a non-retractable tailwheel-type landing gear and other changes.

The C.P.750 has so far been built principally by amateur constructors in Canada, but may also be built in France through the facilities offered by M Choisel at Abbeville.

The example (N7NT) shown in an accompanying illustration was built by Mr Norman Taylor of Ontario, Oregon, over a period of 4 years and 10 months, at a cost of $8,000. Constructed according to plans, with a 160 hp Lycoming O-320 engine, it has an empty weight of 1,332 lb (605 kg), max take-off weight of 1,996 lb (905 kg), cruising speed of 139 knots (160 mph; 257 km/h), landing speed of 52 knots (60 mph; 97 km/h), rate of climb of 1,500 ft (457 m)/min at sea level, take-off and landing run of 475 ft (145 m), and range of 390 nm (450 miles; 725 km) with max fuel.

TYPE: Two-seat aerobatic monoplane.

WINGS: Cantilever low-wing monoplane. Wing section NACA 23012. Dihedral 5° 40′. Incidence 4° 10′. All-wood single-spar structure, made in one piece, with fabric covering. Slotted ailerons and slotted flaps of wood construction with fabric covering.

FUSELAGE: Fabric-covered structure of wood (C.P.70) or welded steel tube (C.P.750).

TAIL UNIT: Cantilever wood structure. Fixed surfaces plywood-covered, control surfaces fabric-covered. Ground-adjustable tab on each elevator.

LANDING GEAR (C.P.70): Non-retractable tricycle type.

LANDING GEAR (C.P.750): Non-retractable tailwheel type. Main wheels size 420 × 150, pressure 24 lb/sq in (1·70 kg/cm²). Hydraulic brakes. Wheel fairings. Steerable tailwheel.

POWER PLANT (C.P.70): One 65 hp Continental C65-8F four-cylinder horizontally-opposed aircooled engine, driving a two-blade wooden propeller. Fuel tank in fuselage, capacity 15·4 Imp gallons (70 litres).

POWER PLANT (C.P.750): One 150 hp Lycoming O-320-E2A four-cylinder horizontally-opposed aircooled engine, driving an EVRA two-blade fixed-pitch wooden propeller. Fuel tank in fuselage, capacity 15·4 Imp gallons (70 litres), with provision for two auxiliary tanks in wings to give total capacity of 30·75 Imp gallons (140 litres). Oil capacity 1·0 Imp gallon (5 litres).

ACCOMMODATION: Two seats in tandem under rearward-sliding transparent canopy. Rear seat of C.P.70 is wide enough to accommodate one adult and a child, or two children.

DIMENSIONS, EXTERNAL:

Wing span:
C.P.70 27 ft 0¾ in (8·25 m)
C.P.750 26 ft 4½ in (8·04 m)
Wing chord at root 4 ft 11 in (1·50 m)
Wing aspect ratio:
C.P.70 5·95
C.P.750 5·85
Length overall:
C.P.70 21 ft 2 in (6·45 m)
C.P.750 22 ft 7¾ in (6·90 m)
Height overall:
C.P.70 5 ft 3 in (1·60 m)
C.P.750 6 ft 10¾ in (2·10 m)
Wheel track:
C.P.70 6 ft 6¾ in (2·00 m)
C.P.750 7 ft 10¼ in (2·40 m)
Propeller diameter 5 ft 11 in (1·80 m)

AREAS:

Wings, gross:
C.P.70 116·8 sq ft (10·85 m²)
C.P.750 118 sq ft (11·00 m²)

WEIGHTS AND LOADINGS:

Weight empty:
C.P.70 705 lb (320 kg)
C.P.750 1,058 lb (480 kg)
Max T-O weight:
C.P.70 1,190 lb (540 kg)
C.P.750 1,675 lb (760 kg)

Max wing loading:
C.P.70 — 10·2 lb/sq ft (50·0 kg/m^2)
C.P.750 — 14·1 lb/sq ft (69·0 kg/m^2)
Max power loading:
C.P.70 — 18·3 lb/hp (8·3 kg/hp)
C.P.750 — 11·0 lb/hp (5·0 kg/hp)

Performance (at max T-O weight):
Max never-exceed speed:
C.P.70 — 118·7 knots (136·7 mph; 220 km/h)
C.P.750 — 183 knots (211 mph; 340 km/h)
Max level speed:
C.P.70 — 95 knots (109 mph; 175 km/h)
C.P.750 — 151 knots (174 mph; 280 km/h)
Max cruising speed (75% power) at 3,940 ft (1,200 m):
C.P.70 — 84 knots (97 mph; 156 km/h)
C.P.750 — 143 knots (165 mph; 265 km/h)
Econ cruising speed (65% power) at 3,940 ft (1,200 m):
C.P.70 — 78 knots (90 mph; 145 km/h)
C.P.750 — 135 knots (155 mph; 250 km/h)
Approach speed, flaps down:
C.P.70 — 54 knots (62·2 mph; 100 km/h)
C.P.750 — 70 knots (81 mph; 130 km/h)
Stalling speed, flaps up:
C.P.70 — 41 knots (47 mph; 75 km/h)
C.P.750 — 54 knots (62·2 mph; 100 km/h)
Stalling speed, flaps down:
C.P.70 — 39 knots (44 mph; 70 km/h)
C.P.750 — 52 knots (59 mph; 95 km/h)
Max rate of climb at S/L:
C.P.70 — 394 ft (120 m)/min
C.P.750 — 1,280 ft (390 m)/min
Service ceiling:
C.P.70 — 9,850 ft (3,000 m)
C.P.750 — 17,060 ft (5,200 m)
T-O run:
C.P.70 — 919 ft (280 m)
C.P.750 — 623 ft (190 m)
T-O to 50 ft (15 m):
C.P.70 — 1,378 ft (420 m)
C.P.750 — 1,148 ft (350 m)
Landing from 50 ft (15 m):
C.P.70 — 919 ft (280 m)
C.P.750 — 1,706 ft (520 m)
Landing run:
C.P.70 — 459 ft (140 m)
C.P.750 — 919 ft (280 m)
Range at econ cruising speed:
C.P.70 — 323 nm (372 miles; 600 km)
C.P.750 — 593 nm (683 miles; 1,100 km)

PIEL C.P.80/ZEF

The C.P.80 was designed as a single-seat racing aircraft for amateur construction. The basic version is made of wood, as described below; but M Calvel of l'Hospitalet du Larzac has adapted the design to enable his C.P.80 Zef to be constructed of laminated plastics. This was the first C.P.80 to fly.

About 20 wooden C.P.80s are under construction by amateurs. The general appearance of the aircraft is shown in the accompanying three-view drawing.

Type: Single-seat amateur-built racing aircraft.

Wings: Cantilever low-wing monoplane. Wing section NACA 23012. Dihedral 3°. Incidence 2° (constant). No sweep at quarter-chord. Conventional single-spar wood structure, plywood-covered and with polyester plastics tips. Ailerons mass-balanced and cable-actuated. No flaps or tabs.

Fuselage: Conventional plywood-covered wood structure of basic rectangular section, with four longerons, nine frames and domed rear decking. Polyester plastics engine cowling. Steel-tube engine mounting attached to fire-proof bulkhead.

Tail Unit: Cantilever plywood-covered all-wood structure, with vertical surfaces swept back at 50° on leading-edge. All-moving constant-chord horizontal surfaces, with centrally-positioned anti-balance and trim tab, and with mass-balance arm projecting forward inside fuselage. Horn-balanced rudder. Control surfaces cable-operated.

Landing Gear: Non-retractable tailwheel type. Main wheels carried on cantilever spring legs of treated AU4SG alloy. Steerable tailwheel carried on steel spring. Hydraulic brakes on main wheels.

Power Plant: One 90 hp Continental C90-8F four-cylinder horizontally-opposed aircooled engine, driving through a short extension shaft a two-blade fixed-pitch wooden propeller. Provision for other engines, including 65 hp Continental. Fuel tank of AG-3 alloy, capacity 8·8 Imp gallons (40 litres), aft of firewall, with refuelling point in top decking.

Accommodation: Pilot only, in enclosed cockpit, under sideways-hinged transparent canopy.

Dimensions, external:
Wing span — 19 ft 8¼ in (6·00 m)
Wing chord at aircraft centreline — 4 ft 5¼ in (1·35 m)
Wing chord at tip — 2 ft 11½ in (0·90 m)
Wing aspect ratio — 5·8
Length overall — 17 ft 4¾ in (5·30 m)
Height overall — 5 ft 7 in (1·70 m)
Tailplane span — 5 ft 2¼ in (1·58 m)
Wheel track — 5 ft 3 in (1·60 m)
Wheelbase — 11 ft 5¾ in (3·50 m)
Propeller diameter — 5 ft 0 in (1·52 m)

Area:
Wings, gross — 66·7 sq ft (6·20 m^2)

Weights and Loadings (90 hp engine):
Weight empty — 573 lb (260 kg)
Max T-O weight — 837 lb (380 kg)
Max wing loading — 12·5 lb/sq ft (61·2 kg/m^2)
Max power loading — 9·3 lb/hp (4·2 kg/hp)

Performance (estimated, with 90 hp engine, at max T-O weight):
Max never-exceed speed — 205 knots (236 mph; 380 km/h)
Max level speed — 167 knots (193 mph; 310 km/h)
Max cruising speed (75% power) at 3,940 ft (1,200 m) — 151 knots (174 mph; 280 km/h)
Econ cruising speed (65% power) at 3,940 ft (1,200 m) — 129·5 knots (149 mph; 240 km/h)
Approach speed — 70 knots (81 mph; 130 km/h)
Stalling speed — 51·5 knots (59 mph; 95 km/h)
Max rate of climb at S/L — 2,362 ft (720 m)/min
Service ceiling — 19,685 ft (6,000 m)
T-O run — 656 ft (200 m)
T-O to 50 ft (15 m) — 1,312 ft (400 m)
Landing from 50 ft (15 m) — 1,181 ft (360 m)
Landing run — 656 ft (200 m)
Range at econ cruising speed — 243 nm (280 miles; 450 km)
Load factors — +8g; −6g

PIEL C.P.90 PINOCCHIO

The C.P.90 Pinocchio is essentially a slightly smaller, single-seat development of the basic Emeraude, intended for aerobatic and general sporting flying.

Wings: Cantilever low-wing monoplane, of similar general planform and construction to Emeraude. Ailerons only, no flaps. Dihedral 5° 40′. Incidence 3°.

Fuselage: Fabric-covered wooden structure of basically rectangular cross-section with domed decking.

Tail Unit: Cantilever fabric-covered wooden structure, similar to that of Emeraude.

Landing Gear: Non-retractable tailwheel type. Streamlined leg and wheel fairings on main units.

Power Plant: One 100 hp Continental O-200 four-cylinder horizontally-opposed aircooled engine, driving a two-blade wooden propeller. Fuel capacity 13·2 Imp gallons (60 litres).

Accommodation: Single seat under fully-transparent canopy.

Dimensions, external:
Wing span — 23 ft 7½ in (7·20 m)
Wing aspect ratio — 5·4
Length overall — 19 ft 8¼ in (6·00 m)
Height overall — 5 ft 11 in (1·80 m)
Wheel track — 5 ft 3 in (1·60 m)
Propeller diameter — 5 ft 11 in (1·80 m)

Area:
Wings, gross — 103·9 sq ft (9·65 m^2)

Weights and Loadings:
Weight empty — 738 lb (335 kg)

Piel C.P.80 Zef with all-plastics fuselage, built by M Calvel (*Aviation Magazine International*)

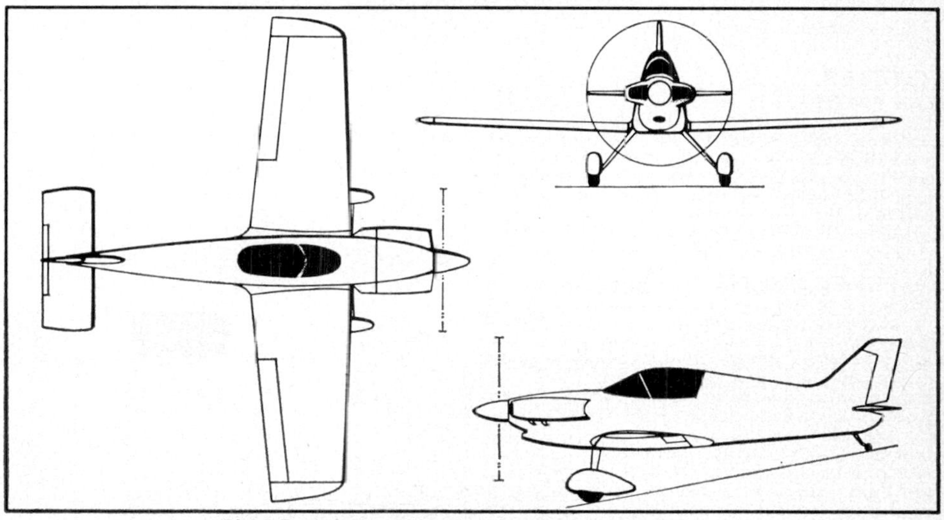
Piel C.P.80 single-seat racing aircraft (*Roy J. Grainge*)

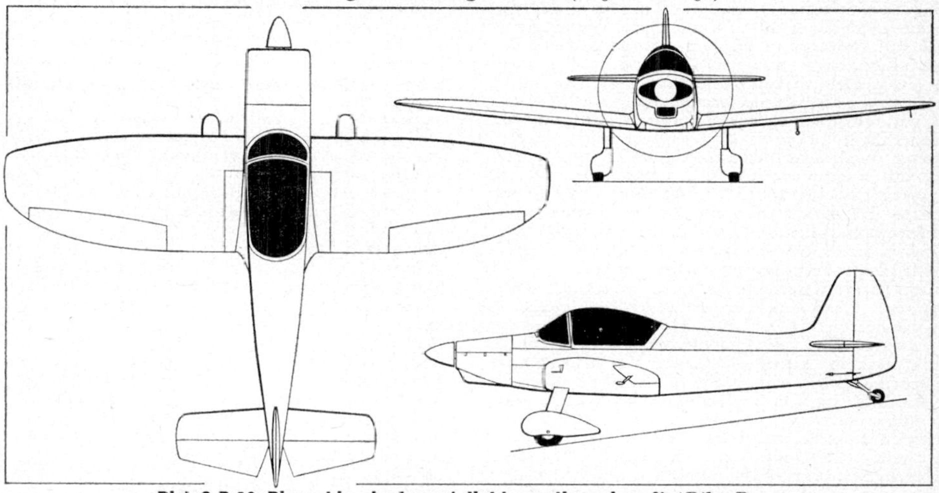
Piel C.P.90 Pinocchio single-seat light sporting aircraft (*Pilot Press*)

Max T-O weight 1,014 lb (460 kg)
Max wing loading 9·8 lb/sq ft (47·7 kg/m²)
Max power loading 10·14 lb/hp (4·6 kg/hp)

PERFORMANCE (estimated, at max T-O weight):
Max never-exceed speed
171 knots (198 mph; 320 km/h)
Max level speed
141 knots (162 mph; 260 km/h)
Max cruising speed (75% power) at 3,940 ft (1,200 m) 132 knots (152 mph; 245 km/h)
Econ cruising speed (65% power) at 3,940 ft (1,200 m) 124 knots (143 mph; 230 km/h)
Approach speed 59 knots (68 mph; 110 km/h)
Stalling speed 41 knots (47 mph; 75 km/h)
Max rate of climb at S/L 1,575 ft (480 m)/min
Service ceiling 19,685 ft (6,000 m)
T-O run 590 ft (180 m)
T-O to 50 ft (15 m) 1,312 ft (400 m)
Landing from 50 ft (15 m) 984 ft (300 m)
Landing run 525 ft (160 m)
Range at econ cruising speed
296 nm (341 miles; 550 km)

PIEL C.P.500

As can be seen in the accompanying illustration, the C.P.500 is a "push and pull" twin-engined aircraft of staggered tandem-wing configuration. Although this gives it some similarity to the Mignet formula, the wings are fixed, and the pilot's controls are conventional.

The strut-braced forward wing has four-section slotted trailing-edge flaps over 75% of the span and 25% of the chord; these can be actuated electrically through 35°. The rear wing carries two elevons, which are actuated by control rods from 40° up to 35° down; these function differentially for roll control and collectively for pitch control. Endplate fins and rudders on the rear wing provide yaw control. The relative position of the wings is expected to permit steep "parachute" descents of the kind possible with Mignet designs.

Wing section is NACA 23015. The front wing has a dihedral of 1° 30′ and incidence of 2° 30′ constant; the rear wing has a constant incidence of 4° 30′ but no dihedral.

The prototype C.P.500 is being built of wood, but provision is made for switching to metal construction for any future series production of the type. In each case, the engine cowlings, wing-tips and fairings are of laminated plastics. Two 150/160 hp Lycoming O-320 four-cylinder horizontally-opposed aircooled engines are specified, with the rear engine driving its propeller through an extension shaft, 5·9 in (15 cm) long. Fuel tanks in the tips of the forward wing have a combined capacity of 66 Imp gallons (300 litres).

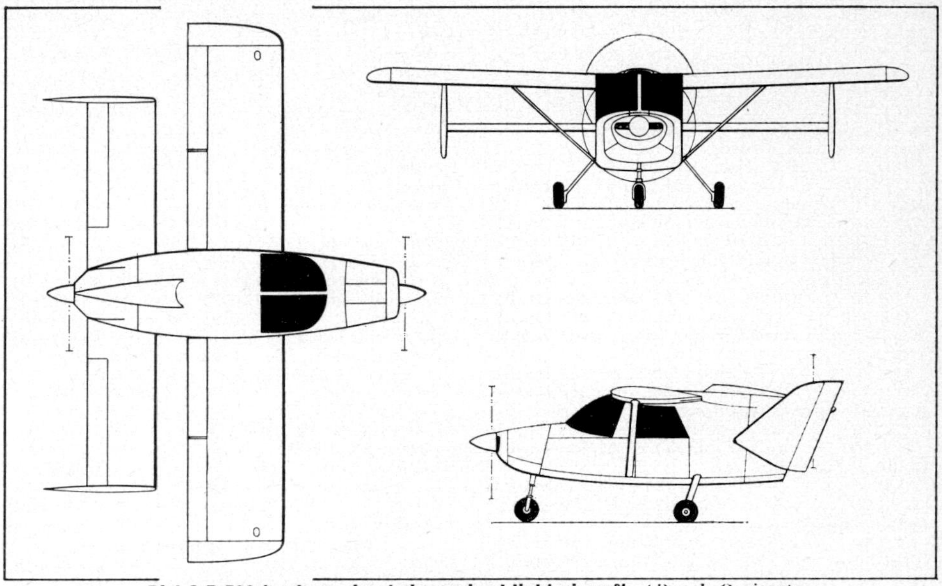

Piel C.P.500 tandem-wing twin-engined light aircraft (*Roy J. Grainge*)

A non-retractable tricycle landing gear is standard, with Wittman-type cantilever steel spring main legs and a steerable nosewheel. Each main wheel is fitted with a hydraulic brake.

Basic accommodation is provided for two persons side by side in front, with optional dual controls, and three passengers on a rear bench seat. Aft of the rear seat is space for a sixth person or a considerable quantity of baggage.

DIMENSIONS, EXTERNAL:
Wing span:
front 28 ft 10½ in (8·80 m)
rear 21 ft 1¼ in (6·43 m)
Wing chord (constant):
front 4 ft 11 in (1·50 m)
rear 3 ft 7¼ in (1·10 m)
Wing aspect ratio:
front 5·85
rear 5·88
Wing stagger 1 ft 6 in (0·46 m)
Length overall 20 ft 0 in (6·10 m)
Height overall 7 ft 4½ in (2·25 m)
Fuselage depth (max) 5 ft 1½ in (1·56 m)
Fuselage width (max) 4 ft 7 in (1·40 m)
Wheel track 8 ft 4¾ in (2·56 m)
Wheelbase 8 ft 6¼ in (2·60 m)

AREAS:
Wings, gross:
front 142·1 sq ft (13·20 m²)
rear 76·42 sq ft (7·10 m²)
Vertical tail surfaces (total) 30·14 sq ft (2·80 m²)
Rudders (total) 9·69 sq ft (0·90 m²)

WEIGHTS:
Weight empty 1,909 lb (866 kg)
Max T-O weight 3,307 lb (1,500 kg)

PERFORMANCE (estimated):
Max level speed 162 knots (186 mph; 300 km/h)
Max level speed, one engine out
129 knots (149 mph; 240 km/h)
Max cruising speed (75% power)
143 knots (165 mph; 265 km/h)
Max cruising speed, one engine out (75% power)
108 knots (124 mph; 200 km/h)
Stalling speed, flaps down
49 knots (56 mph; 90 km/h)
Max rate of climb at S/L 1,770 ft (540 m)/min
Max rate of climb at S/L, one engine out
590 ft (180 m)/min
Service ceiling 22,300 ft (6,800 m)
Service ceiling, one engine out 9,850 ft (3,000 m)
Range with max fuel
647 nm (745 miles; 1,200 km)

POTTIER

JEAN POTTIER

ADDRESS:
Société CARMAM, BP 201, 03001-Moulins

In addition to the light aircraft and sailplanes that he has designed jointly with M Robert Jacquet, his fellow technical director at Société CARMAM, M Pottier is responsible for the purely amateur projects described below and the P.70B racing aircraft built by M Alain Besneux (which see).

POTTIER P.50 BOUVREUIL (BULLFINCH)

Designed by M Jean Pottier, the Bouvreuil is a single-seat racing monoplane, intended for construction by amateurs. Construction is entirely of wood, except for the plastics engine cowling and main-wheel fairings.

The Bouvreuil can be fitted with a variety of engines in the 65-115 hp category. It has also been designed from the start to have either a non-retractable (P.50) or retractable (P.50R) landing gear. Design load factors are ±10.

Six Bouvreuils were known to be under construction in early 1974, numbers 01 and 02 in France, 03 in the Netherlands, 04 in Switzerland, and 05 and 06 in Germany. Four of these aircraft will have a 90 hp Continental C90 engine; 02 will have a 65 hp Continental and 06 an 82 hp Porsche. Numbers 03, 04 and 06 will be P.50Rs, with retractable landing gear, offering a 10% improvement in performance.

Numbers 01 and 04 are expected to fly for the first time in 1975.

TYPE: Single-seat racing monoplane.

WINGS: Cantilever low-wing monoplane. Wing section NACA 23015 at root, NACA 23012 at tip. Dihedral from roots. All-wood structure, with full-span ailerons and flaps. No tabs.

FUSELAGE: Conventional wood semi-monocoque structure, with plastics engine cowling.

TAIL UNIT: Cantilever all-wood structure, with swept vertical surfaces. Trim tab in each elevator.

LANDING GEAR: Alternative retractable or non-retractable tailwheel type. Wheel fairings standard on non-retractable main wheels. Steerable tailwheel. Independent main-wheel brakes.

POWER PLANT: Standard engine is 90 hp Continental C90 "flat-four", driving a two-blade fixed-pitch propeller, with spinner. Other engines of 65 to 115 hp are optional. Fuel capacity 13 Imp gallons (60 litres) for racing, 22 Imp gallons (100 litres) for touring. Provision for carrying one removable auxiliary fuel tank under each wing.

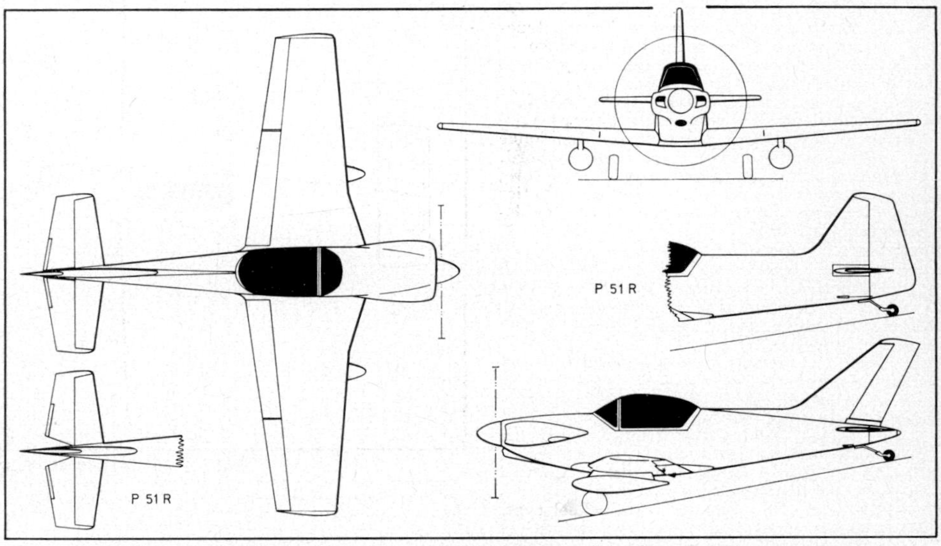

Pottier P.50R Bouvreuil single-seat racing aircraft. Scrap views show tail of P.51R (*Roy J. Grainge*)

ACCOMMODATION: Single seat in enclosed cabin, under large rearward-sliding transparent canopy.

DIMENSIONS, EXTERNAL:
Wing span 20 ft 4 in (6·20 m)
Wing aspect ratio 5·10
Length overall 18 ft 6½ in (5·65 m)

AREA:
Wings, gross 80·7 sq ft (7·50 m²)

WEIGHTS AND LOADING (90 hp engine):
Weight empty 595 lb (270 kg)
Max T-O weight 882 lb (400 kg)
Max wing loading 10·95 lb/sq ft (53·5 kg/m²)

PERFORMANCE (estimated, with 90 hp engine and non-retractable landing gear):
Max level speed
167 knots (192 mph; 310 km/h)
Max cruising speed (75% power)
151 knots (174 mph; 280 km/h)
Min speed 43 knots (50 mph; 80 km/h)

POTTIER P.51R

The P.51R, designed in 1973, is generally similar to the version of the P.50 with retractable landing gear and optional underwing auxiliary tanks, but has unswept vertical tail surfaces. The wings, forward fuselage structure and flying controls of the two types are identical, and the same variety of power plants may be fitted.

Plans of the P.51R are expected to be available in early 1975.

DIMENSIONS, AREA AND WEIGHTS:
As for P.50

PERFORMANCE (estimated):
Max level speed
167 knots (192 mph; 310 km/h)
Max cruising speed (75% power)
151 knots (174 mph; 280 km/h)
Landing speed 43 knots (50 mph; 80 km/h)

POULET *(see under "Dalotel")*

RABOUYT

ADDRESS:
c/o Alpavia SA, 152 Avenue des Champs-Elysées, Paris 8e

RABOUYT D2

First displayed publicly at the Paris Air Show in May/June 1971, the Rabouyt D2 is a two-seat rotorcraft which combines features of both a helicopter and an autogyro. It can take off vertically, like a helicopter; for all other phases of flight the rotor remains in autorotation, and forward propulsion is by means of direct engine drive to a shrouded propeller aft of the fuselage pod. Directional control is exercised, via a control column in the cockpit, solely by tilting the rotor axis to the degree required; ground steering is by pedal-operated linkage between the nosewheel and rudder, which is not used in flight. It is claimed that perfectly safe landing approaches can be made at speeds of less than 16 knots (18 mph; 30 km/h) without the aircraft going into a spin or stall.

The Rabouyt D2 was fitted initially with a low-powered engine for preliminary evaluation. For further tests at the CEV it was to be refitted with a standard aero-engine of about 150 hp.

ROTOR AND PROPULSION SYSTEM: Two-blade semi-rigid rotor, with power transfer from engine via a torque-limiting coupler. Constant-chord blades, of laminated wood construction covered with geodesic glassfibre/epoxy fabric. Except for the vertical take-off phase, the rotor remains constantly in autorotation, so that in the event of a failure of any kind the aircraft can still make a safe landing at zero speed. For horizontal flight the engine drives a four-blade shrouded propeller at the rear of the fuselage, the blades having variable pitch and being synchronised with the rotor pitch.

FUSELAGE: Pod-type structure, of steel-chromium-vanadium with epoxy skin.

TAIL UNIT: Vertical surfaces only, comprising small fin and large rudder supported by boom from underside of fuselage.

LANDING GEAR: Non-retractable tricycle type, with cantilever legs on all units. Streamlined fairings over all three wheels. Nosewheel is linked to rudder via pedal controls in cockpit for ground steering.

ACCOMMODATION: Seats for two persons side by side in fully-enclosed cabin. Access via forward-opening door on each side.

DIMENSIONS, EXTERNAL:
Rotor diameter 32 ft 9½ in (10·00 m)
Length overall (without rotors) 17 ft 4¼ in (5·29 m)
Width overall 7 ft 9 in (2·36 m)
Height overall 8 ft 0½ in (2·45 m)

WEIGHTS:
Max T-O weight 1,653 lb (750 kg)
Max overload T-O weight 1,763 lb (800 kg)

PERFORMANCE (estimated, at max T-O weight, 150 hp engine):
Cruising speed 97 knots (112 mph; 180 km/h)
Minimum speed 16 knots (18 mph; 30 km/h)
Max range 388 nm (447 miles; 720 km)

Rabouyt D2 side-by-side two-seat light autogyro *(Brian M. Service)*

REIMS AVIATION

REIMS AVIATION S A

OFFICE AND WORKS:
Reims-Prunay Airport, BP 2745, 51062-Reims Cédex
Telephone: (26) 49.10.88
Telex: REIMAVIA No 83754

PARIS OFFICE:
18 Quai Alphonse le Gallo, 92100-Boulogne-Billancourt

PRESIDENT DIRECTOR-GENERAL:
Pierre Clostermann

DIRECTOR-GENERAL ADJOINT AND WORKS DIRECTOR: Jean Pichon

FINANCIAL DIRECTOR: Henri Hertz

ADMINISTRATIVE DIRECTOR: Armand Blang

PUBLIC RELATIONS: Frédéric Amanou

CHIEF PILOT: Franck Bardou

Under an agreement signed on 16 February 1960, the Cessna Aircraft Company of Wichita, Kansas, USA, acquired a 49% holding in this company, which was then known as Société Nouvelle des Avions Max Holste.

Reims Aviation has the right to manufacture under licence Cessna designs for sale in Europe, Africa and Asia. By 1 January 1974 it had assembled a total of 1,075 Cessna F-150 and 225 FRA-150 two-seat aircraft, 1,086 F-172 and 457 FR-172 Reims Rocket four-seat aircraft, 94 F-177 RG four-seat aircraft, and 65 F-337, FT-337 and FT-337P six-seat aircraft. Nearly 88% of all products are exported.

The 3,000th aircraft completed by Reims Aviation, a Reims Rocket, left the Reims-Prunay works at the beginning of December 1973. A total of 422 aircraft were delivered in the 1973 calendar year.

Reims Aviation is also taking part in the series production of the Aérospatiale N 262/Frégate twin-turboprop light transport, by manufacturing tail units and fuselage tailcones, wheel fairings, flaps, ailerons, wing leading-edges, wingtips, engine nacelles and instrument panels. It is a subcontractor to Dassault in the Mystère 20/Falcon 10 programme, for which it supplies ailerons and airbrakes. It is also continuing the overhaul and servicing of M.H.1521 Broussard utility monoplanes.

Reims Aviation employed 539 people on 1 January 1974. Its offices and factories at Reims-Prunay Airport have an area of 236,800 sq ft (22,000 m²).

CESSNA F-150 and FRA-150 AEROBAT

Cessna 150 aircraft assembled under licence by Reims Aviation are designated **F-150.** The first example was flown on 22 February 1966. Production was at the rate of 130 aircraft per year in early 1974.

In addition, Reims Aviation produces an aerobatic version known as the **FRA-150** Aerobat. This is a two-seater with a 130 hp Rolls-Royce Continental engine. Production was at a rate of 50 aircraft per year in early 1974.

A full description of the current Cessna 150 and A150 is given in the US section.

Reims-Cessna FRA-150 Aerobat (130 hp Rolls-Royce Continental O-240-A engine)

Reims-Cessna FR-172 Reims Rocket (210 hp Rolls-Royce Continental IO-360-H engine)

CESSNA F-172 and FR-172/FRB-172 REIMS ROCKET

Cessna 172 aircraft assembled under licence by Reims Aviation are designated **F-172.**

Until 1971, Reims Aviation retained a 145 hp Rolls-Royce Continental engine in the F-172, of which the first example was flown on 4 January 1963, with 805 delivered by the end of 1971. The current F-172 has a 150 hp Lycoming O-320-E2D, like the standard Cessna 172, which is described fully in the US section of this edition. Production in 1974 is at the rate of 200 aircraft per year.

First displayed at the 1967 Paris Air Show, the **FR-172** Reims Rocket was developed by Reims Aviation from the F-172. The first Rocket was flown early in 1967; the current rate of production is 90 aircraft per year. Reims produces the Rocket exclusively, for worldwide sale.

The Rocket has a 210 hp Rolls-Royce Continental IO-360-H six-cylinder horizontally-opposed aircooled engine, driving a constant-speed pro-

F

peller. Wing fuel tank capacity is increased to 43·3 Imp gallons (197 litres). There is also a version with a 14·1 Imp gallon (64 litre) auxiliary fuselage tank, increasing total capacity to 57·4 Imp gallons (261 litres).

A number of modifications have been made in the current model, to improve passenger comfort and performance and increase the useful load. These include conical-camber wingtips, re-designed seats, improved baggage door hatch and a more flexible electrical system. Optional items include vertically-adjustable, fully-articulated front seats, foldaway child's seat in the baggage area and glider-towing capability. The 10·5 cu ft (0·3 m^3) baggage compartment aft of the rear seats holds a maximum of 200 lb (90 kg).

In early May 1971, Reims flew the prototype of a STOL version of the Rocket, designated FRA-172 (A for ADAC: Avion de Décollage et Atterrissage Court). Similar modifications are now available on a commercial version designated **FRB-172**. They reduce T-O run to 590 ft (180 m), landing run to 445 ft (135 m), and landing from 50 ft (15 m) to 1,100 ft (335 m).

The following data apply to the standard FR-172 Reims Rocket:

Dimensions, external:
Wing span 35 ft 10 in (10·92 m)
Length overall 26 ft 9½ in (8·17 m)
Height overall 8 ft 9½ in (2·68 m)
Tailplane span 11 ft 4 in (3·45 m)
Wheel track 8 ft 3½ in (2·53 m)
Propeller diameter 6 ft 4 in (1·93 m)

Area:
Wings, gross 175·5 sq ft (16·30 m^2)

Weights and Loadings:
Weight empty 1,430 lb (649 kg)
Max T-O weight 2,550 lb (1,157 kg)
Max wing loading 14·6 lb/sq ft (71·3 kg/m^2)
Max power loading 12·1 lb/hp (5·49 kg/hp)

Performance (at max T-O weight):
Max level speed at S/L 133 knots (153 mph; 246 km/h)
Max cruising speed (75% power) at 5,500 ft (1,675 m) 126 knots (145 mph; 233 km/h)
Econ cruising speed at 10,000 ft (3,050 m) 91 knots (105 mph; 169 km/h)
Stalling speed, power off, flaps up 53 knots (61 mph; 98 km/h)
Stalling speed, power off, flaps down 46 knots (53 mph; 86 km/h)
Max rate of climb at S/L 880 ft (268 m)/min
Service ceiling 17,000 ft (5,182 m)
T-O run 740 ft (226 m)
T-O to 50 ft (15 m) 1,230 ft (375 m)
Landing from 50 ft (15 m) 1,270 ft (387 m)
Landing run 620 ft (189 m)
Range at max cruising speed, no reserve:
standard fuel 503 nm (580 miles; 933 km)
with aux tank 690 nm (795 miles; 1,279 km)
Range at econ cruising speed, no reserve:
standard fuel 642 nm (740 miles; 1,190 km)
with aux tank 877 nm (1,010 miles; 1,625 km)

CESSNA F-177 RG

The Cessna Cardinal RG four-seat light aircraft with retractable landing gear, when assembled by Reims Aviation, has the designation F-177 RG. First example flown on 4 February 1971. Production was at the rate of 30 aircraft per year in early 1974.

CESSNA F-337, FA-337 and FT-337P PRESSURISED SKYMASTER

In 1969 Reims Aviation began the assembly under licence of the Cessna 337 Super Skymaster six-seat twin-engined light aircraft. Primary structures are supplied by Cessna, and engines by Rolls-Royce; smaller components and equipment are French-built.

There are three current French production versions, as follows:

F-337. Standard Cessna 337 as built by Reims Aviation. Two 210 hp Rolls-Royce Continental engines. First flown in 1972.

FA-337. Similar to F-337, but with optional STOL (ADAC) modifications, comprising high-lift trailing-edge flaps which reduce T-O run to 655 ft (200 m), T-O to 50 ft (15 m) to 1,150 ft (350 m), landing from 50 ft (15 m) to 1,115 ft (340 m), and landing run to 495 ft (150 m).

FT-337P. Pressurised Skymaster. Similar to F-337 except for having pressurised cabin and 225 hp Continental turbocharged fuel-injection engines.

Reims-Cessna F-177 RG (200 hp Lycoming IO-360-A1B6 engine)

Reims-Cessna FT-337P Pressurised Skymaster (two 225 hp Continental TSIO-360-C engines)

Reims-Cessna FTB-337 for special duties, with underwing containers

Production was continuing at the rate of 8 F-337s and 5 Pressurised Skymasters per year in early 1974.

Full descriptions of the current models of the Cessna 337 appear in the US section of this edition.

REIMS-CESSNA FTB-337

The airframe of this five/six-seat push-and-pull light twin is basically similar to that of the commercial FA-337 with STOL (ADAC) modifications; but it is powered by two 225 hp Continental IO-360-D engines. Developed at the request of various government agencies, it is not pressurised but can be equipped for maritime or overland patrol duties, sea or land rescue, or other specialised tasks, with four underwing pylons for containers of food and medicine, dinghies and locator beacons, or forest fire patrol equipment. The rear of cabin can be cleared to carry cargo or two stretchers. The aircraft can also be equipped for navigation and IFR training.

Dimensions, external: As Cessna Model 337.

Area:
Wings, gross 202·5 sq ft (18·81 m^2)

Weights and Loading:
Weight empty 3,053 lb (1,385 kg)
Max T-O weight 4,700 lb (2,132 kg)
Max wing loading 23·2 lb/sq ft (113 kg/m^2)

Performance (at max T-O weight):
Max level speed at S/L 217 knots (250 mph; 402 km/h)
Cruising speed (75% power):
at 10,000 ft (3,000 m) 185 knots (214 mph; 344 km/h)
at 20,000 ft (6,000 m) 205 knots (236 mph; 380 km/h)
Max rate of climb at S/L 1,250 ft (381 m)/min
Rate of climb at 10,000 ft (3,000 m) 1,135 ft (346 m)/min
Max certificated operating height, on one or two engines 20,000 ft (6,100 m)
STOL T-O run 738 ft (225 m)
STOL T-O to 50 ft (15 m) 1,245 ft (380 m)
STOL landing from 50 ft (15 m) 1,115 ft (340 m)
STOL landing run 495 ft (150 m)
Max range:
75% power at 20,000 ft (6,000 m) 955 nm (1,100 miles; 1,770 km)
econ power at 10,000 ft (3,000 m) 1,085 nm (1,250 miles; 2,012 km)
econ power at 20,000 ft (6,000 m) 1,150 nm (1,325 miles; 2,132 km)

ROBIN

AVIONS PIERRE ROBIN (CENTRE EST AÉRONAUTIQUE)

Head Office and Works:
Aérodrome Dijon-Darois, BP 38, 21001-Dijon Cédex
Telephone: (80) 35-40-40
Telex: 35-818 Robin

Commercial Management:
Aérodrome de Toussus-le-Noble, 78530-Buc
Telephone: 956-35-14

Service Stations:
Dijon-Darois, La Rochelle Laleu, Paris Toussus-le-Noble

President Director General:
Pierre Robin

Commercial Manager (Paris, Toussus-le-Noble):
P. Meynard

Production Director:
L. Vuillemain

Technical Director:
Michel Brandt

Public Relations:
Mlle Conte

This company was formed in October 1957 as Centre Est Aéronautique to design, manufacture and sell touring aircraft. In 1969 the name of the company was changed to Avions Pierre Robin.

Its founder, M Pierre Robin, in collaboration with M Jean Delemontez, the engineer responsible for the well-known Jodel series of light aircraft, began by developing for production a three-seat high-performance lightplane of wooden construction. This was the Jodel DR 100 Ambassadeur, which flew on 14 July 1958 and was followed by many refined, enlarged and more powerful types embodying the same basic design features. All of these have been described in earlier editions of *Jane's*.

Since 1973, Avions Pierre Robin has manufactured the new 400 series of six wooden light aircraft, all of which represent highly-refined developments of the company's earlier Jodel designs and were first flown in prototype form in 1972. They are described in detail below, together with the company's new range of all-metal light aircraft, some with retractable landing gear.

Under development are a new low-cost aircraft and the 4/6-seat HR 100/4+2, of which a prototype was expected to fly in 1974. Design and development of a new twin-engined six-seater had been suspended in early 1974 because of lower market potential due to the energy crisis.

The company's works currently cover an area of 86,197 sq ft (8,008 m²) and it employs 200 people. A total of 199 aircraft were delivered in 1973, of which 89 were exported.

ROBIN (CENTRE EST) DR 400/2+2

As its name implies, this smallest aircraft in the current Robin 400 series is a refined development of the earlier DR 220 "2+2" and DR 300/108 "2+2 Tricycle" described in the 1972-73 *Jane's*.

Design of the 400 series, and construction of the first example of each type, began towards the end of 1971. New features common to all six designs include a transparent canopy which slides forward to give access to all seats, and lowered walls on each side of the cabin to provide easier access and improved visibility.

The DR 400/2+2 flew for the first time in December 1972 and received SGAC certification on the 19th of that month. Deliveries totalled 24 by February 1974, of which 20 were delivered in 1973.

TYPE: Two/four-seat light aircraft.

WINGS: Cantilever low-wing monoplane. Wing section NACA 23013.5 (modified). Centre-section has constant chord and no dihedral; outer wings have a dihedral of 14°. All-wood one-piece structure, with single box-spar. Leading-edge plywood-covered; polyester-fibre covering overall. Wooden ailerons, covered with polyester-fibre. Aluminium alloy flaps. Ailerons and flaps interchangeable port and starboard. Manually-operated airbrake under spar outboard of landing gear on each side. Picketing ring under each wingtip.

FUSELAGE: Wooden semi-monocoque structure of basic rectangular section, plywood-covered.

TAIL UNIT: Cantilever all-wood structure, covered with polyester-fibre. Sweptback fin and rudder. All-moving one-piece horizontal surface.

LANDING GEAR: Non-retractable tricycle type, with Jodel-Beaune oleo-pneumatic shock-absorbers and Manu hydraulically-actuated drum brakes. All three wheels and tyres are size 380-150, pressure 22·8 lb/sq in (1·6 kg/cm²) on nose unit, 25·6 lb/sq in (1·8 kg/cm²) on main units. Fairings over all three legs and wheels.

POWER PLANT: One 108 hp Lycoming O-235-C2C four-cylinder horizontally-opposed aircooled engine, driving a McCauley IA-BCM-7056 two-blade fixed-pitch metal propeller. Fuel tank in fuselage, capacity 24 Imp gallons (110 litres).

ACCOMMODATION: Basic accommodation for two persons side by side, on adjustable seats, in enclosed cabin, with access via forward-sliding transparent canopy. Bench seat to rear for one or two persons. Dual controls standard. Cabin heated and ventilated.

SYSTEMS AND EQUIPMENT: Standard equipment includes a 40A alternator and pitot de-icing. Radio to customer's requirements.

DIMENSIONS, EXTERNAL:

Wing span	28 ft 7½ in (8·72 m)
Wing chord, centre-section (constant)	5 ft 7½ in (1·71 m)
Wing chord at tip	3 ft 0 in (0·90 m)
Wing aspect ratio	5·6
Length overall	22 ft 10 in (6·96 m)
Height overall	7 ft 3¾ in (2·23 m)
Tailplane span	10 ft 6 in (3·20 m)
Wheel track	8 ft 6¼ in (2·60 m)
Wheelbase	17 ft 0¾ in (5·20 m)
Propeller diameter	5 ft 10 in (1·78 m)

DIMENSIONS, INTERNAL:

Cabin: Length	5 ft 3¾ in (1·62 m)
Max width	3 ft 7¼ in (1·10 m)
Max height	4 ft 0½ in (1·23 m)
Baggage space, volume	13·75 cu ft (0·39 m³)

AREAS:

Wings, gross	146·39 sq ft (13·60 m²)
Ailerons, total	12·38 sq ft (1·15 m²)
Flaps, total	7·53 sq ft (0·70 m²)
Fin	6·57 sq ft (0·61 m²)
Rudder	6·78 sq ft (0·63 m²)
Horizontal tail surfaces, total	31·00 sq ft (2·88 m²)

WEIGHTS AND LOADINGS:

Weight empty, equipped	1,158 lb (525 kg)
Max T-O and landing weight	1,907 lb (865 kg)
Max wing loading	13·03 lb/sq ft (63·6 kg/m²)
Max power loading	17·66 lb/hp (8·0 kg/hp)

PERFORMANCE (at max T-O weight):

Max never-exceed speed	166 knots (191 mph; 308 km/h)
Max level speed at S/L	129 knots (149 mph; 240 km/h)
Max cruising speed at 8,000 ft (2,440 m)	114 knots (131 mph; 211 km/h)
Econ cruising speed at 12,000 ft (3,650 m)	106 knots (122 mph; 197 km/h)
Stalling speed, flaps down	47 knots (54 mph; 87 km/h)
Stalling speed, flaps up	53·5 knots (61·5 mph; 99 km/h)
Max rate of climb at S/L	650 ft (198 m)/min
Service ceiling	14,000 ft (4,265 m)
T-O run	732 ft (240 m)
T-O to 50 ft (15 m)	1,675 ft (510 m)
Landing from 50 ft (15 m)	1,477 ft (450 m)
Landing run	590 ft (180 m)
Range with max fuel	593 nm (683 miles; 1,100 km)

ROBIN (CENTRE EST) DR 400/125 PETIT PRINCE

The prototype of this DR 400 series Petit Prince flew for the first time in May 1972 and received SGAC certification on the 10th of that month, followed by FAA and CAA certification in December 1972. Deliveries totalled 41 by February 1974, of which 25 were delivered during 1973.

TYPE: Three/four-seat light training and touring aircraft.

WINGS, FUSELAGE, TAIL UNIT AND LANDING GEAR: As for DR 400/2+2.

POWER PLANT: One 125 hp Lycoming O-235-F2B four-cylinder horizontally-opposed aircooled engine, driving a McCauley two-blade fixed-pitch metal propeller. Fuel tank in fuselage, capacity 24 Imp gallons (110 litres); optional 11 Imp gallon (50 litre) auxiliary tank. Oil capacity 1·25 Imp gallons (5·7 litres).

ACCOMMODATION: Seats for three or four persons, in pairs, up to a max weight of 340 lb (154 kg) on front pair and 275 lb (125 kg), including baggage, at rear. Otherwise as for DR 400/2+2.

SYSTEMS AND EQUIPMENT: As for DR 400/2+2.

DIMENSIONS, EXTERNAL, INTERNAL, AND WING AREA:

As DR 400/2+2, except:

Length overall	23 ft 3½ in (7·10 m)
Height overall	6 ft 9 in (2·06 m)

WEIGHTS AND LOADINGS:

Weight empty, equipped	1,191 lb (540 kg)
Max T-O and landing weight	1,984 lb (900 kg)
Max wing loading	13·56 lb/sq ft (66·2 kg/m²)
Max power loading	15·9 lb/hp (7·2 kg/hp)

PERFORMANCE (at max T-O weight):

Max never-exceed speed	166 knots (191 mph; 308 km/h)
Max level speed at S/L	129 knots (149 mph; 240 km/h)
Max cruising speed at 8,000 ft (2,440 m)	128 knots (147 mph; 238 km/h)
Econ cruising speed at 12,000 ft (3,650 m)	114 knots (132 mph; 212 km/h)
Stalling speed, flaps down	45 knots (52 mph; 83 km/h)
Stalling speed, flaps up	51 knots (58·5 mph; 94 km/h)
Max rate of climb at S/L	640 ft (195 m)/min
Service ceiling	20,000 ft (6,100 m)
T-O run	837 ft (255 m)
T-O to 50 ft (15 m)	1,755 ft (535 m)
Landing from 50 ft (15 m)	1,510 ft (460 m)
Landing run	657 ft (200 m)
Range with max fuel	593 nm (683 miles; 1,100 km)

ROBIN (CENTRE EST) DR 400/140 MAJOR

Replacing the earlier DR 340, this aircraft introduced the same type of forward-sliding canopy and low-walled cabin as other members of the Robin DR 400 series. The first DR 400/140 flew in October 1972. SGAC and CAA certification was received in December 1972. Deliveries totalled 41 by February 1974, of which 34 were delivered during 1973.

TYPE: Four-seat light monoplane.

WINGS, FUSELAGE, TAIL UNIT, LANDING GEAR: As for DR 400/2+2.

POWER PLANT: One 140 hp Lycoming O-320-E four-cylinder horizontally-opposed aircooled engine, driving a Sensenich two-blade metal fixed-pitch propeller. Otherwise as for DR 400/125.

ACCOMMODATION: Seating for four persons, on two side-by-side adjustable front seats and rear bench seat. Forward-sliding transparent canopy gives access to all seats. Up to 88 lb (40 kg) of baggage can be stowed aft of rear seats when four occupants are carried.

SYSTEMS AND EQUIPMENT: As for DR 400/2+2.

DIMENSIONS, EXTERNAL:

As for DR 400/2+2, except:

Propeller diameter	6 ft 0 in (1·83 m)

DIMENSIONS, INTERNAL: As for DR 400/2+2.

AREAS: As for DR 400/2+2, except:

Flaps (total)	7·53 sq ft (0·70 m²)

WEIGHTS AND LOADINGS:

Weight empty, equipped	1,235 lb (560 kg)
Max T-O and landing weight	2,205 lb (1,000 kg)
Max wing loading	15·05 lb/sq ft (73·5 kg/m²)
Max power loading	15·65 lb/hp (7·1 kg/hp)

PERFORMANCE (at max T-O weight):

Max never-exceed speed	166 knots (191 mph; 308 km/h)
Max level speed at S/L	141 knots (163 mph; 262 km/h)
Max cruising speed at 8,000 ft (2,440 m)	135 knots (156 mph; 251 km/h)
Econ cruising speed at 12,000 ft (3,650 m)	125 knots (144 mph; 232 km/h)
Stalling speed, flaps down	47 knots (54 mph; 87 km/h)
Stalling speed, flaps up	48 knots (55·5 mph; 89 km/h)
Max rate of climb at S/L	748 ft (228 m)/min
Service ceiling	21,000 ft (6,400 m)
T-O run	788 ft (240 m)
T-O to 50 ft (15 m)	1,805 ft (550 m)
Landing from 50 ft (15 m)	1,608 ft (490 m)
Landing run	722 ft (220 m)
Range with max fuel	491 nm (565 miles; 910 km)

ROBIN (CENTRE EST) DR 400/160 CHEVALIER

This four-seat light aircraft replaced the earlier DR 360 Major 160, described in the 1972-73 *Jane's*. It is generally similar to the DR 400 series aircraft listed earlier, but has a more powerful engine and increased fuel capacity. The first DR 400/160 flew in June 1972. It was awarded SGAC certification on 6 September 1972, and both FAA and CAA certification in December of the same year. Deliveries totalled 38 by February 1974, of which 23 were delivered in 1973.

TYPE: Four-seat light aircraft.

WINGS, FUSELAGE, TAIL UNIT, LANDING GEAR: Generally as for DR 400/2+2, but with external baggage door aft of cabin, in top of fuselage on port side.

POWER PLANT: One 160 hp Lycoming O-320-D four-cylinder horizontally-opposed aircooled engine, driving a Sensenich two-blade metal fixed-pitch propeller. Fuel tank in fuselage, capacity 24 Imp gallons (110 litres), and two tanks in wing-root leading-edges, giving total capacity of 41·75 Imp gallons (190 litres). Provision for auxiliary tank, raising total capacity to 52·75 Imp gallons (240 litres). Oil capacity 1·66 Imp gallons (7·55 litres).

ACCOMMODATION: As for DR 400/140.

DIMENSIONS AND AREAS:

As for DR 400/140, plus:

Baggage door: Height	1 ft 6½ in (0·47 m)
Width	1 ft 9½ in (0·55 m)

WEIGHTS AND LOADINGS:

Weight empty, equipped	1,301 lb (590 kg)
Max T-O and landing weight	2,315 lb (1,050 kg)
Max wing loading	15·20 lb/sq ft (74·2 kg/m²)
Max power loading	14·33 lb/hp (6·5 kg/hp)

PERFORMANCE (at max T-O weight):

Max never-exceed speed	166 knots (191 mph; 308 km/h)
Max level speed at S/L	143 knots (165 mph; 265 km/h)
Max cruising speed at 8,000 ft (2,440 m)	137 knots (157 mph; 254 km/h)
Econ cruising speed at 12,000 ft (3,650 m)	127 knots (146 mph; 236 km/h)
Stalling speed, flaps down	50 knots (58 mph; 93 km/h)
Stalling speed, flaps up	56 knots (64 mph; 103 km/h)
Max rate of climb at S/L	925 ft (282 m)/min
Service ceiling	15,000 ft (4,575 m)
T-O run	1,017 ft (310 m)
T-O to 50 ft (15 m)	2,034 ft (620 m)
Landing from 50 ft (15 m)	1,788 ft (545 m)
Landing run	820 ft (250 m)
Range with max fuel	863 nm (994 miles; 1,600 km)

Robin DR 400/180 Régent (180 hp Lycoming O-360-A engine) *(Air Portraits)*

ROBIN (CENTRE EST) DR 400/180 RÉGENT

First flown in May 1972, this most powerful, four/five-seat member of the wooden DR 400 series replaced the earlier DR 253 Régent and DR 380 Prince. It received SGAC certification on 10 May 1972, and both FAA and CAA certification in December 1972. Deliveries totalled 49 by February 1974, of which 29 were delivered in 1973.

The DR 400/180 is generally similar to the DR 400/160 Chevalier, except in the following details:

Power Plant: One 180 hp Lycoming O-360-A four-cylinder horizontally-opposed aircooled engine. Propeller and fuel tankage as for DR 400/160.

Accommodation: Basically as for DR 400/160, but optional seating for three persons on rear bench seat.

Dimensions and Areas:
As for DR 400/160, except:
Length overall 23 ft 6¾ in (7·18 m)
Propeller diameter 6 ft 4 in (1·93 m)

Weights and Loadings:
Weight empty, equipped 1,301 lb (590 kg)
Max T-O and landing weight 2,425 lb (1,100 kg)
Max wing loading 15·91 lb/sq ft (77·7 kg/m²)
Max power loading 13·45 lb/hp (6·1 kg/hp)

Performance (at max T-O weight):
Max never-exceed speed 166 knots (191 mph; 308 km/h)
Max level speed at S/L 149 knots (171 mph; 276 km/h)
Max cruising speed at 8,000 ft (2,440 m) 143 knots (164 mph; 265 km/h)
Econ cruising speed at 12,000 ft (3,650 m) 134 knots (155 mph; 249 km/h)
Stalling speed, flaps down 51·5 knots (59 mph; 95 km/h)
Stalling speed, flaps up 56·5 knots (65 mph; 105 km/h)
Max rate of climb at S/L 825 ft (252 m)/min
Service ceiling 20,000 ft (6,100 m)
T-O run 1,035 ft (315 m)
T-O to 50 ft (15 m) 2,000 ft (610 m)
Landing from 50 ft (15 m) 1,740 ft (530 m)
Landing run 817 ft (249 m)
Range with max fuel 793 nm (913 miles; 1,470 km)

ROBIN (CENTRE EST) DR 400/180R REMORQUEUR

The DR 400/180R is a member of the DR 400 range designed for use as a glider-towing aircraft, although it can also be flown as a normal four-seat tourer. The prototype first flew in November 1972 and received SGAC certification on the 28th of that month. Deliveries totalled 28 by February 1974, of which 24 were delivered in 1973. Details are generally the same as for the DR 400/180 Régent, except for the following items:

Fuselage: No external baggage door.

Power Plant: One 180 hp Lycoming O-360-A four-cylinder horizontally-opposed aircooled engine, driving (for glider-towing) a Sensenich 76 EM 8S5 058 two-blade propeller. For touring operation a Sensenich 76 EM 8S5 064 propeller of the same diameter is fitted. Fuel capacity as for DR 400/2+2.

Weights and Loadings:
Weight empty, equipped 1,279 lb (580 kg)
Max T-O and landing weight 2,205 lb (1,000 kg)
Max wing loading 15·05 lb/sq ft (73·5 kg/m²)
Max power loading 12·35 lb/hp (5·6 kg/hp)

Performance (glider tug, at max T-O weight):
Max never-exceed speed 166 knots (191 mph; 308 km/h)
Max level speed at S/L 124 knots (143 mph; 230 km/h)
Max cruising speed at 8,000 ft (2,440 m) 124 knots (143 mph; 230 km/h)
Econ cruising speed at 12,000 ft (3,650 m) 122 knots (140 mph; 226 km/h)
Stalling speed, flaps down 47 knots (54 mph; 87 km/h)
Stalling speed, flaps up 53·5 knots (61·5 mph; 99 km/h)
Max rate of climb at S/L 1,102 ft (336 m)/min
Service ceiling 25,000 ft (7,620 m)
T-O run 673 ft (205 m)
T-O to 50 ft (15 m) 1,313 ft (400 m)
Landing from 50 ft (15 m) 1,542 ft (470 m)
Landing run 722 ft (220 m)

ROBIN (CENTRE EST) HR 100/210 ROYAL

Some years ago Avions Pierre Robin began studies with a view to the eventual production of an all-metal light aircraft similar in concept to its original range of wooden designs. As a part of this programme, the prototype DR 253 Régent was flown in late 1967 with all-metal wings, and construction of an all-metal prototype aircraft was begun in 1968.

This prototype (F-WPXO), designated HR 100, flew for the first time on 3 April 1969. In 1970 three pre-production aircraft were built, and manufacture of the initial production version, the HR 100/200 with 200 hp Lycoming IO-360-A1D6 engine, began in January 1971. About 30 HR 100/200s were built.

A description of the HR 100/200 appeared in the 1972-73 *Jane's*; that which follows applies to the current HR 100/210, of which production started at the end of 1972. Deliveries totalled 54 by February 1974, of which 37 were delivered in 1973.

Robin HR 100/210 Royal four-seat all-metal light aircraft (210 hp Continental IO-360-D engine)

Type: Four-seat light aircraft.

Wings: Cantilever low-wing monoplane. Wing section NACA 64 series (modified), with max thickness at 45% chord. Constant chord over most of span. Thickness/chord ratio 15%. Dihedral 6° 20′ from roots. No sweepback. All-metal single-spar structure, attached to fuselage by four bolts on each side. Outer skin of flush-riveted Duralinox-Cégédur aluminium alloy. Wingtips, which incorporate navigation and landing lights, are of polyester. All-metal trailing-edge slotted flaps are actuated electrically and have a max setting of 30°. All-metal Frise-type ailerons each have a piano-type hinge on the upper surface; they are controlled by rods and cables.

Fuselage: All-metal box-girder load-bearing structure, covered mainly with flush-riveted Duralinox-Cégédur aluminium alloy. Top-decking, between engine firewall and front of cabin, and from rear of cabin to fin, is of polyester; the forward panels are removable to provide easy access to instruments and controls.

Tail Unit: Cantilever structure, of similar construction to wings, with slight sweepback on fin and rudder. One-piece single-spar all-moving tailplane, with mass-balance and anti-tab. Rudder and tailplane cable-controlled.

Landing Gear: Non-retractable tricycle type, with oleo-pneumatic shock-absorbers. Nosewheel leg is offset to starboard. Single wheel on each unit; all wheels and tyres same size, 420 × 150. Tyre pressures 28·4 lb/sq in (2·0 kg/cm²) on nosewheel, 31·3 lb/sq in (2·2 kg/cm²) on main units. Streamlined leg and wheel fairings on all units. Hydraulic disc brakes.

Power Plant: One 210 hp Continental IO-360-D six-cylinder horizontally-opposed aircooled engine, driving a Hartzell BHC-J2Y-F1-76-63 two-blade constant-speed propeller. Hoffmann three-blade constant-speed propeller optional. Fuel in 25 Imp gallon (113 litre) flexible tank in each leading-edge; total capacity 50 Imp gallons (226 litres). Provision for two auxiliary tanks to double this capacity. Refuelling point above each tank.

Accommodation: Seating for four persons, in pairs, under transparent canopy which slides forward to provide access to all seats. Individual adjustable front seats; bench seat at rear. Baggage space aft of rear seats, accessible internally or by upward-opening external door on port side. Cabin ventilated.

Electronics and Equipment: VHF radio, VOR, navigation and landing lights, and rotating anti-collision beacon standard. Provision for installing full IFR equipment, including autopilot.

Dimensions, external:
Wing span 29 ft 9½ in (9·08 m)
Wing chord (constant) 5 ft 3¼ in (1·61 m)
Length overall 24 ft 3 in (7·39 m)
Height overall 7 ft 5 in (2·26 m)
Tailplane span 10 ft 6 in (3·20 m)
Wheel track 10 ft 6 in (3·20 m)
Wheelbase 5 ft 9¾ in (1·77 m)
Propeller diameter 6 ft 1¾ in (1·87 m)

Area:
Wings, gross 163·6 sq ft (15·2 m²)

Weights and Loadings:
Weight empty 1,565 lb (710 kg)
Max T-O weight 2,755 lb (1,250 kg)
Max wing loading 16·85 lb/sq ft (82·3 kg/m²)
Max power loading 13·12 lb/hp (5·95 kg/hp)

Performance (at max T-O weight):
Max never-exceed speed 175 knots (202 mph; 325 km/h)
Max cruising speed (75% power) at S/L 137 knots (158 mph; 254 km/h)
Max cruising speed (75% power) at 8,000 ft (2,440 m) 146 knots (168 mph; 270 km/h)
Max rate of climb at S/L 1,000 ft (305 m)/min
Service ceiling 16,400 ft (5,000 m)
Max range at 8,000 ft (2,440 m), 75% power:
standard fuel 739 nm (850 miles; 1,370 km)
auxiliary fuel 1,457 nm (1,675 miles; 2,700 km)

ROBIN (CENTRE EST) HR 100/210R ROYAL

This aircraft was intended to differ from the HR 100/210 only in having a retractable tricycle landing gear. Further work on the project has been cancelled.

ROBIN (CENTRE EST) HR 100/235

This aircraft is identical to the HR 100/Tiara, except for having a 235 hp Lycoming O-540-B six-cylinder horizontally-opposed aircooled engine. The prototype (F-WVKA) flew for the first time on 6 March 1974.

Dimensions:
As for HR 100/Tiara, except:
Length overall 24 ft 11¼ in (7·60 m)

Weights and Loadings:
Weight empty 1,851 lb (840 kg)
Max T-O weight 3,020 lb (1,370 kg)
Max wing loading 18·6 lb/sq ft (90·7 kg/m²)
Max power loading 12·85 lb/hp (5·83 kg/hp)

Performance (at max T-O weight):
Max level speed at S/L 162 knots (186 mph; 300 km/h)
Max cruising speed (75% power) at 7,000 ft (2,135 m) 154 knots (178 mph; 286 km/h)
Max rate of climb at S/L 1,005 ft (306 m)/min
Range with max fuel 1,456 nm (1,677 miles; 2,700 km)

ROBIN (CENTRE EST) HR 100/TIARA

This was the first Robin light aircraft to be built with a retractable landing gear. Design began in September 1971 as a further major development stage beyond the HR 100/210, with new vertical tail surfaces, a redesigned wing structure, and a Teledyne Continental Tiara engine. Construction of the prototype (F-WSQV) was started in April 1972 and the first flight was made on 18 November 1972. Certification was expected by April 1974, when the HR 100/Tiara was scheduled to enter production.

The prototype has a 320 hp engine, but production HR 100/Tiaras have a 285 hp engine until the more powerful 6-320 has been certificated. Orders include six for use by the Secrétariat Général a l'Aviation Civile (SGAC) and Service de la Formation Aéronautique (SFA); and one for the Direction des Transports Aériens (DTA).

Type: Four/five-seat all-metal light aircraft.

Wings: Cantilever low-wing monoplane. Wing section NACA 64A515 (modified). Dihedral 6° 18′ from roots. Incidence 4° 41′. No sweepback. Aluminium alloy single-spar structure of constant chord. All-metal Frise-type ailerons and NACA slotted flaps. No tabs.

Fuselage: Aluminium alloy semi-monocoque structure in cabin section. Rear fuselage top decking and engine cowling are of non-stressed polyester.

Tail Unit: Cantilever structure, similar to wings in construction. Sweptback vertical surfaces. One-piece all-moving horizontal surfaces, with automatic anti-tab inboard on each trailing-edge. Trim tab in rudder.

Landing Gear: Retractable tricycle type, with single wheel on each unit. Electro-hydraulic retraction. Nosewheel protrudes slightly when retracted, to reduce damage in a wheels-up landing. Oleo-pneumatic shock-absorbers. Main-wheel tyres size 420 × 150 or 6·50-3, pressure 31·5 lb/sq in (2·2 kg/cm²). Nosewheel tyre size 330 × 130 or 5·00-5. Hydraulic disc brakes.

Power Plant: Prototype has one 320 hp Teledyne Continental Tiara 6-320 six-cylinder horizontally-opposed aircooled engine, driving a Hoffmann three-blade constant-speed metal propeller. Initial production aircraft will have a 285 hp Tiara 6-285B. Four fuel tanks in wings, each with capacity of 25 Imp gallons (113 litres). Total fuel capacity 100 Imp gallons (452 litres).

Accommodation: Two persons side by side in individual front seats. Rear bench seat for two or three passengers. Access via forward-sliding canopy. Baggage space aft of rear seats, accessible internally or by upward-opening external door on port side.

Electronics and Equipment: VHF radio, VOR, navigation and landing lights, and rotating anti-collision beacon at top of fin standard. Provision for installing full IFR equipment, including autopilot.

Dimensions, external:
Wing span 29 ft 9½ in (9·08 m)
Wing chord (constant) 5 ft 6 in (1·675 m)
Wing aspect ratio 5·36
Length overall 24 ft 10¾ in (7·59 m)
Height overall 6 ft 8¼ in (2·04 m)
Tailplane span 10 ft 10 in (3·20 m)
Wheel track 10 ft 7 in (3·225 m)
Wheelbase 7 ft 1 in (2·16 m)
Propeller diameter 6 ft 6¾ in (2·00 m)
Propeller ground clearance 1 ft 1¼ in (0·34 m)

Dimensions, internal:
Cabin: Length 9 ft 2 in (2·80 m)
Max width 3 ft 8 in (1·115 m)
Max height 3 ft 11¼ in (1·20 m)

Areas:
Wings, gross 163·6 sq ft (15·2 m²)
Ailerons, total 10·98 sq ft (1·02 m²)
Trailing-edge flaps, total 16·68 sq ft (1·55 m²)
Fin 10·93 sq ft (1·015 m²)
Rudder 7·21 sq ft (0·67 m²)
Tailplane, incl tabs 29·71 sq ft (2·76 m²)

Weights and Loadings (6-320 engine):
Weight empty 1,764 lb (800 kg)
Max T-O weight 3,086 lb (1,400 kg)
Max wing loading 18·86 lb/sq ft (92·1 kg/m²)
Max power loading 9·65 lb/hp (4·38 kg/hp)

Weights and Loadings (6-285B engine):
Weight empty 1,852 lb (840 kg)
Max T-O weight 3,086 lb (1,400 kg)
Max wing loading 18·86 lb/sq ft (92·1 kg/m²)
Max power loading 10·82 lb/hp (4·91 kg/hp)

Performance (at max T-O weight, with 6-320 engine):
Max level speed at S/L 186 knots (214 mph; 345 km/h)
Max cruising speed at 7,000 ft (2,135 m) 172 knots (199 mph; 320 km/h)
Stalling speed, flaps down 59·5 knots (68·5 mph; 110 km/h)
Max rate of climb at S/L 1,770 ft (540 m)/min
Service ceiling over 19,700 ft (6,000 m)
T-O run 952 ft (290 m)
T-O to 50 ft (15 m) 1,772 ft (540 m)
Landing from 50 ft (15 m) 2,166 ft (660 m)
Landing run 1,150 ft (350 m)
Range with max fuel, three persons and 110 lb (50 kg) baggage 1,240 nm (1,430 miles; 2,300 km)
Range with four persons and 132 lb (60 kg) baggage 865 nm (994 miles; 1,600 km)

Performance (at max T-O weight, with 6-285B engine):
Max level speed at S/L 172 knots (199 mph; 320 km/h)
Max cruising speed (75% power) at 7,000 ft (2,135 m) 165 knots (190 mph; 305 km/h)
Cruising speed (55% power) at 10,000 ft (3,050 m) 148 knots (171 mph; 275 km/h)
Max rate of climb at S/L 1,180 ft (360 m)/min
Range with max fuel 1,348 nm (1,553 miles; 2,500 km)

ROBIN (CENTRE EST) HR 100/4+2

Scheduled to fly before the end of 1974, this aircraft is designed to carry six persons with 52·8 Imp gallons (240 litres) of fuel and no baggage, or four persons with 88 Imp gallons (400 litres) of fuel and 99 lb (45 kg) of baggage.

The wings, tail unit and landing gear are identical to those of the HR 100/Tiara, as is the forward part of the fuselage. The lengthened rear fuselage is entirely different, being a conventional metal structure, with frames and stringers, and without any plastics components. The standard power plant is a 320 hp Teledyne Continental Tiara 6-320 six-cylinder horizontally-opposed aircooled engine, but a 285 hp 6-285B is a suitable alternative.

Dimensions:
As for HR 100/Tiara, except:
Length overall 25 ft 10¾ in (7·89 m)

Weights and Loadings:
Weight empty 1,918 lb (870 kg)
Max T-O weight 3,307 lb (1,500 kg)
Max wing loading 20·3 lb/sq ft (99·3 kg/m²)
Max power loading 10·32 lb/hp (4·68 kg/hp)

Performance (estimated, at max T-O weight, with 6-320 engine):
Max level speed at S/L 180 knots (207 mph; 333 km/h)
Cruising speed:
75% power at 7,000 ft (2,135 m) 172 knots (198 mph; 318 km/h)
65% power at 10,000 ft (3,050 m) 165 knots (190 mph; 305 km/h)
55% power at 10,000 ft (3,050 m) 151 knots (174 mph; 280 km/h)

Robin HR 100/Tiara prototype (320 hp Teledyne Continental Tiara 6-320 engine) (*Photo-Zoom*)

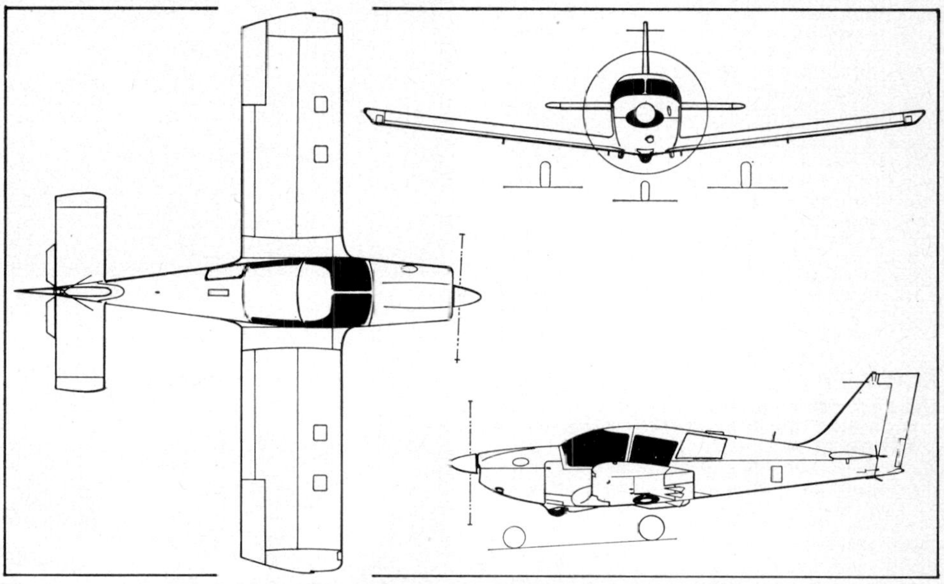

Robin HR 100/Tiara four/five-seat all-metal light aircraft (*Roy J. Grainge*)

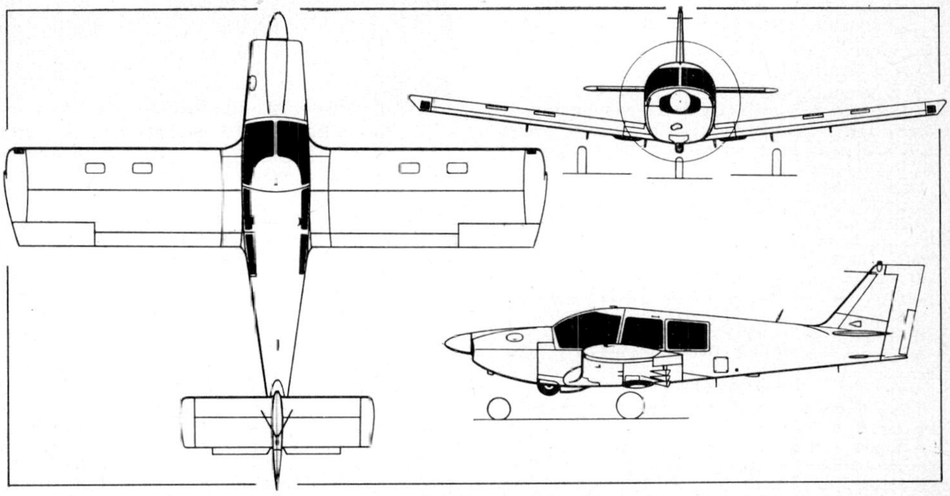

Robin HR 100/4+2 four/six-seat light aircraft (*Pilot Press*)

Stalling speed, flaps down 60 knots (69 mph; 111 km/h)
Max rate of climb at S/L 1,180 ft (360 m)/min
Range with six persons and 240 litres fuel, no reserve:
75% power 588 nm (677 miles; 1,090 km)
55% power 690 nm (795 miles; 1,280 km)
Range with four persons, baggage and 400 litres fuel, no reserve:
75% power 980 nm (1,129 miles; 1,817 km)
55% power 1,160 nm (1,336 miles; 2,150 km)
Max range with 97 Imp gallons (440 litres) fuel, no reserve 1,267 nm (1,460 miles; 2,350 km)

ROBIN (CENTRE EST) HR 200

Although this all-metal two-seat aircraft bears an external resemblance to the HR 100/210, it is an entirely separate design of smaller overall dimensions, intended specifically for clubs and flying schools. Design was started in September 1970. Construction of the prototype began in December 1970 and this aircraft flew for the first time on 30 July 1971.

There are four current versions, as follows:

HR 200/100. Basic version, as described in detail below, with 108 hp Lycoming O-235-H2C engine. Nine delivered by February 1974.

HR 200/120. Version with 125 hp O-235-J2A engine. Five delivered by February 1974.

HR 200/140. Version with 140 hp Lycoming O-320-E engine.

HR 200/160. Version with 160 hp Lycoming IO-320-D engine. One delivered by February 1974.

A fully-aerobatic version of the HR 200 was scheduled to be tested in 1974.

Type: Two-seat light training aircraft.

Wings: Cantilever low-wing monoplane. Wing section NACA 64A515 (modified). Constant chord. Dihedral 6° 18′ from roots. Incidence 6°. No sweepback. All-metal construction, with I-section spar at 40% chord, aluminium stressed skin and ribs; no stringers. Plain Frise-type ailerons, piano-hinged to upper surface; aerodynamically and statically balanced, and cable-operated. Plain trailing-edge flaps, piano-hinged to lower surface and actuated electrically.

Fuselage: Conventional aluminium stressed-skin structure of basic rectangular section with rounded top-decking.

Tail Unit: Cantilever structure, similar to wings in construction. One-piece all-moving horizontal surface of constant chord, with trim and anti-servo tabs. Slightly-swept vertical fin and rudder with aerodynamic balance in upper leading-edge of rudder. Control surfaces aerodynamically and statically balanced, and cable-operated.

Landing Gear: Non-retractable tricycle type, with low-pressure oleo-pneumatic shock-absorbers. Single wheel on each unit; all wheels and tyres same size, 380 × 150. Steerable nosewheel on leg offset to starboard. Hydraulic brakes. Streamlined leg and wheel fairings on all units.

Power Plant: One 108 hp Lycoming O-235-H2C four-cylinder horizontally-opposed engine, driving a McCauley two-blade metal fixed-pitch propeller. Single fuel tank in fuselage, capacity 26·5 Imp gallons (120 litres). Refuelling point in port side of fuselage.

Accommodation: Pilot and passenger side by side, normally on bench seat but with optional individual adjustable seats. Forward-sliding Plexiglas canopy. Room for 55 lb (25 kg) of baggage at rear of cabin.

Systems: Cabin ventilated and heated, with windscreen defrosting standard. Electrical system includes a 12V battery, alternator and starter.

Electronics and Equipment: To customer's requirements.

Dimension, external:
- Wing span — 27 ft 4 in (8·33 m)
- Wing chord (constant) — 4 ft 11 in (1·50 m)
- Length overall — 21 ft 9½ in (6·64 m)
- Height overall — 7 ft 1¾ in (2·18 m)
- Tailplane span — 8 ft 8 in (2·64 m)
- Wheel track — 9 ft 5½ in (2·88 m)
- Wheelbase — 4 ft 10¾ in (1·49 m)
- Propeller diameter — 6 ft 0 in (1·83 m)
- Propeller ground clearance — 10¼ in (26 cm)

Dimension, internal:
- Cabin: Max width — 3 ft 6 in (1·06 m)

Areas:
- Wings, gross — 135·6 sq ft (12·6 m²)
- Ailerons, total — 11·41 sq ft (1·06 m²)
- Trailing-edge flaps, total — 14·42 sq ft (1·34 m²)
- Elevators, incl tabs — 21·85 sq ft (2·03 m²)

Weights (HR 200/100):
- Weight empty, equipped — 1,135 lb (515 kg)
- Max T-O weight — 1,719 lb (780 kg)

Performance (HR 200/100):
- Max never-exceed speed — 178 knots (205 mph; 330 km/h)
- Max level speed — 124 knots (143 mph; 230 km/h)
- Max cruising speed (75% power) at S/L — 116 knots (133 mph; 215 km/h)
- Stalling speed, flaps down — 46·5 knots (53·5 mph; 86 km/h)
- Max rate of climb at S/L — 710 ft (216 m)/min
- Service ceiling — 12,950 ft (3,950 m)
- Range with max fuel — 582 nm (671 miles; 1,080 km)

Robin HR 200/100 (108 hp Lycoming O-235-H2C engine)

SOCATA

SOCIÉTÉ DE CONSTRUCTION D'AVIONS DE TOURISME ET D'AFFAIRES (Subsidiary of AÉROSPATIALE)

Head Office, Works and After-Sales Service:
Aéroport de Tarbes-Ossun-Lourdes, BP 38, 65001-Tarbes
Telephone: (62) 93-97-30
Telex: 52828

Sales:
37 Boulevard de Montmorency, 75781-Paris Cédex 16
Telephone: 525-54-32
Telex: 62059 AIRSPA

Chairman:
Henri Ziegler

This company was formed in 1966, as a subsidiary of Sud-Aviation. It handles development and production of the various versions of the Rallye three/four-seat light aircraft and the four-seat ST 10 Diplomate.

During 1973, Socata sold 302 aircraft of all types, 50 per cent of them for export.

Socata also produces components for the Concorde and A-300 Airbus; the Super Frelon, Puma and Alouette helicopters; and the Corvette and Falcon 10 and 20 business jets. It is responsible for overhaul and repair of MS 760 Paris aircraft.

Socata's works cover an area of 475,230 sq ft (44,150 m²) and employ about 900 people.

SOCATA RALLYE

The Rallye had its origin in a competition organised by the SFATAT in 1958 and was developed originally by the old-established Morane-Saulnier company. The prototype (90 hp MS 880A) Rallye-Club flew on 10 June 1959, and went into production as the MS 880B and the MS 885 Super Rallye. FAA certification of the design was obtained on 21 November 1961.

Production of the MS 885 (212 built) and MS 890 (8 built) with 145 hp Continental engine, MS 881 (12 built) with 105 hp Potez engine, MS 883 (77 built) with 115 hp Lycoming engine and MS 886 (3 built) with 150 hp Lycoming engine has ended.

The current GT models have a new external appearance and greatly improved cabin comfort, as the result of a modernisation programme undertaken at the beginning of 1972. New features include dual wheel control, together with improved aileron efficiency; electrically-controlled flaps offering all positions from 0° to 30°, with two notches preset at 8° and 30°; and a central console grouping the engine controls (throttle, propeller governor and mixture) and the trim and air-conditioning controls in such a way that they are accessible to both pilots. Model GT Rallyes can be fitted with IFR and night flying equipment, following receipt of SGAC approval in June 1973.

Socata Rallye 100 S aerobatic light aircraft supplied to the French Navy Training School at Lanvéoc-Poulmic

The 1974 range of Rallyes is as follows:

Rallye 100 S (=Sport). First flown on 30 March 1973, this version is equipped as a two-seater and is the only aircraft in the Rallye series cleared for spinning. Generally similar to the Rallye 100 T, it received SGAC certification on 6 April 1973. A total of 44 had been built by 1 January 1974. Ten delivered to French Navy Training School at Lanvéoc-Poulmic in April 1974.

Rallye 100 T (=Tourisme). Basic 3/4-seat model with 100 hp Rolls-Royce Continental O-200-A engine and fixed-pitch propeller. Prototype flew on 12 February 1961. Production of a new series, with electrically-controlled wing flaps and more comfortable cabin, was started in 1973. Total of 892 built by 1 January 1974.

Rallye 125. Four-seat version of the Rallye 100 T with 125 hp Lycoming O-235-F2A engine and fixed-pitch propeller. Prototype flew for the first time on 10 February 1972. Rallye 125 received SGAC certification on 31 May 1972, and is in current production.

Rallye 150 GT. Four-seat version with 150 hp Lycoming O-320-E2A engine and fixed-pitch propeller, strengthened structure for increased AUW, larger rudder, larger ailerons, fillets of increased size between wing trailing-edges and fuselage, longer nosewheel leg to give increased propeller clearance, enlarged dorsal fin fairing, modified cockpit canopy and a baggage compartment. Streamlined wheel fairings optional. Prototype flew for the first time on 6 February 1964. Total of 298 built by 1 January 1974.

Rallye 180 GT. Basically similar to 150 GT, but with 180 hp Lycoming O-360-A2A engine and fixed-pitch or constant-speed propeller, giving extra power for duties such as agricultural spraying and dusting, glider and banner towing. Prototype flew for first time on 7 December 1964. French type approval received on 27 April 1965; FAA type approval on 23 June 1971. Total of 531 built by 1 January 1974; 100 ordered by the SFA for duty as glider tugs at French gliding centres.

Rallye 220 GT. Generally similar to 180 GT, but with 220 hp Franklin 6A-350-C1 six-cylinder horizontally-opposed aircooled engine and constant-speed propeller. Prototype first flown on 12 May 1967. Received FAA Type Approval 29 April 1968. Total of 250 built by 1 January 1974.

The Rallye 150 GT, 180 GT and 220 GT are authorised for use as ambulance aircraft carrying a pilot, one stretcher patient and medical attendant. They can also be used for glider towing. Agricultural spraygear can be fitted and tests have been conducted with various models on ski landing gear.

The 2,000th Rallye, a Rallye 220, was delivered on 25 April 1972. Of those sold to date, some 400 are employed in the glider-towing role, including more than 250 in France.

The following details apply to all versions listed above:

Type: Two/four-seat light monoplane.

Wings: Cantilever mid-wing monoplane. Wing section NACA 63A416 (modified). Dihedral 7°. Incidence 4°. All-metal single-spar structure. Wide-chord slotted ailerons. Full-span automatic slats. Long-span slotted flaps. Ailerons and flaps have corrugated metal skin.

Fuselage: All-metal monocoque structure.

Tail Unit: Cantilever all-metal structure with corrugated skin on the mass-balanced control surfaces. Large trim tab on elevator.

LANDING GEAR: Non-retractable tricycle type. ERAM oleo-pneumatic shock-absorbers. Castoring nosewheel. Cleveland hydraulic disc brakes. Provision for fitting skis or floats.

POWER PLANT: One 4/6-cylinder horizontally-opposed aircooled engine (details under entries for individual models above), driving a two-blade fixed-pitch or constant-speed metal propeller. Fuel in two tanks in wings, capacity 21 Imp gallons (96 litres) in Rallye 100 and 125, 37·5 Imp gallons (170 litres) in Rallye 150 and 180, and 48 Imp gallons (220 litres) in Rallye 220. Oil capacity 1·3 Imp gallons (6·0 litres) in Rallye 100 and 125, 1·75 Imp gallons (8 litres) in Rallye 150 and 180, 1·8 Imp gallons (8·3 litres) in Rallye 220.

ACCOMMODATION: Two seats side by side in the Rallye 100 S. All other versions have also a bench seat at rear, under large rearward-sliding canopy. Two persons up to a total weight of 242 lb (110 kg) can occupy rear seat of Rallye 100 T. Other versions are full four-seaters. Dual control columns on Rallye 100 and 125. Dual control wheels on Rallye 150, 180 and 220. Individual adjustable front seats and baggage space aft of rear seats (accessible internally) on the GT models. Heating and ventilation standard.

ELECTRONICS AND EQUIPMENT: The instrument panel is fitted with an anti-glare visor, and is designed to take full radio-navigation equipment to customer's requirements.

DIMENSIONS, EXTERNAL:
Wing span 31 ft 6¼ in (9·61 m)
Wing chord (constant) 4 ft 3 in (1·30 m)
Wing aspect ratio 7·57
Length overall:
100 22 ft 10½ in (6·97 m)
125 23 ft 5¾ in (7·16 m)
150, 180 23 ft 9 in (7·24 m)
220 23 ft 9½ in (7·25 m)
Height overall:
100 T, 125 8 ft 6¼ in (2·60 m)
100 S, 150, 180, 220 9 ft 2¼ in (2·80 m)
Tailplane span 12 ft 0½ in (3·67 m)
Wheel track 6 ft 6½ in (2·00 m)

DIMENSIONS, INTERNAL:
Cabin:
Length 7 ft 4 in (2·25 m)
Width 3 ft 8½ in (1·13 m)

AREAS:
Wings, gross 132 sq ft (12·30 m²)
Vertical tail surfaces 14·96 sq ft (1·39 m²)
Horizontal tail surfaces 37·50 sq ft (3·48 m²)

WEIGHTS:
Weight empty, equipped:
100 992 lb (450 kg)
125 1,125 lb (510 kg)
150 1,213 lb (550 kg)
180 1,257 lb (570 kg)
220 1,389 lb (630 kg)
Max T-O weight:
100 S 1,653 lb (750 kg)
100 T 1,697 lb (770 kg)
125 1,852 lb (840 kg)
150 2,160 lb (980 kg)
180 2,315 lb (1,050 kg)
220 2,425 lb (1,100 kg)

PERFORMANCE (at max T-O weight):
Max never-exceed speed:
100 S 145 knots (167 mph; 270 km/h)
Max level speed at S/L:
100, 125 105 knots (121 mph; 195 km/h)
150 113 knots (130 mph; 210 km/h)
180 129 knots (149 mph; 240 km/h)
220 143 knots (165 mph; 266 km/h)
Cruising speed (75% power) at 5,000 ft (1,500 m):
100 S 94 knots (109 mph; 175 km/h)
100 T 92 knots (105 mph; 170 km/h)
125 97 knots (112 mph; 180 km/h)
150 107 knots (123 mph; 198 km/h)
180 121 knots (139 mph; 224 km/h)
220 132 knots (152 mph; 245 km/h)
Stalling speed, flaps down:
100 41 knots (47 mph; 75 km/h)
125 44 knots (50 mph; 80 km/h)
150 49 knots (56 mph; 90 km/h)
180 50 knots (57·5 mph; 92 km/h)
220 52 knots (59·5 mph; 95 km/h)
Max rate of climb at S/L:
100 S 580 ft (177 m)/min
100 T 541 ft (165 m)/min
125 561 ft (171 m)/min
150 630 ft (192 m)/min
180 787 ft (240 m)/min
220 984 ft (300 m)/min
Service ceiling:
100 S 11,480 ft (3,500 m)
100 T 10,500 ft (3,200 m)
125 8,530 ft (2,600 m)
150 9,840 ft (3,000 m)
180 11,150 ft (3,400 m)
220 13,125 ft (4,000 m)
T-O run:
100 S, 220 393 ft (120 m)
100 T 430 ft (130 m)
125, 150 459 ft (140 m)
180 443 ft (135 m)
Landing run:
100, 220 328 ft (100 m)
125, 150, 180 410 ft (125 m)

Socata Rallye 220 GT with four gliders in tow

Socata Rallye 220 GT equipped for air ambulance duties

Socata ST 10 Diplomate four-seat light aircraft (200 hp Lycoming IO-360-C1B engine)

Range with max fuel:
100 S 405 nm (465 miles; 750 km)
100 T 395 nm (455 miles; 730 km)
125 400 nm (460 miles; 740 km)
150 550 nm (635 miles; 1,020 km)
180 565 nm (650 miles; 1,050 km)
220 860 nm (995 miles; 1,600 km)

SOCATA ST 10 DIPLOMATE

The ST 10 was designed by Socata and was based on a certain number of components common to the earlier GY-80 Horizon, from which it differs chiefly in having a longer fuselage and redesigned cabin. A prototype (F-WOFR), known for a time as the Provence, was flown for the first time on 7 November 1967.

Early in 1969, it was modified to flight test refinements that are standard on production aircraft, including a longer fuselage, a reduction in tailplane span, an increase in rudder area and a shallow "keel" beneath the rear fuselage. In this form the Diplomate received type approval by the SGAC on 26 November 1969. Fifty-six had been delivered by February 1974.

TYPE: Four-seat light cabin monoplane.

WINGS: Cantilever low-wing monoplane. Wing section NACA 4413-6 (modified) at root and NACA 62A-517 (modified) at tip. Dihedral 7°. Incidence 5° at root, 2° 30′ at tip. All-metal single-spar structure with rear auxiliary spar. Entire trailing-edge made up of two Frise-type slotted ailerons and four electrically-operated Fowler flaps of all-metal construction. Ailerons and flaps are interchangeable port/starboard.

FUSELAGE: All-metal structure. Forward section has welded steel-tube structure. Rear section is light alloy semi-monocoque.

TAIL UNIT: Cantilever all-metal structure. All-moving horizontal surfaces with full-span anti-tab. Fin and tailplane halves are interchangeable.

LANDING GEAR: Retractable tricycle type, with single wheel on each unit. Steerable nose-wheel. Electric retraction; nosewheel retracts rearward to lie semi-recessed in fuselage; main wheels retract inward into wings. Oleo-pneumatic shock-absorbers. All three wheels and tyres size 15 × 6·00-6. Main-wheel tyre pressure 31·3 lb/sq in (2·2 kg/cm^2), nose-wheel tyre pressure 25·6 lb/sq in (1·8 kg/cm^2). Parking brake and hydraulically-operated disc brakes.

POWER PLANT: One 200 hp Lycoming IO-360-C1B four-cylinder horizontally-opposed aircooled engine, driving a Hartzell two-blade constant-speed metal propeller. Two fuel tanks in wing-root leading-edges, with total capacity of 44 Imp gallons (200 litres). Oil capacity 1·75 Imp gallons (8 litres).

ACCOMMODATION: Side-by-side adjustable seats for pilot and co-pilot or passenger, with bench seat at rear for two more persons. Dual controls standard. Space for 154 lb (70 kg) of baggage aft of rear seat. Large cabin door and baggage compartment door on starboard side. Cabin heating, ventilation and windscreen de-frosting standard.

ELECTRONICS AND EQUIPMENT: Blind-flying instrumentation standard. Optional equipment includes VHF and HF radio, VOR, ILS, ADF and night-flying equipment. 12V 35Ah battery and 12V 70A alternator.

DIMENSIONS, EXTERNAL:
Wing span 31 ft 9⅞ in (9·70 m)
Wing chord at root 5 ft 8¾ in (1·75 m)
Wing chord at tip 3 ft 3¼ in (1·00 m)
Wing aspect ratio 7·1
Length overall 23 ft 9¾ in (7·26 m)
Height overall 9 ft 5½ in (2·88 m)
Tailplane span 10 ft 4½ in (3·16 m)
Wheel track 9 ft 2¼ in (2·80 m)
Wheelbase 5 ft 9⅝ in (1·77 m)
Propeller diameter 6 ft 2¾ in (1·90 m)

DIMENSIONS, INTERNAL:
Cabin: Length 7 ft 4⅝ in (2·25 m)
Max width 3 ft 8⅞ in (1·14 m)
Max height 4 ft 1¼ in (1·25 m)

AREAS:
Wings, gross 139·93 sq ft (13·00 m^2)
Ailerons (total) 7·96 sq ft (0·74 m^2)
Trailing-edge flaps (total) 15·93 sq ft (1·48 m^2)
Fin 12·92 sq ft (1·20 m^2)
Rudder 5·17 sq ft (0·48 m^2)
Horizontal tail surfaces (total) 29·17 sq ft (2·71 m^2)

WEIGHTS:
Weight empty, equipped 1,594 lb (723 kg)
Max T-O weight 2,690 lb (1,220 kg)

PERFORMANCE (at max T-O weight):
Max level speed at S/L 151 knots (174 mph; 280 km/h)
Cruising speed (75% power) 143 knots (165 mph; 265 km/h)
Stalling speed, flaps down 55 knots (63 mph; 100 km/h)
Max rate of climb at S/L 1,003 ft (306 m)/min
Service ceiling 16,400 ft (5,000 m)
T-O run 886 ft (270 m)
Landing run 820 ft (250 m)
Range with 4 passengers 746 nm (860 miles; 1,385 km)

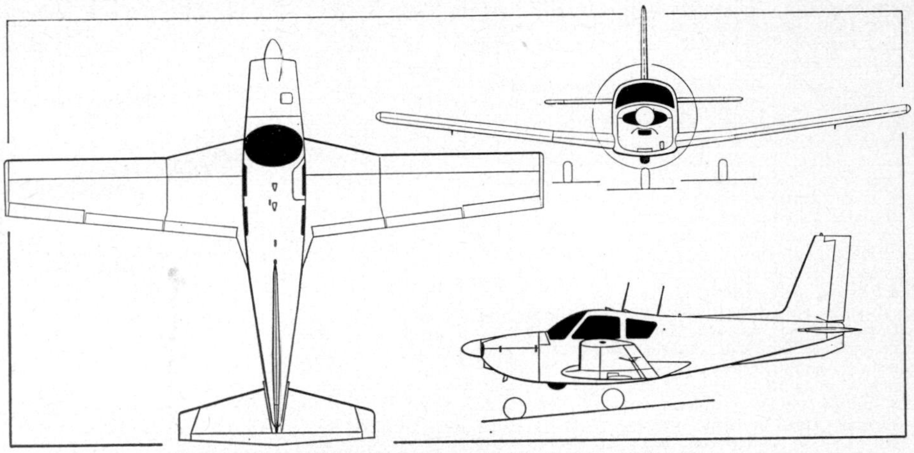

Socata ST 10 Diplomate four-seat light aircraft (*Pilot Press*)

"SURVOL"

"SURVOL"-CHARLES FAUVEL

HEAD OFFICE:
72 Boulevard Carnot, 06400-Cannes AM
Telephone: 39.83.32

In addition to the sailplanes and self-launching sailplanes described in the relevant section of this edition, Charles Fauvel has designed several powered lightplanes. Plans of these are available to amateur constructors.

FAUVEL AV.44

The general appearance of this all-wood side-by-side two-seat, or three-seat, tailless monoplane can be seen in the accompanying illustration. It is a direct development of M Fauvel's AV.10 aircraft which flew for the first time in 1935, with a 75 hp Pobjoy R engine, and subsequently set up altitude records in single-seat and two-seat categories, in competition with aircraft of considerably greater power.

The AV.44 can be powered by a variety of engines in the 90-130 hp range, and is classed as a STOL (ADAC) type. All available details follow:

DIMENSIONS, EXTERNAL:
Wing span 35 ft 1¼ in (10·70 m)
Wing aspect ratio 5·8
Length overall 16 ft 4¾ in (5·00 m)

AREA:
Wings, gross 213·1 sq ft (19·8 m^2)

WEIGHTS:
Weight empty 749 lb (340 kg)
Fuel and oil 198 lb (90 kg)
Normal T-O weight, two-seat 1,331 lb (604 kg)
Max T-O weight, three-seat 1,501 lb (681 kg)

PERFORMANCE (100 hp Continental engine):
Max level speed at S/L 113 knots (130 mph; 210 km/h)
Max cruising speed at S/L 102 knots (118 mph; 190 km/h)
Max rate of climb at S/L 965 ft (294 m)/min
Endurance with max fuel at econ cruising speed 5½ hours

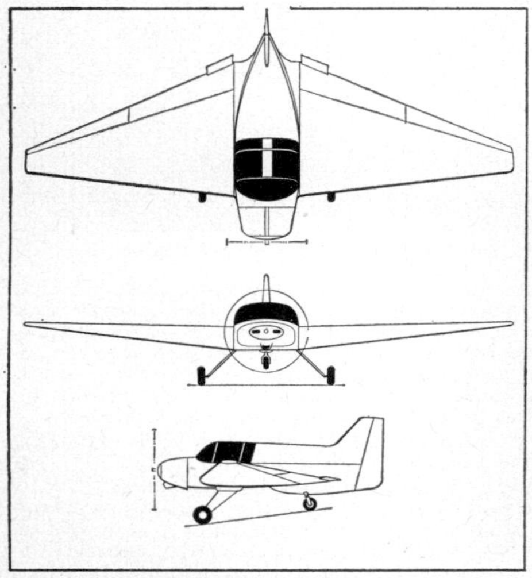

Fauvel AV.44 (*Roy J. Grainge*)

FAUVEL AV.50 (61) LUTIN (ELF)

The AV.50 (61) is a single-seat all-wood light aircraft of tailless configuration. Its wing section can be either Fauvel F2 or a special Wortmann FX-66-H-159 laminar aerofoil. Suitable power plants include a modified Volkswagen motor car engine developing 40 hp and the 55 hp Hirth 0 28 two-cylinder aircooled two-stroke engine. A tandem-wheel, tailwheel or tricycle landing gear can be fitted.

Predecessor of the AV.50 (61) was the AV.60 Leprechaun, of which an example built and flown in the USA is shown in an accompanying illustration. Only details of the AV.50 (61) available in mid-1974 were the following:

DIMENSIONS, EXTERNAL:
Wing span 24 ft 7¼ in (7·50 m)
Wing aspect ratio 5·2
Length overall:
Hirth engine 14 ft 5¼ in (4·40 m)
VW engine 13 ft 5½ in (4·10 m)

AREA:
Wings, gross 116·25 sq ft (10·80 m^2)

WEIGHTS:
Weight empty, equipped:
Hirth engine 352 lb (160 kg)
VW engine 419 lb (190 kg)
Fuel 99 lb (45 kg)
Max T-O weight:
Hirth engine 659 lb (299 kg)
VW engine 725 lb (329 kg)

PERFORMANCE (estimated, at max T-O weight):
Max level speed (Hirth engine):
tandem landing gear 116 knots (134 mph; 215 km/h)
tailwheel landing gear 110 knots (127 mph; 205 km/h)
tricycle landing gear 102 knots (118 mph; 190 km/h)
Max level speed (VW engine):
tandem landing gear 102 knots (118 mph; 190 km/h)
tailwheel landing gear 98 knots (113 mph; 182 km/h)
tricycle landing gear 92 knots (106 mph; 170 km/h)
Max rate of climb at S/L:
Hirth engine 1,085 ft (330 m)/min
VW engine 710 ft (216 m)/min
T-O run:
Hirth engine 230 ft (70 m)
VW engine 330 ft (100 m)
Endurance with max fuel:
Hirth or VW engine 5 hours

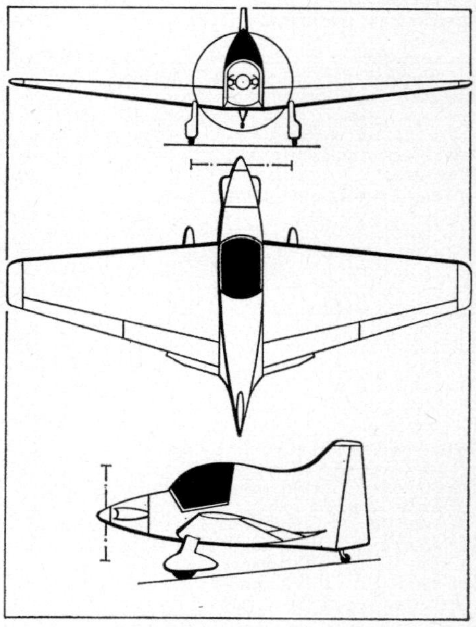

Fauvel AV.50(61) Lutin (*Tony Mitchell*)

Fauvel AV.60 Leprechaun, predecessor of the AV.50 (61) Lutin

WASSMER

WASSMER-AVIATION SA

Head Office, Delivery and After-Sales Service:
BP 7, 63501-Issoire
Telephone: 89-19-15 and 89-01-54

Works:
Route de Parentignat, 63501-Issoire
Telephone: 89-23-86

Director General:
Roger Liévin

Director of Design Studies:
Daniel Pizzolato

This company was founded in 1905 by M Benjamin Wassmer, under the title Société Wassmer, and in its early days was concerned with overhaul and repair of military aircraft and the manufacture of propellers.

When activities were resumed after the second World War, Wassmer was again concerned initially with repair work, later building the designs of other manufacturers under licence. In 1955 a design department was created; its first product was the Jodel-Wassmer D.120 Paris-Nice, and subsequently more than 300 Jodel aircraft were built by Wassmer.

Today, Wassmer's facilities at Issoire occupy a total area of 269,100 sq ft (25,000 m²), including 64,600 sq ft (6,000 m²) of roofed accommodation, comprising one factory for component manufacture and one for repair work and maintenance of army helicopters at the Aérodrome d'Issoire.

Current production is concentrated on the WA 51 Pacific, WA 52 Europa and WA 54 Atlantic all-plastics light aircraft of Wassmer's own design. In addition, Wassmer has formed, with Siren SA, a company known as CERVA (GIE) to develop and market an all-metal derivative of its earlier, wooden WA 4/21 light aircraft, known as the CE.43 Guépard. This is described under the CERVA heading in this section.

Under development by Wassmer is an all-plastics two-seat training aircraft, which it hopes to put in production towards the end of 1975. It is also test flying the prototype WA 28 sailplane, an all-plastics development of its earlier WA 26 Squale, and is developing with Siren SA a two-seat sailplane known as the CERVA CE 75 (see Sailplanes section).

WASSMER WA 51 PACIFIC, WA 52 EUROPA AND WA 54 ATLANTIC

First flown on 22 March 1966, the WA 50 was a prototype four-seat light aircraft of which the airframe was made entirely of plastics. Its development was started in 1962, with official support, and the Société du Verre Textile provided considerable help in selecting the most suitable materials for construction.

The airframe was built up of large components moulded in thin layers of glassfibre, reinforced either by stringers or by a double corrugated skin.

Following flight and ground testing of the prototype WA 50 (see 1969-70 *Jane's*), Wassmer has developed the following production models:

WA 51 Pacific. Differs from WA 50 prototype in having non-retractable landing gear and modifications to the tail-fin and rear cabin windows. First flown on 17 May 1969. Delivery of production aircraft began in 1970. One WA 51 and 12 improved WA 51As were delivered in 1971, followed by 12 more WA 51As in 1972 and 4 in 1973.

WA 52 Europa. Generally similar to WA 51, but powered by a 160 hp engine, driving a variable-pitch propeller, and available with an auxiliary fuel tank, capacity 15·5 Imp gallons (70 litres). Seven delivered in 1971, 27 in 1972 and 19 in 1973.

WA 54 Atlantic. Generally similar to WA 51/52, but powered by a 180 hp Lycoming O-360 four-cylinder horizontally-opposed aircooled engine, driving a two-blade McCauley variable-pitch propeller. Baggage space increased to 35 cu ft (1 m³). New oleo-pneumatic main landing gear, with forks of the kind fitted to the earlier Wassmer Baladou and new fairings. Improved nosewheel steering. New cowling air intake, embodying taxi light. Prototype flew for the first time on 20 February 1973, and production began in June 1973. Ten aircraft were delivered before the end of that year. Length overall 24 ft 3½ in (7·40 m).

The following details apply to the WA 51 Pacific, except where indicated otherwise:

Type: Four-seat light aircraft.

Wings: Cantilever low-wing monoplane. Wing section NACA 63-418. Incidence 4° at root, 1° at tip. Dihedral 6°40′. Structure of each wing comprises a one-piece top surface and leading-edge moulding, a bottom skin panel, main front spar, auxiliary rear spar, ten ribs and stringers, all of plastics. Each mechanically-operated aileron is a simple box structure, with corrugated skin, two end ribs and two internal ribs. Three-position mechanically-operated slotted flaps.

Fuselage: Main fuselage shell and integral fin moulded in two halves from glassfibre, with frames and stringers also of glassfibre.

Tail Unit: Cantilever all-plastics structure, with swept vertical surfaces. All-moving one-piece tailplane, with anti-tab each side.

Landing Gear: Non-retractable tricycle type. ERAM oleo-pneumatic main-wheel shock-absorbers. Steerable nosewheel on telescopic shock-strut, similar to that of earlier Wassmer Baladou. Main-wheel brakes and parking brake fitted.

Power Plant (WA 51): One 150 hp Lycoming O-320-E2A four-cylinder horizontally-opposed aircooled engine, driving a Sensenich two-blade fixed-pitch metal propeller. Integral fuel tank in each swept-forward wing-root leading-edge, with total capacity of 33 Imp gallons (150 litres).

Accommodation: Four seats, in pairs, in enclosed cabin. Front two seats are adjustable. Baggage compartment behind rear seats. Upward-hinged door on each side. Cabin heated and ventilated.

Electronics and Equipment: Electrical equipment includes Delco-Rémy 12V engine starter and 12V 50Ah alternator. VOR and VHF radio standard.

Dimensions, external:

Wing span	30 ft 10 in (9·40 m)
Wing chord at c/l	6 ft 10⅝ in (2·10 m)
Wing chord at tip	3 ft 3¼ in (1·00 m)
Wing mean aerodynamic chord	4 ft 6 in (1·375 m)
Wing aspect ratio	7·15
Length overall	23 ft 11½ in (7·30 m)
Height overall	7 ft 5 in (2·26 m)
Tailplane span	9 ft 10 in (3·00 m)
Wheel track	9 ft 10 in (3·00 m)
Wheelbase	5 ft 5 in (1·65 m)
Propeller diameter	6 ft 0⅞ in (1·85 m)

Area:

Wings, gross	40·68 sq ft (12·40 m²)

Weights:

Weight empty:	
WA 51	1,320 lb (600 kg)
WA 52	1,344 lb (610 kg)
WA 54	1,356 lb (615 kg)
Max T-O weight:	
WA 51	2,292 lb (1,040 kg)
WA 52	2,380 lb (1,080 kg)
WA 54	2,447 lb (1,110 kg)

Performance:

Max never-exceed speed	193 knots (223 mph; 360 km/h)
Max level speed at S/L:	
WA 51	127 knots (146 mph; 235 km/h)
WA 54	151 knots (174 mph; 280 km/h)
Cruising speed:	
WA 51 at 5,500 ft (1,675 m)	120 knots (138 mph; 222 km/h)
WA 52 at 5,500 ft (1,675 m)	135 knots (155 mph; 250 km/h)
WA 54 at 5,500 ft (1,675 m)	140 knots (161 mph; 260 km/h)
Stalling speed:	
WA 51	58 knots (66·5 mph; 107 km/h)
Max rate of climb at S/L:	
WA 51	787 ft (240 m)/min
WA 54	1,180-1,375 ft (360-420 m)/min
Service ceiling:	
WA 51	14,450 ft (4,400 m)
T-O run:	
WA 51	755 ft (230 m)
T-O distance to 50 ft (15 m):	
WA 51	1,215 ft (370 m)
Landing distance from 50 ft (15 m):	
WA 51	1,315 ft (400 m)
Landing run:	
WA 51	655 ft (200 m)
Range with max fuel:	
WA 51	490 nm (565 miles; 910 km)
WA52 and WA 54	755 nm (870 miles; 1,400 km)
Endurance with max fuel:	
WA 54	6 hours

Wassmer WA 54 Atlantic four-seat all-plastics light aircraft

GERMANY
(FEDERAL REPUBLIC)

AEROTECHNIK

AEROTECHNIK ENTWICKLUNG UND APPARATEBAU GmbH

Address:
6 Frankfurt/Main 70, Postfach 700165

Director:
Wolfgang Müller

This German company began work in the early 1960s to develop a low-cost, easy-to-fly helicopter that could be parked or stored in the minimum of space. Three prototypes, designated WGM 21, were completed, and were described in the 1971-72 and 1972-73 *Jane's*. A two-seat version, with enclosed cabin, is under development and is designated WGM 22.

AEROTECHNIK WGM 22

Following successful testing of the single-seat WGM 21 prototypes, Aerotechnik is developing a side-by-side two-seat version, the WGM 22, with an extensively-glazed and fully-enclosed cabin.

The configuration of the WGM 21 and WGM 22 differs essentially from other and more familiar

Mock-up of Aerotechnik's proposed WGM 22 two-seat helicopter

forms of helicopter in having four two-blade rotors, each mounted at the extremity of one of a pair of diametrically-opposed rotor support arms on top of the main rotor column. This configuration allows the entire output of the engine to be transmitted directly to the main rotors, and eliminates the need for tail control surfaces or a tail rotor. The support arms can be folded, enabling the helicopter to be stored in a small area.

It is estimated that the WGM 22, shown in mock-up form in the accompanying photograph, will have a max speed of about 108 knots (124 mph; 200 km/h) and a range of 431 nm (497 miles; 800 km).

AIR-METAL

AIR-METAL FLUGZEUGBAU UND ENTWICKLUNGS-GmbH & CO BETRIEBS-KG

Head Office:
D-8058 Erding, Ringstrasse 17
Telephone: (08122) 23 46
Telex: 5-2491 AMFED
Works:
D-8300 Landshut, Flugplatz Ellermühle
Telephone: (08765) 256
Managing Director:
Wolfgang Grabowski

AIR-METAL AM-C 111

Planned construction of a prototype STOL transport aircraft, designated AMZ-102T, was reported in the 1971-72 *Jane's*. This project has since been abandoned and Air-Metal is constructing instead the prototype of the basic version of a new utility STOL transport, under the designation AM-C 111 Series 100. Developed versions with pressurisation, aft loading ramp, high-density seating and a stretched fuselage are projected.

Construction of the AM-C 111 prototype has started and it is planned that, in addition to production in Germany, components will be manufactured for assembly by 14 overseas licensees. Negotiations with licensees are at an advanced stage.

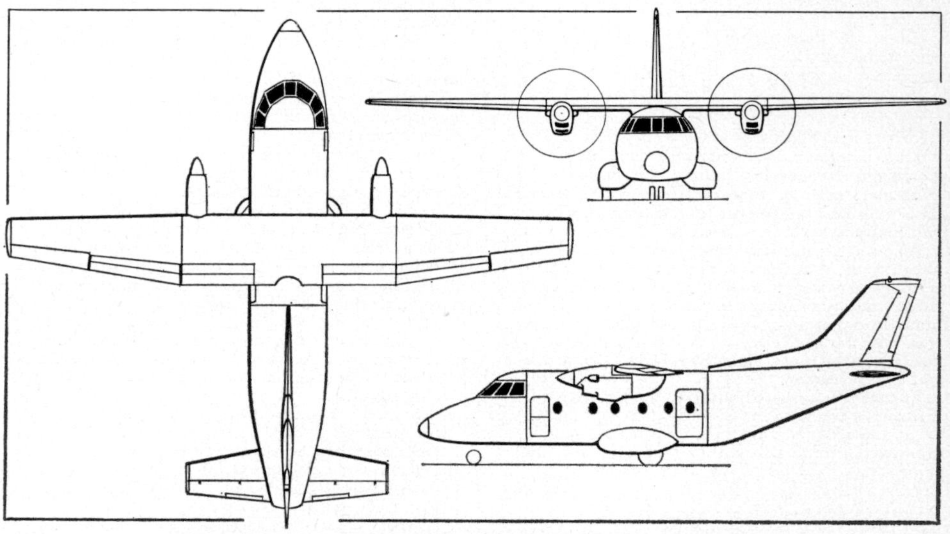

Air-Metal AM-C 111 twin-engined STOL transport (*Pilot Press*)

The description which follows applies in particular to the AM-C 111 Series 400 which has a stretched and pressurised fuselage, with aft loading ramp.

Type: Twin-engined STOL transport and utility aircraft.

Wings: Cantilever high-wing monoplane. Rectangular centre-section of NACA 23015 section. Trapezoidal outer panels of NACA 23015 modified section at root, NACA 23012 modified at tip. Incidence 3°. No dihedral. Conventional two-spar structure of light alloy. Detachable leading-edges. Electrically-operated double-slotted Fowler trailing-edge flaps of light alloy construction, in two sections on each wing, extending from wing root to aileron. Modified single-slotted Frise-type ailerons of light alloy construction. Manually-operated trim tab in port aileron. Glassfibre-reinforced plastics wingtips. Pneumatic de-icing of wing leading-edges.

Fuselage: Semi-monocoque fail-safe structure of light alloy, built in three sections. Forward section comprises unpressurised nose and pressurised cockpit. Nose can accommodate a radar scanner and the standard nose cap is a glassfibre honeycomb radome. Crash wall between flight deck and cabin for passengers or cargo. Aft pressure bulkhead of laminated plastics is removable to facilitate loading of bulky cargo via aft loading ramp.

Tail Unit: Cantilever all-metal structure. Incidence of tailplane variable by dual electric actuators. Manually-operated trim tab in rudder and each elevator. Pneumatic de-icing of fin and tailplane leading-edges.

Landing Gear: Hydraulically-retractable tricycle type of Messier-Hispano design. Nosewheel unit retracts forward and is totally enclosed when retracted. Main wheels retract into fairings on the sides of the fuselage, but only two-thirds of each wheel is enclosed when retracted. Twin nosewheels, with oleo-pneumatic shock-absorption, are steerable to an angle of 60° each side. Single wheel with oleo-pneumatic shock-absorber on each main unit. Emergency extension system operated by hydraulic hand pump, but aircraft can land on the partially exposed main wheels in the event of hydraulic system failure. Nosewheels have tubeless tyres, size 6·00-6, pressure 30 lb/sq in (2·11 kg/cm²). Main wheels have tubeless tyres size 11·0-12, pressure 50 lb/sq in (3·52 kg/cm²). Six-puck hydraulic disc brakes. Anti-skid system optional.

Power Plant: Two 1,122 ehp United Aircraft of Canada PT6A-45 turboprop engines, each driving a Hartzell four-blade metal fully-feathering and reversible-pitch propeller with spinner. Two fuel cells in each wing, total capacity 528 US gallons (1,998 litres), of which 512 US gallons (1,938 litres) are usable. Optional extra fuel cell can be installed in the wing centre-section to provide a maximum usable capacity of 670 US gallons (2,536 litres). Pressure refuelling point in engine nacelle; gravity refuelling point on upper surface of each wing. Electrical de-icing of propellers, spinners and engine air intakes.

Accommodation: Pilot and co-pilot on flight deck. Standard seating for 20-24 passengers, four-abreast with centre aisle. Toilet compartment at aft end of cabin on starboard side. Passenger door with integral airstairs aft of the wing on the port side. Crew door, also with airstairs, forward of the wing on the port side. Hydraulically-operated aft baggage and/or cargo loading door forms loading ramp when lowered. Double-pane cabin windows. Two emergency exits on starboard side. Interior design permits quick change to de luxe executive layout with six passenger seats, steward's seat, table, bar and toilet; mixed executive/cargo configuration; all-cargo interior able to accept LD-1 and LD-3 containers and a range of pallets; or ambulance configuration with up to 15 stretchers and attendants or accommodation for five intensive care patients. Cabin flooring designed for distributed load of 200 lb/sq ft (975 kg/m²). Between the spar frames a load of 250 lb/sq ft (1,220 kg/m²) can be accepted. Vehicles with single-wheel loads of up to 1,102 lb (500 kg) may be carried. Tie-down fittings for containers and pallets. For parachuting or air-dropping of cargo, the standard cargo door/ramp may be replaced by a special ramp incorporating an additional exit which can be opened in flight. In the passenger version detachable baggage racks are installed above the ramp door. Baggage hold in nose. Windscreen de-icing and electrically-operated windscreen wipers standard. Dual controls standard.

Systems: Electrical power supplied by two 200A 30V DC starter/generators, one 115/26V single-phase 400Hz inverter, and two 24V 22Ah nickel-cadmium batteries. External power socket standard. Hydraulic system of 2,000 lb/sq in (140 kg/cm²) is supplied by two engine-driven pumps. Oxygen system for emergency use by flight crew and passengers. Air-conditioning and pressurisation system supplied by engine bleed air, with automatic temperature control and a cabin altitude control system maintaining a normal pressure differential of 5·55 lb/sq in (0·39 kg/cm²). Power plant fire detection and fire extinguishing system.

Equipment: Standard equipment includes fuselage nose cap in form of glassfibre honeycomb radome, heated pitot heads, and two hand-operated fire extinguishers, for flight deck and cabin.

Dimensions, external:
Wing span 62 ft 4 in (19·00 m)
Wing chord, centre-section, constant 7 ft 6 in (2·30 m)
Wing chord, mean 6 ft 5½ in (1·97 m)
Wing aspect ratio 9·63
Length overall 53 ft 7¼ in (16·34 m)
Height overall 21 ft 0 in (6·40 m)
Tailplane span 22 ft 0½ in (6·72 m)
Wheel track 10 ft 8½ in (3·26 m)
Wheelbase 18 ft 11¼ in (5·77 m)
Passenger door (aft, port):
Height 5 ft 1 in (1·55 m)
Width 2 ft 11½ in (0·90 m)
Crew door (fwd, port):
Height 4 ft 2¾ in (1·29 m)
Width 2 ft 0¼ in (0·62 m)
Cargo door (aft fuselage):
Width 6 ft 6¾ in (2·00 m)

Dimensions, internal:
Cabin, excluding flight deck:
Length 19 ft 6 in (5·94 m)
Max width 7 ft 10½ in (2·40 m)
Max height 6 ft 6 in (1·98 m)
Floor area 127·88 sq ft (11·88 m²)
Volume 839 cu ft (23·76 m³)
Baggage rack (aft fuselage):
Volume 88·3 cu ft (2·50 m³)
Baggage hold (nose):
Volume 42·4 cu ft (1·20 m³)

Areas:
Wings, gross 403·6 sq ft (37·50 m²)
Ailerons (total, incl tabs) 24·10 sq ft (2·24 m²)
Trailing-edge flaps (total) 72·98 sq ft (6·78 m²)
Fin 39·29 sq ft (3·65 m²)
Rudder (incl tab) 31·00 sq ft (2·88 m²)

Weights and Loadings (estimated):
Weight empty:
Cargo version 8,007 lb (3,632 kg)
Passenger version, 24 seats 8,227 lb (3,732 kg)
Max T-O and landing weight 14,990 lb (6,800 kg)
Max wing loading 37·1 lb/sq ft (181·3 kg/m²)
Max power loading 6·70 lb/ehp (3·04 kg/ehp)

Performance (estimated, at max T-O weight):
Max cruising speed at S/L 224 knots (258 mph; 415 km/h)
Max cruising speed at 20,000 ft (6,100 m) 216 knots (249 mph; 400 km/h)
Cruising speed, 80% power at S/L 203 knots (234 mph; 377 km/h)
Stalling speed, flaps up 86 knots (99 mph; 158 km/h)
Stalling speed, flaps down 67 knots (77 mph; 123 km/h)
Max rate of climb at S/L 2,000 ft (610 m)/min
Rate of climb at S/L, one engine out 768 ft (234 m)/min
Service ceiling 25,425 ft (7,750 m)
Service ceiling, one engine out 15,250 ft (4,650 m)
T-O run 1,485 ft (452 m)
T-O to 35 ft (10·7 m) 1,665 ft (507 m)
Landing from 50 ft (15 m) 2,005 ft (611 m)
Landing from 50 ft (15 m), with propeller reversal 1,640 ft (500 m)
Landing run 1,130 ft (344 m)
Landing run, with propeller reversal 765 ft (233 m)
Range with 18 passengers at 20,000 ft (6,100 m) 825 nm (950 miles; 1,530 km)
Range, cargo version with 4,409 lb (2,000 kg) payload at 20,000 ft (6,100 m) 565 nm (652 miles; 1,050 km)
Ferry range, no payload 1,940 nm (2,235 miles; 3,600 km)

AKAFLIEG STUTTGART

AKADEMISCHE FLIEGERGRUPPE STUTTGART EV

Address:
7-Stuttgart-80, Pfaffenwaldring 35
Telephone: 784-2443

The flight research group at Stuttgart University has a history of sailplane design extending back to 1928. It has recently built a two-seat lightweight aircraft which has the designation FS-28; this aircraft (D-EAFS) flew for the first time on 20 December 1972.

AKAFLIEG STUTTGART FS-28 AVISPA

Type: Two-seat lightweight sporting and utility aircraft.

Wings: Cantilever mid-wing monoplane. Wing section Eppler 530. Dihedral 4° 30′. Sweepback at quarter-chord 6° 45′. Sandwich structure of glassfibre and rigid foam. Plain ailerons and inboard and outboard Fowler flaps over full span. The inboard flaps extend from the fuselage to the tailbooms, the outboard flaps from the tailbooms to the ailerons. No trim tabs.

FUSELAGE: Nacelle structure of glass-reinforced plastics/honeycomb sandwich, with engine mounted at rear. Semi-annular air intake between cabin and engine bay.

TAIL UNIT: Tailplane/fins, in form of inverted Vee, carried on twin tailbooms. Construction similar to that of wings. Elevators fabric-covered and fitted with spring trim system.

LANDING GEAR: Hydraulically-retractable tricycle type with single wheel on each unit. Steerable nosewheel. Glassfibre shock-absorption. Hydraulic brakes.

POWER PLANT: One 115 hp Lycoming O-235-E2A four-cylinder horizontally-opposed aircooled engine, driving a Hoffmann three-blade metal variable-pitch pusher propeller with spinner. Fuel capacity 25·3 Imp gallons (115 litres).

ACCOMMODATION: Two persons side by side beneath transparent canopy. Access from each side, via upward-opening windows hinged near centreline of cabin roof.

DIMENSIONS, EXTERNAL:
- Wing span: 30 ft 10 in (9·40 m)
- Wing chord at root: 5 ft 4¼ in (1·63 m)
- Wing chord at tip: 3 ft 2⅝ in (0·98 m)
- Wing aspect ratio: 7

Akaflieg Stuttgart FS-28 Avispa light aircraft (115 hp Lycoming O-235-E2A engine)

- Length overall: 23 ft 7½ in (7·20 m)
- Tailplane span: 7 ft 10⅜ in (2·40 m)

AREAS:
- Wings, gross: 136·7 sq ft (12·70 m^2)
- Ailerons (total): 8·61 sq ft (0·80 m^2)
- Tailplane and elevators (horizontal projection): 24·65 sq ft (2·29 m^2)

WEIGHTS AND LOADINGS:
- Weight empty: 1,411 lb (640 kg)
- Max T-O weight: 1,984 lb (900 kg)
- Max wing loading: 14·5 lb/sq ft (71 kg/m^2)
- Max power loading: 17·2 lb/hp (7·8 kg/hp)

PERFORMANCE (at max T-O weight):
- Max never-exceed speed: 182 knots (210 mph; 338 km/h)
- Max level speed: 155 knots (168 mph; 270 km/h)
- Max cruising speed, 75% power: 134 knots (155 mph; 250 km/h)
- Landing speed: 46 knots (53 mph; 85 km/h)
- Range with 30 min reserve: over 538 nm (620 miles; 1,000 km)

DEUTSCHE AIRBUS

DEUTSCHE AIRBUS GmbH

ADDRESS:
D-8 München 19, Leonrodstrasse 68
Telephone: (0811) 1 79 61
Telex: 5215149

CHAIRMAN OF THE BOARD OF DIRECTORS:
Bundesminister a.D. Dr Franz-Josef Strauss

MANAGEMENT:
Dipl Kfm Rolf Siebert
Dipl-Ing Johannes Schäffler

PUBLIC RELATIONS:
Jochen H. Eichen

This company is the German partner in the consortium for development of the European high-capacity A-300 transport aircraft described under the "Airbus" heading in the International section of this edition.

DORNIER

DORNIER GmbH

HEAD OFFICE:
Postfach 317, 7990 Friedrichshafen/Bodensee
Telephone: Immenstaad (07545) 81+
Telex: 0734372

WORKS:
Research and Development: 7759 Immenstaad/Bodensee (near Friedrichshafen)
Production: Postfach 2160, Trimburgstrasse, 8000 München 66

AIRFIELD AND FLIGHT TEST CENTRE:
8031 Oberpfaffenhofen, near München

BONN OFFICE:
Allianzplatz, 5300 Bonn

BOARD OF DIRECTORS:
Dipl-Ing Claudius Dornier Jr (Chairman)
Dipl-Ing Heinz Boldt
Dipl-Ing Dr Bernhard Schmidt
Dipl-Ing Dr jur Karl-Wilhelm Schäfer
Dipl-Betriebswirt Klaus Fischer

PUBLIC RELATIONS:
Gerhard Patt

Dornier GmbH, formerly Dornier-Metallbauten, was formed in 1922 by the late Professor Claude Dornier (who died on 5 December 1969) as the successor to the "Do" division of the former Zeppelin Werke, Lindau, GmbH. It has been operated in the form of a Gesellschaft mit beschränkter Haftung since 22 December 1972.

After 1945, when the design and manufacture of aircraft in Germany was forbidden, Prof Dornier established technical offices in Madrid, Spain, where he designed a general-purpose monoplane known as the Do 25. The advanced development of this aircraft, designated Do 27, was produced in quantity and has been described in earlier editions of *Jane's*.

Manufacture of a twin-engined version of the Do 27, known as the Do 28, ended in 1971 after a total of 120 had been built. Dornier now has in production the Skyservant light utility transport, based on the Do 28. After the delivery of 121 Skyservants to the German Bundeswehr, production continues to meet export orders.

In 1974 the Dornier group employed a total of 7,000 people. Member companies, in addition to Dornier GmbH, include Dornier-Reparaturwerft GmbH at Oberpfaffenhofen (aircraft servicing and maintenance), Dornier System GmbH of Friedrichshafen (spaceflight, new technologies, electronics, management consultancy and contract research) and Lindauer Dornier GmbH of Lindau, which produces machinery for the textile industry and for the manufacture of plastics foils.

Dornier has developed and flight tested an experimental version of the System Kiebitz tethered rotor platform (see "RPVs and Targets" section of this edition), and development of the Do 34 operational version is under way, with the first flight of a prototype anticipated in the Autumn of 1974.

Dornier is collaborating with the Dassault-Breguet group in France in developing the Alpha Jet training/light attack aircraft, described in the International section, the first prototype of which made its first flight on 26 October 1973.

Technical and marketing efforts are continuing on the Do 24/72 amphibian flying-boat project.

Design studies and investigations into technical problems concerning light hoverable aircraft concepts for anti-tank defence were carried out during 1973-74. Tethered flight tests with the Aerodyne E 1 experimental RPV were concluded successfully, and the Viper air-to-air missile development programme entered its prototype fabrication phase. As a follow-up to earlier major programmes, Dornier is involved in licence production of the Sikorsky CH-53G helicopter and in European co-operative production of the Breguet Atlantic. Manufacture of components for the Transall and Phantom has continued.

DORNIER Do 28 D SKYSERVANT

The Skyservant is a completely new design, inheriting only the basic configuration of the earlier Do 28. The prototype (D-INTL) first flew on 23 February 1966. Type approval for the Do 28 D was granted on 24 February 1967, and for the developed Do 28 D-1 on 6 November 1967.

FAA certification of the Do 28 D-1 was granted on 19 April 1968. Military type approval of the Do 28 D-1 was granted in January 1970, and of the Do 28 D-2 in late 1971, in accordance with MIL-specification standards. Initial deliveries of the Skyservant were made in the Summer of 1967, and total sales exceeded 200 by March 1974.

The three production versions of the Skyservant differ as follows:

Do 28 D Skyservant. Initial version, described fully in 1967-68 *Jane's*. Seven built, of which two were later converted to Do 28 D-1.

Do 28 D-1 Skyservant. Production version from 1968, described fully in the 1972-73 *Jane's*. Detail refinements include a 1 ft 7⅝ in (0·50 m) increase in wing span and a 331 lb (150 kg) increase in AUW. Meets FAA Pt 135 requirements, particularly with regard to improved climb on one engine. Produced for the civil market as well as for military use, and delivered to 25 countries. In use for passenger, cargo and troop transport, as a dropping aircraft for paratroops and in many reconnaissance roles, as well as for sea-air rescue, flying laboratory, flying classroom and earth resources investigation.

On 15 March 1972, F. M. Tuytjens set up six international records in a Do 28 D-1 Skyservant in Class C1e for piston-engined business aircraft in the 3,000-6,000 kg weight category. They included an altitude record of 32,687 ft (9,963 m); altitude of 28,294 ft (8,624 m) with a 1,000 kg payload; a record payload of 1,000 kg (2,205 lb) carried to a height of 2,000 m (6,562 ft); and

Survey version of Dornier Do 28 D-1 Skyservant, showing camera doors in the underfuselage

time-to-height records of 6 min 6 sec to 3,000 m (9,843 ft), 12 min 2 sec to 6,000 m (19,685 ft), and 44 min 4 sec to 9,000 m (29,528 ft).

Do 28 D-2 Skyservant. Current production version as described below. Total of 121 delivered to the Federal Republic of Germany, of which 101 allocated to the Luftwaffe for general duties, including light transport and air ambulance, and twenty similar aircraft to the Navy Air Arm for support duties. The D-2 version has a number of aerodynamic and detail refinements, including a 423 lb (192 kg) increase in AUW and more extensive standard equipment such as dual controls, dual brake system, directional slaved gyro, cabin heating, 100A alternators and provisions for de-icing system and IFR com/nav antennae installation.

TYPE: Twin-engined STOL transport and utility aircraft.

WINGS: Cantilever high-wing monoplane. Wing section NACA 23018 (modified), with nose slot in the outer half of each wing. Dihedral 1° 30′. Incidence 4°. All-metal box-spar structure. Double-slotted ailerons and flaps have metal structure, partly Eonnex-covered. Balance tabs on ailerons. Pneumatic de-icing optional.

FUSELAGE: Conventional all-metal stressed-skin structure.

TAIL UNIT: Cantilever all-metal structure, with rudder and horizontal surfaces partly Eonnex-covered. All-moving horizontal surface, with combined anti-balance and trim tab. Trim tab in rudder. Pneumatic de-icing optional.

LANDING GEAR: Non-retractable tailwheel type. Dornier oleo-pneumatic shock-absorbers on main units, glassfibre spring tailwheel unit. Main-wheel tyres size 8·50-10, pressure 49 lb/sq in (3·4 kg/cm²). Twin-contact tailwheel tyre size 5·50-4, pressure 40 lb/sq in (2·81 kg/cm²). Double-disc hydraulic brakes. Fairings on main legs and wheels standard. Wheel-ski gear or floats optional.

POWER PLANT: Two 380 hp Lycoming IGSO-540-A1E six-cylinder horizontally-opposed aircooled engines, mounted on stub-wings and each driving a Hartzell three-blade constant-speed propeller. Fuel tanks in engine nacelles, with total usable capacity of 196·5 Imp gallons (893 litres). Refuelling points above nacelles. Total capacity of separate oil tanks, 7·25 Imp gallons (33 litres).

ACCOMMODATION: Pilot and either co-pilot or passenger side by side on flight deck. Main cabin accommodates up to 12 seats, with aisle, or 13 inward-facing folding seats, or five stretchers and five folding seats, all layouts including toilet and/or baggage compartment and/or darkroom for aerial survey missions aft of cabin. Second baggage compartment in nose-cone. Alternatively, cabin can be stripped for cargo-carrying. Door on each side of flight deck. Emergency exit on starboard side of cabin. Combined two-section passenger and freight door on port side of cabin, at rear.

ELECTRONICS AND EQUIPMENT: IFR instruments and electronics to customer's specifications.

DIMENSIONS, EXTERNAL:
- Wing span: 51 ft 0¼ in (15·55 m)
- Wing chord (constant): 6 ft 2¾ in (1·90 m)
- Wing aspect ratio: 8·3
- Length overall: 37 ft 5¼ in (11·41 m)
- Height overall: 12 ft 9½ in (3·90 m)
- Tailplane span: 21 ft 8¼ in (6·61 m)
- Wheel track: 11 ft 6 in (3·52 m)
- Wheelbase: 28 ft 3¾ in (8·63 m)
- Propeller diameter: 7 ft 9 in (2·36 m)
- Passenger door (port rear):
  - Height: 4 ft 4¾ in (1·34 m)
  - Width: 2 ft 1½ in (0·65 m)
  - Height to sill: 1 ft 11½ in (0·60 m)
- Freight door (port rear):
  - Height: 4 ft 4¾ in (1·34 m)
  - Width: 4 ft 2½ in (1·28 m)

DIMENSIONS, INTERNAL:
- Cabin: Max length: 13 ft 0¼ in (3·97 m)
  - Max width: 4 ft 6 in (1·37 m)
  - Max height: 4 ft 11⅞ in (1·52 m)
  - Floor area: 57·05 sq ft (5·30 m²)
  - Volume: 286 cu ft (8·10 m³)

AREAS:
- Wings, gross: 312·2 sq ft (29·00 m²)
- Ailerons (total): 28·4 sq ft (2·64 m²)
- Trailing-edge flaps (total): 51·6 sq ft (4·80 m²)
- Fin: 50·0 sq ft (4·65 m²)
- Rudder, including tab: 15·1 sq ft (1·40 m²)
- Tailplane, including tab: 82·3 sq ft (7·65 m²)

WEIGHTS AND LOADINGS:
- Weight empty, standard: 5,066 lb (2,298 kg)
- Max T-O and landing weight: 8,470 lb (3,842 kg)
- Max ramp weight: 8,514 lb (3,862 kg)
- Max wing loading: 26·83 lb/sq ft (131 kg/m²)
- Max power loading: 11·13 lb/hp (5·05 kg/hp)

PERFORMANCE (at max T-O weight):
- Max level speed at 10,000 ft (3,050 m): 175 knots (202 mph; 325 km/h)
- Cruising speed, 65% power at 10,000 ft (3,050 m): 148 knots (170 mph; 273 km/h)
- Econ cruising speed, 50% power at 10,000 ft (3,050 m): 130 knots (150 mph; 241 km/h)
- Stalling speed, power off, flaps down: 56·5 knots (65 mph; 104 km/h)

Dornier Do 28 D-2 Skyservant of the Federal German Navy

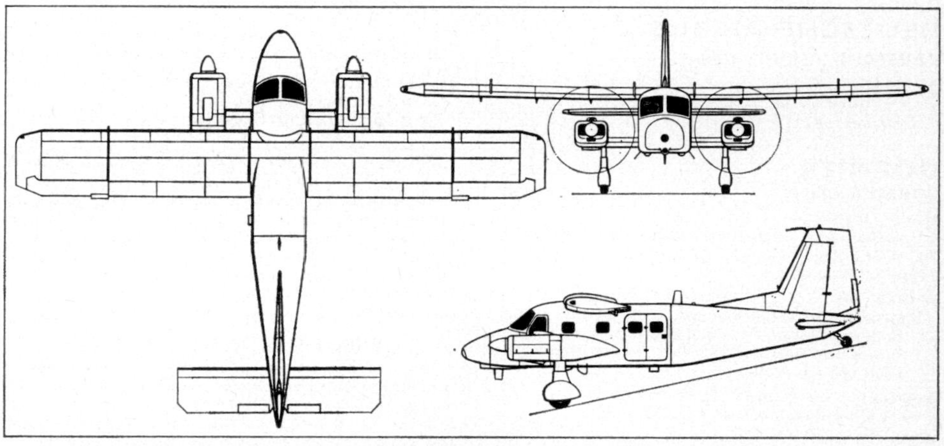

Dornier Do 28 D-1 Skyservant STOL utility transport aircraft *(Pilot Press)*

- Min control speed, power on, flaps down: 35 knots (40 mph; 65 km/h)
- Max rate of climb at S/L: 1,180 ft (360 m)/min
- Service ceiling: 25,200 ft (7,680 m)
- Service ceiling, one engine out: 8,600 ft (2,620 m)
- T-O run: 919 ft (280 m)
- Landing run: 748 ft (228 m)
- Range with max fuel: 1,090 nm (1,255 miles; 2,020 km)

DORNIER Do 24/72

To meet a need expressed by the Spanish Air Force to replace the Grumman HU-16 Albatross amphibians employed on its sea-air rescue services, Dornier has proposed an updated turboprop-powered version of the Do 24T seagoing flying-boat that performed similar duties in Spain for many years. Designated Do 24/72, the new design is generally similar to that of the wartime flying-boat, except for the change in power plant and provision of retractable tricycle landing gear. A decision to begin production is dependent upon sufficient demand and the availability of capital to create a production line.

TYPE: Three-engined amphibian, primarily for sea-air rescue, but suitable for maritime patrol, passenger and cargo transport, ambulance and water bombing operations.

WINGS: Parasol monoplane, with the wing carried on an inverted Vee strut extending from beneath the outboard engine to the stabilising sponson on each side, and on short centre-section struts beneath the centre engine. Conventional all-metal structure. Double-slotted flaps along entire trailing-edge from aileron to aileron. Conventional ailerons, each with trim tab.

HULL: All-metal two-step hull, with sponson on each side to provide lateral stability on the water.

TAIL UNIT: All-metal cantilever structure, with twin endplate fins and rudders. Elevator in two sections. Trim tab in each elevator and rudder.

LANDING GEAR: Retractable tricycle type, with twin wheels on each unit. Nose unit retracts aft into undersurface of hull, main units into housings at the tips of the stabilising sponsons.

POWER PLANT: Three 1,600 shp Lycoming T5321A turboprop engines, mounted in nacelles faired into the leading-edge of the wing.

ACCOMMODATION: Cabin is capable of seating a maximum of 40 persons.

DIMENSIONS, EXTERNAL:
- Wing span: 91 ft 10¼ in (28·00 m)
- Length overall: 78 ft 8 in (23·98 m)
- Height overall: 23 ft 4 in (7·12 m)

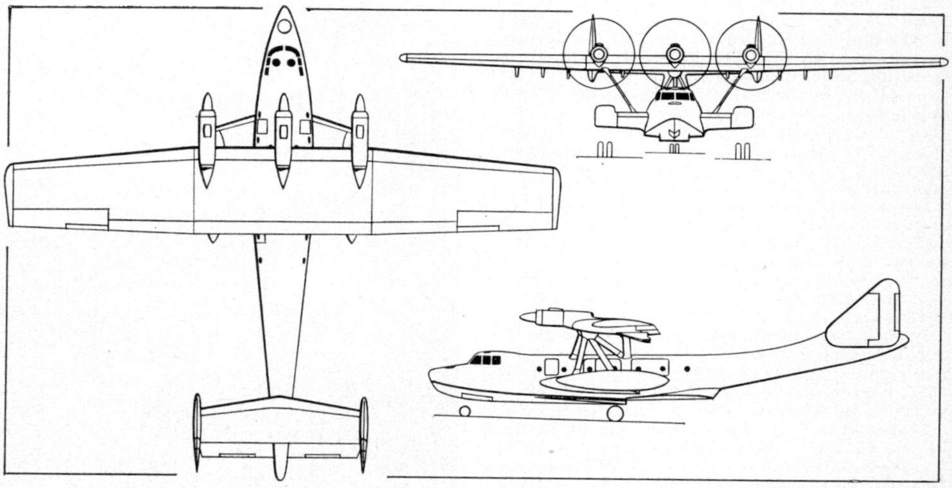

Dornier Do 24/72 three-turboprop general-purpose amphibian *(Pilot Press)*

Width of hull 9 ft 10 in (3·00 m)
Width over sponsons 26 ft 3 in (8·00 m)
Wheel track (c/l of main units) 22 ft 11¾ in (7·00 m)

WEIGHTS (estimated):
Weight empty 24,692 lb (11,200 kg)
Max T-O weight, land or water 41,005 lb (18,600 kg)

PERFORMANCE (estimated):
Max level speed 215 knots (248 mph; 400 km/h)
T-O to 50 ft (15 m) on land 1,804 ft (550 m)
Landing from 50 ft (15 m) on land 1,345 ft (410 m)
T-O time on water 16 sec
Range with max fuel 1,726 nm (1,988 miles; 3,200 km)
Endurance with max fuel 14 hr

FLUWAG BREMEN

FLUGWISSENSCHAFTLICHE ARBEITSGEMEINSCHAFT (FLUWAG) BREMEN

ADDRESS:
Rockwinkeler Landstrasse 33, 28 Bremen Oberneuland

FLUWAG BREMEN ESS 641

Members of the FLUWAG Bremen, including Hans von Engelbrechten and Ulrich Stampa, designed a single-seat glider-towing monoplane known as the ESS 641. This aircraft, registered D-EAVE, was flown for the first time at Ganderkesee airfield near Bremen on 17 September 1971. The main objectives of the design were to improve operating efficiency and reduce initial and operating costs compared with other types of aircraft currently employed in the glider-towing role. Initial flight testing was satisfactory; production was to be considered after an unrestricted C of A had been obtained.

Full details of the ESS 641 can be found in the 1973-74 *Jane's*.

HIRTH

WOLF HIRTH GmbH

ADDRESS:
7311 Nabern/Teck, Am Flugplatz
Telephone: Kirchheim/Teck 5 53 77

HIRTH ACROSTAR Mk III

Wolf Hirth GmbH manufactured the prototype (D-EMKB) of the Acrostar Mk II, a single-seat aircraft designed specifically for advanced competitive aerobatic flying. The Acrostar uses an entirely symmetrical basic aerofoil section, with variable positive and negative camber, and was conceived originally by the Swiss aerobatic champion, Arnold Wagner. The project was sponsored by Herr Wagner, Herr Josef Hössl (the present German aerobatic champion), Herr Walter Wolfrum (a former German champion) and Herr Horst Gehm. Design of the aircraft, which was carried out by Wolf Hirth GmbH under the supervision of Prof Eppler of the Technische Hochschule of Stuttgart, began in the late Summer of 1969. Construction began in December of that year, and the Acrostar Mk II was flown for the first time on 16 April 1970, making a successful appearance in the World Aerobatics Competition at Hullavington, England, three months later. It took part subsequently in international meetings in France and Switzerland, gaining first place at its debut in each country. During 1973 Acrostars took first place in the Scandinavian Cup, Zadar Cup in Yugoslavia, Swiss International Championships, West German Championships and the Coupe Champion Amberieu in France.

The first production aircraft (Serial No. 2) was used for Type Certification tests. Full Type Certification in the Normal and Aerobatic categories, based on the requirements of FAR 23, has been granted by the Luftfahrt Bundesamt.

A new trim system represented the only significant change between the prototype and Mk II production aircraft: two tabs on the inboard ends of the integrated trailing-edge flaps replaced the elevator trim tab of the prototype.

Four Acrostars were completed and delivered by 25 January 1972, and additional deliveries were made in time for the 1972 World Aerobatic Competition.

Since that time a Mk III version has been introduced, embodying more than 50 modifications that reduce weight and improve performance and controllability. These include the provision of lightweight control surfaces, improved fairing at the fuselage/wing junction, and changes in the oil system and engine cooling that permit glider towing without danger of engine overheating. The Acrostar is stressed to $\pm 8g$ ($\pm 12g$ ultimate) with a max aerobatic gross weight of 1,389 lb (630 kg).

TYPE: Single-seat advanced aerobatic aircraft.

WINGS: Cantilever low-wing monoplane. Thick, symmetrical aerofoil section, of 20% thickness/chord ratio, designed by Prof Eppler. Single glassfibre main spar, plastics foam reinforced ribs and plywood covering. Slight sweepback on leading-edge. No dihedral or incidence. Inboard trailing-edge flaps and large proportionally-moving ailerons are coupled to the elevator, providing variable camber as a function of stick position. This gives flight characteristics which are equal in both positive and negative manoeuvres. Trim tab on the inboard end of each trailing-edge flap, which can be positioned independently, to provide both pitch and roll trim.

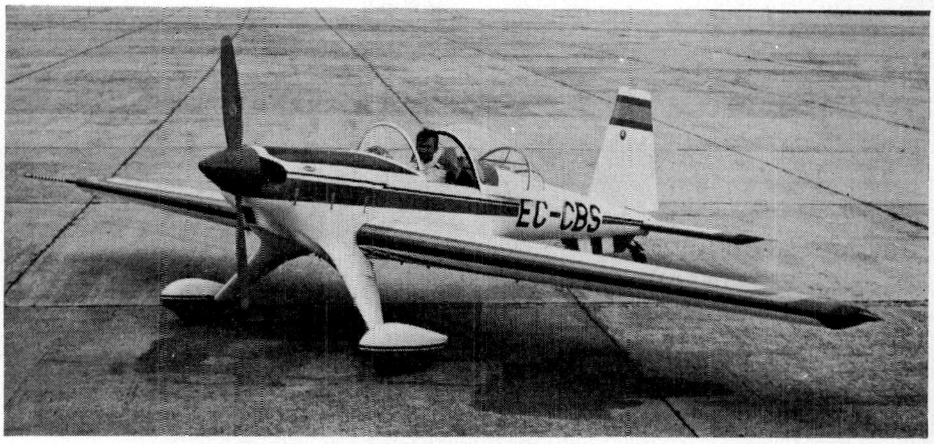

Hirth Acrostar Mk II advanced aerobatic aircraft *(Howard Levy)*

FUSELAGE: Streamlined semi-monocoque structure, of wooden construction except for steel-tube engine mount which is integral with the main landing gear assembly. Fuselage aft of cockpit is detachable for transportation.

TAIL UNIT: Conventional cantilever structure, with single fin and balanced rudder. One-piece elevator. Additional fin area beneath rear fuselage.

LANDING GEAR: Non-retractable tailwheel type, with optional streamline fairings over main wheels and landing gear struts. Main gear legs built integrally with engine mount. Böhler main units and wheels with dual hydraulic brakes. Steerable tailwheel.

POWER PLANT: One 220 hp Franklin 6A-350-C1 six-cylinder horizontally-opposed aircooled engine, driving a Hartzell two-blade constant-speed propeller. Standard fuel capacity for aerobatics 11 Imp gallons (50 litres), contained in wing-root leading-edge tank. Optional cruise tank available, capacity 8·8-13·2 Imp gallons (40-60 litres). Oil system specially modified by Hirth to provide lubrication in all aerobatic manoeuvres.

ACCOMMODATION: Single seat under fully-transparent rearward-sliding canopy which incorporates nose-over protection bars. Space aft of seat for 33 lb (15 kg) of baggage.

SYSTEMS: Hydraulic system for brakes only. No electrical system standard, but an external power socket is fitted as standard to permit use of an electric engine starter. Electrical system to include battery, battery stowage, navigation and internal lights optional.

ELECTRONICS AND EQUIPMENT: Radio rack, antenna, microphone and button control and a selection of com radios available to customers' requirements. Optional equipment includes window in cockpit floor with fire protection cover, stopwatch, cylinder head temperature gauge, rate of climb indicator, sideslip indicator, inverted accelerometer, anatomic control column, baggage compartment, glider tow hook and Hoffmann three-blade propeller.

DIMENSIONS, EXTERNAL:
Wing span 26 ft 3 in (8·00 m)
Wing aspect ratio 6·03
Length overall 19 ft 8¼ in (6·00 m)
Height overall 8 ft 2½ in (2·50 m)

AREA:
Wings, gross 114·1 sq ft (10·60 m²)

WEIGHTS:
Weight empty, standard equipment 992 lb (450 kg)
Weight empty with optional equipment up to 1,091 lb (495 kg)
Max T-O weight for aerobatics 1,389 lb (630 kg)
Max T-O weight for normal flight 1,543 lb (700 kg)

PERFORMANCE (at max T-O weight of 1,543 lb; 700 kg, except where indicated):
Max never-exceed speed 226 knots (261 mph; 420 km/h)
Max level speed at S/L 159 knots (183 mph; 295 km/h)
Max cruising speed, 75% power at 6,000 ft (1,830 m) 157 knots (181 mph; 291 km/h)
Max manoeuvring speed 147 knots (170 mph; 273 km/h)
Econ cruising speed at 10,000 ft (3,050 m) 136 knots (157 mph; 252 km/h)
Stalling speed 52 knots (60 mph; 96 km/h)
Stalling speed inverted 51 knots (59 mph; 94 km/h)
Max rate of climb at S/L 2,360 ft (720 m)/min
Max rate of climb at S/L, at 1,389 lb (630 kg) gross weight 2,950 ft (900 m)/min
T-O run 230 ft (70 m)
T-O to 50 ft (15 m) 425 ft (130 m)
Landing from 50 ft (15 m) 1,050 ft (320 m)
Landing run 360 ft (110 m)
Range with max fuel, no reserve 465 nm (536 miles; 864 km)

HTM

HELICOPTER TECHNIK MÜNCHEN GmbH & CO ANLAGEN KG

ADDRESS:
D-8016 Feldkirchen b. München, Wittelsbacher Strasse 11
Telephone: (89) 9 03 25 41
Telex: 52 39 65

DIRECTORS:
Dr E. Schiek
Chr. Fischer

Helicopter Technik München was founded to produce the Skytrac helicopter which was originally designed and developed by Wagner Helicopter Technik of Friedrichshafen.

When development began in 1960, the objective was to evolve a torque-free basic vehicle, which could be fitted with a variety of cabins and specialised equipment for different applications. The basic Skytrac received German certification in 1969 and FAA certification in 1972.

Specialised equipment in kit form, which has already been developed and certificated, includes a cargo sling installation, dusting equipment, spraying system, floats and night flying equipment.

HTM also produces a kit to convert the multi-purpose Skytrac into a four-seat light passenger helicopter known as the Skyrider, and this is described separately.

HTM FJ-SKYTRAC

TYPE: Lightweight multi-purpose helicopter.

ROTOR SYSTEM: Two identical two-blade contra-rotating rotors of composite construction. Blade section NACA 0012. Each blade consists of a milled light alloy leading-edge spar and a glassfibre/epoxy resin laminate shell with foam core. Blades are each attached to the rotor heads via a grip and tension rod, forming a flapping hinge only. Blades do not fold. A rotor brake is fitted.

ROTOR DRIVE: Power input to special angle gearbox is transmitted through a drive clutch, sprag clutch and torsional damper.

FUSELAGE: Basic structure is a welded steel tube truss framework of rectangular section, supporting the cabin at the front, rotor pylon centrally and power plant at the rear.

TAIL UNIT: Vee tail surfaces carried on a light alloy semi-monocoque tailboom. Incidence varied by aircraft's control system and trimmed by an electrical actuator.

LANDING GEAR: Tubular skid landing gear of light alloy with retractable ground handling wheels. Floats can be attached to the skids for amphibious operation.

POWER PLANT: One flat-rated 260 hp Lycoming IO-540 six-cylinder horizontally-opposed air-cooled engine, mounted horizontally aft of rotor pylon. One fuel cell mounted on each side of fuselage, total capacity 57 Imp gallons (260 litres). Oil capacity 2·4 Imp gallons (11 litres).

ACCOMMODATION: Two seats beneath a transparent cockpit enclosure which slides forward for entry. Conventional controls.

EQUIPMENT: Optional kits available to convert the basic Skytrac for specialised roles including cargo lifting, agricultural dusting and spraying, and for amphibious and night flying operations.

SYSTEMS: Electrical power supplied by engine-driven alternator. 24V battery.

ELECTRONICS: Radio communications and navigation equipment to customer's requirements.

DIMENSIONS, EXTERNAL:

Diameter of rotors (each)	34 ft 1½ in (10·40 m)
Length overall, rotor blades fore and aft	34 ft 1½ in (10·40 m)
Length of fuselage	24 ft 1¼ in (7·35 m)
Height overall	11 ft 9¾ in (3·60 m)
Skid track	6 ft 11½ in (2·12 m)

AREAS:

Main rotor disc	914 sq ft (84·9 m²)
Tail surfaces (total)	19·16 sq ft (1·78 m²)

WEIGHTS AND LOADING:

Weight empty	2,028 lb (920 kg)
Slung payload with fuel for 1 hr	1,100 lb (500 kg)
Max T-O weight	3,306 lb (1,500 kg)
Max disc loading	3·60 lb/sq ft (17·6 kg/m²)

PERFORMANCE (at max T-O weight):

Max cruising speed	86 knots (99 mph; 160 km/h)
Max rate of climb at S/L	1,180 ft (360 m)/min
Service ceiling	12,665 ft (3,860 m)
Max range with standard fuel, 20 min reserve	334 nm (385 miles; 620 km)
Max endurance with standard fuel, 20 min reserve	4 hr

HTM FJ-Skytrac lightweight multi-purpose helicopter

HTM SKYRIDER

The Skyrider, which made its first flight on 21 February 1974, after a power plant change to a Lycoming HIO-540-K1A5 engine, is basically a Skytrac (D-HHTF) with added modification kit to convert the aircraft to four-seat configuration.

The basic structure is identical to that of the Skytrac, except as detailed below:

FUSELAGE: As for Skytrac, except that a glassfibre cabin structure and fairings have been added.

ACCOMMODATION: Single seat for pilot, with bench seat aft to accommodate three passengers. Door on each side of cabin; starboard door at forward end of cabin, port door aft. Baggage compartment in fuselage, aft of rotor pylon, with door on port side of fuselage. Cabin heated and ventilated.

SYSTEMS: Electrical power supplied by engine-driven alternator. 24V battery. Air-conditioning system optional.

ELECTRONICS AND EQUIPMENT: Radio communication and navigation equipment to customer's requirements. Cargo sling optional.

DIMENSIONS, EXTERNAL:

As for Skytrac, except:	
Length of fuselage	24 ft 4½ in (7·43 m)
Passenger door (stbd, fwd):	
Height	3 ft 5¼ in (1·05 m)
Width	2 ft 9½ in (0·85 m)
Height to sill	3 ft 0 in (0·91 m)
Passenger door (port, aft):	
Height	3 ft 5¼ in (1·05 m)
Width	2 ft 5½ in (0·75 m)
Height to sill	3 ft 0 in (0·91 m)
Baggage door:	
Height	1 ft 4½ in (0·41 m)
Width	2 ft 6 in (0·76 m)
Height to sill	4 ft 7 in (1·40 m)

Prototype of HTM's Skyrider four-seat helicopter developed from the FJ-Skytrac

DIMENSIONS, INTERNAL:

Cabin:	
Length	7 ft 4½ in (2·25 m)
Max width	4 ft 5½ in (1·36 m)
Max height	3 ft 11¼ in (1·20 m)
Baggage compartment volume	14·1 cu ft (0·4 m³)

WEIGHTS AND LOADING:

Weight empty	2,237 lb (1,015 kg)
Max T-O weight	3,373 lb (1,530 kg)
Max disc loading	3·69 lb/sq ft (18·02 kg/m²)

PERFORMANCE:

Design max level speed	100 knots (115 mph; 185 km/h)
Max cruising speed	86 knots (99 mph; 160 km/h)
Max rate of climb at S/L	1,180 ft (360 m)/min
Service ceiling	12,665 ft (3,860 m)
Range with max fuel and 727 lb (330 kg) payload, 20 min reserve	334 nm (385 miles; 620 km)
Range with 55% fuel, 915 lb (415 kg) payload and 20 min reserve	215 nm (248 miles; 400 km)

LFU

LEICHTFLUGTECHNIK-UNION GmbH (Subsidiary of Messerschmitt-Bölkow-Blohm GmbH)

ADDRESS:
53 Bonn, Bonn-Center, Bundeskanzlerplatz H1 904
Telephone: (02221) 22 59 81

MANAGERS:
Hans-Otto Fischer
Richard Schreiber

This association was formed in 1963 by Bölkow and its subsidiary Bölkow-Apparatebau GmbH (now part of Messerschmitt-Bölkow-Blohm GmbH); PKT Kunststofftechnik GmbH; and Rhein-Flugzeugbau GmbH, each with a one-third share, as a co-ordinating organisation for research and development of lightweight aircraft. The management is composed of representatives of the three parent companies, assisted in a consultant capacity by a Technical and Scientific Committee.

LFU's principal activity is the continued research into, and development of, the use of lightweight plastics for aircraft construction. This resulted in the design and construction of a prototype aircraft, the LFU-205, embodying the results of studies so far undertaken.

A full description of this aircraft appeared in the 1970-71 *Jane's*.

MBB

MESSERSCHMITT-BÖLKOW-BLOHM GmbH

HEAD OFFICE:
Ottobrunn bei München, 8 München 80, Postfach 801220
Telephone: (0811) 60001
Telex: 0522279 mbbo

WORKS:
Augsburg, Donauwörth, Hamburg-Finkenwerder, Laupheim, Manching, Munich, Nabern/Teck, Ottobrunn, Schrobenhausen and Stade

PRESIDENT:
Dipl-Ing Ludwig Bölkow

EXECUTIVE VICE-PRESIDENT:
Dipl-Ing Werner Blohm

VICE-PRESIDENTS:
Dr Johannes Broschwitz
Gunther Horstkotte
Sepp Hort
Ernst-Georg Pantel
Hans Wallner

PUBLIC RELATIONS:
Eduard Roth

EXECUTIVES:
Ernst-Georg Pantel (Aircraft Division)
Dipl-Ing Werner Blohm (Commercial Aircraft Division)
Günther Kuhlo (Dynamics Division)
Peter Schulz (Surface Transport Division)
Julius Henrici (Space Division)
Kurt Pfleiderer (Helicopter Division)
Kyrill von Gersdorff (Administrative Services Division)

CHAIRMAN OF THE SUPERVISORY BOARD:
Dr Karl Schott

HONORARY CHAIRMAN OF THE SUPERVISORY BOARD:
Prof Dr-Ing E.h. Willy Messerschmitt

In May 1969 the former Messerschmitt-Bölkow GmbH and Hamburger Flugzeugbau GmbH (see 1968-69 *Jane's*) respectively endorsed the merger between their two companies to form a new group known as Messerschmitt-Bölkow-Blohm GmbH. Major shareholder in the new company is the Blohm family, which has a 22·05% interest; other shareholders are Prof Dr Ing E.h. Willy Messerschmitt (16·3%), Dipl-Ing Ludwig Bölkow (13·42%), The Boeing Company and Aérospatiale (8·9% each), Siemens AG (8·35%), the Bavarian State (7·8%), the Bavarian Reconstruction Finance Institute (5·93%) and August Thyssen-Hütte AG (8·35%). The company is the largest aerospace concern in Germany, with a total work force in 1973 of some 19,000 employees, and is affiliated with a number of national and international corporations.

In the military aircraft field, development work on the Panavia MRCA, as Germany's prime contractor, is the company's main activity. MBB has a 42·5% shareholding in Panavia Aircraft GmbH (which see), together with BAC (42.5%) and Aeritalia (15%). MBB participated substantially in licence production of the F-104G Starfighter, a present standard weapon system of the German air force, and the company's Manching facilities are responsible for overhaul of these aircraft, as well as of the F-4 Phantom.

The main civil aircraft programme involves work on the European A-300B Airbus for Airbus Industrie (which see). MBB's share in the development and production of this aircraft is around 30%, which represents 65% of the total German share.

The HFB 320 Hansa, developed and produced in Hamburg, was Germany's first commercial jet transport and executive aircraft.

MBB's BO 105 is the world's first twin-turbine lightweight utility helicopter to enter series production. The glassfibre-reinforced plastics technology developed for its rotor blades has found many applications in engineering fields.

MBB weapon systems include the Kormoran air-to-ship stand-off missile, the Armbrust-300 anti-tank weapon and, in partnership with Aérospatiale of France, the Roland low-level anti-aircraft missile, and the Hot and Milan second-generation anti-tank weapon systems. MBB has produced more than 100,000 Cobra first-generation anti-tank missiles.

Current space project and development work includes systems leadership in the programmes for the German-American Helios solar probe and the COS B research satellite, and substantial participation in the Franco-German Symphonie communications satellite. Four research satellites (Azur, DIAL, HEOS-A1 and HEOS-A2) have already been launched successfully under the company's systems leadership. MBB is bidding as leader of a European consortium for Spacelab, the ESRO space laboratory which will represent a substantial European contribution to the US Space Shuttle programme. Other space activities of the company include rocket engine development, and work on solar cell arrays, cryogenics, control techniques and the construction of check-out systems.

Constantly growing importance is attached by MBB to ground-based forms of transport, and the company has had a major share in the biggest transport study ever undertaken for the Federal Ministry of Transport. This entailed investigation of the need for, and the economics of, a high-performance high-speed transport system (HSB).

The world's first experimental vehicle using the magnetic cushion effect and the linear induction motor is being used at MBB for testing possible components of such a rail system. Another important project for transport operations of the future is the cabin taxi personal rapid transit system being developed by MBB and DEMAG.

The company is also engaged in various other engineering fields, to make optimum use of its aerospace technology in hard- and software for other applications, such as environmental control.

MBB 223 FLAMINGO

The MBB (originally SIAT) 223 Flamingo, which flew for the first time on 1 March 1967, was offered by MBB in two versions, production of which totalled 50 aircraft by the end of January 1972. Manufacture has been transferred to CASA in Spain (which see).

MBB BO 105

As a first stage in the development of this light utility helicopter, Bölkow tested a full-size rotor on a ground rig, under German government contract. Design of the aircraft was started in July 1962 and construction of prototypes began in 1964, under a further government contract.

The rotor system is of rigid unarticulated design, with feathering hinges only, based on a concept by Dipl-Ing E. Weiland, and utilises foldable glassfibre blades. Initial flight tests were made on a Sud-Aviation Alouette II Astazou helicopter, under a programme conducted jointly with Sud-Aviation of France.

The first prototype was fitted with an existing conventional rotor and two Allison 250-C18 turboshaft engines; subsequent aircraft have had the rigid rotor.

The second BO 105 flew for the first time on 16 February 1967, also powered by two Allison 250-C18 turboshaft engines. The third prototype, with MAN-Turbo 6022 engines, was flown on 20 December 1967.

The first two pre-production aircraft (the V4 and V5) were completed in the Spring of 1969, and the V4 flew for the first time on 1 May 1969. It was subsequently fitted with two Allison 250-C20 engines, with which it made its first flight on 11 January 1971. Production aircraft can be fitted, at customer's option, with either Allison 250-C18 or 250-C20 engines.

Autorotation trials with the BO 105 were successfully concluded in the Autumn of 1969. From the Spring of 1970 "droop-snoot" rotor blades of MBB design were introduced.

German LBA type certification with the Allison 250-C18 power plant was granted in October 1970, and FAA certification in March 1971. LBA and FAA certification with the -C20 power plant were granted in August 1971 and April 1972 respectively. Canadian MoT certification for the BO 105 "C" with -C20 power plant was granted in April 1973, and UK CAA certification for the BO 105 "D" in July 1973. Registro Aeronautico Italiano (RAI) certification was received in March 1974.

Instrument Meteorological Condition (IMC) approval for the BO 105 "D" was granted by the CAA in May 1973. Minimum crew for flight is one pilot if T-O and terminal approach are under VFR conditions. Night T-O from offshore platforms is permissible under IMC. If meteorological conditions are too severe to permit VFR, or if flights involve terminal approaches within notified control zones, a crew of two must be carried.

A total of 110 BO 105s had been delivered by 1 February 1974, when production was continuing at a rate of 6 to 8 aircraft per month.

The Federal German government has ordered 20 BO 105s under its "Katastrophenschutz" scheme to provide speedy assistance after major disasters. One BO 105 has also been fitted experimentally with outriggers to carry a total of six Hot anti-tank missiles, three on each side of the cabin, with a stabilised sight above the flight deck on the port side.

Boeing Vertol Company (which see) has exclusive sales rights for the US and other areas of the western hemisphere, and an option to produce the BO 105 under licence.

TYPE: Five-seat light helicopter.

ROTOR SYSTEM: Four-blade main rotor, with folding glassfibre-reinforced plastics blades. MBB-designed "droop-snoot" blades of NACA 23012 asymmetrical section, and having a specially-designed trailing-edge giving improved control in pitching moment. Titanium rotor hub. Two-blade semi-rigid tail rotor, with blades of glassfibre-reinforced plastics. Rotor brake fitted. WMI (EEC) Spraymat electrical de-icing of main and tail rotor blade leading-edges.

ROTOR DRIVE: Main transmission utilises two stages of spur gears and single stage of bevel gearing. Planetary reduction gear, freewheeling clutch and transmission accessory gear. Tail rotor gearbox on fin. Main rotor/engine rpm ratio 1 : 14·1. Tail rotor/engine rpm ratio 1 : 2·7.

FUSELAGE: Conventional light alloy semi-monocoque structure of pod and boom type. Glass-fibre-reinforced cowling over power plant.

TAIL UNIT: Horizontal stabiliser of conventional light alloy construction.

LANDING GEAR: Skids, to which inflatable emergency floats can be attached.

POWER PLANT: Two 317 shp Allison 250-C18 or 400 shp 250-C20 turboshaft engines. One 125 Imp gallon (570 litre) integral fuel tank under cabin floor, with fuelling point on port side of cabin. Provision for fitting auxiliary tanks in freight compartment for ferrying. Oil capacity: engine 8·8 lb (4 kg), gearbox 15·4 lb (7 kg).

ACCOMMODATION: Pilot and passenger on individual front seats. Removable dual controls. Bench seat for three persons. Rear seat removable for cargo and stretcher carrying. Entire rear fuselage aft of seats and under power plant available as freight and baggage space, with access through two clamshell doors at rear. Two standard stretchers can be accommodated in ambulance role. One forward-opening door and one sliding door on each side of cabin. Cabin is ventilated and heated.

SYSTEMS: Hydraulic system for powered controls. 24Ah battery and starter/generator, with provision for external connection.

ELECTRONICS AND EQUIPMENT: Provision for radio, rotating beacon, IFR instrumentation and navigation aids, rescue winch, agricultural equipment, autopilot, cargo hook, swivelling seat at front on port side.

ARMAMENT (Military versions): Provision for a variety of alternative military loads, including six Hot anti-tank missiles and associated stabilised sight.

DIMENSIONS, EXTERNAL:

Diameter of main rotor	32 ft 2¾ in (9·82 m)
Diameter of tail rotor	6 ft 2¾ in (1·90 m)
Distance between rotor centres	19 ft 6¼ in (5·95 m)
Length, excl main rotor	28 ft 0½ in (8·55 m)
Overall height	9 ft 9⅜ in (2·98 m)
Skid track	8 ft 2½ in (2·50 m)
Rear loading doors:	
Height	2 ft 1 in (0·64 m)
Width	4 ft 7 in (1·40 m)

DIMENSIONS, INTERNAL:

Cabin, including cargo compartment:	
Length	14 ft 1 in (4·30 m)
Max width	4 ft 7 in (1·40 m)
Max height	4 ft 1 in (1·25 m)
Floor area (cargo compartment)	23·68 sq ft (2·20 m^2)
Volume	169 cu ft (4·80 m^3)
Cargo compartment	53 cu ft (1·50 m^3)

WEIGHTS AND LOADINGS:

Weight empty	2,447 lb (1,110 kg)
Max T-O weight	5,070 lb (2,300 kg)
Normal disc loading	5·43 lb/sq ft (26·5 kg/m^2)
Max disc loading	6·25 lb/sq ft (30·5 kg/m^2)

PERFORMANCE (at normal T-O weight, Allison 250-C20 engines):

Max never-exceed speed at S/L	145 knots (167 mph; 270 km/h)
Max cruising speed at S/L	125 knots (144 mph; 232 km/h)
Max rate of climb at S/L	1,320 ft (402 m)/min
Rate of climb at S/L, one engine out	150 ft (46 m)/min
Service ceiling	16,500 ft (5,030 m)
Hovering ceiling in ground effect	8,900 ft (2,715 m)
Hovering ceiling out of ground effect	5,700 ft (1,735 m)
Range with standard fuel, no reserves:	
at S/L	315 nm (363 miles; 585 km)
at 5,000 ft (1,525 m)	355 nm (408 miles; 656 km)

MBB BO 105 with inflatable emergency floats attached to landing gear and fuselage-mounted rescue hoist

MBB BO 105 fitted experimentally with six Hot anti-tank missiles and stabilised sight

Max range with auxiliary tanks:
at S/L 556 nm (640 miles; 1,030 km)
at 5,000 ft (1,525 m)
626 nm (720 miles; 1,158 km)
Max endurance with auxiliary tanks 6 hr 35 min

MBB BO 105HGH

An accompanying illustration shows a BO 105 fitted with a rear fuselage fairing, rotor head fairing and four small individual landing gear skids, under a high-speed research programme. Known as the BO 105HGH, this aircraft attained a speed of 200 knots (231 mph; 372 km/h) in a shallow dive at max AUW in September 1973. It was scheduled to resume flight testing in May 1974, after the addition of fixed wings, spanning 19 ft 8¼ in (6·00 m) and with an NACA 230 section varying from 15% thickness/chord ratio at the roots to 12% at the tips. Airbrakes are mounted above and below the leading-edge of each wing; and it is hoped to maintain high manoeuvrability at speeds above 162 knots (186 mph; 300 km/h). Max speed in level flight is 151 knots (174 mph; 280 km/h).

MBB BO 106

First flown on 25 September 1973, the BO 106 is generally similar to the BO 105 but has the cabin widened by 19·7 in (50 cm) to seat two or three persons in front and four on the rear bench. Its uprated Allison 250-C20B engines each develop a maximum of 420 shp and give 50 shp more than the 250-C20 at ISA + 20°C. This gives the BO 106 a performance similar to that of the BO 105 at a higher gross weight of 5,400 lb (2,450 kg).

The prototype was developed with government aid (60%). It is hoped to make available kits to convert existing BO 105s to BO 106 standard, as well as new production aircraft.

MBB HFB 320 HANSA

Design of the Hansa was started in March 1961. The first prototype flew for the first time on 21 April 1964, and was followed by the first production Hansa on 2 February 1966. Versions delivered included VIP aircraft, both civil and military, quick-change passenger/cargo aircraft, pilot trainers, navigation flying classroom and calibration aircraft.

A production series of 50 Hansas was put in hand, of which the first 15 had General Electric CJ610-1 engines. The next 20 were fitted with more powerful CJ610-5 engines. From the 36th aircraft onwards, production Hansas had the further-uprated CJ610-9 model of this engine. A full description of the aircraft in its final form can be found in the 1973-74 *Jane's*.

MBB BO 105HGH, a modified version of the BO 105 for high-speed research

MBB BO 106, a six/seven-seat development of the five-seat BO 105

MYLIUS

ENTWICKLUNGSGEMEINSCHAFT LEICHTFLUGZEUGE DIPL ING HERMANN MYLIUS

ADDRESS:
8011 Brunnthal-Gudrunsiedlung, Kuckucksweg 6

In addition to heading the light aircraft technical development activities of MBB, Dipl Ing Hermann Mylius develops and builds sporting aircraft privately. One such aircraft was the MHK 101, intended as the first of a family of related designs, which flew for the first time on 22 December 1967 and was manufactured by MBB in developed form as the BO 209 Monsun. The MHK 101 was described in the 1968-69 *Jane's*. Details of the BO 209, of which 102 were built, can be found under the MBB entry in the 1972-73 *Jane's*.

In July 1971, Dipl Ing Mylius began privately the development of a single-seat version of the MHK 101, intended for competitive aerobatics. Construction of a prototype was started in December 1971, and the prototype flew for the first time on 7 July 1973. Known as the MY 102 Tornado, it had completed 50 hours of flight testing by March 1974, and had participated successfully in the 1973 German Aerobatic Championships.

MYLIUS MY 102 TORNADO

TYPE: Single-seat sporting and aerobatic aircraft.

WINGS: Cantilever low-wing monoplane. Wing section NACA 64215 at root, NACA 64212 at tip. Dihedral 2° 30′. Incidence 2°. Sweepback 1° 24′ at quarter-chord. Single-spar all-metal structure with glassfibre wingtips. All-metal differentially-operated ailerons. Electrically-operated all-metal plain trailing-edge flaps. By removing three bolts on each side, the wings can be folded back alongside the fuselage to facilitate stowage in a confined space or to permit the aircraft to be towed on ordinary roads behind a car. Control lines to flaps and ailerons disconnect and reconnect automatically during folding and unfolding.

FUSELAGE: Conventional semi-monocoque structure of light alloy, except for engine cowlings which are of glassfibre.

TAIL UNIT: Single fin and rudder, with sweepback on fin leading-edge and dorsal fairing from base of fin to rear of cockpit canopy. Vertical tail surfaces are of all-metal construction. All-moving tailplane, of metal construction with glassfibre tips, has slight taper on leading- and trailing-edges, and is mid-mounted on extreme rear of fuselage, with cable-controlled full-span anti-servo tab.

LANDING GEAR: Tricycle type, with optionally rearward-retracting nosewheel and non-retractable main wheels. Single wheel on each unit. Nosewheel is steerable by means of the rudder pedals, the controls being disconnected automatically during retraction, which is accomplished electrically. Nosewheel can be locked in the down position during flight, if required. Main-gear legs are cantilever steel struts, inclined outwards at 45° from fuselage main bulkhead. Cleveland wheels size 5·00-5; Continental tyres size 5·00-5 on nosewheel and 5·50-5 on main wheels. Streamlined fairings on main wheels. Cleveland hydraulically-actuated brakes. Small skid under rear fuselage, which can be fitted with an adapter for transport by road.

POWER PLANT: One 200 hp Lycoming AIO-360-B1B four-cylinder horizontally-opposed air-cooled engine, driving a Hoffmann type HO-V 123/180R three-blade metal constant-speed propeller with spinner. Fuel in two tanks in wings, each with capacity of 19·4 US gallons (73·4 litres). Total fuel capacity 38·8 US gallons (146·8 litres). Refuelling point in upper surface of each wing.

ACCOMMODATION: Single seat, beneath rearward-sliding tinted canopy.

SYSTEMS: DC electrical system for flaps and nose gear actuation, and engine starting, provided by 40A engine-driven alternator and 12V 33Ah battery. Hydraulic system for brakes only.

ELECTRONICS: Becker AR400 radio.

DIMENSIONS, EXTERNAL:	
Wing span	26 ft 6¾ in (8·10 m)
Wing chord at root	4 ft 7 in (1·40 m)
Wing chord at tip	3 ft 3¼ in (1·00 m)
Wing aspect ratio	6·7
Length overall	21 ft 0 in (6·40 m)
Height overall	7 ft 7 in (2·31 m)
Tailplane span	9 ft 2¼ in (2·80 m)
Wheel track	6 ft 4¼ in (1·94 m)
Wheelbase	4 ft 4¼ in (1·33 m)
Propeller diameter	5 ft 11 in (1·80 m)
AREAS:	
Wings, gross	105·5 sq ft (9·80 m²)
Ailerons (total)	8·61 sq ft (0·80 m²)
Trailing-edge flaps (total)	9·15 sq ft (0·85 m²)
Fin	5·38 sq ft (0·50 m²)
Rudder	5·60 sq ft (0·52 m²)
Tailplane (incl tab)	17·87 sq ft (1·66 m²)
WEIGHTS AND LOADINGS (A: Normal; B: Utility; C: Aerobatic):	
Weight empty	1,168 lb (530 kg)
Max T-O weight:	
A	1,807 lb (820 kg)
B	1,631 lb (740 kg)
C	1,433 lb (650 kg)
Max wing loading:	
A	17·1 lb/sq ft (83·5 kg/m²)
B	15·4 lb/sq ft (75·0 kg/m²)
C	13·6 lb/sq ft (66·5 kg/m²)
Max power loading:	
A	9·04 lb/hp (4·1 kg/hp)
B	8·16 lb/hp (3·7 kg/hp)
C	7·17 lb/hp (3·25 kg/hp)

Mylius MY 102 prototype single-seat sporting monoplane (200 hp Lycoming AIO-360-B1B engine)

PERFORMANCE (at max Normal T-O weight):
Max never-exceed speed
214 knots (246 mph; 396 km/h)
Max level speed at S/L
174 knots (200 mph; 322 km/h)
Max cruising speed
160 knots (184 mph; 296 km/h)
Stalling speed, flaps down
52 knots (60 mph; 97 km/h)
Max rate of climb at S/L 2,400 ft (732 m)/min
Service ceiling 30,000 ft (9,145 m)
T-O run 330 ft (100 m)
Landing run 590 ft (180 m)
Range with max fuel at AUW of 1,653 lb (750 kg), no reserve 517 nm (596 miles; 960 km)

POLIGRAT

POLIGRAT DEVELOPMENT GmbH & Co KG

ADDRESS:
D-8000 München 90

AIRCRAFT DEPARTMENT MANAGER:
Wilhelm Benz

In early 1974 this company, which was formed in 1971, announced details of its first aircraft programmes, involving two twin-engined cargo and passenger transports known as the PD-01 Master Porter and the PC-10 Twin Porter. It is also participating with Pilatus in developing the Module Porter version of the latter's PC-6 Turbo-Porter (which see).

POLIGRAT PD-01 MASTER PORTER

The Master Porter is a twin-turboprop STOL transport aircraft, intended for third-level passenger and/or cargo operations. It has been designed to CAB Pt 298 standards, and Poligrat's ultimate objective is to market it as a product for assembly by approved foreign licensees.

Under contract to Poligrat, Pilatus in Switzerland (assisted by the Federal Aircraft Factory at Emmen) is building two prototypes and a static test airframe. The first prototype is scheduled to fly in September 1975, with certification anticipated in time for production deliveries to begin in the Summer of 1976. An enlarged version seating up to 30 passengers is under consideration.

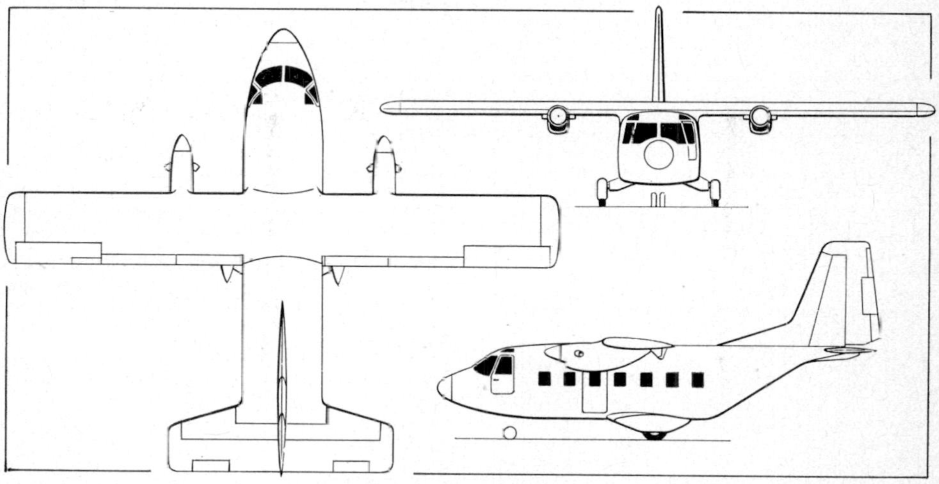

Poligrat PD-01 Master Porter twin-turboprop transport (*Pilot Press*)

TYPE: Twin-turboprop transport aircraft.

WINGS: Cantilever high-wing monoplane of light alloy construction, built in three sections. Constant-chord wings, without dihedral. Wing section NACA 23015. Double-slotted trailing-edge flaps. Trim tab in port aileron.

FUSELAGE: Conventional all-metal semi-monocoque structure of basically rectangular section. Fuselage normally unpressurised, but flight deck pressurisation available at customer's option.

TAIL UNIT: Cantilever structure. Large inset tab in rudder and tab in each half of elevator.

LANDING GEAR: Forward-retracting twin-wheel nose unit. Non-retractable single main wheels, housed in stub-fairings attached to base of fuselage. Designed by Menasco of Montreal.

POWER PLANT: Two 1,120 shp United Aircraft of Canada PT6A-45 turboprop engines, each driving a Hartzell five-blade propeller. Integral fuel tanks in wings.

ACCOMMODATION: Crew of two on flight deck. Three-abreast cabin seating for 19 passengers, or four-abreast for up to 24 passengers in high-density layout, with provision for toilet at front and baggage compartments. Quick-change (30 min) conversion capability to all-cargo configuration, including provision for folding and stowing passenger seats if required. Intermediate combined passenger/cargo layouts also available. Passenger door, with integral steps, ahead of wing on port side. Large rear-loading door, which can be lowered to serve as a ramp or opened upward and inward. Fuselage cross-section can accept standard 88 × 88 in (2·24 × 2·24 m) pallets or LD-1, -3 or -7 containers. Roller conveyor system and crash net available at customer's option.

EQUIPMENT: Standard equipment includes communications radio and cockpit and voice recorders.

DIMENSIONS, EXTERNAL:
Wing span 57 ft 1 in (17·40 m)
Wing aspect ratio 7·98
Length overall 45 ft 3 in (13·79 m)
Height overall 20 ft 8 in (6·30 m)
Tailplane span 22 ft 11½ in (7·00 m)
Wheel track 11 ft 4¾ in (3·50 m)
Wheelbase 14 ft 9 in (4·50 m)
Propeller diameter 9 ft 3 in (2·82 m)
Rear loading door:
Height 7 ft 7 in (2·31 m)
Width 6 ft 3¼ in (1·91 m)

DIMENSIONS, INTERNAL:
Cabin: Max length 20 ft 5½ in (6·24 m)
Max width 7 ft 6½ in (2·30 m)
Max height 6 ft 7½ in (2·02 m)

AREA:
Wings, gross 408·4 sq ft (37·94 m²)

WEIGHTS:
Weight empty 7,253 lb (3,290 kg)
Max T-O weight 14,330 lb (6,500 kg)

PERFORMANCE (estimated, at max T-O weight):
Max level speed at 10,000 ft (3,050 m), max continuous power
230 knots (264 mph; 426 km/h)
Max cruising speed
215 knots (248 mph; 400 km/h)
Econ cruising speed
175 knots (201 mph; 324 km/h)
Stalling speed, wheels and flaps down
66 knots (76 mph; 122 km/h)
Max rate of climb at S/L 2,380 ft (726 m)/min
Service ceiling 27,900 ft (8,500 m)
Service ceiling, one engine out
13,450 ft (4,100 m)
T-O run 804 ft (245 m)
T-O to 50 ft (15 m) 1,510 ft (460 m)
Landing from 50 ft (15 m) 2,198 ft (675 m)
Landing run with reverse thrust
902 ft (275 m)
Range with max fuel
1,295 nm (1,491 miles; 2,400 km)
Range with max payload
108 nm (124 miles; 200 km)

POLIGRAT PC-10 TWIN PORTER

Poligrat has assumed responsibility for development of the Twin Porter transport aircraft, a project originally undertaken by Pilatus (see 1969-70 *Jane's*) and later shelved.

As now envisaged, the current Twin Porter is virtually a new design compared with the original proposal, but it is not intended for production until after the Master Porter is established on the market. Powered by two 680 shp United Aircraft of Canada PT6A-27 turboprop engines, it is designed to FAR 25 standards and will have accommodation for 15-18 passengers or 3,527 lb (1,600 kg) of cargo. The PC-10 will have a wing span of 62 ft 4 in (19·00 m) and empty and max T-O weights of 5,390 lb (2,445 kg) and 10,360 lb (4,700 kg) respectively.

RFB

RHEIN-FLUGZEUGBAU GmbH (Subsidiary of VFW-Fokker GmbH)

HEAD OFFICE AND MAIN WORKS:
405 Mönchengladbach, Flugplatz, Postfach 408
Telephone: (0 21 61) 6 20 31-35
Telex: 08/52506

OTHER WORKS:
505 Porz-Wahn, Flughafen Köln-Bonn, Halle 6; and 2401 Lübeck-Blankensee, Flugplatz

EXECUTIVE DIRECTORS:
Dipl-Volkswirt Wolfgang Kutscher
Dipl-Ing Alfred Schneider

This company, founded in 1956, acquired in 1969 a 50% holding in the stock of Sportavia-Pützer (which see).

RFB is engaged on the development and construction of airframe structural components, with particular reference to wings and fuselages made entirely of glassfibre-reinforced resins. Research and design activities include studies for the Federal German Ministry of Defence.

Current manufacturing programmes include series and individual production of aircraft components and assemblies, made of light alloy, steel and glassfibre-reinforced resin, for aircraft in quantity production by other German companies, as well as spare parts and ground equipment. The company is also concerned in shelter and container construction.

Under contract to the German government, RFB is servicing certain types of military aircraft, and is providing target-towing flights and other services with special aircraft. It operates a factory-certificated service centre for all types of Piper aircraft and the Mitsubishi MU-2 utility transport aircraft. General servicing of other types of all-metal aircraft is undertaken, together with the servicing, maintenance, repair and testing of all kinds of flight instruments, engine instruments and navigation and communications electronics.

RFB/Grumman American Fanliner two-seat light aircraft, powered by a Wankel engine driving a ducted fan (*Brian M. Service*)

In the aircraft propulsion field, RFB has been engaged in the development of specialised applications for ducted propellers, leading to the Fantrainer AWI 2 project, of which brief details can be found in the 1972-73 *Jane's*. In April 1974 it was announced that RFB and Grumman American Aviation (which see) had been collaborating in the development of a new two-seat light aircraft, named the Fanliner, which utilises the ducted-fan propulsion system evolved by RFB.

Under the scientific direction of Dr A. M. Lippisch, the all-plastics X-113 Am Aerofoil Boat has been built and tested.

RFB/GRUMMAN AMERICAN FANLINER

Announced in April 1974, the Fanliner is a two-seat lightweight aircraft developed jointly by RFB of Germany and Grumman American Aviation of the USA. Evolving from RFB's studies of ducted fans, the new aircraft has such a propulsion system and is powered by an NSU Wankel-type engine of 114 hp. Airframe construction benefits from adhesive bonding experience with the Grumman American Trainer and Traveler, and a number of components are common between these aircraft and the Fanliner.

Flight testing of the prototype (D-EJFL) has shown that the ducted fan propulsion system offers a more efficient utilisation of engine power than does a conventional propeller installation. In addition, the rear-mounted engine with central, ducted pusher propeller provides improved visibility, lower cabin noise level, more convenient access for pilot and passenger and, with the propeller shielded by a duct, a reduced ground hazard.

Fanliner flight tests began on 8 October 1973, and both companies were enthusiastic about the results achieved in 75 flying hours up to the end of April 1974. A decision on whether to put the aircraft into production will depend upon evaluation of the full test programme, which was then continuing. Deliveries could begin in 1976.

Type: Two-seat lightweight experimental aircraft.

Wings: Cantilever mid-wing monoplane of light alloy construction, similar to those of Grumman American Traveler. Dihedral from roots. No sweep. Constant chord. Ailerons and trailing-edge flaps of light alloy bonded construction. No tabs.

Fuselage: Semi-monocoque forward structure of light alloy, comprising nose, cockpit and enclosed engine mounting. Aft fuselage, to carry tail unit, consists of a narrow-section structure continuing the upper and lower lines of the forward fuselage, with a bracing beam extending from the trailing-edge of the wing centre-section to the tail unit on each side.

Tail Unit: T-tail of light alloy construction, with swept vertical surfaces. Rudder and elevators of light alloy bonded construction.

Landing Gear: Non-retractable tricycle type. Cantilever main-gear legs. Single wheel and speed fairing on each unit.

Power Plant: One 114 hp Audi NSU Ro 135 Wankel-type two-chamber rotating-piston engine, driving a pusher propeller, with three plastics blades, mounted within an annular duct.

Accommodation: Two seats side by side in enclosed cockpit. Individual upward-opening transparent cockpit canopies, hinged on centre-line. Dual controls standard. Baggage space aft of seats. Provision for coat locker in nose.

Dimensions, external:

Wing span	24 ft 5¼ in (7·45 m)
Wing aspect ratio	6·0
Length overall	20 ft 0 in (6·10 m)
Height overall	6 ft 8 in (2·03 m)

Area:

Wings, gross	100·1 sq ft (9·30 m²)

Weights and Loadings:

Weight empty	1,146 lb (520 kg)
Max T-O weight	1,653 lb (750 kg)
Max wing loading	16·5 lb/sq ft (80·64 kg/m²)
Max power loading	14·51 lb/hp (6·58 kg/hp)

Performance (at max T-O weight):

Max level speed at S/L	119 knots (137 mph; 220 km/h)
Max cruising speed at S/L	97 knots (112 mph; 180 km/h)
Max rate of climb at S/L	650 ft (198 m)/min
Range	356 nm (410 miles; 660 km)

RFB (LIPPISCH) X-113 Am AEROFOIL BOAT

The Aerofoil Boat concept was begun in the United States by Dr A. M. Lippisch, and was first tested in the Collins X-112 craft which was described in the 1964-65 *Jane's*.

Since 1967 further development of the concept has been undertaken by RFB, with assistance from the German Federal government, under the designation X-113, as a preliminary to experiments with larger craft of the same type. Dr Lippisch remains the technical and scientific manager of the project. The present X-113 Am, which is a single-seat craft, underwent its first airworthiness test from Lake Constance in October 1970, and flight characteristics and performance have proved satisfactory. Since that time, tests carried out in the North Sea have shown that the Aerofoil Boat can be operated successfully in rough water conditions. Development work was continuing in early 1974.

The X-113 Am is powered by a 48 hp (derated to 40 hp) Nelson H63-CP four-cylinder horizontally-opposed two-stroke engine, driving a two-blade wooden propeller. The airframe is of a special glassfibre sandwich construction, with a core of tubular or foam plastics. The general appearance of the X-113 Am can be seen in the accompanying illustration.

Dimensions, external:

Wing span	19 ft 3¾ in (5·89 m)
Length overall	27 ft 8 in (8·43 m)
Height overall	6 ft 9½ in (2·07 m)
Propeller diameter	3 ft 10 in (1·17 m)

Weights:

Weight empty	562 lb (255 kg)
Max T-O weight	760 lb (345 kg)

RFB (Lippisch) X-113 Am Aerofoil Boat in flight over Lake Constance

SPORTAVIA

SPORTAVIA-PÜTZER GmbH u Co KG

Head Office and Works:
D-5377 Dahlem-Schmidtheim, Flugplatz Dahlemer Binz

Telephone: (02447) 277/8

Telex: 08 33 602

Sales Manager: Alfons Pützer

This company was formed in 1966 by Comte Antoine d'Assche, director of the French company Alpavia SA, and Mr Alfons Pützer, to take over from Alpavia manufacture of the Avion-Planeur series of light aircraft designed by M René Fournier.

In 1969, RFB (which see), a subsidiary of VFW-Fokker GmbH, acquired a 50 per cent holding in Sportavia.

Recently, the company has designed and built two prototypes of a new lightweight 2+2-seat sporting aircraft designated RF6, details of which follow:

Sportavia Fournier RF6 Sportsman (125 hp Lycoming O-235 engine)

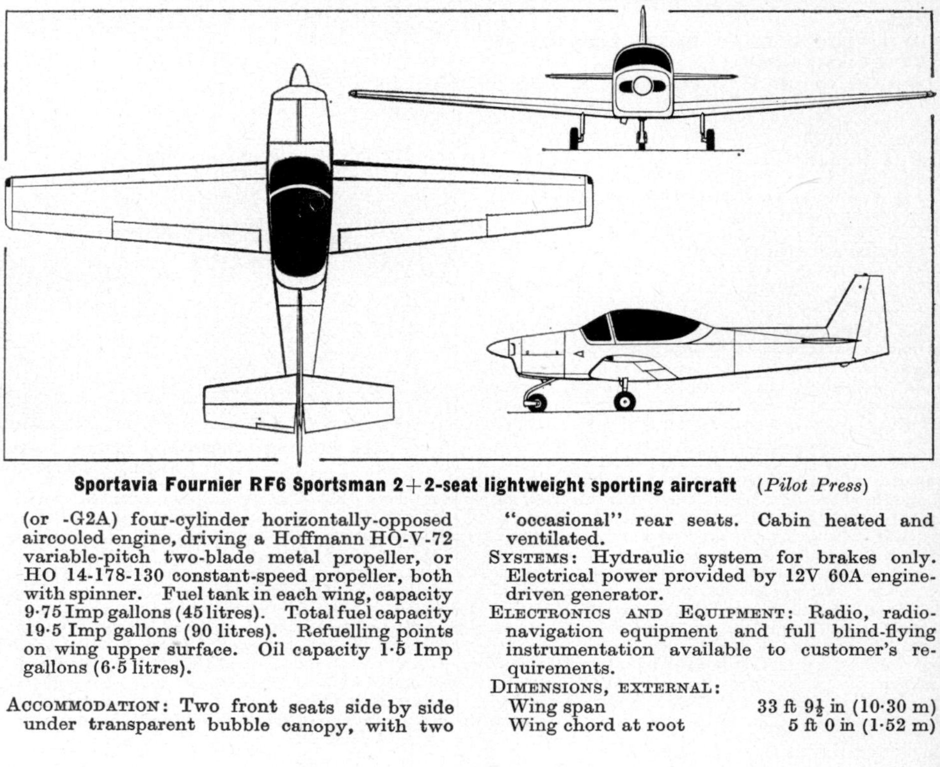

Sportavia Fournier RF6 Sportsman 2+2-seat lightweight sporting aircraft *(Pilot Press)*

SPORTAVIA FOURNIER RF6 SPORTSMAN

M René Fournier began design of the RF6 in December 1970. Construction of the first of two prototypes started fourteen months later, and this aircraft made its first flight on 1 March 1973.

The following details apply to the prototype: details of the RF6 Sportsman and RF6B Club proposed production versions are given in the Addenda. A prototype of the RF6B (F-WPXV) flew for the first time, in France, on 12 March 1974.

Type: 2+2-seat lightweight sporting aircraft.

Wings: Cantilever low-wing monoplane. Wing section NACA 23015 at root, NACA 23012 at tip. Dihedral 4°. All-wood single-spar structure, with plywood and fabric covering. Frise-type ailerons of wooden construction, with fabric covering. Trailing-edge flaps of wooden construction, fabric-covered. No trim tabs.

Fuselage: All-wood oval structure, plywood-covered.

Tail Unit: Cantilever wood structure. Fixed-incidence tailplane. Flettner trim tab in elevators.

Landing Gear: Non-retractable tricycle type. Main units have oleo-pneumatic shock-absorption. Nosewheel carried on strut of E 6150 steel tube, with large free-swivelling fork. Single wheel on each unit. Cleveland single-disc hydraulic brakes.

Power Plant: One 125 hp Lycoming O-235-F2A (or -G2A) four-cylinder horizontally-opposed aircooled engine, driving a Hoffmann HO-V-72 variable-pitch two-blade metal propeller, or HO 14-178-130 constant-speed propeller, both with spinner. Fuel tank in each wing, capacity 9·75 Imp gallons (45 litres). Total fuel capacity 19·5 Imp gallons (90 litres). Refuelling points on wing upper surface. Oil capacity 1·5 Imp gallons (6·5 litres).

Accommodation: Two front seats side by side under transparent bubble canopy, with two "occasional" rear seats. Cabin heated and ventilated.

Systems: Hydraulic system for brakes only. Electrical power provided by 12V 60A engine-driven generator.

Electronics and Equipment: Radio, radio-navigation equipment and full blind-flying instrumentation available to customer's requirements.

Dimensions, external:

Wing span	33 ft 9½ in (10·30 m)
Wing chord at root	5 ft 0 in (1·52 m)

Wing chord at tip	2 ft 8¾ in (0·83 m)
Wing aspect ratio	8·44
Length overall	23 ft 0¼ in (7·02 m)
Height overall	7 ft 8¾ in (2·36 m)
Tailplane span	10 ft 8½ in (3·26 m)
Propeller diameter	5 ft 10 in (1·78 m)
Propeller ground clearance	9¾ in (0·25 m)

Areas:

Wings, gross	135·3 sq ft (12·57 m²)
Ailerons (total)	12·49 sq ft (1·16 m²)
Trailing-edge flaps (total)	16·58 sq ft (1·54 m²)
Fin	11·30 sq ft (1·05 m²)
Rudder	3·77 sq ft (0·35 m²)
Horizontal surfaces, including tab	28·42 sq ft (2·64 m²)

Weights and Loadings (estimated):

Weight empty, equipped	992 lb (450 kg)
Max T-O and landing weight	1,708 lb (775 kg)
Max wing loading	12·6 lb/sq ft (61·7 kg/m²)
Max power loading	13·67 lb/hp (6·2 kg/hp)

Performance (estimated, at max T-O weight):

Max level speed at S/L	135 knots (155 mph; 250 km/h)
Max cruising speed at S/L	108 knots (124 mph; 200 km/h)
Stalling speed, flaps down	47·5 knots (55 mph; 88 km/h)
Max rate of climb at S/L	689 ft (210 m)/min
Service ceiling	18,050 ft (5,500 m)
Range with max fuel and max payload	431 nm (497 miles; 800 km)

TAIFUN

TAIFUN FLUGZEUGBAU GmbH

Head Office: Weiden, Bayern

Other Offices:
8 München 90, Hans-Milich-Strasse 7

Prof Dr-Ing E.h. Willy Messerschmitt and Dipl-Ing Ludwig Bölkow, associates in the German aircraft company Messerschmitt-Bölkow-Blohm, have plans to put into production an improved version of the Messerschmitt Bf (Me) 108 Taifun.

The first prototype of the original Bf 108 (D-ILIT) flew in early 1934. The design featured all-metal stressed-skin construction, a patented single-spar cantilever wing, trailing-edge flaps, automatic leading-edge slots, and retractable main landing gear. The six prototypes and Bf 108As were each powered by a 255 hp Hirth HM 8U or 210 hp Argus As 17 aircooled in-line engine. The improved Bf 108B, introduced in 1935, had a 270 hp Argus As 10 eight-cylinder inverted-vee aircooled engine and was given the name Taifun (Typhoon). A total of 885 Bf 108s was built before the second World War ended, and several of these aircraft are still flying.

Taifun GmbH intends to develop a modern version of this aircraft with retractable tricycle landing gear, a 300 hp Lycoming aircooled engine, and other improvements to provide a four/six-seat cabin monoplane competitive with such aircraft as the Cessna Centurion, Beechcraft Bonanza and Piper Cherokee SIX.

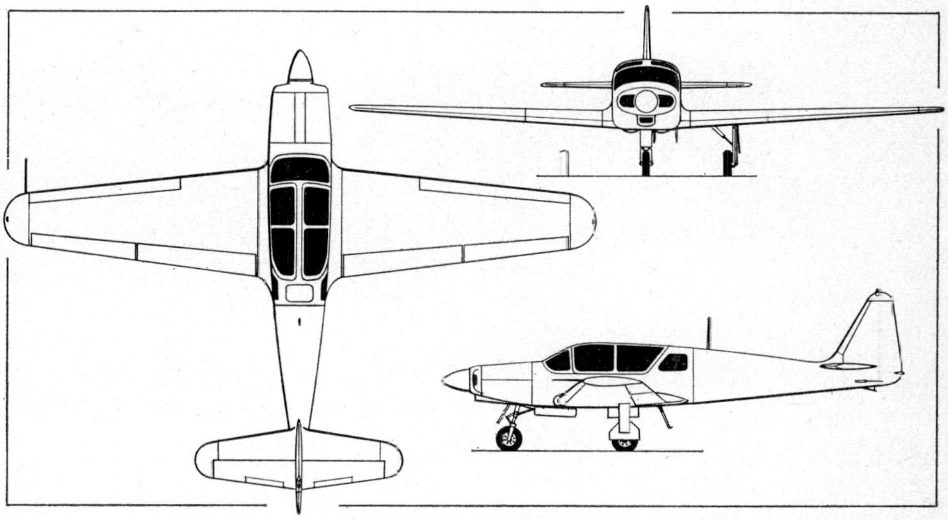

Taifun Me 108F, an updated development of the Messerschmitt Bf 108 *(Pilot Press)*

TAIFUN Me 108F TAIFUN (TYPHOON)

Type: Four/six-seat cabin monoplane.

Wings: Cantilever low-wing monoplane. Conventional structure of light alloy. Ailerons, trailing-edge flaps and leading-edge slots of light alloy construction.

Fuselage: Semi-monocoque structure of light alloy.

Tail Unit: Cantilever all-metal structure. Trim tab in each elevator.

Landing Gear: Retractable tricycle type with single wheel on each unit. Nosewheel retracts aft, main wheels inboard into undersurface of wing. Nosewheel steerable. Hydraulic brakes.

Power Plant: One 300 hp Lycoming IO-540 six-cylinder horizontally-opposed aircooled engine, driving a three-blade metal variable-pitch propeller with spinner.

Accommodation: Enclosed cabin seating a maximum of six people in pairs.

Systems: Electrical and hydraulic systems.

Dimensions, external:

Wing span	36 ft 1 in (11·00 m)
Wing aspect ratio	7·27
Length overall	28 ft 2¾ in (8·60 m)
Height overall	10 ft 1¼ in (3·08 m)

Area:

Wings, gross	179·1 sq ft (16·64 m²)

Weights and Loadings:

Weight empty	1,812 lb (822 kg)
Max T-O weight	3,417 lb (1,550 kg)
Max wing loading	19·1 lb/sq ft (93·14 kg/m²)
Max power loading	11·38 lb/hp (5·16 kg/hp)

Performance (estimated, at max T-O weight):

Max level speed at S/L	180 knots (208 mph; 335 km/h)
Max cruising speed at S/L	170 knots (196 mph; 315 km/h)
Max rate of climb at S/L	1,390 ft (424 m)/min
Service ceiling	19,000 ft (5,790 m)
T-O run	690 ft (210 m)
T-O to 50 ft (15 m)	1,220 ft (372 m)
Landing from 50 ft (15 m)	1,280 ft (390 m)
Landing run	755 ft (230 m)
Max range	690 nm (795 miles; 1,280 km)

VFW-FOKKER

VEREINIGTE FLUGTECHNISCHE WERKE-FOKKER GmbH (Subsidiary of ZENTRALGESELLSCHAFT VFW-FOKKER mbH)

Head Office:
Hünefeldstrasse 1-5, 28 Bremen 1 (Postfach 1206)

Telephone: (0421) 5181

Telex: 245 821

Works:
Bremen, Einswarden, Hoykenkamp, Lemwerder, Speyer and Varel

Executive Directors:
Dipl-Ing A. Niehus
Dr M. Lexis
Prof Dr W. Seibold
Dr F. Wenck
Dr H. R. Büssgen
RA. W. Schaarschmidt

Public Relations Manager: Franz Cesarz

The Vereinigte Flugtechnische Werke GmbH (VFW) was formed at the end of 1963 by a merger of the two Bremen-based aircraft companies of Focke-Wulf GmbH and "Weser" Flugzeugbau GmbH. They were joined in 1964 by Ernst Heinkel Flugzeugbau GmbH. Details of the history and products of these former companies can be found in earlier editions of *Jane's*.

In 1968-69, VFW acquired 65% of the shares of RFB (Rhein-Flugzeugbau GmbH, which see) and a 50% holding in Henschel Flugzeugwerke AG of Kassel.

With effect from 1 January 1969, VFW became an equal partner with Fokker of the Netherlands in a new company known as Zentralgesellschaft VFW-Fokker mbH, with headquarters in Dusseldorf. The two partners continue to operate independently, as subsidiaries of Zentralgesellschaft VFW-Fokker. The name of the VFW company was changed to VFW-Fokker GmbH as a consequence of the amalgamation.

Current activities of VFW-Fokker include development of the VFW 614 twin-turbofan light passenger and freight transport and of the VAK 191B VTOL research aircraft. In addition, VFW is a partner in the Fokker-VFW F.28 transport programme.

Other work includes the overhaul and repair of Noratlas, Albatross, JetStar and Piaggio P.149D aircraft, together with modification work on the F-104G.

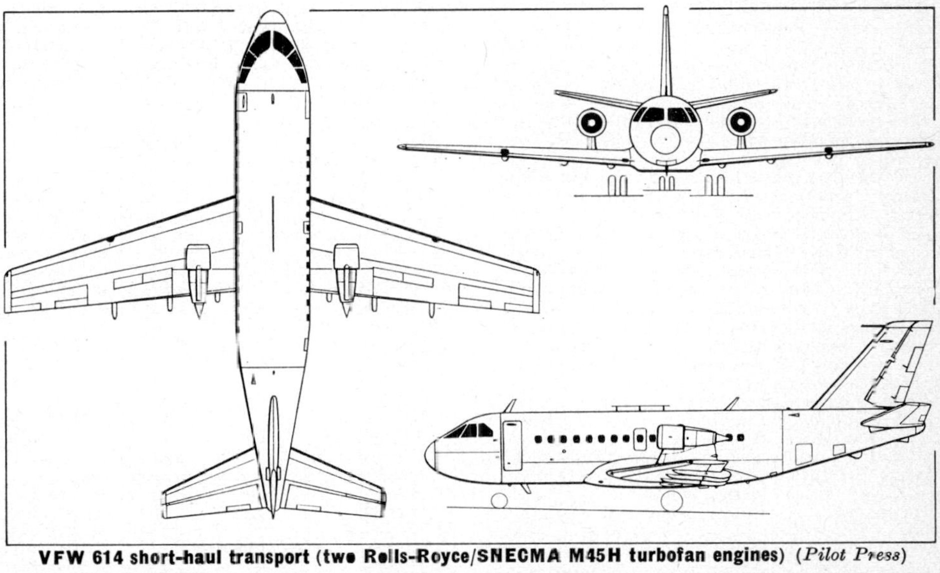

VFW 614 short-haul transport (two Rolls-Royce/SNECMA M45H turbofan engines) *(Pilot Press)*

Through the ERNO Raumfahrttechnik GmbH, in which it has a 60% interest, VFW-Fokker is engaged on studies of high-energy propellants. Study and project work is also in progress in connection with the national space programme and the third stage of the European satellite launcher. VFW-Fokker is also participating in development and manufacturing programmes for the Panavia MRCA and A-300B European Airbus (see International section), and for the Sikorsky CH-53G helicopter.

VFW-FOKKER VFW 614

Development of this twin-turbofan short-haul jet transport was undertaken with the financial backing of the Federal German government. Construction of the first of three prototypes, which were designated G1, G2 and G3, was started on 1 August 1968, and the G1 prototype flew for the first time on 14 July 1971. This aircraft was lost on 1 February 1972.

The G2 prototype (D-BABB) flew for the first time on 14 January 1972, and made its first flight with a boosted elevator control system on 19 August 1972. The first flight of the third prototype (D-BABC) was made on 10 October 1972. VFW-Fokker planned to gain certification of the VFW 614 by mid-1974.

Two airframes were built for static and dynamic fatigue tests. The former have been completed successfully, but dynamic tests were expected to continue until mid-1974.

The following options had been announced by early 1974, with deliveries to begin in early 1975: Sterling Airways (five), Filipinas Orient Airways (two), Bavaria Fluggesellschaft (three), General Air (two), Transportes Aereos Buenos Aires (two), Cimber Air (three), Yemen Airlines (three), Spanish Ministry of Aviation (one), Société de Travail Aérien (two); undisclosed (three). On 29 April 1974, Cimber Air converted its option into a firm order for two aircraft, with a third on option.

VFW-Fokker VFW 614 short-haul transport (two Rolls-Royce/SNECMA M45H Mk 501 turbofan engines)

Manufacture of the VFW 614 is a collaborative venture under the leadership of VFW-Fokker, with participation in the development and production programme by MBB in Germany, Fokker-VFW in the Netherlands, and SABCA and Fairey in Belgium.

TYPE: Twin-turbofan short-haul transport.

WINGS: Cantilever low-wing monoplane. Wing section NACA 63_2A-015 at root, NACA 65_1A-012 at tip. Dihedral 3°. Incidence 3° at root, —1° at tip. Sweepback 15° at quarter-chord. Continuous two-spar fail-safe torsion-box dural structure, consisting of a centre-section integral with the fuselage, and two outer wings. Manually-operated Flettner-type bonded duralumin ailerons, with trim tab of honeycomb construction in port aileron. Hydraulically-operated single-slotted Fowler-type trailing-edge flaps of bonded dural construction. Two split-type flight spoilers and eight ground spoilers, of bonded dural construction. TKS liquid de-icing system.

FUSELAGE: Conventional semi-monocoque fail-safe pressurised structure of circular section, built of high-strength aluminium alloys.

TAIL UNIT: Part-bonded all-swept all-metal structure, with variable-incidence dihedral tailplane. Rudder actuated manually via spring tab with hydraulic boost. Elevators actuated mechanically by two boosters. Elevators may also be actuated manually, and to reduce pilot work load in this mode each elevator has a geared tab. Trim tab in rudder. Electrically-operated tailplane trim, with mechanical backup system. TKS liquid de-icing system for leading-edge of tailplane only.

LANDING GEAR: Hydraulically retractable tricycle type of Dowty Rotol design, with twin wheels on each unit. Steerable nosewheel unit retracts forward. Main units retract inward into fuselage. Oleo-pneumatic telescopic shock-absorbers. All tyres of BF Goodrich manufacture, nosewheels with tyres size 24 × 7·7; main wheels and tyres size 34 × 12-12. Tyre pressure 68 lb/sq in (4·78 kg/cm²) on nose unit, 75 lb/sq in (5·27 kg/cm²) on main units. Goodrich 10×5 disc brakes on main units. Messier anti-skid units.

POWER PLANT: Two Rolls-Royce/SNECMA M45H Mk 501 turbofan engines, each rated at a nominal thrust (without losses) of 7,280 lb (3,302 kg), mounted on overwing pylons aft of the wing rear spar. Fuel in integral wing tanks, with total capacity of 1,363 Imp gallons (6,200 litres). Single-point pressure refuelling point in starboard outer wing. Provision for overwing gravity refuelling. Oil capacity 1·5 Imp gallons (6·82 litres).

ACCOMMODATION: Crew of two on flight deck. Full dual controls and instruments. Standard version provides 40 passenger seats (alternative for 44 passengers) at 32-33 in (81-84 cm) pitch in main cabin, in rows of four with 16 in (41 cm) wide centre aisle. Passenger door, with built-in stairs, at front of cabin on port side. Cargo door for cabin baggage compartment at front on starboard side. Catering service door beside pantry at rear of cabin on starboard side. Cabin baggage compartment at front of cabin (stbd). Toilet on port side, at rear of cabin. Underfloor baggage holds fore and aft of wing. Cabin pressurised and air-conditioned. Seats for an observer and second cabin attendant optional.

SYSTEMS: Garrett-Normalair double air-cycle air-conditioning system, using engine bleed air. Pressure differential 6·55 lb/sq in (0·46 kg/cm²). Two separate hydraulic systems, pressure 3,000 lb/sq in (210 kg/cm²), supplied by a pump on each engine and electrically-powered (DC) auxiliary hydraulic pump, with Skydrol 500B fluid, for nosewheel steering, landing gear, flight and ground spoilers, flaps and brakes. Constant-frequency three-phase 200/115V 400 Hz AC electrical system. Two transformer-rectifiers provide 28V DC power, with batteries for emergency supply. Priority oxygen supply system for flight crew, with second oxygen system for passengers and cabin staff. TKS liquid de-icing system for wings and tailplane. Garrett AiResearch GTCP 36-28 APU, mounted in rear fuselage, provides air supply for engine starting and air-conditioning on ground, and electrical power for pre-flight check of avionics and systems without running engines.

ELECTRONICS AND EQUIPMENT: Standard equipment includes two VHF communications installations, two VOR/ILS, marker, ADF, two compass systems, intercom system, flight data recorder, autopilot/flight director, weather radar and voice recorder. Optional items include an additional ADF, HF communications installation, ATC transponder, DME, radio altimeter, and low weather minima system, digital flight data recorder and altitude alert. Blind-flying instrumentation standard.

DIMENSIONS, EXTERNAL:
- Wing span — 70 ft 6½ in (21·50 m)
- Wing chord at root — 13 ft 11¼ in (4·25 m)
- Wing chord at tip — 5 ft 7¼ in (1·71 m)
- Wing aspect ratio — 7·22
- Length overall — 67 ft 7 in (20·60 m)
- Length of fuselage — 66 ft 1¼ in (20·15 m)
- Height overall — 25 ft 8 in (7·84 m)
- Tailplane span — 29 ft 6¼ in (9·00 m)
- Wheel track — 12 ft 9½ in (3·90 m)
- Wheelbase — 23 ft 0¼ in (7·02 m)
- Passenger door (fwd, port):
  - Height — 6 ft 10¾ in (2·10 m)
  - Width — 2 ft 5½ in (0·75 m)
  - Height to sill — 5 ft 5 in (1·65 m)
- Freight door (fwd, stbd):
  - Height — 3 ft 10 in (1·17 m)
  - Width — 3 ft 7¼ in (1·10 m)
  - Height to sill — 6 ft 6¼ in (1·99 m)
- Catering service door (rear of cabin, stbd):
  - Height — 5 ft 0¼ in (1·53 m)
  - Width — 2 ft 0 in (0·61 m)
  - Height to sill — 6 ft 5¼ in (1·96 m)
- Underfloor baggage door (fwd):
  - Height — 2 ft 6¾ in (0·78 m)
  - Width — 2 ft 9½ in (0·85 m)
  - Height to sill — 4 ft 2½ in (1·28 m)
- Underfloor baggage door (rear):
  - Height — 2 ft 6¾ in (0·78 m)
  - Width — 2 ft 9½ in (0·85 m)
  - Height to sill — 4 ft 1½ in (1·25 m)

DIMENSIONS, INTERNAL:
- Cabin, excluding flight deck:
  - Length — 36 ft 9¼ in (11·21 m)
  - Max width — 8 ft 8¾ in (2·66 m)
  - Max height — 6 ft 3¼ in (1·91 m)
  - Floor area — 248·75 sq ft (23·11 m²)
  - Volume — 1,748 cu ft (49·50 m³)
- Baggage compartment volume:
  - Front fuselage — 79·5 cu ft (2·25 m³)
  - Underfloor (fwd) — 63·2 cu ft (1·79 m³)
  - Underfloor (aft) — 51·2 cu ft (1·45 m³)

AREAS:
- Wings, gross — 688·89 sq ft (64·00 m²)
- Ailerons (total) — 34·87 sq ft (3·24 m²)
- Trailing-edge flaps (total) — 124·86 sq ft (11·60 m²)
- Spoilers (total) — 54·36 sq ft (5·05 m²)
- Fin — 63·08 sq ft (5·86 m²)
- Rudder — 38·64 sq ft (3·59 m²)
- Tailplane — 140·79 sq ft (13·08 m²)
- Elevators — 52·96 sq ft (4·92 m²)

WEIGHTS AND LOADING:
- Operating weight, empty — 26,850 lb (12,180 kg)
- Max design zero-fuel weight — 36,595 lb (16,600 kg)
- Max design taxi weight — 44,200 lb (20,050 kg)
- Max design T-O and landing weight — 43,980 lb (19,950 kg)
- Max wing loading — 63·9 lb/sq ft (312 kg/m²)

PERFORMANCE (estimated, at max design T-O weight; ISA except where indicated):
- Max never-exceed speed — 330 knots (380 mph; 613 km/h) EAS (Mach 0·74)
- Max level speed at 21,000 ft (6,400 m) — 397 knots (457 mph; 735 km/h) TAS
- Max cruising speed at 25,000 ft (7,620 m) — 390 knots (449 mph; 722 km/h) TAS
- Stalling speed, flaps up — 114 knots (131 mph; 210 km/h)
- Stalling speed, flaps down — 88·5 knots (102 mph; 164 km/h)
- Max rate of climb at S/L — 3,100 ft (945 m)/min
- Rate of climb at S/L, one engine out — 875 ft (267 m)/min
- Service ceiling — 25,000 ft (7,620 m)
- Service ceiling, one engine out (at 98% of max T-O weight) — 16,300 ft (4,970 m)
- Min ground turning radius — 41 ft 6 in (12·65 m)
- Runway LCN — 16
- T-O to 35 ft (10·7 m) — 3,136 ft (956 m)
- FAA T-O field length — 4,000 ft (1,220 m)
- FAA landing field length — 3,610 ft (1,100 m)
- Landing from 50 ft (15 m) — 2,160 ft (658 m)
- Range with max fuel, FAR Pt 121·639 reserves with 150 nm (172 mile; 277 km) alternate — 1,085 nm (1,249 miles; 2,010 km)
- Range with 40 passengers, reserves as above — 650 nm (748 miles; 1,205 km)

OPERATIONAL NOISE CHARACTERISTICS:
- T-O noise level at 3·5 nm (4 miles; 6·5 km) from start of T-O run — 89 EPNdB
- Approach noise level at 1 nm (1·15 miles; 1·85 km) from landing threshold on 3° glideslope — 100 EPNdB
- Sideline noise level at 0·25 nm (0·29 miles; 0·46 km) from runway c/l — 96 EPNdB

VFW-FOKKER VAK 191B

The first of three prototypes of the VAK 191B made its first flight on 10 September 1971, following a period of tethered hovering trials. During 1972 the three VAK 191B prototypes took part in an extensive flight test programme, and on 26 October 1972 the first vertical-to-horizontal transition was made successfully. During the test the aircraft flew at a speed of 300 knots (345 mph; 556 km/h), and the RB.162-81 lift-jets were shut down and restarted in flight.

The following "Areas" figures correct those given in the 1973-74 *Jane's*, in which a full description of the VAK 191B can be found:
- Ailerons (total) — 10·76 sq ft (1·00 m²)
- Tailplane — 42·30 sq ft (3·93 m²)

VFW-FOKKER (SIKORSKY) CH-53G

Under a contract placed in 1969 by the Federal Bureau for Weapon Technology and Procurement, a total of 133 Sikorsky CH-53 helicopters were to be built in Germany for the German Army by 1975. This number was reduced to 110 during 1972.

As prime contractor, VFW-Fokker is responsible for final assembly of the helicopters (known in Germany as CH-53G) at its Speyer factory. MBB and Dornier are manufacturing the airframe sections and rotor blades under subcontract. Two Sikorsky-built aircraft were utilised for flight testing at Manching from late 1969; the first flight of a German-built CH-53G took place in October 1971. Delivery of production aircraft began in 1972, and production is expected to continue until June 1975. Details of the basic CH-53 appear under the Sikorsky entry in the American aircraft section (which see).

VFW-Fokker CH-53G with main rotor and tail rotor pylon folded

WILDEN

ING HELMUT WILDEN

Address:
D-5202 Hennef/Sieg 1, Oberkümpel 3

Ing Helmut Wilden, a German architect, has designed and built a two-seat light aircraft which he has designated Vo Wi 8. The first flight was made by Flugkapitän Manfred Scholz on 4 March 1974.

WILDEN Vo Wi 8

Type: Two-seat lightweight sporting or training aircraft.

Wings: Cantilever single-spar mid-wing monoplane. Dihedral from roots. Constant chord. Wide-span trailing-edge flaps. Conventional ailerons.

Fuselage: Glassfibre shell on steel tube frame, with only two bulkheads.

Tail Unit: Cantilever T-tail, with swept vertical surfaces. Trim tab in one-piece horizontal surface.

Landing Gear: Non-retractable tricycle type. Main wheels carried on cantilever struts. Single wheel on each unit. Castoring nosewheel.

Power Plant: One 82 hp Volkswagen-Porsche four-cylinder horizontally-opposed aircooled engine, mounted on a pylon above the fuselage and driving a two-blade pusher propeller. Engine faired by a glassfibre cowling.

Accommodation: Two seats side by side in enclosed cabin with dual controls. Individual transparent cockpit canopies, hinged at centreline and opening upward.

Dimensions, external:

Wing span	28 ft 2¾ in (8·60 m)
Wing aspect ratio	6·7
Length overall	20 ft 4 in (6·20 m)
Height overall	9 ft 2¼ in (2·80 m)

Area:

Wings, gross	118·4 sq ft (11·00 m²)

Weights and Loadings:

Weight empty	749 lb (340 kg)
T-O weight, utility	1,212 lb (550 kg)
Max T-O weight	1,400 lb (635 kg)
Max wing loading	11·8 lb/sq ft (57·7 kg/m²)
Max power loading	17·06 lb/hp (7·74 kg/hp)

Performance (at max T-O weight):

Max level speed at S/L	115 knots (132 mph; 212 km/h)
Max cruising speed at 3,280 ft (1,000 m)	105 knots (121 mph; 194 km/h)
Landing speed	37 knots (42 mph; 68 km/h)
Max rate of climb at S/L	885 ft (270 m)/min
Service ceiling	16,725 ft (5,100 m)
T-O run	575 ft (175 m)
T-O to 50 ft (15 m)	985 ft (300 m)
Landing run	395 ft (120 m)
Max range	458 nm (528 miles; 850 km)

Wilden Vo Wi 8 two-seat training and sporting aircraft *(Brian M. Service)*

GREECE

HAI

HELLENIC AEROSPACE INDUSTRIES

As part of a national defence programme sponsored by the Greek government, it is intended to establish an "aerospace support facility" at Tanagra with the assistance of an international team of aerospace companies. Initially, the major objectives of this facility will be to provide a modern base for depot level maintenance for the Greek Air Force and Greek state services, and for maintenance and manufacturing work on behalf of commercial airlines operating in the Mediterranean area.

In mid-1972 the Greek government selected three companies as the winning team in a competition for the Tanagra project: Lockheed Aircraft Service Company in the US, Avions Marcel Dassault/Breguet Aviation in France, and Olympic Airways, the Greek national airline. Plans at that time were to implement the project in the form of a Greek corporation, Hellenic Aerospace Industries, owned 20 per cent by each of the three team members and 40 per cent by the Greek government. The group's initial proposal was described briefly in the 1973-74 *Jane's*, but in 1973 the Greek government rejected all previous bids and requested that new proposals be submitted. In the Spring of 1974 these new proposals were under evaluation, and an award was expected shortly. The Lockheed proposal is for a 150 acre (60·7 hectare) site incorporating approx 900,000 sq ft (83,613 m²) of covered space for hangars, workshops and offices, and including also large concrete ramp areas, taxiways, connecting roadways and rail services. The eventual work force is expected to total more than 2,000 persons, and the project will take some 2½ years to complete.

INDIA

CIVIL AVIATION DEPARTMENT

TECHNICAL CENTRE, CIVIL AVIATION DEPARTMENT

Head Office:
Civil Aviation Department, R. K. Puram, New Delhi 22

Works:
Technical Centre, opposite Safdarjung Airport, New Delhi 110003

Telephone: 611504

Director General: S. Ramamritham

Director (R&D): K. B. Ganesan

In addition to its work on the design and development of sailplanes, described in the appropriate section of this edition, the Civil Aviation Department has designed and developed a two/three-seat light aircraft named the Revathi.

REVATHI Mk II

The prototype Revathi Mk I (see 1969-70 *Jane's*) flew for the first time on 13 January 1967, and was type certificated in January 1969.

It was subsequently developed into the Revathi Mk II, with constant-chord metal wings, increased fuel capacity and AUW, and other changes. In this form it flew for the first time on 20 May 1970, and was type certificated on 31 October 1972.

Extensive flight tests, including the successful execution of loops, spins, slow rolls and stall turns, were carried out by the Aircraft and Systems Testing Establishment of the Indian Air Force.

In early 1974, conversion of the Revathi Mk II to the standard specified by a customer was under way. The main changes involved are the replacement of the wooden control surfaces by metal ones, and rearrangement of the instrument panel. The aircraft converted to this standard was expected to fly in mid-1974; based on this configuration, a pre-production model is planned.

The Revathi Mk II is intended for use by flying clubs, as a basic trainer for ab initio pilot training, including instruction in spinning, night flying, instrument flying and cross-country navigation; it is also suitable for use as a private aircraft. As a trainer, it is designed to meet the Utility category requirements of FAR Pt 23 Appendix A, with pupil and instructor seated side by side. As a private aircraft it meets the Normal category requirements and can seat three people.

The following description applies to the Revathi Mk II prototype with the modifications referred to above:

Type: Two/three-seat light aircraft.

Wings: Cantilever low-wing monoplane. Wing

section NACA 23015 at root and up to 60·6% of each half-span; NACA 4412 at tip. Dihedral 5°. Incidence 4°. Two-spar stressed-skin structure. The nose cell and, at root, the rear cell also, are covered with aluminium alloy sheet; the remainder of the wing is fabric-covered. Bottom-hinged slotted ailerons and slotted trailing-edge flaps of aluminium alloy construction.

Fuselage: Welded steel tube truss structure, covered with sheet aluminium alloy to rear of cockpit and fabric elsewhere.

Tail Unit: Cantilever horizontal surfaces of aluminium alloy; rear cells of elevators fabric-covered. Sweptback vertical surfaces of steel tube construction, covered with fabric. Fin integral with fuselage. Trim tab in rudder and starboard elevator. Elevator incorporates shielded horn balance; the rudder has an un-shielded horn balance.

Landing Gear: Non-retractable tailwheel type. Rubber rings in tension provide shock-absorption of main units. Dunlop main wheels, size 6·00-6·5, pressure 23-35 lb/sq in (1·75-2·45 kg/cm²). Dunlop hydraulic disc brakes. Castoring tailwheel, with solid tyre, carried on leaf springs, coupled flexibly to rudder.

Power Plant: One 145 hp Rolls-Royce Continental O-300-C six-cylinder horizontally-opposed aircooled engine, driving a Sensenich M74DC54 two-blade fixed-pitch metal propeller. Integral fuel tank in each wing, total capacity 32·6 Imp gallons (148 litres). Auxiliary tank, capacity 11 Imp gallons (50 litres), aft of cockpit. Oil capacity 1·6 Imp gallons (7·5 litres).

Accommodation: Enclosed cabin, seating two persons in front, side by side, and one to the rear. Dual controls standard, including duplicated wheel brake and throttle controls. Jettisonable door on each side. Compartment for baggage.

Electronics and Equipment: Blind- and night-flying instrumentation and Bendix RT-221A-14 380-channel VHF transceiver standard. Bendix RN-222 VHF navigation receiver (with glide-slope supplement), IN-224 VOR/ILS and 204A marker receiver optional. Landing light in each wing leading-edge.

Dimensions, external:
- Wing span 30 ft 10 in (9·40 m)
- Wing chord (constant) 4 ft 11 in (1·50 m)
- Wing aspect ratio 6·27
- Length overall 24 ft 10 in (7·58 m)
- Height overall (tail up) 9 ft 8¾ in (2·97 m)
- Tailplane span 9 ft 0 in (2·74 m)
- Wheel track 6 ft 5 in (1·96 m)
- Wheelbase 17 ft 6 in (5·33 m)
- Propeller diameter 6 ft 2 in (1·88 m)
- Propeller ground clearance 9½ in (0·24 m)
- Cabin doors (each):
  - Height 4 ft 0 in (1·22 m)
  - Width 2 ft 10½ in (0·88 m)

Dimensions, internal:
- Cabin: Length 7 ft 2½ in (2·20 m)
  - Max width 3 ft 1½ in (0·95 m)
  - Max height 3 ft 11¾ in (1·21 m)
- Baggage compartment volume 3 cu ft (0·085 m³)

Areas:
- Wings, gross 151·7 sq ft (14·09 m²)
- Ailerons (total) 10·89 sq ft (1·01 m²)
- Trailing-edge flaps (total) 12·92 sq ft (1·20 m²)
- Fin 8·65 sq ft (0·804 m²)
- Rudder 8·40 sq ft (0·78 m²)
- Tailplane 13·10 sq ft (1·22 m²)
- Elevators, incl tab 13·90 sq ft (1·29 m²)

Weights and Loadings:
- Weight empty, equipped 1,370 lb (623 kg)
- Max T-O and landing weight:
  - Normal 2,120 lb (962 kg)
  - Utility 1,832 lb (831 kg)
- Max wing loading:
  - Normal 13·98 lb/sq ft (68·2 kg/m²)
  - Utility 12·08 lb/sq ft (58·95 kg/m²)
- Max power loading:
  - Normal 14·62 lb/hp (6·63 kg/hp)
  - Utility 12·61 lb/hp (5·72 kg/hp)

Performance (at max T-O weight):
- Max never-exceed speed 140 knots (161 mph; 260 km/h)
- Max level speed at S/L 104 knots (120 mph; 193 km/h)
- Max cruising speed (75% power) at 6,000 ft (1,830 m) 91 knots (105 mph; 169 km/h)
- Stalling speed, flaps down:
  - Normal 44·5 knots (51 mph; 82·5 km/h)
  - Utility 42 knots (48 mph; 77 km/h)
- Max rate of climb at S/L 600 ft (182 m)/min
- Service ceiling 10,000 ft (3,050 m)
- T-O run 750 ft (228 m)
- Landing run 660 ft (201 m)
- Range with wing fuel only, no reserves 347 nm (400 miles; 643 km)
- Range with max fuel (incl auxiliary tank), no reserves 434 nm (500 miles; 804 km)

Revathi Mk II two/three-seat light aircraft, developed by the Technical Centre of the Indian Civil Aviation Department

HAL

HINDUSTAN AERONAUTICS LTD

Address:
Indian Express Building, Vidhana Veedhi, PO Box 5150, Bangalore 1

Telephone: 75004/5/6

Telex: 043-266 HAL BG

Chairman:
M. M. Sen

Directors:
G. K. Abhyankar
Air Marshal H. C. Dewan
Dr V. M. Ghatage
B. R. Mandal
Dr B. D. Nag Chaudhuri
P. M. Reddy
P. L. Tandon
Dr S. R. Valluri
Air Vice-Marshal A. S. Rikhy (Retd) (Managing Director, Bangalore Complex)
Air Cdre C. R. Kurpad (Retd) (Managing Director, MiG Complex)
M. C. Sarin (Finance)

General Managers:
Bangalore Complex:
Gp Capt S. C. Keshu (Aircraft Division)
H. K. Karve (Engine Division)
Gp Capt C. G. Kharas (Overhaul Division)
Raj Mahindra (Helicopter Division)
Kanpur Division: P. D. Chopra
Lucknow Division: Gp Capt B. K. Kapur
Nasik Division: J. Bhandari
Koraput Division: G. Narasimhan
Hyderabad Division: R. M. Nayar

Public Relations:
V. R. Ruthnam

Hindustan Aeronautics Ltd (HAL) was formed on 1 October 1964, amalgamating the former Hindustan Aircraft Ltd (formed 1940) and Aeronautics India Ltd (formed 1963), and now has six Divisions, at Bangalore, Kanpur, Nasik, Koraput, Hyderabad and Lucknow, with a total work force of more than 37,000 persons. Of these the oldest, at the Bangalore Complex, is directly under the control of one of the Managing Directors and is engaged in the manufacture of civil and military aircraft and aero-engines, both under licence and of indigenous design. This Complex also has a large organisation undertaking repair and overhaul of airframes, engines, and allied instruments and accessories.

The Kanpur Division is engaged mainly in the manufacture of Hawker Siddeley 748 transport aircraft under licence. It also produces the Rohini two-seat sailplane, of which details can be found in the "Sailplanes" section.

Nasik, Koraput and Hyderabad form the MiG Complex, which currently undertakes the licence manufacture of Soviet MiG-21 fighters with the collaboration of the USSR.

The Lucknow Division, formed in late 1969, is intended initially to produce aircraft accessories under licence from various manufacturers in the UK, France and the USA, including brake and other hydraulic equipment, flight instruments, air-conditioning, pressurisation and fuel system equipment and ejection seats. The Division began production on 30 August 1973 of landing gear, ejection seats, fuel systems and instruments for the Marut and Kiran.

BANGALORE COMPLEX

Address:
Bangalore-17 (Mysore State)

Telephone: 2320, 5101 and 2418

The Bangalore Complex of HAL consists essentially of the former Hindustan Aircraft Limited, the activities of which, since its formation in 1940, were described in previous editions of *Jane's*. The Complex is subdivided into an Aircraft Division, Helicopter Division, Engine Division, Overhaul Division, Foundry and Forge, and Design Bureau.

Bangalore Complex is engaged in developing and building aircraft and aero-engines of its own design, and also manufactures various aircraft and aero-engines under licence. The Engine Division's activities are described in the appropriate section of this edition. The first aircraft of HAL design to enter production was the HT-2 piston-engined primary trainer (see 1965-66 *Jane's*), followed by the Pushpak and Krishak lightplanes (see 1970-71 *Jane's*). Development of the HF-24 Marut jet fighter and HJT-16 Kiran jet trainer were begun towards the end of 1956 and 1959 respectively, and the Bangalore Complex is also building under licence the Aérospatiale SA 315B Lama and SA 316B Alouette III helicopters.

In early 1971 the Indian Defence Minister announced that an advanced-technology combat aircraft "rivalling the capability of America's Phantom and France's Mirage" was to be developed to enter Indian Air Force service in the 1980s as a replacement for the HF-24. Preliminary design and technical studies were to be undertaken by the Bangalore Complex of HAL, possibly with foreign technical assistance.

The Overhaul Division of Bangalore Complex repairs and overhauls Hawker Siddeley (de Havilland) Dove/Devon aircraft, DHC-4 Caribou, Fairchild C-119 Packet transports and English Electric Canberra bombers. Various piston engines and jet engines are overhauled at the Engine Division. The branch factory in Calcutta is continuing to concentrate on the repair and overhaul of DC-3s belonging to the Indian Air Force and non-scheduled operators.

In collaboration with the National Aeronautical Laboratory, the Design Bureau is working on the design requirements of an all-Indian armed light helicopter, with an AUW in the region of 5,500 lb (2,500 kg) and powered by a turboshaft engine of approx 1,400 shp.

HAL HF-24 MARUT (WIND SPIRIT)

Development of the HF-24 Marut single-seat fighter was started by HAL in 1956, under the design leadership of Dr Kurt Tank, who was responsible for the wartime Focke-Wulf aeroplanes. The first prototype HF-24 Mk I (HF-001; BR-462), powered by two Rolls-Royce Bristol Orpheus 703 turbojet engines, flew for the first time on 17 June 1961. It was followed by the second Mk I prototype (HF-003; BR-463) on 4 October 1962.

The HF-24 is being manufactured to Mk I standard as a ground attack fighter, with Orpheus 703 non-afterburning engines. The first of 18 pre-production Maruts (HF-004; BD-828) flew in March 1963, and a token delivery of two aircraft to the Indian Air Force was made on 10 May 1964. By 1967, 12 more pre-production Mk Is had been handed over to the IAF, the other four being used for test and development programmes. The latter included one aircraft (HF-005; BD-830), designated Mk IA, for early trials in 1966 with an afterburner fitted to its Orpheus 703 engine.

The first series production Mk I (HF-022; BD-844) flew on 15 November 1967, and this version equips Nos. 10 and 220 Squadrons of the Indian Air Force, which used its Maruts successfully, without loss, in the December 1971 war with Pakistan. A total of about 80 Maruts had been built by early 1973, including two prototype **Mk IT** tandem two-seat training versions (HF-046; BD-888 and HF-047; BD-889). The first of these began its flight tests on 30 April 1970, in the hands of Wg Cdr R. D. Sahni, then chief test pilot of the Bangalore Division of HAL. It was followed by the second Mk IT in March 1971 and the two prototypes had completed a total of more than 200 test flights by early 1973. Differences by comparison with the Mk I are minimal. The internal Matra rocket launcher is removed to make way for the second seat; full dual controls are fitted, and a wide choice of equipment enables the Mk IT to be used for several advanced training roles, including instrument flying and armament training. Delivery of Mk ITs to the IAF was expected to begin in 1974.

Development of the Mk IT, and of other versions of the HF-24, has been the responsibility of an all-Indian design team led by Mr S. C. Das since the departure of Dr Tank and his German team in 1967. The other versions include two experimental prototypes (HF-005; BD-830 and HF-032; BD-884), known originally as Mk IRs but now designated **Mk II,** fitted with an afterburning version of the Orpheus 703 engine. One of these prototypes was continuing the flight test programme in early 1973, and four pre-production Marut Mk IIs have been ordered; but the Rolls-Royce/Turboméca Adour is under investigation as an alternative power plant, in afterburning form. In addition, the search continues for an engine that could give the Marut its intended Mach 2 performance in a future HF-24 Mk III version. The HAL designation HSS-73 has been given to a Marut Mk III design study, completed by an MBB team led by Dr Kurt Tank, involving an installation of two Turbo-Union RB.199 turbofan engines and a considerable amount of airframe redesign.

The following description applies to the HF-24 Mk I:

TYPE: Single-seat ground attack fighter, stressed to $+9{\cdot}34g$ (limit).

WINGS: Cantilever low-wing monoplane of thin section. Sweepback approx 45° at quarter-chord. All versions have extended-chord (dog-tooth) leading-edges on outer panels; in addition, overall wing chord is increased on later production aircraft, from HF-048; BD-1192 onwards. Conventional torsion-box structure. Hydraulically-actuated ailerons and trailing-edge flaps, with provision for selecting manual control. No de-icing system.

FUSELAGE: Conventional all-metal semi-monocoque structure, narrowed in accordance with area rule in region of wing trailing-edge. Rear fuselage detaches at transport joint for engine removal. Two hydraulically-operated box-type airbrakes on lower fuselage aft of main-wheel wells, opening downward. Engine air intake, with non-adjustable half-cone centrebody, on each side of cockpit.

TAIL UNIT: Cantilever all-metal structure with sweepback on all surfaces. Hydraulically-operated low-set variable-incidence tailplane with electrical trim facility. Elevators can be operated either hydraulically or manually. Manually-operated rudder, with trim tab, on early models. Some aircraft are fitted with hydraulically-actuated rudder.

LANDING GEAR: Retractable tricycle type, with single Dunlop wheel on each unit, supplied by Dowty Rotol. Hydraulic actuation, nosewheel retracting forward, main units inward into fuselage. Steerable nosewheel. Main-wheel tyres size 29 × 8-15, pressure 100 lb/sq in (7·03 kg/cm²). Nosewheel tyre size 19 × 6·25-9, pressure 140 lb/sq in (9·84 kg/cm²). Maxaret anti-skid system. No brake cooling. RFD-GQ Type LB-52 Mk 2 ring-slot braking parachute, diameter 10 ft 6 in (3·20 m), located in top of rear fuselage.

POWER PLANT: Two HAL-built Rolls-Royce Bristol Orpheus 703 turbojet engines, each rated at 4,850 lb (2,200 kg) st, side by side in rear fuselage. Fuel in main fuselage collector tank, wing centre-section supply tank and two integral wing tanks, with total usable capacity of 549 Imp gallons (2,491 litres). Provision for up to four 100 Imp gallon (454 litre) underwing drop-tanks, and an internal auxiliary tank of 88 Imp gallons (400 litres) capacity in place of the Matra rocket launcher.

ACCOMMODATION: Pilot only, on Martin-Baker Mk S4C zero-altitude ejection seat, under rear-ward-sliding blister canopy. Windscreen heated by sandwiched gold-film electrode. Side screens and canopy demisted by warm air from air-conditioning system.

SYSTEMS: Air-conditioning system includes two air-cycle heat exchangers and cold air unit. Cockpit pressurised to differential of 3·5 lb/sq in (0·25 kg/cm²) between 24,000 and 40,000 ft (7,300 to 12,200 m). Dowty Rotol hydraulic system, pressure 4,000 lb/sq in (280 kg/cm²), supplied by two engine-driven pumps, for all services. Nitrogen system, pressure 3,000 lb/sq in (210 kg/cm²), to provide emergency power for landing gear, airbrakes and flaps. 24V DC single-wire earth return electrical system, with two 24V 25Ah batteries and 4Ah emergency supply battery.

ELECTRONICS AND EQUIPMENT: Standard equipment includes DFA 73 D/F, TA and RA Bendix receiver, 12-channel VHF, and Ferranti ISIS (integrated strike and interception system) two-axis rate gyro gunsight.

ARMAMENT: Four 30 mm Aden Mk 2 guns in nose, with 120 rds/gun, and Matra Type 103 retractable pack of 50 SNEB 68 mm air-to-air rockets in lower fuselage aft of nosewheel unit. Attachments for four 1,000 lb bombs, napalm tanks, Type 116 SNEB rocket packs, clusters of T10 air-to-surface rockets, drop-tanks, or other stores under wings.

DIMENSIONS, EXTERNAL (A: with extended-chord wings; B: without extended-chord wings):

Wing span	29 ft 6¼ in (9·00 m)
Wing chord at root:	
A	14 ft 5¼ in (4·40 m)
B	13 ft 1½ in (4·00 m)
Wing chord at tip:	
A	3 ft 7¼ in (1·10 m)
B	3 ft 3¼ in (1·00 m)
Wing aspect ratio:	
A	2·90
B	3·18
Length overall	52 ft 0¾ in (15·87 m)
Height overall	11 ft 9¾ in (3·60 m)
Tailplane span	16 ft 9 in (5·104 m)
Wheel track	9 ft 2 in (2·80 m)
Wheelbase	18 ft 2⅝ in (5·555 m)

AREAS (A: with extended-chord wings; B: without extended-chord wings):

Wings, gross:	
A	301·4 sq ft (28·00 m²)
B	273·9 sq ft (25·45 m²)
Ailerons (total):	
A	13·50 sq ft (1·254 m²)
B	13·73 sq ft (1·276 m²)
Trailing-edge flaps (total):	
A	26·26 sq ft (2·44 m²)
B	23·90 sq ft (2·22 m²)
Fin:	
A	41·23 sq ft (3·83 m²)
Rudder, incl tab:	
A, B	5·32 sq ft (0·494 m²)
Tailplane:	
A, B	60·24 sq ft (5·596 m²)
Elevators (total):	
A, B	8·22 sq ft (0·764 m²)

WEIGHTS AND LOADINGS (A: with extended-chord wings; B: without extended-chord wings):

Weight empty, equipped:	
A, B (with auxiliary fuel tank in belly)	13,658 lb (6,195 kg)
T-O weight, clean:	
A, B (with auxiliary fuel tank in belly)	19,734 lb (8,951 kg)
Max T-O weight:	
A	24,048 lb (10,908 kg)
B	24,085 lb (10,925 kg)
Max wing loading:	
A	79·95 lb/sq ft (390 kg/m²)
B	88·15 lb/sq ft (430 kg/m²)
Thrust/weight ratio (at T-O weight, clean):	
A, B	0·492

PERFORMANCE:

Max level speed attained at 40,000 ft (12,200 m)	Mach 1·02
Max permitted speed at S/L	600 knots (691 mph; 1,112 km/h) IAS
Stalling speed at AUW of 19,734 lb (8,951 kg):	
flaps and landing gear up	138 knots (159 mph; 256 km/h)
flaps and landing gear down	133 knots (154 mph; 248 km/h)
Normal landing speed	145 knots (167 mph; 268 km/h)
Time to climb from S/L to 40,000 ft (12,200 m) (clean aircraft, ISA + 15°C)	9 min 20 sec
T-O run at S/L	2,790 ft (850 m)
Min ground turning radius	17 ft 2 in (5·22 m)

HAL HF-24 Marut Mk I, in squadron service with the Indian Air Force, equipped with underwing fuel tanks *(Alan W. Hall)*

Prototype of the HAL HF-24 Mk IT two-seat training version of the Marut *(Alan W. Hall)*

HAL HJT-16 Mk I KIRAN (RAY OF LIGHT)

In December 1959, the government of India approved the design and development by HAL of a side-by-side two-seat jet basic trainer designated HJT-16 Mk I, powered by a Rolls-Royce Bristol Viper 11 turbojet.

Detailed design work on the HJT-16 Mk I began in 1961 under the leadership of Dr V. M. Ghatage. The first prototype flew for the first

HAL HJT-16 Mk I Kiran two-seat jet basic trainer (2,500 lb st Viper 11 turbojet engine) *(Air Portraits)*

time on 4 September 1964. It was followed by a second aircraft in August 1965.

A total of 24 pre-production HJT-16 Mk Is were delivered to the Indian Air Force, the initial delivery (of six aircraft) being made in March 1968. The HJT-16 Mk I is now in series production for the IAF and Navy; by early 1973 approx 36 had been delivered, of a reported order for 150. The Kiran is also understood to be undergoing development as a potential light attack aircraft.

TYPE: Two-seat jet basic trainer.

WINGS: Cantilever low-wing monoplane. Wing section NACA 23015 at root, NACA 23012 at tip. Dihedral 4° from roots. Incidence 0° 30′ at root. Conventional all-metal three-spar structure. Frise-type differential ailerons. Hydraulically-actuated split trailing-edge flaps.

FUSELAGE: All-metal semi-monocoque structure of light alloy. Hydraulically-actuated door-type airbrake under centre-fuselage.

TAIL UNIT: Cantilever all-metal structure. Electrically-operated variable-incidence tailplane. Ground-adjustable tab on rudder.

LANDING GEAR: Retractable tricycle type, of HAL manufacture. Hydraulic actuation. Main units retract inward into fuselage; self-centering twin-contact non-steerable nosewheel retracts forward. Oleo-pneumatic shock-absorbers. Main-wheel tyres size 19 × 6·25-9, pressure 90 lb/sq in (6·33 kg/cm²). Nosewheel tyre size 15·4 × 4·6, pressure 70 lb/sq in (4·92 kg/cm²). Hydraulic brakes, without cooling.

POWER PLANT: One 2,500 lb (1,135 kg) st Rolls-Royce Bristol Viper11 turbojet engine. Internal fuel in main saddle tanks in fuselage (two 46 Imp gallon), wing centre-section collector tank (62 Imp gallons) and outboard wing tanks (two 48 Imp gallon), with total capacity of 250 Imp gallons (1,137 litres). Provision for two underwing tanks with total capacity of 100 Imp gallons (454 litres). System permits 30 sec of inverted flight.

ACCOMMODATION: Crew of two side by side in air-conditioned and pressurised cockpit, on Martin-Baker Mk H4 HA zero-altitude fully-automatic ejection seats. Clamshell-type canopy. Dual controls and duplicated blind-flying instruments.

SYSTEMS: Air-conditioning system has max pressure differential of 1·75 lb/sq in (0·12 kg/cm²). Dowty hydraulic system for landing gear, flaps and airbrake, pressure 3,000 lb/sq in (210 kg/cm²). Accumulator for manual emergency system. Electrical system is of 28V DC single-wire earth return type, with two 24V 25Ah batteries. Normalair pressure-demand oxygen system.

ELECTRONICS AND EQUIPMENT: STR 9X/M 10-channel VHF transceiver, AX-3 single-channel VHF standby set and Marconi-Elliott AD-722 ADF manufactured by BEL-India. Landing light in nose.

ARMAMENT: Provision for conversion to armament training or COIN role, carrying two 7·62 mm twin-gun pods, eight T10 3 in rocket projectiles, twelve 68 mm rockets or four 25 lb practice bombs on underwing pylons.

DIMENSIONS, EXTERNAL:
Wing span 35 ft 1¼ in (10·70 m)
Wing chord at root 7 ft 8½ in (2·35 m)
Wing chord at tip 3 ft 4 in (1·02 m)
Wing aspect ratio 6
Length overall 34 ft 9 in (10·60 m)
Height overall 11 ft 11 in (3·635 m)
Tailplane span 12 ft 9½ in (3·90 m)
Wheel track 7 ft 11 in (2·42 m)
Wheelbase 11 ft 6 in (3·50 m)

AREAS:
Wings, gross 204·5 sq ft (19·00 m²)
Ailerons (total) 16·68 sq ft (1·55 m²)
Flaps (total) 25·19 sq ft (2·34 m²)
Vertical tail surfaces (total) 22·60 sq ft (2·10 m²)
Rudder, incl tab 7·69 sq ft (0·714 m²)
Horizontal tail surfaces (total) 40·04 sq ft (3·72 m²)
Elevators 12·27 sq ft (1·14 m²)

WEIGHTS AND LOADINGS:
Weight empty 5,644 lb (2,560 kg)
Normal T-O weight 7,936 lb (3,600 kg)
Max T-O weight (with two 50 Imp gallon drop-tanks) 9,039 lb (4,100 kg)
Max wing loading 38·9 lb/sq ft (190 kg/m²)
Thrust/weight ratio 0·315

PERFORMANCE (at normal T-O weight):
Max level speed at S/L 375 knots (432 mph; 695 km/h)
Max level speed at 30,000 ft (9,150 m) 371 knots (427 mph; 687·5 km/h)
Max cruising speed 175 knots (201 mph; 324 km/h)
Stalling speed, flaps and landing gear up 81 knots (94 mph; 151 km/h)
Stalling speed, flaps and landing gear down 71 knots (82 mph; 132 km/h)
Ceiling 30,000 ft (9,850 m)
Time to 30,000 ft (9,850 m) 20 min
Min ground turning radius 18 ft 0½ in (5·50 m)
T-O run 1,450 ft (442 m)
Endurance on internal fuel at 230 knots (265 mph; 426 km/h) at 30,000 ft (9,150 m) 1 hr 45 min

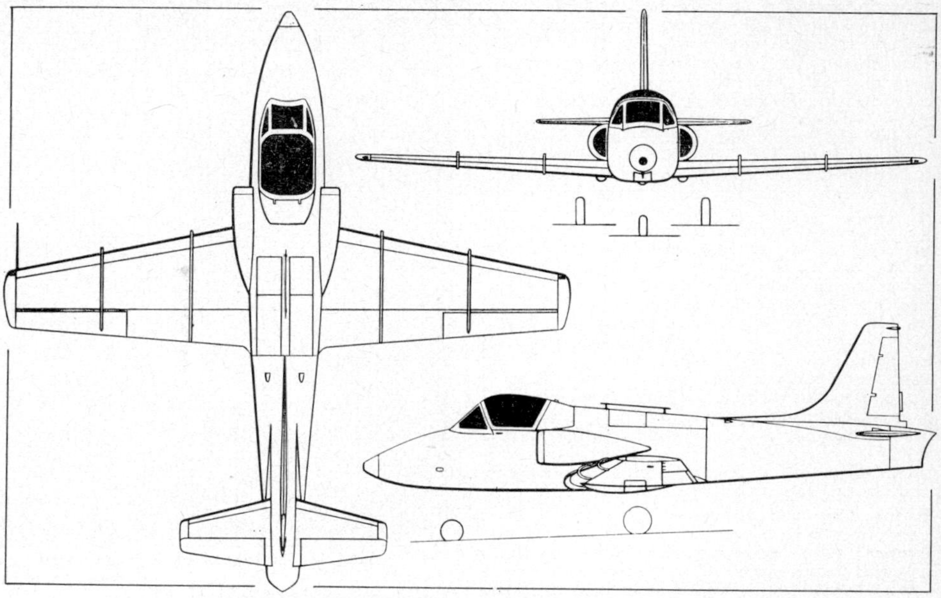

HAL HJT-16 Mk I Kiran jet basic trainer (*Pilot Press*)

HAL (HAWKER SIDDELEY) GNAT Mk I

Development of this single-seat lightweight fighter was started in the UK in 1951 by the former Folland Aircraft Ltd, and the first prototype flew on 18 July 1955. Deliveries of British-built Gnat Mk 1 fighters included 25 to India, plus 15 sets of components, in 1959, and in the same year HAL acquired a licence to manufacture the aircraft in India. The first HAL-built Gnat Mk I was delivered to the Indian Air Force in 1962.

The Gnat Mk I continued in production at HAL's Bangalore Complex until early 1973; production is then reported to have ended with the 215th aircraft.

The description which follows relates to the Gnat Mk I; HAL is currently developing a Mk II version, which is described separately.

TYPE: Single-seat lightweight fighter or fighter-bomber.

WINGS: Cantilever shoulder-wing monoplane. Sweptback wings, of RAE 102 (modified) section. Thickness/chord ratio 8%. Anhedral 5°. Sweepback 40° at quarter-chord. One-piece wing of two-spar thick-skin light alloy construction, fitting into recess in top of fuselage and secured by bolts at four points. Power-operated inboard ailerons, which droop to serve as flaps. No tabs.

FUSELAGE: Light alloy semi-monocoque structure.

TAIL UNIT: Cantilever all-metal structure. One-piece tailplane, operated hydraulically by Hobson actuator.

LANDING GEAR: Retractable tricycle type, all units retracting into fuselage. Hydraulic actuation. Dowty Rotol oleo-pneumatic shock-absorber struts. Wheel well fairings attached to individual landing gear units serve as air-brakes when landing gear is partly lowered, the relative movements of the airbrakes being so adjusted that no change of trim occurs at any speed. A stop on the landing gear airbrake selector prevents gear from being lowered fully when braking only is desired. Main-wheel tyres size 20 × 5·25; twin nosewheel tyres, size 17 × 3·25. Toe-operated Dunlop disc brakes. Braking parachute in fairing at base of fin.

POWER PLANT: One Rolls-Royce Bristol Orpheus 701 (BOr.2) non-afterburning turbojet engine, rated at 4,520 lb (2,050 kg) st. Air intakes in sides of fuselage. Seven (plus two optional) fuselage fuel tanks, with common collector tank and one booster pump. Total internal fuel capacity (nine tanks) 200 Imp gallons (909 litres). Two underwing drop-tanks can be fitted, each of 66 Imp gallons (300 litres) capacity. Compressed-air starting.

ACCOMMODATION: Pilot only, on Folland/Saab lightweight automatic ejection seat, in pressurised cockpit with jettisonable canopy.

SYSTEMS: Normalair pressure and temperature control systems, cold air unit and oxygen breathing equipment. Pressure differential 4 lb/sq in (0·28 kg/cm²).

ARMAMENT AND EQUIPMENT: Two 30 mm Aden cannon in air intake fairings, one on each side of fuselage, with 115 rds/gun. Four underwing hardpoints on which can be carried two 500 lb bombs or up to eighteen 3 in rocket projectiles, and two drop-tanks. VHF radio and standby set, navigation aids, gyro gunsight and radar ranging.

DIMENSIONS, EXTERNAL:
Wing span 22 ft 2 in (6·76 m)
Wing chord (mean) 6 ft 2 in (1·88 m)
Wing aspect ratio 3·575
Length overall 29 ft 9 in (9·07 m)
Height overall 8 ft 10 in (2·69 m)
Tailplane span 9 ft 0 in (2·74 m)
Wheel track 5 ft 1 in (1·55 m)
Wheelbase 7 ft 9 in (2·36 m)

AREAS:
Wings, gross 136·6 sq ft (12·69 m²)
Vertical tail surfaces (total) 14·0 sq ft (1·30 m²)
Horizontal tail surfaces (total) 18·0 sq ft (1·66 m²)

WEIGHTS:
Max T-O weight:
interceptor, clean 6,650 lb (3,016 kg)
tactical version, external tanks and armament 8,885 lb (4,030 kg)

PERFORMANCE:
Max level speed at 20,000 ft (6,100 m) 603 knots (695 mph; 1,118 km/h) (Mach 0·98)
Max level speed at low altitude 620 knots (714 mph; 1,150 km/h)
Max rate of climb at S/L 20,000 ft (6,100 m)/min
Time to 40,000 ft (12,200 m) with underwing tanks 5 min 15 sec
Ceiling more than 50,000 ft (15,250 m)
T-O to 50 ft (15 m):
interceptor 2,620 ft (800 m)
tactical 4,550 ft (1,387 m)
Radius of action with underwing tanks 435 nm (500 miles; 805 km)
Endurance:
normal 1 hr 15 min
with underwing tanks 2 hr 30 min

HAL GNAT Mk II

The Bangalore Complex completed in early 1974 the design of a Mk II version of the Gnat, with improved performance characteristics and equipment. These are: improved communications and navigation systems; more reliable longitudinal control; improved take-off performance, through modifications to the engine; and

HAL Gnat Mk I single-seat fighter of the Indian Air Force (*Ronaldo S. Olive*)

increased combat capability. The last-named characteristic is to be achieved by a redesigned fuel system, which will dispense with the underwing drop-tanks; instead, the Mk II will have integral tanks in the wings for 110 Imp gallons (500 litres) of fuel, so maintaining the overall fuel capacity while at the same time permitting additional underwing armament to be carried in place of the drop-tanks. The Orpheus 701 power plant will be retained, but with a small increase (approx 150 lb; 68 kg) in thrust.

The last two Gnat Mk I aircraft are being converted as prototypes for the Mk II version, which has reportedly been named Ajeet (Unconquerable); first flight was expected to be made in mid-1974.

DIMENSIONS, EXTERNAL:
- Wing span — 22 ft 1 in (6·73 m)
- Length overall — 29 ft 8 in (9·04 m)
- Height overall — 8 ft 10 in (2·69 m)
- Tailplane span — 9 ft 4 in (2·84 m)
- Wheel track — 5 ft 1 in (1·55 m)

WEIGHTS:
- Weight empty — 4,850 lb (2,200 kg)
- Max T-O weight:
  - interceptor — 6,650 lb (3,016 kg)
  - tactical — 8,855 lb (4,016 kg)

PERFORMANCE:
- Combat radius at high altitude — 400 nm (460 miles; 740 km)
- Tactical radius at ground level — 133 nm (153 miles; 246 km)

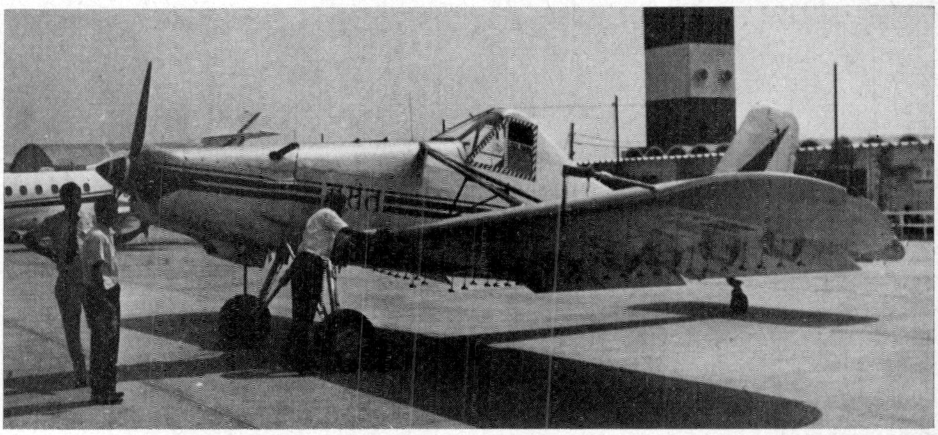

HAL HA-31 Mk II Basant single-seat agricultural aircraft *(Ronaldo S. Olive)*

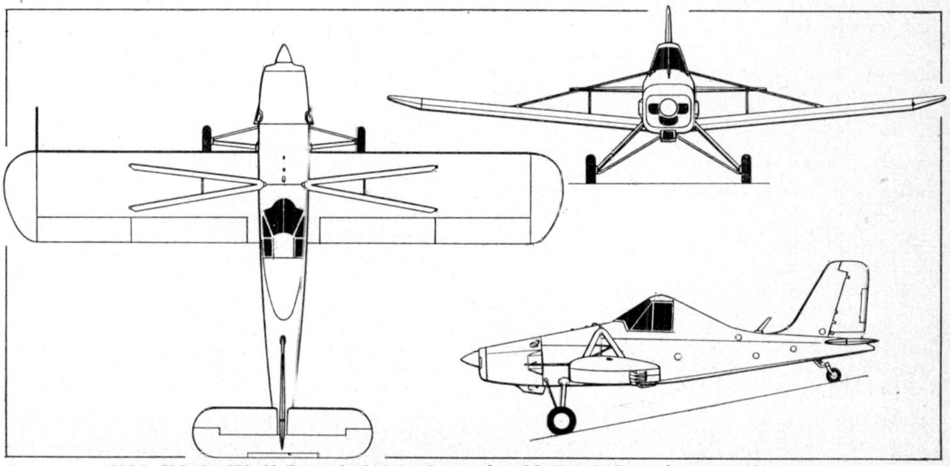

HAL HA-31 Mk II Basant (400 hp Lycoming IO-720-C1B engine) *(Pilot Press)*

HAL HA-31 Mk II BASANT (SPRING)

Design of this agricultural aircraft began in mid-1968. The prototype, designated HAL-31 Mk I, was powered by a 250 hp Rolls-Royce Continental engine, and was described in the 1971-72 *Jane's*. The aircraft was subsequently completely redesigned as the HA-31 Mk II, with a 400 hp engine, and a prototype of this version flew for the first time on 30 March 1972. A second, pre-production prototype flew in September 1972, and certification was in progress in early 1973. A small pre-production batch of Basants (reportedly six) is being built, and is to be followed by an initial production series of 100 aircraft.

The Basant is intended primarily for aerial application of pesticides and fertilisers. It can also be used for aerial survey, fire/patrol duties and cloud seeding.

TYPE: Single-seat agricultural and utility aircraft.

WINGS: Strut-braced low-wing monoplane. Constant-chord wings, of USA 35B section with rounded tips. Thickness/chord ratio 11·6%. Dihedral 5° from roots. No incidence or sweepback. Spars (two) and ribs of light alloy, with fabric covering. Fowler-type trailing-edge flaps and Frise-type ailerons, of similar construction to wings and operated manually. Linked tabs in port and starboard ailerons. Single inverted-Vee bracing strut and cross-strut on each side, attached to fuselage forward of cockpit.

FUSELAGE: Conventional structure, of welded chrome-molybdenum steel tube with fabric covering in most areas. Structure forward of cockpit designed to absorb impact in the event of a crash. The cockpit structure, the seat and its attachment, seat belt and shoulder harness are all designed to withstand 40*g* loads in the event of a crash.

TAIL UNIT: Conventional metal-skinned light alloy structure, with single fin and rudder and wire-braced fixed-incidence tailplane. One-piece elevator, with central trim tab. Trim tab in rudder.

LANDING GEAR: Non-retractable tailwheel type, with HAL oleo-pneumatic shock-absorbers on all units. Size 24·7 × 7·5-10 tyres on main wheels, 11·28 × 4·3·5 on tailwheel. Tyre pressure 35 lb/sq in (2·5 kg/cm²) on main units. Dunlop hydraulic disc brakes.

POWER PLANT: One 400 hp Lycoming IO-720-C1B eight-cylinder horizontally-opposed aircooled engine, driving a Hartzell three-blade constant-speed metal propeller. Two inboard fuel tanks (each 20 Imp gallons; 91 litres) and two outboard tanks (each 14 Imp gallons; 63·5 litres) in each wing, and 2 Imp gallons (9 litres) in collector tank. Total fuel capacity 70 Imp gallons (318 litres). Refuelling point on each tank. Oil capacity (nominal) 4·25 Imp gallons (19·3 litres).

ACCOMMODATION: Single seat in fully-enclosed cockpit. Forward-hinged door on starboard side; emergency door on port side. Cockpit heated and ventilated.

SYSTEMS: Hydraulic motor for crop spraying. Electrical power, from 24V 50A alternator and 24V 25Ah battery, for engine starting, instruments, VHF radio etc.

ELECTRONICS AND EQUIPMENT: VHF radio optional. Glassfibre hopper, installed between engine firewall and front wall of cockpit enclosure, has 33 cu ft (0·93 m³) capacity and can carry up to 1,333 lb (605 kg) of pesticide for Normal category operation and up to 2,000 lb (907 kg) in Restricted category.

DIMENSIONS, EXTERNAL:
- Wing span — 39 ft 4½ in (12·00 m)
- Wing chord (constant) — 6 ft 6½ in (2·00 m)
- Wing aspect ratio — 6·17
- Length overall (tail down) — 29 ft 6¼ in (9·00 m)
- Height overall (tail down) — 8 ft 4½ in (2·55 m)
- Tailplane span — 12 ft 8 in (3·86 m)
- Wheel track — 8 ft 10¼ in (2·70 m)
- Wheelbase — 19 ft 8¼ in (6·00 m)
- Propeller diameter — 7 ft 0 in (2·13 m)
- Propeller ground clearance — 10 in (0·254 m)

AREAS:
- Wings, gross — 251·23 sq ft (23·34 m²)
- Ailerons (total) — 23·03 sq ft (2·14 m²)
- Trailing-edge flaps (total) — 28·18 sq ft (2·618 m²)
- Fin — 11·41 sq ft (1·06 m²)
- Rudder, incl tab — 9·26 sq ft (0·86 m²)
- Tailplane — 26·26 sq ft (2·44 m²)
- Elevator, incl tab — 19·37 sq ft (1·80 m²)

WEIGHTS AND LOADINGS:
- Weight empty — 2,645 lb (1,200 kg)
- Basic operating weight — 4,300 lb (1,954 kg)
- Max T-O weight — 5,000 lb (2,270 kg)
- Max wing loading — 19·92 lb/sq ft (97·25 kg/m²)
- Max power loading — 12·6 lb/hp (5·7 kg/hp)

PERFORMANCE (at basic operating weight):
- Max never-exceed speed — 164 knots (189 mph; 305 km/h)
- Max level speed at S/L — 121 knots (140 mph; 225 km/h)
- Max cruising speed at 8,000 ft (2,625 m) — 100 knots (115 mph; 185 km/h)
- Econ cruising speed — 87 knots (100 mph; 161 km/h)
- Stalling speed, flaps up — 52 knots (60 mph; 96 km/h)
- Stalling speed, flaps down — 49 knots (57 mph; 91 km/h)
- Max rate of climb at S/L — 750 ft (228 m)/min
- Service ceiling — 12,500 ft (3,800 m)
- Min ground turning radius — 22 ft 11 in (7·00 m)
- T-O run — 700 ft (214 m)
- T-O to 50 ft (15 m) — 1,200 ft (365 m)
- Landing from 50 ft (15 m) — 1,000 ft (305 m)
- Landing run — 600 ft (183 m)
- Range with max fuel, no payload — 348 nm (400 miles; 645 km)
- Endurance with max payload, 30 min reserves — 1 hr

HAL (AÉROSPATIALE) SA 315B LAMA
Indian name: Cheetah

The Bangalore Complex's Helicopter Division is building the French Aérospatiale SA 315B Lama five-seat general-purpose helicopter (which see) under licence in India, where it is known as the Cheetah.

The overall programme calls for the completion of 140 aircraft, of which the first 40 are being completed from components and subassemblies imported from France. The remaining 100 are to be built from raw materials, and delivery of these is scheduled to begin in 1976.

The first Indian-assembled Cheetah was flown for the first time on 6 October 1973, and six had been delivered to the Indian Air Force by the beginning of 1974.

HAL (AÉROSPATIALE) SA 316B ALOUETTE III

The Bangalore Complex's Helicopter Division is building under licence the French Aérospatiale SA 316B Alouette III. An initial quantity of 80 is being built, of which the first were delivered in late 1973; HAL also supplies Indian-built components for French-built Alouette IIIs.

KANPUR DIVISION

ADDRESS:
Chakeri, Kanpur

Telephone: HAL PABX 62471-4
Telex: HAL KP 243

When the decision was taken to build the Hawker Siddeley 748 twin-turboprop transport in India, as a replacement for the Dakotas of the Indian Air Force, four hangars at Kanpur were taken over, on 23 January 1960, as the IAF Aircraft Manufacturing Depot. The Depot was incorporated in Aeronautics (India) Ltd in June 1964 and subsequently became the Kanpur Division of Hindustan Aeronautics Ltd.

HAL (HAWKER SIDDELEY) 748

The first set of jigs for the 748 was set up in the Depot by mid-1960, and the first Indian-built 748 flew on 1 November 1961, followed by the second one on 13 March 1963.

The first four Indian 748s were Srs 1 aircraft, utilising components imported from the UK. The first Indian-built Srs 2 flew for the first time on 28 January 1964. Series production of the Srs 2 is continuing at a current rate of nine aircraft a year; by January 1973, 39 Srs 2 aircraft had been built and delivered. Most of the airframe components are manufactured by HAL from raw materials. The aircraft's 2,105 ehp Dart 531 turboprop engines are built by the Bangalore Complex of HAL. Some HF, VHF and other radio equipment is being manufactured by Bharat Electronics Ltd of Bangalore.

Indian Airlines placed an initial order for 14 Srs 2 aircraft; the first of these was delivered on 28 June 1967 and the last in March 1970. Deliveries of a further 10 aircraft ordered by the airline were due to be completed by the end of 1973.

HAL is also producing the aircraft in several versions for the Indian Air Force, which has to date ordered four Srs 1s and 41 Srs 2s. Some of these have already been delivered as executive transports and navigation and signaller trainers. A number of pilot training aircraft are in production, of which first deliveries were scheduled for late 1973.

A prototype military freighter version, developed by Kanpur Division, flew for the first time on 16 February 1972 and successfully completed flight trials with the Indian Air Force. Further environmental trials, conducted from some of the highest airfields in the world, confirmed the suitability of this version for the roles envisaged, and a provisional production order for 48 of this version was placed by the Indian Air Force in 1973. In the Spring of 1974, however, it was reported that the IAF had stated a preference for the de Havilland Canada Buffalo to fulfil its future tactical transport requirement, and that assembly of these aircraft, if ordered, would be undertaken by HAL's Kanpur Division.

HAL-built HS 748 transport aircraft of Indian Airlines (two 2,105 ehp Dart 531 turboprop engines)

MiG COMPLEX

The MiG Complex is formed from the Nasik, Koraput and Hyderabad Divisions of HAL, which build respectively the airframes, power plants and avionics equipment of MiG-21 fighters under licence from the USSR.

HAL (MIKOYAN) MiG-21

Indian Air Force designations: Type 66-400, 66-600, 74, 76, 77 and 88

The following versions of the MiG-21 (NATO code name "Fishbed") have been supplied to or manufactured in India:

MiG-21F. Six Soviet-built MiG-21F ("Fishbed-C") day fighters were supplied to the Indian Air Force in early 1963 and were assigned to No. 28 Squadron. Four more were delivered in mid-1964. IAF designation **Type 74.**

MiG-21PF. Two Soviet-built MiG-21PF ("Fishbed-D") all-weather fighters supplied to IAF (No. 28 Squadron) in mid-1964. Planned import of a further 18 prevented by Indo-Pakistan conflict of September 1965. IAF designation **Type 76.**

MiG-21FL. Soviet export designation of the late-production model MiG-21PF. First version to be manufactured in India, following an initial order for 60 in 1964. Production by HAL, initially from knock-down components and with Soviet-built Tumansky RD-11 engines, began in late 1966; about 100 were assembled in this way, with first deliveries to IAF in 1967. First example built from raw materials, with 60% indigenous content, handed over to IAF on 19 October 1970, and by December 1971 MiG-21s (all versions) were in service with Nos. 1, 4, 8, 28, 29, 30, 45 and 47 Squadrons. Indian production of the FL version, now completed, is believed to have totalled 196. IAF designation **Type 77.**

MiG-21MF ("Fishbed-J"; HAL designation **MiG-21M**). Improved current production version, all except first three (which are to MiG-21PFMA standard) having more powerful Tumansky RD-13 turbojet engine and increased fuel. Total of 150 ordered, for delivery at a planned rate of 30 per year. First aircraft handed over to IAF on 14 February 1973, and about 15 delivered by Spring 1974. IAF designation **Type 88.**

MiG-21U. Tandem two-seat training versions (NATO code name "Mongol"). Small batch of MiG-21U "Mongol-A" delivered from USSR in 1965, these being given the IAF designation **Type 66-400 Series.** Main version in current service is the "Mongol-B" (with broad-chord fin), the IAF designation of which is **Type 66-600 Series.** Total of 42 received.

A full description of the MiG-21 appears in the USSR section of this edition.

HAL-built MiG-21M, the first example of which was completed in February 1973 (*Aviation News*)

INDONESIA

LIPNUR

LIPNUR, LEMBAGA INDUSTRI PENERBANGAN NURTANIO (Department of the Indonesian Air Force, Nurtanio Aircraft Industry)

ADDRESS:
Lanuma Husein Sastranegara (Husein Sastranegara AFB), Bandung

GENERAL DIRECTOR:
Colonel Ir Yuwono

To honour the service of the late Air Marshal Nurtanio Pringgoadisurjo, who was largely responsible for establishing an aircraft industry in Indonesia, the Department of the Air Force of Indonesia named after him the former Institute for Aero Industry Establishment.

The Institute had come into being in August 1961, as a successor to the Indonesian Air Force Design, Development and Production Depot.

LIPNUR has facilities for training aircraft factory workers. Its engineering and production facilities are being used at the present time for the manufacture under licence of the Polish PZL-104 utility aircraft, under the Indonesian name Gelatik.

Lipnur-built PZL-104 Gelatik 32 STOL utility aircraft in Indonesian Air Force insignia

PZL-104 GELATIK 32 (RICE BIRD)

The initial production version of the Gelatik, with 225 hp Continental O-470-13A engine, was described in the 1970-71 *Jane's*.

The current production version is designated Gelatik 32 and has a 230 hp Continental O-470-L or O-470-R engine.

The Gelatik 32 is a licence-built version of the Polish PZL-104 Wilga 32 utility aircraft (see Polish section), with detail changes compared with the current Polish production models.

A total of 39 Gelatiks is being built, of which the first was flown in 1964; 35 had been completed by the Spring of 1974, including six equipped for agricultural duties. The remainder are employed chiefly as passenger or ambulance aircraft, or at flying clubs. The agricultural version received Indonesian certification to BCAR standards on 23 December 1965, and the passenger and ambulance versions on 5 July 1966.

TYPE: STOL general utility aircraft.

WINGS: Cantilever high-wing monoplane. Wing section NACA 2415. Dihedral 1°. Incidence 4° 30′. All-metal single-spar structure, with leading-edge torsion box. Each wing attached to fuselage by three bolts, two at spar and one at forward fitting. All-metal slotted ailerons, which can be drooped to supplement flaps during landing. Mechanically-operated single-slotted all-metal flaps in two sections on each wing. Full-span fixed slats on leading-edges. Ground-adjustable tab on aileron.

FUSELAGE: All-metal stressed-skin semi-monocoque structure. Forward section in upper and lower halves; conical rear section with beaded skin.

TAIL UNIT: Cantilever all-metal structure, with fixed-incidence tailplane. Elevator and rudder are aerodynamically and statically balanced. Ground-adjustable tab in elevator.

LANDING GEAR: Non-retractable tailwheel type. Semi-cantilever main units have oleo-pneumatic shock-absorbers. Castoring and self-centering tailwheel with leaf spring shock-absorber. Tyres size 500 × 150 mm on main wheels and size 200 × 80 mm on tailwheel. Tyre pressure: main wheels 35·6 lb/sq in (2·5 kg/cm²), tailwheel 56·9 lb/sq in (4·0 kg/cm²). Hydraulic brakes. Streamline fairings optional for main wheels and legs.

POWER PLANT: One 230 hp Continental O-470-L or O-470-R six-cylinder horizontally-opposed aircooled engine, driving, respectively, a McCauley 2A34C-50/90A-2 or A-8 two-blade constant-speed metal propeller. Two non-integral fuel tanks in wing torsion box, total usable capacity 42·5 Imp gallons (193 litres). Refuelling points on top of wings, at root. Oil capacity 2·5 Imp gallons (11·5 litres).

ACCOMMODATION: Pilot (front seat, port side) and three passengers, in pairs, or equivalent cargo. Upward-hinged door on each side. Cabin has strengthened honeycomb floor. Baggage compartment aft of seats.

ELECTRONICS AND EQUIPMENT: Motorola or Nova Star VHF transceiver standard. 24V 10Ah battery for engine starting, lights, instruments and radio system. ARC 300 radio standard in agricultural version, ARC 400 in passenger and aeroclub versions. Four AN 3000 Micronair atomisers fitted as standard in agricultural version. Glider towing hook in aeroclub version.

DIMENSIONS, EXTERNAL:
Wing span 36 ft 5 in (11·10 m)
Wing chord (constant) 4 ft 7 in (1·40 m)
Wing aspect ratio 8
Length overall (tail down) 26 ft 6¾ in (8·10 m)
Height overall (tail down) 8 ft 2½ in (2·50 m)
Tailplane span 12 ft 1¾ in (3·70 m)
Wheel track 8 ft 1¼ in (2·47 m)
Wheelbase 21 ft 4¼ in (6·50 m)
Propeller diameter:
O-470-L 7 ft 4 in (2·23 m)
O-470-R 6 ft 10 in (2·08 m)
Propeller ground clearance:
O-470-L 1 ft 6 in (0·46 m)
O-470-R 1 ft 9 in (0·53 m)
Passenger doors (each):
Height 3 ft 1 in (0·94 m)
Width 4 ft 11 in (1·50 m)

DIMENSIONS, INTERNAL:
Cabin: Length 7 ft 2½ in (2·20 m)
Max width 3 ft 9¼ in (1·15 m)
Max height 4 ft 11 in (1·50 m)
Floor area 23 sq ft (2·20 m²)
Volume 85 cu ft (2·40 m³)
Baggage space 17·5 cu ft (0·50 m³)

AREAS:
Wings, gross 166·6 sq ft (15·50 m²)
Ailerons (total) 17·2 sq ft (1·60 m²)
Flaps (total) 21·6 sq ft (2·00 m²)
Fin 15·9 sq ft (1·48 m²)
Rudder 9·8 sq ft (0·91 m²)
Tailplane 13·2 sq ft (1·23 m²)
Elevators (total, incl tab) 23·4 sq ft (2·17 m²)

WEIGHTS AND LOADINGS:
Weight empty 1,624 lb (737 kg)
Max T-O and landing weight 2,711 lb (1,230 kg)
Max wing loading 16·3 lb/sq ft (79·4 kg/m²)
Max power loading 11·8 lb/hp (5·35 kg/hp)

PERFORMANCE (at max T-O weight):
Max never-exceed speed 150 knots (173 mph; 279 km/h)
Max level speed at S/L 110 knots (127 mph; 205 km/h)
Econ cruising speed 81 knots (93 mph; 150 km/h)
Stalling speed, flaps up 30·5 knots (35 mph; 56 km/h)
Max rate of climb at S/L 866 ft (264 m)/min
Time to 12,075 ft (3,680 m) 38 min
Service ceiling 12,075 ft (3,680 m)
T-O run 410 ft (125 m)
T-O to 50 ft (15 m) 787 ft (240 m)
Landing from 50 ft (15 m) 978 ft (298 m)
Landing run 584 ft (178 m)
Range with max fuel 377 nm (435 miles; 700 km)
Range with max payload 337 nm (388 miles; 625 km)

LIPNUR (PAZMANY) PL-2

The Lipnur factory of the Indonesian Air Force has begun the construction of a Pazmany PL-2 light aircraft (see US section), for evaluation as a two-seat military trainer.

It is also understood that tooling has begun for a small initial production batch of these aircraft.

INTERNATIONAL PROGRAMMES

AIRBUS

AIRBUS INDUSTRIE

HEAD OFFICE:
Route de Lectoure, BP No. 33, 31700-Blagnac, France
Telephone: (61) 42 68 68
Telex: AI TO A 53526 F

PARIS OFFICE:
12bis Avenue Bosquet, 75007 Paris, France
Telephone: 551 40 95

AIRFRAME PRIME CONTRACTORS:
Aérospatiale (SNIAS), 37 Boulevard de Montmorency, 75781 Paris-cédex 16, France
Deutsche Airbus GmbH, 8 München 19, Leonrodstrasse 68, Postfach 47, German Federal Republic

CHAIRMAN OF SUPERVISORY BOARD:
Dr Franz-Josef Strauss

PRESIDENT AND CHIEF EXECUTIVE:
Henri Ziegler

EXECUTIVE VICE-PRESIDENT AND CHIEF OPERATING OFFICER:
Roger Beteille

SENIOR VICE-PRESIDENTS:
R. Beteille (Technical)
R. Blanchet (Sales)
F. Feye (Commercial)
F. Kracht (Production)

Airbus Industrie was set up as a "Groupement d'Intérêts Economiques" to manage the development, manufacture and marketing of the twin-engined large-capacity short/medium-range A-300B transport aircraft. It has design leadership and is responsible for the A-300B activities of Aérospatiale of France, Deutsche Airbus (MBB and VFW-Fokker) of Germany, Hawker Siddeley Aviation of the UK, Fokker-VFW of the Netherlands and CASA of Spain.

The associated companies raised the necessary funding in the form of repayable loans from the French, German, Dutch and Spanish governments respectively. Hawker Siddeley Aviation is financing separately a part of the development. A levy on sales of the A-300B will repay the development loans. In addition, a consortium of major French and German banks has been formed to provide finance for sales.

At the end of 1973 Airbus Industrie moved its headquarters from Paris to new accommodation at Toulouse-Blagnac, where construction and flight testing of the A-300B are undertaken.

Aérospatiale is responsible for manufacturing the entire nose section (including the flight deck), lower centre fuselage and engine pylons, and for final assembly. Deutsche Airbus is responsible for manufacturing the forward fuselage, between the flight deck and wing box, the upper centre fuselage, the rear fuselage and the vertical tail surfaces. Hawker Siddeley has design responsibility for the wings, builds the wing fixed structures, and is working in collaboration with Fokker-VFW, which is building the wing moving surfaces. CASA manufactures the horizontal tail surfaces, fuselage main doors and landing gear doors.

AIRBUS A-300B

The Airbus A-300B is basically a wide-bodied aircraft with underwing pods for two turbofan engines. The early history of the project has appeared in previous editions of *Jane's*.

It is currently being offered with two 51,000 lb (23,130 kg) st General Electric CF6-50C turbofans, but the underwing location of the power plant enables the A-300B to use any advanced-technology turbofan engine in the 50,000 lb (22,700 kg) thrust class. The engines at present offered have considerable development potential and are installed in pods interchangeable with those of the McDonnell Douglas DC-10 Series 30.

Six airframes were involved in the certification programme, including one static test specimen and separate components, to cover the complete structure, for fatigue tests.

Construction of the first A-300B, a B1, began in September 1969. This aircraft (F-WUAB, later F-OCAZ) made its first flight on 28 October 1972, and was followed by the second B1 (F-WUAC) on 5 February 1973. Together with the first two A-300B2 aircraft, the B1s flew a total of more than 1,580 hours by the time French and German certification was granted on 15 March 1974. This was followed by FAA certification on 30 May 1974 and covers automatic approach and landing in Category 2 weather conditions. Certification flights for Category 3 were continuing in the Spring of 1974. The first automatic landing was made, by the second B1 development aircraft, on 2 May 1973.

The following major versions have been or are being built:

A-300B1. Initial version, with 49,000 lb (22,226 kg) st CF6-50A engines, overall length of 167 ft 2¼ in (50·97 m) and max seating for 302 passengers. Described in detail in 1971-72 *Jane's*. First and second development aircraft are built to this specification.

A-300B2. Basic production version, to which the following description applies. Third and fourth aircraft (F-WUAD and F-WUAA) are to this configuration, and flew for the first time on 28 June and 20 November 1973 respectively. Next three (ie first three production) aircraft are for Air France; the first of these flew for the first time on 15 April 1974 and was delivered at the end of that month to Air France, with which it entered service on 23 May 1974 on the Paris-London route. Air France aircraft are equipped to accommodate 26 first class and 225 economy class passengers.

A-300B4. Long-range development of B2, with same capacity but increased design weights and fuel capacity. Wing leading-edge aerodynamic refinements to improve take-off performance. Ninth aircraft will be the first built to B4 configuration; first flight was due in 1974, with deliveries scheduled to begin in the Spring of 1975.

Possible future versions currently under consideration in 1974 included the B8 (increased wing span and less powerful engines), B9

Second of two Airbus Industrie A-300B2 development aircraft, shown in the insignia of Air France, with whom this version entered service in 1974

("stretched" version with four more rows of seats than the B4) and B10 (with Rolls-Royce RB.211-524 engines).

To transport large components of the A-300B between the various factories involved, Airbus Industrie acquired a Guppy-201 transport aircraft from the USA, which is operated on its behalf by Aéromaritime.

By 1 May 1974, orders and options totalling 47 aircraft had been signed, as follows:

	Orders	*Options*
Air France	6 B2	10 B2
Air Siam	2 B4	1 B2
Iberia	4 B4	8 B4
Lufthansa	3 B2	4 B2
SATA (Switzerland)	1 B4	—
Sterling Airways (Denmark)	3 B4	—
Transbrasil	2 B2	2 B2
Trans European Airways (Belgium)	1 B2*	—

**lease from Airbus Industrie*

Manufacture of the first 32 production aircraft (Nos. 5-36) is under way, and materials for the next 16 have been ordered. Eight aircraft were due to be delivered by the end of 1974, and 18 more during 1975.

TYPE: Large-capacity short/medium-range transport.

WINGS: Cantilever mid-wing monoplane. Thickness/chord ratio 10·5%. Sweepback 28° at quarter-chord. Primary two-spar box-type structure, integral with fuselage and incorporating fail-safe principles, built of high-strength aluminium alloy. Third spar across inboard sections. Machined skin with open-sectioned stringers. Each wing has three-section leading-edge slats (no slat cutout over the engine pylon), and three Fowler-type double-slotted flaps on trailing-edge; a Krueger flap in the leading-edge wing root (B4 only); an all-speed aileron between inboard flap and outer pair; and a low-speed aileron outboard of the outer pair of flaps. Lift dump facility by combination of three spoilers (outboard) and two airbrakes (inboard) on each wing, forward of outer pair of flaps, plus two additional airbrakes forward of inboard flap. The flaps extend over 84% of each half-span, and increase the wing chord by 25% when fully extended. The datum of the all-speed aileron is deflected downward by up to 10° with flap operation to maintain trailing-edge continuity with deflected flaps. Drive mechanisms for flaps and slats are similar to one another, each powered by twin motors driving ball screwjacks on each surface with built-in protection against asymmetric operation. Three slat positions for take-off and landing. Pre-selection of the airbrake/lift dump lever allows automatic extension of the lift dumpers on touchdown. All flight controls are powered by triplex hydraulic servo-jacks, with no manual reversion. Anti-icing of wing leading-edges, outboard of engine pods, is by hot air bled from engines.

FUSELAGE: Conventional semi-monocoque structure of circular cross-section, with frames and open Z-section stringers. Built mainly of high-strength aluminium alloy, with steel or titanium for some major components. Skin panels integrally machined in areas of high stress. Honeycomb panels or restricted glassfibre laminates for secondary structures.

TAIL UNIT: Cantilever all-metal structure, with sweepback on all surfaces. Variable-incidence tailplane and separately-controlled elevators. Tailplane powered by two motors driving a fail-safe ball screwjack. No anti-icing of leading-edges.

LANDING GEAR: Hydraulically-retractable tricycle type, of Messier-Hispano design, with Messier-Hispano shock-absorbers and wheels. Twin-wheel nose unit retracts forward and main units inward into fuselage. Free-fall extension. Each four-wheel main unit comprises two tandem-mounted bogies, interchangeable left with right, with tyres size 46 × 16-20, pressure 168 lb/sq in (11·8 kg/cm²) on B2, 182 lb/sq in (12·8 kg/cm²) on B4. Nosewheel tyres size 40 × 14-16, pressure 138 lb/sq in (9·7 kg/cm²) on B2, 115 lb/sq in (8·1 kg/cm²) on B4. Steering angles 65°/100°. SNECMA (Hispano) hydraulic disc brakes, with Hispano 286223 cooling system, on all main wheels. Duplex anti-skid units fitted, with a third standby hydraulic supply for wheel brakes.

POWER PLANT (B2 and B4): Two General Electric CF6-50C turbofan engines, each of 51,000 lb (23,130 kg) st, assembled under licence by SNECMA and MTU and mounted in underwing pods, fitted with thrust reversers which are actuated pneumatically by engine bleed air. Nacelles supplied by McDonnell Douglas. Fuel in two integral tanks in each wing, with total usable capacity of 9,460 Imp gallons (43,000 litres) in B2. Max total capacity of 12,450 Imp gallons (56,600 litres) in B4. Two refuelling points standard beneath each wing, outboard of engines.

ACCOMMODATION (B2 and B4): Crew of three on flight deck, with provision for two-man operation. Fourth seat for observer. Provision for a second observer's seat (fifth crew member). Electrical de-icing and demisting of windscreen. Seating for between 220 and 300 passengers in main cabin in six, seven or eight-abreast layout with 31/34 in (79/86 cm) seat pitch. Nine-abreast high-density layout provides up to 345 seats. Typical all-tourist class layout has 281 seats, eight abreast with two aisles, at 34 in (86 cm) seat pitch. This layout includes one galley and one toilet forward, with provision for a second one, and one more galley and four toilets aft. Up to 331 passengers can be carried at 28 in (71 cm) seat pitch in single-class high-density layout. Closed hatracks on each side, forming baggage lockers. Provision for central double-sided rack. Two outward parallel-opening plug-type passenger doors ahead of wing leading-edge on each side, and one on each side at rear. Underfloor baggage/cargo holds fore and aft of wings, with doors on starboard side. The forward hold will accommodate four 88 × 125 × 64 in (224 × 318 × 163 cm) pallets or twelve IATA A1 containers; the rear hold will accommodate eight containers each of 150 cu ft (4·25 m³) capacity. Additional bulk loading of freight provided for in an extreme rear compartment with usable volume of 565 cu ft (16·0 m³). As an option, the latter compartment can be used for the transport of livestock. Entire accommodation is pressurised, including freight, baggage and electronics compartments.

SYSTEMS: Air for air-conditioning system can be provided from engines, the APU or a high pressure ground source. Supply is controlled by separate and parallel bootstrap-type units, each of which includes a flow limiting unit, primary and secondary cooler units, water separator and temperature control unit. In addition, air from each engine passes through a pressure control pre-cooler unit. Distribution in flight deck and three cabin areas, with independent regulation. Two independent automatic systems, with manual override, control the cabin altitude, its rate of change and the differential pressure. Cabin pressure differential for normal operations is 8·25 lb/sq in (0·58 kg/cm²). Hydraulic system comprises three fully-independent circuits, operating simultaneously. Fluid used is a fire-resistant phosphate-ester type, working at a pressure of 3,000 lb/sq in (210 kg/cm²). The three circuits provide triplex power for primary flying controls; if any circuit fails, full control of the aircraft is retained without any necessity for action by the crew. All three circuits supply the all-speed and low-speed ailerons, airbrakes, rudder and elevator; "blue" circuit additionally supplies tail trim, spoilers, slats and rudder variable-gear unit; "green" circuit additionally supplies spoilers, slats, elevator artificial feel units, flaps, steering, wheel brakes and normal landing gear requirements; "yellow" circuit additionally supplies tail trim, lift dumpers, rudder variable-gear unit, elevator artificial feel unit, flaps and steering. Each circuit normally powered by engine-driven self-regulating pumps, one on each engine for the green circuit and one each for the blue and yellow circuits. Dowty Rotol ram-air turbine-driven pump provides standby hydraulic power should both engines become inoperative. Main electrical power is supplied by two Westinghouse three-phase constant-frequency AC generators mounted on the engines. A third identical generator, driven by the APU, can supply power both in flight, to replace a failed engine-driven generator, and on the ground. Supply frequency is 400Hz and voltage is 115/200V. Any one generator can supply sufficient power to operate all equipment and systems necessary for take-off and landing. A conventional generator CSD system is installed, the two units being mounted on opposite sides of the engine gearbox with the CSD driving an air-cooled generator at a constant 8,000 rpm. Each generator is rated at 90kVA, with overload ratings of 135kVA for 5 minutes and 180 kVA for 5 seconds. The APU generator is driven at constant speed through a gearbox. Three unregulated transformer-rectifier units (TRUs) supply 28V DC power. Three 24V 25Ah nickel-cadmium batteries are used for APU starting and fuel control, engine starter control, standby lights and, by selection, emergency busbar. This busbar and a 115V 400Hz static inverter provide standby power in flight if normal power is unavailable. This system is separated completely from the main system. Hot air protection for engine intakes and slat sections on the wings outboard of the engines. The necessity to protect other zones, such as the tailplane and the slat sections inboard of the engines, is the subject of further testing. Garrett AiResearch TSCP 700-5 APU

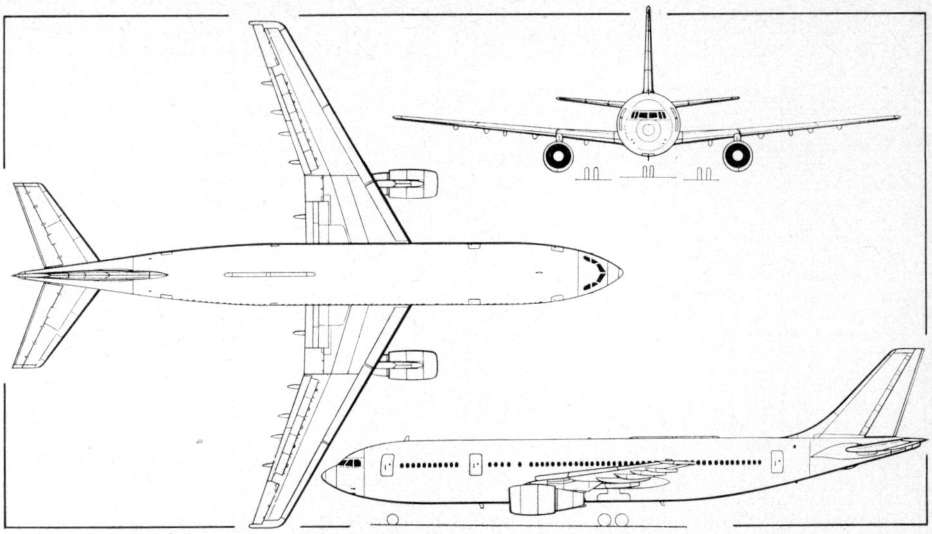

Airbus A-300B2 wide-bodied short/medium-range transport *(Pilot Press)*

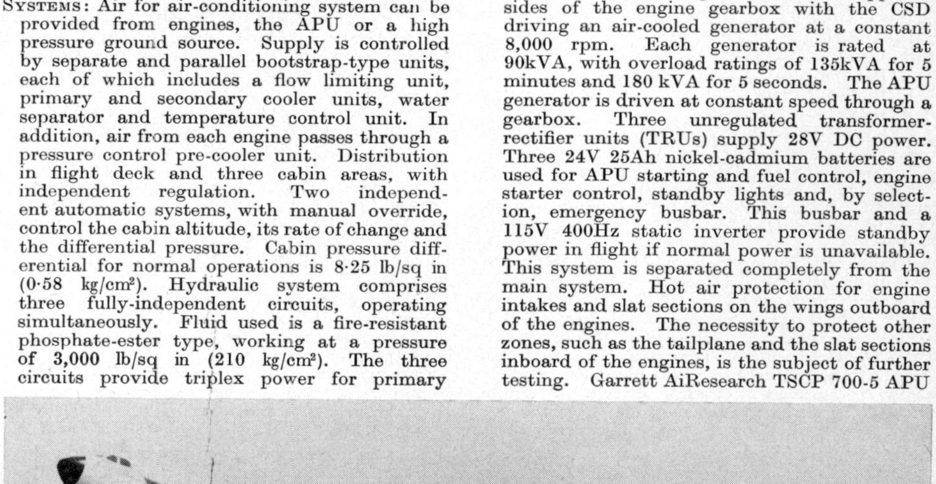

Airbus A-300B2 taking off from Heathrow on the second leg of its first commercial service with Air France

installed in tailcone, exhausting upward. The installation incorporates APU noise attenuation. Fire protection system is self-contained, and firewall panels protect main structure from an APU fire. The APU can be operated on the ground, in flight up to 35,000 ft (10,675 m), and in icing conditions. Relights are possible up to 25,000 ft (7,620 m). Aircraft is completely independent of ground power sources, since all major services can be operated by using the APU.

Electronics and Equipment: Standard communications equipment includes two VHF sets and one Selcal system, plus interphone and passenger address systems. An accident recorder and voice recorder are also installed. Standard navigation equipment includes two VOR, two ILS, two radio altimeters, one marker beacon, two ADF, two DME, two ATC transponders and a weather radar. Most other electronic equipment available to customer's requirements, only those related to the blind landing system (VOR/ILS and radio altimeter) being selected and supplied by the manufacturer. Additional optional equipment includes an HF set, third VHF, second marker beacon, third VOR/ILS, second radar, navigation computer and pictorial display. Both the pilot and co-pilot have an integrated instrument system combining heading and attitude (three SAGEM MGC 10/ARINC 569 are standard in B2, but one or two of these can be replaced by MGC 30/ARINC 571 Mk 1 inertial sensors, which are modular with the MGC 10); SFENA or Sperry STARS flight director system; and radio information. The SFENA/Smiths/Bodenseewerk automatic flight control system includes a comprehensive range of en-route facilities such as VOR coupling, heading select, height acquire, turbulence, rate of descent (if required) and control wheel steering, in addition to the normal height, speed, pitch-and-roll attitude and heading locks.

Dual automatic landing system provides coupled approach and automatic landing facilities suitable for Category 3A operation. The system is designed to allow future extension to Category 3B automatic landing capability.

Dimensions, external (B2 and B4):
Wing span 147 ft 1 in (44·84 m)
Wing aspect ratio 7·71
Length overall 175 ft 11 in (53·62 m)
Length of fuselage 170 ft 8½ in (52·03 m)
Fuselage max diameter 18 ft 6 in (5·64 m)
Height overall 54 ft 2¾ in (16·53 m)
Tailplane span 55 ft 7 in (16·94 m)
Wheel track 31 ft 6 in (9·60 m)
Wheelbase (c/l of shock struts) 61 ft 0 in (18·60 m)
Passengers doors (each):
Height 6 ft 4 in (1·93 m)
Width 3 ft 6 in (1·07 m)
Height to sill:
fwd 15 ft 1 in (4·60 m)
centre 15 ft 9 in (4·80 m)
rear 18 ft 0½ in (5·50 m)
Emergency exits (each):
Height 5 ft 3 in (1·60 m)
Width 2 ft 0 in (0·61 m)
Height to sill 15 ft 10 in (4·87 m)
Underfloor cargo door (fwd):
Height 5 ft 7 in (1·70 m)
Width 8 ft 0 in (2·44 m)
Height to sill 8 ft 4¾ in (2·56 m)
Underfloor cargo door (rear):
Height 5 ft 7 in (1·70 m)
Width 5 ft 11¼ in (1·81 m)
Height to sill 9 ft 8½ in (2·96 m)
Underfloor cargo door (extreme rear):
Height 3 ft 1 in (0·95 m)
Width 3 ft 1 in (0·95 m)
Height to sill 10 ft 10 in (3·30 m)

Dimensions, internal (B2 and B4):
Cabin, excl flight deck:
Length 128 ft 6 in (39·15 m)
Max width 17 ft 7 in (5·35 m)
Max height 8 ft 4 in (2·54 m)
Underfloor cargo hold volume:
forward 2,652 cu ft (75·1 m³)
rear 1,652 cu ft (46·8 m³)
extreme rear 565 cu ft (16·0 m³)
Max total volume for bulk loading 4,869 cu ft (137·9 m³)

Areas (B2 and B4):
Wings, gross 2,799 sq ft (260·0 m²)
Vertical tail surfaces (total) 486·5 sq ft (45·2 m²)
Horizontal tail surfaces (total) 748·1 sq ft (69·5 m²)

Weights and Loadings:
Manufacturer's weight empty:
B2 168,805 lb (76,569 kg)
B4 173,404 lb (78,655 kg)
Typical operating weight empty:
B2 186,975 lb (84,810 kg)
B4 191,690 lb (86,950 kg)
Max payload (structural):
B2 69,865 lb (31,690 kg)
B4 77,270 lb (35,050 kg)
Max T-O weight:
B2 302,000 lb (137,000 kg)
B4 330,700 lb (150,000 kg)
Max ramp weight:
B2 304,015 lb (137,900 kg)
B4 332,675 lb (150,900 kg)
Max landing weight:
B2 281,000 lb (127,500 kg)
B4 293,200 lb (133,000 kg)
Max zero-fuel weight:
B2 256,840 lb (116,500 kg)
B4 269,000 lb (122,000 kg)
Max wing loading:
B2 107·9 lb/sq ft (527 kg/m²)
B4 118·2 lb/sq ft (577 kg/m²)
Max power loading:
B2 2·96 lb/lb st (2·96 kg/kg st)
B4 3·24 lb/lb st (3·24 kg/kg st)

Performance (at max T-O weight except where indicated):
Max operating speed (Vmo):
B2, B4 360 knots (415 mph; 668 km/h) CAS
Max operating Mach number (Mmo):
B2, B4 Mach 0·84
Max cruising speed at 25,000 ft (7,620 m):
B2, B4 505 knots (582 mph; 937 km/h) TAS
Typical high-speed cruise at 30,000 ft (9,145 m):
B2, B4 495 knots (570 mph; 917 km/h) TAS
Typical long-range cruising speed at 31,000 ft (9,450 m):
B2, B4 457 knots (526 mph; 847 km/h) TAS
Approach speed at typical weight:
B2 131 knots (151 mph; 243 km/h)
B4 132 knots (152 mph; 245 km/h)
Max operating altitude:
B2 35,000 ft (10,700 m)
Min ground turning radius (wingtips) 109 ft 11¼ in (33·51 m)
Runway LCN at max T-O weight:
30 in (0·76 m) radius of rigidity:
B2 60
B4 69
40 in (1·02 m) radius of rigidity:
B2 71
B4 81
T-O field length (S/L, ISA + 15°C):
B2 6,445 ft (1,965 m)
B4 9,185 ft (2,800 m)
Landing field length at typical weight:
B2 5,350 ft (1,630 m)
B4 5,445 ft (1,660 m)
Range with 281 passengers and baggage:
B2 1,402 nm (1,615 miles; 2,600 km)
B4 2,098 nm (2,417 miles; 3,890 km)
Range with max fuel:
B2 1,997 nm (2,300 miles; 3,700 km)
B4 2,800 nm (3,225 miles; 5,190 km)

Operational Noise Characteristics:
T-O noise level at 3·5 nm (4 miles; 6·5 km) from start of T-O run:
B2 93 EPNdB
B4 96 EPNdB
Approach noise level at 1·0 nm (1·15 miles; 1·85 km) from landing threshold on 3° glideslope:
B2, B4 101 EPNdB
Sideline noise level at 0·25 nm (0·29 miles; 0·46 km) from runway centre-line:
B2, B4 95 EPNdB

ALPHA JET

Airframe Prime Contractors:

Avions Marcel Dassault/Breguet Aviation, BP 32, 92420-Vaucresson, France
Telephone: 970-75-21
Telex: 0734372

Dornier GmbH, Postfach 317, 7990 Friedrichshafen, German Federal Republic
Telephone: (07545) 81

On 22 July 1969 the French and German governments announced a joint requirement for a new subsonic basic and advanced training aircraft to enter service with the French and German armed forces in the mid-1970s. Each government has a potential requirement for about 200 such aircraft to replace Magister and Lockheed T-33A trainers in service, and two designs were studied during the first half of 1970. These were the Aérospatiale/MBB E 650 Eurotrainer and the Dassault-Breguet/Dornier Alpha Jet.

On 24 July 1970, it was announced that the Alpha Jet design had been selected for development to meet the requirement. The aircraft is also to have a capacity for close air support and battlefield reconnaissance duties, to meet Luftwaffe requirements.

DASSAULT-BREGUET/DORNIER ALPHA JET

The Dassault-Breguet group of France and Dornier of Germany are jointly developing the Alpha Jet, with Dassault-Breguet as main contractor and Dornier as industrial collaborator, the total work load being shared equally between the two groups.

On 15 February 1971 the project definition phase of the Alpha Jet was completed, and design work for the development phase was begun in the Autumn of 1971. This received joint Franco-German government approval in late 1972. Four prototypes are being built, the first and third assembled in France and the second and fourth in Germany.

Flight testing is being carried out predominantly in France, by both French and German pilots, with each prototype making its first few test flights in the country where it is assembled. Prototypes 01 and 02 are being used to finalise systems installations and for flight and performance evaluation; the 03 is representative of the production close-support version, and the 04 of the trainer version. The 01 was completed at St Cloud in mid-June 1973, and the first functional test (of the fuel system) was made on 26 July 1973. This prototype made its first flight, at Istres, on 26 October 1973, followed by the 02 at Oberpfaffenhofen on 9 January 1974. The third Alpha Jet made its first flight on 6 May 1974. The fourth prototype was due to fly in October 1974, followed by the first flight and first deliveries of production aircraft in late 1976.

The French and German versions will be identical as regards airframe, power plant, landing gear and standard equipment; and assembly lines for production Alpha Jets will be set up in each country. The outer wings, tail unit, rear fuselage and cold-flow exhaust will be manufactured in Germany; the forward and centre fuselage (with integrated wing centre-section) will be manufactured in France. Final assembly of the trainer version will take place in France, and of the close-support version in Germany. The power

First prototype of the Dassault-Breguet/Dornier Alpha Jet (two 2,645 lb; 1,200 kg st SNECMA/Turboméca Larzac turbofan engines)

plant prime contractors are Turboméca and SNECMA in France, and MTU and KHD in Germany; and, for the landing gear, Messier-Hispano in France and Liebherr Aero Technik in Germany.

Belgium has also chosen the Alpha Jet as its next military trainer, and is expected to order thirty-three.

TYPE: Tandem two-seat basic, low-altitude and advanced jet trainer and close-support and battlefield reconnaissance aircraft.

WINGS: Cantilever shoulder-wing monoplane, with 6° anhedral from roots. Thickness/chord ratio 10·2% at root, 8·6% at tip. Sweepback 28° at quarter-chord. All-metal numerically- or chemically-milled structure, consisting of two outer wings bolted to a centre frame. Two-section hydraulically-actuated double-slotted flaps on each trailing-edge. Ailerons actuated by double-body hydraulic servo, with trimmable artificial feel system.

FUSELAGE: All-metal semi-monocoque structure, numerically or chemically milled, of basically oval cross-section. Built in three sections: nose (including cockpit), centre-section (including engine air intake trunks and main landing gear housings) and rear (including engine mounts and tail assembly). Electrically-controlled, hydraulically-actuated airbrake on each side of rear upper fuselage, possibly of carbon-fibre-reinforced epoxy resin construction.

TAIL UNIT: Cantilever all-metal type, of similar construction to wings, with 45° sweepback on fin leading-edge. Dorsal spine fairing between cockpit and fin. All-flying tailplane, with trimmable and IAS-controlled artificial feel system. Double-body hydraulic servo-actuated rudder, with trimmable artificial feel system.

LANDING GEAR: Forward-retracting tricycle type, of Liebherr/Messier-Hispano design. All units retract hydraulically, main units into underside of engine air intake trunks. Single wheel and low-pressure tyre (approx 57 lb/sq in; 4·0 kg/cm²) at normal T-O weight) on each unit. Steel disc brakes and anti-skid units on main gear. Emergency braking system. Hydraulic nosewheel steering and arrester hook on German version. Nosewheel offset to starboard to permit ground firing from gun pod.

POWER PLANT: Two SNECMA/Turboméca Larzac 04 turbofan engines, each rated at 2,976 lb (1,350 kg) st for production aircraft, mounted on sides of fuselage. Splitter plate in front of each intake. Fuel in two integral tanks in outer wings, one in centre-section and three fuselage tanks. Internal fuel capacity 303·5 Imp gallons (1,380 litres) in French basic trainer version; 413·5 Imp gallons (1,880 litres) in French low-altitude trainer and German close-support versions. Provision for 68·2 Imp gallon (310 litre) capacity drop-tank on each outer wing pylon. Pressure refuelling standard for all tanks, including drop-tanks. Gravity system optional for fuselage tanks and drop-tanks. Pressure refuelling point near starboard engine air intake. Fuel system incorporates provision for short periods of inverted flying.

ACCOMMODATION: Two persons in tandem, in pressurised cockpit under individual upward-opening canopies. Rear seat (for instructor in trainer versions) is elevated. Prototypes fitted with Martin-Baker Mk 4 ejection seats, operable (including ejection through canopy if necessary) at zero height and speeds down to 90 knots (103 mph; 166 km/h). Cockpits and canopies suitable for installation of Stencel SIIIS or Martin-Baker Mk 10 zero-zero ejection seats.

SYSTEMS: Cockpit air-conditioning and demisting system. Two independent hydraulic systems, each 3,000 lb/sq in (210 kg/cm²), with engine-driven pumps (emergency electric pump on one circuit), for actuating control surfaces, landing gear, brakes, flaps, airbrakes, and (when fitted) nosewheel steering. Pneumatic system, for cockpit pressurisation and air-conditioning, occupants' pressure suits and fuel tank pressurisation, is supplied by compressed air from engines. Main electrical power supplied by two 9kW starter/generators, one on each engine. Circuit includes a 36Ah nickel-cadmium battery and two static inverters for supplying AC current to auxiliary systems. An external ground DC power receptacle is fitted. Hydraulic and electrical systems can be sustained by either engine in the event of the other engine becoming inoperative. Oxygen mask for each occupant, supplied by liquid oxygen converter of 2·2 Imp gallons (10 litres) capacity. Emergency gaseous oxygen bottle for each occupant.

ELECTRONICS AND EQUIPMENT: Dual controls standard. Large electronics bay in rear fuselage, containing most of the radio and navigation equipment. Standard equipment includes VHF and UHF transceivers (optionally, UHF and emergency UHF respectively), IFF-SIF, VOR/ILS and intercom. Optional equipment includes Dornier crash recorder, VOR/ILS with marker, TACAN, navigation computer and radio altimeter.

First prototype of the Dassault-Breguet/Dornier Alpha Jet

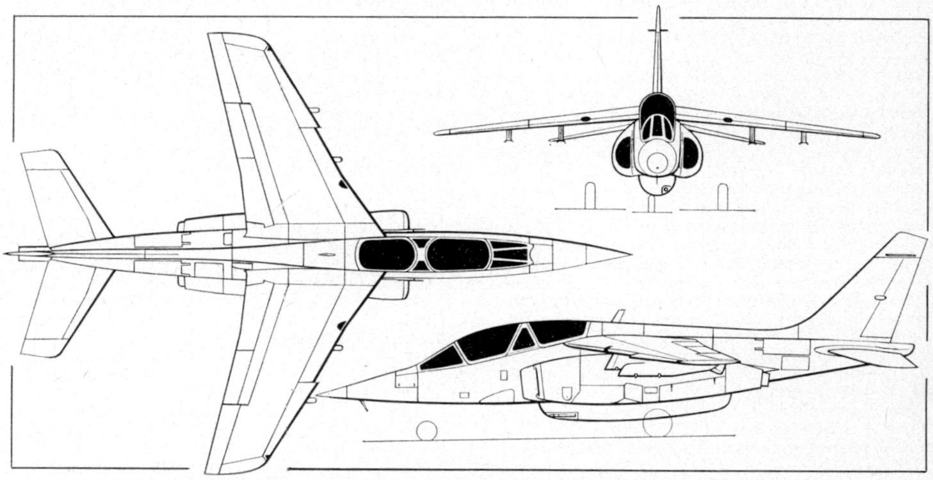

Alpha Jet advanced jet trainer and close-support aircraft (*Pilot Press*)

ARMAMENT AND OPERATIONAL EQUIPMENT: For armament training and light close-support missions, the Alpha Jet can be equipped with an underfuselage detachable pod containing a 30 mm DEFA or 27 mm Mauser cannon with 150 rds, or a pod with two 0·50 in machine-guns and 250 rds/gun. Provision also for one or two hardpoints under each wing, with non-jettisonable pylons, on which can be carried, within the load capacity for each station, pods of thirty-six 2·75 in rockets; HE or incendiary bombs of 50, 125, 250 or 400 kg; practice launchers for bombs or rockets; or drop-tanks. Provision also for carrying target demonstration devices or an underfuselage reconnaissance pod. Max permissible payload for all five stations is 4,850 lb (2,200 kg). Fire control system for air-to-air or air-to-ground firing, dive bombing and low-level bombing. Firing by trainee pilot (in front seat) is governed by a safety interlock system controlled by the instructor, which energises the forward station trigger circuit and illuminates a "fire clearance" indicator in the trainee's cockpit.

DIMENSIONS, EXTERNAL:
- Wing span: 29 ft 11 in (9·12 m)
- Wing aspect ratio: 4·8
- Length overall (excl nose-probe): 40 ft 3¾ in (12·29 m)
- Height overall (at normal T-O weight): 13 ft 9 in (4·19 m)
- Tailplane span: 14 ft 2⅞ in (4·34 m)
- Wheel track: 8 ft 10⅝ in (2·71 m)
- Wheelbase: 15 ft 5¾ in (4·716 m)

AREAS:
- Wings, gross: 188·4 sq ft (17·50 m²)
- Ailerons (total): 11·19 sq ft (1·04 m²)
- Trailing-edge flaps (total): 30·78 sq ft (2·86 m²)
- Airbrakes (total): 7·97 sq ft (0·74 m²)
- Fin: 31·97 sq ft (2·97 m²)
- Rudder: 6·67 sq ft (0·62 m²)
- Horizontal tail surfaces (total): 42·41 sq ft (3·94 m²)

WEIGHTS AND LOADINGS:
- Weight empty, equipped: 6,944 lb (3,150 kg)
- Normal T-O weights:
  - trainer, clean: 9,920 lb (4,500 kg)
  - weapon training or close support: 13,227 lb (6,000 kg)
- Max T-O weight (exceptional): 15,432 lb (7,000 kg)
- Combat wing loading (clean): 47·1 lb/sq ft (230 kg/m²)
- Combat power loading (clean): 1·5 lb/lb st (1·5 kg/kg st)

PERFORMANCE (estimated, at normal (clean) T-O weight, except where indicated):
- Max level speed at high altitude: Mach 0·85
- Max level speed at low altitude: more than 500 knots (576 mph; 927 km/h)
- Landing speed at normal landing weight: less than 100 knots (115 mph; 185 km/h)
- Rate of climb at S/L, one engine out, at 10,542 lb (4,782 kg) AUW, in landing configuration: 984 ft (300 m)/min
- Time to 39,375 ft (12,000 m): less than 10 min
- Service ceiling: 49,200 ft (15,000 m)
- T-O run at 9,920 lb (4,500 kg) AUW: 1,280 ft (390 m)
- T-O to 50 ft (15 m): less than 2,297 ft (700 m)
- Landing run at 7,716 lb (3,500 kg) AUW: 1,310 ft (400 m)
- Endurance, typical low-altitude navigation training mission: 1 hr 40 min
- Max endurance: 2 hr 35 min
- Max range: 1,078 nm (1,242 miles; 2,000 km)
- Ferry range (internal fuel and two 310 litre external tanks): 1,311 nm (1,510 miles; 2,430 km)
- g limits: +12; —6·4

CONCORDE

CONCORDE SUPERSONIC TRANSPORT PROGRAMME

AIRFRAME PRIME CONTRACTORS:

British Aircraft Corporation Ltd, Brooklands Road, Weybridge, Surrey KT13 0RN, England
Telephone: Weybridge (97) 45522

Aérospatiale (SNIAS), 37 Boulevard de Montmorency, 75781 Paris-cédex 16, France
Telephone: 224-84-00

POWER PLANT PRIME CONTRACTORS:

Rolls-Royce (1971) Ltd, PO Box 3, Filton, Bristol, England
Telephone: 0272-693871

Société Nationale d'Etude et de Construction de Moteurs d'Aviation, 150 Boulevard Haussmann, 75361 Paris-cédex 08, France
Telephone: 227-33-94

British-assembled Concorde 202 (second production aircraft), landing after its first flight on 13 February 1974

CONCORDE

Anglo-French negotiations concerning the development of a supersonic transport aircraft culminated on 29 November 1962 in the signing of two agreements, one between the French and British governments, the other between the manufacturers to whom the project was entrusted. The agreements provided for a fair division of the work, responsibility and development costs among the partners, and covered the manufacture of two Concorde prototypes, followed by two pre-production aircraft and two airframes for static and fatigue testing. The static test programme was completed in September 1973.

The planned test programme, involving the two prototypes, two pre-production and the first three production Concordes, will total 3,890 flying hours. By 10 April 1974 the first six of these seven aircraft had totalled 1,161 flights with a total block time of 2,500 hours, nearly 750 hours of which were at supersonic speeds.

After completing only some 800 hours of test flying, BAC and Aérospatiale were convinced that they would be able to guarantee a payload of at least 20,000 lb (9,070 kg) on a Paris-New York flight, under specified conditions, on entry into service. This has been amply demonstrated by Concorde 02 (which see), and the guaranteed entry-into-service figure has since been raised to 26,500 lb (12,020 kg) over this sector.

Initially, delivery positions for 74 Concordes were reserved by 16 airlines, as listed in the 1972-73 *Jane's*, but this option system was abolished on 28 March 1973. The first firm order, for five aircraft, was announced by BOAC on 25 May 1972. It was followed shortly afterwards by announcement of an Air France order for four Concordes and these two contracts were signed on 28 July 1972.

Operationally, development of the new Type 28 aft thrust reverser nozzle promises a continuing substantial reduction in noise levels, and the engine smoke problem is eliminated completely with the installation of Olympus 593 Mk 602 engines in the 02 (second pre-production) and subsequent aircraft.

When sonic boom considerations preclude use of the normal climb technique, sufficient power is available to increase the transonic acceleration height to over 40,000 ft (12,200 m). Normally, however, the aircraft will accelerate and climb from 200 knots (230 mph; 370 km/h) CAS at S/L to 400 knots (460 mph; 740 km/h) CAS at 5,000 ft (1,500 m), then climb at a constant CAS of 400 knots (460 mph; 740 km/h) to 36,000 ft (11,000 m) where its speed will be Mach 1·15, climb and accelerate to Mach 1·8 (530 knots; 610 mph; 980 km/h CAS) at 45,300 ft (13,800 m) and continue climbing at this CAS until the cruise Mach number is reached, finally climbing to cruising height at cruising Mach number.

Airframe development and production of the Concorde is undertaken jointly by Aérospatiale and BAC, with two final assembly lines, at their Toulouse and Filton works respectively. There is no duplication of main production jigs.

Aérospatiale is responsible for development and production of the rear cabin section, wings and wing control surfaces, hydraulic system, flying controls, navigation systems, radio and air-conditioning system. The automatic flight control system is designed by Marconi-Elliott in the UK and SFENA in France, under contract to Aérospatiale. BAC is responsible for the three forward sections of the fuselage, the rear fuselage and vertical tail surfaces, the engine nacelles and ducting, the electrical system, sound and thermal insulation, oxygen system, fuel system, engine installation, and fire warning and extinguishing systems.

The following versions of Concorde have been built:

Concorde 001. First prototype (F-WTSS), assembled by Aérospatiale and first flown on 2 March 1969. Construction started in 1965. Generally similar in most respects to pre-production and production models, but with lower-powered Olympus 593 engines, shorter fuselage (184 ft 6 in; 56·24 m) and design gross weight of 326,000 lb (148,000 kg). Used for sales demonstration tour of South America in September 1971, and for special flight in June 1973 to observe solar eclipse. Described in previous editions of *Jane's*. Retired on 19 October 1973 to French Air Museum at Le Bourget Airport, having made 397 test flights covering 812 hours block time, of which 255 hours were above Mach 1.

Concorde 002. Second prototype (G-BSST), assembled by BAC and first flown on 9 April 1969. Construction started in 1965. Design gross weight and general configuration as 001. Used for sales demonstration tour of Far East between 2 June and 1 July 1972 (details on page 758 of 1972-73 *Jane's*), during which it flew 20 sectors and gave 12 demonstration flights, emphasising its reliability and ease of fitting in to airline operational patterns. Used for "hot and high" trials at Jan Smuts Airport, Johannesburg, in January-February 1973 and for high-temperature certification trials at Torrejon, Spain, in July 1973.

Concorde 01. First pre-production aircraft (G-AXDN), assembled in UK and first flown on 17 December 1971. Fuselage lengthened to 193 ft 0½ in (58·84 m), increasing length of pressurised cabin by 19 ft 3½ in (5·90 m). Fully transparent retractable windscreen visor and increased weights. Powered by 34,730 lb (15,753 kg) st Olympus 593-4 turbojets with Type 11 nozzles.

Concorde 02. Second pre-production aircraft (F-WTSA), assembled in France and first flown on 10 January 1973. First aircraft to incorporate Type 28 aft thrust reverser nozzles; production-standard longer rear fuselage and increased fuel capacity; improvements in wing leading-edge camber (to improve airflow into the engines) and wingtip shape; and modifications to engine exhaust assembly. First to be powered by initial production standard Olympus 593 Mk 602 engines. After its third flight, on 13 January 1973, Concorde 02 made its first fully-automatic landing. On 23 February 1973 it flew non-stop from Toulouse to Iceland and back (3,255 nm; 3,750 miles; 6,035 km) in 3 hr 27 min, including 2 hr 9 min at Mach 2, with an effective payload of 28,000 lb (12,700 kg)—8,000 lb (3,630 kg) more than the then-guaranteed entry-into-service minimum. On 26 September 1973 it flew non-stop from Washington to Paris with a 25,000 lb (11,340 kg) payload in an airborne time of 3 hr 33 min (block time 3 hr 47 min) of which 2 hr 42 min was at supersonic speeds, including 2 hr 16 min at Mach 2. This was the final flight of 02's September 1973 American tour, which took Concorde to the United States for the first time. Used for cold-weather trials at Fairbanks, Alaska, in February 1974.

Concorde Series 200. Initial production version, of which the first two examples were flown on 6 December 1973 at Toulouse (F-WTSB) and 13 February 1974 at Filton (G-BBDG), each attaining a speed of approx 868 knots (1,000 mph; 1,610 km/h) on its first flight. At that time, final building of the next four aircraft was well advanced, and early building was proceeding on another 10. Ordered by British Airways (five) and Air France (four); in addition, preliminary purchasing agreements have been signed by CAAC of China (for three) and Iran Air (for two, with an intention to purchase a third). Certification anticipated in mid-1975.

The following description applies to the initial production Concorde Series 200, except where otherwise indicated:

Type: Four-jet supersonic transport.

Wings: Cantilever low wing of ogival delta planform. Thickness/chord ratio 3% at root, 2·15% from nacelle outboard. Slight anhedral. Continuous camber. Multi-spar torsion-box structure, manufactured mainly from RR.58 (AU2GN) aluminium alloy. Integrally-machined components used for highly loaded members and skin panels. In centre wing, spars are continuous across fuselage, the spars and associated frames being built as single assemblies extending between the engine nacelles. Forward wing sections built as separate components attached to each side of fuselage, spar loads being transferred to cross-members in lower part of main fuselage frames. Three elevons on trailing-edge of each wing, of aluminium alloy honeycomb construction. Each elevon is independently operated by a tandem jack, each half supplied from an independent hydraulic source and controlled by a separate electrical system. Power control units are supplied by Dowty Boulton Paul. Hydraulic artificial feel units protect the aircraft against excessive aerodynamic loads induced by pilot through over-control. Autostabilisation is provided. Autopilot control is by signals fed into

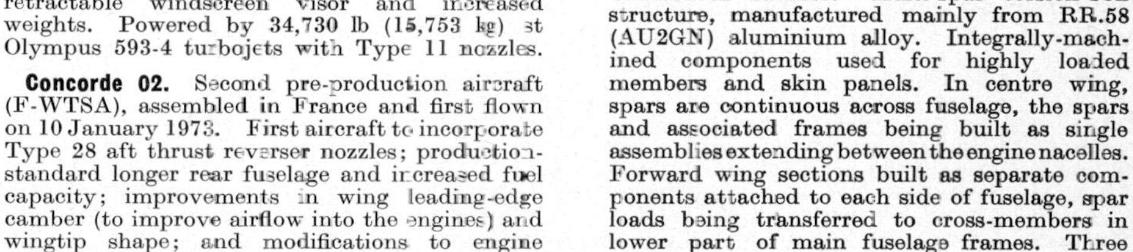

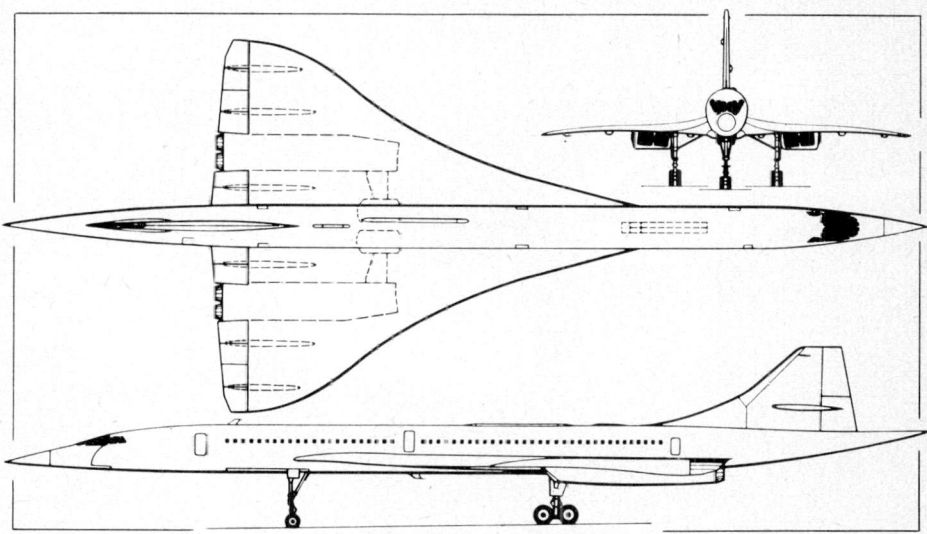

Aérospatiale/BAC Concorde Series 200 supersonic transport (*Pilot Press*)

normal control circuit. No high-lift devices. Leading-edges ahead of air intakes are electrically de-iced.

Fuselage: Mainly-conventional pressurised aluminium alloy semi-monocoque structure of constant cross-section, with unpressurised nose and tail cones. Hoop frames at approx 21·5 in (0·55 m) pitch support integrally-machined panels having closely-pitched longitudinal stringers. Window surrounds in passenger cabin formed of integral skin-stringer panels machined from aluminium alloy planks. Nose is drooped hydraulically to improve forward view during take-off, initial climb, approach and landing. Retractable visor is raised hydraulically to fair in windscreen in cruising flight.

Tail Unit: Vertical fin and rudder only. Fin is multi-spar torsion box of similar construction to wings. Two-section aluminium rudder controlled in same way as elevons. No de-icing system.

Landing Gear: Hydraulically-retractable tricycle type. Messier-Hispano nose and main units, with Dunlop or Kléber wheels and tyres. Twin-wheel steerable nose unit retracts forward. Four-wheel bogie main units retract inward. Oleo-pneumatic shock-absorbers. Main wheels and tyres size 47 × 15·75-22, pressure 184 lb/sq in (12·9 kg/cm²). Nosewheels and tyres size 31 × 10·75-14, pressure 174 lb/sq in (12·25 kg/cm²). Dunlop carbon disc brakes. SNECMA (Hispano) SPAD anti-skid units. Retractable tail bumper.

Engine Nacelles: Each consists of hydraulically-controlled variable-area (by ramp) air intake, engine bay and nozzle support structure. Intakes are of RR.58 or AU2GN aluminium alloy with steel leading-edges. The engine bay has an Inconel centre wall with aluminium alloy forward doors and titanium rear doors. The nozzle bay, aft of the rear spar, is of welded Stresskin sandwich panels and heat-resistant nickel alloys. Reverser buckets, which are also used as a secondary nozzle, are actuated by ball-screw jacks driven by compressed air through flexible shafts. Leading-edges of intake walls, rear ramp sections and intake auxiliary door are electrically de-iced. Engine nose bullet and inlet guide vanes are de-iced by hot engine bleed air.

Power Plant: Four Rolls-Royce/SNECMA Olympus 593 Mk 602 turbojet engines, each rated at 38,050 lb (17,260 kg) st with 17% afterburning and fitted with silencers and Type 28 aft thrust reversers. Fuel system is used also as heat sink and to maintain aircraft trim. All tanks are of integral construction and are in two groups, with total usable capacity of about 25,800 Imp gallons (117,285 litres). Main group comprises five tanks in each wing and four tanks in fuselage and maintains CG automatically in cruising flight. Trim tank group (three tanks) comprises two tanks at the front and a tank of 2,800 Imp gallons (12,730 litres) capacity in fuselage beneath tail fin. This group maintains correct relationship between CG and aerodynamic centre of pressure by transferring fuel rearward during acceleration and forward during return to subsonic flight. Four pressure refuelling points in bottom fairing, two forward of each main landing gear unit. Oil capacity 4·5 Imp gallons (20 litres) per engine.

Accommodation: Pilot and co-pilot side by side on flight deck, with third crew member behind on starboard side. Provision for supernumerary seat behind pilot. Wide variety of four-abreast seating layouts to suit individual requirements of airlines. With all normal toilet and galley service facilities, up to 128 economy class passengers can be carried with 34 in (86 cm) seat pitch. A version with 144 passenger seats at 32 in (81 cm) pitch is available. Toilets at front and rear of cabin. Baggage space under forward cabin and aft of cabin. Passenger doors forward of cabin and amidships on port side, with service doors opposite. Baggage door aft of cabin on starboard side. Emergency exits in rear half of cabin on each side. Two galley areas.

Systems: Hawker Siddeley Dynamics air-conditioning system, comprising four independent subsystems, with Hamilton Standard heat exchangers. Pressure differential 10·7 lb/sq in (0·75 kg/cm²). In each subsystem the air passes through a primary ram-air heat exchanger to an air cycle cold-air unit, and then through secondary air/air and air/fuel heat exchangers. The air is then mixed with hot air and fed to cabins, flight deck, baggage holds, landing gear, equipment and radar bays. Hydraulic services utilise two primary systems and one standby, pressure 4,000 lb/sq in (280 kg/cm²), each actuated by two engine-driven pumps. Temperature of the Oronite M.2V fluid is limited by heat exchangers. Main systems actuate flying control surfaces, artificial feel units, landing gear, wheel brakes, nosewheel steering, windscreen visors, nosecone droop, engine intake ramps and fuel pumps in rear transfer tank. Electrical system powered by four 60kVA engine-driven constant-speed brushless alternators giving 200/115V AC at 400Hz. Four 150A transformer-rectifiers and two 25Ah batteries provide 28V DC supply.

Electronics: SFENA/Marconi-Elliott automatic flight control system (AFCS). Primary navigation system (Litton LTN-72 in Air France aircraft) comprises three identical inertial platforms, each coupled to a digital computer to form three self-contained units, two VOR/ILS systems, one ADF (Marconi-Elliott AD-380 in British Airways aircraft), two DME systems, one marker, two Ekco E390/564 weather radars and two radio altimeters. Plessey flight data recording system. Provision for supplementary system including a long-distance radio fixing system of the Loran C type. Optional equipment includes a second ADF. Basic communications equipment consists of two VHF and two HF transceivers, one Selcal decoder and two ATC transponders. Nose radome by Reinforced Microwave Plastics. Provision for a third VHF transceiver and data link equipment.

Dimensions, external:
Wing span — 83 ft 10 in (25·56 m)
Wing aerodynamic reference chord at root — 90 ft 9 in (27·66 m)
Wing aspect ratio — 1·7
Length overall — 202 ft 3·6 in (61·66 m)
Height overall — 40 ft 0 in (12·19 m)
Fin aerodynamic reference chord at base — 34 ft 9 in (10·59 m)
Wheel track — 25 ft 4 in (7·72 m)
Wheelbase — 59 ft 8¼ in (18·19 m)
Passenger doors (each):
  Height — 5 ft 6 in (1·68 m)
  Width — 2 ft 6 in (0·76 m)
  Height to sill: fwd — 16 ft 3 in (4·95 m)
  amidships — 15 ft 7 in (4·74 m)
Service doors (each):
  Height — 4 ft 0 in (1·22 m)
  Width — 2 ft 0·8 in (0·63 m)
  Height to sill: fwd — 16 ft 3 in (4·95 m)
  amidships — 15 ft 7 in (4·75 m)
Baggage hold door (underfloor):
  Length — 3 ft 3 in (0·99 m)
  Width — 2 ft 2·8 in (0·68 m)
  Height to sill — 11 ft 7 in (3·54 m)
Baggage hold door (rear, stbd):
  Height — 5 ft 0 in (1·52 m)
  Width — 2 ft 6 in (0·76 m)
  Height to sill — 12 ft 11 in (3·94 m)

Dimensions, internal:
Cabin:
  Length, flight deck door to rear pressure bulkhead, including galley and toilets — 129 ft 0 in (39·32 m)
  Width — 8 ft 7½ in (2·63 m)
  Height — 6 ft 5 in (1·96 m)
  Volume — 8,440 cu ft (238·5 m³)
Baggage/freight compartments:
  underfloor — 237 cu ft (6·71 m³)
  rear fuselage (total) — 466 cu ft (13·20 m³)

Areas:
Wings, gross — 3,856 sq ft (358·25 m²)
Elevons (total) — 344·44 sq ft (32·00 m²)
Fin (less dorsal fin) — 365 sq ft (33·91 m²)
Rudder — 112 sq ft (10·40 m²)

Weights and Loadings:
Operating weight, empty — 172,000 lb (78,015 kg)
Typical payload — 25,000 lb (11,340 kg)
Max T-O weight — 389,000 lb (176,445 kg)
Max zero-fuel weight — 203,000 lb (92,080 kg)
Max landing weight — 245,000 lb (111,130 kg)
Max wing loading approx — 100 lb/sq ft (488 kg/m²)
Max power loading — approx 2·5 lb/lb st (2·5 kg/kg st)

Weight and Performance (flight envelope explored by 13 February 1974):
Altitude — 68,000 ft (20,725 m)
Airspeed 553 knots (637 mph; 1,025 km/h) CAS
Mach number — 2·17
Minimum airborne speed — 119 knots (137 mph; 221 km/h)
Incidence — 24·5°
Weight at T-O — 389,490 lb (176,670 kg)
Measured crosswind component — 20 knots (23 mph; 37 km/h)
Landing with nose up and visor up (simulated)
CG in T-O and landing — 51·5% to 53·5%
CG in flight — 51·1% to 59·6%

Performance (production version, estimated, at max T-O weight):
Max cruising speed at 51,300 ft (15,635 m)
  Mach 2·05 or 530 knots CAS, whichever is the lesser, equivalent to TAS of 1,176 knots (1,354 mph; 2,179 km/h)
Max range speed — approx Mach 2·05
Rate of climb at S/L — 5,000 ft (1,525 m)/min
Service ceiling — approx 60,000 ft (18,290 m)
Min ground turning radius — 34 ft 9½ in (10·60 m)
Runway LCN at max T-O weight — 86
T-O to 35 ft (10·7 m) — 10,250 ft (3,124 m)
Landing from 35 ft (10·7 m) — 8,020 ft (2,444 m)
Range with max fuel, FAR reserves and 11,800 lb (5,352 kg) payload — 3,900 nm (4,490 miles; 7,215 km)
Range with max payload, FAR reserves:
  at Mach 0·93 at 30,000 ft (9,100 m), — 2,650 nm (3,050 miles; 4,900 km)
  at Mach 2·05 cruise/climb — 3,450 nm (3,970 miles; 6,380 km)

Operational Noise Characteristics:
T-O noise level at 3·5 nm (4 miles; 6·5 km) from start of T-O run — 114 EPNdB
Approach noise level at 1 nm (1·15 miles; 1·85 km) from landing threshold on 3° glideslope — 115 EPNdB
Sideline noise level at 0·35 nm (0·40 miles; 0·65 km) from runway c/l — 111 EPNdB

French-assembled first production Concorde Series 200 (F-WTSB), which flew for the first time on 6 December 1973

EUROPLANE

EUROPLANE LTD

It was announced in February 1972 that BAC, MBB and SAAB-Scania had agreed to form a new joint company, registered in the UK, to carry out collaborative development work on a QTOL (Quiet Take-Off and Landing) civil aeroplane for short/medium-range operation. CASA of Spain became a member of Europlane in September 1972.

Details of the proposed design were announced at the Paris Air Show in May/June 1973, and were given briefly in the Addenda to the 1973-74 *Jane's*. Work on the project was halted at the end of 1973.

HELI-EUROPE

HELI-EUROPE INDUSTRIES LTD

ADDRESS:
6 Rue Raffet, 75016-Paris, France

Formation of this new joint company was announced on 31 May 1973 by Aérospatiale and Westland. It is registered in England and has its offices in Paris, and has been formed to exploit the existing industrial co-operation between the two companies with regard to future joint designs in the helicopter field. Other European companies are being invited to join the partnership.

MCDONNELL DOUGLAS/ HAWKER SIDDELEY

PARTICIPATING AIRFRAME AND ENGINE MANUFACTURERS:

Hawker Siddeley Aviation Ltd, Richmond Road, Kingston upon Thames, Surrey KT2 5QS, England

McDonnell Aircraft Company, Box 516, St Louis, Missouri 63166, USA

Pratt & Whitney, East Hartford, Connecticut 06108, USA

Rolls-Royce (1971) Ltd, 14-15 Conduit Street, London W1A 4EY, England

ADVANCED HARRIER

US Navy and USMC designation: AV-16A

In December 1973, following an eight-month jointly-financed initial definition phase, proposals were presented to the British and US governments for an advanced version of the Hawker Siddeley Harrier (see UK section).

These proposals were agreed, and by the Spring of 1974 the two governments had received for approval further proposals regarding the cost- and work-sharing for the continuation of the programme. Other development options, including alternative unilateral programmes, were then continuing to be examined by the US participants.

Essentially, the objective of the Advanced Harrier programme is to evolve a version which, without too much of a departure from the existing Harrier airframe, will virtually double the aircraft's weapons payload/combat radius. The major changes envisaged are the adoption of the 24,500 lb (11,112 kg) st Rolls-Royce Pegasus 15 turbofan engine and the employment of a more efficient wing. To accommodate the Pegasus 15 engine, the Advanced Harrier will have enlarged air intakes, and a broader fuselage some 3 ft (0·91 m) longer than the present Harrier. Internal fuel load will be increased from 5,000 lb (2,268 kg) in the AV-8A to 6,500 lb (2,948 kg) in the AV-16A, which will also be able to carry standard 300 US gallon (250 Imp gallon; 1,135 litre) underwing drop-tanks. The exhaust nozzles will be strengthened for VIFF (thrust vectoring in forward flight), and the main landing gear also will be strengthened to cater for the increased gross weight. The outrigger balancer wheel fairings will be moved inboard on the wings, where they will provide a third underwing hardpoint on each side if required. The cockpit canopy will be raised, to improve the all-round field of view. Two alternative wing designs have been developed independently by Hawker Siddeley and McDonnell, the former being a so-called "sonic rooftop" wing and the latter being based on supercritical wing research carried out by NASA. Both are generally similar in sweepback and planform, and have greater span and area than those of the present Harrier.

The Advanced Harrier will be able to carry a wide range of specialised modern operational avionics and equipment, according to the requirements of individual operators. It will have the same centreline stores point and underfuselage gun pod capability as the present Harrier, with either four or six underwing hardpoints as required.

Artist's impression of versions of the Advanced Harrier for (*front to back*) the US Marine Corps, minus the 20 mm underfuselage gun packs and five weapons pylons that it would normally carry; the RAF, with 30 mm gun packs and undernose sensor; Royal Navy and US Navy

Four projected versions of the Advanced Harrier were announced in early 1974. The US Marine Corps, which has stated a requirement for 342 AV-16As for service in the 1980s, is potentially the largest customer at the present time. Its version will have an integrated weapons delivery system (IWDS) of the type now being developed for the AV-8A Harrier and the McDonnell Douglas A-4M Skyhawk II, four underwing hardpoints, and 20 mm underfuselage guns. The proposed RAF version has the full seven stores points, 30 mm Aden gun pods, and an undernose sensor, possibly for a low light level TV scanner. The Royal Navy and US Navy versions will each have a nose-mounted radar; the latter, which is designed for SCS (Sea Control Ship) use, will be equipped to carry Sidewinder or Sparrow air-to-air or Harpoon, Maverick or Condor air-to-surface missiles.

DIMENSIONS, EXTERNAL (approx):

Wing span	30 ft 3½ in (9·23 m)
Wing area, gross	230 sq ft (21·37 m²)
Length overall (flying attitude)	46 ft 6 in (14·17 m)
Height overall (on ground)	12 ft 0 in (3·66 m)

WEIGHTS (approx):

Vertical T-O weight	21,100 lb (9,570 kg)
Max T-O weight	28,000 lb (12,700 kg)

PERFORMANCE (estimated):

Combat speed: 625 knots (720 mph; 1,157 km/h)

Combat radius, with reserves:

VTO with over 2,000 lb (907 kg) payload: 300 nm (345 miles; 555 km)

Rolling T-O with over 4,000 lb (1,815 kg) payload: 300 nm (345 miles; 555 km)

PANAVIA

PANAVIA AIRCRAFT GmbH

HEAD OFFICE:
8 München 86, Postfach 860629, Arabellastrasse 16, German Federal Republic
Telephone: Munich (089) 92171
Telex: 05 29 825

DIRECTORS:
L. Bölkow (Chairman)
H. R. Baxendale
F. Forster-Steinberg
Dr F. Giura (Deputy Chairman)
A. H. C. Greenwood (Deputy Chairman)
F. Marocco
F. W. Page
E. G. Pantel

MANAGING DIRECTOR:
G. Madelung

DEPUTY MANAGING DIRECTOR:
E. Loveless

FUNCTIONAL DIRECTORS:
R. P. Beamont (Flight Operations)
Dr I. A. M. Hall (Programme Management)
B. O. Heath (Systems Engineering, Warton)
H. J. Klapperich (Finance and Contracts)
H. Langfelder (Systems Engineering, Munich)
J. K. Quill (Marketing)
Dr R. Stradella (Production)
J. A. Thornber (Procurement)

PUBLICITY MANAGER:
F. Oelwein

Panavia Aircraft GmbH is an international European industrial company formed on 26 March 1969 to design, develop and produce a multi-role combat aircraft (MRCA) for service from 1977 with the air forces of the United Kingdom, the Federal Republic of Germany and Italy, and the German navy. This programme is one of the largest European industrial programmes ever undertaken. The three component companies of Panavia are British Aircraft Corporation (42½%), Messerschmitt-Bölkow-Blohm (42½%) and Aeritalia (15%).

The German, British and Italian governments have set up a joint organisation known as NAMMO (NATO MRCA Management Organisation). This has its executive agency NAMMA (NATO MRCA Management Agency) in Munich in the same building as Panavia.

The project was the subject of a feasibility study, which ended on 1 May 1969, when the project definition phase began. This saw the completion of the detailed design work and costing.

In mid-1970 the governments announced the satisfactory outcome of the definition phase and the beginning of the development phase, which was to lead to the flight of the first of nine prototypes. A further tri-national governmental review of the programme, begun at the end of 1972 and concluded in March 1973, preceded the production investment phase.

In addition to the MRCA, Panavia is also undertaking, as a joint private venture, studies of a range of other military aircraft complementary to the MRCA.

PANAVIA 200 MRCA

The MRCA is a twin-engined two-seat supersonic aircraft capable of fulfilling the agreed operational requirements of its three sponsoring countries. The use of a variable-geometry wing gives it the necessary flexibility to achieve this.

The aircraft is intended to fulfil six major requirements, some of which are shared by more than one of the partners. These are:
(a) Close air support/battlefield interdiction
(b) Interdictor strike
(c) Air superiority
(d) Interception
(e) Naval role
(f) Reconnaissance

In addition, a trainer version is being built which will also have an operational capability.

The Royal Air Force is expected to order 385 MRCAs initially. These are due to begin entering service with Strike Command in 1977 and will, in the first instance, replace the Vulcan and Buccaneer in the overland strike and reconnaissance roles. Later, the air defence version will succeed the Phantom; and finally it is envisaged that the MRCA will replace the Buccaneer for maritime strike tasks. Some two-thirds of the RAF's front-line aircraft will eventually be MRCAs, according to the Chief of the Air Staff.

The Luftwaffe is to order 202 MRCAs, primarily to replace the Lockheed F-104G and partly the Aeritalia G91 in the battlefield interdiction, air superiority and reconnaissance roles. Four

First prototype of the Panavia MRCA multi-role combat aircraft. A cover plate has been removed to show the port wing pivot

wings and one training squadron are to be equipped, starting in 1978. The 120 for the German Navy will be equipped for strike missions against sea and coastal targets, and for reconnaissance.

The Italian Air Force will use its 100 MRCAs to replace the F-104G and G91Y in the air superiority, ground attack and reconnaissance roles.

Structural design of the prototype MRCA was completed in August 1972. Nine prototype aircraft are being built—four in the UK, three in Germany and two in Italy—and static tests with a complete airframe were under way in the Spring of 1974.

The P-01 first prototype (D-9591), assembled by MBB, was rolled out in April 1974, prior to its first flight in Summer 1974 at Manching in Germany, flown by BAC test pilot Paul Millett. The second and third prototypes were scheduled to fly in 1974, and all nine by the end of 1975. The second and third prototypes will fly at BAC's Warton aerodrome in Lancashire, the fourth at Manching, and the fifth at Caselle in Italy. Two more will fly at Warton, one at Manching and one at Caselle. Within the overall flight test programme, the first aircraft will be used for systems and handling trials; the second for flutter tests; the third will be the first MRCA to be fitted with dual controls; and the fourth will carry out initial testing of the avionics and weapon systems. The nine prototypes will be followed by six pre-production aircraft in advance of the main production stream.

Ground running of the RB.199 power plant began in September 1971; air testing under a Hawker Siddeley Vulcan testbed (XA903) started in April 1973. The 27 mm Mauser cannon is being test-flown in, and fired from, a BAC Lightning fighter. Marshall of Cambridge (see UK section) has modified two Buccaneer aircraft to flight test the nav/attack system.

TYPE: Twin-engined multi-purpose military aircraft.

WINGS: Cantilever shoulder-wing monoplane. All-metal wings, of variable geometry, having a sweep of approx 25° in the fully forward position and approx 65° when fully swept. Wing carry-through box is of electron-beam-welded titanium alloy; majority of remaining wing structure is of aluminium alloy, with integrally stiffened skin. The wings each pivot hydraulically, on Teflon-plated bearings, from a point in the centre-section just outboard of the fuselage. The root of the outer wing mates with the pivot pin through attachment members made of titanium alloy and fixed to the upper and lower light alloy panels of the outer wing box, and a so-called "round rib", also of titanium alloy, transmitting the normal aerodynamic force. Sweep actuators are of the ballscrew type, with hydraulic motor drive. In the event of wing sweep failure, the aircraft can land safely with the wings fully swept. High-lift devices on the outer wings include full-span leading-edge slats (three sections on each side), full-span double-slotted trailing-edge flaps (four sections on each side), and spoilers (two on upper surface on each side). Spoilers give augmented roll control at unswept and intermediate wing positions at low speed, and also act as lift dumpers after touchdown. All flying control surfaces actuated by electrically-controlled tandem hydraulic jacks. There are no ailerons. Entire outer wings, including control surfaces, are Italian-built, Aeritalia having prime responsibility for final assembly and production of these units, assisted by Aermacchi, Aeronavali Venezia, Piaggio, Saca and SIAI-Marchetti as subcontractors. Microtecnica (Italy) is prime subcontractor for the wing sweep system.

FUSELAGE: Conventional all-metal semi-monocoque structure, mainly of aluminium alloy, built in three main sections. MBB in Germany is prime contractor (with participation by VFW-Fokker for the prototype and pre-production aircraft) for the centre fuselage section, including the engine air intake trunks and wing centre-section box and pivot mechanism. This task includes responsibility for the surface interface between the movable wing and the fixed portion, to ensure both a smooth and slender external contour and proper sealing against aerodynamic pressure over a range of wing sweep positions. The present design uses fibre-reinforced plastics in these areas, and an elastic seal between the outer wings and the fuselage sides. Responsibility for the front fuselage, including both cockpits, and for the rear fuselage, including the engine installation, is undertaken by the Military Aircraft Division of British Aircraft Corporation. Radar-transparent nose-cone by AEG-Telefunken, assisted by Aeritalia and BAC, hinges sideways to starboard. Door-type airbrake on each side at top of rear fuselage.

TAIL UNIT: Cantilever all-metal structure, consisting of single sweptback two-spar fin and rudder, and low-set all-moving horizontal surfaces ("tailerons") which operate together for pitch control and differentially for roll control, assisted by use of the wing spoilers when the wings are not fully swept. Rudder and tailerons actuated by electrically-controlled tandem hydraulic jacks. Passive ECM antenna fairing near top of fin. Ram-air intake for heat exchanger at base of fin. Entire tail unit is the responsibility of BAC.

LANDING GEAR: Hydraulically-retractable tricycle type, with forward-retracting twin-wheel steerable nose unit. Single-wheel main units retract forward and upward into centre section of fuselage. Development and manufacture of the complete landing gear and associated hydraulics is headed by Dowty Rotol (UK). Dunlop wheels, brakes, low-pressure tyres (to permit operation from soft, semi-prepared surfaces) and anti-skid units. Runway arrester hook beneath rear of fuselage.

POWER PLANT: Two Turbo-Union RB.199-34R three-spool turbofan engines, each rated at 8,500 lb (3,855 kg) st dry and 14,500 lb (6,577 kg) st with afterburning, fitted with bucket-type thrust reversers and installed in rear fuselage with downward-opening doors for servicing and engine change. Four large "blow-out" doors in top of each trunk, above the wedge-shaped two-dimensional intake. All internal fuel in multi-cell Uniroyal self-sealing integral fuselage tanks and/or wing box tanks, all fitted with press-in fuel sampling and water drain plugs, and all refuelled from a single-point NATO connector. Detachable and retractable in-flight refuelling probe can be mounted on starboard side of fuselage, adjacent to cockpit. System also designed to accept a buddy-to-buddy refuelling pack. Provision for drop-tanks of various sizes to be carried beneath outer wings. Dowty Fuel Systems/Lucas/Microtecnica afterburning fuel control system. AEG-Telefunken intake de-icing system.

ACCOMMODATION: Crew of two on tandem Martin-Baker Mk 10A ejection seats under Kopperschmidt/AIT one-piece canopy, which is hinged at rear and opens upwards. Flat centre windscreen panel and curved side panels, built by Lucas Aerospace, incorporate Sierracote electrically-conductive heating film for de-icing and internal demisting.

SYSTEMS: Nordmicro/HSD/Microtecnica air intake control system, and Dowty Boulton Paul/Liebherr Aerotechnik engine intake ramp control actuators. Two separate independent hydraulic systems, one driven by each engine, provide fully duplicated power for wing sweep, flaps, slats, spoilers, airbrakes, landing gear, tailerons and rudder. Main system includes Vickers pump, Dowty accumulators and Teves power pack. Fairey Hydraulics system for actuation of spoilers, rudder and taileron control. Provision for reversion to single-engine drive of both systems, via a mechanical cross-connection between the two engine auxiliary gearboxes, in the event of a single engine failure. In the event of a double engine flameout, an emergency pump in No. 1 system has sufficient duration for re-entry into the engine cold relight boundary. Flying control circuits are protected from loss of fluid due to leaks in other circuits by isolating valves which shut off the utility circuits if the reservoir contents drop below a predetermined safety limit level. Duplicated AC and DC electrical power is provided by two alternators, each driven by its respective engine auxiliary gearbox, to two separate main AC busbars and one essential AC busbar, and through two fan-cooled transformer-rectifier units (TRUs) to two main DC busbars. Lucas/Siemens 40/60 kVA 200V 400Hz three-phase constant-frequency AC generating system. Either generator can cope with the full demand of the electrical systems in the event of a single generator failure. If both TRUs fail, an on-board Varta battery supplies the essential DC busbar. In the event of a total loss of power the battery also drives an electro-hydraulic pump which provides power for the primary flying controls. Under normal conditions the battery drives the KHD/Microtecnica/Lucas T312 APU for engine starting, but a DC ground supply is provided to assist starting if required. Plessey power systems controller. Normalair-Garrett precooler and cold-air unit, Marston Excelsior intercooler and Teddington temperature control system. Normalair-Garrett/Draegerwerk/OMI demand-type oxygen system, using a LOX converter. KHD accessory drive gearboxes and Rotax/Lucas/Siemens integrated drive generator. Marconi-Elliott flow-metering system. Eichweber fuel gauging system and Flight Refuelling flexible couplings. Graviner fire detection and extinguishing systems. Rotax contactors. Smiths engine speed and temperature indicators.

ELECTRONICS AND EQUIPMENT: Communications equipment includes Plessey (UK and Italy) or Rohde und Schwarz (Germany) UHF/VHF radio; AEG-Telefunken UHF/DF (UK and Germany only); Chelton UHF homer aerial; SIT/Siemens emergency UHF with Rohde und Schwarz switch; BAC HF/SSB aerial tuning unit; Rohde und Schwarz (UK and Germany) or Montedel (Italy) HF/SSB radio; Ultra communications control system; Marconi-Elliott central suppression unit; Epsylon voice recorder; and Chelton communications and landing system aerials.

Primary self-contained nav/attack system includes Texas Instruments multi-mode forward-looking radar (Marconi-Elliott multi-mode airborne interception radar for RAF interceptor version); Ferranti three-axis digital inertial navigation system (DINS) and combined radar display; Decca Type 72 Doppler radar system; Microtecnica air data computer; Litef Spirit 3 16-bit central digital computer; Aeritalia radio/radar altimeter; Smiths electronic head-up display with Davall camera; Ferranti nose-mounted laser ranger and marked target seeker; Marconi-Elliott TV tabular display; Astronautics (USA) bearing distance heading indication and contour map display. Defensive equipment includes Siemens (Germany) or Cossor SSR-3100 (UK) IFF transponder; Elettronica warning radar; and MSDS/Plessey/Decca passive ECM system.

Flight control system includes a Marconi-Elliott command stability augmentation system (CSAS), incorporating fly-by-wire and auto-stabilisation; Marconi-Elliott autopilot and flight director (APFD), using two self-monitoring digital computers; Marconi-Elliott triplex transducer unit (TTU), with analogue computing and sensor channels; Marconi-Elliott terrain-following E-scope (TFE); Fairey/Marconi-Elliott quadruplex electro-hydraulic actuator; and Microtecnica air data set. The APFD provides preselected attitude, heading or barometric height hold, heading and track acquisition, and Mach number or airspeed hold with autothrottle. Flight director operates in parallel with, and can be used as back-up for, the autopilot. Automatic approach, terrain-following and radio height-holding modes are also available. Other instrumentation includes Smiths horizontal situation indicator, vertical speed indicator and standby altimeter; AEG-Telefunken ADF; Lital standby attitude and heading reference system; SEL (with SETAC) or (in UK aircraft) Marconi-Elliott AD2770 (without SETAC) TACAN; Cossor CILS 75 ILS; and Bodenseewerk attitude direction indicator.

Overall responsibility for the avionics rests with the three-nation group Avionica Systems Engineering, combining the activities of EASAMS (UK), ESG (Germany) and SIA (Italy). The avionics systems, while standardised as far as possible, retain the flexibility necessary to perform the various roles required. They provide accurate low- and high-level navigation; precision visual attack on ground targets in blind and poor weather conditions; air-to-ground and air-to-air attack with a wide variety of weapons; manually controlled and automatic attack; and comprehensive on-board checkout and mission data recording; with minimisation of ground support facilities at bases and the front line.

ARMAMENT: All MRCAs are fitted with two 27 mm Mauser cannon, one in each side of the lower forward fuselage. Other armament varies according to version, with emphasis on the ability to carry a wide range of advanced non-nuclear weapons on three underfuselage attachments and up to four swivelling hardpoints beneath the outer wings. A Marconi-Elliott stores management system is fitted, and Sandall Mace 14 in (35·5 cm) ejector release units are standard. Initial weapon systems evaluation will include trials in the fourth prototype of a modified Raytheon Sparrow missile, fitted with a British warhead and fuse. The battlefield interdiction version will be capable of dropping defensive "streuwaffen" (scatter weapons), and of carrying weapons to suit "hard" or "soft" targets. The naval and interdictor strike versions will have provision for carrying additional, externally-mounted fuel tanks. The air superiority version will be able to carry a wide range of guided and semi-active homing air-to-air weapons. Among the weapons already specified for, or suitable for carriage by, the MRCA are the Sparrow and Aspide air-to-air missiles; AS.30, Martel, Kormoran and Jumbo air-to-surface missiles; napalm; BL-755 600 lb cluster bombs; and "smart" or retarded bombs.

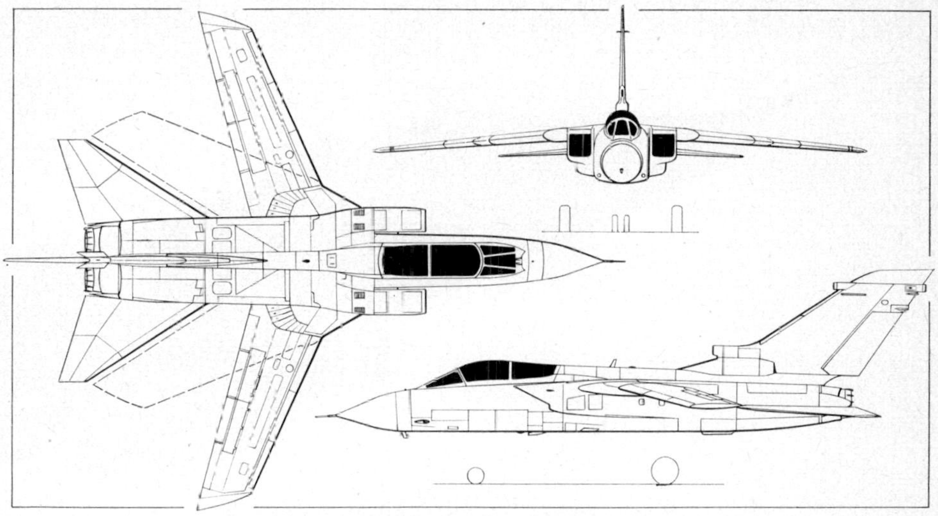

Panavia 200 MRCA, multi-role combat aircraft (*Pilot Press*)

DIMENSIONS, EXTERNAL:
- Wing span:
  - fully spread 45 ft 7¼ in (13·90 m)
  - fully swept 28 ft 2½ in (8·60 m)
- Length overall 54 ft 9½ in (16·70 m)
- Height overall 18 ft 8½ in (5·70 m)

WEIGHTS (estimated):
- Weight empty, equipped 22,000-23,000 lb (9,980-10,430 kg)
- Max T-O weight 38,000-40,000 lb (17,240-18,145 kg)

PERFORMANCE:
- Max level speed at 36,000 ft (11,000 m) above 1,146 knots (1,320 mph; 2,125 km/h)
- Max level speed at low altitude approx 790 knots (910 mph; 1,465 km/h)
- Combat endurance (internal fuel) 70-80 min

SEPECAT
SOCIÉTÉ EUROPÉENNE DE PRODUCTION DE L'AVION E.C.A.T.

AIRFRAME COMPANIES:

British Aircraft Corporation Ltd, Brooklands Weybridge Road, Weybridge, Surrey KT13 0RN, England
Telephone: Weybridge (97) 45522

Avions Marcel Dassault/Breguet Aviation, BP 32, 92420-Vaucresson, France
Telephone: 970-38-50

DIRECTORS:
H. R. Baxendale (alternate Chairman)
J. Barge (alternate Chairman)
J. Fort
F. W. Page
Paul Jaillard
A. H. C. Greenwood
Jeffrey Quill
C. Edelstenne

MANAGEMENT COMMITTEE:
Directors as above, plus:
M. Berjon (Engineering Project Manager)
T. O. Williams (Production)
I. R. Yates (Engineering Project Manager)

PUBLIC RELATIONS:
W. B. Brown (BAC)
C. P. Raffin (Dassault-Breguet)

This Anglo-French company was formed in May 1966 by Breguet Aviation and British Aircraft Corporation, the two partners in the design and production of the Jaguar supersonic strike fighter/trainer for the air forces of France and the UK.

The Jaguar project was initiated by the Defence Ministries of Britain and France on 17 May 1965. The governments of the two countries appointed an official Jaguar Management Committee to look after their interests. SEPECAT is the complementary industrial organisation.

SEPECAT JAGUAR

The Jaguar, which was evolved from the Breguet Br 121 project, was designed by Breguet and BAC to meet a common requirement of the French and British air forces laid down in early 1965. This requirement called for a dual-role aircraft, to be used as an advanced and operational trainer and a tactical support aircraft of light weight and high performance, to enter French service in 1972 and with the RAF in 1973. The Jaguar M French naval version (1972-73 *Jane's*) was abandoned in 1973.

The following versions of the Jaguar are in production:

Jaguar A. French single-seat tactical support version. Prototypes (A-03 and A-04) first flown on 29 March and 27 May 1969. The A-04 has been used for weapon trials. Total of 80 ordered.

By the end of 1973 a total of 20 production Jaguar As had flown. The first operational Armée de l'Air Jaguar unit (Esc.1/7 "Provence") was formed at St Dizier in eastern France on 19 June 1973.

Jaguar B (RAF designation: Jaguar T.Mk 2). British two-seat operational training version. Prototype B-08 (XW566) first flown on 30 August 1971. Total of 37 ordered by early 1974. First T. Mk 2 delivered to RAF was XX137.

Jaguar E. French two-seat advanced training version. Prototypes (E-01 and E-02) first flown on 8 September 1968 and 11 February 1969. Total of 40 ordered by early 1974. First production Jaguar, designated E-1, flew for the first time on 2 November 1971, and deliveries to the CEAM at Air Base 118, Mont de Marsan, began in May 1972. By the end of 1973 a further 18 production Jaguar Es had flown. The first unit to equip with this version is Esc.1/7 "Provence" at St Dizier.

Jaguar S (RAF designation: Jaguar GR.Mk 1). British single-seat tactical support version, basically similar to A but with an advanced inertial navigation and weapon-aiming system which is controlled by a digital computer. Prototypes S-06 and S-07, of which the former (XW560) was first flown on 12 October 1969 and the latter (XW563) on 12 June 1970. The S-06 was subsequently fitted with a taller, larger-area fin, which is standard on all production models. It is equipped with the Marconi-Elliott modular air data computer, and the S-07 with the Marconi-Elliott digital inertial navigation and weapon aiming subsystem (incorporating an MCS 920M computer), projected map display and Smiths head-up display and other equipment, which are fitted to RAF versions of the aircraft. Total of 121 ordered by beginning of 1974. The first production GR. Mk 1 (XX108) flew on 11 October 1972, followed by XX109 on 16 November 1972, and by the end of 1973 14 production aircraft had flown. The first production Jaguar GR.Mk 1 for the RAF (S-4/XX111) was officially handed over at Lossiemouth on 30 May 1973, and was used for ground crew training prior to the formation of the first Jaguar operational conversion team in October. The first for flying training (XX114 and XX115) were deliver-

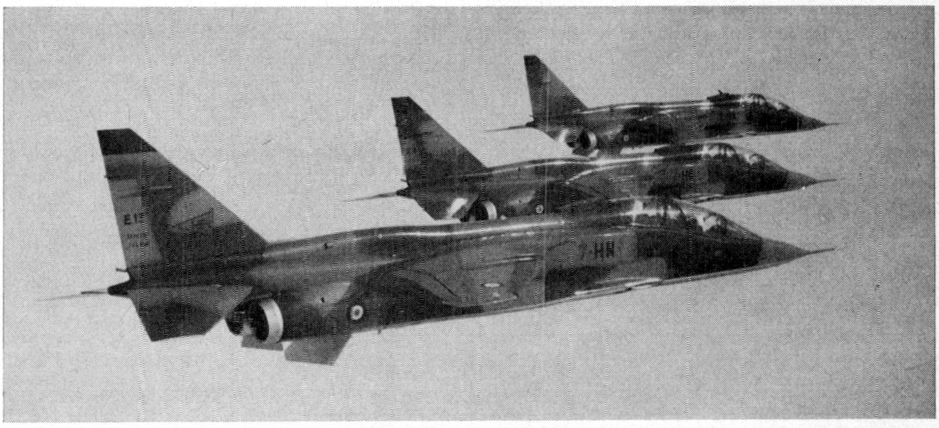

Formation of Jaguar E two-seat advanced training aircraft of the 7e Escadre de Chasse, French Air Force

S-07 prototype for the Jaguar GR.Mk 1 single-seat tactical support aircraft, with four cluster bombs on inboard wing pylons and 1,000 lb bombs outboard and beneath fuselage

ed on 13 September 1973; aircrew conversion training began in January 1974. The first operational RAF Jaguar unit, No. 54 Squadron, formed at Lossiemouth on 29 March 1974, and was scheduled to move later to Coltishall. Second RAF operational unit will be No. 6 Squadron; in all, it is planned to equip eight RAF front-line squadrons with Jaguars.

Training versions will be able to operate from conventional runways only 6,560 ft (2,000 m) long, with full provision for safety in the event of an engine failure at the critical point of take-off.

Under the terms of a production agreement signed by the British and French Defence Ministers on 9 January 1968, an initial series of 400 Jaguars is to be built, 200 for the Royal Air Force and 200 for the French air forces. The first formal production contract, placed in the Autumn of 1969, covered 50 Jaguars for France; the second was for 30 for the RAF. Subsequent contracts had brought the total ordered to 278 by the beginning of 1974, and it was anticipated that further contracts to bring this total up to the initial Anglo-French requirement of 400 Jaguars would be signed by the end of 1974.

Dassault-Breguet factories at Toulouse and Biarritz are responsible for the front and centre fuselage. The Military Aircraft Division of BAC has responsibility for the rear fuselage, air intakes, wings and tail unit. There are final assembly lines for complete aircraft in both Britain and France.

The powered flying controls, developed and supplied by Fairey Hydraulics Ltd, are the most advanced yet designed for a European aircraft, with all functions contained within a single assembly. The Jaguar is fully power-controlled in all three axes and is automatically stabilised as a weapons platform by gyros which sense disturbances and feed appropriate correcting data through a computer to the power control assemblies, in addition to the human pilot manoeuvre demands. The power controls are all of duplex tandem arrangement, with both mechanical and electrical servo-valves of the established Fairey platen design.

Type: Single-seat tactical support aircraft (Jaguar A and S) and two-seat operational or advanced trainer (Jaguar B and E).

Wings: Cantilever shoulder-wing monoplane. Anhedral 3°. Sweepback 40° at quarter-chord. All-metal two-spar torsion-box structure, the skin of which is machined from solid aluminium alloy, with integral stiffeners. Main portion built as single unit, with three-point attachment to each side of fuselage. Outer panels fitted with slat which also gives effect of extended-chord "dog-tooth" leading-edge. No conventional ailerons. Lateral control by two-section spoilers, forward of outer flap on each wing, in association (at low speeds) with differential tailplane. Hydraulically-operated (by screwjack) full-span double-slotted trailing-edge flaps. Leading-edge slats, which can be used in combat, are fitted. Entire wing unit is British-built.

Fuselage: All-metal structure, mainly aluminium, built in three main units and making use of sandwich panels and, around the cockpit(s), honeycomb panels. Local use of titanium alloy in engine bay area. The forward and centre fuselage, up to and including the main undercarriage bays, and including cockpit(s), main systems installations, forward fuel tanks and landing gear, is of French construction.

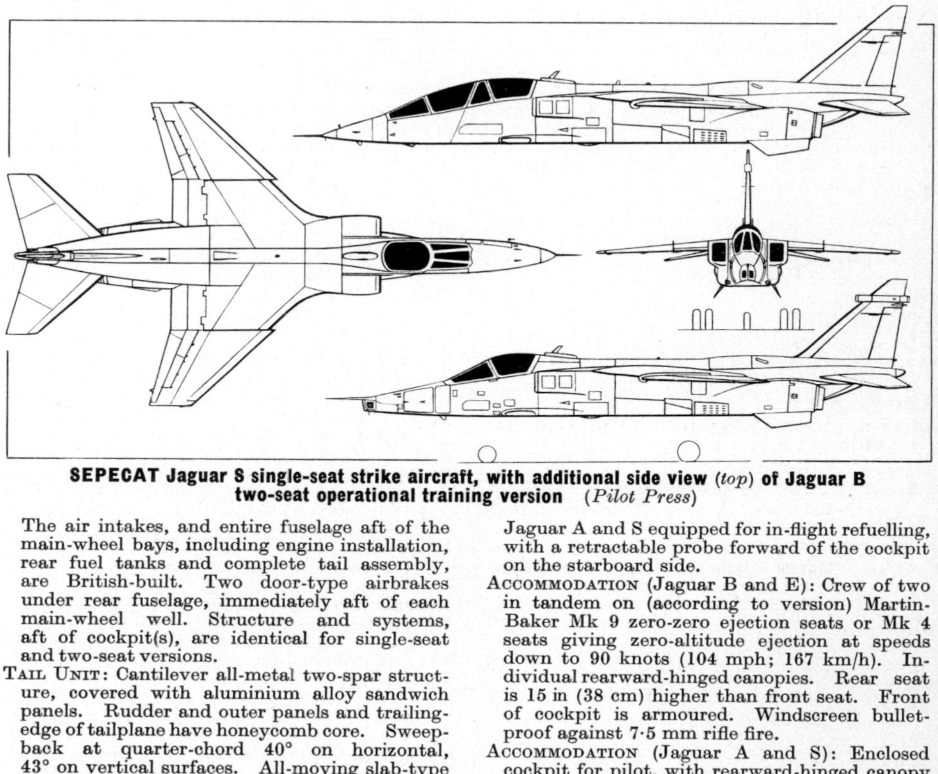

SEPECAT Jaguar S single-seat strike aircraft, with additional side view (*top*) **of Jaguar B two-seat operational training version** (*Pilot Press*)

The air intakes, and entire fuselage aft of the main-wheel bays, including engine installation, rear fuel tanks and complete tail assembly, are British-built. Two door-type airbrakes under rear fuselage, immediately aft of each main-wheel well. Structure and systems, aft of cockpit(s), are identical for single-seat and two-seat versions.

Tail Unit: Cantilever all-metal two-spar structure, covered with aluminium alloy sandwich panels. Rudder and outer panels and trailing-edge of tailplane have honeycomb core. Sweepback at quarter-chord 40° on horizontal, 43° on vertical surfaces. All-moving slab-type tailplane, with 10° of anhedral, the two halves of which can operate differentially to supplement the spoilers. No separate elevators. Auxiliary fins beneath the rear fuselage, aft of the jet pipes. Entire tail unit is British-built.

Landing Gear: Messier-Hispano retractable tricycle type, all units having Dunlop wheels and low-pressure tyres for rough-field operation. Hydraulic retraction, with oleo-pneumatic shock-absorbers. Forward-retracting main units each have twin wheels, tyre size 615 × 225-10, tyre pressure 70 lb/sq in (4·9 kg/cm²). Wheels pivot during retraction to stow horizontally in bottom of fuselage. Single rearward-retracting nosewheel, with tyre size 550 × 250-6 and pressure of 50 lb/sq in (3·5 kg/cm²). Twin landing lights in nosewheel door. Dunlop hydraulic brakes. Anti-skid units and arrester hook standard. Brake parachute (Irvin type for RAF aircraft) housed in fuselage tailcone.

Power Plant: Two Rolls-Royce/Turboméca Adour turbofan engines (each 5,115 lb; 2,320 kg st dry, and 7,304 lb; 3,313 kg st with afterburning). Lateral-type fixed-geometry air intakes, on each side of fuselage aft of cockpit. Fuel in eight tanks, one in each wing and six in fuselage. Armour protection has been provided for critical fuel system components. In the basic tactical sortie the loss of fuel from one tank at the halfway point would not prevent the aircraft from regaining its base. Provision for carrying three auxiliary drop-tanks, each of 264 Imp gallons (1,200 litres) capacity, on fuselage and inboard wing pylons. Jaguar A and S equipped for in-flight refuelling, with a retractable probe forward of the cockpit on the starboard side.

Accommodation (Jaguar B and E): Crew of two in tandem on (according to version) Martin-Baker Mk 9 zero-zero ejection seats or Mk 4 seats giving zero-altitude ejection at speeds down to 90 knots (104 mph; 167 km/h). Individual rearward-hinged canopies. Rear seat is 15 in (38 cm) higher than front seat. Front of cockpit is armoured. Windscreen bullet-proof against 7·5 mm rifle fire.

Accommodation (Jaguar A and S): Enclosed cockpit for pilot, with rearward-hinged canopy and Martin-Baker Mk 9 or Mk 4 ejection seat as described above. Front and underside of cockpit are armoured against light ground fire. Bullet-proof windscreen, as in two-seat versions.

Systems: Air-conditioning and pressurisation systems maintain automatically, throughout the flight envelope, comfortable operating conditions for the crew, and also control the temperature in certain equipment bays. Two independent hydraulic systems, powered by two Vickers engine-driven pumps. Hydraulic pressure 3,000 lb/sq in (210 kg/cm²). First system (port engine) supplies one channel of each actuator for the flying controls, the hydraulic motors which actuate the flaps and slats, the landing gear retraction and extension system, the brakes and anti-skid units. The second system supplies the other half of each flying control actuator, two further hydraulic motors actuating the slats and flaps, the air-brake and landing gear extension jacks, nose-wheel steering system and the wheel brakes. In addition to the duplicated hydraulic power systems, there is an emergency hydraulic power transfer unit. Electrical power provided by two 15kVA AC generators, either of which can sustain functional and operational equipment without load-shedding. DC power provided by two 4kW transformer-rectifiers. Emergency AC power for essential instruments provided by 15Ah battery and static inverter. De-icing, rain clearance and demisting standard. Liquid oxygen system installed, which also pressurises the pilot's anti-*g* suit.

ELECTRONICS AND OPERATIONAL EQUIPMENT (French versions): Equipment of Jaguar E includes VHF/UHF radio, VOR/ILS and IFF; TACAN with Crouzet Type 90 navigation indicator; SFIM 153-6 twin-gyro inertial platform with two SFIM 810 all-attitude roll and pitch spherical indicators; SFIM 511 directional compass; Jaeger ELDIA air data system with Jaeger altitude indicator; CSF RL 50Pj incidence probe with angle of attack indicator; CSF 121 fire control sighting unit with weapon selector and adaptor for sighting head camera. Except for the use of a SFIM 250-1 twin-gyro platform, and the addition of a vector adder to the navigation indicator, this equipment is repeated in the Jaguar A, which has in addition a panoramic camera, Dassault-built Decca RDN 72 Doppler radar, Crouzet Type 90 navigation computer with target selector, CFTH passive radar warning (ECM) detector, a CSF 31 weapon aiming computer and a Dassault fire control computer for Martel anti-radar missiles. Provision for the addition to these basic installations of such other items as terrain-following radar, air-to-air fire control radar or sighting equipment for low light level targets.

ELECTRONICS AND OPERATIONAL EQUIPMENT (British versions): Except for the installation of a panoramic camera in the single-seat version, the basic equipment of both the Jaguar B and S is similar. It includes a Smiths radio altimeter indicator, slip indicator, E2B compass and autostabilising system; Plessey PTR 377 VHF/UHF radio and HF/UHF radios; Cossor ILS system and Honeywell radar altimeter; IFF; TACAN; Marconi-Elliott MCS 920M digital navigation and weapon aiming computer with E.3R three-gyro inertial platform, inertial velocity sensor, navigation control unit and projected-map display; Elliott air data computer; Smiths electronic head-up display; Smiths FS6 horizontal situation indicator and standby compass; Sperry C2J gyro amplifier master unit, compass controller and magnetic detector; Plessey stores management system. Jaguar S fitted with Ferranti laser rangefinder and marked target seeker in modified nose.

ARMAMENT (Jaguar A and S): Two 30 mm cannon (DEFA 553 in Jaguar A, Aden in Jaguar S) in lower fuselage aft of cockpit. One stores attachment point on fuselage centreline and two under each wing. Provision for wingtip attachments for air-to-air missiles. Centreline and inboard wing points can each carry up to 2,000 lb (1,000 kg) of weapons, and the outboard underwing points up to 1,000 lb (500 kg) each. Jaguar As in service can carry the AN 52 tactical nuclear weapon. Typical alternative loads include two Martel AS.37 anti-radar missiles and a 264 Imp gallon (1,200 litre) drop-tank; eight 1,000 lb bombs; various combinations of free-fall and retarded bombs, Sidewinder-type missiles and unguided air-to-air or air-to-surface rockets, including the 68 mm SNEB rocket; a reconnaissance-camera pack with two photo-flare pods; or two drop-tanks. Maximum external weapon load 10,000 lb (4,500 kg).

ARMAMENT (Jaguar B and E): Two 30 mm DEFA 553 cannon in Jaguar E; Jaguar B has single 30 mm Aden cannon on port side. The two-seat versions have similar weapons capability to the tactical models, and can be employed for operational missions as required.

DIMENSIONS, EXTERNAL:

Wing span	28 ft 6 in (8·69 m)
Wing chord at root	11 ft 9 in (3·58 m)
Wing chord at tip	3 ft 8½ in (1·13 m)
Wing aspect ratio	3·12
Length overall:	
A and S	50 ft 11 in (15·52 m)
B and E	53 ft 11 in (16·42 m)
Height overall	16 ft 1½ in (4·92 m)
Tailplane span	14 ft 10½ in (4·53 m)
Wheel track	7 ft 10½ in (2·40 m)
Wheelbase	18 ft 8 in (5·69 m)

AREAS:

Wings, gross	258·33 sq ft (24·00 m²)
Leading-edge slats (total)	11·30 sq ft (1·05 m²)
Trailing-edge flaps (total)	44·35 sq ft (4·12 m²)
Spoilers (total)	11·09 sq ft (1·03 m²)
Vertical tail surfaces (total)	42·00 sq ft (3·90 m²)
Horizontal tail surfaces (total)	83·96 sq ft (7·80 m²)

WEIGHTS AND LOADINGS:

Normal T-O weight	24,000 lb (11,000 kg)
Max T-O weight	34,000 lb (15,500 kg)
Max wing loading	126·3 lb/sq ft (604 kg/m²)
Max power loading	2·14 lb/lb st (2·14 kg/kg st)

PERFORMANCE (initial production aircraft, at max T-O weight, except where indicated):

Max level speed at S/L
729 knots (840 mph; 1,350 km/h) (Mach 1·1)

Max level speed at 36,000 ft (11,000 m)
860 knots (990 mph; 1,593 km/h) (Mach 1·5)

Landing speed 115 knots (132 mph; 213 km/h)

T-O run with typical tactical load
1,900 ft (580 m)

T-O to 50 ft (15 m) with typical tactical load
2,900 ft (885 m)

Landing from 50 ft (15 m) with typical tactical load 2,825 ft (860 m)

Landing run with typical tactical load
1,545 ft (470 m)

Typical attack radius, internal fuel only:
hi-lo-hi 440 nm (507 miles; 815 km)
lo-lo-lo 310 nm (357 miles; 575 km)

Typical attack radius with external fuel:
hi-lo-hi 710 nm (818 miles; 1,315 km)
lo-lo-lo 450 nm (518 miles; 835 km)

Ferry range with external fuel
2,270 nm (2,614 miles; 4,210 km)

Max high-altitude endurance at subsonic speed (B and E) 3 hr 0 min

TRANSALL

ARBEITSGEMEINSCHAFT TRANSALL

ADDRESS (including export office):
Hünefeldstrasse 1-5, 28 Bremen 1, Germany
Telephone: (0421) 5181
Telex: 245821b

Transall (Transporter Allianz) was formed in January 1959 by French and German aircraft companies to undertake the joint development and production of a turboprop military transport known as the Transall C-160. Participating companies were Messerschmitt-Bölkow-Blohm GmbH, Aérospatiale and VFW-Fokker GmbH.

This programme is now completed. It was fully described in the 1972-73 and 1973-74 *Jane's*.

ZENTRALGESELLSCHAFT VFW-FOKKER mbH

ADDRESS:
15 Gartenstrasse, Düsseldorf 4, Germany
Telephone: Düsseldorf 44941
Telex: 8584344 ZGVF-D

BOARD OF MANAGEMENT:
Frederik Jan Leo Diepen
Prof Gerhard Eggers
Dr Walter Habrich
Ir Agni Aldo Holle
Gerrit Cornelis Klapwijk (Deputy Chairman)
Dr Werner Knieper (Chairman)

DIRECTORS:
Dipl-Volksw A. Ackermann
H. H. van Doorn
Dipl-Volksw L. Förster
Ir A. M. Hazen
Dipl-Volksw H. Noever
H. Reichardt
N. P. A. Teunissen
F. Cesarz (Public Relations)
Ir P. van Lent
Dr G. Sadtler

DIRECTORS, FOKKER-VFW INTERNATIONAL BV, AMSTERDAM:
A. R. Buley
Dipl-Volksw S. Hellmann
D. Krook

MANAGERS, ERNO RAUMFAHRTTECHNIK GMBH, BREMEN:
Dipl-Ing H. Schneider
Dr. R. Kappler
RA B. Kosegarten
Dipl-Ing H. Hoffmann

DIRECTOR, HANDELMIJ. AVIO-DIEPEN BV, AMSTERDAM:
D. G. de Rooij

In May 1969 it was announced that NVKNV Fokker of the Netherlands and Vereinigte Flugtechnische Werke GmbH of Germany had decided to combine their activities on a parity basis. To accomplish this, a new central company named Zentralgesellschaft VFW-Fokker mbH was created, with its headquarters in Düsseldorf. The effective operating date of the association, the first of its kind in the European aerospace industry, was made retrospective to 1 January 1969.

Zentralgesellschaft VFW-Fokker mbH has a board of management comprising three directors from each company. The entire group employs just under 17,000 people in some 15 factories and companies, and has also, with Dassault-Breguet of France, a parity interest in the Belgian company SABCA (which see), with factories at Haren and Gosselies.

NV Koninklijke Nederlandse Vliegtuigenfabriek Fokker and VFW-Verwaltungsgesellschaft are the holding companies of Zentralgesellschaft VFW-Fokker mbH. The manufacturing companies, described fully under "Germany" and "Netherlands" respectively, are VFW-Fokker GmbH and Fokker-VFW BV. All marketing and product support of civil aircraft of VFW and Fokker design are undertaken by a separate company, Fokker-VFW International BV, with offices at PO Box 7600, Schiphol-Oost, Holland.

ISRAEL

IAI

ISRAEL AIRCRAFT INDUSTRIES LTD

HEAD OFFICE AND WORKS:
Ben Gurion International Airport, Lydda (Lod)
Telephone: 03-973111
Telex: Isravia 031114

PRESIDENT:
A. W. Schwimmer

EXECUTIVE VICE-PRESIDENTS:
A. Ben Yoseph
I. Roth
E. P. Wohl (Finance)

SENIOR VICE-PRESIDENTS:
S. N. Ariav (Gen Manager, Aircraft Manufacturing Division)
S. Yoran (Gen Manager, Bedek Aviation Division)

VICE-PRESIDENTS:
M. Blumkin (General Manager, Engineering Division)
Z. Yaari (Central Services)
A. Ostrinsky (Personnel and Administration)
S. Mendes (Western Hemisphere Operations)

COMMERCIAL DIRECTOR, ARAVA:
H. Pearlman

COMMERCIAL DIRECTOR, 1123 WESTWIND:
S. Samach

DIRECTOR, SYSTEMS SALES:
N. Rosen

DIRECTOR, GROUP MARKETING CO-ORDINATION:
D. Arnon

DIRECTOR OF EXTERNAL RELATIONS:
Elkana Galli

This company was established in 1953 as Bedek Aircraft Company. The change of name, to Israel Aircraft Industries, was made on 1 April 1967.

IAI employs about 15,000 people in all its facilities, which occupy a total covered floor area of 3,229,170 sq ft (300,000 m²). It is licensed by, among others, the Israel Civil Aviation Administration, US Federal Aviation Administration, British Civil Aviation Authority and the Israeli Air Force as an approved repair station and maintenance organisation.

Israel Aircraft Industries Ltd is composed of several divisions, plants and subsidiary companies as follows:

Bedek Aviation is an internationally approved multi-faceted single-site civil and military aircraft service centre. Present programmes include the turnaround inspection, overhaul, repair, retrofitting, outfitting and testing of 30 types of aircraft, up to the size of the Boeing 707 and McDonnell Douglas DC-8; 28 types of engine up to the 55,000 lb (24,947 kg) st Pratt & Whitney JT9D; and 4,000 types of components, accessories and systems. Offshore workload includes the supply of total technical support to several international operators. The division holds warranty and/or approved service centre approvals from many of the world's leading component manufacturers.

The **Aircraft Manufacturing Division** manufactures and assembles the Arava STOL transport and the 1123 Westwind business jet; diverse spare parts and assemblies for aircraft and engines; ground support equipment, including armament servicing trolleys; and performs subcontracting for leading aerospace companies in Europe and the United States.

A new factory was opened in November 1972 at Bnei-Yehuda, on the Golan Heights, to manufacture metal parts and electronics products. Present production output is entirely for the Israeli Ministry of Defence.

Among other items, flap assemblies for the Dassault Mystère 20/Falcon 20 business jet are built by this Division, which also produces a complete range of ground support equipment for many aircraft, as well as several cargo loading systems.

The **Engineering Division** is responsible for engineering research, design, development and testing of aerospace systems. It provides engineering support in system analysis, aerodynamics, materials and processing, landing and control systems, and in structural, flight and environmental testing. The Division performed modification and production support for the manufacture of the Magister jet trainer for the IAF; and major structural conversions of the Boeing Model 377, for military applications such as swing-tail freighter and hose-refuelling tanker. The Division designed and developed the Arava STOL transport aircraft, and made major modifications on the 1123 Westwind, both of which are now in production.

IAI's diversification has led to the creation of a number of subsidiary companies which produce specialised products:

The company's electronics subsidiary, **Elta**, although wholly owned, is fully autonomous. It is specialising in the design, development and production of sophisticated electronic equipment such as airborne, ground and shipborne communications and radars, transceivers and navigational aids, general communications equipment, automatic test systems, and such electronic medical devices as cardiac resuscitation instruments.

MBT Weapons Systems is concerned with advanced electronic research, design and production; it participated in the development of the Gabriel missile system, among others, as well as of an Electronic Warning Fence and an Audible Bomb Release Altimeter.

SHL Servo-Hydraulics Lod designs, develops and manufactures hydraulic and fuel system components, hydraulic flight control servo-systems, landing gears and brake systems.

TAMAM Precision Industries manufactures and assembles high-precision electromechanical components and servo-systems for such mechanisms as aerosystems, torque motors and gyroscopes.

PML Precision Mechanisms Ltd includes among its products air-actuated chucks, miniature gears, clutches and brakes.

Orlite Engineering Ltd is a custom-moulder of reinforced plastics, and produces parts for aircraft, cabs and trucks, concrete casting moulds and sheet products.

Turbochrome is specialised in the application of corrosion and abrasion resistant coating by the diffusion process.

The **Beer-Sheva** ground equipment plant manufactures ground support equipment and stainless steel tanks.

IAI-101 ARAVA

The Arava was designed to fulfil the need for a light transport with STOL performance and rough-field landing capabilities.

Design work started in 1966 and construction of a prototype began towards the end of the same year. This airframe was used for structural testing; it was followed by a flying prototype (4X-IAI), which made its first flight on 27 November 1969. This aircraft crashed on 19 November 1970 while undergoing flutter tests, after having completed successfully 92 previous test flights totalling 110 flying hours. A second Arava (4X-IAA) began flight trials on 8 May 1971.

A type certificate for the IAI-101 was issued in April 1972.

IAI-201 MILITARY ARAVA

The IAI-201 is the military transport version of the Arava, based upon the original IAI-101. A prototype (4X-IAB) began its flight tests on 7 March 1972, and this version is now in full production. The standard equipment available for the IAI-201 enables a wide variety of missions to be undertaken.

Prior to the "Yom Kippur war" in October 1973, a total of 15 military Aravas had been ordered, 14 of them for export. During the conflict it was reported that three aircraft were being lease-operated by the Israeli Air Force, which was expected to place an official order for the Arava later. By early 1974 five of the export-order Aravas had been delivered to the Mexican Air Force, and one to Nicaragua, from sales made in Latin America.

TYPE: Twin-turboprop STOL light military transport.

WINGS: Braced high-wing monoplane, with single streamline-section bracing strut each side. Wing section NACA 63(215)A 417. Dihedral 1° 30′. Incidence 0° 27′. No sweepback. Light alloy two-spar torsion-box structure. Frise-type light alloy ailerons. Electrically-operated double-slotted light alloy flaps. Scoop-type light alloy spoilers, for lateral control, above wing at 71% chord. Electrically-actuated trim tab in port aileron.

FUSELAGE: Conventional semi-monocoque light alloy structure of stringers, frames and single-skin panels.

TAIL UNIT: Cantilever light alloy structure, with twin fins and rudders, carried on twin booms extending rearward from engine nacelles. Fixed-incidence tailplane. Geared tab and electrically-actuated trim tab in elevator and geared trim tab in each rudder.

LANDING GEAR: Non-retractable tricycle type, of Electro-Hydraulics manufacture, with single main wheels and steerable nosewheel. Main wheels carried on twin struts, incorporating oleo-pneumatic shock-absorbers. Main wheels size 11·00-12. Nosewheel size 9·00-6. Tyre pressure 48 lb/sq in (3·37 kg/cm²) on main units, 45 lb/sq in (3·16 kg/cm²) on nose unit. Disc brakes on main units.

POWER PLANT: Two 750 shp United Aircraft of Canada PT6A-34 turboprop engines, each driving a Hartzell HC-B3TN three-blade hydraulically-actuated fully-feathering reversible-pitch metal propeller. Electrical de-icing of propellers optional. Two integral fuel tanks in each wing, with total usable capacity of 366 Imp gallons (1,663 litres). Four overwing refuelling points. Optional pressure refuelling point in fuselage/strut fairing. Two cabin-mounted tanks, each of 210 Imp gallons (954 litres), are available optionally; these are used for ferrying purposes.

ACCOMMODATION: Crew of one or two on flight deck, with door on starboard side. Main cabin has folding inward-facing metal-framed fabric seats along each side, and can accommodate 24 fully-equipped troops or 16 paratroops and two dispatchers. Outward-opening door at rear of cabin, opposite which, at floor level, is an emergency exit door/cargo door on the starboard side. Aft section of fuselage is hinged to swing sideways through more than 90° to provide unrestricted access to main cabin. Alternative interior configurations available for ambulance role (twelve stretchers and two sitting patients/medical attendants) or as all-freight transport carrying (typically) a jeep-mounted recoil-less rifle and its four-man crew.

SYSTEMS: Hydraulic system (pressure 2,500 lb/sq in; 175 kg/cm²) for brakes and nosewheel steering only. Electrical system includes two 28V 170A DC engine-driven starter/generators, a 28V 40Ah nickel-cadmium battery and two 250VA 115/26V 400Hz static inverters.

ELECTRONICS AND EQUIPMENT: Blind-flying instrumentation standard. Optional equipment includes VHF, VOR/ILS, ADF, marker beacon and PA system.

ARMAMENT: Optional 0·50 in Browning machine-gun pack on each side of fuselage, above a pylon

Civil version of the Israel Aircraft Industries Arava STOL light transport

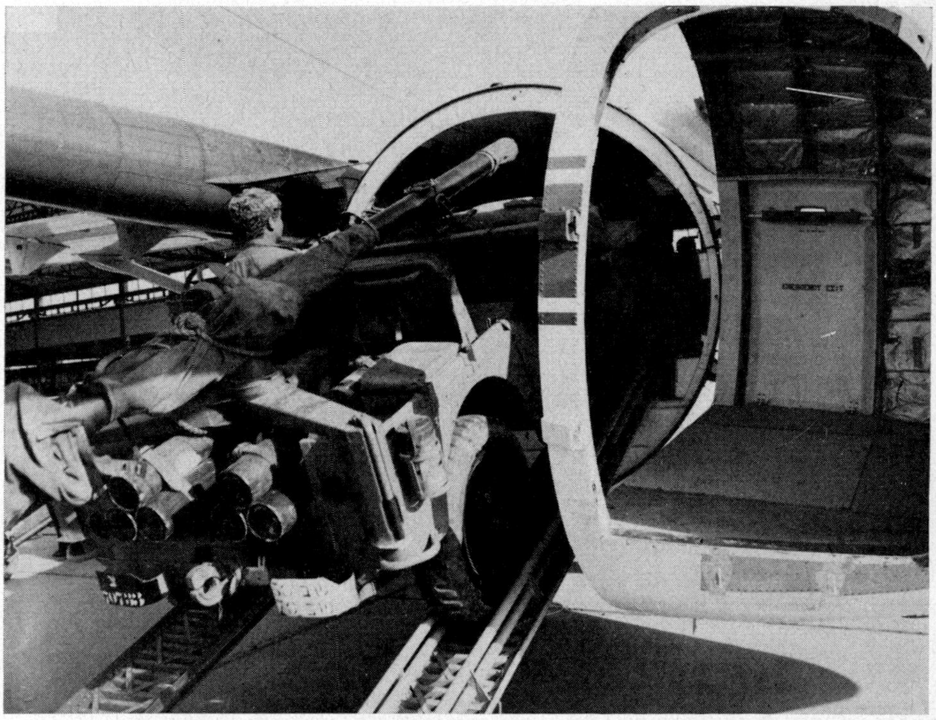

Jeep-mounted artillery weapon being loaded into the hold of an IAI-201 Arava military transport

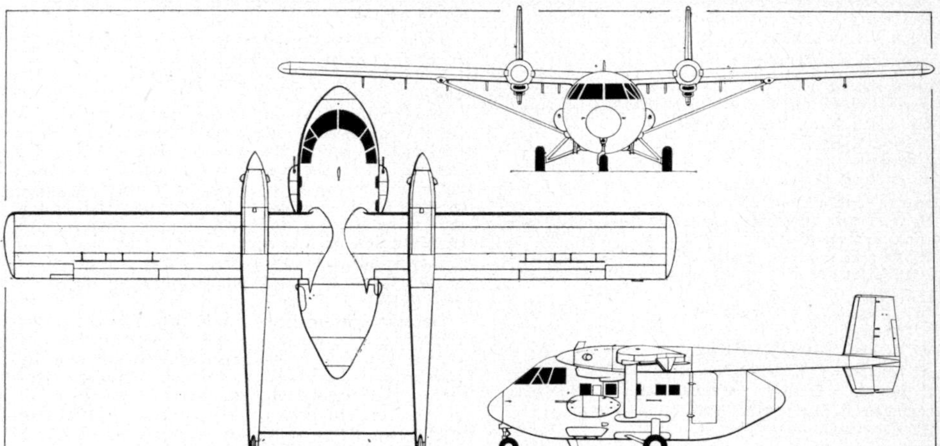

IAI-201 Arava twin-turboprop STOL light military transport (*Pilot Press*)

for a pod containing seven 68 mm rockets. Provision for aft-firing machine-gun. Librascope gunsight.

Dimensions, external:
Wing span 69 ft 6 in (20·88 m)
Wing chord (constant) 6 ft 10½ in (2·09 m)
Wing aspect ratio 10
Length overall 42 ft 7½ in (12·99 m)
Length of fuselage pod 30 ft 7½ in (9·33 m)
Diameter of fuselage 8 ft 2½ in (2·50 m)
Height overall 17 ft 1 in (5·21 m)
Propeller ground clearance 5 ft 9 in (1·75 m)
Tailplane span (c/l of tailbooms) 17 ft 1 in (5·21 m)
Wheel track 13 ft 1½ in (4·00 m)
Wheelbase 15 ft 2 in (4·62 m)
Propeller diameter 8 ft 6 in (2·59 m)
Crew door (fwd, stbd):
Height 2 ft 8 in (0·81 m)
Width 1 ft 6 in (0·46 m)
Passenger door (rear, port):
Height 5 ft 7 in (1·70 m)
Width 2 ft 11 in (0·89 m)
Cargo drop door (rear, port):
Height 7 ft 3 in (2·21 m)
Width 3 ft 2 in (0·97 m)
Emergency/baggage door (rear, stbd):
Height 3 ft 9 in (1·14 m)
Width 2 ft 1¼ in (0·64 m)
Emergency window exits (each):
Height 2 ft 2 in (0·66 m)
Width 1 ft 6¾ in (0·48 m)

Dimensions, internal:
Cabin, excluding flight deck and hinged tail-cone:
Length 12 ft 8½ in (3·87 m)
Max width 7 ft 8 in (2·33 m)
Max height 5 ft 8½ in (1·74 m)
Floor area 77·1 sq ft (7·16 m²)
Volume 466·2 cu ft (13·2 m³)
Baggage compartment volume 91·8 cu ft (2·60 m³)
Cargo door volume 113 cu ft (3·20 m³)

Areas:
Wings, gross 470·2 sq ft (43·68 m²)
Ailerons (total) 18·84 sq ft (1·75 m²)
Trailing-edge flaps (total) 94·72 sq ft (8·80 m²)
Spoilers (total) 9·04 sq ft (0·84 m²)
Fins (total) 52·31 sq ft (4·86 m²)
Rudders (total incl tabs) 37·03 sq ft (3·44 m²)
Tailplane 100·75 sq ft (9·36 m²)
Elevator, including tabs 30·03 sq ft (2·79 m²)

Weights and Loadings:
Basic operating weight 8,900 lb (4,037 kg)
Max payload 5,100 lb (2,313 kg)
Max T-O and landing weight 15,000 lb (6,803 kg)
Max zero-fuel weight 13,500 lb (6,123 kg)
Max wing loading 31·44 lb/sq ft (153·5 kg/m²)
Max power loading 9·32 lb/ehp (4·23 kg/ehp)

Performance (at max T-O weight):
Max never-exceed speed 215 knots (247 mph; 397 km/h)
Max level speed at 10,000 ft (3,050 m) 176 knots (203 mph; 326 km/h)
Max cruising speed at 10,000 ft (3,050 m) 172 knots (198 mph; 319 km/h)
Econ cruising speed at 10,000 ft (3,050 m) 168 knots (193 mph; 311 km/h)
Stalling speed, flaps up 75 knots (87 mph; 140 km/h)
Stalling speed, flaps down 62 knots (71·5 mph; 115 km/h)
Max rate of climb at S/L 1,270 ft (387 m)/min
Rate of climb at S/L, one engine out 180 ft (55 m)/min
Service ceiling 24,000 ft (7,315 m)
Service ceiling, one engine out 9,800 ft (2,985 m)
STOL T-O run 730 ft (223 m)
STOL T-O to 50 ft (15 m) 1,180 ft (360 m)
STOL landing from 50 ft (15 m) 930 ft (283 m)
STOL landing run 390 ft (119 m)
Range with max fuel, 45 min reserves 700 nm (806 miles; 1,297 km)
Range with max payload, 45 min reserves 175 nm (201 miles; 323 km)

IAI BARAK (LIGHTNING)

The refitting of Israeli Air Force Mirage III-CJ combat aircraft with General Electric J79-GE-17 turbojet engines has been reported by various press sources, several of which have stated that the J79-powered version of the Mirage is named Barak (Lightning); it had been reported earlier by other sources under the code name "Black Curtain". The Israeli Air Force is said to have a requirement for 200 aircraft of this type, and one report, in the magazine *Ordnance*, suggested that the Barak was on the point of entering service with the Israeli Air Force in late 1972. The Barak was subsequently reported to have taken part in small numbers in the "Yom Kippur war" in October 1973.

Understandably, IAI is unable to comment upon these reports, or on the Mirage III re-engining programme, but it is known that the company has subcontracted Metal Resources Inc of Gardena, California, USA, to build replacement wing components for Israel's Mirage III-CJs.

IAI 1123 WESTWIND

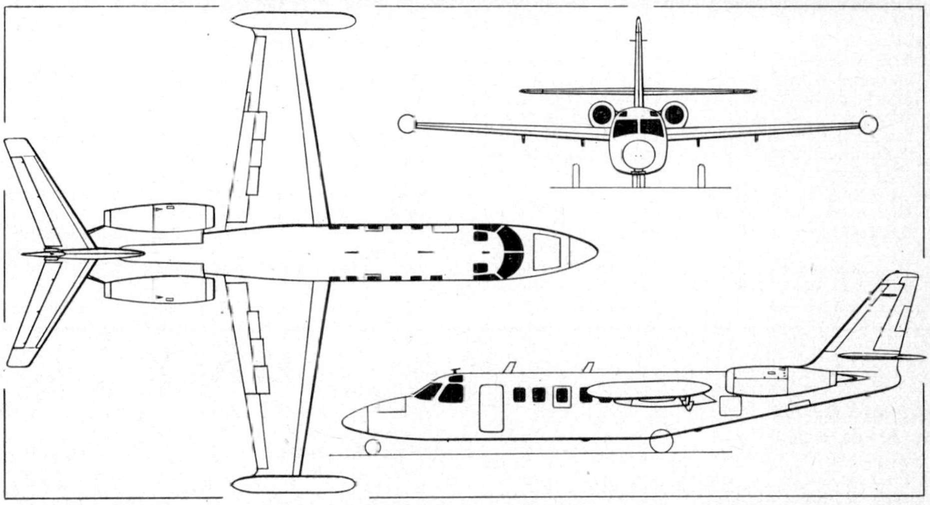

Three-view drawing (*Pilot Press*) and photograph of the IAI 1123 Westwind twin-jet light executive transport

In 1967, Israel Aircraft Industries acquired all production and marketing rights for the Rockwell-Standard Corporation (formerly Aero Commander) Jet Commander business jet transport. The latest, improved version, which is in full production, is known as the 1123 Westwind business jet, and is certificated in the FAA transport category. It was known formerly as the Commodore Jet 1123.

The first of two prototype Jet Commanders (N601J) was flown for the first time in the US on 27 January 1963. The US production line was phased out between 1967 and mid-1969. A total of 150 Commodore Jet/Jet Commander aircraft (US and IAI production) were delivered, in three basic models: the 1121, 1121A and 1121B.

Many modifications and improvements were incorporated by IAI into the original Jet Commander/Commodore Jet 1121. In early 1971 an 1121C model was certificated. Main improvements included an increase in max T-O weight to 18,500 lb (8,391 kg), strengthened landing gear, greater fuel capacity and improved performance.

The current 1123 Westwind, to which the following description applies, has a 1 ft 8 in (0·51 m) longer cabin than the model 1121, wingtip auxiliary fuel tanks, more powerful engines, an APU, strengthened landing gear, simplified electrical system, double-slotted flaps, drooped wing leading-edges and two additional cabin windows. A prototype was flown for the first time on 28 September 1970, and was certificated by the Israel CAA and by the FAA at the end of 1971.

Deliveries of the 1123 Westwind totalled 25 by February 1974, to customers in the US, Canada and Germany. Atlantic Aviation Corporation of Wilmington, Delaware, has sole marketing rights for the aircraft in the USA and Canada.

Type: Twin-jet business transport.

Wings: Cantilever mid-wing monoplane. Wing section NACA 64A212. Dihedral 2°. Incidence 1° at root, —1° at tip. Sweepback 4° 37′ at quarter-chord. All-metal flush-riveted two-spar fail-safe structure. Manually-operated all-metal ailerons. Electrically-operated all-metal double-slotted trailing-edge Fowler-type flaps and detachable drooped leading-edge. Electrically-operated trim tab in port aileron. Hydraulically-actuated speed brake and two lift dumpers above each wing, forward of flap. All skins chemically milled and fully sealed. All primary control surfaces, including tabs, are fully mass-balanced. Pneumatic anti-icing boots standard.

Fuselage: All-metal semi-monocoque flush-riveted structure with pressurised fail-safe cabin and baggage compartment. Built in two main sections and joined at aft pressure bulkhead. Forward section, except for nose-cone, is fully pressurised.

Tail Unit: Cantilever all-metal structure, with 28° sweepback at quarter-chord. Variable-incidence tailplane, actuated electrically. Manually-operated statically-balanced elevators and rudder. Trim tab in rudder. Pneumatic anti-icing boots standard.

Landing Gear: Hydraulically-retractable tricycle type, main wheels retracting outward into wings, twin nosewheels rearward. Oleo-pneumatic shock-absorbers. Single wheels on main units, pressure 155 lb/sq in (10·9 kg/cm²). Nose unit steerable and self-centering. Nose-wheel tyre pressure 50 lb/sq in (3·5 kg/cm²). Goodyear multiple-disc brakes. Fully-modulated anti-skid system has automatic computer/sensor to prevent wheel lock and maintain brake effectiveness. Parking brake fitted.

Power Plant: Two 3,100 lb (1,406 kg) st General Electric CJ610-9 turbojet engines, mounted in pod on each side of rear fuselage. 85% of wing area forms an integral fuel tank, and additional fuel is carried separately in wingtip tanks and rear fuselage tanks. Total usable capacity 1,107 Imp gallons (1,330 US gallons; 5,035 litres), including wingtip tanks. Refuelling points in wingtips and fuselage. Thrust reversers and single-point pressure refuelling available optionally.

Accommodation: Standard seating for two pilots and up to 10 passengers in pressurised cabin. Interior layout to customer's requirements, with galley and toilet standard. Separate pressurised compartment for up to 400 lb (181 kg) of baggage. Passenger door at front on port side; emergency exit on each side, forward of wing. Entire accommodation heated, ventilated and air-conditioned.

Systems: Primary hydraulic system, pressure 2,000 lb/sq in (140 kg/cm²), operates through two engine-driven pumps to actuate landing gear, wheel brakes, nosewheel steering, speed brakes and lift dumpers. Electrically-operated emergency system, pressure 1,000 lb/sq in (70 kg/cm²), for brakes only. DC electrical system with two 350A 24V engine-driven starter/generators and two 21Ah long-life nickel-cadmium batteries. One main bus for each generator, connected to the central battery bus. A 400Hz 115V AC system is installed, and is powered by two solid-state static inverters, each of 1,000VA capacity, with power fed from the main DC buses. Each inverter is independently capable of supplying the entire AC load if required. Pneumatic system for anti-icing of wing and tail leading-edges only. Warm air bled from engines to prevent icing of air intakes. Windscreen is heated electrically. Microturbo Saphir III APU, installed in tailcone, for ground air-conditioning and ground electrical power supply. Cabin air pressure max differential of 8·7 lb/sq in (0·61 kg/cm²) up to 45,000 ft (13,715 m).

Equipment: Full blind-flying instrumentation standard. Radio and avionics to customer's requirements.

Dimensions, external:
Wing span 44 ft 9½ in (13·65 m)
Wing chord at root 10 ft 6 in (3·20 m)
Wing chord at tip 3 ft 6 in (1·07 m)
Wing aspect ratio 6·51

Length overall 52 ft 3 in (15·93 m)
Fuselage: Max width 5 ft 2 in (1·57 m)
Max depth 6 ft 0 in (1·83 m)
Height overall 15 ft 9½ in (4·81 m)
Tailplane span 21 ft 0 in (6·40 m)
Wheel track 11 ft 0 in (3·35 m)
Passenger door:
Height 4 ft 6 in (1·37 m)
Width 2 ft 0 in (0·61 m)
Height to sill 1 ft 8 in (0·51 m)

Dimensions, internal:
Cabin, excluding flight deck:
Length 15 ft 6 in (4·72 m)
Max width 4 ft 9 in (1·45 m)
Max height 4 ft 11 in (1·50 m)
Volume 347 cu ft (9·83 m³)
Baggage compartment volume 25 cu ft (0·71 m³)

Areas:
Wings, gross 308·26 sq ft (28·64 m²)
Ailerons (total) 15·39 sq ft (1·43 m²)
Trailing-edge flaps (total) 41·58 sq ft (3·86 m²)
Fin 48·60 sq ft (4·51 m²)
Rudder, including tab 10·69 sq ft (0·99 m²)
Tailplane 52·42 sq ft (4·87 m²)
Elevators 17·66 sq ft (1·64 m²)

Weights and Loadings:
Weight empty, equipped 9,370 lb (4,250 kg)
Typical basic operating weight 11,300 lb (5,125 kg)
Max payload 2,200 lb (1,000 kg)
Max T-O weight 20,700 lb (9,389 kg)
Max ramp weight 21,000 lb (9,525 kg)
Max zero-fuel weight 13,500 lb (6,123 kg)
Max landing weight 19,000 lb (8,618 kg)
Max cabin floor loading 200 lb/sq ft (976·5 kg/m²)
Max wing loading 67·0 lb/sq ft (327·1 kg/m²)

Performance (at max T-O weight, ISA, except where indicated):
Max operating speed at S/L 360 knots (415 mph; 668 km/h) CAS
Max operating speed at 18,000 ft (5,485 m) 372 knots (428 mph; 689 km/h) CAS
Max speed at 18,000 ft (5,485 m) 471 knots (542 mph; 872 km/h) TAS
Max operating Mach number at 18,000 ft (5,485 m) and above Mach 0·765
Econ cruising speed at 41,000 ft (12,500 m) 365 knots (420 mph; 676 km/h)
Stalling speed, flaps and landing gear down, at max landing weight 97 knots (112 mph; 180 km/h) CAS
Stalling speed, flaps and landing gear down, at 12,000 lb (5,443 kg) AUW 79 knots (91 mph; 146·5 km/h) CAS
Max rate of climb at S/L 4,040 ft (1,231 m)/min
Rate of climb at S/L, one engine out 1,100 ft (335 m)/min
Service ceiling 45,000 ft (13,715 m)
Service ceiling, one engine out 22,500 ft (6,860 m)
T-O to 35 ft (10·7 m) 4,100 ft (1,250 m)
FAA balanced T-O field length 5,350 ft (1,631 m)
Balanced field length at 18,000 lb (8,164 kg) AUW 3,800 ft (1,158 m)
Landing from 50 ft (15 m) at max landing weight 3,400 ft (1,036 m)
Landing from 50 ft (15 m) at 14,000 lb (6,350 kg) AUW 2,650 ft (808 m)
Range with max fuel, 5 passengers and baggage, 45 min reserve 1,840 nm (2,120 miles; 3,410 km)
Range with max payload, 45 min reserve 1,390 nm (1,600 miles; 2,575 km)
IFR range with 6 passengers after T-O from balanced field length of 4,000 ft (1,220 m) 1,233 nm (1,420 miles; 2,285 km)

IAI 1124 WESTWIND

This longer-range version of the Westwind, under development in 1974, is expected to be certificated in time for deliveries to begin at the end of 1975. It has essentially the same airframe and systems as the 1123 Westwind, but is powered by two 3,700 lb (1,678 kg) st Garrett-AiResearch TFE 731-3 turbofan engines, with thrust reversers as a standard fit. Fuel capacity will be the same as for the 1123; but runway requirements will be substantially reduced and max range with nine passengers will be 2,257 nm (2,600 miles; 4,184 km).

Weights:
Basic operating weight (incl two pilots) 12,600 lb (5,715 kg)
Max T-O weight 22,850 lb (10,364 kg)
Max ramp weight 23,000 lb (10,432 kg)
Max landing weight 19,000 lb (8,618 kg)
Max zero-fuel weight 16,000 lb (7,257 kg)

ITALY

AERITALIA

AERITALIA SpA

Head Office:
Piazzale Vincenzo Tecchio 51, 80125 Naples
Telephone: (081) 619522, 619721, 619845, 619149, 619703
Telex: N. 71370 (AERIT)

Office of the Chairman, and External Relations Office:
Via Panama 52, 00198 Rome
Telephone: (06) 853125
Telex: N. 62395 (AERIT)

Branch Office (Commercial):
Via Panama 52, 00198 Rome
Telephone: (06) 851528
Telex: N. 62395 (AERIT)

Board of Directors:
Gen SA (r) Gastone Valentini
Dott Ercole Agosta
Dott Romolo Arena
Dott Ing Riccardo Baldini
Dott Ing Luigi di Giorgio
Dott Ing Luigi Galleani d'Agliano
Dott Ing Franco Giura
Dott Ermanno Pedrana
Dott Ing Amilcare Porro
Gen SA (r) Mario Porru Locci
Dott Ernesto Postiglione
Dott Ing Bruno Ressico
Dott Fabio Massimo Tafuri
Dott Giovanni Mario Rossignolo

Executive Directors:
Dott Ing Amilcare Porro (General Manager)
Dott Ing Alessandro Pagni (External Relations)
Dott Ing Giulio Ciampolini (Technical Affairs)
Dott Ing Ugo Micheletta (Production)
Rag Antonio Fiori (Finance and Budget)
Dott Ing Tiziano Fortunati (Planning)
Dott Michele Crosio (Personnel)
Dott Ing Fausto Cereti (Aircraft Group)
Dott Ing Francesco Gnavi (Avionics, Instruments and Space Group)

Press:
Baldassare Catalanotto

Aeritalia is a joint stock company which was formed on 12 November 1969 by an equal shareholding of Fiat and Finmeccanica-IRI, to combine Fiat's aerospace activities (except that which concerns aero-engines) and those of Aerfer and Salmoiraghi belonging to the Finmeccanica group. The company became fully operational under the new title on 1 January 1972. Aeritalia had a total work force, in 1974, of more than 9,500 persons.

Aeritalia's organisational structure is based upon a central general direction and two operational groups, the Aircraft Group and the Avionics. Instruments and Space Group. The production centres are located in Turin (Corso Marche, Caselle Nord and Caselle Sud), Milan (Nerviano) and Naples (Pomigliano d'Arco and Capodichino). The Italian Interministerial Committee for Economic Planning has approved Aeritalia's plans for the first module of a new industrial plant in the Foggia area.

Aeritalia has a co-operation agreement with Boeing of the US to develop an advanced commercial transport aircraft. This programme began in the Spring of 1971 and was continuing in 1974. More recently, Aeritalia signed a co-operation agreement with Lockheed to market the G222 transport and F-104S fighter aircraft. This agreement also provides for joint development and marketing of the Lancer project for a successor to the F-104S.

AIRCRAFT GROUP

Headquarters:
Via Marina 9, 80125 Naples
Telephone: (081) 517344

Turin Area

Turin Works: Corso Marche 41, 00146 Turin
Telephone: (011) 790166, 720072
Telex: N. 21076 (AERITOR)
Caselle Works: Turin Airport CP, 10100 Turin
Telephone: (011) 991362
Telex: N. 21602 (FIATVOLI)

The Turin Area factories are engaged in the manufacture, assembly and flight testing of the G91Y tactical fighter-bomber and reconnaissance aircraft, F-104S interceptor fighter, and G222 military transport aircraft for the Italian armed forces; in the design and construction of structural components for the Panavia MRCA (see International section); collaboration with Dassault-Breguet of France in the design and construction of part of the structure of the Mercure short-haul commercial transport aircraft; and repair, overhaul and maintenance of test equipment. Other activities include the repair, overhaul and maintenance of F-104G, F-104S, TF-104G and G91Y aircraft.

Naples Area

Pomigliano d'Arco Works (Naples):
80038 Pomigliano d'Arco, Naples
Telephone: (081) 8841544
Telex: N. 71082 (AERITPOM)
Capodichino Works: Via del Riposo alla Doganella, Aeroporto di Capodichino, 80144 Naples
Telephone: (081) 444166

Aeritalia's principal activities in the Naples Area comprise construction of the complete series of fuselage structural panels for the McDonnell Douglas DC-9, and fuselage upper panels and the vertical tail surfaces for the DC-10 commercial airliner; construction of engine support pylons for the Boeing 747; system design and construction of part of structure, final assembly and flight test of the Aeritalia/Aermacchi AM.3C military light aircraft; and construction of parts for the Aeritalia G222, the Aeritalia (Lockheed) F-104S and the Breguet 1150 Atlantic. Other activities include the repair, overhaul and modification of aircraft of various nations, including Italy and the United States, and the repair and maintenance of Caravelle and Fokker-VFW F.27 aircraft.

INSTRUMENT, AVIONICS AND SPACE GROUP

Headquarters:
Via Panama 52, 00198 Rome
Telephone: (06) 853125
Telex: N.62395 (AERIT)

Turin Area

Caselle Works: Turin Airport, 10100 Turin
Telephone: (011) 991363
Telex: 31602 (FIATVOLI)

Avionics:
After earlier work on the concept, design and interface of complex avionics systems and the development of specific equipment for space purposes, Aeritalia has diversified its project activity in the avionics field to include the capability to conceive, design and interface such aerospace systems as satellite attitude control and new systems for civil utility purposes, ie vehicle control, automation of airport functions, and simulation and design of production multi-loop controls. Production activity in this area comprises the manufacture, repair and overhaul of sophisticated avionics and space equipment, either for aircraft and space components of Aeritalia's own production or for the international market.

Foggia Area

Branch Office:
Via Giannone 1, 70100 Foggia
Telephone: (0881) 79641
Telex: N. 81213 (AERITFOG)
Amendola Works:
Under development and construction

Milan Area

Nerviano Works: Viale Europa, 20014 Nerviano, Milan
Telephone: (0331) 587330
Telex: N. 36675 (AERITNER)

The Nerviano works is engaged in the manufacture of avionics and instrumentation, including systems and instruments for aeronautical, missile and space applications such as accelerometers, altimeters, electrical equipment, gyro compasses, gyroscopic platforms, magnetic compasses, pressure, stress and temperature transducers and load amplifiers.

Space Activities:
Aeritalia is a member of the MESH consortium which produces the OTS satellite (which see); it has undertaken studies and manufactured electronic control equipment for this programme, and also builds the satellite structure. The company also participates in the Ariane launcher programme, and is taking part in the development and design definition of the Italian Sirio satellite, with responsibility for the main structure and thermal control, the VHF antenna, and the logic portion of the attitude control system.

AERITALIA G91Y

Announced in the Spring of 1965, the G91Y is a twin-engined development of the earlier single-engined Fiat G91 (see 1966-67 *Jane's*); its structure is based upon the airframe of the G91T. The G91Y has approximately 60% greater take-off thrust than the original G91 at the cost of only a relatively small increase in power plant weight. This makes possible a considerable increase in military load and/or fuel. It is possible to cruise with one engine stopped to extend endurance. The normal T-O distance can be reduced by approx 50% by the use of JATO rockets, and an underfuselage arrester hook enables the aircraft to be used in SATS (Short Airfield for Tactical Support) conditions.

Two G91Y prototypes were built, of which the first flew for the first time on 27 December 1966. The other, first flown in September 1967, was to full operational standard, including armament and navigational equipment. The first of 20 pre-series G91Ys for the Italian Air Force was flown in July 1968. All 20 were delivered to the 1° Group of the 8° Wing of the Italian Air Force.

An initial series production order for 35 was placed subsequently by the Italian Air Force; delivery of these aircraft began in September 1971, and was completed by mid-1973. An additional Italian Air Force order for 10 aircraft was placed in the Spring of 1973, and delivery of these is due to be completed by mid-1975.

Type: Lightweight single-seat tactical fighter-bomber and reconnaissance aircraft.

Wings: Cantilever low-wing monoplane. Laminar-flow section. Sweepback at quarter-chord 37° 40′ 38″. Two-spar structure, with milled skin panels and detachable leading-edge. Ailerons with hydraulic servo control. Electrically-actuated slotted trailing-edge flaps. Automatic full-span leading-edge slats.

Fuselage: Semi-monocoque structure. Rear fuselage detachable for engine replacement. Two door-type airbrakes under centre-fuselage.

Tail Unit: Cantilever structure. Electrically-actuated variable-incidence tailplane. Auxiliary fin beneath each side of rear fuselage.

Landing Gear: Retractable tricycle type of Messier-Hispano design. Hydraulic actuation. Main-wheel tyre pressure 57 lb/sq in (4·0 kg/cm²). Hydraulic brakes. Brake chute housed at base of rudder. Arrester hook under rear fuselage.

Power Plant: Two General Electric J85-GE-13A turbojet engines (each 2,720 lb; 1,235 kg st dry, 4,080 lb; 1,850 kg st with afterburning), mounted side by side in rear fuselage. Provision for JATO units for assisted take-off. Fuel in main tanks in fuselage and inner wing panels with total capacity of 703 Imp gallons (3,200 litres). Provision for underwing auxiliary tanks.

Accommodation: Pilot only, on fully-automatic zero-zero ejection seat, under electrically-actuated rearward-hinged jettisonable canopy. Cockpit armoured, pressurised and air-conditioned.

Armament and Operational Equipment: Two 30 mm DEFA cannon and cameras in nose. Four underwing attachments for 1,000 lb bombs, 750 lb (340 kg) napalm tanks, seven 2 in rocket packs, twenty-eight 2 in rocket packs or four 5 in rocket containers. Nav/attack system includes Computing Devices of Canada 5C-15 position and homing indicator, Sperry SYP twin-axis gyro platform, Bendix RDA-12 Doppler radar and AiResearch air data computer, Ferranti ISIS B gyro-gunsight, Honeywell AN/APN-171 radar altimeter and Marconi-Elliott AD 370 automatic direction-finding equipment.

Dimensions, external:
- Wing span: 29 ft 6½ in (9·01 m)
- Wing chord at root: 8 ft 3½ in (2·526 m)
- Wing chord at tip: 4 ft 2¼ in (1·274 m)
- Wing aspect ratio: 4·475
- Length overall: 38 ft 3½ in (11·67 m)
- Height overall: 14 ft 6 in (4·43 m)
- Tailplane span: 13 ft 1½ in (4·00 m)
- Wheel track: 9 ft 8 in (2·94 m)
- Wheelbase: 11 ft 8 in (3·56 m)

Areas:
- Wings, gross: 195·15 sq ft (18·13 m²)
- Ailerons (total): 18·75 sq ft (1·742 m²)
- Trailing-edge flaps (total): 18·69 sq ft (1·736 m²)
- Fin (excl ventral fins): 18·87 sq ft (1·753 m²)
- Rudder: 4·28 sq ft (0·398 m²)
- Horizontal tail surfaces (total): 30·25 sq ft (2·810 m²)

Weights and Loadings:
- Weight empty: 8,598 lb (3,900 kg)
- Normal T-O weight: 17,196 lb (7,800 kg)
- Max T-O weight (semi-prepared surface): 15,432 lb (7,000 kg)
- Max T-O weight (hard runway): 19,180 lb (8,700 kg)
- Max wing loading: 98·3 lb/sq ft (480 kg/m²)
- Max power loading: 2·35 lb/lb st (2·35 kg/kg st)

Performance (at max T-O weight, except where indicated):
- Max level speed at 30,000 ft (9,145 m): Mach 0·95
- Max level speed at S/L: 600 knots (690 mph; 1,110 km/h)
- Stalling speed, flaps down: 125 knots (143 mph; 230 km/h)
- Max rate of climb at S/L:
  - with afterburning: 17,000 ft (5,180 m)/min
  - without afterburning: 7,000 ft (2,134 m)/min
- Time to 40,000 ft (12,200 m):
  - with afterburning: 4 min 30 sec
  - without afterburning: 11 min
- Service ceiling: 41,000 ft (12,500 m)
- Service ceiling, one engine out (with afterburning): 19,685 ft (6,000 m)
- *T-O run:
  - hard runway: 4,000 ft (1,219 m)
  - semi-prepared surface: 3,000 ft (914 m)
  - semi-prepared surface, with JATO: 1,500 ft (457 m)
- *T-O to 50 ft (15 m):
  - hard runway: 6,000 ft (1,829 m)
  - semi-prepared surface: 4,500 ft (1,372 m)
  - semi-prepared surface, with JATO: 2,500 ft (762 m)
- Landing from 50 ft (15 m): 1,970 ft (600 m)
- Typical combat radius at S/L: 323 nm (372 miles; 600 km)
- Ferry range with max fuel: 1,890 nm (2,175 miles; 3,500 km)

* *See "Weights" above*

Aeritalia G91Y single-seat combat aircraft of the Italian Air Force (two 2,720 lb st J85-GE-13A turbojet engines)

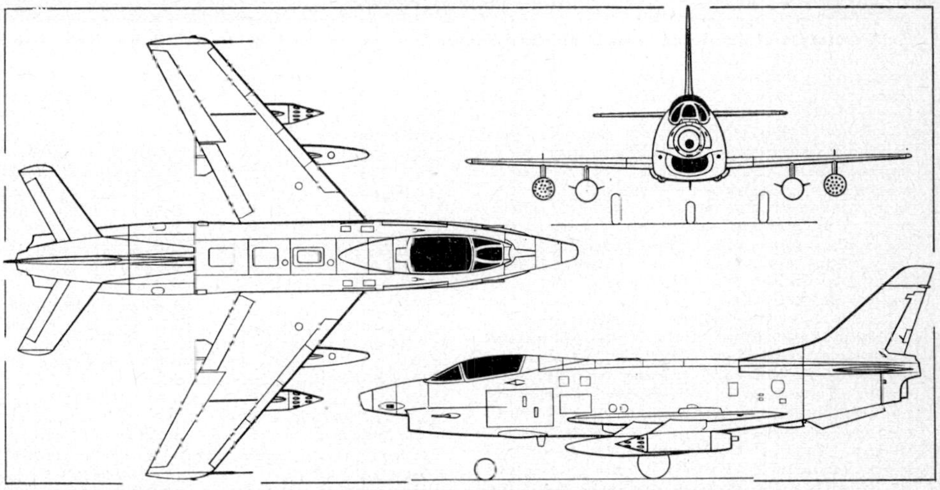

Aeritalia G91Y single-seat twin-engined tactical reconnaissance/fighter-bomber (*Pilot Press*)

AERITALIA G222

The G222 was originally conceived in four separate configurations, three of which were halted at the research project stage. Two prototypes have been built of the military transport version, designated G222 TCM, to which the description applies. The first of these flew for the first time on 18 July 1970 and the second on 22 July 1971. The first prototype was handed over to the Italian Air Force in December 1971 for operational evaluation. An additional airframe has been completed for static fatigue testing.

The Italian Air Force has ordered 44 production G222s: manufacture of these will take place initially at the Turin Area factories and will later be transferred to the new Amendola works now under construction.

The first two production aircraft are due to fly and to be delivered by mid-1975.

Several major Italian airframe companies are sharing in the construction programme, including Aermacchi (outer wings); Piaggio (wing centre-section); SIAI-Marchetti (tail unit); SACA (miscellaneous airframe components); and CIRSEA (landing gear).

Type: Twin-engined general-purpose transport aircraft.

Wings: Cantilever high-wing monoplane. Thickness/chord ratio 15%. Light alloy three-spar fail-safe structure in three portions, the outer panels having taper on the leading- and trailing-edges and slight dihedral. One-piece centre-section fits in recess in top of fuselage and is secured by bolts at six main points. All-metal ailerons and double-slotted flaps, the latter extending over 60% of the trailing-edge. Spoilers ahead of each outboard flap section. Servo tabs on each aileron. Controls are hydraulically powered.

Fuselage: Stressed-skin aluminium alloy fail-safe structure of circular cross-section.

Tail Unit: Cantilever aluminium alloy two-spar structure, with sweptback vertical surfaces. Variable-incidence tailplane. Elevators hydraulically powered. Tabs on each elevator. No rudder tabs.

Landing Gear: Hydraulically-retractable tricycle type, suitable for use from prepared runways or grass fields. Messier-Hispano design, built under licence by CIRSEA (Nardi/Magnaghi). Twin-wheel nose unit retracts forward, tandem-wheel main units rearward into fairings on sides of fuselage. Oleo-pneumatic shock-absorbers. Gear can be lowered by gravity in emergency, the nose unit being aided by aerodynamic action and the main units by the shock-absorbers, which remain compressed in the retracted position. Oleo pressure in shock-absorbers is adjustable to permit variation in height of the cabin floor from the ground. Low-pressure tubeless tyres on all units, pressure 50-57 lb/sq in (3·5-4 kg/cm²).

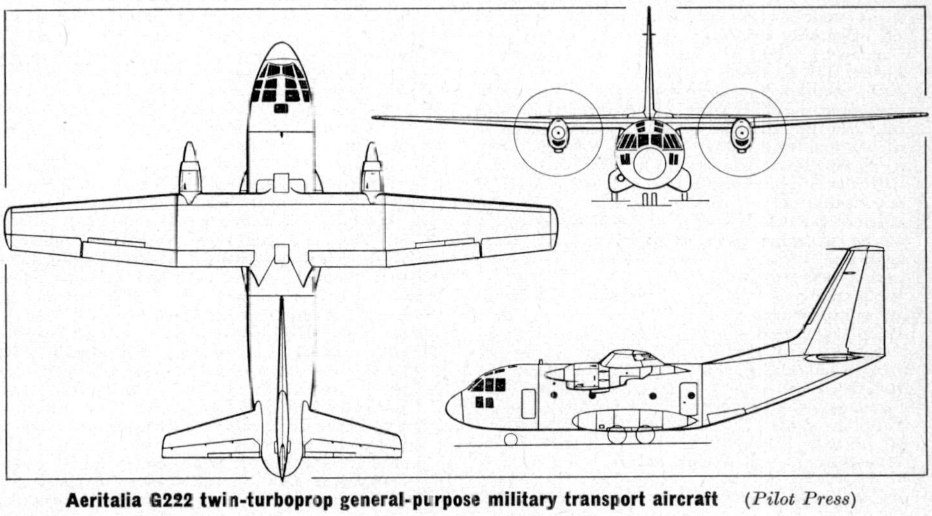

Aeritalia G222 twin-turboprop general-purpose military transport aircraft (*Pilot Press*)

A prototype of the Aeritalia G222 military transport aircraft ordered by the Italian Air Force (two 3,400 shp General Electric T64 turboprop engines)

Hydraulic multi-disc brakes. No anti-skid units.

POWER PLANT: Two 3,400 shp Fiat-built General Electric T64/P4D turboprop engines, each driving a Hamilton Standard 63E60 three-blade variable-pitch metal propeller. Provision in fuselage for eight Aerojet General JATO rockets with total additional thrust of 7,937 lb (3,600 kg) for T-O with extra-heavy loads. Fuel in two outer-wing main tanks, total capacity 1,495 Imp gallons (6,800 litres) and two centre-section auxiliary tanks, total capacity 1,143 Imp gallons (5,200 litres). Total overall fuel capacity 2,638 Imp gallons (12,000 litres).

ACCOMMODATION: Crew of three (two pilots and wireless operator/flight engineer) or four on flight deck. Standard seating for 44 fully-equipped troops or 32 paratroops. Alternative payloads include 36 stretcher patients and eight medical attendants or sitting casualties; or freight. Typical Italian military equipment loads can include two CL-52 light trucks, one CL-52 with a 105 mm L4 howitzer or one-ton trailer, Fiat AR-59 Campagnola reconnaissance vehicle with 106 mm recoil-less gun or 550 lb (250 kg) trailer, or five standard A-22 freight containers. In the ambulance role a second toilet can be installed, and provision can be made to increase the water supply and to install supplementary electrical points and hooks for medical treatment bottles. In the freight role a 3,306 lb (1,500 kg) capacity cargo hoist can be installed, and there is provision for up to 135 cargo tie-down points. Crew door forward of cabin on port side. Doors at front and rear of main cabin on starboard side and at rear on port side. Underside of upswept rear fuselage lowers to form loading ramp, which can be opened in flight for air-drop operations. Provision is made for pressurisation of cabin in production aircraft, but prototypes have air-conditioning only.

SYSTEMS: Starboard main landing gear fairing houses a 152 hp Garrett AiResearch APU for engine starting, hydraulic pump and alternator actuation. Two hydraulic systems, the primary system actuating the flying controls and the secondary system the landing gear, brakes, part of the flying control system and the auxiliaries. Emergency system, fed by APU, can take over from secondary system in flight. Standby hand pump for emergency use to lower landing gear and, on the ground, for propellers and parking brakes.

ELECTRONICS AND EQUIPMENT: Navigation equipment includes inertial PHI system with 12 pre-selectable stations, Doppler, two-axis gyro platform, VOR/ILS, TACAN, radio direction finder, DME, marker beacon, weather radar with secondary navigation capability, radar altimeter and ATC/IFF. Provision for installing head-up display. Communications equipment includes a 3,500-channel UHF/AM radio, a three-channel emergency UHF/AM radio with 1,630 channels, a 930-channel VHF/FM set usable as a direction finder, a 28,000-channel HF/AM SSB CW set, and an intercom acting as mixer and amplifier for all other systems.

DIMENSIONS, EXTERNAL:

Wing span	94 ft 6 in (28·80 m)
Wing aspect ratio	9·15
Wing chord at root	11 ft 1⅛ in (3·40 m)
Wing chord at tip	5 ft 6¼ in (1·685 m)
Length overall	74 ft 5½ in (22·70 m)
Height overall	32 ft 1¾ in (9·80 m)
Fuselage: Max diameter	11 ft 7¾ in (3·55 m)
Tailplane span	40 ft 8¼ in (12·40 m)
Wheel track	12 ft 0½ in (3·67 m)
Wheelbase (to c/l of main units)	20 ft 5½ in (6·235 m)
Propeller diameter	14 ft 6 in (4·42 m)
Distance between propeller centres	31 ft 2 in (9·50 m)

DIMENSIONS, INTERNAL:

Main cabin:	
Length	28 ft 1¾ in (8·58 m)
Width	8 ft 0½ in (2·45 m)
Height	7 ft 4½ in (2·25 m)
Volume	2,613 cu ft (74·0 m³)

AREAS:

Wings, gross	882·6 sq ft (82·00 m²)
Ailerons (total)	39·29 sq ft (3·65 m²)
Trailing-edge flaps (total)	198·06 sq ft (18·40 m²)
Spoilers (total)	17·76 sq ft (1·65 m²)
Vertical tail surfaces (total)	206·67 sq ft (19·21 m²)
Horizontal tail surfaces (total)	255·11 sq ft (23·70 m²)

WEIGHTS AND LOADINGS:

Weight empty	32,165 lb (14,590 kg)
Weight empty, equipped	33,950 lb (15,400 kg)
Max payload	19,840 lb (9,000 kg)
Normal T-O weight	54,013 lb (24,500 kg)
Max T-O weight	58,422 lb (26,500 kg)
Max zero-fuel weight	53,792 lb (24,400 kg)
Max landing weight	58,422 lb (26,500 kg)
Max wing loading	66·2 lb/sq ft (323 kg/m²)
Max cargo floor loading	155 lb/sq ft (750 kg/m²)
Max power loading	8·6 lb/shp (3·9 kg/shp)

PERFORMANCE (at max T-O weight except where indicated):

Max level speed at 15,000 ft (4,575 m)	291 knots (336 mph; 540 km/h)
Cruising speed at 14,750 ft (4,500 m)	194 knots (224 mph; 360 km/h)
Minimum speed	84 knots (96·5 mph; 155 km/h)
Time to 14,750 ft (4,500 m)	8 min 35 sec
Max rate of climb at S/L	2,034 ft (620 m)/min
Rate of climb at S/L, one engine out	410 ft (125 m)/min
Service ceiling	29,525 ft (9,000 m)
T-O run	1,720 ft (525 m)
T-O to 50 ft (15 m)	2,707 ft (825 m)
Landing from 50 ft (15 m)	2,362 ft (720 m)
Landing run at max landing weight	1,444 ft (440 m)
Accelerate-stop distance	3,937 ft (1,200 m)
Min ground turning radius	68 ft 3 in (20·80 m)
Basic mission range with 11,025 lb (5,000 kg) payload	1,591 nm (1,833 miles; 2,950 km)
Ferry range with max fuel	2,670 nm (3,075 miles; 4,950 km)

AERITALIA (LOCKHEED) F-104S

The first of two Lockheed-built F-104S prototypes flew during December 1966. Aeritalia is building 205 under licence for the Italian Air Force, of which the first was flown on 30 December 1968. Deliveries began in the Spring of 1969 and are due to be completed by February 1976.

A programme to modernise the R21G radar system of the F-104S was announced in the Spring of 1974. The improved installation, which will be built under licence by CGE-Fiar in Italy, will incorporate a moving-target indication and tracking capability based upon a Rockwell Missile Systems Division moving-target detection processor which was due to be tested during 1974. CGE-Fiar has itself developed an improved antenna and a number of ECCM (electronic counter-countermeasures) features.

TYPE: Single-seat multi-purpose combat aircraft.

WINGS: Cantilever mid-wing monoplane. Biconvex supersonic wing section with a thickness/chord ratio of 3·36%. Anhedral 10°. No incidence. Sweepback 18° 6′ at quarter-chord. Leading-edge nose radius of 0·016 in (0·041 cm) and razor-sharp trailing-edge. All-metal structure with two main spars, 12 spanwise intermediate channels between spars and top and bottom one-piece skin panels, tapering from thickness of 0·25 in (6·3 mm) at root to 0·125 in (3·2 mm) at tip. Each half-wing measures 7 ft 7 in (2·31 m) from root to tip and is a separate structure cantilevered from five forged frames in fuselage. Full-span electrically-actuated drooping leading-edge. Entire trailing-edge hinged, with inboard sections serving as landing flaps and outboard sections as ailerons. Ailerons are of aluminium, each powered by a servo control system which is irreversible and hydraulically powered, and each actuated by ten small hydraulic cylinders. Trim control is applied to position the aileron relative to the servo control position. An electric actuator positions the aileron trim. Flaps are of aluminium, actuated electrically. Above each flap is the air delivery tube of a boundary layer control system, which ejects air bled from the engine compressor over the entire flap span when the flaps are lowered to the landing position.

FUSELAGE: All-metal monocoque structure. Hydraulically-operated aluminium airbrake on each side of rear fuselage.

TAIL UNIT: T-type cantilever unit with "all-flying" one-piece horizontal tail surface hinged at mid-chord point at top of the sweptback vertical fin and powered by a hydraulic servo. Tailplane has similar profile to wing and is all-metal. Rudder is fully powered by a hydraulic servo. Trim control is applied to position the tailplane relative to the servo control position, by means of an electric actuator. Rudder trim is operated by an electric actuator located in the fin. The rudder itself is trimmed in the same way as the tailplane. Narrow-chord ventral fin on centre-line and two smaller lateral fins under fuselage to improve stability.

LANDING GEAR: Retractable tricycle type with Dowty patent liquid-spring shock-absorbers. Hydraulic actuation. Main wheels raised in and forward. Steerable nosewheel retracts forward into fuselage. Main-wheel legs are hinged on oblique axes so that the wheels lie flush within the fuselage when retracted. Main wheels size 26 × 8·0, with Goodrich tyres size 26 × 8·0 type VIII, pressure 173 lb/sq in (12·16 kg/cm²). Nosewheel tyre size 18 × 5·5 type VII. Bendix hydraulic disc brakes with Goodyear anti-skid units. Arrester hook under rear of fuselage.

POWER PLANT: One General Electric J79-GE-19 turbojet engine (17,900 lb; 8,120 kg st with afterburning). Electrical de-icing elements fitted to air intakes. Most of the aircraft's hydraulic equipment mounted inside large engine bay door under fuselage to facilitate servicing. Internal fuel in five bag-type fuselage tanks with total standard capacity of 896 US gallons (3,392 litres). Provision for external fuel in two 195 US gallon (740 litre) pylon tanks and two 170 US gallon (645 litre) wingtip tanks. Pressure refuelling of all internal and external tanks through single point on upper port fuselage just forward of air intake duct. Gravity fuelling point for internal tanks aft of pressure refuelling point, with individual gravity fuelling of external tanks. In-flight refuelling can be provided through Lockheed-designed probe-drogue system. Probe, mounted below port sill of cockpit, is removable but when installed is non-retractable. Oil capacity 4 US gallons (15 litres).

ACCOMMODATION: Pressurised and air-conditioned cockpit well forward of wings. Canopy hinged to starboard for access. Lockheed Model C-2 ejection seat.

SYSTEMS: Air-conditioning package by AiResearch, using engine bleed air. Pressure differential 5 lb/sq in (0·35 kg/cm²). Two completely separate hydraulic systems, using engine-driven pumps operating at 3,000 lb/sq in (210 kg/cm²). No. 1 system operates one side of tailplane, rudder and ailerons, also the automatic pitch control actuator and autopilot actuators. No. 2 system operates other half of tailplane, rudder and ailerons, also the landing gear, wheel brakes, airbrakes, nosewheel steering and constant-frequency electrical generator. Emergency ram-air turbine supplies emergency hydraulic pump and 4·5kVA 115/200V electric generator. Electrical system supplied by two engine-driven 20kVA 115/200V variable-frequency (320-520Hz) generators. Constant-speed hydraulic motor drives 2·5kVA 115/200V generator to supply fixed-frequency AC. DC power supplied by two batteries and an inverter.

ARMAMENT: Nine external attachment points, at wingtips, under wings and under fuselage, for bombs, rocket pods, auxiliary fuel tanks and Sidewinder air-to-air missiles. Normal primary armament consists of Raytheon Sparrow III air-to-air missiles and permanently-installed M-61 20 mm rotary cannon in port underside of fuselage. Provision for two Sidewinders under fuselage and either a Sidewinder or 170 US gallon (645 litre) fuel tank on each wingtip.

ELECTRONICS AND EQUIPMENT: Integrated electronics system in which various communications and navigation components may be installed as a series of interconnecting but self-sustaining units which may be varied to provide for different specific missions. Equipment includes autopilot with "stick steering", which includes modes for pre-selecting and holding altitude, speed, heading and constant rate of turn; multi-purpose NASARR R21G radar; fixed-reticle gunsight; bombing computer; air data computer; dead reckoning navigation device; TACAN radio air navigation system; provision for data link-time division set and UHF radio; lightweight fully-automatic inertial navigation system; and provision for fitting a camera pod under the fuselage for reconnaissance duties.

DIMENSIONS, EXTERNAL:

Wing span without tip-tanks	21 ft 11 in (6·68 m)
Wing chord (mean)	9 ft 6·6 in (2·91 m)
Wing aspect ratio	2·45
Length overall	54 ft 9 in (16·69 m)
Length of fuselage	51 ft 3 in (15·62 m)
Height overall	13 ft 6 in (4·11 m)
Tailplane span	11 ft 11 in (3·63 m)
Wheel track	8 ft 10¾ in (2·71 m)
Wheelbase	15 ft 0½ in (4·59 m)

AREAS:

Wings, gross	196·1 sq ft (18·22 m²)
Ailerons (total)	9·2 sq ft (0·85 m²)
Trailing-edge flaps (total)	22·7 sq ft (2·11 m²)
Leading-edge flaps (total)	16·2 sq ft (1·51 m²)
Airbrakes (total)	8·25 sq ft (0·77 m²)
Fin	37·7 sq ft (3·50 m²)
Ventral fin (centreline)	5·9 sq ft (0·55 m²)
Rudder, including tab	5·5 sq ft (0·51 m²)
Tailplane	48·2 sq ft (4·48 m²)

WEIGHTS AND LOADING:

Weight empty	14,900 lb (6,760 kg)
T-O weight (clean)	21,690 lb (9,840 kg)
Max T-O weight	31,000 lb (14,060 kg)
Max wing loading	110·7 lb/sq ft (540 kg/m²)

PERFORMANCE (at 21,690 lb; 9,840 kg AUW):

Max never-exceed speed — Mach 2·2

Max level speed at 36,000 ft (11,000 m) Mach 2·2 (1,259 knots; 1,450 mph; 2,330 km/h)

Max level speed at S/L Mach 1·2 (790 knots; 910 mph; 1,464 km/h)

Max cruising speed at 36,000 ft (11,000 m) 530 knots (610 mph; 981 km/h)

Econ cruising speed — Mach 0·85

Service ceiling — 58,000 ft (17,680 m)

Zoom altitude — over 90,000 ft (27,400 m)

Time to accelerate from Mach 0·92 to Mach 2·0 — 2 min

Time to climb to 35,000 ft (10,670 m) — 1 min 20 sec

Time to climb to 56,000 ft (17,070 m) — 2 min 40 sec

Radius with max fuel 673 nm (775 miles; 1,247 km)

Ferry range (excluding flight refuelling) 1,576 nm (1,815 miles; 2,920 km)

AERITALIA AM.3C

The AM.3C (originally M.B.335) is a three/four-seat monoplane designed to meet an Italian Air Force requirement. Development was undertaken jointly by Aerfer (now part of Aeritalia) and Aeronautica Macchi SpA, and it utilises the basic wing of the Aermacchi-Lockheed AL.60. Duties for which it is suitable include forward air control, observation, liaison, transport of passengers and cargo, casualty evacuation, tactical support of ground forces and general duties.

The first of three AM.3 prototypes (assembled at Varese by Aermacchi) flew for the first time on 12 May 1967, followed by the second (assembled by Aerfer) on 22 August 1968. A third airframe was built for static testing.

The two flying prototypes were each powered originally by a 340 hp Continental GTSIO-520-C engine, in which form they were described in the 1969-70 *Jane's*. In 1969 both were refitted with Lycoming GSO-480-B1B6 engines, in which form the aircraft is designated AM.3C.

During 1970 the AM.3C was successfully evaluated by the Italian Army, and evaluation was also carried out at Eglin AFB in the US in 1971, in connection with the USAF's Pave Coin programme for a forward air control aircraft. Beech Aircraft Corporation has retained rights to build the AM.3C under licence in the US.

The AM.3C is now in production by Aeritalia, to meet orders from the South African Air Force (40) and the Rwanda Air Force (3). Delivery of these began in mid-1973 and February 1974 respectively. In the Spring of 1974 negotiations to finalise a firm order with the Italian Army Aviation were under way.

TYPE: Three/four-seat general-purpose monoplane.

WINGS: Strut-braced high-wing monoplane, with one bracing strut each side. Wing section NACA 23016 at root, NACA 4412 at tip. Dihedral 2°. Incidence 1° at root, —1° 54′ at tip. All-metal D-spar torsion-box structure. All-metal piano-hinged ailerons. Manually-operated Fowler flaps of all-metal two-spar construction.

FUSELAGE: Welded chrome-molybdenum steel-tube centre fuselage structure, covered with light alloy skin at front, but with much of the cabin covered with glassfibre-reinforced plastics panels. Light alloy semi-monocoque rear fuselage, attached to centre portion at three points for easy removal.

TAIL UNIT: Conventional cantilever all-metal structure. Variable-incidence tailplane for trimming. Spring tab in rudder.

LANDING GEAR: Non-retractable tailwheel type. Each main leg consists of a tubular strut hinged to lower side of fuselage, with oleo-pneumatic shock-absorber between top of strut and wing-strut pickup point on fuselage. Cast light alloy main wheels, each fitted with a size 6·50-8 4PR type III tyre, pressure 24 lb/sq in (1·69 kg/cm²). Steerable tailwheel, with oleo-pneumatic shock-absorber. Tailwheel tyre size 10·00-6PR type I, pressure 30 lb/sq in (2·11 kg/cm²). Single-disc hydraulic brakes. Provision for fitting floats or Fluidyne Fli-lite MK3000 hydraulically-actuated main wheel-skis and tail ski.

POWER PLANT: One 340 hp Piaggio-built Lycoming GSO-480-B1B6 six-cylinder horizontally-opposed aircooled engine, driving a Piaggio P1033-G4-AD/0691/245 three-blade metal propeller. Two light alloy fuel tanks in each wing, near root. Total fuel capacity 52·5 Imp gallons (238 litres).

ACCOMMODATION: Normal accommodation for two persons in tandem, with dual controls. Provision at rear for two stretchers (one above the other), a rear seat for one or two persons, or freight in place of rear seat. Forward-hinged door by pilot's seat. Large upward-hinged door immediately aft of pilot's door, to open up entire starboard side of cabin. Third door on port side.

ELECTRONICS AND EQUIPMENT: Blind-flying instrumentation standard, also ARINC 546 680-channel VHF transceiver, Collins AN/ARC-54 800-channel VHF-FM transceiver with homing group, AN/ARN-83 ADF, and RMI.

ARMAMENT: Standard version has two underwing pylons, each capable of carrying up to 375 lb (170 kg) of external stores, including a Matra pod containing two 7·62 mm machine-guns and 2,000 rounds of ammunition, a General Electric Minigun pod and 1,500 rounds of ammunition, a Matra 125 pack of six 2·75 in rockets, a Matra 122 pack of seven BPD 50 mm rockets, a 113 kg GP bomb, an AN/M1A2 cluster of six 9 kg fragmentation bombs, an AN/M4A1 cluster of three 10 kg parachute-retarded fragmentation bombs, an M28A2 cluster of twenty-four 2 kg "butterfly" bombs, an AS.11 or AS.12 wire-guided missile, an M84A1 target marker, an M46 photoflash or M26A1 parachute flare, or a 250 lb supply container. Alternatively, a Vinten 70 mm automatic three-camera reconnaissance pack can be carried under the fuselage; or two 70 mm cameras or a three-lens CA-103 camera can be carried inside the fuselage.

DIMENSIONS, EXTERNAL:

Wing span	38 ft 6 in (11·73 m)
Wing chord at root	5 ft 8 in (1·73 m)
Wing chord at tip	4 ft 2½ in (1·28 m)
Wing aspect ratio	7·2
Length overall	28 ft 8 in (8·73 m)

Aeritalia AM.3C (340 hp Lycoming GSO-480-B1B6 engine), ordered by the air forces of South Africa and Rwanda

Aeritalia-built Lockheed F-104S combat aircraft of the Italian Air Force (17,900 lb st General Electric J79-GE-19 turbojet engine)

Height overall (tail down) 8 ft 11 in (2·72 m)
Tailplane span 14 ft 11 in (4·55 m)
Wheel track 8 ft 7 in (2·62 m)
Propeller ground clearance 2 ft 3¼ in (0·695 m)
Pilot's door (starboard):
Mean height 3 ft 1½ in (0·95 m)
Max width 2 ft 1¼ in (0·64 m)
Rear door (starboard):
Height 2 ft 10¾ in (0·88 m)
Max width 5 ft 10¾ in (1·80 m)
Dimensions, internal:
Cabin: Length 8 ft 2 in (2·50 m)
Max width 2 ft 8 in (0·81 m)
Max height 5 ft 3 in (1·60 m)
Areas:
Ailerons (total) 28·20 sq ft (2·62 m^2)
Trailing-edge flaps (total) 40·58 sq ft (3·77 m^2)
Fin, incl dorsal fin 17·44 sq ft (1·62 m^2)
Rudder 10·12 sq ft (0·94 m^2)
Tailplane 59·31 sq ft (5·51 m^2)
Elevators, incl tabs 19·91 sq ft (1·85 m^2)
Weights and Loadings:
Weight empty 2,380 lb (1,080 kg)
Normal T-O weight (2 crew only) 3,306 lb (1,500 kg)
Max T-O weight (underwing weapons) 3,750 lb (1,700 kg)
Max wing loading 18·3 lb/sq ft (89·3 kg/m^2)
Max power loading 11·0 lb/hp (5·00 kg/hp)
Performance (at normal T-O weight):
Max level speed at 8,000 ft (2,440 m) 150 knots (173 mph; 278 km/h)
Max level speed at S/L 141 knots (162 mph; 260 km/h)
Max cruising speed (75% power) at 8,000 ft (2,440 m) 133 knots (153 mph; 246 km/h)
Max rate of climb at S/L 1,378 ft (420 m)/min
Service ceiling 27,550 ft (8,400 m)

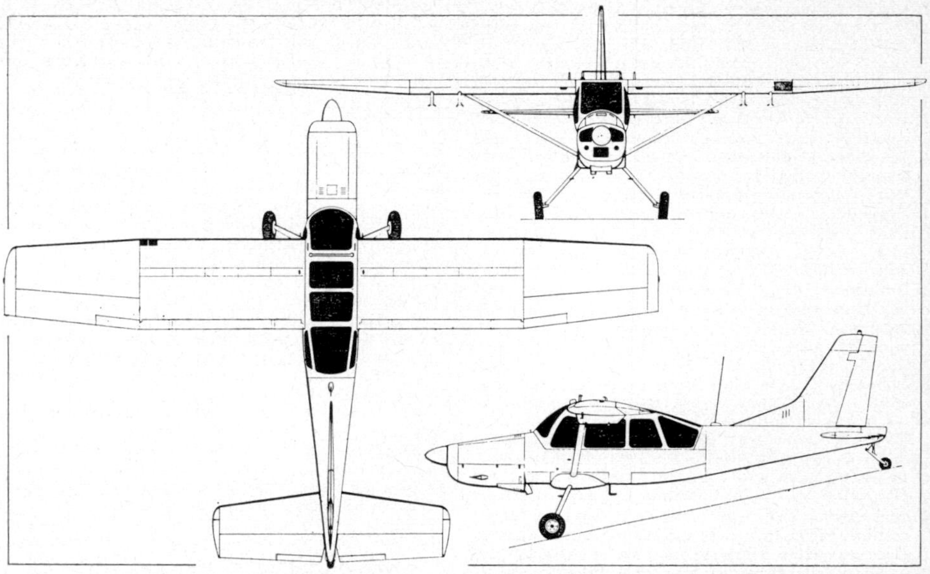

Aeritalia AM.3C three/four-seat general-purpose military aircraft (*Pilot Press*)

T-O run 280 ft (85 m)
T-O to 50 ft (15 m) 558 ft (170 m)
Landing from 50 ft (15 m) 571 ft (174 m)
Landing run 217 ft (66 m)
Max range at 5,000 ft (1,525 m), 30 min reserves 534 nm (615 miles; 990 km)
Endurance at 5,000 ft (1,525 m), 30 min reserves 5 hr 45 min

AERMACCHI

AERONAUTICA MACCHI SpA

Head Office:
Corso Vittorio Emanuele 15, Milan
Offices and Works:
Via Sanvito Silvestro 80, Casella Postale 246, 21100 Varese
Telephone: (0332) 283100
Telex: 38070 Aviomacc
President:
Dott Ing Paolo Foresio
General Managers:
Dott Ing Ermanno Bazzocchi
Dott Fabrizio Foresio
Technical Director:
Dott Ing Alberto Notari
Sales Manager:
Dott Ing Gianni Cattaneo
Press and Public Relations:
Giorgio Apostolo

The Macchi company was founded in 1912 in Varese and its first aeroplane was built in 1913. In addition to its former factory area of 397,200 sq ft (36,900 m^2), a new plant is under construction on Venegono airfield, and about 145,310 sq ft (13,500 m^2) of covered assembly line area was due to be completed in the Autumn of 1974. Aermacchi had about 1,700 employees in 1974.

Lockheed Aircraft International acquired a substantial minority interest in Aermacchi in December 1959, and Aermacchi subsequently built the Lockheed 60 light utility transport as the Aermacchi-Lockheed AL.60. In current production are various single- and two-seat versions of Aermacchi's own design, the M.B. 326.

Also in production, in association with Aeritalia, is the AM.3C military AOP and liaison monoplane, described under the Aeritalia heading.

Aermacchi M.B. 326GB ground attack/training aircraft in the insignia of the Zambian Air Force

AERMACCHI M.B. 326

The first prototype of the original Aermacchi M.B. 326 jet trainer flew for the first time on 10 December 1957, powered by a Rolls-Royce Bristol Viper 8 turbojet engine. The more powerful Viper 11 engine is fitted in the six production versions of the aircraft built for the air forces of Italy (M.B. 326), Tunisia (M.B. 326B), Ghana (M.B. 326F), Australia (M.B. 326H) and South Africa (M.B. 326M), and for Alitalia (M.B. 326D). Of these versions, which have been described in previous editions of *Jane's*, only the M.B. 326M remains in production, by Atlas Aircraft Corporation in South Africa (which see). The South African Air Force version is known as the **Impala.**

Later versions, with more powerful Viper engines, armament and other modifications, are the M.B. 326GB, GC, K and L. These are described separately.

AERMACCHI M.B. 326GB and M.B. 326GC

These dual-role training and counter-insurgency attack versions of the M.B. 326 differ from other versions primarily in having a more powerful Viper turbojet engine. The prototype M.B. 326G flew for the first time in the Spring of 1967, and the similar M.B. 326GB is now in production.

Eight have been ordered by the Argentine Navy, 17 by the air force of the Zaïre Republic and 20 by the Zambian Air Force. In addition, 112 M.B. 326GC are being assembled in Brazil under licence by EMBRAER (which see) for the Brazilian Air Force, as the **AT-26 Xavante.**

The following description applies to both the M.B. 326G and M.B. 326GB:

Type: Two-seat basic trainer and tactical ground attack aircraft.

Wings: Cantilever low/mid-wing monoplane. Wing section NACA 6A series (modified). Thickness/chord ratio 13·7% at root, 12% at tip. Dihedral 2° 55′. Incidence 2° 30′. All-metal two-spar stressed-skin structure in three sections, of which the centre-section is integral with the fuselage. Single fence on each wing at approx two-thirds span. Manually-operated all-metal ailerons and hydraulically-operated slotted flaps. Electrically-actuated balance and trim tab in port aileron. Geared balance tab in starboard aileron.

Fuselage: All-metal semi-monocoque structure. Hydraulically-operated airbrake under centre-fuselage.

Tail Unit: Cantilever all-metal structure. Electrically-actuated trim tab in rudder and each elevator.

Landing Gear: Hydraulically-retractable tricycle type, with oleo-pneumatic shock-absorbers. Nosewheel retracts forward, main units outward into wings. Pirelli main wheels and tyres, size 6·50-10 (8-ply). Steerable and self-centering nosewheel with anti-shimmy device. Dunlop twin-contact nosewheel tyre, size 5·4·5. Hydraulic disc brakes.

Power Plant: One Rolls-Royce Bristol Viper 20 Mk 540 turbojet engine, rated at 3,410 lb (1,547 kg) st. Fuel in flexible rubber main tank in fuselage, capacity 172 Imp gallons (782 litres), and two 67 Imp gallon (305 litre) non-jettisonable wingtip tanks. Total standard fuel capacity 306 Imp gallons (1,392 litres). Provision for two 73 Imp gallon (332 litre) jettisonable underwing tanks, to give total capacity of 452 Imp gallons (2,056 litres). Single-point pressure refuelling receptacle under fuselage. Fuel dump valves permit quick emptying of tip-tanks.

Accommodation: Crew of two in tandem under a one-piece moulded Perspex canopy which hinges sideways to starboard. Pressurised cabin. Dual controls and instruments. Blind-flying screens for pupil. Martin-Baker Mk 04A lightweight ejection seats.

Systems: Air-conditioning and pressurisation system, differential 3 lb/sq in (0·21 kg/cm^2), uses air bled from engine compressor and incorporates turbo-refrigerator unit. Hydraulic system, pressure 2,500 lb/sq in (175 kg/cm^2), for landing gear and doors, flaps, airbrake and wheel brakes. Independent manually-operated hydraulic system for emergency landing gear extension. DC electrical supply from 30V 9kW starter/generator and two 24V 22Ah batteries. Fixed-frequency AC system powered by 750VA main inverter, with 250VA standby unit. 6kVA alternator supplies engine air intake anti-icing system and can feed primary electrical system, via transformer-rectifier, in event of DC generator failure.

Electronics and Equipment: To customer's specification. Standard configuration includes UHF transmitter-receiver type AN/ARC-51BX with 3,500 channels or 26 preset channels, auxiliary UHF system with 5-channel Collins 718B-8C transceiver, AN/AIC-18 interphone, AN/ARN-52(V) TACAN with USAF type AQU-4/A horizontal situation indicator, and AN/ARN-83 ADF, AN/ARA-50 UHF/DF, Collins 51RV-1 (ARINC 547) VOR/ILS and CPU-76/A flight director computer. Standard AN/APX-72 IFF transponder can be replaced by Bendix-FIAR TRA-62A, AN/APX-68 or AN/APX-77 IFF/SIF system.

ARMAMENT (optional): Up to 4,000 lb (1,814 kg) of armament can be carried on six underwing attachments. Typical weapon loads include following alternatives: two LAU-3/A packs each containing nineteen 2·75 in FFAR rockets and two packs each containing eight Hispano-Suiza SURA 80 mm rockets; two 12·7 mm gun pods and four packs each containing six SURA 80 mm rockets; one 7·62 mm Minigun, one 12·7 mm gun pod, two Matra 122 rocket packs and two packs each containing six SURA 80 mm rockets; two 500 lb bombs and eight 5 in HVAR rockets; two AS.12 missiles; one 12·7 mm gun pod, one reconnaissance pack containing four Vinten cameras and two 600 lb (272 kg) drop-tanks, or two Matra SA-10 packs each containing a 30 mm Aden gun and 150 rounds. SFOM type 83 fixed gunsight or Ferranti LFS 5/102A gyro-sight. Gun camera in nose.

DIMENSIONS, EXTERNAL:
- Wing span over tip-tanks: 35 ft 7 in (10·85 m)
- Wing chord at root: 7 ft 11½ in (2·43 m)
- Wing chord at tip: 4 ft 7·1 in (1·40 m)
- Wing aspect ratio: 6·08
- Length overall: 34 ft 11 in (10·64 m)
- Height overall: 12 ft 2½ in (3·72 m)
- Tailplane span: 13 ft 4½ in (4·08 m)
- Wheel track: 7 ft 9¼ in (2·37 m)
- Wheelbase: 13 ft 7¼ in (4·15 m)

AREAS:
- Wings, gross: 208·3 sq ft (19·35 m²)
- Ailerons (total): 14·3 sq ft (1·33 m²)
- Trailing-edge flaps (total): 27·5 sq ft (2·55 m²)
- Fin: 16·7 sq ft (1·55 m²)
- Rudder, incl tab: 7·6 sq ft (0·71 m²)
- Tailplane: 28·2 sq ft (2·62 m²)
- Elevators, incl tabs: 9·5 sq ft (0·88 m²)

WEIGHTS (T: Trainer; A: Attack):
- Basic operating weight, excluding crew:
  - T: 5,920 lb (2,685 kg)
  - *A: 5,640 lb (2,558 kg)
- Max zero-fuel weight:
  - T: 6,280 lb (2,849 kg)
  - *A: 5,820 lb (2,640 kg)
- Max T-O weight (full internal fuel, wingtip and underwing tanks):
  - T: 10,090 lb (4,577 kg)
  - A, no armament: 9,805 lb (4,447 kg)
  - A, with 1,695 lb (769 kg) armament: 11,500 lb (5,216 kg)
- Max T-O weight (max armament):
  - *A, with fuel in fuselage tank only and 4,325 lb (1,962 kg) armament: 11,500 lb (5,216 kg)
- Max wing loading: 55·2 lb/sq ft (269·5 kg/m²)
- Max power loading: 3·37 lb/lb st (3·37 kg/kg st)

*** Without tip-tanks and aft ejection seat**

PERFORMANCE (T: Trainer at typical weight of 8,680 lb (3,937 kg), representing max T-O weight without underwing tanks; AC: Attack version at combat weight of 10,500 lb (4,763 kg); AM: Attack version at max T-O weight):
- Max never-exceed speed:
  - T: Mach 0·82 or 469 knots (541 mph; 871 km/h) EAS
  - AC: Mach 0·75 or 419 knots (483 mph; 778 km/h) EAS
- Max level speed:
  - T: 468 knots (539 mph; 867 km/h)
- Max cruising speed:
  - T: 430 knots (495 mph; 797 km/h)
- Max rate of climb at S/L:
  - T: 6,050 ft (1,844 m)/min
  - AC: 3,550 ft (1,082 m)/min
  - AM: 3,100 ft (945 m)/min
- Time to 10,000 ft (3,050 m):
  - AC: 3 min 10 sec
  - AM: 4 min 0 sec
- Time to 20,000 ft (6,100 m):
  - T: 4 min 10 sec
  - AC: 8 min 0 sec
  - AM: 9 min 20 sec
- Time to 30,000 ft (9,150 m):
  - T: 7 min 40 sec
  - AC: 15 min 0 sec
  - AM: 18 min 40 sec
- Time to 40,000 ft (12,200 m):
  - T: 13 min 5 sec
- Service ceiling:
  - T: 47,000 ft (14,325 m)
  - AC: 39,000 ft (11,900 m)
- T-O run, ISA:
  - T: 1,350 ft (412 m)
  - AC: 2,100 ft (640 m)
  - AM: 2,770 ft (845 m)
- T-O run, ISA + 25°C:
  - T: 1,660 ft (506 m)
  - AC: 2,640 ft (805 m)
  - AM: 3,280 ft (1,000 m)
- T-O to 50 ft (15 m), ISA:
  - T: 1,820 ft (555 m)
  - AC: 2,840 ft (866 m)
  - AM: 3,740 ft (1,140 m)
- T-O to 50 ft (15 m), ISA + 25°C:
  - T: 2,310 ft (704 m)
  - AC: 3,650 ft (1,113 m)
  - AM: 4,630 ft (1,411 m)
- Landing from 50 ft (15 m), ISA:
  - T at landing weight of 7,000 lb (3,175 kg): 2,070 ft (631 m)
  - AC at landing weight of 9,250 lb (4,195 kg): 2,630 ft (802 m)
- Landing from 50 ft (15 m), ISA + 25°C:
  - T at landing weight of 7,000 lb (3,175 kg): 2,200 ft (671 m)
  - AC at landing weight of 9,250 lb (4,195 kg): 2,810 ft (857 m)
- Range (T, with 25 Imp gallons; 113 litres reserve):
  - fuselage and tip-tanks: 998 nm (1,150 miles; 1,850 km)
  - fuselage, tip and underwing tanks: 1,320 nm (1,520 miles; 2,445 km)
- Combat radius (A at max AUW):
  - max fuel, 1,695 lb (769 kg) armament, 200 lb (90 kg) fuel reserve, out at 20,000 ft (6,100 m), return at 25,000 ft (7,620 m): 350 nm (403 miles; 648 km)
  - fuselage tank only, 4,000 lb (1,814 kg) armament, 200 lb (90 kg) fuel reserve, cruise at 10,000 ft (3,050 m), five minutes over target: 69 nm (80 miles; 130 km)
  - max fuel, 1,700 lb (771 kg) armament, 200 lb (90 kg) fuel reserve, cruise at 10,000 ft (3,050 m), 1 hr 50 min patrol at 500 ft (150 m) over target: 49·5 nm (57 miles; 92 km)

AERMACCHI M.B. 326K

The M.B. 326K is a single-seat operational trainer and light ground attack aircraft developed from, and based upon the airframe of, the M.B. 326GB, and retaining most of the structure and systems of the latter aircraft.

Major differences in the M.B. 326K, compared with the M.B. 326GB, include the installation of a more powerful Rolls-Royce Bristol Viper 600 Series turbojet engine; deletion of the rear pilot's station; single-seat front cockpit, which is pressurised and has provision for armour protection from small-arms fire; and additional fuel tanks in the fuselage.

Combat capabilities are enhanced by the installation of two 30 mm cannon in the fuselage, and by increasing to six the number of underwing stations for bombs, rockets or additional fuel tanks.

Provision is made for complete instrumentation for navigation and armament delivery systems, and for self-sealing fuel tanks and armour protection for the pilot and vital engine and fuel system areas.

A prototype of the M.B. 326K (I-AMKK) flew for the first time on 22 August 1970, with a Viper 540 engine. It was followed in 1971 by a second prototype with a more powerful Viper 632 engine, and this version is now in production, an initial export order having been received from an undisclosed customer (reportedly South Africa).

TYPE: Single-seat operational trainer and light ground attack aircraft.

WINGS: As M.B. 326GB/GC, except for strengthened structure and hydraulically servo-powered ailerons. Hydraulically-operated single-slotted flaps.

FUSELAGE: As M.B. 326GB/GC.

TAIL UNIT: As M.B. 326GB/GC.

LANDING GEAR: As M.B. 326GB/GC, except for more powerful wheel brakes. Separate emergency extension system. Tyre pressure as max T-O weight 100 lb/sq in (7 kg/cm²). Dunlop high-capacity hydraulic disc brakes.

POWER PLANT: One 4,000 lb (1,814 kg) st Rolls-Royce Bristol Viper Mk 632-43 turbojet engine. Fuel in three rubber fuselage tanks and two permanent wingtip tanks, total usable capacity 440 US gallons (366 Imp gallons; 1,660 litres). Provision for installing self-sealing fuselage tanks and reticulated foam anti-explosive filling in all tanks, including those at wingtips. Two underwing stations equipped normally to carry jettisonable auxiliary tanks of up to 90 US gallons (75 Imp gallons; 340 litres) each. Single-point pressure refuelling receptacle and auxiliary gravity refuelling points.

ACCOMMODATION: Pilot on Martin-Baker WY-6A zero-zero rocket ejection seat in pressurised, heated and air-conditioned cockpit. Separately-controlled canopy jettison system provided, but seat is fitted with breakers to permit ejection through canopy in extreme emergency. Canopy hinges sideways to starboard.

SYSTEMS: All systems basically as M.B. 326GB/GC, except that pressurisation system operates at a differential of 3·5 lb/sq in (0·25 kg/m²), and hydraulic system operates through a self-regulating engine-driven pump to provide power for landing gear, flap, airbrake, aileron servo and wheel brake actuation.

ELECTRONICS AND EQUIPMENT: Variety of navigational and tactical equipment, to customer's specification, which can include main (3,500-channel) and standby (5-channel) UHF transceivers or two 680-channel VHF transceivers, TACAN, VOR/ILS and marker beacon, flight director computer with integrated instrumentation, ADF, UHF/DF, navigation computer and Doppler radar. Weapon-sighting equipment may range from a fixed reflector gunsight to a gyroscopic lead-computing sight, with provision to install a laser rangefinder and a bombing computer.

ARMAMENT AND OPERATIONAL EQUIPMENT: Standard fixed armament of two 30 mm DEFA electrically-operated cannon in lower front fuselage, with 125 rds/gun. Six underwing pylons, the inboard four stressed to carry up to 1,000 lb (454 kg) each and the outboard pair up to 750 lb (340 kg) each. Max external military load (with reduced fuel) is 4,000 lb (1,814 kg). Each pylon fitted with standard NATO 14 in (35·5 cm) MA-4A stores rack. Typical loads may include two 750 lb and four 500 lb bombs, four napalm containers, two AS.11 or AS.12 air-to-surface missiles, two machine-gun pods, two Matra 550 air-to-air missiles, six SUU-11A/A 7·62 mm Minigun pods, and various Matra or other launchers for 37 mm, 68 mm, 100 mm, 2·75 in or 5 in rockets. A four-camera tactical reconnaissance pod can be carried on the port inner pylon without affecting the weapon capability of the other five stations.

DIMENSIONS, EXTERNAL:
- Wing span over tip-tanks: 35 ft 7 in (10·85 m)
- Length overall: 34 ft 11 in (10·64 m)
- Height overall: 12 ft 2 in (3·71 m)
- Wheel track: 7 ft 7 in (2·31 m)
- Wheelbase: 13 ft 7 in (4·14 m)

AREAS: As M.B. 326GB except:
- Wings, gross: 208·3 sq ft (19·4 m²)

WEIGHTS AND LOADINGS:
- Weight empty, equipped: 6,240 lb (2,830 kg)
- Manufacturer's basic weight empty: 6,300 lb (2,857 kg)
- Operational weight empty: 6,500 lb (2,948 kg)
- T-O weight (clean): 9,680 lb (4,390 kg)
- Typical operational T-O weights:
  - patrol and visual reconnaissance: 11,130 lb (5,048 kg)
  - photographic reconnaissance: 11,270 lb (5,111 kg)

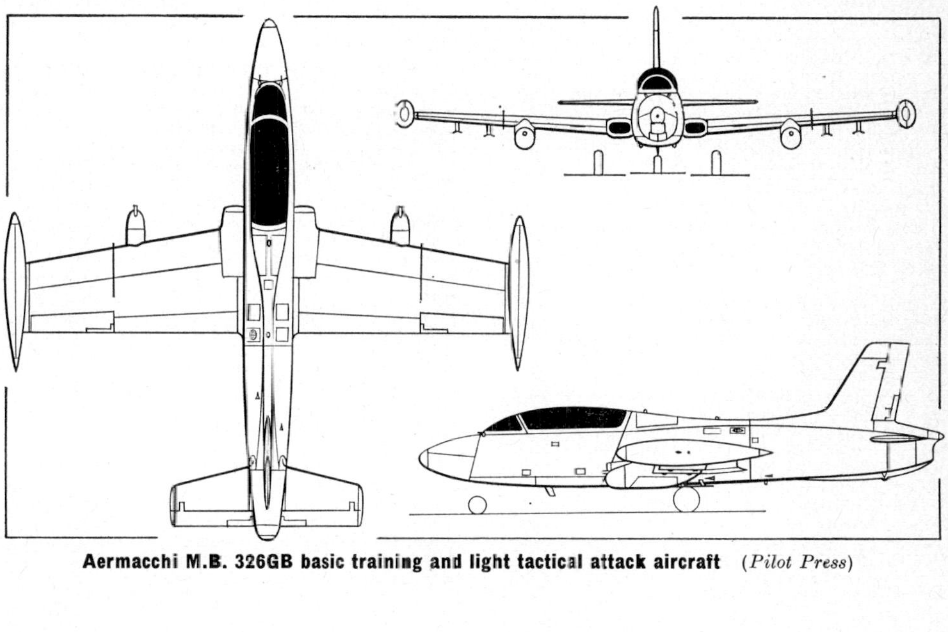

Aermacchi M.B. 326GB basic training and light tactical attack aircraft *(Pilot Press)*

Max T-O weight 12,500 lb (5,670 kg)
Max landing weight 12,000 lb (5,443 kg)
Normal design landing weight
10,000 lb (4,535 kg)
Max wing loading 59·8 lb/sq ft (292 kg/m²)
Max power loading 3·125 lb/lb st (3·125 kg/kg st)

PERFORMANCE (A: aircraft clean, at AUW of 9,680 lb; 4,390 kg; B: armed aircraft at 12,000 lb; 5,443 kg AUW):
Max design limit speed at S/L
500 knots (576 mph; 927 km/h) EAS
Max limiting Mach number 0·82
Max level speed at 5,000 ft (1,525 m):
A 480 knots (553 mph; 890 km/h) TAS
Max level speed at 30,000 ft (9,145 m):
B 370 knots (426 mph; 686 km/h) TAS
Stalling speed, flaps up:
A 102 knots (118 mph; 190 km/h) CAS
B 113 knots (131 mph; 211 km/h) CAS
Stalling speed, flaps down:
A 91 knots (105 mph; 169 km/h) CAS
B 102 knots (118 mph; 190 km/h) CAS
Max rate of climb at S/L:
A 6,500 ft (1,980 m)/min
B 3,750 ft (1,143 m)/min
Time to 35,000 ft (10,670 m):
A 9 min 30 sec
B 23 min 0 sec
Runway LCN at max T-O weight 5
T-O run, ISA:
A 1,350 ft (411 m)
B 2,200 ft (670 m)
T-O run, ISA+20°C:
A 1,700 ft (518 m)
B 2,675 ft (815 m)
T-O to 50 ft (15 m), ISA:
A 1,875 ft (572 m)
B 3,000 ft (914 m)
T-O to 50 ft (15 m), ISA+20°C:
A 2,325 ft (709 m)
B 3,800 ft (1,158 m)
Max rate of descent at touchdown:
at 10,000 lb (4,535 kg) AUW 10 ft (3·05 m)/sec
at 12,000 lb (5,443 kg) AUW 7 ft (2·13 m)/sec
Typical combat radius:
B (internal fuel and 2,822 lb; 1,280 kg external weapons), lo-lo-lo
145 nm (167 miles; 268 km)
B (reduced fuel and 4,000 lb; 1,814 kg external weapons), lo-lo-lo
70 nm (81 miles; 130 km)
visual reconnaissance with two external fuel tanks 400 nm (460 miles; 740 km)
photo reconnaissance with two auxiliary tanks and camera pod, hi-lo-hi
560 nm (644 miles; 1,036 km)
Max ferry range (two underwing tanks)
more than 1,149 nm (1,323 miles; 2,130 km)
g limits +7·33; —3·5

AERMACCHI M.B. 326L

This version of the M.B. 326 family, first announced in 1973, combines the modified airframe of the single-seat M.B. 326K with the standard two-seat cockpit installation, and is intended primarily for the advanced training role.

The description of the M.B. 326GB/GC applies also to the M.B. 326L, except in the following respects:

TYPE: Two-seat jet advanced trainer and tactical ground attack aircraft.

WINGS: As M.B. 326K, including servo-powered ailerons and increased flap extension speed.

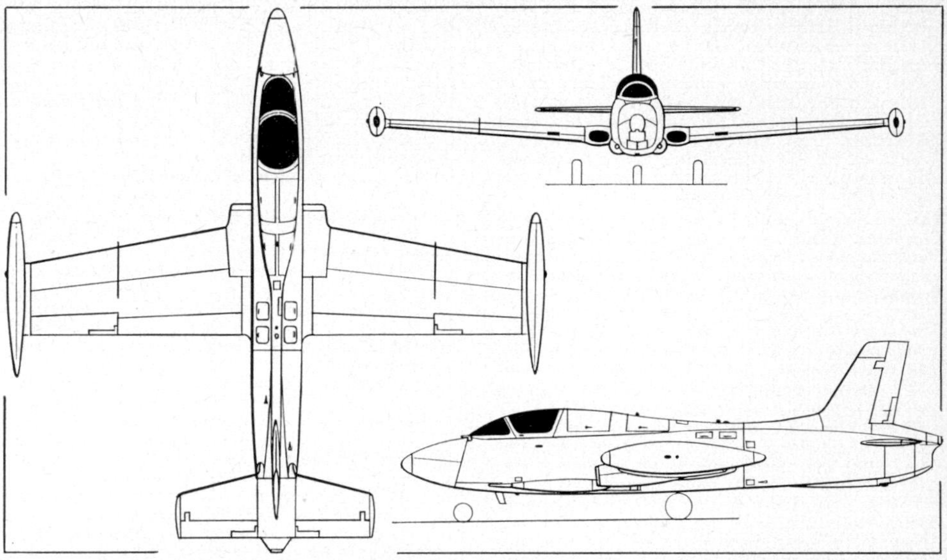

Three-view drawing and photograph of Aermacchi M.B. 326K single-seat light ground attack aircraft. The aircraft photographed is carrying underwing rocket pods and other stores

FUSELAGE AND TAIL UNIT: As M.B. 326GB/GC.

LANDING GEAR: As M.B. 326K, including more powerful wheel brakes.

POWER PLANT: As M.B. 326K. Fuel capacity as M.B. 326GB.

ACCOMMODATION: As M.B. 326GB/GC except for cockpit pressure differential of 3·5 lb/sq in (0·25 kg/cm²).

ELECTRONICS AND EQUIPMENT: As M.B. 326GB/GC, with options at customer's choice. Side cockpit consoles widened to provide space for additional equipment.

ARMAMENT, AND DIMENSIONS, EXTERNAL: As M.B. 326GB/GC.

WEIGHTS AND LOADINGS:
Weight empty, equipped 6,470 lb (2,934 kg)
T-O weight, training configuration
9,285 lb (4,211 kg)
Max T-O weight 12,000 lb (5,443 kg)
Max wing loading 57·3 lb/sq ft (280 kg/m²)
Max power loading 3·0 lb/lb st (3·0 kg/kg st)

PERFORMANCE (at training T-O weight):
Max level speed at S/L
485 knots (558 mph; 898 km/h)
Max level-flight Mach number at 36,000 ft (11,000 m) Mach 0·77
Max rate of climb at S/L
7,000 ft (2,134 m)/min
T-O run 1,360 ft (415 m)
T-O to 50 ft (15 m) 1,830 ft (558 m)

AERMACCHI/LOCKHEED AL.60F5 AND AL.60C5 CONESTOGA

Aermacchi acquired exclusive manufacturing rights, outside the United States, for the Lockheed 60 light utility transport. The first Aermacchi-built example flew on 19 April 1961, and 100 were built before production ended in 1972. The AL.60F5 and AL.60C5 were described and illustrated in the 1972-73 *Jane's*.

AGUSTA

COSTRUZIONI AERONAUTICHE GIOVANNI AGUSTA SpA

HEAD OFFICE AND WORKS:
Casella Postale 193, 21017 Cascina Costa, Gallarate
Telephone: (0331) 20 478
Telex: 31057

CHAIRMAN AND PRESIDENT:
Conte Corrado Agusta

DEPUTY CHAIRMAN:
Dott E. Marelli

PRESIDENT, CHIEF EXECUTIVE OFFICER:
Dott Ing P. Fascione

GENERAL MANAGERS:
Dott Ing M. Masini
Dott Ing G. Brazzelli

TECHNICAL DIRECTOR:
Dott Ing L. Passini

This company was established in 1907 by Giovanni Agusta and built many experimental and production aircraft before the second World War.

In 1952 Agusta acquired a licence to manufacture the Bell Model 47 helicopter and the first Agusta-built Model 47G made its maiden flight on 22 May 1954.

In addition to versions of the Model 47, Agusta is now producing under licence in Italy the Bell Iroquois Models UH-1B and UH-1D/H, as the Agusta-Bell 204B and 205 respectively, the twin-engined Model 212, and the light turbine-powered Model 206 JetRanger helicopter series. Under licence from Sikorsky, production of SH-3D helicopters began in 1967, and production of the HH-3F (S-61R) started in 1974. Agusta is also engaged, together with Meridionali, SIAI-Marchetti and other Italian companies, in quantity production under licence of the Boeing Vertol CH-47C Chinook helicopter (see Meridionali entry).

Details of these aircraft (except the Chinook) are given hereafter, together with descriptions of current helicopters designed by Agusta.

AGUSTA A 106

This aircraft programme has now been terminated. A full description and illustration of the A 106 appeared in the 1973-74 *Jane's*.

AGUSTA A 109 HIRUNDO (SWALLOW)

The Agusta A 109 is a high-speed, high-performance twin-engined helicopter. The basic version accommodates a pilot and seven passengers, and has a large baggage compartment in the rear of the fuselage. Alternatively, the Hirundo can be adapted for freight-carrying, as an ambulance, or for search and rescue. Military loads can also be carried, as indicated in the "Armament" paragraph. Five Hirundos, each armed with four TOW air-to-surface anti-tank missiles, were to be evaluated in this role by the Italian Army in mid-1974. Agusta has also projected and completed a mock-up of an armed helicopter based on the Hirundo; this project has the designation A 129.

The first of three flying prototypes (NC7101) flew for the first time on 4 August 1971. Delivery of production aircraft is scheduled to begin in 1975. Petroleum Helicopters Inc of the US has ordered four.

TYPE: Twin-engined general-purpose helicopter.

ROTOR SYSTEM AND DRIVE: Fully-articulated four-blade single main rotor and two-blade semi-rigid delta-hinged tail rotor. Main transmission assembly is housed in fairing above the passenger cabin, driving the main rotor through a coupling gearbox and main reduction gearbox, and the tail rotor through a 90° gearbox. Main rotor blades can be folded back for stowage. Main rotor/engine rpm ratio 1 : 15·62. Tail rotor/engine rpm ratio 1 : 2.88. Rotor brake fitted.

FUSELAGE AND TAIL UNIT: Pod and boom type, of aluminium alloy construction, built in four main sections: nose, cockpit, passenger cabin and tailboom. Sweptback vertical fin and non-swept elevators mounted on rear of tailboom. Tail rotor on port side.

LANDING GEAR: Retractable tricycle type, with single main wheels and self-centering steerable nosewheel. Hydraulic retraction, nosewheel forward, main wheels upward into fuselage. Emergency manual retraction. Brakes on main wheels, locking mechanism on nosewheel. All tyres are of tubeless type, size 360 × 135-6. Combined wheel/ski gear available optionally.

POWER PLANT: Two Allison 250-C20B turboshaft engines (each 420 shp for T-O, 400 shp max continuous power, 370 shp max cruise power, derated to 346 shp for twin-engine operation), mounted side by side in upper rear fuselage and separated from passenger cabin and from each other by firewalls. Fuel tank in lower rear fuselage, usable capacity 121 Imp gallons (550 litres). Oil capacity 1·2 Imp gallons (5·5 litres) for each engine and 1·6 Imp gallons (7·5 litres) for transmission. For search missions, auxiliary fuel tanks may be fitted.

ACCOMMODATION: Crew of one or two on flight deck, which has a door on each side. Dual controls. Main cabin seats up to six passengers, in two rows of three at 32in (81 cm) pitch, with large space at rear for baggage. A seventh passenger can be carried in lieu of second crew member. Door to passenger cabin on each side. First row of seats removable to permit use as freight transport. Ambulance version can accommodate two stretchers, one above the other, and two medical attendants, in addition to the pilot, when the forward cabin bulkhead is removed. Cabin heating and ventilation standard.

SYSTEMS: Utility hydraulic system for landing gear operation, wheel and rotor braking and nosewheel locking. Two separate hydraulic systems provide for dual flight servo-controls. 28V DC electrical system, using two 150A starter/generators, and one 24V 13Ah battery. 115V 400Hz AC power supplied by 250VA static inverter.

ELECTRONICS AND EQUIPMENT: Standard flight instrumentation and VHF-AM transceiver. Additional instrumentation and equipment to customer's requirements, including provision for VHF-FM, UHF-AM, VOR (with Area Navigation if required), ILS, DME and ADF.

ARMAMENT: The primary machine-gun is the flexible, remotely-controlled (by the co-pilot/gunner) Minitat, with 1,000 rounds of 7·62 mm ammunition. Mamee containers are available for 3,000 and 4,000 rounds. An alternative is an external twin MG-3 installation, flexible in elevation, with 2,500 rounds of 7·62 mm. Stores pylons can be provided for two rocket pods (each of seven 2·75 in or eighteen 50 mm SNIA rockets). Rocket pods and the Minitat can be installed simultaneously. Missile configurations for anti-tank missions include four MGM-71A TOW or four AS.11 missiles. Fire control available includes the SFOM 83A3 or XM-60 (for rockets), APX-334 or XM-58 (for AS.11) and XM-65 (for TOW). The Minitat has its own hand-held, counterbalanced control unit with a polarised ring device.

DIMENSIONS, EXTERNAL:
- Diameter of main rotor: 36 ft 1 in (11·00 m)
- Main rotor blade chord: 1 ft 1 in (0·33 m)
- Diameter of tail rotor: 6 ft 6¾ in (2·00 m)
- Tail rotor blade chord: 8 in (0·20 m)
- Length overall, both rotors turning: 42 ft 11 in (13·082 m)
- Length of fuselage, tail rotor turning: 36 ft 7 in (11·15 m)
- Length of fuselage: 36 ft 0¾ in (10·99 m)
- Height to top of rotor hub: 9 ft 9¾ in (2·99 m)
- Height overall: 10 ft 6 in (3·20 m)
- Fuselage: Max width: 4 ft 8 in (1·42 m)
- Elevator span: 9 ft 5¼ in (2·88 m)
- Width over main wheels: 8 ft 0½ in (2·45 m)
- Passenger doors (each):
  - Width: 3 ft 7 in (1·10 m)

DIMENSIONS, INTERNAL:
- Cabin, excluding flight deck:
  - Length: 5 ft 3¾ in (1·62 m)
  - Width: 4 ft 5½ in (1·36 m)
  - Height: 4 ft 2½ in (1·28 m)
  - Volume: 100 cu ft (2·82 m³)
- Baggage compartment:
  - Volume: 18·4 cu ft (0·52 m³)

AREAS:
- Main rotor disc: 1,022·6 sq ft (95·00 m²)
- Tail rotor disc: 33·80 sq ft (3·14 m²)
- Main rotor blades (each): 19·81 sq ft (1·84 m²)
- Tail rotor blades (each): 2·15 sq ft (0·20 m²)
- Fin: 10·98 sq ft (1·02 m²)
- Elevators (total): 11·41 sq ft (1·06 m²)

WEIGHTS AND LOADINGS:
- Weight empty: 2,998 lb (1,360 kg)
- Max T-O weight: 5,400 lb (2,450 kg)
- Max disc loading: 5·90 lb/sq ft (28·8 kg/m²)
- Max power loading: 6·39 lb/shp (2·9 kg/shp)

PERFORMANCE (at 5,200 lb; 2,360 kg AUW. A: ISA, B: ISA+22°C):
- Max never-exceed speed: 166 knots (191 mph; 308 km/h)
- Max level speed at S/L, max continuous power:
  - A: 151 knots (174 mph; 280 km/h)
  - B: 142 knots (164 mph; 264 km/h)
- Max level speed at 6,560 ft (2,000 m), max continuous power:
  - A: 148 knots (171 mph; 276 km/h)
  - B: 138 knots (159 mph; 256 km/h)
- Optimum cruising speed at S/L:
  - A, B: 141 knots (162 mph; 260 km/h)
- Max rate of climb at S/L:
  - A: 1,675 ft (510 m)/min
  - B: 1,160 ft (354 m)/min
- Rate of climb at S/L, one engine out:
  - A: 118 ft (36 m)/min
- Service ceiling:
  - A, B: 15,625 ft (4,760 m)
- Service ceiling, one engine out:
  - A: 2,625 ft (800 m)
- Hovering ceiling in ground effect:
  - A: 11,150 ft (3,400 m)
  - B: 8,370 ft (2,550 m)
- Hovering ceiling out of ground effect:
  - A: 8,700 ft (2,650 m)
  - B: 5,750 ft (1,750 m)
- Max range at S/L:
  - A, B: 329 nm (379 miles; 610 km)
- Max range at 6,560 ft (2,000 m):
  - A: 380 nm (438 miles; 705 km)
  - B: 378 nm (435 miles; 700 km)
- Max endurance at S/L:
  - A: 3 hr 4 min
  - B: 2 hr 58 min

Third prototype of the Agusta A 109 Hirundo twin-turbine eight-seat helicopter

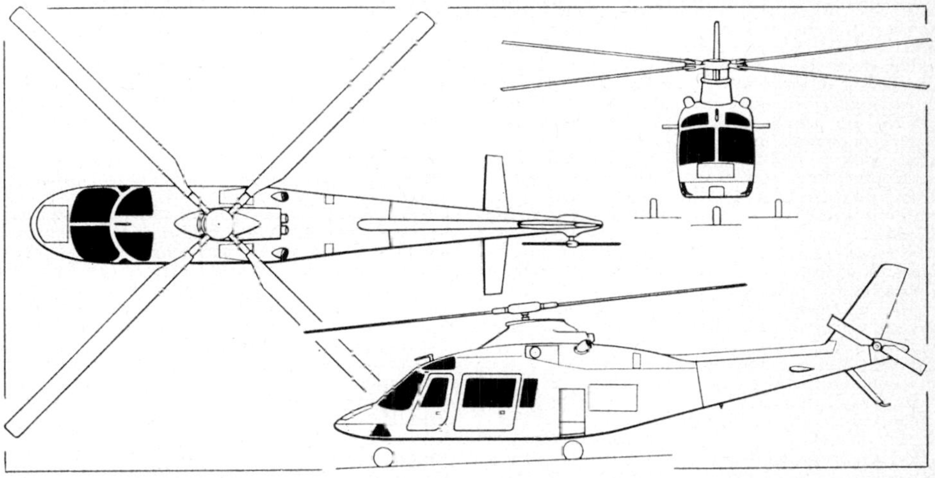

Agusta A 109 Hirundo twin-engined general-purpose helicopter (*Pilot Press*)

AGUSTA-BELL MODEL 47 SERIES

Latest versions of the Bell Model 47 in production by Agusta include the standard Models 47G-3B-1 and -3B-2, 47G-4A, 47G-5 and 47J-2A. In addition, Agusta is building two special variants of its own design, derived from the series 47J, designated 47J-3 and 47J-3B-1.

The 47J-3 differs from the standard 47J-2A in having a modified main transmission able to absorb greater power input, ie 270 hp for take-off and a max continuous output of 260 hp, in lieu of the normal 260 hp and 220 hp respectively. Performance remains similar to that of the 47J-2A, as described under the Bell entry in the US section of the 1966-67 *Jane's*.

A special ASW version of the 47J-3 was evolved for the Italian Navy, for operation from the decks of ships. This version has instrumentation for over-sea operation in reduced visibility, and a high-efficiency rotor brake. Its armament comprises one Mk 44 torpedo.

The 47J-3B-1 is a high-altitude four-seat helicopter, powered by a Lycoming TVO-435-B1A engine, rated at 270 hp for take-off and 220 hp for continuous operation. The engine is equipped with an exhaust-driven supercharger, fitted with an automatic control which maintains sea level conditions up to at least 14,000 ft (4,300 m). The 47J-3B-1 also has a high-inertia rotor and servo-control on both the cyclic and collective pitch control systems.

All versions can be fitted with the full range of optional equipment offered by Bell, including pontoons, stretchers, etc. A total of more than 1,100 had been built in Italy by the end of 1971 and production continues on a limited basis. Further deliveries of Model 47 series helicopters were scheduled to be made during 1974.

WEIGHTS:
- Weight empty:
  - 47J-3: 1,819 lb (825 kg)
  - 47J-3B-1: 1,863 lb (845 kg)
- Max T-O weight:
  - 47J-3 and 3B-1: 2,950 lb (1,340 kg)

PERFORMANCE (47J-3B-1, at max T-O weight):
- Max level speed at S/L: 91 knots (105 mph; 169 km/h)
- Normal cruising speed at 5,000 ft (1,525 m): 75 knots (86 mph; 138 km/h)
- Max rate of climb at S/L: 905 ft (276 m)/min
- Max rate of climb at 14,000 ft (4,300 m): 785 ft (240 m)/min
- Service ceiling: 17,500 ft (5,340 m)
- Hovering ceiling in ground effect: 16,500 ft (5,030 m)
- Hovering ceiling out of ground effect: 12,200 ft (3,720 m)
- Range with max fuel at 5,000 ft (1,525 m), no reserves: 182 nm (210 miles; 338 km)
- Max endurance at 5,000 ft (1,525 m), no reserves: 3 hr 30 min

AGUSTA-BELL 204B and 204AS

The Agusta-Bell 204B is a medium-size utility helicopter, similar to the Bell UH-1B Iroquois, and has been in production since 1961 for the armed services of Italy, Spain, Sweden, Holland, Austria, Turkey and Saudi Arabia, and for

Agusta-Bell 47G-4A helicopter (280 hp Lycoming VO-540 engine)

commercial operators in Italy, Norway, Sweden, Switzerland and Lebanon. By the end of 1973 approx 250 AB 204-series helicopters had been delivered; the production programme was nearing completion in the Spring of 1974. Versions of the AB 204B have been built with 44 ft (13·41 m) and 48 ft (14·63 m) main rotors and with Rolls-Royce Bristol Gnome, Lycoming T53 and General Electric T58 turboshaft engines.

Agusta has designed and built a special version of the AB 204B for ASW operation. Known as the **Agusta-Bell 204AS**, this version was supplied to the Italian and Spanish navies. The 204AS is provided with electronic equipment for automatic stabilisation (ASE) and for automatic approach to hovering (AATH), in addition to complete instrumentation for all-weather flying. It was developed specifically for the anti-submarine search and attack role, for which task it is fitted with sonar, linked to the electronic equipment for stabilisation during search, and can be fitted optionally with AN/APN-195 search radar and two Mk 44 torpedoes.

The latest multi-role version of the AB 204AS, of which a substantial number has been ordered, is capable of operation also against fast surface vessels, for which purpose it is provided with search radar and Aérospatiale AS.12 or similar-type missiles. The AB 204B may be fitted with long-range auxiliary fuel tanks, rescue hoist and emergency flotation gear.

Power plant of the AB 204AS is the General Electric T58-GE-3, with a T-O rating of 1,290 shp. The transmission has been appropriately strengthened, compared with the AB 204B, to allow for the higher rating.

The following data apply to the multi-role version, and the weight and performance data to a typical mission with a normal fuel load of 155 Imp gallons (705 litres):

DIMENSIONS, EXTERNAL:
Main rotor diameter 48 ft 0 in (14·63 m)
Length overall, main rotor turning 57 ft 0 in (17·37 m)
Length of fuselage 41 ft 7 in (12·67 m)

WEIGHTS:
Weight empty, equipped (without armament) 6,481 lb (2,940 kg)
T-O weight (incl armament) for multi-role mission 9,501 lb (4,310 kg)

PERFORMANCE (typical ASW mission at AUW of 9,000 lb; 4,082 kg):
Cruising speed at S/L 90 knots (104 mph; 167 km/h)
Time for sonar search operation (50% hovering OGE, 50% cruise) 1 hr 40 min
Operation radius for above time of search 60 nm (69 miles; 111 km)

AGUSTA-BELL 205 and 205A-1

The Agusta-Bell Model 205 is a multi-purpose utility helicopter, corresponding to the UH-1D/UH-1H versions adopted by the US armed forces. It can be used to transport passengers, equipment and troops, or for casualty evacuation, tactical support, rescue or other missions. Various special installations such as stretchers, floats, snow skids, armament or a rescue hoist can be fitted according to role. The cabin will accommodate a pilot and 14 passengers, and has a clear volume of 220 cu ft (6·2 m³) when stripped for cargo carrying. The AB 205 is fitted with IFR and night flying instruments, and for normal operation only one pilot is carried.

More than 300 AB 205s had been built by early 1974, the current production version having a Lycoming T53-L-13B turboshaft engine, developing a maximum of 1,400 shp for take-off.

The AB 205 is in service with the Italian armed forces and has been ordered by those of Iran, Kuwait, Morocco (24), Saudi Arabia, Spain, Turkey, Zambia (25) and other countries.

In 1969 Agusta began production of a developed version known as the **AB 205A-1**, certificated for commercial and passenger transport operation. The Agusta-Bell 205A-1 can accommodate up to 14 passengers and has a 28·3 cu ft (0·8 m³) baggage compartment in the tailboom. A wide variety of equipment can be fitted to fulfil a number of other roles. Power plant is a 1,400 shp Lycoming T5313B turboshaft engine, derated to 1,250 shp for take-off.

DIMENSIONS, EXTERNAL:
Main rotor diameter 48 ft 0 in (14·63 m)
Tail rotor diameter 8 ft 6 in (2·59 m)
Fuselage length 41 ft 11 in (12·78 m)
Width overall 9 ft 0½ in (2·76 m)
Height overall 14 ft 8 in (4·48 m)

WEIGHTS (AB 205):
Weight empty (standard) 4,800 lb (2,177 kg)
Normal T-O weight 8,500 lb (3,860 kg)
Max T-O weight 9,500 lb (4,310 kg)

WEIGHTS (AB 205A-1):
Weight empty (standard) 5,195 lb (2,356 kg)
Max T-O weight (FAA cert):
internal load 9,500 lb (4,310 kg)
external load 10,500 lb (4,762 kg)

PERFORMANCE (AB 205 at AUW of 8,500 lb; 3,860 kg, with T53-L-13 engine):
Max level speed at S/L 120 knots (138 mph; 222 km/h)
Cruising speed 115 knots (132 mph; 212 km/h)
Max rate of climb at S/L 1,800 ft (548 m)/min
Hovering ceiling in ground effect 17,000 ft (5,180 m)
Hovering ceiling out of ground effect 11,000 ft (3,350 m)
Max range, standard tanks, no reserves 312 nm (360 miles; 58 km
Max endurance, standard tanks, no reserves 3 hr 48 min

PERFORMANCE (AB 205A-1, at max T-O weight with internal load):
Max level speed 120 knots (138 mph; 222 km/h)
Max cruising speed 109 knots (126 mph; 203 km/h)
Max rate of climb at S/L 2,030 ft (619 m)/min
Hovering ceiling in ground effect 11,000 ft (3,350 m)
Hovering ceiling out of ground effect 6,800 ft (2,075 m)
Max range, standard tanks, no reserves 287 nm (331 miles; 532 km)
Max endurance, standard tanks, no reserves 3 hr 18 min

AGUSTA-BELL 206B JETRANGER II

The Agusta-Bell 206 JetRanger has been manufactured under licence from Bell since the end of 1967; production of the Model 206A (see 1973-74 *Jane's*) has now ended.

Deliveries began in 1972 of the Agusta-Bell 206B JetRanger II, which is now the standard Agusta-built version. The AB 206B has a 400 shp (max) Allison 250-C20 engine, derated to 317 shp. The AB 206B has an increased gross weight and an improved performance in "hot and high" conditions.

Production is planned in due course of the seven-seat Model 206L Long Ranger stretched version, with increased gross weight and a 420 shp (max) Allison 250-C20B engine.

By the beginning of 1974 some 700 Agusta-built Model 206-series helicopters had been built and delivered to commercial and military operators, including the armed forces of Iran, Italy, Saudi Arabia, Spain, Sweden and Turkey. The AB 206As for Sweden (Swedish designation HKP 6) have long-leg skid gear and underfuselage weapon racks.

The cabin can accommodate four persons in addition to the pilot; the baggage compartment has a capacity of 250 lb (113 kg) and a usable volume of 16 cu ft (0·45 m³).

The following details refer to the current Agusta-Bell 206B:

DIMENSIONS, EXTERNAL:
Main rotor diameter 33 ft 4 in (10·16 m)
Length overall, rotors turning 39 ft 2 in (11·94 m)
Length of fuselage 31 ft 2 in (9·50 m)

WEIGHTS:
Weight empty (standard) 1,504 lb (682 kg)
Max T-O weight (internal load) 3,200 lb (1,452 kg)
Max T-O weight (external load) 3,350 lb (1,519 kg)

PERFORMANCE (at AUW of 3,200 lb; 1,452 kg, ISA):
Max level speed at S/L 122 knots (140 mph; 226 km/h)
Cruising speed 116 knots (133 mph; 214 km/h)
Max rate of climb at S/L 1,358 ft (414 m)/min
Hovering ceiling in ground effect 11,325 ft (3,450 m)
Hovering ceiling out of ground effect 5,800 ft (1,770 m)
Max range, standard fuel, no reserves 363 nm (418 miles; 673 km)
Max endurance, standard fuel, no reserves 4 hr 0 min

AGUSTA-BELL 206A-1 and 206B-1

The Agusta-Bell 206A-1 and 206B-1, corresponding to the Bell OH-58A Kiowa (see US section), have been developed expressly for military operation, and are in service with the Italian armed forces and other operators. In general configuration they are similar to the AB 206A and B, with accommodation for a pilot and four passengers. Main differences are a larger-diameter main rotor, and appropriate military modifications, such as local strengthening of the airframe, provision for armament and additional cabin doors. The AB 206A-1 and AB 206B-1 are powered respectively by Allison 250-C18 and 250-C20 engines.

Production of the AB 206B-1 began in 1972.

DIMENSIONS, EXTERNAL:
Main rotor diameter 35 ft 4 in (10·77 m)
Length overall, rotors turning 41 ft 0 in (12·50 m)
Length of fuselage 32 ft 4 in (9·85 m)

WEIGHTS:
Weight empty (standard):
206A-1 1,504 lb (682 kg)
206B-1 1,540 lb (698 kg)
Max T-O weight (internal load):
206A-1 3,000 lb (1,360 kg)
206B-1 3,200 lb (1,452 kg)
Max T-O weight (external load):
206A-1 and B-1 3,350 lb (1,519 kg)

PERFORMANCE (at AUW of 3,000 lb; 1,360 kg, ISA for 206A-1; AUW of 3,200 lb; 1,452 kg, ISA for 206B-1):
Max level speed at S/L:
206A-1 114 knots (131 mph; 211 km/h)
206B-1 120 knots (138 mph; 222 km/h)
Cruising speed:
206A-1 110 knots (127 mph; 204 km/h)
206B-1 112 knots (129 mph; 208 km/h)
Max rate of climb at S/L:
206A-1 1,560 ft (475 m)/min
206B-1 1,300 ft (396 m)/min

Agusta-Bell 204AS anti-submarine helicopter of the Italian Navy, with AN/APN-195 search radar in radome above the cabin

Agusta-Bell 205 multi-purpose helicopter in the insignia of the Imperial Iranian Ground Forces

Hovering ceiling in ground effect:
206A-1 10,900 ft (3,325 m)
206B-1 12,000 ft (3,660 m)
Hovering ceiling out of ground effect:
206A-1 6,000 ft (1,825 m)
206B-1 8,000 ft (2,440 m)
Max range, standard fuel, no reserves:
206A-1 319 nm (368 miles; 592 km)
206B-1 290 nm (334 miles; 538 km)
Max endurance, standard fuel, no reserves:
206A-1 4 hr 0 min
206B-1 3 hr 30 min

AGUSTA-BELL 212

The Agusta-Bell 212 is a twin-engined utility transport helicopter particularly suited to passenger transport duties. Deliveries began in the second half of 1971, and by the end of 1973 more than 25 had been built, with others on order, for Italian and other commercial and military operators. The first IFR flight by an AB 212 fitted with a SFENA Helistab autopilot took place at Gallarate on 5 April 1973.

The general configuration of the AB 212 is similar to that of the AB 205/205A-1, but it embodies considerable modifications to the dynamic components, systems and structure.

Power plant is the UACL PT6T-6 Turbo Twin Pac, derated in the AB 212 to 1,290 shp for T-O and a max continuous rating of 1,130 shp. Fuel capacity is 215 US gallons (179 Imp gallons; 813 litres).

Standard accommodation is for a pilot and up to 14 passengers, but the helicopter is readily adaptable to alternative configurations, including a de luxe interior or as a VIP transport.

Optional kits for alternative roles include rescue hoist, cargo hook, auxiliary fuel tanks, stretchers and float landing gear.

An extensively-modified military version, the AB 212ASW, is being produced by Agusta and is described separately.

Dimensions, external:
Diameter of main rotor 48 ft 0 in (14·63 m)
Diameter of tail rotor 8 ft 6 in (2·59 m)
Length overall, rotors turning 57 ft 1 in (17·40 m)
Fuselage length 46 ft 0 in (14·02 m)
Height to top of cabin roof 7 ft 8 in (2·34 m)
Height overall, tail rotor turning 14 ft 5 in (4·40 m)
Elevator span 9 ft 4 in (2·84 m)
Width over skids 8 ft 8 in (2·64 m)

Weights:
Weight empty (standard) 5,800 lb (2,630 kg)
Max T-O weight, internal or external load 11,200 lb (5,081 kg)

Performance (at AUW of 10,000 lb ; 4,536 kg, ISA):
Cruising speed at S/L 110 knots (127 mph; 204 km/h)
Max rate of climb at S/L 1,860 ft (567 m)/min
Service ceiling 17,000 ft (5,180 m)
Hovering ceiling in ground effect 13,000 ft (3,960 m)
Hovering ceiling out of ground effect 10,000 ft (3,050 m)
Max range at 5,000 ft (1,525 m) with standard fuel, no reserves:
on two engines 267 nm (307 miles; 494 km)
on one engine 318 nm (366 miles; 589 km)

AGUSTA-BELL 212ASW

The Agusta-Bell 212ASW helicopter has been developed as a medium-sized twin-engined naval helicopter designed for anti-submarine search and attack missions, and attack missions against surface vessels. It is also suitable for search and rescue and utility roles. It is an extensively modified version of the standard Agusta-Bell 212 (which see), utilising naval operational experience gained with the AB 204AS, and because of its similarity in size to the 204AS can also operate from small ship decks. A prototype has been successfully evaluated, and the AB 212ASW is now being produced and delivered to meet orders from the Italian Navy (28) and from foreign operators.

Apart from some local strengthening and the provision of deck-mooring equipment, the airframe structure remains essentially similar to that of the commercial Model 212 and military UH-1N, described under the Bell entry in the US section. Main differences from the Agusta-Bell 212 are as follows:

Type: Twin-engined anti-submarine and anti-surface-vessel helicopter.

Power Plant: As AB 212, but with protection against salt water corrosion. Provision for one internal or two external auxiliary fuel tanks.

Accommodation: Crew of three or four.

Systems: Standard duplicated hydraulic systems for flight controls, as in AB 212. Either hydraulic system is capable of operating the automatic flight control system. Third, self-contained system for operation of sonar, rescue hoist and other utilities. Electrical system capacity increased to cater for higher power demand; the two standard generators are integrated with a 20kVA alternator.

Electronics and Equipment: Complete instrumentation for day and night sea operation in all weathers. Avionics installed are EAS ERM 710 UHF transceiver, Collins SSB/DSB 718 U-5 HF transceiver, and Agusta AG-03-M intercom, for communications; Marconi-Elliott AD-370B ADF, Hoffman AN/ARN-91 TACAN and Collins AN/ARA-50 homing UHF, for navigation assistance; Aeritalia (Honeywell) AN/APN-171 radar altimeter, Canadian Marconi AN/APN-172(V)2 Doppler radar, Canadian Marconi CMA-708/ASW navigation computer, and automatic flight control system with General Electric SR-3 gyro platform, Agusta ASE-531A automatic stabilisation equipment and Agusta AATH-547A automatic approach to hover, for automatic navigation; Siemens AN/APX-77 IFF/SIF transponder; MEL ARI-5955 search radar and Motorola SST-119X radar transponder; and Bendix AN/AQS-13B sonar for ASW search.

Agusta-Bell 212ASW twin-engined anti-submarine and anti-surface-vessel helicopter

Agusta-Sikorsky SH-3D anti-submarine helicopter in Italian Navy insignia (see page 130)

Armament and Operational Equipment: Weapon system may consist of two Mk 44 or Mk 46 homing torpedoes or two air-to-surface missiles. Provisions for auxiliary installations such as a 595 lb (270 kg) capacity rescue hoist, 5,000 lb (2,270 kg) capacity cargo sling, inflatable emergency pontoons, internal and external auxiliary fuel tanks, according to mission.

ASW Mission: The basic sensor system employed for the ASW search and attack mission is the AN/AQS 13B variable-depth sonar, with a max operating depth of 450 ft (137 m). The automatic navigation system permits the positioning of the helicopter over any desired "dip" point of a complex search pattern. The position of the helicopter, computed by the automatic navigation system, is integrated with sonar target information in the radar tactical display where both the surface and the underwater tactical situations can be continuously monitored. Additional navigation and tactical information is provided by accurate UHF direction-finding equipment, from an A/A mode-capable TACAN and from a radar transponder. The AB 212ASW helicopter's automatic flight control system (AFCS) integrates the basic automatic stabilisation equipment with signal output from the radar altimeter, the Doppler radar, sonar cable angle signals and outputs from the dry cable transducer. The effectiveness of this sytem results in hands-off flight from cruise condition to sonar hover in all weathers and under rough sea conditions. A specially designed cockpit display in the AB 212ASW shows the pilots all flight parameters for each phase of the ASW operation.

The attack mission is carried out with two Mk 44 or Mk 46 homing torpedoes, or with depth charges.

AWW Mission: For this mission the AB 212ASW carries a high-performance long-range search radar, with a very efficient scanner design and installation possessing high discrimination in rough sea conditions. Provisions have also been made to permit incorporation of future radar systems developments. The automatic navigation system and the search radar are integrated to permit a continuously updated picture of the tactical situation. Provisions are also incorporated for the installation of the most advanced ECM systems. The surface attack is performed with air-to-surface wire-guided missiles. In operation, the co-pilot aims and "flies" the missiles to the target through a gyro-stabilised sight system of the XM-58 type.

Dimensions, external: As AB 212, except:
Max width:
with torpedoes 12 ft 11½ in (3·95 m)
with missiles 13 ft 8¼ in (4·17 m)

Weights (A: ASW mission with Mk 44 torpedoes; B: AWW mission with AS.12 missiles; C: search and rescue mission; all at S/L, ISA):
Weight empty, equipped:
A, B, C 7,484 lb (3,395 kg)
Crew of three:
A, B, C 529 lb (240 kg)
Mission equipment:
A (two Mk 44 torpedoes) 846 lb (384 kg)
B (AS.12 installation and XM-58 sight) 491 lb (223 kg)
C (rescue hoist) 88 lb (40 kg)
Full fuel (normal tanks):
A, B, C 1,764 lb (800 kg)
Auxiliary internal tank:
A, B 55 lb (25 kg)
Auxiliary external tanks:
C 70 lb (32 kg)
Auxiliary fuel:
A, B 518 lb (235 kg)
C 785 lb (356 kg)
Max mission T-O weight:
A 11,196 lb (5,079 kg)
B 10,841 lb (4,918 kg)
C 10,720 lb (4,863 kg)

Performance (at max T-O weight, ISA):
Max level speed at S/L 106 knots (122 mph; 196 km/h)
Max cruising speed with armament 100 knots (115 mph; 185 km/h)
Max rate of climb at S/L:
A 1,519 ft (463 m)/min
B 1,197 ft (365 m)/min

Rate of climb at S/L, one engine out:
- A: 423 ft (129 m)/min
- B: 348 ft (106 m)/min

Hovering ceiling in ground effect:
- A: 12,500 ft (3,810 m)

Hovering ceiling out of ground effect:
- A: 4,000 ft (1,220 m)

Search endurance (A) with 50% at 90 knots (103·5 mph; 167 km/h) cruise and 50% hovering out of ground effect, 10% reserve fuel — 3 hr 0 min

Search range (B) with 10% reserve fuel — 323 nm (372 miles; 598 km)

Endurance (B), no reserves — 3 hr 45 min

Endurance (C) at 90 knots (103·5 mph; 167 km/h) search speed — 4 hr 15 min

Max range with auxiliary tanks, 100 knots (115 mph; 185 km/h) cruise at S/L, 15% reserves — 360 nm (414 miles; 667 km)

Max endurance with auxiliary tanks, no reserves — 5 hr 0 min

AGUSTA-SIKORSKY SH-3D

During 1967, Agusta began the construction under licence of an initial batch of 24 Sikorsky SH-3D anti-submarine helicopters for the Italian Navy. Delivery began in 1969. Additional orders have since been placed, both for the Italian armed forces and for the Imperial Iranian Navy (25), in various configurations including ASW, VIP transport and rescue. These aircraft are fitted with Teledyne AN/APN-182 Doppler velocity sensor radar and AN/APN-195 search radar. Thirty-five had been delivered by the end of 1973.

Full details of the SH-3D can be found under the Sikorsky heading in the US section of this edition.

AGUSTA-SIKORSKY HH-3F (S-61R)

In 1974 Agusta began production of this multi-purpose rescue helicopter. Twenty are being built initially, for the Italian Navy and foreign operators.

Details of the HH-3F can be found under the Sikorsky heading in the US section of this edition.

BREDANARDI

BREDANARDI COSTRUZIONI AERONAUTICHE SpA

Head Office and Works*:
Aeroporto Forlanini, 20090 Milan (*pending completion of new facilities at Porto d'Ascoli, in central Italy)
Telephone: 738.52.51
Telex: 33666 NARDI

Rome Office:
Via XXIV Maggio 43/45, 00187 Rome
Telephone: 4660
Telex: 61050

President:
Ing Giovanni Berardi

Managing Director:
Dott Elto Nardi

This company was established on 15 February 1971 by Nardi (which see) and Breda (which is a member company of the EFIM state-owned financial group), to undertake helicopter production under a manufacturing licence from Hughes Helicopters of the US. Breda and Nardi each have a 50% interest.

BredaNardi has obtained jigs and tools to manufacture both the Hughes Model 300C and Model 500C, and all derivatives of both models, and was to begin production at its Milan plant in 1974. Initial production will be of the three-seat Hughes 300C (Italian designation NH-300C) and five-seat Hughes 500C (Italian designation NH-500C) and 500M (Italian designations NH-500M and NH-500MC). An anti-submarine version of the latter aircraft, designated NH-500CASW, has also been announced. Details of the basic Models 300C and 500M can be found under the Hughes heading in the US section of this edition.

The new works now under construction at Porto d'Ascoli in central Italy, to which helicopter production will eventually be transferred, will also be able to undertake the overhaul, repair and manufacture of components for other types of helicopters and other aircraft, and will possess its own airfield facilities. In the meantime, all helicopter overhaul, repair and maintenance continues to be carried out at the Milan facility.

BredaNardi NH-500C (Hughes Model 500) light general-purpose helicopter

BUCCIERO

RENATO BUCCIERO

Address:
Via Tuscolo 8, 00040 Monteporzio (Rome)

Captain Bucciero, an airline pilot with Alitalia, designed a two-seat all-metal light training and touring aircraft known as the SVIT (Studio per un Velivolo da Istruzione e Turismo), which was built with the assistance of Mr Gastone Canal, an Alitalia engineer. This aircraft was described and illustrated in the 1970-71 *Jane's*.

In May 1969 Capt Bucciero began, with the financial help of seven other Alitalia pilots and two flight engineers, to build a developed version with a 100 hp engine, of which details follow:

BUCCIERO SVIT 70

The SVIT 70 is generally similar to the original SVIT prototype (1970-71 *Jane's*), but has a modified landing gear, sliding cockpit canopy and rounded fuselage top-decking. The first aircraft of this type (I-FABO) was exhibited at the Turin Air Show in June 1972 and is illustrated in the accompanying photograph. Static tests for FAR 23 (Utility category) certification have been completed.

A new SVIT is now under construction, with an oleo-pneumatic shock-absorber in the nosewheel leg and modified main landing gear attachments to the fuselage.

Type: Two-seat light training and touring aircraft.

Wings: Cantilever mid-wing monoplane. Wing section NACA 65_2415 (modified). Thickness/chord ratio 16%. Dihedral 2° 30′ from roots. Incidence 2°. No sweepback. Metal-skinned two-spar torsion-box structure of 2024-T3. Slotted flaps and ailerons of 2024-T3.

Fuselage: All-metal (2024-T3) structure, built in four main sections: engine bay, front fuselage, cabin and rear fuselage. Engine bay has a steel-tube basic structure, with cowling panels of non-inflammable plastics. Front fuselage is of steel-tube construction with aluminium alloy covering. Cabin section and rear fuselage are light alloy semi-monocoque structures. Fuselage is of basically rectangular cross-section, with rounded top-decking.

Tail Unit: Cantilever all-metal (2024-T3) structure, with all-moving tailplane and full-span anti-tab. Small dorsal fin fairing; auxiliary fin beneath rear fuselage.

Bucciero SVIT 70 two-seat light aircraft (100 hp Continental O-200-A engine) (*Martin Fricke*)

Landing Gear: Non-retractable tricycle type, with cantilever spring-steel main legs. Nosewheel unit has steel spring shock-absorption. Main wheels size 6·00-5, nosewheel size 5·00-5. Tyre pressure 34 lb/sq in (2·39 kg/cm^2) on all units. Hydraulic disc brakes on main wheels. Nosewheel is steerable.

Power Plant: One 100 hp Continental O-200-A four-cylinder horizontally-opposed aircooled engine, driving a two-blade McCauley metal propeller. Fuel tank in each wing, with total capacity of 23 Imp gallons (105 litres).

Accommodation: Side-by-side seating for two persons under transparent rearward-sliding Plexiglas canopy. Dual controls fitted. Baggage compartment aft of cabin.

Systems: Hydraulic system for actuation of wheel brakes. 12V electrical system includes 20A generator and 24Ah battery.

Equipment: Standard VFR instrumentation.

Dimensions, external:
- Wing span: 24 ft 7¼ in (7·50 m)
- Wing chord (constant): 4 ft 3½ in (1·31 m)
- Wing aspect ratio: 5·84
- Length overall: 18 ft 10¼ in (5·75 m)
- Height overall: 7 ft 10½ in (2·40 m)
- Tailplane span: 9 ft 5½ in (2·88 m)
- Wheel track: 8 ft 0½ in (2·45 m)
- Wheelbase: 7 ft 2¾ in (2·20 m)
- Propeller diameter: 6 ft 1 in (1·85 m)

Areas:
- Wings, gross: 103·76 sq ft (9·64 m^2)
- Ailerons (total): 9·04 sq ft (0·84 m^2)
- Trailing-edge flaps (total): 17·22 sq ft (1·60 m^2)
- Fin: 9·15 sq ft (0·85 m^2)
- Rudder: 3·34 sq ft (0·31 m^2)
- Horizontal tail surfaces (total): 20·45 sq ft (1·90 m^2)

Weights (100 hp engine):
- Weight empty: 925 lb (420 kg)
- Max T-O and landing weight: 1,488 lb (675 kg)

Performance (at max T-O weight, 100 hp engine):
- Max never-exceed speed: 154 knots (177 mph; 286 km/h)
- Max level speed at S/L: 115 knots (132 mph; 213 km/h)
- Max cruising speed at 8,200 ft (2,500 m): 102 knots (117 mph; 189 km/h)
- Stalling speed, flaps up: 37 knots (42 mph; 68 km/h)
- Stalling speed, flaps down: 32 knots (36 mph; 58 km/h)
- Max rate of climb at S/L: 1,200 ft (366 m)/min
- Service ceiling: 13,000 ft (3,962 m)

GENERAL AVIA

COSTRUZIONI AERONAUTICHE GENERAL AVIA

Address:
Via Trieste 24, 20096 Pioltello, Milan
Telephone: 9046774

Technical Director:
Dott Ing Stelio Frati

Secretary-Treasurer:
Lamberto Frati

Public Relations:
Carla Bielli

Dott Ing Stelio Frati is well known for the many successful light aircraft which, as a freelance designer, he has evolved since 1950.

These have been built in prototype and production series by several Italian manufacturers, and have included such aircraft as the two-seat F.4

and three-seat F.7 Rondone, built by Ambrosini; the Caproni F.5 two-seat light jet aircraft and the twin-engined F.6 Airone built for Pasotti; the Aviamilano F.8 Falco and F.14 Nibbio; the Procaer F.15 Picchio, F.400 Cobra and F.480; and the F.250.

The 260 hp developed version of the F.250 is manufactured by SIAI-Marchetti as the SF.260, and is described under that company's heading in this section.

Dott Ing Frati's designs have all possessed considerable aesthetic appeal, and all have been capable of full aerobatic flying, including spinning.

Early in 1970, Dott Ing Frati established the new company of General Avia, of which he is the Technical Director, and has acquired extensive and well-equipped workshops where, since April 1970, prototypes of his current designs are being built.

The F.20 Pegaso, of which General Avia built two prototypes, is to be produced by Italair, and is described under that company's heading in this section. General Avia is currently building a prototype known as the F15F Delfino, derived from the Procaer F15E Picchio (which see); this was due to fly for the first time in October 1974.

Design study is continuing of the F.22 Condor twin-turbofan executive aircraft, to which brief reference was made in the last edition of *Jane's*.

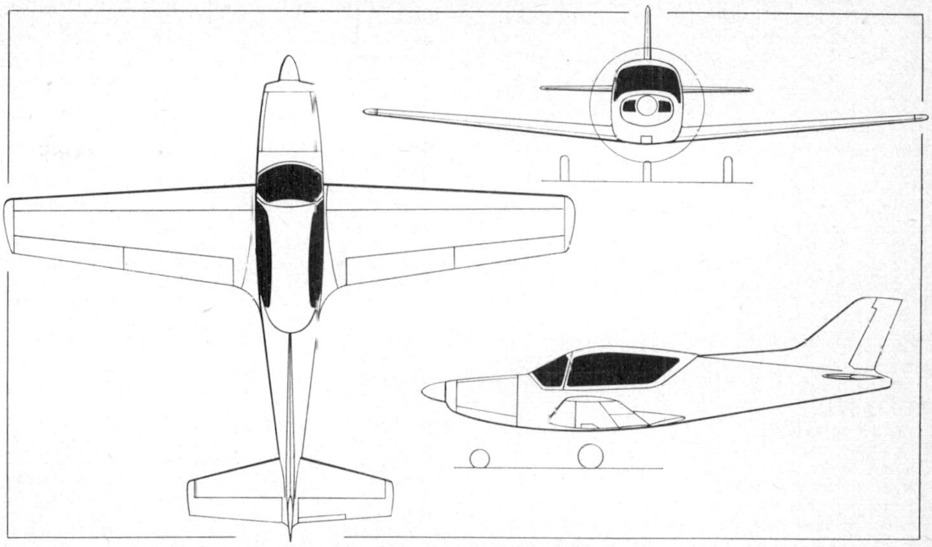

General Avia F15F Delfino, derived from the F15E Picchio (*Pilot Press*)

GENERAL AVIA (PROCAER) F15F DELFINO (DOLPHIN)

The Delfino is a derivative of the Procaer F15E Picchio (which see), designed by Dott Ing Frati. A prototype is under construction, and was due to make its first flight in October 1974.

The description of the F15E is generally applicable also to the F15F, except in the following respects:

Power Plant: One 200 hp Lycoming IO-360-A four-cylinder horizontally-opposed aircooled engine.

Dimensions, external: As F15E except:
Length overall 25 ft 5¼ in (7·75 m)

Weights and Loadings:
Weight empty 1,653 lb (750 kg)
Max T-O weight (Utility category) 2,700 lb (1,225 kg)
Max wing loading 18·8 lb/sq ft (91·7 kg/m²)
Max power loading 13·45 lb/hp (6·1 kg/hp)

Performance (estimated, at max T-O weight):
Max level speed 167 knots (193 mph; 310 km/h)
Cruising speed 151 knots (174 mph; 280 km/h)
Stalling speed 55·5 knots (64 mph; 102 km/h)
Max rate of climb at S/L 885 ft (270 m)/min
Service ceiling 17,050 ft (5,200 m)
T-O run 855 ft (260 m)
Landing run 655 ft (200 m)
Max range 755 nm (870 miles; 1,400 km)

IANNOTTA

DR ING ORLANDO IANNOTTA

Address:
Via Nicolardi 254, 80131 Naples

Dr Ing Iannotta has built a single-seat ultra-light high-wing monoplane (I-IANN), known as the I-66 San Francesco. Test flying took place between the Spring and Autumn of 1969.

A two-seat version is currently under development. The single-seat version was described and illustrated in the 1973-74 *Jane's*.

ITALAIR

ITALAIR SpA

Address and Works:
Via S.Zita 1-11, 16100 Genoa
Telephone: (010) 589026

President and Managing Director:
Mario Del Bianco

Company Secretary:
Elfo Frignani

Dott Mazzocchi, a well-known Italian publisher, initiated the formation of Italair primarily to develop, build and market a range of light aircraft and twin-engined executive aircraft.

The first such design is the F.20 Pegaso.

Second prototype of the Italair F.20 Pegaso (two 300 hp Continental IO-520-K engines)

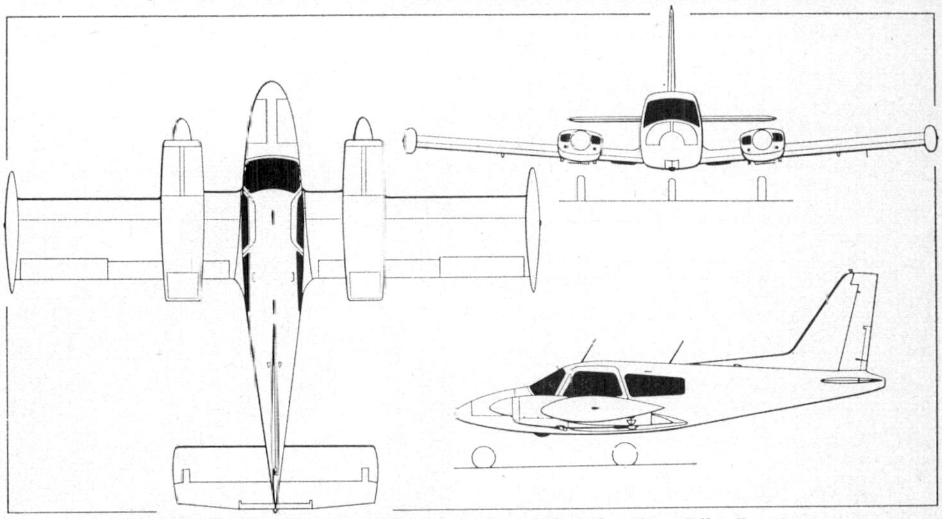

Italair F.20 Pegaso light twin-engined executive aircraft (*Pilot Press*)

ITALAIR F.20 PEGASO (PEGASUS)

The F.20 Pegaso is a six-seat light business twin. Its design, by General Avia, started in January 1970, and construction began in September 1970.

Two prototypes were built by General Avia, of which the first (I-GEAV) was flown for the first time on 21 October 1971 and the second (I-CBIE) on 11 August 1972. These were acquired subsequently by Italair, which planned to build an initial series of ten production Pegasos. The programme for RAI and FAA certification was nearing completion in mid-1974.

The description applies to the second prototype, which has slightly increased overall dimensions and higher weights than the first.

Type: Twin-engined six-seat light executive transport.

Wings: Cantilever low-wing monoplane. Wing section NACA 65_2-415. Dihedral 5°. Incidence 1° 45′. All-metal single-spar structure in light alloy, with flush-riveted stressed skin. Differentially-operated all-metal ailerons and electrically-operated double-slotted metal flaps. Anti-icing equipment planned for production aircraft.

Fuselage: All-metal semi-monocoque structure, with flush-riveted aluminium alloy skin.

Tail Unit: Cantilever all-metal structure with flush-riveted skin. Fixed-incidence tailplane. Trim tabs in rudder and each elevator. Anti-icing equipment planned for production aircraft.

Landing Gear: Retractable tricycle type, with single main wheels. Nosewheel steerable 18° to left and right. Electrical retraction, with manual standby. Oleo-pneumatic shock-absorbers. Main wheels size 7·00-6, nosewheel size 6·00-6.

Power Plant: Two 300 hp Continental IO-520-K six-cylinder horizontally-opposed aircooled engines, each driving a Hartzell fully-feathering constant-speed propeller. Fuel in two wing tanks, each of 35·5 US gallons (135 litres), and two wingtip tanks each of 33 US gallons (125 litres) capacity. Total capacity 137 US gallons (520 litres). Electrical propeller de-icing at customer's option.

Accommodation: Normal seating, in fully-enclosed cabin, for six persons, including pilot. Space for up to 230 lb (104 kg) of baggage in four compartments in forward and rear fuselage and each nacelle. Access to cabin via large door on each side. Normal IFR instrumentation and dual controls. Cabin heated, ventilated and soundproofed with glass-wool insulation. Provision for weather radar in nose at customer's option.

DIMENSIONS, EXTERNAL:

Wing span over tip-tanks	33 ft 11 in (10·34 m)
Wing chord at root	5 ft 5 in (1·65 m)
Wing chord at tip	4 ft 11 in (1·50 m)
Wing aspect ratio	6·67
Length overall	26 ft 10¾ in (8·20 m)
Height overall	11 ft 5¾ in (3·50 m)
Tailplane span	13 ft 5½ in (4·10 m)
Wheel track	11 ft 5¾ in (3·50 m)
Wheelbase	7 ft 10½ in (2·40 m)
Propeller diameter	6 ft 6 in (1·98 m)

AREAS:

Wings, gross	172·4 sq ft (16·02 m²)
Ailerons (total)	15·28 sq ft (1·42 m²)
Trailing-edge flaps (total)	17·13 sq ft (1·59 m²)
Fin	13·35 sq ft (1·24 m²)
Rudder, incl tab	8·50 sq ft (0·79 m²)
Tailplane	26·48 sq ft (2·46 m²)
Elevators, incl tabs	20·99 sq ft (1·95 m²)

WEIGHTS AND LOADINGS:

Weight empty, equipped	3,086 lb (1,400 kg)
Max T-O weight	5,070 lb (2,300 kg)
Max wing loading	29·39 lb/sq ft (143·5 kg/m²)
Max power loading	8·44 lb/hp (3·83 kg/hp)

PERFORMANCE (designed, at max T-O weight):

Max level speed at S/L
216 knots (249 mph; 400 km/h)

Max cruising speed (75% power)
205 knots (236 mph; 380 km/h)

Econ cruising speed (60% power)
194 knots (224 mph; 360 km/h)

Stalling speed, flaps down
63 knots (72 mph; 116 km/h)

Max rate of climb at S/L 2,000 ft (600 m)/min

Rate of climb at S/L, one engine out
492 ft (150 m)/min

Service ceiling (climb at 100 ft; 30·5 m/min)
20,500 ft (6,250 m)

Service ceiling, one engine out (climb at 50 ft; 15·2 m/min) 8,375 ft (2,550 m)

T-O run 656 ft (200 m)

Landing run 853 ft (260 m)

Max range at max cruising speed
917 nm (1,056 miles; 1,700 km)

Max range at econ cruising speed
1,052 nm (1,210 miles; 1,950 km)

MAGNI

VITTORIO MAGNI

ADDRESS:

Via Novara 72, 21017 Samarate (Varese)

Telephone: (0331) 20575

Sr Magni has built four small rotorcraft, of which the first and second were, respectively, single- and two-seat gyro-gliders of the Bensen type. The third aircraft was powered by a Volkswagen engine.

Sr Magni's fourth autogyro has a 60 hp Franklin piston engine and was displayed on the Silvercraft stand at the 1972 Turin Air Show. It was illustrated and briefly described in the 1973-74 *Jane's*.

Sr Magni has purchased from Mr Jukka Tervamäki of Finland (which see) the prototype, and all tooling, moulds and production rights, of the latter's JT-5 single-seat autogyro; this is now being marketed in Italy as the MT5, and production was expected to have begun by the time this edition closed for press.

In addition, Sr Magni has world marketing rights for rotor blades and other components of this aircraft, and rights to sell plans of the aircraft to amateur constructors in French-, Italian- and Spanish-speaking countries. For customers in other countries, plans are supplied by Mr Tervamäki. A description of the JT-5/MT5 appears in the Finnish section of this edition.

Magni-Tervamäki MT5 single-seat autogyro, designed in Finland

MERIDIONALI

ELICOTTERI MERIDIONALI SpA

HEAD OFFICE:

Via Poggio Laurentino, Rome

WORKS:

Via Giovanni Agusta, Frosinone

Telephone: (0775) 23273-23133

Telex: Elmef 62377

PRESIDENT:

Gen Ettore Pellacci

SALES AND PUBLIC RELATIONS MANAGER:

Dr Franco Ostini

SECRETARY GENERAL:

Gen Ernesto Caprioglio

TECHNICAL MANAGER:

Ing Mario Sala

This company was formed with assistance from Agusta (which see) and began to operate in October 1967. Initially, its activities consisted of overhauling helicopters of the Italian armed forces and other organisations, and the manufacture of helicopter components and subassemblies. In April 1968 it was announced that an agreement had been concluded with Boeing in the US, whereby Meridionali acquired rights to undertake co-production, marketing and servicing of the Boeing Vertol CH-47C Chinook transport helicopter for customers in Italy, Austria, Switzerland and the Middle East.

Manufacture of the Chinook began in the Spring of 1970, to meet initial orders for 20 for the Imperial Iranian Army and Air Force. Twenty-six have been ordered by the Italian Army Aviation, and funds for these were released in late 1973.

In addition, Meridionali announced in April 1970 that it was to undertake the series production of a new helicopter known as the EMA 124. This aircraft has been designed by Agusta, and will be built under a licence agreement between the two companies, which are sharing the development work.

Meridionali, whose works occupy a total area of more than 3,229,170 sq ft (300,000 m²), also participates in the manufacturing programme for the Agusta-Bell 206B JetRanger II helicopter (see under Agusta heading in this section).

MERIDIONALI/AGUSTA EMA 124

The three-seat EMA 124 was designed by Costruzioni Aeronautiche Giovanni Agusta, and conforms to FAR Part 27 airworthiness requirements. It is suitable for a variety of duties, including passenger or goods transport, pilot training, survey, reconnaissance, agricultural or other aerial work, policing duties and casualty transportation. The general appearance of the aircraft, which is derived from the Bell 47, can be seen in the accompanying illustration. It flew for the first time in May 1970.

TYPE: Three-seat light helicopter.

ROTOR SYSTEM: Semi-rigid two-blade main rotor, with provision for blade folding. Semi-rigid delta-hinged two-blade tail rotor.

ROTOR DRIVE: Transmission system consists of a main rotor reduction gearbox, tail rotor gearbox and drive shafting. Main gearbox incorporates a centrifugal clutch and a roller-type free-wheeling unit. Collective pitch control is exercised through rigid linkage, cyclic pitch control through rigid linkage with hydraulic boost.

FUSELAGE: Basic welded-tube structure, built in three sections: cabin, centre-section and tailboom.

TAIL UNIT: One-piece elevator mid-mounted on tailboom. Small ventral fin.

LANDING GEAR: Fixed tubular skid type, with two removable ground handling wheels.

POWER PLANT: One 305 hp (derated to 250 hp) Lycoming VO-540-B1B3 six-cylinder horizontally-opposed aircooled engine, mounted aft of cabin. Fuel in two interconnected metal tanks above engine, with total capacity of 33 Imp gallons (150 litres).

ACCOMMODATION: Side-by-side seating for pilot and two passengers in fully-enclosed and fully-transparent cabin. Provision for dual controls.

SYSTEMS: Single hydraulic system, including pump, reservoir, filter, pressure relief valve and irreversible valves, powers the servo-control cylinders. 28V DC electrical system supplied by one 24V 11Ah battery and a 28V 50A generator.

ELECTRONICS AND EQUIPMENT: Provision for installing Narco Mk XII or King KY-95 VHF communications sets, or alternatives to customer's requirements.

DIMENSIONS, EXTERNAL:

Main rotor diameter	31 ft 2 in (9·50 m)
Tail rotor diameter	4 ft 7 in (1·40 m)

WEIGHTS:

Weight empty	1,543 lb (700 kg)
Max T-O weight	2,535 lb (1,150 kg)

Meridionali-built Boeing Vertol CH-47C Chinook in Italian Army insignia

PERFORMANCE (at max T-O weight, ISA):
- Max level speed at S/L: 92 knots (106 mph; 170 km/h)
- Cruising speed at S/L: 78 knots (90 mph; 145 km/h)
- Max rate of climb at S/L: 827 ft (252 m)/min
- Service ceiling: 14,100 ft (4,300 m)
- Hovering ceiling in ground effect: 8,200 ft (2,500 m)
- Hovering ceiling out of ground effect: 5,575 ft (1,700 m)
- Max range at S/L: 225 nm (260 miles; 420 km)

Meridionali EMA 124 three-seat light helicopter (250 hp Lycoming engine)

NARDI

NARDI SA PER COSTRUZIONI AERONAUTICHE

HEAD OFFICE AND WORKS:
Aeroporto Forlanini, 20090 Milan
Telephone: 738.52.51
Telex: 33666

PRESIDENT:
Dott Ing Luigi Nardi

VICE-PRESIDENT, MANAGING DIRECTOR AND COMMERCIAL MANAGER:
Dott Elto Nardi

This company was established by the four Nardi brothers in 1933. Their first product, the FN-305, flew in 1935, and subsequently more than 600 of these aircraft were built by Nardi and, under licence, by Piaggio. They were followed by other Nardi designs, produced in large numbers.

The factory at Loreto was almost completely destroyed during the second World War, but the Milan factory was rebuilt and the prototype of the company's first post-war aircraft, the FN-333 all-metal amphibian, flew there for the first time on 4 December 1952.

For work in the helicopter field, Nardi established in 1971 a new company (BredaNardi, which see) in equal partnership with Breda, another well-known Italian aircraft manufacturer, which now forms one element of the EFIM state-owned financial group.

In addition to aircraft manufacture, Nardi produces wheels, brakes, retractable landing gear, hydraulic and electric aircraft controls, fuel pumps, armament installations and aircraft accessories generally. Among these is the production of landing gear, flaps and other accessories for F-104G Starfighters and other NATO combat aircraft, for the domestic F-104S programme, and for the Panavia MRCA programme.

PARTENAVIA

PARTENAVIA COSTRUZIONI AERONAUTICHE SpA

HEAD OFFICE AND WORKS:
Via Cava, CP 2179, 80026 Casoria (Naples)
Telephone: 596311 (PBX)
Telex: 77199 Partenav

PRESIDENT:
Prof Ing Luigi Pascale

DIRECTORS:
Dott G. Bulgari
Dott G. Fiore
Dott D. Marchiorello
Ing G. Regazzoni

PRODUCTION DIRECTOR:
Ing Nino Pascale

INTERNATIONAL MARKETING:
Ian A. Forbes

This company was founded in 1957 by Prof Ing Luigi Pascale and his brother, Ing Nino Pascale, and has since built a series of light aircraft designed by Prof Ing Pascale.

On 1 March 1974 the company moved from its small factory at Arzano, near Naples, to a 129,165 sq ft (12,000 m²) facility on Capodichino Airport, Naples, where it is now concentrating on the production of the P.68 Victor twin-engined light aircraft.

The P.64B and P.66B Oscar series of single-engined high-wing light aircraft, of which more than 200 have been built since production began in 1966, continue in limited production. Partenavia is also currently developing the P.70 Alpha low-wing single-engined trainer.

PARTENAVIA P.64B OSCAR-180 and OSCAR-200

Design of an improved version of the P.64 Oscar four-seat light aircraft (see 1966-67 *Jane's*) was started in November 1966 and construction of the prototype began in January 1967. The prototype flew in the first half of 1967. Seventy-three **Oscar-180s** (previously known as Oscar-Bs) had been built by 13 February 1974.

Improvements introduced in the Oscar-180 include a "stepped-down" rear fuselage and panoramic rear cabin window, giving an all-round field of vision.

A second version, the **Oscar-200,** has improved performance resulting from the installation of a 200 hp Lycoming IO-360-A1B fuel-injection engine with variable-pitch propeller. First example flown in May 1970; 16 built by February 1974. Orders include three for the Italian state police.

All current Oscar models have an improved engine exhaust system, resulting in a lower noise level, and modified nosewheel steering giving lighter forces on the ground. The standard of interior finish has also been improved.

In addition to production by the parent company, the Oscar-180 was produced by AFIC

Partenavia P.66B Oscar-100 (115 hp Lycoming O-235-C1B engine), described on page 134

(Pty) Ltd of Johannesburg as the **RSA 200 Falcon** (see the South African section of this edition). Production by AFIC has been suspended for the time being.

The two-seat P.66B Oscar-100 and three-seat Oscar-150 are described separately.

The following description applies generally to both the Oscar-180 and Oscar-200, except where indicated:

TYPE: Four-seat light monoplane.

WINGS: Braced high-wing monoplane with single streamline-section bracing strut each side. Wing section NACA 63 series. Thickness/chord ratio 15%. Dihedral 1° 30′. Incidence at root 1° 40′. No sweepback. Stressed-skin single-spar torsion-box structure of aluminium alloy, with glassfibre-reinforced leading-edges. Ailerons and manually-operated slotted trailing-edge flaps of similar construction to wings.

FUSELAGE: Conventional all-metal stressed-skin structure.

TAIL UNIT: Cantilever stressed-skin metal structure with sweptback vertical surfaces. All-moving tailplane in two symmetrical halves joined by steel cross-tube. Anti-balance tab in trailing-edge of tailplane, over 80% of span.

LANDING GEAR: Non-retractable tricycle type, with steerable nosewheel. Cantilever spring steel main legs. Oleo nosewheel shock-absorber. Cleveland main wheels type 40-28, with Pirelli tyres size 6·00-6. Goodyear nosewheel tyre size 5·00-5. Cleveland type 30-18 hydraulic disc brakes.

POWER PLANT: One 180 hp Lycoming O-360-A1A four-cylinder horizontally-opposed aircooled engine (200 hp IO-360-A1B in Oscar-200), driving a Hartzell HC-C2YK-1A two-blade variable-pitch constant-speed metal propeller or (Oscar-180 only) a Sensenich fixed-pitch propeller. Two fuel tanks in wing roots, total usable capacity 41·5 Imp gallons (190 litres). Refuelling points above wings. Oil capacity 1·66 Imp gallons (7·5 litres).

ACCOMMODATION: Enclosed cabin seating four persons in pairs with dual controls; front seats are of the adjustable sliding type. Three forward-hinged doors: one by each front seat and on starboard side at rear. Baggage space aft of rear seats, with separate door on starboard side. Heating, ventilation and sound-proofing standard.

ELECTRONICS AND EQUIPMENT: Optional items include full IFR instrumentation, Grimes rotating beacon, VHF radio, VOR and ADF.

DIMENSIONS, EXTERNAL:
- Wing span: 32 ft 9½ in (9·99 m)
- Wing chord (constant): 4 ft 5½ in (1·36 m)
- Wing aspect ratio: 7·45
- Length overall: 23 ft 8¾ in (7·23 m)
- Height overall: 9 ft 1 in (2·77 m)
- Tailplane span: 10 ft 2 in (3·10 m)
- Wheel track: 6 ft 10¾ in (2·10 m)
- Propeller diameter: 6 ft 2 in (1·88 m)

DIMENSIONS, INTERNAL:
- Cabin: Max width: 3 ft 5¾ in (1·06 m)
- Max height: 3 ft 11¼ in (1·20 m)

AREAS:
- Wings, gross: 144·2 sq ft (13·40 m²)
- Ailerons (total): 13·88 sq ft (1·29 m²)
- Trailing-edge flaps (total): 18·40 sq ft (1·71 m²)

Fin 7·86 sq ft (0·73 m^2)
Rudder 4·84 sq ft (0·45 m^2)
Tailplane, including tab 23·36 sq ft (2·17 m^2)

WEIGHTS AND LOADINGS:
Weight empty:
180 1,477 lb (670 kg)
200 1,521 lb (690 kg)
Max T-O weight:
180 (fixed-pitch prop) 2,425 lb (1,100 kg)
180 (variable-pitch prop), 200 2,546 lb (1,155 kg)
Max landing weight 2,425 lb (1,100 kg)
Max wing loading:
180 (fixed-pitch prop) 16·8 lb/sq ft (82 kg/m^2)
180 (variable-pitch prop), 200 17·6 lb/sq ft (86 kg/m^2)
Max power loading:
180 13·4 lb/hp (6·10 kg/hp)
200 12·7 lb/hp (5·77 kg/hp)

PERFORMANCE (at max T-O weight):
Max never-exceed speed 178 knots (205 mph; 331 km/h)
Max level speed at S/L:
180 141 knots (162 mph; 260 km/h)
200 148·5 knots (171 mph; 275 km/h)
Max cruising speed (75% power) at 7,000 ft (2,150 m):
180 129 knots (149 mph; 240 km/h)
200 135 knots (155 mph; 250 km/h)
Stalling speed, flaps up 58·5 knots (67·5 mph; 108 km/h)
Stalling speed, flaps down 48·5 knots (55·5 mph; 89 km/h)
Max rate of climb at S/L:
180 984 ft (300 m)/min
200 1,180 ft (360 m)/min
Service ceiling:
180 16,400 ft (5,000 m)
200 17,400 ft (5,300 m)
T-O run:
180 869 ft (265 m)
200 805 ft (245 m)
Landing run 656 ft (200 m)
Endurance (75% power):
180 4 hr 30 min
200 4 hr 0 min

PARTENAVIA P.66B OSCAR-100 and OSCAR-150

These all-metal light aircraft are two- and three-seat counterparts of the P.64B Oscar, and many airframe components of the four types are interchangeable.

Differences between the two versions are as follows:

Oscar-100. Two-seater, with 115 hp Lycoming O-235-C1B engine. One hundred and seven built by 13 February 1974.

Oscar-150. Similar to Oscar-100, but with seating for three persons. Power plant is a 150 hp Lycoming O-320-E2A four-cylinder horizontally-opposed aircooled engine, driving a two-blade Sensenich 74DM6S5-2-60 fixed-pitch metal propeller. Seventy-nine built by 13 February 1974.

The structural description of the P.64B applies equally to the P.66B, except for details given below:

TYPE: Two-seat (Oscar-100) or three-seat (Oscar-150) light monoplane.

WINGS: As for P.64B.

FUSELAGE: Forward portion, to rear of cabin, is a welded steel-tube structure, covered with light alloy panels. Rear fuselage is of conventional light alloy stressed-skin construction.

POWER PLANT: One 115 hp Lycoming O-235-C1B four-cylinder horizontally-opposed aircooled engine, driving a Sensenich 76AM6-2-46 two-blade fixed-pitch metal propeller. Two wing fuel tanks, total usable capacity 23·7 Imp gallons (108 litres). Provision for 17·5 Imp gallon (80 litre) auxiliary tank. Refuelling point above each wing.

ACCOMMODATION: Two adjustable sliding seats side by side in enclosed cabin, with forward-hinged door on each side. Dual stick-type controls standard (starboard one quickly removable). Dual wheel-type controls optional. Provision for fitting rear seat for a child weighing up to 90 lb (40 kg). Baggage space aft of seats. Cabin heated, ventilated and soundproofed.

ELECTRONICS AND EQUIPMENT: Provision for full blind-flying instrumentation, VHF nav/com radio, VOR and ADF.

DIMENSIONS, EXTERNAL:
As for P.64B, except:
Length overall 23 ft $3\frac{1}{8}$ in (7·09 m)
Propeller diameter
100 6 ft 2 in (1·88 m)
150 6 ft 0 in (1·83 m)

DIMENSIONS, INTERNAL:
Cabin: Max width 3 ft $5\frac{3}{4}$ in (1·06 m)
Max height 3 ft $9\frac{3}{4}$ in (1·16 m)

WEIGHTS AND LOADINGS:
Weight empty:
100 1,235 lb (560 kg)
150 1,344 lb (610 kg)
Max T-O weight:
100 1,808 lb (820 kg)
150 2,050 lb (930 kg)
Max wing loading:
100 12·53 lb/sq ft (61·2 kg/m^2)
150 14·2 lb/sq ft (69·45 kg/m^2)
Max power loading:
100 15·74 lb/hp (7·14 kg/hp)
150 13·7 lb/hp (6·20 kg/hp)

PERFORMANCE (at max T-O weight):
Max never-exceed speed:
100 166·5 knots (192 mph; 310 km/h)
150 171 knots (197 mph; 317 km/h)
Max level speed at S/L:
100 116 knots (134 mph; 215 km/h)
150 129 knots (149 mph; 240 km/h)
Max cruising speed (75% power) at 7,000 ft (2,150 m):
100 102 knots (118 mph; 190 km/h)
150 116 knots (134 mph; 215 km/h)
Stalling speed, flaps up:
100 45·5 knots (52 mph; 83 km/h)
150 48·5 knots (55·5 mph; 89 km/h)
Stalling speed, flaps down:
100 36 knots (41 mph; 66 km/h)
150 40 knots (45·5 mph; 73 km/h)
Max rate of climb at S/L:
100 728 ft (222 m)/min
150 885 ft (270 m)/min
Service ceiling:
100 13,125 ft (4,000 m)
150 14,775 ft (4,500 m)
T-O run:
100 820 ft (250 m)
150 804 ft (245 m)
Landing run:
100 394 ft (120 m)
150 492 ft (150 m)
Endurance (75% power):
100 3 hr 36 min
150 3 hr 0 min

PARTENAVIA P.68 VICTOR

Designed by Prof Ing Luigi Pascale, the P.68 is a twin-engined high-wing monoplane for private or business flying, air taxi, training or third-level transport duties. The prototype (I-TWIN) made its first flight on 25 May 1970, and the P.68 was certificated by RAI and FAA (Normal category) on 17 November and 7 December 1971 respectively.

Due to limited manufacturing facilities at Arzano, only thirteen pre-production P.68s had been completed by February 1974; these were sold to operators in Denmark, Finland, Israel, Switzerland and Italy, and three of them have been modified for aerial survey photography.

In January 1974 larger-scale manufacture of the production series P.68 began in the new facility at Capodichino Airport, and a production rate of four aircraft per month was expected to be achieved by the end of 1974. Deliveries of the P.68 to Africa, Australia, Brazil, England, France, Germany, Portugal and Sweden began in the Spring of 1974, and production capacity is entirely committed to distributors' requirements well into 1975.

Due to the simplicity of the P.68's construction, Partenavia plans to offer the aircraft in kit form to those countries wishing to start an assembly programme. Two complete aircraft, less engines and propellers, can be loaded for shipping from the port of Naples in a standard 40 ft (12·2 m) container.

The initial production series P.68, to which the description applies, differs from the pre-production batch in having a 6 in (15 cm) extension in the front part of the fuselage and greater width at the instrument panel, resulting in a roomier cockpit. Further improvements include re-grouping of the engine starting controls on the cockpit roof, repositioning of the electrical system panel on the left-hand cockpit wall, and the use of counterweighted crankshaft Lycoming IO-360-A1B6 engines. All aircraft now incorporate the

Partenavia P.66B Oscar-150 (150 hp Lycoming O-320-E2A engine) (*Dr Ulrich Haller*)

Partenavia P.68 Victor six-seat light aircraft (two 200 hp Lycoming IO-360 engines) (*Air Portraits*)

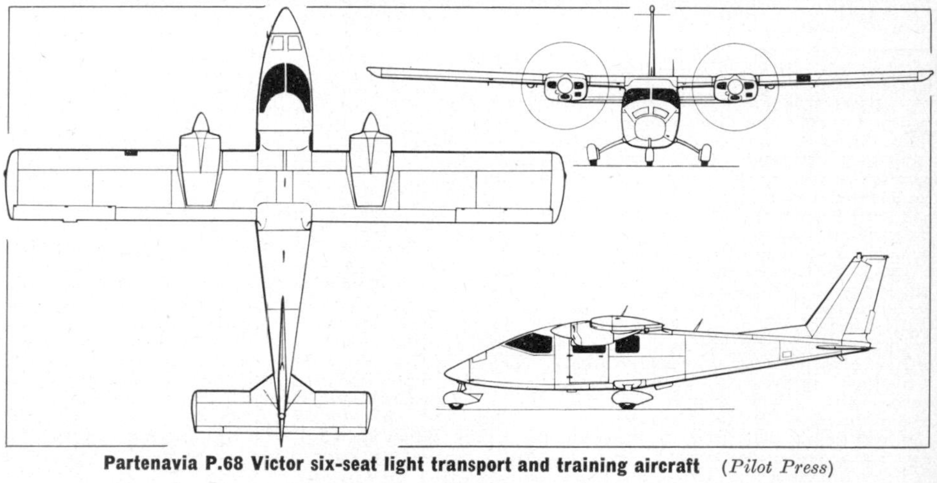

Partenavia P.68 Victor six-seat light transport and training aircraft (*Pilot Press*)

large baggage locker door formerly available as an optional extra. A freight door that will permit the loading of stretchers and very bulky goods is in the design stage. Engineering work for the retractable-gear version of the P.68 is almost complete but, due to manufacturing commitments for the existing fixed-gear version, certification of the retractable-gear version is not expected to be possible until the end of 1975.

TYPE: Six-seat light transport and trainer.

WINGS: Cantilever high-wing monoplane. Wing section NACA 63 series. Thickness/chord ratio 15%. Dihedral 1°. Incidence 1° 30′. No sweepback. Stressed-skin single-spar torsion-box structure, of aluminium alloy except for area forward of main spar (30% of total area) which is of glassfibre-reinforced plastics. All-metal ailerons and electrically-operated single-slotted trailing-edge flaps. Hoerner wingtips.

FUSELAGE: Conventional all-metal semi-monocoque structure of frames and longerons with four main longerons and stressed-skin covering. Fuselage/wing intersection mainly of glassfibre-reinforced plastics.

TAIL UNIT: Cantilever stressed-skin metal structure. All-moving tailplane, in two symmetrical halves joined by steel cross-tube and of constant chord except for increase at leading-edge roots. Balance tab in tailplane trailing-edge, over 80% of span. Sweptback fin and rudder, with small dorsal fin. Trim tab on rudder.

LANDING GEAR: Initial production version has non-retractable tricycle type, with steerable nosewheel. Cantilever spring steel main legs. Oleo-pneumatic shock-absorber on nosewheel. Cleveland main wheels, type 40-96, with Pirelli tyres size 6·00-6. Goodyear nosewheel tyre, size 5·00-5. Cleveland type 30-61 hydraulic disc brakes. Streamlined wheel fairings optional. Future production version is planned with hydraulically-retractable tricycle landing gear, having oleo-pneumatic shock-absorbers and fairings on the fuselage sides to house the retracted main units.

POWER PLANT: Two 200 hp Lycoming IO-360-A1B6 four-cylinder horizontally-opposed air-cooled engines, each driving a Hartzell HC-C2YK-2C/C-7666A-4 two-blade variable-pitch constant-speed fully-feathering propeller. Integral fuel tank in each outer wing, total capacity 107 Imp gallons (485 litres). Refuelling point above each wing. Oil capacity 3·3 Imp gallons (15 litres).

ACCOMMODATION: Seating for six persons in cabin, including pilot, in three rows of two, with space for baggage aft of rear pair. Front seats are of the adjustable sliding type. Access to all seats via large car-type door on port side of cabin. Access to baggage compartment via separate door on starboard side. Dual controls, cabin heating, ventilation and soundproofing standard.

SYSTEMS AND EQUIPMENT: Optional equipment includes full IFR instrumentation, two 360-channel VHF transceivers, two navigation receivers, VOR/ILS, marker beacon, ADF and DME. Electrical power supplied by two 24V 50A alternators. Bendix FCS 810 autopilot system and Goodrich pneumatic de-icing system optional.

DIMENSIONS, EXTERNAL:
- Wing span: 39 ft 4½ in (12·00 m)
- Wing chord (constant): 5 ft 1 in (1·55 m)
- Wing aspect ratio: 7·75
- Length overall: 30 ft 2 in (9·19 m)
- Height overall: 11 ft 1¾ in (3·40 m)
- Tailplane span: 12 ft 9½ in (3·90 m)
- Wheel track (1st prototype): 7 ft 10½ in (2·40 m)
- Wheel track (2nd prototype): 6 ft 6¾ in (2·00 m)
- Wheelbase: 11 ft 5¾ in (3·50 m)
- Propeller diameter: 6 ft 2 in (1·88 m)
- Baggage door, stbd:
  - Height: 2 ft 7½ in (0·80 m)
  - Width: 2 ft 7½ in (0·80 m)

DIMENSIONS, INTERNAL:
- Cabin:
  - Length: 13 ft 1½ in (4·00 m)
  - Max width: 3 ft 9½ in (1·16 m)
  - Max height: 3 ft 11½ in (1·21 m)
- Baggage space: 37 cu ft (1·05 m³)

AREAS:
- Wings, gross: 206·0 sq ft (19·44 m²)
- Ailerons (total): 19·27 sq ft (1·79 m²)
- Trailing-edge flaps (total): 25·51 sq ft (2·37 m²)
- Fin: 17·11 sq ft (1·59 m²)
- Rudder: 4·74 sq ft (0·44 m²)
- Tailplane, including tab: 47·47 sq ft (4·41 m²)

WEIGHTS AND LOADINGS:
- Weight empty: 2,645 lb (1,200 kg)
- Max T-O weight: 4,321 lb (1,960 kg)
- Max landing weight: 4,100 lb (1,860 kg)
- Max wing loading: 21·5 lb/sq ft (105 kg/m²)
- Max power loading: 10·80 lb/hp (4·9 kg/hp)

PERFORMANCE (at max T-O weight):
- *Max level speed at S/L: 175 knots (201 mph; 324 km/h)
- *Max cruising speed (75% power) at 5,575 ft (1,700 m): 166 knots (191 mph; 307 km/h)
- *Econ cruising speed (65% power) at 8,860 ft (2,700 m): 159 knots (183 mph; 294 km/h)

**with wheel fairings fitted*

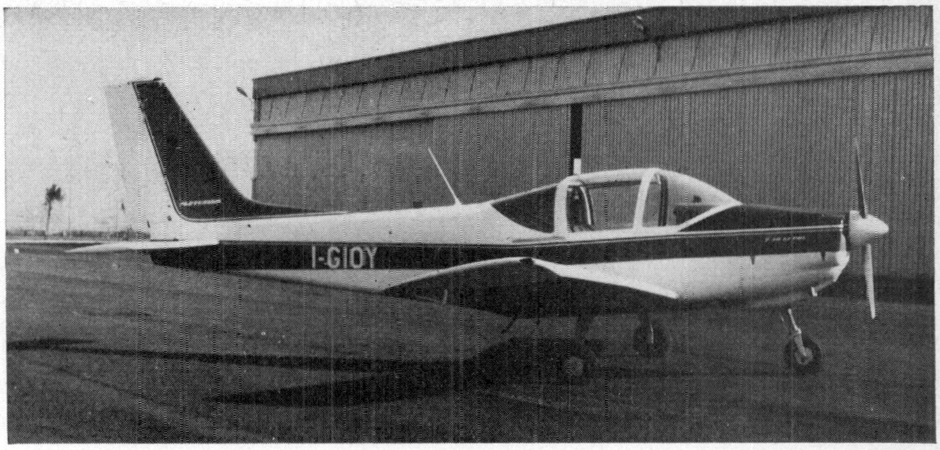

Partenavia P.70 Alpha two-seat training aircraft (100 hp Rolls-Royce Continental O-200 engine)

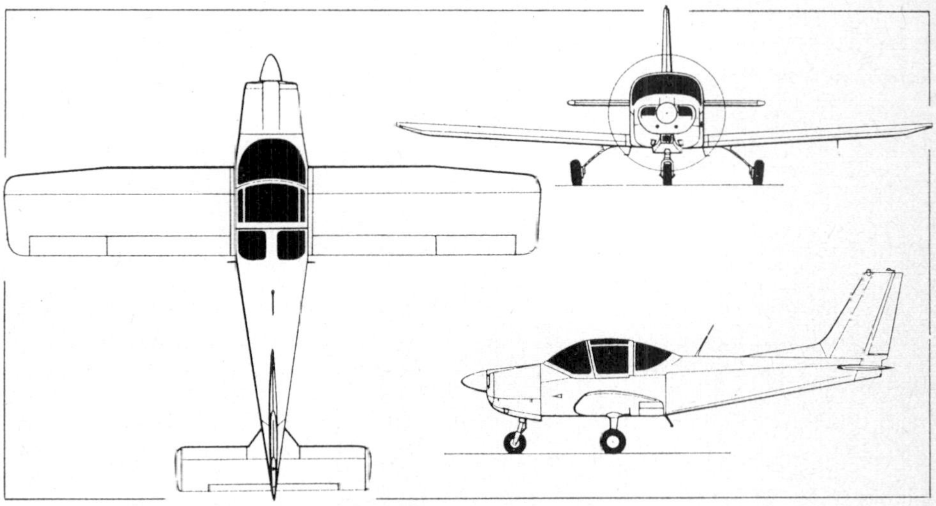

Partenavia P.70 Alpha two-seat fully-aerobatic training aircraft (*Pilot Press*)

- Stalling speed, flaps up: 59 knots (68 mph; 109 km/h)
- Stalling speed, flaps down: 53 knots (61 mph; 97 km/h)
- Max rate of climb at S/L: 1,650 ft (503 m)/min
- Rate of climb at S/L, one engine out: 350 ft (107 m)/min
- Service ceiling: 20,000 ft (6,100 m)
- Service ceiling, one engine out: 7,000 ft (2,135 m)
- T-O run: 860 ft (262 m)
- T-O to 50 ft (15 m): 1,128 ft (344 m)
- Landing from 50 ft (15 m): 1,158 ft (353 m)
- Landing run: 640 ft (195 m)
- Max range at max cruising speed: 825 nm (950 miles; 1,528 km)
- Max range at econ cruising speed: 907 nm (1,045 miles; 1,681 km)

PARTENAVIA P.70 ALPHA

Design of the P.70 light trainer was started in August 1970 by Prof Ing Luigi Pascale, and construction of a prototype began in January 1971. This aircraft (I-GIOY) made its first flight on 24 April 1972.

The P.70, designed to meet FAR Pt 23-III aerobatic requirements ($-6g$; $-3g$ load factors) and to take engines of up to 160 hp, is of simplified metal and plastics construction, approx 50 per cent of the airframe being of glassfibre-reinforced plastics. All metal parts are of flat section, plastics being used for curved components.

Due to heavy production commitments for the P.68 Victor, and to limited manufacturing capacity, the P.70 development programme has necessarily been retarded, and certification is not expected before the end of 1974.

By the Spring of 1974 the prototype had completed about 80 hours of test flying, mostly in the hands of Prof Ing Pascale. Changes made to the aircraft during the test programme have been restricted to an increase in wing dihedral, and installation of integral fuel tanks in the one-piece moulded glassfibre-reinforced plastics leading-edges, in place of the original fuselage tank.

The following description applies to the prototype as being flown in the Spring of 1974:

TYPE: Two-seat light training aircraft.

WINGS: Cantilever low-wing monoplane. Wing section NACA 3412 (modified). Thickness/chord ratio between 12 and 13%. Dihedral 5°. Stressed-skin single-spar torsion-box structure of aluminium alloy, with secondary rear spar and glassfibre-reinforced plastics leading-edges. Bottom-hinged ailerons and electrically-actuated flaps.

FUSELAGE: Basic light alloy structure of longerons and webs, mainly rectangular in section with rounded corners. Top of fuselage, from rear of cabin to tail, tailcone and parts of engine cowling, are of glassfibre-reinforced plastics.

TAIL UNIT: Cantilever metal stressed-skin structure, with tailplane tips and fin leading-edge of glassfibre-reinforced plastics. Fin integral with fuselage. One-piece all-moving tailplane with anti-tabs.

LANDING GEAR: Non-retractable tricycle type. Main units have single leaf-spring shock-absorbers, size 5·00-5 wheels and hydraulic disc brakes. Nose unit has oleo-pneumatic shock-strut, size 5·00-5 wheel, and is steerable.

POWER PLANT: One 100 hp Rolls-Royce Continental O-200-A four-cylinder horizontally-opposed aircooled engine, driving a McCauley two-blade fixed-pitch metal propeller. Integral fuel tank in each wing leading-edge, total usable capacity 26 Imp gallons (118 litres).

ACCOMMODATION: Side-by-side adjustable seats for two persons under rearward-sliding canopy. Baggage space aft of seats. Dual controls.

SYSTEMS AND EQUIPMENT: Electrical power, for flap actuation, lights and instrumentation, and emergency fuel pump, provided by one 12V 60A alternator and a 30Ah battery. Standard provision for VFR or IFR instrumentation, ADF and VOR/ILS.

DIMENSIONS, EXTERNAL:
- Wing span: 27 ft 10¾ in (8·50 m)
- Wing chord: 4 ft 7 in (1·40 m)
- Wing aspect ratio: 6·23
- Length overall: 23 ft 2 in (7·06 m)
- Height overall: 9 ft 10 in (3·00 m)
- Tailplane span: 9 ft 6¼ in (2·90 m)
- Wheel track: 9 ft 4½ in (2·86 m)
- Propeller diameter: 6 ft 2 in (1·88 m)

DIMENSIONS, INTERNAL:
- Cabin: Max width: 3 ft 5 in (1·04 m)
  - Max height: 3 ft 7¼ in (1·10 m)

AREAS:
- Wings, gross: 125 sq ft (11·60 m²)
- Ailerons (total): 8·72 sq ft (0·81 m²)
- Flaps (total): 15·72 sq ft (1·46 m²)
- Fin: 7·75 sq ft (0·72 m²)
- Rudder: 4·74 sq ft (0·44 m²)
- Tailplane, incl tabs: 20·24 sq ft (1·88 m²)

WEIGHTS AND LOADINGS:
- Weight empty: 1,014 lb (460 kg)
- Max T-O and landing weight: 1,543 lb (700 kg)
- Max wing loading: 12·4 lb/sq ft (60·3 kg/m²)
- Max power loading: 15·43 lb/hp (7·0 kg/hp)

PERFORMANCE (prototype, at max T-O weight):
- Max never-exceed speed: 182 knots (210 mph; 338 km/h)

Max level speed at S/L
116 knots (134 mph; 216 km/h)
Max cruising speed (75% power) at 7,000 ft (2,135 m) 107 knots (123 mph; 198 km/h)
Stalling speed, flaps up
47·5 knots (55 mph; 88 km/h)
Stalling speed, flaps down
43 knots (49 mph; 79 km/h)
Max rate of climb at S/L 700 ft (213 m)/min
Service ceiling 12,000 ft (3,660 m)
T-O run 722 ft (220 m)
Landing run 427 ft (130 m)
Range with max fuel
474 nm (546 miles; 880 km)
g limits +6; —3

PERFORMANCE (P.70-160 with 160 hp Lycoming O-320-B engine, estimated at max T-O weight):
Max level speed at S/L
139 knots (160 mph; 257 km/h)
Max cruising speed (75% power) at 7,000 ft (2,135 m) 126 knots (145 mph; 233 km/h)
Max rate of climb at S/L 1,400 ft (427 m)/min
Service ceiling 16,500 ft (5,030 m)

PIAGGIO

INDUSTRIE AERONAUTICHE E MECCANICHE RINALDO PIAGGIO SpA

HEAD OFFICE:
Viale Brigata Bisagno 14, Casella Postale 1396, 16129 Genoa
Telephone: 540.521
Telex: 27695 AERPIAG

BRANCH OFFICE:
Via A. Gramsci 34, Rome

WORKS:
Genoa-Sestri P. (Aircraft Division)
Finale Ligure (Aero-Engine Division)

CHAIRMAN:
Ing Armando Piaggio

VICE-PRESIDENT AND CHIEF EXECUTIVE OFFICER:
Dott Lucio Lotti

MANAGING DIRECTOR:
Dott Rinaldo Piaggio

TECHNICAL CONSULTANT:
Ing Giovanni P. Casiraghi

MARKETING DIRECTOR:
Commander G. B. Pizzinato

PUBLIC RELATIONS MANAGER:
Dott Alceo Gerli

Piaggio began the construction of aeroplanes in its Genoa-Sestri plant in 1916, and later in the Finale Ligure works. A second large plant covering approx 430,000 sq ft (40,000 m²) was built in 1968 at Genoa-Sestri, on the edge of Genoa's Christopher Columbus Airport, for assembly and overhaul of the P.166 twin-engined aircraft and of the PD-808 light twin-jet utility aircraft.

The present company was formed on 29 February 1964, and has since operated as an independent concern. It employs about 1,300 people.

The company is organised into two production Divisions. The P.166 and PD-808 are in production by the Aircraft Division at Genoa-Sestri; current activities of the Aero-Engine Division are described in the appropriate section of this edition.

R. PIAGGIO P.166

The P.166 is a twin-engined light transport aircraft, with standard accommodation for 6/8 passengers. An alternative layout offers seats for 12 passengers, and the aircraft can be used for a variety of different duties.

The P.166 has been produced or is available in several basic versions. Of these, the original P.166 production version (32 built) was described in the 1963-64 *Jane's*; and the military P.166M (51 built), the P.166B Portofino (5 built) and P.166C (2 built) in the 1971-72 *Jane's*. Production of these versions has been completed.

Versions recently produced or currently under development are as follows:

P.166S. Search and surveillance version, developed from P.166. Nose radar, two pilot's doors, cargo door and emergency hatch in cabin roof. Extensive nav/com equipment. Increased fuel capacity. First flight October 1968, RAI type approval 27 February 1969. Total of 20 ordered, of which delivery was completed during 1973.

P.166-BL2. Superseded P.166B as a standard commercial version. Increased fuel capacity in integral wingtip tanks, increased max T-O weight. Two prototypes were under construction in Spring 1974. One of these will be used as a demonstrator; the other will serve as a flying testbed for the various versions in which this aircraft will be made available.

The following description applies to the standard P.166-BL2:

TYPE: Twin-engined light transport.

WINGS: Shoulder gull-wing cantilever monoplane. NACA 230 wing section. Dihedral 21° 30′ on inner portion, 2° 8′ on outer wings. Incidence 2° 43′. All-metal aluminium alloy flush-riveted structure. All-metal slotted ailerons, with geared and trim tab on starboard aileron. All-metal slotted flaps. Rubber boot de-icing of leading-edges optional.

FUSELAGE: All-metal aluminium alloy flush-riveted semi-monocoque structure.

TAIL UNIT: Cantilever all-metal aluminium alloy flush-riveted structure. Geared and trim tab in elevators; trim tab in rudder.

LANDING GEAR: Retractable tricycle type. Magnaghi oleo-pneumatic shock-absorbers. Hydraulic retraction. Nosewheel retracts rearward, main units outward and upward. Goodyear main wheels with size 25·65 × 8·70-10 tyres, pressure 52 lb/sq in (3·66 kg/cm²). Goodyear nosewheel with size 17·5 × 6·30-6 tyre, pressure 42 lb/sq in (2·95 kg/cm²). Goodyear or Magnaghi hydraulic brakes.

POWER PLANT: Two 380 hp Lycoming IGSO-540-A1C six-cylinder horizontally-opposed air-cooled engines, each driving a Hartzell type HC-BZ30-2 BL/L10151-8 three-blade feathering constant-speed pusher propeller. Fuel in two internal tanks in outer wings (each 46·6 Imp gallons; 212 litres), and two external wingtip tanks (each 71 Imp gallons; 323 litres). Total fuel capacity 235·2 Imp gallons (1,070 litres). Total oil capacity 7·5 Imp gallons (34 litres).

ACCOMMODATION: Standard seating for pilot and five passengers in individual seats, with toilet and bar at rear. Alternative layouts include an 8-seat executive version, with two rows of three seats in cabin, facing each other; high-density 10-seat version with three individual seats on each side of central aisle in cabin, and curved rear twin seats in place of toilet and bar; cargo version with stripped cabin; ambulance and air survey versions. Main door in centre of cabin on port side. Separate door to flight deck on starboard side. Outside door to baggage compartment aft of cabin on port side. Dual controls standard.

SYSTEMS: Hydraulic system, pressure 1,840 lb/sq in (125 kg/cm²), operates landing gear, flaps and brakes. 28V engine-driven DC generator for electrical system.

ELECTRONICS AND EQUIPMENT: Optional equipment includes VHF radio, VOR, ADF, marker beacon receiver, glideslope receiver and Sperry SPL 45 autopilot and horizon gyro unit.

DIMENSIONS, EXTERNAL:
Wing span:
without tip-tanks 44 ft 4 in (13·51 m)
with tip-tanks 48 ft 2½ in (14·69 m)
Wing chord at root 7 ft 10¼ in (2·40 m)
Wing chord at tip 3 ft 9¼ in (1·15 m)
Wing aspect ratio 7·3
Length overall 39 ft 3 in (11·90 m)
Height over tail 16 ft 5 in (5·00 m)
Tailplane span 16 ft 9 in (5·10 m)
Wheel track 8 ft 9 in (2·66 m)
Wheelbase 15 ft 5½ in (4·71 m)
Passenger door (port side):
Height 4 ft 10 in (1·47 m)
Width 2 ft 2 in (0·66 m)

DIMENSIONS, INTERNAL:
Cabin: Length 11 ft 8 in (3·55 m)
Max width 5 ft 2 in (1·57 m)
Max height 5 ft 9 in (1·76 m)
Floor area 55·3 sq ft (5·14 m²)
Volume 234·1 cu ft (6·63 m³)
Baggage compartment (front)
27·2 cu ft (0·77 m³)
Baggage compartment (rear) 63·6 cu ft (1·80 m³)

AREAS:
Wings, gross 285·9 sq ft (26·56 m²)
Ailerons (total) 21·00 sq ft (1·95 m²)
Trailing-edge flaps (total) 25·60 sq ft (2·38 m²)
Fin 17·44 sq ft (1·62 m²)
Rudder, incl tab 13·24 sq ft (1·23 m²)
Tailplane 37·67 sq ft (3·50 m²)
Elevators, incl tabs 13·88 sq ft (1·29 m²)

WEIGHTS AND LOADINGS:
Weight empty, equipped 5,556 lb (2,520 kg)
Max payload 2,204 lb (1,000 kg)
Max T-O weight 8,708 lb (3,950 kg)
Max landing weight 8,377 lb (3,800 kg)
Max wing loading 30·45 lb/sq ft (148·7 kg/m²)
Max power loading 11·46 lb/hp (5·20 kg/hp)

PERFORMANCE (at max T-O weight, except where indicated otherwise):
Max never-exceed speed
256 knots (295 mph; 476 km/h)
*Max level speed at 11,300 ft (3,450 m)
214 knots (246 mph; 396 km/h)
*Max cruising speed (75% power) at 15,000 ft (4,550 m) 194 knots (223 mph; 395 km/h)
*Econ cruising speed (45% power) at 15,000 ft (4,550 m) 153 knots (176 mph; 283 km/h)
Stalling speed, flaps and wheels down, at max landing weight
57·5 knots (66 mph; 106 km/h)
Max rate of climb at S/L 1,415 ft (430 m)/min
Service ceiling 27,000 ft (8,230 m)
Service ceiling, one engine out
11,500 ft (3,505 m)
Min ground turning radius 19 ft 8¼ in (6·00 m)
Runway LCN 4·5
T-O run, FAR 23 1,320 ft (402 m)
T-O to 50 ft (15 m), FAR 23 1,930 ft (588 m)
*Landing from 50 ft (15 m), FAR 23
1,400 ft (427 m)
*Landing run, FAR 23 920 ft (280 m)
Range with max fuel, no reserves, at 10,000 ft (3,050 m) 1,300 nm (1,500 miles; 2,410 km)
Range with max payload, no reserves
337 nm (388 miles; 626 km)
**at intermediate flying weight of* 7,715 lb (3,500 kg)

R. PIAGGIO PD-808

The PD-808 is a 6/10-seat light jet utility aircraft suitable for both civil and military use. The Italian Defence Ministry assisted Piaggio by purchasing the two prototypes (each powered by 3,000 lb; 1,360 kg st Viper Mk 525 engines) and by providing test facilities. The first of these prototypes made its first flight on 29 August 1964.

In mid-1965, the Italian Defence Ministry ordered 25 production PD-808s. These aircraft have more powerful Viper Mk 526 engines and differ from the original prototype in having larger tip-tanks, longer dorsal fin and forward-sliding nose fairing.

More than 20 PD-808s had been built by the Spring of 1974, in the following versions:

PD-808 VIP. Six-seat version for the Italian Air Force, used for government and military VIP transport duties.

PD-808 TA. Nine-seat version for military transport duties and navigation training. RAI and FAA certification 19 October 1968.

PD-808 ECM. Electronic countermeasures military version, with accommodation for two pilots and three equipment operators. Details classified.

Four PD-808s are currently being built for the Italian Air Force in the RM (radio calibration) configuration. These will be fitted with appropriate equipment to carry out medium and high altitude calibration of aids to navigation.

Piaggio is continuing the design study of a version with turbofan engines, the PD-808 TF. This was described in the 1972-73 *Jane's*.

The following description applies to the standard production aircraft with Viper Mk 526 engines:

TYPE: Twin-jet light utility aircraft.

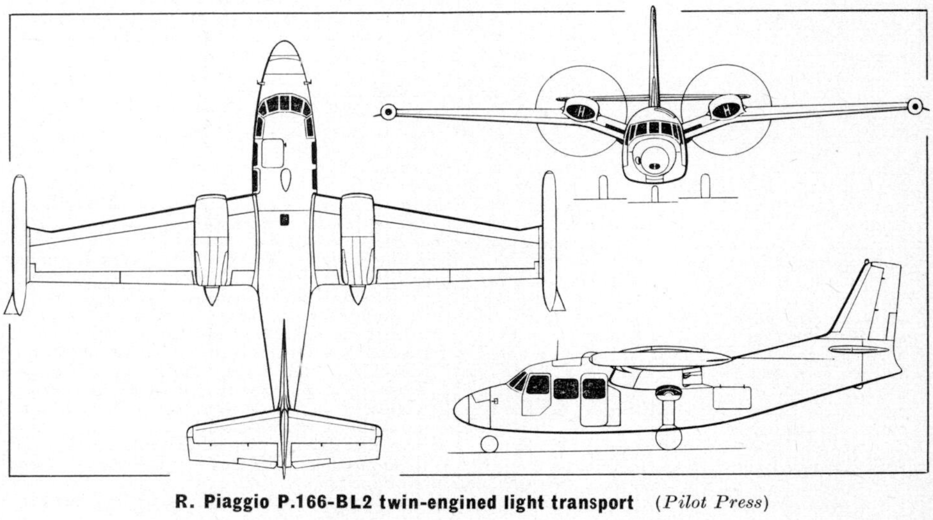

R. Piaggio P.166-BL2 twin-engined light transport (*Pilot Press*)

WINGS: Cantilever low-wing monoplane. Wing section DES 0010-1·1-40/11° (modified) at root, DES 0008-1·1-40/9° (modified) at tip. Dihedral 3°. Incidence 1°. Sweepback 1° 50′ at quarter-chord. All-metal aluminium alloy fail-safe three-spar structure. All-metal ailerons, each with geared and trim tab. Hydraulically-operated single-slotted trailing-edge flaps. Hydraulically-operated spoilers on top of each wing operate on nosewheel contact during landing.

FUSELAGE: Circular-section all-metal fail-safe structure with machined frames. Hydraulically-operated airbrakes under fuselage.

TAIL UNIT: Cantilever all-metal structure, with fixed-incidence tailplane. Trim and geared tabs in elevator, trim tab in rudder.

LANDING GEAR: Retractable tricycle type with single wheel on each unit. Hydraulic retraction, all units retracting forward. Oleo-pneumatic shock-absorbers. Goodyear main wheels and tyres size 24·15 × 7·65-10, pressure 135 lb/sq in (9·49 kg/cm²). Goodyear nosewheel and tyre, size 17·9 × 5·70-8, pressure 135 lb/sq in (9·49 kg/cm²). Aerostatica R.F.91 braking parachute, diameter 7 ft 10½ in (2·40 m). Messier hydraulic brakes. Hydraulic nosewheel steering.

POWER PLANT: Two Rolls-Royce Bristol Viper Mk 526 turbojet engines (each rated at 3,360 lb; 1,524 kg st) mounted on sides of rear fuselage. Fuel in two integral tanks in wings, with total capacity of 425·5 Imp gallons (1,935 litres), and two integral wingtip tanks with total capacity of 394 Imp gallons (1,792 litres). Total fuel capacity 819·5 Imp gallons (3,727 litres). Refuelling points on tip-tanks. Oil capacity 28 lb (13 kg).

ACCOMMODATION (Military versions): In addition to standard transport roles, the aircraft can be used for training and combat duties. The PD-808 TA has one main student station in the co-pilot's seat, with two or three more student stations in the cabin.

ACCOMMODATION (Civil versions): Crew of one or two on flight deck, with dual controls. Standard seating for five passengers in individual chairs, with bar and toilet at front of cabin and baggage space aft of rear seats. Further stowage space in nose, with access by sliding nose forward. Up to nine seats in cabin in high-density version. Executive interiors styled by Pininfarina available. Ambulance version has accommodation for two stretchers, two sitting casualties and medical attendant. With cabin stripped, there is space for 185 cu ft (5·24 m³) of freight, survey camera stations, navigation training equipment etc. Downward-opening plug-type door, with built-in steps, at front of cabin on port side. Cabin air-conditioned and pressurised.

SYSTEMS: AiResearch simple air-cycle air-conditioning and pressurisation system, using engine bleed air. Pressure differential 8·8 lb/sq in (0·62 kg/cm²). Hydraulic system, pressure 3,000 lb/sq in (210 kg/cm²), operates landing gear, flaps, spoilers, airbrakes, nosewheel steering and wheel brakes. Pneumatic de-icing and anti-icing. Electrical system includes two DC generators, three inverters, two AC generators and two batteries.

R. Piaggio PD-808 VIP military transport aircraft of the Italian Air Force

ELECTRONICS AND EQUIPMENT: Standard equipment includes VHF radio, ADF, glideslope and marker beacon receivers. DME and weather radar optional.

DIMENSIONS, EXTERNAL:
Wing span 37 ft 6 in (11·43 m)
Wing span over tip-tanks 43 ft 3½ in (13·20 m)
Wing chord (mean) 8 ft 0 in (2·438 m)
Wing aspect ratio 6·25
Length overall 42 ft 2 in (12·85 m)
Height overall 15 ft 9 in (4·80 m)
Tailplane span 17 ft 9½ in (5·43 m)
Wheel track 12 ft 0¾ in (3·68 m)
Wheelbase 14 ft 9 in (4·50 m)
Passenger door (forward, port):
Height 4 ft 1½ in (1·26 m)
Width 2 ft 1½ in (0·65 m)

DIMENSIONS, INTERNAL:
Cabin: Length 14 ft 8 in (4·47 m)
Max width 5 ft 4½ in (1·64 m)
Max height 4 ft 9 in (1·45 m)
Floor area 50·16 sq ft (4·66 m²)
Volume 291 cu ft (8·24 m³)

AREAS:
Wings, gross 225 sq ft (20·9 m²)
Ailerons (total) 12·10 sq ft (1·12 m²)
Trailing-edge flaps (total) 25·00 sq ft (2·32 m²)
Spoilers (total) 13·45 sq ft (1·25 m²)
Airbrakes 6·00 sq ft (0·56 m²)
Fin 36·0 sq ft (3·34 m²)
Rudder, including tab 5·81 sq ft (0·54 m²)
Tailplane 70·0 sq ft (6·50 m²)
Elevator, including tabs 18·9 sq ft (1·75 m²)

WEIGHTS AND LOADINGS:
Weight empty, equipped 10,650 lb (4,830 kg)
Max payload 1,600 lb (726 kg)
Max T-O weight 18,000 lb (8,165 kg)
Max ramp weight 18,300 lb (8,300 kg)
Max zero-fuel weight 13,000 lb (5,902 kg)
Max landing weight 16,000 lb (7,257 kg)
Max wing loading 80 lb/sq ft (390·6 kg/m²)
Max power loading 2·70 lb/lb st (2·70 kg/kg st)

PERFORMANCE (at max T-O weight, except where indicated):
Max never-exceed speed
425 knots (489 mph; 788 km/h) EAS between S/L and 14,000 ft (4,260 m); Mach 0·85 above 14,000 ft (4,260 m)
Max level speed at 19,500 ft (5,945 m)
460 knots (529 mph; 852 km/h)
Max cruising speed above 36,000 ft (11,000 m)
432 knots (497 mph; 800 km/h)
Econ cruising speed at 41,000 ft (12,500 m)
390 knots (449 mph; 722 km/h)
Stalling speed, landing configuration, at landing weight of 13,000 lb (5,902 kg)
90 knots (104 mph; 167 km/h)
Max rate of climb at S/L at AUW of 15,821 lb (7,176 kg) 5,400 ft (1,650 m)/min
Service ceiling 45,000 ft (13,715 m)
Service ceiling, one engine out
26,000 ft (7,925 m)
Min ground turning radius 22 ft 11¾ in (7·00 m)
Runway LCN 16
T-O run 2,760 ft (841 m)
T-O to 35 ft (10·7 m) 3,180 ft (970 m)
FAR 25 T-O field length 5,560 ft (1,695 m)
FAR 121 landing field length (4 passengers and baggage, 45 min reserve) 4,985 ft (1,520 m)
Landing from 50 ft (15 m), with 4 passengers and baggage, 45 min reserve
2,990 ft (912 m)
Range with max fuel and 840 lb (381 kg) payload, 45 min reserve
1,148 nm (1,322 miles; 2,128 km)

PROCAER

PROGETTI COSTRUZIONI AERONAUTICHE SpA

HEAD OFFICE:
Via Cardinale Ascanio Sforza 85, 20141 Milan
Telephone: 84.93.797

WORKS:
Strada Alzaia Naviglio Pavese 78, Milan

PRESIDENT: Dott Ing Rico Neeff

Production by this company in recent years has concentrated on various versions of the Picchio F15 four-seat light aircraft. The latest Procaer-built version is the F15E, a description of which follows:

PROCAER F15E PICCHIO

The F15E is an all-metal version of the Picchio aerobatic light aircraft, designed by Dott Ing Stelio Frati. Descriptions of the earlier versions have appeared in previous editions of *Jane's*.

The F15E prototype (I-PROM) flew for the first time on 21 December 1968. The aircraft has been certificated by both the RAI and FAA, on 6 November 1970 and 16 July 1971 respectively, and four more F15Es are in various stages of completion.

A prototype of a developed version, known as the **F15F Delfino,** was under construction in 1974 by General Avia (which see).

The following description refers to the F15E:

TYPE: Four-seat light monoplane.

WINGS: Cantilever low-wing monoplane. NACA 64·215/64·210 wing sections. Dihedral 6°. Incidence 4°. One-piece metal structure with single main spar, rear spar carrying aileron and flap hinges, and short front spar to carry landing gear loads. All-metal Frise ailerons and electrically-actuated Fowler flaps.

FUSELAGE: All-metal semi-monocoque structure.

TAIL UNIT: Cantilever all-metal structure. Trim tab in starboard elevator.

LANDING GEAR: Retractable tricycle type. Electrical or mechanical retraction. Oleo-pneumatic shock-absorbers. Main wheels size 6·00-6. Steerable nosewheel size 5·00-5. Hydraulic disc brakes.

Prototype Procaer F15E Picchio four-seat light aircraft (300 hp Continental IO-520-F engine)

POWER PLANT: One 300 hp Continental IO-520-F six-cylinder horizontally-opposed aircooled engine, driving a Hartzell HC.C2YF-1B/8475-6 two-blade constant-speed metal propeller. Fuel in two wing tanks and two wingtip tanks, with a total capacity of 70 Imp gallons (318 litres). Oil capacity 2·5 Imp gallons (11·5 litres).

ACCOMMODATION: Four persons in pairs in enclosed cabin. Forward-opening door on each side. Space for 100 lb (45 kg) of baggage behind rear bench seat; baggage door on port side. Dual controls. Cabin soundproofed, heated and ventilated.

SYSTEMS, ELECTRONICS AND EQUIPMENT: Two 12V 35Ah batteries, connected in series, provide power for landing gear and flap actuation. 600W engine-driven generator. Blind-flying instruments and radio optional.

DIMENSIONS, EXTERNAL:
Wing span over tip-tanks 32 ft 5¾ in (9·90 m)
Wing chord at root 5 ft 8 in (1·72 m)
Wing chord at tip 2 ft 9 in (0·85 m)
Wing aspect ratio 7·37
Length overall 24 ft 7¼ in (7·50 m)
Height overall 9 ft 2¼ in (2·80 m)
Tailplane span 11 ft 8 in (3·55 m)
Wheel track 9 ft 1¼ in (2·78 m)
Wheelbase 5 ft 8¼ in (1·73 m)
Propeller diameter 6 ft 6 in (1·98 m)

DIMENSIONS, INTERNAL:
Cabin: Length 9 ft 0 in (2·75 m)
Max width 3 ft 11¼ in (1·20 m)
Max height 4 ft 5¼ in (1·35 m)

AREAS:
Wings, gross 143·2 sq ft (13·30 m²)
Ailerons (total) 12·81 sq ft (1·19 m²)
Flaps (total) 18·50 sq ft (1·72 m²)
Fin 9·50 sq ft (0·88 m²)
Rudder 5·27 sq ft (0·49 m²)
Tailplane 17·97 sq ft (1·67 m²)
Elevators, incl tab 13·67 sq ft (1·27 m²)

WEIGHTS AND LOADINGS:
Basic weight empty 1,856 lb (842 kg)
Weight empty, equipped 1,900 lb (861 kg)
Max T-O weight:
Normal 3,000 lb (1,360 kg)
Utility 2,700 lb (1,224 kg)
Max wing loading:
Normal 20·85 lb/sq ft (101·8 kg/m²)
Utility 18·85 lb/sq ft (92·0 kg/m²)
Max power loading:
Normal 10·55 lb/hp (4·79 kg/hp)

Utility 9·45 lb/hp (4·29 kg/hp)
PERFORMANCE (N: at max Normal T-O weight; U: at max Utility T-O weight):
Max never-exceed speed:
N 191 knots (220 mph; 354 km/h)
U 200 knots (230 mph; 370 km/h)
Max level speed:
N 173 knots (199 mph; 320 km/h)
U 174 knots (200 mph; 322 km/h)
Max cruising speed:
N, U 165 knots (190 mph; 306 km/h)
Econ cruising speed:
N, U 144 knots (166 mph; 267 km/h)
Stalling speed, flaps and landing gear up:
N 68 knots (78·5 mph; 127 km/h)
U 63 knots (73 mph; 118 km/h)
Stalling speed, flaps and landing gear down:
N 60 knots (69 mph; 111 km/h)
U 55 knots (63·5 mph; 103 km/h)
Service ceiling (N, U) 17,390 ft (5,300 m)
T-O run (N, U) 1,181 ft (360 m)
T-O to 50 ft; 15 m (N, U) 1,837 ft (560 m)
Landing from 50 ft; 15 m (N, U) 2,050 ft (625 m)
Landing run (N, U) 1,230 ft (375 m)
Max range (N, U, no reserves):
at max cruising speed 647 nm (746 miles; 1,200 km)
at econ cruising speed 863 nm (994 miles; 1,600 km)
Max endurance (N, U):
at max cruising speed 5 hr
at econ cruising speed 6 hr

SIAI-MARCHETTI

SIAI-MARCHETTI SOCIETA PER AZIONI

MANAGEMENT AND WORKS:
21018 Sesto Calende (Varese)
Telephone: (0331) 924421
Telex: 32433 Siaiavio Sesto Calende
AERODROME: Vergiate (Varese)
ROME OFFICE: Via Barberini 36, 00187 Rome
PRESIDENT:
Dott Ermenegildo Marelli
MANAGING DIRECTOR:
Dott Ing Giorgio Belli

Founded in 1915, the SIAI-Marchetti company was known originally as Savoia-Marchetti. It has produced a wide range of military and civil landplanes and flying-boats.

Following a reappraisal of its overall activities, SIAI-Marchetti is now concentrating on production of light aircraft for military and commercial applications. The company is actively studying ways of extending the manufacture of these aircraft outside Italy, probably by supplying Italian-built kits or component parts for assembly by foreign licensees. SIAI-Marchetti is increasing its activities in the development of aircraft to meet various military requirements, including the SF.260MX military development of the civil SF.260, the SM.1019 FAC (forward air control) STOL aircraft, and military versions of the S.208 and S.210.

The company's Vertical Flight Division, formed in August 1968 under the direction of Dott Ing Emilio Bianchi, was dissolved for financial reasons in 1973, with the consequent abandonment of the SV-20 winged helicopter programme described in the 1973-74 *Jane's*.

SIAI-Marchetti is engaged on the overhaul and repair of various types of large aircraft (notably the C-119 and C-130) serving with the Italian Air Force. It also participates in national or multinational programmes for the Aeritalia G91Y and G222, Aeritalia (Lockheed) F-104S, Breguet Atlantic and Panavia MRCA.

SIAI-MARCHETTI SF.260MX

The SF.260MX was developed from the basic SF.260 (which see) specifically for military training duties, and was first flown on 10 October 1970.

A total of 141 had been ordered by the Spring of 1974; these are designated as follows:

SF.260AMI. Twenty-five for Italian Air Force.

SF.260M. Thirty-six for Belgian Air Force. Delivery completed.

SF.260MC. Twelve for Zaïre Air Force. Delivery completed.

SF.260MP. Thirty-two for Philippine Air Force, which has also ordered 16 of the SF.260W armed version. Fourteen delivered by February 1974.

SF.260MS. Sixteen for Singapore Air Defence Command. Delivery completed.

SF.260MT. Twelve for Royal Thai Air Force. Eight delivered by February 1974.

SF.260MZ. Eight for Zambian Air Force. Delivery completed.

SF.260W. Developed version of SF.260MX, described separately.

As noted in the description which follows, the SF.260MX incorporates a number of important structural modifications compared with the basic SF.260:

TYPE: Two/three-seat military training aircraft.

WINGS: Cantilever low-wing monoplane. Wing section NACA 64_1-212 (modified) at root, NACA 64_1-210 at tip. Thickness/chord ratio 13% at root, 10% at tip. Dihedral 6° 20′. Incidence 2° 45′ at root, 0° at tip. No sweepback. Increased wing leading-edge radius compared with basic SF.260, with lower datum line, to improve stall characteristics. All-metal light alloy structure, with single main spar and auxiliary rear spar, built in two portions bolted together at centreline and attached to fuselage by six bolts. Press-formed ribs, with dimpled stiffening holes. Skin, which is butt-jointed and flush-riveted, is stiffened by stringers between main and rear spars. Differentially-operating Frise-type light alloy mass-balanced ailerons (travel 24° up, 13° down), and electrically-actuated light alloy single-slotted flaps (max travel 50°). Flaps and ailerons operated by pushrods and cables. Ground-adjustable tab on each aileron.

FUSELAGE: Semi-monocoque structure of frames and stringers, exclusively of light alloy except for welded steel tube engine mounting, glassfibre front panel of engine cowling, and detachable glassfibre tailcone.

SIAI-Marchetti SF.260MX two/three-seat military trainer (260 hp Lycoming O-540 engine) photographed during inverted flight

TAIL UNIT: Cantilever light alloy structure, with sweptback vertical surfaces (approx 20 per cent greater in area than those of basic SF.260), fixed-incidence tailplane and one-piece balanced elevator. Two-spar fin and tailplane, bolted to fuselage; single-spar elevator and balanced rudder. Reinforced tail unit/fuselage joints compared with basic SF.260. Rudder (30° travel to left or right) and elevator (travel 24° up, 16° down) operated by cables. Controllable trim tab in starboard half of elevator; ground-adjustable tab on rudder.

LANDING GEAR: Electrically-retractable tricycle type, with mechanical standby for emergency use. Small tail bumper under rear fuselage. Inward-retracting main wheels and rearward-retracting nosewheel each embody Magnaghi oleo-pneumatic shock-absorber (type 2/22028 on main units). Cleveland P/N 3080A main wheels, with size 6·00-6 tube and tyre (6-ply rating), pressure 35·5 lb/sq in (2·5 kg/cm²). Cleveland P/N 40-77A nosewheel, with size 5·00-5 tube and tyre (6-ply rating), pressure 28·4 lb/sq in (2·0 kg/cm²). Cleveland P/N 3000-500 independent hydraulic single-disc brake on each main wheel. Nosewheel steering (20° to left or right) is operated directly by the rudder pedals, to which it is linked by pushrods. Up-lock secures main gear in retracted position during flight; anti-retraction system prevents main gear from retracting whenever strut is compressed by weight of aircraft. Compared with basic SF.260, the SF.260MX has a reinforced nosewheel drag brace attachment and landing gear retraction supports; increased use of light alloy forgings, instead of welded steel, in certain landing gear structures; and improved retraction locking mechanism.

POWER PLANT: One 260 hp Lycoming O-540-E4A5 six-cylinder horizontally-opposed aircooled engine, driving a Hartzell HC-C2YK-1B/8477-8R two-blade constant-speed metal propeller with spinner. Fuel in two internal light alloy wing tanks, each of 10·9 Imp gallons (49·5 litres), and two wingtip tanks, each of 15·8 Imp gallons (72 litres) capacity. Total fuel capacity 53·4 Imp gallons (243 litres), of which 51·7 Imp gallons (235 litres) are usable. Individual refuelling point for each tank. Oil capacity 22·7 lb (10 kg).

ACCOMMODATION: Side-by-side front seats for instructor and pupil, with third seat centrally at rear. Front seats are individually adjustable fore and aft, and have forward-folding backs and provision for back-type parachute packs. All three seats equipped with aerobatic-type safety belts. Baggage compartment aft of rear seat. One-piece fully-transparent rearward-sliding Plexiglas canopy. Emergency canopy ejection system, instead of the rubber-cord canopy release of the basic SF.260. Steel tube windscreen frame, for protection in the event of an overturn. Cabin is carpeted, air-conditioned, heated and ventilated, and walls are thermally insulated and soundproofed by a glassfibre lining.

SYSTEMS: Hydraulic equipment for main-wheel brakes only. No pneumatic system. 24V DC electrical system, of single-conductor type, including 24V 50A Prestolite engine-mounted alternator/rectifier and 24V 25Ah Varley battery, for engine starting, flap and landing gear actuation, fuel booster pumps, avionics and lighting. Sealed battery compartment in rear of fuselage on port side. External power receptacle on port side at rear. Connection of an external power source automatically disconnects the battery. Heating system for carburettor air intake. Emergency electrical system for extending landing gear if normal electrical actuation fails; provision for mechanical extension in the event of total electrical failure. Cabin heating, and windscreen de-icing and demisting, by heat exchanger using engine bleed air. Additional manually-controlled warm-air outlets for general cabin heating.

ELECTRONICS AND EQUIPMENT: Basic instrumentation and military equipment to customer's requirements. Dual controls standard. Blind-flying instrumentation and communications equipment optional. Landing light in nose, below spinner. Instrument panel can be slid rearward to provide access to rear of instruments. Compared with basic SF.260, the SF.260 MX has various improvements to flight controls, engine controls (duplicated propeller and throttle controls), electrical system, radio, and other equipment installations.

DIMENSIONS, EXTERNAL:
Wing span 27 ft 0¾ in (8·25 m)
Wing span over tip-tanks 27 ft 4¾ in (8·35 m)
Wing chord at root 5 ft 3 in (1·60 m)
Wing chord at tip 2 ft 6¾ in (0·784 m)
Wing mean aerodynamic chord 4 ft 4¼ in (1·325 m)
Wing aspect ratio (without tip-tanks) 6·33
Wing taper ratio 2·24
Length overall 23 ft 3½ in (7·10 m)
Length of fuselage 16 ft 8¾ in (5·10 m)
Fuselage: Max width 3 ft 7¼ in (1·10 m)
Max depth 3 ft 5 in (1·042 m)
Height overall 7 ft 11 in (2·41 m)
Tailplane span 9 ft 10½ in (3·01 m)
Wheel track 7 ft 5½ in (2·274 m)
Wheelbase 5 ft 5¼ in (1·66 m)
Propeller diameter 6 ft 4 in (1·93 m)
Min propeller ground clearance 8 in (0·20 m)

DIMENSIONS, INTERNAL:
Cabin: Length 5 ft 5¼ in (1·66 m)
Max width 3 ft 3¼ in (1·00 m)
Height (seat squab to canopy) 3 ft 0¼ in (0·92 m)
Volume 53 cu ft (1·50 m³)
Baggage compartment volume 6·36 cu ft (0·18 m³)

AREAS:
Wings, gross 108·7 sq ft (10·10 m²)
Ailerons (total) 8·20 sq ft (0·762 m²)
Trailing-edge flaps (total) 12·70 sq ft (1·18 m²)
Fin 8·18 sq ft (0·76 m²)
Rudder, incl tab 6·46 sq ft (0·60 m²)
Tailplane 15·70 sq ft (1·46 m²)
Elevator, incl tab 10·30 sq ft (0·96 m²)

WEIGHTS AND LOADINGS:
Weight empty, equipped 1,587 lb (720 kg)
Max T-O and landing weight:
Aerobatic 2,425 lb (1,100 kg)
Utility 2,645 lb (1,200 kg)
Utility with external load 2,998 lb (1,360 kg)
Max wing loading 27·6 lb/sq ft (134·6 kg/m²)
Max power loading 11·5 lb/hp (5·23 kg/hp)

PERFORMANCE (at max T-O weight of 2,645 lb; 1,200 kg, except where indicated):
Max never-exceed speed 235 knots (271 mph; 436 km/h)
Max level speed at S/L 183 knots (211 mph; 340 km/h)
Max cruising speed (75% power) at 4,925 ft (1,500 m) 161·5 knots (186 mph; 300 km/h)

Stalling speed, flaps up
74 knots (85·5 mph; 137 km/h)
Stalling speed, flaps down, power off
64 knots (73·5 mph; 118 km/h)
Max rate of climb at S/L 1,496 ft (456 m)/min
Time to 4,925 ft (1,500 m) 4 min 0 sec
Time to 7,550 ft (2,300 m) 6 min 50 sec
Time to 9,850 ft (3,000 m) 10 min 0 sec
Service ceiling 16,400 ft (5,000 m)
T-O run at S/L 1,837 ft (560 m)
T-O to 50 ft (15 m) at S/L 2,543 ft (775 m)
Landing from 50 ft (15 m) at S/L
2,264 ft (690 m)
Landing run at S/L 1,132 ft (345 m)
Range with max fuel
777 nm (895 miles; 1,440 km)
g limits:
at max Aerobatic T-O weight +6; —3
at max Utility T-O weight (without external load) +4·4; —2·2

SIAI-MARCHETTI SF.260W

The SF.260W, first flown (I-SJAV) in May 1972, is a developed version of the SF.260MX (which see) combining the structural and technical characteristics of the SF.260MX with the ability to carry external loads, up to a maximum of 660 lb (300 kg), on two underwing pylons. In addition to the range of close-support missions possible with the SF.260MX, the SF.260W can also undertake such roles as low-level strike with rockets, anti-tank missiles, or machine-guns; forward air control; forward area support, with droppable supply containers; armed reconnaissance; camouflage inspection; or liaison.

The SF.260W also meets the requirements of modern primary flying training, including basic flying training; instrument flying; aerobatics, including deliberate spinning and recovery; night flying; navigation flying; and formation flying.

Sixteen SF.260Ws have been ordered by the Philippine Air Force.

ARMAMENT: Typical alternative underwing loads when carrying a crew of two include two Matra MAC AAF1 7·62 mm gun pods; two 50 kg bombs; two Matra F2 launchers, each with six 68 mm SNEB 253 rockets; two Simpres AL 9-70 launchers, each with nine 2·75 in FFAR rockets; two Simpres AL 18-50 launchers, each with eighteen 2 in SNIA ARF/8M2 rockets; or two Alkan 20AP cartridge throwers for Lacroix 74 mm explosive cartridges, flare cartridges, or F.130 smoke cartridges. As a single-seater, two 120 kg bombs can be carried.

SIAI-MARCHETTI SM.1019

The SM.1019 light STOL military aircraft is suitable for observation, light ground attack or utility duties. It is based very largely upon the airframe of the American Cessna L-19/O-1 Bird Dog (see 1964-65 *Jane's*), from which it differs principally in having an Allison 250-B15G turboprop engine in a lengthened nose, and redesigned, angular vertical tail surfaces of greater area. The main fuselage, wings, landing gear and cabin have been extensively modified to meet current operational requirements.

Design of the SM.1019 was started in January 1969, and construction of a prototype began two months later. This aircraft (I-STOL) flew for the first time on 24 May 1969, and was granted Normal category certification by the RAI on 25 October 1969.

A second prototype (I-SJAR), which flew for the first time on 18 February 1971, is designated SM.1019A. It has an improved fuel system, two doors and two instrument panels, and has received RAI certification in the Utility category.

Production was beginning in 1974 of an initial series of 100 aircraft for the Aviazione Leggera dell'Esercito (ALE, or Italian Army Aviation), with deliveries scheduled to begin in 1975.

TYPE: Two-seat STOL light aircraft.

WINGS: Braced high-wing monoplane. Wing section NACA 2412. Dihedral 2° 8'. Incidence 1° 30'. Washout 3°. No sweepback. Wing braced by single strut on each side. Conventional all-metal structure, with metal Frise-type ailerons and electrically-actuated trailing-edge slotted flaps. Trim tab on starboard aileron.

FUSELAGE: Conventional all-metal semi-monocoque stressed-skin structure.

TAIL UNIT: Conventional cantilever all-metal structure, with horizontal surfaces mounted on top of fuselage. Dorsal fairing to fin. Fixed-incidence tailplane. Manually-operated mechanically-actuated trim tab in starboard elevator. Trim tab on rudder.

LANDING GEAR: Non-retractable tailwheel type, with cantilever leaf-type spring steel main-wheel legs. Goodyear 511960 main wheels, with low-pressure tyres, size 7·00-6, pressure 30 lb/sq in (2·11 kg/cm²); Scott 3200A tailwheel, with size 8-3·00 tyre, pressure 35 lb/sq in (2·46 kg/cm²). Goodyear independent hydraulic single-disc brake on each main wheel. Combined wheel/ski gear, with hydraulic operation of skis, optional.

POWER PLANT: One 317 shp Allison 250-B15G (T63) turboprop engine, driving a Hartzell HC-A3VF-5/V10133D-11R reversible-pitch constant-speed three-blade metal propeller. Fuel in two tanks in each wing, each of 17 Imp gallons (20·5 US gallons; 77·5 litres) capacity; total capacity 68 Imp gallons (82 US gallons; 310 litres). Refuelling point for each tank on top of wings. Oil capacity 1·75 Imp gallons (2·1 US gallons; 8 litres).

ACCOMMODATION: Pilot and co-pilot or observer/systems operator seated in tandem in fully-enclosed and extensively-glazed cabin. Two forward-hinged doors on starboard side. Cabin heated and ventilated. Dual controls optional.

SYSTEMS: No pneumatic or air-conditioning systems. 24V DC electrical system power provided by 30V 150A Lear-Siegler P/N23032-0020 starter/generator and 24V 25Ah Sonotone battery. External ground power receptacle. Windscreen defrosting and engine compressor duct heating standard. Oxygen system optional.

ELECTRONICS AND EQUIPMENT: Choice of blind-flying instrumentation, communications and other equipment, to customer's requirements. Twin landing lights in port outer wing leading-edge.

ARMAMENT AND OPERATIONAL EQUIPMENT: Rack installed beneath each wing for bombs, rockets or reconnaissance cameras.

DIMENSIONS, EXTERNAL:
Wing span 36 ft 0 in (10·972 m)
Wing chord at root 5 ft 4 in (1·63 m)
Wing chord at tip 3 ft 7 in (1·09 m)
Wing aspect ratio 7·44
Length overall (tail up) 27 ft $11\frac{1}{2}$ in (8·52 m)
Height overall (tail down) 9 ft $4\frac{1}{2}$ in (2·85 m)
Tailplane span 11 ft $2\frac{3}{4}$ in (3·42 m)
Wheel track 7 ft 6 in (2·29 m)
Wheelbase 20 ft $5\frac{1}{4}$ in (6·23 m)
Propeller diameter 7 ft 6 in (2·29 m)
Propeller ground clearance 9 in (23 cm)
Cabin doors, each:
Height 3 ft $5\frac{3}{4}$ in (1·06 m)
Width 1 ft $11\frac{3}{4}$ in (0·60 m)
Baggage door:
Height 1 ft $6\frac{1}{2}$ in (0·47 m)
Width 1 ft 9 in (0·53 m)
Height to sill 2 ft $0\frac{1}{4}$ in (0·62 m)

DIMENSIONS, INTERNAL:
Cabin: Max length approx 6 ft $6\frac{3}{4}$ in (2·00 m)
Max width approx 2 ft $0\frac{3}{4}$ in (0·63 m)
Max height approx 4 ft $1\frac{1}{4}$ in (1·25 m)
Volume 38·8 cu ft (1·10 m³)
Baggage compartment volume 3·5 cu ft (0·1 m³)

AREAS:
Wings, gross 174·0 sq ft (16·16 m²)
Ailerons (total) 18·30 sq ft (1·70 m²)
Trailing-edge flaps (total) 21·10 sq ft (1·96 m²)
Fin 10·3 sq ft (0·957 m²)
Rudder 13·94 sq ft (1·295 m²)
Tailplane 20·41 sq ft (1·896 m²)
Elevators, incl tab 17·05 sq ft (1·584 m²)

WEIGHTS AND LOADINGS (operational mission, without external stores):
Weight empty, equipped 1,499 lb (680 kg)
Max payload 1,300 lb (590 kg)
Max T-O and landing weight 2,800 lb (1,270 kg)
Max wing loading 16·1 lb/sq ft (78·6 kg/m²)
Max power loading 8·8 lb/shp (4·0 kg/shp)

PERFORMANCE (at max T-O weight, except where indicated):
Max level speed at S/L
154 knots (177 mph; 285 km/h)
Max cruising speed (75% power) at S/L
127 knots (146 mph; 235 km/h)
Max cruising speed (75% power) at 9,850 ft (3,000 m) 129 knots (149 mph; 239 km/h)
Stalling speed, flaps up, power off
51 knots (58 mph; 93 km/h)
Stalling speed, flaps down, power on
25 knots (28 mph; 45 km/h)
Max rate of climb at S/L 1,300 ft (396 m)/min

SIAI-Marchetti SF.260W, armed version of the SF.260MX, with two underwing rocket pods

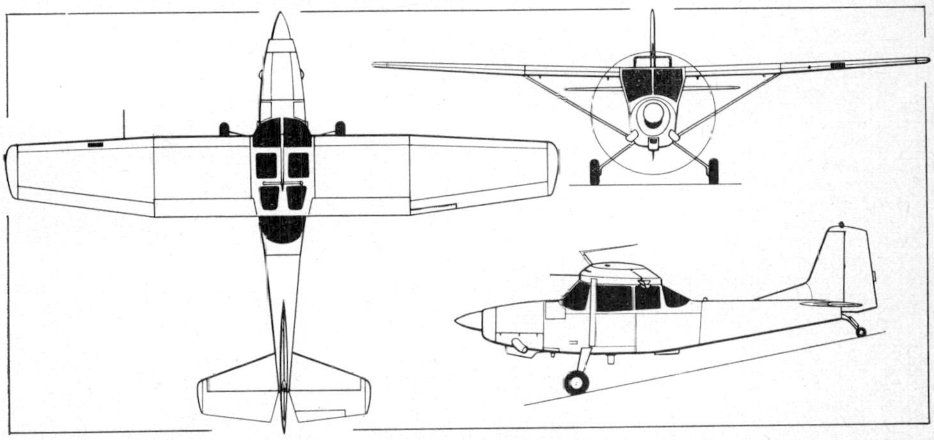

Photograph and three-view drawing (*Pilot Press*) **of the SIAI-Marchetti SM.1019 two-seat STOL light military aircraft**

Rate of climb at 9,850 ft (3,000 m) 120 ft (36 m)/min
Service ceiling 19,675 ft (6,000 m)
T-O run 375 ft (114 m)
T-O to 50 ft (15 m) 740 ft (225 m)
Landing from 50 ft (15 m) 805 ft (246 m)
Landing run 385 ft (118 m)
Max range (AUW of 2,513 lb; 1,140 kg):
at S/L 519 nm (598 miles; 963 km)
at 9,850 ft (3,000 m) 660 nm (761 miles; 1,225 km)
Max endurance at S/L 3 hr 40 min

SIAI-MARCHETTI S.208

First flown on 22 May 1967, the S.208 has some 60% of its structural components in common with the earlier S.205 but has a more powerful engine and is able to carry up to five persons. Production began in the Spring of 1968, and by mid-February 1973 approx 80 had been delivered, to customers in Europe and Africa. Production was continuing in 1974.

Orders include 44 of a version designated **S.208M** for the Italian Air Force. These have a jettisonable cabin door, and are intended for liaison and training duties.

TYPE: Five-seat light aircraft.

WINGS: Cantilever low-wing monoplane. Wing section NACA 63_3618 on aircraft centreline, NACA 63_2415 at tip. Dihedral 5° 42′. Incidence 2° at root, —1° at tip. Sweepback at quarter-chord 2° 1′. All-metal structure, with large honeycomb skin panels. All-metal ailerons and slotted flaps.

FUSELAGE: All-metal semi-monocoque stressed-skin structure.

TAIL UNIT: Cantilever all-metal structure. Trim tab in port elevator.

LANDING GEAR: Electrically-retractable tricycle type. Oleo-pneumatic shock-absorbers. Main wheel tyres size 6·00-6 (6-ply): nosewheel tyre size 5·00-5. Tyre pressure 25 lb/sq in (1·75 kg/cm²). Goodyear hydraulic disc brakes.

POWER PLANT: One 260 hp Lycoming O-540-E4A5 six-cylinder horizontally-opposed air-cooled engine, driving a Hartzell two-blade constant-speed metal propeller. Two wing fuel tanks, total capacity 47 Imp gallons (215 litres), and two auxiliary wingtip tanks (each 25·4 Imp gallons; 115·5 litres), bringing total fuel capacity to 98 Imp gallons (446 litres). Oil capacity 2·5 Imp gallons (11·35 litres).

ACCOMMODATION: Enclosed cabin seating pilot and up to four passengers. Forward-opening cabin door on starboard side (jettisonable on S.208M). Second door, on port side, available optionally. Access to baggage compartment, aft of seats, from inside or outside. Eight warm air outlets, four of which are individual, and two windscreen defroster outlets.

ELECTRONICS AND EQUIPMENT: Provision for full range of HF, VHF, VOR and ADF equipment, to customer's specification. Blind-flying instrumentation, two-axis autopilot and navigation systems optional.

DIMENSIONS, EXTERNAL:
Wing span 35 ft 7½ in (10·86 m)
Wing chord at root 5 ft 3½ in (1·61 m)
Wing chord at tip 3 ft 10 in (1·17 m)
Wing aspect ratio 7·04
Length overall 26 ft 3 in (8·00 m)
Height overall 9 ft 5¾ in (2·89 m)
Tailplane span 11 ft 2½ in (3·42 m)
Wheel track 11 ft 8 in (3·55 m)
Wheelbase 6 ft 2¾ in (1·90 m)
Propeller diameter 6 ft 2 in (1·88 m)
Cabin door:
Height 3 ft 2¼ in (0·97 m)
Width 3 ft 2¼ in (0·97 m)
Baggage compartment door:
Height 1 ft 8¾ in (0·53 m)
Width 1 ft 9¼ in (0·54 m)
Height to sill 2 ft 3½ in (0·70 m)

DIMENSIONS, INTERNAL:
Cabin: Length 5 ft 10¼ in (1·78 m)
Max width 3 ft 8¾ in (1·14 m)
Max height 4 ft 4 in (1·32 m)
Floor area 21·8 sq ft (2·03 m²)
Volume 88·0 cu ft (2·5 m³)

AREAS:
Wings, gross 173 sq ft (16·09 m²)
Ailerons (total) 11·67 sq ft (1·08 m²)
Trailing-edge flaps (total) 23·36 sq ft (2·17 m²)
Fin 12·1 sq ft (1·12 m²)
Rudder 6·6 sq ft (0·61 m²)
Tailplane 24·11 sq ft (2·24 m²)
Elevators, including tab 13·24 sq ft (1·23 m²)

WEIGHTS AND LOADINGS:
Weight empty, equipped 1,785 lb (810 kg)
Max T-O weight 3,306 lb (1,500 kg)
Max wing loading 19·2 lb/sq ft (93·5 kg/m²)
Max power loading 12·79 lb/hp (5·8 kg/hp)

PERFORMANCE (at max T-O weight):
Max never-exceed speed 175 knots (202 mph; 325 km/h)
Max level speed at S/L 173 knots (199 mph; 320 km/h)
Max cruising speed 162 knots (187 mph; 300 km/h)
Econ cruising speed 140 knots (162 mph; 260 km/h)
Stalling speed 50 knots (58 mph; 92 km/h)
Service ceiling 17,725 ft (5,400 m)
T-O run 1,115 ft (340 m)
T-O to 50 ft (15 m) 1,640 ft (500 m)
Landing from 50 ft (15 m) 1,310 ft (400 m)
Landing run 1,065 ft (325 m)
Range with max internal fuel 647 nm (746 miles; 1,200 km)
Range with max fuel (incl tip-tanks) 1,085 nm (1,250 miles; 2,000 km)

SIAI-Marchetti S.208 five-seat cabin monoplane (one 260 hp Lycoming O-540 engine)

S.208M military version of the SIAI-Marchetti S.208, in production for the Italian Air Force

SIAI-MARCHETTI S.210

This is a twin-engined version of the S.205 series, embodying many components of the latter. The prototype (I-SJAP) made its first flight on

SIAI-Marchetti S.210 six-seat light aircraft (two 200 hp Lycoming TIO-360-A engines)

19 February 1970, and the S.210 received RAI type certification on 22 May 1972. The second prototype appeared in S.210M military configuration at the 1971 Paris Air Show, but this version is not in production.

TYPE: Six-seat light aircraft.

WINGS: Cantilever low-wing monoplane. Wing section NACA 63_3618. All-metal structure, with large honeycomb skin panels. All-metal ailerons and slotted flaps.

FUSELAGE: All-metal semi-monocoque structure.

TAIL UNIT: Cantilever all-metal structure. Trim tabs in rudder and each elevator.

LANDING GEAR: Retractable tricycle type. Electrical retraction. Oleo-pneumatic shock-absorbers. Goodyear hydraulic disc brakes.

POWER PLANT: Two 200 hp Lycoming TIO-360-A horizontally-opposed aircooled and turbocharged engines, each driving a Hartzell HC-C2YK-1B/8468-10R two-blade constant-speed metal propeller. Four fuel tanks in wings, with total capacity of 79·2 Imp gallons (360 litres). Provision for tip-tanks. Total oil capacity 3·33 Imp gallons (15 litres).

ACCOMMODATION: Pilot and five passengers in enclosed cabin. One forward-hinged door on each side. Six individual warm air outlets and two windscreen defroster outlets.

ELECTRONICS: Provision for full range of HF, VHF, VOR and ADF equipment to customer's specification. Optional equipment includes blind-flying instrumentation, two-axis autopilot and navigation aids.

DIMENSIONS, EXTERNAL:
Wing span 38 ft 2 in (11·63 m)
Length overall 29 ft 0 in (8·83 m)
Height overall 10 ft 11¼ in (3·33 m)
Tailplane span 15 ft 5 in (4·70 m)
Wheel track 11 ft 8¼ in (3·56 m)
Wheelbase 8 ft 10 in (2·69 m)
Propeller diameter 6 ft 2 in (1·88 m)
Passenger doors (each):
Height 3 ft 2¼ in (0·97 m)
Width 3 ft 2¼ in (0·97 m)

DIMENSIONS, INTERNAL:
Cabin:
Length 7 ft 7¾ in (2·33 m)
Max width 3 ft 8¾ in (1·14 m)
Max height 4 ft 4 in (1·32 m)

AREAS:
Wings, gross 185·5 sq ft (17·23 m²)
Ailerons (total) 11·63 sq ft (1·08 m²)
Trailing-edge flaps (total) 23·47 sq ft (2·18 m²)
Fin 12·25 sq ft (1·14 m²)
Rudder, including tab 9·28 sq ft (0·86 m²)
Tailplane 27·56 sq ft (2·56 m²)
Elevators, including tab 20·88 sq ft (1·94 m²)

WEIGHTS AND LOADINGS:
Weight empty, equipped 2,425 lb (1,100 kg)
Max T-O weight 4,078 lb (1,850 kg)
Max wing loading 21·97 lb/sq ft (107·3 kg/m²)
Max power loading 10·33 lb/hp (4·62 kg/hp)

PERFORMANCE (at max T-O weight):
Max level speed at S/L
169 knots (195 mph; 314 km/h)
Max rate of climb at S/L 1,395 ft (425 m)/min
Service ceiling 25,250 ft (7,700 m)
Service ceiling, one engine out 12,475 ft (3,800 m)
T-O run 920 ft (280 m)
T-O to 50 ft (15 m) 1,310 ft (400 m)
Landing from 50 ft (15 m) 1,800 ft (550 m)
Landing run 770 ft (235 m)
Range with max payload
1,024 nm (1,180 miles; 1,900 km)

SIAI-MARCHETTI SF.260

Designed by Dott Ing Stelio Frati, the SF.260 is certificated for aerobatic flying.

The prototype, known as the F.250, was built by Aviamilano, with a 250 hp Lycoming engine (see 1965-66 *Jane's*), and flew for the first time on 15 July 1964.

The version developed for production was manufactured, initially under licence from Aviamilano, by SIAI-Marchetti, and is designated SF.260. SIAI-Marchetti is now the official holder of the type certificate and of all manufacturing rights in the SF.260. The aircraft received FAA Type Approval on 1 April 1966.

Following delivery of the first 50 production aircraft, a second series of 50 civil SF.260s, incorporating many of the structural and aerodynamic improvements of the military SF.260MX, entered production to fulfil orders from Air France, Sabena and other customers.

The SF.260 holds two FAI speed records in Class C-1-b. The first of these is for a speed of 174 knots (200·4 mph; 322·52 km/h) over a 1,000 km closed circuit near Santa Monica, California, on 25 March 1969. The second, set up on 29 March 1969 near Los Angeles, is for a speed of 199·4 knots (229·6 mph; 369·43 km/h) over a 100 km closed circuit. These records are listed under the aircraft's US type name of "Waco Meteor".

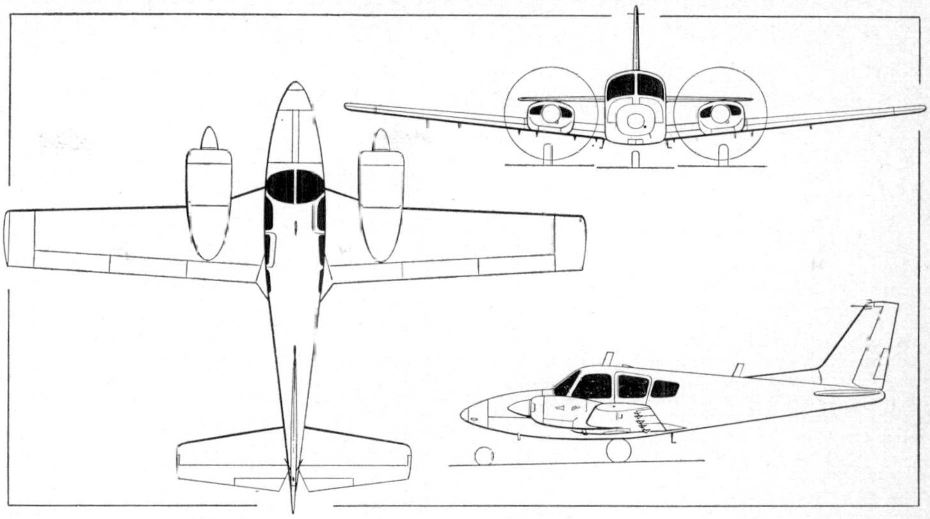

SIAI-Marchetti S.210 twin-engined six-seat light aircraft (*Pilot Press*)

TYPE: Three seat cabin monoplane.

WINGS: Cantilever low-wing monoplane. Wing section NACA 64212 at root, NACA 64210 at tip. Dihedral 5°. All-metal single-spar structure in two portions. All-metal Frise-type ailerons and electrically-operated slotted flaps.

FUSELAGE: All-metal semi-monocoque structure, with comparatively thick skin and few stringers.

TAIL UNIT: Cantilever all-metal structure with swept vertical surfaces. Rudder and elevators statically and dynamically balanced. Controllable trim tab in elevator.

LANDING GEAR: Retractable tricycle type. Electrical retraction with manual emergency actuation. Oleo-pneumatic shock-absorbers. Steerable nosewheel with tyre size 5·00-5. Main wheels and tyres size 6·00-6. Cleveland single-disc hydraulic brakes.

POWER PLANT: One 260 hp Lycoming O-540-E4A5 six-cylinder horizontally-opposed aircooled engine, driving a two-blade Hartzell type HC-C2YK-1B/8467-8R or HC-C2YK-1B/8477-8R constant-speed metal propeller. Fuel in two tanks in wings, total capacity 22 Imp gallons (100 litres), and two on wingtips, total capacity of 31 Imp gallons (140 litres). Overall fuel capacity (four tanks) 53 Imp gallons (240 litres).

ACCOMMODATION: Three seats in enclosed cockpit, two in front, one at rear. Two children with a combined weight not exceeding 250 lb (113 kg) may use rear seat. Rearward-sliding transparent canopy. Baggage compartment capacity 88 lb (40 kg). Cabin soundproofed with glassfibre, heated and ventilated.

EQUIPMENT: Optional equipment includes blind-flying instrumentation, communications radio and oxygen system.

DIMENSIONS, EXTERNAL:
Wing span over tip-tanks 26 ft 11¾ in (8·25 m)
Wing chord at root 5 ft 3 in (1·60 m)
Wing chord at tip 2 ft 6¾ in (0·78 m)
Wing aspect ratio 6·4
Length overall 23 ft 0 in (7·02 m)
Height overall 8 ft 6 in (2·60 m)
Tailplane span 9 ft 9⅞ in (3·00 m)
Wheel track 7 ft 5 in (2·26 m)
Wheelbase 5 ft 3¾ in (1·62 m)
Propeller diameter 6 ft 4 in (1·93 m)

DIMENSIONS, INTERNAL: As SF.260MX

AREAS:
Wings, gross 108·5 sq ft (10·10 m²)
Ailerons (total) 8·50 sq ft (0·79 m²)
Flaps (total) 12·7 sq ft (1·19 m²)
Fin 8·05 sq ft (0·75 m²)
Rudder 5·38 sq ft (0·50 m²)
Tailplane 14·9 sq ft (1·39 m²)
Elevators 10·0 sq ft (0·93 m²)

WEIGHTS AND LOADINGS:
Weight empty, equipped 1,543 lb (700 kg)
Max T-O weight:
Utility 2,430 lb (1,102 kg)
Aerobatic 2,205 lb (1,000 kg)
Max wing loading 22·4 lb/sq ft (109 kg/m²)
Max power loading 9·33 lb/hp (4·23 kg/hp)

PERFORMANCE (at max Utility T-O weight):
Max level speed at S/L
204 knots (235 mph; 375 km/h)
Max cruising speed at 10,000 ft (3,050 m)
186 knots (214 mph; 345 km/h)
Stalling speed, flaps down
57 knots (65 mph; 104 km/h)
Max rate of climb at S/L 1,770 ft (540 m)/min
Service ceiling 21,370 ft (6,500 m)
T-O run on runway 820 ft (250 m)
T-O run on grass 950 ft (290 m)
T-O to 50 ft (15 m) 1,390 ft (425 m)
Landing from 50 ft (15 m) 1,610 ft (490 m)
Landing run 790 ft (240 m)
Range with max fuel (two persons)
1,107 nm (1,275 miles; 2,050 km)

SIAI-Marchetti SF.260 three-seat light aircraft, in Sabena Belgian World Airlines insignia

SILVERCRAFT

SILVERCRAFT SpA

HEAD OFFICE AND WORKS:
Strada del Sempione 114, Casella Postale 37, 21018 Sesto Calende (Varese)
Telephone: (0331) 924842 and 923598

PRESIDENT:
Giovanni Barone Silvestri

PUBLIC RELATIONS MANAGER:
Dott Ing Pier Maria Pellò

Silvercraft was established in early 1962 to develop a light multi-purpose helicopter known as the Silvercraft XY, which flew for the first time in October 1963. This was subsequently developed into the Silvercraft SH-4. The company's Sesto Calende factory is adjacent to the SIAI-Marchetti airfield at Vergiate, and occupies an area of more than 269,100 sq ft (25,000 m²).

SILVERCRAFT SH-4

The SH-4 is a three-seat light helicopter suitable for pilot training, utility, agricultural, survey, police, ambulance, military liaison and observation duties.

The prototype flew for the first time in March 1965, and five pre-production models had been completed by the end of 1967. On 4 September 1968 the SH-4 became the first all-Italian helicopter to receive both FAA and RAI certification, and has since been certificated also in France by the SGAC.

Production of an initial series of 50 aircraft is under way in the Silvercraft works at Sesto Calende with the co-operation of the Aero-Engine Division of Fiat (which see) which produces mechanical components for the rotor transmission system. These 50 aircraft are fully covered by existing orders, and a follow-on series of 200 SH-4s is to be put in hand. Deliveries, to Italian and overseas customers, began in early 1970. Exclusive distribution rights for Latin American countries have been granted to Audi SA of São Paulo, Brazil.

The following versions are currently available:

SH-4. Standard general-purpose version.

SH-4A. Agricultural version. Fitted with 32 ft 9½ in (10·00 m) spraybars, capable of covering a 108 ft (33 m) swath width with liquid chemicals. Max capacity of chemical tanks 53 US gallons (200 litres) up to a max weight of 441 lb (200 kg). Max rate of distribution 24 US gallons (91 litres)/min; chemical tanks can be replenished in 1 minute. Total weight (empty) of spray installation 82 lb (37 kg).

Type: Three-seat light helicopter.

Rotor System: Two-blade semi-rigid main and tail rotors. Blades constructed of laminated wood, with glassfibre covering and (on main rotor) steel weights at blade tips to augment the inertia of the rotor. Aluminium alloy attachment fittings and steel hubs.

Rotor Drive: Rotors driven through steel shafting. Primary gearbox, consisting of two sets of planetary gears (reduction ratio 1 : 0·89), mounted aft of engine; secondary bevel gearboxes at base of main rotor driveshaft (reduction ratio 1 : 0·164) and in rear of tailboom for main and tail rotors respectively. Rotor design eliminates need for stabilisation bars and dampers, and rotor is controlled directly without hydraulic servo-command system. Main rotor/engine rpm ratio 418 : 2,850. Tail rotor/engine rpm ratio 2,434 : 2,850.

Fuselage: Central structure of aluminium alloy, except engine fireproof bulkheads which are of titanium alloy. Semi-monocoque cabin at front and semi-monocoque tailboom are also of aluminium construction. Cabin door frames and window frames of reinforced glassfibre.

Tail Unit: Horizontal stabiliser mid-mounted on tailboom. Ventral stabilising fin beneath tip of tailboom.

Landing Gear: Tubular skid type, with provision to fit ground manoeuvring wheels or skis. Tailskid at base of ventral stabilising fin, to protect tail rotor. Alternative pontoon gear available for amphibious operation.

Power Plant: One 235 hp (derated to 170 hp) Franklin 6A-350-D1B six-cylinder horizontally-opposed aircooled engine, installed horizontally, offset to port. Fuel in two main tanks, one on each side of base of pylon, with total capacity of 28·6 Imp gallons (130 litres). For short-range missions, one tank may be omitted, the remaining tank containing enough fuel for up to 1 hour's flight. Oil capacity 2 Imp gallons (9 litres).

Accommodation: Bench seat for pilot and two passengers side by side in enclosed cabin. Forward-hinged, easily removable car-type door on each side. Roof panels of blue tinted Plexiglas. Large baggage compartment. Agricultural version normally flown as single-seater.

Systems: 12V electrical system includes generator, 37Ah battery and engine starter.

Optional Equipment: Dual controls; radio; cabin heating system; navigation, landing and cabin lights. External cargo hook under engine platform for 441 lb (200 kg) slung load. Baggage container on starboard side of engine platform, aft of cabin. Provision in ambulance version for an enclosed stretcher pannier to be mounted externally on brackets on port side of cabin. Agricultural installation of 32 ft 9½ in (10·00 m) sprayboom and twin tanks, one mounted externally each side of cabin and each containing 26·5 US gallons (100 litres) of liquid chemical.

Dimensions, external:
- Diameter of main rotor: 29 ft 7½ in (9·03 m)
- Diameter of tail rotor: 4 ft 6¾ in (1·39 m)
- Length overall, main rotor fore and aft: 34 ft 4¼ in (10·47 m)
- Length of fuselage, incl tailskid: 25 ft 1¼ in (7·65 m)
- Span of horizontal stabiliser: 6 ft 8¾ in (2·05 m)
- Max width of fuselage: 5 ft 0¾ in (1·54 m)
- Height to top of cabin roof: 5 ft 8⅛ in (1·73 m)
- Height overall: 9 ft 9¼ in (2·98 m)
- Width over skids: 5 ft 8½ in (1·74 m)

Dimensions, internal:
- Cabin:
  - Length: 4 ft 9¾ in (1·47 m)
  - Max height: 4 ft 0¾ in (1·24 m)

Areas:
- Main rotor blades (each): 12·61 sq ft (1·17 m^2)
- Tail rotor blades (each): 0·97 sq ft (0·09 m^2)
- Main rotor disc: 689·32 sq ft (64·04 m^2)
- Tail rotor disc: 16·32 sq ft (1·52 m^2)

Weights and Loadings:
- Weight empty:
  - SH-4: 1,142 lb (518 kg)
- Max T-O weight (Normal): 1,900 lb (862 kg)
- Max disc loading: 2·76 lb/sq ft (13·36 kg/m^2)
- Max power loading: 11·2 lb/hp (5·07 kg/hp)

Performance (at max T-O weight):
- Max level speed at S/L: 87 knots (100 mph; 161 km/h)
- Max cruising speed: 70 knots (81 mph; 130 km/h)
- Econ cruising speed: 63·5 knots (73 mph; 117 km/h)
- Max rate of climb at S/L: 1,180 ft (360 m)/min
- Service ceiling:
  - SH-4: 15,090 ft (4,600 m)
- Hovering ceiling in ground effect:
  - SH-4: 9,845 ft (3,000 m)
- Hovering ceiling out of ground effect:
  - SH-4: 7,875 ft (2,400 m)
- Range with max fuel: 173 nm (200 miles; 320 km)
- Max endurance: 3 hr

Production line-up of Silvercraft SH-4 three-seat light helicopters

JAPAN

CTDC

ZAIDAN HOZIN MINKAN YUSOOKI KAIHATSU KYOKAI (Civil Transport Development Corporation)

Head Office:
Toranomon Daiichi Building, No. 1, Kotohira-cho Shiba, Minato-ku, Tokyo 105
Telephone: Tokyo (03) 503-3211
Telex: 2222863 NAMC J

Directors:
Gakuji Moriya (Chairman)
Reizo Wakasugi (Senior Directing Manager)
Kyoku Hirano (Directing Manager)

The CTDC was established in April 1973 to manage, on behalf of the Japanese government and aerospace industry, the YX programme to design and develop a civil transport aircraft to succeed the NAMC YS-11. In addition to the officers listed above, board members include the chairmen of Mitsubishi Heavy Industries Ltd and Shin Meiwa Industries Co Ltd; and the presidents of All Nippon Airways, Fuji Heavy Industries Ltd, Ishikawajima-Harima Heavy Industries Co Ltd, Japan Aircraft Manufacturing Co Ltd (Nippi), Japan Air Lines, Kawasaki Heavy Industries Ltd, and Toa Domestic Airlines.

YX PROGRAMME

With substantial support from the Japanese government, the Japanese aerospace industry is planning to develop a civil transport aircraft in collaboration with The Boeing Company. The aircraft will be in the short/medium-range category, with a passenger capacity of approx 200.

Activity during 1974 is concerned with exploring the feasibility of developing and producing the new transport aircraft for commercial service in the late 1970s or early 1980s. Exploratory work is being carried out in collaboration with Boeing, under an agreement signed in April 1973. For this initial phase of the programme the Japanese government has voted Y2,100 million to cover 75 per cent of the required budget for the 1974 fiscal year.

FUJI

FUJI JUKOGYO KABUSHIKI KAISHA (Fuji Heavy Industries Ltd)

Head Office:
Subaru Building, 7-2, 1-chome, Nishi-shinjuku, Shinjuku-ku, Tokyo
Telephone: Tokyo (03) 347-2505
Telex: 0-232-2268

Aircraft Factory (Utsunomiya Manufacturing Division):
Utsunomiya City, Tochigi Prefecture
Telephone: Utsunomiya (0286) 58-1111

President:
Eiichi Ohara

Executive Managing Directors:
Nobuhiro Sakata
Sukemitsu Irie

Managing Directors:
Shoji Nagashima
Shigeichi Ota
Iwao Shibuya
Kiyoyuki Kawabata

General Manager of Aircraft Division:
Yoshio Minoda

Manager of Aircraft Sales Department:
Atsushi Kasai

Superintendent of Utsunomiya Aircraft Factory:
Saburo Watanabe

Fuji Heavy Industries Ltd was established on 15 July 1953. It is a successor to the Nakajima Aircraft Company, which was established in 1914 and built 30,000 aircraft up to the end of the second World War.

The present Utsunomiya Manufacturing Division (Aircraft and Rolling Stock Factories) occupies a site of 5,511,870 sq ft (512,070 m^2) including a floor area of 1,738,710 sq ft (161,532 m^2) and in April 1974 employed 3,445 people.

Under a 1953 licence and technical assistance agreement with Beech Aircraft Corporation, Fuji built the Beechcraft Mentor at Utsunomiya. Several modified versions of the Mentor, designated LM-1 Nikko, LM-2, KM and KM-2, were also built by Fuji. Details of these can be found in earlier editions of *Jane's*. Three more KM-2s were ordered for the JMSDF in FY 1974.

Simultaneously, under licence from Cessna, Fuji produced 22 L-19E Bird Dog observation aircraft for the Japan Ground Self-Defence Force.

Under another major agreement, the company is now producing in Japan the Bell Model 204/205 series of helicopters. The first 204B covered by the agreement arrived in Japan in kit form in May 1962 for assembly by Fuji.

First aircraft designed entirely by Fuji was the T-1 intermediate two-seat jet trainer, described fully in the 1967-68 *Jane's*. It was followed by a four-seat light aeroplane known as the FA-200 Aero Subaru, details of which follow.

In early 1970, Fuji began design studies for a twin-engined six/ten-seat aircraft, known as the FA-300, intended as a light business aircraft or for military or civil crew trainer duties.

Fuji was responsible for construction of the VTOL flying testbed designed by the National Aerospace Laboratory (see 1972-73 *Jane's*), and in 1972 began further study of VTOL research aircraft under contract to NAL.

Fuji is currently studying two proposals to meet the JASDF's XT-3 requirement for a basic trainer, acquisition of which is expected to form a part of the 6th defence build-up programme (1982-87). One of these proposals is essentially an improved T-1; the other is an entirely new design.

In 1971 Fuji began to produce Firebee I subsonic target drones for the JMSDF, under a technical and licensing agreement with Teledyne Ryan (see "RPVs and Targets" section).

FUJI FA-200 AERO SUBARU

Fuji began detail design of this light aircraft in 1964 and the prototype flew for the first time on 12 August 1965. Subsequently, refinements were made to the aircraft, and it went into production as the FA-200-160 and FA-200-180 (see 1973-74 *Jane's*). One example was also produced of the FA-203S STOL version, and this was described in the 1970-71 *Jane's*.

Versions in current production are designated as follows:

FA-200-160A. Basic four-seat light aircraft, with 160 hp Lycoming engine. Received Japan Civil Aviation Bureau Normal category type certificate as a four-seater on 1 March 1966, Utility category certification as a three-seater on 6 July 1966 and Aerobatic category certification as a two-seater on 29 July 1967. FAA Type Approval in all three categories followed on 26 September 1967.

FA-200-180A. Developed version with 180 hp Lycoming engine. Certification by JCAB in Normal (four-seat), Utility (four-seat), and Aerobatic (two-seat) categories was received on 28 February 1968, and FAA Type Approval in all three categories on 25 April 1968.

FA-200-180AO. Version with 180 hp Lycoming engine and fixed-pitch propeller . Certificated by JCAB in Normal (four-seat), Utility (four-seat) and Aerobatic (two-seat) categories on 27 September 1973; FAA Type Approval requested in December 1973.

Production of the FA-200 began in March 1968, and 243 had been completed by the end of March 1974, of which 142 were for export.

The following description applies generally to all three current versions, except where a specific version is indicated. "Subaru" is the Japanese name for the Pleiades group of six stars in the constellation of Taurus, and was chosen to represent the six companies which merged to form Fuji Heavy Industries Ltd.

TYPE: Four-seat light monoplane.

WINGS: Cantilever low-wing monoplane. Dihedral 7°. Incidence 2° 30′. All-metal structure, with single extruded main spar at 42% chord. All-metal riveted Frise-type ailerons and single-slotted flaps. Trim tab in each aileron.

FUSELAGE: All-metal semi-monocoque structure of frames and stringers.

TAIL UNIT: Cantilever all-metal structure, with swept vertical surfaces. One-piece horizontal surface. Trim tab in port elevator. Manually-adjustable tab in rudder.

LANDING GEAR: Non-retractable tricycle type. Oleo-pneumatic shock-absorbers on all units. Nosewheel steerable. Tube-type 4-ply tyres size 6·00-6 on main wheels, 5·00-5 on nosewheel. Hydraulic disc brakes. Parking brake. Streamlined wheel fairings optional.

POWER PLANT: One 160 hp Lycoming O-320-D2A (180 hp Lycoming IO-360-B1B in FA-200-180A and 180 hp Lycoming O-360-A5AD in FA-200-180AO) four-cylinder horizontally-opposed aircooled engine, driving a McCauley 1C 160/FGM 7656 two-blade fixed-pitch metal propeller in FA-200-160A (McCauley B2D34C53/74E-0 two-blade constant-speed metal propeller in FA-200-180A, and McCauley 1A 170/EFA 7658 two-blade fixed-pitch metal propeller in FA-200-180AO). Fuel in two integral tanks in inner wings with total capacity of 45 Imp gallons (204·5 litres). Overwing refuelling point on each tank. Oil capacity 1·5 Imp gallons (7 litres).

ACCOMMODATION: Four seats in pairs in enclosed cabin. Individual adjustable front seats, with dual controls. Optional shoulder harness on each of the four seats. Large rearward-sliding canopy. Two tinted roof windows optional. Cabin heating and ventilation, and windscreen defrosting, standard. Baggage compartment in rear of fuselage, capacity 176 lb (80 kg). Baggage shelf aft of rear seats, capacity 44 lb (20 kg).

ELECTRONICS AND EQUIPMENT: Standard electrical equipment includes 14V 50/60A alternator and 12V 38Ah battery. Optional extras include HF and VHF radio, full blind-flying instrumentation, VOR, ADF, ILS, ATC transponder, landing and navigation lights, cabin lights, instrument lights and anti-collision light.

DIMENSIONS, EXTERNAL:

Wing span	30 ft 11 in (9·42 m)
Wing chord (constant)	5 ft 0 in (1·525 m)
Wing aspect ratio	6·02
Length overall	26 ft 9½ in (8·17 m)
Height overall	8 ft 6 in (2·59 m)
Tailplane span	11 ft 4½ in (3·47 m)
Wheel track	8 ft 7½ in (2·63 m)
Wheelbase	5 ft 8¾ in (1·75 m)
Propeller diameter:	
160A	6 ft 4 in (1·93 m)
180A	6 ft 2 in (1·88 m)

DIMENSIONS, INTERNAL:

Cabin: Length	5 ft 8½ in (1·74 m)
Width	3 ft 4½ in (1·03 m)

AREAS:

Wings, gross	150·7 sq ft (14·0 m²)
Ailerons (total)	12·11 sq ft (1·13 m²)
Flaps (total)	20·13 sq ft (1·87 m²)
Fin	16·11 sq ft (1·50 m²)
Rudder, incl tab	9·58 sq ft (0·89 m²)
Tailplane	35·74 sq ft (3·32 m²)
Elevator, incl tab	15·4 sq ft (1·43 m²)

WEIGHTS AND LOADINGS (N: Normal; U: Utility; A: Aerobatic category):

Weight empty:	
160A	1,366 lb (620 kg)
180A	1,433 lb (650 kg)
180AO	1,411 lb (640 kg)
Max T-O weight:	
N (160A)	2,335 lb (1,060 kg)
N (180A)	2,535 lb (1,150 kg)
N (180AO)	2,513 lb (1,140 kg)
U (160A)	2,138 lb (970 kg)
U (180AO/180A)	2,425 lb (1,100 kg)
A (160A)	1,940 lb (880 kg)
A (180AO/180A)	2,072 lb (940 kg)
Max wing loading:	
N (160A)	15·5 lb/sq ft (75·7 kg/m²)
N (180A)	16·8 lb/sq ft (82·1 kg/m²)
Max power loading:	
N (160A)	14·62 lb/hp (6·63 kg/hp)
N (180A)	14·09 lb/hp (6·39 kg/hp)

PERFORMANCE (N: Normal category; A: Aerobatic category, at max T-O weight):

Max level speed at S/L:	
N (160A)	120 knots (138 mph; 222 km/h)
N (180A)	126 knots (145 mph; 233 km/h)
N (180AO)	123 knots (142 mph; 229 km/h)
A (160A)	122 knots (140 mph; 225 km/h)
A (180A)	128 knots (147 mph; 237 km/h)
A (180AO)	126 knots (145 mph; 233 km/h)
Max cruising speed (75% power):	
N (160A) at 5,000 ft (1,525 m)	106 knots (122 mph; 196 km/h)
N (180A) at 5,000 ft (1,525 m)	110 knots (127 mph; 204 km/h)
N (180AO) at 5,000 ft (1,525 m)	112 knots (129 mph; 208 km/h)
A (160A) at 7,500 ft (2,290 m)	114 knots (131 mph; 211 km/h)
A (180A and 180AO) at 7,500 ft (2,290 m)	119 knots (137 mph; 220 km/h)
Econ cruising speed (55% power):	
N (160A) at 5,000 ft (1,525 m)	89 knots (102 mph; 164 km/h)
N (180A) at 5,000 ft (1,525 m)	90 knots (104 mph; 167 km/h)
N (180AO) at 5,000 ft (1,525 m)	92 knots (106 mph; 171 km/h)
A (160A) at 7,500 ft (2,290 m)	96 knots (110 mph; 177 km/h)
A (180A) at 7,500 ft (2,290 m)	100 knots (115 mph; 185 km/h)
A (180AO) at 7,500 ft (2,290 m)	102 knots (118 mph; 190 km/h)
Stalling speed, flaps down:	
N (160A)	49 knots (56 mph; 90 km/h)
N (180A)	53 knots (60 mph; 97 km/h)
N (180AO)	52 knots (59 mph; 95 km/h)
A (160A)	45·5 knots (52·5 mph; 84 km/h)
A (180A and 180AO)	47 knots (54 mph; 87 km/h)
Max rate of climb at S/L:	
N (160A)	680 ft (207 m)/min
N (180A)	760 ft (232 m)/min
N (180AO)	670 ft (204 m)/min
A (160A)	991 ft (302 m)/min
A (180A)	1,129 ft (344 m)/min
A (180AO)	1,020 ft (311 m)/min
Service ceiling:	
N (160A and 180AO)	11,400 ft (3,480 m)
N (180A)	13,700 ft (4,175 m)
A (160A)	15,500 ft (4,725 m)
A (180A)	19,000 ft (5,790 m)
A (180AO)	18,500 ft (5,640 m)
T-O run:	
A (160A)	525 ft (160 m)
A (180A and 180AO)	623 ft (190 m)
T-O to 50 ft (15 m):	
N (160A)	1,530 ft (465 m)
N (180A and 180AO)	1,640 ft (500 m)
A (160A)	1,020 ft (310 m)
A (180A and 180AO)	1,000 ft (305 m)
Landing from 50 ft (15 m):	
N (160A)	1,115 ft (340 m)
N (180A and 180AO)	1,150 ft (350 m)
A (160A)	1,033 ft (315 m)
A (180A and 180AO)	1,066 ft (325 m)
Landing run:	
A (160A)	377 ft (115 m)
A (180A and 180AO)	410 ft (125 m)
Range with max fuel (55% power at 7,500 ft; 2,290 m, no reserves):	
N (160A)	655 nm (755 miles; 1,215 km)
N (180A)	725 nm (835 miles; 1,343 km)
N (180AO)	675 nm (778 miles; 1,252 km)
A (160A)	816 nm (940 miles; 1,512 km)
A (180A)	755 nm (870 miles; 1,400 km)
A (180AO)	748 nm (862 miles; 1,387 km)

Fuji FA-200-180A Aero Subaru four-seat light aircraft (180 hp Lycoming IO-360 engine)

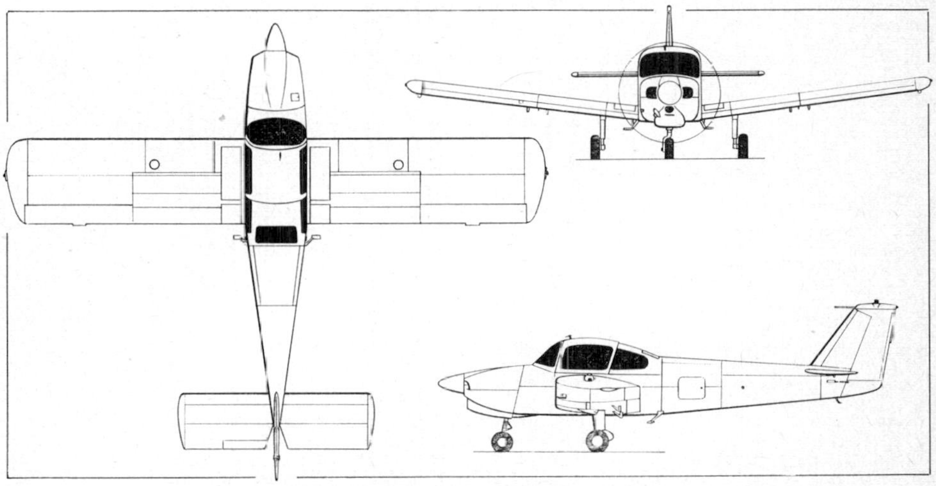

Fuji FA-200-180AO four-seat light aircraft *(Pilot Press)*

FUJI FA-300

The FA-300 is a six/ten-seat twin-engined light aircraft, a small number of prototypes of which are to be built. Power plant is likely to be two Lycoming or Continental engines.

No further details were available at the time of closing for press, the FA-300 then being still in the design development stage. The possibility of joint development in partnership with a US company has been explored.

FUJI-BELL 204B/204B-2 and 205A-1/UH-1H

Fuji is manufacturing Bell Model 204B and UH-1H helicopters under sub-licence from Mitsui and Co Ltd, Bell's Japanese legal licensee. By the end of February 1974, six Fuji-built 204Bs were in service with Asahi Helicopter Company, two with Tokyo Metropolitan Police Board Headquarters, two with the Toa Kokunai Koku Company, three with Nakanihon Koku, one with the Shin Nihon Helicopter Co, one with the Tokyu Kensetsu Co, one with Nihon Norin Helicopter Co and four with the National Police Bureau.

Initial orders for the UH-1B military version of the 204B, from the Japan Ground Self-Defence Force, totalled 36, all of which were delivered by December 1967. By early 1973, 90 UH-1Bs had been delivered to the JGSDF. Subsequent orders are for the UH-1H version, of which the first example flew for the first time on 17 July 1973; 11 were ordered in FY 1974 and 55 are to be delivered by March 1977. The civil 205A-1 will be available to order.

The Fuji-Bell 204B and UH-1H are identical with the versions of these aircraft built by Bell Helicopter Company (see US section). They are powered by 1,100 shp Kawasaki-built Lycoming KT5311A turboshaft engines.

In October 1973 Fuji developed a higher-powered version of the 204B. Powered by a 1,400 shp Lycoming T5313B turboshaft engine, it has the same basic airframe and dynamic components as the 204B, but has a tractor-type tail rotor. The first example of this version, which is designated **204B-2,** was due to be delivered to the Asahi Helicopter Co in early 1974.

The following details apply to the standard Fuji-Bell 204B/204B-2 /UH-1H:

DIMENSIONS, EXTERNAL:
- Diameter of main rotor: 48 ft 0 in (16·63 m)
- Diameter of tail rotor: 8 ft 6 in (2·59 m)
- Length overall, tail rotor turning:
  - 204B/B-2: 44 ft 7¾ in (13·61 m)
  - UH-1H: 44 ft 10 in (13·67 m)
- Length of fuselage:
  - 204B/B-2: 40 ft 4¾ in (12·31 m)
  - UH-1H: 40 ft 7 in (12·37 m)
- Height overall, tail rotor turning: 14 ft 6 in (4·42 m)
- Height to top of rotor hub:
  - 204B/B-2: 12 ft 4½ in (3·77 m)
  - UH-1H: 13 ft 0¾ in (3·98 m)
- Max width over landing skids:
  - 204B/B-2: 8 ft 8 in (2·64 m)
  - UH-1H: 8 ft 6½ in (2·60 m)
- Tailplane span: 9 ft 4 in (2·84 m)

WEIGHTS:
- Weight empty:
  - 204B/B-2: 4,800 lb (2,177 kg)
  - UH-1H: 5,270 lb (2,390 kg)
- Max T-O weight:
  - 204B/B-2: 8,500 lb (3,855 kg)
  - UH-1H: 9,500 lb (4,309 kg)

PERFORMANCE (at max T-O weight):
- Max level and cruising speed: 110 knots (127 mph; 204 km/h)
- Max rate of climb at S/L:
  - 204B: 1,520 ft (463 m)/min
  - 204B-2: 1,930 ft (588 m)/min
  - UH-1H: 1,600 ft (488 m)/min
- Service ceiling:
  - 204B: 14,700 ft (4,480 m)
  - 204B-2: 19,000 ft (5,790 m)
  - UH-1H: 12,600 ft (3,840 m)
- Hovering ceiling in ground effect:
  - 204B: 9,800 ft (2,985 m)
  - 204B-2: 15,200 ft (4,635 m)
  - UH-1H: 13,600 ft (4,145 m)
- Hovering ceiling out of ground effect:
  - 204B: 4,300 ft (1,310 m)
  - 204B-2: 10,500 ft (3,200 m)
  - UH-1H: 1,100 ft (335 m)
- Range at S/L:
  - 204B: 206 nm (237 miles; 381 km)
  - 204B-2: 207 nm (238 miles; 383 km)
  - UH-1H: 252 nm (290 miles; 467 km)

FUJI XMH

The XMH company-owned UH-1B helicopter which Fuji modified as a high-speed research aircraft made its first flight on 11 February 1970.

The first phase of flight testing ended in January 1973, after 87 flights. Further flight testing has been discontinued.

A description and illustration of the XMH appeared in the 1973-74 *Jane's*.

Fuji-Bell UH-1H helicopter in the insignia of the Japan Ground Self-Defence Force

JEAA

JAPAN EXPERIMENTAL AIRCRAFT ASSOCIATION (Chapter 306 of EAA International)

ADDRESS:
2-27 Uehara, Shibuya-ku, Tokyo 151

PRESIDENT:
Asahi Miyahara

Telephone: (03) 467-8522

Various fixed- and rotating-wing aircraft have recently been designed and/or built and flown by members of the JEAA, and several of these have appeared in recent editions of *Jane's*. Construction of the JEAA-S1 designed by Mr Asahi Miyahara (see 1973-74 *Jane's*) has been discontinued due to lack of funds. One homebuilt design not previously recorded, but still flying, is Mr K. Abe's Mizet II, first flown in 1948; brief details of this follow.

Other activities by JEAA members are described in the "Sailplanes" section.

ABE MIZET II

The Mizet II single-seat homebuilt light aircraft was designed in 1942-44 by Mr K. Abe, a school teacher of Kushiro-shi, Hokkaido, and made its first flight on 9 December 1948. It is still flying, as shown in the accompanying photograph. The constant-chord wings are of Göttingen 387 section and are fitted with ailerons. Power plant is a 25 hp Paburica 800 cc two-cylinder four-stroke motor car engine, driving a two-blade wooden pusher propeller.

DIMENSIONS, EXTERNAL:
- Wing span: 24 ft 11¼ in (7·60 m)
- Wing chord (constant): 3 ft 10½ in (1·18 m)
- Wing aspect ratio: 6·5
- Length overall: 18 ft 0½ in (5·50 m)
- Height over tail: 7 ft 2¾ in (2·20 m)
- Propeller diameter: 3 ft 7⅜ in (1·10 m)

AREA:
- Wings, gross: 96·9 sq ft (9·00 m²)

WEIGHTS AND LOADINGS:
- Weight empty: 363 lb (165 kg)
- Max T-O weight: 562 lb (255 kg)
- Max wing loading: 5·8 lb/sq ft (28·2 kg/m²)
- Max power loading: 22·5 lb/hp (10·2 kg/hp)

MAKINO MHO.235

This single-seat all-wood biplane was built by Mr T. Makino, with the assistance of Mr Hirano and Mr Oki. It is powered by a 1·2 litre VW engine.

Mizet II single-seat ultra-light aircraft, designed by Mr K. Abe (*H. Seo*)

MHO.235 single-seat homebuilt biplane built by Mr T. Makino of the JEAA (*Asahi Miyahara*)

DIMENSIONS, EXTERNAL:

Wing span	18 ft 4½ in (5·60 m)
Wing area (gross)	102·3 sq ft (9·50 m²)
Length overall	16 ft 8¾ in (5·10 m)

WEIGHT AND LOADING:

T-O weight	573 lb (260 kg)
Wing loading	5·61 lb/sq ft (27·4 kg/m²)

HAMAO SIOKARA TOMBO

This small single-seat biplane, designed and built by Mr T. Hamao, is powered by a 150 hp Lycoming engine and is shown in an accompanying photograph.

No other details have been received for publication.

Single-seat Siokara Tombo biplane designed and built by Mr T. Hamao of the JEAA (*Asahi Miyahara*)

KAWASAKI

KAWASAKI JUKOGYO KABUSHIKI KAISHA (Kawasaki Heavy Industries Ltd)

HEAD OFFICE:
2-16-1 Nakamachi-Dori, Ikuta-ku, Kobe

TOKYO AND AIRCRAFT GROUP OFFICE:
World Trade Center Building, 4-1, Hamamatsu-cho 2-chome, Minato-ku, Tokyo
Telephone: Tokyo (03) 435-2971
Telex: J22672 and J26888

PRESIDENT:
Kiyoshi Yotsumoto

EXECUTIVE VICE-PRESIDENTS:
Riichi Kato
Kenji Hasegawa

WORKS:
Gifu

GENERAL MANAGER, AIRCRAFT GROUP:
Kenji Uchino

ASST GENERAL MANAGER, AIRCRAFT GROUP:
Hiroharu Tsukamoto

GENERAL MANAGER, AIRCRAFT SALES DIVISION:
Yasushi Tsuboi

With effect from 1 April 1969, Kawasaki Aircraft Co Ltd was amalgamated with the Kawasaki Dockyard Co Ltd, and the Kawasaki Rolling Stock Mfg Co Ltd, to form a new company known as Kawasaki Heavy Industries Ltd. The Aircraft Division of the former Kawasaki Aircraft Co Ltd, which employs some 8,000 people, continues its activities as the Aircraft Group of this company. Kawasaki has a 34% holding in Nippi (which see).

In addition to extensive overhaul work, Kawasaki has built many US aircraft under licence since 1955.

Between 1959 and 1963 Kawasaki delivered 42 Lockheed P2V-7 (P-2H) Neptune anti-submarine aircraft to the Japan Maritime Self-Defence Force, and six more were delivered in 1965. Kawasaki then developed from the Neptune a new anti-submarine aircraft, designated P-2J, which is in production.

Design studies are being undertaken for a new ASW aircraft, provisionally designated PX-L, to succeed the P-2J.

Kawasaki has been producing the Bell Model 47 helicopter under licence since 1953 and had built by 1 January 1974 11 Model 47Ds, 15 Model 47Gs, 180 Model 47G-2s, 33 Model 47G-2As and 207 Model KH-4s developed from the Model 47 by its own design staff.

Kawasaki has exclusive rights to manufacture and sell the twin-engined Boeing Vertol 107 Model II helicopter and its own KV-107/IIA development of it. The Hughes Model 369 (500S and 500M) light observation helicopter is also being assembled by Kawasaki under a licence agreement concluded in October 1967. By early 1974 a total of 100 KV-107 helicopters had been delivered to customers in Japan and other countries, including Sweden, Thailand and the US; and 104 Hughes 500s had been delivered to government and commercial operators in Japan.

Kawasaki built main wings and nacelle structures, including the landing gear, for the NAMC YS-11 turboprop transport. It is now prime contractor for the JASDF's C-1 transport; and builds main wing and tail assemblies under subcontract for Japanese-built (see Mitsubishi entry) F-4EJ Phantom II fighters for the JASDF. Cargo and passenger doors for the Lockheed L-1011 TriStar jet transport are manufactured at the Gifu works, and Kawasaki has a Boeing contract to manufacture outboard trailing-edge flaps for the Boeing 747SP transport aircraft.

Kawasaki is engaged in missile development and production; its aero-engine activities are described in the appropriate section of this edition.

KAWASAKI P-2J

JMSDF designation: P-2J

The P-2J was developed by Kawasaki, originally under the designation GK-210, to meet a JMSDF requirement for a new anti-submarine aircraft to replace its P2V-7 Neptunes in service during the 1970s. Design is based very closely upon that of the P2V-7 (P-2H), and began in October 1961. Work on the conversion of a standard P2V-7 as the P-2J prototype began in June 1965, and this aircraft flew for the first time on 21 July 1966.

The first production P-2J was flown on 8 August 1969, and was delivered to the JMSDF on 7 October. The second aircraft was also flown before the end of 1969, and five current contracts cover the delivery of 54 P-2Js by March 1975. The first 46 P-2Js were delivered to the JMSDF by 31 March 1974. The JMSDF is to purchase an additional 35 of these aircraft, bringing the total to 89.

TYPE: Four-engined anti-submarine and maritime patrol aircraft.

WINGS: Cantilever all-metal mid-wing monoplane, with taper on outer panels. Wing section NACA 2419 (modified) at root, NACA 4410·5 at tip. Dihedral 5° on outer panels. Incidence 3° 30′ at root. No sweepback. Wing designed to give temporary flotation in event of ditching. Centre-section box beam is continuous through fuselage. All-metal ailerons, each incorporating a spring and trim tab. Fowler-type all-metal inboard and outboard trailing-edge flaps. All-metal two-section spoilers in upper surface of outer wing panels, inboard of ailerons. Thermal de-icing of leading-edges.

FUSELAGE: Conventional all-metal unpressurised semi-monocoque structure, basically as P2V-7 (P-2H) but with extra 4 ft 2 in (1·27 m) section inserted between wing leading-edge and cockpit to house improved electronic equipment.

TAIL UNIT: Cantilever all-metal structure, incorporating "Varicam" (variable camber), a movable trimming surface between the fixed tailplane and each elevator which is operated by hydraulically-driven screwjack. Spring tab and trim tab in rudder, balance tab and spring tab in each elevator. Tail unit has thermal de-icing and is virtually unchanged from P2V-7 except for an increase in rudder area by extending the chord by 1 ft (0·30 m) at the top.

LANDING GEAR: Retractable tricycle type, with single steerable nosewheel and twin-wheel main units. Hydraulic retraction, nosewheel rearward, main wheels forward into inboard engine nacelles. Sumitomo Precision oleo-pneumatic shock-absorbers. Goodyear Type VII tubeless tyres on all units, size 9·9 × 34-14 on nosewheel and 13 × 39-16 on main wheels. Tyre pressures 90 lb/sq in (6·3 kg/cm²) on nosewheel, 100 lb/sq in (7·0 kg/cm²) on main wheels. Goodyear disc brakes and on/off-type anti-skid units on main units.

POWER PLANT: Two 2,850 ehp Japanese-built General Electric T64-IHI-10 turboprop engines, mounted on wing centre-section and each driving a Sumitomo Precision 63E60-19 three-blade variable-pitch metal propeller. Outboard of these, on underwing pylons, are two pod-mounted Ishikawajima-Harima J3-IHI-7C turbojets, each rated at 3,085 lb (1,400 kg) st. Fuel in inboard and outboard wing tanks with total capacity of 2,515 Imp gallons (3,020 US gallons; 11,433 litres), plus 333 Imp gallons (400 US gallons; 1,514 litres) in port wingtip tank. For ferry purposes a 583 Imp gallon (700 US gallon; 2,650 litre) auxiliary tank can be installed in the weapons bay. Oil capacity 5·2 Imp gallons (6·2 US gallons; 23·6 litres) for each turboprop and 2·4 Imp gallons (2·9 US gallons; 11·0 litres) for each turbojet engine.

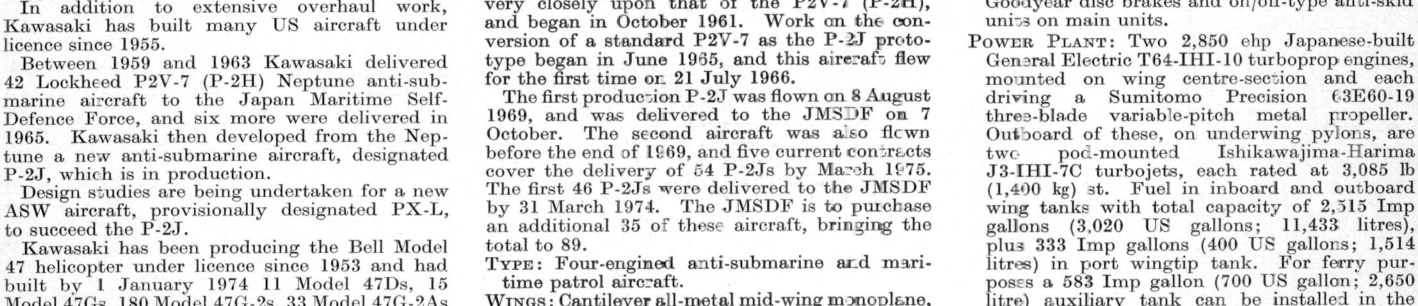

Kawasaki P-2J maritime patrol aircraft of the Japan Maritime Self-Defence Force (*T. Matsuzaki*)

Accommodation: Crew of twelve, including two pilots on flight deck, seven men in tactical compartment in forward fuselage and three aft of centre-section wing box beam. Aft of the tactical compartment, in centre fuselage, are an ordnance room, galley and toilet. Crew escape hatches in flight deck, tactical and ordnance compartments. All accommodation heated, ventilated and air-conditioned.

Systems: Primary hydraulic system, pressure 3,000 lb/sq in (210 kg/cm²), for Varicam (tail unit), landing gear and nosewheel steering. Secondary system, pressure 1,500 lb/sq in (105 kg/cm²), for flaps, spoilers, jet pod doors, main-wheel brakes and propeller braking. Two 40kVA generators provide 115/200V AC power at 400Hz. DC power from three 28V 200A transformer-rectifiers.

Electronics and Equipment: Standard equipment includes HRC-6 VHF radio, HRC-7 HF, AN/ARC-552 UHF and APS-80J search radar. Details of operational equipment are classified, but this is of comparable standard to that carried by the Lockheed P-3 Orion and includes a smoke detector and MAD in the elongated tailcone. Searchlight in starboard wingtip pod.

Dimensions, external:
Wing span 97 ft 8½ in (29·78 m)
Wing span over tip-tanks 101 ft 3½ in (30·87 m)
Wing chord at root 14 ft 7¼ in (4·45 m)
Wing chord at tip 7 ft 3½ in (2·22 m)
Wing aspect ratio 10
Length overall 95 ft 10¾ in (29·23 m)
Height overall 29 ft 3½ in (8·93 m)
Tailplane span 34 ft 0 in (10·36 m)
Wheel track (c/l of shock struts) 25 ft 0 in (7·62 m)
Wheelbase 29 ft 0 in (8·84 m)
Propeller diameter 14 ft 6¼ in (4·43 m)
Distance between propeller centres 25 ft 0 in (7·62 m)

Dimensions, internal (tactical compartment):
Cabin: Length 18 ft 0 in (5·49 m)
Max width 6 ft 8 in (2·03 m)
Max height (at c/l) 5 ft 1 in (1·55 m)
Floor area 120 sq ft (11·15 m²)
Volume 500 cu ft (14·16 m³)

Areas:
Wings, gross 1,000 sq ft (92·9 m²)
Ailerons (total) 63·2 sq ft (5·87 m²)
Trailing-edge flaps (total) 179·6 sq ft (16·70 m²)
Spoilers (total) 15·2 sq ft (1·41 m²)
Fin 190·0 sq ft (17·65 m²)
Rudder, incl tabs 43·5 sq ft (4·04 m²)
Tailplane 231·0 sq ft (21·50 m²)
Elevators, incl tabs and Varicam 91·0 sq ft (8·45 m²)

Weights and Loadings:
Weight empty 42,500 lb (19,277 kg)
Max T-O weight 75,000 lb (34,019 kg)
Max zero-fuel weight 50,900 lb (23,087 kg)
Max landing weight 62,000 lb (28,122 kg)
Max wing loading 75·00 lb/sq ft (366·2 kg/m²)
Max power loading 13·16 lb/ehp (5·97 kg/ehp)

Performance (at max T-O weight):
Max never-exceed speed 350 knots (403 mph; 649 km/h)
Max cruising speed 217 knots (250 mph; 402 km/h)
Econ cruising speed at 10,000 ft (3,050 m) 200 knots (230 mph; 370 km/h)
Stalling speed, flaps down 90 knots (103 mph; 166 km/h)
Max rate of climb at S/L 1,800 ft (550 m)/min
Service ceiling 30,000 ft (9,150 m)
T-O to 50 ft (15 m) 3,600 ft (1,100 m)
Landing from 50 ft (15 m) 2,880 ft (880 m)
Range with max fuel 2,400 nm (2,765 miles; 4,450 km)

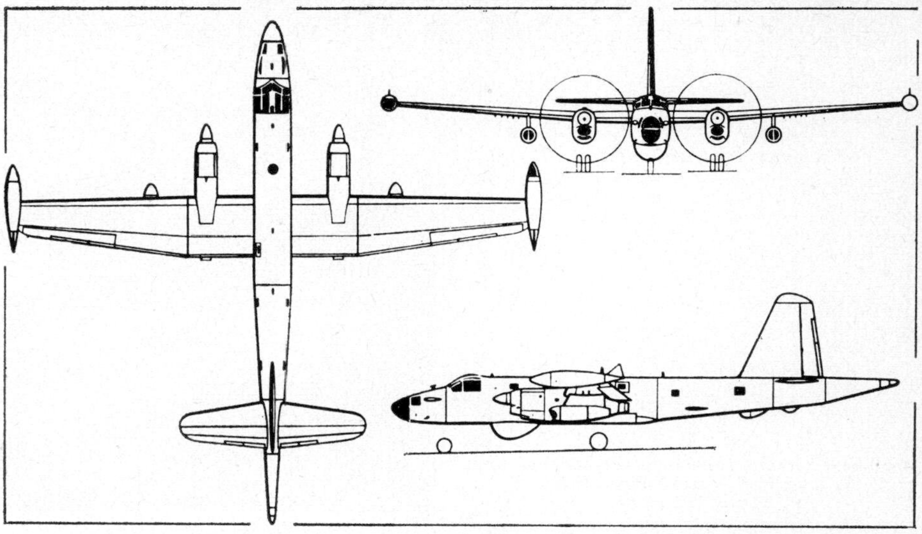

Kawasaki P-2J twin-turboprop development of the Lockheed Neptune *(Pilot Press)*

KAWASAKI C-1

The C-1 is a medium-sized troop and freight transport designed to meet the JASDF's requirement for a replacement for its fleet of Curtiss C-46 transports. Preliminary design was started by NAMC in 1966, and in 1968 a prototype development contract was awarded. Following the completion of a full-size mock-up in March 1968, construction began in the following Autumn of two XC-1 flying prototypes and one airframe for static tests. The first flying prototype, assembled at Kawasaki's Gifu factory, made its first flight on 12 November 1970, followed by the second on 16 January 1971. These prototypes were handed over to the Japan Defence Agency on 24 February and 20 March 1971 respectively. Further development and evaluation tests by the JDA were completed in March 1973.

Two pre-production aircraft and a fatigue test airframe had been delivered by the end of February 1974, at which time one of the prototypes and both pre-production aircraft were being operated by the JASDF Transport Wing at Iruma base.

Eleven production C-1s were ordered in FY 1973, and a further 13 in FY 1974; continued production is anticipated under the 5th defence buildup programme.

Prime contractor in the C-1 programme is Kawasaki, which builds the front fuselage and wing centre-section and undertakes final assembly and flight testing. Major subcontractors are Fuji (outer wing panels); Mitsubishi, which also built the mock-up, builds the centre and aft fuselage sections and the tail surfaces; and Nihon Hikoki (Nippi) builds the flaps, ailerons, pylons and engine pods.

Type: Twin-turbofan medium-range transport.

Wings: Cantilever high-wing monoplane. Wings have moderate sweepback, with slightly increased leading-edge sweep inboard of the engine pylons. 20° sweepback at quarter-chord. Thickness/chord ratio 12% at root, 11% at tip. Anhedral 5° 30′ from centre-section. Conventional two-spar fail-safe structure of aluminium alloy, including control surfaces. Two quadruple-slotted flaps on each trailing-edge, with 75° travel. Forward of these, on each wing, are three flight spoilers and a ground spoiler. Drooping leading-edge slats, in four sections, on each wing. Aileron outboard of each outer flap. Trim tab in one aileron. Flaps are operated hydraulically, ailerons manually. Thermal anti-icing of leading-edges, using engine bleed air.

Fuselage: Conventional semi-monocoque fail-safe structure of aluminium alloy, with a circular cross-section.

Tail Unit: "T" type cantilever structure, of aluminium alloy, with sweepback on all surfaces (30° at fin quarter-chord, 25° at tailplane quarter-chord). Tailplane has 5° anhedral. Variable-incidence tailplane, with elevators. Balance tab in each elevator and anti-balance tab in rudder. Elevators and rudder are each operated by two independent hydro-actuator systems; the elevators can be operated manually in an emergency. Thermal de-icing of tailplane, using electric heater mat.

Landing Gear: Hydraulically-retractable tricycle type, of Sumitomo design. Each main unit has two pairs of wheels in tandem, retracting forward into fairings built on to the sides of the fuselage. Forward-retracting nose unit has twin wheels. Oleo shock-absorbers. Kayaba wheels with Dunlop tyres, which on main units have pressure of 75 lb/sq in (5·27 kg/cm²). Kayaba hydraulic brakes and anti-skid units.

Power Plant: Two 14,500 lb (6,575 kg) st Pratt & Whitney JT8D-9 turbofan engines, installed in pylon-mounted underwing pods and fitted with thrust reversers. Four integral wing fuel tanks with total capacity of 3,344 Imp gallons (15,200 litres). Single pressure-refuelling point for all tanks, plus overwing gravity refuelling point for each tank.

Accommodation: Crew of five, comprising pilot, co-pilot, navigator, flight engineer and load supervisor. Escape hatch in flight deck roof on starboard side. Flight deck and main cabin pressurised and air-conditioned. Standard complements are as follows: troops (max) 60, paratroops (max) 45, stretchers 36 plus attendants. As a cargo carrier, loads can include a 2½ ton truck, a 105 mm howitzer, two ¾ ton trucks or three jeeps. Up to three pre-loaded freight pallets, 7 ft 4 in (2·24 m) wide and 9 ft 0 in (2·74 m) long, designed by Shin Meiwa, can be carried. Floor is stressed for

First pre-production example of the Kawasaki C-1 medium-range military transport for the JASDF (two 14,500 lb st Pratt & Whitney JT8D-9 turbofan engines)

loads of up to 100 lb/sq in (7 kg/cm²). Access to flight deck via downward-opening door, with built-in stairs, on port side of forward fuselage. Paratroop door on each side of fuselage, aft of wing trailing-edge. For air-dropping, the rear-loading ramp/door at the rear of the cabin can be opened in flight to the full cabin cross-section.

SYSTEMS: Pressurisation and air-conditioning systems utilise engine bleed air. APU in front section of starboard landing gear fairing. Three independent hydraulic systems. One APU-driven and two engine-driven AC generators for electrical power.

ELECTRONICS AND EQUIPMENT: Standard equipment includes autopilot, Doppler radar, radio altimeter, HF, VHF and UHF radio, ADF, UHF/DF, marker beacon, VOR/ILS, TACAN, SIF, dual compass system and flight director system. Optional equipment includes LORAN and weather radar.

DIMENSIONS, EXTERNAL:

Wing span	100 ft 4¾ in (30·60 m)
Wing chord at root	20 ft 8 in (6·30 m)
Wing chord at tip	6 ft 6¾ in (2·00 m)
Wing aspect ratio	7·8
Length overall	95 ft 1¾ in (29·00 m)
Length of fuselage	86 ft 11 in (26·50 m)
Height overall	32 ft 9¼ in (9·99 m)
Tailplane span	37 ft 1 in (11·30 m)
Wheel track	14 ft 5¼ in (4·40 m)
Wheelbase	30 ft 7¼ in (9·33 m)
Rear-loading ramp-door:	
Length	8 ft 9 in (2·67 m)
Width	8 ft 10¼ in (2·70 m)
Height to sill	4 ft 1¼ in (1·25 m)

DIMENSIONS, INTERNAL:

Cabin: Max length	34 ft 9¼ in (10·60 m)
Max width	11 ft 9¾ in (3·60 m)
Max height	8 ft 4½ in (2·55 m)
Floor area	308 sq ft (28·6 m²)
Volume (excl ramp area)	2,606 cu ft (73·8 m³)

AREAS:

Wings, gross	1,297 sq ft (120·5 m²)
Ailerons (total)	36·6 sq ft (3·4 m²)
Trailing-edge flaps (total)	246·5 sq ft (22·9 m²)
Spoilers (total)	95·8 sq ft (8·9 m²)
Fin	170·1 sq ft (15·8 m²)
Rudder, including tabs	68·9 sq ft (6·4 m²)
Tailplane	197·0 sq ft (18·3 m²)
Elevators, including tabs	70·0 sq ft (6·5 m²)

WEIGHTS AND LOADINGS:

Weight empty	51,035 lb (23,150 kg)
Weight empty, equipped	53,130 lb (24,100 kg)
Normal payload	17,640 lb (8,000 kg)
Max T-O weight	85,320 lb (38,700 kg)
Max wing loading	65·79 lb/sq ft (321·2 kg/m²)
Max power loading	2·94 lb/lb st (2·94 kg/kg st)

PERFORMANCE (at max T-O weight except where indicated):

Max level speed at 25,000 ft (7,620 m) at 78,150 lb (35,450 kg) AUW
435 knots (501 mph; 806 km/h)

Econ cruising speed at 35,000 ft (10,670 m)
335 knots (386 mph; 621 km/h)

Max rate of climb at S/L 3,500 ft (1,065 m)/min

Service ceiling 38,000 ft (11,580 m)

Service ceiling, one engine out
18,000 ft (5,485 m)

T-O run 2,100 ft (640 m)

Landing run 1,500 ft (455 m)

Range with max fuel and 5,070 lb (2,300 kg) payload 1,810 nm (2,084 miles; 3,353 km)

Range with 17,640 lb (8,000 kg) payload
700 nm (807 miles; 1,300 km)

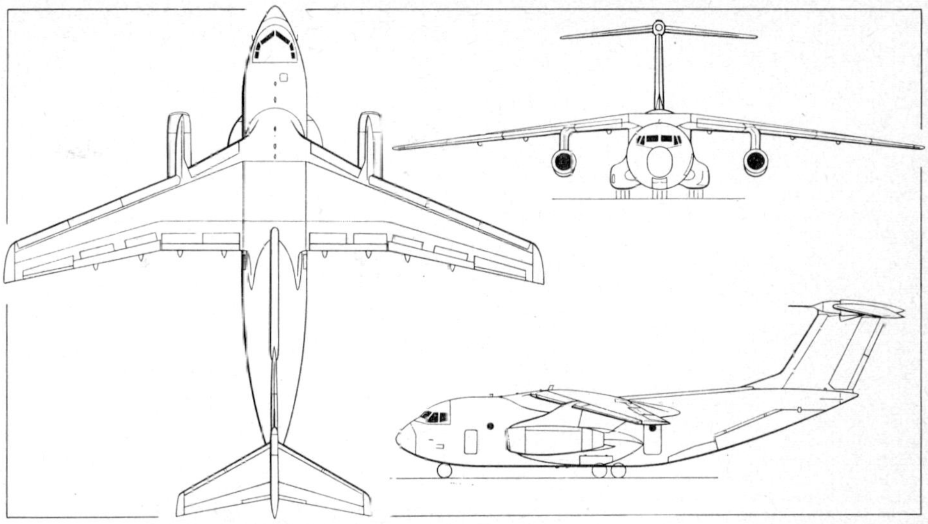

Kawasaki C-1 twin-turbofan medium-range military transport (*Pilot Press*)

Kawasaki KH-4 four-seat helicopter (270 hp Lycoming TVO-435 engine)

KAWASAKI KH-4

JGSDF designation: H-13KH

Developed by Kawasaki from the three-seat Bell Model 47G-3B, the KH-4 is a four-seat light general-purpose helicopter powered by a 270 hp Lycoming TVO-435-D1A six-cylinder horizontally-opposed aircooled engine. The prototype flew for the first time in August 1962 and the KH-4 received JCAB Normal category type approval on 9 November 1962.

A total of 206 KH-4s had been built by 1 January 1974. Of this total, 153 were delivered to civil operators, 19 to the JGSDF, 28 to Thailand, 5 to Korea and 1 to the Philippines.

In addition to changes in the cabin, to accommodate one extra person, the Kawasaki KH-4 has a new instrument layout, modified control system and larger fuel capacity, totalling 46 Imp gallons (209 litres). Kits are available to equip the aircraft with agricultural dusting and spray gear, granular distributor, pontoons, auxiliary fuel tank, cargo sling, stretchers, cabin heater and loudspeaker.

DIMENSIONS, EXTERNAL:

Diameter of main rotor	37 ft 1½ in (11·32 m)
Diameter of tail rotor	5 ft 10½ in (1·78 m)
Distance between rotor centres	21 ft 11¼ in (6·69 m)
Length overall (main rotor fore and aft)	43 ft 2¼ in (13·17 m)
Length of fuselage	32 ft 7¼ in (9·93 m)
Width overall (main rotor fore and aft)	9 ft 5¼ in (2·88 m)
Height to top of rotor hub	9 ft 3½ in (2·84 m)
Skid track	7 ft 6 in (2·29 m)

AREAS:

Main rotor blades (each)	17·14 sq ft (1·59 m²)
Tail rotor blades (each)	1·12 sq ft (0·10 m²)
Main rotor disc	1,083 sq ft (100·61 m²)
Tail rotor disc	25·6 sq ft (2·38 m²)

WEIGHTS AND LOADINGS:

Weight empty	1,890 lb (857 kg)
Max T-O and landing weight	2,850 lb (1,292 kg)
Max disc loading	2·63 lb/sq ft (12·8 kg/m²)
Max power loading	11·0 lb/hp (4·99 kg/hp)

PERFORMANCE (at max T-O weight):

Max level and never-exceed speed
91 knots (105 mph; 169 km/h)

Cruising speed 76 knots (87 mph; 140 km/h)

Max rate of climb at S/L 850 ft (260 m)/min

Service ceiling 18,500 ft (5,640 m)

Hovering ceiling in ground effect
18,000 ft (5,485 m)

Hovering ceiling out of ground effect
15,000 ft (4,570 m)

Range with max fuel
186 nm (214 miles; 345 km)

Max endurance 4 hr

KAWASAKI KH-7

Kawasaki has in the design stage a new 10-seat helicopter designated KH-7. To be powered by a Lycoming turboshaft engine in the 500 shp class, it will have a max T-O weight of about 5,950 lb (2,700 kg) and will have both civil and military applications.

KAWASAKI (BOEING VERTOL) KV-107/II and IIA

Swedish Navy designation: HKP 4C

Kawasaki has exclusive rights to manufacture and sell the Boeing Vertol 107 Model II helicopter. The first KV-107 to be produced by Kawasaki under this licence agreement flew for the first time in May 1962.

In 1965, Kawasaki obtained world-wide sales rights in the KV-107 from The Boeing Company's Vertol Division. In November 1965, it was awarded a type certificate for the KV-107 by the FAA. To meet various requirements, it offers the aircraft in the following versions:

KV-107/II-1. Basic utility helicopter. None yet built.

KV-107/II-2. Basic airline helicopter. Ten built by 31 March 1968, for Thailand (three), Pan American (two, for operation by New York Airways), New York Airways (one) and Air Lift Inc of Japan (formerly Kanki Airlines, two). Remaining two used as company test aircraft.

KV-107/II-3. Mine countermeasures (MCM) helicopter for JMSDF with extended-range fuel tanks, towing winch and cargo sling. Eight ordered, of which seven had been delivered by early 1974, including five of the KV-107/IIA-3 version with uprated power. All of these are fitted with minesweeping and retrieval equipment. The JMSDF's minesweeping unit, the 11th Air Wing, is scheduled to reach a full strength of 12 of these aircraft by the end of the 4th national defence programme.

KV-107/II-4. Tactical cargo/troop transport for JGSDF, with foldable seats for 26 troops or 15 casualty litters. Strengthened floor for carrying heavy vehicles. Orders for 50 placed, of which 46 had been delivered by early 1974, including one equipped as a VIP transport for Cabinet use. The latest four aircraft of the 46 delivered are of the KV-107/IIA-4 version with uprated power.

KV-107/II-5. Long-range search and rescue helicopter for JASDF. Orders for 20 placed, of which 18 had been delivered by early 1974, including one uprated KV-107/IIA-5. Large additional fuel tank each side of fuselage, making total capacity 833 Imp gallons (3,787 litres). Extensive nav/com equipment, four searchlights, domed observation window and rescue hoist. Seven (plus one additional) basically similar aircraft ordered for Swedish Navy have Kawasaki-built airframes and rotor assemblies but have been fitted in Sweden with Rolls-Royce Bristol Gnome H.1200 turboshaft engines and a Decca navigation system. They have a Kawasaki/Boeing automatic flight control system, enabling the aircraft to cruise at pre-selected altitude and speed, descend at a programmed rate and distance, and come to hover at a pre-selected altitude. Also provided are automatic climb-out to the cruise mode; standard distance approach; a turns coupler to a pre-selected heading; altitude sensing, with dual radar altimeters, for added safety in IFR operations; and a vernier flight control to permit critical positioning during rescue hoist operations. Provision for additional features such as a programmed procedural turn for automatic approach to rescue, and automatic approach guided by radio signal from person being rescued. First of these aircraft was delivered to the Swedish Navy on 30 October 1972; all of the original seven had been delivered by late 1973; the eighth was due to have been delivered by March 1974.

KV-107/II-6. De luxe transport version. None yet built.

KV-107/II-7. De luxe VIP transport with 6-11 seats. One sold to Thailand in 1964.

KV-107/IIA. Improved model, available in any of the KV-107/II forms, powered by two 1,400 shp General Electric CT58-140-1 or Ishikawajima-Harima CT58-IHI-140-1 turboshaft engines (max continuous rating 1,250 shp), which give improved performance during VTOL and in "hot and high" conditions. Fuel capacity 350 US gallons; 1,323 litres (standard), 1,000 US gallons; 3,785 litres (max). Prototype (JA9509) first flown 3 April 1968. Awarded type approval by JCAB on 26 September 1968 and by FAA on 15 January 1969.

The following details apply to the commercial KV-107/II-2, except where shown:

Type: Twin-engined transport helicopter.

Rotor System: Two three-blade rotors in tandem, rotating in opposite directions. Each blade is made up of a steel "D" spar to which is bonded a trailing-edge box constructed of aluminium ribs and glassfibre or aluminium skin.

Rotor Drive: Power is transmitted from each engine through individually-overrunning clutches into the aft transmission, which combines the engine outputs, thereby providing a single power output to the interconnecting shaft which enables both rotors to be driven by either engine.

Fuselage: Basically square-section semi-monocoque structure built primarily of high-strength bare and Alclad aluminium alloy. Transverse bulkheads and built-up frames support transmission, power plant and landing gear. Loading ramp forms undersurface of upswept rear fuselage on utility and military models. Baggage container replaces ramp on airliner version. Fuselage is sealed to permit operation from water.

Landing Gear: Non-retractable tricycle type, with twin wheels on all three units. Oleo-pneumatic shock-absorbers. Tubeless tyres, size 18 × 5·5, pressure 150 lb/sq in (10·55 kg/cm²), on all wheels. Disc brakes.

Power Plant: Two 1,250 shp General Electric CT58-110-1 or Ishikawajima-Harima CT58-IHI-110-1 turboshaft engines, mounted side by side at base of rear rotor pylon. Alternatively, two Rolls-Royce Bristol Gnome H.1200 turboshafts (in HKP 4C). Fuel tanks in sponsons, capacity 350 US gallons (1,323 litres). KV-107/IIA has more powerful CT58 engines and provision for increased fuel capacity (see introductory copy).

Accommodation: Standard accommodation for two pilots, stewardess and 25 passengers in airliner version. Seats in eight rows, in pairs on port side and single seats on starboard side (two pairs at rear of cabin) with central aisle. Airliner fitted with parcel rack and a roll-out baggage container, with capacity of approximately 1,500 lb (680 kg), located in underside of rear fuselage. Ramp of utility model is power-operated on the ground or in flight and can be removed or left open to permit carriage of extra-long cargo.

Electronics and Equipment: Standard equipment includes stability augmentation system (SAS) and automatic speed trim system (AST). Optional equipment includes automatic stabilisation equipment (ASE); automatic flight control system (AFCS); Doppler radar; radio altimeter; HF, VHF and UHF radio; ADF; VOR/ILS; TACAN; compass system and attitude director indicator system; and intercom system.

Dimensions, external:
Rotor diameter (each) 50 ft 0 in (15·24 m)
Length overall, blades turning 83 ft 4 in (25·40 m)
Length of fuselage 44 ft 7 in (13·59 m)
Height to top of rear rotor hub 16 ft 8½ in (5·09 m)
Wheel track 12 ft 10½ in (3·92 m)
Wheelbase 24 ft 10 in (7·57 m)
Passenger door (fwd):
Height 5 ft 3 in (1·60 m)
Width 3 ft 0 in (0·91 m)

Dimensions, internal:
Cabin, excluding flight deck:
Length 24 ft 2 in (7·37 m)
Normal width 6 ft 0 in (1·83 m)
Max height 6 ft 0 in (1·83 m)
Floor area 145 sq ft (13·47 m²)
Volume (usable) 865 cu ft (24·5 m³)

Areas:
Rotor blades (each) 37·50 sq ft (3·48 m²)
Rotor discs (total) 3,925 sq ft (364·6 m²)

Weights and Loadings (KV-107/II-2):
Weight empty, equipped 10,732 lb (4,868 kg)
*Max T-O and landing weight 19,000 lb (8,618 kg)
Max disc loading 4·84 lb/sq ft (23·60 kg/m²)
Max power loading 7·8 lb/shp (3·54 kg/shp)
**Alternative gross weight 21,400 lb (9,706 kg)*

Weights (KV-107/IIA): As KV-107/II-2, except:
Weight empty:
Utility model (A-1) 10,118 lb (4,589 kg)
Airliner model (A-2) 11,576 lb (5,250 kg)

Performance (KV-107/II-2 at 19,000 lb; 8,618 kg max T-O weight):
Max never-exceed speed 146 knots (168 mph; 270 km/h)
Max speed (normal rated power) 136 knots (157 mph; 253 km/h)
Cruising speed at 5,000 ft (1,525 m) 130 knots (150 mph; 241 km/h)
Max rate of climb at S/L (normal rated power) 1,520 ft (463 m)/min
Service ceiling (normal rated power) 15,000 ft (4,570 m)
Service ceiling (military power), one engine out, yaw, 248 rpm 350 ft (107 m)
Hovering ceiling in ground effect 9,500 ft (2,895 m)
Hovering ceiling out of ground effect 6,200 ft (1,890 m)
Range with 6,600 lb (3,000 kg) payload, 10% fuel reserve 94 nm (109 miles; 175 km)

Performance (KV-107/IIA at 19,000 lb; 8,618 kg max T-O weight, ISA):
Max never-exceed speed 175 knots (202 mph; 325 km/h)
Max level speed at S/L 148 knots (170 mph; 274 km/h)
Max speed at S/L (normal rated power) 137 knots (158 mph; 254 km/h)
Cruising speed at 5,000 ft (1,525 m) 130 knots (150 mph; 241 km/h)
Max rate of climb at S/L 2,050 ft (625 m)/min
Max vertical rate of climb at S/L 1,250 ft (381 m)/min
Service ceiling 17,000 ft (5,180 m)
Service ceiling, one engine out 5,700 ft (1,740 m)
Hovering ceiling in ground effect 11,700 ft (3,565 m)
Hovering ceiling out of ground effect 8,800 ft (2,680 m)
Min landing area:
Length 126 ft (38 m)
Width 75 ft (23 m)
T-O to 50 ft (15 m) 430 ft (131 m)
Landing from 50 ft (15 m), one engine out 275 ft (84 m)
Range with standard fuel 192 nm (222 miles; 357 km)
Range with max fuel 592 nm (682 miles; 1,097 km)

KAWASAKI (HUGHES) 369/MODEL 500 SERIES
JGSDF and JMSDF designation: OH-6J

A total of 70 Model 369HM helicopters, assembled by Kawasaki under licence from the Hughes Tool Company's Aircraft Division, had been delivered to the JGSDF (67) and JMSDF (3) by 1 January 1974. By the same date, a total of 31 Model 369HS helicopters, including one Model 500C, had been delivered to civil customers in Japan. Power plants are the 317 shp Allison 250-C18A turboshaft engine, built in Japan by Mitsubishi, for the OH-6J and Model 369HS/500; and the 400 shp Allison 250-C20 turboshaft for the Model 369HS/500C.

Dimensions and Areas: As for Hughes Model 369 (see US section)

Weights and Loadings:
Weight empty:
OH-6J, 500 1,185 lb (537 kg)
500C 1,203 lb (545 kg)
Max T-O and landing weight 2,550 lb (1,156 kg)
Design disc loading 4·68 lb/sq ft (22·8 kg/m²)
Design power loading 9·18 lb/shp (4·16 kg/shp)

Performance (at max T-O weight, ISA):
Max level and never-exceed speed 130 knots (150 mph; 241 km/h)
Cruising speed 125 knots (144 mph; 232 km/h)
Max rate of climb at S/L 1,700 ft (518 m)/min
Hovering ceiling in ground effect:
OH-6J, 500 8,200 ft (2,500 m)
500C 12,900 ft (3,930 m)
Hovering ceiling out of ground effect:
OH-6J, 500 5,300 ft (1,615 m)
500C 6,700 ft (2,040 m)
Range with max fuel:
OH-6J, 500 307 nm (353 miles; 568 km)
500C 301 nm (346 miles; 557 km)
Max endurance:
OH-6J, 500 3 hr 36 min
500C 3 hr 24 min

Kawasaki KV-107/IIA-4 tandem-rotor helicopter of the JGSDF, with extended-range (1,000 US gallon) fuel tank

Kawasaki (Hughes) Model 369HS light helicopter (317 shp Allison 250-C18A turboshaft engine)

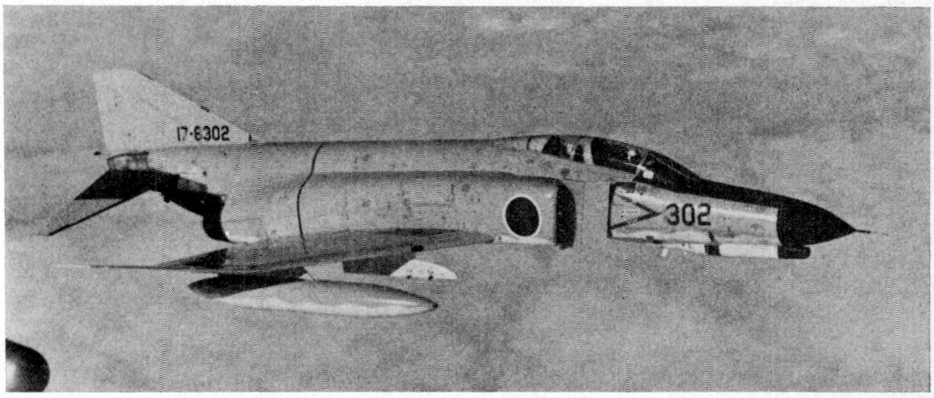

McDonnell Douglas F-4EJ Phantom II, of the type being produced by Mitsubishi for the JASDF

Mitsubishi LR-1, JGSDF photographic version of the twin-turboprop MU-2C utility aircraft

MITSUBISHI

MITSUBISHI JUKOGYO KABUSHIKI KAISHA (Mitsubishi Heavy Industries, Ltd)

HEAD OFFICE:
5-1, Marunouchi 2-Chome, Chiyoda-ku, Tokyo 100
Telephone: Tokyo (03) 212-3111
Telex: J22282 HISHIJU and J22443 HISHIJU

NAGOYA AIRCRAFT WORKS:
10, Oye-cho, Minato-ku, Nagoya 455

CHAIRMAN OF BOARD OF DIRECTORS:
Shigeichi Koga

PRESIDENT:
Gakuji Moriya

EXECUTIVE VICE-PRESIDENTS:
Seiji Watanabe
Shizuka Hayashi

MANAGING DIRECTOR AND GENERAL MANAGER OF AIRCRAFT HEADQUARTERS:
Teruo Tojo

GENERAL MANAGER, AIRCRAFT ADMINISTRATION DEPARTMENT:
Hirotoshi Tanaka

GENERAL MANAGER, AIRCRAFT DEPARTMENT:
Kazuo Iyoda

GENERAL MANAGER, AIRCRAFT EQUIPMENT DEPARTMENT:
Hiroshi Hamada

GENERAL MANAGER, SPACE SYSTEM DEPARTMENT:
Yoshiaki Kato

MANAGER OF MU-2 ADMINISTRATION SECTION:
Kotaro Yoshizawa

GENERAL MANAGER, NAGOYA AIRCRAFT WORKS:
Chushichi Ueda

Mitsubishi began the production of aircraft in the present Oye plant of its Nagoya Engineering Works in 1921, and manufactured a total of 18,000 aircraft of approximately one hundred different types during the 24 years prior to the termination of the second World War in 1945.

The company was also one of the leading aero-engine manufacturers in Japan, and produced a total of 52,000 engines in the 1,000-2,500 hp range.

The conclusion of the Peace Treaty in 1952 enabled the aircraft industry in Japan to recommence, and in December of that year the company constructed its present Komaki South plant.

This factory, together with Mitsubishi's Oye, Daiko and Komaki North plants, has since been separated from the original Nagoya Engineering Works and consolidated as the Nagoya Aircraft Works, with a combined floor area of 2,750,000 sq ft (247,500 m²).

Like other Japanese companies, Mitsubishi restarted with overhaul work for the USAF. Contracts to overhaul F-86 Sabre fighters led, in June 1955, to the selection of Mitsubishi as the company to manufacture 300 F-86F fighters for the Japan Air Self-Defence Force under a licence agreement with North American Aviation Inc.

It subsequently produced a total of 230 Lockheed F-104J and F-104DJ Starfighters, in co-operation with Kawasaki.

In co-operation with Kawasaki, Mitsubishi is producing a total of 128 F-4EJ Phantom fighters for the JASDF, under licence from McDonnell Douglas Corporation. The first two F-4EJs, built by McDonnell Douglas, were delivered to Japan in July 1971. The next eight were assembled from knock-down components, the first of these making its first flight on 12 May 1972. The remaining 118 are being built entirely in Japan. The first JASDF unit to equip with the F-4EJ was the 301st Squadron at Hyakuri, in August 1972, and a total of 34 F-4EJs was scheduled to be delivered to the JASDF by the end of March 1974. Five squadrons in all will be equipped with the F-4EJ.

Mitsubishi's overhaul work on Sikorsky S-55 helicopters, started in 1954, led in December 1958 to a licence agreement for the manufacture of this type in the Oye and Komaki plants, and 44 were delivered for civil and military use. Subsequently, Mitsubishi assembled 20 S-58/HSS-1s for the JMSDF (17), Maritime Safety Agency (2) and Asahi Helicopter Ltd (1).

Today, Mitsubishi holds licence agreements to manufacture the Sikorsky S-61A, S-61A-1, S-61B (HSS-2) and S-61B-1 (HSS-2A) helicopters. By 28 February 1974, Mitsubishi had built two S-61As (for the JMSDF, for use in support of the Japanese Antarctic Expedition) and two S-61Ns for civil operators, and had delivered 54 of an order for 61 S-61Bs (HSS-2s) and S-61B-1s (HSS-2As) to the JMSDF for anti-submarine duties. In five years from 1974, two S-61A-1s for use in support of the Japanese Antarctic Expedition, four S-61A-1s for rescue duties, and 35 S-61B-1s for anti-submarine duties with the JMSDF, are expected to be produced. Mitsubishi had previously delivered 25 S-62As, including 9 to the JASDF, 9 to the JMSDF, 1 to the Maritime Safety Agency, 3 to civil operators, 2 to the Philippines and 1 to Thailand.

Mitsubishi is producing a twin-turboprop utility transport designated MU-2. It also built front and centre fuselage sections of the NAMC YS-11 transport and was responsible for final assembly of this aircraft.

Current activities at the Daiko plant include various aero-engine activities; these are described in the appropriate section of this edition.

In September 1967 the Japan Defence Agency nominated Mitsubishi as prime contractor for development of the T-2 supersonic trainer and FS-T2-KAI close-support combat aircraft for the JASDF, with Fuji, Nippi and Shin Meiwa as principal subcontractors. Mitsubishi is also a subcontractor in the production programme for the Kawasaki C-1 (which see).

MITSUBISHI MU-2

JGSDF designation: LR-1

The MU-2 is a twin-turboprop STOL utility transport, the basic design of which was begun in 1960. Prototype construction began in 1962 and the first aircraft was flown on 14 September 1963. By 31 December 1973, total orders for the MU-2 (all versions) had reached 333, including 304 for export and 29 for Japanese customers. Nine versions have been announced, as follows:

MU-2A. Prototype: three built, one later converted to MU-2B. Full description in 1965-66 *Jane's*.

MU-2B. Thirty-four built. Production completed. Full description in 1967-68 *Jane's*.

MU-2C. Unpressurised liaison and reconnaissance/support version for JGSDF. First flown on 11 May 1967, and first production aircraft delivered on 30 June 1967. Four delivered to JGSDF, whose designation is **LR-1.** On first aircraft only, wingtip fuel tanks were replaced by fuselage tank aft of cabin. Remainder have wingtip tanks as standard. One vertical and one swing-type oblique camera in photographic version. Six more on order, including one with infra-red radar.

MU-2D. Eighteen built. Production completed. Described in 1968-69 *Jane's*.

MU-2E. Search and rescue version for Japan Air Self-Defence Force. Max T-O weight increased to 10,030 lb (4,550 kg). Sixteen built. Production completed. Described in 1972-73 *Jane's*.

MU-2F. Commercial version developed from MU-2D, with uprated AiResearch engines and extra fuel in enlarged wingtip tanks. Ninety-five built. Production completed. Described in 1973-74 *Jane's*.

MU-2G. Stretched version, developed from MU-2F with same power plant, increased fin height and area, and modified landing gear. Forty-one built. Production completed. Described in 1973-74 *Jane's*.

MU-2J. Basically similar to MU-2G, but with more powerful AiResearch engines. First flown August 1970. JCAB certification February 1971, FAA Type Approval May 1971. Eighty-eight delivered by 31 December 1973. Six to be purchased by JASDF for flight calibration duties. In production.

MU-2K. Basically similar to MU-2F, but with more powerful AiResearch engines and higher max cruising speed. First flown in August 1971. JCAB certification February 1972, FAA Type Approval May 1972. Sixty-eight delivered by 31 December 1973. Eight to be purchased by JASDF for rescue duties. In production.

A subsidiary company, Mitsubishi Aircraft International, Inc, in San Angelo, Texas, was established on 1 October 1967 for final assembly in the US of semi-finished MU-2s shipped from Japan and for marketing of the aircraft in the western hemisphere.

The following description applies generally to the MU-2J and K, except where a specific version is indicated:

TYPE: Twin-turboprop utility transport.

WINGS: Cantilever high-wing monoplane. Wing section NACA 64A415 at root, NACA 63A212 (modified) at tip. No dihedral. Incidence 2°. Washout 3°. Sweepback 0°21′ at quarter-chord. One-piece two-spar all-metal structure of light alloy. Spoilers for lateral control, between rear spar and flaps. Electrically-actuated full-span double-slotted flaps of aluminium alloy and plastics construction. Outboard flap section each side incorporates trim aileron. All primary controls manually-operated. Pneumatic de-icing boots.

FUSELAGE: Circular-section aluminium alloy semi-monocoque structure.

TAIL UNIT: Cantilever structure of aluminium alloy, except for top of fin, which is of reinforced plastics. Small auxiliary fin beneath each side of rear fuselage. Trim tab in rudder and each elevator. Pneumatic de-icing boots.

LANDING GEAR (MU-2J): Retractable tricycle type, with single wheel on each main unit and twin-wheel steerable nose unit. All wheels retract electrically, nosewheel forward, main wheels upward into fairings on fuselage sides. Oleo-pneumatic shock-absorbers. Main-wheel tyres Type III, size 8·50-10 (10-ply). Nose-wheel tyres Type III, size 5·00-5 (6-ply). Tyre pressure 40-60 lb/sq in (2·81-4·22 kg/cm²) on main units, 55 lb/sq in (3·87 kg/cm²) on nose unit. Goodrich single-disc nine-spot hydraulic brakes.

LANDING GEAR (MU-2K): Retractable tricycle type, with single wheel on each main unit and twin-wheel steerable nose unit. All wheels retract electrically into fuselage. Oleo-pneumatic shock-absorbers. Main-wheel tyres Type III (tubeless) 8·50-10 (8-ply). Nosewheel tyres Type III 5·00-5 (6-ply). Main-wheel tyre pressure 40-57 lb/sq in (2·81-4·0 kg/cm²), nose-wheel tyre pressure 55 lb/sq in (3·87 kg/cm²). Goodrich single-disc nine-spot hydraulic brakes.

POWER PLANT (MU-2J and MU-2K): Two AiResearch TPE 331-6-251M turboprop engines, each rated at 724 ehp (665 shp plus 148 lb; 67 kg residual thrust) and driving a Hartzell HC-B3TN-5/T10178HB-11 or HE-11 fully-feathering three-blade reversible-pitch constant-speed propeller. Total internal fuel capacity of 155

Imp gallons (706 litres) and two fixed wingtip tanks with total capacity of 150 Imp gallons (682 litres). Max total fuel capacity of 305 Imp gallons (1,388 litres). Oil capacity 2·6 Imp gallons (11·8 litres).

ACCOMMODATION (MU-2J): Seats for pilot and co-pilot or passenger on flight deck. Optional dual controls. Seating in main cabin, on rearward- and forward-facing seats, for 4 to 12 persons. Separate compartment at rear of cabin provides coat locker and baggage compartment. Door at rear of cabin on port side with built-in steps. Emergency exit door under wing leading-edge on starboard side.

ACCOMMODATION (MU-2K): Seats for pilot and co-pilot or passenger on flight deck. Optional dual controls. Typical seating for five passengers in main cabin, two on individual rearward-facing seats, three on forward-facing rear bench seat. Optional arrangements for up to nine persons, including pilot. Pressurised baggage compartment over main-wheel bays, capacity 220 lb (100 kg). Non-pressurised baggage compartment aft of main-wheel bays, capacity 154 lb (70 kg). Space for coats and small baggage at rear of cabin. Door under wing on port side. Emergency exit door opposite main door.

SYSTEMS: Air-cycle pressurisation and air-conditioning system. Differential 5·0 lb/sq in (0·35 kg/cm²). No hydraulic system. 28V DC primary electrical system, supplemented by 115V AC system for instruments and avionics. DC power supplied by two 30V 200A generators and two 24V 34Ah nickel-cadmium batteries. Oxygen system standard.

ELECTRONICS AND EQUIPMENT: Blind-flying instrumentation standard. Radio and radar to customers' requirements. Optional equipment includes VOR/LOC, glideslope, ADF and marker beacon receivers; ATC transponder; DME; VHF or other communications systems; compass systems; autopilot; and weather radar.

DIMENSIONS, EXTERNAL:
Wing span over tip-tanks 39 ft 2 in (11·95 m)
Wing chord (mean) 5 ft 0¾ in (1·54 m)
Wing aspect ratio 7·71
Length overall:
J 39 ft 5⅝ in (12·03 m)
K 33 ft 2¾ in (10·13 m)
Length of fuselage:
J 38 ft 10 in (11·84 m)
K 32 ft 8¾ in (9·98 m)
Height overall:
J 13 ft 8½ in (4·17 m)
K 12 ft 11¼ in (3·94 m)
Tailplane span 15 ft 9 in (4·80 m)
Wheel track:
J 7 ft 10½ in (2·40 m)
K 7 ft 8¾ in (2·36 m)
Wheelbase:
J 14 ft 5¼ in (4·40 m)
K 14 ft 10 in (4·52 m)
Propeller diameter 7 ft 6 in (2·29 m)
Distance between propeller centres 14 ft 9 in (4·50 m)
Cabin door: Height 4 ft 0 in (1·22 m)
Width 2 ft 5½ in (0·76 m)
Emergency exit door:
Height 2 ft 4½ in (0·72 m)
Width 2 ft 3½ in (0·70 m)

DIMENSIONS, INTERNAL (J):
Cabin: Length 11 ft 0 in (3·35 m)
Max width 4 ft 11 in (1·50 m)
Max height 4 ft 3¼ in (1·30 m)
Baggage compartment 43·08 cu ft (1·22 m³)

DIMENSIONS, INTERNAL (K):
Cabin: Length 19 ft 8¼ in (6·00 m)
Max width 4 ft 11 in (1·50 m)
Max height 4 ft 3¼ in (1·30 m)
Baggage compartment 38 cu ft (1·08 m³)

AREAS:
Wings, gross 178 sq ft (16·55 m²)
Flaps (total) 42·0 sq ft (3·90 m²)
Spoilers (total) 5·82 sq ft (0·54 m²)
Fin 30·68 sq ft (2·85 m²)
Rudder, including tab 12·60 sq ft (1·17 m²)
Tailplane 43·26 sq ft (4·02 m²)
Elevators, including tabs 15·04 sq ft (1·39 m²)

WEIGHTS AND LOADINGS:
Weight empty, equipped:
J 6,800 lb (3,084 kg)
K 5,920 lb (2,685 kg)
Max T-O weight:
J 10,800 lb (4,900 kg)
K 9,920 lb (4,500 kg)
Max landing weight:
J 10,260 lb (4,655 kg)
K 9,435 lb (4,280 kg)
Max wing loading:
J 60·6 lb/sq ft (296 kg/m²)
K 55·7 lb/sq ft (272 kg/m²)
Max power loading:
J 7·46 lb/ehp (3·38 kg/ehp)
K 6·85 lb/ehp (3·11 kg/ehp)

PERFORMANCE (J at AUW of 9,200 lb; 4,175 kg. K at AUW of 8,730 lb; 3,960 kg, except where indicated):
Max never-exceed speed:
J 330 knots (380 mph; 611 km/h)
K 315 knots (362 mph; 583 km/h)
Max cruising speed:
J at 15,000 ft (4,575 m) 300 knots (345 mph; 556 km/h)
K at 15,000 ft (4,575 m) 315 knots (363 mph; 584 km/h)
Econ cruising speed at 25,000 ft (7,620 m):
J 265 knots (305 mph; 491 km/h)
K 270 knots (311 mph; 500 km/h)
Stalling speed, flaps up:
J 96 knots (111 mph; 178 km/h)
K 95 knots (109 mph; 176 km/h)
Stalling speed, flaps down:
J 73 knots (84 mph; 135·5 km/h)
K 71 knots (82 mph; 132 km/h)
Max rate of climb at S/L:
J 2,700 ft (820 m)/min
K 3,100 ft (945 m)/min
Rate of climb at S/L, one engine out:
J 845 ft (258 m)/min
K 920 ft (280 m)/min
Service ceiling:
J 30,800 ft (9,390 m)
K 33,200 ft (10,120 m)
Service ceiling, one engine out:
J 18,700 ft (5,700 m)
K 19,800 ft (6,035 m)
T-O to 50 ft (15 m) at max T-O weight:
J 1,870 ft (570 m)
K 1,700 ft (518 m)
Landing from 50 ft (15 m):
J at AUW of 8,620 lb (3,910 kg) 1,670 ft (509 m)
K at AUW of 7,740 lb (3,510 kg) 1,090 ft (333 m)
Max range with wingtip tanks full, 30 min reserves:
J at 25,000 ft (7,620 m) 1,350 nm (1,554 miles; 2,500 km)
K at 25,000 ft (7,620 m) 1,460 nm (1,680 miles; 2,705 km)

MITSUBISHI T-2 and FS-T2-KAI

The T-2, the first supersonic aircraft to be developed by the Japanese aircraft industry, is a twin-engined two-seat jet trainer designed to meet the requirements of the JASDF.

Mitsubishi was selected as prime contractor for the development programme in September 1967. Preliminary and detailed design, under the leadership of Dr Kenji Ikeda, were followed by the completion of a full-size mock-up in January 1969, after which a development contract for prototype construction was awarded. The first XT-2 prototype (19-5101) flew for the first time on 20 July 1971, and flew supersonically for the first time in level flight (Mach 1·03) during its 30th flight, on 19 November 1971. The first flight of the second prototype (25-5102) followed on 2 December 1971. These two aircraft were delivered to the TRDI in December 1971 and March 1972 respectively for further flight testing. A static test airframe was delivered in March 1971.

Meanwhile, in 1970 two additional development aircraft were ordered, for operational flight testing. These had joined the evaluation programme by August 1972, and by mid-January 1974 the four prototypes had completed 753 hours' flying. The flight test programme was scheduled to continue until the end of March 1974. A fatigue test airframe is to be delivered in late 1974.

Initial production orders for 42 T-2s had been placed by March 1974; the first of these is scheduled to fly in early 1975, and JASDF pilots will begin training on the aircraft later that year. The 4th national DBP (defence buildup programme) provides for the eventual purchase of 59 T-2s by 1977. Mitsubishi, as prime contractor, is responsible for fuselage construction, final assembly and flight testing of production aircraft. Major programme subcontractors are Fuji (wings), Nippi (tail unit) and Shin Meiwa (pylons and drop-tanks).

To replace its North American F-86F Sabres, the JASDF has decided to develop a single-seat close-support fighter version, provisionally designated **FS-T2-KAI.** Following the conversion of a T-2 to serve as a prototype, the 4th DBP provides for the eventual purchase of 68 FS-T2-KAIs, of which the first batch is expected to be ordered in FY 1975.

The following description applies to both the T-2 and the FS-T2-KAI, except where a specific version is indicated:

TYPE: Two-seat supersonic jet trainer (T-2) and single-seat close-support fighter (FS-T2-KAI).

WINGS: Cantilever all-metal shoulder-wing monoplane. Thickness/chord ratio 4·8%. Anhedral 9° from roots. Sweepback approx 42° on outer leading-edges, increasing sharply towards roots. Multi-spar torsion-box machined from tapered

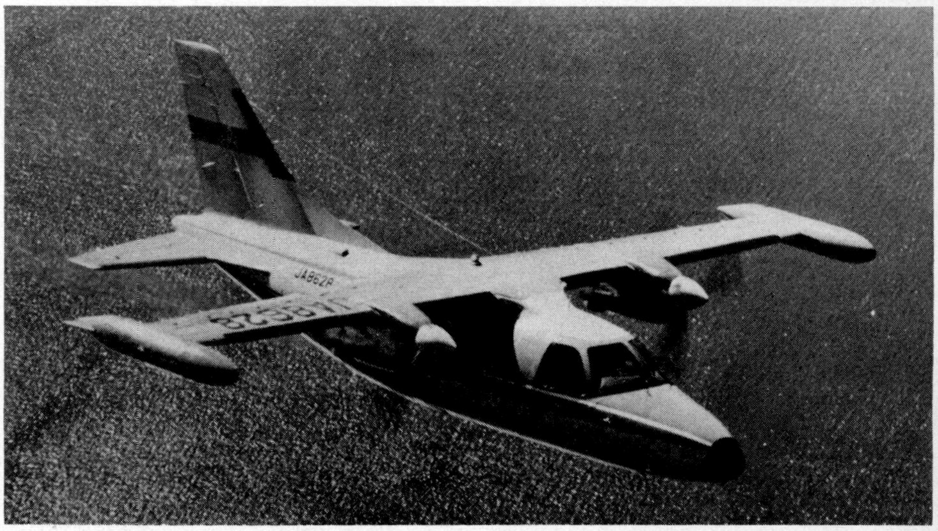

Mitsubishi MU-2K utility transport aircraft (two 724 ehp AiResearch TPE 331-6-251M turboprop engines)

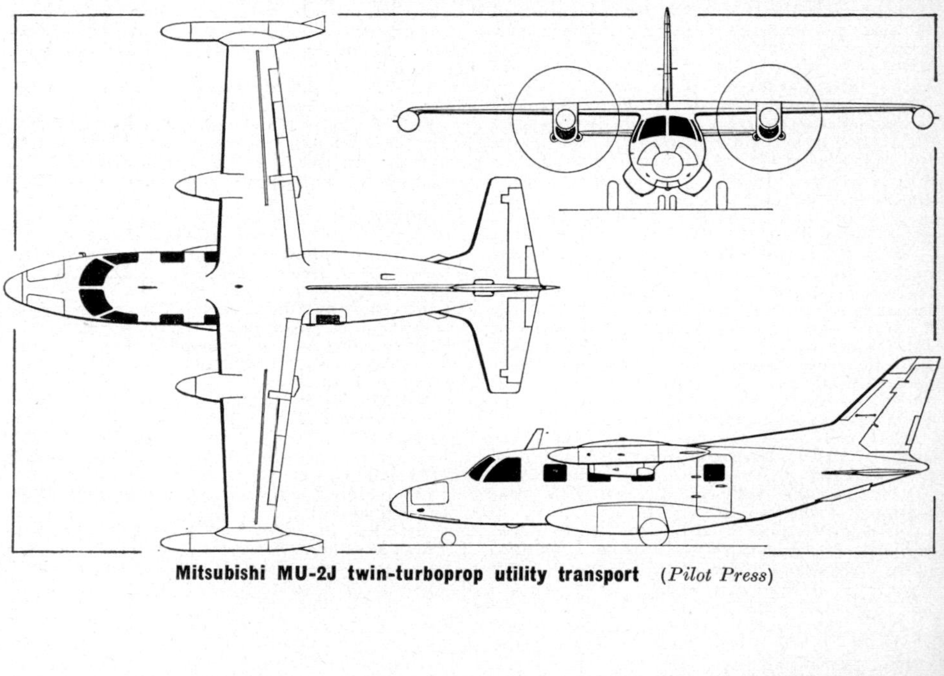

Mitsubishi MU-2J twin-turboprop utility transport (*Pilot Press*)

First prototype of the Mitsubishi T-2 tandem two-seat supersonic jet trainer under development for the JASDF

thick panel. Aluminium honeycomb leading-edge flaps, the outer portions of which have extended chord to give "dog-tooth" effect. Electrically-actuated all-metal single-slotted flaps, with aluminium honeycomb trailing-edges over 70% of each half-span. No conventional ailerons. Lateral control by hydraulically-actuated all-metal two-section spoilers ahead of flaps.

FUSELAGE: Conventional all-metal semi-monocoque structure.

TAIL UNIT: Cantilever all-metal structure. One-piece all-moving swept tailplane, with 15° anhedral. Inner leading-edges of titanium; outer leading-edges of aluminium. Trailing-edges of aluminium honeycomb construction. Small ventral fin under each side of fuselage at rear.

LANDING GEAR: Hydraulically-retractable type, with pneumatic backup for emergency extension. Main units retract forward into fuselage, nose unit rearward. Single wheel on each unit. Oleo-pneumatic shock-absorbers. Hydraulic brakes and anti-skid units. Brake parachute in fuselage tailcone.

POWER PLANT: Two Rolls-Royce/Turboméca Adour turbofan engines, each rated at 7,140 lb (3,238 kg) st with afterburning, mounted side by side in centre of fuselage. (Engines will be licence-built eventually by Ishikawajima-Harima, under designation TF40-IHI-801A.) Fixed-geometry air intake, with auxiliary "blow-in" intake doors, on each side of fuselage aft of rear cockpit. Fuel in seven fuselage tanks with total capacity of 841 Imp gallons (1,010 US gallons; 3,823 litres). Provision for carrying up to three 183·2 Imp gallon (220 US gallon; 833 litre) drop-tanks under wings and fuselage.

ACCOMMODATION (T-2): Crew of two in tandem on Weber ES-7J zero-zero ejection seats in pressurised and air-conditioned cockpits, separated by windscreen. Individual manually-operated rearward-hinged jettisonable canopies. Liquid oxygen equipment.

SYSTEMS: Cockpit air-conditioning system. Two independent hydraulic systems, each 3,000 lb/sq in (210 kg/cm²), for landing gear, spoilers, brakes and anti-skid units. Pneumatic bottle for landing gear emergency extension. Primary electrical power from two 12/15kVA AC generators.

ELECTRONICS AND EQUIPMENT (T-2): Mitsubishi Electric J/ARC-51 UHF. Nippon Electric J/ARN-53 TACAN and Toyo Communication J/APX-101 SIF/IFF. Mitsubishi Electric J/AWG-11 fire control system in nose. General Electric SR-3 attitude/heading reference system.

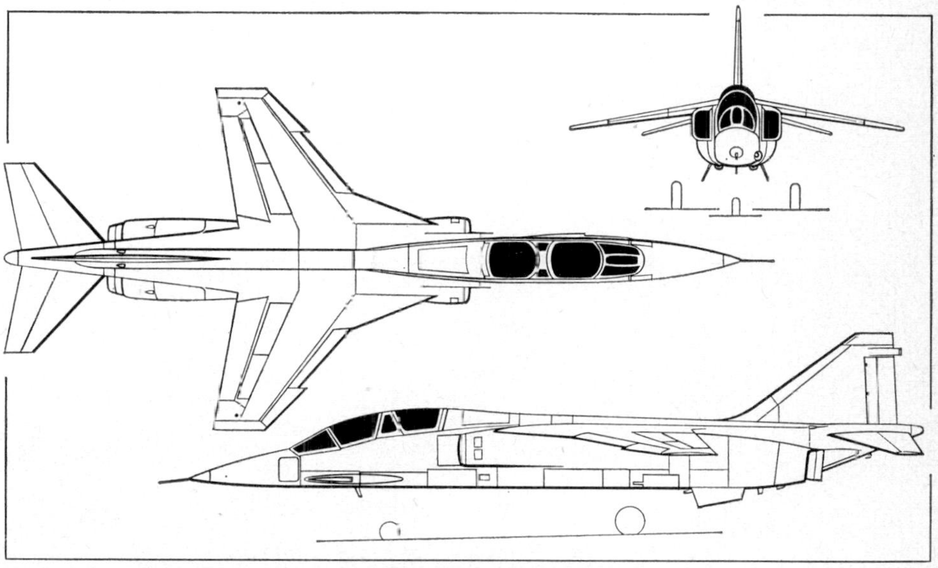

Mitsubishi T-2 tandem two-seat supersonic jet trainer (*Pilot Press*)

ELECTRONICS AND EQUIPMENT (FS-T2-KAI): To include air-to-air and air-to-surface radar, Ferranti inertial navigation system, radio altimeter, data computer, Thomson-CSF head-up display, Mitsubishi Electric bombing computer, optical ranging system and radar warning system.

ARMAMENT (T-2): One Vulcan multi-barrel 20 mm cannon in lower fuselage, aft of cockpit on port side. Attachment point on underfuselage centreline and two under each wing for drop-tanks or other stores. Wingtip attachments for air-to-air missiles.

ARMAMENT (FS-T2-KAI): Single multi-barrel 20 mm cannon, as in T-2. Eight to twelve 500 lb bombs, two or four infra-red air-to-air missiles, two air-to-surface missiles, or rockets, on external attachments.

DIMENSIONS, EXTERNAL:
- Wing span: 25 ft 10 in (7·87 m)
- Length overall: 58 ft 7 in (17·85 m)
- Height overall: 14 ft 7 in (4·445 m)

AREA:
- Wings, gross: 228·0 sq ft (21·18 m²)

WEIGHTS:
- Weight empty (T-2): 13,668 lb (6,200 kg)
- Max T-O weight:
  - T-2, clean: 21,274 lb (9,650 kg)
  - FS-T2-KAI with eight 500 lb bombs: approx 30,865 lb (14,000 kg)

PERFORMANCE (T-2 at max T-O weight, clean, except where indicated):
- Max level speed at 36,000 ft (11,000 m): Mach 1·6
- Service ceiling: 50,025 ft (15,250 m)
- Required field length: 5,000 ft (1,525 m)
- Max ferry range with external tanks: 1,550 nm (1,785 miles; 2,870 km)

PERFORMANCE (FS-T2-KAI, approximate):
- Max level speed at 36,000 ft (11,000 m): Mach 1·6
- Time to 36,000 ft (11,000 m): 2 min
- T-O run: 4,000 ft (1,220 m)
- Combat radius (hi-lo-hi) with eight 500 lb bombs: 300 nm (345 miles; 555 km)

MIYAUCHI

MIYAUCHI MANUFACTURING CO LTD

ADDRESS:
591 Aoyagi Kunitachi-Shi, Tokyo
Telephone: (0425) 23-1541 to 1545

Under the direction of Mr Asahi Miyahara, this company has a licence to produce in Japan the Pazmany PL-2 light aircraft (see US section).

The first Miyauchi-built PL-2 was flown for the first time on 8 October 1972. Production tooling has been completed, and in 1973 Miyauchi was carrying out flight testing and market survey preparatory to licence production of the PL-2.

NAL

NATIONAL AEROSPACE LABORATORY

ADDRESS:
1880 Jindaiji-machi, Chofu City, Tokyo
Telephone: Musashino (0422) 47-5911

DIRECTOR:
Masao Yamanouchi

HEAD OF V/STOL AIRCRAFT DIVISION:
Shun Takeda

The National Aerospace Laboratory (NAL) is a government establishment responsible for research and development in the field of aeronautical and space sciences. Since 1962 it has extended its activity in the field of V/STOL techniques.

NAL VTOL FLYING TESTBED

In order to study the problems associated with the hovering, vertical take-off and landing of VTOL aircraft, a flying testbed (FTB) hovering test rig was developed by NAL and constructed by Fuji Heavy Industries Co Ltd. It was completed in 1968 and made its first flight at Kakuta on 15 December 1970. Flight testing was completed in June 1971, and a description and illustration of the aircraft appeared in the 1972-73 *Jane's*.

Utilising the data gained from this vehicle, NAL is to build a further experimental VTOL research vehicle. The specification, as at the end of 1973, called for a single-seat vehicle having an overall length of 37 ft 6¾ in (11·45 m), a wing span of 33 ft 6¼ in (10·22 m), and a height of 14 ft 11½ in (4·56 m); and a power plant of one 3,100 lb (1,406 kg) st General Electric CJ610-9 turbojet engine for horizontal thrust and four 2,932 lb (1,330 kg) st IHI/NAL JR-100V lift-jets installed in tandem in the centre of the fuselage. It is planned to build two prototypes, one for flight testing and one for static test, by converting the airframes of JASDF Fuji T-1 or Lockheed T-33A aircraft. The flying prototype is scheduled to be completed in 1976 and to begin flight testing in 1977.

NAMC

NIHON KOKUKI SEIZO KABUSHIKI KAISHA
(Nihon Aeroplane Manufacturing Co, Ltd)

HEAD OFFICE:
Toranomon Daiichi Building, No. 1, Kotchira-cho, Shiba, Minato-Ku, Tokyo
Telephone: Tokyo (03) 503-3211
Telex: 222-2863 (NAMC J) and 222-2864 (NAMC)

PRESIDENT:
Yuji Koyama

DIRECTORS:
Fumio Shima
Masaichi Oguri

As detailed in previous editions of *Jane's*, NAMC was responsible for the development and production (now ended) of the YS-11 twin-turboprop transport aircraft. It continues to be responsible for YS-11 after-sales support.

About 50 of the NAMC work force will be transferred to work on the Y-X programme to develop a successor to the YS-11 (see CTDC entry in this section).

NAMC also built the two XC-1 prototypes of the C-1 military transport for the JASDF, described under the Kawasaki heading in this section.

NAMC YS-11

Construction of the first of two YS-11 prototypes began in March 1961 and it flew for the first time on 30 August 1962. The first production YS-11 flew on 23 October 1964, and deliveries began in March 1965.

Manufacture of the YS-11 ceased after completion of the 182nd aircraft, which was delivered to the JMSDF on 1 February 1974.

The following versions of the YS-11 were built:

YS-11-100. Basic 60-seat passenger transport. Two prototypes and 47 production aircraft built. All 49 sold, including four to JASDF and one to JMSDF. Described in 1967-68 *Jane's*.

YS-11A-200. 60-seat passenger version of YS-11A. First flown on 27 November 1967. Ninety-five built, including one for JASDF and four for JMSDF. Described in 1973-74 *Jane's*.

YS-11A-300. Mixed traffic version of YS-11A, with cargo door in port side of forward fuselage. First flown in Summer 1968. Sixteen sold, including one to JASDF. Described in 1973-74 *Jane's*.

YS-11A-400. All-cargo configuration, with reinforced floor and cargo door in port side of aft fuselage. First flight 17 September 1969. Seven built for JASDF and two for JMSDF. Described in 1972-73 *Jane's*.

YS-11A-500. Similar to YS-11A-200, but with increase of 1,105 lb (500 kg) in max T-O weight. Four built. Described in 1973-74 *Jane's*.

YS-11A-600. Similar to YS-11A-300, but with same increased max T-O weight as -500. Nine built, including three for JMSDF. Described in 1973-74 *Jane's*.

Power Plant: Two Rolls-Royce Dart Mk 542-10K (RDa.10/1) turboprop engines, each giving 3,060 ehp with water-methanol injection for take-off. Rotol four-blade propellers. Fuel in wing tanks: two bag-type tanks inboard of engines with total capacity of 490 Imp gallons (2,230 litres), two integral tanks outboard of engines with total capacity of 1,110 Imp gallons (5,040 litres). Total fuel capacity 1,600 Imp gallons (7,270 litres). Gravity fuelling points above wing; pressure refuelling points under wing. Total oil capacity 13·75 Imp gallons (62 litres).

Dimensions, external:	
Wing span	104 ft 11¾ in (32·00 m)
Wing chord at root	13 ft 9½ in (4·20 m)
Wing chord at tip	4 ft 11 in (1·50 m)
Wing aspect ratio	10·8
Length overall	86 ft 3½ in (26·30 m)
Fuselage: Max diameter	9 ft 5½ in (2·88 m)
Height overall	29 ft 5½ in (8·98 m)
Tailplane span	39 ft 4½ in (12·00 m)
Wheel track	28 ft 2½ in (8·60 m)
Wheelbase	31 ft 2½ in (9·52 m)
Propeller diameter	14 ft 6 in (4·42 m)
Areas:	
Wings, gross	1,020·4 sq ft (94·8 m²)
Ailerons (total)	63·80 sq ft (5·92 m²)
Trailing-edge flaps (total)	202·20 sq ft (18·78 m²)
Fin	104·95 sq ft (9·75 m²)
Rudder, including tab	51·13 sq ft (4·75 m²)
Tailplane	180·50 sq ft (16·76 m²)
Elevators, including tabs	57·40 sq ft (5·33 m²)
Weights and Loadings:	
Operating weight, empty:	
200, 500	33,993 lb (15,419 kg)
300, 600	34,899 lb (15,830 kg)
Max payload:	
200	14,508 lb (6,581 kg)
300	13,602 lb (6,170 kg)
500	15,610 lb (7,081 kg)
600	14,704 lb (6,670 kg)
Max T-O weight:	
200, 300	54,010 lb (24,500 kg)
500, 600	55,115 lb (25,000 kg)
Max wing loading:	
200, 300	52·8 lb/sq ft (258 kg/m²)
500, 600	54·1 lb/sq ft (264 kg/m²)
Max power loading:	
200, 300	8·83 lb/ehp (4·00 kg/ehp)
500, 600	9·00 lb/ehp (4·08 kg/ehp)

Performance (at max T-O weight, except where indicated):

Max cruising speed at 15,000 ft (4,575 m):	
200, 300	253 knots (291 mph; 469 km/h)
500, 600	252 knots (290 mph; 467 km/h)
Econ cruising speed at 20,000 ft (6,100 m):	
200, 300	244 knots (281 mph; 452 km/h)
500, 600	241 knots (278 mph; 447 km/h)
Range with max fuel, no reserves (all versions):	
without bag tanks	1,137 nm (1,310 miles; 2,110 km)
with bag tanks	1,736 nm (2,000 miles; 3,215 km)
Range with max payload, no reserves (all versions)	590 nm (680 miles; 1,090 km)

Second prototype NAMC YS-11, now fitted with MAD tail "sting" and underfuselage towed "bird" for service with the Geological Survey of Japan (*T. Matsuzaki*)

NIHON UNIVERSITY

COLLEGE OF SCIENCE AND ENGINEERING (DEPARTMENT OF MECHANICAL ENGINEERING), NIHON UNIVERSITY

Address:
8 Kanda-Surugadai, 1-chome, Chiyoda-ku, Tokyo 101

Telephone: Tokyo (03) 293-3251

Chief Professor: Dr Hidemasa Kimura

Under the leadership of Dr Kimura, students of Nihon University have designed and built several aircraft, including the Okamura N-52 and N-58 Cygnet lightplanes and a STOL lightplane designated N-62, in collaboration with the Itoh company, which built the prototype. The N-62 was put into production by Itoh, as the Eaglet, and was described in the 1968-69 *Jane's*.

This design team was also responsible for a series of successful man-powered aircraft named Linnet, all of which have been described fully in previous editions of *Jane's*. A powered sailplane, the N-70 Cygnus, is described in the appropriate section of this edition.

The latest aircraft of Nihon University design to fly is another man-powered aircraft, the NM-73 New Egret, which is a development of the NM-72 Egret I described in the 1973-74 *Jane's*.

NIHON UNIVERSITY NM-73 NEW EGRET

Design of the New Egret began in February 1973, and construction was started in the following May. The aircraft made its first flight on 30 October 1973 and up to 14 December 1973 had made 19 steady flights, of which the longest covered a distance of 505 ft (154 m).

Type: Single-seat man-powered aircraft.

Wings: Cantilever low-wing monoplane. Wing section Wortmann FX-61-184. Thickness/chord ratio 18%. Constant-chord, no-dihedral centre-section, of 26 ft 3 in (8·00 m) span. Dihedral 6° on outer panels. Incidence 4°. No sweepback at quarter-chord. One-piece wooden structure. Two-spar construction, with spruce flanges and balsa stringers and ribs, covered with styrene paper. Conventional ailerons. No flaps.

Fuselage: Front portion, including cabin and propeller pylon, is a welded chrome-molybdenum steel tube truss structure, covered with styrene paper. Portion aft of cabin, of triangular section, is a spruce truss covered with styrene paper.

Tail Unit: Cantilever wooden structure, of similar construction to wings. Tailplane and elevators, of NACA 0012 section, without tab. Single fin and rudder.

Landing Gear: Two non-retractable bicycle wheels, mounted in tandem and not driven by pedals. No shock-absorbers or brakes.

Power System: Man-power on bicycle pedals, transmitted by rubber belt drive to a two-blade GRP pusher propeller mounted aft of a fairing above and slightly behind the cabin. Foot pedal rpm 90; propeller rpm 180.

Accommodation: Pilot only, in enclosed cabin. Stick control for aileron and horizontal tail actuation. Twist-grip on top of control stick actuates rudder.

Nihon University NM-73 New Egret single-seat man-powered aircraft

DIMENSIONS, EXTERNAL:
- Wing span: 74 ft 5¾ in (22·70 m)
- Wing chord, centre-section (constant): 5 ft 1¼ in (1·558 m)
- Wing chord at tip: 2 ft 0½ in (0·623 m)
- Wing aspect ratio: 18·1
- Length overall: 25 ft 3 in (7·70 m)
- Height overall: 8 ft 2¾ in (2·51 m)
- Tailplane span: 16 ft 4¾ in (5·00 m)
- Wheelbase: 3 ft 11¼ in (1·20 m)
- Propeller diameter: 8 ft 10¼ in (2·70 m)

AREAS:
- Wings, gross: 306·8 sq ft (28·50 m^2)
- Ailerons (total): 33·48 sq ft (3·11 m^2)
- Fin: 11·19 sq ft (1·04 m^2)
- Rudder: 6·03 sq ft (0·56 m^2)
- Tailplane: 21·31 sq ft (1·98 m^2)
- Elevators (total): 14·21 sq ft (1·32 m^2)

WEIGHTS AND LOADING:
- Weight empty: 117 lb (53 kg)
- T-O weight: 249 lb (113 kg)
- Wing loading: 0·82 lb/sq ft (4·0 kg/m^2)

PERFORMANCE:
- Speed: 20·5 knots (23·5 mph; 38 km/h)

NIPPI

NIHON HIKOKI KABUSHIKI KAISHA (Japan Aircraft Manufacturing Company Ltd)

HEAD OFFICE:
No 3175 Showa-machi, Kanazawa-ku, Yokohama 236
Telephone: Yokohama (045) 771-1251
WORKS: Sugita and Atsugi
CHAIRMAN: Masami Takasaki
PRESIDENT: Masao Nagahisa
EXECUTIVE VICE-PRESIDENTS:
Masatoshi Takasaki
Makoto Watanabe
MANAGING DIRECTORS:
Shigeru Kato (Management Planning)
Yoshio Misawa (Business, Contracts and Accounting)
DIRECTORS:
Matsuo Ishiwata (Aircraft Division)
Masanao Morita (Repair and Overhaul Division)
Norio Otomori (Ship Division)
Taketoshi Kitamura (General Affairs Department)
Saburo Sato (Accounting Department)
Gensuke Okada
PUBLIC RELATIONS MANAGER:
Taketoshi Kitamura

Nippi has two works. The Sugita plant, to which the head office was transferred in early 1971, has facilities with a floor area of 462,330 sq ft (42,952 m^2) and accommodates the Aircraft and Ship Divisions with a total work force of 1,007 persons. The Atsugi plant, which employs 1,157 persons, has a floor area of 384,560 sq ft (35,727 m^2) and accommodates the Repair and Overhaul Division. A 34% holding in Nippi is held by Kawasaki.

The Atsugi plant is engaged chiefly in the overhaul, repair and maintenance of various types of aircraft and helicopters, including those of the Japan Defence Agency and Maritime Safety Agency, and carrier-based aircraft of the US Navy. The Sugita plant manufactures components and assemblies for the Kawasaki P-2J and C-1, Mitsubishi T-2, F-4EJ and MU-2, and Shin Meiwa PS-1; airframe and dynamic components for the Kawasaki KV-107; dynamic components for the Fuji-Bell HU-1B and Kawasaki-Hughes OH-6J; body structures for Japanese space satellites; and tail units for Japanese-built rocket vehicles.

SHIN MEIWA

SHIN MEIWA INDUSTRY Co, Ltd

HEAD OFFICE:
1-5-25, Kosone-Cho, Nishinomiya-Shi, Hyogo-Ken
Telephone: Nishinomiya (0798) 47-0331
Telex: 5644493
TOKYO OFFICE:
c/o Shin Ohtemachi Building, 5th Floor, 2-1, 2 chome, Ohtemachi, Chiyoda-ku, Tokyo 100
Telephone: Tokyo (03) 279-3531
Telex: 222 2431 SMICAIR TOK
WORKS (AIRCRAFT DIVISION):
Konan Plant, 1-1-1 Ogi, Higashinada-ku, Kobe 658
Telephone: (078) 431-4151
Itami Plant, 3-7-1 Minowa, Toyonaka, Osaka 560
Telephone: (068) 54-1151
CHAIRMAN OF THE BOARD:
Toshio Itoh
PRESIDENT:
Yoshio Yagi
VICE-PRESIDENT:
Hiroshi Kohno
MANAGING DIRECTOR AND SUPERINTENDENT, AIRCRAFT DIVISION:
Tadao Uno
ASSISTANT GENERAL MANAGERS:
Hajime Kawanishi (Managing Director)
Shiro Katagiri
SENIOR TECHNICAL CONSULTANT:
Dr Koichi Tokuda
CHIEF DESIGNER:
Dr Shizuo Kikuhara
SALES MANAGER AND PUBLIC RELATIONS:
Shigemi Matsui

The former Kawanishi Aircraft Company became Shin Meiwa in 1949 and established itself as a major overhaul centre for Japanese and US military and commercial aircraft.

Shin Meiwa's principal current activities concern the series production of its PS-1 medium-range STOL flying-boat for the JMSDF, development of an amphibious search and rescue version, the PS-1 Mod, and overhaul work on flying-boats and amphibians.

Shin Meiwa is also engaged in the manufacture of components for other aircraft. In particular, it produces nose and tail components for the Kawasaki P-2J, underwing drop-tanks for the Mitsubishi T-2 supersonic jet trainer and the cargo loading system for the Kawasaki C-1 transport aircraft.

SHIN MEIWA SS-2 and SS-2A

JMSDF designations: PS-1 and PS-1 Mod

After seven years of basic study and research, Shin Meiwa was awarded a contract in January 1966 to develop a new anti-submarine flying-boat for the Japan Maritime Self-Defence Force. As part of this programme, the company first rebuilt a Grumman UF-1 Albatross as a dynamically-similar flying scale model of the new design, under the designation UF-XS. This aircraft was described and illustrated in the 1964-65 *Jane's*.

The first SS-2 prototype (5801) flew for the first time on 5 October 1967. It was delivered to the JMSDF on 31 July 1968. The second prototype, which flew on 14 June 1968, was handed over on 30 November 1968. These two aircraft were delivered to the 51st Flight Test Squadron of the JMSDF at Iwakuni. JDA type approval was granted in Autumn 1970.

In addition to the two prototypes, Shin Meiwa had by March 1974 delivered 12 of a total of 14 PS-1 production aircraft ordered for the JMSDF under the 3rd national defence programme. These are in service with the 31st Squadron of the JMSDF. They will be followed, under the 4th national defence programme (1972-76), by nine more PS-1s and three **PS-1 Mod** amphibious search and rescue aircraft (manufacturer's designation SS-2A). Funds for these aircraft have already been allocated.

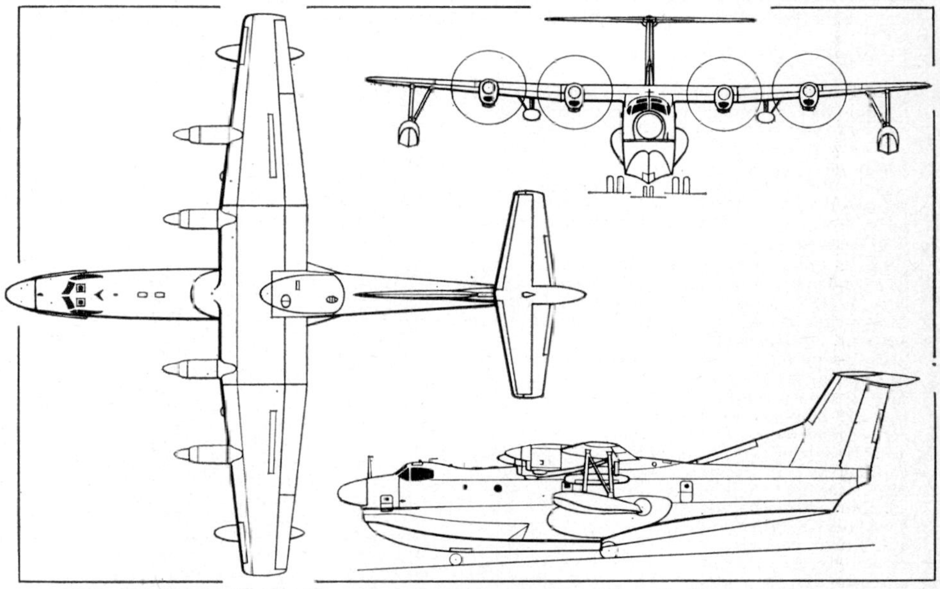

Shin Meiwa PS-1 Mod multi-purpose amphibian, developed from the PS-1 *(Pilot Press)*

Design of the SS-2A (PS-1 Mod) began in June 1970, and the first example was scheduled to fly for the first time in September 1974. Delivery to the JMSDF is scheduled for March 1975, with the second and third aircraft following later that year. The first PS-1 Mod operating unit will be stationed at the Omura base of the JMSDF.

Shin Meiwa is also continuing design study of a STOL transport version of the aircraft.

To make possible very low landing and take-off speeds, the PS-1 has both a boundary layer control system and extensive flaps for propeller slipstream deflection. Control and stability in low-speed flight are enhanced by "blowing" the rudder, flaps and elevators, and by use of an automatic flight control system.

The PS-1 is designed to dip its large sonar deep into the sea during repeated landings and take-offs, and can land on very rough water, in winds of up to 25 knots (29 mph; 47 km/h). Take-offs and landings have been made successfully in seas with wave heights of up to 13 ft (4 m).

The following description applies to both the PS-1 and PS-1 Mod, except where a specific version is indicated:

TYPE: Four-turboprop STOL anti-submarine flying-boat (PS-1) or air/sea rescue amphibian (PS-1 Mod).

WINGS: Cantilever high-wing monoplane. Conventional all-metal, two-spar structure with rectangular centre-section and tapered outer panels. High-lift devices include leading-edge slats extending over nearly 17% of the span and large outer and inner blown trailing-edge flaps extending 60° and 80° respectively. Two spoilers are located in front of the outer flap on each wing. Powered ailerons. Leading-edge de-icing boots.

FUSELAGE: All-metal semi-monocoque hull structure, with high length/beam ratio. Vee-shaped single-step planing bottom, with curved spray suppression strakes along sides of nose and spray suppressor slots in fuselage undersides aft of inboard propeller line. Double-deck interior.

TAIL UNIT: Cantilever all-metal T-type structure. Large dorsal fin. Tailplane has slats and de-icing boots on leading-edge. Blown rudder and elevators.

ALIGHTING AND BEACHING GEAR (PS-1): Hull; and fixed stabilising floats near wingtips. Retractable tricycle-type beaching gear installed, with aft-retracting single-wheel main gear unit on each side of hull and forward-retracting twin steerable nosewheels, making aircraft independent of ground beaching aids.

LANDING GEAR (PS-1 Mod): Hull, as PS-1, plus hydraulically-retractable tricycle landing gear with twin wheels on all units. Oleo-pneumatic shock-absorbers. Main units, housed in bulged fairings on hull sides, have size 40 × 14-22 tyres, pressure 113 lb/sq in (7·95 kg/cm^2). Nosewheel tyres size 25 × 6·75-18, pressure 300 lb/sq in (21 kg/cm^2). Three-rotor hydraulic disc brakes. No anti-skid units.

POWER PLANT: Four 3,060 ehp Ishikawajima-built General Electric T64-IHI-10 turboprop engines, each driving a Hamilton Standard 63E60-19 three-blade constant-speed reversible-pitch propeller. Additionally, one 1,400 shp Ishikawajima-built General Electric T58-IHI-10 gas turbine (1,250 ehp T58-IHI-10-M1 in PS-1 Mod) is housed in the upper centre portion of the fuselage to provide power for boundary layer control system on rudder, flaps and elevators. Fuel in two bladder-type rear-fuselage tanks and five wing tanks, with total usable capacity of 3,938 Imp gallons (17,900 litres) in PS-1. PS-1 Mod fuel is in wing tanks (2,387 Imp gallons; 10,851 litres) and fuselage tanks (2,563 Imp gallons; 11,649 litres); total capacity 4,950 Imp gallons (22,500 litres). Refuelling point near bow hatch. Oil capacity 22·3 Imp gallons (101 litres).

ACCOMMODATION (PS-1): Two pilots and flight engineer on flight deck, which has wide-visibility bulged windows at sides. Aft of this on the upper deck is a tactical compartment, housing two sonar operators, a navigator, MAD operator, radar operator, radio operator and a tactical co-ordinator. Electronic, magnetic and sonic equipment is installed on starboard side, with crew's rest area and bunks on port side. Aft of tactical compartment is the weapons compartment. On the lower deck, from nose to rear, are the electronics compartment, oxygen-bottle bay, main gear bay and two

Shin Meiwa PS-1 four-turboprop STOL anti-submarine flying-boat, twelfth production aircraft for the Japan Maritime Self-Defence Force

fuel tanks. Door on port side of rear fuselage.

Accommodation (PS-1 Mod): Search and rescue version has accommodation for crew of nine and 12 survivors, with 12 stretchers, one auxiliary seat and two observers' seats. Rescue hatch on port side of fuselage, aft of wing. Transport version can seat up to 64 passengers in mainly four-abreast seating with centre aisle; rear portion of cabin convertible to cargo compartment.

Systems: Cabin air-conditioning system. Two independent hydraulic systems, each 3,000 lb/sq in (210 kg/cm^2). Air/sea rescue version has oxygen system for all crew and stretcher stations. AiResearch GTCP85-131J APU provides power for starting main engines and shaft power for 40kVA emergency AC generator. BLC system includes a C-2 compressor, driven by T58-IHI-10 gas turbine, which delivers compressed air at a flow of 30·9 lb (14 kg)/sec and pressure of 27 lb/sq in (1·9 kg/cm^2) for ducting to inner and outer flaps, rudder and elevators. Electrical system includes three-phase 400Hz constant-frequency AC and converted 27V DC. Two 40kVA AC generators, driven by Nos. 2 and 3 main engines. Emergency AC generator driven by APU. Anti-icing, air-conditioning, and fire detection and extinguishing systems, are standard on PS-1 Mod.

Electronics and Equipment (PS-1): AN/ARA-50 UHF direction finder, AN/ARN-52 TACAN, HRN-4 Loran, HPN-101B wave height meter, AN/APN-153 Doppler radar, AN/AYK-2 navigation computer, A/A24G-9 TAS transmitter, AN/APS-80 search radar, HGC-102 teletypewriter, AN/APA-125A indicator group, HRN-101 ADF, N-PT-3 dead reckoning plotting board, AN/APX-68 SIF, N-OA-35/HSA tactical plotting group, HLR-1 countermeasure device, AN/ARR-52A sonobuoy data recorder, AN/ASQ-10A magnetic anomaly detector, N-MX-143/HSQ error voltage monitor, HQS-101B dipping sonar, AN/ASA-20B recorder group, AN/AQA-5 sonobuoy recorder, AN/AQA-1 sonobuoy indicator group, N-R-86/HRA optical group, AN/ASA-16 integrated display system, AN/ASA-50 computer group, HQH-101 sonobuoy data recorder, HSA-1 SDDS, RRC-15 emergency transmitter, HSA-2 automatic magnetic compensator device, N-CU-58/HRC antenna coupler, N-ID-66/HRN BDHI, N-RO-14B BT recorder, HIC-3 interphone and HRC-7 HF.

Electronics and Equipment (PS-1 Mod): HIC interphone, HRC-107 HF, N-CU-58/HRC antenna coupler, HGC-102 teletypewriter, HRC-106 radio, HRC-100 radio, HRN-101 ADF, AN/ARA-50 UHF/DF, HRN-105 TACAN, HRN-104 Loran, HRN-3 marker beacon receiver, AN/APN-171 (N2) radar altimeter, HPN-101B wave height meter, AN/APN-153 Doppler radar, AN/AYK-2 navigation computer, A/A24G-9 TAS transmitter, N-PT-3 dead reckoning plotting board, N-OA-35/HSA tactical plotter group, AN/APS-80N search radar, AN/APA-125N indicator group, AN/APX-68N IFF transponder, RRC-15 emergency transmitter and N-ID-66/HRN BDHI.

Armament and Operational Equipment (PS-1): Weapons bay on upper deck, aft of tactical compartment, in which are stored AQA-3 Jezebel passive long-range acoustic search equipment with 20 sonobuoys and their launchers, Julie active acoustic echo ranging with 30 explosive charges, four 330 lb anti-submarine bombs, and smoke bombs. External armament includes two underwing pods, mounted between each pair of engine nacelles and each containing two homing torpedoes, and a launcher beneath each wingtip for three 5 in air-to-surface rockets. Searchlight below starboard outer wing.

Operational Equipment (PS-1 Mod): Marker launcher, 10 marine markers, 6 green markers, 2 droppable message cylinders, 10 float lights, pyrotechnic pistol, parachute flares, 2 flare storage boxes, binoculars, 2 rescue equipment kits, 2 droppable life-raft containers, rescue equipment launcher, lifeline pistol, lifeline, 3 lifebuoys, portable speaker, hoist unit, floating mat, lifeboat with outboard motor, camera, and 12 stretchers. Stretchers can be replaced by troop seats.

Dimensions, external:
Wing span 108 ft 8¾ in (33·14 m)
Wing chord at root 16 ft 4¾ in (5·00 m)
Wing chord at tip 7 ft 10 in (2·39 m)
Wing aspect ratio 8
Length overall 109 ft 11 in (33·50 m)
Height overall:
PS-1 31 ft 10¼ in (9·715 m)
PS-1 Mod 32 ft 1 in (9·78 m)
Tailplane span 40 ft 6½ in (12·36 m)
Wheel track:
PS-1 10 ft 2 in (3·10 m)
PS-1 Mod 11 ft 8¼ in (3·56 m)
Wheelbase:
PS-1 26 ft 10¾ in (8·20 m)
PS-1 Mod 27 ft 4 in (8·33 m)
Propeller diameter 14 ft 6 in (4·42 m)
Rescue hatch, PS-1 Mod (port side, rear fuselage):
Height 4 ft 7½ in (1·41 m)
Width 2 ft 7 in (0·79 m)

Areas:
Wings, gross 1,462 sq ft (135·8 m^2)
Ailerons (total) 68·9 sq ft (6·40 m^2)
Inner flaps (total) 101·18 sq ft (9·40 m^2)
Outer flaps (total) 152·85 sq ft (14·20 m^2)
Leading-edge slats (total) 64·7 sq ft (6·01 m^2)
Spoilers (total) 22·60 sq ft (2·10 m^2)
Fin 189 sq ft (17·56 m^2)
Dorsal fin 68·03 sq ft (6·32 m^2)
Rudder 75·5 sq ft (7·01 m^2)
Tailplane 248 sq ft (23·05 m^2)
Elevators 94·5 sq ft (8·78 m^2)

Weights and Loadings (PS-1):
Weight empty 58,000 lb (26,300 kg)
Normal T-O weight 79,365 lb (36,000 kg)
Max T-O weight 94,800 lb (43,000 kg)
Max wing loading 64·84 lb/sq ft (316·6 kg/m^2)
Max power loading 7·74 lb/ehp (3·51 kg/ehp)

Weights and Loadings (PS-1 Mod, search and rescue):
Weight empty, equipped 56,218 lb (25,500 kg)
Max oversea operating weight 79,365 lb (36,000 kg)
Max T-O weight on land 99,200 lb (45,000 kg)
Max wing loading 67·9 lb/sq ft (331·4 kg/m^2)
Max power loading 8·11 lb/ehp (3·68 kg/ehp)

Performance (PS-1 at normal T-O weight):
Max level speed at 5,000 ft (1,525 m) 295 knots (340 mph; 547 km/h)
Cruising speed at 5,000 ft (1,525 m):
4 engines 230 knots (265 mph; 426 km/h)
2 engines 170 knots (196 mph; 315 km/h)
Approach speed 47 knots (54 mph; 87 km/h)
Touchdown speed 41 knots (47 mph; 76 km/h)
Stalling speed 40 knots (46 mph; 75 km/h)
Max rate of climb at S/L 2,264 ft (690 m)/min
Service ceiling 29,500 ft (9,000 m)
Time to 10,000 ft (3,050 m) 5 min
T-O run 820 ft (250 m)
Landing run 590 ft (180 m)
Minimum turning radius 82 ft 0 in (25·00 m)
Normal range 1,169 nm (1,347 miles; 2,168 km)
Max range for ferrying 2,560 nm (2,948 miles; 4,744 km)
Endurance 15 hr

Performance (PS-1 Mod, search and rescue version, estimated):
Max level speed 260 knots (299 mph; 481 km/h)
Cruising speed at 10,000 ft (3,050 m) 230 knots (265 mph; 426 km/h)
T-O to 50 ft (15 m) at max T-O weight 2,165 ft (660 m)
Landing from 50 ft (15 m) at 79,365 lb (36,000 kg) AUW 2,950 ft (900 m)
Runway LCN requirement at AUW of 94,798 lb (43,000 kg) 42
Minimum ground turning radius 69 ft 6½ in (21·20 m)
Radius of search operation at AUW of 99,200 lb (45,000 kg), including 2·3 hr search 900 nm (1,035 miles; 1,665 km)

SHOWA

SHOWA HIKOKI KOGYO KABUSHIKI KAISHA (Showa Aircraft Industry Co, Ltd)

Head Office:
No 3, 3-Chome, Nihonbashi-Muromachi, Chuo-ku, Tokyo
Telephone: Tokyo (03) 270-1451

Sales Office:
No 1, 2-Chome, Nihonbashi-Muromachi, Chuo-ku, Tokyo
Telephone: Tokyo (03) 279-1451

Works:
No 600, Tanaka-machi, Akishima-shi, Tokyo

President: Hidesuke Noda

Showa was the first Japanese aircraft manufacturing company to resume post-war operations when it undertook the overhaul and repair of aircraft of the US Air Force.

The company's present activities comprise mainly the manufacture of wingtip floats, tail fin, partition and other doors, torpedo pods and hatches for the Shin Meiwa PS-1 flying-boat; and the supply of aluminium and non-metal honeycomb and honeycomb sandwich panels for aircraft construction. Showa also manufactures a variety of airborne equipment, including galleys, trolleys and containers.

KOREA
(REPUBLIC OF)

ROKAF

REPUBLIC OF KOREA AIR FORCE

Headquarters:
Tae Bandong, Yong Dong Po City

Chief of Staff:
General Kim Sung Yong

The Republic of Korea Air Force, after completing one example of the Pazmany PL-2 two-seat light aircraft (see US section) for evaluation, has subsequently built further examples of this aircraft, of which four were understood to be flying by the beginning of 1974.

MEXICO

AAMSA

AERONAUTICA AGRICOLA MEXICANA SA

ADDRESS:
171 Oriente No. 398, Colonia Agron, Apartado 26783, Mexico 14, DF

ENQUIRIES TO:
Alejo Peralta

WORKS DIRECTOR: J. A. Jansen

As the result of an agreement between Rockwell International Corporation of the US (which see) and Industrias Unidas SA of Mexico, this company was formed in 1971 for the purpose of taking over from the former's Commercial Products Group the manufacture of Aero Commander Quail Commander and Sparrow Commander agricultural aircraft.

Aeronautica Agricola Mexicana SA has purchased the type design, tooling and all production materials for the Sparrow and Quail Commander agricultural aircraft, and is to build them at a new Industrias Unidas manufacturing complex in Pasteje, Mexico. Rockwell retains the right to market these aircraft in the United States.

Rockwell International has a 30% holding in the Mexican company.

Sparrow Commander agricultural aircraft (235 hp Lycoming O-540-B2B5 engine)

AAMSA (AERO COMMANDER) SPARROW COMMANDER

The Sparrow Commander is a small agricultural aircraft with a 170 US gallon (643 litre) hopper and low operating cost.

The entire primary structure of the aircraft is coated with Copon, an epoxy resin catalyst paint which is resistant to all known agricultural chemicals.

The Sparrow Commander can be purchased with any type of dispersal equipment required, ie straight sprayer of either high or low volume, dust dispersal gear, or a quick-change combination dust or spray unit. The units normally offered as optional extras are the Transland Boommaster spray system, Strutmaster spray system with 2 in Simplex pump, invert emulsion spray system, Buckeye bottom loader spray system, Micronair spray system, standard dust spreader, spreader with gate box and agitator, and Transland Swathmaster dry spreader.

TYPE: Single-seat agricultural monoplane.

WINGS: Braced low-wing monoplane. Modified Clark Y wing section. Dihedral 5° 8′. Incidence 0° 20′. Composite structure with spruce wood spars, metal-covered leading-edge and fabric covering on remainder of wing. Multiple steel-tube bracing struts on each side of fuselage. Hoerner wingtips. Wooden ailerons are fabric-covered. Flaps and drooping ailerons.

FUSELAGE: Steel-tube structure with fabric covering. Removable side panels.

TAIL UNIT: Wire-braced steel-tube structure with fabric covering. Wire deflector from canopy to fin.

LANDING GEAR: Non-retractable tailwheel type. CallAir spring shock-absorbers. Cleveland main wheels, with Goodyear tyres, size 8·50-6 (6-ply). Scott 8 in (20 cm) steerable tailwheel. Cleveland toe-actuated brakes. Wire-cutters on main legs.

POWER PLANT: One 235 hp Lycoming O-540-B2B5 six-cylinder horizontally-opposed air-cooled engine, driving a McCauley Type 1A200-DFA9045 two-blade fixed-pitch metal propeller. Two-position adjustable-pitch McCauley Type 2D34CT-84HF two-blade metal propeller optional. All fuel in wing tanks, capacity 40 US gallons (151 litres). Oil capacity 3 US gallons (11 litres).

ACCOMMODATION: Single seat in open-sided cockpit aft of hopper. Side doors. Wire-cutters on windscreen. Cabin heater standard. Capacity of standard hopper 22·5 cu ft (0·64 m³) or 170 US gallons (643 litres).

SYSTEMS: Electrical system includes 50A 24V alternator and 35Ah battery.

ELECTRONICS: Narco Mk III Omnigator radio and other avionics available as optional extras.

EQUIPMENT: Optional equipment includes night lighting system, landing light in nose cowl and AC full-flow oil filter.

DIMENSIONS, EXTERNAL:
- Wing span — 34 ft 9 in (10·59 m)
- Wing chord, constant — 5 ft 2¾ in (1·59 m)
- Length overall — 23 ft 6 in (7·16 m)
- Height overall — 7 ft 7 in (2·31 m)
- Tailplane span — 10 ft 6 in (3·20 m)
- Wheel track — 6 ft 10 in (2·08 m)
- Wheelbase — 17 ft 1 in (5·21 m)
- Propeller diameter:
  - standard — 7 ft 6 in (2·29 m)
  - optional — 7 ft 0 in (2·13 m)

AREAS:
- Wings, gross — 182 sq ft (16·90 m²)
- Ailerons (total) — 21·4 sq ft (1·99 m²)
- Fin — 8·6 sq ft (0·80 m²)
- Rudder — 9·0 sq ft (0·84 m²)
- Tailplane — 15·8 sq ft (1·47 m²)
- Elevators — 14·0 sq ft (1·30 m²)

WEIGHTS AND LOADINGS:
- Weight empty — 1,600 lb (726 kg)
- Max payload — 1,400 lb (635 kg)
- Max T-O weight:
  - CAR.3 — 3,000 lb (1,360 kg)
  - CAR.8 — 3,400 lb (1,542 kg)
- Max wing loading — 16·4 lb/sq ft (80·0 kg/m²)
- Max power loading — 12·8 lb/hp (5·8 kg/hp)

PERFORMANCE (at CAR.8 max T-O weight, except where indicated):
- Max level speed at S/L — 103 knots (119 mph; 191 km/h)
- Max cruising speed (75% power) at 3,000 lb (1,360 kg) AUW — 91 knots (105 mph; 169 km/h)
- Normal operating speed — 78-87 knots (90-100 mph; 145-161 km/h)
- Stalling speed at max T-O weight — 53 knots (60 mph; 97 km/h)
- Stalling speed as usually landed — 35 knots (40 mph; 64 km/h)
- Max rate of climb at S/L — 650 ft (198 m)/min
- Service ceiling — 14,000 ft (4,265 m)
- T-O run — 600 ft (183 m)
- Landing run — 447 ft (136 m)
- Range at max cruising speed (75% power) — 260 nm (300 miles; 483 km)

AAMSA (AERO COMMANDER) QUAIL COMMANDER

The Quail Commander differs from the Sparrow Commander only in having a 290 hp Lycoming IO-540-G1C5 six-cylinder horizontally-opposed aircooled engine and a larger hopper with a capacity of 210 US gallons (795 litres).

Details given for the Sparrow Commander apply also to the Quail Commander, except as follows:

EQUIPMENT: Optional equipment includes also an alternative retractable landing light in the wing and a rotating beacon.

WEIGHTS:
- Max payload — 1,600 lb (726 kg)
- Max T-O weight (CAR.8) — 3,600 lb (1,633 kg)

PERFORMANCE (at CAR.8 max T-O weight, except where indicated):
- Max level speed — 104 knots (120 mph; 193 km/h)
- Cruising speed (75% power) at 3,000 lb (1,360 kg) AUW — 100 knots (115 mph; 185 km/h)
- Operating speed — 78-87 knots (90-100 mph; 145-161 km/h)
- Stalling speed at max T-O weight — 54 knots (62 mph; 100 km/h)
- Stalling speed as usually landed — 35 knots (40 mph; 65 km/h)
- Max rate of climb at S/L — 850 ft (259 m)/min
- Service ceiling — 16,000 ft (4,875 m)
- T-O run — 800 ft (244 m)
- Landing run at normal landing weight — 447 ft (136 m)
- Range (at 50% power) — 260 nm (300 miles; 483 km)

ANAHUAC

FABRICA DE AVIONES ANAHUAC SA

ADDRESS:
Calzada Adolfo López Mateos 478, Aeropuerto Internacional, México 9, DF

Telephone: 558-27-57

PRESIDENT, FOUNDER AND GENERAL ADMINISTRATOR:
Dr Alejandro Elizondo

CHIEF EXECUTIVES:
Ing Arno Gjumlich (Designer and Chief Engineer)
Capt Marcial Sánchez (Chief Production and Flight Test Pilot)
Arq J. Alfonso Menchero (International Public Relations and Purchasing Manager)
Capt Hector Mariscal (Sales Manager)
CPT Luis Picón (General Comptroller)

This company was formed to initiate in Mexico the development of aircraft suited to the particular needs of agricultural aviation in that country, and takes its name from the former Aztec valley where Mexico City is now situated. Anahuac's first product is a single-seat aircraft known as the Tauro 300.

Anahuac Tauro 300 agricultural aircraft (300 hp Jacobs R-755-A2M1 engine)

ANAHUAC TAURO 300 (BULL)

Design of the Tauro was begun in January 1967 by Ing Arno Gjumlich, assisted by Alejandro Betancourt, David Zamora, Rafael Vega and Octavio Climent, graduate engineers from the Instituto Politécnico Nacional. Construction of the prototype started in July of that year, and this aircraft (XB-TAX) was flown for the first time on 3 December 1968 by test pilot Marcial Sánchez.

The first production Tauro was flown on 5 June 1970, and the aircraft was awarded the Mexican DGAC's approved type certificate No. 1. Seven production aircraft, incorporating some engineering modifications, had been completed by the end of 1971, as the initial phase of development and tentative introduction to the internal market.

During 1972 and part of 1973, studies were made for an improved version of the Tauro which will incorporate a number of improvements suggested as a result of early operational use of the aircraft. Mexican government approval was given on 21 December 1972 for financial support for an expansion of the manufacturing programme to meet orders both from Mexican customers and for export. It had not been possible to provide this support by mid-1974.

The following description applies to the standard version; the developed Tauro 350 will have a 350 hp Jacobs R-755-SM seven-cylinder radial engine and a fixed-pitch or constant-speed propeller.

Type: Single-seat agricultural aircraft.

Wings: Strut-braced low-wing monoplane. Wing section US 35B. Thickness/chord ratio approx 10%. Dihedral 5° from roots. Incidence 2°. No sweepback. Braced by inverted Vee-strut above each wing. All-metal (aluminium) spars and ribs, covered with Grade AA cotton fabric. Ailerons, of similar construction, are actuated mechanically by push/pull rods. No flaps or tabs.

Fuselage: Basic structure of 4130 steel tube, covered with removable aluminium side panels. Impact-absorbing structure forward of cockpit.

Tail Unit: Single, slightly-sweptback fin and balanced rudder, and non-swept fixed-incidence tailplane and balanced elevators, of 4130 steel tube construction with fabric covering. Trim tab on port elevator. Horizontal surfaces wire-braced above and below.

Landing Gear: Non-retractable tailwheel type, with spring shock-absorbers on main units, leaf spring on tail unit. Main units have Cleveland 6·00-6 wheels with Goodyear 8·50-6 tyres, pressure 30 lb/sq in (2·1 kg/cm²). Cleveland plate-type brakes.

Power Plant: One 300 hp Jacobs R-755-A2M1 seven-cylinder radial aircooled engine, driving a Sensenich 5404/MA96K two-blade ground-adjustable metal propeller. Aluminium fuel tank in each wing root, total capacity 37 US gallons (31 Imp gallons; 140 litres). Refuelling point above tank in each wing. Provision for optional auxiliary tank in fuselage. Oil capacity 5·28 US gallons (4·4 Imp gallons; 20 litres).

Accommodation: Single adjustable seat for pilot in enclosed cockpit, with downward-hinged window/door on each side. Cabin ventilated.

Systems: Electrical system includes 12V 35Ah Rebat R-35 battery for engine starting.

Electronics and Equipment: King VHF radio optional. No blind-flying instrumentation. Chemical hopper in fuselage, forward of cockpit at CG position, capacity 230 US gallons (191 Imp gallons; 870 litres) of liquid or 1,764 lb (800 kg) of dry chemical. Transland dispersal equipment.

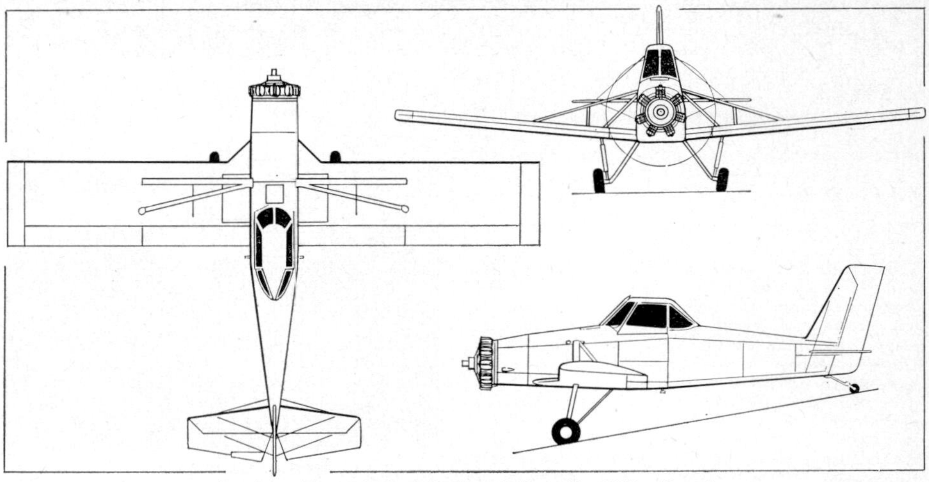

Anahuac Tauro 300 agricultural aircraft *(Pilot Press)*

Dimensions, external:

Wing span	37 ft 6½ in (11·44 m)
Wing chord (constant)	5 ft 9¾ in (1·77 m)
Wing aspect ratio	6·4
Length overall	26 ft 11¼ in (8·21 m)
Height overall	7 ft 8 in (2·34 m)
Tailplane span	11 ft 5¾ in (3·50 m)
Wheel track	8 ft 2½ in (2·50 m)
Propeller diameter	5 ft 0 in (2·44 m)
Propeller ground clearance (in flying attitude)	1 ft 0 in (0·30 m)

Dimensions, internal:

Cabin: Max length	3 ft 8 in (1·12 m)
Max width	2 ft 10 in (0·86 m)
Max height	4 ft 3 in (1·295 m)
Floor area	10 sq ft (0·93 m²)

Areas:

Wings, gross	217·89 sq ft (20·24 m²)
Ailerons (total)	18·0 sq ft (1·67 m²)
Fin	11·0 sq ft (1·02 m²)
Rudder	14·0 sq ft (1·30 m²)
Tailplane	16·0 sq ft (1·49 m²)
Elevators, incl tab	15·0 sq ft (1·39 m²)

Weights and Loadings:

Weight empty	1,973 lb (895 kg)
Max T-O and landing weight	3,542 lb (1,606 kg)
Max wing loading	16·28 lb/sq ft (79·5 kg/m²)
Max power loading	11·79 lb/hp (5·35 kg/hp)

Performance (at max T-O weight):

Max never-exceed speed	121 knots (140 mph; 225 km/h)
Max level speed at S/L	104 knots (120 mph; 193 km/h)
Max cruising speed at S/L	78 knots (90 mph; 145 km/h)
Econ cruising speed at 5,000 ft (1,525 m)	74 knots (85 mph; 137 km/h)
Stalling speed	36·5 knots (42 mph; 68 km/h)
Max rate of climb at S/L	500 ft (152 m)/min
Service ceiling	14,000 ft (4,250 m)
T-O run	1,150 ft (350 m)
T-O to 50 ft (15 m)	1,476 ft (450 m)
Landing from 50 ft (15 m)	1,150 ft (350 m)
Landing run	820 ft (250 m)
Range with max fuel	202 nm (233 miles; 375 km)

NETHERLANDS

FOKKER-VFW

FOKKER-VFW BV (Subsidiary of Zentralgesellschaft VFW-Fokker mbH)

Head Office and Main Factory:
PO Box 7600, Schiphol-Oost (Amsterdam Airport)
Telephone: Amsterdam (020) 73 10 44
Telex: 12227 SIFO NL

Other Factories and Companies:
Fokker-VFW BV, Drechtsteden Division, with plants at Papendrecht and Dordrecht
Fokker-VFW BV, Avio-Fokker Division, with Ypenburg Works (formerly Avio-Diepen) at Ypenburg Air Base, near the Hague; and Woensdrecht Works (formerly Aviolanda) at Woensdrecht Air Base, near Bergen op Zoom
Lichtwerk BV, Hoogeveen
Trading Company Avio-Diepen BV

Supervisory Board:
F. J. L. Diepen
G. C. Klapwijk
Ir A. A. Holle

Management:
Dr J. H. Greidanus
H. J. Grobben
H. Yff

Manager, Public Relations and Sales Promotion:
Brian H. Railton

Fokker-VFW BV, Netherlands Aircraft Factories, is the Dutch manufacturing company of the Zentralgesellschaft VFW-Fokker mbH (see International section), which was formed when the 50-year-old Royal Netherlands Aircraft Factories Fokker and Vereinigte Flugtechnische Werke GmbH of Germany joined forces on a parity basis in 1969. Marketing and product support of civil aircraft produced by the two companies is undertaken by a separate company, Fokker-VFW International BV, whose offices are at PO Box 7600, Schiphol-Oost, The Netherlands.

Fokker-VFW BV forms the entire aircraft industry in the Netherlands, with six plants, in which about 6,000 people are employed. Earlier collaborative ventures, other than those with VFW, have included participation in the manufacturing programmes for the Gloster Meteor, Hawker Hunter and Lockheed F-104G, with final assembly lines at Schiphol; and for the Breguet Atlantic and Canadair (Northrop) CF-5/NF-5.

Some 3,500 people are employed at the Schiphol-Oost works, which accommodates the company headquarters and administration together with the main F.27 and F.28 assembly lines and test flying facilities. Production is continuing of the F.27 and F.28, each in various versions, and components are being produced there for the Airbus A-300B (wing moving surfaces) and Shorts SD3-30 (outer wings and struts). Also at Schiphol are the design offices, research department, numerically-controlled milling department, metal bonding department, electronics division, space division and scientific and administrative computer facilities.

The Drechtsteden plant, formed by the integrated production facilities at Dordrecht and Papendrecht, employs some 1,100 people. Most of these are engaged on detail production and component assembly for the F.27 and F.28, VFW 614, Airbus A-300B and Breguet Atlantic; other work includes the manufacture of antennae and other specialised products. Several types of Aviobridge airport passenger gangways are also manufactured at Papendrecht.

Avio-Fokker is a Division of Fokker-VFW, employing some 1,200 people, and comprises the former Avio-Diepen plant at Ypenburg air base near the Hague and the former Aviolanda plant at Woensdrecht air base. At both facilities maintenance, overhaul, repair and modification work is carried out on a wide variety of military and civil aircraft. In recent years these have included the Fokker S.11, F.27 and F.28, Lockheed Neptune and Starfighter, Convair Coronado, McDonnell Douglas DC-8, Boeing 707, Republic Thunderstreak, Saab 91 Safir, Breguet Atlantic, Morane-Saulnier aircraft and Nike missiles.

Nike radomes, and reinforced plastics components for the Friendship, Fellowship, F-104G Starfighter, Airbus A-300B and Shorts SD3-30 are also manufactured at Ypenburg. Avio-Fokker is also engaged in the "wide-body look" modification of McDonnell Douglas DC-8s.

At Woensdrecht the special ELMO division is engaged on producing electrical and electronic systems and wire harnesses.

At Hoogeveen, Lichtwerk BV employs about 150 people in the manufacture of parts for the aerospace industry, radar and telecommunications and other industries. Quantity production of LD3 freight containers is also undertaken in this factory. Earlier activities included the assembly of Aérospatiale Alouette helicopters for the RNethAF.

FOKKER-VFW F.27 FRIENDSHIP

The Friendship is a medium-sized short/medium-range airliner. Two prototypes were built. The first made its first flight on 24 November 1955, and was designed to accommodate 28 passengers in a 73 ft (22·3 m) long fuselage. The second, which flew on 29 January 1957, was representative of Series 100 production aircraft, with Dart 511 engines and 32 seats in a 76 ft (23·1 m) fuselage. Two further airframes were built for static and fatigue testing.

The F.27 has been in series production for many years, both by Fokker and by Fairchild Industries in the United States. Deliveries by Fokker began in November 1958, and the sale of the 600th Friendship was announced on 1 September 1973. US production of the F-27 and FH-227 has ended, a total of 205 having been sold by Fairchild.

The following F.27 orders by airlines, air forces and government agencies had been announced by 1 April 1974:

Mk 100 (1967-68 *Jane's*; 84 built, incl 2 corporate; orders listed in 1971-72 *Jane's*)

Mk 200 (113 built, incl 1 corporate; orders listed in 1973-74 *Jane's*)

Mk 300 (1967-68 *Jane's*; 13 built; orders listed in 1971-72 *Jane's*)

Mk 400/600 (153 sold, incl 9 corporate)

Aero Trasporti Italiani	5
Air Algérie	3
Air France	2
Air Zaïre	8
Alia, Royal Jordanian Airlines	1
Ansett Transport Industries (Ansett Airlines of Australia 2, Airlines of South Australia 1, Ansett Airlines of Papua/New Guinea 2)	5
Argentine Air Force (incl 8 Troopships)	12
Bangladesh Biman	4
Condor Flugdienst (Lufthansa)	2
Danish Aero Lease	2
DETA (Mozambique)	1
DTA (Angola)	1
Garuda Indonesian Airways	12
Ghana Air Force (incl 5 Troopships)	6
Gulf Aviation Co	1
Iberia	8
Indian Airlines Corporation	2
Imperial Iranian Air Force (incl 10 Troopships and 2 Troopship/cartographic version)	18
Imperial Iranian Navy (incl 2 Troopships)	4
Iran National Geographic Organisation (Troopship/cartographic version)	2

Fokker-VFW F.27 Friendship Mk 400M twin-turboprop transport aircraft in the insignia of the Imperial Iranian Air Force

Republic of the Ivory Coast (incl 1 Troopship)	2
Libyan Arab Airlines	6
Lina Congo	1
Luxair	1
Maersk Air (Denmark)	2
Nigeria Airways	2
Nigerian government (incl 4 Troopships)	6
Pakistan International Airlines	3
Royal Air Inter (Royal Air Maroc)	2
Sobelair (Sabena)	1
Schreiner Airways	1
Sudanese Air Force (4 Troopships)	4
Swissair (for operation by Balair)	2
Trans-Australia Airlines	8
Union of Burma Airways	4
Mk 500 (48 sold, incl 1 corporate)	
Air Inter	10
ALM Dutch Antillean Airlines	2
French Ministère des Postes et Télécommunications (Air France)	15
Korean Air Lines	3
Malaysia-Singapore Airlines/MAS	11
Maersk Air (Denmark)	4
Sterling Airways (Denmark)	2

F-27 (128 built, including 49 corporate; orders listed in 1971-72 *Jane's*)

FH-227 (77 sold, incl 4 corporate; orders listed in 1973-74 *Jane's*)

By 1 April 1974, total sales were 616 (411 by Fokker-VFW and 205 by Fairchild).

Fokker is standardising currently on the Mks 400, 400M, 500 and 600, but any of the following versions of the F.27 are available to order:

F.27 Mk 200. Basic airliner or executive model with Dart RDa.7 Mk 532-7R turboprops. First flight 20 September 1959.

F.27 Mk 400 Combiplane. Cargo or combined cargo/passenger version of Mk 200. Large cargo door. First flight 6 October 1961.

F.27 Mk 400M. Military version, with accommodation for 45 parachute troops, 13,283 lb (6,025 kg) of freight or 24 stretchers and 9 attendants. Large cargo door and enlarged parachuting door on each side. First flight 24 April 1965.

F.27 Mk 400M Cartographic version. Aerial survey version with two super-wide-angle cameras, remotely controlled from central navigation station, and navigation sight. Inertial navigation system, with digital readout at navigation station and recorded on each picture. Photography through optical glass window panes. Electrically-operated window doors. First flight 1973.

F.27 Mk 500. Similar to F.27 Mk 200, but with lengthened fuselage and large cargo door. The 15 aircraft for the French Ministère des Postes et Télécommunications (Air France) have special para-dropping type large doors on both sides. First flight 15 November 1967.

F.27 Mk 500M. Military version, with lengthened fuselage; similar to Mk 400M but with accommodation for 50 paratroops, 14,588 lb (6,617 kg) of freight or 30 stretchers and six attendants.

F.27 Mk 600. Similar to Mk 200, but with a large cargo door. Does not have the reinforced and watertight flooring of the Combiplane. Can be fitted with quick-change interior, featuring roller tracks and palletised seats and/or cargo pallets. First flight 28 November 1968.

Any of the above models can be fitted, at customer's option, with a Dowty Rotol rough-field landing gear having two-stage oleos with a 4 in (10 cm) increase in stroke, giving increased overall height and propeller ground clearance.

Present rate of production by Fokker-VFW is three aircraft every two months.

Type: Twin-turboprop medium-range airliner.

Wings: Cantilever high-wing monoplane. Wing section NACA 64-421 at root, 64-415 at tip. Dihedral 2° 30′. Incidence 3° 30′. All-metal riveted and metal-bonded two-spar stressed-skin structure, consisting of centre-section and two detachable outer sections. Detachable honeycomb-core sandwich leading-edges with rubber-boot de-icers. Glassfibre-reinforced plastics trailing-edges. Mechanically-operated single-slotted flaps, divided by engine nacelles. Electrically-operated trim tab in each aileron.

Fuselage: All-metal stressed-skin structure, built to fail-safe principles, with cylindrical portions metal bonded and conical parts riveted. Fuselage is pressurised between rear bulkhead of nosewheel compartment and circular pressure bulkhead aft of the baggage compartment. Length of pressurised section 53 ft (16·16 m), except for Series 500 in which the pressurised section is 57 ft 11 in (17·66 m) long. The slightly flattened fuselage bottom is reinforced by underfloor members.

Tail Unit: Cantilever all-metal stressed-skin structure. Fin and tailplane, as well as leading-edges of surfaces, are detachable. Trim tab in port elevator. Pneumatic-boot anti-icing.

Landing Gear: Retractable tricycle type. Pneumatic retraction. Dowty oleo-pneumatic shock-absorber struts. Twin-wheel main units retract backward into engine nacelles. Single-wheel steerable nose unit retracts forward into non-pressurised nosecone. Main-wheel tyre pressure 80 lb/sq in (5·62 kg/cm²), nosewheel tyre pressure 55 lb/sq in (3·87 kg/cm²). Pneumatic brakes on main wheels, with Dunlop Maxaret automatic anti-skid system. Provision on all currently-available models for Dowty Rotol rough-field landing gear in which, at 43,500 lb (19,730 kg) AUW, the total stroke in the main gear is lengthened from 12 in (30·5 cm) to 16 in (40·6 cm), increasing the aircraft's static height and propeller ground clearance by 3 in (7·6 cm). Low-pressure main-wheel tyres are fitted, pressure 60 lb/sq in (4·2 kg/cm²) below 40,000 lb (18,143 kg) AUW and 65 lb/sq in (4·57 kg/cm²) at higher operating weights. Nose unit is of levered-suspension type, with tyre pressure of 55 lb/sq in (3·87 kg/cm²).

Power Plant (all current versions): Two Rolls-Royce Dart Mk 532-7R (RDa.7 rating) turboprop engines, each developing 2,140 shp plus 525 lb (238 kg) st for take-off. Four-blade Dowty Rotol propellers. Integral fuel tanks in outer wings, capacity 1,130 Imp gallons (5,140 litres). Optionally, bag tanks for an additional 503·5 Imp gallons (2,290 litres) may be fitted. Overwing fuelling, but pressure refuelling optional. Provision for carrying two 209 Imp gallon (950 litre) external fuel tanks under wings. Methyl-bromide fire-extinguishing system with flame detectors.

Accommodation (Mks 200 and 600): Flight compartment seats two pilots side by side, with folding seat for third crew member if required. Main cabin has standard four-abreast seating for 44 passengers (31·5 in; 80 cm seat pitch in Mk 200, 34·5 in; 87·6 cm in Mk 600); alternative arrangements allow this number to be increased to 48. Passenger door at rear of cabin, on port side, with toilet opposite. Standard cargo door at front of Mk 200 on port side; large cargo door in same position on Mk 600, with sill at truck-bed level. Cargo holds forward and aft of main cabin, size dependent on interior arrangement.

Accommodation (executive and VIP versions): Can be furnished to customer's specification, but a basic layout is available. In this, the cabin is divided into three sections: a conference room with six seats, a rest room with settee and divan, and a lounge with four seats. Toilet, galley, wardrobe, baggage space and seat for attendant in forward fuselage. Second toilet and baggage space at rear.

Accommodation (Mk 400 Combiplane): Principal features of this version are a large cargo loading door forward of the wings on the port side, with the sill at truck-bed height, and a reinforced cargo floor with tiedown rings. Typical layouts include 40 passengers four abreast at 35·5 in (90 cm) seat pitch, plus 218 cu ft (6·17 m³) of cargo space; 28 passengers at same seat pitch in rear of cabin, plus 588 cu ft (16·65 m³) cargo space; or all-cargo version with 1,727 cu ft (48·9 m³) of cargo space. Alternative layouts for up to 48 passengers.

Accommodation (Mk 400M): Folding canvas seats, with safety harnesses, along cabin sides for up to 45 paratroops, with toilet and provision for medical supply box or pantry unit at rear. Ambulance version can accommodate 24 USAF-type stretchers, in eight tiers of three, with seats at front and rear for up to nine medical attendants or sitting casualties. All-cargo version fitted with skid strips, tiedown fittings, protection plates and hinged

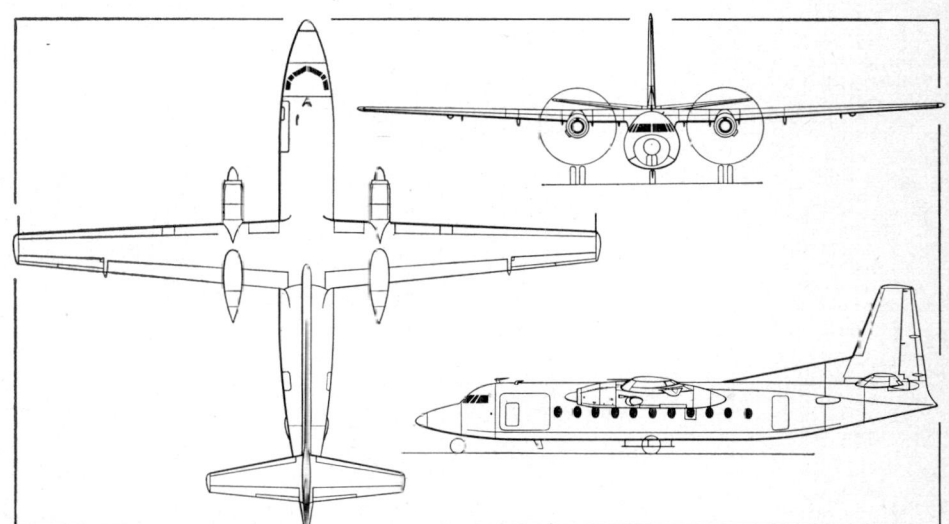

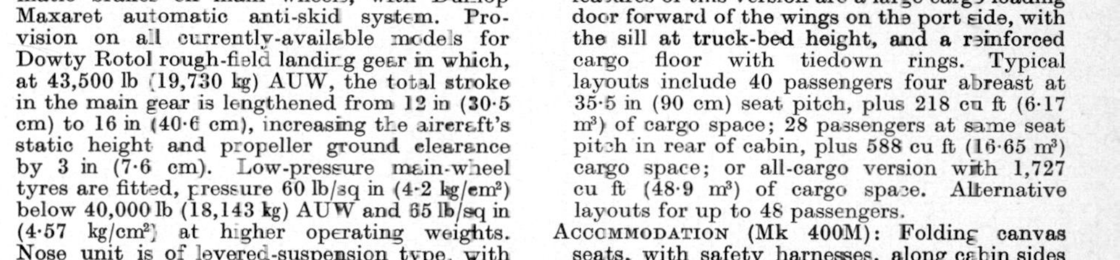

Fokker-VFW F.27 Friendship Mk 500 twin-turboprop medium-range passenger/freighter (*Pilot Press*)

hatracks. Despatch door on each side of fuselage at rear for dropping supplies and personnel.

ACCOMMODATION (Mk 500): Main cabin has standard seating for 52 passengers four abreast at 35·25 in (89·5 cm) seat pitch; alternative layouts enable up to 56 passengers to be carried at 28·5 in (72 cm) pitch.

SYSTEMS: **Pressurisation and air-conditioning system utilises two Rootes-type engine-driven blowers. Choke heating and air-to-air heat exchanger; optional bootstrap cooling system.** Pressure differential 4·16 lb/sq in (0·29 kg/cm²) in Mks 400, 500 and 600; 5·5 lb/sq in (0·39 kg/cm²) in Mk 200. No hydraulic system. Pneumatic system, pressure 3,400 lb/sq in (239 kg/cm²), for landing gear retraction, nosewheel steering and brakes. Emergency pneumatic circuits for landing gear extension and brakes. Primary 28V electrical system supplied by two 375A 28V DC engine-driven generators. Secondary system supplied via two 115V 400Hz AC constant-frequency inverters. Variable-frequency AC power supply, from 120/208V 15kVA engine-driven alternators, for anti-icing and heating. Two 24V 40Ah nickel-cadmium batteries. 39·4 cu ft (1·12 m³) oxygen system for pilots.

ELECTRONICS AND EQUIPMENT: Standard provisions for VHF and HF transceivers, VHF navigation system (including glideslope), ADF, ILS, marker beacon, dual gyrosyn compass system and intercom system. Provision for weather radar, autopilot etc.

DIMENSIONS, EXTERNAL:
- **Wing span** — 95 ft 2 in (29·00 m)
- **Wing chord at root** — 11 ft 4 in (3·45 m)
- **Wing chord at tip** — 4 ft 7 in (1·40 m)
- **Wing aspect ratio** — 12
- **Length overall:**
  - **except Mk 500** — 77 ft 3½ in (23·56 m)
  - **Mk 500** — 82 ft 2½ in (25·06 m)
- **Fuselage: Max width** — 8 ft 10½ in (2·70 m)
  - **Max height** — 9 ft 1¾ in (2·79 m)
- **Height overall, standard landing gear:**
  - **except Mk 500** — 27 ft 11 in (8·50 m)
  - **Mk 500** — 28 ft 7¼ in (8·71 m)
- **Height overall, rough-field landing gear:**
  - **except Mk 500** — 28 ft 2 in (8·59 m)
- **Tailplane span** — 32 ft 0 in (9·75 m)
- Wheel track (c/l shock struts) — 23 ft 7½ in (7·20 m)
- Wheelbase:
  - except Mk 500 — 28 ft 8 in (8·74 m)
  - Mk 500 — 31 ft 11¼ in (9·74 m)
- Propeller diameter — 11 ft 6 in (3·50 m)
- Propeller ground clearance:
  - standard landing gear:
    - except Mk 500 — 3 ft 1 in (0·94 m)
    - Mk 500 — 3 ft 3 in (0·99 m)
  - rough-field landing gear:
    - except Mk 500 — 3 ft 4¼ in (1·02 m)
- **Passenger door (aft, port):**
  - **Height** — 5 ft 5 in (1·65 m)
  - **Width** — 2 ft 5 in (0·74 m)
  - Height to sill — 4 ft 0 in (1·22 m)
- **Service/emergency door (aft, stbd):**
  - **Height** — 3 ft 8 in (1·12 m)
  - **Width** — 2 ft 5 in (0·74 m)
  - Height to sill — 3 ft 3 in (0·99 m)
- Standard cargo door (Mk 200 only):
  - Height — 3 ft 11 in (1·19 m)
  - Width — 3 ft 5 in (1·04 m)
  - Height to sill — 3 ft 3 in (0·99 m)
- Large cargo door (Mks 400, 500 and 600):
  - **Height** — 5 ft 10 in (1·78 m)
  - **Width** — 7 ft 7½ in (2·32 m)
  - Height to sill:
    - except Mk 500 — 3 ft 3 in (0·99 m)
    - Mk 500 — 3 ft 4½ in (1·03 m)
- Despatch doors (Mk 400M only, aft, port and stbd, each):
  - Height — 5 ft 5 in (1·65 m)
  - Width — 3 ft 11 in (1·19 m)
  - Height to sill — 4 ft 0 in (1·22 m)

DIMENSIONS, INTERNAL:
- **Cabin, excluding flight deck:**
  - Length:
    - except Mk 500 — 47 ft 5 in (14·46 m)
    - Mk 500 — 52 ft 4 in (15·96 m)
  - Max width — 8 ft 4½ in (2·55 m)
  - Max height — 6 ft 7½ in (2·02 m)
  - Volume:
    - except Mk 500 — 2,136 cu ft (60·5 m³)
    - Mk 500 — 2,360 cu ft (66·8 m³)
- Freight hold (fwd) max:
  - Mk 200 — 169 cu ft (4·78 m³)
  - Mks 400, 500, 600 — 197 cu ft (5·58 m³)
- Freight hold (aft) max:
  - all versions — 100 cu ft (2·83 m³)

AREAS:
- **Wings, gross** — 753·5 sq ft (70·0 m²)
- **Ailerons (total)** — 37·80 sq ft (3·51 m²)
- **Trailing-edge flaps (total)** — 136·90 sq ft (12·72 m²)
- **Vertical tail surfaces (total)** — 153 sq ft (14·20 m²)
- **Horizontal tail surfaces (total)** — 172 sq ft (16·00 m²)

WEIGHTS AND LOADINGS:
- Manufacturer's weight, empty:
  - Mk 200, 44 seats — 22,436 lb (10,177 kg)
  - Mk 400, 40 seats — 23,290 lb (10,564 kg)
  - Mk 400M — 23,360 lb (10,596 kg)
  - Mk 500, 52-56 seats — 23,578 lb (10,695 kg)
  - Mk 500M — 24,325 lb (11,034 kg)
  - Mk 600, 44 seats — 22,786 lb (10,336 kg)
- Operating weight, empty:
  - Mk 200, 44 seats — 24,612 lb (11,164 kg)
  - Mk 400, 40 seats — 24,875 lb (11,283 kg)
  - Mk 400M, all-cargo — 23,947 lb (10,862 kg)
  - Mk 400M, medical evacuation — 24,880 lb (11,286 kg)
  - Mk 400M, paratrooper — 24,336 lb (11,039 kg)
  - Mk 500, 52-56 seats — 25,915 lb (11,755 kg)
  - Mk 500M, all-cargo — 24,912 lb (11,300 kg)
  - Mk 500M, medical evacuation — 26,023 lb (11,804 kg)
  - Mk 500M, paratrooper — 25,332 lb (11,491 kg)
  - Mk 600, 44 seats — 24,962 lb (11,323 kg)
- Max payload (weight limited):
  - Mk 200, 44 seats — 12,888 lb (5,846 kg)
  - Mk 400, 40 seats — 12,625 lb (5,727 kg)
  - Mk 400M, all-cargo — 13,553 lb (6,148 kg)
  - Mk 400M, medical evacuation — 12,612 lb (5,721 kg)
  - Mk 400M, paratrooper — 13,164 lb (5,971 kg)
  - Mk 500, 52-56 seats — 13,585 lb (6,162 kg)
  - Mk 500M, all-cargo — 14,588 lb (6,617 kg)
  - Mk 500M, medical evacuation — 13,477 lb (6,113 kg)
  - Mk 500M, paratrooper — 14,168 lb (6,427 kg)
  - Mk 600, 44 seats — 12,538 lb (5,687 kg)
- Max T-O weight:
  - all versions — 45,000 lb (20,410 kg)
- Max landing weight:
  - Mks 200, 400, 400M and 600 — 41,000 lb (18,600 kg)
  - Mks 500 and 500M — 42,000 lb (19,050 kg)
- Max zero-fuel weight:
  - Mks 200, 400, 400M and 600 — 37,500 lb (17,010 kg)
  - Mks 500 and 500M — 39,500 lb (17,900 kg)
- Max wing loading:
  - all versions — 59·7 lb/sq ft (291·5 kg/m²)
- Max power loading:
  - all versions — 10·5 lb/shp (4·76 kg/shp)

PERFORMANCE (at weights indicated):
- Normal cruising speed at 20,000 ft (6,100 m) and AUW of 38,000 lb (17,237 kg):
  - all versions — 259 knots (298 mph; 480 km/h)
- Rate of climb at S/L, AUW of 40,000 lb (18,143 kg):
  - all civil versions — 1,480 ft (451 m)/min
  - both military versions — 1,620 ft (494 m)/min
- Service ceiling at AUW of 38,000 lb (17,237 kg):
  - all civil versions — 29,500 ft (8,990 m)
  - both military versions — 30,000 ft (9,145 m)
- Service ceiling, one engine out, at AUW of 38,000 lb (17,237 kg):
  - all civil versions — 11,700 ft (3,565 m)
  - both military versions — 13,300 ft (4,055 m)
- Runway LCN at max T-O weight, standard landing gear — 16
- Required T-O field length (ICAO-PAMC) at AUW of 40,000 lb (18,143 kg), all civil versions:
  - S/L, ISA — 3,250 ft (991 m)
  - S/L, ISA +15°C — 3,560 ft (1,085 m)
  - 3,000 ft (914 m), ISA — 3,980 ft (1,213 m)
- Required T-O field length (military) at AUW of 40,000 lb (18,143 kg), both military versions:
  - S/L, ISA — 2,310 ft (704 m)
  - S/L, ISA +15°C — 2,510 ft (765 m)
  - 3,000 ft (914 m), ISA — 2,750 ft (838 m)
- Required landing field length (ICAO-PAMC) at AUW of 37,500 lb (17,010 kg), all civil versions:
  - S/L — 3,160 ft (963 m)
  - 3,000 ft (914 m) — 3,390 ft (1,033 m)
- Required landing field length (military) at AUW of 37,500 lb (17,010 kg), both military versions:
  - S/L — 1,900 ft (579 m)
  - 3,000 ft (914 m) — 2,040 ft (622 m)
- Range (ISA, zero wind conditions) with FAR 121.645 reserves for diversion, 30 min hold at 10,000 ft (3,050 m) and 10% flight fuel:
  - Mks 200 and 600, 44 passengers — 1,020 nm (1,197 miles; 1,926 km)
  - Mk 400, 40 passengers — 1,025 nm (1,203 miles; 1,935 km)
  - Mk 500, 52 passengers — 935 nm (1,082 miles; 1,741 km)
- Military transport range (ISA, zero wind conditions) at max T-O weight, reserves for 30 min hold at S/L and 5% initial fuel:
  - Mks 400M and 500M, all-cargo, max standard fuel — 1,195 nm (1,375 miles; 2,213 km)
  - Mks 400M and 500M, all-cargo, max possible fuel — 2,370 nm (2,727 miles; 4,389 km)
- Military combat radius, conditions as above:
  - Mks 400M and 500M, all-cargo, max standard fuel — 625 nm (719 miles; 1,158 km)
  - Mks 400M and 500M, all-cargo, max possible fuel — 1,230 nm (1,416 miles; 2,278 km)
- Max endurance at 20,000 ft (6,100 m):
  - Mk 400M, max standard fuel — 7 hr 25 min
  - Mk 400M, max possible fuel — 12 hr 47 min
  - Mk 500M, max standard fuel — 7 hr 14 min
  - Mk 500M, max possible fuel — 12 hr 26 min

OPERATIONAL NOISE CHARACTERISTICS (FAR Pt 36):
- T-O noise level — 89 EPNdB
- Approach noise level — 99 EPNdB
- Sideline noise level — 92·5 EPNdB

FOKKER-VFW F.28 FELLOWSHIP

Announced in April 1962, the F.28 Fellowship twin-turbofan short-haul transport was developed in collaboration with other European aircraft manufacturers and with the financial support of the Netherlands government. One half of the Dutch share of the development cost was supplied through the Netherlands Aircraft Development Board, the other half through a loan guaranteed by the government.

Under agreements signed in the Summer of 1964, production is undertaken by Fokker-VFW in association with MBB and VFW-Fokker in Germany and Short Bros and Harland in the UK.

Fokker-VFW is responsible for the front fuselage, to a point just aft of the flight deck, the centre fuselage and wing-root fairings. MBB builds the fuselage from the wing trailing-edge to the rear pressure bulkhead and the engine nacelles and support stubs. VFW-Fokker is responsible for the rear fuselage and tail unit, and for the cylindrical fuselage section between the wing leading-edge and flight deck. Shorts are responsible for the wings (including the slatted wings for the Mks 5000 and 6000), and other components, including the main-wheel and nosewheel doors.

First flight of the first prototype F.28 (PH-JHG) was made on 9 May 1967, and the second prototype, PH-WEV, flew on 3 August 1967. **The third F.28 (PH-MOL) flew for the first time on 20 October 1967 and was brought up to production standard in the early Summer of 1968.**

The Dutch RLD granted a C of A to the F.28 on 24 February 1969, and the first delivery (of the fourth aircraft, to LTU) was made on the same day. The aircraft received FAA Type Approval on 24 March 1969 and German certification on 30 March 1969. RLD certification for operation from unpaved runways was granted in mid-1972. The Mk 1000 was granted FAA-approved noise certification on 31 December 1971.

A total of 83 Fellowships had been ordered by 28 March 1974, as follows:

Aerolinee Itavia (Italy)	3
Aeroperu	3
Air Gabon (Mk 2000)	2
Air Nauru	2
Ansett Transport Industries (Airlines of NSW and MacRobertson-Miller)	5
Argentine government (Mk 1000)	1
Australian Dept of Civil Aviation	3
Aviaction (Germany)	3
Braathens (Norway)	5
Colombian Air Force	1
Eastex (USA)	1
Fairchild Industries	3
Garuda Indonesian Airways	11
Germanair	4

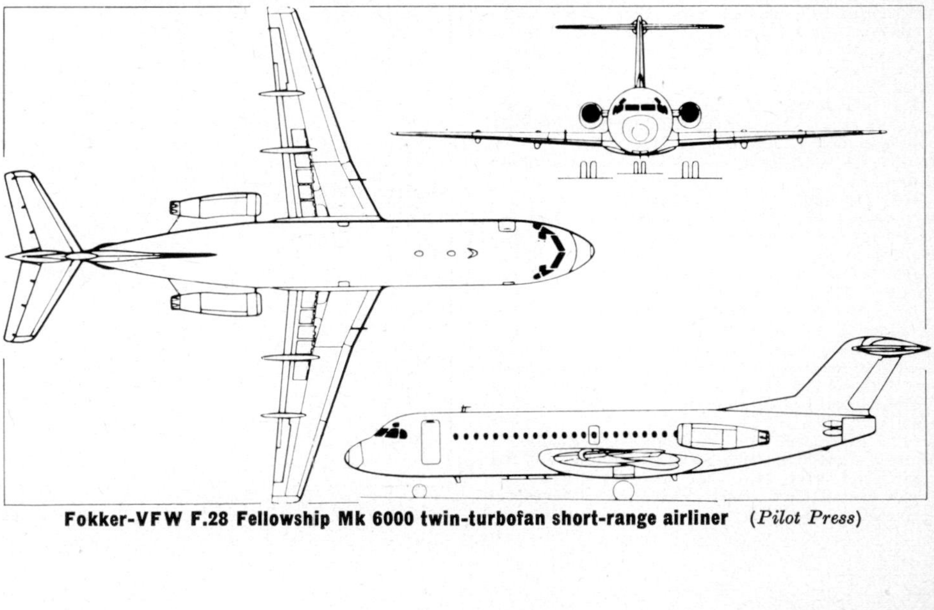

Fokker-VFW F.28 Fellowship Mk 6000 twin-turbofan short-range airliner *(Pilot Press)*

Fokker-VFW F.28 Fellowship Mk 2000 (two 9,850 lb st Rolls-Royce Spey Mk 555-15 turbofan engines) in the insignia of Ghana Airways

Ghana Airways (Mk 2000)	2
Iberia	3
LADE (Argentine) (Mk 1000C)	5
Linjeflyg (Sweden)	3
LTU (Germany)	4
Malaysian government	2
Martinair-Holland	1
Netherlands goverment	1
Nigeria Airways (incl 1 Mk 2000)	3
Nigerian government	1
Pelita/Pertamina	2
THY (Turkey)	5
Touraine Air Transport	1
Transair (Canada)	2
Undisclosed	1

Four versions have been announced, as follows:

Mk 1000. Initial version, in production and service, with seating for up to 65 passengers. First F.28 commercial service was flown by Braathens on 28 March 1969. Available optionally, for all-cargo or mixed passenger/cargo operations, with large freight door at front on port side, aft of passenger door, in which form it is designated **Mk 1000C.**

Mk 2000. Similar to Mk 1000 except for lengthened fuselage, permitting an increase in accommodation for up to 79 passengers in all-tourist layout. F.28 first prototype modified to Mk 2000 standard and flown for first time on 28 April 1971. Dutch certification awarded on 30 August 1972. In production and service.

Mk 5000. Similar to Mk 1000 except for slatted, long-span wings and improved Spey engines. Also to be available with large cargo door.

Mk 6000. Similar to Mk 2000 except for slatted, long-span wings and improved Spey engines. Prototype, modified from F.28 first prototype (previously used for Mk 2000 certification flying) and fitted with modified wings from the second prototype, made its first flight on 27 September 1973. Certification is scheduled for late 1974.

The following details apply generally to all four versions, except where a specific model is indicated:

Type: Twin-turbofan short-range airliner.

Wings: Cantilever low/mid-wing monoplane. Wing section NACA 0000-X 40Y series with camber varying along span. Thickness/chord ratio up to 14% on inner wing, 10% at tip. Dihedral 2° 30′. Sweepback at quarter-chord 16°. Single-cell two-spar light alloy torsion-box structure, comprising centre-section, integral with fuselage, and two outer wings. Fail-safe construction. Lower skin made of three planks. Taper-rolled top skin. Forged ribs in centre-section, built-up ribs in outer panels. Double-skin leading-edge with ducts for hot-air de-icing. Irreversible hydraulically-operated ailerons. Emergency manual operation of ailerons, through tabs. Hydraulically-operated Fowler double-slotted flaps over 70% of each half-span with electrical emergency extension. Five-section hydraulically-operated lift dumpers in front of flaps on each wing. Trim tab in each aileron. Mks 5000 and 6000 have extended-span wings with full-span hydraulically-operated leading-edge slats.

Fuselage: Circular-section semi-monocoque light alloy fail-safe structure, made up of skin panels with Redux-bonded Z-stringers. Bonded doubler plates at door and window cut-outs. Quickly-detachable sandwich (metal/end grain balsa) floor panels. Hydraulically-operated petal airbrakes form aft end of fuselage.

Tail Unit: Cantilever light alloy structure, with hydraulically-actuated variable-incidence T tailplane. Electrical emergency actuation of tailplane. Hydraulically-boosted elevators. Hydraulically-operated rudder with duplicated actuators and emergency manual operation. Honeycomb sandwich skin panels used extensively, in conjunction with multiple spars. Double-skin leading-edges for hot-air de-icing.

Landing Gear: Retractable tricycle type of Dowty-Rotol manufacture, with twin wheels on each unit. Hydraulic retraction, nosewheels forward, main units inward into fuselage. Oleo-pneumatic shock-absorbers. Goodyear wheels, tyres and electronically-controlled braking system. Steerable nosewheel. Mainwheel tyres size 39 × 13, 16-ply rating, pressure 100 lb/sq in (7·0 kg/cm²) on Mk 1000, 102 lb/sq in (7·1 kg/cm²) on Mk 2000, 110 lb/sq in (7·7 kg/cm²) on Mks 5000 and 6000. Nosewheel tyres size 24·5 × 8·5, 10-ply rating, pressure 85 lb/sq in (5·98 kg/cm²) on Mk 1000, 78 lb/sq in (5·5 kg/cm²) on Mk 2000, 80 lb/sq in (5·6 kg/cm²) on Mk 5000 and 75 lb/sq in (5·3 kg/cm²) on Mk 6000. Low-pressure tyres optional on all units.

Power Plant (Mks 1000 and 2000): Two Rolls-Royce RB.183-2 Spey Mk 555-15 turbofan engines with blade-cooling (each 9,850 lb; 4,468 kg st), mounted in pod on each side of rear fuselage. No water injection or thrust reversers. Thermal anti-icing for air intakes. For Mks 5000 and 6000, a Mk 555-15H version of the Spey engine is under development. This will retain the existing nominal thrust rating of the Mk 555-15, but at ambient temperatures up to 28°C, and will be fitted with a five-chute silencing nozzle. Integral fuel tank in each outer wing panel with total usable capacity of 2,143 Imp gallons (9,740 litres) in Mks 1000/2000; 2,130 Imp gallons (9,682 litres) in Mks 5000/6000. Optional seven bladder-type tank units in wing centre-section with total usable capacity of 726 Imp gallons (3,300 litres). Single refuelling point under starboard wing, near root.

Accommodation: Crew of two side by side on flight deck, with jump-seat for third crew member. Electrically-heated windscreen. Pantry/baggage space immediately aft of flight deck on starboard side, followed by entrance lobby with hydraulically-operated airstair door on port side, service and emergency door on starboard side, and seat for stewardess. On Mks 1000 and 5000, an optional upward-opening cargo door, to permit all-cargo or all-passenger operation, can be added aft of the passenger airstair door. Additional emergency door on each side of main cabin, over wing. Main cabin layout of Mks 1000/5000 can be varied to accommodate 55, 60 or 65 passengers five abreast at 37, 32/33 or 31 in (94, 81/84 or 79 cm) seat pitch respectively. In Mks 2000/6000, layout can be varied to accommodate 79 passengers at 31 in (79 cm) seat pitch. Aft of cabin are a wardrobe (port), baggage compartment (port) and toilet compartment (starboard). Underfloor cargo compartments fore and aft of wing, with single door on starboard side of forward hold, with one door on rear hold of each version.

Systems: AiResearch air-conditioning system, using engine bleed air. Max pressure differential 7·45 lb/sq in (0·52 kg/cm²). Two independent hydraulic systems, pressure 3,000 lb/sq in (210 kg/cm²). Primary system for flight controls, landing gear, nosewheel steering and brakes, secondary system for duplication of certain essential flight controls. Flying control hydraulic components supplied by Jarry Hydraulics. All-AC electrical system utilises two 20kVA Westinghouse engine-driven generators to supply three-phase constant-frequency 115/200V 400Hz power. One 20Ah battery for starting APU and for emergency power. AiResearch GTCP 36-4A APU, mounted aft of rear pressure bulkhead, for engine starting, ground air-conditioning and ground electrical power, and to drive a third AC generator for standby use on essential services in flight.

Electronics and Equipment: Standard equipment includes VHF transceivers, VHF navigation system (with glideslope), DME, marker beacon, weather radar, ADF, ATC transponder, dual compass system, interphone and public address systems, Smiths SEP6 autopilot, Collins FD 108 flight director, flight guidance caution system, flight data recorder and voice recorder. Thermal bleed air system for wing leading-edges (slats on Mks 5000/6000), tailplane leading-edge and engine air intakes. Stick pusher system on Mks 5000/6000. Optional equipment to customer's requirements, including equipment for operation in Cat. 2 weather minima.

Dimensions, external:

Wing span:	
1000, 2000	77 ft 4¼ in (23·58 m)
5000, 6000	82 ft 3 in (25·07 m)
Wing chord at root:	
all versions	15 ft 9 in (4·80 m)
Wing chord at tip:	
1000, 2000	5 ft 9¾ in (1·77 m)
Wing aspect ratio:	
1000, 2000	7·27
Length overall:	
1000, 5000	89 ft 10¾ in (27·40 m)
2000, 6000	97 ft 1¾ in (29·61 m)
Length of fuselage:	
1000, 5000	80 ft 6¼ in (24·55 m)
2000, 6000	87 ft 9½ in (26·76 m)

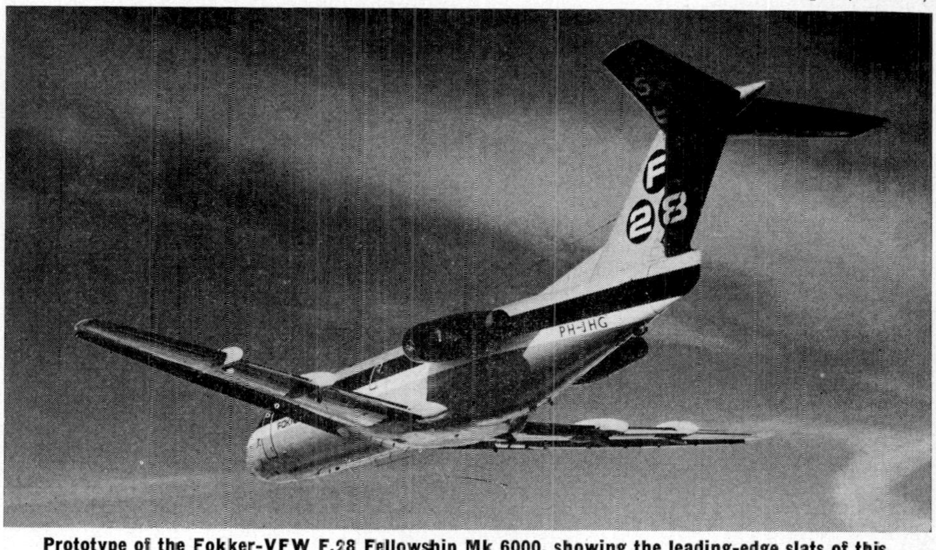

Prototype of the Fokker-VFW F.28 Fellowship Mk 6000, showing the leading-edge slats of this version deployed

Fuselage: Max width 10 ft 10 in (3·30 m)
Height overall 27 ft 9½ in (8·47 m)
Tailplane span 28 ft 4¼ in (8·64 m)
Wheel track (c/l of shock struts) 16 ft 6½ in (5·04 m)
Wheelbase:
1000, 5000 29 ft 2½ in (8·90 m)
2000, 6000 33 ft 11½ in (10·35 m)
Passenger door (fwd, port):
Height 6 ft 4 in (1·93 m)
Width 2 ft 10 in (0·86 m)
Service/emergency door (fwd, stbd):
Height 4 ft 2 in (1·27 m)
Width 2 ft 0 in (0·61 m)
Emergency exits (centre, each):
Height 3 ft 0 in (0·91 m)
Width 1 ft 8 in (0·51 m)
Freight hold doors (each):
Height (fwd, each) 2 ft 11½ in (0·90 m)
Height (aft) 2 ft 7½ in (0·80 m)
Width (fwd, each) 3 ft 1½ in (0·95 m)
Width (aft) 2 ft 11 in (0·89 m)
Height to sill (fwd, each) 4 ft 10 in (1·47 m)
Height to sill (aft) 5 ft 2½ in (1·59 m)
Baggage door (rear, port, optional):
Height 1 ft 11½ in (0·60 m)
Width 1 ft 8 in (0·51 m)
Optional cargo door (fwd, port):
Height 6 ft 1¾ in (1·87 m)
Width 8 ft 2 in (2·49 m)
Height to sill 7 ft 4¼ in (2·24 m)

DIMENSIONS, INTERNAL:
Cabin, excluding flight deck:
Length:
1000, 5000 43 ft 0 in (13·10 m)
2000, 6000 50 ft 3 in (15·31 m)
Max length of seating area:
1000, 5000 35 ft 2¾ in (10·74 m)
2000, 6000 42 ft 6¾ in (12·95 m)
Max width 10 ft 2 in (3·10 m)
Max height 6 ft 7¼ in (2·02 m)
Floor area:
1000, 5000 413·3 sq ft (38·4 m²)
2000, 6000 482·2 sq ft (44·8 m²)
Volume:
1000, 5000 2,525 cu ft (71·5 m³)
2000, 6000 2,931 cu ft (83·0 m³)
Freight hold (underfloor, fwd):
1000, 5000 245 cu ft (6·90 m³)
2000, 6000 308 cu ft (8·70 m³)
Freight hold (underfloor, rear):
1000, 5000 135 cu ft (3·80 m³)
2000, 6000 169 cu ft (4·80 m³)
Baggage hold (aft of cabin) max 80 cu ft (2·265 m³)

AREAS:
Wings, gross:
1000, 2000 822 sq ft (76·40 m²)
5000, 6000 850 sq ft (78·97 m²)
Ailerons (total) 28·74 sq ft (2·67 m²)
Trailing-edge flaps (total) 150·7 sq ft (14·00 m²)
Fuselage airbrakes (total) 38·97 sq ft (3·62 m²)
Fin (incl dorsal fin) 132·4 sq ft (12·30 m²)
Rudder 24·76 sq ft (2·30 m²)
Tailplane 209·9 sq ft (19·50 m²)
Elevators (total) 41·33 sq ft (3·84 m²)

WEIGHTS AND LOADINGS:
Manufacturer's weight empty:
1000, 65 seats 31,954 lb (14,492 kg)
1000C 31,954 lb (14,492 kg)
2000, 79 seats 32,929 lb (14,936 kg)
5000, 65 seats 33,504 lb (15,198 kg)
6000, 79 seats 34,477 lb (15,638 kg)
Operating weight empty:
1000, 65 seats 35,464 lb (16,084 kg)
1000C 35,853 lb (16,263 kg)
2000, 79 seats 36,795 lb (16,690 kg)
5000, 65 seats 37,014 lb (16,790 kg)
6000, 79 seats 38,345 lb (17,393 kg)
Max weight-limited payload:
1000 19,036 lb (8,636 kg)
1000C 18,647 lb (8,457 kg)
2000 17,705 lb (8,030 kg)
5000 17,436 lb (7,930 kg)
6000 17,655 lb (8,007 kg)
Max T-O weight:
1000/2000 65,000 lb (29,485 kg)
5000/6000 70,800 lb (32,115 kg)
Max zero-fuel weight:
1000/2000/5000 54,500 lb (24,720 kg)
6000 56,000 lb (25,400 kg)
Max landing weight:
1000/2000 59,000 lb (26,760 kg)
5000/6000 64,000 lb (29,030 kg)
Max wing loading:
1000/2000 79·1 lb/sq ft (386 kg/m²)
5000/6000 83·3 lb/sq ft (406 kg/m²)
Max cabin floor loading:
all passenger versions 75 lb/sq ft (366 kg/m²)
1000/5000 with large cargo door 125 lb/sq ft (610 kg/m²)
Max power loading:
1000/2000 3·3 lb/lb st (3·3 kg/kg st)
5000/6000 3·6 lb/lb st (3·6 kg/kg st)

PERFORMANCE (ISA, except where indicated):
Max never-exceed speed (all versions) 390 knots (449 mph; 723 km/h) EAS or Mach 0·83
Max permissible operating speed (all versions) 330 knots (380 mph; 611 km/h) EAS or Mach 0·75
Max cruising speed at 23,000 ft (7,000 m) (all versions) 455 knots (523 mph; 843 km/h) TAS
Econ cruising speed at 30,000 ft (9,150 m), AUW of 59,000 lb (26,760 kg):
1000/2000 362 knots (416 mph; 670 km/h) TAS
5000/6000 366 knots (421 mph; 678 km/h) TAS
Threshold speed at max landing weight:
1000/2000 119 knots (137 mph; 220 km/h) EAS
5000/6000 110 knots (127 mph; 204 km/h) EAS
Max cruising altitude:
all versions 35,000 ft (10,675 m)
Min ground turning radius:
1000/5000 31 ft 6 in (9·60 m)
2000/6000 35 ft 9 in (10·90 m)
Runway LCN at max T-O weight (hard runway):
1000, standard tyres 26·5
1000, low-pressure tyres 22
2000, standard tyres 27
2000, low-pressure tyres 22·5
5000, standard tyres 31
5000, low-pressure tyres 27
6000, standard tyres 30
6000, low-pressure tyres 26
Runway LCN at max T-O weight (flexible runway):
1000, standard tyres 21
2000, standard tyres 21·5
5000, standard tyres 25
5000, low-pressure tyres 21
6000, standard tyres 24
6000, low-pressure tyres 20
FAR T-O field length at max T-O weight (1000/2000):
S/L 5,490 ft (1,673 m)
S/L, ISA + 10°C 5,820 ft (1,774 m)
S/L, ISA + 15°C 6,160 ft (1,878 m)
2,000 ft (610 m) 5,970 ft (1,820 m)
3,000 ft (915 m) 6,320 ft (1,926 m)
FAR T-O field length at max T-O weight (5000/6000):
S/L 5,860 ft (1,786 m)
S/L, ISA + 10°C 6,046 ft (1,843 m)
S/L, ISA + 15°C 6,168 ft (1,880 m)
2,000 ft (610 m) 6,120 ft (1,865 m)
3,000 ft (915 m) 6,530 ft (1,990 m)
FAR landing field length at max landing weight (1000/2000):
S/L 3,540 ft (1,079 m)
5,000 ft (1,525 m) 4,010 ft (1,222 m)
FAR landing field length at max landing weight (5000/6000):
S/L 3,120 ft (951 m)
5,000 ft (1,525 m) 3,527 ft (1,075 m)
Range, high-speed schedule, FAR 121.654 reserves:
1000, 65 passengers 1,020 nm (1,174 miles; 1,889 km)
2000, 79 passengers 630 nm (725 miles; 1,167 km)
*5000, 65 passengers 1,210 nm (1,392 miles; 2,240 km)
6000, 79 passengers 900 nm (1,036 miles; 1,667 km)
Range, long-range schedule, FAR 121.654 reserves:
1000, 65 passengers 1,130 nm (1,300 miles; 2,093 km)
2000, 79 passengers 700 nm (806 miles; 1,296 km)
*5000, 65 passengers 1,400 nm (1,611 miles; 2,593 km)
6000, 79 passengers 1,030 nm (1,185 miles; 1,908 km)
* *With wing centre-section tanks*

OPERATIONAL NOISE CHARACTERISTICS (FAR Pt 36):
T-O noise level:
1000/2000 90 EPNdB
5000/6000 (estimated) 88 EPNdB
Approach noise level:
1000 101·2 EPNdB
2000 101·8 EPNdB
5000/6000 (estimated) 97·5 EPNdB
Sideline noise level:
1000/2000 99·5 EPNdB
5000/6000 (estimated) 97 EPNdB

NEW ZEALAND

AEROSPACE

NEW ZEALAND AEROSPACE INDUSTRIES LIMITED

HEAD OFFICE AND WORKS:
Hamilton Airport, R.D.2, Hamilton
Telephone: Hamilton 36-144 and 36-069
Telex: SECOMPRO NZ 2625 AEROSPACE
DIRECTOR AND CHIEF EXECUTIVE:
A. M. Coleman
COMMERCIAL MANAGER:
G. Scheltema
MARKETING MANAGER:
G. Bates
CHIEF DESIGNER:
P. W. C. Monk
WORKS MANAGER:
C. R. S. Wood
QUALITY CONTROL MANAGER:
K. W. James
CHIEF MAINTENANCE ENGINEER:
H. W. Robertson
COMPANY SECRETARY:
J. D. Linch

Aero Engine Services Ltd and Air Parts (NZ) Ltd (see 1972-73 *Jane's*) amalgamated on 1 April 1973 to form a new company operating under the name of New Zealand Aerospace Industries Ltd. The new company has a share capital of $A1·3 million, half of which is held by shareholders of the two constituent companies and the remainder in equal proportions by Air New Zealand and New Zealand National Airways Corporation.

Among the initial tasks of the new company is to integrate production of the (formerly Air Parts) Fletcher agricultural aircraft and the (formerly AESL) Airtrainer CT/4, in a new 17,000 sq ft (1,579 m²) facility at the AESL premises at Hamilton Airport. Descriptions follow of these and other aircraft for which New Zealand Aerospace Industries is responsible:

Airtourer two-seat light aircraft in the insignia of the Aviation Academy of Djakarta, Indonesia (*K. E. Sissons*)

AEROSPACE AIRTOURER

The Airtourer was designed by Henry Millicer, then Chief Aerodynamicist of the Australian Government Aircraft Factories, as an entry for a competition for a light two-seat aircraft held in 1953 by the Royal Aero Club of Great Britain. It won the competition, against 103 other designs.

A prototype Airtourer, built mainly of wood and powered by a 65 hp Continental engine, flew for the first time on 31 March 1959, and was described fully in earlier editions of *Jane's*.

Production Airtourers have an all-metal airframe and were built initially by Victa Ltd of Milperra, NSW, Australia. World manufacturing rights were acquired from Victa by AESL in early 1967, and from October of that year production was undertaken exclusively by the Airtourer Division of AESL in New Zealand.

Glos-Air Ltd of Staverton Airport, Cheltenham, England, was appointed the sole UK distributor for the Airtourer early in 1968. Aircraft are received by Glos-Air in a partially knocked-down condition and are assembled, painted and test-flown at Staverton prior to delivery to UK operators as Glos-Airtourers.

The following versions have been announced, of which all except the Airtourer 100 and T2 are currently available:

Airtourer 100. Initial model with 100 hp Continental O-200-A engine. Production completed. Described in 1969-70 *Jane's*.

Airtourer T2. Version with 115 hp Lycoming O-235-C2A engine and fixed-pitch propeller. Originally known as Airtourer 115. Prototype flew on 17 September 1962 and first production model on 22 February 1963. DCA Type Approval received on 6 July 1963. Production completed. Described in 1973-74 *Jane's*.

Airtourer T3. As T2, but with 130 hp Rolls-Royce Continental engine and fixed-pitch propeller. First flight 27 January 1972. In production.

Airtourer T4. Similar to T2, but with 150 hp Lycoming O-320-E2A engine, fixed-pitch propeller and increased AUWs. Prototype flew in September 1968; first production model delivered to UK in January 1969.

Airtourer T5. Similar to T4, but with O-320-E1A engine, constant-speed propeller and needle-type spinner. Prototype flew in November 1968; first production model delivered in January 1969.

Airtourer T6/12. Similar to T5, but with higher AUWs and 12V electrical system.

Airtourer T6/24. As T6/12, but with 24V electrical system.

A total of 170 Airtourer 100s and 115s had been completed by Victa Ltd when production by that company was suspended in late 1966.

By 1973, a further 80 Airtourers had been built and delivered by AESL. Of this total, 49 had been exported, to the UK, Australia, Fiji and South Africa. Four T6/24s were delivered to the Royal New Zealand Air Force in mid-1970, and fourteen T6/24s have been delivered to Indonesia, Singapore and Thailand under the Colombo Aid Plan. The balance have been delivered to New Zealand customers, mainly aero clubs and flying schools.

TYPE: Two-seat fully-aerobatic light monoplane.

WINGS: Cantilever low-wing monoplane. NACA 5 digit series wing sections. Thickness/chord ratio 12%. Dihedral 6°. Incidence 3° at root, 0° at tip. Taper 3° 26′ on leading-edge. Single-spar light alloy stressed-skin structure, foam-reinforced in tank bay. Glassfibre wingtips. Light alloy ailerons and flaps of NACA type, with fluted skins. Ailerons and flaps are interconnected by rod and mechanical linkages, so that both function simultaneously as ailerons and flaps. Adjustable trim tab on starboard aileron. Electrical actuation of flaps and trim optional.

FUSELAGE: All-metal stressed-skin semi-monocoque type. Glassfibre engine cowling. Split flap under fuselage.

TAIL UNIT: Cantilever light alloy structure. Ground-adjustable tabs on rudder and elevator. Control of rudder by rod and cable linkage, of elevator by rod and mechanical linkage.

LANDING GEAR: Non-retractable tricycle type. Cantilever spring steel main legs. Nosewheel is carried on coil spring and shock-absorber, and is steerable. All three wheels are fitted with Dunlop Australia wheels and tubeless tyres size 5·00-5. Tyre pressure 23 lb/sq in (1·62 kg/cm²) on main units, 16 lb/sq in (1·12 kg/cm²) on nose unit. Dunlop Australia single-disc dual hand-operated hydraulic brakes with parking lock. Landing gear designed to shear prior to any excess impact loading being transmitted to wing, to minimise structural damage in the event of a crash-landing.

POWER PLANT (Airtourer T3): One 130 hp Rolls-Royce Continental O-240-A four-cylinder horizontally-opposed aircooled engine, driving a McCauley fixed-pitch propeller. Fuel in single rubber bag tank centrally placed in wing, with usable capacity of 29 Imp gallons (132 litres). Refuelling point in side of fuselage above wing. Oil capacity 1·25 Imp gallons (5·7 litres).

POWER PLANT (Airtourer T4, T5 and T6): One 150 hp Lycoming O-320 four-cylinder horizontally-opposed aircooled engine (details given under model descriptions) driving a Sensenich two-blade fixed-pitch metal propeller (T4) or Hartzell two-blade constant-speed propeller (T5 and T6). Fuel tankage as for Airtourer T2. Oil capacity 1·75 Imp gallons (8 litres).

ACCOMMODATION: Two seats side by side in enclosed and soundproofed cabin, under rear-ward-sliding Perspex canopy. Dual controls. Heating and ventilation standard. Baggage compartment aft of seats with capacity of 100 lb (45 kg) and baggage tie-down provision.

SYSTEMS: Heating from engine muffler. Hydraulic system, pressure 700 lb/sq in (49 kg/cm²), for brakes. Engine-driven generator, 35A × 12V (24V on T6/24). Alternator fitted on Airtourer T4, T5 and T6.

ELECTRONICS AND EQUIPMENT: Optional equipment includes blind-flying instrumentation, Bendix or AWA Skyphone VHF, or AWA Skyranger HF radio, and Bendix ADF. Rotating beacon.

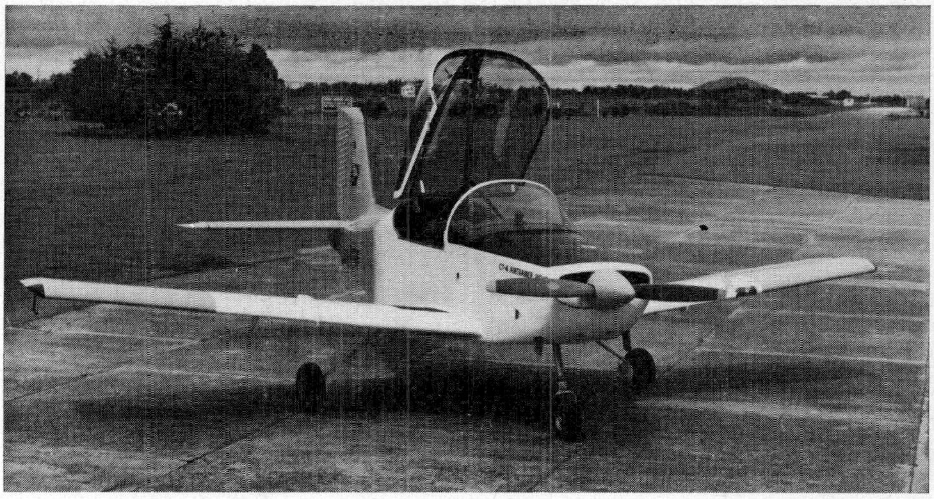

Aerospace Airtrainer CT/4 prototype (210 hp Continental IO-360-D six-cylinder engine)

DIMENSIONS, EXTERNAL:

Wing span	26 ft 0 in (7·92 m)
Wing chord at root	5 ft 9 in (1·75 m)
Wing chord at tip	3 ft 1⅞ in (0·96 m)
Wing aspect ratio	5·65
Length overall:	
T4	21 ft 5⅞ in (6·55 m)
T5, T6	22 ft 0 in (6·71 m)
Height overall	7 ft 0 in (2·13 m)
Max fuselage width	3 ft 5¾ in (1·06 m)
Tailplane span	10 ft 10 in (3·30 m)
Wheel track	9 ft 6 in (2·90 m)
Wheelbase	5 ft 0⅛ in (1·52 m)
Propeller diameter:	
T4, T5, T6	6 ft 0 in (1·83 m)

DIMENSIONS, INTERNAL:

Cabin: Length	5 ft 8 in (1·73 m)
Max width	3 ft 6 in (1·07 m)
Max height	4 ft 2 in (1·27 m)
Baggage space	8 cu ft (0·23 m³)

AREAS:

Wings, gross	120 sq ft (11·15 m²)
Full-span ailerons/flaps:	
as ailerons (total)	26·5 sq ft (2·46 m²)
as flaps (total)	30·5 sq ft (2·83 m²)
Fin	6·60 sq ft (0·61 m²)
Rudder, including tab	5·60 sq ft (0·52 m²)
Tailplane	17·20 sq ft (1·60 m²)
Elevator, including tab	13·80 sq ft (1·28 m²)

WEIGHTS AND LOADINGS:

Weight empty, equipped:	
T4	1,165 lb (528 kg)
T5	1,175 lb (532 kg)
T6/12	1,250 lb (567 kg)
T6/24	1,300 lb (589 kg)
Max T-O weight (Aerobatic):	
T3	1,550 lb (703 kg)
T4, T5	1,650 lb (748 kg)
T6	1,800 lb (816 kg)
Max T-O and landing weight (Normal):	
T3	1,650 lb (748 kg)
T4, T5	1,750 lb (793 kg)
T6	1,900 lb (862 kg)
Max wing loading:	
T4, T5	14·6 lb/sq ft (71·3 kg/m²)
T6	15·4 lb/sq ft (75·2 kg/m²)
Max power loading:	
T4, T5	11·7 lb/hp (5·31 kg/hp)
T6	12·3 lb/hp (5·58 kg/hp)

PERFORMANCE (at max T-O weight):

Max never-exceed speed (structural):	
T3	175 knots (202 mph; 325 km/h)
T4, T5, T6	176 knots (203 mph; 327 km/h)
Max level speed at S/L:	
T3	124 knots (143 mph; 230 km/h)
T4	130 knots (150 mph; 241 km/h)
T5, T6	142 knots (164 mph; 264 km/h)
Max cruising speed at 4,000 ft (1,220 m):	
T4	122 knots (140 mph; 225 km/h)
T5, T6	130 knots (150 mph; 241 km/h)
Econ cruising speed (60% power) at 5,000 ft (1,525 m):	
T3	98 knots (113 mph; 182 km/h)
T4	107 knots (123 mph; 198 km/h)
T5, T6	116 knots (134 mph; 216 km/h)
Stalling speed:	
T3	46 knots (53 mph; 85 km/h)
T4, T5, T6	49 knots (56 mph; 90 km/h)
Max rate of climb at S/L:	
T3	920 ft (280 m)/min
T4	980 ft (299 m)/min
T5	1,100 ft (335 m)/min
T6	1,150 ft (351 m)/min
Time to 10,000 ft (3,050 m):	
T4, T5, T6	11 min
Service ceiling:	
T3	14,000 ft (4,275 m)
T4	15,500 ft (4,725 m)
T5, T6	16,000 ft (4,875 m)
T-O run:	
T4	750 ft (229 m)
T5, T6	700 ft (213 m)
T-O to 50 ft (15 m):	
T4	1,350 ft (411 m)
T5, T6	1,380 ft (421 m)
Landing from 50 ft (15 m):	
T4	1,140 ft (347 m)
T5, T6	1,135 ft (346 m)
Landing run (all versions)	706 ft (215 m)
Range with max fuel, no allowances:	
T4	542 nm (625 miles; 1,005 km)
T5, T6	581 nm (670 miles; 1,075 km)

AEROSPACE AIRTRAINER CT/4

In 1967, Victa Ltd in Australia built and flew a prototype four-seat development of the Airtourer, known as the Aircruiser. This project was shelved when AESL purchased the Airtourer later that year, but AESL retained first option on the Aircruiser, and in mid-1971 purchased the latter project, including the Victa-built prototype. The project was brought to New Zealand, where AESL decided to manufacture a military trainer based on the original Victa Aircruiser.

The Victa aircraft was stressed only for flying between g limits of +3·8 and —1·5; AESL redesigned and restressed the aircraft to make it suitable for aerobatic flying with limits of +6 and —3g. The resulting military version, the Airtrainer CT/4, differs from the original Victa civil Aircruiser in having a hinged, clear-Perspex cockpit canopy; side-by-side seating for two persons, with an optional third seat at the rear; and stick-type (instead of wheel-type) control columns.

A prototype of the Airtrainer CT/4 (ZK-DGY) flew for the first time on 23 February 1972. In July 1972 it was announced by the Australian Minister of Defence that 37 Airtrainer CT/4s would be ordered for the Royal Australian Air Force, and this order was later confirmed. The Royal Thai Air Force has ordered 24 Airtrainers, the first of which was handed over on 23 October 1973; others have been ordered by the RNZAF (13). Enquiries have been received from several other countries in Europe, the Middle and Far East and South America. Deliveries to the Royal Thai Air Force were due to be completed by mid-1974, followed by the first deliveries to the RAAF.

TYPE: Two/three-seat fully-aerobatic light training aircraft.

WINGS: Cantilever low-wing monoplane. Wing section NACA 23012 (modified) at root, NACA 4412 (modified) at tip. Dihedral 6° 45′ at chord line. Incidence 3° at root, 0° at tip. Structure is similar in layout to that of Aircruiser, but with root chord increased by forward sweep of the inboard leading-edges. Single main spar light alloy stressed-skin structure, with glassfibre wingtips which are detachable to permit optional wingtip fuel tanks to be fitted. Single-slotted electrically-actuated flap and aerodynamically-balanced bottom-hinged aileron on each trailing-edge, of light alloy construction with fluted skins. No tabs.

FUSELAGE: All-metal stressed-skin semi-monocoque structure. Glassfibre engine cowling.

TAIL UNIT: Cantilever light alloy structure, with some aerodynamic balance. The one-piece elevator is also statically balanced. Ground-adjustable tab on rudder. Rudder controlled by rod and cable linkage, elevator by rod and mechanical linkage.

LANDING GEAR: Non-retractable tricycle type. Cantilever spring steel main legs. Nosewheel is carried on telescopic strut and oleo shock-absorber, and is steerable. Main units are fitted with Dunlop Australia wheels and tubeless tyres size 6·00-6; nosewheel is fitted with tubeless tyre size 5·00-5. Tyre pressure 23 lb/sq in (1·62 kg/cm²) on main units, 16 lb/sq in (1·12 kg/cm²) on nose unit. Dunlop Australia single-disc toe-operated hydraulic brakes, with hand-operated parking lock. Landing gear designed to shear prior to any excess impact loading being transmitted to wing, to minimise structural damage in the event of a crash landing.

POWER PLANT: One 210 hp Continental IO-360-H six-cylinder horizontally-opposed aircooled engine standard, driving a Hartzell HC-C2YF-1 two-blade metal constant-speed propeller. Total fuel capacity 45 Imp gallons (204·5 litres). Wingtip tanks, each of 17 Imp gallons (77 litres) capacity, available optionally. 200 hp Lycoming IO-360-B four-cylinder engine available optionally.

ACCOMMODATION: Two seats side by side under hinged, fully-transparent Perspex canopy. Space to rear for optional third seat or 115 lb (52 kg) of baggage or equipment. Dual controls standard.

DIMENSIONS, EXTERNAL:
Wing span 26 ft 0 in (7·92 m)
Span over tip-tanks 26 ft 11 in (8·20 m)
Wing chord at root 7 ft 1¼ in (2·17 m)
Wing chord at tip 3 ft 2½ in (0·98 m)
Wing aspect ratio 5·25
Length overall 23 ft 2 in (7·06 m)
Height overall 8 ft 6 in (2·59 m)
Fuselage: Max width 3 ft 8 in (1·12 m)
Max depth 4 ft 7¼ in (1·40 m)
Tailplane span 10 ft 10 in (3·30 m)
Wheel track 9 ft 9 in (2·97 m)
Wheelbase 5 ft 7½ in (1·71 m)
Propeller diameter 6 ft 4 in (1·93 m)
Propeller ground clearance 1 ft 5 in (0·43 m)

DIMENSIONS, INTERNAL:
Cabin: Length 9 ft 0 in (2·74 m)
Max width 3 ft 6½ in (1·08 m)
Max height 4 ft 5 in (1·35 m)

AREAS:
Wings, gross 129·0 sq ft (12·0 m^2)
Ailerons (total) 9·24 sq ft (0·86 m^2)
Flaps (total) 22·60 sq ft (2·10 m^2)
Fin 6·43 sq ft (0·60 m^2)
Rudder, incl tab 6·26 sq ft (0·58 m^2)
Tailplane 15·50 sq ft (1·44 m^2)
Elevator, incl tab 13·60 sq ft (1·26 m^2)

WEIGHTS AND LOADINGS:
Basic weight empty 1,460 lb (662 kg)
Weight empty, equipped 1,490 lb (675 kg)
Max T-O weight 2,400 lb (1,088 kg)
Max wing loading 18·6 lb/sq ft (90·8 kg/m^2)
Max power loading (IO-360-H) 11·43 lb/hp (5·18 kg/hp)

PERFORMANCE (at T-O weight of 2,350 lb; 1,066 kg, ISA, 210 hp engine):
Max never-exceed speed 230 knots (265 mph; 426 km/h)
Max level speed at S/L 155 knots (178 mph; 286 km/h)
Max level speed at 10,000 ft (3,050 m) 142 knots (163 mph; 262 km/h)
Cruising speed at S/L:
75% power 140 knots (161 mph; 259 km/h)
65% power 129 knots (149 mph; 240 km/h)
55% power 118 knots (136 mph; 219 km/h)
Cruising speed at 10,000 ft (3,050 m):
75% power 125 knots (144 mph; 232 km/h)
Stalling speed at S/L:
flaps up 56 knots (64 mph; 103 km/h)
flaps down 44·5 knots (50·7 mph; 82 km/h)
Stalling speed at 10,000 ft (3,050 m):
flaps up 65·5 knots (75 mph; 121 km/h)
flaps down 51·5 knots (59 mph; 95 km/h)
Max rate of climb at S/L 1,350 ft (411 m)/min
Time to altitude of:
3,000 ft (915 m) 2 min 31 sec
5,000 ft (1,525 m) 4 min 36 sec
10,000 ft (3,050 m) 11 min 40 sec
Service ceiling 17,900 ft (5,455 m)
T-O run 733 ft (224 m)
T-O to 50 ft (15 m) 1,237 ft (377 m)
Landing from 50 ft (15 m) 1,100 ft (335 m)
Landing run 510 ft (155 m)
Max range at S/L at 102·5 knots (118 mph; 190 km/h) 767 nm (884 miles; 1,422 km)
Range with 10% reserves (without tip-tanks):
75% power at S/L 595 nm (686 miles; 1,104 km)
75% power at 5,000 ft (1,525 m) 686 nm (790 miles; 1,271 km)
55% power at S/L 645 nm (743 miles; 1,195 km)
65% power at 5,000 ft (1,525 m) 707 nm (815 miles; 1,311 km)
Max endurance with 10% reserves (without tip-tanks):
75% power at S/L 4 hr 15 min
75% power at 5,000 ft (1,525 m) 5 hr 10 min
55% power at S/L 5 hr 28 min
65% power at 5,000 ft (1,525 m) 5 hr 47 min
g limits +6; —3

AEROSPACE AIRCRUISER CT/2

The Aircruiser CT/2 development of the Airtrainer CT/4 differed from the military version primarily in having a four-seat cabin, with a large door on each side, and a wheel-type control column. Like the Airtrainer CT/4, it was to be powered by a 210 hp Continental IO-360 six-cylinder engine, and had 46 Imp gallons (209 litres) fuel capacity. A non-aerobatic prototype (ZK-DAH) was flown in 1972, and was described in the 1973-74 *Jane's*. This programme is no longer active.

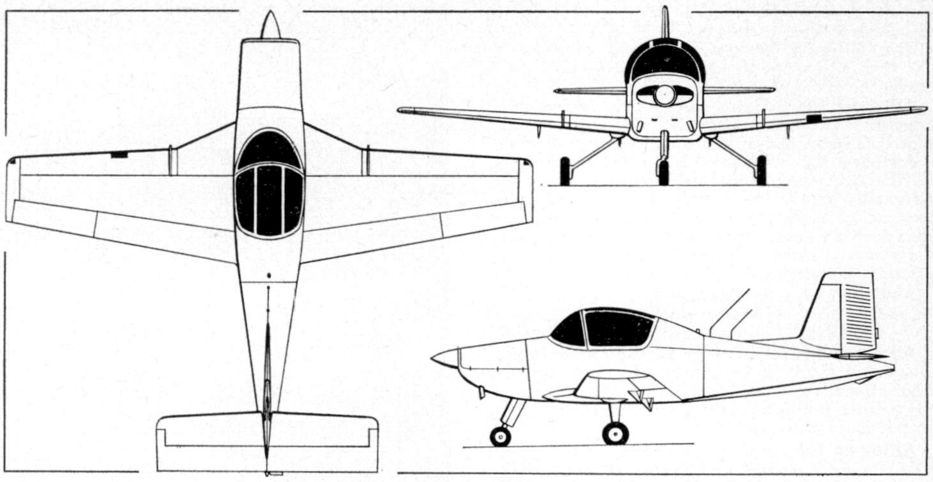

Airtrainer CT/4 two/three-seat aerobatic trainer (*Pilot Press*)

AEROSPACE FLETCHER FU-24 and FU-24-950

The FU-24 was developed by the Sargent-Fletcher Company of El Monte, California, initially for agricultural top-dressing work in New Zealand. The prototype flew in July 1954, followed by the first production aircraft five months later. All manufacturing and sales rights for the FU-24 were acquired by Air Parts (NZ) Ltd in 1964, and production was undertaken subsequently in this company's factory at Hamilton Airport, New Zealand.

The initial production series of 100 was delivered to New Zealand operators for top-dressing work. By February 1974, a total of 190 Fletcher aircraft had been produced, including some for customers in Australia, India, the Pacific Islands, South America and Thailand.

With the availability of piston engines of greater power, Air Parts developed higher-powered versions of the Fletcher FU-24, and there are two current piston-engined models, as follows:

FU-24. Standard agricultural version, with 300 hp Rolls-Royce Continental IO-520-F engine.

FU-24-950. Agricultural version with 400 hp Lycoming IO-720 engine.

In addition, Air Parts developed utility cargo/passenger versions, and three turboprop-engined versions of the FU-24, the latest of which is listed separately.

The following description applies to the standard FU-24 and 400 hp FU-24-950:

TYPE: General utility cabin monoplane.

WINGS: Cantilever low-wing monoplane. NACA 4415 wing section. Dihedral (outer wings) 8°. Incidence 2°. All-metal two-spar structure. All-metal plain-hinged ailerons. All-metal slotted flaps.

FUSELAGE: All-metal semi-monocoque structure. Cockpit area stressed for 18*g* impact.

TAIL UNIT: Cantilever all-metal structure. All-movable horizontal tail with anti-servo tab.

LANDING GEAR: Non-retractable tricycle type, with steerable nosewheel. Fletcher air-oil shock-absorber struts. Cleveland wheels and hydraulic disc brakes on main units. Goodyear tyres, size 8·50-6 (6-ply), pressure range 11-30 lb/sq in (0·77-2·11 kg/cm^2). Wheel fairings optional.

POWER PLANT (FU-24): One 300 hp Rolls-Royce Continental IO-520-F six-cylinder horizontally-opposed aircooled engine, driving a McCauley two-blade constant-speed variable-pitch metal propeller. Fuel tank in each wing-root leading-edge, with total usable capacity of 44 US gallons (166 litres).

POWER PLANT (FU-24-950): One 400 hp Lycoming IO-720-A1A eight-cylinder horizontally-opposed aircooled engine, driving a Hartzell HC-C3YR-1R/8475R three-blade constant-speed variable-pitch metal propeller. Fuel tanks in wing leading-edges; total usable capacity 67 US gallons (253 litres).

ACCOMMODATION (Agricultural models): Enclosed cockpit for pilot and one passenger on side-by-side seats under rearward-sliding canopy. Optional equipment includes large cargo door on port side, additional cargo floor area, small rear door, and dual controls.

ACCOMMODATION (Utility models): Enclosed cabin for pilot and up to five passengers in FU-24 or seven in FU-24-950, or equivalent freight. Dual controls optional. Rearward-sliding hood over front two seats. Large passenger/cargo door on port side.

AGRICULTURAL EQUIPMENT: Hopper outlets for spreading of solids (fertiliser, dry ice, poison bait, etc). Transland Swathmaster for top-dressing, seeding and high-volume spraying. Transland Boommaster for liquid spraying with booms, nozzles, fan-driven pump, etc, for low- and high-volume spraying. Micronair spraying equipment with electrically- or fan-driven pump, varied control systems, side-loading valve for liquids, and special adaptor plate for interchangeability of equipment.

GENERAL OPTIONAL EQUIPMENT (all models): Full blind-flying instrumentation with ADF, VHF, VOR and DME. Full dual controls; dual main wheels and brakes, wheel and leg fairings; long-range fuel tanks.

DIMENSIONS, EXTERNAL:
Wing span 42 ft 0 in (12·81 m)
Wing chord (constant) 7 ft 0 in (2·13 m)
Wing aspect ratio 6
Length overall:
FU-24 31 ft 10 in (9·69 m)
FU-24-950 32 ft 9 in (9·98 m)
Height over tail 9 ft 4 in (2·84 m)
Tailplane span 13 ft 9½ in (4·20 m)
Wheel track 12 ft 2 in (3·71 m)
Wheelbase 7 ft 6 in (2·28 m)
Propeller diameter 7 ft 2 in (2·18 m)
Passenger/cargo door (port, rear):
Height 3 ft 2 in (0·97 m)
Width 3 ft 1 in (0·94 m)
Optional small cargo door (rear):
Height 1 ft 5¼ in (0·44 m)
Width 2 ft 6 in (0·76 m)

DIMENSIONS, INTERNAL:
Cabin: Length 10 ft 5 in (3·18 m)
Max width 4 ft 0 in (1·22 m)

Fletcher FU-24-950 (400 hp Lycoming IO-720 engine) in service at Hokitika Airport, South Island, New Zealand (*Brian M. Service*)

Max height 4 ft 2 in (1·27 m)
Floor area 41·7 sq ft (3·87 m²)

AREAS:
Wings, gross 294 sq ft (27·31 m²)
Ailerons (total) 19·6 sq ft (1·82 m²)
Trailing-edge flaps (total) 34·0 sq ft (3·16 m²)
Fin 13·6 sq ft (1·26 m²)
Rudder 6·9 sq ft (0·64 m²)
Tailplane 43·1 sq ft (4·00 m²)
Tailplane tab 4·9 sq ft (0·45 m²)

WEIGHTS AND LOADINGS (A: FU-24; B: FU-24-950):
Weight empty, equipped:
A 2,210 lb (1,002 kg)
B 2,616 lb (1,186 kg)
Max payload (agricultural):
A 1,870 lb (848 kg)
B 2,320 lb (1,052 kg)
Normal max T-O weight:
A 4,000 lb (1,814 kg)
B 4,860 lb (2,204 kg)
Special T-O weight:
A 4,470 lb (2,027 kg)
B 5,430 lb (2,463 kg)
Cabin floor loading:
A, B 386 lb/sq ft (1,885 kg/m²)
Normal wing loading:
A 13·7 lb/sq ft (66·8 kg/m²)
B 16·5 lb/sq ft (80·6 kg/m²)
Normal power loading:
A 13·3 lb/hp (6·03 kg/hp)
B 12·2 lb/hp (5·53 kg/hp)

PERFORMANCE (at normal max T-O weight. A: FU-24; B: FU-24-950):
Max never-exceed speed:
A, B 143 knots (165 mph; 265 km/h)
Max level speed at S/L:
A 114 knots (131 mph; 211 km/h)
B 126 knots (145 mph; 233 km/h)
Max cruising speed (75% power):
A 97 knots (112 mph; 180 km/h)
B 106 knots (122 mph; 196 km/h)
Stalling speed:
A, B 42 knots (48 mph; 77 km/h)
Max rate of climb at S/L:
A 625 ft (190 m)/min
B 630 ft (192 m)/min
Service ceiling:
A, B 16,000 ft (4,875 m)
T-O run:
A 500 ft (152 m)
B 930 ft (283 m)
T-O to 50 ft (15 m):
A 920 ft (280 m)
B 1,610 ft (491 m)
Landing from 50 ft (15 m):
A 900 ft (275 m)
B 1,340 ft (408 m)
Landing run:
A 500 ft (152 m)
B 720 ft (219 m)
Range with max fuel:
A 322 nm (371 miles; 597 km)
B 382 nm (440 miles; 708 km)

AEROSPACE FLETCHER 1284

Air Parts developed three turboprop-powered versions of the Fletcher FU-24. Of these, the Fletcher 1060 (500 shp PT6A-20 engine) and Fletcher 1160 (530 shp TPE 331 engine) were described in the 1969-70, 1970-71 and 1971-72 editions of *Jane's*.

The third version, designated Fletcher 1284, was powered by a 665 shp AiResearch TPE 331 turboprop engine and was first flown in early 1970.

Only one Fletcher 1284 was built; a description of this appeared in the 1973-74 *Jane's*.

BARR

BARR BROTHERS LTD

ADDRESS:
22-24 Kitchener Street, PO Box 2367, Auckland

MANAGING DIRECTOR:
J. T. Barr

Barr Brothers Ltd, an agricultural operating company, and Marine Helicopters Ltd have formed jointly an associate company known as Flight Engineers Ltd to provide servicing facilities for the two operating companies. As an extension to this business it was decided to undertake the licence assembly in New Zealand of the Transavia Airtruk.

By late May 1973 Flight Engineers Ltd had assembled three of these aircraft, with a fourth nearly complete and a further eight kits to be supplied from Australia by the end of 1973. Arrangements were in hand at that time for Transavia to supply wing and centre-section jigs so that the PL-12 could be built almost entirely in New Zealand, in addition to Australian production by Transavia. At present only the PL-12 agricultural version is being built in New Zealand, but the PL-12-U is not ruled out if a requirement for this version is established.

One of the Transavia Airtruk agricultural aircraft assembled in New Zealand by Flight Engineers Ltd

PAKISTAN

PAKISTAN ARMY AVIATION (No. 503 WORKSHOP)

ADDRESS:
Dhamial, near Rawalpindi, Western Punjab

Two types of aircraft are currently being manufactured at the Dhamial base of the Pakistan Army Aviation, which accommodates, besides No. 503 Workshop, the Army Aviation School and three operational PAA squadrons.

The Pakistan Army received about 60 Cessna O-1 Bird Dog observation and liaison aircraft from the US in the 1950s, and a substantial proportion of these are still in service. Based on its experience of repairing and overhauling these aircraft, and taking advantage of a substantial quantity of spares, the No. 503 Workshop is now manufacturing, apparently without a licence, new-production O-1s for the PAA, at an approximate rate of one per month. About 60% of the components of each aircraft are manufactured locally.

The Workshop is, in addition, manufacturing at about the same rate the Aérospatiale Alouette III helicopter, for which the Pakistan Army originally placed an order in 1968. An initial quantity of French-built Alouette IIIs was followed by the supply of knock-down kits for assembly in Pakistan, and domestically-built examples are currently being supplied to all three branches of the Pakistan armed forces.

Aérospatiale Alouette III helicopter built in Pakistan (*John Fricker*)

Cessna O-1 Bird Dog built at No. 503 Workshop (*John Fricker*)

POLAND

PZL

POLSKIE ZAKLADY LOTNICZE, ZJEDNOCZENIE PRZEMYSLU LOTNICZEGO I SILNIKOWEGO PZL (Polish Aviation Works, Aircraft and Engine Industry Union)

HEAD OFFICE:
ul. Miodowa 5, 00251 Warsaw
Telephone: Warsaw 279985
Telex: 814281

GENERAL MANAGER:
Ing Andrzej Jedynak

VICE-DIRECTORS:
Ing Zbigniew Pawlak (Research and Development)
Ing Kazimierz Brejnak (Technical)
Dr Józef Jablonski (Sales)

The Polish aircraft industry is under the central direction of the Zjednoczenie Przemyslu Lotniczego i Silnikowego PZL (Aircraft and Engine Industry Union).

The principal factories concerned with aircraft manufacture are the WSK-Mielec, WSK-Okecie and WSK-Swidnik. Other Polish factories, engaged in the production of sailplanes and aero-engines, are listed in the relevant sections of this edition.

The Polish aircraft industry manufactures the Soviet Antonov An-2 utility biplane under licence, and is responsible for development and production of the Mil Mi-2 turbine-powered helicopter. Several aircraft of Polish origin are also in production.

The export sales of all Polish aviation products are handled by PEZETEL Foreign Trade Enterprise, whose address is given below.

PEZETEL

PEZETEL Foreign Trade Enterprise

ADDRESS:
ul. Przemyslowa 26, 00450 Warsaw
Telephone: Warsaw 285071
Telex: 813430

GENERAL MANAGER: Dr Józef Jablonski
SALES MANAGER: Janusz Meder
PUBLIC RELATIONS MANAGER:
Wojciech Kielanowski

This organisation is the trade representative of the Polish aviation industry for foreign markets.

IL

INSTYTUT LOTNICTWA (Aeronautical Institute)

ADDRESS:
Al. Krakowska 110/114, 02-256 Warsaw-Okecie
Telephone: Warsaw 460993
Telex: 813537

MANAGING DIRECTOR: Ing Zbigniew Pawlak
SCIENTIFIC DIRECTOR: Dr Czeslaw Skoczylas
CHIEF OF TECHNICAL INFORMATION DIVISION:
Dipl Ing Andrzej Glass

The Instytut Lotnictwa was founded in 1926. It belongs to the PZL Polish Aviation Works group, under the general management of the PZL Aircraft and Engine Industry Union. The IL is responsible for the control of all research and development work in the Polish aircraft industry. It conducts scientific research, including the investigation of problems associated with low-speed and high-speed aerodynamics, static and fatigue tests, development and testing of aero-engines, flight instruments and other equipment, flight tests, and materials technology. It is also responsible for the construction of experimental aircraft and aero-engines. Descriptions of two of the IL's latest experimental aircraft follow:

IL WINGED SM-1

For research purposes, the IL modified and flight tested a winged version of the SM-1 (licence-built Mil Mi-1) helicopter, shown in an accompanying illustration.

A description of the standard SM-1W appeared in the 1966-67 *Jane's*. The winged version had an NACA 23015 wing section, a span of 25 ft 6¼ in (7·78 m) and a wing area of 73·2 sq ft (6·80 m^2). The wings' angle of incidence was adjustable.

The winged SM-1 helicopter developed and flight tested by the Instytut Lotnictwa in Poland

IL LALA-1

As a part of the Polish aircraft industry's general programme for the future development of specialised agricultural aircraft, the Instytut Lotnictwa conducted experiments to determine the feasibility of producing a gas-turbine-engined aircraft for this role. For this purpose it completed a testbed aircraft, known as the Lala-1 (Latajace Laboratorium-1: Flying Laboratory-1), by modifying a WSK-Mielec-built Antonov An-2R agricultural biplane (serial number 12832). This aircraft is also used to test agricultural equipment designed for the WSK-Mielec M-15 (which see).

The Lala-1 retains unaltered the existing An-2 installation of a 1,000 hp Shvetsov ASh-62IR radial piston engine driving an AW-2 four-blade variable-pitch metal propeller. In addition, it is fitted with a 3,306 lb (1,500 kg) st Ivchenko AI-25 turbofan engine, mounted behind the crew compartment. The air intake duct for this engine is mounted centrally on the starboard side of the fuselage, between the wings.

The major modifications to the An-2R airframe were described in the 1973-74 *Jane's*. Design work began in June 1971, and the Lala-1 made its first flight on 10 February 1972, with only the piston engine operating; first flight with both engines operating was made on 26 April 1972.

IL Lala-1 experimental aircraft, based on the airframe of the An-2R agricultural biplane

DIMENSIONS, EXTERNAL:

Wing span:	
upper	59 ft 7¾ in (18·18 m)
lower	46 ft 8½ in (14·24 m)
Length overall:	
tail up	40 ft 0¼ in (12·20 m)
tail down	40 ft 8¼ in (12·40 m)
Height overall:	
tail up	20 ft 7¾ in (6·29 m)
tail down	13 ft 1½ in (4·00 m)
Tailplane span	23 ft 7½ in (7·20 m)
Wheel track	11 ft 3¾ in (3·45 m)
Wheelbase	14 ft 9¼ in (4·50 m)

WEIGHTS:

Weight empty, without agricultural equipment	9,788 lb (4,440 kg)
Max T-O weight	12,125 lb (5,500 kg)
Max landing weight	11,574 lb (5,250 kg)

PERFORMANCE (at AUW of 12,125 lb; 5,500 kg, both engines operating, except where indicated):

Max never-exceed speed	107·5 knots (124 mph; 200 km/h)
Max level speed at S/L	97 knots (112 mph; 180 km/h)
Min flying speed	65 knots (75 mph; 120 km/h)
Stalling speed, flaps down, power on	32·5 knots (37·5 mph; 60 km/h)
Max rate of climb at S/L:	
both engines	1,378 ft (420 m)/min
ASh-62 engine only	196 ft (60 m)/min
Time to 14,760 ft (4,500 m)	approx 10 min
T-O run, on grass	525 ft (160 m)
T-O to 50 ft (15 m)	885 ft (270 m)
Landing from 50 ft (15 m)	1,510 ft (460 m)
Landing run	690 ft (210 m)
Max range, without chemical payload	237 nm (273 miles; 440 km)
Operating time, with 881 lb (400 kg) of chemical	20 min

WSK-MIELEC

WYTWORNIA SPRZETU KOMUNIKACYJNEGO-MIELEC (Transport Equipment Manufacturing Centre, Mielec)

HEAD OFFICE AND WORKS: 39-300 Mielec
Telephone: Mielec 20
Telex: 83214 *and* 83293

GENERAL MANAGER:
Dipl Ing Tadeusz Ryczaj

Largest and best-equipped aircraft factory in Poland, the WSK at Mielec was engaged mainly on licence production of MiG single-seat jet fighters for several years. These aircraft carry the Polish designation of LiM, meaning Licence MiG.

It is believed that, after completion of the production order for LiM-5s (MiG-17s) for the Polish Air Force, licence production of MiG fighters ceased in Poland in about 1959.

Following a reduction in orders for combat aircraft in 1955, Mielec began production in 1956 of the TS-8 Bies basic trainer, described in the 1962-63 *Jane's*. Four years later, the Soviet-designed An-2 general utility biplane went into production at Mielec. In parallel production with the An-2 at the present time is the TS-11 Iskra jet trainer.

There is a design office at the factory for development of original aircraft. Its latest known product is the M-15 agricultural aircraft.

WSK-MIELEC (ANTONOV) An-2

NATO code name: "Colt"

The prototype of this large biplane was designed to a specification of the Ministry of Agriculture and Forestry of the USSR and made its first flight on 31 August 1947. It was powered by a 760 hp ASh-21 engine and was known as the SKh-1 (Selskokhozyaistvennyi-1: agricultural-economic-1). This designation was dropped subsequently and in 1948 the design went into production in the USSR as the An-2, with a 1,000 hp ASh-62 engine.

By 1960, more than 5,000 An-2s had been built in the Soviet Union for service with the Soviet armed forces, Aeroflot and other civilian organisations, and the various Soviet-built versions have been fully described in previous editions of *Jane's*. Many were exported, to all of the Socialist States, and to Greece, Afghanistan, Mali, Nepal, India and Cuba, and licence rights were granted to China, where the first locally-produced An-2 was completed in December 1957.

Since 1960, apart from a small Soviet-built quantity of a developed version known as the An-2M, the continued production of the An-2 has been the responsibility of the Polish WSK factory at Mielec. The first 10 Polish-built An-2s were completed in 1960, and WSK-Mielec has since built considerable numbers of this aircraft for domestic use and for export to the USSR, Bulgaria, Czechoslovakia, the German Democratic Republic, Hungary, North Korea, Romania and Yugoslavia. The 5,000th Polish-built An-2 was delivered to the USSR on 3 February 1973.

By the beginning of 1974 more than 6,000 An-2s (all versions) had been built at Mielec, including 3,300 of the An-2R agricultural version. More than 90 per cent of these were for export, chiefly to the USSR.

The Polish-built versions have different designations from those built in the USSR. These are as follows:

An-2T. Basic general-purpose version, with accommodation for 12 passengers and baggage or 3,306 lb (1,500 kg) of cargo.

An-2TP. Cargo/passenger version, similar to An-2T but with full standard of comfort for passengers.

An-2P. Passenger version, with seating for 12 adult passengers and two children. Compared with Soviet-built An-2P (see 1971-72 *Jane's*) has improvements in passenger cabin layout and comfort, better soundproofing, a new propeller and spinner, and weight-saving instrumentation and equipment. Entered production in 1968.

An-2TD. Paratroop transport and training version. Granted French type certificate No. IM-55 (for import licence) in 1972.

An-2S. Ambulance version, equipped to carry six stretcher patients and their medical attendants.

An-2R. Agricultural version, with 2,976 lb (1,350 kg) capacity hopper or tank for dry or liquid chemicals. Similar to Soviet-built An-2S. One aircraft converted to IL Lala-1 (which see) in 1971 as testbed for M-15 agricultural aircraft. Modernisation of agricultural equipment under way.

An-2M. Twin-float version of An-2T, similar to Soviet-built An-2V.

The following details apply to the WSK-Mielec An-2P:

TYPE: Single-engined general-purpose biplane.

WINGS: Unequal-span single-bay biplane. Wing section RPS 14% (constant). Dihedral, both wings, approx 2° 48′. All-metal two-spar structure, fabric-covered aft of front spar. I-type interplane struts. Differential ailerons and full-span automatic leading-edge slots on upper wings, slotted flaps on both upper and lower wings. Flaps operated electrically, ailerons mechanically by cables and push/pull rods. Electrically-operated trim tab in port aileron.

FUSELAGE: **All-metal stressed-skin semi-monocoque structure of circular section forward of cabin, rectangular in the cabin section and oval in the tail section.**

TAIL UNIT: **Braced metal structure. Fin integral with rear fuselage. Fabric-covered tailplane.** Elevators and rudder operated mechanically by cables and push/pull rods. Electrically-operated trim tab in rudder and port elevator.

LANDING GEAR: Non-retractable split-axle type, with long-stroke oleo shock-absorbers. Main wheel tyres size 800 × 260 mm, pressure 32·7 lb/sq in (2·3 kg/cm²). Pneumatic shoe brakes on main units. Fully-castoring and self-centering tailwheel with electro-pneumatic lock. For rough-field operation the oleo-pneumatic shock-absorbers can be charged from a compressed air cylinder installed in the rear fuselage. Interchangeable ski landing gear available optionally.

POWER PLANT: One 1,000 hp Shvetsov ASh-62IR nine-cylinder radial aircooled engine, driving an AW-2 four-blade variable-pitch metal propeller. Six fuel tanks in upper wings, with total capacity of 264 Imp gallons (1,200 litres). Oil capacity 26·4 Imp gallons (120 litres).

ACCOMMODATION: Crew of two on flight deck, with access via passenger cabin. Standard accommodation for 12 passengers, in four rows of three with centre aisle. Two foldable seats for children in aisle between first and second rows, and infant's cradle at front of cabin on starboard side. Toilet at rear of cabin on starboard side. Overhead racks for up to 352 lb (160 kg) of baggage, with space for coats and additional 88 lb (40 kg) of baggage between rear pair of seats and toilet. Walls of cabin are lined with glass-wool mats and inner facing of plywood to reduce internal noise level. Cabin floor is carpeted. Cabin heating and starboard windscreen de-icing by engine bleed air; port and centre windscreens are electrically de-iced. Cabin ventilation by ram-air intakes on underside of top wings.

WSK-Mielec (Antonov) An-2P 12-seat passenger transport aircraft

SYSTEMS: Compressed air cylinder, of 490 cu in (8 litres) capacity, for pneumatic charging of shock-absorbers and operation of tailwheel lock at 711 lb/sq in (50 kg/cm²) pressure and operation of main-wheel brakes at 142 lb/sq in (10 kg/cm²). Contents of cylinder are maintained by AK-50 M engine-driven compressor, with AD-50 automatic relief device to prevent overpressure. DC electrical system is supplied with basic 27V power (and 36V or 115V where required) by an engine-driven generator and a storage battery. CO_2 fire extinguishing system with automatic fire detector.

ELECTRONICS AND EQUIPMENT: Dual controls and blind-flying instrumentation standard. R-842 short wave and R-860 ultra short wave lightweight radio transceivers, RW-UM radio altimeter, ARK-9 radio compass, MRP-56P marker, GIK-1 gyro compass, GPK-48 gyroscopic direction indicator and SPU-7 intercom.

DIMENSIONS, EXTERNAL:
Wing span:
upper 59 ft 8½ in (18·18 m)
lower 46 ft 8½ in (14·24 m)
Wing chord (constant):
upper 7 ft 10½ in (2·40 m)
lower 6 ft 6¾ in (2·00 m)
Wing aspect ratio:
upper 7·57
lower 7·12
Wing gap 7 ft 1½ in (2·17 m)
Length overall:
tail up 41 ft 9½ in (12·74 m)
tail down 40 ft 8¼ in (12·40 m)
Height overall:
tail up 20 ft 0 in (6·10 m)
tail down 13 ft 1½ in (4·00 m)
Tailplane span 23 ft 7½ in (7·20 m)
Wheel track 11 ft 3¾ in (3·45 m)
Wheelbase 11 ft 0¼ in (3·36 m)
Propeller diameter 11 ft 9¾ in (3·60 m)
Propeller ground clearance 2 ft 3½ in (0·70 m)

AREAS:
Wings, gross:
upper 469 sq ft (43·6 m²)
lower 301 sq ft (28·0 m²)
Ailerons (total) 63·5 sq ft (5·90 m²)
Flaps (total) 103 sq ft (9·60 m²)
Fin 62·97 sq ft (5·85 m²)
Rudder, incl tab 28·52 sq ft (2·65 m²)
Tailplane 132·18 sq ft (12·28 m²)
Elevators (total, incl tab) 50·81 sq ft (4·72 m²)

WEIGHTS AND LOADINGS:
Weight empty 7,605 lb (3,450 kg)
Max T-O weight 12,125 lb (5,500 kg)
Max landing weight 11,574 lb (5,250 kg)
Max wing loading 15·7 lb/sq ft (76·82 kg/m²)
Max power loading 12·13 lb/hp (5·5 kg/hp)

PERFORMANCE (at AUW of 11,574 lb; 5,250 kg):
Max level speed at 5,740 ft (1,750 m)
139 knots (160 mph; 258 km/h)
Econ cruising speed
100 knots (115 mph; 185 km/h)
Min flying speed 49 knots (56 mph; 90 km/h)
T-O speed 43 knots (50 mph; 80 km/h)
Landing speed 46 knots (53 mph; 85 km/h)
Max rate of climb at S/L 689 ft (210 m)/min
Service ceiling 14,425 ft (4,400 m)
Time to 14,425 ft (4,400 m) 30 min
T-O run:
hard runway 492 ft (150 m)
grass 558 ft (170 m)
T-O to 35 ft (10·7 m):
hard runway 984 ft (300 m)
grass 1,050 ft (320 m)
Landing run:
hard runway 558 ft (170 m)
grass 607 ft (185 m)
Range at 3,280 ft (1,000 m) with 1,102 lb (500 kg) payload 485 nm (560 miles; 900 km)

TS-11 ISKRA (SPARK)

Developed by the OKL under the supervision of Docent Ing T. Soltyk, the TS-11 Iskra two-seat jet trainer was produced as a replacement for the piston-engined TS-8 Bies. The prototype, built at the WSK Warsaw-Okecie, began flight trials on 5 February 1960. Quantity production commenced at the WSK-Mielec in 1962. The formal handing over of the first Iskra for service with the Polish Air Force took place in March 1963. Early production aircraft were powered by a 1,760 lb (800 kg) st Type HO-10 Polish-designed axial-flow turbojet engine. Several hundred Iskras had been built by 1973, and production continues. A version with underwing armament pods is designated **Iskra 100.**

In September 1964 an Iskra set up four international records in Class C-1-d, by achieving speeds of 452·7 knots (521·33 mph; 839 km/h) over a 15/25 km course, 386·2 knots (444·71 mph; 715·691 km/h) over a 100 km closed circuit and 394·3 knots (454·03 mph; 730·701 km/h) over a 500 km closed circuit, and a distance of 275·3 nm (317·02 miles; 510·194 km) in a closed circuit.

The following description applies to the current production versions:

TYPE: Fully aerobatic jet primary and basic trainer.

WINGS: Cantilever mid-wing monoplane. Wing section NACA 64209 at root, NACA 64009 at tip. Sweepback at quarter-chord 7°. Marked dihedral. All-metal torsion-box structure with steel main spar and duralumin stressed skin. Hydraulically-servo-assisted ailerons. Two-section double-slotted flaps and airbrakes fitted. One boundary layer fence on each wing.

FUSELAGE: All-metal semi-monocoque structure of pod and boom type.

TAIL UNIT: Cantilever all-metal structure. Fin integral with fuselage. Mass- and aerodynamically-balanced elevators and rudder.

LANDING GEAR: Retractable tricycle type with single wheel on each unit. Nosewheel retracts

WSK-Mielec TS-11 Iskra 100 two-seat jet trainer, armed version with 23 mm nose cannon and underwing practice bombs and rockets

forward, main wheels inward into wing-root air intake trunks. Hydraulic retraction. Main wheels size 600 × 180, tyre pressure 78 lb/sq in (5·5 kg/cm^2). Nosewheel size 400 × 150, tyre pressure 50 lb/sq in (3·5 kg/cm^2). AMG-10 oleo-pneumatic shock-absorbers. Anti-shimmy nosewheel.

Power Plant: One SO-3 turbojet, rated at 2,205 lb (1,000 kg) st, mounted in fuselage aft of cockpit, with nozzle under tailboom. Fuel in two 69 Imp gallon (315 litre) integral wing tanks, one 110 Imp gallon (500 litre) fuselage main tank and one 15·4 Imp gallon (70 litre) fuselage collector tank. Total fuel capacity 264 Imp gallons (1,200 litres).

Accommodation: Crew of two in tandem on lightweight ejection seats, under a one-piece hydraulically-actuated rearward-hinged jettisonable canopy. Cockpit pressurised and air-conditioned. Rear seat slightly raised.

Systems: Hydraulic system pressure 2,000 lb/sq in (140 kg/cm^2). Pneumatic system pressure 1,710 lb/sq in (120 kg/cm^2). 28V electrical system, with 28Ah battery.

Electronics and Equipment: Complete dual controls and instrumentation, including blind-flying panels. R/T, intercom and oxygen equipment standard. Position and homing indicator.

Armament (Iskra 100): Forward-firing 23 mm cannon in nose on starboard side, with gun camera. Four attachments for a variety of underwing stores, including bombs of up to 110 lb (50 kg) and rockets.

Dimensions, external:
Wing span 33 ft 0¼ in (10·07 m)
Wing chord at root 7 ft 4¾ in (2·254 m)
Wing chord at tip 3 ft 9¾ in (1·162 m)
Wing aspect ratio 5·71
Length overall 36 ft 10¾ in (11·25 m)
Height overall 10 ft 8 in (3·25 m)
Tailplane span 12 ft 7¼ in (3·84 m)
Wheel track 11 ft 5 in (3·48 m)
Wheelbase 11 ft 3½ in (3·44 m)

Areas:
Wings, gross 188·37 sq ft (17·5 m^2)
Ailerons (total) 16·15 sq ft (1·50 m^2)
Trailing-edge flaps (total) 18·08 sq ft (1·68 m^2)
Horizontal tail surfaces (total) 38·1 sq ft (3·54 m^2)
Vertical tail surfaces (total) 24·2 sq ft (2·25 m^2)

Weights and Loadings:
Weight empty 5,423 lb (2,460 kg)
Normal T-O weight 8,068 lb (3,660 kg)
Max T-O weight 8,377 lb (3,800 kg)
Max landing weight 7,716 lb (3,500 kg)
Max wing loading 44·5 lb/sq ft (217·1 kg/m^2)
Max power loading 3·8 lb/lb st (3·8 kg/kg st)

Performance (at normal T-O weight except where indicated):
Max never-exceed speed 404 knots (466 mph; 750 km/h) (Mach 0·8)
Max level speed at 16,400 ft (5,000 m) 388 knots (447 mph; 720 km/h)
Normal cruising speed 324 knots (373 mph; 600 km/h)
Landing speed 92 knots (106 mph; 170 km/h)
Stalling speed, power off, flaps down 75·5 knots (87 mph; 140 km/h)
Max rate of climb at S/L 3,150 ft (960 m)/min
Time to 19,685 ft (6,000 m) 9 min 36 sec
Service ceiling 41,000 ft (12,500 m)
T-O run 2,067 ft (630 m)
T-O to 50 ft (15 m) 3,315 ft (1,010 m)
Landing from 50 ft (15 m) 2,885 ft (880 m)
Landing run 1,835 ft (560 m)
Range with max fuel 787 nm (907 miles; 1,460 km)

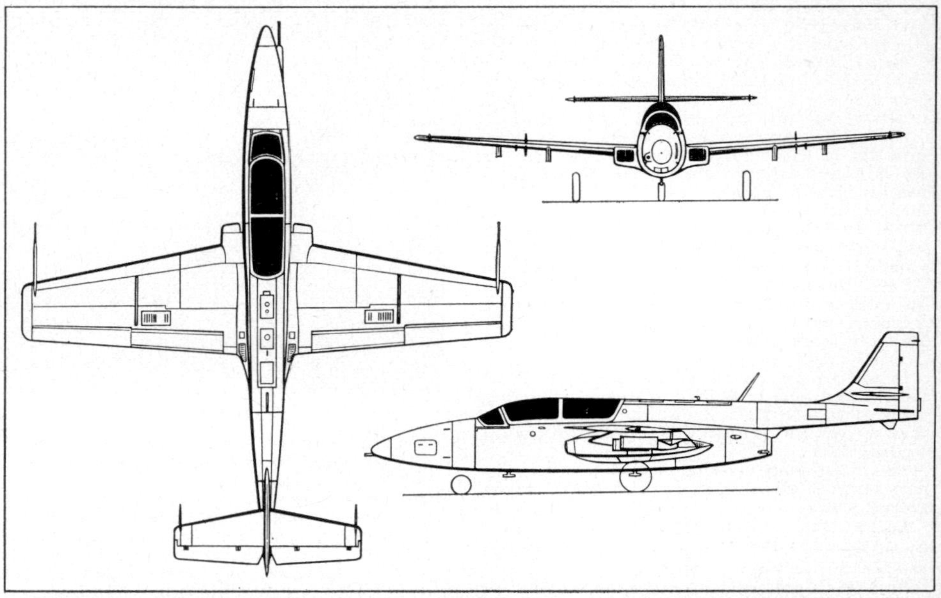

WSK-Mielec TS-11 Iskra 100 jet primary and basic trainer, with underwing weapon attachments (*Pilot Press*)

WSK-MIELEC M-15

On 1 March 1971, an agreement was concluded in Warsaw between the Polish and Soviet governments regarding the development and production of new aviation products, including large and medium-sized agricultural aircraft, light single- and twin-engined helicopters, sailplanes and powered sailplanes. The USSR has not manufactured any specialised agricultural aircraft, apart from a small quantity of An-2Ms, since it transferred production to Poland of the Antonov An-2 in 1960. Consequently, following the 1971 agreement, one subject of discussion between the Polish Ministry of Civil Aviation and the Soviet Ministry of Aircraft Industry was the development of a new, large agricultural aircraft known as the M-15, together with associated agricultural and ground support equipment.

The Soviet government has indicated a requirement for about 3,000 such aircraft, and on 2 December 1971 signed an agreement with the Polish government for large-scale production of the M-15.

Initial design of the M-15 was undertaken by a design bureau at Mielec under Soviet chief consulting engineer R. A. Ismailov and Polish designer K. Gocyla, and staffed by Polish and Soviet specialists. The agricultural equipment for the aircraft is being developed jointly by the Instytut Lotnictwa at Warsaw (which see) and the Soviet Research Institute of Special and Utility Aviation at Krasnodar.

The M-15, a mock-up of which was approved in June 1972, is of biplane configuration. A flying prototype, designated LLP-M15 (Laboratorium Latajace Prototyp M-15: Flying Laboratory Prototype M-15), was flown by Ing Ludwik Natkaniec on 30 May 1973; the first M-15 prototype was completed and rolled out on 12 July 1973 and made its first flight on 9 January 1974. A passenger-carrying version has also been proposed, in which the agricultural hoppers would be replaced by enlarged between-wings fairings, equipped as passenger cabins with nose baggage compartments.

The following description refers to the agricultural version:

Type: Three-seat agricultural aircraft.

Wings: Biplane wings, of mainly metal construction and unequal span, built chiefly of aluminium and steel alloys and glassfibre laminates. The upper wing has a constant-chord centre-section and tapered outer panels; the centre-section is faired to the top of the engine pod. The shorter-span lower wings, which house the agricultural dispersal pipes, are of generally similar planform and are joined to the fuselage nacelle at floor level. The entire trailing-edge of the upper wing is hinged, and is made up of hydraulically-operated double-slotted flaps and single-slotted ailerons. There are automatically-operated slats on the leading-edge. In line with each tailboom, and occupying the full depth of the gap between the upper and lower wings, is a narrow streamlined hopper for agricultural chemical, and there is a single outward-sloping bracing strut outboard of each hopper fairing.

Fuselage: Central semi-monocoque nacelle, of narrow rectangular section, built of same materials as wings.

Tail Unit: Cantilever metal/glassfibre structure, consisting of twin sweptback endplate fins and rudders, bridged by a high-mounted tailplane and full-span elevator, supported on two slender tailbooms located at approx one-quarter span on the trailing-edge of the upper wing.

Landing Gear: Non-retractable tricycle type, with single wheel on each unit. Main wheels and tyres size 720 × 360; nosewheel and tyre size 700 × 250. Nosewheel steerable hydraulically, 50° to left or right. Brakes on main wheels.

Power Plant: One 3,306 lb (1,500 kg) st Ivchenko AI-25 turbofan engine, mounted in a pod on top of the fuselage. Five fuel tanks in the upper wing.

Accommodation: Seat for pilot in fully-enclosed cockpit in extreme nose of fuselage. Two seats in cabin, to rear of pilot's compartment, for carrying ground staff during ferry flights. Cockpit air-conditioning by engine compressor bleed air.

Equipment: Full flight and navigation instrumentation, including stall-warning indicator. VFR radio/navigation equipment optional. The two between-wings hoppers have a combined capacity for 638 Imp gallons (2,900 litres) of liquid or 4,850 lb (2,200 kg) of dry (powdered or granulated) chemical. Ivchenko AI-9 APU, normally removed from aircraft during agricultural operations, provides power for engine starting, ground refuelling and filling of hoppers with liquid chemical.

Dimensions, external:
Wing span:
upper 72 ft 2¼ in (22·00 m)
lower approx 49 ft 2½ in (15·00 m)

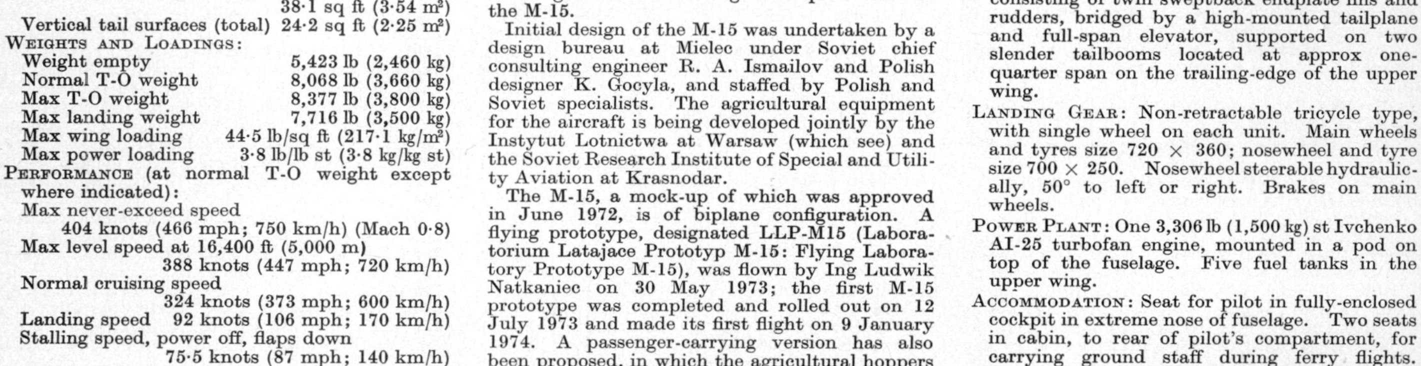

WSK-Mielec LLP-M15 prototype for the M-15 turbofan-engined agricultural biplane

Mean aerodynamic wing chord (upper) 6 ft 0½ in (1·84 m)
Length overall 41 ft 1¼ in (12·53 m)
Height overall 17 ft 0¾ in (5·20 m)
Wheel track 13 ft 9¼ in (4·20 m)
Wheelbase 15 ft 9 in (4·80 m)

Areas:
Wings (total) 723·3 sq ft (67·2 m²)
Ailerons (total) 46·82 sq ft (4·35 m²)
Trailing-edge flaps (total) 69·97 sq ft (6·50 m²)
Fins (total) 64·58 sq ft (6·00 m²)
Rudders (total) 43·06 sq ft (4·00 m²)
Tailplane 64·58 sq ft (6·00 m²)
Elevator, incl tabs 43·06 sq ft (4·00 m²)

Weights and Loading:
Weight empty 5,291 lb (2,400 kg)
Max T-O weight 11,684 lb (5,300 kg)
Max wing loading 16·1 lb/sq ft (78·6 kg/m²)

Performance (estimated, at max T-O weight):
Max cruising speed 146 knots (168 mph; 270 km/h)
Normal operating speed 75·5-97 knots (87-112 mph; 140-180 km/h)
Stalling speed 48 knots (56 mph; 89 km/h)
Max rate of climb at S/L 1,675 ft (510 m)/min
T-O run 607 ft (185 m)
Landing run 344 ft (105 m)
Max range at 9,850 ft (3,000 m) 540 nm (621 miles; 1,000 km)
Swath width 197 ft (60 m)

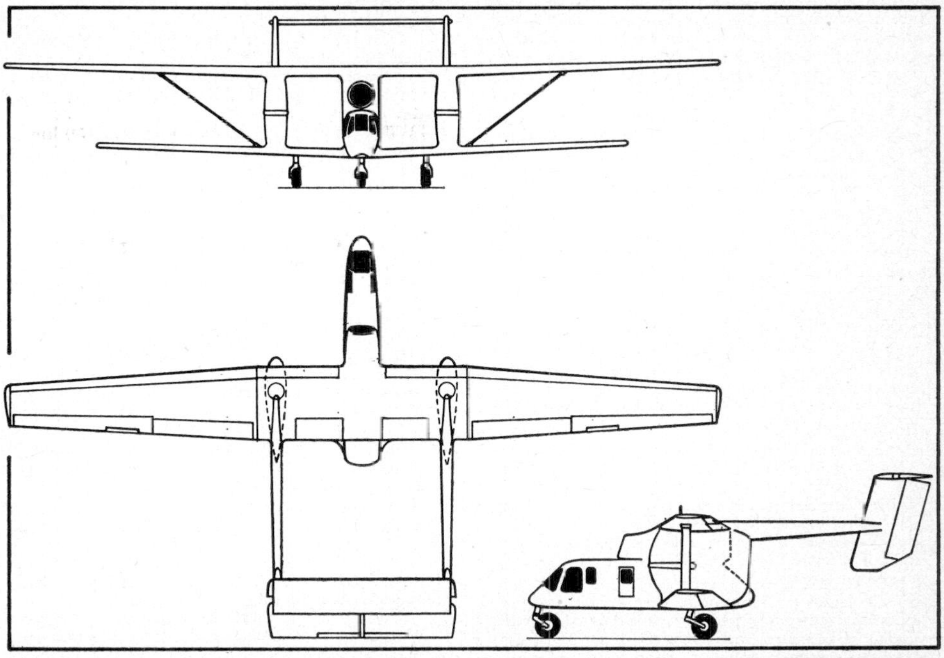

WSK-Mielec M-15 three-seat agricultural aircraft (*Roy J. Grainge*)

WSK-OKECIE

WYTWORNIA SPRZETU KOMUNIKACYJNEGO-OKECIE (Transport Equipment Manufacturing Centre, Okecie)

Head Office and Works:
02-256 Warsaw-Okecie, Al. Krakowska 110/114
Telephone: Warsaw 461173

Managers:
Jerzy Malkinski, Eng MSc (General Manager)
Jerzy Milczarek, Eng (Technical)
Roman Kojder, MSc (Sales)

Public Relations:
Jerzy Pasterski, Eng MSc

The Okecie factory is responsible for light aircraft development and production, and for the design and manufacture of associated agricultural equipment for its own aircraft and for those built at other factories in the Aircraft and Engine Industry Union.

PZL-101A GAWRON (ROOK)

The PZL-101 is a development of the Soviet Yak-12, several versions of which were licence-produced in the WSK at Warsaw-Okecie. The prototype flew for the first time in April 1958 and the first production Gawron in February 1960.

Following extensive evaluation trials in the countries of eastern Europe, including the Soviet Union, the PZL-101 was approved by these countries as the standard agricultural aircraft for the period beginning in 1961. In addition to orders from these countries and domestic orders, a number of PZL-101s were sold to Austria, Finland, India, Spain, Turkey and Vietnam.

More than 330 Gawrons were built in Poland, including about 150 for export to the USSR and elsewhere. Production of the Gawron ended in 1973.

The three production versions of the Gawron are all designated PZL-101A. The standard version, with 260 hp AI-14R engine, is equipped for agricultural duties. The ambulance and utility models are conversions of the standard airframe.

A full description of the PZL-101A appeared in the 1973-74 *Jane's*.

PZL-104 WILGA (THRUSH)

The PZL-104 Wilga is a light general-purpose aircraft intended for a wide variety of general aviation and flying club duties. The original prototype (SP-PAZ), known as the Wilga 1, with a 180 hp WN-6B engine, flew for the first time on 24 April 1962. This aircraft, together with the Wilga 2, C and 3 prototypes, 3A and 3S production versions and other early models, were described in the 1968-69 *Jane's*.

In 1967 the basic design was further modified, with improved cabin comfort, redesigned landing gear and glassfibre tailwheel leg. This version is known as the **Wilga 35** (first flight 28 July 1967) when fitted with a 260 hp AI-14R engine, and as the **Wilga 32** (first flown 12 September 1967) with a 230 hp Continental O-470-K, -L or -R engine and shorter landing gear. Both the Wilga 32 and Wilga 35 received a Polish type certificate on 31 March 1969, having entered production in 1968. A British C of A has been granted for the import of the Wilga 32 into the UK. The current production models are the **32A and 35A** (indicating Aeroclub versions) for paratroop training and glider towing, and some have been sold to Bulgaria, Germany (Democratic Republic), Germany (Federal Republic), Hungary, Romania, the UK and Venezuela. Passenger/liaison (**Wilga 32P and 35P**) and ambulance (**Wilga 32S and 35S**) models are also available.

PZL-104 Wilga 32 general-purpose aircraft (230 hp Continental O-470-L engine)

PZL-104 Wilga 35 four-seat utility aircraft in the insignia of the Polish Air Force

Details of the Wilga 40 and 43 experimental versions were given in the 1972-73 *Jane's*.

By early 1974 more than 170 Wilgas, of all versions, had been built in Poland. A modified version of the Wilga 32 is in production in Indonesia as the Lipnur Gelatik 32 (which see).

The following description applies to the Wilga 32 and 35:

Type: **Single-engined general-purpose monoplane.**

Wings: **Cantilever high-wing monoplane. Wing** section NACA 2415. Dihedral 1°. All-metal single-spar structure, with leading-edge torsion box and beaded metal skin. Each wing attached **to fuselage by three bolts, two at spar and one at forward fitting. All-metal aerodynamically-and mass-balanced slotted ailerons, with beaded metal skin. Ailerons can be drooped to** supplement flaps during landing. Manually-operated all-metal slotted flaps with beaded metal skin. Fixed metal slat on the leading-edge along the full span of the wing and over the fuselage.

Fuselage: All-metal semi-monocoque structure in two portions, riveted together. Forward section incorporates main wing spar carry-through structure. Rear section is in the form of a tailcone. Beaded metal skin. Floor in cabin is of sandwich construction, with a paper core, covered with foam rubber.

Tail Unit: Braced all-metal structure, with sweptback vertical surfaces. Stressed-skin single-spar tailplane attached to fuselage by a single centre fitting and supported by a single aluminium alloy strut on each side. Stressed-skin two-spar fin structure of semi-monocoque construction. Rudder and one-piece elevator are aerodynamically horn-balanced and mass-balanced, with counterweights in the form of metal slats attached to the front section of the elevator. Controllable trim tab in centre of elevator trailing-edge.

LANDING GEAR: Non-retractable tailwheel type. Semi-cantilever main units, of rocker type, have PZL oleo-pneumatic shock-absorbers. Stomil low-pressure tyres size 500 × 150 on main wheels. Hydraulic brakes. Steerable tailwheel, size 200 × 80, carried on sprung leg of glassfibre-reinforced epoxy resin. Retractable metal ski landing gear optional.

POWER PLANT (Wilga 32): One 230 hp Continental O-470-K, -L or -R six-cylinder horizontally-opposed aircooled engine, driving a McCauley 2A346-050-90A two-blade constant-speed metal propeller. Two removable fuel tanks in each wing, with total capacity of 43 Imp gallons (195 litres). Refuelling point on each side of fuselage, at junction with wing. Oil capacity 2·5 Imp gallons (11·5 litres).

POWER PLANT (Wilga 35): One 260 hp Ivchenko AI-14R nine-cylinder aircooled radial engine, driving a US-122000 two-blade constant-speed wooden propeller. Fuel capacity as for Wilga 32; oil capacity 3·5 Imp gallons (16 litres). It is intended in the near future to power this version with an AI-14RC engine having electrical starting.

ACCOMMODATION: Passenger version accommodates four persons in pairs, with adjustable front seats. Baggage compartment aft of seats. Upward-opening door on each side of cabin, jettisonable in emergency. In the parachute training version the starboard door is removed and replaced by a tubular upright with a horizontal strap, and the starboard front seat is rearward-facing. Backrests of the rear seats are removable, and jumps are facilitated by a step on the starboard side and by a parachute hitch. A controllable towing hook can be attached to the tail landing gear permitting the Wilga, in this role, to tow a single glider of up to 1,433 lb (650 kg) weight or two or three gliders with a total combined weight of 2,480 lb (1,125 kg).

SYSTEMS: Hydraulic system pressure 570 lb/sq in (40 kg/cm²) in both models. In the Wilga 32, the electrical system includes a Delco-Rémy generator, 10Ah battery and Eclipse Pioneer electrical starter. In the Wilga 35, engine starting is effected pneumatically by a built-in system of 7 litres capacity with a pressure of 710 lb/sq in (50 kg/cm²); electrical system includes GSK-1500 generator and a 10Ah battery for 24V DC power.

ELECTRONICS AND EQUIPMENT: Standard equipment of Wilga 32s for the UK includes ARK-9 radio compass, directional gyro and stall-warning signal, but these items are optional on all other Wilga 32s. Standard equipment of Wilga 35 includes R 860 VHF radio and blind-flying instrumentation.

DIMENSIONS, EXTERNAL:

Wing span	36 ft 4⅞ in (11·14 m)
Wing chord (constant)	4 ft 7¼ in (1·40 m)
Wing aspect ratio	8
Length overall	26 ft 6¾ in (8·10 m)
Height overall:	
Wilga 32	8 ft 2½ in (2·50 m)
Wilga 35	9 ft 7¾ in (2·94 m)
Tailplane span	12 ft 1¾ in (3·70 m)
Wheel track:	
Wilga 32	8 ft 1¼ in (2·47 m)
Wilga 35	9 ft 4¼ in (2·85 m)
Wheelbase:	
Wilga 32	21 ft 3⅞ in (6·50 m)
Wilga 35	21 ft 11¾ in (6·70 m)
Propeller diameter:	
Wilga 32	7 ft 4 in (2·24 m)
Wilga 35	8 ft 8 in (2·65 m)
Passenger doors (each):	
Height	3 ft 3¼ in (1·00 m)
Width	4 ft 11 in (1·50 m)

DIMENSIONS, INTERNAL:

Cabin: Length	7 ft 2½ in (2·20 m)
Max width	3 ft 10 in (1·20 m)
Max height	4 ft 11 in (1·50 m)
Floor area	23·8 sq ft (2·20 m²)
Volume	85 cu ft (2·40 m³)
Baggage compartment	17·5 cu ft (0·50 m³)

AREAS:

Wings, gross	166·8 sq ft (15·50 m²)
Ailerons (total)	17·0 sq ft (1·60 m²)
Trailing-edge flaps (total)	21·6 sq ft (2·00 m²)
Fin	15·9 sq ft (1·48 m²)
Rudder	9·8 sq ft (0·91 m²)
Tailplane	13·24 sq ft (1·23 m²)
Elevator, including tab	23·36 sq ft (2·17 m²)

WEIGHTS AND LOADINGS:

Weight empty, equipped:	
Wilga 32	1,624 lb (737 kg)
Wilga 35	1,874 lb (850 kg)
Max T-O and landing weight	2,755 lb (1,250 kg)
Max wing loading	16·3 lb/sq ft (79·4 kg/m²)
Max power loading:	
Wilga 32	11·79 lb/hp (5·35 kg/hp)
Wilga 35	10·41 lb/hp (4·72 kg/hp)

PERFORMANCE (at max T-O weight):

Max never-exceed speed	150 knots (173 mph; 279 km/h)
Max level speed:	
Wilga 32	110 knots (127 mph; 205 km/h)
Wilga 35	108 knots (125 mph; 201 km/h)
Max cruising speed:	
Wilga 32	81 knots (93 mph; 150 km/h)
Wilga 35	104 knots (120 mph; 193 km/h)
Econ cruising speed:	
Wilga 32	73 knots (84 mph; 135 km/h)
Wilga 35	69 knots (79 mph; 127 km/h)
Stalling speed, power on	35·5 knots (40·5 mph; 65 km/h)
Max rate of climb at S/L:	
Wilga 32	865 ft (264 m)/min
Wilga 35	1,245 ft (380 m)/min
Service ceiling:	
Wilga 32	12,075 ft (3,680 m)
Wilga 35	15,025 ft (4,580 m)
T-O run:	
Wilga 32	280 ft (85 m)
Wilga 35	410 ft (125 m)
T-O to 50 ft (15 m):	
Wilga 32	625 ft (190 m)
Wilga 35	770 ft (235 m)
Landing from 50 ft (15 m):	
Wilga 32	780 ft (238 m)
Wilga 35	1,070 ft (326 m)
Landing run:	
Wilga 32	430 ft (131 m)
Wilga 35	690 ft (210 m)
Range with max fuel, 30 min reserve:	
Wilga 32	338 nm (390 miles; 630 km)
Wilga 35	366 nm (422 miles; 680 km)

PERFORMANCE AS GLIDER TUG (at max T-O weight):

Rate of climb at S/L towing 1 glider:	
Wilga 32A	785 ft (240 m)/min
Wilga 35A	770 ft (234 m)/min
Rate of climb at S/L towing 2 gliders:	
Wilga 32A	670 ft (204 m)/min
Wilga 35A	750 ft (228 m)/min
Rate of climb at S/L towing 3 gliders:	
Wilga 32A	435 ft (132 m)/min
Wilga 35A	395 ft (120 m)/min
Service ceiling with 1 glider:	
Wilga 32A	14,800 ft (4,510 m)
Wilga 35A	13,125 ft (4,000 m)
Service ceiling with 2 gliders:	
Wilga 32A	10,900 ft (3,320 m)
Wilga 35A	12,800 ft (3,900 m)
Service ceiling with 3 gliders:	
Wilga 32A, 35A	8,200 ft (2,500 m)
Time to reach service ceiling:	
Wilga 32A:	
1 glider	45 min
2 gliders	44 min
3 gliders	42 min
Wilga 35A:	
1 glider	37 min 12 sec
2 gliders	43 min 12 sec
3 gliders	36 min 36 sec
Range:	
Wilga 32A:	
1 glider	333 nm (383 miles; 617 km)
2 gliders	282 nm (324 miles; 522 km)
3 gliders	226 nm (259 miles; 418 km)
Wilga 35A:	
1 glider	344 nm (395 miles; 637 km)
2 gliders	272 nm (313 miles; 504 km)
3 gliders	227 nm (260 miles; 420 km)

PZL-106 KRUK (RAVEN)

The PZL-106 agricultural aircraft, built in seven months, was designed in 1972 by a team led by Dipl Ing Andrzej Frydrychewicz and is intended as a successor to the PZL-101 Gawron. The prototype (SP-PAS) flew for the first time on 17 April 1973, and was officially demonstrated before senior government officials on 27 April. Test pilot for the first flight was Dipl Ing Jerzy Jedrzejewski.

TYPE: Single-engined agricultural aircraft.

WINGS: Braced low-wing monoplane. All-metal two-spar constant-chord structure (wooden on prototype) with metal and fabric covering.

FUSELAGE: Welded steel-tube structure, with glassfibre-reinforced plastics and fabric covering.

TAIL UNIT: Braced T-tail, of duralumin construction with metal-skinned fin and tailplane, fabric-covered rudder and elevator.

LANDING GEAR: Non-retractable tailwheel type. Oleo-pneumatic shock-absorbers and large-diameter low-pressure tyres on main units.

POWER PLANT (prototype): One 400 hp Lycoming IO-720 eight-cylinder horizontally-opposed aircooled engine, driving a three-blade constant-speed metal propeller. Total fuel capacity 79 Imp gallons (360 litres). Provision for radial piston engine of up to 600 hp.

ACCOMMODATION: Pilot only, in enclosed, ventilated and air-conditioned cockpit. Second

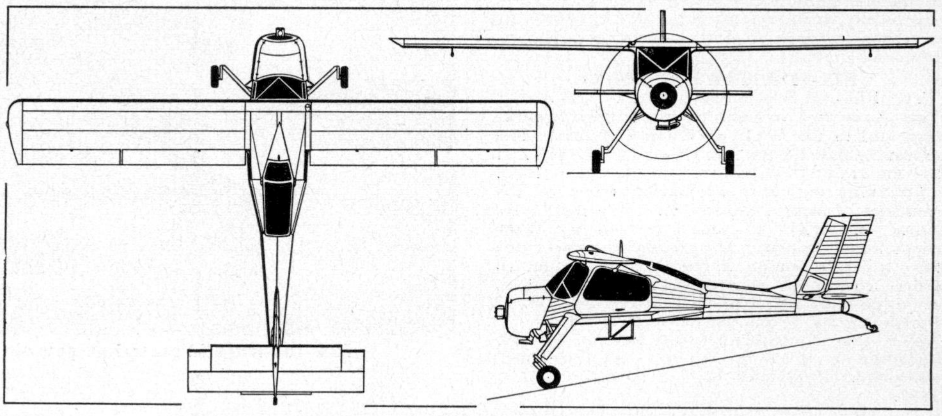

PZL-104 Wilga 35 general-purpose monoplane (*Pilot Press*)

Wilga 35A Aeroclub version of the PZL-104 (260 hp Ivchenko AI-14R engine)

(mechanic's) seat to rear. Door on each side of cabin.

EQUIPMENT: Easily-removable hopper, forward of cockpit, can carry 1,763-2,204 lb (800-1,000 kg) of dry or liquid chemical and has a maximum capacity of 275 Imp gallons (1,250 litres).

DIMENSIONS, EXTERNAL:
Wing span 42 ft 7¾ in (13·00 m)
Length overall 27 ft 6¾ in (8·40 m)
Height overall 9 ft 6¼ in (2·90 m)

AREA:
Wings, gross 317·5 sq ft (29·50 m²)

WEIGHTS:
Weight empty 2,314 lb (1,050 kg)
Max T-O weight 4,960 lb (2,250 kg)

PERFORMANCE:
Cruising speed 97 knots (112 mph; 180 km/h)
Operating speed with 1,763 lb (800 kg) chemical load 65-86 knots (75-100 mph; 120-160 km/h)
Operating height 15-50 ft (5-15 m)
Swath width 100-150 ft (30-45 m)
Rate of climb (prototype) with 1,763 lb (800 kg) chemical load 984 ft (300 m)/min
T-O and landing run 492 ft (150 m)

First prototype of the PZL-106 Kruk agricultural aircraft (400 hp Lycoming IO-720 engine)

WSK-SWIDNIK

WYTWORNIA SPRZETU KOMUNIKACYJNEGO im. ZYGMUNTA PULAWSKIEGO-SWIDNIK (Zygmunt Pulawski's Transport Equipment Manufacturing Centre, Swidnik)

HEAD OFFICE AND WORKS:
Swidnik k/Lublina
Telephone: Lublin 12061
Telex: 84212 and 84302

GENERAL MANAGER:
Dipl Ing Jozef Lipinski

In 1955, when the manufacture of combat aircraft was drastically reduced in Poland, the WSK at Swidnik began licence production of the Soviet-designed Mi-1 helicopter, which was built under the designation of SM-1. A small design office was formed subsequently at the factory to work on variants and developments of the basic SM-1 design and on original projects, including the SM-4 Latka helicopter prototype, of which brief details were given in the 1967-68 *Jane's*.

In September 1957, the WSK-Swidnik works were named after the famous pre-war PZL designer Zygmunt Pulawski.

Details of the SM-1 series, and the developed SM-2, can be found in the 1966-67 *Jane's*. The IL (which see) has recently test-flown an SM-1 fitted with wings. Production at Swidnik is concentrated on various versions of the Soviet-designed Mil Mi-2 turbine-powered helicopter.

The WSK design office is currently working on a new, lightweight general-purpose helicopter with four/five seats and an AUW of about 3,750 lb (1,700 kg). It will have a max speed of 108-135 knots (125-155 mph; 200-250 km/h), and a range of about 270 nm (310 miles; 500 km). Initially, it will have a single Isotov GTD-350 turboshaft engine of the type that powers the Mi-2, but eventually a developed version of this engine, of 500-700 shp, is likely to be used.

WSK-SWIDNIK (MIL) Mi-2

The Mil Mi-2, announced in the Autumn of 1961, was designed in the USSR by the Mikhail L.Mil bureau. It retains the basic configuration of the earlier Mi-1 helicopter, but instead of the latter's single piston engine has two Isotov turboshaft engines mounted side by side above the cabin.

Development of the Mi-2 prototype, usually referred to in the Soviet Union as the V-2, continued in the USSR until the helicopter had completed its initial State trials programme of flying. Then, in accordance with an agreement signed in January 1964, further development, production and marketing of the Mi-2 were assigned exclusively to the Polish aircraft industry.

Production by WSK began in 1965, and this factory has since built many hundreds in a variety of versions. It is undertaking a considerable development programme to improve the Mi-2 during the period up to 1975. As a first stage, the present metal stabiliser, tail rotor blades and main rotor blades will be replaced with similar components made of plastics, to simplify production and improve performance. The new rotor blades were designed, manufactured and tested at the WSK-Swidnik transport equipment plant, with satisfactory results, and preparations were being made in early 1974 to manufacture them in quantity. Stage two involves improvement of the cabin heating and ventilation system and introduction of skid landing gear to improve performance and versatility. Stage three involves the switch to a larger cabin on the major production versions.

There are several versions of the Mi-2, as follows:

(a) Convertible passenger/cargo transport;
(b) Passengers-only version, for six or eight passengers;
(c) Ambulance version;
(d) Agricultural version;

WSK-Swidnik Mi-2 general-purpose helicopter, ambulance version

(e) Search and rescue version, with electrically-operated external hoist;
(f) Freighter version, with external cargo sling;
(g) Pilot training version, designed by WSK-Swidnik;
(h) Photogrammetric version;
(i) Television version (for transmission from the air);
(j) Version with 573 lb (260 kg) capacity hoist;
(k) Version (under development) with inflatable pontoon landing gear.

TYPE: Twin-turbine general-purpose light helicopter.

ROTOR SYSTEM: Three-blade main rotor fitted with hydraulic blade vibration dampers. All-metal blades of NACA 230-13M section. Flapping, drag and pitch hinges on each blade. Main rotor blades and those of two-blade tail rotor each consist of an extruded duralumin spar with bonded honeycomb trailing-edge pockets. Anti-flutter weights on leading-edges, balancing plates on trailing-edges. Hydraulic boosters for longitudinal, lateral and collective pitch controls. Coil spring counterbalance mechanism in main and tail rotor systems. Pitch-change centrifugal loads on tail rotor carried by ribbon-type steel torsion elements. Rotors do not fold. Electrical blade de-icing system for main and tail rotors. Rotor brake fitted.

ROTOR DRIVE: Main rotor shaft driven via gearbox on each engine (reduction ratio 0·246 : 1); three-stage main gearbox, intermediate gearbox and tail rotor gearbox. Main rotor/engine rpm ratio 247 : 24,000; tail rotor/engine rpm ratio 1,445 : 24,000. Main gearbox provides drive for auxiliary systems and take-off for rotor brake. Free-wheel units permit disengagement of a failed engine and also autorotation.

FUSELAGE: Conventional semi-monocoque structure of pod and boom type, made up of three main assemblies: the nose (including cockpit), central section and tailboom. Construction is of sheet duralumin, bonded and spot-welded or riveted to longerons and frames. Main load-bearing joints are of steel alloy.

TAIL UNIT: Variable-incidence horizontal stabiliser controlled by collective-pitch lever.

LANDING GEAR: Non-retractable tricycle type, plus tailskid. Twin-wheel nose unit. Single wheel on each main unit. Oleo-pneumatic shock-absorbers on all units, including tailskid. Main shock-absorbers designed to cope with both normal operating loads and possible ground resonance. Main-wheel tyres size 600 × 180, pressure 64 lb/sq in (4·5 kg/cm²). Nosewheel tyres size 300 × 125, pressure 50 lb/sq in (3·5 kg/cm²). Pneumatic brakes on main wheels.

POWER PLANT: Two 437 shp Isotov GTD-350 turboshaft engines, mounted side by side above cabin. Fuel in single flexible tank, capacity 131 Imp gallons (600 litres), under cabin floor. Provision for carrying a 52·5 Imp gallon (238 litre) external tank on each side of cabin. Refuelling point in starboard side of fuselage. Oil capacity 5·4 Imp gallons (25 litres). Engine air intake de-icing by engine bleed air.

ACCOMMODATION: Normal accommodation for one pilot on flight deck (port side). Seats for up to eight passengers in air-conditioned cabin,

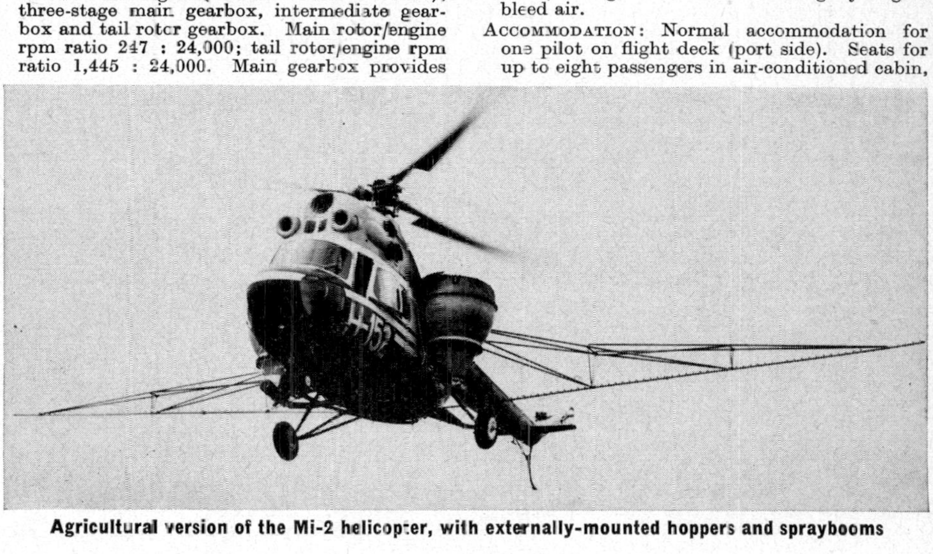

Agricultural version of the Mi-2 helicopter, with externally-mounted hoppers and spraybooms

there being back-to-back bench seats for three persons each, with two optional extra starboard side seats at the rear, one behind the other. All seats are removable for carrying up to 1,543 lb (700 kg) of internal freight. Access to cabin via forward-hinged doors on each side at front of cabin and aft on port side. Pilot's sliding window jettisonable in emergency. Ambulance version has accommodation for four stretchers and a medical attendant or for two stretchers and two sitting casualties. Side-by-side seats and dual controls in pilot training version. Cabin heating, ventilation and air-conditioning standard. Electrical de-icing of windscreen.

Operational Equipment: As an agricultural aircraft, the Mi-2 carries a hopper on each side of the fuselage (total capacity 220 Imp gallons; 1,000 litres) and either a pair of spraybars to the rear of the cabin or a distributor for dry chemicals under each hopper. Swath width covered by the spraying version is 130-150 ft (40-45 m). As a search and rescue aircraft, an electric hoist, capacity 264 lb (120 kg), is fitted. In the freight role an underfuselage hook can be fitted for suspended loads of up to 1,763 lb (800 kg).

Systems: Cabin heating, by engine bleed air, and ventilation; heat exchangers warm atmospheric air for ventilation system during cold weather. Hydraulic system, pressure 855-1,140 lb/sq in (60-80 kg/cm²), for cyclic and collective pitch control boosters. Pneumatic system, pressure 710 lb/sq in (50 kg/cm²), for main-wheel brakes. AC electrical system, with two STG-3 3kW engine-driven starter/generators and 208V 16kVA three-phase alternator. 24V DC system, with two 28Ah lead-acid batteries.

Electronics and Equipment: Standard equipment includes two transceivers (medium and short wave), gyro compass, radio compass, radio altimeter, intercom system and blind-flying panel. Electrically-operated wiper for pilot's windscreen. Fire extinguishing system, for engine bays and main gearbox compartment, is generally similar to, but simpler than, the Freon system fitted to the Soviet Mil Mi-8, and can be actuated automatically or manually.

Dimensions, external:
- Diameter of main rotor: 47 ft 6¾ in (14·50 m)
- Main rotor blade chord (constant, each): 1 ft 3¾ in (0·40 m)
- Diameter of tail rotor: 8 ft 10¼ in (2·70 m)
- Length overall, rotors turning: 57 ft 2 in (17·42 m)
- Length of fuselage: 37 ft 4¾ in (11·40 m)
- Height to top of rotor hub: 12 ft 3½ in (3·75 m)
- Stabiliser span: 6 ft 0¾ in (1·85 m)
- Wheel track: 10 ft 0 in (3·05 m)
- Wheelbase: 8 ft 10¾ in (2·71 m)
- Tail rotor ground clearance: 5 ft 2¾ in (1·59 m)
- Cabin door (port, rear):
  - Height: 3 ft 5¾ in (1·065 m)
  - Width: 3 ft 8 in (1·115 m)
- Cabin door (stbd, front):
  - Height: 3 ft 7¾ in (1·11 m)
  - Width: 2 ft 5½ in (0·75 m)
- Cabin door (port, front):
  - Height: approx 4 ft 7 in (1·40 m)
  - Width: approx 3 ft 11¼ in (1·20 m)

Dimensions, internal:
- Cabin:
  - Length, including flight deck: 13 ft 4¼ in (4·07 m)
  - Length, excluding flight deck: 7 ft 5½ in (2·27 m)
  - Mean width: 3 ft 11¼ in (1·20 m)
  - Mean height: 4 ft 7 in (1·40 m)

Areas:
- Main rotor blades (each): 25·83 sq ft (2·40 m²)
- Tail rotor blades (each): 2·37 sq ft (0·22 m²)
- Main rotor disc: 1,776 sq ft (165·0 m²)
- Tail rotor disc: 61·35 sq ft (5·70 m²)
- Horizontal stabiliser: 7·53 sq ft (0·70 m²)

Weights and Loadings:
- Basic operating weight, empty:
  - single-pilot versions: 5,213 lb (2,365 kg)
  - dual-control version: 5,344 lb (2,424 kg)
- Max payload, excluding pilot, oil and fuel: 1,763 lb (800 kg)
- Normal T-O weight: 7,826 lb (3,550 kg)
- Max T-O weight: 8,157 lb (3,700 kg)
- Max disc loading: 4·3 lb/sq ft (21·0 kg/m²)
- Max power loading: 8·82 lb/shp (4·0 kg/shp)

Performance (at normal T-O weight):
- Max level speed at 1,640 ft (500 m): 113 knots (130 mph; 210 km/h)
- Max cruising speed at 1,640 ft (500 m): 108 knots (124 mph; 200 km/h)
- Econ cruising speed for max range at 1,640 ft (500 m): 102 knots (118 mph; 190 km/h)
- Econ cruising speed for max endurance at 1,640 ft (500 m): 54 knots (62 mph; 100 km/h)
- Max rate of climb at S/L: 885 ft (270 m)/min
- Service ceiling: 13,755 ft (4,200 m)
- Hovering ceiling in ground effect: 6,550 ft (2,000 m)
- Hovering ceiling out of ground effect: 3,275 ft (1,000 m)
- Minimum landing area: 100 × 100 ft (30 × 30 m)
- Range at 1,640 ft (500 m) with max fuel, 30 min reserve: 313 nm (360 miles; 580 km)
- Range at 1,640 ft (500 m) with max payload, 5% fuel reserve: 91 nm (105 miles; 170 km)

CZERNIEJEWSKI

CZESLAW CZERNIEJEWSKI

Address:
ul. Libelta 58c/15, 62200 Gniezno

CZERNIEJEWSKI PIAST

Mr Czerniejewski, assisted by Mr Stanislaw Bechert, has designed and built a light single-seat aircraft of the Mignet Pou du Ciel type which he has named Piast. Construction began in late 1970, and was completed in December 1972. First flight was planned to take place in 1973.

Type: Single-seat ultra-light homebuilt aircraft.

Wings: Wire-braced Mignet-type tandem wings, without ailerons. All-wood two-spar structure. Plywood-covered leading-edges, remainder fabric-covered.

Fuselage: Plywood-covered wooden semi-monocoque structure.

Tail Unit: Rudder only, of fabric-covered wooden construction.

Landing Gear: Non-retractable tailwheel type, with spring shock-absorbers. Main-wheel tyres of 450 mm diameter. No brakes.

Power Plant: One 44 hp FIS 500 cc single-cylinder aircooled motor-cycle engine, driving a two-blade fixed-pitch wooden propeller. Wing fuel tank, capacity 2·6 Imp gallons (12 litres).

Accommodation: Single seat in open cockpit.

Czerniejewski Piast, Polish-built example of the Mignet Pou du Ciel

Dimensions, external:
- Wing span: 19 ft 11 in (6·07 m)
- Length overall: 13 ft 10¼ in (4·22 m)
- Height overall: 5 ft 10 in (1·78 m)
- Tailplane span: 13 ft 1½ in (4·00 m)
- Wheel track: 4 ft 8¼ in (1·43 m)
- Propeller diameter: 4 ft 3¼ in (1·30 m)

Areas:
- Wings, gross:
  - front: 96·2 sq ft (8·94 m²)
  - rear: 58·5 sq ft (5·44 m²)
- Rudder: 12·9 sq ft (1·20 m²)

Weights and Loading:
- Weight empty: 242·5 lb (110 kg)
- Max T-O weight: 425·5 lb (193 kg)
- Max wing loading: 2·75 lb/sq ft (13·4 kg/m²)

DOBRACZYNSKI

TADEUSZ DOBRACZYNSKI

DOBRACZYNSKI WROCLAW

This single-seat ultra-light aeroplane has been built using components from two sailplanes: the fuselage of a Komar and the wings of an ABC. The description which follows is of the aircraft in its Wroclaw-1 form, with standard wings of 9 m span. It can be converted to a short-span configuration by removing the outer wing panels and fitting endplates to the new tips. This reduces the wing span and wing area, and increases the wing loading, to 19 ft 8¼ in (6·00 m), 96·9 sq ft (9·00 m²) and 6·35 lb/sq ft (31·0 kg/m²) respectively, and has the effect of increasing the range by 27 nm (31 miles; 50 km).

Type: Single-seat ultra-light homebuilt aircraft.

Wings: Parasol monoplane. Constant-chord two-spar wings, of Peyret section and 16% thickness/chord ratio, supported above fuselage by centre-section struts forward and aft of cockpit and streamline-section Vee strut on each side. All-wood structure, plywood-covered between spars; fabric-covered ailerons and flaps.

Fuselage: Wooden box structure, with plywood covering.

Tail Unit: Cantilever structure, with plywood-covered tailplane and fin, and fabric-covered elevators and rudder. Fin integral with fuselage. Elevators operated by pushrods, rudder by cables.

Landing Gear: Non-retractable tailwheel type. Split-axle main gear, with rubber-cord shock-absorbers. Main wheels size 300 × 125 mm.

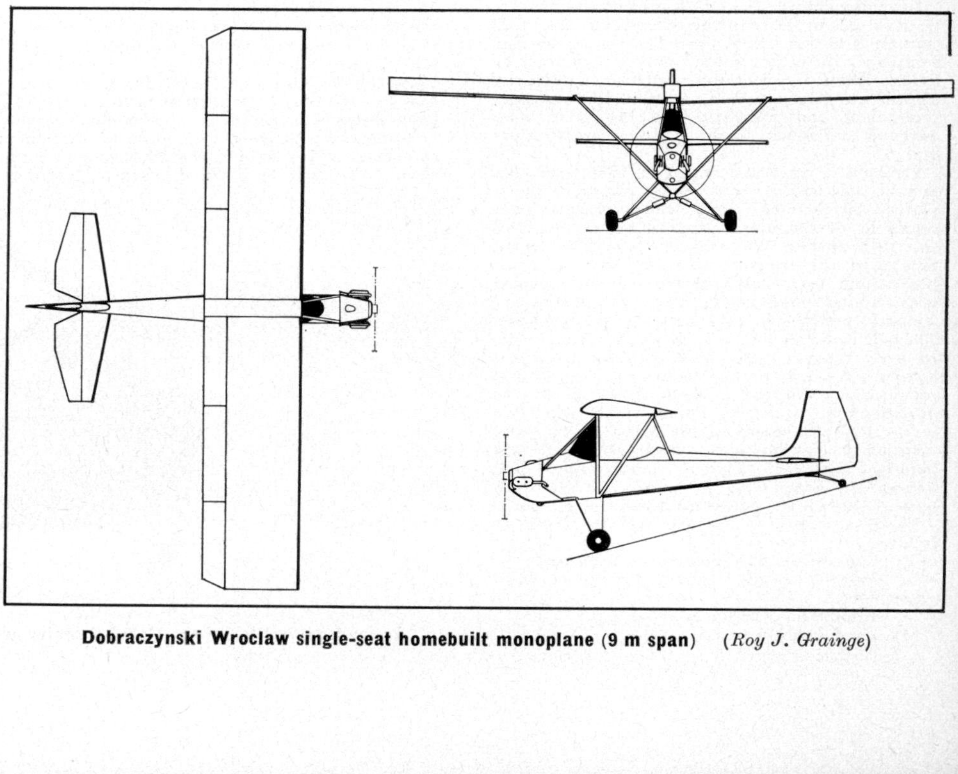

Dobraczynski Wroclaw single-seat homebuilt monoplane (9 m span) (*Roy J. Grainge*)

Power Plant: One 30 hp VW 1200 four-cylinder aircooled engine, driving a two-blade wooden propeller. Fuel tank behind pilot's seat, capacity 4·4 Imp gallons (20 litres).

Accommodation: Single seat in open cockpit behind deep one-piece windscreen. No baggage space.

Dimensions, external:
Wing span 29 ft 6⅜ in (9·00 m)
Wing chord (constant) 4 ft 11 in (1·50 m)
Length overall 17 ft 0¾ in (5·20 m)
Height overall 7 ft 2¾ in (2·20 m)
Wheel track 5 ft 11 in (1·80 m)
Propeller diameter 3 ft 11¼ in (1·20 m)

Areas:
Wings, gross 145·3 sq ft (13·50 m^2)
Ailerons (total) 23·68 sq ft (2·20 m^2)
Vertical tail surfaces (total) 13·99 sq ft (1·30 m^2)
Horizontal tail surfaces (total) 17·98 sq ft (1·67 m^2)

Weights and Loading:
Weight empty 397 lb (180 kg)
Max T-O weight 617 lb (280 kg)
Max wing loading 4·32 lb/sq ft (21·1 kg/m^2)

Performance:
Max never-exceed speed 96·5 knots (111 mph; 180 km/h)
Max level speed 70 knots (81 mph; 130 km/h)
Cruising speed 49 knots (56 mph; 90 km/h)
Stalling speed 30 knots (34·5 mph; 55 km/h)
Max rate of climb at S/L 415 ft (126 m)/min
T-O run 330 ft (100 m)
Landing run 195 ft (60 m)
Range 107 nm (124 miles; 200 km)
g limits +3·5; —2·0

DOBRACZYNSKI MONIKA

The Monika is a simple single-seat biplane with an open fuselage structure; its general appearance can be seen in the accompanying three-view drawing.

Type: Single-seat ultra-light homebuilt aircraft.

Wings: Strut-braced and staggered biplane. Constant-chord two-spar wings, of Peyret section and 16% thickness/chord ratio. Dihedral from centre-section on both wings. All-wood structure, plywood-covered between spars; fabric-covered ailerons on both upper and lower wings.

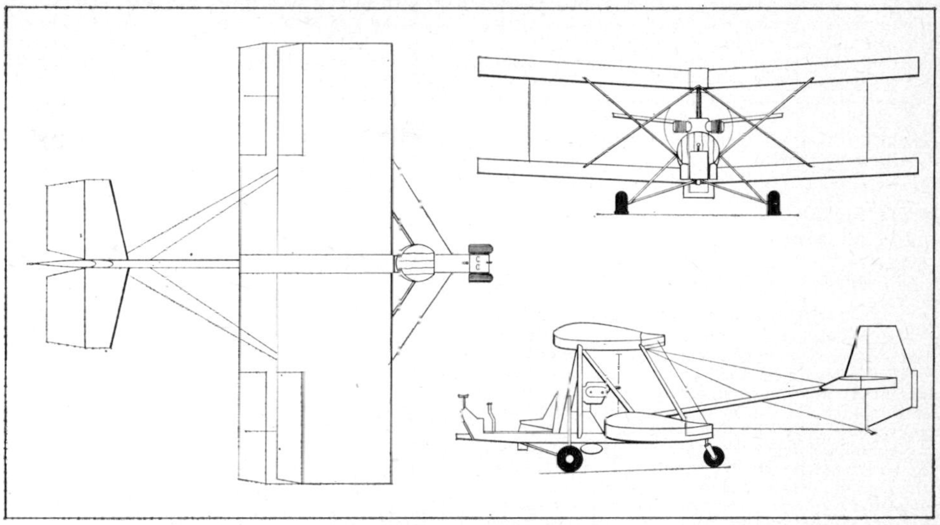

Dobraczynski Monika single-seat homebuilt biplane (*Roy J. Grainge*)

Fuselage: Tubular metal keel structure, with rear boom to support tail unit.

Tail Unit: Plywood-covered tailplane and fin; fabric-covered elevators and rudder. Large trim tab on rudder.

Landing Gear: Non-retractable type, with two main wheels at front and third wheel beneath lower wing at rear. Main-wheel tyre size 300 × 125 mm.

Power Plant: One 30 hp VW 1200 four-cylinder aircooled engine, driving a two-blade pusher propeller. Fuel tank behind pilot's seat, capacity 4·4 Imp gallons (20 litres).

Accommodation: Single open seat, ahead of wings.

Dimensions, external:
Wing span 19 ft 8¼ in (6·00 m)
Length overall 19 ft 0¼ in (5·80 m)
Height overall 6 ft 6¾ in (2·00 m)
Tailplane span 7 ft 2¾ in (2·20 m)
Wheel track 6 ft 2¾ in (1·90 m)
Propeller diameter 3 ft 11¼ in (1·20 m)

Areas:
Wings, gross 193·75 sq ft (18·00 m^2)
Ailerons (total) 36·17 sq ft (3·36 m^2)
Horizontal tail surfaces (total) 21·31 sq ft (1·98 m^2)

Weights and Loading:
Weight empty 441 lb (200 kg)
Max T-O weight 661·5 lb (300 kg)
Max power loading 22·05 lb/hp (10·0 kg/hp)

Performance (at max T-O weight):
Max level speed 54 knots (62 mph; 100 km/h)
Cruising speed 43 knots (50 mph; 80 km/h)
Stalling speed 32·5 knots (37·5 mph; 60 km/h)
Max rate of climb at S/L 395 ft (120 m)/min
T-O run 395 ft (120 m)
Landing run 164 ft (50 m)
Range 80 nm (93 miles; 150 km)
g limits +4·5; —3

JANOWSKI

JAROSLAW JANOWSKI

Address:
Lodz 11, ul. Nowomiejska 2/29

Mr Janowski, assisted by Mr Witold Kalita, has designed and completed a light single-seat amateur-built aircraft, the J-1 Przasniczka, of which brief details follow. Its power plant, the 30 hp Saturn two-cylinder engine, was also designed by Mr Janowski, and built by Mr S. Polawski, and is described in the "Aero-Engines" section of this edition.

A smaller development of the J-1, known as the J-2 Polonez, is also described.

JANOWSKI J-1 PRZASNICZKA

Design and construction of the J-1 was started in 1967, and it flew for the first time on 30 July 1970.

Two additional J-1s are being built by amateur constructors: one by Mr Michal Offierski, a pre-war Polish holder of international powered sailplane records, and one by Mr T. Wood in the UK.

A full description appeared in the 1970-71 *Jane's*.

Power Plant: One 30 hp Janowski Saturn 500 two-stroke two-cylinder horizontally-opposed aircooled engine, mounted at top of fuselage aft of cabin and driving a two-blade fixed-pitch wooden pusher propeller designed by Mr Janowski. Fuel capacity 4·4 Imp gallons (20 litres).

Dimensions, external:
Wing span 24 ft 11¼ in (7·60 m)
Wing chord (constant) 3 ft 3¼ in (1·00 m)
Wing aspect ratio 7·7
Length overall 16 ft 0 in (4·88 m)
Height overall 4 ft 7 in (1·40 m)
Tailplane span 6 ft 8¾ in (2·05 m)
Wheel track 3 ft 9¼ in (1·15 m)
Propeller diameter 3 ft 5¾ in (1·06 m)

Areas:
Wings, gross 80·7 sq ft (7·50 m^2)
Ailerons (total) 7·75 sq ft (0·72 m^2)
Fin 5·60 sq ft (0·52 m^2)
Rudder 3·23 sq ft (0·30 m^2)
Tailplane 7·43 sq ft (0·69 m^2)
Elevator 6·89 sq ft (0·64 m^2)

Weights and Loadings:
Weight empty 330 lb (150 kg)
Max T-O weight 595 lb (270 kg)
Max wing loading 7·37 lb/sq ft (36·0 kg/m^2)
Max power loading 19·84 lb/hp (9·0 kg/hp)

Performance (at max T-O weight):
Max never-exceed speed 96·5 knots (111 mph; 180 km/h)
Max level speed at S/L 70 knots (81 mph; 130 km/h)
Cruising speed 59 knots (68 mph; 110 km/h)
Stalling speed 32·5 knots (37·5 mph; 60 km/h)
Max rate of climb at S/L 590 ft (180 m)/min
Service ceiling 9,850 ft (3,000 m)
Range 134 nm (155 miles; 250 km)
g limits +4·0; —1·5

JANOWSKI J-2 POLONEZ

Mr Janowski designed in 1971 an amateur-built single-seat aircraft known as the J-2 Polonez. This is smaller than the J-1, but is of generally similar configuration except for its mid-mounted wings and a T tail. An aerodynamic model of the J-2 underwent wind-tunnel tests at the Warsaw Technical University in 1972, and a prototype is believed to be under construction.

Type: Single-seat ultra-light aircraft.

Wings: Cantilever mid-wing monoplane. Wing section NACA 23015. Constant-chord wings. All-wood single-spar structure. Leading-edge plywood-covered, rest of wing fabric-covered. Fabric-covered ailerons. No tabs.

Model of the Janowski J-2 Polonez light aircraft (*Z. Szulc*)

Janowski J-1 Przasniczka single-seat ultra-light homebuilt aeroplane

FUSELAGE: Pod and boom type. Enclosed cabin faired into front fuselage. Wooden single-boom structure supporting tail unit.

TAIL UNIT: Cantilever wooden structure, with T tailplane. Sweptback vertical surfaces and constant-chord non-swept horizontal surfaces. No tabs.

LANDING GEAR: Non-retractable single main wheel and tailskid.

POWER PLANT: One 30 hp Janowski Saturn 500 two-stroke two-cylinder horizontally-opposed aircooled engine, mounted at top of fuselage aft of cabin and driving a two-blade fixed-pitch wooden pusher propeller. The aircraft may be fitted with any other suitable engine of 25-40 hp.

DIMENSIONS, EXTERNAL:

Wing span	21 ft 0 in (6·40 m)
Wing chord (constant)	3 ft $3\frac{1}{4}$ in (1·00 m)
Wing aspect ratio	6·4
Length overall	15 ft 9 in (4·80 m)
Height overall	4 ft $3\frac{1}{4}$ in (1·30 m)

AREA:

Wings, gross	68·4 sq ft (6·35 m²)

WEIGHTS:

Weight empty	242 lb (110 kg)
Normal T-O weight	452 lb (205 kg)

POLNIAK

LEON POLNIAK

ADDRESS:

ul Czerwinskiego 5a/1, 40-123 Katowice

POLNIAK LP DEDAL-2

Mr Polniak began design studies of a single-seat man-powered aircraft, designated Dedal-1, in 1966. It was scheduled to fly in 1972, but was unfortunately damaged during road transit when it was only 50% complete. A brief description appeared in the 1972-73 *Jane's*.

Mr Polniak decided, as a result of the mishap, to build instead an improved version known as the Dedal-2, which is shown in the accompanying illustration. The following description applies to the Dedal-2, construction of which was under way in the Spring of 1974:

TYPE: Single-seat man-powered aircraft.

WINGS: Wire-braced mid-wing monoplane. Eiffel 400 wing section, thickness/chord ratio 13·1%. Six-piece single-spar spruce/balsa structure, with slight forward sweep. Incidence and outer-wing dihedral can be varied, the latter raising wingtips up to 39·4 in (100 cm) above centre-section datum line. No flaps or ailerons: lateral control by pilot's body movement.

FUSELAGE: Spruce (cabin) and balsa structure.

TAIL UNIT: One-piece balsa tailplane, aft of fuselage, incidence of which is adjustable on ground. Oval balsa rudder aft of tailplane. No fin.

LANDING GEAR: Non-retractable balsa monowheel with size 12·5-2·25 pneumatic tyre, and small tailwheel.

POWER PLANT: Muscle-power (leg and arm), transmitted by belt drive from monowheel to a two-blade fixed-pitch propeller.

ACCOMMODATION: Pilot only, in enclosed cockpit.

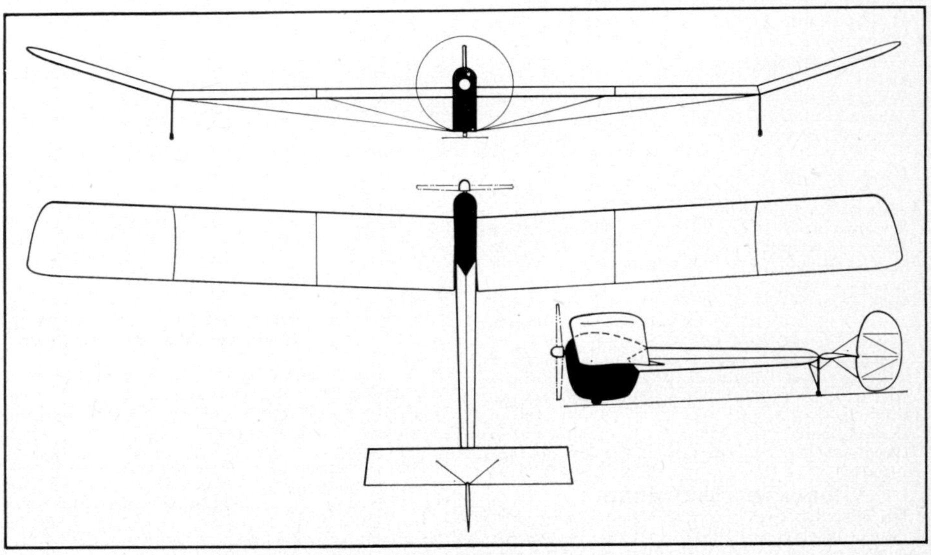

Polniak Dedal-2 man-powered aircraft (*Roy J. Grainge*)

DIMENSIONS, EXTERNAL:

Wing span	75 ft $5\frac{1}{2}$ in (23·00 m)
Wing chord (constant)	6 ft $2\frac{3}{4}$ in (1·90 m)
Wing aspect ratio	approx 12
Length overall	30 ft $2\frac{1}{4}$ in (9·20 m)
Length of fuselage	22 ft $5\frac{3}{4}$ in (6·85 m)
Height overall	6 ft $10\frac{3}{4}$ in (2·10 m)
Tailplane span	17 ft $4\frac{3}{4}$ in (5·30 m)
Propeller diameter	8 ft $6\frac{1}{4}$ in (2·60 m)

DIMENSIONS, INTERNAL:

Cabin: Length	2 ft $8\frac{3}{4}$ in (0·83 m)
Width	2 ft $0\frac{1}{4}$ in (0·62 m)
Height	5 ft 9 in (1·75 m)

AREAS:

Wings, gross	430·6 sq ft (40·00 m²)
Rudder	24·22 sq ft (2·25 m²)
Tailplane	57·00 sq ft (5·30 m²)

WEIGHTS AND LOADING:

Weight empty	44 lb (20 kg)
T-O weight	187 lb (85 kg)
Wing + tailplane loading	approx 0·41 lb/sq ft (2·0 kg/m²)

PERFORMANCE:

Speed (estimated)	11 knots (12·75 mph; 20·5 km/h)

STUDENCKIE BIURO KONSTRUKCYJNE

KOLA NAUKOWEGO LOTNIKOW STUDENTOW POLITECHNIKI WARSZAWSKIEJ

ADDRESS:

Politechnika Warszawska (Warsaw Technical University), Warsaw, ul. Nowowiejska 24

A team of students from the Aeronautical Department of Warsaw Technical University, under the leadership of Dipl Ing Edward Marganski, has designed a two-seat all-metal light aircraft known as the EM-5A.

MARGANSKI EM-5A DUDUŚ KUDLACZ

The EM-5A was designed in 1969-71, as a two-seat training aircraft, and construction began in September 1972 at the WSK-Mielec factory. Two flight test prototypes and a static test airframe are being built. The first flight was expected to take place in 1974. The general appearance of the EM-5A can be seen in the accompanying three-view drawing.

TYPE: Two/three-seat light aircraft.

WINGS: Cantilever mid-wing monoplane. Wing section NACA 66-215. No anhedral, dihedral or sweepback. Incidence 2°. Constant-chord single-spar all-metal wings. All-metal ailerons and flaps, with beaded alloy skin. No tabs.

FUSELAGE: All-metal semi-monocoque stressed-skin central nacelle and twin tailbooms.

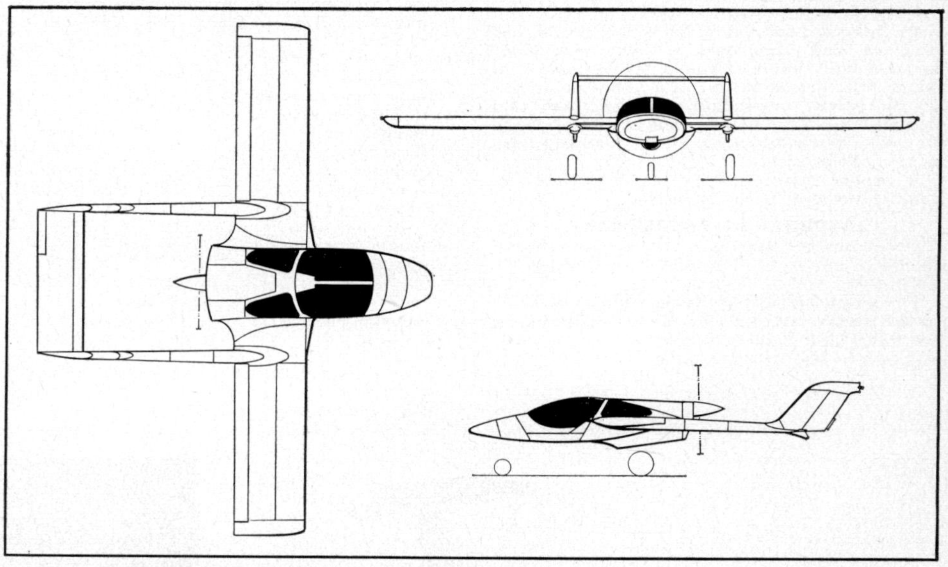

Marganski EM-5A Duduś Kudlacz two/three-seat light aircraft (*Roy J. Grainge*)

TAIL UNIT: Cantilever all-metal structure, with twin sweptback fins and rudders. Mass-balanced all-moving horizontal surface, with electrically-actuated balance tab in port half. Trim tab on port rudder.

LANDING GEAR: Retractable tricycle type, with electrical actuation. Main units retract inward, nosewheel forward. Nosewheel self-centering. Oleo-pneumatic shock-absorber on each unit. Main wheels from Zlin 526 F, tyre size 420 × 150 mm, pressure 42·7 lb/sq in (3·0 kg/cm²). Nosewheel from SZD-12A Mucha 100 sailplane, tyre size 300 × 125 mm, pressure 28·4 lb/sq in (2·0 kg/cm²). Aircooled and power-assisted hydraulic brake system from Zlin 526 F.

POWER PLANT: One 160 hp Walter Minor 6-III or 180 hp Avia M 137 inverted six-cylinder aircooled in-line engine, with low-pressure injection pump, driving a three-blade controllable-pitch metal pusher propeller from an L-200 Morava. Four integral fuel tanks, two in wing centre-section and one in each outer panel, total capacity 68 Imp gallons (310 litres). Individual refuelling point on top of each tank. Oil capacity 2·64 Imp gallons (12 litres).

ACCOMMODATION: Individual side-by-side seats for two persons in enclosed cabin. Canopy opens forward and upward. Dual controls. Space for 66 lb (30 kg) of baggage, or third seat, aft of front seats. Cabin heated and ventilated.

SYSTEMS: Hydraulic braking system. Electrical system (27·5V 500W AC, and 24V DC battery) for engine starting and landing gear and balance tab actuation. No pneumatic or oxygen system.

ELECTRONICS AND EQUIPMENT: R-860 VHF transceiver, ARK-9 radio compass, gyro-magnetic compass, MRP-66 marker, and gyro horizon.

DIMENSIONS, EXTERNAL:

Wing span	30 ft 10 in (9·40 m)
Wing chord (constant)	4 ft $1\frac{1}{4}$ in (1·25 m)
Wing aspect ratio	7·5
Length overall	22 ft $3\frac{3}{4}$ in (6·80 m)
Height overall	5 ft 7 in (1·70 m)
Tailplane span	8 ft $2\frac{1}{2}$ in (2·50 m)
Wheel track	8 ft $10\frac{1}{4}$ in (2·70 m)
Wheelbase	7 ft $10\frac{1}{2}$ in (2·40 m)
Propeller diameter	5 ft 7 in (1·70 m)
Propeller ground clearance	1 ft $3\frac{3}{4}$ in (0·40 m)

DIMENSIONS, INTERNAL:

Cabin: Max length	5 ft 3 in (1·60 m)
Max width	3 ft $11\frac{1}{4}$ in (1·20 m)
Max height	2 ft $4\frac{1}{4}$ in (0·72 m)

AREAS:

Wings, gross	126·5 sq ft (11·75 m²)
Ailerons (total)	8·07 sq ft (0·75 m²)
Trailing-edge flaps (total)	8·07 sq ft (0·75 m²)
Fins (total)	10·55 sq ft (0·98 m²)
Rudders (total, incl tab)	5·81 sq ft (0·54 m²)
Tailplane, incl tab	21·53 sq ft (2·00 m²)

WEIGHTS AND LOADINGS:

Weight empty	1,389 lb (630 kg)
Max T-O and landing weight:	
semi-aerobatic	1,984 lb (900 kg)
non-aerobatic	2,315 lb (1,050 kg)
Max wing loading	15·7 lb/sq ft (76·6 kg/m²)
Max power loading	11·02 lb/hp (5·0 kg/hp)

PERFORMANCE (estimated, at 1,984 lb; 900 kg T-O weight with M 137 engine except where indicated):
Max never-exceed speed
269 knots (310 mph; 500 km/h)
Max level speed at S/L
194 knots (224 mph; 360 km/h)
Max cruising speed at 9,850 ft (3,000 m)
162 knots (186 mph; 300 km/h)
Econ cruising speed at 9,850 ft (3,000 m)
135 knots (155 mph; 250 km/h)
Stalling speed, flaps up
60 knots (69 mph; 110 km/h)
Stalling speed, flaps down
52 knots (59 mph; 95 km/h)
Max rate of climb at S/L 1,380 ft (420 m)/min
Service ceiling 21,325 ft (6,500 m)
T-O and landing run 590 ft (180 m)
T-O to 50 ft (15 m) 950 ft (290 m)
Landing from 50 ft (15 m) 985 ft (300 m)
Max range, with 45 min reserve:
with 22 Imp gallons (100 litres) in centre-section tanks and outer tanks empty
323 nm (372 miles; 600 km)
with full fuel at max T-O weight of 2,315 lb (1,050 kg) 1,187 nm (1,367 miles; 2,200 km)

PORTUGAL

OGMA

OFICINAS GERAIS DE MATERIAL AERONÁUTICO (GENERAL AERONAUTICAL MATERIAL WORKSHOPS)

WORKS:
Alverca do Ribatejo
Telephone: 258803

DIRECTOR:
Brigadier Engineer Alberto Fernandes

ASSISTANT DIRECTOR:
Colonel Engineer Rui do Carmo da Conceição Espadinha

OGMA was first organised in 1918 and has been in continuous operation since then. It is a department of the Secretary of State for Aeronautics and is charged with the responsibility of maintaining and repairing all flying equipment, ground equipment, communications and radar equipment of the Portuguese Air Force. It also undertakes the manufacture of training aircraft and spare parts.

OGMA has a total floor space of 1,192,340 sq ft (110,772 m²), to which are being added new installations totalling 279,054 sq ft (25,925 m²). It has a personnel strength of 4,190.

OGMA is currently engaged on considerable conversion and re-manufacturing work, and performs IRAN inspection of F-86F, G91, T-6, T-33, T-37C, C-45, C-47, C-54, C-118, P-2E, Noratlas, Broussard, Chipmunk, Dornier Do 27 and DC-6 aircraft and Alouette II/III and SA 330 helicopters.

Sizeable installations have been established for the repair of F-104G Starfighter aircraft and the overhaul of J79 turbojet engines. As a preliminary step, a new training centre was built and equipped with mock-ups, cutaway components of various aircraft, and a new English-language training laboratory.

In addition to major overhaul and IRAN work on aircraft, aero-engines and components for the Portugese Air Force, OGMA performs maintenance work on Transall C-160 transport aircraft for the Federal German Air Force. Under a contract signed in 1959, it also undertakes IRAN, refurbishing and rehabilitation and periodic inspection of C-1A, C-47 and C-117D aircraft, and emergency maintenance and crash repair of A-7A Corsair, C-121M, C-130, E-1B, E-2B, EKA-3B, F-4B, P-3A and RA-5C aircraft for the USAF and US Navy.

OGMA is established as an industrial organisation operating on private industry principles. Initial funds were provided for self-contained administration, but the Air Force and other contractors are charged for work done.

In the latter half of 1973 OGMA announced preliminary details of a STOL utility transport which it had designed, to be powered by two 480 shp Turboméca Astazou II turboprop engines and to carry 18-24 passengers or equivalent freight. Of shoulder-wing layout, it has front and rear loading doors, a triple tail unit and a four-wheel landing gear. Dimensions include a wing span of 72 ft 2¼ in (22·00 m), an overall length of 48 ft 8¾ in (14·85 m) and a wing area of 473·6 sq ft (44·00 m²); design max T-O weight is 13,227 lb (6,000 kg), and estimated cruising speed 227 knots (261 mph; 420 km/h).

ROMANIA

CIAR

CENTRALA INDUSTRIALA AERONAUTICA ROMANA (Industrial Centre for Romanian Aviation)

HEADQUARTERS: 133 Calea Victoriei, Sector 1, Bucharest

Romania has had a tradition of aviation since the earliest days of flying, dating from the first monoplane built in France in early 1906 by the Romanian engineer Traian Vuia, the original monoplane of Aurel Vlaicu which, on 17 June 1910, became the first nationally-designed aeroplane to be flown in Romania, and the famous aeroplanes designed and built in France and Britain by Henri Coanda in 1910-14.

Since that time the Romanian aircraft industry (IAR) has produced some 80 different types of landplane (of which 70 were Romanian-designed) and three types of seaplane (two being of Romanian design), and has developed and manufactured 39 different types of sailplane. In addition, many other achievements in the fields of theoretical and experimental aerodynamics have been made by teams of Romanian engineers led by Prof Elie Carafoli, Prof Ion Stroiescu, Prof Ion Grosu, Ing Radu Manicatide, Ing Iosif Silimon and others.

Before the second World War the Romanian aircraft industry employed more than 20,000 people, the most important centres being the IAR (Industria Aeronautica Romana) at Brasov, with 8,000 employees, SET at Bucharest, and ICAR, also at Bucharest. The IAR factory, destroyed by bombing in 1944, was rebuilt after the war for the manufacture of tractors, and resumed its aeronautical activities with the IAR-811 training aircraft designed by Dipl Ing Radu Manicatide and flown for the first time in March 1949. Known until 1959 as URMV-3 (aircraft component repair factory 3), the Brasov factory during that period produced more than 200 aircraft of different types (designed by Dipl Ing Manicatide) and more than 20 types of sailplane (designed by Dipl Ing Iosif Silimon). At the same time a number of sailplanes were produced at the Combinatul de Lemn (wood factory) at Reghin by Vladimir Novitzchi; and two repair factories, subordinate to the Ministry of Military Forces, were set up at Medias (ARMV-1) and Bucharest (ARMV-2).

A major reorganisation took place in 1959, when the URMV-3 at Brasov was dissolved and its staff were divided into two teams. One of these was placed under the leadership of Dipl Ing Manicatide at ARMV-2, which was then renamed IRMA (Intreprinderea de Reparat Material Aeronautic). The other, led by Dipl Ing Silimon, was set up at Ghimbav as a division of IIL-Brasov, to concentrate on sailplane design. Up to 1968 IRMA, which was then responsible to the Ministry of Transport, built more than 140 aircraft for ambulance, training, agricultural and other duties.

The Romanian aeronautical industry was reorganised in 1968, and its activities are now undertaken, within the Ministry of Machine Tool Building Industry and Electrotechnics, by the CIAR (Industrial Centre for Romanian Aviation).

The major activities of CIAR are carried out in two factories: Intreprinderea de Reparat Material Aeronautic (IRMA-Bucuresti) and Intreprinderea de Constructii Aeronautice (ICA-Brasov). Research and development in the aeronautical field are undertaken by the Institute of Fluid Mechanics and Aerospace Construction (IMFCA-Bucuresti).

For the selection and training of specialist workers, an Engineering Faculty for Aerospace Construction has been established at the Polytechnic Institute of Bucharest. This Faculty has three sections, devoted to aircraft, propulsion systems and avionics.

In 1974 the Romanian aircraft industry was collaborating with SOKO of Yugoslavia (which see) in the design and construction of a twin-jet (Rolls-Royce Viper 623) fighter and ground attack aircraft. Known provisionally as the "JuRom" (*Jugoslavia-Romania*), it is being developed to meet a requirement of the air forces of the two countries.

The current products and activities of the IRMA and ICA factories, which have a combined work force of about 5,000 persons, are as follows:

IRMA-BUCURESTI

INTREPRINDEREA DE REPARAT MATERIAL AERONAUTIC (Aircraft Component Repair Factory)

ADDRESS:
Baneasa Airport, Bucharest

As indicated in the introductory copy for CIAR, IRMA was formed in 1959 from part of the former URMV-3 at Brasov, having also an aircraft design and production centre under the leadership of Dipl Ing Radu Manicatide. It currently specialises in the repair and overhaul of various types of large and small aircraft and aero-engines on behalf of various airlines, including Tarom, the Romanian state airline. It is also the agent and repair centre for Lycoming engines. IRMA was responsible for series production of the IAR-818 ambulance and agricultural aircraft (1965-66 *Jane's*) and, more recently, the IAR-821 and 821B. It was also responsible for building the IAR-822 and 822B prototypes described under the ICA-Brasov heading. In addition, IRMA-Bucuresti is manufacturing under licence the Britten-Norman BN-2A Islander.

Britten-Norman BN-2A Islander of Tarmaco Services Ltd, Zaïre Republic, built in Romania by IRMA (*P. J. Bish*)

IAR-821

Design of the IAR-821 agricultural and utility monoplane began at IRMA, under the leadership of Dipl Ing Radu Manicatide, in August 1965, and construction of the prototype was started in 1966. This aircraft flew for the first time in 1967. Twenty production aircraft were built, the first of which flew for the first time in 1968.

A full description and illustration appeared in the 1973-74 *Jane's*.

IAR-821B

The IAR-821B is a tandem two-seat version of the IAR-821 for primary training and for the specialised training of agricultural aircraft pilots.

The prototype flew for the first time in August 1968, and was certificated in the following month.

A description and illustration appeared in the 1973-74 *Jane's*.

IRMA (BRITTEN-NORMAN) ISLANDER

In 1968 it was announced that the Britten-Norman BN-2A Islander (see UK section) was to be manufactured under licence in Romania, and the aircraft is now in production by IRMA.

The initial agreement with IRMA is for the production of 215 Islanders, and the first Romanian-built example flew for the first time at Baneasa Airport, Bucharest, on 4 August 1969. A total of 84 had been completed by the end of 1972.

A further 30 were built in 1973, with production scheduled to increase to 40 in 1974 and 50 in 1975.

Since September 1972 the production of Islanders has continued in co-operation with the new Fairey Group Britten-Norman company, with which Romania also plans to collaborate in other projects.

ICA-BRASOV

INTREPRINDEREA DE CONSTRUCTII AERONAUTICE (Aircraft Construction Factory)

ADDRESS:
Brasov

ICA-Brasov, created in 1968, continues the work begun in 1926 by IAR-Brasov and continued in 1950-59 as URMV-3 Brasov. Today, it manufactures aircraft and sailplanes of its own design, including the IS-24, of which a description follows; and the IS-28 and IS-29 series of sailplanes, described in the appropriate section of this edition.

In addition, ICA-Brasov undertakes the repair and overhaul of light aircraft; it participated in the manufacturing programme for the Britten-Norman BN-2A Islander; manufactures the Aérospatiale SA 316B Alouette III helicopter under licence in Romania; and is also responsible for building the production-series IAR-822 and -822B agricultural and training aircraft and the prototypes of the IAR-823 training and IAR-826 agricultural aircraft.

In 1970, ICA-Brasov was awarded a Diploma of Honour by the FAI in recognition of its work in the field of aeronautical construction.

IS-23A

Design of the IS-23A, led by Dipl Ing Iosif Silimon, began at Brasov in the Summer of 1967, and construction was started in the following Autumn. The prototype (YR-ISA) flew for the first time on 24 May 1968, and a certificate of airworthiness was granted in August 1971.

No production of the IS-23A was undertaken. A full description and illustration appeared in the 1973-74 *Jane's*.

IS-24

Design of the IS-24, under the leadership of Dipl Ing Iosif Silimon, began at ICA-Brasov in the Winter of 1969 and is based largely upon that of the IS-23A (see 1973-74 *Jane's*). The IS-24 prototype (YR-ISB) flew for the first time on 24 May 1971, and certification was granted on 13 May 1972.

TYPE: Six-seat light executive and utility aircraft.

WINGS: Cantilever high-wing monoplane. Wing section NACA 64_2-413·5 (constant). No dihedral or sweepback. Two-spar constant-chord all-metal structure of ribs and stringers, with light alloy skin. Automatic leading-edge slats over almost full span. Electrically-operated trailing-edge flaps. Rod- and cable-actuated ailerons, which can be operated differentially or in conjunction with flaps. No tabs.

FUSELAGE: Corrosion-protected aluminium alloy semi-monocoque structure. Engine cowling of metal and glassfibre.

TAIL UNIT: Cantilever metal structure, with variable-incidence tailplane, one-piece elevator and sweptback fin and rudder. Balanced elevator and rudder, with fluted skins. Elevator controlled by rods, tailplane and rudder by cables. Trim tab in rudder.

LANDING GEAR: Non-retractable tricycle type, with hydraulic telescopic shock-absorber on each main unit. Nosewheel steerable by rudder pedals. Main-wheel tyres size 600 × 180; nosewheel tyre size 440 × 130. Hydraulic main-wheel brakes.

POWER PLANT: One 290 hp Lycoming IO-540-C1D5 six-cylinder horizontally-opposed air-cooled engine, driving a Hartzell HC.92.WK.1D-W9350-4·6 two-blade constant-speed metal propeller. Integral fuel tank in wing spar box, capacity 71·5 Imp gallons (325 litres). Reserves in wingtip tanks.

ACCOMMODATION: Enclosed, heated, ventilated and soundproofed cabin, accommodating in standard passenger version up to six persons. Passenger seats may be removed for cargo carrying.

DIMENSIONS, EXTERNAL:

Wing span	40 ft 8¼ in (12·40 m)
Wing chord (constant)	6 ft 4 in (1·90 m)
Wing aspect ratio	6·6
Length overall	29 ft 10½ in (9·10 m)
Height overall	11 ft 3½ in (3·44 m)
Wheel track	10 ft 10 in (3·30 m)
Wheelbase	7 ft 6½ in (2·30 m)

AREAS:

Wings, gross	254 sq ft (23·60 m²)
Ailerons (total)	25·83 sq ft (2·40 m²)
Trailing-edge flaps (total)	27·56 sq ft (2·56 m²)
Horizontal tail surfaces (total)	43·06 sq ft (4·00 m²)
Vertical tail surfaces (total)	16·79 sq ft (1·56 m²)

WEIGHTS AND LOADING:

Weight empty	2,733 lb (1,240 kg)
Payload	1,102 lb (500 kg)
Max T-O weight	4,188 lb (1,900 kg)
Max wing loading	16·7 lb/sq ft (81·5 kg/m²)

PERFORMANCE (at max T-O weight):

Max level speed at S/L	110 knots (127 mph; 205 km/h)
Max cruising speed at S/L	97 knots (112 mph; 180 km/h)
Stalling speed	40·5 knots (47 mph; 75 km/h)
Max rate of climb at S/L	591 ft (180 m)/min
Service ceiling	9,850 ft (3,000 m)
T-O run	623 ft (190 m)
Landing run	361 ft (110 m)
Max range	485 nm (559 miles; 900 km)

Prototype of the ICA-Brasov IS-24 general-purpose monoplane (290 hp Lycoming IO-540 engine)

IAR-822 single-seat agricultural aircraft (290 hp Lycoming IO-540 engine)

IAR-826 all-metal version of the IAR-822, with underfuselage dispenser for chemicals

IAR-822 and IAR-826

Design of the **IAR-822** was initiated at IMFCA in October 1968, by a team under the leadership of Dipl Ing Radu Manicatide, and the prototype, built by IRMA, flew for the first time in March 1970. Certification of the standard version was granted in October 1971, and of the agricultural version in January 1972.

In 1971 manufacture was begun at ICA-Brasov, which is responsible for series production, of the present series of 200 IAR-822s. The first production aircraft was flown for the first time in August 1971, and by early 1973 a total of 20 had been built. These were of mixed construction; as from 1973, the aircraft became available also in all-metal form as the **IAR-826.** The structural details below cover both models. The weights and performance figures apply to the IAR-822, but are generally similar for the IAR-826. A developed version, known as the **IAR-827,** is described separately.

Production is both for Romanian use and for export. Applications of the aircraft, in addition to agricultural duties, include highway de-icing, firefighting, aerial survey work, glider towing (up to three gliders), power and pipeline inspection, geological survey, fishery patrol, training, and the transport of up to 1,543 lb (700 kg) of mail or other cargo.

TYPE: Single/two-seat utility aircraft, designed primarily for agricultural operations.

WINGS: Cantilever low-wing monoplane. Wing section NACA 23014. Constant-chord safe-life wings, with 0° dihedral on centre-section and 5° on outer panels. Incidence 5°. Centre-section is a welded chrome-molybdenum steel tube structure, with metal skin. Outer panels, which are attached to centre-section at three points, are either of single-spar all-wood construction (Romanian spruce) with birch plywood skin, varnished on the inside and protected externally by a fabric coating; or of all-metal single-spar construction with duralumin skin. Mechanically-actuated single-slotted wood or metal flaps and ailerons. Ground-adjustable tab.

FUSELAGE: Welded chrome-molybdenum steel tube truss-type structure, of basically rectangular section with rounded top-decking. Air-tight fabric covering. Fuselage is designed to collapse progressively from the front and is fitted with a steel tube overturn structure to protect the pilot in the event of a crash.

TAIL UNIT: Cantilever all-metal or wood/fabric structure, of similar construction to outer wings. Fixed-incidence braced tailplane, of constant chord and NACA 0012 section. One automatic trim tab and one controllable tab in elevators. Ground-adjustable tab on rudder.

LANDING GEAR: Non-retractable tailwheel type, with main units interchangeable left/right. Main units, with fork legs and Vee bracing struts, have oleo-pneumatic shock-struts located in the centre-section. Rubber shock-absorber on tailwheel. Main wheels and tyres size 600 × 180 mm, tyre pressure 50 lb/sq in (3·5 kg/cm²); self-centering, fully-steerable tailwheel, size 290 × 110 mm. Hydraulic brakes. Optional ski gear.

POWER PLANT: One 290 hp Lycoming IO-540-G1D5 six-cylinder horizontally-opposed air-cooled engine, driving a Hartzell HC 92 WK-1D-9349-4-6 two-blade constant-speed variable-pitch metal propeller. Fuel tank in each outer wing, total capacity 44 Imp gallons (200 litres). Refuelling point above each wing. Optional auxiliary tank, capacity 27·5 Imp gallons (125 litres), can be mounted in hopper. Oil capacity 2·5 Imp gallons (11·4 litres).

Accommodation: Single adjustable seat in specially-strengthened enclosed cockpit with steel overturn structure. Upward-hinged door on port side. Cockpit designed to remain substantially undamaged in a low-speed crash. Provision for fitting jump-seat below and behind pilot, to accommodate mechanic or loader. Cabin heated, ventilated and sound-proofed.

Electronics: Standard equipment includes an electrical system for engine starting, pitot heating and flying instruments, a 24V 30Ah battery, and complete instrumentation for agricultural operation and for long-distance flights between operations. Optional equipment includes Bendix RT 221-AE transceiver, position lights, and blind- and night-flying instrumentation.

Operational Equipment: Chemical is carried in an epoxy-treated riveted duralumin-sheet hopper in forward fuselage, located at the CG point to avoid trim changes as the load is reduced. The hopper, which is loaded through a rubber-sealed door on the top of the fuselage, has an internal volume of 28·25 cu ft (0·8 m³) and can accommodate up to 132 Imp gallons (600 litres) of liquid or up to 1,389 lb (630 kg) of dry (powdered or granulated) chemicals. The corners are rounded to avoid dust catchment. Wide range of application equipment available, including a windmill-driven centrifugal pump and spraybars, which can be changed in less than 30 min "in the field" for a venturi-type solid chemical distributor. Rotary atomisers optional. Entire hopper load can be jettisoned in an emergency.

Dimensions, external:

Wing span	42 ft 0 in (12·80 m)
Wing chord (constant)	6 ft 10¾ in (2·10 m)
Wing aspect ratio	6·3
Wing centre-section span	12 ft 0 in (3·656 m)
Length overall	30 ft 10 in (9·40 m)
Height overall (tail up)	10 ft 2 in (3·10 m)
Height overall (tail down)	8 ft 6¼ in (2·60 m)
Wheel track	9 ft 7¾ in (2·94 m)
Wheelbase	19 ft 7¾ in (5·99 m)
Propeller diameter	7 ft 3 in (2·20 m)

Areas:

Wings, gross	279·86 sq ft (26·00 m²)
Ailerons (total)	29·92 sq ft (2·78 m²)
Flaps (total)	39·18 sq ft (3·64 m²)
Fin	7·21 sq ft (0·67 m²)
Rudder, incl tab	15·72 sq ft (1·46 m²)
Tailplane	27·12 sq ft (2·52 m²)
Elevators, incl tabs	21·31 sq ft (1·98 m²)

Weights and Loadings:

Weight empty:	
IAR-822	2,380 lb (1,080 kg)
IAR-826	2,469 lb (1,120 kg)
Max T-O weight	4,188 lb (1,900 kg)
Max wing loading	14·95 lb/sq ft (73·0 kg/m²)
Max power loading	14·44 lb/hp (6·55 kg/hp)

Performance (IAR-822. S: standard, no external agricultural equipment, at 2,866 lb; 1,300 kg AUW. A: agricultural version, with equipment, at 4,188 lb; 1,900 kg AUW):

Max never-exceed speed:	
A	134·5 knots (155 mph; 250 km/h)
Max level speed at S/L:	
S	121 knots (139 mph; 224 km/h)
A	97 knots (112 mph; 180 km/h)
Max cruising speed (75% power) at S/L:	
S	112 knots (129 mph; 208 km/h)
A	89 knots (103 mph; 165 km/h)
Operating speed:	
A	65-86 knots (75-99 mph; 120-160 km/h)
Stalling speed, flaps up:	
S, power on	32·5 knots (37·5 mph; 60 km/h)
A, power on	49 knots (56 mph; 90 km/h)
S, power off	42·5 knots (48·5 mph; 78 km/h)
A, power off	52·5 knots (60·5 mph; 97 km/h)
Stalling speed, 40° flap:	
S, power on	27 knots (31 mph; 50 km/h)
A, power on	40 knots (46 mph; 74 km/h)
S, power off	36·5 knots (42 mph; 67 km/h)
A, power off	48 knots (55 mph; 88 km/h)
Max rate of climb at S/L:	
S	984 ft (300 m)/min
A	689 ft (210 m)/min
Service ceiling:	
S	17,050 ft (5,200 m)
A	9,850 ft (3,000 m)
T-O run, on grass:	
S	262 ft (80 m)
A	591 ft (180 m)
T-O to 50 ft (15 m):	
S	722 ft (220 m)
A	1,181 ft (360 m)
Landing from 50 ft (15 m):	
S	656 ft (200 m)
A	984 ft (300 m)
Landing run:	
S	262 ft (80 m)
A	459 ft (140 m)
Max range, no reserves:	
S	323 nm (372 miles; 600 km)
A	242 nm (279 miles; 450 km)
Max endurance, no reserves:	
S, A	3 hr
Swath width (A):	
sprayer	66-82 ft (20-25 m)
granule duster	39-59 ft (12-18 m)
powder duster	98-131 ft (30-40 m)

IAR-822B

The IAR-822B is a tandem two-seat version of the IAR-822, design of which began at IMFCA in February 1972. It is intended for training, glider towing and simulated agricultural operations.

Construction of a prototype began at IRMA in May 1972, and this aircraft flew for the first time in December 1972. Production by ICA-Brasov has begun; five aircraft were due to be completed by early 1974.

The description of the IAR-822 applies also to the IAR-822B, except in the following respects:

Type: Two-seat training, glider towing and agricultural training aircraft.

Accommodation: Enclosed cabin, with fully glazed canopy, seating two persons in tandem. Fuselage structure modified to take second cockpit at front, in place of chemical hopper. Both seats adjustable and can accept parachutes. Two upward-hinged doors on port side.

Equipment: Dual controls are standard, and aircraft can be fully controlled from either seat. Optionally, to simulate agricultural operations, aircraft can be fitted with dispersal equipment of IAR-822, together with a reduced-capacity hopper (22 Imp gallons; 100 litres) located under front seat. Can also be fitted with release gear for glider towing.

Dimensions, external, and Areas:

As for IAR-822, except:	
Length overall	31 ft 4 in (9·55 m)
Wheel track	8 ft 10¼ in (2·70 m)

Weights and Loading:

Weight empty	2,403 lb (1,090 kg)
Max T-O weight	3,196 lb (1,450 kg)
Max wing loading	11·5 lb/sq ft (56·0 kg/m²)

Performance (at max T-O weight):

Max never-exceed speed	140 knots (161 mph; 260 km/h)
Max level speed at S/L	128 knots (148 mph; 238 km/h)
Max cruising speed (75% power) at S/L	116 knots (134 mph; 215 km/h)
Stalling speed, flaps up:	
power on	35·5 knots (40·5 mph; 65 km/h)
power off	43·5 knots (50 mph; 80 km/h)
Stalling speed, flaps down:	
power on	30 knots (34·5 mph; 55 km/h)
power off	38 knots (43·5 mph; 70 km/h)
Max rate of climb at S/L	984 ft (300 m)/min
Service ceiling	17,050 ft (5,200 m)
T-O run	312 ft (95 m)
T-O to 50 ft (15 m)	820 ft (250 m)
Landing from 50 ft (15 m)	722 ft (220 m)
Landing run	295 ft (90 m)
Max range, no reserves	340 nm (391 miles; 630 km)
Max endurance, no reserves	3 hr

IAR-823

The IAR-823 is a two/five-seat training or touring light aircraft, with retractable landing gear. It was designed at IMFCA, work beginning in May 1970, by a team led by Dipl Ing Radu Manicatide. Construction of a prototype began at ICA-Brasov in the Autumn of 1971, and this aircraft made its first flight in July 1973. The first production aircraft was due to fly in early 1974.

As a two-seater, the IAR-823 is fully aerobatic and is intended for training duties. With a rear bench seat for up to three more persons it is suitable as an executive, taxi or touring aircraft. Provision is made for two underwing pylons for the carriage of special equipment.

Type: Two/five-seat cabin monoplane.

Wings: Cantilever low-wing monoplane. Wing section NACA 23012 (modified). Dihedral 7° from roots. Incidence 3° at root, 1° at tip. All-metal structure, with single main spar and rear auxiliary spar; three-point attachment to fuselage. Riveted spars, ribs and skin of corrosion-proof aluminium alloy. Leading-edges riveted, and sealed to ribs and main spar to form main torsion box and integral fuel tanks. Electrically-actuated all-metal single-slotted flaps and fabric-covered metal ailerons. Ground-adjustable tab.

Fuselage: All-metal semi-monocoque structure. Glassfibre engine cowling.

Tail Unit: Cantilever metal structure. Two-spar duralumin-covered fin and tailplane; fabric-covered duralumin balanced rudder and elevators. Electrically-actuated automatic trim tabs in elevators; controllable tab on rudder.

Landing Gear: Retractable tricycle type, with steerable nosewheel. Electrical retraction, main units inward, nose unit rearward. Emergency manual actuation. Oleo-pneumatic shock-absorbers. Main-wheel tyres size 6·00-6, pressure 42·5 lb/sq in (3·0 kg/cm²). Nose-wheel tyre size 355 × 150 mm. Independent hydraulic main-wheel brakes, pedal-controlled from left front seat.

Power Plant: One 290 hp Lycoming IO-540-G1D5 six-cylinder horizontally-opposed air-cooled engine, driving a Hartzell two-blade constant-speed metal propeller. Fuel in four integral wing tanks, total capacity 79 Imp gallons (360 litres).

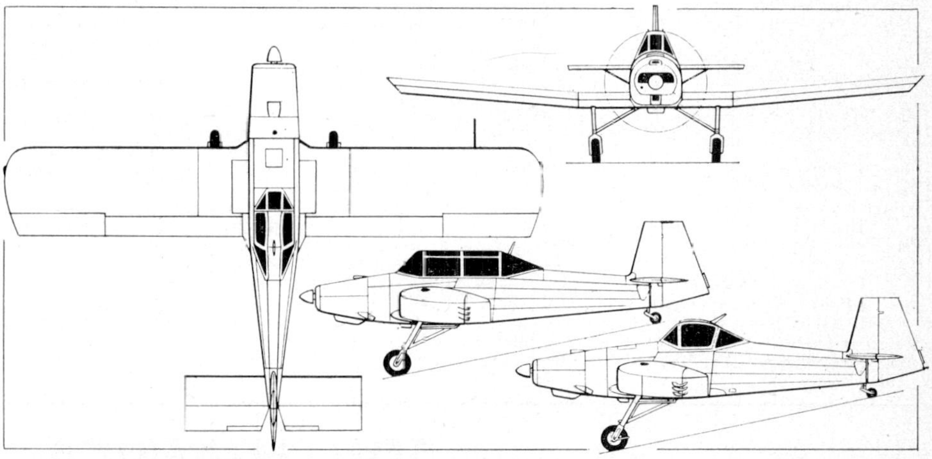

IAR-822 single-seat agricultural aircraft, with additional side view (*centre*) of two-seat IAR-822B (*Pilot Press*)

Two-seat IAR-822B, developed from the IAR-822 for flying simulated agricultural missions

Accommodation: Fully-enclosed cabin, seating two persons side by side on individual adjustable front seats, with removable bench seat at rear for up to three more people. Upward-hinged door (optionally jettisonable) on each side of cabin, which is soundproofed, heated and ventilated. Compartment at rear of cabin for 88 lb (40 kg) of baggage. Equipment and layout can be varied for use as air taxi, executive or freight transport, ambulance, liaison or photographic aircraft.

Systems and Equipment: Electrical system, including 50A alternator and 24V 30Ah battery, for engine starting, elevator tab and landing gear actuation, radio communications, landing and navigation lights and cabin and instrument lighting. Dual controls standard in training version, optional in other versions. Other standard equipment includes VFR instrumentation and Bendix RT 221-AE transceiver. Optional equipment, according to mission, includes blind-flying instrumentation and, in civil transport version, marker beacon, nav/com radio, VOR/ILS, ADF and autopilot.

Dimensions, external:
Wing span 32 ft 9¾ in (10·00 m)
Wing chord at c/l 6 ft 6¾ in (2·00 m)
Wing chord at tip 3 ft 3¼ in (1·00 m)
Wing aspect ratio 6·66
Length overall 27 ft 0¼ in (8·24 m)
Height overall 8 ft 3¼ in (2·52 m)
Wheel track 7 ft 4¼ in (2·24 m)
Wheelbase 6 ft 1¼ in (1·86 m)
Propeller diameter 7 ft 4 in (2·23 m)

Areas:
Wings, gross 161·5 sq ft (15·00 m²)
Ailerons (total) 12·92 sq ft (1·20 m²)
Trailing-edge flaps (total) 19·16 sq ft (1·78 m²)
Horizontal tail surfaces (total) 35·52 sq ft (3·30 m²)
Vertical tail surfaces (total) 16·15 sq ft (1·50 m²)

Weights and Loadings (A: Aerobatic; U: Utility category):
Weight empty:
A 1,984 lb (900 kg)
U 2,006 lb (910 kg)
Max T-O weight:
A 2,623 lb (1,190 kg)
U 3,042 lb (1,380 kg)
Max permissible weight for special missions 3,307 lb (1,500 kg)
Max normal wing loading:
A 16·2 lb/sq ft (79·0 kg/m²)
U 18·8 lb/sq ft (92·0 kg/m²)
Max normal power loading:
A 9·15 lb/hp (4·15 kg/hp)

Performance (at 3,086 lb; 1,400 kg AUW):
Max never-exceed speed (limited) 215 knots (248 mph; 400 km/h)
Max level speed at S/L 167 knots (192·5 mph; 310 km/h)
Max cruising speed (75% power) at 5,750 ft (1,750 m) 162 knots (186 mph; 300 km/h)
Econ cruising speed (60% power) at 10,000 ft (3,050 m) 156 knots (180 mph; 290 km/h)
Stalling speed, flaps up 62·5 knots (71·5 mph; 115 km/h)
Stalling speed, 30° flap 54·5 knots (62·5 mph; 100 km/h)
Max rate of climb at S/L 1,378 ft (420 m)/min
Service ceiling 19,025 ft (5,800 m)
T-O run 755 ft (230 m)
Landing run 656 ft (200 m)
Range, according to mission and payload, 1 hr reserve 431-863 nm (497-994 miles; 800-1,600 km)
Endurance, according to mission and payload 3-7 hr

IAR-827

The IAR-827 is a developed version of the all-metal IAR-826 (which see), and represents a new generation of Romanian agricultural aircraft, having an increased payload, more powerful engine and improved flying and operating characteristics.

Type: Single-seat agricultural aircraft.

Power Plant: One 400 hp Lycoming IO-720 eight-cylinder horizontally-opposed aircooled engine, with fuel injection, driving a Hartzell three-blade variable-pitch metal propeller. Total fuel capacity 48 Imp gallons (220 litres).

Dimensions, external:
Wing span 45 ft 11¼ in (14·00 m)
Length overall 31 ft 7½ in (9·64 m)
Height overall 8 ft 8 in (2·64 m)
Wheel track 11 ft 9¾ in (3·60 m)

Area:
Wings, gross 312·15 sq ft (29·00 m²)

Weights:
Weight empty 2,667 lb (1,210 kg)
Chemical payload for 2 hr mission 1,984 lb (900 kg)
Max payload (FAR 21) 2,204 lb (1,000 kg)
Max T-O weight 5,180 lb (2,350 kg)

Performance (estimated. S: standard, no external agricultural equipment, at 3,306 lb; 1,500 kg AUW. A: agricultural version, with equipment, at 5,180 lb; 2,350 kg AUW):
Max level speed:
S 124 knots (143 mph; 230 km/h)
A 104 knots (120 mph; 193 km/h)
Cruising speed:
S 114 knots (132 mph; 212 km/h)
A 94 knots (109 mph; 175 km/h)
Stalling speed, flaps down, power off:
S 40·5 knots (47 mph; 75 km/h)
A 49 knots (56 mph; 90 km/h)
Max rate of climb at S/L:
S 984 ft (300 m)/min
A 770 ft (235 m)/min
Operational ceiling:
A 6,560 ft (2,000 m)
Service ceiling:
S 16,400 ft (5,000 m)
A 9,850 ft (3,000 m)
T-O run:
A 738 ft (225 m)
T-O to 50 ft (15 m):
A 1,476 ft (450 m)
Max range:
S 323 nm (372 miles; 600 km)
Max endurance:
A 2 hr 30 min

IAR-823 prototype light touring and training aircraft, built by ICA-Brasov

ICA-Brasov-built Aérospatiale SA 316B Alouette III helicopter

ICA (AÉROSPATIALE) ALOUETTE III

It was announced in 1971 that ICA and Aérospatiale had concluded an agreement for an initial quantity of 50 SA 316B Alouette III helicopters (see French section) to be built in Romania. Production of these is now under way, and Romanian-built components are also being supplied for incorporation in French-built Alouette IIIs.

SOUTH AFRICA

AFIC

AFIC (PTY) LTD

Head Office:
PO Box 8816, Johannesburg
Telephone: Johannesburg 51-2367

Works:
"L" Hangar, c/o Atlas Aircraft Corporation of South Africa, Kempton Park, Transvaal

Directors:
P. Henman-Laufer
A. G. Mechin

This company was formed in 1967 to produce a modified version of the Italian Partenavia P.64B Oscar-B, designated RSA 200, of which details appeared in the 1972-73 *Jane's*.

Production of the RSA-200 has been suspended pending the completion of arrangements for new manufacturing facilities.

AIR NOVA

AIR NOVA (PTY) LTD

Address:
PO Box 6125, Durban North, Durban 4016
Telephone: Durban 837518

Directors:
H. G. Brown (Manufacture)
Capt J. H. Rautenbach, DFC, DFM (Operations)
Dr Maitland Reed, PrEng, BScEng(SA), MScEng, PhD, CEng, FIMechE, AFRAeS (Technical)
G. P. M. Stege

Dr Maitland Reed was formerly the Head of the Dept of Mechanical Engineering at the University of Natal. With Capt J. H. Rautenbach as consultant on flight matters, and assisted by seven final-year students, he began in 1965 the design of an aerobatic biplane named the Rooivalk (Kestrel), a description of which appeared in the 1970-71 and 1972-73 *Jane's*.

The aircraft was later redesigned to such an extent that it was renamed Falcon.

With three associates, Dr Reed has now formed Air Nova (Pty) Ltd, to market plans and kits of the Falcon and also to manufacture the complete aircraft in single- and two-seat versions with power plants of up to 260 hp.

In addition, Air Nova operates service and sales centres for Beechcraft and Piper aircraft, and manufactures a new type of universal (high volume and ultra low volume) aerial spray nozzle developed by Capt Rautenbach and featuring quick adjustment in setting and very low drag.

REED FALCON

The Falcon is a further redesign of the modified Rooivalk prototype ZS-UDU (1972-73 *Jane's*), construction of which began in November 1972. It is basically a single-seat aircraft, designed for unlimited aerobatics, but is to be made available also as a two-seater.

The wings are the outer panels from the original Rooivalk, fitted with balanced ailerons; the fuselage is shorter than before, but wider.

The following description applies to the single-seat prototype Falcon, which was acquired from the University of Natal by Air Nova in April 1974:

TYPE: Single-seat aerobatic biplane.

WINGS: Strut-braced biplane. Wing section NACA 0012. No anhedral or dihedral. Incidence 0°. Sweepback 10° at quarter-chord. Sitka spruce main spars and ribs, covered with Dacron. Single "I" bracing strut each side, faired to upper and lower wings; centre-section of upper wing supported by a pair of inverted Vee struts forward of cockpit. Internally-balanced ailerons, of spruce and ply, on both upper and lower wings. No tabs.

FUSELAGE: Welded chrome-molybdenum steel tube (4130) structure, Dacron-covered.

TAIL UNIT: Single fin and rudder, with wire-braced tailplane. Welded steel tube structure, Dacron-covered. Trim tab in each elevator. No rudder tab.

LANDING GEAR: Non-retractable tailwheel type. Vee-type independently-sprung main legs, with rubber-cord shock-absorption. Cleveland main wheels and tyres, size 5·00-5, pressure 30 lb/sq in (2·11 kg/cm²). Cleveland hydraulic brakes on main units. Streamline fairings over main wheels.

POWER PLANT (from Rooivalk): One Continental IO-360-C six-cylinder horizontally-opposed air-cooled engine, rated at 210 hp, driving a two-blade constant-speed propeller. Three fuel tanks in fuselage, total capacity 28 Imp gallons (127 litres), including one 14 Imp gallon (63·6 litre) tank for ferry purposes. Oil capacity 2 Imp gallons (9·1 litres).

ACCOMMODATION: Single cockpit, with fully-transparent rearward-sliding canopy. Design can be adapted to two-seat configuration.

DIMENSIONS, EXTERNAL:

Wing span (upper and lower)	19 ft 3 in (5·87 m)
Wing chord (constant, each)	3 ft 10 in (1·17 m)
Length overall	19 ft 3 in (5·87 m)
Height overall	7 ft 0 in (2·13 m)

AREA:

Wings (total)	134·0 sq ft (12·45 m²)

WEIGHTS:

Weight empty	900 lb (408 kg)
Max T-O weight	1,450 lb (657 kg)

PERFORMANCE (estimated, 210 hp engine):

Max never-exceed speed	195 knots (225 mph; 362 km/h)
Max level speed	148 knots (170 mph; 274 km/h)
Stalling speed	51·5 knots (59 mph; 95 km/h)
Max rate of climb at S/L	2,400 ft (732 m)/min
Range with max fuel	450 nm (515 miles; 830 km)

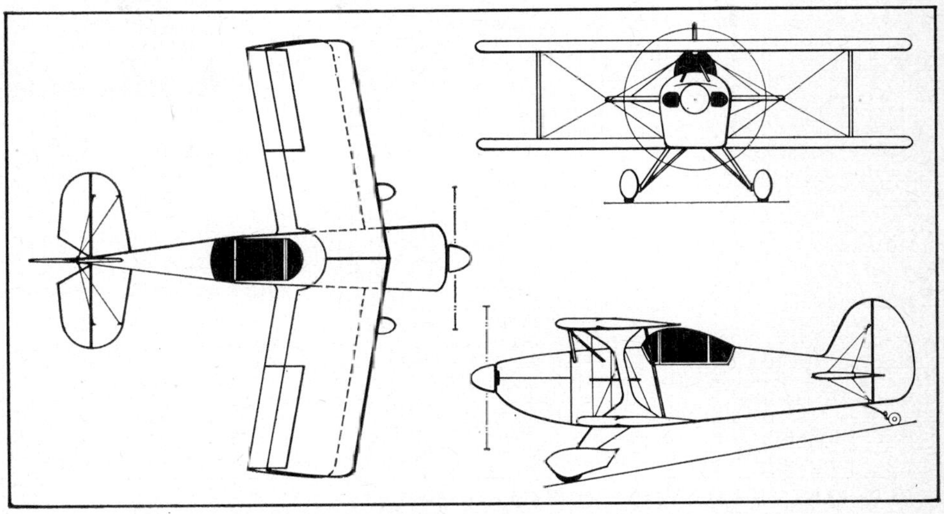

Reed Falcon single-seat biplane for competitive aerobatics (*Roy J. Grainge*)

ATLAS

ATLAS AIRCRAFT CORPORATION OF SOUTH AFRICA (PTY) LIMITED

HEAD OFFICE AND WORKS:
PO Box 11, Atlas Road, Kempton Park, Transvaal
Telephone: 973-0111
Telex: J7965

DIRECTORS:
V. P. Verster (Chairman)
L. W. Dekker
Dr W. J. de Villiers
P. A. Earle
J. F. H. Jagoe
Dr L. B. Knoll
J. S. van Vollenhoven

GENERAL MANAGER:
F. Nel

GROUP MANAGER, SALES:
N. F. Harrison

Atlas's present programme entails licence construction of the Aermacchi M.B. 326 jet trainer. In addition, Atlas undertakes the maintenance and overhaul of South African Air Force aircraft.

It has been reported that an advanced version of the Atlas Impala, possibly the single-seat Aermacchi M.B. 326K, is to be built in South Africa.

Preparations are also to be made for the assembly by Atlas's parent company, the Armaments Development and Production Corporation, of a light military aircraft, possibly the Aeritalia/Aermacchi AM.3C, of which 40 are on order for the South African Army Air Corps.

Atlas is understood to be making preparations for the licence assembly of components for Dassault Mirage F1 multi-purpose combat aircraft. The first South African-built Mirage F1 is expected to be completed in 1977.

ATLAS IMPALA

"Impala" is the name given to the South African version of the Aermacchi M.B. 326M currently being produced for delivery to the SAAF. Full structural and performance details of the M.B. 326M can be found in the Italian section of the 1970-71 *Jane's*. It has been reported that nearly 200 Impalas had been built by early 1973.

Atlas Impala (Aermacchi M.B. 326M) jet trainer of the South African Air Force

CSIR

COUNCIL FOR SCIENTIFIC AND INDUSTRIAL RESEARCH (Aeronautics Research Unit, National Mechanical Engineering Research Institute)

ADDRESS:
PO Box 395, Pretoria
Telephone: 74-6011

HEAD OF AERONAUTICS RESEARCH UNIT:
Dr C. G. van Niekerk, FRAeS

SENIOR PROJECT LEADERS:
Dr. W. J. van der Elst, AFRAeS (Low-speed aerodynamics)
M. S. Hunt, FRAeS (Aircraft structures)
A. J. van Wyk, AFRAeS (High-speed aerodynamics and Aircraft propulsion)

Initially, the CSIR concentrated on the spin-off from aeronautical research. This work led to the establishment in 1952 of a small aerodynamics division, within a research unit which has since become the National Mechanical Engineering Research Institute. By 1960 the division had become involved in various operational and other aeronautical projects, and was re-formed as an aeronautics division to provide research assistance when needed by the emerging South African aircraft manufacturing industry. This division grew into what is now the Aeronautics Research Unit, established in 1968.

Facilities at the ARU include supersonic and low-speed wind tunnels, a computer-controlled data handling system (capacity 20,000 bits/sec), a colour Schlieren system, and free-flight tunnel testing equipment.

Current ARU activities include research into lifting rotors, airframe fatigue, synthetic materials, separation of underwing stores, aircraft and missile stability, atmospheric turbulence, and aircraft noise problems.

The ARU has also designed and is developing a two-seat experimental autogyro, which flew for the first time in late 1972.

CSIR EXPERIMENTAL AUTOGYRO II

The CSIR (ARU) autogyro was designed to have a minimum level flight speed of 23·5 knots (27 mph; 43 km/h), a maximum level speed of 86 knots (99 mph; 160 km/h), a rate of climb of 905 ft (276 m)/min and an endurance of 3 hr. The design was started in March 1965, and construction of a prototype began in April 1967. This aircraft (ZS-UGL), after tethered tests from a lorry platform, made its first free flight at Swartkop air force base, near Pretoria, on 30 November 1972, piloted by Capt J. H. Rautenbach.

As a result of initial flight trials various modifications were subsequently made, and the description which follows applies to the aircraft as it was in late February 1973. In early 1974 the prototype was still being flight tested and subjected to an extensive evaluation programme, and updated performance figures were not available at that time.

TYPE: Two-seat experimental autogyro.

ROTOR SYSTEM: Single two-blade teetering rotor. Blades, which are of constant chord and NACA 8-H-12 section, each consist of a light alloy extruded spar and a foam-filled, light-alloy-skinned rear section; each is attached to the hub by a single teeter hinge. Metal trim tab on each trailing-edge, near tip. No rotor brake.

ROTOR DRIVE: For rotor spin-up only, the aircraft has a belt/clutch power take-off, connected to a dog clutch on the rotor by steel tube shafting via a two-stage 90° gearbox. Rotor/engine rpm ratio 1 : 10.

FUSELAGE: Box-type structure of light alloy construction with fairings of glassfibre-reinforced plastics.

TAIL UNIT: Twin fins and rudders, bridged by a fixed-incidence tailplane and supported on twin strut-braced tailbooms. All tail surfaces of light alloy stressed-skin construction. Full-span trim tab on tailplane.

LANDING GEAR: Non-retractable tricycle type. Shock-absorption by bungee rubber bands and nosewheel oleo leg. Nosewheel steerable and self-centering. Small skid beneath each fin.

POWER PLANT: One 180 hp Lycoming O-360-A four-cylinder horizontally-opposed aircooled engine, driving a Hartzell two-blade constant-speed pusher propeller. Power take-off for rotor spin-up. Rubber bag-type fuel tank in fuselage, capacity 30 Imp gallons (136 litres). Refuelling point on top of fuselage. Oil capacity 2 Imp gallons (9 litres).

ACCOMMODATION: Crew of two, with dual controls,

on side-by-side seats in extensively-glazed cabin. Forward-opening door, with glazed panels, on each side. Two spaces for baggage above and behind seats. Cabin is not heated, ventilated or air-conditioned.

SYSTEMS AND EQUIPMENT: 12V battery and radio equipment fitted.

DIMENSIONS, EXTERNAL:
Rotor diameter 36 ft $6\frac{1}{4}$ in (11·13 m)
Rotor blade chord (constant, each) 1 ft $0\frac{1}{4}$ in (0·31 m)
Propeller diameter 6 ft 0 in (1·83 m)
Length of fuselage 15 ft 3 in (4·65 m)
Width of fuselage 3 ft $11\frac{1}{4}$ in (1·20 m)
Height to top of rotor hub 9 ft $2\frac{1}{4}$ in (2·80 m)
Wheel track 8 ft $0\frac{1}{2}$ in (2·45 m)
Wheelbase 6 ft $6\frac{3}{4}$ in (2·00 m)
Cabin doors (each):
Max height 3 ft $1\frac{1}{2}$ in (0·95 m)
Max width 3 ft $1\frac{1}{2}$ in (0·95 m)
Height to sill 2 ft $7\frac{1}{2}$ in (0·80 m)

DIMENSIONS, INTERNAL:
Cabin:
Max width 3 ft $10\frac{1}{2}$ in (1·18 m)
Max height 3 ft $3\frac{1}{4}$ in (1·00 m)

AREAS:
Rotor disc 1,046·25 sq ft (97·20 m^2)
Rotor blades (each) 17·98 sq ft (1·67 m^2)
Fins (total) 13·99 sq ft (1·30 m^2)
Rudders (total) 6·46 sq ft (0·60 m^2)
Tailplane 12·38 sq ft (1·15 m^2)

*WEIGHT:
Max T-O weight 1,851 lb (840 kg)

*PERFORMANCE (estimated, at max T-O weight):
Max never-exceed speed 104 knots (119 mph; 193 km/h)
Max level speed 83 knots (95·5 mph; 154 km/h)

CSIR Experimental Autogyro II (180 hp Lycoming O-360-A engine)

Normal cruising speed 74·5 knots (85·5 mph; 138 km/h)
Econ cruising speed 66 knots (75·5 mph; 122 km/h)
Min level flight speed 26 knots (30 mph; 48 km/h)
Max rate of climb at S/L 800 ft (244 m)/min
Service ceiling 14,000 ft (4,267 m)
Min landing area circle of 98 ft 6 in (30 m) diameter
T-O run 200 ft (61 m)
T-O to 50 ft (15 m) 550 ft (168 m)
Landing from 50 ft (15 m) 250 ft (76 m)
Landing run 30 ft (9 m)

**Up to February 1974 final weights, loadings and performance figures could not be given*

REED/UNIVERSITY OF NATAL—*See "Air Nova"*

SPAIN

AISA

AERONAUTICA INDUSTRIAL, SA

HEAD OFFICE:
Plaza de las Cortes 2, Apartado 984, Madrid 14
Telephone: 222 75 80
Telex: 23593 Madrid

WORKS AND AERODROME:
Cuatro Vientos (Carabanchel Alto), Madrid 25
Telephone: 208 52 40 and 208 96 40

PRESIDENT:
Manuel Loring, Conde de Mieres

VICE-PRESIDENT:
Fernando Beltrán

MANAGING DIRECTOR:
Gonzalo Suárez

PLANT MANAGER:
José A. Delgado

DESIGN MANAGER:
Angel Sánchez

SALES MANAGER:
Rodrigo García

ADMINISTRATION MANAGER:
Manuel Algarra

This concern has since 1923 been engaged in the manufacture, repair and maintenance of fixed-wing aircraft and helicopters.

During recent years, the AISA design office has been responsible for several liaison, training and sporting aircraft, including the I-11, I-11B, AVD-12 (in collaboration with M Dewoitine) and I-115.

AISA is also engaged in IRAN repair and maintenance of several types of US aircraft, in particular the North American T-6 trainers operated by the Spanish Air Force.

Since 1962, AISA has been awarded several US government contracts for IRAN repair work on Sikorsky S-55 (H-19) and S-58 (H-34) helicopters. It is also engaged on the repair and overhaul of Bell 47, 204 and 205 and Hughes 300 helicopters of the Spanish Army, Spanish Air Force and civilian operators.

The present facility at Cuatro Vientos has a covered area of 430,556 sq ft (40,000 m^2) and employs a work force of some 775 persons.

AISA I-11B

Spanish Air Force designation: L.8C

The original I-11, of which two prototypes were built, had a tricycle landing gear and first flew in 1951. The I-11B, with tailwheel landing gear, was developed in response to the request of would-be owners for a traditional layout, and the first of two prototypes of this version flew for the first time on 16 October 1953.

Production of the I-11B began in 1954, and a total of 180 was built. The first six of these, with only basic flying instruments, were sold to civilian customers. The remainder, fitted with a full blind-flying panel, were delivered to the Spanish Air Force, by whom they were operated in the liaison and training roles under the designation L.8C. Some aircraft were fitted with the 93 hp ENMA Flecha engine.

In about 1970 the L.8Cs were withdrawn from Spanish Air Force service and transferred to the Real Aero Club de España, which in the Spring of 1974 was distributing them to Spanish flying clubs after a complete engine and fuselage overhaul.

A description and illustration of the I-11B can be found in the 1973-74 *Jane's*.

Model of the projected AISA-GN autogyro

AISA-GN AUTOGYRO

AISA, which in 1927 built some of the earliest Cierva Autogiros, is currently working on a new autogyro of its own design. Flight testing of the prototype was scheduled to begin in late 1974.

Its general appearance is shown in the accompanying photograph of a model of the aircraft. It will be a four-seat autogyro of all-metal construction, with twin tailbooms, twin fins and rudders and a non-retractable tricycle landing gear. The rotor will be of the four-blade articulated type. Power plant will be a 300 hp air-cooled engine, driving a two-blade pusher propeller.

The autogyro will have jump take-off capability. A special version is to be developed for agricultural use.

DIMENSIONS, EXTERNAL:
Rotor diameter 42 ft 0 in (12·80 m)
Wing span 8 ft $6\frac{1}{4}$ in (2·60 m)
Length of fuselage 21 ft 4 in (6·50 m)
Height overall 10 ft 6 in (3·20 m)

WEIGHTS:
Weight empty 1,560 lb (708 kg)
Max payload 915 lb (415 kg)
Max T-O weight 2,645 lb (1,200 kg)

PERFORMANCE (estimated, at max T-O weight):
Max level speed at S/L 129 knots (149 mph; 240 km/h)
Cruising speed at S/L 114 knots (132 mph; 212 km/h)
Min level speed 24 knots (27·5 mph; 44 km/h)
Max rate of climb 1,280 ft (390 m)/min
Landing run (zero wind) 0-16·5 ft (0-5 m)
Normal range:
standard fuel 323 nm (372 miles; 600 km)
with auxiliary fuel tank 431 nm (497 miles; 800 km)

CASA

CONSTRUCCIONES AERONAUTICAS SA

HEAD OFFICE:
Rey Francisco 4, Apartado 193, Madrid 8
Telephone: 247 25 00
Telex: 27418

WORKS:
Getafe, Seville, San Pablo, Cádiz, Madrid and Ajaloir

HONORARY PRESIDENT:
José Ortiz Echagüe

CHAIRMAN OF THE BOARD:
Lt Gen Enrique Jimenez Benamú

PRESIDENT:
Dr Emilio González García

VICE-PRESIDENT, FINANCE AND PROGRAMMES:
Dr Enrique de Guzmán de Ozamiz

VICE-PRESIDENT, ENGINEERING AND MANUFACTURING:
Eugenio Aguirre Castillo

GENERAL SECRETARY:
C. Marín

This company was formed in March 1923 for the primary purpose of producing metal aircraft for the Spanish Air Force. It began by building under licence the Breguet XIX and has since

manufactured many other aircraft of foreign design. The latest of these was the Northrop F-5 fighter, for which the company received a contract in early 1966.

CASA's own Project Office has designed and produced several transport aircraft under contract to the Spanish Air Ministry. The latest of these is the C.212 Aviocar, which is currently in production.

The Project Office also undertakes design and development work for foreign companies and has, for example, collaborated in the design of the MBB HFB 320 Hansa light twin-jet executive transport; HFB co-operated in the design of the CASA C.212 Aviocar. In 1973 the Project Office of CASA collaborated with Dassault-Breguet and MBB in the design of a four-turboprop STOL military transport aircraft, known as the CASA-401.

Under contract to Dassault-Breguet (which see), CASA is responsible for manufacturing certain sections of the Mercure twin-turbofan transport (forward fuselage up to the wing attachment point) and the Falcon 10 light business aircraft (outer wings). CASA is a full member (4·2%) of Airbus Industrie (see International section), and manufactures the horizontal tail surfaces, landing gear doors and forward passenger doors for the Airbus A-300B wide-bodied transport aircraft. In addition, CASA is a member (25% share) of the Europlane consortium (see International section).

CASA has carried out maintenance and modernisation work for the Spanish Air Force and, since 1954, for the US Air Force in Europe, as described in the 1972-73 *Jane's*. Its principal present activities of this kind concern the overhaul and maintenance of McDonnell Douglas F-4 aircraft and Bell 47G, 204 and 205 and Sikorsky H-19 helicopters.

In 1972 the former Hispano Aviación SA (see 1972-73 *Jane's*) was merged with CASA, the latter company taking over all of Hispano's offices and other facilities, aircraft production programmes and personnel. In June 1973 ENMASA (Empresa Nacional de Motores de Aviación) was merged into CASA, and now constitutes the CASA División de Motores (see "Aero-Engines" section). CASA has six factories, employing a total of 6,830 people in early 1974. Including Hispano production, the company had by that time manufactured 3,445 aircraft and overhauled 5,435. CASA has a total covered area in the region of 2,120,490 sq ft (197,000 m²); majority shareholder in the company is the INI (Instituto Nacional de Industria).

CASA C.212 AVIOCAR

Spanish Air Force designation: T.12

The C.212 Aviocar twin-turboprop light utility STOL transport was evolved by CASA to fulfil a variety of military or civil rôles, but primarily to replace the mixed fleet of Junkers Ju 52/3m (T.2), Douglas DC-3 (T.3) and CASA-207 Azor (T.7) transport aircraft in service with the Spanish Air Force.

The C.212 is at present proposed in six main versions—as a 16-seat paratroop transport, military freighter, ambulance, photographic aircraft, crew trainer or 18-seat passenger transport —and is being certificated to joint military and civil standards laid down by the Instituto Nacional de Técnica Aeroespacial (INTA), which is also responsible for the flight test programme. It has a STOL capability that enables it to use unprepared landing strips of about 1,310 ft (400 m) in length, and other applications at present envisaged include those of forest fire patrol and (with a hopper installed) of dispensing chemicals for pest control.

On 24 September 1968, CASA was awarded a contract by the Ministerio del Aire for the development and construction of two flying prototypes and one structural test airframe. The first flight took place on 26 March 1971; the second prototype flew for the first time on 23 October 1971.

Production is under way of an initial quantity of 12 pre-production Aviocars; the first of these made its first flight on 17 November 1972, and 11 had flown by February 1974.

For the Spanish Air Ministry, six of the pre-production aircraft will be equipped for photographic survey and two for navigation training; four will be used for commercial development. A further 32 Aviocars (29 paratroop transports and three navigation trainers) have been ordered by the Spanish Air Force; the Portuguese Air Force has ordered 28, with a further 12 on option. CASA has a co-operative agreement with the Commercial Aircraft Division of MBB whereby the German company is contributing to the development and manufacture of the wing centre-section for the Aviocar, including the engine nacelles, flaps and flap controls.

Type: Twin-turboprop STOL utility transport.

Wings: Cantilever high-wing monoplane. Wing section NACA 65_3-218. Incidence 2° 30′. No dihedral or sweepback. All-metal light alloy fail-safe structure. All-metal ailerons and double-slotted trailing-edge flaps. Trim tab in port aileron. Rubber-boot de-icing of leading-edges.

Fuselage: Semi-monocoque fail-safe structure of light alloy construction.

Tail Unit: Cantilever two-spar all-metal structure, with dorsal fairing forward of fin. Tailplane mid-mounted on rear of fuselage. Trim tab in rudder and each elevator. Rubber-boot de-icing of leading-edges.

Landing Gear: Non-retractable tricycle type, with single main wheels and single steerable nosewheel. CASA oleo-pneumatic shock-absorbers. Dunlop wheels and tyres, main units size 11·00-12 (8-ply) Type III, nose unit size 8·00-7 Type III. Tyre pressure (all units) 45 lb/sq in (3·16 kg/cm²). Dunlop hydraulic disc brakes on main wheels.

Power Plant: Two 776 ehp AiResearch TPE 331-5-251C turboprop engines, each driving a Hartzell HC-B4TN-5CL/LT10282HB+4 four-blade constant-speed (Beta-mode on ground) metal propeller (three-blade HC-B3TN-5E in prototype and early pre-series aircraft). Fuel in four outer-wing tanks, with total capacity of 462 Imp gallons (2,100 litres). Oil capacity 1·32 Imp gallons (6 litres) per engine.

Accommodation: Crew of two on flight deck. For the paratroop role, the main cabin can be fitted with 16 inward-facing seats along the cabin walls, to accommodate 15 paratroops and an instructor/jumpmaster. As an ambulance, the cabin would normally be equipped to carry 10 stretcher patients and 3 sitting casualties, plus medical attendants, but an alternative layout provides for up to 18 stretchers to be carried if necessary. As a freighter, the Aviocar can carry up to 4,410 lb (2,000 kg) of cargo in the main cabin, including light vehicles. Photographic version is equipped with two cameras and a darkroom. Aircrew training version accommodation consists of individual desks for an instructor and five pupils, in two rows, fitted with appropriate instrument installations. The civil passenger transport version has standard seating for 18 persons in five rows of three (one to port and two to starboard of centre aisle) at 33 in (83 cm) pitch, plus three seats side by side at rear of cabin. Access to main cabin is via two doors on the port side, one aft of (and providing access to) the flight deck and one aft of the wing trailing-edge. In addition, there is a two-section underfuselage loading ramp/door aft of the main cabin; this door is openable in flight for the discharge of paratroops or cargo, and is fitted with external wheels, to allow the door to remain open during ground manoeuvring. There is an emergency exit door aft of the wing trailing-edge on the starboard side. All versions have a toilet at the forward end of the main cabin on the starboard side, with a baggage compartment opposite on the port side. In the civil transport version, the interior of the rear-loading door can be used for additional baggage stowage. Lucas Aerospace electrically-heated laminated acrylic windscreen.

Systems: Unpressurised cabin. Hydraulic system, pressure 2,000 lb/sq in (140 kg/cm²), operates main-wheel brakes, flaps and nose-wheel steering. Electrical system is supplied by two 3kW starter/generators.

Electronics and Equipment: Radio and radar equipment includes Bendix RTA 41B VHF, AN/ARC 34C UHF, VOR/ILS and one ADF. Blind-flying instrumentation standard. Optional equipment includes TACAN, SIF/IFF, Collins 618S-4 HF and a second ADF.

Dimensions, external:

Wing span	62 ft 4 in (19·00 m)
Wing chord at root	8 ft 2½ in (2·50 m)

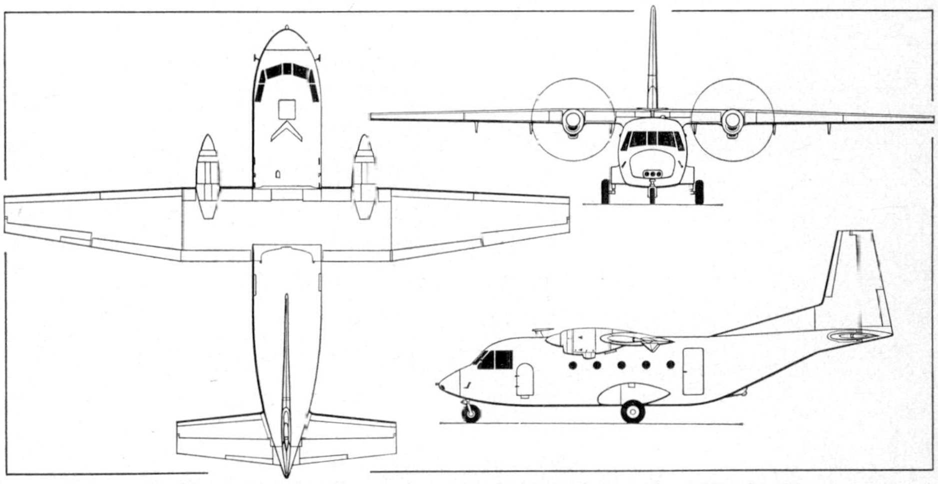

CASA C.212 Aviocar twin-turboprop light transport aircraft (*Pilot Press*)

CASA C.212 Aviocar military transport and general-purpose aircraft for the Spanish Air Force (two 776 ehp AiResearch TPE 331-5-251C turboprop engines)

Wing chord at tip 4 ft 1¼ in (1·25 m)
Wing aspect ratio 9
Length overall 49 ft 10½ in (15·20 m)
Height overall 20 ft 8 in (6·30 m)
Tailplane span 24 ft 3¼ in (7·40 m)
Wheel track 10 ft 2 in (3·10 m)
Wheelbase 17 ft 10½ in (5·45 m)
Propeller diameter 8 ft 11½ in (2·73 m)
Distance between propeller centres
17 ft 4¾ in (5·30 m)
Passenger door (port, aft):
Max height 5 ft 2¼ in (1·58 m)
Max width 2 ft 3½ in (0·70 m)
Crew and servicing door (port, fwd):
Max height 3 ft 7¼ in (1·10 m)
Max width 1 ft 11⅝ in (0·60 m)
Rear-loading door:
Max length 13 ft 1½ in (4·00 m)
Max width 5 ft 7 in (1·70 m)

DIMENSIONS, INTERNAL:
Cabin (between flight deck and rear-loading door):
Length 16 ft 4¾ in (5·00 m)
Width 6 ft 10¾ in (2·10 m)
Height 5 ft 7 in (1·70 m)
Volume 618 cu ft (17·5 m^3)

AREAS:
Wings, gross 430·56 sq ft (40·0 m^2)
Ailerons (total) 26·37 sq ft (2·45 m^2)
Trailing-edge flaps (total) 79·44 sq ft (7·38 m^2)
Fin 45·75 sq ft (4·25 m^2)
Rudder, incl tab 31·74 sq ft (2·02 m^2)
Tailplane 79·22 sq ft (7·36 m^2)
Elevators, incl tabs 38·32 sq ft (3·56 m^2)

WEIGHTS AND LOADINGS:
Manufacturer's weight empty
8,157 lb (3,700 kg)
Weight empty, equipped 8,609 lb (3,905 kg)
Max payload 4,410 lb (2,000 kg)
Max T-O weight 13,889 lb (6,300 kg)
Max zero-fuel weight 12,952 lb (5,875 kg)
Max landing weight 13,448 lb (6,100 kg)
Max wing loading 32·3 lb/sq ft (157·5 kg/m^2)
Max power loading 9·19 lb/ehp (4·17 kg/ehp)

PERFORMANCE (at max T-O weight except where indicated):
Max never-exceed speed
240 knots (276 mph; 445 km/h) EAS
Max level speed at 12,000 ft (3,660 m)
199 knots (230 mph; 370 km/h)
Max cruising speed at 12,000 ft (3,660 m)
194 knots (223 mph; 359 km/h)
Econ cruising speed at 12,000 ft (3,660 m)
170 knots (196 mph; 315 km/h)
Stalling speed, flaps up, AUW of 13,448 lb (6,100 kg) 72 knots (83 mph; 133 km/h)
Stalling speed, flaps down
62 knots (72 mph; 116 km/h)
Max rate of climb at S/L 1,800 ft (548 m)/min
Max rate of climb at S/L, one engine out
350 ft (106 m)/min
Service ceiling 28,025 ft (8,540 m)
Service ceiling, one engine out
13,250 ft (4,035 m)
T-O run 1,050 ft (320 m)
T-O to 50 ft (15 m) 1,410 ft (430 m)
Landing from 50 ft (15 m) 1,050 ft (320 m)
Landing run 590 ft (180 m)
Range at 12,000 ft (3,660 m):
with max fuel and 2,303 lb (1,045 kg) payload
949 nm (1,093 miles; 1,760 km)
with max payload
258 nm (298 miles; 480 km)

CASA 223A1 two-seat light aircraft, supplied to the Spanish Under-Secretary of Civil Aviation

CASA 223K1 single/two-seat aerobatic training aircraft in military insignia

CASA (MBB) 223 FLAMINGO

The former Hispano Aviación acquired from MBB in Germany sole rights for further manufacture of the latter's MBB 223 Flamingo light aircraft. The first Hispano-built Flamingo was flown for the first time on 14 February 1972, and a current series of 50 is being built in Spain.

The Flamingo is available in either of the following versions:

CASA 223A1. Basic two-seat utility version, intended primarily for training airline pilots. Ten built by MBB for Swissair and others (reportedly 15) for the Turkish Air Force. Can be equipped under Normal category conditions as a "2+2" three/four-seat touring aircraft and as an agricultural aircraft dispensing liquid or dry chemicals. Four delivered in 1973 by CASA to the Spanish Under-Secretary of Civil Aviation.

CASA 223K1. Fully-aerobatic as single-seater, with specially-modified version of IO-360-C1B engine and stressed for load factors between $+6g$ and $-4g$. Thirty to be delivered in 1974 to the air force of an undisclosed foreign country, which has a further 10 on option. The remaining six aircraft from the series of 50 being built by CASA have been offered to the Spanish Under-Secretary of Civil Aviation.

TYPE: One/four-seat light aircraft.

WINGS: Cantilever low-wing monoplane. Wing section NACA 64$_2$A215. Dihedral 3°. No sweepback. All-metal two-spar structure. Main spars inserted through fuselage sides and bolted together at centreline. Rear spars attached to sides of fuselage. Removable plastics wingtips. All-metal Frise-type ailerons and electrically-operated flaps have corrugated skin and extend over the full span. Trim tab in starboard aileron.

FUSELAGE: Conventional all-metal semi-monocoque structure of frames and stringers with riveted skin.

TAIL UNIT: Cantilever all-metal structure, with corrugated skin on control surfaces. Trim tab in port elevator and rudder.

LANDING GEAR: Non-retractable tricycle type. Rubber shock-absorption. Steerable and self-centering nosewheel. All three wheels and tyres size 6·00-6. Toe-operated independent hydraulic disc brakes. Parking brake.

POWER PLANT: One 200 hp Lycoming IO-360-C1B four-cylinder horizontally-opposed aircooled fuel-injection engine (200 hp AIO-360 in aerobatic version), driving a Hartzell two-blade constant-speed propeller. Fuel in integral tanks in wings with total capacity of 48 Imp gallons (220 litres).

ACCOMMODATION: Two seats side by side under large rearward-sliding jettisonable canopy. Removable dual controls. Cabin is soundproofed, heated and ventilated. Space for 200 lb (90 kg) of baggage aft of seats, with internal and external access. Provision for fitting a folding seat for one adult or two children in the baggage area.

SYSTEMS: 24V electrical system, with two 50Ah batteries.

ELECTRONICS AND EQUIPMENT: Provision for radio, radio compass, additional IFR instrumentation and glider-towing attachment.

DIMENSIONS, EXTERNAL:
Wing span 27 ft 2 in (8·28 m)
Wing aspect ratio 6
Length overall 24 ft 4½ in (7·43 m)
Height over tail 8 ft 10¼ in (2·70 m)
Tailplane span 10 ft 6 in (3·20 m)
Wheel track 8 ft 0¼ in (2·70 m)
Wheelbase 5 ft 3 in (1·60 m)
Propeller diameter 5 ft 11 in (1·80 m)

DIMENSIONS, INTERNAL:
Cabin:
Length 7 ft 2½ in (2·20 m)
Width 3 ft 8 in (1·12 m)
Height 3 ft 11¼ in (1·20 m)

AREAS:
Wings, gross 123·8 sq ft (11·50 m^2)
Ailerons (total) 8·25 sq ft (0·766 m^2)
Trailing-edge flaps (total) 10·12 sq ft (0·94 m^2)
Vertical tail surfaces (total)
19·81 sq ft (1·84 m^2)
Horizontal tail surfaces (total)
26·37 sq ft (2·45 m^2)

WEIGHTS AND LOADINGS:
Weight empty, equipped 1,510 lb (685 kg)
Max T-O weight:
A1 (Normal) 2,315 lb (1,050 kg)
A1 (Utility) 2,160 lb (980 kg)
K1 1,810 lb (821 kg)
Max wing loading:
A1 (Normal) 18·72 lb/sq ft (91·3 kg/m^2)
A1 (Utility) 17·47 lb/sq ft (85·2 kg/m^2)
K1 14·64 lb/sq ft (71·4 kg/m^2)
Max power loading:
A1 (Normal) 11·57 lb/hp (5·25 kg/hp)
A1 (Utility) 10·80 lb/hp (4·90 kg/hp)
K1 9·04 lb/hp (4·10 kg/hp)

PERFORMANCE (at max T-O weight):
Max never-exceed speed
205 knots (236 mph; 380 km/h)
Max level speed:
A1 (Normal) 131 knots (151 mph; 243 km/h)
A1 (Utility) 132 knots (152 mph; 245 km/h)
K1 135 knots (155 mph; 249 km/h)
Cruising speed (75% power):
A1 (Normal) 116 knots (134 mph; 216 km/h)
A1 (Utility) 118 knots (136 mph; 219 km/h)
K1 120 knots (138 mph; 222 km/h)
Landing speed:
A1 (Normal) 62 knots (71 mph; 115 km/h)
A1 (Utility) 54 knots (62 mph; 100 km/h)
K1 49 knots (56 mph; 91 km/h)
Max rate of climb at S/L:
A1 (Normal) 846 ft (258 m)/min
A1 (Utility) 886 ft (270 m)/min
K1 1,220 ft (372 m)/min
Service ceiling:
A1 (Normal) 12,300 ft (3,750 m)
A1 (Utility) 14,100 ft (4,300 m)
K1 17,390 ft (5,300 m)
Min ground turning radius 18 ft 0½ in (5·50 m)
T-O run:
A1 (Normal) 722 ft (220 m)
A1 (Utility) 705 ft (215 m)
K1 590 ft (180 m)
T-O to 50 ft (15 m):
A1 (Normal) 1,312-1,558 ft (400-475 m)
Landing from 50 ft (15 m):
A1 (Normal) 869-1,115 ft (265-340 m)
Landing run:
A1 (Normal) 689 ft (210 m)
Range with 30 min reserves:
A1 (Normal) 475 nm (547 miles; 880 km)
A1 (Utility) 269 nm (310 miles; 500 km)
Range with max fuel:
A1 (Normal) 620 nm (715 miles; 1,150 km)

SWEDEN

ANDREASSON

BJÖRN ANDREASSON

ADDRESS:
c/o Saab-Scania, Box 463, S-201 24, Malmö 1

Mr Andreasson has designed eleven different types of light aircraft. Of these, the BA-7 was built in series by AB Malmö Flygindustri as the MFI-9B Trainer/Militrainer and by MBB in Germany as the BO 208 C Junior (see 1970-71 *Jane's*).

An earlier design, the BA-4 biplane, was modernised by Mr Andreasson for members of the Swedish branch of the Experimental Aircraft Association, and a prototype was built by apprentices of the MFI apprentice school as part of their training programme. To distinguish it from the original BA-4, it is designated BA-4B.

Mr Andreasson took part in the design of the Swiss Trainer, described under the Dätwyler heading in the Swiss section of this edition. His latest design is the BA-11.

ANDREASSON BA-4B

The prototype BA-4B, built by MFI apprentices, was of all-metal construction. The design provides for alternative all-wooden wings.

Six BA-4Bs are now flying in Sweden and the UK.

World manufacturing rights in the BA-4B are held by Mr. P. J. C. Phillips of Down House, Cocking, Midhurst, Sussex, and the aircraft is built in the UK by Crosby Aviation Ltd (which see). Plans for homebuilders continue to be available from Mr Andreasson.

TYPE: Single-seat fully-aerobatic light biplane.

WINGS: Braced biplane type, with a single streamline-section interplane strut each side. A streamline-section bracing strut runs from the bottom fuselage longeron on each side to the top of the interplane strut, and an N-type cabane structure supports the centre-section. Incidence, upper wing 3°, lower wing 4°. Stagger 20°. Dihedral, upper wing 2°, lower wing 4°. Alternative all-metal structure or all-wood structure, with solid spars, covered with heavy plywood skin. Pop-riveted ailerons, of simplified sheet metal construction, on lower wings only. No flaps. Provision for fitting detachable plastics wingtips.

FUSELAGE: Sheet metal structure, with external stringers, making extensive use of pop-riveting. Turtledeck either sheet metal or reinforced plastics.

TAIL UNIT: Cantilever structure of pop-riveted sheet metal construction.

LANDING GEAR: Non-retractable tailwheel type. Cantilever spring-steel main legs. Main wheels size 5·00-4 or 5·00-5. Hydraulic brakes. Steerable tailwheel carried on leaf spring.

POWER PLANT: Prototype has 100 hp Rolls-Royce Continental O-200-A four-cylinder horizontally-opposed aircooled engine. Provision for other engines, including Volkswagen conversions. Standard fuel tank, capacity 11 Imp gallons (50 litres), forward of cockpit. Provision for carrying external "bullet" tank of 11 Imp gallons (50 litres) capacity under fuselage.

ACCOMMODATION: Single seat in open cockpit.

ELECTRONICS AND EQUIPMENT: Provision for battery, VHF radio and IFR instrumentation.

DIMENSIONS, EXTERNAL:
- Wing span:
  - upper: 17 ft 7 in (5·34 m)
  - lower: 16 ft 11 in (5·14 m)
- Wing chord (upper and lower, constant): 2 ft 7½ in (0·80 m)
- Wing aspect ratio (upper and lower): 6
- Length overall: 15 ft 0 in (4·60 m)
- Tailplane span: 6 ft 6 in (2·00 m)

AREAS:
- Wings, total: 90 sq ft (8·3 m²)
- Fin: 3·25 sq ft (0·3 m²)
- Rudder: 3·25 sq ft (0·3 m²)
- Tailplane: 6·5 sq ft (0·6 m²)
- Elevators: 5·4 sq ft (0·5 m²)

WEIGHT:
- Max T-O weight: 827 lb (375 kg)

Andreasson BA-4B single-seat aerobatic homebuilt biplane

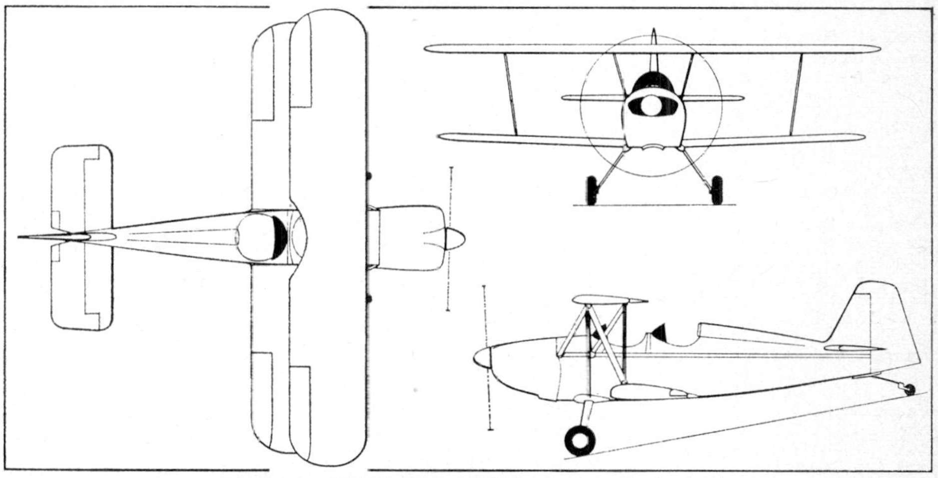

Andreasson BA-11 two-seat biplane (*Roy J. Grainge*)

PERFORMANCE (prototype, at max T-O weight):
- Max level speed: 122 knots (140 mph; 225 km/h)
- Max cruising speed: 104 knots (120 mph; 193 km/h)
- Min flying speed: 35 knots (40 mph; 64 km/h)
- Max rate of climb at S/L: 2,000 ft (600 m)/min
- T-O and landing run: less than 330 ft (100 m)
- Range with standard fuel: 152 nm (175 miles; 280 km)

ANDREASSON BA-11

The BA-11 is an all-metal biplane, intended for single-seat aerobatic, two-seat training or competition flying. It is designed generally to FAR Pt 23 Appendix A category A (aerobatic) requirements, but will have enhanced limiting load factors. These will be +9 to —6g as a single-seater, and in excess of +6 to —3g as a two-seater. A prototype was scheduled to fly in 1974.

WINGS: Biplane type, braced with dual sets of streamlined tie-rods. Ailerons, of simplified pop-riveted sheet metal construction, on both upper and lower wings. Positive stagger.

FUSELAGE: Metal structure, with one-piece moulded glassfibre turtledeck.

TAIL UNIT: All-metal structure. Control surfaces of similar construction to ailerons.

LANDING GEAR: Non-retractable tailwheel type. Main legs consist of two steel leaf springs attached to bottom of fuselage. Size 5·50-5 main wheels, with hydraulic disc brakes. Tailwheel also uses leaf spring and is steerable.

POWER PLANT: Designed for one 200 hp Lycoming fuel-injection engine, driving a 6 ft 2 in (1·88 m) diameter Hartzell constant-speed propeller. Main fuel tank in upper front fuselage, capacity approx 13 Imp gallons (60 litres). Auxiliary fuel tank, capacity approx 11 Imp gallons (50 litres), in upper wing centre-section.

ACCOMMODATION: Two seats in tandem, each designed to accommodate a back-type parachute. Basic instrumentation only in forward cockpit. Instrument panel of rear cockpit is large enough to accommodate a limited IFR panel in addition to the normal engine instruments. Electrical equipment, including starter, alternator and battery, can be fitted.

EKSTRÖM

STAFFAN W. EKSTRÖM

ADDRESS:
Tivedsvägen 1, S-181 64 Lidingö
Telephone: (08) 7663448

EKSTRÖM HUMLAN 2

Mr Ekström began the design of this single-seat autogyro in June 1971. Construction began in April 1972, and it flew for the first time in June 1973.

TYPE: Single-seat light autogyro.

ROTOR SYSTEM: Single two-blade semi-rigid rotor, attached to hub by a single bolt. Ztan Zee rotor blades. No rotor brake.

ROTOR DRIVE: Flexible shaft for rotor spin-up only. Via gearbox and two Vee-belts.

FUSELAGE: Cruciform chassis of 6061 T6 square-section aluminium tube, on which is mounted a pod-type nacelle.

TAIL UNIT: Conventional single fin and rudder, and fixed tailplane with dihedral, built of 4 mm and 8 mm aluminium sheet.

LANDING GEAR: Non-retractable tricycle type, with additional small wheel beneath tail. Rubber shock-absorption on tailwheel only. Go-kart wheels on main and nose units, tyre pressure 12·8 lb/sq in (0·9 kg/cm²). Nosewheel is steerable, self-centering, and is fitted with cycle-type brake.

POWER PLANT: One 90 hp McCulloch AF 100-X3 four-cylinder engine, driving a two-blade fixed-pitch pusher propeller. Fuel tank, capacity 10·5 Imp gallons (48 litres), behind pilot's seat. Fuel is a petrol/oil mixture, with 4% oil.

ACCOMMODATION: Single seat in open cockpit. One-piece curved windscreen. Shoulder harness fitted.

DIMENSIONS, EXTERNAL:
- Rotor diameter: 22 ft 3¾ in (6·80 m)
- Rotor blade chord: 7 in (0·18 m)
- Length overall: 11 ft 2¾ in (3·42 m)
- Height overall: 6 ft 6 in (1·98 m)
- Width over wheels: 5 ft 5 in (1·65 m)
- Propeller diameter: 3 ft 11¼ in (1·20 m)

AREAS:
- Main rotor disc: 390·9 sq ft (36·32 m²)
- Fin: 2·91 sq ft (0·27 m²)
- Rudder: 3·44 sq ft (0·32 m²)
- Tailplane: 2·15 sq ft (0·20 m²)

WEIGHTS AND LOADINGS:
- Weight empty: 321 lb (145 kg)
- Normal max T-O weight: 573 lb (260 kg)

Max T-O weight 661 lb (300 kg)
Normal max disc loading 1·47 lb/sq ft (7·16 kg/m²)
Normal max power loading 6·37 lb/hp (2·89 kg/hp)

PERFORMANCE (at 573 lb; 260 kg AUW):
Max never-exceed speed 97 knots (111·5 mph; 180 km/h)
Max cruising speed 81 knots (93 mph; 150 km/h)
Econ cruising speed 70 knots (80·5 mph; 130 km/h)
Max rate of climb at S/L 984 ft (300 m)/min
T-O run 197 ft (60 m)
T-O to 50 ft (15 m) 328 ft (100 m)
Landing from 50 ft (15 m), zero wind 98 ft (30 m)
Landing run, zero wind 16 ft (5 m)
Max range 140 nm (161 miles; 260 km)

Ekström Humlan 2 single-seat light autogyro (90 hp McCulloch four-cylinder engine)

SAAB-SCANIA

SAAB-SCANIA AKTIEBOLAG

HEAD OFFICE:
S-581 88 Linköping
Telephone: 013-115400
Telex: 50040 *SAABLG S*

PRESIDENT:
Curt Mileikowsky

EXECUTIVE VICE-PRESIDENTS:
T. Arnheim
T. Lidmalm

Aerospace Division
Telephone: 013-129020
HEAD OF DIVISION: T. Gullstrand
HEAD OF AIRCRAFT SECTION: H. Schröder
HEAD OF MISSILE AND ELECTRONICS SECTION: I. K. Olsson
INFORMATION: Hans G. Andersson

Datasaab Division
Telephone: 013-111500
HEAD OF DIVISION: R. Nyman

Scania Division
Telephone: 0755-34140
HEAD OF DIVISION: I. Eriksson

Saab Car Division
Telephone: 0155-80700
HEAD OF DIVISION: T. Arnheim

Nordarmatur Division
Telephone: 013-129060
HEAD OF DIVISION: Å. Schillström

The original Svenska Aeroplan AB was founded at Trollhättan in 1937 for the production of military aircraft. In 1939 this company was amalgamated with the Aircraft Division (ASJA) of the Svenska Järnvägsverkstäderna rolling stock factory in Linköping, which had been manufacturing and developing military and civil aircraft since 1930. Following this merger, Saab moved its head office and engineering departments to Linköping, which has since become the company's main factory.

In 1950, Saab acquired a factory at Jönköping for development and manufacture of airborne equipment. Other post-war expansions include a bombproof underground factory in Linköping, as well as important new production and engineering facilities in Linköping, Jönköping, Trollhättan and Gothenburg.

To reflect the growing diversity of the company's activities, its name was changed to Saab Aktiebolag in May 1965.

During 1968 a decision was taken to merge the company with another large Swedish automotive concern, Scania-Vabis, to strengthen the two companies' position in automotive product development, production and export. In that year also, Malmö Flygindustri (MFI) and Nordarmatur (NAF) were acquired.

The present Saab-Scania company has more than 32,000 employees, organised in five separate Divisions. Of these, nearly 5,000 are employed by the Aerospace Division.

Saab-Scania's current aerospace products include the Saab 37 Viggen supersonic multi-purpose STOL combat aircraft, the Saab 35X Draken single-seat all-weather fighter-bomber, the Saab 105 multi-purpose military aircraft and the Saab-MFI 15/17 light piston-engined trainer and army co-operation aircraft. Since 1968 the company has received export orders from Denmark and Finland for 51 and 12 Drakens respectively and from Austria for 40 Saab 105Ös.

The company also has a Scandinavian dealership for Hughes helicopters.

Saab-Scania has greatly expanded its activities in the electronics field. Current production items include general-purpose computers, automatic pilots and fire control and bombing systems for piloted aircraft, and components for guided missiles. A major production programme is the airborne computer for the Saab 37, and many toss-bomb sights have been bought by the United States, France, Switzerland and Denmark.

Saab-Scania is main Swedish Air Board contractor for licence production of Hughes Falcon air-to-air missiles in both radar homing (RB27) and infra-red homing (RB28) versions. It is also manufacturing the Saab 305 (RB05A) air-to-surface missile for the Swedish Air Force and a modernised RB04E version of the Air Force RB04 homing anti-shipping missile to be carried by the AJ 37 Viggen.

In addition, Saab-Scania is a member of the MESH space technology consortium which has delivered the TD-1A solar research satellite to ESRO. In 1973 ESRO ordered from MESH the OTS satellite.

SAAB 37 VIGGEN (THUNDERBOLT)

Swedish Air Force designations: AJ 37, JA 37, SF 37, SH 37 and SK 37

The Saab 37 Viggen multi-mission combat aircraft is the major component in the System 37 manned weapon system for the Swedish Air Force.

In brief, System 37 comprises the Saab 37 aircraft with power plant, airborne equipment, armament, ammunition and photographic equipment; special ground servicing equipment, including test equipment; and special training equipment, including simulators. Particular attention is paid to the optimum adaptation of System 37 to the SwAF base organisation and air defence control system (STRIL 60).

The Saab 37 is designed as a basic platform which can be readily adapted to fulfil the four primary roles of attack, interception, reconnaissance and training. The aircraft has an advanced aerodynamic configuration, using a foreplane, fitted with flaps, in combination with a main delta wing to confer STOL characteristics.

By employing a Swedish supersonic development of the American Pratt & Whitney JT8D turbofan engine, with a very powerful Swedish-designed afterburner, the Saab 37 can cruise economically at extremely low altitudes and, at

Saab AJ 37 Viggen single-seat attack aircraft of the Swedish Air Force with Saab RB04E homing missile on underfuselage pylon

the same time, possesses the acceleration and climb performance required for interception duties. The combination of advanced aerodynamic features with this powerful engine, thrust reverser, automatic speed control during landing, and head-up display, enables the aircraft to operate from narrow runways of about 1,640 ft (500 m) length.

The first of seven prototypes of the Saab 37 flew for the first time on 8 February 1967, and by April 1969 all six single-seat prototypes were flying. The seventh Viggen was the prototype for the two-seat SK 37 trainer. A number of airframe parts have also been completed for static testing.

Five versions have so far been announced, as follows:

AJ 37. Single-seat all-weather attack version, with secondary interceptor capability. Initial production version, which began to replace the A 32A Lansen from mid-1971. First production AJ 37 flew on 23 February 1971 and deliveries began 21 June 1971; first unit was F7 Wing at Såtenäs. No other units equipped with AJ 37 up to early 1974.

JA 37. Single-seat interceptor, with Smiths electronic head-up display and secondary capability for attack missions. Under development. Preliminary design work began in 1968. Flight testing of selected systems, including the radar, was initiated in early 1973 in a modified Saab 32 Lansen development aircraft. By early 1974, four modified AJ 37s were being used in the JA 37 development programme. A true JA 37 prototype is scheduled to fly in mid-1975. Volvo Flygmotor RM8B engine, of improved performance, is under development for this version and has been successfully run in a test rig.

SF 37. Single-seat all-weather armed photographic reconnaissance version to replace the S 32C version of the Lansen. A production contract was awarded in early 1973. Intended normally for overland reconnaissance, the SF 37 will be fitted with cameras and other equipment permitting reconnaissance at any hour of the day or night, at high or low altitudes and at long distances from the target. First flown on 21 May 1973.

SH 37. Single-seat all-weather armed sea surveillance version, to replace the S 35E Draken. Production ordered at same time as the SF 37. Primarily intended to survey, register and report activities in the neighbourhood of Swedish territory. Can also be used for attack missions. Prototype first flown on 10 December 1973.

SK 37. Tandem two-seat training version, in which rear cockpit takes the place of some electronics and forward fuselage fuel tank, and is fitted with bulged hood and periscope. Prototype first flown on 2 July 1970. First production SK 37 delivered June 1972. In service with F7 Wing at Såtenäs.

Initially, 175 aircraft of the AJ 37, SF/SH 37 and SK 37 versions were ordered for the Swedish Air Force; in December 1973 it was announced that five more aircraft (AJ 37s) were to be built within the same overall budget cost.

The following details refer specifically to the AJ 37 version, except where indicated otherwise:

Type: Single-seat all-weather attack aircraft, stressed for ultimate load factor of 12*g*.

Wings: Tandem arrangement of canard foreplane, with trailing-edge flaps, and a rear-mounted delta main wing with two-section hydraulically-actuated powered elevons on each trailing-edge, which can be operated differentially or in unison. Main wing has compound sweep on leading-edge. Outer sections have extended ("dog-tooth") leading-edge. Extensive use of metal-bonded honeycomb panels for wing control surfaces, foreplane flaps and main landing gear doors.

Fuselage: Conventional all-metal semi-monocoque structure, of similar construction to that of Draken, using light metal forgings and heat-resistant plastics bonding. Local use of titanium for engine firewall and other selected areas. Four plate-type airbrakes, one on each side and two below fuselage, are of metal-bonded honeycomb construction, which is also used for other selected areas of centre fuselage. Quick-release handle permits nosecone to be pulled forward on tracks to give access to radar compartment.

Tail Unit: Vertical surfaces only, comprising main fin and powered rudder, supplemented by a small ventral fin. Rudder of metal-bonded honeycomb construction. The main fin can be folded downward to port.

Landing Gear: Retractable tricycle type of Saab origin, built by Motala Verkstad and designed for a max rate of sink of 985 ft (300 m)/min. Power-steerable twin-wheel nose unit retracts forward. Each main unit has two main wheels in tandem and retracts inward into main wing and fuselage. Main oleos shorten during retraction. Nosewheel tyres size 18 × 5·5, pressure 155 lb/sq in (10·9 kg/cm²). Main-wheel tyres size 26 × 6·6, pressure 215 lb/sq in (15·1 kg/cm²). Goodyear wheels and brakes. Dunlop anti-skid system.

Saab AJ 37 Viggen in new Swedish Air Force camouflage

SF 37 photo-reconnaissance version of the Saab 37 Viggen, with ventral camera pod and other external stores

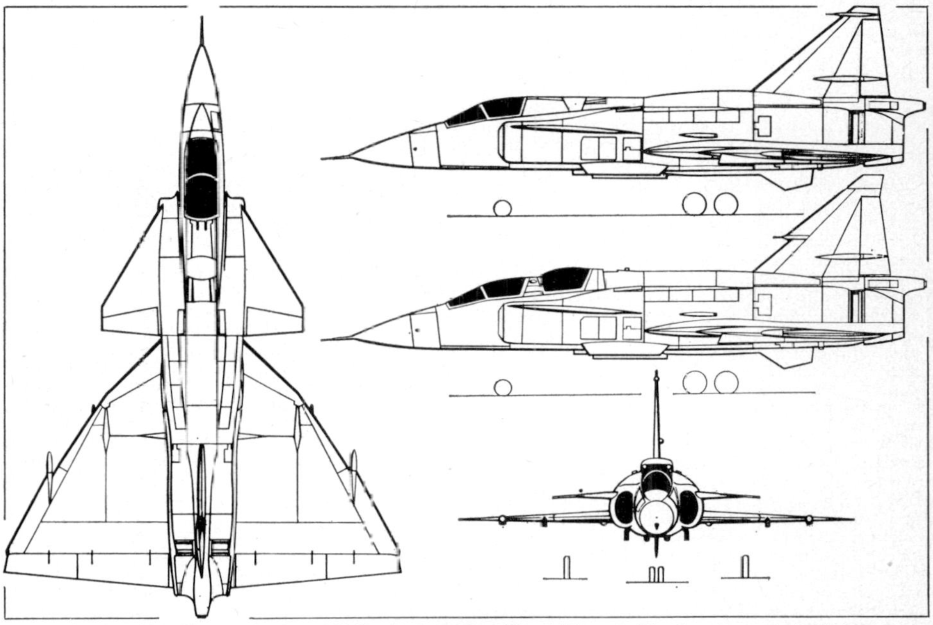

Saab AJ 37 Viggen single-seat attack aircraft, with additional side view (*centre*) of SK 37 two-seat training version (*Pilot Press*)

Power Plant: One Volvo Flygmotor RM8A (supersonic development of the Pratt & Whitney JT8D-22) turbofan engine, fitted with a Swedish-developed afterburner and thrust reverser. This engine has a static thrust of 14,770 lb (6,700 kg) dry and 26,000 lb (11,800 kg) with afterburning. Thrust reverser doors are actuated automatically by the compression of the oleos as the main landing gear strikes the runway, the thrust being deflected forward via three annular slots in the ejector wall. The ejector is normally kept open at subsonic speeds to reduce fuselage base drag; at supersonic speeds, with the intake closed, the ejector serves as a supersonic nozzle. Fuel is contained in one tank in each wing, a saddle tank over the engine, one tank in each side of the fuselage, and one aft of the cockpit. Electrically-powered pumps deliver fuel to the engine from the central fuselage tank, which is kept filled continuously from the peripheral tanks. Pressure refuelling point beneath starboard wing. Provision for jettisonable external auxiliary tank on centre pylon under fuselage.

Accommodation: Pilot only, on Saab fully-adjustable rocket-assisted ejection seat beneath rearward-hinged clamshell canopy. Cockpit pressurisation, heating and air-conditioning by engine bleed air via Delaney Gallay heat exchangers, cooling turbines and water separator. Birdproof windscreen. JA 37 cockpit will be redesigned and optimised for fighter mission.

Systems: Two independent hydraulic systems, of 3,000 lb/sq in (210 kg/cm²) pressure, each with engine-driven pump and with auxiliary electrically-operated standby pump for emergency use. Three-phase AC electrical system supplies 210/115V 400Hz power via a General Electric 60kVA liquid-cooled brushless generator, which also provides 28V DC power via 24V nickel-cadmium batteries and rectifier. Emergency standby power from 6kVA turbo-generator, which is extended automatically into the airstream in the event of a power failure or when the landing gear is extended. External power receptacle on port side of fuselage. Graviner fire detection system.

Electronics and Flight Equipment: Altogether, about 50 avionics packages, with a total weight of approx 1,323 lb (600 kg), are installed in the Saab 37. Flight equipment includes an automatic speed control system, SRA (in AJ 37) or Smiths (JA 37) electronic head-up display. AGA aircraft attitude instruments and radio, Phillips air data computer and instruments, L. M. Ericsson radar, Honeywell radar altimeter, Decca Doppler Type 72 navigation equipment, SATT radar warning system, Svenska Radio radar display system and electronic countermeasures, and AIL Tactical Instrument Landing System (TILS), a microwave scanning beam landing guidance system. Most of the electronic equipment in the Saab 37 is connected to the CK-37 airborne digital computer, which is programmed to check out and monitor these systems both on the ground and during flight.

Armament and Operational Equipment (AJ 37): All armament is carried externally on seven permanent attachment points, three under the fuselage and two under each wing, with standard 30 in (75 cm) store ejection racks. Wings can be fitted with two additional hardpoints if required. Primary armament is the Swedish RB04E air-to-surface homing missile for use against naval targets or the Saab RB05A air-to-surface missile for use against ground and naval targets, plus various types of Bofors air-to-surface rockets, bombs, 30 mm Aden guns and mines. The attack version can be adapted to perform interception missions armed with air-to-air missiles. Computations in connection with various phases of an attack, including navigation, target approach and fire control calculations, are handled by a Saab CK-37 miniaturised digital computer. This computer, which performs 48 specific tasks within the aircraft and is capable of 200,000 calculations per second, also provides data to the head-up display in the cockpit, thus freeing the pilot for concentration on other aspects of a flight. For a typical attack mission, the pilot would feed into the computer the position of the target and flight-path waypoints; the exact time of the attack; details of intended and alternative landing bases; and the type and method of delivery of the weapons to be carried. The CK-37 computer would then calculate and present to him information regarding engine start and take-off times, navigation and approach to the target (including any deviations from the time schedule), weapon aiming and release, climb-out, return flight path and landing. Continuous monitoring of the flight paths and fuel situation is provided throughout the mission, and the computer can also, when required, release the weapons automatically.

Armament and Operational Equipment (SF 37 and SH 37): Both reconnaissance versions can carry two air-to-air missiles, on the outboard wing stations, for self-defence. Equipment in the SF 37 includes a special optical sight, data camera, tape recorder and other registration equipment. The data camera collects and store on its film co-ordination figures, aircraft position, course, altitude, target location and other data. Four vertical or oblique low-level cameras, one long-range vertical high-altitude camera and an infra-red camera are installed in the nose, together with the camera sight and ECM registration equipment. Systems configuration also makes possible the detection of camouflaged targets and horizon-to-horizon (180°) photo coverage. Typical external mission equipment, in addition to air-to-air missiles, includes a drop-tank and two night reconnaissance pods (night cameras and illumination equipment) on the underfuselage stations, and an active or passive ECM pod on each of the inboard underwing pylons. Internal equipment of the SH 37 includes a nose-mounted surveillance radar, a camera for photographing the radar display, ECM registration equipment and various other registration systems including a data camera and a tape recorder. The inboard and outboard wing pylons can be occupied, respectively, by active or passive ECM pods and air-to-air missiles, as on the SF 37; the underfuselage attachments can carry a drop-tank on the centreline pylon, a night reconnaissance pod on the port pylon and a camera pod on the starboard pylon.

Armament and Operational Equipment (JA 37): Internally-mounted 30 mm Oerlikon long-range cannon, with improved gunsight. Advanced target search and tracking system, based on a high-performance L. M. Ericsson long-range radar, with good low-level performance and resistance to ECM. Weapons system will include long-range homing air-to-air missiles.

Dimensions, external:
Main wing span 34 ft 9¼ in (10·60 m)
Main wing aspect ratio 2·45
Foreplane span 17 ft 10½ in (5·45 m)
Length overall (incl probe) 53 ft 5¾ in (16·30 m)
Length of fuselage 50 ft 8¼ in (15·45 m)
Height overall 18 ft 4½ in (5·60 m)
Height overall, main fin folded
13 ft 1½ in (4·00 m)
Wheel track 15 ft 7½ in (4·76 m)
Wheelbase (c/l of shock struts)
18 ft 2 in (5·54 m)

Areas:
Main wings, gross 495·1 sq ft (46·00 m²)
Foreplanes, outside fuselage 72·12 sq ft (6·70 m²)

Weight:
T-O weight with normal armament
approx 35,275 lb (16,000 kg)

Performance:
Max level speed:
at high altitude Mach 2
at 300 ft (100 m) above Mach 1·1
Approach speed:
approx 119 knots (137 mph; 220 km/h)
Time to 36,000 ft (11,000 m) from brakes off
approx 2 min
T-O run approx 1,310 ft (400 m)
Landing run approx 1,475 ft (450 m)
Required landing field length:
conventional landing 3,280 ft (1,000 m)
no-flare landing 1,640 ft (500 m)
Tactical radius with external armament:
hi-lo-hi over 540 nm (620 miles; 1,000 km)
lo-lo-lo over 270 nm (310 miles; 500 km)

Saab SK 37 tandem two-seat trainer version of the Viggen for the Swedish Air Force

SAAB 35 DRAKEN

Swedish Air Force designations: J 35, S 35 and SK 35

The Saab 35 Draken single-seat fighter was originally designed to intercept bombers in the transonic speed range, and carries radar equipment to accomplish this under all weather conditions. It is able also to carry substantial weapon loads for attack duties or cameras for photographic reconnaissance.

The first of three prototypes made its maiden flight on 25 October 1955, and the first version, the J 35A, entered service with the Swedish Air Force at the beginning of 1960. Subsequently the Draken went through several stages of development, and continuously-improved versions for the Swedish Air Force included the J 35B, D and F fighter versions, the SK 35C trainer version and the S 35E reconnaissance version. Production of these models, described in earlier editions of *Jane's*, has been completed. Altogether, the Swedish Air Force ordered more than 500 Drakens.

A new 705 lb (320 kg) underfuselage photo-reconnaissance pod, giving 120° stereo coverage across the line of flight at an altitude of 300 ft (100 m) and a speed of 630 knots (725 mph; 1,167 km/h), has been ordered for the S 35E Drakens of the Swedish Air Force. Equipment in these pods, of which 20 sets have been ordered, includes three synchronised 70 mm Vinten cameras with infra-red-corrected lenses and a 10kVA EG & G electronic flash system. Using these pods, the S 35E will be able to undertake night and low light level reconnaissance missions.

The following version of the Draken continues in production:

Saab 35X. Long-range fighter/attack/reconnaissance version developed for the export market. Externally similar to the J 35F (1972-73 *Jane's*), but has greatly increased attack capability (max external load 9,920 lb; 4,500 kg) and range. For reconnaissance duties, a nose similar to that of the S 35E is fitted. T-O run with nine 1,000 lb bombs is 4,030 ft (1,210 m).

In 1968-69 the Danish Defence Ministry ordered 46 aircraft of this type, designated **Saab 35XD,** for the Royal Danish Air Force. Details of these aircraft, which were delivered in 1970-71, were given in the 1972-73 *Jane's*. A further five two-seat TF-35s were ordered in late 1973.

In April 1970, 12 Drakens (designated **Saab 35S**) were ordered by Finland. These are being assembled in Finland by Valmet Oy (which see),

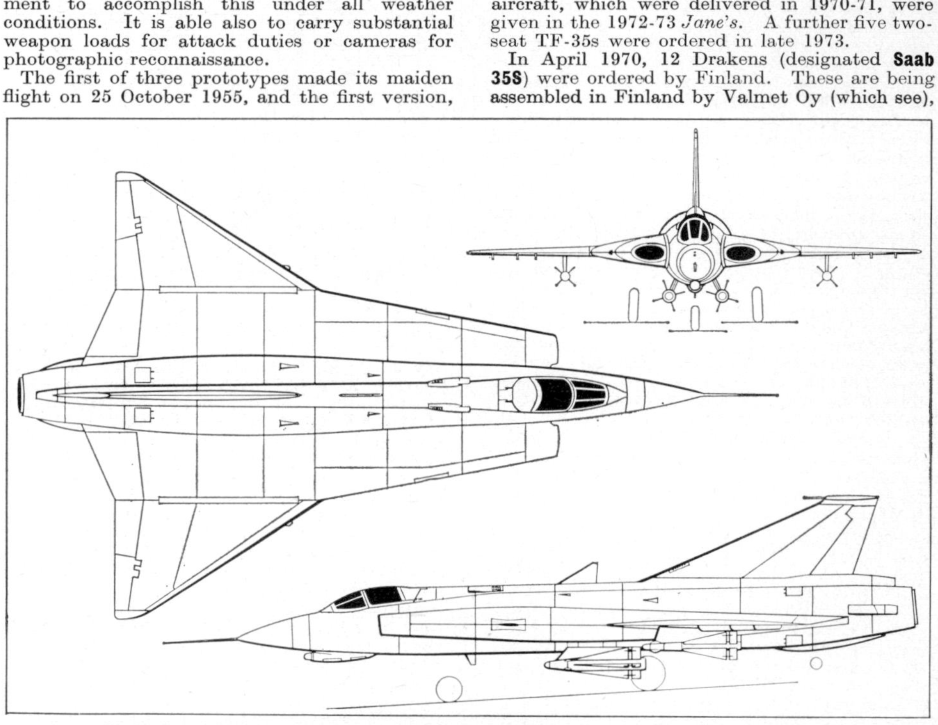

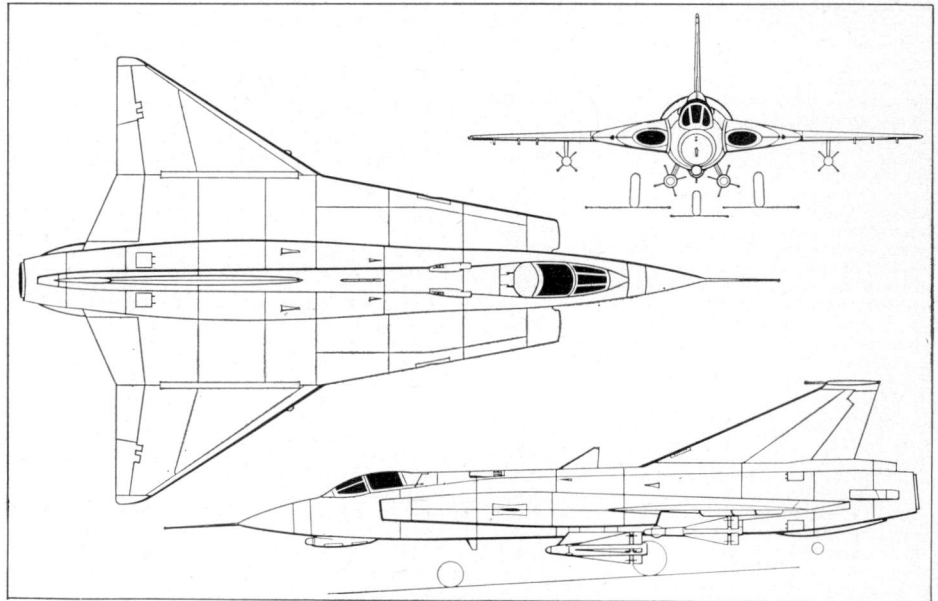

Saab J 35F Draken armed with RB27 and RB28 Falcon missiles (*Pilot Press*)

One of the six Saab 35BS Drakens leased from Sweden by the Finnish Air Force for training

for delivery during 1974-75. For familiarisation purposes, six Saab 35B Drakens (designated Saab 35BS) have meanwhile been leased to Finland by the Swedish Air Force.

The total number of Drakens built or on order for Sweden, Denmark and Finland is more than 600.

The following description refers to the basic Saab 35X:

TYPE: Single-seat supersonic all-weather fighter, reconnaissance and attack aircraft.

WINGS: Cantilever "double delta" mid-wing monoplane. Sweepback on centre wing leading-edge 80°, on outer wing leading-edge 57°. Thickness/chord ratio 5%. Central wing integral with fuselage. All-metal stressed-skin structure, with some bonding. Outer wing panels, attached to centre wing with a bolt joint, have relatively thick skin on a framework of spars and ribs and can be detached for transportation by road.

FUSELAGE: All-metal structure, in front and rear main sections, connected to each other by a bolt joint. Fuselage front section integral with front of centre wing structure. Two pairs of airbrakes, above and below rear fuselage.

CONTROL SURFACES: Conventional delta-shape fin and rudder. Elevons on wing trailing-edge comprise two inboard and two outboard surfaces, the latter being mass-balanced. Each control surface servo-operated by two hydraulic tandem jacks, fed by two separate hydraulic systems. No part of load on control surfaces is fed into stick and rudder pedals. Stick forces are generated artificially. Three-axis stabilisation system.

LANDING GEAR: Retractable tricycle type. Hydraulic actuation. Main units retract outward, the legs shortening during retraction to reduce the space required inside wing. Nosewheel retracts forward and is steerable. Tyre pressures 142-185 lb/sq in (10-13 kg/cm²) on nose unit, 171-242 lb/sq in (12-17 kg/cm²) on main units. Goodyear double-disc brakes and Dunlop anti-skid brake units. Dual retractable tailwheels. Brake parachute in fairing above rear fuselage. Arrester hook optional.

POWER PLANT: One Volvo Flygmotor (Rolls-Royce licence) Avon 300-series engine (Swedish Air Force designation RM 6C) with Swedish-developed afterburner. Static thrust approximately 12,790 lb (5,800 kg) dry and 17,650 lb (8,000 kg) with afterburner. Internal fuel in integral tanks in inner wings and fuselage bag tanks. Total internal fuel capacity 880 Imp gallons (4,000 litres). Provision for external tanks under fuselage and wings, increasing total capacity to 1,980 Imp gallons (9,000 litres). Additional internal tanks can be fitted in place of guns for ferry purposes. Single-point pressure fuelling system, capacity 185 Imp gallons (840 litres) per minute.

ACCOMMODATION: Pressurised and air-conditioned cockpit, with fully-automatic Saab 73SE-F rocket-assisted ejection seat and GQ parachute system permitting ejection within the normal flight envelope and down to 54 knots (62 mph; 100 km/h) on the ground. Rearward-hinged canopy.

SYSTEMS: Duplicated hydraulic system, with two independent pumps, for control surface and landing gear actuation. Third pump, for emergency use, is driven by ram air in case of engine failure. Three-phase AC electrical system supplies 200/115V 400Hz power via a 20kVA engine-driven generator or, in emergency, via a 3·5kVA generator in emergency power unit. Equipment requiring DC power is fed from these AC systems via two rectifiers giving 2·2kW at 29V. One 24V 22Ah accumulator acts as a buffer. The power permits three engine starting attempts.

ELECTRONICS AND EQUIPMENT: Complete radar equipment with nose scanner and pilot's scope, as well as Saab S7 collision-course fire-control equipment. Saab FH5 autopilot, with air data system, stick-steering and various following modes. Vertical tape instruments. Aga FR 21 VHF. DME.

ARMAMENT: Nine attachment points (each 1,000 lb; 454 kg) for external stores: three under each wing and three under fuselage. Stores can consist of air-to-air missiles and unguided air-to-air rocket pods (19 × 7·5 cm), 12 × 13·5 cm Bofors air-to-ground rockets, nine 1,000 lb or fourteen 500 lb bombs, or fuel tanks. Two or four RB24 Sidewinder air-to-air missiles can be carried under wings and fuselage. Two 30 mm Aden cannon (one in each wing) can be replaced by extra internal fuel tanks. With two 280 Imp gallon (1,275 litre) and two 110 Imp gallon (500 litre) drop-tanks, two 1,000 lb or four 500 lb bombs can be carried.

DIMENSIONS, EXTERNAL:
Wing span 30 ft 10 in (9·40 m)
Wing aspect ratio 1·77
Width, outer wing panels removed 14 ft 5 in (4·40 m)
Length overall 50 ft 4 in (15·35 m)
Height overall 12 ft 9 in (3·89 m)
Wheel track 8 ft 10½ in (2·70 m)
Wheelbase 13 ft 1 in (4·00 m)

AREAS:
Wings, gross 529·6 sq ft (49·20 m²)
Fin 56·51 sq ft (5·25 m²)
Rudder 10·23 sq ft (0·95 m²)

WEIGHTS:
T-O weight clean 25,130 lb (11,400 kg)
T-O weight with two 1,000 lb bombs and two 280 Imp gallon drop-tanks 32,165 lb (14,590 kg)
Max T-O weight 33,070 lb (15,000 kg)
Max overload T-O weight 35,275 lb (16,000 kg)
Normal landing weight 19,400 lb (8,800 kg)

PERFORMANCE (A: AUW of 25,130 lb; B: AUW of 32,165 lb):
Max level speed with afterburning:
A Mach 2
B Mach 1·4
Max rate of climb at S/L with afterburning:
A 34,450 ft (10,500 m)/min
B 22,650 ft (6,900 m)/min
Time to 36,000 ft (11,000 m) with afterburning:
A 2 min 36 sec
Time to 49,200 ft (15,000 m) with afterburning:
A 5 min 0 sec
T-O run with afterburning:
A 2,130 ft (650 m)
B 3,840 ft (1,170 m)
T-O to 50 ft (15 m) with afterburning:
A 3,150 ft (960 m)
B 5,080 ft (1,550 m)
Landing run at normal landing weight:
A and B 1,740 ft (530 m)
Radius of action (hi-lo-hi), internal fuel only:
A 343 nm (395 miles; 635 km)
Radius of action (hi-lo-hi) with two 1,000 lb bombs and two drop-tanks:
B 541 nm (623 miles; 1,003 km)
Ferry range with max internal and external fuel 1,754 nm (2,020 miles; 3,250 km)

SAAB 105

The Saab 105 is a twin-jet multi-purpose military aircraft, designed originally for training and ground attack duties, with reconnaissance, target flying and liaison as secondary roles. It normally seats two pilots side by side on ejection seats in a pressurised cabin; four fixed seats can be installed in place of the ejection seats.

The design was developed as a private venture by Saab (now Saab-Scania). The first of two prototypes flew for the first time on 29 June 1963, and the second on 17 June 1964.

Seven versions have so far been announced, of which the SK 60A, B and C versions (150 built) for the Swedish Air Force were described in the 1969-70 *Jane's*; the projected Saab 105XH in the 1971-72 *Jane's*; and the Saab 105XT prototype and Saab 105Ö production version for Austria (40 built) in the 1972-73 *Jane's*.

Development and flight testing of the following version is continuing:

Saab 105G. Current version, developed from Saab 105Ö, with increased armament capability (max external load 5,180 lb; 2,350 kg); more advanced avionics, including a high-precision nav/attack and weapon delivery system; modified wing leading-edges; provision for external fuel tanks on the inboard wing pylons; and increased flap deflection for steeper glideslope. Prototype flown for the first time on 26 May 1972.

The following description refers to the Saab 105G:

TYPE: Multi-purpose twin-jet military aircraft.

WINGS: Cantilever shoulder-wing monoplane. Sweepback 12° 48′ at quarter-chord. Anhedral 6°. Thickness/chord ratio 9·5% at root, 10·9% at tip. One-piece stressed-skin structure with two continuous spars. New "peaky profile" leading-edge, compared with earlier versions, gives improved manoeuvrability at high Mach numbers. Ailerons, of bonded honeycomb

Saab 105G close-support and training aircraft (two General Electric J85-GE-17B turbojet engines)

construction, are statically and aerodynamically balanced and have hydraulically-actuated servo assistance, with provision for reversion to manual control in the event of a hydraulic failure. Geared servo tab in each aileron; starboard tab adjustable mechanically for trimming. Hydraulically-operated single-slotted flaps of honeycomb construction. Two small fences on upper surface of each wing.

FUSELAGE: All-metal stressed-skin semi-monocoque structure. Hydraulically-operated perforated airbrakes pivoted in transverse slots in lower fuselage aft of landing gear.

TAIL UNIT: Cantilever all-metal T-tail. Control surfaces of bonded honeycomb construction, statically and aerodynamically balanced. Elevators have hydraulically-actuated servo control, with provision for reversion to manual control in the event of a hydraulic failure. Electrical elevator trimming. Electrically-operated trim tab in rudder. A pneumatic yaw-damper is also fitted. Geared servo tab in each elevator. Small ventral fin.

LANDING GEAR: Retractable tricycle type. Hydraulic actuation. Main units retract into fuselage, and have provision for gravity extension in an emergency. Forward-retracting hydraulically-steerable nosewheel, with shimmy damper. Oleo-pneumatic shock-absorbers. Hydraulic disc brakes with anti-skid system.

POWER PLANT: Two General Electric J85-GE-17B turbojet engines, each rated at 2,850 lb (1,293 kg) st, mounted on sides of fuselage. Engine starting by internal battery. Fuel in two fuselage tanks (combined capacity 202·4 Imp gallons; 920 litres) and two wing tanks (combined capacity 237·6 Imp gallons; 1,080 litres). Total internal fuel capacity 440 Imp gallons (2,000 litres). Pressure refuelling point in starboard wingtip. Provision for gravity refuelling through overwing points. Internal fuel load can be augmented by auxiliary drop-tanks carried on the inboard underwing pylons.

ACCOMMODATION: Two side-by-side ejection seats, though attack missions are normally flown as a single-seater from the left-hand seat. Alternative provision for four fixed seats, which may be of upholstered type or suitable for use with parachute and rescue packs. Provision for armour protection in attack role. Birdproof windscreen. Electrically-actuated rearward-hinged canopy of double-curved acrylic glass. Dual controls standard. Four-seat version can be used for liaison role or as navigation trainer with instructor/pilot and three students.

SYSTEMS: Air-conditioning system includes refrigeration unit. Nominal cabin pressure differential of 3·4 lb/sq in (0·24 kg/cm²). Hydraulic system, pressure 3,000 lb/sq in (210 kg/cm²), has two pumps (one on each engine) and actuates landing gear, nosewheel steering, brakes, flaps, airbrakes and aileron servo control. System can be operated from one pump only. DC electrical system has two 300A 28V starter/generators and two 22Ah batteries. External power connector installed. AC system provides 3-phase power at 200/115V 400Hz from two 750A converters. *G*-suit connections. Oxygen system, with two 4·5 litre bottles. Fire warning system and fire extinguishers in each engine bay.

ELECTRONICS AND EQUIPMENT: A wide range of navigational and communications equipment can be installed. The standard installation, according to mission, includes two VHF, or two UHF, or one VHF and one UHF; one ADF/DME and VOR/ILS with marker beacon, or TACAN, or Decca Doppler 72 radar with Sperry SGP 500 platform, TANS computer and roller map display; Marconi-Elliott air data computer, with probes; Ferranti ISIS F-105/125 gyro sighting head (with or without depressed sight line); Saab BT9R ballistic computer with laser rangefinder; pre-flight and in-flight control box; one transponder.

ARMAMENT AND OPERATIONAL EQUIPMENT: Three attachment points under each wing, the outer points each capable of supporting a 606 lb (275 kg) load, and the other four capable of supporting 992 lb (450 kg) each. Maximum total weapons load, with reduced fuel, is 5,180 lb (2,350 kg); with full internal fuel, up to 3,748 lb (1,700 kg) of external stores can be carried. Wide range of operational loads includes: six 500 lb bombs; four 750 lb bombs and two Sidewinder air-to-air missiles; four 1,000 lb bombs and two Sidewinders; four 500 lb bombs and two 106 US gallon (88 Imp gallon; 400 litre) drop-tanks; two 750 lb bombs, two Sidewinders and two 106 US gallon tanks; four 500 lb bombs and two 30 mm gun pods; twelve 13·5 cm rockets; eight 13·5 cm rockets and two 30 mm gun pods; camera pod (on port outer pylon), two Sidewinders and two 106 US gallon tanks; two drop-tanks only (liaison mission); or tow reel (port centre pylon), target launcher (port outer pylon) and two 106 US gallon tanks (target flying mission). For reconnaissance missions, aircraft can be fitted either with a panoramic camera in a special nose housing, which can be used in conjunction with any combination of ground attack armament, or with a wing-mounted camera pod. This pod contains one forward-looking and four sideways/downward-looking cameras (or a two-camera alternative installation for high-altitude photography); a flashlight pod is available for night photography. Gyro gunsight is standard. The Saab 105G can also be fitted with specialised equipment for advanced weapon training, target towing, ECM training, radar warning training, passive and active radar signal augmentation training, and for collection of radioactive atmospheric samples.

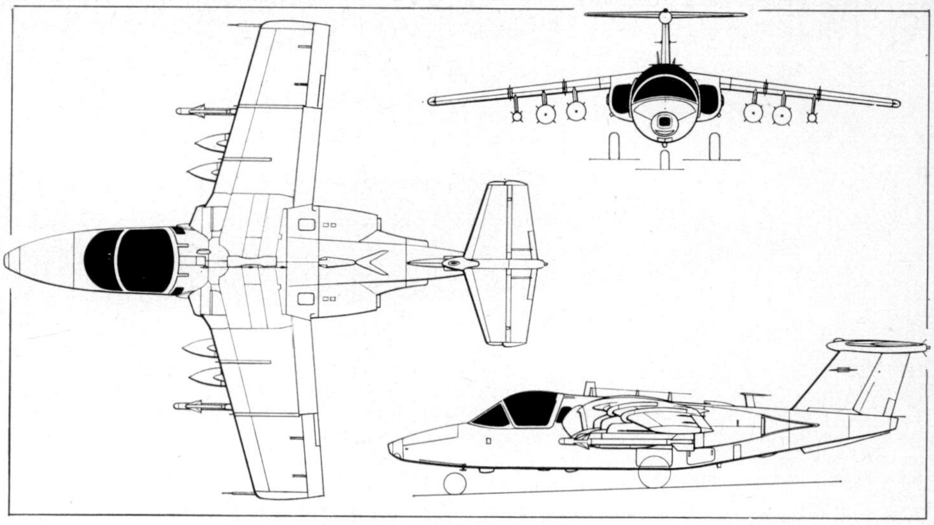

Saab 105G multi-purpose attack/training aircraft (*Pilot Press*)

DIMENSIONS, EXTERNAL:

Wing span	31 ft 2 in (9·50 m)
Length overall	35 ft 5¼ in (10·80 m)
Height overall	8 ft 10 in (2·70 m)
Wheel track	6 ft 6¾ in (2·00 m)
Wheelbase	12 ft 9½ in (3·90 m)

AREA:

Wings, gross	175 sq ft (16·3 m²)

WEIGHTS:

Weight empty	6,834 lb (3,100 kg)
T-O weight:	
trainer, clean	10,714 lb (4,860 kg)
liaison, with two drop-tanks	12,731 lb (5,775 kg)
with target gear and two drop-tanks	12,760 lb (5,788 kg)
with camera pod, two Sidewinders and two drop-tanks	12,908 lb (5,855 kg)
with six 500 lb bombs	13,893 lb (6,302 kg)
with max external armament	14,330 lb (6,500 kg)

PERFORMANCE (at weights indicated):

Max never-exceed speed (all weights) Mach 0·86

Max level speed at S/L:
- at 9,546 lb (4,330 kg), clean: 518 knots (597 mph; 960 km/h)
- at 12,731 lb (5,775 kg): 475 knots (547 mph; 880 km/h)

Max level speed at 32,800 ft (10,000 m):
- at 9,546 lb (4,330 kg), clean: 469 knots (541 mph; 870 km/h)
- at 12,731 lb (5,775 kg): 442 knots (510 mph; 820 km/h)

Max rate of climb at S/L:
- at 10,582 lb (4,800 kg) 11,155 ft (3,400 m)/min
- at 13,893 lb (6,302 kg) 5,971 ft (1,820 m)/min

Time to 32,800 ft (10,000 m):
- at 10,582 lb (4,800 kg): 5 min 30 sec
- at 13,893 lb (6,302 kg): 11 min 50 sec

Service ceiling: 42,650 ft (13,000 m)

T-O run:
- at 10,714 lb (4,860 kg): 1,345 ft (410 m)
- at 13,893 lb (6,302 kg): 2,723 ft (830 m)

T-O to 50 ft (15 m):
- at 10,714 lb (4,860 kg): 2,297 ft (700 m)
- at 13,893 lb (6,302 kg): 4,167 ft (1,270 m)

Landing from 50 ft (15 m):
- at 7,936 lb (3,600 kg): 3,215 ft (980 m)

Landing run:
- at 7,936 lb (3,600 kg): 2,214 ft (675 m)

Typical attack radius, including 2½ min combat:
- with six 500 lb bombs:
  - hi-lo-hi, 5% reserves: 375 nm (431 miles; 695 km)
  - lo-lo-lo, 10% reserves: 161 nm (186 miles; 300 km)
- with four 500 lb bombs and two drop-tanks:
  - hi-lo-hi, 5% reserves: 536 nm (618 miles; 995 km)
  - lo-lo-lo, 10% reserves: 223 nm (257 miles; 415 km)

Range at 39,375 ft (12,000 m) at 378 knots (435 mph; 700 km/h), 20 min reserves:
- internal fuel only: 1,068 nm (1,230 miles; 1,980 km)
- with two drop-tanks: 1,365 nm (1,572 miles; 2,530 km)

Ferry range at S/L, no reserves:
- at 10,934 lb (4,960 kg): 458 nm (528 miles; 850 km)
- at 12,698 lb (5,760 kg), incl two drop-tanks: 593 nm (683 miles; 1,100 km)

Ferry range at 39,375 ft (12,000 m), no reserves:
- at 10,934 lb (4,960 kg): 1,173 nm (1,351 miles; 2,175 km)
- at 12,698 lb (5,760 kg), incl two drop-tanks: 1,456 nm (1,677 miles; 2,700 km)

SAAB-MFI 15

The Saab-MFI 15 is intended as a primary trainer and utility aircraft. It can be fitted with either a non-retractable tricycle landing gear or a tailwheel landing gear.

The prototype (SE-301) flew for the first time on 11 July 1969 with a 160 hp engine. Subsequently, its original low-mounted horizontal tail surfaces were replaced by new ones mounted at the top of the fin to prevent interference or damage by snow and debris when operating in winter from rough airfields. After being re-engined with a 200 hp Lycoming, it resumed flying on 26 February 1971.

The Saab-MFI 15 is in production, and two were delivered to Sierra Leone in April 1973.

A developed version for armed military and other uses, designated Saab-MFI 17, is described separately.

TYPE: Two/three-seat light aircraft, stressed for flight load factors of + 4·4*g* and —1·76*g* (Utility) and +6·0*g* and —3·0*g* (Aerobatic).

WINGS: Braced shoulder-wing monoplane, with single bracing strut each side. Thickness/chord ratio 10%. Dihedral 1° 30′. All-metal structure, swept forward 5° from roots. Mass-balanced all-metal ailerons. Electrically-operated all-metal plain flaps. No tabs.

FUSELAGE: All-metal box structure.

TAIL UNIT: Cantilever all-metal T tail comprising swept fin and rudder and one-piece mass-balanced horizontal "stabilator" with large anti-servo and trimming tab. Trim tab in rudder.

LANDING GEAR: Non-retractable tricycle or tail-wheel type. Cantilever composite spring main legs on both versions. Goodyear 6·00-6 main wheels and either a 5·00-5 nosewheel or a tailwheel. Cleveland disc brakes on main units. Landes or Finncraft skis, or Edo floats, optional on both versions.

POWER PLANT: One 200 hp Lycoming IO-360-A1B four-cylinder horizontally-opposed aircooled engine, driving a Hartzell two-blade constant-speed metal propeller. Two integral wing fuel tanks, total capacity 41·8 Imp gallons (190 litres). Oil capacity 1·6 Imp gallons (7·5 litres).

ACCOMMODATION: Side-by-side adjustable seats, with provision for back-type or seat-type parachutes, for two persons beneath fully-transparent upward-hinged canopy. Space aft of front seats for 220 lb (100 kg) of baggage or, optionally, a rearward-facing third seat. Upward-hinged door, with window, beneath wing on port side. Heated and ventilated.

SYSTEMS: 28V 50A DC electrical system.

ELECTRONICS AND EQUIPMENT: Dual controls standard. Provision for full blind-flying instrumentation and radio.

DIMENSIONS, EXTERNAL:

Wing span	29 ft 0½ in (8·85 m)
Wing chord (outer panels, constant)	4 ft 5½ in (1·36 m)
Length overall:	
nosewheel	22 ft 11½ in (7·00 m)

tailwheel 22 ft 5¾ in (6·85 m)
Height overall:
nosewheel 7 ft 10½ in (2·40 m)
tailwheel (tail down) 6 ft 2¾ in (1·90 m)
Tailplane span 9 ft 2¼ in (2·80 m)
Wheel track:
nosewheel 7 ft 6½ in (2·30 m)
tailwheel 6 ft 7¾ in (2·025 m)
Wheelbase:
nosewheel 5 ft 2¾ in (1·59 m)
tailwheel 15 ft 7 in (4·75 m)
Cabin door (port):
Height 2 ft 6¾ in (0·78 m)
Width 1 ft 8½ in (0·52 m)

Dimensions, internal:
Cabin: Max width 3 ft 7¼ in (1·10 m)
Max height (from seat squab) 3 ft 3¼ in (1·00 m)

Areas:
Wings, gross 127 sq ft (11·80 m^2)
Ailerons (total) 10·55 sq ft (0·98 m^2)
Flaps (total) 16·68 sq ft (1·55 m^2)
Fin 8·29 sq ft (0·77 m^2)
Rudder, incl tab 7·86 sq ft (0·73 m^2)
Horizontal tail surfaces (total) 22·6 sq ft (2·10 m^2)

Weights and Loadings:
Weight empty, VFR equipped 1,322 lb (600 kg)
Max T-O weight:
Normal 2,204 lb (1,000 kg)
Utility 1,984 lb (900 kg)
Aerobatic 1,818 lb (825 kg)
Max wing loading:
Normal 18·0 lb/sq ft (88 kg/m^2)
Utility 16·2 lb/sq ft (79 kg/m^2)
Aerobatic 14·7 lb/sq ft (72 kg/m^2)
Max power loading:
Normal 11·02 lb/hp (5·0 kg/hp)
Utility 9·92 lb/hp (4·5 kg/hp)
Aerobatic 9·04 lb/hp (4·1 kg/hp)

Performance (at max T-O weight, Utility category, nosewheel version):
Max never-exceed speed 196 knots (226 mph; 364 km/h)
Max level speed at S/L 138·5 knots (160 mph; 257 km/h)
Cruising speed 126 knots (145 mph; 233 km/h)
Stalling speed, flaps down 51·5 knots (59 mph; 95 km/h)
Max rate of climb at S/L 1,329 ft (405 m)/min
Time to 6,560 ft (2,000 m) 5 min 50 sec
Cruise ceiling 19,525 ft (5,950 m)
T-O to 50 ft (15 m) 755 ft (230 m)
Landing from 50 ft (15 m) 1,030 ft (314 m)
Max endurance (65% power) at S/L, 10% reserves 5 hr 10 min

SAAB-MFI 17

The basic configuration of the Saab-MFI 15 (which see) offers a good ground clearance for carrying external loads. Saab-Scania is therefore offering a developed version of the aircraft, designated Saab-MFI 17, with 660 lb (300 kg) external load-carrying ability.

The second Saab-MFI 15 was modified to Saab-MFI 17 standard, making its first flight in the new form on 6 July 1972.

The airframe and power plant are the same in each aircraft, but the Saab-MFI 17 has six underwing stations for external stores. This enables it to undertake, in addition to the roles of the Saab-MFI 15, agricultural operations (carrying two spray pods); transport of supplies in droppable containers; and military operations with such weapons as air-to-ground rockets, two pods each housing two machine-guns, or six Bantam wire-guided anti-tank missiles.

In April 1974, under the direction of Count Carl Gustav von Rosen, three Saab-MFI 17s were being used in an extensive famine relief operation in Ethiopia. Approx 13,230 lb (6,000 kg) of sorghum seed per day was being air-dropped in underwing containers, the aircraft flying at about 59 knots (68 mph; 110 km/h) at heights from 3 to 15 ft (1·5 m) above the ground, each with a 551 lb (250 kg) load.

Dimensions and Areas:
As for Saab-MFI 15

Weights, Loadings and Performance (Normal, Utility and Aerobatic categories):
As for Saab-MFI 15

Weights and Loadings (Restricted category, aircraft clean):
Max T-O weight 2,425 lb (1,100 kg)
Max landing weight 2,204 lb (1,000 kg)
Max wing loading 19·9 lb/sq ft (97 kg/m^2)
Max power loading 12·13 lb/hp (5·5 kg/hp)

Performance (at AUW of 2,204 lb; 1,000 kg):
Max never-exceed speed 196 knots (226 mph; 364 km/h)
Max level speed at S/L 138·5 knots (160 mph; 257 km/h)
Cruising speed 126 knots (145 mph; 233 km/h)
Stalling speed, flaps down 51·5 knots (59 mph; 95 km/h)
Max rate of climb at S/L 1,100 ft (335 m)/min
Time to 6,560 ft (2,000 m) 7 min 18 sec
Cruise ceiling 17,050 ft (5,200 m)
T-O to 50 ft (15 m) 919 ft (280 m)
Landing from 50 ft (15 m) 1,135 ft (346 m)
Max endurance (65% power) at S/L, 10% reserves 5 hr 10 min

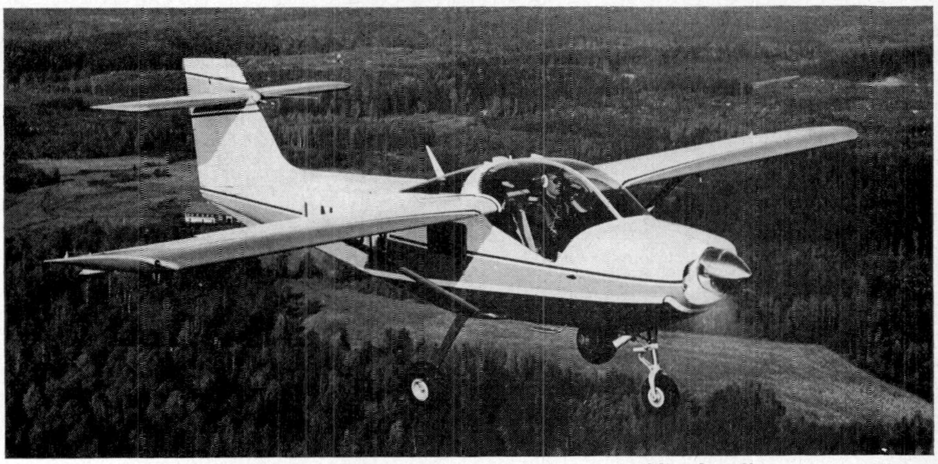

Saab-MFI 15 two/three-seat primary trainer and utility aircraft

One of the Saab-MFI 17s used for famine relief in Ethiopia, with droppable underwing load

Saab-MFI 17, exhibited at the 1974 Hanover Air Show with underwing weapons, wheel-ski landing gear and drogue target towing equipment *(Brian M. Service)*

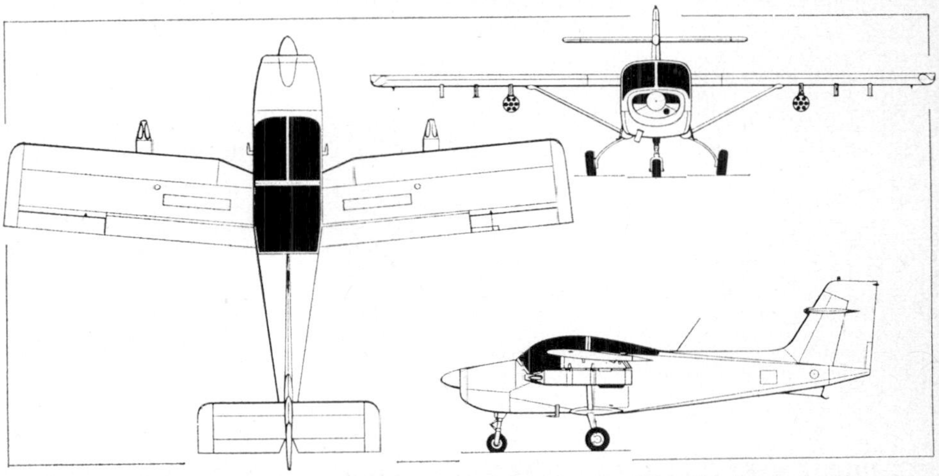

Saab-MFI 17 two/three-seat army co-operation and training aircraft, with underwing stores *(Pilot Press)*

SWITZERLAND

BERGER

HANS BERGER

ADDRESS:
Casa Piccolo Menderli, CH-6575 San Nazzaro

BERGER BX-110

Mr Berger has designed and built a small two-seat helicopter, the BX-110, the general appearance of which can be seen in the accompanying illustration. It has a 115 hp Wankel rotating-piston engine, driving a three-blade main rotor and two-blade tail rotor.

Berger BX-110 two-seat homebuilt light helicopter (115 hp Wankel engine)

BRÜGGER

MAX BRÜGGER

ADDRESS:
1751 Villarsel-le-Gibloux, CH Fribourg
Telephone: (037) 31 16 20

Brief details of the Brügger Colibri 1 single-seat ultra-light aircraft, which flew for the first time on 30 October 1965, were given in the 1967-68 and 1971-72 *Jane's*.

A more recent design is the Colibri 2, of which a number have been or are being built by amateur constructors.

BRÜGGER MB-2 COLIBRI 2

Mr Brügger began design of the Colibri 2 in January 1966. Construction was started a year later, and the first of two prototypes flew for the first time on 1 May 1970. In the Spring of 1974, about 10 more Colibri 2s were under construction by amateur builders in Switzerland.

TYPE: Single-seat homebuilt light aircraft.

WINGS: Cantilever low-wing monoplane. Wing section NACA 23012. Dihedral from roots. Two-spar constant-chord wings. Wings and ailerons built of spruce with fabric covering. No flaps or tabs.

FUSELAGE: Plywood-covered wooden structure.

TAIL UNIT: Cantilever all-wood structure. Rudder only: no fin. All-moving horizontal surfaces, with Flettner-type elevators.

LANDING GEAR: Non-retractable tailwheel type, with coil spring shock-absorption on main units. Main wheels size 400 × 100, with streamline fairings. Tailwheel mounted on leaf spring. Mechanically-operated disc brakes.

POWER PLANT: One 40 hp 1,600 cc Volkswagen engine (Brügger modification), driving a Brügger two-blade fixed-pitch wooden propeller with plastics-coated blades. Fuel in single fuselage tank, capacity 7·25 Imp gallons (33 litres). Oil capacity 0·55 Imp gallons (2·5 litres).

ACCOMMODATION: Single seat under one-piece moulded transparent canopy, with quarter-lights to rear.

Brügger MB-2 Colibri 2 single-seat homebuilt light aircraft (*Dr Ulrich Haller*)

DIMENSIONS, EXTERNAL:

Wing span	19 ft 8¼ in (6·00 m)
Wing chord (constant)	4 ft 7 in (1·40 m)
Length overall	15 ft 9 in (4·80 m)
Height overall	5 ft 3 in (1·60 m)
Tailplane span	6 ft 6¾ in (2·00 m)
Wheel track	5 ft 11 in (1·80 m)
Propeller diameter	4 ft 6⅓ in (1·38 m)

AREAS:

Wings, gross	88·25 sq ft (8·20 m²)
Ailerons (total)	9·69 sq ft (0·90 m²)
Rudder	7·10 sq ft (0·66 m²)
Horizontal tail surfaces (total)	7·75 sq ft (0·72 m²)

WEIGHTS:

Weight empty	474 lb (215 kg)
Max T-O and landing weight	727 lb (330 kg)

PERFORMANCE (at max T-O weight):

Max speed at 13,125 ft (4,000 m)	97 knots (111 mph; 180 km/h)
Econ cruising speed (70% power) at 13,125 ft (4,000 m)	86 knots (99 mph; 160 km/h)
Stalling speed	32·5 knots (37·5 mph; 60 km/h)
Max rate of climb at S/L	590 ft (180 m)/min
Service ceiling	14,760 ft (4,500 m)
T-O and landing run	656 ft (200 m)
Range with max fuel	270 nm (310 miles; 500 km)

DÄTWYLER

MAX DÄTWYLER & CO

HEAD OFFICE AND WORKS:
Flugplatz, CH-3368 Bleienbach-Langenthal
Telephone: 063 2 06 32
Telex: 68218 mdc ch

CHIEF DESIGNER:
Siegfried F. Stiemer

Dätwyler & Co is a servicing organisation which has specialised in the repair and modification of Piper aircraft, particularly war-surplus Cubs. A specialised glider-tug known as the MDC-Trailer was described in the 1966-67 *Jane's*. A version of the Bücker Jungmann, named the Lerche, built by Dätwyler to the design of Ing Frits Dubs, was described in the 1969-70 *Jane's*.

Current activities of this company include the manufacture of components for the Pilatus Porter STOL transport and B4-PC11 sailplane, and for the Dassault Mercure transport aircraft; and development of a simple two-seat trainer of original design, of which all available details follow:

DÄTWYLER SWISS TRAINER

After some years of study, Dätwyler announced during 1967-68 some preliminary details of a new two-seat basic training aircraft called the Swiss Trainer. The basic design was evolved by a team under the leadership of Hans Farner and the Swedish designer Björn Andreasson. A prototype is being built under the direction of Dätwyler's German chief designer, Siegfried Stiemer, and a feature of the aircraft will be simplicity of repair and maintenance.

Single-seat glider-towing and four-seat touring versions, each powered by a 220 hp Franklin engine, are also projected.

The following details apply to the prototype two-seat training version:

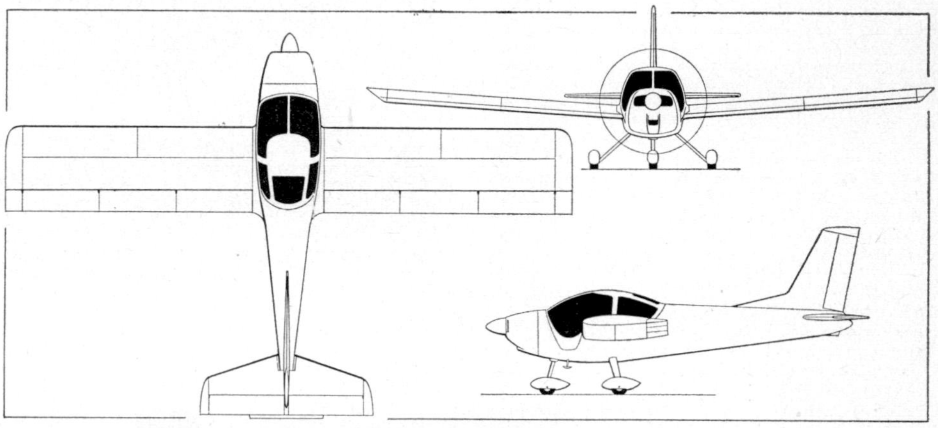

Dätwyler Swiss Trainer two-seat basic training aircraft (*Pilot Press*)

TYPE: Two-seat basic training aircraft, stressed to +6 *g* and —3 *g* for aerobatic flying.

WINGS: Cantilever mid-wing monoplane. Constant-chord wings, with full-span flaps and ailerons.

FUSELAGE: Semi-monocoque structure.

TAIL UNIT: Single sweptback fin and rudder, with dorsal fairing. Tailplane has sweepback on leading-edge. One-piece elevator, with balance tab.

LANDING GEAR: Non-retractable tricycle type, with cantilever legs on all units. Single wheel, with streamlined fairing, on each unit.

POWER PLANT: One 115-160 hp Lycoming horizontally-opposed aircooled engine, driving a two-blade propeller.

ACCOMMODATION: Side-by-side seats for two persons, under large rearward-hinged transparent moulded canopy.

DIMENSIONS, EXTERNAL:

Wing span	32 ft 1¾ in (9·80 m)
Length overall	22 ft 5¼ in (6·84 m)

AREA:

Wings, gross	158·23 sq ft (14·70 m²)

WEIGHTS (estimated):

Weight empty	1,014 lb (460 kg)
Max T-O weight	1,587 lb (720 kg)

FEDERAL AIRCRAFT FACTORY—*See "Swiss Federal Aircraft Factory"*

FFA

FLUG- & FAHRZEUGWERKE AG ALTENRHEIN

Head Office and Works:
CH-9422 Staad b/Rorschach
Telephone: (071) 41 41 41
Telex: 77 230

President:
Dr C. Caroni

Director:
Dipl Ing H. Eisenring

Works Director:
O. Wick

Chief Engineer:
Dipl Ing P. Spalinger

This company, known formerly as AG für Dornier Flugzeuge, was originally the Swiss branch of the German Dornier company. It is now an entirely Swiss company.

FFA developed a glassfibre sailplane named Diamant, of which details were given in the Sailplanes section of the 1972-73 *Jane's*. Current activities include production of the AS.202 Bravo light aircraft, and the overhaul, modification and servicing of military and civil aircraft.

The company has about 1,000 employees, approximately half of whom are engaged in its aviation activities.

FFA AS.202 BRAVO

Following an agreement concluded with SIAI-Marchetti of Italy, FFA is engaged in production and development of the AS.202 Bravo light trainer and sporting aircraft.

The previously-announced AS.202/10 version (see 1973-74 *Jane's*) has now been abandoned. Two versions are currently envisaged, as follows:

AS.202/15. Two/three-seat initial production version, with 150 hp Lycoming O-320-E2A engine. Optional third seat. In production.

AS.202/18A. Two/three-seat version with a 180 hp Lycoming IO-360-B1F engine, Hartzell HC-C2YK-1BF/7666-2 two-blade constant-speed propeller and inverted oil system. Under development.

The first Bravo to fly was a Swiss-assembled AS.202/15 prototype (HB-HEA), which flew for the first time on 7 March 1969. The Italian-built second prototype flew on 7 May 1969. The third aircraft (HB-HEC) made its first flight on 16 June 1969, and the first production aircraft on 22 December 1971. Swiss certification of the AS.202/15 was granted on 15 August 1972; FAA certification was awarded on 16 November 1973.

The first 50 production Bravos are of the AS.202/15 version, to which the following description applies:

Type: Two/three-seat light aircraft.

Wings: Cantilever low-wing monoplane. Wing section NACA 63_2618 (modified) at centreline, 63_2415 at tip. Thickness/chord ratio 17·63% at root, 15% at tip. Dihedral 5° 43′ from roots. Incidence 3°. Sweepback at quarter-chord 0° 40′. Conventional aluminium single-spar fail-safe structure, with honeycomb laminate skin. Aluminium single-slotted flaps and single-slotted ailerons. Ground-adjustable tab on each aileron.

Fuselage: Conventional aluminium semi-monocoque fail-safe structure, with several glassfibre fairings.

Tail Unit: Cantilever aluminium single-spar structure with sweptback vertical surfaces. Rudder mass-balanced, with provision for anti-collision beacon. Fixed-incidence tailplane. Two-piece elevator with full-span trim tab on starboard half. Ground-adjustable tab on rudder.

Landing Gear: Non-retractable tricycle type, with steerable nosewheel. Rubber-cushioned shock-absorber struts of SIAI-Marchetti design. Main-wheel tyres size 6·00-6; nosewheel tyre size 5·00-5. Tyre pressure (all units) 35 lb/sq in (2·5 kg/cm²). Independent hydraulically-operated disc brake on each main wheel.

Power Plant: One 150 hp Lycoming O-320-E2A four-cylinder horizontally-opposed aircooled engine, driving a McCauley 1C172 MGM two-blade fixed-pitch metal propeller. Two wing leading-edge fuel tanks with total capacity of 30·5 Imp gallons (140 litres). Refuelling point above each wing. Oil capacity 1·6 Imp gallons (7·6 litres).

Accommodation: Seats for two persons side by side, in Aerobatic version, under rearward-sliding jettisonable transparent canopy. Space at rear in Utility version for a third seat or 220 lb (100 kg) of baggage. Dual controls, cabin ventilation and heating standard.

Systems: Hydraulic system for brake actuation. One 12V 60A engine-driven alternator and one 25Ah battery provide electrical power for engine starting, lighting, instruments, communications and navigation installations.

Electronics and Equipment: Provision for VHF radio, VOR, ADF, blind-flying instrumentation or other special equipment at customer's option. Clutch-and-release mechanism for glider towing optional.

Dimensions, external:

Wing span	31 ft 11¾ in (9·75 m)
Wing chord at root	6 ft 2 in (1·88 m)
Wing chord at tip	3 ft 9½ in (1·16 m)
Wing aspect ratio	6·51
Length overall	24 ft 7¼ in (7·50 m)
Length of fuselage	23 ft 5½ in (7·15 m)
Height overall	9 ft 2¾ in (2·81 m)
Tailplane span	12 ft 0½ in (3·67 m)
Wheel track	7 ft 4½ in (2·25 m)
Wheelbase	5 ft 10 in (1·78 m)
Propeller ground clearance	1 ft 0½ in (0·31 m)
Propeller diameter	6 ft 2 in (1·88 m)

Dimensions, internal:

Cabin: Max length	7 ft 0½ in (2·15 m)
Max width	3 ft 4¼ in (1·02 m)
Max height	3 ft 7¼ in (1·10 m)
Floor area	23·14 sq ft (2·15 m²)

Areas:

Wings, gross	149 sq ft (13·86 m²)
Ailerons (total)	11·7 sq ft (1·09 m²)
Trailing-edge flaps (total)	16·04 sq ft (1·49 m²)
Fin	18·08 sq ft (1·68 m²)
Rudder, incl tab	10·12 sq ft (0·94 m²)
Tailplane	29·0 sq ft (2·69 m²)
Elevator, incl tab	8·18 sq ft (0·76 m²)

Weights and Loadings:

Weight empty, equipped:	
AS.202/15	1,388 lb (630 kg)
Max payload:	
AS.202/15, Aerobatic	386 lb (175 kg)
AS.202/15, Utility	595 lb (270 kg)
Max T-O and landing weight:	
AS.202/15, Aerobatic	1,951 lb (885 kg)
AS.202/15, Utility	2,202 lb (999 kg)
AS.202/18A	2,292 lb (1,040 kg)
Max wing loading:	
AS.202/15	14·8 lb/sq ft (72·2 kg/m²)
AS.202/18A	15·36 lb/sq ft (75 0 kg/m²)
Max power loading:	
AS.202/15	14·7 lb/hp (6·66 kg/hp)
AS.202/18A	12·74 lb/hp (5·78 kg/hp)

Performance (AS.202/15, Utility version at max T-O weight):

Max never-exceed speed	173·5 knots (200 mph; 322 km/h)
Max level speed at S/L	114 knots (131 mph; 211 km/h)
Max cruising speed (75% power) at 8,000 ft (2,440 m)	114 knots (131 mph; 211 km/h)
Econ cruising speed (66% power) at 10,000 ft (3,050 m)	109·5 knots (126 mph; 203 km/h)
Stalling speed, flaps up	59·5 knots (68·5 mph; 110 km/h)
Stalling speed, flaps down	48·5 knots (55·5 mph; 89 km/h)
Max rate of climb at S/L	633 ft (193 m)/min
Service ceiling	14,000 ft (4,265 m)
T-O run	590 ft (180 m)
T-O to 50 ft (15 m)	1,520 ft (463 m)
Landing from 50 ft (15 m)	1,360 ft (415 m)
Landing run	425 ft (130 m)
Range with max fuel, no reserves	498 nm (574 miles; 925 km)

Performance (AS.202/18A, estimated):

Max never-exceed speed	173·5 knots (200 mph; 322 km/h)
Max level speed at S/L	124 knots (143 mph; 230 km/h)
Stalling speed, flaps up	62 knots (71 mph; 113 km/h)
Stalling speed, flaps down	49 knots (56 mph; 90 km/h)
Max rate of climb at S/L	1,000 ft (305 m)/min
Service ceiling	18,050 ft (5,500 m)
T-O to 50 ft (15 m)	1,200 ft (365 m)
Landing from 50 ft (15 m)	1,395 ft (425 m)

FFA AS.202/15 Bravo two/three-seat light aircraft (150 hp Lycoming O-320 engine)

MORAND

ATELIERS DE PRÉCISION MORAND

Address:
CH-1635, La Tour-de-Trême
Telephone: (029) 2 90 01

MORAND/BÜCKER Bü 131A JUNGMANN

On behalf of the Aero Club of Switzerland, to which the Swiss Air Force has donated all its remaining airworthy Bücker Bü 131A Jungmann trainers (approx 25 aircraft), Morand is undertaking the conversion of these aircraft by replacing their existing 105 hp Hirth engines with 150 hp Lycoming engines. The conversions, which cost some 43,000 SF each, are authorised on condition that the modified aircraft are offered for sale to Swiss customers only.

Power Plant: One 150 hp Lycoming IO-320-E2A four-cylinder horizontally-opposed aircooled engine, driving a Hoffmann HO-23 188/125 propeller. Fuel capacity 19·4 Imp gallons (88 litres).

Dimensions, external:

Wing span	24 ft 3¼ in (7·40 m)
Length overall	21 ft 8¾ in (6·62 m)
Height overall	7 ft 9¼ in (2·37 m)
Propeller diameter	6 ft 2 in (1·88 m)

Weight:

Max T-O weight	1,477 lb (670 kg)

Four Bücker Bü 131A Jungmann biplanes fitted by Morand with 150 hp Lycoming engines

Performance (at max T-O weight):

Max level speed	110·5 knots (127 mph; 205 km/h)
Max cruising speed (75% power)	97 knots (112 mph; 180 km/h)
Stalling speed	51·5 knots (59·5 mph; 95 km/h)
Max rate of climb at S/L	more than 1,000 ft (300 m)/min
Service ceiling	16,400 ft (5,000 m)
T-O run	492 ft (150 m)
Landing run	164 ft (50 m)
Range	242 nm (280 miles; 450 km)

Pilatus PC-6 Porter (340 hp Lycoming GSO-480 engine) with Edo twin-float landing gear

Pilatus PC-6/B2 Turbo-Porter equipped for experiments in quiet STOL operation

PILATUS

PILATUS FLUGZEUGWERKE AG

HEAD OFFICE AND WORKS:
CH-6370, Stans, near Lucerne
Telephone: (041) 61 14 46
Telex: 78 329

GENERAL MANAGER:
S. Balmer

MANAGERS:
Dr K. Zimmermann (Chief of Instruments and Vehicles, PR and Propaganda)
D. Klöckner (Chief of Aircraft Department, Development and Sales)
W. Gubler (Production Manager)
P. Ebner (Chief Administrator, Finances and Personnel)

Pilatus Flugzeugwerke AG was formed in December 1939, and began work in September 1941. A founder's syndicate had been formed in 1938 under the leadership of M. E. Bührle, the Swiss industrialist and owner of the Oerlikon company, of which the Pilatus company is now a subsidiary.

The current Pilatus products are the PC-6/B1 and B2 Turbo-Porter single-engined utility transports, a description of which follows; and the B4-PC11 sailplane, described in the "Sailplanes" section.

Pilatus is also building two prototypes of the PD-01 Master Porter twin-turboprop transport aircraft, a description of which can be found under the Poligrat heading in the German section of this edition.

PILATUS PC-6 PORTER AND TURBO-PORTER

The Pilatus PC-6 is a single-engined utility aircraft, with STOL characteristics permitting operation from small airfields. It can be converted rapidly from a pure freighter to a passenger transport, and can also be adapted for ambulance duties (two stretchers and seats for five persons, including crew), aerial photography, supply dropping, parachute training, agricultural dusting and spraying, etc.

Design work began in 1957, and the first of five PC-6 prototypes made its first flight on 4 May 1959. Swiss certification of the pre-series PC-6, with 340 hp Lycoming engine, was received in December 1959, and the entire batch of 20 aircraft was delivered by the Summer of 1961.

All aircraft delivered up to mid-1966 had double doors, without a central pillar, on the starboard side of the cabin; these doors were non-structural, and the aircraft could be flown without them. A further door on the port side was optional. Subsequent production aircraft have a forward-opening door on each side of the cockpit, a large rearward-sliding door on the starboard side of the cabin, and a double door on the port side of the cabin.

The basic PC-6 airframe has been built with a variety of piston and turboprop engines. Swiss-built piston-engined variants have the name Porter, and turboprop-powered variants are known as Turbo-Porters. In the US, where the PC-6 is manufactured by Fairchild, it is known simply as the Porter, irrespective of the type of power plant fitted.

The following variants have been announced; designation suffixes H1 and H2 indicate max T-O weights of 4,444 lb (2,015 kg) and 4,850 lb (2,200 kg) respectively:

PC-6 Porter. Initial production version, with 340 hp Lycoming GSO-480-B1A6 piston engine and Hartzell HC-B3X20-1B/9333C non-feathering constant-speed propeller. Oil capacity 2·9 Imp gallons (3·5 US gallons; 13 litres). Original certification 1 December 1959; later models, with increased AUW, are designated PC-6-H1 and PC-6-H2, certificated on 10 December 1963 and 26 August 1964 respectively.

PC-6/350 Porter. Version with 350 hp Lycoming IGO-540-A1A piston engine and Hartzell HC-B3Z30-2B/9349 constant-speed feathering propeller. Oil capacity as for PC-6. Original certification 12 September 1962; later models, with increased AUW, are designated PC-6/350-H1 and PC-6/350-H2, certificated on 10 December 1963 and 26 August 1964 respectively.

PC-6/A Turbo-Porter. Version with 523 shp Turboméca Astazou IIE or IIG turboprop engine and Ratier Figeac FH 76-1-07/FH 76.207 electrically-controllable fully-feathering reversible-pitch propeller. Oil capacity 1·8 Imp gallons (2·2 US gallons; 8 litres). First flown on 2 May 1961. Original certification 26 November 1962; later models, with increased AUW, are designated PC-6/A-H1 and PC-6/A-H2, certificated on 10 December 1963 and 26 August 1964 respectively.

PC-6/A1 Turbo-Porter. Version with 573 shp Turboméca Astazou XII turboprop engine and Hamilton Standard 23LF-351/1017A hydraulically-controllable fully-feathering reversible-pitch propeller. Oil capacity 2·6 Imp gallons (3·1 US gallons; 12 litres). Certificated as PC-6/A1-H2 on 29 February 1968.

PC-6/A2 Turbo-Porter. Version with 573 shp Turboméca Astazou XIVE turboprop engine. Other details as for PC-6/A1. Certificated as PC-6/A2-H2 on 22 January 1971.

PC-6/B Turbo-Porter. Version with 550 shp United Aircraft of Canada PT6A-6A turboprop engine and Hartzell HC-B3TN-3C/T-10173CH hydraulically-controllable fully-feathering reversible-pitch constant-speed propeller. Oil capacity 2·9 Imp gallons (3·5 US gallons; 13 litres). First flown 1 May 1964. Certificated as PC-6/B-H2 on 8 June 1965.

PC-6/B1 Turbo-Porter. Current production version, similar to PC-6/B but with 550 shp PT6A-20 turboprop engine and HC-B3TN-3D/T-10173 or /T-10178 propeller. First flight May 1966. Certificated as PC-6/B1-H2 on 6 August 1966.

PC-6/B2 Turbo-Porter. Current production version, similar to PC-6/B1 but with 550 shp PT6A-27 turboprop engine and HC-B3TN-3D/T-10178 propeller. Certificated as PC-6/B2-H2 on 30 June 1970.

PC-6/C Turbo-Porter. Version with 575 shp AiResearch TPE 331-25D turboprop engine and Hartzell HC-B3TN-3D/T-10178 hydraulically-controllable fully-feathering reversible-pitch constant-speed propeller. Oil capacity 2·4 Imp gallons (2·9 US gallons; 11 litres). Prototype, built by Fairchild, USA, first flown in October 1965; first Pilatus-built example flown on 4 March 1966. Certificated as PC-6/C-H2 on 1 December 1966.

PC-6/C1 Turbo-Porter. Similar to PC-6/C but with 576 shp TPE 331-1-100 turboprop engine. Certificated as PC-6/C1-H2 on 15 July 1970.

PC-6/C2-H2 Porter. Version under development by Fairchild with 650 ehp AiResearch TPE 331-101F turboprop engine. First flight expected in Spring 1974, with certification planned for mid-1974.

PC-6/D-H3 Porter. Prototype with 500 hp Lycoming TIO-720 turbocharged engine and larger, sweptback vertical tail surfaces and modified wingtips. Described and illustrated in 1971-72 *Jane's*. No production, as suitable engine not available.

By 1 January 1974, Pilatus had built a total of 233 production aircraft, comprising 63 PC-6, 8 PC-6/350, 42 PC-6/A series, 111 PC-6/B series and 9 PC-6/C series.

Pilatus also markets a Q-STOL (Quiet STOL) conversion kit for the B1 and B2 Turbo-Porters fitted with PT6A-20 or -27 engines. This includes a reversal system whereby propeller speed can be altered independently of the engine power setting, and is claimed to reduce the noise level by more than 10 dB for T-O and 20 dB for landing.

The basic structural description which follows is generally applicable to all PC-6 variants; dimensions, weights and performance of individual models are as indicated. Details of the Turbo-Porter when adapted for agricultural duties are given separately.

TYPE: Single-engined STOL utility transport.

WINGS: Braced high-wing monoplane, with single streamline-section bracing strut each side. Wing section NACA 64-514 (constant). Dihedral 1°. Incidence 2°. Single-spar all-metal structure. Entire trailing-edge hinged, inner sections consisting of electrically-operated all-metal double-slotted flaps and outer sections of all-metal single-slotted ailerons. No air-brakes or de-icing equipment. Trim tabs and/or Flettner tabs on ailerons optional; fixed tabs are mandatory if these are not fitted.

FUSELAGE: All-metal semi-monocoque structure.

TAIL UNIT: Cantilever all-metal structure. Variable-incidence tailplane. Trim tab on rudder, optional Flettner tabs on elevator; fixed tabs are mandatory if these are not fitted.

LANDING GEAR: Non-retractable tailwheel type. Oleo shock-absorbers of Pilatus design on all units. Steerable tailwheel. Goodyear Type II main wheels and GA 284 tyres size 24 × 7 or 7·50 × 10 (pressure 32 lb/sq in; 2·2 kg/cm²); oversize Goodyear Type III wheels and tyres optional, size 11·0 × 12, pressure 12·8 lb/sq in (0·9 kg/cm²). Goodyear tailwheel with size 5·00-4 tyre. Goodyear disc brakes. Alternative Pilatus wheel/ski gear or Edo 58-4580 floats may be fitted.

POWER PLANT: One piston or turboprop engine (details under model descriptions in introductory copy). Standard fuel in integral wing tanks, capacity 105·5 Imp gallons (127 US gallons; 480 litres) normal, 142 Imp gallons

(170 US gallons; 644 litres) maximum. Two underwing auxiliary tanks, each of 42 Imp gallons (50 US gallons; 190 litres), available optionally.

ACCOMMODATION: Cabin has pilot's seat forward on port side, with one passenger seat alongside, and is normally fitted with six quickly-removable seats, in pairs, to the rear of these for additional passengers. Up to 10 persons can be carried in high-density layout. Floor is level, flush with door sill, and is provided with seat rails. Forward-opening door beside each front seat. Large rearward-sliding door on starboard side of main cabin. Double doors, without central pillar, on port side. Hatch in floor 1 ft 10¾ in × 2 ft 11½ in (0·58 × 0·90 m), openable from inside cabin, for installation of aerial camera or for supply dropping. Hatch in cabin rear wall 1 ft 7 in × 2 ft 7 in (0·50 × 0·80 m) permits stowage of six passenger seats or accommodation of freight items up to 16 ft 5 in (5·0 m) in length. Walls lined with lightweight soundproofing and heat-insulation material. Adjustable heating and ventilation systems provided. Dual controls optional.

SYSTEMS: Cabin heated by bleed air from engine compressor. Scott 8500 oxygen system optional. 200A 30V starter/generator and 24V 34Ah nickel-cadmium battery.

DIMENSIONS, EXTERNAL:
Wing span 49 ft 8 in (15·13 m)
Wing span over navigation lights 49 ft 10½ in (15·20 m)
Wing chord (constant) 6 ft 3 in (1·90 m)
Wing aspect ratio 7·96
Length overall:
PC-6 33 ft 5½ in (10·20 m)
PC-6/A series 36 ft 4½ in (11·08 m)
PC-6/B series 36 ft 1 in (11·00 m)
PC-6/C series 35 ft 9 in (10·90 m)
Height overall (tail down) 10 ft 6 in (3·20 m)
Elevator span 16 ft 9½ in (5·12 m)
Wheel track 9 ft 10 in (3·00 m)
Wheelbase 25 ft 10 in (7·87 m)
Propeller diameter:
PC-6, PC-6/350 7 ft 9 in (2·36 m)
PC-6/A 8 ft 2½ in (2·50 m)
PC-6/A1, PC-6/A2 8 ft 6 in (2·59 m)
PC-6/B, PC-6/B1, PC-6/B2, PC-6/C, PC-6/C1 8 ft 5 in (2·56 m)
Cabin double door (port) and sliding door (starboard):
Height 3 ft 5 in (1·04 m)
Width 5 ft 2¼ in (1·58 m)

DIMENSIONS, INTERNAL:
Cabin, from back of pilot's seat to rear wall:
Length 7 ft 6½ in (2·30 m)
Max width 3 ft 9½ in (1·16 m)
Max height (at front) 4 ft 2½ in (1·28 m)
Height at rear wall 3 ft 10½ in (1·18 m)
Floor area 28·6 sq ft (2·67 m²)
Volume 107 cu ft (3·28 m³)

AREAS:
Wings, gross 310 sq ft (28·80 m²)
Ailerons (total) 41·2 sq ft (3·83 m²)
Flaps (total) 40·5 sq ft (3·76 m²)
Fin 18·3 sq ft (1·70 m²)
Rudder, incl tab 10·3 sq ft (0·96 m²)
Tailplane 43·4 sq ft (4·03 m²)
Elevator, incl tabs 45·4 sq ft (4·22 m²)

WEIGHTS AND LOADINGS:
Weight empty, equipped:
PC-6-H2 2,755 lb (1,250 kg)
PC-6/A2-H2 2,623 lb (1,190 kg)
PC-6/B2-H2 2,601 lb (1,180 kg)
PC-6/C1-H2 2,612 lb (1,185 kg)
Max T-O and landing weight:
H1 versions 4,444 lb (2,015 kg)
H2 versions 4,850 lb (2,200 kg)
Max cabin floor loading (all versions) 100 lb/sq ft (488 kg/m²)
Max wing loading (all versions) 15·57 lb/sq ft (76 kg/m²)
Max power loading:
PC-6-H2 14·3 lb/hp (6·5 kg/hp)
PC-6/A2-H2 8·4 lb/shp (3·8 kg/shp)
PC-6/B2-H2 8·8 lb/shp (4·0 kg/shp)
PC-6/C1-H2 8·4 lb/shp (3·8 kg/shp)

PERFORMANCE (at max T-O weight):
Max never-exceed speed (all versions) 151 knots (174 mph; 280 km/h) IAS
Max cruising speed at 10,000 ft (3,050 m):
PC-6-H2 116 knots (134 mph; 216 km/h) TAS
PC-6/A2-H2 145 knots (167 mph; 268 km/h) TAS
PC-6/B2-H2 140 knots (161 mph; 259 km/h) TAS
PC-6/C1-H2 142 knots (164 mph; 264 km/h) TAS
Econ cruising speed at 10,000 ft (3,050 m):
PC-6-H2 102 knots (118 mph; 190 km/h) TAS
PC-6/A2-H2 117 knots (135 mph; 217 km/h) TAS
PC-6/B2-H2 129 knots (150 mph; 240 km/h) TAS
PC-6/C1-H2 125 knots (144 mph; 231 km/h) TAS
Stalling speed, flaps up:
all versions 51 knots (58 mph; 94 km/h)
Stalling speed, flaps down:
all versions 45 knots (52 mph; 83 km/h)
Max rate of climb at S/L:
PC-6-H2 550 ft (168 m)/min
PC-6/A2-H2, PC-6/C1-H2 1,607 ft (490 m)/min
PC-6/B2-H2 1,580 ft (482 m)/min
Service ceiling:
PC-6-H2 17,400 ft (5,300 m)
PC-6/A2-H2 32,000 ft (9,750 m)
PC-6/B2-H2 30,025 ft (9,150 m)
PC-6/C1-H2 27,875 ft (8,500 m)
T-O run:
PC-6-H2 700 ft (213 m)
PC-6/A2-H2, PC-6/C1-H2 350 ft (107 m)
PC-6/B2-H2 360 ft (110 m)
T-O to 50 ft (15 m):
PC-6-H2 1,270 ft (387 m)
PC-6/A2-H2, PC-6/C1-H2 600 ft (183 m)
PC-6/B2-H2 620 ft (189 m)
Landing from 50 ft (15 m):
PC-6-H2 1,000 ft (305 m)
PC-6/A2-H2 540 ft (165 m)
PC-6/B2-H2 560 ft (171 m)
PC-6/C1-H2 550 ft (168 m)
Landing run:
PC-6-H2 502 ft (153 m)
PC-6/A2-H2, PC-6/C1-H2 220 ft (67 m)
PC-6/B2-H2 240 ft (73 m)
Max range:
PC-6-H2, normal internal fuel 810 nm (932 miles; 1,500 km)
PC-6/A2-H2, max internal fuel 685 nm (790 miles; 1,270 km)
PC-6/B2-H2, max internal fuel 550 nm (634 miles; 1,020 km)
PC-6/C1-H2, max internal fuel 594 nm (683 miles; 1,100 km)
*Max range with max internal fuel and two 190 litre underwing drop-tanks:
PC-6/A2-H2 1,080 nm (1,243 miles; 2,000 km)
PC-6/B2-H2 875 nm (1,006 miles; 1,620 km)
PC-6/C1-H2 906 nm (1,044 miles; 1,680 km)
Endurance:
PC-6-H2, normal internal fuel 7 hr 45 min
PC-6/A2-H2, max internal fuel 5 hr 50 min
PC-6/B2-H2, max internal fuel 4 hr 15 min
PC-6/C1-H2, max internal fuel 4 hr 35 min
*Endurance with max internal fuel and two 190 litre underwing drop-tanks:
PC-6/A2-H2 9 hr 13 min
PC-6/B2-H2 6 hr 45 min
PC-6/C1-H2 7 hr 18 min

**Operation with auxiliary fuel during overweight condition permitted under Restricted category (CAM8) only*

PILATUS PC-6 TURBO-PORTER (AGRICULTURAL VERSIONS)

The Turbo-Porter can, if required, be equipped for agricultural duties, the necessary equipment being easily removable when not required, to permit the use of the aircraft for other work.

For liquid spraying, a stainless steel tank (capacity 249 Imp gallons; 299 US gallons; 1,133 litres) is installed behind the two front seats, and 62-nozzle spraybooms are fitted beneath the wings. In this configuration the aircraft can cover a swath width of 148 ft (45 m). An ultra-low-volume system, using four to six atomisers or two to four Micronairs, is also available, permitting increase in swath width up to 1,310 ft (400 m).

For dusting with granulated materials, the lower part of the standard tank can be replaced by a discharge and dispersal door permitting coverage of a swath width of up to 65·6 ft (20 m). A Transland spreader can be fitted for dust application (swath up to 100 ft; 30 m). Effective swath width of these versions is 43-131 ft (13-40 m), the optimum being approx 66 ft (20 m).

Both versions are fitted with small doors in the fuselage sides, giving access to the tank/hopper for servicing, removal or replenishment, and two single seats or a bench seat for three persons can be installed aft of the tank. Optional items include an engine air intake screen and a loading door for chemicals in the top of the fuselage.

Approximately 25 of the agricultural version had been built by the beginning of 1974.

ELECTRONICS AND EQUIPMENT: Optional equipment includes Decca Mk 8A navigator, Decca Hi-Fix radio, Decca Doppler 72 radar, gyrosyn CL-11 compass and SR 54A radio altimeter.

WEIGHTS (L: liquid spray system; D: dry chemicals system):
Weight empty:
L, D 2,579 lb (1,170 kg)
Agricultural installation:
L 293 lb (133 kg)
D 231 lb (105 kg)
Chemical:
L 2,592 lb (1,176 kg)
D 2,665 lb (1,209 kg)
Fuel, oil and pilot:
L, D 630 lb (286 kg)
Max T-O weight:
L, D 6,106 lb (2,770 kg)
Max landing weight:
L, D 4,850 lb (2,200 kg)

PERFORMANCE (liquid spray version, PT6A-20 engine, at max T-O weight):
Operating speed approx 86 knots (99 mph; 160 km/h)
Operating height 20-26 ft (6-8 m)
Spraying duration with full spray tank 6 min

PILATUS MODULE PORTER

In collaboration with Poligrat of Germany (which see) Pilatus is studying the market for a Module Porter version (or conversion) of the Turbo-Porter, involving aerodynamic refinements to the fuselage and tail unit, the fitting of a 680 shp PT6A-27 turboprop engine, and the installation of an extra row of seats. The production version of the Module Porter, of which a prototype has been flown, would have empty and max T-O weights of 2,950 lb (1,338 kg) and 6,173 lb (2,800 kg) respectively.

PC-6/B1 Turbo-Porter fitted with Micronair AU-3000 crop-spraying gear

SCHRETZMANN

WALTER SCHRETZMANN

ADDRESS:
Obere Mattstrasse 24, CH-8713 Uerikon

SCHRETZMANN S.W.1 PEGASUS

The Pegasus is a single-seat homebuilt light aircraft, designed and built by Herr Walter Schretzmann. Construction began in early April 1968, and the aircraft (HB-YAA) made its first flight on 4 November 1972, powered by a 100 hp modified Chevrolet Corvair motor car engine. It proved to be somewhat underpowered with this power plant, and has since been fitted with a 115 hp Lycoming engine. It was hoped to resume flying with the new engine in mid-1974.

TYPE: Single-seat homebuilt light aircraft.

WINGS: Cantilever all-wood low-wing monoplane. Entire wings, including ailerons and trailing-edge flaps, are plywood-covered.

FUSELAGE: Plywood-covered wooden structure.

TAIL UNIT: Cantilever all-wood structure, with small dorsal fin fairing.

LANDING GEAR: Non-retractable tailwheel type.

Oleo-pneumatic shock-absorbers. Streamlined fairings on main wheels and legs.

Power Plant: One 115 hp Lycoming O-235 four-cylinder horizontally-opposed aircooled engine, driving a two-blade propeller. Electric starter.

Dimensions, external:
- Wing span: 21 ft 6¼ in (6·56 m)
- Wing chord (constant): 4 ft 4 in (1·32 m)
- Wing aspect ratio: 5
- Length overall: 17 ft 8¾ in (5·40 m)
- Height overall: 6 ft 11½ in (2·12 m)
- Propeller diameter: 4 ft 9½ in (1·46 m)

Area:
- Wings, gross: 96·88 sq ft (9·00 m²)

Weights (Chevrolet engine):
- Weight empty: 970 lb (440 kg)
- Max T-O weight: 1,389 lb (630 kg)

Performance (at max T-O weight, Chevrolet engine):
- Max level speed: 132 knots (152 mph; 245 km/h)
- Cruising speed (70% power): 113 knots (130 mph; 210 km/h)
- Stalling speed: 51·5 knots (59 mph; 95 km/h)
- T-O run: 984 ft (300 m)
- Landing run: 820 ft (250 m)
- Range: 540 nm (620 miles; 1,000 km)

S.W.1 Pegasus single-seat homebuilt light aircraft designed and built by Herr Walter Schretzmann

SWISS FEDERAL AIRCRAFT FACTORY

EIDGENÖSSISCHES FLUGZEUGWERK — FABRIQUE FÉDÉRALE D'AVIONS — FABBRICA FEDERALE D'AEROPLANI

Head Office and Works:
CH-6032 Emmen
Telephone: (041) 50 55 11
Telex: 7 84 80 fwead ch

Director:
Lucien Othenin-Girard

Deputy Director:
Dr Peter Burkhardt

Chief Designer:
Heinz Rhomberg

Head of Research Department:
Heini Kamber

F+W is the Swiss government's official aircraft establishment for research, development and production of military aircraft. It was prime contractor for the production of 60 Aérospatiale SA 316S Alouette III helicopters for the Swiss Army, delivery of which was completed in the Spring of 1974. It is a collaborating contractor of Dassault-Breguet for development of the engine nacelles of the Mercure jet transport. It has produced prototype nacelles, including some versions with noise-suppressing air intakes, and is manufacturing the first batch of production nacelles for the Mercures ordered by Air Inter.

F+W is subcontractor to Hawker Siddeley for the final assembly of, and application of Swiss modifications to, 60 refurbished Hunter Mk 58A aircraft ordered by the Swiss Air Force.

F+W developed, primarily for fighters but also for private aircraft, an assisted take-off device known as POHWARO (Pulsated Over-Heated WAter ROcket). Several sizes, ranging from 2,500 lb (1,134 kg) sec to 70,000 lb (31,750 kg) sec impulse, were designed and tested. One of the models (5,500 lb; 2,495 kg sec) was demonstrated on a Pilatus Porter aircraft at the 1972 Hanover Air Show. Other models are at present in use for the acceleration of sleds on test tracks in France and Germany.

Testing and research facilities at F+W, which include five wind tunnels for speeds up to Mach 4·5, test cells for piston engines and turbojet engines with afterburners, and modern data acquisition and processing systems, are utilised also by foreign research and aircraft industries.

An important activity is research work in the field of aeronautical fatigue. Extensive specimen tests are carried out to determine the fatigue behaviour of light alloys and steels. After the completion of a full-scale test of a de Havilland Venom Mk 4 airframe, a similar test with an entire Mirage III-S airframe was being prepared in the Spring of 1974.

Swiss Air Force Dassault Mirage III-S, fitted with two F + W POHWARO assisted take-off rockets

Swiss-built SA 316S Alouette III, fitted with skis developed by F + W

F+W C-3605

The C-3605 is a turboprop conversion of the EKW C-3603 fighter-bomber, which has been in Swiss Air Force service since 1942 and of which 144 were built up to 1944.

The prototype conversion flew for the first time on 19 August 1968, and 23 more aircraft were subsequently converted to C-3605 standard; delivery of these to the Swiss Air Force was completed in January 1973.

A full description of the C-3605 appeared in the 1972-73 *Jane's*.

F + W (AÉROSPATIALE) SA 316 ALOUETTE III

The first of 60 SA 316S Alouette III helicopters for the Swiss Army built under licence by F+W was delivered on 22 March 1972, and delivery was completed in early 1974. A description of the Alouette III appears under the Aérospatiale heading in the French section of this edition.

F+W (DE HAVILLAND) VENOM

A number of Venom F.B Mks 4 and 50 aircraft (possibly as many as 200) of the Swiss Air Force have recently been modernised by F+W. Brief details of this programme were given in the 1973-74 *Jane's*.

TAIWAN

AIDC/CAF

AERO INDUSTRY DEVELOPMENT CENTER—CHINESE AIR FORCE

Address:
PO Box 7173, Taichung, Taiwan 400
Telephone: Taichung 23051
Telex: 51140

Director: Lieutenant General Y. C. Lee

Deputy Directors:
Major General C. Y. Lee (Manufacturing)
Dr T. C. Lee, PhD (Engineering and Research)

Aeronautical Research Laboratory

Address:
PO Box 7174, Taichung, Taiwan

Director:
Dr T. C. Lee, PhD

The Aero Industry Development Center was established on 1 July 1969. It is a successor to the Bureau of Aircraft Industry (BAI), which was established in 1946 in Nanking and moved to Taiwan in 1948.

In October 1968 the Aeronautical Research Laboratory, then a branch of BAI, constructed the first Chinese-built PL-1A (see 1970-71 *Jane's*), which was a slightly modified version of the US Pazmany PL-1 powered by a 125 hp Lycoming

O-290-D engine. The PL-1A flew for the first time on 26 October 1968. After flight tests and further modifications, 35 PL-1B Chienshou production models were built by AIDC in 1970, and a further 10 in the Spring of 1972. These have since been used extensively as primary trainers for CAF air cadets. The PL-1B continues in production, with a number of more recent modifications.

Under an agreement reached in 1969, the AIDC is now producing in Taiwan the Bell UH-1H (Bell Model 205) helicopter under licence for the Chinese Army. The AIDC-Bell UH-1H is almost identical with the UH-1H version built by Bell Helicopter Company (see US section). The original contract was for 50 UH-1Hs, to which was added in 1972 a follow-on order for a further 24 of these aircraft.

The AIDC has also completed preparations for the production under licence, for the Chinese Nationalist Air Force, of the Northrop F-5E Tiger II combat aircraft.

Since 1970, the AIDC has been developing the XT-CH-1A, a turboprop-powered secondary trainer of its own design with two seats in tandem. This prototype began flight testing in 1973; a second, designated XT-CH-1B, was due for completion by the end of 1974.

AIDC XT-CH-1A

This aircraft is a tandem two-seat secondary trainer, the design of which was started by AIDC in November 1970. Two prototypes have been ordered, designated XT-CH-1A and XT-CH-1B; construction began in January 1972.

The first aircraft was completed in September 1973 and was flown for the first time on 23 November 1973. In early 1974 it was undergoing an extensive flight test programme. The second (XT-CH-1B) aircraft, which is a modified version of the XT-CH-1A, is under construction and was scheduled for completion by the end of 1974.

The following description applies to the XT-CH-1A:

Type: Turboprop-powered secondary trainer.

Wings: Cantilever low-wing monoplane. Wing section NACA 64-2A215 (constant). Dihedral 8° from roots. Incidence 2°. No sweepback. Conventional aluminium alloy stressed-skin structure, with aluminium alloy ailerons and slotted trailing-edge flaps. Link-balance type trim tab in each aileron.

Fuselage: Conventional semi-monocoque structure of aluminium alloy.

Tail Unit: Cantilever aluminium alloy structure, with fixed-incidence tailplane. Dorsal fin. Link-balance type trim tabs in rudder and each elevator.

Landing Gear: Retractable tricycle type. Hydraulic retraction, main wheels inward into wings, nosewheel rearward. Telescopic shock-absorbers. Goodyear brakes. Small tail bumper under rear fuselage.

Power Plant: One 1,450 ehp Lycoming T53-L-701 turboprop engine, driving a Hamilton Standard 53C51-27 three-blade metal propeller with spinner. Fuel in two tanks in each wing and one in fuselage, with total capacity of 255 US gallons (212 Imp gallons; 963 litres). Oil capacity 8 US gallons (6·6 Imp gallons; 30 litres).

Accommodation: Crew of two in tandem. Rearward-sliding fully-transparent canopy over each cockpit. Cockpits heated and ventilated.

Systems: Midland-Ross Corporation heating and ventilating system. 115V 300A system provides AC electrical power at 250VA 400Hz. 28V DC system includes 24V 34Ah battery. Oxygen bottle with volume of 2,100 cu in (3·5 litres).

Electronics and Equipment: Collins AN/ARC-51BX UHF radio and Collins AN/ARN-83 ADF.

Dimensions, external:

Wing span	40 ft 0 in (12·19 m)
Wing chord at root	8 ft 0 in (2·44 m)
Wing chord at tip	5 ft 0 in (1·52 m)
Wing aspect ratio	6
Length overall	33 ft 8 in (10·26 m)
Height overall	12 ft 0 in (3·66 m)
Tailplane span	16 ft 0 in (4·88 m)
Wheel track	12 ft 8 in (3·86 m)
Wheelbase	7 ft 10 in (2·39 m)
Propeller diameter	10 ft 0 in (3·05 m)
Propeller ground clearance	2 ft 5 in (0·74 m)

Areas:

Wings, gross	271·0 sq ft (25·18 m²)
Ailerons (total)	26·0 sq ft (2·42 m²)
Flaps (total)	54·0 sq ft (5·02 m²)
Fin	18·0 sq ft (1·67 m²)
Rudder, incl tab	12·0 sq ft (1·11 m²)
Elevators, incl tabs	16·0 sq ft (1·49 m²)

Weights and Loadings:

Weight empty, equipped	7,250 lb (3,288 kg)
Max T-O weight	9,200 lb (4,173 kg)
Max landing weight	7,050 lb (3,197 kg)
Max wing loading	34·0 lb/sq ft (166 kg/m²)
Max power loading	6·34 lb/ehp (2·88 kg/ehp)

Performance (at AUW of 7,600 lb; 3,447 kg):

Max never-exceed speed	370 knots (426 mph; 685 km/h)
Max level speed at 15,000 ft (4,570 m)	320 knots (368 mph; 592 km/h)
Max cruising speed at 15,000 ft (4,570 m)	220 knots (253 mph; 407 km/h)
Econ cruising speed at 15,000 ft (4,570 m)	170 knots (196 mph; 315 km/h)
Stalling speed	50 knots (58 mph; 93 km/h)
Max rate of climb at S/L	3,400 ft (1,036 m)/min
Service ceiling	32,000 ft (9,755 m)
T-O run	800 ft (244 m)
T-O to 50 ft (15 m)	1,100 ft (335 m)
Landing from 50 ft (15 m)	1,300 ft (396 m)
Landing run	900 ft (274 m)
Range with max fuel	1,085 nm (1,250 miles; 2,010 km)

First Taiwan-built example of the Bell UH-1H Iroquois helicopter, which first flew in 1971

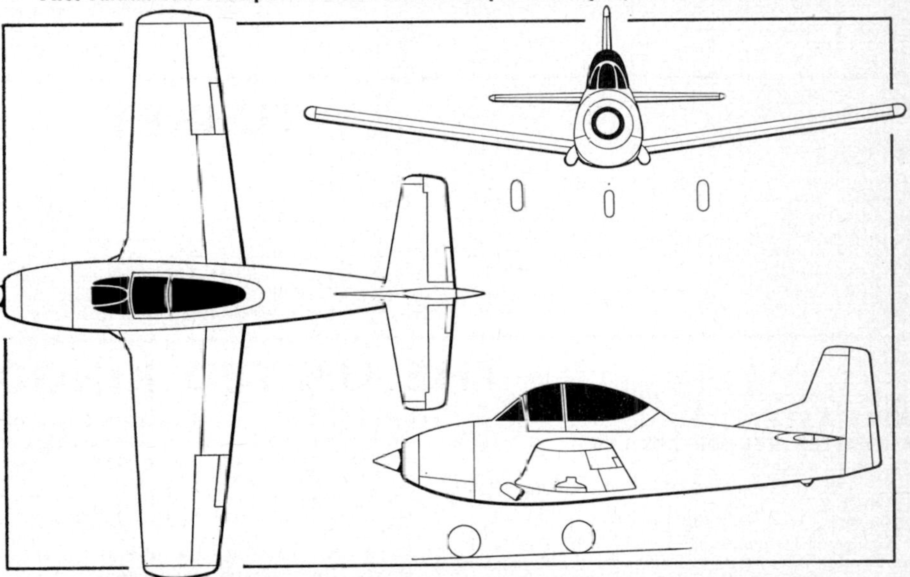

AIDC XT-CH-1A tandem two-seat turboprop-powered trainer (*Michael Badrocke*)

AIDC XT-CH-1A secondary trainer (1,450 ehp Lycoming T53-L-701 turboprop engine)

AIDC (PAZMANY) PL-1B CHIENSHOU (LONG LIFE)

A description of the PL-1A prototype appeared in the 1970-71 *Jane's*. The PL-1B is the version modified for production, of which 35 were built in 1970 and a further 10 in the Spring of 1972. Significant improvements compared with the PL-1A include a wider cockpit, larger rudder and more powerful engine.

The PL-1B continues in production, currently with additional modifications to the engine cowling, tail unit, flaps control and pilot seats.

Type: Two-seat light aircraft.

Wings: Cantilever low-wing monoplane. Wing section NACA 63_2615. Dihedral 3° from roots. Incidence —1° 20′. All-metal single-spar structure in one piece, with leading-edge torsion box. Plain piano-hinged ailerons and flaps of all-metal construction. No trim tabs.

Fuselage: Conventional all-metal semi-monocoque structure, with flat or single-curvature skins.

Tail Unit: Cantilever all-metal structure. One-piece horizontal surface, with anti-servo tab which serves also as a trim tab.

Landing Gear: Non-retractable tricycle type, with all three oleo-pneumatic shock-absorbers interchangeable. Goodyear wheels and tyres size 5·00-5; tyre pressure 31 lb/sq in (2·18 kg/cm²). Goodyear brakes. Steerable nosewheel.

Power Plant: One 150 hp Lycoming O-320-E2A four-cylinder horizontally-opposed aircooled engine, driving a McCauley IA100/MCM 6668 two-blade fixed-pitch metal propeller. Fuel in two glassfibre wingtip tanks, each of 10·4 Imp gallons (12·5 US gallons; 47 litres) capacity. Total fuel capacity 20·8 Imp gallons (25 US gallons; 94 litres). Oil capacity 1·7 Imp gallons (2 US gallons; 7·5 litres).

Accommodation: Two seats side by side, under rearward-sliding transparent canopy. Dual controls. Space for 40 lb (18 kg) baggage aft of seats. Heater and airscoops for ventilation.

Electronics and Equipment: VHF radio standard.

Dimensions, external:

Wing span	28 ft 0 in (8·53 m)

Wing chord (constant)	4 ft 2 in (1·27 m)
Wing aspect ratio	6·72
Length overall	19 ft 8⅛ in (5·99 m)
Height overall	7 ft 4 in (2·24 m)
Tailplane span	8 ft 0 in (2·44 m)
Wheel track	8 ft 2½ in (2·50 m)
Wheelbase	4 ft 3 in (1·30 m)
DIMENSIONS, INTERNAL:	
Cabin: Length	4 ft 2 in (1·27 m)
Max width	3 ft 6½ in (1·07 m)
Max height	3 ft 4 in (1·02 m)
AREAS:	
Wings, gross	116 sq ft (10·78 m^2)
Ailerons (total)	10·54 sq ft (0·98 m^2)
Flaps (total)	17·36 sq ft (1·61 m^2)
Fin	7·30 sq ft (0·68 m^2)
Rudder	4·20 sq ft (0·39 m^2)
Tailplane, incl tab	18·00 sq ft (1·67 m^2)
WEIGHTS AND LOADINGS:	
Weight empty, equipped	950 lb (431 kg)
Max T-O weight	1,440 lb (653 kg)
Max wing loading	12·4 lb/sq ft (60·5 kg/m^2)
Max power loading	9·6 lb/hp (4·35 kg/hp)
PERFORMANCE (at max T-O weight):	
Max never-exceed speed	178 knots (205 mph; 330 km/h)
Max level speed at S/L	130 knots (150 mph; 241 km/h)
Max cruising speed at S/L	113 knots (130 mph; 209 km/h)
Econ cruising speed at S/L	100 knots (115 mph; 185 km/h)
Stalling speed, flaps down	47 knots (54 mph; 87 km/h)
Max rate of climb at S/L	1,600 ft (488 m)/min
T-O run	560 ft (171 m)
T-O to 50 ft (15 m)	950 ft (290 m)
Landing from 50 ft (15 m)	1,100 ft (335 m)
Landing run	550 ft (167 m)
Range with max fuel	350 nm (405 miles; 650 km)

AIDC/CAF (Pazmany) PL-1B Chienshou primary trainer for the Chinese Air Force

TURKEY

TUSAS

Preliminary steps have been taken by the Turkish government to establish an aircraft manufacturing facility, to be known as TUSAS, in that country, financed jointly by the Turkish government (55%) and the Turkish Air Forces Foundation (45%).

TUSAS was officially established with effect from 11 July 1973 with an initial capital of 300 million Turkish lire.

Plans are for a programme for the manufacture in Turkey of some 200 aircraft as replacements for the Turkish Air Force. Detailed proposals are being considered from major aerospace companies: BAC and Hawker Siddeley Aviation from the UK, and Lockheed Aircraft Corporation, Northrop Corporation and LTV from the US. The evaluation of contenders is being co-ordinated by the Turkish Air Forces Foundation, which was expected to make its recommendations to the Turkish government during 1974.

The initial stage of the TUSAS programme will be the licence production of an existing type of military aircraft, selection of which had not been announced at the time of closing for press.

THE UNITED KINGDOM

AIRMASTER

AIRMASTER HELICOPTERS LTD

ADDRESS:
c/o Bering Ltd, Doman Road, Camberley, Surrey
Telephone: Camberley (027) 64191

Airmaster Helicopters Ltd was formed in 1971 to develop the lightest, smallest, simplest and lowest-cost two-seat helicopter possible, and its constructors consider that they have successfully achieved this objective.

AIRMASTER H2-B1

Construction of the Airmaster H2-B1 (G-AYNS) was begun in September 1970 and completed in January 1972. Ground-running tests have been completed, and the first flight was made in February 1972 under a Permit to Fly issued in the same month. The H2-B1, which is described in detail below, is the prototype for an H2-B2 version now in the design stage, which will have a fully-streamlined fuselage with a monocoque tailboom.

TYPE: Two-seat ultra-light helicopter.

ROTOR SYSTEM: Single two-blade main rotor and two-blade tail rotor. Main rotor blades, of NACA 0012 section, are attached to hub by five shear bolts. Leading- and trailing-edges are aluminium extrusions, joined by aluminium skins; the whole assembly is metal bonded and safety riveted. Tail rotor is of formed aluminium skin, riveted on trailing-edges; attachment points are aluminium extrusions. No rotor brake is fitted, and the blades do not fold.

ROTOR DRIVE: Simple gearbox, incorporating two helical spur gears. Main rotor/engine rpm ratio 5·5 : 1. Tail rotor/engine rpm ratio 1 : 1.

FUSELAGE: Welded safe-life tubular structure with aluminium skin.

TAIL UNIT: Welded tubular elevators and vertical fin.

LANDING GEAR: Skid type, with rubber shock-absorption. Wheels (tyre pressure 30 lb/sq in; 2·11 kg/cm^2) fitted for ground handling only.

POWER PLANT: One 100 hp Rolls-Royce Continental O-200-A four-cylinder horizontally-opposed aircooled engine. Fuel in two externally-mounted tanks, each of 7 Imp gallons (31·5 litres) capacity. Refuelling point on top of each tank. Oil capacity 1·5 Imp gallons (6·8 litres).

ACCOMMODATION: Seats for pilot and one passenger. Door on each side of cabin.

SYSTEMS AND EQUIPMENT: Electrical power from engine generator and battery. Standard air/ground communications equipment.

DIMENSIONS, EXTERNAL:	
Main rotor diameter	23 ft 0 in (7·01 m)
Tail rotor diameter	4 ft 0 in (1·22 m)
Main rotor blade chord (each)	8 in (20·3 cm)
Length overall	25 ft 3 in (7·70 m)
Length of fuselage	19 ft 4 in (5·89 m)
Height to top of rotor hub	7 ft 7 in (2·31 m)
Height overall	8 ft 1 in (2·46 m)
Skid track	6 ft 2 in (1·88 m)
Cabin doors (each):	
Height	3 ft 1 in (0·94 m)
Width	2 ft 11 in (0·89 m)
Height to sill	2 ft 2 in (0·66 m)
DIMENSIONS, INTERNAL:	
Cabin: Length	4 ft 10 in (1·47 m)
Max width	3 ft 7 in (1·09 m)
Max height	4 ft 0 in (1·22 m)
AREAS:	
Main rotor blades (each)	7·25 sq ft (0·67 m^2)
Tail rotor blades (each)	0·42 sq ft (0·04 m^2)
Main rotor disc	1,120·0 sq ft (104·0 m^2)
Tail rotor disc	17·7 sq ft (1·64 m^2)
Fin	2·0 sq ft (0·19 m^2)
Elevators	4·0 sq ft (0·37 m^2)
WEIGHTS AND LOADINGS:	
Weight empty, equipped	738 lb (334 kg)
Max payload	340 lb (154 kg)
Max T-O and landing weight	1,200 lb (544 kg)
Max disc loading	1·01 lb/sq ft (4·93 kg/m^2)
Max power loading	12·0 lb/hp (5·44 kg/hp)
PERFORMANCE (at max T-O weight):	
Max never-exceed speed	104 knots (120 mph; 193 km/h)
Max level speed at S/L	82·5 knots (95 mph; 153 km/h)
Max cruising speed at 1,000 ft (305 m)	78 knots (90 mph; 145 km/h)
Econ cruising speed at 1,000 ft (305 m)	74 knots (85 mph; 137 km/h)
Max rate of climb at S/L	1,800 ft (549 m)/min
Max vertical rate of climb at S/L	580 ft (177 m)/min
Service ceiling	10,000 ft (3,050 m)
Hovering ceiling in ground effect	7,000 ft (2,135 m)
Hovering ceiling out of ground effect	4,000 ft (1,220 m)
Range with max fuel	200 nm (230 miles; 370 km)

Prototype Airmaster H2-B1 light helicopter

AJEP

AJEP DEVELOPMENTS

ADDRESS:
The Lodge, Marden Hill Farm, nr Hertford, Hertfordshire
Telephone: 433-5936

MANAGING DIRECTOR:
A. J. E. Perkins

AJEP (WITTMAN) TAILWIND

AJEP is marketing in the UK plans and construction kits for a modified version of the Wittman Tailwind light aircraft (see US section), and has completed one aircraft (G-AYDU) as a UK demonstrator. Both complete and partial kits are available to amateur constructors. Partial kits, intended for experienced engineers, have a complete welded airframe, but no power plant is supplied and fabrication of such major components as the wings requires a higher degree of constructional skill than does the assembly of the completed components of the standard kit.

AJEP's prototype is powered by a 100 hp Continental PC60 (GPU) piston engine, but recommended power plants include the 95 hp Rolls-Royce Continental C90 or 100 hp O-200-A four-cylinder horizontally-opposed aircooled engines.

The basic description of the Wittman Tailwind in the US section applies also to the British version, but there are detail changes. The most noticeable externally is a revised tail unit with swept vertical and horizontal surfaces, but others include modifications to engine cowlings and door size, and a revised wing aerofoil section. Internal changes include modifications to the seating position, instrument panel and cockpit layout.

By comparison with the US basic version, the AJEP Tailwind has a cruising speed of 140 knots (161 mph; 259 km/h), but wing section and tail unit changes have reduced stalling speed to 43 knots (50 mph; 80 km/h).

AJEP Developments Wittman Tailwind prototype (100 hp Continental PC60 (GPU) engine)

ATEL

AVIATION TRADERS (ENGINEERING) LTD

OFFICES AND WORKS:
Municipal Airport, Southend-on-Sea, Essex SS2 6XZ
Telephone: Southend (0702) 49471
Telex: 99132
and
Stansted Airport, Essex
Telephone: Stansted 2031

DIRECTORS:
The Hon Anthony Cayzer (Chairman)
R. W. Cantello (Vice-Chairman)
G. H. C. Fisher (Managing Director)
P. E. B. de Buriatte (Financial)
C. W. Murrell (Technical)
S. B. F. Oates (General Manager, Aircraft Division)
J. R. Batt
P. N. Buckley
R. L. Cumming
H. W. Denman
A. F. Nickalls

SALES MANAGER:
M. D. Ellis

Aviation Traders (Engineering) Ltd was formed in 1949 and became a member company of Air Holdings Ltd in 1961. The company has aircraft maintenance bases at Stansted and Southend Airports engaged on line and base maintenance of aircraft types which range from light trainers to four-engined jets. At Southend there are also design, component overhaul, parts manufacture, technical training and ground equipment manufacturing departments. The facilities are Ministry of Defence, CAA and FAA approved.

Activities of the aircraft maintenance and component overhaul departments include work on Britannia, CL-44, Vanguard, Boeing 707, 727, 737, BAC One-Eleven, Herald, DC-4, DC-6, DC-7, DC-8, Caravelle and TriStar aircraft. The design and aircraft conversion departments have carried out work for the Concorde, VC10, Boeing 707 and Saunders ST-27 aircraft, and for Wessex, JetRanger and BO 105 helicopters.

ATEL has extensive manufacturing facilities for airport and airline ground support equipment, and holds manufacturing and distribution licences from Fokker-VFW relating to various models of covered passenger gangways and from the Cochran-Western Corporation embracing a wide range of baggage and cargo handling equipment suitable for Boeing 747, DC-10, TriStar and other aircraft. Orders for ground equipment have been obtained from the British Airports Authority, Manchester Airport, the German Ministry of Defence and major airlines, including British Airways, MEA, Aer Lingus, VARIG, Egyptair, TWA, PanAm, Lebanese Air Transport, British Caledonian, Air France, KLM and ALIA.

BAC

BRITISH AIRCRAFT CORPORATION LTD

HEAD OFFICE:
Brooklands Road, Weybridge, Surrey KT13 0RN
Telephone: Weybridge (0932) 45522
Telex: 27111

DIRECTORS:
Sir George R. Edwards, OM, CBE, FRS, BSc(Eng), Hon DSc, CEng, Hon FRAeS, Hon FAIAA (Chairman)
A. H. C. Greenwood, CBE, JP, FRAeS (Deputy Chairman)
G. E. Knight, CBE (Vice-Chairman)
G. R. Jefferson, CBE, BSc, CEng, MIMechE, FRAeS (Managing Director, Guided Weapons)
F. W. Page, CBE, MA, CEng, FRAeS (Managing Director, Aircraft)
J. E. Armitage, FCMA (Commercial Director)
E. G. Barber, BSc, CEng, AFRAeS, MIPM (Director of Personnel and Training)
H. R. Baxendale, OBE, ACMA (Deputy Chairman and Managing Director, Military Aircraft Division)
Handel Davies, CB, MSc, CEng, FRAeS, FIAeS, FAIAA (Technical Director)
G. T. Gedge, CBE, CEng, FIProdE (Director of Manufacturing)
T. B. Pritchard, FCA (Financial Director)
J. Ferguson Smith, FCA (Deputy Chairman and Managing Director, Commercial Aircraft Division)

SECRETARY: B. Cookson, LLB

TREASURER: J. D. Hanson, LLB, FCA

PUBLICITY MANAGER: C. J. T. Gardner, OBE, AFRAeS

Incorporated in 1963, British Aircraft Corporation Ltd was formed to take over the business formerly carried out by its predecessor companies' subsidiaries, Bristol Aircraft Ltd, English Electric Aviation Ltd, Vickers-Armstrongs (Aircraft) Ltd and Hunting Aircraft Ltd. The undertaking is ultimately owned by the General Electric Company Ltd (50%) and Vickers Ltd (50%), and has been rationalised progressively into three Divisions: the Commercial Aircraft Division, the Military Aircraft Division and the Guided Weapons Division, each managed by an individual management company with its own Board of Directors.

The Corporation has the following overseas subsidiaries: British Scandinavian Aviation AB, British Aircraft Corporation (Australia) Pty Ltd and British Aircraft Corporation (USA) Inc; and the following UK subsidiaries: British Aircraft Corporation (Insurance Brokers) Ltd, British Aircraft Corporation (Insurance) Ltd, British Aircraft Corporation (Pension Fund Trustees) Ltd, and British Aircraft Corporation (AT) Ltd. Its associated companies are SEPECAT (formed in May 1966 by BAC and Breguet Aviation to control the development and production of the Jaguar light strike fighter and trainer) and Panavia Aircraft GmbH (formed in March 1969 by BAC, MBB and Aeritalia to foster the development and production of the Multi-Role Combat Aircraft).

COMMERCIAL AIRCRAFT DIVISION

ADDRESS:
Brooklands Road, Weybridge, Surrey KT13 0RN
Telephone: Weybridge (0932) 45522
Telex: 27111
and
Filton House, Filton, Bristol
Telephone: Bristol (0272) 693831
Telex: 44163

DIRECTORS:
F. W. Page, CBE, MA, CEng, FRAeS (Chairman)
J. Ferguson Smith, FCA (Deputy Chairman and Managing Director)
Sir Geoffrey Tuttle, KBE, CB, DFC, FRAeS (Vice Chairman)
W. R. Coomber (Chief Executive, Weybridge)
G. Hanby, FCA, FCWA (Commercial Director)
J. T. Jefferies, CEng, FIProdE (Chief Executive, Filton)
D. J. John, MA (Oxon) (Sales Director)
E. E. Marshall, CBE, CEng, FRAeS (Director of Engineering)
H. Smith, FCA (Financial Director)
Dr W. J. Strang, CBE, PhD, BSc, CEng, FRAeS (Technical Director)
E. B. Trubshaw, CBE, MVO, FRAeS (Director of Flight Test)
M. G. Wilde, OBE, BSc, DipAe, CEng, FRAeS (Project Director, Concorde)

SECRETARY: H. T. Fream

With effect from 1 June 1971 the former Filton and Weybridge Divisions of BAC were replaced by a Commercial Aircraft Division which includes the Filton, Hurn and Weybridge factories and the Fairford flight test centre.

Weybridge, with approximately 6,000 employees, is responsible for the manufacture of all Concorde flight deck and forward fuselage sections, and all rear fuselage, fin and rudder assemblies. In addition it is involved in a variety of subcontract work in support of programmes managed by other BAC Divisions and other aerospace manufacturers, as well as design studies for new subsonic transports.

The factory at Hurn, near Bournemouth, has approximately 2,500 employees and is responsible for BAC One-Eleven final assembly, the production of all Concorde droop nose and visor sections, the assembly of the complete electrical wiring harness for all Concordes and numerous subcontract work programmes. There is also a steady flow of One-Elevens passing through Hurn which are being reconfigured to customers' requirements. Both Weybridge and Hurn are responsible for supporting many hundreds of aircraft in service throughout the world. They include not only One-Elevens, but Viscounts, Vanguards, VC10s, Super VC10s and the Hunting Prince/Pembroke series, all of which have been described in earlier editions of *Jane's*.

Filton, with 6,000 employees (excluding those on guided weapons and space work), is responsible for design and development of the Concorde supersonic transport, in partnership with Aérospatiale of France, and is the location of the British Concorde final assembly centre. Filton is also carrying out a number of subcontract work programmes, and provides after-sales support for former Bristol aircraft which remain in service.

Fairford, in Gloucestershire, is the site of the Division's Flight Test Centre, and is the base from which the British Concorde flight test programme is controlled.

BAC/AÉROSPATIALE CONCORDE

Details of the Concorde programme can be found in the International section of this edition.

BAC ONE-ELEVEN

Details of the One-Eleven were announced on 9 May 1961, simultaneously with the news that British United Airways had ordered ten. Design and manufacture are shared between three BAC factories, at Weybridge, Filton and Hurn.

There are five commercial versions, as follows:

Series 200. First production model, for applications demanding both short and medium range. Two 10,330 lb (4,686 kg) st Rolls-Royce Spey-25 Mk 506 turbofan engines. BAC-owned prototype flew for first time on 20 August 1963, followed by first production Model 201 on 19 December 1963. ARB certification received 6 April 1965; FAA Type Approval 20 April 1965. First services operated by BUA and Braniff, on 9 and 25 April 1965 respectively.

Series 300. Physically similar to Series 200 but developed for applications demanding range with high payload. Two 11,400 lb (5,171 kg) st Rolls-Royce Spey Mk 511 turbofan engines in 4 in (10 cm) longer nacelles. Increased standard fuel tankage (centre-section tank). Heavier wing planks and shear webs and strengthened landing gear to cater for increased AUW. Enlarged capacity wheel brakes.

Series 400. Generally similar to Series 300, but modified to meet requirements of US operators. Standard items as for Series 300, plus lift dumpers and dropout oxygen systems. First Srs 400 flew for first time on 13 July 1965. FAA Type Approval 22 November 1965; ARB certification 10 December 1965.

Series 475. Combines standard fuselage and accommodation of Series 400 with wings and power plant of Series 500 and a modified landing gear system, using low-pressure tyres, to permit operation from secondary low-strength runways with poorer-grade surfaces. The Srs 400/500 development aircraft (G-ASYD) was converted to serve as prototype and flew for the first time on 27 August 1970. First production Series 475 (G-AYUW) flew for the first time on 5 April 1971. Certification and first production delivery (to Faucett of Peru) in July 1971. The three Srs 475s ordered by the Sultan of Oman's Air Force have a quick-change passenger/cargo interior layout and a 10 ft 0 in × 6 ft 1 in (3·05 × 1·85 m) forward freight door.

Series 500. Derived from Series 300/400, this version incorporates a lengthened fuselage (100 in; 2·54 m fwd of wing, 62 in; 1·57 m aft) which accommodates 97-119 passengers, with a flight crew of two. Wingtip extensions increase span by 5 ft (1·52 m). Take-off performance improved by increased wing area and by installation of two Rolls-Royce Spey Mk 512 DW turbofans, each rated at 12,550 lb (5,692 kg) st. Main landing gear strengthened and heavier wing plank stringers used to cater for increased AUW.

Prototype, converted from Srs 400 development aircraft (G-ASYD), flew for first time on 30 June 1967. First Srs 500 production aircraft (G-AVMH) flew on 7 February 1968. ARB certification 15 August 1968. Deliveries to BEA began on 29 August 1968, and regular services on 17 November 1968.

Executive and freighter versions of the One-Eleven are available.

A One-Eleven "hush kit", comprising an intake duct lining, a by-pass duct lining, an acoustically-lined jetpipe, and a fluted jet mixing exhaust silencer, was flown for the first time, on the Srs 475 development aircraft G-ASYD, on 14 June 1974. It is designed to reduce the area within the 90 EPNdB noise contour by approximately 50 per cent, giving a noise footprint equivalent to that of a twin-turboprop aircraft. Production "hush kits" should be available for retrofitting towards the end of 1975.

Orders for 215 One-Elevens had been received by 19 June 1974, of which 209 had been delivered. Totals of the various series sold by that date are as follows:

Series 200	56
Series 300	9
Series 400	69
Series 475	8
Series 500	73
	215

Operators of the One-Eleven in mid-1974 were as follows:

Series 200	
Aer Lingus	4
Allegheny	31
BCAL	7
Braniff	1
Zambian Airways	2
Executive and military operators	8
Series 300	
Dan-Air	2
Laker Airways	5
Quebecair	2
Series 400	
American Airlines	12
Austral	4
Bahamasair	2
Bavaria Flug	4
British Airways	5
Dan-Air	3
Gulf Air	2
LACSA	1
Quebecair	1
TACA	3
Tarom	7
VASP	2
Executive and military operators	18
Series 475	
Air Malawi	1
Air Pacific	2
Faucett (Peru)	2
Sultan of Oman's Air Force	3*
**Delivery to begin in late* 1974	
Series 500	
Austral	3
AVIATECA	1
Bavaria Flug	3
BCAL	14
British Airways	18
Court Line	10
Germanair	6
LACSA	4
LIAT	2
PAL	3*
Phoenix	1
Transbrasil	5

**2 more due for delivery in mid-*1974

Type: Twin-engined short/medium-range turbofan transport.

Wings: Cantilever low-wing monoplane. Modified NACA cambered wing section. Thickness/chord ratio 12½% at root, 11% at tip. Dihedral 2°. Incidence 2° 30′. Sweepback 20° at quarter-chord. All-metal structure of copper-based aluminium alloy, built on fail-safe principles.

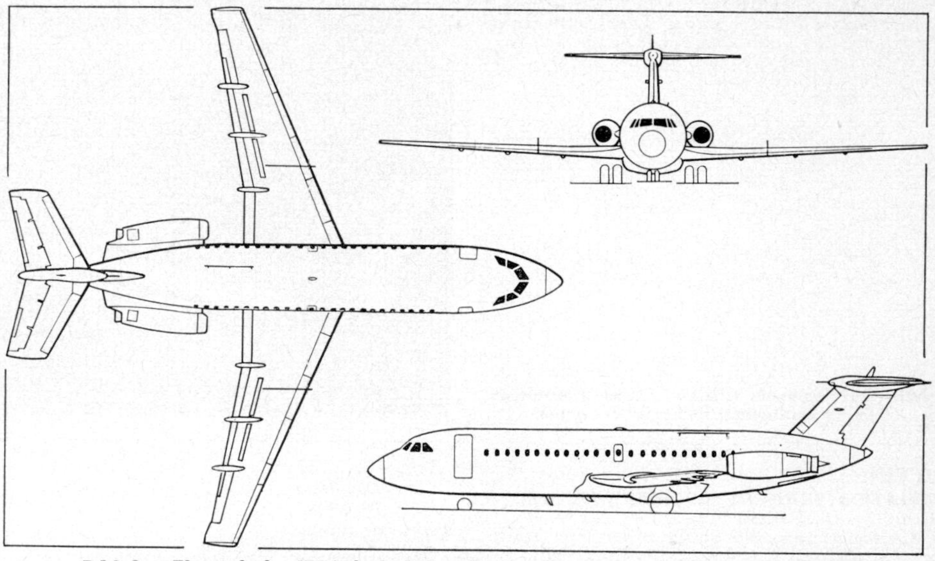

BAC One-Eleven Series 475 twin-turbofan short/medium-range airliner *(Pilot Press)*

BAC One-Eleven Series 475 in the insignia of Air Pacific

Three-shear-web torsion box with integrally-machined skin/stringer panels. Ailerons of Redux-bonded light alloy honeycomb, manually operated through servo tabs. Port servo tab used for trimming. Light alloy Fowler flaps hydraulically operated through Hobson actuators. Light alloy spoiler/air-brakes on upper surface of wing, operated hydraulically through Dowty Boulton Paul actuators. Hydraulically-actuated lift dumpers, inboard of spoilers, are standard on Srs 400, 475 and 500; structural provision for them on Srs 300. Flaps on Series 475 have a glass-fibre coating. Thermal de-icing of wing leading-edges with engine bleed air.

Fuselage: Conventional circular-section all-metal fail-safe structure with continuous frames and stringers. Skin made from copper-based aluminium alloy.

Tail Unit: Cantilever all-metal fail-safe structure, with variable-incidence T tailplane, controlled through duplicated Hobson hydraulic units. Fin integral with rear fuselage. Elevators and rudder actuated hydraulically through Dowty Boulton Paul tandem jacks. Leading-edges of fin and tailplane de-iced by engine bleed air.

Landing Gear: Retractable tricycle type, with twin wheels on each unit. Hydraulic retraction, nose unit forward, main units inward. Oleo-pneumatic shock-absorbers manufactured by BAC. Hydraulic nosewheel steering. Dunlop wheels, tubeless tyres and 4-plate heavy-duty hydraulic disc brakes on Srs 200, 300 and 400; 5-plate heavy-duty hydraulic disc brakes on Srs 475 and 500. Maxaret anti-skid units on Srs 200 and 300. Hytrol Mk III anti-skid units on Srs 400, 475 and 500. Main-wheel tyres size 40 × 12, pressure (Srs 200) 128 lb/sq in (9·00 kg/cm²); (Srs 300, 400) 141 lb/sq in (9·92 kg/cm²); (Srs 500) 160 lb/sq in (11·25 kg/cm²). Dunlop 44 × 16 tyres on Srs 475, pressure 83 lb/sq in (5·8 kg/cm²). Nosewheel tyres size 24 × 7·25, pressure (Srs 200) 100 lb/sq in (7·03 kg/cm²); (Srs 300, 400, 500) 110 lb/sq in (7·73 kg/cm²). Dunlop 24 × 7·7 tyres on Srs 475, pressure 105 lb/sq in (7·38 kg/cm²). All tyre pressures are given for aircraft at mid-CG position and operating at max taxi weight.

Power Plant: Two turbofan engines, mounted in pod on each side of rear fuselage (details under "Series" descriptions). Fuel in integral wing tanks of 2,235 Imp gallons (10,160 litres) and centre-section tank (optional on Srs 200) of 850 Imp gallons (3,864 litres) capacity; total fuel capacity 3,085 Imp gallons (14,024 litres). Optional 350 Imp gallon (1,591 litre) and 700 Imp gallon (3,182 litre) fuel tanks are available to increase total fuel capacity. Pressure refuelling point in fuselage forward of wing on starboard side. Provision for gravity refuelling. Oil capacity (total engine oil) 3 Imp gallons (13·66 litres) per engine).

Accommodation (all versions except Srs 500): Crew of two on flight deck and up to 89 passengers in main cabin. Single class or mixed class layout, with movable divider bulkhead to permit any first/tourist ratio. Typical mixed class layout has 16 first class (four abreast) and 49 tourist (five abreast) seats. Galley units normally at front on starboard side. Coat space available on port side aft of flight deck and, on Srs 200 and 300, at rear vestibule. One toilet at rear on stbd side in Srs 200. Two toilets in Srs 300, 400 and 500, in front and rear combinations (Srs 300 has one front port, one rear stbd; Srs 400 and 500 have one each side at rear). Ventral entrance with hydraulically-operated airstair. Forward passenger door on port side incorporates optional power-operated airstair. Galley service door forward on starboard side. Two baggage and freight holds under floor, fore and aft of wings, with doors on starboard side. Forward freight door on Srs 475s for Sultan of Oman's Air Force. Entire accommodation air-conditioned.

Accommodation (Srs 500): Crew of two on flight deck and up to 119 passengers in main cabin. Two additional overwing emergency exits, making two on each side. Otherwise generally similar to other versions.

Systems: Fully-duplicated air-conditioning and pressurisation systems with main components by Normalair-Garrett. Air bled from engine compressors through heat exchangers. Max pressure differential 7·5 lb/sq in (0·53 kg/cm²). Hydraulic system, pressure 3,000 lb/sq in (210 kg/cm²), operates flaps, spoilers, rudder, elevators, tailplane, landing gear, brakes, nosewheel steering, ventral and forward airstairs and windscreen wipers. No pneumatic system. Electrical system utilises two 30kVA Plessey/Westinghouse AC generators, driven by Plessey constant-speed drive and starter units, plus a similar generator mounted on the APU and shaft-driven. AiResearch gas-turbine APU in tailcone to provide ground electrical power, air-conditioning and engine starting, also some system checkout capability. APU is run during take-off to eliminate performance penalty of bleeding engine air for cabin air-conditioning.

Electronics and Equipment: Communications and navigation equipment generally to customers' individual requirements. Typical installation includes dual VHF communications equipment to ARINC 546, dual VHF navigation equipment to ARINC 547A, including glideslope receivers, marker receiver, flight/service interphone system, Marconi AD 370, Bendix DFA 73 or Collins DF 203 ADF, ATC transponder to ARINC 532D, Collins 860 E2 DME, Ekco E 190 or Bendix RDR 1E weather radar. Sperry C9 or CL11 compass systems and Collins FD 108 flight director system (dual) are also installed. The autopilot is the Elliott 2000 Series system and provision is made on the Srs 500 for additional equipment, including automatic throttle control, for low weather minima operation.

DIMENSIONS, EXTERNAL:
- Wing span:
  - Srs 200, 300, 400 — 88 ft 6 in (26·97 m)
  - Srs 475, 500 — 93 ft 6 in (28·50 m)
- Wing chord at root — 16 ft 5 in (5·01 m)
- Wing chord at tip — 5 ft 3½ in (1·61 m)
- Wing aspect ratio:
  - Srs 200, 300, 400 — 8
  - Srs 475, 500 — 8·5
- Length overall:
  - except Srs 500 — 93 ft 6 in (28·50 m)
  - Srs 500 — 107 ft 0 in (32·61 m)
- Length of fuselage:
  - except Srs 500 — 83 ft 10 in (25·55 m)
  - Srs 500 — 97 ft 4 in (29·67 m)
- Height overall — 24 ft 6 in (7·47 m)
- Tailplane span — 29 ft 6 in (8·99 m)
- Wheel track — 14 ft 3 in (4·34 m)
- Wheelbase:
  - except Srs 500 — 33 ft 1 in (10·08 m)
  - Srs 500 — 41 ft 5 in (12·62 m)
- Passenger door (fwd, port):
  - Height — 5 ft 8 in (1·73 m)
  - Width — 2 ft 8 in (0·82 m)
  - Height to sill — 7 ft 0 in (2·13 m)
- Ventral entrance:
  - Height — 6 ft 0 in (1·83 m)
  - Width — 2 ft 2 in (0·66 m)
  - Height to sill — 7 ft 0 in (2·13 m)
- Freight door (fwd, starboard):
  - Height (projected) — 2 ft 7 in (0·79 m)
  - Width — 3 ft 0 in (0·91 m)
  - Height to sill — 3 ft 7 in (1·09 m)
- Freight door (rear, starboard):
  - Height (projected) — 2 ft 2 in (0·66 m)
  - Width — 3 ft 0 in (0·91 m)
  - Height to sill — 4 ft 3 in (1·30 m)
- Galley service door (fwd, starboard):
  - Height (projected) — 4 ft 0 in (1·22 m)
  - Width — 2 ft 3 in (0·69 m)
  - Height to sill — 7 ft 0 in (2·13 m)

DIMENSIONS, INTERNAL (except Srs 500):
- Cabin, excluding flight deck:
  - Length — 56 ft 10 in (17·31 m)
  - Max width — 10 ft 4 in (3·16 m)
  - Max height — 6 ft 6 in (1·98 m)
  - Floor area — approx 506 sq ft (47·0 m²)
- Freight hold, fwd — 354 cu ft (10·02 m³)
- Freight hold, rear:
  - Srs 200, 300, 400 — 180 cu ft (5·10 m³)
  - Srs 475 — 156 cu ft (4·42 m³)

DIMENSIONS, INTERNAL (Srs 500):
- Cabin, excluding flight deck:
  - Length — 70 ft 4 in (21·44 m)
  - Total floor area — approx 665 sq ft (61·78 m²)
- Freight holds (total volume) 687 cu ft (19·45 m³)

AREAS:
- Wings, gross:
  - except Srs 475, 500 — 1,003 sq ft (93·18 m²)
  - Srs 475, 500 — 1,031 sq ft (95·78 m²)
- Ailerons (total) — 30·8 sq ft (2·86 m²)
- Flaps (total) — 175·6 sq ft (16·30 m²)
- Spoilers (total) — 24·8 sq ft (2·30 m²)
- Vertical tail surfaces (total) 117·4 sq ft (10·90 m²)
- Rudder, incl tab — 32·8 sq ft (3·05 m²)
- Horizontal tail surfaces (total) — 257·0 sq ft (23·90 m²)
- Elevators, incl tab — 70·4 sq ft (6·55 m²)

WEIGHTS AND LOADINGS:
- Operating weight empty:
  - Srs 200 — 46,405 lb (21,049 kg)
  - Srs 300 — 48,722 lb (22,100 kg)
  - Srs 400 — 49,587 lb (22,493 kg)
  - Srs 475 — 51,731 lb (23,464 kg)
  - Srs 500 — 54,582 lb (24,758 kg)
- Max payload:
  - Srs 200 — 19,095 lb (8,661 kg)
  - Srs 300 — 22,278 lb (10,105 kg)
  - Srs 400 — 21,413 lb (9,713 kg)
  - Srs 475 — 21,269 lb (9,647 kg)
  - Srs 500 — 26,418 lb (11,983 kg)
- Max T-O weight:
  - Srs 200 — 79,000 lb (35,833 kg)
  - Srs 300, 400 — 87,000-88,500 lb (39,462-40,143 kg)
  - Srs 475 — 92,000-98,500 lb (41,730-44,678 kg)
  - Srs 500 — 99,650-104,500 lb (45,200-47,400 kg)
- Max ramp weight:
  - Srs 200 — 80,500 lb (36,514 kg)
  - Srs 300, 400 — 89,000 lb (40,370 kg)
  - Srs 475 — 99,000 lb (44,905 kg)
  - Srs 500 — 105,000 lb (47,625 kg)
- Max landing weight:
  - Srs 200 — 71,000 lb (32,205 kg)
  - Srs 300, 400 — 78,000 lb (35,381 kg)
  - Srs 475 — 84,000-87,000 lb (38,100-39,462 kg)
  - Srs 500 — 87,000 lb (39,462 kg)
- Max zero-fuel weight:
  - Srs 200 — 65,500 lb (29,710 kg)
  - Srs 300, 400 — 71,000 lb (32,206 kg)
  - Srs 475 — 73,000 lb (33,112 kg)
  - Srs 500 — 81,000 lb (36,741 kg)
- Max wing loading:
  - Srs 200 — 78·8 lb/sq ft (384·7 kg/m²)
  - Srs 300, 400 — 86·7 lb/sq ft (423 kg/m²)
  - Srs 475 — 89·2 lb/sq ft (435·5 kg/m²)
  - Srs 500 — 96·7 lb/sq ft (472 kg/m²)
- Max power loading:
  - Srs 475 — 3·66 lb/lb st (3·66 kg/kg st)

PERFORMANCE (at max T-O weight):
- Max never-exceed speed (structural):
  - Srs 200 — 399 knots (460 mph; 740 km/h) EAS
  - Srs 300, 400, 475, 500 — 410 knots (472 mph; 760 km/h) EAS
- Max level and cruising speed at 21,000 ft (6,400 m):
  - all versions — 470 knots (541 mph; 871 km/h) TAS
- Fuel econ cruising speed at 25,000 ft (7,620 m):
  - all versions — 400 knots (461 mph; 742 km/h) TAS
- Stalling speed (T-O flap setting):
  - Srs 200 — 107 knots (123·5 mph; 199 km/h)
  - Srs 300, 400 — 114 knots (131 mph; 211 km/h)
  - Srs 475 — 99 knots (114 mph; 184 km/h) EAS
  - Srs 500 — 105 knots (121 mph; 195 km/h)
- Rate of climb at S/L at 300 knots (345 mph; 555 km/h) EAS:
  - Srs 200 — 2,500 ft (762 m)/min
  - Srs 300, 400 — 2,580 ft (786 m)/min
  - Srs 475 — 2,480 ft (756 m)/min
  - Srs 500 — 2,280 ft (695 m)/min
- Max cruising height:
  - all versions — 35,000 ft (10,670 m)
- Min ground turning radius:
  - Srs 200, 300, 400 — 54 ft 0 in (16·46 m)
  - Srs 475 — 56 ft 0 in (17·07 m)
  - Srs 500 — 59 ft 0 in (17·98 m)
- Runway LCN at max weight, rigid pavement (1: 40):
  - Srs 200 — 41
  - Srs 300, 400 — 45
  - Srs 475 — 32
  - Srs 500 — 53
- T-O run at S/L, ISA:
  - Srs 200 — 6,500 ft (1,981 m)
  - Srs 300 — 7,500 ft (2,286 m)
  - Srs 400 — 7,200 ft (2,195 m)
  - Srs 475 — 5,500 ft (1,676 m)
  - Srs 500 — 6,500 ft (1,981 m)
- Balanced T-O to 35 ft (10·7 m) at S/L, ISA:
  - Srs 200 — 6,850 ft (2,088 m)
  - Srs 300 — 8,000 ft (2,438 m)
  - Srs 400 — 7,600 ft (2,316 m)
  - Srs 475 — 5,900 ft (1,798 m)
  - Srs 500 — 7,300 ft (2,225 m)
- Landing distance (BCAR) at S/L, ISA, at max landing weight:
  - Srs 475 — 4,720 ft (1,439 m)
- Landing run at S/L, ISA at max landing weight:
  - Srs 475 — 2,710 ft (826 m)
- Still-air range with max fuel, ISA, with reserves for 200 nm (230 miles; 370 km) diversion and 45 min hold:
  - Srs 200 — 1,849 nm (2,130 miles; 3,430 km)
  - Srs 300, 400 — 2,100 nm (2,420 miles; 3,894 km)
  - Srs 475 — 1,997 nm (2,300 miles; 3,700 km)
  - Srs 500 — 1,880 nm (2,165 miles; 3,484 km)
- Still-air range with typical capacity payload, ISA, reserves as above:
  - Srs 200 — 759 nm (875 miles; 1,410 km)
  - Srs 300, 400 — 1,241 nm (1,430 miles; 2,300 km)
  - Srs 475 at 98,500 lb (44,678 kg) — 1,619 nm (1,865 miles; 3,000 km)
  - Srs 500 at 104,500 lb (47,400 kg) — 1,480 nm (1,705 miles; 2,744 km)
  - Srs 475 executive aircraft with additional 700 Imp gallons (3,182 litres) fuel has equivalent range of — 2,549 nm (2,936 miles; 4,725 km)

BAC One-Eleven Series 500 twin-turbofan transport in the insignia of Court Line

MILITARY AIRCRAFT DIVISION

ADDRESS:
Warton Aerodrome, Preston PR4 1AX, Lancashire
Telephone: Preston (0772) 633333
Telex: 67627

DIRECTORS:
F. W. Page, CBE, MA, CEng, FRAeS (Chairman)
H. R. Baxendale, OBE, ACWA (Deputy Chairman and Managing Director)
A. F. Atkin, OBE, BSc(Hons), DipAe (Hull), CEng, FIMechE, FRAeS (Assistant Managing Director)
R. P. Beamont, CBE, DSO, DFC, FRAeS (Director of Flight Operations)
R. F. Creasey, OBE, BSc(Eng), FAIAA (Director of Advanced Systems and Technology)
F. D. Crowe, BSc, CEng, FRAeS (Director and Chief Engineer)
B. O. Heath, BSc, DIC, CEng, AFRAeS (Director, MRCA)
F. E. Roe, DIC, BSc, CEng, ACGI, FRAeS (Director of Resources)
Air Chief Marshal Sir Frederick Rosier, GCB, CBE, DSO (Director and Military Adviser)
R. H. Sawyer, FCA, FCMA, JDipMA (Financial Director)
T. O. Williams, MA, CEng, FIMechE, MIEE (Production Director)
I. R. Yates, BEng, CEng, FRAeS, AMIMechE (Director and Project Manager, Jaguar)

SPECIAL DIRECTORS:
R. Dickson, MA(Cantab), CEng, FRAeS (Chief of Research)
P. Grocock (Commercial Manager)
G. M. Hobday, OBE, AFRAeS (Sales and Service Manager)
R. Hothersall (Works Manager, Aircraft Experimental)
J. K. Quill, OBE, AFC (Sales Director, SEPECAT, and Director of Marketing, Panavia)

SECRETARY: L. F. Trueman, FCCA

CHIEF OF SYSTEMS ANALYSIS:
P. J. Midgley, BSc, CEng, AFRAeS

CHIEF OF PROJECT TECHNOLOGY:
T. W. Smith, BSc, FBIS

MANAGER, PANAVIA FLIGHT OPERATIONS:
Wg Cdr J. L. Dell, OBE

PRINCIPAL ENGINEER, LIGHTNING AND JET PROVOST:
T. W. Robinson

PROJECT MANAGER, CANBERRA:
M. W. Cara, CEng, MIMechE

PUBLICITY MANAGER:
A. F. Johnston

This Division includes the Preston, Warton and Samlesbury works and has 11,000 employees. It is responsible for production of the BAC 167, for the refurbishing of Canberra aircraft for overseas customers, after-sales service for operators of this aircraft, and service support of Lightnings and Jet Provosts.

Current programmes also include those for the Panavia MRCA and SEPECAT Jaguar military aircraft, as described in the International section.

BAC JET PROVOST

Under a three-year programme involving 157 aircraft, BAC is installing VOR and DME equipment in Jet Provost T. Mk 3 and T. Mk 5 aircraft in service with the RAF. The refurbished aircraft are designated T.Mk 3A and T. Mk 5A respectively.

BAC LIGHTNING

A total of 338 English Electric/BAC Lightning prototype and production aircraft were built, made up of two P.1A prototypes (WG760 and WG763); one structural test airframe; three P.1B prototypes (XA847, XA853 and XA856); 20 P.1B development aircraft (XG307-313 and XG325-337, of which XG310 became development aircraft for the F.Mk 3); one static test airframe; 20 F.Mk 1 and 28 F. Mk 1A (serials commencing XM134); 14 F. Mk 2 (commencing XN723; five converted to F. Mk 52) and 30 F. Mk 2A (converted from F. Mk 2); 63 F. Mk 3 (commencing XP693, of which XP697 became development aircraft for the F. Mk 6; one converted to F. Mk 53); two T. Mk 4 prototypes (XL628-629); 20 production T. Mk 4 (commencing XM966, of which XM967 became development aircraft for the T. Mk 5; two converted to T. Mk 54); 22 T. Mk 5 (commencing XS416; one converted to T. Mk 55); 62 F. Mk 6 (commencing XR752 and XS893); 45 F. Mk 53 (plus one converted from F. Mk 3; commencing 53-666); and seven T. Mk 55 (plus one converted from T. Mk 5; commencing 55-710).

BAC 167 STRIKEMASTER

The BAC 167 Strikemaster was developed from the BAC 145 series (see 1972-73 *Jane's*). It has the same airframe, but is powered by a Rolls-Royce Viper Mk 535 turbojet engine (3,410 lb; 1,547 kg st) and has eight underwing hardpoints, enabling it to carry up to 3,000 lb (1,360 kg) of stores. This makes it particularly suitable for counter-insurgency combat operations.

The first BAC 167 (G-27-8) was flown for the first time on 26 October 1967, and the aircraft continues in production. Most of those ordered had been delivered by early 1973, but deliveries of the more recent orders were scheduled to continue until the latter part of 1974.

A total of 129 Strikemasters had been ordered by mid-1974, as follows:

Mk 80. For Royal Saudi Air Force. Twenty-five ordered in 1966. Deliveries began in 1968 and were completed in September 1969.

Mk 80A. Further order, for ten aircraft, for Royal Saudi Air Force.

Mk 81. For South Yemen People's Republic. Four ordered in December 1966; delivery completed in May 1969.

Mk 82. For Sultan of Oman's Air Force. Twelve ordered by October 1968; delivery completed in December 1969.

Mk 82A. For Sultan of Oman's Air Force. Eight ordered.

Mk 83. For Kuwait Air Force. First order, for six, placed in October 1968; deliveries began in 1969. Order subsequently increased to 12, the last of which was delivered in July 1971.

Mk 84. For Singapore Air Defence Command. Sixteen ordered by July 1968; delivery completed in September 1970.

Mk 87. For Kenya Air Force. Six ordered.

Mk 88. For Royal New Zealand Air Force. Ten ordered in November 1970; delivery completed in October 1972. In service with No. 14 Squadron of RNZAF. Six more ordered in Spring 1974.

Mk 89. For Ecuadorean Air Force. Initial order for eight (later increased to 12), of which delivery had begun by early 1973.

Eight more aircraft (four each for two undisclosed existing operators of Strikemasters) were ordered in Spring 1974. Four of these are reported to be for Ecuador and four for Oman.

The following description applies primarily to later variants of the Strikemaster, such as the Mk 88, but is also substantially applicable to earlier versions:

Type: Two-seat ab initio, basic and advanced trainer, armament trainer and tactical support aircraft.

Wings: Cantilever low-wing monoplane. Wing section NACA 23015 (modified) at root, NACA 4412 (modified) at tip. Dihedral 6°. Incidence 3° at root, 0° at tip. All-metal structure, with main and subsidiary spars, having three-point attachment to fuselage. Metal-covered ailerons with balance tabs. Hydraulically-operated slotted flaps. Hydraulically-operated airbrakes and lift spoilers on wings at rear spar position ahead of flaps.

Fuselage: All-metal semi-monocoque stressed-skin structure, built in three parts, comprising bulkheads, built-up frames and longerons covered with light alloy panels. Hinged nose cap provides access to pressurisation, oxygen, radio and electrical equipment.

Tail Unit: Cantilever all-metal structure. One-piece tailplane, interchangeable elevators, fin and rudder. Fixed surfaces covered with smooth and movable surfaces with fluted alloy skin. Combined trim and balance tab in starboard elevator; balance tabs in port elevator and rudder.

Landing Gear: Hydraulically-retractable tricycle type. Main wheels retract inward into wings, nosewheel forward. Dowty oleo-pneumatic shock-absorbers. Dunlop wheels and tubeless tyres. Dunlop hydraulic disc brakes.

Power Plant: One Rolls-Royce Bristol Viper Mk 535 turbojet engine (3,410 lb; 1,547 kg st) in fuselage aft of cockpit. Lateral intake on each side of forward fuselage. Internal fuel capacity (one integral tank outboard and three bag tanks inboard in each wing) is 270 Imp gallons (1,227 litres). Refuelling point near each wingtip. Two wingtip fuel tanks, total capacity 96 Imp gallons (436 litres), are a standard fit at all times. All tanks in wings are interconnected. System designed to permit 18 sec of inverted flight. Oil capacity 1·75 Imp gallons (8 litres).

Accommodation: Two persons side by side in pressurised cabin, on Martin-Baker automatic ejection seats suitable for use down to ground level and 90 knots (104 mph; 167 km/h). Power-operated rearward-sliding canopy. Dual controls standard.

Systems: Pressurisation and air-conditioning system by Normalair and Tiltman Langley, differential 3 lb/sq in (0·21 kg/cm²), using engine bleed air. Hydraulic system, pressure 2,100 lb/sq in (147 kg/cm²), for landing gear, flaps, airbrakes, lift spoilers and wheel brakes. Engine-driven generator provides 28V DC supply. Three 25Ah batteries. Two inverters supply phased AC to flight instruments and fire warning system. Automatically-controlled gaseous oxygen system for each crew member.

Radio and Navigation Equipment: Varies in different Mks to meet individual customer's requirements. The following radio equipment has been installed in various combinations: ARC 51 BX and ARC 52 UHF; PV 141 UHF homer; D 403 UHF standby; PTR 175 UHF/VHF; Collins 61BM VHF; Collins 618 FIA VHF standby; ARI 18120/2 Violet Picture; Sunair ASB 100 and SA 14-RA HF; and PTR 446, SSR 1600 and SSR 2100 IFF. The following navigation equipment has been installed in various combinations: Bendix CNS 220B UHF; Bendix CNS 240B VHF; RCA AVQ-75 DME; AD 370B and ADF 722 ADF; Bendix 221 VOR/ILS; and ARN B4, ARN 52 and ARN 65 TACAN.

Armament (optional): Two 7·62 mm FN machine-guns, with 550 rds/gun; one in the nose of each engine air intake duct. Later variants have SFOM gunsights; GM2L reflector gunsights fitted to some earlier models. Provision for a G90 gun camera and a Specto camera sight recorder. Four underwing strongpoints for the carriage of external stores. Typical underwing loads include two 75 and two 50 Imp gallon (341 and 227 litre) drop-tanks; four Matra launchers each containing eighteen 68 mm SNEB rockets; four 540 LAU 68 rocket launchers, each with seven rockets; four 540 lb ballistic or retarded bombs; four 250 kg or 500 kg bombs; four PMBR carriers, each with six practice bombs; light-series bomb carriers to carry 8·5, 19 or 25 lb practice bombs; BAC/Vinten five-camera reconnaissance pod; or banks of SURA 80 mm rockets, with four

First Canberra T.Mk 22 for the Royal Navy, converted from a PR.Mk 7, which flew for the first time on 28 June 1973. Deliveries were completed in 1974

BAC 167 Strikemaster on patrol with armament of SURA 80 mm rockets and 245 kg bombs

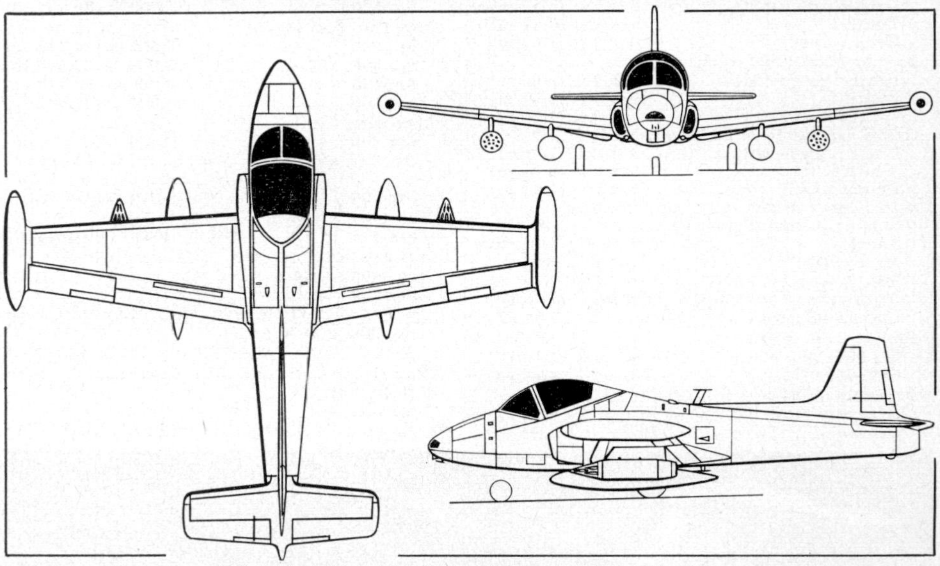

BAC 167 Strikemaster light attack aircraft (*Pilot Press*)

rockets per bank. Other armament, to specific customer requirements, can include napalm tanks, 65 or 125 kg bombs, 2·75 in or 3 in rockets, and 7·62 mm or 20 mm gun packs. Max T-O weight of 11,500 lb (5,215 kg) includes one pilot only, full usable fuel (internal and wingtip tanks) and 2,650 lb (1,200 kg) of external stores. Max possible external stores load 3,000 lb (1,360 kg).

DIMENSIONS, EXTERNAL:
Wing span over tip-tanks 36 ft 10 in (11·23 m)
Wing chord at root 7 ft 8 in (2·33 m)
Wing chord at tip 4 ft 2 in (1·27 m)
Wing aspect ratio 5·84
Length overall 33 ft 8½ in (10·27 m)
Height overall 10 ft 11½ in (3·34 m)
Tailplane span 13 ft 6 in (4·11 m)
Wheel track 10 ft 8·9 in (3·27 m)
Wheelbase 9 ft 7·4 in (2·93 m)

AREAS:
Wings, gross 213·7 sq ft (19·85 m²)
Ailerons (total) 19·06 sq ft (1·77 m²)
Trailing-edge flaps (total) 24·80 sq ft (2·30 m²)

WEIGHTS:
Operating weight empty, equipped, including crew 6,195 lb (2,810 kg)
Typical T-O weights:
pilot conversion training, 2 crew, full internal fuel 9,303 lb (4,219 kg)
armament training, 2 crew, full internal fuel, practice armament (bombs and racks) 10,300 lb (4,808 kg)
ferry role, 2 crew, full internal fuel plus inboard and outboard drop-tanks 11,493 lb (5,213 kg)
*Max T-O weight 11,500 lb (5,215 kg)
**See note under "Armament" paragraph*

PERFORMANCE (at max T-O weight except where indicated):
Max never-exceed speed 450 knots (518 mph; 834 km/h)
Max level speed, with 50% fuel, clean:
at S/L 391 knots (450 mph; 724 km/h)
at 18,000 ft (5,485 m) 418 knots (481 mph; 774 km/h)
at 20,000 ft (6,100 m) 410 knots (472 mph; 760 km/h)
Stalling speed at 9,500 lb (4,309 kg) AUW:
flaps up 98·5 knots (113 mph; 182 km/h)
flaps down 85·5 knots (98 mph; 158 km/h)
Max rate of climb at S/L (training, full internal fuel) 5,250 ft (1,600 m)/min
Time to height (training, full internal fuel):
to 30,000 ft (9,150 m) 8 min 45 sec
to 40,000 ft (12,200 m) 15 min 30 sec
T-O to 50 ft (15 m):
at 7,930 lb (3,579 kg) AUW (training) 1,900 ft (579 m)
at 11,500 lb (5,216 kg) AUW (combat) 3,500 ft (1,067 m)
Landing from 50 ft (15 m):
at 6,500 lb (2,948 kg) AUW (training) 2,400 ft (732 m)
at 11,250 lb (5,103 kg) AUW (aborted armed sortie) 4,250 ft (1,295 m)
Combat radius (hi-lo-hi), 5 min over target, 10% reserves:
with 3,000 lb (1,360 kg) weapons load 215 nm (247 miles; 397 km)
with 2,000 lb (907 kg) weapons load 355 nm (408 miles; 656 km)
with 1,000 lb (454 kg) weapons load 500 nm (575 miles; 925 km)
Combat radius (lo-lo-lo, at S/L), 5 min over target, 10% reserves:
with 3,000 lb (1,360 kg) weapons load 126 nm (145 miles; 233 km)
with 2,000 lb (907 kg) weapons load 175 nm (201 miles; 323 km)
with 1,000 lb (454 kg) weapons load 240 nm (276 miles; 444 km)
reconnaissance mission 300 nm (345 miles; 555 km)
Range with 200 lb (91 kg) fuel reserve:
at 8,355 lb (3,789 kg) AUW (training) 629 nm (725 miles; 1,166 km)
at 10,500 lb (4,558 kg) AUW (combat) 1,075 nm (1,238 miles; 1,992 km)
at 11,500 lb (5,215 kg) AUW (max T-O) 1,200 nm (1,382 miles; 2,224 km)

BRITTEN-NORMAN

BRITTEN-NORMAN (BEMBRIDGE) LTD (Member of the Fairey Group)

HEAD OFFICE:
Bembridge Airport, Bembridge, Isle of Wight PO35 5PR
Telephone: Bembridge 2511/5
Telex: 86277

DIRECTORS:
R. W. Holder, MA (Chairman)
F. R. J. Britten, CBE
N. D. Norman, CBE
D. A. Berryman
I. G. Tylee, CA(R)
A. C. Hayward, MBIM
A. Talbott

CHIEF DESIGNER:
A. J. Coombe

WORKS MANAGER:
J. W. Sullivan

SALES MANAGER:
P. A. Hatswell

MILITARY SALES MANAGER:
G. W. Paul

CUSTOMER SERVICE MANAGER:
M. J. Benjamin

COMMERCIAL MANAGER:
P. P. Graham

PUBLICITY MANAGER:
B. T. Bennett

Britten-Norman became a member of the Fairey Group on 31 August 1972, when the assets of Britten-Norman (Bembridge) Limited (see 1972-73 *Jane's*) were acquired by The Fairey Company. The announcement assured the future of the business after some doubt following the original company's financial difficulties which had arisen in 1971.

The Fairey Group has experience in aviation going back to 1915, and is diversified, with marine, nuclear and other interests. One of the largest companies within the Group is Fairey SA at Gosselies, Belgium (which see).

One of Britten-Norman's major problems had been a lack of "in-house" production facilities, and this was overcome with the formation of a holding company, Fairey Britten-Norman, which looks after the mutual interests of Fairey SA and Britten-Norman (Bembridge) Limited. A new Islander/Trislander production line was established at Gosselies, and Romanian Islander production by IRMA (which see) is also continuing.

John Britten and Desmond Norman, co-founders of the business, have joined the boards of Britten-Norman (Bembridge) Limited, Fairey SA and Fairey Britten-Norman. Under their guidance, final finishing of all aircraft to the specific requirements of individual customers, design, marketing and product support continue at Bembridge.

A feasibility study for a 100-seat short/medium-range transport, known as the Fairey Britten-Norman Mainlander, has been announced, and plans for expansion of Islander/Trislander production and range, as a result of increased demand, are being put into effect.

Britten-Norman BN-2A Islander twin-engined utility transport (two 260/300 hp Lycoming O-540 engines)

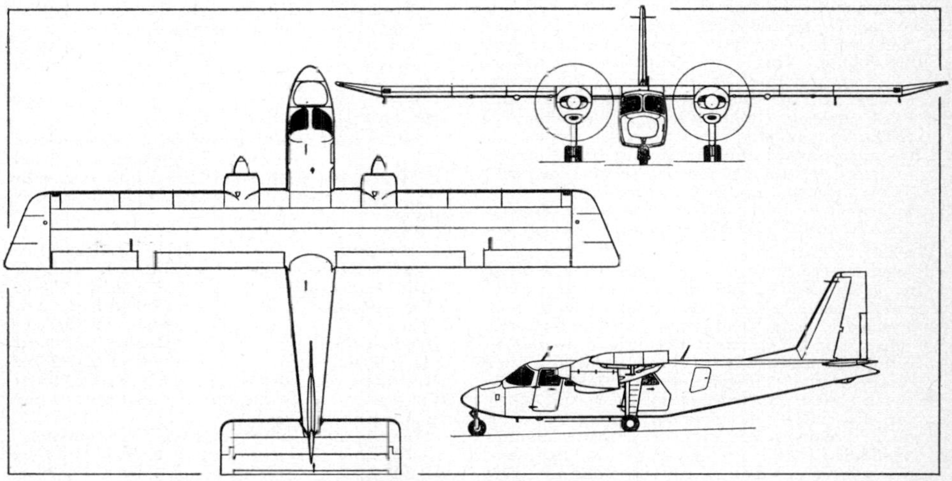

Britten-Norman Islander with extended-span wing (*Pilot Press*)

BRITTEN-NORMAN BN-2A ISLANDER

The Islander is a modern replacement for aircraft in the class of the de Havilland Dragon Rapide. Detail design work began in April 1964 and construction of the prototype (G-ATCT) was started in September of the same year. It flew for the first time on 13 June 1965, powered by two 210 hp Rolls-Royce Continental IO-360-B engines and with wings of 45 ft (13·72 m) span. Subsequently, the prototype was re-engined with more powerful Lycoming O-540 engines, with which it flew for the first time on 17 December 1965. The wing span was also increased by 4 ft (1·22 m) to bring the prototype to production standard.

The production prototype BN-2 Islander (G-ATWU) flew for the first time on 20 August 1966. The Islander received its domestic C of A on 10 August 1967 and an FAA type certificate on 19 December 1967.

Deliveries of Islanders began in August 1967, and by the Spring of 1974 more than 460 aircraft of the various models had been delivered to operators in 67 countries. Orders totalled more than 520 by mid-1974, and in one week alone, at the SBAC Display at Farnborough in September 1972 (immediately following the company's joining the Fairey Group), new orders were announced for more than 40 Islanders.

Initial production aircraft, described in previous editions of *Jane's*, are designated **BN-2.** Those built since 1 June 1969 are known as **BN-2A,** and the following description applies to this version, which continues in production. A military version, known as the **Defender,** and the three-engined **Trislander** development are described separately.

A new model of the Islander, originally designated **BN-2A-8S,** made its first flight on 22 August 1972 and was announced at Farnborough in September 1972. This version had an extended nose, incorporating 28 cu ft (0·79 m³) of additional baggage space, which is now available as an option on the BN-2A.

The basic BN-2A Islander is available with a choice of two alternative power plants (see details following) and either standard 49 ft 0 in (14·94 m) span wings or wingtip extensions having raked tips and containing auxiliary fuel tanks. The company has introduced a series of modification kits which are available as standard or optional fits on new production aircraft and which can also be supplied to operators in the field for retrospective fitting to existing aircraft.

The version of the Islander with 300 hp fuel-injection engines was first introduced in 1970, deliveries beginning in November of that year.

A Rajay turbocharging installation was developed in the United States by Jonas Aircraft, the New York based distributor for Britten-Norman in the western hemisphere.

The Rajay installation is a bolt-on unit, for manual operation, which can be fitted on to standard 260 hp engines. The superchargers have the effect of increasing the single-engined ceiling to 12,500 ft (3,810 m) and twin-engined ceiling to 26,000 ft (7,925 m). Cruising speed is also increased, from 139 knots (160 mph; 257 km/h) at 7,000 ft (2,135 m) to 146 knots (168 mph; 270 km/h) at 10,000 ft (3,050 m). By the Spring of 1974, ten Islanders fitted with Rajay installations were operating successfully in Mexico.

TYPE: Twin-engined feederline transport.

WINGS: Cantilever high-wing monoplane. NACA 23012 constant wing section. No dihedral. Incidence 2°. No sweepback. Conventional riveted two-spar torsion-box structure in one piece, using L72 aluminium-clad aluminium alloys. Flared-up wingtips of Britten-Norman design. Slotted ailerons and single-slotted flaps of metal construction. Flaps operated electrically, ailerons by pushrods and cables. Ground-adjustable tab on starboard aileron. BTR-Goodrich pneumatic de-icing boots optional.

FUSELAGE: Conventional riveted four-longeron semi-monocoque structure of pressed frames and stringers and metal skin, using L72 aluminium-clad aluminium alloys. Optional 3 ft 9½ in (1·16 m) nose extension for baggage stowage.

TAIL UNIT: Cantilever two-spar structure, with pressed ribs and metal skin, using L72 aluminium-clad aluminium alloys. Fixed-incidence tailplane and mass-balanced elevator. Rudder and elevator are actuated by pushrods and cables. Trim tabs in rudder and elevator. Pneumatic de-icing of tailplane and fin optional.

LANDING GEAR: Non-retractable tricycle type, with twin wheels on each main unit and single steerable nosewheel. Cantilever main legs mounted aft of rear spar. All three legs fitted with Lockheed oleo-pneumatic shock-absorbers. All five wheels and tyres size 16 × 7-7, supplied by Goodyear. Tyre pressure: main 35 lb/sq in (2·46 kg/cm²); nose 29 lb/sq in (1·00 kg/cm²). Foot-operated aircooled Cleveland hydraulic brakes on main units. Parking brake. Retractable wheel/ski gear available optionally.

POWER PLANT: Two Lycoming six-cylinder horizontally-opposed aircooled engines, each driving a Hartzell HC-C2YK-2B or -2C two-blade metal constant-speed feathering propeller. Standard power plant is the 260 hp O-540-E4C5, but the 300 hp IO-540-K1B5 can be fitted at customer's option. Optional Rajay turbocharging installation on 260 hp engines, to improve high-altitude performance. Integral fuel tank between spars in each wing, outboard of engine. Total fuel capacity (standard) 114 Imp gallons (137 US gallons; 518 litres). With auxiliary tanks in wingtip extensions, total capacity is increased to 163 Imp gallons (196 US gallons; 741 litres). Additional pylon-mounted underwing auxiliary tanks, each of 50 Imp gallons (60 US gallons; 227 litres) capacity, available optionally. Refuelling point in upper surface of wing above each internal tank. Total oil capacity 5 Imp gallons (22·75 litres).

ACCOMMODATION: Up to 10 persons, including pilot, on side-by-side front seats and four bench seats. No aisle. Seat backs fold forward. Access to all seats via three forward-opening doors, forward of wing and at rear of cabin on port side and forward of wing on starboard side. Baggage compartment at rear of cabin, with port-side loading door in standard versions. Exit in emergency by removing door windows. Special executive layouts available. Can be operated as freighter, carrying more than a ton of cargo; in this configuration the passenger seats can be stored in the rear baggage bay. In ambulance role, up to three stretchers and two attendants can be accommodated. Other layouts possible, including photographic and geophysical survey, parachutist transport or trainer (with accommodation for up to eight parachutists and a dispatcher), or public health spraying. A 130 Imp gallon (590 litre) chemical tank can be installed in the cabin, supplying liquid to wing-mounted rotary atomiser spray units. Aircraft with this type of equipment have operated successfully in the Far East and with the Desert Locust Control Organisation at Asmara, Ethiopia.

SYSTEMS: Southwind cabin heater standard. 45,000 BTU Stewart Warner combustion unit, with circulating fan, provides hot air for distribution at floor-level outlets and at windscreen demisting slots. Fresh air, boosted by propeller slipstream, is ducted to each seating position for on-ground ventilation. Electrical DC power, for instruments, lighting and radio, from one or two engine-driven 24V 50A self-rectifying alternators and a controller to main busbar and circuit-breaker assembly in nose bay. Emergency busbar with automatic changeover provides a secondary route for essential services. 24V 17Ah heavy-duty lead-acid battery for independent operation. Ground power receptacle provided. Optional electrical de-icing of propellers and windscreen, and pneumatic de-icing of wing and tail unit leading-edges. Intercom system, including second headset, and passenger address system are standard. Oxygen system available optionally for all versions.

ELECTRONICS AND EQUIPMENT: Standard items include blind-flying instrumentation, autopilot, dual flying controls and brake system, and a wide range of VHF or HF communications and navigation equipment.

DIMENSIONS, EXTERNAL:
Wing span:
standard — 49 ft 0 in (14·94 m)
with extended tips — 53 ft 0 in (16·15 m)
Wing chord (constant) — 6 ft 8 in (2·03 m)
Wing aspect ratio:
standard — 7·4
with extended tips — 7·95
Length overall:
standard — 35 ft 7¾ in (10·86 m)
optional nose extension — 39 ft 5¼ in (12·02 m)
Fuselage:
Max width — 3 ft 11½ in (1·21 m)
Max depth — 4 ft 9¾ in (1·46 m)
Height overall — 13 ft 8¾ in (4·18 m)
Tailplane span — 15 ft 4 in (4·67 m)
Wheel track (c/l of shock struts) — 11 ft 10 in (3·61 m)
Wheelbase:
standard — 13 ft 1¼ in (3·99 m)
optional nose extension — 16 ft 0¾ in (4·90 m)
Propeller diameter — 6 ft 8 in (2·03 m)
Cabin door (front, port):
Height — 3 ft 7½ in (1·10 m)
Width — 2 ft 1¼ in (0·64 m)
Height to sill — 1 ft 11¼ in (0·59 m)
Cabin door (front, starboard):
Height — 3 ft 7½ in (1·10 m)
Max width — 2 ft 10 in (0·86 m)
Height to sill — 1 ft 10½ in (0·57 m)
Cabin door (rear, port):
Height — 3 ft 7 in (1·09 m)
Width:
top — 2 ft 1 in (0·635 m)
bottom — 3 ft 11 in (1·19 m)
Height to sill — 1 ft 8½ in (0·52 m)
Baggage door (rear, port):
Height — 2 ft 3 in (0·69 m)

DIMENSIONS, INTERNAL:
Passenger cabin, aft of pilot's seat:
Length — 10 ft 0 in (3·05 m)
Max width — 3 ft 7 in (1·09 m)
Max height — 4 ft 2 in (1·27 m)
Floor area — 32 sq ft (2·97 m²)
Volume — 130 cu ft (3·68 m³)
Baggage space aft of passenger cabin:
standard — 30 cu ft (0·85 m³)
maximum — 49 cu ft (1·39 m³)
Nose baggage compartment (optional) — 22 cu ft (0·62 m³)
Freight capacity:
aft of pilot's seat, inc rear cabin baggage space — 166 cu ft (4·70 m³)
with four bench seats folded into rear cabin baggage space — 130 cu ft (3·68 m³)

AREAS:
Wings, gross:
standard — 325·0 sq ft (30·19 m²)
with extended tips — 337·0 sq ft (31·25 m²)
Ailerons (total) — 25·6 sq ft (2·38 m²)
Flaps (total) — 39·0 sq ft (3·62 m²)
Fin — 36·64 sq ft (3·41 m²)
Rudder, incl tab — 17·2 sq ft (1·60 m²)
Tailplane — 73·0 sq ft (6·78 m²)
Elevator, incl tabs — 33·16 sq ft (3·08 m²)

WEIGHTS AND LOADINGS (A: standard wings, B: extended wings):
Weight empty, equipped (without avionics):
260 hp — 3,588 lb (1,627 kg)
300 hp — 3,738 lb (1,695 kg)
Max T-O weight (A, B) — 6,600 lb (2,993 kg)
Max zero-fuel weight (BCAR):
A, 260 hp and 300 hp — 6,300 lb (2,855 kg)
B, 260 hp and 300 hp — 6,200 lb (2,810 kg)
Max landing weight (A, B) — 6,300 lb (2,855 kg)
Max wing loading:
A — 20·3 lb/sq ft (99·1 kg/m²)
B — 19·6 lb/sq ft (95·7 kg/m²)
Max floor loading, without cargo panels — 120 lb/sq ft (586 kg/m²)

PERFORMANCE (at max T-O weight, ISA):
Max never-exceed speed:
A — 177 knots (203 mph; 327 km/h) IAS
B — 184 knots (211 mph; 340 km/h) IAS
Max level speed at S/L:
260 hp — 147 knots (170 mph; 273 km/h)
300 hp — 156 knots (180 mph; 290 km/h)
Cruising speed (75% power) at 7,000 ft (2,135 m):
260 hp — 139 knots (160 mph; 257 km/h)
300 hp — 147 knots (170 mph; 273 km/h)
Cruising speed (67% power) at 9,000 ft (2,750 m):
260 hp — 137 knots (158 mph; 254 km/h)
300 hp — 146 knots (168 mph; 270 km/h)
Cruising speed (59% power) at 13,000 ft (3,960 m):
260 hp — 133 knots (153 mph; 246 km/h)
300 hp — 143 knots (164 mph; 264 km/h)
Stalling speed, flaps up:
260 hp — 50 knots (57 mph; 92 km/h) IAS
Stalling speed, flaps down:
260 hp — 40 knots (46 mph; 74 km/h)
Max rate of climb at S/L:
260 hp — 970 ft (296 m)/min
300 hp — 1,140 ft (347 m)/min
Rate of climb at S/L, one engine out:
260 hp — 190 ft (58 m)/min
300 hp — 200 ft (61 m)/min
Absolute ceiling:
260 hp — 15,200 ft (4,635 m)
300 hp — 19,750 ft (6,020 m)
Service ceiling:
260 hp — 13,200 ft (4,025 m)
Service ceiling, one engine out:
260 hp, standard wings — 5,800 ft (1,770 m)
260 hp, extended wings — 6,700 ft (2,040 m)
300 hp, standard wings — 6,200 ft (1,890 m)
300 hp, extended wings — 7,150 ft (2,180 m)
Min ground turning radius — 31 ft 0 in (9·45 m)
T-O run at S/L, zero wind, hard runway:
260 hp — 555 ft (169 m)
300 hp — 660 ft (201 m)
T-O run at 5,000 ft (1,525 m):
300 hp — 936 ft (285 m)
T-O to 50 ft (15 m) at S/L, zero wind, hard runway:
260 hp — 1,090 ft (332 m)
300 hp — 1,100 ft (335 m)
T-O to 50 ft (15 m) at 5,000 ft (1,525 m):
300 hp — 1,560 ft (475 m)
Landing from 50 ft (15 m) at S/L, zero wind, hard runway:
260 hp, 300 hp — 960 ft (292 m)
Landing distance at 5,000 ft (1,525 m):
300 hp — 1,150 ft (350 m)
Landing run at 5,000 ft (1,525 m):
300 hp, ISA + 20°C — 555 ft (169 m)
Landing run at S/L, zero wind, hard runway:
260 hp, 300 hp — 450 ft (137 m)
Range at 75% power at 7,000 ft (2,135 m):
260 hp, standard wings — 622 nm (717 miles; 1,153 km)
260 hp, extended wings — 903 nm (1,040 miles; 1,673 km)
Range at 67% power at 9,000 ft (2,750 m):
260 hp, standard wings — 713 nm (822 miles; 1,322 km)
260 hp, extended wings — 1,036 nm (1,193 miles; 1,920 km)
Range at 59% power at 13,000 ft (3,960 m):
260 hp, standard wings — 755 nm (870 miles; 1,400 km)
260 hp, extended wings — 1,096 nm (1,263 miles; 2,032 km)

BRITTEN-NORMAN DEFENDER

The Defender is a variant of the civil Islander which can be adapted for a wide variety of government and military roles such as search and rescue, internal security, long-range patrol, forward air control, troop transport, logistic support and casualty evacuation.

The Defender was first shown at the 1971 Paris Air Show, and has since completed an intensive development programme in the UK. The aircraft is available with the same choice of power plant and wing configuration as the current civil version and can be equipped with a wide range of highly sophisticated avionics, including nose-mounted weather radar, providing the aircraft with a marine search capability. Optional equipment includes four NATO standard underwing pylons for a variety of external stores, the inboard pair each carrying up to 700 lb (317·5 kg) and the outboard pair up to 450 lb (204 kg).

Typical underwing loads include twin 7·62 mm machine-guns in pod packs, 250 lb or 500 lb GP bombs, Matra rocket packs, SURA rocket clusters, wire-guided missiles, 5 in reconnaissance flares, anti-personnel grenades, smoke bombs, marker bombs and 60 US gallon (227 litre) drop-tanks.

Internal capacity for passengers, stretcher cases or cargo is the same as that of the civil Islander. Static and air-to-ground firing trials were successfully completed in 1971, during which the forward and beam firing of two pairs of 7·62 mm machine-guns and the forward firing of 68 mm SNEB rocket installations were cleared for operation.

Britten-Norman Defenders are in service with the Abu Dhabi Defence Force, British Army Parachute Association, Ghana Air Force, Guyana Defence Force, Jamaica Defence Force, Malagasy Air Force, Presidential Flight of the Mexican Air Force and the Royal Hong Kong Auxiliary Air Force. Eight were ordered for the Sultan of Oman's Air Force in March 1974.

The description given for the BN-2A Islander applies also to the Defender, except as detailed below:

POWER PLANT: Two 300 hp Lycoming IO-540-K1B5 six-cylinder horizontally-opposed aircooled engines standard.

ELECTRONICS: Typical installation comprises King 360-channel VHF nav/com transceivers with VOR/LOC and VOR/ILS, ADF, marker beacon, KT76 transponder, Sunair ASB 100A HF transceiver, RCA or Bendix radar and Brittain B5 three-axis autopilot.

WEIGHTS:

Weight empty	3,708 lb (1,682 kg)
Max T-O weight	6,600 lb (2,993 kg)
Max landing weight	6,300 lb (2,855 kg)

PERFORMANCE (at max T-O weight, ISA. A: no stores on pylons; B: pylons loaded):

Max level speed:	
A	153 knots (176 mph; 283 km/h)
B	146 knots (168 mph; 270 km/h)
Cruising speed, 67% power at 10,000 ft (3,050 m):	
A	143 knots (165 mph; 265 km/h)
B	136 knots (157 mph; 252 km/h)
Cruising speed, 59% power at 2,000 ft (610 m):	
A	128 knots (147 mph; 237 km/h)
B	121 knots (139 mph; 224 km/h)
Stalling speed, flaps down:	
A, B	39 knots (45 mph; 73 km/h)
Max rate of climb at S/L:	
A	1,300 ft (396 m)/min
B	1,170 ft (357 m)/min
Service ceiling:	
A, B	17,000 ft (5,180 m)
Absolute ceiling:	
A, B	20,000 ft (6,100 m)
T-O to 50 ft (15 m):	
A, B	1,050 ft (320 m)
Landing from 50 ft (15 m):	
A, B	995 ft (303 m)
Range with max payload:	
A	363 nm (418 miles; 672 km)
B	326 nm (375 miles; 603 km)
Range with standard fuel:	
A	1,096 nm (1,260 miles; 2,027 km)
B	1,000 nm (1,150 miles; 1,850 km)
Max range with auxiliary fuel, no reserve, at full mission weight with max endurance power setting	1,497 nm (1,723 miles; 2,772 km)

Britten-Norman Defender, military version of the BN-2A Islander

BRITTEN-NORMAN BN-2A Mk III-1 and -2 TRISLANDER

In the Autumn of 1970 Britten-Norman introduced an enlarged development of the twin-engined Islander, having a third engine mounted at the rear and a lengthened fuselage seating up to 17 passengers. This version is known as the BN-2A Mk III Trislander.

The prototype Trislander was produced by converting the second prototype of the twin-engined Islander (G-ATWU), adding a 7 ft 6 in (2·29 m) length of parallel-section fuselage forward of the wing, reinforcing the rear fuselage and fitting a new main landing gear with larger wheels and tyres. The tail unit was modified to act as a mount for the third engine. This aircraft made its first flight on 11 September 1970, appearing in public for the first time at the SBAC Display at Farnborough later the same day. Production aircraft have additional fin area above the rear engine.

The prototype was later dismantled and its fuselage used for structural testing. By the end of 1970 construction had begun of three production aircraft by converting standard Islander airframes from the current production line, and this system has been adopted for all production aircraft, thus maintaining maximum flexibility on what is now a completely integrated Islander/Trislander assembly line. The first production Trislander (G-AYTU) was flown on 6 March 1971, and the first delivery (to Aurigny Air Services in the Channel Islands) was made on 29 June 1971.

ARB certification of the Trislander, granted on 14 May 1971, approved the aircraft for both VFR and IFR operation and for full public transport with one pilot and up to 17 passengers. FAA certification followed on 4 August 1971, to FAR Pt 23 and to the latest air taxi requirements of SFAR Pt 23 and Appendix A of FAR Pt 135. The Appendix A standard is higher than that met by most other commuter aircraft currently offered on world markets, and is achieved primarily because of continued take-off capability and fatigue-free structure.

Trislander production and sales were affected more by the company's financial difficulties than those of the Islander, but by the Spring of 1974 12 had been delivered (six in the UK, two each to Africa and Australia and one each to the USA and Canada); all of these were successfully in operation, and the company has established a Trislander production line at Gosselies in Belgium to meet increasing demands. Orders totalled 24 by mid-1974. The extended baggage nose of the Islander is also available as a Trislander option, with which the designation changes to Trislander Mk III-2.

TYPE: Three-engined feederline transport.

WINGS: Cantilever high-wing monoplane. NACA 23012 constant wing section. No dihedral. Incidence 2°. No sweepback. Conventional riveted two-spar torsion-box structure in one piece, using aluminium-clad aluminium alloys. Increases in skin gauges and spar laminates compared with twin-engined versions. Structure is strictly "safe-life", but exhibits several fail-safe features and principles. Flared-up wingtips of Britten-Norman design, with raked tips. Slotted ailerons and electrically-operated single-slotted permanently-drooped flaps of metal construction. Ground-adjustable tab on starboard aileron. BTR-Goodrich pneumatic de-icing boots optional.

FUSELAGE: Conventional riveted four-longeron semi-monocoque structure of pressed frames and stringers and metal skin, using L72 aluminium-clad aluminium alloys. Some reinforcement of fuselage aft of wing to support weight of rear engine. Structure is strictly "safe-life", but exhibits several fail-safe features and principles. Optional extension of nose by 3 ft 9¼ in (1·15 m).

TAIL UNIT: Cantilever structure, using L72 aluminium-clad aluminium alloys, with low aspect ratio main fin which also acts as mount for the third engine. Fixed-incidence tailplane (with raked tips) and elevators are similar in construction to those of twin-engined Islander. Trim tab in rudder. BTR-Goodrich pneumatic de-icing boots for tailplane optional.

LANDING GEAR: Non-retractable tricycle type, with twin main-wheel units and single steerable nosewheel. Cantilever main legs mounted aft of rear spar. All five wheels and tyres are Cleveland size 7·00-6. Tyre pressure 45 lb/sq in (3·16 kg/cm²) on main units, 29 lb/sq in (2·04 kg/cm²) on nose unit. Cleveland foot-operated aircooled hydraulic disc brakes on main units. Parking brake. No anti-skid units. Fairings fitted to main gear extension tubes below the engine nacelle and above the shock-absorber attachment bolts.

POWER PLANT: Three 260 hp Lycoming O-540-E4C5 six-cylinder horizontally-opposed air-cooled engines (two mounted on wings and one on vertical tail), each driving a Hartzell HC-C2YK-2G/C8477-4 two-blade constant-speed fully-feathering metal propeller. Fuel in two integral tanks between front and rear wing spars, outboard of the engine nacelles, and two tanks in wingtips. Total fuel capacity 154 Imp gallons (185 US gallons; 700 litres). Overwing refuelling point above each tank. Oil capacity 7·5 Imp gallons (9 US gallons; 34 litres).

ACCOMMODATION: Up to 18 persons, including pilot, in pairs on bench seats at approx 31 in (79 cm) pitch. Access to all seats provided by five broad-hinged rearward-opening car-type doors, two on port side and three on starboard side. Baggage compartment at rear of cabin, with external baggage door on port side. Exit in emergency by removing window panels

Britten-Norman BN-2A Mk III-1 Trislander 18-seat feederline transport aircraft

in front four passenger doors. Heating, ventilation and sound insulation standard. Ambulance or VIP interior layouts at customer's option.

Systems and Equipment: One Southwind cabin heater fitted as standard. DC electrical system includes two 24V 50A self-rectifying alternators, supplying the instruments, lighting and radio, and a 24V 17Ah battery. No hydraulic or pneumatic systems, except for self-contained hydraulic brakes. Optional equipment includes Bendix M4C or Mitchell Century III autopilot; a wide range of Bendix, King or Narco VHF or HF communications and navigational equipment, including ADF and DME; de-icing systems for propellers (electric), airframe (pneumatic) and windscreen; and dual controls, second cabin heater, anti-collision strobe beacons, emergency exit beta lights and cargo tiedowns.

Dimensions, external:
Wing span — 53 ft 0 in (16·15 m)
Wing chord (constant) — 6 ft 8 in (2·03 m)
Wing aspect ratio — 7·95
Length overall:
standard — 43 ft 9 in (13·34 m)
with extended nose — 47 ft 6¼ in (14·48 m)
Fuselage:
Max width — 3 ft 11½ in (1·21 m)
Max depth — 4 ft 9¾ in (1·46 m)
Height overall — 14 ft 2 in (4·32 m)
Tailplane span — 21 ft 3 in (6·48 m)
Wheel track (c/l of shock struts) — 11 ft 0 in (3·35 m)
Wheelbase:
standard — 20 ft 7¼ in (6·28 m)
with extended nose — 23 ft 4¼ in (7·12 m)
Propeller diameter — 6 ft 8 in (2·03 m)
Propeller ground clearance — 2 ft 3 in (0·69 m)
Distance between propeller centres (wing engines) — 11 ft 10 in (3·61 m)
Passenger doors (stbd, fwd and centre):
Height — 3 ft 7½ in (1·10 m)
Max width — 2 ft 10·9 in (0·89 m)
Height to sill — 1 ft 10½ in (0·57 m)
Passenger doors (port, fwd and rear):
Height — 3 ft 7 in (1·09 m)
Max width — 3 ft 11·9 in (1·21 m)
Height to sill — 1 ft 10½ in (0·57 m)
Passenger door (stbd, rear):
Height — 3 ft 7 in (1·09 m)
Width — 2 ft 5½ in (0·75 m)
Baggage compartment door (rear, port):
Height — 2 ft 1·95 in (0·66 m)
Width — 1 ft 5·2 in (0·44 m)
Nose baggage compartment door (port, optional):
Width — 2 ft 7 in (0·79 m)

Dimensions, internal:
Cabin:
Length, excluding flight deck but including rear baggage compartment — 27 ft 0½ in (8·24 m)
Max width — 3 ft 7 in (1·09 m)
Max height — 4 ft 2 in (1·27 m)
Floor area — 84·45 sq ft (7·85 m²)
Volume — 327·4 cu ft (9·27 m³)
Rear baggage compartment volume — 25·0 cu ft (0·71 m³)
Nose baggage compartment volume (optional) — 22 cu ft (0·62 m³)

Areas:
Wings, gross — 337·0 sq ft (31·25 m²)
Ailerons (total) — 25·6 sq ft (2·38 m²)
Trailing-edge flaps (total) — 39·0 sq ft (3·62 m²)
Fin — 62·7 sq ft (5·83 m²)
Rudder, incl tab — 12·2 sq ft (1·13 m²)
Tailplane — 90·0 sq ft (8·36 m²)
Elevators — 26·0 sq ft (2·42 m²)

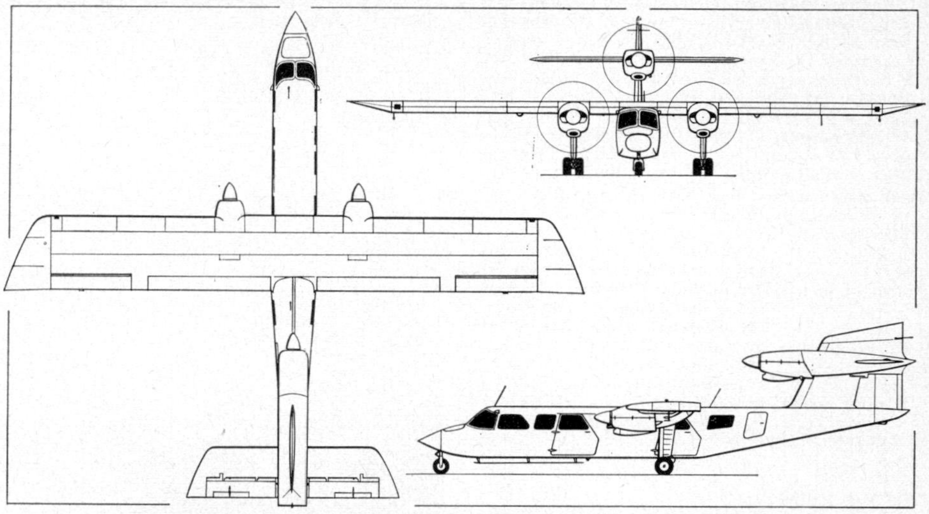

Britten-Norman BN-2A Mk III-1 Trislander feederline transport (*Pilot Press*)

Weights and Loadings:
Weight empty, equipped (without avionics) — 5,745 lb (2,605 kg)
Max T-O and landing weight — 10,000 lb (4,536 kg)
Max wing loading — 29·67 lb/sq ft (144·8 kg/m²)
Max power loading — 12·8 lb/hp (5·82 kg/hp)

Performance (at max T-O weight, ISA):
Max level speed at S/L — 156 knots (180 mph; 290 km/h)
Cruising speed (75% power) at 6,500 ft (1,980 m) — 144 knots (166 mph; 267 km/h)
Cruising speed (67% power) at 9,000 ft (2,740 m) — 139 knots (160 mph; 257 km/h)
Cruising speed (59% power) at 13,000 ft (3,960 m) — 135 knots (155 mph; 249 km/h)
Max rate of climb at S/L — 980 ft (298 m)/min
Rate of climb at S/L, one engine out — 283 ft (86 m)/min
Absolute ceiling — 14,600 ft (4,450 m)
Service ceiling — 13,150 ft (4,010 m)
Service ceiling, one engine out — 6,900 ft (2,105 m)
T-O run at S/L, zero wind, hard runway — 1,290 ft (393 m)
T-O to 50 ft (15 m) at S/L, zero wind, hard runway — 1,950 ft (594 m)
Landing from 50 ft (15 m) at S/L, zero wind, hard runway — 1,445 ft (440 m)
Landing run at S/L, zero wind, hard runway — 852 ft (260 m)
Max still-air range at 59% cruising power — 868 nm (1,000 miles; 1,610 km)

BRITTEN-NORMAN BN-3 NYMPH

The Nymph is a four-seat light aircraft, the design of which is such that it can be marketed in kit form for assembly by approved licensees. A Britten-Norman-built prototype (G-AXFB) flew for the first time on 17 May 1969 with a 115 hp Lycoming O-235 engine. This was subsequently replaced by a 160 hp O-320 engine; the aircraft is also suitable for use with a 130 hp Rolls-Royce Continental.

A full description of the Nymph appeared in the 1972-73 *Jane's*; a final decision on marketing this aircraft had not been taken when this edition closed for press, but the project was still under active consideration.

Britten-Norman BN-3 Nymph four-seat light aircraft (160 hp Lycoming O-320 engine)

CAMPBELL

CAMPBELL AIRCRAFT LTD

Head Office and Works:
Membury Airfield, Lambourn, Newbury, Berkshire
Telephone: Lambourn 770 or 511

Directors:
A. M. W. Curzon-Herrick (Chairman)
J. P. Metcalfe (Managing Director)
G. Whatley, MInstPI

Secretary:
C. G. Horwood, ACA

Campbell produces the Cricket single-seat autogyro, of which all available details follow, and has completed the prototype of a new autogyro known as the Cougar.

Alliance Aviation (which see) represents Campbell Aircraft in France. It will introduce the Cougar autogyro into France as soon as British certification is obtained, and may eventually manufacture the Cougar under licence in France.

CAMPBELL CRICKET

The Cricket is a single-seat light autogyro of Campbell design. Construction of a prototype began in June 1969, and it flew for the first time during the following month. Crickets are flyable under a Board of Trade permit issued on 14

Campbell Cricket single-seat autogyro (modified Volkswagen engine) (*P. J. Bish*)

November 1969. Seven of those ordered were for shrimp-spotting duties in Kuwait.

Campbell also developed a version of the Cricket for crop-spraying duties, using ultra-low-volume (ULV) insecticides. The first of this type was flown on 21 January 1971.

A total of 47 Crickets had been built by 1 April 1972.

In France, AA (which see) is setting up a training school for light gyroplanes near Paris, using the Campbell-Bensen Gyro-Glider and the Campbell Cricket.

The following description applies to the standard Cricket:

Type: Single-seat light autogyro.

Rotor System: Two-blade autorotating main rotor. All-metal blades of hollow section with single steel spar, solid extruded leading-edge, bonded and flush-riveted, and attached to aluminium alloy hub by blocks and four bolts on each blade. Rotor brake fitted. Pre-spin device, which rotates the rotor to 200 rpm, is available optionally.

Rotor Drive: Optional mechanical drive from engine, by means of rubber-latch type friction clutch, for rotor spin-up only. Rotor/engine rpm ratio 1:20.

Fuselage: All-metal steel tube cruciform structure, with engine mounts of T45 tube, argon arc-welded, and glassfibre nacelle.

Tail Unit: Fin and rudder only, of Aerolam aluminium alloy sandwich construction, supported by single-spar tailboom. Automatic rudder offset.

Landing Gear: Non-retractable tricycle type, with small tailwheel or bumper. No shock-absorbers. Same size (5 in; 12·7 cm) nylon wheels, with Avon tyres and tubes, on each unit. Tyre pressure (all units) 14 lb/sq in (68 kg/cm²). Campbell drum brake on nosewheel. Steerable and self-centering nosewheel, linked to rudder control.

Power Plant: One 72 hp modified Volkswagen 1·6 litre four-cylinder engine, driving a Hordern Richmond fixed-pitch propeller. Hot-air de-icing of carburettor. Single fuel tank, capacity 7·25 Imp gallons (33 litres), aft of pilot's seat. Oil capacity 4·25 Imp pints (2·4 litres).

Accommodation: Single seat in open cockpit. Nacelle and windscreen afford adequate protection from elements.

Equipment: Battery-operated light VHF radio optional. Special camera mount available for aerial photographic work. Equipment in agricultural version includes an engine-driven pump, tank for chemicals, and six electrically-actuated spraying nozzles.

Dimensions, external:

Diameter of rotor	21 ft 9 in (6·63 m)
Rotor blade chord (each)	7 in (17·8 cm)
Length of fuselage	11 ft 3 in (3·43 m)
Height to top of rotor hub	6 ft 10 in (2·08 m)
Wheel track	5 ft 2½ in (1·59 m)
Propeller diameter	4 ft 2 in (1·27 m)

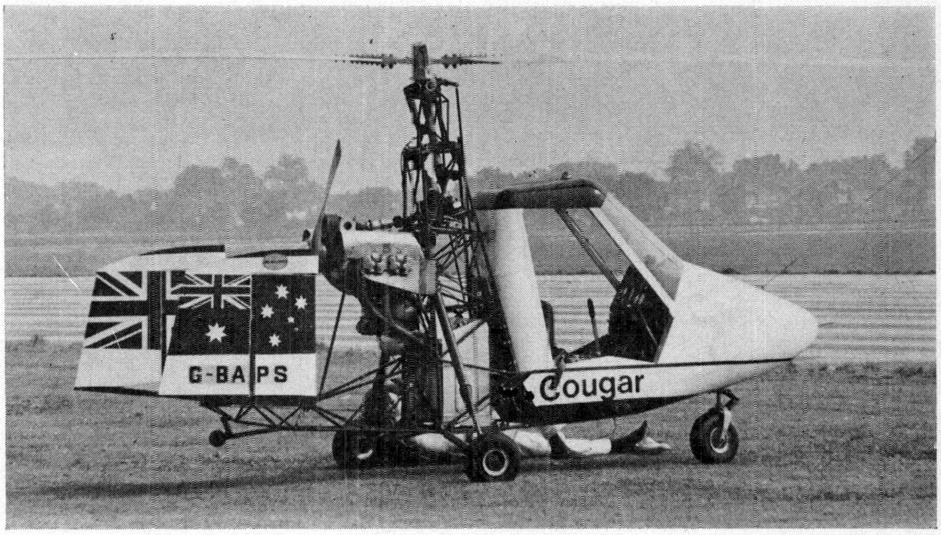

Prototype Campbell Cougar single/two-seat light autogyro *(Dr Alan Beaumont)*

Area:

Main rotor disc	371·5 sq ft (34·51 m²)

Weights and Loading:

Weight empty, less rotor	295 lb (133·5 kg)
Weight empty, incl rotor	329 lb (149 kg)
Max T-O and landing weight	600 lb (272 kg)
Max disc loading	1·9 lb/sq ft (9·3 kg/m²)

Performance (at max T-O weight):

Max never-exceed speed	78 knots (90 mph; 144 km/h)
Max level speed at S/L	69 knots (80 mph; 129 km/h)
Max cruising speed at S/L	56 knots (65 mph; 105 km/h)
Econ cruising speed at S/L	52 knots (60 mph; 97 km/h)
Climb-out speed	43 knots (50 mph; 80 km/h)
Max rate of climb at S/L	500 ft (152 m)/min
Service ceiling	5,000 ft (1,524 m)
T-O run: with spin-up	270 ft (83 m)
without spin-up	600 ft (183 m)
Landing run	0-15 ft (0-4·6 m)
Range with max fuel	122 nm (140 miles; 225 km)
Endurance	2 hr

CAMPBELL COUGAR

The Cougar is a single/two-seat autogyro which has been developed to meet the needs not only of private owners but to fulfil a variety of utility roles such as border patrol, police work, line inspection, ultra-low-volume crop spraying and general surveillance.

Construction of a prototype began in December 1971; this aircraft (G-BAPS) first flew on 20 April 1973 and made its first public appearance at the Paris Air Show in May/June 1973.

Rotor Drive: Mechanical, hydraulic and electronic system for spin-up only, to 400 rpm.

Power Plant: One 130 hp Rolls-Royce Continental O-240-A four-cylinder horizontally-opposed aircooled engine. Fuel capacity 18 Imp gallons (82 litres).

Accommodation: One or two seats side by side in enclosed, carpeted and heated cabin.

Dimensions, external:

Rotor diameter	27 ft 7 in (8·41 m)
Rotor blade chord (each)	9 in (23 cm)
Length overall	15 ft 4 in (4·67 m)
Height overall	8 ft 7 in (2·62 m)
Wheelbase	9 ft 0 in (2·74 m)
Wheel track	7 ft 11 in (2·41 m)
Propeller diameter	5 ft 6 in (1·68 m)

Weights and Loading:

Weight empty	650 lb (295 kg)
Max T-O weight	1,000 lb (454 kg)
Max disc loading	1·84 lb/sq ft (8·98 kg/m²)

Performance (estimated, at max T-O weight):

Max never-exceed speed	78 knots (90 mph; 144·5 km/h)
Cruising speed	65 knots (75 mph; 121 km/h)
Landing speed	21 knots (24 mph; 38·5 km/h)
Max rate of climb at S/L	700 ft (213 m)/min
Ceiling	10,000 ft (3,050 m)
T-O run	30-60 ft (9-18 m)
Landing run	0-30 ft (0-9 m)
Range	195 nm (225 miles; 362 km)

CIERVA

CIERVA ROTORCRAFT LTD

Address:
South Block, Redhill Aerodrome, Surrey RH1 5JY

Telephone: (01) 682-3325

Directors:
The Hon Dr G. A. Weir, BA, SM, PhD (Chairman)
N. M. Niven
J. S. Shapiro, Dipl Ing, MIMechE, FRAeS (Technical Director)
G. R. L. Weir (Commercial Director and Secretary)

Cierva has been a familiar name in the British rotorcraft industry since 1926, when Mr (later Air Cdre) James G. Weir invited the Spanish pioneer Juan de la Cierva to Britain. The Cierva Autogiro Co Ltd was formed at Hanworth, Middlesex, and the company's C.30 Autogiros were built by Avro and others (including foreign licensees) for the RAF and civilian flying clubs. Having rejected a licence to build the German Focke-Wulf Fw 61 helicopter, Mr Weir set up his own team with C. G. Pullin in Scotland, where the Weir W-5 helicopter first flew in 1938, becoming the second helicopter in the history of aviation to fly under perfect control. The successful two-seat W-6 followed in 1939. Meanwhile, in 1936 Weir had assisted in the formation of Power Jets Ltd, the company formed to develop the first Whittle turbojet engines, and a number of his employees joined this company in 1940 when helicopter activity was discontinued in Britain after the outbreak of the second World War.

Cierva Autogiro Ltd was revived in 1943, its first products being the W-9 and the three-rotor W-10 Air Horse, then the world's largest helicopter. In 1951 the company retrenched into model-testing activity, directed personally by Mr Weir, in efforts to develop an inherently non-stalling rotor. At about the same time Mr J. S. Shapiro was forming Servotec Ltd, to undertake research and development and contract design work for the aviation and light engineering industries. Among this company's early studies were small "foolproof" helicopters and an experimental version of the twin-engined, co-axial rotor Grasshopper. In 1960 Shapiro and F. G. Mitchell of the Mitchell Engineering Group formed Rotorcraft Ltd to undertake the development of a helicopter embodying the principles so far explored. Two years later this emerged as the Servotec-built Grasshopper I prototype, which flew for the first time on 11 March 1962, followed on 26 November the same year by the more powerful Grasshopper II; but financial support was no longer available after the death of Mr Mitchell in 1962.

Throughout the 1950s and 1960s Mr Weir maintained a working association with Mr Shapiro, and in 1962-63 Servotec built a man-carrying helicopter model to embody Mr Weir's ideas of a non-stalling rotor, which had moved towards the concept of contra-rotating co-axial rotors. In the course of this collaboration Mr Weir became aware of the CR Twin development, and in 1965 decided to give it financial support. The Cierva Autogiro Co therefore took over Rotorcraft Ltd, changing its name to Cierva Rotorcraft Ltd, of which the major shareholders were Mr Weir and Mr Shapiro. The former died on 7 November 1973. In 1967 the Ministry of Technology awarded a research contract for the four-seat helicopter (as it then was), as a partial contribution towards testing some of its novel design features; prototype construction began in the same year.

In 1969, Servotec Ltd also became a part of Cierva Rotorcraft Ltd, and in August of that year the prototype CR Twin made its first flight. Servotec, with its design and inspection approval, continues design and development work on the CR Twin, and its work under contract to other aerospace organisations including Canadair, Boeing Vertol, Sikorsky and Bell.

CIERVA CR TWIN

The CR Twin is a twin-engined light utility helicopter utilising a co-axial contra-rotating rotor system. This maintains torque balance without the need for a tail rotor, and the aircraft can fly safely on one engine. Among advantages inherent in the design are a low operating noise level, high rotor efficiency due to an unusually close rotor separation, and straightforward overhaul and maintenance. The aircraft is adaptable to a variety of operational roles, and is the result of many years of research into twin-engined co-axial rotor layouts in an attempt to establish a formula for a simple, reasonably inexpensive and safe helicopter. Design of the helicopter began in April 1965 and construction of the first of two prototypes in September 1967. The early history of the project is given in the introductory copy.

The CR.LTH-1, as the prototype was originally known, was shown publicly for the first time at the SBAC Flying Display and Exhibition at Farnborough in 1970. Preliminary hovering trials began in 1969 with the second aircraft (G-AWRP); the first prototype (G-AXFM, powered by 145 hp Rolls-Royce Continental O-300-C engines and first flown on 18 August 1969) underwent a number of control system modifications prior to taking over the flight test programme from the second aircraft. Construction of a pre-production aircraft began in August 1971, and this was being fitted initially with 210 hp Continental IO-360-D engines, but progress has been slow pending finance negotiations. Production aircraft, to which the following description applies, are designated **CR420** and **CR640**, and will have, respectively, Rolls-Royce Continental TSIO-360-A engines of 210 hp each or T6-320 Tiara engines of 320 hp each.

TYPE: Twin-engined light utility helicopter.

ROTOR SYSTEM: Semi-rigid teetering system, with two co-axial contra-rotating two-blade rotors. Blades, of NACA 00 series symmetrical section, are of plastics construction, are tapered and are attached to steel hubs by "see-saw" hinges. Rotor brake fitted. No blade folding or tail rotor.

ROTOR DRIVE: Single-stage reduction via central spiral bevel gearbox. Patented system of "see-saw" beams, constrained by direct linkage, provides starting safety in high or gusty winds by transmitting parallel motion from one rotor to the other, contra-rotating, rotor. Directional control is by simultaneous reversed increments of torque and lift of the two rotors. Pitch lever has a twist-grip for throttle control of both engines, and a thumb lever to equalise cruising boost. Rotor/engine rpm ratio 7 : 47 on CR420, 9 : 47 on CR640.

FUSELAGE: Semi-monocoque pod-and-boom structure, incorporating a number of fail-safe features. Power plant/rotor system installed in a welded steel-tube frame on anti-vibration mounts, attached to a main platform structure of sheet aluminium alloy which supports the semi-monocoque tailboom, landing gear, instrument console and cabin structure. Cabin, engine cowlings and tailboom fairing panels are of epoxy resin-impregnated glass-cloth, and are detachable.

TAIL UNIT: Single fin and rudder; prototypes have small underfin. Fixed-incidence horizontal stabiliser, approx midway along tailboom.

LANDING GEAR: Tubular steel twin-skid type, with two 3·5 × 6·0 in ground handling wheels. Tyre pressure 75-80 lb/sq in (5·3-5·6 kg/cm²). Float gear optional.

POWER PLANT: Prototypes have two 145 hp Rolls-Royce Continental O-300-C six-cylinder horizontally-opposed aircooled engines. Production aircraft will have 210 hp Rolls-Royce Continental TSIO-360-A (CR420) or 320 hp Rolls-Royce Continental T6-320 Tiara turbocharged engines (CR640). Fuel in two tanks consisting of four interconnected flexible bags in fuselage platform, total usable capacity 65 Imp gallons (295·5 litres). Refuelling point on starboard side of fuselage. Oil capacity 2 Imp gallons (9 litres).

ACCOMMODATION: Seats for pilot and co-pilot or passenger in front of extensively-glazed cabin, with seats for three more passengers at rear. Two forward-opening car-type doors on each side. Baggage compartment at rear of cabin, beneath engine mounting, with external door on starboard side. Rear bench seat can be removed for carriage of freight. Cabin heated and ventilated. Dual controls optional.

SYSTEMS: Electrical system includes two 12V 60A alternators.

ELECTRONICS AND EQUIPMENT: All radio, radar and special equipment to customer's requirements. Optional equipment includes Decca navigator and MADGE. Standard instrument panel can accommodate full IMC equipment.

DIMENSIONS, EXTERNAL:

Rotor diameter (each)	33 ft 0 in (10·06 m)
Rotor blade mean chord	8 in (20·3 cm)
Rotor separation	2 ft 3 in (0·69 m)
Length overall	36 ft 2 in (11·02 m)
Length of fuselage	28 ft 2 in (8·58 m)
Height to top of rotor hub	9 ft 11 in (3·02 m)
Skid track	6 ft 8 in (2·03 m)
Passenger doors (front, each):	
Mean height	3 ft 1 in (0·94 m)
Mean width	2 ft 0 in (0·61 m)
Height to sill	2 ft 2 in (0·66 m)
Passenger doors (rear, each):	
Height	3 ft 3 in (0·99 m)
Width	2 ft 4 in (0·71 m)
Height to sill	2 ft 2 in (0·66 m)
Baggage door (starboard):	
Height	1 ft 5 in (0·43 m)
Width	3 ft 0 in (0·91 m)
Height to sill	1 ft 9 in (0·53 m)

DIMENSIONS, INTERNAL:

Cabin: Max length	8 ft 6 in (2·59 m)
Max width	5 ft 2 in (1·57 m)
Max height	4 ft 5 in (1·35 m)
Floor area	34 sq ft (3·16 m²)
Volume	112·5 cu ft (3·19 m³)
Cabin freight compartment:	
Volume	40 cu ft (1·13 m³)
Baggage compartment (aft of cabin):	
Volume	16 cu ft (0·45 m³)

AREAS:

Rotor disc	855·3 sq ft (79·46 m²)
Rotor blades (each)	9·0 sq ft (0·84 m²)
Fin	4·0 sq ft (0·37 m²)
Rudder	5·25 sq ft (0·49 m²)
Horizontal stabiliser	7·0 sq ft (0·65 m²)

WEIGHTS AND LOADINGS:

Weight empty:	
CR420	2,036 lb (923 kg)
CR640	2,212 lb (1,003 kg)
Max T-O and landing weight:	
CR420, CR640	3,450 lb (1,564 kg)
Max disc loading:	
CR420, CR640	4·04 lb/sq ft (19·7 kg/m²)
Max power loading (engines derated to 165 hp each):	
CR420, CR640	10·22 lb/hp (4·63 kg/hp)

PERFORMANCE (CR420 and CR640, estimated, at max T-O weight, ISA):

Max level speed at S/L
120 knots (138 mph; 222 km/h)

Max cruising speed at S/L
110 knots (127 mph; 204 km/h)

Econ cruising speed at S/L
104 knots (120 mph; 193 km/h)

Max rate of climb at S/L 1,300 ft (396 m)/min

Service ceiling more than 20,000 ft (6,100 m)

Hovering ceiling out of ground effect
more than 9,500 ft (2,895 m)

Single-engine hovering ceiling out of ground effect (CR640 only) 9,500 ft (2,895 m)

Range with max fuel, 30 min reserves
390 nm (449 miles; 722 km)

Range with max payload, no reserves
390 nm (449 miles; 722 km)

Prototype Cierva CR Twin twin-engined light helicopter

CLUTTON-TABENOR

ERIC CLUTTON

ADDRESS:

92, Newlands Street, Shelton, Stoke-on-Trent, Staffordshire ST4 2RF

Mr E. Clutton and Mr E. Sherry designed and built a single-seat light aircraft designated FRED, of which details were given in the 1967-68 *Jane's*. A description of it in its Series 2 form appeared in the 1971-72 *Jane's*.

A later aeroplane, the Easy Too, has been designed by Mr Clutton and Mr Tabenor to make full use of a geared Volkswagen engine flight-tested on FRED Series 2 and described briefly in the "Aero-Engines" section.

CLUTTON-TABENOR E.C.2 EASY TOO

The Easy Too design was started in 1969 to utilise the geared Volkswagen power plant developed by Mr Clutton and Mr Tabenor. It is a single-seat aircraft, plywood-covered with a polyester resin finish and having foldable wings, and is stressed for aerobatics. A prototype is under construction, but its completion has been delayed by other work. A first flight is not anticipated until 1975.

The general appearance of Easy Too can be seen in the accompanying three-view drawing. The prototype is to have the new geared 1,500 cc Volkswagen engine, but the aircraft is equally suited to a direct-drive VW engine. The outer wing panels can be folded back by one person, by withdrawing pins and replacing them by an irreversible screwjack arrangement which locks them in position. The ailerons and flaps are coupled automatically. The folding hinge and support is entirely separate from the flying fittings, and the aeroplane can be towed on the road behind a motor-car. The wingtips, of glassfibre, are of similar type and size to those fitted to the Rollason Turbulent and the Taylor Monoplane. A one-piece sliding cockpit canopy is fitted. Wing span of Easy Too is 23 ft 4 in (7·11 m) and the estimated empty weight is 485 lb (220 kg). It is intended to make plans of the aircraft available after the successful conclusion of flight testing.

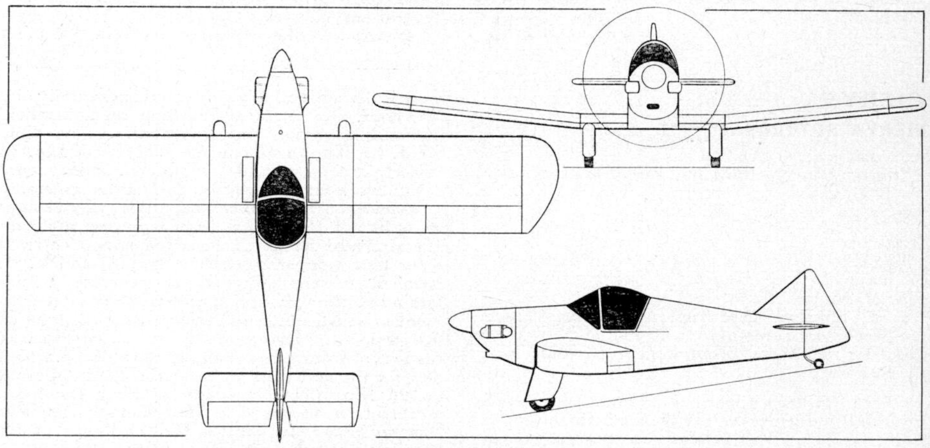

E.C.2 Easy Too light aircraft designed by Mr Eric Clutton (*Pilot Press*)

COATES

J. R. COATES

ADDRESS:

The Spinney, Breachwood Green, Hitchin, Hertfordshire

Mr Coates has designed and built a two-seat light aircraft known as the S.A.II Swalesong. Drawings for amateur construction are not available, but Mr Coates is designing a simplified version, the S.A.III, which will be suitable for homebuilding and will have a choice of wooden or metal construction.

COATES S.A.II SWALESONG

The Swalesong was designed for sporting and touring purposes, with an emphasis on a good short-field performance, to enable the aircraft to operate from unprepared surfaces. The prototype (G-AYDV) made its first flight on 2 September 1973.

TYPE: Two-seat light aircraft.

WINGS: Cantilever low-wing monoplane. Wing section NACA 23013·5. Dihedral 5° 30′. Incidence 3° 30′. All-wood (spruce) structure, with plywood covering. Built in three pieces, with 4-bolt attachment to fuselage at front and rear spars. Frise-type ailerons and slotted trailing-edge flaps, all of plywood-covered wooden construction.

FUSELAGE: Semi-monocoque spruce structure, with plywood covering.

TAIL UNIT: Cantilever structure, with sweptback vertical surfaces. Tailplane incidence adjustable on ground. One-piece fabric-covered wooden elevator, with spring tab.

LANDING GEAR: Non-retractable tricycle type, with spring and rubber shock-absorbers on main units, rubber only on nose unit. Light alloy wheels and same-size 15 × 5-5 tyres, pressure 17 lb/sq in (1·2 kg/cm²) on main units, 14 lb/sq in (0·98 kg/cm²) on nose unit. Cable-operated drum brakes.

POWER PLANT: One 90 hp Continental C90 four-cylinder horizontally-opposed aircooled engine, driving a two-blade wooden fixed-pitch propeller. Fuel in main tank in nose, capacity 14 Imp gallons (64 litres), with 10 Imp gallon (45 litre) reserve tank aft of seats. Refuelling point in front of windscreen. Oil capacity 1 Imp gallon (4·5 litres).

ACCOMMODATION: Side-by-side seating for pilot and one passenger in fully-enclosed cockpit, access to which was originally via a front-hinged window on each side. These were subsequently replaced by a rearward-sliding canopy. Cabin heated and ventilated.

Coates S.A.II Swalesong, showing new rearward-sliding cockpit canopy

DIMENSIONS, EXTERNAL:

Wing span	26 ft 5 in (8·05 m)
Wing chord at root	4 ft 9 in (1·45 m)
Wing chord at tip	4 ft 0 in (1·22 m)
Length overall	19 ft 0 in (5·79 m)
Height overall	7 ft 3 in (2·21 m)
Height over cabin roof	5 ft 3 in (1·60 m)
Tailplane span	8 ft 3 in (2·51 m)
Wheel track	6 ft 6 in (1·98 m)
Wheelbase	4 ft 0 in (1·22 m)
Propeller diameter	5 ft 2 in (1·52 m)
Propeller ground clearance	10 in (25 cm)

DIMENSION, INTERNAL:

Cabin: Max length	3 ft 4 in (1·01 m)

AREAS:

Wings, gross	120 sq ft (11·15 m²)
Ailerons (total)	12 sq ft (1·11 m²)
Flaps (total)	14 sq ft (1·30 m²)
Fin	5 sq ft (0·46 m²)
Rudder	6 sq ft (0·56 m²)
Tailplane	10·5 sq ft (0·97 m²)
Elevator, incl tab	9·5 sq ft (0·88 m²)

WEIGHTS AND LOADINGS:

Weight empty	660 lb (299 kg)
Max design T-O weight	1,150 lb (521 kg)
Max wing loading	9·5 lb/sq ft (46·4 kg/m²)
Max power loading	12·5 lb/hp (5·67 kg/hp)

PERFORMANCE (estimated, at max T-O weight):

Max never-exceed speed	147 knots (170 mph; 273 km/h)
Max level speed at 1,000 ft (305 m)	108 knots (125 mph; 201 km/h)
Max cruising speed at 1,000 ft (305 m)	95 knots (110 mph; 177 km/h)
Econ cruising speed at 1,000 ft (305 m)	82·5 knots (95 mph; 153 km/h)
Stalling speed	46 knots (53 mph; 86 km/h)
Max rate of climb at S/L	850 ft (260 m)/min
Min ground turning radius	14 ft 6 in (4·42 m)
T-O run	450 ft (137 m)
Landing from 50 ft (15 m)	900 ft (274 m)
Landing run	300 ft (92 m)
Range with max fuel	390 nm (450 miles; 724 km)

CROSBY

CROSBY AVIATION LTD

ADDRESS:
Archery House, Leycester Road, Knutsford, Cheshire

Telephone: 0565-4254

DIRECTORS:
John Crosby
P. J. C. Phillips

CROSBY (ANDREASSON) BA-4B

The Andreasson BA-4B single-seat biplane, described in the Swedish section, is being produced in the UK by Crosby Aviation. Mr P. J. C. Phillips holds the world rights for commercially-manufactured examples of this aircraft, and has vested these rights in Crosby Aviation, of which he is a director. Crosby also markets plans and kits for amateur constructors wishing to build their own aircraft, and plans (only) can also be obtained from the BA-4B's Swedish designer, Mr Björn Andreasson.

Two versions are available from Crosby Aviation:

BA-4B. Basic model with 100 hp Rolls-Royce Continental O-200-A four-cylinder horizontally-opposed aircooled engine. Standard fuel capacity 12·4 Imp gallons (56·3 litres). Provision for carrying an external "bullet" tank of 11 Imp gallons (50 litres) capacity.

Super BA-4B. Structurally identical to BA-4B, but powered by a 130 hp Rolls-Royce Continental O-240-A four-cylinder horizontally-opposed aircooled engine.

The description of the BA-4B given in the Swedish section applies also to the aircraft produced in the UK, except in the following details:

ELECTRONICS AND EQUIPMENT: Aircraft can be equipped with electric starter for engine, engine-driven alternator, battery, 360-channel VHF com radio, cabin heater, disc brakes, fully-castoring tailwheel, corrosion proofing and *g*-meter.

DIMENSIONS, EXTERNAL (A: BA-4B; B: Super BA-4B):

Wing span	18 ft 6 in (5·64 m)
Length overall:	
A	15 ft 4 in (4·67 m)
B	15 ft 6 in (4·72 m)

AREA:

Wings, gross	90 sq ft (8·36 m²)

WEIGHTS AND LOADINGS (A: BA-4B; B: Super BA-4B):

Weight empty, basic:	
A	650 lb (295 kg)
B	670 lb (304 kg)
T-O weight, aerobatic	996 lb (451 kg)
Max T-O weight	1,014 lb (460 kg)
Wing loading, aerobatic	11·06 lb/sq ft (54·0 kg/m²)
Max wing loading	11·2 lb/sq ft (54·7 kg/m²)
Max power loading:	
A	10·14 lb/hp (4·60 kg/hp)
B	7·8 lb/hp (3·54 kg/hp)

PERFORMANCE (at max T-O weight. A: BA-4B; B: Super BA-4B):

Max never-exceed speed:	
A, B	161 knots (186 mph; 299 km/h)
Max level speed at S/L:	
A	130 knots (150 mph; 241 km/h)
B	139 knots (160 mph; 257 km/h)
Max cruising speed, 75% power at 7,000 ft (2,135 m):	
A	117 knots (135 mph; 217 km/h)
B	126 knots (145 mph; 233 km/h)
Stalling speed, power off:	
A, B	51 knots (58 mph; 94 km/h)
Stalling speed, power on:	
A, B	39 knots (45 mph; 73 km/h)
Max rate of climb at S/L:	
A	1,200 ft (366 m)/min
B	1,800 ft (549 m)/min
Range, standard fuel, 75% power:	
A	282 nm (325 miles; 523 km)
B	273 nm (315 miles; 507 km)
Range, max optional fuel, 75% power:	
A	529 nm (610 miles; 981 km)
B	521 nm (600 miles; 965 km)

EKIN

W. H. EKIN (ENGINEERING) CO LTD

ADDRESS:
Crumlin, Co Antrim BT29 4XL, Northern Ireland

Telephone: Crumlin 52222

DIRECTORS:
W. H. Ekin, BSc(Hons), CEng, MIMechE
M. J. H. Ekin

This company was formed in March 1969 to undertake the production of six McCandless Mk IV Gyroplanes (see 1972-73 *Jane's*) and the first of these made its first flight in February 1972. For various reasons, an extensive redesign of the McCandless Mk IV was embarked upon by Ekin in Autumn 1971 and a new prototype flew for the first time on 1 February 1973. The modified aircraft, which is available in kit or ready-built form, is now known by the name of WHE Airbuggy. Two were flying and four more under construction in early 1974. Main details of the factory-built version are as follows:

WHE AIRBUGGY

TYPE: Single-seat light autogyro.

ROTOR SYSTEM AND DRIVE: Two-blade semi-rigid teetering rotor with blades secured to hub by bolts. Each blade has solid extruded leading-edge of light alloy with L72 or equivalent light alloy sheet for top and bottom skins. Rotor spin-up effected via Vee-belt drive to 9·667 : 1 worm reduction gearbox and universal and sliding joints.

FUSELAGE: Space-frame of T.35 and T.45 steel tube, assembled by sifbronze welding.

TAIL UNIT: Fin, rudder and tailplane formed from $\frac{1}{16}$ in, $\frac{1}{4}$ in, $\frac{1}{16}$ in plywood sandwich. Ground-adjustable trim tab on rudder. End-plate auxiliary fins on tailplane of latest aircraft.

WHE Airbuggy single-seat autogyro, developed from the McCandless Mk IV Gyroplane

LANDING GEAR: Non-retractable tricycle type. All three wheels have rubber bungee for shock-absorption. Nosewheel steerable. Main wheels with tyres sized from 12 × 2-5 to 13-5 × 5-8 and nosewheel from 12 × 2-5 to 12 × 3-8 according to surface from which aircraft operates. Internal expanding drum brakes.

POWER PLANT: One 75 hp 1,600-1,800 cc modified Volkswagen engine, driving a Hoffmann two-blade pusher propeller. Fuel capacity 6·5 Imp gallons (29·5 litres), in gravity tank mounted above engine, with refuelling point on top of tank. Oil capacity $4\frac{1}{2}$ Imp pints (2·5 litres).

ACCOMMODATION: Single seat in open cockpit.

ELECTRONICS: Prototype has Parkair Nipper 24-channel com transceiver.

DIMENSIONS, EXTERNAL:

Diameter of rotor	21 ft 9 in (6·63 m)
Rotor blade chord	7 in (0·18 m)
Propeller diameter	4 ft 9 in (1·45 m)
Length overall	11 ft 6 in (3·51 m)

Height overall 7 ft 3 in (2·21 m)
Wheel track 5 ft 4 in-5 ft 6 in (1·63 m-1·68 m)
Wheelbase 4 ft 4 in (1·32 m)
AREAS:
Rotor blades (each) 5·6 sq ft (0·52 m²)
Rotor disc 405 sq ft (37·63 m²)
Fin plus endplates 7·9 sq ft (0·73 m²)
Rudder 5·3 sq ft (0·49 m²)
WEIGHTS AND LOADINGS:
Weight empty 355 lb (161 kg)
Max T-O and landing weight 650 lb (295 kg)
Max disc loading 1·75 lb/sq ft (8·5 kg/m²)
Max power loading 8·7 lb/hp (3·95 kg/hp)
PERFORMANCE (at max T-O weight):
Max never-exceed speed 69 knots (80 mph; 128 km/h)
Max level speed at S/L 69 knots (80 mph; 128 km/h)
Max cruising speed 61 knots (70 mph; 113 km/h)
Econ cruising speed 52 knots (60 mph; 97 km/h)
Max rate of climb at S/L 1,000 ft (305 m)/min
T-O run 150-300 ft (46-92 m)
Landing run, still air 30 ft (9 m)
Landing run in 13 knot (15 mph; 24 km/h) wind 0 ft (0 m)
Range with max fuel, no allowances 121 nm (140 miles; 225 km)
Range with max payload, no allowances 86 nm (100 miles; 161 km)

HAWKER SIDDELEY

HAWKER SIDDELEY GROUP LTD

REGISTERED OFFICE:
18, St James's Square, London SW1Y 4LJ

Telephone: 01-930-6177

Telex: 919011

DIRECTORS:
Sir Arnold Hall, FRS (Chairman and Managing Director)
Sir John Lidbury, FRAeS (Vice-Chairman)
Air Chief Marshal Sir Harry Broadhurst, GCB, KBE, DSO, DFC, AFC, RAF (Retd)
F. V. Brook, CBE
R. R. Kenderdine, CEng, FIPE
A. Stewart Kennedy
A. J. Laurence, FCA (Finance)
Sir Joseph Lockwood
C. D. MacQuaide, FCA
M. Parkinson, MA
The Rt Hon Lord Shawcross, PC, QC
Sir Thomas Sopwith, CBE, Hon FRAeS (Founder President)
F. H. Wood, CEng, FIMechE

SECRETARY: C. B. White, MA

Hawker Siddeley Group, with over 80,000 employees, is one of the largest industrial organisations in the world; of this total approximately 46,000 are employed in the Group's aerospace activities. Turnover amounts to more than £465 million per year; capital employed is more than £140 million. Hawker Siddeley Aviation and Hawker Siddeley Dynamics together form one of the largest aerospace manufacturing organisations in Europe. Hawker Siddeley Diesels is a leading manufacturer of diesel engines; its products are in use throughout the world. Hawker Siddeley Electric is a major supplier of power generation and distribution plant, and manufactures a comprehensive range of electrical equipment. High Duty Alloys Ltd produces many aviation components, including Hiduminium 58 (French designation AU2GN) aluminium-alloy components for the Anglo-French Concorde supersonic transport.

Overseas subsidiaries include The de Havilland Aircraft of Canada Ltd, Hawker de Havilland Australia Pty Ltd, and Hawker Siddeley Canada Ltd.

HAWKER SIDDELEY AVIATION LTD

HEAD OFFICE:
Richmond Road, Kingston upon Thames, Surrey KT2 5QS

Telephone: 01-546-7741
Telex: 23726

DIRECTORS:
Sir Arnold Hall, FRS (Chairman)
Sir John Lidbury, FRAeS (Deputy Chairman and Managing Director)
A. Stewart Kennedy, CA
Air Chief Marshal Sir Harry Broadhurst, GCB, KBE, DSO, DFC, AFC, RAF (Retd) (Deputy Managing Director)
Air Chief Marshal Sir Peter Fletcher, KCB, OBE, DFC, AFC, RAF(Retd)
J. L. Glasscock, BA, FCIS, JP (Director and General Manager, Kingston)
A. J. Laurence, FCA
R. L. Lickley, BSc, DIC, CEng, FIMechE, FRAeS (Assistant Managing Director)
E. G. Rubython (Director and General Manager)
J. L. Thorne (Director and General Manager, Hatfield)
J. T. Stamper, MA, CEng, FRAeS (Technical Director)
P. Jefferson, CEng, AFRAeS, MIMechE (Production Director)
J. H. A. Wood, MA (Director and General Manager, Manchester)
J. P. Smith, CEng, FRAeS (Director and Chief Engineer, Civil)
B. P. Laight, OBE, CEng, MSc, MIMechE, FRAeS (Director and Chief Project Engineer, Military)
E. F. T. Jenkins, BCom (Commercial Director)
A. S. Watson (Marketing Director)
L. G. Wilgoss (Financial Director)

EXECUTIVE DIRECTORS:
R. G. Adolphus, BSc, CEng, AFRAeS (Production, Kingston)
H. R. Beattie, BSc(Eng), CEng, AFRAeS, AMBIM (Commercial, Manchester)
C. F. Bethwaite, BSc (Hons), CEng, FRAeS (HS 146, Hatfield)
R. D. Boot, BSc(Eng), FRAeS (Chief Engineer, Brough)
M. J. Brennan, BSc, FIMechE, FRAeS (Special Projects, Head Office)
G. W. Carr, FCIS, AFRAeS (General Manager, Brough)
B. J. Champion, CA(SA) (Finance, Chester)
C. M. Chandler, ACWA (Commercial, Kingston)
R. A. Courtman, MIProdE (Manufacturing, Head Office)
J. Cunningham, CBE, DSO, DFC, DL, FRAeS (Chief Test Pilot, Hatfield)
P. Edwards (Production, Chester)
K. Essex-Crosby, CEng, FRAeS (Deputy Chief Engineer, Brough)
J. W. Fozard, DCAe, BSc(Hons), CEng, FRAeS (Deputy Chief Engineer, Kingston)
J. Garston, OBE, CEng, AFRAeS (General Manager, Chester)
M. J. Goldsmith, DIC, CEng, AFRAeS (Airbus, Hatfield)
R. S. Hooper, DCAe, DAe, CEng, MIMechE, AFRAeS (Chief Engineer, Kingston)
J. Hosie, FIWM (General Manager, Bitteswell)
E. C. T. Humberstone, FInstPS (Purchasing, Head Office)
W. B. Irvine, CA (Financial Control, Head Office)
J. A. Johnstone, OBE, CEng, FRAeS, AMSLAET (Marketing, Hatfield)
W. Lambert, FCA (Finance, Hatfield)
A. E. Lane (General Manager, Hamble)
P. H. Lightfoot, MICM (Production, Manchester)
J. McGregor Smith, ACWA (Finance, Manchester)
F. Murphy, OBE, DFC, AFRAeS (Military Sales, Head Office)
D. R. Newman, CEng, FRAeS (Assistant Chief Engineer, Hatfield)
P. R. Owen, CEng, FRAeS (Deputy Chief Engineer, Hatfield)
J. B. Scott-Wilson, MA, AFRAeS (Deputy Chief Engineer, Manchester)
A. Sewart, OBE, CEng, FIProdE, FRAeS, JP (Manchester)
A. C. Spencer (Production, Brough)
B. F. W. Tull, CBE (Marketing, Manchester)
J. F. White, FCA, MBIM, AFRAeS (Finance, Kingston)
G. A. Whitehead, CBE, FIMechE, CEng, FRAeS, AMCT (Chief Engineer, Manchester)
G. R. Wilkinson (Production, Hatfield)
J. C. Wimpenny, CEng, FRAeS (Research, Head Office)

SECRETARY: R. D. Smith Wright, FCA

Hawker Siddeley Aviation Ltd is responsible for all aircraft design, development, production and supply activities of the Hawker Siddeley Group.

The Aviation Head Office at Kingston upon Thames administers company policy and co-ordinates the activities of the eleven establishments in the United Kingdom. At present three civil aircraft types, the HS 125 business jet, the HS 748 turboprop transport and the Trident short/medium-range jet airliner; and three military aircraft types, the Harrier V/STOL strike fighter, the Buccaneer low-level strike/reconnaissance aircraft and the Nimrod turbofan-powered maritime reconnaissance aircraft, are in production.

Under development at Kingston is the Hawker Siddeley Hawk multi-purpose jet trainer for the Royal Air Force, and at Hatfield the HS 146 short-haul feederliner.

In addition, the refurbishing of Hunter fighters for foreign governments continues. Latest orders include one from Switzerland for 60 refurbished Hunters for delivery between the Autumn of 1972 and Autumn of 1974.

Conversion work is continuing of Handley Page Victors to K.Mk 2 tanker configuration (reportedly involving approx 30 aircraft, for Nos. 55, 57 and 214 Squadrons) and of Argosy C.Mk 1 freighters to T.Mk 2 crew trainers. The first Victor K.2 was delivered to No. 232 OCU at Marham, Norfolk, on 7 May 1974.

Two separate agreements have been made between Hawker Siddeley Aviation and McDonnell Douglas Corporation in the US. In these, the American company has responsibility for support and any licence production of the Harrier in the United States, and Hawker Siddeley, as weapon system sister design company, has responsibility for in-service support and modification of the McDonnell Douglas F-4K and F-4M Phantoms serving with the Royal Navy and Royal Air Force.

In addition, Hawker Siddeley Aviation and Beech Aircraft Corporation in the US have joined forces to design, build and market a family of business jet aircraft. This agreement was initiated by the transfer to Beech of all marketing for the HS 125 in North America, where it is now known as the Beechcraft Hawker 125.

Hawker Siddeley Aviation is also working in close conjunction with Airbus Industrie, the European company designing and manufacturing the A-300 high-capacity short-haul airliner. Under the participation agreement, Hawker Siddeley has responsibility for design of the wing and manufacture of the wing main structure, and is working in close co-operation with Fokker-VFW in the Netherlands, which manufactures the wing moving surfaces.

HAWKER SIDDELEY 125/BEECHCRAFT HAWKER BH 125

RAF name: Dominie T. Mk 1

The Hawker Siddeley (formerly de Havilland) 125 is a twin-jet business aircraft which is also suitable for use by armed forces in the communications role, as a troop carrier, as an ambulance aircraft, for airways inspection, and as an economical trainer for pilots, navigators and specialised radio and radar operators. All Series of HS 125s can operate from unpaved runways without modification.

The HS 125 was developed as a private venture, and the first of two prototypes flew for the first time on 13 August 1962. Deliveries to customers began in September 1964. The 100th aircraft came off the assembly line at Hawker Siddeley Aviation's Chester factory in July 1966, and sales passed the 300 mark in October 1972.

By 1 February 1974 a total of 345 HS 125s had been sold, more than 80 per cent of them for export, including 201 in North America. One British company operates 11 HS 125s, and 12 other operators have fleets of two or more aircraft. The Series 2 navigation trainer version serves as the **Dominie T. Mk 1** with the RAF, whose No. 32 Squadron also operates, in the communications role, four HS 125 Series 400 under the designation **CC. Mk 1** and two Series 600 under the designation **CC. Mk 2.** The HS 125 has also been supplied in the communications role to the air forces of Brazil (eleven), Ghana (one), Malaysia (two), South Africa (seven, known in SAAF service as the **Mercurius**), and to the Argentine Navy. Qantas purchased two HS 125 Series 3s for pilot training. Aircraft supplied to the Australian Department of Civil Aviation, the Brazilian government and the South African Department of Civil Aviation are extensively equipped for airways inspection and calibration of radio aids.

In December 1969 it was announced that Hawker Siddeley Aviation and Beech Aircraft Corporation of the US (which see) had joined forces to design, build and market a family of jet executive aircraft, starting with the joint marketing of the HS 125 Series 400, which in America is known as the **Beechcraft Hawker BH 125-400.** The companies are now concentrating on the larger, faster and higher-powered HS 125 Series 600 (BH 125-600).

Production of the Hawker Siddeley 125 Series 1 (8 built), 1A (64 built), 1B (13 built), 2 (RAF Dominie T. Mk 1, 20 built), 3 (2 built), 3A (12 built), 3B (15 built), 3A-R and 3A-RA (20 built), and 3B-RA (16 built), has ended, and these versions have been described in previous editions of *Jane's*. The latest versions are:

Hawker Siddeley 125 Series 600 (Beechcraft Hawker BH 125-600) twin-engined business jet transport

HS 125 Srs 400A (BH 125-400) and 400B. Developments of Srs 3A-RA (for US, Canadian and Mexican markets, where it is known as the BH 125-400) and Srs 3B-RA (world markets except the US, Canada and Mexico) respectively. Integral airstair door, and improvements to flight deck, cabin, vestibule and exterior appearance. First announced September 1968. Max T-O weight 23,300 lb (10,568 kg). A total of 69 Srs 400A and 47 Srs 400B were built before production ended in 1972. Sales included 32 to Beech for equipment and furnishing as BH 125-400s. Described in 1972-73 *Jane's*.

HS 125 Srs 600A (BH 125-600) and 600B. Larger, faster development of Srs 400, with 20 per cent more payload, for North American markets (Srs 600A/BH 125-600) and the rest of the world (Srs 600B). Changes compared with Srs 400 include more powerful Viper 601 engines, strengthened wings with modified control surfaces, lengthened fuselage (seating a maximum of 14 passengers), taller main fin and extended ventral fin, additional fuel tank in extended dorsal fin, deletion of cockpit canopy fairing, and other detail improvements. First of two development aircraft (G-AYBH) flew for the first time on 21 January 1971, and second (G-AZHS) on 25 November 1971. Certificated by ARB (Special category) on 4 August 1971, and by FAA (600A) on 17 August 1972. In production, with first deliveries in early 1973. Orders up to 1 February 1974 totalled 61, including two (XX507 and XX508) as CC. Mk 2s for No. 32 Squadron, RAF, 11 for civilian customers in the UK and 41 (with five more on option) for Beech Aircraft Corporation. The BH 125-600s are furnished and equipped under Beech contract to individual customer requirements.

The following description applies specifically to the Series 600 version:

Type: Twin-jet business transport aircraft.

Wings: Cantilever low-wing monoplane. Thickness/chord ratio 14% at root, 11% at tip. Dihedral 2°. Incidence 2° 6′ at root, —0° 24′ at tip. Sweepback 20° at quarter-chord. Wings built in one piece and dished to pass under fuselage, to which they are attached by four vertical links, a side link and a drag spigot. All-metal two-spar fail-safe structure, with partial centre spar of approx two-thirds span, sealed to form integral fuel tankage which is divided into two compartments by centreline rib. Skins are single-piece units on each of the upper and lower semi-spans. Detachable leading-edges. Fence on each upper surface at approx two-thirds span. Mass-balanced ailerons, operated manually by cable linkage. Trim tab and geared tab in port aileron, two geared tabs in starboard aileron. Aileron fences to improve lateral stability. Large, four-position double-slotted flaps (45° travel compared with 50° on Srs 400), actuated hydraulically via a screwjack on each flap. Mechanically-operated hydraulic cutout prevents asymmetric operation of the flaps. Flat-plate spoilers above and below each wing, forming part of flap shrouds, provide lift-dumping facility during landing, and have interconnected controls to prevent asymmetric operation. TKS liquid system, using porous stainless steel leading-edge panels, for de-icing or anti-icing.

Fuselage: All-metal semi-monocoque fail-safe structure, making extensive use of Redux bonding. Constant circular cross-section over much of its length. Compared with Srs 400, the Srs 600 has an extra 2 ft 0 in (0·61 m) cabin section added forward of the wings, and 12 cabin windows instead of 10; the nose radome is redesigned and is 6 in (15 cm) longer.

Tail Unit: Cantilever all-metal structure, with fixed-incidence tailplane mounted on fin. Small fairings on tailplane undersurface to eliminate turbulence around elevator hinge cutouts. Triangular ventral fin, and extended dorsal fin. Control surfaces operated manually via cable linkage. Tabs in rudder and each elevator. TKS liquid de-icing or anti-icing of fin and tailplane leading-edges.

Landing Gear: Retractable tricycle type, with twin wheels on each unit. Hydraulic retraction of all units into fuselage, nosewheels forward, main wheels inward. Oleo-pneumatic shock-absorbers. Fully-castoring nose unit, steerable 45° to left or right. Dunlop main wheels and 10-ply tyres, size 23 × 7-12, pressure 120 lb/sq in (8·44 kg/cm²). Dunlop nosewheels and 6-ply tyres, size 18 × 4·25-10, pressure 75 lb/sq in (5·27 kg/cm²). Dunlop double-disc hydraulic brakes with Maxaret anti-skid units on all main wheels.

Power Plant: Two Rolls-Royce Bristol Viper 601-22 turbojet engines, each rated at 3,750 lb (1,701 kg) st, pod-mounted on sides of rear fuselage. Hot-air anti-icing of intake lips and bullets. Integral fuel tanks in wings, with total capacity of 1,028 Imp gallons (4,673 litres). Overwing refuelling point near each wingtip. Rear underfuselage tank of 112 Imp gallons (509 litres) capacity, with refuelling point on starboard side, and 51 Imp gallon (231 litre) dorsal fin tank, raising overall total capacity to 1,191 Imp gallons (1,430 US gallons; 5,414 litres), of which 1,181 Imp gallons (1,418 US gallons; 5,368 litres) are usable. Self-contained engine re-oiling system, capacity 27 Imp pints (15·5 litres).

Accommodation: Crew of two on flight deck, which is fully soundproofed, insulated and air-conditioned. Optional seat for third crew member. Standard executive layout has seating for eight passengers, with forward baggage compartment, refreshment bar and coat compartment (forward) and toilet (aft). Compared with Srs 400, there are smoother-line roof panels, with individual recessed lights and air louvres. Cabin restyling offers the operator a choice of interchangeable furnishing units to suit individual requirements. The new, wider seats, which on the Srs 600A swivel through 180°, are adjustable fore and aft and sideways, have adjustable lumbar support, and can be reclined hydraulically up to 40°. Typical executive furnishing includes a couch for three persons and five individual seats, foldaway conference table and individual foldaway wall tables. Alternative high-density layout is available, seating up to 14 passengers. Outward-opening door at front on port side, with integral airstairs. Emergency exit over wing on starboard side. Windscreen demisting by engine bleed air; electrical windscreen anti-icing, with methanol spray backup.

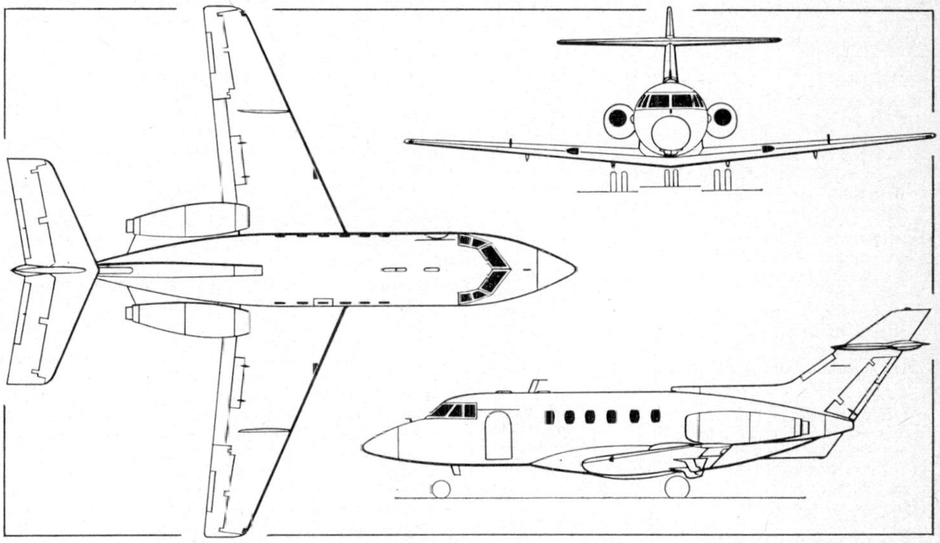

Hawker Siddeley 125 Srs 600 light twin-jet business transport (*Pilot Press*)

Systems: AiResearch air-conditioning and pressurisation system. Max cabin differential 8·35 lb/sq in (0·59 kg/cm²), maintaining S/L cabin pressure up to 21,500 ft (6,550 m). Oxygen system standard, with drop-out masks for passengers. Hydraulic system, pressure 2,300-3,000 lb/sq in (160-210 kg/cm²), for operation of landing gear, main-wheel doors, flaps, spoilers, nosewheel steering, main-wheel brakes and anti-skid units. Two accumulators provide emergency hydraulic power for wheel brakes in case of a main system failure. Independent auxiliary system for lowering landing gear and flaps in the event of a main system failure. DC electrical system utilises two 300A 9kW engine-driven starter/generators and two 24V 25Ah batteries. A 24V 3·5Ah battery provides separate power for igniter and starter control circuits. AC electrical system includes two 115V 2·5kVA 400Hz three-phase rotary inverters and one 250VA solid-state standby inverter for avionics, and one engine-driven 115V 3kVA frequency-wild alternator for windscreen anti-icing. Ground power receptacle on starboard side at rear of fuselage for 28V external DC supply. AiResearch GTCP-30-92 auxiliary power unit is standard on Srs 600B; Solar T-62T-39 is optional on Srs 600A. Engine ice protection system supplied by engine bleed air. Graviner triple FD Firewire fire warning system and two BCF engine fire extinguishers.

Electronics and Equipment: Standard equipment includes full dual controls, full blind-flying instrumentation, complete ice protection system, stick-shaker stall warning, and electrically-heated rudder auto-bias to apply corrective rudder during asymmetric engine power conditions. A spring and g weight are included in the elevator circuit to reduce variations in stick force to a minimum over a wide CG range. Compared with the Srs 400, the layout of flight deck instrumentation has been completely redesigned, all systems (including the electrical and ice protection systems) have been refined, and a new central warning system is incorporated. A combined slot/stereo tape unit and FM/AM self-seeking radio are fitted as standard in Srs 600B, together with storage for additional tape cartridges, magazines and stationery. Comprehensive electronics, available to customer's requirements, include an automatic flight system comprising autopilot (typically, Sperry SP40C or Bendix PB60 for Srs 600A, Collins AP104 for Srs 600A and 600B), flight director and compass; dual VHF nav/com; HF com; dual ADF; marker; ATC transponder; DME; and weather radar. Doppler, Decca Navigator, flight data recorder, and passenger address system may also be installed. Equipment for ICAO Category 2 low weather minima operation will be available as an option. A feature console is provided for fitting customer-specified optional items such as digital readouts and a telephone.

DIMENSIONS, EXTERNAL:
Wing span 47 ft 0 in (14·33 m)
Wing chord (mean) 7 ft 6¼ in (2·29 m)
Wing aspect ratio 6·25
Length overall 50 ft 6 in (15·39 m)
Height overall 17 ft 3 in (5·26 m)
Fuselage: Max diameter 6 ft 4 in (1·93 m)
Tailplane span 20 ft 0 in (6·10 m)
Wheel track (c/l of shock struts) 9 ft 2 in (2·79 m)
Wheelbase 20 ft 9½ in (6·34 m)
Passenger door (fwd, port):
Height 4 ft 3 in (1·30 m)
Width 2 ft 3 in (0·69 m)
Height to sill 3 ft 6 in (1·07 m)
Emergency exit (overwing, stbd):
Height 3 ft 0 in (0·91 m)
Width 1 ft 8 in (0·51 m)

DIMENSIONS, INTERNAL:
Cabin (excluding flight deck):
Length 21 ft 4 in (6·50 m)
Max width 5 ft 11 in (1·80 m)
Max height 5 ft 9 in (1·75 m)
Floor area 55·0 sq ft (5·11 m^2)
Volume 628·0 cu ft (17·8 m^3)
Baggage compartment 29·6 cu ft (0·84 m^3)

AREAS:
Wings, gross 353·0 sq ft (32·8 m^2)
Ailerons (total) 29·76 sq ft (2·76 m^2)
Trailing-edge flaps (total) 56·06 sq ft (5·21 m^2)
Fin, incl dorsal fin 57·15 sq ft (5·31 m^2)
Ventral fin 6·61 sq ft (0·61 m^2)
Horizontal tail surfaces (total) 100 sq ft (9·29 m^2)

WEIGHTS AND LOADINGS:
Weight empty 12,530 lb (5,683 kg)
Typical operating weight, empty 13,555 lb (6,148 kg)
Max payload 1,995 lb (905 kg)
Max T-O and ramp weight 25,000 lb (11,340 kg)
Max zero-fuel weight 15,550 lb (7,053 kg)
Max landing weight 22,000 lb (9,979 kg)
Max wing loading 70·8 lb/sq ft (346 kg/m^2)
Max power loading 3·33 lb/lb st (3·33 kg/kg st)

PERFORMANCE (initial certification, at max T-O weight except where indicated):
Max never-exceed speed 375 knots (432 mph; 695 km/h) IAS
Max design Mach number in dive 0·85
Max operating speed:
fuselage fuel tanks empty 320 knots (368 mph; 592 km/h) IAS
fuel in fuselage fuel tanks 280 knots (322 mph; 519 km/h) IAS
Max operating Mach number 0·78
Max cruising speed at 28,000 ft (8,534 m) 454 knots (522 mph; 840 km/h)
Econ cruising speed at 39,000 ft (11,890 m) 403 knots (464 mph; 747 km/h)
Rough-air speed 230 knots (265 mph; 426 km/h) IAS
Landing gear operation speed 220 knots (253 mph; 407 km/h) IAS
Flap operating speed:
T-O 220 knots (253 mph; 407 km/h) IAS
approach 175 knots (201·5 mph; 324 km/h) IAS
landing 160 knots (184 mph; 296·5 km/h) IAS
Stalling speed 83 knots (96 mph; 155 km/h) EAS
Max rate of climb at S/L 4,900 ft (1,493 m)/min
Rate of climb at S/L, one engine out 1,380 ft (420 m)/min
Service ceiling 41,000 ft (12,500 m)
T-O run 4,400 ft (1,341 m)
T-O balanced field length 5,350 ft (1,631 m)
Landing from 50 ft (15 m) at typical landing weight, unfactored 2,130 ft (649 m)
Landing run (scheduled performance):
BH 125-600 at typical landing weight 3,400 ft (1,036 m)
BH 125-600 at max landing weight 4,250 ft (1,295 m)
Srs 600B at 15,800 lb (7,167 kg) landing weight 3,730 ft (1,137 m)
Min ground turning radius (inside wheel) 15 ft 5 in (4·70 m)
Runway LCN requirement at max T-O weight 10
Typical range with 1,000 lb (454 kg) payload, 45 min reserves plus allowances for T-O, approach, landing and taxying 1,650 nm (1,900 miles; 3,057 km)
Range with max fuel and max payload, reserves as above 1,560 nm (1,796 miles; 2,891 km)

HAWKER SIDDELEY 146

Announcement of government support for the HS 146 four-turbofan quiet-operating transport aircraft was made on 29 August 1973, and the first pre-production aircraft, a Series 100, is expected to fly for the first time in December 1975.

The basic aims of the HS 146 are to provide a passenger seating standard comparable with present wide-bodied transports, combined with competitive operating costs, good airfield performance and low operating noise levels.

Two versions will be available:

Series 100. Designed to operate from short semi-prepared airstrips with minimal ground facilities, with a normal seating capacity of 71-88. A mixed passenger/freight version will be available.

Series 200. For operation from paved runways only, with seating capacity of 82-102 and greater range. Fuselage lengthened by four frame pitches (7 ft 3½ in; 2·22 m). Increased maximum T-O weight and zero-fuel weight. Underfloor cargo volume increased by 30%. Reduced max operating speed.

Construction of the first pre-production aircraft was scheduled to begin in mid-1974, with full transport category CAA certification of the Series 100 anticipated in early 1977.

Freight-carrying and military versions are being studied.

The following description applies to the HS 146 Series 100, except where indicated:

TYPE: Four-turbofan short-range transport aircraft.

WINGS: Cantilever high-wing monoplane. Hawker Siddeley high-lift aerofoil section. Thickness/chord ratio 15·3% adjacent to fuselage, 12·2% at tip. Anhedral 3° at trailing-edge. Incidence 3° 6′ at fuselage side, 0° at tip. Sweepback 15° at quarter-chord. All-metal fail-safe structure of light alloy with machined skins, integrally machined spars and ribs. Single-section hydraulically-actuated tabbed Fowler flaps of light alloy spanning 66% of each wing trailing-edge. Mechanically-actuated balanced ailerons, with hydraulically-operated power boost spoilers on upper surfaces. Trim and spring tab in each aileron. No leading-edge lift devices. Hot-air anti-icing of leading-edges.

FUSELAGE: All-metal fail-safe pressurised semi-monocoque structure. Flight deck and tailcone areas free of stringers. Remainder of structure has "top hat" stringers bonded to skins above keel area. "Z" section stringers "wet" assembled with bonding agent and riveted to skin in keel area. Chemically-etched skins of light alloy. Petal-type airbrakes form tailcone when closed.

TAIL UNIT: Cantilever sweptback T-tail, of all-metal construction. Chemically-etched light alloy skins bonded to "top hat" section stringers. Fixed-incidence tailplane. Balanced elevators, each with trim and spring tab. Powered rudder. Hot-air anti-icing of tailplane leading-edges.

LANDING GEAR: Hydraulically-retractable tricycle type, of Dowty Rotol design, with twin wheels on each unit. Main units retract inward into fairings on fuselage sides; nose unit retracts forward. Oleo-pneumatic shock-absorbers with wheels mounted on trailing axle. Simple telescopic nosewheel strut. Main wheel tyres size 12·50-16 Type III, pressure (Series 100) 105 lb/sq in (7·38 kg/cm^2). Nosewheel tyres size 7·50-10 Type III, pressure (Series 100) 89 lb/sq in (6·26 kg/cm^2). Low-pressure tyres optional. Multi-disc type brakes operated by duplicated hydraulic systems. Brake cooling optional. Anti-skid units in both primary and secondary brake systems.

POWER PLANT: Four Avco Lycoming ALF 502H turbofan engines, each rated at 6,500 lb (2,948 kg) st, installed in pylon-mounted underwing pods. Fuel in two integral wing tanks and integral centre-section tank (the latter with a vented and drained sealing diaphragm above passenger cabin), having a combined capacity of 2,540 Imp gallons (11,547 litres). Optional auxiliary tanks in wing-root fairings, with combined capacity of 300 Imp gallons (1,363 litres), giving total optional capacity of 2,840 Imp gallons (12,910 litres). Single-point pressure refuelling, with coupling situated in starboard wing outboard of outer engine.

ACCOMMODATION: Crew of two pilots on flight deck, and two or three cabin staff. Series 100 has accommodation in main cabin for 71 passengers with five-abreast seating at 33 in (84 cm) pitch, and a maximum of 88 seats at 31 in (79 cm) pitch. Series 200 will have maximum capacity for 102 passengers with six-abreast seating at 31 in (79 cm) pitch. Various alternative layouts for mixed passenger/freight configurations. All seating layouts have two toilets and galley as standard. One outward-opening passenger door forward and one aft on port side of cabin. Built-in airstairs optional. Servicing doors, one forward and one aft, on starboard side of cabin. Freight and baggage holds under cabin floor. All accommodation air-conditioned.

SYSTEMS: Cabin air-conditioning and pressurisation from engine bleed air. Electro-pneumatic pressurisation control with discharge valves at fore and aft of cabin. Max differential 6·5 lb/sq in (0·46 kg/cm^2). Hydraulic system, duplicated for essential services, for landing gear, flaps, rudder, roll and lift spoilers, airbrakes, nosewheel steering, brakes and auxiliary fuel pumps; pressure 3,000 lb/sq in (210 kg/cm^2). Electrical system powered by two integrated drive alternators to feed 115/200V 3-phase 400Hz primary systems. Hydraulically-powered emergency electrical power unit. APU for ground air-conditioning and electrical power generation optional. High-pressure gaseous oxygen system, pressure 1,800 lb/sq in (127 kg/cm^2).

ELECTRONICS: Full complement of nav/com equipment to meet IFR requirements; Cat 2 minima optional. Standard ARINC interfaces.

DIMENSIONS, EXTERNAL:
Wing span 86 ft 6 in (26·37 m)
Wing aspect ratio 8·98
Length overall:
Series 100 85 ft 10 in (26·16 m)
Series 200 93 ft 1½ in (28·38 m)
Height overall 27 ft 11 in (8·51 m)
Tailplane span 36 ft 4 in (11·07 m)
Wheel track 15 ft 6 in (4·72 m)
Wheelbase 33 ft 1½ in (10·10 m)
Passenger doors (port, fwd and rear):
Height 6 ft 3 in (1·91 m)
Width 2 ft 8 in (0·81 m)
Height to sill 6 ft 4 in (1·93 m)
Servicing doors (stbd, fwd and rear):
Height 5 ft 3 in (1·60 m)
Width 2 ft 8 in (0·81 m)
Height to sill 6 ft 4 in (1·93 m)

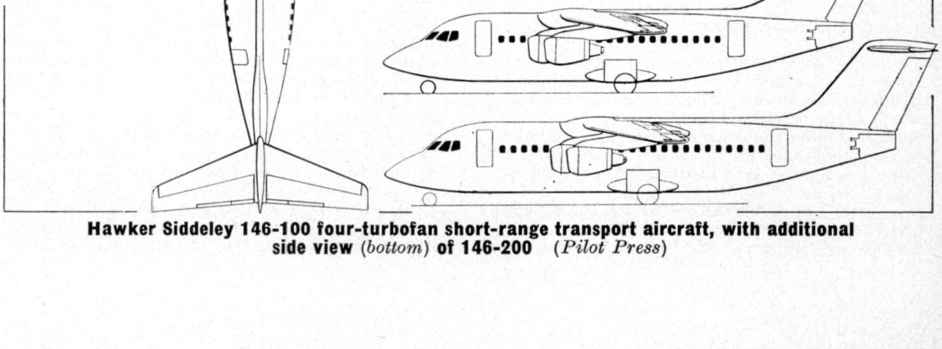

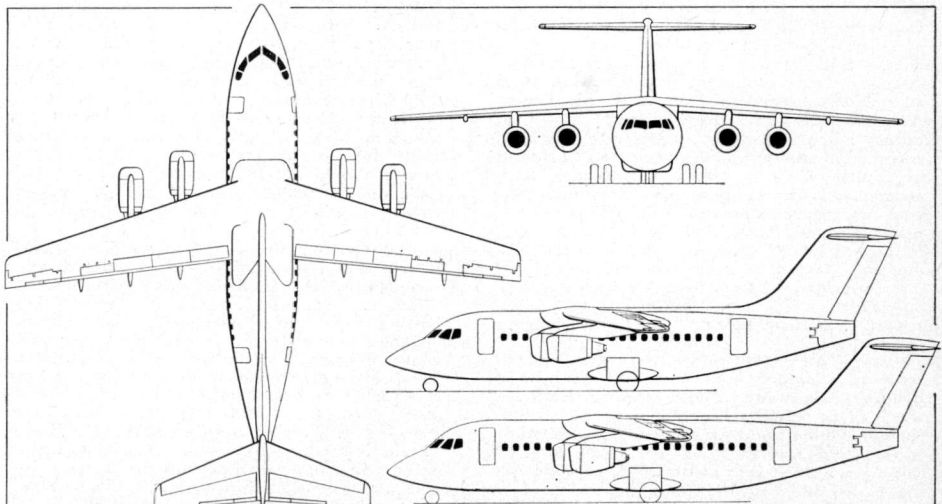

Hawker Siddeley 146-100 four-turbofan short-range transport aircraft, with additional side view (*bottom*) **of 146-200** (*Pilot Press*)

Underfloor freight hold door (stbd, fwd):
Height 3 ft 6 in (1·07 m)
Width 4 ft 0 in (1·22 m)
Height to sill 2 ft 10 in (0·86 m)
Underfloor freight hold door (stbd, aft):
Height 3 ft 6 in (1·07 m)
Width 3 ft 0 in (0·91 m)
Height to sill 3 ft 6 in (1·07 m)

DIMENSIONS, INTERNAL:
Cabin (excluding flight deck, including galley and toilets):
Length:
Series 100 50 ft 7 in (15·42 m)
Series 200 57 ft 10 in (17·63 m)
Max width 11 ft 0 in (3·35 m)
Max height 6 ft 8½ in (2·04 m)
Floor area:
Series 100 530 sq ft (49·24 m²)
Series 200 607 sq ft (56·39 m²)
Baggage/freight holds, underfloor:
Series 100 500 cu ft (14·16 m³)
Series 200 654 cu ft (18·52 m³)

AREAS:
Wings, gross 832 sq ft (77·30 m²)
Ailerons (total) 38 sq ft (3·53 m²)
Trailing-edge flaps (total) 208 sq ft (19·32 m²)
Spoilers (total) 104 sq ft (9·66 m²)
Fin 125 sq ft (11·61 m²)
Rudder 99 sq ft (9·20 m²)
Tailplane 168 sq ft (15·61 m²)
Elevators, incl tab 108 sq ft (10·03 m²)

WEIGHTS AND LOADINGS (estimated):
Operating weight, empty:
Series 100 42,930 lb (19,472 kg)
Series 200 45,485 lb (20,632 kg)
Max payload:
Series 100 18,320 lb (8,310 kg)
Series 200 23,015 lb (10,440 kg)
Max T-O weight:
Series 100 73,850 lb (33,497 kg)
Series 200 87,500 lb (39,690 kg)
Max ramp weight:
Series 100 74,350 lb (33,724 kg)
Series 200 88,000 lb (39,916 kg)
Max zero-fuel weight:
Series 100 61,250 lb (27,782 kg)
Series 200 68,500 lb (31,070 kg)
Max landing weight:
Series 100 71,850 lb (32,590 kg)
Series 200 77,000 lb (34,926 kg)
Max wing loading:
Series 100 88·8 lb/sq ft (433·6 kg/m²)
Series 200 105·2 lb/sq ft (513·6 kg/m²)
Max power loading:
Series 100 0·35 lb/lb st (0·35 kg/kg st)
Series 200 0·297 lb/lb st (0·297 kg/kg st)

PERFORMANCE (estimated, at max T-O weight, except where indicated):
Max operating speed:
Series 100
315 knots (363 mph; 584 km/h) CAS
Series 200
300 knots (345 mph; 555 km/h) CAS
Max cruising speed:
Series 100 at 22,000 ft (6,705 m)
427 knots (492 mph; 791 km/h) TAS
Series 200 at 24,000 ft (7,315 m)
422 knots (486 mph; 782 km/h) TAS
Econ cruising speed, Series 100 and 200 at 30,000 ft (9,145 m)
364 knots (419 mph; 674 km/h) TAS
Stalling speed, 40° flap:
Series 100 91 knots (105 mph; 169 km/h) EAS
Series 200 99 knots (114 mph; 183 km/h) EAS
Stalling speed, 45° flap, at max landing weight:
Series 100 87 knots (101 mph; 162 km/h) EAS
Series 200 90 knots (104 mph; 168 km/h) EAS
T-O to 35 ft (10·7 m), S/L, ISA:
Series 100 3,690 ft (1,125 m)
Series 200 5,100 ft (1,554 m)
FAR landing distance from 50 ft (15 m), S/L, ISA:
Series 100 3,730 ft (1,137 m)
Series 200 3,960 ft (1,207 m)
Range with max fuel, incl 820 lb (372 kg) fuel for ground and airborne manoeuvres, plus fuel for 150 nm (173 miles; 278 km) diversion and 45 min hold at 5,000 ft (1,525 m):
Series 100 1,540 nm (1,773 miles; 2,853 km)
Series 200 1,730 nm (1,992 miles; 3,205 km)
Range with max payload, allowances as above:
Series 100 600 nm (691 miles; 1,112 km)
Series 200 1,280 nm (1,474 miles; 2,372 km)

OPERATIONAL NOISE CHARACTERISTICS (estimated):
T-O noise level at 3·5 nm (4 miles; 6·5 km) from start of T-O roll:
Series 100 85·2 EPNdB
Series 200 93·5 EPNdB
Approach noise level at 1·0 nm (1·15 miles; 1·85 km) from landing threshold on 3° glideslope:
Series 100 97·4 EPNdB
Series 200 98·0 EPNdB
Sideline noise level at 0·35 nm (0·40 miles; 0·65 km) from runway centreline:
Series 100 and 200 89·4 EPNdB

HAWKER SIDDELEY 748 SERIES 2A

Design of the Hawker Siddeley (originally Avro) 748 short/medium-range turboprop airliner started in January 1959. The first prototype flew on 24 June 1960, followed by a second on 10 April 1961. Production of the Series 1 (18 built) and 2 (including two Andover CC.Mk 2s for The Queen's Flight and four for Air Support Command), described in previous editions of *Jane's*, has been completed, except for the manufacture of components for Indian assembly.

The Series 2A, which superseded the Series 2 in production from mid-1967, differs only in having 2,280 ehp Dart RDa.7 Mk 532-2L or -2S turboprop engines, giving improved performance. Production continuing in 1974, total sales (including 31 Andover C.Mk 1s for the RAF: see 1968-69 *Jane's*) totalling 296 by 22 April 1974, including 242 for export. Of these, 272 had been delivered. Two aircraft supplied to the Royal Australian Navy have Dart RDa.8 engines and navigational and electronic training equipment.

The Series 2A is also available optionally with a large rear freight door which has an aperture size of 8 ft 9 in by 5 ft 7¾ in (2·67 m × 1·72 m), and a strengthened cabin floor capable of supporting an overall floor loading of 200 lb/sq ft (976·5 kg/m²). An air-transportable cargo hoist is an optional extra. The large door can be opened in flight and gives the aircraft air-dropping capability. A modified Series 2A aircraft (G-AZJH) with the large door modification flew for the first time on 31 December 1971 and has since undergone extensive air and ground trials, including the dropping of parachutists and supplies. The first order for HS 748s fitted with the large freight door was for six of these aircraft for the Brazilian Air Force.

The HS 748 is the subject of a manufacturing agreement with the Indian government. The first five IAF aircraft (four Series 1s and one Series 2) were delivered unassembled from England; the first Indian-assembled Srs 1 flew on 1 November 1961, and the first Srs 2 on 28 January 1964.

A further 64 aircraft, all Series 2s, are being assembled, from British-built components, by the Kanpur Division of Hindustan Aeronautics Ltd (which see). Twenty-four of these are for Indian Airlines and 40 for the Indian Air Force. A military freighter version developed by HAL flew for the first time on 16 February 1972.

The latest development proposals for the HS 748 include a coastal patrol and surveillance version. For this role the aircraft would have an advanced search radar and an accurate long-range navigation system. Selection from a range of optional equipment, including additional internal fuel tanks, would allow expansion of the operational and performance capabilities of the basic surveillance aircraft.

Orders for the HS 748 by August 1973, excluding Indian production, were listed in the 1972-73 and 1973-74 *Jane's*; additional orders during the past year include the following:

748 Series 2 and 2A

Belgian Air Force	3
Bouraq Airlines (Indonesia)	2
Brazilian Air Force	6
British Airways	2
Cape Verde Air Transport	2
Mount Cook Airlines	1
Nepal Royal Flight	1
United Republic of Tanzania	1
Undisclosed	1

Hawker Siddeley 748 Series 2A with optional large rear freight door

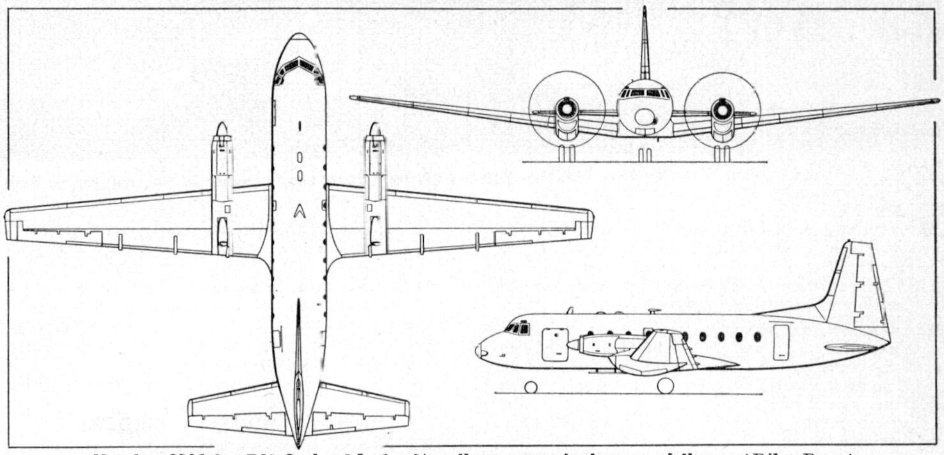

Hawker Siddeley 748 Series 2A short/medium-range turboprop airliner (*Pilot Press*)

The following details apply to the HS 748 Series 2A:

TYPE: Twin-engined passenger or freight transport.

WINGS: Cantilever low-wing monoplane. Wing section NACA 23018 at root, NACA 4412 at tip. Dihedral 7°. Incidence 3°. Sweepback 2° 54′ at quarter-chord. All-metal two-spar fail-safe structure. No cutouts in spars for engines or landing gear. All-metal set-back hinge, shielded horn-balance, manually-operated ailerons and electrically-actuated Fowler flaps. Geared tab in each aileron. Trim tab in starboard aileron. Pneumatic leading-edge de-icing boots.

FUSELAGE: All-metal semi-monocoque riveted fail-safe structure, of circular section.

TAIL UNIT: Cantilever all-metal structure. Fixed-incidence tailplane. Manually-operated controls. Trim tabs in elevators and rudder. Spring tab in rudder.

LANDING GEAR: Retractable tricycle type, with hydraulically-steerable nose unit. All wheels retract forward hydraulically. Main wheels retract into bottom of engine nacelles forward of front wing spar. Dowty Rotol shock-absorbers. Twin wheels, with Dunlop tyres, on all units. Main wheels size 32 × 10·75-14. Nosewheels 25·65 × 8·5-10. Standard tyre pressures: main wheels 73 lb/sq in (5·13 kg/cm²), nosewheels 55 lb/sq in (3·87 kg/cm²). Minimum tyre pressures: main wheels 65 lb/sq in (4·57 kg/cm²), nosewheels 50 lb/sq in (3·52 kg/cm²). Dunlop disc brakes with Maxaret anti-skid units. No brake cooling.

POWER PLANT: Two 2,280 ehp Rolls-Royce Dart RDa.7 Mk 532-2L or -2S turboprop engines, each driving a Dowty Rotol four-blade constant-speed fully-feathering propeller. Fuel in two integral wing tanks, with total capacity of 1,440 Imp gallons (6,550 litres). Underwing pressure refuelling and overwing gravity refuelling. Oil capacity 25 Imp pints (14·2 litres) per engine.

ACCOMMODATION: Crew of two on flight deck, and cabin attendant. Normal accommodation for 40-58 passengers in paired seats on each side of central gangway. Baggage compartment forward of cabin, with provision for steward's seat. Galley, toilet and baggage compartment aft of cabin. Forward baggage compartment and steward's seat can be replaced by freight hold with moving partition between hold and passenger cabin. Main passenger door, on port side at rear, with smaller door on starboard side to serve as baggage door and emergency exit. Crew and freight door on port side at front. Hydraulically-operated stairs.

SYSTEMS: Normalair pressurisation and air-conditioning system, giving equivalent altitude of 8,000 ft (2,440 m) at 25,000 ft (7,600 m). Pressure differential 5·5 lb/sq in (0·4 kg/cm²). Hydraulic system, pressure 2,500 lb/sq in (175 kg/cm²), for landing gear retraction, nose-wheel steering, brakes and propeller brakes. No pneumatic system. One 9kW 28V DC generator and one 22kVA alternator on each engine. Two 1,800VA inverters.

Hawker Siddeley 748 Srs 2A twin-turboprop airliner in the insignia of Cape Verde Air Transport

ELECTRONICS AND EQUIPMENT: Collins or Bendix solid-state radio and radar. Blind-flying instrumentation and weather radar. Smiths SEP2E autopilot. Provision for flight director system and flight data recorder.

DIMENSIONS, EXTERNAL:
- Wing span: 98 ft 6 in (30·02 m)
- Wing chord at root: 11 ft $5\frac{1}{4}$ in (3·49 m)
- Wing chord at tip: 4 ft 5 in (1·34 m)
- Wing aspect ratio: 11·967
- Length overall: 67 ft 0 in (20·42 m)
- Fuselage:
  - Max diameter: 8 ft 9 in (2·67 m)
- Height over tail: 24 ft 10 in (7·57 m)
- Tailplane span: 36 ft 0 in (10·97 m)
- Wheel track: 24 ft 9 in (7·54 m)
- Wheelbase: 20 ft 8 in (6·30 m)
- Propeller diameter: 12 ft 0 in (3·66 m)
- Propeller ground clearance: 2 ft 0 in (0·61 m)
- Passenger door (port, rear):
  - Height: 5 ft 2 in (1·57 m)
  - Width: 2 ft 6 in (0·76 m)
  - Height to sill: 6 ft $0\frac{1}{2}$ in (1·84 m)
- Freight and baggage door (fwd):
  - Height: 4 ft 6 in (1·37 m)
  - Width: 4 ft 0 in (1·22 m)
  - Height to sill: 6 ft $0\frac{1}{2}$ in (1·84 m)
- Baggage door (rear, stbd):
  - Height: 4 ft 1 in (1·24 m)
  - Width: 2 ft 1 in (0·64 m)
  - Height to sill: 6 ft $0\frac{1}{2}$ in (1·84 m)
- Optional freight door (rear, port):
  - Height: 5 ft $7\frac{3}{4}$ in (1·72 m)
  - Width: 8 ft 9 in (2·67 m)

DIMENSIONS, INTERNAL:
- Cabin, excluding flight deck:
  - Length: 46 ft 6 in (14·17 m)
  - Max width: 8 ft 1 in (2·46 m)
  - Max height: 6 ft $3\frac{1}{2}$ in (1·92 m)
  - Floor area: 296 sq ft (27·5 m^2)
  - Volume: 1,936 cu ft (54·82 m^3)
- Max total freight holds: 337 cu ft (9·54 m^3)

AREAS:
- Wings, gross: 810·75 sq ft (75·35 m^2)
- Ailerons (total): 42·90 sq ft (3·98 m^2)
- Trailing-edge flaps (total): 159·80 sq ft (14·83 m^2)
- Fin: 105·64 sq ft (9·81 m^2)
- Rudder, including tabs: 39·36 sq ft (3·66 m^2)
- Tailplane: 188·9 sq ft (17·55 m^2)
- Elevators, including tabs: 54·10 sq ft (5·03 m^2)

WEIGHTS AND LOADINGS:
- Basic operating weight, including crew: 27,000 lb (12,247 kg)
- Max payload: 11,500 lb (5,216 kg)
- Max T-O weight: 46,500 lb (21,092 kg)
- Max zero-fuel weight: 38,500 lb (17,460 kg)
- Max landing weight: 43,000 lb (19,500 kg)
- Max wing loading: 57·3 lb/sq ft (279·8 kg/m^2)
- Max power loading: 10·1 lb/ehp (4·58 kg/ehp)

PERFORMANCE (at max T-O weight except where indicated):
- Max cruising speed (at AUW of 40,000 lb; 18,145 kg): 242 knots (278 mph; 448 km/h)
- Max rate of climb at S/L (at AUW of 40,000 lb; 18,145 kg): 1,320 ft (402 m)/min
- Service ceiling: 25,000 ft (7,620 m)
- Min ground turning radius: 39 ft 0 in (11·89 m)
- Runway LCN requirement, depending on surface and tyre pressure: 9 to 18
- T-O run: 3,380 ft (1,030 m)
- T-O to 50 ft (15 m): 4,060 ft (1,237 m)
- Landing from 50 ft (15 m) at max landing weight: 2,035 ft (620 m)
- Landing run at max landing weight: 1,280 ft (390 m)
- Range with max fuel, with reserves for 200 nm (230 mile; 370 km) diversion and 45 min hold: 1,730 nm (1,992 miles; 3,205 km)
- Range with max payload, reserves as above: 729 nm (840 miles; 1,351 km)

OPERATIONAL NOISE CHARACTERISTICS:
- T-O noise level at 3·5 nm (4·0 miles; 6·5 km) from start of T-O roll: 92·5 EPNdB
- Approach noise level at 1·0 nm (1·15 miles; 1·85 km) from landing threshold on 3° glideslope: 103·8 EPNdB
- Sideline noise level at 0·25 nm (0·29 miles; 0·46 km) from runway centreline: 96·3 EPNdB

HAWKER SIDDELEY TRIDENT

The Hawker Siddeley (originally de Havilland D.H.121) Trident was ordered into production initially to meet BEA's requirements for a short-haul 520 knot (600 mph; 965 km/h) airliner for service from 1963-64 onwards. Design was started in 1957 and construction of the first airframe began on 29 July 1959. The first Trident (G-ARPA), a production aircraft for BEA, flew for the first time on 9 January 1962.

Five versions of the Trident have been ordered, of which the Trident 1 and 1E have been fully described in previous editions of *Jane's*. Current versions are as follows:

Trident 2E. Developed version; 15 ordered by BEA in August 1965, with accommodation for up to 115 passengers. Two others ordered subsequently by Cyprus Airways, and 33 by CAAC, the national airline of the Chinese People's Republic. Overall length unchanged. Fuel capacity and max T-O weight increased, and take-off performance improved by use of more powerful (11,960 lb; 5,425 kg st) Spey RB.163-25 Mk 512-5W turbofan engines. Leading-edge slats, as in Trident 1E, and increased wing span. Low-drag (Küchemann) wingtips. Some strengthening of undercarriage, and of wing and fuselage by use of thicker panels. British Airways aircraft carry 97 tourist class passengers, compared with 88 in this operator's Trident 1s. The first Trident 2E (G-AVFA) flew for the first time on 27 July 1967, and the first for BEA (G-AVFC) was delivered on 15 February 1968. British Airways aircraft, known as Trident Twos, began scheduled services on 18 April 1968. A high-density version is available, having a maximum of 149 seats.

Trident 2Es were delivered with autoland installed at triplex level and were the first airliners in the world with complete all-weather-operation instrumentation of this kind. ARB certification for Trident autolands in Category 2 weather (100 ft decision height, 400 m RVR) was received in February 1969. Full Category 2 operation was first performed by BEA Tridents in December 1970. AiResearch APU, similar to that in Trident 3B, being fitted retrospectively to all British Airways Trident 2Es.

Trident 3B. High-capacity short-haul development of Trident 1E, with fuselage lengthened by 16 ft 5 in (5·00 m) to accommodate from 128 to 180 passengers. Wing span as Trident 2E, but wing area, wing incidence and flap span increased. Powered by same mark of Spey turbofan as Trident 2E, but with Rolls-Royce RB.162-86 turbojet in tail for improved T-O performance. First flight, on 11 December 1969, was made by G-AWYZ without an operational RB.162 engine fitted. The RB.162 was fitted in February 1970, the first flight with this engine operating being made on 22 March 1970. BEA ordered 26, with options on 10 more, and the first of these entered service on 1 April 1971. Trident 3B autoland operation down to 12 ft decision height 270 m RVR, and take-offs in RVR of 90 m (full Category 3A conditions) were certificated by the ARB (now the CAA) in December 1971, and in May 1972 the Authority approved the start of such operations by BEA. All these Tridents, now in the British Airways fleet, were fitted retrospectively to this standard by the Winter of 1972-73.

Super Trident 3B. Announced in late 1972, following an order for two of this version by CAAC (Civil Aviation Administration of China). Externally identical to British Airways Trident 3B; major differences are an increase in passenger seating capacity to 152, and increases in fuel capacity, max T-O and max zero-fuel weights, and an effective range increase of 373 nm (430 miles; 692 km). The additional 380 Imp gallons (1,727 litres) of fuel is carried in the wing centre-section tank, and increases the total usable fuel capacity to 6,000 Imp gallons (27,275 litres).

Orders for the Trident 2E, 3B and Super 3B announced by February 1974 were as follows:

Trident 2E
- BEA (British Airways): 15
- Cyprus Airways: 2
- CAAC: 33

Trident 3B
- BEA (British Airways): 26

Super Trident 3B
- CAAC: 2

The following details apply to the Trident 2E and 3B:

TYPE: Short/medium-range turbofan-engined airliner.

WINGS: Cantilever low-wing monoplane. Wing sections designed with high critical drag rise Mach number for economical operation at ultimate subsonic cruising speeds. Mean thickness/chord ratio approx 9·8%. Dihedral 3°. Incidence 6° 30′ at root, 1° 30′ at tip. Sweepback at quarter-chord 35°. Main wing is continuous from wingtip to wingtip, and comprises a six-cell centre-section box extending across the fuselage, a two-cell box from the wing root out to 40% of the semi-span, and from there a single-cell box to the wingtip. The entire wing box is subdivided to form integral fuel tanks. Skins and stringers are of aluminium alloy, as are the leading-edge and trailing-edge flaps. Extensive use is made of Reduxing between skins and stringers. Structure is fail-safe, except for slat and flap tracks which are safe-life components tested to at least six times the aircraft life. Conventional all-metal ailerons actuated by triplexed power control system without manual reversion. Three independent hydraulic systems work continuously in parallel and power three separate jacks of Fairey manufacture at each primary flying control surface. Two all-metal double-slotted trailing-edge flaps on each wing. Krueger leading-edge flap at each wing-root. All flaps operated by screwjacks and hydraulic motors of Hobson manufacture. One all-metal spoiler on 2E, two on 3B, forward of outer flap on each wing, act also as airbrakes/lift dumpers. Lift dumpers forward of inner flaps. No trim tabs. Both 2E and 3B have full-span leading-edge slats, in four sections per wing, operated by screwjacks and extending on curved titanium tracks. Thermal anti-icing system.

FUSELAGE: Consists of a pressure shell extending back to the engines and a rear fuselage carrying the engines and tail unit. Semi-monocoque fail-safe structure of aluminium/copper alloys, using Redux bonding to attach stringers to skin throughout the pressure cell. No structural bulkheads in pressure cell. Unpressurised cut-outs for nose and main landing gear and wing centre-section.

TAIL UNIT: Cantilever all-metal T-tail. All-moving tailplane with geared slotted flap on trailing-edge to assist in providing high negative lift coefficient for take-off and landing. No trim tabs. Power control system as for ailerons. Thermal anti-icing of leading-edges.

LANDING GEAR: Retractable tricycle type. Hydraulic retraction. Hawker Siddeley (main units) and Lockheed (nose) oleo-pneumatic shock-absorbers. Each main unit consists of two twin-tyred wheels mounted on a common axle: during retraction the leg twists through nearly 90° and lengthens by 6 in (15 cm), enabling wheels to stow within the circular cross-section of the fuselage. Nose unit has twin wheels and is offset 2 ft 0 in (61 cm) to port, retracting transversely. Dunlop wheels, tyres and multi-plate disc brakes, with Maxaret anti-skid units. Trident 3B has main wheel tyres size 36 × 10, pressure 165 lb/sq in (11·60 kg/cm²), and nosewheel tyres size 29 × 8, pressure 124 lb/sq in (8·72 kg/cm²).

POWER PLANT: Three Rolls-Royce Spey turbofan engines (details under model descriptions). Two in pods, one on each side of rear fuselage; one inside rear fuselage. Additionally, Trident 3B has a 5,250 lb (2,381 kg) st Rolls-Royce RB.162-86 turbojet installed in tail, below the rudder, to boost T-O and climb-out. Five integral fuel tanks, four in wings and one in centre-section. Total usable fuel capacity: Trident 2E, 6,400 Imp gallons (29,094 litres); Trident 3B, 5,620 Imp gallons (25,548 litres). For operators requiring greater range/payload capability, Trident 3B has provision for an additional wing centre-section tank of 380 Imp gallons (1,727 litres) capacity. This tank is fitted in the Super 3B. One pressure refuelling point under each wing. Oil capacity 3 Imp gallons (13·5 litres) per engine.

ACCOMMODATION (Trident 2E): Crew of three on flight deck. Mixed-class version has galley (stbd) and toilet (port) at front, then a 12-seat first class compartment, with seats in pairs on each side of central aisle, two galleys (port), 79-seat tourist class cabin with three-seat units on each side of aisle, and two toilets at rear. British Airways' all-tourist version has 97 seats, six abreast, with galley and toilet at front and two toilets at rear. Provision can be made for 132 passengers in high-density seating arrangement, or 149 passengers with some seven-abreast. Two inward-opening plug-type passenger doors, at front and centre of cabin on port side, with provision for built-in airstairs. Doors for crew and servicing at front and amidships on starboard side. Large underfloor baggage holds forward and aft of wing. All crew and passenger accommodation air-conditioned. Provision for air-conditioning forward part of forward baggage hold for animals.

ACCOMMODATION (Trident 3B): Basically as for Trident 2E, with four-abreast first class seats at 38 in (96·5 cm) pitch and six-abreast tourist seating at 31 in (79 cm) pitch. Mixed class version has toilet (port) and two galleys (port and stbd) at front, 14-seat first class cabin, and 122-seat tourist cabin, with two galleys and two toilets (one each port and stbd) at rear. All-tourist version has 152 seats at 30 in (76 cm) pitch, no coat stowage and only one galley (stbd) instead of two at rear, but is otherwise similar. High-density versions can have up to 180 seats (with seven-abreast seating in centre fuselage) at 28 in (71 cm) pitch and no rear galley, but are otherwise similar to the 152-seat version.

SYSTEMS: Hawker Siddeley Dynamics air-conditioning and pressurisation system, differential 8·25 lb/sq in (0·58 kg/cm²). Two independent supplies, each capable of maintaining full cabin pressurisation, with emergency ram-air system for use below 8,000 ft (2,440 m). Three independent hydraulic systems operating all flying controls, landing gear, nosewheel steering, brakes and windscreen wipers. Each system powered by separate engine-driven pump, operating continuously in parallel at 3,000 lb/sq in (210 kg/cm²), using Skydrol fluid. Back-up hydraulic power supplied by two electrically-driven pumps, and emergency power from drop-out air turbine, capable of feeding any one system. Pneumatic system for toilet flushing, forward water system, stall recovery system and for pressurising hydraulic reservoirs. Electrical system comprises three separate channels, supplied by three 27·5kVA brushless generators. Emergency 30 min AC and DC supply available from 24V battery. AiResearch GTCP 85C APU for engine starting and cabin air-conditioning, driving generator to provide 40kVA of electrical power from which hydraulic systems can also be actuated through standby pumps.

ELECTRONICS AND EQUIPMENT: To customer's specification. Provision for duplicated VOR/ILS, including a third localiser for three-channel automatic landing guidance; integration of navigational aids with flight system, providing coupling facilities for all flight modes except take-off; duplicated ADF, VHF and HF with selective calling; C- or X-band weather radar; triplicated radio altimeters for automatic landing; Doppler; DME and transponder.

DIMENSIONS, EXTERNAL:

Wing span (2E, 3B)	98 ft 0 in (29·87 m)
Wing geometric mean chord:	
3B	15 ft $2\frac{3}{4}$ in (4·65 m)
Wing aspect ratio:	
3B	6·43
Length of fuselage:	
3B	119 ft 11 in (36·55 m)
Length overall:	
2E	114 ft 9 in (34·97 m)
3B	131 ft 2 in (39·98 m)
Height overall:	
2E	27 ft 0 in (8·23 m)
3B	28 ft 3 in (8·61 m)
Tailplane span	34 ft 3 in (10·44 m)
Wheel track (c/l of shock-struts)	19 ft $1\frac{1}{4}$ in (5·83 m)
Wheelbase:	
2E	44 ft 0 in (13·41 m)
3B	52 ft $6\frac{1}{2}$ in (16·01 m)
Passenger doors (both):	
Height	5 ft 10 in (1·78 m)
Width	2 ft 4 in (0·71 m)
Min height to sill	9 ft 5 in (2·87 m)
Max height to sill	10 ft 3 in (3·12 m)
Crew and service doors (fwd stbd on 2E; fwd, centre and rear stbd on 3B. Optional fourth door rear port side on high-density 3B):	
Height	4 ft $0\frac{1}{4}$ in (1·22 m)
Width	2 ft 0 in (0·61 m)
Height to sill	approx 9 ft 0 in (2·74 m)
Emergency exits (above centre-section, port and stbd):	
Height	3 ft 4 in (1·03 m)
Width	1 ft 8 in (0·51 m)
Baggage hold doors (fwd, stbd):	
Height (vertical)	2 ft 11 in (0·89 m)
Width	4 ft 0 in (1·22 m)
Height to sill	4 ft 6 in (1·37 m)
Baggage hold door (rear, port):	
Mean height (vertical)	2 ft 8 in (0·81 m)
Width	2 ft 11 in (0·89 m)
Height to sill	4 ft 6 in (1·37 m)

DIMENSIONS, INTERNAL:

Cabin, excluding flight deck:	
Length:	
2E	67 ft $1\frac{1}{2}$ in (20·46 m)
3B	83 ft 5 in (25·43 m)
Max width	11 ft $3\frac{1}{2}$ in (3·44 m)
Max height:	
2E	6 ft $7\frac{1}{2}$ in (2·02 m)
3B	6 ft 8 in (2·03 m)
Floor area:	
2E	708 sq ft (65·77 m²)
3B	1,043 sq ft (96·9 m²)
Volume:	
2E	4,440 cu ft (125·7 m³)
3B	5,600 cu ft (158·57 m³)
Freight hold (fwd):	
2E	490 cu ft (13·88 m³)
3B	633 cu ft (17·92 m³)
Freight hold (rear):	
2E	270 cu ft (7·65 m³)
3B	477 cu ft (13·51 m³)

AREAS:

Wings, gross:	
2E	1,462 sq ft (135·82 m²)
3B	1,493 sq ft (138·7 m²)
Ailerons (total)	52·5 sq ft (4·89 m²)
Trailing-edge flaps (total):	
3B	291·9 sq ft (27·12 m²)
Spoilers	15·3 sq ft (1·42 m²)
Fin	202 sq ft (18·76 m²)
Rudder	52·1 sq ft (4·84 m²)
Tailplane	310 sq ft (28·80 m²)

WEIGHTS AND LOADINGS:

Operating weight, empty:	
2E	73,200 lb (33,203 kg)
3B (152-seat)	81,778 lb (37,090 kg)
Super 3B (152-seat)	82,143 lb (37,259 kg)
Max payload:	
2E	26,800 lb (12,156 kg)
3B (152-seat)	33,722 lb (15,296 kg)
Super 3B (152-seat)	35,357 lb (16,037 kg)

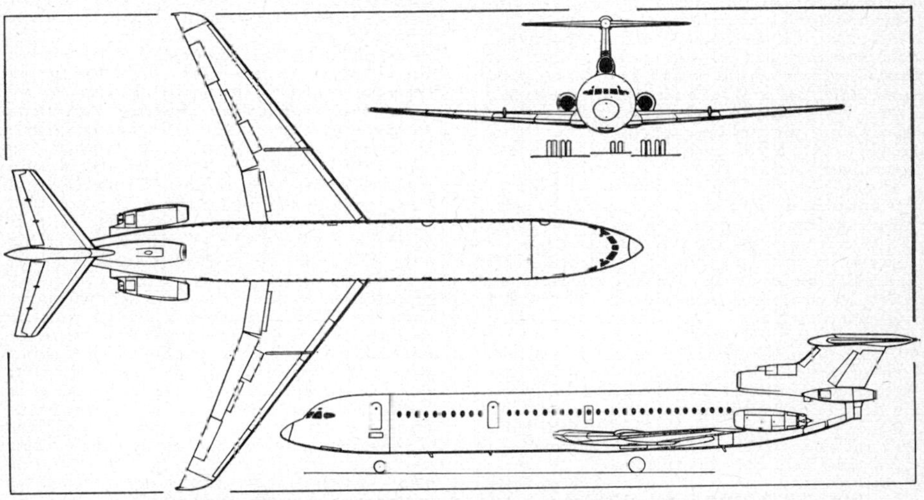

Hawker Siddeley Trident 3B high-capacity short-haul airliner (*Pilot Press*)

Hawker Siddeley Trident 2E short/medium-range three-turbofan transport in the insignia of CAAC of China

Max T-O weight:
2E 143,500 lb (65,090 kg)
3B 150,000 lb (68,040 kg)
Super 3B 158,000 lb (71,667 kg)
Max ramp weight:
3B 150,500 lb (68,267 kg)
Max zero-fuel weight:
2E 100,000 lb (45,359 kg)
3B 115,500 lb (52,395 kg)
Super 3B 117,500 lb (53,296 kg)
Max landing weight:
2E 113,000 lb (51,261 kg)
3B 128,500 lb (58,285 kg)
Super 3B 130,000 lb (58,965 kg)
Max wing loading:
3B 100·5 lb/sq ft (490·7 kg/m²)
Max power loading:
3B 3·65 lb/lb st (3·65 kg/kg st)

PERFORMANCE (2E at max T-O weight):
Max never-exceed speed (design limit) Mach 0·95
Typical high-speed cruise at 27,000 ft (8,230 m) 525 knots (605 mph; 972 km/h) (Mach 0·88)
Econ cruising speed at 30,000 ft (9,150 m) 518 knots (596 mph; 959 km/h) (Mach 0·88)
T-O field length for 1,000 miles (1,610 km) stage, with 21,378 lb (9,697 kg) payload 6,400 ft (1,950 m)
Minimum ground turning radius 52 ft 0 in (15·85 m)
Runway LCN requirement at max weight 58
Range with max fuel* and 16,020 lb (7,266 kg) payload 2,171 nm (2,500 miles; 4,025 km)
Range with typical space-limited payload* of 21,378 lb (9,679 kg) 2,110 nm (2,430 miles; 3,910 km)

PERFORMANCE (Super 3B, at max T-O weight except where stated):
Max never-exceed speed (design limit) Mach 0·95
Max cruising speed at 28,300 ft (8,625 m) 522 knots (601 mph; 967 km/h)
Typical high-speed cruise at 25,000 ft (7,620 m) 505 knots (581 mph; 936 km/h)
Econ cruising speed at 29,000-33,000 ft (8,800-10,000 m) 463 knots (533 mph; 858 km/h)
Stalling speed (at max landing weight, flaps down) 112 knots (129 mph; 208 km/h) EAS
T-O to 35 ft (10 m) 8,900 ft (2,715 m)
Landing from 30 ft (9 m) at max landing weight 5,680 ft (1,730 m)
Minimum ground turning radius 61 ft 0 in (18·60 m)
Runway LCN requirement at max weight 66
Range with max fuel* and 28,200 lb (12,791 kg) payload 2,050 nm (2,360 miles; 3,798 km)
Range with max payload* 1,550 nm (1,785 miles; 2,872 km)

**Reserves for 217 nm (250 mile; 450 km) diversion, 45 min hold at 15,000 ft (4,570 m), final reserve, 4·5% en route allowance and allowances for taxi prior to take-off, circuit approach and land at destination, and taxi after landing.*

OPERATIONAL NOISE CHARACTERISTICS (2E, estimated):
T-O noise level at 3·5 nm (4·0 miles; 6·5 km) from start of T-O run 109 EPNdB
Approach noise level at 1·0 nm (1·15 miles; 1·85 km) from landing threshold on 3° glide-slope 109·5 EPNdB
Sideline noise level at 0·25 nm (0·29 miles; 0·46 km) from runway centreline 106 EPNdB

OPERATIONAL NOISE CHARACTERISTICS (3B, estimated):
T-O noise level at 3·5 nm (4·0 miles; 6·5 km) from start of T-O run 105 EPNdB
Approach noise level at 1·0 nm (1·15 miles; 1·85 km) from landing threshold on 3° glide-slope 110·5 EPNdB
Sideline noise level at 0·25 nm (0·29 miles; 0·46 km) from runway centreline 108 EPNdB

HAWKER SIDDELEY HAWK

After examining designs submitted by BAC and Hawker Siddeley to meet an RAF requirement for a basic and advanced jet trainer, the Ministry of Defence announced in October 1971 that the Hawker Siddeley 1182 had been selected to meet this requirement. Selection of a non-afterburning version of the Rolls-Royce/Turbo-méca Adour to power the aircraft was announced on 2 March 1972, and later in the same month the Ministry of Defence confirmed an order for 176 HS 1182s, which were given the RAF name of Hawk. These will consist of one pre-production aircraft, which was scheduled to fly in mid-1974, and 175 production aircraft of which deliveries are due to begin in late 1976. There will be no separate prototypes; instead, the first five production aircraft are scheduled to take part in the development programme.

The Hawk has been designed to be fully aerobatic (it is stressed to +8 and —4*g*) and to have a fatigue life of 6,000 hours. It will eventually replace the Jet Provost, Gnat Trainer and Hunter in RAF service for pre-wings and advanced flying training, and for radio, navigation and weapons training. The basic design is capable of development for other operational roles, and studies of a number of variants have been made.

TYPE: Two-seat basic and advanced jet trainer, with capability for close-support role.

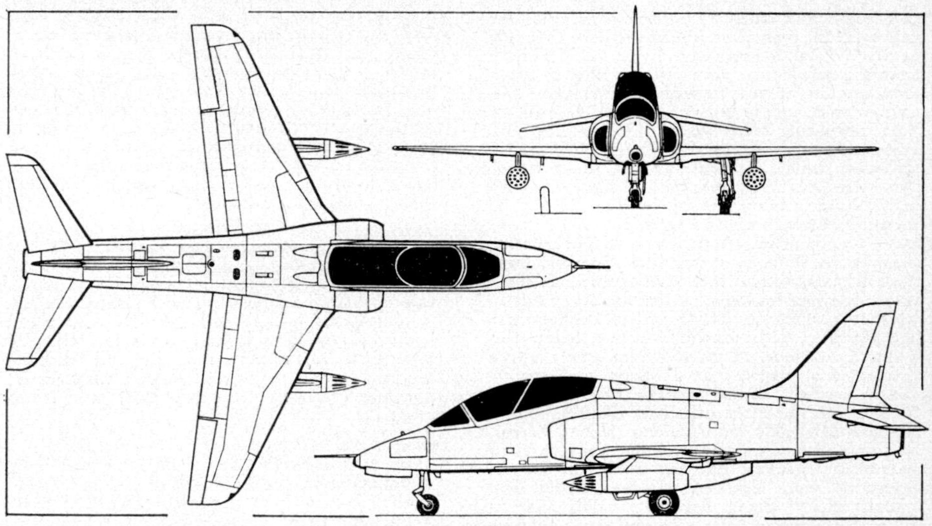

Hawker Siddeley Hawk two-seat advanced training aircraft, equipped with gun and rocket pods
(*Pilot Press*)

WINGS: Cantilever low-wing monoplane. Thickness/chord ratio 10·9% at root, 9% at tip. Slight dihedral. Sweepback 26° on leading-edge, 21° 30′ at quarter-chord. One-piece wing, with six-bolt attachment to fuselage, employing a machined spars-and-skin torsion box, the greater part of which forms an integral fuel tank. Hydraulically-operated double-slotted flaps and ailerons, the latter operated by Lockheed tandem actuators.

FUSELAGE: Conventional all-metal structure of frames and stringers, cut out to accept the one-piece wing. Large airbrake under rear of fuselage, aft of wing.

TAIL UNIT: Cantilever all-metal structure, with sweepback on all surfaces. One-piece all-moving power-operated anhedral tailplane, with Lockheed tandem hydraulic actuators. Mechanically-operated rudder, with electrically-actuated trim tab.

LANDING GEAR: Wide-track retractable tricycle type, with single wheel on each unit. Hydraulic actuation, using Lockheed jacks. Main units retract inward into wing, ahead of front spar; nosewheel retracts forward. Tail bumper fairing under rear fuselage. Anti-skid wheel brakes.

POWER PLANT: One Rolls-Royce/Turboméca RT.172-06-11 Adour 151 non-afterburning turbofan engine, rated at 5,340 lb (2,422 kg) st. Air intake on each side of fuselage, forward of wing leading-edge. Engine starting by integral gas turbine starter. Fuel in one fuselage bag tank (180 Imp gallons; 818 litres) and integral wing tank (175 Imp gallons; 795 litres); total fuel capacity 355 Imp gallons (1,613 litres). Pressure refuelling point near front of port engine air intake trunk. Provision for carrying one 100 Imp gallon (454 litre) drop-tank on each inboard underwing pylon.

ACCOMMODATION: Crew of two in tandem under one-piece fully-transparent sideways-opening canopy. Fixed front windscreen and separate internal windscreen in front of rear cockpit. Rear seat elevated. Martin-Baker Mk 10B zero-zero rocket-assisted ejection seats, with MDC (miniature detonation cord) system to break canopy before seats eject. The MDC can also be operated from outside the cockpit in case of a ground emergency. Dual controls standard. Entire accommodation pressurised, heated and air-conditioned.

SYSTEMS: Hawker Siddeley Dynamics cockpit air-conditioning and pressurisation systems, using engine bleed air. Duplicated hydraulic systems, each 3,000 lb/sq in (210 kg/cm²), for actuation of control jacks, flaps, airbrake, landing gear and anti-skid wheel brakes. Compressed nitrogen accumulators provide emergency power for flaps, landing gear and brakes. No pneumatic system. DC electrical power from single brushless generator, with two static inverters to provide AC power and two batteries for standby power. Gaseous oxygen system for crew. Pop-up ram-air turbine in upper rear fuselage provides emergency power for flying controls in the event of an engine or No. 2 pump failure.

ELECTRONICS AND EQUIPMENT: Flight instrumentation includes Ferranti gyros and inverter, two Sperry Gyroscope RAI-4 4 in remote attitude indicators and a magnetic detector unit, and Louis Newmark compass system. Radio and navigation equipment includes Sylvania UHF and VHF, Cossor CAT.7000 TACAN, Cossor ILS with CILS.75/76 localiser/glideslope receiver and marker receiver, and IFF/SSR.

ARMAMENT AND OPERATIONAL EQUIPMENT: Ferranti F.195 weapon sight and camera recorder in each cockpit. Trainer version has underfuselage centreline-mounted 30 mm Aden gun and ammunition pack, similar to that in use on the Harrier, and two inboard underwing points each capable of carrying a 1,000 lb (454 kg) stores load. Typical underwing armament training loads include two Matra 155 launchers, each with eighteen 2·75 in air-to-surface rockets, or two clusters of four practice bombs. Provision for two outboard underwing pylons, and a pylon in place of the ventral gun pack, also each capable of a 1,000 lb load (i.e. 5,000 lb; 2,270 kg total external stores load), for close-support role. In RAF training roles the normal max external load will probably be about 1,500 lb (680 kg).

DIMENSIONS, EXTERNAL:
Wing span 30 ft 10 in (9·40 m)
Length overall (incl probe) 39 ft 2½ in (11·95 m)
Height overall 13 ft 5 in (4·09 m)

AREA:
Wings, gross 180 sq ft (16·72 m²)

WEIGHTS:
Weight empty 7,450 lb (3,379 kg)
T-O weight:
trainer, clean 10,250 lb (4,649 kg)
trainer, armed 12,000 lb (5,443 kg)
Max T-O weight approx 16,500 lb (7,483 kg)

PERFORMANCE (estimated):
Design max speed at 36,000 ft (11,000 m) 516 knots (595 mph; 1,102 km/h) (Mach 0·9)
Endurance (trainer, clean) approx 1 hr 30 min
Ferry range approx 1,500 nm (1,725 miles; 2,780 km)

HAWKER SIDDELEY HARRIER

RAF designations: Harrier GR.Mk 1, 1A and 3; and T. Mk 2, 2A and 4

USMC designations: AV-8A and TAV-8A

The Harrier is the western world's only operational fixed-wing V/STOL strike fighter. Developed from six years of operating experience with the P.1127/Kestrel series of aircraft (see 1968-69 *Jane's*), the Harrier is an integrated V/STOL weapons system, incorporating the Ferranti FE 541 inertial navigation and attack system and Smiths head-up display. The first of six single-seat prototypes flew for the first time on 31 August 1966. The major current production version is the single-seat AV-8A (Harrier Mk 50) for the US Marine Corps.

By February 1974, some 180 aircraft of the Harrier family had been built, and had made more than 300,000 lift-offs and landings from a variety of surfaces such as grass, tarmac, concrete, dirt and gravel strips, snow- and ice-covered runways. They had also operated from the decks of 18 ships, including US, Argentinian, Spanish, Indian, French and British aircraft carriers, Italian and British cruisers, and US amphibious support ships. The aircraft had been flown by more than 300 Air Force, Navy, Marine and Army pilots from the UK, the US and the German Federal Republic.

The following versions of the Harrier have been built:

Harrier GR. Mk 1, 1A and 3. Single-seat close-support and tactical reconnaissance versions, in quantity production for the Royal Air Force. First of 77 production aircraft ordered initially (XV738) flew on 28 December 1967. Entered service, with the RAF at Wittering, on 1 April 1969. Delivered to No. 1 Squadron at Wittering and Nos. 3, 4 and 20 in Germany. Harriers of No. 1 Squadron carried out operational trials on board HMS *Ark Royal* in May 1971.

A Harrier GR. Mk 1A, piloted by Sqn Ldr T. L. Lecky-Thompson, set up two international time-to-height records after VTO, in Class H for jet-lift aircraft, on 5 January 1971. The aircraft, after a vertical take-off, reached 9,000 m (29,528 ft) in 1 min 44·7 seconds and 12,000 m (39,370 ft) in 2 min 22·7 seconds. The same RAF pilot also set up a Class H altitude record of 46,063 ft (14,040 m) in a Harrier GR. Mk 1A on 2 January 1971.

The Harrier has, in non-record-attempt flights, been flown to altitudes in excess of 50,000 ft (15,240 m).

Harrier GR. Mk 1 aircraft were fitted initially with 19,000 lb (8,620 kg) st Pegasus 101 engines, but no aircraft powered by these engines remain in service. The designation GR. Mk 1A applies to those subsequently refitted with the 20,000 lb (9,071 kg) st Pegasus 102 engine. Aircraft currently being retrofitted with the more powerful Pegasus 103 engine are designated GR. Mk 3. By early 1973, GR. Mk 3s were in service with Nos. 4 and 20 Squadrons of the RAF. A further 15 Harriers, believed to be GR. Mk 3s, were ordered for the RAF in March 1973.

Harrier T. Mk 2, 2A and 4. Two-seat versions, retaining the full combat capability of the single-seater in terms of equipment fit and weapon carriage. There is a large degree of commonality in structure and system components, ground support equipment and flight and ground crew training. Differences include a new, longer nose section forward of the wing leading-edge, with two cockpits in tandem; a tailcone approx 6 ft (1·83 m) longer than that of the single-seat model; and enlarged fin surfaces. The two-seat Harrier may be used operationally with the rear seat and compensating tail ballast removed, thus minimising the weight penalty over its single-seat counterpart. First development aircraft flew on 24 April 1969, followed by the second on 14 July 1969 and the first production aircraft on 3 October 1969. Current orders are for 15 of this version (including two development aircraft), and the first of these entered RAF service in July 1970.

The Harrier T. Mk 2, like the GR. Mk 1, was powered originally by the Pegasus 101 engine. The designations T. Mk 2A and T. Mk 4 apply to aircraft retrofitted with, respectively, the Pegasus 102 and 103.

Harrier Mk 50 (USMC designation AV-8A). Single-seat close-support and tactical reconnaissance version for the US Marine Corps. Dimensionally the same as GR. Mk 3, but with modifications to customer's specification, including provision for the carriage of Sidewinder missiles. Initial quantity of 12 ordered in 1969. Subsequent firm orders had brought this total to 102 by early 1974. The last fiscal order for USMC aircraft included eight Harrier **Mk 54s** with Pegasus 103 engines, a two-seat version designated **TAV-8A** for operational training.

The first AV-8A was delivered to the USA on 26 January 1971. The first 10 AV-8As had Pegasus 102 engines; the next 92 aircraft are powered by Pegasus 103s, which are also being fitted retrospectively to the earlier aircraft. McDonnell Douglas has licence rights to manufacture "any significant numbers" ordered if the US government decides to build in the USA.

The AV-8As equip three USMC combat squadrons: VMA 513 and VMA 542 at Beaufort, South Carolina, and VMA 231 at Cherry Point, North Carolina. A training squadron is also provided for. Six AV-8As and two TAV-8As have been ordered, through the USA, for the Spanish Navy.

Harrier Mk 52. One aircraft built as a demonstrator using HSA and equipment suppliers' private funding. It is similar to the Harrier T. Mk 4, and is fitted with a Pegasus 103 engine; in recognition of its status as the first civil-registered jet V/STOL aircraft in the UK, it has been granted the civil registration G-VTOL. First flight was made on 16 September 1971, with a Pegasus 102 fitted initially.

An Advanced Harrier study was completed in December 1973 by Hawker Siddeley, Rolls-Royce, McDonnell Douglas and Pratt & Whitney. This was funded jointly by the UK and US governments on behalf of the RAF, RN, USMC and USN, and is described in the International section.

Also during 1973, a project definition study was completed on a maritime version of the Harrier. Powered by the Pegasus 103 engine, this would meet the needs of the RN for operation from the new Invincible Class through-deck cruisers in the late 1970s and the 1980s. Development of the Maritime Harrier had not been approved by July 1974, although it was known that the weapons system meets all of the Royal Navy's operational requirements.

The following details apply generally to the Harrier GR. Mk 3 and T. Mk 4, except where a specific version is indicated:

Type: V/STOL close-support and reconnaissance aircraft.

Wings: Cantilever shoulder-wing monoplane. Aerofoil section of HSA design. Thickness/chord ratio 10% at root, 5% at tip. Anhedral 12°. Incidence 1° 45′. Sweepback at quarter-chord 34°. One-piece aluminium alloy three-spar safe-life structure with integrally-machined skins, manufactured by Brough factory of HSA, with six-point attachment to fuselage. Plain ailerons and flaps, of bonded aluminium alloy honeycomb construction. Ailerons irreversibly operated by Fairey tandem hydraulic jacks. Jet reaction control valve built into

Hawker Siddeley Harrier GR. Mk 1 with laser rangefinder in modified nose

Single-seat Hawker Siddeley Harrier of No. 1 Squadron RAF in snow camouflage scheme

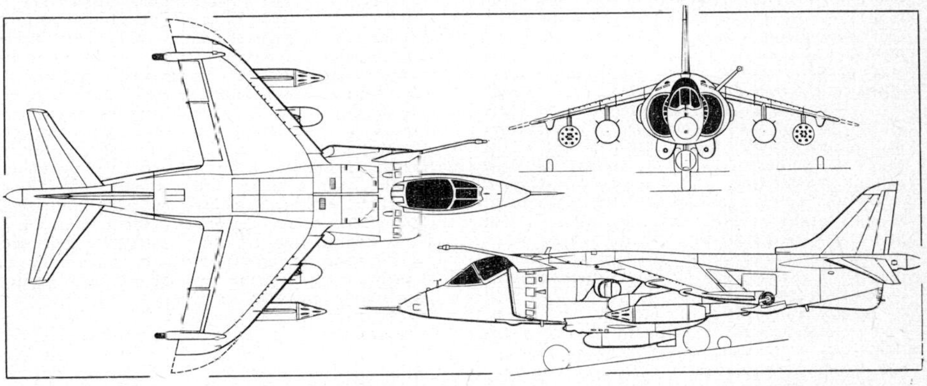

Hawker Siddeley Harrier GR. Mk 3 single-seat V/STOL close-support and reconnaissance aircraft
(*Pilot Press*)

Hawker Siddeley Harrier two-seat combat trainer of the RAF's No. 233 Squadron

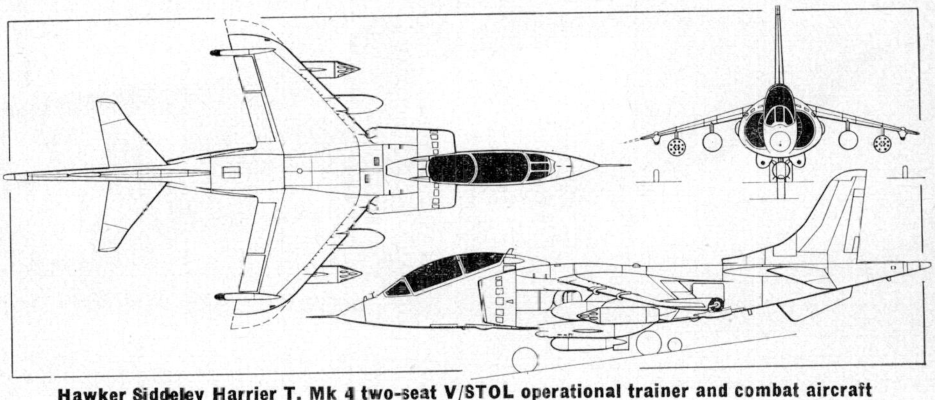

Hawker Siddeley Harrier T. Mk 4 two-seat V/STOL operational trainer and combat aircraft
(*Pilot Press*)

front of each outrigger wheel fairing. Entire wing unit removable to provide access to engine. For ferry missions, the normal "combat" wingtips can be replaced by bolt-on extended tips to increase ferry range.

Fuselage: Conventional semi-monocoque safe-life structure of frames and stringers, mainly of aluminium alloy, but with titanium skins at rear and some titanium adjacent to engine and in other special areas. Access to power plant through top of fuselage, ahead of wing. Jet reaction control valves in nose and in extended tailcone. Large forward-hinged air-brake under fuselage, aft of main-wheel well.

Tail Unit: One-piece variable-incidence tail-plane, with 15° of anhedral, irreversibly operated by Fairey tandem hydraulic jack. Rudder and trailing-edge of tailplane are of bonded aluminium honeycomb construction. Rudder is operated manually. Trim tab in rudder. Ventral fin under rear fuselage. Fin tip carries suppressed VHF aerial.

Landing Gear: Retractable bicycle type of Dowty Rotol manufacture, permitting operation from rough unprepared surfaces of CBR as low as 3% to 5%. Hydraulic actuation, with nitrogen bottle for emergency extension of landing gear. Single steerable nosewheel retracts forward, twin coupled main wheels rearward, into fuselage. Small outrigger units retract rearward into fairings slightly inboard of wingtips. Nosewheel leg is of levered-suspension Liquid Spring type. Dowty Rotol telescopic oleo-pneumatic main and outrigger gear. Dunlop wheels and tyres, size 26·00 × 8·75-11 (nose unit), 26·00 × 7·75-13 (main units) and 13·50 × 6·4 (outriggers). GR. Mk 1, 1A and 3 pressures 90 lb/sq in (6·33 kg/cm²) on nose and main units, 95 lb/sq in (6·68 kg/cm²) on outriggers. T. Mk 2, 2A and 4 tyre pressures 100 lb/sq in (7·03 kg/cm²) on nose unit, 95 lb/sq in (6·68 kg/cm²) on main and outrigger units. Dunlop multi-disc brakes and Dunlop-Hytrol adaptive anti-skid system.

Power Plant: One Rolls-Royce Bristol Pegasus Mk 103 vectored-thrust turbofan engine (21,500 lb; 9,752 kg st), with four exhaust nozzles of the two-vane cascade type, rotatable through 98° from fully-aft position. Engine bleed air from HP compressor used for jet reaction control system and to power duplicated air motor for nozzle actuation. The low-drag intake cowls, with inward-cambered lips, each have 8 automatic suction relief doors aft of the leading-edge to improve intake efficiency by providing extra air for the engine at low forward or zero speeds. Fuel in five integral tanks in fuselage and two in wings, with total capacity of approx 630 Imp gallons (2,865 litres). This can be supplemented by two 100 Imp gallon (455 litre) jettisonable combat tanks or two 330 Imp gallon (1,500 litre) ferry tanks on the inboard wing pylons. Ground refuelling point in port rear nozzle fairing. Provision for in-flight refuelling probe above the port intake cowl.

Accommodation: Crew of one (Mk 3) or two (Mk 4) on Martin-Baker Type 9A Mk 1 zero-zero rocket ejection seats which operate through the miniature detonating cord equipped canopy of the pressurised, heated and air-conditioned cockpit. AV-8A Harriers of the USMC will be retrofitted with Stencel SIIIS-3 ejection seats. Manually-operated canopy, rearward-sliding on single-seat, sideways-opening (to starboard) on two-seat versions. Bird-proof windscreen, with hydraulically-actuated wiper. Windscreen de-icing.

Systems: Pressurisation system of HSA design, with Normalair-Garrett and Marston major components; max pressure differential 3·5 lb/sq in (0·25 kg/cm²). Duplicated hydraulic systems, each of 3,000 lb/sq in (210 kg/cm²), actuate flying controls, landing gear and nosewheel steering and include a retractable ram-air turbine inside top of rear fuselage, driving a small hydraulic pump for emergency power. AC electrical system with transformer-rectifiers to provide required DC supply. One 12kVA Lucas alternator. Two 28V 25Ah batteries, one of which energises a 24V motor to start Lucas gas-turbine starter/APU. This unit drives a 6kVA auxiliary alternator for ground readiness servicing and standby. Normalair-Garrett liquid oxygen system of 1 Imp gallon (5 litres) capacity. Bootstrap-type cooling unit for equipment bay, with intake at base of dorsal fin.

Electronics and Equipment: Plessey U/VHF, Ultra standby UHF, Hoffman TACAN and Cossor IFF, Ferranti FE 541 inertial navigation and attack system (INAS), with Sperry C2G compass, Smiths electronic head-up display of flight information and Smiths air data computer. INAS can be aligned equally well at sea or on land. The weapon aiming computer provides a general solution for manual or automatic release of free-fall and retarded bombs, and for the aiming of rockets and guns, in dive and straight-pass attacks over a wide range of flight conditions with very considerable freedom of manoeuvre in elevation. Communication equipment ranges through VHF in the 100-156 MHz band to UHF in the 220-400MHz band.

Armament and Operational Equipment: Optically-flat panel in nose, on port side, for F.95 oblique camera, which is carried as standard. A cockpit voice recorder with in-flight playback facility supplements the reconnaissance cameras, and facilitates rapid briefing and mission evaluation. No built-in armament. Combat load is carried on four underwing and one underfuselage pylon, all with ML ejector release units. The inboard wing points and the fuselage point are stressed for loads of up to 2,000 lb (910 kg) each, and the outboard underwing pair for loads of up to 650 lb (295 kg) each; the two strake fairings under the fuselage can each be replaced by a 30 mm Aden gun pod and ammunition. At present, the Harrier is cleared for operations with a maximum external load exceeding 5,000 lb (2,270 kg), but has flown with a weapon load of 8,000 lb (3,630 kg). The Harrier is able to carry 30 mm guns, bombs, rockets and flares of UK and US designs, and in addition to its fixed reconnaissance camera can also carry a five-camera reconnaissance pod on the underfuselage pylon. A typical combat load comprises a pair of 30 mm Aden gun pods, a 1,000 lb bomb on the underfuselage pylon, a 1,000 lb bomb on each of the inboard underwing pylons, and a Matra 155 launcher with 19 × 68 mm SNEB rockets on each outboard underwing pylon. A Sidewinder installation is provided in the AV-8A version, to give the aircraft an effective air-to-air capability in conjunction with the two 30 mm Aden guns.

Dimensions, external:

Wing span:	
combat	25 ft 3 in (7·70 m)
ferry	29 ft 8 in (9·04 m)
Wing chord at root	11 ft 8 in (3·56 m)
Wing chord at tip	4 ft 1½ in (1·26 m)
Wing aspect ratio:	
combat	3·175
ferry	4·08
Length overall:	
single-seat	45 ft 6 in (13·87 m)
two-seat	55 ft 9½ in (17·00 m)
Height overall:	
single-seat	approx 11 ft 3 in (3·43 m)
two-seat	approx 13 ft 8 in (4·17 m)
Tailplane span	13 ft 11 in (4·24 m)
Outrigger wheel track	22 ft 2 in (6·76 m)
Wheelbase, nosewheel to main wheels	approx 11 ft 4 in (3·45 m)

Areas:

Wings, gross:	
combat	201·1 sq ft (18·68 m²)
ferry	216 sq ft (20·1 m²)
Ailerons (total)	10·5 sq ft (0·98 m²)
Trailing-edge flaps (total)	13·9 sq ft (1·29 m²)
Fin (excluding ventral fin):	
single-seat	25·8 sq ft (2·40 m²)
two-seat	38·4 sq ft (3·57 m²)
Rudder, including tab	5·3 sq ft (0·49 m²)
Tailplane	47·5 sq ft (4·41 m²)

Weights and Loading:

Basic operating weight, empty, with crew:	
GR.Mk 1 and Mk 50	12,200 lb (5,533 kg)
T.Mk 2 (solo for combat)	13,000 lb (5,896 kg)
T.Mk 2 (dual)	13,600 lb (6,168 kg)
Max T-O weight (single-seat)	over 25,000 lb (11,339 kg)
Max wing loading (single-seat)	125 lb/sq ft (610 kg/m²)

Performance:

Speed at low altitude	over 640 knots (737 mph; 1,186 km/h) EAS
Mach number (in a dive)	approaching 1·3
Ceiling	more than 50,000 ft (15,240 m)
Endurance, with one in-flight refuelling	more than 7 hr
Range with one in-flight refuelling	more than 3,000 nm (3,455 miles; 5,560 km)

HAWKER SIDDELEY BUCCANEER

The Hawker Siddeley (originally Blackburn) Buccaneer strike aircraft flew for the first time on 30 April 1958, and was produced initially for the Royal Navy (20 development aircraft, 40 S.Mk 1 and 84 S.Mk 2) and the South African Air Force (16 S.Mk 50). Descriptions of these versions were given in the 1970-71 *Jane's*.

Most Royal Navy S.Mk 2s were later transferred to the RAF, the first four being delivered to No. 12 Squadron at RAF Honington on 1 October 1969. Those operated by the RAF are designated **S.Mk 2A** (without Martel capability) and **S.Mk 2B** (with Martels). Other airframe and equipment differences exist between these models, but the capability to carry Martel air-to-ground missiles is the fundamental definition of aircraft standard. The RAF, in addition to the ex-RN aircraft, has ordered 43 new-production S.Mk 2Bs, the first of which flew on 8 January 1970. Delivery of these is due to be completed in late 1975. All Mk 2As are being brought up to Mk 2B standard. First RAF units to be completely equipped with the Buccaneer S.Mk 2B were Nos. 15 and 16 Squadrons based at Laarbruch in Germany.

Buccaneers remaining in Royal Navy service are now designated **S.Mk 2C** without, and **S.Mk 2D** with, Martel capability.

Three S.Mk 2Bs (XW986-988) have been specially built for the Royal Aircraft Establishment, and will be used for development trials of various weapons. Two other Buccaneers are being modified by Marshall of Cambridge (which see) as a part of the Panavia MRCA development programme.

The following details apply to the Buccaneer S.Mk 2A/2B:

Type: Two-seat strike and reconnaissance aircraft.

Wings: Cantilever mid-wing monoplane. Sweep-back at quarter-chord: 40° at root, decreasing first to 38° 36′ and then to 30° 12′. Thin section. No dihedral. Incidence 2° 30′. Structure is of all-metal multi-spar design with integrally-stiffened thick skins machined from the solid. Inner wings each have an aluminium alloy auxiliary spar and two steel main spars which are bolted to three spar rings in centre fuselage. Outer wings have two aluminium alloy spars. Electrically-actuated ailerons, powered by Dowty Boulton Paul duplicated tandem actuators, can be drooped in conjunction with the inboard

One of three Hawker Siddeley Buccaneers for RAE weapons trials. Yellow, green and white paint scheme aids tracking cameras

flaps to provide a full-span trailing-edge flap system. No trim tabs. Resin-bonded glassfibre tips on wings and ailerons. "Supercirculation" boundary layer control, with air outlet slots near leading-edges and forward of the drooping ailerons and plain flaps. This system also provides thermal de-icing of the engines and intakes; use of the boundary layer system supplies sufficient heat to de-ice the wing and tailplane leading-edges under most operational conditions. Outer wings fold upward hydraulically for stowage.

FUSELAGE: All-metal semi-monocoque structure, bulged at rear end in conformity with area rule. Built in three main sections, comprising cockpit, centre fuselage and rear fuselage, plus nosecone and tailcone. Upper section of centre fuselage contains the fuel tanks, lower section contains the weapons bay. Engine and jet-pipe firewalls and heat shields are titanium. Equipment bay in rear fuselage has strengthened floor to absorb stresses when arrester hook is used and transfer them to main structure. Tailcone is made up of two petal-type airbrakes, hydraulically actuated to hinge sideways into the airstream; these can be opened fully or to any intermediate position. For stowage the resin-bonded glasscloth nosecone hinges sideways to port and the airbrakes are fully opened.

TAIL UNIT: Cantilever all-metal T-tail. Large dorsal fin faired into fuselage dorsal fairing. All-moving tailplane attached to tip of fin, which is pivoted to move with it. Electrically-actuated tailplane trim flap is used only when ailerons are deflected. Flying control surfaces powered by Dowty Boulton Paul duplicated tandem actuators. "Super-circulation" boundary layer control system, with air outlet slots in underskin of tailplane, just aft of leading-edge.

LANDING GEAR: Retractable tricycle type of Dowty manufacture. Hydraulic retraction, main wheels inward into jet-pipe nacelles, nosewheel rearward into front fuselage. Oleo shock-absorbers and single wheels on all units. Goodyear or Dunlop wheels and tubeless tyres, size 24 × 6·6 on nose unit, 35 × 10 on main units. Hydraulically steerable nosewheel. Goodyear or Dunlop double-disc hydraulic brakes, with anti-skid system. Sting-type arrester hook under rear fuselage.

POWER PLANT: Two 11,100 lb (5,035 kg) st Rolls-Royce RB.168-1A Spey Mk 101 turbofan engines, housed in nacelle on each side of the fuselage. Standard internal fuel in eight integral tanks in upper part of centre fuselage, total capacity 1,560 Imp gallons (7,092 litres), with provision for cross-feed of all fuel to either engine. In addition, a 425 Imp gallon (1,932 litre) bomb-door fuel tank can be fitted, without detriment to the aircraft's bomb-carrying capability. Provision for additional 440 Imp gallon (2,000 litre) auxiliary tank in weapons bay, and/or two 250 or 430 Imp gallon (1,136 or 1,955 litre) underwing drop-tanks on the inboard pylons. Detachable flight refuelling probe standard. In the tanker role (max capacity 2,815 Imp gallons; 12,797 litres) the inboard starboard pylon is occupied by a 140 Imp gallon (636 litre) Mk 20B or 20C refuelling pod fed continuously from the main fuel system.

ACCOMMODATION: Crew of two in tandem on Martin-Baker zero-zero ejection seats in pressurised cockpit under single electrically-actuated rearward-sliding blown Perspex canopy. Canopy can be jettisoned separately, if necessary, by explosive charge. Windscreen anti-icing by gold film electrical heating system.

SYSTEMS: Liquid oxygen breathing system. Normalair pressurisation and air-conditioning system. Main hydraulic system pressure 4,000 lb/sq in (280 kg/cm²); secondary system, for flying controls, pressure 3,300 lb/sq in (232 kg/cm²). Two 30kVA alternators, one driven by each engine, provide 200V 400Hz three-phase AC electrical power. For certain equipment this is phased through a 115V 400Hz transformer. Two 4·5kW rectifiers supply a 28V battery to provide DC power for certain other systems. Emergency battery provides 20 min of power in the event of failure of main generating system.

ELECTRONICS, ARMAMENT AND OPERATIONAL EQUIPMENT: Standard equipment includes single-sideband HF and UHF/VHF communications equipment with centralised audio selection and telebriefing, air data system, Doppler radar navigation system, master reference gyro, search and fire control radar incorporating terrain warning, and strike sighting and computing system. The rotating weapons bay door can carry four 1,000 lb HE Mk 10 bombs, a 440 Imp gallon (2,000 litre) fuel tank, or a reconnaissance pack containing one vertical F97 night camera and six F95 day cameras (three vertical, two oblique and one forward) with low or high altitude 4 in or 12 in (10 cm or 30·5 cm) lenses. Other possible reconnaissance equipment includes linescan, electronic flash gear and different camera arrangements. Each of the four wing pylon stations can be adapted to carry a wide variety of external stores. Typical loads for any one pylon include one 1,000 lb HE Mk N1 or Mk 10 bomb; two 500 lb or 540 lb bombs on tandem carriers; one 18-tube 68 mm rocket pod; one 36-tube 2 in rocket pod; 3 in rockets; or an HSD/Matra Martel air-to-surface missile (maximum 3 missiles and a Martel systems pod). Each pylon is also suitable for carrying three 1,000 lb stores on triple release ejection units, or six 500 lb stores on multiple ejection release units, with only small restrictions on the flight envelope. In addition to a Mk 20 in-flight refuelling pod, when operating in the tanker role, an airborne low-pressure starter pod can be carried on an inner pylon; 250 Imp gallon (1,136 litre) or 430 Imp gallon (1,955 litre) drop-tanks can also be carried on these positions. Maximum internal and external stores load is 16,000 lb (7,257 kg).

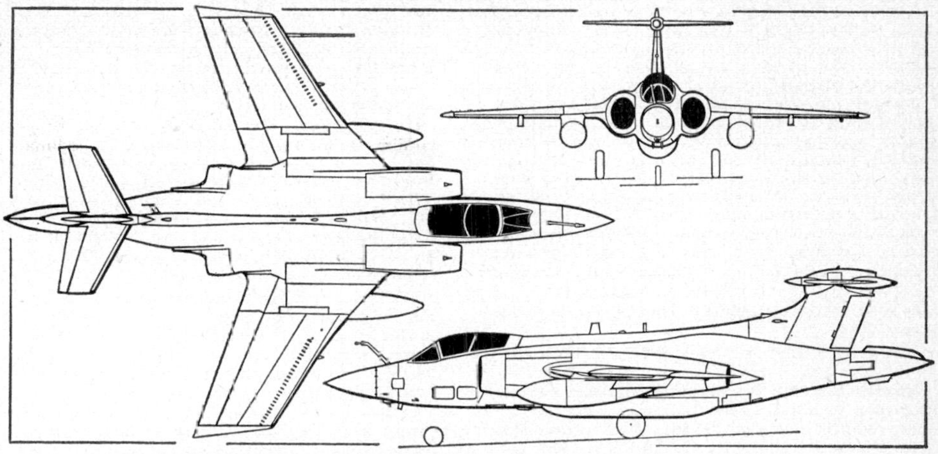

Hawker Siddeley Buccaneer S.Mk 2B twin-engined strike aircraft (*Pilot Press*)

DIMENSIONS, EXTERNAL:

Wing span	44 ft 0 in (13·41 m)
Wing span (folded)	19 ft 11 in (6·07 m)
Wing span (folded, over tank fairings)	20 ft 5 in (6·22 m)
Wing chord at root	13 ft 7 in (4·14 m)
Wing chord at tip	8 ft 0 in (2·44 m)
Wing chord (mean)	11 ft 11½ in (3·65 m)
Wing aspect ratio	3·55
Length overall	63 ft 5 in (19·33 m)
Length folded	51 ft 10 in (15·79 m)
Height overall	16 ft 3 in (4·95 m)
Height folded	16 ft 8 in (5·08 m)
Tailplane span	14 ft 3 in (4·34 m)
Wheel track	11 ft 10½ in (3·62 m)
Wheelbase	20 ft 8 in (6·30 m)

AREAS:

Wings, gross	514·70 sq ft (47·82 m²)
Ailerons (total)	54·80 sq ft (5·09 m²)
Trailing-edge flaps (total)	23·30 sq ft (2·16 m²)
Fin	68·60 sq ft (6·37 m²)
Rudder	10·74 sq ft (1·00 m²)
Tailplane, gross	75·52 sq ft (7·02 m²)
Tailplane trim flap	22·20 sq ft (2·06 m²)

WEIGHTS:

Typical take-off weights	46,000 lb (20,865 kg) to 56,000 lb (25,400 kg)
Max T-O weight	62,000 lb (28,123 kg)
Typical landing weight	35,000 lb (15,876 kg)

PERFORMANCE:

Max design level speed at 200 ft (61 m)
560 knots (645 mph; 1,038 km/h) (Mach 0·85)

T-O run at S/L, ISA:
at 46,000 lb (20,865 kg) AUW — 2,360 ft (720 m)
at 56,000 lb (25,400 kg) AUW — 3,800 ft (1,160 m)

Landing run at 35,000 lb (15,876 kg) landing weight, S/L, ISA — 3,150 ft (960 m)

Typical strike range
2,000 nm (2,300 miles; 3,700 km)

Endurance, with two in-flight refuellings 9 hr

HAWKER SIDDELEY ARGOSY

Hawker Siddeley Aviation announced on 28 February 1974 the receipt of a contract from the Ministry of Defence covering the conversion initially of 14 Argosy C.1s to serve as flying classrooms for RAF Training Command. Under the designation **T.Mk 2,** they will be used for the training of navigators and for other in-flight operations, replacing Vickers Varsity T.1s that are being phased out of service.

Design of the modifications was carried out at HSA Manchester. Conversion is being undertaken at Bitteswell, where the Argosies were assembled originally.

Major modifications include a dual nose window, where both instructor and pupil can operate in a prone position; an enlarged nose radome; equipping of the fuselage with consoles and desks for pupil navigators; and installation of avionic equipment relays. The Argosy T.2s are scheduled to enter RAF service in the Spring of 1975.

HAWKER SIDDELEY HS 801 NIMROD

RAF designations: Nimrod MR.Mks 1 and 2 and R. Mk 1

The Nimrod is a derivative of the Comet 4C, and has replaced completely the Shackleton maritime reconnaissance aircraft of RAF Strike Command. It has a 6 ft 6 in (1·98 m) shorter, modified fuselage with a new unpressurised, underslung pannier for operational equipment and weapons, and the original Avon engines are replaced by Rolls-Royce Spey turbofans. Other external changes include wider air intakes, to allow for the greater mass flow of the Spey turbofan engines, enlarged pilot's windscreen, ECM and MAD equipment fairings, and a searchlight in the starboard pinion tank.

Design of the Nimrod began in June 1964. It was designed to combine the advantages of high-altitude, fast transit speed with good low-speed manoeuvring capabilities when operating in the ASW role. When required, two of the four Spey engines can be shut down to extend endurance. A wide range of weapons can be carried in the approx 50 ft (15·35 m) bomb bay, and large numbers of sonobuoys and markers can be

Artist's impression of Hawker Siddeley Argosy T. Mk 2 flying classroom for the RAF

carried and released from the pressurised fuselage area. Spare space is available to accommodate future developments in avionics equipment. The radar is housed in a streamlined fairing which forms the forward extension of the bomb bay.

In addition to its surveillance and ASW roles, the Nimrod can carry out day or night photography and has a stand-off surface missile capability. The aircraft can also carry 16 additional personnel for the self-support role, or 45 persons after removal of some equipment in the aft section of the fuselage.

The first prototype, which had Spey engines, flew on 23 May 1967, and was used for aerodynamic investigations. The second, powered by Avon engines, was flown on 31 July 1967 and was used for development of the special maritime equipment.

The following production versions have been announced:

Nimrod MR. Mk 1. Major production version described in detail below. Initial order for 38, subsequently increased to 46. First production MR. Mk 1 (XV226) flew on 28 June 1968 and deliveries began on 2 October 1969. The MR. Mk 1 was delivered initially to No. 236 OCU, RAF Strike Command, at St Mawgan, Cornwall, and is now in service with Nos. 42, 120, 201 and 206 Squadrons of RAF Strike Command in the UK, No. 203 Squadron of the Near East Air Force based in Malta, and a detachment operating from Singapore as part of the ANZUK force.

Nimrod R.Mk 1. Designation of three aircraft (additional to the Nimrod MR. Mk 1s ordered for RAF Strike Command) built for No. 51 Squadron. These aircraft (XW644-646) are replacements for Comet 2 aircraft, said to be employed for electronic reconnaissance and to monitor hostile radio and radar transmissions, although official statements have referred only to radio/radar calibration duties connected with RAF equipment. They can be identified by absence of an MAD tailboom.

Nimrod MR.Mk 2. The RAF's Nimrod MR.Mk 1 fleet is scheduled to be retrofitted with new electronics systems from 1977 onwards, and the aircraft will then be designated Nimrod MR. Mk 2. Their equipment will include an advanced EMI radar offering greater range and sensitivity coupled with a higher data processing rate. Additionally, a new acoustic processing system is being developed by Marconi-Elliott Avionics Systems, and this is intended to be compatible with a wide range of existing and projected sonobuoys, including the joint Australian/UK BARRA long-range buoy.

Type: Four-turbofan maritime reconnaissance aircraft.

Wings: Cantilever low/mid-wing monoplane, of metal construction. Sweepback 20° at quarter-chord. All-metal two-spar structure, comprising a centre-section, two stub-wings and two outer panels. Extensive use of Redux metal-to-metal bonding. All-metal ailerons, operated through duplicated hydraulic and mechanical units. Trim tab in each aileron. Plain flaps outboard of engines, operated hydraulically. Hot-air anti-icing system.

Fuselage: All-metal semi-monocoque structure. The circular-section cabin space is fully pressurised. Below this is an unpressurised pannier housing the bomb bay, radome and additional space for operational equipment. Segments of this pannier are free to move relative to each other, so that structural loads in the weapons bay are not transmitted to the pressure-cell. A glassfibre nose radome and tailboom are provided.

Tail Unit: Cantilever all-metal structure. Rudder and elevators operated through duplicated hydraulic and mechanical units. A glassfibre pod on top of the fin houses ECM equipment. Trim tab in each elevator. Hot-air anti-icing system.

Landing Gear: Retractable tricycle type, similar to Comet 4C but with strengthened main leg and axle beams, stronger wheels and hydraulic brakes of increased capacity. Four-wheel tandem-bogie main units, with size 36 × 10-18 Dunlop tyres, pressure 185 lb/sq in (13·0 kg/cm²). Twin-wheel nose unit, with size 30 × 9-15 Dunlop tyres, pressure 90 lb/sq in (6·33 kg/cm²). No brake cooling.

Power Plant: Four Rolls-Royce RB.168 Spey Mk 250 turbofan engines (each 12,000 lb; 5,443 kg st). Reverse thrust fitted on outboard engines. The 192,000 lb (87,090 kg) AUW version carries extra fuel in removable bomb-bay tanks.

Accommodation: Normal crew of twelve, with three on flight deck, and two navigators and seven sensor operators in forward cabin. Flight deck has large side windows and "eyebrow" windows. Main cabin is fitted out as a tactical compartment, containing detection equipment. Hemispherical observation windows, giving 180° field of view, are provided. Galley and rest quarters in centre section of fuselage; ordnance area in rear cabin. Bomb-bay may be utilised for the carriage of freight. Provision is made for a trooping role, and in this configuration 45 passengers can be accommodated. Two normal doors, emergency door and four emergency exits.

Systems: Air-conditioning by engine bleed air; Smith-Kollsman pressurisation system, max differential 8·75 lb/sq in (0·61 kg/cm²). Anti-icing and bomb-bay heating by engine bleed air. Lockheed hydraulic system, pressure 2,500 lb/sq in (175 kg/cm²), for duplicated flying control power units, landing gear shock-absorbers, steering and door jacks, weapons bay door jacks, camera aperture door jacks, and self-sealing couplings for water charging, ground test, engine bay and ancillary services. Rover APU provides high-pressure air for engine starting. Electrical system utilises four 60kVA engine-driven alternators, with English Electric constant-speed drives, to provide 200V 400Hz three-phase AC supply. Secondary AC comes from two 115V three-phase static transformers, with duplicate 115/26V two-phase static transformers which also feed a 1kVA frequency changer providing a 115V 1,600Hz single-phase supply for radar equipment. Emergency supplies for flight instruments are provided by a 115V single-phase static inverter. DC supply is by four 28V transformer-rectifier units backed up by two nickel-cadmium batteries.

Electronics and Equipment: Routine navigation by Decca Doppler Type 67/Marconi-Elliott E3 inertial system incorporating data computer and twin-gyro compass, and operating in conjunction with Ferranti vertical projector. Tactical navigation by Marconi-Elliott nav/attack system, utilising Marconi-Elliott 920B computer and data processing equipment. ASW equipment includes SONICS IC sonar and a new long-range sonar system, ASV 21 air-to-surface-vessel detection radar, Autolycus ionisation detector, and ECM gear. MAD (magnetic anomaly detector) in extended tail "sting". Searchlight in starboard external wing fuel tank. Smiths SFS.6 flight system and SEP.6 autopilot. U/VHF and Marconi-Elliott AD 470 HF radio and ILS glideslope indicator. Yaw damper and Mach trim standard.

Armament: Bay for active and passive sonobuoys in pressurised part of rear fuselage. Ventral weapons bay, approx 50 ft (15 m) long, can accommodate full range of ASW weapons including bombs, mines, depth charges and torpedoes. Pylon beneath each wing at approx one-third span, on which can be carried AS.12 or other weapons as required.

Dimensions, external:

Wing span	114 ft 10 in (35·00 m)
Wing chord at root	29 ft 6 in (9·00 m)
Wing chord at tip	6 ft 9 in (2·06 m)
Wing aspect ratio	6·2
Length overall	126 ft 9 in (38·63 m)
Height overall	29 ft 8½ in (9·08 m)
Tailplane span	47 ft 7¼ in (14·51 m)
Wheel track	28 ft 2½ in (8·60 m)
Wheelbase	46 ft 8½ in (14·24 m)

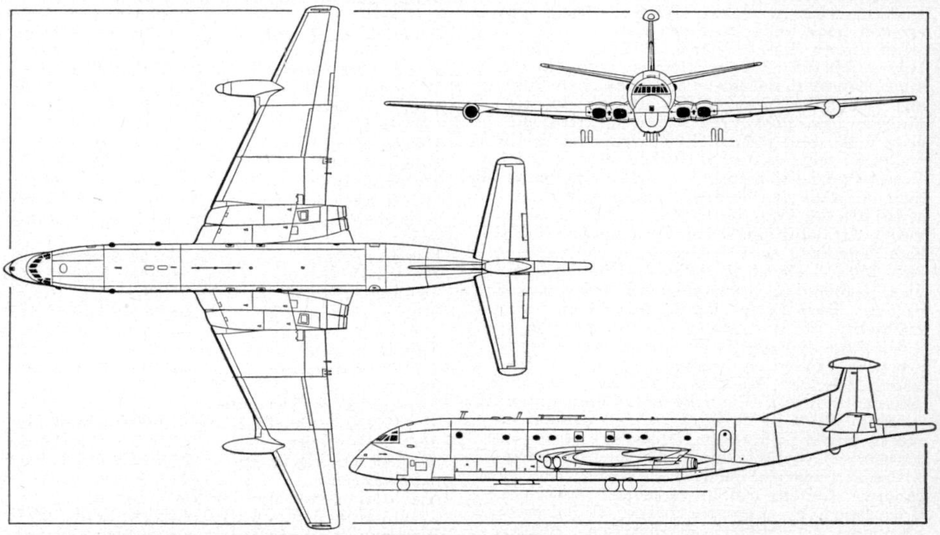

Hawker Siddeley Nimrod MR.Mk 1 four-turbofan maritime reconnaissance aircraft (*Pilot Press*)

Hawker Siddeley Nimrod MR. Mk 1 four-turbofan maritime reconnaissance aircraft of RAF Strike Command

DIMENSIONS, INTERNAL:
Cabin (including flight deck, navigation and ordnance areas, galley and toilet):
Length 88 ft 0 in (26·82 m)
Max width 9 ft 8 in (2·95 m)
Max height 6 ft 10 in (2·08 m)
Volume 4,384 cu ft (124·14 m³)
AREAS:
Wings, gross 2,121 sq ft (197·0 m²)
Ailerons (total) 60·6 sq ft (5·63 m²)
Trailing-edge flaps (total) 251·6 sq ft (23·37 m²)
Fin and rudder (above tailplane centreline) 118 sq ft (10·96 m²)
Dorsal fin 61 sq ft (5·67 m²)
Tailplane 435 sq ft (40·41 m²)
Elevators (including tabs) 135·3 sq ft (12·57 m²)
WEIGHTS:
Typical weight empty 92,000 lb (41,730 kg)
Max disposable payload 11,500 lb (5,216 kg)
Typical T-O weights 175,500 lb (79,605 kg) to 192,000 lb (87,090 kg)
PERFORMANCE:
Max speed for operational necessity, ISA + 20°C 500 knots (575 mph; 926 km/h)
Max transit speed, ISA + 20°C 475 knots (547 mph; 880 km/h)
Econ transit speed, ISA + 20°C 425 knots (490 mph; 787 km/h)
Min ground turning radius 89 ft 0 in (27·1 m)
Runway LCN at T-O weight of 182,000 lb (82,550 kg) 50
T-O run at 177,500 lb (80,510 kg) AUW, ISA at S/L 4,800 ft (1,463 m)
Unfactored landing distance at 120,000 lb (54,430 kg) AUW, ISA at S/L 3,500 ft (1,067 m)
Typical ferry range 4,500-5,000 nm (5,180-5,755 miles; 8,340-9,265 km)
Typical endurance 12 hr

HPA

HERTFORDSHIRE PEDAL AERONAUTS

ADDRESS:
48 Orchard Drive, Park Street, St Albans, Hertfordshire

OFFICERS:
M. S. Pressnell, BSc, CEng, AFRAeS (Chairman)
P. R. Sladden, BSc (Vice-Chairman)
R. E. Harris, BSc (Treasurer)
R. F. Lambert, BSc(Eng), CEng, AFRAeS (Hon Secretary)
Derrick G. Welch (Press Officer)

The Hertfordshire Pedal Aeronauts group was formed in September 1965, mainly from engineers of Handley Page Ltd, to design and build a man-powered aircraft to compete for the Kremer prizes. With the aid of a grant from the Royal Aeronautical Society, construction of the group's first aircraft began in April 1967 and was completed in mid-1972. Taxying trials began on 16 June 1972, and the aircraft (named Toucan, the pun being deliberate) made its first flight at Radlett on 23 December 1972. Three flights were made on that date, the longest of them covering 204 ft (62 m); the pilot on that occasion was Mr Bryan Bowen, with Mr Derek May as crewman. The Toucan was then grounded for a short time for minor modifications, including a reduction in outer-wing dihedral, before further flight trials were undertaken. On 3 July 1973, the same crew flew 2,100 ft (640 m) at a height of 15-20 ft (4·5-6 m).

This original version, now known as the Toucan Mk 1, was the largest man-powered aircraft then to have flown, and also the first two-man-powered aircraft to fly.

An extended-span version, designated Toucan Mk 2, was due to fly in 1974.

Toucan Mk 1 two-seat man-powered aircraft, built by HPA, in flight

HPA TOUCAN Mk 1

TYPE: Two-seat man-powered aircraft.

WINGS: Cantilever mid-wing monoplane. Wing section NACA 63_3618. Dihedral 6° (originally 10°) on outer panels. Incidence 8°. Spars have spruce booms and plywood webs. Balsa ribs. Leading-edges and other forward areas of wing are covered with expanded polystyrene. Melinex plastics film covering overall. Slot-lip ailerons, of similar construction to wings. No flaps. Yaw control by extreme movement of ailerons.

FUSELAGE: Braced structure of spruce and balsa, with Melinex plastics film covering. Crew supported on 30SWG L72 light alloy box framework.

TAIL UNIT: Cantilever structure of Melinex-covered balsa. One-piece non-reversible trimming tailplane, cable-operated through a spiral cam, for pitch control. Fin extends above and below fuselage. No rudder.

LANDING GEAR: Main wheel (with Raleigh RSW wheel and 16 × 2 in diameter balloon tyre, pressure 60 lb/sq in; 4·22 kg/cm²) and nosewheel on fuselage centreline, in tandem; outrigger wheels under wings, at ends of flat centre-section. Wheels do not retract, but are recessed into fuselage. Twin lightweight bicycle-type brakes.

POWER PLANT: Two-man crew provide, by pedalling, power via an alloy chain to a road wheel and a shaft to a two-blade fixed-pitch pusher propeller mounted aft of the tail unit. Propeller rpm 180 at cruise. For test purposes only, aircraft has been fitted with a Merco 60 model glow-plug engine, mounted under the wing.

ACCOMMODATION: Pilot (on rear seat) and second crewman, in tandem, under transparent lift-off canopy. Aperture in front fuselage fairing for breathing and cooling air.

INSTRUMENTS: Ultra-low-speed (0-26 knots; 0-30 mph; 0-48 km/h) ASI and yaw meter.

DIMENSIONS, EXTERNAL:
Wing span 123 ft 0 in (37·49 m)
Wing chord at root 6 ft 0 in (1·83 m)
Wing chord at tip 2 ft 4½ in (0·73 m)
Wing aspect ratio 25
Length overall 28 ft 8 in (8·74 m)
Height overall 13 ft 6 in (4·11 m)
Tailplane span 18 ft 0 in (5·49 m)
Wheelbase 4 ft 0 in (1·22 m)
Propeller diameter 10 ft 0 in (3·05 m)
AREAS:
Wings, gross 600·0 sq ft (55·7 m²)
Fin (total) 48·0 sq ft (4·46 m²)
Tailplane 54·0 sq ft (5·02 m²)
WEIGHTS AND LOADING:
Weight empty 210 lb (95 kg)
Max T-O weight 528 lb (239 kg)
Max wing loading 0·88 lb/sq ft (4·30 kg/m²)
PERFORMANCE:
Max never-exceed speed 29·5 knots (34 mph; 54·5 km/h)
Max cruising speed at 0-5 ft (0-1·5 m) 17·5 knots (20 mph; 32 km/h)
T-O run approx 100 ft (30 m)
Landing run approx 150 ft (46 m)

HPA TOUCAN Mk 2

The Toucan Mk 2 is essentially the Mk 1 aircraft with an extended wing span. It was expected to make its first flight in 1974.

Differences from the Toucan Mk 1 are as follows:

DIMENSIONS, EXTERNAL:
Wing span 139 ft 0 in (42·37 m)
Wing aspect ratio 27·76
AREA:
Wings, gross 696 sq ft (64·66 m²)
WEIGHT:
Max T-O weight approx 550 lb (249 kg)

ISAACS

JOHN O. ISAACS

ADDRESS:
42 Landguard Road, Southampton, Hampshire SO1 5DP
Telephone: Southampton 25853

Mr Isaacs designed and built a single-seat light aircraft, the airframe of which is basically a $\frac{7}{10}$th scale wooden version of that of the Hawker Fury fighter of the 1930s. Constructional drawings are available to amateur builders.

He has also designed and is building an all-wood scaled-down version of the Supermarine Spitfire single-seat fighter of the second World War.

Prototype Isaacs Fury II, with spinner removed, in flight off Land's End

ISAACS FURY II

Design of the Isaacs Fury was started in January 1961 and construction of the aircraft began in April 1961. It flew for the first time on 30 August 1963, powered by a 65 hp Walter Mikron engine (see 1965-66 *Jane's*).

In 1966-67 Mr Isaacs modified the Fury prototype to Mk II standard, by re-stressing the airframe and installing a 125 hp Lycoming O-290 engine, and flew the aircraft in this form in the Summer of 1967. It was acquired subsequently by Mr W. Raper of Wrotham, Kent, who made further refinements, including the addition of blister fairings over the engine cylinders. It is now owned by Mr D. Toms, and is based at Land's End airfield.

Several other Furies are under construction in the UK; three are known to be under construction in New Zealand; one in Jersey; and others in the USA and Canada. The first Canadian-built Fury II made a successful first flight on 23 October 1972 and was illustrated in the 1973-74 *Jane's*.

TYPE: Single-seat ultra-light biplane, stressed to 9*g* for aerobatics.

WINGS: Staggered biplane, with N type interplane strut each side and two N strut assemblies supporting centre-section of top wing above fuselage. Conventional wire bracing. Wing section RAF 28. Thickness/chord ratio 9·75%. Dihedral 1° on top wing, 3° 30′ on bottom wings. Incidence 3° 20′ on top wing, 3° 50′ on bottom wings. Spruce "plank" spars and Warren girder ribs, with fabric covering. Fabric-covered spruce ailerons on top wing only. No flaps.

FUSELAGE: Spruce structure, covered with birch plywood.

TAIL UNIT: Strut-braced spruce structure of "plank" spars and girder ribs, fabric-covered. Ground-adjustable tab in port elevator.

LANDING GEAR: Non-retractable type, with tailskid. Cross-axle tied to Vees with rubber-cord shock-absorption. Main wheels consist of WM.2 14 in (35·5 cm) rims spoked to home-made hubs. Dunlop tyre, size 3·25-14, pressure approx 33 lb/sq in (2·32 kg/cm²). Brakes optional.

POWER PLANT (prototype): One 125 hp Lycoming O-290 four-cylinder horizontally-opposed aircooled engine. Two-blade fixed-pitch propeller. Fuel tank in fuselage, aft of fireproof bulkhead, capacity 10 Imp gallons (45·5 litres) or 12 Imp gallons (54·5 litres).

ACCOMMODATION: Single seat in open cockpit. Small door above top longeron on port side opens downward. Space for light baggage aft of seat. Radio optional.

DIMENSIONS, EXTERNAL:
- Wing span:
  - upper 21 ft 0 in (6·40 m)
  - lower 18 ft 2 in (5·54 m)
- Wing chord (both, constant) 3 ft 6 in (1·07 m)
- Wing aspect ratio (upper) 6
- Length overall 19 ft 3 in (5·87 m)
- Height over tail (flying attitude) 7 ft 1 in (2·16 m)
- Tailplane span 7 ft 0 in (2·13 m)
- Wheel track 4 ft 2 in (1·27 m)

AREAS:
- Wings (total) 123·8 sq ft (11·50 m²)
- Ailerons (total) 10·56 sq ft (0·98 m²)
- Fin 2·90 sq ft (0·27 m²)
- Rudder 4·83 sq ft (0·45 m²)
- Tailplane 10·50 sq ft (0·97 m²)
- Elevators 5·70 sq ft (0·53 m²)

WEIGHTS AND LOADINGS (125 hp Lycoming):
- Weight empty 710 lb (322 kg)
- Max permissible T-O weight 1,000 lb (450 kg)
- Max wing loading 8·05 lb/sq ft (39·3 kg/m²)
- Max power loading 8·00 lb/hp (3·63 kg/hp)

PERFORMANCE (with uncowled 125 hp engine):
- Max level speed 100 knots (115 mph; 185 km/h)
- Stalling speed 33 knots (38 mph; 61 km/h)
- Max rate of climb at S/L 1,600 ft (488 m)/min

ISAACS SPITFIRE

Construction of this prototype $\frac{6}{10}$-scale Spitfire (G-BBJI) began in the Summer of 1969, and work on it continues. Construction is well advanced, and it was hoped to achieve completion by early 1975. The airframe is stressed to meet the aerobatic requirements of $+9g$ and $-4.5g$ (factored) as laid down in BCAR.

TYPE: Single-seat homebuilt sporting aircraft.

WINGS: Cantilever low-wing monoplane of semi-elliptical planform. Wing section NACA 2200 series. Thickness/chord ratio 13·2% at root, 6% at tip. Dihedral 6°. Incidence 2° at root, —30′ at tip. Two-spar wing built in one piece, mainly of spruce, with birch plywood covering, except for ailerons which are fabric-covered.

FUSELAGE: Spruce structure, covered with birch plywood.

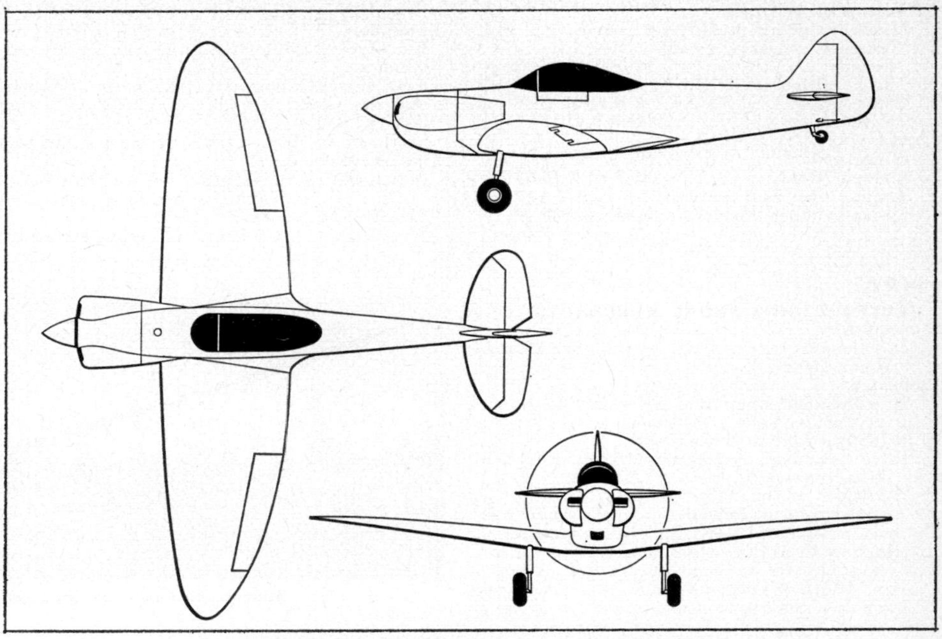

Isaacs Spitfire single-seat light sporting aircraft

TAIL UNIT: Cantilever structure of plywood-covered spruce.

LANDING GEAR: Non-retractable tailwheel type on prototype. Cantilever main legs.

POWER PLANT: One 100 hp Continental O-200 four-cylinder horizontally-opposed aircooled engine, or alternative engine in same category.

ACCOMMODATION: Single seat under blister-type transparent canopy.

DIMENSIONS, EXTERNAL:
- Wing span 22 ft 1½ in (6·75 m)
- Wing chord at root 5 ft 0 in (1·52 m)
- Length overall 19 ft 3 in (5·88 m)
- Height overall 5 ft 3 in (1·60 m)
- Tailplane span 6 ft 3½ in (1·92 m)
- Wheel track 5 ft 11 in (1·80 m)

AREA:
- Wings, gross 87 sq ft (8·08 m²)

WEIGHT AND LOADINGS:
- Max T-O weight 1,000 lb (454 kg)
- Max wing loading 11·5 lb/sq ft (56 kg/m²)
- Max power loading 10 lb/hp (4·54 kg/hp)

PERFORMANCE (estimated, at max T-O weight):
- Max level speed 130 knots (150 mph; 240 km/h)
- Stalling speed 49 knots (56·5 mph; 90 km/h)

JUPITER

PROJECT JUPITER (Royal Air Force Halton Man-Powered Aircraft)

ADDRESS:

Computer Squadron, RAF College, Cranwell, Sleaford, Lincolnshire NG34 8HB

Telephone: Cranwell (040 06) 201, extn T231

OFFICER IN CHARGE OF PROJECT:

Flt Lt J. Potter, MA, MSc, RAF

Under the direction of Flt Lt J. Potter a group of 100 staff and apprentices at No. 1 School of Technical Training, RAF Halton, built a single-seat man-powered aircraft named Jupiter. The original aircraft was designed in 1960 by Mr C. H. Roper of Woodford, Essex; but in 1969, when nearly completed, it was seriously damaged by fire. The remains were acquired in September 1970 by the Halton group, who rebuilt it completely.

The Jupiter made its first flight, of approx 200 yd (183 m), at RAF Benson on 9 February 1972, piloted by Flt Lt Potter. On 19 March 1972, also piloted by Flt Lt Potter, it made a 45-second flight of some 500 yd (457 m) at an altitude of 25-30 ft (7·5-9 m).

During the first half of 1972 the aircraft was flown regularly for distances of more than half a mile (0·4 nm; 0·8 km), including one flight (not officially observed) of 1,350 yd (1,234 m). On 29 June 1972 the Jupiter, flown by Flt Lt Potter, set up (subject to confirmation) new world and British national records for distance and duration by a man-powered aircraft. The flight lasted for 1 min 47·4 sec and covered a distance of 1,171 yd (1,071 m). The previous record distance, of 993 yd (908 m), was set up in the HMPAC Puffin in 1962.

Jupiter single-seat man-powered aircraft built by apprentices at RAF Halton

Towards the end of the 1972 trials, an electrical attitude indicator was fitted, which assisted precise pitch control and thus helped the pilot to fly steadily at the minimum power cruise conditions.

A full description of the Jupiter has appeared in the 1972-73 and 1973-74 *Jane's*. Work on the programme was suspended between August 1972 and November 1973 while the Project Officer completed post-graduate work. At Cranwell in the Spring of 1974 he formed a new man-powered aircraft group, and shortly afterwards acquired the Weybridge man-powered aircraft (which see). It was hoped to fly this in the Summer of 1974.

LIVERPOOL UNIVERSITY

UNIVERSITY OF LIVERPOOL, DEPARTMENT OF MECHANICAL ENGINEERING (Engineering Design and Production)

ADDRESS:

PO Box 147, Liverpool L69 3BX

Telephone: 051 709-6022

PROJECT DIRECTOR:

Dr Keith Sherwin

LIVERPUFFIN

Under the leadership of Dr Keith Sherwin a team of students at the University of Liverpool designed, built and flew a single-seat man-powered aircraft known as the Liverpuffin. It was developed from the salvaged remains of the HMPAC Puffin II man-powered aircraft (see 1963-64 *Jane's*), and was described and illustrated in the 1972-73 *Jane's*.

In April 1972 the aircraft was transported to the USA (where it remained in early 1974) for exhibition: first at Transpo '72 at Dulles Airport, Washington, and subsequently at the Franklin Institute, Philadelphia, and Princeton University.

LIVESEY

DAVID M. LIVESEY

ADDRESS:

"Rawhiti", 12 Kenwood Drive, Burwood Park, Walton on Thames, Surrey KT12 5AU

LIVESEY D.L.5

The D.L.5 has been designed for amateur construction by Mr David Livesey, who had begun construction of a prototype by the Spring of 1974. Design was started in 1971, to a "minimum aeroplane" concept that could be easily accomplished by unskilled constructors, using easily obtainable materials and a minimum of basic tools.

TYPE: Single-seat ultra-light homebuilt aircraft.

WINGS: Cantilever low-wing monoplane. Wing section NACA 632-615. Dihedral 7° from roots. Incidence 3°. Constant-chord wings. No sweep. Sitka spruce primary structure, covered mainly in marine plywood, with rigid foam filling. Trailing-edge plain flaps (optional) and ailerons of glassfibre, with foam filling. No tabs: trimming is by variable tension on control column.

FUSELAGE: Basic wooden keel structure of 11 in (279 mm) square constant section, bearing nacelle-type cockpit and tail surfaces. Spruce primary structure, with plywood skin.

TAIL UNIT: Cantilever surfaces, fin and tailplane

each having a central ply panel, to which are glued half-ribs with foam core infills. Conventional rudder and one-piece elevator, without tabs.

Landing Gear: Non-retractable tailwheel type. Main gear on single curved cantilever unit of laminated ash, moulded round a circular former and reinforced with glassfibre. Main wheels and tyres size 5·00-5, with go-kart hubs and brakes. Steerable tailwheel.

Power Plant: One 1,300-1,600 cc modified Volkswagen engine, driving a two-blade fixed-pitch wooden propeller. Single 8 Imp gallon (36 litre) fuel tank forward of instrument panel.

Accommodation: Single seat in open cockpit with large one-piece curved windscreen. Cockpit heated by air supply from engine.

Dimensions, external:
Wing span 25 ft 0 in (7·62 m)
Wing chord (constant) 4 ft 0 in (1·22 m)
Wing aspect ratio 6
Length overall 17 ft 0 in (5·18 m)
Width, wings removed 5 ft 3 in (1·60 m)
Height overall 6 ft 2 in (1·88 m)
Tailplane span 8 ft 0 in (2·44 m)
Wheel track 5 ft 6 in (1·68 m)
Wheelbase 12 ft 3 in (3·73 m)
Propeller ground clearance 1 ft 0 in (0·305 m)

Areas:
Wings, gross 100·0 sq ft (9·29 m^2)
Ailerons (total) 8·0 sq ft (0·74 m^2)
Trailing-edge flaps (if fitted, total) 6·6 sq ft (0·61 m^2)
Fin 3·8 sq ft (0·35 m^2)
Rudder 5·0 sq ft (0·46 m^2)
Tailplane 10·2 sq ft (0·95 m^2)
Elevator 6·8 sq ft (0·63 m^2)

Weights and Loadings:
Weight empty 450 lb (204 kg)
Max T-O weight 650 lb (295 kg)

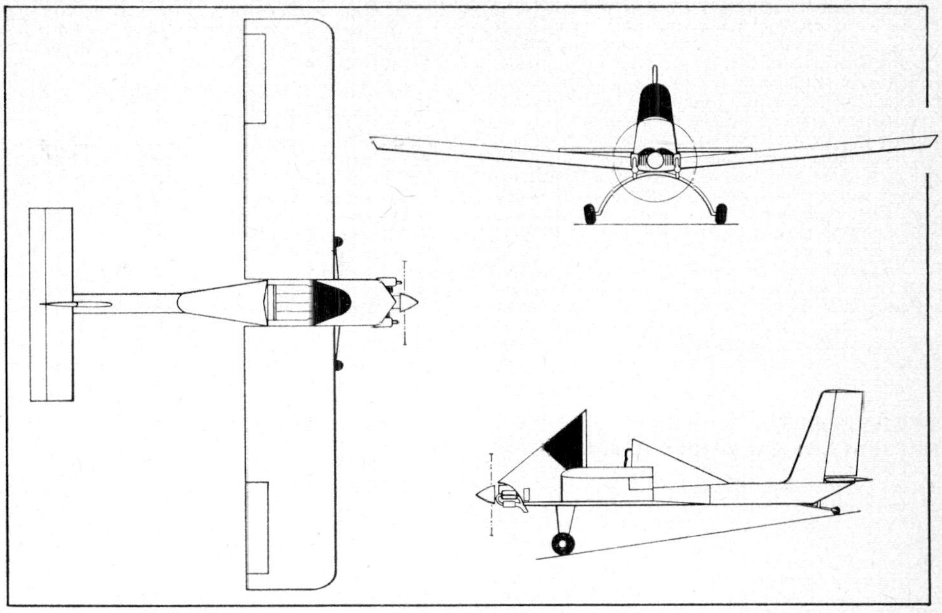

Livesey D.L.5 single-seat ultra-light homebuilt aircraft (*Roy J. Grainge*)

Max wing loading 6·5 lb/sq ft (31·7 kg/m^2)
Max power loading 16 lb/hp (7·26 kg/hp)

Performance (estimated, at max T-O weight):
Max never-exceed speed 104 knots (120 mph; 193 km/h)
Max cruising speed at S/L 85 knots (98 mph; 158 km/h)
Econ cruising speed at S/L 65 knots (75 mph; 121 km/h)
Stalling speed, without flaps 35 knots (40 mph; 64·5 km/h)
Max rate of climb at S/L 550 ft (168 m)/min

LOCKSPEISER

LOCKSPEISER AIRCRAFT LTD

Registered Office:
652 Grand Buildings, Trafalgar Square, London WC2 5HN
Telephone: 01-839 2777

Enquiries to:
Toad Hall, Highfield, Christhurst Lane, Shalford, Guildford, Surrey

Managing Director:
David Lockspeiser, AFRAeS, CEng

Company Secretary:
Christopher E. Bean, FCA

LOCKSPEISER LDA-01

Mr David Lockspeiser has designed a utility aeroplane known as the LDA, or Land Development Aircraft, the production version of which is intended for operation as a passenger, freight or vehicle transport, as an agricultural, ambulance, survey or firefighting aircraft, or for other duties.

The basic concept of the LDA is that of an "aerial Land-Rover", offering a wide variety of applications, low initial cost and economy of operation, and capable of being easily assembled, inspected and repaired. Many of the major components are interchangeable; the aircraft can carry a complete set of its own spares, including wings and foreplane, and is capable of licence assembly by semi-skilled labour in underdeveloped countries or in factories with limited facilities.

A 70% scale prototype, registered G-AVOR and known as the LDA-01, was flown for the first time by Mr Lockspeiser on 24 August 1971, when it took off in less than 300 ft (91 m).

Since that time the wing dihedral angle has been reduced from 8° to 3°; the height of the twin rudders has been increased by 9 in (23 cm), giving them horn balance as well as increased area and aspect ratio; in 1973 the original 80 hp Continental C85-12 engine was replaced by a 160 hp Lycoming O-320-D1A engine; the aircraft also now has a tricycle landing gear, with larger rear wheels, tyres and brakes than before, though the ability to fit two front wheels is retained.

A feature of the LDA-01 design is a flush-fitting removable ventral container which serves as an interchangeable "mission pack" and facilitates the quick conversion of the aircraft from one role to another. The landing gear is designed to permit easy manoeuvring of the aircraft on the ground, to pick up a pre-loaded container.

Aerodynamic studies, including further wind tunnel testing, have defined the proposed full-size LDA-1 as a 290 hp Lycoming-engined aircraft, with a disposable load of 1,985 lb (900 kg) and an NACA 2412 wing section. As an alternative to the removable "mission pack" of the LDA-01, the LDA-1 may have a side-loading double door on the port side and be fitted with a conventional tricycle landing gear, as shown in the accompanying three-view drawing.

The description which follows applies to the LDA-01 prototype with the O-320 engine prior to the start of flight testing in 1974. A description of it with the original 85 hp Continental engine appeared in the 1972-73 *Jane's*.

Type: Single-seat general utility aeroplane.

Wings: Canard surfaces, consisting of strut-braced main wings at rear and cantilever foreplane at front. Main wings and foreplane are of constant NACA 23012 section and constant chord. Dihedral 3° on main wings, 0° on foreplane. Main wing incidence 3°, foreplane 2° (adjustable on ground). Conventional all-metal alloy construction, with parallel main and rear spars and pop-riveted stressed-skin covering. Built in three basically identical and interchangeable units, two forming the main wings and the third being used as the foreplane. Each panel has four strongpoints at the centre. These serve as attachment points to the fuselage when the panel is positioned as a foreplane; when it is positioned as a port or starboard mainplane they serve as fin-post attachments or as lift-strut and picketing points. They can also be located on a "luggage rack" under the fuselage when a panel is carried as a spare by an aircraft of the same type. Main wings have trailing-edge flaps inboard and ailerons outboard; in addition to their normal function these can be operated in unison to perform the function of an elevator. The foreplane is fitted with a screw-jack-operated flap which, in addition to its conventional function, also doubles as a pitch trimmer. This system of control, as distinct from one employing an elevator on the foreplane, gives greater safety at the stall. The foreplane is fitted with leading-edge breaker strips and is designed to stall before the main wings. A single fence is fitted on each main wing, at approx one-third span, to contain vortex disturbance from the foreplane tips.

Fuselage: Conventional box-shaped structure, consisting of a space frame of $\frac{3}{4}$ in (1·9 cm) square 22 gauge T.35 steel, welded on a flat jig and covered with an easily removable fabric bag. Nosecone and cowling panels are of glassfibre. Ventral detachable payload container, which fits flush with the basic structure, is of welded steel and light alloy.

Tail Unit: Twin wire-braced fins and twin rudders, above and below main wings, of welded steel-tube construction with fabric covering.

Landing Gear: Non-retractable tricycle type,

Lockspeiser LDA-01 prototype general utility aeroplane (160 hp Lycoming O-320-D1A engine)

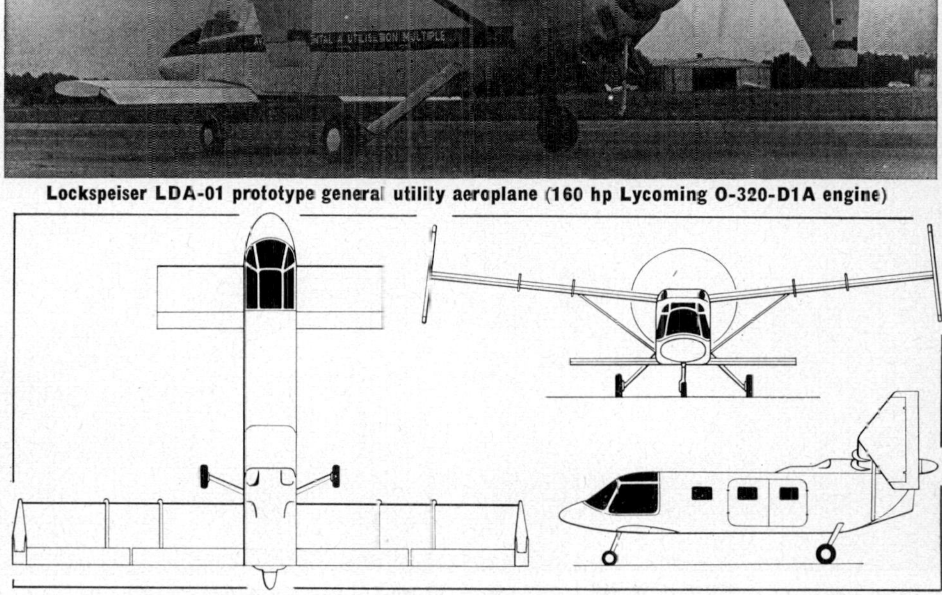

Proposed LDA-1 side-loading version of the Lockspeiser Land Development Aircraft (*Pilot Press*)

with cantilever main-gear legs at rear, inclined forwards. Rubber shock-absorbers. All wheels originally same size, with Goodyear 6·00-4 tyres, pressure 15 lb/sq in (1·05 kg/cm²) on front wheel and 25 lb/sq in (1·76 kg/cm²) on rear pair. Goodyear hydraulic brakes on rear wheels; Ackerman steering on front wheel.

Power Plant: One 160 hp Lycoming O-320-D1A four-cylinder horizontally-opposed aircooled engine, at rear of fuselage, driving a Hoffmann two-blade variable-pitch constant-speed metal pusher propeller. Fuel tank in fuselage, capacity 15·2 Imp gallons (69 litres). Refuelling point on starboard side.

Accommodation: Pilot only, in enclosed cabin. Sideways-opening canopy, hinged on port side. Removable payload container in lower centre of fuselage. Production version will have a gantry running along the roof for hoisting and carrying items not suitable for carriage in the ventral container, and access via the roof so that conventional loaders can be used when the aircraft is employed in an agricultural role.

Systems and Equipment: 12V electrical system. Murphy four-channel radio.

Dimensions, external:

Main wing span	29 ft 0 in (8·84 m)
Foreplane span	13 ft 0 in (3·96 m)
Main wing chord, constant	3 ft 9 in (1·14 m)
Foreplane chord, constant	3 ft 9 in (1·14 m)
Main wing aspect ratio	7
Foreplane aspect ratio	4·5
Length overall	22 ft 6 in (6·86 m)
Fuselage: Max width	3 ft 0 in (0·91 m)
Max depth	3 ft 6 in (1·07 m)
Height overall	10 ft 3 in (3·12 m)
Wheel track, inside of wheels	6 ft 8 in (2·03 m)
Wheelbase	9 ft 4 in (2·84 m)
Propeller diameter	5 ft 6 in (1·68 m)
Propeller ground clearance	2 ft 4 in (0·71 m)
Removable payload container:	
Length	6 ft 6 in (1·98 m)
Width	3 ft 0 in (0·91 m)
Depth	1 ft 3 in (0·38 m)

Dimension, internal:

Centre fuselage: total internal volume	60 cu ft (1·7 m³)

Areas:

Main wings, gross	108·8 sq ft (10·11 m²)
Foreplane, gross	48·8 sq ft (4·53 m²)

Weights and Loadings:

T-O weight, early test flights	1,300 lb (590 kg)
Max T-O weight	1,500 lb (680 kg)
Max wing loading	14·0 lb/sq ft (68·4 kg/m²)
Max power loading	9·4 lb/hp (4·26 kg/hp)

Performance:

No details available for publication

MARSHALL

MARSHALL OF CAMBRIDGE (ENGINEERING) LTD

Head Office and Works:
Airport Works, Cambridge CB5 8RX
Telephone: Cambridge (0223) 61133
Telex: 81208

Managing Director:
Sir Arthur Marshall, OBE

Commercial Director:
R. D. Horsbrough

Chief Engineer:
R. O. Gates

The Aircraft Division of this company (known as Marshalls Flying School Ltd until 1962) has specialised for many years in the modification, overhaul and repair of military and commercial aircraft, including the design and installation of interior furnishing for executive transports.

The company's design department is both CAA and MoD(PE) approved. As the appointed service and repair centre for the Grumman Gulfstream business transport aircraft, Marshall of Cambridge also has FAA approval covering most types of American aircraft. The company's conversion, modification and overhaul facilities, which include some of the largest heated hangars in England, with workshop support to full aircraft factory standard, have enabled it to undertake numerous major programmes of work on Viscounts, Britannias, Comets, VC10s, Canberras and a vast number of other civil and military aircraft.

In 1966, Marshall of Cambridge was appointed the designated centre for the Royal Air Force Hercules C.Mk 1 transport aircraft, being responsible for controlling all technical data, special modifications and development, together with the preparation of these aircraft and painting before delivery to the Service. In 1973, Marshall completed the conversion of an RAF Hercules C. Mk 1 to W. Mk 2 configuration.

During 1966 also, Marshall of Cambridge was selected to design and manufacture the variable-geometry nose and visor for the pre-production Concorde aircraft, and to design and manufacture the Concorde flight deck and associated electrics, and ground equipment.

Additions to the factory now include a separate hangar for specialised painting of the largest aircraft, and a sculpture milling shop for manufacture of major aircraft components.

In the Spring of 1974, Marshall was undertaking the conversion of two Hawker Siddeley Buccaneer Mk 2s for use as trials aircraft in connection with the Panavia MRCA development programme. This conversion involved aircraft design, airworthiness, avionics installation, monitoring displays, instrumentation, and the provision of required environmental systems for the aircraft and equipment.

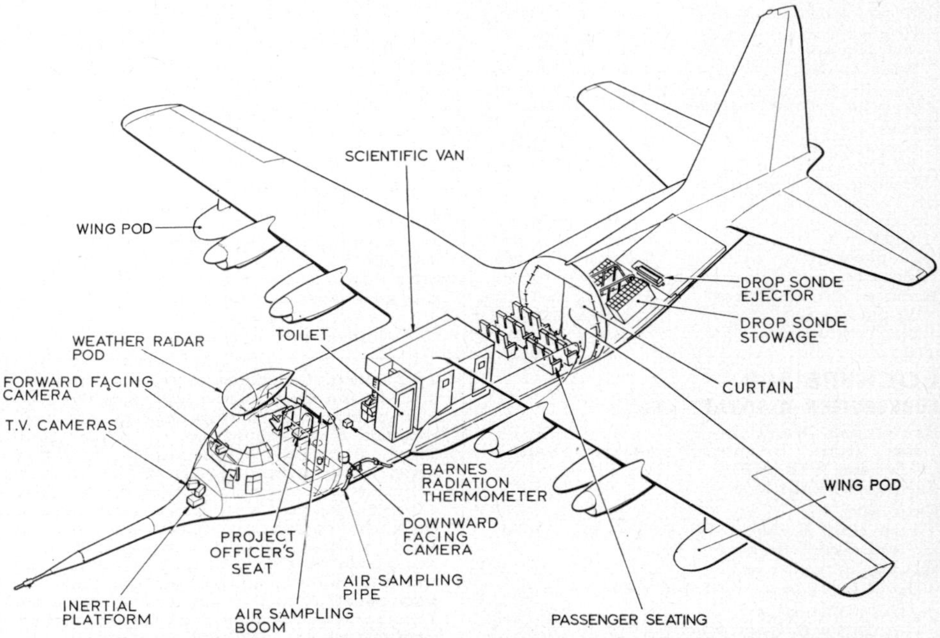

Cutaway drawing showing the essential internal and external equipment of the Hercules W. Mk 2

MARSHALL (LOCKHEED) HERCULES W. Mk 2 CONVERSION

The Hercules W. Mk 2 is a long-range meteorological aircraft, adapted by Marshall from a Lockheed Hercules C. Mk 1 (XV208) which has been procured by the Ministry of Defence for the RAF's Meteorological Research Flight at the RAE, Farnborough, Hampshire, to replace a Vickers Varsity used by the Flight.

The W. Mk 2 flew for the first time on 21 March 1973, and entered service on 3 January 1974. Among its early tasks will be participation in the multi-national Project GATE in 1975.

The outward appearance of the W. Mk 2 is shown in the accompanying photograph. Extensive modification to the nose of the aircraft, to incorporate an 18 ft (5·49 m) long nose boom, necessitated mounting the Ekco 280 weather radar scanner in a pod above the flight deck. Instrumentation pods can also be fitted on the wings, outboard of the engine nacelles.

The nose boom carries, at its forward end, a Rosemount instrumentation boom which comprises a pitot-static head and four yaw and pitch wind vanes. Further aft on the boom are mounted two total temperature sensors, that on the starboard side being capable of being heated electrically.

The interior of the aircraft is equipped with a variety of photographic and scientific equipment, including a closed-circuit television system to provide a remote display of the panorama in front of the aircraft, and a forward-facing and a downward-facing camera; an air sampling pipe, with removable instrument section; and an air sampling boom carriage upon which a variety of booms may be fitted. The instrument section of the pipe, and the boom on the carriage, may be changed while the aircraft is pressurised. A hygrometer installation, which is part of the air sampling system, is installed on the starboard side between fuselage stations 245 and 280, its sensor head being mounted on a blanking plate in a window aperture on the starboard side of the cargo hold. A Barnes radiation thermometer is installed below the cargo hold floor on the port side, at fuselage station 347. Absolute pressure sensors are mounted in the television camera compartment.

Hercules W. Mk 2, modified by Marshall of Cambridge from a C. Mk 1 for the RAF Meteorological Research Flight

In the central part of the fuselage hold is secured a mobile van approx 6 ft (1·83 m) high and 12 ft (3·66 m) long, equipped as a laboratory and fitted with an air-conditioning system. Mounted on two main wheels and a landing bogie, this van has two consoles fitted with altimeters, airspeed indicators, TV display units, a recorder control and display panel, and controls and indicators for all meteorological equipment.

Aft of the mobile van are rearward-facing seats for 15 passengers. A folding seat for a project officer is provided on the flight deck, behind the first pilot's seat.

To the rear of the passenger seats a curtain divides off the rear cargo compartment in which is located, on the underfuselage ramp/door, an operator's seat and stowage for sixty radio sondes. In the rear cargo door is installed a rotating, electrically controlled and hydraulically driven radio sonde ejection system.

Much of the instrumentation is of British manufacture. The dimensions, weights and performance of the Hercules C. Mk 1 (Lockheed C-130K), as given in the US section of this edition, apply generally also to the W. Mk 2, except in the following respects:

Landing Gear: Main-wheel tyres size 54 × 20·5-24·25, pressure 105 lb/sq in (7·38 kg/cm²). Nosewheel tyres size 37 × 13·5-18·5, pressure 60 lb/sq in (4·22 kg/cm²).

Dimensions, external:

Length overall, incl boom	120 ft 0 in (36·58 m)
Height overall	38 ft 5 in (11·71 m)

Weights:

Weight empty	70,678 lb (32,059 kg)
Weight empty, equipped	81,900 lb (37,149 kg)
Max normal T-O weight	155,000 lb (70,310 kg)
Max zero-fuel weight	128,800 lb (58,422 kg)
Max landing weight	130,000 lb (58,970 kg)

McCANDLESS—*see "Ekin"*

MITCHELL-PROCTER

The Mitchell-Procter team was dissolved in October 1968. The prototype Mitchell-Procter Kittiwake I light aircraft was acquired by Procter Aircraft Associates, and is described under that heading in this section.

MITCHELL

Dr C. G. B. MITCHELL

Address: "Clouds", 17 Tavistock Road, Fleet, Hampshire

Dr. C. G. B. Mitchell, formerly associated with Mr Roy G. Procter in Mitchell-Procter Aircraft Ltd, designed both the Kittiwake I and Kittiwake II light sporting aircraft.

Dr. Mitchell is no longer connected with either of these aircraft. Details of the Kittiwake I may be found under the Procter heading in this section. Rights in the Kittiwake II have passed to a company which was not yet ready to release details of its plans for the aircraft in mid-1974.

NIPPER

NIPPER KITS AND COMPONENTS LTD

Head Office:
East Midlands Airport, Castle Donington, Derby
Telephone: Derby 810621, extension 257
Managing Director: D. P. L. Antill

Complete world-wide rights for the Nipper aircraft were purchased from Belgium in 1966, and the aircraft was marketed in both factory-built form and in the form of several stages of kits for amateur construction.

The former Nipper Aircraft Ltd went into receivership in May 1971. Prior to this Mr D. P. L. Antill, formerly Managing Director of Nipper Aircraft Ltd, acquired all rights in the Nipper aircraft, and on 20 October 1971 formed a new company, Nipper Kits and Components Ltd, to supply spares for existing aircraft and to encourage and support amateur construction of the Nipper. Plans and an advisory service for amateur constructors continue to be available.

Nipper Aircraft Ltd developed a 24-channel solid-state transceiver for light aircraft, known as the Model 20/4 Nipper radio, which could be powered by dry batteries or from an aircraft's 14V DC supply. Radios and accessories are still available from the new company.

Nipper Mk III single-seat ultra-light aircraft (45 hp Rollason Ardem X engine)

NIPPER Mk III and IIIA

From 1966, many improvements were made to the standard factory-built Nipper Mk III, as detailed in previous editions of *Jane's*.

The Mk III Nipper is powered by a 1·5 litre Rollason Ardem engine; when fitted with the 1·6 litre Ardem engine it is known as the Mk IIIA. The Nipper may also be fitted with wingtip fuel tanks which almost double the standard fuel capacity. With these tanks fitted, but empty, the aircraft remains aerobatic. Flutter tests have been completed satisfactorily at speeds up to 156 knots (180 mph; 290 km/h).

Production of factory-built aircraft has ceased (see introductory copy), but Nippers are available in several stages of kits for amateur construction, and can be built at home for operation on a Permit to Fly basis.

Type: Single-seat ultra-light monoplane.

Wings: Cantilever shoulder-wing monoplane. Modified NACA 43012A wing section. Dihedral 5° 30′. Incidence 2°. All-wood one-piece single-spar structure, with plywood-covered leading-edge and overall fabric covering. Wooden ailerons with fabric covering. No flaps. Portion of port wing-root trailing-edge is made of light alloy and hinged, with built-in footrest, so that it can be folded down to assist access to cockpit. Wing is quickly removable, to permit aircraft to be towed behind a motor car.

Fuselage: Welded steel tube structure. Underfuselage fairing of glassfibre. Rear fuselage fabric-covered.

Tail Unit: Braced tailplane and elevators of wood construction. No fin. Rudder of steel-tube construction with fabric covering.

Landing Gear: Non-retractable tricycle type. Nieman transverse rubber-ring shock-absorbers. Steerable nosewheel. Continental tyres, size 4·00-4, pressure 26 lb/sq in (1·8 kg/cm²). Disc brakes.

Power Plant: Standard power plant is one 45 hp Rollason Ardem X four-cylinder horizontally-opposed aircooled engine, driving a two-blade fixed-pitch wooden propeller with glassfibre spinner. More powerful versions of Ardem engine are available optionally. Fuel tank between engine and cockpit, capacity 7·5 Imp gallons (34 litres). Provision for two 3·6 Imp gallon (16·5 litre) wingtip fuel tanks. Oil capacity 0·77 Imp gallons (3·5 litres).

Accommodation: Single seat under blown Perspex sliding canopy. Small baggage space aft of seat.

Electronics: Nipper, Pye Bantam, Bayside BEI 990P and various other radio installations available.

Dimensions:

Wing span (without tip-tanks)	19 ft 8 in (6·00 m)
Wing span (with tip-tanks)	20 ft 6 in (6·25 m)
Wing chord at c/l	4 ft 7¼ in (1·40 m)
Wing chord at tip	3 ft 7¼ in (1·10 m)
Wing aspect ratio	4·8
Length overall	15 ft 0 in (4·56 m)
Height overall	6 ft 3 in (1·91 m)
Tailplane span	7 ft 0 in (2·14 m)
Wheel track	4 ft 7 in (1·40 m)
Wheelbase	3 ft 8 in (1·13 m)

Areas:

Wings, gross	80·70 sq ft (7·50 m²)
Ailerons (total)	8·93 sq ft (0·83 m²)
Rudder	7·50 sq ft (0·70 m²)
Tailplane	9·30 sq ft (0·86 m²)
Elevators	5·80 sq ft (0·54 m²)

Weights and Loadings:

Weight empty	465 lb (210 kg)
Max T-O weight:	
Aerobatic	685 lb (310 kg)
Normal	750 lb (340 kg)
Max wing loading	9·3 lb/sq ft (45·4 kg/m²)
Max power loading	16·6 lb/hp (7·5 kg/hp)

Performance (at max T-O weight):

Max never-exceed speed	126 knots (146 mph; 235 km/h)
Max level speed at S/L: without tip-tanks	93 knots (107 mph; 173 km/h)
with tip-tanks	83 knots (96 mph; 155 km/h)
Max cruising speed (75% power) at S/L: without tip-tanks	81 knots (93 mph; 150 km/h)
Econ cruising speed at S/L	78 knots (90 mph; 145 km/h)
Stalling speed, power off	33 knots (38 mph; 61 km/h)
Max rate of climb at S/L	650 ft (198 m)/min
Service ceiling	12,000 ft (3,660 m)
T-O run	280 ft (85 m)
T-O to 50 ft (15 m)	1,110 ft (338 m)
Landing from 50 ft (15 m)	1,500 ft (457 m)
Landing run	360 ft (110 m)
Range with max internal fuel, 30 min reserve	173 nm (200 miles; 320 km)
Range with tip-tanks	390 nm (450 miles; 720 km)

ORD-HUME

ARTHUR W. J. G. ORD-HUME

Address:
14 Elmwood Road, Chiswick, London W4

Mr Ord-Hume was a co-founder and (until 1962) a director of Phoenix Aircraft Ltd, which was responsible for redesigning the pre-war Luton Minor and Luton Major aircraft. As an amateur aircraft constructor, he was one of the first in the UK to construct his own aircraft after the second World War and has since built or restored 11 aeroplanes.

Mr Ord-Hume also designed an all-wood ultra-light aircraft, the O-H 7, details of which were given in the 1972-73 *Jane's*.

ORD-HUME GY-201 MINICAB

Ord-Hume GY-20 Minicab, built and flown in the United Kingdom (*Air Portraits*)

The original two-seat GY-20 Minicab was designed in France by M Yves Gardan and flew for the first time in February 1949. Production Minicabs were built by Constructions Aéronautiques du Béarn, until that company's dissolution following the death of its Chief Engineer and General Manager. Mr Ord-Hume subsequently acquired original drawings for the GY-20 and redrafted them to make the aircraft suitable for amateur construction. They were first introduced in this revised form in 1963.

and amateur construction of Minicabs to the English plans, for which Mr Ord-Hume holds the exclusive rights, is now approved in the US, Canada, Australia, New Zealand and the UK. Several examples of the Minicab built to the English plans are currently flying in Australia, Canada, the US, the UK and Europe, and many more are under construction.

Owing to non-availability of Sitka spruce in Australia and New Zealand, aircraft built in that part of the world from local materials are unable to achieve the normal max T-O weight of 1,235 lb (560 kg). For these countries only, therefore, the design has been re-stressed for a max T-O weight of 1,400 lb (635 kg), for which weight a 100 hp Continental engine is mandatory. Australian DCA approval at this higher weight was anticipated in the Spring of 1974.

The standard Ord-Hume Minicab embodies as standard the so-called GY-201 and JB-01 modifications for increased fuel capacity and spar strengthening for increased AUW.

A full structural description of the Béarn GY-20 Minicab was given in the 1956-57 edition of *Jane's*; the following data apply to the Ord-Hume version:

TYPE: Two-seat light monoplane.

POWER PLANT: One 65 hp Continental four-cylinder horizontally-opposed aircooled engine. Modified plans also available for installation of 90 hp (or, in Australia and New Zealand, 100 hp) Continental engine. Fuel capacity 11 Imp gallons (50 litres) in fuselage tank aft of engine firewall. Provision for auxiliary fuel tank.

ACCOMMODATION: Side-by-side seating for two persons under forward-hinged canopy. Space for 25 lb (11 kg) of baggage aft of seats.

DIMENSIONS, EXTERNAL:
- Wing span: 25 ft 0 in (7·62 m)
- Length overall: 17 ft 10 in (5·44 m)
- Height overall: 5 ft 5 in (1·65 m)

AREA:
- Wings, gross: 107·6 sq ft (10·0 m²)

WEIGHTS AND LOADINGS:
- Weight empty: 595 lb (270 kg)
- Max T-O weight (except Australia and NZ): 1,235 lb (560 kg)
- *Max T-O weight (Australia and NZ only): 1,400 lb (635 kg)
- Max wing loading: 9·84 lb/sq ft (48·5 kg/m²)
- Max power loading: 16·28 lb/hp (7·38 kg/hp)

**awaiting confirmation in Spring 1974*

PERFORMANCE:
- Max level speed at S/L: 108 knots (124 mph; 200 km/h)
- Cruising speed at S/L: 97 knots (112 mph; 180 km/h)
- Stalling speed, flaps up: 41 knots (47 mph; 76 km/h)
- Max rate of climb at S/L: 680 ft (207 m)/min
- Service ceiling: 13,100 ft (4,000 m)
- Range with standard fuel: 404 nm (466 miles; 750 km)

PHOENIX

PHOENIX AIRCRAFT LTD

ENQUIRIES TO:
James L. Bainbridge, "Wykeham", St Nicholas Avenue, Cranleigh, Surrey
Telephone: Cranleigh (048 66) 3970

Phoenix Aircraft Ltd was formed in 1958 to produce light aircraft and engines. It acquired licence rights in the pre-war designs of Luton Aircraft Ltd and brought up to date the designs of the Luton Minor and Major. It also evolved a two-seat version of the former aircraft known as the Phoenix Duet (originally Minor III).

The company specialised in the supply of sets of plans and instructions, kits of materials and components for amateur constructors to build either the Luton Minor or Major, and the Currie Wot light biplane; and was appointed sole agent for the British Commonwealth for the supply of drawings of the French Jodel D.9 and D.11 and American EAA Biplane light aircraft.

In 1971 a new company, Phoenix Aircraft (Development and Holdings) Ltd, was formed to take over the assets of Phoenix Aircraft Ltd, which had a 51% holding in the new company; but the former company went into involuntary liquidation on 15 January 1972. Phoenix Aircraft Ltd, however, retains the rights in the Luton Major, Luton Minor and Duet, although for the time being the company has no staff and has ceased trading. Rights in the Currie Wot are held by Dr John Urmston, under whose name the aircraft is described in this section. Development of the Duet, which made a successful first flight in mid-1973, is under the direction of Gp Capt A. S. Knowles, who was closely associated with Phoenix Aircraft in the design of this aircraft.

PHOENIX (LUTON) L.A.4a MINOR

The first Luton Minor flew in 1936 and proved entirely suitable for construction and operation by amateur builders and pilots. Examples were built pre-war in England and other parts of the world.

In 1960, the design was modernised and re-stressed completely to the latest British Airworthiness Requirements, allowing for a power increase to 55 hp and a maximum flying weight of 750 lb (340 kg).

By December 1969, 149 sets of plans for the Luton Minor had been sold. Minors are under construction in many parts of the world, and several amateur-built examples have been completed and flown successfully since mid-1962. At least one of them, built in Australia by R. A. Pearman and H. Nash, has obtained a full Certificate of Airworthiness.

TYPE: Single-seat light monoplane.

WINGS: Strut-braced parasol monoplane. Wing section RAF 48. No dihedral. Wooden two-spar structure in two halves, attached to the fuselage by tubular centre-section pylons and braced by parallel lift struts of streamline-section steel tubing. Wings removable for ground transport and storage. Leading-edge and tips plywood-covered, remainder fabric-covered. Plain ailerons of wood construction, fabric-covered. No flaps.

FUSELAGE: Rectangular all-wood structure. Sides and bottom plywood-covered. Curved decking aft of cockpit fabric-covered.

TAIL UNIT: Cantilever all-wood structure, fabric-covered. Fixed fin. Aerodynamically-balanced rudder.

LANDING GEAR: Non-retractable tailwheel type with divided main legs of tubular-steel construction. Rubber disc shock-absorbers. Brakes and wheel fairings optional. Fully-castoring tailwheel.

POWER PLANT: One aircooled engine in the 37-65 hp range, driving a two-blade fixed-pitch wooden propeller. Fuel tank forward of cockpit, capacity 6·5 Imp gallons (29·5 litres). Provision for additional tanks in wings.

ACCOMMODATION: Single seat in open cockpit. Coupé top optional. Luggage space aft of seat.

DIMENSIONS, EXTERNAL:
- Wing span: 25 ft 0 in (7·62 m)
- Wing chord (constant): 5 ft 3 in (1·60 m)

Luton L.A.4a Minor (65 hp Continental A65-8F engine) built by Mr Tom Regan (*Air Portraits*)

- Wing aspect ratio: 5
- Length overall: 20 ft 9 in (6·32 m)

AREA:
- Wings, gross: 125 sq ft (11·6 m²)

WEIGHTS:
- Weight empty: 390 lb (177 kg)
- Max T-O weight: 750 lb (340 kg)

PERFORMANCE (37 hp Aeronca-JAP J.99 engine, at normal T-O weight):
- Max level speed at S/L: 74 knots (85 mph; 137 km/h)
- Max cruising speed: 65 knots (75 mph; 121 km/h)
- Stalling speed: 25 knots (28 mph; 45 km/h)
- Max rate of climb at S/L: 450 ft (137 m)/min
- T-O run: 240 ft (73 m)
- Landing run: 120 ft (36·5 m)
- Range with standard fuel: 155 nm (180 miles; 290 km)
- Range with auxiliary tanks: 340 nm (400 miles; 645 km)

PHOENIX PM-3 DUET

The Duet, known originally as the Minor III, is a version of the L.A.4a Minor with side-by-side seating for two persons, and was developed by Gp Capt A. S. Knowles in close association with Phoenix Aircraft Ltd. Differences from the L.A.4a include increased wing span, a 65 hp engine and an AUW of 1,140 lb (517 kg). The prototype (G-AYTT) made its first flight on 22 June 1973. No news of it has been received since that time.

LUTON L.A.5a MAJOR

The prototype Luton Major flew on 12 March 1939, and was demonstrated at several pre-war flying displays. Phoenix Aircraft Ltd brought the design up to date, including restressing to current British Airworthiness Requirements, and offered sets of plans to amateur constructors. A total of 53 sets had been sold by the end of 1969, and many Majors are being built throughout the world. The first was completed in February 1965 by S. G. and T. G. Stott of Wincanton, Somerset.

TYPE: Two-seat cabin monoplane.

WINGS: Braced high-wing monoplane wings of similar construction to those of Luton Minor. Vee bracing struts. RAF 48 wing section. Dihedral 2°. Wings fold back along sides of fuselage.

FUSELAGE: Wooden structure with plywood covering.

TAIL UNIT: Cantilever wooden structure, fabric-covered. Trim tab in elevators.

LANDING GEAR: Fixed tailwheel type with divided main legs. Rubber disc shock-absorbers. Fully-castoring tailwheel. Brakes optional.

POWER PLANT: Normally one 62 hp Walter Mikron Series II four-cylinder in-line aircooled engine. Alternative engines include 83 hp Agusta G.A.70, 55 hp and 65 hp Lycoming, 65 hp Continental A65 and 85 hp Continental C85. Fuel capacity 11 Imp gallons (50 litres).

ACCOMMODATION: Enclosed cabin seating two persons in tandem, with dual controls. Door on starboard side.

DIMENSIONS, EXTERNAL:
- Wing span: 35 ft 2 in (10·72 m)
- Wing chord (constant): 5 ft 3 in (1·60 m)
- Wing aspect ratio: 7·55
- Length overall: 23 ft 9 in (7·24 m)
- Width, wings folded: 11 ft 8 in (3·55 m)

Prototype Phoenix Duet side-by-side two-seat light aircraft evolved from the Luton Minor (*P. J. Bish*)

AREA:
Wings, gross 163 sq ft (15·14 m²)
WEIGHTS:
Weight empty 700 lb (318 kg)
Max T-O weight 1,300 lb (590 kg)
PERFORMANCE (at max T-O weight):
Max level speed at S/L 87 knots (100 mph; 161 km/h)
Max cruising speed 80 knots (92 mph; 148 km/h)
Stalling speed 33 knots (38 mph; 61 km/h)
Max rate of climb at S/L 650 ft (198 m)/min
T-O run 250 ft (76 m)
Landing run 160 ft (49 m)
Range with max fuel 260 nm (300 miles; 483 km)

Phoenix Luton L.A.5a Major two-seat high-wing cabin monoplane (*R. W. Cranham*)

PRACTAVIA

PRACTAVIA LTD

ADDRESS:
c/o *Pilot* magazine, The White House, Church Road, Claygate, Surrey

This company was formed to market plans and kits of a two-seat all-metal aerobatic aircraft known as the Sprite, the design of which was initiated by *Pilot* magazine.

PILOT SPRITE

Initial design work on the Sprite was started by the staff of *Pilot* magazine in early 1968, after consultation with many experienced light aircraft constructors, and a design and development panel was set up to foster the project. Detailed design began in November 1968. Mr Brian Healey, former editor of *Pilot* magazine, is project executive, and Mr Lloyd Jenkinson and Mr Peter Sharman, lecturers at Loughborough University, are the designers.

Two prototypes are being constructed by British Airways apprentices, under their instructor, Mr Bert Page, at London Airport. Plans are available for amateur construction, and more than 60 sets had been sold by early 1971. Kits are also being made available.

TYPE: Two-seat all-metal aerobatic aircraft, suitable for amateur construction.

WINGS: Cantilever low-wing monoplane. Wing section NACA 64315. Dihedral 6° on outer panels only. No incidence or sweepback. All-metal structure of aluminium alloy. Single main spar with light rear spar forming central torsion box. Skins and ribs of L72 alloy, extrusions of L65 alloy and spar caps of L73 alloy. Single-slotted full-span flaps and ailerons of L72 alloy. No trim tabs. Outer wing panels detachable for transit.

FUSELAGE: All-metal semi-monocoque structure, with no double curvature. Longerons of L65 aluminium alloy, skins and frames of L72 alloy. Sides and top curved to avoid drumming.

TAIL UNIT: Cantilever all-metal structure with swept vertical surfaces, constructed of L72 alloy. Fixed-incidence tailplane. Trim tab in centre of elevator trailing-edge, of one-third span; outer one-third on each side comprises anti-balance tab.

LANDING GEAR: Non-retractable tricycle type standard, although design of wing structure will allow for fitment of retractable gear as a future development. Shock-absorption by rubber in compression. Wheels and tyres size 5·00-5. Hydraulic disc brakes.

POWER PLANT: One 130 hp Rolls-Royce Continental O-240-A or 130 hp Franklin Sport 4B engine, driving a two-blade fixed-pitch propeller. Other suitable power plants include a 115 or 150 hp Lycoming or a 100 hp Rolls-Royce Continental engine. Fuel contained in one fuselage tank, aft of firewall, capacity 12 Imp gallons (54·5 litres). Wingtip fuel tanks optional, capacity 12 Imp gallons (54·5 litres) each. Maximum total capacity 36 Imp gallons (163·5 litres). Oil capacity 1 Imp gallon (4·5 litres).

ACCOMMODATION: Two seats, side by side, in enclosed cockpit, with rearward-sliding transparent canopy. Space for baggage behind seats.

SYSTEMS: Air-conditioning. Hydraulic system for brakes only. 12V electrical system.

ELECTRONICS AND EQUIPMENT: Radio, blind-flying instrumentation and special equipment to individual builder's requirements.

DIMENSIONS, EXTERNAL:
Wing span 24 ft 0 in (7·32 m)
Wing span over tip-tanks 27 ft 0 in (8·23 m)
Wing chord (constant) 4 ft 0 in (1·22 m)
Wing aspect ratio 6
Length overall 20 ft 0 in (6·10 m)
Width, outer panels removed 8 ft 0 in (2·44 m)
Height overall 8 ft 3 in (2·51 m)
Tailplane span 8 ft 0 in (2·44 m)
Wheel track 7 ft 6 in (2·29 m)
Wheelbase 4 ft 7 in (1·40 m)

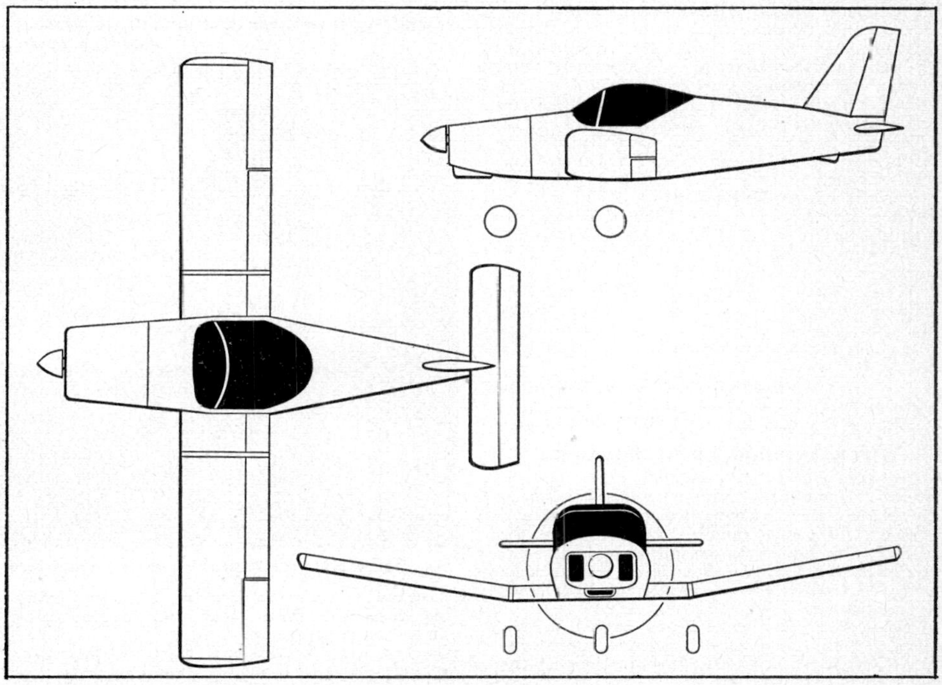

Pilot Sprite two-seat light aircraft for amateur construction (*Sherwood Designs Ltd*)

DIMENSIONS, INTERNAL:
Cabin:
Max width 3 ft 10 in (1·17 m)
Max height 3 ft 2 in (0·97 m)
AREAS:
Wings, gross 96 sq ft (8·92 m²)
Ailerons (total) 8 sq ft (0·74 m²)
Trailing-edge flaps (total) 16 sq ft (1·49 m²)
Fin 10·5 sq ft (0·98 m²)
Rudder 3·5 sq ft (0·33 m²)
Tailplane 18·0 sq ft (1·67 m²)
Elevator, including tabs 9·0 sq ft (0·84 m²)
WEIGHTS AND LOADINGS (100 hp engine):
Weight empty 850 lb (385 kg)
Max T-O weight 1,400 lb (635 kg)
Max wing loading 14·6 lb/sq ft (71·2 kg/m²)
Max power loading 12·2 lb/hp (5·53 kg/hp)
PERFORMANCE (estimated, at max T-O weight with 125 hp engine):
Max never-exceed speed 212 knots (245 mph; 394 km/h)
Max cruising speed 111 knots (128 mph; 206 km/h)
Stalling speed, flaps down 48 knots (55 mph; 89 km/h)

PROCTER

PROCTER AIRCRAFT ASSOCIATES LTD

HEAD OFFICE:
Greenball, Crawley Ridge, Camberley, Surrey GU15 2AJ
Telephone: Camberley 25566

DIRECTORS:
Roy G. Procter, CEng, AFRAeS
Roger H. White-Smith
Mrs Barbara Alexander

SECRETARY:
Mrs Ann Procter

This company changed its name from Mitchell-Procter Aircraft Ltd in November 1968. The latter company comprised a group of enthusiasts who designed and built the prototype Kittiwake I, plans and parts for which are available from Procter Aircraft Associates and also from Yorkshire Sailplanes Ltd (see "Sailplanes" section). Aircraft of this type are currently under construction in the UK, USA and Canada.

Procter Aircraft Associates has designed a larger aircraft on the same lines, known as the Petrel.

PROCTER PETREL

This two-seat light aircraft is based upon the Kittiwake I single-seat lightplane with increased wing area; it has many components in common with the single-seater and has also been optimised for glider towing. It is powered by a Rolls-Royce Continental O-240 engine and has a number of improvements and simplifications to the detail mechanical design, compared with Kittiwake I. Materials used throughout are L72 clad dural and S510 mild steel.

Construction of the prototype Petrel was originally subcontracted to Miles Aviation and Transport (R & D) Ltd, but construction was later transferred to Southborough Engineering Ltd of West Byfleet, Surrey. Following the liquidation of Phoenix (D & H) Ltd in 1972, completion of this aircraft was again suspended for a time, but arrangements have now been made for its completion by Yorkshire Sailplanes Ltd. In addition to the prototype, two other Petrels were under construction in 1974 by apprentice organisations.

It is intended to offer the Petrel for amateur construction.

TYPE: Two-seat light aircraft.

WINGS: Cantilever low-wing monoplane. Wing section NACA 3415. Dihedral 5° on outer panels. No sweepback or washout. All-metal constant-chord structure, built in three sections: centre-section, integral with fuselage, to which outer panels are each attached with three bolts. Single main spar at 30% chord and lightweight auxiliary spar at 66% chord. Multiple ribs, with no spanwise stiffeners. All-metal NACA slotted flaps and ailerons. Flaps are operated manually by pushrod and torque tube; ailerons are mass-balanced and operated by cables.

FUSELAGE: All-metal structure. Four-longeron basic structure, with flat sides and bottom and single-curvature top-decking. Integral wing centre-section forms seat and main landing gear attachment structure.

Tail Unit: Cantilever all-metal structure. Fixed-incidence tailplane. Manually-operated tab in starboard elevator. Control surfaces mass-balanced and operated by cables.

Landing Gear: Non-retractable tricycle type. Nose unit is an oleo-pneumatic strut with Goodyear 5·00-6 wheel, and is steerable from the rudder pedals. Main gear is of cantilever spring type, with Goodyear 6·00-6 wheels and hydraulic disc brakes. Tyre pressure (all) 25 lb/sq in (1·75 kg/cm^2).

Power Plant: One 130 hp Rolls-Royce Continental O-240 four-cylinder horizontally-opposed aircooled engine, driving a McCauley fixed-pitch two-blade metal propeller. Fuel capacity 16 Imp gallons (73 litres).

Accommodation: Two persons side by side, on seats with individually-adjustable backs. Baggage space aft of seats.

Equipment: Starter, generator and basic instrumentation. Radio, navigation and other equipment to builder's requirements.

Dimensions, external:

Wing span	30 ft 0 in (9·14 m)
Wing chord (constant)	4 ft 6½ in (1·38 m)
Wing aspect ratio	6·6
Length overall	20 ft 8 in (6·30 m)
Height overall	7 ft 8 in (2·33 m)
Tailplane span	9 ft 2 in (2·79 m)
Wheel track	7 ft 4 in (2·24 m)
Wheelbase	5 ft 0 in (1·52 m)

Areas: As Kittiwake I except:

Wings, gross	135·0 sq ft (12·5 m^2)
Tailplane	23·0 sq ft (2·14 m^2)
Elevators, incl tab	12·2 sq ft (1·13 m^2)

Weights:

Weight empty	1,137 lb (515·5 kg)
Max T-O weight	1,680 lb (762 kg)

Performance (at max T-O weight: estimated, based on measured performance of Kittiwake I):

Max level speed 113 knots (130 mph; 209 km/h)
Cruising speed 104 knots (120 mph; 193 km/h)
Max rate of climb at S/L 1,000 ft (305 m)/min

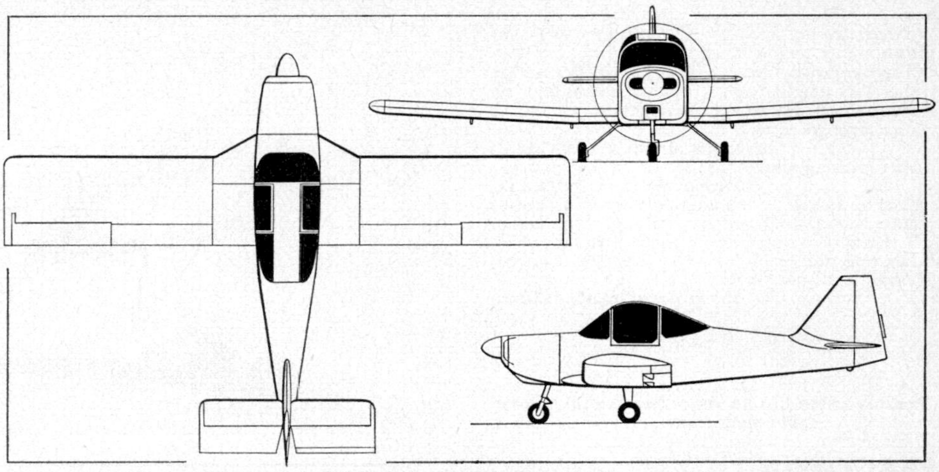

Procter Petrel two-seat light aircraft for amateur construction in its current form, with revised landing gear and other changes (*Pilot Press*)

MITCHELL-PROCTER KITTIWAKE I

The Kittiwake I was designed by Dr C. G. B. Mitchell to make full use of modern materials and constructional techniques while retaining a simplicity of design making it possible for the aircraft to be built without special tooling. The wings attach directly to the sides of the fuselage, so that construction and storage can take place in a normal-sized garage.

Design of the Kittiwake I was started in February 1965. Construction of the prototype (G-ATXN) began in June 1965 and it flew for the first time on 23 May 1967.

Dr Mitchell no longer retains the design rights in the Kittiwake I. Plans of the aircraft, and parts or kits for its construction, are currently available either from Procter Aircraft Associates or from Yorkshire Sailplanes Ltd, whose address is given in the "Sailplanes" section. Kittiwake Is are under construction in the UK, USA and Canada. One, built by the Royal Navy Air Engineering School at Gosport, Hampshire, has the serial number XW784 and was flown for the first time at RNAS Lee-on-Solent on 21 October 1971.

The details that follow apply to the prototype in its original form. It was later fitted with a Lycoming O-290 engine, in a glassfibre cowling, and a new nosewheel leg with rubber-in-compression shock-absorption.

The prototype Kittiwake I in its current form, with Lycoming O-290 engine (*Foto Hunter*)

Type: Single-seat glider-towing and sporting light aircraft.

Wings: Cantilever low-wing monoplane. Wing section NACA 3415. Dihedral 5°. Incidence 2° 30′. No washout. All-metal (L72 and L64 aluminium alloys) structure, with single main spar at 30% chord and light false spar at 66%. Multiple ribs. No spanwise stiffeners. Wings attach at fuselage sides; centre-section is integral with fuselage. All-metal (L72) NACA single-slotted flaps.

Fuselage: All-metal (L72) structure. Four-longeron box with flat sides and bottom, and single-curvature top decking. Integral wing centre-section forms seat and landing gear attachment structure.

Tail Unit: Cantilever all-metal (L72) structure. Fixed-incidence tailplane. Manually-operated tab on elevator.

Landing Gear: Non-retractable tricycle type. Cantilever spring-steel main legs. Nose unit has rubber torsion-bush shock-absorption. All three units fitted with Goodyear wheels and tyres, size 5·00-5. Tyre pressure 25 lb/sq in (1·75 kg/cm^2). Goodyear hydraulically-operated disc brakes on main wheels.

Power Plant: One 100 hp Rolls-Royce Continental O-200-A four-cylinder horizontally-opposed aircooled engine, driving a McCauley 69CM52 two-blade fixed-pitch metal propeller for general use or a McCauley 76CM36 two-blade fixed-pitch metal propeller for glider towing. Two integral leading-edge fuel tanks, total capacity 22 Imp gallons (100 litres). Space for 12 Imp gallon (54·5 litre) tank forward of instrument panel. Oil capacity 1·5 Imp gallons (7 litres).

Accommodation: Single seat under rearward-sliding canopy.

Electronics and Equipment: Prototype has full blind-flying instrumentation and electrical system, but no radio.

Dimensions, external:

Wing span	24 ft 0 in (7·32 m)
Wing chord (constant)	4 ft 6½ in (1·38 m)
Wing aspect ratio	5·28
Length overall	19 ft 7 in (5·97 m)
Height overall	7 ft 6 in (2·29 m)
Tailplane span	8 ft 0 in (2·44 m)
Wheel track	5 ft 9 in (1·75 m)
Wheelbase	5 ft 0 in (1·52 m)
Propeller diameter:	
69CM52	5 ft 9 in (1·75 m)
76CM36	6 ft 4 in (1·93 m)

Dimensions, internal:

Cabin: Length	5 ft 0 in (1·52 m)
Max width	2 ft 1 in (0·64 m)
Max height, seat to canopy	3 ft 5 in (1·04 m)

Areas:

Wings, gross	105 sq ft (9·75 m^2)
Ailerons (total)	9·30 sq ft (0·86 m^2)
Trailing-edge flaps (total)	14·00 sq ft (1·30 m^2)
Fin	14·30 sq ft (1·33 m^2)
Rudder	5·20 sq ft (0·48 m^2)
Tailplane	21·50 sq ft (2·00 m^2)
Elevators, incl tab	10·00 sq ft (0·93 m^2)

Weights and Loadings (prototype, incl some test equipment):

Weight empty, equipped	910 lb (413 kg)
Max T-O and landing weight	1,350 lb (612 kg)
Max aerobatic weight	1,250 lb (567 kg)
Max wing loading	12·9 lb/sq ft (63·0 kg/m^2)
Max power loading	13·5 lb/hp (6·12 kg/hp)

Performance (at AUW of 1,250 lb; 567 kg):

Max level speed 114 knots (131 mph; 211 km/h)
Max cruising speed (75% power) 106 knots (122 mph; 196 km/h)
Max rate of climb at S/L:
69CM52 propeller 850 ft (259 m)/min
76CM36 propeller 1,050 ft (320 m)/min
Range at 100 knots (115 mph; 185 km/h) 425 nm (490 miles; 790 km)
Range at 80 knots (92 mph; 148 km/h) 468 nm (540 miles; 870 km)

ROLLASON

ROLLASON AIRCRAFT AND ENGINES LTD

Head Office and Works:
Brighton, Hove and Worthing Joint Municipal Airport, Shoreham-by-Sea, Sussex BN4 5FJ
Telephone: Shoreham-by-Sea 62680

Aircraft Sales Department:
Redhill Aerodrome, Surrey
Telephone: 682-2212

Directors:
Norman Jones (Chairman)
F. R. Hounslow (General Manager)
D. M. J. Jones (Sales Manager and Secretary)

Well known for many years as an aircraft and engine overhaul, repair and sales organisation, this company entered the manufacturing field in 1957. It built under licence the French Druine Turbulent, and has also undertaken conversion of the Ardem 4CO2 engine for this aircraft. The company also manufactures Turbulent components to assist amateur constructors of this aircraft.

The Rollason-built Druine Condor two-seat light aircraft is now Rollason's main production type.

Development and construction of the Luton Beta light aircraft continues.

ROLLASON (DRUINE) D31 and D31A TURBULENT

The standard Rollason-built D31 Turbulent is powered by a 45 hp 1,500 cc Ardem (Volkswagen) Mk IV or 55 hp Ardem Mk V four-cylinder horizontally-opposed aircooled engine, the conversion of which from a standard motor car engine is undertaken by Rollason. It operates with a Special Category C of A and is available to order.

The first Rollason-built Turbulent flew on 1 January 1958, and 30 had been built by 1 January 1974.

In general, the Rollason-built Turbulent is similar to the standard Druine design. Main differences are that it has wheels of slightly greater size and a tailskid instead of a tailwheel, although a tailwheel is available optionally.

The fitting of optional wheel spats and a sliding canopy increases speed by about 7 knots (8 mph; 13 km/h).

Rollason built a slightly modified (D31A) Turbulent, registered G-ARLZ, which was awarded a full Certificate of Airworthiness in 1966. Only major modification is an improved wing main spar, but D31As intended for C of A approval must be fitted, like G-ARLZ, with a CAA-approved 45 hp 1,500 cc Ardem Mk X engine, with which the max T-O weight is 700 lb (316 kg). Three D31As had been built by 1 January 1974.

The following data apply to the D31 Turbulent:

TYPE: Single-seat ultra-light monoplane.

WINGS: Cantilever low-wing monoplane. Wing section NACA 23012. Dihedral 4°. Incidence 3° 40′. All-wood two-spar structure of grade A spruce and birch ply, covered with fabric. Built-in leading-edge slot on outer 45% of half-span. Wooden slotted ailerons with fabric covering. No flaps or tabs.

FUSELAGE: Conventional rectangular four-longeron spruce structure with domed decking. Plywood-covered.

TAIL UNIT: Cantilever wooden structure of spruce and plywood. Fixed surfaces plywood-covered, movable surfaces fabric-covered. No tabs.

LANDING GEAR: Non-retractable two-wheel type, with tailskid or (optionally) tailwheel. Rollason compression-spring shock-absorbers. Dunlop or Goodyear main wheels and tyres, size 14 × 3, pressure 28 lb/sq in (1·97 kg/cm²). Vespa mechanical brakes. Wheel spats, taxying and parking brakes available optionally. Skis or floats may be fitted as alternative to wheels.

POWER PLANT: One 45 hp Rollason Ardem 4CO2 Mk IV or 55 hp Ardem Mk V four-cylinder horizontally-opposed aircooled engine, driving a Permali type Z/3405 two-blade fixed-pitch wooden propeller. Fuel tank in fuselage forward of cockpit, capacity 8·5 Imp gallons (39 litres). Oil capacity 0·5 Imp gallons (2·25 litres).

ACCOMMODATION: Pilot only, in open cockpit. Sliding canopy available as optional extra. Baggage locker aft of seat, capacity 25 lb (11·5 kg).

ELECTRONICS: Provision for lightweight radio. VHF radio has been fitted to some aircraft.

DIMENSIONS, EXTERNAL:

Wing span	21 ft 7 in (6·58 m)
Wing chord (constant)	3 ft 11 in (1·90 m)
Wing aspect ratio	5·4
Length overall	17 ft 6 in (5·33 m)
Height overall	5 ft 0 in (1·52 m)
Tailplane span	6 ft 6 in (1·98 m)
Wheel track	5 ft 8 in (1·73 m)
Wheel/tailskid base	12 ft 6 in (3·81 m)

AREAS:

Wings, gross	77·5 sq ft (7·20 m²)
Ailerons (total)	7·6 sq ft (0·71 m²)
Fin	1·3 sq ft (0·12 m²)
Rudder	3·2 sq ft (0·30 m²)
Tailplane	6·1 sq ft (0·57 m²)
Elevators	5·5 sq ft (0·51 m²)

WEIGHTS AND LOADINGS:

Weight empty	395 lb (179 kg)
Max T-O weight	620 lb (281 kg)
Max wing loading	8·0 lb/sq ft (39·1 kg/m²)
Max power loading	13·8 lb/hp (6·25 kg/hp)

PERFORMANCE (with 45 hp engine, at max T-O weight):

Max never-exceed speed	108 knots (125 mph; 202 km/h)
Max level speed	95 knots (109 mph; 176 km/h)
Max cruising speed	87 knots (100 mph; 161 km/h)
Econ cruising speed	76 knots (87 mph; 141 km/h)
Stalling speed	39 knots (44 mph; 71 km/h)
Max rate of climb at S/L	450 ft (137 m)/min
Service ceiling	9,000 ft (2,740 m)
T-O run from grass	310 ft (95 m)
T-O to 50 ft (15 m) from grass	410 ft (125 m)
Landing from 50 ft (15 m) on grass	320 ft (98 m)
Landing run on grass	170 ft (52 m)
Range with max fuel, normal allowances	217 nm (250 miles; 400 km)

ROLLASON (DRUINE) D62 CONDOR

Rollason has developed a slightly modified version of the Druine D62 Condor two-seat light aircraft, which has flown in the following forms:

D62. Prototype Rollason Condor (G-ARHZ) with 90 hp Continental C90 engine. Described in 1972-73 *Jane's*.

D62A. Pre-production version. Two built, with 100 hp Rolls-Royce Continental O-200-A engine. Described in 1972-73 *Jane's*.

D62B. Standard production version. Two examples, G-ASRB and G-ASRC, built originally as D62As and modified into D62Bs. G-ASRB flew in December 1964, G-ASRC in January 1965. Two more (G-ATAU and G-ATAV) flew in August and October 1965 respectively. These first four aircraft were without flaps, but subsequent D62Bs are fitted with flaps.

D62C. Version powered by 130 hp Rolls-Royce Continental O-240 engine. Specially equipped for glider towing, with wingtip endplates, larger wheels (7·00-6·5) and raised cockpit canopy. The first D62C flew in March 1970; by March 1974 nine had been produced, four of them by converting existing D62Bs.

A total of 51 Condors of all marks had been delivered by the Spring of 1974, and flight development has resulted in clearances for spinning.

Further planned developments will include a version with removable auxiliary fuel tanks for long-distance ferrying or touring.

The following details refer to the D62B:

TYPE: Two-seat light monoplane.

WINGS: Cantilever low-wing monoplane. Dihedral 3° 10′ on top of spar booms. Incidence 5° at root, 3° 6′ at tip. All-wood two-spar structure of grade A spruce and birch ply, covered with fabric. Frise ailerons and flaps of wooden construction, with fabric covering.

FUSELAGE: Conventional rectangular four-longeron spruce structure with domed decking. Plywood-covered.

TAIL UNIT: Cantilever wooden structure of spruce and plywood. Fin plywood-covered. Tailplane and movable surfaces fabric-covered. Controllable tab in port elevator. Fixed tab on rudder.

LANDING GEAR: Non-retractable tailwheel type. Jodel-Rollason cantilever main legs. Dunlop main wheels and tyres, size 6·00-6·5, pressure 24 lb/sq in (1·69 kg/cm²). Lockheed hydraulic twin-shoe brakes.

POWER PLANT: One 100 hp Rolls-Royce Continental O-200-A four-cylinder horizontally-opposed aircooled engine, driving a Permali type Z 5793 two-blade fixed-pitch propeller. Fuel tank in fuselage forward of cabin, capacity 15 Imp gallons (68 litres). Oil capacity 1 Imp gallon (4·5 litres).

ACCOMMODATION: Pilot and passenger side by side in enclosed cabin. Door on each side, hinged to open upward. Baggage shelf at rear of cabin.

ELECTRONICS AND EQUIPMENT: Blind-flying instrumentation and full night-flying equipment standard. Narco radios to customer's requirements.

DIMENSIONS, EXTERNAL:

Wing span	27 ft 6 in (8·38 m)
Wing chord at root	5 ft 7½ in (1·72 m)
Wing chord at tip	3 ft 3½ in (1·00 m)
Wing aspect ratio	6·3
Length overall	22 ft 6 in (6·86 m)
Height overall	7 ft 9 in (2·36 m)
Tailplane span	10 ft 8 in (3·25 m)
Wheel track	10 ft 6 in (3·20 m)
Wheelbase	16 ft 6 in (5·03 m)
Cabin doors:	
Height	2 ft 3 in (0·69 m)
Width	2 ft 2 in (0·66 m)
Height of sill above wing	1 ft 3 in (0·38 m)

AREAS:

Wings, gross	119·8 sq ft (11·13 m²)
Ailerons (total)	9·8 sq ft (0·91 m²)
Trailing-edge flaps (total)	18·4 sq ft (1·71 m²)
Fin	5·8 sq ft (0·54 m²)
Rudder, incl tab	6·6 sq ft (0·61 m²)
Tailplane	15·3 sq ft (1·42 m²)
Elevators, incl tab	9·75 sq ft (0·91 m²)

WEIGHTS AND LOADINGS:

Weight empty	920 lb (417 kg)
Max T-O weight	1,475 lb (670 kg)
Max wing loading	14·6 lb/sq ft (71·3 kg/m²)
Max power loading	14·75 lb/hp (6·70 kg/hp)

PERFORMANCE (at max T-O weight):

Max never-exceed speed	146 knots (169 mph; 272 km/h)
Max level speed	110 knots (127 mph; 204 km/h)
Max cruising speed	100 knots (115 mph; 185 km/h)
Econ cruising speed	93 knots (107 mph; 172 km/h)
Stalling speed	40 knots (46 mph; 74 km/h)
Max rate of climb at S/L	610 ft (185 m)/min
Service ceiling	12,000 ft (3,650 m)
T-O run from grass	410 ft (125 m)
T-O to 50 ft (15 m) from grass	580 ft (177 m)
Landing from 50 ft (15 m) on grass	450 ft (137 m)
Landing run on grass	280 ft (58 m)
Range with max fuel and max payload, normal allowances	285 nm (328 miles; 528 km)

ROLLASON/LUTON GROUP BETA

Development and construction of the Beta was taken over by Rollason from the Luton Group (see 1966-67 *Jane's*) and the following versions are now available:

Beta B1. 65 hp Continental A65 engine. Prototype, first flown on 21 April 1967, later converted to B2 standard. Further development included fitting of a new streamlined cowling and nose extension, which added approx 8·7 knots (10 mph; 16 km/h) to the max level speed. This was done to assist the promotion of Formula I racing in the UK, and is now standard in production aircraft.

Beta B2. 90 hp Continental C90 engine. Construction of three B2s started by Rollason during 1968; first of these (G-AWHV) flew for first time on 15 February 1969. Production B2s have a cleaner canopy line, shorter main gear with wheel fairings and improved interior and exterior finish. Four B2s fitted with spring steel main landing gear legs, mounted on the fuselage forward of the wing main spar. With these modifications, the aircraft is designated B2(A); height overall is reduced to 4 ft 9 in (1·45 m) and wheel track to 4 ft 0 in (1·22 m). The modification, which is officially approved, is primarily a racing one and adds 5 knots (6 mph; 10 km/h) to the max and cruising speeds.

Beta B4. With 100 hp Continental O-200 engine, starter/generator and radio.

Rollason had sold 55 sets of Beta plans to

Rollason D62C Condor light aircraft, showing wingtip endplates (*Peter Basden*)

Rollason Beta B2 single-seat sporting monoplane (90 hp Continental engine)

amateur constructors by the beginning of 1974, and had supplied parts and materials for others to amateur constructors.

TYPE: Single-seat ultra-light sporting aircraft.

WINGS: Cantilever low-wing monoplane. Wing section NACA 23012. Dihedral 7° on outer wings. Incidence 3° at root, 1° at tip. All-wood torsion-box structure in three sections: constant-chord centre-section and detachable tapered outer wings. Single main spar and auxiliary rear spar. Plywood-covered. Mass-balanced wooden ailerons, covered with fabric aft of spar. Optional plain flaps of similar construction to ailerons. No tabs.

FUSELAGE: All-wood semi-monocoque structure with frames, stringers and plywood covering. Welded steel-tube engine mounting.

TAIL UNIT: Cantilever all-wood structure with sweptback vertical surfaces. Fin and tailplane plywood-covered; rudder and elevators fabric-covered aft of spar.

LANDING GEAR: Non-retractable tailwheel type, with steerable tailwheel. Cantilever main legs, with rubber-in-compression shock-absorption. Goodyear or Dunlop tyres, size 5·00-5, pressure 28 lb/sq in (1·97 kg/cm²). Goodyear brakes. Main-wheel fairings standard.

POWER PLANT: One four-cylinder horizontally-opposed aircooled engine (details under individual model descriptions), driving a two-blade fixed-pitch propeller. One metal fuel tank in fuselage aft of firewall, capacity 10·5 Imp gallons (48 litres).

ACCOMMODATION: Single seat in enclosed cockpit. Side-hinged canopy. Baggage compartment aft of seat.

DIMENSIONS, EXTERNAL:
Wing span 20 ft 5 in (6·22 m)
Wing chord at root 3 ft 9 in (1·14 m)
Wing chord at tip 2 ft 3½ in (0·70 m)
Wing aspect ratio 6·15
Length overall 16 ft 8 in (5·08 m)
Width with outer wings removed for road transport 6 ft 8 in (2·03 m)
Height overall 5 ft 0 in (1·52 m)
Tailplane span 6 ft 0 in (1·83 m)
Wheel track 4 ft 10 in (1·47 m)
Wheelbase 11 ft 2 in (3·40 m)

AREAS:
Wings, gross 66 sq ft (6·13 m²)
Ailerons (total) 9·6 sq ft (0·89 m²)
Trailing-edge flaps (optional; total) 5·4 sq ft (0·50 m²)
Fin 2·9 sq ft (0·27 m²)
Rudder 4·4 sq ft (0·41 m²)
Tailplane 10·5 sq ft (0·98 m²)
Elevators 5·0 sq ft (0·46 m²)

WEIGHTS AND LOADINGS:
Weight empty:
B1, B2 575 lb (260 kg)
Max T-O and landing weight 850 lb (385 kg)
Max wing loading 13·1 lb/sq ft (64·0 kg/m²)
Max power loading:
B1 13·1 lb/hp (5·94 kg/hp)

PERFORMANCE (at max T-O weight; data for B4 estimated):
Max never-exceed speed 195 knots (225 mph; 362 km/h)
Max level speed at S/L:
B1 129 knots (149 mph; 240 km/h)
B2 182 knots (210 mph; 338 km/h)
B4 160 knots (185 mph; 298 km/h)
Max cruising speed at 7,000 ft (2,150 m):
B1 122 knots (140 mph; 225 km/h)
B2, B4 144 knots (166 mph; 267 km/h)
Stalling speed:
B1, B2, without flaps 53 knots (60 mph; 97 km/h)
Max rate of climb at S/L:
B1 1,000 ft (305 m)/min
B2, B4 1,800 ft (548 m)/min
Service ceiling:
B1 15,000 ft (4,575 m)
B2 20,000 ft (6,100 m)
T-O run, without flaps:
B1 900 ft (274 m)
B2 600 ft (183 m)
Landing run, without flaps:
B1, B2 1,000 ft (305 m)
Range with max fuel at max cruising speed, no reserves:
B1 217 nm (250 miles; 400 km)
B2 277 nm (320 miles; 515 km)

SCOTTISH AVIATION

SCOTTISH AVIATION LTD (Member company of the Laird Group)

HEAD OFFICE AND WORKS:
Prestwick International Airport, Ayrshire KA9 2RW
Telephone: Prestwick (0292) 79888
Telex: 77432

OTHER WORKS:
Cumnock

LONDON OFFICE:
60 Buckingham Palace Road, London SW1W 0RR
Telephone: (01) 730-5187

DIRECTORS:
J. A. Gardiner (Chairman)
T. D. M. Robertson, CBE (Deputy Chairman)
H. W. Laughland (Managing Director)
W. L. Denness (Programme Director)
D. McConnell (Commercial)
G. S. Nelson
Dr W. G. Watson (Technical)
J. R. Woods (Works)

SECRETARY: W. L. Denness, CA

WORKS ACCOUNTANT: J. Baird

MARKETING MANAGER: R. L. Porteous

Scottish Aviation Ltd was formed in 1935 to provide opportunities for employment in the various branches of aviation in Scotland. In doing so, the company developed Prestwick International Airport and on it established an aircraft design and manufacturing industry.

The company's five-seat Prestwick Pioneer first flew in 1950 and was followed by the 16-seat Twin Pioneer in 1955. A total of 150 aircraft of these types were built. Details can be found in earlier editions of *Jane's*.

Scottish Aviation's activities are currently concentrated on five main programmes. These are: maintenance and modification of CF-104 Starfighter aircraft for the Canadian Armed Forces; production of components for, and overhaul of, Rolls-Royce piston and jet engines; manufacture of major airframe components, including major fuselage sections for the Lockheed C-130 Hercules and doors for the Lockheed TriStar; production and development of Bulldog training aircraft; and production and development of the Jetstream light transport and aircrew training aircraft.

The company's design facilities are CAA- and AQD-approved, and maintenance services are covered by CAA, AQD and FAA approvals.

A separate division of the company, Scottish Air Engine Services, also based at Prestwick Airport, undertakes the overhaul of Pratt & Whitney, Avco Lycoming and Teledyne Continental piston engines.

The Bulldog Series 120 and Jetstream Series 200 are now in full production. In addition, Scottish Aviation offers product support facilities for the Beagle Pup, B.206 and Basset.

SCOTTISH AVIATION BULLDOG SERIES 120

RAF designation: Bulldog T.Mk 1

The Bulldog originated in 1968 as a military trainer version of the Beagle Pup. It differs substantially, however, from the Pup in having a fully-transparent canopy, increased wing span, and strengthened construction to allow full aerobatic operation.

First flight of the Beagle-built prototype (G-AXEH) was made on 19 May 1969. A second prototype (G-AXIG), completed by Scottish Aviation, was flown on 14 February 1971, and a third airframe was completed for static and fatigue tests.

All versions ordered so far are basically similar, except for the equipment fitted. The first production Bulldog, completed by Scottish Aviation, flew for the first time on 22 June 1971 and received full ARB certification on 30 June 1971. The first 98 production Bulldogs were of the Series 100 version (78 Model 101, 15 Model 102 and five Model 103); production of these was as described in the 1972-73 *Jane's*. In addition the second prototype was refurbished, issued with a Normal category C of A, and delivered to a private owner under the designation Model 104.

Production is now concentrated on the Series 120 version, which features an increased fully-aerobatic weight, semi-aerobatic ability at max T-O weight, and a deepened instrument panel. Full CAA certification of the Series 120 was awarded on 12 February 1973.

By Spring 1974 orders for the Bulldog Series 120 were as follows:

Model 121. For Royal Air Force, by whom it is designated **T. Mk 1.** Total of 130 on order, of which the first (XX513) flew for the first time on 30 January 1973 and was delivered to the A & AEE at Boscombe Down on 20 February 1973. The first RAF training unit to equip with Bulldogs was No. 2 FTS, at Church Fenton, in 1973.

Model 122. For Ghana Air Force. Six ordered. Delivery completed September 1973.

Model 123. For Nigerian Air Force. Twenty ordered. Delivery began in January 1974.

Model 124. One aircraft (G-ASAL) used as company demonstration aircraft.

Model 125. For Jordanian Royal Academy of Aeronautics. Five ordered, for delivery in mid-1974.

The following description applies to the Bulldog Series 120:

TYPE: Two/three-seat primary trainer.

WINGS: Cantilever low-wing monoplane. Wing section NACA 63_2615. Dihedral 6° 30′. Incidence 1° 9′ at root. Conventional single-spar

Scottish Aviation Bulldog T. Mk 1 (Model 121) of the Royal Air Force

Scottish Aviation's Model 124 Bulldog demonstrator, equipped with underwing rocket pods

Scottish Aviation Jetstream T. Mk 1 of the Royal Air Force (two 996 ehp Turboméca Astazou XVI D turboprop engines)

two-cell riveted stressed-skin structure of light alloy. Electrically-operated slotted trailing-edge flaps and slotted ailerons of similar construction. Fixed tab in starboard aileron.

FUSELAGE: Conventional light alloy stressed-skin semi-monocoque structure.

TAIL UNIT: Cantilever two-spar light alloy stressed-skin structure. Fixed-incidence tailplane. Full-span trim tab in starboard elevator. Manually-operated trim tab in rudder. Fixed ventral fin.

LANDING GEAR: Non-retractable tricycle type, with single wheel on each unit. Steerable nosewheel with Lockheed oleo-pneumatic shock-absorber and Goodyear wheel and tyre, size 5·00-5, pressure 40 lb/sq in (2·81 kg/cm²). Main gear has Lockheed oleo-pneumatic shock-absorbers and Goodyear wheels and tyres, size 6·00-6, pressure 30 lb/sq in (2·11 kg/cm²). Goodyear hydraulic disc brakes on main wheels. Optional ski landing gear.

POWER PLANT: One 200 hp Lycoming IO-360-A1B6 four-cylinder horizontally-opposed air-cooled engine, driving a Hartzell HC-C2YK-4/C7666A-2 two-blade constant-speed metal propeller. Four removable metal fuel tanks, two in each wing, with total usable capacity of 32 Imp gallons (145·5 litres). Refuelling point on top of each wing. Oil capacity 2 Imp gallons (9 litres).

ACCOMMODATION: Enclosed cabin seating pilot and co-pilot or trainee side by side with dual controls, with space at rear for observer's seat or up to 120 lb (54 kg) of baggage. Rearward-sliding jettisonable transparent canopy. Cabin heated and ventilated.

SYSTEMS: Heat exchanger for cabin heating. Hydraulic system, pressure 450 lb/sq in (31·65 kg/cm²), for main-wheel brakes only. Vacuum-type pneumatic system available optionally. 24V DC power from engine-driven alternator and 24V 25Ah storage battery. No oxygen or de-icing systems.

ELECTRONICS AND EQUIPMENT: Radio to individual customer's requirements; panel can accommodate dual VHF and navaids. Blind-flying instrumentation and dual controls standard. Glider towing attachment optional.

ARMAMENT: Standard aircraft is unarmed, but has provision for installation of four underwing hardpoints to which can be attached various weapon loads if required. Maximum underwing load 640 lb (290 kg).

DIMENSIONS, EXTERNAL:
Wing span 33 ft 0 in (10·06 m)
Wing chord at root 4 ft 11¼ in (1·51 m)
Wing chord at tip 2 ft 9¾ in (0·86 m)
Wing aspect ratio 8·4
Length overall 23 ft 3 in (7·09 m)
Height overall 7 ft 5¾ in (2·28 m)
Tailplane span 11 ft 0 in (3·35 m)
Wheel track 6 ft 8 in (2·03 m)
Wheelbase 4 ft 7 in (1·40 m)
Propeller diameter 6 ft 2 in (1·88 m)
Propeller ground clearance 8 in (20 cm)

DIMENSIONS, INTERNAL:
Cabin: Length 6 ft 11 in (2·11 m)
Max width 3 ft 9 in (1·14 m)
Max height 3 ft 4 in (1·02 m)

AREAS:
Wings, gross 129·4 sq ft (12·02 m²)
Ailerons (total) 9·4 sq ft (0·87 m²)
Trailing-edge flaps (total) 13·95 sq ft (1·30 m²)
Vertical tail surfaces (total) 22·72 sq ft (2·11 m²)
Horizontal tail surfaces (total) 27·50 sq ft (2·55 m²)

WEIGHTS AND LOADINGS:
Basic empty weight 1,420 lb (644 kg)
Max T-O weight:
normal and semi-aerobatic 2,350 lb (1,066 kg)
fully aerobatic 2,238 lb (1,015 kg)
Max wing loading 18·15 lb/sq ft (88·6 kg/m²)
Max power loading 11·75 lb/hp (5·33 kg/hp)

PERFORMANCE (at max T-O weight):
Max never-exceed speed (structural) 210 knots (241 mph; 389 km/h)
Max level speed at S/L 130 knots (150 mph; 241 km/h)
Max cruising speed at 4,000 ft (1,220 m) 120 knots (138 mph; 222 km/h)
Econ cruising speed at 4,000 ft (1,220 m) 105 knots (121 mph; 194 km/h)
Stalling speed, flaps down 54 knots (62 mph; 100 km/h) EAS
Max rate of climb at S/L 1,006 ft (306 m)/min
Service ceiling 17,000 ft (5,180 m)
Min ground turning radius 24 ft 0 in (7·32 m)
T-O run 920 ft (280 m)
T-O to 50 ft (15 m) 1,440 ft (439 m)
Landing from 50 ft (15 m) 1,190 ft (363 m)
Landing run 500 ft (153 m)
Range with max fuel 540 nm (621 miles; 1,000 km)
g limits:
semi-aerobatic +4·4; —1·8
fully aerobatic +6; —3

SCOTTISH AVIATION JETSTREAM SERIES 200
RAF designation: Jetstream T. Mk 1

The original H.P. 137 Jetstream was designed and developed between 1966 and 1970 by Handley Page Ltd, and was described in *Jane's* at that time. A number of Handley Page-built Jetstream Mk 1s are in service with operators in Canada, France, the UK and the USA.

The current version of the Jetstream is the Series 200. This model originated with Handley Page, was developed subsequently by Jetstream Aircraft Ltd (see 1972-73 *Jane's*), and is now in production by Scottish Aviation. A full UK type certificate in the transport category (passenger), for operations in performance group C, was awarded on 22 November 1972.

Scottish Aviation will offer the civil Jetstream Series 200 for sale in due course, but at present production is concentrated upon the 26 military Series 200s (Model 201) for the Royal Air Force, ordered in February 1972. The first of these (XX 475) flew for the first time on 13 April 1973, eight months after construction began, and was delivered to the A & AEE, Boscombe Down, in July 1973. The RAF aircraft, which are designated Jetstream **T. Mk 1**, are generally similar to the civil Series 200 except for having Astazou XVI D engines, "eyebrow" windows above the flight deck, and different instrumentation and avionics installations. They will be used as trainers for pilots of multi-engined aircraft, superseding the Vickers Varsity in this role. The third production Model 201 was delivered to the Central Flying School at Little Rissington and on 12 December 1973 to No. 5 FTS. Five Jetstreams had been delivered to No. 5 FTS by mid-1974, when the first course was due to begin training on the type.

TYPE: Twin-turboprop light transport and aircrew trainer.

WINGS: Cantilever low-wing monoplane. Wing section NACA 63A418 at root, NACA 63A412 at tip. Dihedral 7° from roots. Incidence 2° at root, 0° at tip. Sweepback 0° 34′ at quarter-chord. Aluminium alloy fail-safe structure. Aluminium alloy manually-operated Frise-type ailerons. Hydraulically-operated aluminium alloy double-slotted flaps, with glassfibre slat. No slots or leading-edge flaps. Trim tab in each aileron. Goodrich pneumatic rubber-boot de-icing system for leading-edges.

FUSELAGE: Conventional aluminium alloy semi-monocoque fail-safe structure, with chemically-milled skin panels. Fully pressurised.

TAIL UNIT: Cantilever two-spar aluminium alloy structure. Fixed-incidence tailplane. Manually-operated control surfaces. Trim tabs

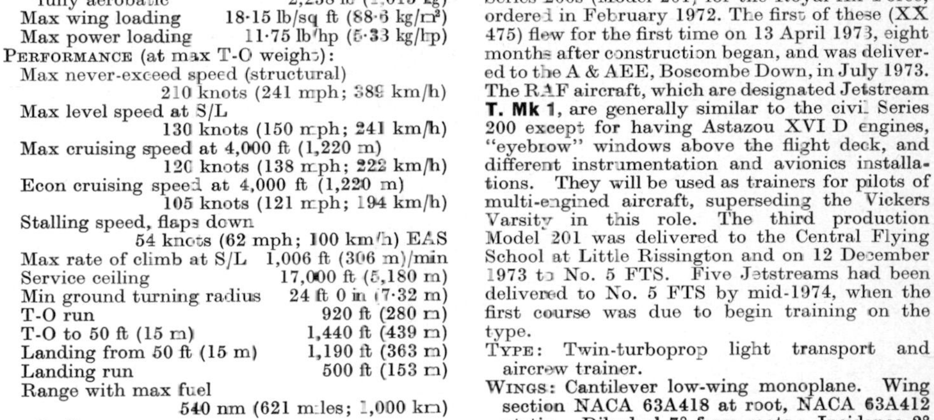

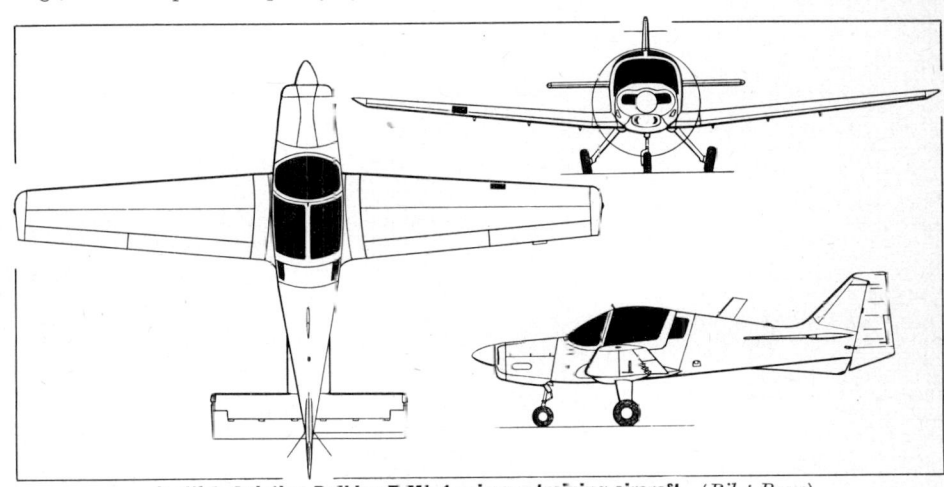

Scottish Aviation Bulldog T.Mk 1 primary training aircraft (*Pilot Press*)

in rudder and each elevator. Goodrich pneumatic rubber-boot de-icing system for leading-edges.

LANDING GEAR: Retractable tricycle type, with nosewheel steering. Hydraulic retraction, main wheels inward into wings, twin nosewheels forward. Electro-Hydraulics oleo-pneumatic shock-absorbers. Dunlop wheels, tyres and disc brakes on all units. Main-wheel tyres size 28 × 9·00-12, pressure 34 lb/sq in (2·39 kg/cm^2). Nosewheel tyres size 6·00-6, pressure 57 lb/sq in (4·01 kg/cm^2). No brake cooling. Dunlop anti-skid units.

POWER PLANT: Two 996 ehp Turboméca Astazou XVI C2 turboprop engines (Astazou XVI D in Model 201), each driving a Hamilton Standard Type 23LF-371 three-blade variable- and reversible-pitch fully-feathering metal propeller. Fuel in integral tank in each wing, total capacity 384 Imp gallons (461 US gallons; 1,745 litres). Refuelling point on top of each outer wing. Oil capacity 2·09 Imp gallons (2·51 US gallons; 9·50 litres) per engine. Hot-air de-icing of engine air intakes, electrical de-icing of propellers and spinners.

ACCOMMODATION: Two seats side by side on flight deck, with provision for dual controls, though aircraft can be approved (subject to local regulations) for single-pilot operation. Main cabin can be furnished in executive layout for up to 12 passengers, with individual swivel seats and settees and full galley and toilet facilities; or in airliner layout, for up to 18 passengers at 29 in (74 cm) seat pitch, with toilets but no galley. RAF T. Mk 1 accommodation includes two pilot seats, four passenger seats, and toilet. Universal seat rails fitted. Downward-opening passenger door, with integral stairs, at rear of cabin on port side. Emergency exit over wing on starboard side. Baggage compartment in rear of cabin, aft of main door. Entire accommodation pressurised, heated, ventilated and air-conditioned. Windscreen de-iced electrically.

SYSTEMS: AiResearch dual air cycle air-conditioning system, using engine bleed air. Cabin pressure control, with rate of pressure control which can be set to either 6·5 or 5·5 lb/sq in (0·46 or 0·39 kg/cm^2). Duplicated hydraulic systems, each of 2,000 lb/sq in (140 kg/cm^2) pressure, for actuation of flaps, landing gear, brakes and nosewheel steering. Electrical system includes two 3kW 28V DC starter/generators, two 7·5kVA 208V AC 400Hz alternators and two 25Ah batteries, all of Plessey manufacture. Piped oxygen system, with optional dropout masks.

ELECTRONICS AND EQUIPMENT: All instruments and avionics to customer's specification. Equipment in RAF T. Mk 1 includes Sperry STARS flight director system, Decca VHF nav/com system, Collins 51-series VOR/ILS with marker beacon, Marconi-Elliott AD 370B ADF, Decca DME, Bendix M.4C autopilot, Cossor 1520 transponder and S. G. Brown intercom.

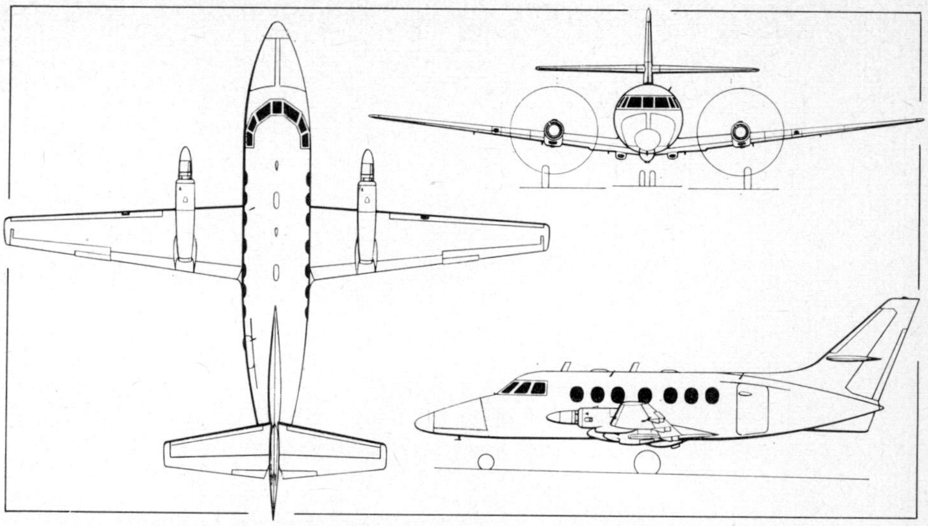

Scottish Aviation Jetstream twin-turboprop light transport (*Pilot Press*)

DIMENSIONS, EXTERNAL:
- Wing span: 52 ft 0 in (15·85 m)
- Wing chord at root: 7 ft $2\frac{1}{2}$ in (2·19 m)
- Wing chord at tip: 2 ft $7\frac{1}{4}$ in (0·80 m)
- Wing aspect ratio: 10
- Length overall: 47 ft $1\frac{1}{2}$ in (14·37 m)
- Length of fuselage: 43 ft 5 in (13·20 m)
- Height overall: 17 ft $5\frac{1}{2}$ in (5·32 m)
- Fuselage: Max diameter: 6 ft 6 in (1·98 m)
- Tailplane span: 21 ft 8 in (6·60 m)
- Wheel track: 19 ft 6 in (5·94 m)
- Wheelbase: 15 ft 1 in (4·60 m)
- Propeller diameter: 8 ft 6 in (2·59 m)
- Passenger door:
  - Height: 4 ft 8 in (1·42 m)
  - Width: 2 ft 10 in (0·86 m)
- Emergency exit:
  - Height: 3 ft 0 in (0·91 m)
  - Width: 1 ft 10 in (0·56 m)

DIMENSIONS, INTERNAL:
- Cabin, excluding flight deck:
  - Length: 24 ft 0 in (7·32 m)
  - Max width: 6 ft 1 in (1·85 m)
  - Max height: 5 ft 11 in (1·80 m)
  - Floor area: 90 sq ft (8·35 m^2)
  - Volume: 638 cu ft (18·05 m^3)
- Baggage compartment volume (according to layout): 40-60 cu ft (1·13-1·70 m^3)

AREAS:
- Wings, gross: 270 sq ft (25·08 m^2)
- Ailerons, aft of hinge line (total): 16·4 sq ft (1·52 m^2)
- Trailing-edge flaps (total): 35·0 sq ft (3·25 m^2)
- Fin: 33·3 sq ft (3·09 m^2)
- Rudder, incl tab: 23·0 sq ft (2·14 m^2)
- Tailplane: 55·25 sq ft (5·13 m^2)
- Elevators, incl tabs: 27·55 sq ft (2·56 m^2)

WEIGHTS AND LOADINGS:
- Manufacturer's weight empty: 7,562 lb (3,430 kg)
- Max payload: 3,814 lb (1,730 kg)
- Max T-O and landing weight: 12,566 lb (5,700 kg)
- Max ramp weight: 13,228 lb (6,000 kg)
- Max zero-fuel weight: 12,250 lb (5,556 kg)
- Max wing loading: 46·3 lb/sq ft (226 kg/m^2)
- Max power loading: 6·3 lb/ehp (2·86 kg/ehp)

PERFORMANCE (at max T-O weight, ISA):
- Max never-exceed speed (structural): 300 knots (345 mph; 555 km/h)
- Max level and cruising speed at 10,000 ft (3,050 m): 245 knots (282 mph; 454 km/h)
- Econ cruising speed at 15,000 ft (4,575 m): 234 knots (269 mph; 433 km/h)
- Stalling speed, flaps down: 76 knots (87·5 mph; 141 km/h)
- Max rate of climb at S/L: 2,500 ft (762 m)/min
- Rate of climb at S/L, one engine out: 600 ft (182 m)/min
- Service ceiling: 26,000 ft (7,925 m)
- Service ceiling, one engine out: 10,000 ft (3,050 m)
- Min ground turning radius: 25 ft 0 in (7·62 m)
- T-O run: 1,900 ft (579 m)
- T-O to 50 ft (15 m): 2,500 ft (762 m)
- Landing from 50 ft (15 m): 2,310 ft (702 m)
- Range with max fuel, reserves for 45 min hold and 5% total fuel: 1,200 nm (1,380 miles; 2,224 km)

SHIELD

G. W. SHIELD, BSc

ADDRESS:
Grammar School, Maple Road, Mexborough, Yorkshire WR, S64 9SD
Telephone: Mexborough 2108

SHIELD XYLA and XYPHI

Mr Shield has designed and built a single-seat light aircraft named Xyla. Construction began in the Autumn of 1968, and the aircraft (G-AWPN) made its first flight on 30 October 1971. A Restricted category C of A was awarded on 10 July 1972.

Since test flying began, the tail-surface hinge lines have been sealed with fabric, to prevent leakage of air; the fin has been relocated at an angle of 4° to port; and a 5 ft 3 in (1·60 m) diameter three-blade wooden propeller has been fitted. The aircraft otherwise remains as described in the 1972-73 *Jane's*, except for the performance figures which follow.

By early 1974 Mr Shield had completed a series of calculations and sketches for a new aircraft designated Xyphi. This will be generally similar to the Xyla, but with semi-elliptical wings and tail surfaces, flaps and, possibly, retractable landing gear. Construction had not begun at that time.

Shield Xyla single-seat homebuilt light aircraft (*W. Hill*)

DIMENSIONS, EXTERNAL (Xyla):
- Wing span: 27 ft 3 in (8·31 m)
- Length overall: 19 ft 3 in (5·87 m)
- Height overall: 5 ft 4 in (1·63 m)

WEIGHT AND LOADING (Xyla):
- Max T-O and landing weight: 1,000 lb (454 kg)
- Max wing loading: 8·0 lb/sq ft (39·1 kg/m^2)
- Max power loading: 10·9 lb/hp (4·94 kg/hp)

PERFORMANCE (Xyla, at max T-O weight):
- Max never-exceed speed: 150 knots (172 mph; 277 km/h)
- Max cruising speed: 96 knots (110 mph; 177 km/h)
- Econ cruising speed at S/L: 85 knots (98 mph; 157 km/h)
- Stalling speed: 41 knots (47 mph; 76 km/h)
- Max rate of climb at S/L: approx 400 ft (122 m)/min
- Landing run: 150 ft (46 m)

SHORTS

SHORT BROTHERS & HARLAND LTD

HEAD OFFICE, WORKS AND AERODROME:
PO Box 241, Airport Road, Belfast BT3 9DZ, Northern Ireland
Telephone: 0232-58444
Telex: 74688

OTHER FACTORIES:
Newtownards, Castlereagh, Belfast (2)

LONDON OFFICE:
Berkeley Square House, Berkeley Square, W1

CHAIRMAN:
Air Marshal Sir Edouard Grundy, KBE, CB

MANAGING DIRECTOR:
P. F. Foreman, CBE

DIRECTORS:
F. F. H. Charlton
D. W. G. L. Haviland, CB
Dr Llewellyn Smith, CBE
H. E. Trevan-Hawke

SECRETARY:
Gordon Bruce, MA

EXECUTIVE COMMERCIAL DIRECTOR:
D. N. B. McCandless

EXECUTIVE DIRECTOR, ENGINEERING:
T. D. R. Carroll

EXECUTIVE FINANCIAL DIRECTOR:
N. L. Galloway

GENERAL MANAGER (AIRCRAFT):
A. F. C. Roberts, OBE

GENERAL MANAGER (MANUFACTURING AND AERO-STRUCTURES):
K. W. Tyson

Shorts Skyvan 3M of No. 121 Squadron, Singapore Air Defence Command. Note the pair of Schermuly flare containers in fairing on side of fuselage at rear

Manager, Missile Systems Division:
E. G. Collinson
Manager, Flying Services Division:
Wg Cdr T. C. Chambers, AFC
Chief Test Pilot:
D. B. Wright
Publicity Manager:
G. H. Edgar

The original firm of Short Brothers was established at Battersea in 1903, to manufacture balloons. In 1909 it was moved to Leysdown, becoming the first manufacturer of aeroplanes in the UK when it received a contract to build six Wright biplanes. The company later transferred its works to Eastchurch and then to Rochester.

In June 1936 Short Brothers, in collaboration with Harland & Wolff Ltd, formed a new company known as Short & Harland Ltd to build aircraft in Belfast, and in 1947 activities were concentrated in Belfast under the name Short Bros & Harland Ltd.

In 1954 the Bristol Aeroplane Co Ltd acquired a financial interest and the company is now owned by the British government, Rolls-Royce and Harland & Wolff, with the government holding a 69½% controlling interest. In 1973 the company received the Queen's Award to Industry for the seventh year in succession. It had 5,800 employees in March 1974.

The company's current products include the Skyvan and Skyliner turboprop STOL light transports, developed as a private venture and now in use throughout the world for passenger, freight, survey, military and miscellaneous operations.

In September 1972 details were announced of the SD3-30, a 30-passenger feederliner designed to meet the needs of the mid-1970s, and this was due to make its first flight in August 1974.

Internationally, Shorts is collaborating as risk-sharing partner with Fokker-VFW, MBB and VFW-Fokker in production of the F.28 Fellowship transport, with responsibility for the wings; and holds contracts to produce ailerons, spoilers, wingtips, landing gear doors, galley doors, environmental control system doors and tail unit rib assemblies for the Lockheed L-1011 TriStar, and landing gear doors for the Boeing 747. During 1967, Shorts began the design and manufacture of pods for Rolls-Royce jet engines, and now has an agreement for podding Rolls-Royce RB.211 turbofan engines for the TriStar. Deliveries of these direct to Lockheed at Palmdale began in the early Summer of 1970. To cope with its involvement in the TriStar programme, Shorts has installed some of Europe's most advanced facilities for the hot-forming of titanium and the manipulation of high-temperature creep-resistant alloys. It is producing M45H turbofan pods for the VFW-Fokker VFW 614 and ALF 502H turbofan pods for the Hawker Siddeley 146 transport aircraft, and is conducting advanced research into jet-engine noise reduction and metal bonding. Shorts is also quality-approved subcontractor to many major US and UK aerospace companies.

In addition to its activities in the field of piloted aircraft, Shorts is engaged on missile development and production, production of supersonic target drones, and development of the Skyspy remote control aerial surveillance vehicle.

The company's Flying Services Division operates maintenance units and airfields for various civil and military organisations, and flies and maintains aircraft and target drones for the Ministry of Defence. This includes operation of the Llanbedr target aircraft base, and the target service, supply and recovery flight at the Woomera range in Australia.

SHORTS SC.7 SKYVAN

Design of the SC.7 Skyvan was started as a private venture in 1959, and construction of the first prototype began in 1960. This aircraft (G-ASCN) flew for the first time on 17 January 1963, with two 390 hp Continental GTSIO-520 piston engines, and completed its flight trials by mid-1963. It was then re-engined with 520 shp Astazou II turboprops and first flew in its new form on 2 October 1963.

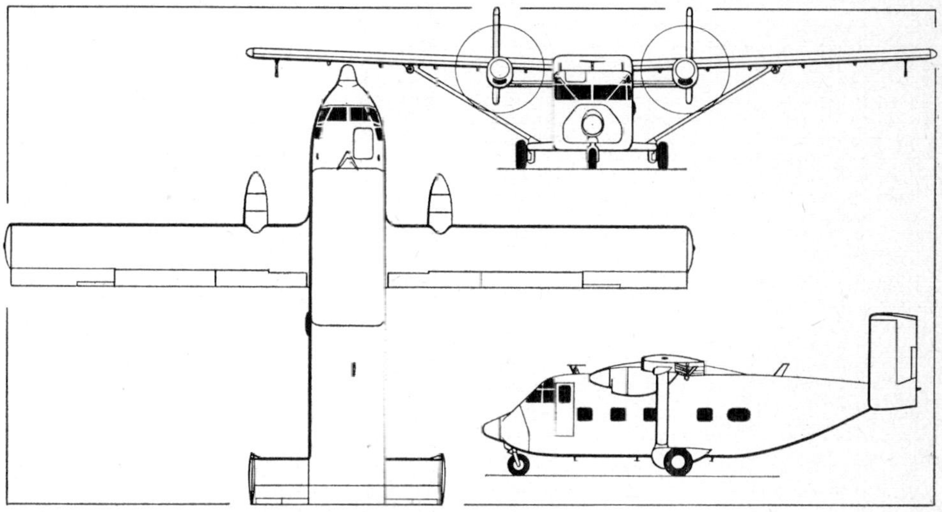

Shorts Skyvan Series 3M military transport with nose radome (*Pilot Press*)

The following versions of the Skyvan have been announced:

Skyvan Srs 1 and Srs 1A. Designation of first prototype, with Continental engines (Srs 1) and later with Astazou IIs (Srs 1A).

Skyvan Srs 2. Designation of three development aircraft (G-ASCO/ASZI/ASZJ) and sixteen initial production aircraft, with 730 ehp Astazou XII turboprop engines. The first of these flew on 29 October 1965. Several subsequently re-engined to Srs 3 standard. Descriptions in 1968-69 and 1970-71 *Jane's*.

Skyvan Srs 3. Current civil production version, which superseded Srs 2 in 1968. First Srs 3 to fly was the second development aircraft, G-ASZI, which had been equipped originally with Astazous. The first flight with AiResearch engines was made on 15 December 1967, and a second aircraft (G-ASZJ) re-engined with TPE 331s flew on 20 January 1968. Total of 47 ordered by 1 April 1974.

Skyvan Srs 3A. In September 1970 the maximum design T-O weight of the civil version of the Skyvan was increased above the 12,500 lb (5,670 kg) limit, enabling the aircraft to comply with British Civil Airworthiness Requirements, Passenger Transport Category, in Performance Group A. This version is designated Skyvan Series 3A and has a max T-O weight of 13,700 lb (6,215 kg) and max landing weight of 13,400 lb (6,075 kg). Total of nine ordered by 1 April 1974.

Skyvan Srs 3M. Military version of Srs 3, modified internally to accept optional equipment for typical military missions. Prototype (G-AXPT) flew for the first time in early 1970. Suitable for paratrooping and supply dropping, assault landing, troop transport, casualty evacuation, staff transport, and vehicle or ordnance transport. Initial order for two placed in February 1969.

A total of 47 had been ordered by 1 April 1974, for 11 armed services, including the Austrian Air Force (two), the Sultan of Oman's Air Force (sixteen), the Indonesian Air Force (three), the Argentine Naval Prefectura (five), the Royal Nepalese Army (two), the Royal Thai Police (three), the Ecuador Army Air Force (one), Singapore Air Defence Command (six) and the Ghana Air Force (six). Three of the Singapore aircraft are equipped for search and rescue duties. Those of the Indonesian Air Force are equipped to civil standard and operate social services on behalf of the Ministry of the Interior.

Skyliner. All-passenger version, described separately.

A feasibility study has been completed for a counter-insurgency version of the Skyvan carrying rocket and machine-gun pods, four Short Hellcat air-to-surface missiles or reconnaissance flares under the wings, and having provision for fuselage-mounted pyrotechnic devices and internally-mounted machine-guns or automatic cannon.

Total orders for Series 3/3A/3M Skyvans and Skyliners had reached 103 by 1 April 1974. In February 1970 the Skyvan became the first aircraft to be certificated under the British Air Registration Board's new Civil Airworthiness Requirements for STOL operations.

The following description applies to the standard civil Srs 3 and military Srs 3M in current production:

Type: Light civil or military STOL utility transport.

Wings: Braced high-wing monoplane. Wing section NACA 63A series (modified). Thickness/chord ratio 14%. Dihedral 2° 2′. Incidence 2° 30′. Light alloy structure consisting of a two-cell box with wing skins made up of a uniform outer sheet bonded to a corrugated inner sheet. All-metal single-slotted ailerons. Geared tabs on port and starboard ailerons, with manual trim on starboard aileron. All-metal single-slotted flaps. Provision for sintered leading-edge de-icing system.

Fuselage: Light alloy structure. Nose and crew cabin section is of conventional skin/stringer design. Elsewhere, the fuselage structure consists of double-skin panels (flat outer sheets bonded to inner corrugated sheets), stabilised by frames.

Tail Unit: Cantilever all-metal two-spar structure, with twin fins and rudders. Fixed-incidence tailplane. Geared trim tabs in outer elevators and rudders. Provision for sintered leading-edge de-icing system.

Landing Gear: Non-retractable tricycle type. Single wheel on each unit. Steerable nosewheel. Main units carried on short sponsons. Electro-

Hydraulics oleo-pneumatic shock-absorbers. Main-wheel tyres size 11·00-12, nosewheel tyre size 7·50-10. Tyre pressure (all units) 40 lb/sq in (2·81 kg/cm²). Hydraulically-operated disc brakes, with differential braking for steering. Provision for fitting skis and low-pressure tyres.

Power Plant: **Two 715 shp Garrett AiResearch TPE 331-201 turboprop engines, each** driving a Hartzell HC-B3TN-5/T10282H three-blade (optionally four-blade) variable-pitch propeller. Fuel in four tanks in pairs on top of fuselage between wing roots, each pair consisting of one tank of 40 Imp gallons (182 litres) capacity and one of 106·5 Imp gallons (484 litres) capacity. Total fuel capacity of 293 Imp gallons (1,332 litres). Provision for increase in total fuel capacity to 390 Imp gallons (1,773 litres) by installing four specially-designed tanks in spaces between fuselage frames on each side, beneath main fuel tank. Oil capacity 1·7 Imp gallons (7·73 litres).

Accommodation: **Crew of one, with provision for two. Accommodation (Srs 3) for up to 19 passengers, or 12 stretcher patients and attendants, or 4,600 lb (2,085 kg) of freight, vehicles or agricultural equipment. Srs 3M can accommodate 22 equipped troops; 16 paratroops and a despatcher;** 12 stretcher cases and two medical attendants, or 5,200 lb (2,358 **kg) of freight. It carries its own lightweight vehicle loading ramps and has a one-piece military door which leaves the fuselage threshold entirely clear of appendages. Executive version provides luxury accommodation and equipment for nine passengers. Full-width rear loading door, and forward door on each side of crew compartment. Rear door can be opened in flight to permit the parachuting of loads up to 4 ft 6 in (1·37 m) in height. Cockpit** and cabin heated by engine bleed air mixed **with fresh air from intake in nose. Cabin unpressurised. Some aircraft fitted with Rolamat cargo loading equipment.**

Systems: **Hydraulic system, pressure 2,500 lb/sq in (175 kg/cm²), operates flaps and wheel brakes. No pneumatic system. Electrical system utilises two busbars, operating independently, each connected to a 28V 125A** DC starter/generator, a battery and a 115V 400Hz static inverter. General services are 28V DC; some radio and instruments 115V AC.

Electronics and Equipment: **Radio optional. Typical installation for operations in Europe and USA consists of duplicated VHF, duplicated VOR/ILS, marker beacon and ADF. Provision** for HF, DME, transponder, Bendix M4C autopilot and weather radar. Blind-flying instrumentation standard.

Equipment (Srs 3M): Port-side blister window for an air despatcher; two anchor cables for parachute static lines; a guard rail beneath the tail to prevent control surface fouling by the static lines; inward-facing paratroop **seats with safety nets; parachute signal light; mounts for NATO-type stretchers; and roller conveyors for easy loading and paradropping of pallet-mounted supplies.**

Dimensions, external:
Wing span 64 ft 11 in (19·79 m)
Wing chord (constant) 5 ft 10 in (1·78 m)
Wing aspect ratio 11
Length overall:
Srs 3 40 ft 1 in (12·21 m)
Srs 3M, with radome 41 ft 4 in (12·60 m)
Height over tail 15 ft 1 in (4·60 m)
Tailplane span 17 ft 4 in (5·28 m)
Wheel track 13 ft 10 in (4·21 m)
Wheelbase 14 ft 10 in (4·52 m)
*Propeller diameter 8 ft 6 in (2·59 m)
Propeller ground clearance 5 ft 0 in (1·52 m)
Crew and passenger doors (fwd, port and stbd):
Height 5 ft 0 in (1·52 m)
Width 1 ft 8 in (0·51 m)
Height to sill 3 ft 9 in (1·14 m)
Rear loading door:
Height 6 ft 6 in (1·98 m)
Width 6 ft 5 in (1·96 m)
Height to sill 2 ft 5 in (0·74 m)

**Optional four-blade propellers of 8 ft 3 in* (2·51 *m) diameter*

Dimensions, internal:
Cabin, excluding flight deck:
Length 18 ft 7 in (5·67 m)
Max width 6 ft 6 in (1·98 m)
Max height 6 ft 6 in (1·98 m)
Floor area 120 sq ft (11·15 m²)
Volume 780 cu ft (22·09 m³)

Areas:
Wings, gross 373 sq ft (34·65 m²)
Ailerons (total) 32·3 sq ft (3·00 m²)
Trailing-edge flaps (total) 63·1 sq ft (5·86 m²)
Fins 82·0 sq ft (7·62 m²)
Rudders, incl tabs 26·8 sq ft (2·49 m²)
Tailplane 81·0 sq ft (7·53 m²)
Elevators, incl tabs 39·0 sq ft (3·62 m²)

Weights and Loadings (with 293 Imp gallons; 1,332 litres of fuel):
Basic operating weight:
Srs 3 7,314 lb (3,318 kg)
Srs 3M 7,400 lb (3,356 kg)
Typical operating weight as frighter:
Srs 3 7,600 lb (3,447 kg)
Srs 3M 7,620 lb (3,456 kg)
Typical operating weight with passengers or troops:
Srs 3 8,100 lb (3,674 kg)
Srs 3M 8,330 lb (3,778 kg)
Max payload for normal T-O weight:
Srs 3 4,600 lb (2,086 kg)
Srs 3M 5,200 lb (2,358 kg)
Max payload for overload T-O weight:
Srs 3M 6,000 lb (2,721 kg)
Max T-O weight:
Srs 3, normal 12,500 lb (5,670 kg)
Srs 3M, normal 13,700 lb (6,214 kg)
Srs 3M, overload 14,500 lb (6,577 kg)
Max landing weight:
Srs 3 12,500 lb (5,670 kg)
Srs 3M 13,500 lb (6,123 kg)
Max wing loading:
Srs 3 33·5 lb/sq ft (163·6 kg/m²)
Srs 3M 36·2 lb/sq ft (176·7 kg/m²)

Performance (at max T-O weight, with 293 Imp gallons; 1,332 litres of fuel):
Max never-exceed speed
240 knots (277 mph; 445 km/h) EAS
Max cruising speed at 10,000 ft (3,050 m):
max continuous power
176 knots (203 mph; 327 km/h) TAS
cruise power
169 knots (195 mph; 314 km/h) TAS
Econ cruising speed at 10,000 ft (3,050 m)
150 knots (173 mph; 278 km/h) TAS
Stalling speed, flaps down:
Srs 3 60 knots (69 mph; 111 km/h) EAS
Srs 3M 62 knots (71 mph; 115 km/h) EAS
Max rate of climb at S/L:
Srs 3 1,640 ft (500 m)/min
Srs 3M 1,530 ft (466 m)/min
Service ceiling (100 ft; 30 m/min climb):
Srs 3 22,500 ft (6,858 m)
Srs 3M 22,000 ft (6,705 m)
Service ceiling, one engine out (50 ft; 15 m/min climb):
Srs 3 12,500 ft (3,810 m)
Srs 3M 9,500 ft (2,895 m)
Min ground turning radius 12 ft 4 in (3·76 m)
Runway LCN at AUW of 12,500 lb (5,670 kg):
standard tyres 3·5
low-pressure tyres 3·0
T-O run, STOL, unfactored:
Srs 3 850 ft (259 m)
Srs 3M 780 ft (238 m)
T-O run (normal):
Srs 3 (BCAR) 1,680 ft (512 m)
T-O to 50 ft (15 m), STOL, unfactored:
Srs 3, 3M 1,260 ft (384 m)
T-O to 50 ft (15 m):
Srs 3 (BCAR, normal) 2,000 ft (610 m)
Srs 3 (BCAR, STOL) 1,580 ft (482 m)
Srs 3 (FAR Pt 23) 1,600 ft (488 m)
Landing from 50 ft (15 m):
Srs 3 (BCAR, normal) 2,040 ft (622 m)
Srs 3 (BCAR, STOL) 1,860 ft (567 m)
Srs 3 (FAR Pt 23) 1,480 ft (451 m)
Srs 3M (STOL, unfactored) 1,395 ft (425 m)
Landing from 30 ft (9 m):
Srs 3 (STOL, unfactored) 1,150 ft (351 m)
Srs 3 (BCAR, STOL) 1,640 ft (500 m)
Landing run:
Srs 3M (STOL, unfactored) 695 ft (212 m)
Range at long-range cruising speed, 45 min reserves:
Srs 3 600 nm (694 miles; 1,115 km)
Srs 3M 580 nm (670 miles; 1,075 km)
Range (typical freighter) at long-range cruising speed, 45 min reserves:
Srs 3 with 4,000 lb (1,814 kg) payload
162 nm (187 miles; 300 km)
Srs 3M with 5,000 lb (2,268 kg) payload
208 nm (240 miles; 386 km)

SHORTS SKYLINER SERIES 1

Concurrent with certification of the Skyvan Series 3A to Performance Group A standards, Shorts unveiled at the 1970 Farnborough Air Show an all-passenger version, known as the Skyliner. The Skyliner takes full advantage of the internal capacity of the Skyvan, and the increase in max take-off weight, to provide a spacious all-passenger cabin, furnished to de luxe standard, including the provision of overhead baggage lockers. This version can be equipped for up to 19 passengers; optional features include a galley and an airstair passenger door.

The principal structural alterations are the provision of a large door in each side of the fuselage at the rear, for ease of passenger boarding. The large cargo-loading door of the basic Skyvan can be replaced by a smaller door which allows access to a large rear baggage compartment.

Up to April 1974 Skyliners had been ordered by British Airways—Scottish (two), Gulf Air (one), Airexecutive Norway (one), Ednasa Hong Kong (two) and Yokohama Air. Orders are included in Skyvan totals.

A special VIP version, the Skyliner Executive, was announced concurrently with the commercial passenger version; one has since been delivered to the Royal Air Flight of Nepal.

External dimensions and most systems of the Skyliner are identical to those of the Skyvan Series 3.

The following are the salient features of the Skyliner:

Accommodation: Crew of two, with provision for steward or stewardess. Accommodation for up to 19 passengers. Standard optional equipment includes a toilet with washing facilities and a small galley for buffet service.

Dimensions, external: As Skyvan Srs 3 except:
Passenger doors (rear, port and stbd):
Height 4 ft 9 in (1·45 m)
Width 2 ft 6 in (0·76 m)

Dimensions, internal:
Cabin, excluding flight deck and baggage compartment:
Max length 20 ft 0 in (6·10 m)
Max width 6 ft 6 in (1·98 m)
Max height 6 ft 6 in (1·98 m)
Volume 830 cu ft (23·5 m³)
Baggage compartment (basic aircraft, excluding overhead baggage lockers in cabin)
148 cu ft (4·20 m³)

Weights:
Typical operating weight 8,940 lb (4,055 kg)
Max T-O weight 13,700 lb (6,210 kg)
Max landing weight 13,400 lb (6,070 kg)

Performance (Group A, ISA at S/L):
T-O to 35 ft (10·7 m) 3,350 ft (1,020 m)
Landing from 50 ft (15 m) 3,320 ft (1,010 m)
Range at high-speed cruise, reserves for 50 nm (57 miles; 92 km) diversion and 45 min hold
170 nm (196 miles; 315 km)

SHORTS SD3-30

The SD3-30 is a 30-passenger twin-turboprop transport aircraft designed primarily for commuter and regional air service operators whose current 18/20-seat aircraft will require replacement in the mid-1970s by larger aircraft.

Design of the SD3-30 is derived from that of the Skyvan STOL utility transport, and it retains many of the latter type's well-proven characteristics, including the large cabin cross-section. The same fail-safe concept and design philosophy is employed in the structural components. The cabin, including the toilet and galley compartments, is 12 ft 5 in (3·78 m) longer than that of the Skyvan Srs 3.

The SD3-30 will be certificated at first to FAR Pt 25 (US) and CAR Section D, Group A (UK) requirements. In addition, it will conform with CAB Pt 298 (US) and will meet the noise requirements of FAR Pt 36 by a substantial margin. Unrestricted maximum-weight operation will be achievable at S/L ambient temperatures up to ISA+20°C.

A military version, the **SD3-M**, has also been announced. This will be capable of a variety of

Shorts Skyliner 19-passenger commuter transport aircraft, in the insignia of British Airways' Scottish Division

roles, including the tactical transportation of troops, cargo and vehicles, paratrooping, supply dropping, casualty evacuation and search and rescue, and will be able to carry up to 34 troops or 8,000 lb (3,630 kg) of cargo.

Two prototypes and the first two production aircraft will be used for the development programme. The first flight was scheduled for 7 August 1974, with certification by September 1975.

The following description applies to both the SD3-30 and the SD3-M, except where a specific version is indicated:

TYPE: Twin-turboprop civil and military transport aircraft.

WINGS: Braced high-wing monoplane, of all-metal fail-safe construction, built in three sections. Wing sections NACA 63A series (modified). Thickness/chord ratio 18% at root, 14% on outer panels. Dihedral 3° on outer panels. Centre-section, integral with top of centre-fuselage, has taper on leading- and trailing-edges, and is a two-spar single-cell box structure of light alloy with conventional skin and stringers on the undersurface. The strut-braced outer panels, which are pin-jointed to the centre-section, are reinforced Skyvan constant-chord units, built of light alloy, and each consists of a two-cell box; they, and the centre-section upper surface, have wing skins made up of a smooth outer skin bonded to a corrugated inner skin. All-metal single-slotted ailerons. Geared tabs in port and starboard ailerons, with manual trim on starboard aileron. All-metal single-slotted flaps, each in three sections. Primary control surfaces are rod-actuated.

FUSELAGE: Light alloy structure, built in two main portions: nose (including flight deck, nosewheel bay and forward baggage compartment); and the centre (including main wing spar attachment frames and lower transverse beams which carry the main landing gear and associated fairings) and rear portion (including aft baggage compartment, optional rear-loading door and tail unit attachment frames). The nose and rear underfuselage are of conventional skin/stringer design. The remainder is composed of a smooth outer skin bonded to a corrugated inner skin and stabilised by frames.

TAIL UNIT: Cantilever all-metal two-spar structure with twin fins and rudders, basically similar to that of the Skyvan. Fixed-incidence tailplane, with reinforced leading-edge. Full-span elevator, aerodynamically balanced by set-back hinges. Rudders each have an unshielded horn aerodynamic balance. Primary control surfaces are rod-actuated; elevator has hydraulic trim assist. Geared trim tabs in elevator and rudders.

LANDING GEAR: Menasco retractable tricycle type, with single wheel on each unit. Main units carried on short sponsons, into which the wheels retract hydraulically. Oleo-pneumatic shock-absorbers. Main wheels are standard Fokker-VFW Friendship units; the nosewheel is steerable. Normal tyre pressures: main units 75 lb/sq in (5·27 kg/cm²), nose unit 58 lb/sq in (4·08 kg/cm²). Special requirements for rough-field operation have been catered for in the design.

POWER PLANT: Two 1,120 shp (max continuous rating 1,020 shp) United Aircraft of Canada PT6A-45 turboprop engines, each driving a Hartzell five-blade low-speed propeller. Fuel in main tanks in wing centre-section/fuselage fairing, total capacity 480 Imp gallons (2,182 litres). Normal cross-feed provisions to allow for pump failure. Provision to increase total fuel capacity for special requirements.

ACCOMMODATION (SD3-30): Crew of two on flight deck, plus cabin attendant. Standard seating for 30 passengers, in ten rows of three at 30 in (76 cm) pitch, with wide aisle. Seat rails fitted to facilitate changes in configuration. Galley, toilet and cabin attendant's seat at rear, all of which are removable. Large overhead baggage lockers. Entire accommodation soundproofed and air-conditioned. Baggage compartments in nose (45 cu ft; 1·27 m³) and to rear of cabin (100 cu ft; 2·83 m³), each with external access and capable of holding a combined total of 1,000 lb (454 kg) of baggage. Passenger door is at rear of cabin on port side. Passenger version has two emergency exits on the starboard side, one on port side and one in the flight deck roof. Mixed-traffic version has full access to these emergency exits. For mixed passenger/freight operation a bulkhead divides the cabin into a rear passenger area (typically for 18 persons) and a forward cargo compartment, the latter being loaded through a large port-side door, capable of admitting ATA "D" type containers. In all-cargo configuration the cabin can accommodate up to seven "D" type containers, with ample space around them for additional freight. Cabin floor is flat throughout its length, and is designed to support loadings of 400 lb (181 kg) per foot run at 125 lb/sq ft (610·3 kg/m²). Locally-reinforced areas of higher strength are also provided. Seat rails can be used as cargo lashing points. Freight loading is facilitated by the low-level cabin floor.

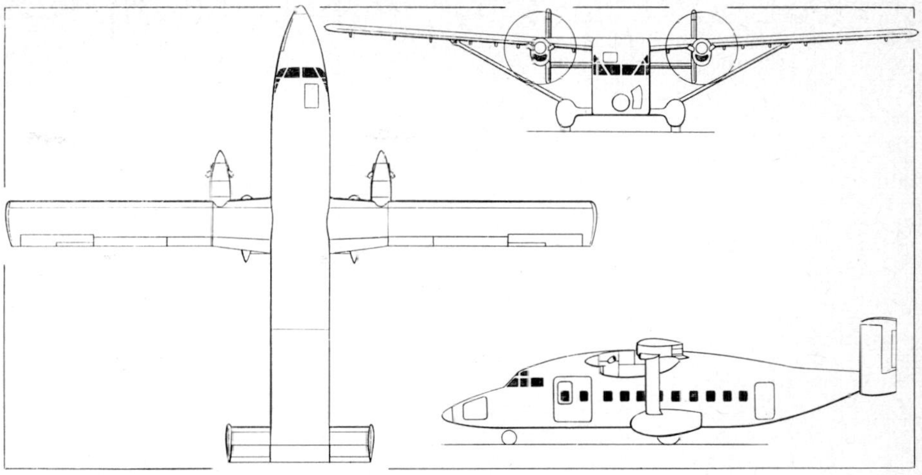

Shorts SD3-30 twin-turboprop commercial and military transport *(Pilot Press)*

ACCOMMODATION (SD3-M): Generally similar to SD3-30, but with large rear-loading doors. It is capable of accommodating up to 34 fully-equipped troops, or 26 fully-armed paratroops and a despatcher, when used for personnel transport. Freighter version can carry up to 8,000 lb (3,630 kg) of cargo, and more than 7,000 lb (3,175 kg) of supplies can be air-dropped. With load spreaders, the SD3-M can also be operated as a vehicle transport, carrying Land-Rovers or similar vehicles; for casualty evacuation, carrying 18 stretchers and three medical attendants; for search and rescue, with up to 9 hr endurance; as a VIP STOL transport; and for aerial survey, border and coastal patrol.

SYSTEMS: Hydraulic system of 3,000 lb/sq in (210 kg/cm²), supplied by engine-driven pumps, operates landing gear, nosewheel steering, flaps and brakes (at lower pressure), and elevator trim assistance, and includes emergency accumulators. Main electrical system, for general services, is 28V DC and is of the split-busbar type with cross-coupling for essential services. Special AC sources of 115V and 26V available at 400Hz for certain instruments. De-icing/anti-icing system for wing and tail leading-edges. Inertial anti-icing system for engine intake ducts; electric mat de-icing for inlet lips and propellers; electrically-heated windscreen; full air-conditioning system.

ELECTRONICS AND EQUIPMENT: Dual controls, anti-icing system, air-conditioning system and passenger safety equipment standard. Wide range of radio and navigation equipment available to customer's requirements. Typical standard equipment would comprise duplicated VHF communications and navigation systems, two glideslope/markers, two ILS repeaters, two radio magnetic indicators, one ADF, one transponder, one DME, PA system, flight data recorder, voice recorder and weather radar.

DIMENSIONS, EXTERNAL:
- Wing span — 74 ft 9 in (22·78 m)
- Wing chord (standard mean) — 6 ft 0·7 in (1·85 m)
- Length overall — 58 ft 0½ in (17·69 m)
- Height overall — 15 ft 8 in (4·775 m)
- Propeller diameter — 9 ft 0 in (2·74 m)
- Propeller ground clearance — 6 ft 1 in (1·85 m)
- Cabin floor: height above ground — 3 ft 1 in (0·94 m)
- Passenger door (port, rear):
  - Height — 4 ft 8 in (1·42 m)
  - Width — 2 ft 4 in (0·71 m)
- Forward cargo door (port):
  - Height — 5 ft 6 in (1·68 m)
  - Width — 4 ft 7 in (1·40 m)

DIMENSIONS, INTERNAL:
- Cabin: Max length — 31 ft 1 in (9·47 m)
  - Max width — 6 ft 6 in (1·98 m)
  - Max height — 6 ft 6 in (1·98 m)
  - Volume (all-cargo) — 1,230 cu ft (34·83 m³)
- Baggage compartments volume (total usable) — 145 cu ft (4·11 m³)

AREA:
- Wings, gross — 453·0 sq ft (42·1 m²)

WEIGHTS:
- Weight empty, equipped (incl crew of three):
  - 3-30 for 30 passengers — 13,890 lb (6,300 kg)
- Fuel:
  - standard tanks only — 3,840 lb (1,741 kg)
  - with long-range tanks — 5,000 lb (2,268 kg)
- Max payload for normal max T-O weight:
  - 3-30 with 30 passengers and baggage — 5,940 lb (2,694 kg)
  - 3-30 freighter — 7,500 lb (3,400 kg)
  - 3-M — 8,000 lb (3,630 kg)
- Payload for max range, standard tanks:
  - 3-M, normal max T-O weight — 4,950 lb (2,245 kg)
  - 3-M, overload max T-O weight — 6,750 lb (3,060 kg)
- Max T-O weight:
  - 3-30 — 21,700 lb (9,843 kg)
  - 3-M, normal — 21,700 lb (9,843 kg)
  - 3-M, overload — 23,500 lb (10,660 kg)
- Max landing weight:
  - all versions — 21,400 lb (9,706 kg)

PERFORMANCE (estimated, at normal max T-O weight, ISA at S/L, except where indicated):
- Max never-exceed speed:
  - 3-30, 3-M — 244 knots (281 mph; 452 km/h)
- Max cruising speed at 10,000 ft (3,050 m), AUW of 20,000 lb (9,072 kg):
  - 3-30, 3M — 198 knots (228 mph; 367 km/h)
- Econ cruising speed at 10,000 ft (3,050 m), AUW of 20,000 lb (9,072 kg):
  - 3-30, 3-M — 160 knots (184 mph; 296 km/h)
- Stalling speed, flaps and landing gear up:
  - 3-30, 3-M — 92 knots (106 mph; 171 km/h)
- Stalling speed, flaps and landing gear down:
  - 3-30, 3-M — 74 knots (85 mph; 137 km/h)
- Max rate of climb at S/L:
  - 3-30 — 1,420 ft (433 m)/min
- Service ceiling, one engine out, AUW of 19,000 lb (8,618 kg):
  - 3-30, 3-M — 13,800 ft (4,205 m)
- T-O run:
  - 3-M (STOL) — 1,170 ft (357 m)
- T-O distance (FAR Pt 25 and BCAR Go A):
  - 3-30 — 3,850 ft (1,173 m)
  - 3-30, ISA + 15°C — 4,300 ft (1,310 m)
- T-O to 50 ft (15 m):
  - 3-M (STOL) — 1,820 ft (555 m)
- Landing distance, AUW of 19,000 lb (8,618 kg):
  - 3-30, BCAR — 3,470 ft (1,058 m)
  - 3-30, FAR — 3,080 ft (939 m)
  - 3-M (STOL) — 1,775 ft (541 m)
- Landing run, AUW of 19,000 lb (8,618 kg):
  - 3-M (STOL minimum) — 740 ft (226 m)
- Runway LCN at max T-O weight — 9·9
- Range with max payload, cruising at 10,000 ft (3,050 m), no reserves:
  - 3-30 (passenger) — 435 nm (500 miles; 805 km)
- Range at 10,000 ft (3,050 m) with alternative payloads, no reserves:
  - 3-30 (passenger) with 4,000 lb (1,815 kg) payload — 903 nm (1,040 miles; 1,673 km)
  - 3-30 (freighter) with 5,500 lb (2,495 kg) payload — 846 nm (975 miles; 1,569 km)
  - 3-M with 8,000 lb (3,630 kg) payload — 160 nm (185 miles; 297 km)
  - 3-M with 8,000 lb (3,630 kg) payload at overload max T-O weight — 590 nm (680 miles; 1,094 km)
- Max range with long-range tanks:
  - 3-M — 1,190 nm (1,370 miles; 2,205 km)
- Max endurance:
  - 3-M, standard tanks — 7 hr 30 min
  - 3-M, long-range tanks — 10 hr 0 min

SIZER

JOHN A. SIZER

ADDRESS:
69 The Avenue, Lowestoft, Suffolk

Mr Sizer has designed a single-seat light monoplane known as the Sapphire, and two basically similar biplanes, the Rosette and Continental Rosette.

Mr Sizer's own construction of a Sapphire prototype has been shelved for the time being, but plans and instructions for building all three aircraft are available to other interested amateur constructors.

Mr Sizer is also working on the design of a two-seat flying-boat known as the Seagull.

SIZER SAPPHIRE

TYPE: Single-seat homebuilt light aircraft.

WINGS: Strut-braced low-wing monoplane. RAF 38 wing section, with thickness/chord ratio of 12%. Dihedral 2°. Incidence 2° 30′. All-wood structure, with sealed-gap ailerons. No flaps. Braced to fuselage main longeron on each side by two parallel struts. Ground-adjustable tabs on ailerons.

FUSELAGE: Braced-girder wooden structure.

TAIL UNIT: Conventional all-wood structure, with fixed-incidence tailplane. Ground-adjustable tabs on elevators and rudder.

LANDING GEAR: Non-retractable two-wheel type, with sprung shock-absorption. Main wheels size 16 in × 4 in, tyre pressure 12 lb/sq in (0·8 kg/cm²). Cable-operated brakes. Spring steel leaf-type tailskid.

POWER PLANT: One 40 hp Peacock (Volkswagen) engine, driving a Sizer-Hutchins two-blade propeller. Fuel tank, capacity 6 Imp gallons (27 litres), in front fuselage aft of engine firewall. Oil capacity 0·77 Imp gallons (3·5 litres).

ACCOMMODATION: Single seat in open cockpit.

DIMENSIONS, EXTERNAL:

Wing span	22 ft 0 in (6·71 m)
Wing chord (constant)	4 ft 2 in (1·27 m)
Wing aspect ratio	4·75
Length overall	16 ft 6 in (5·03 m)
Height overall (tail down)	6 ft 6 in (1·98 m)
Tailplane span	6 ft 0 in (1·83 m)
Wheel track	4 ft 2 in (1·27 m)
Propeller diameter	4 ft 6 in (1·37 m)

AREAS:

Wings, gross	101·0 sq ft (9·38 m²)
Ailerons (total)	12·10 sq ft (1·12 m²)
Fin	3·05 sq ft (0·28 m²)
Rudder	2·02 sq ft (0·19 m²)
Tailplane	10·00 sq ft (0·93 m²)
Elevators	6·50 sq ft (0·60 m²)

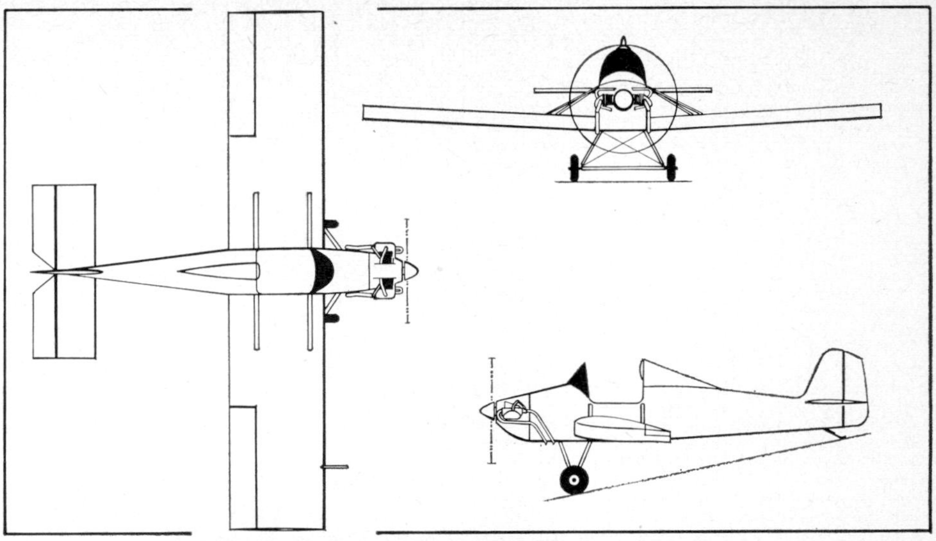

Sizer Sapphire single-seat homebuilt monoplane (*Roy J. Grainge*)

WEIGHTS AND LOADINGS (estimated):

Weight empty, equipped	380 lb (172 kg)
Max T-O weight	600 lb (272 kg)
Max wing loading	5·95 lb/sq ft (29·3 kg/m²)
Max power loading	15·0 lb/hp (6·8 kg/hp)

PERFORMANCE (estimated, at max T-O weight):

Max never-exceed speed (structural)	104 knots (120 mph; 193 km/h)
Max level speed at S/L	71 knots (82 mph; 132 km/h)
Max cruising speed	65 knots (75 mph; 121 km/h)
Econ cruising speed	61 knots (70 mph; 113 km/h)
Stalling speed, power on	36·5 knots (42 mph; 68 km/h)
Max rate of climb at S/L	600 ft (183 m)/min
Service ceiling	10,000 ft (3,050 m)
T-O run	380 ft (116 m)

SIZER ROSETTE and CONTINENTAL ROSETTE

Descriptions of these two single-seat biplane designs can be found in the 1973-74 *Jane's*. Neither type is yet under construction.

TAYLOR

Mrs JOHN F. TAYLOR

ADDRESS: 25, Chesterfield Crescent, Leigh-on-Sea, Essex SS9 5PD

Telephone: Southend (0702) 521063

The late Mr John Taylor, AMIED, an amateur constructor, designed and built the prototype of a single-seat ultra-light sporting monoplane, designated J.T.1. His object was to produce the airframe for not more than £100. Construction took about 14 months, and it flew for the first time on 4 July 1959.

A second design by Mr Taylor, the J.T.2 Titch, was awarded second prize in the Midget Racer Design Competition organised by Mr Norman Jones of the Rollason company in 1964. A prototype was built and flown successfully, but crashed on 16 May 1967, killing its designer.

Mrs J. F. Taylor is continuing to market plans of both these aircraft to amateur constructors.

TAYLOR MONOPLANE J.T.1

The prototype of this small fully-aerobatic single-seat monoplane was designed for, and originally fitted with, a British-built JAP engine. The basically-similar US Aeronca E.113 engine is equally suitable and the design can be modified slightly to take 65 hp Continental and Lycoming engines. Any of the modified Volkswagen engines now on the market can also be fitted and the prototype was, in fact, re-engined with the latest type of 1·5 litre Ardem engine, by Rollason Aircraft, in the Spring of 1964. It was also fitted with a one-piece sideways-hinged (to starboard) windscreen-canopy assembly.

Plans of the Taylor Monoplane have been made available to amateur constructors and many sets have been sold to customers in the United Kingdom and nearly 20 other countries in all parts of the world. Thirty-five J.T.1s are known to be flying, including four in the UK, seven in Canada, 15 in the US, two in Australia and three in New Zealand.

Aircraft currently flying or under construction are fitted with a variety of engines, including the 40 hp Aeronca E 113, 65 hp Continental A65, 65 hp Lycoming, 72 hp two-stroke McCulloch and the modified Volkswagen series. Aircraft with the 65 hp engines have a 4 in (10 cm) longer nose and 10 in (25 cm) longer rear fuselage to maintain the correct CG position.

TYPE: Single-seat ultra-light monoplane.

WINGS: Cantilever low-wing monoplane. Wing section RAF 48. Constant chord. Dihedral on outer panels 4°. Incidence 3°. Wooden two-spar structure, comprising centre-section and outer panels. Plywood and fabric covering. Differential ailerons. Split trailing-edge flaps. No tabs.

FUSELAGE: Conventional plywood-covered wood structure of four main longerons and curved formers. Centre-section integral with fuselage.

TAIL UNIT: Cantilever fin and fixed-incidence tailplane are plywood-covered wood structures. Elevators and rudder are fabric-covered wood structures.

LANDING GEAR: Non-retractable two-wheel type. Cantilever main legs, with coil spring shock-absorption. Wheels fitted with tailwheel tyres from an Avro Anson aircraft. Leaf spring tailskid with steerable skid-pad. One example, built by Mr R. Ladd in the US (see 1972-73 *Jane's*), has manually-actuated inward-retracting main gear.

POWER PLANT: One 38 hp JAP two-cylinder horizontally-opposed aircooled engine, driving a modified Flottorp two-blade wooden fixed-pitch propeller. Fuel tank aft of firewall, capacity 6 Imp gallons (27 litres).

ACCOMMODATION: Single seat under transparent Perspex canopy. Aerobatic harness. Small locker aft of seat.

DIMENSIONS, EXTERNAL:

Wing span	21 ft 0 in (6·40 m)
Wing aspect ratio	6
Length overall	15 ft 0 in (4·57 m)
Height over tail	4 ft 10 in (1·47 m)
Tailplane span	6 ft 6 in (1·98 m)
Wheel track	5 ft 0 in (1·52 m)

AREAS:

Wings gross	76 sq ft (7·06 m²)
Ailerons (total)	8 sq ft (0·74 m²)
Fin	1·48 sq ft (0·14 m²)
Rudder	4·56 sq ft (0·42 m²)
Tailplane	6 sq ft (0·56 m²)
Elevators	5·75 sq ft (0·51 m²)

WEIGHTS AND LOADINGS:

Weight empty	410 lb (186 kg)
Max T-O weight	610 lb (276 kg)
Max wing loading	8 lb/sq ft (39 kg/m²)
Max power loading	16 lb/hp (78 kg/hp)

PERFORMANCE:

Max never-exceed speed	113 knots (130 mph; 209 km/h)
Max level speed at S/L	91 knots (105 mph; 169 km/h)
Econ cruising speed	78 knots (90 mph; 145 km/h)
Never-exceed speed with flaps down	56 knots (65 mph; 105 km/h)
Stalling speed, flaps up	40 knots (46 mph; 75 km/h)
Stalling speed, flaps down	33 knots (38 mph; 62 km/h)

Taylor Monoplane built by Mr Christopher Healey in New Zealand, with 1,600 cc Volkswagen engine

Taylor Titch built in the US by Mr Jim Mellor of Kansas City, Mo. It won awards for outstanding workmanship, best finish and paint design (*Howard Levy*)

Max rate of climb at S/L	1,000 ft (305 m)/min
Range	200 nm (230 miles; 370 km)
g limits	+9; —9

TAYLOR J.T.2 TITCH

Construction of the prototype Titch was started in February 1965 and it flew for the first time on 22 January 1967.

Ten Titches are known to be flying, including four in the US, three in New Zealand, and one each in France and Rhodesia; plans have been supplied to amateur constructors in Brasil, Iceland, Italy, Mexico and Spain.

The following details apply to the prototype:

TYPE: Single-seat light monoplane.

WINGS: Cantilever low-wing monoplane. Taylor-modified NACA 23012 wing section. Dihedral 5° on top surface. Incidence 3°. Spruce structure with main box-spar and "plank" auxiliary spar. Plywood and fabric covering. Plain manually-operated ply-covered flaps over half-span and fabric-covered differential ailerons.

FUSELAGE: All-wood structure, with four main longerons, four secondary longerons and double-curvature ply covering. Aluminium cockpit side panels.

TAIL UNIT: All-wood structure, with fixed-incidence tailplane. Fixed surfaces plywood-covered, control surfaces fabric-covered.

LANDING GEAR: Non-retractable tailwheel type. Steerable tailwheel. Chrome-vanadium compression coil-spring shock-absorbers. Wheels of own manufacture with 4-ply tyres size 5·00-4 and drum brakes.

POWER PLANT: One 85 hp Continental C85 four-cylinder horizontally-opposed aircooled engine, driving a Hegy wooden two-blade scimitar propeller. Glassfibre fuel tank between firewall and instrument panel, capacity 10 Imp gallons (45·5 litres).

ACCOMMODATION: Single seat, with aerobatic harness, under bubble canopy hinged along starboard side.

DIMENSIONS, EXTERNAL:

Wing span	18 ft 9 in (5·72 m)
Wing chord at root	4 ft 6 in (1·37 m)
Wing chord at tip	3 ft 0 in (0·91 m)
Wing aspect ratio	5·14
Length overall	16 ft 1½ in (4·91 m)
Height overall	4 ft 8 in (1·42 m)
Tailplane span	6 ft 6 in (1·98 m)
Wheel track	5 ft 0 in (1·52 m)
Propeller diameter	5 ft 0 in (1·52 m)

AREAS:

Wings, gross	68 sq ft (6·32 m²)
Ailerons (total)	7·00 sq ft (0·65 m²)
Trailing-edge flaps (total)	3·40 sq ft (0·32 m²)
Fin	1·53 sq ft (0·14 m²)
Rudder	2·70 sq ft (0·25 m²)
Tailplane	4·60 sq ft (0·43 m²)
Elevators	4·70 sq ft (0·44 m²)

WEIGHTS (A: 85 hp Continental engine; B: Volkswagen engine):

Weight empty:	
A	500 lb (227 kg)
B	410 lb (185 kg)
Max T-O weight:	
A	745 lb (338 kg)
B	640 lb (290 kg)

PERFORMANCE (prototype, at max T-O weight, except where indicated):

Max never-exceed speed	195 knots (225 mph; 362 km/h)
Max level speed	174 knots (200 mph; 322 km/h)
Normal cruising speed	135 knots (155 mph; 250 km/h)
Econ cruising speed	95·5 knots (110 mph; 177 km/h)
Best approach speed	65 knots (75 mph; 121 km/h)
Stalling speed, flaps up:	
A	50·5 knots (58 mph; 93·5 km/h)
B	46 knots (53 mph; 86 km/h)
Stalling speed, flaps down:	
A	43·5 knots (50 mph; 80·5 km/h)
B	40 knots (46 mph; 74 km/h)
Unstick speed	54 knots (62 mph; 100 km/h)
Touchdown speed	48 knots (55 mph; 89 km/h)
Max rate of climb at S/L	1,100 ft (335 m)/min

URMSTON

Dr J. H. B. URMSTON, BA (Cantab), MRCS, LRCP

ADDRESS:
7 Winchester Street, Botley, Southampton, Hampshire SO3 2EB

CURRIE WOT

This aircraft was designed originally by Mr J. R. Currie in 1937. Two examples were built at Lympne in that year, but were destroyed in a wartime bombing raid. Mr V. H. Bellamy took over the design after the war, at the Hampshire Aeroplane Club, and the first Wot built by members of this club (G-APNT) flew for the first time on 11 September 1958. The second example built at the Club (G-APWT) was powered by a 60 hp Walter Mikron four-cylinder in-line aircooled engine. Both aircraft have been described in earlier editions of *Jane's*.

Further Wots have since been completed, including Dr Urmston's G-ARZW with a 65 hp Walter Mikron III engine ("Hotter Wot").

Dr Urmston purchased all rights in the design from Mr Bellamy and subsequently had the aircraft re-stressed, in anticipation of meeting the British Aerobatic requirement of 6*g* at an AUW of 900 lb (408 kg).

The following details refer to Dr Urmston's Wot, built to standard plans. Data on the versions with Aeronca-JAP and 60 hp Mikron engines can be found in the 1961-62 *Jane's*.

TYPE: Single-seat fully-aerobatic light biplane.

WINGS: Braced biplane type, with two parallel interplane struts each side and N-type centre-section support struts. Wing section Clark Y. Dihedral (both wings) 3°. No incidence. Conventional spruce and plywood structure, with fabric covering. Fabric-covered ailerons on lower wings only. No flaps.

FUSELAGE: All-wood structure. Plywood-box construction, with overall fabric covering.

TAIL UNIT: Cantilever structure of spruce and plywood, with fabric covering. Fixed-incidence tailplane. Adjustable tab on rudder. Trim tab in port elevator.

Mr R. W. Hart's Currie Wot, with 65 hp Continental A65 engine (*Austin J. Brown*)

LANDING GEAR: Non-retractable two-wheel type. Rubber-cord shock-absorbtion. Main wheels fitted with Dunlop tyres, size 400 × 8, pressure 18 lb/sq in (1·27 kg/cm²). No brakes.

POWER PLANT: One 65 hp Walter Mikron III four-cylinder in-line aircooled engine, driving a two-blade fixed-pitch wooden propeller. Fuel tank aft of firewall, capacity 12 Imp gallons (54·5 litres). Oil capacity 1·5 Imp gallons (7 litres).

ACCOMMODATION: Single seat in open cockpit.

DIMENSIONS, EXTERNAL:

Wing span (both)	22 ft 1 in (6·73 m)
Wing chord (both, constant)	3 ft 6 in (1·07 m)
Wing aspect ratio	6·3
Length overall	18 ft 3½ in (5·58 m)
Height overall	6 ft 9 in (2·06 m)
Wheel track	4 ft 6½ in (1·38 m)

AREA:

Wings, gross	140 sq ft (13·0 m²)

WEIGHTS:

Weight empty	550 lb (250 kg)
Max T-O weight	900 lb (408 kg)

PERFORMANCE (at max T-O weight):

Max never-exceed speed	112 knots (130 mph; 209 km/h)
Max level speed at 2,000 ft (610 m)	83 knots (95 mph; 153 km/h)
Max cruising speed at 2,000 ft (610 m)	78 knots (90 mph; 145 km/h)
Econ cruising speed at 2,000 ft (610 m)	69 knots (80 mph; 129 km/h)
Stalling speed	35 knots (40 mph; 65 km/h)
Max rate of climb at S/L	600 ft (183 m)/min
Range with max fuel	208 nm (240 miles; 385 km)

WALLIS

WALLIS AUTOGYROS LTD

HEAD OFFICE:
Reymerston Hall, Norfolk NOR 28X
Telephone: Mattishall 418

DIRECTORS:
Wing Cdr K. H. Wallis, CEng, AFRAeS
P. M. Wallis

By adopting a completely new design approach to the mechanical details of the single-seat ultra-light autogyro, Wing Cdr Wallis has produced a much-refined aircraft which can be flown quite safely "hands and feet off". The Wallis prototype (G-ARRT, flown for first time in August 1961) introduced many patented features, including a rotor head with offset gimbal system to provide hands and feet off stability and to eliminate pitch-up and "tuck-under" hazards; a high-speed flexible rotor spin-up shaft with positive disengagement during flight; an automatic system of controlling rotor drive on take-off which allows power to be applied until the last moment; centrifugal stops to control rotor blade teetering; and a novel safe starting arrangement.

All Wallis autogyros are at present built for special purposes, and are not on public sale.

WALLIS WA-116 and WA-116-T

Designation of the original Wallis design, of which the prototype (G-ARRT) flew for the first time on 2 August 1961, powered by a 72 hp

Wallis WA-116 autogyro fitted with a Franklin 2A-120-A engine

modified McCulloch 4318 piston engine. Four more WA-116s were built by Beagle and five by Wg Cdr Wallis, as described in the 1973-74 *Jane's*. The last of these was later dismantled for construction of G-AXAS, a tandem two-seat version which was designated WA-116-T and flew for the first time on 3 April 1969.

Descriptions of, and details of earlier achievements by, the WA-116 and WA-116-T have appeared in the 1970-71, 1971-72 and 1972-73 *Jane's*. The WA-116 has remained potentially one of the most promising of the Wallis autogyro designs, particularly following the refitting of G-ASDY in 1971 with a 60 hp Franklin 2A-120-A engine.

It is currently fitted with a Franklin 2A-120-B engine, and suffix designations have now been introduced to indicate the type of engine fitted to various Wallis autogyros. Thus the two-seat WA-116-T is now known as the WA-116/Mc-T, and the Franklin-engined aircraft as WA-116/F.

The WA-116/F continues to perform well, with progressive refinements which include, on the latest Franklin conversions, a four-blade propeller. One WA-116/F conversion under way in the Spring of 1974 was that of the WA-116/Mc previously registered in Ceylon as 4R-ACK. This has now resumed its former British registration G-ATHM and is the subject of a more extensive conversion than its predecessors, mainly to increase fuel capacity and pilot comfort to fit it for special long-range flights. An overload tank will also be fitted, and aerodynamic cleanness improved. It is hoped to use this aircraft, in preference to the more powerful WA-120, for long-range record attempts, possibly in 1974.

WALLIS WA-117

Started in 1964, the WA-117 was intended to combine proven features of the WA-116 airframe with a fully-certificated engine, the 100 hp Rolls-Royce Continental O-200-B. An experimental test vehicle (G-ATCV) flew for the first time on 24 March 1965; this was later dismantled for the construction of a true WA-117 prototype (G-AVJV), which made its first flight on 28 May 1967. This aircraft took part in the Loch Ness investigations in 1970 and, as described in the 1972-73 *Jane's*, was evaluated as a carrying vehicle for HSD Linescan 212 infra-red sensor equipment. A third WA-117 (G-AXAR) was sold to Airmark Ltd for a test and certification programme prior to intended marketing by Airmark. Built by Wg Cdr Wallis's cousin, it had a larger cockpit than the other WA-117s, and a larger (14 Imp gallon; 63·6 litre) fuel tank; but it was lost in a crash at the 1970 SBAC Display at Farnborough. The G-AVJV prototype, which with its special silencers and "quiet" propeller is one of the quietest autogyros yet built, continues to operate as a camera platform for various experimental projects. Recent work for the Department of the Environment, carrying a multi-spectral four-camera pack, has been very successful, and an extension of this work is planned.

WEIGHT:
Max T-O weight approx 700 lb (317 kg)

WA-121, the smallest Wallis autogyro yet flown

PERFORMANCE:
Max level speed 104 knots (120 mph; 193 km/h)
Cruising speed 78 knots (90 mph; 145 km/h)
Max rate of climb approx 1,000 ft (305 m)/min

WALLIS WA-118 METEORITE

Design of the WA-118 Meteorite (G-ATPW) was started in April 1965. Construction began in October 1965 and it flew for the first time on 6 May 1966. It is intended for a long-term test programme, with the emphasis on high-speed and high-altitude research.

The 120 hp supercharged Italian Meteor Alfa 1 engine of this research aircraft was brought up to the latest modification standards during 1969-70, and has been further modified by Wallis Autogyros Ltd to fit it for autogyro operation.

The aircraft, intended for speeds of up to 174 knots (200 mph; 322 km/h), was also fitted with a bubble canopy, reclining cockpit and other modifications and was rebuilt as G-AVJW, making its first flight in this new form on 9 August 1969. It is currently being used as a testbed for modifications to the Alfa 1 engine intended for the WA-121/M.

WALLIS WA-120

Construction of the WA-120 began in early 1970, under the original designation WA-117-S. It subsequently developed into more than a re-engined version of the WA-117, so justifying the use of a new designation.

The WA-120 (G-AYVO) is powered by a 130 hp Rolls-Royce Continental O-240-A "flat-four" engine and flew for the first time on 13 June 1971. Flight operation continues, and after tests in varying climatic conditions the horizontal tail surface has now been removed.

The WA-120 has a forward-sliding transparent cockpit canopy, and can be flown at speeds of up to 60 knots (69 mph; 111 km/h) with this canopy partly open.

WALLIS WA-121

The WA-121, currently in the flight development stage, is the smallest and lightest Wallis autogyro to date. At present, three versions are envisaged: a high-speed version (WA-121/Mc) with a Wallis-McCulloch engine of about 100 hp; a cross-country version (WA-121/F) with a 60 hp Franklin 2A-120-B engine; and a high-altitude version (WA-121/M Meteorite 2) with a supercharged 120 hp Meteor Alfa radial two-stroke engine.

The prototype (G-BAHH) has a high-mounted tailplane and an open cockpit, and made its first flight on 28 December 1972. With the McCulloch engine, it has already exceeded unofficially the speed and altitude records set up by the WA-116 prototype G-ARRT. It employs a number of new features in the rotor head and suspension system, and further improvements are planned.

The next version to be built will be the WA-121/M, employing a transistorised-ignition version of the Meteor Alfa 1 engine; construction is planned for the Winter of 1974-75. The WA-121/F design is expected to benefit from experience gained with the interim WA-116/F conversion G-ATHM.

WESTLAND

WESTLAND AIRCRAFT LTD

HEAD OFFICE, WORKS AND AERODROME:
Yeovil, Somerset BA20 2YB

LONDON OFFICE:
8 The Sanctuary, Westminster, London SW1P 3JU

CHAIRMAN:
D. C. Collins, CBE, CEng, FIMechE, FIProdE, FRAeS

EXECUTIVE VICE-CHAIRMEN:
Walter Oppenheimer, FCA
G. S. Hislop, PhD, BSc, ARCST, CEng, FIMechE, FRAeS, FRSA

DIRECTORS:
The Rt Hon Lord Aberconway
B. D. Blackwell, MA, BSc(Eng), CEng, FIMechE, FRAeS, FBIM
F. E. J. Hallett
Sir Christopher Hartley, KCB, CBE, DFC, AFC, BA
Sir Ronald H. Melville, KCB, MA
Sir Eric Mensforth, CBE, MA, HonDEng, CEng, FIMechE, FRAeS, FIProdE
W. T. C. Miller, MA, CEng, MIMechE, MInstM
S. W. Wiltshire

SECRETARY:
M. Barnes, FCA

PUBLIC RELATIONS EXECUTIVE:
John Teague, CEng, AFRAeS, MInstM, MIPR

Westland Aircraft Ltd was formed in July 1935, to take over the aircraft branch of Petters Ltd, previously known as the Westland Aircraft Works, which had been engaged in aircraft design and construction since 1915.

Westland entered the helicopter industry in 1947 by acquiring the licence to build the Sikorsky S-51, of which it produced 133 under the name Westland Dragonfly. This technical association with Sikorsky has continued, and it was decided subsequently to concentrate the company's resources on the design, development and construction of helicopters.

In 1959, Westland acquired Saunders-Roe Ltd. In 1960, it further acquired the Helicopter Division of Bristol Aircraft Ltd and Fairey Aviation Ltd, as a result of which it is the only major organisation engaged in helicopter design and manufacture in the United Kingdom.

Since 1 October 1966, the company's helicopter business has been conducted through a wholly-owned company named Westland Helicopters Ltd.

Through the British Hovercraft Corporation Ltd, Westland is continuing development of the Hovercraft type of vehicle pioneered by Saunders-Roe, in association with the National Research Development Corporation.

One of Westland's subsidiary companies, Normalair-Garrett Ltd, specialises in the design, development and production of aircraft pressure control, air-conditioning, oxygen breathing and hydraulic systems. Able to supply complete aircraft installations, Normalair-Garrett Ltd is recognised as the foremost European authority in this field. Most British pressurised aircraft, civil and military, use Normalair-Garrett equipment, as do the Panavia MRCA and many aircraft of foreign design. In addition, this company produces data loggers, trace readers and hydraulic equipment for aircraft flying controls.

WESTLAND HELICOPTERS LTD

HEAD OFFICE, WORKS AND AERODROME:
Yeovil, Somerset BA20 2YB
Telephone: Yeovil (0935) 5222
Telex: 46277

CHAIRMAN:
D. C. Collins, CBE, CEng, FIMechE, FIProdE, FRAeS

MANAGING DIRECTOR:
B. D. Blackwell, MA, BSc(Eng), CEng, FIMechE, FRAeS, FBIM

DEPUTY MANAGING DIRECTOR:
J. Speechley, MSc, CEng, FRAeS

FINANCE DIRECTOR:
A. R. B. Hobbs, FCCA

RESEARCH DIRECTOR:
J. P. Jones, PhD, BSc(Eng), CEng, FRAeS

COMMERCIAL DIRECTOR:
A. V. N. Reed, BSc(Tech), CEng, FRAeS, AMBIM

WORKS DIRECTOR:
B. Baxter, BEng, CEng, MI MechE

TECHNICAL DIRECTOR:
V. A. B. Rogers, MSc, CEng, FRAeS, FIMechE

SALES DIRECTOR:
D. N. de Mattos, BSc(Eng), CEng, FIEE, MIMechE, MBIM

DIRECTORS:
Sir Christopher Hartley, KCB, CBE, DFC, AFC, BA
G. S. Hislop, PhD, BSc, ARCST, CEng, FIMechE, FRAeS, FRSA
Walter Oppenheimer, FCA

SECRETARY:
M. S. Double, MA, ACA

YEOVIL DIVISION
TECHNICAL DIRECTOR:
V. A. B. Rogers, MSc, CEng, FRAeS, FIMechE
GENERAL WORKS MANAGER (YEOVIL):
C. F. Read
WORKS MANAGER, AIRCRAFT DIVISION:
C. V. Olsen
WORKS MANAGER, MECHANICAL COMPONENTS DIVISION:
J. Vardé

Helicopters in current production at the Yeovil headquarters of Westland Helicopters are the Sea King, Gazelle and Lynx. The Gazelle and Lynx, together with the Puma, form part of the Anglo-French helicopter co-operation programme.

Gazelle helicopters are in production for both the British and French armed forces. Ten Lynx prototypes have flown, and further prototypes are under construction. The initial production go-ahead for the Lynx was announced by Westland in May 1973, and deliveries of production aircraft will start in 1975. Forty Pumas have been delivered to the RAF, and Westland is now actively involved with the production of component sets for the Pumas built by Aérospatiale.

WESTLAND SEA KING

The Sea King was developed originally by Westland to meet the Royal Navy's requirement for an advanced anti-submarine helicopter with prolonged endurance. It can also undertake a number of secondary roles, such as search and rescue, tactical troop transport, casualty evacuation, cargo carrying and long-range self-ferry. A land-based general-purpose version, known as the Commando, is described separately.

The Sea King development programme stemmed from a licence agreement for the S-61 helicopter concluded originally with Sikorsky in 1959. This permitted Westland to utilise for the Royal Navy Sea King the basic airframe and rotor system of the Sikorsky SH-3D, of which a description can be found in the US section. Considerable changes were made in the power plant and in specialised equipment, to meet British requirements.

The fuselage is essentially similar to that of the basic Sikorsky aircraft, and is of the watertight-hull type which allows water landing in an emergency. The main landing gear, which is retractable, is housed in sponsons braced to the fuselage by fixed struts. To improve the lateral stability and flotation capability of the helicopter with the rotor stopped, inflatable buoyancy bags are fitted to the outside of each sponson.

The following versions of the Sea King had been announced up to mid-1974:

Sea King HAS. Mk 1. ASW version for Royal Navy. A £24 million order for Sea Kings for the Royal Navy was placed in 1967, and a pattern aircraft was imported from the USA for conversion to Sea King prototype standard as XV370. Three sets of components were also imported, and assembled by Westland as pre-production aircraft.

The first production Sea King HAS. Mk 1 (XV642) was flown for the first time on 7 May 1969 and in August 1969 the Royal Navy's first Sea King unit, No. 700S Intensive Flying Trials Squadron, was commissioned. The first operational Sea King squadron was No. 824, and the second No. 826. A total of 56 Sea King HAS. Mk 1s was built, and delivery of these was completed in May 1972. In service with Nos. 814, 819, 820, 824 and 826 Squadrons.

Sea King Mk 41. Search and rescue version for Federal German Navy. First example (89 + 50) flown for first time on 6 March 1972. Twenty-two ordered, of which production and delivery was due for completion in mid-1974. First unit to equip with these aircraft is MFG.5, based at Kiel-Holtenau.

Sea King Mk 42. ASW version for Indian Navy. Original order for six, which are in service with No. 330 Squadron. Delivery of a further six was due to be completed by early 1974.

Sea King Mk 43. SAR version for Norwegian Air Force. Ten ordered, all of which were delivered in 1972. In service with No. 330 Squadron at Bodø.

Sea King Mk 45. ASW version for Pakistan Navy, in production in early 1973. Six ordered, of which delivery was due to begin in mid-1974.

Sea King Mk 48. SAR version for Belgian Air Force. Five ordered, of which delivery is due to be completed by the end of 1975.

Sea King Mk 50. Version, developed from Mk 1, for Royal Australian Navy, which has ordered 10. Production, which includes offset manufacture in Australia to 30% of the contract value, began in 1973, and delivery was due to begin in the Autumn of 1974. This version has 1,590 shp (max contingency rating) Gnome H.1400-1 engines, uprated transmission, a six-blade tail rotor and a max T-O weight of 21,000 lb (9,525 kg). It will be capable of operation in the roles of anti-submarine search and strike, tactical troop lift, search and rescue, casualty evacuation, and self-ferry.

In addition, some Sea Kings are included in the order for 30 helicopters placed by Saudi Arabia on behalf of the Egyptian government, bringing to 153 the total number of Sea King and Commando aircraft ordered up to 1 May 1974.

POWER PLANT: Two 1,500 shp (except Sea King Mk 50 version) Rolls-Royce Gnome H.1400 turboshaft engines. To meet Royal Navy requirements these engines feature the full authority electronic engine governing system. This provides precise control of rotor speed in steady-state and transient manoeuvres. Standard fuel system has a maximum capacity of 704 Imp gallons (3,200 litres), contained in bag tanks beneath the cabin floor, arranged to provide two completely independent main systems and an auxiliary system. The system may be pressure or gravity refuelled and defuelled and provision is made for fuel jettison. An increased-capacity system of 800 Imp gallons (3,636 litres) is available, involving the addition of an extra underfloor tank. One or two long-range ferry tanks can be accommodated in the main cabin. Each of these has a maximum fuel capacity of 1,500 lb (680 kg), but as this system utilises cabin space it is intended primarily for the self-ferry role.

SYSTEMS: Three main hydraulic systems. Primary and auxiliary systems operate main rotor control. Utility system (3,000 lb/sq in; 210 kg/cm²) for main landing gear, sonar and rescue winches and blade folding. Pressure for windscreen wipers 1,250 lb/sq in (88 kg/cm²). Electrical system includes two 20kVA 200V three-phase 400Hz engine-driven generators, a 26V single-phase AC supply fed from the aircraft's 22Ah nickel-cadmium battery through an inverter, and DC power provided as a secondary system from two 200A transformer-rectifier units.

OPERATIONAL EQUIPMENT (ASW models): As equipped for this role, the Sea King is a fully-integrated all-weather hunter-killer weapons system, capable of operating independently of surface vessels, and has the following equipment and weapons to achieve this task: Plessey Type 195 dipping sonar, Marconi-Elliott AD 580 Doppler navigation system, AW 391 search radar in dorsal radome, transponder beneath rear fuselage, Honeywell AN/APN 171 radio altimeter, Sperry GM7B Gyrosyn compass system, Louis Newmark Mk 31 automatic flight control system, two No. 4 marine markers, four No. 2 Mk 2 smoke floats, up to four Mk 44 homing torpedoes, or four Mk 11 depth charges or one Clevite simulator. Observer/navigator has tactical display on which sonar contacts are integrated with search radar and navigational information. Radio equipment comprises Plessey PTR 377 UHF/VHF and homer, Ultra D 403M standby UHF, Collins 618-T3 HF radio, Ultra UA 60M intercom, Telebrief system and IFF provisions. For secondary role a mounting is provided on the aft frame of the starboard door for a general-purpose machine-gun. The Mk 31 AFCS provides radio altitude displays for both pilots; artificial horizon displays; three-axis stabilisation in pilot-controlled manoeuvres; attitude hold, heading hold and height hold in cruising flight; controlled transition manoeuvres to and from the hover; automatic height control and plan position control in the hover; and an auxiliary trim facility.

OPERATIONAL EQUIPMENT (Search and rescue and transport models): Standard radio and navigational equipment includes Plessey PTR 377 UHF/VHF with UHF homing, Ultra D 403M standby UHF, Collins 618-T3 HF, Ultra UA 60M intercom, Honeywell AN/APN-171 radio altimeter, Marconi-Elliott AD 580 Doppler navigation system, Sperry compass system, AW 391 search radar, Marconi-Elliott AD 370S ADF, Collins 51R-8B VOR/ILS, Collins 51V-5 glideslope receiver and Collins 51Z-4 marker receiver. Sea Kings equipped for search and rescue have in addition a Breeze BL 10300 variable-speed hydraulic rescue hoist of 600 lb (272 kg) capacity mounted above the starboard-side cargo door. Automatic main rotor blade folding and spreading is standard with this version, and for shipboard operation the tail pylon can also be folded. With search radar fitted, a total of 18 survivors and medical staff can be carried; this total can be increased to 22 if the search radar is omitted. In the casualty evacuation role, the Sea King can accommodate up to 9 stretchers and two medical attendants, or intermediate combinations of seats and stretchers; a typical layout might provide for 14 seats and two stretchers. In the troop transport role, the Sea King can accommodate 22 troops, with the majority of seats at 16·5 in (42 cm) pitch, and can carry this load over a range of 300 nm (345 miles; 555 km) under ISA sea level conditions. As a cargo transport, the aircraft has an internal capacity of 6,000 lb (2,720 kg) or a max external load capacity of 8,000 lb (3,630 kg) when a low-response sling is fitted.

Westland Sea King Mk 41, one of 22 being delivered to the Federal German Navy and already in service with Marinefliegergruppe 5 at Kiel-Holtenau

DIMENSIONS, EXTERNAL:
Diameter of main rotor 62 ft 0 in (18·90 m)
Diameter of tail rotor 10 ft 4 in (3·16 m)
Length overall (rotors turning) 72 ft 8 in (22·15 m)
Length of fuselage 55 ft $9\frac{3}{4}$ in (17·01 m)
Length overall (main rotor folded) 57 ft 2 in (17·42 m)
Length overall (rotors and tail folded) 47 ft 3 in (14·40 m)
Height overall (rotors turning) 16 ft 10 in (5·13 m)
Height overall (rotors spread and stationary) 15 ft 11 in (4·85 m)
Height to top of rotor hub 15 ft 6 in (4·72 m)
Width overall (rotors folded):
with flotation bags 16 ft 4 in (4·98 m)
without flotation bags 15 ft 8 in (4·77 m)
Wheel track (c/l of shock struts) 13 ft 0 in (3·96 m)
Cabin door (port):
Height 5 ft 6 in (1·68 m)
Width 3 ft 0 in (0·91 m)
Cargo door (stbd):
Height 5 ft 0 in (1·52 m)
Width 5 ft 8 in (1·73 m)
Height to sill 3 ft 9 in (1·14 m)

DIMENSIONS, INTERNAL:
Cabin: Length:
ASW 19 ft 3 in (5·87 m)
SAR 24 ft 11 in (7·59 m)
Max width 6 ft 6 in (1·98 m)
Max height 6 ft $3\frac{1}{2}$ in (1·92 m)

WEIGHTS (A: anti-submarine, B: SAR, C: troop transport, D: casualty evacuation, E: internal cargo):
Basic weight:
A, C, D, E 12,975 lb (5,885 kg)
B 12,900 lb (5,851 kg)
Manufacturer's weight empty:
Mk 50 13,181 lb (5,978 kg)
Weight, equipped:
A 15,474 lb (7,019 kg)
B 13,660 lb (6,196 kg)
C 12,491 lb (5,666 kg)
D 14,418 lb (6,540 kg)
E 13,430 lb (6,092 kg)
Max T-O weight:
all versions except Mk 50 20,500 lb (9,300 kg)
Mk 50 21,000 lb (9,525 kg)

PERFORMANCE (at max T-O weight, all versions except Mk 50):
Max never-exceed speed 124 knots (143 mph; 230 km/h)
Normal operating speed 114 knots (131 mph; 211 km/h)
Max endurance speed 75 knots (86 mph; 138 km/h)
Max rate of climb at S/L 1,770 ft (540 m)/min
Max rate of climb at S/L, one engine out 324 ft (99 m)/min
Approved ceiling 10,000 ft (3,050 m)
Ferry/transit range (SAR model):
standard fuel 520 nm (598 miles; 963 km)
auxiliary fuel 750 nm (863 miles; 1,390 km)

PERFORMANCE (Mk 50 at max T-O weight):
Max level speed 132 knots (152 mph; 245 km/h)
Normal operating speed 110 knots (127 mph; 204 km/h)

WESTLAND COMMANDO

First announced by Westland on 14 July 1971, the Commando is a tactical helicopter based on the Sea King.

The payload/range performance and endurance capabilities of the Sea King have been optimised in the design of the Commando, which is intended to operate with maximum efficiency in the primary roles of tactical troop transport, logistic support and cargo transport, and casualty evacuation. In addition, the Commando can operate effectively in the secondary roles of air-to-surface strike and search and rescue.

The first five Commandos, part of a larger order placed on behalf of Egypt by the Saudi Arabian government, were of the **Mk 1** version, a minimally-modified version able to transport up to 25 troops. The first two Commando Mk 1s were flown for the first time on 12 and 13 September 1973, and were delivered to Egypt in January/February 1974.

The major production version, to which the following description applies, is the **Commando Mk 2.** The Saudi Arabian order for 30 Sea King/Commando helicopters includes a number of Mk 2s. In addition, two Mk 2s have been ordered by another, undisclosed Middle Eastern country.

TYPE: Twin-turboshaft tactical military helicopter.

ROTOR SYSTEM: Five-blade single main rotor and six-blade tail rotor. Main rotor blades, of NACA 0012 section, attached to hub by multiple bolted joint. Blade construction consists of a light alloy extruded spar, with light alloy trailing-edge pockets. Tail rotor blades are of similar construction. Rotor brake fitted. Tail section folds for stowage; main rotor blades do not.

ROTOR DRIVE: Twin input four-stage reduction main gearbox, with single bevel intermediate and tail gearboxes. Main rotor/engine rpm ratio 93·43; tail rotor/engine rpm ratio: 15·26.

FUSELAGE: Light alloy stressed-skin structure, unpressurised.

TAIL UNIT: Similar to Sea King, with starboard-side half-tailplane at top of tail rotor pylon.

LANDING GEAR: Non-retractable tailwheel type, with twin-wheel main units. Oleo-pneumatic shock-absorbers. Main-wheel tyres size 6·50-10, tailwheel tyre size 6·00-6.

POWER PLANT: Two 1,590 shp (max contingency rating) Rolls-Royce Gnome H.1400-1 turboshaft engines, mounted side by side above cabin. Fuel in underfloor bag tanks, total capacity 800 Imp gallons (3,636 litres). Internal auxiliary tank may be fitted for long-range ferry purposes. Pressure refuelling point on starboard side, two gravity points on port side.

ACCOMMODATION: Crew of two on flight deck. Seats along cabin sides, and single jump seat, for total of 28 troops. Two-piece airstair door at front on port side, cargo door at rear on starboard side. Entire accommodation heated and ventilated. Cockpit doors and windows, and two windows each side of main cabin, are jettisonable in an emergency.

SYSTEMS: Primary and secondary hydraulic systems for flight controls. No pneumatic system. Electrical system includes two 20kVA alternators.

ELECTRONICS AND EQUIPMENT: Blind-flying instrumentation standard. Wide range of radio, radar and navigation equipment available to customer's requirements. Cargo sling and rescue hoist optional.

ARMAMENT: Wide range of guns, missiles, etc may be carried, according to customer's requirements.

DIMENSIONS, EXTERNAL:
Diameter of main rotor 62 ft 0 in (18·90 m)
Diameter of tail rotor 10 ft 4 in (3·16 m)
Distance between rotor centres 36 ft 5 in (11·10 m)
Main rotor blade chord 1 ft $6\frac{1}{4}$ in (0·46 m)
Length overall (rotors turning) 72 ft 8 in (22·15 m)
Length of fuselage 55 ft 10 in (17·02 m)
Height overall (rotors turning) 16 ft 10 in (5·13 m)
Height to top of rotor hub 15 ft 6 in (4·72 m)
Wheel track (c/l of shock struts) 13 ft 0 in (3·96 m)
Wheelbase 23 ft 8 in (7·21 m)
Passenger door (fwd, port):
Height 5 ft 6 in (1·68 m)
Width 3 ft 0 in (0·91 m)
Cargo door (aft, stbd):
Height 5 ft 0 in (1·52 m)
Width 5 ft 8 in (1·73 m)

DIMENSIONS, INTERNAL:
As Sea King (SAR version)

AREAS:
Main rotor disc 3,019 sq ft (280·5 m^2)
Tail rotor disc 83·86 sq ft (7·79 m^2)
Main rotor blades (each) 44·54 sq ft (4·14 m^2)
Tail rotor blades (each) 2·46 sq ft (0·23 m^2)
Tailplane 19·40 sq ft (1·80 m^2)

WEIGHTS:
Operating weight empty (troop transport, 2 crew) 12,222 lb (5,543 kg)
Max T-O and landing weight 21,000 lb (9,525 kg)

PERFORMANCE (at 21,000 lb; 9,525 kg AUW, ISA):
Cruising speed at S/L 112 knots (129 mph; 208 km/h)
Max rate of climb at S/L 2,020 ft (616 m)/min
Vertical rate of climb at S/L 390 ft (119 m)/min
Service ceiling, one engine out 4,000 ft (1,220 m)
Hovering ceiling in ground effect 5,000 ft (1,525 m)
Hovering ceiling out of ground effect 3,200 ft (975 m)
Range with max payload (28 troops), reserves for 30 min stand-off and T-O 305 nm (351 miles; 564 km)
Range with max normal fuel 664 nm (764 miles; 1,230 km)
Ferry range with max normal and auxiliary fuel 814 nm (937 miles; 1,507 km)

WESTLAND/AÉROSPATIALE LYNX

The Lynx is one of three types of aircraft (Puma, Gazelle and Lynx) covered by the Anglo-French helicopter agreement first proposed in February 1967 and confirmed on 2 April 1968. On 1 December 1972 a long-term agreement was signed between Westland Helicopters and Aérospatiale to formalise and strengthen the existing collaboration programme. Westland has design leadership in the Lynx, which is a medium-sized helicopter intended to fulfil general-purpose, naval and civil transport roles. It is the first British aircraft to be designed entirely on a metric basis.

First Commando Mk 1 troop transport helicopter, developed from the Westland Sea King

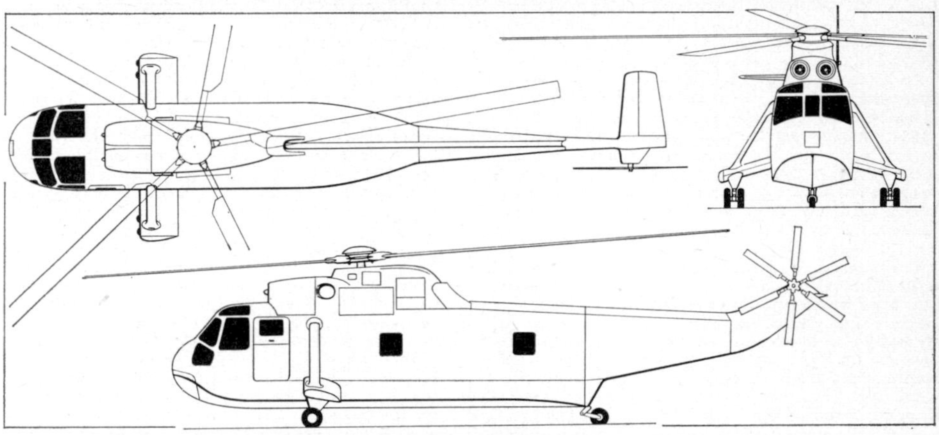

Westland Commando Mk 2 twin-turboshaft tactical military helicopter *(Pilot Press)*

Five basic aircraft are being used by Westland to prove the fundamental design parameters. Following flight testing of two Scout helicopters fitted with scaled-down versions of the Lynx rotor system, the first Lynx prototype (XW835) flew for the first time on 21 March 1971 and was followed by XW837, the third prototype (second Lynx to fly), on 28 September 1971. Third to fly was the fourth Lynx (XW838, on 9 March 1972), the first to have the monobloc rotor head designed for production aircraft. Then followed, on 24 March 1972, the first flight of the second aircraft (XW836), which had previously been used for ground vibration testing. The fifth Lynx to fly (XX153, on 12 April 1972) is a development aircraft for the British Army AH. Mk 1 version. In addition to these five aircraft, a sixth Lynx (XX907, first flight 20 May 1973) was allocated to Rolls-Royce for engine development. Other airframes have been built for static, fatigue and electrical testing.

On 20 and 22 June 1972 respectively, piloted by Roy Moxam, XX153 set up Class E1e international speed records of 173·61 knots (199·92 mph; 321·74 km/h) over a 15/25 km straight course and 171·868 knots (197·909 mph; 318·504 km/h) over a 100 km closed circuit. During the flight test programme the Lynx has been rolled at more than 100° per second, dived at 200 knots (230 mph; 370 km/h), and flown backwards at 70 knots (80 mph; 130 km/h).

A further seven aircraft are being used for the main military development programme. First of these to fly was XX469, first prototype for the Royal Navy HAS. Mk 2 version, which made its first flight on 25 May 1972. The second Royal Navy prototype, XX510, flew for the first time on 6 March 1973. The first French Navy prototype (XX904) made its first flight on 6 July 1973, and the second (XX911) on 18 September 1973. The three remaining prototypes, all of which were due to have flown by the Spring of 1974, comprise one more Royal Navy version, one common naval version, and one basic version.

The following versions of the Lynx have been announced:

Lynx AH. Mk 1. General-purpose and utility version for the British Army, due to enter service in the Autumn of 1976. Development aircraft XX153 and XX907. Capable of operation on tactical troop transport, logistic support, armed escort of troop-carrying helicopters, anti-tank strike, search and rescue, casualty evacuation, reconnaissance and command post duties.

Lynx HAS. Mk 2. Version for Royal Navy, for advanced shipborne anti-submarine and other duties. Due to enter service in early 1976, following first production deliveries in 1975. Ferranti Seaspray search and tracking radar in modified nose. Capable of operation on anti-submarine classification and strike, air to surface vessel search and strike, search and rescue, reconnaissance, troop transport, fire support, communication and fleet liaison, and vertical replenishment duties. Two development aircraft (XX469 and XX510) originally, of which the former carried out deck landing trials at RAE Bedford and, on 4 August 1972, on board the French destroyer *Tourville* in harbour. This aircraft was subsequently lost in an accident and was to be replaced by one of the final three prototypes. Sea trials on board the helicopter support ship RFA *Engadine*, by XX510, began on 29 June 1973, and air launches of dummy Skua weapons have been made. A further series of trials on board the *Tourville* was completed under operational conditions at sea in the Spring of 1974.

The Argentine Navy has expressed its intention to order two aircraft of a similar type.

Lynx (French Navy). Naval version, generally similar to British HAS. Mk 2 but with more advanced target detection equipment. Two development aircraft (XX904 and XX911), both of which were handed over to Aérospatiale in the Autumn of 1973 for equipment to Aéronavale standard and continuation of testing in France.

Lynx HT. Mk 3. Training version for Royal Air Force.

Sea Lynx. Name given by Sikorsky Aircraft to a proposed version to meet the US Navy's LAMPS (Light Airborne Multi-Purpose System) requirement for a successor to the Kaman SH-2 Seasprite. Westland and Sikorsky are negotiating an agreement for a marketing programme to present the Sea Lynx as the Sikorsky candidate in this programme. Preliminary tests, using a Lynx mock-up, were initiated by Sikorsky in April 1972.

Civil Lynx. Westland plans to market a civil Lynx, based on the general-purpose version, from about 1976. Layouts being studied include an eight-seat executive transport version. Max accommodation would be for pilot and 13 passengers or 3,000 lb (1,360 kg) of internal or slung cargo.

The first Lynx production order, covering the setting up of production facilities and ordering of materials for more than 100 aircraft, was placed by the Ministry of Defence in May 1973; confirmation of this contract, which covers aircraft for the British and French Navies and the British Army, was announced in February 1974. On 30 July 1973 Ferranti announced receipt of a contract for 100 Seaspray radars for installation in the British naval version. Lynx production will be shared in the ratio of 70% by Westland to 30% by Aérospatiale.

The following description applies generally to the basic military general-purpose and naval versions, except where a specific version is indicated:

TYPE: Twin-engined multi-purpose helicopter.

ROTOR SYSTEM: Single four-blade semi-rigid main rotor and four-blade tail rotor. The main rotor blades, which are interchangeable, are of cambered aerofoil section and embody mass taper. Each blade consists of a two-piece, two-channel stainless steel D-shaped box-spar, to which is bonded a glassfibre-reinforced plastics rear skin stabilised by a Nomex plastics honeycomb core. Blade tips are of moulded glassfibre-reinforced plastics, with a stainless steel anti-erosion sheath forward of the 50% chord line. Each blade is attached to the main rotor hub by titanium root attachment plates and a flexible arm; the inboard portion of each arm accommodates most of the flapping movement of each blade, while the outer portion provides freedom in the lag plane. The rotor hub and inboard portions of the flexible arms are built as a complete unit, in the form of a titanium monobloc forging. A feathering hinge, comprising double needle bearings, is incorporated between the inboard and outboard flexible arms. The feathering hinge bearings are relieved of centrifugal loading by a flexible torsion bar which joints the inboard and outboard section of each arm. A two-pin jaw for blade attachment and manual blade folding is provided. Each of the tail rotor blades has a light alloy spar, machined integrally with the root attachment, which forms the nose portion of the aerofoil section and has a flush-fitting stainless steel sheath on the leading-edge. The rear section of each blade is of similar construction to that of the main rotor blades. The tail rotor hub has conventional flapping and feathering hinges, and incorporates torsionally flexible tiebars which carry the centrifugal loads inboard to the flapping hinges. Tail rotor blades are replaceable in matched pairs, and each blade is attached to the hub by the outboard tiebar pin and a six-bolt root-end flanged joint. Main rotor blades of both versions can be folded, and tail rotor pylon of naval version can be folded and spread manually, to reduce overall length for stowage.

ROTOR DRIVE: Transmission consists of three interconnected gearboxes, transmitting power to the main and tail rotors. The engines are mounted from extensions of the gearbox casing through gimbal and flexible couplings which permit a degree of angular misalignment. The drives are taken from the front of the engines into the main gearbox, which is mounted above the cabin forward of the engines. This gearbox interconnects the two engines, with the speed reduction being carried out in two stages. The first stage uses an involute-form spiral bevel pinion and gear. The second stage comprises a conformal pinion meshing with a gear fixed directly to the main rotor drive-shaft. In flight, the accessory gears, which are all at the front of the main gearbox, are driven by one of the two through shafts from the first-stage reduction gears. For system checking on the ground without the rotor turning, the accessories can be driven by the port engine via a through shaft, a lockout freewheel unit being selected manually to isolate the main rotor transmission from the port engine input drive. Freewheel units are mounted in each engine gearbox shaft, and also within the accessory drive chain of gears. Rotor head controls are actuated by three identical tandem servojacks, trunnion-mounted from the main rotor gearbox and powered by two independent hydraulic systems. The collective jack is mounted centrally on the forward end of the main gearbox, with the cyclic jacks positioned at 45° on each side. Duplex autostabiliser actuators are integral with each jack. Cyclic and collective inputs from the three control jacks are translated to the lower bearing housing of a four-arm spider which is located within, and rotates with, the main rotor shaft. The spider is mounted universally within a splined section of the main shaft, above its bearing housing, and is linked to the blade pitch-change levers by four adjustable-length track rods. Rod and lever control runs are employed on both the cyclic and collective systems, and are carried within protective ducts below the cockpit floor, up to cabin roof level on both sides of the aircraft, and finally to the rotor head. Yaw control runs are initially by rod and lever, and then to cables which transmit pedal movements along the tailboom to the tail rotor control jack, which in turn effects blade pitch changes. Spring feel units and electric trim motors for the cyclic control channels are installed below the cockpit floor. Yaw control pedals are adjustable separately over a wide speed range. Control system incorporates a simple stability augmentation system, which acts in a single channel to provide improved stability in pitch. Provision is made for in-flight blade tracking. Each engine embodies an independent control system

Lynx prototype XX907, used formerly as an engine testbed and now acting as development aircraft for the British Army AH. Mk 1 version

Two Lynx naval prototypes: XX510 for the Royal Navy in foreground, with the French Navy aircraft XX904 in flight at rear

which provides full-authority rotor speed governing, pilot control being limited to selection of the desired rotor speed range. In the event of an engine failure, this system will restore power up to single-engine maximum contingency rating to maintain the power turbine/rotor governed speed within the prescribed limits. A single, centrally-mounted rotor speed select lever, with a limited authority, sets the datum of the power turbine/rotor speed governing system. This system meters fuel to maintain the selected speed throughout the flight condition range. A fine-adjustment trimming control is provided to facilitate accurate matching of each engine. On the naval versions, the main rotor can provide negative thrust to increase stability on deck after touchdown. Tail rotor drive is taken from the main ring gear. A hydraulically-operated rotor brake is mounted on the main gearbox at the tail rotor drive-shaft coupling, the shaft continuing aft to the single-stage, bevel reduction type intermediate and tail rotor gearboxes. Pitch variation of the tail rotor blades is controlled by a spider, actuated by hydraulic jack via a pushrod which extends through the centre of the tail rotor gearbox.

Fuselage and Tail Unit: Conventional semi-monocoque pod and boom structure, mainly of light alloy, including a cantilever floor structure with unobstructed surface. Glassfibre components used for access panels, doors and fairings. The forward fuselage is free from bulkheads, giving an unrestricted field of view. Three large windows in each of the main cabin sliding doors. Provision for internally-mounted defensive armament, and for universal flange mountings on each side of the exterior to carry weapons or other stores. Tailboom is a light alloy monocoque structure bearing the sweptback vertical fin/tail rotor pylon, which has a half-tailplane near the tip on the starboard side. Tailplane leading- and trailing-edges, and bullet fairings of tail rotor gearbox, are of glassfibre.

Landing Gear (general-purpose version): Non-retractable tubular skid type. Provision for a pair of adjustable ground handling wheels on rear of each skid. Flotation gear optional.

Landing Gear (naval version): Non-retractable oleo-pneumatic tricycle type. Single-wheel main units, mounted on sponsons near rear of main fuselage, are fixed at 27° toe-out for deck landing, and can be manually turned into line and locked fore and aft for movement of aircraft into and out of ship's hangar. Twin-wheel nose unit can be castored hydraulically through 90° by the pilot. Designed for high shock-absorption to facilitate take-off from, and landing on, small decks under severe sea and weather conditions. Sprag brakes (wheel locks) fitted to each wheel prevent rotation on landing or inadvertent deck roll. These locks are disengaged hydraulically and will automatically re-engage in the event of hydraulic failure. Friction brakes may be fitted for shore use. Flotation gear, and hydraulically-actuated harpoon deck-lock securing system, optional.

Power Plant: Two Rolls-Royce BS.360-07-26 Gem turboshaft engines. Each has a max continuous rating of 750 shp, a take-off and inter-contingency rating of 830 shp, and a max contingency rating (2½ min) of 900 shp. Engines are mounted side by side on top of the fuselage upper decking, aft of the main rotor shaft and gearbox, and are separated from the fuselage, transmission area and each other by firewalls. Engine air intakes are de-iced electrically. Fuel in five crashproof bag-type tanks, all within the fuselage structure, comprising two main tanks each of 450 lb (204 kg) capacity, two side-by-side collector tanks each of 204·5 lb (93 kg) capacity, and a 326 lb (148 kg) capacity underfloor tank at the forward end of the cabin. Total fuel capacity 1,635 lb (742 kg). Cross-feed system allows fuel to be supplied from both collector tanks to one engine or from one tank to both engines. If required, ferry range can be increased by installing in the rear of the cabin two metal auxiliary tanks with a combined capacity of 1,600 lb (726 kg). Single-point pressure refuelling (55 lb/sq in; 3·87 kg/cm² max) and defuelling; two points for gravity refuelling. A removable 25 Imp gallons (114 litres)/min pressure refuelling/defuelling pack can be fitted in the cabin which, with the port engine running, can be used to refuel the aircraft from dump stocks on the ground or containers suspended from the hoist. It is also possible to raise fuel about 15 ft (5 m) while the aircraft is hovering. Fuel jettison capability for main and forward tanks. Provision for self-sealing of both collector tanks (except in Royal Navy version) to provide protection against small-arms fire. Engine oil tank capacity 1·5 Imp gallons (6·8 litres). Main rotor gearbox oil capacity 4 Imp gallons (18 litres).

Accommodation: Pilot and co-pilot or observer on side-by-side seats which can accommodate back-type dinghies and are adjustable fore and aft and for height. Inertia-reel shoulder harness for pilot and co-pilot. Additional crew members (eg, gunner, hoist operator) according to role. Individual forward-hinged cockpit door and large rearward-sliding cabin door on each side; all four doors are jettisonable. Cockpit is accessible from cabin area. Maximum high-density layout (general-purpose version) for one pilot and 10 armed troops or paratroops, on lightweight bench seats in soundproofed cabin. Alternative VIP layouts for four to seven passengers, with additional cabin soundproofing. Seats can be removed quickly to permit the carriage of up to 2,000 lb (907 kg) of freight internally. Tie-down rings are provided at approx 20 in (508 mm) intervals on main cabin floor, which is stressed for loads of up to 200 lb/sq ft (976 kg/m²). Alternatively, loads of up to 3,000 lb (1,360 kg) can be carried externally on a freight hook mounted below the cabin floor and fitted, in naval version, with an electrically-operated emergency release system. In the casualty evacuation role, with a crew of two, the Lynx can accommodate three standard stretchers and a medical attendant; electrically-heated casualty bags can be provided. Both versions have secondary capability for search and rescue (up to nine survivors) and other roles (see introductory copy and "Equipment" paragraphs). An 8/13-seat civil transport version is being studied.

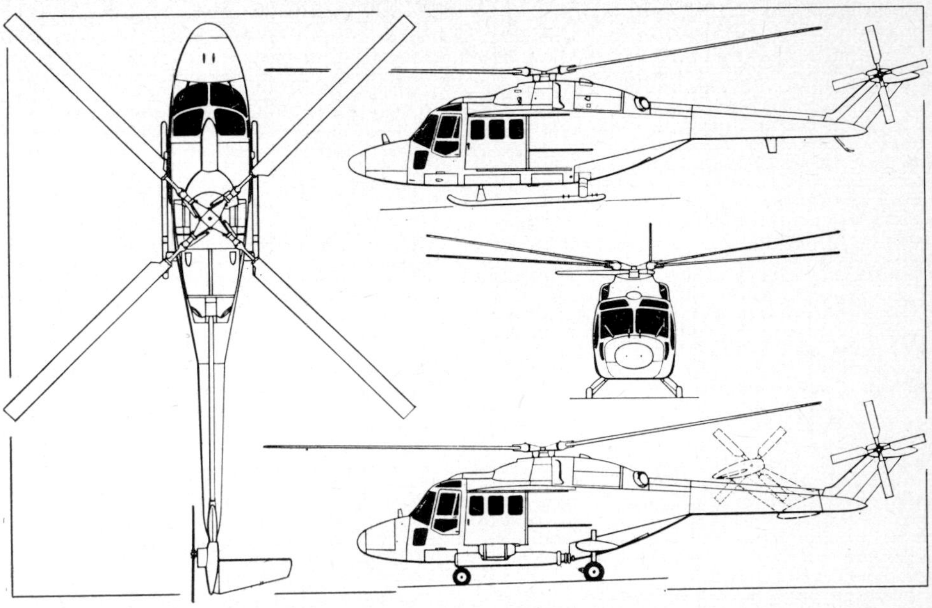

Westland Lynx AH. Mk 1 light general-purpose helicopter, with additional side view (*bottom*) **of Lynx HAS.Mk 2** (*Pilot Press*)

Systems: Two independent hydraulic systems in all versions, pressure 2,050 lb/sq in (144 kg/cm²). Pumps are powered by accessory drive from main rotor gearbox, enabling full power to be drawn from both main systems in the event of an engine failure. If either No. 1 or No. 2 main system fails, the other maintains adequate flying control. No. 1 system, additionally, actuates the tail rotor yaw control and the rotor brake. Tail rotor operation reverts to mechanical control if No. 1 system fails. A third hydraulic system, at the same pressure, is provided in the naval version when sonar equipment, MAD or a hydraulic winch system are installed. When this third hydraulic system is installed, the deck-lock harpoon is also operated by this system. No pneumatic system. 28V DC electrical power is supplied by two 6kW engine-driven starter/generators and an alternator. Engines can also be started from an external 28V DC power source. A 24V 23Ah (optionally 40Ah) nickel-cadmium battery is fitted for essential services and emergency engine starting. 200V three-phase AC power is available at 400Hz from two 15kVA transmission-driven alternators. AC and DC external ground power sockets are fitted on starboard side of fuselage. Graviner Triple FD engine fire detection system; two separate fire suppression systems are fitted, but are interconnected to permit contents of both bottles to be directed to one engine if necessary. All versions are fitted with a centralised standard warning system which provides visual and audio warnings of major emergencies, visual warnings for secondary failure, and visual indications of an advisory nature. Optional cabin heating and ventilation system, using a mixing unit combining engine bleed air with outside air. Optional supplementary cockpit heating system. Electrical anti-icing and demisting of windscreen, and electrically-operated windscreen wipers, are standard; windscreen washing system is optional.

Electronics and Flight Equipment: Main equipment bays are in nose (under upward-hinged door) and at rear of cabin. All versions equipped as standard with navigation, cabin and cockpit lights; adjustable landing light under nose; anti-collision beacon; first aid kit(s); and hand-type fire extinguishers for cabin. Optional equipment common to all roles (general-purpose and RN versions) includes simplex four-axis cross-country autopilot system; Plessey PTR 377 UHF/VHF transceiver with homing; Ultra D 403M standby UHF; S.G. Brown three-position crew intercom. Optional role equipment or installations for both versions include Marconi-Elliott automatic flight control system (AFCS); AN/ARC-44 VHF(FM); Collins 718 UA HF; VOR/ILS; DME; AN/ARN-52 TACAN (general-purpose version only); X-band transponder (naval version only); Sperry C2J or GM9B Gyrosyn compass system; Sperry E2C standby compass; Plessey PTR 446 IFF transponder; AD 360 radio compass (general-purpose version only); Honeywell AN/APN-198 radar altimeter; dual controls; Decca Tactical Air Navigation System (TANS) with Decca Type 71 Doppler radar; Decca Mk 19 flight log; and vortex-type sand filter for engine air intakes. Additional AFCS units in general-purpose version permit automatic turns and radio height hold; in naval version, when sonar is fitted, these units are extended to provide automatic transition to the hover and automatic Doppler hold in the hover. Other optional equipment (both versions) includes signal pistol and cartridges, Aldis lamp and stowage.

Armament and Operational Equipment: For armed escort, anti-tank or air-to-surface strike missions, the general-purpose version can be equipped with one 20 mm AME 621 or similar cannon, with 1,500 rds, or a pintle-mounted 7·62 mm GEC Minigun inside the cabin; or a Minigun beneath the cabin, in an Emerson Minitat installation, with 3,000 rds. An external pylon can be fitted on each side of the cabin for a variety of stores, including two Minigun or other self-contained gun pods; two pods of fourteen and two of seven 2 in rockets; pods of 68 mm SNEB rockets; or up to six BAC Hawkswing or Aérospatiale AS.11, or eight Aérospatiale/MBB Hot or Hughes TOW, or similar air-to-surface missiles. An additional six or eight missiles can be carried in the cabin, for re-arming in forward areas, and an Avimo-Ferranti 530 lightweight stabilised sight is fitted for target detection and missile direction. The Lynx can also transport mobile anti-tank teams consisting of three gunners with missiles and launchers. For the search and rescue role, with a crew of three, both versions can be fitted with a waterproof floor, four 5 in flares (three in naval version), and a 600 lb (272 kg) capacity electrically-operated "clip-on" hoist in the starboard side of the cabin. Alternative option of hydraulically-operated hoist in naval version when third hydraulic system is installed. The hoist, which can lift a load through 250 ft (76 m) at 100 ft (30·5 m)/min, can be swung back into the cabin when not in use, permitting the sliding door to be closed. The general-purpose version can also be equipped for several other duties, including firefighting and crash rescue, reconnaissance, military command post, liaison, customs and border control, and pilot and operational training. Optional equipment, according to role, can include lightweight sighting system with alternative target magnification, vertical and/or oblique cameras, up to six 5 in flares for night operation, low light level TV, infra-red linescan, searchlight, and specialised communications equipment. The naval version can carry out a number of these roles, but has specialised equipment for its primary duties. For the ASW role, this includes two Mk 44 or Mk 46 homing torpedoes, one each on an external pylon on each side of the fuselage, and six marine markers; or two Mk 11 depth charges. Detection of the submarine can either be carried out by the parent ship (in which case the Lynx carries retractable classification and localisation equipment), or the Lynx can itself be equipped for this function, with Alcatel D.U.A.V.4 lightweight dunking sonar, and hydraulically-powered winch and cable hover mode facilities within the AFCS. Ferranti Seaspray lightweight search and tracking radar, for detecting small surface targets in low visibility/high sea conditions, Armament includes BAC CL834 Skua semi-active homing missiles for attacking light surface craft; alternatively, four AS.12 or similar wire-guided missiles can be employed in conjunction with an AF 530 or APX-334 lightweight stabilised optical sighting system.

DIMENSIONS, EXTERNAL (A: general-purpose version; N: naval version):
Diameter of main rotor (A, N) 42 ft 0 in (12·802 m)
Diameter of tail rotor (A, N) 7 ft 3 in (2·21 m)
Main rotor blade chord (A, N, constant, each) 1 ft 3·4 in (0·39 m)
Tail rotor blade chord (A, N, constant, each) 7·1 in (180 mm)
Length overall, both rotors turning (A, N) 49 ft 9 in (15·163 m)
Length overall:
A, main rotor blades folded 43 ft 2·3 in (13·165 m)
N, main rotor blades and tail folded 34 ft 10 in (10·618 m)
Length of fuselage, nose to tail rotor centre:
A 39 ft 6·8 in (12·06 m)
N 39 ft 1·3 in (11·92 m)
Width overall, main rotor blades folded:
A, N 9 ft 7·75 in (2·94 m)
N, main wheels fore and aft 10 ft 0 in (3·05 m)
Height overall, both rotors turning:
A, N 12 ft 0 in (3·66 m)
Height overall, both rotors stopped:
A 11 ft 6 in (3·504 m)
N 11 ft 0·5 in (3·365 m)
Height to top of rotor hub:
A 9 ft 8·7 in (2·964 m)
Height overall, main rotor blades and tail folded:
N 10 ft 6 in (3·20 m)
Tail rotor ground clearance:
A 4 ft 7·5 in (1·41 m)
N 4 ft 6·3 in (1·38 m)
Tailplane half-span (from fuselage c/l):
A, N 5 ft 9·9 in (1·776 m)
Skid track (A) 6 ft 8 in (2·032 m)
Wheel track (N) 9 ft 1·4 in (2·778 m)
Wheelbase (N) 9 ft 10·7 in (3·014 m)
Cabin door openings (A, N, each):
Mean width 4 ft 6 in (1·372 m)
Height 3 ft 11 in (1·194 m)

DIMENSIONS, INTERNAL:
Cabin, from back of pilots' seats:
Min length 6 ft 9 in (2·057 m)
Max width 5 ft 10 in (1·778 m)
Width at rear 4 ft 7·5 in (1·409 m)
Max internal floor width 5 ft 7·5 in (1·715 m)
Max height 4 ft 8 in (1·422 m)
Floor area 40·04 sq ft (3·72 m²)
Volume 184 cu ft (5·21 m³)

WEIGHTS (A: general-purpose version, N: naval version):
Manufacturer's bare weight:
A 5,225 lb (2,370 kg)
N 5,507 lb (2,498 kg)
Manufacturer's basic weight:
A 5,395 lb (2,474 kg)
N 5,744 lb (2,605 kg)
Operating weight empty, equipped:
A, troop transport (pilot and 10 troops) 5,641 lb (2,558 kg)
A, anti-tank strike (incl weapon pylons, firing equipment and sight) 6,313 lb (2,863 kg)
A, search and rescue (crew of three) 6,168 lb (2,797 kg)
N, anti-submarine strike 6,481 lb (2,939 kg)
N, reconnaissance (crew of two) 6,409 lb (2,907 kg)
N, anti-submarine classification and strike 6,641 lb (3,012 kg)
N, air to surface vessel search and strike (crew of two and four AS.12s) 6,789 lb (3,079 kg)
N, search and rescue (crew of three) 6,517 lb (2,956 kg)
N, dunking sonar search and strike 7,218 lb (3,274 kg)
Max T-O weight:
A 9,250 lb (4,196 kg)
N 9,500 lb (4,309 kg)

PERFORMANCE (at AUW of 9,100 lb; 4,128 kg at S/L, ISA, except where indicated. A: general-purpose version; N: naval version):
Max never-exceed speed (A, N) at 8,000 lb (3,628 kg) AUW 180 knots (207 mph; 333 km/h)
Max continuous cruising speed:
A 153 knots (176 mph; 284 km/h)
N 150 knots (172 mph; 278 km/h)
A (ISA + 20° C) 144 knots (166 mph; 267 km/h)
N (ISA + 20° C) 141 knots (163 mph; 262 km/h)
Max continuous cruising speed (1 hr), one engine out:
A 142 knots (163·5 mph; 263 km/h)
N 128 knots (148 mph; 238 km/h)
A (ISA + 20° C) 131 knots (151 mph; 243 km/h)
N (ISA + 20° C) 115 knots (132 mph; 213 km/h)
Speed for max endurance:
A, N (ISA and ISA + 20° C) 70 knots (81 mph; 130 km/h)
Min flying speed (max contingency rating), one engine out:
A, N 25 knots (29 mph; 46 km/h)
A, N (ISA + 20° C) 35 knots (41 mph; 65 km/h)
Max forward rate of climb:
A 2,370 ft (722 m)/min
N 2,270 ft (692 m)/min
A (ISA + 20° C) 2,030 ft (618 m)/min
N (ISA + 20° C) 1,980 ft (603 m)/min
Max forward rate of climb (1 hr power), one engine out:
A 910 ft (277 m)/min
N 800 ft (244 m)/min
A (ISA + 20° C) 500 ft (152 m)/min
N (ISA + 20° C) 420 ft (128 m)/min
Max vertical rate of climb:
A, N 1,540 ft (469 m)/min
A, N (ISA + 20° C) 820 ft (250 m)/min
Hovering ceiling out of ground effect:
A, N above 12,000 ft (3,650 m)
Typical range, with reserves:
A, troop transport 304 nm (350 miles; 563 km)
A, search and rescue 164 nm (188 miles; 303 km)
Radius of action, out and back at 150 knots (173 mph; 278 km/h), max hover weight at pick-up of 9,100 lb (4,128 kg), reserves for T-O and landing, 15 min loiter in search area, 2 min hover for each survivor, and 20 min loiter at end of mission:
N, search and rescue (crew of three and two survivors) 148 nm (170 miles; 274 km)
N, search and rescue (crew of three and eight survivors) 135 nm (155 miles; 250 km)
Time on station at 50 nm (58 miles; 93 km) radius, out and back at 150 knots (173 mph; 278 km/h), with two torpedoes and six marine markers, reserves for T-O, landing, and 20 min loiter at end of mission:
N, anti-submarine classification and strike, loiter speed on station 2 hr 20 min
N, anti-submarine strike, loiter speed on station 2 hr 20 min
N, dunking sonar search and strike, 50% loiter speed and 50% hover on station 56 min
Time on station at 50 nm (58 miles; 93 km) radius, out at 135 knots (155 mph; 250 km/h), back at 145 knots (167 mph; 268 km/h), with crew of two and four AS.12s, reserves as above:
N, air to surface vessel strike, en-route radar search and loiter speed on station 2 hr 20 min
Max range:
A 411 nm (473 miles; 761 km)
N 363 nm (418 miles; 673 km)
A (ISA + 20° C) 420 nm (483 miles; 778 km)
N (ISA + 20° C) 374 nm (430 miles; 693 km)
Max endurance:
A, N (ISA and ISA + 20° C) 3 hr 45 min
Max ferry range with auxiliary cabin tanks:
A, N 748 nm (861 miles; 1,386 km)

WESTLAND/AÉROSPATIALE SA 330 PUMA

The Puma, which is described fully under the Aérospatiale heading in the French section, is one of the three helicopters forming part of the Anglo-French helicopter agreement ratified in 1967. Joint production, for the British and French armed forces, is shared between Westland and the Marignane factory of Aérospatiale. The first joint production SA 330 flew in September 1968.

In 1968, production began of 40 Puma HC. Mk 1 helicopters for the RAF. Following the completion of the British production order in 1972 (see 1973-74 *Jane's*), Westland is building Puma component sets for the French production line.

WESTLAND/AÉROSPATIALE SA 341 GAZELLE

The Gazelle, described fully under the Aérospatiale heading in the French section, is in joint production in Britain and France under the same Anglo-French agreement as the Puma. The Gazelle has been ordered by the British Army (99 **AH.Mk 1**), Royal Navy (30 **HT.Mk 2**) and Royal Air Force (13 **HT.Mk 3** and **HCC.Mk 4**).

The first production Gazelle was flown on 6 August 1971, and the first HT.Mk 2 (XW845) on 6 July 1972. The first civil Gazelle (G-BAGJ) was delivered to Point-to-Point Helicopters Ltd, on 27 March 1973, and the first HT. Mk 3 to the RAF Central Flying School at Tern Hill on 16 July 1973.

WESTLAND WASP

Wasp HAS.Mk 1. Version for Royal Navy, developed from Scout (1970-71 *Jane's*) with folding tail and special landing gear for deck operations.

First Wasp HAS.Mk 1 for Royal Navy flew on 28 October 1962, and deliveries began in second half of 1963. Wasps still in Royal Navy service are to be fitted with APX Bézu M.260 gyro-stabilised periscopic weapons sights, built under licence by BAC's Guided Weapons Division's Precision Product Group. Other countries which have Wasps for naval duty are South Africa (10), Brazil (3), New Zealand (3) and the Netherlands (12, designated AH-12A). Production of an additional seven Wasps for South Africa was nearing completion in early 1974.

All versions have a constant-speed rotor/turbine control system, with pre-select facility.

TYPE: **Five/six-seat general-purpose helicopter.**

ROTOR SYSTEM: **Four-blade main rotor, with all-metal blades, carried on fully-articulated hub with drag and flapping hinges. Torsion-bar blade-suspension system. Two-blade tail rotor with metal blades and single central flapping hinge. Main rotor blades fold for stowage. Rotor brake standard.**

ROTOR DRIVE: **Rotors driven through steel shafting. Primary gearbox at rear of engine, secondary gearbox at base of pylon, angle gearbox at base of fin, tail rotor gearbox at top of fin. Main rotor/engine rpm ratio 1 : 71. Tail rotor/engine rpm ratio 1 : 15.**

FUSELAGE: **Conventional aluminium alloy stressed-skin structure, manufactured in two main sections. Front section forms the cabin, fuel tank bays and aft compartment. Rear section is a tapered boom terminating in a fin which carries the tail rotor.**

TAIL SURFACE: Horizontal stabiliser, of light alloy construction, mounted on starboard side of fin, opposite tail rotor.

LANDING GEAR: Non-retractable four-wheel type. All four wheels castor and are carried on Lockheed shock-absorber struts. All wheels and tubeless tyres are Dunlop, size 15 × 4·75-6·5, pressure 60 lb/sq in (4·22 kg/cm²). Dunlop dog clutch brakes. Flotation gear standard.

POWER PLANT: **One 710 shp (derated) Rolls-Royce Bristol Nimbus 503 turboshaft engine, mounted above fuselage to rear of cabin. Fuel in three interconnected flexible tanks in fuselage below main rotor, with total capacity of 155 Imp gallons (705 litres). Refuelling point on starboard side of decking. Oil capacity 1·5 Imp gallons (7 litres).**

ACCOMMODATION: **Two seats side by side at front of cabin, with bench seat for three persons at rear. Four doors, by front and rear seats on each side of cabin. Rear seats removable for cargo carrying. Heater standard.**

The first civil Westland-built Gazelle helicopter, in the insignia of Point-to-Point Helicopters Ltd

Systems: Delaney Galley/Westland 1kW cabin heating and windscreen demisting system. Hydraulic system, pressure 1,050 lb/sq in (74 kg/cm^2), operating servojacks for rotor head controls and rotor brake. No pneumatic system. 28V DC electrical supply from engine-driven generator. Limited supply by 15Ah or 23Ah battery. Three-phase 115V 400Hz AC provided by inverter.

Electronics and Equipment: PTR 170 and PV 141 UHF and UHF homing radio, and standby UHF. Intercom taken from side tone of UHF T/R. Blind-flying instrumentation standard. Equipment includes autostabilisation/autopilot system, with radio altimeter.

Dimensions, external:
- Diameter of main rotor — 32 ft 3 in (9·83 m)
- Diameter of tail rotor — 7 ft 6 in (2·29 m)
- Distance between rotor centres — 20 ft 5½ in (6·24 m)
- Length overall, rotors turning — 40 ft 4 in (12·29 m)
- Length of fuselage — 30 ft 4 in (9·24 m)
- Width, rotors folded — 8 ft 8 in (2·64 m)
- Height to top of rotor hub — 8 ft 11 in (2·72 m)
- Overall height, tail rotor turning — 11 ft 8 in (3·56 m)
- Wheel track — 8 ft 0 in (2·44 m)
- Wheelbase — 8 ft 0 in (2·44 m)
- Cabin doors (fwd, each):
  - Height — 3 ft 8½ in (1·13 m)
  - Width — 3 ft 1 in (0·94 m)
  - Height to sill — 2 ft 5 in (0·74 m)
- Cabin doors (rear, each):
  - Height — 3 ft 8½ in (1·13 m)
  - Width — 3 ft 6 in (1·07 m)
  - Height to sill — 2 ft 5 in (0·74 m)

Dimensions, internal:
- Cabin: Length — 6 ft 0½ in (1·84 m)
  - Max width — 5 ft 1 in (1·55 m)
  - Max height — 4 ft 5 in (1·35 m)

Areas:
- Main rotor blades (each) — 15·5 sq ft (1·44 m^2)
- Tail rotor blades (each) — 1·82 sq ft (0·17 m^2)
- Main rotor disc — 816·86 sq ft (75·90 m^2)
- Tail rotor disc — 44·16 sq ft (4·10 m^2)
- Tailplane (semi-span) — 3·32 sq ft (0·31 m^2)

Weights and Loading:
- Manufacturer's weight empty — 3,452 lb (1,566 kg)
- Max payload, external cargo — 1,500 lb (680 kg)
- Max fuel load — 1,240 lb (562 kg)
- Max T-O and landing weight — 5,500 lb (2,495 kg)
- Max disc loading — 6·70 lb/sq ft (32·71 kg/m^2)

Performance (at max T-O weight):
- Max never-exceed speed — 109 knots (126 mph; 203 km/h)
- Max level speed at S/L — 104 knots (120 mph; 193 km/h)
- Max and econ cruising speed — 96 knots (110 mph; 177 km/h)
- Max rate of climb at S/L — 1,440 ft (439 m)/min
- Vertical rate of climb at S/L — 600 ft (183 m)/min
- Practical manoeuvring ceiling — 12,200 ft (3,720 m)
- Hovering ceiling in ground effect — 12,500 ft (3,810 m)
- Hovering ceiling out of ground effect — 8,800 ft (2,682 m)
- Max range with standard fuel — 263 nm (303 miles; 488 km)
- Range with max fuel, including allowances of 5 min for T-O and landing, and 15 min cruising at best cruising height, with 4 passengers — 234 nm (270 miles; 435 km)

Westland Wasp anti-submarine helicopter, one of 17 built for the South African Navy

WESTON DIVISION

Works:
Old Mixon Works, Weston-super-Mare, Somerset BS24 9AB

General Manager: E. J. Frost

This division is responsible for building a number of components for current Westland production aircraft and for repair and construction of new parts for aircraft currently in operation.

WEYBRIDGE MPAG

WEYBRIDGE MAN POWERED AIRCRAFT GROUP

Address:
4 Park View, Hollies Court, Addlestone, Surrey KT15 2LZ

Chairman:
P. K. Green, BSc(Eng), GradRAeS

Weybridge Man Powered Aircraft Group was formed in September 1967 to design, build and fly a man-powered aircraft. The Royal Aeronautical Society donated money to buy materials, and building space was provided by British Aircraft Corporation.

WEYBRIDGE MAN POWERED AIRCRAFT

The Weybridge Man Powered Aircraft is a single-seat low-wing monoplane with a pusher propeller. The design was started in July 1967, and construction began in June 1968. The aircraft was completed at the end of 1970 and flew for the first time at Weybridge on 18 September 1971, piloted by Mr Christopher Lovell of the Surrey Gliding Club; it covered a distance of about 50 yd (46 m) at a height of approximately 3 ft (0·9 m). Following the first flight, modifications were made to the rudder and transmission system to improve control and reliability.

For various reasons, no subsequent flights had been made up to the Spring of 1974; but the aircraft was then acquired by the group owning Jupiter (which see) and it was hoped to resume trials later in the year.

The following description applies to the aircraft as it was at the end of March 1972:

Type: Single-seat man-powered aircraft.

Wings: Cantilever low-wing monoplane. Wortmann wing sections: FX68-M-180 at root, FX68-M-160 at mid-span, FX68-M-140 at tip. Dihedral 11° 12′. Incidence 3° 18′. Single Warren-girder main spar, of L63 aluminium alloy tubing, with balsa ribs and leading- and trailing-edges. Melinex covering. Differential wing incidence change instead of ailerons.

Fuselage: Basic framework of L63 aluminium alloy tubing, with balsa frames and stringers and Melinex covering.

The single-seat man-powered aircraft built by the Weybridge MPAG

Tail Unit: Plywood and spruce box-spar structure, with balsa ribs and leading- and trailing-edges and Melinex covering. Cable-operated all-moving tailplane and fin.

Landing Gear: Non-retractable tandem arrangement, using standard bicycle wheels (size 18 in × 1⅜ in) and brakes. No shock-absorbers. Front wheel is chain-driven from the pedal axle.

Power Plant: Man power on bicycle pedals, driving a two-blade laminated balsa pusher propeller (weight 3 lb; 1·4 kg) aft of the tail unit. Bevel gears on the pedal axle drive the propeller through a ¾ in (1·9 cm) outside diameter aluminium alloy shaft. Estimated cruising power 0·3 to 0·4 hp.

Accommodation: Pilot only, in enclosed cockpit.

Dimensions, external:
- Wing span — 120 ft 4 in (36·68 m)
- Wing chord at root — 5 ft 8 in (1·73 m)
- Wing chord at tip — 2 ft 4 in (0·71 m)
- Wing aspect ratio — 30
- Length overall — 21 ft 0 in (6·40 m)
- Height overall — 11 ft 6 in (3·51 m)
- Tailplane span — 13 ft 9 in (4·19 m)
- Wheelbase — 4 ft 0 in (1·22 m)
- Propeller diameter — 7 ft 0 in (2·13 m)
- Propeller ground clearance — 1 ft 0 in (0·305 m)

Areas:
- Wings, gross — 485·0 sq ft (45·06 m^2)
- Fin — 32·0 sq ft (2·97 m^2)
- Tailplane — 41·25 sq ft (3·83 m^2)

Weights and Loadings:
- Weight empty — 125 lb (56·5 kg)
- Max T-O weight — 280 lb (127 kg)
- Max wing loading — 0·58 lb/sq ft (2·83 kg/m^2)
- Max power loading — approx 1,000 lb/hp (454 kg/hp)

Performance (estimated):
- Max level speed — 14 knots (16 mph; 25·5 km/h)
- Stalling speed — 10 knots (11 mph; 18 km/h)
- T-O run — approx 300 ft (91 m)

WRIGHT

PETER WRIGHT

Address:
3 The Close, Burton Lazars, Melton Mowbray, Leicestershire

Telephone: Melton Mowbray 4361

Mr Wright has designed, built and flown a man-powered aircraft known as the MPA Mk 1. All available details follow:

WRIGHT MPA Mk 1

Design of the MPA Mk 1 began in January 1971, and construction started in the following June. In February 1972 it made its first flight, covering 120 yards (110 m) at a height of 1 ft (0·30 m) above the ground. Propeller pitch trials were carried out in 1973, but continuation of flight trials is at present awaiting transfer to a more suitable operating site.

A full description of the MPA Mk 1 appeared in the 1973-74 *Jane's*.

Dimensions, external:
- Wing span — 71 ft 0 in (21·64 m)
- Wing aspect ratio — 10·3
- Length overall — 20 ft 0 in (6·10 m)
- Height overall — 8 ft 6 in (2·59 m)
- Propeller diameter — 7 ft 0 in (2·13 m)

AREAS:
- Wings, gross 486·0 sq ft (45·15 m²)
- Fins (total) 8·00 sq ft (0·74 m²)
- Rudder 8·00 sq ft (0·74 m²)
- Tailplane 36·00 sq ft (3·34 m²)

WEIGHTS:
- Weight empty 95 lb (43 kg)
- Max T-O weight 225 lb (102 kg)

PERFORMANCE:
- Max level speed 13 knots (15 mph; 24 km/h)
- Cruising speed 12·2 knots (14 mph; 22·5 km/h)
- Stalling speed 11·4 knots (13 mph; 21 km/h)

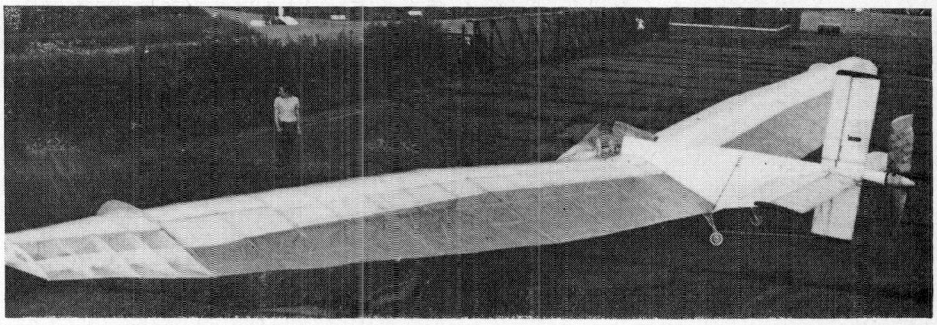

Wright MPA Mk 1 single-seat man-powered aircraft (*R. G. Moulton*)

THE UNITED STATES OF AMERICA

ACE

ACE AIRCRAFT MANUFACTURING CO

ADDRESS:
106 Arthur Road, Asheville, North Carolina 28806

OWNER: Thurman G. Baird

SALES AND PUBLIC RELATIONS MANAGER:
V. P. Baird

This company is the successor to the original Corben Aircraft Company, which was established in 1923 and began manufacturing the Baby Ace single-seat ultra-light monoplane in kit form in 1931.

The Corben assets were acquired in 1953 by Mr Paul Poberezny, President of the Experimental Aircraft Association. With Mr S. J. Dzik, a former WACO engineer, he completely redesigned the Baby Ace, with the intention of offering it in the form of plans and kits of parts for amateur construction. All rights in the new version, known as the Model C, were sold to Mr Cliff DuCharme of West Bend, Wisconsin, to dispel any suggestions of the Experimental Aircraft Association being concerned with a profit-making venture. Again the Baby Ace was redesigned, as the Model D, and special tools were built to produce Baby Ace components in quantity. At the same time, the side-by-side two-seat Junior Ace was redesigned as the Junior Ace Model E.

In 1961, the company was acquired by Mr Edwin T. Jacob of McFarland, Wisconsin, from whom all rights were purchased by the present owner in 1965. Plans, kits and parts are available to amateur builders.

It is estimated that there are about 350 Baby Aces flying today and hundreds more being built.

Ace Aircraft Manufacturing Co also has full rights in the American Flea Ship and Heath Parasol light aircraft, of which plans are available; descriptions of these two aircraft appeared in the 1970-71 *Jane's*.

The company reports that it has two more aircraft under development, one of which is a small single-seat biplane with a span of 21 ft (6·40 m). The second, a single-seat wire-braced parasol-wing monoplane with a span of 32 ft (9·75 m), is intended to be powered by a Volkswagen engine.

BABY ACE MODEL D

The prototype of the redesigned Baby Ace Model D flew for the first time on 15 November 1956. Large numbers have since been built by amateurs, some of whom have introduced authorised refinements to the basic design. At least one Baby Ace is flying with a float landing gear. That shown in the accompanying illustration was built by EAA Chapter 60 of Janesville, Wisconsin. The floats were constructed of glassfibre, using a wood pattern and glassfibre mould, and have spruce struts wrapped in glassfibre, with cast aluminium end fittings. Twin water rudders are fitted for surface handling, and performance is claimed to be comparable with that of a Piper Cub seaplane with 65 hp engine.

TYPE: Single-seat ultra-light monoplane.

WINGS: Braced parasol monoplane. Wing section Clark Y (modified). Dihedral 1°. Incidence 1°. Fabric-covered two-spar wood structure. Fabric-covered wood ailerons. No flaps.

FUSELAGE: Welded steel tube structure, fabric-covered.

TAIL UNIT: Wire-braced steel tube structure, fabric-covered.

LANDING GEAR: Non-retractable tailwheel type. Combination special tubing and spring shock-absorption. Goodrich 8·00-4 main wheels. Scott hydraulic brakes. Wheel spats optional. Steerable tailwheel. Alternatively Edo 1140 floats on seaplane version.

POWER PLANT: One Continental A65, A85, C65 or C85 four-cylinder horizontally-opposed air-cooled engine of 65-85 hp, driving a two-blade wood fixed-pitch propeller. Fuel in tank aft of firewall with capacity of 16·8 US gallons (63·6 litres). Oil capacity 1 US gallon (3·8 litres).

ACCOMMODATION: Single seat in open cockpit. Wide door on starboard side. Space for 10 lb (4·5 kg) baggage.

DIMENSIONS, EXTERNAL:
- Wing span 26 ft 5 in (8·05 m)
- Wing chord (constant) 4 ft 6 in (1·37 m)
- Wing aspect ratio 5·95
- Length overall 17 ft 8¾ in (5·40 m)
- Height overall 6 ft 7¾ in (2·02 m)
- Tailplane span 7 ft 0 in (2·13 m)
- Wheel track 6 ft 0 in (1·83 m)
- Wheelbase 13 ft 0 in (3·96 m)

DIMENSION, INTERNAL:
- Baggage space 2·2 cu ft (0·06 m³)

AREAS:
- Wings, gross 112·3 sq ft (10·43 m²)
- Ailerons (total) 10·2 sq ft (0·95 m²)
- Fin 3·5 sq ft (0·33 m²)
- Rudder 4·5 sq ft (0·42 m²)
- Tailplane 10·75 sq ft (1·00 m²)
- Elevators 6·5 sq ft (0·30 m²)

WEIGHTS:
- Weight empty, equipped 575 lb (261 kg)
- Max T-O weight:
  - 65 hp 950 lb (431 kg)
  - 85 hp landplane or seaplane 1,150 lb (522 kg)

PERFORMANCE (65 hp engine, at max T-O weight):
- Max level speed at S/L 96 knots (110 mph; 177 km/h)
- Max cruising speed 87-91 knots (100-105 mph; 160-169 km/h)
- Stalling speed 30 knots (34 mph; 54·7 km/h)
- Max rate of climb at S/L 1,200 ft (365 m)/min
- Service ceiling 16,000 ft (4,875 m)
- T-O run 200 ft (60 m)
- Landing run 250 ft (76 m)
- Range with max fuel 303·5 nm (350 miles; 560 km)

JUNIOR ACE MODEL E

The Junior Ace Model E differs from the Baby Ace Model D in being a side-by-side two-seater. It is powered usually by an 85 hp Continental C85 four-cylinder horizontally-opposed aircooled engine, and the data below refer to an aircraft with this power plant that was built by Mr Louis C. Seno of Melrose Park, Illinois.

First flown on 2 August 1966, it has a cockpit 3 in (7·5 cm) wider and 4 in (10 cm) deeper than that of the standard Model E, full electrical system and increased fuel capacity of 22·5 US gallons (85 litres).

DIMENSIONS, EXTERNAL:
- Wing span 26 ft 0 in (7·92 m)
- Wing chord (constant) 4 ft 6 in (1·37 m)
- Wing aspect ratio 5·95
- Length overall 18 ft 0 in (5·50 m)
- Height overall 6 ft 7 in (2·00 m)

WEIGHTS:
- Weight empty 809 lb (367 kg)
- Max T-O weight 1,335 lb (606 kg)

PERFORMANCE:
- Max level speed at S/L 113 knots (130 mph; 209 km/h)
- Cruising speed 91 knots (105 mph; 169 km/h)
- Landing speed 57 knots (65 mph; 105 km/h)
- Service ceiling 10,000 ft (3,050 m)
- T-O run 400 ft (122 m)
- Landing run 600 ft (183 m)
- Range with max fuel 303·5 nm (350 miles; 560 km)

Baby Ace Model D seaplane built by EAA Chapter 60 at Janesville, Wisconsin (*Howard Levy*)

AEROCAR

AEROCAR, INC

HEAD OFFICE AND WORKS:
Box 1171, Longview, Washington 98632
Telephone: (206) 423-8260

PRESIDENT AND GENERAL MANAGER:
Moulton B. Taylor

Aerocar, Inc has been developing since February 1948 a flying automobile designed by Mr M. B. Taylor. The prototype Aerocar, with a Lycoming O-290 engine, was completed in October 1949. It was followed by a pre-production Aerocar Model I, with Lycoming O-320 engine, and this was used for tests which led to FAA airworthiness certification of the Aerocar on 13 December 1956.

Four additional Model I Aerocars were completed subsequently for demonstration tours of the United States and for sale to customers. One of these is fitted with the more powerful Lycoming O-360 engine and has also been certificated by the FAA.

The accumulated road mileage on the six Model I Aerocars is well over 200,000 miles and they have logged a total of more than 5,000 flying hours. No further production of this model is planned.

Development of the Aerocar has continued, and many changes have been made to the hand-built Model Is, enhancing both the flight performance and the road operation. A prototype of the refined Model III Aerocar has also been built and is shown in an accompanying illustration.

Details of the Aerocar Model III were given in the 1970-71 *Jane's*. It was intended to be followed by a four-seat Aerocar IV, which would be based on an automobile in the class of the Ford Pinto and would have a normal cruising speed in flight of 150 knots (172 mph; 278 km/h). Current and projected US government safety and environmental requirements for automobiles suggest that an Aerocar able to conform with them would be so heavy and expensive that it could be neither practical nor economical. As a result, Aerocar Inc has continued to devote most of its activity to other projects, including a two-seat aircraft known as the Imp which embodies features of the Aerocar and is suitable for amateur construction.

In 1966 Aerocar built the prototype of a light flying-boat for a private customer. It was followed by two further machines named the Coot, on similar lines but provided with tricycle landing gear for amphibious operation. Many sets of plans for the Coot have been sold to amateur constructors.

AEROCAR SOOPER-COOT MODEL A AND COOT MODEL B

A prototype of the Coot Model B, a small side-by-side two-seat amphibian, was completed in June 1969. A variant known originally as the Coot Model A, but since re-named Sooper-Coot Model A, is similar except that it has a conventional rear fuselage and single fin instead of the twin-boom configuration of the Model B.

The first prototype of the Sooper-Coot Model A flew for the first time in February 1971. It logged approximately 100 hours powered by a 120 hp Franklin 225 engine, driving a Sensenich fixed-pitch metal propeller. This has since been replaced by a 180 hp Franklin 335 engine, driving a Hartzell constant-speed metal propeller, and the aircraft was flown extensively during 1972 with this more powerful engine.

The "float-wing" configuration of the Coot permits rough-water operation and, since the close proximity of the wings to the water forms a "pressure wedge", unusually low take-off and landing speeds are possible without recourse to flaps or other lift-enhancing devices.

The structure is basically of wood, with the exception of the twin-boom tail of the Coot-B, which must necessarily be of all-metal construction. The conventional single tail of the Sooper-Coot A, however, can be of steel tube and fabric, wood monocoque or all-metal construction. The rearward-folding wings, of NACA 4415 section, can be folded by one person. The fabric-covered ailerons are of metal construction and statically balanced. There are no tip floats. Construction of the hull, which has only seven bulkheads, is straightforward, without the complication of wheel-well doors. Tailplane and elevators of Sooper-Coot A fold, and both models have elevator trim tabs. All control surfaces are statically balanced. The tricycle-type landing gear is manually retractable into the wings, but an alternative powered retraction system is shown on the plans.

The Coot was designed to use any engine of 100-150 hp, and the prototype Coot-B, built by Dick Liljegren of Kelso, Washington, is powered by a 125 hp Continental C-125 four-cylinder horizontally-opposed aircooled engine. Maximum fuel capacity is 50 US gallons (189 litres). The first two Coot-As built by Aerocar had 125 hp Franklin Sport 4R engines, but these have since been replaced by 180 hp Franklin 335 engines.

Some amateur builders of Sooper-Coot As are installing a 220 hp Continental IO-360 for operation in places like the high Andes and Alaska.

Following the sale of the Coot-B prototype to another pilot, the tail unit of this machine was modified by Aerocar to improve longitudinal and directional stability. The modifications included 1 ft 6 in (0·46 m) extensions to the horizontal surfaces, outboard of each vertical tail surface, and an increase in the height and chord of the rudders. Despite these changes, the flight characteristics of this aircraft have failed to satisfy Aerocar, and further modifications were being made in early 1974.

As the vertical tail surfaces of the Coot-B are out of the propeller slipstream, turning out of wind is difficult in strong surface winds. Consequently, Aerocar is encouraging prospective builders to select the Sooper-Coot A version.

Certain component parts, including the glassfibre engine cowls, glassfibre hull shell for Sooper-Coot A, foredeck, instrument panel, tail fairings, engine cooling-fan blades and spring steel main landing gear legs, and plans are available to amateur constructors. The company also maintains a list of recommended suppliers of welded assemblies and machined components.

DIMENSIONS, EXTERNAL:
- Wing span (Model A): 36 ft 0 in (10·97 m)
- Wing span (Model B): 37 ft 0 in (11·28 m)
- Wing chord (constant): 5 ft 0 in (1·52 m)
- Length overall: 20 ft 0 in to 22 ft 0 in (6·10 to 6·71 m)
- Height overall: 8 ft 0 in (2·44 m)
- Width folded: 8 ft 0 in (2·44 m)
- Tailplane span (Model A): 10 ft 0 in (3·04 m)
- Tailplane span (Model B): 11 ft 0 in (3·35 m)

AREA:
- Wings, gross: 180 sq ft (16·72 m²)

WEIGHTS:
- Weight empty (Model A): 1,100 lb (499 kg)
- Weight empty (Model B prototype): 1,200 lb (544 kg)
- Max T-O weight (Model A): 1,950 lb (884 kg)

Aerocar Model III in flight configuration

- Max T-O weight (Model B prototype): 1,900 lb (862 kg)

PERFORMANCE (A: Sooper-Coot A with 180 hp engine; B: Coot-B with 125 hp engine):
- Max never-exceed speed:
  - A: 120 knots (139 mph; 223 km/h)
- Max cruising speed:
  - A: 113 knots (130 mph; 209 km/h)
  - B: 104 knots (120 mph; 193 km/h)
- Econ cruising speed:
  - A, at 50% power: 95·5 knots (110 mph; 177 km/h)
  - B: 87 knots (100 mph; 161 km/h)
- Stalling speed:
  - B: 37-39 knots (42-45 mph; 68-73 km/h)
- Max rate of climb at S/L:
  - A at AUW of 1,950 lb (884 kg): 1,250 ft (381 m)/min
  - B: 600-800 ft (183-245 m)/min
- T-O run (land):
  - A at AUW of 1,950 lb (884 kg): 200 ft (61 m)
- T-O (water):
  - A at AUW of 1,950 lb (884 kg): 6-8 sec
  - B: 12 sec

AEROCAR IMP

Most recent of Mr Taylor's projects is the Imp (an acronym derived from Independently Made Plane), of which design began in January 1972.

Mr Taylor's aim has been to evolve an aircraft suitable for the homebuilder, that can be constructed easily and quickly. The Imp incorporates many design features of the Aerocar, including folding wings and torsion-bar type wheel suspension to allow easy and fast towing, and a pusher propeller aft of the tail unit. All-metal construction, using pop-rivets, bolt-together assemblies and limited welding, is specified to reduce building time, which Mr Taylor estimates will average approximately 750 hours.

Construction of the prototype began in August 1972, and the first flight was expected to be made in the early Summer of 1973. This was delayed by further investigation into the torsion and vibration characteristics of the long propeller shaft, as well as by design of new-technology wings employing the results of recent NASA research. It is likely that the prototype will be fitted with wings of GA(W)-1 or GAO-410 aerofoil section after initial flight testing with the existing wings of NACA 4415 section. In late March 1974 the company was awaiting delivery of a glassfibre propeller of supercritical aerofoil section.

Following successful flight testing, it is intended that plans, kits of constructional materials and/or

Aerocar Sooper-Coot Model A lightweight homebuilt amphibian

First Aerocar Coot Model B, prior to modification of the tail unit

Scale radio-controlled model of the Aerocar Imp

difficult-to-make components will be made available to amateur constructors.

TYPE: Two-seat homebuilt light aircraft.

WINGS: Cantilever high-wing monoplane. Wing section initially NACA 4415. No dihedral. Incidence 4°. No sweepback. All-metal structure of constant chord. Wings fold aft, alongside fuselage, for towing or storage. All-metal ailerons, each with trim tab. No flaps.

FUSELAGE: All-metal structure with glassfibre shell.

TAIL UNIT: Inverted "Vee" type of all-metal construction, with trim tab on each rudder/elevator.

LANDING GEAR: Electrically-retractable tricycle type, main units retracting inward. Torsion-bar type suspension. Special highway-type wheels and 6-ply tyres suitable for road towing. Tyre pressure 40 lb/sq in (2·81 kg/cm²). Wheel fenders for road-towing. Rosenhan wheel brakes. Nosewheel retracts separately from main wheels for road towing.

POWER PLANT: One 120 hp Franklin Sport 4R four-cylinder horizontally-opposed aircooled engine, driving a two-blade controllable-pitch Beech Roby pusher propeller. One fuel tank of 14 US gallons (53 litres) capacity in each wing root. Total fuel capacity 28 US gallons (106 litres). Refuelling points in upper surface of wings, inboard of wing fold. Oil capacity 2 US gallons (7·5 litres).

ACCOMMODATION: Two seats, side by side, under transparent cockpit canopy which opens upward and forward. Space for baggage aft of seats.

SYSTEM: Electrical system powered by 12V 60A engine-driven alternator.

ELECTRONICS: Narco Escort 110 radio and Type 50A transponder.

DIMENSIONS, EXTERNAL:
- Wing span: 29 ft 0 in (8·84 m)
- Wing chord, constant: 4 ft 0 in (1·22 m)
- Wing aspect ratio: 7
- Length overall: 20 ft 0 in (6·10 m)
- Width, wings folded: 7 ft 8 in (2·34 m)
- Height overall (propeller blades horizontal): 5 ft 6 in (1·68 m)
- Tailplane span: 8 ft 0 in (2·44 m)
- Wheel track: 5 ft 10 in (1·78 m)
- Wheelbase: 7 ft 0 in (2·13 m)
- Propeller diameter: 6 ft 0 in (1·83 m)
- Propeller ground clearance: 1 ft 8 in (0·51 m)

DIMENSION, INTERNAL:
- Cockpit:
  - Max width: 3 ft 8 in (1·12 m)

AREAS:
- Wings, gross: 112 sq ft (10·41 m²)
- Ailerons (total): 10 sq ft (0·93 m²)
- Fixed tail surfaces (total): 12 sq ft (1·11 m²)
- Movable tail surfaces (total): 8 sq ft (0·74 m²)

WEIGHTS AND LOADINGS (estimated):
- Weight empty: 950 lb (431 kg)
- Max T-O and landing weight: 1,550 lb (703 kg)
- Max wing loading: 13·8 lb/sq ft (67·4 kg/m²)
- Max power loading: 12·9 lb/hp (5·85 kg/hp)

PERFORMANCE (estimated):
- Max cruising speed: more than 130 knots (150 mph; 241 km/h)
- Stalling speed: 44 knots (50 mph; 81 km/h)
- Max rate of climb at S/L: 800 ft (244 m)/min

AERONCA

AERONCA, INC, AEROSPACE GROUP

ADDRESS:
1712 Germantown Road, Middletown, Ohio 45042
Telephone: (513) 422-2751

VICE-PRESIDENT, ENGINEERING: Sumner Alpert
VICE-PRESIDENT, MARKETING:
Fred Stein

AERONCA SUPER PINTO

This company worked in conjunction with American Jet Industries (which see) to produce a light strike COIN version of the Super Pinto developed by the latter company. Under an agreement signed between the two companies, Aeronca Inc was to have been responsible for construction of any production aircraft.

Three versions were projected, and details of these were given in the 1973-74 *Jane's*.

AERO RESOURCES

AERO RESOURCES INC

ADDRESS:
Gardena, California

This company is now responsible for the J-2 gyroplane, designed originally by Mr D. K. Jovanovich and described under the McCulloch Aircraft Corporation entry in the 1972-73 *Jane's*.

AERO RESOURCES J-2

The J-2 is a side-by-side two-seat light autogyro, of which the prototype flew for the first time in June 1962. It received FAA certification on 6 May 1970 and is in production.

A version known as the **Super J-2** has been developed; this is powered by a 200 hp Lycoming IO-360 engine.

TYPE: Two-seat light autogyro.

ROTOR SYSTEM: One three-blade rotor with fully-articulated blades of all-metal construction. Blades are built up of an aluminium extrusion and wrap-around skin, bonded together to form fail-safe structures. Aerofoil section NACA 0015. Blades attached to steel hub through lag and flapping hinges. Rotor unpowered in flight.

ROTOR DRIVE: Auxiliary transmission of ring and pinion type, belt-driven, to spin-up rotor on ground prior to take-off.

WINGS: Short mid-set cantilever wings, carrying tailbooms and main landing gear. Dihedral 5°. Incidence 3°. All-metal construction.

FUSELAGE: Aluminium tube chassis-type structure with glassfibre shell.

TAIL UNIT: Cantilever light alloy structure, with twin fins and rudders, carried on slim tailbooms.

LANDING GEAR: Non-retractable tricycle type with single wheel on each unit. Oleo-pneumatic shock-absorbers. Cleveland wheels with B.F. Goodrich Uniroyal tyres size 5·00-5. Tyre pressure 48 lb/sq in (3·37 kg/cm²). Steerable and self-centering nosewheel. Cleveland disc brakes on main wheels. Wheel fairings optional.

POWER PLANT: One 180 hp Lycoming O-360-A2D four-cylinder horizontally-opposed aircooled engine, mounted horizontally in rear fuselage and driving a Sensenich two-blade wooden fixed-pitch propeller. Super J-2 has one 200 hp Lycoming IO-360 engine. Fuel tanks in wingtips, capacity 24 US gallons (90·8 litres). Refuelling points in upper surface of wings. Oil capacity 2·25 US gallons (8·5 litres), of which 2 US gallons (7·5 litres) are usable.

ACCOMMODATION: Two seats side by side in enclosed cabin. Forward-hinged door on each side. Standard equipment includes nylon safety belts. Baggage space under seats. Cockpit heated and ventilated.

ELECTRONICS AND EQUIPMENT: Standard equipment includes outside air temperature gauge, navigation lights, 60A alternator, battery, de luxe cabin interior and nylon safety belts. Optional equipment includes electric turn and bank indicator, 12-hour clock, dual controls, engine hour indicator, rotating beacon and landing light. Optional radio equipment includes Bendix RT221A transceiver and Bendix IN-222A or 223A VOR.

Aero Resources Super J-2 two-seat autogyro (200 hp Lycoming IO-360 engine) (*Air Portraits*)

DIMENSIONS, EXTERNAL:
- Diameter of rotor: 26 ft 0 in (7·92 m)
- Rotor blade chord, constant: 6·8 in (17·3 cm)
- Wing chord, constant: 2 ft 5½ in (0·75 m)
- Wing span: 11 ft 2 in (3·40 m)
- Length overall: 16 ft 0 in (4·88 m)
- Height overall: 8 ft 6 in (2·59 m)
- Wheel track: 6 ft 6 in (1·98 m)
- Wheelbase: 6 ft 5½ in (1·97 m)
- Propeller diameter: 6 ft 0 in (1·83 m)
- Cabin doors (each):
  - Height: 5 ft 0 in (1·52 m)
  - Width: 2 ft 6 in (0·76 m)
  - Height to sill: 2 ft 4 in (0·71 m)

DIMENSIONS, INTERNAL:
- Cabin:
  - Max width: 3 ft 7 in (1·09 m)
  - Max height: 4 ft 2 in (1·27 m)

AREAS:
- Rotor blades (each): 7·4 sq ft (0·69 m²)
- Rotor disc: 533 sq ft (49·52 m²)
- Wings, gross (effective): 33·2 sq ft (3·08 m²)
- Fins (each): 4·55 sq ft (0·42 m²)
- Rudders (each): 2·23 sq ft (0·21 m²)

WEIGHTS AND LOADINGS (A: J-2; B: Super J-2):
- Weight empty:
  - A: 1,000 lb (453 kg)
  - B: 1,090 lb (494 kg)
- Max T-O and landing weight:
  - A: 1,500 lb (680 kg)
  - B: 1,600 lb (725 kg)
- Max disc loading:
  - A: 2·82 lb/sq ft (13·8 kg/m²)
  - B: 3·0 lb/sq ft (14·6 kg/m²)
- Max power loading:
  - A: 8·33 lb/hp (3·78 kg/hp)
  - B: 8·0 lb/hp (3·63 kg/hp)

PERFORMANCE (at max T-O weight. A: J-2; B: Super J-2):
- Max never-exceed speed:
  - A, B: 105 knots (122 mph; 196 km/h)
- Max level speed at S/L:
  - A, B: 96 knots (110 mph; 177 km/h)
- Max cruising speed at S/L:
  - A: 82·5 knots (95 mph; 153 km/h)
- Max rate of climb at S/L:
  - A: 700 ft (213 m)/min
  - B: 985 ft (300 m)/min
- Service ceiling:
  - A: 10,000 ft (3,050 m)
- T-O run:
  - A: 100 ft (30·5 m)
  - B: 280 ft (85 m)
- T-O to 50 ft (15 m):
  - A: 700 ft (213 m)
  - B: 820 ft (250 m)
- Landing from 50 ft (15 m):
  - A: 500 ft (152 m)
- Landing run:
  - A, B: 50 ft (15 m)
- Range with max payload and max fuel:
  - A: 173 nm (200 miles; 321 km)
  - B: 191 nm (220 miles; 354 km)

AERO SPACELINES

AERO SPACELINES INC (Subsidiary of Twin Fair Inc)

HEAD OFFICE AND WORKS:
495B South Fairview Avenue, Goleta, California 93017
Telephone: (805) 967-4571

PRESIDENT:
V. Read
VICE-PRESIDENT AND GENERAL MANAGER:
K. S. Irwin

This company was responsible initially for the construction of two conversions of Boeing Stratocruiser/C-97 transport aircraft, under the names of Pregnant Guppy and Super Guppy respectively, to provide specialised transportation of large booster stages and other items used in America's national space programmes. The Pregnant Guppy retained the original piston engines of the Stratocruiser; the Super Guppy is turboprop-powered. Details of both aircraft can be found in earlier editions of *Jane's*.

The conversions were performed entirely with private capital and with no prior contracts or other commitments. The US government subsequently contracted for the exclusive use of both aircraft, and heavy utilisation by NASA and the Department of Defense has precluded their use for commercial transportation of outsize cargoes.

To meet a potential commercial requirement, Aero Spacelines next built the prototype of a third Stratocruiser conversion, known as the Mini Guppy. Piston-engined, like the original Pregnant Guppy, this aircraft was described in the 1972-73 *Jane's*.

New advanced versions of the Super Guppy and Mini Guppy were announced in late 1968. One of these, designated Guppy-201, completed FAA certification in 1971 and was sold to Airbus Industrie for the airlift of major components of the A-300B Airbus and Concorde SST from various points of manufacture in Europe to assembly facilities at Toulouse, France. A second Guppy-201 was sold to Airbus Industrie in 1973.

Aero Spacelines operated formerly as a US Air Carrier under FAA certification and was authorised as a worldwide common carrier by the CAB, operating B-377PG, B-377SG, B-377MG and 377SGT (Guppy-201) aircraft. This activity has now ended, but the company continues to carry out aircraft modification and manufacture under subcontract. It had a total of 50 employees in January 1974.

AERO SPACELINES 377SGT GUPPY-201

Design of the Guppy-201 began in January 1968 and the first flight of this heavy transport aircraft was made on 24 August 1970. Following certification it was sold to and is operated by Airbus Industrie in Europe. A second aircraft was completed in 1972 and sold to Airbus Industrie in mid-1973.

Details of the Guppy-201 and the somewhat smaller Guppy-101 can be found in the 1973-74 *Jane's*.

AEROSPORT

AEROSPORT INC

ADDRESS:
Box 278, Holly Springs Airport, North Carolina 27540

Telephone: (919) 552-6375

Mr H. L. Woods, formerly chief engineer of Bensen Aircraft Corporation, has designed and built a number of aircraft and air cushion vehicles, including flex-wing and rotating-wing aircraft, a variety of gliders and the Wager V-1 and ACV No. 3 experimental ACVs, described in the 1960-61 and 1962-63 editions of *Jane's* respectively.

In 1970 Mr Woods formed a new company, known as Aerosport Inc, to design, manufacture and maintain aircraft, and to continue the sale of plans and kits. His latest designs, marketed by this company, are described below.

Aerosport Woody Pusher built in Canada (65 hp Continental engine) (*Neil A. Macdougall*)

AEROSPORT WOODY PUSHER

The prototype Woody Pusher was designed originally with a fuselage of wooden construction, plywood-covered, with fabric covering overall, and was powered by a 65 hp Lycoming engine. Mr Woods subsequently redesigned the fuselage and landing gear and increased the engine power.

Several hundred sets of construction plans for the Woody Pusher have been sold, and at least 12 aircraft have been completed and flown.

TYPE: Two-seat amateur-built light aircraft.

WINGS: Braced parasol monoplane, with Vee streamline-section main bracing struts each side and multi-strut centre-section cabane structure. Wing section NACA 4412. Two-spar wood structure, with metal leading-edge and fabric covering overall. Conventional ailerons and trailing-edge flaps.

FUSELAGE: Welded steel tube structure with fabric covering.

TAIL UNIT: Wire and strut-braced type. Ground-adjustable tab on rudder.

LANDING GEAR: Non-retractable tailwheel type. Cantilever spring steel main gear. Champion wheels. Wheel fairings on main gear.

POWER PLANT: One 75 hp Continental four-cylinder horizontally-opposed aircooled engine, driving a two-blade wooden fixed-pitch pusher propeller type LYL 36-68 SEN. Provision for other engines in 65-85 hp range. Fuel tank above wing, forward of engine, capacity 12 US gallons (45 litres).

ACCOMMODATION: Two seats in tandem in open cockpit.

DIMENSIONS, EXTERNAL:

Wing span	29 ft 0 in (8·84 m)
Wing chord	4 ft 6 in (1·37 m)
Length overall	20 ft 5 in (6·22 m)
Height overall	7 ft 0 in (2·13 m)
Tailplane span	8 ft 7½ in (2·62 m)

AREA:

Wings, gross	130 sq ft (12·07 m²)

WEIGHTS:

Weight empty	630 lb (285 kg)
Max T-O weight	1,150 lb (522 kg)

PERFORMANCE (at max T-O weight):

Max level speed at S/L	85 knots (98 mph; 158 km/h)
Cruising speed	76 knots (87 mph; 140 km/h)
Stalling speed	39 knots (45 mph; 72 km/h)
Max rate of climb at S/L	600 ft (183 m)/min
T-O to 50 ft (15 m)	1,500 ft (457 m)
Landing from 50 ft (15 m)	1,000 ft (305 m)
Endurance with max fuel	2 hr 30 min

AEROSPORT RAIL

In January 1970 Mr Woods set out to design an aircraft that would be as simple as possible for construction by amateur builders, requiring no specialised knowledge of constructional techniques or the need for a comprehensive selection of tools. In finalising the design emphasis was placed on evolving an aircraft that would also be safe, easy to fly and maintain, and economic in operation.

Construction of the prototype began in May 1970 and the first flight was made on 4 November of that year. FAA certification in the Experimental category was awarded on 24 June 1971.

An unusual aspect of the design is the utilisation of a completely new power plant. In conjunction with Rockwell Manufacturing Company, Aerosport has developed a new lightweight two-stroke engine by derating a Rockwell-designed snowmobile power plant. Weighing about 56 lb (25·4 kg), this engine develops 33 hp at a peak rpm of 4,300.

Plans, a construction manual and kits of materials and components are available to amateur constructors.

TYPE: Single-seat homebuilt lightweight aircraft.

WINGS: Cantilever low-wing monoplane. Wing section NACA 23015. Dihedral 4°. Incidence 3°. No sweepback. All-metal two-spar structure of 2024-T3 and 6061-T6 light alloy. Plain ailerons of light alloy construction with piano hinge at upper surface. No flaps. No trim tabs. Endplates at wingtips.

FUSELAGE: Consists of a 2 in by 5 in (5 cm by 12·5 cm) extruded fuselage boom of 6061-T6 light alloy. Boom folds sideways aft of wing.

TAIL UNIT: Cantilever T-tail of light alloy construction. Fixed-incidence tailplane. Elevator trimmed by spring-loading of control column. Trim tab on rudder.

LANDING GEAR: Non-retractable tricycle type. Cantilever spring main gear struts of light alloy. Nosewheel shock-absorption by rubber in compression. Main-wheel tyres 14 in (35·5 cm) in diameter. Nosewheel tyre 8 in (20·5 cm) in diameter. Tyre pressure 24 lb/sq in (1·69 kg/cm²). Barrel-type wheel brakes. Nosewheel steerable.

POWER PLANT: Two 33 hp Aerosport-Rockwell JLO LB-600/2 two-cylinder horizontally-opposed two-stroke aircooled engines, strut-mounted aft of main spar and driving Aerial fixed-pitch two-blade pusher propellers. Fuel tank mounted aft of pilot, capacity 10·8 US gallons (40 litres). Filler cap on top of tank.

ACCOMMODATION: Open seat for pilot.

SYSTEM: Electrical power available from one 60W alternator on each engine.

DIMENSIONS, EXTERNAL:

Wing span	23 ft 3½ in (7·10 m)
Wing chord, constant	3 ft 6 in (1·07 m)
Wing aspect ratio	6·7
Length overall	15 ft 9 in (4·80 m)
Length, fuselage folded	8 ft 0 in (2·44 m)
Height overall	6 ft 0 in (1·83 m)
Tailplane span	6 ft 0 in (1·83 m)
Wheel track	5 ft 0 in (1·52 m)
Wheelbase	4 ft 0 in (1·22 m)
Propeller diameter	3 ft 5 in (1·04 m)
Propeller ground clearance	2 ft 0 in (0·61 m)
Distance between propeller centres	3 ft 7 in (1·09 m)

AREA:

Wings, gross	81·5 sq ft (7·57 m²)

WEIGHTS AND LOADINGS:

Weight empty	438 lb (198 kg)
Max T-O and landing weight	710 lb (322 kg)
Max wing loading	8·1 lb/sq ft (39·5 kg/m²)
Max power loading	11·4 lb/hp (5·17 kg/hp)

PERFORMANCE (at max T-O weight):

Max never-exceed speed	108 knots (125 mph; 201 km/h) IAS
Max level speed at S/L	83 knots (95 mph; 153 km/h)
Max cruising speed at 2,000 ft (610 m)	69 knots (80 mph; 129 km/h)
Econ cruising speed	57 knots (66 mph; 106 km/h)
Stalling speed	39 knots (45 mph; 72·5 km/h) IAS
Max rate of climb at S/L	800 ft (244 m)/min
Max rate of climb at S/L, one engine out	more than 10 ft (3·05 m)/min
Service ceiling	12,000 ft (3,660 m)

Aerosport Rail prototype (two 33 hp Aerosport-Rockwell JLO LB-600/2 engines) (*Howard Levy*)

Service ceiling, one engine out 3,000 ft (914 m)
T-O run 230 ft (70 m)
T-O to 50 ft (15 m) 730 ft (223 m)
Landing from 50 ft (15 m) 800 ft (244 m)
Landing run 300 ft (91 m)
Range, with max fuel, no reserve 104 nm (120 miles; 193 km)

AEROSPORT QUAIL

Though very different in appearance to the Rail, the Quail has a similar wing and the same type of landing gear. Its design also began in January 1970, and construction of the prototype was started in July 1971. It flew for the first time in December 1971.

The prototype had an all-moving tailplane, but Mr Woods designed a fixed-incidence tailplane with elevators before plans were made available to amateur constructors.

TYPE: Single-seat lightweight homebuilt cabin monoplane.

WINGS: Cantilever high-wing monoplane, otherwise as described for Rail except for slightly increased span and trailing-edge flaps. Endplates on prototype; optional for later aircraft.

FUSELAGE: Semi-monocoque all-metal structure of 2024-T3 light alloy.

TAIL UNIT: Cantilever all-metal structure of light alloy, with swept vertical surfaces. Fixed-incidence tailplane. Trim tab on rudder and elevator of prototype; optional for later aircraft.

LANDING GEAR: As for Rail. Optional wheel fairings.

POWER PLANT: One 1,600 cc modified Volkswagen motor car engine, driving an Aymar 54-34 two-blade fixed-pitch wooden propeller. Provision for installation of Volkswagen engines from 1,500 cc to 1,800 cc capacity. Fuel tank in fuselage nose, aft of firewall, capacity 8 US gallons (30·5 litres). Refuelling point on upper fuselage, forward of windscreen.

ACCOMMODATION: Single seat in enclosed cabin, which is heated. Door on starboard side is hinged at top and opens upwards. Stowage for 20 lb (9 kg) baggage.

SYSTEMS: Electrical power supplied by 60W engine-driven alternator.

EQUIPMENT: Electric starter for engine.

DIMENSIONS, EXTERNAL:
Wing span 24 ft 0 in (7·32 m)
Wing chord, constant 3 ft 6 in (1·07 m)
Wing aspect ratio 6·87
Length overall 15 ft 11 in (4·85 m)
Height overall 5 ft 6½ in (1·69 m)
Tailplane span 6 ft 0 in (1·83 m)
Wheel track 5 ft 0 in (1·52 m)
Wheelbase 4 ft 0 in (1·22 m)
Propeller diameter 4 ft 6 in (1·37 m)

AREA:
Wings, gross 84 sq ft (7·8 m^2)

WEIGHTS AND LOADINGS:
Weight empty 534 lb (242 kg)
Normal T-O weight 762 lb (345 kg)
Max T-O weight 792 lb (359 kg)
Normal wing loading 9·1 lb/sq ft (44·4 kg/m^2)
Normal power loading 15·2 lb/hp (6·89 kg/hp)

PERFORMANCE (at max T-O weight):
Max level speed at S/L 113 knots (130 mph; 209 km/h)
Max cruising speed 100 knots (115 mph; 185 km/h)
Econ cruising speed 95·5 knots (110 mph; 177 km/h)
Max manoeuvring speed 78 knots (90 mph; 145 km/h)
Stalling speed, flaps down 42 knots (48 mph; 78 km/h)
Max rate of climb at S/L 850 ft (259 m)/min
Service ceiling (estimated) 12,000 ft (3,660 m)
T-O run 300 ft (91 m)
Landing run 400 ft (122 m)
Range with max fuel, no reserve 200 nm (230 miles; 370 km)

AEROSPORT SCAMP

Most recent of Mr Woods' designs, the prototype of the single-seat all-metal Scamp flew for the first time on 21 August 1973.

The intention was to evolve an aircraft that could be operated from grass strips, and tricycle landing gear was chosen because Mr Woods feels that this is more rational for a generation of amateur pilots who received their initial flight training on aircraft equipped with landing gear of this configuration. Stressed to +6*g* and —3*g*, the Scamp can be used for limited aerobatics; and emphasis has been placed on simple construction techniques to make it an easy project for the homebuilder.

Aerosport Quail homebuilt lightweight cabin monoplane (*Howard Levy*)

Prototype Aerosport Scamp homebuilt aerobatic biplane (60 hp Volkswagen 1,834 cc modified motor car engine) (*Howard Levy*)

Plans and kits of parts, except for the Volkswagen engine, are available to amateur constructors.

TYPE: Single-seat homebuilt light aircraft.

WINGS: Braced biplane structure, with Vee-type interplane strut each side. Flying and landing wires of streamline section. Single 2 in by 5 in (5 cm by 12·5 cm) extruded section of 6061-T6 light alloy forms a pylon to support the centre-section of the upper wing. All-metal two-spar structures of light alloy. Plain ailerons of light alloy construction, with piano hinge at upper surface, on upper wing only. No flaps. No trim tabs.

FUSELAGE: Semi-monocoque all-metal structure of light alloy.

TAIL UNIT: Braced T-tail of light alloy construction. Single bracing strut on each side. Fixed-incidence tailplane. Ground-adjustable trim tab on rudder.

LANDING GEAR: Non-retractable tricycle type. Cantilever spring main-gear struts of light alloy. Wheel fairing on each unit.

POWER PLANT: Prototype has one 1,834 cc 60 hp Volkswagen modified motor car engine. Design suitable for Volkswagen engine of 1,600 cc to 2,100 cc. Aymar 54-38 two-blade fixed-pitch wooden propeller. Fuel tank in fuselage nose, aft of firewall, capacity 8 US gallons (30·5 litres). Refuelling point on fuselage upper surface, forward of windscreen.

ACCOMMODATION: Single seat in open cockpit.

DIMENSIONS, EXTERNAL:
Wing span 17 ft 6 in (5·33 m)
Length overall 14 ft 0 in (4·27 m)
Height overall 5 ft 6½ in (1·69 m)

AREA:
Wings, gross 102·5 sq ft (9·52 m^2)

WEIGHTS AND LOADINGS (prototype):
Weight empty 520 lb (236 kg)
Max T-O weight 768 lb (348 kg)
Max wing loading 7·49 lb/sq ft (36·6 kg/m^2)
Max power loading 12·8 lb/hp (5·81 kg/hp)

PERFORMANCE:
Max never-exceed speed 108 knots (125 mph; 201 km/h)
Max level speed 82 knots (95 mph; 153 km/h)
Cruising speed 74 knots (85 mph; 137 km/h)
Max manoeuvring speed 72 knots (83 mph; 134 km/h)
Stalling speed 39 knots (45 mph; 73 km/h)
Service ceiling (estimated) 12,000 ft (3,660 m)
T-O run 300 ft (91 m)
Landing run 400 ft (122 m)
Range at cruising speed 130 nm (150 miles; 241 km)

AGRINAUTICS

AGRICULTURAL AVIATION ENGINEERING COMPANY

POSTAL ADDRESS:
PO Box 11045, McCarran Airport, Las Vegas, Nevada 89111

WORKS:
1333 Patrick Lane, McCarran Airport, Las Vegas, Nevada 89119

Telephone: (702) 736-3794

Agrinautics is one of the leading companies engaged in the design and manufacture of aerial dispersal systems for both fixed- and rotating-wing aircraft. Established for more than fifteen years, the company has completed military R & D contracts and has designed and built systems for military use.

On 1 June 1972 Agrinautics announced the development of a new self-contained spray system for the Bell Model 205A helicopter. Weighing only 456 lb (211 kg), it comprises a 500 US gallon (1,892 litre) chemical tank of glassfibre, a gas-engine-powered high-capacity pump system, a 54 ft (16·5 m) standard boom system with two 5 ft (1·5 m) boom extensions, and an electrical valve control system with all controls accessible to the pilot, the boom on-off switch being mounted on the cyclic control stick. The basic engine control box is fastened to the console between the pilot's and co-pilot's seats.

The chemical tank can be filled from either side of the aircraft and, being mounted around the transmission enclosure, has little effect on the aircraft's CG whether full or empty.

The spray system engine can be started during the ferry flight to a working area, but it is more usual to start it on the ground after loading, and then to leave it idling until spraying is due to begin. Maximum output is 240 US gallons (908 litres)/min, with flow rates adjustable by varying the engine speed or by the selection of alternative nozzle orifices.

Agrinautics states that an alternative two-stroke engine, of similar power output to that used in the standard system, could reduce weight by more than twenty per cent.

During 1973 a similar self-contained spray system has been developed for the Bell Model 212 Twin Two-Twelve. The most significant feature of this new system is that it can be installed in the Model 212 without any modification of the airframe.

AJI

AMERICAN JET INDUSTRIES INC

HEAD OFFICE AND WORKS:
7701 Woodley Avenue, Van Nuys, California
PRESIDENT: Allen E. Paulson
DIRECTOR OF MARKETING:
Charles Dusheck

Since the 1973-74 edition of *Jane's* was compiled, American Jet Industries (AJI) has been involved in an expansion programme. All of its production facilities are now located on a 38-acre site at Van Nuys Airport, California, occupying more than 500,000 sq ft (46,450 m²) of offices and hangars used formerly by Lockheed Aircraft Corporation for the Cheyenne helicopter programme.

Founded in 1951, AJI specialises in the modification and repair of all types of executive and airline transport aircraft. The company is also converting Convair and Lockheed turboprop transport aircraft to all-cargo or passenger/cargo configuration; installing cargo doors and floors in Fairchild Hiller FH-227 aircraft; and converting Cessna Model 401, 402 and 414 aircraft to turboprop power plants.

In order to speed the transport of damaged aircraft to the works at Van Nuys Airport, AJI announced on 6 March 1974 that it had purchased from Aero Spacelines Inc the latter company's Pregnant Guppy and Mini-Guppy aircraft. These two aircraft will also be available for the transport of outsize cargo on a charter or lease basis.

AJI announced on 31 December 1973 that it had received a $1 million contract from Allegheny and Wien Airlines to modify to convertible passenger/cargo configuration four Fairchild Hiller FH-227s which Wien is purchasing from Allegheny. This involves the installation of cargo doors and cargo flooring and, in addition, a complete major overhaul of each aircraft. Two F-27 aircraft of Wien Airlines are also being reworked to have convertible passenger/cargo interiors. Another contract, worth $800,000, announced on 7 January 1974, covers the conversion of four Convair 640 aircraft to all-cargo configuration for Zantop Air Transport Inc.

A new palletised cargo system designed specifically for the Lockheed Electra includes a 6 ft 9 in (2·06 m) by 11 ft 10 in (3·61 m) hydraulically-operated outward-opening forward cargo door, emergency access, pressurised cargo interior, smoke detection system, floor strengthened to allow a loading of 300 lb/sq ft (1,465 kg/m²) and provision of a pallet loading system with 7,000 lb (3,175 kg) cargo capacity per pallet. In this new configuration, the Lockheed Electra is able to carry a 35,000 lb (15,875 kg) payload over a range of 1,700 nm (1,957 miles; 3,149 km) at a cruising speed of 350 knots (403 mph; 649 km/h). Fred Olsen Airtransport of Oslo, Norway, has taken delivery of the first of an initial batch of five Electras fitted with this Compatible Cargo System.

Prototype of the American Jet Industries Turbo Star 402 conversion

AJI TURBO STAR 402

In November 1969, American Jet Industries began conversion of a standard Cessna 402 to turbine power. This involved removal of its Continental piston engines and their replacement by two 400 shp Allison 250-B17 turboprop engines, each driving a Hartzell Type HCA3VF-7 three-blade metal constant-speed fully-feathering reversible propeller with Beta control.

The conversion offered an overall saving of 505 lb (229 kg) in terms of empty weight, giving increased performance, range and payload by comparison with the standard Cessna 402.

The first flight of the Turbo Star 402, as AJI named the conversion, was made on 10 June 1970. Since that time a number of additional modifications have been introduced. Gross weight has been increased to 6,525 lb (2,959 kg), an automatic propeller feathering system has been added, minimum control speed has been reduced by 12·6%, and fuel capacity increased from 126 US gallons (477 litres) to 200 US gallons (757 litres). Recertification of the Turbo Star 402 in this form, in January 1974, was announced by the company on 25 March 1974, simultaneously with news that two of these conversions had been sold to Scenic Airlines of Las Vegas, Nevada.

The following details apply to the Turbo Star 402 as now in production:

WEIGHTS AND LOADINGS:
Weight empty 3,214 lb (1,458 kg)
Max T-O weight 6,525 lb (2,959 kg)
Max zero-fuel weight 6,300 lb (2,857 kg)
Max landing weight 6,200 lb (2,812 kg)
Max wing loading 33·5 lb/sq ft (163·6 kg/m²)
Max power loading 8·16 lb/shp (3·70 kg/shp)

PERFORMANCE (at max T-O weight):
Max level speed at 9,500 ft (2,895 m) 233 knots (268 mph; 431 km/h)
Max cruising speed at 12,000 ft (3,660 m) 223 knots (257 mph; 414 km/h)
Econ cruising speed at 20,000 ft (6,100 m) 208 knots (240 mph; 386 km/h)
Approach speed 90·5 knots (104 mph; 167 km/h) CAS
Min control speed, one engine out 77·5 knots (89 mph; 144 km/h) CAS
Max rate of climb at S/L 2,095 ft (639 m)/min
Max rate of climb, one engine out 485 ft (148 m)/min
Operational ceiling 25,000 ft (7,620 m)
Service ceiling, one engine out 12,700 ft (3,870 m)
T-O run 832 ft (254 m)
T-O to 50 ft (15 m) 1,445 ft (440 m)
Accelerate-stop distance 1,984 ft (605 m)
Balanced field length 1,984 ft (605 m)
Landing from 50 ft (15 m), with propeller reversal, at max landing weight 1,104 ft (336 m)
Landing run, with propeller reversal, at max landing weight 450 ft (137 m)
Range at max cruising speed, no reserve 1,149 nm (1,324 miles; 2,130 km)
Max range at econ cruising speed, no reserve 1,397 nm (1,609 miles; 2,589 km)

AJI TURBO STAR PRESSURISED 414

American Jet Industries announced on 17 April 1974 that the company was well advanced with its conversion programme for Cessna Model 414 pressurised aircraft, with the first flight scheduled for mid-May 1974.

The programme is generally similar to that developed for conversion of Cessna Model 402 aircraft, but differs by introducing an uprated version of the Allison turboprop engine, the 250-B17B which develops 420 shp for take-off, and a newly developed hydraulically-driven "fail-safe" pressurisation system offering significant weight reduction. It is anticipated that the conversion will allow a Cessna Model 414 to equal the performance of the more expensive Cessna 421B Golden Eagle.

Preliminary specification details of the Turbo Star Pressurised 414 are as follows:

WEIGHTS AND LOADINGS:
Weight empty 3,505 lb (1,590 kg)
Max T-O weight 6,525 lb (2,959 kg)
Max zero-fuel weight 6,300 lb (2,857 kg)
Max landing weight 6,200 lb (2,812 kg)
Max wing loading 33·5 lb/sq ft (163·6 kg/m²)
Max power loading 7·77 lb/shp (3·52 kg/shp)

PERFORMANCE (estimated at max T-O weight):
Max level speed at 10,000 ft (3,050 m) 238 knots (274 mph; 441 km/h)
Max cruising speed at 16,000 ft (4,875 m) 226 knots (260 mph; 418 km/h)
Econ cruising speed at 20,000 ft (6,100 m) 208 knots (240 mph; 386 km/h)
Approach speed 90·5 knots (104 mph; 167 km/h) CAS
Min control speed, one engine out 77·5 knots (89 mph; 144 km/h) CAS
Max rate of climb at S/L 2,180 ft (664 m)/min
Max rate of climb at S/L, one engine out 510 ft (155 m)/min
Operational ceiling 25,000 ft (7,620 m)
Service ceiling, one engine out 13,800 ft (4,205 m)
T-O run 792 ft (241 m)
T-O to 50 ft (15 m) 1,396 ft (426 m)
Accelerate-stop distance 1,940 ft (591 m)
Balanced field length 1,940 ft (591 m)
Landing from 50 ft (15 m), with propeller reversal, at max landing weight 1,104 ft (336 m)
Landing run, with propeller reversal, at max landing weight 450 ft (137 m)
Range at max cruising speed, no reserve 1,112 nm (1,281 miles; 2,061 km)
Max range at econ cruising speed, no reserve 1,327 nm (1,528 miles; 2,459 km)

ANDERSON

EARL W. ANDERSON

PO Box 101, North Windham, Maine 04062

Mr Earl Anderson, a Boeing 747 captain flying for Pan American World Airways, has designed and built an original light amphibian which he has named EA-1 Kingfisher. The project occupied a period of nine years from start of design to completion, at a cost of around $5,500, and the first flight was made on 24 April 1969. After completing 50 hours of flight, as required by FAA regulations, Mr Anderson flew the Kingfisher to Canada and back on a fishing trip.

Since that time, Mr Anderson has replaced the original 100 hp Continental O-200 engine by a 115 hp Lycoming O-235-C1, driving a Sensenich Type M76AM-4-44 propeller. With this power plant the Kingfisher has an empty weight of 1,092 lb (495 kg), a max T-O weight of 1,600 lb (725 kg) and improved performance.

Plans available to amateur constructors cover this increase in weight. The Kingfisher was designed originally to accept alternative power plants up to a maximum of 140 hp, but since completing successfully more than 100 hours of flight with the 115 hp Lycoming engine, Mr Anderson is discouraging homebuilders from installing more powerful engines than this.

By March 1974 approximately 200 sets of plans had been sold, and more than 100 Kingfishers were under construction in the USA, Canada, Mexico, Sweden, Germany and Panama. At least two homebuilt Kingfishers are known to be flying.

The following details apply to Mr Anderson's Kingfisher in its original configuration:

ANDERSON EA-1 KINGFISHER

TYPE: Two-seat light amphibian.

WINGS: Braced high-wing monoplane with streamline-section Vee bracing struts each side (standard Piper Cub wing). Stabilising floats mounted beneath wings, adjacent to wingtips, are constructed of ⅜ in square mahogany stringers, covered with $\frac{1}{16}$ in mahogany plywood coated with glassfibre. Each float weighs 4·25 lb (2 kg).

FUSELAGE: Conventional flying-boat hull of wooden construction with spruce frames and longerons, covered with $\frac{1}{16}$ in and ¼ in mahogany plywood coated with glassfibre.

TAIL UNIT: Conventional strut-braced tail unit.

LANDING GEAR: Retractable tailwheel type. Each main unit is retracted forward, manually and individually, with spring-loaded assist mechanism.

POWER PLANT: One 100 hp Continental O-200 four-cylinder horizontally-opposed aircooled engine, driving a fixed-pitch two-blade tractor propeller. Single fuel tank in hull, immediately forward of windscreen, capacity 20 US gallons (76 litres).

ACCOMMODATION: Two seats, side by side, in enclosed cabin. Piper Tri-Pacer windscreen.

Anderson EA-1 Kingfisher amphibian (115 hp Lycoming O-235-C1 engine)

DIMENSIONS, EXTERNAL:
- Wing span 36 ft 1 in (11·00 m)
- Length overall 23 ft 6 in (7·16 m)
- Height overall 8 ft 0 in (2·44 m)
- Wheel track 5 ft 0 in (1·52 m)

WEIGHTS:
- Weight empty 1,032 lb (468 kg)
- Max T-O weight 1,500 lb (680 kg)

PERFORMANCE (at max T-O weight):
- Cruising speed 74 knots (85 mph; 136 km/h)
- Max rate of climb at S/L 500-600 ft (150-180 m)/min
- Service ceiling 10,000 ft (3,050 m)

AVIATION SPECIALTIES

AVIATION SPECIALTIES INTERNATIONAL

HEAD OFFICE:
4930 East Falcon Drive, Falcon Field, Mesa, Arizona 85205
Telephone: (602) 832-0600

MARKETING DIRECTOR:
Floyd D. Stilwell

Aviation Specialties has developed a turbine-powered conversion of the Sikorsky S-55 helicopter, and this was awarded FAA certification in the Transport Category on 19 January 1971. The large cabin of this helicopter makes it ideal for deployment in ambulance and rescue roles. Production of at least 100 conversions is anticipated.

AVIATION SPECIALTIES (SIKORSKY) S-55T

The S-55T conversion entails removing the existing Wright R-1300 or Pratt & Whitney R-1340 piston engine and replacing it with a Garrett-AiResearch TSE 331-3U-303 turboshaft engine of 840 shp derated to 650 shp. This is mounted at an angle of approximately 35°, with the exhaust outlet facing to starboard, so that in flight it partially unloads the tail rotor. The new engine is connected to the engine mount by three gearbox mount fittings, and this in turn mates to the original attachment fittings on the firewall of the helicopter structure. The output-flange of the turbine connects directly to the existing fluid-drive clutch unit. The throttle-collective interconnection system has been redesigned to eliminate the interconnection, so that the throttle can be connected to the underspeed governor shaft of the engine's fuel control.

Various mechanical and electronic components formerly located in the tailboom of the S-55 have been resited in the forward compartment. This improves accessibility for maintenance and allows a wider range of loads to be carried within the CG limitations. A weight saving of approximately 900 lb (408 kg) is made by the conversion.

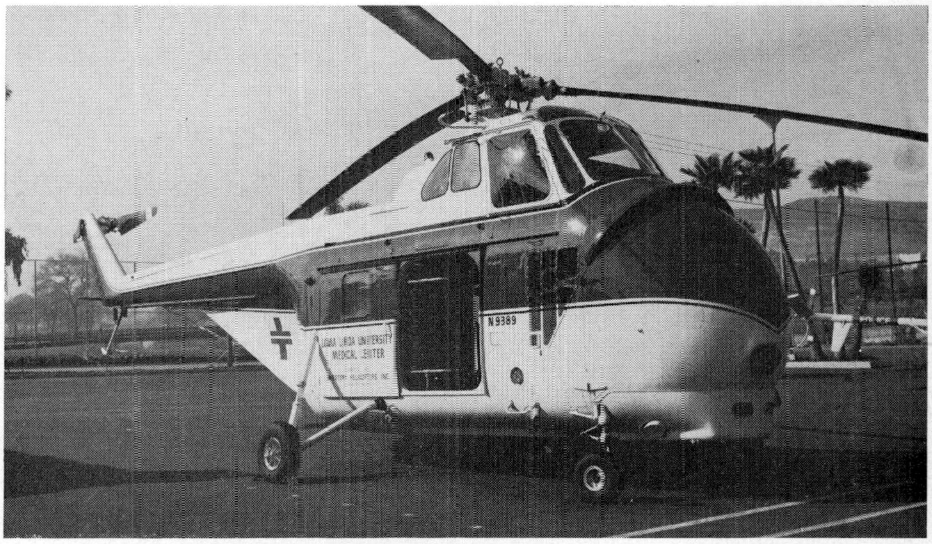

Ambulance version of Aviation Specialties S-55T operated by the Loma Linda University Medical Center, near Riverside, California (*Howard Levy*)

Twenty-eight S-55T conversions had been completed by early February 1974, of which 12 were operational in Canada, and the others in Alaska, Europe, South America and the US.

WEIGHTS AND LOADINGS:
- Weight empty, equipped 4,700 lb (2,132 kg)
- Max T-O and landing weight 7,200 lb (3,265 kg)
- Max disc loading 3·33 lb/sq ft (16·25 kg/m²)
- Max power loading 10·3 lb/shp (4·67 kg/shp)

PERFORMANCE (at max T-O weight):
- Max level speed at S/L 99 knots (114 mph; 183 km/h)
- Econ cruising speed at S/L 85 knots (98 mph; 157 km/h)
- Max rate of climb at S/L 1,200 ft (365 m)/min
- Max vertical rate of climb at S/L 800 ft (244 m)/min
- Service ceiling 12,400 ft (3,780 m)
- Hovering ceiling in ground effect 10,000 ft (3,050 m)
- Hovering ceiling out of ground effect 6,700 ft (2,040 m)
- Range with 180 US gallons (681 litres) fuel, 20 min reserve 321 nm (370 miles; 595 km)

BAKENG

BAKENG AIRCRAFT

ADDRESS:
19025 92nd W, Edmonds, Washington 98020

Mr Gerald Bakeng designed and built a two-seat high-performance parasol-wing monoplane known as the Duce, which received the EAA's "Outstanding New Design" and "Design Improvement" awards in 1971. It was followed in 1972 by a tandem two-seat biplane known as the Double Duce.

Plans of both aircraft are available to other builders.

BAKENG DUCE

Design and construction of the original Duce began in October 1969; it was completed six months later at a cost of approximately $1,500. The first flight was made on 2 April 1970. Plans are available to amateur constructors, and more than 200 sets had been sold by February 1974.

TYPE: Two-seat homebuilt light sporting aircraft.

WINGS: Braced parasol-wing monoplane, with Vee bracing struts each side. Streamline centre-section struts. Wing section Clark Y modified. Dihedral 1°. Incidence 3°. No sweepback. Composite structure of spruce and 4130 steel tube, fabric-covered. Frise-type ailerons of wooden construction, fabric-covered. Trailing-edge flaps of wooden construction, fabric-covered. Ground-adjustable tabs on ailerons.

FUSELAGE: Welded 4130 steel tube Warren truss structure, with fabric covering.

TAIL UNIT: Conventional wire-braced structure of welded 4130 steel tube, fabric-covered. Incidence of tailplane ground-adjustable. Ground-adjustable trim tab on rudder.

LANDING GEAR: Non-retractable tailwheel type. Cantilever spring steel main units. Main-wheel tyres size 6·00-6, pressure 5 lb/sq in (0·35 kg/cm²). Goodyear puck-type wheel brakes. Glassfibre wheel fairings on main units. Design may be adapted for float or ski landing gear.

POWER PLANT: One 125 hp Lycoming O-290-G (GPU) four-cylinder horizontally-opposed air-cooled engine in prototype, driving a Sensenich two-blade fixed-pitch metal propeller with spinner. Design suitable for other engines in 75-125 hp range. One fuel tank in wing centre-section, capacity 11 US gallons (42 litres), and one tank in forward fuselage, immediately aft of

Bakeng Duce two-seat homebuilt sporting monoplane (*Peter M. Bowers*)

firewall, capacity 17 US gallons (64 litres). Total fuel capacity 28 US gallons (106 litres). Refuelling points on upper surface of wing centre-section and front fuselage. Oil capacity 2 US gallons (7·5 litres).

ACCOMMODATION: Two persons in tandem in open cockpits. Fold-down doors on starboard side.

DIMENSIONS, EXTERNAL:

Wing span	30 ft 4 in (9·25 m)
Wing chord, constant	4 ft 6 in (1·37 m)
Length overall	20 ft 9 in (6·32 m)
Height overall	8 ft 0 in (2·44 m)
Tailplane span	8 ft 0 in (2·44 m)
Wheel track	7 ft 0 in (2·13 m)
Wheelbase	16 ft 0 in (4·88 m)
Propeller diameter	6 ft 2 in (1·88 m)
Propeller ground clearance	1 ft 0 in (0·31 m)

DIMENSION, INTERNAL:

Max width	2 ft 1¼ in (0·64 m)

AREAS:

Wings, gross	138 sq ft (12·8 m²)
Ailerons (total)	6 sq ft (0·56 m²)
Trailing-edge flaps (total)	6 sq ft (0·56 m²)
Fin	5 sq ft (0·46 m²)
Rudder, including tab	6 sq ft (0·56 m²)
Tailplane	8 sq ft (0·74 m²)
Elevators	7 sq ft (0·65 m²)

WEIGHTS AND LOADINGS:

Weight, empty	898 lb (407 kg)
Max T-O and landing weight	1,500 lb (680 kg)
Max wing loading	10·87 lb/sq ft (53·1 kg/m²)
Max power loading	12 lb/hp (5·44 kg/hp)

PERFORMANCE (at max T-O weight):
Max never-exceed speed
130 knots (150 mph; 241 km/h)

Bakeng Double Duce two-seat sporting biplane (220 hp Continental R-670 radial engine) *(Peter M. Bowers)*

Max level speed at S/L
126 knots (145 mph; 233 km/h)
Max cruising speed at S/L
122 knots (140 mph; 225 km/h)
Econ cruising speed at S/L
91 knots (105 mph; 169 km/h)
Stalling speed, flaps down
31·5 knots (36 mph; 58 km/h)

Max rate of climb at S/L	2,000 ft (610 m)/min
Service ceiling	17,000 ft (5,180 m)
T-O run	150 ft (46 m)
Landing run	150 ft (46 m)

Range with max fuel
260 nm (300 miles; 482 km)

BAKENG DOUBLE DUCE

The Double Duce is similar to the Duce in all respects except for its biplane configuration. It has a fabric-covered steel tube fuselage and wooden wings, braced with N-type interplane struts and with ailerons on all four wings. The power plant can be almost any horizontally-opposed or radial engine in the 125-220 hp range.

No other details are yet available.

BARNETT

BARNETT ROTORCRAFT COMPANY

ADDRESS:
4307 Olivehurst Avenue, Olivehurst, California 95961
Telephone: (916) 742-7416
PROPRIETOR AND DESIGNER: K. J. Barnett

This company has designed and built prototypes of two generally-similar ultra-light gyroplanes, designated J-3M and J-4B. The basic difference between the two lies in the power plant and the degree of skill needed to construct them. Plans, materials and kits of parts are available to amateur constructors.

In early 1974, Barnett Rotorcraft was developing a 95 hp Barnett-Corvair engine for installation on the basic J-4B airframe. It is also working on the design of a two-seat autogyro, of which no details are yet available.

BARNETT J-3M and J-4B

The essential differences between these two versions of the Barnett gyroplane are as follows:

J-3M. Utility model with 65 hp Continental A65 engine and flat-sided fabric-covered cabin enclosure.

J-4B. Higher-performance version, with 85 hp Continental C85 engine and more-streamlined glassfibre nacelle, resulting in some changes to overall dimensions.

The following details apply generally to both models:

TYPE: Single-seat light autogyro.

ROTOR SYSTEM: Single two-blade autorotating main rotor. Offset gimbal control head. Rotor blades of spruce with single internal steel spar and glassfibre covering. Optional aluminium blades with steel spar. Pre-spin device, to spin up the rotor to about 250 rpm, to be made available as a bolt-on optional extra. Normal rotor rpm: J-3M 400; J-4B 425.

FUSELAGE: All-metal structure of welded 4130 steel tube. Bolt-together aluminium airframe under development for J-4B. Nacelle of J-3M has streamlined glassfibre nose, and fabric covering elsewhere. J-4B has all-glassfibre streamlined nacelle.

TAIL UNIT: Fin, rudder and fixed one-piece horizontal surfaces, carried on tubular steel extension from main fuselage structure. All surfaces of welded 4130 steel tube, with fabric covering.

LANDING GEAR: Non-retractable tricycle type, with small tailwheel or bumper. No shock-absorbers. Steerable nosewheel linked to rudder pedals. Main-wheel tyres size 5·30 × 4·50-6. Nosewheel tyre size 4·10 × 3·50-4. Disc brakes. Light alloy or plastics floats to be made available as optional items. Parking brake.

Barnett J-4B single-seat autogyro (85 hp Continental C85 engine). A fixed fin has now been added forward of the rudder

POWER PLANT: J-3M has one 65 hp Continental A65 four-cylinder horizontally-opposed air-cooled engine, driving a Barnett two-blade resin-laminated birch fixed-pitch propeller. J-4B has one 85 hp Continental C85 four-cylinder horizontally-opposed aircooled engine, driving a Barnett two-blade wooden fixed-pitch propeller of 56 in (142 cm) pitch. Single aluminium fuel tank under pilot's seat. J-3M tank has capacity of 7 US gallons (26·5 litres); J-4B tank a capacity of 12 US gallons (45·5 litres).

ACCOMMODATION: Single seat in open or fully enclosed cockpit. Moulded Plexiglas windscreen and optional cockpit canopy. Door can be fitted to fully-enclosed version.

DIMENSIONS, EXTERNAL (A: J-3M; B: J-4B):

Diameter of rotor: A, B	23 ft 0 in (7·01 m)
Rotor blade chord (each): A, B	7¼ in (0·18 m)
Length overall:	
A	11 ft 4 in (3·45 m)
B	12 ft 2 in (3·71 m)
Height overall:	
A	7 ft 2 in (2·18 m)
B	7 ft 8 in (2·34 m)
Wheel track: A, B	6 ft 6¾ in (2·00 m)
Wheelbase: A, B	6 ft 5 in (1·96 m)
Propeller diameter: B	4 ft 10 in (1·47 m)

AREA:

Rotor disc: A, B	415·5 sq ft (38·6 m²)

WEIGHTS (A: J-3M; B: J-4B):

Weight empty:	
A	400 lb (181 kg)
B	441 lb (200 kg)
Max T-O weight:	
A	650 lb (294 kg)
B	750 lb (340 kg)

PERFORMANCE (A: J-3M; B: J-4B):

Max level speed:	
A	74 knots (85 mph; 137 km/h)
B	100 knots (115 mph; 185 km/h)
Cruising speed:	
A	61 knots (70 mph; 113 km/h)
B	78 knots (90 mph; 145 km/h)
Max rate of climb at S/L:	
A	500 ft (152 m)/min
B	700 ft (213 m)/min
Service ceiling:	
A	6,000 ft (1,830 m)
B	14,000 ft (4,265 m)
T-O run: A, B	200 ft (61 m)
Landing run: A, B	0-20 ft (0-6 m)
Range:	
A	104 nm (120 miles; 193 km)
B	217 nm (250 miles; 402 km)

BARNEY OLDFIELD

BARNEY OLDFIELD AIRCRAFT CO

ADDRESS:
PO Box 5974, Cleveland, Ohio 44101
Telephone: (216) 449-6300
PRESIDENT: Harvey R. Swack

On 23 February 1972 Mr Harvey Swack announced formation of this new company, following sale of the Great Lakes Aircraft Company to Windward Aviation Inc of Enid, Oklahoma. This latter company is continuing to operate under the name of Great Lakes Aircraft Co (which see).

Barney Oldfield Aircraft Co continues to market plans and material kits for the single-seat sporting biplane known formerly as the Baby Great Lakes and now known as the Barney Oldfield Lakes. This is a scaled-down version of the Great Lakes Sport Trainer, the original prototype of which was designed and built by Mr Andrew Oldfield, who died during 1970. A total of 515 were under construction and about 40 had been completed by March 1974. Examples are being built in many parts of the world, including

Africa, Australia, Italy and the United Kingdom.

The company intends to test alternative Volkswagen power plants in this aircraft at a later date. It considers that the Barney Oldfield Lakes powered by a fuel-injection engine would provide amateur pilots with an ideal aerobatic aircraft for competition up to intermediate levels.

BARNEY OLDFIELD LAKES

TYPE: Single-seat amateur-built sporting biplane.

WINGS: Braced biplane, with N-type interplane struts, double landing and flying wires and N-type centre-section support struts. Wing section modified M6, tapering to USA 27 18 in (46 cm) from tips. Incidence 2° 30′ on top wing, 1° 30′ on bottom wing. Wood structure of spruce spars and Warren truss ribs, with overall fabric covering. Ailerons on lower wings only. No flaps.

FUSELAGE: Welded steel tube structure, fabric-covered.

TAIL UNIT: Wire-braced welded steel tube structure, fabric-covered.

LANDING GEAR: Non-retractable tailwheel type. Oleo main legs with size 5·00-4 wheels. Steerable tailwheel.

POWER PLANT: One 80 hp Continental A80 four-cylinder horizontally-opposed aircooled engine, driving a two-blade fixed-pitch propeller. Provision for alternative engines of between 50 and 100 hp, and several aircraft now under construction will have 1,500 and 1,600 cc Volkswagen engines. Fuel tank in front fuselage, capacity 12 US gallons (45 litres).

ACCOMMODATION: Single seat in open cockpit.

Barney Oldfield Lakes sporting biplane (65 hp Continental engine) built by John Peel of Lake Stevens, Washington (*Peter M. Bowers*)

DIMENSIONS, EXTERNAL:

Wing span: top	16 ft 8 in (5·08 m)
Wing chord (both wings, constant)	3 ft 0 in (0·91 m)
Length overall	13 ft 9 in (4·19 m)
Height overall	4 ft 6 in (1·37 m)

AREA:

Wings, gross	86 sq ft (7·99 m²)

WEIGHTS (A80 engine):

Weight empty	475 lb (215 kg)
Max T-O weight	850 lb (285 kg)

PERFORMANCE (A80 engine, at max T-O weight):

Max level speed at S/L	117 knots (135 mph; 217 km/h)
Cruising speed at S/L	102 knots (118 mph; 190 km/h)
Stalling speed	43·5 knots (50 mph; 81 km/h)
Max rate of climb at S/L	2,000 ft (610 m)/min
Service ceiling	17,000 ft (5,200 m)
T-O run	300 ft (91 m)
Landing run (no brakes)	400 ft (122 m)
Max range	217 nm (250 miles; 400 km)

BEDE

BEDE AIRCRAFT, INC

HEAD OFFICE:
Newton Municipal Airport, Newton, Kansas 67114

Telephone: (316) 283-8870

PRESIDENT: James R. Bede

As a successor to the former Bede Aviation Corporation, Mr James R. Bede formed Bede Aircraft Inc, to continue development of plans and kits of parts for construction of his BD-4 two/four-seat light aircraft. Since then he has devoted further efforts to the development of sport aircraft for the homebuilder, and the range of designs now available includes a lightweight monoplane known as the Bede BD-5 Micro, a jet-powered version designated BD-5J, and a single-seat version of the BD-4 which has the designation BD-6.

Mr Bede is also continuing development of his BD-2 Love One aircraft for an attempted non-stop unrefuelled round-the-world flight. Combining the basic airframe of a Schweizer sailplane with a specially-adapted Continental piston engine, this unique aircraft has already established a world record for distance in a closed circuit. It was described and illustrated on pages 445-6 of the 1972-73 *Jane's*.

BEDE BD-4

The Bede BD-4 can be built as a two-seater with a 108 hp engine or as a four-seater with an engine of 150-200 hp. By 1973, more than 2,000 sets of plans for the BD-4 had been sold; 575 were under construction, and 70 completed aircraft were known to have flown. At least one has a non-standard tailwheel-type landing gear.

TYPE: Two/four-seat sporting and utility monoplane for amateur construction.

WINGS: Cantilever high-wing monoplane. Wing section NACA 64-415 (modified). No dihedral. Incidence 3°. Each wing is built up of 12 glassfibre "panel-ribs" which are slid over a 6½ in (16·5 cm) diameter extruded aluminium tubular spar, to which they are secured by epoxy resin and large-diameter tube clamps. Each 10 ft (3·05 m) wing section then slides for 1 ft (0·30 m) over a smaller-diameter 2024-T3 centre-section tube. Identical and interchangeable trailing-edge flaps and ailerons are attached to the trailing-edges of the ribs. Design allows for either removable or folding wings.

FUSELAGE: All-metal structure of bolt-together design. Formed 2024-T3 aluminium angle-sections, made from 0·063 in sheet stock in 2 in × 2 in, 1½ in × 1½ in and 1 in × 1 in sizes, are used for the basic structure of the fuselage. Simple metal gussets are used to form joints, bolted together with AN3 bolts and AN509 flush screws and lock nuts. Skin of either aluminium sheet or glassfibre panels can be pop-riveted or bonded to the primary structure. Cabin door on each side, under wing.

TAIL UNIT: Cantilever all-metal structure with swept vertical surfaces. All-moving tailplane, consisting of a single 2¼ in (5·85 cm) diameter tubular spar, with six metal ribs and aluminium skin. Fin and rudder are constructed on U-section metal spars, with aluminium skin. Rudder pivots on a one-piece piano hinge. All control surfaces statically mass-balanced.

Bede BD-4, showing optional wheel fairings completely enclosing wheels

LANDING GEAR: Non-retractable tricycle type. Each main leg is formed from a single piece of 2024-T3 aluminium plate, which rotates on a pivot point inside the fuselage. Shock loads are absorbed by rubber in compression. Main wheels size 6·00-6 with 15 in (0·38 m) diameter tubed tyres. Non-steerable fully-castoring nosewheel carried on a 1½ in (3·81 cm) diameter 4130 steel tube which pivots on the firewall and has similar shock-absorption to the main legs. Nosewheel of either 8 in or 10 in (0·20 m or 0·25 m) diameter. Hydraulic brakes. Optional wheel fairings, with wheel covers that retract for take-off and landing, and which are lowered to enclose the wheels completely in flight. These fairings add 14·7 knots (17 mph; 27 km/h) to the aircraft's max cruising speed.

POWER PLANT: One 108 hp Lycoming O-235-C1 four-cylinder horizontally-opposed aircooled engine, driving a McCauley 1B-90/CM two-blade fixed-pitch propeller for two-seat configuration; or one 150 hp Lycoming O-320 engine, driving a Sensenich type 74DM6-0-60 fixed-pitch propeller; or one 180 hp Lycoming O-360 engine, driving a Hartzell 7666-A2 constant-speed propeller for four-seat configuration. Alternative engines of up to 200 hp, and McCauley or Hartzell constant-speed propellers, are optional. Propeller spinner standard. Simple three-piece cowling with glassfibre nose section. Engine mounting of swing-out type for easy maintenance. Fuel contained between wing panel ribs, with standard capacity of 25·8 US gallons (97 litres) in each wing. Total standard fuel capacity 51·6 US gallons (195 litres). Max fuel capacity 85 US gallons (322 litres). Refuelling points above each wing.

ACCOMMODATION: Two or four seats, in pairs, in enclosed cabin.

SYSTEMS: Hydraulic system for brakes only. Electrical system includes engine-driven generator, 12V battery and navigation lights.

DIMENSIONS, EXTERNAL:

Wing span	25 ft 7 in (7·80 m)
Wing chord (constant)	4 ft 0 in (1·22 m)
Wing aspect ratio	6·4
Length overall	21 ft 4½ in (6·52 m)
Width, wings folded	7 ft 2½ in (2·20 m)
Height overall	7 ft 2¾ in (2·20 m)
Tailplane span	7 ft 3½ in (2·22 m)
Wheel track	7 ft 0 in (2·13 m)
Propeller diameter:	
108 hp	5 ft 9 in (1·75 m)
150 hp	6 ft 2 in (1·88 m)
180 hp	6 ft 4 in (1·93 m)

DIMENSIONS, INTERNAL:

Cabin:	
Length	7 ft 5 in (2·26 m)
Max width	3 ft 6 in (1·07 m)
Max height	3 ft 5 in (1·04 m)

AREAS:

Wings, gross	102·33 sq ft (9·51 m²)
Ailerons, total	3·5 sq ft (0·33 m²)
Trailing-edge flaps, total	8·0 sq ft (0·74 m²)
Fin	6·9 sq ft (0·64 m²)
Rudder	1·5 sq ft (0·14 m²)
Tailplane	21·3 sq ft (2·00 m²)

WEIGHTS AND LOADINGS (A: 108 hp, B: 150 hp, C: 180 hp, D: 200 hp):

Weight empty:	
A	960 lb (435 kg)
B	1,010 lb (458 kg)
C	1,080 lb (489 kg)
D	1,125 lb (510 kg)
Max T-O weight:	
A	1,600 lb (725 kg)
B, C, D	2,000 lb (907 kg)

Max wing loading:
A 15·15 lb/sq ft (74·0 kg/m²)
B, C, D 19·06 lb/sq ft (93·0 kg/m²)
Max power loading:
A 14·35 lb/hp (6·5 kg/hp)
B 12·00 lb/hp (5·4 kg/hp)
C 10·83 lb/hp (4·9 kg/hp)
D 10·00 lb/hp (4·54 kg/hp)

PERFORMANCE (at max T-O weight; A: 108 hp, B: 150 hp, C: 180 hp, D: 200 hp):
Max level speed at S/L:
A 135 knots (156 mph; 251 km/h)
B 149 knots (172 mph; 277 km/h)
C 159 knots (183 mph; 295 km/h)
D 176 knots (203 mph; 327 km/h)
Cruising speed (75% power):
A 126 knots (145 mph; 233 km/h)
B 143 knots (165 mph; 266 km/h)
C 151 knots (174 mph; 280 km/h)
D 167 knots (192 mph; 309 km/h)
Cruising speed (65% power):
A 118 knots (136 mph; 219 km/h)
B 135 knots (155 mph; 249 km/h)
C 147 knots (169 mph; 272 km/h)
D 156 knots (180 mph; 290 km/h)
Stalling speed, flaps up:
A 50·5 knots (58 mph; 93·5 km/h)
B 55 knots (63 mph; 101·5 km/h)
C 57 knots (65 mph; 105 km/h)
D 59 knots (67 mph; 108 km/h)
Stalling speed, flaps down:
A 47 knots (54 mph; 87 km/h)
B 50·5 knots (58 mph; 93·5 km/h)
C 53 knots (61 mph; 98·2 km/h)
D 55 knots (63 mph; 102 km/h)
Max rate of climb at S/L:
A 900 ft (274 m)/min
B 1,250 ft (381 m)/min
C 1,400 ft (427 m)/min
D 1,700 ft (518 m)/min
T-O run:
A, B 650 ft (198 m)
C, D 600 ft (183 m)
T-O to 50 ft (15 m):
A 1,200 ft (366 m)
B 1,100 ft (335 m)
C 1,000 ft (305 m)
D 750 ft (229 m)
Landing run:
A 500 ft (152 m)
B, C, D 600 ft (183 m)
Max range, 45 min reserve:
A, B, C, D 781 nm (900 miles; 1,448 km)

BEDE BD-5B MICRO

Design of this unusual single-seat sporting monoplane began in February 1967, and construction of the prototype was started in December 1970. First flight of the BD-5 was made on 12 September 1971. Two versions were available: the BD-5A with a short-span wing, and the BD-5B with a wing of greater span. In early 1974, however, Bede Aircraft decided to discontinue the short-span wing and the 40 hp power plant that had been used in the prototype. The basic model then became the BD-5B with 55 hp engine, with the 70 hp engine optional.

As a result of early flight tests the original "butterfly" tail unit was replaced by a conventional fin and rudder, with an all-moving horizontal "stabilator" on the lower portion of the rear fuselage.

Bede Aircraft reported that by the end of January 1973 it had received more than 4,000 orders for plans and kits of the BD-5 Micro.

The details which follow apply to the BD-5B:

TYPE: Single-seat lightweight homebuilt monoplane.

WINGS: Cantilever low-wing monoplane. Wing section NACA 64_1-212 at root, 64_3-218 at tip. Dihedral 5°. Incidence 1°. Sweepback 0°. Light alloy structure. Plain ailerons and trailing-edge flaps of light alloy construction. No trim tabs.

FUSELAGE: Light alloy. Aft end of fuselage terminates as a deep knife-edge section to provide directional stability.

TAIL UNIT: Conventional cantilever light alloy structure, comprising fin, rudder and all-moving tailplane. Trim tab and anti-servo tab.

LANDING GEAR: Manually-retractable tricycle type. Nosewheel retracts aft, main wheels inward. Shock-absorption of main gear by glassfibre cantilever struts. Main-wheel and nosewheel tyres size 2·80-4. Disc brakes.

POWER PLANT: One 55 or 70 hp Hirth two-cylinder aircooled two-stroke engine, mounted in aft fuselage and driving a Sensenich two-blade fixed-pitch wooden pusher propeller. Fuel in two inboard wing tanks, each of 14 US gallons (53 litres) capacity. Total fuel capacity 28 US gallons (106 litres). Refuelling point in rear fuselage. Special air intakes.

ACCOMMODATION: Single seat under upward-opening transparent canopy. Cockpit heated and ventilated.

SYSTEM: Electrical power supplied by 12V DC battery.

DIMENSIONS, EXTERNAL:
Wing span 21 ft 6 in (6·55 m)
Wing aspect ratio 9·8
Length overall, excl nose probe 13 ft 6¾ in (4·13 m)

James Bede with a prototype BD-5B Micro single-seat light aircraft

Prototype Bede BD-5J, the jet-powered version of the Micro

Height overall 4 ft 2½ in (1·28 m)
Tailplane span 7 ft 4 in (2·24 m)
Wheel track 3 ft 8 in (1·12 m)
Propeller diameter, max 3 ft 8 in (1·12 m)

AREAS:
Wings, gross 47·4 sq ft (4·40 m²)
Ailerons (total) 2·64 sq ft (0·24 m²)
Trailing-edge flaps (total) 6·17 sq ft (0·57 m²)
Fin 5·00 sq ft (0·46 m²)
Rudder 1·66 sq ft (0·15 m²)
Tailplane (including tab) 10·50 sq ft (0·98 m²)

WEIGHTS AND LOADINGS (A: 55 hp, B: 70 hp):
Weight empty 355 lb (161 kg)
Max T-O weight 660 lb (299 kg)
Max wing loading 13·9 lb/sq ft (67·9 kg/m²)
Max power loading:
A 12 lb/hp (5·44 kg/hp)
B 9·4 lb/hp (4·26 kg/hp)

PERFORMANCE (at max T-O weight. A: 55 hp, B: 70 hp):
Max level speed at S/L:
A 185 knots (213 mph; 343 km/h)
B 201 knots (232 mph; 373 km/h)
Cruising speed at 7,500 ft (2,285 m):
A 182 knots (210 mph; 337 km/h)
B 199 knots (229 mph; 369 km/h)
Manoeuvring speed:
A, B 122 knots (140 mph; 225 km/h) IAS
Stalling speed, flaps up:
A, B 54 knots (62 mph; 100 km/h)
Stalling speed, flaps down:
A, B 48 knots (55 mph; 89 km/h)
Max rate of climb at S/L:
A 1,480 ft (451 m)/min
B 1,920 ft (585 m)/min
Service ceiling (estimated):
A 23,000 ft (7,010 m)
B 26,000 ft (7,925 m)
T-O run:
A 670 ft (204 m)
B 590 ft (180 m)
T-O to 50 ft (15 m):
A 830 ft (253 m)
B 740 ft (226 m)
Landing from 50 ft (15 m):
A, B 830 ft (253 m)
Landing run:
A, B 530 ft (162 m)
Range at 75% power with 30 min reserve:
A 612 nm (705 miles; 1,134 km)
B 500 nm (575 miles; 925 km)
Optimum range with 30 min reserve:
A 1,055 nm (1,215 miles; 1,955 km)
B 812 nm (935 miles; 1,504 km)

BEDE BD-5D

The interest aroused by the original BD-5A/B proposals was such that Bede Aircraft received innumerable requests from those who wished to buy a production BD-5, as opposed to building a -5A or -5B for themselves.

To meet this demand a production line has been established, and the resulting version of what is essentially a BD-5B with the 70 hp Hirth engine as standard has the designation BD-5D. It is certificated in the Utility category under FAR Part 23.

The description given for the BD-5B applies also to the BD-5D, except that the latter, being a production aircraft, has certain standard equipment. Optional items include advanced instrumentation, with communications and navigation radios to suit individual requirements. An unusual option is an enclosed trailer, in effect a portable hangar for the aircraft.

Specification and performance of the BD-5D are the same as for the BD-5B with 70 hp engine, except for the following:

WEIGHTS:
Weight empty 385 lb (174 kg)
Max T-O weight 710 lb (322 kg)

PERFORMANCE (at max T-O weight):
Max rate of climb at S/L 1,350 ft (411 m)/min
Range at 65% power 516 nm (595 miles; 957 km)

BEDE BD-5J

This designation identifies a jet-powered version of the BD-5 which was introduced in the Summer of 1973. Similar to the BD-5B, it differs by having a wing of reduced span, increased "wet wing" fuel capacity, engine intakes on each side of the fuselage, over the wing, and power plant that consists of a US-built French Sermel TRS 18 lightweight axial-flow turbojet of 200 lb (91 kg) st.

Plans, materials and certain finished components and assemblies are available to amateur constructors. It is intended also to build the BD-5J as a production aircraft.

The description of the BD-5B applies also to this version, except in the following respects:

WINGS: As for BD-5B, except span reduced by 4 ft 6 in (1·37 m).

FUSELAGE: As for BD-5B, except for provision of engine air intakes in each side of fuselage, above the wing.

POWER PLANT: One 200 lb (91 kg) st Sermel TRS 18 lightweight turbojet engine, mounted in rear fuselage with tailpipe extending below and aft of rudder. Integral fuel tank in each wing, with total capacity of 34·8 US gallons (131·7 litres), plus 15 US gallon (57·8 litre) fuselage tank. Total fuel capacity 49·8 US gallons (188·5 litres).

Systems: Automatic electrically-operated fuel control system. Electrical system supplied by 28V engine-driven generator.

Electronics and Equipment: Optional avionics include nav/com transceiver with 360-channel com and 200-channel nav; VOR/LOC heading indicator with glideslope and marker beacon; transponder; and DME. Standard equipment of production aircraft will include full blind-flying instrumentation, *g* meter, complete electrical system, wingtip strobe lights and seat belts. Optional equipment includes instrument, navigation and landing lights.

Dimensions, external: As BD-5B except:
Wing span 17 ft 0 in (5·18 m)
Wing aspect ratio 7·64
Length overall 12 ft 4¾ in (3·78 m)
Height overall 6 ft 0 in (1·83 m)

Dimensions, internal:
Cabin: Length 5 ft 4 in (1·63 m)
Max width 1 ft 11½ in (0·60 m)
Max height 3 ft 0 in (0·91 m)

Areas: As BD-5B except:
Wings, gross 37·8 sq ft (3·50 m²)
Ailerons (total) 1·8 sq ft (0·17 m²)
Trailing-edge flaps (total) 4·9 sq ft (0·46 m²)
Rudder 5·0 sq ft (0·465 m²)

Weights and Loadings:
Weight empty 425 lb (192 kg)
Max T-O weight 910 lb (412 kg)
Max wing loading 24 lb/sq ft (117·2 kg/m²)
Max power loading 4·55 lb/lb st (4·55 kg/kg st)

Performance (at max T-O weight):
Max level speed at S/L 288 knots (332 mph; 534 km/h)
Cruising speed at 15,000 ft (4,575 m) 282 knots (325 mph; 523 km/h)
Cruising speed at 25,000 ft (7,620 m) 255 knots (294 mph; 473 km/h)
Stalling speed, flaps up 71 knots (81 mph; 131 km/h)
Stalling speed, flaps down 62 knots (71 mph; 115 km/h)
Max rate of climb at S/L 2,400 ft (732 m)/min
Service ceiling 30,000 ft (9,145 m)
Absolute ceiling 32,000 ft (9,755 m)
T-O run 1,100 ft (335 m)
Landing run 800 ft (244 m)
Range at max cruising speed at 24,000 ft (7,315 m) 451 nm (520 miles; 836 km)
Optimum range at 24,000 ft (7,315 m), with allowance for start, taxi, T-O, descent, landing and 30 min reserve 477 nm (550 miles; 885 km)

BEDE BD-6

Simultaneously with the announcement of the BD-5J came news of what is essentially a single-seat development of the BD-4, with reduced overall dimensions and power.

Type: Single-seat lightweight homebuilt sporting aircraft.

Wings: Similar to those of BD-4, except dimensions reduced.

Fuselage and Tail Unit: Similar to those of BD-4.

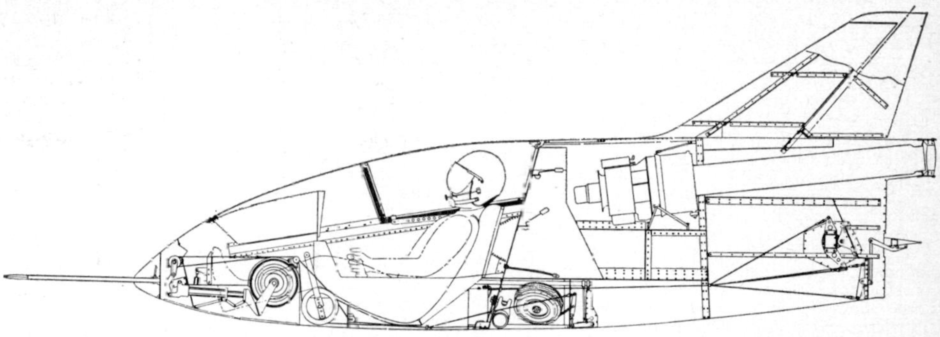

Sectional drawing of the BD-5J jet-powered version of the Bede Micro homebuilt light aircraft

Landing Gear: Non-retractable tricycle type. Cantilever main-gear struts of glassfibre construction. Non-steerable fully-castoring nose-wheel. Hydraulic brakes.

Power Plant: One 55 or 70 hp Hirth two-cylinder horizontally-opposed aircooled two-stroke engine, driving a two-blade metal fixed-pitch propeller with spinner. Fuel contained between wing panel ribs, with total capacity of 21 US gallons (79·4 litres).

Accommodation: Single seat in enclosed cabin. Baggage space aft of seat.

Dimensions, external:
Wing span 21 ft 6 in (6·55 m)
Wing aspect ratio 8·32
Length overall 16 ft 9 in (5·11 m)
Height overall 6 ft 6 in (1·98 m)

Dimensions, internal:
Cabin: Length 5 ft 10 in (1·78 m)
Max width 2 ft 0 in (0·61 m)
Max height 3 ft 6 in (1·07 m)

Area:
Wings, gross 55·5 sq ft (5·16 m²)

Weights and Loadings (A: 55 hp; B: 70 hp):
Weight empty 375 lb (170 kg)
Max T-O weight 650 lb (295 kg)
Max wing loading 11·7 lb/sq ft (57·1 kg/m²)
Max power loading:
A 11·8 lb/hp (5·4 kg/hp)
B 9·3 lb/hp (4·2 kg/hp)

Performance (estimated, at max T-O weight; A: 55 hp; B: 70 hp):
Max level speed at S/L more than 122 knots (140 mph; 225 km/h)
Cruising speed at 7,500 ft (2,285 m) more than 122 knots (140 mph; 225 km/h)
Stalling speed, flaps down:
A 43·5 knots (50 mph; 80·5 km/h)
B 46 knots (53 mph; 85 km/h)
Max rate of climb at S/L:
A 900 ft (274 m)/min
B more than 900 ft (274 m)/min
Service ceiling:
A 14,000 ft (4,265 m)
B over 14,000 ft (4,265 m)
T-O run:
A 600 ft (183 m)
B 500 ft (152 m)
Landing run:
A 400 ft (122 m)
B 450 ft (137 m)
Range at 75% power with 30 min reserve:
A more than 390 nm (450 miles; 724 km)
B more than 347 nm (400 miles; 644 km)

Prototype of the Bede BD-6 single-seat lightweight homebuilt aircraft

BEECHCRAFT

BEECH AIRCRAFT CORPORATION

Head Office and Main Works:
Wichita, Kansas 67201
Telephone: (316) 689-7111

Branch Divisions:
Liberal, Kansas; Salina, Kansas; and Boulder, Colorado

Chairman of the Board:
Mrs O. A. (Walter H.) Beech

President:
Frank E. Hedrick

Vice-Presidents:
E. C. Burns (Operations)
Seymour Colman
Harold W. Deets (Materiel)
J. A. Elliott (Treasurer)
R. W. Fisher (Administration)
Leddy L. Greever (Corporate Director)
J. E. Isaacs (Industrial Relations)
James N. Lew (Engineering)
Jack L. Marinelli (Aircraft Research and Development)
Roy H. McGregor (Marketing)
M. G. Neuburger (International Division)
E. C. Nikkel (Aerospace Programmes)
Austin Rising (Corporate Planning and Distribution Development)
Darrell L. Schneider (Government Relations)

Secretary:
L. Winters

Assistant Secretary:
I. Alumbaugh

Assistant Treasurer:
P. M. Vann

Director, Advertising and Sales Promotion:
R. James Yarnell

Director, Public Relations:
Bill Robinson

Founded jointly in 1932 by Mrs Clive Ann Beech and the late Walter H. Beech, pioneer designer and builder of light aeroplanes in the United States, the Beech Aircraft Corporation is currently engaged in the production of civil and military aircraft, missile targets, aircraft and missile components and cryogenic equipment for spacecraft.

Deliveries by Beech in 1973 were made up of 3 Beechcraft 99 Airliners, 140 King Airs, 13 Queen Airs, 42 Dukes, 337 Barons, 351 Bonanzas, 62 Sierras, 82 Sundowners, 72 Sports and 9 Beechcraft Hawker BH 125 jets. By the end of 1973 Beech had delivered well over 1,000 pressurised aircraft since introducing the King Air 90 in 1964, a record exceeding that of any other general aviation manufacturer.

Production continues under a succession of contracts awarded by Bell Helicopter Company since 1968 for manufacture of airframes for the turbine-powered Bell JetRanger helicopter. The contracts, covering production of airframes for both military and commercial JetRangers, have been assigned to Beech Aircraft's Wichita Plant III. Included in the contracts are airframes for the Bell light observation helicopter (OH-58A). Beech Aircraft is responsible for fuselage, skid gear, tailboom, spar, stabiliser and two rear fairing assemblies. Initial deliveries of JetRanger airframes began in December 1968, with first deliveries of OH-58A airframes in the preceding month; by 1 January 1974 a total of 3,319 JetRanger and OH-58A airframes had been delivered. Units are shipped to Fort Worth, where Bell completes assembly.

In December 1973, Beech received a $6·5 million add-on contract for continued production of airframes for the commercial JetRanger II, extending production until the end of 1975. Bell Helicopter has an option for additional orders which could extend this subcontracting programme into 1976.

Beech production of subassemblies for the McDonnell Douglas F-4 Phantom II fighter has entered its twelfth consecutive year.

Beech Aircraft and Hawker Siddeley Aviation Ltd, of Kingston upon Thames, England, announced in December 1969 a combining of their efforts to design, develop, manufacture and market a family of next-generation corporate jet aircraft. This resulted in the formation, during 1970, of a Beech Aircraft subsidiary known as Beechcraft Hawker Corporation. Simultaneously, Beech Aircraft assumed marketing responsibilities for North America for the Hawker Siddeley 125, which is known as the Beechcraft Hawker 125 (BH 125) in this area.

Business executive jet aircraft produced jointly by the two companies are known as Beechcraft Hawker types, and include the larger and faster version of the BH 125 designated BH 125-600 (see, as HS 125 Srs 600, in UK section).

In late 1972, Beech ordered 50 BH 125s for delivery in the US over a three-year period. Upon receipt, these aircraft receive custom interiors, avionics installations and exterior paint design at the Beechcraft Jet Completion Center in Wichita.

The BH 125-600 was introduced in the US in September 1972 and was then demonstrated extensively in the US, Canada and Mexico during

1973. The first delivery of the type was made in November 1972, and additional aircraft have been undergoing completion at Wichita and delivery to customers throughout 1973 and 1974.

Beech is developing and manufacturing target drones for the US military services and details of these can be found in the "RPVs and Targets" section of this edition.

Beech Aircraft occupies 2,514,748 sq ft (233,628 m^2) of plant area at its four major facilities in Wichita, Liberal and Salina, Kansas, and Boulder, Colorado.

The Salina division supplies all wings used in Wichita production and is responsible for manufacture and final assembly of the six-seat Beechcraft Duke.

All assembly, flight testing and delivery of the Beechcraft Sierra, Sundowner and Sport are carried out at the Liberal Division.

In an expanded marketing programme in the light aircraft field, Beech began franchising Beech Aero Centers in 1972 to ensure optimum sales and service of the Sierra, Sundowner and Sport. By November 1973 one hundred of these Centers had been appointed.

Work at Boulder involves space vehicle or missile applications, and included design, development, final assembly and testing of the cryogenic gas storage system for NASA's Apollo spacecraft. This same system was utilised in the Apollo spacecraft for NASA's Skylab programme during 1973-74. Boulder engineers have developed for NASA cryogenic tanks with the capacity of supporting space missions of as long as six months. These tanks can store 50 times as much oxygen and 120 times as much hydrogen as those used in the Apollo programme.

In January 1974 Beech was awarded a subcontract to produce the power reactant storage assembly for NASA's Space Shuttle orbiter. The assembly includes two liquid oxygen and two liquid hydrogen tanks to supply the orbiter's fuel cells and environmental control/life support system. Design, development, test and production will be carried out at the Boulder Division, with deliveries scheduled to continue until the end of 1979.

As a direct result of its work for the US space programme, Beech has developed a cryogenic automotive fuel system which uses liquefied natural gas as a fuel source and is designed to utilise liquid hydrogen ultimately, one of the world's most abundant fuel resources. The Beech system has undergone extensive laboratory testing, and field testing in both private and commercial road vehicles is underway. Test results indicate that the system has a life expectancy of more than 10 years, and that liquefied natural gas offers greater overall operating economy and safety than petroleum fuel. Prototype development and laboratory testing is being carried out at the Boulder Division.

Boulder also produces aircraft assemblies for other Beech divisions and the AQM-37A missile target system for the US Navy (see "RPVs and Targets" section).

Wholly-owned subsidiaries of the parent company include Beech Acceptance Corporation, Inc, which is engaged in business aircraft retail finance and leasing; Beechcraft Hawker Corporation Inc, which markets the BH 125 in North America; Beechcraft AG, which has its headquarters in Zurich, Switzerland, and supports in Europe the sales, liaison and other activities of the parent company; Travel Air Insurance Company Ltd, a Bermuda-based company organised during 1972 to provide aircraft liability insurance; Fuel and Line Service, Inc, Wichita, Kansas, and Broomfield, Colorado, established in 1972 to provide aircraft fuel and service; Beech Holdings Inc, which provides marketing support to the parent company; Beech International Sales Corporation, Wichita, through which all Beech export sales are made; and the following product distributorships: Houston-Beechcraft, Inc, Houston, Texas; Denver-Beechcraft, Inc, Denver, Colorado; United Beechcraft, Inc, Wichita, Kansas; Beechcraft West, Hayward, Van Nuys and Fresno, California; Mission Beechcraft, Santa Ana, California; Indiana Beechcraft Inc, Indianapolis, Indiana; and Beechcraft East, Inc, Farmingdale, New York.

BEECHCRAFT TURBO MENTOR

US Navy designation: YT-34C

In March 1953 the USAF selected the Beechcraft Model 45 as its new primary trainer and, under the designation T-34A Mentor, a total of 450 were eventually acquired. Power plant consisted of a 225 hp Continental O-470-13 six-cylinder horizontally-opposed aircooled engine.

Just over a year after the Air Force adopted the Beech Model 45 as its primary trainer, the US Navy reached a similar decision, and a total of 423 T-34B Mentors were built for that service.

Experience in both the USAF and USN showed the Mentor to be a rugged and reliable aircraft, and in 1973 Beech received a USN R & D contract to modify two T-34Bs to see whether the type could be upgraded for a continuing training role. This involved the installation of a turboprop engine and the latest avionics equipment, the primary object being to let student pilots have experience of operating turbine-powered aircraft from the beginning of their flight training.

The power plant selected was the 715 shp United Aircraft of Canada PT6A-25 turboprop, which has a torque limiter in this application to restrict engine output to 400 shp. This will not only ensure long engine life, but will also provide constant performance over a wide range of temperature and altitude.

Design of the modifications to update the aircraft began in March 1973, and work on two T-34Bs started in May of the same year. Designated YT-34C, the first of these aircraft flew for the first time on 21 September 1973, and the test programme was continuing in the early Summer of 1974.

By comparison with the original Mentor, the new YT-34C has a 1,000 lb (454 kg) increase in gross weight, which has meant that structural modifications have also had to be made to strengthen the fuselage and tail unit. Additional strength for other assemblies and components has been achieved largely by adopting off-the-shelf parts from other Beech aircraft.

Type: Two-seat turbine-powered primary training aircraft.

Wings: Cantilever low-wing monoplane. Wing section NACA 23016.5 (modified) at root, NACA 23012 at tip. Dihedral 7°. Incidence 4° at root, 1° at tip. No sweepback. Conventional box beam structure of light alloy. Ailerons of light alloy construction. Single-slotted trailing-edge flaps of light alloy. Manually operated trim/servo tab in port aileron.

Fuselage: Semi-monocoque light alloy structure.

Tail Unit: Cantilever structure of light alloy. Fixed-incidence tailplane. Manually-operated trim tabs in elevators and rudder.

Landing Gear: Electrically-retractable tricycle type. Main units retract inward, nosewheel aft. Beech oleo-pneumatic shock struts. Single wheel on each unit. Main wheels and tyres size 6·50-8. Nosewheel and tyre size 5·00-5. Goodyear multiple-disc hydraulic brakes.

Power Plant: One 715 shp United Aircraft of Canada PT6A-25 turboprop engine, torque limited to 400 shp, driving a Hartzell three-blade metal constant-speed fully-feathering propeller. Two bladder-type fuel cells in each wing, with a combined usable capacity of 142 US gallons (537·5 litres). Oil capacity 3·5 US gallons (13·2 litres).

Accommodation: Pilot and pupil in tandem beneath rearward-sliding cockpit canopy. Cockpit ventilated, and heated by engine bleed air.

Systems: Hydraulic system for brakes only. Pneumatic system for emergency opening of cockpit canopy. Diluter demand gaseous oxygen system, pressure 1,500 lb/sq in (105 kg/cm^2). Electrical power supplied by 200A starter/generator. Air-conditioning system planned for production aircraft but not installed in prototypes.

Electronics and Equipment: Dual controls and blind-flying instrumentation standard. Engine intake de-iced by bleed air. Electrically-heated pitot and angle of attack indicator. UHF com, Omni, DME, LF/DF and transponder. Intercom. Fluxgate compass system.

Armament: An armament system similar to that of the Model PD 249 "Pave Coin" Bonanza, detailed in the 1973-74 *Jane's*, could be provided.

Dimensions, external:
- Wing span: 33 ft 6 in (10·21 m)
- Wing chord at root: 8 ft 4½ in (2·55 m)
- Wing chord at tip: 3 ft 5¼ in (1·05 m)
- Wing aspect ratio: 6·22
- Length overall: 28 ft 8½ in (8·75 m)
- Height overall: 9 ft 10 in (3·00 m)
- Tailplane span: 12 ft 2 in (3·71 m)
- Wheel track: 9 ft 6½ in (2·91 m)
- Wheelbase: 7 ft 11 in (2·41 m)
- Propeller diameter: 7 ft 6 in (2·29 m)
- Propeller ground clearance: 1 ft 5¾ in (0·45 m)

Dimensions, internal:
- Cabin: Length: 9 ft 0 in (2·74 m)
  - Max width: 2 ft 10 in (0·86 m)
  - Max height: 4 ft 0 in (1·22 m)

Areas:
- Wings, gross: 179·9 sq ft (16·71 m^2)
- Ailerons (total): 11·4 sq ft (1·06 m^2)
- Trailing-edge flaps (total): 21·3 sq ft (1·98 m^2)
- Fin: 14·1 sq ft (1·31 m^2)
- Rudder, incl tab: 8·16 sq ft (0·76 m^2)
- Tailplane: 31·8 sq ft (2·95 m^2)
- Elevators, incl tab: 16·2 sq ft (1·50 m^2)

Weights and Loading:
- Weight empty: 2,630 lb (1,193 kg)
- Max T-O and landing weight: 4,000 lb (1,814 kg)
- Max wing loading: 22·2 lb/sq ft (108·3 kg/m^2)

Performance (preliminary results at max T-O weight):
- Max never-exceed speed: 250 knots (288 mph; 463·5 km/h)
- Max level speed at 17,500 ft (5,335 m): 223 knots (257 mph; 414 km/h)
- Max cruising speed at 17,500 ft (5,335 m): 223 knots (257 mph; 414 km/h)
- Stalling speed, without flaps: 55 knots (63·3 mph; 102 km/h)
- Max rate of climb at S/L: 1,696 ft (517 m)/min
- Service ceiling: over 30,000 ft (9,145 m)

BEECHCRAFT SIERRA 200, SUNDOWNER 180 and SPORT 150

In December 1971, Beech introduced a new light aircraft marketing programme centered around three models, which were given individual exterior paint schemes and re-named from their previous Musketeer designations (see 1971-72 *Jane's*).

For 1974 these designations were changed again to indicate the engine horsepower rating. The new names are Beechcraft Sierra 200 (formerly Model A24R Musketeer Super R), Sundowner 180 (Model C23, formerly Musketeer Custom), and Sport 150 (Model B19, formerly Musketeer Sport). The Sierra 200 was recertificated for 1974 and redesignated Model B24R, due to the installation of a new engine, improved cowling and redesign of control features. The Sierra 200 has also elliptical entry steps, a new firewall-mounted oil cooler, added airscoop on the engine cowling, weighted engine crankshaft and a new Hartzell propeller. The fourth aircraft in the former Musketeer line, the Super, was discontinued at the end of 1971 after a total of 368 had been built.

The three current aircraft have a cabin door on the port side of the fuselage, the Sport 150 thus becoming the only US low-wing trainer with cabin doors on each side. Standard equipment includes a new quadrant for the engine controls, new low-profile instrument panel to improve visibility, padded glareshield, safety contour door handles and improved door-latching system, automotive-type inner door-latch handles, inertia-reel shoulder restraint belts for front seats, and restyled Bonanza-type interiors. The Sierra 200 features a 24 × 36 in (0·61 × 0·91 m) rear door on the port side of the fuselage for easier passenger or cargo loading.

Details of the current models are as follows:

Sundowner 180. Basic four-seat version with 180 hp Lycoming O-360-A4J engine, driving a Sensenich Type 76EM865-0-60 two-blade fixed-pitch metal propeller, and non-retractable landing gear. Aerobatic version is approved for rolls,

Beechcraft YT-34C Turbo Mentor (715 shp United Aircraft of Canada PT6A-25 turboprop engine)

Immelmann turns, loops, spins, chandelles and other manoeuvres, carrying two persons.

Sport 150. Two/four-seat sporting and training version with 150 hp Lycoming O-320-E3D engine, driving a Sensenich 74OM6S5-0-54 two-blade fixed-pitch metal propeller, and non-retractable landing gear. Aerobatic version is approved for rolls, Immelmann turns, loops, spins, chandelles and other manoeuvres, carrying two persons.

Sierra 200. Generally similar to the Sundowner but with accommodation for four to six persons, a 200 hp Lycoming IO-360-A1B6 engine, driving a Hartzell Type HC-M2YR-1BF/F766A-2R two-blade metal constant-speed propeller, and retractable tricycle landing gear. Electrically-actuated hydraulic system based on a self-contained unit in the rear fuselage, comprising electrically-driven hydraulic pump, fluid reservoir and valves. An emergency valve, sited adjacent to the pilot's feet, allows selection of the landing gear to free-fall within three seconds. Main wheels retract outward into wings; nosewheel turns through 90° as it retracts rearwards. Four windows standard on each side of cabin.

Factory-installed optional equipment packages are as follows:

Weekender. Includes sun visors; lighting group comprising rotating beacon, navigation, cabin dome, overhead instrument and map lights; cabin boarding steps; dual controls and pedal-operated brakes for co-pilot; adding 17 lb (7·7 kg) to basic empty weight.

Holiday. As above, plus wing-mounted landing light; 35A battery; instrument group comprising 3 in horizon and directional gyros with vacuum system, turn co-ordinator, rate-of-climb indicator, 8-day clock, and outside air temperature gauge; adding 38 lb (17·2 kg) to basic empty weight.

Professional. As above, plus wing-mounted taxi light; heated pitot tube; electrically-operated tailplane trim and control wheel switch; tinted windscreen and windows; two headrests and instrument post lights; adding 45 lb (20·4 kg) to basic empty weight.

Factory-installed optional avionics packages are as follows (a cabin speaker, microphone with jack, antennae and wiring are common to all seven):

No 1. Narco Com 10A 360-channel communications transceiver with Nav 10 200-channel navigation frequency selector, and VOR/LOC indicator, adding 8 lb (3·6 kg) to basic empty weight.

No 2. Narco Com 11A 360-channel transceiver, Narco Nav 11 200-channel navigation receiver/converter and VOR/LOC indicator, Narco AT-50A transponder, Narco PDF-35 ADF system with remote indicator, Edo-Aire Mitchell Century I stabilisation system, adding 22 lb (10 kg) to basic empty weight.

No 3. As No 1 plus No 2, with Narco CP-25B audio panel, amplifier and radio tracker for stabilisation system, adding 33 lb (15 kg) to basic empty weight.

No 4. Dual Narco Com 11A 360-channel transceivers, Narco Nav 11 200-channel navigation receiver/converter and VOR/LOC indicator, Narco Nav 12 200-channel navigation receiver/converter and VOR/ILS indicator. Narco UGR-2A glideslope receiver, Narco MBT-12R marker beacon receiver, Narco CP-25B audio panel, amplifier and 3-light marker beacon receiver, Narco AT-50A transponder, Narco PDF-35 ADF system with remote indicator, and Edo-Aire Mitchell Century I stabilisation system with radio tracker, adding 38 lb (17·2 kg) to basic empty weight.

No 5. King KX-170B nav/com (720-channel communications and 200-channel navigation) with KI-201C VOR/LOC converter-indicator, adding 12 lb (5·4 kg) to basic empty weight.

No 6. As No 5, plus King KT-78 transponder, King KR-86 ADF with indicator and Edo-Aire Mitchell Century I stabilisation system, adding 26 lb (11·8 kg) to basic empty weight.

No 7. Dual King KX-170B nav/coms (720-channel communications and 200-channel navigation) with dual KI-201C VOR/LOC converter-indicators, King KMA-20 audio panel, amplifier and 3-light marker beacon receiver, King KT-78 transponder, King KR-86 ADF and Edo-Aire Mitchell Century I stabilisation system with radio tracker, adding 40 lb (18 kg) to basic empty weight.

Production is centred in Beech's Liberal, Kansas, plant. A total of 2,675 Musketeers, Sundowners, Sports and Sierras had been delivered by the end of 1973. They included 20 aircraft delivered to the Mexican government for military pilot training, as well as 25 for the Canadian Armed Forces which were delivered in 1971.

The following details apply to all three current models:

Type: Two, four or six-seat cabin monoplane.

Wings: Cantilever low-wing monoplane. Wing section NACA 63_2A415. Dihedral 6° 30'. Incidence 3° at root, 1° at tip. Single extruded main spar at 50% chord. Aluminium skin and stringers are bonded to honeycomb Trussgrid ribs on forward 50% of wing; rear 50% of wing is riveted. Slotted all-metal riveted ailerons and mechanically-controlled (optionally electrically-actuated) flaps have corrugated skin. No trim tabs. Plastics wingtips.

Beechcraft Sport 150 two/four-seat training and sporting aircraft

Beechcraft Sundowner 180 four-seat light aircraft (180 hp Lycoming O-360-A4J engine)

Fuselage: Cabin section has basic keel formed by floor and lower skin, with rolled skin side panels, stringers, a minimum number of bulkheads and structural top. Conventional semi-monocoque rear fuselage.

Tail Unit: Cantilever all-metal structure, with swept vertical surfaces. One-piece all-moving horizontal surface with full-span anti-servo tab. Optional electric tailplane trim. Rudder and aileron controls interconnected for easy cross-country flying.

Landing Gear (Sundowner and Sport): Non-retractable tricycle type. Beech rubber-disc shock-absorbers. Tube-type tyres size 15 × 6·00-6, pressure 40 lb/sq in (2·8 kg/cm²). Optional size 17·5 × 6·00-6 tyres, pressure 32 lb/sq in (2·25 kg/cm²). Cleveland disc-type hydraulic brakes. Steerable nosewheel. Parking brake.

Landing Gear (Sierra): Retractable tricycle type with electrically-actuated hydraulic retraction. Main units retract outwards and upwards into wing wells; nosewheel unit turns through 90° and retracts rearward to fold flat into a fairing behind the nosewheel strut. Steerable self-centering nosewheel. Beech rubber-disc shock-absorbers. Main wheels with tube-type tyres size 17·5 × 6·00-6, pressure 32 lb/sq in (2·25 kg/cm²). Nosewheel tyre size 14·2 × 5·00-5, pressure 35 lb/sq in (2·46 kg/cm²), Cleveland disc-type hydraulic brakes with toe-operated control. Parking brake.

Power Plant: One four-cylinder horizontally-opposed aircooled engine (details under model listings above). Fuel in two tanks in inboard wing leading-edges, with usable capacity of 52 US gallons (196·8 litres). Refuelling points above tanks. Oil capacity 2 US gallons (7·5 litres).

Accommodation (Sundowner and Sierra): Pilot and three or five passengers, in pairs, in enclosed cabin. Door on each side of cabin. Compartment for 270 lb (122 kg) baggage, with external door on port side. In-flight adjustable seats, pilot's storm window, windscreen defroster, instrument panel glare shield, air vents, map stowage, wall-to-wall carpeting. Optional aerobatic kit for Sundowner includes *g* meter and quick-release door.

Accommodation (Sport): Generally as for other versions except pilot and one to three passengers in pairs. Optional aerobatic kit includes *g* meter and quick-release door.

Systems: Electrical system supplied by 60A alternator, 12V 25Ah battery. 35Ah battery optional. Hydraulic system for brakes only, except on Sierra which has electro-hydraulic retraction system for landing gear. Vacuum system for instruments optional.

Electronics and Equipment: Standard equipment includes stall warning system, ventilation, heating and defrosting system; towbar; tie-down rings; control locks and pitot cover. Optional equipment and avionics as listed earlier. Additional optional equipment includes rear cabin "family seat" installation, cabin fire extinguisher, Hobbs hour meter, true airspeed indicator, mixture indicator, strobe lights, instrument post lights, external power socket, urethane paint, internal corrosion proofing, heavy-duty tyres (except Sierra) and electrically-operated flaps.

Dimensions, external:

Wing span	32 ft 9 in (9·98 m)
Wing chord (constant)	4 ft 4¾ in (1·34 m)
Wing aspect ratio	7·5
Length overall	25 ft 8½ in (7·84 m)
Height overall	8 ft 3 in (2·51 m)
Tailplane span	10 ft 8 in (3·25 m)
Wheel track:	
Sundowner, Sport	11 ft 10 in (3·61 m)
Sierra	12 ft 8 in (3·86 m)
Wheelbase:	
Sundowner, Sport	6 ft 4 in (1·93 m)
Sierra	6 ft 0¼ in (1·83 m)
Propeller diameter:	
Sundowner, Sierra	6 ft 4 in (1·93 m)
Sport	6 ft 2 in (1·88 m)
Propeller ground clearance:	
Sundowner	1 ft 1½ in (0·34 m)
Sport	1 ft 2½ in (0·37 m)
Sierra	1 ft 1 in (0·33 m)
Cabin doors:	
Height	3 ft 2 in (0·97 m)
Width	3 ft 4 in (1·03 m)
Baggage compartment door:	
Sundowner:	
Height	1 ft 6½ in (0·47 m)
Width	1 ft 11¾ in (0·60 m)
Sierra:	
Height	3 ft 0 in (0·91 m)
Width	1 ft 11½ in (0·60 m)

Dimensions, internal:

Cabin, aft of instrument panel:	
Length:	
Sundowner, Sierra	7 ft 11 in (2·41 m)
Sport	5 ft 11 in (1·80 m)
Max width	3 ft 8 in (1·18 m)
Max height	4 ft 0¼ in (1·22 m)
Floor area:	
Sundowner, Sierra	25·84 sq ft (2·4 m²)
Volume:	
Sundowner, Sierra	103·2 cu ft (2·92 m³)
Baggage compartment:	
Sundowner, Sierra	19·5 cu ft (0·55 m³)
Sport	28·8 cu ft (0·82 m³)

Areas:

Wings, gross	146 sq ft (13·57 m²)

Ailerons (total) 9·9 sq ft (0·92 m²)
Flaps (total) 18·7 sq ft (1·74 m²)
Fin 10·61 sq ft (0·99 m²)
Rudder 4·62 sq ft (0·43 m²)
Tailplane, incl anti-servo tab 27·0 sq ft (2·51 m²)

WEIGHTS AND LOADINGS:
Weight empty (includes oil and unusable fuel):
Sundowner 1,500 lb (680 kg)
Sport 1,433 lb (650 kg)
Sierra 1,711 lb (776 kg)
Max T-O weight:
Sundowner 2,450 lb (1,111 kg)
Sport 2,150 lb (975 kg)
Sierra 2,750 lb (1,247 kg)
T-O weight, Utility category:
Sundowner, Sport 2,030 lb (920 kg)
Max wing loading:
Sundowner 16·78 lb/sq ft (81·9 kg/m²)
Sport 14·73 lb/sq ft (71·9 kg/m²)
Sierra 18·84 lb/sq ft (91·9 kg/m²)
Max power loading:
Sundowner 13·61 lb/hp (6·17 kg/hp)
Sport 14·33 lb/hp (6·50 kg/hp)
Sierra 13·75 lb/hp (6·24 kg/hp)

PERFORMANCE (at max T-O weight):
Max level speed at S/L:
Sundowner 120 knots (138 mph; 222 km/h)
Sport 109 knots (126 mph; 203 km/h)
Sierra 140 knots (161 mph; 259 km/h)
Max cruising speed:
Sundowner 118 knots (136 mph; 219 km/h)
Sport 108 knots (124 mph; 200 km/h)
Sierra 131 knots (151 mph; 243 km/h)
Econ cruising speed:
Sundowner 93 knots (107 mph; 172 km/h)
Sport 84 knots (97 mph; 156 km/h)
Sierra 111 knots (128 mph; 206 km/h)
Stalling speed, flaps down, power off:
Sundowner 52 knots (59 mph; 95 km/h)
Sport 49 knots (56 mph; 91 km/h)
Sierra 55 knots (63 mph; 102 km/h)
Max rate of climb at S/L:
Sundowner 792 ft (241 m)/min
Sport 680 ft (207 m)/min
Sierra 893 ft (272 m)/min
Service ceiling:
Sundowner 12,600 ft (3,840 m)
Sport 11,650 ft (3,550 m)
Sierra 14,342 ft (4,370 m)
Min ground turning radius 22 ft 4 in (6·81 m)
T-O run:
Sundowner 1,130 ft (344 m)
Sport 1,030 ft (314 m)
Sierra 1,169 ft (356 m)
T-O to 50 ft (15 m):
Sundowner 1,955 ft (596 m)
Sport 1,635 ft (498 m)
Sierra 1,804 ft (550 m)
Landing from 50 ft (15 m):
Sundowner 1,484 ft (452 m)
Sport 1,693 ft (516 m)
Sierra 1,519 ft (463 m)
Landing run:
Sundowner 703 ft (214 m)
Sport 824 ft (251 m)
Sierra 803 ft (245 m)
Range at 75% power with max fuel, allowances for warm-up, T-O, climb and 45 min fuel reserve:
Sundowner 459 nm (529 miles; 851 km)
Sport 552 nm (636 miles; 1,023 km)
Sierra 561 nm (646 miles; 1,040 km)
Max cruising range:
Sundowner 508 nm (585 miles; 941 km)
Sport 577 nm (665 miles; 1,070 km)
Sierra 592 nm (682 miles; 1,097 km)

Beechcraft Sierra 200 four/six-seat light aircraft (200 hp Lycoming IO-360-A1B6 engine)

BEECHCRAFT BONANZA MODEL V35B

The prototype Bonanza flew for the first time on 22 December 1945 and the type went into production in 1947. Beech had delivered a total of 9,556 V-tail Bonanzas by 1 January 1974, in which year the Bonanza Model 35 series entered its 27th consecutive year of production.

The current version, designated Model V35B, is described in detail below.

The Bonanza Model A36 utility aircraft, and Model F33 series with conventional tail unit, are described separately.

The Bonanzas for 1974 are equipped with a dual-duct fresh air system to increase cabin airflow, flush-mounted overhead console, a new method of installing the aft bulkhead to simplify removal and access for maintenance, and safety features which include a three-light strobe system and double-strap safety shoulder harness with inertia reel for front seat occupants. Two new optional factory-installed IFR avionics packages include dual communication, navigation, marker beacon, glideslope, DME, and transponder. One package meets FAA Technical Standard Order (TSO). Beech was in 1972 the first general aviation manufacturer to acquire IFR approval of factory installation of area navigation equipment on production aircraft with this new equipment.

In 1974 Beech was offering four "Super Utility" packages of optional equipment, as detailed below:

Package No 1: Mitchell Century I autopilot with VOR/LOC tracker; 3 in directional gyro and gyro horizon with pressure system; alternate static source; 74 gallon (280 litre) extended-range fuel tanks; heated pitot tube; super soundproofing; King KR-85 ADF with KI-225 indicator; adding 54 lb (24·5 kg) to basic empty weight.

Package No 2: As above less Century I autopilot and gyros, plus Mitchell Century III autopilot, which includes roll, pitch and heading control, altitude hold, pitch trim, radio and glideslope couplers and Mitchell 3 in directional gyro and gyro horizon. This installation requires an optional glideslope receiver. Adding 68 lb (31 kg) to basic empty weight.

Package No 3: As package No 2, but replaces Mitchell Century III by Mitchell Century IV, this including Edo-Aire Mitchell DG-360 directional gyro in place of Mitchell directional gyro. Adding 73 lb (33 kg) to basic empty weight.

Package No 4: As package No 1, less Century I autopilot and gyros, plus Bendix FCS-810 autopilot, which includes roll, pitch and heading control, altitude hold, pitch trim, radio and glideslope couplers and Bendix 3 in directional gyro and gyro horizon. This installation requires an optional glideslope receiver. Adding 84 lb (38 kg) to basic empty weight.

Other optional extras available on the current Bonanza include the Beech-designed "Magic Hand" introduced in May 1965. Designed to eliminate the possibility of wheels-up landing or inadvertent retraction of the landing gear on the ground, it lowers the gear automatically on approach when the engine manifold pressure falls below approximately 20 in (50 cm) and airspeed has been reduced to 104 knots (120 mph; 193 km/h). On take-off, it keeps the gear down until the aircraft is airborne and has accelerated to 78 knots (90 mph; 145 km/h) IAS. The system can be switched off by the pilot at will.

TYPE: Four/six-seat light cabin monoplane.

WINGS: Cantilever low-wing monoplane. Wing section Beech modified NACA 23016·5 at root, modified NACA 23012 at tip. Dihedral 6°. Incidence 4° at root, 1° at tip. Sweepback 0° at quarter-chord. Each wing is a two-spar semi-monocoque box-beam of conventional aluminium alloy construction. Symmetrical-section ailerons and single-slotted flaps of aluminium alloy construction. Ground-adjustable trim tab in each aileron.

FUSELAGE: Conventional aluminium alloy semi-monocoque structure. Hat-section longerons and channel-type keels extend forward from cabin section, making the support structure for the engine and nosewheel an integral part of the fuselage.

TAIL UNIT: "Butterfly" type, consisting of tailplane and elevators set at 33° dihedral angle. Semi-monocoque construction. Fixed surfaces have aluminium alloy structure and skin. Control surfaces, aft of the light alloy spar, are primarily of magnesium alloy, with large controllable trim tab in each. Tail surfaces are interchangeable port and starboard, except for tabs and actuator horns. Electrically-operated elevator trimming optional.

LANDING GEAR: Electrically-retractable tricycle type, with steerable nosewheel. Main wheels retract inward into wings, nosewheel aft. Beech oil-air shock-absorbers on all units. Cleveland main wheels and tyres, size 6·00-6, pressure 30 lb/sq in (2·11 kg/cm²). Cleveland nosewheel and tyre, size 5·00-5, pressure 40 lb/sq in (2·81 kg/cm²). Cleveland ring-disc hydraulic brakes. Parking brake.

POWER PLANT: One 285 hp Continental IO-520-BA six-cylinder horizontally-opposed aircooled engine, driving a McCauley two-blade metal constant-speed propeller. Three-blade McCauley propeller optional. Manually-adjustable engine cowl flaps. Two standard fuel tanks in wing leading-edges, with total usable capacity of 44 US gallons (166·5 litres). Optionally, these can be replaced by tanks with total usable capacity of 74 US gallons (280 litres). Refuelling points above tanks. Oil capacity 3 US gallons (11·5 litres).

ACCOMMODATION: Enclosed cabin seating four, five or six persons on individual seats. Centre windows open for ventilation on ground and have release pins to permit their use as emergency exits. Pilot's storm window, port side. Cabin structure reinforced for protection in turnover. Space for up to 270 lb (122·5 kg) of baggage aft of seats. Passenger door and baggage access door both on starboard side. Cabin heated and ventilated.

SYSTEMS: Electrical system supplied by 70A alternator, 12V 35Ah battery. Hydraulic system for brakes only. Pneumatic system for instrument gyros.

ELECTRONICS AND EQUIPMENT: Standard equipment includes heating, ventilation and defrosting system; electric turn co-ordinator; 8-day clock; outside air temperature gauge; flap position indicator; stall warning system; electroluminescent sub-panel lighting; landing light; taxi light; navigation lights; cabin dome and instrument lights; passengers' reading lights; ultra-violet-proof windscreen and windows; wall-to-wall carpeting; glove compartment; sun visors; pilot's foul weather window; armrests; headrest; assist straps; utility shelf; towbar; pitot tube cover; control lock and winterisation kit. Standard avionics comprise King KX-170B 720-channel nav/com system with KI-201C VOR/LOC converter-indicator, microphone, headset, cabin speaker, Beechcraft B11-1 nav/com/GS antenna and emergency locator transmitter. Optional items include nav/com equipment by Bendix, King, Narco,

Beechcraft's V-tailed Bonanza Model V35B (285 hp Continental IO-520-BA engine)

Sunair and Pantronics, including marker beacon receiver, ADF, DME, VOR/LOC transmitter-receiver and glideslope receiver, full oxygen system, super soundproofing, co-pilot's toe-operated brakes, internally lighted instruments, instrument post lights, exhaust temperature gauge, control wheel map light, alternate static source, heated pitot tube, standby generator system, external power socket, cabin door courtesy light, electric elevator trim, dual control wheels, rotating beacons, headrests and fifth and sixth seats.

DIMENSIONS, EXTERNAL:
Wing span 33 ft 5½ in (10·20 m)
Wing chord at root 7 ft 0 in (2·13 m)
Wing chord at tip 3 ft 6 in (1·07 m)
Wing aspect ratio 6·2
Length overall 26 ft 4½ in (8·04 m)
Height over tail 7 ft 7 in (2·31 m)
Tailplane span 10 ft 1½ in (3·08 m)
Wheel track 9 ft 7 in (2·93 m)
Wheelbase 7 ft 0 in (2·13 m)
Propeller diameter:
Two-blade 7 ft 0 in (2·13 m)
Three-blade 6 ft 8 in (2·03 m)
Passenger door:
Height 3 ft 0 in (0·91 m)
Width 3 ft 1 in (0·94 m)
Baggage compartment door:
Height 1 ft 6½ in (0·47 m)
Width 1 ft 10½ in (0·57 m)

DIMENSIONS, INTERNAL:
Cabin, aft of instrument panel:
Length 8 ft 6 in (2·59 m)
Max width 3 ft 6 in (1·07 m)
Max height 4 ft 2 in (1·27 m)
Volume 117 cu ft (3·31 m³)
Baggage space 35 cu ft (0·99 m³)

AREAS:
Wings, gross 181 sq ft (16·80 m²)
Ailerons (total) 11·4 sq ft (1·06 m²)
Trailing-edge flaps (total) 21·3 sq ft (1·98 m²)
Fixed tail surfaces 23·8 sq ft (2·20 m²)
Movable tail surfaces, including tabs 14·4 sq ft (1·34 m²)

WEIGHTS AND LOADINGS:
Weight empty, equipped 2,031 lb (921 kg)
Max T-O and landing weight 3,400 lb (1,542 kg)
Max wing loading 18·80 lb/sq ft (91·8 kg/m²)
Max power loading 11·96 lb/hp (5·42 kg/hp)

PERFORMANCE (at max T-O weight):
Max level speed at S/L 182 knots (210 mph; 338 km/h)
Max cruising speed (75% power) at 6,500 ft (1,980 m) 176 knots (203 mph; 327 km/h)
Econ cruising speed (45% power) at 12,000 ft (3,660 m) 142 knots (164 mph; 264 km/h)
Stalling speed, wheels and flaps up 65 knots (74 mph; 119 km/h)
Stalling speed, wheels and flaps down 55 knots (63 mph; 102 km/h)
Max rate of climb at S/L 1,136 ft (346 m)/min
Service ceiling 17,500 ft (5,335 m)
Absolute ceiling 19,200 ft (5,850 m)
Min ground turning radius 12 ft 2½ in (3·72 m)
T-O run 1,115 ft (340 m)
T-O to 50 ft (15 m) 1,870 ft (570 m)
Landing from 50 ft (15 m) 1,505 ft (459 m)
Landing run 797 ft (243 m)
Range, 45% power at 12,000 ft (3,660 m) with max fuel and allowances for warm-up, T-O, climb and 45 min reserve 874 nm (1,007 miles; 1,620 km)

BEECHCRAFT BONANZA MODEL F33A/C

The **F33A** version of the Bonanza is a four/six-seat single-engined executive aircraft, similar in general configuration to the Bonanza Model V35B, but distinguished by a conventional tail unit with sweptback vertical surfaces. The prototype flew for the first time on 14 September 1959, and the production models were known as Debonairs until 1967.

The **F33C** is generally similar to the A, but approved for both aerobatic and utility operation.

The Model G33, generally similar to the F33A but with reduced wing span and powered by a 260 hp Continental IO-470-N engine, was first flown in April 1971. Delivery of this version was discontinued in early 1973 after 49 had been produced.

A total of 1,794 Model 33s had been built by the end of 1973. Twenty-one are used for pilot training by Lufthansa in Germany, and Pacific Southwest Airlines operates ten G33s for airline crew training. Orders received in 1973 for F33As and aerobatic F33Cs to equip foreign air forces were as follows: Imperial Air Force of Iran, 12 F33Cs; Mexican Air Force, 20 F33Cs; Spanish Air Ministry, 12 F33As and 12 F33Cs.

In 1971, the Bonanza F33A's interior layout was revised, providing cabin space equal to that of the Model V35B. The additional 1 ft 7 in (0·48 m) of interior length makes possible the introduction of optional fifth and sixth forward-facing seats. This model introduces also the improvements noted for the Bonanza V35B.

Optional extras include the "Magic Hand" automatic landing gear control system and other items described under the Model V35B Bonanza entry.

TYPE: Four/six-seat cabin monoplane.

WINGS: As for V35B Bonanza.

FUSELAGE: As for Bonanza V35B series.

TAIL UNIT: Conventional cantilever all-metal stressed-skin structure, primarily of aluminium alloy but with corrugated magnesium skin on elevators. Large trim tab in each elevator. Fixed tab in rudder.

LANDING GEAR: As for Bonanza V35B series. Main wheels size 6·00-6, pressure 30 lb/sq in (2·11 kg/cm²); nosewheel size 5·00-5, pressure 40 lb/sq in (2·81 kg/cm²).

POWER PLANT: One 285 hp Continental IO-520-B six-cylinder horizontally-opposed aircooled engine, driving a McCauley two-blade metal constant-speed propeller. The fuel tanks and capacity are as described for the V35B. Refuelling points on wing upper surface. Oil capacity 3 US gallons (11·5 litres).

ACCOMMODATION: Enclosed cabin with four individual seats in pairs as standard, plus optional forward-facing fifth and sixth seats. Baggage compartment and hat shelf aft of seats. Passenger door and baggage compartment door on starboard side. Heater standard. Large cargo door, on starboard side of fuselage, optional.

SYSTEMS: Electrical system supplied by 70A alternator. 12V 35Ah battery. Hydraulic system for brakes only. Pneumatic system for instrument gyros.

ELECTRONICS AND EQUIPMENT: As for V35B.

DIMENSIONS, EXTERNAL:
Wing span 33 ft 5½ in (10·20 m)
Wing chord at root 7 ft 0 in (2·13 m)
Wing chord at tip 3 ft 6 in (1·07 m)
Wing aspect ratio 6·2
Length overall 25 ft 6 in (7·77 m)
Height over tail 8 ft 3 in (2·51 m)
Tailplane span 12 ft 2 in (3·71 m)
Wheel track 9 ft 6¾ in (2·91 m)
Wheelbase 7 ft 5¼ in (2·27 m)
Propeller diameter 7 ft 0 in (2·13 m)
Passenger door:
Height 3 ft 0 in (0·91 m)
Width 3 ft 1 in (0·94 m)
Baggage compartment door:
Height 1 ft 8 in (0·51 m)
Width 2 ft 0 in (0·61 m)

DIMENSIONS, INTERNAL:
Cabin, aft of firewall:
Length 10 ft 1 in (3·07 m)
Max width 3 ft 6 in (1·07 m)
Max height 4 ft 2 in (1·27 m)
Volume 111·7 cu ft (3·16 m³)
Baggage compartment 35 cu ft (0·99 m³)

AREAS:
Wings, gross 181 sq ft (16·8 m²)
Ailerons (total) 11·4 sq ft (1·06 m²)
Trailing-edge flaps (total) 21·3 sq ft (1·98 m²)
Fin 9·1 sq ft (0·85 m²)
Rudder, incl tab 4·6 sq ft (0·43 m²)
Tailplane 18·82 sq ft (1·75 m²)
Elevators, incl tabs 13·36 sq ft (1·24 m²)

WEIGHTS AND LOADINGS:
Weight empty 2,000 lb (907 kg)
Max T-O and landing weight 3,400 lb (1,542 kg)
Max wing loading 18·8 lb/sq ft (91·8 kg/m²)
Max power loading 11·96 lb/hp (5·42 kg/hp)

PERFORMANCE:
Max level speed at S/L 181 knots (208 mph; 335 km/h)
Max cruising speed, 75% power at 6,500 ft (1,980 m) 174 knots (200 mph; 322 km/h)
Econ cruising speed, 45% power at 12,000 ft (3,655 m) 136 knots (157 mph; 253 km/h)
Stalling speed, wheels and flaps up 64·5 knots (74 mph; 119 km/h)
Stalling speed, wheels and flaps down 55 knots (63 mph; 101·5 km/h)
Max rate of climb at S/L 1,136 ft (346 m)/min
Service ceiling 17,500 ft (5,335 m)
Min ground turning radius 12 ft 2½ in (3·72 m)
T-O run 1,115 ft (340 m)
T-O to 50 ft (15 m) 1,870 ft (570 m)
Landing from 50 ft (15 m) 1,505 ft (459 m)
Landing run 797 ft (243 m)
Range at econ cruising speed with max fuel, allowances for warm-up, T-O, climb and 45 min reserve 847 nm (976 miles; 1,570 km)

BEECHCRAFT BONANZA MODEL A36

This version of the Bonanza, introduced in mid-1968, is a full six-seat utility aircraft developed from the Bonanza Model V35B. It is generally similar to the V35B, but is distinguished by a conventional tail unit with sweptback vertical surfaces, similar to that of the F33 series of Bonanzas (formerly known as Debonairs), and has large double doors on the starboard side of the fuselage aft of the wing root, to facilitate loading and unloading of bulky cargo when used in a utility role. The cabin area is increased by 6 cu ft (0·17 m³) compared with the V35B.

The Model A36, as all Bonanza models, is licensed in the FAA Utility category at full gross weight, with no limitation of performance. A total of 527 civil versions of the Model 36/A36 had been built by the end of 1973.

The current version of the Bonanza Model A36 introduced the improvements noted for the Bonanza V35B as well as new options which include a club-seating interior layout with rear-facing third and fourth seats, executive writing desk, headrests for third and fourth seats, reading lights and fresh air outlets for fifth and sixth seats. Optional extras include the "Magic Hand" automatic landing gear control system and all other items mentioned under the Model V35B Bonanza entry, except for the large cargo door.

TYPE: Six-seat utility light cabin monoplane.

WINGS: As for Model V35B.

FUSELAGE: As for Model V35B but lengthened by 10 in (26 cm).

TAIL UNIT: Conventional cantilever all-metal stressed-skin structure, primarily of aluminium alloy but with corrugated magnesium skin on elevators. Large trim tab in each elevator. Fixed tab in rudder.

LANDING GEAR: Electrically-retractable tricycle type, similar to that of Baron. Main units retract inward into wings, nosewheel rearward. Beech air-oil shock-absorbers. Steerable nosewheel. Cleveland main wheels with tyres size 18·75 × 7-7·5, pressure 30 lb/sq in (2·1 kg/cm²). Nosewheel tyre size 14·2 × 4·95-6·5, pressure 40 lb/sq in (2·8 kg/cm²). Cleveland ring-disc hydraulic brakes.

POWER PLANT: As for Model V35B.

ACCOMMODATION: Enclosed cabin seating six persons on individual seats in pairs. Two rear removable seats and two folding seats permit rapid conversion to utility configuration. Optional club-seating layout with rear-facing third and fourth seats, executive writing desk, headrests for third and fourth seats, reading lights and fresh air outlets for fifth and sixth seats. Double doors of bonded aluminium honeycomb construction on starboard side facilitate loading of cargo. Used as an air ambulance, one stretcher can be accommodated with ample room for a medical attendant and/or other passengers. Extra windows provide improved visibility for passengers. Stowage for 400 lb (181 kg) of baggage.

SYSTEMS: Electrical system supplied by 70A alternator, 12V 35Ah battery. Hydraulic system for brakes only. Pneumatic system for instrument gyros.

ELECTRONICS AND EQUIPMENT: Standard equipment includes King KX-170B 720-channel nav/com, with KI-201C VOR/LOC Omni conv/ind

Beechcraft Bonanza F33A four/six-seat light executive aircraft

and Beechcraft antenna, but a wide range of optional avionics equipment is available. Optional items of equipment are as detailed for the V35B Bonanza.

DIMENSIONS, EXTERNAL:

Wing span	33 ft 5½ in (10·2 m)
Length overall	27 ft 6 in (8·38 m)
Height overall	8 ft 5 in (2·57 m)
Wheel track	9 ft 6¾ in (2·91 m)
Wheelbase	9 ft 1¼ in (2·78 m)
Forward passenger door:	
Height	3 ft 0 in (0·91 m)
Width	3 ft 1 in (0·94 m)
Rear passenger/cargo door:	
Height	3 ft 4 in (1·02 m)
Width	3 ft 9 in (1·14 m)

AREA:

Wings, gross	181 sq ft (16·8 m²)

WEIGHTS AND LOADINGS:

Weight empty, equipped	2,096 lb (950 kg)
Max T-O weight	3,600 lb (1,633 kg)
Max wing loading	19·9 lb/sq ft (97·2 kg/m²)
Max power loading	12·6 lb/hp (5·7 kg/hp)

PERFORMANCE:

Max level speed at S/L 177 knots (204 mph; 323 km/h)
Max cruising speed (75% power) at 6,000 ft (1,830 m) 170 knots (196 mph; 315 km/h)
Cruising speed (65% power) at 10,000 ft (3,050 m) 162 knots (187 mph; 301 km/h)
Cruising speed (55% power) at 12,000 ft (3,655 m) 148 knots (170 mph; 274 km/h)
Stalling speed, power off, wheels and flaps up 63 knots (72 mph; 116 km/h)
Stalling speed, power off, wheels down and 30° flap 52·5 knots (60 mph; 97 km/h)
Max rate of climb at S/L 1,015 ft (309 m)/min
Service ceiling 16,000 ft (4,875 m)
Absolute ceiling 17,800 ft (5,425 m)
Min ground turning radius 13 ft 9½ in (4·20 m)
T-O run 1,257 ft (383 m)
T-O to 50 ft (15 m) 2,167 ft (660 m)
Landing from 50 ft (15 m) 1,575 ft (480 m)
Landing run 833 ft (254 m)
Range with max fuel, with allowances for warm-up, T-O, climb and 45 min fuel reserve:
55% power at 10,000 ft (3,050 m) 769 nm (886 miles; 1,425 km)
65% power at 10,000 ft (3,050 m) 749 nm (863 miles; 1,388 km)
75% power at 6,500 ft (1,980 m) 694 nm (800 miles; 1,287 km)

Beechcraft Bonanza A36 (285 hp Continental IO-520-BA engine)

BEECHCRAFT BARON MODELS B55 and E55
US Army designation: T-42A Cochise

The Baron was introduced in November 1960 as a development of the earlier Travel Air with more power, better all-weather capability and airframe refinements that included a swept tail-fin. It first flew in prototype form on 29 February 1960.

The original Model 95-55 Baron was a four/five-seater, but optional five-seat and six-seat layouts are available on the following current versions:

Model B55. With two 260 hp Continental IO-470-L engines. Received FAA Type Approval in September 1963.

Model E55. With two 285 hp Continental IO-520-C engines.

The 1974 Barons have interior features as described for the Bonanza, a single-point refuelling system at each wing, like that introduced on the Baron 58, a new four-light landing gear position indicator, and manually-operated engine cowl flaps. Avionics packages, one TSO'd, and a choice of fully integrated automatic flight director systems, are offered as optional items.

It was announced in February 1965 that the US Army had selected the B55 Baron as winner of its competition for a twin-engined fixed-wing instrument trainer. Subsequently, 65 Barons were ordered, under the designation T-42A. During 1971 Beech delivered an additional five T-42As to the US Army, for service with the army of Turkey, under the Military Assistance Programme. Export deliveries of the Baron B55 during 1972 included seven for the Spanish Air Ministry and six for the Civil Aviation Bureau of Japan. These aircraft are being used as instrument trainers.

A total of 2,677 civil and military Model 55 Barons had been built by the beginning of 1974.

TYPE: Four/six-seat cabin monoplane.

WINGS: Cantilever low-wing monoplane. Wing section NACA 23016·5 at root, NACA 23010·5 at tip. Dihedral 6°. Incidence 4° at root, 0° at tip. Each wing is a semi-monocoque box beam of aluminium alloy construction. Plain ailerons of aluminium construction. Electrically-operated single-slotted aluminium alloy flaps. Manually-operated trim tab in port aileron. Pneumatic rubber de-icing boots optional.

FUSELAGE: **Semi-monocoque aluminium alloy structure. E55 has nose extended by 11·6 in (0·29 m).**

TAIL UNIT: **Cantilever all-metal structure. Two trim tabs in elevators, one in rudder. Pneumatic rubber de-icing boots optional.**

LANDING GEAR: Electrically-retractable tricycle type. **Main units retract inward into wings, nosewheel rearward. Beech air-oil shock-absorbers. Steerable nosewheel with shimmy damper.** Cleveland wheels, with main-wheel tyres 6·50-8; pressure 50-54 lb/sq in (3·5-3·8 kg/cm²) on B55, 52-56 lb/sq in (3·7-3·9 kg/cm²) on E55. Nosewheel tyre size 5·00-5; pressure 48-52 lb/sq in (3·4-3·7 kg/cm²) on B55, 55-60 lb/sq in (3·9-4·2 kg/cm²) on E55. Cleveland ring-disc hydraulic brakes. Parking brake.

POWER PLANT: Two six-cylinder horizontally-opposed aircooled engines (details under model listings), driving McCauley or Hartzell two-blade constant-speed fully-feathering propellers. Optional Hartzell or McCauley three-blade propellers. Manually-operated cowl flaps. Fuel in four tanks in wings with total usable capacity of 100 US gallons (378 litres). Different wing tanks may be fitted to give total usable capacity of 136 US gallons (514 litres) in B55 and E55, or up to 166 US gallons (628 litres) usable in E55. Oil capacity 6 US gallons (23 litres). Propeller de-icing optional.

ACCOMMODATION: Standard model has four individual seats in pairs in enclosed cabin, with door on starboard side. Optional wider door for cargo. Folding airline-style fifth and sixth seats optional. Baggage compartments aft of cabin and in nose, both with external doors and with capacity of 400 lb (181 kg) and 300 lb (136 kg) respectively. E55 has also an extended rear compartment providing for an additional 120 lb (54 kg) of baggage; this is optional on B55. Pilot's storm window, port side. Cabin heated and ventilated. Windscreen defrosting standard. Alcohol de-icing for port side of windscreen optional.

SYSTEMS: Cabin heated by Janitrol 50,000 BTU heater. Oxygen system of 49 cu ft (1·39 m³) or 65 cu ft (1·84 m³) capacity optional. Electrical system includes two 24V 25A generators on B55 (24V 50A alternators on E55), one 24V 17Ah battery; two 12V 24Ah batteries optional. Hydraulic system for brakes only. Pneumatic system for instrument gyros.

ELECTRONICS AND EQUIPMENT: Standard equipment includes blind-flying instrumentation; electric turn co-ordinator; outside air temperature gauge; 8-day clock; vacuum gauge; flap position indicator; heated pitot tube; heated fuel vents; silent ventilation system; ultra-violet-proof windscreen and windows; soundproofing; wall-to-wall carpeting; glove compartment; sun visors; in-flight storage pockets; armrests; headrests; two landing lights; navigation lights; alternator failure lights (E55); cabin door courtesy light (E55); cabin dome, instrument and map lights; two cabin reading lights for each passenger; full-flow oil filters (E55); towbar; control locks; and winterisation kit. Standard avionics comprise 720-channel communications transceiver; 200-channel navigation receiver with VOR/LOC converter-indicator; emergency locator transmitter; microphone; headset; cabin speaker and nav/com GS antenna. (E55 has, in addition, ADF and indicators.) Optional avionics include a wide range of nav/coms by ARC, Bendix, Collins, King, Narco and RCA, and ADF and DME. Optional equipment includes rotating beacons, dual controls, executive writing desk, oxygen installation, engine and flight hour recorders, exhaust temperature gauge, internally lighted instruments, instrument post lights, control-wheel chronograph, three-light strobe system, nosewheel taxi light, wing ice lights, cabin door courtesy light (B55), lightweight automatic de-icer installation, alternate static source, propeller unfeathering accumulators, propeller synchroniser, co-pilot brakes, external power socket, super soundproofing and seat headrests. Extended baggage compartment and 50A alternators optional for B55. Bendix FCS-810 or Edo-Aire Mitchell Century IV autopilots, latter with heading lock, altitude hold, automatic pitch trim, and VOR/ILS coupling; Bendix FCS-810 or Mitchell Century IV flight director/autopilot systems and RCA AVQ-47 or AVQ-55, or King KWX-40 radar are also available optionally for both B55 and E55.

DIMENSIONS, EXTERNAL:

Wing span	37 ft 10 in (11·53 m)
Wing chord at root	7 ft 0 in (2·13 m)
Wing chord at tip	2 ft 11·6 in (0·90 m)
Wing aspect ratio	7·16
Length overall:	
B55	28 ft 0 in (8·53 m)
E55	29 ft 0 in (8·84 m)
Height over tail:	
B55	9 ft 7 in (2·92 m)
E55	9 ft 2 in (2·79 m)
Tailplane span:	
B55	13 ft 9¼ in (4·20 m)
E55	15 ft 11¼ in (4·86 m)
Wheel track	9 ft 7 in (2·93 m)
Wheelbase:	
B55	7 ft 0 in (2·13 m)
E55	8 ft 1 in (2·46 m)

Beechcraft Baron Model E55 (two 285 hp Continental IO-520-C engines)

Propeller diameter 6 ft 6 in (1·98 m)
Passenger door:
Height 3 ft 1 in (0·94 m)
Width 3 ft 0 in (0·91 m)
Height to step 1 ft 1 in (0·33 m)
Baggage door (fwd):
Height 1 ft 10 in (0·56 m)
Width 2 ft 1 in (0·64 m)
Baggage door (rear):
Standard:
Height 1 ft 10½ in (0·57 m)
Width 1 ft 6½ in (0·47 m)
Height to sill 2 ft 4 in (0·71 m)
Optional:
Height 1 ft 10½ in (0·57 m)
Width 3 ft 2 in (0·97 m)

Dimensions, internal:
Cabin: Length (including rear baggage compartment):
B55 10 ft 1 in (3·07 m)
E55 11 ft 9 in (3·58 m)
Max width 3 ft 6 in (1·07 m)
Max height 4 ft 2 in (1·27 m)
Baggage compartment (fwd):
B55 12 cu ft (0·34 m³)
E55 18 cu ft (0·51 m³)
Baggage compartment (rear) 35 cu ft (0·99 m³)
Extension to rear baggage compartment (optional on B55) 10 cu ft (0·28 m³)

Areas:
Wings, gross 199·2 sq ft (18·50 m²)
Ailerons (total) 11·40 sq ft (1·06 m²)
Trailing-edge flaps (total) 25·70 sq ft (2·39 m²)
Fin 11·00 sq ft (1·02 m²)
Rudder, including tab: 11·60 sq ft (1·08 m²)
Tailplane:
B55 48·06 sq ft (4·46 m²)
E55 53·30 sq ft (4·95 m²)
Elevators, including tabs:
B55 16·20 sq ft (1·51 m²)
E55 19·80 sq ft (1·84 m²)

Weights and Loadings:
Weight empty:
B55 3,155 lb (1,431 kg)
E55 3,189 lb (1,446 kg)
Max T-O and landing weight:
B55 5,100 lb (2,313 kg)
E55 5,300 lb (2,405 kg)
Max ramp weight:
B55 5,121 lb (2,322 kg)
E55 5,324 lb (2,415 kg)
Max wing loading:
B55 25·6 lb/sq ft (120·5 kg/m²)
E55 26·6 lb/sq ft (130·0 kg/m²)
Max power loading:
B55 9·8 lb/hp (4·45 kg/hp)
E55 9·3 lb/hp (4·22 kg/hp)

Performance (at max T-O weight):
Max level speed at S/L:
B55 205 knots (236 mph; 380 km/h)
E55 210 knots (242 mph; 390 km/h)
Max cruising speed, 75% power at 7,000 ft (2,135 m):
B55 195 knots (225 mph; 362 km/h)
E55 200 knots (230 mph; 370 km/h)
Cruising speed, 55% power at 12,000 ft (3,660 m):
B55 180 knots (207 mph; 333 km/h)
E55 181 knots (208 mph; 335 km/h)
Stalling speed (power off, wheels and flaps down):
B55 73 knots (84 mph; 135·5 km/h) IAS
E55 72 knots (83 mph; 134 km/h) IAS
Max rate of climb at S/L:
B55, E55 1,670 ft (510 m)/min
Rate of climb at S/L, one engine out:
B55 318 ft (97 m)/min
E55 335 ft (102 m)/min
Service ceiling:
B55 19,700 ft (6,000 m)
E55 20,900 ft (6,370 m)
Service ceiling, one engine out:
B55 7,000 ft (2,135 m)
E55 7,100 ft (2,165 m)
Min ground turning radius:
B55 12 ft 2 in (3·71 m)
E55 14 ft 0 in (4·27 m)
Runway LCN:
B55, E55 2
T-O run:
B55 1,340 ft (409 m)
E55 1,337 ft (408 m)
T-O to 50 ft (15 m):
B55 1,675 ft (511 m)
E55 1,631 ft (497 m)
Landing from 50 ft (15 m):
B55 1,840 ft (561 m)
E55 1,798 ft (548 m)
Landing run:
B55 940 ft (287 m)
E55 908 ft (277 m)
Cruising range, 65% power, including allowances for warm-up, taxi, T-O, climb to altitude and 45 min reserve:
B55 at 10,500 ft (3,200 m) with 136 US gallons (514 litres) fuel 942 nm (1,085 miles; 1,746 km)
E55 at 11,000 ft (3,350 m) with 136 US gallons (514 litres) fuel 833 nm (960 miles; 1,545 km)
E55 with 166 US gallons (628 litres) fuel 1,052 nm (1,212 miles; 1,950 km)

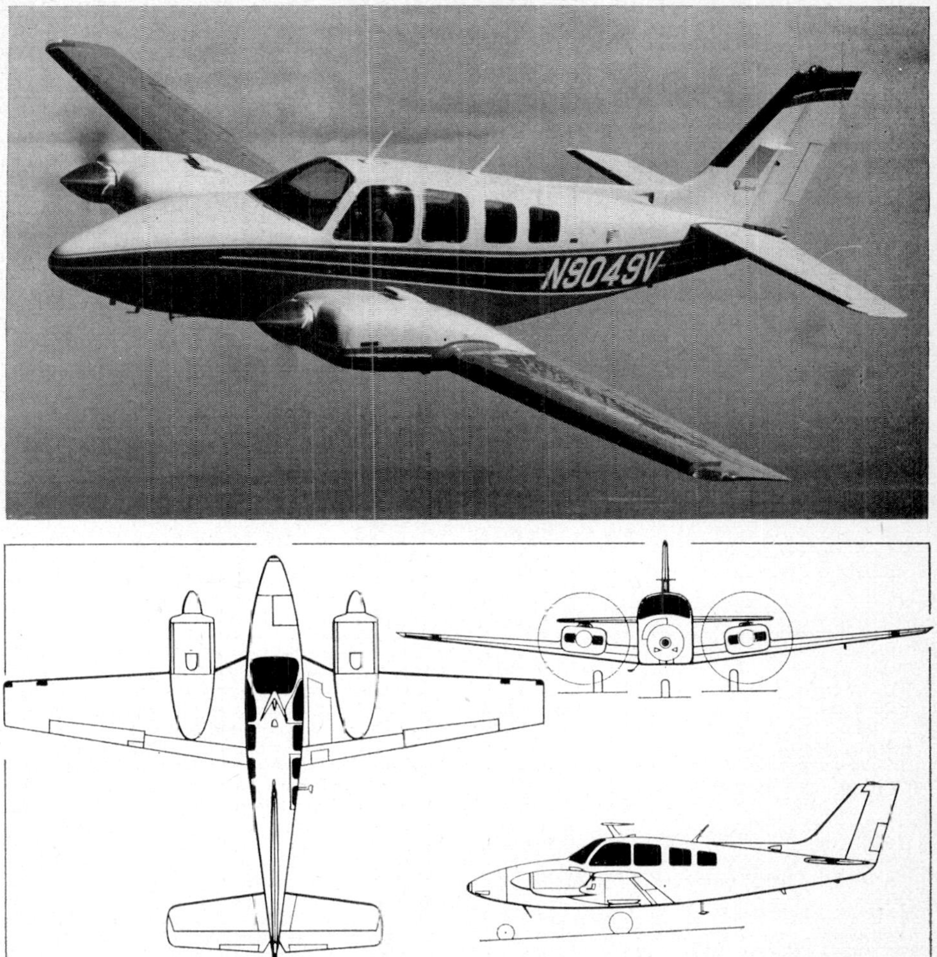

Photograph and three-view drawing (*Pilot Press*) of the Beechcraft Baron 58 four/six-seat cabin monoplane

BEECHCRAFT BARON 58

In December 1969 Beech added to the twin-engined 4/6-seat Baron series of aircraft a new model designated Baron 58. It differs from the earlier versions by having the forward fuselage extended by 10 in (0·25 m), double passenger/cargo doors on the starboard side of the fuselage, a fourth window on each side of the cabin and redesigned engine nacelles. By moving forward the instrument panel, cabin door and two front seats, it has been possible to provide a more spacious cabin without disturbing the wing location and main spar. The wheelbase has also been extended and gives improved ground handling.

Other improvements include the introduction of more contoured seats, a pilot's storm window, extended propeller hubs to improve engine cooling, re-siting of starter and magneto switches on the pilot's sub-panel, a three-deck circuit breaker console on the pilot's sidewall, colour-coded switches, a simplified fuel selector and a number of new paint schemes and interior trims.

Design of this version started on 16 August 1968. Construction of the first prototype began in March 1969 and first flight was made in June 1969. First flight of a production aircraft was made in November and FAA certification was granted on 19 November 1969.

The current version of the Baron 58 introduced high-capacity heavy-duty air compressors to power instrument gyros and new options which include alcohol de-icing for the port side of the windscreen, a club-seating arrangement with rear-facing third and fourth seats, headrests and reading lights for these seats, an executive writing desk, reading lights for the optional fifth and sixth seats and electrically-operated elevator trim control.

By the beginning of 1974, 419 Baron 58s had been delivered.

Type: Four/six-seat cabin monoplane.

Wings: Cantilever low-wing monoplane. Wing section NACA 23016·5 at root, NACA 23010·5 at tip. Dihedral 6°. Incidence 4° at root, 0° at tip. No sweepback. Each wing is a two-spar semi-monocoque box beam of aluminium alloy construction. Plain ailerons with corrugated aluminium skins. Trim and balance tab in port aileron. Electrically-operated single-slotted trailing-edge flaps with corrugated aluminium skins. Pneumatic rubber de-icing boots optional.

Fuselage: Semi-monocoque aluminium alloy structure, with nose extended 10 in (0·25 m) more than on the Model E55. Avionics compartment in nose, capacity 7 cu ft (0·20 m³).

Tail Unit: Cantilever all-metal structure. Trim tab in each elevator, one in rudder. Pneumatic rubber de-icing boots optional. Electrically-operated elevator trim control optional.

Landing Gear: Electrically-retractable tricycle type. Main units retract inward into wings, nosewheel rearward. Beech air-oil shock-absorbers. Steerable nosewheel. Cleveland main wheels and tyres size 6·50-8, pressure 56 lb/sq in (3·9 kg/cm²). Nosewheel and tyre size 5·00-5, pressure 60 lb/sq in (4·2 kg/cm²). Cleveland ring-disc hydraulic brakes. Parking brake.

Power Plant: Two 285 hp Continental IO-520-C six-cylinder horizontally-opposed aircooled engines, each driving a McCauley or Hartzell metal two-blade constant-speed fully-feathering propeller. McCauley or Hartzell three-blade propeller optional. Manually-operated cowl flaps. Fuel in four tanks in wings with standard usable capacity of 136 US gallons (514 litres). Two optional fuel tanks may be fitted to provide total usable capacity of 166 US gallons (628 litres). Single refuelling point in each wing. Non-electrical fuel sight gauge allows partial fuelling accuracy. Oil capacity 6 US gallons (23 litres). Electric or fluid propeller de-icing optional.

Accommodation: Standard model has four individual seats in pairs in enclosed cabin. Folding fifth and sixth seats optional. Club seating with aft-facing third and fourth seats optional. Pilot's storm window, port side. Forward-hinged door at front of cabin on starboard side. Double passenger/cargo doors on starboard side, aft of wing trailing-edge; forward door hinged to open forward, aft door hinged to open aft. Forward baggage compartment, capacity 300 lb (136 kg), with external access door in nose, forward of windscreen. Rear baggage compartment, capacity 400 lb (181 kg), and space for 120 lb (54 kg) baggage in extended rear compartment. Window adjacent to third and fourth seats can be used as emergency exit. Cabin heated and ventilated.

Systems: Electrical system supplied by two 24V 50A alternators; 24V 17Ah battery. Two 12V 24Ah batteries optional. Hydraulic system for brakes only. Cabin heated by Janitrol 50,000 BTU heater. Pneumatic system for instrument gyros and optional surface de-icing boots. Oxygen system of either 49 cu ft (1·39 m³) or 65 cu ft (1·84 m³) capacity optional.

Electronics and Equipment: Standard equipment is as for the E55 Baron, plus a heated stall warning vane and a door-ajar light. Standard and optional avionics and optional equipment are as detailed for the E55 Baron, except that the cargo door is standard on the B58 Baron.

Dimensions, external:

Wing span	37 ft 10 in (11·53 m)
Wing chord at root	7 ft 0 in (2·13 m)
Wing chord at tip	2 ft 11·6 in (0·90 m)
Wing aspect ratio	7·16
Length overall	29 ft 10 in (9·09 m)
Height overall	9 ft 6 in (2·90 m)
Tailplane span	15 ft 11 in (4·85 m)
Wheel track	9 ft 7 in (2·92 m)
Wheelbase	8 ft 11 in (2·72 m)
Propeller diameter:	
Two-blade	6 ft 6 in (1·98 m)
Three-blade	6 ft 4 in (1·93 m)
Forward passenger door:	
Height	3 ft 0 in (0·91 m)
Width	3 ft 1 in (0·94 m)
Rear passenger/cargo door:	
Height, max	3 ft 4 in (1·02 m)
Width	3 ft 9 in (1·14 m)
Nose baggage door:	
Height	1 ft 10 in (0·56 m)
Width	2 ft 1 in (0·64 m)
Emergency exit window:	
Height	1 ft 9 in (0·53 m)
Width	2 ft 0 in (0·61 m)

Dimensions, internal:

Cabin, including rear baggage area:	
Length	12 ft 7 in (3·84 m)
Max width	3 ft 6 in (1·07 m)
Max height	4 ft 2 in (1·27 m)
Floor area	40 sq ft (3·72 m²)
Volume	135·9 cu ft (3·85 m³)
Baggage compartment (fwd)	18 cu ft (0·51 m³)
Baggage compartment (aft)	37 cu ft (1·05 m³)
Extended rear baggage compartment	10 cu ft (0·28 m³)

Areas:

Wings, gross	199·2 sq ft (18·50 m²)
Ailerons (total)	11·40 sq ft (1·06 m²)
Trailing-edge flaps (total)	25·70 sq ft (2·39 m²)
Fin	11·00 sq ft (1·02 m²)
Rudder, including tab	11·60 sq ft (1·08 m²)
Tailplane	53·3 sq ft (4·95 m²)
Elevators, including tabs	19·8 sq ft (1·84 m²)

Weights and Loadings:

Weight empty	3,268 lb (1,482 kg)
Max T-O and landing weight	5,400 lb (2,449 kg)
Max wing loading	27·1 lb/sq ft (132·3 kg/m²)
Max power loading	9·5 lb/hp (4·3 kg/hp)

Performance (at max T-O weight):

Max never-exceed speed	223 knots (257 mph; 414 km/h)
Max level speed at S/L	210 knots (242 mph; 390 km/h)
Max cruising speed, 75% power at 7,000 ft (2,135 m)	200 knots (230 mph; 370 km/h)
Cruising speed, 65% power at 11,000 ft (3,350 m)	195 knots (225 mph; 362 km/h)
Cruising speed, 55% power at 12,000 ft (3,660 m)	180 knots (207 mph; 333 km/h)
Stalling speed, power off, landing gear and flaps down	74 knots (85 mph; 137 km/h)
Max rate of climb at S/L	1,694 ft (516 m)/min
Rate of climb at S/L, one engine out	382 ft (116 m)/min
Service ceiling	17,800 ft (5,425 m)
Service ceiling, one engine out	7,150 ft (2,180 m)
Min ground turning radius	15 ft 0 in (4·57 m)
Runway LCN	2
T-O run	1,403 ft (428 m)
T-O to 50 ft (15 m)	1,706 ft (520 m)
Landing from 50 ft (15 m)	2,070 ft (631 m)
Landing run	1,044 ft (318 m)
Cruising range, 65% power at 11,000 ft (3,350 m) with 166 US gallons (628 litres) fuel and allowances for warm-up, taxi, T-O, climb to altitude and 45 min reserve	1,052 nm (1,212 miles; 1,950 km)

BEECHCRAFT DUKE B60

Design work on the original version of this 4/6-seat pressurised and turbocharged light twin-engined transport started in early 1965. Construction of the prototype began in January 1966, and the first flight was made on 29 December 1966. FAA Type Approval was granted on 1 February 1968.

The 1974 B60 version has an engine overboost relief valve serving as a backup to the automatic system, redesigned engine intake valves, nickel-cadmium battery failure detection system, improved fuel injection system, an almost level rear cabin floor for the fifth and sixth seats, and cabin length increased by 6 in (0·15 m), achieved by moving the pressurisation valves to the aft side of the rear bulkhead.

A total of 250 Dukes had been produced by 1 January 1974.

Type: Four/six-seat cabin monoplane.

Wings: Cantilever low-wing monoplane. Wing section NACA 23016·5 at root, NACA 23010·5 at tip. Thickness/chord ratio 13·7% at root, 10·5% at tip. Dihedral 6°. Incidence 4° at root, 0° at tip. Each wing is a two-spar semi-monocoque box-beam of conventional aluminium alloy construction. Overhang-balance ailerons constructed of aluminium alloy. Conventional hinged trim tab in port aileron. Electrically-operated single-slotted aluminium alloy flaps. Pneumatic rubber de-icing boots optional.

Fuselage: Semi-monocoque aluminium alloy structure. Heavy-gauge chemically-milled aluminium alloy skins.

Tail Unit: Cantilever all-metal structure. Aluminium spars and end ribs; magnesium alloy skins reinforced with metal bonded honeycomb stiffeners running chordwise. Dorsal fin. Swept vertical and horizontal surfaces. Tailplane dihedral 10°. Trim tabs in rudder and port elevator. Pneumatic rubber de-icing boots optional.

Landing Gear: Electrically-retractable tricycle type. Main units retract inward, nosewheel aft; all three units have fairing doors. Beechcraft air-oil shock-absorbers. Goodrich main wheels and tyres size 19·50 × 6·75-8 10-ply rating, pressure 80 lb/sq in (5·6 kg/cm²). Goodyear steerable nosewheel with shimmy damper, tyre size 15 × 6·00-6, pressure 50 lb/sq in (3·5 kg/cm²). Goodrich single-disc hydraulic brakes. Parking brake.

Power Plant: Two 380 hp Lycoming TIO-541-E1C4 six-cylinder horizontally-opposed air-cooled turbocharged engines, each driving a Hartzell three-blade metal constant-speed and fully-feathering propeller. Propeller unfeathering accumulators and electric anti-icing optional. Electrically-operated engine cowl flaps. Two interconnected fuel cells in each wing containing 71 US gallons (269 litres); total capacity 142 US gallons (538 litres). Optionally, four interconnected fuel cells in each wing containing 103 US gallons (390 litres); total capacity 206 US gallons (780 litres). Refuelling points in leading-edge of each wing, near wingtip. Oil capacity 6·5 US gallons (24·5 litres).

Accommodation: Standard model has four individual seats in pairs, with centre aisle, in enclosed cabin. Door, hinged at forward edge, on port side at rear of cabin. Baggage hold in the nose, capacity 32 cu ft (0·91 m³), with external access door on port side of nose. Additional stowage for 28·25 cu ft (0·80 m³) of baggage at rear of cabin. Optional extras include fifth and sixth seats, rearward-facing third and fourth seats, headrests, curtain separating passenger and pilot seating, writing desks, refreshment cabinets, toilet, windscreen electrical de-icing and cabin fire extinguishers.

Systems: Cabin pressurisation system, differential 4·6 lb/sq in (0·32 kg/cm²), supplied by engine turbocharger bleed air, maintains cabin altitude equivalent to 10,000 ft (3,050 m) at 24,800 ft (7,560 m). Optional engine-driven vapour-cycle air-conditioning system of 14,000 BTU and combustion heater of 45,000 BTU. Automatic altitude controller for cabin pressurisation system optional. Oxygen system optional, with 11 cu ft (0·31 m³), 22 cu ft (0·62 m³) or 49 cu ft (1·39 m³) bottle. Hydraulic system for brakes only. Pneumatic system for pressure-operated instruments and de-icing boots only. 24V 125A generators standard; 24V 13Ah aircooled nickel-cadmium battery.

Electronics and Equipment: Standard equipment includes full-flow oil filters, alternate static source, blind-flying instrumentation, electric turn co-ordinator, outside air temperature gauge, eight-day clock, heated pitot tube, external power socket, fuel vent anti-icer, heated stall warning device, dual landing lights, navigation lights, rotating beacons, taxi light, map light, passengers' reading lights, cabin dome light, instrument post lights, instrument floodlights, entrance light, nose baggage compartment light, ventilation installation with provisions for air-conditioning, tinted cabin side windows, super soundproofing, wall-to-wall carpeting, sun visors, cabin storage pockets, foul weather window for pilot, armrests, headrests, baggage straps, retracting exterior step, and aircraft towbar. Optional equipment includes de luxe instrument panel with duplicated blind-flying instrumentation for co-pilot, instantaneous vertical speed indicator, tachometer with synchroscope, flight and engine hour recorders, pilot's control wheel chronometer, control wheel map light, cabin altitude programmer, co-pilot toe brakes, wing ice lights, propeller synchroniser, urethane paint, pilot's relief tube and strobe lights. Standard avionics installation comprises RCA AVC-110A main VHF transceiver with integral control and B3 com antenna; RCA AVN-210A manual Omni No. 1 with VOR/ILS converter-indicator, B12 nav antenna, B16 marker antenna and A-326A GS antenna; King KA-25 amplifier; marker beacon; glideslope; Beech metal radio panel; static wicks; single audio switch panel; microphone key button in pilot's control wheels; white lighting; microphone, headset and cockpit speaker; avionics master switch; annunciator panel; and emergency locator transmitter. Optional avionics include an extensive range of RCA, King, Collins, Bendix, Wilcox and Beech equipment.

Dimensions, external:

Wing span	39 ft 3 in (11·96 m)
Wing chord at fuselage c/l	9 ft $2\frac{1}{8}$ in (2·80 m)
Wing chord at tip	2 ft $11\frac{3}{8}$ in (0·90 m)

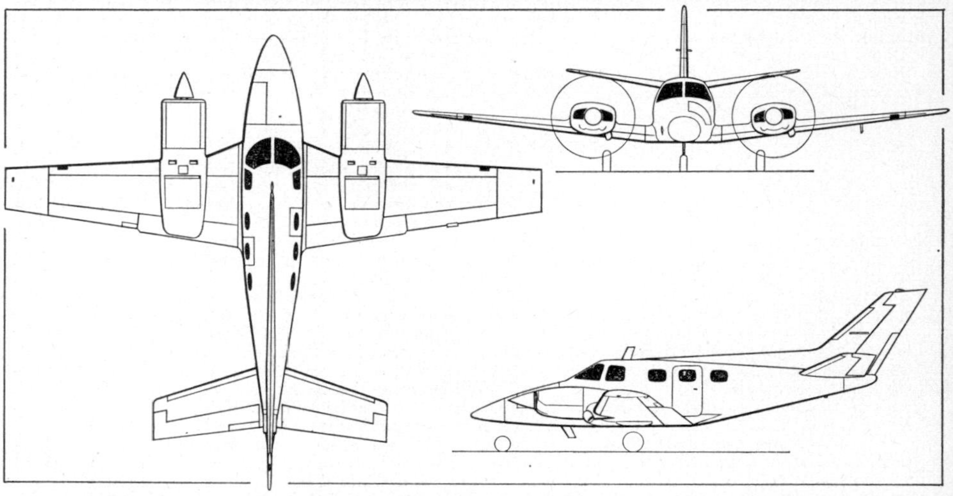

Photograph and three-view drawing (*Pilot Press*) of the Beechcraft Duke B60 4/6-seat pressurised transport (two 380 hp Lycoming TIO-541-E1C4 engines)

Wing aspect ratio 7·243
Length overall 33 ft 10 in (10·31 m)
Height overall 12 ft 4 in (3·76 m)
Tailplane span 17 ft 0 in (5·18 m)
Wheel track 11 ft 2 in (3·40 m)
Wheelbase 9 ft 3 in (2·82 m)
Propeller diameter 6 ft 2 in (1·88 m)
Passenger door:
  Height 3 ft 11½ in (1·21 m)
  Width 2 ft 2½ in (0·67 m)
  Height to sill 2 ft 8 in (0·81 m)
Baggage compartment door:
  Height 1 ft 11½ in (0·60 m)
  Width 3 ft 1½ in (0·96 m)
  Height to sill 3 ft 1½ in (0·95 m)

Dimensions, internal:
Cabin:
  Length 11 ft 10 in (3·61 m)
  Max width 4 ft 2 in (1·27 m)
  Max height 4 ft 4 in (1·32 m)
  Floor area 36·2 sq ft (3·36 m^2)
  Volume 169·6 cu ft (4·80 m^3)

Areas:
Wings, gross 212·9 sq ft (19·78 m^2)
Ailerons (total) 11·4 sq ft (1·06 m^2)
Trailing-edge flaps (total) 29·7 sq ft (2·76 m^2)
Fin 16·38 sq ft (1·52 m^2)
Rudder, including tab 12·4 sq ft (1·15 m^2)
Tailplane 45·6 sq ft (4·24 m^2)
Elevators, including tab 16·4 sq ft (1·52 m^2)

Weights and Loadings:
Weight empty, equipped 4,265 lb (1,934 kg)
Max ramp weight 6,819 lb (3,093 kg)
Max T-O and landing weight 6,775 lb (3,073 kg)
Max wing loading 31·8 lb/sq ft (155·3 kg/m^2)
Max power loading 8·9 lb/hp (4·04 kg/hp)

Performance (at max T-O weight):
Max never-exceed speed
  235 knots (270 mph; 434·5 km/h) IAS
Max level speed at 23,000 ft (7,010 m)
  248 knots (286 mph; 460 km/h)
Max cruising speed:
  79% power at 25,000 ft (7,620 m)
    242 knots (279 mph; 449 km/h)
  79% power at 20,000 ft (6,100 m)
    230 knots (265 mph; 426 km/h)
  79% power at 15,000 ft (4,570 m)
    219 knots (252 mph; 406 km/h)
Cruising speed:
  75% power at 25,000 ft (7,620 m)
    236 knots (272 mph; 438 km/h)
  75% power at 20,000 ft (6,100 m)
    225 knots (259 mph; 417 km/h)
  75% power at 15,000 ft (4,570 m)
    214 knots (247 mph; 398 km/h)
  65% power at 25,000 ft (7,620 m)
    221 knots (255 mph; 410 km/h)
  65% power at 20,000 ft (6,100 m)
    211 knots (243 mph; 391 km/h)
  65% power at 15,000 ft (4,570 m)
    201 knots (232 mph; 373 km/h)
  45% power at 25,000 ft (7,620 m)
    182 knots (210 mph; 338 km/h)
  45% power at 20,000 ft (6,100 m)
    178 knots (205 mph; 330 km/h)
  45% power at 15,000 ft (4,570 m)
    171 knots (197 mph; 317 km/h)
Stalling speed, wheels and flaps up, power off
  86 knots (98 mph; 157 km/h)
Stalling speed, wheels and flaps down, power off
  76 knots (87 mph; 140 km/h)
Max rate of climb at S/L 1,601 ft (488 m)/min
Rate of climb at S/L, one engine out
  307 ft (94 m)/min
Service ceiling 30,800 ft (9,390 m)
Service ceiling, one engine out
  15,100 ft (4,600 m)
Runway LCN 4
T-O run 2,006 ft (611 m)
T-O to 50 ft (15 m) 2,626 ft (800 m)
Landing from 50 ft (15 m) 3,065 ft (934 m)
Landing run 1,318 ft (402 m)
Range, with max optional fuel and allowances for warm-up, taxi, take-off, climb to altitude and 45 min fuel reserve at 45% power, ISA:
  75% power at 25,000 ft (7,620 m)
    837 nm (963 miles; 1,550 km)
  75% power at 20,000 ft (6,100 m)
    825 nm (950 miles; 1,529 km)
  75% power at 15,000 ft (4,570 m)
    809 nm (931 miles; 1,498 km)
  65% power at 25,000 ft (7,620 m)
    936 nm (1,077 miles; 1,733 km)
  65% power at 20,000 ft (6,100 m)
    919 nm (1,058 miles; 1,702 km)
  65% power at 15,000 ft (4,570 m)
    903 nm (1,040 miles; 1,673 km)
  45% power at 25,000 ft (7,620 m)
    1,022 nm (1,176 miles; 1,892 km)
  45% power at 20,000 ft (6,100 m)
    1,031 nm (1,187 miles; 1,910 km)
  45% power at 15,000 ft (4,570 m)
    1,022 nm (1,177 miles; 1,894 km)

BEECHCRAFT QUEEN AIR B80 AND QUEEN AIRLINER B80

The prototype of the original Queen Air 80, which introduced more powerful engines than those of the A65, flew for the first time on 22 June 1961 and received its FAA Type Certificate on 20 February 1962. It was followed in January 1964 by the Queen Air A80, with increased wing span and AUW, new interior styling, increased fuel capacity and redesigned nose compartment, giving more space for radio. The A80 was followed in turn by the improved B80 and eleven-seat Queen Airliner B80, to which the details below apply.

Beechcraft Queen Air B80 (two 380 hp Lycoming IGSO-540-A1D engines) in Venezuelan insignia

For 1974 Beech has introduced two optional equipment packages for factory installation:

Executive Package. Comprising quickly removable forward partition with magazine rack and accordion door separating cockpit from cabin; quickly removable aft cabin partition and door; private lavatory, aft installation with relief tube; four executive cabin chairs with inboard folding armrests, or two such chairs and one four-seat couch (exchange for five commuter chairs with fixed armrests); and aft coat hanger rod installation; adding 43 lb (19·5 kg) to basic empty weight.

Airliner Package. Comprising seven floor-mounted chairs with inboard folding armrests and removable upholstery, two aft folding chairs with removable upholstery, extended seat tracks, four additional fresh air outlets and reading lights (exchange for five standard chairs); extended aft baggage compartment with baggage restraints; aft baggage door with safety light; fourth cabin window on starboard side; 39Ah nickel-cadmium battery (exchange for 13Ah battery); metal map case under pilot's seat; cockpit fire extinguisher; cockpit separation half-curtain; second outboard fuel filler caps with dipstick (one each side); coat hanger bar; and upholstery for nose baggage compartment; adding 172 lb (78 kg) to basic empty weight.

By the beginning of 1974, Beech had built a total of 473 Queen Air 80s, A80s, B80s and Queen Airliner B80s, of which 39 per cent had been exported.

Type: Six/eleven-seat business aircraft, commuter airliner and utility aircraft.

Wings: Cantilever low-wing monoplane. Wing section NACA 23020 at root, NACA 23012 outboard of joint between outer panel and wingtip. Dihedral 7°. Incidence 3° 55′ at root, 0° 1′ at tip. Two-spar all-metal structure of aluminium alloy. All-metal ailerons of magnesium. Trim tab in port aileron. Single-slotted aluminium alloy flaps. Pneumatic rubber de-icing boots optional.

Fuselage: Aluminium alloy semi-monocoque structure.

Tail Unit: Cantilever all-metal structure of aluminium alloy, with sweptback vertical surfaces. Tailplane dihedral 7°. Trim tabs in rudder and elevators. Pneumatic rubber de-icing boots optional.

Landing Gear: Electrically-retractable tricycle type. Main units retract forward, nosewheel aft. Beechcraft air-oil shock-absorbers. Goodyear main wheels and tyres, size 8·50-10, 8-ply rating, pressure 48 lb/sq in (3·4 kg/cm^2). Goodyear steerable nosewheel with tyre size 6·50-10, 6-ply rating, pressure 42 lb/sq in (3·0 kg/cm^2). Goodyear heat sink and aircooled single-disc hydraulic brakes. Parking brakes.

Power Plant: Two 380 hp Lycoming IGSO-540-A1D six-cylinder horizontally-opposed air-cooled geared and supercharged engines, each driving a Hartzell three-blade fully-feathering constant-speed propeller. Propeller synchrophasers optional. Fuel in two inboard wing tanks, each with capacity of 44 US gallons (166 litres) and two outboard tanks, each 63 US gallons (238·5 litres). Total standard fuel capacity 214 US gallons (809 litres). Provision for two optional auxiliary tanks in wings to bring total capacity to 264 US gallons (1,000 litres). Refuelling points above wings. Oil capacity (total) 8 US gallons (30 litres).

Accommodation: Crew of one or two on flight deck and four to nine passengers in cabin. Basic layout has five commuter passenger seats; executive layout has four lounge chairs, fore and aft partitions and lavatory; airliner layout has seven commuter and two folding passenger seats, extended aft baggage compartment and door, map case, cabin fire extinguisher and fourth cabin window. Door on port side of cabin at rear; optionally, double-width cargo doors. Optional toilet and baggage compartment opposite door, capacity 350 lb (160 kg). Other optional items include sofa, tables, refreshment cabinets and external cargo pod.

Systems: Optional electrically-driven vapour-cycle air-conditioning system with combustion heater. Standard model has 100,000 BTU heater and ventilating system. Hydraulic system for brakes only. Two 28V 150A DC engine-driven generators and 24V 13Ah nickel-cadmium battery for electrical system. 39Ah nickel-cadmium battery optional. Oxygen system of 64 cu ft (1·81 m^3) capacity optional.

Electronics and Equipment: Standard avionics comprise Narco Com 11A 360-channel transceiver with Nav 12 200-channel nav receiver/converter, VOR/ILS indicator, B3 com antenna and B17 nav/GS antenna; Narco Com 11A 360-channel transceiver with Nav 11 200-channel nav receiver/converter, VOR/LOC indicator and B3 com antenna; Collins 356F-3 speaker amplifier and Collins 356C-4 isolation amplifier; Bendix T-12D ADF with 551RL indicator, voice range filter and sense antenna; Narco MBT-24R marker beacon with B16 marker antenna and panel-mounted marker lights; Narco UGR-2A glideslope with B35 glideslope antenna; Beech metal radio panel, accessories and static wicks; edge-lighted audio switch panel; white lighting; dual microphones, headsets and single cockpit speaker; emergency locator transmitter; and avionics master switch. Standard equipment includes dual controls, blind-flying instrumentation, outside air temperature gauge, 8-day clock, flap position indicator, dynamic brake on landing gear, landing gear warning system, heated stall warning system, dual heated pitot heads, cabin door "unlocked" warning light, external power socket, two landing lights, navigation lights, dual rotating beacons, cabin door and indirect overhead lighting, reading lights for each passenger, map light, aft compartment dome light, primary and secondary instrument light systems, windscreen defroster, dual storm windows, sun visors, map pockets, four-way adjustable pilot and co-pilot seats, "No smoking—Fasten seat belt" sign, carpeted floor, provisions for removable cabin partitions and toilet, window curtains, emergency exit, coat rack, towbar, control lock assembly and heated fuel vents. A wide range of avionics and equipment is available to customer's requirements, including Collins, King, Bendix, Sunair, Narco or RCA radar and radio packages; King RNav; RCA weather-avoidance radar; Beech or Mitchell autopilot; de luxe instrument panel carrying duplicate blind-flying instruments, exhaust temperature gauge, flight hour recorder; control-wheel chronograph and map light installation, nosewheel taxi light, three-light strobe system, wing ice lights, alcohol or electric propeller and windscreen anti-icing, dual windscreen wipers, propeller unfeathering accumulators, nose compartment light, super soundproofing, external power socket, cabin and cockpit fire extinguishers, cargo door, and photographic installation.

DIMENSIONS, EXTERNAL:
Wing span 50 ft 3 in (15·32 m)
Wing chord at root 7 ft 0½ in (2·15 m)
Wing chord at tip 3 ft 6 in (1·07 m)
Wing aspect ratio 7·51
Length overall 35 ft 6 in (10·82 m)
Height overall 14 ft 8 in (4·47 m)
Tailplane span 17 ft 2¾ in (5·25 m)
Wheel track 12 ft 9 in (3·89 m)
Wheelbase 12 ft 3½ in (3·75 m)
Propeller diameter 7 ft 9 in (2·36 m)
Standard passenger door:
Height 4 ft 3¾ in (1·31 m)
Width 2 ft 3 in (0·69 m)
Height to sill 3 ft 10 in (1·17 m)
Optional cargo door:
Height 4 ft 3¾ in (1·31 m)
Width 4 ft 6 in (1·37 m)
Height to sill 3 ft 10 in (1·17 m)

DIMENSIONS, INTERNAL:
Cabin, including flight deck and baggage area:
Length 19 ft 7 in (6·97 m)
Max width 4 ft 6 in (1·37 m)
Max height 4 ft 9 in (1·45 m)
Volume 335·4 cu ft (9·5 m³)
Standard aft baggage compartment 53 cu ft (1·50 m³)
Nose baggage compartment 24 cu ft (0·68 m³)
Optional extension to aft baggage compartment 17 cu ft (0·48 m³)

AREAS:
Wings, gross 293·9 sq ft (27·3 m²)
Ailerons (total) 13·90 sq ft (1·29 m²)
Trailing-edge flaps (total) 29·30 sq ft (2·72 m²)
Fin 23·67 sq ft (2·20 m²)
Rudder, including tab 14·00 sq ft (1·30 m²)
Tailplane 47·25 sq ft (4·39 m²)
Elevators, including tabs 17·87 sq ft (1·66 m²)

WEIGHTS AND LOADINGS:
Weight empty, equipped 5,277 lb (2,393 kg)
Max T-O and landing weight 8,800 lb (3,992 kg)
Max ramp weight 8,855 lb (4,016 kg)
Max wing loading 29·9 lb/sq ft (146·0 kg/m²)
Max power loading 12·2 lb/hp (5·53 kg/hp)

PERFORMANCE (at max T-O weight, except where indicated):
Max level speed at 11,500 ft (3,500 m) at average AUW 215 knots (248 mph; 400 km/h)
Cruising speed, 70% power at 15,000 ft (4,570 m) at average AUW 195 knots (225 mph; 362 km/h)
Econ cruising speed, 45% power at 15,000 ft (4,570 m) at average AUW 159 knots (183 mph; 294 km/h)
Stalling speed, wheels and flaps up 85 knots (97 mph; 157 km/h) IAS
Stalling speed, wheels and flaps down 71 knots (81 mph; 131 km/h) IAS
Max rate of climb at S/L 1,275 ft (388 m)/min
Rate of climb at S/L, one engine out 210 ft (64 m)/min
Service ceiling 26,800 ft (8,168 m)
Service ceiling, one engine out 11,800 ft (3,596 m)
Min ground turning radius 38 ft 0 in (11·58 m)
Runway LCN 3·5
T-O run 2,007 ft (612 m)
T-O to 50 ft (15 m) 2,556 ft (779 m)
Landing from 50 ft (15 m) at max landing weight 2,572 ft (784 m)
Landing run at max landing weight 1,620 ft (494 m)
Range with max optional fuel, allowances for warm-up, taxi, T-O and climb to altitude, with 45 min reserve:
70% power at 15,000 ft (4,570 m) 957 nm (1,102 miles; 1,773 km)
65% power at 17,000 ft (5,180 m) 1,076 nm (1,239 miles; 1,994 km)
45% power at 15,000 ft (4,570 m) 1,317 nm (1,517 miles; 2,441 km)

BEECHCRAFT KING AIR MODEL C90
USAF designation: VC-6B

This model of the King Air is a pressurised 6/10-seat business aircraft powered by two United Aircraft of Canada PT6A-20 turboprop engines. It has superseded the original Models 90, A90 and B90 King Air.

Introduced in September 1970, the C90 King Air utilises the more advanced cabin pressurisation and heating system of the King Air 100. This comprises a dual engine bleed air system for cabin pressurisation, with a max differential of 4·6 lb/sq in (0·32 kg/cm²), maintaining a sea level cabin environment to a height of 10,500 ft (3,200 m), and a 10,000 ft (3,050 m) environment to an altitude of 24,700 ft (7,530 m). It has also a 27,000 BTU auxiliary electrical heating system which allows the cabin to be preheated prior to engine start. It can be used in conjunction with the standard automatic 45,000 BTU dual bleed air heating system if extremely low external air temperatures are experienced. Standard equipment includes also an electrically-heated windscreen, polarised windows, airframe and engine anti-icing, a comprehensive avionics package, including a remote compass system, DME and transponder, and four cabin chairs in club-seating arrangement. The C90 is available with either new engines, or UACL factory-overhauled engines at reduced price.

A total of 701 King Air 90s had been delivered by the beginning of 1974, including one for the USAF's 1,254th Special Air Missions Squadron at Andrews AFB, Maryland, for VIP transport duties under the designation VC-6B. In late 1973 the Spanish Air Ministry ordered six King Air C90s for instrument training and liaison transportation. They were scheduled for delivery by the end of March 1974.

TYPE: Six/ten-seat twin-turboprop business aircraft.

WINGS: Cantilever low-wing monoplane. Wing section NACA 23014·1 (modified) at root, NACA 23016.22 (modified) at outer end of centre-section, NACA 23012 at tip. Dihedral 7°. Incidence 4° 48′ at root, 0° at tip. No sweepback at quarter-chord. Two-spar aluminium alloy structure. All-metal ailerons of magnesium, with adjustable trim tab on port aileron. Single-slotted aluminium alloy flaps. Automatic pneumatic de-icing boots on leading-edges standard.

FUSELAGE: Aluminium alloy semi-monocoque structure.

TAIL UNIT: Cantilever all-metal structure with sweptback vertical surfaces. Fixed-incidence tailplane, with 7° dihedral. Trim tabs in rudder and each elevator. Automatic pneumatic de-icing boots on leading-edges of fin and tailplane.

LANDING GEAR: Electrically-retractable tricycle type. Nosewheel retracts rearward, main wheels forward into engine nacelles. Main wheels protrude slightly beneath nacelles when retracted, for safety in a wheels-up emergency landing. Steerable nosewheel with shimmy damper. Beech air-oil shock-absorbers. BF Goodrich main wheels with tyres size 8·50-10, pressure 55 lb/sq in (3·9 kg/cm²). BF Goodrich nosewheel with tyre size 6·50-10, pressure 52 lb/sq in (3·7 kg/cm²). Goodrich heat-sink and aircooled multi-disc hydraulic brakes. Parking brakes.

POWER PLANT: Two 550 ehp United Aircraft of Canada PT6A-20 turboprop engines, each driving a Hartzell three-blade constant-speed fully-feathering propeller. Propeller electrothermal anti-icing standard. Fuel in two tanks in engine nacelles, each with capacity of 61 US gallons (231 litres), and bladder type auxiliary tanks in outer wings, each with capacity of 131 US gallons (496 litres). Total fuel capacity 384 US gallons (1,454 litres). Refuelling points in top of each engine nacelle and in wing leading-edge outboard of each nacelle. Oil capacity 3·5 US gallons (13·2 litres). Engine anti-icing system standard.

ACCOMMODATION: Two seats side by side in cockpit with dual controls standard. Normally, four reclining seats are provided in the main cabin, in pairs facing each other fore and aft. Standard furnishings include cabin forward partition, with fore and aft partition curtain, hinged nose baggage compartment door and coat rod. Optional arrangements seat up to eight persons, some with two- or three-place couch and refreshment cabinets. Baggage racks at rear of cabin on starboard side, with optional toilet on port side. Door on port side aft of wing, with built-in airstairs. Emergency exit on starboard side of cabin. Entire accommodation pressurised and air-conditioned. Electrically-heated windscreen standard.

SYSTEMS: Pressurisation provided by dual engine bleed air system with maximum pressure differential of 4·6 lb/sq in (0·32 kg/cm²). Cabin heated by 45,000 BTU dual engine bleed air system and auxiliary 27,000 BTU electrical heating system. Electrical system utilises two 28V 250A starter/generators, 24V 45Ah air-cooled nickel-cadmium battery. Complete de-icing and anti-icing equipment. Oxygen system, 22 cu ft (0·62 m³), 49 cu ft (1·39 m³) or 64 cu ft (1·81 m³) capacity, optional. Vacuum system for flight instruments.

ELECTRONICS AND EQUIPMENT: Standard avionics for the King Air C90 include King KX-175B main and standby VHF transceivers, each with KA-39 power adapter and B3 antenna; King KN-77 Omni No. 1 VOR/ILS converter, Collins 331A-3G indicator, King KN-73 GS and B17 antenna; King KN-77 Omni No. 2 VOR/ILS converter, KNI-520 indicator and B17 antenna; King KR-85 ADF with KI-225 indicator and sense antenna; Bendix TPR-660 transponder with B18 antenna; King KN-65 DME with KI-265 indicator, Nav 1-Nav 2 switching and B18 antenna; King KMA-20 audio system, less marker lights; King KA-40 marker lights and B16 antenna; Collins PN-101 compass system, electric gyro horizon, co-pilot's 3 in CF gyro horizon and directional gyro; dual 100VA Flite-Tronics PC-14C inverters with failure light; de luxe instrument panel with dual flight instrumentation and vertical engine instruments display; white lighting; Beech metal radio panel, accessories and static wicks; microphone key buttons in pilot's and co-pilot's control wheels; dual microphones, headsets and cockpit speakers and avionics master switch. A wide range of optional avionics, available as individual items or in standard packages, can be supplied to customer's requirements. Standard equipment includes heated stall warning system, dual heated pitot heads, external power socket, wing ice lights, two landing lights, taxi light, navigation lights, dual rotating beacons, dual map lights, indirect cabin lighting, reading lights, cabin door light, aft compartment dome light, primary and secondary instrument light systems, white cockpit lighting, fresh air outlets, double glazed windows, curtains and shades, soundproofing, carpeted floor, "No smoking—Fasten seat belt" sign, windscreen defroster, engine anti-icing system with inertial separators, dual storm windows, sun visors, map pockets, windscreen wipers, heated fuel vents, cabin coat rack, pictorial navigation indicator, electric directional gyro, outside air temperature gauge, vacuum gauge, oxygen pressure and de-icing pressure gauges, cabin rate of climb indicator, cabin altitude and differential pressure indicators, edge-lighted control panels, emergency locator transmitter, tow-bar and control lock assembly. Optional equipment includes flight hour recorder, chronograph in pilot's control wheel, 24-hour GMT clock in co-pilot's control wheel, reversible-pitch propellers with synchrophaser or automatic propeller feathering system with reversible-pitch propellers and synchrophasers, three-light strobe system, engine fire detection and fire extinguishing systems, electrically-operated elevator trim, cabin fire extinguisher, low profile toilet installation, instantaneous vertical speed indicator and cabin door step lights.

DIMENSIONS, EXTERNAL:
Wing span 50 ft 3 in (15·32 m)
Wing chord at root 7 ft 0½ in (2·15 m)
Wing chord at tip 3 ft 6 in (1·07 m)
Wing aspect ratio 8·57
Length overall 35 ft 6 in (10·82 m)
Height overall 14 ft 2½ in (4·33 m)
Tailplane span 17 ft 2½ in (5·25 m)
Wheel track 12 ft 9 in (3·89 m)
Wheelbase 12 ft 3½ in (3·75 m)
Propeller diameter 7 ft 9 in (2·36 m)

Three of six Beechcraft King Air C90s for delivery to the Spanish Air Ministry

Passenger door:
- Height 4 ft 3¾ in (1·31 m)
- Width 2 ft 3 in (0·69 m)
- Height to sill 3 ft 10 in (1·17 m)

DIMENSIONS, INTERNAL:
- Total pressurised length 17 ft 10 in (5·43 m)
- Cabin:
  - Length 12 ft 8 in (3·86 m)
  - Max width 4 ft 6 in (1·37 m)
  - Max height 4 ft 9 in (1·45 m)
  - Floor area 70 sq ft (6·50 m^2)
  - Volume 314 cu ft (8·89 m^3)
- Baggage compartment, aft 53·5 cu ft (1·51 m^3)

AREAS:
- Wings, gross 293·94 sq ft (27·31 m^2)
- Ailerons (total) 13·90 sq ft (1·29 m^2)
- Trailing-edge flaps (total) 29·30 sq ft (2·72 m^2)
- Fin 23·67 sq ft (2·20 m^2)
- Rudder, including tab 14·00 sq ft (1·30 m^2)
- Tailplane 47·25 sq ft (4·39 m^2)
- Elevators, including tabs 17·87 sq ft (1·66 m^2)

WEIGHTS AND LOADINGS:
- Weight empty 5,630 lb (2,553 kg)
- Max T-O weight 9,650 lb (4,377 kg)
- Max ramp weight 9,705 lb (4,402 kg)
- Max landing weight 9,168 lb (4,159 kg)
- Max wing loading 32·8 lb/sq ft (160·1 kg/m^2)
- Max power loading 8·8 lb/ehp (3·99 kg/ehp)

PERFORMANCE (at max T-O weight, except where stated otherwise):
- Max cruising speed at 12,000 ft (3,660 m) 221 knots (254 mph; 409 km/h)
- Max cruising speed at 16,000 ft (4,880 m) at AUW of 8,365 lb (3,794 kg) 220 knots (253 mph; 407 km/h)
- Max cruising speed at 21,000 ft (6,400 m) at AUW of 8,365 lb (3,794 kg) 217 knots (250 mph; 402 km/h)
- Approach speed at AUW of 9,168 lb (4,159 kg) 83 knots (95 mph; 153 km/h)
- Stalling speed, wheels and flaps up, power off 80 knots (92 mph; 148 km/h) IAS
- Stalling speed, wheels and flaps down, power off 72 knots (82 mph; 132 km/h) IAS
- Max rate of climb at S/L 2,000 ft (610 m)/min
- Rate of climb at S/L, one engine out 555 ft (169 m)/min
- Service ceiling 25,600 ft (7,800 m)
- Service ceiling, one engine out 14,100 ft (4,298 m)
- Min ground turning radius 38 ft 0 in (11·58 m)
- Runway LCN 4
- T-O to 50 ft (15 m) 1,960 ft (597 m)
- Accelerate-stop distance 3,601 ft (1,098 m)
- Landing from 50 ft (15 m) without propeller reversal at AUW of 9,168 lb (4,159 kg) 2,010 ft (613 m)
- Landing run, without propeller reversal at AUW of 9,168 lb (4,159 kg) 980 ft (299 m)
- Range with max fuel at max cruising speed, including allowance for starting, taxi, take-off, climb, descent and 45 min reserve at max range power, ISA, at:
  - 21,000 ft (6,400 m) 1,148 nm (1,321 miles; 2,126 km)
  - 16,000 ft (4,875 m) 1,012 nm (1,165 miles; 1,875 km)
  - 12,000 ft (3,660 m) 914 nm (1,052 miles; 1,693 km)
- Max range at econ cruising power, allowances as above, at:
  - 21,000 ft (6,400 m) 1,256 nm (1,446 miles; 2,327 km)
  - 16,000 ft (4,875 m) 1,162 nm (1,337 miles; 2,151 km)
  - 12,000 ft (3,660 m) 1,083 nm (1,247 miles; 2,006 km)

BEECHCRAFT KING AIR E90

On 1 May 1972 Beech announced an addition to the King Air range of business aircraft. Designated King Air E90, this combines the airframe of the King Air C90 with the 680 ehp United Aircraft of Canada PT6A-28 turboprop engines that power the King Air A100, each flat rated to 550 ehp.

The description of the King Air C90 in this edition applies also to the King Air E90, except as detailed below:

LANDING GEAR: As King Air C90, except main-wheel tyre pressure 57 lb/sq in (4·0 kg/cm^2).

POWER PLANT: Two 680 ehp United Aircraft of Canada PT6A-28 turboprop engines, flat rated to 550 ehp, each driving a Hartzell three-blade metal fully-feathering and reversible constant-speed propeller. Standard fuel capacity 474 US gallons (1,794 litres).

ELECTRONICS AND EQUIPMENT: Standard electronics include RCA AVC-111A main VHF transceiver with B3 antenna; RCA AVC-110A standby VHF transceiver with B3 antenna; RCA AVN-220A manual Omni No. 1 with glideslope, marker beacon receiver, Collins 331A-3G indicator, single marker lights, B17 nav antenna, B16 marker antenna and B35 glideslope antenna; RCA AVN-211A manual Omni No. 2 on B17 antenna; King KR-85 ADF with KI-225 indicator, voice range filter and sense antenna; RCA AVQ-47 radar with 12 in phased array antenna and standard scope; Bendix TPR-660 transponder with B18 antenna; King KN-65 DME with KI-265 indicator, KA-43 converter, Nav 1 and Nav 2 switching and B18 antenna; Collins 356C-4 isolation amplifier and 356F-3 speaker amplifier with single set audio switches in edge-lighted panel; Collins PN-101 compass system; standard electric gyro horizon; 3 in CF gyro horizon and directional gyro for co-pilot; and 100VA Flite-Tronics PC-14C inverters with failure light; white lighting; radio accessories; static wicks; Beech metal radio panel; microphone button in pilot and co-pilot control wheels; dual microphones, headsets and cockpit speakers; avionics master switch; and emergency locator transmitter. Standard equipment includes engine-driven fuel boost pumps, vertically-arranged engine instruments, polarised cabin windows, alternate static source and items as detailed for King Air C90. Optional equipment includes the items detailed for the King Air C90, plus an extensive range of optional avionics.

WEIGHTS AND LOADINGS:
- Weight empty 5,876 lb (2,635 kg)
- Max T-O weight 10,100 lb (4,581 kg)
- Max ramp weight 10,160 lb (4,608 kg)
- Max landing weight 9,700 lb (4,400 kg)
- Max wing loading 34·4 lb/sq ft (168·0 kg/m^2)
- Max power loading 9·2 lb/ehp (4·17 kg/ehp)

PERFORMANCE (at max T-O weight, unless detailed otherwise):
- Max cruising speed, at 12,000 ft (3,655 m) 249 knots (287 mph; 462 km/h)
- Cruising speed, at max recommended cruise power:
  - At 16,000 ft (4,875 m) 247 knots (285 mph; 459 km/h)
  - At 21,000 ft (6,400 m) 245 knots (282 mph; 454 km/h)
- Cruising speed for max range 197 knots (227 mph; 365 km/h)
- Stalling speed, power off, wheels and flaps up 86 knots (99 mph; 159 km/h) IAS
- Stalling speed, power off, wheels and flaps down 77 knots (89 mph; 143 km/h) IAS
- Max rate of climb at S/L 1,870 ft (570 m)/min
- Rate of climb at S/L, one engine out 470 ft (143 m)/min
- Service ceiling 27,620 ft (8,419 m)
- Service ceiling, at 8,000 lb (3,629 kg) AUW 30,910 ft (9,421 m)
- Service ceiling, one engine out 14,390 ft (4,386 m)
- Service ceiling, one engine out, at 8,000 lb (3,629 kg) AUW 20,400 ft (6,218 m)
- Min ground turning radius 38 ft 0 in (11·58 m)
- Runway LCN 4·5
- T-O run 1,553 ft (473 m)
- T-O to 50 ft (15 m) 2,024 ft (617 m)
- Landing distance, 5° approach angle, full flaps, at max landing weight:
  - Landing from 50 ft (15 m) 2,110 ft (643 m)
  - Landing run 1,030 ft (314 m)
- Accelerate/stop distance, including 2 sec failure recognition time 3,736 ft (1,139 m)
- Cruising range at max recommended cruise power:
  - At 16,000 ft (4,875 m) 1,125 nm (1,295 miles; 2,084 km)
  - At 21,000 ft (6,400 m) 1,309 nm (1,507 miles; 2,425 km)
- Cruising range at max range power:
  - At 16,000 ft (4,875 m) 1,480 nm (1,704 miles; 2,742 km)
  - At 21,000 ft (6,400 m) 1,625 nm (1,871 miles; 3,011 km)
- Range, at max T-O weight, max recommended power at 21,000 ft (6,400 m), 45 min reserve, five occupants, 258 lb (117 kg) baggage and 3,176 lb (1,440 kg) fuel before engine start 1,309 nm (1,507 miles; 2,425 km)

BEECHCRAFT B99 AIRLINER

The Beechcraft B99 Airliner is an unpressurised high-performance 17-seat twin-turboprop airliner designed specifically for the scheduled airline and scheduled air taxi market. The prototype of the original Model 99 flew for the first time in July 1966 and the first delivery of a production aircraft was made on 2 May 1968.

By 1 January 1974 a total of 153 of these aircraft had been delivered to 47 operators.

Beechcraft King Air E90 (two 550 ehp United Aircraft of Canada PT6A-28 turboprop engines)

Installation of an optional forward-hinged cargo door forward of the standard airstair door permits the Airliner to be used for all-cargo or combined cargo-passenger operations, with a movable bulkhead separating freight and passengers in the latter configuration.

Two versions are currently available:

B99 Airliner. Standard model with gross weight of 10,900 lb (4,944 kg) and powered by two 680 ehp United Aircraft of Canada PT6A-27 turboprop engines, as described below.

B99 Executive. Basically the same as the standard model, but offering optional seating arrangements for eight to 17 persons and various corporate interiors.

Earlier versions were the 99 Airliner, with two 550 ehp United Aircraft of Canada PT6A-20 turboprop engines, and the 99A Airliner with two 680 ehp United Aircraft of Canada PT6A-27 turboprop engines, flat rated to 550 ehp.

Nine examples of the latter aircraft were supplied to the Chilean Air Force, for search and rescue and navigational training.

TYPE: Twin-turboprop light passenger, freight or executive transport.

WINGS: Cantilever low-wing monoplane. Wing section NACA 23018 at root, NACA 23016·5 at centre-section joint with outer panel, NACA 23012 at tip. Dihedral 7°. Incidence 4° 48′ at root, 0° at tip. Two-spar all-metal aluminium alloy structure. All-metal ailerons of magnesium. Trim tab in port aileron. Single-slotted aluminium alloy flaps. Optional automatic pneumatic de-icing boots.

FUSELAGE: All-metal semi-monocoque structure.

TAIL UNIT: Cantilever all-metal structure, with sweptback vertical surfaces and a ventral stabilising fin. Variable-incidence tailplane. Trim tab in rudder. Pneumatic de-icing boots optional.

LANDING GEAR: Retractable tricycle type with single steerable nosewheel and twin wheels on each main unit. Electrical retraction, nosewheel rearward, main units forward into engine nacelles. Beech oleo-pneumatic shock-absorbers. Goodrich wheels and tyres. Main-wheel tyres size 18 × 5·5, pressure 92-96 lb/sq in (6·5-6·75 kg/cm^2). Nosewheel tyre size 6·50 × 10, pressure 50-55 lb/sq in (3·5-3·9 kg/cm^2). BF Goodrich heat-sink and aircooled single-disc hydraulic brakes. Parking brake. Shimmy damper on nosewheel.

POWER PLANT: Two 680 ehp United Aircraft of Canada PT6A-27 turboprop engines, each driving a Hartzell three-blade fully-feathering and reversible-pitch constant-speed propeller. Automatic feathering system standard. Rubber fuel tanks in wings, with total capacity of 368 US gallons (1,393 litres).

ACCOMMODATION: Crew of two side by side on flight deck, with full dual controls and blind-flying instrumentation. Half-curtain or bulkhead between flight deck and cabin. Standard version has 15 removable high-density cabin chairs, two-abreast with centre aisle (single chair opposite door). Executive version has six standard seats in cabin, the two forward seats facing rearwards. Baggage space aft of rear seats, with external door. Nose baggage compartment with two external doors. An optional underfuselage baggage/cargo pod with a volume of 35·5 cu ft (1·01 m^3) and structural capacity of 800 lb (363 kg) is available, and this does not affect speed appreciably. Airstair door on port side of cabin at rear. Optional forward-hinged cargo door forward of passenger door, to give wide unobstructed opening for cargo loading. Emergency exit on each side at forward end of cabin. A wide selection of corporate interiors and removable chemical or electrical flushing toilet optional.

SYSTEMS: Automatic 100,000 BTU heating system and high-capacity ventilation system, with individual fresh air outlets, standard. Optional 24,000 BTU air-conditioning system. Hydraulic system for brakes only. 28V DC electrical system, with two 200A generators, 40Ah nickel-cadmium battery and dual solid-state inverters.

Beechcraft B99 Airliner 17-seat light transport (two 680 ehp United Aircraft of Canada PT6A-27 turboprop engines)

Electronics and Equipment: Standard avionics (domestic aircraft) include dual 360-channel VHF transceivers; dual 200-channel nav receivers, with VOR/ILS indicators; ADF with voice range filter; three-light marker beacon; 40-channel glideslope receiver; 200-channel DME with Nav 1 and Nav 2 switching; transponder; pilot-to-cabin paging, with four speakers; dual 120VA inverters with failure light; pilot's electric gyro horizon; dual microphones, headsets and cockpit speakers; microphone key buttons in pilot's and co-pilot's control wheels; and avionics master switch. The standard export avionics package includes a second ADF and a 10-channel HF transceiver in lieu of DME and transponder. Standard equipment includes electric propeller anti-icing, landing and taxi lights, wing ice lights, cabin instrument and map lights, dual rotating beacons, and fire detection system. Optional equipment includes high-pressure oxygen system, air-conditioning system with Freon compressor, engine fire extinguishing system, weather radar, propeller synchronisers, high-intensity anti-collision lights, autopilot, electrical windscreen anti-icing system and auxiliary engine bleed air heater.

Dimensions, external:
Wing span 45 ft 10½ in (14·00 m)
Wing chord at root 7 ft 0½ in (2·15 m)
Wing chord at tip 3 ft 6 in (1·07 m)
Wing aspect ratio 7·51
Length overall 44 ft 6¾ in (13·58 m)
Height overall 14 ft 4¼ in (4·38 m)
Tailplane span 22 ft 4½ in (6·82 m)
Wheel track 13 ft 0 in (3·96 m)
Wheelbase 17 ft 11¾ in (5·48 m)
Propeller diameter 7 ft 9½ in (2·37 m)
Propeller ground clearance 1 ft 1½ in (0·34 m)
Passenger door:
Height 4 ft 3½ in (1·31 m)
Width 2 ft 3 in (0·69 m)
Cargo double-door (optional):
Height 4 ft 3½ in (1·31 m)
Width 4 ft 5½ in (1·36 m)

Dimensions, internal:
Cabin, including flight deck:
Length 25 ft 4 in (7·72 m)
Max width 4 ft 7 in (1·40 m)
Max height 4 ft 9 in (1·45 m)
Volume 423·6 cu ft (12·0 m^3)
Baggage space (nose) volume 43·9 cu ft (1·24 m^3)
Baggage space (rear) volume 21·1 cu ft (0·60 m^3)

Weights and Loadings (A: 99 Airliner, B: 99A Airliner, C: B99 Airliner):
Weight empty, equipped:
A 5,722 lb (2,595 kg)
B 5,749 lb (2,607 kg)
C 5,777 lb (2,620 kg)
Max T-O weight:
A, B 10,400 lb (4,717 kg)
C 10,900 lb (4,944 kg)
Max design taxi weight:
C 10,955 lb (4,969 kg)
Max wing loading:
C 38·97 lb/sq ft (190·3 kg/m^2)
Max power loading:
C 8·02 lb/ehp (3·64 kg/ehp)

Performance (A: 99 Airliner, B: 99A Airliner, C: B99 Airliner, at max T-O weight unless stated otherwise):
Max cruising speed at AUW of 9,500 lb (4,309 kg):
A at 8,000 ft (2,440 m) 221 knots (254 mph; 409 km/h)
A at 12,000 ft (3,650 m) 219 knots (252 mph; 406 km/h)
B at 8,000 ft (2,440 m) 243 knots (280 mph; 451 km/h)
B at 12,000 ft (3,650 m) 247 knots (284 mph; 457 km/h)
C at 8,000 ft (2,440 m) 246 knots (283 mph; 455 km/h)
243 knots (280 mph; 451 km/h)
C at 12,000 ft (3,650 m) 247 knots (285 mph; 459 km/h)
Max rate of climb at S/L:
A, B 1,700 ft (518 m)/min
C 2,090 ft (637 m)/min
Rate of climb at S/L, one engine out:
C 561 ft (171 m)/min
Service ceiling:
A 23,650 ft (7,210 m)
B 26,200 ft (7,986 m)
C 26,313 ft (8,020 m)
Service ceiling, one engine out:
A 8,100 ft (2,470 m)
B 13,200 ft (4,025 m)
C 13,000 ft (3,960 m)
Min ground turning radius 40 ft 0 in (12·2 m)
Runway LCN 4·5
T-O run:
A, B 1,728 ft (527 m)
C 1,660 ft (506 m)
Accelerate/stop distance:
A, B 3,731 ft (1,137 m)
C 3,674 ft (1,120 m)
Landing from 50 ft (15 m), without propeller reversal:
A, B 2,680 ft (817 m)
C 2,793 ft (851 m)
Range at max cruise speed, at 8,000 ft (2,440 m), with max fuel, 45 min reserve:
A 788 nm (907 miles; 1,459 km)
B 765 nm (881 miles; 1,417 km)
C 722 nm (832 miles; 1,339 km)
Range at max cruise speed, at 8,000 ft (2,440 m), with 17 occupants and 480 lb (218 kg) baggage, 45 min reserve:
A 367 nm (422 miles; 679 km)
B 333 nm (383 miles; 616 km)
C 461 nm (530 miles; 853 km)

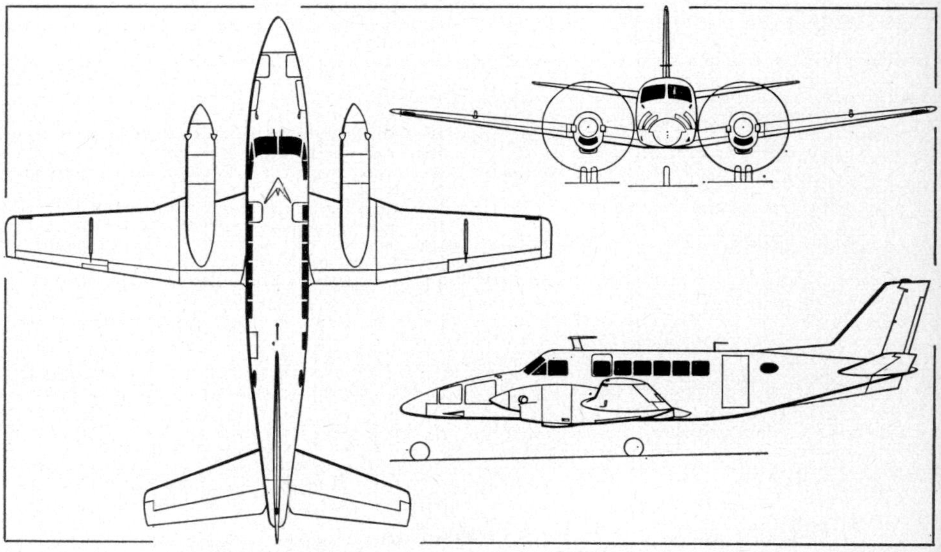

Beechcraft B99 Airliner 17-seat light transport *(Pilot Press)*

BEECHCRAFT KING AIR 100 and A100

US Army designation: U-21F

Beech Aircraft announced on 26 May 1969 the addition of a new version of the King Air to its fleet of corporate transport aircraft. Designated King Air 100, this is a pressurised transport with increased internal capacity and more powerful engines, enabling it to carry a useful load of more than two short tons. By comparison with the King Air 90 series, it has a fuselage 4 ft 2 in (1·27 m) longer, reduced wing span, larger rudder and elevator and twin-wheel main landing gear. It is available in a variety of interior configurations, seating six to eight in executive versions, or up to 13 in high-density arrangement, plus crew of two.

The King Air 100 has been approved for Category II landing minima by the FAA. Initial deliveries were made in August 1969, following FAA certification. A total of 184 King Air 100s had been delivered by the beginning of January 1974.

First deliveries of the advanced model A100, comprising five U-21Fs for the Department of the Army, began in October 1971. Supplied under a $2·5 million contract, they represent the first pressurised aircraft in the Army's inventory.

During 1972 Beech delivered five specially-equipped King Air A100s to the Canadian Department of Transport and two to the Mexican Secretaria de Comunicaciones y Transportes. Designated UNACE (Universal Aircraft Com/Nav Evaluation) aircraft, the configuration was developed by Beech as an economical means of conducting flight inspections and scheduled calibration of aviation navigation aids and facilities. UNACE configuration King Airs are also operated in Algeria and Malaysia.

In 1973 Beech received orders for six A100s for the Royal Moroccan Air Force and two for the Spanish Air Ministry.

TYPE: Twin-turboprop light passenger, freight or executive transport.

WINGS: As for Beechcraft 99 Airliner. Pneumatic de-icing boots standard.

FUSELAGE: As for King Air C90, except length extended by 2 ft 6 in (0·76 m) forward of the wing, and 1 ft 8 in (0·51 m) aft of the wing.

TAIL UNIT: Cantilever all-metal structure with swept vertical surfaces and a ventral stabilising fin. Trim tab in rudder. Electrically-operated adjustment of tailplane incidence.

LANDING GEAR: As for Beechcraft 99 Airliner. Dual main wheels and tubeless tyres size 17·9 × 5·70-8, pressure 101-105 lb/sq in (7·1-7·4 kg/cm²). Nosewheel with tubeless tyre size 22·1 × 5·70-8, pressure 101-105 lb/sq in (7·1-7·4 kg/cm²). BF Goodrich heat sink and aircooled single-disc hydraulic brakes.

POWER PLANT: Two 680 ehp United Aircraft of Canada PT6A-28 turboprop engines, each driving a Hartzell three-blade fully-feathering and reversible-pitch constant-speed propeller, or four-blade propeller on the King Air A100. Rubber fuel cells in wings, with total capacity of 374 US gallons (1,415 litres) on King Air 100; A100 has two additional fuel cells in each outer wing panel, providing a total fuel capacity of 470 US gallons (1,779 litres). Automatic fuel heating systems; inertial engine inlet de-icing system; engine inlet lips de-iced by electro-thermally heated boots. Goodrich electric propeller anti-icing system.

ACCOMMODATION: Crew of two side by side on flight deck, with full dual controls and instruments. Easily removable partition with sliding door between flight deck and cabin. Six fully-adjustable individual cabin chairs standard, with removable headrests, with a variety of alternative layouts, for up to 13 passengers in commuter role. Dual storm windows. Fully-carpeted floor. External access door to forward radio compartment. Aft fuselage maintenance access door. Plug-type emergency exit at forward end of cabin on starboard side. Passenger door at rear of cabin on port side, with integral airstair. Easily removable aft cabin partition with sliding doors. Lavatory installation and stowage for up to 410 lb (186 kg) luggage in aft fuselage. Other standard cabin equipment includes reading lights and fresh air outlets for all passengers, cabin coat rack and dual "No smoking—Fasten seat belt" signs. Electro-thermally heated windscreen, hot air windscreen defroster and windscreen wipers standard. Optional equipment includes cabin fire extinguisher, additional cabin window, flush toilet and a variety of interior cabinets.

SYSTEMS: Cabin pressurisation by dual engine bleed air with a maximum differential of 4·6 lb/sq in (0·32 kg/cm²). Cabin heated by 45,000 BTU dual engine bleed air system and auxiliary 27,000 BTU electrical heating system. Oxygen system for flight deck and 22 cu ft (0·62 m³) oxygen system for cabin standard. Cabin oxygen system of 49·2 cu ft (1·39 m³) or 65·6 cu ft (1·86 m³) optional. Dual vacuum system for instruments. Hydraulic system for brakes only. Pneumatic system for wing and tail unit de-icing only. Two 250A starter/generators. Nickel-cadmium 28V 45Ah battery.

EQUIPMENT: Standard equipment includes stall warning system, heated nose-mounted pitot heads, full blind-flying instrumentation, wing ice lights, dual nose-mounted landing lights, nose gear taxi light, adjustable cabin reading lights, cabin door, baggage compartment, aisle and map lights, blue-white cockpit lighting, primary and secondary instrument lights, rheostat-controlled white cockpit lighting, navigation lights, upper and lower rotating beacons, map pockets, dual adjustable sun visors and polarised cabin windows to reduce external light intensity and glare, super soundproofing and towbar. Optional items include a variety of interior layouts and seating, engine fire extinguisher system, propeller synchrophaser, smoke detection system for radio compartment, flight hour meter, safe-flight-speed control indicator, three-light strobe system, and automatic propeller feathering. Oversize dual main wheels and tyres are available to replace the standard dual main wheels and tyres.

ELECTRONICS: Standard system comprises King KTR-900A main VHF transceiver with dual Gables controls and B-3 antenna; King KTR-900A standby transceiver with Gables control and B-3 antenna; King KNR-600A manual Omni No 1 with Collins 331A-3G indicator, Gables control and B-17 Nav/GS antenna; King KNR-660A automatic Omni No 2 with Collins 331H-3G indicator and Gables control; dual Omni range filters; Collins KDF-800 ADF less indicator, with KFS-580 control, voice-range filter and Beech flush sense antenna; King KGM-691 No. 1 glideslope and marker beacon receiver with dual marker lights and B-16 antenna; King KGS-681 No 2 glideslope receiver; RCA AVQ-47 radar with 12 in antenna and standard scope; Sperry C14-23 compass system with pilot's servo amplifier; AAR 2105D-B-6 RMI with VOR 2 and ADF; King KXP-750A transponder with Gables control and B-18 antenna; King KN-65 DME with KI-265 indicator, KA-43 converter, B-18 antenna, Nav 1-Nav 2 switching and DME hold; dual 400VA OECO inverters with failure light; de luxe sectional instrument panel; AIM 500ECF pilot's electric gyro horizon; co-pilot's 3 in CF gyro horizon and directional gyro; Beech edge-lighted radio panel, radio accessories, microphone key button in pilot's and co-pilot's control wheels, static wicks and white lighting; dual microphones, headsets and cabin speakers; and avionics master switch.

DIMENSIONS, EXTERNAL:

Wing span	45 ft 10½ in (13·98 m)
Wing chord at root	7 ft 0½ in (2·15 m)
Wing chord at tip	3 ft 6 in (1·07 m)
Wing aspect ratio	7·51
Length overall	39 ft 8½ in (12·10 m)
Height overall	15 ft 4½ in (4·68 m)
Tailplane span	22 ft 4½ in (6·81 m)
Wheel track	13 ft 0 in (3·96 m)
Wheelbase	14 ft 11 in (4·55 m)
Propeller diameter:	
Three-blade	7 ft 9½ in (2·37 m)
Four-blade	7 ft 6 in (2·29 m)
Propeller ground clearance:	
Four-blade	1 ft 1½ in (0·34 m)

WEIGHTS AND LOADINGS (A: King Air 100, B: King Air A100):

Weight empty:	
A	6,405 lb (2,905 kg)
B	6,748 lb (3,061 kg)
Max ramp weight:	
A	10,668 lb (4,838 kg)
B	11,568 lb (5,247 kg)
Max T-O weight:	
A	10,600 lb (4,808 kg)
B	11,500 lb (5,216 kg)
Max zero-fuel weight:	
B	9,600 lb (4,354 kg)
Max landing weight:	
B	11,210 lb (5,084 kg)

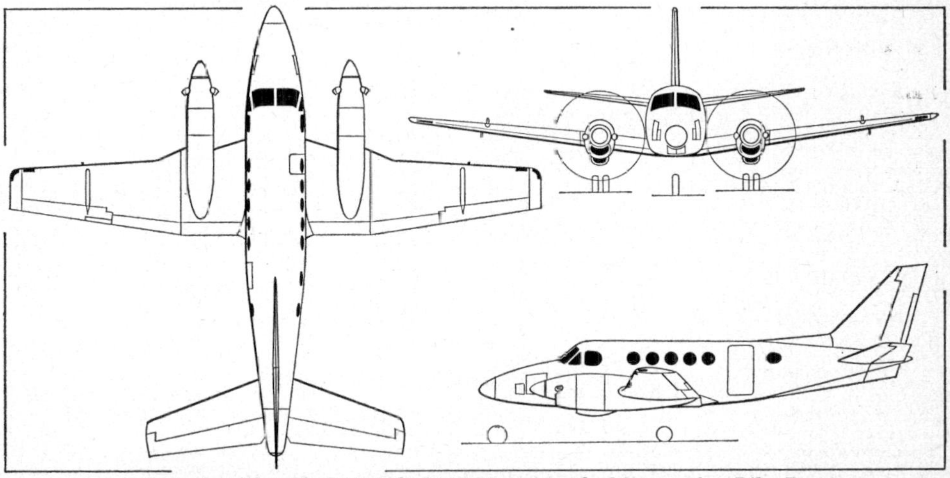

Beechcraft King Air A100 twin-turboprop pressurised transport (*Pilot Press*)

Beechcraft King Air A100 eight/fifteen-seat pressurised light transport (two 680 ehp United Aircraft of Canada PT6A-28 turboprop engines)

Beechcraft Super King Air 200 (two 850 shp United Aircraft of Canada PT6A-41 turboprop engines)

Max wing loading:
B 40·8 lb/sq ft (199 kg/m²)
Max power loading:
B 8·38 lb/ehp (3·80 kg/ehp)

PERFORMANCE (A: King Air 100 at max T-O weight of 10,600 lb: 4,808 kg; B: King Air A100 at max T-O weight of 11,500 lb: 5,216 kg, unless otherwise quoted):
Max cruising speed:
A, at 9,500 lb (4,309 kg) AUW:
at 21,000 ft (6,400 m)
239 knots (275 mph; 443 km/h)
at 16,000 ft (4,875 m)
245 knots (282 mph; 454 km/h)
at 10,000 ft (3,050 m)
248 knots (285 mph; 459 km/h)
B, at 10,500 lb (4,762 kg) AUW:
at 21,000 ft (6,400 m)
235 knots (271 mph; 436 km/h)
at 16,000 ft (4,875 m)
243 knots (280 mph; 450 km/h)
at 10,000 ft (3,050 m)
248 knots (285 mph; 459 km/h)
Cruising speed, low cruise power:
A, at 9,500 lb (4,309 kg) AUW:
at 21,000 ft (6,400 m)
226 knots (260 mph; 418 km/h)
at 16,000 ft (4,875 m)
234 knots (269 mph; 433 km/h)
at 12,000 ft (3,660 m)
237 knots (273 mph; 439 km/h)
B, at 10,500 lb (4,762 kg) AUW:
at 21,000 ft (6,400 m)
221 knots (254 mph; 409 km/h)
at 16,000 ft (4,875 m)
231 knots (266 mph; 428 km/h)
at 10,000 ft (3,050 m)
236 knots (272 mph; 438 km/h)
Stalling speed, power off, wheels and flaps down:
A 76 knots (87·5 mph; 141 km/h)
B 75 knots (86·5 mph; 139 km/h)
Stalling speed, power off, wheels and flaps up:
A 92 knots (106 mph; 170·5 km/h)
B 90 knots (104 mph; 167·5 km/h)
Max rate of climb at S/L:
A 2,200 ft (671 m)/min
B 1,963 ft (598 m)/min
Rate of climb at S/L, one engine out:
A 608 ft (185 m)/min
B 452 ft (138 m)/min
Service ceiling:
A 25,900 ft (7,895 m)
B 24,850 ft (7,575 m)
Service ceiling, one engine out:
A 11,800 ft (3,595 m)
B 9,300 ft (2,835 m)
Min ground turning radius 40 ft 0 in (12·2 m)
Runway LCN 4·5
T-O run:
A (using flaps) 1,452 ft (443 m)
B (no flaps) 2,060 ft (628 m)
T-O to 50 ft (15 m):
A (using flaps) 1,729 ft (527 m)
B (no flaps) 3,245 ft (989 m)
Landing from 50 ft (15 m) at max landing weight, without propeller reversal:
A 2,138 ft (652 m)
B 2,246 ft (685 m)
Landing run at max landing weight, without propeller reversal:
A 1,240 ft (378 m)
B 1,302 ft (397 m)
*Accelerate/stop distance, flaps up:
B 4,275 ft (1,303 m)
*Accelerate/stop distance, 30% flaps:
B 3,877 ft (1,182 m)
Range at high cruise power, A with 374 US gallons (1,415 litres) fuel, B with 470 US gallons (1,779 litres) fuel, includes allowances for starting, taxi, take-off, climb, descent and 45 min reserve:
at 21,000 ft (6,400 m):
A 945 nm (1,089 miles; 1,752 km)
B 1,201 nm (1,384 miles; 2,227 km)
at 16,000 ft (4,875 m):
A 830 nm (956 miles; 1,538 km)
B 1,064 nm (1,225 miles; 1,971 km)
at 10,000 ft (3,050 m):
A 706 nm (813 miles; 1,308 km)
B 900 nm (1,036 miles; 1,667 km)
Range, at low cruise power, fuel and allowances as above:
at 21,000 ft (6,400 m):
A 1,005 nm (1,158 miles; 1,863 km)
B 1,287 nm (1,482 miles; 2,385 km)
at 16,000 ft (4,875 m):
A 895 nm (1,031 miles; 1,659 km)
B 1,149 nm (1,323 miles; 2,129 km)
at 10,000 ft (3,050 m):
A 762 nm (878 miles; 1,413 km)
B 982 nm (1,130 miles; 1,818 km)

**Includes allowance for failure recognition*

BEECHCRAFT SUPER KING AIR 200

Latest addition to the King Air range of business/corporate aircraft, the Super King Air is regarded by the company as an expansion of its product line and is not intended as a replacement for any existing model.

Design began in October 1970, construction of the first prototype and first pre-production aircraft starting simultaneously a year later. The first prototype, serial BB-1, flew for the first time on 27 October 1972, the second aircraft, BB-2, on 15 December 1972. Since that time an intensive test programme has been flown, which Beech claims to be the most extensive carried out for any product of the company. While the flight tests and testing of a static fuselage were under way, construction of the first production aircraft began in June 1973. FAA certification under FAR Part 23 was awarded on 14 December 1973, the aircraft satisfying also the icing requirements of FAR Part 25.

By comparison with the King Air 100, the new aircraft has increased wing span, basically the same fuselage, a new T-tail, more powerful engines, additional fuel capacity, increased cabin pressurisation and a higher gross weight. By the end of February 1974 Beech had received orders for 107 Super King Airs. The first commercial delivery was made to Mr Arthur K. Watson, a director of IBM Corporation, in March 1974.

TYPE: Twin-turboprop passenger or executive light transport.

WINGS: Cantilever low-wing monoplane. Wing section NACA 23018·5 (modified) at root, NACA 23011·3 at tip. Dihedral 6°. Incidence 3° 48′ at root, —1° 7′ at tip. No sweepback at quarter-chord. Two-spar light alloy structure. Conventional ailerons of light alloy construction, with trim tab in port aileron. Single-slotted trailing-edge flaps of light alloy construction. Pneumatic de-icing boots standard.

FUSELAGE: Light alloy semi-monocoque structure of safe-life design.

TAIL UNIT: Conventional cantilever T-tail structure of light alloy with swept vertical and horizontal surfaces. Fixed-incidence tailplane. Trim tab in each elevator. Anti-servo tab in rudder. Pneumatic de-icing boots standard, on leading-edge of tailplane only.

LANDING GEAR: Electrically-retractable tricycle type, with twin wheels on each main unit. Single wheel on steerable nose unit, with shimmy damper. Main units retract forward, nosewheel aft. Beech oleo-pneumatic shock-absorbers. Goodrich main wheels and tyres size 18 × 5·5, pressure 102 lb/sq in (7·2 kg/cm²). Goodrich nosewheel and tyre size 6·50 × 10, pressure 57 lb/sq in (4·0 kg/cm²). Goodrich or Goodyear hydraulic multiple-disc brakes. Parking brake.

POWER PLANT: Two 850 shp United Aircraft of Canada PT6A-41 turboprop engines, each driving a three-blade metal constant-speed fully-feathering and reversible propeller. Bladder type fuel cells in each wing, with main system capacity of 386 US gallons (1,461 litres) and auxiliary system capacity of 158 US gallons (598 litres). Total fuel capacity 544 US gallons (2,059 litres). Two refuelling points in upper surface of each wing. Oil capacity 7·8 US gallons (29·5 litres). Anti-icing of engine air intakes by hot air from engine exhaust is standard. Electro-thermal anti-icing for propellers.

ACCOMMODATION: Pilot only, or crew of two side by side, on flight deck, with full dual controls and instruments as standard. Six cabin seats standard, with alternative layouts for a maximum of 13 passengers in cabin and 14th beside pilot. Partition with sliding door between cabin and flight deck, and partition at rear of cabin. Door at rear of cabin on port side, with integral airstair. Inward-opening emergency exit on starboard side over wing. Lavatory and stowage for up to 410 lb (186 kg) baggage in aft fuselage. Maintenance access door in rear fuselage; radio compartment access door in nose. Standard equipment includes reading lights and fresh air outlets for all passengers, triple cabin windows with polarised glare control, fully-carpeted floor, "No smoking—Fasten seat belt" sign, cabin coat rack, fluorescent cabin lighting, aisle and door courtesy lights. Electrically-heated windscreens, hot air windscreen defroster, dual storm windows, sun visors, map pockets and windscreen wipers. Cabin is air-conditioned and pressurised, and can be provided with optional radiant heat panels.

SYSTEMS: Cabin pressurisation by engine bleed air, with a maximum differential of 6·0 lb/sq in (0·42 kg/cm²), maintaining a sea level cabin altitude to 13,820 ft (4,210 m). Cabin air-conditioner of 34,000 BTU, with 24,000 BTU cooling system. Auxiliary cabin heating by radiant panels optional. Oxygen system for flight deck, and 22 cu ft (625 litre) oxygen system for cabin, standard; system of 49 cu ft (1,390 litres) or 64 cu ft (1,810 litres) optional. Dual vacuum system for instruments. Hydraulic system for brakes only. Pneumatic system for wing and tail unit de-icing. Electrical system has two 250A 28V starter/generators and 24V 34Ah aircooled nickel-cadmium battery. AC power provided by dual 600VA inverters.

ELECTRONICS: Standard King Gold Crown avionics package includes King KTR-900A main and standby VHF transceivers with Gables controls and B3 antennae; King KNR-600A manual Omni No. 1 with Collins 331A-3G indicator, Gables control and B17 nav antenna; King KNR-660A automatic Omni No. 2 with Collins 331H-3G indicator and Gables control; dual Omni range filters; Collins dual 356F-3 audio amplifiers with dual 356C-4 isolation amplifiers with dual audio switches; King KDF-800 ADF less indicator, with KFS-580 control, voice range filter and Beech flush sense antenna; King KGM-691 No. 1 glideslope and marker beacon receiver with dual marker lights, B16 antenna and B35 glideslope antenna; King KGS-681 No. 2 glideslope receiver; RCA AVQ-47 radar with 12 in phased array antenna and standard scope; Sperry C-14-23 compass system with servo amplifier; AAR 2105D-B-6 RMI with ADF on single needle and VOR 2 on double needle; King KXP-750A transponder with Gables control and B18 antenna; King KN-65 DME with KI-265 indicator, KA-43 converter, Nav 1 and Nav 2 switching and B18 antenna; dual 600VA Flite-Tronics PC-17 inverters with failure light; sectional instrument panel; dual flight instrumentation; standard electric gyro horizon; co-pilot's 3 in CF gyro horizon and directional gyro; Beech edge-lighted radio panel, radio accessories, microphone key button in pilot's and co-pilot's control wheels, static wicks and white lighting; dual microphones, headsets and cockpit speakers; emergency locator transmitter; and avionics master switch. An extensive range of optional avionics by ARC, Collins, King, RCA and Sperry is available to customer's requirements.

EQUIPMENT: Standard equipment includes an automatic fuel heater system, engine fire detection system, propeller synchroscope indicator, max permissible airspeed indicator, outside air temperature gauge, eight-day clock, chronograph clock, cabin rate of climb indicator, cabin altitude and differential pressure indicator, annunciator panel, heated stall warning system, dual heated pitot heads, external power socket, heated fuel vents, wing ice lights, dual landing lights, taxi light, rotating beacons, dual map lights, cabin dome lights, primary and secondary instrument lighting systems, blue-white flight deck lights, internal corrosion-proofing, super soundproofing, low profile glare-shield, urethane paint, towbar, and control lock assembly. Optional equipment includes instantaneous vertical speed indicator, flight hour recorder, propeller synchrophaser, oversize wheels and tyres, three-light strobe system, electrically-powered elevator trim, two- and four-seat couches with and without stowage drawer, folding armrests for couch, sixth starboard cabin window, forward-facing instead of standard toilet, Sherwood flushing toilet, cabin fire extinguisher, aft baggage partition, approach plate/map cases, cabin table, chair covers, entrance door step lights, fin illumination light, a variety of cabinets and a range of galley equipment.

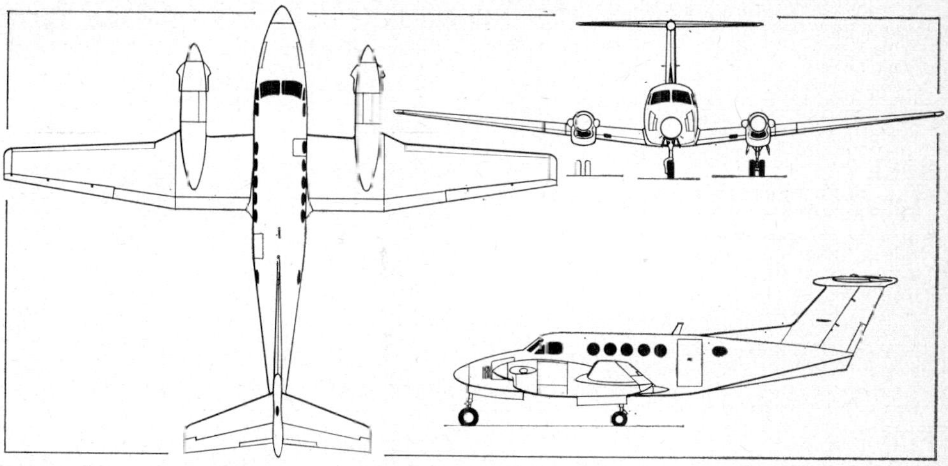

Beechcraft Super King Air 200 twin-turboprop transport (*Pilot Press*)

DIMENSIONS, EXTERNAL:
- Wing span: 54 ft 6 in (16·61 m)
- Wing chord at root: 7 ft 1¾ in (2·18 m)
- Wing chord at tip: 2 ft 11⅝ in (0·90 m)
- Wing aspect ratio: 9·8
- Length overall: 43 ft 9 in (13·34 m)
- Height overall: 14 ft 11½ in (4·56 m)
- Tailplane span: 18 ft 5 in (5·61 m)
- Wheel track: 17 ft 2 in (5·23 m)
- Wheelbase: 14 ft 11½ in (4·56 m)
- Propeller diameter: 8 ft 2½ in (2·50 m)
- Propeller ground clearance: 1 ft 2½ in (0·37 m)
- Distance between propeller centres: 17 ft 2 in (5·23 m)
- Passenger door:
  - Height: 4 ft 3½ in (1·31 m)
  - Width: 2 ft 2¾ in (0·68 m)
  - Height to sill: 3 ft 10 in (1·17 m)
- Nose avionics service doors (port and stbd):
  - Max height: 1 ft 10½ in (0·57 m)
  - Width: 2 ft 1 in (0·63 m)
  - Height to sill: 4 ft 6 in (1·37 m)
- Emergency exit door (stbd):
  - Height: 2 ft 2 in (0·66 m)
  - Width: 1 ft 7¾ in (0·50 m)

DIMENSIONS, INTERNAL:
- Cabin (from forward to aft pressure bulkhead):
  - Length: 22 ft 0 in (6·71 m)
  - Max width: 4 ft 6 in (1·37 m)
  - Max height: 4 ft 9 in (1·45 m)
  - Floor area: 84 sq ft (7·80 m²)
  - Volume: 392 cu ft (11·10 m³)
- Baggage hold, rear of cabin:
  - Volume: 54 cu ft (1·53 m³)

AREAS:
- Wings, gross: 303 sq ft (28·15 m²)
- Ailerons (total): 18·0 sq ft (1·67 m²)
- Trailing-edge flaps (total): 44·9 sq ft (4·17 m²)
- Fin: 37·2 sq ft (3·46 m²)
- Rudder, including tab: 15·1 sq ft (1·40 m²)
- Tailplane: 48·7 sq ft (4·52 m²)
- Elevators, including tabs: 19·3 sq ft (1·79 m²)

WEIGHTS AND LOADINGS:
- Weight empty: 7,315 lb (3,318 kg)
- Max T-O and landing weight: 12,500 lb (5,670 kg)
- Max ramp weight: 12,590 lb (5,710 kg)
- Max zero-fuel weight: 10,400 lb (4,717 kg)
- Max wing loading: 41·3 lb/sq ft (201·6 kg/m²)
- Max power loading: 7·4 lb/shp (3·36 kg/shp)

PERFORMANCE (at max T-O weight, ISA, unless specified):
- Max never-exceed speed: 270 knots (310 mph; 600 km/h) CAS or Mach 0·483
- Max level speed at 15,000 ft (4,570 m): 289 knots (333 mph; 536 km/h)
- Max cruising speed, average cruise weight at 25,000 ft (7,620 m): 278 knots (320 mph; 515 km/h)
- Econ cruising speed, average cruise weight at 25,000 ft (7,620 m): 273 knots (314 mph; 505 km/h)
- Stalling speed, flaps up: 102 knots (117 mph; 189 km/h) CAS
- Stalling speed, flaps down: 80 knots (92 mph; 148 km/h) CAS
- Max rate of climb at S/L: 2,450 ft (747 m)/min
- Rate of climb at S/L, one engine out: 740 ft (226 m)/min
- Service ceiling: 32,800 ft (10,000 m)
- Service ceiling, one engine out: 19,150 ft (5,835 m)
- T-O run, 40% flap: 1,855 ft (565 m)
- T-O to 50 ft (15 m), flaps up: 3,340 ft (1,018 m)
- T-O to 50 ft (15 m), 40% flaps: 2,580 ft (786 m)
- Landing from 50 ft (15 m), full flap, without propeller reversal: 2,845 ft (867 m)
- Landing run, full flap, without propeller reversal: 1,760 ft (536 m)
- Range with max fuel at 27,000 ft (8,230 m); allowances for start, taxi, T-O, climb to altitude and descent, with 45 min reserve: 1,802 nm (2,075 miles; 3,338 km)
- Range with max payload, conditions and allowances as above: 915 nm (1,053 miles; 1,695 km)

BEETS

GLENN BEETS

Mr G. Beets of Riverside, California, has designed and built a lightweight sporting aircraft which he has named the G/B Special. Construction of the prototype occupied two years and cost approximately $2,500, the first flight being made on 25 July 1973. Plans of the G/B Special are available to amateur constructors, and Mr Beets intends also to supply kits of components and materials.

BEETS G/B SPECIAL

TYPE: Single-seat homebuilt sporting aircraft.

WINGS: Braced parasol-wing monoplane. Vee bracing struts each side with auxiliary struts. N-type cabane struts. Conventional wood structure with spruce spars and truss ribs, Dacron covered. Plain ailerons of similar construction. No trim tabs. Cut-out in wing trailing-edge.

FUSELAGE: Welded structure of 4130 steel tube with Dacron covering.

TAIL UNIT: Cantilever structure of wood, with foam filling and covering of 1/16 in mahogany plywood.

LANDING GEAR: Non-retractable tailwheel type, with main wheels carried on braced tubular steel struts. Glassfibre wheel fairings on main wheels.

POWER PLANT: One 70 hp Volkswagen 1,641 cc modified motor car engine, driving a two-blade fixed-pitch propeller.

Beets G/B Special lightweight homebuilt sport aircraft (70 hp Volkswagen engine) (*Henry Artof*)

ACCOMMODATION: Single seat in open cockpit.
DIMENSIONS, EXTERNAL:

Wing span	25 ft 0 in (7·62 m)
Wing chord	4 ft 2 in (1·27 m)
Length overall	16 ft 4 in (4·98 m)
Height overall	6 ft 0 in (1·83 m)

WEIGHTS:

Weight empty	625 lb (284 kg)
Max T-O weight	925 lb (420 kg)

PERFORMANCE (at max T-O weight):

Max level speed at S/L	135 knots (156 mph; 251 km/h)
Cruising speed	104 knots (120 mph; 193 km/h)
Landing speed	51 knots (58 mph; 94 km/h)
Max rate of climb at S/L	1,000 ft (305 m)/min
T-O run	200 ft (61 m)
Landing run	300 ft (92 m)
Range	520 nm (600 miles; 965 km)

BELL

BELL AEROSPACE COMPANY DIVISION OF TEXTRON INC

HEAD OFFICE AND WORKS:
Buffalo, New York 14240
Telephone: (716) 297-1000
PRESIDENT:
William G. Gisel
EXECUTIVE VICE-PRESIDENTS:
Lawrence P. Mordaunt (Operations)
Norton C. Willcox (Administration)
VICE-PRESIDENTS:
Dr Clifford F. Berninger (Research and Engineering)
John R. Clark Jr (Eastern Region)
James L. Decker (Bell Aerospace Canada)
John F. Gill (Product Assurance)
Adolph Kastelowitz (Manufacturing)
John J. Kelly (Vice-President and General Manager, New Orleans Operations)
Joseph R. Piselli (Marketing)
Delmar E. Wilson (Western Region)

Bell Aerospace is active in aircraft, missile, propulsion and electronics systems development and advanced technology for aerospace and defence programmes. Its research and development programmes include air cushion vehicles and air cushion landing systems. It is producing an advanced upper-stage propulsion system for the USAF's Minuteman III ICBM. Designated the Post Boost Propulsion System (PBPS), this has attained a high record of reliability since production began in 1968.

Production of liquid-propellant rocket engines for Lockheed's Agena satellite programme continues and is described in the "Aero-Engines" section.

Major propulsion systems and components research and development programmes cover the investigation of high-energy and powdered propellants, advanced engine cooling techniques, and new positive expulsion propellant storage and delivery systems.

Bell is competing currently for a number of shuttle orbit manoeuvring and reaction control propulsion contracts, working under several technology contracts awarded in 1972.

As an outgrowth of its AN/SPN-42 Automatic Carrier Landing System (ACLS), now in operation on board US Navy aircraft carriers, Bell is updating land-based versions at US Naval air stations where the systems are being used to train pilots and operators in the use of the carrier-based system. In 1972 the company's land-based AN/SPN-42T2 at Cecil Field NAS was certified for Mode 1 landings on all runways. In 1973, Bell completed a Naval Electronic Systems Command contract for the installation of a system at the Whidbey Island NAS near Seattle, Washington. Both the land- and carrier-based systems permit fully-automatic hands-off landings, and can handle up to 120 aircraft an hour.

Early in 1972, Bell, teamed with the Bendix Corporation, won a Phase I contract from the FAA to begin work on the development of an automatic landing system for airports. Through a series of phases, the FAA will eventually select one of the competing teams of companies for production of the Microwave Landing System.

A major landing system programme completed by Bell in 1973 was the development of a man-transportable unit for the Marine Corps. This will be used to guide approaches and landings by V/STOL aircraft in remote areas where landing facilities are limited. Known as MRAALS (Marine Remote Area Approach and Landing System) the 88 lb (40 kg) unit transmits range information up to 40 nm (46 miles; 74 km), and azimuth and glideslope data up to 17·4 nm (20 miles; 32 km).

Other electronics work is concerned with precision inertial guidance/navigation equipment, transoceanic satellite-relay air traffic control systems, and airborne target location and fire control systems.

BELL AIR CUSHION LANDING SYSTEM (ACLS)

Bell Aerospace first began development of an air cushion landing system (ACLS) as a company-funded research project in December 1963. In 1966 the company was awarded a $99,000 contract by the USAF Flight Dynamics Laboratory for wind-tunnel testing of the project. Subsequent Air Force contracts included a $99,500 feasibility study in 1966, a $98,700 model test programme in 1967 and a $66,300 flight test programme in 1968.

The initial intention was to find the best way of providing an ACLS for cargo transports, and the flight test programme was carried out with a modified Lake LA-4 four-seat amphibian. Details of this may be found in the 1970-71 *Jane's*. Bell has also studied the feasibility of using an ACLS on Space Shuttle vehicles, under NASA contract. Details were given in the 1972-73 *Jane's*.

de Havilland Canada XC-8A research aircraft in flight with ACLS inflated

Current activities are being conducted under a joint United States/Canadian programme to adapt the ACLS for military transport aircraft. This would allow such aircraft to operate from a variety of surfaces, including rough fields, soft soils, swamps, water, ice and snow. A contract for the first phase, covering programme definition and air cushion trunk fabrication, was awarded to Bell by the USAF Flight Dynamics Laboratory in November 1970.

It was decided to use a de Havilland Canada XC-8A Buffalo STOL military transport aircraft, loaned by the Canadian Department of National Defence, as the testbed aircraft for this programme.

The ACLS is based on the ground effect principle that employs a layer of air instead of wheels as an aircraft's ground contacting medium. The system's trunk, a large inner-tube-like arrangement, encircles the underside of the aircraft's fuselage. Upon inflation, the trunk provides an air duct and seal for the air cushion.

The cushion air pressure is provided by an on-board auxiliary compressor, and the underside of the rubberised trunk is perforated with hundreds of vent holes through which the air is allowed to escape to form the air cushion.

Because the ACLS distributes the weight of an aircraft over a considerably larger area than conventional wheeled systems, and itself exerts a ground pressure of less than 3 lb/sq in (0·20 kg/cm^2), the concept permits operations on surfaces with very low bearing strengths.

As can be seen in the accompanying photograph, balancer floats have been mounted on struts beneath each wing for operation on and from water. Beneath the floats are sprung skids for use in operations from land.

United Aircraft of Canada Ltd was made responsible for development and flight qualification of the auxiliary power system, and de Havilland Aircraft of Canada Ltd modified the XC-8A testbed aircraft to take the ACLS installation. The Canadian government funded the work of these two companies.

BELL JET FLYING BELT

Developed for the US Army, under a $3 million contract sponsored by DoD's Advanced Research Projects Agency, this is an experimental one-man back-pack flying system powered by a miniature jet engine.

A total of 430 lb (195 kg) thrust is provided by a single Williams Research Corporation WR-19 high-bypass turbojet engine measuring approximately 1 ft (0·30 m) in diameter by 2 ft (0·61 m) in length, and which features a high thrust-to-weight ratio and low specific fuel consumption.

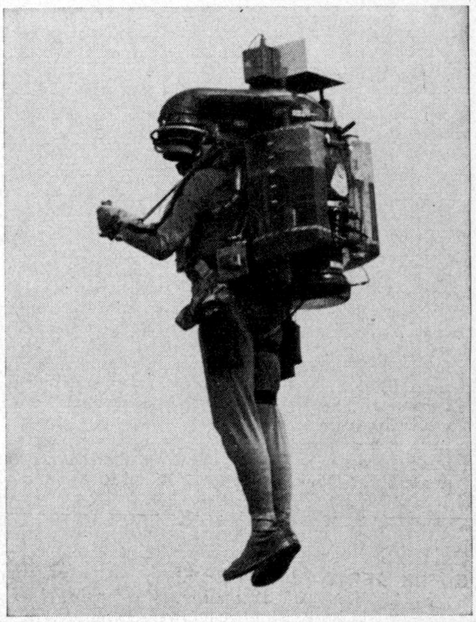

Bell Aerospace Jet Flying Belt in free flight

The bypass concept, in which a proportion of engine intake air is diverted through a chamber around the core of the engine and mixed with the primary flow of hot exhaust gases, insulates the operator and fuel tanks from primary engine heat.

The system burns standard JP-4 fuel, carried in transparent plastic tanks which wrap around the engine. A helmet vibrator warns the pilot when fuel contents have been consumed to a reserve level.

Potential military applications for such a mobility system include flying over barbed wire and minefields, reconnaissance, counter-guerilla warfare, assault, perimeter guard and amphibious landings. Some potential civil applications are for riot control, powerline and pipeline patrols, photographic news coverage, rescue operations, traffic surveillance and microwave tower inspections.

Bell has granted to the Williams Research Corporation, Walled Lake, Michigan, a licence to manufacture, use and sell certain small lift device systems, including the Jet Flying Belt.

BELL HELICOPTER COMPANY

Head Office:
PO Box 482, Fort Worth, Texas 76101
Telephone: (817) 280-2011

President:
James F. Atkins

Senior Vice-Presidents:
Hans Weichsel Jr
Bartram Kelley (Engineering)

Vice-Presidents:
Manuel A. Atkins (Manufacturing)
Edwin L. Farmer (Finance)
M. R. Barcellona (Materiel)
John Finn (Industrial Relations)
James C. Fuller (Public Relations)
Leonard M. Horner (Operations)
William L. Humphrey (General Manager, Amarillo Facility)
Joseph Mashman (Special Projects)
Warren T. Rockwell (Washington Operations)
Dwayne K. Jose (Commercial Marketing)
Clifford J. Kalista (Advanced Attack Helicopter)
Charles R. Rudning (Programme Management)
Frank M. Sylvester (International Marketing)

Bell Helicopter Company is the largest operating division of Textron Inc.

Present production at Fort Worth is concerned primarily with military and commercial single- and twin-engined versions of the turbine-powered UH-1 Iroquois, the AH-1 HueyCobra armed helicopter developed from the UH-1, and military and commercial versions of the Model 206 JetRanger. The Bell 47, in continuous production in the US for more than 25 years, after receiving the first helicopter Approved Type Certificate from the CAA on 8 March 1946, is not on Bell's 1974 production schedule. Versions of the Model 47 continue in production, however, by Agusta in Italy and Kawasaki in Japan (which see).

Versions of the UH-1 are built under licence by Agusta in Italy and Fuji in Japan (which see). Bell also has licence agreements with the Republic of China, covering co-production of Model 205 general-purpose helicopters, and with the government of Australia, covering the production of Model 206B-1 Kiowas for the Australian Army. Prime contractor in Australia is the Commonwealth Aircraft Corporation (which see).

On 23 April 1974, Bell celebrated delivery of its 20,000th helicopter, a US Army UH-1H. The total included more commercial helicopters than the number built by all other US manufacturers combined.

Since 1958, when Bell's Model XV-3 tilt-rotor research aircraft achieved the first full in-flight conversion by a machine of this configuration, Bell engineers have continued research in this field and have completed recent US Army/USAF/NASA contracts to investigate proprotor and folding proprotor technology. The contracts included manufacture and wind tunnel testing of examples of both types of rotor.

A full-scale folding proprotor of 25 ft (7·62 m) diameter was built. During 1971 it completed whirl, folding and shake tests. In early 1972 power testing in the NASA wind tunnel at Ames Research Center was carried out, during which the complete stop/fold sequence and blade folding at up to 175 knots (202 mph; 325 km/h) were achieved. Stability was excellent to a speed of more than 195 knots (225 mph; 362 km/h), the maximum attainable wind tunnel speed, and all test requirements were met or exceeded.

Towards the end of 1972, Bell and one other company received contracts from NASA and the US Army for the design of a tilt-rotor VTOL research vehicle. In May 1973 Bell announced that its Model 301 proposal had been selected for development. Two prototypes are to be built, and have been allocated the US Army designation XV-15.

It is proposed to mount proprotors at the tips of a medium-span high-mounted wing. For take-off the rotors (shaft-driven by turboshaft engines) will be used as those of a conventional helicopter. Once airborne, the rotors will be tilted forward through 90 degrees until they serve as propellers, allowing forward speeds of up to 300 knots (345 mph; 556 km/h) for short/medium-range flights. For speeds in excess of this figure, the proprotors would be stopped and folded back to a minimum drag configuration, forward propulsion being provided by the engines operating as turbofans and lift being developed by the wing.

Also under investigation, and already tested extensively, is a method of varying a rotor's diameter in flight. Maximum diameter would provide lift for vertical take-off and climb, with minimum diameter being used when the rotor was serving as a conventional tractor propeller, thus increasing cruise efficiency.

During 1972 Bell achieved a major breakthrough in the elimination of vibration in helicopters with what is known as the nodalisation concept, flight test data and analytical results suggesting that 70 to 90 per cent vibration isolation was practicable.

The new concept is based on the scientific fact that any beam subjected to vertical vibratory forces, such as those induced by a rotor, will develop flexing to produce a wave form. Points of no relative motion, called the nodal points, appear at equal distances from the centre of the induced wave form, and it is from these points that Bell decided to try suspending a helicopter fuselage. Since the nodes have no relative motion, it seemed likely that the fuselage would be virtually free from rotor-induced vibration.

Early flight tests of a Model 206 JetRanger with its fuselage suspended from a nodalised beam were so convincing that Bell considered it would be able to meet or exceed the latest vibration requirements for military and commercial helicopters. Flight testing of this "Noda-Matic" concept on larger Bell helicopters continued throughout 1973, and it was decided to utilise the technique on new production helicopters, beginning with the Model 206L Long Ranger.

Under contract to the Army Air Mobility Research and Development Laboratory, the company has been carrying out endurance tests of elastomeric bearings on helicopter rotor systems. These bearings, which consist of alternate layers of elastomer and steel, require no lubrication or seals, and are expected to offer improved safety and maintenance features. In flight tests, UH-1 rotor hubs with prototype elastomeric bearings exceeded 4,000 hours. Showing no apparent indication of wear, they suggested that production bearings would offer a service life in excess of 2,000 hours. As a result, flapping bearing kits have been ordered by the US Army for installation on AH-1 and UH-1 helicopter gunships.

Approximately 8,400 people were employed by Bell in mid-1974.

Bell's full-scale 25 ft (7·62 m) diameter folding proprotor during wind tunnel tests at NASA's Ames Research Center

BELL MODEL 47G-3B-2A and 47G-5A

No version of the Bell Model 47 is included in the company's manufacturing programme for 1974. The most recent commercial production versions were as follows:

Model 47G-3B-2A. Three-seater, with Lycoming TVO-435-F1A supercharged engine, uprated to 280 hp, and increased fuel capacity by comparison with earlier 47G-3. Cabin widened by 8 in (20 cm) to 5 ft 0 in (1·52 m), and AUW increased by 100 lb (45 kg). A 10 lb (4·5 kg) weight added to each blade-tip improves autorotation characteristics and manoeuvrability.

Model 47G-5A. Powered by 265 hp Lycoming VO-435-B1A engine, this model has the same cabin as the 47G-3B-2A, almost a foot wider than that of the Model 47G-5 which it replaced. Standard items include tinted Plexiglas canopy, doors, heavy-duty battery, 12V 70A alternator, synchronised elevator and twin 28·5 US gallon (108 litre) fuel tanks. Other features include an automotive electrical system and compact low-profile instrument pedestal. A rotating beacon, landing light and full range of Model 47 optional extras were available.

The description which follows refers to both the 47G-3B-2A and the 47G-5A:

Type: Three-seat general-utility helicopter.

Rotor System: Two-blade semi-rigid main rotor, with interchangeable blades of all-metal bonded construction and stabilising bar below and at right-angles to blades. Conventional swashplate assembly for cyclic-pitch and collective-pitch control. Blades do not fold. Two-blade all-metal tail rotor. Brake on main rotor optional.

Rotor Drive: Through centrifugal clutch and two-stage planetary transmission. Shaft drive to tail rotor. Main rotor rpm 333-355.

Fuselage: In three sections: centre, tail and cabin. Centre section has a welded steel tube structure to carry the engine and cabin. Rear section is also a steel tube structure, is triangular in cross-section and serves as a support for the tail rotor drive-shaft.

Tail Surface: Small synchronised elevator at rear end of fuselage responds to the fore and aft motion of the cyclic-pitch control, to provide better stability and allow a greatly increased CG travel.

Landing Gear: Tubular skid type with small ground handling wheels and tie-down and towing attachments. Cross-tubes serve as supports for external loads such as litters or cargo bins. For amphibious operation, two air-inflated nylon floats are easily attached.

Power Plant: One vertically-mounted Lycoming VO-435-B1A (Model 47G-5A) or TVO-435-F1A (Model 47G-3B-2A) six-cylinder horizontally-opposed fancooled engine with clutch, drive shaft and rotor assembly in an integral unit. Two interconnected saddle-mounted fuel tanks (57 US gallons; 216 litres total capacity) on CG and with gravity feed.

Accommodation: Side-by-side seats for three in cabin enclosed by a blue-tinted free-blown Plexiglas canopy. Door on each side, with sliding windows. For fair weather or specialised operations the doors are quickly removable. Can carry 1,000 lb (455 kg) cargo externally on underfuselage hook.

Electronics and Equipment: Standard equipment includes complete VFR flight and engine instruments, hydraulic boost controls, 28V 50A generator, electric starter, ground handling wheels, heavy-duty battery, etc. Additional accessories available in FAA-approved kits include pontoons, night flying equipment, dusting and spraying equipment, cargo carriers, litters, dual controls, heater-defroster, rotor brake, inertia reel and shoulder harness, ARC, King or Narco 360-channel VHF transceivers, fire extinguisher, first aid kit, etc.

Dimensions, external:

Diameter of main rotor	37 ft 1½ in (11·32 m)
Main rotor blade chord	11 in (28 cm)
Diameter of tail rotor	5 ft 10⅛ in (1·78 m)
Length overall (rotors turning)	43 ft 7½ in (13·30 m)
Length of fuselage	31 ft 7 in (9·63 m)
Width, rotors fore and aft	9 ft 6 in (2·90 m)
Width over skids	7 ft 6 in (2·29 m)
Height to top of rotor hub	9 ft 3$\frac{11}{16}$ in (2·84 m)

Dimensions, internal:

Cabin: Length	4 ft 11 in (1·50 m)
Max width	5 ft 0 in (1·52 m)
Max height	4 ft 6 in (1·37 m)

Areas:

Main rotor blade (each)	17·14 sq ft (1·59 m^2)
Tail rotor blade (each)	1·20 sq ft (0·11 m^2)

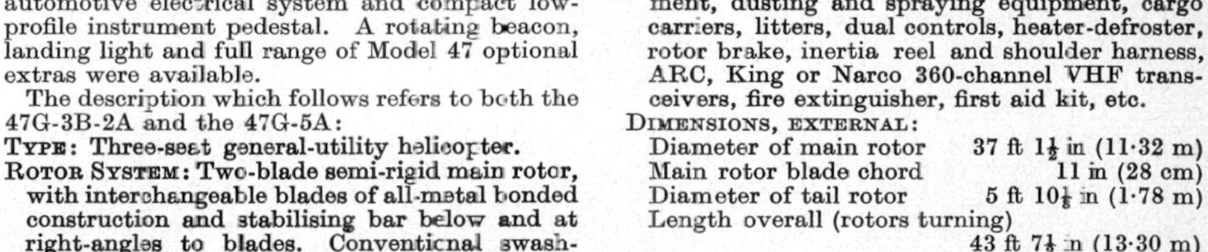
Bell Model 47G-3B-2A three-seat utility helicopter

Main rotor disc 1,083 sq ft (100·61 m^2)
Tail rotor disc 26·8 sq ft (2·49 m^2)

WEIGHTS:
Weight empty, with oil and equipped:
47G-3B-2A 1,893 lb (858 kg)
47G-5A 1,732 lb (785 kg)
Max T-O weight:
47G-3B-2A 2,950 lb (1,338 kg)
47G-5A 2,850 lb (1,293 kg)

PERFORMANCE (at max T-O weight, except where indicated):
Max level speed at S/L:
91 knots (105 mph; 169 km/h)
Recommended cruising speed at 5,000 ft (1,525 m):
47G-3B-2A 73 knots (84 mph; 135 km/h)
47G-5A 74 knots (85 mph; 137 km/h)
Max rate of climb at S/L:
47G-3B-2A 990 ft (302 m)/min
47G-5A 860 ft (262 m)/min
Service ceiling:
47G-3B-2A 19,000 ft (5,790 m)
47G-5A 10,500 ft (3,200 m)
Hovering ceiling in ground effect:
47G-3B-2A 17,700 ft (5,395 m)
47G-5A 5,900 ft (1,800 m)
Hovering ceiling out of ground effect:
47G-3B-2A 12,700 ft (3,870 m)
47G-5A 1,400 ft (427 m)
Range with max fuel at 6,000 ft (1,830 m), no reserves:
47G-3B-2A 214 nm (247 miles; 397 km)
Range with max fuel at 5,000 ft (1,525 m), no reserves:
47G-5A 222 nm (256 miles; 411 km)

BELL UH-1 HELMS

On 18 June 1971 Bell Helicopter announced that a UH-1C and a UH-1M helicopter had been modified to UH-1 HELMS (Helicopter Multi-function System) standard with rotor blade radar.

Rotor blade radar is designed to give helicopters unrestricted flight capability at night and in poor visibility conditions, and is planned for integration into helicopter night attack systems.

The basic concept involves use of the helicopter main rotor blade as a scanning radar antenna. The resulting large horizontal antenna provides a narrow azimuth beam with high resolution that shows clearly water/land demarcation, fields, fence rows, tree-lines, roads and vehicles. It provides a lighter, more reliable and less expensive system than conventional radars. Combined with an elevation-sensing (monopulse) antenna/receiver mounted on the nose of the helicopter, the system provides fire-control and obstacle-sensing capability, as well as terrain avoidance and bad weather detection, allowing helicopter pilots to navigate and make approaches in zero visibility.

Produced and installed under contract from the US Army Electronics Command, the HELMS subsystems comprise leading-edge rotor-blade antennae, basic high-resolution radar, nose-mounted elevation antenna/receiver, Honeywell AN-APN/171-V radar altimeter, M-21 armament (Miniguns) with radar interface, and an articulated wave-guide coupling system, developed for Bell by Alpha Industries, mounted on the rotor head. Texas Instruments was radar subcontractor.

The two UH-1 helicopters were delivered to the Army in May 1971, and in July began a lengthy period of tests to evaluate their military potential. US Army testing continued throughout 1973.

BELL MODEL 205

US military designations: UH-1D/H and HH-1H Iroquois

Canadian military designation: CH-118 Iroquois

Although basically similar to the earlier Model 204 (see 1971-72 *Jane's*), the Model 205 introduced a longer fuselage, increased cabin space to accommodate a much larger number of passengers, and other changes. The following military versions have been built:

UH-1D. This US Army version of the Model 205 Iroquois has a 1,100 shp Lycoming T53-L-11 turboshaft, 48 ft (14·63 m) rotor, normal fuel capacity of 220 US gallons (832 litres) and overload capacity of 520 US gallons (1,968 litres). Relocation of the fuel cells increases cabin space to 220 cu ft (6·23 m^3), providing sufficient room for a pilot and twelve troops, or six litters and a medical attendant, or 4,000 lb (1,815 kg) of freight. A contract for a service test batch of seven YUH-1Ds was announced in July 1960 and was followed by further very large production orders from the US Army and from many other nations of the non-Communist world. First YUH-1D flew on 16 August 1961 and delivery to US Army field units began on 9 August 1963, when the second and third production UH-1Ds went to the 11th Air Assault Division at Fort Benning, Georgia. The UH-1D was superseded in production for the US Army by the UH-1H, but 352 UH-1Ds were built subsequently under licence in Germany for the German Army and Air Force. Prime contractor was Dornier.

UH-1H. Following replacement of the original T53-L-11 turboshaft by the 1,400 shp T53-L-13, the version of the Model 205 currently in production by Bell for the US Army is designated UH-1H. Deliveries of an initial series of 319 aircraft for the US Army began in September 1967. Subsequent orders included 300 more for the Army in January 1971, and nine for the RNZAF.

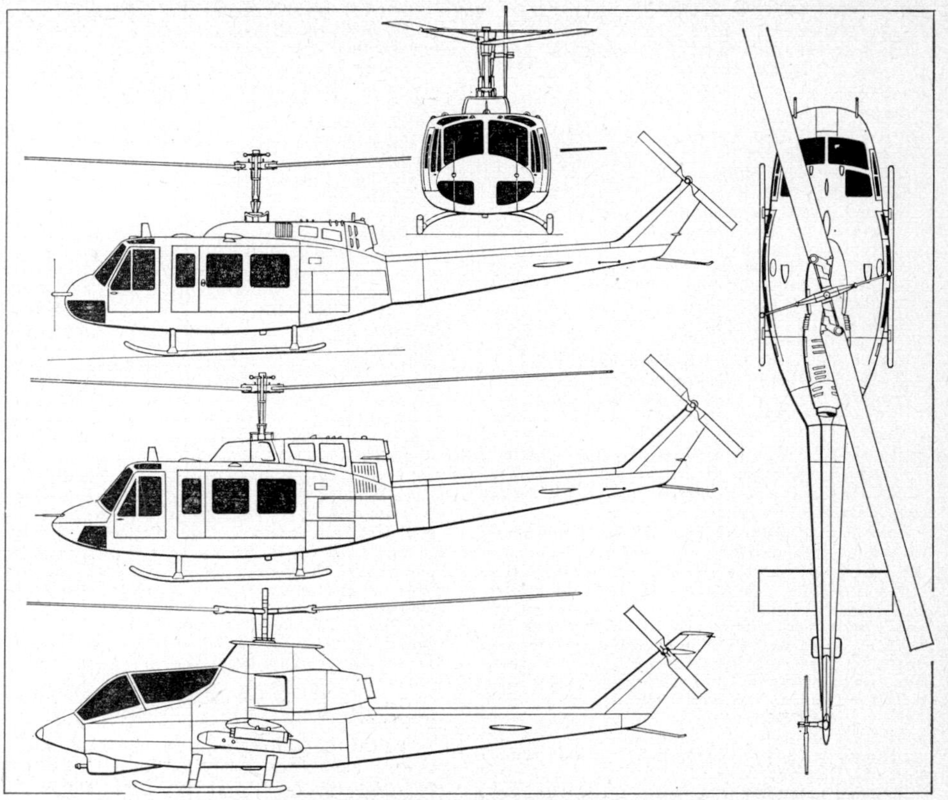

Bell UH-1H Iroquois, with additional side views of UH-1N (centre) and AH-1G HueyCobra (bottom) (*Pilot Press*)

An additional order announced in December 1971, from the US Army Aviation Systems Command, called for 136 UH-1Hs, with deliveries scheduled to begin in February 1973. The fixed price incentive contract, worth \$21·5 million, included an option for an additional 44 aircraft. This option was exercised in 1972, plus an additional option making a total of 48 aircraft, with delivery extending to early 1974. A further US Army order for 180 UH-1Hs, to be delivered in 1974, was announced in March 1973, and an option was exercised for 16 more. In December 1973 the US Army ordered a further 180 UH-1Hs for delivery in 1975.

Under a licensing agreement concluded in 1969, the Republic of China is producing UH-1Hs for the Nationalist Chinese Army, with much of the manufacturing and assembly process being carried out at Taichung, Taiwan. The initial production programme was for 50 helicopters, already delivered. Subsequent orders have increased the total procurement to 118.

CH-118. Similar to UH-1H, for Mobile Command, Canadian Armed Forces. First of ten delivered on 6 March 1968. Originally designated CUH-1H.

HH-1H. It was announced on 4 November 1970 that a fixed price contract worth more than \$9·5 million had been received from the USAF for 30 HH-1H aircraft (generally similar to the UH-1H) for use as local base rescue helicopters. Deliveries were completed during 1973.

The commercial Model 205A-1 is described separately.

The 7,000th Model 205/205A helicopter was completed in 1973.

The following details refer specifically to the military UH-1H:

TYPE: Single-rotor general-purpose helicopter.

ROTOR SYSTEM: Two-blade all-metal semi-rigid main rotor with interchangeable blades, built up of extruded aluminium spars and laminates. Stabilising bar above and at right angles to main rotor blades. Underslung feathering axis hub. Two-blade all-metal tail rotor of honeycomb construction. Blades do not fold.

ROTOR DRIVE: Shaft-drive to both main and tail rotors. Transmission rating 1,100 shp. Main rotor rpm 294-324.

FUSELAGE: Conventional all-metal semi-monocoque structure.

TAIL SURFACE: Small synchronised elevator on rear fuselage is connected to the cyclic control to increase allowable CG travel.

LANDING GEAR: Tubular skid type. Lock-on ground handling wheels and inflated nylon float-bags available.

POWER PLANT: One 1,400 shp Lycoming T53-L-13 turboshaft mounted aft of the transmission on top of the fuselage and enclosed

Bell HH-1H Iroquois local base rescue helicopter in USAF service

in cowlings. Five interconnected rubber fuel cells, total capacity 220 US gallons (832 litres). Overload fuel capacity of 520 US gallons obtained by installation of kit comprising two 150 US gallon (568 litre) internal auxiliary fuel tanks interconnected with the basic fuel system.

ACCOMMODATION: Cabin space of 220 cu ft (6·23 m³) provides sufficient room for pilot and 11-14 troops, or six litters and a medical attendant, or 3,880 lb (1,759 kg) of freight. Crew doors open forward and are jettisonable. Two doors on each side of cargo compartment; front door is hinged to open forward and is removable, rear door slides aft. Forced air ventilation system.

EQUIPMENT: Bleed air heater and defroster, comprehensive range of engine and flight instruments, power plant fire detection system, 30V 300A DC starter/generator, navigation, landing and anti-collision lights, controllable searchlight, hydraulically-boosted controls. Optional equipment includes external cargo hook, auxiliary fuel tanks, rescue hoist, 150,000 BTU muff heater.

ELECTRONICS: FM, UHF, VHF radio sets, IFF transponder, Gyromatic compass system, direction finder set, VOR receiver and intercommunications set standard. Optional nav/com systems.

DIMENSIONS, EXTERNAL:
- Diameter of main rotor 48 ft 0 in (14·63 m)
- Main rotor blade chord 21 in (53·3 cm)
- Diameter of tail rotor 8 ft 6 in (2·59 m)
- Tail rotor blade chord 8·4 in (21·3 cm)
- Length overall (main rotor fore and aft) 57 ft 1 in (17·40 m)
- Length of fuselage 41 ft 10¾ in (12·77 m)
- Overall height 14 ft 6 in (4·42 m)

AREAS:
- Main rotor disc 1,809 sq ft (168·06 m²)
- Tail rotor disc 56·7 sq ft (5·27 m²)

WEIGHTS AND LOADINGS:
- Weight empty 4,667 lb (2,116 kg)
- Basic operating weight (troop carrier mission) 5,557 lb (2,520 kg)
- Mission weight 9,039 lb (4,100 kg)
- Max T-O and landing weight 9,500 lb (4,309 kg)
- Max zero-fuel weight 8,070 lb (3,660 kg)
- Max disc loading 5·25 lb/sq ft (25·6 kg/m²)
- Max power loading 8·63 lb/hp (3·91 kg/hp)

PERFORMANCE (at max T-O weight):
- Max never-exceed speed 110 knots (127 mph; 204 km/h)
- Max level speed 110 knots (127 mph; 204 km/h)
- Max cruising speed 110 knots (127 mph; 204 km/h)
- Econ cruising speed at 5,700 ft (1,735 m) 110 knots (127 mph; 204 km/h)
- Max rate of climb at S/L 1,600 ft (488 m)/min
- Service ceiling 12,600 ft (3,840 m)
- Hovering ceiling in ground effect 13,600 ft (4,145 m)
- Hovering ceiling out of ground effect 1,100 ft (335 m)
- Range with max fuel, no allowances, no reserves, at S/L at 9,500 lb (4,309 kg) AUW 276 nm (318 miles; 511 km)

BELL MODEL 205A-1

The Model 205A-1 is a fifteen-seat commercial utility helicopter, developed from the UH-1H, with 1,400 shp Lycoming T5313A turboshaft, derated to 1,250 shp for take-off. It is designed for rapid conversion for alternative air freight, flying crane, ambulance, rescue and executive roles. Total cargo capacity is 248 cu ft (7·02 m³) including baggage space in tailboom, with 7 ft 8 in (2·34 m) by 4 ft 1 in (1·24 m) door openings on each side of the cabin to facilitate loading of bulky freight. External load capacity in flying crane role is 5,000 lb (2,268 kg). The ambulance version can accommodate six litter patients and one or two medical attendants.

Normal fuel capacity is 215 US gallons (814 litres); optional capacity 395 US gallons (1,495 litres).

The Model 205A-1 is produced under licence in Italy by Agusta (which see) as the AB 205A-1.

The description of the Bell UH-1H applies also to the Model 205A-1, except for the following details:

TYPE: Fifteen-seat commercial utility helicopter.

ELECTRONICS AND EQUIPMENT: Standard equipment includes vertical gyro system, 5 in gyro attitude indicator, gyro compass, master caution panel, bleed air heater, force trim hydraulic boost controls, soundproof headliner, dual windscreen wipers, cabin and engine fire extinguishers, map case and retractable passenger boarding steps. Optional items include dual controls, float landing gear, rotor brake, external cargo suspension, rescue hoist, auxiliary fuel tanks, litter installations, high-output cabin heater, protective covers and customised interiors. Standard electronics comprise 360-channel VHF transceiver and intercom system. An extensive range of optional nav/com systems is available.

DIMENSIONS, EXTERNAL:
- Length of fuselage 41 ft 6 in (12·65 m)
- Height overall 14 ft 4¾ in (4·39 m)

WEIGHTS:
- Weight empty, equipped 5,197 lb (2,357 kg)
- Normal T-O weight 9,500 lb (4,309 kg)
- Max T-O weight, external load 10,500 lb (4,763 kg)

PERFORMANCE (at normal T-O weight):
- Max level speed at S/L 110 knots (127 mph; 204 km/h)
- Max level speed at 3,000 ft (915 m) 110 knots (127 mph; 204 km/h)
- Max cruising speed at S/L 110 knots (127 mph; 204 km/h)
- Max cruising speed at 8,000 ft (2,440 m) 96 knots (111 mph; 179 km/h)
- Max rate of climb at S/L 1,680 ft (512 m)/min
- Max vertical rate of climb at S/L 850 ft (259 m)/min
- Service ceiling 14,700 ft (4,480 m)
- Hovering ceiling in ground effect 10,400 ft (3,170 m)
- Hovering ceiling out of ground effect 6,000 ft (1,830 m)
- Range at S/L, at max cruising speed 270 nm (311 miles; 500 km)
- Range at 8,000 ft (2,440 m) at max cruising speed, no reserves 298 nm (344 miles; 553 km)

BELL MODEL 206A JETRANGER
US Navy designation: TH-57A SeaRanger
US Army designation: OH-58A Kiowa

Production of the Model 206A JetRanger ended during 1972, after a total of 688 had been delivered. This version is generally similar to the current Model 206B JetRanger II, except that its power plant consists of a 317 shp Allison 250-C18A turboshaft engine.

The Model 206A was described in the 1972-73 and 1973-74 *Jane's*. The OH-58A Kiowa version is described after the entry on the Model 206B JetRanger II which follows.

BELL MODEL 206B JETRANGER II

In the Spring of 1971, Bell began delivery of the more powerful Model 206B JetRanger II, and this has since replaced in production the original Model 206A JetRanger. Military 206B-1 Kiowas being assembled in Australia are to Model 206B standard.

Power plant of the Model 206B JetRanger II is the 400 shp Allison 250-C20 turboshaft engine, which Bell was able to install with minimal modification of the basic airframe to meet requests for higher performance under hot-day/high-altitude conditions. This power plant increases power-limited airspeeds by 4·3 knots (5 mph; 8 km/h) at S/L ISA, and by as much as 25 knots (29 mph; 46·5 km/h) at 10,000 ft (3,050 m) in a 95°F ambient temperature. Hovering weights are increased by approximately 400 lb (181 kg) at the same altitude, and hovering ceilings by approximately 4,000 ft (1,220 m) at the same gross weights.

Bell is producing an airframe modification kit to convert Model 206As to JetRanger II standard and Allison made available late in 1971 a conversion kit to modify 250-C18 engines to 250-C20 standard.

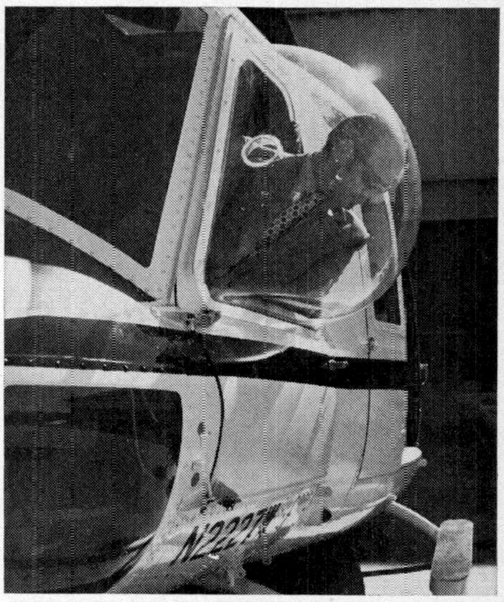

Blown window, for logging operations, on Bell Model 212 (*Henry Artof*)

In late 1972, Bell announced that it was flying a demonstration Model 206 JetRanger in which the fuselage was suspended from a nodalised beam. Details of this "Noda-Matic" concept are given in this company's introductory copy.

Under a five-year programme, covered by contracts valued at more than $75 million, Beech Aircraft produced airframes for both the commercial and military versions of the JetRanger and JetRanger II, the first airframe being delivered to Bell on 1 March 1968. A follow-on contract, valued at $8·6 million, was awarded to Beech in December 1972, extending production to August 1974, and an additional follow-on contract was announced during 1973. The work involves manufacture of the fuselage, skid gear, tailboom, spar, stabiliser and two rear fairing assemblies.

By May 1974, Bell and its licensees had manufactured more than 3,500 of the Model 206 series for military and commercial customers. Largest commercial operator is Petroleum Helicopters Inc, which has ordered a total of more than 115 JetRangers and JetRanger IIs. Military operators of the JetRanger II include the Brazilian Navy, with eighteen.

TYPE: Turbine-powered general-purpose light helicopter.

ROTOR SYSTEM: Two-blade semi-rigid see-saw type main rotor, employing pre-coning and underslinging to ensure smooth operation. Blades are of standard Bell "droop-snoot"

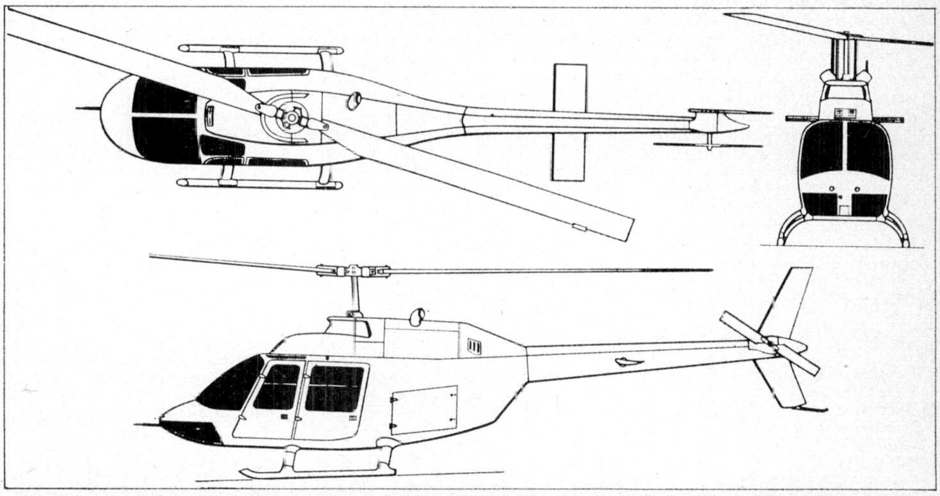

Three-view drawing (*Pilot Press*) **and photograph of the Bell 206B JetRanger II light utility helicopter (400 shp Allison 250-C20 turboshaft engine)**

section. They have a D-shape aluminium spar, bonded aluminium alloy skin, honeycomb core and a trailing-edge extension. Each blade is connected to the hub by means of a grip, pitch-change bearings and a tension-torsion strap assembly. Two tail rotor blades have bonded aluminium skin but no core. Main rotor blades do not fold, but modification to permit manual folding is possible. Rotor brake available as optional kit.

ROTOR DRIVE: Rotors driven through tubular steel alloy shafts with spliced couplings. Initial drive from engine through 90° spiral bevel gear to single-stage planetary main gearbox. Shaft to tail rotor single-stage bevel gearbox. Free-wheeling unit ensures that main rotor continues to drive tail rotor when engine is disengaged. Main rotor/engine rpm ratio 1:15; main rotor rpm 374-394. Tail rotor/engine rpm ratio 1:2·3.

FUSELAGE: Forward cabin section is made up of two aluminium alloy beams and 1 in (2·5 cm) thick aluminium honeycomb sandwich. Rotor, transmission and engine are supported by upper longitudinal beams. Upper and lower structures are interconnected by three fuselage bulkheads and a centre-post to form an integrated structure. Intermediate section is of aluminium alloy semi-monocoque construction. Aluminium monocoque tailboom.

TAIL UNIT: Fixed stabiliser of aluminium monocoque construction, with inverted aerofoil section. Fixed vertical tail-fin in sweptback upper and ventral sections, made of aluminium honeycomb with aluminium alloy skin.

LANDING GEAR: Aluminium alloy tubular skids bolted to extruded cross-tubes. Tubular steel skid on ventral fin to protect tail rotor in tail-down landing. Special high skid gear (10 in; 25 cm greater ground clearance) available for use in areas with high brush. Inflated bag-type pontoons or stowed floats capable of in-flight inflation available as optional kits.

POWER PLANT: One 400 shp Allison 250-C20 turboshaft engine. Fuel tank below and behind passenger seat, capacity 76 US gallons (288 litres). Refuelling point on starboard side of fuselage, aft of cabin. Oil capacity 5·5 US quarts (5·2 litres).

ACCOMMODATION: Two seats side by side in front and rear bench seat for three persons. Two forward-hinged doors on each side, made of formed aluminium alloy with transparent panels. Baggage compartment aft of rear seats, capacity 250 lb (113 kg), with external door on port side.

SYSTEMS: Hydraulic system, pressure 600 lb/sq in (42 kg/cm^2), for cyclic, collective and directional controls. Electrical supply from 150A starter/generator. One 24V 13Ah nickel-cadmium battery.

ELECTRONICS: Full range of electronics available in form of optional kits, including VHF communications and omni navigation kit, glideslope kit, ADF, DME, marker beacon, transponder and intercom and speaker system.

EQUIPMENT: Standard equipment includes night lighting equipment, dynamic flapping restraints, door locks, fire extinguishers and first aid kit. Optional items include dual controls, custom seating, external cargo sling with 1,200 lb (545 kg) capacity, heater, high-intensity night lights, turn and slip indicator, clock, engine oil vent, fire detection system, engine fire extinguisher, fairing kit, camera access door, engine hour meter, internal litter kit and stability and control augmentation system.

DIMENSIONS, EXTERNAL:
- Diameter of main rotor 33 ft 4 in (10·16 m)
- Main rotor blade chord 13 in (33 cm)
- Diameter of tail rotor 5 ft 2 in (1·57 m)
- Distance between rotor centres 19 ft 6½ in (5·96 m)
- Length overall, blades turning 38 ft 9½ in (11·82 m)
- Length of fuselage 31 ft 2 in (9·50 m)
- Height overall 9 ft 6½ in (2·91 m)
- Stabiliser span 6 ft 5½ in (1·96 m)
- Width over skids 6 ft 3½ in (1·92 m)

DIMENSIONS, INTERNAL:
- Cabin: Length 7 ft 0 in (2·13 m)
  - Max width 4 ft 2 in (1·27 m)
  - Max height 4 ft 3 in (1·28 m)
- Baggage compartment 16 cu ft (0·45 m^3)

AREAS:
- Main rotor blades (total) 36·1 sq ft (3·35 m^2)
- Tail rotor blades (total) 2·26 sq ft (0·21 m^2)
- Main rotor disc 873 sq ft (81·1 m^2)
- Tail rotor disc 20·97 sq ft (1·95 m^2)
- Stabiliser 9·65 sq ft (0·90 m^2)

WEIGHTS:
- FAA empty weight 1,455 lb (660 kg)
- Max T-O weight 3,200 lb (1,451 kg)

PERFORMANCE (at max T-O weight):
- Max level speed at S/L 122 knots (140 mph; 225 km/h)
- Max level speed at 5,000 ft (1,525 m) 116 knots (134 mph; 216 km/h)
- Max cruising speed at S/L 118 knots (136 mph; 219 km/h)
- Max cruising speed at 5,000 ft (1,525 m) 120 knots (138 mph; 222 km/h)
- Econ cruising speed at 5,000 ft (1,525 m) 120 knots (138 mph; 222 km/h)
- Max rate of climb at S/L 1,260 ft (384 m)/min
- Vertical rate of climb at S/L 280 ft (85 m)/min
- Service ceiling over 20,000 ft (6,095 m)
- Hovering ceiling in ground effect 11,300 ft (3,445 m)
- Hovering ceiling out of ground effect 5,800 ft (1,770 m)
- Range with max fuel and max payload at S/L, no reserves 299 nm (345 miles; 555 km)
- Range with max fuel and max payload at 5,000 ft (1,525 m), no reserves 337 nm (388 miles; 624 km)

Bell OH-58A Kiowa turbine-powered light observation helicopter in US Army service (*Norman Taylor*)

BELL KIOWA

US Army designation: OH-58A

Canadian military designation: CH-136

On 8 March 1968 the US Army named Bell as winner of its reopened light observation helicopter competition, and awarded the company the first increment of a planned total order for 2,200 OH-58A Kiowa aircraft generally similar to the Model 206A.

The first OH-58A was delivered to the US Army on 23 May 1969 and deployment in Vietnam began in the early Autumn of 1969.

On 1 May 1970 it was announced that 74 COH-58As had been ordered for the Canadian Armed Forces. The first of these was handed over officially at Uplands Airport, Ottawa, on 16 December 1971, and deliveries (from US Army production) were completed in October 1972. In January 1973 the US Army ordered an additional 74 OH-58As, but these represented replacements for the COH-58As delivered to the Canadian Armed Forces and the total US Army order remained at 2,200 aircraft; the delivery of these was completed by the end of 1973. The Canadian aircraft are now designated CH-136.

In early 1971 it was announced that Bell Helicopter Company and the Australian government had entered upon a co-production programme under which 75 Model 206B-1 Kiowa military light observation helicopters (similar to the OH-58A) would be delivered over an eight-year period. The initial 12 206B-1s were built by Bell, and the first of these was handed over officially at Eagle Farm Airport, Brisbane, on 22 November 1971. Commonwealth Aircraft Corporation (which see) is prime Australian licensee, with responsibility for final assembly of the remainder. Only the engines and avionics are being supplied from US sources.

Major difference between the OH-58A Kiowa and JetRanger concerns the main rotor, which has an increased diameter. There are also differences in the internal layout and electronics.

TYPE: Turbine-powered light observation helicopter.

ROTOR SYSTEM, ROTOR DRIVE: As for Model 206A, except main rotor/engine rpm ratio 1:17.44; main rotor rpm 354. Tail rotor/engine rpm ratio 1:2.353.

FUSELAGE, TAIL UNIT AND SKID LANDING GEAR: As for Model 206A.

POWER PLANT: One 317 shp Allison T63-A-700 turboshaft engine. Fuel tank below and behind the aft passenger seat, total usable capacity 73 US gallons (276 litres). Refuelling point on starboard side of fuselage, aft of cabin. Oil capacity 1·5 US gallons (5·64 litres).

ACCOMMODATION: Forward crew compartment seats pilot and co-pilot/observer side by side. Entrance to this compartment is provided by single door on each side of fuselage. The cargo/passenger compartment, which has its own access doors, one on each side, provides approximately 40 cu ft (1·13 m^3) of cargo area, or provisions for two passengers by installation of two seat cushions, seat belts and shoulder harnesses.

SYSTEMS: As Model 206A, except that directional controls are not hydraulically-powered.

ELECTRONICS: C-6533/ARC intercommunication subsystem, AN/ARC-114 VHF-FM, AN/ARC-115 VHF-AM, AN/ARC-116 UHF-AM, AN/ARN-89 ADF, AN/ASN-43 gyro magnetic compass, AN/APX-72 transponder, TSEC/KY-28 communications security set, C-8157/ARC control indication, MT-3802/ARC mounting, TS-1843/APX transponder test set and mounting, KIT-1A/TSEC computer and mounting, and duplicate AN/ARC-114.

ARMAMENT: Standard equipment is the XM-27 armament kit, utilising the 7·62 mm Minigun.

DIMENSIONS, EXTERNAL:
- As Model 206A except:
  - Diameter of main rotor 35 ft 4 in (10·77 m)
  - Length overall, blades turning 40 ft 11¾ in (12·49 m)
  - Length of fuselage 32 ft 7 in (9·93 m)

AREAS:
- As Model 206A except:
  - Main rotor blades (total) 38·26 sq ft (3·55 m^2)
  - Main rotor disc 978·8 sq ft (90·93 m^2)

WEIGHTS AND LOADING:
- Weight empty 1,464 lb (664 kg)
- Operating weight 2,313 lb (1,049 kg)
- Max T-O and landing weight 3,000 lb (1,360 kg)
- Max zero-fuel weight 2,525 lb (1,145 kg)
- Max disc loading 30·7 lb/sq ft (14·9 kg/m^2)

PERFORMANCE (estimated at observation mission gross weight of 2,768 lb; 1,255 kg, ISA, except where indicated otherwise):
- Max never-exceed speed at S/L 120 knots (138 mph; 222 km/h)
- Cruising speed for max range 102 knots (117 mph; 188 km/h)
- Loiter speed for max endurance 49 knots (56 mph; 90·5 km/h)
- Max rate of climb at S/L 1,780 ft (543 m)/min
- Service ceiling 18,900 ft (5,760 m)
- Hovering ceiling in ground effect 13,600 ft (4,145 m)
- Hovering ceiling out of ground effect 8,800 ft (2,682 m)
- Hovering ceiling out of ground effect (armed scout mission at 3,000 lb; 1,360 kg) 6,000 ft (1,828 m)
- Max range at S/L, 10% reserves 259 nm (299 miles; 481 km)
- Max range at S/L, armed scout mission at 3,000 lb (1,360 kg), no reserves 264 nm (305 miles; 490 km)
- Endurance at S/L, no reserves 3 hr 30 min

BELL MODEL 206L LONG RANGER

First announced on 25 September 1973, Bell's Long Ranger is intended to satisfy a requirement for a turbine-powered general-purpose light helicopter in a size and performance range between the five-seat JetRanger II and 15-seat Model 205A-1.

Developed from the JetRanger II, it has a fuselage which is 2 ft 1 in (0·64 m) longer, an Allison 250-C20B engine with a take-off rating of 420 shp and continuous rating of 370 shp, new rotor, and transmission system rated at 428 shp. It is the first production helicopter to incorporate Bell's new Noda-Matic cabin suspension system, described in the introductory copy to this company's entry.

An increase of 22 US gallons (83·3 litres) in fuel capacity, to a total of 98 US gallons (371 litres), extends range by over 39 nm (45 miles; 72 km) at a maximum take-off weight of 3,900 lb (1,769 kg). With a useful load of 2,006 lb (910 kg), this represents increases of 700 lb (318 kg) and 334 lb (151 kg), respectively, by comparison with the JetRanger II.

The company's latest developments in transmission technology provide a power rating increase of more than one-third over the present light-turbine transmission, while adding only 8 lb (3·6 kg) to component weight.

The Noda-Matic transmission suspension system not only gives a substantial reduction in rotor-induced vibration, particularly noticeable in high-speed cruise and manoeuvring conditions, but also, through the use of elastomerics, isolates structure-borne noise from the cabin environment. This results in a standard of comfort comparable with that of turboprop-powered fixed-wing aircraft.

With a cabin volume of 83 cu ft (2·35 m³), compared with the 49 cu ft (1·39 m³) of the JetRanger II, utility is enhanced by innovations that allow the maximum use of this area. For example, the port forward passenger seat has a folding back to allow loading of a container measuring 8 ft × 3 ft × 1 ft (2·44 m × 0·91 m × 0·30 m), making possible the carriage of such items as survey equipment, skis, and long components that cannot be accommodated in any other light helicopter. Double doors on the port side of the cabin provide an opening 5 ft 0 in (1·52 m) in width, for easy straight-in loading of litter patients or utility cargo; in an ambulance or rescue role two litter patients and two ambulatory patients/attendants may be carried. With a crew of two, the standard cabin layout accommodates five passengers in two canted aft-facing seats and three forward-facing seats. An optional executive cabin layout has four individual passenger seats.

Detail improvements include a redesigned instrument panel, pedestal and glare shield, to give the pilot improved visibility over the nose and through the lower forward windows. To simplify maintenance, the Long Ranger's forward upper engine cowling is hinged and the tail rotor gearbox has an easy-access cover.

A prototype of the Model 206L is flying, and initial deliveries of production aircraft are scheduled to be made in early 1975. Optional kits to be made available will include emergency flotation gear, a 2,000 lb (907 kg) cargo hook, and an engine bleed air environmental control unit.

Preliminary specification for the Model 206L Long Ranger is as follows:

DIMENSIONS, EXTERNAL:
Diameter of main rotor 37 ft 0 in (11·28 m)
Main rotor rpm 394

WEIGHTS:
Weight empty, standard configuration 1,894 lb (859 kg)
Max T-O weight 3,900 lb (1,769 kg)

PERFORMANCE (ISA at max T-O weight):
Max level speed at S/L 130 knots (150 mph; 241 km/h)
Cruising speed at S/L 118 knots (136 mph; 219 km/h)
Service ceiling at max cruise power 12,700 ft (3,870 m)
Hovering ceiling in ground effect 7,500 ft (2,285 m)
Hovering ceiling out of ground effect 1,800 ft (550 m)
Range at S/L 298 nm (344 miles; 553 km)
Range at 5,000 ft (1,525 m) 321 nm (370 miles; 595 km)

BELL MODEL 209 HUEYCOBRA (single-engined)
US Army designations: AH-1G, AH-1Q
Spanish Navy designation: Z-16

First flown on 7 September 1965, six months after its development was started, the Model 209 HueyCobra is a development of the UH-1B/C Iroquois intended specifically for armed helicopter missions. It combines the basic transmission and rotor system and (in its standard form) the power plant of the UH-1C with a new streamlined fuselage designed for maximum speed, armament load and crew efficiency.

The prototype was sent to Edwards AFB for US Army evaluation in December 1965. On 11 March 1966, the Army announced its intention to order the HueyCobra into production.

Three production versions have been announced so far, as follows:

AH-1G. Standard version for US Army, powered by 1,400 shp (derated to 1,100 shp) Lycoming T53-L-13 turboshaft, driving a two-blade wide-chord Model 540 "door-hinge" rotor of the kind fitted to the UH-1C. Main rotor rpm is 294-324. A development contract for two pre-production prototypes was placed on 4 April 1966, followed on 13 April by an initial contract for 110 production aircraft plus long lead-time spares. Subsequent contracts raised the total on order to 838 by October 1968. On 30 January 1970 the US Army ordered a further 170 AH-1Gs for delivery between July 1971 and August 1972, followed by a further order for 70 in mid-1971. Eight have been delivered to the Spanish Navy for anti-shipping strike duties.

Deliveries of the original production series began in June 1967 and operational deployment to Vietnam began in the early Autumn of 1967. The US Marine Corps acquired 38 AH-1Gs during 1969, for transition training and initial deployment, pending delivery of the AH-1J; these are included in the above totals.

AH-1J. Twin-turbine version for US Marine Corps. Described separately.

AH-1Q. Anti-armour version of the AH-1G HueyCobra, equipped to fire Hughes TOW anti-tank missiles. The first of eight pre-production examples was delivered to the US Army in early 1973. Scheduled for deployment with European-based units in mid-1974, it was anticipated that about half of the US Army's current total of approximately 600 AH-1Gs would be modified to AH-1Q standard. Initial orders under a $59·2 million contract awarded in January 1974 cover the conversion of 101 aircraft. Each AH-1Q installation consists of eight TOW missile containers, disposed as two two-round pods on each of the outboard underwing pylons, plus a helmet sight subsystem produced by the Univac Division of Sperry Rand. The inboard wing weapon pylons are still available for other stores. TOW/Cobras produced under this programme demonstrated their anti-armour proficiency in Vietnam in 1972, as well as in a joint US/Canadian/West German test programme in Germany.

Relatively small, the HueyCobra has a low silhouette and narrow profile, with a fuselage width of only 38 in (0·965 m). These features make it easy to conceal with small camouflage nets or to move under cover of trees. Tandem seating for the crew of two provides maximum field of view for the pilot and forward gunner. The skid landing gear is non-retractable. Stub-wings carry armament and help to offload the rotor in cruising flight.

Emerson Electric designed and developed for the HueyCobra the TAT-102A tactical armament turret, which was faired into the front fuselage undersurface and housed a GAU-2B/A (formerly XM-134) Minigun six-barrel 7·62 mm machine-gun, with 8,000 rounds. This turret has been superseded on the AH-1G by the XM-28 subsystem, mounting either two Miniguns, with 4,000 rounds each; two XM-129 (similar to the XM-75) 40 mm grenade launchers, each with 300 rounds; or one Minigun and one XM-129. Two rates of fire are provided for the TAT-102A and XM-28 Miniguns, namely 1,600 and 4,000 rounds per minute. The lower rate is for searching or registry fire, while the higher rate is used for attack, the rate of fire being controlled by the gunner's trigger. The XM-129 fires at a single rate of 400 rounds per minute. Structural provisions have been incorporated in the airframe to accept a turret subsystem capable of firing the M-61A1 20 mm Vulcan gun at a firing rate of 750 rounds per minute, the XM-197 three-barrel 20 mm gun, or a three-barrel 30 mm gun.

Four external stores attachments under the stub-wings accommodate various loads, including a total of 76 2·75 in rockets in four XM-159 packs, 28 similar rockets in four XM-157 packs, or two XM-18E1 Minigun pods.

In late 1969 an XM-35 20 mm cannon kit was added to the weapons available for the AH-1G, and an initial batch of six aircraft equipped with the XM-35 was delivered to the US Army in December 1969. A total of 350 kits was ordered subsequently by the Army.

Designed jointly by Bell and General Electric, the XM-35 armament subsystem consists of a six-barrel 20 mm automatic cannon, two ammunition boxes and certain structural and electrical modifications. Mounted on the inboard stores attachment of the port stub-wing, the XM-35 has a firing rate of 750 rounds per minute. Two ammunition boxes faired flush to the fuselage below the stub wings accommodate 1,000 rounds. Total installed weight of the system is 1,172 lb (531 kg).

In normal operation, the co-pilot/gunner controls and fires the turret armament, using a hand-held pantograph-mounted sight to which the turret is slaved. The gunner can fire throughout a field of 230° (± 115° both sides of the aircraft centreline) and can depress the turreted weapons 50° and elevate them 25°. Velocity jump compensation automatically computes the lead angle with respect to the relative motion of aircraft and target. In addition, the gunner has the capability of firing the wing stores.

The pilot can fire the turreted weapons only in the stowed position, dead ahead. The turret returns to the stowed position automatically when the gunner releases his grip on the slewing switch.

The pilot normally fires the wing stores, utilising the XM-73 adjustable rocket sight. Rockets are fired in pairs, made up of one rocket from each opposing wing station. Any desired number of pairs from one to nineteen can be preselected on the cockpit-mounted intervalometer. The inboard wing stores are equipped to fire either the XM-18 or XM-18E1 Minigun pod. All wing stores are symmetrically or totally jettisonable.

The crew of the HueyCobra are protected by seats and side panels made of NOROC armour, manufactured by the Norton Company. Other panels protect vital areas of the aircraft.

On missions of 50 nm (57 miles; 92 km) radius the HueyCobra can reach the target area in half the time taken by a UH-1B and operate in the target area for three times as long. During flight tests it has been dived at a speed of 214 knots (246 mph; 397 km/h). Normal fuel capacity is 268 US gallons (1,014 litres).

In November 1970 three AH-1G HueyCobras equipped with prototypes of a day/night fire control system known as SMASH (South-east Asia Multi-sensor Armament System for HueyCobra) were delivered to the US Army for tests. Major elements of the system included a nose-mounted Sighting System Passive Infra-red (SSPI) sensor developed by Aerojet Electro-Systems Company, a Moving Target Indicator (MTI) radar (which is an AN/APQ-137B high-resolution radar system developed by Emerson Electric) mounted on the starboard wing station, pilot and co-pilot/gunner displays and consoles, and an Interface Control Unit (ICU) that electronically "married" the fire control sub-

Bell Model 206L Long Ranger seven-seat general-purpose light helicopter

Prototype of the Bell AH-1Q TOW/Cobra during qualification testing

system sensing, control and display units to the aircraft's armament.

DIMENSIONS, EXTERNAL:

Diameter of main rotor	44 ft 0 in (13·41 m)
Main rotor blade chord	27 in (68·6 cm)
Diameter of tail rotor	8 ft 6 in (2·59 m)
Tail rotor blade chord	8·4 in (21·3 cm)
Wing span	10 ft 4 in (3·15 m)
Length overall (main rotor fore and aft)	52 ft 11½ in (16·14 m)
Length of fuselage	44 ft 5 in (13·54 m)
Overall height	13 ft 5¼ in (4·10 m)
Width over skids	7 ft 0 in (2·13 m)

AREAS:

Main rotor disc	1,520·4 sq ft (141·2 m^2)
Tail rotor disc	56·8 sq ft (5·27 m^2)

WEIGHTS:

Operating weight	6,073 lb (2,754 kg)
Mission weight	9,407 lb (4,266 kg)
Max T-O and landing weight	9,500 lb (4,309 kg)

PERFORMANCE (at max T-O weight):

Max never-exceed speed	190 knots (219 mph; 352 km/h)
Max level speed	190 knots (219 mph; 352 km/h)
Max rate of climb at S/L	1,230 ft (375 m)/min
Service ceiling	11,400 ft (3,475 m)
Hovering ceiling in ground effect	9,900 ft (3,015 m)
Max range at S/L, max fuel, 8% reserves	310 nm (357 miles; 574 km)

BELL MODEL 209 HUEYCOBRA (twin-engined)
US Marine Corps designation: AH-1J SeaCobra

This is a modified version of the Bell AH-1G, initially for the US Marine Corps. A batch of 49 AH-1Js was ordered for the USMC (by which they are known as SeaCobras) in May 1968, and a pre-production aircraft was displayed to representatives of the US armed forces at Enless, Texas, on 14 October 1969.

Delivery of the Marine AH-1Js began in mid-1970 and was completed in the following year. Twenty more were ordered in early 1973, for delivery to the USMC between April 1974 and February 1975.

Bell announced on 22 December 1972 the receipt of a further order for 202 AH-1Js from the US Army, with an initial funding of $38·5 million. They are being acquired by Iran through the US government, and will be similar to the 49 aircraft delivered to the US Marine Corps.

The AH-1J differs from the single-engined AH-1G in having an 1,800 shp United Aircraft of Canada T400-CP-400 coupled free-turbine turboshaft power plant (a military version of the PT6T-3 Turbo Twin Pac power plant as described for the Model 212/UH-1N). Engine and transmission are flat-rated for 1,100 shp continuous output, with increase to 1,250 shp for take-off or 5 min emergency power. To cater for the increased power, the tail rotor pylon has been strengthened and the tail rotor blade chord increased.

An electrically-driven 20 mm turret system, developed by the General Electric Company, is faired into the forward lower fuselage, and houses an XM-197 three-barrel weapon, which is a lightweight version of the General Electric M-61 cannon. The firing rate is 750 rounds per minute, but a 16-round burst limiter is incorporated in the firing switch. The gun has a tracking capability of 220° in azimuth, 50° depression and 18° elevation, and can be slewed at a rate of 80° per second. A barrel length of 5 ft (1·52 m) makes it imperative that the XM-197 is centralised before wing stores are fired. An ammunition container of 750-round capacity is located in the fuselage directly aft of the turret. Four external stores attachment points under the stub-wings can accommodate various loads, including XM-18E1 7·62 mm Minigun pods as well as 2·75 in folding-fin rockets in either seven-tube (XM-157) or 19-tube (XM-159) packs.

The USMC SeaCobra also differs from the AH-1G in having Marine avionics.

DIMENSIONS, EXTERNAL:

As for AH-1G except:

Tail rotor blade chord	11·5 in (29·2 cm)
Length overall (main rotor fore and aft)	53 ft 4 in (16·26 m)
Length of fuselage	44 ft 7 in (13·59 m)
Width of fuselage	3 ft 2½ in (0·98 m)
Height overall	13 ft 8 in (4·15 m)

WEIGHTS:

Operating weight, including 400 lb (181 kg) crew, fluids, avionics and armour	6,816 lb (3,091 kg)
Mission weight	9,637 lb (4,371 kg)
Max T-O and landing weight	10,000 lb (4,535 kg)

PERFORMANCE (at max T-O weight, except as detailed):

Max never-exceed speed	180 knots (207 mph; 333 km/h)
Max level speed	180 knots (207 mph; 333 km/h)
Max rate of climb at S/L	1,090 ft (332 m)/min
Service ceiling	10,550 ft (3,215 m)
Hovering ceiling in ground effect	12,450 ft (3,794 m)
Max range, no reserves	311 nm (359 miles; 577 km)

Bell AH-1J SeaCobra in the insignia of the Imperial Iranian Army Aviation Service

Bell Model 212 fifteen-seat general-purpose commercial helicopter

BELL MODEL 212 TWIN TWO-TWELVE
US military designation: UH-1N
Canadian military designation: CH-135

Bell announced on 1 May 1968 that the Canadian government had approved development of a twin-engined UH-1 helicopter to be powered by a United Aircraft of Canada PT6T power plant. Subsequently, on 19 September 1969, Bell stated that the Canadian government had ordered 50 of these aircraft (designated **CUH-1N**) for the Canadian Armed Forces, with options on 20 more. Simultaneously, orders totalling 141 aircraft for the United States services were announced, comprising 79 for the USAF, 40 for the USN and 22 for the USMC, all having the designation **UH-1N.** Subsequent orders have covered the delivery of 72 more UH-1Ns to the US Navy and Marine Corps in 1973-75.

Initial deliveries for the USAF began in 1970, and the first CUH-1N for the Canadian Armed Forces was handed over officially at Uplands Airport, Ottawa, on 3 May 1971; the Canadian order was completed one year later. Deliveries to the USN and USMC began during 1971. Canadian aircraft are now designated CH-135.

A commercial version, known as the Twin Two-Twelve, is also in full-scale production. This received FAA type certification in October 1970, and on 30 June 1971 the Two-Twelve was granted FAA Transport Type Category A certification.

More than 100 commercial Model 212s had been delivered by the end of 1973.

The Model 212/UH-1N utilises a Bell 205A/UH-1H airframe, and civil and military versions have basically the same configuration, but differ in mission kits and avionics. They each accommodate a pilot and 14 passengers or, in cargo configuration, provide 220 cu ft (6·23 m^3) of internal capacity. The Model 212 has the capability of carrying an external load of 5,000 lb (2,268 kg), and the military UH-1N a load of 3,383 lb (1,534 kg).

Power plant is a United Aircraft of Canada PT6T-3 Turbo Twin Pac, which consists of two PT6 turboshaft engines coupled to a combining gearbox with a single output shaft. Producing 1,800 shp, the Twin Pac is flat-rated to 1,250 shp for T-O and 1,100 shp for continuous operation. In the event of an engine failure, the remaining engine is capable of delivering 900 shp for 30 minutes or 765 shp continuously, which is adequate to maintain cruise performance at maximum gross weight.

On 6 March 1972 a UH-1N helicopter of the US Navy Antarctic Development Squadron Six (VXE-6) stationed at McMurdo carried parachute rigger Hendrick V. Gorick to a height of 20,500 ft (6,248 m), from which altitude he jumped to set a new parachute jump record for the Antarctic continent.

Bell announced in January 1973 that two Twin Two-Twelves had been modified and flown in a programme to gain IFR certification from the UK's CAA and America's FAA. Conversion of the Model 212 from VFR to IFR configuration requires a new avionics package, new instrument panel and aircraft stabilisation controls. The Model 212 has also qualified for IFR certification by the Norwegian DCA and the Canadian MoT.

The new avionics include dual King KTR-900A com transceivers; dual King KNR-660A VOR/LOC/RMI receivers; King KDF-800 ADF; King KMD-700A DME; King KXP-750A transponder; King KGM-690 marker beacon/glideslope receiver; and dual Sperry Tarsyn-444 three-axis gyro units. The new panel has blue-white lighted instruments, and the pilot's and co-pilot's 5 in attitude director indicator and horizontal situation indicator are as used in Astronautics Corporation's Model 11300 flight director system. Installation of a mechanical Stability Control Augmentation System (SCAS), an automatic flight control system, separation of the two DC generator circuits and provision of a triple-redundant AC power system completes the IFR installation.

Bell announced simultaneously with the above that Helicopter Service AS of Oslo, Norway, had ordered six Model 212s equipped for IFR, which were to be used in support of offshore oil operations in the North Sea. Delivery was completed in 1973, and the first of four IFR 212s ordered by the Japan Maritime Safety Agency was delivered in November 1973. By the end of that year a total of 20 IFR-configured 212s had been delivered.

The Bell Helicopter Company's largest single order for non-military helicopters was received from the government of Peru in October 1973. Valued at more than $11·5 million, it covered the purchase of 14 Model 212s, plus spares and technical services. One of the helicopters, assigned to the Peruvian Air Force Group 3, will be used on commercial contracts in support of oil exploration, drilling and production operations. With delivery scheduled for completion by mid-1974, the helicopters supplement three Model 212s purchased earlier by Peru.

The description given for the Bell UH-1H applies generally to the Model 212, but the twin-engined power plant makes considerable changes to the specification, which is detailed below for both the Model 212 and UH-1N:

DIMENSIONS, EXTERNAL:

Diameter of main rotor (with tracking tips)	48 ft 2¼ in (14·69 m)
Main rotor blade chord	2 ft 4⅜ in (0·72 m)
Diameter of tail rotor	8 ft 6 in (2·59 m)
Tail rotor blade chord	11·5 in (35·0 cm)
Length overall (main rotor fore and aft)	57 ft 3¼ in (17·46 m)
Length of fuselage	42 ft 4¾ in (12·92 m)
Height overall	14 ft 4¾ in (4·39 m)

WEIGHTS (A: Model 212, B: UH-1N):

FAA empty weight plus usable oil:

A	5,549 lb (2,517 kg)

Max T-O weight and mission weight:

A	11,200 lb (5,080 kg)
B	10,500 lb (4,762 kg)

PERFORMANCE (at max T-O weight):
Max never-exceed speed at S/L:
A, B 109 knots (126 mph; 203 km/h)
Max level speed at S/L:
A, B 109 knots (126 mph; 203 km/h)
Max rate of climb at S/L:
A, B 1,745 ft (532 m)/min
Service ceiling:
A 17,400 ft (5,305 m)
B 15,000 ft (4,570 m)
Hovering ceiling in ground effect:
A 14,700 ft (4,480 m)
B 12,900 ft (3,930 m)
Hovering ceiling out of ground effect:
A 10,600 ft (3,230 m)
B 4,900 ft (1,495 m)
Max range at S/L, no reserves:
A 237 nm (273 miles; 439 km)
B 216 nm (248 miles; 400 km)

BELL MODEL 214 HUEY PLUS

Bell Helicopter announced on 12 October 1970 that it had built the prototype of an improved version of its military UH-1H, known as the Model 214 Huey Plus.

Designed to improve the lift capability of the UH-1H, it also offered improved safety and reliability. It utilised a Model H airframe with strengthened main beams, pylon structure and aft fuselage, including the tailboom attachment. The tailboom carried push/pull control tubes instead of conventional cables. A large increase in horsepower resulted from the installation of a 1,900 shp Lycoming T53-L-702 turboshaft engine.

The main rotor, of 50 ft (15·2 m) diameter, had blades of 27 in (0·69 m) chord, each with a double-swept blade tip to reduce noise and improve high-speed performance. This rotor was a development of the Model 540 "door-hinge" rotor introduced on the UH-1C. Rotor transmission was of the type designed for the earlier HueyTug and was rated at 2,000 shp. The rotor hub was strengthened and incorporated elastomeric and Teflon faced bearings which required no lubrication. The tail rotor was of tractor configuration and its drive system was uprated in power.

The Model 214 had a mission T-O gross weight of 11,000 lb (4,989 kg), an increase of 1,500 lb (680 kg) over the single-engine Huey family. It could carry 10 troops with a crew of four, capacity of the cabin being increased by replacing the two jump seats aft of the pilot and co-pilot with a five-man seat, without other cabin modifications.

At mission T-O gross weight the Huey Plus could hover out of ground effect at 4,000 ft (1,220 m) at 35°C. Under these gross weight and atmospheric conditions it had a cruising speed of 135 knots (155 mph; 250 km/h) and a maximum speed of 165 knots (190 mph; 305 km/h).

BELL MODEL 214A

On 22 December 1972, Bell announced that it had received an order for 287 advanced Model 214A 16-seat utility helicopters from the US Army. With an initial funding of $63 million, these are being acquired by Iran through the US government.

Developed from the Model 214 Huey Plus, the 214A is powered by a 2,930 shp Lycoming LTC4B-8D turboshaft engine, an improved version of the T55-L-7C that was fitted in the original Model 214A demonstrator when it went to Iran. It has the 2,050 shp transmission and rotor drive systems developed for the KingCobra experimental gunship helicopter, described in the 1973-74 *Jane's*, and embodies Bell's Noda-Matic nodalised beam concept to minimise vibration.

At a max T-O weight of 13,000 lb (5,896 kg), the Model 214A has a cruising speed of 130 knots (150 mph; 241 km/h) and a range of 260 nm (299 miles; 481 km). It has an external load max T-O weight of 15,000 lb (6,803 kg).

The first Model 214A for Iran flew for the first time on 13 March 1974. Deliveries are scheduled to begin in early 1975, building up to a rate of ten a month within a year.

BELL MODEL 214B

Bell announced on 4 January 1974 that a commercial version of the Model 214A, known as the Model 214B, will become available in 1975, emphasising that it will have a lift capability better than any existing commercial helicopter in the medium category.

To be powered by a 2,930 shp Lycoming T5508D turboshaft engine, it will have the same rotor drive and transmission system as the Model 214A. The transmission will be rated at 2,050 shp for take-off, with a maximum continuous power output of 1,850 shp. The main rotor will have swept tips, and an advanced rotor hub with elastomeric bearings on the flapping axis. The tail rotor will also have swept tips and a hub that requires no lubrication. Other features will include an automatic flight control system, with stability augmentation and attitude retention; nodalised suspension; separate dual hydraulic systems; and a large engine deck that will serve as a maintenance platform. Differences by comparison with the military Model 214A will include the addition of an engine fire extinguishing system, push-out escape windows in the cargo doors, and commercial avionics.

It is estimated that the Model 214B will be able to cruise at 130 knots (150 mph; 241 km/h) with an internal load of 4,000 lb (1,814 kg). Alternative loads will include 14 men, nearly four US tons of chemicals in an agricultural role, or 800 US gallons (3,025 litres) of water or suppressant in a firefighting role. It will be able to haul an external load of 7,000 lb (3,175 kg) on its cargo hook.

DIMENSIONS, EXTERNAL:
Main rotor diameter 50 ft 0 in (15·24 m)
Main rotor blade chord 2 ft 9 in (0·84 m)
Tail rotor diameter 9 ft 8 in (2·95 m)
Tail rotor blade chord 1 ft 0 in (0·305 m)
WEIGHT:
Max T-O weight 16,000 lb (7,257 kg)

BELL MODEL 222

In April 1974, Bell announced its intention of developing the Model 222, described as the first commercial light twin-engined helicopter to be built in the USA. The prototype is scheduled to fly for the first time at the end of 1975, with deliveries of production aircraft planned to begin in 1978.

The general appearance of the Model 222 is shown in the accompanying illustration. Before taking a development decision, Bell displayed a full-scale concept mockup, designated D306, at the annual convention of the Helicopter Association of America, in San Diego, in January 1974. The response of potential operators encouraged the development go-ahead, and customer suggestions were embodied in the definitive Model 222 design. In particular, the lower glazing of the flight deck was revised to provide increased visibility for rooftop landings, and the cabin was both lengthened and widened at the rear to give more spacious accommodation in high-density passenger-carrying configuration. There is now 124 cu ft (3·51 m³) of cabin space and another 46 cu ft (1·30 m³) in the baggage compartment.

The main cabin is 12 ft 6 in (3·81 m) long from the rear of the baggage compartment to the rear of the flight deck, to which the passengers have full access. Alternative configurations range from six-person super executive to ten-person high-density, with provision for rapid conversion from passenger to utility arrangements. As an ambulance the Model 222 will accommodate two NATO/Stokes litters, two attendants and two crew.

The Model 222 is powered by two 600 shp Avco Lycoming LTS 101-650C turboshaft engines, mounted in a streamlined housing above the cabin and aft of the rotor pylon. The airframe incorporates Bell's focused pylon and nodalisation for smoothness, and will isolate structure-borne vibration by mounting the pylon and engines in elastomeric rubber. The landing gear is retractable, with provision for emergency flotation gear and likely availability of skids as an option for operations in varied terrain.

Safety features include dual electrical and hydraulic systems, fail-safe structures and redundancy throughout the systems. The completely dry main rotor hub has conical elastomerics. When equipped with the appropriate avionics, the Model 222 is intended to qualify for IFR certification.

WEIGHTS:
Weight empty, equipped 3,770 lb (1,710 kg)
Max T-O weight 6,500 lb (2,950 kg)
PERFORMANCE (estimated):
Speed at max continuous power
156 knots (180 mph; 290 km/h)
Normal cruising speed
over 130 knots (150 mph; 240 km/h)
Service ceiling, one engine out
over 10,000 ft (3,050 m)
Range, with 30 min reserve
370 nm (425 miles; 685 km)

BELL MODEL 301
US Army designation: XV-15

Bell Helicopter announced in May 1973 that it had been chosen by NASA and the US Army to build and test two twin-engined tilt-rotor research aircraft. Estimated cost of the four-year programme is $26·4 million.

The company has been working on tilt-rotor technology since the mid-1950s, proving the concept feasible with its XV-3 prototype, described in the 1962-63 *Jane's*. Since that time development of tilt-rotor systems has progressed steadily, leading to the Model 301 which Bell proposed to meet the NASA/Army requirement. The two research prototypes have been allocated the official designation XV-15. They will have fuselages and tail units built under subcontract by Rockwell International's Tulsa Division.

As shown in the accompanying three-view drawing of the XV-15, the airframe structure is basically that of a conventional fixed-wing aircraft. However, the wingtip-mounted engines and rotors can be swivelled to a vertical position for VTOL operations, and are then moved forward gradually to provide transition to cruising

Bell Model 214A in Iranian camouflage (2,930 shp Lycoming LTC4B-8D turboshaft engine)

Mockup of Bell's Model 222 twin-engined light helicopter

flight at speeds in excess of 300 knots (345 mph; 556 km/h).

Power plant comprises two uprated versions of the Lycoming T53-L-13B turboshaft engine, each of which provides a contingency rating of 1,760 shp. Qualified to operate in the vertical mode, they have been redesignated LTC1K-4K. The three-blade rotors are stiff in plane and gimballed, with an elastomeric hub spring to increase control power and damping. The blades are a high-twist design, with wide chord, suitable for both helicopter and high-speed aircraft flight modes. Interconnect drive-shafts and redundant tilting mechanisms permit single-engine operation and fail-safe tilt capability.

The XV-15 is fitted with a stability and control augmentation system, and an automatic flight control system to improve the handling qualities and enhance pilot efficiency. Ejection seats will be installed as a safety feature during flight trials.

Future commercial and military aircraft which might be derived from the XV-15 would have a wing span of about 35 ft (10·67 m) and fuselage length of 41 ft (12·50 m). They would carry 15 troops in military service or 12 passengers as civil transports.

The programme is being funded and managed jointly by the NASA Ames Research Center and the US Army's Air Mobility Research and Development Laboratory. The two XV-15s, when available, will be used in a research programme to prove the concept, explore the limits of the operational flight envelope and assess its application to military and civil transport needs.

The first XV-15 will be tested in the 40 ft × 80 ft (12 m × 24 m) wind tunnel at NASA's Ames Research Center prior to the first flight, by the second aircraft, which is scheduled for mid-1976.

DIMENSIONS:
- Rotor diameter (each) 25 ft 0 in (7·62 m)
- Rotor blade chord 1 ft 2 in (0·36 m)

WEIGHTS:
- Design max T-O weight:
  - VTOL 13,000 lb (5,897 kg)
  - STOL 15,000 lb (6,804 kg)

PERFORMANCE (estimated):
- Max never-exceed speed (structural) over 360 knots (415 mph; 667 km/h)
- Design cruising speed over 310 knots (357 mph; 574 km/h)

Full-scale mockup of the Bell YAH-63 advanced attack helicopter

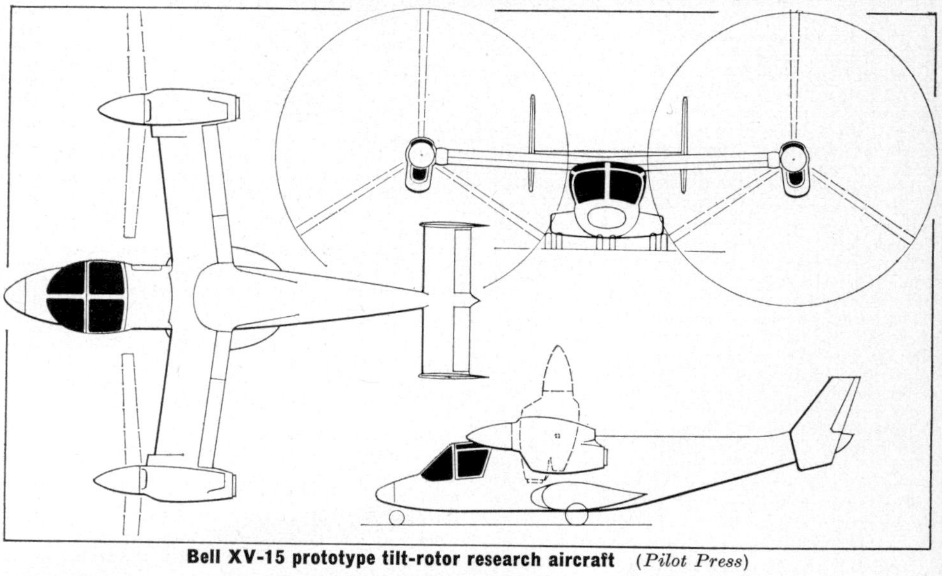

Bell XV-15 prototype tilt-rotor research aircraft (*Pilot Press*)

BELL MODEL 309 KINGCOBRA

Following the success of its AH-1G and AH-1J armed helicopters, Bell built two prototypes of a more advanced design known as the Model 309 KingCobra. This was described and illustrated in the 1973-74 *Jane's*.

Bell intended to offer the KingCobra to the US Marines and Army in slightly differing versions to meet their specific requirements. However, in late 1972 the company received a request for proposal from the US Army, to compete in its new Advanced Attack Helicopter (AAH) development programme. This resulted in Bell's receiving a contract for the Model 409 (YAH-63) AAH, which is described separately. The two KingCobras will continue in use as company research vehicles, in support of this and other programmes.

BELL MODEL 409
US Army designation: YAH-63

Bell Helicopter Company announced on 22 June 1973 that it had received a contract valued at $44·7 million from the US Army to begin development of an Advanced Attack Helicopter. Total development funding was considered likely to exceed $120 million.

The US Army's request for proposals, issued in November 1972, resulted in submissions from Bell, Boeing Vertol, Hughes, Lockheed and Sikorsky. Those from Bell and Hughes were selected for development, and each company is to build two flight test prototypes and a ground test vehicle. A three-year programme, terminating in a fly-off competition, will enable the Army to select a final contractor for this helicopter, for which it has established a design-to-cost objective of $1·4 to 1·6 million for each production aircraft.

Bell's proposal, which has the company designation Model 409 and Army designation YAH-63, was evolved from the Model 309 KingCobra. It is a twin-turbine helicopter, seating a crew of two in tandem, with the pilot in front; but differs externally from the KingCobra in having a lower profile, extended ventral fin and (replacing the aft-fuselage elevator of the Huey family) a horizontal surface at the tip of the upper fin.

Maximum manoeuvrability is to be ensured by utilising a zero *g* main rotor hub, with flapping axis moment springs to give instant fuselage response to cyclic control, with no fear of control reversal during terrain-hugging operations. The two main rotor blades are to have dual stainless steel spars to enhance combat survivability; and use of nodalised dynamic beams in the rotor pylon suspension system will reduce crew fatigue, extend airframe component and subsystems life, and provide a more stable gun platform.

The fuselage is to be of conventional semi-monocoque construction; the non-retractable tailwheel-type landing gear will have high-flotation shock struts, with a single wheel on each main unit and twin nosewheels. Power plant will consist of two 1,500 shp General Electric T700-GE-700 advanced technology turboshaft engines, mounted one on each side of the fuselage just aft of the stub wings.

Intended for deployment against enemy armour by day or night, or in bad weather, armament will comprise launchers for TOW anti-tank missiles or 2·75 in folding-fin rockets beneath the stub wings, and a three-barrel 30 mm cannon. The cannon is to be mounted in an undernose turret, forward of the pilot, who aims it with a direct-view helmet sight for close-in defence. This installation has been chosen in preference to the more usual chin-mount, since it not only allows greater elevation of the weapon, but reduces the effect of gun muzzle blast on systems and airframe. The TOW missiles will be guided by the stabilised telescopic sight by day, and by an infra-red vision system at night. The navigation equipment is to include Loran C/D.

No further details of the YAH-63 were available up to mid-1974.

PERFORMANCE (primary mission, at 4,000 ft; 1,220 m and at 35°C):
- Sustained cruising speed 145-175 knots (167-202 mph; 269-325 km/h)
- Min vertical rate of climb at 95% power 500 ft (152 m)/min
- Endurance 1·9 hr

BELLANCA

BELLANCA AIRCRAFT CORPORATION

HEAD OFFICE AND WORKS:
Box 624, Municipal Airport, Alexandria, Minnesota 56308

Telephone: (612) 762-1501

CHAIRMAN: J. K. Downer
VICE-CHAIRMAN: James N. Miller
PRESIDENT: Robert DePalma
EXECUTIVE VICE-PRESIDENT:
Donald J. O'Mara (General Manager)
VICE-PRESIDENTS:
Rod Absher
James L. Brown
John J. McCarten
Mrs T. E. "Marge" Mitchell
R. C. Vogel (Marketing and Sales)
Russel R. Wilson
SECRETARY: C. R. Bentley
TREASURER: Russel R. Wilson
GENERAL SALES MANAGER: F. O. Thompson
COMMUNICATIONS MARKETING MANAGER:
N. D. Dunn

Bellanca Super Viking 300A four-seat light aircraft (*Ronaldo S. Olive*)

Known originally as International Aircraft Manufacturing, Inc (Inter-air), Bellanca Sales Company (a subsidiary of Miller Flying Service) acquired the assets of Champion Aircraft Corporation on 30 September 1970. Following the merger, the name Bellanca Aircraft Corporation was adopted, and Bellanca now markets both its own products and those of Champion Aircraft.

In addition to continued production of the four-seat Viking series, Bellanca markets the two-seat Citabria, a utility version known as the Scout, and an advanced aerobatic aircraft named the Decathlon. A new version of the Scout, designated Model 8GCBC, was nearing the end of its certification programme in early 1974. Also under development is a side-by-side two-seat trainer based on the pre-war Aeronca Chief.

Sales during the 1973 fiscal year totalled 671 aircraft, compared with 451 in 1972.

BELLANCA VIKING SERIES

There are three current aircraft in the Viking series, developed from the earlier Bellanca 260C and Standard Viking 300 (see 1971-72 *Jane's*), as follows:

Model 17-30A Super Viking 300A. Powered by a 300 hp Continental IO-520-K six-cylinder horizontally-opposed aircooled engine, driving a McCauley two- or three-blade metal constant-speed propeller. Total of 511 delivered by 1 November 1972.

Model 17-31A Super Viking 300A. This is identical to the foregoing version except for the installation of a 300 hp Lycoming IO-540-K1E5 engine, driving a Hartzell three-blade constant-speed propeller. Total of 102 delivered by 1 November 1972.

Model 17-31ATC Turbo Viking 300A. Powered by a 300 hp Lycoming IO-540-K1E5 engine with two Rajay turbochargers. Hartzell three-blade constant-speed propeller. Deliveries of this version totalled 45 on 1 November 1972.

A Super Viking 300 delivered on 1 November 1972 was the 1,000th Bellanca aircraft completed by the company. At that time Viking production was at a rate of 17 aircraft per month.

Type: Four-seat light business aircraft.

Wings: Cantilever low-wing monoplane. Bellanca B wing section. Dihedral 4° 30′. Incidence 0° at root, —3° at tip. Structure consists of two laminated Sitka spruce spars, mahogany plywood and spruce ribs and mahogany plywood skin, covered with Dacron. Ailerons and electrically-actuated flaps are Dacron-covered wooden structures.

Fuselage: Welded 4130 steel tube structure, covered with Dacron. Two-piece glassfibre engine cowling, suspended from firewall.

Tail Unit: Strut-braced welded 4130 steel tube structure, covered with Dacron. Sweptback vertical surfaces. Trim tab in port elevator.

Landing Gear: Tricycle type, with Auto-Axion electro-hydraulic retraction, which lowers gear automatically during approach if pilot omits to do so, and prevents accidental retraction on ground. Manual emergency extension. Nosewheel protrudes slightly in "up" position to reduce damage in a wheels-up landing. Nosewheel retracts rearward, main wheels forward into underwing fairings, optionally enclosed by doors. Spring-air-oil shock-absorbers. Main-wheel tyres size 6·00-6 6-ply. Steerable nosewheel. Goodyear type 2-747 hydraulic disc brakes.

Power Plant: One six-cylinder horizontally-opposed aircooled engine (details under model descriptions above). Two fuel tanks in wings and one in fuselage, aft of cabin, with total usable capacity of 60 US gallons (227 litres). Optional auxiliary fuel tank in fuselage, increasing max usable capacity to 75 US gallons (283 litres). Refuelling points above each wing and on starboard side of fuselage. Oil capacity 3 US gallons (11·5 litres).

Accommodation: **Four seats in pairs in enclosed cabin.** Dual controls standard, with brakes on port side only. Moulded glassfibre door on starboard side of cabin. Tinted glass. Baggage space, capacity 186 lb (84 kg), aft of rear seats, with glassfibre external door and in-flight access. Provision for tube for carrying skis, max weight 20 lb (9 kg). Heating and ventilation standard.

Systems: 12V electrical system, with Prestolite 60A alternator, solid-state regulator and 33Ah battery. Landing, taxi and navigation lights standard.

Electronics and Equipment: Standard equipment includes artificial horizon, directional gyro, electric turn co-ordinator, rate of climb indicator, vacuum gauge, 8-day clock, outside air temperature gauge, tinted glass, sun visor, towbar, stall warning device, soundproofing, custom interior, tie-down straps. With factory-installed radio equipment the following additional equipment is standard: Narco omni antenna, electroVoice microphone, power cable, Narco VP-10 broad-band transmitting antenna and microphone jacks. Mitchell Century I, II or III autopilot optional, with optional accessories which include radio tracker, radio coupler and automatic trim for Century II or III, glideslope coupler for Century III, electric trim and switch kits. Optional radio and navigation equipment includes Bendix, King and Narco VHF transceivers, transponders and marker beacon receivers, Bendix, King, Kett and Narco ADF radio receivers, King and Narco DME and Narco course line computer. Miscellaneous optional equipment includes Alcor engine analyser and EGT meter, heated pitot tube, auxiliary power source, stereo tape player, oxygen system, true air speed indicator, alternative paint schemes, 3 in gyros, strobes, quick oil drain, alternative static source, shoulder harness for front seat, dual brakes and map pockets.

Dimensions, external:
Wing span 34 ft 2 in (10·41 m)
Length overall 26 ft 4 in (8·02 m)
Height overall 7 ft 4 in (2·24 m)
Tailplane span 12 ft 2 in (3·71 m)
Wheel track 9 ft 0 in (2·74 m)
Wheelbase 6 ft 8 in (2·03 m)
Propeller diameter 6 ft 3 in (2·03 m)
Cabin door:
Height 2 ft 10 in (0·86 m)
Max width 2 ft 9 in (0·84 m)
Baggage compartment door:
Height 2 ft 0 in (0·61 m)
Width 1 ft 8½ in (0·51 m)

Dimensions, internal:
Cabin: Length, firewall to rear wall 10 ft 2 in (3·10 m)
Max width 3 ft 7 in (1·09 m)
Max height 3 ft 11 in (1·19 m)
Baggage compartment volume 12·08 cu ft (0·34 m³)

Areas:
Wings, gross 161·5 sq ft (15·00 m²)
Ailerons (total) 11·77 sq ft (1·09 m²)
Trailing-edge flaps (total) 16·16 sq ft (1·50 m²)

Weights (A: IO-520, B: IO-540, C: turbocharged IO-540):
Weight empty:
A 2,191 lb (994 kg)
B 2,225 lb (1,009 kg)
C 2,320 lb (1,052 kg)
Max T-O weight 3,325 lb (1,508 kg)

Performance (at max T-O weight, A: IO-520, B: IO-540, C: turbocharged IO-540):
Max never-exceed speed:
A, B, C 196 knots (226 mph; 363 km/h) IAS
Max cruising speed (75% power):
A 162 knots (187 mph; 301 km/h)
B 165 knots (190 mph; 305 km/h)
C at 24,000 ft (7,315 m) 193 knots (223 mph; 358 km/h)
Cruising speed (65% power):
A 156 knots (180 mph; 290 km/h)
B 160 knots (184 mph; 296 km/h)
C at 24,000 ft (7,315 m) 175 knots (202 mph; 325 km/h)
Stalling speed, wheels and flaps down:
A, B, C 61 knots (70 mph; 113 km/h) CAS
Max rate of climb at S/L:
A, B, C 1,170 ft (356 m)/min
Service ceiling:
A 17,000 ft (5,180 m)
B 18,200 ft (5,550 m)
C 24,000 ft (7,315 m)
T-O to 50 ft (15 m):
A, B, C 1,420 ft (433 m)
Landing from 50 ft (15 m):
A, B, C 1,340 ft (409 m)
Range, standard fuel, 75% power:
A, B 521 nm (600 miles; 965 km)
C 603 nm (695 miles; 1,118 km)
Range, auxiliary fuel, 65% power:
A, B 755 nm (870 miles; 1,400 km)
C 851 nm (980 miles; 1,577 km)

BELLANCA TRAINER

One of the designs which Bellanca acquired through its purchase of Champion Aircraft was the Aeronca Chief, a side-by-side two-seat light aircraft built in considerable numbers before the second World War. It has now updated the design to form the basis of a low-cost training aircraft, of which the prototype flew for the first time on 26 October 1973. Production was scheduled to begin before the end of 1974.

The general appearance of the trainer, unnamed in mid-1974, is shown in the accompanying illustrations. It differs from the pre-war Chief in having a tricycle landing gear, with faired wheels on cantilever legs, an angular sweptback fin and rudder, and much-refined interior. Construction follows the standard Bellanca/Champion pattern, with a Ceconite-covered steel tube fuselage and Vee-braced wooden-spar wings of NACA 4412 section. The power plant is a 115 hp Lycoming O-235-C1 four-cylinder horizontally-opposed aircooled engine, driving a two-blade fixed-pitch propeller. Production aircraft are expected to have flaps, although none are fitted to the prototype. They will also have 360° field of vision through wraparound windows, dual control wheels and a full professional instrument panel as standard.

Dimensions, external:
Wing span 34 ft 6 in (10·52 m)
Wing chord (constant) 5 ft 0 in (1·52 m)
Wing aspect ratio 6·9
Wing dihedral 2°
Wing incidence 1°
Length overall 22 ft 4¾ in (6·83 m)
Height overall 6 ft 9 in (2·06 m)

Prototype Bellanca Trainer (115 hp Lycoming O-235-C1 engine)

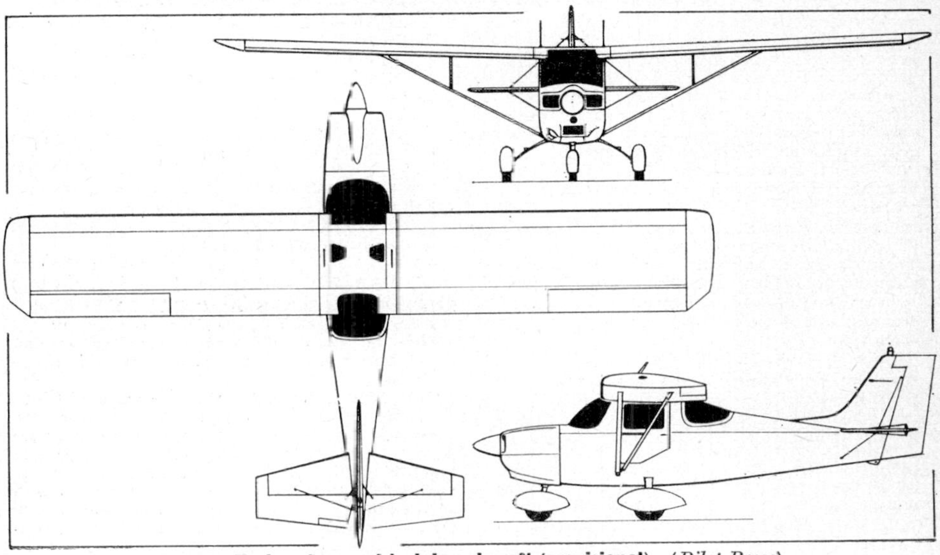

Bellanca Trainer two-seat training aircraft (provisional) (*Pilot Press*)

AREA:
Wings, gross 165 sq ft (15·33 m²)

WEIGHTS AND LOADINGS:
Weight empty 960 lb (435 kg)
Max T-O weight 1,650 lb (748 kg)
Max wing loading 10 lb/sq ft (48·8 kg/m²)
Max power loading 16·5 lb/hp (7·48 kg/hp)

PERFORMANCE (at max T-O weight):
Max never-exceed speed
156 knots (180 mph; 290 km/h)
Max level speed at S/L
108 knots (125 mph; 201 km/h)
Design cruising speed
117 knots (135 mph; 217 km/h)
Stalling speed, flaps up
39 knots (45 mph; 73 km/h)
Stalling speed, flaps down
34 knots (39 mph; 63 km/h)
Max rate of climb at S/L 720 ft (220 m)/min
Service ceiling 13,000 ft (3,960 m)
Range, 75% power at 7,500 ft (2,285 m), with 26 US gallons (98·5 litres) of fuel, no reserve
480 nm (553 miles; 890 km)

CHAMPION (BELLANCA) MODEL 7ECA/7GCAA/ 7KCAB CITABRIA

The Citabria ("airbatic" spelled backwards) represents Bellanca's advanced development of the Model 7 Champion airframe. There are four current versions, as follows:

Model 7ECA. Basic version, with 115 hp Lycoming O-235-C1 engine and standard wings. Design and prototype construction started on 1 January 1964. Prototype flew for first time on 1 May 1964 and first production model on 18 August 1964. FAA certification received 5 August 1964. During 1969 the Model 7ECA received FAA certification for operation with Edo floats.

Model 7GCAA. Generally similar to Model 7ECA but with 150 hp Lycoming O-320-A2B engine. Design started 15 February 1965. Construction of prototype began on 1 May 1965, and it flew on 30 May, followed by the first production model on 20 July 1965. FAA certification received 30 July 1965.

Model 7GCBC Scout. Generally similar to Model 7ECA but with 150 hp Lycoming O-320-A2B engine and flaps. Described separately.

Model 7KCAB. Generally similar to Model 7ECA but with 150 hp Lycoming IO-320-E2A engine. Currently certificated with a special fuel and oil system for prolonged inverted flying.

TYPE: Two-seat light cabin monoplane. Load factors +5*g* and —2*g*.

WINGS: Braced high-wing monoplane. NACA 4412 wing section. Dihedral 2°. Incidence 1°. Two spruce spars, aluminium ribs, Dacron covering. Steel-tube Vee bracing struts. Single-spar Dacron-covered metal ailerons. Glassfibre-reinforced polyester wingtips.

FUSELAGE: Welded chrome-molybdenum steel-tube structure, covered with Dacron.

TAIL UNIT: Wire-braced welded steel-tube structure, with Dacron covering. Fixed-incidence tailplane. Counterbalanced elevators. Controllable trim tab in elevator.

LANDING GEAR: Non-retractable tailwheel type. All aircraft produced from January 1968 have cantilever spring steel main gear with 6·00-6 wheels and tyres as standard. Tyre pressure 24 lb/sq in (1·69 kg/cm²), Cleveland disc brakes. Wheel fairings optional. Pee Kay 1800 floats available on 7ECA. Federal A-2000-A skis available on Model 7ECA. Edo floats available on Model 7ECA.

POWER PLANT: One four-cylinder horizontally-opposed aircooled engine, as described under model listings above. McCauley two-blade fixed-pitch metal propeller: type 1C90ALM on 115 hp model and type 1C172AGM on 150 hp models. Two aluminium fuel tanks in wings, total capacity 36 US gallons (136 litres). Refuelling points above tanks. Oil capacity 1·5 US gallons (5·75 litres) on versions with 115 hp engine, 2 US gallons (7·5 litres) on 150 hp versions.

ACCOMMODATION: Enclosed cabin seating two persons in tandem. Dual controls. Heater standard. Quick-jettison door on starboard side. Space for 100 lb (45 kg) baggage.

SYSTEMS: Hydraulic system for brakes only. Electrical system powered by engine-driven generator.

ELECTRONICS AND EQUIPMENT: Wide range of King and Narco radio equipment optional, including omni, ILS and ADF. Blind-flying instrumentation optional. Standard equipment includes landing and navigation lights.

DIMENSIONS, EXTERNAL:
Wing span:
7ECA, 7GCAA, 7KCAB 33 ft 5 in (10·19 m)
Wing chord (constant) 5 ft 0 in (1·52 m)
Wing aspect ratio:
7ECA, 7GCAA 6·72
Length overall:
7ECA, 7GCAA, 7KCAB 22 ft 8 in (6·91 m)
Height overall 6 ft 7¾ in (2·02 m)
Wheel track 6 ft 4 in (1·93 m)
Wheelbase 16 ft 1 in (4·90 m)
Cabin door: Height 3 ft 1 in (0·94 m)
Width 3 ft 1 in (0·94 m)
Height to sill 1 ft 5½ in (0·44 m)

Champion Citabria two-seat aerobatic light aircraft

AREAS:
Wings, gross:
7ECA, 7GCAA, 7KCAB 165 sq ft (15·33 m²)
Ailerons (total) 16·5 sq ft (1·53 m²)
Fin 7·02 sq ft (0·65 m²)
Rudder 6·83 sq ft (0·63 m²)
Tailplane 12·25 sq ft (1·14 m²)
Elevators, including tab 14·58 sq ft (1·35 m²)

WEIGHTS AND LOADINGS:
Weight empty, equipped:
7ECA 1,034 lb (469 kg)
7GCAA 1,107 lb (502 kg)
Max T-O and landing weight:
landplanes 1,650 lb (748 kg)
Max wing loading:
7ECA, 7GCAA, 7KCAB 10 lb/sq ft (48·8 kg/m²)
Max power loading:
7ECA 15·3 lb/hp (6·94 kg/hp)
7GCAA, 7KCAB 11·0 lb/hp (5·00 kg/hp)

PERFORMANCE (at max T-O weight):
Max never-exceed speed
140 knots (162 mph; 261 km/h)
Max level speed at S/L:
7ECA 102 knots (117 mph; 188 km/h)
7ECA seaplane 75 knots (86 mph; 138 km/h)
7GCAA 113 knots (130 mph; 209 km/h)
7KCAB 116 knots (133 mph; 214 km/h)
Max cruising speed (75% power) at optimum height:
7ECA 103 knots (119 mph; 191 km/h)
7GCAA, 7KCAB
114 knots (132 mph; 212 km/h)
Cruising speed (65% power):
7ECA 100 knots (115 mph; 185 km/h)
7GCAA, 7KCAB
108 knots (125 mph; 201 km/h)
Stalling speed:
all models 44·5 knots (51 mph; 82 km/h)
Max rate of climb at S/L:
7ECA 725 ft (221 m)/min
7ECA seaplane 515 ft (157 m)/min
7GCAA, 7KCAB 1,120 ft (341 m)/min
Service ceiling:
7ECA 12,000 ft (3,660 m)
7GCAA, 7KCAB 17,000 ft (5,180 m)
T-O run:
7ECA 450 ft (137 m)
7GCAA, 7KCAB 375 ft (114 m)
T-O to 50 ft (15 m):
7ECA 890 ft (271 m)
7GCAA, 7KCAB 630 ft (192 m)
Landing from 50 ft (15 m):
7ECA 775 ft (236 m)
7GCAA, 7KCAB 755 ft (230 m)
Landing run:
7ECA, 7GCAA, 7KCAB 400 ft (121 m)
Range at max cruising speed:
7ECA 495 nm (570 miles; 917 km)
7GCAA, 7KCAB 395 nm (455 miles; 732 km)

CHAMPION (BELLANCA) MODEL 7GCBC SCOUT

First announced in December 1970, this utility version of the basic Citabria introduces several new features to make it suitable for a wide range of duties.

Of particular interest is the optional equipment available to enable the Scout to be used as a crop sprayer. This comprises a Sorensen glassfibre belly tank of 90 US gallons (340 litres) capacity, this tank having internal plumbing, a side-loading port, a 28 sq in (180·6 cm²) safety dump valve and an instant-release mechanism that allows the tank to be jettisoned in emergency. For distribution of the spray, 16-nozzle tapered booms are provided.

The description of the basic Citabria applies also to the Scout, except as detailed below:

WINGS: As for Citabria, except increased wing span and provision of fabric-covered trailing-edge flaps of metal construction.

FUSELAGE: Removable metal skin panels on undersurface.

LANDING GEAR: Non-retractable tailwheel type. Cantilever spring steel main gear with wheels and tyres size 7·00-6. Heavy-duty Scott tailwheel. Wire cutters on main landing gear. Ski installations approved are Fluidyne 2000 and Airglas Landis 2000A; approved floats are Edo 2000, Pee Kay 2000 and Canadian Aircraft Products 2000A. Hydraulic disc brakes. Parking brake.

POWER PLANT: 150 hp Lycoming O-320-A2B four-cylinder horizontally-opposed aircooled engine, driving a Sensenich two-blade metal fixed-pitch propeller. Two fuel tanks in wings with a total fuel capacity of 36 US gallons (136 litres). Refuelling points above tanks. Oil capacity 2 US gallons (7·5 litres).

ACCOMMODATION: Enclosed cabin seating two persons in tandem. Dual controls and heater standard. Quick-jettison door on starboard side. Shoulder harness and heavy-duty seat belt standard for front seat. Tinted windscreen. Front seat heater. Space for 100 lb (45 kg) cargo or baggage. Rear seat and control column quickly removable for carriage of bulk cargo. Heavy-duty cargo tie-downs standard.

EQUIPMENT: Standard equipment includes fire extinguisher, crash locator beacon, landing light, navigation lights, de luxe interior trim, two-colour external paint scheme and seaplane corrosion proofing.

DIMENSIONS, EXTERNAL:
Wing span 34 ft 5·4 in (10·50 m)
Wing chord (constant) 5 ft 0 in (1·52 m)
Wing aspect ratio 6·97
Length overall 22 ft 8 in (6·91 m)
Height overall 6 ft 7¾ in (2·02 m)
Cabin door: Height 3 ft 1 in (0·94 m)
Width 3 ft 1 in (0·94 m)
Height to sill 1 ft 5½ in (0·44 m)

AREAS:
Wings, gross 170·2 sq ft (15·81 m²)
Ailerons (total) 16·5 sq ft (1·53 m²)
Flaps (total) 18·4 sq ft (1·71 m²)
Fin 7·02 sq ft (0·65 m²)
Rudder 6·83 sq ft (0·63 m²)
Tailplane 12·25 sq ft (1·14 m²)
Elevators, including tab 14·58 sq ft (1·35 m²)

WEIGHTS:
Weight empty, equipped:
Aerobatic version 1,136 lb (515 kg)
Sprayer 1,150 lb (522 kg)
Max T-O weight:
Aerobatic version 1,650 lb (758 kg)
Sprayer 2,325 lb (1,054 kg)

PERFORMANCE (at max T-O weight in standard landplane configuration):
Max level speed at S/L
111 knots (128 mph; 206 km/h)
Max cruising speed (75% power) at optimum height 114 knots (132 mph; 212 km/h)
Cruising speed (65% power)
108 knots (125 mph; 201 km/h)
Stalling speed, flaps up
44·5 knots (51 mph; 82 km/h)
Stalling speed, 35° flaps
39 knots (45 mph; 73 km/h)

Max rate of climb at S/L 1,145 ft (349 m)/min
Service ceiling 17,000 ft (5,180 m)
T-O to 50 ft (15 m) 860 ft (262 m)
Landing from 50 ft (15 m) 690 ft (210 m)
Landing run 200 ft (61 m)
Range at max cruising speed
395 nm (455 miles; 732 km)

BELLANCA MODEL 8GCBC SCOUT

This slightly larger version of the 7GCBC Scout, with a 180 hp Lycoming engine, received type approval on 30 April 1974, and went into immediate production to meet large orders.

The description of the 7GCBC Scout applies also to the new version, except for the following details:

WINGS: As for 7GCBC, but span increased and dihedral reduced to 1°. Hoerner wingtips. 27° high-lift flaps.

TAIL UNIT: As for 7GCBC, but areas increased.

POWER PLANT: One 180 hp Lycoming O-360-C2A four-cylinder horizontally-opposed aircooled engine, driving a McCauley two-blade metal fixed-pitch propeller. Fuel capacity 36 US gallons (136 litres).

ACCOMMODATION: Enclosed cabin seating two persons in tandem.

EQUIPMENT: Optional items include a 90 US gallon (340 litre) Sorensen belly tank and underwing spraybooms, glider towing hook, skis and Edo 2000 floats.

DIMENSIONS, EXTERNAL:
Wing span 36 ft 3 in (11·05 m)
Wing chord (constant) 5 ft 0 in (1·52 m)
Length overall, tail up 22 ft 9 in (6·92 m)
Tailplane span 10 ft $2\frac{1}{4}$ in (3·10 m)
Wheel track 6 ft $10\frac{1}{2}$ in (2·10 m)
Wheelbase, tail up 16 ft $5\frac{1}{2}$ in (5·02 m)
Propeller diameter 6 ft 8 in (2·03 m)

AREAS:
Wings, gross 180 sq ft (16·7 m^2)
Vertical tail surfaces 16·5 sq ft (1·53 m^2)
Horizontal tail surfaces 26 sq ft (2·42 m^2)

WEIGHTS:
Weight empty 1,320 lb (598 kg)
Normal category payload 830 lb (376 kg)
Restricted category payload 1,060 lb (480 kg)
Max T-O weight:
Normal 2,150 lb (975 kg)
Restricted 2,540 lb (1,152 kg)

PERFORMANCE (at Normal category T-O weight):
Max never-exceed speed
140 knots (162 mph; 260 km/h) CAS
Max level speed at S/L
117 knots (135 mph; 217 km/h)
Design cruising speed
113 knots (130 mph; 209 km/h) CAS
Stalling speed, flaps down, power off
45 knots (52 mph; 84 km/h)
Max rate of climb at S/L 1,100 ft (335 m)/min
T-O run, flaps up 485 ft (148 m)

Bellanca Model 8GCBC Scout two-seat light aircraft (180 hp Lycoming O-360-C2A engine)

CHAMPION (BELLANCA) MODEL 8KCAB DECATHLON

The Champion Model 8KCAB Decathlon is an aerobatic competition aircraft designed for loads of $+6\,g$ and $-5\,g$, and has been arbitrarily cleared for two minutes of inverted flight, although the aircraft has been flown inverted in excess of four minutes without loss of oil or oil pressure. FAA certification under FAR 23, for both Normal and Aerobatic categories, was granted on 16 October 1970.

Following immediate sale of the first hand-built production batch of 14 aircraft, with the first aircraft being delivered on 24 February 1971, Bellanca decided to begin full-scale production with the 15th aircraft, thus making the Decathlon the only unlimited aerobatic competition aircraft to enter production in the US. At the time of writing maximum permissible speed was limited to 156 knots (180 mph; 289 km/h), but redesign of the windscreen was expected to increase this figure to 173 knots (200 mph; 321 km/h).

Champion Decathlon two-seat light aircraft (150 hp Lycoming IO-320-E1A engine)

Generally similar to the 150 hp Model 7 Citabrias, all available details of the Decathlon follow:

TYPE: Two-seat light cabin monoplane.

WINGS: Braced high-wing monoplane. Wing section NACA 1412 modified. Dihedral 1°. Incidence 1° 30′. Size of front spar substantially increased and ribs stronger and more closely-spaced by comparison with Citabria. Trusses added between front and rear spars in aileron area. Aluminium (front) and steel-tube (rear) Vee bracing struts each side, of enlarged section.

FUSELAGE: Welded steel-tube structure, fabric covered.

TAIL UNIT: Wire-braced welded steel-tube structure. Fixed-incidence tailplane. Trim tab in elevator.

LANDING GEAR: Non-retractable tailwheel type. Cantilever spring steel main gear. Fairings on main wheels.

POWER PLANT: One 150 hp Lycoming IO-320-E1A four-cylinder horizontally-opposed aircooled engine, driving a Hartzell type HC-C2YL-4/C7663-4 two-blade metal counterweighted constant-speed propeller. Two wing fuel tanks, with total usable capacity of 40 US gallons (151·4 litres). Oil capacity 2 US gallons (7·5 litres).

ACCOMMODATION: Enclosed cabin seating two persons in tandem. Quick-jettison door on starboard side. Space for 100 lb (45 kg) baggage.

DIMENSIONS, EXTERNAL:
Wing span 32 ft 0 in (9·75 m)
Wing chord (constant) 5 ft 4 in (1·63 m)
Length overall 22 ft 8 in (6·91 m)
Height overall 7 ft 8 in (2·34 m)
Wheel track 6 ft 4 in (1·93 m)
Wheelbase 16 ft 4 in (4·98 m)

AREAS:
Wings, gross 169 sq ft (15·7 m^2)
Ailerons (total) 20·68 sq ft (1·92 m^2)
Fin 7·02 sq ft (0·65 m^2)
Rudder 6·83 sq ft (0·63 m^2)
Tailplane 12·25 sq ft (1·14 m^2)
Elevators, including tab 14·58 sq ft (1·35 m^2)

WEIGHTS AND LOADINGS:
Weight empty 1,225 lb (555 kg)
Max T-O weight 1,800 lb (815 kg)
Max wing loading 10·7 lb/sq ft (52·2 kg/m^2)
Max power loading 12·0 lb/hp (5·44 kg/hp)

PERFORMANCE (at max T-O weight):
Max never-exceed speed
156 knots (180 mph; 289 km/h)
Max level speed
126 knots (145 mph; 233 km/h)
Max cruising speed, 75% power at 8,000 ft (2,450 m) 121 knots (140 mph; 225 km/h)
Cruising speed (65% power)
114 knots (132 mph; 212 km/h)
Stalling speed 46 knots (53 mph; 86 km/h)
Max rate of climb at S/L 1,025 ft (312 m)/min
Service ceiling 16,000 ft (4,875 m)
Range, 75% power at 8,000 ft (2,450 m)
461 nm (531 miles; 854 km)

BELLANCA

BELLANCA AIRCRAFT ENGINEERING, INC

HEAD OFFICE AND WORKS:
PO Box 70, Scott Depot, Nr Charleston, West Virginia 25560
Telephone: (304) 755-4354
PRESIDENT: August T. Bellanca
MANAGING DIRECTOR:
Henry E. Payne

The original Bellanca Aircraft Corporation of New Castle, Delaware, merged with companies not engaged in aircraft manufacture and lost its identity in 1959. This new company, formed by Mr August Bellanca and his father, the late G. M. Bellanca, bought all of the original Bellanca aircraft designs with the exception of the Model 14-19.

Since 1956, Bellanca Aircraft Engineering has carried out extensive research into the use of glassfibre composite materials for airframe construction. Following the successful testing of full-scale structures, embodying a variety of different design and fabrication techniques, it is now developing the prototype of an aircraft known as the Bellanca Model 19-25 Skyrocket, constructed of high-strength glassfibre-epoxy laminates.

On 1 December 1971 the company was re-organised and acquired corporate offices and production plant at Scott Depot, West Virginia. Construction of the Skyrocket prototype was well advanced in February 1973, but the decision to

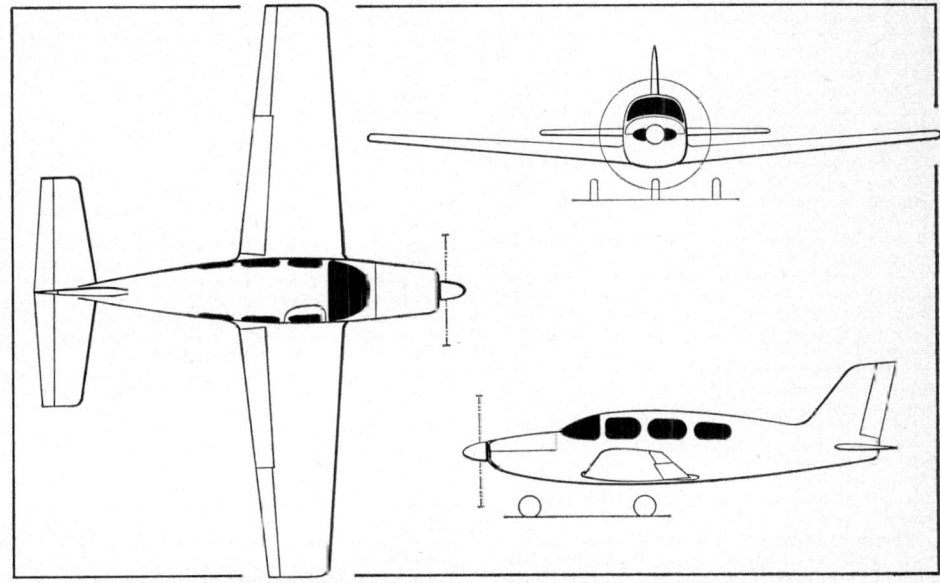

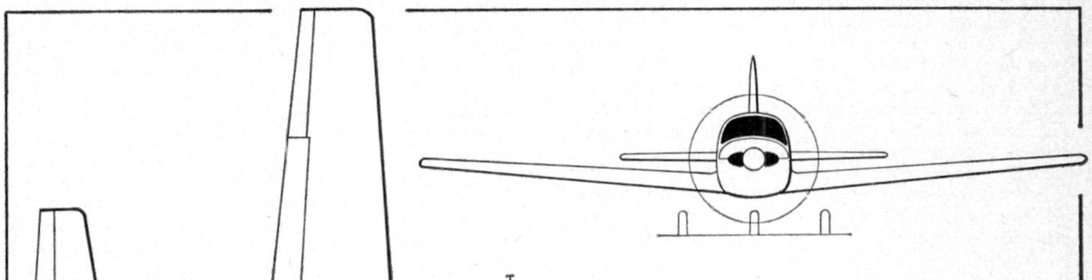

Bellanca Model 19-25 Skyrocket six-seat light aircraft (*Roy J. Grainge*)

install a 435 hp Continental engine, instead of the 400 hp Lycoming IO-720-A1A as specified originally, was expected to delay the first flight until the Autumn of 1974.

BELLANCA MODEL 19-25 SKYROCKET

Research and design of this aircraft was initiated in 1956 by the late G. M. Bellanca and his son, August T. Bellanca. Construction of a prototype began in 1962 and development and testing of this aircraft is continuing in consultation with the FAA. Complete aerodynamic testing in a 7 ft by 10 ft (2·13 m by 3·05 m) wind tunnel was completed successfully in 1967. Production tooling was 90% complete in March 1968, and the prototype was expected to fly for the first time during 1974.

The early decision to fabricate this aircraft from glassfibre composites resulted from much research and testing. Basically, the advantages are that smooth aerodynamic surfaces are obtained, together with high strength. The materials used in the Model 19-25 Skyrocket have a higher strength-to-weight ratio than aluminium, with better durability and fatigue resistance.

Type: Six-seat light cabin monoplane.

Wings: Cantilever low-wing monoplane. Laminar-flow wing section. Incidence 2°. Moulded as two half-shells, with two glassfibre spars.

Fuselage: Semi-monocoque structure of glassfibre epoxy laminate. Glassfibre stringers. Fuselage is moulded in two halves, each with an integral wing root, vertical fin half and tailplane root.

Tail Unit: Cantilever glassfibre epoxy laminated structure. Variable-incidence tailplane. No trim tabs.

Landing Gear: Retractable tricycle type, hydraulically-operated. Oleo-pneumatic shock-absorbers. Main wheels and tyres size 15 × 6·00-6.

Power Plant: One 435 hp Continental GTSIO-520-F six-cylinder horizontally-opposed air-cooled engine, flat rated to 19,000 ft (5,790 m), driving a Hartzell three-blade constant-speed propeller. Integral fuel tank in each wing, capacity 60 US gallons (227 litres). Total fuel capacity 120 US gallons (454 litres). Oil capacity 3·75 US gallons (14·2 litres).

Accommodation: Pilot and five passengers in enclosed cabin. Door on starboard side. Stowage for 200 lb (90·7 kg) of baggage.

Dimensions, external:

Wing span	35 ft 0 in (10·67 m)
Length overall	28 ft 11 in (8·81 m)
Height overall	9 ft 3 in (2·82 m)
Propeller diameter	6 ft 8 in (2·03 m)

Area:

Wings, gross	182·6 sq ft (16·96 m²)

Weights and Loadings (estimated):

Weight empty	2,150 lb (975 kg)
Max T-O weight	3,775 lb (1,712 kg)
Max wing loading	20·6 lb/sq ft (100·6 kg/m²)
Max power loading	9·5 lb/hp (4·31 kg/hp)

Performance (estimated):

Max level speed at S/L 226 knots (260 mph; 418 km/h)

Max cruising speed, 75% power at 8,000 ft (2,440 m) 215 knots (248 mph; 399 km/h)

Cruising speed, 65% power at 8,500 ft (2,590 m) 203 knots (234 mph; 377 km/h)

Stalling speed, wheels and flaps down 56·5 knots (65 mph; 105 km/h)

Max rate of climb at S/L	1,900 ft (579 m)/min
Service ceiling	26,000 ft (7,925 m)
T-O run	900 ft (274 m)
T-O to 50 ft (15 m)	1,790 ft (546 m)
Landing from 50 ft (15 m)	1,665 ft (507 m)
Landing run	790 ft (241 m)

Range, 75% power at 6,500 ft (1,980 m) 1,055 nm (1,215 miles; 1,955 km)

Range, 65% power at 8,500 ft (2,590 m) 1,270 nm (1,465 miles; 2,355 km)

BENSEN

BENSEN AIRCRAFT CORPORATION

Head Office and Works:
PO Box 2746, Raleigh-Durham Airport, Raleigh, North Carolina 27602
Telephone: (919) 787-4224/0945

President: Igor B. Bensen

The Bensen Aircraft Corporation was formed by Dr Igor B. Bensen, formerly Chief of Research of the Kaman company, to develop a series of lightweight helicopters and rotary-wing gliders suitable for production in kit form for amateur construction as well as in ready-to-fly condition.

Research into, and design of, new models was under way in early 1974, at which time Bensen production was centred on the B-8M/V and Super Bug Gyro-Copter powered autogyros, the twin-engined B-16S Gyro-Copter, the B-8MA Agricopter agricultural spraying version and various land and waterborne versions of the B-8 rotor-kite.

BENSEN MODEL B-8 GYRO-GLIDER
USAF designation: X-25

The Gyro-Glider is a simple unpowered rotor-kite which can be towed behind even a small motor car and has achieved free gliding with the towline released. It is available as either a completed aircraft or kit of parts for amateur construction. Alternatively, would-be constructors can purchase a set of plans, with building and flying instructions. No pilot's licence is required to fly it in the United States and many hundreds of kits and plans have been sold. Application has been made for an Approved Type Certificate.

The original Model B-7 Gyro-Glider was described in the 1958-59 edition of *Jane's*. It has been followed by the Model B-8, which is offered as either a single-seater or two-seater, the latter version being suitable for use as a pilot trainer.

The Model B-8 consists basically of an inverted square-section tubular aluminium T-frame structure, of which the forward arm supports the lightweight seat, towing arm, rudder bar and landing gear nosewheel. The rear arm supports a large stabilising fin and rudder, with the main landing gear wheels carried on a tubular axle near the junction of the T-frame. The free-turning two-blade rotor is universally-mounted at the top of the T-frame and is normally operated directly by a hanging-stick control. A floor-type control column is available as optional equipment. A movable rudder with pedal controls is standard.

The standard Gyro-Glider rotor is of laminated plywood construction, with steel spar. Factory-built all-metal rotor blades, and metal tail surfaces, are available as optional items.

The two-seat trainer version of the Gyro-Glider is fitted with castoring crosswind landing gear and has an extra-wide wheel track. It will maintain level flight down to 16·5 knots (19 mph; 30·5 km/h).

Under contract to the USAF, Bensen delivered a single-seat and a two-seat Gyro-Glider to the USAF Flight Dynamics Laboratory at Wright-Patterson AFB, Dayton, Ohio, where, designated X-25, they have been used to explore the feasibility of using tilting rotors on a Discretionary Descent Vehicle (DDV).

A new concept in rescue devices, the DDV would have a set of rotor blades folded into an ejection system, in addition to the normal parachute, enabling a pilot to attain any pre-selected site within gliding range.

Dimensions, external:

Diameter of rotor	20 ft 0 in (6·10 m)
Length of fuselage	11 ft 4 in (3·45 m)
Height overall	6 ft 3 in (1·90 m)

BENSEN MODEL B-8W HYDRO-GLIDER

The basic structure of this floatplane rotor-kite is similar to that of the B-8 Gyro-Glider and conversion from one to the other is simple. Main change is that the nosewheel landing gear is replaced by two floats. The original round-type floats have been superseded by flat-bottomed pontoons of polyurethane foam covered by glassfibre, which give better planing, with less spray.

The Hydro-Glider is towed by a motorboat.

Bensen Model B-8MW Hydro-Copter (72 hp McCulloch 4318E or 90 hp 4318G engine)

BENSEN MODEL B-8M, B-8V and SUPER BUG GYRO-COPTERS and B-8MW HYDRO-COPTER

First flown on 6 December 1955, the Gyro-Copter is a powered autogyro conversion of the Gyro-Glider, designed for home construction from kits or plans. When fitted with floats it is known as a Hydro-Copter.

The current **B-8M** version of the Gyro-Copter has a more powerful engine than the original B-7M and can be equipped with an optional mechanical rotor drive. By engaging this drive, the rotor can be accelerated to flying speed while the aircraft is stationary. Then, by transferring the power to the pusher propeller, it is possible to take off in only 50 ft (15 m), with the rotor autorotating normally. Alternatively, a 1 hp Ohlsson & Rice Compact III two-stroke engine can be attached to the rotor for pre-rotation, automatically disengaging itself at take-off rpm.

Other non-standard items available optionally include a 90 hp engine instead of the normal 72 hp engine, a larger-diameter rotor, an offset gimbal rotor head, a floor-type control column instead of the normal overhead type of column, dual ignition, nosewheel arrester and Bensen-manufactured pontoons of polyurethane foam covered with glassfibre. All-metal rotor blades and tail surfaces are available as alternatives to the standard wooden components.

The prototype Model B-8M Gyro-Copter flew for the first time on 8 July 1957 and the first production model on 9 October 1957.

The B-8M is roadable, requiring no removal of, or changes in, its equipment for transition from air to ground travel. The rotor is merely stopped in a fore-and-aft position by a lock. Gyro-Copters have been driven on highways and have negotiated heavy city traffic with ease in a number of public demonstrations in the USA.

The **B-8V**, which flew for the first time in the Autumn of 1967, is basically a standard B-8M, but is powered by a 1,600 cc Volkswagen engine. In unmodified form the VW1600 yields just adequate flight performance at 600 lb (272 kg) gross weight. Since Bensen engineers considered that most Gyro-Copters would not have a gross weight as high as 600 lb, the VW engine justified inclusion as an alternative power plant to the standard McCulloch engine.

Kits and parts for the B-8V, excluding engine and mounting, are available, as are plans and an instruction manual for converting the B-8M to a B-8V, or for mounting a VW engine on a standard B-8 airframe.

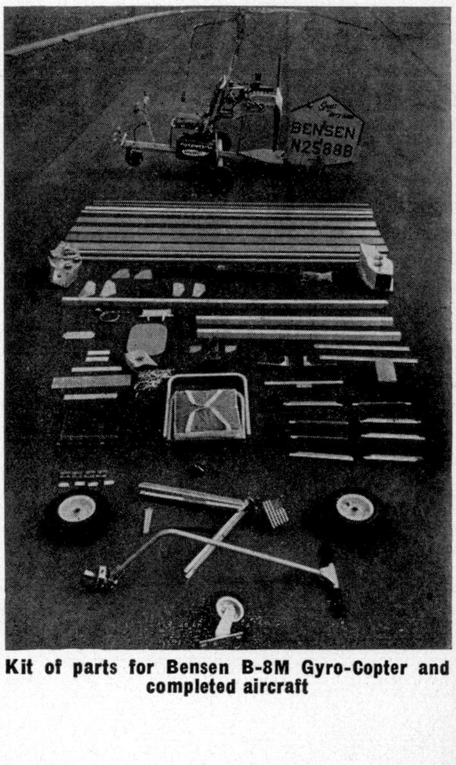

Kit of parts for Bensen B-8M Gyro-Copter and completed aircraft

In May 1971, Bensen announced introduction of the **Super Bug,** an advanced version of the standard Model B-8M. This features a twin-engine installation to spin up the rotor prior to take-off. Bensen claims this as an intermediate step towards full VTOL capability, as this more powerful pre-rotation enables the Super Bug to take off and clear a 50 ft (15 m) obstacle within 450 ft (137 m) of starting its T-O run in zero wind conditions at max T-O weight. Other new standard equipment of the Super Bug includes rotor brake, parking brake on main wheels, single control of rudder and nosewheel steering, soft suspension of the auxiliary tailwheel and an increase of 100 lb (45·5 kg) in max T-O weight.

The following description applies to the Models B-8M, B-8V and B-8MW:

TYPE: Single-seat light autogyro,

ROTOR SYSTEM: B-8M has single two-blade rotor of laminated plywood construction, with steel spar (optional all-metal rotor). Blade section Bensen G2. Teetering hub, with no lag hinges or collective pitch control. A similar rotor, of all-metal construction, is provided for the B-8V. A larger-diameter rotor is not available as an alternative for this latter model. No anti-torque rotor. Rotor speed 400 rpm.

ROTOR DRIVE (optional): An auxiliary 1 hp Ohlsson & Rice engine is available to spin up the rotor.

FUSELAGE: Square-section tubular 6061-T6 aluminium structure.

TAIL SURFACES: Vertical fin and rudder of ¼ in plywood. Optional all-metal tail surfaces.

LANDING GEAR: Non-retractable tricycle type, with auxiliary tailwheel. No shock-absorbers. Steerable nosewheel. General Tire wheels, size 12-4 in (30·5-10·15 cm). Tyre pressure 10 lb/sq in (0·70 kg/cm²). Brake on nosewheel.

POWER PLANT: One 72 hp McCulloch Model 4318E four-cylinder horizontally-opposed air-cooled two-stroke engine (or, optionally, a 90 hp McCulloch 4318G engine of similar weight and dimensions), driving a two-blade wooden fixed-pitch Aero Prop Model BA 48-A2 pusher propeller with leading-edges covered with stainless steel. Alternatively, one 64 hp Volkswagen 1,600 cc four-cylinder horizontally-opposed aircooled four-stroke engine, driving a Troyer Model 50-24-65 two-blade wooden fixed-pitch pusher propeller. Fuel tank under pilot's seat, capacity 6·0 US gallons (22·75 litres). Can be fitted with auxiliary tank for ferrying.

ACCOMMODATION: Open seat for pilot, with overhead azimuth stick and rudder pedal controls. Optional floor-type control column. Safety belt.

DIMENSIONS, EXTERNAL:

Diameter of rotor:	
standard	20 ft 0 in (6·10 m)
optional (on B-8M and B-8MW)	22 ft 0 in (6·70 m)
Rotor blade chord	7 in (18·8 cm)
Length of fuselage	11 ft 4 in (3·45 m)
Height overall	6 ft 3 in (1·90 m)
Wheel track	5 ft 0 in (1·52 m)
Propeller diameter:	
72 hp McCulloch	4 ft 0 in (1·22 m)
64 hp Volkswagen	4 ft 2 in (1·27 m)

AREAS (Standard rotor):

Rotor blade (each)	5·83 sq ft (0·54 m²)
Rotor disc	314 sq ft (29·17 m²)

WEIGHTS (Standard rotor):

Weight empty:	
B-8M	247 lb (112 kg)
B-8V	348 lb (158 kg)
Max T-O weight:	
B-8M	500 lb (227 kg)
B-8V	600 lb (272 kg)

PERFORMANCE (at max T-O weight, with standard rotor):

Max level speed at S/L:	
B-8M	74 knots (85 mph; 137 km/h)
B-8V	52 knots (60 mph; 96·5 km/h)
Max cruising speed at S/L:	
B-8M	52 knots (60 mph; 96·5 km/h)
B-8V	43 knots (50 mph; 80·5 km/h)
Econ cruising speed:	
B-8M, B-8V	39 knots (45 mph; 72·5 km/h)
Min speed in level flight:	
B-8M	13 knots (15 mph; 24 km/h)
B-8V	17·4 knots (20 mph; 32 km/h)
T-O speed at S/L:	
B-8M	17·4 knots (20 mph; 32 km/h)
B-8V	22 knots (25 mph; 40 km/h)
Landing speed:	
B-8M	6 knots (7 mph; 11·5 km/h)
B-8V	9 knots (10 mph; 16 km/h)
Max rate of climb at S/L:	
B-8M	1,000 ft (305 m)/min
B-8V	650 ft (198 m)/min
Service ceiling:	
B-8M	12,500 ft (3,800 m)
B-8V	8,000 ft (2,440 m)
T-O run, unpowered rotor, zero wind:	
B-8M	300 ft (92 m)
B-8V	400 ft (122 m)
T-O run, powered rotor, zero wind:	
B-8M	50 ft (15·2 m)
Landing run in 10 mph (16 km/h) wind:	
B-8M, B-8V	0 ft
Landing run in zero wind:	
B-8M	20 ft (6 m)
B-8V	25 ft (7·5 m)
Normal range:	
B-8M	86 nm (100 miles; 160 km)
B-8V	130 nm (150 miles; 241 km)
Ferry range:	
B-8M	260 nm (300 miles; 482 km)
B-8V	345 nm (400 miles; 643 km)
Endurance:	
B-8M	1·5 hrs
B-8V	2·25 hrs

Bensen B-8MA Agricopter with spraybooms and tail-mounted spray nozzle

Bensen Model B-16S, a development of the B-8M Gyro-Copter (two 48 hp Kiekhaefer KAM 525 snowmobile engines)

BENSEN MODEL B-8MA AGRICOPTER

Bensen announced first in 1970 the introduction of an agricultural version of the B-8M Gyro-Copter. Known as the B-8MA Agricopter, this is basically the same as the B-8M but has a 5 US gallon (19 litre) tank for chemicals mounted beneath the engine. Introduction of ultra-low-volume insecticides has made it possible for this small-capacity system to offer effective cover of an area of from 160 to 400 acres during a single 40-minute flight. When first introduced, the Agricopter had only a single spray nozzle mounted at the tip of a tail "stinger". This has been supplemented by conventional spraybooms, allowing the aircraft to apply agricultural chemicals at the low altitudes normal for a spray-control role.

First flight of the prototype was made in September 1969.

Up to the present time, the Agricopter has received FAA certification only in an Experimental (Market Survey) Category, to permit its demonstration in the US. Bensen is hoping to gain certification in four utility fields of the FAA Restricted category, namely aerial survey, aerial application, forest patrol and pipeline patrol. At the present time operators of such aircraft in the USA must hold an agricultural aircraft operator's certificate.

The description of the B-8M applies also to the Model B-8MA except in the following details:

POWER PLANT: One 90 hp McCulloch 4318G four-cylinder horizontally-opposed aircooled two-stroke engine, driving an Aerial Prop Model BA 48-A8-90 two-blade wooden fixed-pitch propeller.

DIMENSIONS, EXTERNAL:

Diameter of rotor	21 ft 8 in (6·60 m)
Length of fuselage	13 ft 3 in (4·04 m)
Propeller diameter	4 ft 0 in (1·22 m)

WEIGHT:

Max T-O and landing weight	600 lb (272 kg)

PERFORMANCE (at AUW of 500 lb; 227 kg):

As for the Model B-8M with standard rotor

BENSEN MODEL B-16S GYRO-COPTER

Latest version of the Bensen Model B-8M Gyro-Copter, the B-16S is described as the world's first flying snowmobile when equipped with skis. Basically a B-8M, it is converted to the new configuration by installation of twin Kiekhaefer snowmobile engines, and ski landing gear, a larger-diameter rotor, snow baffle on the tail, new plastics fuel tank and pipelines, gimbal head and double-tube mast.

The B-16S can be used on wheels, skis or floats, and conversion from wheel to ski landing gear can be accomplished in ten minutes. It is claimed to be particularly economical in operation, as the Kiekhaefer engines run on low-octane automobile fuel.

The description of the B-8M applies also to the B-16S, except as detailed below:

ROTOR SYSTEM: As B-8M, except rotor diameter increased. Rotor speed 380 rpm.

LANDING GEAR: Ski landing gear; optionally

wheel gear as described for the B-8M, or floats.

POWER PLANT: Two 48 hp Kiekhaefer KAM 525 snowmobile engines, mounted side by side aft of the rotor mast, each driving a two-blade wooden fixed-pitch pusher propeller. Plastics fuel tank beneath pilot's seat, capacity 6 US gallons (22·5 litres). Provision for fitting second tank of same capacity for extended range.

DIMENSIONS, EXTERNAL:
Rotor diameter 22 ft 8½ in (6·92 m)
Length overall 11 ft 7¼ in (3·54 m)
Height overall 6 ft 6 in (1·98 m)
Width, rotor blades fore and aft 5 ft 9½ in (1·77 m)

WEIGHTS:
Weight empty 450 lb (204 kg)
Max T-O weight 700 lb (317 kg)

PERFORMANCE (at max T-O weight):
Max level speed at S/L 69 knots (80 mph; 129 km/h)
Cruising speed 43·5 knots (50 mph; 80·5 km/h)
Landing speed 6 knots (7 mph; 11·5 km/h)
T-O run on skis 600 ft (183 m)
Landing run under 100 ft (30 m)
Range, standard fuel 52 nm (60 miles; 96 km)

BOEING

THE BOEING COMPANY

HEAD OFFICE:
PO Box 3707, Seattle, Washington 98124

ESTABLISHED: July 1916

CHAIRMAN OF THE BOARD AND CHIEF EXECUTIVE OFFICER:
T. A. Wilson

PRESIDENT:
Malcolm T. Stamper

SENIOR VICE-PRESIDENTS:
J. E. Prince (Administration)
H. W. Haynes (Finance)

VICE-PRESIDENTS:
Robert E. Bateman (Washington Representative)
H. K. Hebeler (Corporate Business Development)
S. M. Little (Industrial and Public Relations)
H. W. Neffner (Contracts)
B. M. Wheat (Operations Staff)
Other Vice-Presidents are listed under Divisions

TREASURER: J. B. L. Pierce

CONTROLLER: V. F. Knutzen

PUBLIC RELATIONS AND ADVERTISING DIRECTOR:
R. P. Bush

Boeing Commercial Airplane Company:

ADDRESS:
PO Box 707, Renton, Washington 98055

PRESIDENT:
E. H. Boullioun

EXECUTIVE VICE-PRESIDENT:
W. M. Maulden

VICE-PRESIDENTS:
W. W. Buckley (General Manager 707/727/737 Division)
W.L. Hamilton (Requirements and Marketing)
K. F. Holtby (General Manager 7X7 Programme)
G. D. Nible (Customer Support)
E. A. Ochel (General Manager Fabrication and Services Division)
J. E. Steiner (Programme Operations)
J. F. Sutter (General Manager 747 Division)
R. W. Welch (Finance and Contracts)
C. F. Wilde (Sales)
H. W. Withington (Engineering)

Boeing Aerospace Company:

ADDRESS:
Kent, Washington

PRESIDENT:
O. C. Boileau

VICE-PRESIDENTS:
D. A. Cole (General Manager Naval Systems Division)
D. E. Graves (Manager Aeronautical and Information Systems Division)
H. E. Hurst (Prototype Airplane Operations, Aeronautical and Information Systems Division)
J. C. Maxwell (General Manager Operations and Planning)
M. L. Pennell (Manager Exploratory Development)
B. T. Plymale (General Manager Space and Ballistic Missiles Group)
R. W. Taylor (General Manager Military Systems Group)

Wichita Division:

ADDRESS:
3801 South Oliver, Wichita, Kansas 67210

VICE-PRESIDENT AND GENERAL MANAGER:
O. H. Smith

Boeing Vertol Company:

ADDRESS:
Boeing Centre, PO Box 16858, Philadelphia, Pa, 19142

PRESIDENT:
H. N. Stuverude

VICE-PRESIDENT AND ASST GENERAL MANAGER:
C. W. Ellis

In May 1961 The Boeing Airplane Company changed its proprietary name to The Boeing Company as a recognition of the company's diversified interests. The change did not imply any decreased interest in the design and manufacture of aircraft.

On 19 December 1972 it was announced that three of the operating organisations of The Boeing Company had been designated as companies, comprising Boeing Commercial Airplane Company, Renton, Washington; Boeing Aerospace Company, Kent, Washington; and Boeing Vertol Company, Philadelphia, Pennsylvania.

The Wichita Division at Wichita, Kansas, continues modification programmes, 737 and 747 parts fabrication, research, programmes on military aircraft currently in use with the armed forces (B-52 and KC-135) and other support functions for the company. A new factory with an area of 807,300 sq ft (75,000 m²) was opened on 9 November 1971 at St James-Assiniboia Airport, near Winnipeg, to produce 747 components.

BOEING COMMERCIAL AIRPLANE COMPANY

The Boeing Commercial Airplane Company, with headquarters at the company's Renton, Washington, facility just south of Seattle, has four divisions. The 707/727/737 Division and 747 Division continue to manufacture aircraft of those series; the Fabrication and Services Division handles central fabrication services from its Auburn, Washington, plant, and other services such as CAG facilities; and the Engineering and Operations Division is responsible for such functions as technology, quality control and flight operations.

The 747 Division is at Everett, Washington, 30 miles north of Seattle; and the 707/727/737 and E and O Divisions are based at Renton.

Boeing delivered its 2,500th commercial jet transport, an Advanced 737 for Transavia of the Netherlands, on 17 May 1974.

BOEING MODEL 707

US Air Force designation: VC-137

The prototype of the Boeing Model 707 was the first jet transport to be completed and flown in the United States. It made its first flight on 15 July 1954.

Designated Model 367-80, it was built as a private venture and was used to demonstrate the potential of commercial and military developments of the design for a period of more than 15 years. During its early test programme, it was fitted with a flight refuelling boom, to prove the capability of this type of aircraft for refuelling present and future jet bombers, fighters and reconnaissance aircraft at or near their operational altitudes and speeds. As a result, a developed version was ordered in large numbers for the USAF under the designation KC-135.

Boeing announced on 25 April 1972 that the Model 367-80, widely known as the "Dash-Eighty", was to be given to the Smithsonian Institution.

On 13 July 1955 Boeing was given clearance by the USAF to build commercial developments of the prototype concurrently with the production of military KC-135 tanker-transports. These transport aircraft have the basic designations of Boeing 707 and 720, but were made available in many versions, of which a total of 892 had been sold and 880 delivered by 1 June 1974. These totals include five specially-equipped aircraft delivered to the USAF under the designations VC-137A (now VC-137B) and VC-137C, and two AWACS (Airborne Warning And Control System) aircraft which were used, under the designation EC-137D, for competitive trials of downward-looking radars. They are now being used in the next phases of the E-3A programme (which see).

The versions of the 707 available in 1974 are as follows:

707-320B Intercontinental. Development of 707-320 with four Pratt & Whitney JT3D-7 turbofan engines (each 19,000 lb; 8,618 kg st), fitted with double thrust reversers. New leading and trailing-edge flaps, low-drag wingtips and other refinements. First 707-320B flew on 31 January 1962. FAA Type Approval received on 31 May 1962, and the type entered service with Pan American in June 1962.

707-320C Convertible. Cargo or mixed cargo-passenger version of 707-320B with 91 in × 134 in (2·31 m × 3·4 m) forward cargo door and Boeing-developed cargo loading system, using pallets or containers. Cargo space comprises 7,415 cu ft (210 m³) on full upper deck and 1,700 cu ft (48 m³) in two lower-deck holds. Accommodation for up to 219 passengers. Received FAA Type Approval on 30 April 1963, and first entered service with Pan American in June 1963. Five were delivered to the Canadian Armed Forces during 1970-71 to serve as troop and staff transports and military cargo carriers. Two of these are equipped as flight refuelling tankers, utilising wingtip pods containing a hinged boom and trailing hose and drogue manufactured by Beech.

707-320C Freighter. All-cargo version of the Convertible. Passenger facilities eliminated, increasing payload by 2,736 lb (1,241 kg). The full upper deck will accommodate 7,612 cu ft (215·5 m³) of cargo, and 1,770 cu ft (50 m³) can be loaded on two lower decks. The cargo system can carry thirteen 88 in × 125 in (2·24 m × 3·68 m) or 88 in × 108 in (2·24 m × 2·74 m) "A" Type containers. There is a crew rest area aft of the flight deck.

Boeing 707-3K1C commercial transport aircraft in the insignia of Tarom

The following additional orders for the Boeing 707 have been received since the 1973-74 *Jane's* went to press:

Model 707-320

Egyptair	1	707-366C
Iraqi Airways	3	707-370C
Sudan Airways	2	707-3J8C
Unidentified operator	2	707-320C

The following description applies in general to current models of the Boeing 707:

TYPE: Four-turbofan airliner.

WINGS: Cantilever low-wing monoplane. Dihedral 7°. Incidence 2°. Sweepback at quarter-chord 35°. All-metal two-spar fail-safe structure. Centre-section continuous through fuselage. Normal outboard aileron and small inboard aileron on each wing, built of aluminium honeycomb panels. Two Fowler flaps and one fillet flap of aluminium alloy on each wing. Full-span leading-edge flaps. Four hydraulically-operated aluminium alloy spoilers on each wing, forward of flaps. Primary flying controls are aerodynamically balanced and manually-operated through spring tabs. Lateral control at low speeds by all four ailerons, supplemented by spoilers which are interconnected with the ailerons. Lateral control at high speeds by inboard ailerons and spoilers only. Operation of flaps adjusts linkage between inboard and outboard ailerons to permit outboard operation with extended flaps. Spoilers may also be used symmetrically as speed brakes. Thermal anti-icing of wing leading-edges.

FUSELAGE: All-metal semi-monocoque fail-safe structure with cross-section made up of two circular arcs of different radii, the larger above, faired into smooth-contoured ellipse.

TAIL UNIT: Cantilever all-metal structure. Anti-balance tab and trim tab in rudder. Trim and control tabs in each elevator. Electrically and manually operated variable-incidence tailplane. Powered rudder.

LANDING GEAR: Hydraulically-retractable tricycle type. Main units are four-wheel bogies which retract inward into underside of thickened wing-root and fuselage. Dual nosewheel unit retracts forward into fuselage. Landing gear doors close when legs fully extended. Gear can be extended in flight to give maximum rate of descent of 15,000 ft/min (4,570 m/min) when used in conjunction with spoilers. Boeing oleo-pneumatic shock-absorbers. Main wheels and tyres size 46 × 16. Nosewheels and tyres size 39 × 13. Tyre pressures: main wheels 180 lb/sq in (12·66 kg/cm²), nosewheels 115 lb/sq in (8·10 kg/cm²). Multi-disc brakes by Goodyear. Hydro-Aire flywheel detector type anti-skid units.

POWER PLANT: Currently four turbofan engines in pods under wings. Fuel in four main, two reserve and one centre main integral wing tanks. Total fuel capacity varies with individual model, but max standard capacity of 707-320B and -320C is 23,855 US gallons (90,299 litres). Provision for both pressure and gravity refuelling. Total oil capacity 707-320B, -320C 30 US gallons (114 litres).

ACCOMMODATION: Max accommodation for 189 economy class passengers in 707-320B. 707-320C can seat up to 219 passengers due to provision of two extra emergency exits aft of wing. Typical arrangement has 14 first class seats, a 4-seat lounge and 133 coach class seats, with four galleys and five toilets. There are two passenger doors, forward and aft on port side. Galley servicing doors forward and aft on starboard side. Baggage compartments fore and aft of wing in lower segment of fuselage below cabin floor. Entire accommodation, including baggage compartments, air-conditioned and pressurised.

SYSTEMS: Air-cycle vapour-cycle air-conditioning and pressurisation system, using three AiResearch engine-driven turbocompressors. Pressure differential 8·6 lb/sq in (0·60 kg/cm²). Hydraulic system, pressure 3,000 lb/sq in (210 kg/cm²), for landing gear retraction, nosewheel steering, brakes, flaps, flying controls and spoilers. Electrical system includes four 30kVA or 40kVA 115/200V 3-phase 400Hz AC alternators and four 75A transformer-rectifiers giving 28V DC. No APU.

ELECTRONICS AND EQUIPMENT: To customer's specification.

DIMENSIONS, EXTERNAL:

Wing span	145 ft 9 in (44·42 m)
Wing chord at root	33 ft 10·7 in (10·33 m)
Wing chord at tip	9 ft 4 in (2·84 m)
Wing aspect ratio	7·056
Length overall	152 ft 11 in (46·61 m)
Length of fuselage	145 ft 6 in (44·35 m)
Width of fuselage	12 ft 4 in (3·76 m)
Height overall	42 ft 5 in (12·93 m)
Tailplane span	45 ft 9 in (13·95 m)
Wheel track	22 ft 1 in (6·73 m)
Wheelbase	59 ft 0 in (17·98 m)
Passenger doors (each):	
Height	6 ft 0 in (1·83 m)
Width	2 ft 10 in (0·86 m)
Height to sill:	
fwd	10 ft 6 in (3·20 m)
aft	10 ft 8 in (3·25 m)
Cargo door (707-320C only):	
Height	7 ft 7 in (2·31 m)
Width	11 ft 2 in (3·40 m)
Height to sill	10 ft 6 in (3·20 m)
Forward baggage compartment door:	
Height	4 ft 2 in (1·27 m)
Width	4 ft 0 in (1·22 m)
Height to sill	5 ft 1 in (1·55 m)
Rear baggage compartment door (fwd):	
Height	4 ft 1 in (1·24 m)
Width	4 ft 0 in (1·22 m)
Height to sill	5 ft 3 in (1·60 m)
Rear baggage compartment door (aft):	
Height	2 ft 11 in (0·89 m)
Width	2 ft 6 in (0·76 m)
Height to sill	6 ft 5 in (1·96 m)

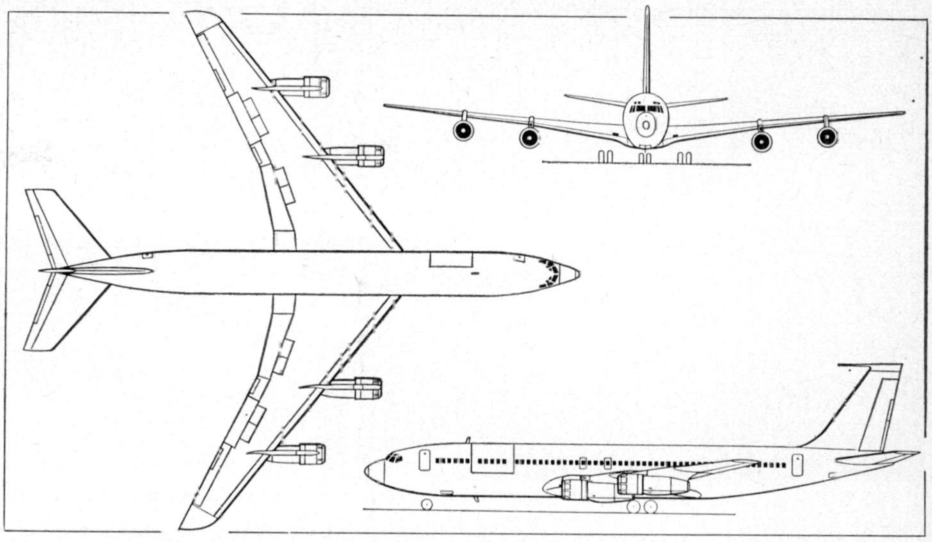

Boeing 707-320C four-turbofan passenger/cargo transport aircraft (*Pilot Press*)

DIMENSIONS, INTERNAL:

Cabin, excluding flight deck:	
Length	111 ft 6 in (33·99 m)
Max width	11 ft 8 in (3·55 m)
Max height	7 ft 7 in (2·31 m)
Floor area	1,143 sq ft (106·18 m²)
Volume:	
320B	7,983 cu ft (226 m³)
320C Convertible	8,074 cu ft (228·6 m³)
Baggage compartment (fwd):	
320B	870 cu ft (24·65 m³)
320C Convertible	835 cu ft (23·65 m³)
Baggage compartment (rear):	
320B	905 cu ft (25·62 m³)
320C Convertible	865 cu ft (24·50 m³)

AREAS:

Wings, gross	3,050 sq ft (283·4 m²)
Ailerons (total)	121 sq ft (11·24 m²)
Trailing-edge flaps (total)	476 sq ft (44·22 m²)
Leading-edge flaps	154 sq ft (14·31 m²)
Fin	328 sq ft (30·47 m²)
Rudder, including tabs	102 sq ft (9·48 m²)
Tailplane	625 sq ft (58·06 m²)
Elevators, including tabs	151 sq ft (14·03 m²)

WEIGHTS AND LOADINGS:

Basic operating weight, empty:	
320B	141,100 lb (64,000 kg)
320C (Passenger)	146,000 lb (66,224 kg)
320C (Cargo)	138,610 lb (62,872 kg)
Max payload:	
320B	53,900 lb (24,448 kg)
320C (Passenger)	84,000 lb (38,100 kg)
320C (Cargo)	91,390 lb (41,453 kg)
Max T-O weight:	
320B, 320C	333,600 lb (151,315 kg)
Max ramp weight:	
320B, 320C	336,000 lb (152,405 kg)
Max zero-fuel weight:	
320B	195,000 lb (88,450 kg)
320C	230,000 lb (104,330 kg)
Max landing weight:	
320B, 320C	247,000 lb (112,037 kg)
Max wing loading:	
320B, 320C	110·0 lb/sq ft (537·1 kg/m²)
Max power loading:	
320B, 320C	4·59 lb/lb st (4·59 kg/kg st)

PERFORMANCE (at average cruising weight. A: JT3D-3 or -3B engines; B: JT3D-7 engines):

Max never-exceed speed:	
All versions	Mach 0·95
Max level speed:	
A 320B, 320C	545 knots (627 mph; 1,010 km/h)
Max cruising speed at 25,000 ft (7,620 m):	
A 320B, 320C	521 knots (600 mph; 966 km/h)
B 320B, 320C	525 knots (605 mph; 973 km/h)
Econ cruising speed:	
A 320B, 320C	478 knots (550 mph; 886 km/h)
Stalling speed (flaps down, at max landing weight):	
A 320B, 320C	105 knots (121 mph; 195 km/h)
Max rate of climb at S/L:	
A 320B, 320C	3,550 ft (1,082 m)/min
B 320B, 320C	4,000 ft (1,219 m)/min
Service ceiling:	
A 320B, 320C	38,500 ft (11,735 m)
B 320B, 320C	39,000 ft (11,885 m)
CAR T-O to 35 ft (10·7 m):	
A 320B, 320C	10,900 ft (3,322 m)
B 320B, 320C	10,020 ft (3,054 m)
CAR landing from 50 ft (15 m):	
A 320B, 320C	6,250 ft (1,905 m)
Landing run:	
A 320B, 320C	2,575 ft (785 m)
Range with max fuel, allowances for climb and descent, no reserve:	
A 320B, 320C	6,493 nm (7,475 miles; 12,030 km)
Range with max payload, allowances for climb and descent, no reserve:	
A 320B	5,420 nm (6,240 miles; 10,040 km)
A 320C	3,735 nm (4,300 miles; 6,920 km)

BOEING MODEL 727

On 5 December 1960, Boeing announced its intention to produce a short/medium-range transport designated Boeing 727. Design work had been under way since June 1959 and component manufacture had been started in October 1960.

Simultaneously with the Boeing announcement, Eastern and United Air Lines each signed agreements to purchase 727s.

A major innovation, compared with this company's earlier designs, was the choice of a rear-engined layout, with two Pratt & Whitney JT8D turbofan engines mounted on the sides of the rear fuselage and a third at the base of the T-tail assembly.

In other respects the 727 bears a resemblance to the 707 and 720 series. It has an identical upper fuselage section and many parts and systems are interchangeable between the three types.

The 727-100, 727-100C, 727-100QC and 727-100 Business Jet versions of the Model 727 are no longer in production; details of these can be found in the 1973-74 *Jane's*. Two versions remain in production, as follows:

727-200. "Stretched" version announced on 5 August 1965 with basic accommodation for 163 passengers and maximum capacity of 189 passengers. Fuselage extended by 10 ft (3·05 m) both forward and aft of main undercarriage wheel well. Structural modification corresponding to higher loads. Revised centre engine air intake. Three JT8D-9 turbofans, each flat rated at 14,500 lb (6,577 kg) st to 84°F, are standard. Optionally, JT8D-11s rated at 15,000 lb (6,804 kg) st, JT8D-15s rated at 15,500 lb (7,030 kg) st, or JT8D-17s rated at 16,000 lb (7,257 kg) st can be fitted. Construction of the first 727-200 began in September 1966 and the first flight was made on 27 July 1967. FAA certification was awarded on 30 November 1967.

Advanced 727-200. On 12 May 1971, Boeing announced it was offering the Advanced 727-200 at 191,000 lb (86,635 kg) gross ramp weight and with sound suppression characteristics that would make this aircraft quieter than any other commercial jet transport then in use; initial deliveries of this version began in June 1972. Increased fuel capacity gives a range capability at least 694 nm (800 miles; 1,287 km) greater than that of the earlier 727-200. The interior features the "Superjet-look".

A later version, first ordered by Sterling Airways in May 1972, has Pratt & Whitney JT8D-15 engines, ramp weight of 208,000 lb (94,350 kg) and more fuel.

The following additional orders for the 727

Boeing Model 727-277 three-turbofan short/medium-range airliner in service with Ansett Airlines of Australia

series have been announced since the 1973-74 *Jane's* went to press:

Air Algérie	2	727-2D6
Air Canada	5	727-233
Alia (Jordan)	3	727-2D3
All Nippon	8	727-281
American	14	727-223
Ansett	2	727-277
Braniff	13	727-227
Condor	3	727-230
CP Air	2	727-217
Delta	14	727-232
Dominicana	1	727-51C
Eastern	2	727-225
Iberia	13	727-256
Iran	3	727-286
JAT (Yugoslavia)	6	727-2H9
Libyan Arab	3	727-200
Lufthansa	12	727-230
Mexicana	5	727-264
National Aircraft Leasing	2	727-2J7
Pacific Southwest	1	727-214
Royal Air Maroc	1	727-2B6
TAP (Portugal)	2	727-282
THY (Turkey)	4	727-2F2
Trans-Australia	2	727-276
Trans World Airlines	17	727-231
Tunis Air	2	727-2H3
Western	10	727-247

Hawker de Havilland in Australia has, since January 1972, manufactured as sole source supplier rudders and main wing ribs for the Model 727 Series 200.

A total of 1,151 727s had been sold by 1 June 1974, of which 1,038 had been delivered. The 727 is the only commercial transport aircraft to have exceeded a sales figure of one thousand.

Type: Three-turbofan airliner.

Wings: Cantilever low-wing monoplane. Special Boeing aerofoil sections. Thickness/chord ratio from 9% to 13%. Dihedral 3°. Incidence 2°. Sweepback at quarter-chord 32°. Primary structure is a two-spar aluminium alloy box with conventional ribs. Upper and lower surfaces are of riveted skin-stringer construction. There are no chordwise splices in the primary structure from the fuselage to the wingtip. Advanced 727-200s at gross weight options have modified stringers and in-spar webs, as well as upper and lower surface wing skins of increased gauge. Structure is fail-safe. Hydraulically-powered aluminium ailerons, in inboard (high speed) and outboard (low speed) units, operate in conjunction with flight spoilers. Triple-slotted trailing-edge flaps constructed primarily of aluminium and aluminium honeycomb. Four aluminium leading-edge slats on outer two-thirds of wing. Three Krueger leading-edge flaps on inboard third of wing, made from magnesium or aluminium castings. Seven aluminium (plus some magnesium) spoilers on each wing, consisting of five flight spoilers outboard and two ground spoilers inboard. Spoilers function also as airbrakes. Balance tab on each outboard aileron; control tab on each inboard aileron. Controls are hydraulically-powered dual systems with automatic reversion to manual control. Actuators manufactured primarily by Weston, National Water Lift and Bertea. Thermal anti-icing of wing leading-edges by engine bleed air.

Fuselage: Semi-monocoque fail-safe structure, with aluminium alloy skin reinforced by circumferential frames and longitudinal stringers.

Tail Unit: Cantilever structure, built primarily of aluminium alloys, with tailplane mounted near tip of fin. Dual-powered variable-incidence tailplane, with direct manual reversion. Hydraulically-powered dual elevator control system with control tab manual reversion. Hydraulically-powered rudders, utilising two main systems with backup third system for lower rudder. Anti-balance tabs; rudder trim by displacing system neutral.

Landing Gear: Hydraulically-retractable tricycle type, with twin wheels on all three units. Nosewheels retract forward, main gear inward into fuselage. Boeing oleo-pneumatic shock-absorbers. B.F. Goodrich nose-gear wheels, tyres and brakes are standard on all models. Goodrich and Bendix are both approved suppliers of main-gear wheels, tyres and brakes for all Model 727s. Nosewheels and tyres are size 32 × 11·5 Type VIII. Main-gear wheels and tyres size 49 × 17 Type VII are standard on all models, with size 50 × 21 optional on the 727-200. Increased gross weight versions of 183,000 lb (83,000 kg) and over have 50 × 21 main-wheel tyres as standard equipment.

Power Plant: Three Pratt & Whitney JT8D turbofan engines (details under individual model listings) with thrust reversers. Each has individual fuel system fed from integral tanks in wings, but all three tanks are interconnected. Optional fuselage fuel tanks can be installed, displacing forward and/or aft cargo compartment volume. Standard total fuel capacity 8,186 US gallons (30,985 litres). Modular design bladder cell tanks with dual fuel barrier can be installed to contain up to approximately 2,480 US gallons (9,387 litres). Single pressure fuelling point, rated at 600 US gallons (2,271 litres)/min, near wing leading-edge on underside of starboard wing at mid-span. Total usable oil capacity 12 US gallons (45·5 litres).

Accommodation: Crew of three on flight deck. Basic accommodation for 163 passengers, six-abreast. Max capacity 189 passengers. Two galleys forward and/or aft. One toilet forward and two aft. Other layouts to customer's specification. A "Superjet-look" passenger interior design is standard. The wide-body effect is achieved (without any change in cross-section dimensions) by lighting and architectural redesign. Retrofit kits for the "Superjet-look" are offered. Entry via hydraulically-operated integral aft stairway under centre engine and door at front on port side with optional Weber Aircraft electrically-operated airstairs. Two Type III emergency exits in mid-cabin on each side and aft service door on each side. The starboard forward service door is opposite the port forward passenger door. Two heated and pressurised baggage and freight compartments under floor, forward and aft of main landing gear bay. Each compartment has one outward-opening cargo door; a second cargo door is optional for the aft compartment.

Systems: AiResearch air-conditioning and pressurisation system, using engine bleed air combined with air-cycle refrigeration. Pressure differential 8·6 lb/sq in (0·60 kg/cm²). Three independent 3,000 lb/sq in (210 kg/cm²) hydraulic systems, utilising Boeing Material Specification BMS 3-11 hydraulic fluid, provide power for flying controls, landing gear and aft airstairs. Electrical system includes three 40kVA 400Hz constant-frequency AC generators, three 50A transformer-rectifier units, one 22Ah battery. AiResearch APU provides electrical power and compressed air for engine starting, air-conditioning and electrical systems on ground.

Electronics and Equipment: Standard equipment includes two ARINC 546 VHF communications installations, Collins selcal, flight and service attendants' interphone, passenger address system, ARINC 542 flight recorder with remote encoder, three ARINC 547 VHF navigation systems with glideslope, one ARINC 550 ADF, two ARINC 521D DME, two ARINC 532D ATC, Collins marker beacon receiver, Bendix RDR-1E X-band weather radar, Sperry SP-50 single-channel Mod. Blk. IV autopilot, two yaw dampers, two vertical gyros, two Sperry C-9D compasses, without latitude correction, ARINC 557 voice recorder, ARINC 552 radio altimeter, instrument comparison and warning system, central air data system, variable instrument switching and two Collins FD-108 flight directors (with glideslope gain programming). Optional equipment includes dual ARINC 540 and 543 Doppler, dual ARINC 552 radio altimeters, Loran, dual HF, third vertical gyro, third VHF transceiver, auto throttles, speed command, engine failure warning light and automatic bleed air shut-off, and Sperry SP-50 Mod. Blk.IV autopilot with dual pitch channels, roll monitor and flare coupler.

Dimensions, external:

Wing span	108 ft 0 in (32·92 m)
Wing chord at root	25 ft 3 in (7·70 m)
Wing chord at tip	7 ft 8 in (2·34 m)
Wing aspect ratio	7·2
Length overall	153 ft 2 in (46·69 m)
Length of fuselage	136 ft 2 in (41·51 m)
Height overall	34 ft 0 in (10·36 m)
Tailplane span	35 ft 9 in (10·90 m)
Wheel track	18 ft 9 in (5·72 m)
Wheelbase	63 ft 3 in (19·28 m)
Passenger door (ventral):	
Height	6 ft 4 in (1·93 m)
Width	2 ft 8 in (0·81 m)
Passenger door (fwd):	
Height	6 ft 0 in (1·83 m)
Width	2 ft 10 in (0·86 m)
Height to sill	8 ft 9 in (2·67 m)
Service door (each):	
Height	5 ft 0 in (1·52 m)
Width	2 ft 6 in (0·76 m)

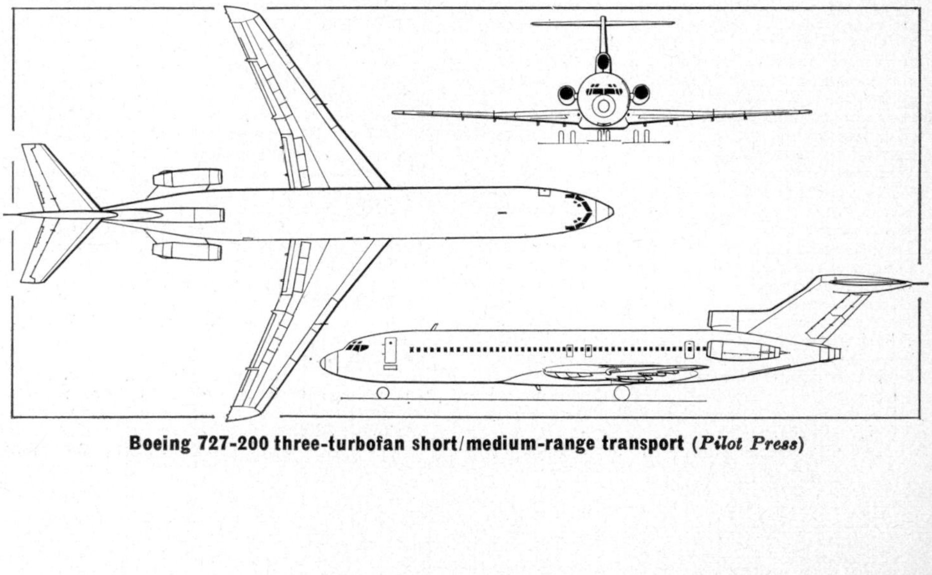

Boeing 727-200 three-turbofan short/medium-range transport (*Pilot Press*)

Baggage hold door (fwd):
Height 3 ft 6 in (1·07 m)
Width 4 ft 6 in (1·37 m)
Baggage hold door (aft):
Height 3 ft 8 in (1·12 m)
Width 4 ft 6 in (1·37 m)

DIMENSIONS, INTERNAL:
Cabin (aft of flight deck to rear pressure bulkhead):
Length 92 ft 8 in (28·24 m)
Max width 11 ft 8 in (3·55 m)
Max height:
727 standard 7 ft 2 in (2·18 m)
727 "Superjet-look" 6 ft 11 in (2·11 m)
Floor area 980 sq ft (91·05 m²)
Volume 6,652 cu ft (188·4 m³)
Baggage hold (fwd) 690 cu ft (19·54 m³)
Baggage hold (aft):
standard 795 cu ft (22·51 m³)
with optional 2nd door 745 cu ft (21·10 m³)

AREAS:
Wings, gross 1,700 sq ft (157·9 m²)
Ailerons (total) 57 sq ft (5·30 m²)
Trailing-edge flaps, retracted (total) 281 sq ft (26·10 m²)
Trailing-edge flaps, extended (total) 388 sq ft (36·04 m²)
Flight spoilers (total) 79·8 sq ft (7·41 m²)
Fin 356 sq ft (33·07 m²)
Rudder, including tabs 66 sq ft (6·13 m²)
Tailplane 376 sq ft (34·93 m²)
Elevators, including tabs 95 sq ft (8·83 m²)

WEIGHTS AND LOADINGS (A: AUW of 173,000 lb (78,470 kg), B: brake release weight of 184,800 lb (83,820 kg), C: brake release weight of 190,500 lb (86,405 kg), D: brake release weight of 207,500 lb (94,120 kg)):
Operating weight empty (basic specification):
727-200 (A) 97,591 lb (44,266 kg)
727-200 (B) 99,398 lb (45,086 kg)
727-200 (C) 100,648 lb (45,650 kg)
Operating weight empty (typical airline):
727-200 (A, B, C) 99,000 lb (44,905 kg)
Max payload (structural, based on airline operating weight empty):
727-200 (A, B) 37,000 lb (16,782 kg) or 39,000 lb (17,690 kg)
727-200 (C) 41,000 lb (18,597 kg)
Max T-O weight:
727-200 (A) 172,000 lb (78,015 kg)
727-200 (B) 184,800 lb (83,820 kg)
727-200 (C) 190,500 lb (86,405 kg)
727-200 (D) 207,500 lb (94,120 kg)
Max ramp weight:
727-200 (A) 173,000 lb (78,470 kg)
727-200 (B) 185,800 lb (84,275 kg)
727-200 (C) 191,000 lb (86,635 kg)
727-200 (D) 208,000 lb (94,350 kg)
Max zero-fuel weight:
727-200 (A) 136,000 lb (61,690 kg) or 138,000 lb (62,595 kg)
727-200 (B) 138,000 lb (62,595 kg)
727-200 (C) 140,000 lb (63,500 kg)
727-200 (D) 144,000 lb (65,315 kg)
Max landing weight:
727-200 (A) 150,000 lb (68,035 kg) or 154,500 lb (70,080 kg) or 160,000 lb (72,575 kg)
727-200 (B, C) 154,500 lb (70,080 kg) or 160,000 lb (72,575 kg)
727-200 (D) 160,000 lb (72,575 kg)
Max wing loading:
727-200 (A) 101·2 lb/sq ft (494·1 kg/m²)
727-200 (B) 108·7 lb/sq ft (530·7 kg/m²)
727-200 (C) 111·5 lb/sq ft (544·4 kg/m²)
727-200 (D) 122 lb/sq ft (595·7 kg/m²)
Max power loading:
727-200 (A) 3·9 lb/lb st (3·9 kg/kg st)
727-200 (B) 4·2 lb/lb st (4·2 kg/kg st)
727-200 (C) 4·1 lb/lb st (4·1 kg/kg st)
727-200 (D) 4·5 lb/lb st (4·5 kg/kg st)

PERFORMANCE (727-200 (B) at brake release weight of 184,800 lb (83,820 kg), 727-200 (C) at brake release weight of 190,500 lb (86,405 kg), and 727-200 (D) at brake release weight of 208,000 lb (94,120 kg), except where indicated):
Max never-exceed speed Mach 0·95
Max level speed:
727-200 (B) at 21,600 ft (6,585 m) 549 knots (632 mph; 1,017 km/h)
727-200 (C, D) at 20,500 ft (6,250 m) 539 knots (621 mph; 999 km/h)
Max cruising speed:
727-200 (B) at 22,000 ft (6,705 m) 514 knots (592 mph; 953 km/h)
727-200 (C, D) at 24,700 ft (7,530 m) 520 knots (599 mph; 964 km/h)
Econ cruising speed at 30,000 ft (9,145 m) 495 knots (570 mph; 917 km/h)
Stalling speed at S/L, flaps up:
727-200 (B) 171 knots (197 mph; 317 km/h)
Stalling speed at S/L, flaps down:
at 160,000 lb (72,575 kg) 106 knots (122 mph; 197 km/h)
Max rate of climb at S/L:
727-200 (B) 2,500 ft (762 m)/min
727-200 (C) 2,600 ft (793 m)/min
Service ceiling:
727-200 (B) 33,000 ft (10,060 m)
727-200 (C) 33,500 ft (10,210 m)
Min ground turning radius (Advanced 727-200) 80 ft 4 in (24·49 m)

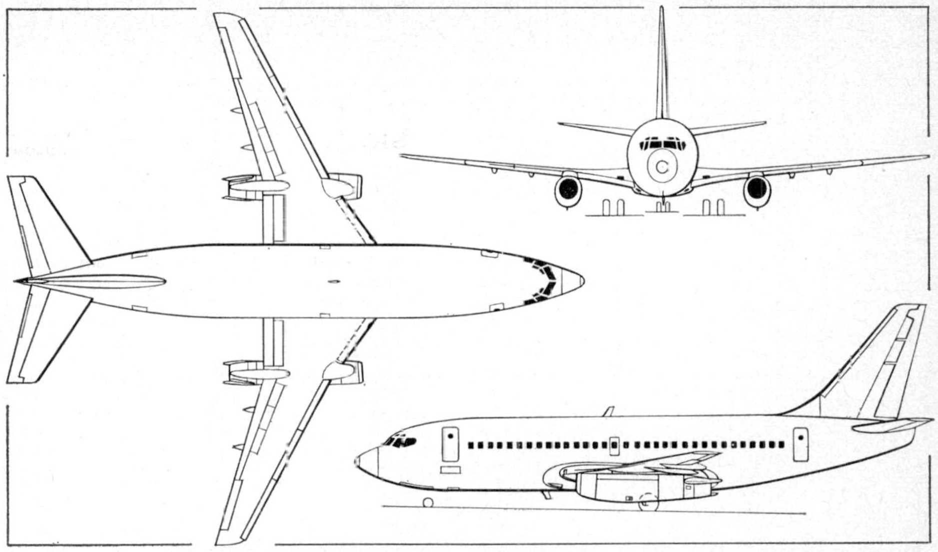

Boeing 737-200 twin-turbofan short-range transport (*Pilot Press*)

Runway LCN (Advanced 727-200) at max weight of 191,000 lb (86,635 kg), optimum tyre pressure and 20 in (50·8 cm) flexible pavement:
50 × 21 tyres 74
T-O run:
727-200 (B) 8,250 ft (2,515 m)
727-200 (C) 7,550 ft (2,301 m)
CAR T-O distance to 35 ft (10·7 m):
727-200 (B) 9,340 ft (2,847 m)
727-200 (C) 8,500 ft (2,591 m)
CAR landing distance from 50 ft (15 m):
at 160,000 lb (72,575 kg) 4,690 ft (1,430 m)
Landing run:
at 160,000 lb (72,575 kg) 2,800 ft (853 m)
Range at long-range cruising speed, with fuel and load as specified, ATA domestic reserve:
727-200 (B) with 8,986 US gallons (34,014 litres) fuel, brake release weight of 184,200 lb (83,550 kg) and payload of 25,400 lb (11,521 kg) 2,300 nm (2,645 miles; 4,260 km)
727-200 (C) with 9,786 US gallons (37,042 litres) fuel, brake release weight of 190,500 lb (86,405 kg) and payload of 26,400 lb (11,974 kg) 2,475 nm (2,850 miles; 4,585 km)
Range with max payload at long-range cruising speed, with load specified, ATA domestic reserve:
727-200 (B) at brake release weight of 184,200 lb (83,550 kg) 1,450 nm (1,670 miles; 2,685 km)
727-200 (C) at brake release weight of 190,500 lb (86,405 kg) 1,605 nm (1,845 miles; 2,970 km)
727-200 (D) at brake release weight of 207,500 lb (94,120 kg) approx 2,500 nm (2,880 miles; 4,635 km)

OPERATIONAL NOISE CHARACTERISTICS (Advanced 727-200):
T-O noise level at 3·5 nm (4 miles; 6·5 km) from start of T-O roll, at brake release weight of 190,500 lb (86,405 kg) 100 EPNdB
Approach noise level at 1 nm (1·15 miles; 1·85 km) from landing threshold on 3° glide-slope, at 154,500 lb (70,080 kg) landing weight and 30° flaps 100·4 EPNdB
Sideline noise level at 0·35 nm (0·40 miles; 0·65 km) from runway c/l 102·2 EPNdB

BOEING MODEL 737

US Air Force designation: T-43

The decision to build this short-range transport was announced by Boeing on 19 February 1965. Simultaneously, a first order for 21 aircraft was placed by Lufthansa.

Initial five versions in service are as follows:

737-100. To carry normally 103 passengers and baggage with 34 in pitch seating, or up to 115 passengers in 31 in pitch seating with no reduction in cabin facilities. JT8D-7 engines (each 14,000 lb; 6,350 kg st). Optionally JT8D-9 engines (each 14,500 lb; 6,575 kg st).

737-200. Generally similar to 737-100, but with fuselage lengthened by 6 ft 4 in (1·93 m). Accommodates normally 115 passengers and baggage with 34 in pitch seating, or up to 130 passengers in 29 in pitch seating with no reduction in cabin facilities. JT8D-9 engines standard; JT8D-15 and JT8D-17 engines optional.

737-200C. Convertible passenger/cargo version of 737-200.

737-200QC. Same as 737-200C, except that conversion is made much quicker by use of palletised passenger seats.

737-200 Business Jet. Version of the 737-200 with custom styled luxury interior. Additional fuel tankage in lower cargo compartment for extended range.

Continuous refinement of the Boeing 737 led The Boeing Company to introduce a number of improvements in stages from 1969 to 1971. The first series of modifications to improve performance was made on the production line during 1969; the second series came into effect in 1971 and further optional improvements were offered on the **Advanced Model 737-200.**

The 1969 refinements were effective from the 135th production aircraft and were concerned with improving the specific range by decreasing drag, and improving the effectiveness of the thrust reversers. Target-type reversers replaced the earlier clamshell type and this change was accompanied by a 45 in (1·14 m) aft extension of the engine pod, which helped to reduce drag. Small changes were made to the wing vortex generators, and the sealing of the lower leading-edges of the flaps and slats, when retracted, was improved. In addition to being introduced on the production line, these modifications were offered in kit form to operators of the first 134 aircraft, free of charge.

An additional change introduced on the production line at this time allows Model 737-200 aircraft to use an increased take-off flap setting of 25°, and strengthening of the flap tracks allows unrestricted use of a 40° setting for landing. Previously, Series 200 aircraft with landing weights of below 98,000 lb (44,450 kg) could not use this setting.

The three Advanced 737 versions, which became available from May 1971, permit short-field operation. Similar to earlier 737-200 series aircraft, the Advanced 737s have an improved high-lift system, comprising modified leading-edge slats, Krueger flaps and engine nacelle fairings, as well as better stopping capabilities which include automatic brakes, a changed anti-skid system and a revised metering pin in the main landing gear shock strut. In addition, Pratt & Whitney JT8D-15 turbofan engines, rated at 15,500 lb (7,030 kg) st, became available in September 1971, and JT8D-17 engines of 16,000 lb (7,255 kg) st during 1973. Introduction of these improvements allows the Advanced 737s to operate from runways as short as 4,000 ft (1,220 m). These models, the only versions of the 737 now in production, are identified as follows:

Advanced 737-200. Current standard model has max ramp weight of 116,000 lb (52,605 kg) and max T-O weight of 115,500 lb (52,390 kg), with JT8D-9 engines as standard (JT8D-15 or JT8D-17 engines optional) and basic fuel capacity of 5,151 US gallons (19,498 litres). This model accommodates normally 115 passengers and baggage, with 34 in (86 cm) pitch seating, or up to 130 passengers in 29 in (74 cm) pitch seating with no reduction in cabin facilities. A high gross weight option with a max ramp weight of 117,500 lb (53,295 kg) and max T-O weight of 117,000 lb (53,070 kg) is also available.

Boeing announced in May 1971 receipt of an $87·1 million contract from the USAF for 19 Model 737-200 aircraft, with options on 10 more, for use as **T-43A** navigation trainers. These are described separately on pages 290-291.

Advanced 737-200C/QC. Standard convertible passenger/cargo model with strengthened fuselage and floor, and a large two-position upper-deck cargo door, size 7 ft 2 in × 11 ft 2 in (2·18 m × 3·40 m). The quick-change (QC) feature allows more rapid conversion by using palletised passenger seating and other special interior furnishings. A high gross weight option with a max ramp weight of 117,500 lb (53,295 kg) and max T-O weight of 117,000 lb (53,070 kg) is also available.

Advanced 737-200 Business Jet. Same as the standard model of the 737-200, except certain airline-type furnishings are not installed, to allow post-delivery installation of luxury interior to customer's requirements. Additional fuel capacity offered by installation of fuel cells in lower cargo compartments. With max fuel this model can carry 20 passengers up to 3,475 nm (4,000 miles; 6,437 km).

The following additional orders for the Boeing 737 have been received since the 1973-74 *Jane's* went to press:

Aer Lingus	1	737-248C
Aerolineas Argentinas	4	737-287
Air Algérie	3	737-2D6C
Cruzeiro	6	737-200
DETA	1	737-2B1
Frontier	1	737-200
Indian Airlines	4	737-2A8
MAS	1	737-2H6
NAC New Zealand	1	737-222
Pacific Western	4	737-275
Sahsa	1	737-2K6
Saudia	2	737-268
Southwest	1	737-2H4
Transair	1	737-2A9
Transavia	3	737-2K2C
Varig	10	737-241
VASP	5	737-2A1
Wien Air Alaska	2	737-210C

The Model 737 was designed to utilise many components and assemblies already in production for the Boeing 727. Design work began on 11 May 1964, and the first Model 737 flew for the first time on 9 April 1967. Deliveries began before the end of 1967, following FAA certification on 15 December. Sales of the 737 totalled 414 on 14 June 1974, of which 357 had been delivered.

Boeing developed a gravel runway kit for the Model 737, and obtained FAA certification for operation of this aircraft from unpaved or gravel runways.

The kit includes a vortex dissipator for each engine, which consists of a short hollow boom protruding from under each engine's forward edge. The boom is capped by a plug with downward-facing orifices. Pressurised engine bleed air forced through these orifices destroys any ground-level vortex and prevents small pieces of gravel being ingested by the engines. Other items include a gravel deflection "ski" on the nosewheel, deflectors between the main landing gear wheels, protective shields over hydraulic tubing and speed brake cable on the main gear strut, glassfibre reinforcement of lower inboard flap surfaces, application of Teflon-base paint to fuselage and wing undersurfaces and provision of more robust DME, ATC and VHF antennae and a retractable rotating beacon on the lower fuselage.

TYPE: Twin-turbofan short-range transport.

WINGS: Cantilever low-wing monoplane. Special Boeing wing sections. Average thickness/chord ratio 12·89%. Dihedral 6°. Incidence 1° at root. Sweepback at quarter-chord 25°. Aluminium alloy dual-path fail-safe two-spar structure. Ailerons of aluminium honeycomb construction. Boeing-developed triple-slotted trailing-edge flaps, all of aluminium with trailing-edges of aluminium honeycomb. Aluminium alloy Krueger flaps on leading-edge, inboard of nacelles. Three leading-edge slats of aluminium alloy with aluminium honeycomb trailing-edge on each wing from engine to wingtip. Two-section aluminium honeycomb flight spoilers on each outer wing serve as both airbrakes in the air and for lateral control, in association with ailerons. Two section aluminium honeycomb ground spoilers on each wing, inboard of engine, are used only during landing. Ailerons are hydraulically powered by two hydraulic systems with manual reversion. Trailing-edge flaps are hydraulically powered, with electrical backup. Leading-edge slats and Krueger flaps are symmetrically powered by two hydraulic systems each. Flight spoilers are symmetrically powered by the two main individual hydraulic systems. Engine bleed air for anti-icing supplied to engine nose cowls and all wing leading-edge slats.

FUSELAGE: Aluminium alloy semi-monocoque fail-safe structure.

TAIL UNIT: Cantilever aluminium alloy multi-spar structure. Variable-incidence tailplane. Elevator has dual hydraulic power, with manual reversion. Rudder is powered by a dual actuator from two main hydraulic systems, with a standby hydraulic actuator and system. Tailplane trim has dual electric drive motors, with manual backup. Elevator control tabs for manual reversion are locked out during hydraulic actuation.

LANDING GEAR: Hydraulically-retractable tricycle type, with free-fall extension. Nosewheels retract forward, main units inward. No main gear doors: wheels form wheel-well seal. Twin wheels on each main and nose unit. Boeing oleo-pneumatic shock-absorbers. Main wheels and tyres size 40 × 14 (low-pressure 40 × 18-17 tyres, or 40 × 14-21 cantilever tyres with heavy-duty wheel brakes, are available optionally. Nosewheels and tyres size 24 × 7·7 (low pressure 24·5 × 8·5 tyres available optionally). Bendix multi-disc brakes. Hydro-Aire Mk III anti-skid units standard.

POWER PLANT: Two Pratt & Whitney JT8D turbofan engines (details under individual model listings), in underwing pods. High-performance target-type thrust reversers installed on all aircraft delivered after February 1969, in place of a thrust reverser of earlier design. High gross weight models have fuel capacity of up to 5,151 US gallons (19,498 litres), by utilising integral fuel cells in wing centre-section, as well as standard two integral wing tanks and centre wing cells. Single-point pressure refuelling through leading-edge of starboard wing. Fuelling rate 300 US gallons (1,135 litres)/min. Auxiliary overwing fuelling points. Total oil capacity 11 US gallons (41·5 litres).

ACCOMMODATION: Crew of two side by side on flight deck. Details of passenger accommodation given under individual model descriptions. Passenger versions are equipped with forward airstair; an aft airstair is optional. Convertible passenger/cargo versions have the aft airstair as standard and forward airstair optional. One plug-type door at each corner of cabin, of which passenger doors are on port side and service doors on starboard side. Overwing escape hatches on each side. Basic passenger cabin has two lavatories aft and two galleys forward, opposite passenger door, or lavatories and galleys forward and aft. Flexibility is provided for a large variety of interior arrangements. Freight holds forward and aft of wing, under floor.

SYSTEMS: Air-conditioning and pressurisation system utilises engine bleed air. Max differential 7·5 lb/sq in (0·53 kg/cm²). Two independent hydraulic systems, using fire-resistant hydraulic fluid, for flying controls, flaps, slats, landing gear, nosewheel steering and brakes; pressure 3,000 lb/sq in (210 kg/cm²). No pneumatic system. Electrical supply provided by engine-driven generators. AiResearch APU for air supply and electrical power in flight and on the ground, as well as engine starting.

ELECTRONICS AND EQUIPMENT: Equipment to satisfy FAA category II low weather minimum criteria is standard. Autopilot, specially designed for ILS localiser and glideslope control, features control wheel steering.

DIMENSIONS, EXTERNAL:

Wing span	93 ft 0 in (28·35 m)
Wing chord at root	15 ft 5·6 in (4·71 m)
Wing chord at tip	5 ft 3 in (1·60 m)
Wing aspect ratio	8·83
Length overall	100 ft 0 in (30·48 m)
Length of fuselage	96 ft 11 in (29·54 m)
Height overall	37 ft 0 in (11·28 m)
Tailplane span	36 ft 0 in (10·97 m)
Wheel track	17 ft 2 in (5·23 m)
Wheelbase	37 ft 4 in (11·38 m)
Main passenger door (port, front):	
Height	6 ft 0 in (1·83 m)
Width	2 ft 10 in (0·86 m)
Height to sill	8 ft 7 in (2·62 m)
Passenger door (port, rear):	
Height	6 ft 0 in (1·83 m)
Width	2 ft 6 in (0·76 m)
Width with airstair	2 ft 10 in (0·86 m)
Height to sill	8 ft 11 in (2·72 m)
Galley service door (stbd, front):	
Height	5 ft 5 in (1·65 m)
Width	2 ft 6 in (0·76 m)
Height to sill	8 ft 7 in (2·62 m)
Service door (stbd, rear):	
Height	5 ft 5 in (1·65 m)
Width	2 ft 6 in (0·76 m)
Height to sill	8 ft 11 in (2·72 m)
Freight hold door (stbd, fwd):	
Height	4 ft 3 in (1·30 m)
Width	4 ft 0 in (1·22 m)
Height to sill	4 ft 3 in (1·30 m)
Freight hold door (stbd, rear):	
Height	4 ft 0 in (1·22 m)
Width	4 ft 0 in (1·22 m)
Height to sill	4 ft 9 in (1·45 m)

DIMENSIONS, INTERNAL:

Cabin, including galley and toilet:	
Length	68 ft 6 in (20·88 m)
Max width	11 ft 6½ in (3·52 m)
Max height	7 ft 2 in (2·18 m)
Floor area	687 sq ft (63·8 m²)
Volume	4,636 cu ft (131·28 m³)
Freight hold (fwd) volume	370 cu ft (10·48 m³)
Freight hold (rear) volume	505 cu ft (14·30 m³)

AREA:

Wings, gross	980 sq ft (91·05 m²)

WEIGHTS AND LOADINGS (at brake release weight of 115,500 lb; 52,390 kg):

Operating weight empty:	
737-200	60,210 lb (27,310 kg)
737-200C all passenger	63,110 lb (28,625 kg)
737-200C all cargo	60,650 lb (27,510 kg)
737-200QC all passenger	66,000 lb (29,937 kg)
737-200QC all cargo	61,650 lb (27,964 kg)
737 Business Jet	62,500 lb (28,350 kg)
Max payload:	
737-200	34,790 lb (15,780 kg)
737-200C all passenger	31,890 lb (14,465 kg)
737-200C all cargo	34,350 lb (15,580 kg)
737-200QC all passenger	29,000 lb (13,154 kg)
737-200QC all cargo	33,350 lb (15,127 kg)
737 Business Jet	5,000 lb (2,267 kg)
Max T-O weight:	
All models	115,500 lb (52,390 kg)
Max ramp weight:	
All models	116,000 lb (52,615 kg)
Max zero-fuel weight:	
All models	95,000 lb (43,091 kg)
Max landing weight:	
All models	103,000 lb (46,720 kg)
Max wing loading:	
All models	117·9 lb/sq ft (575·6 kg/m²)
Max power loading:	
All models	3·72 lb/lb st (3·72 kg/kg st)

PERFORMANCE (ISA, with JT8D-9 engines):

Max never-exceed speed, all models, at 20,000 ft (6,100 m) 545 knots (628 mph; 1,010 km/h)

Max level speed, all models, at 23,500 ft (7,165 m) 509 knots (586 mph; 943 km/h)

Max cruising speed, 737-200 at an average cruise weight of 90,000 lb (40,823 kg) at 22,600 ft (6,890 m) 500 knots (576 mph; 927 km/h)

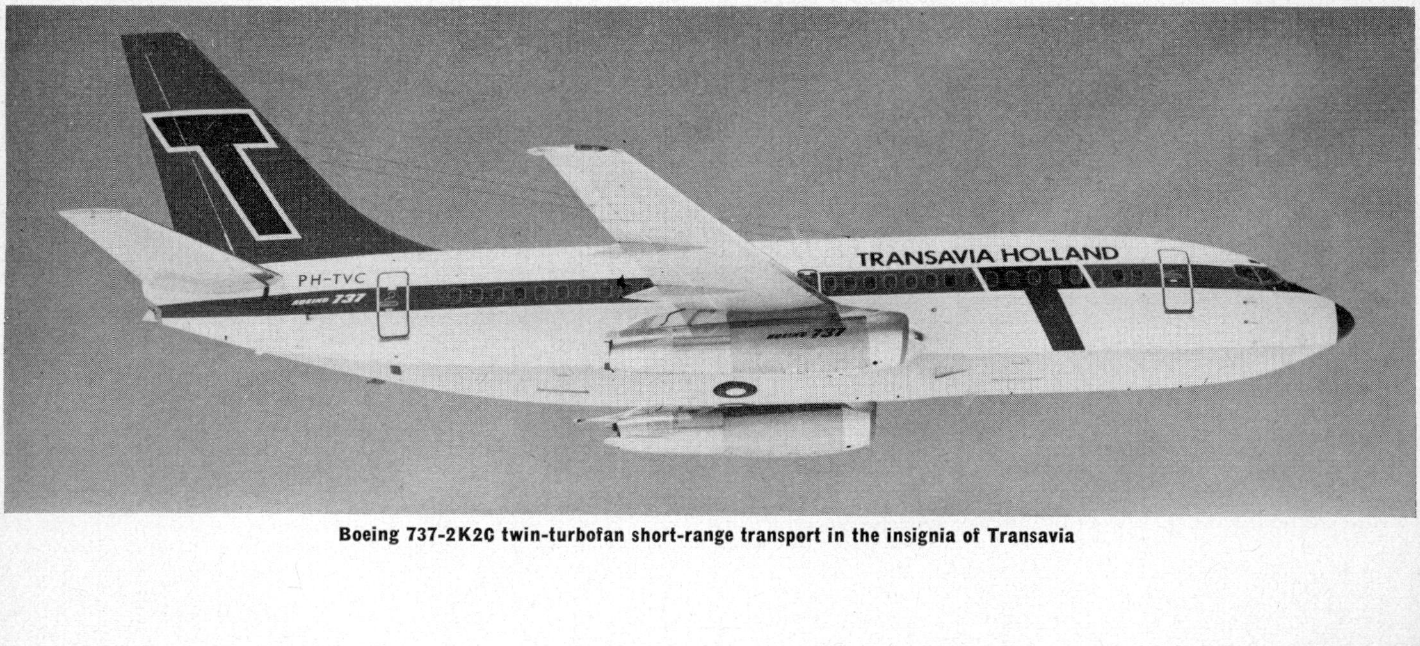

Boeing 737-2K2C twin-turbofan short-range transport in the insignia of Transavia

JA8117, the first Boeing 747SR-46 short-range version of the 747 for Japan Air Lines

Econ cruising speed at 30,000 ft (9,145 m) Mach 0·78
Stalling speed, flaps down, at max landing weight 97 knots (111 mph; 179 km/h)
Rate of climb at S/L, all models, at 100,000 lb (45,355 kg) AUW 3,760 ft (1,146 m)/min
Runway LCN (Advanced 737-200 at max taxi weight of 116,000 lb; 52,615 kg, optimum tyre pressure and 20 in flexible pavement):
- 40 × 14-16 tyres 52
- 40 × 14-21 tyres 52
- 40 × 18-17 tyres 37

FAR T-O distance to 35 ft (10·7 m), 737-200 at 109,000 lb (49,435 kg) AUW:
- JT8D-9 engines 6,700 ft (2,040 m)
- JT8D-17 engines 5,300 ft (1,615 m)

FAR landing distance from 50 ft (15 m), 737-200 at max landing weight 4,300 ft (1,310 m)
Minimum ground turning radius 56 ft 5 in (17·20 m)
Range with max fuel, cruising at 30,000 ft (9,145 m), including reserves for 174 nm (200 miles; 321 km) flight to alternate airport and 45 min continued cruise, 737-200 at 116,000 lb (52,615 kg) taxi weight with 107 passengers 2,200 nm (2,530 miles; 4,075 km)
Range with max payload, conditions as above, 737-200 with 115 passengers 2,060 nm (2,370 miles; 3,815 km)

Operational Noise Characteristics (Advanced 737-200 with JT8D-9 engines and nacelle acoustic treatment, per FAR 36 regulations):
- T-O, at 115,500 lb (52,390 kg) brake release weight 95·3 EPNdB
- Sideline, at 115,500 lb (52,390 kg) brake release weight 100·6 EPNdB
- Approach, at 103,000 lb (46,720 kg) max landing weight 102·4 EPNdB

BOEING MODEL 747

USAF designation: E-4

First details of this very large commercial transport were announced on 13 April 1966, simultaneously with the news that Pan American World Airways had placed a $525 million contract for 25 Boeing 747s, including spares.

There was no prototype and the first 747 was rolled out from the factory on 30 September 1968, making its first flight on 9 February 1969 from Paine Field, 20 miles north of Seattle. The certification flight test programme was completed and FAA certification granted on 30 December 1969. More than 1,400 flight test hours were flown by five 747s at several test sites, including Boeing Field, adjacent to the company's headquarters in Seattle; Grant County Airport, Eastern Washington; Roswell, New Mexico; and Edwards AFB, California.

The first 747 to be delivered was received by Pan American late in 1969, and this company inaugurated commercial service with the type on its New York/London route on 22 January 1970. Orders for the seven basic versions of the 747 totalled 276 by 10 July 1974, by which date 236 had been delivered.

Boeing announced that by 1 May 1974 more than 63 million passengers had been carried in 747s, that flight hours had exceeded 2·0 million and that the airliners had flown more than 1,001 million miles (1,611 million km).

The initial version of the 747-100 had a max gross ramp weight of 713,000 lb (323,400 kg), with a max T-O weight of 710,000 lb (322,050 kg). A version is now available at a max taxi weight of 738,000 lb (334,750 kg) and a max T-O weight of 735,000 lb (333,390 kg).

In late November 1968, Boeing announced the Model 747-200B, with a max T-O weight of 775,000 lb (351,540 kg), and this is being produced in passenger, freighter (747F) and convertible (747C) versions. Versions of the Boeing 747 are, therefore, available as follows:

747-100. Two versions, each of which seats up to 500 passengers. Typical configuration accommodates 48 first class and 337 tourist passengers. Versions with max taxi weights of 713,000 lb (323,400 kg) and 738,000 lb (334,750 kg) are available.

747SP. Lighter-weight derivative of the 747-100, designed for longer range/lower density routes. Described separately.

747SR. This short-range version of the 747-100 embodies structural changes required for high take-off and landing cycles. The purchase of four 747SRs by Japan Air Lines was announced on 30 October 1972, and these aircraft have max taxi weights of 603,000 lb (273,515 kg) and 523,000 lb (237,230 kg). The first delivery of this version was made during September 1973.

747-200B. Passenger version, with same accommodation as 747-100. Increased max T-O weight of 775,000 lb (351,540 kg) and increased fuel capacity. Available now with 48,570 lb (22,030 kg) st JT9D-7A engines and max T-O weight of 785,000 lb (356,070 kg).

747-200C. A version of the 747-200B which can be converted from all-passenger to all-cargo, or a combination of both. The first 747-200C was delivered to World Airways in April 1973.

747-200F. Freighter version, capable of delivering 200,000 lb (90,720 kg) of palletised cargo over a range of 3,744 nm (4,312 miles; 6,940 km). Certification of the first 747-200F, which is described separately, was awarded by the FAA on 7 March 1972.

747-200B(CF6). Passenger version, similar to the 747-200B, but with General Electric CF6-50E turbofan engines, each of 52,500 lb (23,810 kg) st. Max T-O weight increased to 800,000 lb (362,870 kg). In a collaborative programme with General Electric Company, Boeing re-engined the original 747 development aircraft experimentally with four CF6-50 turbofans. The aircraft flew for the first time with its new power plant on 26 June 1973 and completed the planned 129 hr 18 min of testing in February 1974. During these flights, it reached a maximum speed of Mach 0·97, a maximum altitude of 45,200 ft (13,775 m), and took off at weights up to 720,000 lb (326,590 kg). Final certification was anticipated by October 1974.

747-200C(CF6). Version of the 747-200B(CF6) which can be converted from all-passenger to all-cargo configuration, or to a combination of both.

747-200F(CF6). Freighter version of the 747-200B(CF6), described separately.

The Advanced Airborne Command Post version of the 747, developed for the USAF as the Boeing **E-4**, is described separately.

Orders announced by 1 July 1974 for various versions of the Model 747 were as follows:

Air Canada	5	747-133
Air Canada	1	747-233B
Air France	14	747-128
Air France	1	747-228F
Air-India	4	747-237B
Alitalia	2	747-143
Alitalia	3	747-243B
American Airlines	16	747-123
Braniff	1	747-127
British Airways	17	747-136
CP Air	4	747-217B
Condor	2	747-230B
Continental	4	747-124
Delta Air Lines	5	747-132
Eastern Air Lines	4	747-131
El Al	3	747-258B
Iberia	2	747-156
Iberia	1	747-256B
Iran Air	3	747SP-86
Irish International	2	747-148
Japan Air Lines	8	747-146
Japan Air Lines	12	747-246B
Japan Air Lines	7	747SR-46
Japan Air Lines	1	747-246F
KLM	7	747-206B
Korean Air Lines	2	747-2B5B
Lufthansa	3	747-130
Lufthansa	2	747-230B
Lufthansa	1	747-230F
Middle East Airlines	3	747-200B
National Airlines	2	747-135
Northwest Orient	10	747-151
Northwest Orient	5	747-251B
Olympic Airways	2	747-284B
Pan American	33	747-121
Pan American	5	747SP-21
Qantas	11	747-238B
SAS	2	747-283B
Sabena	2	747-129
Seaboard World	3	747-245F
Singapore	4	747-212B
South African Airways	5	747-244B
South African Airways	3	747SP-44
Swissair	2	747-257B
TAP Portugal	4	747-282B
TWA	15	747-131
USAF	4	747-E4A
United Air Lines	18	747-122
Wardair	1	747-1D1
World Airways	3	747-273C

The following details apply specifically to the basic Model 747 passenger airliner:

Type: Four-turbofan heavy commercial transport.

Wings: Cantilever low-wing monoplane. Special Boeing wing sections. Thickness/chord ratio 13·44% inboard, 7·8% at mid-span, 8% outboard. Dihedral 7°. Incidence 2°. Sweepback 37° 30′ at quarter-chord. Aluminium alloy dual-path fail-safe structure. Low-speed outboard ailerons; high-speed inboard ailerons. Triple-slotted trailing-edge flaps. Six aluminium honeycomb spoilers on each wing, comprising four flight spoilers outboard and two ground spoilers inboard. Ten variable-camber leading-edge flaps outboard and three-section Krueger flaps inboard on each wing leading-edge. All controls fully powered.

Fuselage: Conventional semi-monocoque structure, consisting of aluminium alloy skin, longitudinal stiffeners and circumferential frames. Structure is of fail-safe design, utilising riveting, bolting and structural bonding.

Tail Unit: Cantilever aluminium alloy dual-path fail-safe structure. Variable-incidence tailplane. No trim tabs. All controls fully powered.

Landing Gear: Hydraulically-retractable tricycle type. Twin-wheel nose unit retracts forward. Main gear comprises four four-wheel bogies: two, mounted side by side under fuselage at wing trailing-edge, retract forward; two mounted under wings retract inward. Cleveland Pneumatic oleo-pneumatic shock-absorbers. All 18 wheels and tubeless tyres of model 747-100 are size 46 × 16 Type VII. Tyre pressure: main wheels 204 lb/sq in (14·34 kg/cm²), nosewheels 165 lb/sq in (11·6 kg/cm²). Main wheels and tyres size 49 × 17 on 747-200B model, pressure 185 lb/sq in (13·0 kg/cm²). Disc brakes on all main wheels, with individually-controlled anti-skid units.

Power Plant: Four Pratt & Whitney JT9D turbofan engines in pods pylon-mounted on wing leading-edges. All current versions of the 747 are structurally capable of accepting JT9D-3, JT9D-3W, JT9D-7, JT9D-7A, JT9D-7AW or JT9D-7W turbofan engines and have QEC capability. Corresponding thrust for the above engines is 43,500, 45,000, 45,500, 46,950, 48,570 and 47,000 lb (19,730, 20,410, 20,635, 21,296, 22,030 and 21,320 kg). The General Electric CF6-50E turbofan engine, rated at 52,500 lb (23,813 kg) st, can also be installed in the 747-200 models. Fuel in seven integral tanks. Capacity of centre wing tank varies according to version: 747-100 12,890 US gallons (48,790 litres); 747-200B and 747-200F 16,680 US gallons (63,139 litres). Remaining tanks common to all versions: two inboard main tanks, each 12,240 US gallons (46,333 litres); two outboard main tanks, each 4,420 US gallons (16,731 litres); two outboard reserve tanks, each 500 US gallons (1,892 litres). Total capacity 747-100 47,210 US gallons (178,702 litres); 747-200B and 747-200F 51,000 US gallons (193,051 litres). Refuelling point on each wing between inboard and outboard engines. Total usable oil capacity 5 US gallons (19 litres).

ACCOMMODATION: Normal operating crew of three, on flight deck above level of main deck. Observer station and provision for second observer station are provided. Basic accommodation for 385 passengers, made up of 48 first class, which includes a 16-passenger upper deck lounge, and 337 economy class. Alternative layouts accommodate 447 economy class passengers in nine-abreast seating or 500 ten-abreast. All versions have two aisles. Five passenger doors on each side, of which two forward of wing on each side are normally used. Freight holds under floor, forward and aft of wing, with doors on starboard side. One door on forward hold, two on rear hold. Aircraft is designed for fully-mechanical loading of baggage and freight. An optional side cargo door is available for both passenger and freighter versions of the Model 747. Installed aft of door 4 on the port side of the fuselage, it provides a clear opening 11 ft 2 in (3·40 m) wide and 10 ft 0 in (3·05 m) in height. This door makes it possible to carry main-deck cargo on passenger versions. Addition of this door to the freighter makes available an extra 2,500 cu ft (70·78 m³) of cargo space aft of the flight deck, and also makes possible simultaneous nose and side cargo handling.

SYSTEMS: Air-cycle air-conditioning system. Pressure differential 8·9 lb/sq in (0·63 kg/cm²). Electrical supply from four aircooled 60kVA generators mounted one on each engine. Two 60kVA generators (supplemental cooling allows 90kVA each) mounted on APU for ground operation and to supply primary electrical power when engine-mounted generators are not operating. Three-phase 400Hz constant-frequency AC generators, 115/200V output. 28V DC power obtained from transformer-rectifier units. 24V 30Ah nickel-cadmium battery for selected ground functions and as in-flight backup. Gas-turbine APU for pneumatic and electrical supplies.

ELECTRONICS AND EQUIPMENT: Standard avionics include two ARINC 566 VHF communications systems, two ARINC 566 satellite communications systems, ARINC 531 selcal, two ARINC 547 VOR/ILS navigation systems, two ARINC 550 ADF, marker beacon, two ARINC 521D DME, two ARINC 532D ATC, two ARINC 552 low-range radio altimeters, two ARINC 564 weather radar units, two ARINC 561 inertial navigation systems, two heading reference systems, ARINC 412 interphone, passenger address system, passenger entertainment system, ARINC 573 flight recorder, ARINC 557 cockpit voice recorder, integrated electronic flight control system to provide automatic stabilisation, path control and pilot assist functions for category II and III landing conditions, two ARINC 565 central air data systems, stall warning system, central instrument warning system, attitude and navigation instrumentation, and standby attitude indication. Provision for two ARINC 533A HF communications systems.

DIMENSIONS, EXTERNAL:
Wing span 195 ft 8 in (59·64 m)
Wing chord at root 54 ft 4 in (16·56 m)
Wing chord at tip 13 ft 4 in (4·06 m)
Wing aspect ratio 6·96
Length overall 231 ft 4 in (70·51 m)
Length of fuselage 225 ft 2 in (68·63 m)
Height overall 63 ft 5 in (19·33 m)
Tailplane span 72 ft 9 in (22·17 m)
Wheel track 36 ft 2 in (11·02 m)
Wheelbase 83 ft 11½ in (25·59 m)
Passenger doors (ten, each):
Height 6 ft 4 in (1·93 m)
Width 3 ft 6 in (1·07 m)
Height to sill approx 16 ft 0 in (4·88 m)
Baggage door (front hold):
Height 5 ft 8 in (1·73 m)
Width 8 ft 8 in (2·64 m)
Height to sill approx 8 ft 8 in (2·64 m)
Baggage door (forward door, aft hold):
Height 5 ft 8 in (1·73 m)
Width 8 ft 8 in (2·64 m)
Height to sill approx 8 ft 10 in (2·69 m)
Bulk loading door (rear door on aft hold):
Height 4 ft 0 in (1·22 m)
Width 3 ft 8 in (1·12 m)
Height to sill approx 9 ft 6 in (2·90 m)
Optional cargo door (port):
Height 10 ft 0 in (3·05 m)
Width 11 ft 2 in (3·40 m)

DIMENSIONS, INTERNAL:
Cabin, including toilets and galleys:
Length 185 ft 0 in (56·39 m)
Max width 20 ft 0 in (6·10 m)
Max height 8 ft 4 in (2·54 m)

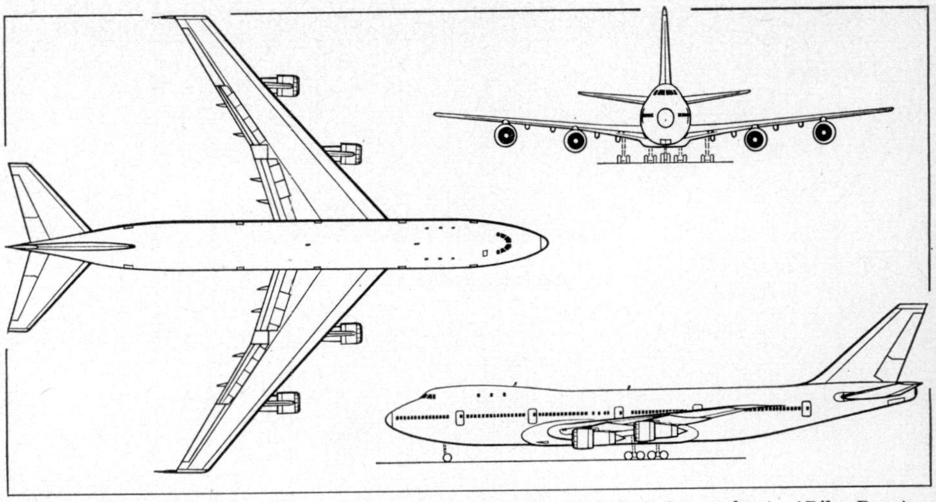

Boeing 747 heavy transport aircraft (four Pratt & Whitney JT9D turbofan engines) (*Pilot Press*)

Floor area, passenger deck 3,529 sq ft (327·9 m²)
Volume, passenger deck 27,860 cu ft (789 m³)
Baggage hold (fwd, containerised) volume 2,768 cu ft (78·4 m³)
Baggage hold (aft, containerised) volume 2,422 cu ft (68·6 m³)
Bulk volume 1,000 cu ft (28·3 m³)

AREAS:
Wings, reference area 5,500 sq ft (511 m²)
Ailerons (total) 222 sq ft (20·6 m²)
Trailing-edge flaps (total) 847 sq ft (78·7 m²)
Leading-edge flaps (total) 518 sq ft (48·1 m²)
Spoilers (total) 331 sq ft (30·8 m²)
Fin 830 sq ft (77·1 m²)
Rudder 247 sq ft (22·9 m²)
Tailplane 1,470 sq ft (136·6 m²)
Elevators 350 sq ft (32·5 m²)

WEIGHTS (Weights given for the 747-100, 747-200B, 747-200C, 747-200F and 747SR are for aircraft fitted with JT9D-7A engines without water injection. Versions of the 747-100, 747-200B, 747-200C and 747-200F are available with water injection, which increases the operating weight empty by approximately 500 lb (227 kg). 747-100(W) and 747-100(X) denote respectively the versions with max ramp weight of 713,000 lb and 738,000 lb; 747SR(Y) and 747SR(Z) denote respectively the versions with max ramp weight of 523,000 lb and 603,000 lb):
Operating weight, empty:
747-100 (W) 354,224 lb (160,673 kg)
747-100 (X) 354,382 lb (160,744 kg)
747SR 345,405 lb (156,673 kg)
747-200B, basic 363,068 lb (164,684 kg)
747-200C, all-passenger 375,128 lb (170,155 kg)
747-200C, all-cargo 335,018 lb (151,961 kg)
747-200B(CF6), basic 367,672 lb (166,773 kg)
747-200C(CF6), all-passenger 379,327 lb (172,060 kg)
747-200C(CF6), all-cargo 343,028 lb (155,594 kg)
Max payload:
747-100 (W) 172,276 lb (78,143 kg)
747-100 (X) 172,118 lb (78,071 kg)
747SR (Y) 129,595 lb (58,783 kg)
747SR (Z) 139,595 lb (63,319 kg)
747-200B, basic 163,432 lb (74,131 kg)
747-200C, all-passenger 151,372 lb (68,661 kg)
747-200C, all-cargo 254,982 lb (115,657 kg)
747-200B(CF6), basic 158,828 lb (72,043 kg)
747-200C(CF6), all-passenger 147,173 lb (66,756 kg)
747-200C(CF6), all-cargo 246,972 lb (112,024 kg)
Max T-O weight:
747-100 (W) 710,000 lb (322,050 kg)
747-100 (X) 733,000 lb (332,480 kg)
747SR (Y) 520,000 lb (235,865 kg)
747SR (Z) 600,000 lb (272,155 kg)
*747-200B, basic 775,000 lb (351,530 kg)
*747-200C, both versions 775,000 lb (351,530 kg)
747-200B(CF6), basic 800,000 lb (362,870 kg)
747-200C (CF6), both versions 800,000 lb (362,870 kg)
**optionally* 785,000*lb* (356,070*kg*) *since May* 1973
Max ramp weight:
747-100 (W) 713,000 lb (323,400 kg)
747-100 (X) 738,000 lb (334,750 kg)
747SR (Y) 523,000 lb (237,225 kg)
747SR (Z) 603,000 lb (273,515 kg)
747-200B, C 778,000 lb (352,895 kg)
747-200B, C(CF6) 803,000 lb (364,230 kg)
Max zero-fuel weight:
747-100 (W, X), 747-200B 526,500 lb (238,815 kg)
747SR (Y) 475,000 lb (215,455 kg)
747SR (Z) 485,000 lb (219,990 kg)
747-200C, 747-200C(CF6), all-passenger 526,500 lb (238,815 kg)
747-200C, 747-200C(CF6), all-cargo 590,000 lb (267,620 kg)
Max landing weight:
747-100 (W, X), 747-200B, 747-200B (CF6) 564,000 lb (255,825 kg)
747SR (Y) 505,000 lb (229,060 kg)
747SR (Z) 525,000 lb (238,135 kg)
747-200C, 747-200C(CF6), all-passenger 564,000 lb (255,825 kg)
747-200C, 747-200C(CF6), all-cargo 630,000 lb (285,760 kg)

PERFORMANCE:
Max level speed:
747-100 at 30,000 ft (9,150 m) at AUW of 600,000 lb (272,155 kg) 517 knots (595 mph; 958 km/h)
747-200B at 30,000 ft (9,150 m) at AUW of 600,000 lb (272,155 kg) 528 knots (608 mph; 978 km/h)
Cruise ceiling, all versions 45,000 ft (13,715 m)
Minimum ground turning radius 75 ft 0 in (22·86 m)
Runway LCN (A: 713,000 lb; 323,410 kg, B: 738,000 lb; 334,750 kg, C: 778,000 lb; 352,895 kg max taxi weight, on h=20 in; 51 cm flexible pavement):
A 79
B 81
C 83
Runway LCN (weights as above, on l=40 in; 102 cm rigid pavement):
A 87
B 88
C 90
FAR T-O distance to 35 ft (10·7 m) at S/L, ISA, 747-100 at T-O weight of 733,000 lb (332,480 kg), 747-200B at 785,000 lb (356,070 kg):
747-100 9,450 ft (2,880 m)
747-200B 10,500 ft (3,200 m)
FAR landing field length, at max landing weight:
747-100, 747-200B 6,170 ft (1,880 m)
Range (long-range cruise, FAR 121,645 reserves):
747-100 at 733,000 lb (332,480 kg), with 385 passengers and baggage 4,930 nm (5,677 miles; 9,136 km)
747-200B at 785,000 lb (356,070 kg), with 385 passengers and baggage 5,400 nm (6,218 miles; 10,005 km)
Ferry range (long-range cruise, FAR 121,645 reserves):
747-200B 6,400 nm (7,370 miles; 11,860 km)

OPERATIONAL NOISE CHARACTERISTICS (A: JT9D-7A engines at brake release weight (BRW) of 733,000 lb; 332,480 kg. B: JT9D-7A (wet) engines at BRW of 785,000 lb; 356,070 kg):
T-O noise level at 3·5 nm (4 miles; 6·5 km) from start of T-O roll:
A, B, C 107 EPNdB
Approach noise level at 1 nm (1·15 miles; 1·85 km) from landing threshold on 3° glideslope:
A 107 EPNdB
B 106 EPNdB
Sideline noise level at 0·35 nm (0·40 miles; 0·65 km) from runway c/l:
A 99 EPNdB
B 98 EPNdB

BOEING MODEL 747SP

The Boeing Company announced on 3 September 1973 that it intended to proceed "incrementally" with development of a lower-weight longer-range version of the basic Model 747, for use on lower-density routes. A week later came the news that Pan American had placed an order for 10 747SP (Special Performance) aircraft, with an option on 15 more. Subsequently, Iran Air ordered three of these aircraft, and the Pan American order was amended to five.

Retaining a 90 per cent commonality of components with the standard Model 747, the major change is a reduction in overall length of 46 ft 9 in (14·25 m). Construction of the first production aircraft was scheduled to begin in April 1974, with first flight in July 1975 and FAA certification following in December 1975.

The description of the basic Model 747 applies also to the 747SP, except for the following details:

WINGS: As Model 747, except that trailing-edge flaps are of single-slotted variable pivot type, and wing structural materials are of reduced gauge.

FUSELAGE: As Model 747, except length reduced.

TAIL UNIT: Similar to 747, but tailplane span increased by 10 ft (3·05 m). Two-segment elevators. Height of fin increased.

LANDING GEAR: As Model 747, except structural weight reduced. Main-wheel tyres size 16-46, pressure 185 lb/sq in (13 kg/cm²). Nosewheel tyres size 17-49, pressure 230 lb/sq in (16·2 kg/cm²). Modified 747-100 steel brakes by Bendix.

POWER PLANT: Four Pratt & Whitney JT9D-7A turbofan engines, each of 46,150 lb (20,933 kg) st. Fuel system, fuel capacity and oil capacity as for Model 747-100.

ACCOMMODATION: Normal operating crew of three on flight deck above level of main deck. Observer station and provision for second observer station are provided. Basic accommodation for 289 passengers on main deck, with 28 first class seats in forward area and ten-abreast seating throughout the major part of the main cabin. Seating for 16 passengers in upper-deck first class lounge optional, giving total optional capacity of 305 passengers. Alternative nine-abreast layout providing an optional total capacity of 281 passengers. Four doors on each side, two forward and two aft of the wing. Crew door on starboard side giving access to upper deck. Freight holds under floor, forward and aft of wing box, each with one door on starboard side.

SYSTEMS, ELECTRONICS AND EQUIPMENT: As for 747.

DIMENSIONS, EXTERNAL: As for Model 747 except:
- Length overall 184 ft 7 in (56·26 m)
- Height overall 65 ft 5 in (19·94 m)
- Tailplane span 82 ft 9 in (25·22 m)
- Wheelbase 67 ft 4 in (20·52 m)

DIMENSIONS, INTERNAL:
- Cabin, including toilets and galleys:
  - Length 136 ft 8 in (41·66 m)
  - Max width 20 ft 0 in (6·10 m)
  - Max height 8 ft 4 in (2·54 m)
  - Floor area, passenger deck 2,725 sq ft (253·2 m²)
  - Volume, passenger deck 21,660 cu ft (613·34 m³)
- Baggage hold volume (fwd) 1,730 cu ft (48·99 m³)
- Baggage hold volume (aft, containerised) 1,730 cu ft (48·99 m³)
- Bulk compartment volume (aft) 400 cu ft (11·33 m³)

AREAS: As for Model 747 except:
- Ailerons (total) 219·3 sq ft (20·37 m²)
- Trailing-edge flaps (total) 848 sq ft (78·78 m²)
- Fin 885 sq ft (82·22 m²)
- Tailplane 1,534 sq ft (142·51 m²)

WEIGHTS:
- Operating weight empty 316,000 lb (143,335 kg)
- Max payload 94,000 lb (42,637 kg)
- Max T-O weight 660,000 lb (299,370 kg)
- Max ramp weight 663,000 lb (300,730 kg)
- Max zero-fuel weight 410,000 lb (185,970 kg)
- Max landing weight 450,000 lb (204,115 kg)

PERFORMANCE (at max T-O weight, except as detailed):
- Max never-exceed speed Mach 0·92
- Max level speed, AUW of 500,000 lb (226,795 kg) at 30,000 ft (9,145 m) 529 knots (609 mph; 980 km/h)
- Service ceiling 45,100 ft (13,745 m)
- Minimum ground turning radius over outer wingtip 73 ft 0 in (22·25 m)
- Runway LCN (at max ramp weight, h = 20 in; 51 cm flexible pavement) 73
- Runway LCN (at max ramp weight, l = 40 in; 102 cm rigid pavement) 74

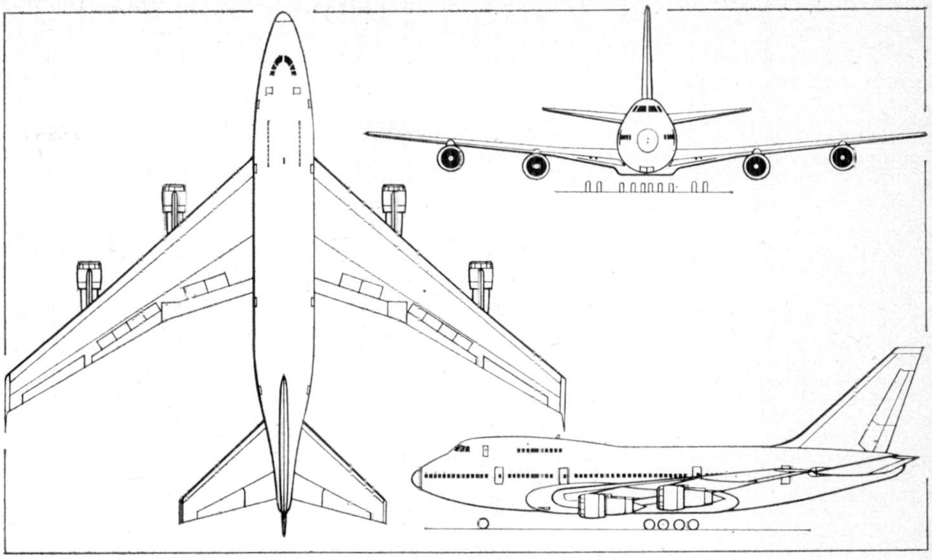

Boeing 747SP short-fuselage long-range version of the 747 (*Pilot Press*)

- FAR T-O distance to 35 ft (10·7 m) at S/L, ISA 7,100 ft (2,165 m)
- FAR landing field length, at max landing weight 5,600 ft (1,705 m)
- Range (long-range step cruise, FAR 121,645 reserves) with 305 passengers and baggage 5,712 nm (6,578 miles; 10,586 km)
- Ferry range (long-range step cruise, FAR 121,645 reserves) 7,253 nm (8,352 miles; 13,441 km)

BOEING MODEL 747-200F FREIGHTER

The Boeing Model 747-200F is a freighter version of the standard Model 747-200, capable of delivering 200,000 lb (90,720 kg) of containerised or palletised cargo over a range of 3,744 nm (4,312 miles; 6,940 km).

Certification of the first 747-200F was awarded on 7 March 1972 and this aircraft was delivered to Lufthansa later in the same month.

To ensure maximum utilisation, the 747-200F has a special loading system that enables two men to handle and stow the maximum load of up to 270,208 lb (122,560 kg) in 30 min. This system comprises rollers, castors, rails and drive-wheels which are powered from the aircraft's electrical system, utilising the APU, or from an external power source.

As cargo reaches the nose-door sill area it is steered by the loading manager from a master control station. Loads are propelled by the drive wheels, under control from a series of local control stations, along roller tracks to their assigned positions, where they are locked in place.

An on-board computer-controlled weight and balance system measures, computes and displays all necessary loading data via a series of transducers mounted inside the landing gear axles, providing the operator with very precise CG location and weight readings.

If, as a result of incorrect loading, the CG location is outside a pre-set limit, a visible internal and audible external alarm is actuated. Simultaneously, electric power to the deck cargo-handling system is isolated, halting the loading operation.

The 747-200F can carry up to 29 containers measuring 10 ft long, 8 ft high and 8 ft wide

Nose-loading of the Boeing Model 747-230F freighter being demonstrated

Boeing Model 747-245F freighter in the insignia of Seaboard World Airlines

(3·05 × 2·44 × 2·44 m), plus 30 lower-lobe containers, each of 173 cu ft (4·90 m^3) capacity, and 800 cu ft (22·65 m^3) of bulk cargo. The main deck can accommodate ANSI/ISO containers of up to 40 ft (12·19 m) in length, and many combinations of pallets and igloos. The lower hold can accommodate combinations of IATA-A1 or -A2, and ATA LD-1 or -3 half-width containers, full-width or main-deck baggage containers, as well as many combinations of pallets and igloos.

The nose loading door, which is hinged just below the flight deck to allow it to swing forward and upward, gives clear access to the main deck to facilitate the handling of long or large loads.

The description of the Model 747-200B applies also to the Model 747-200F except as detailed:

TYPE: Four-turbofan heavy commercial freighter.

FUSELAGE: As for Model 747-200B, except nose cargo loading door with max width of 11 ft 4 in (3·45 m) and max height of 8 ft 2 in (2·49 m), which is hinged at the top and opens forward and upward.

ACCOMMODATION: Normal operating crew of three on flight deck. Nose cargo loading door, hinged at top. Lower lobe cargo doors, on starboard side, one forward and one aft of wing. Bulk compartment cargo door, on starboard side, aft of lower lobe cargo door. Two doors for crew on port side of aircraft. Aircraft is designed for fully-mechanical loading of freight.

DIMENSIONS, EXTERNAL: As for Model 747-200B except:
Crew doors (two, each):
Height 6 ft 4 in (1·93 m)
Width 3 ft 6 in (1·07 m)
Height to sill, approx 16 ft 0 in (4·88 m)
Nose cargo loading door:
Height 8 ft 2 in (2·49 m)
Width at top (min) 8 ft 8 in (2·64 m)
Height to sill, approx 16 ft 1 in (4·90 m)

DIMENSIONS, INTERNAL:
Main cargo deck:
Height 8 ft 4 in (2·54 m)
Width, max 19 ft 5 in (5·92 m)
Lower lobe:
Width at floor level 10 ft 5 in (3·18 m)
Total cargo volume 23,690 cu ft (670·83 m^3)

AREAS: As for Model 747-200B

WEIGHTS:
Operating weight empty (not including container and pallet tare) 319,812 lb (145,064 kg)
Max payload (including tare) 270,188 lb (122,555 kg)
Normal max T-O weight 775,000 lb (351,530 kg)
Optional max T-O weight 785,000 lb (356,070 kg)
Normal max ramp weight 778,000 lb (352,895 kg)
Optional max ramp weight 788,000 lb (357,430 kg)
Max zero-fuel weight 590,000 lb (267,615 kg)
Max landing weight 630,000 lb (285,760 kg)

PERFORMANCE (at max T-O weight):
Max level speed at AUW of 600,000 lb (272,155 kg), at 30,000 ft (9,150 m) 528 knots (608 mph; 978 km/h)
Cruise ceiling 45,000 ft (13,715 m)
Min ground turning radius 75 ft 0 in (22·86 m)
FAR T-O distance to 35 ft (10·7 m) at S/L, ISA 10,900 ft (3,322 m)
FAR landing field length, at max landing weight 7,270 ft (2,216 m)
Range, long-range cruise, FAR 121,645 reserve, with 257,858 lb (116,962 kg) payload 2,501 nm (2,880 miles; 4,630 km)
Ferry range with max fuel, long-range cruise, FAR 121,645 reserve 6,903 nm (7,949 miles; 12,790 km)

BOEING MODEL 747-200F(CF6) FREIGHTER

The Model 747-200F(CF6) is generally similar to the 747-200F, except that it is intended to be powered by General Electric CF6-50E turbofan engines, each of 52,500 lb (23,810 kg) st, which will permit a maximum take-off weight of 800,000 lb (362,870 kg). The figures given below are estimated:

WEIGHTS:
Operating weight empty (not including container and pallet tare) 324,011 lb (146,968 kg)
Max payload 265,989 lb (120,650 kg)
Max T-O weight 800,000 lb (362,870 kg)
Max ramp weight 803,000 lb (364,230 kg)
Max zero-fuel weight 590,000 lb (267,620 kg)
Max landing weight 630,000 lb (285,760 kg)

BOEING AEROSPACE COMPANY

The Boeing Aerospace Company has its headquarters at the company's space centre at Kent, Washington, some 12 miles south of Seattle. It consists of Operations and Planning, Research and Engineering Division, Field Operations and Support Division, Space and Ballistic Missiles Group, Naval Systems Division and Military Systems Group. Responsible for much of Boeing's military, space and diversification efforts, it has a labour force of approximately 20,000. Among its principal current activities are the SRAM missile programme, Minuteman modernisation, advanced surface transportation programmes, military applications of commercial transports, and space projects which have included the Apollo programme's Saturn V first stage and the Lunar Rover Vehicle. Another important activity involves development of hydrofoil marine vessels, including NATO Patrol Hydrofoil Missile ships (PHMs) and several Jetfoils, the latter being commercial passenger-carrying hydrofoils. Both military and civil versions have fully submerged foils, water jet propulsion and automatic stabilisation systems.

BOEING AWACS

USAF designations: EC-137D and E-3A

The E-3A AWACS (Airborne Warning And Control System) aircraft being developed for USAF service in the late 1970s will be equipped with extensive sensing, communications, display and navigational devices.

In concept, an AWACS offers the potential of long-range high- or low-level surveillance of all air vehicles, manned or unmanned, in all weathers and above all kinds of terrain. Its data storage and processing capability would provide real-time assessment of enemy action, and also of the status and position of friendly resources. By centralising the co-ordination of complex, diverse and simultaneous air operations, such an aircraft would be able to command and control the total air effort: strike, air superiority, support, airlift, reconnaissance and interdiction.

The primary use of such an aircraft, as deployed by Aerospace Defence Command, will be as a survivable early-warning airborne command and control centre for identification, surveillance and tracking of airborne enemy forces, and for the command and control of NORAD (North American Air Defense) forces. Similar aircraft, operated by Tactical Air Command, will be used as airborne command and control centres for quick-reaction deployment and tactical operations.

Boeing's Aerospace Group was one of two competitors for the AWAC System (the other being McDonnell Douglas), and was awarded an initial contract as prime contractor and systems integrator for the programme on 23 July 1970. Boeing's submission was based on the airframe of the Model 707-320B commercial jet transport. In Phase 1 of the development programme, two of these aircraft, with the prototype designation EC-137D, were modified initially for comparative trials with prototype downward-looking radars designed, respectively, by Hughes Aircraft Company and Westinghouse Electric Corporation.

The first flight by one of these aircraft was made on 9 February 1972. After more than five months of radar test flights, during which each radar accumulated over 290 hours of airborne operating time, Boeing completed its evaluation, and the Westinghouse radar was selected on 5 October 1972. Following successful completion of the radar competition, additional data processing equipment and two tracking displays were installed in the Westinghouse-equipment test aircraft, and a new series of flight tests was conducted to demonstrate the ability of the radar and data processor to detect and maintain continuous tracking of airborne targets. In addition, the capability of the system to maintain several simultaneous tracks was evaluated. These tests also proved successful, and were completed by 6 November 1972.

On 26 January 1973, the USAF announced that, following satisfactory completion of Phase 1, approval had been given for full-scale development of the AWACS aircraft under Phase 2 of the programme. To reduce costs, two major changes were made from the original Phase 2 proposal. The previously planned power plant of eight General Electric TF34-GE-2 turbofan engines was superseded by four Pratt & Whitney TF33-P-7 turbofans, each of 21,000 lb (9,525 kg) st; and only four test aircraft were ordered instead of the six originally envisaged.

Phase 2 of the development programme involves systems integration demonstration, and initial operational test and evaluation. Additional subsystems are being installed in one of the two existing EC-137D test aircraft, so that it can demonstrate full AWACS capability. At a later date the USAF plans to use three fully-configured E-3A AWACS prototypes. including the second of the original EC-137D test airframes, for a development/operational test and evaluation programme. Following successful demonstration of the full AWAC system, a production (Phase 3) decision is scheduled for December 1974. If production is approved, it is intended that the four integration demonstration and development/operational test aircraft shall be refurbished and will enter the operational inventory. Phase 3, if approved, will also cover the manufacture of production aircraft, of which 42 were due to be built under plans announced in 1970.

In addition to meeting military requirements, AWACS aircraft could be used in many civil applications. A large-scale emergency, such as posed by earthquake or flood, needs rapid air delivery of relief materials and produces immediately an air traffic control problem. The highly mobile AWACS would be able to cope with such a situation quickly. It could be used also for air traffic control operations over the busy North Atlantic traffic lanes that lack mid-ocean control, improving route efficiency and safety margins. Such aircraft might prove invaluable for tracking tornadoes and marshalling relief forces in their wake.

The existing Boeing 707-320 requires relatively minor adaptation to accommodate the AWAC system. External changes include the rotodome assembly, which is mounted on two large struts rooted into the fuselage structure aft of the wing, new engine pylon fairings, specially located windows, doors and hatches, and provisions for in-flight refuelling. Essential antennae will be installed within the wings, fin, tailplane and fuselage, and internal changes require floor reinforcement, provision of crew compartments, and revised cooling and wiring systems.

TYPE: Airborne early-warning and command post aircraft.

WINGS, FUSELAGE, TAIL UNIT, AND LANDING GEAR: Basically as Boeing 707-320B, with strengthened fuselage structure and installation of rotodome.

POWER PLANT: Prototypes retained their existing power plants during Phase 1. Pre-production and production aircraft will be powered by four Pratt & Whitney TF33-P-7 turbofan engines, redesignated TF33-PW-100/100A in their AWACS-modified configuration. Each rated at 21,000 lb (9,525 kg) st, they are mounted in pods beneath the wings.

ACCOMMODATION: Basic operational crew of 17 includes a flight crew complement of four plus thirteen AWACS specialists, though this latter number can vary for tactical and defence missions. Aft of flight deck, from front to rear of fuselage, on the System Integration Demonstration aircraft are communications, data processing and other equipment bays; multi-purpose consoles; communications, navigation and identification equipment; and crew rest area.

ELECTRONICS AND EQUIPMENT: Prominent above the fuselage is the elliptical cross-section rotodome which is 30 ft (9·14 m) in diameter and 6 ft (1·83 m) in depth. It comprises four essential elements: a strut-mounted turntable, supporting the rotary joint assembly to which are attached sliprings for electrical and wave-

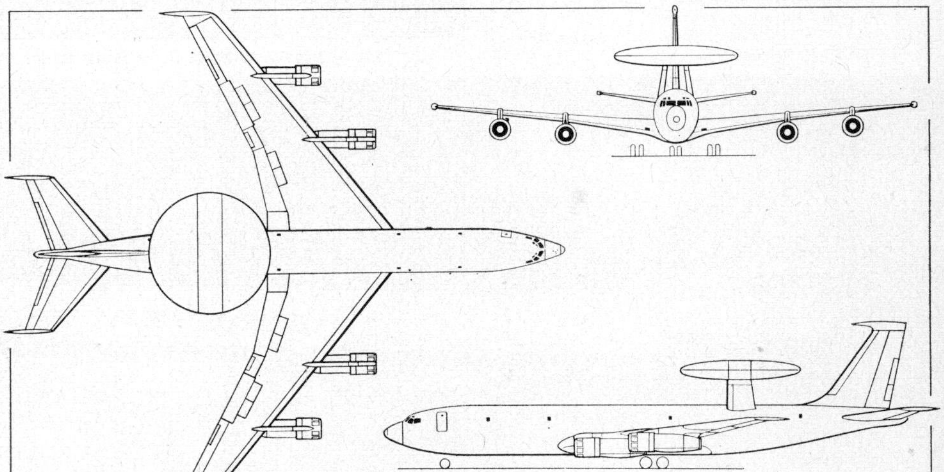

Boeing E-3A airborne warning and control system aircraft (*Pilot Press*)

Boeing EC-137D testbed aircraft for the USAF's Airborne Warning And Control System (AWACS) programme

guide continuity between rotodome and fuselage; a structural centre section of aluminium skin and stiffener construction, which supports the surveillance radar and IFF/TADIL C antennae, radomes, auxiliary equipment for radar operation and environmental control of the rotodome interior; liquid cooling of the radar antenna; and two radomes constructed of multi-layer glassfibre sandwich material, one for the surveillance radar and one for the IFF/TADIL C array. For surveillance operations the rotodome is hydraulically driven at 6 rpm, but during non-operational flights it is rotated at only ¼ rpm, to keep the bearings lubricated. The Westinghouse radar operates in the S band; by use of pulse Doppler technology, with a high pulse repetition frequency, this radar features long range and accuracy in addition to a normal downlook capability. Its antenna, spanning about 24 ft (7·32 m), and 5 ft (1·52 m) deep, scans mechanically in azimuth, and electronically from ground level up into the stratosphere. Heart of the data processing is an IBM 4 Pi CC-1 high-speed computer, the entire group consisting of arithmetic control units, input/output units, main storage units, peripheral control units, mass memory drums, magnetic tape transports, punched tape reader, line printer, and an operator's control panel. Processing speed is in the order of 740,000 operations/sec; input/output data rate has a maximum of 710,000 words/sec; main memory size is 114,688 words (expandable to 180,224), and mass memory size 802,816 words (expandable to 1,204,224). An interface adapter unit developed by Boeing is the key integrating element interconnecting functional data between AWACS avionics subsystems, data processing group, radar, communications, navigation/guidance, display, azimuth and identification. Data display and control is provided by Hazeltine Corporation multi-purpose consoles (MPC) and auxiliary display units (ADU); in present configuration each AWACS aircraft carries nine MPCs and two ADUs. Navigation/guidance relies upon three principal sources of information: dual Delco Carousel IV inertial navigation sets; Northrop ARN-99 Omega navigation; and a Ryan APM-200 Doppler velocity sensor. Communications equipment, supplied by Collins Radio, Electronic Communications Inc, and Hughes Aircraft, provides HF, VHF and UHF communication channels by means of which information can be transmitted or received in clear or secure mode, in voice or digital form. Identification is based on an AN/APX-103 interrogator set being developed by Cutler-Hammer's AIL Division. It is the first airborne IFF interrogator set to offer complete AIMS Mk X SIF air traffic control and Mk XII military identification friend or foe (IFF) in a single integrated system. Simultaneous Mk X and Mk XII multi-target and multi-mode operations will allow the operator to obtain instantaneously the range, azimuth and elevation, code identification, and IFF status of all targets within radar range.

SYSTEMS: A liquid cooling system provides protection for the radar transmitter. An air-cycle pack system and a closed-loop ram-cooled environmental control system ensure a suitable environment for crew and avionics equipment. Electrical power generation has a 600kVA capability. The distribution centre for mission equipment power and remote electronics is located in the lower forward cargo compartment. The aft cargo compartment houses the radar transmitter and an APU. External sockets allow intake of power when the aircraft is on the ground. Two separate and independent hydraulic systems power flight-essential and mission-essential equipment, but either system has the capability of satisfying the requirements of both equipment groups in an emergency.

BOEING 707-LRPA

On 1 November 1972 the Canadian government issued a request for proposals for a long-range patrol aircraft (LRPA) to replace the fleet of Canadair CL-28 Argus piston-engined aircraft that currently fulfil this role in the Canadian Armed Forces' Maritime Air Command. To obtain maximum utility from this $750 million programme, the Canadians desire that the new aircraft should, in addition to the basic maritime reconnaissance role, be capable of other duties that range from Arctic surveillance to wildlife management and cataloguing tasks, including land-resources exploration, troop transport and flight refuelling of fighter aircraft. It is reported that Australia is interested in a similar type of aircraft to replace its force of Lockheed SP-2H Neptunes.

To meet the Canadian requirement, The Boeing Company proposed a specially-developed version of its Model 707-320C; and to demonstrate the potential of such an aircraft it modified a Model 720 acquired from a charter operator. Details of the Model 720, which is basically similar in construction to the 707-320C, can be found in the 1970-71 *Jane's*.

The current ASW mission calls for an aircraft able to operate for long periods at extreme low altitudes, but it is envisaged that the advanced ASW missions of the 1980s will require also adequate performance in a high-altitude environment. Flight tests completed as a company-financed programme by the 720 testbed aircraft have demonstrated both capabilities. It has flown for long periods at only 200 ft (61 m) above the ocean surface, performed 40° banks, dropped sonobuoys successfully from altitudes up to 40,000 ft (12,200 m) at a speed of 400 knots (460 mph; 740 km/h), and has demonstrated the capability of remaining on station for 8-10 hr at a range of 1,000 nm (1,150 miles; 1,850 km) from its base.

Aware of the pending requirement of the Canadian government, Boeing acquired the secondhand Model 720 in the Autumn of 1971 and immediately began to prepare it as a testbed aircraft. More than four months were devoted to structural modifications and the installation of new equipment to provide magnetic anomaly detection (MAD), sonobuoy storage and launch facilities, new automatic flight control and navigation systems, tactical crew stations and crew comfort accommodation. Flight testing in the new configuration began on 6 April 1972; since then, in addition to completing the first phase of the military flight test programme, the 720 has demonstrated its versatility by gathering ocean current data for a research project being carried out by the Canadian Department of Environment.

The requirement for MAD has been met by installation of dual wingtip-mounted booms, the tips of which are designed to accept either AN/ASQ 10 or AN/ASQ 501 detector heads. Tests have been made with three different boom lengths, allowing location of each detector 5 ft, 8 ft or 10 ft (1·52 m, 2·44 m or 3·05 m) aft of the wing trailing-edge. It has been established that this dual system gives improved target detection and localisation capability by comparison with the usual single tail "sting". CAE nine-term compensating systems are installed, with all system controls located at the electronic sensor operator's station.

Search equipment, to customer's requirements, can include radar in a nose installation or medium-resolution side-looking radar, which would offer almost all-weather capability for searches in the Arctic.

Two sonobuoy launch tubes, of Boeing design and construction, have been installed. One of these is mounted vertically and the other at 30° to the vertical, and storage racks are provided for up to 100 sonobuoys. Thirty entirely successful in-flight launches have been made, including cartridge-assisted launches at altitudes between 1,000 and 40,000 ft (300 and 12,200 m) and at speeds up to 400 knots (460 mph; 740 km/h) TAS, and free-fall launches at altitudes below 3,000 ft (915 m) at airspeeds from 180 to 240 knots (207-276 mph; 333-444 km/h). Satisfactory separation from the aircraft has been obtained under all conditions.

To enhance safe operation and reduce the pilot's work load, particularly during long periods of low-level tactical operation, Boeing has evolved a new automatic flight control system, using as its basis the advanced Sperry SPZ-1 autopilot developed for the Boeing 747. The system has two independent channels, each deriving its input from independent sensors, an inertial

Boeing 720 testbed modified to demonstrate the potential of the company's ASW projects, which would be based on the basically-similar 707-320C airframe

platform and an air data computer. These independent channels drive dual hydraulic control servos, which ensure a fail-passive condition in the event of a system failure. The system has demonstrated excellent handling characteristics during prolonged low-level manoeuvres with the control-wheel steering and altitude-hold modes. Accurate altitude control has been demonstrated during rapid manoeuvres and during changes to power or flap settings.

Dual flight-path angle and radar altimeter inputs serve to operate a low-altitude monitor and warning system, installed to increase safety during let-down and low-level operation. In addition, the SPZ-1 offers such facilities as all-weather autoland, compatibility with an inertial navigation system (INS), cruise altitude hold and airways navigation performance.

Another component of the flight control system is a turn co-ordinator which reduces sideslip effectively up to the maximum roll rate; this feature is combined with a yaw damper. An autothrottle is provided, to control the airspeed through the entire flight envelope.

Navigation equipment in the testbed aircraft includes dual INS, Doppler, Omni UHF ADF (sonobuoy), dual air data computers, a flight director and a vertical camera for position fixing. Controls and associated displays are installed at the radar navigator's console. A cathode ray tube display developed by IBM is installed in the test aircraft. Its future fully-developed counterpart is intended to provide information to improve the precision of tactical manoeuvres, assist descent to a surface target and aid all-weather landings.

The lower cargo bays of the 707 provide ample room for sensors or other equipment requiring a downward look; and the large cabin could accommodate some cargo in addition to the installed specialised equipment. To provide for the carriage of troops, it is intended that some of the equipment should be easily removable.

No provision is to be made for the carriage of installed armament; but four underwing pylons inboard of the engines would be able to accommodate a variety of stores, including bombs, missiles and surveillance pods.

The accompanying photograph depicts the Model 720 testbed aircraft. Alternative versions have been projected by Boeing, including an ASW aircraft with search radar in a "droop-nose" radome.

The interior drawing shows the cabin layout of the Model 707-LRPA as it was proposed in February 1974, but it is possible that further revisions will be made.

BOEING B-52G/H STRATOFORTRESS

Under a $212 million programme, Boeing B-52G and H Stratofortresses of the USAF's Strategic Air Command are being equipped with an AN/ASQ-151 Electro-optical Viewing System (EVS) to improve low-level flight capability.

Clearly seen in the accompanying photograph are the two steerable chin turrets that house the new sensors. That on the starboard side contains a Hughes Aircraft AAQ-6 forward-looking infra-red scanner (FLIR), while the port turret houses a Westinghouse AVQ-22 low-light-level TV camera.

After six months of operational service the reliability of the equipment has exceeded the specification issued by the Air Force Logistics Command's Oklahoma City Logistics Center, the first seven B-52s to be equipped with EVS recording a mean time between failure of 37·4 hours. This represents only 13 equipment failures in an accumulated 486 flight hours, and demonstrates that the 1,110-hour production reliability test that preceded the first installation served its purpose adequately. In this test, a facsimile of the EVS was subjected to temperature, humidity and vibration conditions that duplicated those of the B-52.

More than 270 EVS kits are being produced, with the last scheduled for delivery in the first quarter of 1976.

BOEING T-43A

Experience gained during the war in Vietnam alerted the USAF to the need to increase its supply of trained navigators. To meet this requirement and to improve the standard of training, it was decided to replace the existing fleet of Convair T-29 piston-engined trainers by more modern aircraft of greater capacity.

Boeing's Model 737-200 was selected as the most suitable off-the-shelf basic aircraft for this role, and 19 of these, modified to meet the military requirement, were ordered with the designation T-43A under an $82·4 million contract.

Generally similar to the commercial model, they differ primarily in having only two doors, one on each side of the fuselage; nine windows only on each side; strengthened floor to carry avionics consoles; provision of overhead sextant viewing ports; and installation of an 800 US gallon (3,027 litre) auxiliary fuel tank in the aft cargo compartment.

The first of these navigational trainers was rolled out at Boeing's Renton, Washington, factory on 2 March 1973, and made its first flight on 10 April 1973, prior to obtaining FAA certification in the new configuration. Following certification, this first T-43A was delivered to Mather AFB, California, for operational test and evaluation by the USAF. Seven had been delivered by 1 February 1974, and deliveries were scheduled to continue at a rate of two per month until completion of the order in July 1974.

At Mather the T-43As are replacing 77 T-29s which have been in use for navigation training. Only 19 T-43As are needed to replace this fleet as they each accommodate up to twelve trainee navigators, four navigator proficiency students and three instructors, and are expected to have double the utilisation factor of the T-29s.

They are being used in conjunction with Honeywell T-45 electronic simulators to form a new Undergraduate Navigator Training System. The new ground-based equipment provides

Boeing B-52H fitted with AN/ASQ-151 Electro-optical Viewing System

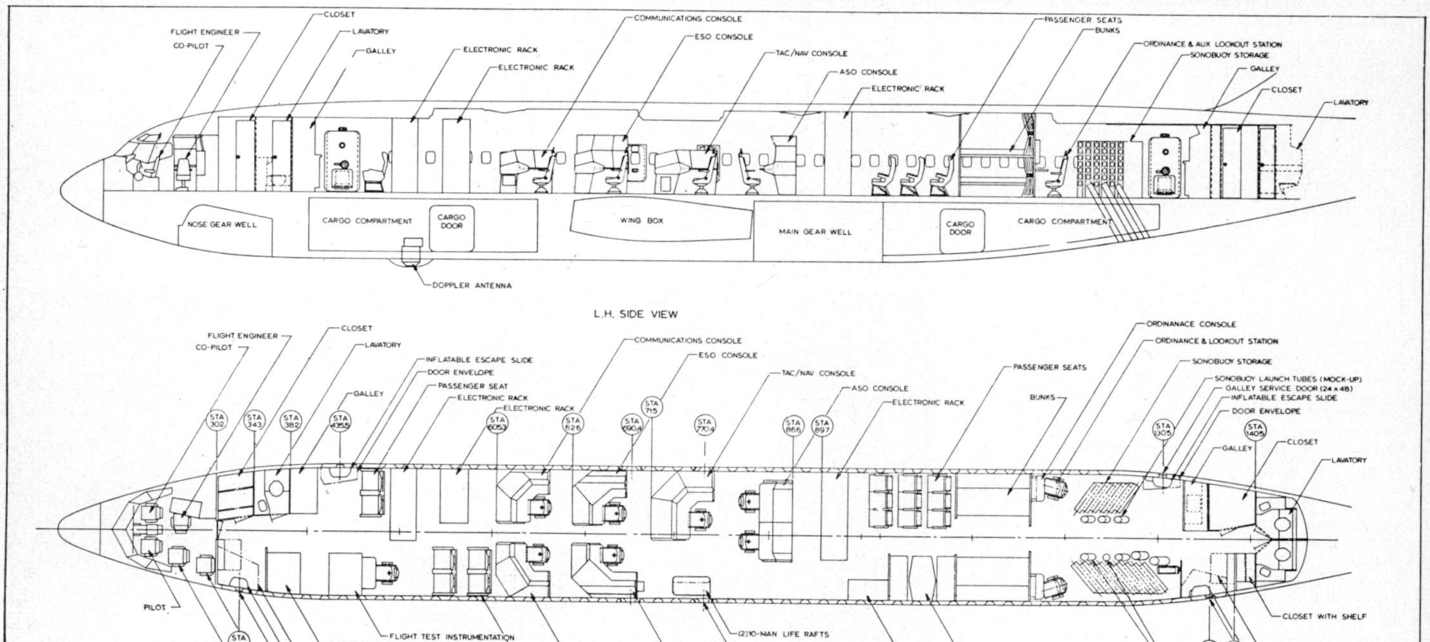

Cabin layout of the Boeing Model 707-LRPA, as proposed in February 1974

simulation of a wide range of missions, including low-level flights over land and water, night flights, airways navigation, high-altitude operations up to 70,000 ft (21,340 m) and at speeds of up to Mach 2. On-board avionics equipment of the T-43As is the same as that used in the most advanced USAF operational aircraft, including celestial, radar and inertial navigation systems, LORAN and other radio systems.

The specification and performance figures quoted for the Boeing Model 737-200 equipped with Pratt & Whitney JT8D-9 turbofan engines apply in general to the T-43A, except as detailed below:

PERFORMANCE:
Econ cruising speed at 35,000 ft (10,670 m) Mach 0·7
Operational range, MIL-C-5011A reserves 2,600 nm (2,995 miles; 4,820 km)
Endurance 6 hr

Boeing T-43A navigational trainer, evolved from the Model 737-200

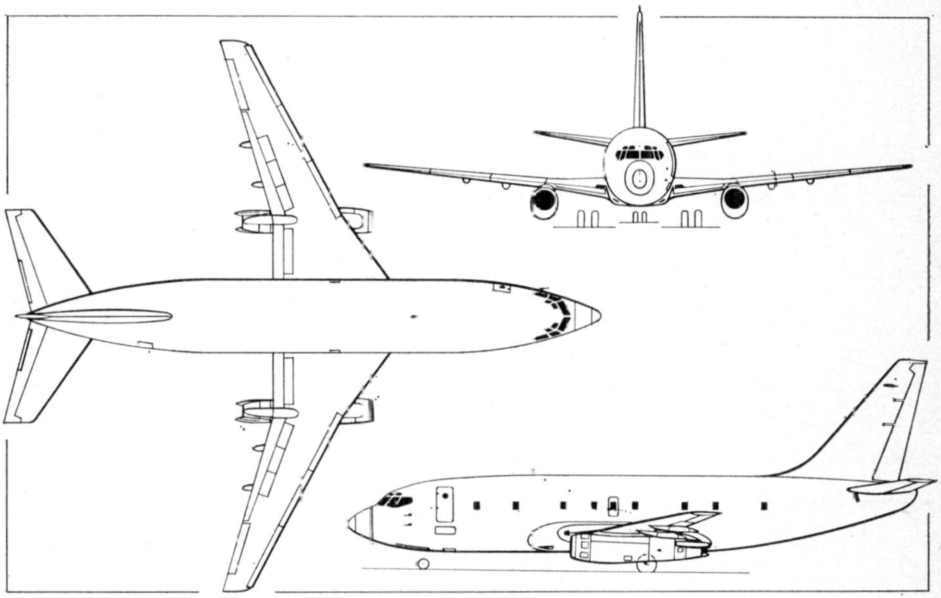

Boeing T-43A navigational trainer (two Pratt & Whitney JT8D-9 turbofan engines) (*Pilot Press*)

The third Boeing E-4A advanced airborne command post version of the Model 747B, with F103-GE-100 turbofan engines

BOEING ADVANCED AIRBORNE COMMAND POST

USAF designation: E-4

On 28 February 1973 the USAF's Electronic Systems Division announced from its headquarters at Hanscom Field, Bedford, Massachusetts, that it had awarded The Boeing Company a $59 million fixed-price contract for the supply of two Model 747Bs to be adapted as **E-4A** airborne command posts under the 481B Advanced Airborne Command Post (AABNCP) programme. The contract specified only an option on a third aircraft, but the USAF hoped to obtain Congressional approval for the purchase of four more E-4As to make a fleet of seven aircraft. Since that time, a contract valued at more than $27·2 million has been awarded, in July 1973, for the third aircraft; in December 1973 the fourth aircraft was contracted at $39 million.

The third and fourth aircraft differ from the first two in having General Electric F103-GE-100 turbofan engines, each rated at 52,500 lb (23,815 kg) st, instead of the JT9Ds fitted normally to aircraft of the 747 series. The fourth will also be fitted with more advanced equipment (see below) and will be designated **E-4B.** The first three aircraft will be modified eventually to a similar standard.

They are to replace the EC-135 Airborne Command Posts of the National Military Command System and the Strategic Air Command, which are military variants of the Model 707. E-Systems Inc of Greenville, Texas, won a contract to install interim equipment in the first three aircraft. This involved transfer and integration of equipment removed from EC-135s. In this condition these aircraft can be used with an expanded battle staff, allowing a more flexible response capability than was possible with the older aircraft.

Anticipating the order, Boeing had completed final assembly of two aircraft for this role prior to receipt of the USAF contract. The first of these E-4As was delivered in July and the second in December 1973.

In early 1974, Boeing and a team comprising Computer Sciences Corp, of Falls Church, Virginia; Electrospace Systems Inc of Richardson, Texas; and E-Systems Inc, won the contract to design and install the advanced command post equipment in the remainder of the fleet and, eventually, to replace the equipment in the first three aircraft.

On their entry into service the first three aircraft will be stationed at Andrews AFB. It is planned that the remainder will operate from Offutt AFB. The aircraft have three decks, the upper deck of the commercial 747 serving as the crew rest area. The two lower decks, one forward and one aft of the wing, carry communications and data processing equipment. The main deck, 185 ft (56·39 m) long and 19 ft 6 in (5·94 m) maximum width, provides command and staff work areas, plus rest, eating and sleeping areas. Unrefuelled endurance of the E-4A is 12 hours.

BOEING YC-14 (AMST)

Looking ahead for potential replacements for its fleet of Lockheed C-130 Hercules transport aircraft, the USAF issued requests for proposals to nine US aerospace companies in early 1972. Responses were received from Bell Aerospace, Boeing, Fairchild Industries, a combined Lockheed-Georgia/North American Rockwell team and McDonnell Douglas. From these proposals, those of Boeing and McDonnell Douglas (which see) were selected, and on 10 November 1972 these two companies were each awarded a contract to develop, construct and flight test two prototype aircraft to compete in a prototype fly-off competition.

The advanced medium short take-off and landing transport (AMST) programme is under the management of the Prototype Program Office of the USAF Systems Command's Aeronautical Systems Division, Wright-Patterson AFB, Ohio. Boeing's entry, the two prototypes of which have been allocated the USAF designation YC-14, is being built under a $105·9 million contract. Its Phase 1 requirement, which had a 90-day completion period, demanded the submission of additional design/performance analysis. Both companies completed this stage of the contract in just over a month, and this enabled the USAF to give a go-ahead for Phase 2 of the contract some 30 days ahead of schedule. Phase 2 covers a 45-month period, during which each company will build and fly two prototypes, emphasis being placed on performance and cost goals rather than rigid adherence to specification requirements.

The first flight of Boeing's first YC-14 prototype was scheduled for September 1975, that of the second aircraft about two months later. Since the programme originated, however, Congress set a limit of $25 million on the YC-14 and YC-15 in the FY 1974 budget, instead of the figure of $65·2 million which the USAF had requested. It was anticipated that the Air Force would request a funding of $55 million in FY 1975, but this means that although the programme is continuing the first flight date for the first prototype has had to be deferred to mid-1976. When the competing aircraft become available it is anticipated that evaluation tests could last for about a year.

A significant feature of the Boeing YC-14 is the use of a relatively small supercritical wing, with an overwing installation of the power plant. Benefits accruing from this layout include the presentation of a low infra-red signature to ground-based detectors; an uncluttered underwing surface, simplifying the carriage of external stores, including RPVs; efficient thrust reversal; and a reduced noise footprint. Significant improvement of cargo compartment loading efficiency will result from the adoption of the wide-body fuselage concept, which is now a familiar feature of civil air transports.

Type: Advanced military STOL transport.

Wings: Cantilever shoulder-wing monoplane. Comparatively small supercritical wing of tapered planform, incorporating advanced concepts to enhance STOL capability. Wing upper-surface blowing concept requires the engines to be mounted above and forward of the wing, so that they exhaust over the wing upper surface. Wide-span leading-edge and Coanda-type trailing-edge flaps will, when extended, induce the high-speed airflow from the engines to cling to the surface of the wing-flap system and direct it downward, generating powered lift. Boeing claims that wind tunnel tests of the system have shown it to be superior to other powered lift concepts, such as externally blown flaps or vectored thrust.

Fuselage: Conventional semi-monocoque all-metal structure.

Tail Unit: Cantilever all-metal structure with high T-tail. Double-hinged rudder and elevators.

Landing Gear: Retractable tricycle type. Twin wheels on nose unit. Each main unit is of the four-post levered type, with twin wheels in tandem. Main wheels and nosewheels have tyres size 40 × 18-16.

Power Plant: Two General Electric CF6-50D two-shaft high by-pass ratio turbofan engines, each with a max rating of approx 50,000 lb (22,680 kg) st. Mounting of the engines above and forward of the wing is expected to offer significant noise reduction. Mission fuel load 25,000 lb (12,340 kg), less reserves.

Accommodation: Able to carry 150 troops, or approximately 27,000 lb (12,247 kg) cargo in STOL operations or 65,000 lb (29,500 kg) in conventional operation. Passenger doors on each side of fuselage. Cargo loading ramp in undersurface of rear fuselage. Undersurface of fuselage retracts upward inside fuselage aft of ramp. Digital flight controls are triple-redundant and fail-operational.

Dimensions, external:
Wing span 129 ft 0 in (39·32 m)

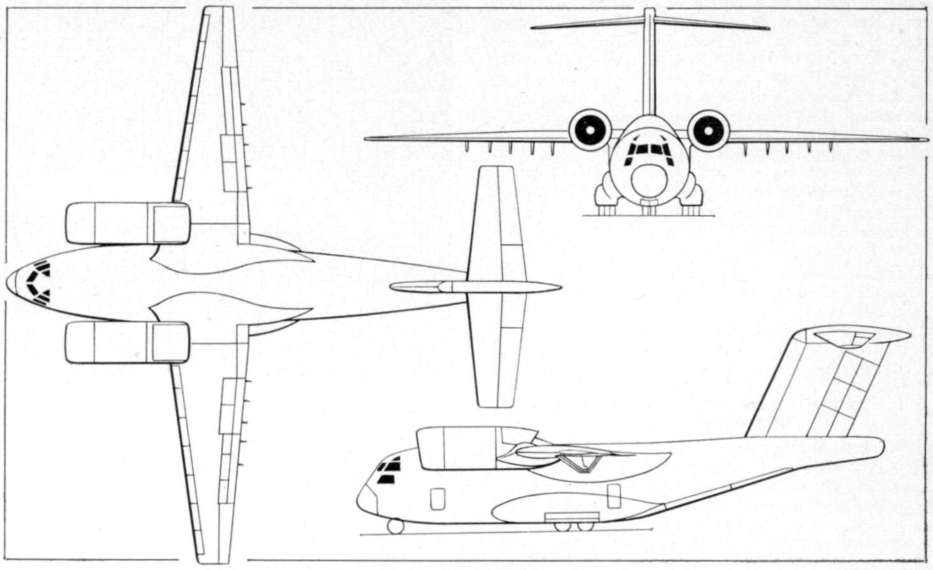

Boeing YC-14 advanced medium STOL transport (*Pilot Press*)

Length overall 131 ft 8 in (40·13 m)
Height overall 48 ft 8 in (14·83 m)
Tailplane span 55 ft 0 in (16·76 m)
Wheel track 18 ft 7 in (5·66 m)
Wheelbase 41 ft 0 in (12·50 m)

Dimensions, internal:
Cargo compartment:
Length 47 ft 0 in (14·33 m)
Width 11 ft 6 in to 11 ft 8 in (3·50-3·55 m)
Height 11 ft 2 in to 12 ft 0 in (3·40-3·66 m)

Area:
Wings, gross 1,762 sq ft (163·7 m²)

Weights:
Design max T-O weight:
STOL operation 172,000 lb (78,020 kg)
Conventional operation 216,000 lb (97,975 kg)

Performance (estimated at STOL max T-O weight, except where indicated):
Max level speed at 30,000 ft (9,150 m) 400 knots (460 mph; 740 km/h)
Landing speed 86 knots (99 mph; 159 km/h)
T-O to and landing from 50 ft (15 m) 2,000 ft (610 m)
Range with max payload:
STOL operation 1,000 nm (1,150 miles; 1,850 km)
Conventional operation 1,100 nm (1,265 miles; 2,040 km)
Range with max fuel, zero payload:
STOL operation 2,300 nm (2,650 miles; 4,260 km)
Conventional operation 2,600 nm (3,000 miles; 4,820 km)

BOEING VERTOL COMPANY

Boeing Vertol Company produces the CH-47 Chinook helicopter for the US Army. Research and development work on heavy-lift helicopters resulted in the company being awarded a contract worth an estimated $76 million to conduct the first phase of the development of a heavy lift helicopter. The company has also demonstrated the BO 105 light helicopter to the US Navy. Boeing has marketing rights for this aircraft in the United States and other parts of the western hemisphere, and has an option to manufacture it in the US. The BO 105 was developed and is manufactured in Germany by Messerschmitt-Bölkow-Blohm GmbH (which see), the largest German aerospace company, in which Boeing has a holding of just under 10%.

BOEING VERTOL MODEL 114
US Army designation: CH-47 Chinook

Development of the CH-47 Chinook series of helicopters began in 1956, when the Department of the Army announced its intention to replace its piston-engined transport helicopters with a new generation of turbine-powered helicopters. As a result of a systems capability analysis by a joint Army/Air Force Selection Board, the Boeing Vertol company was awarded an initial contract for five YCH-47As (formerly YHC-1B) by the US Army in June 1959. The first YCH-47A was completed on 28 April 1961. The first hovering flight was made on 21 September 1961. Since then, the effectiveness of the CH-47 has been increased by successive product improvement programmes. A total of 713 Chinooks had been delivered (US Army 688, Australia 12, Iran 7, Italy 4 and Spain 2) by December 1973, at which time US Army CH-47s had flown over 1·3 million hours; of this total more than three-quarters had been accumulated under combat conditions in Southeast Asia.

The CH-47 was designed to meet the US Army's requirement for an all-weather medium transport helicopter and, depending upon the series model, is capable of transporting specified payloads under severe combinations of altitude and temperature conditions. The primary mission radius criterion established by the US Army is 100 nm (115 miles; 185 km). The primary mission take-off gross weight is based on the capability of hovering out of ground effect at 6,000 ft/95°F (1,830 m/35°C). The CH-47C has demonstrated its ability to hover out of ground effect with a useful load of 25,250 lb (11,453 kg) at sea level under standard atmospheric conditions.

Boeing Vertol announced that a CH-47 Chinook had flown on 30 April 1969 with composite material rotor blades. These 60 ft (18·29 m) diameter blades, constructed of glassfibre with an aluminium honeycomb core, were the largest composite material blades built up to that time.

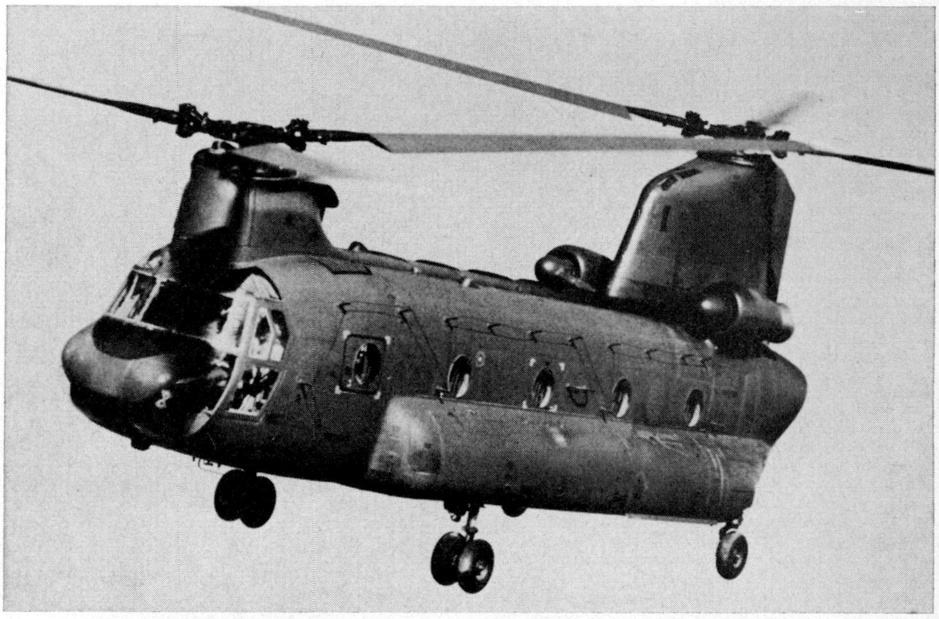

Boeing CH-47C Chinook twin-engined medium transport helicopter

Glassfibre rotor blades of improved aerodynamic capability, reliability and maintainability were being developed in 1974 for use on future improved Chinooks.

Three versions of the Chinook have been produced:

CH-47A. Initial production version, powered by two 2,200 shp Lycoming T55-L-5 or 2,650 shp T55-L-7 turboshaft engines. Operation of the CH-47A by the Vietnamese Air Force (VNAF) began in 1971.

CH-47B. Developed version with 2,850 shp T55-L-7C turboshaft engines, redesigned rotor blades with cambered leading-edge, blunted rear rotor pylon, and strakes along rear ramp and fuselage for improved flying qualities. First of two prototypes flew for the first time in early October 1966. Deliveries began on 10 May 1967.

CH-47C. This latest model achieves its increased performance from a combination of strengthened transmissions, two 3,750 shp T55-L-11A engines and increased integral fuel capacity totalling 1,093 US gallons (4,137 litres). First flight of the CH-47C was made on 14 October 1967, and deliveries of production aircraft began in the Spring of 1968. They were first deployed in Vietnam in September 1968.

Extensive development work for a Crashworthy Fuel System (CFS), and an Integral Spar Inspection System (ISIS) has been carried out, and these safety features were made available during 1973. Incorporation of the CFS on US Army CH-47Cs is being accomplished by retrofit kits, delivery of which began in March 1973. All Chinooks delivered to Australia have this system and the Canadian aircraft are being similarly equipped. Fuel capacity with these tanks is 1,042 US gallons (3,944 litres).

Rotor blades with ISIS, as well as improved corrosion protection, have been approved for use on US Army, Australian and Canadian aircraft; all new blades for initial installation, or supplied as spares, embody these improvements. By the end of 1973, more than 2,900 CH-47A rotor blades had been modified to embody ISIS. Blades in service or already delivered can have ISIS incorporated by means of a kit, deliveries of which were scheduled to begin in early 1974; improved corrosion protection can be applied at the first blade overhaul.

Following delivery of the CH-47A to the US

Army in December 1962, for service testing and pilot training, the helicopter participated in the Army's team exercises for the evaluation of air mobility and became fully operational with the First Cavalry Division (Air Mobile), formerly the 11th Air Assault Division. The Chinook was classified in October 1963 as Standard A (the US Army's designation for its standard medium transport helicopter).

By the end of 1972, more than 550 CH-47 Chinooks had been deployed in Vietnam. On one occasion, no fewer than 147 refugees and their possessions were evacuated on a single flight; and more than 11,500 disabled aircraft worth more than $3·0 billion had been recovered by Chinooks and flown to repair bases by that date.

On 6 March 1972 the Australian government announced an order for 12 CH-47Cs for the RAAF, and these were delivered during 1973. The Spanish Army has ordered six CH-47Cs; delivery began in December 1972 and extended into 1974. Eight were ordered by Canada in August 1973, and deliveries of these were scheduled to start in the latter half of 1974.

It is reported that all of the US Army's surviving CH-47As and -47Bs are to be modified to CH-47C standard.

CH-47 helicopters are in service at many locations, including Alaska, Australia, Germany, Hawaii, Iran, Italy, Korea, Spain, Thailand and Vietnam, as well as at numerous US National Guard and US Army installations within the continental United States.

Type: Twin-engined medium transport helicopter.

Rotor System (CH-47A): Two three-blade rotors, rotating in opposite directions and driven through interconnecting shafts which enable both rotors to be driven by either engine. Blades have a steel "D" spar, to which trailing-edge boxes constructed of aluminium ribs and glass-fibre skin are bonded. They have a modified NACA 0012 section, and have provision for a chemical de-icing system. Two blades of each rotor can be folded manually. Rotor heads are fully articulated, with pitch, flapping and drag hinges. All bearings are submerged completely in oil.

Rotor System (CH-47B/C): Blades have cambered leading-edge, a strengthened steel spar structure and honeycomb-filled trailing-edge boxes, and are approximately 6 in (15 cm) longer than those of the CH-47A.

Rotor Drive: Power is transmitted from each engine through individual overrunning clutches, into the combiner transmission, thereby providing a single power output to the interconnecting shafts. Rotor/engine rpm ratio 66 : 1 for the A and B models, and 64 : 1 for the CH-47C.

Fuselage: Square-section all-metal semi-monocoque structure. Loading ramp forms undersurface of upswept rear fuselage. Fairing pods along bottom of each side are made of metal honeycomb sandwich and are sealed and compartmented, as is the underfloor section of the fuselage, for buoyancy during operation from water.

Landing Gear: Non-retractable quadricycle type, with twin wheels on each forward unit and single wheels on each rear unit. Oleo-pneumatic shock-absorbers on all units. Rear units fully castoring and steerable; power steering installed on starboard rear unit. All wheels are government-furnished size 24 × 7·7-VII, with tyres size 8·50-10-III, pressure 67 lb/sq in (4·71 kg/cm²). Two single-disc hydraulic brakes. Provision for fitting detachable wheel-skis.

Power Plant: Two Lycoming T55 turboshaft engines (details given under model listings), mounted on each side of rear rotor pylon. Self-sealing fuel tanks in external pods on sides of fuselage. Total fuel capacity is 621 US gallons (2,350 litres) for the CH-47A/B; and 1,093 US gallons (4,137 litres), or 1,042 US gallons (3,944 litres) when equipped with Crashworthy Fuel System, for the CH-47C. Refuelling points above tanks. Total oil capacity 3·7 US gallons (14 litres).

Accommodation: Two pilots on flight deck, with dual controls. Jump seat is provided for crew chief or combat commander. Jettisonable door on each side of flight deck. Depending on seating arrangement, 33 to 44 troops can be accommodated in main cabin, or 24 litters plus two attendants, or vehicles and freight. Typical loads include a complete artillery section with crew and ammunition. All components of the Pershing missile system are transportable by Chinooks. Extruded magnesium floor designed for distributed load of 300 lb/sq ft (1,465 kg/m²) and concentrated load of 2,500 lb (1,136 kg) per wheel in tread portion. Floor contains eighty-three 5,000 lb (2,270 kg) tie-down fittings and eight 10,000 lb (4,540 kg) fittings. Rear loading ramp can be left completely or partially open, or can be removed to permit transport of extra-long cargo and in-flight parachute or free-drop delivery of cargo and equipment. Main cabin door, at front on starboard side, comprises upper hinged section which can be opened in flight and lower section with integral steps. Lower section is jettisonable.

Systems: Cabin heated by 200,000 BTU heater-blower. Hydraulic system provides pressures of 3,000 lb/sq in (210 kg/cm²) for flying controls, and 4,000 lb/sq in (280 kg/cm²) for engine starting. Electrical system includes two 20kVA alternators driven by transmission drive system. Solar T62 APU runs accessory gear drive, thereby operating all hydraulic and electrical systems.

Electronics and Equipment: All government furnished, including UHF communications and FM liaison sets, transponder, intercom, omni-receiver, ADF and marker beacon receiver. Blind-flying instrumentation standard. Special equipment includes dual electro-hydraulic stability augmentation system, automatic/manual speed trim system, hydraulically-powered winch for rescue and cargo handling purposes, cargo and rescue hatch in floor, external cargo hook of 20,000 lb (9,072 kg) capacity, integral work stands and steps for maintenance, rearview mirror, provisions for paratroops' static lines and for maintenance davits for removal of major components.

Dimensions, external:

Diameter of rotors (each):	
CH-47A	59 ft 1¼ in (18·02 m)
CH-47B/C	60 ft 0 in (18·29 m)
Main rotor blade chord:	
CH-47A	1 ft 11 in (58·4 cm)
CH-47B/C	2 ft 1¼ in (63·5 cm)
Distance between rotor centres	39 ft 2 in (11·94 m)
Length overall, rotors turning:	
CH-47A	98 ft 1·3 in (29·90 m)
CH-47B/C	99 ft 0 in (30·18 m)
Length of fuselage	51 ft 0 in (15·54 m)
Width, rotors folded	12 ft 5 in (3·78 m)
Height to top of rear rotor hub	18 ft 7 in (5·67 m)
Wheelbase	22 ft 6 in (6·86 m)
Passenger door (fwd, stbd):	
Height	5 ft 6 in (1·68 m)
Width	3 ft 0 in (0·91 m)
Height to sill	3 ft 7 in (1·09 m)
Rear loading ramp entrance:	
Height	6 ft 6 in (1·98 m)
Width	7 ft 7 in (2·31 m)
Height to sill	2 ft 7 in (0·79 m)

Dimensions, internal:

Cabin, excluding flight deck:	
Length	30 ft 2 in (9·20 m)
Width	7 ft 6 in (2·29 m)
Height	6 ft 6 in (1·98 m)
Floor area	226 sq ft (21·0 m²)
Usable volume	1,474 cu ft (41·7 m³)

Areas:

Rotor blades (each):	
CH-47A	56·6 sq ft (5·26 m²)
CH-47B/C	63·1 sq ft (5·86 m²)
Main rotor discs (total):	
CH-47A	5,486 sq ft (509·6 m²)
CH-47B/C	5,655 sq ft (525·3 m²)

Weights and Performance:
See adjoining table

CH-47 CHINOOK WEIGHTS AND PERFORMANCE

	Condition 1	Condition 2	Condition 3
Take-off weight:			
CH-47A	28,400 lb (12,882 kg)	28,550 lb (12,950 kg)	33,000 lb (14,969 kg)
CH-47B	31,350 lb (14,220 kg)	33,000 lb (14,969 kg)	40,000 lb (18,144 kg)
CH-47C	39,200 lb (17,781 kg)	33,000 lb (14,969 kg)	46,000 lb (20,865 kg)
Weight empty:			
CH-47A	17,932 lb (8,133 kg)	17,932 lb (8,133 kg)	18,112 lb (8,216 kg)
CH-47B	19,375 lb (8,788 kg)	19,375 lb (8,788 kg)	19,555 lb (8,870 kg)
CH-47C	20,616 lb (9,351 kg)	20,616 lb (9,351 kg)	20,785 lb (9,428 kg)
Payload:			
CH-47A	6,000 lb (2,722 kg)	6,150 lb (2,790 kg)	13,400 lb (6,078 kg)
CH-47B	7,200 lb (3,266 kg)	8,850 lb (4,014 kg)	18,600 lb (8,437 kg)
CH-47C	13,212 lb (5,992 kg)	7,262 lb (3,294 kg)	23,212 lb (10,528 kg)
Mission radius:			
CH-47A	100 nm (115 miles; 185 km)	100 nm (115 miles; 185 km)	20 nm (23 miles; 37 km)
CH-47B	93 nm (107 miles; 172 km)	92 nm (106 miles; 171 km)	20 nm (23 miles; 37 km)
CH-47C	100 nm (115 miles; 185 km)	100 nm (115 miles; 185 km)	20 nm (23 miles; 37 km)
Average cruising speed:			
CH-47A	130 knots* (150 mph; 241 km/h)	130 knots* (150 mph; 241 km/h)	115 knots* (132 mph; 212 km/h)
CH-47B	141 knots (162 mph; 261 km/h)	141 knots (162 mph; 261 km/h)	119 knots (137 mph; 220 km/h)
CH-47C	139 knots (160 mph; 257 km/h)	137 knots (158 mph; 254 km/h)	114 knots (131 mph; 211 km/h)
Max speed at S/L, normal rated power:			
CH-47A	130 knots* (150 mph; 241 km/h)	130 knots* (150 mph; 241 km/h)	110 knots* (127 mph; 204 km/h)
CH-47B	156 knots (180 mph; 290 km/h)	155 knots (178 mph; 286 km/h)	125 knots (144 mph; 232 km/h)
CH-47C	156 knots* (180 mph; 290 km/h)	164 knots (189 mph; 304 km/h)	123 knots* (142 mph; 229 km/h)
Max rate of climb at S/L, standard temperature, normal rated power:			
CH-47A	2,180 ft (664 m)/min	2,160 ft (658 m)/min	1,595 ft (486 m)/min
CH-47B	2,225 ft (678 m)/min	2,010 ft (613 m)/min	1,285 ft (392 m)/min
CH-47C	2,045 ft (623 m)/min	2,880 ft (878 m)/min	1,320 ft (402 m)/min
Hovering ceiling out of ground effect, max power, standard temperature:			
CH-47A	12,500 ft (3,810 m)	12,300 ft (3,750 m)	7,300 ft (2,225 m)
CH-47B	12,400 ft (3,780 m)	10,700 ft (3,260 m)	1,700 ft (520 m)
CH-47C	9,600 ft (2,925 m)	14,750 ft (4,495 m)	Sea Level
Service ceiling, normal rated power, standard temperature:			
CH-47A	11,900 ft (3,625 m)	11,900 ft (3,625 m)	9,200 ft (2,805 m)
CH-47B	15,000 ft (4,570 m)	14,000 ft (4,265 m)	9,000 ft (2,745 m)
CH-47C	10,200 ft (3,110 m)	15,000 ft (4,570 m)	8,000 ft (2,440 m)
Max ferry range (integral and internal auxiliary fuel only). Cruise at optimum altitude and standard temperature. No payload. 10% fuel reserve.			
CH-47A	—	—	835 nm (962 miles; 1,548 km)
CH-47B	—	—	1,086 nm (1,250 miles; 2,021 km)
CH-47C	—	—	1,223 nm (1,409 miles 2,267 km)

Condition 1 Criteria: Take-off gross weight equals gross weight to hover out of ground effect at 6,000 ft/95°F (1,830 m/35°C). Radius of action of 100 nm (115 miles; 185 km). Fuel reserve of 10%. Payload is carried internally.

Condition 2 Criteria: Take-off gross weight equals design gross weight. Radius of action of 100 nm (115 miles; 185 km). Fuel reserve of 10%. Payload is carried internally.

Condition 3 Criteria: Take-off gross weight equals alternative design gross weight. Radius of action of 20 nm (23 miles; 37 km). Fuel reserve of 10%. Payload is carried externally. Except for the mission average cruise speed, all other performance is predicated on internal loading of cargo.

*Current flight envelope.

BOEING VERTOL YUH-61A

The US Department of Defense announced on 30 August 1972 that it had awarded a $91 million contract to the Boeing Vertol Company to design, build and test three prototypes under the US Army's Utility Tactical Transport Aircraft System (UTTAS) programme.

Each of these aircraft, designated YUH-61A, is a twin-engined single-rotor helicopter, designed to carry 11 troops and a crew of three. It is intended for use as a troop transport or for medical evacuation and logistics duties. UTTAS aircraft are scheduled to replace the US Army's UH-1H Iroquois in the assault transport role in the late 1970s.

The development programme will emphasise reliability and maintainability features, in order to keep life-cycle costs to a minimum. Stringent production cost goals have been established and have been made an incentive feature of the development contract.

The YUH-61A incorporates many advances in helicopter technology which should contribute to a substantial reduction in costs, while at the same time improving safety, reliability, performance and flight characteristics. As an example, the use of a simplified hingeless rotor of composite materials will bring a significant reduction in working parts by comparison with previous designs, as well as resulting in superior aircraft stability and safety. Built-in work platforms, direct access to all major components and modularised design will offer improved maintainability and should increase the productivity of the aircraft.

The power plant comprises two 1,500 shp General Electric T700-GE-700 turboshaft engines. All transmission components are supplied by Litton Systems, Power Transmission Division.

First flight of the prototype YUH-61A was scheduled for November 1974. Following an evaluation competition between UTTAS prototypes developed by Boeing Vertol and Sikorsky Aircraft, it was expected that a production contract would be awarded to one of these companies.

BOEING VERTOL MODEL 179

Boeing Vertol's Model 179 is a commercial derivative of the YUH-61A helicopter designed to meet the US Army's UTTAS requirement.

A twenty-passenger twin-turbine single-rotor helicopter, the Model 179 will be in the 17,500 lb (7,937 kg) gross weight class and will have full IFR capability. Advanced technology features developed for the YUH-61A will ensure that this new aircraft has high standards of reliability and safety, coupled with low vibration and noise levels, and substantial reductions in operating costs for a helicopter in this weight category.

A prototype was under construction in early 1974, with the first flight scheduled to take place in early 1975.

BOEING VERTOL XCH-62

In November 1970, the US Department of Defense issued to nine aerospace manufacturers requests for proposals for the advanced technology components of the Heavy Lift Helicopter (HLH) programme. From five tenders received, that submitted by Boeing Vertol was selected and the company was awarded a $67 million contract on 25 June 1971 for the first phase of the development of an HLH.

The objective of the first phase of the programme was to demonstrate component technology, to reduce the development risks applicable to an HLH with a design mission payload of 22·5 tons, and with the ability to carry up to 35 tons for shorter distances. The Boeing Vertol design uses tandem rotors and a transmission not greatly larger than systems in current use, in order to ensure the lowest possible technical risk, as well as lower costs for development and production.

Boeing Vertol has designed, built and started testing of all selected advanced technology components. These include a titanium and glassfibre rotor blade with Boeing-developed aerofoil section, a titanium hub with elastomeric bearing blade retention, a drive system using advanced gear materials and integral transmission lubricating systems, a fly-by-wire flight control system, and a cargo handling system incorporating dual winches.

An Allison T701-AD-700 power plant has been selected for the HLH. Allison 501-M62B test engines have been delivered to Boeing Vertol for installation on a dynamic system test rig, which was constructed to provide early verification of rotor and transmission design. It is limited to the aft rotor, and is powered by three turboshaft engines driving through a combiner transmission and an aft transmission, the load of the forward rotor being simulated by the interconnecting shaft driving a dynamic water brake.

On 29 January 1973 the Boeing Vertol Company was awarded a contract to build a single prototype, designated XCH-62, and to conduct the initial flight test programme. This phase of the programme will permit flight demonstration of the advanced technology components, and will also provide a basis for both technical and cost projections of an operational HLH. The first flight is scheduled for August 1975.

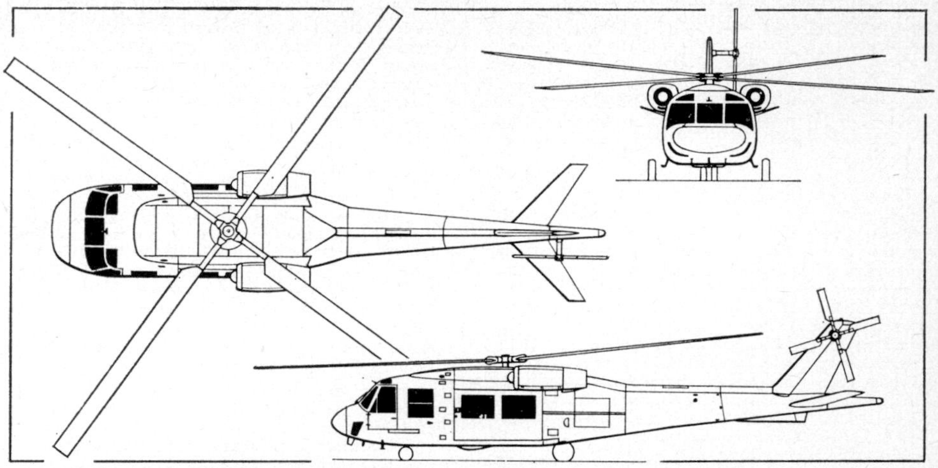

Boeing Vertol YUH-61A Utility Tactical Transport Aircraft System (UTTAS) (*Pilot Press*)

Full-scale mockup of the Boeing Vertol Model 179

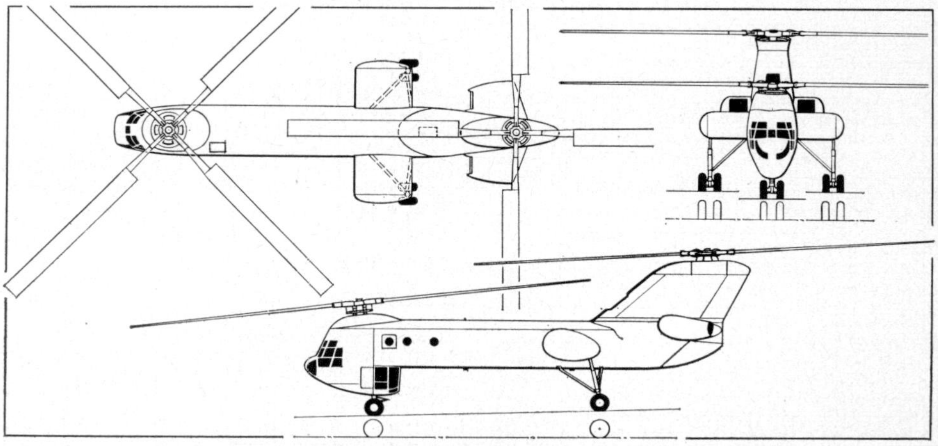

Boeing Vertol XCH-62 heavy lift helicopter (*Pilot Press*)

Boeing Vertol Model 347 HLH advanced technology demonstration aircraft, with fly-by-wire control system and retractable underfuselage capsule to evaluate the load-controlling crewman's station and functions

Boeing Vertol announced on 28 February 1974 that it had completed testing of a full-scale HLH cargo handling system integrated test rig. Consisting of a twin tower structure 70 ft (21·34 m) in height, the rig carried the winches, pneumatic hoist drives, dual tension member suspension system, cargo couplings, and control and display systems, that will be installed in the XCH-62. The test programme included hoisting, pneumatic braking, load acquisition and release, and static load holding to simulate cruise flight. In service, the HLH system will be expected to handle external cargo loads of up to 28 tons at 2·5*g*. It was tested with loads of up to 50 US tons.

The general appearance of the HLH is shown in the accompanying three-view drawing. Responsibility for developing this aircraft has been assigned to the US Army, with Navy participation in the programme, although the aircraft has to meet the shore-based heavy lift requirements of all the US services.

TYPE: Three-engined heavy transport helicopter.

ROTOR SYSTEM: Two four-blade rotors turning in opposite directions and driven through an interconnecting shaft. Each composite-structure blade is of advanced aerofoil section. The leading-edge of the glassfibre spar is protected by a formed titanium nose cap, while the trailing-edge comprises a subassembly of glassfibre/Nomex honeycomb. The blades have redundant load paths and incorporate diagnostic warning and pneumatic failure warning systems. The titanium rotor hub has elastomeric bearing blade retention. The rotor system has an estimated mean time between replacements of 2,000 hours.

ROTOR DRIVE: The combining transmission has an output rating of 17,700 shp. Power is transmitted from each turboshaft engine into the combiner transmission, thereby providing a single power output through interconnecting shafts to each rotor transmission. All gearboxes have integral cooling, dual lubrication, self-sealing sumps and casing, diagnostic and failure warning systems. New design offers reduced noise levels, and the estimated mean time between replacements is 2,000 hours. Rotor rpm is 156, equivalent to a tip speed of 750 ft (229 m)/sec.

FUSELAGE: Square-section all-metal honeycomb sandwich structure.

LANDING GEAR: Non-retractable tricycle type, with twin wheels on each unit. Oleo-pneumatic shock-absorber on each unit. The landing gear provides approximately 14 ft (4·27 m) of headroom between the fuselage undersurface and the ground, to permit loading of large containers.

POWER PLANT: Three Allison XT701-AD-700 turboshaft engines, each with an intermediate max rating of 8,079 shp. One engine is mounted on each side of the rear rotor pylon, the third centrally within the fuselage structure. Maximum integral fuel capacity 20,100 lb (9,117 kg).

ACCOMMODATION: Crew of two on flight deck in side-by-side seats; aft-facing load controlling crewman, flight engineer and crew chief.

SYSTEMS: Flight control system relies upon fly-by-wire techniques to enhance combat survivability. Central data computer, automatic flight control system with precision hover subsystem, and full IFR capability. External cargo system provided for single or dual suspension by means of pneumatically-operated winches. Provision for in-flight load levelling capability, vision augmentation, and discharge of static electricity.

DIMENSIONS, EXTERNAL:
- Diameter of rotors (each): 92 ft 0 in (28·04 m)
- Rotor blade chord: 3 ft 4 in (1·02 m)
- Length overall, rotors turning: 162 ft 3 in (49·45 m)
- Length of fuselage: 89 ft 3 in (27·20 m)
- Height to top of rear rotor hub: 38 ft 7½ in (11·77 m)
- Wheel track: 25 ft 4 in (7·72 m)
- Wheelbase: 44 ft 7 in (13·59 m)

AREAS:
- Rotor blades (each): 153 sq ft (14·2 m²)
- Rotor discs (total): 13,295 sq ft (1,235 m²)

WEIGHTS AND LOADING (design):
- Weight empty: 58,929 lb (26,729 kg)
- Design mission fuel weight: 11,723 lb (5,318 kg)
- Design payload: 45,000 lb (20,412 kg)
- Design gross weight: 118,000 lb (53,529 kg)
- Max alternate gross weight: 148,000 lb (67,129 kg)
- Disc loading at design gross weight: 8·9 lb/sq ft (43·45 kg/m²)

BOWERS

PETER M. BOWERS

ADDRESS:
13826 Des Moines Way South, Seattle, Washington 98168

Mr Peter Bowers, an aeronautical engineer with Boeing in Seattle, is a principal source of detailed information on vintage aircraft in the United States, and has provided much of the data for a number of replicas of 1914-18 War aircraft now under construction or flying.

Among several aircraft built by Mr Bowers is a full-scale replica of the Wright Model EX of 1911, the first aeroplane to cross the American continent. This machine was tested as a towed sailplane in the Autumn of 1961 and during 1967/68 was converted into a replica of the Wright Model "A", the US Army's first aeroplane. Powered by a 25 hp Ford Model "T" engine, it was intended to take part in celebrations to mark the anniversary of the 1908/09 flights of the original machine.

In addition to this work on replicas, Mr Bowers has designed and built a single-seat light aircraft known as the Fly Baby, of which full details are given below.

Mr Bowers has almost completed the prototype of a new two-seat light aircraft of his own design. Named Namu II, after Seattle's famous captive whale, as well as for its bulky appearance by comparison with the Fly Baby, it was expected to be completed by June 1974. Meanwhile, another Namu II, with different canopy, has been completed by Richard Lowe and Tom Godbey of Seattle.

Bowers Fly Baby 1-A built by Mr Ray Lee of Seattle, Washington. Its early-model Continental A65 engine has upward-facing exhaust ports

Two-seat version of the Bowers Fly Baby 1-A built by students of Ash Fork High School, Arizona

BOWERS FLY BABY 1-A

The prototype Fly Baby monoplane was produced to compete in an Experimental Aircraft Association design contest, organised to encourage the development of a simple, low-cost, easy-to-fly aeroplane that could be built by inexperienced amateurs for recreational flying. It was built in 720 working hours, at a cost of $1,050, and flew for the first time on 27 July 1960. As only one other aircraft was completed by the specified closing date, the contest was postponed for two years.

Following a crash in April 1962, when a pilot borrowed the Fly Baby and became lost in mountain country in bad weather, an entirely new fuselage was built. This is 6 in (15 cm) longer than the original and features minor structural improvements. In addition, the original Continental A65 engine, converted to give 75 hp, was replaced by a C75 engine converted to give 85 hp, and the capacity of the fuel tank was increased from 12 to 16 US gallons (60·5 litres).

When the EAA contest was finally held in the Summer of 1962, Fly Baby was placed first and won a prize of $2,500. Home construction plans of the aircraft are available and 3,496 sets had been sold by late March 1974. Construction of well over 600 Fly Babies is known to have been undertaken, of which 165 had been completed and flown by 31 March 1974, including some based on detailed drawings and instructions published in *Sport Aviation*, journal of the EAA.

The Fly Baby monoplane has been tested as a twin-float seaplane, in which configuration it has a max AUW of 1,000 lb (454 kg) and cruising speed of 84 knots (97 mph; 156 km/h).

During 1968, Mr Bowers designed and built interchangeable biplane wings for the Fly Baby, and he has since designated the monoplane version as the Fly Baby 1-A, and the biplane as the Fly Baby 1-B.

Mr Bowers received repeated requests to provide plans for a two-seat version of the Fly Baby, but declined initially on the grounds that an extensive redesign would be necessary to maintain structural integrity. Despite this a number of homebuilders completed two-seat versions, usually by confining their modifications to increased fuselage width, for side-by-side seats and a single, central control column.

Mr Bowers amended his plans during 1973 to allow for construction of a two-seat version of the Fly Baby. The changes include a 3 ft 2 in (0·97 m) wide fuselage, a 5 ft 0 in (1·52 m) span wing centre-section to support a shock-absorbing landing gear similar to that of the Ryan ST/PT-22 of 1934-42, the use of heavier flying wires with swaged fork ends, a raised aft turtledeck to offset the drag of the larger cockpit and a recommendation to use an engine of 85 to 107 hp. The outer wing panels are unchanged, giving the two-seat Fly Baby a span of 31 ft 0 in (9·45 m) and wing area of 133·5 sq ft (12·4 m²).

The following description applies to the original single-seat Fly Baby 1-A. The Fly Baby 1-B biplane is described separately.

TYPE: Single-seat light monoplane.

WINGS: Wire-braced low-wing monoplane. Double ⅛ in 1 × 19 stainless steel bracing wires. Wing section NACA 4412. Wooden two-spar structure, covered with Dacron fabric and finished with two coats of nitrate dope and one coat of automotive enamel. Wings rotate about a special fitting to fold back alongside the fuselage for towing.

FUSELAGE: Conventional plywood-covered wood structure of rectangular section. Decking behind cockpit, including pilot's headrest, is removable and can be replaced with higher transparent section matched with a sliding transparent cockpit canopy for enclosed cockpit operation.

TAIL UNIT: Wire-braced wood structure, fabric-covered.

LANDING GEAR: Non-retractable tailwheel type. Main landing gear struts of laminated wood, braced by crossed steel wires. Steel-tube straight-across axle faired with streamline-section steel tube. Ends of axles project beyond wheel hubs to serve as anchor points for wing bracing wires. Shock-absorption by low-pressure 8·00-4 tyres, carried on Piper Cub wheels, with hydraulic brakes.

POWER PLANT: One 85 hp Continental C75 four-cylinder horizontally-opposed aircooled engine, driving a two-blade fixed-pitch propeller. Fuel tank from Piper J-3 Cub, capacity 16 US gallons (60·5 litres).

ACCOMMODATION: Single seat in open or enclosed cockpit. Baggage in underfuselage "tank" which can be removed and carried like a suitcase.

DIMENSIONS, EXTERNAL:
- Wing span: 28 ft 0 in (8·53 m)
- Wing chord (constant): 4 ft 6 in (1·37 m)
- Length overall: 18 ft 6 in (5·64 m)
- Height, wings folded: 6 ft 6 in (1·98 m)

WEIGHTS:
- Weight empty: 605 lb (274 kg)
- Max T-O weight: 924 lb (419 kg)

PERFORMANCE (at max T-O weight):
- Max level speed at S/L: over 104 knots (120 mph; 193 km/h)
- Cruising speed: 91-96 knots (105-110 mph; 169-177 km/h)
- Landing speed: 39 knots (45 mph; 72·5 km/h)
- Max rate of climb at S/L: 1,100 ft (335 m)/min
- T-O run: 250 ft (76 m)

Landing run 250 ft (76 m)
Range with max fuel
277 nm (320 miles; 515 km)

BOWERS FLY BABY 1-B

During 1968 Mr Bowers designed and built a set of interchangeable biplane wings for the original prototype Fly Baby and with these fitted it flew for the first time on 27 March 1969.

The new wings have the same aerofoil section and incidence as those of the monoplane version, but the rib webs are made of $\frac{1}{16}$ in instead of $\frac{1}{8}$ in plywood and the wingtip bows are formed from $\frac{1}{2}$ in aluminium tube instead of laminated wood strips. This lightweight construction limits weight increase to only 46 lb (20 kg) for an increase of 30 sq ft (2·79 m²) in wing area. Span is reduced by 6 ft (1·83 m) and chord by 1 ft (0·30 m). Ailerons are fitted to the lower wings only.

To facilitate entry to the cockpit the upper wing has been located well forward, and in order to bring the new centre of lift in line with the original CG, both planes have been given 11° of sweepback. Changeover from monoplane to biplane configuration can be accomplished by two people in approximately one hour.

The description of the Fly Baby 1-A applies also to the 1-B, except in the following details:

TYPE: Single-seat light biplane.

WINGS: Forward-stagger single-bay biplane with N-type interplane and centre-section struts. Landing and flying bracing wires. Sweepback 11°. Wooden structure with Dacron covering. Rib webs constructed of $\frac{1}{16}$ in plywood, wingtip bows formed of $\frac{1}{2}$ in aluminium tube. Ailerons on lower wings only.

POWER PLANT: One 85 hp Continental C85 four-cylinder horizontally-opposed aircooled engine.

DIMENSIONS, EXTERNAL:
Wing span 22 ft 0 in (6·71 m)
Wing chord, both wings (constant)
3 ft 6 in (1·07 m)
Height overall 6 ft 10 in (2·08 m)

AREA:
Wings, gross 150 sq ft (13·94 m²)

WEIGHTS AND LOADING:
Weight empty 651 lb (295 kg)
Max T-O weight 972 lb (440 kg)
Max wing loading 6·5 lb/sq ft (31·74 kg/m²)

PERFORMANCE (at max T-O weight):
Cruising speed 75·5 knots (87 mph; 140 km/h)
Max rate of climb at S/L 875 ft (267 m)/min

Bowers Fly Baby 1-B biplane, out of service in mid-1974 for installation of a modified Corvair motor car engine

With bubble canopy and 150 hp Lycoming O-320 engine, modified Bowers Namu II built by Richard Lowe and Tom Godbey of Seattle, Washington

BOWERS NAMU II

TYPE: Two-seat amateur-built sporting aircraft.

WINGS: Cantilever low-wing monoplane. Wing section NACA 4415 at root, NACA 4412 at tip. Wing centre-section has anhedral, outer wing has dihedral. Composite three-piece monospar structure. The spar has laminated spruce flanges and $\frac{1}{8}$ in mahogany marine plywood webs. The leading-edge torsion box is a sandwich of two sheets of 2024-T3 aluminium with glassfibre cloth between, epoxy-cemented together and formed over $\frac{3}{8}$ in mahogany marine plywood nose ribs. The ribs aft of the spar are cut from $\frac{1}{8}$ in plywood and have $\frac{1}{4}$ in by $\frac{1}{2}$ in slotted spruce cap strips. The structure is Dacron-covered. Slotted ailerons. No flaps. No trim tabs.

TAIL UNIT: Dacron-covered wooden structure. Controllable trim tab in starboard elevator.

LANDING GEAR: Non-retractable tailwheel type. Main wheels are mounted in symmetrical bent-steel forks welded directly to the cantilever main legs. Main wheels size 6·00-6. Steerable tailwheel. Disc-type hydraulic brakes. Glass-fibre fairings on main wheels.

POWER PLANT: One 125 hp Lycoming O-290-G (GPU) four-cylinder horizontally-opposed air-cooled engine. One fuselage fuel tank, mounted immediately aft of the firewall, capacity 32 US gallons (121 litres).

ACCOMMODATION: Two seats side by side under transparent canopy. Dual controls. Stowage for 100 lb (45 kg) baggage under and aft of the seats.

DIMENSIONS, EXTERNAL:
Wing span 33 ft 0 in (10·06 m)
Length overall 21 ft 6 in (6·55 m)

AREA:
Wings, gross 150 sq ft (13·9 m²)

WEIGHTS AND LOADINGS (estimated):
Weight empty 1,050 lb (476 kg)
Max T-O weight 1,750 lb (793 kg)
Max wing loading 11·66 lb/sq ft (56·9 kg/m²)
Max power loading 14 lb/hp (6·35 kg/hp)

PERFORMANCE (estimated at max T-O weight):
Max level speed
117 knots (135 mph; 217 km/h)
Cruising speed 104 knots (120 mph; 193 km/h)
Landing speed 43·5 knots (50 mph; 80·4 km/h)
Max rate of climb at S/L 850 ft (259 m)/min
Service ceiling 15,000 ft (4,570 m)
Range with max fuel
434 nm (500 miles; 804 km)

BRANTLY

BRANTLY OPERATORS INC

HEAD OFFICE AND WORKS:
PO Box 1046, Frederick, Oklahoma 73542
Telephone: (405) 335-2256

PRESIDENT: Michael K. Hynes

All rights in Brantly helicopters have been acquired by this company, the president of which, Mr M. K. Hynes, owns the Type Certificates for the Brantly B-2, B-2A, B-2B and Model 305. Details of the B-2A appear in the 1963-64 *Jane's* and of the B-2B, B-2E and Model 305 in the 1970-71 *Jane's*.

First concern of the new company has been to initiate production of urgently needed components, under the supervision of Mr N. O. Brantly at the original manufacturing location in Frederick, Oklahoma. This factory, which had originally a working area of 7,200 sq ft (669 m²), was expanded to 102,000 sq ft (9,476 m²) during 1973 in preparation for re-establishment of a production line.

It was anticipated that the Model B-2B would be put back into production in the Autumn of 1974 and that production of the Model 305 would begin about six months later.

Brantly Operators Inc has received FAA approval of its construction of main rotor blades for the B-2 series and Model 305, and in February 1973 dealers and distributors were being selected for the US, South America and Europe.

BROKAW-JONES

BERGON F. BROKAW, MD, FACFP, and ERNEST R. JONES, PhD

ADDRESS:
Route 3, PO Box 58B, Leesburg, Florida 32748
Telephone: (904) 787-2339/1324

BROKAW-JONES BJ-520

Dr B. F. Brokaw, a former US Navy pilot, and Dr E. Jones, who has a PhD in aeronautical engineering, have combined talents to design and build a two-seat low-wing monoplane which could prove to be the world's fastest homebuilt. Dr Brokaw has been concerned primarily with overall design and construction, Dr Jones with stress analysis and structural design.

Design emphasis was to evolve a high-speed all-weather two-seat homebuilt suitable for cross-country flying. Aerobatic potential was of secondary consideration, but the BJ-520 is stressed to $\pm 6g$ for aerobatics and $9g$ ultimate.

Design began in September 1966 and construction of the prototype started five months later. First flight of the BJ-520 was made on 18 November 1972, and during the Summer of 1973 work was carried out to clean up the airframe to achieve the full potential of the design. This included the provision of wheel-well doors, and attention to reduce the drag of the engine cooling system, achieved by the use of baffles, ducts and direct ram air cooling. It was intended in early

Brokaw-Jones BJ-520 homebuilt cabin monoplane (285 hp Continental TSIO-520-B engine)

1974 to modify the profile of the windscreen to improve aerodynamic efficiency.

An information package and plans are available to amateur constructors.

TYPE: Two-seat homebuilt sporting aircraft.

WINGS: Cantilever low-wing monoplane. Laminar-flow wing section: NACA 64_1A212 at root, NACA 64_1A210 at tip. Dihedral 3°. Incidence 1° at root, —2° at tip. Conventional structure of 2024-T3 light alloy. Ailerons and trailing-edge flaps of light alloy.

FUSELAGE: Semi-monocoque structure of light alloy.

TAIL UNIT: Cantilever light alloy structure. Fixed-incidence tailplane. Electrically-operated trim tabs in elevators and rudder.

LANDING GEAR: Hydraulically-retractable tricycle type. Main and nose units and associated hydraulic system are from a Navion aircraft. Single wheel on each unit, with 6·00 × 15 low-profile tyre, pressure 65 lb/sq in (4·57 kg/cm²). Goodyear hydraulic brakes on main wheels.

POWER PLANT: One 285 hp Continental TSIO-520-B turbocharged six-cylinder horizontally-opposed aircooled fuel-injection engine, driving a McCauley three-blade metal constant-speed propeller with spinner. Four integral wing fuel tanks, with usable capacity of 66 US gallons (250 litres). Refuelling points at wingtips. Oil capacity 3 US gallons (11·3 litres).

ACCOMMODATION: Two seats in tandem beneath transparent individual canopies. Port half of each canopy hinged at centreline, to open upwards. Baggage space aft of rear seat. Cabin heated and ventilated.

SYSTEMS: Hydraulic system at 1,500 lb/sq in (105 kg/cm²) for landing gear retraction and brakes. 24V electrical system. Oxygen system for pilot and passenger, with capacity in excess of 4 hours.

ELECTRONICS AND EQUIPMENT: Full IFR instrumentation, including DGO 10, DME 70, dual 360-channel transceivers and dual VORs, ADF, transponder, marker beacon and ILS. Landing gear warning lights, navigation lights and external power socket.

DIMENSIONS, EXTERNAL:
Wing span 20 ft 6 in (6·25 m)
Wing chord at root 5 ft 0 in (1·52 m)
Length overall 22 ft 6 in (6·86 m)
Height overall 9 ft 4 in (2·84 m)
Tailplane span 8 ft 0 in (2·44 m)

AREAS:
Wings, gross 78·8 sq ft (7·32 m²)
Fin 5·13 sq ft (0·48 m²)
Rudder, including tab 5·25 sq ft (0·49 m²)
Tailplane 13·05 sq ft (1·21 m²)
Elevators, including tab 7·63 sq ft (0·71 m²)

WEIGHTS AND LOADINGS:
Weight empty 2,105 lb (955 kg)
Max T-O weight 2,920 lb (1,324 kg)
Max wing loading 37·5 lb/sq ft (183·1 kg/m²)
Max power loading 10·2 lb/hp (4·6 kg/hp)

PERFORMANCE (at max T-O weight):
Max never-exceed speed 274 knots (315 mph; 507 km/h)
Max cruising speed at 20,000 ft (6,100 m) 257 knots (296 mph; 476 km/h)
Econ cruising speed at 20,000 ft (6,100 m) 220 knots (253 mph; 407 km/h)
Stalling speed, flaps down 75 knots (87 mph; 140 km/h)
Max rate of climb at S/L 1,800 ft (549 m)/min
Service ceiling 25,000 ft (7,620 m)
T-O run 1,400 ft (427 m)
T-O to 50 ft (15 m) 2,500 ft (762 m)
Landing from 50 ft (15 m) 2,700 ft (823 m)
Landing run 1,500 ft (457 m)
Range with max fuel, with reserve 900 nm (1,036 miles; 1,667 km)

BUSHBY

BUSHBY AIRCRAFT INC

ADDRESS:
Route 1, PO Box 13, Minooka, Illinois 60447

Mr Robert W. Bushby, a research engineer with Sinclair Oil Co, began by building a Midget Mustang single-seat sporting monoplane, using drawings, jigs and certain components produced by the aircraft's designer, the late David Long. He has since produced the aircraft in kit form and also offers sets of plans of the Midget Mustang and a two-seat derivative known as the Mustang II to amateur constructors.

BUSHBY/LONG MM-I MIDGET MUSTANG

The prototype of the Midget Mustang was completed in 1948 by David Long, then chief engineer of the Piper company. He flew it in the National Air Races that year, and in 1949 was placed fourth in the Continental Trophy Race at Miami.

Two basic versions have been developed by Robert Bushby, as follows:

MM-1-85. Powered by 85 hp Continental C85-8FJ engine. Flew for first time on 9 September 1959.

MM-1-125. Powered by 135 hp Lycoming O-290-D2 engine. Otherwise similar to MM-1-85. Flew for first time in July 1963. New propeller introduced during 1973 has improved max speed and cruising speed.

At least 80 Midget Mustangs had been completed by the Spring of 1974 and there were 700 more under construction throughout the world. Several of those now flying are powered by a 150 hp Lycoming O-320 engine, providing a cruising speed of 234 knots (270 mph; 435 km/h) at 8,000 ft (2,440 m). Some have been fitted with retractable main landing gear.

The following details apply to the two basic versions:

TYPE: Single-seat fully-aerobatic sporting monoplane.

WINGS: Cantilever low-wing monoplane. Wing section NACA 64A212 at root, NACA 64A210 at tip. Dihedral 5°. Incidence 1° 30′. Two-spar flush-riveted stressed-skin aluminium structure. Aluminium statically-balanced ailerons and plain trailing-edge flaps.

FUSELAGE: Aluminium flush-riveted stressed-skin monocoque structure.

TAIL UNIT: Cantilever all-metal structure. Controllable trim tab in port elevator.

LANDING GEAR: Non-retractable tailwheel type. Cantilever spring steel main legs. Steerable tailwheel. Goodyear wheels and tyres, size 5·00-5, pressure 18 lb/sq in (1·27 kg/cm²). Goodyear hydraulic disc brakes.

POWER PLANT (MM-1-85): One 85 hp Continental C85-8FJ or -12 four-cylinder horizontally-opposed aircooled engine, driving a McCauley two-blade metal fixed-pitch propeller. Fuel tank aft of firewall, capacity 15 US gallons (57 litres). Optional integral wing fuel tanks, each with capacity of 15 US gallons (57 litres). Optional wingtip tanks, each with capacity of 3·5 US gallons (13 litres). Oil capacity 1 US gallon (3·75 litres).

POWER PLANT (MM-1-125): One 135 hp Lycoming O-290-D2 four-cylinder horizontally-opposed aircooled engine, driving a Sensenich two-blade metal fixed-pitch propeller. Fuel tank aft of firewall, capacity 15 US gallons (57 litres). No provision for wingtip tanks. Oil capacity 1·5 US gallons (5·75 litres).

ACCOMMODATION: Single seat in enclosed cabin. Canopy hinged on starboard side. Space for 12 lb (5·5 kg) of baggage aft of seat. Room for back parachute.

ELECTRONICS AND EQUIPMENT: Radio optional. No provision for blind-flying instrumentation. Electrical system available on MM-1-85 only.

DIMENSIONS, EXTERNAL:
Wing span 18 ft 6 in (5·64 m)
Span over tip-tanks (MM-1-85) 19 ft 8 in (5·99 m)
Wing chord at root 5 ft 0 in (1·53 m)
Wing chord at tip 2 ft 6 in (0·76 m)

Bushby/Long Midget Mustang built by Mr W. F. Cassidy of Dallas, Texas (100 hp Continental O-200 engine)

Bushby M-II Mustang II built by Mr B. Edwards

Wing aspect ratio 4
Length overall 16 ft 5 in (5·00 m)
Height overall 4 ft 6 in (1·37 m)
Tailplane span 6 ft 6 in (1·98 m)
Wheel track 5 ft 1 in (1·55 m)

DIMENSIONS, INTERNAL:
Cabin: Length 3 ft 11 in (1·19 m)
Max width 1 ft 10 in (0·56 m)
Max height 4 ft 0 in (1·22 m)
Baggage space 2 cu ft (0·057 m³)

AREAS:
Wings, gross 68 sq ft (6·32 m²)
Ailerons (total) 4·8 sq ft (0·45 m²)
Trailing-edge flaps (total) 7·5 sq ft (0·70 m²)
Fin 3·5 sq ft (0·33 m²)
Rudder 3·36 sq ft (0·31 m²)
Tailplane 8·78 sq ft (0·82 m²)
Elevators, including tab 5·12 sq ft (0·48 m²)

WEIGHTS AND LOADINGS:
Weight empty:
MM-1-85 575 lb (261 kg)
MM-1-125 590 lb (268 kg)
Max T-O and landing weight:
MM-1-85 875 lb (397 kg)
MM-1-125 900 lb (408 kg)
Max wing loading:
MM-1-85 12·9 lb/sq ft (63·00 kg/m²)
MM-1-125 13·2 lb/sq ft (64·45 kg/m²)
Max power loading:
MM-1-85 10·0 lb/hp (4·53 kg/hp)
MM-1-125 7·2 lb/hp (3·26 kg/hp)

PERFORMANCE (at max T-O weight):
Max never-exceed speed: 243 knots (280 mph; 450 km/h)
Max level speed at S/L:
MM-1-85 165 knots (190 mph; 306 km/h)
MM-1-125 195 knots (225 mph; 362 km/h)
Max cruising speed:
MM-1-85 152 knots (175 mph; 281 km/h)
MM-1-125 182 knots (210 mph; 338 km/h)
Econ cruising speed:
MM-1-85 129 knots (148 mph; 238 km/h)
MM-1-125 143 knots (165 mph; 265 km/h)
Stalling speed, flaps down:
MM-1-85 50 knots (57 mph; 92 km/h)
MM-1-125 53 knots (60 mph; 97 km/h)
Max rate of climb at S/L:
MM-1-85 1,750 ft (533 m)/min
MM-1-125 2,200 ft (670 m)/min
Service ceiling:
MM-1-85 over 16,000 ft (4,875 m)
MM-1-125 19,000 ft (5,790 m)
T-O run:
MM-1-85 450 ft (137 m)
MM-1-125 400 ft (122 m)
T-O to 50 ft (15 m):
MM-1-85 900 ft (274 m)
MM-1-125 700 ft (213 m)
Landing from 50 ft (15 m) 1,200 ft (365 m)
Landing run 500 ft (152 m)
Range with max fuel:
MM-1-85 347 nm (400 miles; 640 km)
MM-1-125 325 nm (375 miles; 603 km)
Range with max fuel and tip-tanks:
MM-1-85 651 nm (750 miles; 1,200 km)

BUSHBY M-II MUSTANG II

Design of this side-by-side two-seat derivative of the Midget Mustang was started in 1963. Construction of a prototype began in 1965 and it flew for the first time on 9 July 1966. During 1968 Mr Bushby designed an alternative non-retractable tricycle landing gear for the Mustang II, and amateur constructors have the option of either configuration. Over 500 examples were being built by amateurs in the Spring of 1974, at which time at least 20 Mustang IIs were flying.

The Mustang II illustrated was built by Mr B. Edwards. It differs from standard by having glassfibre wingtips and engine cowling, a small dorsal fin and a 180 hp Lycoming O-360-A1A engine, driving a two-blade metal constant-speed propeller. It won the "Outstanding Mustang II" award for its owner at the 1970 EAA Fly-in.

The details below apply to the de luxe model, and the empty weight quoted includes IFR instrumentation and nav/com equipment. The M-II can also be operated as an aerobatic aircraft in what Bushby Aircraft calls the "Sport" configuration. This is identical to the de luxe model except that the electrical system, radio and additional IFR instrumentation are deleted. The "Sport" model has an empty weight of 750 lb (340 kg) and T-O weight of 1,250 lb (567 kg).

Type: Two-seat amateur-built light aircraft.

Wings: Cantilever low-wing monoplane. Outer wings similar to those of Midget Mustang, attached to new constant-chord centre-section of short span. Wing section NACA 64A212 at root, NACA 64A210 at tip. Dihedral 5° on outer wings only. Incidence 1° 30′. Two-spar flush-riveted stressed-skin aluminium structure. Aluminium statically-balanced ailerons and plain trailing-edge flaps. No trim tabs.

Fuselage: Aluminium flush-riveted stressed-skin monocoque structure.

Tail Unit: Cantilever all-metal structure. Fixed-incidence tailplane. Controllable trim tab in starboard elevator.

Landing Gear: Standard version has non-retractable tailwheel type. Cantilever spring steel main legs. Goodyear 5·00-5 main wheels and tyres, pressure 20 lb/sq in (1·41 kg/cm²). Goodyear hydraulic disc brakes. Steerable tailwheel. Alternatively, non-retractable tricycle type. Cantilever spring steel main legs. Cleveland or Goodyear wheels and tyres size 5·00-5. Non-steerable nose-wheel, mounted on oleo-pneumatic shock strut and free to swivel up to 16° either side. Goodyear wheel and tyre size 5·00-5. Goodyear or Cleveland hydraulic disc brakes. Wheel fairings optional on either type of landing gear.

Power Plant: Normally one 160 hp Lycoming O-320 four-cylinder horizontally-opposed air-cooled engine, driving a two-blade fixed-pitch metal propeller. Provision for other engines including a 125 hp Lycoming O-290 engine, driving a two-blade fixed-pitch metal propeller. Fuel tank aft of firewall, capacity 25 US gallons (94·6 litres). Optional integral wing fuel tanks, each with a capacity of 12 US gallons (45 litres). Refuelling point on starboard side of fuselage aft of firewall. Provision for wingtip tanks. Oil capacity 2 US gallons (7·5 litres).

Accommodation: Two seats side by side, under large rearward-sliding transparent canopy. Dual controls. Baggage space aft of seats, capacity 75 lb (34 kg).

Systems: 12V electrical system, supplied by Delco-Remy 15A generator and Exide 33A battery.

Electronics and Equipment: Provision for full IFR instrumentation and dual nav/com system.

Dimensions, external:
- Wing span — 24 ft 2 in (7·37 m)
- Wing chord at root — 4 ft 10 in (1·47 m)
- Wing chord at tip — 2 ft 7 in (0·79 m)
- Wing aspect ratio — 5·5
- Length overall — 19 ft 6 in (5·94 m)
- Height overall — 5 ft 3 in (1·60 m)
- Tailplane span — 7 ft 6 in (2·29 m)
- Wheel track — 6 ft 10 in (2·08 m)
- Propeller diameter:
  - 125 hp — 5 ft 8 in (1·73 m)
  - 160 hp — 6 ft 0 in (1·82 m)

Dimensions, internal:
- Cabin:
  - Length, incl baggage compartment — 5 ft 2 in (1·57 m)
  - Max width — 3 ft 4 in (1·02 m)
  - Max height — 3 ft 5 in (1·04 m)
- Baggage space — 5·5 cu ft (0·16 m³)

Areas:
- Wings, gross — 97·12 sq ft (9·02 m²)
- Ailerons (total) — 4·8 sq ft (0·45 m²)
- Flaps (total) — 9·1 sq ft (0·85 m²)
- Fin — 4·25 sq ft (0·39 m²)
- Rudder — 4·1 sq ft (0·38 m²)
- Tailplane — 9·28 sq ft (0·86 m²)
- Elevators, incl tab — 5·42 sq ft (0·50 m²)

Weights:
- Weight empty, equipped (N: nosewheel, T: tailwheel landing gear):
  - N 125 hp engine — 911 lb (413 kg)
  - T 125 hp engine — 900 lb (408 kg)
  - N 160 hp engine — 938 lb (425 kg)
  - T 160 hp engine — 927 lb (420 kg)
- *Max T-O and landing weight 1,500 lb (680 kg)

*Except for countries that restrict max wing loading to 15 lb/sq ft (73·2 kg/m²), where T-O weight of 1,450 lb (658 kg) applies

Performance (with tailwheel, at max T-O weight):
- Max never-exceed speed:
  - 125 hp — 173 knots (200 mph; 322 km/h)
  - 160 hp — 211 knots (243 mph; 391 km/h)
- Max level speed at S/L:
  - 125 hp — 148 knots (170 mph; 274 km/h)
  - 160 hp — 171 knots (197 mph; 317 km/h)
- Max cruising speed at 7,500 ft (2,285 m):
  - 125 hp — 152 knots (175 mph; 282 km/h)
  - 160 hp — 161 knots (185 mph; 297 km/h)
- Stalling speed, flaps down:
  - 125 hp — 47 knots (54 mph; 87 km/h)
  - 160 hp — 51 knots (58 mph; 94 km/h)
- Stalling speed, flaps up:
  - 125 hp — 51 knots (58 mph; 94 km/h)
  - 160 hp — 53 knots (60 mph; 96 km/h)
- Max rate of climb at S/L:
  - 125 hp — 1,000 ft (305 m)/min
  - 160 hp — 1,400 ft (425 m)/min
- Service ceiling:
  - 125 hp — 16,000 ft (4,875 m)
  - 160 hp — 18,000 ft (5,485 m)
- T-O run — 650 ft (198 m)
- T-O to 50 ft (15 m):
  - 125 hp — 1,050 ft (320 m)
  - 160 hp — 1,000 ft (305 m)
- Landing from 50 ft (15 m):
  - 125 hp — 950 ft (290 m)
  - 160 hp — 1,000 ft (305 m)
- Landing run:
  - 125 hp — 700 ft (215 m)
  - 160 hp — 750 ft (228 m)
- Range with standard fuel (75% power):
  - 125 hp — 416 nm (480 miles; 770 km)
  - 160 hp — 373 nm (430 miles; 692 km)
- Range with optional wingtip tanks:
  - 160 hp — 542 nm (625 miles; 1,005 km)

BUSHMASTER

BUSHMASTER AIRCRAFT CORPORATION

Head Office:
2701 E. Wardlow Road, Long Beach, California 90807

Telephone: (213) 427-5405

President: Ralph P. Williams

Vice-Presidents:
Peter L. DeLuca
Walter D. Greer

Secretary-Treasurer:
George Gaulding Jr

A modernised version of the Ford Tri-Motor transport aircraft was built by Aircraft Hydro-Forming Inc, of which Mr. Ralph P. Williams was President. On 27 February 1969 Aircraft Hydro-Forming was sold to Whittaker Corporation, this sale including rights to the Bushmaster 2000. In August 1970 Bushmaster Aircraft Corporation was formed and the Bushmaster 2000 project was re-purchased from Whittaker Corporation.

The Bushmaster 2000 is now in production in the company's facility, a 4½ acre site at the west end of Long Beach Airport.

Prototype Bushmaster 2000, a modernised version of the Ford Tri-Motor, in the insignia of Cherokee Airlines (*Duane A. Kasulka*)

BUSHMASTER 2000

The original Ford Tri-Motor was first produced in the 1920s by the Stout Metal Airplane Company, a division of the Ford Motor Company. After more than 40 years of service, several Tri-Motors are still in commercial operation.

The late Mr William B. Stout conceived the idea of modernising the design and putting it back into production as a simple and economical transport aircraft able to operate from grass surfaces. The Bushmaster 2000, of which the prototype was completed in 1966, is the end product of this programme.

New features compared with the original Tri-Motor include more powerful and lighter Pratt & Whitney R-985-AN-1 or AN-14B engines, each rated at 450 hp, with improved cowlings for better engine temperature control; Hartzell HC-B3R30-2E fully-feathering three-blade constant-speed propellers; 24V 50A engine-driven generator; aileron, elevator and rudder trim tabs; oleo-pneumatic main landing gear shock-absorbers; B.F. Goodrich main wheels and tubeless tyres, size 15·00 × 10-ply rating; Hayes Industries tailwheel and US Rubber tyre, size 17·00 × 8-ply rating; B.F. Goodrich single-disc brakes; modernised cockpit with larger windows; fully-swivelling tailwheel; re-routing of control cables internally; addition of a large cargo door; strengthened floor for concentrated loads; a larger tail fin; and redesigned elevators which are now interchangeable with each other and with the rudder. Later production models will be fitted with wing flaps.

Construction remains all-metal, but the corrugated skin panels are now made of new, lighter and stronger aluminium sheet, riveted to the flanges of structural members. The wing is built around three main spars, with five auxiliary spars to reinforce the corrugated skin. Inter-spar stress distribution is accomplished by struts and diagonals instead of ribs.

The Bushmaster normally accommodates 15 passengers, or equivalent freight, and a crew of two, but can be operated by a single pilot; a high-density seating arrangement will accommodate a pilot and 23 passengers. Optional items include a 600 US gallon (2,272 litre) tank for firefighting, forest dusting, etc, and a large floor hatch for loading extra-long items such as oil rig equipment. The normal wheel landing gear can be replaced by floats or skis. Standard fuel capacity is 360 US gallons (1,363 litres), with provision for auxiliary tanks.

FAA certification at a max T-O weight of 12,500 lb (5,670 kg) has been received, but Bushmaster is exploring the possibility of a variation in the Type Certificate to allow domestic operation above 12,500 lb gross weight.

Dimensions, external:
- Wing span — 77 ft 11 in (23·75 m)
- Length overall — 50 ft 8 in (15·44 m)
- Height overall — 13 ft 5 in (4·09 m)
- Wheel track — 19 ft 7¾ in (5·99 m)
- Cabin door (stbd, rear):
  - Width — 5 ft 0 in (1·52 m)
  - Height — 5 ft 0 in (1·52 m)

Dimensions, internal:
- Cabin: Length — 21 ft 8 in (6·60 m)
  - Average width — 5 ft 0 in (1·52 m)
  - Average height — 7 ft 0 in (2·13 m)
  - Volume — 735 cu ft (20·81 m³)

Area:
- Wings, gross — 851·7 sq ft (79·13 m²)

Weights:
- Weight empty — 7,500 lb (3,401 kg)
- Max T-O weight — 12,500 lb (5,670 kg)

Performance (at max T-O weight):
- Max level speed — 111 knots (128 mph; 206 km/h) IAS
- Stalling speed — 48 knots (55 mph; 88·5 km/h) IAS
- T-O run — 850 ft (259 m)
- Range with max fuel — 607 nm (700 miles; 1,125 km)

CALSPAN

CALSPAN CORPORATION

Head Office:
PO Box 235, Buffalo, New York 14221

Telephone: (716) 632-7500

Telex: 91-270

On 17 November 1972, Cornell Aeronautical Laboratory changed its name to Calspan Corporation, but the company is continuing its traditional research and development activities.

TOTAL IN-FLIGHT SIMULATOR

USAF designation: NC-131H

Calspan Corporation, under a $6 million contract awarded by the USAF Flight Dynamics Laboratory at Wright-Patterson AFB, Ohio, modified a Convair C-131H to serve as a Total In-Flight Simulator (TIFS). This involved construction of a second cockpit attached to the nose of the aircraft, the provision of movable control surfaces mounted vertically on the wings, and a servo-operated trailing-edge flap on each wing, extending between the inboard Fowler flap and the aileron. The vertical surfaces on the wings provide direct control of side forces; the new rapid-operating flaps provide direct control of lift.

Designation of the aircraft was changed to NC-131H following the installation of Allison turboprop engines.

The separate easily-detachable forward cockpit duplicates the configuration of the aircraft being simulated and is manned by evaluation pilots who control the aircraft through a fly-by-wire system. The three conventional control surfaces and the engine throttles are driven by hydraulic servos acting in parallel with the normal mechanical control system. An on-board computer processes the control actions of the evaluation pilots and determines the appropriate commands to the six TIFS motion controllers by processing the computed motion itself, and by comparing actual motion with the computed motion of the aeroplane that is being simulated. The command pilots, who engage and monitor the TIFS system on the original flight deck, have overall responsibility for the safety of the aircraft and can, at any time, override action initiated by the system, by operation of the aircraft's conventional control system, which is retained intact.

Design of the TIFS aircraft began in November 1966, and modification of the basic airframe started in March of the following year. First flight was made on 8 July 1970.

Flight testing of the TIFS and its control system was carried out in the Autumn of 1970; following successful completion of this, an $816,000 flight research programme was sponsored by the USAF's Flight Dynamics Laboratory.

For this 16-month programme, the TIFS onboard computer was programmed with the flight characteristics of a large multi-engined jet aircraft having supersonic capabilities and an advanced control system. Two phases of the research programme evaluated landing approach characteristics with low Dutch roll frequencies and pitch-up tendencies.

In 1972, three programmes were conducted in the approach and landing phases of flight. One made a study of static longitudinal stability boundaries for delta-wing SSTs; another provided a simulation of the Space Shuttle orbiter. The FAA and NASA's Manned Spaceflight Center, working through the Air Force Flight Dynamics Laboratory, were the respective sponsors. The Flight Dynamics Laboratory conducted the third programme, concerning direct side force for STOL crosswind landings.

In 1972 the USAF conducted in TIFS the first known flight tests of multiplex hardware in an aircraft flight control system.

NC-131H Total In-Flight Simulator, operated by Calspan on behalf of the USAF and other agencies

A new contractual arrangement with the USAF began in 1973, enabling that service, other government agencies, and organisations outside the government, to arrange through the Flight Dynamics Laboratory to conduct investigations using the TIFS with a minimum of time delay. A B-1 flight control system study was conducted during the Summer of 1973, involving the landing approach, in-flight refuelling and low-level, high-speed regions of the flight envelope. In late 1973, NASA's Langley Research Center began preparations for tests of passenger ride qualities using the ten-passenger TIFS configuration, in which the evaluation cockpit is replaced by a nose fairing.

Details of the basic Convair C-131E may be found in the 1959-60 *Jane's*.

TYPE: TIFS research aircraft.

WINGS: As C-131E, except movable control surfaces mounted vertically above and below each wing, outboard of engines, approximately at semi-span. A rapid-operating servo-operated trailing-edge flap has been added to each wing, extending between the inboard Fowler flap and the aileron. Miller actuators on all controls, with Moog servo-valve controls. Max rate of flap movement 60°/sec.

FUSELAGE: As C-131H.

TAIL UNIT: As C-131H, except Miller actuators and Moog servo-valves for operation of control surfaces.

LANDING GEAR, POWER PLANT: As C-131H.

ACCOMMODATION: Crew of eight, comprising pilot, co-pilot, evaluation pilot and co-pilot, two test engineers to operate analogue computer and digital data recording equipment, and two observers. Three double seats at forward end of cabin, on port side. Computer, recording equipment and hydraulic system occupy most of rear cabin. Conventional passenger door is structurally sealed. Cargo door used for access to cabin. For tests not requiring an evaluation cockpit, such as RPV or ride qualities work, a crew of four plus twelve passengers can be accommodated..

SYSTEMS: As C-131H, plus hydraulic power for variable-stability system and AC/DC electrical power conversion.

ELECTRONICS AND EQUIPMENT: Special equipment includes full blind-flying instrumentation. Special electronics include radar altimeter, variable-stability system, 1000 amplifier analogue computer with 60-channel digital data recording equipment, and full six degrees-of-freedom motion sensing.

DIMENSIONS, INTERNAL, EXTERNAL AND AREAS: As C-131H

WEIGHTS AND LOADING:

Weight empty, equipped	46,000 lb (20,865 kg)
Max T-O weight	54,600 lb (24,766 kg)
Max zero-fuel weight	49,000 lb (22,226 kg)
Max landing weight	50,600 lb (22,951 kg)
Max wing loading	59·4 lb/sq ft (290 kg/m²)

PERFORMANCE (at max T-O weight):

Max never-exceed speed 295 knots (339 mph; 546 km/h)

Max level speed at 10,000 ft (3,050 m) 280 knots (322 mph; 518 km/h)

Max cruising speed 240 knots (276 mph; 444 km/h)

Stalling speed, flaps up 115 knots (133 mph; 214 km/h)

Stalling speed, flaps down 88 knots (101·5 mph; 163·5 km/h)

Max rate of climb at S/L 2,100 ft (640 m)/min

Range with max fuel 500 nm (575 miles; 925 km)

CAMAIR

CAMAIR AIRCRAFT CORPORATION

HEAD OFFICE:
PO Box 231, Remsenburg, Long Island, New York 11960
Telephone: (516) 325-0120

PRESIDENT:
Fred Garcia, Jr

CAMAIR TWIN NAVION

The Camair Twin Navion is a twin-engined version of the North American/Ryan Navion light aircraft. It embodies structural modifications to cater for the increased power and weight, together with design and aerodynamic refinements which provide improved performance, comfort and styling. Versions are as follows:

CTN-A. Prototype only. Built and flown in 1953 with two 225 hp Continental engines.

CTN-B. Powered by two 240 hp Continental O-470-B engines. First flown in early 1954. Total of 28 delivered in 1955-59.

CTN-C. First flown in 1960, with two 260 hp Continental IO-470-D engines. A number of Model "Bs" have been converted to Model "C" configuration.

CTN-D. The prototype of this version was powered originally by two 260 hp Continental TSIO-470-B six-cylinder horizontally-opposed aircooled turbocharged engines, and had increased fuel capacity and gross weight. It has since had two 300 hp Continental IO-520 engines installed.

Production of new aircraft has been suspended; but Camair is able to modify B and C models to the latest model D configuration, and continues to supply spares to Twin Navion owners.

The following details apply specifically to the CTN-D:

TYPE: Twin-engined four-seat cabin monoplane.

WINGS: Cantilever low-wing monoplane. Wing section NACA 4415R at root, NACA 6410R at tip. Dihedral 7° 30′. Incidence 2° at root, —1° at tip. All-metal structure. All-metal mass-balanced ailerons and hydraulically-operated flaps.

FUSELAGE: All-metal semi-monocoque structure.

TAIL UNIT: Cantilever all-metal structure. Controllable trim tabs on rudder and elevators. Optional electrically-powered elevator trim control.

LANDING GEAR: Hydraulically-retractable tricycle type. Main units retract inward, nose unit aft. Oleo-pneumatic shock-absorbers. Main-wheel tyres size 7·00-8, Type III. Steerable nosewheel, tyre size 6·00-6, Type III. Hydraulic disc brakes.

POWER PLANT: Two 300 hp Continental IO-520 six-cylinder horizontally-opposed aircooled engines, each driving a Hartzell three-blade constant-speed fully-feathering propeller. Two 20 US gallon (75·5 litre) aluminium alloy fuel tanks in the wing roots, two 35 US gallon (132 litre) wingtip tanks and two 35 US gallon (132 litre) rubber fuel cells located in the aft overwing engine nacelles. Total standard fuel capacity 180 US gallons (679 litres). Optional auxiliary fuselage fuel tank containing 20 US gallons (75·5 litres). Oil capacity 3 US gallons (11·5 litres) per engine.

ACCOMMODATION: Enclosed cabin seating pilot and co-pilot on individually adjustable and reclining front seats and two passengers on individual rear seats. Rearward-sliding canopy with transverse web which seals the baggage compartment and provides a shelf when the canopy is closed. Dual controls. Cabin soundproofing, air-conditioning and heating. Windscreen defogger. Baggage compartment aft of cabin, with outside access, for 180 lb (82 kg); and forward compartment for equipment and baggage in nose, capacity 100 lb (45 kg). Total baggage capacity 280 lb (127 kg).

SYSTEMS: Hydraulic system supplied by two engine-driven pumps to operate flaps, landing gear and brakes. Dual engine-driven vacuum pumps. Dual engine-driven alternators power a 24V electrical system, which has also an external power socket. Oxygen system optional.

ELECTRONICS AND EQUIPMENT: Optional items include complete dual radio, full IFR instrumentation and navigation equipment, plus integrated flight system, weather radar and autopilot. Standard equipment includes dual retractable taxi lights, dual landing lights, triple strobe lights and rotating beacon. Alcohol propeller de-icing system optional.

DIMENSIONS, EXTERNAL:

Wing span	34 ft 8 in (10·57 m)
Wing chord at root	7 ft 2½ in (2·20 m)
Wing chord at tip	3 ft 11 in (1·19 m)
Wing aspect ratio	6·04
Length overall	28 ft 0 in (8·53 m)
Height overall	10 ft 8 in (3·25 m)
Wheel track	8 ft 8½ in (2·65 m)
Wheelbase	7 ft 8½ in (2·35 m)

AREAS:

Wings, gross	184·34 sq ft (17·13 m²)

Camair Twin Navion CTN-D (two 300 hp Continental IO-520 engines)

Ailerons (total)	10·32 sq ft (0·96 m²)
Trailing-edge flaps (total)	29·23 sq ft (2·72 m²)
Fin	18·20 sq ft (1·69 m²)
Rudder	8·20 sq ft (0·76 m²)
Tailplane	43·05 sq ft (4·0 m²)
Elevators	14·10 sq ft (1·31 m²)

WEIGHTS AND LOADINGS:

Weight empty	3,000 lb (1,360 kg)
Max T-O weight	4,500 lb (2,041 kg)
Max landing weight	4,323 lb (1,960 kg)
Max wing loading	24·4 lb/sq ft (119·1 kg/m²)
Max power loading	7·5 lb/hp (3·40 kg/hp)

PERFORMANCE (at AUW of 3,500 lb; 1,590 kg):
Max level speed at S/L
187 knots (215 mph; 346 km/h)
Max cruising speed, 75% power at 6,500 ft (1,980 m) 174 knots (200 mph; 322 km/h)
Stalling speed 52·5 knots (60 mph; 97 km/h)
Max rate of climb at S/L 2,000 ft (610 m)/min
Rate of climb at S/L, one engine out
500 ft (152 m)/min
Service ceiling 22,000 ft (6,705 m)
Service ceiling, one engine out
10,000 ft (3,050 m)
T-O run 400 ft (122 m)
Landing run 600 ft (183 m)

CASSUTT

THOMAS K. CASSUTT

ADDRESS:
11718 Persuasion Drive, San Antonio, Texas 78216

While employed as an airline pilot, Capt Tom Cassutt designed and built in 1954 a small single-seat racing monoplane known as the Cassutt Special I (No. 111), in which he won the 1958 National Air Racing Championships. In 1959, he completed a smaller aircraft on the same lines, known as the Cassutt Special II (No. 11).

Plans of both aircraft, and of a sporting version of No. 111 with a larger cockpit, are available to amateur constructors. As a result, many Cassutt Specials are flying and under construction, and brief details of a number of these are given in the accompanying table.

Following his retirement from airline flying, Tom Cassutt plans to develop a number of different aircraft to meet Formula I specifications. No details of these are yet available.

First Australian-built Cassutt Special, being flown by its builder, Peter Furlong of Traralgon, Victoria

CASSUTT SPECIAL I

The original Cassutt Special I (No. 111), named *Jersey Skeeter*, is described in detail below.

Airmark Ltd in the UK built several slightly modified examples of the Cassutt Special I; these are known as Airmark/Cassutt 111Ms in Britain. First Cassutt Special to be completed in Australia was built during 1973 by Peter Furlong, an aircraft maintenance engineer at the Latrobe Valley Airfield near Traralgon, Victoria. Powered by a 100 hp Rolls-Royce Continental engine, this aircraft flew for the first time in early 1974.

TYPE: Single-seat racing monoplane.

WINGS: Cantilever mid-wing monoplane. Wing section Cassutt 1107. No incidence or dihedral. All-wood two-spar structure with spruce ribs, solid spars and plywood skin, fabric-covered. Ailerons are of welded steel tube construction, fabric-covered. No flaps.

FUSELAGE: Steel tube structure, fabric-covered.

TAIL UNIT: Cantilever steel tube structure, with fabric covering.

LANDING GEAR: Non-retractable tailwheel type. Wittman cantilever spring steel main legs. Main-wheel tyres size 5·00-5. Wheel fairings standard.

POWER PLANT: One Continental C85-8F four-cylinder horizontally-opposed aircooled engine, rated normally at 85 hp but capable of developing 112-115 hp in racing trim. Sensenich two-blade fixed-pitch propeller. Fuel capacity 15 US gallons (57 litres). Oil capacity 1 US gallon (3·8 litres).

ACCOMMODATION: Single seat in enclosed cockpit.

DIMENSIONS, EXTERNAL:

Wing span	14 ft 11 in (4·54 m)
Wing chord (mean)	4 ft 6 in (1·37 m)
Wing aspect ratio	3·37
Length overall	16 ft 0 in (4·88 m)
Height overall	4 ft 3 in (1·30 m)
Tailplane span	3 ft 11 in (1·19 m)
Wheel track	4 ft 6 in (1·37 m)

AREAS:

Wings, gross	66·0 sq ft (6·13 m²)
Ailerons (total)	7·5 sq ft (0·70 m²)
Fin	2·4 sq ft (0·22 m²)
Rudder	2·1 sq ft (0·195 m²)
Tailplane	5·3 sq ft (0·49 m²)
Elevators	3·1 sq ft (0·29 m²)

WEIGHTS:

Weight empty	516 lb (234 kg)
Max T-O weight	730 lb (331 kg)

PERFORMANCE (at max T-O weight):
Max level speed
200 knots (230 mph; 370 km/h)
Max cruising speed
165 knots (190 mph; 306 km/h)
Stalling speed 61 knots (70 mph; 113 km/h)
Max rate of climb at S/L 2,000 ft (610 m)/min
Endurance with max fuel 3 hours

CASSUTT SPECIAL II

TYPE: Single-seat racing monoplane.

WINGS: Cantilever mid-wing monoplane. Wing section Cassutt 13106. No incidence or dihedral. All-wood structure. No flaps.

FUSELAGE: Steel tube structure, fabric-covered.

TAIL UNIT: Cantilever steel tube structure, fabric-covered. The prototype (No 11) has small centre fin and auxiliary fins on the tailplane tips.

LANDING GEAR: Non-retractable tailwheel type. Wittman cantilever spring steel main legs. Main-wheel tyre size 5·00-5. Wheel fairings standard.

POWER PLANT AND ACCOMMODATION: As for Cassutt Special I.

DIMENSIONS, EXTERNAL:

Wing span	13 ft 8 in (4·16 m)
Wing chord (constant)	4 ft 10 in (1·47 m)
Wing aspect ratio	2·83
Length overall	16 ft 0 in (4·88 m)
Height overall	3 ft 10 in (1·16 m)
Tailplane span	3 ft 9 in (1·14 m)
Wheel track	3 ft 2 in (0·97 m)

AREAS:

Wings, gross	66 sq ft (6·13 m²)
Ailerons (total)	6 sq ft (0·56 m²)
Fin	1·0 sq ft (0·09 m²)
Rudder	1·6 sq ft (0·15 m²)
Tailplane	4·3 sq ft (0·40 m²)
Elevators	2·4 sq ft (0·22 m²)

WEIGHTS:

Weight empty	433 lb (196 kg)
Max T-O weight	800 lb (363 kg)

PERFORMANCE (at max T-O weight):
Max level speed at S/L
204 knots (235 mph; 378 km/h)
Max cruising speed
174 knots (200 mph; 322 km/h)
Stalling speed 54 knots (62 mph; 100 km/h)
Max rate of climb at S/L 3,000 ft (915 m)/min
Endurance with max fuel 3 hours

Builder (B) *Owner* (O)	*Name of aircraft*	*Racing Number*	*Wing Span*	*Length Overall*	*Height Overall*	*Normal Loaded Weight*	*Max Speed*
(B, O) Marion Baker & Associates	Boo-Ray	81	15 ft 0 in (4·57 m)	16 ft 8 in (5·08 m)	4 ft 0 in (1·22 m)	750 lb (340 kg)	182 knots (210 mph; 337 km/h)
(B, O) Ken Burmeister	Firefly	4	13 ft 8 in (4·17 m)	17 ft 1 in (5·21 m)	4 ft 3 in (1·30 m)	738 lb (335 kg)	N.A.
(B) R. Grieger (O) E. E. Stover	Ole Yaller	58	15 ft 0 in (4·57 m)	16 ft 6 in (5·03 m)	4 ft 11 in (1·50 m)	834 lb (378 kg)	N.A.
(B) D. Hoffman R. Philbrick (O) Harold Lund	Chabasco	76	13 ft 8 in (4·17 m)	16 ft 6½ in (5·04 m)	N.A.	774 lb (351 kg)	182 knots (210 mph; 337 km/h)
(B, O) Ray O. Morris	Miss A-Go-Go	12	14 ft 11 in (4·55 m)	16 ft 0 in (4·88 m)	4 ft 6 in (1·37 m)	642 lb (291 kg)	195 knots (225 mph; 362 km/h)
(B, O) Fred Wofford	Gold Dust	7	14 ft 4 in (4·37 m)	17 ft 3 in (5·26 m)	4 ft 3½ in (1·31 m)	787 lb (357 kg)	169 knots (195 mph; 314 km/h)
(B, O) James H. Wilson	Snoopy	—	14 ft 6 in (4·42 m)	16 ft 9 in (5·11 m)	4 ft 2 in (1·27 m)	800 lb (363 kg)	208 knots (240 mph; 386 km/h)

CESSNA

CESSNA AIRCRAFT COMPANY

HEAD OFFICE AND WORKS:
Wichita, Kansas 67201
Telephone: (316) 685-9111

CHAIRMAN OF THE BOARD AND CHIEF EXECUTIVE OFFICER:
Dwane L. Wallace

PRESIDENT:
Delbert L. Roskam

EXECUTIVE VICE-PRESIDENTS:
Malcolm S. Harned
Russell W. Meyer, Jr

SENIOR VICE-PRESIDENTS:
R. L. Lair (Commercial Aircraft Marketing)
R. P. Bauer (Treasurer and Controller)

VICE-PRESIDENTS:
Max E. Bleck (Aircraft Divisions)
Pierre Clostermann (President, Reims Aviation)
Derby D. Frye (Military Relations Director)
Shelby Law (Fluid Power Division)
James B. Taylor (Commercial Jet Marketing Division)
Bill Worford (Personnel Relations)

GENERAL MANAGERS:
Robert D. Dickerson (Wallace Division)
Lee Zuker (Aircraft Radio Corporation)
John W. Dussault (McCauley Accessory Division)

CONTROLLER AND ASSISTANT TREASURER:
Homer G. Nester

SECRETARY: Vincent E. Moore

PUBLIC RELATIONS DIRECTOR:
Jerry Kell

Cessna Aircraft Company was founded by the late Clyde V. Cessna, a pioneer in US aviation in 1911, and was incorporated on 7 September 1927.

By the end of January 1974 the company had produced a total of 111,871 aircraft, of which 12,040 were for military use.

Cessna has four plants in Wichita engaged on the production of commercial and military aircraft, and The Fluid Power Division in Hutchinson, Kansas, which manufactures fluid power systems.

Subsidiary companies owned by Cessna are Aircraft Radio Corporation at Boonton, New Jersey, the McCauley Industrial Corporation of Dayton, Ohio, Cessna Fluid Power Ltd of Glenrothes, Fife, Scotland, and Cessna Finance Corporation in Wichita. It has a 49% interest in Reims Aviation of France.

In early 1974 Cessna had in production 39 types of commercial aircraft. In addition, it is continuing to produce the T-37B twin-engined jet trainer and A-37 strike aircraft for the USAF and the T-37C for the US Military Assistance Programme.

During 1973 Cessna commercial sales totalled 7,262 aircraft, including units assembled in France by Reims Aviation (which see). It was anticipated that these figures would be exceeded in 1974.

Military subcontract programmes include manufacture of assemblies, including missile ejection racks, wing tank and missile pylons, for the McDonnell Douglas F-4 Phantom II, and crew door subassemblies for Bell helicopters.

CESSNA MODEL 150

The prototype of the Model 150 flew for the first time in September 1957, and Cessna re-entered the two-seat light aircraft market by putting it into production in August 1958. By 31 January 1974 a total of 19,231 Model 150s had been delivered, including aircraft built in France by Reims Aviation as F-150s.

The current American-built Model 150 is available in standard, trainer, Aerobat (described separately) and commuter versions. The trainer has as standard equipment dual controls, a Cessna 300 Series 100-channel nav/com installation, rate of climb indicator, sensitive altimeter, electric clock, outside air temperature gauge, rearview mirror, sun visors, a turn co-ordinator that provides visual presentation of turn information, and landing lights.

The commuter has the same equipment as the trainer, plus a vacuum system with directional and horizon gyros, wheel fairings, individually adjustable bucket seats, interior carpet, conical-camber wingtips, heated pitot and "omni-flash" beacon.

The 1974 version of the Model 150 has an improved control column shaft bearing on the starboard side which gives smoother control operation; improved wheel fairings and exterior styling; new seats to improve visibility and headroom; folding seatbacks to simplify baggage handling; increased forward seat travel; new control wheels of glass-filled nylon with urethane foam padded centre section; and new interior and exterior styling.

The original Model 150 received FAA Type Approval on 10 July 1958.

TYPE: Two-seat cabin monoplane.

WINGS: Braced high-wing monoplane. Wing section NACA 2412 (tips symmetrical). Dihedral 1°. Incidence 1° at root, 0° at tip. All-metal structure, with conical-camber glass-fibre tips on commuter (optional on other models). Modified Frise all-metal ailerons. Electrically-actuated NACA single-slotted all-metal flaps.

FUSELAGE: All-metal semi-monocoque structure.

TAIL UNIT: Cantilever all-metal structure, with sweptback vertical surfaces. Trim tab in starboard elevator. Ground-adjustable rudder trim tab.

LANDING GEAR: Non-retractable tricycle type. Land-O-Matic cantilever main legs, each comprising a one-piece machined conically-tapered spring steel tube. Steerable nose-wheel on oleo-pneumatic shock-absorber strut. Size 6·00-6 wheels, with nylon tube-type tyres, on main wheels; size 5·00-5 nosewheel, with nylon tube-type tyre. Tyre pressure 30 lb/sq in (2·11 kg/cm²). Toe-operated single-disc hydraulic brakes. Optional wheel fairings for all three units (standard on commuter). Parking brake.

POWER PLANT: One 100 hp Continental O-200-A four-cylinder horizontally-opposed aircooled engine, driving a McCauley two-blade metal fixed-pitch propeller. Two all-metal fuel tanks in wings. Total standard fuel capacity 26 US gallons (98 litres), of which 22·5 US gallons (85 litres) are usable. Optional long-range tanks increase total capacity to 38 US gallons (143·8 litres), of which 35 US gallons (132·5 litres) are usable. Oil capacity 1·5 US gallons (5·7 litres).

ACCOMMODATION: Enclosed cabin seating two side by side. Baggage compartment behind seats, backs of which hinge forward. Baggage capacity 120 lb (54 kg). Alternatively, "family seat" can be fitted in baggage space, for two children not exceeding 120 lb (54 kg) total weight. Door, with opening window, on each side. Heating and ventilation standard. Windscreen defroster standard. Winterisation kit optional. Optional overhead skylights.

SYSTEMS: Hydraulic system for brakes only. Electrical power supplied by 12V 60A alternator and 12V battery.

ELECTRONICS AND EQUIPMENT: Optional equipment includes Cessna 300 Series nav/com with 360-channel com and 160-channel nav with remote VOR indicator, 300 Series transceiver with 360 com channels, 300 Series nav/com with 360-channel com, 200-channel nav with remote VOR/LOC or VOR/ILS indicator, Series 300 ADF, marker beacon with three lights and aural signal, and transponder with 4096 code capability; blind-flying instrumentation (standard on commuter model); dual controls, rate of climb indicator, turn co-ordinator indicator, outside air temperature gauge, rearview mirror, sun visors, cowl-mounted landing light (all standard in trainer and commuter); and "omni-flash" beacon (standard on commuter). Standard equipment includes a stall warning indicator, control locks, cabin dome light, variable intensity instrument panel red floodlights, windscreen defroster, navigation lights, map compartment, baggage retaining net, and safety belts. Optional extras include a winterisation kit, control-wheel mounted map light, electric clock and sensitive altimeter (standard for trainer and commuter), directional and horizon gyros with vacuum (standard for commuter), true air speed and turn and bank indicators, directional gyro with movable heading index, flight hour recorder, cabin fire extinguisher, emergency locator transmitter, overhead skylights, full-flow oil filter, internal corrosion proofing, heated pitot (standard on commuter), glider tow hook, tinted windows, cowl-mounted landing lights, conical-camber wingtips and omni-flash beacon (both standard on commuter), white strobe lights, advanced-design dry vacuum pump, ground service socket for external battery connection, handle and step for easier refuelling, and a quick-drain oil system.

DIMENSIONS, EXTERNAL:
- Wing span:
  - Standard, Trainer: 32 ft 8½ in (9·97 m)
  - Commuter: 33 ft 2 in (10·11 m)
- Wing chord at root: 5 ft 4 in (1·63 m)
- Wing chord at tip: 3 ft 8½ in (1·12 m)
- Wing aspect ratio: 7·0
- Length overall: 23 ft 9 in (7·24 m)
- Height overall: 8 ft 0 in (2·44 m)
- Tailplane span: 10 ft 0 in (3·05 m)
- Wheel track: 7 ft 7¼ in (2·32 m)
- Wheelbase: 4 ft 10 in (1·47 m)
- Propeller diameter: 5 ft 9 in (1·75 m)
- Passenger doors (each):
  - Width: 2 ft 10 in (0·86 m)

AREAS:
- Wings, gross:
  - Standard, Trainer: 157 sq ft (14·59 m²)
  - Commuter: 159·5 sq ft (14·82 m²)
- Ailerons (total): 17·88 sq ft (1·66 m²)
- Trailing-edge flaps (total): 18·56 sq ft (1·72 m²)
- Fin: 7·55 sq ft (0·70 m²)
- Rudder: 6·50 sq ft (0·60 m²)
- Tailplane: 17·06 sq ft (1·58 m²)
- Elevators, including tab: 11·46 sq ft (1·06 m²)

WEIGHTS AND LOADINGS:
- Weight empty, equipped, standard tanks:
  - Standard: 995 lb (451 kg)
  - Trainer: 1,015 lb (460 kg)
  - Commuter: 1,060 lb (480 kg)
- Max T-O weight: 1,600 lb (726 kg)
- Max wing loading:
  - Standard, Trainer: 10·2 lb/sq ft (49·8 kg/m²)
  - Commuter: 10·0 lb/sq ft (48·9 kg/m²)
- Max power loading: 16·0 lb/hp (7·26 kg/hp)

PERFORMANCE (all models, at max T-O weight):
- Max never-exceed speed: 140 knots (162 mph; 261 km/h)
- Max level speed at S/L: 106 knots (122 mph; 196 km/h)
- Max cruising speed (75% power) at 7,000 ft (2,135 m): 102 knots (117 mph; 188 km/h)
- Econ cruising speed at 10,000 ft (3,050 m): 81 knots (93 mph; 149 km/h)
- Stalling speed, flaps up, power off: 48 knots (55 mph; 89 km/h)
- Stalling speed, flaps down, power off: 42 knots (48 mph; 78 km/h)
- Max rate of climb at S/L: 670 ft (204 m)/min
- Service ceiling: 12,650 ft (3,850 m)
- T-O run: 735 ft (224 m)
- T-O to 50 ft (15 m): 1,385 ft (422 m)
- Landing from 50 ft (15 m): 1,075 ft (328 m)
- Landing run: 445 ft (136 m)
- Range at econ cruising speed, normal tankage, no reserve: 490 nm (565 miles; 909 km)
- Range at econ cruising speed, long-range tanks, no reserve: 764 nm (880 miles; 1,416 km)
- Range at max cruising speed, normal tankage, no reserve: 412 nm (475 miles; 737 km)
- Range at max cruising speed, long-range tanks, no reserve: 629 nm (725 miles; 1,166 km)

CESSNA MODEL A150 AEROBAT

Introduced in 1970, the Model A150 Aerobat was designed to combine the economy and versatility of the standard Model 150 with aerobatic capability. Structural changes allow the Aerobat to perform "unusual attitude" manoeuvres and it is licensed in the aerobatic category for load factors of plus six and minus three *g* at full gross weight, permitting the performance of barrel and aileron rolls, snap rolls, loops, Immelmann turns, Cuban eights, spins, vertical reversements, lazy eights and chandelles.

Equipment of the Aerobat differs only slightly from the standard aircraft. Quick-release cabin doors, removable seat cushions and backs, quick-release lap belts, and shoulder harnesses are standard, as are two tinted skylights which offer extra visibility; a ground-adjustable rudder trim tab is fitted and distinct external styling provides immediate recognition of the A150's aerobatic role. The 1974 version of the Aerobat introduces a new propeller with blades of Clark Y section, as well as the improvements detailed for the standard Model 150. The new propeller gives improved performance, with increased speeds and a higher service ceiling. Optional equipment includes an accelerometer, 3 in lightweight non-tumbling gyros, conical-camber glass-fibre wingtips, steps and handles to simplify refuelling, and a quick-drain oil valve.

Structural changes have increased the empty weight slightly, by comparison with the standard Model 150.

DIMENSIONS, EXTERNAL:
- Wing span: 32 ft 8½ in (9·97 m)
- Length overall: 23 ft 9 in (7·24 m)
- Height overall: 8 ft 0 in (2·44 m)

AREA:
- Wings, gross: 157 sq ft (14·59 m²)

WEIGHTS AND LOADINGS:
- Weight empty, equipped, standard tanks: 1,040 lb (471 kg)
- Max T-O weight: 1,600 lb (726 kg)
- Max wing loading: 10·2 lb/sq ft (49·8 kg/m²)
- Max power loading: 16·0 lb/hp (7·26 kg/hp)

PERFORMANCE (at max T-O weight):
- Max level speed at S/L: 108 knots (124 mph; 200 km/h)
- Max cruising speed (75% power) at 7,000 ft (2,135 m): 103 knots (119 mph; 192 km/h)
- Econ cruising speed at 10,000 ft (3,050 m): 83 knots (96 mph; 154 km/h)
- Stalling speed, flaps up, power off: 48 knots (55 mph; 89 km/h)
- Stalling speed, flaps down, power off: 42 knots (48 mph; 77 km/h)
- Max rate of climb at S/L: 670 ft (204 m)/min
- Service ceiling: 14,000 ft (4,265 m)
- T-O run: 735 ft (224 m)
- T-O to 50 ft (15 m): 1,385 ft (422 m)
- Landing from 50 ft (15 m): 1,075 ft (328 m)
- Landing run: 445 ft (136 m)
- Range at max cruising speed, standard tanks, no reserve: 421 nm (485 miles; 780 km)
- Range at max cruising speed, optional long-range tanks, no reserve: 638 nm (735 miles; 1,182 km)
- Range at econ cruising speed, at 10,000 ft (3,050 m), standard tanks, no reserve: 503 nm (580 miles; 933 km)
- Range at econ cruising speed, at 10,000 ft (3,050 m), optional long-range tanks, no reserve: 781 nm (900 miles; 1,448 km)

CESSNA XMC RESEARCH AIRCRAFT

Cessna announced on 22 January 1971 that a new research aircraft designated XMC (Experimental Magic Carpet) had recently made its first flight. In general appearance it was similar in configuration to the Super Skymaster, but had only a single rear-mounted engine driving a pusher propeller, a non-retractable tricycle landing gear, and two seats side by side.

No further information has been released beyond that which appeared in the 1973-74 *Jane's*.

CESSNA MODEL 172

USAF designation: T-41A Mescalero

With the introduction of the Skyhawk II for 1974, the current version of the Model 172 is available in three commercial forms:

Model 172. Standard version.

Skyhawk/Skyhawk II. De luxe versions of 172, described separately.

Cessna Model A150 Aerobat, the aerobatic version of the basic Model 150

In addition, a version designated F-172 is being produced in France by Reims Aviation.

On 31 July 1964, the USAF ordered 170 earlier-type Model 172s, under the designation **T-41A**, for delivery between September 1964 and July 1965. USAF student pilots complete about 30 hours of basic training on the T-41A before passing on to the T-37B jet primary trainer. Eight T-41As have been bought by the Ecuadorean Air Force, and 26 by the Peruvian government. The USAF ordered more in July 1967 and a total of 237 had been built by December 1973. The more powerful T-41B/C/D (R172E) are described separately.

A total of 20,961 aircraft in the Model 172/Skyhawk series had been built by 31 January 1974, including 947 F-172s built in France. This exceeds the production total for any other single commercial aircraft model.

The 1974 version of the Model 172 has improved air distribution from the cabin heater and defroster outlets, redesigned wheel and brake fairings, more comfortable seating, improved interior side panel life and a stronger door latch assembly.

Type: Four-seat cabin monoplane.

Wings: Braced high-wing monoplane. NACA 2412 wing section. Dihedral 1° 44′. Incidence 1° 30′ at root, —1° 30′ at tip. All-metal structure, except for conical-camber glassfibre wingtips. Single bracing strut on each side. Modified Frise all-metal ailerons. Electrically-controlled NACA all-metal single-slotted flaps inboard of ailerons.

Fuselage: All-metal semi-monocoque structure.

Tail Unit: Cantilever all-metal structure. Sweepback on fin 35° at quarter-chord. Trim tab in starboard elevator. Ground-adjustable trim tab in rudder.

Landing Gear: Non-retractable tricycle type. Cessna Land-O-Matic cantilever main legs, each comprising a one-piece machined conically-tapered spring steel tube. Nosewheel is carried on an oleo-pneumatic shock-strut and is steerable with rudder up to 10° and controllable up to 30° on either side. Cessna main wheels size 6·00-6 and nosewheel size 5·00-5 (optionally 6·00-6), with nylon cord tube-type tyres. Tyre pressure: main wheels 23 lb/sq in (1·62 kg/cm^2), nosewheel 26 lb/sq in (1·83 kg/cm^2). Hydraulic disc brakes. Optional wheel fairings. Alternative float and ski gear.

Power Plant: One 150 hp Lycoming O-320-E2D four-cylinder horizontally-opposed aircooled engine, driving a two-blade fixed-pitch metal propeller. One fuel tank in each wing, total capacity 42 US gallons (159 litres). Usable fuel 38 US gallons (143·8 litres). Provision for long-range tanks, giving total capacity of 52 US gallons (197 litres), of which 48 US gallons (182 litres) are usable. Oil capacity 2 US gallons (7·5 litres).

Accommodation: Cabin seats four in two pairs, with optional fully-articulating front seats. Baggage space aft of rear seats, capacity 120 lb (54 kg). An optional foldaway seat can be fitted in baggage space, for one or two children not exceeding 120 lb (54 kg) total weight. Door on each side of cabin giving access to all seats and to simplify loading if rear seats are removed and cabin used for freight. Pilot's window opens; opening co-pilot's side window is optional. Baggage door on port side. Combined heating and ventilation system. Glassfibre soundproofing. Optional overhead skylights.

Systems: Electrical system includes a 60A 12V alternator, automatic alternator cutout, electric engine starter and 12V battery.

Electronics and Equipment: Optional extras include Cessna Series 300 360-channel transceiver, 360-channel nav/com with remote VOR indicator, 360-channel nav/com with remote VOR/LOC indicator or VOR/ILS indicator, ADF, marker beacon with three lights and aural signal, transponder with 4096 code capability, DME, 10-channel HF transceiver, Nav-O-Matic autopilot with heading control plus VOR, and Series 400 glideslope receiver, boom microphone with control-wheel switch, control-wheel map light, dual controls, sensitive altimeter, directional gyro with movable heading index, electric clock, outside air temperature gauge, landing light, rate of climb indicator, turn co-ordinator, map and instrument panel light, carburettor air temperature gauge, true airspeed indicator, turn and bank indicator, horizon and directional gyros with vacuum system, sun visors, towbar, flight hour recorder, cabin fire extinguisher, headrests, courtesy lights, rearview mirror, child's foldaway seat, rear seats with individual reclining backs, front seats with articulating recline and vertical adjustment, utility shelf, safety belts for third and fourth seats, overhead skylights, portable stretcher, emergency locator transmitter, rear-seat ventilation system, hinged window on starboard side, full-flow oil filter, engine primer system, alternative static source, wing-strut and fuselage steps and handles for easy refuelling, quick-drain oil valve, internal corrosion proofing, navigation light detectors, floatplane kit, external power socket, pitot heating system, glider tow hook, omni-flash beacon, dual cowl-mounted landing lights, wingtip strobe lights, tailplane abrasion boots, tinted windows and winterisation kit.

Skyhawk II, de luxe version of the Cessna Model 172 introduced for 1974

Dimensions, external (L: landplane; F: floatplane):
Wing span 35 ft 10 in (10·92 m)
Wing chord at root 5 ft 4 in (1·63 m)
Wing chord at tip 3 ft 8½ in (1·12 m)
Wing aspect ratio 7·52
Length overall: L 26 ft 11 in (8·20 m)
F 27 ft 0 in (8·23 m)
Height overall: L 8 ft 9½ in (2·68 m)
F 9 ft 11 in (3·02 m)
Tailplane span 11 ft 4 in (3·45 m)
Wheel track: L 8 ft 3½ in (2·53 m)
Wheelbase: L 5 ft 4 in (1·63 m)
Propeller diameter:
L 6 ft 3 in (1·91 m)
F 6 ft 8 in (2·03 m)
Passenger doors (each):
Height 3 ft 3¾ in (1·01 m)
Width 2 ft 11 in (0·89 m)

Areas:
Wings, gross 174 sq ft (16·17 m^2)
Ailerons (total) 18·3 sq ft (1·70 m^2)
Trailing-edge flaps (total) 21·20 sq ft (1·97 m^2)
Fin 11·24 sq ft (1·04 m^2)
Rudder 7·30 sq ft (0·68 m^2)
Tailplane 20·16 sq ft (1·87 m^2)
Elevators, including tab 16·15 sq ft (1·50 m^2)

Weights and Loadings (L: landplane; F: floatplane):
Weight empty, equipped:
L 1,300 lb (589 kg)
F 1,450 lb (657 kg)
Max T-O weight:
L 2,300 lb (1,043 kg)
F 2,220 lb (1,007 kg)
Max wing loading:
L 13·2 lb/sq ft (64·45 kg/m^2)
F 12·7 lb/sq ft (62·0 kg/m^2)
Max power loading:
L 15·3 lb/hp (6·94 kg/hp)
F 14·8 lb/hp (6·71 kg/hp)

Performance (L: landplane; F: floatplane, at max T-O weight):
Max never-exceed speed:
L 151 knots (174 mph; 280 km/h)
Max level speed at S/L:
L 122 knots (140 mph; 225 km/h)
F 98 knots (113 mph; 182 km/h)
Max cruising speed (75% power):
L at 8,000 ft (2,440 m) 117 knots (135 mph; 217 km/h)
F at 7,500 ft (2,285 m) 97 knots (112 mph; 180 km/h)
Econ cruising speed at 10,000 ft (3,050 m):
L 101 knots (116 mph; 187 km/h)
F 86 knots (99 mph; 159 km/h)
Stalling speed, flaps up:
L 50 knots (57 mph; 92 km/h)
F 48 knots (55 mph; 88·5 km/h)
Stalling speed, flaps down:
L 43 knots (49 mph; 79 km/h)
F 43·5 knots (50 mph; 80·5 km/h)
Max rate of climb at S/L:
L 645 ft (196 m)/min
F 715 ft (218 m)/min
Service ceiling:
L 13,100 ft (3,995 m)
F 12,000 ft (3,660 m)
T-O run:
L 865 ft (264 m)
F 1,620 ft (494 m)
T-O to 50 ft (15 m):
L 1,525 ft (465 m)
F 2,390 ft (729 m)
Landing from 50 ft (15 m):
L 1,250 ft (381 m)
F 1,345 ft (410 m)
Landing run:
L 520 ft (158 m)
F 590 ft (180 m)
Range at max cruising speed, standard tanks, no reserve:
L, at 8,000 ft (2,440 m) 551 nm (635 miles; 1,022 km)
F, at 7,500 ft (2,285 m) 456 nm (525 miles; 845 km)
Range at max cruising speed, optional long-range tanks, no reserve:
L, at 8,000 ft (2,440 m) 690 nm (795 miles; 1,279 km)
F, at 7,500 ft (2,285 m) 573 nm (660 miles; 1,062 km)
Range at econ cruising speed, standard tanks, no reserve:
L, at 10,000 ft (3,050 m) 603 nm (695 miles; 1,118 km)
F, at 10,000 ft (3,050 m) 499 nm (575 miles; 925 km)
Range at econ cruising speed, optional long-range tanks, no reserve:
L, at 10,000 ft (3,050 m) 755 nm (870 miles; 1,400 km)
F, at 10,000 ft (3,050 m) 629 nm (725 miles; 1,166 km)

CESSNA SKYHAWK and SKYHAWK II

The Skyhawk is a de luxe version of the Model 172, to which it is generally similar; the Skyhawk II, introduced for 1974, includes as standard equipment many further items which are optional on the Skyhawk. Details are as follows:

Skyhawk. Generally similar to Model 172, but including as standard full blind-flying instrumentation, including a turn co-ordinator indicator, and lightweight 3 in gyros, sun visors, landing and taxi lights, map and instrument panel light, electric clock, speed fairings on the wheels, all-over paint scheme including racing stripes, and towbar. The 1974 Skyhawk introduces the improvements detailed for the Model 172 and has, in addition, an engine cowling with redesigned internal baffles and cooling air exit opening which increases cruising speed by 5 knots (6 mph; 10 km/h).

Skyhawk II. As Skyhawk, but including as standard equipment a 300 Series nav/com with 360-channel com and 160-channel nav, dual controls, true airspeed indicator, navigation light detectors, heated pitot, courtesy lights, omni-flash beacon, alternate static source and an emergency locator transmitter.

The Skyhawk is certificated for operation as a floatplane, and can be fitted with skis.

Dimensions:
As for Model 172

Weights and Loadings (L: landplane; F: floatplane):
As for Model 172, except:
Weight empty, equipped:
Skyhawk:
L 1,345 lb (610 kg)
F 1,485 lb (673 kg)
Skyhawk II 1,370 lb (621 kg)

Performance (Skyhawk landplane, Skyhawk II, at max T-O weight):
As for Model 172, except:
Max level speed at S/L 125 knots (144 mph; 232 km/h)
Max cruising speed (75% power) at 8,000 ft (2,440 m) 120 knots (138 mph; 222 km/h)
Econ cruising speed at 10,000 ft (3,050 m) 102 knots (117 mph; 188 km/h)
Range at max cruising speed, standard tanks, no reserve 564 nm (650 miles; 1,046 km)
Range at max cruising speed, optional long-range tanks, no reserve 707 nm (815 miles; 1,311 km)
Range at econ cruising speed at 10,000 ft (3,050 m), standard tanks, no reserve 607 nm (700 miles; 1,126 km)
Range at econ cruising speed, at 10,000 ft (3,050 m), long-range tanks, no reserve 759 nm (875 miles; 1,408 km)

CESSNA MODEL R172E

US Army designation: T-41B Mescalero
US Air Force designations: T-41C/D Mescalero

The Cessna Model R172E is a more powerful version of the 172. Its design was started in late 1963, and a prototype was then built, with a 180 hp Continental O-360 engine. Type approval was received in 1964, but the original power plant has been replaced in the production Model R172E by a fuel-injection IO-360 engine, as described below.

In August 1966, the US Army ordered 255 aircraft of this type, under the designation **T-41B,** for training and installation support duties. Delivery of these was completed in March 1967.

In October 1967, the US Air Force ordered 45 of these aircraft, with a fixed-pitch propeller, under the designation **T-41C,** for cadet flight training at the USAF Academy in Colorado. A total of 52 had been produced by 31 January 1974. Thirty **T-41Ds,** with a constant-speed propeller and 28V electrical system, were ordered initially for the Colombian Air Force, and deliveries of this version to all operators totalled 226 by 31 January 1974.

In addition, a version known as the Reims Rocket is being produced by Reims Aviation in France (which see). A total of 447 Rockets had been delivered by 31 January 1974.

The description of the Model 172 applies also to the R172E, except for the following details:

Power Plant: One 210 hp Continental IO-360-D six-cylinder horizontally-opposed aircooled engine, driving a McCauley D2A34C67/76S constant-speed propeller. Two fuel tanks in wings with total capacity of 52 US gallons (197 litres), of which 46 US gallons (174 litres) are usable. Provision for long-range tanks, giving total usable capacity of 63 US gallons (238 litres). Refuelling points above wing. Oil capacity 10 US quarts (9·5 litres).

Accommodation: Basically as for Model 172. T-41B has special crew seatbacks and shoulder harness, with forward-hinged door on each side of cabin by crew seats. Baggage capacity 200 lb (90·5 kg).

Electronics and Equipment: The T-41B, C and D have variations in their electronics and other equipment consistent with their intended roles.

Dimensions, external:
Propeller diameter 6 ft 4 in (1·93 m)

Weights and Loadings:
Weight empty, equipped 1,405 lb (637 kg)
Max T-O and landing weight 2,550 lb (1,156 kg)
Max wing loading 14·6 lb/sq ft (71·3 kg/m²)
Max power loading 12·1 lb/hp (5·49 kg/hp)

Performance (at max T-O weight):
Max never-exceed speed 158 knots (182 mph; 293 km/h)
Max level speed at S/L 133 knots (153 mph; 246 km/h)
Max cruising speed at 5,500 ft (1,675 m) 126 knots (145 mph; 233 km/h)
Econ cruising speed at 10,000 ft (3,050 m) 91 knots (105 mph; 169 km/h)
Stalling speed, flaps up 55·6 knots (64 mph; 103 km/h)
Stalling speed, flaps down 46 knots (53 mph; 85 km/h)
Max rate of climb at S/L 880 ft (268 m)/min
Service ceiling 17,000 ft (5,180 m)
T-O run 740 ft (226 m)
T-O to 50 ft (15 m) 1,230 ft (375 m)
Landing from 50 ft (15 m) 1,270 ft (387 m)
Landing run 620 ft (189 m)
Range with max fuel at econ cruising speed at 10,000 ft (3,050 m) 877 nm (1,010 miles; 1,625 km)

CESSNA MODEL 177

On 30 September 1967, Cessna introduced its Model 177, a single-engined four-seat aircraft with a cantilever wing, then powered by a 150 hp Lycoming engine, and intended as a luxury addition to its range of single-engined two- and four-seat models. Increased engine power was provided in 1969 by installation of the 180 hp Lycoming O-360 engine as standard.

The 1974 version of the Model 177 has more comfortable seating, a new tailplane abrasion boot and a new optional boom microphone headset.

A total of 2,050 Model 177/Cardinals had been built by 31 January 1974. Three commercial versions are currently available:

Model 177. Standard version, described below.

Cardinal. De luxe version of 177, described separately.

Cardinal RG. Version with retractable landing gear, described separately.

Type: Four-seat cabin monoplane.

Wings: Cantilever high-wing monoplane. Wing section modified NACA 2400 series. Dihedral 1° 30′. Incidence 3° 30′ at root, 0° 30′ at tip. All-metal structure except for conical-camber glassfibre wingtips. Modified Frise all-metal ailerons. Electrically-operated wide-span all-metal slotted flaps.

Fuselage: All-metal semi-monocoque structure of low profile.

Tail Unit: Cantilever all-metal structure. Sweepback on fin 35° at quarter-chord. All-moving tailplane, with large controllable trim tab. Controllable rudder trim tab.

Landing Gear: Non-retractable tricycle type. Improved Cessna Land-O-Matic cantilever main legs, each comprising a one-piece machined conically-tapered steel tube. Nosewheel is carried on a short-stroke oleo-pneumatic shock-strut, with hydraulic damper, and is steerable with rudder up to 12° each side and controllable up to 45° on each side. Cessna main wheels size 6·00-6 and nosewheel size 5·00-5, with nylon cord tube-type tyres. Tyre pressure 30 lb/sq in (2·11 kg/cm²). Single-caliper hydraulic disc brakes. Parking brake locks both main wheels. Wheel fairings optional.

Power Plant: One 180 hp Lycoming O-360-A1F6 four-cylinder horizontally-opposed air-cooled engine, driving a two-blade constant-speed metal propeller. Pointed aluminium spinner. Fuel is carried in a 25 US gallon (94·5 litre) integral fuel tank in each wing, vented at the wingtip. Total usable fuel 49 US gallons (185 litres). Optional fuel system of 61 US gallons (230 litres) capacity, of which 60 US gallons (227 litres) are usable. Refuelling point on top of each wing. Oil capacity 2 US gallons (7·5 litres).

Accommodation: Cabin seats four in two pairs. Optional seat for two children aft of rear seats. Baggage compartment in rear fuselage, capacity 120 lb (54 kg) with large forward-hinged external access door in port side of fuselage. Forward-hinged door on each side of cabin, forward of main landing gear. Combined heating and ventilation system. Glassfibre soundproofing.

Systems: Electrical supply from 12V 60A alternator. 12V 25Ah battery. 12V 33Ah battery optional.

Electronics and Equipment: Optional items include Cessna Series 300 360-channel transceiver, 360-channel nav/com with remote VOR/LOC indicator or VOR/ILS indicator, ADF, marker beacon with three lights and aural signal, transponder with 4096 code capability, DME, 10-channel HF transceiver, Nav-O-Matic autopilot with heading control plus VOR, Series 400 glideslope receiver, boom microphone with control wheel switch, control wheel map light, dual controls, sensitive altimeter, directional gyro with movable heading index, carburettor air temperature gauge, true airspeed indicator, economy mixture indicator, turn and bank indicator, flight hour recorder, cabin fire extinguisher, headrests, electric clock, outside air temperature gauge, landing light, rate-of-climb indicator, turn co-ordinator indicator, sun visors, horizon and directional gyros with vacuum system, emergency locator transmitter, alternate static source, tailcone lift handles, towbar, rearview mirror, child's seat, individual articulating and vertically adjustable front seats, individual reclining rear seats, safety belts for third and fourth seats, stretcher, rear seat ventilation system, internal corrosion proofing, navigation light detectors, external power socket, engine primer system, quick-drain oil valve, cowl-mounted landing lights, pitot heating system, courtesy lights, wingtip strobe lights, tinted windows, wing leveller system and engine winterisation kit. Standard equipment includes omni-flash beacon, windscreen defroster, stall warning indicator, control locks, full-flow oil filter and navigation lights.

Dimensions, external:
Wing span 35 ft 6 in (10·82 m)
Wing chord at root 5 ft 6 in (1·68 m)
Wing chord at tip 4 ft 0 in (1·22 m)
Wing aspect ratio 7·31
Length overall 27 ft 3 in (8·31 m)
Height overall 8 ft 7 in (2·62 m)
Tailplane span 11 ft 10 in (3·61 m)
Wheel track 8 ft 3½ in (2·53 m)
Wheelbase 6 ft 4½ in (1·94 m)
Propeller diameter 6 ft 4 in (1·93 m)
Passenger doors (each):
Height 3 ft 8 in (1·12 m)
Width 4 ft 0 in (1·22 m)
Height to sill 2 ft 3 in (0·69 m)

Dimensions, internal:
Cabin:
Length 14 ft 7½ in (4·46 m)
Maximum width 4 ft 0 in (1·22 m)
Maximum height 3 ft 8½ in (1·13 m)

Areas:
Wings, gross 174·0 sq ft (16·2 m²)
Ailerons (total) 18·86 sq ft (1·75 m²)
Trailing-edge flaps (total) 29·50 sq ft (2·74 m²)
Fin 11·02 sq ft (1·02 m²)
Rudder 6·41 sq ft (0·60 m²)
Tailplane, including tab 35·01 sq ft (3·25 m²)

Weights and Loadings:
Weight empty, equipped 1,455 lb (660 kg)
Max T-O weight 2,500 lb (1,133 kg)
Max wing loading 14·4 lb/sq ft (70·3 kg/m²)
Max power loading 13·9 lb/hp (6·30 kg/hp)

Performance (at max T-O weight, with wheel fairings):
Max level speed at S/L 135 knots (156 mph; 251 km/h)
Max cruising speed, 75% power at 8,000 ft (2,440 m) 124 knots (143 mph; 230 km/h)
Econ cruising speed at 10,000 ft (3,050 m) 109 knots (125 mph; 201 km/h)
Stalling speed, flaps up 55 knots (63 mph; 101·5 km/h)
Stalling speed, flaps down 46 knots (53 mph; 85·5 km/h)
Max rate of climb at S/L 840 ft (256 m)/min
Service ceiling 14,600 ft (4,450 m)
T-O run 750 ft (229 m)
T-O to 50 ft (15 m) 1,400 ft (427 m)
Landing from 50 ft (15 m) 1,220 ft (372 m)
Landing run 600 ft (183 m)
Range at max cruising speed, standard fuel, no reserve 603 nm (695 miles; 1,118 km)
Range at econ cruising speed, standard fuel, no reserve 686 nm (790 miles; 1,271 km)
Range at max cruising speed, optional fuel, no reserve 742 nm (855 miles; 1,376 km)
Range at econ cruising speed, optional fuel, no reserve 838 nm (965 miles; 1,553 km)

CESSNA CARDINAL

The Cardinal is a de luxe version of the Model 177, to which it is generally similar. Standard equipment includes sensitive altimeter, electric clock, speed fairings on the wheels, external air temperature gauge, full blind-flying instrumentation with vacuum system, rate of climb indicator, turn co-ordinator, special interior appointments, landing light, all-over two-tone paint scheme, sun visors and towbar.

Under a US Navy contract granted to Curtiss-Wright Corporation, a Cessna Cardinal has had a Curtiss-Wright Wankel-type engine installed as power plant in an experimental "quiet aeroplane" programme. The Navy-sponsored programme is intended to obtain acoustical flight evaluation of the rotating combustion engine for possible use in light tactical aircraft.

Since noise reduction is a primary aim, the Cardinal in which the engine was installed had a three-blade propeller, 8 ft 4 in (2·54 m) in diameter, with wide-chord blades, and an extensive exhaust and muffling system which ejected the exhaust above the aircraft.

Cessna was subcontracted to fly the aircraft.

Dimensions:
Same as for Model 177

Weights and Loadings:
Same as for Model 177, except:
Weight empty, equipped 1,505 lb (682 kg)

Performance (at max T-O weight):
Same as for Model 177

CESSNA CARDINAL RG

On 3 December 1970 Cessna announced a new version of its Cardinal single-engined four-seat cabin monoplane, with hydraulically-retractable tricycle-type landing gear, a more powerful fuel-injection engine and a number of new standard and optional items.

The landing gear is retracted by a simplified self-contained hydraulic system, with an electrically-powered hydraulic pump that provides a maximum system pressure of 1,500 lb/sq in (105 kg/cm²). The hand pump, for emergency retraction or extension of the gear, is designed to

Cessna Cardinal, de luxe version of the Model 177 (180 hp Lycoming O-360-A1F6 engine)

eliminate the need for complex sequencing valves in the hydraulic power pack. When the landing gear is retracted the nose unit is faired by wheel doors; the main gear is retained flush with the fuselage and has no wheel doors.

The 1974 version of the Cardinal RG has a new cabin heating and ventilation system, more comfortable seating, a panel-mounted selector for landing gear retraction, new interior and exterior styling, a shoulder harness stowage tray for front seat occupants, and miniaturised marker beacon lights. New options available on the Cardinal RG include a combination microphone/headset and the Cessna 200A Nav-O-Matic single-axis autopilot.

By 31 January 1974 a total of 485 Cardinal RGs had been delivered, the total including 87 produced by Reims Aviation in France.

Type: Four-seat cabin monoplane.

Wings: Cantilever high-wing monoplane. Wing section NACA 64A215 at root, NACA 64A412 at tip. Dihedral 1° 30′. Incidence 4° 7′ at root, 0° 43′ at tip. All-metal structure except for glassfibre wingtips. All-metal ailerons. Electrically-operated all-metal trailing-edge flaps.

Fuselage: All-metal semi-monocoque structure of low profile.

Tail Unit: Cantilever all-metal structure with swept vertical surfaces. All-moving tailplane with large controllable trim tab.

Landing Gear: Hydraulically-retractable tricycle type. Tubular spring steel main gear struts, retracting rearward into fuselage. Nosewheel, which retracts rearward, is carried on a short-stroke oleo-pneumatic shock-strut with hydraulic damper, and is steerable. Nosewheel enclosed by doors when retracted. Hydraulic brakes. Parking brake.

Power Plant: One 200 hp Lycoming IO-360-A1B6 four-cylinder horizontally-opposed air-cooled engine, driving a two-blade constant-speed metal propeller. Pointed metal spinner. One 30·5 US gallon (115 litre) integral fuel tank in each wing. Total fuel capacity 61 US gallons (230 litres), of which 60 US gallons (227 litres) are usable. Refuelling point in top of each wing. Oil capacity 2 US gallons (7·5 litres).

Accommodation: Cabin seats four in two pairs. Forward-hinged door on each side of cabin, forward of main landing gear. Cabin heated and ventilated. Baggage compartment in rear fuselage, capacity 120 lb (54 kg), with large forward-hinged external access door on port side of fuselage.

Systems: Electrical system powered by a 14V 60A alternator and 12V battery for operation of wing flaps, hydraulic motor, avionics and lighting. Hydraulic system for landing gear retraction and brakes.

Electronics and Equipment: Optional items are as detailed for the Model 177, plus Cessna Series 400 360-channel transceiver, 360-channel nav/com with remote VOR/LOC indicator or VOR/ILS indicator, ADF with digital tuning, transponder with 4096 code capability. Standard equipment includes inertia safety belts for pilot and co-pilot and omni-flash beacon at tip of fin.

Dimensions, external:

Wing span	35 ft 6 in (10·82 m)
Wing chord at root	5 ft 6 in (1·68 m)
Wing chord at tip	4 ft 0 in (1·22 m)
Length overall	27 ft 3 in (8·31 m)
Height overall	8 ft 7 in (2·62 m)
Tailplane span	11 ft 10 in (3·61 m)
Wheel track	7 ft 10 in (2·39 m)
Propeller diameter	6 ft 6 in (1·98 m)
Passenger doors (each): Width	4 ft 0 in (1·22 m)

Area:

Wings, gross	174·0 sq ft (16·2 m²)

Weights and Loadings:

Weight empty	1,665 lb (755 kg)
Max T-O weight	2,800 lb (1,270 kg)
Max wing loading	16·1 lb/sq ft (78·6 kg/m²)
Max power loading	14·0 lb/hp (6·4 kg/hp)

Performance (at max T-O weight):

Max level speed at S/L 156 knots (180 mph; 290 km/h)

Max cruising speed (75% power) at 7,000 ft (2,135 m) 149 knots (171 mph; 275 km/h)

Econ cruising speed at 10,000 ft (3,050 m) 121 knots (139 mph; 223 km/h)

Stalling speed, flaps up 57 knots (66 mph; 106 km/h)

Stalling speed, flaps down 50 knots (57 mph; 92 km/h)

Max rate of climb at S/L	925 ft (282 m)/min
Service ceiling	17,100 ft (5,210 m)
T-O run	890 ft (271 m)
T-O to 50 ft (15 m)	1,585 ft (483 m)
Landing from 50 ft (15 m)	1,350 ft (411 m)
Landing run	730 ft (223 m)

Range at max cruising speed, no reserve 820 nm (945 miles; 1,520 km)

Range at econ cruising speed, no reserve 1,050 nm (1,210 miles; 1,945 km)

Cessna Cardinal RG (200 hp Lycoming IO-360-A1B6 engine)

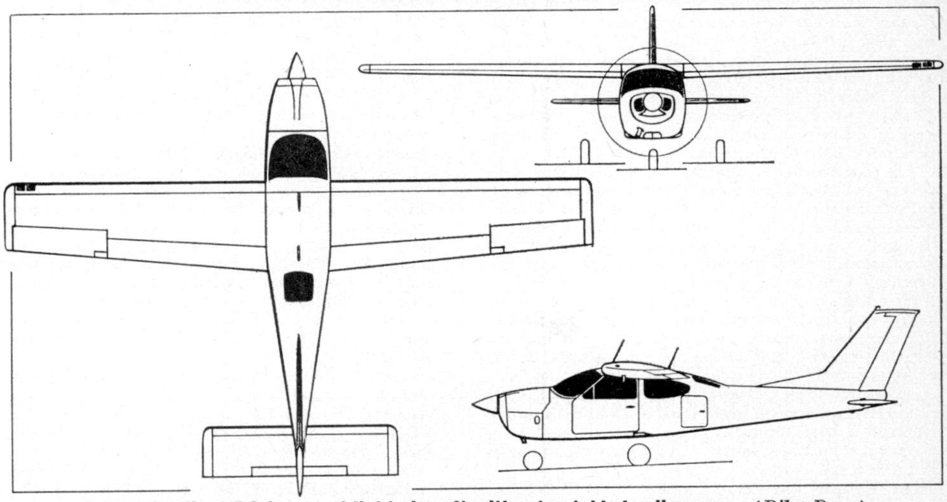

Cessna Cardinal RG four-seat light aircraft with retractable landing gear (*Pilot Press*)

CESSNA MODEL 180 SKYWAGON

The Model 180 Skywagon has a typical Cessna braced high-wing monoplane layout, but with a tailwheel type of landing gear.

The 1974 version introduces new landing/taxi light switching and a redesigned vertical fin attachment to the aft tailcone. New options include rudder pedal extensions, blue/white instrument post lights and additional window area totalling 1,197 sq in (7,722 cm²). Of this total nearly 800 sq in (5,161 cm²) comes from 2 ft 2 in by 1 ft 3¼ in (0·66 m by 0·38 m) tinted windows in the lower half of each cabin door, the remainder from two tinted skylights each 1 ft 11¾ in by 8¾ in (0·60 m by 0·22 m). In addition, optional domed upper windows are available to replace the flat openable windows in each door. Of green-tinted free-blown plastics, these provide much improved vertical and horizontal visibility for the front-seat occupants.

A total of 5,424 Model 180s had been built by 31 January 1974.

Type: One/six-seat cabin monoplane.

Wings: Generally similar in construction to those of Model 172. Dihedral 1° 45′.

Fuselage: All-metal semi-monocoque structure. Identical to fuselage of Cessna 185, except for firewall and mounting brackets for dorsal fin.

Tail Unit: Unswept cantilever all-metal structure with adjustable-incidence tailplane. Normally no trim tabs; but manually-operated rudder trim is optionally available.

Landing Gear: Non-retractable tailwheel type. Cessna cantilever spring steel main legs. Tailwheel has tapered tubular spring. Main wheels and nylon tube-type tyres size 6·00-6 (optionally 8·00-6). Scott tailwheel with 8 in (20 cm) tyre. Tyre pressure, main wheels 28 lb/sq in (1·97 kg/cm²), tailwheel 55-65 lb/sq in (3·87-4·57 kg/cm²) according to load. Hydraulic disc brakes. Parking brake. Alternative Edo Model 628-296 floats, snow ski or amphibian gear.

Power Plant: One 230 hp Continental O-470-R six-cylinder horizontally-opposed aircooled engine, driving a McCauley 2A34C50/90A8 constant-speed metal propeller. Two fuel tanks in wings, with total standard capacity of 65 US gallons (246 litres) and usable capacity of 60 US gallons (227 litres). Optional long-range tanks with total capacity of 84 US gallons (318 litres), of which 79 US gallons (299 litres) are usable. Oil capacity 3 US gallons (11·5 litres).

Accommodation: Standard seating is for a pilot only, with a choice of three optional arrangements. Maximum seating is for six persons in three pairs, without baggage space. With fewer seats there is space at rear of cabin for up to 400 lb (181 kg) of baggage. Door on each side of cabin, plus optional cargo door and baggage compartment door on port side. Starboard door has quick-release hinge pins so that it can be removed when loading bulky cargo. Passenger seats can all be removed when aircraft is to be used for freight carrying. Hinged window each side. Instrument lighting controls are transistorised. Heating and ventilation standard. Fully-articulating seats for pilot and co-pilot, fold-away child's seat for the rear cabin and safety belts for rear-seat passengers are available optionally.

Systems: Hydraulic system for brakes only. Electrical system powered by 14V 60A alternator. 12V 33Ah battery. Oxygen system, 48 cu ft (1·36 m³) capacity, optional.

Electronics and Equipment: Optional electronics include Cessna Series 300 360-channel com transceiver, 360-channel nav/com with remote VOR/LOC indicator or VOR/ILS indicator, ADF with digital tuning, marker beacon with three lights and aural signal, transponder with 4096 code capability, DME, 10-channel HF transceiver, Nav-O-Matic single-axis autopilot with heading control and VOR intercept and track; or Series 400 360-channel com transceiver, 360-channel nav/com with remote VOR/LOC indicator or VOR/ILS indicator, transponder with 4096 code capability, glideslope receiver and ADF with digital tuning. Standard equipment includes audible stall warning indicator, instrument panel red floodlights, control locks, windscreen defroster, cabin dome light, landing and taxi lights, and baggage restraint net. Optional equipment includes blind-flying instrumentation, boom microphone, electric clock, control wheel with map light and microphone switch, dual controls, carburettor air temperature gauge, outside air temperature gauge, true airspeed indicator, economy mixture indicator, turn co-ordinator, turn and bank indicator, flight hour recorder, pilot and co-pilot headrests, map and auxiliary instrument light, courtesy lights, co-pilot's seat, stretcher installation, sun visors, emergency locator transmitter, tinted windows, heated pitot, non-congealing oil cooler, oil dilution system, engine winterisation kit, internal corrosion proofing, navigation light detectors, external power socket, omni-flash beacon, quick oil drain valve, overall paint scheme, photographic provisions, agricultural sprayer system, tailplane abrasion boots, static dischargers, alternate static source and cabin fire extinguisher.

Dimensions, external:

Wing span	35 ft 10 in (10·92 m)
Wing chord at root	5 ft 4 in (1·63 m)
Wing chord at tip	3 ft 7¾ in (1·11 m)
Wing aspect ratio	7·52
Length overall:	
Landplane, skiplane	25 ft 9 in (7·85 m)
Floatplane	27 ft 0 in (8·23 m)
Amphibian	27 ft 6 in (8·38 m)
Height overall:	
Landplane, skiplane	7 ft 9 in (2·36 m)
Floatplane	12 ft 2 in (3·71 m)
Amphibian	12 ft 8 in (3·86 m)
Tailplane span	10 ft 10 in (3·30 m)

Wheel track, landplane 7 ft 8 in (2·33 m)
Propeller diameter:
Landplane, skiplane 6 ft 10 in (2·08 m)
Floatplane, amphibian 7 ft 4 in (2·24 m)
Passenger doors (each):
Height 3 ft 3¾ in (1·01 m)
Width 2 ft 11 in (0·89 m)

AREAS:
Wings, gross 174 sq ft (16·16 m²)
Ailerons (total) 18·3 sq ft (1·70 m²)
Trailing-edge flaps (total) 21·23 sq ft (1·97 m²)
Fin 9·01 sq ft (0·84 m²)
Dorsal fin 2·04 sq ft (0·19 m²)
Rudder 7·29 sq ft (0·68 m²)
Tailplane 20·94 sq ft (1·94 m²)
Elevators 15·13 sq ft (1·40 m²)

WEIGHTS AND LOADINGS:
Weight empty, equipped:
Landplane 1,560 lb (707 kg)
Floatplane 1,870 lb (848 kg)
Skiplane 1,700 lb (771 kg)
Amphibian 2,110 lb (957 kg)
Max T-O weight:
Landplane, skiplane 2,800 lb (1,270 kg)
Floatplane, amphibian 2,950 lb (1,338 kg)
Max wing loading:
Landplane, skiplane 16·1 lb/sq ft (78·6 kg/m²)
Floatplane, amphibian 17·0 lb/sq ft (83·0 kg/m²)
Max power loading:
Landplane, skiplane 12·2 lb/hp (5·53 kg/hp)
Floatplane, amphibian 12·8 lb/hp (5·80 kg/hp)

PERFORMANCE (at max T-O weight):
Max never-exceed speed:
Landplane 167 knots (192 mph; 309 km/h)
Max level speed at S/L:
Landplane 148 knots (170 mph; 274 km/h)
Floatplane, amphibian, skiplane 129 knots (149 mph; 240 km/h)
Max cruising speed (75% power) at 6,500 ft (1,980 m):
Landplane 141 knots (162 mph; 261 km/h)
Floatplane, amphibian 128 knots (147 mph; 237 km/h)
Skiplane 125 knots (144 mph; 232 km/h)
Econ cruising speed at 10,000 ft (3,050 m):
Landplane 105 knots (121 mph; 195 km/h)
Floatplane 99 knots (114 mph; 183 km/h)
Amphibian 99 knots (114 mph; 183 km/h)
Skiplane 88 knots (101 mph; 162 km/h)
Stalling speed, flaps up, power off:
All versions 53 knots (61 mph; 98·5 km/h)
Stalling speed, flaps down, power off:
All versions 48 knots (55 mph; 88·5 km/h)
Max rate of climb at S/L:
Landplane 1,090 ft (332 m)/min
Floatplane, amphibian 990 ft (302 m)/min
Service ceiling:
Landplane 19,600 ft (5,975 m)
Floatplane, amphibian 16,000 ft (4,877 m)
T-O run:
Landplane 625 ft (190 m)
Floatplane 1,280 ft (390 m)
Amphibian, on land 1,360 ft (415 m)
Amphibian, on water 1,280 ft (390 m)
T-O to 50 ft (15 m):
Landplane 1,205 ft (367 m)
Floatplane 2,070 ft (631 m)
Amphibian, on land 2,185 ft (666 m)
Amphibian, on water 2,070 ft (631 m)
Landing from 50 ft (15 m):
Landplane 1,365 ft (416 m)
Floatplane 1,720 ft (524 m)
Amphibian, on land 1,490 ft (454 m)
Amphibian, on water 1,720 ft (524 m)
Landing run:
Landplane 480 ft (146 m)
Floatplane 735 ft (224 m)
Amphibian, on land 1,025 ft (312 m)
Amphibian, on water 735 ft (224 m)
Range at econ cruising speed, with long-range tanks, no reserve:
Landplane 1,055 nm (1,215 miles; 1,955 km)
Floatplane 946 nm (1,090 miles; 1,754 km)
Amphibian 946 nm (1,090 miles; 1,754 km)
Skiplane 829 nm (955 miles; 1,537 km)
Range at max cruising speed, standard fuel, no reserve:
Landplane 603 nm (695 miles; 1,118 km)
Floatplane, amphibian 547 nm (630 miles; 1,014 km)
Skiplane 538 nm (620 miles; 998 km)
Range at max cruising speed, with long-range tanks, no reserve:
Landplane 803 nm (925 miles; 1,489 km)
Floatplane, amphibian 725 nm (835 miles; 1,344 km)
Skiplane 712 nm (820 miles; 1,320 km)

CESSNA MODEL 182

The 1974 version of the Model 182 has an improved cabin heating and ventilation system, more comfortable seating, a more efficient constant-speed propeller and new inside door handles as standard, together with improvements to the front doorpost and the seal of the pilot's openable window. New options include the 200A Nav-O-Matic autopilot, and a combination microphone/headset.

A total of 13,778 Model 182/Skylanes had been built by 31 January 1974.

The Model 182 is built also, under licence, by the FMA in the Argentine (which see).

TYPE: Four-seat cabin monoplane.

WINGS: Braced high-wing monoplane. Wing section NACA 2412, modified. Incidence at root 0° 47′, at tip —2° 50′. Dihedral 1° 44′. Wing structure similar to Model 172, except metal-to-metal bonded leading-edge.

FUSELAGE: All-metal semi-monocoque structure.

TAIL UNIT: Cantilever all-metal structure with swept fin and rudder. Trim tab in starboard elevator.

LANDING GEAR: Non-retractable tricycle type. Land-O-Matic cantilever main legs, each comprising a one-piece machined conically-tapered spring steel tube. Steerable nosewheel with oleo-pneumatic shock-absorption. Cessna main wheels and tyres size 6·00-6, pressure 32 lb/sq in (2·25 kg/cm²). Cessna nosewheel and tyre size 5·00-5, pressure 45 lb/sq in (3·16 kg/cm²). Cessna hydraulic disc brakes. Parking brake. Optional wheel fairings.

POWER PLANT: Similar to that of Model 180, except for McCauley propeller type 2A36C/90M-8.

ACCOMMODATION: Generally similar to Model 172. Baggage space aft of rear seats, capacity 200 lb (91 kg), with external baggage door. Safety belts for rear seats and leather seating available optionally, as is the cargo pack as described for Model 185 Skywagon.

SYSTEMS: Electrical system powered by 60A 14V engine-driven alternator. 12V battery. Hydraulic system for brakes only. Oxygen system of 48 cu ft (1·36 m³) capacity optional.

ELECTRONICS AND EQUIPMENT: Optional electronics include Cessna 200 Series 200A Nav-O-Matic autopilot, 300 Series 360-channel com transceiver, 360-channel nav/com with remote VOR/LOC or VOR/ILS indicator, ADF with digital tuning, marker beacon with three lights and aural signal, transponder with 4096 code capability, DME, 10-channel HF transceiver, Nav-O-Matic single-axis autopilot with heading control plus VOR intercept and track, 400 Series 360-channel com transceiver, 360-channel nav/com with remote VOR/LOC or VOR/ILS indicator, glideslope receiver, ADF with digital tuning and transponder with 4096 code capability. Standard equipment includes audible stall warning indicator, variable-intensity instrument panel red floodlights, pedestal lights, control locks, armrests, windscreen defrosters, cabin dome light, baggage restraint net, adjustable cabin ventilators, tinted windscreen and windows, landing, taxi and navigation lights and cabin steps. Optional equipment includes blind-flying instrumentation, electric clock, outside air temperature gauge, turn co-ordinator indicator, rate of climb indicator, dual controls, control wheel with map light and microphone switch, carburettor air temperature gauge, economy mixture indicator, true airspeed indicator, instrument post lights, flight hour recorder, rear window curtain, sun visors, cabin fire extinguisher, headrests, rearview mirror, safety belts for rear seats, child's seat, skylights, stretcher installation, utility shelf, emergency locator transmitter, rear seat ventilation system, external power socket, non-congealing oil cooler, full-flow oil filter, quick-drain oil valve, engine winterisation kit, engine priming system, overall paint scheme, towbar, internal corrosion proofing, navigation light detectors, heated stall warning transmitter and pitot, glider tow hook, omni-flash beacon, courtesy lights, wingtip strobe lights, tailplane abrasion boots, static dischargers, alternate static source and tailcone lift handles.

DIMENSIONS, EXTERNAL:
Wing span 35 ft 10 in (10·92 m)
Wing chord at root 5 ft 4 in (1·63 m)
Wing chord at tip 3 ft 7 in (1·09 m)
Length overall 28 ft 2 in (8·59 m)
Height overall 9 ft 1½ in (2·78 m)
Tailplane span 11 ft 8 in (3·55 m)
Wheel track 9 ft 1 in (2·77 m)
Wheelbase 5 ft 6½ in (1·69 m)
Propeller diameter 6 ft 10 in (2·08 m)
Passenger doors (each):
Height 3 ft 4¼ in (1·02 m)
Width 2 ft 11¼ in (0·90 m)

AREAS:
Wings, gross 174 sq ft (16·16 m²)
Ailerons (total) 18·3 sq ft (1·70 m²)
Trailing-edge flaps (total) 21·20 sq ft (1·97 m²)
Fin 11·62 sq ft (1·08 m²)
Rudder 6·95 sq ft (0·65 m²)
Tailplane 22·96 sq ft (2·13 m²)
Elevators 15·85 sq ft (1·47 m²)

WEIGHTS AND LOADINGS:
Weight empty, equipped 1,595 lb (723 kg)
Max T-O weight 2,950 lb (1,338 kg)
Max wing loading 16·9 lb/sq ft (82·5 kg/m²)
Max power loading 12·8 lb/hp (5·8 kg/hp)

PERFORMANCE (at max T-O weight):
Max level speed at S/L 146 knots (168 mph; 270 km/h)
Max cruising speed, 75% power at 6,500 ft (1,980 m) 139 knots (160 mph; 257 km/h)
Econ cruising speed at 10,000 ft (3,050 m) 100 knots (115 mph; 185 km/h)
Stalling speed, flaps up 56 knots (64 mph; 103 km/h)
Stalling speed, flaps down 50 knots (57 mph; 92 km/h)
Max rate of climb at S/L 890 ft (271 m)/min
Service ceiling 17,700 ft (5,395 m)
T-O run 705 ft (215 m)
T-O to 50 ft (15 m) 1,350 ft (411 m)
Landing from 50 ft (15 m) 1,350 ft (411 m)
Landing run 590 ft (180 m)
Range at max cruising speed, standard fuel, no reserve 599 nm (690 miles; 1,110 km)
Range at max cruising speed, with long-range fuel tanks, no reserve 790 nm (910 miles; 1,460 km)
Range at econ cruising speed, standard fuel, no reserve 768 nm (885 miles; 1,424 km)
Range at econ cruising speed, with long-range fuel tanks, no reserve 1,007 nm (1,160 miles; 1,865 km)

CESSNA SKYLANE

The Skylane is a de luxe version of the Model 182 and was first introduced in January 1958. The 1974 version features the improvements detailed for the Model 182.

It was announced on 1 June 1971 that the Venezuelan Air Force had purchased 12 Model 182/Skylanes from Salta CA, Caracas, Cessna's Venezuelan distributor. Delivered in July 1971, they are used as personnel transports, and for training and FAC duties.

ELECTRONICS AND EQUIPMENT: As detailed for the Model 182, except standard equipment includes full blind-flying instrumentation, sensitive altimeter, electric clock, outside air temperature gauge, turn co-ordinator indicator, rate of climb indicator, rear window curtain, sun visors, wheel fairings, overall paint scheme and towbar. A turn and bank indicator is available optionally.

DIMENSIONS, EXTERNAL:
As for Model 182

WEIGHTS AND LOADINGS:
As for Model 182, except:
Weight empty, equipped 1,645 lb (746 kg)

PERFORMANCE (at max T-O weight):
As for Model 182

CESSNA MODEL 185 SKYWAGON
US military designation: U-17

The prototype of the Model 185 Skywagon flew for the first time in July 1960 and the first production model was completed in March 1961.

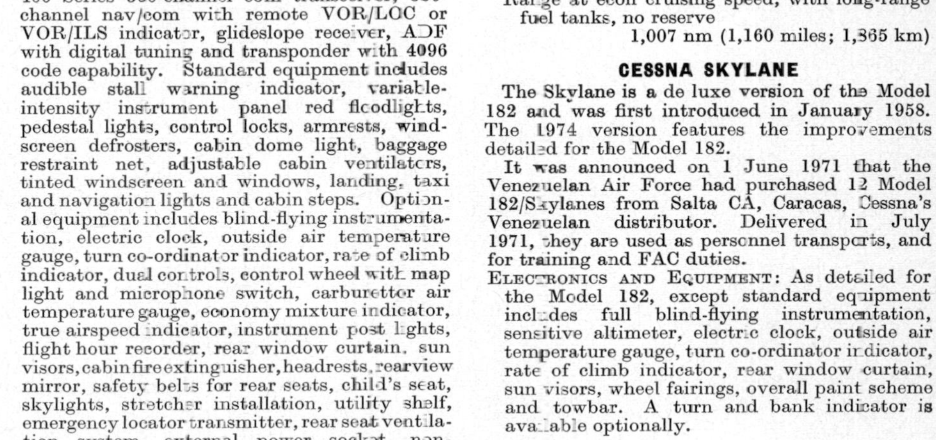

Cessna Model 180 Skywagon one/six-seat cabin monoplane (230 hp Continental O-470-R engine)

T

It is generally similar to the Model 180 Skywagon, except for installation of a 300 hp Continental IO-520 engine.

The 1974 version has the same improvements as those detailed for the Model 180.

Cessna has received important contracts to supply U-17A/B Skywagons to the US Air Force for delivery to overseas countries, under the US Military Assistance Programme.

A total of 2,321 Model 185 Skywagons, including U-17A/Bs, had been built by 31 January 1974.

The Model 185 Skywagon can be fitted with Edo 628-2960 floats, or Edo Model 597 amphibious floats, or Fli-Lite skis, and is suitable for agricultural duties, using quickly-removable Sorensen spray gear. It can carry under its fuselage a detachable glassfibre Cargo-Pack, more than 9 ft long and 2 ft 7 in wide (2·75 m × 0·79 m), with a volume of 21·5 cu ft (0·61 m³) and capacity of 300 lb (136 kg). The Pack incorporates loading doors on the side and at the rear.

TYPE: One/six-seat cabin monoplane.

WINGS AND FUSELAGE: Similar to Model 180.

TAIL UNIT: Same as for Model 180, except for fin of increased area and manually-operated rudder trim as standard equipment.

LANDING GEAR: Similar to Model 180, except for tyre pressures: Main wheels (6·00-6) 35 lb/sq in (2·46 kg/cm²), main wheels (8·00-6) 25 lb/sq in (1·76 kg/cm²), tailwheel 55-70 lb/sq in (3·87-4·92 kg/cm²) depending on load. Manual tailwheel lock standard. Optional amphibian, float or ski gear.

POWER PLANT: One 300 hp Continental IO-520-D six-cylinder horizontally-opposed aircooled engine, driving a McCauley constant-speed metal propeller. Fuel in two tanks in wings, total capacity 65 US gallons (246 litres), of which 62 US gallons (235 litres) are usable. Extended-range tanks available as optional equipment in place of standard tanks, total capacity 84 US gallons (318 litres), of which 81 US gallons (306·5 litres) are usable. Oil capacity 3 US gallons (11·4 litres).

ACCOMMODATION, ELECTRONICS AND EQUIPMENT: Same as for Model 180, except omni-flash beacon standard.

DIMENSIONS:
Same as for Model 180, except:
Propeller diameter:
Landplane 6 ft 10 in (2·08 m)
Floatplane, amphibian, skiplane 7 ft 2 in (2·18 m)

AREAS:
Same as for Model 180, except:
Fin 13·86 sq ft (1·29 m²)

WEIGHTS AND LOADINGS:
Weight empty, equipped:
Landplane 1,600 lb (725 kg)
Floatplane 1,910 lb (866 kg)
Amphibian 2,150 lb (975 kg)
Skiplane 1,740 lb (789 kg)
Max T-O weight:
Landplane, skiplane 3,350 lb (1,519 kg)
Floatplane 3,320 lb (1,506 kg)
Amphibian, land take-off 3,265 lb (1,481 kg)
Amphibian, water take-off 3,100 lb (1,406 kg)
Max wing loading:
Landplane, skiplane 19·3 lb/sq ft (94·2 kg/m²)
Floatplane 19·1 lb/sq ft (93·3 kg/m²)
Amphibian 18·8 lb/sq ft (91·8 kg/m²)
Max power loading:
Landplane, skiplane 11·2 lb/hp (5·08 kg/hp)
Floatplane 11·1 lb/hp (5·0 kg/hp)
Amphibian 10·9 lb/hp (4·9 kg/hp)

PERFORMANCE (at max T-O weight):
Max never-exceed speed:
Landplane 182 knots (210 mph; 338 km/h)
Max level speed at S/L:
Landplane 155 knots (178 mph; 286 km/h)
Floatplane 141 knots (162 mph; 261 km/h)
Amphibian 135 knots (156 mph; 251 km/h)
Skiplane 136 knots (157 mph; 252 km/h)
Max cruising speed (75% power) at 7,500 ft (2,285 m):
Landplane 147 knots (169 mph; 272 km/h)
Floatplane 135 knots (156 mph; 251 km/h)
Amphibian 129 knots (149 mph; 240 km/h)
Skiplane 133 knots (153 mph; 246 km/h)
Econ cruising speed at 10,000 ft (3,050 m):
Landplane 112 knots (129 mph; 208 km/h)
Floatplane 94 knots (108 mph; 174 km/h)
Amphibian 88 knots (101 mph; 162 km/h)
Skiplane 109 knots (126 mph; 203 km/h)
Stalling speed, flaps up, power off:
Landplane, skiplane, floatplane 56·5 knots (65 mph; 105 km/h)
Amphibian 55 knots (63 mph; 102 km/h)
Stalling speed, flaps down, power off:
Landplane, skiplane 49 knots (56 mph; 90·5 km/h)
Amphibian 51 knots (58 mph; 94 km/h)
Floatplane 52·5 knots (60 mph; 97 km/h)
Max rate of climb at S/L:
Landplane 1,010 ft (308 m)/min
Floatplane 960 ft (293 m)/min
Amphibian 970 ft (296 m)/min
Service ceiling:
Landplane 17,150 ft (5,229 m)
Floatplane 16,400 ft (5,000 m)
Amphibian 15,300 ft (4,663 m)
T-O run:
Landplane 770 ft (235 m)
Floatplane 1,105 ft (337 m)
Amphibian, on land 670 ft (204 m)
Amphibian, on water 885 ft (270 m)
T-O to 50 ft (15 m):
Landplane 1,365 ft (416 m)
Floatplane 1,740 ft (530 m)
Amphibian, on land 1,275 ft (389 m)
Amphibian, on water 1,430 ft (436 m)
Landing from 50 ft (15 m):
Landplane 1,400 ft (427 m)
Floatplane 1,530 ft (466 m)
Amphibian, on land 1,240 ft (378 m)
Amphibian, on water 1,480 ft (450 m)
Landing run:
Landplane 480 ft (146 m)
Floatplane 640 ft (195 m)
Amphibian, on land 780 ft (238 m)
Amphibian, on water 600 ft (183 m)
Range at econ cruising speed at 10,000 ft (3,050 m), long-range tanks, no reserve:
Landplane 898 nm (1,035 miles; 1,665 km)
Floatplane 807 nm (930 miles; 1,496 km)
Amphibian 755 nm (870 miles; 1,400 km)
Skiplane 777 nm (895 miles; 1,440 km)
Range at max cruising speed, standard tanks, no reserve (amphibian and floatplane only 59 US gallons; 223 litres usable):
Landplane 573 nm (660 miles; 1,062 km)
Amphibian 482 nm (555 miles; 893 km)
Floatplane 503 nm (580 miles; 933 km)
Skiplane 516 nm (595 miles; 957 km)
Range at max cruising speed, long-range tanks, no reserve:
Landplane 720 nm (830 miles; 1,335 km)
Floatplane 664 nm (765 miles; 1,231 km)
Amphibian 638 nm (735 miles; 1,182 km)
Skiplane 651 nm (750 miles; 1,207 km)

Cessna Skylane, de luxe version of the Model 182 (230 hp Continental O-470-R engine), described on page 305

CESSNA AGPICKUP, AGWAGON AND AGTRUCK

On 8 December 1971, Cessna announced introduction of four new agricultural aircraft, three of which are based on the earlier Agwagon. The fourth model, a high-wing monoplane designated AGcarryall, is described separately.

The AGpickup, AGwagon and AGtruck are of all-metal construction and have special corrosion proofing. All have heavy-duty spring steel Land-O-Matic landing gear and Cessna's Camber-Lift wing to provide better control during low-speed operations. Wing fences are used to smooth airflow over the wing. Special attention has been paid to safety features, and these include ensolite padding on the upper instrument panel, urethane padding on tubular structures in the cabin area and around doors, safe flush switch and control locations and quick-release door hinges. Other standard features include wide wing walks, large hopper loading doors and a fresh-air scoop that slightly pressurises the cockpit to prevent the ingress of dust and fumes.

Optional equipment available for the AGwagon and AGtruck includes a special night operations package to provide brilliant illumination for night operations. This comprises a 100A 24V alternator, taxi/landing lights, instrument panel lights, overhead floodlight, two 600W retractable spray lights, lighting angle control for spray lights, wingtip turning lights, hopper quantity light and a control stick grip incorporating light switches.

The current versions of all three of these agricultural aircraft introduced aerodynamic improvements to the wing struts and strut fairings, improving airflow over the wing and reducing drag. All have new exterior styling, and the AGtruck has polyurethane paint styling as standard. New options for all three aircraft include a simplified hydraulic motor, dispersal spray pump and connecting coupling, quick-cleanable chemical strainer, disposable hydraulic fluid filter and a variable-intensity hopper light.

The following production versions are available:

AGpickup. Basic model, powered by a 230 hp Continental O-470-R six-cylinder horizontally-opposed aircooled engine, and equipped with a 200 US gallon (757 litre) hopper, and liquid and dry material dispersal control system as standard.

AGwagon. As basic model, but powered by a 300 hp Continental IO-520-D six-cylinder horizontally-opposed aircooled engine, driving a constant-speed propeller. Standard equipment includes cockpit canopy with all-round vision, tailplane abrasion boots, oversize 8·00-8 × 22 main-wheel tyres, 10 in tailwheel tyre, wire cutters, cable deflector, tailcone lift handles, hopper side-loading system on port side, navigation lights, four-way adjustable pilot's seat, control stick lock, quick oil drain, auxiliary fuel pump, steerable tailwheel and remote fuel strainer drain control.

AGtruck. As AGwagon, except for 280 US gallon (1,060 litre) hopper. Additional standard equipment includes a 22-nozzle engine-driven hydraulic spray system with electrically-controlled spray valve and gatebox without agitator, wing fuel tanks, extended conical-cambered wingtips, automatic inertia reel for the safety belt system, sensitive altimeter, pilot's foul weather windows, four-way adjustable pilot's seat, strobe lights, instrument panel lights, landing and taxi lights, three-colour exterior styling, oversize 10 in main and tailwheel tyres and overall polyurethane paint scheme.

By 31 January 1974 deliveries totalled 1,201 AGwagons, 39 AGpickups and 221 AGtrucks.

TYPE: Single-seat agricultural monoplane.

WINGS: Braced low-wing monoplane, with single streamline-section bracing strut each side. Wing section NACA 2412, modified. All-metal structure with NACA all-metal single-slotted flaps inboard of Frise all-metal ailerons. Aileron leading-edge gaps sealed. Wing fences immediately outboard of bracing strut attachment points. Conical-cambered wingtips, extended on AGtruck.

Cessna AGwagon agricultural aircraft (300 hp Continental IO-520-D engine)

Fuselage: Rectangular-section welded steel tube structure with removable metal skin panels forward of cabin. All-metal semi-monocoque rear fuselage.

Tail Unit: Cantilever all-metal structure. Fixed-incidence tailplane. Trim tab in starboard elevator.

Landing Gear: Non-retractable tailwheel type. Land-O-Matic cantilever main legs of heavy-duty spring steel. Tapered tubular tailwheel spring shock-absorber. Main wheels and tyres size 8·00-6 on AGpickup, other versions as detailed in model listings. Hydraulic disc brakes and parking brake.

Power Plant: One 230 or 300 hp Continental six-cylinder horizontally-opposed aircooled engine, as detailed in model listings, driving a McCauley two-blade metal fixed-pitch or constant-speed propeller. Metal fuel tank aft of firewall for AGpickup and AGwagon, capacity 37 US gallons (140 litres) or, optionally on AGwagon and standard for AGtruck, two 28 US gallon (106 litre) wing fuel tanks, total capacity 56 US gallons (212 litres). Oil capacity 3 US gallons (11·4 litres).

Accommodation: Pilot only, on vertically and longitudinally adjustable seat, in enclosed cabin. Steel overturn structure. Combined window and door on each side, hinged at bottom. Heating and ventilation standard.

System: Electrical system has a 60A 12V alternator and 12V 24Ah battery as standard. A 60A 24V alternator is available optionally for all three versions, or a 100A 24V alternator for the AGtruck and AGwagon only.

Electronics and Equipment: Standard equipment is as detailed in model listings. Optional equipment includes fan-driven or engine-driven hydraulic spray systems; 22, 44 or 64 nozzle sprayboooms; and two spreader systems for either medium or high-volume applications. Optional equipment specifically for AGpickup includes navigation lights, tinted rear cabin window and skylights, wire cutters, cable deflector, 7 ft 4 in (2·24 m) diameter constant-speed propeller and propeller control, quick oil drain, external power socket, tailcone lifting handles, four-way pilot's seat, propeller spinner, 10 in diameter steerable tailwheel, oversize tyres and remote quick-loading hopper valve.

Dimensions, external (A: AGpickup; B: AGwagon; C: AGtruck):
Wing span:
A, B — 40 ft 8½ in (12·41 m)
C — 41 ft 8 in (12·70 m)
Height overall:
A — 7 ft 8½ in (2·35 m)
B, C — 7 ft 9½ in (2·37 m)
Propeller diameter:
A (fixed-pitch) — 7 ft 6 in (2·29 m)
A (constant-speed) — 7 ft 4 in (2·24 m)
B, C — 6 ft 10 in (2·08 m)

Areas (A: AGpickup; B: AGwagon; C: AGtruck):
Wings, gross:
A, B — 202 sq ft (18·77 m²)
C — 205 sq ft (19·05 m²)

Weights and Loadings (A: AGpickup; B: AGwagon; C: AGtruck):
Empty weight, approx, with no dispersal equipment installed:
A (fixed pitch) — 1,835 lb (832 kg)
A (constant-speed) — 1,855 lb (841 kg)
B — 1,930 lb (875 kg)
C — 2,020 lb (916 kg)
Empty weight, with liquid dispersal system, gatebox and engine-driven hydraulic pump:
A (fixed-pitch) — 1,950 lb (884 kg)
A (constant-speed) — 1,985 lb (900 kg)
B — 2,060 lb (934 kg)
C — 2,150 lb (975 kg)
Gross T-O weight, Normal category:
A, B, C — 3,300 lb (1,496 kg)
Max T-O weight, Restricted category:
A — 3,800 lb (1,723 kg)
B — 4,000 lb (1,814 kg)
C — 4,200 lb (1,905 kg)
Wing loading, Normal category:
A, B — 16·3 lb/sq ft (79·6 kg/m²)
C — 16·1 lb/sq ft (78·6 kg/m²)
Power loading, Normal category:
A — 14·3 lb/hp (6·49 kg/hp)
B, C — 11·0 lb/hp (4·99 kg/hp)

Performance (at 3,300 lb; 1,496 kg. A: AGpickup; B: AGwagon; C: AGtruck):
Max level speed at S/L:
A (fixed-pitch) 91 knots (105 mph; 169 km/h)
A (constant-speed) 97 knots (112 mph; 180 km/h)
B, C 105 knots (121 mph; 195 km/h)
Max cruising speed, 75% power:
A (fixed-pitch, at 5,000 ft; 1,525 m) 78 knots (90 mph; 145 km/h)
A (constant-speed, at 6,500 ft; 1,980 m) 88 knots (101 mph; 163 km/h)
B, C, at 6,500 ft (1,980 m) 98 knots (113 mph; 182 km/h)
Stalling speed, flaps up:
A, B, C — 53 knots (61 mph; 98·5 km/h)
Stalling speed, flaps down:
A, B, C — 49·5 knots (57 mph; 92 km/h)
Max rate of climb at S/L:
A (fixed-pitch) — 400 ft (122 m)/min

Cessna AGcarryall utility aircraft (300 hp Continental IO-520-D engine)

A (constant-speed) — 505 ft (154 m)/min
B, C — 690 ft (210 m)/min
Service ceiling:
A (fixed-pitch) — 6,500 ft (1,980 m)
A (constant-speed) — 8,400 ft (2,560 m)
B, C — 11,100 ft (3,385 m)
T-O run:
A (fixed-pitch) — 1,120 ft (341 m)
A (constant-speed) — 940 ft (287 m)
B, C — 680 ft (207 m)
T-O to 50 ft (15 m):
A (fixed-pitch) — 1,920 ft (585 m)
A (constant-speed) — 1,620 ft (494 m)
B, C — 1,090 ft (332 m)
Landing from 50 ft (15 m):
A, B, C — 1,265 ft (386 m)
Landing run:
A, B, C — 420 ft (128 m)
Range at 75% power, standard fuel, no reserve:
A (fixed-pitch at 5,000 ft; 1,525 m) 204 nm (235 miles; 378 km)
A (constant-speed), B 225 nm (260 miles; 418 km)
Range at 75% power, long-range fuel, no reserve
B, C at 6,500 ft (1,980 m) 338 nm (390 miles; 625 km)

CESSNA AGCARRYALL

Fourth of the series of agricultural aircraft announced by Cessna on 8 December 1971, the AGcarryall represented a new multi-purpose concept in this specialised category of aircraft. It is intended for use as a demonstrator of spraying techniques, as a runabout for moving people, equipment or cargo when operating in the field, as a backup aircraft for peak seasonal work-loads, as an agricultural pilot trainer, and for use by the farmer who requires spraying capability plus transportation.

Based upon the Model 185, the AGcarryall has dual seating as standard, and optional seating for four additional passengers, and is provided with sprayboooms and a 151 US gallon (571 litre) chemical tank.

The 1974 version has the optional increased window area as specified for the Model 180. A total of 18 had been delivered by 31 January 1974.

Type: One/six-seat agricultural utility monoplane.

Wings: Generally similar to Model 185. Provision for attachment of streamline-section Vee struts on undersurface of each wing to support outer end of sprayboom.

Fuselage and Tail Unit: As for Model 185.

Landing Gear: Non-retractable tailwheel type. Land-O-Matic cantilever main legs of heavy-duty spring steel. Tapered tubular tailwheel spring shock-absorber. Hydraulic disc brakes. Parking brake. Wire cutters on main legs.

Power Plant: As for Model 185.

Accommodation: Standard seating is for a pilot and passenger, side by side, on four-way adjustable seats. Optional seating for four additional passengers, in two pairs. Door on each side of cabin with quick-release hinges. Extended baggage floor. Cabin heated and ventilated. Wire cutters on windscreen.

System: Electrical system with 60A 12V engine-driven alternator and 12V 24Ah battery standard.

Equipment: Standard equipment includes corrosion proofing, windscreen defrosting system, remote fuel strainer drain control, interior lights, landing and taxi lights, navigation lights, aft cabin baggage net, cable deflector, two-colour external acrylic paint scheme, and wind-driven spray system with associated 30-nozzle boom, liquid material controls, underfuselage chemical tank with capacity of 151 US gallons (571 litres), omni-flash beacon, overhead flood-light, stowable rudder pedals, safety belts for pilot and co-pilot. Pilot and co-pilot seats, adjustable fore and aft, have reclining backs.

Dimensions, external: As for Model 185

Areas: As for Model 185

Weights and Loadings:
Weight empty, approx — 1,835 lb (832 kg)
Max T-O weight — 3,350 lb (1,519 kg)
Max wing loading — 19·3 lb/sq ft (94·2 kg/m²)
Max power loading — 11·2 lb/hp (5·08 kg/hp)

Performance (at max T-O weight):
*Max level speed at S/L 129 knots (148 mph; 238 km/h)
*Max cruising speed at 2,500 ft (762 m) 117 knots (135 mph; 217 km/h)
*Max cruising speed at 7,500 ft (2,285 m) 122 knots (141 mph; 227 km/h)
Stalling speed, flaps up 57 knots (65 mph; 105 km/h)
Stalling speed, flaps down 49 knots (56 mph; 91 km/h)
Max rate of climb at S/L — 845 ft (258 m)/min
Service ceiling — 13,400 ft (4,085 m)
T-O run — 885 ft (270 m)
T-O to 50 ft (15 m) — 1,450 ft (442 m)
Landing from 50 ft (15 m) — 1,400 ft (427 m)
Landing run — 480 ft (146 m)
Range, 75% power at 7,500 ft (2,285 m), standard fuel, no reserve 456 nm (525 miles; 845 km)
Range, 75% power at 7,500 ft (2,285 m), long-range fuel, no reserve 594 nm (685 miles; 1,102 km)

*With sprayboooms removed, max level speed and cruising speed are increased by 8·7 knots (10 mph; 16 km/h).

CESSNA STATIONAIR

Cessna re-named the former U206 Skywagon and TU206 Turbo-Skywagon as the Stationair and Turbo-Stationair respectively, to emphasise the considerable differences between these six-seat cargo/utility aircraft and the Model 185 Skywagon. In particular, they have swept vertical tail surfaces, a tricycle landing gear, a tailplane of greater span, wide-span flaps, and double cargo doors on the starboard side of the fuselage which permit the easy loading and unloading of a crate more than 4 ft long, 3 ft wide and 3 ft deep (1·22 m × 0·91 m × 0·91 m).

The two basic versions of the Stationair are as follows:

Stationair. Standard cargo utility model with 300 hp Continental IO-520-F engine and double loading doors, as described in detail above and below.

Turbo-Stationair. Similar to the Stationair but with 285 hp Continental TSIO-520-C turbocharged engine in modified cowling and provided with a manifold pressure relief valve to prevent overboost.

A utility version of the Stationair is also available, with a single seat for the pilot as standard, vinyl floor covering, two-colour paint scheme and no wheel fairings. Up to five passenger seats can be supplied optionally.

The 1974 models of the two basic Stationair versions embody the improvements detailed for the Model 182, plus a simplified auxiliary fuel pump system, relocated marker beacon antenna, new interior styling, improved electric trim response by providing a more direct drive, and installation of new engine baffle seals.

A total of 2,894 Model 206 Skywagons and Stationairs had been built by 31 January 1974, including 643 de luxe Super Skylanes of similar basic design.

Type: Single-engined cargo/utility aircraft.

Wings: Braced high-wing monoplane. Single streamline-section bracing strut each side. Wing section NACA 2412, modified. Dihedral 1° 44′. Incidence 1° 30′ at root, —1° 30′ at tip. All-metal structure. Glassfibre conical camber tips. Modified Frise-type wide-chord ailerons. Electrically-operated long-span NACA single-slotted flaps. No tabs.

Fuselage: Conventional all-metal semi-monocoque structure.

Tail Unit: Cantilever all-metal structure, with sweptback vertical surfaces. Large trim tab in starboard elevator. Electrical operation of trim tab optional.

Landing Gear: Non-retractable tricycle type. Cessna Land-O-Matic cantilever spring steel main legs. Steerable nosewheel with oleo-pneumatic shock-absorbers. Cessna wheels, tubeless tyres and hydraulic disc brakes. Parking brake. Main wheels and tyres size 6·00-6, pressure 42 lb/sq in (2·95 kg/cm²).

Nosewheel and tyre size 5·00-5, pressure 45 lb/sq in (3·16 kg/cm²). Optional 8·00-6 main-wheel tyres, 6·00-6 nosewheel tyre. Available with floats and hydraulically-operated wheel-skis.

POWER PLANT: One Continental six-cylinder horizontally-opposed aircooled engine (details given under model listings), driving a McCauley D2A34C58/90AT-8 two-blade metal constant-speed propeller (several different three-blade propellers optional). Two fuel cells in wings, with total standard capacity of 65 US gallons (246 litres), of which 63 US gallons (238·5 litres) are usable. Optional capacity of 84 US gallons (318 litres), of which 80 US gallons (302·8 litres) are usable. Oil capacity 3 US gallons (11·4 litres).

ACCOMMODATION: Standard seating for pilot, co-pilot and up to four passengers, front seats with inertia safety belts. Pilot's door on port side. Large double cargo doors on starboard side; forward door hinged to open forward, rear door hinged to open rearward. Aircraft can be flown with cargo doors removed for photography, air dropping of supplies or parachuting. Fully articulating seats for pilot and co-pilot and safety harness for four rear seats optional. Cabin heated and ventilated.

SYSTEMS: Electrical system powered by an engine-driven 60A 14V alternator. 12V 33Ah battery. 28V electrical system optional. Hydraulic system for brakes and optional wheel-skis. Oxygen system of 74 cu ft (2·10 m³) capacity standard on Turbo-Stationair; 48 cu ft (1·36 m³) system optional for Stationair. Vacuum system optional.

ELECTRONICS AND EQUIPMENT: Optional avionics as detailed for the Model 182, plus Series 400 Nav-O-Matic two-axis autopilot with heading control, VOR intercept and track and altitude control. Standard equipment as for the Model 182, plus sensitive altimeter, electric clock, turn co-ordinator indicator, outside air temperature gauge, glareshield, overall paint scheme, and sun visors. Optional equipment, less the above items, is as detailed for the Model 182, plus ambulance kits, casket kit, photographic provisions and skydiving kit. The child's seat and skylights are not available for the Stationair. The Turbo-Stationair has an overboost control valve, absolute pressure controller, pressurised fuel system, non-congealing oil cooler, full-flow oil filter and alternate static source as standard.

DIMENSIONS, EXTERNAL (L: landplane; F: floatplane; S: skiplane):
- Wing span — 35 ft 10 in (10·92 m)
- Wing chord at root — 5 ft 4 in (1·63 m)
- Wing chord at tip — 3 ft 7 in (1·09 m)
- Wing aspect ratio — 7·63
- Length overall:
  - L, S — 28 ft 0 in (8·53 m)
  - F — 28 ft 5½ in (8·67 m)
- Height over tail:
  - L, S — 9 ft 7½ in (2·93 m)
  - F — 13 ft 11½ in (4·25 m)
- Tailplane span — 13 ft 0 in (3·96 m)
- Wheel track: L — 8 ft 1¾ in (2·48 m)
- Propeller diameter:
  - L — 6 ft 10 in (2·08 m)
  - F — 7 ft 2 in (2·18 m)
- Pilot's door (port):
  - Height, mean — 3 ft 4 in (1·03 m)
- Cargo double door (stbd):
  - Height — 3 ft 2½ in (0·98 m)
  - Width — 3 ft 8½ in (1·13 m)
  - Height to sill — 2 ft 1 in (0·64 m)

DIMENSIONS, INTERNAL:
- Cabin: Length — 12 ft 0 in (3·66 m)
  - Max width — 3 ft 8 in (1·12 m)
  - Max height — 4 ft 1½ in (1·26 m)
  - Volume available for payload — 101·2 cu ft (2·87 m³)

AREAS:
- Wings, gross — 174·0 sq ft (16·17 m²)
- Ailerons — 17·32 sq ft (1·60 m²)
- Trailing-edge flaps — 28·35 sq ft (2·63 m²)
- Fin — 11·62 sq ft (1·08 m²)
- Rudder, including tab — 6·95 sq ft (0·65 m²)
- Tailplane — 24·84 sq ft (2·31 m²)
- Elevators, including tab — 20·08 sq ft (1·86 m²)

WEIGHTS AND LOADINGS (L: landplane; F: floatplane; S: skiplane):
- Weight empty, one seat only:
  - Stationair: L — 1,745 lb (791 kg)
  - F — 2,105 lb (954 kg)
  - S — 1,995 lb (905 kg)
  - Turbo-Stationair: L — 1,845 lb (836 kg)
  - S — 2,095 lb (950 kg)
- Max T-O and landing weight:
  - Stationair: L — 3,600 lb (1,633 kg)
  - F — 3,500 lb (1,588 kg)
  - S — 3,300 lb (1,496 kg)
  - Turbo-Stationair: L — 3,600 lb (1,633 kg)
  - S — 3,300 lb (1,496 kg)
- Max wing loading:
  - Stationair: L — 20·7 lb/sq ft (101 kg/m²)
  - F — 20·1 lb/sq ft (98 kg/m²)
  - S — 19.0 lb/sq ft (93 kg/m²)
  - Turbo-Stationair:
    - L — 20·7 lb/sq ft (101 kg/m²)
    - S — 19·0 lb/sq ft (93 kg/m²)

Cessna Stationair one/six-seat cargo/utility aircraft (300 hp Continental IO-520-F engine)

- Max power loading:
  - Stationair: L — 12·0 lb/hp (5·4 kg/hp)
  - F — 11·7 lb/hp (5·3 kg/hp)
  - S — 11·0 lb/hp (5·0 kg/hp)
  - Turbo-Stationair: L — 12·6 lb/hp (5·7 kg/hp)
  - S — 11·6 lb/hp (5·26 kg/hp)

PERFORMANCE (L: landplane; F: floatplane; S: skiplane):
- Max level speed:
  - Stationair at S/L:
    - L — 151 knots (174 mph; 280 km/h)
    - F — 135 knots (156 mph; 251 km/h)
    - S — 121 knots (139 mph; 224 km/h)
  - Turbo-Stationair at 19,000 ft (5,790 m):
    - L — 174 knots (200 mph; 322 km/h)
    - S — 145 knots (167 mph; 269 km/h)
- Max cruising speed (75% power):
  - Stationair at 6,500 ft (1,980 m):
    - L — 142 knots (164 mph; 264 km/h)
    - F — 131 knots (151 mph; 243 km/h)
    - S — 119 knots (137 mph; 220 km/h)
  - Turbo-Stationair: L at 24,000 ft (7,320 m) — 160 knots (184 mph; 296 km/h)
  - S at 20,000 ft (6,100 m) — 132 knots (152 mph; 245 km/h)
- Econ cruising speed:
  - Stationair at 10,000 ft (3,050 m):
    - L — 114 knots (131 mph; 211 km/h)
    - F — 98 knots (113 mph; 182 km/h)
    - S — 92 knots (106 mph; 171 km/h)
  - Turbo-Stationair at 15,000 ft (4,575 m):
    - L — 121 knots (139 mph; 224 km/h)
    - S — 102 knots (118 mph; 190 km/h)
- Stalling speed, flaps up, power off:
  - Stationair: L — 61 knots (70 mph; 113 km/h)
  - F — 55 knots (63 mph; 102 km/h)
  - S — 59 knots (68 mph; 110 km/h)
  - Turbo-Stationair:
    - L — 61 knots (70 mph; 113 km/h)
    - S — 59 knots (68 mph; 110 km/h)
- Stalling speed, flaps down, power off:
  - Stationair: L — 53 knots (61 mph; 98 km/h)
  - F — 49 knots (56 mph; 91 km/h)
  - S — 51 knots (58 mph; 94 km/h)
  - Turbo-Stationair:
    - L — 53 knots (61 mph; 98 km/h)
    - S — 51 knots (58 mph; 94 km/h)
- Max rate of climb at S/L:
  - Stationair: L — 920 ft (280 m)/min
  - F — 855 ft (260 m)/min
  - S — 800 ft (244 m)/min
  - Turbo-Stationair: L — 1,030 ft (314 m)/min
  - S — 920 ft (280 m)/min
- Service ceiling:
  - Stationair: L — 14,800 ft (4,511 m)
  - F — 13,900 ft (4,237 m)
  - S — 11,500 ft (3,505 m)
  - Turbo-Stationair: L — 26,300 ft (8,020 m)
  - S — 23,500 ft (7,163 m)
- T-O run:
  - Stationair:
    - L — 900 ft (274 m)
    - F — 1,445 ft (440 m)
  - Turbo-Stationair:
    - L — 910 ft (277 m)
- T-O to 50 ft (15 m):
  - Stationair
    - L — 1,780 ft (543 m)
    - F — 2,475 ft (754 m)
  - Turbo-Stationair:
    - L — 1,810 ft (552 m)
- Landing from 50 ft (15 m):
  - Stationair:
    - L — 1,395 ft (425 m)
    - F — 1,570 ft (479 m)
  - Turbo-Stationair:
    - L — 1,395 ft (425 m)
- Landing run:
  - Stationair:
    - L — 735 ft (224 m)
    - F — 695 ft (212 m)
  - Turbo-Stationair:
    - L — 735 ft (224 m)
- Range, 75% power, normal fuel, no reserve:
  - Stationair: L at 6,500 ft (1,980 m) — 564 nm (650 miles; 1,045 km)
  - F at 6,500 ft (1,980 m) — 521 nm (600 miles; 966 km)
  - S at 6,500 ft (1,980 m) — 473 nm (545 miles; 877 km)
  - Turbo-Stationair:
    - L at 24,000 ft (7,320 m) — 607 nm (700 miles; 1,127 km)
    - S at 20,000 ft (6,100 m) — 495 nm (570 miles; 917 km)
- Range, 75% power, long-range tanks, no reserve:
  - Stationair: L at 6,500 ft (1,980 m) — 720 nm (830 miles; 1,335 km)
  - F at 6,500 ft (1,980 m) — 664 nm (765 miles; 1,231 km)
  - S at 6,500 ft (1,980 m) — 603 nm (695 miles; 1,118 km)
  - Turbo-Stationair:
    - L at 24,000 ft (7,320 m) — 772 nm (890 miles; 1,432 km)
    - S at 20,000 ft (6,100 m) — 642 nm (740 miles; 1,190 km)
- Range at econ cruising speed, long-range tanks, no reserve:
  - Stationair at 10,000 ft (3,050 m):
    - L — 885 nm (1,020 miles; 1,640 km)
    - F — 872 nm (1,005 miles; 1,617 km)
    - S — 725 nm (835 miles; 1,343 km)
  - Turbo-Stationair at 15,000 ft (4,575 m):
    - L — 911 nm (1,050 miles; 1,690 km)
    - S — 703 nm (810 miles; 1,303 km)

CESSNA SKYWAGON 207 AND TURBO-SKYWAGON T207

On 19 February 1969 Cessna announced two new seven-seat versions of its Skywagon utility aircraft. Generally similar to the earlier Model 206 Super Skywagon, the new Skywagon had been "stretched" to provide improved load-carrying ability while retaining the single engine and operating economy of the Model 206.

In addition to the longer fuselage, new features included a door for the co-pilot or passenger on the starboard side at the front of the cabin, and a separate baggage compartment forward of the cabin, accessible through an external door, also on the starboard side of the fuselage.

Design of this model started in November 1967 and the prototype flew for the first time on 11 May 1968. The first production aircraft, a Model 207, was completed on 13 December 1968 and made its first flight on 3 January 1969, followed three days later by the first flight of a T207 Turbo-Skywagon. Both models received FAA certification on 31 December 1968. A total of 236 Model 207s had been completed by 31 January 1974.

The 1974 version of the Model 207 introduces a new door handle assembly for the two forward cabin doors, a reduced-weight glareshield together with a new instrument panel and panel cover which offers a weight saving of 4 lb (1·8 kg), improved glove box latch, a simplified auxiliary fuel pump system, improved and regrouped marker beacon lights and a new flush marker beacon antenna, and new interior and exterior styling.

There are two current versions, as follows:

Skywagon 207. Standard passenger/cargo utility model with 300 hp Continental IO-520-F engine.

Turbo-Skywagon T207. Generally similar to Skywagon 207, but with 300 hp Continental TSIO-520-G turbocharged engine, driving a McCauley D2A34C78/90AT-8·5 two-blade metal constant-speed propeller. Three-blade propeller optional. Absolute pressure controller, pressurised fuel system, non-congealing oil cooler, full-flow oil filter, overboost control valve, alternate static source and oxygen system standard.

The following description applies to the Skywagon 207, except where stated otherwise:

TYPE: Single-engined utility aircraft.

WINGS: Braced high-wing monoplane. Single streamline-section bracing strut each side. Wing section NACA 2412 from root to just inboard of tip; wingtip is symmetrical. Dihedral 1° 44′. Incidence 1° 30′ at root, —1° 30′ at tip. All-metal structure. Glassfibre conical-camber tips. Modified Frise-type all-metal wide-chord ailerons. Electrically-operated long-span NACA single-slotted all-metal flaps. No trim tabs.

FUSELAGE: Conventional all-metal semi-monocoque structure.

TAIL UNIT: Cantilever all-metal structure, with sweptback vertical surfaces. Tailplane fixed with —3° incidence. Large trim tab in starboard elevator. Electrical operation of trim tab optional. Rudder trimmed by adjustment of rubber bungee.

LANDING GEAR: Non-retractable tricycle type. Improved Cessna Land-O-Matic cantilever main legs of one-piece tapered steel tube. Steerable nosewheel with Cessna oleo-pneumatic shock-absorber and hydraulic shimmy damper. Cessna wheels, tubeless tyres and hydraulic disc brakes. Main wheels and tyres size 6·00-6, pressure 55 lb/sq in (3·87 kg/cm²). Nosewheel and tyre size 5·00-5, pressure 49 lb/sq in (3·45 kg/cm²). Optional 8·00-6 main-wheel tyres, pressure 35 lb/sq in (2·96 kg/cm²), nosewheel tyre size 6·00-6, pressure 29 lb/sq in (2·04 kg/cm²), and wheel fairings.

POWER PLANT: One 300 hp Continental IO-520-F six-cylinder horizontally-opposed aircooled engine, driving a McCauley D2A34C58/90AT-8 two-blade metal constant-speed propeller. A bladder-type fuel tank, capacity 32·5 US gallons (123 litres), is located in the inboard section of each wing. Total fuel capacity 65 US gallons (246 litres), of which 58 US gallons (220 litres) are usable. Optional tankage increases capacity to 42 US gallons (159 litres) in each wing, giving a total capacity of 84 US gallons (318 litres), of which 77 US gallons (292 litres) are usable. Refuelling points in upper surface of each wing. Oil capacity 3 US gallons (11·4 litres).

ACCOMMODATION: Pilot's seat only standard. Optional individual seats for up to seven persons, arranged in three pairs, two-abreast, with a single seat at the rear of cabin. Pilot's door on port side, co-pilot's door on starboard side at front. Large double cargo doors on starboard side of rear cabin; forward door hinged to open forward, rear door hinged to open rearward. Aircraft can be flown with cargo doors removed for photography, air dropping of supplies or parachuting; optional equipment includes a spoiler for use when the aircraft is flown in this configuration. Hinged window, port side. Separate baggage compartment, forward of cabin, capacity 120 lb (54 kg), accessible through top-hinged door on starboard side. External glassfibre cargo pack, capacity 300 lb (136 kg), carried beneath the fuselage, is available as an optional extra.

SYSTEMS: Hydraulic system for brakes. Electrical system powered by a 14V 60A engine-driven alternator. 12V 33Ah battery. 24V electrical system optional. Oxygen system of 76 cu ft (2·15 m³) capacity standard on T207; 48 cu ft (1·36 m³) system optional on 207.

ELECTRONICS AND EQUIPMENT: As described for the Model 180, except electric clock, sensitive altimeter, outside air temperature gauge, flap position indicator, rate of climb indicator, turn co-ordinator, elevator and rudder trim controls, cabin steps, electro-luminescent lights for switch and comfort control panels, instrument panel glareshield light, triple dome lights, sun visors, tinted windscreen and windows, dual-beam landing lights and towbar standard. Additional optional items include Series 400 transponder with 4096 code capability, instrument post lights, ambulance kit, comprising stretcher, oxygen and attendant's seat, heated stall warning transmitter and pitot, centre armrests, rearview mirror, articulating and vertically adjustable front seats, shoulder harness for five passenger seats, glider tow hook and skydiving kit.

DIMENSIONS, EXTERNAL:
Wing span 35 ft 10 in (10·92 m)
Wing chord at root 5 ft 4 in (1·63 m)
Wing chord at tip 3 ft 8 in (1·12 m)
Wing aspect ratio 7·46
Length overall 31 ft 9 in (9·68 m)
Height overall 9 ft 6½ in (2·91 m)
Tailplane span 13 ft 0 in (3·96 m)
Wheel track 10 ft 0 in (3·05 m)
Wheelbase 6 ft 11¼ in (2·11 m)
Propeller diameter:
Two-blade:
207 6 ft 10 in (2·08 m)
T207 6 ft 9½ in (2·07 m)
Three-blade 6 ft 8 in (2·03 m)
Forward cabin doors (each):
Height 3 ft 5½ in (1·05 m)
Width 2 ft 11½ in (0·89 m)
Height to sill 2 ft 4 in (0·71 m)
Cargo double doors (stbd):
Height 3 ft 2 in (0·97 m)
Width 3 ft 8½ in (1·13 m)
Height to sill 2 ft 6 in (0·76 m)
Baggage door (stbd):
Height 2 ft 0 in (0·61 m)
Width 1 ft 1½ in (0·34 m)
Height to sill 3 ft 4 in (1·02 m)

DIMENSIONS, INTERNAL:
Cabin:
Length 14 ft 0 in (4·27 m)
Max width 3 ft 8½ in (1·13 m)
Max height 4 ft 1 in (1·24 m)
Floor area 47·1 sq ft (4·38 m²)
Volume 155·5 cu ft (4·40 m³)
Forward baggage compartment:
Length 1 ft 5 in (0·43 m)
Max width 3 ft 5½ in (1·05 m)
Max height 2 ft 3 in (0·69 m)
Floor area 4·9 sq ft (0·46 m²)
Volume 9·5 cu ft (0·27 m³)
Underfuselage cargo pack 12·0 cu ft (0·34 m³)

AREAS:
Wings, gross 174·0 sq ft (16·17 m²)
Ailerons 17·32 sq ft (1·60 m²)
Trailing-edge flaps 26·60 sq ft (2·46 m²)
Fin 9·04 sq ft (0·84 m²)
Rudder 6·95 sq ft (0·65 m²)
Tailplane 24·84 sq ft (2·31 m²)
Elevators, including tab 20·08 sq ft (1·83 m²)

WEIGHTS AND LOADINGS:
Weight empty, one seat only:
207 1,900 lb (861 kg)
T207 2,005 lb (909 kg)
Max T-O and landing weight:
207 and T207 3,800 lb (1,724 kg)
Max wing loading:
207 and T207 21·8 lb/sq ft (106·4 kg/m²)
Max power loading:
207 and T207 12·7 lb/hp (5·7 kg/hp)

PERFORMANCE (at max T-O weight and with optional wheel fairings, which increase speed by 1 mph):
Max never-exceed speed:
207 and T207 182 knots (210 mph; 338 km/h)
Max level speed:
207 at S/L 146 knots (168 mph; 270 km/h)
T207 at 17,000 ft (5,180 m)
164 knots (189 mph; 304 km/h)
Normal cruising speed (75% power):
207 at 6,500 ft (1,980 m)
138 knots (159 mph; 256 km/h)
T207 at 10,000 ft (3,050 m)
142 knots (163 mph; 262 km/h)
T207 at 20,000 ft (6,100 m)
153 knots (176 mph; 283 km/h)
Econ cruising speed:
207 at 10,000 ft (3,050 m)
114 knots (131 mph; 211 km/h)
T207 at 20,000 ft (6,100 m)
135 knots (156 mph; 251 km/h)
Stalling speed, flaps up, power off:
207 and T207 65·5 knots (75 mph; 121 km/h)
Stalling speed, 30° flaps, power off:
207 and T207 58·5 knots (67 mph; 108 km/h)
Max rate of climb at S/L:
207 810 ft (247 m)/min
T207 885 ft (270 m)/min
Service ceiling:
207 13,300 ft (4,054 m)
T207 24,200 ft (7,376 m)
T-O run:
207 and T207 1,100 ft (335 m)
T-O to 50 ft (15 m):
207 and T207 1,970 ft (600 m)
Landing from 50 ft (15 m):
207 and T207 1,500 ft (457 m)
Landing run:
207 and T207 765 ft (233 m)
Range (at normal cruising speed, standard fuel, no reserves):
207 at 137 knots (158 mph; 254 km/h) at 6,500 ft (1,980 m)
508 nm (585 miles; 941 km)
T207 at 151 knots (174 mph; 280 km/h) at 20,000 ft (6,100 m)
529 nm (610 miles; 982 km)
T207 at 140 knots (161 mph; 259 km/h) at 10,000 ft (3,050 m)
490 nm (565 miles; 909 km)
Range (at normal cruising speed, auxiliary fuel, no reserves):
207 at 137 knots (158 mph; 254 km/h) at 6,500 ft (1,908 m)
673 nm (775 miles; 1,247 km)
T207 at 151 knots (174 mph; 280 km/h) at 20,000 ft (6,100 m)
712 nm (820 miles; 1,320 km)
T207 at 140 knots (161 mph; 259 km/h) at 10,000 ft (3,050 m)
655 nm (755 miles; 1,215 km)
Range (at econ cruising speed, auxiliary fuel, no reserves):
207 at 114 knots (131 mph; 211 km/h) at 10,000 ft (3,050 m)
803 nm (925 miles; 1,489 km)
T207 at 135 knots (156 mph; 251 km/h) at 20,000 ft (6,100 m)
790 nm (910 miles; 1,445 km)

CESSNA MODEL 210 CENTURION I AND CENTURION II

The original prototype Model 210, which flew in January 1957, followed the general formula of the Cessna series of all-metal high-wing monoplanes, but was the first to have a retractable tricycle landing gear.

Later versions of the Model 210 have a fully-cantilever wing, eliminating the bracing struts used on earlier models. Their design was started on 24 October 1964 and construction of a prototype began on 29 November 1964. The first T210 with the new wing flew on 18 June 1965.

On 3 December 1970 Cessna announced the introduction of two new versions of the Model 210 to be known as Centurion II and Turbo-Centurion II. These differ from the Centurion I and Turbo-Centurion I by having as standard equipment a factory-installed IFR avionics package which offers a cost saving of 19% on avionics equipment,

Cessna Skywagon 207 one/seven-seat utility aircraft (300 hp Continental IO-520-F engine)

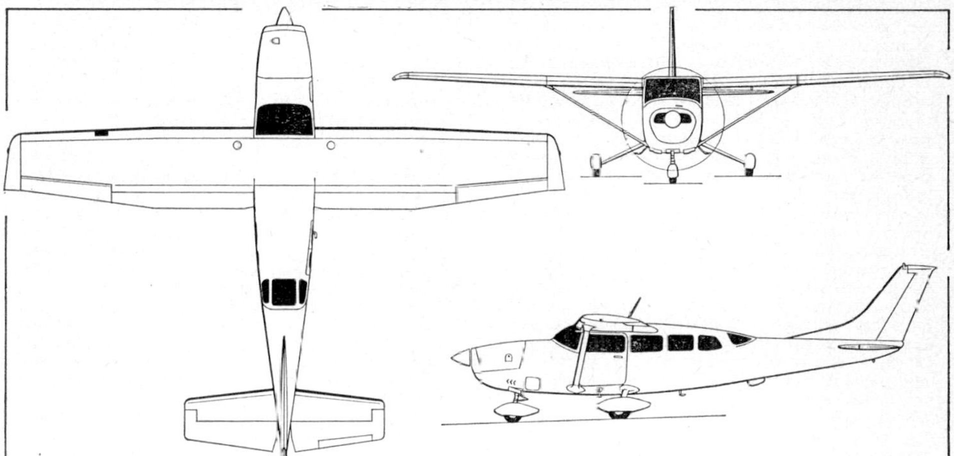

Cessna Skywagon 207 utility aircraft (*Pilot Press*)

plus a gyro panel, dual controls, articulating front seats, all-purpose control wheel and three-blade propeller.

Improvements in the 1974 versions include more responsive electric elevator trim, a new baggage door latch, improved engine baffle seals to simplify maintenance and enhance engine cooling, simplified auxiliary fuel pump switching, a new cowl nose cap on the Turbo Centurion I and II to increase airflow to the cabin heater and turbocharger, together with a matching recontoured propeller spinner, an improved anti-precipitation static kit, reduced cabin noise level by attention to door and window seals, a redesigned openable window for the cabin doors, new interior and exterior styling, plus new optional equipment.

The four current production versions of the Centurion are, therefore, as follows:

210 Centurion I. Standard model, with 300 hp Continental IO-520-L six-cylinder horizontally-opposed aircooled engine, driving a McCauley E2A34C73/90AT-8 two-blade metal propeller or, optionally, a McCauley D3A32C88/82NC-2 three-blade metal propeller.

T210 Turbo-Centurion I. Generally similar to Centurion I, but powered by a 285 hp Continental TSIO-520-H turbocharged engine, driving a McCauley E2A34C70/90AT-8 two-blade metal propeller or, optionally, a McCauley D3A32C88/82NC-2 three-blade metal propeller. Absolute pressure controller, full-flow oil filter, non-congealing oil cooler and overboost control valve standard.

210 Centurion II. Identical to Centurion I but with a 360-channel Cessna Series 300 nav/com, ADF, transponder, all-purpose control wheel, instrument post lights, constant-speed three-blade propeller, navigation light detectors, heating system for pitot and stall warning transmitter, omni-flash beacon, two courtesy lights and alternate static source as standard.

T210 Turbo-Centurion II. Identical to Turbo-Centurion I but with additional standard equipment as detailed above for Centurion II.

The Turbo-Centurion I version holds an international altitude record for aircraft of this class with a height of 42,344 ft (12,906·5 m).

The original versions received FAA Type Approval on 23 August 1966. A total of 3,585 Model 210s had been delivered by 31 January 1974.

TYPE: Six-seat cabin monoplane.

WINGS: Cantilever high-wing monoplane. Wing section NACA 64_2A215 at root, NACA 64_1A412 (A=0·5) at tip. Dihedral 1° 30′. Incidence 1° 30′ at root, —1° 30′ at tip. All-metal structure, except for glassfibre conical-camber tips. All-metal Frise-type ailerons. Electrically-actuated all-metal Fowler-type flaps. Ground-adjustable tab in each aileron. Pneumatic de-icing system optional.

FUSELAGE: All-metal semi-monocoque structure.

TAIL UNIT: Cantilever all-metal structure with 36° sweepback on fin. Fixed-incidence tailplane. Controllable trim tabs in rudder and starboard elevator. Electric operation of elevator tab optional. Pneumatic de-icing system optional.

LANDING GEAR: Hydraulically-retractable tricycle type with single wheel on each unit. Nose unit retracts forward, main units aft and inward. Wheel doors close when wheels are up or down. Chrome vanadium tapered steel tube main legs. Steerable nosewheel with oleo-pneumatic shock-absorber. Cessna main wheels and tube-type tyres, size 6·00-6, pressure 42 lb/sq in (2·95 kg/cm²). Cessna nosewheel and tyre, size 5·00-5, pressure 45 lb/sq in (3·16 kg/cm²). Cessna hydraulic disc brakes. Parking brake.

POWER PLANT: One six-cylinder horizontally-opposed aircooled engine, as described under model listings above. Electrical de-icing system for propeller optional. Integral fuel tanks in wings, with max total capacity of 90 US gallons (340 litres). Refuelling points above wing. Wing fuel drains optional. Oil capacity 2·5 US gallons (9·5 litres) in 210, 2·75 US gallons (10·5 litres) in T210.

ACCOMMODATION: Six persons in pairs in enclosed cabin. Front two seats of fully-articulating type on Centurion II and Turbo-Centurion II (pilot's seat only on other versions). Fifth and sixth seats have folding backs to accommodate articles up to 6 ft 7 in (2·01 m) long. Optional four-seat executive interior with a fully-reclining couch-type rear seat. Hinged window on port side. Dual controls standard on Centurion II and Turbo-Centurion II (optional on other models). Forward-hinged door on each side of cabin. Baggage space aft of rear seats, with outside door on port side, capacity 300 lb (136 kg). Combined heating and ventilation system.

SYSTEMS: Integral hydro-electrical unit for landing gear retraction. Hydraulic system for brakes. Electrical power supplied by 24V 60A engine-driven alternator. 24V battery. Oxygen system standard on Turbo-Centurion, optional for Centurion.

Cessna Centurion II one/six-seat cabin monoplane (one 300 hp Continental IO-520-L engine)

ELECTRONICS AND EQUIPMENT: Optional avionics as for Stationair, except that Series 300 or 400 integrated flight control system is available when the Series 300 or 400 Nav-O-Matic autopilot is replaced by the Series 400A two-axis autopilot, which has automatic pitch trim and an optional ILS coupler. Standard equipment includes sensitive altimeter, electric clock, outside air temperature gauge, audible landing gear and stall warning indicators, turn co-ordinator indicator, electroluminescent lights for switch and comfort control panels, glareshield lights, variable-intensity instrument panel red floodlights, control locks, armrests, windscreen defroster, dome and map lights, baggage restraint net, sun visors, adjustable cabin air ventilation, tinted windscreen and windows, landing lights, taxi light, navigation lights, overall paint scheme, cabin steps and towbar. Optional equipment includes dual controls, a gyro panel, fully-articulating co-pilot seat, all-purpose control wheel and three-blade propeller for Centurion I and Turbo-Centurion I, plus control wheel map light, economy mixture indicator, true airspeed indicator, turn and bank indicator, instrument post lights, boom microphone, flight hour recorder, cabin fire extinguisher, headrests, rearview mirror, alternate static source, stretcher installation, emergency locator transmitter, ice detector light, external power socket, engine priming system, internal corrosion proofing, navigation light detectors, heated stall warning transmitter and pitot, glider tow hook, omni-flash beacon, courtesy lights, wingtip-mounted strobe lights, tailplane abrasion boots, static dischargers and electric elevator trim system. Optional for the Centurion I and II only are an alternate static source, full-flow oil filter, non-congealing oil cooler, and engine winterisation kit.

DIMENSIONS, EXTERNAL:
- Wing span: 36 ft 9 in (11·20 m)
- Wing chord at root: 5 ft 6 in (1·68 m)
- Wing chord at tip: 4 ft 0 in (1·22 m)
- Wing aspect ratio: 7·66
- Length overall: 28 ft 3 in (8·61 m)
- Height overall: 9 ft 8 in (2·95 m)
- Tailplane span: 13 ft 0 in (3·96 m)
- Wheel track: 8 ft 8 in (2·64 m)
- Wheelbase: 5 ft 9 in (1·75 m)
- Propeller diameter (two-blade): 6 ft 10 in (2·08 m)
- Passenger doors (each):
  - Height: 3 ft 4¼ in (1·02 m)
  - Width: 2 ft 11½ in (0·90 m)
  - Height to sill: 3 ft 0 in (0·91 m)
- Baggage compartment door:
  - Height: 1 ft 10½ in (0·57 m)
  - Width: 2 ft 5 in (0·74 m)

DIMENSIONS, INTERNAL:
- Cabin:
  - Length: 11 ft 6 in (3·50 m)
  - Max width: 3 ft 6½ in (1·08 m)
  - Max height: 4 ft 0½ in (1·23 m)
  - Floor area: 29·0 sq ft (2·69 m²)
  - Volume: 139·9 cu ft (3·96 m³)
- Baggage space: 16·25 cu ft (0·46 m³)

AREAS:
- Wings, gross: 175 sq ft (16·25 m²)
- Ailerons (total): 18·86 sq ft (1·75 m²)
- Trailing-edge flaps (total): 29·50 sq ft (2·74 m²)
- Fin, including dorsal fin: 10·26 sq ft (0·95 m²)
- Rudder, including tab: 6·95 sq ft (0·65 m²)
- Tailplane: 18·57 sq ft (1·73 m²)
- Elevators, including tab: 20·08 sq ft (1·87 m²)

WEIGHTS AND LOADINGS:
- Weight empty (approx):
  - Centurion I: 2,120 lb (961 kg)
  - Centurion II: 2,195 lb (995 kg)
  - Turbo-Centurion I: 2,235 lb (1,013 kg)
  - Turbo-Centurion II: 2,310 lb (1,047 kg)
- Max T-O and landing weight:
  - All versions: 3,800 lb (1,723 kg)
- Max wing loading:
  - All versions: 21·7 lb/sq ft (106 kg/m²)
- Max power loading:
  - Centurion I, II: 12·7 lb/hp (5·76 kg/hp)
  - Turbo-Centurion I, II: 13·3 lb/hp (6·03 kg/hp)

PERFORMANCE (at max T-O weight):
- Max level speed:
  - Centurion I, II at S/L: 174 knots (200 mph; 322 km/h)
  - Turbo-Centurion I, II at 19,000 ft (5,800 m): 200 knots (230 mph; 370 km/h)
- Max cruising speed:
  - Centurion I, II, 75% power at 7,500 ft (2,285 m): 163 knots (188 mph; 303 km/h)
  - Turbo-Centurion I, II, 75% power at 24,000 ft (7,300 m): 190 knots (219 mph; 352 km/h)
- Econ cruising speed:
  - Centurion I, II at 10,000 ft (3,050 m): 134 knots (154 mph; 248 km/h)
  - Turbo-Centurion I, II at 24,000 ft (7,300 m): 152 knots (175 mph; 282 km/h)
- Stalling speed, flaps up, power off:
  - All versions: 66 knots (75 mph; 121 km/h)
- Stalling speed, flaps down, power off:
  - All versions: 57 knots (65 mph; 105 km/h)
- Max rate of climb at S/L:
  - Centurion I, II: 860 ft (262 m)/min
  - Turbo-Centurion I, II: 930 ft (283 m)/min
- Service ceiling:
  - Centurion I, II: 15,500 ft (4,725 m)
  - Turbo-Centurion I, II: 28,500 ft (8,685 m)
- T-O run:
  - Centurion I, II: 1,100 ft (335 m)
  - Turbo-Centurion I, II: 1,170 ft (357 m)
- T-O to 50 ft (15 m):
  - Centurion I, II: 1,900 ft (579 m)
  - Turbo-Centurion I, II: 2,030 ft (619 m)
- Landing from 50 ft (15 m):
  - All versions: 1,500 ft (457 m)
- Landing run:
  - All versions: 765 ft (233 m)
- Range at max cruising speed, max fuel, no reserves:
  - Centurion I, II: 925 nm (1,065 miles; 1,713 km)
  - Turbo-Centurion I, II: 1,016 nm (1,170 miles; 1,882 km)
- Range at econ cruising speed, max fuel, no reserves:
  - Centurion I, II: 1,085 nm (1,250 miles; 2,011 km)
  - Turbo-Centurion I, II: 1,155 nm (1,330 miles; 2,140 km)

CESSNA MODEL 310 and 310 II
USAF designation: U-3

The Model 310 is a twin-engined five/six-seat cabin monoplane, the prototype of which flew on 3 January 1953. It went into production in 1954. The Turbo-System Model 310 was added in late 1968, and the first production model was delivered in December 1968. On 21 December 1973 Cessna announced two new versions of the Model 310, known as the 310 II and the Turbo 310 II, which have factory installed IFR avionics plus other comfort and convenience features as standard. A total of 3,737 examples of the Model 310 had been completed by 31 January 1974.

There are four current versions of the Mode 310, as follows:

310. Standard model, as described in detail below, powered by two 260 hp Continental IO-470-VO six-cylinder horizontally-opposed air-cooled engines, driving McCauley two-blade metal fully-feathering constant-speed propellers.

Turbo-System T310. Similar to 310, but with two 285 hp Continental TSIO-520-B turbocharged engines, with automatic propeller synchronisation, full-flow oil filters, absolute and pressure ratio controllers, overboost control valves and engine cowl flaps as standard.

310 II. Identical to 310, but having as standard equipment dual 300 Series nav/com with 360-channel com, 200-channel nav, VOR/LOC and VOR/ILS indicators; marker beacon; ADF with digital tuning; 400 Series glideslope receiver; transponder; 400A Nav-O-Matic autopilot with approach coupler; associated antennae; six individual seats; dual controls; starboard landing light; taxi light; rotating beacon; outside air temperature gauge; external power socket; and large baggage door.

Turbo-System T310 II. Identical to T310, but with the additional standard equipment as detailed for the 310 II.

The 1974 versions of the Model 310 introduced a number of improvements including a dual electrical bus system which is installed as standard when avionics are ordered, and which isolates all avionics equipment from other electrical components and incorporates a radio master switch; airspeed indicator calibrated in knots; new interior and exterior styling; white epoxy coated landing gear components for improved abrasion resistance; and new options that include a higher wattage taxi light, inertia reel shoulder harness restraint system for pilot and co-pilot, and a new angle of attack indicator.

The Cessna 310 has been in service with the USAF since 1957, when it won a competition for a light twin-engined administrative liaison and cargo aircraft. Initial orders for a total of 160 "off-the-shelf", under the designation U-3A (formerly L-27A), were followed by a contract for 36 later models, designated U-3B, which were delivered between December 1960 and June 1961.

Type: Twin-engined five- or six-seat monoplane.

Wings: **Cantilever low-wing monoplane. Wing section NACA 23018 at centreline, NACA 23009 at tip. Dihedral 5°. Incidence 2° 30′ at root, —0° 30′ at tip. All-metal structure. Electrically-operated split flaps. Trim tab in port aileron. Pneumatic de-icing system optional.**

Fuselage: **All-metal semi-monocoque structure.**

Tail Unit: **Cantilever all-metal structure, with 40° sweepback on fin at quarter-chord. Small ventral fin. Trim tabs in rudder and starboard elevator. Electrically-operated elevator trim optional. Pneumatic de-icing system optional.**

Landing Gear: **Retractable tricycle type. Electro-mechanical retraction. Cessna oleo shock-absorber struts. Nosewheel steerable to 15° and castoring from 15° to 55° each side. Main wheels size 6·50-10, tyre pressure 60 lb/sq in (4·22 kg/cm²). Nosewheel size 6·00-6, tyre pressure 24 lb/sq in (1·69 kg/cm²). Goodyear single-disc hydraulic brakes.** Parking brake.

Power Plant: Two six-cylinder horizontally-opposed aircooled engines, as described under model listings above. Three-blade propellers, automatic propeller unfeathering system and propeller de-icing optional; automatic propeller synchroniser standard for T310 and T310 II, optional for 310 and 310 II. Standard fuel in two permanently attached canted wingtip tanks, each holding 51 US gallons (193 litres), of which 50 US gallons (189 litres) are usable. Cross-feed fuel system. Optional fuel comprises two 20·5 US gallon (77·5 litre) rubber fuel cells installed between the wing spars outboard of each engine nacelle, two 11·5 US gallon (43·5 litre) rubber fuel cells further outboard in each wing, and two 20·5 US gallon (77·5 litre) wing locker fuel tanks, providing a maximum fuel capacity of 207 US gallons (783 litres), of which 203 US gallons (768 litres) are usable. Oil capacity: 310, 6 US gallons (22·7 litres); T310, 6·5 US gallons (24·6 litres).

Accommodation: **Cabin normally seats five, two in front and three on cross-bench behind. Four alternative seating arrangements are available, with up to six individual seats in pairs, all of which can tilt and have fore and aft adjustment, individual air vents, reading lights and magazine pockets. Inertia seat-belts for two front seats (optional for rear seats). Pilot's storm window, port side. Cabin windows are double-glazed to reduce noise level. Large door on starboard side giving access to all seats. Optional 3 ft 4 in (1·02 m) long cargo door for loading of bulky items. Baggage compartment at rear of cabin, capacity 360 lb (163 kg), with internal and external access. Locker for a further 120 lb (54·5 kg) of baggage in the rear of each engine nacelle. Total baggage capacity 600 lb (272 kg).** Optional cabin accessories include writing desk, window curtains, electrical adjustment of pilot and co-pilot seats, all-leather seats, oxygen system and photographic survey provisions. Windscreen defrosting standard; windscreen alcohol de-icing system optional.

Systems: 50A 28V engine-driven alternators (100A alternators optional). Two 12V 24Ah batteries. Oxygen system of 76·6 cu ft (2·17 m³) optional. Janitrol 35,000 BTU thermostatically-controlled blower-type heater for cabin heating and windscreen defrosting. Cabin air-conditioning system rated at 12,000 BTU optional. Vacuum system for flight instruments. Hydraulic system for brakes only. Goodrich pneumatic de-icing system optional.

Electronics and Equipment: Optional avionics include Series 300 nav/com transceiver with 360-channel com and 200-channel nav with remote VOR/LOC or VOR/ILS indicator, ADF with digital tuning, marker beacon with three lights and aural signal, DME, 10-channel HF transceiver and integrated flight control system; Series 400 360-channel com transceiver, 200-channel nav receiver, nav/com transceiver with 360-channel com and 200-channel nav with remote VOR/LOC or VOR/ILS indicator, 40-channel glideslope, ADF with digital tuning and BFO, transponder with 4096 code capability, Nav-O-Matic 400 or 400A two-axis autopilot and integrated flight control system with optional RMI or HSI; or Series 800 720-channel com transceiver, 200-channel nav receiver with remote VOR/ILS indicator, 40-channel glideslope/marker beacon receiver, ADF with digital tuning and BFO, RMI, DME and integrated flight control system. Additional avionics options include PN-101 pictorial navigation system, X-band weather radar, single side-band HF transceiver, boom microphone and headset. Standard equipment includes sensitive altimeter, electric clock, blind-flying instrumentation, audible landing gear and stall warning indicators, heater overheat light, variable-intensity emergency floodlight, map light, alternator failure lights, instrument post lights, control locks, armrests, reading lights, pilot and co-pilot safety belts, hat shelf, super soundproofing, cabin radio speaker, baggage straps, sun visors, adjustable cabin air ventilators, emergency exit window, aft omni-vision window, tinted dual-pane windows, non-congealing oil coolers, navigation light detectors, nosewheel fender, heated pitot, heated fuel vents and stall-warning transmitter, retractable landing light, navigation lights, quick-drain fuel valves, overall paint scheme, retractable cabin step and tow-bar. Optional equipment includes GMT clock, dual controls, flight hour recorder, co-pilot's blind-flying instrumentation, true airspeed indicator, economy mixture indicator, outside air temperature gauge, instantaneous rate of climb indicator, electroluminescent panel lighting, turn co-ordinator, cabin curtain, rear window curtains, writing desk, engine fire detection and extinguishing system, cabin fire extinguisher, nacelle baggage compartment courtesy lights, rudder pedal locks, electrically-adjustable pilot and co-pilot seats, all-leather seats, emergency locator transmitter, external power socket, internal corrosion proofing, fuselage ice protection plates, ice detection light, rotating beacon, second retractable landing light, wing walk and cabin step lights, three-light strobe system, taxi light, polyurethane paint, photographic provisions, dual pitot system, heated dual static source, static dischargers and radome nose. Additional optional items for the Model 310 and 310 II only include augmentor exhaust systems, full-flow oil filters, automatic propeller synchroniser and engine winterisation kit.

Dimensions, external:
Wing span 36 ft 11 in (11·25 m)
Wing chord at root 5 ft 7½ in (1·72 m)
Wing chord at tip 3 ft 10¼ in (1·18 m)
Wing aspect ratio 7·3
Length overall 29 ft 3 in (8·92 m)
Height overall 10 ft 6 in (3·20 m)
Tailplane span 17 ft 0 in (5·18 m)
Wheel track 12 ft 0 in (3·66 m)
Wheelbase 8 ft 10½ in (2·71 m)
Propeller diameter 6 ft 9 in (2·06 m)

Dimensions, internal:
Baggage compartment (fuselage) 26·1 cu ft (0·74 m³)
Baggage compartments (nacelles, total) 18·5 cu ft (0·52 m³)

Areas:
Wings, gross 179 sq ft (16·63 m²)
Ailerons (total) 11·44 sq ft (1·06 m²)
Trailing-edge flaps (total) 22·9 sq ft (2·13 m²)
Fin 14·30 sq ft (1·33 m²)
Rudder 11·76 sq ft (1·09 m²)
Tailplane 32·15 sq ft (2·99 m²)
Elevators 22·10 sq ft (2·05 m²)

Weights and Loadings:
Weight empty:
310 3,214 lb (1,457 kg)
310 II 3,392 lb (1,538 kg)
T310 3,292 lb (1,493 kg)
T310 II 3,471 lb (1,574 kg)
Max T-O weight:
310 5,300 lb (2,404 kg)
T310 5,500 lb (2,494 kg)
Max landing weight:
T310 5,400 lb (2,449 kg)
Max wing loading:
310 29·6 lb/sq ft (145 kg/m²)
T310 30·73 lb/sq ft (150 kg/m²)
Max power loading:
310 10·2 lb/hp (4·63 kg/hp)
T310 9·65 lb/hp (4·38 kg/hp)

Performance (at max T-O weight):
Max level speed:
310 at S/L 205 knots (236 mph; 379 km/h)
T310 at 16,000 ft (4,875 m) 238 knots (274 mph; 441 km/h)
Max cruising speed:
310, 75% power at 6,500 ft (1,980 m) 192 knots (221 mph; 356 km/h)
T310, 75% power at 20,000 ft (6,100 m) 225 knots (259 mph; 417 km/h)
Econ cruising speed:
310 at 10,000 ft (3,050 m) 159 knots (183 mph; 295 km/h)
Minimum control speed (V_{MC}):
310 75 knots (86 mph; 138·5 km/h) IAS
T310 82 knots (94 mph; 151·5 km/h) IAS
Stalling speed:
310 63 knots (72 mph; 116 km/h) IAS
T310 68 knots (78 mph; 126 km/h) IAS
Max rate of climb at S/L:
310 1,495 ft (546 m)/min
T310 1,790 ft (456 m)/min
Max rate of climb at S/L, one engine out:
310 327 ft (100 m)/min
T310 408 ft (124 m)/min
Service ceiling:
310 19,500 ft (5,943 m)
T310 28,200 ft (8,595 m)
Service ceiling, one engine out:
310 6,680 ft (2,036 m)
T310 17,550 ft (5,350 m)
T-O run:
310 1,519 ft (463 m)
T310 1,306 ft (398 m)
T-O to 50 ft (15 m):
310 1,795 ft (547 m)
T310 1,662 ft (507 m)
Landing from 50 ft (15 m):
310 1,697 ft (517 m)
T310, at 5,400 lb (2,449 kg) 1,790 ft (546 m)
Landing run:
310 582 ft (177 m)
T310, at 5,400 lb (2,449 kg) 640 ft (195 m)
Range at max cruising speed, 600 lb (272 kg) usable fuel, no reserves:
310 672 nm (774 miles; 1,245 km)
T310 713 nm (822 miles; 1,322 km)
Range at max cruising speed, 978 lb (443 kg) usable fuel, no reserves:
310 1,092 nm (1,258 miles; 2,024 km)
T310 1,164 nm (1,341 miles; 2,158 km)
Range at max cruising speed, 1,218 lb (552 kg) usable fuel, no reserves:
310 1,359 nm (1,565 miles; 2,518 km)
T310 1,449 nm (1,669 miles; 2,686 km)
Max range at econ cruising speed, 1,218 lb (552 kg) usable fuel, no reserves:
310 1,693 nm (1,950 miles; 3,138 km)
T310 1,711 nm (1,971 miles; 3,172 km)

CESSNA MODEL 318

USAF designation: T-37

The T-37 was the first jet trainer designed as such from the start to be used by the USAF. The first of two prototype XT-37s made its first flight on 12 October 1954, and the first of an evaluation batch of 11 T-37As flew on 27 September 1955.

A total of 1,247 T-37s had been delivered by 1 March 1974, with production continuing. **In addition to aircraft supplied to the USAF, there have been substantial deliveries to foreign governments by direct purchase, or through the Military Assistance Programme.**

Three versions have been built in quantity:

T-37A. Initial production version with Continental J69-T-9 turbojets (each 920 lb; 417 kg st). 534 built. Converted to T-37B standard by retrospective modification.

Cessna Model 310 five/six-seat cabin monoplane (two 260 hp Continental IO-470-VO engines)

T-37B. Two Continental J69-T-25 turbojets (each 1,025 lb; 465 kg st). New Omni navigational equipment, UHF radio and instrument panel. First T-37B was accepted into service with the USAF in November 1959. The T-37B has also been supplied to the Royal Thai Air Force and the Cambodian, Chilean and Pakistan Air Forces. Forty-seven ordered by the Federal German government are being used to train Luftwaffe pilots at Sheppard AFB in Texas.

Equipment can be added to the T-37B to enable it to perform military surveillance and low-level attack duties, in addition to training. Range can be extended by two 65 US gallon (245 litre) wingtip fuel tanks. Two armed T-37Bs were evaluated at the USAF Special Air Warfare Center, and were followed by two prototypes of the more powerful and more heavily armed YAT-37D (see entry on A-37). Thirty-nine T-37Bs were later converted to A-37A standard. To replace these and to meet further requirements, the USAF placed further contracts for the T-37B in 1967 and again in 1968, bringing the total on order to 447.

T-37C. Basically similar to T-37B, but with provision for both armament and wingtip fuel tanks. Initial order for 34 placed by USAF for supply to foreign countries under Military Assistance Programme. Portugal has 30, of which 18 were supplied under this Programme, Peru has 15 and others have been supplied to Chile, Greece, Pakistan, Thailand, Turkey, Brazil and Colombia. In production. Total orders exceed 250.

Following 133 bird strikes encountered in 1965-70, the USAF ordered the original windscreens for more than 800 T-37s to be replaced with a birdproof type. Developed by Cessna, using General Electric-developed Lexan polycarbonate plastics, the material is formed by Texstar of Dallas, Texas, and Cessna fabricates the complete windscreen assembly. The new screens are 0·5 in (1·27 cm) thick, weigh about 35 lb (16 kg) and can resist the impact of a 4 lb (1·8 kg) bird at a speed of 250 knots (288 mph; 463 km/h).

The following details refer to the T-37B:

TYPE: Two-seat primary trainer.

WINGS: Cantilever low-wing monoplane. Wing section NACA 2418 at root, NACA 2412 at tip. Dihedral 3°. Incidence at root 3° 30′. Two-spar aluminium alloy structure. Hydraulically-operated all-metal high-lift slotted flaps inboard of ailerons.

FUSELAGE: All-metal semi-monocoque structure. Hydraulically-actuated speed brake below forward part of fuselage in region of cockpit.

TAIL UNIT: Cantilever all-metal structure. Fin integral with fuselage. Tailplane mounted one-third of way up fin. Movable surfaces all have electrically-operated trim tabs.

LANDING GEAR: Hydraulically-retractable tricycle type. Bendix oleo-pneumatic shock-absorbers. Steerable nosewheel. Tyres by General Tire and Rubber Co. Main-wheel tyres size 20×4·4. Nosewheel tyre size 16×4·4. General Tire and Rubber Co multiple-disc hydraulic brakes.

POWER PLANT: Two Continental J69-T-25 turbojet engines (each 1,025 lb; 465 kg st). Six rubber-cell interconnected fuel tanks in each wing, feeding main tank in fuselage aft of cockpit. Total usable fuel capacity 309 US gallons (1,170 litres). Automatic fuel transfer by engine-driven pumps and a submerged booster pump. Provision for two 65 US gallon (245 litre) wingtip fuel tanks on T-37C only. Oil capacity 3·12 US gallons (11·8 litres).

ACCOMMODATION: Enclosed cockpit seating two side by side with dual controls. Ejection seats and jettisonable clamshell type canopy. Standardised cockpit layout, with flaps, speed brakes, trim tabs, radio controls, etc, positioned and operated as in standard USAF combat aircraft.

ELECTRONICS: Standard USAF UHF radio; Collins VHF navigation equipment and IFF.

ARMAMENT AND EQUIPMENT (T-37C only): Provision for two jettisonable underwing pods, manufactured by General Electric, each containing an 0·50 in machine-gun with 200 rounds, two 2·75 in folding-fin rockets and four 3 lb practice bombs. Alternatively two 250 lb bombs or four Sidewinder missiles can be fitted in place of armament pods. Associated equipment includes K14C computing gunsight and AN-N6 16 mm gun camera. For reconnaissance duties, KA-20 or KB-10A cameras, or HC217 cartographic camera, can be mounted in fuselage.

DIMENSIONS, EXTERNAL:

Wing span	33 ft 9·3 in (10·3 m)
Wing chord (mean)	5 ft 7 in (1·70 m)
Wing aspect ratio	6·2
Length overall	29 ft 3 in (8·92 m)
Height overall	9 ft 2 in (2·8 m)
Tailplane span	13 ft 11½ in (4·25 m)
Wheel track	14 ft 0½ in (4·28 m)
Wheelbase	7 ft 9 in (2·36 m)

AREAS:

Wings, gross	183·9 sq ft (17·09 m²)
Ailerons (total)	11·30 sq ft (1·05 m²)
Trailing-edge flaps (total)	15·10 sq ft (1·40 m²)
Fin	11·54 sq ft (1·07 m²)
Rudder, including tab	6·24 sq ft (0·58 m²)
Tailplane	34·93 sq ft (3·25 m²)
Elevators, including tabs	11·76 sq ft (1·09 m²)

Cessna T-37B two-seat primary jet trainer (two 1,025 lb st Continental J69-T-25 turbojet engines)

WEIGHTS AND LOADINGS (A: T-37B; B: T-37C):

Max T-O weight:

A	6,574 lb (2,982 kg)
B	8,007 lb (3,632 kg)

Max wing loading:

A	35·7 lb/sq ft (174·3 kg/m²)
B	43·5 lb/sq ft (212·4 kg/m²)

Max power loading:

A	3·21 lb/lb st (3·21 kg/kg st)
B	3·91 lb/lb st (3·91 kg/kg st)

PERFORMANCE (at max T-O weight except as noted. A: T-37B; B: T-37C):

Max level speed:
A, at 20,000 ft (6,100 m) — 369 knots (425 mph; 684 km/h)
B, at 15,000 ft (4,570 m) — 312 knots (359 mph; 578 km/h)

Normal cruising speed:
A, at 35,000 ft (10,670 m) — 313 knots (360 mph; 579 km/h)
B, at 25,000 ft (7,620 m) — 278 knots (320 mph; 515 km/h)

Stalling speed:

A	74 knots (85 mph; 137 km/h)
B	78 knots (90 mph; 145 km/h)

Max rate of climb at S/L:

A	3,370 ft (1,027 m)/min
B	2,100 ft (640 m)/min

Service ceiling:

A	39,200 ft (11,948 m)
B	27,100 ft (8,260 m)

Service ceiling, one engine out:

A	25,000 ft (7,620 m)
B	6,700 ft (2,040 m)

T-O to 50 ft (15 m):

A	2,000 ft (610 m)
B	2,750 ft (838 m)

Landing from 50 ft (15 m):

A	2,545 ft (775 m)
B, at 7,200 lb (3,265 kg)	2,400 ft (732 m)

Range, T-37B at 313 knots (360 mph; 579 km/h) standard tankage — 755 nm (870 miles; 1,400 km)

Range, T-37B at 289 knots (333 mph; 536 km/h) at 35,000 ft (10,670 m), standard tankage, with 5% reserve — 809 nm (932 miles; 1,500 km)

Range, T-37C at 278 knots (320 mph; 515 km/h) at 25,000 ft (7,620 m), max fuel including two 65 US gallon (245 litre) wingtip tanks, T-O at max T-O weight, allowances for taxi, T-O and climb — 732 nm (843 miles; 1,356 km)

Range, T-37C at 234 knots (269 mph; 433 km/h) at 25,000 ft (7,620 m), fuel and allowances as above, with 5% reserve — 722 nm (831 miles; 1,337 km)

CESSNA MODEL 318

USAF designation: A-37

The A-37 is a development of the T-37 trainer, intended for armed counter-insurgency (COIN) operations from short unimproved airstrips. Two YAT-37D prototypes were produced initially, for evaluation by the USAF, by modifying existing T-37 airframes. The first of these flew for the first time on 22 October 1963, powered by two 2,400 lb (1,090 kg) st General Electric J85-GE-5 turbojets. There are two production versions, as follows:

A-37A (Model 318D). First 39 aircraft, with derated (2,400 lb; 1,090 kg) engines. Converted from T-37B trainers under letter contract received from USAF Systems Command in August 1966. Deliveries began on 2 May 1967 and a squadron of 25 A-37As was sent to South Vietnam for a four-month computerised evaluation of their ability to perform six basic missions. After the test period, the A-37As remained in service with the 604th Air Commando Squadron at Bien Hoa air base, and early in 1968 they completed their 10,000th combat sortie in Vietnam. In 1973 they were being operated by AFRes.

A-37B (Model 318E). The A-37B is the production version, design of which began in January 1967. Construction of the prototype started in the following month and it flew for the first time in September 1967. The A-37B has two General Electric J85-GE-17A turbojets which offer more than double the take-off power available for the T-37, permitting an almost-doubled take-off weight. A total of 415 had been delivered by April 1973. As the result of a further USAF contract, additional deliveries of A-37Bs were scheduled to begin in August 1974.

The following details apply to the production A-37B:

TYPE: Two-seat light strike aircraft.

WINGS: Cantilever low-wing monoplane. Wing section NACA 2418 (modified) at root, NACA 2412 (modified) at tip. Dihedral 3°. Incidence

Cessna A-37B light strike aircraft of the New York Air National Guard *(Howard Levy)*

3°38′ at root, 1° at tip. No sweep at 22½% chord. Two-spar aluminium alloy structure. Conventional all-metal ailerons, with forward skin of aluminium alloy and aft skin of magnesium alloy. Electrically-operated trim tab on port aileron with force-sensitive boost tabs on both ailerons, plus hydraulically-operated slot-lip ailerons forward of the flap on the outboard two-thirds of flap span. Hydraulically-operated all-metal slotted flaps of NACA 2h type. No de-icing equipment.

FUSELAGE: All-metal semi-monocoque structure. Hydraulically-operated speed brake, measuring 3 ft 9 in (1·14 m) by 1 ft 0 in (0·30 m), below forward fuselage immediately aft of nosewheel well. Mountings for removable probe for in-flight refuelling on upper fuselage in front of cockpit.

TAIL UNIT: Cantilever all-metal structure. Fin integral with fuselage. Fixed-incidence tailplane mounted one-third of way up fin. Electrically-operated trim tabs in port elevator and rudder. No de-icing equipment.

LANDING GEAR: Retractable tricycle type. Cessna oleo-pneumatic shock-absorber struts on all three units. Hydraulic actuation, main wheels retracting inward, nosewheel forward. Steerable nosewheel. Goodyear tyres and single-disc brakes. Main-wheel tyres size 7·00-8 (14PR). Nosewheel tyre size 6·00-6 (6PR). Tyre pressure: main wheels 110 lb/sq in (7·73 kg/cm²), nosewheel 37 lb/sq in (2·60 kg/cm²).

POWER PLANT: Two General Electric J85-GE-17A turbojet engines, each rated at 2,850 lb (1,293 kg) st. Fuel tank in each wing, each with capacity of 113 US gallons (428 litres); two non-jettisonable tip-tanks, each of 95 US gallons (360 litres) capacity; sump tank in fuselage, aft of cockpit, capacity 91 US gallons (344 litres). Total standard usable fuel capacity 507 US gallons (1,920 litres). Single-point refuelling through in-flight refuelling probe, with adaptor. Alternative refuelling through flush gravity filler cap in each wing and each tip-tank. Four 100 US gallon (378 litre) auxiliary tanks can be carried on underwing pylons. Provision for in-flight refuelling through nose-probe. Total oil capacity 2·25 US gallons (9 litres).

ACCOMMODATION: Enclosed cockpit seating two side by side, with dual controls, dual throttles, full flight instrument panel on port side, partial panel on starboard side, engine instruments in between. Full blind-flying instrumentation. Jettisonable canopy hinged to open upward and rearward. Standardised cockpit layout as in standard USAF combat aircraft. Cockpit air-conditioned but not pressurised. Flak-curtains of layered nylon are installed around the cockpit. Windscreen defrosted by engine bleed air.

SYSTEMS: AiResearch air-conditioning system of expansion turbine type, driven by engine bleed air. Hydraulic system, pressure 1,500 lb/sq in (105 kg/cm²), operates landing gear, main landing gear doors, flaps, thrust attenuator, nosewheel steering system, speed-brake, stall spoiler, inlet screen. Pneumatic system, pressure 2,000 lb/sq in (140 kg/cm²), utilises nitrogen-filled 50 cu in (819 cm³) air bottle for emergency landing gear extension. Electrical system includes two 28V DC 300A starter/generators, two 24V nickel-cadmium batteries, and provision for external power source. One main inverter (2,500VA 3-phase 115V 400Hz), and one standby inverter (750VA 3-phase 115V 400Hz), to provide AC power.

ELECTRONICS: Radio and radar installations include UHF communications (AN/ARC-109A), FM communications (FM-622A), TACAN (AN/ARN-65), ADF (AN/ARN-83), IFF (AN/APX-72), direction finder (AN/ARA-50) and interphone (AIC-18).

ARMAMENT AND OPERATIONAL EQUIPMENT: GAU-2B/A 7·62 mm Minigun installed in forward fuselage. Each wing has four pylon stations, the two inner ones carrying 870 lb (394 kg) each, the intermediate one 600 lb (272 kg) and the outer one 500 lb (227 kg). The following weapons, in various combinations, can be carried on these underwing pylons: SUU-20 bomb and rocket pod, MK-81 or MK-82 bomb, BLU/32/B fire bomb, SUU-11/A gun pod, CBU-24/B or CBU-25/A dispenser and bomb, M-117 demolition bomb, LAU-3/A rocket pod, CBU-12/A, CBU-14/A or CBU-22/A dispenser and bomb, BLU-1C/B fire bomb, LAU-32/A or LAU-59/A rocket pod, CBU-19/A canister cluster and SUU-25/A flare launcher. Associated equipment includes an armament control panel, Chicago Aerial Industries CA-503 non-computing gunsight, KS-27C gun camera and KB-18A strike camera.

DIMENSIONS, EXTERNAL:

Wing span, over tip-tanks	35 ft 10½ in (10·93 m)
Wing chord at root	6 ft 7·15 in (2·01 m)
Wing chord at tip	4 ft 6 in (1·37 m)
Wing aspect ratio	6·2
Length overall, excluding refuelling probe	29 ft 3 in (8·92 m)
Height overall	8 ft 10½ in (2·70 m)
Tailplane span	13 ft 11½ in (4·25 m)
Wheel track	14 ft 0½ in (4·28 m)
Wheelbase	7 ft 10 in (2·39 m)

Cessna O-2A forward air control aircraft, with underwing rocket pods *(Howard Levy)*

AREAS:

Wings, gross	183·9 sq ft (17·09 m²)
Ailerons (total)	11·30 sq ft (1·05 m²)
Trailing-edge flaps (total)	15·10 sq ft (1·40 m²)
Fin	11·54 sq ft (1·07 m²)
Rudder, including tab	6·24 sq ft (0·58 m²)
Tailplane	34·93 sq ft (3·25 m²)
Elevators, including tab	11·76 sq ft (1·09 m²)

WEIGHTS AND LOADINGS:

Weight empty, equipped	6,211 lb (2,817 kg)
Max T-O and landing weight	14,000 lb (6,350 kg)
Normal landing weight	7,000 lb (3,175 kg)
Max zero-fuel weight	10,710 lb (4,858 kg)
Max wing loading	65·4 lb/sq ft (319·3 kg/m²)
Max power loading	2·1 lb/lb st (2·1 kg/kg st)

PERFORMANCE (at max T-O weight, except as detailed otherwise):

Max never-exceed speed (Mach limitation) 455 knots (524 mph; 843 km/h)
Max level speed at 16,000 ft (4,875 m) 440 knots (507 mph; 816 km/h)
Max cruising speed at 25,000 ft (7,620 m) 425 knots (489 mph; 787 km/h)
Stalling speed at max landing weight, wheels and flaps down 98·5 knots (113 mph; 182 km/h)
Stalling speed at normal landing weight, wheels and flaps down 75 knots (86·5 mph; 139 km/h)
Max rate of climb at S/L 6,990 ft (2,130 m)/min
Service ceiling 41,765 ft (12,730 m)
Service ceiling, one engine out 25,000 ft (7,620 m)
T-O run 1,740 ft (531 m)
T-O to 50 ft (15 m) 2,596 ft (792 m)
Landing from 50 ft (15 m) at max landing weight 6,600 ft (2,012 m)
Landing run at max landing weight 4,150 ft (1,265 m)
Landing run at normal landing weight 1,710 ft (521 m)
Range with max fuel, including four 100 US gallon (378 litre) drop-tanks, at 25,000 ft (7,620 m) with reserves 878 nm (1,012 miles; 1,628 km)
Range with max payload, including 4,100 lb (1,860 kg) ordnance 399 nm (460 miles; 740 km)

CESSNA MODEL 337 SKYMASTER

USAF designation: O-2

This unique all-metal 4/6-seat business aircraft resulted from several years of study by Cessna aimed at producing a twin-engined aeroplane that would be simple to fly, low in cost, safe and comfortable, while offering all the traditional advantages of two engines. Construction of a full-scale mock-up was started in February 1960 and completed two months later. The prototype flew for the first time on 28 February 1961, followed by the first production model in August 1962. FAA Type Approval was received on 22 May 1962 and deliveries of the original Model 336 Skymaster, with non-retractable landing gear, began in May 1963.

A total of 195 Model 336 Skymasters had been built by January 1965. In the following month, this version was superseded by the Model 337 Skymaster, with increased wing incidence, retractable landing gear, and other changes, making it virtually a new aeroplane. A total of 1,485 Model 337 Skymasters had been built by 31 January 1974, and an additional 42 Reims Skymasters have been built by Reims Aviation in France.

The 1974 version of the Skymaster introduces a number of improvements, including a new hydraulic mechanism for more positive operation of the airstair door; redesigned long-range fuel system; an improved control lock collar; changes to reduce friction in the elevator and aileron controls; and provision of a rear propeller viewing mirror, shoulder harness stowage trays, and miniaturised marker beacon lights. New options include a wall-mounted rear seat table, approach plate holder and light, new propeller synchrophaser, improved baggage net, a flush-mounted glide-slope antenna, and a revised inertia reel shoulder restraint for front seat occupants.

In addition, two military versions have been delivered to the USAF, as follows:

O-2A. Equipped for forward air controller missions, including visual reconnaissance, target identification, target marking, ground-air co-ordination and damage assessment. Dual controls standard. Four underwing pylons for external stores, including rockets, flares or other light ordnance, such as a 7·62 mm Minigun pack. Modified 60A electrical system to support special electronics systems, including UHF, VHF, FM, ADF, TACAN and APX transponder.

Initial contract, dated 29 December 1966, called for 145 O-2As; a follow-on contract awarded in June 1967 brought the total on order to 192, all of which had been delivered by early 1968. A further contract was announced on 26 June 1968, for 45 O-2As, together with modification services and spares, and this was amended in September 1968 to increase the quantity to 154 aircraft. The additional 109 O-2As have lightweight electronics. Early in 1970 Cessna delivered 12 O-2As to the Imperial Iranian Air Force for training, liaison and observation duties.

O-2B. Generally similar to the commercial version, but equipped for psychological warfare missions. Advanced communications system and high-power air-to-ground broadcasting system, supplied by University Sound division of LTV Ling Altec and utilising three 600W amplifiers with highly directional speakers. Manual dispenser fitted, for leaflet dropping. Initial contract for 31 placed on 29 December 1966, and the programme was initiated by the repurchase of 31 commercial aircraft, six of which were used for pilot training at Eglin AFB, Florida. First O-2B accepted by USAF on 31 March 1967 and was assigned to Vietnam. A combined total of 510 O-2As and O-2Bs were delivered by December 1970.

The following details apply to the standard commercial Skymaster:

TYPE: Tandem-engined cabin monoplane.

WINGS: Braced high-wing monoplane, with single streamlined bracing strut each side. Wing section NACA 2412 at root, NACA 2409 at tip. Dihedral 3°. Incidence 4° 30′ at root, 2° 30′ at tip. Conventional all-metal two-spar structure. Conical-camber glassfibre wing-tips. All-metal Frise ailerons. Electrically-operated all-metal single-slotted flaps. Ground-adjustable tab in port aileron. Pneumatic de-icing system optional.

FUSELAGE: Conventional all-metal semi-monocoque structure.

TAIL UNIT: Cantilever all-metal structure with twin fins and rudders, carried on two slim metal booms. Trim tab in elevator, with optional electric actuation. Optional pneumatic de-icing system.

LANDING GEAR: Hydraulically-retractable tricycle type. Cantilever spring steel main legs. Steerable nosewheel with oleo-pneumatic shock-absorber. Main wheels and tyres size 6·00-6. Nosewheel and tyre size 5·00-5. Main-wheel tyre pressure 45 lb/sq in (3·16 kg/cm²). Hydraulic disc brakes. Parking brake. Oversize wheels and heavy-duty brakes optional.

POWER PLANT: Two 210 hp Continental IO-360-C six-cylinder horizontally-opposed aircooled engines, each driving a McCauley two-blade fully-feathering constant-speed metal propeller. Electrically-operated cowl flaps. Propeller de-icing optional for forward propeller. Fuel in two main tanks in each outer wing, with total usable capacity of 92 US gallons (348 litres), and two optional auxiliary tanks in inner wings with total usable capacity of 36 US gallons (136 litres). Total usable capacity with auxiliary tanks 128 US gallons (484 litres). Refuelling points above wings. Oil capacity 5 US gallons (19 litres).

Accommodation: Standard accommodation for pilot and co-pilot on fully-articulating individual seats, with rear bench seat for two passengers. Alternative arrangements utilise four, five or six individual seats. Optional cabin equipment includes fully-articulating individual seats for passengers and matching headrests. Space for 365 lb (165 kg) of baggage in four-seat version. Airstair door on starboard side. Baggage door at rear of cabin on starboard side. Cabin is heated, ventilated and soundproofed. Adjustable air vents and reading lights available to each passenger. Provision for carrying glassfibre cargo pack, with capacity of 300 lb (136 kg), under fuselage; this reduces cruising speed by only 2·6 knots (3 mph; 5 km/h).

Systems: Electrical system supplied by two 38A 28V engine-driven alternators. 24V battery. Hydraulic system for landing gear retraction and brakes.

Electronics and Equipment: Standard equipment includes sensitive altimeter, electric clock, outside air temperature gauge, audible stall warning device, engine synchronisation indicator, turn co-ordinator indicator, elevator and aileron control locks, windscreen defroster, dome light, map light, reading lights, baggage net, sun visors, hinged window starboard side, all-weather window, tinted windscreen and windows, omni-flash beacon, taxi light, navigation light detectors, retractable tie-down rings, towbar and quick drain fuel tank valves. Optional avionics include Cessna Series 300 nav/com with 360-channel com and 200-channel nav with remote VOR/LOC or VOR/ILS indicator, ADF with digital tuning, marker beacon with three lights and aural signal, transponder with 4096 code capability, DME, 10-channel HF transceiver, and Nav-O-Matic single-axis autopilot and integrated flight control system; or Series 400 com with 360 channels, nav/com with 360-channel com and 200-channel nav with VOR/LOC or VOR/ILS indicator, 40-channel glideslope receiver, ADF with digital tuning and BFO, transponder with 4096 code capability, Nav-O-Matic 400 or 400A two-axis autopilot and integrated flight control system, with optional RMI. Optional equipment includes all-purpose control wheel with provision for map light, boom microphone switch, pitch trim switch, autopilot/electric trim disengage switch, dual controls, blind-flying instrumentation, economy mixture indicator, true airspeed indicator, instrument post lights, approach plate holder, flight hour recorder, alternate static source, cabin fire extinguisher, baggage net, wall-mounted table, safety belts for 3rd, 4th, 5th and 6th seats, oxygen system, portable stretcher, cargo tie-down installation, full-flow oil filters, oil dilution system, second hydraulic pump, external power socket, propeller synchrophaser, winterisation kit, internal corrosion proofing, ice detection system, white strobe lights, photographic provisions, static wicks, windscreen anti-icing panel, pitot heating system, flush glideslope antenna, cargo pack, and emergency exit window for port side.

Dimensions, external:
- Wing span: 38 ft 2 in (11·63 m)
- Wing chord at root: 6 ft 0 in (1·83 m)
- Wing chord at tip: 4 ft 0 in (1·22 m)
- Wing aspect ratio: 7·18
- Length overall: 29 ft 9 in (9·07 m)
- Height overall: 9 ft 2 in (2·79 m)
- Tailplane span: 10 ft 0$\frac{3}{8}$ in (3·06 m)
- Wheel track: 8 ft 2 in (2·49 m)
- Wheelbase: 7 ft 10 in (2·39 m)
- Propeller diameter:
  - Front: 6 ft 6 in (1·98 m)
  - Rear: 6 ft 4 in (1·93 m)
- Passenger door:
  - Height: 3 ft 10 in (1·17 m)
  - Width: 3 ft 0 in (0·91 m)
- Baggage door:
  - Height: 1 ft 9$\frac{1}{2}$ in (0·55 m)
  - Width: 1 ft 7 in (0·48 m)

Dimensions, internal:
- Cabin: Length: 9 ft 11 in (3·02 m)
  - Max width: 3 ft 8$\frac{1}{4}$ in (1·12 m)
  - Max height: 4 ft 3$\frac{1}{4}$ in (1·30 m)
  - Volume: 138 cu ft (3·91 m³)
- Baggage space: 17 cu ft (0·50 m³)

Areas:
- Wings, gross: 202·5 sq ft (18·81 m²)
- Ailerons (total): 15·44 sq ft (1·43 m²)
- Trailing-edge flaps (total): 36·88 sq ft (3·43 m²)
- Fins (total): 30·68 sq ft (2·85 m²)
- Rudders (total): 10·70 sq ft (0·99 m²)
- Tailplane: 36·27 sq ft (3·37 m²)

Weights and Loadings:
- Weight empty, approx: 2,705 lb (1,227 kg)
- Max T-O weight: 4,630 lb (2,100 kg)
- Max landing weight: 4,400 lb (1,995 kg)
- Max wing loading: 22·9 lb/sq ft (112 kg/m²)
- Max power loading: 11·0 lb/hp (5·0 kg/hp)

Performance (at max T-O weight):
- Max level speed at S/L: 179 knots (206 mph; 332 km/h)
- Max cruising speed, 75% power at 5,500 ft (1,675 m): 170 knots (196 mph; 315 km/h)
- Econ cruising speed at 10,000 ft (3,050 m): 128 knots (147 mph; 237 km/h)
- Stalling speed, flaps up: 70 knots (80 mph; 129 km/h)
- Stalling speed, flaps down: 61 knots (70 mph; 113 km/h)
- Max rate of climb at S/L: 1,100 ft (335 m)/min
- Rate of climb at S/L, front engine only: 270 ft (82 m)/min
- Rate of climb at S/L, rear engine only: 320 ft (98 m)/min
- Service ceiling: 18,000 ft (5,490 m)
- Service ceiling, front engine only: 6,100 ft (1,860 m)
- Service ceiling, rear engine only: 7,100 ft (2,160 m)
- T-O run: 1,000 ft (305 m)
- T-O to 50 ft (15 m): 1,675 ft (510 m)
- Landing from 50 ft (15 m): 1,650 ft (503 m)
- Landing run: 700 ft (213 m)
- Range at max cruising speed, standard fuel, no reserve: 677 nm (780 miles; 1,255 km)
- Range at max cruising speed, long-range fuel, no reserve: 881 nm (1,015 miles; 1,633 km)
- Range at econ cruising speed, standard fuel, no reserve: 872 nm (1,005 miles; 1,617 km)
- Range at econ cruising speed, long-range fuel, no reserve: 1,120 nm (1,290 miles; 2,076 km)

CESSNA MODEL T337 PRESSURISED SKYMASTER

On 8 December 1971 Cessna introduced a pressurised version of the Skymaster. Design and construction of the prototype began in January 1971, and the first prototype made its initial flight on 23 July 1971. Construction of pre-production and production aircraft began simultaneously in May 1971, and FAA certification was granted on 2 February 1972. Deliveries began in May 1972, and two prototypes and 128 production aircraft had been built by 31 January 1974. Cessna claims the T337 to be the world's cheapest twin-engined pressurised aircraft.

The pressurised version is distinguished easily from the standard Skymaster in having four, instead of three, windows on each side of the cabin. Pressurisation is provided from the turbocharged engines, either of which can maintain full pressurisation and air-conditioning. With a maximum differential of 3·35 lb/sq in (0·24 kg/cm²), a cabin altitude of 10,000 ft (3,050 m) can be maintained to 20,000 ft (6,100 m). Pilot setting of departure and landing field altitudes on the pressurisation controls is all that is necessary for the system to begin automatic operation.

Type: Tandem-engined pressurised cabin monoplane.

Wings: As Model 337 Skymaster.

Fuselage: Conventional all-metal semi-monocoque structure, with fail-safe structure in the pressurised section extending between the two engine bulkheads, but excluding aft lower area below cabin floor.

Tail Unit: As Model 337, except areas of horizontal surfaces changed.

Landing Gear: Hydraulically-retractable tricycle type, main units retracting aft, nosewheel forward. Cantilever spring steel main units. Steerable nosewheel with oleo-pneumatic shock-absorber. Main wheels with Cleveland tyres size 17·5 × 6·30-7·5, pressure 55 lb/sq in (3·85 kg/cm²). Nosewheel with Cleveland tyre size 15·2 × 6·30-7·5, pressure 42 lb/sq in (2·95 kg/cm²). Cleveland hydraulic disc brakes. Parking brake. Heavy-duty wheels, brakes and tyres optional.

Power Plant: Two 225 hp Continental TSIO-360-C turbocharged six-cylinder horizontally-opposed aircooled engines, each driving a McCauley two-blade metal constant-speed fully-feathering propeller. Propeller de-icing optional for forward propeller. Three interconnected fuel tanks in each wing with a combined capacity of 62·5 US gallons (236·5 litres). Total fuel capacity 125 US gallons (473 litres). Refuelling points in wing upper surfaces. Oil capacity 5·5 US gallons (20·5 litres).

Accommodation: Standard accommodation for pilot and co-pilot on fully articulating individual seats, with rear bench seat for two passengers. A third passenger seat at rear of cabin is optional. Space for 365 lb (165 kg) of baggage in four-seat version. Bench seat folds to port to provide easy access to baggage area. Two-section door on starboard side, lower half opening downward and incorporating airstairs. Upper half opens upward. Cabin is heated and ventilated. Double-pane windows. Individual adjustable air ventilators and reading lights for passengers. Windscreen defrosting standard. Windscreen de-icing optional.

Systems: Electrical system powered by two 28V 38A engine-driven self-rectifying alternators. 24V battery. Electrically-driven hydraulic pump for landing gear retraction. Vacuum system optional for blind-flying instrumentation. Oxygen system optional. Cabin pressurised by engine bleed air, max differential 3·35 lb/sq in (0·24 kg/cm²). Cabin heated by 25,000 BTU gasoline heater and/or hot air from the compression section of the pressurisation system.

Electronics and Equipment: Optional avionics are as detailed for the Model 337 Skymaster. Standard equipment is the same as for the Skymaster, plus a manual cabin altitude control, cabin rate-of-change gauge, propeller synchrophaser and altitude warning light. Optional equipment includes a true airspeed computer, emergency locator beacon, solid-state oxygen system, engine priming system, and automatic propeller unfeathering system, in addition to the options detailed for the Skymaster.

Dimensions, external:
- As for Model 337 except:
- Length overall: 29 ft 10 in (9·09 m)
- Propeller ground clearance:
  - Front: 9 in (0·23 m)
  - Rear: 1 ft 8 in (0·51 m)
- Passenger door:
  - Height: 3 ft 9$\frac{1}{4}$ in (1·15 m)
  - Width: 2 ft 11$\frac{1}{4}$ in (0·90 m)
  - Height to sill: 1 ft 10 in (0·56 m)

Dimensions, internal:
- Cabin: Length: 9 ft 11 in (3·02 m)
  - Max width: 3 ft 7$\frac{3}{4}$ in (1·11 m)
  - Max height: 4 ft 2$\frac{3}{4}$ in (1·29 m)
  - Floor area: 22·6 sq ft (2·10 m²)
  - Volume: 128 cu ft (3·62 m³)
- Baggage space: 17 cu ft (0·50 m³)

Areas:
- As for Model 337 except:
- Tailplane: 32·82 sq ft (3·05 m²)
- Elevator, including tab: 12·72 sq ft (1·18 m²)

Weights and Loadings:
- Weight empty: 2,950 lb (1,338 kg)
- Max T-O weight: 4,700 lb (2,131 kg)
- Max landing weight: 4,465 lb (2,025 kg)
- Max wing loading: 23·2 lb/sq ft (113·3 kg/m²)
- Max power loading: 10·4 lb/hp (4·72 kg/hp)

Performance (at max T-O weight):
- Max level speed at 20,000 ft (6,100 m): 217 knots (250 mph; 402 km/h)
- Max cruising speed at 20,000 ft (6,100 m): 205 knots (236 mph; 380 km/h)
- Cruising speed, 75% power at 16,000 ft (4,875 m): 198 knots (228 mph; 367 km/h)
- Stalling speed, flaps and wheels up: 69·5 knots (80 mph; 129 km/h)
- Stalling speed, flaps and wheels down: 62 knots (71 mph; 114·5 km/h)
- Max rate of climb at S/L: 1,250 ft (381 m)/min
- Rate of climb at S/L, one engine out: 375 ft (114 m)/min
- Max operating altitude: 20,000 ft (6,100 m)
- Service ceiling, one engine out: 18,700 ft (5,700 m)
- Min ground turning radius: 8 ft 4 in (2·54 m)
- T-O run: 945 ft (288 m)
- T-O to 50 ft (15 m): 1,500 ft (457 m)

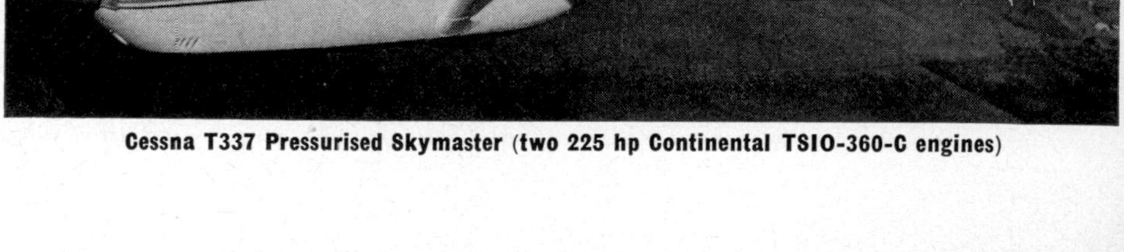

Cessna T337 Pressurised Skymaster (two 225 hp Continental TSIO-360-C engines)

Landing from 50 ft (15 m) at max landing weight 1,675 ft (511 m)
Landing run at max landing weight 795 ft (242 m)
Range with max fuel, at max cruising speed, no allowances 955 nm (1,100 miles; 1,770 km)
Range with max fuel, at econ cruising speed, no allowances 1,305 nm (1,505 miles; 2,420 km)

CESSNA MODEL 340 and 340 II

Cessna announced on 8 December 1971 the introduction of a pressurised twin-engined business aircraft designated Model 340.

Developed from the Model 310, it has a wing and landing gear generally similar to those of the Model 414, a pressurised fuselage of fail-safe design, and a tail unit similar to that of the Model 310.

On 21 December 1973 Cessna announced the Model 340 II, a version of the 340 that has factory-installed avionics as standard. Two versions are therefore available, as follows:

340. Standard model, as described in detail below.

340 II. Identical to Model 340, but with dual Series 300 nav/coms with 360-channel com and 200-channel nav and VOR/LOC and VOR/ILS indicators, ADF, DME, marker beacon, and Series 400 glideslope, transponder and 400A two-axis autopilot as standard. Other standard equipment includes dual controls, external power socket, starboard landing light, taxi light, outside air temperature gauge and all necessary antennae for on-board avionics.

The 1974 versions of the Model 340 have frameless foul-weather windows, white epoxy finish on landing gear components for improved abrasion protection, and an airspeed indicator calibrated in knots. New options include a more powerful nosewheel-mounted taxi light, inertia reel shoulder restraints for pilot and co-pilot, a new lightweight high-capacity air-conditioning system and a new angle of attack indicator.

A total of 233 Model 340s had been delivered by 31 January 1974.

TYPE: Six-seat pressurised business aircraft.

WINGS: Cantilever low-wing monoplane, with "Stabila-tip" fixed wingtip fuel tanks. Wing section NACA 23018 (modified) at aircraft centreline, NACA 23015 (modified) at centre-section/outer wing junction, NACA 23009 (modified) at tip. Dihedral 5° on outer panels. Incidence 2° 30′ at root, —0° 30′ at tip. All-metal two-spar structure. All-metal ailerons of single-spar construction; controllable trim tab in starboard aileron. Electrically-actuated all-metal split trailing-edge flaps, of single-spar construction with lower skin, comprising an inboard and outboard panel on each wing. Optional pneumatic de-icing system.

FUSELAGE: All-metal semi-monocoque structure. The pressurised cabin section, extending from station 100·00 aft to station 252·00, is of fail-safe construction, designed to provide pressurisation to the exterior skin of 4·2 lb/sq in (0·30 kg/cm²). All openings are reinforced with doublers and frame members, and longitudinal continuity is provided by lightweight extruded "T"-section stringers.

TAIL UNIT: Cantilever all-metal structure with swept vertical surfaces. Fixed-incidence tailplane of conventional two-spar construction. Elevators of single-spar construction, with controllable trim tab in starboard elevator. Rudder, built up on a formed channel spar and transverse ribs, has a controllable trim tab. Optional pneumatic de-icing system.

LANDING GEAR: Retractable tricycle type, with single wheel on each unit. Electro-mechanical retraction, main units inward into wings and faired by doors when retracted, nose unit rearward into the fuselage nose and faired by two doors when retracted. Mechanically-operated emergency gear extension system. Cessna oleo-pneumatic shock-absorbers. Steerable nosewheel with shimmy damper and self-centering device. Main-wheel tyres size 6·50-10 (8-ply); nosewheel tyre size 6·00-6 (6-ply). Single-disc hydraulic brakes. Parking brake.

POWER PLANT: Two 285 hp Continental TSIO-520-K six-cylinder horizontally-opposed air-cooled turbocharged fuel-injection engines, each driving a McCauley Type D2AF34C71-02/84JF-3 two-blade metal constant-speed and fully-feathering propeller. Three-blade propellers optional. Fuel system, max usable capacity 203 US gallons (768 litres), as described for Model 310. Manifold pressure relief valves to prevent engines from overboosting are standard equipment.

ACCOMMODATION: Standard seating for pilot and co-pilot on tilting and individually adjustable seats. Individual seats for four passengers, two forward-facing on the port side, one aft-facing and one forward-facing on starboard side. Door, on port side aft of wing, is two-piece type with built-in airstairs in bottom portion. Plug-type emergency escape hatch on starboard side of cabin, over wing. Foul-weather window for pilot. Baggage accommodated in nose compartment with external access doors, capacity 350 lb (159 kg), two wing lockers, capacity 120 lb (54·5 kg) each, and in rear cabin area, capacity 340 lb (154 kg). Total baggage capacity 930 lb (422 kg). Cabin pressurised, heated and ventilated. Air-conditioning optional. Windscreen defroster standard; windscreen de-icing optional.

Cessna Model 340 lightweight pressurised business aircraft (two 285 hp Continental TSIO-520-K engines)

SYSTEMS: Electrical system powered by two 28V 50A engine-driven alternators. Two 12V 24Ah batteries. Vacuum system supplied by two engine-driven pumps. Hydraulic system for brakes only. Cabin pressurised by engine bleed air, max differential 4·2 lb/sq in (0·30 kg/cm²). Cabin heated by Stewart Warner 45,000 BTU gasoline heater. Lightweight air-conditioning system optional.

ELECTRONICS AND EQUIPMENT: Standard equipment of Model 340 includes sensitive altimeter, Accru-Measure fuel gauging system, blind-flying instrumentation, audible stall warning device, variable intensity floodlights and instrument post lights, aileron and elevator control lock, courtesy lights, individual reading lights, safety belts for pilot and co-pilot, super soundproofing, cabin radio speaker, sun visors, full-flow oil filters, propeller synchroniser, navigation lights with flasher unit, heating system for fuel vents, pitot and stall warning device, retractable landing light in port wing, heater overheat indicator light, "Not Locked" light for cabin door, all-over paint scheme, two rotating beacons, and towbar. Optional for the Model 340 but standard for the 340 II are the items detailed in the model listing. Optional items common to both versions include turn co-ordinator, economy mixture and instantaneous rate of climb indicators, flight hour recorder, true airspeed indicator, rudder pedal lock, cabin writing desk, window curtains, flight deck divider curtain, 11·0 cu ft (0·31 m³) or 76·6 cu ft (2·17 m³) oxygen system, cabin fire extinguisher, boom microphone, propeller unfeathering system, 100A alternators, engine fire detection and extinguishing system, GMT clock, blind-flying instrumentation for co-pilot, baggage courtesy lights, all-leather seats, emergency locator transmitter, tinted double-pane cabin windows, heated static source, polyurethane paint, nosewheel fender, ice detection lights, taxi light, white strobe lights, propeller de-icing system, windscreen alcohol de-icing system, fuselage ice impact panels, internal corrosion proofing, static wicks, and dual pitot system. Optional avionics for the Model 340 are as detailed for the Model 310.

DIMENSIONS, EXTERNAL:
Wing span 38 ft 1·3 in (11·62 m)
Wing chord, mean aerodynamic 5 ft 1·68 in (1·57 m)
Wing aspect ratio 7·2
Length overall 34 ft 4 in (10·46 m)
Height overall 12 ft 6·8 in (3·83 m)
Tailplane span 17 ft 0 in (5·18 m)
Wheel track 12 ft 10·7 in (3·93 m)
Propeller diameter 6 ft 9 in (2·06 m)
Propeller ground clearance 7·2 in (0·18 m)
Passenger door:
Height 3 ft 10½ in (1·18 m)
Width 1 ft 9 in (0·53 m)
Emergency hatch:
Height 1 ft 7 in (0·48 m)
Width 2 ft 2 in (0·66 m)

DIMENSIONS, INTERNAL:
Cabin:
Length, including baggage compartment 12 ft 8 in (3·86 m)
Max width 3 ft 10½ in (1·18 m)
Max height 4 ft 1 in (1·24 m)
Volume (total) 162·4 cu ft (4·6 m³)
Baggage space:
Cabin 18·5 cu ft (0·52 m³)
Nose 15·5 cu ft (0·44 m³)
Engine nacelles (each) 4·625 cu ft (0·13 m³)

AREAS:
Wings, gross 184·7 sq ft (17·16 m²)
Ailerons (total) 11·44 sq ft (1·06 m²)
Trailing-edge flaps (total) 23·06 sq ft (2·14 m²)
Fin 16·20 sq ft (1·51 m²)
Rudder (including tab) 11·76 sq ft (1·09 m²)
Tailplane 32·15 sq ft (2·99 m²)
Elevators (including tab) 21·25 sq ft (1·97 m²)

WEIGHTS AND LOADINGS:
Weight empty, approx:
340 3,730 lb (1,692 kg)
340 II 3,857 lb (1,749 kg)
Max T-O weight 5,975 lb (2,710 kg)
Max wing loading 32·47 lb/sq ft (158·5 kg/m²)
Max power loading 10·48 lb/hp (4·75 kg/hp)

PERFORMANCE (at max T-O weight):
Max level speed at S/L 192 knots (221 mph; 356 km/h)
Max level speed at 16,000 ft (4,875 m) 226 knots (260 mph; 418 km/h)
Max cruising speed, 75% power at 20,000 ft (6,100 m) 209 knots (241 mph; 388 km/h)
Econ cruising speed at 25,000 ft (7,620 m) 192 knots (221 mph; 356 km/h)
Max rate of climb at S/L 1,500 ft (457 m)/min
Rate of climb at S/L, one engine out 250 ft (76 m)/min
Service ceiling 26,500 ft (8,075 m)
Service ceiling, one engine out 12,100 ft (3,690 m)
T-O run 1,760 ft (536 m)
T-O to 50 ft (15 m) 2,430 ft (741 m)
Landing from 50 ft (15 m) 1,840 ft (561 m)
Landing run 765 ft (233 m)
Range, 75% power at 10,000 ft (3,050 m), with 600 lb (272 kg) fuel, no reserve 575 nm (663 miles; 1,067 km)
Range, 75% power at 10,000 ft (3,050 m), with 978 lb (443 kg) fuel, no reserve 937 nm (1,079 miles; 1,736 km)
Range, 75% power at 20,000 ft (6,100 m), with 600 lb (272 kg) fuel, no reserve 630 nm (726 miles; 1,168 km)
Range, 75% power at 20,000 ft (6,100 m), with 978 lb (443 kg) fuel, no reserve 1,029 nm (1,185 miles; 1,907 km)
Range, 75% power at 20,000 ft (6,100 m), with 1,218 lb (552 kg) fuel, no reserve 1,280 nm (1,475 miles; 2,373 km)
Max range at econ cruising speed, with 1,218 lb (552 kg) fuel, no reserve 1,425 nm (1,641 miles; 2,641 km)

CESSNA MODEL 401

Announced on 1 November 1966, the Model 401 is a six/eight-seat executive transport. The prototype flew for the first time on 26 August 1965 and type approval was received on 20 September 1966. A total of 404 had been built by May 1972. Production has now ended; a description of the Model 401 can be found in the 1972-73 *Jane's*.

CESSNA MODEL 402

The original Model 402 was announced simultaneously with the Model 401, both having a similar airframe and power plant. The Model 402, however, was designed for the third-level airline market, with a convertible cabin and reinforced cabin floor of bonded crushed honeycomb construction, enabling it to be changed quickly from a ten-seat commuter to a light cargo transport.

On 8 December 1971 Cessna announced an extension to the 400 Series, re-naming the original Model 402 as Model 402 **Utililiner**, and introducing a version known as the Model 402 **Businessliner.**

This latter model has standard seating for six, with optional seating arrangements for up to eight persons. The standard airstair door may be complemented with an optional side-hinged door, to provide a total loading door width of 3 ft 4 in (1·02 m). Optional refinements available specifically for the Businessliner include fold-out business desks, stereo equipment, refreshment centre and cabin dividers.

The 1974 versions of the Model 402 have all-new interior and exterior styling, an airspeed indicator calibrated in knots, and white epoxy coated landing gear components to improve abrasion resistance. New options include an inertia reel shoulder restraint system for pilot and co-pilot, a more powerful taxi light, a new angle of attack indicator and a lightweight air-conditioning system.

The same prototype served for Models 401 and 402, and the FAA type certificate, awarded on 20 September 1966, also covered both types. A total of 560 Model 402s had been built by 31 January 1974.

American Jet Industries (which see) has developed a turboprop conversion of the Model 402, known as the Turbo Star 402.

Type: Ten-seat (optional nine-seat) convertible passenger/freight transport (Utililiner) or six/eight-seat business aircraft (Businessliner).

Wings: Cantilever low-wing monoplane, with "Stabila-tip" fixed wingtip fuel tanks. Wing section NACA 23018 at aircraft centreline, NACA 23015 at centre-section/outer wing junction, NACA 23009 at tip. Dihedral 5° on outer panels. Incidence 2° at root, —0° 30′ at tip. All-metal two-spar structure. All-metal ailerons and electrically-actuated split flaps. Trim tab in port aileron. Optional pneumatic de-icing system.

Fuselage: All-metal semi-monocoque structure.

Tail Unit: Cantilever all-metal structure, with 40° sweepback on fin at quarter-chord. Fixed-incidence tailplane. Trim tabs in rudder and starboard elevator. Electric operation of trim tabs optional. Optional Goodrich pneumatic de-icing system.

Landing Gear: Retractable tricycle type, with single wheel on each unit. Electro-mechanical retraction, main units inward into wings, nose unit rearward. Cessna oleo-pneumatic shock-absorbers. Cleveland Aircraft Products wheels, with Cessna tyres size 6·50-10 on main wheels, size 6·00-6 on nosewheel. Tyre pressures: main, 62 lb/sq in (4·36 kg/cm²); nose, 40 lb/sq in (2·81 kg/cm²). Cleveland single-disc hydraulic brakes. Parking brake.

Power Plant: Two 300 hp Continental TSIO-520-E six-cylinder horizontally-opposed air-cooled engines, each driving a McCauley three-blade metal constant-speed fully-feathering propeller. Propeller synchronisation, automatic unfeathering and electric de-icing systems optional. Fuel system with max usable capacity of 203 US gallons (768 litres), as described for the Model 310. Oil capacity 6·5 US gallons (24·6 litres). Manifold pressure relief valves to prevent engine overboosting are standard.

Accommodation: Two seats side by side in pilot's compartment. Four individual seats in pairs and two bench seats, each accommodating two passengers, in main cabin of Utililiner version. Businessliner has four individual seats as standard, two additional seats optional, in the main cabin. Passenger reading lights optional. Door with built-in airstair on port side of cabin at centre. Storm windows for pilot and co-pilot. Tinted cabin windows. An emergency escape hatch is provided on the starboard side of cabin. Optional cargo door and crew access door available. Baggage area, at rear of cabin, with capacity of up to 500 lb (226 kg). Nose baggage compartment, with optional carpeting, is accessible from either side and has capacity of 350 lb (159 kg). Articles up to 6 ft 5 in (1·96 m) in length may be carried in the nose compartment. Avionics or baggage compartment in nose, separate from forward baggage compartment, and accessible through an "over the top" 180° cam-locked door, has a capacity of 250 lb (113 kg). Optional side access door. Wing lockers, at rear of each engine nacelle, each have capacity of 120 lb (54 kg). Total baggage capacity 1,340 lb (606 kg), if no avionics are carried in the forward nose compartment. Cabin heated and ventilated. Windscreen defrosting standard. Electric anti-icing of pilot's window or alcohol anti-icing of pilot and co-pilot windows optional.

Systems: Electrical system powered by two 24V 50A alternators. 24V 25Ah battery. 100A alternators optional. Hydraulic system for brakes only. Vacuum system provided by two engine-driven vacuum pumps. Oxygen system of 44 cu ft (1·25 m³) or 114·9 cu ft (3·25 m³) capacity optional. Air-conditioning system optional. Heating and ventilation system with 45,000 BTU gasoline heater standard.

Electronics and Equipment: Optional avionics as detailed for Model 310. Standard equipment includes sensitive altimeter, electric clock, variable intensity floodlight, outside air temperature gauge, full blind-flying instrumentation, audible stall warning and landing gear indicators, cabin door "Not Locked" light, map light, heater overheat warning light, alternator failure lights, variable intensity instrument post lights, aileron and elevator control lock, sun visors, armrests, pilot and co-pilot safety belt system, super soundproofing, cabin radio speaker, adjustable cabin air ventilators, navigation light detectors, courtesy light, retractable landing light, navigation lights, two rotating beacons, all-over paint scheme and towbar. Optional equipment includes GMT clock, dual controls, inertial shoulder restraint system for pilot and co-pilot, co-pilot's blind-flying instrumentation, economy mixture indicator, instantaneous rate of climb indicator, true airspeed indicator, rudder pedal locks, flight hour recorder, turn co-ordinator, cabin fire extinguisher, emergency locator transmitter, Utililiner or Businessliner interiors which include flight deck divider curtains, window curtains, headrests, reading lights, "Seat Belt" and "No Smoking" signs and various arrangements of seats, tables, refreshment units and toilets, heavy-duty brakes, internal corrosion proofing, external power socket, ice detection light, second retractable landing light, taxi light, three-light strobe system, locator beacon, nosewheel fender, polyurethane paint, dual heated static source and static dischargers.

Dimensions, external:
Wing span over tip-tanks 39 ft 10¼ in (12·15 m)
Wing chord at root 5 ft 7½ in (1·71 m)
Wing chord at tip 3 ft 9½ in (1·16 m)
Wing aspect ratio 7·5
Length overall 36 ft 1 in (11·0 m)
Height overall 11 ft 8 in (3·56 m)
Tailplane span 17 ft 0 in (5·18 m)
Wheel track 14 ft 8 in (4·47 m)
Wheelbase 10 ft 5½ in (3·19 m)
Propeller diameter 6 ft 4½ in (1·94 m)
Passenger door (standard):
Height 3 ft 11½ in (1·21 m)
Width 1 ft 11 in (0·58 m)
Height to sill 3 ft 11½ in (1·21 m)
Cargo door (optional):
Height 3 ft 11½ in (1·21 m)
Width 3 ft 3½ in (1·00 m)
Height to sill 3 ft 11½ in (1·21 m)
Nose baggage doors (each):
Height 1 ft 8 in (0·51 m)
Width 2 ft 7½ in (0·80 m)
Nacelle baggage doors (each):
Height 1 ft 0 in (0·30 m)
Width 2 ft 0½ in (0·62 m)

Dimensions, internal:
Cabin:
Length 15 ft 10 in (4·83 m)
Max width 4 ft 8 in (1·42 m)
Max height 4 ft 3 in (1·30 m)
Volume 222·4 cu ft (6·30 m³)

Areas:
Wings, gross 195·72 sq ft (18·18 m²)
Ailerons (total) 11·44 sq ft (1·06 m²)
Trailing-edge flaps (total) 22·90 sq ft (2·13 m²)
Fin 37·89 sq ft (3·52 m²)
Rudder, including tab 17·77 sq ft (1·65 m²)
Tailplane 60·70 sq ft (5·64 m²)
Elevators, including tab 17·63 sq ft (1·64 m²)

Weights and Loadings:
Weight empty:
Utililiner 3,746 lb (1,699 kg)
Businessliner 3,742 lb (1,697 kg)
Max T-O weight 6,300 lb (2,857 kg)
Max landing weight 6,200 lb (2,812 kg)
Max wing loading 32·2 lb/sq ft (157·2 kg/m²)
Max power loading 10·5 lb/hp (4·76 kg/hp)

Performance (at max T-O weight):
Max level speed at S/L 198 knots (228 mph; 367 km/h)
Max level speed at 16,000 ft (4,875 m) 227 knots (261 mph; 420 km/h)
Max cruising speed, 75% power at 10,000 ft (3,050 m) 189 knots (218 mph; 351 km/h)
Max cruising speed, 75% power at 20,000 ft (6,100 m) 208 knots (240 mph; 386 km/h)
Max rate of climb at S/L 1,610 ft (491 m)/min
Rate of climb at S/L, one engine out 225 ft (69 m)/min
Service ceiling 26,180 ft (7,980 m)
Service ceiling, one engine out 11,320 ft (3,450 m)
T-O run 1,695 ft (517 m)
T-O to 50 ft (15 m) 2,220 ft (677 m)
Landing from 50 ft (15 m) at max landing weight 1,765 ft (538 m)
Landing run at max landing weight 777 ft (237 m)
Range, 75% power at 10,000 ft (3,050 m), no reserve:
600 lb (272 kg) fuel 549 nm (633 miles; 1,018 km)
978 lb (443 kg) fuel 897 nm (1,033 miles; 1,662 km)
1,218 lb (552 kg) fuel 1,116 nm (1,286 miles; 2,069 km)
Range, 75% power at 20,000 ft (6,100 m), no reserve:
600 lb (272 kg) fuel 601 nm (692 miles; 1,113 km)
978 lb (443 kg) fuel 979 nm (1,128 miles; 1,815 km)
1,218 lb (552 kg) fuel 1,220 nm (1,405 miles; 2,261 km)
Max range at 25,000 ft (7,620 m), 1,218 lb (552 kg) fuel, no reserve 1,423 nm (1,639 miles; 2,637 km)

CESSNA MODEL 414

Cessna announced on 10 December 1969 introduction of the pressurised twin-engined Model 414, intended as a "step-up" aircraft for owners of Cessna or other light unpressurised twins.

It combines the basic fuselage and tail unit of the Model 421 with the wing of the Model 402 and has 310 hp turbocharged Continental engines. Newly-developed flush intakes in the engine cowlings provide improved air cooling of the engine installation, and cabin heating and pressurisation are provided by a new Garrett AiResearch engine bleed air system, either engine being able to maintain full pressurisation down to 60 per cent power. A "radiant heating" system circulates heated air beneath the cabin floor and up the side walls, and an optional 45,000 BTU heater is available to provide heating on the ground or for use during extremely low temperatures. The aircraft is equipped with Cessna's Accru-Measure fuel monitoring system which provides a linear readout in both pounds and gallons to an accuracy of plus or minus 3 per cent.

A choice of eight seating layouts provides accommodation for up to seven persons, including crew, and seats incorporate armrests, tapered backs and headrests.

The prototype of the Model 414 flew for the first time on 1 November 1968 and FAA certification was granted on 18 August 1969. A total of 261 had been built by 31 January 1974.

The 1974 version of the Model 414 introduces the improvements detailed for the Model 402, plus new manual dump valves for the pressurisation system and redesigned overhead consoles as standard.

Type: Six/seven-seat pressurised light transport.

Wings: Cantilever low-wing monoplane, with "Stabila-tip" fixed wingtip fuel tanks. Wing section NACA 23018 (modified) at aircraft centreline, NACA 23015 (modified) at centre-section/outer wing junction, NACA 23009 (modified) at tip. Dihedral 5° on outer panels. Incidence 2° at root. All-metal two-spar structure with stamped ribs and surface skins reinforced with spanwise stringers. All-metal ailerons and electrically-actuated split flaps. Trim tab in starboard aileron. Optional pneumatic de-icing system.

Fuselage: Conventional all-metal semi-monocoque structure, with fail-safe structure in the pressurised section.

Cessna Model 402 Businessliner six/eight-seat business aircraft (two 300 hp Continental TSIO-520-E engines)

TAIL UNIT: Cantilever all-metal structure, with sweptback vertical surfaces. Fixed-incidence tailplane. Trim tabs in rudder and starboard elevator. Optional pneumatic de-icing system.

LANDING GEAR: Retractable tricycle type. Electro-mechanical retraction, main units inward into wings, nosewheel unit rearward. Manual system for emergency retraction or extension. Oleo-pneumatic shock-absorbers. Steerable nosewheel. Magnesium wheels. Mainwheel tyres size 6·50-10 (8-ply), nosewheel tyre size 6·00-6 (6-ply). Goodyear single-disc hydraulic brakes. Parking brakes.

POWER PLANT: Two 310 hp Continental TSIO-520-J six-cylinder horizontally-opposed air-cooled turbocharged engines, each driving a McCauley 3AF32C93/82NC metal three-blade constant-speed fully-feathering propeller. Unfeathering pressure accumulator and electrical blade de-icing system optional. Fuel system with max usable capacity of 203 US gallons (768 litres), as described for the Model 310. Oil capacity 6·5 US gallons (24·6 litres).

ACCOMMODATION: Two seats side by side in pilot's compartment. Optional curtain, or solid divider with curtain, to separate pilot's compartment from main cabin. Standard seating arrangement for four forward-facing passenger seats. Optional arrangements provide for front passenger seats to face aft and a forward-facing seventh seat. Individual consoles each include reading light and ventilator. Optional items include executive writing desk, tables, hat shelf, stereo equipment, electrically-adjustable pilot and co-pilot seats, refreshment and Thermos units, fore and aft cabin dividers, electric shaver converter, all-leather seats, passenger instrument console (clock, true air-speed indicator and altimeter) and intercom. Door is two-piece type with built-in airstairs in bottom portion, on port side of cabin at rear. Plug-type emergency escape hatch on starboard side of cabin. Double-pane cabin windows. Foul-weather windows for pilot and co-pilot, on each side of fuselage. Electrically de-iced windscreen optional. Baggage accommodated in nose compartment with external access doors, capacity 350 lb (159 kg), two wing lockers, capacity 120 lb (54·5 kg) each, and in rear cabin area, capacity 500 lb (226 kg). Total baggage capacity 1,090 lb (494 kg).

SYSTEMS: Cabin pressurisation system, max differential 4·2 lb/sq in (0·30 kg/cm²). Electrical system powered by two engine-driven 28V 50A alternators. 24V 25Ah battery. 28V 100A alternators optional. Hydraulic system for brakes only. Vacuum system for blind-flying instrumentation and optional wing and tail unit de-icing system. Oxygen system of 114·9 cu ft (3·25 m³) capacity, or emergency oxygen system of 11·0 cu ft (0·31 m³) capacity optional. Air-conditioning system optional.

ELECTRONICS AND EQUIPMENT: Standard equipment includes sensitive altimeter, electric clock, dual controls, windscreen defroster, outside air temperature gauge, blind-flying instrumentation, audible stall warning device, instrument post lights, alternator failure lights, aileron and elevator control lock, aircraft systems monitoring device, heater overheat light, cabin door "Not Locked" light, armrests, aft cabin light, adjustable cabin air ventilators, non-congealing oil coolers, quick-drain fuel valves, heated stall warning transmitter, pitot and fuel vents, navigation light detectors, retractable landing light, overall paint scheme, propeller synchronisers, window curtains, courtesy lights, reading lights, super soundproofing, sun visors, full-flow oil filters, navigation lights, rotating beacons and towbar. Optional avionics include Cessna Series 400 360-channel com transceiver, 200-channel nav receiver, 360-channel nav/com with 200-channel nav with remote VOR/LOC or VOR/ILS indicator, 40-channel glideslope, ADF with digital tuning and BFO, transponder with 4096 code capability, 400A Nav-O-Matic two-axis autopilot, and integrated flight control system with optional RMI; Series 800 720-channel com transceiver, 200-channel nav receiver with remote VOR/ILS indicator, 40-channel marker beacon/glideslope receiver, transponder with 4096 code capability, ADF with digital tuning and BFO, RMI, DME and integrated flight control system; PN-101 pictorial navigation system, X-band weather radar, single sideband HF transceiver and aft cabin intercom system. Optional equipment includes electric elevator trim, GMT clock, blind-flying instrumentation for co-pilot, nose-wheel fender, polyurethane paint, true airspeed indicator, economy mixture and instantaneous rate of climb indicators, rudder pedal lock, boom microphone, flight hour recorder, turn co-ordinator, electric or alcohol windscreen anti-icing, cabin fire extinguisher, "Fasten seat belt" and "Oxygen" signs, toilet with privacy curtain, flight deck/cabin divider or curtain, executive table, refreshment centre, 8-track stereo installation, ventilating fan system, tinted windows, internal corrosion proofing, external power socket, locator beacon, fuselage ice impact panels, ice detection lights, retractable starboard wingtip landing light, strobe lights, taxi light, dual pitot system, radome nose, engine nacelle fire detection and extinguishing system, heavy-duty brakes and static wicks.

Cessna Model 414 six/seven-seat pressurised light transport (two 310 hp Continental TSIO-520-J engines)

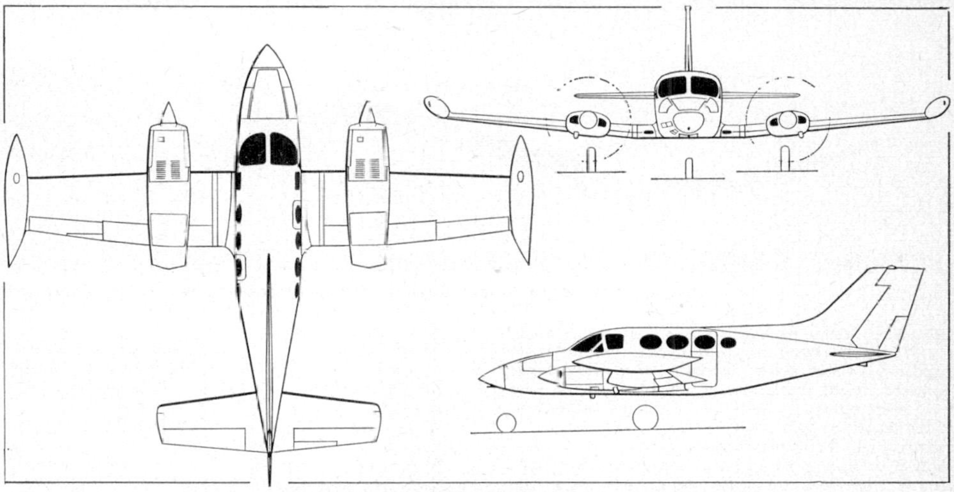

Cessna Model 414 pressurised light transport *(Pilot Press)*

DIMENSIONS, EXTERNAL:

Wing span over tip-tanks	39 ft 10¼ in (12·15 m)
Wing chord, c/l to nacelles (constant)	5 ft 7½ in (1·71 m)
Wing chord at tip	3 ft 9½ in (1·16 m)
Wing aspect ratio	7·5
Length overall	33 ft 9 in (10·29 m)
Height overall	11 ft 10 in (3·61 m)
Tailplane span	17 ft 0 in (5·18 m)
Wheel track	14 ft 8¼ in (4·48 m)
Wheelbase	10 ft 5¾ in (3·19 m)
Propeller diameter	6 ft 4½ in (1·94 m)
Passenger door:	
Height	3 ft 11½ in (1·21 m)
Width	1 ft 11 in (0·58 m)
Height to sill	3 ft 11½ in (1·21 m)

DIMENSIONS, INTERNAL:

Cabin:	
Length	14 ft 6 in (4·42 m)
Max width	4 ft 7 in (1·40 m)
Max height	4 ft 3 in (1·29 m)
Volume	215·6 cu ft (6·11 m³)

AREAS:

Wings, gross	195·72 sq ft (18·18 m²)
Ailerons (total)	11·44 sq ft (1·06 m²)
Trailing-edge flaps (total)	22·90 sq ft (2·13 m²)
Fin	37·89 sq ft (3·52 m²)
Rudder, including tab	17·77 sq ft (1·65 m²)
Tailplane	60·70 sq ft (5·64 m²)
Elevators, including tab	17·63 sq ft (1·64 m²)

WEIGHTS AND LOADINGS:

Weight empty	4,046 lb (1,835 kg)
Max T-O weight	6,350 lb (2,880 kg)
Max landing weight	6,200 lb (2,812 kg)
Max wing loading	32·4 lb/sq ft (158 2 kg/m²)
Max power loading	10·24 lb/hp (4·64 kg/hp)

PERFORMANCE (at max T-O weight):

Max level speed at S/L	197 knots (227 mph; 365 km/h)
Max level speed at 20,000 ft (6,100 m)	236 knots (272 mph; 438 km/h)
Cruising speed, 75% power at 25,000 ft (7,620 m)	219 knots (252 mph; 405 km/h)
Cruising speed, 75% power at 10,000 ft (3,050 m)	191 knots (220 mph; 354 km/h)
Econ cruising speed at 25,000 ft (7,620 m)	195 knots (225 mph; 362 km/h)
Max rate of climb at S/L	1,580 ft (482 m)/min
Rate of climb at S/L, one engine out	240 ft (73 m)/min
Service ceiling	30,100 ft (9,175 m)
Service ceiling, one engine out	11,350 ft (3,460 m)
T-O run	1,695 ft (517 m)
T-O to 50 ft (15 m)	2,350 ft (716 m)
Landing from 50 ft (15 m) at max landing weight	1,865 ft (568 m)
Landing run at max landing weight	805 ft (245 m)
Range, 75% power at 10,000 ft (3,050 m), no reserve:	
600 lb (272 kg) fuel	559 nm (644 miles; 1,036 km)
978 lb (443 kg) fuel	911 nm (1,050 miles; 1,690 km)
1,218 lb (552 kg) fuel	1,135 nm (1,308 miles; 2,105 km)
Range, 75% power at 25,000 ft (7,620 m), no reserve:	
600 lb (272 kg) fuel	638 nm (735 miles; 1,182 km)
978 lb (443 kg) fuel	1,040 nm (1,198 miles; 1,928 km)
1,218 lb (552 kg) fuel	1,296 nm (1,493 miles; 2,402 km)
Range, maximum at 10,000 ft (3,050 m), no reserve:	
600 lb (272 kg) fuel	669 nm (771 miles; 1,240 km)
978 lb (443 kg) fuel	1,091 nm (1,257 miles; 2,023 km)
1,218 lb (552 kg) fuel	1,359 nm (1,565 miles; 2,518 km)
Range, maximum at 25,000 ft (7,620 m), no reserve:	
600 lb (272 kg) fuel	691 nm (796 miles; 1,281 km)
978 lb (443 kg) fuel	1,126 nm (1,297 miles; 2,087 km)
1,218 lb (552 kg) fuel	1,402 nm (1,615 miles; 2,599 km)

CESSNA MODEL 421

On 28 October 1965, Cessna announced a new pressurised twin-engined business aircraft designated Model 421, the prototype of which had flown for the first time on 14 October 1965. FAA type approval was received on 1 May 1967 and deliveries began in the same month.

Subsequently two new versions of the Model 421 were introduced:

Model 421B Golden Eagle. First announced on 10 December 1969, this is an improved version of the Model 421A. Principal changes from the earlier model comprise an increase of 2 ft 4 in (0·71 m) in overall length as a result of enlarging the nose section of the fuselage to provide more baggage and avionics capacity, an extension of 2 ft 0 in (0·61 m) in wing span to maintain take-off and cruise performance without the need to increase engine power, and strengthening of the landing gear to cater for a gross weight which has

Cessna Model 421B Golden Eagle pressurised transport (two 375 hp Continental GTSIO-520-H engines)

increased from 6,840 lb (3,102 kg) to 7,450 lb (3,379 kg). Other improvements include introduction of an Accru-Measure fuel monitoring system; flight instruments mounted in the basic T arrangement; new easy-to-read instruments with standard faces, larger lettering and numerals; instrument white post lighting; new lighting console providing precise control of all cockpit lighting; a systems annunciator panel; and more comfortable seating. New optional equipment includes a high-intensity strobe light system; CAA conversion for UK operators; crew shoulder harnesses and dual heated pitot system.

Model 421B Executive Commuter. First announced on 16 February 1970, this is a ten-seat version of the above model, designed specifically for the commuter airline, commercial and corporate flying markets. It differs by having lightweight, easily-removable seating to provide alternative passenger/cargo configuration; standard fuel capacity of 175 US gallons (662 litres), with optional tanks to allow a maximum fuel capacity of 225 US gallons (852 litres); and deleted rear cabin baggage area, resulting in a total avionics and baggage capacity of 1,000 lb (453 kg).

The 1974 versions of the Model 421B Golden Eagle and Model 421B Executive Commuter introduce the refinements detailed for the Model 402, plus restyled seating for passengers and crew and a new optional radio/telephone system.

A total of 762 Model 421s had been delivered by 31 January 1974.

The description which follows applies to the Model 421B Golden Eagle:

TYPE: Six/eight-seat pressurised light transport.

WINGS: Generally the same as for Model 414, except different aspect ratio and increased wing chord from c/l to nacelles.

FUSELAGE, TAIL UNIT AND LANDING GEAR: As for Model 414.

POWER PLANT: Two 375 hp Continental GTSIO-520-H six-cylinder horizontally-opposed air-cooled geared and turbocharged engines, each driving a McCauley three-blade metal fully-feathering constant-speed propeller. Standard usable fuel capacity is 170 US gallons (643 litres) contained in "Stabila-tip" fixed wingtip fuel tanks and two auxiliary wing tanks. Optional auxiliary wing and wing locker tanks offer a maximum total usable capacity of 248 US gallons (939 litres). Oil capacity 6·5 US gallons (24·6 litres).

ACCOMMODATION: Generally the same as for Model 414, except passenger cabin will accommodate up to six passengers; seats have tapered backs and headrests. The nose compartment can contain a total of 600 lb (272 kg) of baggage and avionics, and two wing lockers an additional 200 lb (91 kg) each, plus 500 lb (226 kg) in the rear cabin area, making a total capacity of 1,500 lb (680 kg).

SYSTEMS, ELECTRONICS AND EQUIPMENT: Generally as for Model 414, except cabin pressurisation system max differential 5·0 lb/sq in (0·35 kg/cm²).

DIMENSIONS, EXTERNAL:
As for Model 414, except:
Wing span over tip-tanks 41 ft 10¼ in (12·76 m)
Wing chord at root 5 ft 9·86 in (1·77 m)
Wing chord at tip 3 ft 9·6 in (1·16 m)
Wing aspect ratio 7·37
Length overall 36 ft 1 in (11·00 m)
Wheel track 16 ft 11 in (5·16 m)
Propeller diameter 7 ft 6 in (2·29 m)

AREA:
Wings, gross 211·65 sq ft (19·66 m²)

WEIGHTS AND LOADINGS:
Weight empty (approx) 4,428 lb (2,008 kg)
Max T-O weight 7,450 lb (3,379 kg)
Max landing weight 7,200 lb (3,266 kg)
Max wing loading 35·20 lb/sq ft (171·9 kg/m²)
Max power loading 9·93 lb/hp (4·50 kg/hp)

PERFORMANCE (at max T-O weight, unless specified otherwise):
Max level speed at S/L 206 knots (237 mph; 381 km/h)
Max level speed at 18,000 ft (5,485 m) 245 knots (282 mph; 454 km/h)
Max cruising speed, 75% power at 25,000 ft (7,620 m) 234 knots (270 mph; 435 km/h)
Max rate of climb at S/L 1,850 ft (564 m)/min
Rate of climb at S/L, one engine out 305 ft (93 m)/min
Service ceiling 31,100 ft (9,480 m)
Service ceiling, one engine out 13,000 ft (3,960 m)
T-O run 1,977 ft (603 m)
T-O to 50 ft (15 m) 2,507 ft (764 m)
Landing from 50 ft (15 m) at max landing weight 2,178 ft (664 m)
Landing run at max landing weight 720 ft (219 m)
Range, 75% power at 10,000 ft (3,050 m), no reserve:
1,020 lb (463 kg) usable fuel 800 nm (922 miles; 1,483 km)
1,176 lb (533 kg) usable fuel 923 nm (1,063 miles; 1,710 km)
1,488 lb (675 kg) usable fuel 1,167 nm (1,344 miles; 2,163 km)
Range, 75% power at 25,000 ft (7,620 m), no reserve:
1,020 lb (463 kg) usable fuel 918 nm (1,057 miles; 1,701 km)
1,176 lb (533 kg) usable fuel 1,058 nm (1,219 miles; 1,961 km)
1,488 lb (675 kg) usable fuel 1,339 nm (1,542 miles; 2,481 km)
Max range, at 10,000 ft (3,050 m), no reserve:
1,020 lb (463 kg) usable fuel 956 nm (1,101 miles; 1,772 km)
1,176 lb (533 kg) usable fuel 1,102 nm (1,269 miles; 2,042 km)
1,488 lb (675 kg) usable fuel 1,394 nm (1,606 miles; 2,584 km)
Max range, at 25,000 ft (7,620 m), no reserve:
1,020 lb (463 kg) usable fuel 1,021 nm (1,176 miles; 1,892 km)
1,176 lb (533 kg) usable fuel 1,177 nm (1,356 miles; 2,182 km)
1,488 lb (675 kg) usable fuel 1,490 nm (1,716 miles; 2,761 km)

CESSNA CITATION 500 SERIES

On 7 October 1968 Cessna announced that it was developing a new eight-seat pressurised executive turbofan aircraft named Fanjet 500, which would be able to operate from most airfields used by light and medium twin-engined aircraft.

After the first flight of the prototype, on 15 September 1969, it was announced that the aircraft's name had been changed to Citation. Subsequently, the gross weight was increased from 9,500 lb (4,310 kg) to 10,350 lb (4,695 kg) and several other changes were made. These included a lengthened front fuselage, movement of the engine nacelles further aft, larger vertical tail, and resiting of, and introduction of dihedral on, the tailplane.

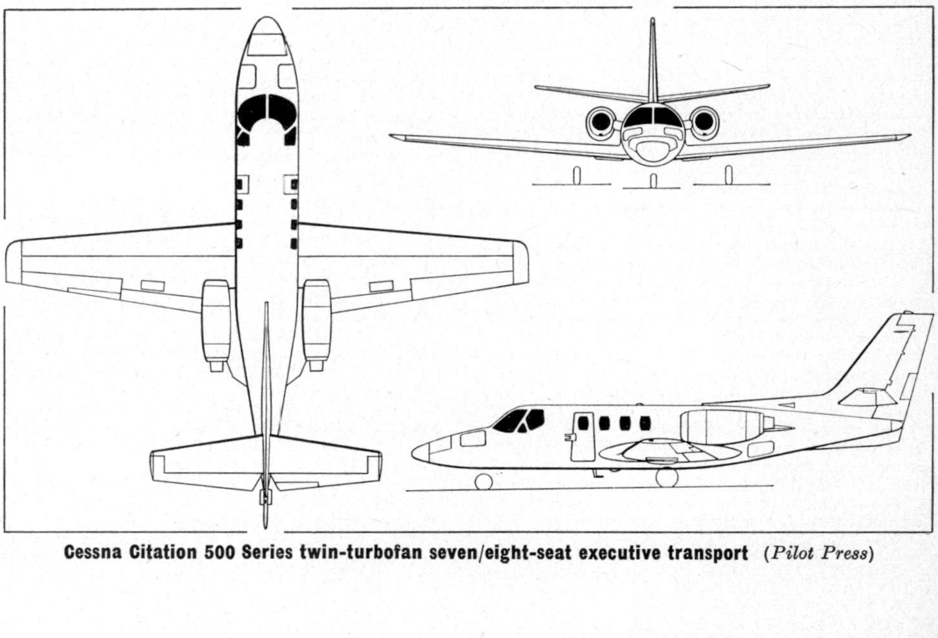

Cessna Citation 500 Series twin-turbofan seven/eight-seat executive transport (*Pilot Press*)

The second Citation flew on 23 January 1970, and by mid-February 1971 the two prototypes had accumulated almost 800 hours of flight time in nearly 600 flights. Two further airframes were built for cyclic and static testing, and by 11 February 1971 all major structural tests had been accepted by the FAA.

On 1 July 1971 Cessna announced that the first production Citation 0001 (N502CC) had recently made its first flight. Final FAA certification under FAR Part 25 was awarded on 9 September 1971.

The Citation is designed to fly from runways as little as 2,500 ft (762 m) in length, and is able also to fly into and out of many unpaved airfields which are not suitable for other commercial jet aircraft. Official tests have shown that the Citation has noise levels at take-off, sideline and approach which are at least 15 EPNdB below the allowable values specified by the FAA's FAR Part 36 noise certification requirements. The Citation is offered on a direct company-to-customer basis in the basic standard configuration or as a complete business aircraft package, including factory-installed interior and avionics, ground and flight training, and one year of computerised maintenance service. Cessna states that factory installation of interior and avionics allows greater payload and also ensures that proper attention is given to the weight distribution of installed equipment.

In February 1972 the Citation was certificated at a maximum T-O weight of 10,850 lb (4,921 kg), and it was subsequently announced, on 30 June 1972, that beginning with production aircraft No. 71, the certificated max ramp weight would be 11,650 lb (5,284 kg), with a max T-O weight of 11,500 lb (5,215 kg). It was anticipated that certification would be granted in March 1973, following which Cessna would make available a modification kit to provide the new gross weight capability for production aircraft prior to No. 71.

A total of 52 Citations were delivered during 1972, the first full year of production. Production was stepped up in 1973 and a total of 136 aircraft had been delivered by 31 January 1974.

TYPE: Twin-turbofan executive transport.

WINGS: Cantilever low-wing monoplane without sweepback. Wing section at c/l NACA 23014 (modified), at wing station 247·95 NACA 23012. Incidence at c/l 2° 30′, at wing station 247·95 —0° 30′. Dihedral 4°. All-metal fail-safe structure with two primary spars, an auxiliary spar, three fuselage attachment points and conventional ribs and stringers. Manually-operated ailerons, with manual trim on port aileron. Electrically-operated single-slotted trailing-edge flaps. Hydraulically-operated aerodynamic speed brakes.

FUSELAGE: All-metal pressurised structure of circular section. Fail-safe design, providing multiple load paths.

TAIL UNIT: Cantilever all-metal structure. Horizontal surfaces have dihedral of 9°. Large dorsal fin and smaller ventral fin. Manually-operated control surfaces. Electric elevator trim with manual override; manual rudder trim.

LANDING GEAR: Hydraulically-retractable tricycle type with single wheel on each unit. Main units retract inward into the wing, nose gear forward into fuselage nose. Free-fall and pneumatic emergency extension systems. Goodyear main wheels and tyres of 16 in diameter, pressure 79 lb/sq in (5·5 kg/cm²), on aircraft Serial No. 0001-0050; aircraft subsequent to Serial No. 0050 have 20 in diameter main-wheel tyres, pressure 90 lb/sq in (6·3 kg/cm²). Steerable nosewheel with Goodyear wheel and tyre of 20 in diameter, pressure 120 lb/sq in (8·4 kg/cm²). Goodyear hydraulic brakes. Parking brake and pneumatic emergency brake system. Skid warning system optional.

POWER PLANT: Two Pratt & Whitney JT15D-1 turbofan engines, each rated at 2,200 lb (998 kg) st for take-off, mounted in pods on each side of rear fuselage. Integral fuel tanks in wings, with capacity of 3,645 lb (1,653 kg).

ACCOMMODATION: Crew of two on separate flight deck. Fully-carpeted main cabin equipped with two individual forward-facing seats aft, one single forward-facing seat centre port, one single aft-facing seat centre starboard and a fifth aft-facing corner lounge chair at front of cabin on starboard side, all with headrests. Toilet compartment and main baggage area at rear of cabin. Refreshment unit at front of cabin. Second baggage area in nose. Cabin is pressurised, heated and ventilated. Individual reading lights and air inlets for each passenger. Drop-out constant-flow oxygen system for emergency use. Plug-type door with integral airstair at front on port side and one emergency exit on starboard side. Doors on each side of nose baggage compartment. Tinted windows, each with curtains. Optional eight-seat layout for crew of two and six passengers, executive table, flush toilet replacing standard toilet, electric razor socket and 110V converter and choice of interior trims.

SYSTEMS: Pressurisation system supplied with engine bleed air, max pressure differential 7·6 lb/sq in (0·53 kg/cm²). Hydraulic system, pressure 1,500 lb/sq in (105 kg/cm²), with two pumps to operate landing gear and speed brakes. Electrical system supplied by two 400A 28V DC starter/generators, with two 600VA inverters and 24V 39Ah nickel-cadmium battery. Oxygen system of 22 cu ft (0·62 m³) capacity includes two crew demand masks and five drop-out constant-flow masks for passengers.

ELECTRONICS AND EQUIPMENT: Standard avionics equipment included in the fully-equipped standard Citation comprises Bendix FGS-70 autopilot/flight director; King KDF-800 ADF; dual RCA AVC-110 VHF transceivers; dual RCA AVN-220 VHF nav receivers, marker beacon and glideslope; dual RCA AVI-200 RMI; dual RCA AVA-310 audio amplifier; Bendix CB-70 compass system; Collins PN-101 HSI and compass system; RCA AVQ-21 radar; RCA AVQ-85 DME; RCA AVQ-95 transponder and all related antennae and equipment. Provision for advanced instrumentation and avionics to customer's specification. Standard equipment includes automatic engine start system; engine fire warning and extinguishing systems; inlet anti-icing; birdproof windscreen with de-fog system; windscreen anti-icing; gust locks; stall warning system; two anti-collision beacons; entry light; emergency exit lights; storm lights; instrument standby lights; tail-cone compartment light; "No Smoking, Fasten Seat Belts" sign; wing ice, taxi, navigation and landing lights; external power receptacle; flight deck sunshades; baggage tie-down kit; cabin fire extinguisher; and standard blind-flying instruments. Optional items include high-capacity oxygen system, surface de-icing system, ice detection system, anti-skid warning system, strobe lights, angle-of-attack indicator, engine fan synchroniser, navigation chart case, hat rack/storage shelf, strobe lights, refreshment cabinets, storage drawers, executive tables and flush toilets.

DIMENSIONS, EXTERNAL:

Wing span	43 ft 9 in (13·33 m)
Wing aspect ratio	6·6
Length overall	43 ft 6 in (13·26 m)
Height overall	14 ft 4 in (4·37 m)
Tailplane span	18 ft 10 in (5·74 m)
Wheel track	12 ft 7 in (3·84 m)
Wheelbase	15 ft 8 in (4·78 m)
Cabin door (port):	
Height	4 ft 2¾ in (1·29 m)
Width	1 ft 11½ in (0·60 m)
Emergency exit (starboard):	
Height	3 ft 1¼ in (0·95 m)
Width	1 ft 10 in (0·56 m)

DIMENSIONS, INTERNAL:

Cabin:	
Length, front to rear bulkhead	17 ft 6 in (5·33 m)
Max width	4 ft 11 in (1·50 m)
Max height	4 ft 4 in (1·32 m)
Baggage space:	
Cabin	43 cu ft (1·22 m³)
Nose	17 cu ft (0·48 m³)

AREA:

Wings, gross	260 sq ft (24·2 m²)

WEIGHTS AND LOADINGS (subsequent to aircraft Serial No. 70):

Weight empty (including avionics)	6,390 lb (2,898 kg)
Max ramp weight	11,650 lb (5,284 kg)
Max T-O weight	11,500 lb (5,215 kg)
Max landing weight	11,000 lb (4,989 kg)
Max zero-fuel weight	8,400 lb (3,810 kg)
Optional max zero-fuel weight	9,500 lb (4,309 kg)
Wing loading	44·2 lb/sq ft (215·8 kg/m²)
Power loading	2·61 lb/lb st (2·61 kg/kg st)

PERFORMANCE (at max T-O weight, except as detailed otherwise):

Maximum operating speed, S/L to 14,000 ft (4,265 m) 260 knots (299 mph; 481 km/h) CAS

Maximum operating speed, 14,000 to 26,000 ft (4,265 to 7,925 m) 287 knots (330 mph; 531 km/h) CAS

Maximum operating speed above 26,000 ft (7,925 m) Mach 0·7

Cruising speed, ± 3% at max T-O weight, max cruise thrust, ISA at 25,400 ft (7,740 m) 348 knots (400 mph; 644 km/h) TAS

Flap extension speed, at 15° extension 200 knots (230 mph; 370 km/h) CAS

Flap extension speed, at 40° extension 174 knots (200 mph; 322 km/h) CAS

Landing gear operating and extended speed 174 knots (200 mph; 322 km/h) CAS

Stalling speed, in landing configuration at max landing weight 82 knots (94 mph; 152 km/h)

Max certificated altitude 35,000 ft (10,670 m)

Min ground turning radius 56 ft 10¾ in (17·34 m)

Balanced field length, FAR 25, ± 5% at S/L, ISA at max T-O weight 3,275 ft (998 m)

Landing field length, FAR 25, ± 5% at S/L, ISA at landing weight of 8,100 lb (3,674 kg) 1,860 ft (567 m)

Landing field length from 50 ft (15 m), FAA FAR 25, max landing weight at S/L 2,300 ft (701 m)

Range with crew, five passengers with 30 lb (13·6 kg) baggage per person, maximum cruise thrust at 35,000 ft (10,670 m), allowance for T-O, climb and 45 min reserve, and based on dry empty weight of 6,390 lb (2,898 kg) 1,140 nm (1,312 miles; 2,110 km)

OPERATIONAL NOISE CHARACTERISTICS:

T-O noise level at 3·5 nm (4 miles; 6·5 km) from start of T-O roll 78 EPNdB

Approach noise level at 1 nm (1·15 miles; 1·85 km) from landing threshold on 3° glideslope 88 EPNdB

Sideline noise level at 0·35 nm (0·40 miles; 0·65 km) from runway c/l 87 EPNdB

Cessna Citation 500 Series seven/eight-seat twin-turbofan executive transport (two Pratt & Whitney JT15D-1 turbofan engines) *(Mick West)*

CHRIS TENA

CHRIS TENA AIRCRAFT ASSOCIATION

ADDRESS:
PO Box 1, Hillsboro, Oregon 97123
Telephone: (503) 985-7612

Chris Tena Aircraft has designed a lightweight all-metal single-seat sporting aircraft which is known as the Mini Coupe. Design originated in June 1968, and construction of the first prototype began in July 1970. This aircraft made its first flight in September 1971 and FAA certification in the Experimental category was awarded on 2 June 1972. Kits of components and materials, less engine, are available to amateur constructors. Four aircraft had flown and 20 more were under construction by 1 February 1974.

Chris Tena Mini Coupe lightweight sporting monoplane (1,600 cc Volkswagen engine) built by Jerry Johnson *(Howard Levy)*

CHRIS TENA MINI COUPE

TYPE: Single-seat lightweight sporting aircraft.

WINGS: Cantilever low-wing monoplane. Aerofoil section Clark Y. Thickness/chord ratio 7%. Incidence 0°. Conventional all-metal stressed-skin structure of constant chord. Plain all-metal ailerons. No flaps. No trim tabs.

FUSELAGE: All-metal semi-monocoque structure.

TAIL UNIT: Cantilever all-metal structure with twin endplate fins and rudders of constant chord. Fixed-incidence tailplane. Manually controlled trim tab in centre of elevator.

LANDING GEAR: Non-retractable tricycle type. Shock-absorption on all units depends on use of oversize tyres. Main wheels with tyres size 14 × 6·00-6, pressure 8 lb/sq in (0·56 kg/cm²). Nosewheel tyre size 12 × 6·00-5, pressure 5 lb/sq in (0·35 kg/cm²). Asuze drum and band brakes.

POWER PLANT: One 65 hp modified Volkswagen 1,600 cc motor car engine, driving a Reese-Shores two-blade fixed-pitch wooden propeller. One metal fuel tank in fuselage, immediately aft of firewall, capacity 13 US gallons (49 litres). Refuelling point on fuselage upper surface, forward of windscreen.

ACCOMMODATION: Single seat for pilot in open cockpit. Transparent cockpit canopy optional. Baggage compartment aft of headrest, volume 3 cu ft (0·085 m³).

DIMENSIONS, EXTERNAL:

Wing span	22 ft 4 in (6·81 m)
Wing chord, constant	3 ft 6 in (1·07 m)
Length overall	16 ft 4 in (4·98 m)
Height overall	5 ft 0 in (1·52 m)
Tailplane span	6 ft 0 in (1·83 m)
Wheel track	6 ft 0 in (1·83 m)
Wheelbase	3 ft 2 in (0·97 m)
Propeller diameter	4 ft 6 in (1·37 m)
Propeller ground clearance	10 in (0·25 m)

AREAS:

Wings, gross	78·4 sq ft (7·28 m²)
Ailerons (total)	8 sq ft (0·74 m²)
Fins (total)	3 sq ft (0·28 m²)
Rudders (total)	6 sq ft (0·56 m²)
Tailplane	4·5 sq ft (0·42 m²)
Elevator	6 sq ft (0·56 m²)

WEIGHTS AND LOADINGS:

Weight empty	494 lb (224 kg)
Max T-O weight	825 lb (374 kg)
Max wing loading	10·39 lb/sq ft (50·7 kg/m²)
Max power loading	12·6 lb/hp (5·72 kg/hp)

PERFORMANCE (at max T-O weight with 1,600 cc engine):

Max never-exceed speed	125 knots (143·5 mph; 231 km/h)
Max level speed at 2,000 ft (610 m)	91 knots (105 mph; 169 km/h)
Max cruising speed at 2,000 ft (610 m)	78 knots (90 mph; 145 km/h)
Stalling speed:	
power off	42 knots (48 mph; 78 km/h)
power on	38 knots (43 mph; 70 km/h)
Max rate of climb at S/L	700 ft (213 m)/min
Service ceiling	12,500 ft (3,810 m)
Min ground turning radius	25 ft 0 in (7·62 m)
T-O run	400 ft (122 m)
T-O to 50 ft (15 m)	900 ft (274 m)
Landing from 50 ft (15 m)	900 ft (274 m)
Landing run	500 ft (152 m)
Range with max fuel, 20 min reserve	260 nm (300 miles; 482 km)

COMPCOP

COMPCOP INC

ADDRESS:
PO Box 1267, 435 Stanford Avenue, Redwood City, California 94064
Telephone: (415) 365-6621
PRESIDENT:
Stephen R. Geraghty

Compcop Inc, a manufacturer and supplier of aircraft accessories and materials, has acquired all rights to the manufacture and sale of kits, parts, plans and information packages on the Volkswagen-powered Boon Jr, of which the prototype was designed and built by 76-year-old Art Weilage. The earlier Boon helicopter designed and built by Mr Weilage was described in the 1966-67 *Jane's*.

Design of the Boon Jr began in 1958, but it was not until 1968 that construction of the prototype started, and the first flight came two years later. The slow rate of progress is explained by the designer's concern to create a structure that would be simple for homebuilders, resulting in a bolt-together airframe of light alloy tubing and channel.

Compcop (Weilage) Boon Jr lightweight homebuilt helicopter (97 hp Volkswagen engine)

COMPCOP (WEILAGE) BOON JR

TYPE: Single-seat lightweight homebuilt helicopter.

ROTOR SYSTEM: Two-blade main rotor with built-up bonded blades. A light alloy skin is wrapped around and bonded to a C-section leading-edge spar, the resulting upper and lower skin then being bonded to a thin Vee strip that forms the trailing-edge. Tail rotor of similar construction. Both rotors of teetering type with main rotor controlled through a swashplate. Blades do not fold.

ROTOR DRIVE: Multiple Vee-belt drive. Main rotor rpm 460; tail rotor rpm 3,200.

FUSELAGE: Bolt-together structure of light alloy tube and channel.

LANDING GEAR: Simple skids with no shock-absorption. Ground handling wheels.

POWER PLANT: One 97 hp Volkswagen modified motor car engine. Fuel tank mounted on port side of rotor pylon, capacity 12 US gallons (45·4 litres).

ACCOMMODATION: Single seat in semi-enclosed cockpit.

DIMENSIONS, EXTERNAL:

Diameter of main rotor	22 ft 0 in (6·71 m)
Diameter of tail rotor	3 ft 4 in (1·02 m)
Main rotor blade chord	7½ in (0·19 m)
Tail rotor blade chord	3½ in (0·09 m)
Length overall	18 ft 0 in (5·49 m)
Height overall	7 ft 0 in (2·13 m)
Skid track	5 ft 0 in (1·52 m)

AREAS:

Main rotor disc	379·9 sq ft (35·3 m²)
Tail rotor disc	8·7 sq ft (0·81 m²)

WEIGHTS AND LOADINGS:

Weight empty	544 lb (247 kg)
Max T-O weight	900 lb (408 kg)
Max disc loading	2·36 lb/sq ft (11·52 kg/m²)
Max power loading	9·3 lb/hp (4·22 kg/hp)

PERFORMANCE (at max T-O weight):

Max level speed at S/L	74 knots (85 mph; 137 km/h)
Cruising speed	72 knots (83 mph; 134 km/h)
Econ cruising speed	61 knots (70 mph; 113 km/h)
Service ceiling	approx 12,000 ft (3,660 m)
Range	182 nm (210 miles; 338 km)

CONTINENTAL COPTERS

CONTINENTAL COPTERS, INC

ADDRESS:
PO Box 13284, Cardinal Road, Fort Worth, Texas 76118
Telephone: (817) BU1-2330
PRESIDENT: John L. Scott

Continental Copters has developed and is producing a series of specialised single-seat agricultural conversions of various versions of the Bell Model 47 helicopter, under the name El Tomcat. Design work on the original conversion began in 1959 and the prototype El Tomcat Mk II flew in April of that year, receiving an FAA Supplementary Type Certificate shortly afterwards.

The prototype of the improved El Tomcat Mk III flew for the first time in April 1965. Further refinement of the design produced the El Tomcat Mk IIIA in January 1966; details and a picture of this version can be found in the 1966-67 *Jane's*. It was superseded in 1967 by the El Tomcat Mk IIIB, which introduced a number of improvements and was described in the 1968-69 *Jane's*.

In 1968 Continental Copters produced the El Tomcat Mk IIIC, an improved version of the IIIB with cleaner nose profile, wraparound side windows in the roof of the cabin for rear-quarter visibility, and refuelling capability from either side of the aircraft. Also in 1968 the company delivered its first El Tomcat Mk V, generally similar to the IIIC but with a change in power plant.

The Mk V was succeeded subsequently by the Mk V-A, based on the Model 47G-2, with a 260 hp Lycoming VO-435-A1F engine and a 24V electrical system; and the Mk V-B, with a 265 hp Lycoming VO-435-B1A and 24V electrical system.

Next came the El Tomcat Mk VI, based on the Bell Model 47G-3B with turbocharged engine. Variants are the Mks VI-A and VI-B.

During 1973, deliveries of eight helicopters were made, either complete or in kit form, made up of one Mk IIIC, three Mk V-A, one Mk V-B, two Mk VI-A and one Mk VI-B. Conversions in hand in March 1974 included three Mk V-As and one Mk VI-B. A full Type Certificate for the Mk V-A was awarded by the FAA in May 1973.

In addition, Continental Copters has for some years been producing passenger helicopters conforming to the Bell 47G and G-2 types. These are assembled from spare and/or surplus parts and are listed in the FAA Helicopter Specification H-1. Other helicopters, not included in this list, have been delivered to Latin America.

CONTINENTAL COPTERS EL TOMCAT Mk IIIC and Mk V-B

Each of these versions of the El Tomcat is basically a Bell Model 47G-2 helicopter which has been converted into a specialised single-seat agricultural aircraft. Payload is increased by deletion of unnecessary structure and equipment. In particular, the original cabin is replaced by a simple functional cab for the pilot.

The two versions are generally similar, except for the following details:

El Tomcat Mk IIIC. Powered by either a 200 hp Franklin 6V4-200-C32, 210 hp 6V-335-A or 235 hp 6V-350-A engine. Standard Bell Model 47D-1 fuel system, with a capacity of 29 US gallons (109 litres). Refuelling point at each side of aircraft. Oil capacity 4 US gallons (15 litres). First flown in May 1968.

El Tomcat Mk V-B. Powered by 265 hp Lycoming VO-435-B1A engine. Fuel system as for Mk IIIC. Oil capacity 3 US gallons (11 litres). Has the 24V electrical system of the Bell Model 47G-2.

In the current El Tomcat Mk IIIC and V-B, the windscreen has been further reduced in area and moved closer to the pilot compared with earlier versions. The glassfibre nose has been modified to ensure easy accessibility to all instruments, the battery and other equipment. It provides a flush mounting for two 600W landing lights which are controllable in elevation by the pilot during flight, landing-light switches being mounted on the collective stick, immediately below the throttle. The cabin roof is of glassfibre, lower than on earlier versions of El Tomcat, and incorporates wraparound side windows for rear-quarter visibility. An FAA-approved folding jump-seat has been developed to permit carriage of a flagman to distant work-sites when large fields are being sprayed. Standard equipment includes hydraulic boost controls and pilot's shoulder harness.

El Tomcat has a revised control system. The collective control has been altered to conform to standard collective geometry, but Continental retains ball bearings in the collective jack shaft, instead of brass bushings, to provide smoother operation. A Harley Davidson throttle control is fitted. The flying controls are hydraulically-boosted.

The chemical hoppers now take the form of two streamlined blister tanks which fit flush against the sides of the fuselage immediately aft of the cabin. A fan-driven pump is mounted adjacent to each tank, aft of the spraybar supports. A filtered ventilation system for the cockpit minimises toxic spray ingress during spraying operations. Types of spraygear fitted include the Bell Agmaster, Simplex Lo Profile and special designs developed by customers.

Apart from the changes noted above, the basic structural description of the standard Bell Model 47 applies also to El Tomcat.

DIMENSIONS:

As for standard Bell Model 47G-2

WEIGHTS:

Weight empty, less specialised equipment:	
IIIC	1,200 lb (544 kg)
V-A	1,375 lb (323 kg)
Max T-O weight:	
IIIC, V-A	2,450 lb (1,111 kg)

PERFORMANCE:

As for standard Bell Model 47G-2 except:

Range (with fuel reserve for 30 min):	
IIIC	112 nm (130 miles; 209 km)
V-A	86 nm (100 miles; 160 km)

CONTINENTAL COPTERS EL TOMCAT Mk VI

The original El Tomcat Mk VI was a conversion of the Bell Model 47G-3B, with a turbocharged Lycoming TVO-435 engine, developing 270 hp, and Bell 47-110-250-23 main rotor blades. The increased length of these blades made it necessary to extend the basic Mk V-A centre frame both fore and aft. The extension aft (as on later production Bell 47s) was needed to provide adequate clearance between main and tail rotor blades, and extension forward to compensate for the resulting rearward movement of the CG.

As in the Mk V-A, the battery was accommodated in the nose of the cab. In addition, the engine oil tank was placed in the nose; an airscoop on top of and an outlet on the bottom of the nose were installed to allow ram air to carry away the heat radiated by the tank. The standard El Tomcat in-flight-adjustable landing lights were installed.

Only this prototype of the El Tomcat Mk VI was completed and was supplied to an operator in the Rocky Mountain area for spraying operations at high altitude. FAA certification was not obtained prior to delivery.

The prototype was claimed to be very stable, and flight tests demonstrated its ability to hover directly into the wind with the pilot's hands and feet off the controls.

A prototype of the Mk VI-B, which has a component similarity to the Bell Model 47G-5, was subsequently completed and flown, and was awarded an FAA Supplemental Type Certificate in the Standard Category. The FAA required installation of a compass and altimeter to meet certification standards, and Continental Copters anticipated that instrument panel and windscreen changes would be required on subsequent machines to facilitate installation of these instruments.

The hydraulic reservoir/regulator unit for the Simplex Lo-Profile sprayer system fitted to the Mk VI-B shown in the accompanying illustration has been mounted forward on the port side of the centre frame instead of in the usual rear position. This enables the pilot to see the hydraulic pressure gauge easily and also offsets the normal aft CG condition of the Tomcat.

Empty weight of the El Tomcat Mk VI-B is 1,487 lb (674 kg) and max T-O weight 2,850 lb (1,293 kg). Maximum permissible speed has been limited to 61 knots (70 mph; 113 km/h) to minimise the airspeed calibration test. In other respects the flight envelope of the Mk VI-B is identical to that of the Bell 47G-5.

Conversion kits for the Mk VI-B installation are available, and Continental Copters states that by using the data gained from this programme Supplemental Type Certification of conversions of Bell Model 47G-2A, -3B and -4 helicopters can be carried out with a minimum of FAA testing.

Prototype of Continental Copters El Tomcat Mk VI-B (270 hp Lycoming TVO-435-B1A engine)

COOK

COOK AIRCRAFT CORPORATION

ADDRESS:

Box 1013, Walteria, Torrance, California 90505

Telephone: (213) 325-3222

MANAGER: William J. Gallon

Cook Aircraft Corporation was formed in 1968 to develop and market initially a four-seat light cabin monoplane of which the basic design was produced by the company's original president, the late John Cook.

With many years experience as an aeronautical engineer and pilot, Mr Cook considered there would be a demand for a low-price strongly-built aircraft in this category, and design of what is now known as the JC-1 Challenger began in July 1967. Its structural strength is such that it can be utilised in an aerobatic role with two persons on board.

Four complete airframes have been built to date, one of which was used for static test purposes and finally tested to failure.

The first flying prototype (N21CA) made its first flight in May 1969, but was destroyed in an accident in April 1970, when the test programme was nearing completion. This necessitated construction of the third airframe (N72CA) which was used to continue the certification programme. Its first flight was made on 17 November 1971; but it, too, was destroyed in an accident on 6 January 1972, in which the aircraft's designer, John Cook, was killed.

Since that date a third flying prototype (N123CA) has been completed. Structural changes involve only the addition of dorsal and ventral fin fillets. The aft limit of the CG envelope has also been moved forward, to prevent the kind of trouble experienced with the earlier aircraft. In this form the aircraft first flew on 1 November 1972, and by 12 March 1973 had accumulated 52½ flying hours. The certification programme has been slowed by the need to comply with an FAA FAR 23.572 requirement for fatigue testing of the wing carry-through structure.

Third prototype of the Cook JC-1 Challenger four-seat light cabin monoplane *(Henry Artof)*

Cook Aircraft Corporation was also working on a Formula One racing aircraft during 1973, designed jointly by Mr Cook and J. G. Parker, the company's chief pilot. No details are available except that the aircraft is of all-metal semi-monocoque construction and is expected to be highly competitive.

COOK JC-1 CHALLENGER

TYPE: Four-seat cabin monoplane.

WINGS: Cantilever low-wing monoplane. Wing section NACA 23015. Dihedral 5° from roots. Incidence 3° 15′. No sweepback, except on wing-root leading-edges. Two-spar structure of light alloy. Plain all-metal ailerons. All-metal NACA slotted trailing-edge flaps. All-metal Handley Page automatic leading-edge slats, in two sections on each wing.

Fuselage: Semi-monocoque structure of light alloy.

Tail Unit: Cantilever light alloy structure with swept vertical surfaces. All-moving horizontal surface with anti-servo tab, adjustable for trim. Dorsal fin faired into vertical fin. Small ventral fin.

Landing Gear: Non-retractable tricycle type. Oleo-pneumatic shock-absorbers on all units. Single wheel, size 6·00-6, on each unit, pressure 28 lb/sq in (1·97 kg/cm²). Cleveland hydraulically-operated disc brakes. Reinforced plastics wheel fairings.

Power Plant: One 150 hp Lycoming O-320-E2A four-cylinder horizontally-opposed aircooled engine, driving a Sensenich two-blade fixed-pitch metal propeller. One 20 US gallon (75·5 litre) metal fuel tank in each wing. Total fuel capacity 40 US gallons (151 litres). Refuelling point in upper surface of each wing. Oil capacity 2 US gallons (7·5 litres).

Accommodation: Enclosed cabin seating four persons in pairs. Door, hinged at forward edge, on port side of fuselage standard; door on starboard side optional. Baggage compartment aft of rear seats, capacity 80 lb (36 kg). Cabin heated and ventilated.

Systems: Hydraulic system for brakes only. Electrical system supplied by 60A engine-driven alternator.

Electronics and Equipment: Various communications and navigation systems available, to customer's requirements. Blind-flying instrumentation optional.

Dimensions, external:
- Wing span: 27 ft 0 in (8·23 m)
- Wing chord at root: 5 ft 6 in (1·68 m)
- Wing chord at tip: 4 ft 8 in (1·42 m)
- Wing aspect ratio: 5·7
- Length overall: 22 ft 0 in (6·71 m)
- Height overall: 8 ft 0 in (2·44 m)
- Tailplane span: 8 ft 6 in (2·59 m)
- Wheel track: 10 ft 10 in (3·30 m)
- Wheelbase: 6 ft 0 in (1·83 m)
- Propeller diameter: 6 ft 2 in (1·88 m)
- Propeller ground clearance: 8 in (0·20 m)
- Cabin doors:
  - Height: 2 ft 10 in (0·86 m)
  - Width: 3 ft 3 in (0·99 m)
  - Height to sill: 3 ft 1 in (0·94 m)

Dimensions, internal:
- Cabin: Length: 6 ft 0 in (1·83 m)
  - Max width: 3 ft 5 in (1·04 m)
  - Max height: 3 ft 6 in (1·07 m)

Areas:
- Wings, gross: 131·2 sq ft (12·2 m²)
- Ailerons (total): 13·3 sq ft (1·24 m²)
- Trailing-edge flaps (total): 17·6 sq ft (1·64 m²)
- Leading-edge slats (total): 12·5 sq ft (1·16 m²)
- Fin: 5·6 sq ft (0·52 m²)
- Rudder: 4·0 sq ft (0·37 m²)
- Tailplane, including tab: 24·55 sq ft (2·28 m²)

Weights and Loadings:
- Basic operating weight: 1,180 lb (535 kg)
- Max T-O and landing weight: 2,150 lb (975 kg)
- Max wing loading: 16·5 lb/sq ft (80·6 kg/m²)
- Max power loading: 14·3 lb/hp (6·48 kg/hp)

Performance (at max T-O weight):
- Max never-exceed speed: 160 knots (185 mph; 297 km/h)
- Max level speed: 130 knots (150 mph; 241 km/h)
- Max cruising speed at 5,500 ft (1,675 m): 126 knots (145 mph; 233 km/h)
- Econ cruising speed at 7,000 ft (2,135 m): 109 knots (125 mph; 201 km/h)
- Stalling speed, flaps down: 47 knots (54 mph; 87 km/h)
- Max rate of climb at S/L: 700 ft (213 m)/min
- Service ceiling: 15,000 ft (4,575 m)
- T-O run: 620 ft (189 m)
- T-O to 50 ft (15 m): 1,020 ft (311 m)
- Landing from 50 ft (15 m): 1,020 ft (311 m)
- Landing run: 400 ft (122 m)
- Range with max fuel: 600 nm (691 miles; 1,112 km)

COSMIC

COSMIC AIRCRAFT CORPORATION

Head Office and Works:
1618 Westheimer Drive, Norman, Oklahoma 73069
Telephone: (405) 329-5080

General Manager: E. Robert Heatley

In 1950 Mr Don D. Funk founded the D. D. Funk Aviation Company Inc to manufacture a specialised agricultural aircraft designated F-23. In May 1970 all rights in this aircraft were acquired by Cosmic Aircraft Corporation, which is continuing to produce the F-23.

COSMIC F-23

Two versions of the F-23 are available, differing only in the installed power plant:

F-23A. With 240 hp Continental W-670 seven-cylinder radial aircooled engine.

F-23B. With 275 hp Jacobs R-755 seven-cylinder radial aircooled engine.

Type: Single-seat agricultural aircraft.

Wings: Cantilever low-wing monoplane. Constant-chord wing of all-metal construction, comprising a wide-span centre-section and two interchangeable outer panels. Dihedral on outer panels only. All four leading-edge sections quickly removable and interchangeable, except for minor items. Interchangeable Ceconite-covered ailerons. No flaps.

Fuselage: Welded steel tube structure, designed to absorb shock of impact by progressive collapse. Fuselage sides covered entirely by quickly removable panels.

Tail Unit: Cantilever metal structure. Elevators and rudder Ceconite-covered. Elevators interchangeable. Tailplane halves interchangeable, except for minor items. Wire deflector from tip of fin to cockpit overturn structure.

Landing Gear: Non-retractable tailwheel type. Cantilever main units. Main wheels fitted with nylon-reinforced tyres size 8·50-10. Parking brake.

Power Plant: One radial aircooled engine as detailed in model listings above, driving a two-blade metal propeller. Propeller blade pitch ground-adjustable. Fuel tanks in wings, with total capacity of 47 US gallons (178 litres). Oil capacity: F-23A 4·2 US gallons (16 litres); F-23B 4·4 US gallons (16·5 litres).

Accommodation: Single adjustable seat under large transparent canopy. Seat belts and shoulder harness standard. Overturn structure of 4130 steel tube. No protruding objects in cockpit area. Instrument panel located forward of hopper. Large window which forms starboard side of canopy hinges downward for access. Optional wire deflector for windscreen.

Cosmic F-23 single-seat agricultural aircraft

Equipment: Epoxy glassfibre hopper in fuselage, forward of cockpit, with capacity of 215 US gallons (814 litres). Transland Boommaster pump standard. Hopper throat, size 2 ft 1 in × 9½ in (63·5 cm × 24 cm), fits all Transland equipment and most other types of spraygear. Provision for quick change from liquids to solids and vice versa. Spraybooms enclosed in wing leading-edges.

Dimensions, external:
- Wing span: 40 ft 6 in (12·34 m)
- Wing chord, constant: 7 ft 0 in (2·13 m)
- Length overall:
  - F-23A: 26 ft 4 in (8·03 m)
  - F-23B: 27 ft 2 in (8·28 m)
- Height overall: 8 ft 6 in (2·59 m)

Areas:
- Wings, gross: 280 sq ft (26·01 m²)
- Ailerons (total): 35·8 sq ft (3·33 m²)
- Fin: 6·2 sq ft (0·58 m²)
- Rudder: 13·2 sq ft (1·23 m²)
- Tailplane: 26·9 sq ft (2·50 m²)
- Elevators: 13·5 sq ft (1·25 m²)

Weights and Loadings:
- Weight empty, sprayer:
  - F-23A: 2,250 lb (1,020 kg)
  - F-23B: 2,280 lb (1,035 kg)
- Licenced hopper load: 1,500 lb (680 kg)
- Max T-O weight: 4,300 lb (1,950 kg)
- Max wing loading: 15 lb/sq ft (73·2 kg/m²)
- Max power loading:
  - F-23A: 17·6 lb/hp (7·98 kg/hp)
  - F-23B: 15·6 lb/hp (7·08 kg/hp)

Performance (at max T-O weight, except as indicated):
- Max never-exceed speed:
  - F-23A/B: 122 knots (140 mph; 225 km/h)
- Max level speed at S/L:
  - F-23A: 100 knots (115 mph; 185 km/h)
  - F-23B: 109 knots (125 mph; 201 km/h)
- Cruising speed at S/L:
  - F-23A: 83 knots (95 mph; 153 km/h)
  - F-23B: 87 knots (100 mph; 161 km/h)
- Working speed:
  - F-23A: 70-83 knots (80-95 mph; 129-153 km/h)
  - F-23B: 70-87 knots (80-100 mph; 129-161 km/h)
- Stalling speed, power on:
  - F-23A/B: 49·5 knots (57 mph; 92 km/h)
- Stalling speed, empty:
  - F-23A/B: 39 knots (45 mph; 73 km/h)
- Max rate of climb at S/L:
  - F-23A: 350 ft (107 m)/min
  - F-23B: 515 ft (157 m)/min
- Service ceiling, empty:
  - F-23A: 16,500 ft (5,030 m)
  - F-23B: 19,000 ft (5,800 m)
- T-O run:
  - F-23A: 925 ft (282 m)
  - F-23B: 850 ft (260 m)
- Range with max fuel, at 75% power:
  - F-23A: 304 nm (350 miles; 560 km)
  - F-23B: 261 nm (300 miles; 480 km)

CUNNING

CUNNING AIRCRAFT

Address:
585 North Main, Clearfield, Utah
Telephone: (801) 825-8347

Mr Grant S. Cunning has built and flown a lightplane which is generally similar to the Evans VP-1, except for having a tricycle landing gear, and is designated Cunning Volksplane. Design of the aircraft began on 3 July 1970, construction beginning two months later. The first flight, and FAA certification in the Experimental category, were both achieved in November 1971.

CUNNING VOLKSPLANE

Type: Single-seat lightweight sporting aircraft.

Wings: Braced low-wing monoplane with two bracing struts each side. Wing section NACA 4412. Dihedral 7°. Conventional two-spar structure with spruce spars and mahogany plywood ribs, Ceconite covered. Ailerons constructed of marine plywood with Ceconite covering. No flaps. No trim tabs.

Fuselage: Truss structure of wood with spruce longerons and side skins of mahogany.

Tail Unit: Cantilever structure of wood with Ceconite covering. No fixed fin. All-moving tailplane. Ground-adjustable trim tab on rudder. Adjustable trim tab in tailplane.

Landing Gear: Non-retractable tricycle type. Main-gear legs, which are wire-braced, have no shock-absorption. Shock-absorption of nosewheel strut by rubber in compression. Mainwheel and nosewheel tyres all size 5·00-5, pressure 28 lb/sq in (1·97 kg/cm²). Industrial Dynamics disc-type hydraulic brakes. Nosewheel steerable.

Power Plant: One 65 hp Continental A65-8 four-cylinder horizontally-opposed aircooled engine, driving a Flottorp type 70-A-50 two-blade wooden fixed-pitch propeller. One fuel tank in forward fuselage, immediately aft of firewall, capacity 8·5 US gallons (32 litres), and one in fuselage aft of cockpit, capacity 2 US gallons (7·5 litres). Total usable capacity 10·5 US gallons (39·5 litres). Refuelling points on upper surface of fuselage above fuel tanks. Oil capacity 1·25 US gallons (4·75 litres).

Accommodation: Pilot only in open cockpit. Space for 20 lb (9 kg) baggage in compartment aft of pilot's seat if rear fuselage fuel tank is not filled.

SYSTEM: Hydraulic system for brakes only.
ELECTRONICS: Battery-powered Alpha 200 nav/com transceiver.
DIMENSIONS, EXTERNAL:
Wing span 24 ft 0 in (7·32 m)
Wing chord (constant) 4 ft 2 in (1·27 m)
Length overall 19 ft 8½ in (6·01 m)
Height overall 7 ft 3 in (2·21 m)
Tailplane span 7 ft 0 in (2·13 m)
Wheel track 5 ft 0 in (1·52 m)
Wheelbase 4 ft 3½ in (1·31 m)
Propeller diameter 5 ft 10 in (1·78 m)
Propeller ground clearance 7¼ in (0·18 m)
AREAS:
Wings, gross 105 sq ft (9·75 m²)
Ailerons (total) 10·8 sq ft (1·00 m²)
Vertical tail surface 8·45 sq ft (0·79 m²)
Tailplane, including tab 15·16 sq ft (1·41 m²)
WEIGHTS AND LOADINGS:
Weight empty 614 lb (278 kg)
Max T-O weight 950 lb (431 kg)
Max wing loading 9·47 lb/sq ft (46·24 kg/m²)
Max power loading 14·6 lb/hp (6·62 kg/hp)
PERFORMANCE (at max T-O weight):
Max never-exceed speed 104 knots (120 mph; 193 km/h)
Max level speed at 7,000 ft (2,135 m) 77 knots (89 mph; 143 km/h)
Max cruising speed at 10,500 ft (3,200 m) 82 knots (95 mph; 153 km/h)
Econ cruising speed at 7,000 ft (2,135 m) 65 knots (75 mph; 121 km/h)

Cunning Volksplane light sporting aircraft (65 hp Continental A65-8 engine)

Stalling speed at 5,300 ft (1,615 m) 42 knots (48 mph; 78 km/h)
Service ceiling 10,500 ft (3,200 m)
T-O run at 5,300 ft (1,615 m) airfield altitude 300 ft (91 m)
T-O to 50 ft (15 m) at 5,300 ft (1,615 m) airfield altitude 750 ft (229 m)
Landing from 50 ft (15 m) 1,100 ft (335 m)
Landing run 600 ft (183 m)
Range with max fuel at max level speed 192 nm (222 miles; 357 km)

CVJETKOVIC

ANTON CVJETKOVIC

ADDRESS:
624 Fowler Avenue, PO Box 323, Newbury Park, California 91320

When living in Yugoslavia, Mr Anton Cvjetkovic designed a single-seat light aeroplane designated CA-51 and powered by a modified Volkswagen engine. A prototype was built by members of Zagreb Aeroclub in 1951, and was followed by five more aircraft of the same type (details and photograph in 1967-68 *Jane's*).

After moving to the United States, Mr Cvjetkovic began work, in May 1960, on the design of an improved light aircraft which he designated CA-61. Construction of a prototype was started in February 1961 and it flew for the first time in August 1962. Plans of both single-seat and two-seat all-wood versions are available to amateur constructors, together with plans of a two-seat aircraft designated CA-65, of which the prototype was completed in 1965. Since then Mr Cvjetkovic has also completed the design of an all-metal version of the CA-65, which is designated CA-65A, and plans of this are available.

By March 1974 a total of approximately 300 sets of plans for these aircraft had been sold, and completed aircraft were flying in Canada, South Africa and the United States.

CVJETKOVIC CA-61/-61R MINI ACE

The CA-61 can be built as a single-seat or side-by-side two-seat light aircraft, with any Continental engine of between 65 and 85 hp. Alternatively, the single-seater can be fitted with a modified Volkswagen engine. Construction takes less than 1,000 hours.

The design was modified during 1973 to allow for installation of retractable landing gear; when constructed in this form, the aircraft is designated **CA-61R**.

The following details refer specifically to the single-seat CA-61 prototype:

TYPE: Single-seat light aircraft.

WINGS: Cantilever low-wing monoplane. Wing section NACA 4415. Dihedral 3°. No incidence. Structure consists of two spruce spars, each built in one piece, built-up spruce girder-type ribs and plywood-covered leading-edge torsion box, with fabric covering overall. Fabric-covered spruce ailerons. No flaps.

FUSELAGE: Conventional wooden structure of basic square section, plywood-covered.

TAIL UNIT: Cantilever wooden structure, covered with plywood. Fixed-incidence tailplane. Trim tab in elevator.

LANDING GEAR: Non-retractable tailwheel type. Cantilever main legs, with helical spring shock-absorption. Goodyear main wheels and tyres, size 5·00-5 Type III, and Model L5 brakes. Steerable tailwheel.

POWER PLANT: One 65 hp Continental A65 four-cylinder horizontally-opposed aircooled engine, driving a Flottorp 63-55 two-blade fixed-pitch propeller. Fuel in two steel tanks in fuselage, with capacities of 12 US gallons (45 litres) and 5 US gallons (19 litres) respectively. Total fuel capacity 17 US gallons (64 litres). Oil capacity 1·25 US gallons (4·5 litres).

ACCOMMODATION: Single seat in enclosed cockpit.

ELECTRONICS AND EQUIPMENT: Prototype fitted with Nova Star radio and omni.

DIMENSIONS, EXTERNAL:
Wing span 27 ft 6 in (8·38 m)
Wing chord (constant) 4 ft 7 in (1·40 m)
Wing aspect ratio 6·0
Length overall 18 ft 11 in (5·77 m)

Cvjetkovic CA-61R, with retractable landing gear and neatly-cowled engine installation

Height overall (in flying position) 6 ft 10 in (2·08 m)
Wheel track:
Single-seat 8 ft 2 in (2·49 m)
Two-seat 8 ft 7 in (2·62 m)
AREA:
Wings, gross 126·5 sq ft (11·75 m²)
WEIGHTS AND LOADINGS:
Weight empty:
Single-seat 606 lb (275 kg)
Two-seat 800 lb (363 kg)
Max T-O weight:
Single-seat 950 lb (430 kg)
Two-seat 1,300 lb (590 kg)
Max wing loading:
Single-seat 7·5 lb/sq ft (36·6 kg/m²)
Two-seat 10·25 lb/sq ft (50·0 kg/m²)
PERFORMANCE:
Max level speed at S/L 104 knots (120 mph; 193 km/h)
Normal cruising speed 87 knots (100 mph; 161 km/h)
Min flying speed:
Single-seat 37 knots (42 mph; 67·5 km/h)
Two-seat 44 knots (50 mph; 80·5 km/h)
Range with max fuel:
Single-seat 369 nm (425 miles; 685 km)
Two-seat 321 nm (370 miles; 595 km)

CVJETKOVIC CA-65

Design work on this side-by-side two-seat light aircraft was started in September 1963. Construction of the prototype began in March 1964 and it flew for the first time in July 1965. Plans are available to other constructors.

The CA-65 closely resembles the CA-61 in general appearance, but has a more powerful engine and retractable landing gear. A folding-wing version was introduced during 1967.

TYPE: Two-seat light aircraft.

WINGS: Cantilever low-wing monoplane. Modified NACA 4415 wing section. Dihedral 0° on

Cvjetkovic CA-65 two-seat light aircraft (125 hp Lycoming O-290-G engine)

centre-section, 3° on outer wings. Structure consists of two spruce spars, each built in one piece, and built-up spruce girder-type ribs, completely plywood-covered. Fabric-covered spruce ailerons. On the folding-wing version, the outer wings fold upward from their junction with the centre-section.

FUSELAGE: Conventional wooden structure of basically square section, plywood-covered. Manually-operated landing flap under fuselage.

TAIL UNIT: Cantilever wooden structure. Fixed surfaces covered with plywood. Elevator and rudder fabric-covered. Fixed-incidence tail-plane.

LANDING GEAR: Mechanically-retractable tail-wheel type. Main wheels retract inward. Goodyear main wheels and tyres, size 5·00-5 Type III. Goodyear type L5 brakes. Steerable tailwheel.

POWER PLANT: One 125 hp Lycoming O-290-G four-cylinder horizontally-opposed aircooled engine, driving a Sensenich 66-68 two-blade fixed-pitch propeller. Two aluminium fuel tanks in fuselage, each with capacity of 14 US gallons (53 litres). Total fuel capacity 28 US gallons (106 litres).

ACCOMMODATION: Two seats side by side in enclosed cockpit, with dual controls; although hydraulic brakes can be operated only by the pilot. Forward-opening canopy.

RADIO: Bayside BEI-990 radio fitted in prototype.

DIMENSIONS, EXTERNAL:
- Wing span: 25 ft 0 in (7·62 m)
- Width, wings folded: 9 ft 0 in (2·74 m)
- Length overall: 19 ft 0 in (5·79 m)
- Height overall (in flying position): 7 ft 4 in (2·24 m)
- Height, wings folded: 10 ft 0 in (3·05 m)
- Wheel track: 6 ft 11 in (2·11 m)
- Propeller diameter: 5 ft 8 in (1·73 m)

AREA:
- Wings, gross: 108 sq ft (10·03 m²)

WEIGHTS AND LOADINGS:
- Weight empty: 900 lb (408 kg)
- Max T-O weight: 1,500 lb (680 kg)
- Max wing loading: 13·9 lb/sq ft (67·9 kg/m²)
- Max power loading: 12·0 lb/hp (5·44 kg/hp)

PERFORMANCE (at max T-O weight):
- Max level speed: 139 knots (160 mph; 257 km/h)
- Normal cruising speed: 117 knots (135 mph; 217 km/h)
- Stalling speed: 48 knots (55 mph; 89 km/h)
- Max rate of climb at S/L: 1,000 ft (305 m)/min
- Service ceiling: 15,000 ft (4,575 m)
- Take-off run: 450 ft (137 m)
- Landing run: 600 ft (183 m)
- Range with max fuel: 434 nm (500 miles; 804 km)

CVJETKOVIC CA-65A

This is essentially similar to the all-wood CA-65; it differs by having a tail unit with a swept vertical surface and is of all-metal construction. It is designed for +9 and −6g ultimate loading.

The general description of the CA-65 applies also to the CA-65A, except in the following details:

WINGS: The wing structure consists of a single main spar and an auxiliary wing spar, with aluminium sheet ribs and skin, riveted throughout. The main wing spar cap is made of extruded and bent-up sheet aluminium angles, tapered towards the tip to produce a wing of uniform bending strength. Ribs are formed from 0·025 in aluminium sheet. Wing skin is of 2024-T3 aluminium alloy sheet.

FUSELAGE: All-metal structure with four aluminium angle longerons and built-up frames. Fuselage skin is of 0·025-0·032 in 2024-T3 aluminium alloy sheet. To simplify formation of the curvature on the upper fuselage, the skins are broken up into small sections of flat panels.

TAIL UNIT: Cantilever all-metal structure, with swept vertical surfaces. Construction similar to that of the wings.

POWER PLANT: The structure is designed to accommodate a Lycoming engine of 108-150 hp.

DIMENSIONS, EXTERNAL: As for Model CA-65 except:
- Wing span: 25 ft 5 in (7·75 m)
- Length overall: 19 ft 8 in (5·99 m)
- Height overall: 7 ft 6 in (2·29 m)

AREA:
- Wings, gross: 109·4 sq ft (10·16 m²)

LOADING:
- Max wing loading: 13·7 lb/sq ft (66·9 kg/m²)

PERFORMANCE (150 hp engine):
- Max level speed: 151 knots (174 mph; 280 km/h)
- Normal cruising speed: 130 knots (150 mph; 241 km/h)
- Stalling speed: 48 knots (55 mph; 89 km/h)
- Max rate of climb at S/L: 1,530 ft (466 m)/min
- Service ceiling: 15,000 ft (4,570 m)
- T-O run: 325 ft (99 m)
- Landing run: 600 ft (183 m)
- Range with max fuel: 460 nm (530 miles; 853 km)

D'APUZZO

NICHOLAS E. D'APUZZO

ADDRESS:
1029 Blue Rock Lane, Blue Bell, Pennsylvania 19422

Telephone: (215) 646-4792

Mr D'Apuzzo, who was formerly employed by the Naval Air Development Center, Warminster, Pennsylvania, as a project manager on specialised projects, retired from the Navy Department during 1973. He retains an association with the Navy on a consultant basis.

He has designed several sporting aircraft for amateur construction, among the best known of which are the Denight Special midget racer, described in the 1962-63 *Jane's*, and the PJ-260 single-seat aerobatic biplane described under the "Parsons-Jocelyn" heading in this edition.

His other designs include the Senior Aero Sport, which is a two-seat version of the PJ-260, and the smaller single-seat Junior Aero Sport.

D'APUZZO D-260 SENIOR AERO SPORT

This is a two-seat dual-control version of the PJ-260 aerobatic biplane described under the "Parsons-Jocelyn" heading in this section.

In February 1974 a total of 26 PJ-260s and Senior Aero Sports were known to have been completed by amateur constructors in the United States, with a further 94 under construction.

At the 1968 EAA International Fly-in at Rockford, Illinois, a Senior Aero Sport (N4030Q) built by Mr Tom Luckey of Ambler, Pennsylvania, was selected as the "Grand Champion" homebuilt, and a similar aircraft (N112JF), built by Mr Jim Frankenfield of Hatfield, Pennsylvania, was runner-up.

There are five basic versions of the Senior Aero Sport, as follows:

D-260(1). With Lycoming O-435 series engine.

D-260(2). With Continental O-470/E-185 series engine. Construction of prototype started by Mr C. L. McHolland of Sheridan, Wyoming, in May 1962 and first flight made on 17 July 1965, with a 225 hp E-185 (modified) engine, driving an Aeromatic F-200H-O-85 propeller. Fuel in one 16 US gallon (60·5 litre) tank in fuselage and one 21 US gallon (79·5 litre) streamlined external tank under fuselage.

D-260(3). With Lycoming GO-435 series engine. Construction of prototype started by Mr G. A. Shallbetter of Minneapolis in April 1961 and first flight made on 17 July 1965, with a 260 hp GO-435-C2 engine, driving a Hartzell controllable-pitch propeller of 7 ft 6 in (2·29 m) diameter. Four fuel tanks in fuselage, with total capacity of 36 US gallons (136 litres). Second D-260(3), completed by Mr Alfred Fessenden of Lafayette, New York, is fitted with a Hartzell constant-speed propeller.

D-260(4). With Ranger 6-440-C six-cylinder inverted aircooled engine.

D-260(5). With 300 hp Lycoming R-680-E3 engine. Prototype built by Mr Henry Neys of Lake Stevens, Washington.

The general description of the PJ-260 applies equally to all five versions of the Senior Aero Sport, with the following exceptions:

TYPE: Two-seat sporting biplane.

LANDING GEAR: Non-retractable tailwheel type. Cantilever spring steel main units. Goodyear 6·00-6 main wheels and tyres, pressure 20 lb/sq in (1·41 kg/cm²). Goodyear disc brakes.

D'Apuzzo D-260(2) Senior Aero Sport built by Mr H. Calloway of Atlanta, Georgia

POWER PLANT: One six-cylinder horizontally-opposed aircooled engine. Details under individual model listings above.

ACCOMMODATION: Two seats in tandem in open cockpits. Baggage space behind headrest.

SYSTEM: 12V electrical system, with optional starter and navigation lights.

ELECTRONICS: Prototypes fitted with two-way radio and omni.

DIMENSIONS, EXTERNAL:
Same as PJ-260, except:
- Wheel track: 8 ft 5 in (2·57 m)
- Wheelbase: 15 ft 9 in (4·80 m)

AREAS:
Same as PJ-260, except:
- Wings, gross: 185 sq ft (17·2 m²)

WEIGHTS AND LOADINGS:
- Normal T-O weight:
  - D-260 (2): 2,050 lb (930 kg)
  - D-260 (3): 2,150 lb (975 kg)
- Max T-O and landing weight:
  - All versions: 2,150 lb (975 kg)
- Max wing loading:
  - All versions: 11·5 lb/sq ft (56·1 kg/m²)
- Max power loading:
  - D-260 (2): 9·77 lb/hp (4·43 kg/hp)
  - D-260 (3): 9·00 lb/hp (4·08 kg/hp)

PERFORMANCE (D-260 (3) at max T-O weight. D-260 (2) comparable):
- Max never-exceed speed: 165 knots (190 mph; 305 km/h)
- Max level speed at 7,000 ft (2,135 m): 135 knots (155 mph; 250 km/h)
- Max cruising speed at 7,000 ft (2,135 m): 122 knots (140 mph; 225 km/h)
- Econ cruising speed at 7,000 ft (2,135 m): 113 knots (130 mph; 209 km/h)
- Stalling speed: 48 knots (55 mph; 89 km/h)
- Max rate of climb at S/L: 2,000 ft (610 m)/min
- Service ceiling: 20,000 ft (6,100 m)
- T-O run: 400 ft (122 m)
- T-O to 50 ft (15 m): 700 ft (213 m)
- Landing from 50 ft (15 m): 900 ft (275 m)
- Landing run: 600 ft (183 m)
- Range with max fuel and max payload: 434 nm (500 miles; 805 km)

D'APUZZO D-200 JUNIOR AERO SPORT

The Junior Aero Sport is a smaller single-seat version of the PJ-260. Its design was started in September 1963 and construction of two prototypes began in September 1964. The first of these was almost completed in early 1973 when the building in which it was being constructed was destroyed by fire. Fortunately the D-200 prototype was not damaged severely, and it was expected to make its first flight in late 1974.

TYPE: Single-seat sporting biplane.

WINGS: Conventional braced biplane type. Wing section NACA M-12 (mod). Dihedral 0° on top wing, 0° 30′ on bottom wing. Incidence 2° on both wings. No sweepback. Spruce spars, wooden ribs and light alloy nose skin, with fabric covering. Fabric-covered aluminium alloy ailerons. No flaps.

FUSELAGE: Welded steel tube structure, with aluminium alloy panels forward of cockpit and fabric covering aft.

TAIL UNIT: Wire-braced welded steel tube struc-

Artist's impression of D'Apuzzo Junior Aero Sport

ture with fabric covering. Fixed-incidence tailplane. Trim tab in each elevator.
LANDING GEAR: Non-retractable tailwheel type. Cantilever spring steel main legs. Goodrich-Hayes main wheels and tyres, size 5·00-4, pressure 20 lb/sq in (1·40 kg/cm²). Goodrich-Hayes brakes.
POWER PLANT: One 180 hp Lycoming O-360 four-cylinder horizontally-opposed aircooled engine, driving a Hartzell two-blade constant-speed metal propeller. Fuel tank in fuselage, capacity 20 US gallons (75 litres). Oil capacity 2 US gallons (7·5 litres).
ACCOMMODATION: Single seat in open cockpit.
DIMENSIONS, EXTERNAL:

Wing span (both)	21 ft 8 in (6·60 m)
Wing chord (constant)	3 ft 4 in (1·02 m)
Wing aspect ratio	4·2
Length overall	18 ft 3 in (5·56 m)
Height overall	6 ft 4 in (1·93 m)
Tailplane span	7 ft 2 in (2·18 m)
Wheel track	5 ft 0 in (1·52 m)
Wheelbase	13 ft 6 in (4·11 m)

AREAS:

Wings, gross	140 sq ft (13·00 m²)
Ailerons (total)	16·5 sq ft (1·53 m²)
Fin	5·0 sq ft (0·46 m²)
Rudder	5·0 sq ft (0·46 m²)

WEIGHTS:

Weight empty	840 lb (381 kg)
Max T-O and landing weight	1,275 lb (578 kg)

PERFORMANCE (estimated, at max T-O weight):

Max never-exceed speed	191 knots (220 mph; 354 km/h)
Max level speed at 7,000 ft (2,135 m)	139 knots (160 mph; 257 km/h)
Max cruising speed at 7,000 ft (2,135 m)	122 knots (140 mph; 225 km/h)
Stalling speed	48 knots (55 mph; 89 km/h)
Max rate of climb at S/L	2,500 ft (762 m)/min
Service ceiling	20,000 ft (6,100 m)
T-O run	400 ft (122 m)
T-O to 50 ft (15 m)	650 ft (198 m)
Landing from 50 ft (15 m)	850 ft (260 m)
Landing run	550 ft (168 m)
Range with max fuel	260 nm (300 miles; 480 km)

DAVIS

LEEON D. DAVIS

ADDRESS:
PO Box 1006, McCamey, Texas 79752

Mr Davis designed and built his first light aircraft, the DA-1A five-seat high-wing monoplane, fourteen years ago. Details can be found in the 1960-61 *Jane's*.

He completed subsequently a prototype of a two-seat low-wing monoplane designated DA-2A, of which plans are available to other builders.

Mr Davis advised in February 1974 that he had formed a group to build a new aircraft, and that details were to be released later in the year. Lack of time has prevented completion of the DA-3, a four-seat development of the DA-2A of which details appeared in the 1973-74 *Jane's*.

DAVIS DA-2A

This side-by-side two-seat light aircraft was flown for the first time on 21 May 1966, after 18 months of spare-time work and an expenditure of $1,600. At the Experimental Aircraft Association's annual Fly-in a few weeks later, it gained the awards for both the most outstanding design and the most popular aircraft. Plans are available to other amateur constructors.

By February 1974 the prototype had flown a total of 780 hours, and the fourteen DA-2As that were then flying had accumulated approximately 2,500 flying hours. It is believed that about 100 other DA-2As are under construction.

The DA-2A is of simple all-metal construction and has an all-moving Vee-tail (included angle 100°), like Mr Davis's earlier DA-1A. The wings are of constant chord, without flaps. Aspect ratio 4.48. Dihedral is 5°. The non-retractable tricycle landing gear has cantilever spring steel main legs and a steerable nosewheel. Power plant is a 65 hp Continental A65-8 four-cylinder horizontally-opposed aircooled engine; but the DA-2A is stressed for engines of up to 100 hp. Total fuel capacity is 20 US gallons (75 litres) and oil capacity 1 US gallon (3·75 litres).

There is baggage space aft of the side-by-side seats or, alternatively, a child's seat may be located in this position.

Davis DA-2A built by Mr Herbert Spilker of Dundas, Ontario (*Howard Levy*)

The DA-2A shown in the accompanying illustration was built by Mr Herbert Spilker of Dundas, Ontario, and took only seven months to complete at a cost of $4,000. Powered by a 100 hp Continental O-200-A engine, it has an empty weight of 720 lb (327 kg) and max T-O weight of 1,250 lb (567 kg). Max level speed is 126 knots (145 mph; 233 km/h), cruising speed 113 knots (130 mph; 209 km/h), landing speed 61 knots (70 mph; 113 km/h), and max rate of climb at S/L 1,000 ft (305 m)/min.

DIMENSIONS, EXTERNAL:

Wing span	19 ft 2¾ in (5·86 m)
Wing chord (constant)	4 ft 3½ in (1·31 m)
Length overall	17 ft 10¼ in (5·44 m)
Height overall	5 ft 5 in (1·65 m)

DIMENSIONS, INTERNAL:
Cabin:

Length	4 ft 6¾ in (1·49 m)
Max width	3 ft 5 in (1·04 m)
Max height	3 ft 8¾ in (1·14 m)

AREAS:

Wings, gross	82·5 sq ft (7·66 m²)
Tail surfaces (total)	12·75 sq ft (1·18 m²)

WEIGHTS AND LOADINGS:

Weight empty	610 lb (277 kg)
Max T-O weight	1,125 lb (510 kg)
Max wing loading	14·5 lb/sq ft (70·7 kg/m²)
Max power loading	17·3 lb/hp (7·8 kg/hp)

PERFORMANCE (at max T-O weight):

Max level speed at S/L	104 knots (120 mph; 193 km/h)
Cruising speed	100 knots (115 mph; 185 km/h)
Landing speed	54 knots (62 mph; 100 km/h)
Range with max fuel	390 nm (450 miles; 725 km)

DOUGLAS (*see "McDonnell Douglas"*)

DSK

DSK AIRMOTIVE

ADDRESS:
126 Georgia Place, Fort Walton Beach, Florida 32548
Telephone: (904) 243-4160

Mr Richard Killingsworth, a USAF Chief Master Sergeant, designed and built a single-seat sporting aircraft which he designated DSK-1 Hawk. Interest in the design was such that he has formed DSK Airmotive to market plans and partial kits to amateur constructors.

The fuselage structure of the prototype is basically a surplus Air Force/Navy 200 US gallon drop-tank; but Mr Killingsworth's plans provide for alternative bulkhead/stressed-skin construction for builders unable to obtain a suitable drop-tank. In this form the aircraft is designated **DSK-2 Hawkette.**

The Hawk flew for the first time on 26 May 1973 powered by a 65 hp Lycoming engine, but the installation will accept power plants of up to 125 hp. Mr Killingsworth intends to evaluate several different wings on the prototype, with the intention of producing two follow-on designs: the DSK-3 Eagle, a side-by-side two-seat aircraft, and the DSK-4 Hawk II, a tandem two-seat "stretched" version of the DSK-1.

By early February 1974 the prototype DSK-1 had flown for more than 80 hours. Orders for plans then exceeded 300 and seven aircraft were known to be under construction. The description which follows applies to the prototype:

DSK AIRMOTIVE DSK-1 HAWK

TYPE: Single-seat homebuilt sporting aircraft.
WINGS: Cantilever low-wing monoplane. Clark Y section. Thickness/chord ratio 15%. Slight dihedral on outer panels. No incidence. Conventional two-spar structure of 2024T-3 light alloy. Trailing-edge flaps of light alloy construction extend from inner edge of ailerons and continue beneath fuselage. Plain ailerons of light alloy construction. Optional plans for aileron droop and drooped, raked wingtips. No tabs. Structure stressed to 9*g* ultimate.
FUSELAGE: All-metal structure utilising a surplus military drop-tank as its basis, with 2024T-3 alloy sheet and 6061T-6 structural angle reinforcement. Structure stressed to 9*g* ultimate.
TAIL UNIT: Cantilever all-metal structure with swept vertical surfaces. Incidence of tailplane ground-adjustable. Trim tab on elevator.
LANDING GEAR: Non-retractable tricycle type. All units have a tubular steel strut with compression springs for shock-absorption. Nosewheel and main-wheel tyres size 14 × 5·00-4, pressure 30 lb/sq in (2·11 kg/cm²). Mechanical disc brakes. Parking brake. Wheel fairings optional.
POWER PLANT: Prototype has one 65 hp Lycoming O-145-B2 four-cylinder horizontally-opposed aircooled engine, driving a two-blade metal fixed-pitch propeller of McCauley design and manufacture, refurbished by Aero Prop. Fuel contained in forward fuselage tank, capacity 9 US gallons (34 litres). Aft fuselage tank of 12 US gallons (45·4 litres) capacity optional. Refuelling point for front tank forward of

DSK Airmotive DSK-1 Hawk homebuilt sporting aircraft (65 hp Lycoming O-145-B2 engine) (*Howard Levy*)

windscreen, for rear tank in turtledeck aft of cockpit. Oil capacity 1·25 US gallons (4·7 litres).

ACCOMMODATION: Single seat for pilot in enclosed cockpit. Canopy slides aft for access. Baggage space aft of pilot's seat. Cockpit heated and ventilated.

SYSTEM: Simple air-driven alternator under design by DSK Airmotive.

ELECTRONICS: Battery-powered Narco VHT-3 nav/com and Omni.

DIMENSIONS, EXTERNAL:
Wing span 20 ft 4½ in (6·21 m)
Wing chord, constant 3 ft 2 in (0·97 m)
Wing aspect ratio 6·4
Length overall 15 ft 0 in (4·57 m)
Height overall 6 ft 0 in (1·83 m)
Tailplane span 6 ft 2 in (1·88 m)
Wheel track 5 ft 4 in (1·63 m)
Wheelbase 3 ft 9 in (1·14 m)
Propeller diameter 5 ft 3 in (1·60 m)
Propeller ground clearance 8 in (0·20 m)

AREAS:
Wings, gross 64 sq ft (5·95 m^2)
Ailerons (total) 3 sq ft (0·28 m^2)
Trailing-edge flaps (total) 6 sq ft (0·56 m^2)
Vertical tail surfaces 4·7 sq ft (0·44 m^2)
Tailplane 6·2 sq ft (0·58 m^2)
Elevator (including tab) 3·2 sq ft (0·30 m^2)

WEIGHTS AND LOADINGS:
Weight empty 525 lb (238 kg)
Max T-O and landing weight 893 lb (405 kg)
Max wing loading 13·95 lb/sq ft (68·1 kg/m^2)
Max power loading 13·7 lb/hp (6·21 kg/hp)

PERFORMANCE (at max T-O weight):
Max level speed at 5,000 ft (1,525 m) 127 knots (146 mph; 235 km/h)
Max cruising speed at 5,000 ft (1,525 m) 114 knots (131 mph; 211 km/h)
Econ cruising speed at 5,000 ft (1,525 m) 96 knots (110 mph; 177 km/h)
Stalling speed, flaps up 52·5 knots (60 mph; 97 km/h)
Stalling speed, flaps down 44 knots (50 mph; 81 km/h)
Max rate of climb at S/L 1,500 ft (457 m)/min
Service ceiling 12,000 ft (3,660 m)
T-O run 600 ft (183 m)
T-O to 50 ft (15 m) 800 ft (244 m)
Landing from 50 ft (15 m) 750 ft (229 m)
Landing run 550 ft (168 m)
Endurance with standard fuel 3 hr

DYKE

JOHN W. DYKE

ADDRESS:
2840 Old Yellow Springs Road, Fairborn, Ohio 45324

DYKE JD-2 DELTA

Mr Dyke was the designer and builder of a then-unique delta-wing aircraft, designated JD-1 Delta, which was described in the 1964-65 *Jane's*. This was of welded steel tube construction with glassfibre covering. His later JD-2 version is generally similar, but has metal skins. Plans are available to amateur constructors, and at the end of 1972 it was reported that 170 were under construction and that seven had been completed and were flying.

Typical of those now flying is that built by Mr Bill Brubacher and shown in the accompanying illustration. Constructed in Canada over a two-year period, at a cost of approximately $4,500, it has a steel tube main spar, and stainless steel ribs; all skins are of light alloy except for the fin, rudder and elevons which are fabric-covered. Power plant of Mr Brubacher's two-seat version is a 160 hp Lycoming O-320-B.

DIMENSIONS, EXTERNAL:
Wing span 22 ft 0 in (6·71 m)
Length overall 19 ft 0 in (5·79 m)
Height overall 6 ft 0 in (1·83 m)

WEIGHTS:
Weight empty 930 lb (421 kg)
Max T-O weight 1,500 lb (680 kg)

PERFORMANCE (at max T-O weight):
Max level speed 165 knots (190 mph; 306 km/h)
Cruising speed 139 knots (160 mph; 257 km/h)
Landing speed 65 knots (75 mph; 121 km/h)
Max rate of climb at S/L 1,000 ft (305 m)/min
T-O run 800 ft (244 m)
Landing run 1,000 ft (305 m)
Range 607 nm (700 miles; 1,126 km)

Dyke JD-2 Delta built by Mr Bill Brubacher of Greensville, Ontario (*Howard Levy*)

EAA

EXPERIMENTAL AIRCRAFT ASSOCIATION INC

ADDRESS:
PO Box 229, Hales Corners, Wisconsin 53130
Telephone: (414) 425-4860

PRESIDENT: Paul H. Poberezny
VICE-PRESIDENT: Ray Scholler
SECRETARY: S. H. Schmid
TREASURER: Arthur Kilps

As a service to its members, the EAA decided in 1955 to develop a modern single-seat sporting biplane suitable for home construction by amateurs. The design drawings were prepared by Mr J. D. Stewart and Mr T. Seely of the Allison Division, General Motors Corporation, with the assistance of Mr Paul H. Poberezny, President of the EAA, and this aircraft became known as the EAA Biplane. It was followed in 1972 by the Acro-Sport, an aerobatic aircraft designed by Mr Paul Poberezny. These two designs were supplemented in 1973 by a more advanced aerobatic aircraft, the Super Acro-Sport.

A report received from the EAA at the end of February 1974 gave news of a new ultra-light design by the EAA President. Known as the Pober Pixie, it is basically a parasol monoplane with many of the design features of the Heath Parasol. The prototype, which was under construction in early 1974, is to be powered by a modified Volkswagen motor car engine. It is intended that the design will be suitable for Volkswagen or Hirth engines, and it was anticipated that the first flight would be made in the early Summer of 1974.

EAA BIPLANE

The prototype of the EAA Biplane was built between 1957 and May 1960 as a classroom project by students of St Rita's High School, Chicago, under the supervision of Mr Robert Blacker. It flew for the first time on 10 June 1960, powered by a 65 hp Continental A65 engine. Due to the fact that the N-shape cabane and I-type interplane struts had not been constructed properly, and that in a change from the original plans a high turtledeck had been added, performance was below expectations. After modification to the struts, flight testing was resumed on 26 November 1960.

Subsequently, a new metal propeller was fitted, the engine cooling was improved and a cockpit canopy was installed. The prototype was then taken over by the EAA, and further changes were made, including installation of an 85 hp engine, removal of the cockpit canopy, reduction in size of the cockpit opening, raising of the engine cowling, installation of a new turtledeck and headrest, and fitting of a new instrument panel.

Mr Poberezny subsequently introduced further modifications, including lighter wing spars and fittings, which reduced the empty weight of the aircraft, together with increases in the area of the tail surfaces and many other improvements. This modified version is known as the EAA Biplane Model P.

Over 7,000 sets of plans of the EAA Biplane had been sold by January 1974 and many examples are flying and under construction.

The following details apply to the standard EAA Biplane Model P:

TYPE: Single-seat sporting biplane.

WINGS: Braced biplane, with N-shape streamline-section cabane struts and interplane struts. Dihedral 0° on upper wing, 2° on lower wings. Incidence 2° on upper wing, 2° on lower wings. All-wood two-spar structure, with aluminium leading-edge and overall fabric covering. Ailerons of similar construction to wings, on lower wings only. No flaps.

FUSELAGE: Welded steel tube structure, fabric-covered.

TAIL UNIT: Wire-braced welded steel tube structure, fabric-covered.

LANDING GEAR: Non-retractable tailwheel type, modified from standard Piper J-3 components. Rubber cord shock-absorption. Brakes on main wheels. Wheel fairings optional. Piper J-3 steerable tailwheel.

POWER PLANT: Prototype Model P has an 85 hp Continental C85-8 four-cylinder horizontally-opposed aircooled engine, driving a two-blade metal fixed-pitch propeller. Provision for engines of up to 150 hp; but most Model Ps have a 125 hp Lycoming. Piper J-3 fuel tank aft of firewall in fuselage, capacity 18 US gallons (68 litres).

ACCOMMODATION: Single seat in open cockpit.

DIMENSIONS, EXTERNAL:
Wing span 20 ft 0 in (6·10 m)
Wing chord, both (constant) 3 ft 0 in (0·91 m)
Length overall 17 ft 0 in (5·18 m)
Height overall 6 ft 0 in (1·83 m)

AREA:
Wings, gross 108 sq ft (10·03 m^2)

WEIGHTS (85 hp engine):
Weight empty 710 lb (322 kg)
Max T-O weight 1,150 lb (522 kg)

PERFORMANCE (85 hp engine, at max T-O weight):
Max level speed at S/L 109 knots (125 mph; 201 km/h)

EAA Biplane Model P single-seat homebuilt sporting aircraft

Econ cruising speed 96 knots (110 mph; 177 km/h)
Stalling speed 44 knots (50 mph; 80 km/h)
Max rate of climb at S/L 1,000 ft (305 m)/min
Service ceiling 11,500 ft (3,500 m)
T-O run 500 ft (152 m)
Landing run 800 ft (245 m)
Range with max fuel 304 nm (350 miles; 560 km)

EAA ACRO-SPORT

The Acro-Sport was designed by Mr Paul Poberezny, President of the EAA, specifically for construction by school students, as a pupils' project. The EAA considers that such a project enables those who participate to discover their capabilities and potential in the manual crafts necessary to build an aircraft, possibly helping the individual to choose a career more wisely.

First flight of the prototype Acro-Sport (N1AC) was made on 11 January 1972, only 352 days after its design was started, although it represented a completely new design, unrelated to the EAA Biplane.

The prototype has demonstrated good flight characteristics, and represents a versatile aircraft for sport or aerobatic use. The provision of ailerons on both wings gives positive aileron response and a high rate of roll.

Plans and construction manuals are available to homebuilders, and a total of over 400 were known to be under construction in January 1974.

The following details apply to the prototype with 180 hp engine:

Type: Single-seat homebuilt aerobatic biplane.

Wings: Braced single-bay biplane, with single streamline-section interplane strut each side. N-type centre-section struts. Double streamline-section flying and landing wires. Wing section M-6. Dihedral: upper 0°, lower 2°. Incidence, both 1° 30′. Conventional two-spar structures, with spruce spars and ribs, single wire drag and anti-drag truss, fabric-covered. Glassfibre wingtips. Ailerons, on all four wings, of wood construction with fabric covering. No flaps. Cutout in trailing-edge of upper wing.

Fuselage: Composite structure of welded steel tube, with wooden stringers, fabric-covered. Glassfibre nose cowl and light alloy engine cowlings.

Tail Unit: Wire-braced welded steel tube structure with fabric covering. Controllable trim tab on port side of elevator, servo tab on starboard side.

Landing Gear: Non-retractable tailwheel type, modified from Piper J-3 components. Two side Vees and half axles. Rubber bungee shock-absorption. Main-wheel tyres size 5·00-5, pressure 27-28 lb/sq in (1·90-1·97 kg/cm²). Cleveland or Goodyear hydraulic brakes. Glassfibre wheel fairings. Steerable tailwheel. Parking brake.

Power Plant: Prototype has a 180 hp Lycoming engine, driving a Sensenich two-blade metal fixed-pitch propeller with spinner. Basic power plant is to be a 100 hp Continental O-200 four-cylinder horizontally-opposed aircooled engine. Single fuel tank immediately aft of firewall, capacity 20 US gallons (104 litres). Refuelling point on upper surface of fuselage. Small smoke oil tank, capacity 5 US gallons (19 litres), forward of instrument panel, could also be used for fuel.

Accommodation: Single seat in open cockpit, which is large enough to accommodate a pilot 6 ft 5 in (1·95 m) tall and weighing 250 lb (115 kg). Baggage space behind headrest, capacity 35 lb (16 kg).

Dimensions, external:
Wing span, upper 19 ft 7 in (5·97 m)
Wing span, lower 19 ft 1 in (5·82 m)
Wing chord, constant, both 3 ft 0 in (0·91 m)
Wing aspect ratio, upper 6·6
Length overall 17 ft 6 in (5·33 m)
Height overall 6 ft 0 in (1·83 m)
Tailplane span 7 ft 1 in (2·16 m)
Wheel track 5 ft 10 in (1·78 m)
Propeller diameter 6 ft 4 in (1·93 m)

Areas:
Wings, gross 115·5 sq ft (10·73 m²)
Ailerons (total) 14·25 sq ft (1·32 m²)

Weights and Loadings:
Weight empty, equipped 733 lb (332 kg)
Max T-O and landing weight 1,350 lb (612 kg)
Max wing loading 11·68 lb/sq ft (57·0 kg/m²)
Max power loading 7·5 lb/hp (3·4 kg/hp)

Performance (at max T-O weight):
Max never-exceed speed 156 knots (180 mph; 289 km/h)
Max level speed 132 knots (152 mph; 245 km/h)
Max cruising speed 113 knots (130 mph; 209 km/h)
Econ cruising speed 91 knots (105 mph; 169 km/h)
Stalling speed 43·5 knots (50 mph; 80·5 km/h)
Max rate of climb at S/L 3,500 ft (1,067 m)/min
T-O run 150 ft (46 m)
T-O to 50 ft (15 m) 350 ft (107 m)
Landing from 50 ft (15 m) 875 ft (267 m)
Landing run 800 ft (244 m)
Range with max fuel 260 nm (300 miles; 482 km)

EAA SUPER ACRO-SPORT

The design of a developed version of the Acro-Sport was started in January 1971. Construction began in the following year and the first flight of this prototype was made on 28 March 1973. Known as the Super Acro-Sport, it is intended for unlimited International Class aerobatic competition at a world championship level. Generally similar in external appearance to the Acro-Sport, it has a more powerful engine, nearly symmetrical aerofoil sections, and an improved rate of roll and inverted flight capability.

The differences by comparison with the standard Acro-Sport are covered in a supplement to the basic plans. The description of the Acro-Sport applies also to the Super Acro-Sport, except as follows:

Type: Single-seat homebuilt advanced aerobatic biplane.

Wings: As Acro-Sport, except wing section NACA 23012.

Tail Unit: As Acro-Sport, except controllable trim tab on starboard side of elevator, servo tab on port side.

Landing Gear: As Acro-Sport, except Cleveland hydraulic brakes. Steerable tailwheel has a solid tyre.

Power Plant: Prototype has a 200 hp Lycoming IO-360-A2A four-cylinder horizontally-opposed aircooled engine, driving a Sensenich two-blade metal fixed-pitch propeller type 76EM8-0-60 with spinner. Fuel system and capacity as for Acro-Sport. Oil capacity 2 US gallons (7·5 litres).

Dimensions, External: As for Acro-Sport, except:
Length overall 17 ft 4½ in (5·30 m)

Weights and Loadings:
Weight empty 884 lb (401 kg)
Max T-O weight 1,350 lb (612 kg)
Max wing loading 11·68 lb/sq ft (57·0 kg/m²)
Max power loading 6·75 lb/hp (3·06 kg/hp)

Performance (at max T-O weight):
Max never-exceed speed 156 knots (180 mph; 289 km/h)
Max level speed at S/L 135 knots (156 mph; 251 km/h)
Max cruising speed 117 knots (135 mph; 217 km/h)
Stalling speed 43·5 knots (50 mph; 80·5 km/h)
Max rate of climb at S/L 3,700 ft (1,128 m)/min
Service ceiling 15,000 ft (4,570 m)
T-O run 125 ft (38 m)
T-O to 50 ft (15 m) 300 ft (91 m)
Landing from 50 ft (15 m) 900 ft (274 m)
Landing run 800 ft (244 m)
Range with max fuel 260 nm (300 miles; 482 km)

EAA Super Acro-Sport aerobatic biplane (200 hp Lycoming engine)

E & P
ELSTON AND PRUITT

Address:
723 McDonald, Flint, Michigan 48507
Telephone: (313) 742-6408

Messrs Elston and Pruitt combined forces to design and build two examples of an original mid-wing sporting monoplane.

Design and construction of the first aircraft began in September 1969. This was completed in September 1972, the second in April 1973.

E & P SPECIAL

Type: Single-seat sporting aircraft.

Wings: Braced mid-wing monoplane with Vee bracing struts each side. Dihedral 1°. Incidence 1° 30′. No sweepback. Conventional wood structure with fabric covering. Plain ailerons of wood construction, fabric-covered. No flaps. No trim tabs.

Fuselage: Welded structure of 4130 steel tube with fabric covering.

Tail Unit: Braced structure of 4130 steel tube, fabric covered. Tailplane incidence ground-adjustable. No trim tabs.

Landing Gear: Non-retractable tailwheel type. Cantilever spring steel main gear. Steerable tailwheel. Main wheels and tyres size 5·00-5 or 6·00-6. Tailwheel size 2·00-6. Hydraulic brakes. Glassfibre wheel fairings.

Power Plant: One 65 hp Continental A65-8 four-cylinder horizontally-opposed aircooled engine, driving a two-blade fixed-pitch propeller. Fuselage fuel tank immediately aft of firewall, capacity 15 US gallons (56·5 litres). Refuelling point on fuselage upper surface, forward of windscreen. Oil capacity 0·25 US gallons (0·94 litres).

Accommodation: Single seat beneath aft-sliding

Elston and Pruitt E & P Special lightweight sporting aircraft (65 hp Continental A65-8 engine)

transparent canopy. Space for 20 lb (9 kg) baggage in headrest.

SYSTEMS: Hydraulic system for brakes only. Electrical power supplied by wind-driven generator.

ELECTRONICS: Com transceiver with 12V supply.

DIMENSIONS, EXTERNAL:

Wing span	23 ft 0 in (7·01 m)
Wing chord (constant)	4 ft 0 in (1·22 m)
Wing aspect ratio	5·75
Length overall	17 ft 11 in (5·46 m)
Tailplane span	6 ft 8 in (2·03 m)
Wheel track	5 ft 6 in (1·68 m)
Propeller diameter	5 ft 9 in (1·75 m)

AREAS:

Wings, gross	92 sq ft (8·55 m²)
Horizontal tail surfaces	14 sq ft (1·3 m²)

WEIGHTS AND LOADINGS:

Weight empty	845 lb (383 kg)
Max T-O weight	1,053 lb (477 kg)
Max wing loading	11·4 lb/sq ft (55·7 kg/m²)
Max power loading	16·2 lb/hp (7·35 kg/hp)

PERFORMANCE (at max T-O weight):

Max level and never-exceed speed	121 knots (140 mph; 225 km/h)
Max cruising speed	104 knots (120 mph; 193 km/h)
Econ cruising speed	100 knots (115 mph; 185 km/h)
Stalling speed	48 knots (55 mph; 89 km/h)
Max rate of climb at S/L	900 ft (274 m)/min
T-O and landing run	475 ft (145 m)
Range with max fuel	278 nm (320 miles; 515 km)

ECTOR

ECTOR AIRCRAFT COMPANY

ADDRESS:
414 East Hillmont, Odessa, Texas 79760
Telephone: (915) 362-1841
PRESIDENT: Alvin H. Parker

ECTOR L-19 MOUNTAINEER and SUPER MOUNTAINEER

The Ector Aircraft Company has in production a civil version of the Cessna L-19 Bird Dog (last described in the 1964-65 *Jane's*), to which it has given the name Mountaineer. This is available in two models:

Mountaineer. Standard model, with 213 hp Continental O-470-11 engine and fixed-pitch propeller. Continental O-470-11-13 (cruising speed increased to 108 knots; 125 mph; 201 km/h at 55% power) or O-470-11-13-15 engine and constant-speed propeller (104 knots; 120 mph; 193 km/h at 57% power) optional.

Super Mountaineer. More powerful version with a 240 hp Lycoming O-540-A4B5 engine, driving a Hartzell Type HC-C2YK-1B two-blade metal constant-speed propeller, and with additional equipment as standard.

Ector Super Mountaineer, a civil version of the Cessna L-19 Bird Dog

Generally similar to the original Cessna L-19, Ector's Mountaineers are rebuilt completely from new off-the-shelf or serviceable components. The entire airframe is corrosion-proofed with zinc chromate before assembly, mounting brackets for floats are built into the basic airframe and all four side windows can be opened in flight. The rear seat is removable to permit the carriage of cargo.

The Mountaineer is in service with various organisations as a glider tug and for patrol and general-purpose duties; it is also in demand as a sporting aircraft.

A total of 27 Mountaineers had been produced by early February 1974.

TYPE: Two-seat lightweight cabin monoplane.

WINGS: Braced high-wing monoplane. Single streamline-section bracing strut each side. Wing section NACA 2412. Dihedral 2° 8′. Incidence 1° 30′ at root, —1° 30′ at tip. All-metal single-spar structure, with metal skin. Frise-type all-metal ailerons. Fowler all-metal trailing-edge flaps. No tabs.

FUSELAGE: Conventional all-metal semi-monocoque structure.

TAIL UNIT: Cantilever all-metal structure. Trim tab in elevator. Small auxiliary fins are attached to tailplane tips of floatplane version.

LANDING GEAR: Non-retractable tailwheel type. Cantilever spring steel main legs. Goodyear main wheels with tyres size 6·00-6. Scott steerable tailwheel. Single-disc hydraulic brakes. Floats, skis or tandem landing gear for rough terrain optional.

POWER PLANT: One Continental or Lycoming six-cylinder horizontally-opposed aircooled engine as detailed in model listings, driving a two-blade fixed-pitch or constant-speed propeller. One fuel tank in each wing root, total capacity 40 US gallons (151·4 litres). Optionally, fuel cells in each wing with a total capacity of 65 US gallons (246 litres). Refuelling points on wing upper surface. Oil capacity 2·5 US gallons (9·4 litres).

ACCOMMODATION: Two seats in tandem in enclosed cabin with 360° field of vision. Door on starboard side. All four cabin side windows can be opened fully. Six skylights in roof. Space for baggage behind rear seats. With rear seat removed, 30 cu ft (0·85 m³) of space is available for freight. Cabin heated and ventilated.

SYSTEMS: Hydraulic system for brakes only. Electrical system powered by 24V 50A engine-driven generator. Super Mountaineer has a 12V electrical system.

ELECTRONICS AND EQUIPMENT: Radio equipment available to customer's requirements. Navigation and landing lights, and heated pitot, standard. External power socket optional. Stall warning indicator, Hobbs hour meter and Whelen three-light strobe system standard on Super Mountaineer. Wing racks optional.

DIMENSIONS, EXTERNAL:

Wing span	36 ft 0 in (10·97 m)
Wing chord (root)	5 ft 4 in (1·63 m)
Wing chord (tip)	3 ft 7 in (1·09 m)
Wing aspect ratio	7·35
Length overall	25 ft 9½ in (7·86 m)
Height overall	7 ft 6 in (2·29 m)
Tailplane span	10 ft 6½ in (3·21 m)
Propeller diameter	7 ft 6 in (2·29 m)
Propeller ground clearance	9 in (0·23 m)
Door:	
Height	2 ft 1 in (0·64 m)
Width	2 ft 8 in (0·81 m)
Height to sill	3 ft 8 in (1·12 m)

WEIGHTS (standard Mountaineer):

Weight empty, equipped	1,450 lb (658 kg)
Max T-O weight	2,300 lb (1,043 kg)

PERFORMANCE (A: Mountaineer with O-470-11 engine and fixed-pitch propeller; B: Super Mountaineer):

Max level speed at S/L:	
A	87 knots (100 mph; 161 km/h) TAS
B	112 knots (129 mph; 208 km/h) IAS
Max cruising speed:	
B at 7,000 ft (2,135 m)	139 knots (160 mph; 257 km/h) TAS
Econ cruising speed:	
B at 9,500 ft (2,895 m)	109 knots (125 mph; 201 km/h) IAS
Stalling speed, flaps down:	
B	45·5 knots (52 mph; 84 km/h)
Max rate of climb at S/L:	
A	1,200 ft (366 m)/min
B	1,800 ft (549 m)/min
Service ceiling:	
A	22,900 ft (6,980 m)
T-O run:	
A	400 ft (122 m)
Landing run:	
A	320 ft (98 m)
Range, max fuel, no reserve:	
A	651 nm (750 miles; 1,207 km)

EMAIR

EMAIR (a division of Murrayair Ltd)

ADDRESS:
Harlingen Air Park, Harlingen, Texas 78550

Under contract to Murrayair Ltd of Hawaii, Air New Zealand engineers began in September 1968 the construction of a single-seat agricultural aircraft, which first flew on 27 July 1969. Subsequently it was dismantled and shipped to Honolulu to complete its trials for FAA certification. FAA Type Approval in the Restricted category was granted on 14 April 1970 at an AUW of 6,250 lb (2,834 kg).

The aircraft is now known as the Agronemair MA-1 Paymaster, and is in production at Harlingen, Texas.

AGRONEMAIR MA-1 PAYMASTER

Although evolved from the Boeing-Stearman Kaydet, the current MA-1 is a very different aeroplane, designed specifically for an agricultural role. For ease of maintenance and repair the fuselage comprises four bolt-together sections, covered by removable glassfibre side panels. Increased gap and stagger of the biplane wings improve pilot visibility and ensure easy access to the hopper; and the wide-track main landing gear ensures adequate stability for operations from rough fields.

The cockpit, which is fully enclosed, has a bench seat for the pilot and can accommodate also a loader/mechanic. A shaped engine cowling, as illustrated, is available optionally but is not normally fitted.

The hopper, which forms an integral part of the front fuselage, has two outlets, each with an adapter. For granular dispersal a stainless steel rotating gate is attached to each of these adapters; for spray distribution one adapter carries the wind-driven spray pump and control valve, the other carries the bottom-loading connector and liquid jettison door. Spraybooms are mounted in a low-drag area at the trailing-edge of the lower wings.

The initial batch of six MA-1s was operational by mid-1973. Ten aircraft had been completed by February 1974, and production was continuing at a rate of two aircraft per month.

TYPE: Single-seat agricultural biplane.

WINGS: Strut-braced biplane with forward-staggered wings of unequal span. NACA 4412 (modified) wing section. Dihedral 1° 30′ on upper wings, 3° on lower wings. Incidence 4° 30′ on upper wings, 4° on lower wings. No sweepback. Stagger 31°. Upper wing carried on streamline steel tube struts. Conventional two-spar structure. Centre-section of upper wing is of aluminium construction. Outer panels of top wing, and both lower wing panels, have spruce laminated spars and ribs, with duralumin channel-section compression struts and steel tie-rod internal bracing, and fabric covering. Ailerons, of aluminium construction with fabric covering, on both upper and lower wings, linked by struts. No trim tabs or slats. Butt fittings and inboard compression members of the lower wing are fabricated from stainless steel. Glassfibre wingtips.

FUSELAGE: Rectangular welded chrome-molybdenum steel tube framework in four separate bolt-together sections, with glassfibre side panels.

TAIL UNIT: Conventional single fin and rudder, of welded chrome-molybdenum steel tube construction with fabric covering. Wire-braced fixed-incidence tailplane and fin. Trim tab in each elevator.

LANDING GEAR: Non-retractable tailwheel type with single wheel on each main unit. Each main-wheel leg incorporates a torque-resisting hydraulically-damped pneumatic spring, enclosed in a streamlined metal fairing. Harvard main wheels, with 8-ply nylon tyres size 27 × 9-14, pressure 35 lb/sq in (2·5 kg/cm²). Steerable tailwheel with solid tyre size 12 × 4·6. Hayes shoe-type hydraulic main-wheel brakes.

POWER PLANT: One 600 hp Pratt & Whitney R-1340-AN1 Wasp nine-cylinder radial aircooled engine, on a steel tube mounting, driving a Hamilton Standard 12.D.40 two-blade adjustable-pitch constant-speed metal propeller. Fuel tank in upper wing centre-section, capacity 108 US gallons (408 litres). Refuelling point above upper wing. Oil capacity 6·7 Imp gallons (8 US gallons; 30·5 litres). Cowling for engine optional.

ACCOMMODATION: Pilot on bench-type seat which provides sufficient room for carriage of a loader/mechanic on short-duration flights. Fully enclosed ventilated cockpit in centre of fuselage, with reinforced overturn structure aft of cockpit. Sliding side-screens of cockpit canopy retract into cockpit wall.

Operational Equipment: Between the cockpit and the engine is mounted a glassfibre hopper for dust or liquid, with a capacity of 62·5 cu ft (1·77 m^3) or 450 US gallons (1,703 litres), the largest of its kind ever fitted to a single-engine aircraft. It is built around the fuselage tubing, which in this area is of stainless steel to resist chemical corrosion. As a further precautionary measure, the hollow steel support struts for the hopper, and all other fuselage tubes, are filled with linseed oil. Any sign of oil seeping from the tubes provides an early warning of corrosion.

Dimensions, external:

Wing span (upper)	41 ft 8 in (12·70 m)
Wing span (lower)	35 ft 0 in (10·67 m)
Wing chord (both, constant)	5 ft 3 in (1·60 m)
Wing aspect ratio (upper)	7·9
Wing aspect ratio (lower)	6·7
Wing stagger	3 ft 11 in (1·19 m)
Wing gap	6 ft 6 in (1·98 m)
Length overall (tail up)	28 ft 8 in (8·74 m)
Height overall (tail down)	11 ft 3 in (3·43 m)
Propeller diameter	9 ft 0 in (2·74 m)
Propeller ground clearance (tail up)	1 ft 2 in (0·36 m)
Tailplane span	12 ft 6 in (3·81 m)
Wheel track	8 ft 8 in (2·64 m)
Wheelbase	22 ft 0 in (6·71 m)
Hopper opening, above fuselage:	
Length	2 ft 0 in (0·61 m)
Width	1 ft 6 in (0·46 m)

Areas:

Wings, gross (both)	400 sq ft (37·16 m^2)
Ailerons (total)	55·2 sq ft (5·13 m^2)
Fin	3·14 sq ft (0·29 m^2)
Rudder	11·83 sq ft (1·10 m^2)
Tailplane	21·16 sq ft (1·97 m^2)
Elevators, incl tabs	14·14 sq ft (1·31 m^2)

Agronemair MA-1 Paymaster heavy-duty agricultural aircraft (600 hp Pratt & Whitney R-1340-AN1 engine)

Weights and Loadings:

Weight empty	3,746 lb (1,699 kg)
Hopper load	3,000 lb (1,360 kg)
Structural design T-O and landing weight	6,250 lb (2,834 kg)
Max T-O weight (agricultural)	7,000 lb (3,175 kg)
Max wing loading	15·7 lb/sq ft (76·65 kg/m^2)
Max power loading	10·4 lb/hp (4·72 kg/hp)

Performance (prototype):

Max never-exceed speed	128 knots (148 mph; 238 km/h) CAS
Max cruising and manoeuvring speed	102 knots (117 mph; 188 km/h) CAS
Stalling speed (loaded)	51·5 knots (59 mph; 95 km/h)
Min ground turning radius	30 ft (9·14 m)

ENSTROM

THE ENSTROM HELICOPTER CORPORATION

Head Office and Works:
PO Box 277, Menominee County Airport, Menominee, Michigan 49858
Telephone: (906) 863-9971
Telex: 263451

Senior Vice-President:
Paul L. Shultz

In its original form, as the R. J. Enstrom Corporation, this company was formed in 1959 to develop an experimental light helicopter built by Rudolph J. Enstrom. This helicopter flew for the first time on 12 November 1960. There followed a design and development programme on a new helicopter, designated F-28, the first of which flew for the first time in May 1962. A limited number of F-28s were built, and were followed by the improved Model F-28A in 1968.

The company was acquired by the Purex Corporation in October 1968 and was operated for a time as part of the Pacific Airmotive Aerospace group. Under this ownership, a turbocharged F-28B version was developed, as well as a Model T-28 turbine-powered version.

The activities of this group ended in February 1970; but with transfer of ownership of the Purex interest to F. Lee Bailey in January 1971 the present company resumed manufacture of the Model F-28A, which is being marketed throughout the world. A total of 200 F-28A helicopters had been built by April 1974, at which time the company was expanding its production to meet new orders for 53 helicopters.

During 1973 an advanced version of the F-28A known as the **Model 280 Shark** was developed. It is generally similar to the Model F-28A, except for the cabin area, which has improved aerodynamic contours, and sweptback vertical and horizontal tail stabilising surfaces. Certification of this version was proceeding with the 205 hp Lycoming HIO-360 fuel-injection engine. When this has been gained, it is intended to obtain certification with a turbocharged version of the same engine.

ENSTROM MODEL F-28A

Type: Three-seat light helicopter.

Rotor System: Fully-articulated metal three-blade main rotor. Blades are of bonded light alloy construction, each attached to rotor hub by retention pin and drag link. Blade section NACA 00135. Two-blade teetering tail rotor, with blades of bonded light alloy construction. Blades do not fold. No rotor brake.

Rotor Drive: Poly vee-belt drive system. Right-angle drive reduction gearbox. Main rotor/engine rpm ratio 1 : 8·78. Tail rotor/engine rpm ratio 1 : 1·226.

Fuselage: Glassfibre and light alloy cab structure, with welded steel tube centre-section Semi-monocoque aluminium tailcone structure.

Landing Gear: Skids carried on Enstrom oleo-pneumatic shock-absorbers. Air Cruiser inflatable floats available optionally.

Power Plant: One 205 hp Lycoming HIO-360-C1A four-cylinder horizontally-opposed air-cooled engine. Two fuel tanks, each of 15 US gallons (56·5 litres). Total fuel capacity 30 US gallons (113 litres). Oil capacity 2 US gallons (7·5 litres).

Accommodation: Pilot and two passengers, side by side on bench seat. Door on each side of cabin. Baggage space aft of engine compartment, with external access door. Cabin heated and ventilated.

Systems: Electrical power provided by 12V 70A engine-driven alternator.

Electronics and Equipment: Nav/com equipment available to customer's requirements. Cargo hook, floats and litters optional.

Dimensions, external:

Diameter of main rotor	32 ft 0 in (9·75 m)
Diameter of tail rotor	4 ft 8 in (1·42 m)
Distance between rotor centres	18 ft 3 in (5·56 m)
Main rotor blade chord	9·5 in (24 cm)
Length overall	29 ft 6 in (8·99 m)
Height to top of rotor hub	9 ft 2 in (2·79 m)
Skid track	7 ft 0 in (2·13 m)
Cabin doors (each):	
Height	3 ft 7 in (1·09 m)
Width	3 ft 4 in (1·02 m)
Height to sill	2 ft 0 in (0·61 m)
Baggage door:	
Height	1 ft 9½ in (0·55 m)
Width	1 ft 3½ in (0·39 m)
Height to sill	2 ft 10 in (0·86 m)

Dimensions, internal:

Max width of cabin	5 ft 1 in (1·55 m)

Enstrom F-28A three-seat light helicopter (205 hp Lycoming HIO-360-C1A engine)

Prototype of Enstrom's Model 280 Shark (205 hp Lycoming HIO-360 turbocharged engine)

Volume of baggage hold 8 cu ft (0·23 m³)
Areas:
Main rotor disc 804 sq ft (74·69 m²)
Tail rotor disc 17·06 sq ft (1·58 m²)
Weights and Loadings:
Weight empty 1,450 lb (657 kg)
Max T-O weight 2,150 lb (975 kg)
Max disc loading 2·67 lb/sq ft (13·04 kg/m²)
Max power loading 10·49 lb/hp (4·76 kg/hp)
Performance (at max T-O weight):
Max level speed at S/L 97 knots (112 mph; 180 km/h)
Max cruising speed at S/L 87 knots (100 mph; 161 km/h)
Max rate of climb at S/L 950 ft (290 m)/min
Service ceiling 12,000 ft (3,660 m)
Hovering ceiling in ground effect 5,600 ft (1,705 m)
Hovering ceiling out of ground effect 3,400 ft (1,035 m)
Range with max fuel 205 nm (237 miles; 381 km)

EVANGEL

EVANGEL AIRCRAFT CORPORATION

Head Office:
PO Box 201, Orange City, Iowa 51041
Telephone: (712) 737-4400
Vice-President, Sales:
Willard R. Elton

EVANGEL 4500-300

The Evangel Aircraft Corporation manufactures a twin-engined STOL aircraft designated Evangel 4500-300. The aircraft is intended specifically for heavy-duty bush operations, and this is reflected in its boxlike fuselage and rugged appearance. Ease of maintenance was a prime consideration, and surface skins are of 2024-T3 light alloy to permit easy repairs in the field.

Design of the prototype started in 1962 and construction began in the following year. First flight was made in June 1964 and the first production aircraft flew in January 1969, with FAA certification being granted on 21 July 1970. It is intended to obtain certification for operation on floats or skis. A turbocharged version, which has an increased max T-O weight of 5,700 lb (2,585 kg), was awarded a Supplemental Type Certificate on 8 March 1973 and is known as the **4500-300-II**.

Seven production aircraft had been completed by January 1974, and demand for the aircraft is such that Evangel planned to increase production to three aircraft per month by November 1974.

Type: Nine-seat light passenger/cargo aircraft.

Wings: Cantilever low-wing monoplane. Dihedral on outer panels 9° 30′. Incidence 3° 15′. Conventional all-metal light alloy structure. Cambered wingtips. Frise-type light alloy ailerons. Single-slotted trailing-edge flaps of light alloy construction. Ground-adjustable trim tabs on ailerons.

Fuselage: Rectangular-section all-metal structure.

Tail Unit: Cantilever all-metal structure. Large dorsal fin faired into upper surface of fuselage. Dihedral on tailplane. Horn-balanced elevators. Controllable trim tabs in rudder and elevators.

Landing Gear: Tailwheel type, main units only retracting rearward into undersurface of wings. Hydraulic retraction. Hand-pump for emergency retraction or extension. Allied Machinist oleo-pneumatic shock-absorbers on main units. Goodyear main wheels and tyres size 24 × 7·7, pressure 40 lb/sq in (2·81 kg/cm²). Castoring tailwheel with Cleveland wheel and tyre size 40-77, pressure 35 lb/sq in (2·46 kg/cm²). Goodyear hydraulic brakes.

Power Plant: Two 300 hp Lycoming IO-540-K1B5 six-cylinder horizontally-opposed air-cooled fuel-injection engines, each driving a Hartzell two-blade constant-speed fully-feathering metal propeller with spinner. Alternatively, a version designated 4500-300-II with Rajay turbochargers is available. Two integral wing fuel tanks, total capacity 111 US gallons (420 litres). Refuelling points in upper surface of wings. Oil capacity 6 US gallons (23 litres).

Accommodation: Pilot and eight passengers in enclosed cabin. In initial layout two passengers accommodated on forward-facing seats, remaining passengers seated on inward-facing seats. Cockpit doors on each side of fuselage, hinged at forward edge. Large cabin doors, one on each side of fuselage, at rear of cabin, hinged at forward edge. Cockpit and cabin heated and ventilated.

Systems: Hydraulic system, for operation of flaps and main landing gear, supplied by electrically-driven hydraulic pump. Electrical system powered by 12V 50A engine-driven generators.

Electronics and Equipment: Full IFR instrumentation standard. Narco and King nav/com radios to customer's requirements.

Dimensions, external:
Wing span 41 ft 3 in (12·52 m)
Wing chord, constant 6 ft 0 in (1·83 m)
Wing aspect ratio 6·83
Length overall 31 ft 6 in (9·60 m)
Height overall 9 ft 6 in (2·90 m)
Tailplane span 14 ft 6½ in (4·43 m)
Wheel track 11 ft 2 in (3·40 m)
Wheelbase 20 ft 4 in (6·20 m)
Propeller diameter 6 ft 8 in (2·03 m)
Propeller ground clearance 10 in (0·25 m)
Cockpit doors (fwd):
Height 2 ft 8½ in (0·82 m)
Width 1 ft 9 in (0·53 m)
Height to sill 4 ft 9 in (1·45 m)
Cabin doors (aft):
Height 2 ft 11 in (0·89 m)
Width 3 ft 9 in (1·14 m)
Height to sill 2 ft 0 in (0·61 m)

Dimensions, internal:
Cabin, excluding flight deck:
Length 10 ft 0 in (3·05 m)
Max width 3 ft 8 in (1·12 m)
Max height 3 ft 8 in (1·12 m)
Floor area 36·7 sq ft (3·41 m²)
Volume 135 cu ft (3·82 m³)

Areas:
Wings, gross 251 sq ft (23·32 m²)
Ailerons (total) 32·0 sq ft (2·97 m²)
Trailing-edge flaps (total) 28·4 sq ft (2·64 m²)
Fin 31·5 sq ft (2·93 m²)
Rudder, including tab 34·2 sq ft (3·18 m²)
Tailplane 62·0 sq ft (5·76 m²)
Elevators 27·5 sq ft (2·55 m²)

Weights and Loadings (A: standard version, B: turbocharged version):
Weight empty:
A 3,530 lb (1,601 kg)
Max T-O and landing weight:
A 5,500 lb (2,495 kg)
B 5,700 lb (2,585 kg)
Max zero-fuel weight:
A 4,834 lb (2,192 kg)
B 5,335 lb (2,420 kg)
Max wing loading:
A 21·9 lb/sq ft (107 kg/m²)
B 22·7 lb/sq ft (110·8 kg/m²)
Max power loading:
A 9·17 lb/hp (4·16 kg/hp)

Performance (at max T-O weight, A: standard version, B: turbocharged version):
Max never-exceed speed:
A, B 199·5 knots (230 mph; 370 km/h)
Max cruising speed, 75% power at 6,000 ft (1,830 m):
A 158 knots (182 mph; 293 km/h)
Econ cruising speed at 65% power:
A at 10,000 ft (3,050 m) 152 knots (175 mph; 282 km/h)
B at 25,000 ft (7,620 m) 169 knots (195 mph; 314 km/h)
Long-range cruising speed, 55% power at 14,000 ft (4,275 m):
A 149 knots (171 mph; 275 km/h)
Stalling speed, flaps down:
A 58·5 knots (67 mph; 108 km/h)
Max rate of climb at S/L:
A 1,500 ft (457 m)/min
B 1,000 ft (305 m)/min
Rate of climb at S/L, one engine out:
A 225 ft (69 m)/min
B 130 ft (40 m)/min
Certificated max operating altitude:
B 25,000 ft (7,620 m)
Service ceiling:
A 21,030 ft (6,410 m)
Service ceiling, one engine out:
A 6,200 ft (1,890 m)
B 11,000 ft (3,350 m)
Absolute ceiling:
B 30,600 ft (9,325 m)
Absolute ceiling, one engine out:
B 12,500 ft (3,810 m)
Min ground turning radius:
A, B 11 ft 0 in (3·35 m)
T-O run:
A 500 ft (152 m)
B 665 ft (203 m)
T-O to 50 ft (15 m):
A 1,125 ft (343 m)
B 1,490 ft (454 m)
Landing from 50 ft (15 m):
A 1,140 ft (347 m)
B 1,180 ft (360 m)
Landing run:
A 475 ft (145 m)
Range with max fuel (A):
75% power at 6,000 ft (1,830 m) 553 nm (637 miles; 1,025 km)
65% power at 10,000 ft (3,050 m) 607 nm (700 miles; 1,126 km)
55% power at 14,000 ft (4,275 m) 651 nm (750 miles; 1,207 km)

Evangel 4500-300-II nine-seat light passenger/cargo aircraft with turbocharged engines

EVANS

EVANS AIRCRAFT

Address:
PO Box 744, La Jolla, California 92037

Mr W. S. Evans, while a design engineer with the Convair division of General Dynamics Corporation, set out to design for the novice home-builder an all-wood aircraft that would be easy to build and safe to fly. He was prepared to sacrifice both appearance and performance to achieve this aim. Two years of spare-time design and a year of construction produced a strut-braced low-wing monoplane with an all-moving tail unit, powered by a 40 hp Volkswagen engine, which Mr Evans called the VP (originally Volksplane).

The prototype was subsequently re-engined

with a 53 hp Volkswagen, giving a rate of climb of 600 ft (183 m)/min at sea level.

Mr Evans has since developed a two-seat version of the VP; this is generally similar to the single-seat model which is now designated VP-1. The two-seat VP-2 is powered by a 60/65 hp Volkswagen engine, but in other respects has only minor constructional variations from the VP-1.

Plans of both models are available to amateur constructors.

EVANS VP-1

TYPE: Single-seat homebuilt aircraft.

WINGS: Strut-braced low-wing monoplane. Two streamline-section bracing struts on each side. Wing section NACA 4412. Square tips. Dihedral 5°. Conventional wood structure with two rectangular spar beams, internal wooden compression struts and diagonal wire bracing, dispensing with the need for a complicated box spar. Fabric covering. Ailerons of wooden construction, fabric covered. No trim tabs. No flaps.

FUSELAGE: Rectangular-section all-wood stressed-skin structure, consisting essentially of three bulkheads, four longerons and plywood skin. Stressed-skin design eliminates the need for any diagonal bracing. Glassfibre fairing aft of pilot's seat.

TAIL UNIT: No fixed fin. The rudder is constructed of plywood ribs clamped to a 2 in (5·08 cm) aluminium tube which is mounted vertically through the rear fuselage and pivots in two nylon bushes. Leading- and trailing-edges are of wood and the whole unit is fabric-covered. The fabric-covered all-moving tailplane is a wooden cantilever structure, comprising ply ribs blocked and glued to a simple constant-section box spar. Both rudder and tailplane have anti-servo tabs.

LANDING GEAR: Non-retractable main wheels and tailskid. Main wheels carried on a bent section of heavy-gauge 24ST-3 aluminium bar, wire-braced by diagonal cables. Shock-absorption by low-pressure tyres. Main wheels and tyres size 6·00-6. Tyre pressure 12 lb/sq in (0·84 kg/cm²). Hydraulic brakes operated by single hand lever.

POWER PLANT: One 40 hp, 53 hp or 60 hp modified Volkswagen motor car engine, driving a Hegy two-blade propeller, with pitch of 24 in (0·61 m) for 40 hp engine, 30 in (0·76 m) for 53 hp and 36 in (0·91 m) for 60 hp. Glassfibre fuel tank aft of firewall and integral with the forward fuselage cowlings, capacity 8 US gallons (30 litres). Filling point on top of fuselage, forward of windscreen.

ACCOMMODATION: Single seat in open cockpit. No baggage stowage.

DIMENSIONS, EXTERNAL:	
Wing span	24 ft 0 in (7·32 m)
Wing chord (constant)	4 ft 2 in (1·27 m)
Length overall	18 ft 0 in (5·49 m)
Height overall	5 ft 1½ in (1·56 m)
Tailplane span	7 ft 0 in (2·13 m)
Wheel track	4 ft 11 in (1·50 m)
Propeller diameter	4 ft 6 in (1·37 m)
AREAS:	
Wings, gross	100 sq ft (9·29 m²)
Rudder, including tab	7·6 sq ft (0·71 m²)
Tailplane, including tab	15·0 sq ft (1·39 m²)
WEIGHTS:	
Weight empty	440 lb (200 kg)
Max T-O weight	750 lb (340 kg)

Evans VP-1 single-seat amateur-built aircraft (*Air Portraits*)

Evans VP-2 two-seat homebuilt monoplane (60 hp Volkswagen engine)

PERFORMANCE (with 40 hp engine, at T-O weight of 650 lb; 295 kg):	
Max never-exceed speed	104 knots (120 mph; 193 km/h)
Stalling speed	40 knots (46 mph; 74 km/h)
Max rate of climb at S/L	400 ft (122 m)/min
T-O run (average breeze)	450 ft (137 m)
Landing run (average breeze)	200 ft (61 m)

EVANS VP-2

TYPE: Two-seat homebuilt aircraft.

WINGS: Generally similar to VP-1, except for NACA 4415 wing section and increased wing span and chord.

FUSELAGE: Similar to VP-1, but width increased by 1 ft 0 in (0·305 m).

TAIL UNIT: Similar to VP-1. No fin. Increased rudder area; all-moving tailplane of increased span and chord.

LANDING GEAR: Similar to VP-1. Wheel track increased by 9 in (0·23 m).

POWER PLANT: One 60 hp (1,834 cc) or 65 hp (2,100 cc) modified Volkswagen motor car engine, driving a two-blade propeller. Glassfibre fuel tank aft of firewall, capacity 14 US gallons (53 litres).

ACCOMMODATION: Two seats side by side in open cockpit.

DIMENSIONS, EXTERNAL:	
Wing span	27 ft 0 in (8·23 m)
Wing chord (constant)	4 ft 10 in (1·47 m)
Length overall	19 ft 3 in (5·87 m)
Tailplane span	8 ft 0 in (2·44 m)
Wheel track	5 ft 8 in (1·73 m)
Propeller diameter	5 ft 0 in (1·52 m)
AREAS:	
Wings, gross	130 sq ft (12·08 m²)
Rudder, including tab	9·6 sq ft (0·89 m²)
Tailplane, including tab	19·0 sq ft (1·77 m²)
WEIGHTS:	
Weight empty	640 lb (290 kg)
Max T-O weight	1,040 lb (471 kg)
PERFORMANCE (60 hp engine, at max T-O weight):	
Max never-exceed speed	104 knots (120 mph; 193 km/h)
Max level speed	87 knots (100 mph; 161 km/h)
Max cruising speed	65 knots (75 mph; 121 km/h)
Stalling speed	35 knots (40 mph; 64·5 km/h)
Max rate of climb at S/L (pilot only)	700 ft (213 m)/min
Max rate of climb at S/L (pilot and passenger)	400 ft (122 m)/min

EXCALIBUR

EXCALIBUR AVIATION COMPANY

ADDRESS:

PO Box 32007, San Antonio, Texas 78216

Excalibur Aviation, which for some time has been responsible for production of the improved versions of the Beechcraft Queen Air and Twin-Bonanza marketed by Swearingen Aircraft, acquired all rights of this conversion programme on 1 October 1970, and is continuing to produce these aircraft at San Antonio International Airport. The only change brought about by the new ownership is use of the name Queenaire 800 for the former Swearingen 800.

EXCALIBUR QUEENAIRE 800

The Excalibur modification of Queen Air 65s and 80s includes installation of two 400 hp Lycoming IO-720 eight-cylinder engines, each driving a Hartzell three-blade metal propeller; new engine mountings; new exhaust system; new low-drag engine nacelles; new (or zero-time overhauled and certified) accessories, including Lear Siegler 90A generators; and Excalibur fully-enclosed wheel-well doors. These modifications qualify the Queenaire 800 for a maximum T-O weight of 7,900 lb (3,583 kg).

EXCALIBUR 800

The Excalibur 800 is basically a series D50 Twin-Bonanza fitted with 400 hp Lycoming IO-720-A1A fuel-injection engines in place of the original 295 hp Lycoming GO-480s. The new engines are housed in low-drag glassfibre cowlings and have revised exhaust systems. Each drives a fully-feathering Hartzell three-blade metal propeller.

Excalibur (Beechcraft) Queenaire 800 (two 400 hp Lycoming IO-720 engines)

Many additional and optional improvements are offered by Excalibur to bring the aircraft to full Excalibur 800 standards. These include the fitting of fairings to enclose the main landing gear when retracted, an increase in total fuel capacity from 180 US gallons (681 litres) to 230 US gallons (870 litres), and refinements to the interior and exterior trim.

DIMENSIONS, EXTERNAL:	
Wing span	45 ft 11⅜ in (14·00 m)
Length overall	31 ft 6½ in (9·61 m)
Height overall	11 ft 4 in (3·45 m)
Propeller diameter	7 ft 6 in (2·29 m)
WEIGHT:	
Max T-O weight	7,600 lb (3,447 kg)
PERFORMANCE (at max T-O weight):	
Max cruising speed (75% power) at 8,300 ft (2,530 m)	213 knots (245 mph; 394 km/h)

Econ cruising speed (55% power) at 10,000 ft (3,050 m) 191 knots (220 mph; 354 km/h)
Stalling speed, wheels and flaps up 80 knots (92 mph; 148 km/h)
Stalling speed, wheels and flaps down 72 knots (82 mph; 132 km/h)
Max rate of climb at S/L 1,870 ft (570 m)/min
Rate of climb at S/L, one engine out 440 ft (134 m)/min
Service ceiling at AUW of 7,000 lb (3,175 kg) 22,200 ft (6,760 m)
Single-engine ceiling at AUW of 7,000 lb (3,175 kg) 11,800 ft (3,600 m)
Range with max fuel, 30 gallon reserve, at max cruising speed 929 nm (1,070 miles; 1,720 km)
Range with max fuel, 30 gallon reserve, at econ cruising speed 1,120 nm (1,290 miles; 2,075 km)

Excalibur 800 conversion of the Beechcraft Twin-Bonanza

FAIRCHILD INDUSTRIES

FAIRCHILD INDUSTRIES, INC

EXECUTIVE OFFICE:
Germantown, Maryland 20767
Telephone: (301) 428-6000
PRESIDENT AND CHIEF EXECUTIVE OFFICER:
Edward G. Uhl
EXECUTIVE VICE-PRESIDENT:
Charles Collis
VICE-PRESIDENTS:
Ralph Bonafede
Wernher von Braun
John F. Dealy
Paul R. Fitez
Emanuel Fthenakis
Norman Grossman
Wilber L. Pritchard
J. Edward Sheridan
Donald J. Strait
Thomas Turner
TREASURER AND DIRECTOR OF FINANCE:
Joseph H. Dugan
COMPTROLLER: Franklin M. Beall
SECRETARY: William A. Jackson

Fairchild Republic Company
PRESIDENT: Charles Collis

Fairchild Republic Division
DIVISIONAL OFFICE AND WORKS:
Farmingdale, Long Island, New York 11735
VICE-PRESIDENT AND GENERAL MANAGER:
Donald J. Strait
HAGERSTOWN, MARYLAND FACILITY:
GENERAL MANAGER: Leo LaBell

Fairchild Aircraft Service Division
DIVISIONAL OFFICE AND WORKS:
Crestview, Florida 32536
GENERAL MANAGER: R. C. Woods
ST AUGUSTINE, FLORIDA FACILITY:
St Augustine, Florida 32084
FACILITY MANAGER: J. Gurnow

Fairchild Space and Electronics Company
Germantown, Maryland 20767
PRESIDENT: Wilber L. Pritchard

Fairchild Aircraft Marketing Company
Germantown, Maryland 20767
PRESIDENT: George Attridge

Swearingen Aviation Corporation
San Antonio, Texas 78216
PRESIDENT: Constantine Stathis

Fairchild Stratos Division
Manhattan Beach, California 90266
GENERAL MANAGER: F. T. Serjeant

Fairchild Industrial Products Division
Winston-Salem, North Carolina 27107
GENERAL MANAGER: Richard G. Orr

Fairchild Burns Company
Winston-Salem, North Carolina 27107
GENERAL MANAGER: A. L. Esposito

American Satellite Corporation
Germantown, Maryland 20769
PRESIDENT: Emanuel Fthenakis

S. J. Industries, Inc
Alexandria, Virginia 22304
PRESIDENT: R. F. Julius

Fairchild KLIF, Inc
Radio Station KLIF, Dallas, Texas 75201
GENERAL MANAGER: Al Lurie

Fairchild Minnesota, Inc
Radio Stations WYOO and WRAH (FM), Richfield, Minnesota 55423
GENERAL MANAGER: Michael R. Sigelman

Fairchild Industries is a diversified aerospace company with interests in communications, satellite systems, radio broadcasting, industrial products and land development.

The Fairchild Republic Company combines all of Fairchild's military aircraft research, design, manufacture and repair and overhaul facilities and personnel into one organisation. Facilities are located at Farmingdale, Long Island, New York; Hagerstown, Maryland; and at Crestview and St Augustine, Florida.

Fairchild Republic Company is proceeding with full-scale development and flight test of the A-10A close-support aircraft for the USAF. It is also manufacturing under subcontract aft fuselages, fin and tailcone assemblies, rudders, tailplanes and engine access doors for the McDonnell Douglas F-4 Phantom II tactical fighter as well as the twin vertical fins for the Grumman F-14A Tomcat fighter. The company is a major subcontractor in the Boeing 747 programme, manufacturing ailerons, spoilers, and wing trailing-edge and leading-edge flaps. This work is performed at the Farmingdale and Hagerstown facilities.

Fairchild Republic Company is also a major subcontractor to Rockwell International's Space Division, and is manufacturing the vertical tail of the Space Shuttle.

Other programmes in which the company is involved include the development and construction of radar site monitoring equipment for the Safeguard anti-ballistic missile system.

Wing structures for Swearingen Aviation Corporation's Merlin and Metro series are manufactured at Hagerstown. This facility also provides support for the F-27 and FH-227 twin-turboprop transport aircraft that were manufactured under licence from Fokker-VFW, as well as for the F.28 Fellowship and the FH-1100 five-passenger turbine-powered helicopter. The Porter STOL aircraft, manufactured under licence from Pilatus of Switzerland, as well as a military version of that aircraft known as the Peacemaker, are built at Hagerstown.

The Florida-based Fairchild Aircraft Service Division is engaged in the maintenance, repair, modification and support of a wide variety of aircraft. These include the C-119 and C-123 transports, the AC-119G and AC-119K gunships, and F-105 tactical fighter. It also modifies T-28B aircraft to T-28D-10 fighter-bomber configuration under USAF contract, and F-102As to PQM-102A drone aircraft configuration.

The Fairchild Space and Electronics Company directs the company's efforts in the design, development and manufacture of spacecraft, spacecraft subsystems, rocket payload projects, electronic systems, letter and parcel handling equipment for the US Postal Service and remotely piloted vehicles (RPVs). It was responsible for design and manufacture of NASA's Applications Technology Satellite (ATS) F (see Spaceflight section).

Fairchild Space and Electronics Company provides design, analysis, fabrication, testing and launch support services as a prime contractor and subcontractor to NASA, the Department of Defense, Atomic Energy Commission, COMSAT/INTELSAT and international organisations. As part of this effort the Company has conducted a number of advanced spacecraft studies, including nuclear-powered multi-mission spacecraft, and advanced concepts for communications and applications satellites. It is also a major supplier of deployable/retractable tubular structures and their mechanisms, of the type used as antennae and gravity stabilisation booms for spacecraft. Other spacecraft subsystems include thermal control louvres, heat pipes, solar array panels complete with solar cells, and components for such spacecraft as the OAO, Nimbus, ERTS, IMP, LES series, Skylab, VO'75 and sounding rockets.

The Division is active in the design and manufacture of search and meteorological/weather radar systems, and in intelligence data acquisition and management. Its auxiliary data annotation systems (ADAS) are in use in RF-4, RF-101, P-3 and OV-1C and -1D reconnaissance aircraft.

An integrated armament control or stores management system developed by the Division provides F-111D pilots with an inventory control and monitoring unit by integrating, on only two cockpit panels, the displays and controls of all the various weapons and stores. A similar system is being provided for F-14A and B-57G aircraft.

S. J. Industries, a subsidiary of the above Company, is engaged in silicon solar cell laydown techniques and power conditioning systems, and completed a multi-million dollar programme for NASA-MSFC on the Apollo Telescope Mount/Skylab programme.

The Fairchild Stratos Division specialises in the development and manufacture of aerospace and commercial aircraft subsystems, accessories and components. Products for the US space programmes include intricate cryogenic valves, fluid disconnects and gas regulators. Contracts included some seventy components for the Apollo/Saturn space vehicle. The self-sealing disconnects pioneered by the Division were used on the Lunar Modules. Stratos Division is now manufacturing valves and other components for the Space Shuttle.

Commercial products manufactured by the Division include lower lobe galley modules and food service carts for Boeing 747 and McDonnell Douglas DC-10 transports. Fairchild Stratos also supplies the complete food, beverage and waste cart system for the Lockheed L-1011 TriStar. The Division designs and manufactures an extensive line of military and commercial ground and airborne air-conditioning systems, together with air-turbine secondary power systems, subsystems and associated components.

Traditionally, this Division is a major producer of military airborne stores dispensing systems, for both lethal and non-lethal stores such as underwater sound sources, sonobuoys, flares, small bombs, and psychological warfare items for all US military services.

Fairchild Burns Company is one of the world's principal suppliers of commercial aircraft seating.

American Satellite Corporation, a subsidiary of Fairchild Industries, is developing a US domestic communications satellite system under authority from the Federal Communications Commission. The initial Earth stations for the nationwide system are located at sites near New York City, Chicago, Dallas and Los Angeles, and the service was scheduled to become operational during 1974.

Swearingen Aviation Corporation, a subsidiary in which Fairchild Industries has a ninety per cent holding, manufactures the Merlin series of turboprop-powered executive aircraft and the Metro 19-passenger aircraft for commuter airlines.

The Corporation has also the following subsidiaries: Fairchild Arms International Ltd, Germantown, Maryland; Fairchild Aviation (Asia) Ltd, Bangkok, Thailand; Fairchild Aviation (Holland) NV, Amsterdam, The Netherlands; and Fairchild-Germantown Development Co, Inc, Germantown, Maryland, a participant in the new Century XXI office centre surrounding the company's corporate headquarters.

FAIRCHILD INDUSTRIES F-27 and FH-227

Fairchild Industries was responsible for building several different models of the F-27 and FH-227, of which it sold a total of 205. Production of these has ended; a full structural description of both types can be found in the 1970-71 *Jane's*. Production in various versions of the original Dutch-built F.27, by Fokker-VFW, is continuing, and is described in the Netherlands section of this edition.

FAIRCHILD INDUSTRIES/PILATUS PORTER AND PEACEMAKER

USAF designation: AU-23A

Fairchild Industries is producing Porter STOL utility aircraft under licence from Pilatus Flugzeugwerke AG of Switzerland. These aircraft are available with a 680 shp United Aircraft of Canada PT6A-27 turboprop engine, flat rated to 550 shp. Alternative installation of the AiResearch TPE 331-101F turboprop engine was under development in early 1974, and this will be flat rated at 575 shp.

Flat rating is adopted on these engines in order to obtain improved hot-day and/or high-altitude performance.

The first production Fairchild Industries Porter (with PT6A-20 engine) was rolled out on 3 June 1966.

A militarised version of the Porter, known as the Peacemaker, has been developed for counter-insurgency operations, including transport, light armed and photographic reconnaissance, leaflet dropping and loudspeaker broadcasting. This version has an underfuselage hardpoint capable of carrying a 590 lb (268 kg) store, and four underwing hardpoints, of which the inboard pair can carry 510 lb (231 kg) each, and the outboard pair 350 lb (159 kg) each. However, total external load on each wing may not exceed 700 lb (318 kg).

Powered by the TPE 331-1-101F engine, the Peacemaker has a complete military nav/com system, including VHF, UHF, HF and FM electronics, an armament control system, dual controls, and high-flotation tyres for rough-field operation.

Alternative installations include two MXU-470 fixed side-firing Miniguns, with 2,000-round magazines, in the main cabin; SUU-11A/A Minigun pods on the inboard wing stations and LAU-59A rocket pods (each 7 × 2·75 in rockets) or 250 lb general-purpose bombs on the outer wing attachments; M19-19A6 machine-guns on fixed side-firing mounts; pintle-mounted GAU-2B/A Minigun with belt feed; an AEM-SYS-ZA 1,400W 20-speaker broadcasting pod on an inner wing hardpoint; a pod containing three P-2 70 mm cameras, and universal 5 in store dispensers each carrying eight flares of two million candlepower.

In early 1970, Fairchild demonstrated another version of the Peacemaker, by the successful installation and firing of an XM-197 side-firing flexibly-mounted manually-operated 20 mm cannon. Fifteen were acquired by the USAF for evaluation under its Credible Chase programme, in competition with the Helio AU-24A. Their designation is AU-23A. One of these aircraft was lost; thirteen were supplied to Thailand and one was retained by the USAF.

Full details of the basic Pilatus Porter can be found in the Swiss section of this edition.

FAIRCHILD INDUSTRIES MODEL FH-1100

The FH-1100 is a refined development of the OH-5A helicopter which Hiller designed for the US Army's LOH (light observation helicopter) competition.

Design of the OH-5A was started on 13 November 1961. Construction began in May 1962 and the first prototype flew on 26 January 1963. FAA certification was received on 20 July 1964. The decision to put the FH-1100 into production was announced in February 1965. The first production model was rolled out on 3 June 1966, and 250 were built.

A full description of the FH-1100 can be found in the 1973-74 *Jane's*.

FAIRCHILD INDUSTRIES M484
USAF designation: C-119K

Fairchild Industries modified a C-119 military transport to YC-119K standard, by adding two pylon-mounted auxiliary turbojets and installing a more powerful version of the existing piston engines. Design of the conversion was started in May 1966 and the prototype aircraft flew for the first time in February 1967.

The YC-119K is powered by two 3,700 hp (wet) Wright R-3350-999 TC18EA2 engines and two General Electric J85-GE-17 auxiliary turbojets, each rated at 2,850 lb (1,293 kg) st.

Fairchild announced on 26 February 1970 that it had received a contract from the USAF to modify an initial batch of five C-119G aircraft to C-119K configuration, including inspection and repair, and installation of anti-skid braking units; a contract for the modification of three additional aircraft was awarded in January 1971, and all eight aircraft were delivered subsequently to Ethiopia. Since that time, six C-119Gs have been modified to C-119K standard for Jordan.

Details of the standard C-119 last appeared in the 1957-58 *Jane's*.

WEIGHTS:
- Weight empty 44,747 lb (20,300 kg)
- Basic operating weight 45,435 lb (20,610 kg)
- Max payload 20,000 lb (9,070 kg)
- Max T-O and landing weight 77,000 lb (34,925 kg)

PERFORMANCE (at max T-O weight):
- Max level speed at 10,000 ft (3,050 m) 211 knots (243 mph; 391 km/h)
- Max cruising speed at 10,000 ft (3,050 m) 162 knots (187 mph; 300 km/h)
- Stalling speed, wheels and flaps down 98 knots (112 mph; 180 km/h)
- Rate of climb at S/L, one engine out 1,050 ft (320 m)/min
- Service ceiling, one engine out 18,100 ft (5,515 m)
- T-O run 1,501 ft (458 m)
- T-O to 50 ft (15 m) 2,100 ft (640 m)
- Landing from 50 ft (15 m) 3,200 ft (975 m)
- Ferry range with four 500 US gal (1,890 litre) Benson tanks 3,004 nm (3,460 miles; 5,570 km)
- Range with max payload 859 nm (990 miles; 1,595 km)

FAIRCHILD INDUSTRIES AC-119 GUNSHIP
USAF designations: AC-119G and AC-119K

To meet an Air Force requirement, Fairchild Aircraft Service Division modified 52 C-119 aircraft into gunships, with the designations AC-119G and AC-119K. Both models were used operationally in Vietnam, where the concept of arming large transport aircraft for interdiction and suppression of enemy ground attack proved very effective. Such gunships have the advantage of long endurance and an ability to carry a large load of equipment, sensors, guns and ammunition needed to locate and attack enemy material and personnel.

The first series of 26 AC-119G aircraft retain two Wright R-3350-89B engines and are fitted with four side-firing 7·62 mm General Electric Miniguns, a pallet-mounted airborne illuminator light set housed in the rear fuselage on the port side, with a LAU 74/A flare launcher on the starboard side. A light-intensifying night observation system is carried on the port side of the fuselage, forward of the wing, and other equipment includes a 60kVA auxiliary power unit, pilot's gunsight, analogue gunfire control computer system and protective armour for the crew.

The second series of 26 AC-119Ks have all the equipment of the AC-119Gs, plus two General Electric J85 auxiliary jet engines, each rated at 2,850 lb (1,293 kg) st, to improve performance, reduce take-off run and increase payload. Additional equipment includes a forward-looking infra-red sensor, side- and forward-looking radar and more nav/com. Armament is strengthened by the addition of two 20 mm cannon.

The Fairchild AC-119Gs and AC-119Ks were used operationally by the USAF under the designations "Shadow" and "Stinger" respectively. All have been transferred to the Vietnamese Air Force.

WEIGHTS:
- Weight empty 58,282 lb (26,436 kg)
- Basic operating weight 60,955 lb (27,649 kg)
- Max payload 4,838 lb (2,194 kg)
- Max T-O and landing weight 80,400 lb (36,468 kg)

PERFORMANCE (at max T-O weight):
- Max level speed at 10,000 ft (3,050 m) 217 knots (250 mph; 402 km/h)
- Max cruising speed at 10,000 ft (3,050 m), with auxiliary turbojets operating 190 knots (219 mph; 352 km/h)
- Max cruising speed at 10,000 ft (3,050 m), with auxiliary turbojets inoperative 150 knots (173 mph; 278 km/h)
- Stalling speed, wheels and flaps down 88 knots (101 mph; 163 km/h)
- Rate of climb at S/L, one engine out 900 ft (274 m)/min
- Service ceiling, one engine out 23,500 ft (7,163 m)
- T-O run 1,580 ft (482 m)
- T-O to 50 ft (15 m) 1,820 ft (555 m)
- Landing from 50 ft (15 m) 1,245 ft (379 m)
- Range with max payload 1,720 nm (1,980 miles; 3,186 km)

FAIRCHILD STRATOS MODEL 616 AERCAB

The Fairchild Stratos Division is one of two companies under contract to the US Navy to investigate an integrated aircrew escape/rescue capability (AERCAB) for combat aircraft. After a ½-scale model of the Fairchild Model 616 had been tested successfully by the Navy in a wind tunnel, a full-scale prototype model was built and negotiations were concluded for construction of a full-scale flying prototype. Flight feasibility demonstration of this was staged at El Centro, California, in early 1971. Development was continuing in 1974.

The US Navy issued a work objective for the AERCAB on 27 August 1968 through the Naval

Fairchild AU-23A Peacemaker, with side-firing gun in cabin doorway and underwing stores

Fairchild Industries AC-119K gunship, an armed conversion of the C-119 transport aircraft

Air Development Center. The purpose of AERCAB is to permit recovery of aircrew who eject from their aircraft over enemy territory and to provide capability to fly the ejection seat up to 43 nm (50 miles; 80 km) at up to 100 knots (115 mph; 185 km/h) prior to vertical descent by personal parachute.

A summary of the NADC requirements lists the following points:

- Safe ejection at velocities up to 600 knots (691 mph; 1,112 km/h);
- Sequencing to provide automatic deployment after ejection;
- A climb rate of 1,000 ft (305 m) per minute for three minutes after deployment;
- Cruise at 100 knots (115 mph; 185 km/h) for 30 minutes;
- Operating altitudes from sea level to 10,000 ft (3,050 m);
- Man/AERCAB separation and vertical descent by personal parachute at end of flight;
- Completely automatic operation from time of aircraft ejection to man/AERCAB separation (with provision for manual override);
- Minimum packaged or folded volume to allow for installation in the A-7 and F-4 aircraft with minimum aircraft modifications;
- Uncompromised normal ejection mode if conditions warrant (automatically sensed by on-board equipment);
- Incorporation of all normal aircrew survival equipment.

The AERCAB would be used in situations where the disabled aircraft was at more than 800 ft (243 m) and in an upright attitude. Below this height, or in an adverse attitude, conventional seat ejection would be used; an on-board ejection sequencer would automatically select the correct mode.

Fairchild's concept can be considered basically as a light aeroplane. It consists of a seat, tailboom, wing, jet engine and inflatable nose fairing. The seat, of conventional design including catapult thrusters and sustainer rockets, forms the basic structure for the entire vehicle.

The nose fairing will be a double-walled inflatable structure which when deflated stows under the pilot's legs against the front of the seat. It protects the occupant from the airstream and provides a low-drag profile for the vehicle. A tank in the seat provides a source of compressed air to inflate the nose structure and a tubular framework extends forward from the seat to support it when inflated.

Three tubular telescoping sections make up the tailboom and position the tail surfaces far enough aft for aerodynamic stability. The outer section of the boom is fixed and forms the primary structural member and the innermost boom section contains and carries the tail surfaces.

The wing of the Model 616 is designed on the Princeton sailwing principle, with a rigid spar to support the leading-edge and tip, and the trailing-edge tensioned by wire. Top and bottom surfaces are covered by a fabric of Dacron sailcloth. Wing lift is gained from the predictable deformation of the fabric between the leading-edge and the tensioned trailing-edge catenary. Fuel is stored in the leading-edge spar, which is of NACA symmetrical aerofoil section; when stowed, the spar folds in the middle and hinges back.

Test version of the Fairchild Stratos Model 616 AERCAB

A small turbofan engine, of the type developed by Continental Motors or Williams, is proposed as the power plant. The required thrust is 160 lb (72·5 kg).

A wholly-automatic deployment and recovery sequence is planned, with provision for pilot override at all times. Initiation of deployment starts with stabilisation of the seat by the drogue chute in the airstream, and as soon as the seat has slowed to 150 knots (172 mph; 277 km/h) IAS. Deployment is achieved through mechanical linkages to the drogue chute line and the AERCAB will be in the climb condition, at full engine thrust, in 6-10 seconds after ejection.

An autopilot will fly the AERCAB to a predetermined altitude and will then trim it to cruise at 100 knots (115 mph; 185 km/h) on a pre-selected heading, programmed into the autopilot prior to the start of the mission. After engine shut-down, the AERCAB glides to a preset altitude, sensed by radar altimeter, and the pilot is then ejected by deploying his personal parachute. Using manual override or in the event of engine malfunction, the pilot can fly the Model 616 as a glider, when its best glide ratio is 8.

The accompanying photograph shows AERCAB in the test form current in early 1974. Although the wings fold, all other components have been made rigid to withstand the rigours of many take-offs and landings required by the development programme. In due course the landing gear will be removed, and the transparent plastics nose fairing will be replaced by the definitive inflatable rubber shield.

DIMENSIONS (deployed):	
Span	15 ft 5½ in (4·70 m)
Wing aspect ratio	6·9
Wing dihedral	6°
Length	15 ft 0½ in (4·57 m)
Height	2 ft 6½ in (0·77 m)
Tailplane span	4 ft 2 in (1·27 m)
Tailplane anhedral or dihedral	30°
AREAS:	
Wings, gross	36 sq ft (3·34 m²)
Tailplane area	6·68 sq ft (0·62 m²)
Vertical fin area	3·34 sq ft (0·31 m²)
WEIGHTS AND LOADINGS:	
Empty weight	304 lb (138 kg)
Useful load	296 lb (134 kg)
Max gross weight	600 lb (272 kg)
Wing loading	16·6 lb/sq ft (81·1 kg/m²)
Power loading	3·75 lb/lb st (3·75 kg/kg st)

FAIRCHILD REPUBLIC COMPANY

PRESIDENT: Charles Collis

Fairchild Republic Division

Farmingdale, Long Island, New York 11735

VICE-PRESIDENT AND GENERAL MANAGER:
Donald J. Strait

VICE-PRESIDENT AND ASSISTANT GENERAL MANAGER:
Dr N. Grossman

DIRECTOR OF OPERATIONS:
R. Bernitt

CHIEF ENGINEER: J. Williamson

DIRECTOR OF MARKETING: W. Morris

Founded on 17 February 1931, as the Seversky Aircraft Company, Republic operated as Republic Aviation Corporation from 1939 until September 1965, when it became a division of Fairchild Hiller Corporation, now Fairchild Industries Inc.

Production of the F-105 Thunderchief supersonic fighter-bomber has been completed, but Republic has important contracts to improve the operational capabilities of F-105s in service, and has developed a new bombing system for the F-105D, known as the T-Stick II.

In early 1973 the Fairchild Republic Company was named the winner of the A-X competition for the development of a new close-support aircraft for the USAF. Designated A-10A, it is the first US aircraft designed specifically for this role. Other major contracts cover the manufacture of assemblies for the McDonnell Douglas F/RF-4 Phantom II fighter and the Boeing 747. For the 747, the Division is manufacturing all the wing control surfaces, including ailerons, spoilers, leading-edge flaps and trailing-edge flaps.

FAIRCHILD REPUBLIC A-10A

USAF designation: A-10A

On 18 December 1970, Fairchild Republic was selected as one of two companies that were each to build two prototypes for evaluation under the USAF's A-X programme for a close-support aircraft. The first Fairchild Republic prototype, designated A-10A, flew for the first time on 10 May 1972, followed by the second prototype on 21 July 1972. USAF flight evaluation in competition with Northrop's A-9A began on 10 October and was completed on 9 December 1972. On 18 January 1973 it was announced that the A-10A had been selected as the winner, and the company later received a contract for six pre-production aircraft, of which the first was due to be delivered in December 1974. An initial order for 30 production A-10As was expected in Summer 1974.

The following description applies to the production version:

TYPE: Single-seat close-support aircraft.

WINGS: Cantilever low-wing monoplane of

Prototype of the Fairchild Republic A-10A single-seat close-support aircraft

all-metal construction. Dihedral on wing outer panels, which have cambered tips. Sweepback on leading-edge of outer panels. Wide-chord wings of deep aerofoil section to provide low wing loading. Wide-span interchangeable ailerons, made up of dual upper and lower surfaces that separate to serve as airbrakes. Two-segment trailing-edge flaps. Small leading-edge slats inboard of wheel fairings. Triple-redundant and armour-protected flight control system. Electrically-operated trim tab in each aileron.

FUSELAGE: All-metal semi-monocoque structure. Pilot's compartment in nose, well forward of wing leading-edge.

TAIL UNIT: Cantilever all-metal structure, with twin fins and interchangeable rudders mounted at the tips of constant-chord tailplane. Interchangeable elevators, each with an electrically-operated trim tab. Triple-redundant and armour-protected flight control system.

LANDING GEAR: Tricycle type, with a single forward-retracting wheel on each unit. Interchangeable main-wheel units retract into pod fairings attached to the lower surface of the wings. When fully retracted approximately half of each main wheel protrudes from the fairing. Nosewheel offset to starboard to clear centrally-installed gun.

POWER PLANT: Two General Electric TF34-GE-100 high by-pass ratio turbofan engines, each of 9,065 lb (4,111 kg) st, enclosed in armoured pods and pylon-mounted to the upper rear fuselage, at a point approximately midway between the wing trailing-edge and the tailplane leading-edge. Fuel contained in four tear-resistant and self-sealing fuel cells, the two main cells in the fuselage, plus a smaller cell in each inboard wing panel. Maximum internal fuel capacity 10,650 lb (4,830 kg). All fuel cells are internally filled with, and externally cradled in, reticulated foam, and all fuel systems pipework is contained within the cells, except for the feeds to the engines, which have self-sealing covers. Three jettisonable auxiliary tanks can be carried on underwing and fuselage centreline pylons, and the fuel system includes flight refuelling capability.

ACCOMMODATION: Enclosed titanium armour-plated cockpit for pilot only, well forward of wing, with large transparent bubble canopy to provide all-round visibility. Basic design work for a two-seat version has been completed.

SYSTEMS: Two primary hydraulic flight control systems, with manual backup. Electrical system. Auxiliary power unit. Environmental control system.

ELECTRONICS AND EQUIPMENT: Head-up display giving airspeed, altitude, and dive angle; weapons delivery package with dual reticle optical sight for use in conjunction with laser aiming; target penetration aids; associated equipment for Maverick and other missile systems; IFF/SIF (AIMS); UHF/AM; VHF/AM; VHF/FM; HF/SSB; secure voice communications; TACAN; UHF/DF; VOR/ILS; LORAN C/D; X-band transponder; heading and altitude reference system (HARS); radar homing and warning (RHAW); armament control panel, and gun camera.

ARMAMENT: Seven-barrel General Electric GAU-8/A 30 mm gun, pallet-mounted in the nose. The gun and the handling system for the linkless ammunition are mechanically synchronised and driven by two hydraulic motors fed from the aircraft's system. The magazine has a capacity of 1,350 rounds, and the firing rate is from 2,100 to 4,200 rounds per minute. Five stores pylons under each wing (two inboard and three outboard of main-wheel fairing) and one under fuselage for max external load of 16,000 lb (7,257

Fairchild Republic A-10A close-support aircraft (two General Electric TF34 turbofan engines)

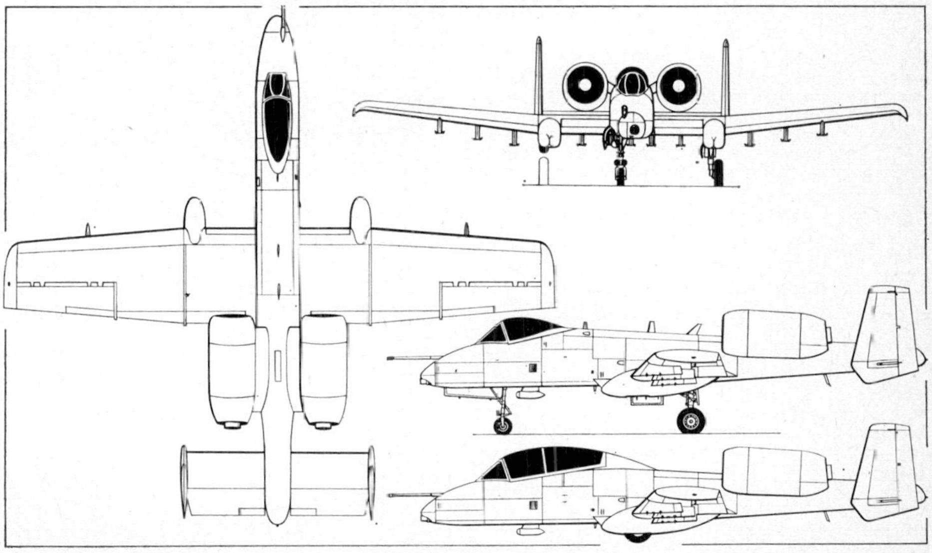

Fairchild Republic A-10A single-seat twin-engined close-support aircraft. The lower side view shows a projected two-seat version (*Pilot Press*)

kg). The centreline pylon has a capacity of 5,000 lb (2,268 kg), the two inner pylons on each wing 3,500 lb (1,587 kg) each, the centre wing pylons 2,500 lb (1,134 kg) each and the two outboard pylons on each wing 1,000 lb (453 kg) each. These allow carriage of a wide range of stores including 24 × 500 lb Mk-82 LDGP, 24 × 500 lb Mk-82 retarded, 16 × 750 lb M-117 LDGP, 16 × 750 lb M-117 retarded or 4 × 2,000 lb Mk-84 general-purpose bombs; 8 BLU-1 or BLU-27/8 incendiary bombs; 4 SUU-25 or SUU-42 flare launchers; 20 Rockeye 11 cluster bombs, 16 CBU-24/49, 8 CBU-43, or 12 CBU-60 dispenser weapons; 9 AGM-65 Maverick and 2 AIM-9E/J Sidewinder missiles; Mk-82 and Mk-84 laser-guided bombs; Mk-84 EO-guided bombs; 2 SUU-23 or recoilless gun pods.

DIMENSIONS, EXTERNAL:

Wing span	55 ft 0 in (16·76 m)
Length overall, incl probe	53 ft 4 in (16·23 m)
Height overall	14 ft 8 in (4·47 m)
Tailplane span	18 ft 10 in (5·74 m)
Wheel track	17 ft 2½ in (5·25 m)
Wheelbase	17 ft 8¾ in (5·40 m)

AREAS:

Wings, gross	488 sq ft (45·3 m²)
Ailerons (total, incl tabs)	52·14 sq ft (4·84 m²)
Trailing-edge flaps (total)	80·2 sq ft (7·45 m²)
Leading-edge slats (total)	10·56 sq ft (0·98 m²)
Airbrakes (total)	86·0 sq ft (7·99 m²)
Fins (total)	85·1 sq ft (7·91 m²)
Rudders (total)	22·4 sq ft (2·08 m²)
Tailplane	87·3 sq ft (8·11 m²)
Elevators, incl tabs	31·1 sq ft (2·89 m²)

WEIGHTS:

Max T-O weight	45,560 lb (20,665 kg)
Forward airstrip weight	30,344 lb (13,763 kg)

PERFORMANCE (A at max T-O weight; B at forward airstrip weight):

Max never-exceed speed
450 knots (518 mph; 834 km/h)
Combat speed, clean, at S/L
390 knots (449 mph; 723 km/h)
Combat speed at 5,000 ft (1,525 m), with 6 Mk-82 bombs 385 knots (443 mph; 713 km/h)
Cruising speed at S/L
300 knots (345 mph; 555 km/h)
Stabilised 45° dive speed
260 knots (299 mph; 481 km/h)
T-O distance:
A 3,850 ft (1,173 m)
B 1,130 ft (344 m)
Landing distance:
A 2,140 ft (652 m)
B 1,085 ft (331 m)
Close air support radius, with 2 hr loiter and 20 min reserve 250 nm (288 miles; 463 km)
Escort radius 258 nm (297 miles; 478 km)
Reconnaissance radius
406 nm (467 miles; 751 km)
Ferry range 2,365 nm (2,723 miles; 4,382 km)

FARRINGTON

FARRINGTON AIRCRAFT CORPORATION

HEAD OFFICE:
PO Box 9, Paducah, Kentucky 42001
Telephone: (502) 444-6611

PRESIDENT: I. D. Farrington Jr

Farrington Aircraft Corporation has produced an improved version of the Model 18-A light autogyro that was designed and developed originally by the Umbaugh Aircraft Corporation in the period 1957-62.

Farrington Aircraft has modified the Model 18-A further by the installation of a strengthened nose landing gear strut and provision of a variable collective pitch trim system, and has obtained an FAA Supplementary Type Certificate for the modified version. This includes also as standard equipment tubeless tyres, improved soundproofing, night flying kit and beacons and, in this form, is not restricted from night flying operations.

At present the company is offering these modifications for application to existing Model 18-As; but in 1975 it is planned to begin production of an improved version with a 200 hp Lycoming IO-360 engine and a rotor of 37 ft 2 in (11·33 m) diameter with glassfibre blades. It is planned also to redesign the exhaust system and engine cowlings to reduce noise and improve cooling and at the same time a cabin heater and windscreen defroster will become standard. Windscreen wipers will be optional. It is intended also to make increased use of glassfibre in non-structural areas. In this form, the new model will have a maximum AUW of 2,000 lb (907 kg).

The description which follows applies to the existing Model 18-A, as modified:

FARRINGTON MODEL 18-A

The President of Farrington Aircraft Corporation established two international speed records in FAI Class E3, for autogyros, on 1 May 1971, with average speeds of 94·395 knots (108·698 mph; 174·932 km/h) over a 15/25 km course and 88·693 knots (102·132 mph; 164·365 km/h) over a 100 km closed circuit.

TYPE: Two-seat light autogyro.

ROTOR SYSTEM: Three-blade fully-articulated rotor, with blades of laminated wood, covered with glassfibre. Blade aerofoil section NACA 0012. Longitudinal and lateral control effected by mechanically tilting the rotor plane. Electrically-controlled variable collective pitch trim system. Hydraulic clutch for pre-rotation of rotor for jump-starts. Rotor brake.

FUSELAGE: Built in three sections. Forward fuselage and tailboom are stressed-skin light alloy structures. Centre section, carrying landing gear, rotor pylon and engine, is a welded 4130 steel tube structure.

TAIL UNIT: Cantilever all-metal structure. Two fixed fins at tips of tailplane and all-moving central fin.

LANDING GEAR: Non-retractable tricycle type. Long-travel Ronson oleo-pneumatic shock-absorber struts. Goodyear main wheels and tyres size 6·00-6. Goodyear nosewheel and tyre size 5·00-4. Goodyear wheel brakes.

POWER PLANT: One 180 hp Lycoming O-360-A1D four-cylinder horizontally-opposed aircooled engine, driving a Hartzell Type HC-92ZK/L8447A-8 two-blade metal constant-speed pusher propeller. Fuel tank in centre fuselage with capacity of 28·3 US gallons (107 litres), of which 27·8 US gallons (105 litres) are usable. Refuelling point on port side of fuselage, aft of cabin. Oil capacity 2 US gallons (7·5 litres).

ACCOMMODATION: Two seats in tandem in enclosed cabin. Large door on starboard side, hinged at forward edge. Dual controls standard, but only occupant of forward seat has control of wheel brakes. Space for 100 lb (45 kg) baggage.

SYSTEMS: Hydraulic system for de-pitch controls and wheel brakes. 12V electrical system supplied by 50A engine-driven generator with inverter and converter.

ELECTRONICS AND EQUIPMENT: Radio and inter-com optional. Standard equipment includes VFR flight instruments, navigation lights, strobe lights and instrument panel lights. Provision for fitting rocket tubes to side of cabin of proposed military version.

DIMENSIONS, EXTERNAL:

Rotor diameter	35 ft 0 in (10·67 m)
Rotor blade chord	1 ft 0½ in (0·32 m)
Length of fuselage	19 ft 10½ in (6·06 m)
Height overall	9 ft 8 in (2·95 m)
Width overall	9 ft 1½ in (2·78 m)
Wheel track	9 ft 0 in (2·74 m)
Wheelbase	9 ft 4¼ in (2·85 m)

AREAS:

Rotor disc	963 sq ft (89·47 m²)
Rotor blades (each)	20 sq ft (1·86 m²)

WEIGHTS AND LOADINGS:

Weight empty	1,315 lb (597 kg)
Max T-O weight	1,800 lb (816 kg)
Max disc loading	1·87 lb/sq ft (9·13 kg/m²)
Max power loading	10 lb/hp (4·54 kg/hp)

PERFORMANCE (at max T-O weight):

Max never-exceed speed 95·5 knots (110 mph; 177 km/h) IAS

Max cruising speed, 75% power at 4,000 ft (1,220 m) 80 knots (92 mph; 148 km/h)

Min level flight speed 23·5 knots (27 mph; 43·5 km/h)

Max rate of climb at S/L 770 ft (235 m)/min

Service ceiling 10,000 ft (3,050 m)

T-O run at density altitude of up to 4,000 ft (1,220 m) Nil

T-O run at density altitudes of 4,000-8,000 ft (1,220-2,440 m) 120 ft (37 m)

Landing run 0-50 ft (0-15 m)

Range, with reserve 173 nm (200 miles; 322 km)

Max endurance, at airspeed of 43 knots (50 mph; 80·5 km/h) 3½ hr

Farrington Model 18-A light autogyro (180 hp Lycoming O-360-A1D engine) (*Brian M. Service*)

FIKE

WILLIAM J. FIKE

ADDRESS:

PO Box 683, Anchorage, Alaska 99510

Telephone: (907) 272-7069

Mr W. J. Fike, whose 16,000 hours logged as a pilot include thousands of hours of "bush flying" in Alaska, has designed and built five light aircraft since 1929. His Model "B" of 1935 was a tiny parasol-wing single-seat monoplane, powered by a 35 hp Long Harlequin engine and with an empty weight of only 300 lb (136 kg). In the following year he produced the Model "C" of similar configuration. A later design was the single- or two-seat Model "D" high-wing cabin monoplane, of which full details were given in the 1961-62 *Jane's*.

This was followed by the Model "E", completed in 1970, a description of which follows. In January 1974 Mr Fike was well advanced with the construction of a new lightweight cabin monoplane which he has designated Model "F". This is a braced high-wing monoplane which may be powered by engines of 40-100 hp. A 65 hp Continental A65-8 has been installed in the prototype, which was scheduled to make its first flight during the Summer of 1974.

Plans of the Model "D" and Model "E" are available to amateur constructors.

FIKE MODEL "E"

In 1953 Mr Fike began design of an aircraft to evaluate the flight characteristics of a low aspect ratio (3·0) wing of only 9% thickness/chord ratio when applied to a low-power monoplane of high-wing configuration. The wing, of wooden geodetic construction, is so designed that various wingtips may be installed for evaluation. A standard Piper J-3 tail unit is utilised, but this is modified by keeping the tailplane span within the 8 ft (2·44 m) limit allowed by US highway regulations for towed vehicles.

A secondary objective of the Model "E" project was to develop a low-cost easy-to-build two-seat lightplane. The wing can be removed within ten minutes to enable the aircraft to be towed by a motor vehicle or for storage in an ordinary garage.

Mr Fike's former heavy commitments as an airline pilot were responsible for the extended construction time, over a period of seven years; but construction was completed in early 1970 and the first flight was made on 22 March 1970.

During 1971 Mr Fike re-engined the Model "E" with an 85 hp Continental C85-8 engine, and it was first flown with this power plant on 6 June 1971. It had accumulated a total of 176 flight hours by early 1974.

TYPE: High-wing sporting monoplane.

WINGS: Cantilever high-wing monoplane. Wing section NACA 4409. No dihedral. Incidence 1° 15′. No sweepback. All-wood geodetic structure, fabric-covered. Conventional wooden ailerons. No flaps. No trim tabs.

Fike Model "E" lightweight cabin monoplane (85 hp Continental C85-8 engine) (*Howard Levy*)

FUSELAGE: Welded steel tube structure; fabric-covered.

TAIL UNIT: Cantilever welded steel tube structure with fabric covering. Adjustable-incidence tailplane. No trim tabs.

LANDING GEAR: Standard Piper J-3 gear of non-retractable tailwheel type, with rubber-cord shock-absorption. Main wheels and tyres size 8·00-4, pressure 15-20 lb/sq in (1·05-1·4 kg/cm²). Max speed can be increased by 7 knots (8 mph; 13 km/h) by fitting 5·00-4 wheels, tyres and tubes. Goodrich toe-operated hydraulic brakes. Federal A-1500 skis available optionally.

POWER PLANT: One 85 hp Continental C85-8 four-cylinder horizontally-opposed aircooled engine, driving a Sensenich Type 76AK two-blade fixed-pitch metal propeller. One (Cessna 140 type) fuel tank in each wing, capacity 12·5 US gallons (47·5 litres). Total fuel capacity 25 US gallons (95 litres). Refuelling point on top of each wing. Oil capacity 1 US gallon (3·8 litres).

ACCOMMODATION: Pilot (with provision for passenger seated in tandem) in enclosed cabin. Door on each side of fuselage, hinged at forward edge. Cabin heated and ventilated. Baggage compartment aft of cabin. Overhead control assembly permits sleeping in the cabin after removing or collapsing seat.

EQUIPMENT: Radair 10 10-channel VHF communications transceiver.

DIMENSIONS, EXTERNAL:

Wing span	20 ft 0 in (6·10 m)
Wing chord (constant, except for tips)	6 ft 8 in (2·03 m)
Wing chord at tip	5 ft 8 in (1·73 m)
Wing aspect ratio	3·0
Length overall	19 ft 2 in (5·84 m)
Height overall	5 ft 8 in (1·73 m)
Tailplane span	7 ft 10 in (2·39 m)
Wheel track	6 ft 0 in (1·83 m)
Wheelbase	14 ft 2 in (4·32 m)
Propeller diameter	6 ft 2 in (1·88 m)
Doors (each):	
Height	2 ft 8 in (0·81 m)
Width	1 ft 8 in (0·51 m)
Height to sill	2 ft 4 in (0·71 m)

DIMENSIONS, INTERNAL:

Cabin: Length	5 ft 6 in (1·68 m)
Max width	2 ft 0 in (0·61 m)
Max height	3 ft 8 in (1·12 m)
Floor area	10 sq ft (0·93 m²)
Volume	35 cu ft (0·99 m³)
Baggage compartment	12 cu ft (0·34 m³)

AREAS:

Wings, gross	132·3 sq ft (12·29 m²)
Ailerons (total)	19·5 sq ft (1·81 m²)
Fin	6·7 sq ft (0·62 m²)
Rudder	6·5 sq ft (0·60 m²)
Tailplane	13·0 sq ft (1·21 m²)
Elevators	10·0 sq ft (0·93 m²)

WEIGHTS AND LOADINGS:

Weight empty	675 lb (306 kg)
Normal T-O weight	1,100 lb (499 kg)
Max wing loading	8·3 lb/sq ft (40·5 kg/m²)
Max power loading	13 lb/hp (5·90 kg/hp)

PERFORMANCE (with 85 hp engine and 5·00-4 wheels, at normal T-O weight):

Max level speed at S/L 104 knots (120 mph; 193 km/h)

Cruising speed 82·5 knots (95 mph; 153 km/h)

Landing speed 30·4 knots (35 mph; 56 km/h)

Max rate of climb at S/L 1,000 ft (305 m)/min

Service ceiling over 10,000 ft (3,050 m)

T-O run 250-300 ft (76-92 m)

Landing run under 300 ft (92 m)

Range with max fuel, 15 min reserve 390 nm (450 miles; 724 km)

FLAGLOR

FLAGLOR AIRCRAFT

ADDRESS:

1550A Sanders Road, Northbrook, Illinois 60062

The latest of a series of light aircraft designed and built by Mr K. Flaglor is an ultra-light sporting monoplane named the Scooter. Design work began in July 1965, and construction was started in November of the same year. The Scooter was powered originally by an 18 hp Cushman golf-kart engine, and it was with this power plant that the first flight was made in June 1967. Performance was marginal and, as a result, Mr Flaglor replaced the Cushman with a nominal 36 hp (25-28 hp output) Volkswagen engine. Current power plant is a 1,500 cc Volkswagen engine developing 40 hp. When flown to the 1967 EAA meet at Rockford, Illinois, the Scooter won the "Outstanding Ultra-light" and "Outstanding Volkswagen-Powered Airplane" awards. Plans are available to amateur constructors from Ace Aircraft Manufacturing Company (see page 241).

The accompanying illustration shows a Flaglor Scooter built by Mr Toshimaru Maeda, of Fukui on the Honshu Island of Japan. Powered by a 40 hp Volkswagen 1,500 cc engine, it appears to conform to Mr Flaglor's plans, but is a little heavier than the prototype, with an empty weight of 441 lb (200 kg).

FLAGLOR SCOOTER

TYPE: Ultra-light sporting monoplane.

WINGS: High-wing monoplane, braced by wires attached to fuselage and to kingpost mounted above centre-section. Wing section NACA 23012. Dihedral 2°. Incidence 3°. Two-spar all-wood structure with wood drag and anti-drag bracing. Aluminium leading-edge and plywood covering. Conventional wooden ailerons. No flaps. No trim tabs.

FUSELAGE: Wooden structure, plywood-covered in the forward cockpit area, fabric-covered aft. Fuselage of triangular section aft of the wing. Wing centre-section and engine mounting constructed of 4130 steel tube.

TAIL UNIT: All-wooden construction with strut bracing. No fixed fin. No trim tabs.

LANDING GEAR: Non-retractable tailwheel type. Fixed spring steel main units. Steerable tail-wheel. Main wheels of Go-Kart type, size 4·10 × 3·50-5. Tyre pressure 20 lb/sq in (1·41 kg/cm²). Vespa or Sears motor scooter brakes.

POWER PLANT: One 40 hp Volkswagen 1,500 cc four-cylinder horizontally-opposed aircooled engine, driving a two-blade Troyer 54-28 propeller. Single fuel tank in fuselage nose, capacity 5 US gallons (19 litres). Filling point on top of fuselage forward of windscreen. Oil capacity 2·5 US quarts (2·37 litres).

ACCOMMODATION: Single seat in cockpit protected by deep windscreen.

DIMENSIONS, EXTERNAL:

Wing span	28 ft 0 in (8·64 m)
Wing chord (constant)	4 ft 2 in (1·27 m)
Wing aspect ratio	6·7
Length overall	15 ft 8 in (4·78 m)
Height overall	7 ft 0 in (2·13 m)
Tailplane span	7 ft 2 in (2·18 m)
Wheel track	4 ft 6 in (1·37 m)

AREAS:

Wings, gross	115 sq ft (10·68 m²)
Ailerons (total)	12·5 sq ft (1·16 m²)
Rudder	5·6 sq ft (0·52 m²)
Tailplane	10·8 sq ft (1·00 m²)
Elevators	7·7 sq ft (0·72 m²)

WEIGHTS AND LOADINGS:

Weight empty	390 lb (177 kg)
Max T-O and landing weight	650 lb (295 kg)
Max wing loading	5·7 lb/sq ft (27·8 kg/m²)
Max power loading	1·6 lb/hp (0·73 kg/hp)

PERFORMANCE:

Max never-exceed speed	82 knots (95 mph; 153 km/h)
Max level speed	78 knots (90 mph; 145 km/h)
Max cruising speed	69 knots (80 mph; 129 km/h)
Econ cruising speed	56 knots (65 mph; 105 km/h)
Stalling speed	30 knots (34 mph; 55 km/h)
Max rate of climb at S/L	600 ft (183 m)/min
T-O run	250 ft (76 m)
Landing run	250 ft (76 m)
Range with max fuel	152 nm (175 miles; 282 km)

Flaglor Scooter built by Mr Toshimaru Maeda of Fukui, Japan (*H. Seo*)

FLIGHT DYNAMICS

FLIGHT DYNAMICS INC

ADDRESS:
PO Box 5070, State College Station, Raleigh, North Carolina 27607
Telephone: (919) 834-6806

PRESIDENT:
Thomas H. Purcell Jr

Flight Dynamics Inc has designed, built and developed an unusual two-seat lightweight amphibian of which plans are available to amateur constructors. It can be built in Stage 1 configuration with a flexible wing and without power plant, and be towed into the air by a water-ski tow boat. In Stage II configuration a power plant is added, enabling the aircraft to be flown from land or water. The final Stage III configuration substitutes a conventional fixed wing in place of the flexible wing.

Flight Dynamics claims that the simplified method of construction enables the homebuilder to get the aircraft into the air in a minimum of time, and that it can be completed in more sophisticated form as time and finances allow.

The design of the Flightsail VII, as this aircraft is known, began in January 1966, with construction of the prototype starting in March 1967, and the first flight was made in October 1970. The details which follow apply to the aircraft in Stage III configuration, with fixed wing and power plant:

FLIGHT DYNAMICS FLIGHTSAIL VII

TYPE: Two-seat lightweight homebuilt amphibian.

WINGS: Braced high-wing monoplane, with Vee bracing struts and auxiliary struts on each side. Wing section NACA 23012. Dihedral 2°. Incidence 6°. No sweepback. Built-up light alloy main spar, bolted together; aerofoil of solid sculptured styrofoam; the whole covered in glassfibre. Plain trailing-edge flaps and ailerons of styrofoam construction, glassfibre covered. No trim tabs.

FUSELAGE: Light alloy structure bolted together, stiffened with styrofoam and covered with glassfibre. Specially designed floats, one each side of fuselage undersurface, are integral with fuselage structure. Fuselage terminates in twin booms, wire-braced.

TAIL UNIT: Twin fins and rudders mounted on fuselage booms. Narrow-chord fixed horizontal surface braces tailbooms to each other. Large balanced elevator.

LANDING GEAR: Mechanically-retractable tricycle type. Shock-absorption by coil spring. Modified commercial wheels. Main-wheel tyre pressure 50 lb/sq in (3·52 kg/cm²). Hearst-Aerheart wheel brakes.

POWER PLANT: One 90 hp Continental C90 four-cylinder horizontally-opposed aircooled engine, carried on two pylons above the wing, and driving a two-blade fixed-pitch pusher propeller. Provision for engines of 85-125 hp. Present fuel tank has capacity of 20 US gallons (75·5 litres), but optimum size not yet determined. Oil capacity 1·25 US gallons (4·7 litres).

ACCOMMODATION: Two seats side by side in enclosed cockpit. Transparent canopy hinged at top, opening upward. Provision for cockpit heating system.

SYSTEMS: Hydraulic system for brakes only. Electrical system powered by engine-driven generator.

ELECTRONICS: Com transceiver only.

DIMENSIONS, EXTERNAL:

Wing span	39 ft 0 in (11·89 m)
Wing chord (constant)	5 ft 0 in (1·52 m)
Wing aspect ratio	7·8
Length overall	25 ft 0 in (7·62 m)
Height overall	8 ft 9½ in (2·68 m)
Elevator span	16 ft 0 in (4·88 m)
Wheel track	7 ft 6 in (2·29 m)
Wheelbase	8 ft 7 in (2·62 m)
Propeller diameter	6 ft 2 in (1·88 m)

DIMENSIONS, INTERNAL:

Cockpit: Length	7 ft 1 in (2·16 m)
Max width	5 ft 10 in (1·78 m)
Max height	3 ft 0 in (0·91 m)

AREAS:

Wings, gross	195 sq ft (18·1 m²)
Ailerons (total)	20 sq ft (1·86 m²)
Trailing-edge flaps (total)	20 sq ft (1·86 m²)
Fins (total)	8 sq ft (0·74 m²)
Rudders (total)	12 sq ft (1·11 m²)
Fixed horizontal surface	2 sq ft (0·19 m²)
Elevator	35 sq ft (3·25 m²)

WEIGHTS AND LOADINGS:

Weight empty	1,200 lb (544 kg)
Max T-O weight	1,700 lb (771 kg)
Max wing loading	8·7 lb/sq ft (42·5 kg/m²)
Max power loading	18·8 lb/hp (8·53 kg/hp)

PERFORMANCE (at max T-O weight):

Max never-exceed speed	112 knots (130 mph; 209 km/h)
Max level speed at S/L	82 knots (95 mph; 153 km/h)
Max cruising speed	74 knots (85 mph; 137 km/h)
Stalling speed, flaps down	35 knots (40 mph; 65 km/h)
Max rate of climb at S/L	500 ft (152 m)/min
Service ceiling	12,000 ft (3,660 m)
T-O time on water	20 sec
T-O to 50 ft (15 m)	1,100 ft (335 m)
Landing from 50 ft (15 m)	1,000 ft (305 m)
Landing run	400 ft (122 m)
Range with max fuel	260 nm (300 miles; 482 km)
Range with max payload	173 nm (200 miles; 321 km)

Flight Dynamics Flightsail VII homebuilt amphibian (90 hp Continental C90 engine)

FRAKES

FRAKES AVIATION INC

ADDRESS:
PO Box 159, Angwin, California 94508
Telephone: (707) 965-2405

SECRETARY-TREASURER: Joe Frakes

FRAKES TURBO-MALLARD

During 1969 Frakes Aviation purchased from Northern Consolidated Airways of Alaska a Grumman Mallard amphibian. This aircraft had been used in 1964 to demonstrate the feasibility of converting from piston engines to turboprop engines. The original Pratt & Whitney R-1340 engine was removed from the starboard wing and replaced by a United Aircraft of Canada PT6A-9 turboprop; the R-1340 engine was retained on the port side and flight tests were carried out with this mixed power plant. After 15 hours of flight testing, during which the conversion was found to be satisfactory, the piston engine was re-installed on the starboard side and the Mallard resumed service with Northern Consolidated Airways.

This same aircraft was acquired by Frakes in 1969, and has been converted to turbine power by the installation of two United Aircraft of Canada PT6A-27 turboprop engines, flat-rated at 715 ehp. It flew for the first time in this configuration in September 1969, and an FAA Supplemental Type Certificate in the Transport category was awarded in October 1970.

The Turbo-Mallard is available with either PT6A-27 or PT6A-34 turboprop engines, each flat-rated at 715 ehp. Frakes has developed for this power plant an inertial separator type of air intake, with normal and anti-icing modes, and has installed an automatic propeller feathering system which is designed to be operative from the start of the take-off run to a 400 ft (122 m) altitude. With one propeller feathered, it is impossible for the second propeller to auto-feather even if the engine fails.

Standard fuel system comprises two main wing tanks, each of 190 US gallons (719 litres) capacity, and two wingtip float tanks, each of 50 US gallons (189 litres). Total standard fuel capacity is 480 US gallons (1,816 litres). Two optional auxiliary fuel tanks, each of 83 US gallons (314 litres) can be installed in the wings, giving a maximum fuel capacity of 646 US gallons (2,444 litres).

B. F. Goodrich Type 21 pneumatic de-icing boots are standard on wing and tail unit leading-edges; the propellers, engine air intakes and windscreen have electrical de-icing.

WEIGHTS AND LOADINGS:
- Weight empty, equipped: 8,750 lb (3,969 kg)
- Max T-O weight: 14,000 lb (6,350 kg)
- Max landing weight: 13,500 lb (6,124 kg)
- Max wing loading: 31·53 lb/sq ft (153·9 kg/m²)
- Max power loading: 9·79 lb/ehp (4·44 kg/ehp)

PERFORMANCE (at max T-O weight):
- Max never-exceed speed up to 10,000 ft (3,050 m): 208 knots (240 mph; 386 km/h) IAS
- Max cruising speed at S/L: 191 knots (220 mph; 354 km/h)
- Econ cruising speed between 10,000 and 14,000 ft (3,050-4,265 m): 187 knots (215 mph; 346 km/h)
- Stalling speed, flaps up: 76 knots (87 mph; 140 km/h)
- Stalling speed, flaps down: 66 knots (76 mph; 122·5 km/h)
- Max rate of climb at S/L: 1,350 ft (411 m)/min
- Rate of climb at S/L, one engine out: 350 ft (107 m)/min
- Service ceiling: 24,500 ft (7,470 m)
- Service ceiling, one engine out: 11,500 ft (3,500 m)
- T-O to 50 ft (15 m):
  - Land: 3,700 ft (1,128 m)
  - Water: 4,900 ft (1,494 m)
- Landing from 50 ft (15 m) at max landing weight:
  - Land: 4,350 ft (1,326 m)
  - Water: 4,500 ft (1,372 m)
- Range with max fuel, no reserve: 1,400 nm (1,612 miles; 2,594 km)
- Range with max payload, no reserve: 750 nm (863 miles; 1,388 km)

Frakes Turbo-Mallard, a turboprop conversion of the Grumman Mallard

GARRISON

PETER GARRISON

ADDRESS:
c/o *Flying* magazine, 1 Park Avenue, New York, NY 10016

Mr Garrison was a contributor to the initial design of the *Pilot* Sprite (of which plans and kits are marketed by Practavia Ltd; see UK aircraft section) when employed in London by the *Pilot and Light Aeroplane* magazine. Since his return to the US he has modified and developed this basic design, and first flight of the resulting aircraft, which he has named "Melmoth", was made on 6 September 1973.

Comparison of the designs reveals to a small degree their common parentage; but whereas the Sprite is a simply-constructed lightplane for amateur builders, Mr Garrison's Melmoth could be described more accurately as a lightplane research prototype. It includes such aerodynamic features as double-slotted Fowler trailing-edge flaps, adjustable-incidence ailerons and airbrakes. Special systems and equipment include automatic fuel balancing, integrated cockpit audio system, remote compass, Century I autopilot, full IFR panel and extensive communication radios.

Garrison OM-1 Melmoth before modification of tail unit in early 1974

GARRISON OM-1 MELMOTH

Details below apply to Melmoth in the T-tail configuration adopted by Mr Garrison after early flight tests.

TYPE: Two-seat homebuilt lightplane.

WINGS: Cantilever low-wing monoplane. Wing section NACA 65A-316. Dihedral 8° on outer panels only. Incidence 1°. No sweepback. Constant-chord wing of two-spar light alloy construction. Plain all-metal ailerons with piano-type hinge at lower surface. Aileron incidence variable in flight from +10° to —10°. Double-slotted Fowler-type trailing-edge flaps of light alloy construction. Airbrakes in each wing, of aluminium honeycomb construction.

FUSELAGE: Conventional semi-monocoque structure of light alloy. Glassfibre nose cowl and fairings.

TAIL UNIT: Cantilever light alloy structure. T-tail configuration with all-moving tailplane of single-spar construction. Anti-servo tab in tailplane. Ground-adjustable trim tab on rudder.

LANDING GEAR: Hydraulically-retractable tricycle type. Main units retract inward into fully-enclosed wheel wells in wing centre-section. Nosewheel retracts aft. Oleo-pneumatic shock-absorber on each unit. All three tyres size 5·00-5. Cleveland hydraulic disc brakes.

POWER PLANT: One 210 hp Continental IO-360-A six-cylinder horizontally-opposed aircooled engine, driving a Hartzell two-blade metal constant-speed propeller, with 7¾ in (19·7 cm) hub extension. One integral fuel tank in each outer wing panel, with capacity of 41 US gallons (155 litres). One glassfibre wingtip tank on each wing, capacity 30 US gallons (113·5 litres). Total fuel capacity 142 US gallons (537 litres). Refuelling points in upper surface of each wing and on top of tip-tanks. Oil capacity 2½ US gallons (9·4 litres).

ACCOMMODATION: Two seats side by side beneath transparent canopy. Each side window is hinged at top centre, opening outward and upward to provide access. Space for 150 lb (68 kg) baggage aft of seats. Cabin is heated and ventilated.

SYSTEMS: Electrical system powered by a 28V 30A engine-driven alternator. External power socket. Electrically-driven hydraulic pump provides pressure of 360 lb/sq in (25·3 kg/cm²) for landing gear and flaps. Constant-flow oxygen system, capacity 32 cu ft (0·91 m³) at pressure of 1,800 lb/sq in (126·5 kg/cm²).

ELECTRONICS AND EQUIPMENT: Communication radios, Mitchell Century I autopilot with couplers, full blind-flying instrumentation, navigation lights, strobe lights, heated pitot and angle of attack transmitter, and electronically-timed fuel switching for fuel balancing.

DIMENSIONS, EXTERNAL:
- Wing span: 23 ft 1 in (7·04 m)
- Wing chord, constant: 4 ft 0 in (1·22 m)
- Wing aspect ratio: 5·78
- Length overall: 21 ft 4 in (6·50 m)
- Height overall: 8 ft 5 in (2·57 m)
- Tailplane span: 8 ft 10 in (2·69 m)
- Wheel track: 10 ft 8 in (3·25 m)
- Wheelbase: 6 ft 0 in (1·83 m)
- Propeller diameter: 6 ft 4 in (1·93 m)
- Propeller ground clearance: 9 in (0·23 m)

DIMENSIONS, INTERNAL:
- Cabin: Length: 8 ft 0 in (2·44 m)
  - Max width: 3 ft 8 in (1·12 m)
  - Max height: 3 ft 4 in (1·02 m)
- Baggage hold, volume: 30 cu ft (0·85 m³)

AREAS:
- Wings, gross: 92 sq ft (8·55 m²)
- Ailerons (total): 8 sq ft (0·74 m²)
- Trailing-edge flaps (total): 14 sq ft (1·30 m²)
- Airbrakes (total): 1·6 sq ft (0·15 m²)
- Fin: 10·8 sq ft (1·00 m²)
- Rudder, incl tab: 5·1 sq ft (0·47 m²)
- Tailplane, incl tab: 18·5 sq ft (1·72 m²)

WEIGHTS AND LOADINGS:
- Weight empty, equipped: 1,300 lb (589 kg)
- Max T-O and landing weight: 2,700 lb (1,224 kg)
- Max wing loading: 29·4 lb/sq ft (143·5 kg/m²)
- Max power loading: 12·86 lb/hp (5·83 kg/hp)

PERFORMANCE (at T-O weight of 2,100 lb; 952 kg):
- Max never-exceed speed: 260 knots (300 mph; 481 km/h)
- Max level speed at S/L: 180 knots (207 mph; 333 km/h)
- Max cruising speed at 6,000 ft (1,830 m): 170 knots (196 mph; 315 km/h)
- Econ cruising speed at 10,000 ft (3,050 m): 148 knots (170 mph; 274 km/h)
- Stalling speed, flaps down: 65 knots (75 mph; 121 km/h)
- Max rate of climb at S/L: 1,500 ft (457 m)/min
- T-O run: 800 ft (244 m)
- Landing run: 600 ft (183 m)
- Range with max fuel, no reserve: 2,550 nm (2,936 miles; 4,725 km)

GATES LEARJET

GATES LEARJET CORPORATION

CORPORATE OFFICES, AIRCRAFT DIVISION:
Municipal Airport, PO Box 1280, Wichita, Kansas 67201
Telephone: (316) 722-5640
Telex: 417441

JET ELECTRONICS AND TECHNOLOGY INC:
5353 52nd Street, Grand Rapids, Michigan 49508

FIXED BASE OPERATIONS:
Hangar 7, Stapleton International Airport, Denver, Colorado 80207

CHAIRMAN OF THE BOARD:
Charles C. Gates, Jr

PRESIDENT: H. B. Combs

EXECUTIVE VICE-PRESIDENTS:
A. J. Brizzolara (J.E.T.)
R. E. Cloughley (Fixed Base Operations)
W. M. Conlin (Aircraft Division)

VICE-PRESIDENTS:
L. C. Barry (Industrial Relations)
C. E. Dyas (Marketing Support)
D. J. Grommesh (Engineering)
S. Kvassay (International Marketing)
J. W. Poston (Manufacturing)
R. E. Wolin (Domestic Marketing and Governmental Relations)

TREASURER: W. H. Webster

SECRETARY: R. C. Troll

DIRECTOR, PUBLIC RELATIONS: Allan K. Higdon

Founded in 1960 by William P. Lear Sr, this company was known originally as the Swiss American Aviation Corporation, which was formed to manufacture a high-speed twin-jet executive aircraft known as the Learjet 23 (formerly SAAC-23). Most of the tooling for production of this aircraft was completed in Europe and then, in 1962, all company activities were re-located at Wichita, Kansas; shortly afterwards the company became known as Lear Jet Corporation. In 1967 all of Mr Lear's interests in the company (approximately 60 per cent) were acquired by The Gates Rubber Company of Denver, Colorado, and in January 1970 the company name was changed to Gates Learjet Corporation.

In January 1973 the tenth anniversary of the incorporation of Learjet was celebrated, and in October the 400th Learjet was delivered, just a decade since the first flight of the prototype Learjet in October 1963. During the year Gates Learjet announced plans for two new models, the turbofan-powered Learjet 35 and Learjet 36. By the end of 1973 the worldwide corporate fleet had exceeded 800,000 flight hours. The company's backlog of orders exceeded 60 units at the end of 1973, and production was being maintained at six new aircraft per month.

Other significant events during the year included certification and initial deliveries of thrust reversers on new aircraft, installation of a dual camera modification for the full-time photo-mapping activities of a Brazilian operator, and receipt of the first order from the UK.

More than 2,000 persons were employed by the company at 31 December 1973.

GATES LEARJET 24D

The prototype Lear Jet twin-jet executive transport flew for the first time on 7 October 1963 and deliveries of production Learjet 23 aircraft began on 13 October 1964. After a total of 104 of this version had been delivered, it was superseded by the Learjet 24, which was certificated under Federal Air Regulations Part 25 (formerly CAR 4B), as have been all subsequent models produced by the company. Deliveries of the Learjet 24 began in March 1966, and a total of 80 were built. This was replaced by a developed version with more powerful engines, known as the Learjet 24B, which received FAA certification on 17 December 1968.

The current version, easily identified externally by deletion of the non-structural bullet at the junction of the tailplane and fin, was redesignated Gates Learjet 24D. Improvements announced on 12 September 1972, for immediate introduction on the production line, included a recognition light in the nose of the starboard wingtip tank; a variable-authority nosewheel steering system to improve low-speed taxying; battery isolation switch to turn off either battery; battery temperature indicators; a depressurisation limiter valve; a depressurisation warning light; sideways slides for individual cabin seats, to improve leg and headroom; and a skin temperature sensor to improve operation of the automatic cabin heating system. The model **24D/A** is essentially similar, but is limited to a max T-O weight of 12,499 lb (5,669 kg).

Type: Twin-jet light executive transport.

Wings: Cantilever low-wing monoplane. Wing section NACA 64A 109. Dihedral 2° 30′. Incidence 1°. Sweepback 13° at quarter-chord. All-metal eight-spar structure with chemically-milled alloy skins. Manually-operated, aerodynamically-balanced all-metal ailerons. Hydraulically-actuated all-metal single-slotted flaps. Hydraulically-actuated all-metal spoilers mounted on trailing-edge ahead of flaps. Trim tab in port aileron. Balance tabs in both ailerons. Anti-icing by engine bleed air ducted into leading-edges.

Fuselage: All-metal flush-riveted semi-monocoque fail-safe structure.

Tail Unit: Cantilever all-metal sweptback structure, with electrically-actuated variable-incidence T-tailplane and small ventral fin. Conventional manually-operated control surfaces. Trim tab in rudder. Electrically-heated thermal de-icing of the tailplane leading-edge.

Landing Gear: Retractable tricycle type of Cleveland Pneumatic Tool Co design, with twin wheels on each main unit and single steerable nosewheel. Hydraulic actuation, with back-up pneumatic extension. Oleo-pneumatic shock-absorbers. Main wheels fitted with Goodyear 18 × 5·50 10-ply tyres, pressure 115 lb/sq in (8·08 kg/cm²). Nosewheel fitted with Goodyear Dual Chine tyre size 18 × 4·40 10-ply rating, pressure 105 lb/sq in (7·38 kg/cm²). Goodyear multiple-disc hydraulic brakes. Anti-skid units.

Power Plant: Two General Electric CJ610-6 turbojet engines (each rated at 2,950 lb; 1,340 kg st) mounted in pod on each side of fuselage aft of wings. Fuel in integral wing and wingtip tanks with a total fuel capacity of 840 US gallons (3,180 litres). Oil capacity 1 US gallon (3·75 litres) per engine.

Accommodation: Two seats side by side on flight deck, with dual controls. Up to six passengers in cabin, with one on inward-facing bench seat on starboard side at front, then two on forward or aft-facing armchairs with centre aisle, and three on forward-facing couch. Toilet and stowage space under front inward-facing seat, which can be screened from remainder of cabin by curtain. Refreshment cabinet opposite this seat. Baggage compartment aft of cabin. With back of rear bench seat folded down, baggage compartment and rear of cabin can be used to carry cargo or stretchers. Table at rear. In full cargo version, the rearward-facing armchair seats are also removed. Two-piece door, with upward-hinged portion and downward-hinged portion with integral steps, on port side of cabin at front. Emergency exit on starboard side.

Systems: Air-conditioning and pressurisation system, with air-cycle refrigeration system, has differential of 8·77 lb/sq in (0·62 kg/cm²). Windscreen primary anti-icing system by engine bleed air, with alcohol system as backup.

Electronics and Equipment: Four different nav/com systems, to full airline standard, are available to customer's requirements, comprising Collins, Bendix, Sperry or Export equipment. All have Learjet autopilot as standard. A new option introduced in 1972 is a second battery package, to provide an emergency battery pack.

Dimensions, external:

Span over tip-tanks	35 ft 7 in (10·84 m)
Wing chord at root	9 ft 0 in (2·74 m)
Wing chord at tip	4 ft 7 in (1·40 m)
Wing aspect ratio	5·01
Length overall	43 ft 3 in (13·18 m)
Length of fuselage	41 ft 0 in (12·50 m)
Height over tail	12 ft 3 in (3·73 m)
Tailplane span	14 ft 8 in (4·47 m)
Wheel track (c/l shock-struts)	8 ft 3 in (2·51 m)
Wheelbase	16 ft 2 in (4·93 m)
Cabin door:	
Height	3 ft 9 in (1·14 m)
Standard width	2 ft 0 in (0·61 m)
Optional width	3 ft 0 in (0·91 m)
Emergency exit:	
Height	2 ft 4 in (0·71 m)
Width	1 ft 7 in (0·48 m)

Dimensions, internal:

Cabin, between pressure bulkheads:	
Length	17 ft 4 in (5·28 m)
Max width	4 ft 11 in (1·50 m)
Max height	4 ft 4 in (1·32 m)
Volume, including baggage compartment	246 cu ft (6·97 m³)
Baggage compartment	40·0 cu ft (1·13 m³)

Areas:

Wings, gross	231·77 sq ft (21·53 m²)
Ailerons (total)	11·70 sq ft (1·08 m²)
Trailing-edge flaps (total)	36·85 sq ft (3·42 m²)
Spoilers	7·05 sq ft (0·66 m²)
Fin	37·37 sq ft (3·47 m²)
Rudder, including tab	7·18 sq ft (0·67 m²)
Tailplane	54·00 sq ft (5·02 m²)
Elevators	14·13 sq ft (1·31 m²)

Weights and Loadings:

Weight empty, equipped	6,988 lb (3,169 kg)
Operating weight empty	7,388 lb (3,351 kg)
Max payload	4,012 lb (1,820 kg)
Max T-O weight	13,500 lb (6,124 kg)
Max ramp weight	13,800 lb (6,260 kg)
Max zero-fuel weight	11,400 lb (5,170 kg)
Max landing weight	11,880 lb (5,389 kg)
Max wing loading	58·3 lb/sq ft (284·6 kg/m²)
Max power loading	2·29 lb/lb st (2·29 kg/kg st)

Performance (at max T-O weight):

Max never-exceed speed	Mach 0·86
Max operating speed at 31,000 ft (9,450 m)	473 knots (545 mph; 877 km/h)
Max operating speed at 45,000 ft (13,720 m)	464 knots (534 mph; 859 km/h)
Econ cruising speed at 45,000 ft (13,720 m)	418 knots (481 mph; 774 km/h)
Stalling speed, clean	126 knots (145 mph; 234 km/h)
Stalling speed at max landing weight, wheels and flaps down	99 knots (114 mph; 184 km/h)
Max rate of climb at S/L	6,800 ft (2,073 m)/min
Service ceiling	45,000 ft (13,720 m)
Service ceiling, one engine out	26,000 ft (7,925 m)
Min ground turning radius	34 ft 4 in (10·46 m)
T-O run	2,607 ft (795 m)
T-O to 35 ft (10·7 m) FAA balanced field length	3,917 ft (1,194 m)
Landing from 50 ft (15 m) at max landing weight	3,352 ft (1,022 m)
Landing run at max landing weight	1,881 ft (573 m)
Range with 4 passengers, max fuel, 45 min reserve	1,605 nm (1,848 miles; 2,974 km)

Operational Noise Characteristics (estimated):

T-O noise level at 3·5 nm (7·5 km) from start of T-O roll	94 EPNdB
Approach noise level at 1·0 nm (2·13 km) from landing threshold on 3° glideslope	92 EPNdB
Sideline noise level at 0·25 nm (0·53 km) from runway c/l	103 EPNdB

GATES LEARJET 25B

First flown on 12 August 1966 as the Learjet 25, this version is 4 ft 2 in (1·27 m) longer than the series 24 aircraft, and will accommodate eight passengers and a crew of two. FAA certification in the air transport category (FAR 25) was obtained on 10 October 1967 and the initial delivery was made in November 1967. British CAA certification was received on 26 June 1974.

The 1970 version, which introduced a number of refinements, was redesignated Gates Learjet 25B. A wingtip tank fuel dump system, introduced as an option in 1972, can jettison 750 lb (340 kg) of fuel from each tip-tank in four minutes. The description of the Learjet 24D applies also to the model 25B, except in the following details:

Dimensions, external:

As for Learjet 24D except:	
Length overall	47 ft 7 in (14·50 m)
Wheelbase	19 ft 2 in (5·84 m)

Dimensions, internal:

As for Learjet 24D except:	
Cabin, between pressure bulkheads:	
Length	20 ft 7 in (6·27 m)
Volume, including baggage compartment	299 cu ft (8·47 m³)

Gates Learjet 24D twin-jet light executive transport (two General Electric CJ610-6 turbojet engines)

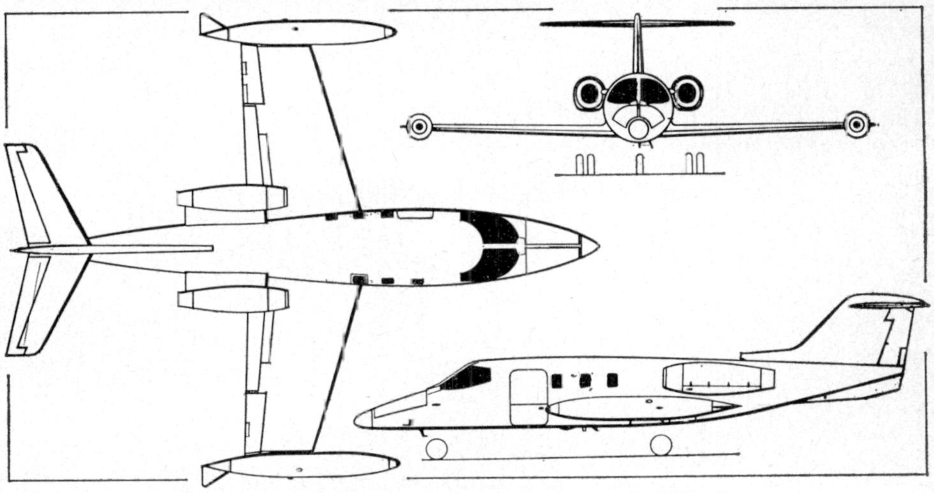

Gates Learjet 24D twin-jet light executive transport (*Pilot Press*)

Weights and Loadings:
- Weight empty, equipped 7,355 lb (3,336 kg)
- Operating weight empty 7,755 lb (3,517 kg)
- Max payload 3,645 lb (1,653 kg)
- Max T-O weight 15,000 lb (6,803 kg)
- Max ramp weight 15,500 lb (7,030 kg)
- Max landing weight 13,300 lb (6,032 kg)
- Max wing loading 64·7 lb/sq ft (315·9 kg/m²)
- Max power loading 2·54 lb/lb st (2·54 kg/kg st)

Performance (at max T-O weight):
- As for Learjet 24D except:
- Max cruising speed at 41,000 ft (12,500 m) 473 knots (545 mph; 877 km/h); Mach 0·81
- Stalling speed, wheels and flaps down, at max landing weight 104 knots (120 mph; 193 km/h)
- Max rate of climb at S/L 6,050 ft (1,844 m)/min
- Max rate of climb at S/L, one engine out 1,750 ft (533 m)/min
- Service ceiling, one engine out 24,500 ft (7,470 m)
- Min ground turning radius 37 ft 6 in (11·43 m)
- T-O run 3,822 ft (1,165 m)
- T-O to 35 ft (10·7 m) FAA balanced field length 5,186 ft (1,580 m)
- Landing from 50 ft (15 m) at max landing weight 3,715 ft (1,132 m)
- Landing run at max landing weight 2,658 ft (810 m)
- Range with 7 passengers, max fuel, 45 min reserve 1,540 nm (1,773 miles; 2,853 km)

Operational Noise Characteristics:
- As for Learjet 24D

GATES LEARJET 25C

This longer-range version of the basic Learjet 25 entered production in 1970. With the addition of a 204 US gallon (772 litre) fuselage fuel tank, the 25C has a non-stop range in excess of 2,000 nm (2,300 miles; 3,700 km), plus fuel reserve. The cabin of this version is optionally convertible from a four- or six-seat configuration to a two-bed sleeper compartment. It is otherwise the same as the Learjet 25B, and the description of this aircraft and of the Learjet 24D applies also to the 25C except as detailed below:

Dimensions, internal:
- Volume, including baggage compartment 259 cu ft (7·33 m³)

Weights:
- Weight empty, equipped 7,233 lb (3,280 kg)
- Operating weight empty 7,633 lb (3,462 kg)
- Max payload 3,767 lb (1,708 kg)

Performance (at max T-O weight):
- Long-range cruising speed at 41,000 ft (12,500 m) 418 knots (481 mph; 774 km/h); Mach 0·73
- Max certificated operating altitude 45,000 ft (13,720 m)
- Range with 2 passengers, max fuel, 45 min reserve 2,108 nm (2,427 miles; 3,905 km)

GATES LEARJET 35 and 36

It was announced first at the Paris Air Show, in May 1973, that the company intended to produce two new business jets, identified as the Learjet 35 Transcontinental and Learjet 36 Intercontinental, each to be powered by two 3,500 lb (1,587 kg) st AiResearch TFE 731-2 turbofan engines. A prototype for the Learjet 35 and 36 (known originally as the Learjet Model 26) made its first flight with TFE 731-2 engines on 4 January 1973.

Generally similar in basic configuration to the other members of the Learjet family of aircraft, the Learjet 35 and 36 are slightly larger in size than the Learjet 25B, previously the largest of those in production. The two new aircraft are almost identical, differing in fuel capacity and accommodation. Two prototypes have been built and the certification programme was scheduled for completion in the late Summer of 1974.

Gates Learjet 25C, longer-range version of the basic Learjet 25

The description of the Learjet 24D applies also to the Learjet 35 and 36, except in the following details:

Type: Twin-turbofan light executive transport.

Wings: As for Learjet 24D, except span increased.

Fuselage: As for Learjet 24D, except length increased.

Tail Unit and Landing Gear: As for Learjet 24D.

Power Plant: Two AiResearch TFE 731-2 turbofan engines, each rated at 3,500 lb (1,587 kg) st, mounted in pod on each side of rear fuselage. Fuel in integral wing and wingtip tanks and a fuselage tank, with a combined usable capacity (Learjet 35) of 921 US gallons (3,486 litres). Learjet 36 has a larger fuselage tank, giving a combined usable total of 1,109 US gallons (4,198 litres). Refuelling point on upper surface of each wingtip tank. Engine nacelle leading-edges anti-iced by engine bleed air.

Accommodation: Crew of two on flight deck, with dual controls. Up to eight passengers in Learjet 35; one on inward-facing bench seat on starboard side at front, then two pairs of forward-facing armchairs with centre aisle, and three on forward-facing couch at rear of cabin. Learjet 36 can accommodate up to six passengers, one pair of forward-facing armchairs being removed. Toilet and stowage space under front inward-facing seat which can be screened from remainder of cabin. Refreshment cabinet opposite this seat, aft of passenger door. Baggage compartment with capacity of 500 lb (226 kg) aft of cabin. Two-piece clamshell door at forward end of cabin on port side, with integral steps built into lower half. Emergency exit on starboard side of cabin.

Systems: Environmental control system comprises cabin pressurisation, ventilation, heating and cooling. Heating and pressurisation are provided by engine bleed air, with a maximum pressure differential of 8·9 lb/sq in (0·625 kg/cm²), maintaining a cabin altitude of 8,000 ft (2,440 m) to an actual altitude of 45,000 ft (13,715 m). Freon R12 vapour cycle cooling system supplemented by a ram-air heat exchanger. Anti-icing system includes distribution of engine bleed air for wing, tailplane and engine nacelle leading-edges and windscreen; electrical heating of pitot heads, stall warning vanes and static ports; and alcohol spray on windscreen and nose radome. Hydraulic system supplied by two engine-driven pumps, each pump capable of maintaining alone the full system pressure of 1,500 lb/sq in (105 kg/cm²), for operation of landing gear, brakes, flaps and spoilers. Electrically-driven hydraulic pump for emergency operation of all hydraulic services. Pneumatic system of 1,800 to 3,000 lb/sq in (126 to 210 kg/cm²) pressure for emergency extension of landing gear and operation of brakes.

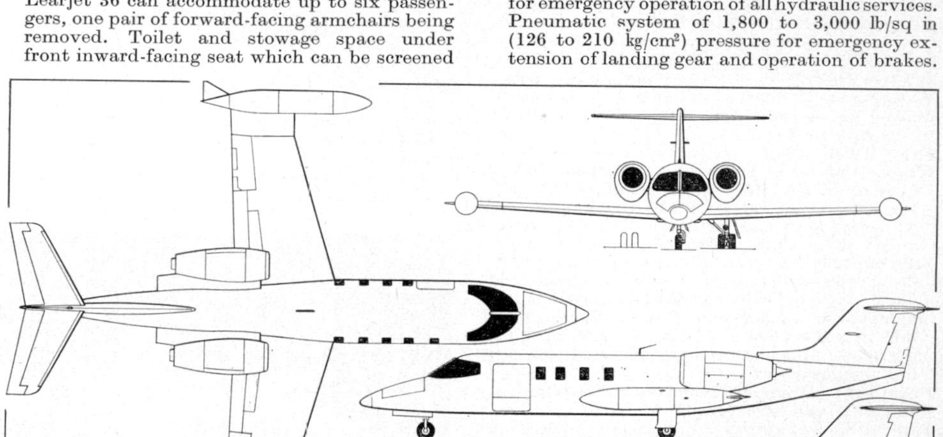

Gates Learjet 35 with optional cargo door. Additional side view (*bottom*) **shows Learjet 25B**
(*Pilot Press*)

Prototype Learjet 35 ten-seat twin-turbofan light executive transport

Electrical system powered by two 30V 400A brushless generators, two 1,000VA solid-state inverters to provide AC power, and two 24V 22Ah nickel-cadmium batteries. Oxygen system for emergency use with crew demand masks and dropout masks for each passenger.

ELECTRONICS: A standard avionics package is available, comprising two Collins VHF-20 transceivers, two Collins VIR-30 VOR/ILS/GS/MB with Dorne-Margolin antenna, Avtech 1250 and 1251 compression audio systems, RCA AVQ-85 DME, Wilcox 1014A transponder, RCA AVQ-21 weather radar, Collins DF-206 ADF, two Collins 332C-10 RMI with single or dual switching, Collins FD-108Y flight director indicator with altitude hold, Collins/J.E.T. PN-101/5-4000 co-pilot's flight indicators, two J.E.T. VG-206 vertical gyros, two J.E.T. DN-101D directional gyros, IDC System 2, and J.E.T. PS-823B/AI-804 standby power pack and attitude gyro. Alternatively to this pre-engineered optional package, customers may select avionics equipment to meet specific requirements.

EQUIPMENT: Standard equipment includes engine fire extinguishers, jacking pads, internal corrosion-proofing, soundproofing, ice detector lights, battery overheat warning system, anti-collision beacons, landing/taxi lights, navigation lights, map lights, instrument panel and floodlights, baggage compartment lights, cabin reading lights, cabin entry light, engine fire warning lights, angle of attack indicator, cabin rate of climb indicator, two clocks, wing and tailplane temperature indicators, alternate static source, lightning protection, fire axe, crew and passenger flotation jackets, cabin fire extinguisher, external power source and control locks.

DIMENSIONS, EXTERNAL:
Wing span over tip-tanks 39 ft 6 in (12·04 m)
Wing chord at root 9 ft 0 in (2·74 m)
Wing chord at tip 5 ft 1 in (1·55 m)
Wing aspect ratio 5·74
Length overall 48 ft 8 in (14·83 m)
Height overall 12 ft 3 in (3·73 m)
Tailplane span 14 ft 8 in (4·47 m)
Wheel track 8 ft 3 in (2·51 m)
Passenger door:
Standard:
Height 5 ft 2½ in (1·59 m)
Width 2 ft 0 in (0·61 m)
Optional:
Height 5 ft 2½ in (1·59 m)
Width 3 ft 0 in (0·91 m)
Emergency exit:
Height 2 ft 4 in (0·71 m)
Width 1 ft 7 in (0·48 m)

DIMENSIONS, INTERNAL (A: Learjet 35; B: Learjet 36):
Cabin: Length, incl flight deck:
A 21 ft 8 in (6·60 m)
B 18 ft 11 in (5·77 m)
Max width 4 ft 11 in (1·50 m)
Max height 4 ft 3½ in (1·31 m)
Volume:
A 268 cu ft (7·59 m³)
B 228 cu ft (6·46 m³)
Baggage compartment 40 cu ft (1·13 m³)

AREA:
Wings, gross 253·3 sq ft (23·53 m²)

WEIGHTS AND LOADINGS (A: Learjet 35; B: Learjet 36):
Weight empty, equipped:
A 8,802 lb (3,992 kg)
B 8,762 lb (3,974 kg)
Max payload:
A 3,298 lb (1,496 kg)
B 3,338 lb (1,514 kg)
Max T-O weight:
A, B 17,000 lb (7,711 kg)
Max zero-fuel weight:
A, B 12,500 lb (5,670 kg)
Max landing weight:
A, B 13,300 lb (6,032 kg)
Max wing loading:
A, B 67·1 lb/sq ft (327·6 kg/m²)
Max power loading 2·43 lb/lb st (2·43 kg/kg st)

PERFORMANCE (at max T-O weight, A: Learjet 35; B: Learjet 36):
Max never-exceed speed Mach 0·87
Max cruising speed 476 knots (548 mph; 882 km/h)
Normal cruising speed 441 knots (508 mph; 817 km/h)
Econ cruising speed 418 knots (481 mph; 774 km/h)
Stalling speed, wheels and flaps down 111 knots (128 mph; 206 km/h)
Max rate of climb at S/L 5,150 ft (1,570 m)/min
Rate of climb at S/L, one engine out 1,475 ft (450 m)/min
Service ceiling 42,500 ft (12,950 m)
Service ceiling, one engine out 25,500 ft (7,770 m)
T-O to 50 ft (15 m) 3,500 ft (1,065 m)
Landing from 50 ft (15 m) 3,625 ft (1,105 m)
Range with max fuel:
A 2,632 nm (3,030 miles; 4,876 km)
B 3,149 nm (3,626 miles; 5,835 km)
Range with max payload:
A 1,475 nm (1,698 miles; 2,732 km)
B 1,500 nm (1,727 miles; 2,779 km)

Prototype Learjet 36 eight-seat twin-turbofan light executive transport

GENERAL AIRCRAFT

GENERAL AIRCRAFT CORPORATION

HEAD OFFICE:
822 Connecticut Avenue NW, Washington, DC 20006
Telephone: (202) 638-5927

CHAIRMAN AND CHIEF EXECUTIVE:
Dr Lynn L. Bollinger

PRESIDENT:
Robert B. Kimnach

TRANSPORT DIVISION TECHNICAL OFFICES:
3777 Gaines Street, San Diego, California 92110
Telephone: (714) 297-2997

ENGINEERING MANAGER:
Kornel J. Feher

General Aircraft Corporation designed a 36/40-seat four-turboprop transport aircraft, designated GAC-100, aimed primarily at the third-level, commuter and local airline market. It featured advanced high-lift devices (some under licence from Helio Aircraft Corporation) for low-speed operation from unimproved airstrips, and was described in the 1970-71 *Jane's*.

Information received from the company in March 1973 indicated that a twin-engined 30-seat commuter development of the GAC-100 had recently been designed; it was then hoped that construction of a prototype of this version, designated GAC-100-2, would begin in late 1973. Since that time there has been a change in the corporation's plans, and it was announced in February 1974 that General Aircraft's production capacity was committed to the Helio Aircraft Corporation (which see) Super Courier model throughout 1974. Remaining corporation resources were then being concentrated on establishing increased production facilities for the Model H-550A Stallion, for which government orders were pending. Construction of the GAC-100-2 prototype has been suspended for the current year.

GENERAL DYNAMICS

GENERAL DYNAMICS CORPORATION

HEAD OFFICE:
Pierre Laclede Center, St Louis, Missouri 63105
Telephone: (314) 862-2440

CHAIRMAN AND CHIEF EXECUTIVE OFFICER:
David S. Lewis

EXECUTIVE VICE-PRESIDENTS:
Gorden E. MacDonald
Gene K. Beare
James M. Beggs

VICE-PRESIDENTS:
Leonard F. Buchanan (General Manager, Pomona Division)
M. C. Curtis (Deputy General Manager, Electric Boat Division)
Otto J. Glasser (International)
Max Golden (Contracts)
Algie A. Hendrix (Industrial Relations)
E. J. LeFevre (GD Field Offices)
Edward E. Lynn (General Counsel)
Frank Nugent (President, Freeman Coal Mining Corporation and The United Electric Coal Companies)
Joseph D. Pierce (General Manager, Electric Boat Division)
P. Takis Veliotis (President and General Manager, Quincy Shipbuilding Division)
Wayne Wells (Treasurer)

Convair Aerospace Division:
Fort Worth, Texas
San Diego, California

PRESIDENT: Frank W. Davis

VICE-PRESIDENTS:
G. L. Hansen (General Manager, San Diego Operation)
R. E. Adams (General Manager, Fort Worth Operation)
R. H. Widmer (Research and Engineering)
L. C. Josephs (YF-16 Programme)
J. T. Cosby (Sales)
H. C. Jones (Contracts and Pricing)
E. E. Hatchett (Management Analysis and Controller)
N. B. Robbins (111 Programmes)
A. Kalitinsky (Long-range Planning)

Prior to 22 September 1970 the aerospace activities of General Dynamics Corporation had been the responsibility of three operating units known as the Fort Worth, Pomona and Convair divisions. All three were components of the former Convair Division, which had its origin in the Consolidated Aircraft Corporation, incorporated on 29 May 1923.

The Company today conducts its US aerospace activities at three divisions: Convair Aerospace, with operations at Fort Worth, Texas, and San Diego, California; the Pomona Division, at Pomona, California; and the Electronics Division, with headquarters in San Diego and an operating unit at Orlando, Florida.

The Convair Aerospace Division is responsible for the design, development and production of military and commercial aircraft and of systems for space exploration. The Pomona Division is engaged in tactical missile and other ordnance programmes. The Electronics Division is engaged in advanced radar development, and produces ocean data and navigation systems, anti-submarine warfare sonobuoy receivers and ground support equipment.

In addition to development and production of the F-111 series of combat aircraft, Convair Aerospace is responsible for production of a major portion of the fuselage for the McDonnell Douglas DC-10 commercial transport aircraft.

Under development for the USAF is a new lightweight fighter which has the designation YF-16.

Convair Aerospace Division retains detailed tooling for high-usage spares for the Convair-Liner 240/340/440 series of piston-engined transports, and Convair 880 and 990 jet transports, and is manufacturing components for operators of these types.

GENERAL DYNAMICS F-111

Following a detailed evaluation of design proposals submitted by General Dynamics and Boeing, the US Department of Defense announced on 24 November 1962 that General Dynamics had been selected as prime contractor for development of the F-111 variable-geometry tactical fighter (known originally by the designation TFX), with Grumman Aircraft as an associate. An initial contract was placed for 23 development aircraft (18 F-111As for the USAF, five F-111Bs for the US Navy), of which the first were scheduled for delivery within 2½ years. Subsequently, further orders were placed, covering F-111D, E and F improved tactical fighters for the USAF, 24 F-111Cs for the Royal Australian Air Force, and the FB-111A strategic bomber version for the USAF.

A total of 562 F-111s of all types, including the 23 development models, are being delivered under these current contracts. Twelve more have been authorised for manufacture in 1976.

Versions are as follows:

F-111A. USAF two-seat tactical fighter-bomber. Development models built with two P & W TF30-P-1 turbofan engines; production version has TF30-P-3 engines and Mk I avionics. Manufacture of parts, components and sub-systems began in 1963. First F-111A was completed at GD Fort Worth plant 16 October 1964 and flew for the first time (with wings locked at sweepback of 26°) on 21 December 1964. Contracts covered the 18 development aircraft and 141 production models for the USAF Tactical Air Command. Production completed.

EF-111A. ECM version of the F-111A, of which two prototypes were projected in mid-1973.

YF-111A. Two strike/reconnaissance fighters completed prior to cancellation of the British government's order for 50 aircraft, under the designation F-111K, were subsequently assigned to the USAF for use in its research, development, test and evaluation programme, with the designation YF-111A. Included in F-111A total of 141 production aircraft.

F-111B. US Navy version, designed for carrier-based fleet defence duties with armament of six Hughes AIM-54 Phoenix air-to-air missiles. Greater wing span and area than F-111A. Powered initially by TF30-P-1 turbofan engines; production models were programmed to have more powerful TF30-P-12 engines. First F-111B, assembled by Grumman, flew for the first time on 18 May 1965. Original orders covered five development aircraft and 24 production models for the US Navy. The sixth aircraft, the first to be fitted with TF30-P-12 engines, flew on 29 June 1968. The seventh (and last) is used as a testbed for the Phoenix missile. Continued development, production and support of the F-111B were halted by Congress in mid-1968.

F-111C. Strike aircraft. Outwardly similar to FB-111A, with Pratt & Whitney TF30-P-3 engines, Mk I avionics, cockpit ejection module and eight underwing attachments for stores. 24 built for RAAF.

F-111D. Similar to F-111A, but with Mk II avionics, offering improvements in navigation and in air-to-air weapon delivery. TF30-P-9 engines. Delivery of 96 completed in February 1973. Equips 27th Tactical Fighter Wing, Cannon AFB, New Mexico.

F-111E. Superseded F-111A from 160th aircraft. Modified air intakes improve engine performance above Mach 2·2. Total of 94 built; followed by F-111D. The first two aircraft of a wing of 72 F-111Es, for deployment by the 20th Tactical Fighter Wing, USAFE, in support of NATO, arrived at RAF Upper Heyford, Oxon, on 12 September 1970.

F-111F. Fighter-bomber. Generally similar to F-111D, but with avionics that combine the best features of the F-111E and FB-111A systems, to provide effective tactical avionics at the lowest possible cost. TF30-P-100 engines, producing 25% more thrust than the basic TF30 and providing a significant improvement in T-O performance, single-engine rate of climb, payload capability, acceleration and max speed at low level without use of afterburning. 94 ordered for Tactical Air Command. It was reported in January 1972 that 30 F-111Fs were being delivered to the 366th TFW at Mountain Home AFB, Idaho, with TF30-P-9 turbofans pending availability of the TF30-P-100. The more powerful engines were retrofitted at a later date.

It was announced in late 1970 that all F-111F aircraft would have a boron-epoxy doubler applied to the wing pivot fitting to increase fatigue life. The doubler will be retrofitted to all tactical F-111 aircraft already in service during each aircraft's inspect-and-repair-as-needed (IRAN) programme.

F-111K. See YF-111A.

FB-111A. Two-seat strategic bomber version for USAF Strategic Air Command with Mk IIB advanced avionics and TF30-P-7 engines. Requirement for 210 announced by US Secretary of Defense on 10 December 1965, to replace B-52C/F versions of the Stratofortress and B-58A Hustler. Initial contract for 64 signed in Spring of 1967. Subsequently, on 20 March 1969, the US Secretary of Defense stated that FB-111A production would total 76 aircraft. First of two prototypes converted from development F-111As flew on 30 July 1967, followed by first production FB-111A on 13 July 1968 (fitted temporarily with TF30-P-3 engines). Long-span wings. Strengthened landing gear. Increased braking capacity. Max load of six nuclear bombs, or six SRAM missiles (four under wings, two in weapons bay), or combinations of these weapons. Conventional weapon loadings of up to 31,500 lb (14,288 kg) of bombs can also be delivered.

First FB-111A was delivered to the 340th Bomb Group, a training unit of Strategic Air Command, at Carswell AFB, Texas, on 8 October 1969. FB-111A units (each two squadrons) are the 509th Bomb Wing at Pease AFB, New Hampshire, and the 380th Strategic Aerospace Wing at Plattsburgh AFB, New York. Production completed.

RF-111A. Reconnaissance conversion of No. 11 F-111A, tested in prototype form. No further development planned.

The specification to which the F-111 was designed called for a maximum speed of about Mach 2·5, capability of supersonic speed at sea level, short take-off capability from rough airfields in forward areas and short landing capability. The F-111 had to be able to fly between any two airfields in the world in one day and to carry a full range of conventional and nuclear weapons including the latest air-to-surface tactical weapons.

Subcontractors on the programme have included General Electric Co, for attack radars, flight control systems and portions of the armament system; Westinghouse Electric Corp for electrical generating systems; Litton Industries for the navigation and attack system and astrocompass; Sanders Associates for ECM group; Avco Corp for countermeasures receiving sets; Navigation and Control Division of Bendix Corp for air data computer units; Collins Radio for high-frequency radio and antenna coupler; AiResearch Manufacturing Company for air-conditioning and pressurisation equipment; Texas Instruments for terrain-following radar; GPL Division of General Precision Inc for Doppler radar; Motorola for X-band transponder; Honeywell for the low-altitude radar altimeter: Textron for the radar homing and warning system; and Autonetics Division of Rockwell International for Mk II/IIB avionics.

General Dynamics F-111E fighter-bomber of the USAF *(Stephen P. Peltz)*

The following details apply to the F-111A except where otherwise indicated:

TYPE: Two-seat variable-geometry multi-purpose fighter.

WINGS: Cantilever shoulder wing. Wing section of NACA 63 series, with conventional washout. Sweepback of outer portions variable in flight or on the ground from 16° to 72° 30′. Wing-actuating jacks by Jarry Hydraulics. Five-spar structure, with stressed and sculptured skin panels, each made in one piece between leading and trailing-edge sections, from root to tip. Leading and trailing-edge sections of honeycomb sandwich. Airbrake/lift dumpers above wing operate as spoilers for lateral control at low speeds. Full-span variable-camber leading-edge slats and full-span double-slotted trailing-edge flaps. General Electric flight control system.

FUSELAGE: Semi-monocoque structure, mainly of aluminium alloy, with honeycomb sandwich skin. Some steel and titanium. Main structural member is a T-section keel, under the arms of which the engines are hung.

TAIL UNIT: Conventional cantilever sweptback surfaces, utilising honeycomb sandwich skin panels, except for tailplane tips and central area of fin on each side. All-moving horizontal surfaces operate both differentially and symmetrically to provide aileron and elevator functions. Two long narrow ventral stabilising fins.

LANDING GEAR: Hydraulically-retractable tricycle type. Single wheel on each main leg. Twin-wheel nose unit retracts forward. Main gear is a triangulated structure with hinged legs which are almost horizontal when the gear is extended. During retraction, the legs pivot downward, the wheels tilt to lie almost flat against them, and the whole gear rotates forward so that the wheels are stowed side by side in fuselage between engine air intake ducts. Low-pressure tyres on main wheels, size 47-18 in (42-13 in on F-111C and FB-111A). Disc brakes, with anti-skid system. Main landing gear door, in bottom of fuselage, hinges down to act as speed brake in flight.

POWER PLANT: Two Pratt & Whitney TF30-P-3 turbofan engines, each giving 18,500 lb (8,390 kg) st with afterburning. Fuel tanks in wings and fuselage. Pressure fuelling point in port side of fuselage, forward of engine air intake. Gravity fuel filler/in-flight refuelling receptacle in top of fuselage aft of cockpit. Hamilton Standard hydro-mechanical air intake system with movable shock-cone.

ACCOMMODATION: Crew of two side by side in air-conditioned and pressurised cabin. Portion of canopy over each seat is hinged on aircraft centreline and opens upward. Zero-speed, zero-altitude (including underwater) emergency escape module developed by McDonnell Douglas Corpn and utilising a 40,000 lb (18,140 kg) st Rocket Power Inc rocket motor. Emergency

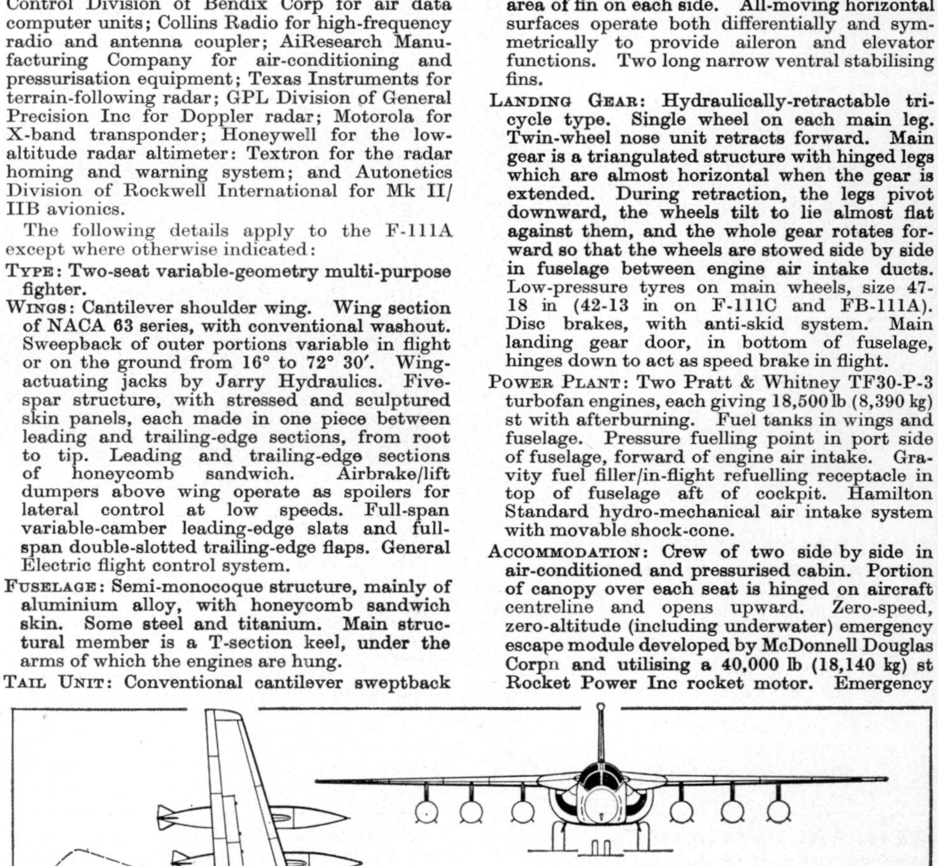

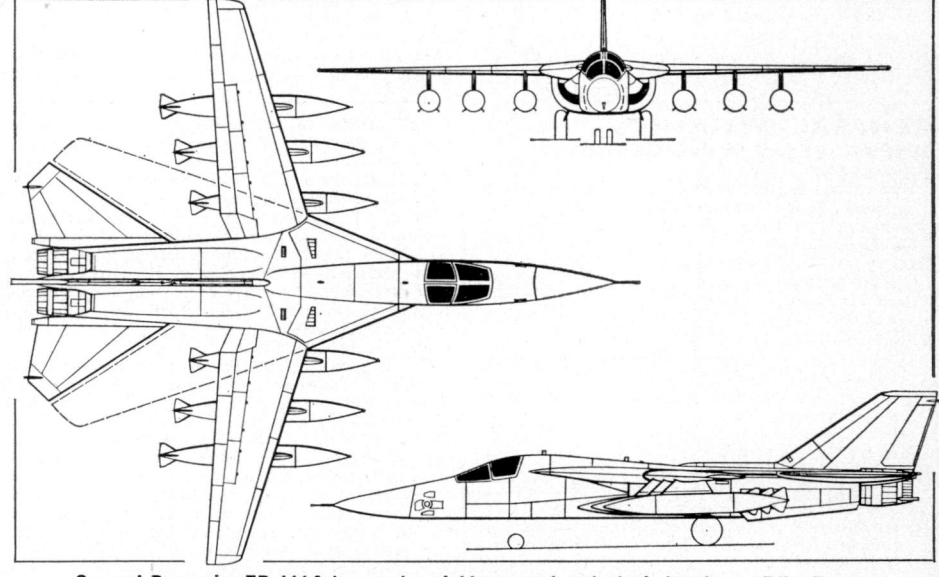

General Dynamics FB-111A two-seat variable-geometry strategic bomber *(Pilot Press)*

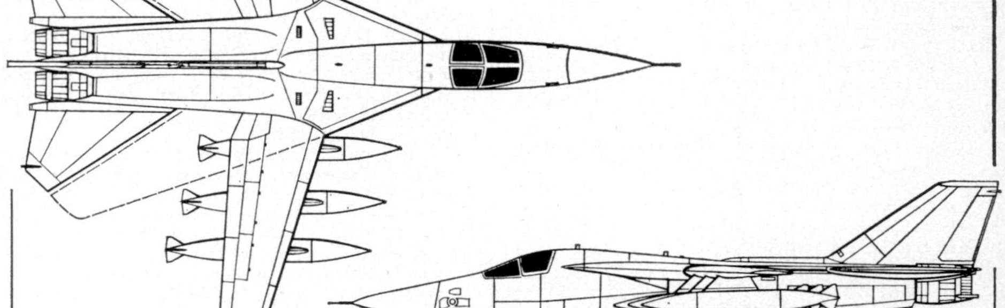

General Dynamics FB-111A for USAF Strategic Air Command

procedure calls for both crew members to remain in capsule cabin section, which is propelled away from aircraft by rocket motor and lowered to ground by parachute. Airbags **cushion impact and form flotation gear** in water. Entire capsule forms survival shelter.

ARMAMENT: Tactical fighter versions carry one M61 multi-barrel 20 mm gun or two 750 lb bombs in internal weapon bay. External stores are carried on four attachments under each wing. The two inboard pylons on each side pivot as the wings sweep back, to keep the stores parallel with the fuselage. The two outboard pylons on each wing are jettisonable and non-swivelling.

DIMENSIONS:
Wing span:
F-111A, F-111D, F-111E, F-111F:
spread 63 ft 0 in (19·20 m)
fully swept 31 ft 11·4 in (9·74 m)
F-111B, F-111C, FB-111A:
spread 70 ft 0 in (21·34 m)
fully swept 33 ft 11 in (10·34 m)
Wing chord at root 6 ft 11 in (2·11 m)
Length overall:
F-111A, F-111C, F-111D, F-111E, F-111F, FB-111A 73 ft 6 in (22·40 m)
Height overall:
F-111A, F-111C, F-111D, F-111E, F-111F, FB-111A 17 ft 1·4 in (5·22 m)

WEIGHTS (F-111A):
Weight empty 46,172 lb (20,943 kg)
Max T-O weight 91,500 lb (41,500 kg)

PERFORMANCE (F-111A):
Max speed at height Mach 2·2
Max speed at S/L Mach 1·2
Service ceiling over 51,000 ft (15,500 m)
T-O and landing run under 3,000 ft (915 m)
Range with max internal fuel over 2,750 nm (3,165 miles; 5,093 km)

General Dynamics YF-16 single-seat lightweight fighter, second prototype

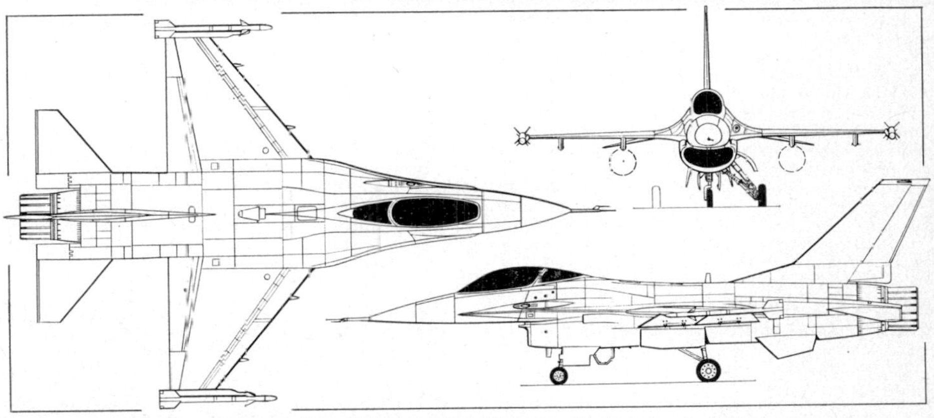

General Dynamics YF-16 (Pratt & Whitney F100-PW-100 afterburning turbofan) (*Pilot Press*)

GENERAL DYNAMICS MODEL 401

USAF designation: YF-16

In April 1972, General Dynamics Corporation and Northrop Corporation were each awarded a contract to build prototypes for the USAF's Lightweight Fighter (LWF) Prototype Program. Intended to determine the viability of a small, lightweight, low-cost air superiority fighter, these prototypes are expected to aid evaluation of the operational potential of such an aircraft, as well as establishing its operational role.

In the technical evaluation of the five proposals submitted originally for the programme, the General Dynamics Model 401 took first place, Northrop's P-600 (which now has the USAF designation YF-17) was runner-up, and the proposals received from The Boeing Company, LTV Aerospace and Lockheed were third, fourth and fifth respectively.

Under its contract, worth more than $37·9 million, General Dynamics has built two prototypes for evaluation in a twelve-month 300-hour flight programme being directed by the USAF Aeronautical Systems Division's Prototype Programs Office, at Wright-Patterson AFB, Ohio, under the overall control of Colonel Lyle W. Cameron.

Whilst the LWF policy is, in effect, a reversion to the old-time US prototyping concept, without any guarantee of production contracts for the winning design, it is considered that the escalating unit costs of air superiority fighters currently under development might well lead to substantial contracts for the successful contender.

Design priorities for this programme recognised cost as being equal in importance with schedule of performance. The USAF specified that the prototype aircraft must provide accurate information in respect of both cost to develop and cost to produce. Thus, the manufacturer has had to consider how best to use advanced technology to provide very high performance within a price range considered acceptable to USAF planners. The concept chosen for the Model 401 blends advanced technology with a basically conservative configuration and a power plant offering high thrust-to-weight ratio.

The selection of a single-engine configuration meant that emphasis had to be placed on weight saving if the critical performance categories of high acceleration rates, high rate of climb and exceptional manoeuvrability were to be met. This dictated limitation of aircraft size, and the use of advanced concepts to obtain optimum lift.

Another source of weight reduction has been tapped by specifying graphite composite material for the tail unit, General Dynamics having gained considerable manufacturing and flight experience in the use of this material from its application in the F-111. In other respects the structure is conventional, keeping material costs to a minimum; it utilises approximately 33% 7050 and 2124 light alloy for integrally-machined components, 39% 2024 light alloy for formed sheet and extrusions, 2% full-depth aluminium honeycomb core, 2% 641V titanium, 9% 200 grade maraging steel, 4% graphite composites, 1% reinforced plastics, and 10% other materials.

Further cost savings stem from the use of identical and interchangeable horizontal tail surfaces, ventral fins, and wing flap/ailerons. Eighty per cent of the main landing gear components are also interchangeable port and starboard.

More than 1,200 hours of wind tunnel testing of over 50 configurations led to the present design, with special emphasis on development of an optimum relationship between the wing leading-edges and the forebody strakes which provide vortex control. Similar in-depth study of potential requirements of an LWF resulted in the selection of manufacturing breaks, methods of attachment of external aerodynamic shapes and surfaces, structural provisions, and internal space so that full advantage could be taken of any new features or concepts that might originate during progress of the prototype programme. This has ensured that changes can be made easily to a particular component, with minimum structural disruption to the rest of the airframe. The forward section of the engine air inlet, wings, tail surfaces and forebody strakes are examples of readily removable structures. This modular approach provides great flexibility, and makes it possible to flight test on the YF-16 components such as supercritical wings, advanced composite wings, growth versions of the F100 engine, advanced armament, a more advanced high-*g* cockpit and a variable-geometry engine air intake.

USAF, NASA, and company research all contributed to the technological advances built into the YF-16. They include vortex control, variable wing camber, a high-*g* cockpit, fly-by-wire control system, and a blended wing/body.

Vortex control is provided by sharp wing leading-edges and highly-swept strakes extending along the fuselage forebody. Benefits include the ability to use a lower aspect ratio wing, with significant reductions in wing area, and improved handling qualities through greater stability at high angles of attack.

Variable wing camber is achieved by the use of automatic leading-edge manoeuvring flaps, which increase wing camber to maintain effective lift coefficients at high angles of attack. The trailing-edges carry large combined flap/ailerons. The rate of flap movement is 35°/sec, which is compatible with the aircraft's response in pitch, and is programmed automatically as a function of Mach number and angle of attack.

In the high-*g* cockpit, the seat is inclined 30° aft, with a raised heel-rest position to enhance the pilot's ability to perform efficiently while subjected to sustained high gravity forces during combat manoeuvres. It has been found also that this seat position makes it easier for the pilot to see aft through the bubble canopy. While this canopy imposes a supersonic drag penalty, it is considered to be more than offset by the improved rear view afforded to the pilot. The bubble canopy, developed by Sierracin Corporation of Sylmar, California, is made of polycarbonate, a virtually indestructible advanced plastics material. The windscreen and forward canopy are an integral unit, separated from the aft canopy by a simple support structure, which serves also as the hinge-point where the forward section pivots upward and aft to give access to the cockpit. This new windscreen/canopy design provides 360° all round, 260° side to side, 195° fore and aft, 40° down over the side, and 15° down over the nose vision.

The cockpit has a triple-redundant system for emergency exit. In normal operation the canopy is pivoted upward and aft by hydraulic power. Explosive bolts release the canopy in the event of hydraulic failure; but should both these systems fail, the pilot is able to unlatch the canopy manually, so that the airstream forces it into the open position.

A side control stick is provided, with a suitable armrest, to allow precise control inputs during combat manoeuvres. The McDonnell Douglas Escapac seat chosen for the YF-16 will provide safe ejection capability at ground level from 0 to 600 knots (0-690 mph; 0-1,110 km/h) during high sink-rate conditions.

In the fly-by-wire control system, electrical circuits replace the conventional mechanical linkages, conveying direct electrical commands from the pilot's controls to servo motors that operate the control surfaces. There is no mechanical backup to the system in the YF-16, but four electric channels provide quadruple redundancy. The fly-by-wire system is integrated into the basic aerodynamic configuration in a manner which exploits the total capabilities of flight control system technology through the control configured vehicle (CCV) principle. CCV in this application is concerned with the relationship of aircraft balance to static longitudinal stability, allowing the CG to be moved further aft than is normally possible with a conventional configuration. This results in a significant reduction in drag, especially at high load factors and at supersonic speeds. The effect is to reduce trim drag, which includes both the tail drag and the change in drag on the wing due to changes in wing lift required to balance the down load on the tail.

The blended wing/body concept adopted for the YF-16 is achieved by flaring the wing/body intersection. This not only provides lift from the body at high angles of attack, but also gives less wetted area and increased internal fuel volume. In addition, thickening of the wing root gives increased rigidity of the structure, with a weight saving of some 250 lb (113 kg).

The Pratt & Whitney F100-PW-100 afterburning turbofan engine chosen to power the YF-16 provides a thrust-to-weight ratio of approximately 1·5 : 1. A fixed-geometry air intake was chosen for the prototypes as it was calculated that it would be 400 lb (181 kg) lighter than a variable-geometry intake designed for optimum performance. It could be changed without difficulty at a later date if desirable to improve performance. The intake is mounted beneath the fuselage, where the airflow suffers least disturbance throughout the entire range of aircraft manoeuvres, and minimises the problem of gun gas ingestion. To reduce the risk of foreign objects being drawn into the engine during ground operations, the nosewheel is located aft of the intake. Because of the thin wing section, both main and nose landing gear units retract into the fuselage, the nosewheel turning during retraction to lie horizontally under the intake duct.

The prototypes carry minimal avionics to restrict weight and costs, but ample space has been made available for installation of suitable equipment at a later date. It was planned to utilise as much off-the-shelf equipment as possible in the prototypes. The horizontal tail and flap/aileron actuators, and electro-mechanical servos in the control system, are modified versions of units used on the F-111. The nose-mounted air data probe, feeding an air data converter and a central air data computer, is similar to that of the Lockheed SR-71. The stick-grip, embodying control force transducers, is a modified version of that used on the LTV A-7; and the cockpit air-conditioning system similar to that used on the A-7 or Northrop F-5. To provide electrical power for the YF-16, Sundstrand Corporation's Aviation Division has developed a constant-speed drive for an integrated drive generator rated at 50kVA.

Armament, which is specified only for the second prototype, comprises a single M61 20 mm multi-barrel cannon with 500 rounds, mounted in the port side of the fuselage, and an infra-red missile carried on each wingtip. There are four underwing hardpoints for the carriage of stores such as auxiliary fuel tanks and ECM pods.

The first of the two YF-16 prototypes was rolled out at Fort Worth, Texas, on 13 December 1973, and was ferried in a USAF C-5 to Edwards AFB on 8 January 1974. This aircraft (72-01567) made an unscheduled first flight on 20 January 1974, when test pilot Philip Oestricher elected to take to the air after the all-moving tailplane was damaged during high-speed taxi tests. Official first flight was made on 2 February 1974, and on 5 February a speed in excess of Mach 1 was recorded. A level speed of Mach 2 at 40,000 ft (12,190 m) was attained on 11 March 1974. The second prototype (72-01568) was ferried to Edwards AFB on 27 February 1974, where it flew for the first time on 9 May 1974.

TYPE: Single-seat lightweight fighter prototype.

WINGS: Cantilever mid-wing monoplane, basically of light alloy construction. Wing blended into fuselage. Full-span automatic leading-edge manoeuvring flaps. Flap/aileron on each trailing-edge. Mountings at wingtips for carriage of infra-red air-to-air missiles.

FUSELAGE: Semi-monocoque all-metal structure. Highly-swept vortex control strakes mounted along the fuselage forebody. An airfield arrester hook can be mounted in the rear fuselage, between the ventral fins.

TAIL UNIT: Cantilever structure with swept surfaces, constructed largely of graphite composite material. Small dorsal fin, conventional rudder and interchangeable ventral fins. Interchangeable all-moving horizontal surfaces. Split speed-brake inboard of rear portion of horizontal tail surface, to each side of nozzle.

LANDING GEAR: Hydraulically-retractable tricycle type, main units retracting forward and nose unit aft into fuselage. Single wheel on each unit. Eighty per cent of main unit components interchangeable.

POWER PLANT: One Pratt & Whitney F100-PW-100 turbofan engine of approximately 25,000 lb (11,340 kg) st with afterburning, mounted within the rear fuselage. Fixed-geometry air intake beneath fuselage. Standard fuel contained in wing-root and fuselage cells, auxiliary fuel in tanks on underwing and underfuselage hardpoints.

ACCOMMODATION: Pilot only, in air-conditioned cockpit, on McDonnell Douglas Escapac type IE-2 zero-zero ejection seat, under polycarbonate transparent canopy. Forward portion of canopy opens upward and aft hydraulically.

SYSTEMS: Electrical system powered by engine-driven integrated drive generator, rated at 50kVA. Quadruple-redundant fly-by-wire control system. Hydraulic system for undercarriage retraction, operation of cockpit canopy and airfield arrester hook. Air-conditioning unit for cockpit, utilising engine bleed air.

ARMAMENT: One M61A-1 20 mm multi-barrel cannon with 500 rounds. Provision for carriage of one infra-red air-to-air missile on each wingtip. Underwing hardpoints for miscellaneous stores. "Snap-shoot" gunsight.

DIMENSIONS, EXTERNAL:

Wing span	30 ft 0 in (9·14 m)
Length overall	47 ft 0 in (14·32 m)
Height overall	16 ft 3 in (4·95 m)

WEIGHTS:

Weight empty	approx 12,000 lb (5,443 kg)
Mission weight	approx 17,500 lb (7,938 kg)
Design T-O weight	27,000 lb (12,245 kg)

PERFORMANCE:

Max speed	in excess of Mach 2·0
Radius of action	more than 500 nm (575 miles; 925 km)
Ferry range	more than 2,000 nm (2,303 miles; 3,705 km)

GREAT LAKES

GREAT LAKES AIRCRAFT COMPANY

HEAD OFFICE:
PO Box 11132, Wichita, Kansas 67202

EUROPEAN OFFICE:
89 Augsburg 21, Berg Street 1C, Federal Republic of Germany

PRESIDENT:
Douglas L. Champlin

GENERAL MANAGER:
Brad Shelman

On 23 February 1972, Mr Douglas Champlin announced the purchase of Great Lakes Aircraft Company from Mr Harvey R. Swack.

Great Lakes Aircraft Company is building the well-known Sport Trainer at Wichita, Kansas. Certificated components and assemblies are available to amateur constructors, but plans are no longer available.

GREAT LAKES SPORT TRAINER MODEL 2T-1A-1

Great Lakes Sport Trainer Model 2T-1A-1 (140 hp Lycoming O-320-E2A engine)

The Great Lakes Sport Trainer was produced with Cirrus and Menasco engines by the original Great Lakes Company, founded on 2 January 1929.

Certification of the **Model 2T-1A-1** with 140 hp Lycoming engine was obtained in May 1973, and delivery of production aircraft began in October 1973. Delivery of the **Model 2T-1A-2,** with a 180 hp Lycoming fuel-injection engine, driving a constant-speed propeller, and with four ailerons and inverted fuel and oil systems as standard, was scheduled to begin in June 1974. Sport Trainers were undergoing certification in Germany and the United Kingdom in February 1974.

The following description applies to the Model 2T-1A-1:

TYPE: Two-seat sporting biplane.

WINGS: Braced biplane, with N-type interplane struts, wire bracing and N-type centre-section support struts. Dual streamline-section landing and flying wires. Wing section M-12. No dihedral on upper wing, 2° on lower wings. Sweepback on upper wing 9° 13′. Composite structure, with Douglas fir spars, metal ribs and overall fabric covering. Ailerons on lower wings only. No flaps or tabs.

FUSELAGE: Welded chrome-molybdenum steel tube Warren girder structure, with fabric covering.

TAIL UNIT: Wire-braced welded chrome-molybdenum steel tube structure, fabric-covered. Tailplane incidence manually adjustable. No controllable tabs.

LANDING GEAR: Non-retractable type, with steerable Scott tailwheel. Divided main legs with spring-oleo shock-absorbers standard. Main wheels size 6·00-6 with hydraulic disc brakes. Parking brake. 7·00-6 tyres optional. Wheel fairings optional.

POWER PLANT: One 140 hp Lycoming O-320-E2A four-cylinder horizontally-opposed aircooled engine, driving a McCauley two-blade fixed-pitch propeller type 1C160/EGM 7654. Aluminium fuel tank in centre-section of upper wing, capacity 26 US gallons (98·5 litres). Refuelling point in upper wing surface. Propeller spinner and inverted fuel and oil systems optional.

ACCOMMODATION: Two seats in tandem in open cockpits. Dual controls standard. Compass, airspeed indicator, altimeter and engine speed indicator standard in rear cockpit, optional for front cockpit. Enclosed canopy for front and rear cockpit, and cockpit heating, optional. Baggage compartment aft of rear cockpit, capacity 40 lb (18 kg), optional.

SYSTEMS: Engine-driven generator for electric supply to navigation lights, two rotating beacons and rear cockpit instrument lights standard. Hydraulic system for brakes only.

ELECTRONICS AND EQUIPMENT: Emergency locator transmitter standard. Escort 110 com radio, intercom, and Edo-Aire RT-553 with or without auto Omni optional. Standard equipment includes map case, seat belts and shoulder harness, and a choice of four paint trims. Optional equipment includes turn and bank indicator, rate of climb indicator, manifold pressure gauge, cylinder head temperature gauge and accelerometer for rear cockpit, and cockpit canopies.

DIMENSIONS, EXTERNAL:

Wing span	26 ft 8 in (8·13 m)
Length overall	20 ft 4 in (6·20 m)
Height overall	7 ft 4 in (2·24 m)
Wheel track	5 ft 10 in (1·78 m)

AREAS:

Wings, gross	187·6 sq ft (17·43 m²)
Ailerons (two, total)	13·5 sq ft (1·25 m²)
Fin	5·87 sq ft (0·55 m²)
Rudder	6·81 sq ft (0·63 m²)
Tailplane	15·44 sq ft (1·43 m²)
Elevators	10·68 sq ft (0·99 m²)

WEIGHTS AND LOADINGS:

Weight empty	1,140 lb (517 kg)
Max T-O weight	1,750 lb (793 kg)
Max wing loading	9·32 lb/sq ft (45·5 kg/m²)
Max power loading	12·5 lb/hp (5·67 kg/hp)

PERFORMANCE (at max T-O weight):

Max level speed at S/L	104 knots (120 mph; 193 km/h)
Max cruising speed	91 knots (105 mph; 169 km/h)
Stalling speed	47 knots (54 mph; 87 km/h)
Max rate of climb at S/L	720 ft (219 m)/min
Service ceiling	12,400 ft (3,780 m)
T-O run	575 ft (175 m)
Landing run	400 ft (122 m)
Range with max fuel	260 nm (300 miles; 482 km)

GRUMMAN

GRUMMAN CORPORATION

HEAD OFFICE:
Bethpage, New York 11714

Telephone: (516) 575-0574

CHAIRMAN OF THE BOARD:
E. Clinton Towl

PRESIDENT:
John C. Bierwirth

VICE-PRESIDENTS:
Edward Balinsky (Investment Management)
John F. Carr (Administration)
Patrick J. Cherry (Controller)
Robert G. Freese (Treasurer)

Lawrence M. Pierce (General Counsel)
John B. Rettaliata (Public Affairs)
Peter E. Viemeister (Development)
SECRETARY: Robert W. Bradshaw

GRUMMAN AEROSPACE CORPORATION
See below

GRUMMAN ALLIED INDUSTRIES, INC
HEAD OFFICE AND WORKS:
600 Old Country Road, Garden City, New York 11530
Telephone: (516) 741-3500
CHAIRMAN OF THE BOARD:
Wallace B. Spielman
PRESIDENT:
Robert F. Loar
VICE-PRESIDENTS:
Wells A. Darling (Recreational Products and Special Vehicles)
Robert J. Farren (Facilities)
James L. Maxwell (General Manager, Metal Boat Division)
J. J. Serota (Secretary)
William H. Shaw (Pearson Yacht Division)
Robert W. Somerville (Automotive)
TREASURER: Robert G. Landon

GRUMMAN AMERICAN AVIATION CORPORATION
See pages 349-352

GRUMMAN AVIO SYSTEMS CORPORATION
HEAD OFFICE AND WORKS:
2501 East Arkansas Lane, Grand Prairie, Texas 75050
PRESIDENT: Joseph G. Stalk Jr
TREASURER: Robert G. Freese
SECRETARY: Lawrence M. Pierce

GRUMMAN DATA SYSTEMS CORPORATION
HEAD OFFICE AND WORKS:
Bethpage, New York 11714
Telephone: (516) 575-0574
CHAIRMAN OF THE BOARD:
E. Clinton Towl
PRESIDENT:
Robert A. Nafis
VICE-PRESIDENTS:
James M. Conners (Division Management)
Derwin C. DeForest (Network Services)
Dominic J. DiFalco (Grumman Account)
Robert T. Pearson (Products)
Burton Stern (Finance)
Walter C. Wood Jr (Commercial Systems)
TREASURER: James M. Pettit
SECRETARY: Robert W. Bradshaw

GRUMMAN ECOSYSTEMS CORPORATION
HEAD OFFICE AND WORKS:
Bethpage, New York 11714
Telephone: (516) 575-0574
CHAIRMAN OF THE BOARD:
E. Clinton Towl
PRESIDENT AND TREASURER:
Wm. T. Schwendler Jr
VICE-PRESIDENTS:
Thomas W. Attridge Jr (Operations, Environmental and Mapping Division)
Clifford F. Jessberger (Operations, Pollution Control Division)
William T. Malloy (General Manager, Environmental and Mapping Division)
Edward A. Sargent (Sales, Pollution Control Division)
SECRETARY: Robert W. Bradshaw
CONTROLLER: Raymond E. Montano

GRUMMAN INTERNATIONAL, INC
HEAD OFFICE:
Bethpage, New York 11714
Telephone: (516) 575-1101
CHAIRMAN OF THE BOARD:
E. Clinton Towl
PRESIDENT:
Robert L. Townsend
VICE-PRESIDENTS:
Thomas A. Brancati
Peter B. Oram
Joseph Y. Rodriguez
Edwin V. Zolkoski
TREASURER: Patrick J. Cherry
SECRETARY: Mellor A. Gill

GRUMAIR EXPORT SALES CORPORATION
HEAD OFFICE:
Bethpage, New York 11714
Telephone: (516) 575-0574
PRESIDENT: John F. Carr
TREASURER: Patrick J. Cherry
SECRETARY: Lawrence M. Pierce

PAUMANOCK DEVELOPMENT CORPORATION
HEAD OFFICE:
Bethpage, New York 11714
Telephone: (516) 575-0574
CHAIRMAN OF THE BOARD:
E. Clinton Towl
PRESIDENT:
Chester M. Parker
VICE-PRESIDENT:
Thomas D. Gill
TREASURER: Robert G. Freese
SECRETARY: John E. Galligan
CONTROLLER: Gerard J. Vanella

PAUMANOCK INSURANCE COMPANY LTD
HEAD OFFICE:
PO Box 660, Belvedere Building, Hamilton, Bermuda
Telephone: 2-4355/6/7
PRESIDENT:
Robert G. Freese
VICE-PRESIDENTS:
John F. Carr
Edward B. Jacobs
Donald H. Middleton
TREASURER: James J. Reilly
SECRETARY: Robert W. Bradshaw

PAUMANOCK LEASING SERVICES INC
HEAD OFFICE:
Bethpage, New York 11714
Telephone: (516) 575-3421
CHAIRMAN OF THE BOARD:
E. Clinton Towl
PRESIDENT:
Robert G. Freese
VICE-PRESIDENT:
Raymond G. Nightengale (Operating Manager)
TREASURER: James J. Reilly
SECRETARY: Thomas L. Genovese

The Grumman Aircraft Engineering Corporation was incorporated on 6 December 1929. Important changes in the corporate structure of the company were announced in 1969, resulting in the formation of Grumman Corporation, a small holding company, with Grumman Aerospace Corporation, Grumman Allied Industries Inc, Grumman Data Systems Corporation, Grumman International Inc and Montauk Aero Corporation as subsidiaries. A new organisation known as Grumman Ecosystems Corporation was brought into operation in January 1971, and in the Autumn of 1972 a merger was planned with American Aviation Corporation of Cleveland, Ohio. This became effective on 2 January 1973 when Grumman American Aviation Corporation was announced as a new subsidiary of Grumman Corporation. During 1973 Montauk Aero Corporation ceased to operate, and Grumman Corporation has three new subsidiaries: Paumanock Development Corporation, Paumanock Insurance Company Ltd, and Paumanock Leasing Services Inc.

It was announced on 7 May 1973 that Grumman Corporation and the Federal German aerospace company of VFW-Fokker GmbH had formed a new joint venture, incorporated as Grumman Avio Systems Corporation, and based at Grand Prairie, Texas. This company is licenced to manufacture, sell and service the Aviobridge system designed originally by the Fokker-VFW Drechtsteden division in the Netherlands. An initial US order from the Massachusetts Port Authority was announced simultaneously, covering the supply and installation of ten Mk 5M apron drive Aviobridges at Boston's Logan International Airport.

It was announced in April 1974 that Grumman was collaborating with Rhein-Flugzeugbau GmbH of West Germany (which see), a subsidiary of VFW-Fokker GmbH, in the design and development of a Wankel-powered ducted-fan light aircraft which has been named the Fanliner. All available details of this are given under Rhein-Flugzeugbau GmbH in the German aircraft section.

GRUMMAN AEROSPACE CORPORATION
HEAD OFFICE AND WORKS:
Bethpage, New York 11714
Telephone: (516) 575-0574
CHAIRMAN OF THE BOARD AND PRESIDENT:
Joseph G. Gavin Jr
VICE-CHAIRMAN OF THE BOARD:
William M. Zarkowsky
SENIOR VICE-PRESIDENT:
Ira G. Hedrick (Advanced Systems Technology)
ADMINISTRATIVE VICE-PRESIDENT:
John O'Brien (Resources)
VICE-PRESIDENTS:
A. D. Alexandrovich (Product Technology Development)
John M. Buxton (President, Grumman Houston Corporation)
Edward Dalva (Operations Manager, Bethpage)
Thomas W. Johnson (Manufacturing Operations)
Thomas J. Kelly (Space Programmes)
Lawrence M. Mead Jr (Technical Operations)
Ross S. Mickey (Aircraft and Other Programmes)
Robert C. Miller (EA-6B and EF-111 Programmes)
Gordon H. Ochenrider
Michael Pelehach (F-14 Programme)
G. Thomas Rozzi (Security and Personnel)
L. M. Satterfield
George M. Skurla (General Manager, Calverton)
Ralph H. Tripp (Corporate Systems)
A. James Zusi (Operations Quality)
TREASURER: Carl A. Paladino
SECRETARY AND GENERAL COUNSEL:
Raphael Mur

Current products of this subsidiary of Grumman Corporation include versions of the A-6 Intruder, EA-6B Prowler, E-2C Hawkeye and F-14 Tomcat for the US Navy.

At the beginning of January 1974 Grumman Aerospace Corporation had a total of approximately 23,500 employees.

Grumman E-2C advanced early-warning aircraft, latest version of the Hawkeye

GRUMMAN HAWKEYE

US Navy designation: E-2

The E-2 Hawkeye was evolved as a carrier-borne early-warning aircraft, but is suitable also for land-based operations from unimproved fields. The prototype flew for the first time on 21 October 1960, since when the following versions have been built:

E-2A (formerly W2F-1). Initial production version, the first of which, equipped with full early-warning and command electronics system, flew on 19 April 1961. Delivery to the US Navy began officially on 19 January 1964, when the first Hawkeye was accepted at San Diego for training of air and ground crews of airborne early warning squadron VAW-11. This unit became operational on USS *Kitty Hawk* in 1965. Second Hawkeye unit was VAW-12. Total of 62 built; delivery completed in Spring 1967.

E-2B. The prototype of this version flew for the first time on 20 February 1969. It differs from the E-2A by having a Litton Industries L-304 microelectronic general-purpose computer. A retrofit programme, completed in December 1971, updated all operational E-2As to E-2B standard. In service with VAW-113, VAW-116, VAW-125 and VAW-126 in 1974.

E-2C. First of two E-2C prototypes flew on 20 January 1971. Production began in mid-1971; 28 are scheduled for delivery by the end of 1975, of which 10 had been delivered by March 1974. The E-2C utilises an advanced form of Grumman/General Electric-developed radar that is capable of detecting airborne targets in a land-clutter environment. Improvements for increased reliability and easier maintenance have been provided. Entered service, with airborne early-warning squadron VAW-123 at NAS Norfolk, Va, in November 1973.

Teams of Hawkeyes are able to maintain patrols on naval task force defence perimeters in all weathers, and are capable of detecting and assessing any threat from approaching high-Mach-number enemy aircraft early enough to ensure successful interception. To make this possible highly sophisticated equipment is carried by the aircraft, including a Randtron Systems AN/APA-171 antenna system housed in a 24 ft (7·32 m) diameter saucer-shaped rotodome mounted above the rear fuselage of the aircraft. The rotodome revolves in flight at 6 rpm, and can be lowered 1 ft 10¼ in (0·64 m) to facilitate aircraft stowage on board ship. The Yagi type radar arrays within the rotodome are interfaced to the on-board electronic systems, providing radar sum and difference signals plus IFF.

Major detection capability stems from the General Electric AN/APS-120 radar and OL-93/AP radar detector processor (RDP). The radar is able to spot distant airborne targets despite heavy sea or land echo "clutter", as well as surface targets. It is linked to the tracking and intercept computer via the RDP, which carries out automatic detection and signals target reports which the computer needs for automatic tracking.

To provide the Combat Information Center (CIC) staff with the essential man/machine interface, the Hazeltine Corporation's AN/APA-172 control indicator group consists of three identical display stations, each with a 10 in (25·4 cm) main and a 5 in (12·7 cm) auxiliary display. The main display shows target track information, while the auxiliary provides alpha-numeric information with random-write capability. Station controls allow each of the three CIC operators to select independently specific information for their displays, so that each may have the same or a different perspective on any tactical situation. Other Hazeltine equipment includes an OL-76/AP IFF detector processor, providing automatic Mk X SIF processing capability in a single integrated system. Signals generated by the OL-76/AP enable the CIC operators to obtain instant range, azimuth and altitude positions of a friendly target. In order to identify that target as friend or foe, an RT-988/A IFF interrogator "challenges" and identifies the aircraft, feeding its information direct to the OL-76/AP for processing.

Accurate navigation is critical for an aircraft which, after hours on patrol, needs to find without delay its mobile carrier base. Such a requirement is catered for by Litton Industries' AN/ASN-92 (LN-15C) carrier aircraft inertial navigation system (CAINS), an important feature being its capability of rapid alignment and orientation following take-off from a rolling and pitching carrier deck. Litton's Amecom division's AN/ALR-59 passive detection system provides early-warning capability. Able to capture short-duration signals in real time, its four-band simultaneous coverage ensures highly-accurate direction finding, even in an environment cluttered with enemy signals.

Linking all this advanced equipment is Litton Data Systems division's L-304 computer, which processes radar, Link 4 and Link 11 communications, navigation and passive detection data in real time. It comprises two L-304 processors, eight 8,192-word memory units (expandable to ten), power supplies, a recorder producer, power converter, system test module, a 4,096 word refresh memory for the displays, input/output buffers for each function, plus display, radar, navigation, communications and passive detection converter modules.

In addition to the L-304 computer, the E-2C has also a Conrac Corporation CP-1085/AS air data computer (ADC). Combining solid-state pressure transducers with a special preprogrammed digital computer, it provides outputs of altitude, altitude hold, indicated airspeed, true airspeed and Mach number in analogue and digital format to interface with the navigation, flight control and display subsystems.

The following details apply to the E-2C Hawkeye:

Type: Airborne early-warning aircraft.

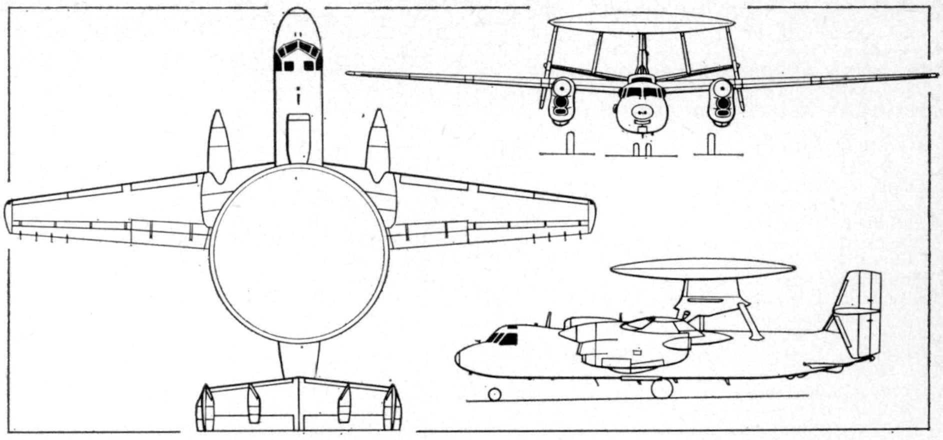

Grumman E-2C Hawkeye twin-turboprop airborne early-warning aircraft (*Pilot Press*)

Wings: Cantilever high-wing monoplane of all-metal construction. Centre-section is a structural box consisting of three beams, ribs and machined skins. Hinged leading-edge is non-structural and provides access to flying and engine controls. The outer panels fold rearward about skewed axis-hinge fittings mounted on the rear beams, to stow parallel with the rear fuselage on each side. Folding is done through a double-acting hydraulic cylinder. Trailing-edges of outer panels and part of centre-section consist of long-span ailerons and hydraulically-actuated Fowler flaps. When flaps are lowered, ailerons are drooped automatically. All control surfaces of E-2C are power-operated and incorporate devices to produce artificial feel forces. Automatic flight control system (AFCS) can be assigned sole control of the system hydraulic actuators, or AFCS signals can be superimposed on the pilot's mechanical inputs for stability augmentation. Pneumatically-inflated rubber de-icing boots on leading-edges.

Fuselage: Conventional all-metal semi-monocoque structure.

Tail Unit: Cantilever structure, with four fins and three double-hinged rudders. Tailplane dihedral 11°. Portions of tail unit made of glassfibre to reduce radar reflection. Power control and artificial feel systems as for ailerons. Pneumatically-inflated rubber de-icing boots on all leading-edges.

Landing Gear: Hydraulically-retractable tricycle type. Pneumatic emergency extension. Steerable nosewheel unit retracts rearward. Main wheels retract forward, and rotate to lie flat in bottom of nacelles. Twin wheels on nose unit only. Oleo-pneumatic shock-absorbers. Main-wheel tyres size 36 × 11 Type VII 24-ply, pressure 260 lb/sq in (18·28 kg/cm²) on ship, 210 lb/sq in (14·76 kg/cm²) ashore. Hydraulic brakes. Hydraulically-operated retractable tailskid. A-frame arrester hook under tail.

Power Plant: Two 4,910 ehp Allison T56-A-422 turboprop engines, driving Aeroproducts N41 four-blade fully-feathering reversible-pitch constant-speed propellers. Spinners and blade cuffs incorporate electrical anti-icers.

Accommodation: Crew of five on flight deck and in ATDS compartment in main cabin, consisting of pilot, co-pilot, combat information centre officer, air control officer and radar operator. Downward-hinged door, with built-in steps, on port side of centre fuselage.

Electronics: AN/APA-171 rotodome and antenna, AN/APS-120 search radar, IFF interrogator type RT-988/A, OL-93/AP radar detector processor, OL-76/AP IFF detector processor, AN/APA-172 control indicator group, OL-77/ASQ computer programmer, L-304 airborne computer, ARC-158 UHF data link, ARQ-34 HF data link, ASM-440 in-flight performance monitor, ARC-51A UHF com, ARQ-34 HF com, AIC-14A intercom, AN/ASN-92 (LN-15C) CAINS carrier aircraft inertial navigation system, CP-1085/AS air data computer, APN-153 (V) Doppler, ASN-50 heading and attitude reference system, ARN-52(V) TACAN, ARA-50 UHF ADF, ASW-25B ACLS and APN-171(V) radar altimeter.

Dimensions, external:

Wing span	80 ft 7 in (24·56 m)
Length overall	57 ft 7 in (17·55 m)
Height overall	18 ft 4 in (5·59 m)
Diameter of rotodome	24 ft 0 in (7·32 m)
Propeller diameter	13 ft 6 in (4·11 m)

Area:

Wings, gross	700 sq ft (65·03 m²)

Weights:

Weight empty	37,678 lb (17,090 kg)
Max fuel (internal)	12,400 lb (5,624 kg)
Max T-O weight	51,569 lb (23,391 kg)

Performance (at max T-O weight):

Max level speed	325 knots (374 mph; 602 km/h)
Cruising speed	269 knots (310 mph; 499 km/h)
Stalling speed (landing configuration)	71 knots (82 mph; 132 km/h)
Service ceiling	30,800 ft (9,390 m)
T-O run	1,890 ft (576 m)
T-O to 50 ft (15 m)	2,520 ft (768 m)
Ferry range	1,394 nm (1,605 miles; 2,583 km)

GRUMMAN INTRUDER AND PROWLER

US Navy designations: A-6, EA-6 and KA-6

The basic A-6A (originally A2F-1) Intruder was conceived as a carrier-borne low-level attack bomber equipped specifically to deliver nuclear or conventional weapons on targets completely obscured by weather or darkness. Performance is subsonic, but the Intruder possesses outstanding endurance and carries a heavier and more varied load of stores than any previous US naval attack aircraft.

Competition for the original A-6 contract was conducted from May to December 1957, among eight aircraft companies. Of the 11 designs submitted, Grumman's was adjudged the best on 31 December 1957. The A-6 was developed subsequently under the first "cost plus incentive fee" contract placed by the US Navy, and seven variants of the basic design have been announced to date, as follows:

A-6A Intruder. Initial carrier-based attack bomber, described in 1972-73 *Jane's*. The first A-6A flew on 19 April 1960, and this version entered service officially on 1 February 1963, when the first aircraft was accepted for the US Navy's VA-42 squadron at NAS Oceana. A total of 482 were built, the last delivery taking place in December 1969. A-6As saw considerable service with the Navy and Marine Corps in Vietnam. Most other versions of the Intruder are modifications of A-6As.

Grumman has US Navy contracts covering the modernisation of A-6As by fitting A-6E advanced weapon systems. It is anticipated that the programme could continue until all remaining A-6As in the inventory have been modified to A-6E standard.

EA-6A. First flown in prototype form in 1963, this version retains partial strike capability, but is equipped primarily to support strike aircraft and ground forces by suppressing enemy electronic activity and obtaining tactical electronic intelligence within a combat area. Elements of the A-6A's bombing/navigation system are deleted and the EA-6A carries more than 30 different antennae to detect, locate, classify, record and jam enemy radiation. Externally-evident features include a radome at the top of the tail-fin, and attachment points under the wings and fuselage for ECM pods, fuel tanks and/or weapons. A total of 27 EA-6As were built for the US Marine Corps, including six A-6As modified into EA-6As.

EA-6B Prowler. Development of EA-6A for which Grumman received a prototype design and development contract in the Autumn of 1966. Nose is 40 in (1·02 m) longer than that of EA-6A to accommodate enlarged cockpits housing a crew of four under two separate upward-opening canopies. The two additional crewmen operate the much more advanced ECM equipment. Major subcontractor was Airborne Instruments, a subsidiary of Cutler-Hammer Corporation, responsible for developing the electronic countermeasures system. Prototype EA-6B flew for the first time on 25 May 1968.

The US Administration Fiscal 1969 defence budget allocated a sum of $139 million for the purchase of eight EA-6Bs for the US Navy, and funding for 12 additional aircraft was included in the FY 1970 budget request. The FY 1971, 1972 and 1973 budgets called for 11, 10 and 6 aircraft respectively.

A-6B Intruder. Conversion of the A-6A to provide Standard ARM missile capability. Though primarily an avionics modification, it has three different configurations ranging from limited to full strike capability. A total of 19 A-6As were modified to A-6B configuration.

A-6C Intruder. Derived from the A-6A but differing externally by having an underfuselage turret housing forward-looking infra-red (FLIR) sensors and (low-light-level television camera, providing additional night attack capability. This equipment is intended to permit detailed identification and acquisition of targets not discernible by the aircraft's radar. A total of 12 A-6As were modified to the A-6C configuration.

KA-6D Intruder. An A-6A was modified into a prototype flight refuelling tanker, with hose and reel in the rear fuselage, and flew for the first time on 23 May 1966. The KA-6D production model is fitted with TACAN and can transfer more than 21,000 lb (9,500 kg) of fuel immediately after take-off or 15,000 lb (6,800 kg) at a distance of 250 nm (288 miles; 463 km) from its carrier base. In addition, the KA-6D could act as a control aircraft for air-sea rescue operations or as a day bomber. A total of 54 A-6As were modified to KA-6D configuration.

A-6E Intruder. An advanced conversion of the A-6A with multi-mode radar and an IBM computer similar to that first tested in the EA-6B. First flight of an A-6E was made on 27 February 1970. First squadron deployment was made in September 1972, and the A-6E was approved officially for service use in December 1972. By the end of that month 24 A-6Es had been delivered to the US Navy, and 12 more were ordered for 1973 delivery. Funding currently approved for a further 21 aircraft, giving a total of 57 by the end of March 1975. Described separately.

GRUMMAN A-6E INTRUDER

Development of the A-6E began with the substitution of a single simultaneous multi-mode navigation and attack radar, developed by the Norden Division of United Aircraft Corporation, for the two earlier radar systems in the A-6A. Following the concepts of the EA-6B, the IBM Corporation and Fairchild Camera and Instrument Corporation have supplied a new attack and navigation computer system and an interfacing data converter. Conrac Corporation has designed an armament control unit and RCA has developed a video tape recorder for post-strike assessment of attacks.

The Norden Division's AN/APQ-148 multi-mode radar provides simultaneous ground mapping; identification, tracking, and range-finding of fixed or moving targets; and terrain-clearance or terrain-following manoeuvres. It can also detect, locate and track radar beacons used by forward air controllers when providing close support for ground forces. The APQ-148 has mechanical scanning in azimuth and utilises a newly-developed electronics system for simultaneous vertical scanning. There are two cockpit displays, one for the pilot and one for the bombardier/navigator, and terrain data is also presented on a vertical display indicator ahead of the pilot. Built-in test equipment (BITE), that provides automatic fault location, is an integral part of the system, permitting repairs to be carried out at squadron level.

IBM's AN/ASQ-133 solid-state digital computer is coupled to the A-6E's radar, inertial and Doppler navigational equipment, communications and automatic flight control system. This computer receives its inputs from programmes written specifically for the A-6E and stored in the computer's memory circuits. As mission data is measured in flight by on-board aerodynamic and electronic sensors, the computer compares the data with the programmed information, computes any differences, and provides corrective data that can be used to alter the parameters of the mission. Pedestal control and digital display units form part of the complete computer subsystem. The digital display unit shows the basic parameters needed for operation of the system. The pedestal control, mounted at the navigator's position, has a slew stick which is used to place radar display cursors on the selected target for tracking purposes. Input keys mounted on top of the pedestal can be used to update or add to mission information to be factored into the flight path by the computer subsystem. The entire subsystem also features BITE circuitry to simplify maintenance at squadron level.

Fairchild Camera and Instrument Corporation's AN/ASQ-133 signal data converter for the A-6E accepts analogue input data from up to sixty sensors, and converts that information to a digital output that is fed into the computer of the navigation and attack system. A necessary interface between the analogue sensors and displays and the digital computer, it is in effect an interpretation system able to communicate in both analogue and digital language, and can translate from one to the other almost instantaneously. Updating (the processing of complete successive sets of data for comparison with previous information) is accomplished ten times a second. Like the other electronic equipment of the A-6E, the ASQ-133 converter has BITE circuitry.

Conrac Corporation's armament control unit (ACU) for the A-6E provides in a single unit all the inputs and outputs necessary to select and release the Intruder's weapons. It receives and sends appropriate signals to arm, control and release weapons individually or simultaneously in any of the standard attack patterns. The master arming switch has a "practice" position that allows the ACU to be cycled up to the point of firing command. Safety circuits in the unit prevent accidental firing during the practice mode.

The multi-mode AN/AVA-1 display developed by Kaiser Aerospace and Electronics Corporation serves as a primary flight aid for navigation, approach, landing and weapons delivery. The basic vertical display indicator (VDI) is an 8 in (20·3 cm) cathode-ray tube which shows a synthetic landscape, sky, and electronically-generated command flight path that move to simulate the motion of these features as they would be seen by the pilot through the windscreen of the aircraft. Symbols are superimposed to augment the basic attitude data, and for attack a second set of superimposed information provides a target symbol, steering symbol, and release and pull-up markers. A solid-state radar data scan converter can provide on the same display an apparent real-world perspective of terrain, ten shades of grey defining terrain elevation at ten different segmented contour intervals up to 8·7 nm (10 miles; 16 km) ahead of the aircraft. This makes it possible for the pilot to fly the Intruder in either a terrain-following or terrain-avoidance mode at low altitude. Flight path and attack symbols can be superimposed over the terrain elevation data on the VDI, enabling the pilot to make his attack while avoiding or following terrain in the target area. Kaiser has also developed a micromesh filter to prevent "wash-out" of the data displayed on the VDI in sunlight conditions. Naval pilots currently use the VDI as a primary flight instrument, for precise steering in navigation, and for weapons cues, progress, and status information during an attack. For carrier landing the unit is used as a flight director and, linked to the APQ-148 radar, it presents steering information, allowing the pilot to select a descent angle for the final approach.

The first **A-6E TRAM** (target recognition attack multisensor) version of the A-6E flew for the first time on 22 March 1974. This conversion adds a turreted electro-optical sensor package, containing both infra-red and laser equipment, to a full-system Intruder. The sensor package provides lower hemispheric coverage for laser-guided weapons delivery.

TYPE: Two-seat carrier-based attack bomber.

WINGS: Cantilever mid-wing monoplane, with 25° sweepback at quarter-chord. All-metal structure. Hydraulically-operated almost-full-span leading-edge and trailing-edge flaps, with inset spoilers (flaperons) of same span as flaps forward of trailing-edge flaps. Trailing-edge of each wingtip, outboard of flap, splits to form speed-brakes which project above and below wing when extended. Two short fences above each wing. Outer panels fold upward and inward.

FUSELAGE: Conventional all-metal semi-monocoque structure. Bottom is recessed between engines to carry semi-exposed store.

TAIL UNIT: Cantilever all-metal structure. All-moving tailplane, without separate elevators. Electronic antenna in rear part of fin, immediately above rudder.

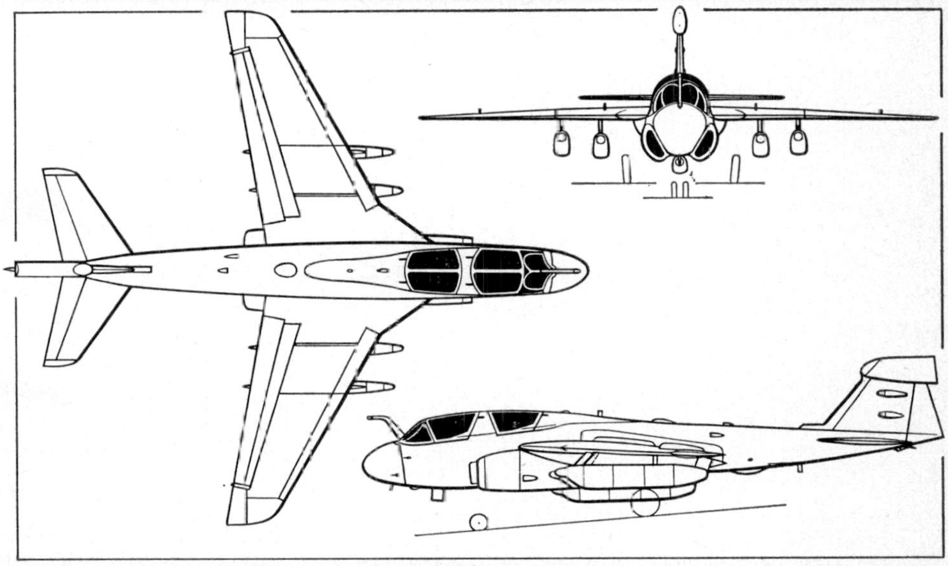

Photograph (*Stephen P. Peltz*) **and three-view drawing** (*Pilot Press*) **of the Grumman EA-6B Prowler four-seat all-weather electronic countermeasures aircraft**

Grumman KA-6D Intruder tanker of US Navy Squadron VA-145, based on the USS *Ranger* (*Peter M. Bowers*)

Landing Gear: Hydraulically-retractable tricycle type. Twin-wheel nose unit retracts rearwards. Single-wheel main units retract forward and inward into air intake fairings. A-frame arrester hook under rear fuselage.

Power Plant: Two 9,300 lb (4,218 kg) st Pratt & Whitney J52-P-8A turbojet engines. Provision for up to four external fuel tanks under wings. Removable flight refuelling probe projects upward immediately forward of windscreen.

Accommodation: Crew of two on Martin-Baker Mk GRU7 ejection seats, which can be reclined to reduce fatigue during low-level operations. Bombardier/navigator slightly behind and below pilot to starboard. Hydraulically-operated rearward-sliding canopy.

Systems: AiResearch environmental control system for cockpit and avionics bay. Electrical system powered by two AiResearch constant-speed drive starters that combine engine starting and electrical power generation, each delivering 30kVA. An AiResearch ram-air turbine, mounted so that it can be projected into the airstream above the port wing-root, provides in-flight emergency electrical power for essential equipment. Dual hydraulic systems for operation of flight controls, leading-edge and trailing-edge flaps, wingtip speed-brakes, landing gear brakes and cockpit canopy. One electrically-driven hydraulic pump provides restricted flight capability by supplying the tailplane and rudder actuators only.

Armament: Five weapon attachment points, each with a 3,600 lb (1,633 kg) capacity. Typical weapon loads are thirty 500 lb bombs in clusters of six, or three 2,000 lb general purpose bombs plus two 300 US gallon (1,135 litre) drop-tanks.

Dimensions, external:
- Wing span: 53 ft 0 in (16·15 m)
- Wing chord, mean aerodynamic: 10 ft 10¾ in (3·32 m)
- Width folded: 25 ft 4 in (7·72 m)
- Length overall: 54 ft 7 in (16·64 m)
- Height overall: 16 ft 2 in (4·93 m)
- Height folded: 16 ft 3 in (4·95 m)
- Tailplane span: 20 ft 4½ in (6·21 m)
- Wheel track: 10 ft 10½ in (3·32 m)

Areas:
- Wings, gross: 528·9 sq ft (49·1 m^2)
- Flaperons (total): 41·0 sq ft (3·81 m^2)
- Trailing-edge flaps (total): 104·0 sq ft (9·66 m^2)
- Leading-edge slats (total): 49·8 sq ft (4·63 m^2)
- Fin: 62·93 sq ft (5·85 m^2)
- Rudder: 16·32 sq ft (1·52 m^2)

Weights and Loading:
- Weight empty: 25,630 lb (11,625 kg)
- Max payload: 17,280 lb (7,838 kg)
- Max T-O weight:
  - catapult: 58,600 lb (26,580 kg)
  - field: 60,400 lb (27,397 kg)
- Max zero-fuel weight: 44,460 lb (20,166 kg)
- Max landing weight:
  - carrier: 36,000 lb (16,329 kg)
  - field: 45,000 lb (20,411 kg)
- Max wing loading: 114·2 lb/sq ft (557·6 kg/m^2)

Performance (no stores):
- Max never-exceed speed: 694 knots (799 mph; 1,285 km/h)
- Max level speed at S/L: 563 knots (648 mph; 1,043 km/h)
- Max cruising speed: 419 knots (482 mph; 776 km/h)
- Stalling speed, flaps up: 132 knots (152 mph; 245 km/h)
- Stalling speed, flaps down: 92 knots (106 mph; 171 km/h)
- Max rate of climb at S/L: 8,600 ft (2,621 m)/min
- Rate of climb at S/L, one engine out: 3,000 ft (914 m)/min
- Service ceiling: 44,600 ft (13,595 m)
- Service ceiling, one engine out: 29,000 ft (8,840 m)
- T-O to 50 ft (15 m): 2,630 ft (802 m)
- Landing from 50 ft (15 m): 2,100 ft (640 m)
- Landing run: 1,500 ft (457 m)
- Combat range: 1,880 nm (2,164 miles; 3,482 km)
- Range with max payload, 5% reserve plus 20 min at S/L: 936 nm (1,077 miles; 1,733 km)

A-6E TRAM (target recognition attack multisensor) version of the A-6E Intruder

GRUMMAN TOMCAT

US Navy designation: F-14

Grumman announced on 15 January 1969 that it had been selected as winner of the design competition for a new carrier-based fighter for the US Navy. Known as the VFX during the competitive phase of the programme, this aircraft was later designated officially F-14.

First flight of the F-14A Tomcat prototype took place on 21 December 1970, more than a month ahead of schedule. It was lost in a non-fatal accident, and flight testing was resumed on 24 May 1971 with the second aircraft. Seven more F-14As were flying before the end of 1971 and by early 1973 20 aircraft had logged almost 3,000 hours in more than 1,500 flights. Weapons system testing accounted for half of the total flight time.

The F-14 is designed to fulfil three primary missions. The first of these, fighter sweep/escort, involves clearing contested airspace of enemy fighters and protecting the strike force, with support from early-warning aircraft, surface ships and communications networks to co-ordinate penetration and escape.

Second mission is to defend carrier task forces via Combat Air Patrol (CAP) and Deck Launched Intercept (DLI) operations. Third role is secondary attack of tactical targets on the ground, supported by electronic countermeasures and fighter escort.

Emphasis has been placed on producing a high-performance aircraft able to fulfil both "dogfight" and air defence roles, and offering significant advantages compared with other current US and Soviet first-line combat aircraft. In terms of airframe design, the F-14 uses advanced constructional techniques and titanium for optimum strength/weight ratio. Structural strength and a high thrust/weight ratio enable it to combine a maximum speed in excess of Mach 2 with great agility in close-in air-to-air combat. Development time and risk were reduced by use of an already-existing avionics system, a landing gear evolved from that of the A-6 Intruder and proven high-performance engines in the initial version. Armament includes an M61 multi-barrel gun, and the F-14/Phoenix missile system has been demonstrated successfully against air-to-surface and surface-to-surface missiles, extreme high-altitude/high-speed interceptors, and in a simultaneous four-missile launch against four targets.

The Pratt & Whitney F401-PW-400 after-burning turbofan engine is under development for the F-14B and is expected to produce 28-30,000

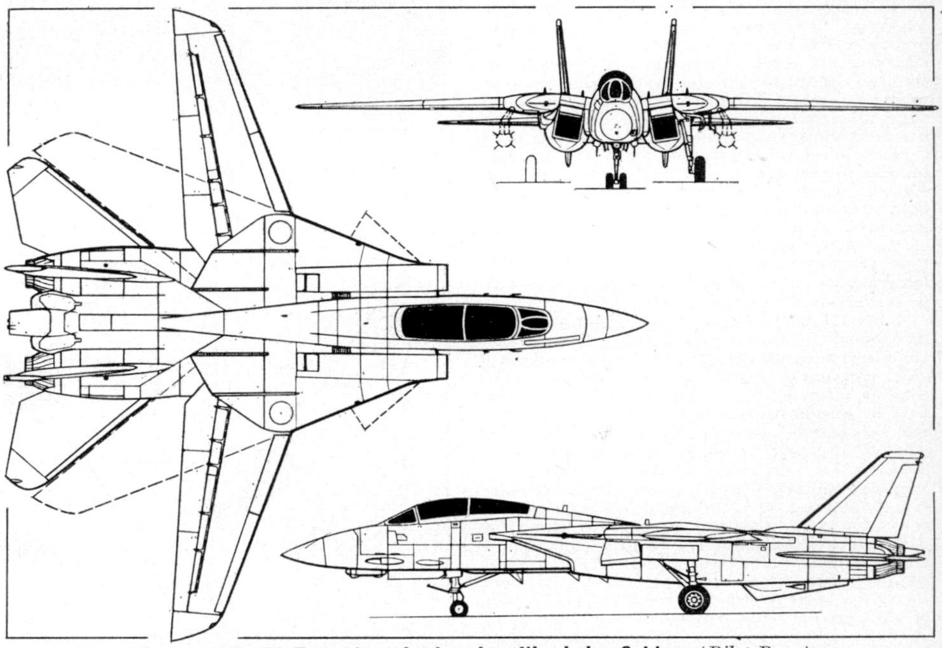

Grumman F-14A Tomcat carrier-based multi-mission fighter *(Pilot Press)*

This Grumman F-14A of US Navy Squadron VF-1 was the first Tomcat delivered to a combat unit *(Robert L. Lawson)*

lb st (12,700-13,600 kg st). It weighs some 600 lb (272 kg) less than the Pratt & Whitney TF30-P-412 engines which power the prototype and current production models.

The configuration of the F-14 is unique, with variable-geometry wings, small foreplanes which are extended as the wings sweep back to control centre-of-pressure shift, leading-edge slats and manoeuvring flaps to create a lower effective wing loading, and twin outward-canted fins and rudders.

The variable-geometry wing in particular has contributed to exceptional aerodynamic performance. F-14s have made field take-offs in less than 1,000 ft (305 m); landings in under 1,500 ft (457 m) at normal 20° sweep and under 5,000 ft (1,525 m) at full 68° sweep; and have been manoeuvred at speeds below 75 knots (86·5 mph; 139 km/h) at an angle of attack of 77°, with no tendency towards uncontrolled flight.

Optimum sweep of the wing is controlled automatically by a Mach Sweep Programmer, which relates sweep to speed and altitude.

The engines are mounted in ducts under the fixed inner wings, with simple inlets and straight-line airflow for maximum efficiency over a wide range of altitudes and Mach numbers. The ducts have multiple-shock ramp systems for good pressure-recovery at high Mach numbers.

Three versions of the F-14 have been projected:

F-14A. Current version, as described in detail below.

F-14B. Airframe and avionics basically the same as those of the F-14A, but powered by Pratt & Whitney F401 turbofans. Expected to be capable of acceleration from Mach 0·8 to Mach 1·8 in 1·27 minutes. Flown for first time on 12 September 1973.

F-14C. Development of F-14B, with new avionics and weapons. Fiscal restraints have retarded development of the avionics systems, and there are no current plans for F-14C production.

Under the initial contracts, Grumman was required to provide the US Navy with a mock-up of the F-14A in May 1969, and to build 12 research and development aircraft. Subsequently, the US Navy ordered an initial series of 26 production F-14As, and is now expected to acquire a total of 334 Tomcats, including the 12 development aircraft. Carrier trials were started in June 1972, and initial deployment with the fleet began in October 1972. Readiness Unit VF-124 at Miramar NAS, San Diego, California, was responsible for working up ground and air crews for the new aircraft, and the first two operational squadrons, VF-1 and VF-2, were serving on board the USS *Enterprise* in early 1974.

The Imperial Iranian Air Force has ordered a total of 80 F-14s.

TYPE: Two-seat carrier-based multi-role fighter.

WINGS: Variable-geometry mid-wing monoplane, with 20° of sweep in the fully-forward position and 68° when fully swept. Oversweep position of 75° for carrier stowage. Wing position is programmed automatically for optimum performance throughout the flight régime, but manual override is provided. A short movable wing section, needing only a comparatively light pivot structure, results from utilisation of a wide fixed centre-section "glove", with pivot points 8 ft 11 in (2·72 m) from the centreline of the airframe. The inboard wing sections, adjacent to the fuselage, are upward slightly to minimise cross-sectional area and wave drag, and consist basically of a one-piece electron beam-welded titanium assembly, 22 ft (6·70 m) in span, made from Ti-6Al-4V titanium alloy. Small canard surfaces, known as glove vanes, swing out from the leading-edge of the fixed portion of the wing as sweep of outer panels is increased. Spoilers on upper surfaces of wing centre-section. Stabilisation in pitch, provided by the canard surfaces, leaves the differential tailplane free to perform its primary control function. Trailing-edge control surfaces extend over almost entire span. Leading-edge slats.

First prototype of the Grumman F-14B Tomcat carrier-based multi-role fighter

FUSELAGE: The centre-fuselage section is a simple, fuel-carrying box structure; forward fuselage section comprises cockpit and nose. The aft section has a tapered aerofoil shape to minimise drag, with a fuel dump pipe projecting from the rear. Speed brakes located on the upper and lower surfaces, between the bases of the vertical tail fins.

TAIL UNIT: Twin vertical fins, mounted at the rear of each engine nacelle; a small pod at the top of each houses electronic countermeasures equipment. Outward-canted ventral fin under each nacelle. The all-flying horizontal surfaces have skins of boron-epoxy composite material.

LANDING GEAR: Retractable tricycle type. Twin-wheel nose unit retracts rearward. Single-wheel main units retract forward and upward. Arrester hook under rear fuselage, housed in small ventral fairing. Nose-tow catapult attachment on nose unit.

ENGINE INTAKES: Straight two-dimensional external compression inlets. A double-hinged ramp extends down from the top of each intake, and these are programmed to provide the correct airflow to the engines automatically under all flight conditions. Each intake is canted slightly away from the fuselage, from which it is separated by some 10 in (0·25 m) to allow sufficient clearance for the turbulent fuselage boundary layer to pass between fuselage and intake without causing turbulence within the intake. Engine inlet ducts and aft nacelle structures are designed and manufactured by Rohr Corporation. The inlet duct, constructed largely of aluminium honeycomb, is about 14 ft (4·27 m) long, while the aft nacelle structure, of bonded titanium honeycomb, is about 16 ft (4·88 m) in length.

POWER PLANT: Two Pratt & Whitney TF30-P-412A turbofan engines of 20,900 lb (9,480 kg) thrust with afterburning, mounted in ducts which open to provide 180° access for ease of maintenance. AiResearch ATS200-50 air-turbine starter.

ACCOMMODATION: Pilot and naval flight officer seated in tandem on Martin-Baker GRU-7A rocket-assisted zero-zero ejection seats, under a one-piece bubble canopy, hinged at the rear and offering all-round visibility. Provision for internal attachment of armour plate for crew protection.

ARMAMENT: One General Electric M61-A1 Vulcan 20 mm gun mounted in the port side of forward fuselage. Four Sparrow air-to-air missiles mounted partially submerged in the underfuselage. Two wing pylons, one under each fixed wing section, will carry four Sidewinder missiles, the latter being mounted one on either side of each pylon. For Phoenix and later missiles, Grumman has developed a concept in which removable pallets can be attached to the present Sparrow missile positions, the missiles then being attached to the pallets. Various combinations of missiles and bombs to a max external weapons load of 14,500 lb (6,577 kg). A tactical reconnaissance pod to be carried on an underwing pylon is being developed by Grumman, and this can accommodate a number of high- or low-altitude cameras and advanced electro-optical sensors.

ELECTRONICS: Hughes AN/AWG-9 weapons control system. Kaiser Aerospace AN/AVA-12 vertical and head-up display system.

DIMENSIONS, EXTERNAL:

Wing span: unswept	64 ft 1·5 in (19·54 m)
swept	38 ft 1·9 in (11·63 m)
overswept	32 ft 11·5 in (10·05 m)
Wing aspect ratio	7·28
Length overall	61 ft 11·9 in (18·89 m)
Height overall	16 ft 0 in (4·88 m)
Tailplane span	33 ft 3·5 in (10·15 m)
Distance between fin tips	10 ft 8 in (3·25 m)
Wheel track	16 ft 5 in (5·00 m)
Wheelbase	22 ft 10·25 in (6·97 m)

AREAS:

Wings, gross	565·0 sq ft (52·49 m²)
Horizontal tail surfaces (total)	140·0 sq ft (13·01 m²)
Vertical tail surfaces (total)	118·0 sq ft (10·96 m²)

WEIGHTS:

Weight empty	37,500 lb (17,010 kg)
Fuel (usable):	
internal	16,445 lb (7,459 kg)
external	3,632 lb (1,647 kg)
Normal T-O weight	55,000 lb (24,948 kg)
Max T-O weight	72,000 lb (32,658 kg)
Design landing weight	49,000 lb (22,225 kg)

PERFORMANCE:

Max design speed	Mach 2·34
Service ceiling	above 56,000 ft (17,070 m)
Min T-O distance at 59,000 lb 26,762 kg) AUW	1,200 ft (366 m)
Min landing distance	1,500 ft (458 m)

GRUMMAN AMERICAN AVIATION CORPORATION

HEAD OFFICE AND WORKS:
318 Bishop Road, Cleveland, Ohio 44143
Telephone: (216) 449-2200
Telex: 980-245

CHAIRMAN OF THE BOARD:
E. Clinton Towl

PRESIDENT:
Corwin H. Meyer

EXECUTIVE VICE-PRESIDENT:
Alan B. Lemlein

VICE-PRESIDENTS:
Roy C. Garrison (Commercial Light Aircraft Marketing)
Arnold D. Palmer (Public Relations)
William C. Seidel (General Manager, Cleveland Operations)
Charles G. Vogeley (Commercial Jet Marketing)
Harry S. Wilson (Finance)

TREASURER:
Robert G. Freese

SECRETARY:
Fred D. Kidder

This subsidiary of Grumman Corporation builds the Trainer, Tr-2 and Traveler, of which more than 1,200 were produced by the former American Aviation Corporation, and is responsible for manufacture and marketing of the Grumman-designed Gulfstream II. It markets the Grumman-designed Super Ag-Cat, built by Schweizer Aircraft (which see).

Sales in 1973 totalled 235 two-seat Trainers and Tr-2s, 234 four-seat Travelers, 19 Gulfstream IIs and 175 Super Ag-Cats.

GRUMMAN AMERICAN GULFSTREAM II
US Coast Guard designation: VC-11A

The decision to start production of this twin-turbofan executive transport was announced by Grumman on 17 May 1965, and 141 aircraft had been delivered by early 1974. The first production Gulfstream II (no prototype was built) flew for the first time on 2 October 1966. FAA certification was gained on 19 October 1967, and the first production aircraft was delivered to National Distillers & Chemical Corporation on 6 December 1967. The current production schedule calls for 1·25 aircraft per month during 1974. Custom interiors and avionics, with the exception of the Sperry SP-50G automatic flight control system, which is standard, are installed by specialist agencies.

Grumman has a noise abatement programme underway to meet FAR Part 36 Appendix C requirements.

A single Gulfstream II operates with the US Coast Guard under the designation **VC-11A.**

TYPE: Twin-turbofan executive transport aircraft.

WINGS: Cantilever low-wing monoplane of all-metal construction. Thickness/chord ratio 12% at wing station 50, 9·5% at wing station 145 and 8·5% at wing station 414. Dihedral 3°. Incidence 3° 30′ at wing station 50, 1° 30′ at wing station 145 and —0° 30′ at wing station 414. Sweepback 25° at quarter-chord. One-piece single-slotted Fowler-type trailing-edge flaps. Spoilers forward of flaps assist in lateral control and can be extended for use as air-brakes. All control surfaces actuated by dual independent hydraulic systems with manual backup.

FUSELAGE: Conventional all-metal semi-monocoque structure. Glassfibre nose-cone hinged for access to radar, etc.

TAIL UNIT: Cantilever all-metal T-tail. All surfaces sweptback. Trim tab in rudder. Powered controls (see under "Wings" paragraph).

LANDING GEAR: Retractable tricycle type, with twin wheels on each unit. Inward-retracting main units, with tyres size 34 × 8·25-32, pressure 150 lb/sq in (10·5 kg/cm²). Forward-retracting steerable nose unit. Nosewheel tyres size 21 × 7·25-22, pressure 95 lb/sq in (6·7 kg/cm²). Goodyear aircooled brakes with Goodyear fully-modulating anti-skid units.

POWER PLANT: Two Rolls-Royce Spey Mk 511-8 turbofan engines (each 11,400 lb; 5,171 kg st), mounted in pod on each side of rear fuselage. Rohr target-type thrust reversers form aft portions of nacelles when in stowed position. All fuel in integral tanks in wings, capacity 23,300 lb (10,568 kg).

ACCOMMODATION: Crew of two or three. Certificated for 19 passengers in pressurised and air-conditioned cabin. Large baggage compartment at rear of cabin, capacity 2,000 lb (907 kg). Integral airstair door at front of cabin on port side.

SYSTEMS: Two independent hydraulic systems.

Grumman American Gulfstream II executive transport (two Rolls-Royce Spey Mk 511-8 turbofan engines)

All flying controls hydraulically powered, with manual reversion. APU in tail compartment.

DIMENSIONS, EXTERNAL:

Wing span	68 ft 10 in (20·98 m)
Length overall	79 ft 11 in (24·36 m)
Length of fuselage	71 ft 4 in (21·74 m)
Height overall	24 ft 6 in (7·47 m)
Tailplane span	27 ft 0 in (8·23 m)
Wheel track	13 ft 8 in (4·16 m)
Wheelbase	33 ft 4 in (10·16 m)
Passenger door:	
Height	5 ft 2 in (1·57 m)
Width	3 ft 0 in (0·91 m)
Baggage door:	
Height	2 ft 4 in (0·71 m)
Width	2 ft 10 in (0·86 m)
Ventral door:	
Width	1 ft 6 in (0·46 m)
Length	2 ft 4 in (0·71 m)

DIMENSIONS, INTERNAL:

Cabin: Length	33 ft 11 in (10·34 m)
Height	6 ft 1 in (1·85 m)
Volume	1,300 cu ft (36·8 m³)
Baggage compartment	160 cu ft (4·53 m³)

AREA:

Wings, gross	793·5 sq ft (73·72 m²)

WEIGHTS AND LOADING:

Max T-O weight	62,000 lb (28,122 kg)
Max ramp weight	62,500 lb (28,349 kg)
Max landing weight	58,500 lb (26,535 kg)
Max zero-fuel weight	42,000 lb (19,050 kg)
Max wing loading	78 lb/sq ft (380·8 kg/m²)

PERFORMANCE (at max T-O weight):

Max cruising speed at 25,000 ft (7,620 m) Mach 0·85: 511 knots (588 mph; 946 km/h)
Econ cruising speed at 43,000 ft (13,105 m) Mach 0·76
Approach speed 144 knots (166 mph; 267 km/h)
Max rate of climb at S/L 4,350 ft (1,325 m)/min
Rate of climb at S/L, one engine out 1,525 ft (465 m)/min
Service ceiling 43,000 ft (13,100 m)
Service ceiling, one engine out 25,000 ft (7,620 m)
Min ground turning radius 45 ft 0 in (13·72 m)
FAA T-O field length 5,000 ft (1,524 m)
FAA landing field length 3,190 ft (972 m)
Range with max fuel 3,375 nm (3,886 miles; 6,254 km)

OPERATIONAL NOISE CHARACTERISTICS:

T-O noise level at 3·5 nm (4 miles; 6·5 km) from start of T-O roll, with thrust cutback 94·4 EPNdB
Approach noise level at 1·0 nm (1·15 miles; 1·85 km) from landing threshold on 3° glide-slope 99·5 EPNdB
Sideline noise level at 0·25 nm (0·29 miles; 0·46 km) from runway centreline 107·5 EPNdB

GRUMMAN AMERICAN AA-1B TRAINER

Designed originally as a specialised trainer version of the American Aviation AA-1 American Yankee, the prototype AA-1A Trainer first flew on 25 March 1970; FAA certification in the Normal and Utility categories was granted on 14 January 1971. The 1974 model, which has the designation AA-1B, introduces new bucket seats. Flight instruments and other accessories are repositioned, and cabin noise is reduced by using new front and rear canopy seals and bonded windscreen/canopy bars. A durable polyurethane two-tone exterior finish and white vinyl interior trim are standard.

Three versions of the Trainer are available, differing in installed equipment, any item of which may be added as optional to the Standard Trainer.

Standard Trainer. As described below.

Basic Trainer. As Standard Trainer, plus sensitive altimeter, electric clock, dual controls, Narco Escort 110 nav/com radio with M-700 microphone, headset, and antenna, de luxe propeller spinner, tinted windows, turn co-ordinator and rate of climb indicators.

Advanced Trainer. As Basic Trainer, plus vacuum system, de luxe interior, landing light, omni-flash beacon, outside air temperature gauge, heated pitot, true airspeed indicator, turn and bank indicator, and towbar.

TYPE: Two-seat trainer/utility monoplane.

WINGS: Cantilever low-wing monoplane. Wing section NACA 64_2415 (modified). Dihedral 5°. Incidence 1° 25′. No sweep. Alclad aluminium skin and ribs, attached to main spar by adhesive bonding. Tube-type circular-section main spar serves as integral fuel tank. Plain ailerons of bonded construction, with honeycomb ribs and Alclad aluminium skin. Electrically-actuated plain trailing-edge flaps of bonded construction, with honeycomb ribs and aluminium skin, and RAE Motors Corporation actuators. Ground-adjustable trim tab on each aileron.

FUSELAGE: Aluminium honeycomb cabin section and aluminium semi-monocoque rear fuselage structure, utilising adhesive bonding. The use of honeycomb eliminates false floors, resulting in greater usable cabin space relative to cross-sectional area.

TAIL UNIT: Cantilever adhesive-bonded aluminium structure. Movable surfaces built up of honeycomb ribs bonded to sheet aluminium. All three fixed surfaces interchangeable. Combined trim and anti-servo tab in starboard elevator. Ground-adjustable rudder trim tab.

LANDING GEAR: Non-retractable tricycle type. Nose gear of 4340 tubular steel, with large free-swivelling fork. Main legs are cantilever leaf springs of glassfibre. US Royal main wheels and tyres Type III, size 17 × 6·00-6, pressure 19 lb/sq in (1·34 kg/cm²). US Royal nosewheel tyre Type III LP, size 5·00-5, pressure 22 lb/sq in (1·55 kg/cm²). Cleveland single-disc hydraulic brakes. Parking brake. Optional shock-mounted wheel fairings available.

POWER PLANT: One 108 hp Lycoming O-235-C2C four-cylinder horizontally-opposed aircooled engine, driving a McCauley two-blade fixed-pitch propeller type 1A105/SCM 7157 for cruise or 1A105/SCM 7154 for climb performance, with spinner. Two integral fuel tanks in wing spar, with total capacity of 24 US gallons (91 litres), of which 22 US gallons (83 litres) are usable. Refuelling points at wingtips. Oil capacity 1·5 US gallons (5·7 litres).

ACCOMMODATION: Two individual seats side by side in enclosed cabin, under large transparent sliding canopy. Aircraft certificated for open-canopy flight. Optional seat for child. Cabin heated and ventilated, with windscreen defroster on pilot's side. Centre console, between seats, accommodates trim wheel and electric flap operating switch. Space for 100 lb (45 kg) baggage aft of seats.

SYSTEMS: Hydraulic system for brakes only. Electrical system includes 60A 14V engine-driven alternator and 25Ah battery to supply flap motor, lights, navigation/communication equipment and flight instrumentation.

ELECTRONICS AND EQUIPMENT: Standard equipment includes windscreen defroster, aileron and elevator control lock, cabin dome light, instrument lights, navigation lights, audible stall warning device, cabin heating system, air ventilators, cargo tie-down rings, seat belts, shoulder harness, baggage straps, chart holders, instrument panel glare shield, wheel hub covers, map holder and glove compartment. Optional items include sensitive altimeter, dual controls, blind-flying instrumentation, engine-driven vacuum pump and suction gauge, eight-day or electric clock, outside air temperature gauge, hour recorder, cabin-mounted fire extinguisher, pitot heating system, landing light, omniflash

Grumman American AA-1B Advanced Trainer (108 hp Lycoming O-235-C2C engine)

beacon, high intensity strobe lights, external power socket, canopy cover, alternative propeller for improved cruising performance, internal corrosion-proofing, towbar, canopy sun curtain, tinted windows, dual windscreen defrosters, wing leveller system and winterisation kit. Optional electronics include Narco Escort 110-channel VHF transceiver and 110-channel nav receiver with integral VOR/LOC indicator; Narco Spectrum COM 10A/NAV 10 or COM 11A/NAV 11 360-channel VHF transceiver and 200-channel VOR/LOC remote navigation indicator; Narco Spectrum COM 11A/NAV 12 360-channel VHF transceiver plus 200-channel VOR/ILS remote navigation indicator with glideslope display plus UGR-2A glideslope receiver; Narco Spectrum COM 11A/NAV 14/DGO-10 360-channel VHF transceiver plus 200-channel VOR/ILS remote navigation indicator with glideslope receiver plus DGO-10 pictorial navigation display; Narco Spectrum AT-50A 4096 code ATC transponder; Narco MBT marker beacon receiver; Narco ADF-31AB and PDF-35 automatic direction finder; King KX-170B/KI-214 360-channel VHF transceiver plus 200-channel VOR/ILS indicator with glideslope receiver and display; King KI-201C VOR/LOC indicator; King KR-85 ADF; King KT-78 4096 code ATC transponder; King KMA-20 audio switch panel with marker beacon; King KX-175 TSO'd transceiver with 360-channel com and 200-channel nav; Narco CP-125 audio switch panel; and emergency locator transmitter.

DIMENSIONS, EXTERNAL:

Wing span	24 ft 6 in (7·47 m)
Wing chord (constant)	4 ft 1¼ in (1·25 m)
Wing aspect ratio	5·975
Length overall	19 ft 3 in (5·86 m)
Height overall	7 ft 7¼ in (2·32 m)
Tailplane span	7 ft 8¼ in (2·34 m)
Wheel track	8 ft 3 in (2·45 m)
Wheelbase	4 ft 4½ in (1·33 m)
Propeller diameter	5 ft 11 in (1·80 m)
Propeller ground clearance	8¾ in (0·22 m)

DIMENSIONS, INTERNAL:

Cabin: Length	4 ft 6 in (1·37 m)
Max width	3 ft 5 in (1·04 m)
Max height	3 ft 9¼ in (1·15 m)
Floor area	16·7 sq ft (1·55 m²)

AREAS:

Wings, gross	100·92 sq ft (9·38 m²)
Ailerons (total)	5·20 sq ft (0·48 m²)
Trailing-edge flaps (total)	5·44 sq ft (0·50 m²)
Fin	4·76 sq ft (0·44 m²)
Rudder	3·61 sq ft (0·34 m²)
Tailplane	9·52 sq ft (0·88 m²)
Elevators, including tab	7·22 sq ft (0·67 m²)

WEIGHTS AND LOADINGS:

Weight empty	980 lb (445 kg)
Max T-O and landing weight	1,560 lb (707 kg)
Max zero-fuel weight	1,368 lb (620 kg)
Max wing loading	15·5 lb/sq ft (75·7 kg/m²)
Max power loading	14·4 lb/hp (6·53 kg/hp)

PERFORMANCE (at max T-O weight. A: standard propeller, B: with optional cruise propeller):

Max never-exceed speed 170 knots (195 mph; 313 km/h)

Max level speed at S/L:

A	120 knots (138 mph; 222 km/h)
B	125 knots (144 mph; 232 km/h)

Max cruising speed (75% power) between 3,500 and 8,000 ft (1,070 and 2,440 m):

A	109 knots (126 mph; 203 km/h)
B	116 knots (134 mph; 216 km/h)

Econ cruising speed at 10,000 ft (3,050 m):

A	97 knots (112 mph; 180 km/h)
B	99 knots (114 mph; 183 km/h)

Stalling speed, flaps up 54 knots (62 mph; 100 km/h)

Stalling speed, flaps down 52·5 knots (60 mph; 97 km/h)

Max rate of climb at S/L:

A	705 ft (215 m)/min
B	660 ft (201 m)/min

Service ceiling:

A	12,750 ft (3,885 m)
B	11,550 ft (3,520 m)

T-O run:

A	810 ft (247 m)
B	890 ft (271 m)

T-O to 50 ft (15 m):

A	1,550 ft (472 m)
B	1,590 ft (485 m)
Landing from 50 ft (15 m)	1,100 ft (335 m)
Landing run	410 ft (125 m)

Range with max fuel at max cruising speed, no reserves:

A	377 nm (435 miles; 700 km)
B	402 nm (463 miles; 745 km)

Range with max fuel, no reserves, at 10,000 ft (3,050 m):

A	425 nm (490 miles; 788 km)
B	441 nm (508 miles; 817 km)

GRUMMAN AMERICAN Tr-2

Generally similar to the Grumman American Trainer, the Tr-2 is intended to satisfy a dual requirement: as an advanced trainer or as a sports aircraft with de luxe equipment.

It is generally similar to the Advanced Trainer version of the AA-1B, but has in addition the following equipment as standard: carpeted floor to cabin and baggage area, de luxe vinyl/fabric interior, and polyurethane external trim in five combinations; Narco COM 10A/NAV 10 radio in lieu of Escort 110, with M-700 microphone, headset, loudspeaker and antenna. The 57 in pitch McCauley cruise propeller is standard on the Tr-2, the climb propeller as fitted to the AA-1B being available optionally. A three-tone exterior finish is also standard on this model.

WEIGHTS:

Weight empty	1,035 lb (469 kg)
Max T-O and landing weight	1,560 lb (708 kg)
Max zero-fuel weight	1,368 lb (620 kg)

PERFORMANCE: As for AA-1B with optional cruise propeller

GRUMMAN AMERICAN AA-5 TRAVELER

This is an enlarged version of the AA-1B, with increased wing span, a more powerful engine, and an extended fuselage to provide accommodation for a pilot and three passengers. The first flight of the original AA-5 was made on 21 August 1970, and FAA certification was awarded on 12 November 1971.

The 1974 model of the AA-5 introduces the improvements detailed for the AA-1B. In addition, the occupants' visibility is improved as the result of a 1 ft 0 in (0·30 m) extension in the aft side windows; there is an enlarged baggage compartment with hat rack, an external access door to the baggage compartment on the port side of the fuselage, and a newly styled dorsal fin.

Two versions of the AA-5 are available, as follows:

AA-5 Traveler. Standard version, as described below.

AA-5 Traveler Deluxe. As standard version, plus the following additional equipment: sensitive altimeter, omni-flash beacon, dual controls, vacuum system, landing light, outside air temperature gauge, heated pitot, tinted windows, turn co-ordinator and rate of climb indicators, and towbar.

Narco COM 10A/NAV 10 nav/com transceiver with VOR/LOC indicator, M-700 microphone, speaker and antenna, single-axis autopilot (wing leveller with nav tracker option), exhaust temperature gauge and high intensity strobe lights.

The general description of the AA-1B applies also to the AA-5, except as detailed below:

TYPE: Four-seat cabin monoplane.

WINGS: Generally as for AA-1B, except that wing span and chord are increased, and flap electrical actuators supplied by Commercial Aircraft Products.

FUSELAGE: As for AA-1B, except length increased.

TAIL UNIT: As for AA-1B, except general dimensions increased, and the addition of dorsal and ventral fins, and spin fillets on inboard leading-edges of tailplane. Combined trim and anti-servo tab in port and starboard elevators.

LANDING GEAR: As for AA-1B.

Grumman American Tr-2 sporting aircraft/advanced trainer

Grumman American AA-5 Traveler four-seat lightplane (150 hp Lycoming O-320-E2G engine)

POWER PLANT: One 150 hp Lycoming O-320-E2G four-cylinder horizontally-opposed aircooled engine, driving a McCauley fixed-pitch two-blade metal propeller with spinner. Two integral fuel tanks in wing spars, with a total capacity of 38 US gallons (144 litres), of which 37 US gallons (140 litres) are usable. Refuelling point in upper surface of each wing. Oil capacity 2 US gallons (7·5 litres).

ACCOMMODATION: Pilot and three passengers in enclosed cabin on four separate seats, in pairs. Baggage area aft of rear seats, which may be folded forward when unoccupied to increase baggage space, providing a capacity of 41·5 cu ft (1·18 m³) for maximum load of 340 lb (154 kg). Max normal baggage load 120 lb (54·4 kg).

SYSTEMS: As for AA-1B.

ELECTRONICS AND EQUIPMENT: Standard equipment includes baggage straps, chart holders, coat hook, cabin heating system, soundproofing for cabin and baggage area, windscreen defroster, cabin air ventilators, carpeting, fold-down rear seat, glove compartment, aileron and elevator control lock, armrests, hat shelf, instrument panel glare shield, headrests, seat belts, shoulder harness, baggage tie-down rings, cabin dome lights, navigation lights, instrument lights, quick fuel tank drains and audible stall warning device.

DIMENSIONS, EXTERNAL:
- Wing span: 31 ft 6 in (9·60 m)
- Wing chord (constant): 4 ft 5¼ in (1·35 m)
- Wing aspect ratio: 7·10
- Length overall: 22 ft 0 in (6·71 m)
- Height overall: 7 ft 10 in (2·39 m)
- Tailplane span: 8 ft 8½ in (2·65 m)
- Wheel track: 8 ft 3 in (2·51 m)
- Wheelbase: 5 ft 4½ in (1·64 m)
- Propeller diameter: 6 ft 1 in (1·85 m)
- Propeller ground clearance: 9 in (0·23 m)

DIMENSIONS, INTERNAL:
- Cabin: Length: 6 ft 6 in (1·98 m)
  - Max width: 3 ft 5 in (1·04 m)
  - Max height: 4 ft 0¼ in (1·23 m)
  - Floor area: 23·5 sq ft (2·18 m²)
- Baggage space: 12 cu ft (0·34 m³)

AREAS:
- Wings, gross: 140·12 sq ft (13·02 m²)
- Ailerons (total): 7·74 sq ft (0·72 m²)
- Trailing-edge flaps (total): 16·26 sq ft (1·51 m²)

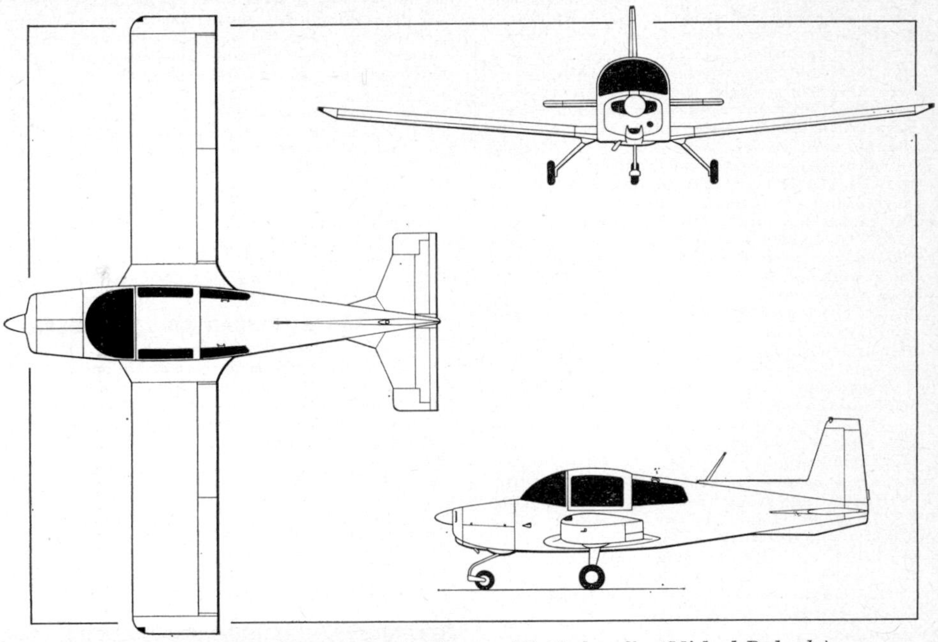

Grumman American AA-5 Traveler four-seat light aircraft *(Michael Badrocke)*

- Fin: 4·76 sq ft (0·44 m²)
- Rudder: 3·61 sq ft (0·34 m²)
- Tailplane: 9·50 sq ft (0·88 m²)
- Elevators, including tabs: 10·68 sq ft (0·99 m²)

WEIGHTS AND LOADINGS:
- Weight empty: 1,200 lb (544 kg)
- Max T-O weight: 2,200 lb (998 kg)
- Max zero-fuel weight: 1,984 lb (900 kg)
- Max wing loading: 15·7 lb/sq ft (76·6 kg/m²)
- Max power loading: 14·7 lb/hp (6·67 kg/hp)

PERFORMANCE (at max T-O weight):
- Max level speed at S/L: 130 knots (150 mph; 241 km/h)
- Max cruising speed, 75% power at 9,000 ft (2,745 m): 122 knots (140 mph; 225 km/h)
- Econ cruising speed, 65% power at 9,000 ft (2,745 m): 112 knots (129 mph; 207 km/h)
- Stalling speed, flaps up: 54 knots (62 mph: 100 km/h)
- Stalling speed, flaps down: 50·5 knots (58 mph; 93·5 km/h)
- Max rate of climb at S/L: 660 ft (201 m)/min
- Service ceiling: 12,650 ft (3,855 m)
- T-O run: 880 ft (268 m)
- T-O to 50 ft (15 m): 1,600 ft (488 m)
- Landing from 50 ft (15 m): 1,100 ft (335 m)
- Landing run: 380 ft (116 m)
- Range at max cruising speed, 45 min reserve: 390 nm (450 miles; 724 km)
- Range at econ cruising speed, 45 min reserve: 434 nm (500 miles; 805 km)

HAMILTON

HAMILTON AIRCRAFT COMPANY INC

HEAD OFFICE:
PO Box 11427, Tucson International Airport, Tucson, Arizona 85706
Telephone: (602) 294-3481

PRESIDENT:
Gordon B. Hamilton

CHIEF ENGINEER:
John D. Burnham Jr

Hamilton Aircraft Company, which is engaged primarily in the procurement and overhaul of various types of military aircraft for foreign governments, is also building and marketing turboprop conversions of the Beech Model 18 (last described in the 1969-70 *Jane's*). Two versions are available, known as the Westwind III and Westwind II STD; these differ in power plant, internal layout and in the arrangement of passenger and cargo doors.

HAMILTON WESTWIND III

The Westwind III is a passenger/cargo aircraft, in which the passenger seats can be removed easily to make the whole cabin space available for cargo. Design began in 1961 and the prototype flew for the first time in 1963. FAA certification under CAR Part 3 was awarded in 1964, and the company had produced 42 conversions by February 1974.

The Westwind III can have agricultural or military applications.

TYPE: Utility passenger/cargo commuter airliner.

WINGS, FUSELAGE, TAIL UNIT: As for Beech Model 18.

LANDING GEAR: Electrically-retractable tailwheel type. Oleo-pneumatic shock-absorbers on all units. Main wheels retract aft. Main-wheel tyre pressure 60 lb/sq in (4·22 kg/cm²). Tailwheel tyre pressure 80 lb/sq in (5·62 kg/cm²). Goodyear single-disc multi-puck hydraulic brakes. Main wheels fully enclosed by wheel-well doors when retracted.

POWER PLANT: Two 579 ehp United Aircraft of Canada PT6A-20 turboprop engines standard. Optional power plants include two 715 ehp (derated to 630 ehp) United Aircraft of Canada PT6A-27s, two 715 ehp (derated to 630 ehp) United Aircraft of Canada PT6A-28s or two 610 ehp Lycoming LTP-101s. Hartzell three-blade metal fully-feathering constant-speed propellers. Standard fuel capacity 408 US gallons (1,544 litres), contained in outer wing, inner wing and centre-section tanks. Optional total fuel in larger-capacity tanks 740 US gallons (2,801 litres). Refuelling points on wing upper surface.

Hamilton Westwind III conversion of the Beech Model 18 (two United Aircraft of Canada PT6A-27 derated turboprop engines)

Engine air intakes have an inertial separator system, including foreign object and hail by-pass and heating of the leading-edges by engine bleed air.

ACCOMMODATION: Pilot and co-pilot on flight deck, with cabin seating eight passengers. Door on port side, aft of wing, with built-in airstair, can be replaced by larger cargo door. Separate door to flight deck, on port side of fuselage, is optional. Emergency exit (push-out type) on starboard side of cabin. Passenger seating quickly removable for conversion to all-cargo role. Baggage or cargo space aft of cabin and in extended fuselage nose. Cabin is heated by bleed air, and can be cooled by a bleed air converter. Windscreen de-icing standard.

SYSTEMS: Cabin cooling by AiResearch engine bleed air converter. Cabin heater manufactured by Hamilton Aircraft. Pneumatic system, for flight instruments and wing and tail unit de-icing, supplied by engine bleed air. Electrical system powered by two 200A starter/generators and nickel-cadmium battery. Oxygen system optional.

ELECTRONICS AND EQUIPMENT: Radio com/nav and radar to customer's requirements. Blind-flying instrumentation standard.

ARMAMENT: Optional armament for military versions includes a cargo pod containing two General Electric Miniguns, and hardpoints on the wings for the carriage of bombs or rockets.

DIMENSIONS, EXTERNAL:
- Wing span: 46 ft 0 in (14·02 m)
- Wing chord at root: 13 ft 9 in (4·19 m)
- Wing chord at tip: 3 ft 6 in (1·07 m)
- Wing aspect ratio: 6·5
- Length overall: 35 ft 7¼ in (10·85 m)
- Tailplane span: 14 ft 11½ in (4·56 m)
- Passenger door (port, aft):
  - Height: 4 ft 0 in (1·22 m)
  - Width: 1 ft 10 in (0·56 m)
  - Height to sill: 2 ft 7 in (0·79 m)
- Cargo door (port, aft, optional):
  - Max height (forward edge): 4 ft 11¾ in (1·52 m)
  - Min height (rear edge): 3 ft 11 in (1·19 m)
  - Width: 4 ft 9¾ in (1·47 m)
  - Height to sill: 2 ft 7 in (0·79 m)
- Emergency exit (stbd):
  - Height: 2 ft 1 in (0·64 m)
  - Width: 1 ft 7 in (0·48 m)

DIMENSIONS, INTERNAL:
- Cabin (bare cargo configuration):
  - Length: 15 ft 0 in (4·57 m)
  - Max width: 4 ft 4 in (1·32 m)
  - Max height: 5 ft 1 in (1·55 m)
  - Floor area: 84 sq ft (7·80 m²)
- Baggage/cargo hold (aft cabin): 30 cu ft (0·85 m³)
- Baggage/cargo hold (fuselage nose): 54 cu ft (1·53 m³)

AREAS:
- Wings, gross: 326·4 sq ft (30·32 m²)
- Ailerons (total): 26·6 sq ft (2·47 m²)
- Trailing-edge flaps (total): 37·6 sq ft (3·49 m²)
- Fins (total): 32·6 sq ft (3·03 m²)
- Rudders (total): 34·56 sq ft (3·21 m²)
- Tailplane: 65·4 sq ft (6·08 m²)
- Elevator: 27·22 sq ft (2·53 m²)

WEIGHTS AND LOADINGS:
- Weight empty: 5,500 lb (2,495 kg)
- Max payload: 4,000 lb (1,814 kg)

Max T-O weight 11,230 lb (5,094 kg)
Max zero-fuel weight 10,700 lb (4,854 kg)
Max landing weight 10,500 lb (4,763 kg)
Max wing loading 34·4 lb/sq ft (167·9 kg/m²)
Max power loading 19·4 lb/ehp (8·8 kg/ehp)

PERFORMANCE (at max T-O weight, except as detailed otherwise. A: PT6A-20 engines; B: PT6A-27):
Max level speed at 12,000 ft (3,660 m):
A 234 knots (270 mph; 435 km/h)
B 269 knots (310 mph; 499 km/h)
Max cruising speed at 12,000 ft (3,660 m):
A 217 knots (250 mph; 402 km/h)
B 252 knots (290 mph; 467 km/h)
Econ cruising speed at 10,000 ft (3,050 m):
A 204 knots (235 mph; 378 km/h)
B 234 knots (270 mph; 435 km/h)
Max rate of climb at S/L:
A 1,800 ft (549 m)/min
B 2,700 ft (823 m)/min
Rate of climb at S/L, one engine out:
A 600 ft (183 m)/min
B 1,100 ft (335 m)/min
Service ceiling:
A 24,000 ft (7,315 m)
B 28,000 ft (8,535 m)
Service ceiling, one engine out:
A 9,000 ft (2,745 m)
B 13,000 ft (3,960 m)
T-O run:
A 1,800 ft (549 m)
B 1,200 ft (366 m)
T-O to 50 ft (15 m):
A 3,300 ft (1,005 m)
B 2,400 ft (731 m)
Landing from 50 ft (15 m):
A, B 1,800 ft (549 m)
Landing run:
A, B 1,200 ft (366 m)
Range with max optional fuel:
A 3,240 nm (3,731 miles; 6,004 km)
Range with max payload:
A 810 nm (933 miles; 1,501 km)

HAMILTON WESTWIND II STD

The Westwind II STD is a stretched version of the Beech 18, providing accommodation for a maximum of 17 passengers. Otherwise it is generally similar to the Westwind III except that a version with tricycle landing gear is available optionally. The Westwind II STD is intended primarily as a commuter airliner, but is convertible for freight carrying or military uses. Certification of this model was anticipated in July 1974.

The description of the Westwind III applies also to the Westwind II STD, except as detailed below:

LANDING GEAR: Retractable tricycle type available optionally.

POWER PLANT: Two 840 ehp United Aircraft of Canada PT6A-34 turboprop engines, derated to 630 ehp, are standard, each driving a Hartzell constant-speed fully-feathering and reversible-pitch propeller. Optional power plants include two 776 ehp AiResearch TPE 331-3-251 or two 1,100 ehp Lycoming T5307A turboprop engines, in each case derated to 630 ehp.

ACCOMMODATION: Pilot and co-pilot or passenger on flight deck, with seating in main cabin for a maximum of 17 passengers. Two emergency exits on starboard side of fuselage.

DIMENSIONS, EXTERNAL:
As for Westwind III, except:
Length overall (standard) 45 ft 0 in (13·72 m)
Length overall (tricycle landing gear) 44 ft 2 in (13·46 m)

DIMENSIONS, INTERNAL:
As for Westwind III, except:
Cabin: Length 20 ft 0 in (6·10 m)

WEIGHTS AND LOADING (estimated):
Weight empty 6,000 lb (2,712 kg)
Max payload 4,500 lb (2,041 kg)
Max T-O weight 12,495 lb (5,667 kg)
Max zero-fuel weight 11,500 lb (5,217 kg)
Max landing weight 11,500 lb (5,217 kg)
Max wing loading 38·3 lb/sq ft (186·9 kg/m²)

PERFORMANCE (estimated at max T-O weight):
Max level speed at 14,000 ft (4,265 m) 278 knots (320 mph; 515 km/h)
Max cruising speed at 12,000 ft (3,660 m) 261 knots (300 mph; 483 km/h)
Econ cruising speed at 22,000 ft (6,705 m) 234 knots (270 mph; 435 km/h)
Stalling speed, flaps up 87 knots (100 mph; 161 km/h)
Stalling speed, flaps down 74 knots (85 mph; 137 km/h)
Max rate of climb at S/L 3,100 ft (945 m)/min
Rate of climb at S/L, one engine out 900 ft (274 m)/min
Service ceiling 32,000 ft (9,755 m)
Service ceiling, one engine out 18,000 ft (5,485 m)
T-O run 1,400 ft (427 m)
T-O to 50 ft (15 m) 3,400 ft (1,036 m)
Landing from 50 ft (15 m):
Without propeller reversal 2,200 ft (671 m)
With propeller reversal 1,100 ft (335 m)
Range with max optional fuel 3,240 nm (3,731 miles; 6,004 km)
Range with max payload 810 nm (933 miles; 1,501 km)

HATZ

JOHN D. HATZ

ADDRESS:
Merrill Airways, Municipal Airport, Merrill, Wisconsin 54452

Mr Hatz has designed and built a two-seat lightweight biplane, designated CB-1, of which plans are available to amateur constructors. Design and construction started in September 1959, and FAA certification in the Amateur-built category was awarded on 18 April 1968. First flight of the CB-1 was made on the following day, powered by an 85 hp Continental C85-12 engine, but this has since been replaced by a 150 hp Lycoming O-320. Sixteen examples of the CB-1 were believed to be under construction at the end of 1973.

Hatz CB-1 homebuilt two-seat biplane (150 hp Lycoming O-320 engine)

HATZ CB-1 BIPLANE

TYPE: Two-seat lightweight homebuilt biplane.

WINGS: Braced single-bay biplane, with N-type interplane struts each side. N-type centre-section struts and streamline-section flying and landing wires. Wing section Clark Y. Dihedral 2°, on lower wings only. Incidence (both wings) 2°. Wooden two-spar structure with fabric covering. Cutout in trailing-edge of upper wing. Plain unbalanced ailerons of wood construction, with fabric covering, on both wings. No flaps. No trim tabs.

FUSELAGE: Welded steel tube structure, with fabric covering.

TAIL UNIT: Wire-braced welded steel tube structure, with fabric covering. Tailplane incidence adjustable by screwjack.

LANDING GEAR: Non-retractable tailwheel type. Two side Vees and half-axles hinged to fuselage structure. No shock-absorption. Main wheels from Piper J-3 Cub, with Goodyear tyres size 8·00-4, pressure 15 lb/sq in (1·05 kg/cm²). Wheel brakes from J-3 Cub. Glassfibre fairings on main wheels.

POWER PLANT: One 150 hp Lycoming O-320 four-cylinder horizontally-opposed aircooled engine, driving a Sensenich Type M74DM two-blade metal fixed-pitch propeller. Two fuel tanks in centre-section of upper wing, each with capacity of 16 US gallons (60·5 litres). Total fuel capacity 32 US gallons (121 litres). Refuelling points on upper surface of upper wing centre-section. Oil capacity 2 US gallons (7·5 litres).

ACCOMMODATION: Two seats in tandem in open cockpits.

SYSTEM: Electrical system, with 12V 12A DC engine-driven generator and 12V battery, for engine starting, navigation and instrument lights.

DIMENSIONS, EXTERNAL:
Wing span (both) 26 ft 0 in (7·92 m)
Wing chord (constant, both) 4 ft 6 in (1·37 m)
Wing aspect ratio 5·77
Length overall 18 ft 6 in (5·64 m)
Height overall 7 ft 10 in (2·39 m)
Tailplane span 9 ft 0 in (2·74 m)
Wheel track 6 ft 0 in (1·83 m)
Propeller diameter 6 ft 2 in (1·88 m)
Propeller ground clearance 1 ft 6 in (0·46 m)

AREA:
Wings, gross 190 sq ft (17·65 m²)

WEIGHTS AND LOADINGS:
Weight empty 966 lb (438 kg)
Max T-O weight 1,600 lb (726 kg)
Max wing loading 8·42 lb/sq ft (41·1 kg/m²)
Max power loading 10·7 lb/hp (4·9 kg/hp)

PERFORMANCE (at max T-O weight):
Max never-exceed speed 130 knots (150 mph; 241 km/h)
Max cruising speed 87 knots (100 mph; 161 km/h)
Stalling speed 39 knots (45 mph; 72·5 km/h)
Max rate of climb at S/L 1,200 ft (366 m)/min
T-O run approx 400 ft (122 m)
Range with max fuel, 30 min reserve 234 nm (270 miles; 434 km)

HELIO

HELIO AIRCRAFT COMPANY (a division of General Aircraft Corporation)

HEAD OFFICE:
Hanscom Field, Civilian Terminal Area, Bedford, Massachusetts 01730
Telephone: (617) 274-9130

WORKS:
Pittsburg, Kansas

CHAIRMAN AND CHIEF EXECUTIVE OFFICER:
Dr L. L. Bollinger

PRESIDENT:
R. B. Kimnach

DIRECTOR OF ENGINEERING:
R. L. Devine

CONTROLLER: J. R. Cray

SALES AND PUBLIC RELATIONS:
H. A. Wheeler Jr (Asst to the President)

The original Helio Aircraft Corporation was founded in 1948 by Dr Lynn L. Bollinger of the Harvard Graduate School of Business Administration and Professor Otto C. Koppen of the Massachusetts Institute of Technology, to develop a light aircraft in the STOL category. In 1969 this company became a division of General Aircraft Corporation and was renamed Helio Aircraft Company.

After considerable flight testing of a prototype, converted from a Piper Vagabond light aircraft, Helio designed the original Courier prototype, which first flew in 1953. The first production Courier was the four-seat Model H-391B, which was certificated in 1954. It was followed by the 4/5-seat Model H-395 in 1958 and the Model H-395A in 1959. These models were superseded by the 250 hp six-seat Model H-250 in 1964 and the H-295 in 1965. Production of the Model H-250 has ended, but the H-295 Super Courier continues in production in an improved form, an alternative version with a non-retractable tricycle landing gear having been introduced in 1974.

The Super Courier is an all-metal cantilever high-wing monoplane incorporating full-span automatic leading-edge slats, an augmented lateral control system and high-lift flap system, and crash-resistant tubular steel cabin structure.

Also in production is the 8/10-seat turboprop H-550A Stallion, which incorporates the same aerodynamic features as the Super Courier and is specifically designed for safe operation from unprepared fields. In December 1971 the USAF ordered a number of the armed version of the H-550A Stallion, and these were delivered during 1972.

Helio refers to all its products as C/STOL aircraft, signifying "controlled short take-off and landing".

Over 500 Helio Courier and Stallion aircraft of all types have been sold and are in service throughout the world. More than 150 have been delivered to the USAF, others are used by various US and foreign government agencies.

HELIO SUPER COURIER MODEL H-295

USAF designation: U-10

The original version of the Super Courier was flown for the first time in 1958 and received FAA Type Approval on 17 November that year. Three were supplied to the USAF for evaluation, under the designation L-28A. Further substantial orders were received subsequently, some aircraft being assigned to Tactical Air Command for counter-insurgency duties.

Design and construction of the prototype H-295 began in late 1964 and it flew for the first time on 24 February 1965. FAA certification was received in the following month.

The current commercial versions of the Super Courier are the Model **H-295** with non-retractable tailwheel landing gear and the Model **H-295T** with non-retractable tricycle-type landing gear.

USAF Super Couriers are of three types, as follows:

U-10A. Standard model with fuel capacity of 60 US gallons (227 litres).

U-10B. Long-range version with standard internal fuel capacity of 120 US gallons (455 litres). This version has been operated in South-east Asia, South America, and in other parts of the world, on a wide variety of military missions and has an endurance of more than 10 hours. Paratroop doors standard.

U-10D. Improved long-range version with max AUW increased to 3,600 lb (1,633 kg). Standard internal fuel capacity of 120 US gallons (455 litres). Accommodation for pilot and five passengers.

The following details refer to the standard commercial Super Courier:

TYPE: Six-seat light STOL personal, corporate and utility monoplane.

WINGS: Cantilever high-wing monoplane. NACA 23012 wing section. Dihedral 1°. Incidence 3°. All-metal single-spar structure. Frise ailerons have duralumin frames and fabric covering and are supplemented by Arc-type aluminium spoilers, located at 15·5% chord on upper surface of each wing and geared to ailerons for control at low speeds. Ground-adjustable tab on ailerons. Full-span automatic all-metal Handley Page leading-edge slats. Electrically-operated NACA slotted all-metal trailing-edge flaps over 74% of span. No anti-icing equipment.

FUSELAGE: All-metal structure. Cabin section has welded steel tube framework, covered with aluminium; rear section is an aluminium monocoque.

TAIL UNIT: Cantilever all-metal structure. All-moving one-piece horizontal surface is fitted with trim and anti-balance tabs. Electrically-operated elevator trim optional.

LANDING GEAR (H-295): Non-retractable tail-wheel type. Cantilever main legs. Oleo-pneumatic shock-absorbers of Helio design and manufacture on all three units. Goodyear crosswind landing gear with main-wheel tyres size 6·50-8, pressure 28 lb/sq in (1·97 kg/cm²). Goodyear 10 in (25 cm) tailwheel tyre, pressure 40 lb/sq in (2·81 kg/cm²). Goodyear hydraulic disc brakes. Edo 582-3430 floats, Edo Flying Dolphin amphibious floats or AirGlas Model LW3600 glassfibre wheel-skis optional.

LANDING GEAR (H-295T): Non-retractable tricycle type. Cantilever spring steel main gear, with wheels and tyres size 8·00-6, pressure 35 lb/sq in (2·46 kg/cm²). Nosewheel carried on oleo-pneumatic shock-strut, with wheel and tyre size 6·00-6, pressure 42 lb/sq in (2·95 kg/cm²).

POWER PLANT: One 295 hp Lycoming GO-480-G1D6 six-cylinder horizontally-opposed air-cooled geared engine, driving a Hartzell three-blade constant-speed propeller. Rajay turbo-charger system optional. Two 30 US gallon (113·7 litre) bladder-type fuel tanks in wings. Two further 30 US gallon (113·7 litre) tanks may be fitted to give total fuel capacity of 120 US gallons (455 litres). Oil capacity 3 US gallons (11·4 litres).

ACCOMMODATION: Cabin seats six in three pairs. Front and centre pair of seats individually adjustable. Rear pair comprises double sling seat. FAA standard instrument panel. Special over-strength cabin and seats, stressed to 15*g* and all fitted with safety harness, are based on Flight Safety Foundation recommendations. Two large doors, by pilot's seat on port side and opposite centre row of seats on starboard side. Baggage compartment aft of rear seats. Second- and third-row seats are removable for carrying over 1,000 lb (454 kg) freight.

ELECTRONICS AND EQUIPMENT: Radio and blind-flying instrumentation to customer's requirements.

DIMENSIONS, EXTERNAL:

Wing span	39 ft 0 in (11·89 m)
Wing chord (constant)	6 ft 0 in (1·83 m)
Wing aspect ratio	6·58
Length overall	31 ft 0 in (9·45 m)
Height overall	8 ft 10 in (2·69 m)
Tailplane span	15 ft 6 in (4·72 m)
Wheel track	9 ft 0 in (2·74 m)
Wheelbase	23 ft 5 in (7·14 m)
Propeller diameter	8 ft 0 in (2·44 m)
Cabin door (fwd, port):	
Height	3 ft 5 in (1·04 m)
Width	2 ft 9½ in (0·85 m)
Height to sill	3 ft 0 in (0·91 m)
Cabin door (stbd, rear):	
Height	3 ft 2½ in (0·98 m)
Width	2 ft 9½ in (0·85 m)
Height to sill	2 ft 2½ in (0·67 m)

DIMENSIONS, INTERNAL:

Cabin: Length	10 ft 0 in (3·05 m)
Max width	3 ft 9 in (1·14 m)
Max height	4 ft 0 in (1·22 m)
Floor area	30 sq ft (2·79 m²)
Volume	140 cu ft (3·96 m³)
Baggage space	15 cu ft (0·42 m³)

AREAS:

Wings, gross	231 sq ft (21·46 m²)
Ailerons (total)	20·7 sq ft (1·92 m²)
Flaps (total)	38·1 sq ft (3·54 m²)
Leading-edge slats (total)	31·3 sq ft (2·91 m²)
Spoilers (total)	1·68 sq ft (0·16 m²)
Fin	15·2 sq ft (1·41 m²)
Rudder	10·6 sq ft (0·99 m²)
Tailplane	37·5 sq ft (3·48 m²)

WEIGHTS AND LOADINGS:

Weight empty	2,080 lb (943 kg)
Max T-O and landing weight	3,400 lb (1,542 kg)
Max wing loading	14·7 lb/sq ft (71·8 kg/m²)
Max power loading	11·5 lb/hp (5·22 kg/hp)

PERFORMANCE (at max T-O weight):

Max never-exceed speed	174 knots (200 mph; 322 km/h)
Max level speed at S/L	145 knots (167 mph; 269 km/h)
Max cruising speed (75% power) at 8,500 ft (2,600 m)	143 knots (165 mph; 265 km/h)
Econ cruising speed (60% power)	130 knots (150 mph; 241 km/h)
Min speed, power on	26 knots (30 mph; 48 km/h)
Max rate of climb at S/L	1,150 ft (350 m)/min
Service ceiling	20,500 ft (6,250 m)
T-O run	335 ft (102 m)
T-O to 50 ft (15 m)	610 ft (186 m)
Landing from 50 ft (15 m)	520 ft (158 m)
Landing run	270 ft (82 m)
Range with standard tanks	573 nm (660 miles; 1,062 km)
Range with optional tanks	1,198 nm (1,380 miles; 2,220 km)

HELIO STALLION MODEL H-550A

USAF designation: AU-24A

Design of the turboprop Stallion was started in July 1963 and construction of the prototype Model HST-550 began in November 1963. First flight took place on 5 June 1964 and FAA certification was received in August 1965.

Construction of the first production version, known as the Stallion Model H-550A, began in April 1966 and FAA certification of this was received in August 1969.

The Model H-550A has full-span automatic leading-edge slats, an augmented lateral control system, slotted flaps to enhance STOL performance, and crash-resistant cabin structure. It is designed to operate over a wide speed range, to allow flexibility in operation.

The AU-24A armed version of the Stallion, acquired by the USAF, has an increased max T-O weight of 6,300 lb (2,857 kg) and incorporates a number of modifications to meet specific military requirements. These include two hardpoint pylons under each wing and a fuselage centreline hardpoint for the mounting of MA4A bomb racks. Each outboard wing station has a capacity of 350 lb (158 kg), each inboard station 500 lb (227 kg), and the fuselage station has a 600 lb (272 kg) capacity. Equipment includes an armament control panel, gunsight, a cabin mounting for a side-firing gun as large as the M-197 20 mm cannon and ammunition magazines, and complete military VHF, UHF, FM and HF electronics. Numerous combinations of rockets, bombs and flares can be carried on the five external stores stations, and the cantilever high-wing design provides a virtually unobstructed field of fire for cabin-mounted rapid-firing guns.

The AU-24A can be configured for a variety of missions, including armed reconnaissance, COIN operations, close air support transportation, and other special missions including forward air control.

A squadron comprising fourteen AU-24As was supplied to Cambodia by the USAF.

The following details refer to the commercial version of the Model H-550A:

TYPE: Eight/ten-seat general-utility STOL turboprop aircraft.

WINGS: Cantilever high-wing monoplane. Wing section slatted NACA 23012 (constant). Dihedral 1°. Incidence 3°. No sweepback. All-aluminium single-spar structure. Each wing unbolts at side of fuselage. Dacron-covered Frise balanced metal ailerons. NACA high-lift slotted all-metal flaps, electrically-actuated. Arc-type all-metal spoilers at front of wing upper surface, interconnected with ailerons. Ground-adjustable tab on starboard aileron. Fully-automatic Handley Page full-span leading-edge slats.

FUSELAGE: Aluminium semi-monocoque structure, with welded steel tube framework forward of pilot's position.

TAIL UNIT: Cantilever all-aluminium structure, with sweptback vertical surfaces. All-moving

Helio H-295T version of the Super Courier with fixed tricycle landing gear

Helio Model H-295 Super Courier six-seat STOL monoplane (295 hp Lycoming GO-480-G1D6 engine)

one-piece horizontal surface with combined trim and anti-balance tab and separate flap trim interconnect tab.

LANDING GEAR: Non-retractable tailwheel type. Rearwardly-inclined cantilever main legs. Oleo-pneumatic shock-absorbers, designed and manufactured by Helio, on all three units. Goodyear tyres. Main wheels size 7·50-10, tyre pressure 22 lb/sq in (1·55 kg/cm²). Steerable tailwheel with 5·00-5 Type II tyre, pressure 55 lb/sq in (3·87 kg/cm²). Goodyear disc brakes. Wheel-ski landing gear available.

POWER PLANT: One 680 ehp United Aircraft of Canada PT6A-27 turboprop engine, driving a Hartzell three-blade reversible-pitch propeller. Fuel tanks in wings, with total capacity of 120 US gallons (455 litres). Refuelling points above wing. Oil capacity 2·3 US gallons (8·75 litres).

ACCOMMODATION: Pilot and co-pilot or passenger side by side at front, on fully-adjustable seats. Eight passengers in three rows, or up to six passengers in individual seats with reclining backs and headrests, two-abreast. All passenger seats can be removed for cargo carrying. Full-length rails in floor for cargo restraint. Jettisonable door on port side of cabin by pilot. Similar door on starboard side optional. Double door, without central pillar, on port side of main cabin. Forward section of this door is hinged, rear portion slides. When sliding section is in place, forward section can be used alone as forward-hinged door. When rear (sliding) section is moved aft, the entire double door opening, size 61 in × 43 in (1·55 m × 1·09 m), is available for cargo loading. In the air, the sliding section moves aft to provide a parachuting or cargo-drop doorway. Similar double door on starboard side optional. Doors are non-structural. Hatches in wall of rear cabin enable pieces of freight up to 12 ft (3·65 m) long to be carried. Hatch size 23 in × 40 in (0·58 m × 1·02 m) in floor. Seats and harness stressed for 15*g*. Walls lined with fireproofing and soundproofing. Heating and ventilation standard.

SYSTEMS: Hydraulic system for brakes only. No pneumatic system. 24V electrical system supplied by 150A (optionally 200A) generator.

ELECTRONICS AND EQUIPMENT: Avionics to customer's requirements.

DIMENSIONS, EXTERNAL:
- Wing span: 41 ft 0 in (12·50 m)
- Wing span over tip-tanks: 41 ft 9 in (12·72 m)
- Wing chord (constant): 6 ft 0 in (1·83 m)
- Wing aspect ratio (without tip-tanks): 6·93
- Length overall: 39 ft 7 in (12·07 m)
- Height overall: 9 ft 3 in (2·81 m)
- Tailplane span: 18 ft 0 in (5·49 m)
- Wheel track: 9 ft 8 in (2·94 m)
- Wheelbase: 24 ft 8 in (7·52 m)
- Propeller diameter: 8 ft 0 in (2·44 m)
- Pilot's compartment doors (each):
  - Height: 4 ft 5 in (1·35 m)
  - Width: 3 ft 4 in (1·03 m)
  - Height to sill (mean): 3 ft 9 in (1·14 m)
- Hinged portion of double-door:
  - Height: 4 ft 0 in (1·22 m)
  - Width: 2 ft 7 in (0·79 m)
  - Height to sill: 2 ft 11 in (0·89 m)
- Sliding portion of double-door:
  - Height: 3 ft 8 in (1·12 m)
  - Width: 2 ft 7 in (0·79 m)
  - Height to sill: 3 ft 0 in (0·91 m)

DIMENSIONS, INTERNAL:
- Cabin: Length: 13 ft 6 in (4·11 m)
  - Max width: 4 ft 2¼ in (1·28 m)
  - Max height: 5 ft 1¼ in (1·56 m)
  - Floor area: 43·4 sq ft (4·03 m²)
  - Volume: 181·4 cu ft (5·14 m³)

AREAS:
- Wings, gross: 242 sq ft (22·48 m²)
- Wings, with tip-tanks: 248 sq ft (23·04 m²)
- Ailerons (total): 20·7 sq ft (1·92 m²)
- Trailing-edge flaps (total): 40·32 sq ft (3·75 m²)
- Leading-edge slats (total): 38·3 sq ft (3·56 m²)
- Spoilers (total): 3·1 sq ft (0·29 m²)
- Fin: 17·0 sq ft (1·58 m²)
- Rudder, including tab: 19·62 sq ft (1·82 m²)
- Tailplane, including tabs: 57·43 sq ft (5·33 m²)

WEIGHTS AND LOADINGS:
- Weight empty: 2,360 lb (1,297 kg)
- Max payload (with 120 US gallons; 455 litres fuel and pilot): 1,290 lb (585 kg)
- Max T-O and landing weight: 5,100 lb (2,313 kg)
- Max wing loading: 21·1 lb/sq ft (103·0 kg/m²)
- Max power loading: 7·5 lb/hp (3·4 kg/hp)

PERFORMANCE (at max T-O weight):
- Max never-exceed speed: 190 knots (218 mph; 351 km/h) CAS
- Max level speed at 10,000 ft (3,050 m): 188 knots (216 mph; 348 km/h)
- Max cruising speed at 10,000 ft (3,050 m): 179 knots (206 mph; 332 km/h)
- Econ cruising speed at 10,000 ft (3,050 m): 139 knots (160 mph; 257 km/h)
- Min fully-manoeuvrable descent speed, power on: 37 knots (42 mph; 68 km/h)
- Max rate of climb at S/L: 2,200 ft (671 m)/min
- Service ceiling: 25,000 ft (7,620 m)
- T-O run: 320 ft (98 m)
- T-O to 50 ft (15 m): 660 ft (201 m)
- Landing from 50 ft (15 m): 750 ft (229 m)
- Landing run: 250 ft (76 m)
- Range with max fuel, allowances for warm-up, taxying, take-off and climb to 10,000 ft (3,050 m): 557 nm (641 miles; 1,031 km)
- Range with max payload, allowances as above: 386 nm (445 miles; 716 km)

Helio Stallion Model H-550A eight/ten-seat general-utility STOL aircraft

Helio AU-24A armed version of the Stallion, with LAU-68A/A rocket launcher and B-37K-1 bomb container beneath the wing

HILL

JOHN S. HILL

ADDRESS: Enid, Oklahoma

HILL TINY HAWK

Mr John Hill has built a scale replica of a Curtiss P-6E military biplane of the early 1930s, which he has named Tiny Hawk. Although built at a cost of only $1,200, construction has occupied an eleven-year period. No performance or specification details were available at the time of closing for press.

TYPE: Single-seat homebuilt scale replica of Curtiss P-6E Hawk.

WINGS: Braced single-bay biplane. N-type interplane and centre-section struts. Streamline bracing wires. Conventional structure with fabric covering. Ailerons on both wings.

FUSELAGE: Welded steel tube structure with fabric covering.

TAIL UNIT: Conventional wire-braced structure. Fixed-incidence tailplane.

LANDING GEAR: Non-retractable tailwheel type. Wheel fairings on main wheels.

POWER PLANT: One 130 hp Lycoming O-290 four-cylinder horizontally-opposed aircooled engine, driving a homebuilt three-blade metal fixed-pitch propeller.

ACCOMMODATION: Single seat in open cockpit.

Tiny Hawk, a scale replica of a Curtiss P-6E Hawk, built by Mr John S. Hill of Enid, Oklahoma
(*Howard Levy*)

HOVEY

R. W. HOVEY

ADDRESS:
PO Box 1074, Saugus, California 91350
Telephone: (805) 252-4054

Mr Hovey has designed and built an ultra-lightweight biplane of which plans are available to amateur constructors. His objective was to produce an aircraft which would require minimal construction time and have STOL performance, and which could be quickly disassembled for transportation. To achieve these ends the design has some unusual features, such as wing warping for roll control, use of an aluminium tube tail-boom which has high-strength light alloy sheet and urethane foam stiffening, and the use of styrofoam core sandwiched in craft paper for horizontal and vertical tail surfaces.

Design began in October 1970, construction starting in the following month. First flight was made in February 1971, at which time the aircraft, known as Whing Ding II, received FAA certification in the Experimental category.

The original prototype was sold in Japan where considerable interest has been aroused among homebuilders. A second prototype was completed subsequently. More than 2,400 sets of plans had been sold and at least 200 Whing Dings were under construction in February 1974. At that time, Mr Hovey was working on the design of an enclosed single-seat mid-wing monoplane. To be powered by a 42 hp Snowmobile engine, it has the designation WD-V.

A practical demonstration of the light weight and mobility of the Hovey Whing Ding II

HOVEY WHING DING II (WD-II)

TYPE: Single-seat ultra-lightweight homebuilt biplane.

WINGS: Braced single-bay biplane with parallel streamline-section interplane struts. Aircraft's fuselage, into which wing spars are socketed, gives location of inboard ends of wings. Landing and flying wires, the rear flying wires being used to control warping of upper wing. Wing section Hovey-10. Thickness/chord ratio 10%. Dihedral, both 1°. Incidence, both 4°. No sweepback. Wooden two-spar structure with ribs formed of $\frac{3}{8}$ in (0·95 cm) light alloy tube. Wingtip bows of $\frac{3}{8}$ in (0·95 cm) light alloy tube. Leading-edge faired in with rigid urethane foam. Wing structure fabric-covered, tension of which retains the ribs in position. A plasticised fabric dope is used to ensure adequate flexibility for wing warping. No ailerons. No flaps. No trim tabs.

FUSELAGE: A closed box structure of $\frac{1}{8}$ in mahogany plywood glued to $\frac{1}{2}$ in square pine stringers, which is filled with urethane foam to stiffen and stabilise the plywood skin. This narrow fuselage provides attachment points for the seat, rudder bar and controls, and sockets for the wing spars. A reinforced extension at the top of the fuselage carries the engine. Aluminium tube tailboom is reinforced by high-strength alloy sheet at the forward end, this being wrapped around the tube and bonded with epoxy resin. The entire tube is filled with free-foam urethane.

TAIL UNIT: Strut-braced structure with all-moving tailplane. Tailplane consists of one piece of Foam Core sheet, which has a styrofoam core sandwiched between high-strength craft paper. Leading- and trailing-edges are pressed together and taped to form a streamline shape. Tailplane attached to tail-boom by piano hinge. Stressed areas reinforced by $\frac{1}{8}$ in plywood sheet. Fin and rudder of similar construction, utilising Foam Core reinforced with $\frac{1}{8}$ in plywood sheet. Rudder attached to fin by cloth hinges. No trim tabs.

LANDING GEAR: Non-retractable tailwheel type. Main wheels carried on spring-type strut of laminated fir covered with a layer of polyester glassfibre. Go-Kart type main wheels with 11 in (28 cm) diameter tyres. Tyre pressure 20 lb/sq in (1·4 kg/cm²). Tailwheel has solid rubber tyre. Alternative steel tube landing gear available.

POWER PLANT: One 14 hp McCulloch 101A single-cylinder two-stroke aircooled Go-Kart engine, driving a two-blade hand-carved laminated birch or beechwood fixed-pitch pusher propeller. Fuel tank integral with engine, capacity 0·5 US gallons (1·9 litres).

ACCOMMODATION: Pilot only on open seat.

EQUIPMENT: Basic instrumentation only, comprising airspeed and engine speed indicators and cylinder head temperature gauge.

DIMENSIONS, EXTERNAL:	
Wing span (both)	17 ft 0 in (5·18 m)
Wing chord (both, constant)	3 ft 0 in (0·91 m)
Wing aspect ratio	5·66
Length overall	14 ft 0 in (4·27 m)
Height overall	5 ft 6 in (1·68 m)
Tailplane span	6 ft 4 in (1·93 m)
Wheel track	4 ft 0 in (1·22 m)
Wheelbase	9 ft 9 in (2·97 m)
Propeller diameter	4 ft 0 in (1·22 m)
AREAS:	
Wings, gross	98 sq ft (9·10 m²)
Fin	2·3 sq ft (0·21 m²)
Rudder	3·0 sq ft (0·28 m²)
Tailplane	10·4 sq ft (0·97 m²)
WEIGHTS AND LOADINGS:	
Weight empty, including fuel	123 lb (55·5 kg)
Max T-O weight	310 lb (140 kg)
Max wing loading	3·22 lb/sq ft (15·7 kg/m²)
Max power loading	22·2 lb/hp (10·07 kg/hp)
PERFORMANCE (at max T-O weight):	
Max never-exceed speed	52 knots (60 mph; 96·5 km/h)
Max level speed at S/L	43·5 knots (50 mph; 80·5 km/h)
Econ cruising speed at S/L	35 knots (40 mph; 64·5 km/h)
Stalling speed	23 knots (26 mph; 42 km/h)
Service ceiling	4,000 ft (1,220 m)
T-O run	250 ft (76 m)
T-O to 50 ft (15 m)	350 ft (107 m)
Landing from 50 ft (15 m)	250 ft (76 m)
Landing run	150 ft (46 m)
Range	17 nm (20 miles; 32 km)

HUGHES

HUGHES HELICOPTERS (Division of Summa Corporation)

HEAD OFFICE AND WORKS:
Culver City, California 90230
Telephone: (213) 390-4451

VICE-PRESIDENT AND GENERAL MANAGER:
Thomas R. Stuelpnagel

VICE-PRESIDENTS:
William E. Rankin (Finance)
C. D. Perry (Marketing)

DIRECTORS:
W. J. Blackburn (Manufacturing)
E. J. Brandreth (Commercial Sales)
R. E. Brix (Ordnance Engineering)
J. N. Kerr (Military Helicopters)
L. P. Sonsini (Quality Assurance)
F. C. Strible (Commercial Helicopters)

PUBLIC RELATIONS AND ADVERTISING MANAGER:
Harold S. Stall

Following reorganisation of Hughes Tool Company as the Summa Corporation, its former Aircraft Division is now known as Hughes Helicopters.

Products comprise light helicopters powered by reciprocating and turboshaft engines. Current research activities include work on jet-flap aerodynamic devices for NASA and a quiet helicopter for the Advanced Research Projects Agency.

Kawasaki Heavy Industries Ltd in Japan (which see) has assembled a number of model 369HM helicopters, this being the designation of the uprated version of the Hughes OH-6 available to foreign military customers.

In the Summer of 1973 Hughes was awarded a US Army contract for the development of two Advanced Attack Helicopter prototypes to compete against those being developed by Bell Helicopter.

Hughes Model 300C in operation in an agricultural spraying role

HUGHES MODEL 300

US Army designation: TH-55A Osage

Design and development of the original Hughes Model 269 two-seat light helicopter began in September 1955 and the first of two prototypes was flown 13 months later.

The design was then re-engineered for production, with the emphasis on simplicity and ease of maintenance. The resulting Model 269A offered an overall life of over 1,000 hours for all major components.

Five Model 269A pre-production helicopters were purchased by the US Army under the designation YHO-2HU, and completed a highly successful evaluation programme in the command and observation roles.

The Model 269A was then put into production and deliveries began in October 1961. The design has since undergone considerable development, leading to new versions, the latest commercial and military models being as follows:

Model 300. Three-seat version developed under the engineering designation 269B. Received FAA Type Approval 30 December 1963. In production at a rate of one a day by 1964. Hughes engineers have perfected a quiet tail rotor (QTR) for the Model 300, which reduces the sound level of the aircraft by 80%. At cruise rpm, the QTR-equipped version operates at a noise level comparable with that of a fixed-wing light aircraft. QTR has been standard factory-installed equipment on production Model 300s since June 1967, and retrofit kits are available to all Model 269A and 300 owners.

Model 300C. This three-seat version of the Hughes Model 300 was developed under the engineering designation 269C. It is described separately.

TH-55A. The Hughes 269A was selected by

the US Army as a light helicopter primary trainer in mid-1964, under the designation TH-55A. A total of 792 were eventually delivered, production being completed by the end of March 1969.

It was reported in March 1973 that Hughes had been evaluating a TH-55A powered by a 185 hp Wankel RC 2-60 rotating-piston engine.

TYPE: One-, two- or three-seat light helicopter.

ROTOR SYSTEM (all models): Fully-articulated metal three-blade main rotor. Blades are of bonded construction, with constant-section extruded aluminium spar, wraparound skin and a trailing-edge section. Blade section NACA 0015. Two-blade teetering tail rotor, each blade comprising a steel tube spar with glassfibre skin. Blades do not fold. No rotor brake.

ROTOR DRIVE: Vee-belt drive system eliminates need for conventional clutch. Metal-coated and hard-anodised sheaves. Spiral bevel angular drive-shaft. Tail rotor shaft-driven directly from belt-drive. Main rotor/engine rpm ratio 1 : 6.

FUSELAGE: Welded steel tube structure, with aluminium and Plexiglas cabin and one-piece aluminium tube tailboom.

TAIL UNIT: Horizontal and vertical fixed stabilisers made up of aluminium ribs and skin.

LANDING GEAR: Skids carried on Hughes oleo-pneumatic shock-absorbers. Two cast magnesium ground handling wheels with 10 in (25 cm) balloon tyres, pressure 60-75 lb/sq in (4·22-5·27 kg/cm²). Model 300 is available on floats made of polyurethane coated nylon fabric, 15 ft 5 in (4·70 m) long and with total installed weight of 60 lb (27·2 kg).

POWER PLANT: One 180 hp Lycoming HIO-360-A1A (HIO-360-B1A in TH-55A) four-cylinder horizontally-opposed aircooled engine, mounted horizontally below seats. Aluminium fuel tank, capacity 30 US gallons (103·5 litres), mounted externally aft of cockpit. Provision for aluminium auxiliary fuel tank, capacity 19 US gallons (72 litres), mounted opposite standard tank. Oil capacity 2 US gallons (7·5 litres).

ACCOMMODATION: Two seats (TH-55A) or three seats (Model 300) side by side in Plexiglas-enclosed cabin. Door on each side. Dual controls optional. Baggage capacity 100 lb (45 kg). Exhaust muff or gasoline-heating and ventilation kits available.

ELECTRONICS AND EQUIPMENT (Model 300): Optional equipment includes King KY 90 radio, welded aluminium Stokes litter kit, cargo rack, external load sling of 600 lb (272 kg) capacity.

ELECTRONICS AND EQUIPMENT (TH-55A): Provision for ARC-524M VHF radio.

DIMENSIONS, EXTERNAL:
- Diameter of main rotor: 25 ft 3½ in (7·71 m)
- Main rotor blade chord: 6·83 in (17·35 cm)
- Diameter of tail rotor: 3 ft 10 in (1·17 m)
- Distance between rotor centres: 14 ft 1 in (4·29 m)
- Length overall: 28 ft 10¾ in (8·80 m)
- Length of fuselage: 21 ft 11¾ in (6·80 m)
- Height overall: 8 ft 2¾ in (2·50 m)
- Skid track: 6 ft 6½ in (2·00 m)
- Cabin doors (each):
  - Height: 3 ft 8 in (1·12 m)
  - Width: 2 ft 8 in (0·81 m)
  - Height to sill: 2 ft 11 in (0·89 m)

DIMENSIONS, INTERNAL:
- Cabin: Length: 4 ft 7 in (1·40 m)
  - Max width: 4 ft 3 in (1·30 m)
  - Max height: 4 ft 4 in (1·32 m)
  - Floor area: 13·0 sq ft (1·21 m²)

AREAS:
- Main rotor blades (each): 7·1 sq ft (0·66 m²)
- Tail rotor blades (each): 0·77 sq ft (0·07 m²)
- Main rotor disc: 503 sq ft (46·73 m²)
- Tail rotor disc: 8·70 sq ft (0·81 m²)
- Fin: 1·22 sq ft (0·11 m²)
- Horizontal stabiliser: 3·44 sq ft (0·32 m²)

WEIGHTS AND LOADINGS:
- Weight empty:
  - 300: 958 lb (434 kg)
  - TH-55A: 1,008 lb (457 kg)
- Max certificated T-O and landing weight:
  - 300, TH-55A: 1,670 lb (757 kg)
- Max recommended weight (restricted operation):
  - 300, TH-55A: 1,850 lb (839 kg)
- Max disc loading (at certificated AUW):
  - 300, TH-55A: 3·3 lb/sq ft (16·1 kg/m²)
- Max power loading (at certificated AUW):
  - 300, TH-55A: 9·3 lb/hp (4·22 kg/hp)

PERFORMANCE (at max certificated T-O weight):
- Max never-exceed speed:
  - 300: 75·5 knots (87 mph; 140 km/h)
  - TH-55A: 75 knots (86 mph; 138 km/h)
- Max level speed at S/L:
  - 300: 75·5 knots (87 mph; 140 km/h)
  - TH-55A: 75 knots (86 mph; 138 km/h)
- Max cruising speed:
  - 300: 69 knots (80 mph; 129 km/h)
  - TH-55A: 65 knots (75 mph; 121 km/h)
- Econ cruising speed:
  - 300, TH-55A: 57 knots (66 mph; 106 km/h)
- Max water contact speed (on floats): 17 knots (20 mph; 32 km/h)
- Max water taxying speed (on floats): 9 knots (10 mph; 16 km/h)
- Max rate of climb at S/L:
  - 300: 1,140 ft (347 m)/min
  - TH-55A (mission weight): 1,140 ft (347 m)/min
- Service ceiling:
  - 300: 13,000 ft (3,960 m)
  - TH-55A (mission weight): 11,900 ft (3,625 m)
- Hovering ceiling in ground effect:
  - 300: 7,700 ft (2,350 m)
  - TH-55A: 5,500 ft (1,675 m)
- Hovering ceiling out of ground effect:
  - 300: 5,800 ft (1,770 m)
  - TH-55A: 3,750 ft (1,145 m)
- Range with max fuel, no reserve:
  - 300: 260 nm (300 miles; 480 km)
  - TH-55A: 177 nm (204 miles; 328 km)
- Endurance with max fuel:
  - 300: 3 hr 30 min
  - TH-55A: 2 hr 35 min

Hughes Model 300CQ "quiet" version of the established Model 300C

HUGHES MODEL 300C

This is a developed version of the Model 300, with improvements to allow an increase in payload of 45 per cent. Construction of the prototype started in July 1968, and this made its first flight in August 1969, followed by the first production model in December 1969. FAA certification was received in May 1970.

The introduction of a more powerful engine and an increase of main rotor diameter required a number of related structural changes, including use of a larger tail rotor and fin of greater area. The main rotor mast and tailboom had to be lengthened to accommodate the longer and heavier rotor blades.

Following upon the research that produced a modified version of the OH-6A known as "The Quiet One", Hughes has used similar techniques to develop and obtain full FAA certification of a quiet version of the Model 300, and this has the designation Model **300CQ**. In this new configuration, emission of audible sound is 75 per cent less than with earlier models, and it is possible for the necessary modifications to be retrofitted to existing 300Cs. Max T-O weight of the 300CQ is 1,925 lb (873 kg), with a useful load of 875 lb (397 kg), and there is little change in range and endurance by comparison with the standard Model 300C.

The description of the standard Model 300 applies also to the Model 300C, except in the following details:

ROTOR SYSTEM: As Model 300 except that limited folding is possible. Tracking tabs on main rotor blades at three-quarters radius.

ROTOR DRIVE: Combination Vee-belt/pulley and reduction gear drive system. Main rotor and tail rotor gearbox has spiral bevel right-angle drive. Main rotor/engine rpm ratio 1 : 6·8. Tail rotor/engine rpm ratio 0·97 : 1.

POWER PLANT: One 190 hp Lycoming HIO-360-D1A four-cylinder horizontally-opposed air-cooled engine. Oil capacity 2·5 US gallons (9·5 litres).

ACCOMMODATION: Three persons seated side by side on sculptured and cushioned bench seat.

ELECTRONICS AND EQUIPMENT: Optional electronics include King KY95 VHF radio and headsets. Optional equipment includes amphibious floats, litters, cargo rack, external load sling of 600 lb

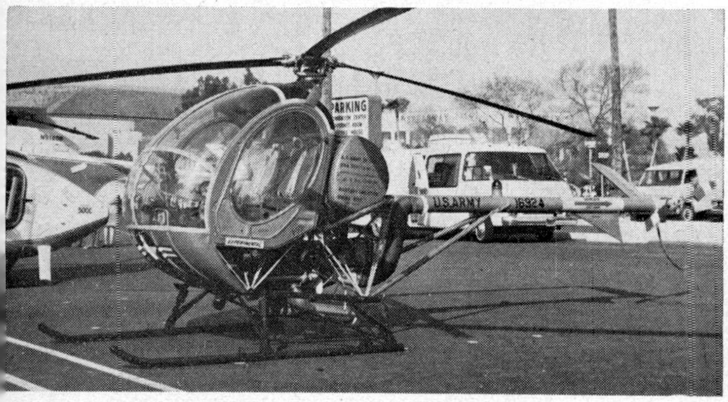

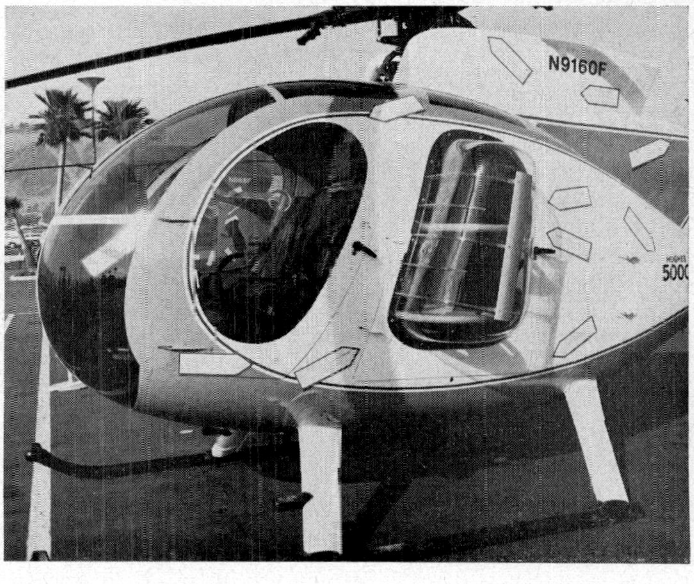

Above:

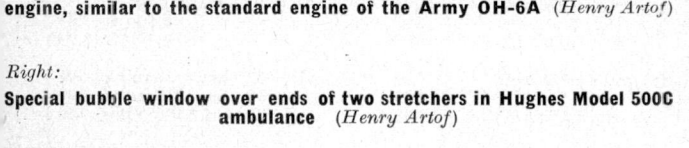

Hughes TH-55A (modified) with 317 shp Allison Model 250-C18 turboshaft engine, similar to the standard engine of the Army OH-6A *(Henry Artof)*

Right:

Special bubble window over ends of two stretchers in Hughes Model 500C ambulance *(Henry Artof)*

(272 kg) capacity, agricultural spray or dry powder dispersion kits, 19 US gallon (72 litre) auxiliary fuel tank, fire extinguisher, dual baggage case, night flying kit, external power socket, dual controls, all-weather cover, heavy-duty skid plates, exhaust muffler, main rotor tie-down kit, door lock, dual oil cooler, tinted glass for cabin windows, gasoline or exhaust manifold cabin heating.

DIMENSIONS, EXTERNAL:
Diameter of main rotor 26 ft 10 in (8·18 m)
Main rotor blade chord 6·75 in (17·1 cm)
Diameter of tail rotor 4 ft 3 in (1·30 m)
Length overall 30 ft 11 in (9·42 m)
Width, rotor partially folded 8 ft 0 in (2·44 m)
Skid track 6 ft 3 in (1·91 m)
Passenger doors (each):
Height 3 ft 7 in (1·09 m)
Width 3 ft 2 in (0·97 m)
Height to sill 3 ft 0 in (0·91 m)

AREAS:
Main rotor blades (each) 7·55 sq ft (0·70 m²)
Tail rotor blades (each) 0·86 sq ft (0·08 m²)
Main rotor disc 565·5 sq ft (52·5 m²)
Tail rotor disc 14·2 sq ft (1·32 m²)
Fin 2·8 sq ft (0·26 m²)
Horizontal stabiliser 3·44 sq ft (0·32 m²)

WEIGHTS AND LOADING:
Weight empty 1,039 lb (471 kg)
Max T-O and landing weight 1,900 lb (861 kg)
Max disc loading 3·36 lb/sq ft (16·4 kg/m²)

PERFORMANCE (at max T-O weight):
Max level speed
91 knots (105 mph; 169 km/h) TAS
Max cruising speed at 5,000 ft (1,525 m)
87 knots (100 mph; 161 km/h) TAS
Econ cruising speed at 5,000 ft (1,525 m)
70 knots (81 mph; 130 km/h) TAS
Service ceiling 12,000 ft (3,658 m)
Hovering ceiling in ground effect
6,900 ft (2,103 m)
Hovering ceiling out of ground effect
4,250 ft (1,295 m)
Range with max fuel, five min engine warm-up, econ cruising speed at 5,000 ft (1,525 m), no reserve 202 nm (232 miles; 373 km)

HUGHES OH-6

US Army designation: OH-6A (formerly HO-6) Cayuse

This aircraft was chosen for development following a US Army design competition for a light observation helicopter in 1961. Five prototypes were ordered for evaluation in competition with the Bell OH-4A and Hiller OH-5A, and the first of these flew on 27 February 1963.

On 26 May 1965 it was announced that the OH-6A had been chosen, as a result of the evaluation, and an initial order for 714 was placed by the US Army; this was increased by subsequent orders to a total of 1,434, all of which were delivered by August 1970.

In March and April 1966, US Army and civilian pilots set up 23 international records in OH-6A helicopters. Among Class E-1 (covering all classes of helicopters) records established was one for a distance of 1,922 nm (2,213 miles; 3,561·55 km) in a straight line (California to Florida) non-stop with one pilot.

On 8 April 1971 Hughes announced the existence of a modified OH-6A light observation helicopter known as "The Quiet One". Product of a research project funded by the Department of Defense Advanced Research Projects Agency, Hughes claims that it is the world's quietest helicopter.

Modifications include the installation of a five-blade main rotor, four-blade tail rotor and engine exhaust muffler; sound blanketing of the complete power plant assembly, including engine air intake; and re-shaping of the tips of the main rotor blades. The modified aircraft can operate with engine and rotor speeds reduced to 67 per cent of normal in-flight levels and is able to offer a 600 lb (272 kg) increase in payload and 20 knot (23 mph; 37 km/h) increase in airspeed.

A similar aircraft, designated **OH-6C** and powered by a 400 hp Allison 250-C20 turboshaft engine, has achieved a speed of 173 knots (200 mph; 322 km/h) during tests at Edwards AFB.

Full-scale production of the Hughes 500 commercial and 500M international military versions of the OH-6A (which are described separately) began in November 1968.

TYPE: Turbine-powered light observation helicopter.

ROTOR SYSTEM: Four-blade fully-articulated main rotor, with blades attached to laminated strap retention system by means of folding quick-disconnected pins. Each blade consists of an extruded aluminium spar hot-bonded to one-piece wraparound aluminium skin. Trim tab outboard on each blade. Main rotor blades can be folded. Two-blade tail rotor, each blade comprising a swaged steel tube spar and glass-fibre skin covering. No rotor brake.

ROTOR DRIVE: Three sets of bevel gears, three drive-shafts and one overrunning clutch. Main rotor/engine rpm ratio 1 : 12·806. Tail rotor/engine rpm ratio 1 : 1·987.

FUSELAGE: Aluminium semi-monocoque structure of pod and boom type. Clamshell doors at rear of pod give access to engine and accessories.

Anti-submarine version of the Hughes 500M in Spanish Navy insignia

TAIL UNIT: Fixed fin, horizontal stabiliser and ventral fin.

LANDING GEAR: Tubular skids carried on Hughes single-acting shock-absorbers.

POWER PLANT: One 317 shp Allison T63-A-5A turboshaft engine, derated to 252·5 shp for take-off and 214·5 shp max continuous rating. Two 50% self-sealing bladder fuel tanks under rear cabin floor, capacity 61·5 US gallons (232 litres). Refuelling point aft of cargo door on starboard side. Oil capacity 1·25 US gallons (4·75 litres).

ACCOMMODATION: Crew of two side by side in front of cabin. Two seats in rear cargo compartment can be folded to make room for four fully-equipped soldiers, seated on floor. Crew door and cargo compartment door on each side. Fourteen cargo tie-down points.

ELECTRONICS AND EQUIPMENT: Government-furnished electronics and avionics. Sylvania SLAE avionics package installed in 1969/70 production aircraft. ARC-114 VHF-FM and ARC-116 UHF radios, ARN-89 ADF, ASN-43 gyro compass, ID 1351 bearing-heading indicator and ARC-6533 intercoms are standard. ARC-115 may be substituted for ARC-116.

ARMAMENT: Provision for carrying packaged armament on port side of fuselage, comprising XM-27 7·62 mm machine-gun, with 2,000-4,000 rds/min capability, or XM-75 grenade launcher.

DIMENSIONS, EXTERNAL:
Diameter of main rotor 26 ft 4 in (8·03 m)
Main rotor blade chord 6·75 in (17·15 cm)
Diameter of tail rotor 4 ft 3 in (1·30 m)
Distance between rotor centres
15 ft 0¼ in (4·58 m)
Length overall, rotors fore and aft
30 ft 3¾ in (9·24 m)
Length of fuselage 23 ft 0 in (7·01 m)
Height to top of rotor hub 8 ft 1½ in (2·48 m)
Skid track 6 ft 9 in (2·06 m)
Cabin door (fwd, each):
Height 3 ft 11 in (1·19 m)
Width 2 ft 11 in (0·89 m)
Cargo compartment door (each):
Height 3 ft 5 in (1·04 m)
Width 2 ft 10½ in (0·88 m)
Height to sill 1 ft 10½ in (0·57 m)

DIMENSIONS, INTERNAL:
Cabin: Length 8 ft 0 in (2·44 m)
Max width 4 ft 6 in (1·37 m)
Max height 4 ft 3½ in (1·31 m)

AREAS:
Main rotor blades (each) 7·41 sq ft (0·69 m²)
Tail rotor blades (each) 0·85 sq ft (0·079 m²)
Main rotor disc 544·63 sq ft (50·60 m²)
Tail rotor disc 14·19 sq ft (1·32 m²)
Fin 5·65 sq ft (0·52 m²)
Horizontal stabiliser 7·70 sq ft (0·72 m²)

WEIGHTS AND LOADINGS:
Weight empty, equipped 1,229 lb (557 kg)
Design gross weight 2,400 lb (1,090 kg)
Overload gross weight 2,700 lb (1,225 kg)
Design disc loading 4·4 lb/sq ft (21·48 kg/m²)
Design power loading 9·5 lb/shp (4·31 kg/shp)

PERFORMANCE (at design gross weight):
Never-exceed speed and max cruising speed at S/L
130 knots (150 mph; 241 km/h)
Cruising speed for max range at S/L
116 knots (134 mph; 216 km/h)
Max rate of climb at S/L (military power)
1,840 ft (560 m)/min
Max rate of climb at S/L (max continuous power) 1,250 ft (381 m)/min
Service ceiling 15,800 ft (4,815 m)
Hovering ceiling in ground effect
11,800 ft (3,595 m)
Hovering ceiling out of ground effect
7,300 ft (2,225 m)
Normal range at 5,000 ft (1,500 m)
330 nm (380 miles; 611 km)
Ferry range (1,300 lb; 590 kg fuel)
1,354 nm (1,560 miles; 2,510 km)

HUGHES MODEL 500, 500C and 500M

These are the commercial and foreign military counterparts of the OH-6A military helicopter, as follows:

Model 500. Commercial helicopter, with accommodation for pilot and four passengers or equivalent freight. Optional accommodation for seven with litter kit in use or with four in passenger compartment.

Model 500C. As Model 500, except for installation of 400 shp engine for improved hot-day/altitude performance.

Model 500M. Uprated version of OH-6A, available to foreign military customers. First deliveries to Colombian Air Force in April 1968. Now in service also in Japan, Argentina, Denmark, Spain, Mexico and the Philippines.

The Model 500Ms delivered to the Spanish Navy for ASW duties have an AN/ASQ-81 magnetic anomaly detector installed on the starboard side of the fuselage, and can carry two Mk 44 torpedoes beneath the fuselage. Control boxes for the MAD equipment are mounted on the instrument panel and centre pedestal, and special instrumentation includes a 6 in attitude indicator and radar altimeter.

Although similar in basic design and construction to the OH-6A, the Model 500s have been substantially uprated. The 317 shp Allison Model 250-C18A turbine engine (civil version of the T63-A-5A), installed in the 500 and 500M, is derated only to 278 shp for T-O and has a maximum continuous rating of 243 shp. The Model 500C is powered by a 400 shp Allison Model 250-C20 turboshaft engine; this also is derated to 278 shp for T-O and has a maximum continuous rating of 243 shp. The Models 500 and 500C have a fuel capacity of 64 US gallons (242 litres); the Model 500M has a capacity of 60 US gallons (227 litres).

Optional equipment available for the Model 500 includes shatterproof glass, heating system, radios and intercom, attitude and directional gyros, rate of climb indicator, inertia reels and shoulder harnesses for pilot and co-pilot, fire extinguisher, dual controls, cargo hook, hoist, auxiliary fuel system, heated pitot tube, extended landing gear, blade storage rack, litter kit, emergency inflatable floats, inflated utility floats, rotor brake, seating for four in passenger compartment and first aid kit. Standard equipment includes engine hour meter, navigation lights, clock and ground handling wheels.

DIMENSIONS AND AREAS:
Same as for OH-6A

WEIGHTS:
Weight empty:
500 1,088 lb (493 kg)
500C 1,105 lb (501 kg)
500M 1,130 lb (512 kg)
Max normal T-O weight 2,550 lb (1,157 kg)
Max overload T-O weight 3,000 lb (1,360 kg)

PERFORMANCE (at max T-O weight):
Max level speed at 1,000 ft (305 m):
500, 500C, 500M
132 knots (152 mph; 244 km/h)
Cruising speed for max range at S/L:
500, 500M 117 knots (135 mph; 217 km/h)
500C 124 knots (143 mph; 230 km/h)
Max rate of climb at S/L:
500, 500C, 500M 1,700 ft (518 m)/min
Service ceiling:
500, 500C, 500M 14,400 ft (4,390 m)
Hovering ceiling in ground effect:
500, 500M 8,200 ft (2,500 m)
500C 12,900 ft (3,930 m)
Hovering ceiling out of ground effect:
500, 500M 5,300 ft (1,615 m)
500C 6,700 ft (2,040 m)
Range at 4,000 ft (1,220 m):
500 327 nm (377 miles; 606 km)
500C 328 nm (378 miles; 608 km)
500M 318 nm (366 miles; 589 km)

HUGHES ADVANCED ATTACK HELICOPTER
US Army designation: YAH-64

On 22 June 1973 the US Army announced that it had awarded to Hughes Helicopters and Hughes Aircraft Co of Culver City, California, a $70·3 million contract to build two flight test and one ground test prototype helicopters for competitive evaluation against Bell Helicopter's submission for the Advanced Attack Helicopter (AAH) programme. Bell's contract is valued at $44·7 million, the disparity being explained by the fact that Hughes had done less preliminary development work and that final unit costs are more important than those for prototype development. This factor was emphasised in mid-July when the Defense Department authorised the Army to proceed with the validation phase of the programme, but insisted that the recurring fly-away cost per unit must remain within a target figure of $1·6 million.

Development and testing of the AAH contenders is expected to extend over at least a five-year period, with extensive fly-off trials lasting three years. Competitive flight testing of the Bell and Hughes prototypes is scheduled to begin in December 1975. Selection of the winning design is not anticipated before 1979; it is believed that production contracts might eventually total $500 million.

Hughes' programme director has stated that his company is teamed with Teledyne Ryan Aeronautical of San Diego, California, as a major subcontractor. Ryan will build the fuselage structure, which will undergo systems installation at the Hughes plant.

Primary role of the AAH is that of a tank killer, but it will be equipped also with armament to provide close support for ground combat troops. Hughes believes that its specialisation in aircraft weapon systems will offer considerable advantages in the competition. The forward-mounted 30 mm chain gun developed by Hughes has weight, cost and drag criteria about half those of the General Electric XM-188 Gatling-type gun that was to be fitted initially, and has a potential rate of fire of approximately 1,000 rds/min. In addition, a forward-looking infra-red (FLIR) and visionics system developed by Hughes Aircraft Company will enable the new helicopter to operate by day or night and in adverse weather conditions.

Drawing upon combat experience with the OH-6A Cayuse, which accumulated over 2 million flight hours in Vietnam, the company's approach to the AAH is one of straightforward functional design, using sheet metal in lieu of expensive composite materials in construction of the airframe, with emphasis on ease of maintenance in the field.

Type: Prototype armed helicopter.

Rotor System: Wide-chord four-blade main rotor, with a strap retention system similar to that of the OH-6A. Advanced high-lift rotor blades constructed of laminated stainless steel. Four-blade tail rotor mounted on port side of pylon/fin structure with blades not at 90° to each other but at optimum quiet setting.

Fuselage: Conventional semi-monocoque metal structure. Tail folds to port to reduce overall length for storage and transport.

Wings: Cantilever mid-wing monoplane of short span, mounted aft of the cockpit. Underwing pylons for the carriage of mixed ordnance. Wings are removable, and attach to sides of cabin for transport and storage.

Tail Unit: Fixed fin and cantilever horizontal stabiliser.

Landing Gear: Tailwheel type, with single wheel on each unit. Main legs fold rearward to reduce overall height for storage and transport.

Power Plant: Two 1,500 shp General Electric T700-GE-700 turboshaft engines, derated for normal operations to provide reserve power for combat emergencies. Engines mounted on each side of fuselage, above stub wings.

Accommodation: Crew of two in tandem, with pilot aft on an elevated seat, co-pilot/gunner forward. Large transparent cockpit enclosure for optimum visibility.

Armament: Hughes-developed 30 mm chain gun with 800 rounds of ammunition. Up to eight Hughes BGM-71A tube-launched optically-tracked wire-guided (TOW) anti-tank missiles, housed in redesigned streamlined pods carried on underwing pylons. TOW missiles can be carried in addition to 2·75 in aerial rockets, or a total of 76 rockets without TOW missiles.

Dimension, external:
- Main rotor diameter 48 ft 0 in (14·63 m)

Area:
- Main rotor disc 1,809 sq ft (168·06 m²)

Weights (estimated):
- Weight empty 9,500 lb (4,309 kg)
- Primary gross weight 13,600 lb (6,169 kg)

Performance (estimated, at 13,600 lb; 6,169 kg AUW):
- Rate of climb at S/L under "hot-day" conditions 1,140 ft (347 m)/min
- Endurance at 4,000 ft (1,220 m) at temperature of 35°C 1·9 hr

Full-scale mockup of the Advanced Attack Helicopter (AAH) to be built by Hughes

INTERCEPTOR
INTERCEPTOR CORPORATION

Head Office:
PO Box 800, Longmont, Colorado 80501
Telephone: (303) 772-5540

President:
E. Malpass

Sales Manager: P. P. Luce

The original Interceptor Corporation was formed on 18 November 1968 for the purpose of designing, manufacturing, distributing and servicing aircraft for the general aviation market. It had a manufacturing plant at Max Westheimer Field, Norman, Oklahoma.

First aircraft to be produced by that company was the Interceptor 400, an advanced turbine-engined development of what was known originally as the Meyers 200B and was produced subsequently by Aero Commander as its Model 200. Interceptor Corporation acquired all design drawings, production jigs and tools for this latter aircraft and redesigned the power plant installation and tail unit. Construction of the prototype started in January 1969 and the first flight was made on 27 June 1969. FAA certification was received on 20 August 1971.

The first Interceptor 400 was sold to a Mr F. Lee Bailey who leased it back to the company for demonstration flights. Following a forced landing the company ran into financial difficulties, but it has now been re-formed with Mr Ted Malpass as President.

The new Interceptor Corporation has taken over the works at Norman, Oklahoma, and a new demonstrator has been built. It was stated in April 1974 that the volume of orders was such that delivery was then quoted as 12 to 14 months.

INTERCEPTOR 400

The details below refer to the current demonstrator. Production Interceptor 400s will have a more powerful (840 shp) engine, flat rated at 400 shp, and higher performance.

Type: Four-seat light cabin monoplane.

Wings: Cantilever low-wing monoplane. Wing section NACA 23015 at root, NACA 23012 at station 62, NACA 4412 at tip. Dihedral 6°. Incidence 2° at root, 2° at station 62, —3° at tip. Sweepback at quarter-chord approx 1°. Root section outboard to station 62 of welded steel tube construction with aluminium skins. Outer wings are of conventional two-spar flush-riveted light alloy construction. Conventional all-metal ailerons with ground-adjustable trim tab. All-metal Fowler trailing-edge flaps. Wing leading-edge de-icing optional.

Fuselage: All-metal structure. Cabin section of welded steel tube, with overturn structure and light alloy covering. Light alloy semi-monocoque flush-riveted rear fuselage. Fuselage pressurised from firewall to fuselage station 110.

Tail Unit: Cantilever all-metal structure. Fixed-incidence tailplane. Rudder and elevator have controllable trim tabs. De-icing of tail unit leading-edges optional.

Landing Gear: Hydraulically-retractable tricycle type. Nose unit retracts aft, main units inward. Interceptor oleo-pneumatic shock-absorber struts; single wheel on each unit. Goodyear main wheels and tyres size 7·00-6, 6-ply rating, pressure 38 lb/sq in (2·67 kg/cm²). Goodyear nosewheel and tyre size 5·00-5, 6-ply rating, pressure 49 lb/sq in (3·45 kg/cm²). Goodyear caliper drum brakes.

Power Plant: One 665 shp Garrett-AiResearch TPE 331-1-101 turboprop engine, flat rated to 400 shp and driving a Hartzell three-blade metal constant-speed fully-feathering reversible-pitch propeller with spinner. Fuel contained in integral tank in each outer wing panel, with total capacity of 145 US gallons (548 litres). Oil capacity 3·9 US gallons (14·8 litres). Propeller de-icing optional.

Accommodation: Four seats in pairs in enclosed cabin. Door on starboard side, above wing, hinged at forward edge. Baggage compartment aft of cabin with external door on starboard side. Baggage capacity 200 lb (90·5 kg). Cabin air-conditioned and pressurised.

Systems: AiResearch air-cycle air-conditioning and pressurisation by engine bleed air; max differential 2·8 lb/sq in (0·2 kg/cm²). Pneumatic system for pressurisation control and instruments. Hydraulic system, pressure 1,000-1,300 lb/sq in (70-91 kg/cm²), for operation of flaps, landing gear and passenger step, which retracts simultaneously with landing gear. Electrical DC power supplied by 28V 100A starter/generator and two 22Ah nickel-cadmium batteries. Oxygen system optional.

Electronics and Equipment: Nav/com transceivers, ADF, DME, transponder and autopilot are available to customer's requirements. Optional equipment includes Grimes 3-light strobe system, electric propeller de-icing, wing and tail unit de-icing and 4-outlet oxygen system. Full IFR instrumentation standard.

Dimensions, external:
- Wing span 30 ft 6 in (9·29 m)
- Wing chord at root 7 ft 6 in (2·29 m)
- Wing chord at tip 3 ft 4 in (1·02 m)
- Wing aspect ratio 5·81
- Length overall 27 ft 4¾ in (8·35 m)
- Height overall 10 ft 6 in (3·20 m)
- Tailplane span 14 ft 8 in (4·47 m)
- Wheel track 8 ft 11 in (2·72 m)
- Wheelbase (approx) 6 ft 9½ in (2·07 m)

Interceptor 400 pressurised four-seat light aircraft (400 shp AiResearch TPE 331-1-101 turboprop engine)

Propeller diameter 7 ft 2 in (2·18 m)
Cabin door (approx):
Height 3 ft 4 in (1·02 m)
Width 3 ft 0 in (0·91 m)
Baggage compartment door (approx):
Height 1 ft 8 in (0·51 m)
Width 1 ft 11 in (0·58 m)
Height to sill 2 ft 6 in (0·76 m)
DIMENSIONS, INTERNAL:
Cabin:
Length 7 ft 0 in (2·13 m)
Max width 3 ft 6 in (1·07 m)
Max height 4 ft 0 in (1·22 m)
Floor area 24 sq ft (2·23 m²)
Volume 60 cu ft (1·70 m³)
Baggage hold 10 cu ft (0·28 m³)
AREAS:
Wings, gross 160 sq ft (14·86 m²)
Ailerons (total) 10·8 sq ft (1·00 m²)
Trailing-edge flaps (total) 22·4 sq ft (2·08 m²)
Fin (approx) 8·94 sq ft (0·83 m²)
Rudder, incl tab (approx) 7·06 sq ft (0·66 m²)
Tailplane 24·88 sq ft (2·31 m²)
Elevators, incl tab 13·10 sq ft (1·22 m²)
WEIGHTS AND LOADINGS:
Weight empty, equipped 2,400 lb (1,088 kg)
Max payload with full fuel and IFR equipment 600 lb (272 kg)
Max T-O weight 4,030 lb (1,828 kg)
Max wing loading 25·18 lb/sq ft (122·94 kg/m²)
Max power loading 10·7 lb/hp (4·85 kg/hp)
PERFORMANCE (at max T-O weight):
Max never-exceed speed 260 knots (300 mph; 481 km/h)
Max level speed at 16,000 ft (4,875 m) 250 knots (287 mph; 463 km/h)
Max cruising speed at 18,000 ft (5,485 m) 243 knots (280 mph; 450 km/h)
Stalling speed, flaps and landing gear down 59 knots (68 mph; 110 km/h)
Max rate of climb at S/L 1,500 ft (457 m)/min
Service ceiling 24,000 ft (7,315 m)
T-O run 860 ft (262 m)
T-O to 50 ft (15 m) 1,410 ft (430 m)
Landing from 50 ft (15 m) 1,200 ft (366 m)
Landing run 510 ft (155 m)
Range at max cruising speed, with allowances for warm-up, taxi, T-O, climb and 45 min reserve 868 nm (1,000 miles; 1,610 km)
Max range, allowances as above 998 nm (1,150 miles; 1,850 km)
Range with max payload, allowances as above 738 nm (850 miles; 1,368 km)

ISON

WAYNE ISON

ISON PDQ-2

Mr Wayne Ison of Elkhart, Indiana, has designed and built a lightweight sporting aircraft of which plans are available to amateur constructors. It is claimed that the PDQ-2, as Mr Ison has named his aircraft, is cheap, easy and fast to build. The prototype was built in four months at a cost of $350, excluding the cost of the engine, and flew for the first time on 29 May 1973.

The unusual layout of the PDQ-2 can be seen in the accompanying illustration: a welded tubular steel landing gear/fuselage structure, carrying a kingpost to which the monoplane wing is attached and to which it is wire-braced. A horizontal beam aft from the kingpost carries a wire-braced T-tail. The power plant, a 38 hp Aerosport-Rockwell JLO-600-2 two-cylinder horizontally-opposed aircooled engine, is mounted on top of the kingpost, and drives a two-blade pusher propeller. Maximum T-O weight of the PDQ-2 is 425 lb (193 kg), cruising speed 61 knots (70 mph; 113 km/h) and landing speed 35 knots (40 mph; 64 km/h).

Ison PDQ-2 lightweight homebuilt sporting aircraft (38 hp Aerosport-Rockwell JLO-600-2 engine) *(Howard Levy)*

JAMESON

RICHARD J. JAMESON

ADDRESS:
124-C North Stanford Avenue, Fullerton, California 92631

Mr Richard J. Jameson of Fullerton, California, has designed a single-seat all-metal light aircraft, of which he intends to make plans available to amateur constructors. Design emphasis has been on simplicity of construction, light alloy angle being used to fabricate the wing spar, as well as the basic structures of the fuselage and tail unit. Designated RJJ-1 Gypsy Hawk, its construction occupied three and a half years at a cost of under $2,000. By the end of February 1974 the RJJ-1 prototype had accumulated a total of approximately 200 flying hours.

In early 1974 Mr Jameson was working on the design and construction of a new sporting aircraft, to be powered by a Volkswagen engine, but no details were available at the time of closing for press.

JAMESON RJJ-1 GYPSY HAWK

TYPE: Single-seat homebuilt sporting aircraft.
WINGS: Cantilever low-wing monoplane. Wing section NACA 747A315. Constant-chord wing. All-metal structure. Wing spar built up from light alloy angle. Light alloy skins. Conventional ailerons of light alloy construction.
FUSELAGE: Semi-monocoque all-metal structure of light alloy.
TAIL UNIT: Cantilever light alloy structure with swept vertical surfaces. All-moving tailplane with anti-servo tab.
LANDING GEAR: Non-retractable tricycle type.
POWER PLANT: One 65 hp Continental A65 four-cylinder horizontally-opposed aircooled engine, driving a two-blade fixed-pitch propeller with spinner. Integral fuel tanks, one in the outer panel of each wing, have a total capacity of approximately 20 US gallons (75·7 litres).
ACCOMMODATION: Single seat for pilot under transparent cockpit canopy.

Jameson Gypsy Hawk single-seat homebuilt light aircraft *(Henry Artof)*

DIMENSIONS, EXTERNAL:
Wing span 18 ft 8 in (5·69 m)
Wing chord, constant 3 ft 4¾ in (1·03 m)
Length overall 16 ft 1 in (4·90 m)
Height overall 6 ft 9 in (2·06 m)
Wheelbase 4 ft 1¼ in (1·25 m)
WEIGHTS:
Weight empty 520 lb (236 kg)
Max T-O weight 820 lb (372 kg)
PERFORMANCE:
Max level speed 109 knots (125 mph; 201 km/h)
Cruising speed 100 knots (115 mph; 185 km/h)
Landing speed 65-69 knots (75-80 mph; 121-129 km/h)
Stalling speed 57 knots (65 mph; 105 km/h)
Max rate of climb at S/L 900 ft (274 m)/min
T-O run 800 ft (244 m)
Endurance 4 hours

JAVELIN

JAVELIN AIRCRAFT COMPANY, INC

ADDRESS:
9175 East Douglas, Wichita, Kansas 67207
Telephone: (316) 682-0111
PRESIDENT: David D. Blanton

Javelin Aircraft Company was founded on 1 March 1953 to manufacture a low-cost automatic pilot for small aircraft; this was followed by equipment manufacture, and aircraft development work. Following restoration of a Curtiss Robin between 1957 and 1961, which won the National Championship award for the best restored antique aircraft in 1961, Javelin sought an Arrow Sport biplane for similar treatment. Unable to find a suitable aircraft, the company began design and development of a biplane on 1 January 1964.

The resulting aircraft, designated Wichawk, has structural geometry similar to the Stearman biplane, as well as some of its aerodynamic features, and is stressed for +12 and —6*g*. It flew for the first time on 24 May 1971 and has received FAA certification in the homebuilt category. Javelin Aircraft does not build the Wichawk, but plans, wing ribs and fuel tanks are available to amateur constructors. At the end of December 1973 it was known that more than 100 Wichawks were under construction.

JAVELIN WICHAWK

TYPE: Two/three-seat homebuilt sporting biplane.
WINGS: Braced single-bay biplane, with N-shape streamline-section cabane and interplane struts. Streamline-section landing and flying wires. Wing section NACA 23015. 2° dihedral on lower wing only. Incidence 0°. No sweepback. Composite structure, with two wood spars and 2024T3 light alloy ribs, fabric-covered. Simple sealed ailerons on lower wing only. No flaps. Geared trim tab.
FUSELAGE: Welded structure of 4130 chrome-molybdenum steel tube with light alloy tubular stringers, fabric-covered.
TAIL UNIT: Wire-braced welded structure of 4130 chrome-molybdenum steel tube with fabric covering. Fixed-incidence tailplane. Trim tab in starboard elevator.
LANDING GEAR: Non-retractable tailwheel type. Main wheels carried on side Vees hinged to lower fuselage longerons. Shock-absorption by automotive-type shock-struts, similar to those

of Piper PA-20, and rubber shock cord. Main wheels and tyres size 6·00-6. Cleveland toe brakes. Steerable tailwheel. Fittings available for float or ski landing gear.

Power Plant: Prototype has one 180 hp Lycoming O-360 four-cylinder horizontally-opposed aircooled engine, driving a Sensenich two-blade fixed-pitch propeller type 76EM8-0-56. McCauley propellers optional. Provision for alternative engines up to 210 hp, and Javelin can provide installation drawings for various horizontally-opposed or radial engines. Fuel tank of 25 US gallon (94·5 litre) capacity in upper wing centre-section, and one of 14 US gallon (56·5 litre) capacity in fuselage aft of firewall. Refuelling points above tanks. Oil capacity of prototype 2 US gallons (7·5 litres).

Accommodation: Two seats, side by side, in open cockpit. Provision for tandem two-seat or three-seat configurations. Drawings available for rearward-sliding transparent cockpit canopy. Dual controls standard. Baggage compartment aft of seats, capacity 120 lb (54 kg). Hat and purse locker, in turtleback, capacity 20 lb (9 kg).

Systems: Electrical system powered by 12V 50A engine-driven generator. Hydraulic system for brakes only.

Dimensions, external:	
Wing span (upper)	24 ft 0 in (7·32 m)
Wing chord (constant, both)	4 ft 2 in (1·27 m)
Wing aspect ratio	5·76
Length overall	19 ft 3 in (5·87 m)
Height overall	7 ft 2 in (2·18 m)
Tailplane span	8 ft 0 in (2·44 m)
Wheel track	6 ft 1½ in (1·87 m)
Propeller diameter	6 ft 4 in (1·93 m)
Propeller ground clearance	10½ in (0·27 m)
Dimensions, internal:	
Max width	3 ft 0½ in (0·93 m)
Baggage compartment	12 cu ft (0·34 m³)
Area:	
Wings, gross	185 sq ft (17·2 m²)
Weights and Loadings (prototype with 180 hp engine):	
Weight empty	1,280 lb (580 kg)
Max T-O weight	2,000 lb (907 kg)
Max wing loading	10·8 lb/sq ft (52·7 kg/m²)
Max power loading	11·1 lb/hp (5·03 kg/hp)
Performance (prototype with 180 hp engine):	
Max never-exceed speed	156 knots (180 mph; 289 km/h)
Max level speed at S/L	121·5 knots (140 mph; 225 km/h)
Max cruising speed	110 knots (127 mph; 204 km/h)
Landing speed	39 knots (45 mph; 72·5 km/h)
Max rate of climb at S/L	1,700 ft (518 m)/min
T-O run	150 ft (46 m)

Javelin Wichawk two-seat homebuilt biplane (180 hp Lycoming O-360 engine)

KAMAN

KAMAN AEROSPACE CORPORATION
(a subsidiary of Kaman Corporation)

Head Office:
Old Windsor Road, Bloomfield, Connecticut 06002
Telephone: (203) 242-4461

President:
William R. Murray

Vice-Presidents:
David W. Demers (Contracts and Marketing)
Robert L. Martin (Operations)
W. N. Stone (Engineering)
G. F. McDonough (Industrial Relations)
J. T. King Jr (Finance and Procurement)

Secretary: J. S. Murtha

Comptroller: Walter R. Kozlow

Manager, Washington Office:
T. E. Glass Jr

Public Relations Manager:
W. A. McLaughlin Jr

The original Kaman Aircraft Corporation was founded in 1945 by Mr Charles H. Kaman, who continues as President and Chairman of the Board of Kaman Corporation. Its initial programme was to develop and test a novel servo-flap control system for helicopter rotors, and the Kaman K-125 of 1947 was the first in a series of "synchropter" designs with intermeshing contra-rotating rotors and the servo-flap control system.

The HH-43B/F turbine-powered local base rescue helicopter was the last design embodying both of these concepts. This aircraft continues in service with the USAF Aerospace Rescue and Recovery Service and with the air services of Burma, Iran, Morocco, Thailand and Pakistan. Production of spare parts continues. Details of this helicopter can be found in the 1965-66 *Jane's*.

The later H-2 Seasprite naval utility helicopter, which utilises the servo-flap control system on a conventional single main rotor, is described below. Conversion to twin-engined configuration of all H-2s in the US Navy's inventory was completed in early 1972.

Under a succession of US Navy contracts which began in 1970, and which totalled approximately $35 million by Spring 1974, Kaman is modifying and converting 105 earlier model H-2 helicopters to SH-2D/F configuration for the Navy's LAMPS (Light Airborne Multi-Purpose System) programme, which teams these aircraft with frigates, destroyers and escorts for broader capabilities in anti-submarine warfare (ASW) and anti-ship missile defence (ASMD). By February 1974 a total of 20 SH-2D and 37 SH-2F versions had been delivered. Deliveries of the SH-2F version have been funded and programmed to continue through 1975, by which time all available H-2s in the Navy's inventory will have been converted.

In recent years the parent Kaman Corporation has diversified its activities considerably, offering products and services in six principal markets: aerospace, science and technology, general aviation, music, bearings, and industrial supplies and services. These operations produced total corporate sales of approximately $137 million in 1973, of which $47 million resulted from aerospace activities.

Kaman is anticipating further production of the SH-2 following completion of the SH-2F modification programme. New SH-2s would be qualified for a maximum gross weight of 13,300 lb (6,032 kg), compared to the 12,800 lb (5,805 kg) of the current SH-2F. Capacity of the external auxiliary fuel tanks would be almost doubled, at about 120 US gallons (454 litres) each, to offer increased endurance. The electrical and fuel systems would be modernised and improved, and a number of changes suggested by Fleet experience would be introduced to improve maintainability and reliability.

Kaman Aerospace operates three plants in Connecticut, located at Bloomfield, Windsor Locks and Moosup. Its capabilities include major production work in the fields of airframe structures, sheet metal, glassfibre, reinforced honeycomb bonding and chemical milling. It is also a leading company in the field of helicopter dynamics, research and development, and in the application of new materials and technology.

Kamatics Corporation (formerly Kacarb Products Corporation), a subsidiary of Kaman Corporation, was reorganised in January 1973 to reflect its developing potential in the bearings industry. Products include bearings for a variety of aerospace applications, as well as for marine vehicles such as hydrofoils, including self-lubricating high-temperature bearings, and self-lubricating high-load corrosion-resistant bearings.

In research and development, Kaman Aerospace is working on several advanced concepts which will have future impact on rotary-wing technology, particularly on aerodynamics, application of materials and production techniques, and vibration isolation. One of the most promising research programmes is the study of a Circulation Control Rotor (CCR) concept, under a Naval Air Systems Command contract awarded in June 1973. This project is concerned with a slotted rotor blade through which compressed air is blown to enhance aerodynamic performance and improve the lift characteristics of the retreating blade. Several of these R & D programmes are under sponsorship of the US Army Air Mobility Research and Development Laboratory, Eustis Directorate, Fort Eustis, Virginia. They include a controllable twist rotor (CTR); dynamic anti-resonant vibration isolator; glassfibre tail rotor; repairable/expendable main rotor blade concept; advanced structural concepts for aircraft fuselage fabrication; maintainability of major helicopter components; elastic pitch beam tail rotor; fan-in-fuselage concept; and new design, fabrication and inspection techniques for helicopter structures.

For the Office of Naval Research, Kaman is under contract to design, build and demonstrate the feasibility of the Ship Tethered Aerial Platform (STAPL), a ship-towed drone autogyro with automatic flight controls and data recording equipment, which is visualised as an elevated sensor or instrument platform. A similar analysis of a tethered drone helicopter concept for battlefield surveillance is being carried out for Eustis Directorate.

For NASA's Langley Research Center, Hampton, Virginia, Kaman is developing by computer study new testing methods for space vehicles, to simulate dynamic stresses and vibrations during

Kaman NHH-2D, a modified UH-2C, assigned to the Beartrap/Harpoon programme

zero-gravity free flight. The testing methods may have application to NASA's Space Shuttle programme.

Kaman is also continuing development of a stowable aircrew vehicle escape rotoseat (SAVER) which first began under a contract awarded by the US Naval Air Development Center. Follow-on contracts brought this project to the stage of a powered flight test vehicle qualified for manned flight. Testing began in December 1971 and was completed in January 1972. The system is being prepared for flight deployment testing, the final phase of the experimental feasibility demonstration.

Kaman Aerospace is engaged in several major airframe programmes under subcontract. In July 1972 Rockwell International selected the company to build rudders and the tailplane fairing assembly for the three authorised prototypes of the USAF's B-1 strategic bomber, plus test articles. This was followed in December by an additional contract for three aircraft sets of engine access doors. In December 1973, Fairchild Republic awarded Kaman a contract covering tooling for and construction of aft fuselage sections for the A-10A close-support aircraft.

Kaman is an associate contractor with Grumman on the US Navy's F-14 Tomcat fighter, and is constructing flaps, slats, spoilers and cove doors for the outer VG wing. Kaman has delivered wing control surfaces for the first 86 F-14s, and has been authorised to build an additional 98 aircraft sets on an accelerated delivery schedule. Other major airframe contracts have included production of components for the Lockheed C-5A and C-130; Grumman A-6, EA-6B and OV-1; McDonnell Douglas DC-8 and DC-9; and Boeing B-52; thrust reversers for the General Electric TF39 turbofan engine; and portions of space hardware under subcontracts to General Electric and Perkin Elmer.

In May 1971 Kaman was awarded a $7·5 million contract by the USAF's Electronic Systems Division, Air Force Systems Command, for the design, fabrication and testing of the Airborne Weather Reconnaissance System (AWRS). This is a system of both advanced and off-the-shelf equipment for the improved collection, measurement, analysis, recording and communication of meteorological data intended to increase substantially the accuracy of predicting the force and direction of hurricanes, typhoons and lesser storms.

AWRS contains integrated atmospheric/meteorological and electronic sensors, redundant on-board data processing capacity, the world's first integral Omega-inertial navigation system, an advanced-technology meteorological dropsonde and improved communications, including data link. Aircraft modification of the USAF Air Weather Service WC-130B Hercules aircraft consisted of the design, fabrication and installation of instrument consoles for the meteorologist mission controller and dropsonde operator; improved aircraft electrical and environmental control systems; design and installation of external sensors and nav/com antennae, and the addition of viewing bubbles for cloud observations.

Modification of the prototype WC-130B was completed at Kaman's Windsor Locks facility in September 1972, and the aircraft made its first flight in this configuration on 4 October 1972. Contractor testing was completed in September 1973, and USAF pre-acceptance flight testing was substantially completed by January 1974. The prototype was scheduled to enter operational use with the Air Weather Service weather reconnaissance squadron in early 1974. If the prototype unit is successful, AWRS may be installed in additional Air Weather Service WC-130s for worldwide coverage of weather phenomena.

Based on the predicted results of the new AWRS, the US Commerce Department's National Oceanic and Atmospheric Administration (NOAA) contracted Kaman in June 1973 for similar modification of a C-130 operated by NOAA's Research Flight Facility. Delivered to Kaman's Windsor Locks factory for modification on 19 January 1974, it was scheduled for completion in time to participate in the international GATE programme in the Summer of 1974.

Kaman announced in October 1972 that, under a $648,000 contract from the US Naval Engineering Center, Philadelphia, an HH-2D Seasprite was to be modified for the installation, testing and evaluation of Beartrap and Harpoon rapid-capture and securing systems to make possible helicopter landings on small, non-aviation ships in high sea states. Beartrap, manufactured by Dominion Aluminium Fabricating Co of Toronto, Canada, is currently in use by the Canadian Armed Forces. Harpoon, which is in use by the French Navy, is manufactured by Aérospatiale. Differing in detail, both systems are designed to deploy a strong fly-down cable between ship and helicopter to stabilise the latter in hover. Initial testing of the two systems was carried out at the Naval Air Test Facility, Lakehurst, New Jersey, during the Summer of 1973. Tests on board a destroyer at sea were scheduled for early 1974.

Prototype WC-130B Hercules fitted with Kaman AWRS (Airborne Weather Reconnaissance System)

On 8 February 1973 Kaman received a $58,000 contract from the US Army's Air Mobility Research and Development Laboratory at Fort Eustis, Virginia, for evaluation of the COZID (cable operated zero impedance decoupler) developed by Kaman. COZID is designed to eliminate a resonant condition described as "vertical bounce" which can develop when vibration from a helicopter's rotor is transmitted to an underslung cargo load. Kaman's contract calls for analytical and experimental evaluation of the COZID's application to a variety of military helicopters utilising cargo hook systems.

Kaman Sciences Corporation, with headquarters at Colorado Springs, Colorado, is engaged in nuclear research, weapons studies, advanced aerodynamics, computer programming and time sharing, neutron generators, advanced materials, measuring devices and systems analysis. Kaman's general aviation subsidiaries comprise AirKaman Inc, a fixed-base operator at Bradley International Airport, Windsor Locks, Connecticut; Air Kaman of Omaha, Nebraska, and Air Kaman of Jacksonville, Florida, all of which provide sales and service of light and twin-engined business aircraft, repairs, fuel sales, charter service, flight training and airline services.

At the end of February 1974 total corporate employment was approximately 3,300, of whom about 1,500 were engaged in aerospace activities.

KAMAN SEASPRITE

US Navy designations: UH-2 (formerly HU2K-1), HH-2 and SH-2

The prototype Seasprite flew for the first time on 2 July 1959, and the following versions have since been produced for the US Navy:

UH-2A. Initial production version. Entered US Navy service on 18 December 1962, when deliveries began to Helicopter Utility Squadron 2. First shipboard service as HU-2 Detachment 62 on USS *Independence* on 4 June 1963. Total of 88 built.

UH-2B. Development of UH-2A, for operation under VFR conditions. Differed only in the non-installation of certain electronic navigation equipment, although provision for fitting this equipment was retained. Entered shipboard service with Detachment 46 of HU-4, on USS *Albany*, on 8 August 1963. Total of 102 built. All single-engined A and B models later converted to twin-engine configuration, the last being delivered from the Pensacola, Florida, SAR detachment in early 1972.

UH-2C. Seasprites were converted to twin-engined configuration, with this designation, under a US Navy contract. Each has two 1,250 shp General Electric T58-GE-8B turboshaft engines in place of the former single T58. Deliveries began in August 1967 and 57 were delivered by the end of 1970.

NUH-2C. Designation of a single UH-2C modified to have launch racks for Sparrow III and Sidewinder missiles and fire directional control equipment. Tests were carried out at the US Navy's Pacific Missile Range at Point Mugu, California, by the Naval Air Test Center and the Raytheon Company, of Bedford, Massachusetts, to evaluate the helicopter as a missile launch platform with a view to enhancing its combat capability for the LAMPS ASMD mission. Four Sparrow III missiles and several Sidewinders were launched in flight at moving surface targets. In 1973 this aircraft was uprated and redesignated **NHH-2D,** and was the test aircraft assigned to the Beartrap/Harpoon programme. A missile launch capability has not yet been specified as a LAMPS requirement.

HH-2C. Armed and armoured version of the standard UH-2C for search and rescue missions. It differed from the UH-2C by having a chin-mounted Minigun turret, waist-mounted machine-guns, extensive armour around the cockpit and other vital areas, a four-blade tail rotor, dual wheels on the main landing gear and a transmission uprating and gross weight increase to 12,500 lb (5,670 kg). Six of these aircraft were delivered to the US Navy for combat search and rescue operations from DLGs in Southeast Asia. Helicopter Combat Support Squadron 7 (HC-7), NAS Imperial Beach, California, and Subic Point, RP, which had operated HH-2Cs (and earlier armed UH-2A/Bs) from frigates in the Gulf of Tonkin, retired these machines at the beginning of 1972. All have been converted to SH-2s.

HH-2D. Announced in late 1969, this version was identical to the HH-2C, except that the armament and armour were deleted. A total of 67 HH-2Ds were retrofitted from earlier single-engine models. Deliveries to the US Navy, at NAS Lakehurst, began in February 1970 and were concluded in February 1972. While awaiting their scheduled modification to SH-2Fs, these aircraft (and remaining UH-2Cs) are actively engaged with Navy search and rescue (SAR) detachments at Naples, Italy; Rota, Spain; Sigonella, Sicily; Pensacola, Florida; Oceana, Virginia; Memphis, Tennessee; and Meridian, Missouri. In addition, they are assigned as fleet utility aircraft aboard cruisers, cargo and support ships, and are on special assignments that include hydrographic and geodetic surveys. They have also been stationed aboard US Coast Guard cutters and icebreakers for polar exploration.

Two HH-2Ds were modified in 1971 at the US Naval Air Development Center, Warminster, Pennsylvania, for preliminary testing in the ASMD (anti-ship missile defence) portion of the LAMPS mission. These aircraft, each fitted with a Texas Instruments APS-115 experimental undernose radar (instead of the Canadian Marconi LN 66HP fitted to the first 20 LAMPS SH-2Ds), were tested on board the USS *Fox* on the US west coast under the Navy's DV-98 programme. Also under this programme, two more HH-2Ds were modified for ASW tests on board the USS *Wainwright* and USS *Belknap* on the east coast. The systems tested were embodied subsequently into Kaman's LAMPS SH-2Ds.

An HH-2D was also used to test a large-aperture retractable radar antenna in an inflatable radome configuration designed and developed by Cubic

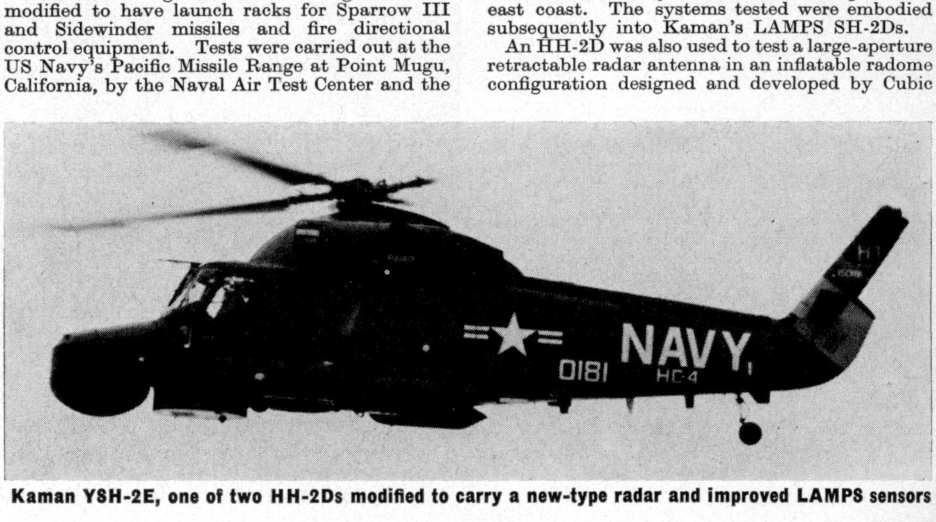

Kaman YSH-2E, one of two HH-2Ds modified to carry a new-type radar and improved LAMPS sensors

Corporation of San Diego, California. Suitable for use with the Canadian Marconi LN 66HP radar system, it is inflated by engine bleed air and, when extended, has a diameter of 6 ft 8 in (2·03 m) and depth of 4 ft 4 in (1·32 m). An improved radar for Mark III LAMPS is still under development.

SH-2D. LAMPS (Light Airborne Multi-Purpose System) version of the HH-2D, for ASW and anti-ship missile defence. The US Navy announced in October 1970 the award of a $2 million contract to Kaman Aerospace for the modification of 10 HH-2Ds, and 10 more were ordered in July 1971. The first SH-2D made its first flight at Bloomfield, Connecticut, on 16 March 1971, and by March 1972 Kaman had completed the modification of all 20 of these aircraft. This involved the installation of Canadian Marconi LN 66 high-power surface search radar in a glassfibre honeycomb dome under the chin; ASQ-81 MAD deployed by winch from a pylon on the starboard side of the fuselage; 15 AN/SSQ-47 active or AN/SSQ-41 passive sonobuoys launched by a small explosive charge from a removable rack on the port side; ALR-54 electronic support measure; eight Mk 25 marine flares/smoke markers; data link; tactical navigation system, and associated command/control units, recorders, displays and antennae. Auxiliary fuel tank mounts on each side of the fuselage have been hardened for the added purpose of launching Mk 44 and Mk 46 ASW homing torpedoes.

As the LAMPS helicopters became operational, the Navy reorganised two squadrons to provide detachments to fleet units and to train additional personnel to operate and maintain them. Helicopter Combat Support Squadron 4 (HC-4) at Naval Air Station Lakehurst, New Jersey, was renamed Helicopter Antisubmarine Squadron Light 30 (HSL-30), and HC-5 at NAS Imperial Beach, California, became HSL-31. During 1973, HSL-30 was transferred to NAS Norfolk, Virginia, and an additional LAMPS squadron, HSL-32, was formed at that station. Two additional LAMPS squadrons were formed at the home station of HSL-31, NAS Imperial Beach, California. These were HSL-33 and HSL-35, commissioned on 31 July 1973 and 15 January 1974 respectively. These new squadrons are being equipped with SH-2Fs.

Operational deployment of SH-2Ds began on 7 December 1971, with assignment of the first unit from HSL-30 to the guided missile frigate USS *Belknap* (DLG-26), the detachment reporting on board in Crete. The second detachment, from HSL-31, was assigned to the guided missile frigate USS *Sterett* (DLG-31) and deployed to the Pacific in January 1972. The USS *Joseph Hewes* (DE-1078) was the first Atlantic Fleet ocean escort of the DE-1052 "Knox" class to become operational with a LAMPS detachment, and the USS *Harold E. Holt* (DE-1074) was the first of this class in the Pacific. First DE-1040 "Garcia" class escorts operational with LAMPS were the USS *O'Callahan* (DE-1051) in the Pacific and USS *Edward McDonnell* (DE-1043) in the Atlantic. By the end of 1973, 25 LAMPS detachments had been deployed (not simultaneously) in the Mediterranean and in the Pacific.

YSH-2E. While delivery of the 20 SH-2Ds was being completed, Kaman also delivered, in March 1972, two HH-2Ds modified with a new type of radar and other improved LAMPS sensors. These aircraft were designated YSH-2E and were assigned to HC-5 (now HSL-31) at Imperial Beach NAS for testing on board the USS *Fox* (DLG-33) in the Pacific. With their specialised equipment, these aircraft were to have been forerunners of a growth version of LAMPS, designated Mk II, with successive LAMPS H-2s similarly configured. On the basis of data provided by operations from the *Fox*, the Navy cancelled the Mk II configuration, and utilised the information in drawing up specifications for a Mk III LAMPS, inviting helicopter companies to submit updated proposals for a new-generation LAMPS aircraft. The two YSH-2Es were returned to Naval Air Development Center, Warminster, Pennsylvania, in November 1972 for further testing, and are now participating in the Mark III LAMPS development programme as testbeds for equipment installation and integration.

SH-2F. In February 1973, Kaman announced the receipt of additional Navy contracts for the third increment of 25 LAMPS helicopters. Deliveries of the SH-2F began in May 1973 and the first unit became operational with squadron HSL-33, deployed to the Pacific on board USS *Bagley* (DE-1069), on 11 September 1973. By February 1974 a total of 37 SH-2Fs had been delivered, with deliveries continuing at a rate of three per month. Modification and conversion of 55 H-2s to SH-2F configuration has been funded and programmed, and long lead time funding received for the conversion of the final 30 by the end of 1975. The earlier SH-2D LAMPS models will probably be uprated to SH-2F configuration.

The SH-2F is fitted with Kaman's "101" rotor, developed through funding by both the company and the US Navy and qualified for installation on the entire H-2 inventory. This rotor provides substantially increased performance in all flight regimes, while practically eliminating rotor vibrations at all speeds and weights, thus improving system reliability and maintainability. The new simplified rotor control system utilises titanium hub and retention assemblies, reduces the number of control elements by two-thirds, and offers a 3,000-hour life from blade tip to blade tip.

Other features of the SH-2F include increased-strength landing gear; a shortened wheelbase by relocation of the tailwheel; twin 1,350 shp General Electric T58-GE-8F turboshaft engines; an improved LN 66HP radar, improved tactical navigation and communications systems and other modifications. In January-February 1973 Kaman flight-tested the prototype for flight qualification to a maximum gross weight of 13,300 lb (6,033 kg), which is 800 lb (363 kg) more than the SH-2D. This may be utilised as increased payload, or in the form of additional fuel in larger auxiliary tanks to provide extended range and endurance in a new production version of the SH-2.

The following details apply to the SH-2D and SH-2F versions of the Seasprite:

Type: Naval anti-submarine warfare and anti-missile defence helicopter, with secondary capability for search and rescue, observation and utility missions.

Rotor System: Four-blade main and tail rotors. Blades of aluminium and glassfibre construction, with servo-flap controls. Blades folded manually. Main rotor rpm 287. Performance figures given are for SH-2F aircraft with the Kaman "101" rotor modification.

Fuselage: All-metal semi-monocoque structure, with flotation hull housing main fuel tanks. Nose fairing split on centreline, to fold rearward on each side to reduce stowage space required. Fixed horizontal stabiliser on tail rotor pylon.

Landing Gear: Tailwheel type, with forward-retracting dual main wheels and non-retractable tailwheel. Liquid spring shock-absorbers.

Power Plant: Two 1,350 shp General Electric T58-GE-8F turboshaft engines, mounted on each side of rotor pylon structure. Normal fuel capacity of 396 US gallons (1,499 litres), including external auxiliary tanks with a capacity of 120 US gallons (454·6 litres).

Accommodation: Crew of three, consisting of pilot, co-pilot and sensor operator. One passenger or litter patient with LAMPS equipment installed; four passengers or two litters with sonobuoy launcher removed. Provision for transportation of internal or external cargo.

Dimensions, external:
- Diameter of main rotor: 44 ft 0 in (13·41 m)
- Main rotor blade chord: 21·6 in (55 cm)
- Diameter of tail rotor: 8 ft 2 in (2·49 m)
- Tail rotor blade chord: 9·3 in (23·6 cm)
- Length overall (blades turning): 52 ft 7 in (16·03 m)
- Length overall, nose and blades folded: 38 ft 4 in (11·68 m)
- Height overall (blades turning): 15 ft 6 in (4·72 m)
- Height to top of rotor head: 13 ft 7 in (4·14 m)
- Stabiliser span: 9 ft 9 in (2·97 m)
- Wheel track (outer wheels): 10 ft 10 in (3·30 m)
- Wheelbase:
  - SH-2D: 22 ft 7 in (6·88 m)
  - SH-2F: 16 ft 9 in (5·11 m)

Weights:
- Weight empty:
  - SH-2D: 6,953 lb (3,153 kg)
  - SH-2F: 7,040 lb (3,193 kg)
- Normal T-O weight:
  - SH-2D: 12,500 lb (5,670 kg)
- Overload T-O weight:
  - SH-2D, SH-2F*: 12,800 lb (5,805 kg)

**Although not yet certificated for a T-O gross weight of 13,300 lb (6,033 kg), all testing has been accomplished at that weight*

Performance (at normal AUW, except where indicated):
- Max level speed at S/L:
  - SH-2D, SH-2F: 143 knots (165 mph; 265 km/h)
- Normal cruising speed: 130 knots (150 mph; 241 km/h)
- Max rate of climb at S/L:
  - SH-2D: 2,440 ft (744 m)/min
- Service ceiling:
  - SH-2D: 22,500 ft (6,858 m)
- Hovering ceiling in ground effect:
  - SH-2D: 18,600 ft (5,670 m)

Kaman SH-2F, latest version of the Seasprite in LAMPS configuration

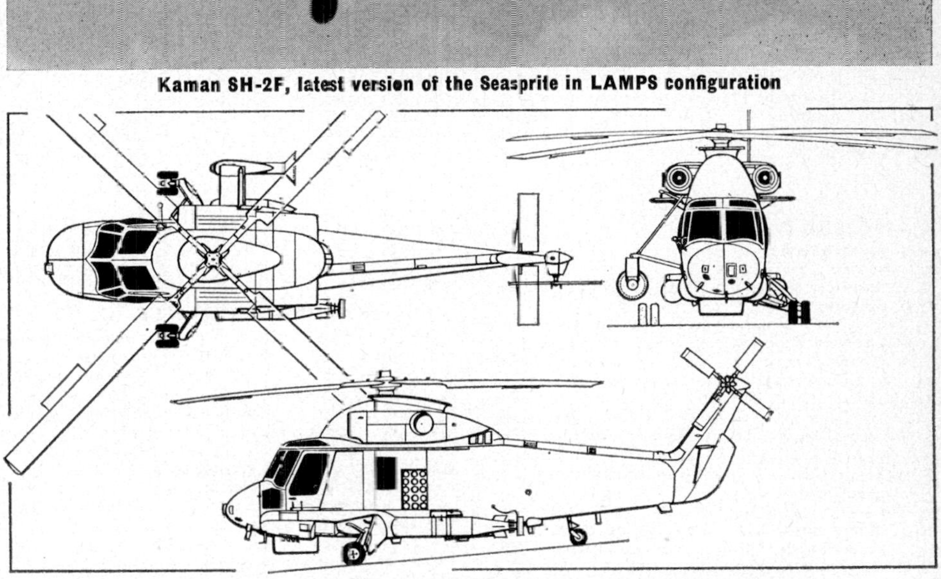

Kaman SH-2F Seasprite Light Airborne Multi-Purpose System (LAMPS) helicopter *(Pilot Press)*

Hovering ceiling out of ground effect:
SH-2D 15,400 ft (4,695 m)
Normal range with max fuel:
SH-2D, SH-2F 367 nm (422 miles; 679 km)

KAMAN KSA-100 SAVER

Combat experience in Vietnam emphasised the need to provide aircrew with a means of escape from the vicinity of crashed aircraft. This resulted in Kaman being awarded a contract by the US Naval Air Development Center to carry out concept definition and preliminary design of a flying rescue seat designated AERCAB (Aircrew Escape/Rescue Capability).

Kaman's proposed vehicle to meet this requirement is a turbofan-powered gyroplane nicknamed SAVER (Stowable Aircrew Vehicle Escape Rotoseat). It is intended to provide pilots of high-performance aircraft such as the F-14, F-4 and A-7 with the means of escape from their disabled machine.

SAVER is basically a gyroplane with an unpowered rotor, having stowable and telescoping blades which, together with its small turbofan engine and controls, will fold into a compact pilot seat for normal use.

In an emergency the pilot would eject from the aircraft as with a conventional ejection seat; but within a second of initiating his escape, a small drogue parachute would be deployed to slow the seat and simultaneously withdraw the folded rotor. Within a total elapsed time of four seconds the seat would have become a rotor-glider, and two seconds later, with the turbofan brought up to full power, the seat would become a gyroplane.

Such a vehicle would enable a pilot to fly to a safer rescue site within a radius of some 50 nm (57 miles; 92 km) or, by remaining airborne, he could communicate with helicopter rescue crews for a co-ordinated meeting and rescue. At the end of flight the pilot would be separated from SAVER and landed by parachute. Alternatively, the rotor system could be jettisoned and the pilot could make a normal parachute descent from the seat. Events for such a parachute escape would also be performed automatically.

Kaman has already carried out more than 1,500 air-drops of self-deploying rotor systems that have demonstrated the feasibility of stowed rotor systems capable of deployment at subsonic, transonic and supersonic speeds, and has also demonstrated a 24 ft (7·32 m) diameter rotor system with telescoping blades.

SAVER is designed to operate from a minimum ejection altitude of 1,000 ft (305 m). Stowed in its pilot seat configuration it measures 1 ft 6 in (0·46 m) in width, 3 ft 9 in (1·14 m) in depth, and 4 ft 5 in (1·35 m) in height, and the deployed rotor is 14 ft 0 in (4·27 m) in diameter.

Preliminary design parameters call for a range of 50 nm (57 miles; 92 km), speed of 100 knots (115 mph; 185 km/h), a rate of climb of 1,000 ft (305 m)/min, endurance of 30 min and a glide lift/drag ratio of 3·05.

It is intended that the SAVER seat will embody automatic flight and homing equipment, an automatic locator beacon, survival kits and restraint harness.

A full-scale unpowered model of SAVER was tested at the NASA Ames Research Laboratory in the Autumn of 1970. These wind tunnel tests included steady-state aerodynamic runs and dynamic deployments of the rotor alone, dynamic unfolding of the rotor from its behind-the-seat stowage and deployment on the seat/airframe, transition from the post-ejection configuration to the autogyro mode, and steady-state aerodynamic tests of SAVER as an autogyro. The rotor was tested at wind tunnel speeds up to 180 knots (207 mph; 333 km/h); deployment was performed at 160 knots (184 mph; 296 km/h), and SAVER was operated in the autogyro mode at up to 110 knots (127 mph; 204 km/h).

Following wind tunnel tests, SAVER was equipped in a test configuration with ground handling apparatus, tricycle landing gear, an electrical system, and basic flight and engine instruments. In this form it has a control stick for cyclic pitch, manual throttle control, and

Kaman KSA-100 SAVER equipped with telescoping rotor blades

twin rudders operated by foot pedals. For control on the ground, main-wheel braking and nosewheel steering are also accomplished by foot pedals.

In this form SAVER was operated in towed flight on 28 December 1971; on the following day the first free flight was made with a 16 ft 0 in (4·88 m) diameter non-telescoping rotor. The first free flight of SAVER with the designed 14 ft 0 in (4·27 m) diameter telescoping rotor was made on 10 January 1972. It became airborne at 55 knots (63·5 mph; 102 km/h) and attained a maximum speed of 75 knots (86·5 mph; 139 km/h), using only half the available power of its turbofan engine.

The Williams WRC-19 turbofan engine was selected for the SAVER prototype as it was the only off-the-shelf engine available, but has much more power than would be needed for a production version. Kaman calculates that an engine of only 290 lb (132 kg) st would be adequate for an operationally-configured SAVER without landing gear.

Installation of remote control equipment, preparatory to unmanned air-launched deployment transition tests to complete the feasibility demonstration, was under way in early 1974.

Type: Aircraft-stowable gyroplane escape device.

Rotor System: Unpowered direct-tilt two-blade rotor with telescoping blades and zero-offset flapping hinges for deployment and decelerator phase governing. The zero-twist blades are fixed at a 4° positive pitch angle. Rotor and vehicle control are via longitudinal and lateral direct tilt of rotor hub. The two-section telescoping rotor blades are light alloy epoxy resin-bonded assemblies. The outboard blade is constructed with a solid light alloy nose section, an intermediate C-channel spar, trailing-edge spline, and skin panels. The inboard blade (into which the outboard blade telescopes) has a light alloy C-section nose spar, Y-shaped trailing-edge element, and skin panels. The nose spar and trailing-edge members of both blade sections are designed to overlap and stop the outboard blade at full extension after deployment. Stop impact forces are controlled by extension dampers. The hub assembly consists of the rotating hub element, two spindle bearings, stationary spindle, and retainers. Blades attach to the hub on the axis of rotation, giving zero offset for minimum control loads; the spindle is offset to place the rotational axis slightly behind the pitch tilt axis for rotor angle-of-attack stability. Zero-offset flapping hinges allow the blades to fold upward 90° for stowage. Rotor deployment system comprises a drogue parachute and lanyard, deployment springs, and explosive cutters. The rotor system is attached to the seat structure by an A-frame support structure, the arm of which pivots almost 180° to bring the blades from stowed to flight position.

Seat/Airframe: This consists of a seat structure assembly, ejection system, restraint harness, life support and survival gear, and personnel recovery parachute. The turbofan engine and rotor are attached to the seat structure. The parachute is carried in the headrest assembly. A lumbar pack forms the seat back and houses a life raft and survival gear. Controls for harness emergency release, harness inertia and take-up reel, and seat position adjustment, are located on the seat's bucket sides. Ejection initiation mechanism and face curtain are part of the headrest assembly.

Power Plant: Prototype has one Williams Research Corporation WRC-19 turbofan engine, developing 430 lb (195 kg) st, normally stowed behind the seat headrest. Production version would need only some 290 lb (132 kg) st. After ejection the engine, mounted on a linkage system, deploys to its flight attitude; the mount linkage system then self-locks to provide a firm engine mounting. A direct-impingement cartridge starter is used to provide quick light-up and acceleration. Starting is automatic, with manual backup, and when the engine is running the throttle is advanced automatically to the flight power setting. Fuel is contained in a self-sealing tank, mounted under the seat pan and filled with 97% reticulated foam.

Systems: The ejection system includes an initiation of sequence unit, dual catapults, sustainer rockets, DART stabilisation, and timers to sequence events at both high and low speeds. Automatic flight control system is designed to fly SAVER in a stable manner at an altitude of 3,000 ft (914 m) and will be able to home on a radio beacon.

Dimensions, external:
Rotor diameter (deployed) 14 ft 0 in (4·27 m)
Rotor blade length (telescoped) 4 ft 0 in (1·22 m)
Rotor blade chord (mean) 7½ in (19 cm)

Weights (prototype):
Weight empty 444 lb (201 kg)
Normal gross weight 710 lb (322 kg)

Performance (estimated):
Max level speed 100 knots (115 mph; 185 km/h)
Range (still air) 50 nm (57 miles; 92 km)

KAMINSKAS

RIM KAMINSKAS

Address:
312 Camino de las Colinas, Redondo Beach, California 90277

First aircraft designed and built by Mr Kaminskas was a single-seat sporting biplane named the Papoose Jungster I, which was a scaled-down replica of the well-known Bücker Bü 133 Jungmeister.

It was followed by a parasol-wing single-seater named the Jungster II, and sets of plans of both designs are available to amateur constructors from K and S, Alberta, Canada (which see), which has acquired from Mr Kaminskas all rights for the above-mentioned aircraft.

Mr Kaminskas has since designed another single-seat sporting biplane, named Jungster III, of which details follow.

Three prototypes of an updated and improved version of the Jungster III, designated Jungster VI, were under construction in Los Angeles in 1972, but no details of this new model have been received.

KAMINSKAS JUNGSTER III

Design of this single-seat biplane was started in July 1967 and construction of the prototype began in the following month. First flight was made on 1 September 1968. The Jungster III had then a gull-wing upper plane to improve forward visibility. Mr Kaminskas has since modified the Jungster III extensively, replacing the upper gull-wing by one more similar to that of the Jungster II, carried on a single braced interplane strut on each side and four centre-section struts. The details which follow apply to the prototype in its modified form with new upper wing:

Type: Single-seat sporting and racing biplane.

Wings: Strut-braced biplane. Conventional upper wing and semi-cantilever lower wings. Aerofoil section NACA 64212 at root, NACA 64209 at tip. Anhedral 2° on top wing. Dihedral 1° on bottom wings. Incidence 0° both wings. Sweepback at quarter-chord 15° on upper wing, 7° lower wings. Conventional all-wood structure with plywood skin. No flaps. Ailerons of wood construction, with plywood skin, on lower wings only. Square wingtips.

Fuselage: All-wood structure of spruce with fabric covering.

Tail Unit: Cantilever all-wood structure with plywood skins. Fixed-incidence tailplane. No trim tabs.

Landing Gear: Non-retractable tailwheel type. Main legs of fixed steel tube bolted to the firewall. Shock-absorption by rubber in compression. Main wheels and tyres size 5·00-5. Hydraulic brakes.

Power Plant: One 125 hp Lycoming O-290 (modified) four-cylinder horizontally-opposed aircooled engine, driving a special two-blade propeller with spinner. Two wing fuel tanks, each of 8 US gallons (30·3 litres) capacity, and one fuselage tank, capacity 5 US gallons (18·9 litres). Total capacity 21 US gallons (79·5 litres).

Accommodation: Single seat in open cockpit.

Dimensions, external:

Wing span	17 ft 0 in (5·18 m)
Wing chord at root (both)	3 ft 0 in (0·91 m)
Wing chord at tip (both)	2 ft 8 in (0·81 m)
Length overall	15 ft 0 in (4·57 m)
Tailplane span	5 ft 4 in (1·63 m)
Wheel track	4 ft 0 in (1·22 m)
Propeller diameter	5 ft 8 in (1·73 m)

Areas:

Wings, gross	81 sq ft (7·53 m²)
Ailerons (total)	6·3 sq ft (0·59 m²)
Fin	2·18 sq ft (0·20 m²)
Rudder	3·4 sq ft (0·32 m²)
Tailplane	4·0 sq ft (0·37 m²)
Elevators	5·32 sq ft (0·49 m²)

Weights and Loadings:

Weight empty	550 lb (249 kg)
Max T-O weight	900 lb (408 kg)
Max wing loading	12 lb/sq ft (58·6 kg/m²)
Max power loading	6·5 lb/hp (2·95 kg/hp)

Kaminskas Jungster III in current form, with new upper wing

Performance (at max T-O weight):

Max never-exceed speed
213 knots (245 mph; 394 km/h)

Max level speed at S/L
154 knots (178 mph; 286 km/h)

Max cruising speed at S/L
139 knots (160 mph; 257 km/h)

Stalling speed 56·5 knots (65 mph; 105 km/h)

KELEHER

JAMES J. KELEHER

Address:
4321 Ogden Drive, Fremont, California 94538

In the early 1960s Mr J. Keleher designed and built a mid-wing sporting monoplane which he called the Lark. The design was revised in 1963, and the current model, for which plans are available to amateur constructors, is designated Lark-1B.

The description which follows applies to the Lark-1B with a 65 hp Continental engine installed. Others are flying with 75 hp A75-8 and 100 hp O-200 Continental engines.

The accompanying illustration shows the Lark-1B built by Mr Parker Warren of Pompano Beach, Florida. Constructed over a five-year period at a cost of approximately $4,000, Mr Warren's Lark differs from standard Keleher plans by having a modified tail planform. Powered by a 100 hp Continental O-200 engine, it has an empty weight of 765 lb (347 kg) and max T-O weight of 1,050 lb (476 kg). Max level speed is 130 knots (150 mph; 241 km/h), cruising speed 109 knots (125 mph; 201 km/h), and landing speed 61 knots (70 mph; 113 km/h). With a sea level rate of climb of 1,000 ft (305 m)/min, service ceiling is over 12,700 ft (3,870 m).

KELEHER LARK-1B

Type: Single-seat amateur-built sporting monoplane.

Wings: Braced mid-wing monoplane with streamline-section Vee bracing struts each side. Wing section NACA $2R_2 12$. No dihedral. Incidence 4° at root, 2° 30′ at tip. All-wood structure of Sitka spruce, with built-up I beam front spar and ribs, fabric-covered. Stressed to 6*g* plus. Fabric-covered wooden ailerons; no trim tabs or flaps.

Fuselage: Welded steel tube structure, fabric-covered, stressed to 6*g* plus.

Tail Unit: Wire-braced welded steel tube structure with sheet steel ribs and fabric covering. Adjustable - incidence tailplane. Swept fin. No trim tabs.

Landing Gear: Non-retractable tailwheel type. Divided main landing gear with shock-absorption by rubber cord in fuselage. Cleveland main wheels and tyres size 5·00-5, pressure 20-25 lb/sq in (1·41-1·76 kg/cm²). Cleveland disc brakes. Wheel fairings optional.

Power Plant: Provision for alternative four-cylinder horizontally-opposed aircooled engines of 65-100 hp, driving a two-blade metal fixed-pitch propeller. One galvanised steel fuel tank in the fuselage, aft of the firewall, capacity 15 US gallons (56 litres). Refuelling point on top of cowl, forward of windscreen. Oil capacity 1·5 US gallons (5·7 litres).

Accommodation: Single seat in enclosed cockpit under sliding canopy. Lowered turtledeck and bubble canopy optional. Stowage for 20 lb (9 kg) baggage aft of seat.

Dimensions, external:

Wing span	23 ft 0 in (7·01 m)
Wing chord, constant	4 ft 0 in (1·22 m)
Wing aspect ratio	5·75
Length overall	17 ft 0 in (5·18 m)
Height overall	5 ft 5 in (1·65 m)
Tailplane span	6 ft 8 in (2·03 m)
Wheel track	5 ft 2 in (1·57 m)
Propeller diameter:	
A65-8	5 ft 7 in (1·70 m)
A75-8	5 ft 5½ in (1·66 m)

Areas:

Wings, gross	80·5 sq ft (7·48 m²)
Ailerons (total)	9·0 sq ft (0·84 m²)
Fin	2·9 sq ft (0·27 m²)
Rudder	3·5 sq ft (0·33 m²)
Tailplane	8·3 sq ft (0·77 m²)
Elevators	5·2 sq ft (0·48 m²)

Weights and Loadings (65 hp engine):

Weight empty	550 lb (249 kg)
Max T-O and landing weight	855 lb (387 kg)
Max wing loading	10·61 lb/sq ft (51·8 kg/m²)
Max power loading	13·15 lb/hp (5·96 kg/hp)

Performance (with 65 hp engine, at max T-O weight):

Max never-exceed speed
160 knots (185 mph; 297·5 km/h)

Max level speed
115 knots (132 mph; 212 km/h)

Max cruising speed
103 knots (119 mph; 192 km/h)

Stalling speed	48 knots (55 mph; 89 km/h)
Max rate of climb at S/L	900 ft (274 m)/min
Service ceiling	19,500 ft (5,950 m)
T-O run	600 ft (183 m)

Range with max payload, with reserve
303 nm (350 miles; 563 km)

Keleher Lark-1B built by Mr Parker Warren of Pompano Beach, Florida *(Howard Levy)*

LAKE

LAKE AIRCRAFT DIVISION OF CONSOLIDATED AERONAUTICS, INC

Executive Offices:
PO Box 399, Tomball, Texas 77375

Sales Offices:
David Hooks Memorial Airport, Tomball, Texas 77375

Telephone: (713) 376-5421
Telex: 76-2054 Lake Air Hou

President:
John J. O'Toole

Executive Vice-President:
M. L. Alson

Sales Manager: Laurin Darrell

Secretary: B. A. Sigsbee

Treasurer: Herbert P. Lindblad

In 1962 Consolidated Aeronautics merged with Lake Aircraft Corporation of Sanford, Maine, as a result of which it operates Lake Aircraft as a division.

It is continuing production of the LA-4 amphibian, which Lake Aircraft developed from the original Colonial C-2 Skimmer IV after purchasing manufacturing rights from Colonial Aircraft Corporation in October 1959.

LAKE LA-4-200 BUCCANEER

Design of the original C-1 Skimmer was started in August 1946. Construction of the prototype began in January 1947 and it flew for the first time in May 1948. Versions of the Lake LA-4 developed from the improved C-2 Skimmer IV have included the LA-4, LA-4A, LA-4P, LA-4S and LA-4T, as described in previous editions of *Jane's*.

The LA-4-200 current production version, as described below, received FAA certification in 1970.

A total of 600 LA-4s of all versions had been built by the end of February 1974.

Type: Single-engined four-seat amphibian.

Wings: Cantilever shoulder-wing monoplane with tapered wing panels attached directly to sides of hull. Wing section NACA 4415 at root, NACA 4409 at tip. Dihedral 5° 30′. Incidence 3° 15′. Structure consists of duralumin leading- and trailing-edge torsion boxes separated by a single duralumin main spar. All-metal ailerons and hydraulically-operated slotted flaps over 80% of span. Ground-adjustable trim tabs on ailerons.

Lake LA-4-200 Buccaneer amphibian (200 hp Lycoming IO-360-A1B engine)

HULL: Single-step all-metal structure, with double-sealed boat hull. Alodined and zinc chromated inside and out against corrosion; hot-enamel painted.

TAIL UNIT: Cantilever all-metal structure. Outboard elevator section separate from inboard section and actuated hydraulically for trimming.

LANDING GEAR: Hydraulically - retractable tricycle type. Consolidated oleo-pneumatic shock-absorbers on main gear, which retracts inward into wings. Long-stroke nosewheel oleo retracts forward. Goodyear main wheels and tyres, size 6·00-6, pressure 35 lb/sq in (2·46 kg/cm²). Goodrich nosewheel and tyre size 5·00-5, pressure 20 lb/sq in (1·41 kg/cm²). Goodyear disc brakes. Nosewheel is free to swivel 30° each way. Floats are aluminium alloy monocoque structures.

POWER PLANT: One 200 hp Lycoming IO-360-A1B four-cylinder horizontally-opposed aircooled engine, mounted on pylon above hull and driving a Hartzell constant-speed pusher propeller. US Rubber DL10 fuel tank in hull, capacity 40 US gallons (151 litres). Refuelling point above hull. Auxiliary fuel in stabilising floats, 7·5 US gallons (28·4 litres) each, optional. Total fuel capacity with optional tanks 55 US gallons (208 litres). Oil capacity 2 US gallons (7·5 litres).

ACCOMMODATION: Enclosed cabin seating pilot and three passengers. Dual controls. Entry through two forward-hinged windscreen sections. Baggage compartment, capacity 200 lb (90·5 kg), aft of cabin.

SYSTEMS: Vacuum system for flight instruments. Hydraulic system, pressure 1,250 lb/sq in (88 kg/cm²), for flaps, horizontal trim and landing gear actuation. Engine-driven 12V 60A alternator and battery. Janitrol B-1500 15,000 BTU heater optional.

ELECTRONICS AND EQUIPMENT: Standard equipment includes full blind-flying instrumentation, outside air temperature gauge, eight-day clock, stall warning indicator, dual controls, tinted windscreen and windows, instrument lights, windscreen defrosting system, heated pitot, landing lights, rotating beacon and paddle. A cabin speaker, microphone, VHF antennae and broad-band com antenna are standard. Basic avionics include Narco 11A 360-channel com transceiver, Narco 11 200-channel nav receiver, 31AB ADF and ELT SHARC 7.

DIMENSIONS, EXTERNAL:
- **Wing span** 38 ft 0 in (11·58 m)
- **Wing chord, mean** 4 ft 5·1 in (1·35 m)
- Wing aspect ratio 8·67
- **Length overall** 24 ft 11 in (7·60 m)
- **Height overall** 9 ft 4 in (2·84 m)
- **Tailplane span** 10 ft 0 in (3·05 m)
- **Wheel track** 11 ft 2 in (3·40 m)
- **Wheelbase** 8 ft 10 in (2·69 m)
- Propeller diameter 6 ft 2 in (1·88 m)

DIMENSIONS, INTERNAL:
- **Cabin: Length** 5 ft 2 in (1·57 m)
  - **Max width** 3 ft 5½ in (1·05 m)
  - **Max height** 3 ft 11½ in (1·32 m)
  - **Floor area** approx 16·5 sq ft (1·53 m²)
  - **Volume** approx 60·0 cu ft (1·70 m³)
- Baggage hold 8·5 cu ft (0·24 m³)

AREAS:
- **Wings, gross** 170 sq ft (15·8 m²)
- **Ailerons (total)** 12·5 sq ft (1·16 m²)
- **Trailing-edge** flaps **(total)** 24·5 sq ft (2·28 m²)
- **Fin** 13·5 sq ft (1·25 m²)
- **Rudder** 8·5 sq ft (0·79 m²)
- **Tailplane** 15·6 sq ft (1·45 m²)
- **Elevators** 8·4 sq ft (0·78 m²)

WEIGHTS AND LOADINGS:
- **Weight empty, equipped** 1,600 lb (726 kg)
- Max T-O and landing weight 2,690 lb (1,220 kg)
- Max wing loading 15·2 lb/sq ft (74·2 kg/m²)
- Max power loading 13·0 lb/hp (5·90 kg/hp)

PERFORMANCE (at max T-O weight):
- Max level speed at S/L 126·5 knots (146 mph; 235 km/h)
- Normal cruising speed, 75% power at 8,000 ft (2,440 m) 130 knots (150 mph; 241 km/h)
- Stalling speed 39 knots (45 mph; 72·5 km/h)
- Max rate of climb at S/L 1,200 ft (366 m)/min
- Service ceiling 14,700 ft (4,480 m)
- T-O run on land 600 ft (183 m)
- T-O run on water 1,100 ft (335 m)
- Landing run on land 475 ft (145 m)
- Alighting run on water 600 ft (183 m)
- Range with max fuel, at normal cruising speed, with reserve 564 nm (650 miles; 1,046 km)
- Max range with max fuel, with reserve 735 nm (847 miles; 1,363 km)

LAS

LOCKHEED AIRCRAFT SERVICE COMPANY (Division of Lockheed Aircraft Corporation)

HEAD OFFICE AND WORKS:
Ontario International Airport, Ontario, California 91761
Telephone: (714) 988-2411

Bases:
John F. Kennedy International Airport, Jamaica, New York
Luke Air Force Base, Arizona

SPECIAL DEVICES DIVISION:
Ontario, California

MARINE SERVICES DIVISION:
Ontario, California

JETPLAN AVIATION SERVICES:
Ontario, California

PRESIDENT:
Charles T. Thum

VICE-PRESIDENTS:
M. H. Greene (Asst to President)
M. Helzel (International Marketing)
K. E. Neudoerffer (Operations)
R. L. Vader (International Operations)
R. C. Zinn (Special Programmes)

DIRECTOR OF PUBLIC RELATIONS:
John R. Dailey

Lockheed Aircraft Service Company is claimed to be the world's largest independent aircraft maintenance and modification company. It has designed and installed major modifications for such aircraft as the Boeing KC-135 and 707; Douglas C-133; and Lockheed C-130, L-188 Electra, C-121 and L-1649. It has also designed and installed interiors for various transport aircraft.

LAS has diversified into many other fields, including aircraft maintenance training devices, aircraft maintenance recording systems and airborne integrated data systems, marine anti-corrosion systems, aircraft ground support equipment and special-purpose vehicles for marginal terrain usage.

The company introduced the new Model 209 digital flight recorder during 1970, and by 1 March 1974 had sold nearly 500 of these units to equip wide-body jets. LAS has also developed JETPLAN, a computerised flight planning and worldwide weather service for airlines and corporate jet operations, and this became available on a world-wide basis in 1971.

In late 1972 the company delivered the third of three L-188 Electra cargo conversions for Ansett Airlines of Australia. Details of this conversion scheme can be found in the 1970-71 *Jane's*. In January 1974 the company received a contract from the Argentine Naval Service to convert three L-188 Electras to a passenger/cargo configuration, with completion of the programme required by February 1975. Brief details of the company's C-130 conversion programme and all available details of the LAS/McDonnell Douglas A-4S Skyhawk conversion follow:

LOCKHEED C-130 CONVERSIONS

LAS specialises in complex aircraft modification, and recent work included conversion of Lockheed C-130E Hercules aircraft to DC-130E drone launch configuration for the US Air Force. The converted aircraft can each launch and control up to two RPVs for reconnaissance operations. The LAS modification programme included design, structural strengthening of the aircraft's wings, installation of drone pylons, extension of the nose to accommodate a chin radome housing a drone control antenna, and installation of a noise abating operations compartment, a two-man launch operator's console and a two-man tracking and control station within the compartment, and a stellar inertial Doppler navigation system, as well as related avionics equipment for command and control of the RPVs.

LAS/McDonnell Douglas A-4S Skyhawk for the Singapore Air Defence Command

LAS/MCDONNELL DOUGLAS A-4S SKYHAWK CONVERSION

Expansion of the Singapore Air Defence Command's operational element began in mid-1972 when 40 ex-United States Navy McDonnell Douglas A-4B Skyhawks were ordered, these being taken from storage at Davis-Monthan Air Force Base in Arizona. The first eight were sent to the LAS works at Ontario for the embodiment of more than 100 modifications, where they were also refurbished, repaired as necessary, and received a full inspection of the entire airframe. First flight of an A-4S took place on 14 July 1973.

The remaining 32 aircraft were dismantled at Davis-Monthan AFB for shipment direct to Singapore, where they were to be refurbished and equipped to A-4S standard at the LAS facility on the island. The first five aircraft to be modified in Singapore were being worked on in mid-February 1974.

An extensively modified version of the A-4B (formerly A4D-2), the A-4S has improved electronics, weapon delivery capability and performance which make it comparable with present-generation aircraft. Primary changes include the addition of split wing spoilers above the flaps, a braking parachute canister beneath the aft fuselage, a longer nose to house advanced electronics equipment of British origin, so that the aircraft will be compatible with Singapore ADC's Hawker Hunters, and replacement of the 20 mm guns in the wing roots by 30 mm Aden cannon. The newly installed equipment includes a Ferranti lightweight lead-computing gunsight, and solid-state electronics packages for the communications, radio and navigation systems. The cockpit has been completely redesigned to accommodate the new instrumentation and control boxes; and the original 7,700 lb (3,493 kg) st Curtiss-Wright J65-W-16A turbojet engine has been replaced by an 8,400 lb (3,810 kg) st J65-W-20.

The initial batch of eight aircraft which were modified at Ontario is being used in a pilot training programme, carried out with the support of LAS at Lemoore NAS, California, since the company's contract called also for maintenance, pilot training and logistics support. When all 40 aircraft have been modified they will then equip two fighter-bomber squadrons on the Singapore ADC airfield at Changi.

The description of the McDonnell Douglas A-4M in this edition applies also to the A-4S, except as follows:

FUSELAGE: As for A-4M, except fixed nose with detachable nose radome over communications and navigation equipment. Integral flak-resistant armour in cockpit area, including internal armour plate below, forward and aft of cockpit.

POWER PLANT: As for A-4M, except one 8,400 lb (3,810 kg) st Wright J65-W-20 turbojet engine.

ACCOMMODATION: Pilot on zero-zero lightweight ejection seat.

SYSTEMS: Dual hydraulic system with manual backup. Electrical system powered by a 9kVA generator, with wind-driven generator to provide emergency power.

ELECTRONICS: Plessey PTR-377 UHF/VHF radio transceiver, with UHF homing; Collins ARC-159 UHF radio transceiver; Plessey PTR-442 IFF; Collins DF-206 low frequency ADF; Arvin ARN-52 TACAN; Rodale APN-141 radar altimeter; Stewart-Warner APQ-145 air-to-ground mapping and ranging radar; Decca Type 72 Doppler and TANS digital navigation computer system; Lear Siegler AJB-7 AHRS; Ferranti ISIS D-101 lead-computing gunsight, weapons release programmer and weapons delivery computer.

EQUIPMENT: Ring-slotted-type braking parachute, 16 ft (4·88 m) in diameter, contained in canister secured in aft fuselage below engine efflux duct. Arrester hook for SATS operation.

ARMAMENT: As for A-4M, except no provision for Bullpup air-to-surface missiles. Two 30 mm Mk 4 Aden cannon in wing roots replace the 20 mm Mk 12 cannon of the A-4M, each with 150 rounds of ammunition.

DIMENSIONS, EXTERNAL:
- Wing span 27 ft 6 in (8·38 m)
- Wing chord at root 15 ft 6 in (4·72 m)
- Length overall (excl flight refuelling probe) 39 ft 5 in (12·01 m)
- Height overall 15 ft 0 in (4·57 m)
- Tailplane span 11 ft 3¼ in (3·44 m)
- Wheel track 7 ft 9½ in (2·38 m)

AREAS:
- Wings, gross 260 sq ft (24·16 m²)

Vertical tail surfaces (total) 50 sq ft (4·65 m²)
Horizontal tail surfaces (total) 48·85 sq ft (4·54 m²)

WEIGHTS:
Weight empty 9,603 lb (4,356 kg)
Max T-O weight 22,500 lb (10,206 kg)
Max landing weight 16,000 lb (7,257 kg)

PERFORMANCE (at design T-O weight except where indicated):
Max level speed 573 knots (660 mph; 1,062 km/h)
T-O run at max T-O weight 3,895 ft (1,187 m)
Landing distance (at 14,500 lb; 6,577 kg AUW):
without braking parachute 3,450 ft (1,052 m)
with braking parachute 2,070 ft (631 m)
Max ferry range 1,680 nm (1,935 miles; 3,114 km)

LOCKHEED

LOCKHEED AIRCRAFT CORPORATION

HEAD OFFICE:
Burbank, California 91520
Telephone: (213) 847-6121

CHAIRMAN OF THE BOARD:
Daniel J. Haughton

PRESIDENT: A. C. Kotchian

DIRECTORS:
Roy A. Anderson
Michael Berberian
Cyril Chappellet
D. M. Cochran
James E. Cross
C. S. Gross
Robert W. Haack
Daniel J. Haughton
Willis M. Hawkins
Louis J. Hector
H. L. Hibbard (Honorary)
J. K. Horton
C. L. Johnson
A. C. Kotchian
Leslie M. Shaw
Fred M. Vinson Jr
Ralph A. Weller
M. Norvel Young

EXECUTIVE VICE-PRESIDENT:
W. B. Rieke

SENIOR VICE-PRESIDENTS:
Roy A. Anderson (Finance)
W. M. Hawkins (Science and Engineering)
James D. Hodgson (Corporate Relations)
C. L. Johnson
R. J. Osborn
W. R. Wilson (Marketing)
Duane O. Wood (President, Lockheed-California Company)

GROUP VICE-PRESIDENTS:
S. W. Burriss (President, Lockheed Missiles and Space Company)
L. O. Kitchen (President, Lockheed-Georgia Company)

CORPORATE VICE-PRESIDENTS:
K. Anderson (Government Contracts and Pricing)
F. A. Cleveland (Engineering)
Richard R. Cook (Washington Area)
A. M. Folden (Chairman, Lockheed Shipbuilding and Construction Co; Executive Vice-President and Assistant to the President, L-1011, Lockheed-California Co)
Robert A. Fuhrman (Executive Vice-President, Lockheed Missiles and Space Co Inc)
R. R. Heppe (Executive Vice-President, Lockheed-California Co)
R. R. Kearton (Executive Vice-President, Lockheed Missiles and Space Co Inc)
J. Fred Lashley (Executive Vice-President, Lockheed-California Co)
E. G. Mattison (Industrial Relations)
W. G. Myers (Government Marketing)
Dr F. C. E. Oder (General Manager, Space Systems Division of Lockheed Missiles and Space Co Inc)
W. D. Perreault Snr (Public Relations)
R. Smelt (Chief Scientist)
William D. Stevenson (President, Lockheed Electronics Co Inc)
D. A. Stuart (General Manager, Missile Systems Division)
C. T. Thum (President, Lockheed Aircraft Service Co)
E. P. Wheaton (General Manager, Research and Development Division of Lockheed Missiles and Space Co Inc)
G. G. Whipple (President, Lockheed Propulsion Co and Murdock Machine and Engineering Co of Texas)

SECRETARY:
James J. Ryan (Assistant General Counsel)

VICE-PRESIDENT AND GENERAL COUNSEL:
J. E. Cavanagh

CHIEF COUNSEL AND ASST SECRETARY:
John H. Martin

VICE-PRESIDENT AND CONTROLLER:
V. N. Marafino

VICE-PRESIDENT AND TREASURER:
R. N. Waters

ASST TREASURER:
L. T. Barrow

DIVISIONS:

LOCKHEED-CALIFORNIA COMPANY:
Burbank, California 91520
PRESIDENT: D. O. Wood

LOCKHEED-GEORGIA COMPANY:
Marietta, Georgia 30063
PRESIDENT: L. O. Kitchen

LOCKHEED AIRCRAFT SERVICE COMPANY:
Ontario, California 91761
PRESIDENT: Charles T. Thum

LOCKHEED PROPULSION COMPANY:
Redlands, California 92373
PRESIDENT: G. G. Whipple

SUBSIDIARIES:

AVIQUIPO INC:
New York, NY 10004
PRESIDENT:
Walter L. Weber

LOCKHEED AIR TERMINAL INC:
Burbank, California 91505
PRESIDENT: D. M. Simmons

LOCKHEED AIRCRAFT INTERNATIONAL INC:
Los Angeles, California 90014
PRESIDENT: G. C. Prill

LOCKHEED ELECTRONICS COMPANY INC:
Plainfield, New Jersey 07061
PRESIDENT: W. A. Stevenson

LOCKHEED MISSILES AND SPACE COMPANY INC:
Sunnyvale, California 94088
PRESIDENT: S. W. Burriss

LOCKHEED PETROLEUM SERVICES LTD:
New Westminster, British Columbia, Canada
PRESIDENT: J. W. Hopkins

LOCKHEED SHIPBUILDING AND CONSTRUCTION COMPANY:
Seattle, Washington 98134
CHAIRMAN: A. M. Folden
PRESIDENT: M. L. Ingwersen

MURDOCK MACHINE & ENGINEERING CO OF TEXAS:
Irving, Texas 75060
PRESIDENT: G. G. Whipple

Built by the brothers Allan and Malcolm Lockheed, the first Lockheed aircraft, a tractor seaplane, first flew in 1913. Three years later the brothers established a company at Santa Barbara, California, to manufacture a twin-engined flying-boat, two seaplanes for the Navy and a small sport biplane that was a forerunner of the true streamlined aeroplane. Lockheed Aircraft Co, formed in 1926, moved to Burbank, California, in 1928 and was reorganised as Lockheed Aircraft Corporation in 1932.

On 30 November 1943, the Vega Aircraft Corporation, which had been formed in 1937 as an affiliate and in 1941 became a wholly-owned subsidiary of the Lockheed Aircraft Corporation, was absorbed and the name Vega abandoned.

Lockheed's aircraft and missile activities are now handled by three separate companies, which were evolved from the former California, Georgia and Missiles and Space Divisions in the Summer of 1961.

The current products of the Lockheed-California and Lockheed-Georgia Companies are described below under the individual company headings.

The activities of Lockheed Propulsion Company (formerly Grand Central Rocket Company) are described in the "Aero-Engines" section.

Lockheed has diversified into many fields of industry since 1959. Following the acquisition of Stavid Engineering Inc, it combined this company and its own Electronics and Avionics Division into the Lockheed Electronics Company.

Lockheed Air Terminal Inc (LAT), a wholly-owned subsidiary, manages, operates and maintains the Hollywood-Burbank Airport, acquired in 1940, as well as providing fuelling and related services at 25 other locations in 11 states. Lockheed Aircraft Service Co (LAS) designs and manufactures products for the aerospace and marine industries, and Lockheed Aircraft International Inc maintains interest in international joint ventures, licensing programmes and direction of foreign manufacturing operations.

Since April 1959 Lockheed has also had an interest in shipbuilding and heavy construction, following its purchase of the Puget Sound Bridge and Dry Dock Company (now Lockheed Shipbuilding and Construction Co).

The total number of people employed by Lockheed Aircraft Corporation at the end of 1973 was 66,900.

LOCKHEED-CALIFORNIA COMPANY

Burbank, California 91520

Lockheed-California has responsibility for the land-based P-3 Orion and carrier-based S-3A Viking naval anti-submarine aircraft, and the YF-12A/SR-71 military aircraft. Also in production is the L-1011 TriStar three-turbofan transport.

LOCKHEED F-104 STARFIGHTER

The Starfighter continues in production, under licence, by Aeritalia of Italy (which see).

LOCKHEED YF-12 and SR-71

Procurement of this aircraft was authorised after consideration of competitive designs from Boeing, General Dynamics, Lockheed and North American, and detail design of the Lockheed submission began in 1959. Known then by the designation A-11, its original purpose was almost certainly to supersede the Lockheed U-2 for long-range high-altitude surveillance missions. Like the U-2, it was designed by a small team led by C. L. Johnson, Lockheed's Vice-President for Advanced Development Projects, in the ADP building at Burbank known as the "Skunk Works". For its construction, a new titanium alloy known as Beta B-120 was evolved specially by Lockheed and the Titanium Metals Corporation, and 93 per cent by weight of the A-11's structure is built of this alloy, which has a tensile strength of up to 200,000 lb/sq in (14,060 kg/cm²).

Existence of the A-11 was not revealed officially until 29 February 1964, when President Lyndon Johnson stated at a news conference that it had already been tested in sustained flight at speeds of more than 1,735 knots (2,000 mph; 3,220 km/h) and at heights in excess of 70,000 ft (21,350 m) at Edwards Air Force Base, California.

The following versions of the aircraft have been built:

YF-12A. The first three A-11 aircraft (60-6934 to 60-6936), ordered on a USAF contract in FY 1960, were redesignated YF-12A in 1964, during which year they were evaluated as experimental all-weather fighters in the USAF's IMI (Improved Manned Interceptor) programme. First flight took place at Watertown Strip, in the Nevada desert, on 26 April 1962.

The YF-12A was displayed publicly for the first time at Edwards AFB on 30 September 1964, and from this base on 1 May 1965 the first and second YF-12As, flown by USAF pilots, set up three world records and six international class records. Col Robert L. Stephens and Lt Col Daniel Andre achieved 1,797·718 knots (2,070·102 mph; 3,331·507 km/h) over a 15/25 km course at unlimited altitude, and a sustained height of 80,257·91 ft (24,462·596 m) in horizontal flight. Maj Walter F. Daniel and Maj Noel T. Warner averaged 1,426·851 knots (1,643·042 mph; 2,644·220 km/h) over a 500 km closed circuit. Maj Daniel and Capt James P. Cooney averaged 1,466·666 knots (1,688·890 mph; 2,718·006 km/h) over a 1,000 km closed circuit, with a 2,000 kg payload, an absolute world record and qualifying also for records without payload and with a 1,000 kg payload. The 500 km and 1,000 km closed-circuit records were later beaten by the Soviet MiG-25.

A brief description of the YF-12A has appeared in previous editions of *Jane's*. It was nicknamed "Blackbird" from the special high-heat-emissive black paint in which the aircraft were finished. Major flight evaluation for the interceptor role ended in 1966, but the second and third YF-12As were allocated in late 1969 to the joint USAF/NASA AST (Advanced Supersonic Technology) programme. This programme, spread over several years, is intended to seek data on altitude-hold at supersonic speeds; boundary layer noise and skin friction; base drag of future hypersonic wing designs; heat transfer under high speed conditions; propulsion system interactions involving effects of engine intake performance; and other performance and handling characteristics. Preliminary parameters in the programme included cruising at altitudes between 80,000 and 120,000 ft (24,400 and 36,575 m) and speeds of between Mach 3 and 4. Aerospace Defense Command of the USAF was responsible for the first phase (operational combat research), which began flight test in 1970 and terminated at the end of 1971; during this phase, on 24 June 1971, aircraft 60-6936 was lost in a crash. The second phase, which began in mid-1972, is controlled by NASA, which allocated a sum of $10 million to finance the programme until the end of 1974. The place of the crashed YF-12A is taken in this phase of the programme by aircraft 60-6937, the sole YF-12C. An alternating schedule keeps one aircraft on flight status most of the time, while the other undergoes installation and checkout of test systems and instrumentation; an average of three flights per month is made, each of two to three hours' duration. The areas occupied originally in the YF-12A by the missiles and fire control radar are taken up in the AST aircraft by research instruments. These include infra-red TV scanners in the port-side wing/body chine, to monitor temperature at the inlet on that side and along the wing leading-edge inboard of the inlet. Other sensors are for monitoring inlet unstart problems at high Mach numbers, and to indicate possible ways of improving inlet tolerance without creating unstart conditions. (A supersonic inlet is temperamental; if the airflow is disturbed from the exact design condition, the internal shock may be expelled, with gross breakdown of flow and sudden collapse of engine thrust, in what is termed an inlet unstart.) In one experiment, completed in the Autumn of 1973, one aircraft was partly disassembled and put through tests to distinguish between aerodynamic and thermal loads on the airframe.

YF-12C. Designation of the fourth aircraft (60-6937), ordered on the same contract as the three A-11/YF-12As and completed as the prototype for the SR-71 version. Subsequently allocated to the USAF/NASA Advanced Supersonic Technology programme, as described under the YF-12A heading.

SR-71A. Strategic photographic and electronic reconnaissance aircraft, developed from the YF-12A via the YF-12C prototype. Development began in February 1963, and the first production SR-71A (61-7950) made its first flight at Edwards AFB on 22 December 1964. Existence first revealed officially, by President Johnson, on 24 July 1964.

As in the YF-12C, the SR-71A fuselage is slightly longer than that of the YF-12A, the wing/body chine fairings extend fully forward to meet at the extreme nose, and there are no ventral fins. The SR-71A is substantially heavier than the YF-12A, carries considerably more fuel, and has a longer range. Evaluation by Strategic Air Command began in 1965, and deliveries of production SR-71As, for working up, were made to the 9th (formerly the 4200th) Strategic Reconnaissance Wing at Beale AFB, California, beginning in January 1966. Subsequent operations have reportedly included surveillance of the Suez Canal region in 1970 and, by aircraft detached to Kadena AB, Okinawa, of the Chinese mainland prior to 1971. The SR-71A and the Teledyne Ryan AQM-34L RPV were the only USAF reconnaissance aircraft permitted to overfly North Vietnam after the cessation of bombing on 15 January 1973. One aircraft was operated in the Middle East during and after the Yom Kippur war in late 1973. The SR-71s, although painted dark blue overall, are also referred to unofficially as "Blackbirds".

The initial SR-71A/SR-71B order, placed in FY 1961, is believed to have been for 21 aircraft (61-7950 to 61-7970). An option for six more was taken up in the Spring of 1966, and published photographs have revealed serial numbers up to 61-7980, suggesting that at least 10 more beyond the initial order may have been built. In service, the YF-12/SR-71 series of aircraft have performed several thousand supersonic flights, of which some 40 per cent have been at Mach 3·0 or above. Because of budget constraints, a large percentage of the SR-71 fleet is in storage, but the number of aircraft on active status was increased slightly in late 1973.

SR-71B. Original tandem two-seat operational training version of the SR-71A, with second cockpit elevated aft of front (pilot's) cockpit. Fixed ventral tail-fins under nacelles reintroduced. Two aircraft known (61-7951 and '56), the first of which was delivered to SAC's 9th (formerly 4200th) Strategic Reconnaissance Wing at Beale AFB, California, on 7 January 1966; one aircraft was subsequently lost in a crash.

SR-71C. Revised training version, modified from an SR-71A after the loss of one SR-71B in an accident.

The following description applies primarily to the SR-71A, but is generally applicable to all YF-12 and SR-71 models except where a specific version is indicated:

Type (SR-71A): Two-seat strategic reconnaissance aircraft.

Wings: Cantilever low/mid-wing monoplane, of basically delta planform with rounded tips. Wings have a bi-convex section, a thickness/chord ratio of 3·2%, and a small negative angle of incidence. Leading-edges have 60° sweepback, trailing-edges 10° forward taper. Multi-spar fail-safe structure, predominantly of Lockheed/TMC B-120 series titanium alloy and incorporating engine nacelle ring carry-through structure. Upper and lower skins are bonded to spars, and have preformed chordwise corrugations to aid the airflow in conditions of prolonged thermal soaking. Entire wing structure is designed to withstand sustained skin temperatures of up to about 260°C, and locally up to about 427°C. The leading-edges inboard of the engine nacelles are extended forward along the fuselage sides in blended wing/body chine fairings, which act as a fixed canard surface to reduce trim drag, improve directional stability and provide additional lifting area. On the YF-12C and SR-71 models these chines extend to, and meet at, the extreme nose; on the YF-12A they are cut back to aft of the nose radome, approximately in line with the front cockpit. The leading-edges outboard of the nacelles have marked conical camber, and there is a smaller chine fairing along the outboard side of each nacelle. The outer wings, and the outer half of each nacelle, hinge upward to provide access to the engines. Hydraulically-actuated plain elevons on trailing-edge, inboard and outboard of engine nacelles, each with 12° travel up or down and a triangular cutout adjacent to the nacelle; these are operated in unison or differentially for control and trim in both pitch and roll. No slats,

Lockheed SR-71A strategic reconnaissance aircraft

flaps, spoilers, tabs or other movable surfaces.

Fuselage: Pressurised fail-safe structure, predominantly of B-120 series titanium alloy, designed to withstand sustained skin temperatures of up to about 260°C, and locally up to about 315°C. Nose, forward of cockpits, is tilted upward 2° to reduce trim drag; the YF-12A has a larger nose than the SR-71A, with a plastics radome. The SR-71 models have an extended tailcone, compared with the YF-12A, to improve boat-tail drag.

Tail Unit: Cantilever fail-safe structure, predominantly of B-120 series titanium alloy, designed to withstand sustained skin temperatures of up to about 315°C. No horizontal surfaces, control in pitch being effected by use of the elevons. On top of each engine nacelle is a fixed stub-fin surmounted by a slab-type all-moving fin, these being inclined inward 15° from the vertical to reduce roll effect during deployment. The movable fins have up to 20° travel to left or right, are actuated hydraulically, and can be operated separately or in unison as required. In addition the YF-12A has a fixed underfin beneath each nacelle, inclined outward at 15°, to offset its larger nose radome and shorter wing/body chines; these fins are fitted also to the SR-71B. In its original form the YF-12A also had a centreline ventral fin beneath the rear fuselage, which folded upward to port through 90° for ground clearance when the landing gear was extended. The ventral fins were fitted originally to offset a loss of stability at high speed, resulting from the increased nose cross-section of the YF-12A; the centreline underfin is not fitted to the YF-12s currently flying.

Landing Gear: Retractable tricycle type. Three-wheel main units retract inward into wing/body chine fairings; twin-wheel steerable nose unit retracts forward into fuselage. Oleo-pneumatic shock-absorbers. Taxying light on each oleo leg; landing light on nose-wheel leg. Treadless tyres. Anti-skid system. Braking parachute.

Air Intakes: Each engine is fed by an axisymmetric circular air inlet with an electro-hydraulically actuated translating central spike. At low Mach numbers the spike is locked fully forward, where it diverts or spills excess airflow ahead of the inlet and provides a minimum, fairly large, throat area at the inlet lip. At 30,000 ft (9,145 m) altitude the spike is unlocked, and starts to translate aft at Mach 1·6. The inlet should have self-started by this time, although this can be delayed until as late as Mach 2·1. As the spike retracts, the throat moves aft to the station of the cowl shock trap bleed, where cowl boundary layer is bled off (to stabilise the internal shock, and also to cool the engine and nozzle) through 33 fixed solid-wall axial ducts. Centrebody (spike) boundary layer is bled off inward through a porous section of centrebody, and expelled overboard via the centrebody support struts. Rearward translation of the spike closes down throat area by 54 per cent, compared with the Mach 1·0 setting, but increases the area of the captured stream tube by 112 per cent. Engine operation is also critically dependent upon the forward by-pass doors, which are a series of large apertures in a broad band in the outer cowl wall just downstream of the throat. Rotation of this band progressively uncovers matching apertures in the duct itself, allowing airflow to escape overboard through louvres. The doors are open on the ground, but rotate to the fully-closed position upon retraction of the landing gear. At speeds above Mach 1·4 the by-pass may modulate as required to maintain a scheduled pressure ratio between selected pitot and static pressures. The complete inlet system is controlled by Hamilton Standard fail-safe powered systems, with manual emergency operation, with computer control according to sensed flight Mach number, angle of attack, angle of sideslip and normal acceleration, thus providing an automatic restart cycle to recover from inlet unstarts. Variation in forward by-pass can exert an enormous influence on aircraft drag, especially noticeable as pronounced yaw if one by-pass modulates while the other remains shut. When operating perfectly, the inlet system generates a pressure ratio of more than 40 : 1 at the cruising Mach number. At low speeds the inlet generates little forward thrust; at Mach 2·2 it generates only 13 per cent of the total propulsive thrust, whereas at about Mach 3·2 it generates 54 per cent, compared with only 17·6 per cent for the engine at that Mach number. An inlet shock stabiliser system, developed by NASA'S Lewis Research Center, was being tested on the YF-12 in 1974. This system is based on a pressure valve which monitors the movement of the shock wave in the inlet and corrects it automatically by moving the inlet spike or inlet dump doors. A new turbine inlet gas temperature (TIGT) sensor has also been developed for evaluation in the YF-12.

Power Plant: All versions of the YF-12 and SR-71 are powered by two Pratt & Whitney JT11D-20B (J58) by-pass turbojets (also correctly described as turbo-ramjet engines), each rated at approx 23,000 lb (10,430 kg) st dry and 32,500 lb (14,740 kg) st at sea level with afterburning. Each engine has a very high capacity by-pass duct system which pipes fourth-stage air to the afterburner to cool the jetpipe and increase the compressor stall margin. The engine discharges through an ejector nozzle, which is part of the airframe and is of purely aerodynamic design. The primary nozzle is a ring of blow-in doors which provide tertiary air to fill in the ejector at Mach numbers below 1·1. This tertiary air is provided by suck-in doors around the nacelle, augmented by the cowl (shock trap) bleed and aft by-pass bleed. The main ejector is supported downstream on streamline struts and a ring of Rene 41 alloy, on which are hinged free-floating trailing-edge flaps of Hastelloy X alloy. These open up progressively between Mach 0·9 and Mach 2·4 to provide a divergent shroud around the primary nozzle and the secondary stream. At low Mach numbers the ejector adds nothing to engine thrust; at Mach 2·2 it provides 14 per cent of the total propulsive thrust, and at about Mach 3·2 it provides 28·4 per cent. The power plant also incorporates suck-in doors, to provide tertiary flow, and secondary by-pass doors around the plane of the engine inlet face. The nacelle structure is designed to withstand sustained skin temperatures of up to about 593°C. The fuel used is a special low vapour pressure hydrocarbon known as JP-7. Insulated integral tanks, five occupying the entire upper part of the fuselage and others in the inner portion of each wing, have a total capacity of more than 80,000 lb (36,290 kg) of fuel. This fuel is used as the main heat-sink for the whole aircraft, and is thus heated until at delivery to the engine its temperature is 320°C. Final fuel injection to the engines is made at 130 lb/sq in (9·14 kg/cm²). An automatic fuel feed system maintains CG adjustment as the tanks are depleted; for thermodynamic reasons, due to the high ratio of surface area to volume, the wing tanks are used first, ie in climb. A nitrogen atmosphere is used to pressurise and inert the tanks. All versions of the aircraft have a receptacle on top of the fuselage, aft of the rear cockpit, for in-flight refuelling from KC-135 tanker aircraft.

Accommodation (SR-71A): Crew of two (pilot and reconnaissance systems officer) on ejection seats in separate tandem cockpits, each under a clamshell canopy which is hinged at the rear and opens upward. Canopies are opaque except for a rectangular window in each side. Front cockpit has a knife-edge windscreen formed by two triangular quarter-lights. Crew members wear Gemini-type *g* suits, and both cockpits are fully pressurised, heated and air-conditioned. Crew escape system is operable from speeds of more than Mach 3·0 at 100,000 ft (30,500 m) down to zero speed at ground level. Duties of the RSO include those of a co-pilot, flight engineer and navigator, and the aircraft can be flown from the rear cockpit if required. This cockpit is elevated in a pronounced "step" in the SR-71B and C, in which versions it is occupied by the instructor.

Systems: Cockpit air-conditioning by heat exchanger system, using engine bleed air pre-cooled by the fuel system. Two independent hydraulic systems for actuation of landing gear, elevons, all-moving fins and, with electrical servo assist, the air inlet spikes. In the event of a control system malfunction the inlet spikes can be controlled manually, provided that hydraulic pressure is available and that the spike linear voltage differential transducer (LVDT) is functioning. If the spike LVDT fails, the spikes can be moved fully forward by means of a solenoid.

Electronics and Equipment: Astro-inertial navigation system, providing automatic star tracking even in daylight. Honeywell air data computer and automatic flight control system (AFCS). The latter comprises a three-axis stability augmentation system (SAS), autopilot and Mach trim system, and is designed primarily to provide optimum handling qualities during take-off and landing, in-flight refuelling, subsonic cruise between 25,000 and 50,000 ft (7,625 and 15,250 m), and Mach 3 cruise above 60,000 ft (18,300 m). The SAS incorporates triple-redundant sensors, electronics and gain-scheduling, and is engaged in the yaw and pitch modes at all times to counteract inlet unstarting. A Hamilton Standard control system governs automatically the variable inlets, fuel supply and variable-area nozzles. The pitch axis has two dual-tandem series servos, each driving one inboard elevon; the roll axis has dual redundancy, and a separate channel to drive each inboard elevon; and the yaw axis has four series servos, two for each fin. Triple display indicator (TDI) gives a digital readout of Mach number, altitude, and knots equivalent airspeed (KEAS), and is used for transition to, and cruising at, supersonic speed. Conventional flight director system, modified to present angle of attack information during cruise on the glideslope portion of the attitude display indicator (ADI). Instrumentation duplicated in the rear (RSO's) cockpit includes basic flight instruments, fuel monitoring systems, annunciator warning panels, systems instruments and most communications instruments. Operational equipment in the SR-71A is classified, but includes provision for a wide variety of advanced observation equipment ranging from simple battlefield surveillance systems to multiple-sensor high-performance systems for interdiction reconnaissance and strategic systems capable of specialised surveying of 60,000 sq miles (155,400 km²) in one hour from an altitude of 80,000 ft (24,400 m). Photographic, infrared and electronic sensors are housed in the forward portions of the wing/body chine fairings.

Armament: All SR-71 models are unarmed. Details of armament formerly fitted to the YF-12A were given in the 1972-73 *Jane's*.

Dimensions, external (SR-71A):
Wing span 55 ft 7 in (16·95 m)
Length overall 107 ft 5 in (32·74 m)
Height overall 18 ft 6 in (5·64 m)
Wheel track (c/l of shock-struts)
approx 17 ft 0 in (5·18 m)
Wheelbase approx 34 ft 0 in (10·36 m)

Area (SR-71A):
Wings, nominal 1,800 sq ft (167·23 m²)

Weights (SR-71A, approx):
Weight empty 60,000 lb (27,215 kg)
Fuel load more than 80,000 lb (36,290 kg)
Max T-O weight 170,000 lb (77,110 kg)

Performance (SR-71A, approx):
Max level speed at 78,740 ft (24,000 m)
more than 1,735 knots (2,000 mph; 3,220 km/h) (more than Mach 3·0)
Max level speed at 30,000 ft (9,145 m)
more than 1,146 knots (1,320 mph; 2,125 km/h) (more than Mach 2·0)
Typical unstick speed
200 knots (230 mph; 370 km/h)
Typical subsonic climb speed
400 knots (460 mph; 741 km/h)
Typical approach speed
180 knots (207 mph; 334 km/h)
Typical touchdown speed
150 knots (173 mph; 278 km/h)
Operational ceiling above 80,000 ft (24,400 m)
Air turning radius at 1,735 knots (2,000 mph; 3,220 km/h)
78-104 nm (90-120 miles; 145-193 km)
Fuel consumption
8,000 US gallons (6,661 Imp gallons; 30,282 litres)/hr
Max lift/drag ratio, trimmed:
below Mach 1·0 approx 11·5
at Mach 3·0 and above 6·5
T-O run at 140,000 lb (63,505 kg) AUW
5,400 ft (1,646 m)
T-O to 50 ft (15 m) at 140,000 lb (63,505 kg) AUW
9,000 ft (2,745 m)
Landing from 50 ft (15 m) at 60,000 lb (27,215 kg)
6,000 ft (1,830 m)
Landing run at 60,000 lb (27,215 kg)
3,600 ft (1,097 m)
Typical operational radius
1,040 nm (1,200 miles; 1,930 km)
Range at Mach 3·0 at 78,740 ft (24,000 m), without refuelling
2,589 nm (2,982 miles; 4,800 km)
Max endurance at Mach 3·0 at 78,740 ft (24,000 m), without refuelling 1 hr 30 min

LOCKHEED MODEL 185 ORION

US Navy designation: P-3

In April 1958 it was announced that Lockheed had been successful in winning with a developed version of the civil Electra four-turboprop airliner a US Navy competition for an "off-the-shelf" ASW aircraft. The two original contracts provided for initial research, development and pre-production activities, while further contracts provided for purchase by the Navy of a standard commercial Electra and its modification, development and testing as a tactical testbed for anti-submarine warfare systems.

An aerodynamic prototype, produced by modifying the airframe of the third civil Electra, flew for the first time on 19 August 1958. A second aircraft, designated YP-3A (formerly YP3V-1), with full electronics, flew on 25 November 1959.

Several production versions have been announced, as follows:

P-3A Orion. Initial production version for US Navy, with 4,500 ehp (with water-alcohol injection) Allison T56-A-10W turboprop engines. First P-3A flew for the first time on 15 April 1961. Deliveries to the US Navy began on 13 August 1962, to replace the P-2 Neptune. Later models (from the 110th aircraft) are known as Deltic P-3As, as they are fitted with the Deltic system, including more sensitive ASW detection devices and improved tactical display equipment. Production completed.

WP-3A Orion. Weather reconnaissance version of P-3A, of which four were delivered to US Navy during 1970 to re-equip squadron previously flying WC-121Ns. The WP-3A has meteorological equipment of the type used in the WC-121Ns and a radome of different configuration.

P-3B Orion. Follow-on production version with 4,910 ehp Allison T56-A-14 turboprop engines, which do not need water-alcohol injection. USN contracts covered 286 P-3As and P-3Bs. In addition, five P-3Bs were delivered to the Royal New Zealand Air Force in 1966, ten to the Royal Australian Air Force during 1968 and five to Norway in the Spring of 1969. USN P-3Bs have been modified to carry Bullpup missiles. Others became **EP-3Bs.**

P-3C Orion. Advanced version with the A-NEW system of sensors and control equipment, built around a Univac digital computer, that integrates all ASW information and permits retrieval, display and transmission of tactical data in order to eliminate routine log-keeping functions. This increases crew effectiveness by allowing them sufficient time to consider all tactical data and devise the best action to resolve the problem. First flight of this version was made on 18 September 1968 and the P-3C entered service in 1969. A total of 109 of this version had been delivered to the US Navy by the end of January 1974.

Five of the eight international records for turboprop aircraft, set up in a P-3C by Cdr Donald H. Lilienthal in early 1971, had not been beaten by the Spring of 1974. They include a speed of 434·97 knots (500·89 mph; 806·10 km/h) over a 15/25 km course; and four time-to-climb records, to 3,000 m in 2 min 51·75 sec; 6,000 m in 5 min 46·36 sec; 9,000 m in 10 min 26·12 sec; and 12,000 m in 19 min 42·24 sec.

RP-3D Orion. One P-3C was reconfigured during the course of manufacture for a five-year mission to map the Earth's magnetic field, under Project Magnet, which is controlled by the US Naval Oceanographic Office. Crew of 17. Range increased to more than 5,000 nm (5,755 miles; 9,265 km) by installation of 1,200 US gallon (4,545 litre) fuel tank in weapons bay. ASW equipment removed, making way for dual inertial navigation systems, dual computers for recording and analysis of magnetic data and for providing co-ordinate readout of Loran A and C, a satellite tracker, an Omega navigation system, a gyro-stabilised sextant capable of giving six lines of position almost simultaneously, highly sensitive magnetometers, and equipment for time correlation by cesium beam time standard. Seven bunks are provided for off-duty crew.

The RP-3D is operated by the US Navy's Oceanographic Development Squadron 8 (VXN-8) based at the Naval Air Test Center, Patuxent River, Maryland. On 4 November 1972, Cdr Philip R. Hite used it to set up an international closed-circuit distance record for turboprop aircraft, covering 5,451·97 nm (6,278·03 miles; 10,103·51 km).

EP-3E Orion. Ten P-3As and two EP-3Bs were converted to EP-3E configuration to replace Lockheed EC-121s in service with VQ-1 and

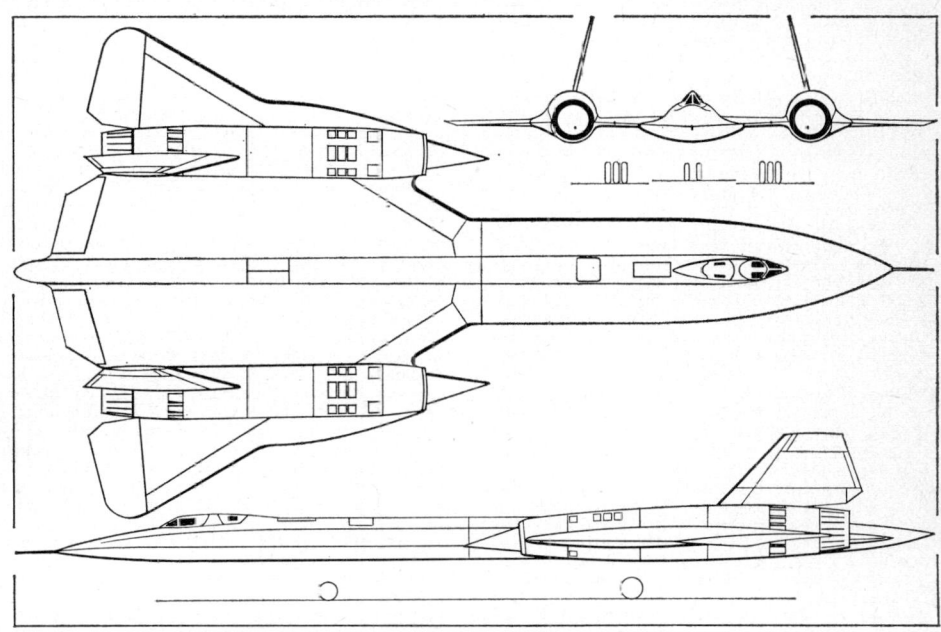

Lockheed SR-71A two-seat strategic reconnaissance aircraft (*Pilot Press*)

Lockheed P-3C Orion four-turboprop naval ASW aircraft

VQ-2 squadrons. They can be identified by large canoe radars on the upper and lower surfaces of the fuselage and a ventral radome forward of the wing.

P-3F. Long-range maritime patrol version of the Orion of which six have been ordered for service with the Imperial Iranian Air Force. Similar to the US Navy's P-3Cs, they are to have much of the P-3C's advanced ASW equipment, but the ASQ-114 computer, ASQ-81 MAD and active sonar will be deleted. To be used initially for long-range surface surveillance, they are intended to be used subsequently also for manually-controlled ASW missions. Delivery of the first aircraft was scheduled for July 1974.

By the end of 1973 Lockheed-California had delivered 402 P-3s of all versions. The following data refer to the P-3C, but are generally applicable to other versions, except for the details noted:

Type: Four-turboprop naval ASW aircraft.

Wings: Cantilever low-wing monoplane. Wing section NACA 0014 (modified) at root, NACA 0012 (modified) at tip. Dihedral 6°. Incidence 3° at root, 0° 30′ at tip. Fail-safe box beam structure of extruded integrally-stiffened aluminium alloy. Lockheed-Fowler trailing-edge flaps. Hydraulically-boosted aluminium ailerons. Anti-icing by engine bleed air ducted into leading-edges.

Fuselage: Conventional aluminium alloy semi-monocoque fail-safe structure.

Tail Unit: Cantilever aluminium alloy structure with dihedral tailplane and dorsal fin. Fixed-incidence tailplane. Hydraulically-boosted rudder and elevators. Leading-edges of fin and tailplane have electrical anti-icing system.

Landing Gear: Hydraulically-retractable tricycle type, with twin wheels on each unit. All units retract forward, main wheels into inner engine nacelles. Oleo-pneumatic shock-absorbers. Main wheels have size 40-14 type VII 26-ply tubeless tyres. Nosewheels have size 28-7·7 type VII tubeless tyres. Hydraulic brakes. No anti-skid units.

Power Plant: Four 4,910 ehp Allison T56-A-14 turboprop engines, each driving a Hamilton Standard 54H60 four-blade constant-speed propeller. Fuel in one tank in fuselage and four wing integral tanks, with total usable capacity of 9,200 US gallons (34,826 litres). Four overwing gravity fuelling points and central pressure refuelling point. Oil capacity (min usable) 29·4 US gallons (111 litres) in four tanks. Electrically de-iced propeller spinners.

Accommodation: Normal ten-man crew. Flight deck has wide-vision windows, and circular windows for observers are provided fore and aft in the main cabin, each bulged to give 180° visibility. Main cabin is fitted out as a five-man tactical compartment containing advanced electronic, magnetic and sonic detection equipment, an all-electric galley and large crew rest area.

Systems: Air-conditioning and pressurisation system supplied by two engine-driven compressors. Pressure differential 5·4 lb/sq in (0·38 kg/cm²). Hydraulic system, pressure 3,000 lb/sq in (210 kg/cm²), for flaps, control surface boosters, landing gear actuation, brakes and bomb-bay doors. Pneumatic system, pressure 3,000/1,200 lb/sq in (210/85 kg/cm²), for ASW store launchers (P-3A/B only). Electrical system utilises three 60kVA generators for 120/208V 400Hz AC supply. 24V DC supply. Integral APU with 60kVA generator for ground air-conditioning and electrical supply and engine starting.

Electronics and Equipment (P-3A/B): Communications and navigation equipment comprises two ARC-94 HF transceivers, ARC-84 VHF transmitter, two ARC-84 VHF receivers, two ARC-51A UHF transceivers, AIC-22 interphone, TT-264/AG teletypewriter, UNH-6 communications tape recorder, two CU-351 HF couplers, ASN-42 inertial navigation system, APN-153 Doppler navigation system, ASA-47 Doppler air mass computer, ASN-50 AHRS, APN-70 Loran, ARN-52 TACAN, DF-202 radio compass, ARN-32 marker beacon receiver APN-141 radar altimeter, ARA-50 UHF direction finder, two ARN-87 VOR installations, two HSI, A/A24G-9 true airspeed computer, PB-20N autopilot, ID-888/U latitude/longitude indicator, and APQ-107 radar altitude warning system. ASW equipment includes ASA-16 tactical display, two APS-80 radar antennae for 360° coverage, APA-125A radar display, ASR-3 trail detector, two ARR-52A sonobuoy signal receivers, AQA-1 sonobuoy indicator, AQA-7 acoustic processer (DIFAR), ASA-20A sonobuoy recorder (Julie), ASQ-10A magnetic anomaly detector in plastics tail "sting", modified ALD-2B ECM direction finder for detecting and locating electronic emissions from submarines, ULA-2 ECM signal analyser, APX-6 IFF identification, APX-7 IFF recognition, APA-89 IFF coder group, AQH-1(V) tactical tape recorder, ASA-50 ground speed and bearing computer, R-1047/A on-top position indicator, TD-441/A intervalometer, PT396/AS ground track plotter, ASA-13 tactical plot board, bearing-distance-heading indicator and KY 364 video decoder. Equipment for day or night photographic reconnaissance. Searchlight under starboard wing.

Electronics and Equipment (P-3C): The ASQ-114 general-purpose digital computer is the heart of the P-3C system. Together with the AYA-8 data processing equipment and computer-controlled display systems, it permits rapid analysis and utilisation of electronic, magnetic and sonic data. Nav/com system comprises two ASN-84 inertial navigation systems, with latitude and longitude indicators; APN-187 Doppler; ARN-81 Loran A and C; ARN-52 TACAN; two ARN-87 VOR receivers; ARN-32 marker beacon receiver; ARN-83 LF-ADF; ARA-50 UHF direction finder; AJN-15 flight director indicator for tactical directions; HSI for long-range flight directions; glideslope indicator; on-top position indicator; two ARC-142 HF transceivers; two ARC-143 UHF transceivers; ARC-101 VHF receiver/transmitter; AGC-6 teletype and high-speed printer; HF and UHF secure communication units; ACQ-5 data link communication set and AIC-22 interphone set; APX-72 IFF transponder and APX-76 SIF interrogator. Electronic computer-controlled display equipment includes ASA-70 tactical display; ASA-66 pilot's display; ASA-70 radar display and two auxiliary readout (computer-stored data) displays. ASW equipment includes two ARR-72 sono receivers; two AQA-7 DIFAR sonobuoy indicator sets; hyperbolic fix unit; acoustic source signal generator; time code generator and AQH-4(V) sonar tape recorder; ASQ-81 magnetic anomaly detector; ASA-64 submarine anomaly detector; ASA-65 magnetic compensator; ALQ-78 electronic countermeasures set; APS-115 radar set (360° coverage); ASA-69 radar scan converter; AXR-13 low light level television (displayed on both ASA-70s); KA-74 forward computer-assisted camera; KB-18A automatic strike assessment camera with horizon-to-horizon coverage; RO-308 bathythermograph recorder. Additional equipment includes APN-141(V) radar altimeter; two APQ-107 radar altimeter warning systems; A/A24G-9 true airspeed computer and ASW-31 automatic flight control system. P-3Cs for delivery in 1975 will have the avionics package updated by addition of an extra 393K memory drum and fourth logic unit, Omega navigation, new magnetic tape transport, and an ASA-66 tactical display for the sonar operators. To accommodate the new systems a new operational software computer programme will be written in CMS-2 language.

Armament: Bomb-bay, 80 in wide, 34·5 in deep and 154 in long (2·03 m × 0·88 m × 3·91 m), forward of wing, can accommodate a 2,000 lb MK 25/39/55/56 mine, three 1,000 lb MK 36/52 mines, three MK 57 depth bombs, eight MK 54 depth bombs, eight MK 43/44/46 torpedoes or a combination of two MK 101 nuclear depth bombs and four MK 43/44/46 torpedoes. There are ten underwing pylons for stores. Two under centre-section each side can carry torpedoes or 2,000 lb mines. Three under outer wing each side can carry respectively (inboard to outboard) a torpedo or 2,000 lb mine (or searchlight on starboard wing), a torpedo or 1,000 lb mine or rockets singly or in pods; a torpedo or 500 lb mine or rockets singly or in pods. Torpedoes can be carried underwing only for ferrying; mines can be carried and released. Search stores, such as sonobuoys and sound signals, are launched from inside cabin area in the P-3A/B. In the P-3C sonobuoys are loaded and launched externally and internally. Max total weapon load includes six 2,000 lb mines under wings and a 7,252 lb (3,290 kg) internal load made up of two MK 101 depth bombs, four MK 44 torpedoes, pyrotechnic pistol and 12 signals, 87 sonobuoys, 100 MK 50 underwater sound signals (P-3A/B), 18 MK 3A marine markers (P-3A/B), 42 MK 7 marine markers, two B.T. buoys, and two MK 5 parachute flares. Sonobuoys are ejected from P-3C aircraft with explosive cartridge actuating devices (CAD), eliminating the need for a pneumatic system.

Dimensions, external:

Wing span	99 ft 8 in (30·37 m)
Wing chord at root	18 ft 11 in (5·77 m)
Wing chord at tip	7 ft 7 in (2·31 m)
Wing aspect ratio	7·5
Length overall	116 ft 10 in (35·61 m)
Height overall	33 ft 8½ in (10·29 m)
Fuselage outside diameter	11 ft 4 in (3·45 m)
Tailplane span	42 ft 10 in (13·06 m)
Wheel track (c/l shock-struts)	31 ft 2 in (9·50 m)
Wheelbase	29 ft 9 in (9·07 m)
Propeller diameter	13 ft 6 in (4·11 m)
Cabin door:	
Height	6 ft 0 in (1·83 m)
Width	2 ft 3 in (0·69 m)

Dimensions, internal:

Cabin, excluding flight deck and electrical load centre:	
Length	69 ft 1 in (21·06 m)
Max width	10 ft 10 in (3·30 m)
Max height	7 ft 6 in (2·29 m)
Floor area	658 sq ft (61·13 m²)
Volume	4,260 cu ft (120·6 m³)

Areas:

Wings, gross	1,300 sq ft (120·77 m²)
Ailerons (total)	90 sq ft (8·36 m²)
Trailing-edge flaps (total)	208 sq ft (19·32 m²)
Fin, with dorsal fin	116 sq ft (10·78 m²)
Rudder, including tab	60 sq ft (5·57 m²)
Tailplane	241 sq ft (22·39 m²)
Elevators, including tabs	81 sq ft (7·53 m²)

Weights (P-3B/C):

Weight empty	61,491 lb (27,890 kg)
Max expendable load	20,000 lb (9,071 kg)
Max normal T-O weight	135,000 lb (61,235 kg)
Max permissible weight	142,000 lb (64,410 kg)
Design landing weight	114,000 lb (51,709 kg)

Performance (P-3B/C, at max T-O weight, except where indicated otherwise):

Max level speed at 15,000 ft (4,570 m) at AUW of 105,000 lb (47,625 kg)	411 knots (473 mph; 761 km/h)
Econ cruising speed at 25,000 ft (7,620 m) at AUW of 110,000 lb (49,895 kg)	328 knots (378 mph; 608 km/h)
Patrol speed at 1,500 ft (457 m) at AUW of 110,000 lb (49,895 kg)	206 knots (237 mph; 381 km/h)
Stalling speed, flaps up	133 knots (154 mph; 248 km/h)
Stalling speed, flaps down	112 knots (129 mph; 208 km/h)
Max rate of climb at 1,500 ft (457 m)	1,950 ft (594 m)/min
Service ceiling	28,300 ft (8,625 m)
Service ceiling, one engine out	19,000 ft (5,790 m)
T-O run	4,240 ft (1,290 m)
T-O to 50 ft (15 m)	5,490 ft (1,673 m)
Landing from 50 ft (15 m) at design landing weight	2,770 ft (845 m)

Max mission radius (no time on station) at 135,000 lb (61,235 kg)
2,070 nm (2,383 miles; 3,835 km)
Mission radius (3 hr on station at 1,500 ft; 457 m) 1,346 nm (1,550 miles; 2,494 km)

LOCKHEED VIKING

US Navy designation: S-3A

On 4 August 1969 Lockheed announced the receipt of a $461 million contract from the US Navy to develop a new anti-submarine aircraft under the designation S-3A. Development has been carried out by Lockheed in partnership with Vought Systems Division of LTV Aerospace, and Univac Federal Systems Division of Sperry Rand. LTV has designed and is building the wing, engine pods, tail unit and landing gear, and Univac is responsible for the digital computer, the heart of the weapon system, which provides high-speed processing of data essential for the S-3A's ASW role. Lockheed is building the fuselage, integrating the avionics, and is responsible for final assembly at Burbank, California.

The selection of Lockheed-California as contractor for this aircraft followed more than a year of intensive competition between North American Rockwell, McDonnell Douglas, Grumman, Convair Division of General Dynamics, and Lockheed-California in conjunction with LTV Aerospace. Proposals submitted by these companies in April 1968 were evaluated by Naval Air Systems Command (NASC), and in August 1968 General Dynamics and Lockheed were requested to provide additional contract definition and to make further refinements to their proposals.

The final proposals of these two companies were submitted in late December 1968, and a detailed technical evaluation was carried out by NASC. Prior experience with Navy programmes was taken into consideration, and finally the Service Selection Authority of NASC awarded the contract to Lockheed-California.

The Lockheed team has been responsible for development, test and demonstration of the aircraft and its weapon systems. The first prototype was rolled out on schedule on 8 November 1971 at Burbank, California, and the first flight was made on 21 January 1972, well in advance of the first flight deadline of 15 March. An increased ceiling of $494 million on the contract, funded over a five-year period, provided for production of eight research and development aircraft in two lots, with an option for the Navy to procure a nominal 186 production models of the S-3A in four lots.

On 4 May 1972 the US Navy announced an order for the first production lot of 13 S-3As, and Lockheed stated that seven of the aircraft would be delivered in 1973, the remaining six during the first quarter of 1974. Follow-on orders for 35 and 45 S-3As were received in April and October 1973 respectively. The 35 aircraft comprising the second production batch are scheduled for delivery by January 1975, the remainder by the end of that year. Lockheed expects to deliver an additional 86 Vikings by December 1977.

The first four production aircraft were delivered to the USN in October 1973, for board of inspection and survey tests.

Seven of the eight test aircraft were flying by the beginning of March 1973, the one remaining example being delivered shortly after. The first was used to investigate flight and performance characteristics and to evaluate the power plant. The second, the structural test vehicle, was used to expand the flight envelope, carrying required weight loads through specified ranges of altitude, speed and manoeuvres. The third, equipped with full ASW electronic equipment, served to integrate the avionics with the airframe; it tracked its first submarine on 23 August 1972. The fourth test Viking, based at the Naval Air Test Center, Patuxent River, Maryland, completed ten months of carrier suitability tests, and demonstrated acceleration from zero to 120 knots (138 mph; 222 km/h) in 2·2 sec, and landing deceleration from 100 knots (115 mph; 185 km/h) to zero in less than 300 ft (91·5 m). The fifth Viking was used to test aircraft systems, including use in a flight refuelling tanker role, and the sixth for ordnance testing. The seventh and eighth aircraft have been used to test braking, pneumatic and electrical systems, to demonstrate armament, radar, electronic countermeasures, navigation and communications equipment, and for a variety of other tasks.

By 30 January 1973 the US Navy had completed three of five Preliminary Evaluations during which 106 hours had been recorded in 24 flights. This evaluation provided the Navy with its first experience of the Viking as a complete weapons system, including all elements of the mission avionics. In November 1973, two Vikings accumulated a total of 40 flight hours during operations from the USS *Forrestal*. In this period these aircraft made 144 touch and go landings, 58 arrested landings and 58 catapult launches, including seven night launches and recoveries. Four of the touch and go landings and one arrested landing were made with one engine out. These aircraft were flown at weights ranging from 35,000 lb (15,875 kg) up to a maximum gross weight of 52,500 lb (23,815 kg), the latter figure being 10,000 lb (4,535 kg) more than the normal ASW mission T-O weight. A further series of carrier tests aboard the USS *Enterprise* were scheduled to take place during April 1974.

By February 1974 the Vikings of the first production batch had accumulated a total of 4,000 flying hours, of which 3,200 had been flown by Lockheed pilots and 800 by Navy pilots. At that time the development programme was 99 per cent complete.

The Viking was introduced into the Fleet officially on 20 February 1974, during ceremonies held at North Island NAS, near San Diego, California. Initial deliveries were made to squadron VS-41, the S-3A training squadron which is based at North Island NAS.

The S-3A is intended for operation from aircraft carriers and has a crew of four, comprising a pilot, co-pilot, tactical co-ordinator (Tacco) and acoustic sensor operator (Senso). The pilot maintains command of the aircraft, while the Tacco formulates strategy and instructs the pilots on the necessary manoeuvres for a successful submarine attack. In addition to flying duties, the co-pilot is responsible for the non-acoustic sensors (such as radar and infra-red) and navigation: the Senso controls the acoustic sensors.

The development of quieter submarines has led to the design of sonobuoys of increased sensitivity, and advanced cathode ray tube displays are provided in the S-3A to maintain flexibility of operation with a limited crew. In particular, a cathode ray tube is utilised to monitor the acoustic sensors. The information formerly stowed in roll form from paper plotters is now stored in the Univac 1832A computer and is available for instant recall. Other functions of the computer include weapon trajectory calculations and pre-flight navigation. Magnetic anomaly detection (MAD) equipment of increased sensitivity makes it possible to detect submarines at greater depths than has been possible until the present time.

Before the S-3A was delivered to the fleet in February 1974, its avionic systems had undergone nearly 2½ years of flight testing on board a specially modified P-3A Orion.

Shipboard maintenance is simplified by the provision of computerised fault-finding equipment, built-in test equipment (BITE), and versatile avionic shop test (VAST) compatibility. Complete deck-level servicing accessibility contributes to the attainment of a quick turnaround time.

The performance characteristics of the S-3A will make possible future design variants, including tanker, utility transport, ASW command and control, and a variety of electronic countermeasures aircraft. To cater for future growth, the airframe is stressed for a maximum take-off weight in excess of 50,000 lb (22,680 kg) and the fuselage volume is such as to allow for a 50 per cent expansion of avionics equipment.

TYPE: Twin-turbofan carrier-borne anti-submarine aircraft.

WINGS: Cantilever shoulder-wing monoplane. Sweepback at quarter-chord 15°. All-metal

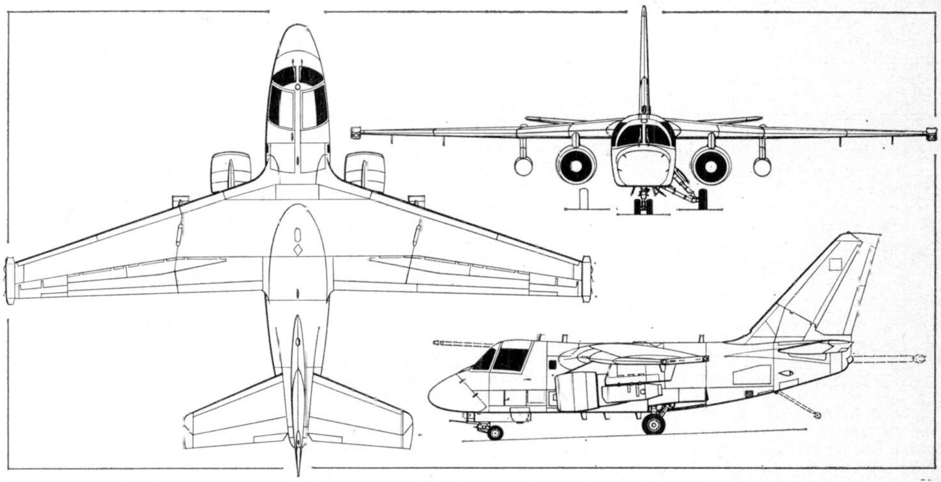

Lockheed S-3A Viking carrier-based anti-submarine aircraft (*Pilot Press*)

Lockheed S-3A Viking taking off from USS *Forrestal* during US Navy tests

fail-safe structure. Wings fold upward and inward hydraulically, outboard of engine pylons, for carrier stowage. Single-slotted Fowler-type trailing-edge flaps, operated by hydraulic power with an integral electric motor for emergency operation. Electrically-operated leading-edge flaps, extending from engine pylons to wingtips, are fully extended after 15° of trailing-edge flap movement. Ailerons augmented by under- and over-wing spoilers for roll control. All primary flight control surfaces are actuated by irreversible servos powered by dual hydraulic systems. Loss of either hydraulic system results in loss of half the available hinge movement, but the remaining system can meet all control requirements. Automatic reversion to manual control in the event of failure of both hydraulic systems. In emergency operation the spoilers are inoperative. Wing anti-icing by engine bleed air, but portions of wing leading-edges are cyclically heated to reduce consumption of bleed air.

FUSELAGE: Semi-monocoque all-metal fail-safe structure, incorporating split weapons bays with clamshell doors. Two parallel beams form a keelson from nose gear to tail-hook, strengthening the fuselage and improving cabin structural integrity by distributing catapult and arrester loads throughout the airframe. Launch tubes for 60 sonobuoys in belly. No provision for in-flight reloading of these launch tubes. Frangible canopies in top of fuselage are so designed that the crew can eject through them in emergency. Avionics bays with external access doors in forward and aft fuselage. An illuminated in-flight refuelling probe, mounted within the fuselage on the top centreline, is operated by an electric drive and protected by a positive-seal door. It can be extended or retracted in emergency by a hand crank. MAD boom, extensible in flight, housed in fuselage tail.

TAIL UNIT: Cantilever all-metal structure with swept vertical and horizontal surfaces. Fin and rudder are folded downward by hydraulic servos for carrier stowage. During fin-folding sequence the pedal input to the rudder servo is disconnected to allow the pilot to steer the nosewheel by the rudder pedals. Variable-incidence tailplane, electrically controlled. Elevator and rudder controlled by hydraulic servos. Trim tabs in elevator and rudder. Anti-icing of tailplane leading-edges by engine bleed air.

LANDING GEAR: Hydraulically-retractable tricycle type. Main units, similar to those of the LTV F-8 Crusader, are fitted with single wheels and retract rearward into wheel wells immediately aft of the split weapons bays. Nose unit similar to that of the LTV A-7 Corsair II, with twin wheels and catapult towbar, retracts rearward into fuselage. Nosewheel steering by hydraulic power. Hydraulic brakes. Arrester hook.

POWER PLANT: Two General Electric TF34-GE-2 high by-pass ratio turbofan engines, each rated at 9,275 lb (4,207 kg) st, pylon-mounted beneath the wings. Fuel in integral wing tanks, entirely within the wing box beam, one on each side of the fuselage centreline and inboard of the wing fold-line. Usable fuel capacity approximately 1,900 US gallons (7,192 litres). Two 300 US gallon (1,136 litre) jettisonable fuel tanks can be carried on underwing pylons. Single-point pressure refuelling adapter located on starboard side of fuselage aft of main landing gear door. Internal tanks may also be gravity fuelled through overwing connections. Fuel jettison system. Anti-icing of engine inlet nozzles by engine bleed air.

ACCOMMODATION: Crew of four. Pilot and co-pilot side by side on flight deck with transparent canopy. Tacco and Senso accommodated in aft cabin, with individual polarised side windows. All crew on McDonnell Douglas Escapac 1-E zero-zero ejection seats. Each seat has a rigid seat survival kit (RSSK), which can be opened during descent for inflation of life raft. Electric windscreen wipers. Windscreen surfaces electrically heated; side canopy is de-fogged with conditioned air. Liquid rain-repellent system to augment action of windscreen wipers. Cabin pressurised and air-conditioned, and each crewman's anti-exposure suit is ventilated with conditioned air from this system.

SYSTEMS: Garrett-AiResearch environmental control system, with engine bleed air supply and air-cycle refrigeration unit. Pressurisation system operates on a differential of 6·8 lb/sq in (0·42-0·56 kg/cm²), maintaining a cabin altitude of 5,000 ft (1,525 m) to a height of 25,000 ft (7,620 m) and 11,500 ft (3,505 m) cabin altitude to 40,000 ft (12,190 m). Two engine-driven pumps supply hydraulic power for two completely independent 3,000 lb/sq in (210 kg/cm²) systems. Port system supplies landing gear, flaps, brakes, wing and tail fold, arrester hook and weapons bay doors. Its secondary function is to power one side of the primary flight control servos. Starboard system powers only the primary flight controls, energising one side of the dual servo actuators; port system energises the other. Electrical system includes two 75kVA generators supplying 115-120V AC at a frequency of 400Hz. Secondary DC power is obtained from two transformer-rectifiers that deliver 28V DC at 200A. Williams Research Corporation gas turbine APU has a 5kVA generator for emergency electric power, providing 115-120V AC at 400Hz to the essential AC bus and 28V DC at 30A through the transformer-rectifiers. Emergency electric power is adequate only for essential capabilities such as those required for night flight under instrument conditions.

ELECTRONICS: ASW data processing, control and display includes Univac 1832A general-purpose digital computer, acoustic data processor, sonobuoy receiver, command signal generator, and analogue tape recorder. Non-acoustic sensors comprise AN/APS-116 high-resolution radar, OR-89/AA forward-looking infra-red (FLIR) scanner in retractable turret, AN/ASQ-81 MAD and compensation equipment, and ALR-47 passive ECM receiving and instantaneous frequency-measuring system housed in wingtip pods. Primary navigation system composed of ASN-92(V) CAINS inertial navigator, AN/APN-200 Doppler ground velocity system (DGVS), AYN-5 airspeed altitude computing set (AACS), ASN-107 attitude heading reference system (AHRS), ARS-2 sonobouy reference system (SRS), APN-201 radar altimeter and altitude warning system (RAAWS), ARN-83 LF/ADF and ARA-50 UHF/DF radio navigation aids, ARN-84(V) TACAN, and the aircraft's flight displays and interface system (FDIS). Communications equipment includes a 1,000W ARC-153 HF transceiver for long-range communication, dual ARC-156 UHF transceivers, AN/ARA-63 receiver/decoder set for use with shipboard ILS, data terminal set (DTS), OK-173 integral intercom system (ICS) and APX-72 IFF/APX-76A SIF units with altitude reporting, and AN/ASW-25B automatic carrier landing system (ACLS) communication set. Search stores are designated as LOFAR (SSQ-41), R/O (SSQ-47), DIFAR (SSQ-53), CASS (SSQ-50), DICASS (SSQ-62) and BT (SSQ-36) sonobuoys.

ARMAMENT: Split weapons bays equipped with BRU-14/A bomb rack assemblies can deploy either four MK-36 destructors, four MK-46 torpedoes, four MK-82 bombs, two MK-57 or four MK-54 depth bombs, or four MK-53 mines. BRU-11/A bomb racks installed on the two wing pylons permit carriage of SUU-44/A flare launchers, MK-52, MK-55 or MK-56 mines, MK-20-2 cluster bombs, Aero 1D auxiliary fuel tanks, or two rocket pods of type LAU-68/A (7 FFAR 2·75 in), LAU-61/A (19 FFAR 2·75 in), LAU-69/A (19 FFAR 2.75 in), or LAU-10A/A (4 FFAR 5·0 in). Alternatively, installation of TER-7 triple ejector racks on the BRU-11/A bomb racks makes it possible to carry three rocket pods, flare launchers, MK-20 cluster bombs, MK-82 bombs, MK-36 destructors, or MK-76-5 or MK-106-4 practice bombs under each wing.

DIMENSIONS, EXTERNAL:	
Wing span	68 ft 8 in (20·93 m)
Wing span, wings folded	29 ft 6 in (8·99 m)
Length overall	53 ft 4 in (16·26 m)
Length overall, tail folded	49 ft 5 in (15·06 m)
Height overall	22 ft 9 in (6·93 m)
Height overall, tail folded	15 ft 3 in (4·65 m)
Tailplane span	27 ft 0 in (8·23 m)
DIMENSIONS, INTERNAL:	
Max height	7 ft 6 in (2·29 m)
Max width	7 ft 2 in (2·18 m)
AREA:	
Wings, gross	598 sq ft (55·56 m²)
WEIGHTS (estimated):	
Weight empty	26,600 lb (12,065 kg)
Normal ASW T-O weight	42,500 lb (19,277 kg)
Max carrier landing weight	37,700 lb (17,100 kg)
PERFORMANCE (estimated):	
Max level speed	440 knots (506 mph; 814 km/h)
Max cruising speed	over 350 knots (403 mph; 649 km/h)
Loiter speed	160 knots (184 mph; 257 km/h)
Stalling speed	84 knots (97 mph; 157 km/h)
Max rate of climb at S/L	over 4,200 ft (1,280 m)/min
Service ceiling	above 35,000 ft (10,670 m)
Combat range	more than 2,000 nm (2,303 miles; 3,705 km)
Ferry range	more than 3,000 nm (3,454 miles; 5,558 km)

LOCKHEED L-1011-1 (MODEL 385) TRISTAR

In January 1966, Lockheed-California began a study of future requirements in the short/medium-haul airliner market. The design which emerged, known as the L-1011 (Lockheed Model 385 TriStar), was influenced by the published requirements of American Airlines, which specified optimum payload/range performance over the Chicago-Los Angeles route, coupled with an ability to take off from comparatively short runways with full payload.

The original design centred around a twin-turbofan configuration. Discussions which followed with American domestic carriers led to the eventual selection of a three-engined configuration, and the Rolls-Royce RB.211 high by-pass ratio turbofan was chosen as power plant.

In June 1968 the L-1011 TriStar moved to the production design stage. Construction of the first aircraft began in March 1969, and this was rolled out in September 1970. The first flight was made on 16 November 1970. On 22 December 1971 a class II provisional Type Certification was received, permitting delivery of aircraft to customers for route proving and demonstration purposes.

In early 1972 TriStar test aircraft completed successfully icing and cold-weather tests, minimum unstick speed and rejected take-off tests; and evacuation of 345 passengers and crew from the aircraft was demonstrated successfully on 6 February 1972.

Initial delivery of the L-1011 TriStar, to Eastern Air Lines for crew training, was made on 6 April, followed by a similar delivery to TWA. FAA certification was granted in the same month and the first passenger service with the TriStar was flown by Eastern on 15 April. Scheduled services began eleven days later.

By the end of 1973 Lockheed had delivered 56 TriStars to Air Canada, All Nippon Airways, Court Line, Delta Air Lines, Eastern Air Lines, Lufttransport Unternehmen and Trans World Airlines.

Approximately 15,000 workers were employed on the L-1011 programme in early 1974, at which time orders and options for 199 aircraft had been received, as follows:

	Orders	Options
Air Canada	10	9
All Nippon Airways	14	7
British Airways	9	9
Court Line Aviation	2	3
Delta Air Lines	18	12
Eastern Air Lines	37	13
Haas/Turner Investment Group	2	0
L-1011 Oreg Ltd	0	3
Lufttransport Unternehmen	1	1
Pacific Southwest Airlines	3	2
Trans World Airlines	33	11

The description which follows applies to the L-1011-1 TriStar in its initial operational form. For details of the longer-range **L-1011-100** TriStar, ordered by Saudia (2) and Cathay Pacific Airways (2), see Addenda.

TYPE: Three-turbofan commercial transport.

WINGS: Cantilever low-wing monoplane. Special Lockheed aerofoil sections. Dihedral at trailing-edge: 7° 31′ on inner wings, 5° 30′ outboard. Sweepback at quarter-chord 35°. The wing consists of a centre-section, passing through the lower fuselage, and an outer wing panel on each side. It is of conventional fail-safe construction, with aluminium surfaces, ribs and spars, and integral fuel tanks. Hydraulically-powered aluminium ailerons of conventional two-spar box construction, with aluminium honeycomb trailing-edge, in inboard and outboard sections on each wing, operate in conjunction with flight spoilers. The low-speed ailerons extend from approximately 80% of semi-span to within 10 in (25·4 cm) of the wingtips, the high-speed ailerons extend from approximately WBL 387 to WBL 480 on each wing. Double-slotted Fowler trailing-edge flaps, constructed of aluminium and aluminium honeycomb. Each flap segment consists of a honeycomb trailing-edge, a front spar, ribs, skin panels, carriages, and tracks mounted on the forward segment to provide for extension and rotation of the aft segment. A sheet metal vane surface, actuated by a linkage system during flap rotation, forms the forward section of the extended flap. Four aluminium leading-edge slats outboard of engine pylon on each wing. Each segment is mounted to two roller-supported tracks and extends in a circular motion down and forward for take-off and landing. Three leading-edge slats inboard of engine pylon on each wing, made of aluminium alloy honeycomb and sheet metal fairings. Six spoilers on the upper surface of each wing, two inboard and four outboard of the inboard aileron, constructed from bonded aluminium tapered honeycomb. No trim tabs. Flight controls fully powered. Each control surface system is controlled by a multiple redundant servo actuator system that is powered by four independent and separate hydraulic sources. Thermal de-icing of outboard wing leading-edge slats by engine bleed air.

FUSELAGE: Semi-monocoque structure of aluminium alloy. Constant cross-sectional diameter of 19 ft 7 in (5·97 m) for most of the length. Bonding utilised in skin joints, for attaching skin-doublers at joints and around openings to improve fatigue life. Skins and stringers supported by frames spaced at 20 in (0·51 m) intervals, with fail-safe straps midway between frames. These frames, with the exception of

Lockheed L-1011-1 TriStar short/medium-range transport (three Rolls-Royce RB.211-22B turbofan engines) in the insignia of All Nippon Airways

main frames and door-edge members, are 3 in (7·62 cm) deep at the sides of the cabin, increasing progressively to a depth of 6 in (15·24 cm) at the top of the fuselage and below the floor.

TAIL UNIT: Conventional cantilever structure, consisting of variable-incidence horizontal tailplane-elevator assembly and vertical fin and rudder. Primary loads of the fin are carried by a conventional box-beam structure, with ribs spaced at approx 20 in (0·51 m) centres. The rudder comprises forward and aft spars, glassfibre trailing-edges, hinge and actuator backup ribs, sheet metal formers, box surface panels and leading-edge fairings. Elevators are of similar construction. Truss members for the tailplane centre-section are built up from forged and extruded sections. Outboard of the centre-section, construction is similar to that of the fin box-beam, leading- and trailing-edges, except that the surface structure is integrally stiffened. The elevators are linked mechanically to the tailplane actuation gear, to modify its camber and improve its effectiveness. No trim tabs. Controls are fully powered, the hydraulic servo actuators receiving power from four independent hydraulic sources, under control of avionic flight control system. Control feel is provided, with the force gradient scheduled as a function of flight condition. No de-icing equipment.

LANDING GEAR: Hydraulically-retractable tricycle type, produced by Menasco Manufacturing. Twin-wheel units in tandem on each main gear; twin wheels on nose gear, which is steerable 65° on each side. Nosewheels retract forward into fuselage. Main wheels retract inward into fuselage wheel-wells. Oleo-pneumatic struts in main and nose landing gear. B. F. Goodrich forged aluminium alloy wheels of split construction. Main wheels have tubeless tyres size 50 × 20-20, Type VIII, pressure 150-165 lb/sq in (10·5-11·6 kg/cm²) for short- to medium-range operational weights, 180 lb/sq in (12·7 kg/cm²) for max-range weight. Nosewheels have tubeless tyres size 36 × 11-16, Type VII, pressure 185 lb/sq in (13·0 kg/cm²). Hydraulically-operated brakes, controlled by the rudder pedals. Anti-skid units, with individual wheel skid and modulated control, installed in the normal and alternative braking systems.

POWER PLANT: Three Rolls-Royce RB.211-22B three-shaft turbofan engines, each rated at 42,000 lb (19,050 kg) st. Two engines mounted in pods on pylons under the wings, the third mounted in the rear fuselage at the base of the fin. Engine bleed air is used to anti-ice the engine inlet lips. Two integral fuel tanks in each wing; inboard tank capacity 8,079 US gallons (30,581 litres), outboard tank capacity 3,828 US gallons (14,489 litres). Total fuel capacity 23,814 US gallons (90,140 litres). Pressure refuelling points in wing leading-edges. Oil capacity approx 9 US gallons (34 litres) per engine.

ACCOMMODATION: Crew of 13. First class and coach mixed accommodation for 256 passengers, with a maximum of 400 in all-economy configuration. Alternative intermediate seating capacities are provided by using eight seat-tracks which permit 6, 8, 9 or 10-abreast seating, with two full-length aisles. Underfloor galley. Seven lavatories are provided, two forward and five aft. Three Type A passenger doors of the upward-opening plug type on each side of the fuselage, one pair immediately aft of flight deck, one pair forward of wing, one pair aft of wing. Two Type I emergency exit doors, one each side of fuselage, at rear of cabin, replaced by two Type A doors with 10-abreast seating. Baggage and freight compartments beneath the floor, each able to accommodate eight containers, totalling 2,528 cu ft (71·58 m³) and 700 cu ft (19·8 m³) bulk cargo.

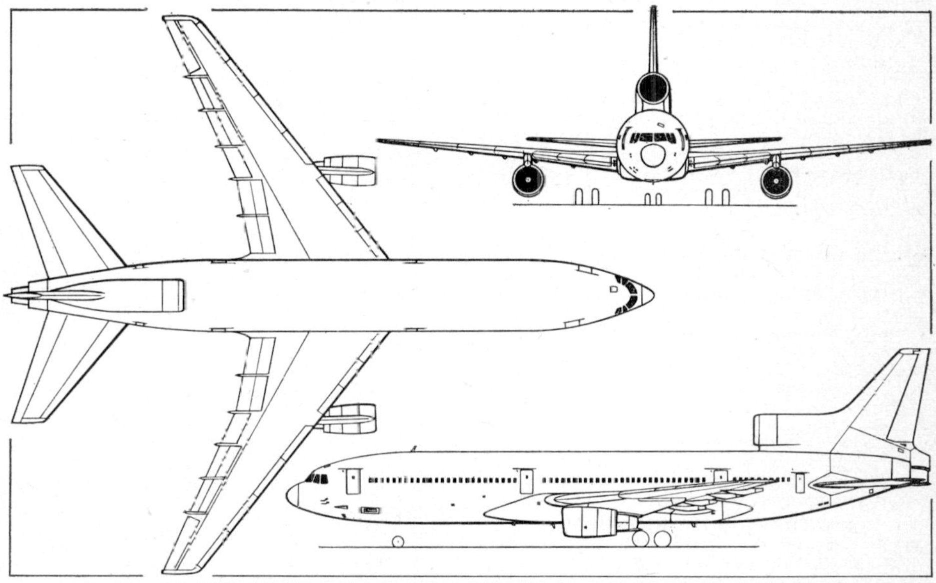

Lockheed L-1011-1 TriStar wide-bodied short/medium-range transport *(Pilot Press)*

SYSTEMS: Air-conditioning and pressurisation system, using engine bleed air or APU air combined with air-cycle refrigeration. Pressurisation system maintains equivalent of 8,000 ft (2,440 m) conditions to 42,000 ft (12,800 m). Normal cabin pressure differential 8·44 lb/sq in (0·59 kg/cm²). Four independent 3,000 lb/sq in (210 kg/cm²) hydraulic systems provide power for the primary flight control surfaces, normal brake power, landing gear retraction and nosewheel steering, etc. Electrical system includes four 120/208V 400Hz alternators, one on each engine and one driven by the APU, which is sited in the aft fuselage. APU provides ground and in-flight power, to an altitude of 30,000 ft (9,145 m), producing both shaft and pneumatic power for utilisation by the electric, environmental control and hydraulic systems. Integral electric heaters

Self-contained hydraulically-operated stairway available on the TriStar

are used to anti-ice windscreens, pitot masts and total temperature probes.

Electronics and Equipment: Standard equipment includes two ARINC 546 VHF communication transceivers, two ARINC 547 VHF navigation systems, two ARINC 568 interrogator units, an ARINC 564 weather radar system, two ARINC 572 air traffic control transponders, partial provision for a dual collision system, three vertical gyros, and full blind-flying instrumentation. Space is provided for future installation of two ARINC 533A HF transceivers and of a dual SATCOM system.

Dimensions, external:

Wing span	155 ft 4 in (47·34 m)
Wing chord at root	34 ft 4 in (10·46 m)
Wing chord at tip	10 ft 3 in (3·12 m)
Wing aspect ratio	6·95
Length overall	178 ft 8 in (54·35 m)
Height overall	55 ft 4 in (16·87 m)
Tailplane span	71 ft 7 in (21·82 m)
Wheel track	36 ft 0 in (10·97 m)
Wheelbase	70 ft 0 in (21·34 m)
Passenger doors (6):	
Height	6 ft 4 in (1·93 m)
Width	3 ft 6 in (1·07 m)
Height to sill	15 ft 1 in (4·60 m)
Emergency passenger doors (2):	
Height	5 ft 0 in (1·52 m)
Width	2 ft 0 in (0·61 m)
Height to sill	15 ft 1 in (4·60 m)
Baggage and freight compartment doors (forward and centre):	
Height	5 ft 8 in (1·73 m)
Width	5 ft 10 in (1·78 m)
Height to sill	8 ft 11 in (2·72 m)
Baggage and freight compartment doors (aft):	
Height	4 ft 0 in (1·22 m)
Width	3 ft 8 in (1·12 m)
Height to sill	9 ft 7 in (2·92 m)

Dimensions, internal:

Cabin, excluding flight deck and underfloor galley:	
Length	135 ft 11 in (41·43 m)
Max width	18 ft 11 in (5·77 m)
Max height	7 ft 11 in (2·41 m)
Floor area	2,320 sq ft (215·52 m²)
Volume	16,000 cu ft (453 m³)
Baggage holds, underfloor, containerised:	
Volume	2,528 cu ft (71·58 m³)
Freight hold, underfloor, bulk cargo:	
Volume	700 cu ft (19·8 m³)

Areas:

Wings, gross	3,456 sq ft (320·0 m²)
Ailerons (total)	160 sq ft (14·86 m²)
Trailing-edge flaps (total)	536 sq ft (49·80 m²)
Leading-edge slats (total):	
Inboard slats	124 sq ft (11·52 m²)
Outboard slats	236 sq ft (21·93 m²)
Spoilers (total)	214 sq ft (19·88 m²)
Fin	550 sq ft (51·10 m²)
Rudder	128 sq ft (11·89 m²)
Tailplane	1,282 sq ft (119·10 m²)

Weights and Loading:

Manufacturer's empty weight	222,941 lb (101,124 kg)
Operating empty weight	238,817 lb (108,325 kg)
Max payload	86,183 lb (39,092 kg)
Max T-O weight	430,000 lb (195,050 kg)
Max ramp weight	432,000 lb (195,955 kg)
Max zero-fuel weight	325,000 lb (147,420 kg)
Max landing weight	358,000 lb (162,390 kg)
Max wing loading	124·5 lb/sq ft (607·9 kg/m²)

Performance (at max T-O weight):

Max never-exceed speed (structural)	Mach 0·95 or 435 knots (500 mph; 806 km/h) CAS
Max level speed at 30,000 ft (9,145 m)	Mach 0·9
Max cruising speed at 35,000 ft (10,670 m)	Mach 0·85
Long-range cruising speed at 35,000 ft (10,670 m)	Mach 0·82
Stalling speed (T-O configuration)	125 knots (144 mph; 232 km/h) EAS
Stalling speed (cruise configuration)	166 knots (190 mph; 306 km/h) EAS
Max rate of climb at S/L	2,800 ft (853 m)/min
Service ceiling	42,000 ft (12,800 m)
Min ground turning radius	141 ft 3 in (43·05 m)
FAR take-off field length	7,590 ft (2,313 m)
FAR landing field length	5,660 ft (1,725 m)
Range with max fuel and 40,000 lb (18,145 kg) payload at Mach 0·85	3,880 nm (4,467 miles; 7,189 km)
Range with max payload (86,183 lb; 39,092 kg) at Mach 0·82	2,324 nm (2,677 miles; 4,308 km)

Operational Noise Characteristics:

T-O noise level at 3·5 nm (4 miles; 6·5 km) from start of T-O roll	97·0 EPNdB
Approach noise level at 1 nm (1·15 miles; 1·85 km) from landing threshold on 3° glideslope	103·0 EPNdB
Sideline noise level at 0·25 nm (0·29 miles; 0·47 km) from runway c/l	95·0 EPNdB

LOCKHEED L-1011-2

On 29 May 1973 Lockheed Aircraft Corporation announced plans to develop a new extended-range version of the L-1011 TriStar, under the designation L-1011-2.

This aircraft will be powered by the new Rolls-Royce RB.211-524 engine, which has a T-O rating of 48,000 lb (21,772 kg) st, providing nearly 15 per cent more power than the engines currently installed in the L-1011-1 TriStar. Max T-O weight of this version will be 516,000 lb (234,052 kg), including about 50% more fuel than the L-1011-1. With a full complement of 256 passengers it will have a range of 4,603 nm (5,300 miles; 8,530 km).

LOCKHEED-GEORGIA COMPANY

86 South Cobb Drive, Marietta, Georgia 30063

Lockheed-Georgia's main building at Marietta covers 76 acres and is one of the world's largest aircraft production plants under a single roof. Aircraft in current production on its assembly lines are the C-130 Hercules turboprop transport and its commercial counterpart, the L 100. Manufacture of the C-5 Galaxy heavy logistics transport, the largest aeroplane yet ordered into production anywhere in the world, has been completed.

Lockheed-Georgia had a total of approximately 9,600 employees at the end of 1973.

Lockheed C-130E combat transport aircraft in service with the Brazilian Air Force (*Ronaldo S. Olive*)

LOCKHEED C-130 HERCULES

USAF designations: C-130, AC-130, DC-130, HC-130, JC-130, RC-130 and WC-130
US Navy designations: C-130, EC-130 and LC-130
US Marine Corps designation: KC-130
US Coast Guard designations: EC-130 and HC-130
Canadian Armed Forces designation: CC-130
RAF designations: Hercules C.Mk 1 and W.Mk 2

The C-130 was designed to a specification issued by the USAF Tactical Air Command in 1951. Lockheed was awarded its first production contract for the C-130A in September 1952, and a total of 461 C-130As and C-130Bs was manufactured. Details of these basic versions and their many variants for special duties can be found in the 1967-68 *Jane's*. Later military versions of the C-130 are as follows:

C-130E (Lockheed Model 382-44). Extended-range development of C-130B, with four 4,050 ehp T56-A-7 turboprop engines and two 1,360 US gallon (5,145 litre) underwing fuel tanks. Normal max T-O weight is 155,000 lb (70,310 kg). Take-off at overload gross weight of 175,000 lb (79,380 kg) increases the range and endurance capabilities, with certain operating restrictions at this higher weight. Deliveries of this version began in April 1962, and by February 1974 all but one of 503 C-130Es had been delivered. Details of the basic C-130E can be found in the 1973-74 *Jane's*.

DC-130E. Version modified by LAS (which see) for drone control duties.

EC-130E. Special version of C-130E for US Coast Guard.

WC-130E. Weather reconnaissance version operated by the USAF.

C-130F (formerly GV-1U). Seven for transport duties with US Navy. Similar to KC-130F, but without underwing pylons and internal refuelling equipment. AUW 135,000 lb (61,235 kg).

KC-130F (formerly GV-1). Forty-six for US Marine Corps. Deliveries completed in November 1962. Assault transport, basically similar to C-130B, with four 4,050 ehp Allison T56-A-7 turboprops. All aircraft were re-engined subsequently with 4,508 ehp Allison T56-A-16 engines. Equipped for in-flight refuelling to service two jet aircraft simultaneously. Entire refuelling equipment can be quickly and easily installed and removed. Two C-130As loaned to USMC in the Summer of 1957 for flight refuelling tests. The production tanker version, first flown on 22 January 1960, has a tankage capacity of 3,600 US gallons (13,620 litres) in its cargo compartment. Able to fly 868 nm (1,000 miles; 1,600 km) at cruise ceiling at 295 knots (340 mph; 547 km/h), and transfer 31,000 lb (14,060 kg) of fuel at 25,000 ft (7,620 m) at a refuelling speed of 308 knots (355 mph; 571 km/h) with normal military reserves. Normal crew of five to seven.

Lockheed EC-130Q command communications aircraft of the US Navy (*T. Matsuzaki*)

C-130H. Similar to earlier Hercules models except for more powerful engines: T56-A-15 turboprops rated at 4,910 ehp for take-off, but limited to 4,508 ehp. By January 1974 a total of 360 C-130Hs, or variants, were on order or had been delivered, including 66 for the UK. A total of 20 countries have ordered versions of the C-130H.

AC-130H. A close-support conversion of the Hercules.

HC-130H. Lockheed was awarded two initial contracts in September 1963 for this extended-range air search, rescue and recovery version to be utilised by the Aerospace Rescue and Recovery Service of the USAF for aerial recovery of personnel or equipment and other duties. The US Coast Guard subsequently ordered three. New folding nose-mounted recovery system makes possible repeated pickups from ground of persons or objects weighing up to 500 lb (227 kg) including the recoverable gear. Four 4,910 ehp (limited to 4,500 ehp) Allison T56-A-15 turboprop engines, each driving a Hamilton Standard 54H60-91 four-blade constant-speed propeller. Normal fuel tankage as for C-130H. Provision for installing two 1,800 US gallon (6,184 litre) tanks in cargo compartment. Normal crew of 10, consisting of pilot, co-pilot, navigator, 2 flight mechanics, radio operator, 2 loadmasters and 2 pararescue technicians, with provision for additional pilot and navigator for long missions. Standard equipment includes four 6-man rafts, two litters, bunks, 16 personnel kits, recovery winches, 10 flare launchers. Total of 66 delivered, of which the first one flew on 8 December 1964.

C-130K (C.Mk 1). This version is basically a C-130H, modified for use by the Royal Air Force. Much of the electronics and instrumentation are of UK manufacture. Sixty-six delivered for service with RAF Air Support (now Strike) Command. First of these flew on 19 October 1966. One has since been modified by Marshall of Cambridge (Engineering) Ltd in the UK (which see), for use by the RAF Meteorological Research Flight. It entered service during the Summer of 1973 under the designation W. Mk 2.

HC-130N. Search and rescue version for recovery of aircrew and retrieval of space capsules after re-entry, using advanced direction-finding equipment. Fifteen ordered for USAF in 1969.

HC-130P. Twenty HC-130Hs have been modified into HC-130Ps with capability of refuelling helicopters in flight, and for mid-air retrieval of parachute-borne payloads. Modification involves the addition of refuelling drogue pods and associated plumbing. A typical helicopter refuelling mission will involve taking off at an AUW of 155,000 lb (70,310 kg), with 73,600 lb (33,385 kg) of fuel on board, rendezvousing with the helicopters at a radius of 575 miles (925 km), transferring 48,500 lb (22,000 kg) of fuel to the helicopters and returning 575 miles (925 km) to the point of origin.

EC-130Q. Operated by the US Navy for command communications.

KC-130R. A tanker version of the C-130H on order for the US Marine Corps. Major changes from the earlier KC-130F include engines of 4,508 ehp, increased T-O and landing weights, pylon-mounted fuel tanks to provide an additional 2,720 US gallons (10,296 litres) of fuel, plus a removable 3,600 US gallon (13,627 litre) fuel tank located in the cargo compartment.

LC-130R. Basically a C-130H with wheel-ski gear for US Navy. Main skis each approximately 20 ft 0 in (6·10 m) long by 5 ft 6 in (1·68 m) wide. The nose ski is approximately 10 ft 0 in (3·05 m) long by 5 ft 6 in (1·68 m) wide. The total ski installation weighs approximately 5,600 lb (2,540 kg). The main skis have 8° nose-up and nose-down pitch and the nose skis have 15° nose-up and nose-down pitch, to enable them to follow uneven terrain. The load-bearing surfaces of the skis are coated with Teflon plastic to reduce friction and resist ice adhesion. Provision is made for fitting JATO units.

There are also commercial versions of the Hercules and these are described separately.

The C-130 is able to deliver single loads of up to 25,000 lb (11,340 kg) by the ground proximity extraction method. This involves making a fly-past 4-5 ft (1·2-1·5 m) above the ground with the rear loading ramp open. The aircraft trails a hook which is attached by cable to the palletised cargo. The hook engages a steel cable on the ground and the cargo is extracted from the aircraft and brought to a stop on the ground in about 100 ft (30 m) by an energy absorption system manufactured by All American Engineering of Wilmington, Delaware. An alternative extraction technique involves deploying a 22 ft (6·70 m) ribbon parachute to drag the pallet from the cabin. Loads of up to 50,000 lb (22,680 kg) have been delivered by this method.

By February 1974 firm orders for all versions of the C-130 totalled 1,387, of which 1,254 had been delivered. Production rate, then three a month, was to be almost doubled during 1974-75.

The following details refer specifically to the C-130H, except where indicated otherwise:

TYPE: Medium/long-range combat transport.

WINGS: Cantilever high-wing monoplane. Wing section NACA 64A318 at root, NACA 64A412 at tip. Dihedral 2° 30′. Incidence 3° at root, 0° at tip. Sweepback at quarter-chord 0°. All-metal two-spar stressed-skin structure, with integrally-stiffened tapered machined skin panels up to 48 ft 0 in (14·63 m) long. Conventional aluminium alloy ailerons have tandem-piston hydraulic boost, operated by either of two independent hydraulic systems. Lockheed-Fowler aluminium alloy trailing-edge flaps. Trim tabs on ailerons. Leading-edge anti-iced by hot air bled from engines.

FUSELAGE: Semi-monocoque structure of aluminium and magnesium alloys.

TAIL UNIT: Cantilever all-metal stressed-skin structure. Fixed-incidence tailplane. Trim tabs on elevator and rudder. Elevator tabs use AC electrical power as primary source and DC as emergency source. Control surfaces have tandem-piston hydraulic boost. Hot-air anti-icing of tailplane leading-edge, by engine bleed air.

LANDING GEAR: Hydraulically-retractable tricycle type. Each main unit has two wheels in tandem, retracting into fairings built on to the sides of the fuselage. Nose unit has twin wheels and is steerable through 60° each side of centre. Oleo shock-absorbers. Main-wheel tyres size 56 × 20-20, pressure 80 lb/sq in (5·6 kg/cm²). Nosewheel tyres size 39 × 13·16, pressure 60 lb/sq in (4·25 kg/cm²). Goodyear aircooled hydraulic brakes with anti-skid units. Retractable combination wheel-skis available.

AC-130H gunship conversion, equipped with one 105 mm howitzer, one 40 mm cannon, two 20 mm cannon, two 7·62 mm machine-guns, FLIR, LLLTV and laser target designator

POWER PLANT: Four 4,508 ehp Allison T56-A-15 turboprop engines, each driving a Hamilton Standard type 54H60 four-blade constant-speed fully-feathering reversible-pitch propeller. Eight Aerojet-General 15KS-1000 JATO units (each 1,000 lb; 455 kg st for 15 sec) can be carried. Fuel in six integral tanks in wings, with total capacity of 6,960 US gallons (26,344 litres) and two underwing pylon tanks, each with capacity of 1,360 US gallons (5,146 litres). Total fuel capacity 9,680 US gallons (36,636 litres). Single pressure refuelling point in starboard wheel well. Fillers for overwing gravity fuelling. Oil capacity 48 US gallons (182 litres).

ACCOMMODATION: Crew of four on flight deck, comprising pilot, co-pilot, navigator and systems manager. Provision for fifth man to supervise loading. Sleeping quarters for relief crew, and galley. Flight deck and main cabin pressurised and air-conditioned. Standard complements are as follows: troops (max) 92, paratroops (max) 64, litters 74 and 2 attendants. As a cargo carrier, loads can include heavy equipment such as a 26,640 lb (12,080 kg) type F.6 refuelling trailer or a 155 mm howitzer and its high-speed tractor. Up to six pre-loaded pallets of freight can be carried. Hydraulically-operated main loading door and ramp at rear of cabin. Paratroop door on each side aft of landing gear fairing.

SYSTEMS: Air-conditioning and pressurisation system max pressure differential 7·5 lb/sq in (0·53 kg/cm²). Two independent hydraulic systems, pressure 3,000 lb/sq in (210 kg/cm²). Electrical system supplied by four 40kVA AC generators, plus one 20kVA auxiliary generator driven by APU. AiResearch gas-turbine APU for engine starting, engine pre-heat, ground air-conditioning and driving air-turbine motor with alternator.

DIMENSIONS, EXTERNAL:

Wing span	132 ft 7 in (40·41 m)
Wing chord at root	16 ft 0 in (4·88 m)
Wing chord, mean	13 ft 8½ in (4·16 m)
Wing aspect ratio	10·09
Length overall:	
all except HC-130H	97 ft 9 in (29·78 m)
HC-130H, recovery system folded	98 ft 9 in (30·10 m)
HC-130H, recovery system spread	106 ft 4 in (32·41 m)
Height over tail	38 ft 3 in (11·66 m)
Tailplane span	52 ft 8 in (16·05 m)
Wheel track	14 ft 3 in (4·35 m)
Wheelbase	32 ft 0¾ in (9·77 m)
Propeller diameter	13 ft 6 in (4·11 m)
Main cargo door (rear of cabin):	
Height	9 ft 1 in (2·77 m)
Width	10 ft 0 in (3·05 m)
Height to sill	3 ft 5 in (1·03 m)
Paratroop doors (each):	
Height	6 ft 0 in (1·83 m)
Width	3 ft 0 in (0·91 m)
Height to sill	3 ft 5 in (1·03 m)

DIMENSIONS, INTERNAL:

Cabin, excluding flight deck:	
Length without ramp	41 ft 5 in (12·60 m)
Length with ramp	51 ft 8½ in (15·73 m)
Max width	10 ft 3 in (3·13 m)
Max height	9 ft 2¾ in (2·81 m)
Floor area, excluding ramp	425 sq ft (39·5 m²)
Volume, including ramp	4,300 cu ft (121·7 m³)

AREAS:

Wings, gross	1,745 sq ft (162·12 m²)
Ailerons (total)	110 sq ft (10·22 m²)
Trailing-edge flaps (total)	342 sq ft (31·77 m²)
Fin	225 sq ft (20·90 m²)
Rudder, including tab	75 sq ft (6·97 m²)
Tailplane	381 sq ft (35·40 m²)
Elevators, including tabs	155 sq ft (14·40 m²)

WEIGHTS AND LOADINGS:

Weight empty, equipped	75,621 lb (34,300 kg)
Max payload	43,521 lb (19,740 kg)
Max normal T-O weight	155,000 lb (70,310 kg)
Max overload T-O weight	175,000 lb (79,380 kg)
Max zero-fuel weight	119,142 lb (54,040 kg)
Max landing weight	130,000 lb (58,970 kg)
Max wing loading	89 lb/sq ft (434·5 kg/m²)
Max power loading	8·6 lb/ehp (3·9 kg/ehp)

PERFORMANCE (at max T-O weight, unless indicated otherwise):

Max level speed	333 knots (384 mph; 618 km/h)
Max cruising speed:	
C-130H	326 knots (375 mph; 603 km/h)
HC-130H	318 knots (366 mph; 589 km/h)
Econ cruising speed	295 knots (340 mph; 547 km/h)
Stalling speed	100 knots (115 mph; 185 km/h)
Max rate of climb at S/L:	
C-130H	1,900 ft (579 m)/min
HC-130H	1,820 ft (555 m)/min
Service ceiling at 130,000 lb (58,970 kg) AUW	33,000 ft (10,060 m)
Service ceiling, one engine out, at 130,000 lb (58,970 kg) AUW	26,500 ft (8,075 m)
Min ground turning radius	63 ft (19·2 m)
Runway LCN at 155,000 lb (70,310 kg) AUW:	
asphalt	37
concrete	42
T-O run	3,580 ft (1,091 m)
T-O to 50 ft (15 m)	5,160 ft (1,573 m)
Landing from 50 ft (15 m) at 100,000 lb (45,360 kg) AUW	2,430 ft (741 m)
Landing from 50 ft (15 m) at max landing weight	2,750 ft (838 m)
Landing run at max landing weight	1,750 ft (533 m)
Range with max payload, with 5% reserve and allowance for 30 min at S/L	2,160 nm (2,487 miles; 4,002 km)
Range with max fuel, including external tanks, 20,000 lb (9,070 kg) payload and reserve of 5% initial fuel plus 30 min at S/L	4,460 nm (5,135 miles; 8,264 km)

LOCKHEED L 100 SERIES COMMERCIAL HERCULES

Following the production of early C-130 military Hercules aircraft, Lockheed-Georgia decided to offer a commercial version of this heavy transport, since when several models have appeared. Details of these follow:

Model 382. First commercial Hercules, with the civil registration N1130E, used for FAA certification and demonstration. FAA Type Certificate for Class A cargo was received on 16 February 1965. Derived from the military C-130E, it was powered by Allison 501-D22 turboprop engines. Converted subsequently to an L 100-20, it flew for the first time in this configuration on 19 April 1968. The Model 382 is no longer available.

Lockheed L 100-30 Hercules commercial transport in the insignia of Saturn Airways *(Norman E. Taylor)*

Model 382B (and L 100). Certificated on 5 October 1965 for Class E cargo, the Model 382B retained all features of the Model 382, while slight differences in cargo loading systems produced the L 100. Operators have included Alaska Airlines, Delta Air Lines, Interior Airways, Pacific Western Airlines, Pakistan International Airlines and Zambian Air Cargoes. This model is no longer available, though several are still in service.

Model 382E (L 100-20). Certificated on 4 October 1968, this "stretched" version of the Hercules is re-designated L 100-20 and has a 100 in (2·54 m) fuselage extension. It has a 60 in (1·52 m) fuselage plug inserted aft of the forward crew door and a 40 in (1·02 m) plug aft of the paratroop doors. It is powered by Allison 501-D22A engines. Operators include Alaska International Air, Delta Air Lines, Saturn Airways and Southern Air Transport in the US; Pacific Western Airlines in Canada; SATCO in Peru; Safair Freighters in the Republic of South Africa; the Kuwait Air Force; the Peruvian Air Force; and the Philippine government.

Model 382F (L 100-20). An L-100-20 powered by Allison 501-D22 engines. This model is no longer in production, but individual aircraft with the lower-rated engine may still be in service. A Model 382F is redesignated 382E when engines are updated to the power output of the Allison 501-22A.

Model 382G (L 100-30). First proposed in October 1969, this aircraft is generally similar to the Model 382E, but has had the fuselage extended a further 80 in (2·03 m). Rear cargo windows, paratroop doors and provision for JATO have been eliminated. Saturn Airways was the first operator of this model, with services beginning in December 1970. Safair Freighters and Southern Air Transport also operate 382Gs, and one is on order for the Republic of Gabon.

The details given for the C-130H apply also to the L 100-20 and L 100-30 except as follows:

Type: Medium/long-range commercial transport.

Landing Gear: As for C-130, except main-wheel tyre pressure 47-107 lb/sq in (3·3-7·5 kg/cm²) and nosewheel tyre pressure 60 lb/sq in (4·2 kg/cm²).

Power Plant: Either four 4,050 ehp Allison 501-D22 or four 4,508 ehp Allison 501-D22A turboprop engines.

Dimensions, external:
Wing span 132 ft 7 in (40·41 m)
Length overall:
L 100-20 106 ft 0½ in (32·32 m)
L 100-30 112 ft 8½ in (34·35 m)
Height overall 38 ft 3 in (11·66 m)
Tailplane span 52 ft 8 in (16·05 m)
Wheel track 14 ft 3 in (4·34 m)
Wheelbase:
L 100-20 37 ft 1¼ in (11·31 m)
L 100-30 40 ft 4¾ in (12·31 m)
Crew door (integral steps):
Height 3 ft 10 in (1·17 m)
Width 2 ft 6 in (0·76 m)
Height to sill 3 ft 5 in (1·04 m)
Rear cargo door:
Height 9 ft 1 in (2·77 m)
Width 10 ft 0 in (3·05 m)
Height to sill 3 ft 5 in (1·04 m)

Dimensions, internal:
Cabin, excluding flight deck:
Length:
L 100-20 49 ft 1½ in (14·97 m)
L 100-30 55 ft 5¼ in (16·90 m)
Max width 10 ft 3 in (3·12 m)
Max height 9 ft 0 in (2·74 m)
Floor area, ramp 103 sq ft (9·57 m²)
Floor area, excluding ramp:
L 100-20 499 sq ft (46·36 m²)
L 100-30 563 sq ft (52·30 m²)

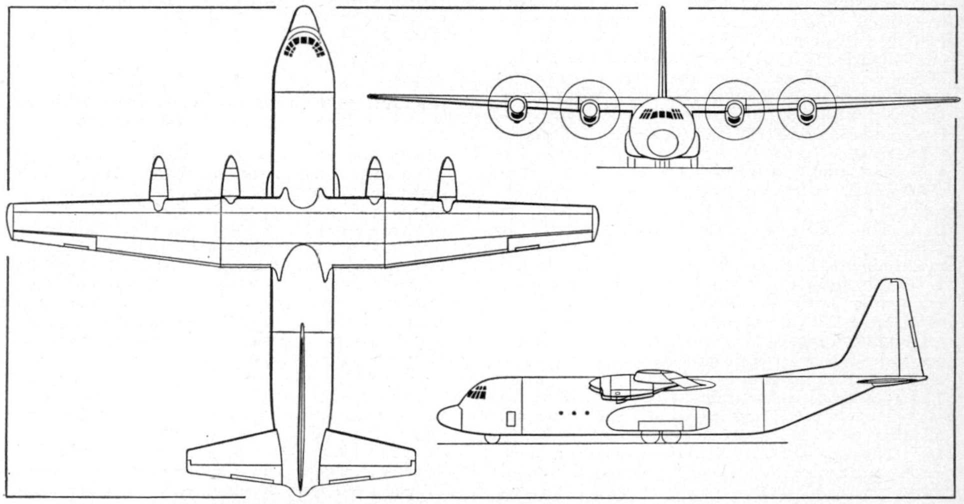

Lockheed L 100-30 (Model 382G) stretched version of the commercial Hercules *(Pilot Press)*

Volume, including ramp:
L 100-20 5,307 cu ft (150·28 m³)
L 100-30 6,057 cu ft (171·5 m³)

Areas:
Wings, gross 1,745 sq ft (162·12 m²)
Ailerons (total) 110 sq ft (10·22 m²)
Trailing-edge flaps (total) 342 sq ft (31·77 m²)
Fin 225 sq ft (20·90 m²)
Rudder, including tab 75 sq ft (6·97 m²)
Tailplane 381 sq ft (35·40 m²)
Elevators, including tab 155 sq ft (14·40 m²)

Weights and Loadings:
Operating weight, empty:
L 100-20 72,945 lb (33,087 kg)
L 100-30 73,598 lb (33,383 kg)
Max payload:
L 100-20 47,055 lb (21,343 kg)
L 100-30 51,402 lb (23,315 kg)
Max zero-fuel weight:
L 100-20 120,000 lb (54,430 kg)
L 100-30 125,000 lb (56,700 kg)
Max T-O weight:
L 100-20, L 100-30 155,000 lb (70,308 kg)
Max ramp weight:
L 100-20, L 100-30 155,800 lb (70,670 kg)
Max landing weight:
L 100-20 130,000 lb (58,970 kg)
L 100-30 135,000 lb (61,235 kg)
Max wing loading 88·8 lb/sq ft (433·5 kg/m²)
Max power loading:
L 100-20, L 100-30 8·6 lb/ehp (3·90 kg/ehp)

Performance (at max T-O weight):
Max cruising speed at 20,000 ft (6,100 m) at 120,000 lb (54,430 kg) AUW:
L 100-20, L 100-30
327 knots (377 mph; 607 km/h)
Landing speed:
L 100-20 126 knots (145 mph; 233 km/h)
L 100-30 128 knots (147 mph; 237 km/h)
Max rate of climb at S/L:
L 100-20, L 100-30 1,900 ft (579 m)/min
Min ground turning radius:
L 100-20 88 ft (26·8 m)
L 100-30 90 ft (27·5 m)
Runway LCN:
Asphalt 37
Concrete 42
FAA T-O field length:
L 100-20, L 100-30 6,000 ft (1,829 m)
FAA landing field length, at max landing weight:
L 100-20 4,760 ft (1,450 m)
L-100-30 4,830 ft (1,472 m)
Range with max payload, 45 min fuel reserve:
L 100-20 2,220 nm (2,556 miles; 4,113 km)
L 100-30 1,815 nm (2,090 miles; 3,363 km)
Range with zero payload, 45 min fuel reserve:
L 100-20 4,100 nm (4,721 miles; 7,597 km)
L 100-30 4,081 nm (4,699 miles; 7,562 km)

Operational Noise Characteristics (L 100-20, -30):
T-O noise level at 3·5 nm (4 miles; 6·5 km) from start of T-O roll 95·0 EPNdB
Approach noise level at 1 nm (1·15 miles; 1·85 km) from landing threshold on 3° glide-slope 101·5 EPNdB
Sideline noise level at 0·35 nm (0·40 miles; 0·65 km) from runway C/L 97·8 EPNdB

LOCKHEED MODEL 1329 JETSTAR

USAF designation: C-140

First announced in March 1957, the JetStar is a jet-powered utility transport with normal accommodation for a crew of two and eight to ten passengers. The first prototype, built as a private venture, flew on 4 September 1957, only 241 days after its design was started.

The two prototype JetStars were each powered originally by two Bristol Siddeley Orpheus turbojets, mounted on each side of the rear fuselage. One of them was re-engined in December 1959 with four Pratt & Whitney J60-P-5 (JT12-6) turbojets mounted in lateral pairs in the same position. This power plant was standardised for the production version, which first flew in the Summer of 1960 and received FAA Type Approval in August 1961.

By mid-1973, 162 JetStars had been delivered for corporate and private use throughout the world, including ten delivered during the previous year. These represent all of the planned production of the Model 1329. Active consideration was already being given to a new longer-range version, with uprated turbofan engines, and it was reported that Garrett Corporation would produce independently a prototype JetStar conversion with AiResearch TFE 731-3 turbofans, flat-rated at 3,700 lb (1,678 kg) st to 76°F. Lockheed announced subsequently that a new version, designated JetStar II, would enter production in 1974, and this is described separately.

Two versions of the JetStar continue to serve with the USAF, as follows:

C-140A. Five delivered to the Air Force Communications Service, which is responsible for inspecting worldwide military navigation aids. First delivered in Summer of 1962.

VC-140B. Eleven transport versions for operation by the special air missions wing of MAC. Cabin layout of this version accommodates a crew of three and eight passengers. First delivered in late 1961.

A full description of the JetStar can be found in the 1973-74 *Jane's*.

LOCKHEED MODEL 1329-25 JETSTAR II

The Lockheed JetStar II, which was first announced in the Summer of 1973, has an airframe generally similar to that of the earlier JetStar (1973-74 *Jane's*), but with detail changes in configuration and equipment.

Design of the Model 1329-25 began in October 1972, and the major change involved the selection of four AiResearch TFE 731-3 turbofan engines, flat-rated at 3,700 lb (1,678 kg) st to 76°F (24·4°C), to replace the 3,300 lb (1,497 kg) st Pratt & Whitney JT12 turbojet engines of the JetStar. The new power plant offers significant improvement in both range and noise levels, as well as allowing an increase in maximum take-off weight.

Production of the JetStar II, at Lockheed-Georgia's Marietta plant, was scheduled to begin in mid-1974, and deliveries of first production aircraft should begin in late 1975. In addition, AiResearch offers a re-engining scheme to convert early JetStars to JetStar II standard.

Type: Four-jet light utility transport.

Wings: Cantilever low-wing monoplane. Wing section NACA 63A112 at root, NACA 63A309 (modified) at tip. Dihedral 2°. Incidence 1° at root, —1° at tip. Sweepback at quarter-chord 30°. Conventional fail-safe stressed-skin structure of high-strength aluminium. Bending loads carried by integral skin/stringer extrusion and sheet ribs, shear loads by three beams. Plain aluminium alloy ailerons; trim tab located near the centre of the trailing-edge of the port aileron. An electrically-powered dual trim actuator is located within the aileron directly forward of the trim tab. Hydraulically-boosted aileron controls are powered by both normal and standby hydraulic systems, either of which is capable of operating the ailerons independently. Manual aileron control is possible in the event of complete hydraulic failure. Aileron booster actuators manufactured by National Waterlift Company. Double-slotted all-metal trailing-edge flaps. Hinged leading-edge flaps. No spoilers. Rubber-boot de-icers on leading-edge.

Fuselage: Semi-monocoque fail-safe structure of light alloy. The nose section, crew compartment and cabin are pressurised. The aft section, where most of the aircraft's system components are mounted, is unpressurised. Hydraulically-operated speed-brake on underside of fuselage aft of pressurised compartment.

Tail Unit: Cantilever light alloy structure with tailplane mounted part-way up fin. Variable incidence is achieved by the fin being pivoted, thus allowing an electro-mechanical dual actuator to move the entire tail unit to rotate the tailplane. No trim tabs in elevators. Mechanically-operated elevator control system is hydraulically-boosted, using a National Waterlift Company actuator, sited in the aft fuselage equipment area. The rudder is mechanically controlled, with servo tab assistance. Two pneumatic cylinders, biased by engine bleed air, automatically assist directional control in the event of a power loss from either engine. Details of tail unit de-icing system not yet finalised.

Landing Gear: Hydraulically-retractable tricycle type, with twin wheels on all units. Pneumatic emergency extension. Main units retract inward, nosewheels forward. Oleo-pneumatic shock-absorbers. Main wheels with tubeless tyres size 26 × 6·60, EHP Type VII, 14-ply rating with reinforced tread, pressure 220 lb/sq in (15·5 kg/cm²). Nosewheels with tubeless chine tyres size 18 × 4·40, EHP Type VII, 12-ply rating with reinforced tread, pressure 220 lb/sq in (15·5 kg/cm²). Hytrol fully-modulated anti-skid units.

Power Plant: Four AiResearch TFE 731-3 turbofan engines, flat-rated at 3,700 lb (1,678 kg) st to 76°F (24·4 °C), mounted in lateral pairs on sides of rear fuselage. Thrust reversers fitted. Air intake anti-icing provided by engine bleed air. Fuel in four integral wing tanks and two non-removable external auxiliary tanks glove-mounted on the wings. Capacity of numbers 1 and 4 internal tanks each 375 US gallons (1,420 litres); numbers 2 and 3 internal tanks each 390 US gallons (1,476 litres), auxiliary tanks each 565 US gallons (2,139 litres). Total fuel capacity 2,660 US gallons (10,070 litres). Gravity refuelling point above each tank, or optional single-point pressure refuelling from starboard wing root. Oil capacity 6·4 US gallons (24·2 litres).

Accommodation: Normal accommodation for crew of two and ten passengers, with wardrobe, galley and toilet aft of cabin and baggage compartments fore and aft. Layout and furnishing can be varied to suit customer's requirements. Optional jump-seat available for crew compartment. Door at forward end of fuselage, on port side, opens by moving inward and sliding aft. The fourth window aft on each side of the cabin is a CAR Type IV emergency exit, of plug type and removed inward. Accommodation heated, ventilated, air-conditioned and pressurised. High-pressure oxygen system for passengers and crew standard. Integral electric heaters for windscreen anti-icing and demisting.

Systems: Air-conditioning and pressurisation system not yet finalised. Two independent hydraulic systems with engine-driven pumps, pressure 3,000 lb/sq in (210 kg/cm²), to operate landing gear, wheel brakes, nosewheel steering, flight control booster units, flaps, speed-brake and thrust reversers. Separate pneumatic systems installed for emergency extension of the landing gear. Air bottles can be manually discharged into the down ports of the landing gear actuators. Two pneumatic cylinders provided to assist directional control if engine power lost. Four 28V 300A engine-driven starter/generators power main DC buses. Two high-discharge 24V 34Ah nickel-cadmium batteries for engine starting and emergency power. Three 3,000VA single-phase 400Hz 115V rotary inverters provide AC power for electronics equipment, flight and engine instruments, and windscreen anti-icing, two being on-load and one on standby. High-pressure oxygen system, 1,800 lb/sq in (126·6 kg/cm²) reduced to 70-90 lb/sq in (4·92 to 6·33 kg/cm²) at the cylinder, provides selective dilution demand or 100 per cent positive pressure demand for crew. A separate 100 per cent demand system with safety pressure and manual control for dilution is installed for passengers. An altitude control valve activates the passenger system when cabin altitude exceeds 14,000 feet, the masks being presented automatically. APU for ground air-conditioning and electrical power is optional.

Dimensions, external:

Wing span	54 ft 5 in (16·60 m)
Wing chord at root	13 ft 7¾ in (4·16 m)
Wing chord at tip	5 ft 1 in (1·55 m)
Wing aspect ratio	5·27
Length overall	60 ft 5 in (18·42 m)
Length of fuselage	58 ft 9½ in (17·92 m)
Height overall	20 ft 5 in (6·23 m)
Tailplane span	24 ft 9 in (7·55 m)
Wheel track	12 ft 3½ in (3·75 m)
Wheelbase	20 ft 7 in (6·28 m)
Cabin door:	
Height	4 ft 11 in (1·50 m)
Width	2 ft 2½ in (0·67 m)
Height to sill	approx 4 ft 6 in (1·37 m)
Servicing door (underfuselage), diameter	2 ft 0 in (0·61 m)
Emergency exits, each:	
Height	1 ft 7¼ in (0·49 m)
Width	2 ft 2½ in (0·66 m)

Dimensions, internal:

Cabin, excluding flight deck:	
Length	28 ft 2½ in (8·59 m)
Max width	6 ft 2½ in (1·89 m)
Max height	6 ft 1 in (1·85 m)
Volume	850 cu ft (24·07 m³)
Baggage hold volume:	
stbd forward	43·1 cu ft (1·25 m³)
port forward	29·8 cu ft (0·84 m³)
centre aft	37·0 cu ft (1·05 m³)

Areas:

Wings, gross	542·5 sq ft (50·40 m²)
Ailerons (total)	48·8 sq ft (4·53 m²)
Trailing-edge flaps (extended, total)	62·6 sq ft (5·82 m²)
Leading-edge flaps (total)	34·0 sq ft (3·16 m²)
Speed-brake	9·2 sq ft (0·85 m²)
Fin	94·0 sq ft (8·73 m²)
Rudder, including tab	16·2 sq ft (1·51 m²)
Tailplane	117·8 sq ft (10·94 m²)
Elevators	31·2 sq ft (2·90 m²)

Weights and Loadings:

Basic operating weight	24,178 lb (10,967 kg)
Max payload	2,822 lb (1,280 kg)
Max T-O weight	43,750 lb (19,844 kg)
Max ramp weight	44,000 lb (19,958 kg)
Max zero-fuel weight	27,000 lb (12,247 kg)
Max landing weight	36,000 lb (16,329 kg)
Max wing loading	80·8 lb/sq ft (394·3 kg/m²)
Max power loading	2·96 lb/lb st (2·96 kg/kg st)

Performance (at max T-O weight except where indicated):

Max never-exceed speed	Mach 0·90
Max level and cruising speed at 23,000 ft (7,010 m)	479 knots (552 mph; 888 km/h)
Econ cruising speed at 35,000 ft (10,670 m)	441 knots (508 mph; 817 km/h)
Stalling speed, T-O flap setting	123 knots (142 mph; 229 km/h)
Max rate of climb at S/L	4,100 ft (1,250 m)/min
Rate of climb at S/L, one engine out	2,450 ft (747 m)/min
Service ceiling	38,000 ft (11,580 m)
Service ceiling, one engine out	30,000 ft (9,145 m)
T-O to 50 ft (15 m)	5,250 ft (1,600 m)
Landing from 50 ft (15 m) at max landing weight	3,900 ft (1,189 m)
Landing run at max landing weight	2,550 ft (777 m)
Range with max fuel, 30 min reserve	2,770 nm (3,189 miles; 5,132 km)

First 731 JetStar re-engined with TFE 731-3 turbofans by AiResearch Aviation Company. The JetStar II will be generally similar

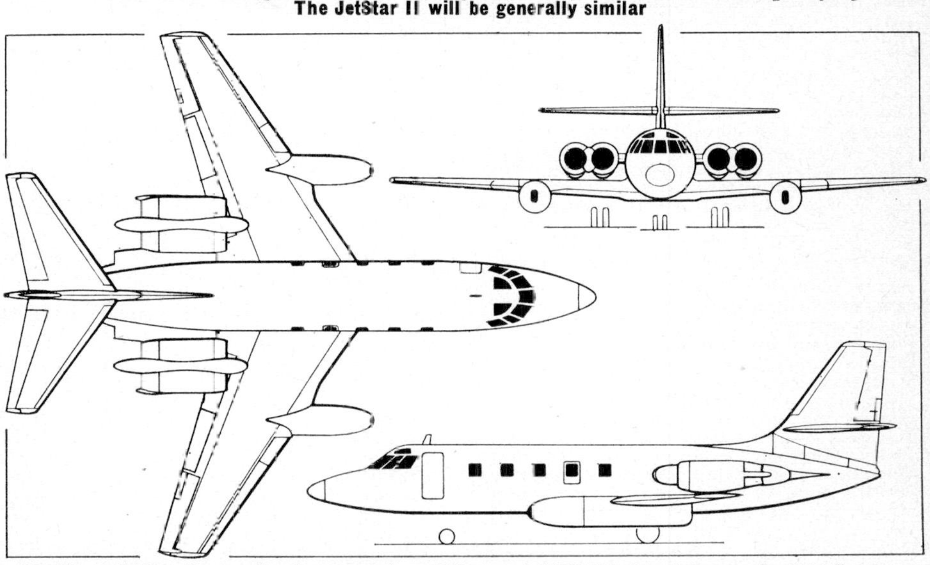
Lockheed JetStar II executive transport (four AiResearch TFE 731-3 turbofan engines) (*Pilot Press*)

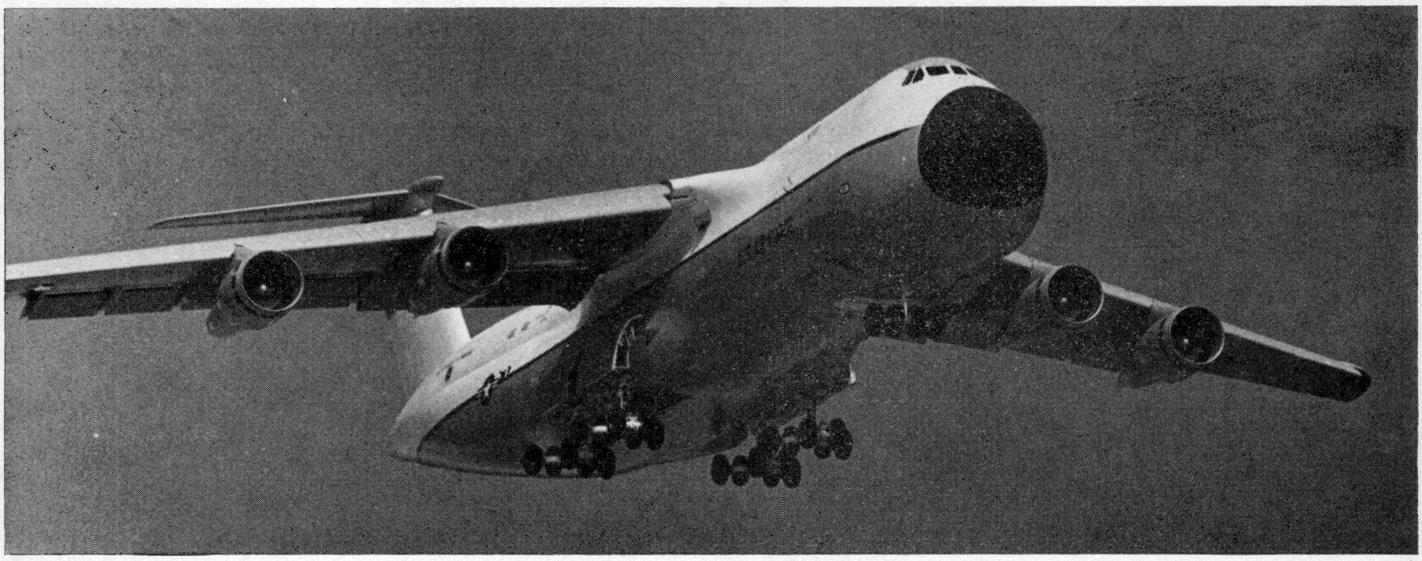

Lockheed C-5A Galaxy long-range military heavy transport (four General Electric TF39-GE-1 turbofan engines)

Range with max payload, 30 min reserve
2,600 nm (2,994 miles; 4,818 km)

LOCKHEED C-5 GALAXY

USAF designation: C-5A

Design studies for a very large logistics transport for Military Airlift Command (then MATS) began in 1963, when the requirement was for a 600,000 lb (272,200 kg) aircraft known by the designation CX-4. Eventually, this and other requirements evolved into a specification known as CX-HLS (Cargo, Experimental-Heavy Logistics System).

Following an initial design competition in May 1964, contracts were awarded to Boeing, Douglas and Lockheed to develop their designs further. At this time, the requirement was for an aircraft with a gross weight of about 700,000 lb (317,500 kg), to which the definitive designation C-5A and the name Galaxy were allocated. Large contracts also went to Pratt & Whitney and General Electric, to finance the development of prototype power plants for the C-5A.

In August 1965, the General Electric GE1/6 turbofan was selected for continued development. In October, Lockheed was nominated as prime contractor for the airframe. Construction of the first C-5A was started in August 1966, and it flew for the first time on 30 June 1968; the first operational aircraft (the ninth C-5A built) was delivered to Military Airlift Command on 17 December 1969. Lockheed-Georgia and the USAF assigned the first eight aircraft to a flight test programme that extended into mid-1971. Contracts were placed covering the manufacture of 81 C-5As for the USAF. About 50% of the work, in terms of payments, was subcontracted.

In May 1973 the 81st C-5A was delivered, and by the end of 1973 the fleet had accumulated more than 136,000 flight hours. The value of the C-5A for rapid movement of large and/or heavy pieces of equipment has been demonstrated frequently since these aircraft became operational. Loads such as two M-48 tanks, each weighing 99,000 lb (45,000 kg), or three CH-47 Chinook helicopters, have been airlifted over transoceanic ranges.

TYPE: Heavy logistics transport aircraft.

WINGS: Cantilever high-wing monoplane. Wing section NACA 0012 (mod) at 20% span, NACA 0011 (mod) at 43·7% and 70% span. Anhedral 5° 30′ at quarter-chord. Incidence 3° 30′ at root. Sweepback at quarter-chord 25°. Conventional fail-safe box structure of built-up spars and machined aluminium alloy extruded skin panels. Statically-balanced aluminium alloy ailerons. Modified Fowler-type aluminium alloy trailing-edge flaps. Simple hinged aluminium alloy spoilers forward of flaps. No trim tabs. Sealed inboard slats and slotted outboard slats on leading-edges. Ailerons and spoilers operated by hydraulic servo actuators. Trailing-edge flaps and leading-edge slats actuated by ball screwjack and torque tube system.

FUSELAGE: Conventional semi-monocoque fail-safe structure of 7079-T6 and 7075-T6 aluminium alloy and titanium alloy.

TAIL UNIT: Cantilever all-metal T-Tail. All surfaces swept; anhedral on tailplane. All components are single-cell box structures with integrally-stiffened aluminium alloy skin panels. Variable-incidence tailplane. Elevators in four sections; rudder in two sections. No trim tabs. Rudder and elevators operated through hydraulic servo actuators. Tailplane actuated through hydraulically-powered screwjack. No anti-icing equipment.

LANDING GEAR: Retractable nosewheel type. Nose unit retracted rearward by hydraulically-driven ballscrews. Main units rotated through 90° and retracted inward via hydraulically-driven gearbox. Single nose shock-strut and four main-gear shock-struts are of Bendix oleo-pneumatic dual-chamber type. Four wheels on nose unit. Four main units (two in tandem on each side) each comprise a "triangular footprint" six-wheel bogie made up of a pair of wheels forward of the shock-strut and two pairs aft. All 28 tyres size 49 × 17-20 type VII 26-ply. Tyre pressures: main 111 lb/sq in (7·80 kg/cm²), nose 137 lb/sq in (9·63 kg/cm²) with in-flight deflation capability. Goodyear aircooled beryllium disc brakes, with fully-modulating anti-skid units. Crosswind positioning of all units 20° to port or starboard by servo-controlled hydraulically-powered cylinders. Ground manoeuvrability enhanced by castoring forward main units.

POWER PLANT: Four General Electric TF39-GE-1 turbofan engines, each rated at 41,100 lb (18,642 kg) st. Twelve integral fuel tanks in wings between front and rear spars, comprising four main tanks (each 3,625 US gallons; 13,721 litres), four auxiliary tanks (each 4,625 US gallons: 17,507 litres) and four extended-

A Lockheed C-5A Galaxy of the USAF accepts what is, for it, part of a conventional load

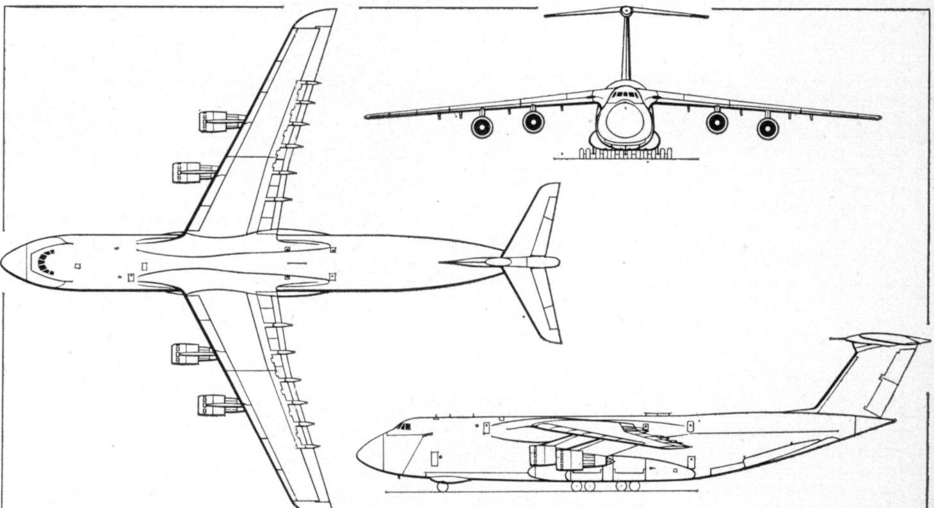

Lockheed C-5A Galaxy four-turbofan military heavy transport aircraft (*Pilot Press*)

range tanks (each 4,000 US gallons; 15,142 litres). Total usable capacity 49,000 US gallons (185,480 litres). Two refuelling points each side, in forward part of main landing gear pods. Flight refuelling capability, via inlet in upper forward fuselage, over flight engineer's station (compatible with KC-135 tanker). Oil capacity 36·4 US gallons (138 litres).

ACCOMMODATION: Normal crew of five, consisting of pilot, co-pilot, flight engineer, navigator and loadmaster, with rest area for 15 people (relief crew, couriers, etc) at front of upper deck. Basic version has seats for 75 troops on rear part of upper deck, aft of wing box. Provision for carrying 270 troops on lower deck, but aircraft is intended primarily as freighter. Typical freight loads include two M-60 tanks or sixteen ¾ ton lorries; or one M-60 and two Bell Iroquois helicopters, five M-113 personnel carriers, one M-59 2½ ton truck and an M-151 ¼ ton truck; or 10 Pershing missiles with tow and launch vehicles; or 36 standard 463L load pallets. "Visor" type upward-hinged nose, and loading ramp, permit straight-in loading into front of hold, under flight deck. Rear straight-in loading via ramp which forms undersurface of rear fuselage. Side panels of rear fuselage, by ramp, hinge outward to improve access on ground but do not need to open for air-drop operations in view of width of ramp. Provision for Aerial Delivery System (ADS) kits for paratroops or cargo. Two passenger doors on port side, at rear end of upper and lower decks. Two crew doors on port side, at forward end of upper and lower decks. Entire accommodation pressurised and air-conditioned.

SYSTEMS: Electronically-controlled air-conditioning and pressurisation systems: pressure differential 8·2 lb/sq in (0·58 kg/cm²). Four separate hydraulic systems, pressure 3,000 lb/sq in (210 kg/cm²) each, supply flying control and utility systems. Electrical system includes four 60/80kVA AC engine-driven generators. Two APUs to provide auxiliary pneumatic, hydraulic and electrical power.

ELECTRONICS AND EQUIPMENT: Communications and navigation radio to military requirements. Norden radar. Nortronics inertial navigation system. Special equipment includes electronic Malfunction Detection, Analysis and Recording subsystem (MADAR) which scans and analyses over 800 test points.

DIMENSIONS, EXTERNAL:
Wing span 222 ft 8½ in (67·88 m)
Wing chord at root 45 ft 5·3 in (13·85 m)
Wing chord at tip 15 ft 4 in (4·67 m)
Wing aspect ratio 7·75
Length overall 247 ft 10 in (75·54 m)
Length of fuselage 230 ft 7¼ in (70·29 m)
Height overall 65 ft 1½ in (19·85 m)
Tailplane span 68 ft 8½ in (20·94 m)
Wheel track (between outer wheels) 37 ft 5½ in (11·42 m)
Wheelbase (c/l main gear to c/l nose gear) 72 ft 11 in (22·23 m)
Crew door (lower deck):
Height 5 ft 11 in (1·80 m)
Width 3 ft 4 in (1·02 m)
Height to sill 12 ft 11 in (3·94 m)
Passenger door (lower deck):
Height 6 ft 0 in (1·83 m)
Width 3 ft 0 in (0·91 m)
Height to sill 11 ft 8 in (3·56 m)
Aft loading opening (ramp lowered):
Max height 12 ft 10¾ in (3·93 m)
Max width 19 ft 0 in (5·79 m)
Aft straight-in loading:
Max height 9 ft 6 in (2·90 m)
Max width 19 ft 0 in (5·79 m)

DIMENSIONS, INTERNAL:
Cabins, excluding flight deck:
Length:
upper deck, forward 39 ft 4 in (11·99 m)
upper deck, aft 59 ft 8½ in (18·20 m)
lower deck, without ramp 121 ft 1 in (36·91 m)
lower deck, with ramp 144 ft 7 in (44·07 m)
Max width:
upper deck, forward 13 ft 9½ in (4·20 m)
upper deck, aft 13 ft 0 in (3·96 m)
lower deck 19 ft 0 in (5·79 m)
Max height:
upper deck 7 ft 6 in (2·29 m)
lower deck 13 ft 6 in (4·11 m)
Floor area:
upper deck, forward 540 sq ft (50·17 m²)
upper deck, aft 776·1 sq ft (72·10 m²)
lower deck, without ramp 2,300·9 sq ft (213·76 m²)
Height to floor (kneeled):
forward 4 ft 4¾ in (1·34 m)
aft 4 ft 9 in (1·45 m)
Volume:
upper deck, forward 2,010 cu ft (56·91 m³)
upper deck, aft 6,020 cu ft (170·46 m³)
lower deck 34,795 cu ft (985·29 m³)

AREAS:
Wings, gross 6,200 sq ft (576·0 m²)
Ailerons (total) 252·8 sq ft (23·49 m²)
Trailing-edge flaps (total) 991·7 sq ft (92·13 m²)
Leading-edge slats (total) 648·5 sq ft (60·25 m²)
Spoilers (total) 430·7 sq ft (40·01 m²)
Fin 961·1 sq ft (89·29 m²)
Rudder 226·7 sq ft (21·06 m²)
Tailplane 965·8 sq ft (89·73 m²)
Elevators 258·7 sq ft (24·03 m²)

WEIGHTS AND LOADINGS (for 2·25g):
Basic operating weight 337,937 lb (153,285 kg)
Design payload 220,967 lb (100,228 kg)
Max T-O weight 769,000 lb (348,810 kg)
Max ramp weight 769,000 lb (348,810 kg)
Max zero-fuel weight 558,904 lb (253,515 kg)
Max landing weight 635,850 lb (288,416 kg)
Max wing loading 124·0 lb/sq ft (605·4 kg/m²)
Max power loading 4·69 lb/lb st (4·69 kg/kg st)

PERFORMANCE (at max T-O weight, except where indicated):
Max never-exceed speed 409·5 knots (472 mph; 760 km/h) CAS or Mach 0·875
Max level speed at 25,000 ft (7,620 m) 496 knots (571 mph; 919 km/h)
High-speed cruise at 25,000 ft (7,620 m) at normal rated thrust 460-480 knots (530-553 mph; 853-890 km/h)
Average cruising speed 450 knots (518 mph; 834 km/h)
Aerial delivery drop speed 130-150 knots (150-173 mph; 241-278 km/h)
Stalling speed, 40° flap at max landing weight 104 knots (120 mph; 194 km/h) EAS
Rate of climb at S/L, ISA, at maximum rated thrust 1,800 ft (549 m)/min
Service ceiling at AUW of 615,000 lb (278,950 kg) 34,000 ft (10,360 m)
Min ground turning radius 75 ft 0 in (22·86 m)
Runway LCN:
Concrete 40
Asphalt 64
T-O run 7,000 ft (2,134 m)
T-O to 50 ft (15 m) 8,400 ft (2,560 m)
Landing from 50 ft (15 m) 3,600 ft (1,097 m)
Landing run 2,230 ft (680 m)
Range with 220,967 lb (100,228 kg) payload 3,256 nm (3,749 miles; 6,033 km)
Range with 112,600 lb (51,074 kg) payload 5,670 nm (6,529 miles; 10,505 km)
Ferry range 6,940 nm (7,991 miles; 12,860 km)

LTV

LTV AEROSPACE CORPORATION (a subsidiary of THE LTV CORPORATION)

HEAD OFFICE:
PO Box 5907, Dallas, Texas 75222
Telephone: (214) 266-4171
CHAIRMAN AND CHIEF EXECUTIVE OFFICER:
W. P. Thayer
PRESIDENT: Sol Love
VICE-PRESIDENTS:
J. B. Allyn (Washington Operations)
R. S. Buzard
D. G. Gilmore (Operations)
Dr G. M. Monroe
E. M. Reyno
E. R. Spiegel Jr (Controller)
J. J. Welch Jr
CORPORATE DIRECTOR OF PUBLIC RELATIONS AND ADVERTISING:
Beal Box
DIVISIONS OF LTV AEROSPACE CORPORATION:

Vought Systems Division
DIVISION HEADQUARTERS:
PO Box 5907, Dallas, Texas 75222
PRESIDENT: Sol Love
VICE-PRESIDENTS:
J. B. Andrasko (Administration)
D. P. Appleby (Materials)
R. S. Buzard (Engineering)
J. W. Casey (Logistics)
E. F. Cvetko (Manufacturing)
D. G. Gilmore (Operations)
J. E. Martin (Advanced Ground Transportation Systems)
F. W. Randell (Advance Systems)
E. M. Reyno (International Marketing)
E. R. Spiegel Jr (Financial and Controller)
G. T. Upton (Engineering)
J. J. Welch Jr (Programmes)

Vought Service Center
DIVISION HEADQUARTERS:
PO Box 5907, Dallas, Texas 75222
ACTING MANAGER: R. S. Buzard

Hampton Technical Center
HEADQUARTERS:
3221 N. Armistead Avenue, Hampton, Virginia 23366
MANAGER: Jack McLain

Michigan Division
DIVISION HEADQUARTERS:
PO Box 909, Warren, Michigan 48090
VICE-PRESIDENT AND GENERAL MANAGER:
B. M. Smith

Advanced Technology Center Inc
HEADQUARTERS:
PO Box 6144, Dallas, Texas 75222
CHAIRMAN OF THE BOARD AND PRESIDENT:
F. W. Fenter

Kentron Hawaii Ltd
HEADQUARTERS:
233 Keawe Street, Honolulu, Hawaii 96813
PRESIDENT:
A. H. Perry

The former Chance Vought Aircraft, Inc, founded in 1917 and a leading producer of aircraft for the US Navy throughout its history, became the Chance Vought Corporation on 31 December 1960. On 31 August 1961, Chance Vought Corporation merged with Ling-Temco Electronics, Inc, to form a new combined company known as Ling-Temco-Vought, Inc.

What had been Chance Vought Corporation was renamed the Aerospace Division of LTV. In February 1965, the Vought Aeronautics Division, Astronautics Division, Range Systems Division, Michigan Division and Kentron Hawaii Ltd were all grouped to form LTV Aerospace Corporation as a new subsidiary of LTV. In 1972, LTV Aerospace Corporation became a wholly-owned subsidiary of the LTV Corporation (formerly Ling-Temco-Vought, Inc), responsible for all aerospace activities of the Corporation.

The LTV Corporation had more than 36,000 employees at the beginning of 1974, of whom 14,500 were employed by LTV Aerospace Corporation.

In September 1972 a reorganisation of the aerospace orientated divisions and subsidiaries of LTV Aerospace Corporation entered its first phase with a merger of Vought Aeronautics Company and Vought Missiles and Space Company into a new Vought Systems Division. The reorganisation continued into early 1974, resulting in a merger of the Ground Transportation Division with Vought Systems Division, the sale of Vought Helicopter Incorporated to Aérospatiale of France, and the creation of Vought Service Center, a division to handle the company's support service programmes. Thus, the divisions and subsidiaries of LTV Aerospace now consist of Vought Systems Division, Michigan Division, Hampton Technical Center, Vought Service Center, Advanced Technology Center Inc, and Kentron Hawaii Ltd.

As a division of the LTV Aerospace Corporation, Vought Systems has responsibility for all aircraft and spacecraft work, aerospace support and training equipment; production of wings, engine nacelles, pylons, aft fuselage, tail unit and landing gear for the S-3A Viking, and responsibility for assurance of carrier suitability (in conjunction with Lockheed-California, which see); construction of Boeing 747 tail assemblies, McDonnell Douglas DC-10 tailplanes and elevators, Lockheed C-130 and P-3 control surfaces. Additionally, the division has in production the A-7D fighter and A-7E attack aircraft for the USAF and USN respectively. Under a company-funded programme, Vought Systems has completed the modification of a Navy A-7E Corsair II as the first two-seat version of the A-7 series, under the designation YA-7H. Other current products of Vought Systems include the Scout launch vehicle for NASA; components for manned and unmanned space vehicles; advanced missile, guidance, control and environmental, and extra-vehicular systems; astronaut equipment; advanced thermal protection materials; and electro-optical traffic monitoring and related systems. Vought Systems Division produced the Airtrans automatic transit system for the Dallas/Fort Worth Airport and is developing variations of that system for domestic and foreign markets. The division is also developing personal rapid transit (PRT) and tracked air-cushion vehicle (TACV) systems for commercial and government utilisation.

In January 1974 Vought Systems Division was awarded a $1 million contract by the US Navy for continued work on the Cruise Missile. A highly versatile vehicle, this is designed for launch from submarines, but is adaptable for aircraft and surface applications. It is sized to fit a standard torpedo tube, which is 21 in (0·53 m) in diameter and 21 ft (6·40 m) in length. The US Navy contract calls for advanced design and development work on the airframe subsystem of the missile. A similar contract was awarded to General Dynamics Corporation of San Diego, California.

The Michigan Division of LTV Aerospace is prime contractor for the US Army's Lance battlefield missile system.

Kentron Hawaii Ltd, an LTV subsidiary, provides service for missile and space test range operations in the Pacific, and electronic equipment maintenance, repair and calibration service for military and commercial activities in the Pacific. Additionally, Kentron provides support services to NASA for the Manned Spacecraft Center at Houston, Texas, and a telemetry station for ESRO in Alaska. Advanced Technology Center Inc is concerned with fundamental and advanced research.

LTV AEROSPACE CORSAIR II
US military designation: A-7

On 11 February 1964 the US Navy named LTV Aerospace Corporation winner of a design competition for a single-seat carrier-based light attack aircraft. The requirement was for a subsonic aircraft able to carry a greater load of non-nuclear weapons than the A-4E Skyhawk. To keep costs to a minimum and speed delivery it was decided that the new aircraft should be based on an existing design.

LTV's design study was based on the F-8 Crusader and an initial contract to develop and build three aircraft, under the designation A-7A, was awarded on 19 March 1964; the first flight was made on 27 September 1965.

Since that time a number of versions of the A-7 have been produced, as Corsair IIs, for both the US Navy and the USAF, as follows:

A-7A. Initial attack version for the US Navy, powered by a Pratt & Whitney TF30-P-6 turbofan engine, rated at 11,350 lb (5,150 kg) st, a simplified non-afterburning version of the engine developed for the General Dynamics F-111. The first four were delivered to US Naval Air Test Center, Patuxent River, Maryland, on 13-15 September 1966. Deliveries to user squadrons began on 14 October 1966. The A-7A went into combat for the first time with Squadron VA-147 on 3 December 1967, off the USS *Ranger* in the Gulf of Tonkin. Delivery of 199 A-7As to the US Navy was completed in the Spring of 1968.

A-7B. Developed version for the US Navy with non-afterburning TF30-P-8 engine, rated at 12,200 lb (5,534 kg) st. First production aircraft flew on 6 February 1968 and A-7B entered combat in Vietnam on 4 March 1969. Last of 196 A-7Bs was delivered to the US Navy on 7 May 1969.

A-7C. Designation applied in late 1971 to the first 67 A-7Es (which see) to eliminate confusion with subsequent Allison-powered A-7Es.

TA-7C. Forty A-7Bs and 41 A-7Cs are being converted into tandem two-seat trainers, with operational capability, under this designation, in 1975-79. Gun and weapon pylons retained. Configuration similar to YA-7H.

A-7D. Tactical fighter version for the USAF, with a continuous-solution navigation and weapon delivery system, including the capability of all-weather radar bomb delivery. First two were powered by TF30-P-8 engine. Subsequent aircraft have an Allison TF41-A-1 (Spey) turbofan engine. First flight of an A-7D was made on 5 April 1968, and first flight with the TF41 engine on 26 September 1968. First A-7D was accepted by the USAF on 23 December 1968. First unit equipped with the A-7D was the 54th Tactical Fighter Wing at Luke AFB, Arizona. The A-7D entered combat in Southeast Asia in October 1972 with the 354th Tactical Fighter Wing, deployed from Myrtle Beach AFB, South Carolina. Delivery of A-7Ds to Air National Guard units in New Mexico, Colorado and Ohio began in 1973, representing the first new aircraft received by these units in more than 20 years. Production continues. This model is described in detail below.

A-7E. Developed version for the US Navy equipped as a light attack/close air-support/interdiction aircraft. First 67 aircraft (since redesignated A-7C, as indicated) powered by TF-30-P-8 turbofan engine; 68th and subsequent aircraft by Allison TF41-A-2 (Spey) turbofan engine rated at 15,000 lb (6,800 kg) st. Max internal fuel 1,500 US gallons (5,678 litres), max external fuel 1,200 US gallons (4,542 litres). Max speed at S/L 562 knots (647 mph; 1,041 km/h) and ferry range up to 2,800 nm (3,224 miles; 5,188 km). First flight of an A-7E was made on 25 November 1968 and deliveries began on 14 July 1969. Airframe and equipment are virtually identical to those of the A-7D, except that the gas-turbine self-starter is replaced by an air-turbine starter. Weight empty is 19,048 lb (8,640 kg). The primary navigation/weapon delivery systems for the A-7E are identical to those of the A-7D except for a different ASCU, type C-8185/AWE. The automatic controls differ only to include the AN/ASN-54 approach power compensator. Radio communications sets include the following: AN/ARC-51A UHF radio; AN/ARR-69 auxiliary UHF receiver; AN/ARN-51 Tacan; AN/APX-72 IFF transponder; AN/ADN-154 radar beacon; AN/ARA-50 ADF; AN/AIC-25 audio system and AN/ASW-25 data link. ECM equipment consists of APR-25 and -27 internal homing and warning systems and ALR-100 active ECM, also external pod-mounted systems compatible with the aircraft internal systems. The A-7E entered combat service in Southeast Asia with Attack Squadrons 146 and 147 in May 1970, operating from the aircraft carrier USS *America*. Production continues.

YA-7H. A single prototype of a two-seat version, with potential as an advanced trainer or for tactical operations, produced as a company funded project by modification of a US Navy A-7E. It is described separately.

The following description, which applies in particular to the A-7D, is generally applicable to other versions of the A-7 except as detailed above:

TYPE: Subsonic single-seat tactical fighter.

WINGS: Cantilever high-wing monoplane. Wing section NACA 65A007. Anhedral 5°. Incidence —1°. Wing sweepback at quarter-chord 35°. Outer wing sections fold upward to allow best utilisation of revetments at combat airfields. All-metal multi-spar structure with integrally-stiffened aluminium alloy upper and lower skins. Plain sealed inset aluminium ailerons, outboard of wing fold, are actuated by fully-triplicated hydraulic system. Leading-edge flaps. Large single-slotted trailing-edge flaps. Spoiler above each wing forward of flaps.

FUSELAGE: All-metal semi-monocoque structure. Large door-type ventral speed-brake under centre fuselage.

TAIL UNIT: Large vertical fin and rudder, swept back at 44·28° at quarter-chord. One-piece horizontal "slab" tailplane, swept back at 45° at quarter-chord and set at dihedral angle of 5° 25′. Tailplane and rudder are operated by triplicated hydraulic systems.

LANDING GEAR: Hydraulically-retractable tricycle type, with single wheel on each main unit and twin-wheel nose unit. Main wheels retract forward into fuselage, nosewheels aft. Main wheels and tyres size 28 × 9-12; nosewheels and tyres size 22 × 5·50. Sting-type arrester hook under rear fuselage for emergency landings or aborted take-offs. Anti-skid brake system and MLG tyres.

POWER PLANT: One Allison TF41-A-1 (Rolls-Royce Spey 168-62) non-afterburning turbofan engine, rated at 14,250 lb (6,465 kg) st. Engine has self-start capability through the medium of battery-powered electric motor that spins an air-breathing gas-turbine starter. The starter unit includes a turbine-driven compressor that compresses air for combustion, a free turbine for accelerating the engine to a self sustaining speed, and an integral control system. The engine has self-contained ignition for start/airstart, automatic relight and selective ignition. Integral fuel tanks in wings and additional fuselage tanks. Maximum internal fuel 1,425 US gallons (5,394 litres). Maximum external fuel 1,200 US gallons (4,542 litres). All fuel tanks filled with polyurethane fire-suppressing foam. Some fuselage tanks and fuel lines self-sealing. Alternate fuel feed system Flight refuelling capability of first 26 A-7Ds provided by a probe and drogue system. 27th and subsequent aircraft have boom receptacle above fuselage on port side in line with wing leading-edge. Boron carbide (HFC) engine armour.

ACCOMMODATION: Pilot on McDonnell Douglas Escapac rocket-powered ejection system, complete with USAF life support system, that provides a fully-inflated parachute three seconds after sequence initiation; positive seat/man separation and stabilisation of the ejected seat and pilot. Boron carbide (HFC) cockpit armour.

SYSTEMS: Triple-redundant hydraulic system for flight controls; double-redundant system for flaps, brakes and landing gear retraction. Electrical system includes storage batteries for engine starting and maintenance of ground-alert radio communications without need for the engine to be running. Liquid oxygen system. An air-conditioning unit using engine bleed air provides pressurisation and cooling for the cockpit and cooling for certain avionics compo-

LTV Aerospace A-7D Corsair II tactical fighter of the USAF

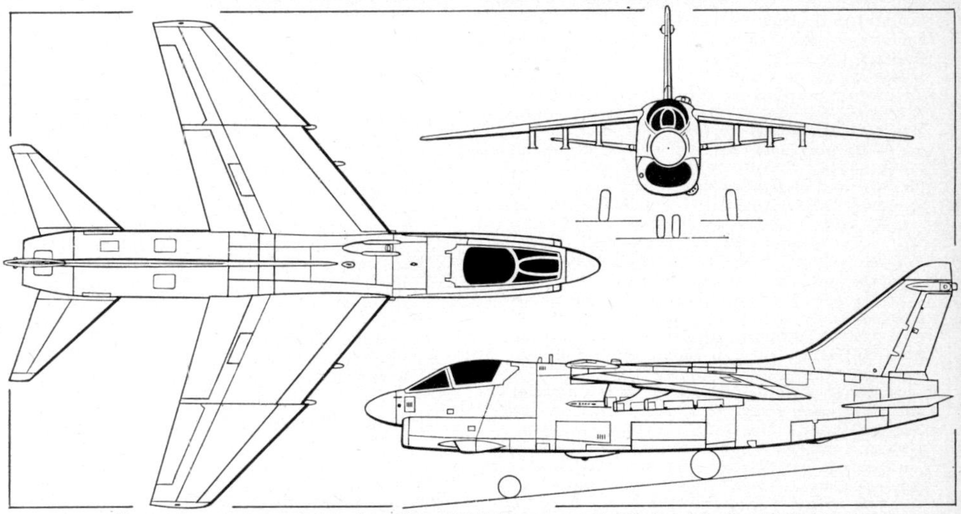
General arrangement drawing of the LTV Aerospace A-7D Corsair II (*Pilot Press*)

LTV Aerospace A-7E Corsair II close air-support/interdiction aircraft of the US Navy

nents. Automatic flight control system provides control-stick steering, altitude hold, heading hold, heading pre-select and attitude hold. Ram-air turbine provides hydraulic pressure and electrical power down to airspeeds below those used in normal landing approaches.

ELECTRONICS AND EQUIPMENT: The primary navigation/weapon-delivery system comprises AN/APQ-126 forward-looking radar, which is utilised for air-to-ground ranging for weapons delivery, ground mapping for navigation or adverse-weather bombing, manual terrain following and terrain avoidance, circular polarisation to enhance adverse-weather penetration; beacon mode for use in conjunction with AN/APN-134 rendezvous beacons in other aircraft; direct-view storage tube (DVST) for Walleye or radar presentation; AN/ASN-91 digital computer; AN/APN-141 radar altimeter; AN/AVQ-7 head-up display (HUD) by Marconi-Elliott (UK); CP-953/A air data computer; AN/ASN-90 inertial measuring set; CV-2622/ASN-99 projected map; AN/APN-190 Doppler radar; C-8230/AWE armament station and control unit (ASCU); and provisions for Loran. Automatic controls comprise nose-gear steering and AN/ASW-30 automatic flight control system. Radio communication and navigation aids include FM-622 VHF radio; AN/ARC-51 BX UHF radio; AN/ARR-69 auxiliary UHF receiver; AN/ARN-52 Tacan; AN/APX-72 IFF transponder; AN/ARN-58A ILS; AN/APN-154 radar beacon; CPU-80A flight director computer; AN/ARA-50 ADF and AN/AIC-26 audio system. ECM equipment consists of internal homing and warning systems and external pod-mounted systems compatible with the aircraft's internal systems.

ARMAMENT: A wide range of stores, to a total weight of more than 15,000 lb (6,805 kg), can be carried on six underwing pylons and two fuselage weapon stations. Two outboard pylons on each wing can each accommodate a load of 3,500 lb (1,587 kg). Inboard pylon on each wing can carry 2,500 lb (1,134 kg). Two fuselage weapon stations, one on each side, can each carry load of 500 lb (227 kg). Weapons carried include air-to-air and air-to-ground missiles; general-purpose bombs; rockets; gun pods and auxiliary fuel tanks. In addition, an M61-A1 Vulcan 20 mm cannon is mounted in the port side of the fuselage. This has 1,000-round ammunition storage and selected firing rates of 4,000 or 6,000 rds/min. Strike camera in lower rear fuselage for damage assessment.

DIMENSIONS, EXTERNAL:

Wing span	38 ft 9 in (11·80 m)
Width, wings folded	23 ft 9 in (7·24 m)
Wing chord at root	15 ft 6 in (4·72 m)
Wing chord at tip	3 ft 10¼ in (1·18 m)
Wing aspect ratio	4
Length overall	46 ft 1½ in (14·06 m)
Height overall	16 ft 0¾ in (4·90 m)
Tailplane span	18 ft 1¼ in (5·52 m)
Wheel track	9 ft 6 in (2·90 m)

AREAS:

Wings, gross	375 sq ft (34·83 m²)
Ailerons (total)	19·94 sq ft (1·85 m²)
Trailing-edge flaps (total)	43·48 sq ft (4·04 m²)
Leading-edge flaps (total)	48·74 sq ft (4·53 m²)
Spoiler	4·60 sq ft (0·43 m²)
Deflector	3·44 sq ft (0·32 m²)
Fin	111·20 sq ft (10·33 m²)
Rudder	15·04 sq ft (1·40 m²)
Horizontal tail surfaces	56·39 sq ft (5·24 m²)
Speed-brake	25·00 sq ft (2·32 m²)

WEIGHTS:

Weight empty	19,781 lb (8,972 kg)
Max T-O weight	42,000 lb (19,050 kg)

PERFORMANCE:

Max level speed at S/L	606 knots (698 mph; 1,123 km/h)
T-O run at max T-O weight	5,000 ft (1,525 m)
Ferry range: max internal fuel	1,981 nm (2,281 miles; 3,671 km)
max internal and external fuel	2,494 nm (2,871 miles; 4,621 km)

LTV AEROSPACE CORSAIR II₂
US military designation: YA-7H

Vought Systems Division, under a company funded project and by modification of an aircraft furnished by the US Navy, designed and built the prototype of a two-seat version of the A-7 Corsair II. Envisaged as an advanced trainer, or as a new operational configuration for tactical duties such as electronic countermeasures, it was known originally as the Vought Project V-519, but now has the designation YA-7H.

The YA-7H has the same basic structure and equipment as the A-7, with a 1 ft 4 in (0·41 m) longer nose section to make room for the second cockpit. A 1 ft 6 in (0·46 m) section is inserted in the rear fuselage, in line with the trailing-edge of the wing, and the overwing fairings are modified to maintain the fuselage profile. The aft fuselage is also modified to cant upward 1° 19′, so making possible approach and landing attitudes identical to those of other A-7s, despite the longer fuselage.

The new cockpit section has two McDonnell Douglas Escapac ejection seats in tandem, under an electrically-actuated sideways-opening (to starboard) cockpit canopy. It is intended that ejection would be made through the canopy; so the seat headrests carry strikers to shatter the canopy and provide a clear egress. Each cockpit has full flying controls, communications and navigation equipment. The rear cockpit, occupied by an instructor or check pilot, has a repeater-type head-up display, and the seat is raised slightly above the level of the front seat to enhance forward visibility. A brake parachute has been installed to permit short-field operations.

The YA-7H, which was the first production A-7E fitted with the Allison TF41-A-2 (Spey) turbofan engine, was modified at the Vought Systems Division's works in Dallas. It was not fitted with an in-flight refuelling probe or gun, to save both time and money, but is able to accept such equipment at a later date if required.

First flight of the YA-7H was made on 29 August 1972. Despite an increase in empty weight, there is little difference in performance between the YA-7H and the A-7E.

DIMENSIONS, EXTERNAL:

Wing span	38 ft 9 in (11·80 m)
Length overall	48 ft 2 in (14·68 m)
Height overall	16 ft 5 in (5·00 m)

WEIGHTS:

Weight empty	19,705 lb (8,938 kg)
Normal T-O weight (no military stores)	30,259 lb (13,725 kg)

PERFORMANCE (at T-O weight of 34,062 lb; 15,450 kg):

Max level speed at S/L	537 knots (618 mph; 994 km/h)
Catapult T-O speed	142 knots (164 mph; 264 km/h)
T-O run	3,600 ft (1,097 m)
Landing run: without brake parachute	3,150 ft (960 m)
with brake parachute	2,200 ft (670 m)
Radius of action	405 nm (466 miles; 750 km)
Ferry range (no external stores)	1,970 nm (2,268 miles; 3,650 km)

LTV Aerospace YA-7H prototype two-seat version of the A-7 Corsair II

MacDONALD
ROBERT A. MacDONALD

ADDRESS:
40 Creek Lane, Sonoma, California 95476
Telephone: (707) 996-7897

Mr MacDonald, an aircraft engineer, has designed and built a single-seat lightweight sporting aircraft of which plans are available to amateur constructors. His aim was to evolve a design that would be simple to build, easy to fly and economical in operation. It is of all-metal construction, and fabrication is simplified by extensive use of pop rivets.

Design and construction of the aircraft, which is designated MacDonald S-20, began simultaneously in March 1969. First flight was made on 9 March 1972. At the time the S-20 was constructed Mr MacDonald lived in Belmont, Massachusetts, and he flew the aircraft from there to the 1972 EAA Fly-in at Oshkosh, Wisconsin, a distance of 1,040 nm (1,200 miles; 1,930 km).

The designation S-20 applies to the prototype, which is described below, and aircraft built to Mr MacDonald's plans have the designation **S-21**.

MacDONALD S-20

TYPE: Single-seat homebuilt lightweight sporting aircraft.

WINGS: Cantilever low-wing monoplane. Wing section NACA 747A315. Small centre-section without dihedral. Dihedral on outer wing panels 5°. Incidence 1°. No sweepback. Constant-chord light alloy structure, with main and auxiliary spars and skins of 2024-T3 aluminium. Modified Frise-type ailerons of 2024-T3 light alloy. No flaps. No trim tabs.

FUSELAGE: Forward fuselage of welded steel tube truss construction. Aft fuselage has light alloy bulkheads and longerons. Skin is of 2024-T3 light alloy.

TAIL UNIT: Cantilever light alloy structure of 2024-T3 aluminium, with two spars in both fin and tailplane. Fixed-incidence tailplane. Combination trim and anti-servo tab on starboard elevator. Ground-adjustable tab on rudder (integral with port-side skin on S-21).

LANDING GEAR: Non-retractable tailwheel type. Shock-absorption of main-gear struts by neoprene discs in compression. Go-Kart wheels with tyres size 4·00-5. Mechanical caliper wheel brakes.

POWER PLANT: One 1,500 cc Volkswagen modified motor car engine, developing 53 hp and driving a Hegy two-blade wooden fixed-pitch propeller. Aluminium fuel tank in fuselage, immediately aft of firewall, capacity 9·8 US gallons (37 litres). Refuelling point on fuselage upper surface, forward of windscreen. Oil capacity 0·34 US gallons (1·27 litres).

ACCOMMODATION: Single seat for pilot in open cockpit. Space for baggage aft of seat, nominally 20 lb (9 kg) capacity, but prototype has storage battery and radio weighing 11 lb (5 kg) stowed in this area.

ELECTRONICS: Battery-powered Genave Alpha 100 com transceiver in prototype.

DIMENSIONS, EXTERNAL:

Wing span	25 ft 0 in (7·62 m)
Wing chord, constant	3 ft 9 in (1·14 m)
Wing aspect ratio	6·65
Length overall	18 ft 6 in (5·64 m)
Height overall	5 ft 3 in (1·60 m)
Tailplane span	7 ft 0 in (2·13 m)
Wheel track	5 ft 2 in (1·57 m)
Wheelbase	15 ft 5 in (4·70 m)
Propeller diameter	4 ft 5 in (1·35 m)
Propeller ground clearance	1 ft 0 in (0·31 m)

AREAS:

Wings, gross	94 sq ft (8·73 m²)
Ailerons (total)	10·0 sq ft (0·93 m²)
Fin	4·1 sq ft (0·38 m²)
Rudder, including tab	4·6 sq ft (0·43 m²)
Tailplane	7·0 sq ft (0·65 m²)
Elevators, including tab	7·0 sq ft (0·65 m²)

WEIGHTS AND LOADINGS:

Weight empty	456 lb (206 kg)

MacDonald S-20 homebuilt sporting aircraft (53 hp Volkswagen 1,500 cc modified motor car engine)

Design gross weight 720 lb (326 kg)
Design wing loading 7·66 lb/sq ft (37·4 kg/m²)
Design power loading 13·5 lb/hp (6·12 kg/hp)
PERFORMANCE (at T-O weight of 690 lb; 313 kg):
Max never-exceed speed
140 knots (162 mph; 260 km/h)
Max level speed, from S/L to 2,000 ft (610 m)
96 knots (110 mph; 177 km/h)
Max cruising speed, from S/L to 2,000 ft (610 m)
78 knots (90 mph; 145 km/h)
Econ cruising speed, from S/L to 2,000 ft (610 m)
69·5 knots (80 mph; 129 km/h)
Stalling speed 33 knots (38 mph; 61·5 km/h)
Max rate of climb at S/L 850 ft (259 m)/min
T-O run 300 ft (91 m)
Landing run approx 300 ft (91 m)
Range with max fuel, no reserve
218 nm (251 miles; 404 km)

MARTIN MARIETTA

MARTIN MARIETTA CORPORATION

AEROSPACE HEADQUARTERS:
International Club Building, 1800 K Street NW, Washington, DC 20006
DENVER DIVISION:
PO Box 179, Denver, Colorado 80201
Telephone: (303) 794-5211
OFFICERS: See "Missiles" section

Martin Marietta has been engaged in lifting-body research and development since 1959, during which time more than two million man-hours have been devoted to engineering design studies, materials investigation and wind-tunnel testing. Its current activities in this field are aimed towards the development of manoeuvring manned re-entry vehicles able to perform as spacecraft in orbit, fly in Earth's atmosphere like aircraft and land at conventional airports.

The small unmanned X-23A (described in the 1967-68 *Jane's*) first proved the aerodynamic characteristics of the design evolved by Martin Marietta. In three flights from orbital altitude and hypersonic speed, the X-23A's stability and manoeuvrability were demonstrated successfully through re-entry conditions down to a speed of Mach 2 and altitude of 100,000 ft (30,480 m). It was followed by a manned, rocket-powered research aircraft known as the X-24A, which was ordered by the USAF in May 1966, to begin where the X-23A models ended, by exploring the lower end of the speed scale.

An illustrated description of the X-24A appeared in the 1972-73 *Jane's*. The aircraft logged a total of 28 flights from Edwards AFB, California, being air-launched from under the wing of a B-52 "mother-plane". Several of the flights were supersonic, and a maximum speed of Mach 1·62 and altitude of 71,407 ft (21,765 m) were attained in 1971.

It was announced by NASA on 29 July 1971 that the X-24A was to be stripped down to its basic structure and rebuilt as the X-24B with completely new external lines. This work started in January 1972 and was completed in October of the same year. Following the first unpowered flight of the X-24B, made on 1 August 1973, the new research aircraft had made four more unpowered tests and two highly successful powered flights by the Spring of 1974.

MARTIN MARIETTA X-24B

The unique "double-delta" form of this wingless research aircraft is shown in the accompanying illustration. It is designed to be air-launched from beneath the wing of a B-52 "mother-plane".

Martin Marietta X-24B lifting-body research vehicle

TYPE: Lifting-body research aircraft.

FUSELAGE: Light alloy structure, primarily of 2024 aluminium. Triangular cross-section, with flat bottom and rounded top. The whole of the fuselage is pressurised.

TAIL UNIT AND CONTROL SURFACES: Light alloy triple-finned tail unit. Fixed centre fin. Each outer fin carries a pair of split rudders. The upper rudders control the vehicle in yaw. The lower rudders are not controlled by the pilot but act as trim surfaces, positioning themselves automatically in proportion to the aircraft's speed. Upper and lower flaps at extreme tail, between fins, serve as elevators and for pitch trim. Ailerons, outboard of the fins, function for both roll and pitch control. All control surfaces are fully powered by irreversible dual hydraulic systems, and have thick trailing-edges. A redundant three-axis stability augmentation system is fitted.

LANDING GEAR: Manually-retracted tricycle type, pneumatically extended. Nose unit, with twin wheels, retracts forward. Main units, each with a single wheel, retract aft. All units have oleo-pneumatic shock-absorbers. Hydraulic disc brakes.

POWER PLANT: One 8,000 lb (3,625 kg) st Thiokol XLR-11 four-chamber regeneratively-cooled turborocket engine. Cylindrical propellant tanks to contain the liquid oxygen and ethyl-alcohol-water mixture are housed longitudinally side by side in the centre fuselage. Total propellant capacity 4,500 lb (2,041 kg). Two 400 lb (181 kg) st Bell LLRV optional landing rockets.

ACCOMMODATION: Pilot only on zero-zero ejection seat beneath jettisonable transparent bubble canopy, which is hinged at rear and opens upward and aft. Conventional control stick and rudder/brake pedals.

SYSTEMS: Air-conditioning and pressurisation system, with max differential of 3·5 lb/sq in (0·25 kg/cm²). Duplicated hydraulic system, pressure 3,000 lb/sq in (210 kg/cm²), for operation of flying control surfaces and brakes. Pneumatic system, pressure 3,000 lb/sq in (210 kg/cm²), for landing gear extension. All electrical power provided from storage battery. Oxygen system standard.

ELECTRONICS: Com transceiver.

DIMENSIONS, EXTERNAL:
Width overall 19 ft 2 in (5·84 m)
Length overall 37 ft 6 in (11·43 m)
Height overall 10 ft 4 in (3·15 m)
AREA:
Double-delta planform 330 sq ft (30·66 m²)
WEIGHTS:
Weight empty equipped, without propellants
7,800 lb (3,538 kg)
Max T-O weight 13,000 lb (5,896 kg)
PERFORMANCE (estimated):
Max level speed at 60,000 ft (18,300 m)
868 knots (1,000 mph; 1,609 km/h)
Service ceiling 90,000 ft (27,430 m)

MAULE

MAULE AIRCRAFT CORPORATION

HEAD OFFICE AND WORKS:
Spence Air Base, Moultrie, Georgia 31768
Telephone: (912) 985-2045
PRESIDENT: B. D. Maule
VICE-PRESIDENT: Mrs B. D. (June) Maule (Treasurer and Purchasing Manager)
PROJECT ENGINEER:
Charles E. Henkel Jr

This company was formed to manufacture the Maule M-4 four-seat light aircraft in various versions. It transferred to new facilities in Moultrie, Georgia, in September 1968.

In early 1973 Maule Aircraft announced that two prototypes of an advanced STOL development of the M-4 Strata-Rocket had been completed and were due to begin flight tests. The new aircraft is known as the M-5 Lunar Rocket and is described separately.

The company has also designed auxiliary fuel transfer tanks for installation in the outboard wing bays of both M-4 and M-5 aircraft. Providing a total usable additional fuel capacity of 23 US gallons (87 litres), these tanks offer owners of the M-4 or M-5 a minimum payload range of 650 nm (750 miles; 1,200 km). FAA approval of the modification was given on 31 October 1973.

In the Spring of 1974 Maule had 90 employees and was building three aircraft each week, with a planned increase to four per week by the end of the year.

MAULE M-4 JETASEN AND ROCKET

Design of the M-4 was started in 1956. Construction of the prototype began in 1960 and it flew for the first time on 8 September 1960. Production began in early 1962 and four versions are now available, as follows:

M-4 Jetasen. Basic model with 145 hp Continental O-300-A engine and McCauley fixed-pitch propeller.

Maule M-4 Rocket, showing current cambered wingtips

M-4 Astro-Rocket. De luxe version of Jetasen, powered by a 180 hp Franklin 6A-335-B1A six-cylinder horizontally-opposed aircooled engine, driving a McCauley two-blade metal constant-speed propeller.

M-4 Rocket. Announced in 1964, this version has a 210 hp Continental IO-360-A engine and McCauley constant-speed propeller, giving improved short-field capability and all-round performance increases. Received FAA Type Approval 24 September 1964. Seaplane version became available in 1967, with ability to take off in seven seconds, cruise at over 122 knots (140 mph; 225 km/h) and land at 35 knots (40 mph; 65 km/h).

M-4 Strata-Rocket. Generally similar to Rocket, but powered by 220 hp Franklin 6A-350-C1 engine, driving McCauley constant-speed propeller.

The following structural description refers specifically to the M-4 Strata-Rocket, but is generally applicable to the other versions except for the power plant details:

TYPE: Four-seat light aircraft.

WINGS: Braced high-wing monoplane. Streamline-section Vee bracing strut each side. USA 35B (modified) wing section. Dihedral 1°. Incidence 30′. All-metal two-spar structure with metal covering and glassfibre tips. All-metal ailerons and two-position flaps.

Ailerons linked with rudder tab, so that aircraft can be controlled in flight by using only the control wheel in the cockpit. Cambered wingtips standard on all but Jetasen.

FUSELAGE: Welded 4130 steel tube structure. Covered with glassfibre, except for metal doors and aluminium skin around cabin.

TAIL UNIT: Wire-braced steel tube structure, covered with glassfibre. Trim tabs in port elevator and rudder. Rudder tab linked to ailerons.

LANDING GEAR: Non-retractable tailwheel type. Oleo main shock-absorbers. Cleveland main wheels type 0-2000, size 6·00-6 (4-ply), pressure 22 lb/sq in (1·55 kg/cm²). Maule SFS-P8-1-2 steerable tailwheel. Cleveland hydraulic brakes. Parking brake. Fairings aft of main wheels. Provision for fitting Fli-Lite Model 3000 Mk IIIA or Federal Model A2000A skis, hydraulically actuated Federal Model C2200H skis, C.A.P. floats, Edo floats, Fleet floats (Rocket only), or oversize tyres.

POWER PLANT: One 220 hp Franklin 6A-350-C1 six-cylinder horizontally-opposed aircooled engine, driving a McCauley two-blade constant-speed propeller. Glassfibre cowlings. Two fuel tanks in wings, with total capacity of 42 US gallons (159 litres). Optional auxiliary fuel tanks in outer wings, each with usable capacity of 11·5 US gallons (43·5 litres). Refuelling points in wing leading-edges. Oil capacity 2·2 US gallons (8·3 litres).

ACCOMMODATION: Four persons in pairs in enclosed cabin, with dual controls. Front seats adjustable. Rear bench seat. Forward-hinged doors on each side at front and on port side at rear of cabin. Space for 100 lb (45 kg) baggage aft of rear seat, with external door on port side. Provision for removing passenger seats so that aircraft can be used for cargo, ambulance and agricultural duties. Double cargo door optional on Jetasen, standard on other models. Cabin heater and windscreen defroster.

SYSTEMS: Hydraulic system for brakes. 35A engine-driven generator, 12V battery. 55A alternator on Astro-Rocket and Strata-Rocket.

ELECTRONICS AND EQUIPMENT: Standard equipment on Astro-Rocket, Rocket and Strata-Rocket includes stall warning system, dual controls, cabin soundproofing, 8-day clock, cabin steps, tie-down rings, ventilation under dash, navigation lights, landing lights, instrument and dome lights and cabin console speaker. Provision for full range of radio equipment to customer's requirements, including Narco and King 1½ systems and ADF. Other optional equipment includes Flite Lite flashing beacons, dual landing lights, blind-flying instrumentation, autopilot, carburettor air temperature gauge, heated pitot, glider tow, and dual brakes.

DIMENSIONS, EXTERNAL:	
Wing span, cambered tips	30 ft 10 in (9·40 m)
Wing chord, constant	5 ft 3 in (1·60 m)
Wing aspect ratio	5·65
Length overall	22 ft 0 in (6·71 m)
Height overall	6 ft 2½ in (1·89 m)
Tailplane span	9 ft 8¾ in (2·97 m)
Wheel track	6 ft 0 in (1·83 m)
Wheelbase	15 ft 10 in (4·82 m)
Propeller diameter	6 ft 2 in (1·88 m)
Cabin doors (fwd, each):	
Height	2 ft 9 in (0·84 m)
Width	2 ft 6 in (0·76 m)
Height to sill	3 ft 1 in (0·94 m)
Cabin door (cargo type, rear, stbd):	
Height	2 ft 5½ in (0·75 m)
Width	4 ft 4 in (1·32 m)
Height to sill	2 ft 4 in (0·71 m)
DIMENSIONS, INTERNAL:	
Cabin: Length	8 ft 4 in (2·54 m)
Max width	3 ft 6½ in (1·08 m)
Max height	3 ft 10½ in (1·18 m)
AREAS:	
Wings, gross	152·5 sq ft (14·17 m²)
Ailerons (total)	14·5 sq ft (1·35 m²)
Trailing-edge flaps (total)	14·6 sq ft (1·36 m²)
Fin	11·15 sq ft (1·04 m²)
Rudder, including tab	5·23 sq ft (0·49 m²)
Tailplane	12·60 sq ft (1·17 m²)
Elevators, including tab	14·00 sq ft (1·30 m²)

WEIGHTS AND LOADINGS (A: Jetasen, B: Astro-Rocket, C: Rocket, D: Strata-Rocket):

Weight empty:	
A	1,100 lb (499 kg)
B, D	1,250 lb (566 kg)
C	1,220 lb (553 kg)
Max T-O and landing weight:	
A	2,100 lb (953 kg)
B, C, D	2,300 lb (1,043 kg)
Max wing loading:	
A	13·75 lb/sq ft (67·13 kg/m²)
B, C, D	15·1 lb/sq ft (73·7 kg/m²)
Max power loading:	
A	14·5 lb/hp (6·58 kg/hp)
B	12·75 lb/hp (5·78 kg/hp)
C	11·00 lb/hp (4·99 kg/hp)
D	10·45 lb/hp (4·74 kg/hp)

PERFORMANCE (at max T-O weight. A: Jetasen, B: Astro-Rocket, C: Rocket, D: Strata-Rocket):

Max cruising speed at optimum altitude:	
A	130 knots (150 mph; 241 km/h)
B	139 knots (160 mph; 257 km/h)
C	143 knots (165 mph; 265 km/h)
D	156 knots (180 mph; 290 km/h)
Stalling speed, full flaps:	
A, B, C, D	35 knots (40 mph; 65 km/h)
Max rate of climb at S/L:	
A	700 ft (213 m)/min
B	1,000 ft (305 m)/min
C, D	1,250 ft (380 m)/min
Service ceiling:	
A	12,000 ft (3,650 m)
B	17,000 ft (5,180 m)
C	18,000 ft (5,500 m)
D	19,000 ft (5,790 m)
Absolute ceiling:	
B	19,000 ft (5,790 m)
C	20,000 ft (6,100 m)
D	21,000 ft (6,400 m)
T-O run:	
A	700 ft (213 m)
B	500 ft (152 m)
C	430 ft (131 m)
D	400 ft (122 m)
T-O to 50 ft (15 m):	
A	900 ft (274 m)
B	700 ft (213 m)
C	650 ft (198 m)
D	600 ft (183 m)
Landing from 50 ft (15 m):	
A, B, C, D	600 ft (183 m)
Landing run:	
A	450 ft (137 m)
B, C, D	390 ft (119 m)
Range with max standard fuel:	
A	607 nm (700 miles; 1,125 km)
B	542 nm (625 miles; 1,005 km)
C, D	590 nm (680 miles; 1,090 km)

MAULE M-5-210C/M-5-220C LUNAR ROCKET

Developed from the M-4 Strata-Rocket, this aircraft has a 30% increase in flap area and enlarged tail surfaces to improve field performance and rate of climb. Two prototypes were built, one powered by a 220 hp Franklin 6A-350-C1 engine being known as the M-5-220C Lunar Rocket. The second, with a 210 hp Continental IO-360-D engine, is designated M-5-210C. The first flight of the M-5-220C prototype was made on 1 November 1971, followed by the first M-5-210C on 16 October 1973; FAA certification was awarded on 28 December 1973. By 1 March 1974 20 M-5-210Cs had been delivered, and orders were in hand for a further 50 M-5-210Cs and 10 M-5-220Cs.

The M-5-210C/M-5-220C is a STCL aircraft, the "C" in its designation implying that it is intended specifically for cargo carrying. Four cabin doors facilitate the loading of cargo. Otherwise it is generally similar to the M-4 Strata-Rocket, and the description of that aircraft applies also to the M-5-210C/M-5-220C, except as follows:

TAIL UNIT: Braced steel tube structure with glassfibre covering. Trim tabs in port elevator and rudder.

LANDING GEAR: Non-retractable tailwheel type. Maule oleo-pneumatic shock-absorbers on main units. Maule steerable tailwheel. Cleveland main wheels with Goodyear, General or Schenuit tyres size 17 × 6·00-6, pressure 26 lb/sq in (1·82 kg/cm²). Tailwheel tyre size 8 × 3·50-4, pressure 15-20 lb/sq in (1·05-1·41 kg/cm²). Cleveland hydraulic disc brakes. Parking brake. Oversize tyres, size 20 × 7·50-6 (pressure 18 lb/sq in; 1·26 kg/cm²), and fairings aft of main wheels optional. Provisions for fitting optional Edo floats Model 248B2440 or Federal skis Model C2200H.

POWER PLANT: M-5-210C has one 210 hp Continental IO-360-D six-cylinder horizontally-opposed aircooled engine, M-5-220C one 220 hp Franklin 6A-350-C1 six-cylinder horizontally-opposed aircooled engine driving a McCauley two-blade metal constant-speed propeller. Two fuel tanks in wings with total usable capacity of 40 US gallons (151 litres). Optional auxiliary fuel tanks in outer wings, each with usable capacity of 11·5 US gallons (43·5 litres). Maximum usable fuel capacity 63 US gallons (238 litres). Refuelling points on wing upper surface. Oil capacity 2·2 US gallons (8·3 litres).

ACCOMMODATION: Pilot and three passengers on two front bucket seats and rear bench seat, or optional quickly-removed rear sling seat. One door on port side of fuselage, hinged at front edge and opening forward. Three doors on starboard side of fuselage, the forward and centre doors hinged at the front edge, the rear baggage door hinged at the rear edge. The centre and aft doors can be opened together to provide an opening 4 ft 1 in (1·24 m) wide to facilitate loading of bulky cargo. Accommodation heated and ventilated.

SYSTEMS: Hydraulic system for brakes only. Electrical system powered by 60A engine-driven alternator.

ELECTRONICS AND EQUIPMENT: A wide range of King, Genave and Narco communication and navigation equipment is available to customer's requirements. Blind-flying instrumentation, autopilot, wing levelling system, automatic glideslope and systems failure detector optional.

DIMENSIONS, EXTERNAL:	
As M-4 Strata-Rocket, except:	
Wing aspect ratio	5·71
Length overall	22 ft 7 in (6·88 m)
Tailplane span	10 ft 9 in (3·28 m)
Propeller ground clearance	10 in (0·25 m)
Cabin door (centre, stbd):	
Height	2 ft 5½ in (0·75 m)
Width	2 ft 3 in (0·69 m)
Height to sill	2 ft 6 in (0·76 m)
Baggage door (aft, stbd):	
Height	1 ft 11 in (0·58 m)
Width	1 ft 10 in (0·56 m)
Height to sill	2 ft 0 in (0·61 m)
AREAS:	
Wings, gross	157·9 sq ft (14·67 m²)
Ailerons (total)	12·8 sq ft (1·19 m²)
Trailing-edge flaps (total)	18·8 sq ft (1·75 m²)
Fin	13·14 sq ft (1·22 m²)
Rudder, including tab	5·83 sq ft (0·54 m²)
Tailplane	14·2 sq ft (1·32 m²)
Elevators, including tab	17·0 sq ft (1·58 m²)
WEIGHTS AND LOADINGS:	
Basic operating weight	1,325 lb (601 kg)
Max T-O and landing weight	2,300 lb (1,043 kg)
Max wing loading	14·6 lb/sq ft (71·3 kg/m²)
Max power loading (M-5-210C)	10·9 lb/hp (4·94 kg/hp)

PERFORMANCE (at max T-O weight. A: M-5-210C, B: M-5-220C):

Max never-exceed speed:	
A, B	173 knots (200 mph; 320 km/h) TAS
Max level speed at 8,000 ft (2,440 m):	
A, B	156 knots (180 mph; 290 km/h) TAS
Max cruising speed, 75% power at 8,000 ft (2,440 m):	
A	144 knots (166 mph; 267 km/h) CAS
B	152 knots (175 mph; 282 km/h) CAS

Maule M-5-220C Lunar Rocket, a utility version of the M-4 Strata-Rocket

Econ cruising speed, 65% power at 8,000 ft (2,440 m):
A 135 knots (155 mph; 249 km/h) CAS
B 143 knots (165 mph; 265 km/h) CAS
Stalling speed, flaps up:
A, B 44 knots (50 mph; 80·5 km/h)
Stalling speed, flaps down:
A 35 knots (41 mph; 66 km/h)
Max rate of climb at S/L:
A, B 1,250 ft (380 m)/min
Service ceiling:
A 18,000 ft (5,485 m)
B 19,000 ft (5,790 m)
Absolute ceiling:
B 21,000 ft (6,400 m)
T-O run:
A, B 400 ft (122 m)
T-O to 50 ft (15 m):
A, B 600 ft (183 m)
Landing from 50 ft (15 m):
A, B 600 ft (183 m)
Landing run:
A 400 ft (122 m)
B 390 ft (119 m)
Range with max fuel, 30 min reserve:
A 910 nm (1,047 miles; 1,685 km)
Range with max standard fuel:
B 590 nm (680 miles; 1,090 km)

MCDONNELL DOUGLAS

MCDONNELL DOUGLAS CORPORATION

HEAD OFFICE AND WORKS:
Box 516, St Louis, Missouri 63166
Telephone: (314) 232-0232

DIRECTORS:
Charles R. Able
John C. Brizendine
George H. Capps
Donald W. Douglas Jr
George S. Graff
Harold H. Helm
Edwin S. Jones
Richard Lloyd Jones Jr
Robert C. Little
James S. McDonnell (Chairman)
John F. McDonnell
Sanford N. McDonnell (President)
Dolor P. Murray
William R. Orthwein Jr
Frederic M. Peirce

CHAIRMAN:
James S. McDonnell

PRESIDENT AND CHIEF EXECUTIVE OFFICER:
Sanford N. McDonnell

CORPORATE EXECUTIVE VICE-PRESIDENT:
Dolor P. Murray Jr

CORPORATE OFFICERS:
Charles R. Able (Vice-President)
John R. Allen (Vice-President, Eastern Region)
David C. Arnold (Vice-President)
Alvin L. Boyd (Assistant Secretary)
John C. Brizendine (Vice-President)
Ben G. Bromberg (Vice-President)
John H. Carroll Jr (Assistant Secretary)
Joseph H. Cinnater (Vice-President, Treasurer)
Richard J. Davis (Vice-President, External Relations)
Newman L. Dotson (Assistant Secretary)
C. Warren Drake (Vice-President, Manufacturing, Quality Assurance and Facilities)
John E. Forry (Vice-President, Controller)
George S. Graff (Vice-President)
Gordon M. Graham (Vice-President, Far East)
Arthur W. Hyland (Assistant Controller)
Robert L. Johnson (Vice-President, Engineering and Research)
Robert H. Koenig (Assistant Treasurer)
Robert C. Krone (Vice-President, Personnel)
Robert C. Little (Vice-President, Marketing)
John F. McDonnell (Vice-President, Finance and Planning)
James T. McMillan (Vice-President)
Donald Malvern (Vice-President)
John R. Moore (Vice-President)
Harry W. Oldeg (Assistant Treasurer)
William R. Orthwein Jr (Vice-President)
Albert J. Redway Jr (Vice-President, Washington, DC)
Robert D. Richmond (Vice-President)
John T. Sant (Vice-President, Legal, and Secretary)
William E. Schowengerdt (Asst Controller)
Stanley J. Sheinbein (Asst Treasurer)
Harry I. Sieferman (Tax Officer)
Albert H. Smith Jr (Vice-President, Contracts and Pricing)

STAFF OFFICERS:
Russell G. Adamson (Vice-President, Personnel MDC West)
Joseph W. Antonides (Vice-President, Material)
Jerry G. Brown (Vice-President, Financial Planning)
O. Ruffin Crow (Vice-President, Corporate Auditor)
Charles A. Gaskill (Vice-President, Properties and Facilities)
Alfred V. Guillou (Vice-President, Corporate Planning)
Arthur W. Hyland (Vice-President, Accounting)
Gilbert D. Masters (Vice-President, Manufacturing)
James S. McDonnell III (Vice-President, Marketing)
Howard C. Todt (Vice-President, Quality Assurance)

McDonnell Douglas Research Laboratories
Box 516, St Louis, Missouri 63166
DIRECTOR: Dr Donald P. Ames

McDonnell Douglas Corporation was formed on 28 April 1967, by the merger of the former Douglas Aircraft Company Inc and McDonnell Company. It encompasses both of the original companies and their subsidiaries.

There are six major operating components of the McDonnell Douglas Corporation, as follows:

Douglas Aircraft Company
See pages 387-395 of this section

McDonnell Douglas Astronautics Company
See "RPVs", "Missiles" and "Spaceflight" sections

McDonnell Aircraft Company
See below

McDonnell Douglas Automation Company
Box 516, St Louis, Missouri 63166
PRESIDENT AND CHIEF EXECUTIVE OFFICER:
William R. Orthwein Jr

McDonnell Douglas Electronics Company
St Charles, Missouri
CHAIRMAN:
John R. Moore
PRESIDENT AND CHIEF EXECUTIVE OFFICER:
David C. Arnold

McDonnell Douglas—Tulsa
Tulsa, Oklahoma
VICE-PRESIDENT AND GENERAL MANAGER:
O. Lee Howser

Subsidiaries:
Subsidiaries of McDonnell Douglas Corporation include Actron Industries Inc, Monrovia, California; Douglas Aircraft Company of Canada Ltd, Malton, Ontario; McDonnell Douglas (Japan) Ltd, Tokyo; McDonnell Douglas International Sales Corporation, St Louis, Missouri; Douglas Development Company, Irvine, California; and McDonnell Douglas Finance Corporation, Long Beach, California.

At 31 March 1974, McDonnell Douglas employed a total of 76,940 people, working in 38 communities in 19 states, the District of Columbia and Toronto. Total office, engineering, laboratory and manufacturing floor area was 27,672,975 gross sq ft (2,570,900 m²).

MCDONNELL AIRCRAFT COMPANY (A Division of McDonnell Douglas Corporation)

HEADQUARTERS:
Box 516, St Louis, Missouri 63166
Telephone: (314) 232-0232
CHAIRMAN: Sanford N. McDonnell
PRESIDENT AND CHIEF EXECUTIVE OFFICER:
George S. Graff
EXECUTIVE VICE-PRESIDENT:
Donald Malvern
VICE-PRESIDENTS:
Aksel R. Anderson (Avionics Engineering)
William J. Blatz (Engineering Technology)
Alvin L. Boyd (Fiscal Management)
Chester V. Braun (General Manager F-15)
Denver D. Clark (Marketing)
Robert F. Cortinovis (Material)
Robert H. Koenig (Controller)
Nate Molinarro (Personnel)
Herbert Perlmutter (Manufacturing)
Madison L. Ramey (Engineering)
William S. Ross (Laboratory and Flight)
John N. Schuler (Contracts and Pricing)
John F. Sutherland (Product Support)

Production at St Louis continues to be concentrated on versions of the F-4 Phantom II and the F-15 Eagle air superiority fighter for the USAF.

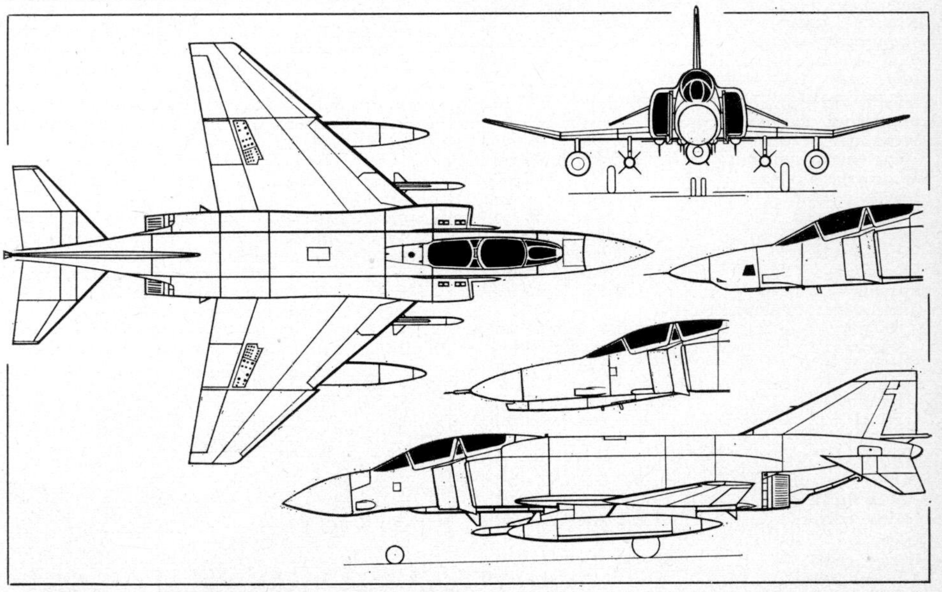

McDonnell Douglas F-4D Phantom II tactical fighter, with additional scrap views of noses of RF-4E (upper) and F-4E (lower) (*Pilot Press*)

MCDONNELL DOUGLAS PHANTOM II
US Navy and USAF designations: F-4 and RF-4

The Phantom II was developed initially as a twin-engined two-seat long-range all-weather attack fighter for service with the US Navy. A letter of intent to order two prototypes was issued on 18 October 1954, at which time the aircraft was designated AH-1. The designation was changed to F4H-1 on 26 May 1955, with change of mission to missile fighter. Early production aircraft were to be F4H-1Fs with additional external weapon carrying ability. A camera-equipped reconnaissance version was ordered as the F4H-1P.

The following production versions have been developed:

F-4A (formerly F4H-1): Flew for the first time on 27 May 1958. Designed for a speed of Mach 2, it achieved Mach 2·6 during its flight trials. This version was armed with four semi-submerged Sparrow III missiles and equipped with Westinghouse APQ-72 air interception radar. During one test, it also carried a total of twenty-two 500 lb bombs under its fuselage and inner wings. Further F-4As were subsequently equipped to F-4B standard. After evaluation of this version, the USAF decided to order land-based versions of the F-4B under the designation F-4C. Basic power plant of the F-4A comprised two General Electric J79-GE-2 turbojet engines, with afterburning.

F-4B (formerly F4H-1F). All-weather fighter for US Navy and Marine Corps, powered by two General Electric J79-GE-8 turbojet engines. A total of 696 F-4As and F-4Bs were built (including 12 F-4Gs, which see).

QF-4B. See "RPVs and Targets".

RF-4B (formerly F4H-1P). Multi-sensor reconnaissance version of F-4B for US Marine Corps. No dual controls or armament. Reconnaissance system the same as for RF-4C. J79-GE-8 engines. High-frequency single sideband radio. Twelve ordered initially under 1963 fiscal year budget. First one flew on 12 March 1965. Overall length increased to 63 ft (19·2 m). Total of 46 built.

F-4C (formerly F-110A). Two-seat fighter for USAF, developed from F-4B, with J79-GE-15 turbojets, cartridge starting, wider-tread low-pressure tyres size 30 × 11·5, larger brakes, Litton type LN-12A/B (ASN-48) inertial navigation system, APQ-100 radar, APQ-100 PPI scope, LADD timer, Lear Siegler AJB-7 bombing system, GAM-83 controls, dual controls and boom flight refuelling instead of drogue (receptacle in top of fuselage, aft of cockpit). Folding wings and arrester gear retained. For close support and attack duties with Tactical Air Command, PACAF and USAFE. First F-4C flew on 27 May 1963. 36 supplied to Spanish Air Force. The last of 583 was delivered to TAC on 4 May 1966. Replaced in production by F-4D.

RF-4C (formerly RF-110A). Multi-sensor reconnaissance version of F-4C for USAF, with radar and photographic systems in modified nose which increases overall length by 2 ft 9 in (0·84 m). Three basic reconnaissance systems are: side-looking radar to record high-definition radar picture of terrain on each side of flight path on film; infra-red detector to locate enemy forces under cover or at night by detecting exhaust gases and other heat sources; forward and side-looking cameras, including panoramic models with moving-lens elements for horizon-to-horizon pictures. Systems are operated from rear seat. HF single sideband radio. This version was produced to replace RF-101 aircraft in USAF service. YRF-4C flew on 9 August 1963. First production RF-4C flew on 18 May 1964. Production ended in December 1973, at which time a total of 505 had been built.

F-4D. Development of F-4C for USAF, with J79-GE-15 turbojets, APQ-109 fire-control radar, ASG-22 servoed sight, ASQ-91 weapon release computer, ASG-22 lead computing amplifier, ASG-22 lead computing gyro, 30kVA generators, and ASN-63 inertial navigation system. First F-4D flew on 8 December 1965. Two squadrons of F-4Ds (32 aircraft) were delivered to the Imperial Iranian Air Force and 18 to the Republic of Korea. Production completed. A total of 825 were built.

F-4E. Multi-role fighter for USAF, capable of performing air superiority, close-support and interdiction missions. Has internally-mounted M-61A1 20 mm multi-barrel gun, improved (AN/APQ-120) fire-control system and J79-GE-17 turbojets (each 17,900 lb; 8,120 kg st). Increased radius of action is provided by an additional fuselage fuel cell. First production F-4E delivered to USAF for initial testing on 3 October 1967. Supplied to the Israeli Air Force, Hellenic Air Force, Turkish Air Force and Imperial Iranian Air Force. All F-4Es will be fitted retrospectively with leading-edge slats as developed for F-4F.

In early 1973 F-4Es were being fitted with Northrop's target identification system electro-optical (TISEO). Essentially a vidicon TV camera with a zoom lens, it aids positive visual identification of airborne or ground targets at long range. The ASX-1 TISEO is mounted in a cylindrical housing on the leading-edge of the port wing of the F-4E. This new optical IFF system is being evaluated also for use on the US Navy's F-14s and certain US Army helicopters.

F-4EJ. On 1 November 1968, the Japan Defence Agency selected the F-4E as the main fighter for the JASDF. Except for the first two, these 104 aircraft are being built in Japan under a licence agreement, with some components being supplied from St Louis. The first US-built F-4EJ flew on 14 January 1971. Equipment includes tail warning radar and launchers for Mitsubishi AAM-2 air-to-air missiles.

RF-4E. Multi-sensor reconnaissance version for the Federal Republic of Germany. Generally similar to the RF-4C, it differs by having the J79-GE-17 turbojets of the F-4E and different reconnaissance equipment. An order for 88 aircraft was completed in 1971. Fourteen ordered by Japan in April 1973.

F-4F. Two-seat fighter, with leading-edge slats to improve manoeuvrability. Selected by Federal Germany for the Luftwaffe; 175 ordered. First one rolled out on 24 May 1973.

F-4G. Development of F-4B for US Navy, with AN/ASW-21 data link communications equipment. In service over Vietnam with Squadron VF-213 from USS *Kitty Hawk* in Spring of 1966. Only 12 were built and these are included in the total quoted for F-4B production.

(F-4H designation not used, to avoid confusion with original F4H)

F-4J. Development of F-4B for US Navy and Marine Corps, primarily as interceptor but with full ground attack capability. J79-GE-10 turbojets. Use of 16½° drooping ailerons and slotted tail gives reduced approach speed in spite of increased landing weight. Westinghouse AWG-10 pulse Doppler fire-control system. Lear Siegler AJB-7 bombing system; 30kVA generators. First F-4J demonstrated publicly on 27 May 1966. Production completed in December 1972.

F-4K. Development of F-4B for Royal Navy, with improvements evolved for F-4J plus other changes. The Westinghouse AN/AWG-10 pulse Doppler fire-control radar system has been modified to allow the antenna to swing around with the radome. This "foldable radome" reduces the length of the aircraft, making it compatible with the deck elevators on British aircraft carriers. Two Rolls-Royce Spey RB.168-25R Mk 201 turbofans (each rated at 12,500 lb; 5,670 kg st dry) with 70% afterburning. Air intake ducts are 6 in (15·2 cm) wider than on US models to cater for these more powerful engines. Drooped ailerons. Tailplane has leading-edge fixed slot. Strengthened main landing gear. Nose landing gear strut extends to 40 in (1·02 m), compared to 20 in (0·51 m) on the F-4J, to permit optimum-incidence catapulting. Martin-Baker ejection seats. Weapons include Sparrow air-to-air missiles. Decision to order this aircraft taken in February 1964. Initial contracts for two YF-4Ks and two F-4Ks. First flight 27 June 1966. 24 ordered as Phantom FG.Mk 1. First three aircraft were delivered to the Royal Navy on 25 April 1968 and the Navy's first Phantom training unit, 767 Squadron, was commissioned at RNAS Yeovilton on 14 January 1969, followed by the first operational Phantom unit, 892 Squadron, also commissioned at RNAS Yeovilton, on 31 March 1969.

McDonnell Douglas F-4F Phantom II, with leading-edge slats

McDonnell Douglas F-4J Phantom II from the aircraft carrier USS *America* (*T. Matsuzaki*)

F-4M. Version for Royal Air Force. Generally similar to F-4K, but with larger brakes and low-pressure tyres of F-4C. Folding wings and arrester gear retained. Orders for F-4K and F-4M totalled 170, with up to 50% of the components manufactured in the UK. First F-4M flew on 17 February 1967. Deliveries began on 23 August 1968, and by January 1969 crew training was under way with No. 228 Operational Conversion Unit, based at RAF Coningsby. RAF designation is Phantom FGR. Mk 2.

F-4N. The US Navy is updating 178 F-4Bs under this designation. The first (150430) was delivered on 21 February 1973.

A total of 4,398 Phantoms had been delivered by 31 December 1973.

The Phantom II has set up many official records since December 1959, including world speed and height records of 1,395·108 knots (1,606·48 mph; 2,585·425 km/h) and 98,556 ft (30,040 m) respectively. Records still standing at the time of closing for press were as follows:

On 28 August 1961, a speed record of 783·92 knots (902·72 mph; 1,452·777 km/h: Mach 1·2) was set up over a hazardous 3 km low-level course (maximum altitude 100 m; 328 ft) by Lt Hunt Hardisty and Lt E. De Esch in one of the F-4As. This exceeded the previous (subsonic) record, set up eight years earlier, by over 130 knots (149 mph; 240 km/h).

Between 21 February and 3 March 1962, the following time-to-height records were set up by US Navy pilots in an F-4B:

To 3,000 m (9,840 ft) 34·50 sec
To 6,000 m (19,680 ft) 48·78 sec
To 9,000 m (29,520 ft) 61·68 sec
To 12,000 m (39,360 ft) 1 min 17·14 sec
To 15,000 m (49,200 ft) 1 min 54·54 sec

It was announced in April 1972 that, under a programme directed by the USAF's Flight Dynamics Laboratory, McDonnell Douglas had modified an F-4 Phantom to have a Survivable Flight Control System (SFCS) including fly-by-wire control. The initial flight, made on 29 April, represented the first flight of fly-by-wire on a high-performance fighter aircraft.

It was announced subsequently, on 22 January 1973, that this Phantom had been flight tested successfully with pure fly-by-wire flight control. Previous SFCS tests had been carried out with the conventional flight controls available as a backup. The SFCS has electrical sensors to measure pilot stick and pedal commands and the aircraft's responses to these commands in pitch, roll and yaw. On-board computers process the sum of the sensor's inputs and provide electrical impulses which move the primary control surfaces to produce the desired change in the aircraft's flight path. The computer's signals to the controls are carried over four redundant channels.

The following details apply to the F-4B:

TYPE: Twin-engined two-seat all-weather fighter.

WINGS: Cantilever low-wing monoplane. Average thickness/chord ratio 5·1%. Sweepback 45°. Outer panels have extended chord, giving "dog-tooth" leading-edge, and dihedral of 12°. Centre-section and centre wings form one-piece structure from wing fold to wing fold. Portion that passes through fuselage comprises a torsion-box between the front and main spars (at 15% and 40% chord) and is sealed to form two integral fuel tanks. Spars are machined from large forgings. Centre wings also have forged rear spar. Centreline rib, wing-fold ribs, two intermediate ribs forward of main spar and two aft of main spar are also made from forgings. Wing skins machined from aluminium panels 2½ in (6·35 cm) thick, with integral stiffening. Trailing-edge is a one-piece aluminium honeycomb structure. Flaps and ailerons of all-metal construction, with aluminium honeycomb trailing-edges. Inset ailerons limited to down movement only, the "up" function being supplied by hydraulic-

McDonnell Douglas Phantom FGR. Mk 2 of No. 54 Squadron, Royal Air Force, with underfuselage reconnaissance pack, four rocket pods and Sparrow missiles

ally-operated spoilers on upper surface of each wing. Ailerons and spoilers fully powered by two independent hydraulic systems. Hydraulically-operated trailing-edge flaps and leading-edge flap on outboard half of each inner wing panel are "blown". Hydraulically-operated airbrake under each wing aft of wheel well. Outer wing panels fold upward for stowage.

FUSELAGE: All-metal semi-monocoque structure, built in forward, centre and rear sections. Forward fuselage fabricated in port and starboard halves, so that most internal wiring and finishing can be done before assembly. Keel and rear sections make extensive use of steel and titanium. Double-wall construction under fuel tanks and for lower section of rear fuselage, with ram-air cooling.

TAIL UNIT: Cantilever all-metal structure, with 23° of anhedral on one-piece all-moving horizontal surfaces. Ribs and stringers of horizontal surfaces are of steel, skin of titanium and trailing-edge of steel honeycomb. Rudder interconnected with ailerons at low speeds.

LANDING GEAR: Hydraulically-retractable tricycle type, main wheels retracting inward into wings, nose unit rearward. Single wheel on each main unit, with tyres size 30 × 7·70; twin wheels on nose unit which is steerable and self-centering, and can be lengthened pneumatically to increase the aircraft's angle of attack for take-off. Brake-chute housed in fuselage tail-cone.

POWER PLANT: Two General Electric J79-GE-8 turbojet engines (each 17,000 lb; 7,711 kg st with afterburning). Variable-area inlet ducts monitored by air data computer. Integral fuel tankage in wings, between front and main spars, and in six fuselage tanks, with total capacity of 2,000 US gallons (7,569 litres). Provision for one 600 US gallon (2,270 litre) external tank under fuselage and two 370 US gallon (1,400 litre) underwing tanks. Equipment for probe-and-drogue and "buddy tank" flight refuelling, with retractable probe in starboard side of fuselage.

ACCOMMODATION: Crew of two in tandem on Martin-Baker Mk H7 ejection seats, under individual rearward-hinged canopies. Optional dual controls.

SYSTEMS: Three independent hydraulic systems, pressure 3,000 lb/sq in (210 kg/cm²). Pneumatic system for canopy operation, nosewheel strut extension and ram-air turbine extension. Primary electrical source is AC generator. No battery.

ARMAMENT: Six Sparrow III, or four Sparrow III and four Sidewinder, air-to-air missiles on four semi-submerged mountings under fuselage and two underwing mountings. Provision for carrying alternative loads of up to about 16,000 lb (7,250 kg) of nuclear or conventional bombs and missiles on five attachments under wings and fuselage. Typical loads include eighteen 750 lb bombs, fifteen 680 lb mines, eleven 1,000 lb bombs, seven smoke bombs, eleven 150 US gallon napalm bombs, four Bullpup air-to-surface missiles or fifteen packs of air-to-surface rockets.

ELECTRONICS: Eclipse-Pioneer dead-reckoning navigation computer, Collins AN/ASQ-19 communications-navigation-identification package, AiResearch A/A 24G central air data computer, Raytheon radar altimeter, General Electric ASA-32 autopilot, RCA data link, Lear attitude indicator and AJB-3 bombing system. Westinghouse APQ-72 automatic radar fire-control system in nose. ACF Electronics AAA-4 infra-red detector under nose.

DIMENSIONS, EXTERNAL:
Wing span 38 ft 5 in (11·70 m)
Width, wings folded 27 ft 6½ in (8·39 m)
Length overall 58 ft 3 in (17·76 m)
Height overall 16 ft 3 in (4·96 m)
Wheel track 17 ft 10½ in (5·30 m)

AREA:
Wings, gross 530 sq ft (49·2 m²)

WEIGHTS:
T-O weight (clean) 46,000 lb (20,865 kg)
Max T-O weight 54,600 lb (24,765 kg)

PERFORMANCE:
Max level speed with external stores over Mach 2
Approach speed 130 knots (150 mph; 240 km/h)
T-O run (interceptor) 5,000 ft (1,525 m)
Landing run (interceptor) 3,000 ft (915 m)
Combat radius:
interceptor over 781 nm (900 miles; 1,450 km)
ground attack over 868 nm (1,000 miles; 1,600 km)
Ferry range 1,997 nm (2,300 miles; 3,700 km)

MCDONNELL DOUGLAS F-15 EAGLE

The USAF first requested development funding for a new air superiority fighter in 1965, and in due course design proposals were sought from three airframe manufacturers: Fairchild Hiller Corporation, McDonnell Douglas Corporation, and North American Rockwell Corporation. On 23 December 1969 it was announced that McDonnell Douglas had been selected as prime airframe contractor. The contract called for the design and manufacture of 20 aircraft for development testing, these to comprise 18 single-seat **F-15As** and two **TF-15A** two-seat trainers, with production scheduled at a rate of one aircraft every other month. A production go-ahead for the first 30 operational aircraft (FY 1973 funds) followed on 1 March 1973. The FY 1974 Defense Procurement Bill authorised production of 62 aircraft and a production rate buildup to 9 aircraft per month. The FY 1975 Executive Department budget requested production funding for 72 aircraft. The FY 1973/1974 production contracts include 13 of the two-seat TF-15A version. The combat-capable two-seat trainer will be used for pilot training, but the USAF is studying the use of two-seat versions for reconnaissance and advanced attack missions.

The contract between the USAF and McDonnell Douglas is based on a combination of cost-plus-incentives with successive target costs, plus specific stages in the development of the aircraft which have been translated into 24 demonstration milestones. The contractor must demonstrate to the USAF the successful attainment of each stage of aircraft development within the pre-determined cost limitations. In this way credit is received for completion of that particular milestone before being allowed to pass to the next stage.

In determining these stages the USAF has related them to release of funding, and decides whether or not the contractor is maintaining a satisfactory rate of progress. If a particular stage is behind schedule, the programme can be extended or re-orientated; in the extreme it could be terminated. If performance should fall below the specification requirement, the additional cost of achieving that level would be balanced against the necessity of matching exactly the original specification figures. To hold down cost and discourage any temptation to introduce design changes, the contractor cannot obtain additional funding without giving the USAF 17 months notice. Any additional cost incurred must be company funded.

The demonstration milestone plan was carefully developed and set to a time schedule well in advance of the F-15 contract award in January 1970. The original McDonnell Douglas milestone schedule was finalised for the USAF in January 1969. Some adjustments have been made since by the USAF to accommodate later changes in ground test requirements. Nonetheless, McDonnell Douglas has managed to adhere essentially to the original 1969 milestone schedule, despite additional work, and all milestone requirements were due to be completed in 1974. The last milestone, No. 24, will be accomplished with delivery of the first F-15 aircraft to Tactical Air Command (TAC) in November 1974.

Structural fatigue testing of the airframe and landing gear has been completed to four lifetimes, and airborne equipment testing has progressed sufficiently to ensure that all aircraft-installed equipment will have been qualified by the time the first F-15 is delivered to TAC.

First flight of the F-15A was made on 27 July 1972, and the first flight of a two-seat TF-15A trainer on 7 July 1973. By mid-March 1974 thirteen aircraft had attained flight status, with two aircraft delivered to the USAF for the beginning of Category II flight testing and evaluation. A total of approximately 1,500 flight hours had been accumulated by mid-March 1974 without any serious problems being encountered. Aircraft performance has met or exceeded the design parameters in all respects.

Design of the F-15 has remained very stable from the outset, with relatively few changes introduced. Two significant changes have been made as a result of flight experience, involving improvements to the landing gear and provision of a larger airbrake. Maximum speed in excess of Mach 2·5 is coupled with the high manoeuvrability demanded of a true air superiority fighter. The basic control system has been refined during the flight test programme to optimise the Eagle's air combat tracking capabilities. The results of combat exercises conducted by USAF and contractor pilots have demonstrated a tracking capability far superior to that of other known fighter aircraft.

Designed specifically as an air superiority aircraft, the F-15A Eagle is proving to be equally suitable for air-to-ground missions without degradation of its primary role. It is able to carry a variety of air-to-air and air-to-ground weapons. Standard armament of the Eagle is an internal, wing-mounted rapid-firing cannon. With an advanced radar and fire control system, coupled with a sophisticated communications system, the F-15 is claimed to provide an extremely flexible and highly self-sufficient vehicle which can be utilised effectively in any weather. Growth potential of the aircraft to meet future demands is considered adequate to ensure viability as a front-line fighter for some years to come.

Initial production was maintained at a rate of one aircraft bi-monthly, increasing to one aircraft per month, and it is intended to increase this steadily if potential sales to other nations are realised.

The F-15A is a single-seat fixed-wing twin-turbofan fighter in the 40,000 lb (18,145 kg) weight class. The airframe comprises 35·8%

McDonnell Douglas F-15A Eagle air superiority fighter for the USAF. The airbrake and horizontal tail surfaces have been modified since this photograph was taken

Prototype McDonnell Douglas TF-15A tandem two-seat training version of the Eagle

aluminium, 26·9% titanium and 37·3% composites and other materials.

The F-15 airframe is being developed concurrently with its turbofan engines. Following initial engine development contracts awarded to General Electric and Pratt & Whitney in August 1968, for the development of two engines based on a common core but with differing characteristics, to power the F-15 and the USN's F-14B fleet defence fighter, it was announced on 27 February 1970 that the latter company had been selected as prime contractor. Pratt & Whitney's F100-PW-100 advanced technology turbofan for the F-15 has a thrust rating in the 25,000 lb (11,340 kg) class, providing a thrust-to-weight ratio greater than 1 : 1. The engine completed USAF qualification test requirements in October 1973.

On 23 July 1971 McDonnell Douglas Corporation announced that it had been awarded an $8·2 million contract by the USAF to build and fly an F-15 prototype wing constructed of advanced composite materials. Under a four-year contract from the Air Force Materials Laboratory, McDonnell Douglas Corporation will fabricate the wing from boron and graphite filaments embedded in epoxy resin. This form of structure is expected to reduce total wing weight by some 500 lb (227 kg), providing greater strength and fatigue resistance than a conventional metal wing.

Although the manufacturer is not yet permitted to release details of the capabilities of the F-15, information based on subcontracts awarded gives some indication of the potential of this new fighter:

TYPE: Single-seat twin-turbofan air superiority fighter.

WINGS: Cantilever shoulder-wing monoplane. Leading-edge swept back at approximately 45°. Outboard aileron actuators by Ozone Metal Products.

FUSELAGE: All-metal semi-monocoque structure.

TAIL UNIT: All-metal structure with twin fins and rudders. All-moving horizontal tail surfaces outboard of fins, with extended chord on outer leading-edges. Rudder servo actuators by Ronson Hydraulic Units Corporation. Actuators for horizontal surfaces by National Water Lift Company. Boost and pitch compensator for control stick by Moog Inc, Controls Division.

LANDING GEAR: Hydraulically-retractable tricycle type, with single wheel on each unit. Nose and main landing gear by Cleveland Pneumatic Tool Company. Wheels and brake assemblies by Goodyear Tire and Rubber Company. Main and nosewheel tyres by B. F. Goodrich Company. Wheel braking skid control system by Hydro-Aire Division of Crane Company. All units retract forward.

POWER PLANT: Two Pratt & Whitney F100-PW-100 turbofan engines of approximately 25,000 lb (11,340 kg) st. Fuel tanks by Goodyear Aviation Products Division. Refuelling control valve by Ronson Hydraulic Units Corporation. Fuel tank valves and check valves by Parker Hannifin Corporation. Fuel gauge system by Simmonds Precision Products Inc. Fuel tank pressure regulators by Vap-Air Division of Vapor Corporation.

ENGINE INTAKES: Straight two-dimensional external compression inlets, on each side of the fuselage. Air inlet controllers by Hamilton Standard Division of United Aircraft Corporation. Air inlet actuators by National Water Lift Company.

ACCOMMODATION: Pilot only, on ejection seat developed by McDonnell Douglas. Polycarbonate canopy and acrylic-clad polycarbonate windscreen by Sierracin Corporation. Windscreen anti-icing valve by Dynasciences Corporation.

SYSTEMS: Electric power generating system by Lear Siegler Power Equipment Division; transformer-rectifier by Electro Development Corporation; and generator constant-speed drive units by Sundstrand Corporation, Aviation Division. Hydraulic system powered by engine-driven pumps supplied by Abex Corporation; modular hydraulic packages by Hydraulic Research and Manufacturing Company. The oxygen system includes a liquid oxygen indicator by Simmonds Precision Products Inc. Air-conditioning system by AiResearch Manufacturing Company. Automatic flight control system by General Electric, Aircraft Equipment Division. Auxiliary power unit for engine starting, and for the provision of electric or hydraulic power on the ground independently of the main engines, supplied by AiResearch Manufacturing Company.

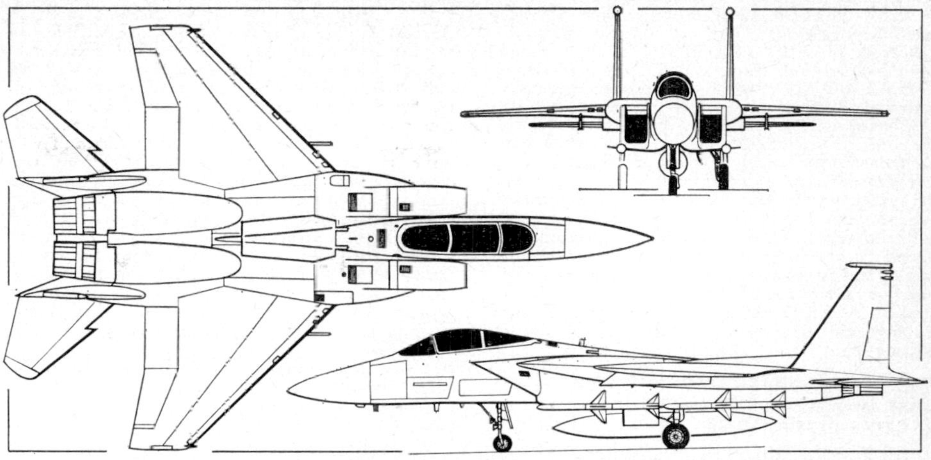

McDonnell Douglas F-15A Eagle twin-turbofan air superiority fighter *(Pilot Press)*

EQUIPMENT: Tachometer, fuel and oil indicators by Bendix Corporation, Flight and Engine Instrument Division. Feel trim actuators by Plessey Airborne Corporation.

ELECTRONICS: Lightweight pulse-Doppler radar system developed by Hughes Aircraft Company provides long-range detection and tracking of small high-speed targets operating at all altitudes down to treetop level, and feeds accurate tracking information to the airborne central computer to ensure effective launch of the aircraft's missiles or the firing of its internal gun. For close-in dogfights, the radar automatically acquires the target on a head-up display. International Business Machines, Electronic Systems Center, is subcontractor for the central computer, and McDonnell Douglas Electronics Company for the head-up display. This latter unit projects all essential flight information in the form of symbols on to a combining glass positioned above the instrument panel at pilot's eye level. The display presents the pilot with all the information required to intercept and destroy an enemy aircraft without need for him to remove his eyes from the target. The display also provides navigation and other steering control information under all flight conditions; as well as built-in test information to pinpoint faults in the aircraft's systems. A transponder for the IFF system, developed by Teledyne Electronics Company, informs ground stations and other suitably equipped aircraft that the F-15 is a friendly aircraft. It also supplies data on the F-15's range, azimuth, altitude and identification to air traffic controllers. The F-15 carries an AN/APX-76 interrogator receiver-transmitter, built by Hazeltine Corporation, to inform the pilot if an aircraft seen visually or on radar is friendly. A reply evaluator for the IFF system, which operates with the AN/APX-76, was developed by Litton Systems Inc, Van Nuys. A vertical situation display set, that uses a cathode-ray tube to present radar, electro-optical identification and attitude director indicator formats to the pilot, has been developed by Sperry Rand Corporation, Sperry Flight Systems Division. This permits inputs received from the aircraft's sensors and the central computer to be visible to the pilot under any light conditions. This company has also developed an air data computer for the F-15, as well as an attitude and heading reference set to provide information on the aircraft's pitch, roll and magnetic heading that is fed to cockpit displays. This latter unit also serves as a backup to the inertial navigation set developed by Litton Systems Inc. This provides the basic navigation data and is the aircraft's primary attitude reference, enabling the F-15 to navigate anywhere in the world. In addition to giving the aircraft's position at all times, the inertial navigation system provides pitch, roll, heading, acceleration and velocity information.

Other specialised equipment for flight control, navigation and communications includes a micro-miniaturised TACAN system by Hoffman Electronics Corporation; a horizontal situation indicator to present aircraft navigation information on a symbolic pictorial display, by Collins Radio Company, which is also responsible for the ADF and ILS receivers, UHF transceiver and UHF auxiliary-fix receiver. The communications sets have cryptographic capability. Dorne and Margolin Aviation Products are responsible for the glideslope localiser antenna, and Teledyne Avionics Company for angle of attack sensors. A special nose radome has been developed by Brunswick Corporation, Technical Products Division. This is fabricated from syntactic foam material sandwiched between outer skins, and offers a weight saving of 35% by comparison with conventional radome structures, as well as providing heat resistance up to 500°F (260°C), undistorted passage for signals from the nose radar and the strength of a primary structure.

An internal countermeasures set is supplied by Hallicrafters Company; radar warning systems by Loral Electronic Systems; and an electronic warfare warning set by Magnavox.

ARMAMENT: Provision for carriage and launch of a variety of air-to-air weapons over short and medium ranges, including four AIM-9L Sidewinders, four AIM-7F Sparrows, and a 20 mm M-61A1 six-barrel gun. A lead-computing gunsight has been developed by the General Electric Co. To keep the pilot informed of the status of his weapons and provide for their management, an integrated stores monitoring and management system has been developed by Dynamic Controls Corporation. Five weapon stations allow for the carriage of up to 12,000 lb (5,443 kg) of ordnance or additional ECM equipment.

DIMENSIONS, EXTERNAL:
- Wing span: 42 ft 9¾ in (13·05 m)
- Length overall: 63 ft 9¾ in (19·45 m)
- Height overall: 18 ft 7½ in (5·68 m)
- Tailplane span: 28 ft 3¾ in (8·63 m)

AREA:
- Wings, gross: 608 sq ft (56·5 m²)

WEIGHT:
- Max T-O weight (interceptor): 40,000 lb (18,145 kg)

PERFORMANCE:
- Max level speed: more than Mach 2·5; more than 800 knots (921 mph; 1,482 km/h) CAS
- Approach speed: 125 knots (144 mph; 232 km/h) CAS
- T-O run (interceptor): 900 ft (274 m)
- Landing run (interceptor), without braking parachute: 2,500 ft (762 m)
- Absolute ceiling: 66,900 ft (20,390 m)
- Ferry range: more than 2,500 nm (2,878 miles; 4,631 km)

DOUGLAS AIRCRAFT COMPANY (a Division of McDonnell Douglas Corporation)

HEADQUARTERS: 3855 Lakewood Boulevard, Long Beach, California 90801
Telephone: (213) 593-5511

CHAIRMAN: Sanford N. McDonnell

PRESIDENT:
John C. Brizendine

EXECUTIVE VICE-PRESIDENTS:
Charles M. Forsyth
Robert E. Hage (Marketing)

VICE-PRESIDENTS:
Ray E. Bates (Engineering Design and Development)
Harold Bayer (Product Support)
Howard W. Cleveland (Manufacturing)
John E. Crosthwait (Government Marketing)
Edward Curtis (Contracts and Pricing)
Joseph S. Dunning (Administration)
Joseph J. Dysart (Product Support and Programme Management)
Gilbert G. Fleming (Production)
Tom Gabbert (Fiscal Management)
Charles S. Glasgow (Engineering)
William T. Gross (Programme Manager DC-10)
Robert C. P. Jackson (Planning)
John C. Londelius (Flight and Laboratory Development)
Marvin D. Marks (Programme Manager YC-15)
Harold E. Showalter (Controller)
Howell L. Walker (Commercial Sales)
William R. Worrell (Material)

CHIEF COUNSEL: John H. Carroll Jr

DIRECTOR, EXTERNAL RELATIONS: Raymond L. Towne

The Douglas Aircraft Company operates plants at Long Beach, Palmdale and Torrance, California.

On 4 April 1972 McDonnell Douglas announced that the company had completed qualification testing of a new combat aircraft ejection seat known as ACES (Advanced Concept Escape System). Developed under USAF contract, the seat unit has built into it an escape rocket, launching guide rails, stabilising and safety devices, and the parachute. All are operated automatically when a crew member initiates the sequence by pulling seat-mounted ejection handles. The control system has its own electrical power supply, and its speed and altitude sensing devices are independent of the aircraft's systems. As the seat emerges from the aircraft, environmental sensors provide airspeed and altitude information to an electronic programmer, which selects and initiates the most appropriate one of three recovery modes, covering low, medium or high speed/altitude. It is estimated that an ACES would allow a safe ejection from an inverted aircraft at an altitude as low as 200 ft (61 m).

MCDONNELL DOUGLAS DC-9

USAF designations: C-9A and VC-9C
US Navy designation: C-9B

Design study data on the DC-9, then known as the Douglas Model 2086, were released in 1962. Preliminary design work began during that year. Fabrication was started on 26 July 1963 and assembly of the first airframe began on 6 March 1964. It flew for the first time on 25 February 1965 and five DC-9s were flying by the end of June 1965. These aircraft were of the basic version now known as the DC-9 Series 10. The full range of DC-9 variants currently available is as follows:

Series 10 Model 11. Initial version, powered by two 12,250 lb (5,556 kg) st Pratt & Whitney JT8D-5 turbofan engines. Max accommodation for 80 passengers at 34 in (86 cm) seat pitch, with normal facilities, or 90 passengers with limited facilities. This version received FAA Type Approval on 23 November 1965 and entered scheduled service with Delta Air Lines on 8 December 1965.

Series 10 Model 15. Generally similar to Srs 10 Model 11 but with 14,000 lb (6,350 kg) st JT8D-1 turbofan engines, increased fuel capacity and increased all-up weight.

Series 20. Developed version for operation in hot climate/high-altitude conditions, combining long-span wings of Series 30 with short fuselage of Series 10. Up to 90 passengers. Two 14,500 lb (6,575 kg) st JT8D-9 turbofans. The Series 20 flew for the first time on 18 September 1968, and was certificated on 11 December 1968. The first Series 20 was delivered to SAS on the same day and entered commercial service on 23 January 1969.

Series 30. Developed version, initially with 14,000 lb (6,350 kg) st JT8D-7s, increased wing span, longer fuselage accommodating up to 105 (normal) or 115 (with limited facilities) passengers, and new high-lift devices including full-span leading-edge slats and double-slotted flaps. First Srs 30 flew for first time on 1 August 1966. First delivery, to Eastern Air Lines, was made on 27 January 1967 and scheduled services began on 1 February 1967. Engine options available include JT8D-9 of 14,500 lb (6,575 kg) st; JT8D-11 of 15,000 lb (6,804 kg) st; and JT8D-15 of 15,500 lb (7,031 kg) st. All engines have sound-treated nacelles that comply with FAA FAR Pt 36 noise regulations.

Series 40. As Series 30, but with 14,500 lb (6,575 kg) st JT8D-9 or 15,500 lb (7,031 kg) st -15 turbofans, increased fuel capacity, longer fuselage accommodating up to 125 passengers, and greater AUW. First flight was made on 28 November 1967 and FAA certification was received on 27 February 1968. The first Series 40 was delivered to SAS on 29 February 1968 and entered commercial service with this airline on 12 March 1968.

Series 50. Stretched short/medium-range development of the Series 30, first announced on 5 July 1973. High-density seating for up to 139 passengers made possible by a 12 ft 7¼ in (3·84 m) fuselage extension. A "new look" interior will feature enclosed overhead racks for carry-on baggage, sculptured wall panels, acoustically-treated ceiling panels and indirect lighting. Available with either Pratt & Whitney JT8D-15 or -17 turbofan engines, rated at 15,500 lb (7,031 kg) and 16,000 lb (7,257 kg) st respectively, and embodying sound-absorption materials as developed for the engines and nacelles of the DC-10, the Series 50 will meet FAR Pt 36 noise requirements. The engines will be smokeless and will have thrust reversers rotated 17° from the vertical to reduce the possibility of exhaust gas ingestion. The landing gear is to be fitted with an improved anti-skid braking system. Max T-O weight of this version will be 121,000 lb (54,885 kg) and max landing weight 110,000 lb (49,895 kg). It was announced simultaneously that Swissair had ordered ten aircraft of this series, with JT8D-17 engines. First deliveries are scheduled for the Summer of 1975.

All versions are offered in passenger, cargo (**DC-9F**), convertible (**DC-9CF**) or passenger-cargo (**DC-9RC**) configurations. The cargo and convertible models have a main cabin cargo door measuring 11 ft 4 in (3·45 m) wide and 6 ft 9 in (2·06 m) high. An executive transport version is also offered, with increased fuel, enabling up to 15 persons to be carried non-stop over 2,865 nm (3,300 mile; 5,300 km) transcontinental or transocean stages. First delivery of an all-cargo model, a DC-9 Srs 30F, was made to Alitalia on 13 May 1968. This model has 4,313 cu ft (122·1 m³) of cargo space in main cabin, plus the underfloor hold, enabling it to carry eight full cargo pallets and two half-pallets with total weight of nearly 40,000 lb (18,144 kg).

There are also three military versions of the DC-9, as follows:

C-9A Nightingale. Aeromedical airlift transport, of which eight were ordered in 1967 for operation by the 375th Aeromedical Wing of the USAF Military Airlift Command. Essentially an "off-the-shelf" DC-9 Srs 30 commercial transport, but with JT8D-9 engines, the C-9A is able to carry 30 to 40 litter patients, more than 40 ambulatory patients or a combination of the two, together with two nurses and three aeromedical technicians. The interior includes a special-care compartment, with separate atmospheric and ventilation controls. Galleys and toilets are provided fore and aft. There are three entrances, two with hydraulically-operated stairways. The third has a forward door 6 ft 9 in (2·06 m) high and 11 ft 4 in (3·45 m) wide, with a hydraulically-operated ramp, to facilitate loading of litters. First C-9A was rolled out on 17 June 1968 and was delivered to the US Air Force at Scott Air Force Base on 10 August 1968. Orders for the C-9A totalled 21, which had been delivered by February 1973.

C-9B Skytrain II. Fleet logistic support transport, of which five were ordered by the USN under a $25·3 million contract announced on 19 April 1972, increased subsequently to eight. Described separately.

VC-9C. A special configuration ordered in December 1973 by the USAF for service in the Special Air Missions Wing based at Andrews DC-9-30 type aircraft are scheduled for delivery AFB, Maryland, near Washington, DC. Three in 1975.

Totals of orders and leases for the commercial DC-9 announced up to 1 June 1974 are as follows:

Series 10	137
Series 20	10
Series 30	568
Series 40	49
Series 50	26
Leased	1

A total of 730 DC-9s (including 21 C-9As and 8 C-9Bs) had been delivered by 17 June 1974.

Under a then-unique participation plan for major subcontractors, component manufacturers accepted deferred payment for developing and producing their portions of the aircraft. Each participant used his own capital to finance the engineering, tooling, qualification testing and work in process on the components he produced. Douglas then purchased these components under a firm fixed-price contract covering a specific number of units. Payment was completed upon delivery of the aircraft to airline customers.

First manufacturer to announce participation in this scheme was de Havilland Aircraft of Canada, which produced wings, rear fuselage and tail unit assemblies for the DC-9, until Douglas Aircraft Company of Canada took over responsibility for this work and leased that portion of the de Havilland plant devoted to DC-9 production. Agreements still in being were concluded with Garrett-AiResearch for air-conditioning and ice protection systems, Rohr Corporation for engine pods and thrust reversers, Sperry Phoenix Company for the aircraft's automatic flight control system, Menasco Manufacturing Company for the landing gear, Westinghouse Aerospace Electrical Division for the electric power generating system, Goodyear Tire and Rubber Company for the wheels and brakes, Sundstrand Corporation for constant-speed mechanisms and Hydro-Aire Division of Crane Company for anti-skid braking units.

In June 1966, the FAA certificated three Category 2 all-weather landing systems for the DC-9, comprising the Collins FD-108 flight director system, Sperry AD-200 flight director system, and coupled approach utilising the Sperry SP-50A autopilot.

The following structural details apply to the DC-9 Series 10:

TYPE: Twin-turbofan short/medium-range airliner.

WINGS: Cantilever low-wing monoplane. Mean thickness/chord ratio 11·6%. Sweepback 24° at quarter-chord. All-metal construction, with three spars inboard, two spars outboard and spanwise stringers riveted to skin. Glassfibre

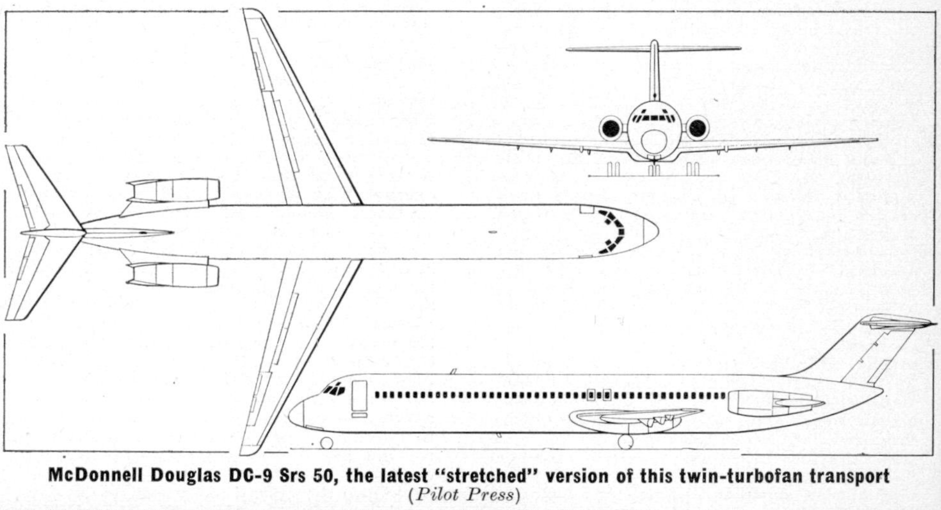

McDonnell Douglas DC-9 Srs 50, the latest "stretched" version of this twin-turbofan transport
(*Pilot Press*)

McDonnell Douglas DC-9 Srs 30 in the insignia of Aeromexico ,the first to be delivered with JT8D-15 engines

McDonnell Douglas DC-9 Srs 40 in the insignia of Toa Domestic Airlines of Japan

trailing-edges on wings, ailerons and flaps. Hydraulically-controlled ailerons, each in two sections, outer sections used at low speed only. Wing-mounted speed brakes. Hydraulically-actuated double-slotted flaps over 67% of semi-span. (Leading-edge slats on Srs 20/30/40/50.) Single boundary-layer fence (vortillon) under each wing. Detachable wingtips. Thermal anti-icing of leading-edges.

Fuselage: Conventional all-metal semi-monocoque structure.

Tail Unit: Cantilever all-metal structure with hydraulically-actuated variable-incidence T-tailplane. Manually-controlled elevators with servo tabs. Hydraulically-controlled rudder with manual override. Glassfibre trailing-edges on control surfaces.

Landing Gear: Retractable tricycle type of Menasco manufacture, with steerable nose-wheel. Hydraulic retraction, nose unit forward, main units inward. Twin Goodyear wheels on each unit. Main-wheel tyres size 40 × 14. Nosewheel tyres size 26 × 6·60. Goodyear brakes. Hydro-Aire Hytrol Mk II anti-skid units.

Power Plant: Two Pratt & Whitney JT8D turbofan engines (details given under individual model listings), mounted on sides of rear fuselage. Engines fitted with 40% target-type thrust reversers for ground operation only. Standard fuel capacity 2,786 US gallons (10,546 litres) in Srs 10 Model 11, 3,700 US gallons (14,000 litres) in Srs 10 Model 15, 3,679 US gallons (13,925 litres) in Srs 20, 30 and 40.

Accommodation (Srs 10): Crew of two on flight deck, plus cabin attendants. Accommodation in main cabin for 56-68 first class passengers four-abreast, or up to 90 tourist class five-abreast. Mixed class versions include one with 16 first class and 40 tourist seats. Fully pressurised and air-conditioned. Toilets at rear of cabin. Provision for galley. Passenger door at front of cabin on port side, with electrically-operated built-in airstairs. Optional ventral stairway. Servicing and emergency exit door opposite on starboard side. Underfloor freight and baggage holds, with forward door on starboard side, rear door on port side.

Dimensions, external:
Wing span:
Srs 10 — 89 ft 5 in (27·25 m)
Srs 20, 30, 40, 50 — 93 ft 5 in (28·47 m)
Wing aspect ratio:
Srs 10 — 8·25
Srs 20, 30, 40, 50 — 8·71
Length overall:
Srs 10, 20 — 104 ft 4¾ in (31·82 m)
Srs 30 — 119 ft 3½ in (36·37 m)
Srs 40 — 125 ft 7¼ in (38·28 m)
Srs 50 — 133 ft 7¼ in (40·72 m)
Height overall:
Srs 10, 20, 30 — 27 ft 6 in (8·38 m)
Srs 40 — 28 ft 0 in (8·53 m)
Tailplane span:
Srs 10, 50 — 36 ft 10¼ in (11·23 m)
Wheel track:
Srs 10, 20, 30, 40, 50 — 16 ft 6 in (5·03 m)
Wheelbase:
Srs 10, 20 — 43 ft 8½ in (13·32 m)
Srs 30 — 53 ft 2½ in (16·22 m)
Srs 40 — 56 ft 1¼ in (17·10 m)
Srs 50 — 60 ft 11 in (18·56 m)
Passenger door (port, fwd):
Height — 6 ft 0 in (1·83 m)
Width — 2 ft 9½ in (0·85 m)
Height to sill — 7 ft 2 in (2·13 m)
Servicing door (stbd, fwd):
Height — 4 ft 0 in (1·22 m)
Width — 2 ft 3 in (0·69 m)
Height to sill — 7 ft 2 in (2·18 m)
Freight and baggage hold doors:
Height — 4 ft 2 in (1·27 m)
Width:
fwd — 4 ft 5 in (1·35 m)
rear — 3 ft 0 in (0·91 m)
Height to sill — 3 ft 6 in (1·07 m)

Dimensions, internal:
Cabin (Srs 10): Length — 55 ft 9 in (16·99 m)
Max width — 10 ft 1 in (3·07 m)
Floor width — 9 ft 5 in (2·87 m)
Max height — 6 ft 9 in (2·06 m)
Floor area — 510 sq ft (47·4 m²)
Volume — 3,450 cu ft (97·7 m³)
Carry-on baggage compartment:
Srs 10, 20 — 50 cu ft (1·42 m³)
Freight hold (underfloor):
Srs 10, 20 — 600 cu ft (17·0 m³)
Srs 30 — 895 cu ft (25·3 m³)
Srs 40 — 1,019 cu ft (28·9 m³)
Srs 50 — 1,003 cu ft (28·4 m³)

Areas:
Wings, gross:
Srs 10 — 934·3 sq ft (86·77 m²)
Srs 20, 30, 40, 50 — 1,000·7 sq ft (92·97 m²)
Ailerons (total):
Srs 50 — 38·0 sq ft (3·53 m²)
Trailing-edge flaps (total):
Srs 50 — 210·8 sq ft (19·58 m²)
Leading-edge slats (total):
Srs 50 — 120·8 sq ft (11·22 m²)
Spoilers (total):
Srs 50 — 34·7 sq ft (3·22 m²)
Fin:
Srs 50 — 161·0 sq ft (14·96 m²)
Rudder:
Srs 50 — 65·3 sq ft (6·07 m²)
Tailplane:
Srs 10, 50 — 275·6 sq ft (25·60 m²)
Elevators, incl tabs:
Srs 50 — 105·8 sq ft (9·83 m²)

Weights and Loadings:
Manufacturer's empty weight:
Srs 10 Model 11 — 45,300 lb (20,550 kg)
Srs 10 Model 15 — 47,750 lb (21,660 kg)
Srs 20 — 49,900 lb (22,620 kg)
Srs 30 — 52,935 lb (24,011 kg)
Srs 40 — 55,690 lb (25,261 kg)
Max space-limited payload:
Srs 10 Model 11 — 18,050 lb (8,188 kg)
Srs 10 Model 15 — 21,381 lb (9,698 kg)
Srs 20 — 21,885 lb (9,925 kg)
Max weight-limited payload:
Srs 30 — 26,156 lb (11,864 kg)
Srs 40 — 34,195 lb (15,510 kg)
Max T-O weight:
Srs 10 Model 11 — 77,700 lb (35,245 kg)
Srs 10 Model 15 — 90,700 lb (41,140 kg)
Srs 20, 30 — 98,000 lb (44,450 kg)
Srs 40 — 114,000 lb (51,710 kg)
Srs 50 — 121,000 lb (54,885 kg)
Max ramp weight:
Srs 10 Model 11 — 78,500 lb (35,605 kg)
Srs 10 Model 15 — 91,500 lb (41,500 kg)
Srs 20, 30 — 98,800 lb (44,815 kg)
Srs 40 — 115,000 lb (52,168 kg)
Max zero-fuel weight:
Srs 10 Model 11 — 66,400 lb (30,120 kg)
Srs 10 Model 15 — 71,400 lb (32,385 kg)
Srs 20 — 78,000 lb (35,380 kg)
Srs 30 — 82,000 lb (37,195 kg)
Srs 40 — 93,000 lb (42,184 kg)
Max landing weight:
Srs 10 Model 11 — 74,000 lb (33,565 kg)
Srs 10 Model 15 — 81,700 lb (37,060 kg)
Srs 20, 30 — 93,400 lb (42,365 kg)
Srs 40 — 102,000 lb (46,265 kg)
Srs 50 — 110,000 lb (49,895 kg)
Max wing loading:
Srs 10 Model 11 — 83·2 lb/sq ft (406·2 kg/m²)
Max power loading:
Srs 10 Model 15 — 3·24 lb/lb st (3·24 kg/kg st)

Performance (at max T-O weight, except where indicated):
Max never-exceed speed:
Srs 50 — 537 knots (618 mph; 994 km/h)
Max level speed:
Srs 50 — 500 knots (576 mph; 927 km/h)
Max cruising speed at 25,000 ft (7,620 m):
Srs 10 Model 11 and 15 — 487 knots (561 mph; 903 km/h)
Srs 20 at 80,000 lb (36,290 kg) AUW — 487 knots (561 mph; 903 km/h)
Srs 30 — 491 knots (565 mph; 909 km/h)
Srs 40 — 487 knots (561 mph; 903 km/h)
Srs 50 — 485 knots (558 mph; 898 km/h)
Max rate of climb at S/L:
Srs 10 Model 11 — 2,750 ft (838 m)/min
Srs 50 — 2,850 ft (869 m)/min
FAA T-O field length:
Srs 10 Model 11 — 5,300 ft (1,615 m)
Srs 20 — 5,750 ft (1,750 m)
Srs 30 — 6,800 ft (2,075 m)
Srs 40 (at 100,000 lb; 45,359 kg AUW) — 8,080 ft (2,462 m)
FAR T-O distance to 35 ft (10·7 m):
Srs 50 — 7,750 ft (2,362 m)
FAA landing field length:
Srs 10 Model 11 — 4,630 ft (1,411 m)
Srs 20 — 4,780 ft (1,460 m)
Srs 30 — 4,920 ft (1,500 m)
Srs 40 — 4,780 ft (1,456 m)
FAR landing distance from 50 ft (15 m):
Srs 50 — 4,720 ft (1,439 m)
Range at Mach 0·8, with reserves for 200 nm (230 mile; 370 km) flight to alternate and 60 min hold at 10,000 ft (3,050 m):
Srs 10 Model 11 at 25,000 ft (7,620 m) with 50 passengers and baggage — 864 nm (995 miles; 1,601 km)
Srs 20 at 25,000 ft (7,620 m) with 50 passengers and baggage — 1,213 nm (1,397 miles; 2,250 km)
Srs 30 at 30,000 ft (9,150 m) — 1,288 nm (1,484 miles; 2,388 km)
Srs 40 at 25,000 ft (7,620 m) — 1,035 nm (1,192 miles; 1,918 km)
Range at long-range cruising speed at 30,000 ft (9,150 m), reserves as above:
Srs 10 Model 11 with 50 passengers — 1,138 nm (1,311 miles; 2,110 km)
Srs 20 with 50 passengers — 1,600 nm (1,843 miles; 2,970 km)
Srs 30 — 1,498 nm (1,725 miles; 2,775 km)
Srs 40 — 1,463 nm (1,685 miles; 2,710 km)
Range with max fuel:
Srs 50 — 2,195 nm (2,527 miles; 4,066 km)
Range with max payload:
Srs 50 — 810 nm (932 miles; 1,500 km)

McDONNELL DOUGLAS C-9B SKYTRAIN II

The US Navy's C-9B Skytrain II is a special convertible passenger/cargo version of the DC-9 Series 30 commercial transport named after the long-enduring Navy R4D Skytrain, a DC-3 variant of which 624 were procured by that service.

The contract for five (increased subsequently to eight) C-9Bs was signed by Naval Air Systems Command on 24 April 1972, and the first of these aircraft made its initial flight on 7 February 1973, two months ahead of schedule. The first two aircraft were delivered on 8 May 1973, to Fleet Tactical Support Squadrons 1 (VR-1) at NAS Norfolk, Virginia, and 30 (VR-30) at NAS Alameda, California. All eight were delivered during 1973.

A compromise between the DC-9 Series 30 and 40, the C-9B has the overall dimensions of the former, and the 14,500 lb (6,575 kg) st Pratt & Whitney JT8D-9 turbofan engines of the latter, as well as the optional 11 ft 4 in (3·45 m) by 6 ft 9 in (2·06 m) cargo door, which is situated at the port forward end of the cabin. This allows loading of standard military pallets measuring 7 ft 4 in (2·24 m) by 9 ft 0 in (2·74 m), and in an all-cargo configuration eight of these can be accommodated, representing a total cargo load of 32,444 lb (14,716 kg). When loading, each pallet is first elevated to door sill height, and then rolled forward on to a ball transfer system before being positioned finally by means of roller tracks.

Normal flight crew consists of pilot, co-pilot, crew chief and two cabin attendants, and standard accommodation is for 90 passengers on five-abreast seating at 38 in (97 cm) pitch, or up to 107 passengers at 34 in (86 cm) pitch. In a typical passenger/cargo configuration, three pallets are carried in the forward area, with 45 passengers in the rear section. A galley and toilet are located at each end of the cabin. In all-cargo or mixed passenger/cargo configuration, a cargo barrier net can be erected at the forward end of the cabin; in the latter configuration a smoke barrier curtain is placed between the cargo section and the passengers.

Normal passenger access is by means of forward port and aft ventral doors, each with hydraulically-operated airstairs to make the C-9B independent of ground facilities. The ventral door allows passengers to board while cargo is being loaded in the forward area. Two Type III emergency exits, each 3 ft 0 in (0·91 m) by 1 ft 8 in (0·51 m), are positioned on each side of the fuselage to permit overwing escape, and four 25-man life rafts are carried in stowage racks. To complete the C-9B's independence of ground facilities, an auxiliary power unit provides both electrical and hydraulic services when the aircraft is on the ground. An environmental control system maintains a sea level cabin altitude to a height of 18,500 ft (5,640 m) and an 8,000 ft (2,440 m) cabin altitude to 35,000 ft (10,670 m).

A maximum fuel capacity of 5,929 US gallons (22,443 litres) provides a ferry range of 2,953 nm (3,400 miles; 5,472 km), the standard wing fuel tanks being supplemented by a 1,250 US gallon (4,732 litre) tank in the forward underfloor freight hold, and a 1,000 US gallon (3,785 litre) tank in the aft hold.

Advanced nav/com equipment is installed, including Omega and inertial navigation systems, and FAA certification has been received for both manual and automatic approaches under Category II weather conditions.

DIMENSIONS, EXTERNAL:
As for DC-9 Series 30

DIMENSIONS, INTERNAL:

Cabin: Length	68 ft 0 in (20·73 m)
Width	10 ft 0 in (3·05 m)
Volume (cargo)	4,200 cu ft (118·9 m³)
Baggage holds (underfloor):	
forward	298 cu ft (8·44 m³)
aft	135 cu ft (3·82 m³)

WEIGHTS:

Operating weight, empty:	
passenger configuration	65,283 lb (29,612 kg)
cargo configuration	59,706 lb (27,082 kg)
Max ramp weight	111,000 lb (50,350 kg)
Max T-O weight	110,000 lb (49,900 kg)
Max landing weight	99,000 lb (44,906 kg)

PERFORMANCE (at max T-O weight unless otherwise specified):
Max cruising speed
500 knots (576 mph; 927 km/h)
Long-range cruising speed
438 knots (504 mph; 811 km/h)
Military critical field length 6,400 ft (1,951 m)
Landing distance, at max landing weight
2,500 ft (762 m)
Range, long-range cruising speed at 30,000 ft (9,145 m) with 10,000 lb (4,535 kg) payload
2,538 nm (2,923 miles; 4,704 km)

MCDONNELL DOUGLAS DC-10

In April 1966, American Airlines circulated to seven airframe manufacturers a statement of the company's requirements, based on traffic forecasts. They appreciated that increasing airport congestion would be alleviated by the introduction of commercial transport aircraft of greater passenger-carrying capacity, but considered it essential that such aircraft should not be restricted to operation from those airports with very long runways. At that time, they visualised a twin-turbofan aircraft with dimensions and performance tailored specifically for operation from smaller airports. During the evolutionary period, the major change was a decision to use three instead of two turbofan engines.

The aircraft which McDonnell Douglas evolved to meet this specification was designated DC-10, an all-purpose commercial transport able to operate economically over ranges from 260 nm to 5,300 nm (300 to 6,100 miles; 480 to 9,815 km), according to Series, and able to carry 270 mixed class passengers, or a maximum of 380 passengers in an all-economy configuration.

It is being produced in three versions, as follows:

Series 10. Initial version, powered by three General Electric CF6-6D or -6D1 turbofan engines, each rated at 40,000 lb (18,143 kg) st or 41,000 lb (18,597 kg) st respectively. Intended for service on domestic routes of 260-3,125 nm (300-3,600 miles; 480-5,795 km). First ordered by American Airlines on 19 February 1968.

Series 30. Extended-range version for intercontinental operations, powered by three General Electric CF6-50A or -50C turbofan engines, each rated at 49,000 lb (22,226 kg) and 51,000 lb (23,133 kg) st respectively with exhaust nozzles. Increased fuel capacity. Wing span increased by 10 ft 0 in (3·05 m). Landing gear supplemented by additional dual-wheel unit, mounted on the fuselage centreline between the four-wheel bogie main units.

Series 40. As Series 30, but power plant is three Pratt & Whitney JT9D-20 turbofan engines, each rated at 49,400 lb (22,407 kg) st with water injection and exhaust nozzle installed. Japan Air Lines has ordered six Srs 40s for delivery in 1976, these to be equipped with JT9D-59A engines rated at 53,000 lb (24,040 kg) st.

There is also a convertible cargo version designated the Model 30CF, which is described separately.

By 9 February 1974 orders and options totalled 252 aircraft (206 orders, 46 options) for the following airlines:

Aeromexico	Series 30
Air Afrique	Series 30
Air New Zealand	Series 30
Air Zaïre	Series 30
Alitalia	Series 30
American Airlines	Series 10
Continental Air Lines	Series 10/10CF
Delta Air Lines	Series 10
Finnair	Series 30
Iberia	Series 30
Japan Air Lines	Series 40
KLM	Series 30
Korean Air Lines	Series 30
Laker Airways	Series 10
Lufthansa	Series 30
Martinair Holland	Series 30CF
National Airlines	Series 10
National Airlines	Series 30
Northwest Airlines	Series 40
Overseas National Airways	Series 30CF
Pakistan International Airlines	Series 30
Philippine Air Lines	Series 30
Sabena	Series 30CF
Scandinavian Airlines System	Series 30
Swissair	Series 30
Trans International Airlines	Series 30CF
Turkish Airlines	Series 10
Union de Transports Aériens	Series 30
United Air Lines	Series 10
VARIG	Series 30
VIASA	Series 30
Western Airlines	Series 10

Manufacture of the first aircraft started on 6 January 1969, and assembly at the McDonnell Douglas plant at Long Beach, California, began in the Summer of 1969. The first DC-10 Srs 10 made its first flight on 29 August 1970.

On 29 July 1971 simultaneous deliveries of the first two McDonnell Douglas DC-10 Srs 10 commercial transport aircraft were made to American Airlines and United Air Lines at Long Beach, California. The FAA awarded the company a type certificate and production certificate for the Srs 10 on the same day.

First scheduled passenger flight of the DC-10 Srs 10 was made on 5 August 1971, when American Airlines began a daily DC-10 service between Los Angeles and Chicago.

First flight of the Series 40 (known originally as Series 20) was made on 28 February 1972. During the period 8-14 October 1972, this aircraft set three non-stop flight records for Los Angeles to Hong Kong, Honolulu to Buenos Aires, and Rio de Janeiro to Long Beach while making a 26,409 nm (30,411 mile; 48,941 km) demonstration tour of Asia and South America. FAA certification for the Series 40 was received on 20 October 1972, and the first delivery of a production aircraft, to Northwest Orient Airlines, was made on 10 November 1972.

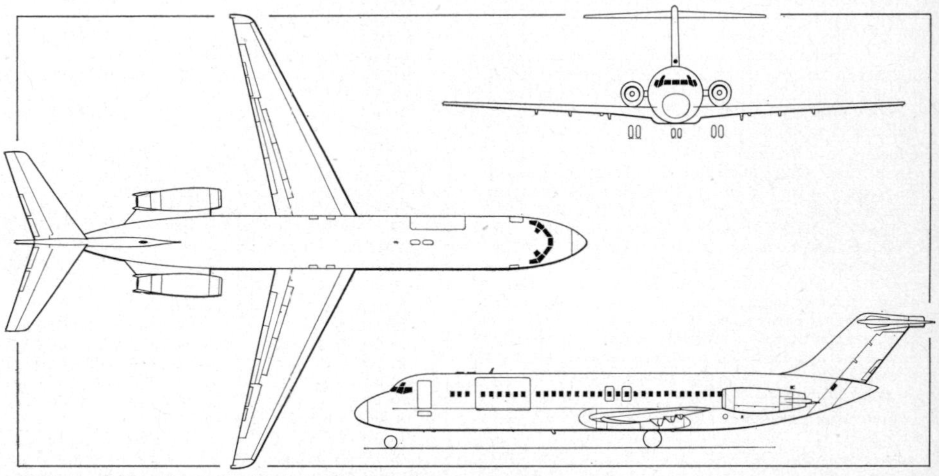

McDonnell Douglas C-9B Skytrain II convertible passenger/cargo transport, based on the DC-9 Srs 30 (*Michael Badrocke*)

McDonnell Douglas C-9B Skytrain II (two 14,500 lb st Pratt & Whitney JT8D-9 turbofan engines)

McDonnell Douglas DC-10 Series 40 (three Pratt & Whitney JT9D turbofan engines) in service with Northwest Orient Airlines

First flight of the Series 30 was made on 21 June 1972. FAA certification was granted on 21 November 1972, simultaneously with the first deliveries of production aircraft to KLM and Swissair.

The DC-10 manufacturing plan calls for subassemblies and components to be brought together at Long Beach for final assembly. Certain major subassemblies are produced at other divisions of McDonnell Douglas. The nose is built at McDonnell Douglas Astronautics Company, Santa Monica, California; McDonnell Aircraft Company, St Louis, Missouri is responsible for design and development of the wing, and production of certain control surface components. Douglas Aircraft Company of Canada, Ltd, a McDonnell Douglas subsidiary, builds the wing structure at Malton, Ontario.

Convair Division of General Dynamics Corporation at San Diego, California, was selected as subcontractor for the fuselage, being responsible for five sections totalling 128 ft (39·01 m).

Other subcontractors engaged in the DC-10 programme include Rohr Corporation for engine pods and sound suppression; Menasco, main landing gear units; AiResearch, auxiliary power unit and environmental system; Abex and Dowty Rotol, nose landing units; Vought Systems, tailplane and elevators; Aerfer, Italy, upper fin and rudder; and Mitsubishi, Japan, the tailcone and actuators for the main landing gear doors. Sundstrand Corporation provides constant-speed drive mechanisms; Aerospace Electrical Division of Westinghouse, electrical generating systems; Bendix Navigation and Control Division, the integrated autopilot/flight director unit; Amimech Division of Aircraft Mechanics, crew seats of advanced design; Goodyear, wheels and brakes; and Sperry Flight Systems, automatic throttle and speed control system.

TYPE: Three-turbofan commercial transport.

WINGS: Cantilever low-wing monoplane of all-metal fail-safe construction. Several different wing sections of Douglas design are used between wing root and tip. Thickness/chord ratio varies from slightly more than 12·2% at root to less than 8·4% at tip. Dihedral 5° 14·4′ inboard, 3° 1·8′ outboard. Incidence ranges from positive at wing root to negative at tip. Sweepback at quarter-chord 35°. All-metal inboard and outboard ailerons, the former used conventionally, the latter only when the leading-edge slats are extended. Double-slotted all-metal trailing-edge flaps mounted on external hinges, with an inboard and outboard flap panel on each wing. On Series 30 and 40 aircraft the inboard ailerons droop symmetrically with the flaps to a maximum of 13° 12′: their differential operation as ailerons is superimposed on top of their symmetrical deployment as flaps. Five all-metal spoiler panels on each wing, at the rear edge of the fixed wing structure, forward of the flaps. All spoilers operate in unison as lateral control, speed brake, direct lift control and ground spoilers. Full-span two-position all-metal leading-edge slats. Ailerons are powered by hydraulic actuators manufactured by Bertea Corporation, spoilers by hydraulic actuators manufactured by Parker-Hannifin Corporation. Each aileron is powered by either of two hydraulic systems; each spoiler is powered by a single system. All leading-edge slat segments outboard of the engines are anti-iced with engine bleed air.

FUSELAGE: Aluminium semi-monocoque fail-safe structure of circular cross-section. Except for auxiliary areas the entire fuselage is pressurised.

TAIL UNIT: Cantilever all-metal structure. Variable-incidence tailplane, actuated by Vickers hydraulic motors. Longitudinal and directional controls are fully powered and comprise inboard and outboard elevators, each segment powered by a Bertea tandem actuator; upper and lower rudder each powered by a Bertea actuator. Rudder standby power supplied by two transfer motor pumps manufactured by Abex Corporation.

LANDING GEAR (Srs 10): Hydraulically-retracted tricycle type, with gravity free-fall for emergency extension. Nosewheel unit retracts forward, main units inward into fuselage. Twin-wheel steerable nose unit. Main gear comprises two four-wheel bogies. Oleo-pneumatic shock-absorbers on all units. Goodyear nosewheels and tyres size 37 × 14-14, pressure 160 lb/sq in (11·2 kg/cm²). Goodyear main wheels and tyres size 50 × 20-20, pressure 170 lb/sq in (12·0 kg/cm²). Goodyear disc brakes and anti-skid system, with individual wheel control.

This photograph shows well the additional, centreline main landing gear unit that is fitted to the DC-10 Series 30 and 40

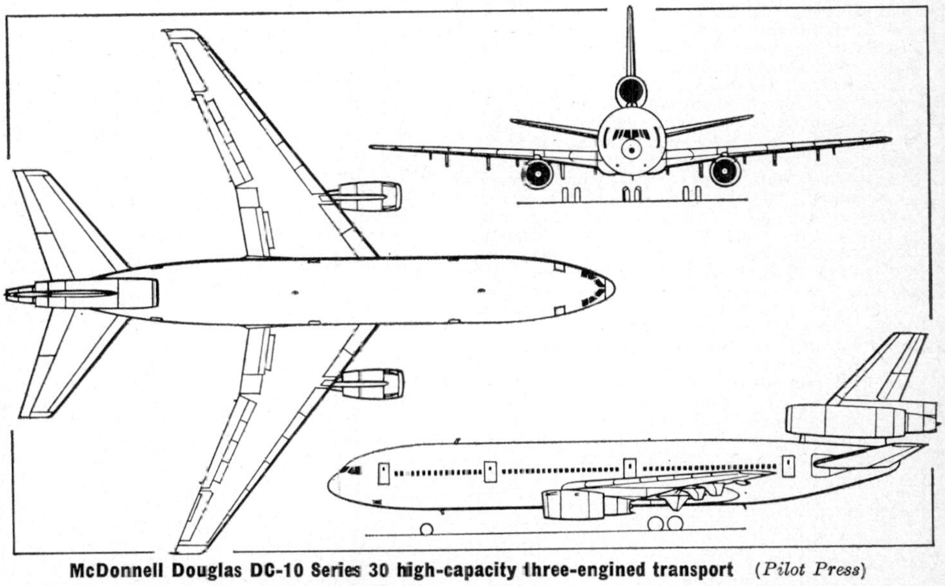

McDonnell Douglas DC-10 Series 30 high-capacity three-engined transport (*Pilot Press*)

LANDING GEAR (Srs 30 and 40): These versions have an additional dual-wheel main unit mounted on the fuselage centreline between the four-wheel bogie units, and this retracts forward. Goodyear nosewheels and tyres size 40 × 15·5-16, pressure 180 lb/sq in (12·7 kg/cm²). Four-wheel bogie main units and centreline unit have Goodyear wheels and tyres size 52 × 20·5-23. The former have a pressure of 165 lb/sq in (11·6 kg/cm²), the latter 140 lb/sq in (9·8 kg/cm²). Otherwise as Srs 10.

POWER PLANT: Three turbofan engines, two of which are mounted on underwing pylons, the third above the rear fuselage at the base of the fin (details under Series descriptions). All engines are fitted with both fan and turbine reversers for ground operation. Engine air inlets have load-carrying acoustically-treated panels for noise attenuation, and each engine fan case and fan exhaust is similarly treated. Three integral wing fuel tanks with a total capacity of approximately 21,800 US gallons

McDonnell Douglas DC-10 Srs 30CF convertible passenger/freight transport in the insignia of Sabena

(82,518 litres). Four standard pressure refuelling adapters, two in each wing outboard of the engine pylons. Series 30 and 40 aircraft have four integral wing fuel tanks and an auxiliary tank in the wing centre-section with a connected structural compartment fitted with a bladder cell, giving increased total capacity of approximately 35,800 US gallons (135,510 litres). Oil capacity, Series 10 and 30: 9 usable US gallons (34·1 litres); Series 40: 15 usable US gallons (56·8 litres).

ACCOMMODATION: Crew of five (pilot, first officer, flight engineer, two observers) plus cabin attendants. Standard seating for 255 or 270 in mixed class versions, with a maximum of 380 passengers in an economy class arrangement. Two aisles run the length of the cabin, which is separated into sections by cloakroom dividers. In the first class section, with three pairs of reclining seats abreast, the aisles are 2 ft 7 in (0·78 m) wide. In the coach class section, four pairs of seats, with a table between the centre pairs, also have two aisles, these being 1 ft 8 in (0·51 m) wide. One pair of seats is exchanged for a three-seat unit in the nine-abreast high-density layout. Up to nine lavatories located throughout the passenger cabin. Cloakrooms of standard and elevating type distributed throughout the cabin. Cabin windows, 11 in × 16 in (0·28 × 0·41 m), are spaced at 20 in (0·51 m) centres. Overhead stowage modules, fully enclosed and providing stowage for passengers' personal effects, are located on the sidewalls and extend the full length of the cabin. Eight passenger doors, four on each side, open by sliding inward and upward into the above-ceiling area. Containerised or bulk cargo compartments located immediately forward and aft of the wing, with outward-opening doors on the starboard side. A bulk cargo compartment is located in the lower aft section of the fuselage, with its door on the port side. Entire accommodation is fully air-conditioned, with five separate control zones for the standard below-floor galley configuration. Series 30 and 40 aircraft have an optional main cabin galley to replace the lower galley, and in this configuration there are four separate control zones for the air-conditioning. The lower-deck galley is provided with eight high-temperature ovens, refrigerators, storage space for linen, china and other accessories. Serving carts are taken to cabin level by two electric elevators, to a buffet service centre, from where stewardesses serve passengers. To permit quick turnround at terminals, without interference to passenger movement in the main cabin, the kitchen is provisioned through the cargo doors at ground level.

SYSTEMS: Three parallel continuously-operating and completely separate hydraulic systems supply the fully-powered flight controls and wheel brakes. Two of these systems supply power for nosewheel steering. Normally, one of the systems supplies power for landing gear actuation; two reversible motor pumps deliver power from the other two systems for standby operation of landing gear. Each hydraulic system is powered by two identical engine-driven pumps, capable of delivering a total of 70 US gallons (265 litres)/min at 3,000 lb/sq in (210 kg/cm²) at take-off. An AiResearch TSCP-700-4 APU provides ground electrical and pneumatic power, including main engine starting, and auxiliary electric power in flight.

ELECTRONICS AND EQUIPMENT: A dual fail-operative landing system is installed to meet Category IIIA weather minima. Digital air data computer meeting ARINC 576 requirements on Srs 10. Triple inertial navigation system with dual area navigation on Srs 30. Triple inertial navigation system meeting ARINC 561 requirements on Srs 40.

DIMENSIONS, EXTERNAL:

Wing span:	
Series 10	155 ft 4 in (47·34 m)
Series 30, 40	165 ft 4·4 in (50·41 m)
Wing chord at root	35 ft 1·8 in (10·71 m)
Wing chord at tip:	
Series 10	10 ft 6½ in (3·21 m)
Series 30, 40	8 ft 11½ in (2·73 m)
Wing aspect ratio:	
Series 10	6·8
Series 30, 40	7·5
Length overall:	
Series 10 (-6D engines)	181 ft 5 in (55·30 m)
Series 10 (-6D1 engines)	182 ft 5 in (55·60 m)
Series 30, 40	182 ft 1 in (55·50 m)
Length of fuselage	170 ft 6 in (51·97 m)
Height overall	58 ft 1 in (17·70 m)
Tailplane span	71 ft 2 in (21·69 m)
Wheel track	35 ft 0 in (10·67 m)
Wheelbase:	
Series 10, 40	72 ft 5 in (22·07 m)
Series 30	72 ft 4 in (22·05 m)

DIMENSIONS, INTERNAL:

Cabin: Length, from aft bulkhead of flight deck to aft cabin bulkhead	approx 136 ft 0 in (41·45 m)
Max width	18 ft 9 in (5·72 m)
Height (basic)	7 ft 11 in (2·41 m)
Series 10, 30, 40 in lower-galley configuration:	
Forward baggage and/or freight hold (forward of wing):	
Containerised volume	960 cu ft (27·2 m³)
Bulk volume	1,375 cu ft (38·9 m³)
Centre baggage and/or freight hold (aft of wing):	
Containerised volume	1,280 cu ft (36·2 m³)
Bulk volume	1,585 cu ft (44·9 m³)
Aft hold:	
Bulk volume	805 cu ft (22·8 m³)
Series 30, 40 in upper-galley configuration:	
Forward baggage and/or freight hold (forward of wing):	
Containerised volume	2,560 cu ft (72·5 m³)
Bulk volume	3,045 cu ft (86·2 m³)
Centre baggage and/or freight hold (aft of wing):	
Containerised volume	1,600 cu ft (45·3 m³)
Bulk volume	1,935 cu ft (54·8 m³)
Aft hold:	
Bulk volume	510 cu ft (14·4 m³)

AREAS:

Wings, gross:	
Series 10	3,861 sq ft (358·7 m²)
Series 30, 40	3,958 sq ft (367·7 m²)
Ailerons, inboard (total)	82·7 sq ft (7·68 m²)
Ailerons, outboard (total)	105·1 sq ft (9·76 m²)
Trailing-edge flaps (total)	668·2 sq ft (62·1 m²)
Leading-edge slats (total):	
Series 10	452·6 sq ft (42·05 m²)
Series 30, 40	471·9 sq ft (43·84 m²)
Spoilers (total)	137·0 sq ft (12·73 m²)
Fin	494·29 sq ft (45·92 m²)
Rudders (total)	110·71 sq ft (10·29 m²)
Tailplane	1,040·2 sq ft (96·6 m²)
Elevators (total)	298·1 sq ft (27·7 m²)

WEIGHTS AND LOADINGS:

Basic operating weight:	
Series 10	233,300 lb (105,820 kg)
Series 30	263,500 lb (119,520 kg)
Series 40	267,250 lb (121,220 kg)
Max payload:	
Series 10	101,700 lb (46,130 kg)
Series 30	104,500 lb (47,400 kg)
Series 40	100,750 lb (45,700 kg)

McDonnell Douglas DC-10 Srs 30 (three General Electric CF6 turbofan engines) operated by Aeromexico

Max T-O weight:
Series 10 440,000 lb (199,580 kg)
Series 30 555,000 lb (251,744 kg)
Series 40 (-20 engines) 555,000 lb (251,744 kg)
Series 40 (-59A engines) 572,000 lb (259,450 kg)
Max ramp weight:
Series 10 443,000 lb (200,940 kg)
Series 30, 40 558,000 lb (253,105 kg)
Max zero-fuel weight:
Series 10 335,000 lb (151,953 kg)
Series 30, 40 368,000 lb (166,922 kg)
Max landing weight:
Series 10 363,500 lb (164,880 kg)
Series 30, 40 403,000 lb (182,798 kg)
Max wing loading:
Series 10 124 lb/sq ft (605·4 kg/m²)
Series 30, 40 152·2 lb/sq ft (743·1 kg/m²)

Performance (at max T-O weight unless specified):
Max never-exceed speed Mach 0·95
Max level speed at 25,000 ft (7,620 m) Mach 0·88, or 530 knots (610 mph; 982 km/h)
Max cruising speed at 30,000 ft (9,145 m):
Series 10 (-6D engines) 499 knots (575 mph; 925 km/h)
Series 10 (-6D1 engines) 501 knots (577 mph; 928 km/h)
Series 30 502 knots (578 mph; 930 km/h)
Series 40 (-20 engines) 489 knots (563 mph; 906 km/h)
Series 40 (-59A engines) 490 knots (564 mph; 908 km/h)
T-O speed (V_2):
Series 10 (-6D engines) 168 knots (193 mph; 311 km/h)
Series 10 (-6D1 engines) 163 knots (188 mph; 302 km/h)
Series 30 (-50A engines) 181 knots (208 mph; 335 km/h)
Series 30 (-50C engines) 175 knots (202 mph; 325 km/h)
Series 40 (-20 engines) 183·5 knots (211 mph; 340 km/h)
Series 40 (-59A engines) 180·6 knots (208 mph; 334 km/h)
Landing speed at max landing weight:
Series 10 136 knots (157 mph; 252 km/h)
Series 30 145 knots (167 mph; 269 km/h)
Series 40 (-20 engines) 146·5 knots (168·5 mph; 271 km/h)
Series 40 (-59A engines) 147 knots (169 mph; 272 km/h)
Max rate of climb at S/L:
Series 10 (-6D engines) 2,680 ft (817 m)/min
Series 10 (-6D1 engines) 2,750 ft (838 m)/min
Series 30 3,000 ft (914 m)/min
Series 40 (-20 engines) 2,720 ft (829 m)/min
Series 40 (-59A engines) 2,540 ft (774 m)/min
Service ceiling:
Series 10, -6D engines, at 425,000 lb (192,775 kg) AUW 34,800 ft (10,605 m)
Series 10, -6D1 engines, at 425,000 lb (192,775 kg) AUW 35,200 ft (10,730 m)
Series 30, at 540,000 lb (244,940 kg) AUW 34,000 ft (10,365 m)
Series 40 (-20 engines) at 535,000 lb (242,670 kg) AUW 21,700 ft (6,615 m)
Series 40 (-59A engines) 32,700 ft (9,965 m)
En-route climb altitude, one engine out:
Series 10 at 430,000 lb (195,045 kg) AUW 13,600 ft (4,145 m)
Series 30 at 545,000 lb (247,205 kg) AUW 14,900 ft (4,540 m)
Series 40 (-20 engines) at 545,000 lb (247,205 kg) AUW 11,700 ft (3,565 m)
Series 40 (-59A engines) at 560,000 lb (254,010 kg) AUW 16,850 ft (5,135 m)
FAR T-O distance to 35 ft (10·7 m):
Series 10 (-6D engines) 9,800 ft (2,987 m)
Series 10 (-6D1 engines) 9,000 ft (2,743 m)
Series 30 (-50A engines) 11,670 ft (3,557 m)
Series 30 (-50C engines) 10,630 ft (3,240 m)
Series 40 (-20 engines) 12,250 ft (3,734 m)
Series 40 (-59A engines) 11,300 ft (3,444 m)
FAR landing distance from 50 ft (15 m) at max landing weight:
Series 10 5,830 ft (1,777 m)
Series 30 5,960 ft (1,817 m)
Series 40 6,020 ft (1,835 m)
Range with max fuel:
Series 10 5,150 nm (5,930 miles; 9,543 km)
Series 30 6,250 nm (7,197 miles; 11,580 km)
Series 40 (-20 engines) 5,800 nm (6,679 miles; 10,750 km)
Series 40 (-59A engines) 6,100 nm (7,024 miles; 11,305 km)
Range with max payload:
Series 10 2,350 nm (2,706 miles; 4,355 km)
Series 30 3,800 nm (4,375 miles; 7,040 km)
Series 40 (-20 engines) 3,500 nm (4,030 miles; 6,485 km)
Series 40 (-59A engines) 4,050 nm (4,663 miles; 7,505 km)

MCDONNELL DOUGLAS DC-10 MODEL 30CF

The Model 30CF is a convertible freighter version of the McDonnell Douglas DC-10 transport. Generally similar to the basic DC-10 Series 30 and 40, it is designed for easy conversion to either passenger or cargo configuration. Its payload can consist of 380 passengers and baggage or 143,000 lb (64,860 kg) of cargo over full intercontinental range; or up to 155,700 lb (70,626 kg) of cargo on domestic transcontinental routes.

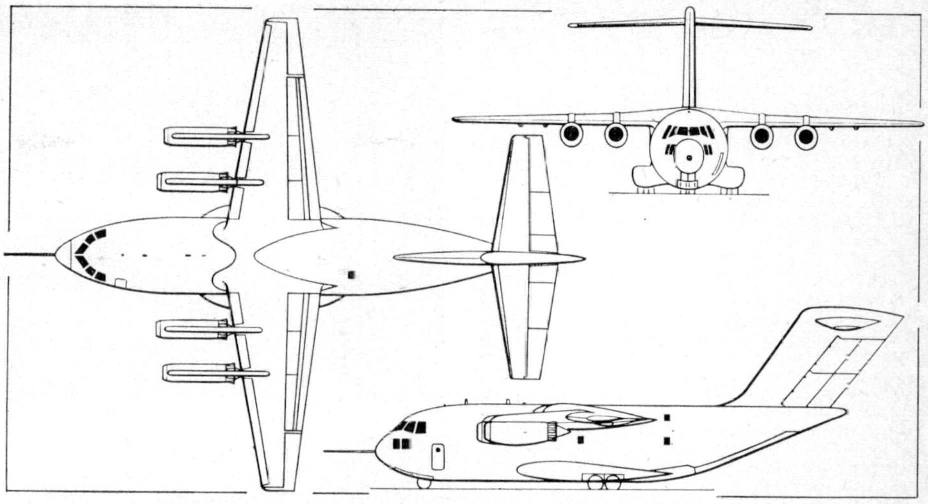

McDonnell Douglas YC-15 advanced medium STOL transport prototype *(Pilot Press)*

The Model 30CF is powered by three General Electric CF6-50A turbofans. It flew for the first time on 28 February 1973 and initial deliveries were made to Overseas National Airways and Trans International Airlines on 17 April 1973.

In the passenger configuration, interior layout is generally similar to that of the DC-10, but the Model 30CF was designed to permit overnight conversion to an all-cargo configuration. This entails removal of seats, overhead baggage racks, forward food service centre, cloakrooms and carpeting from the main cabin, and installation of freight loading tracks and rollers, a cargo tie-down system and restraint nets. Coffee service fixtures and lavatories in the aft cabin may also be removed but are retained normally for regular cargo flights.

The cargo loading system for the Model 30CF is based on that in use in the DC-8 Super Sixty Series freighters. A two-channel network of roller conveyors, adjustable guide rails and pallet restraint fittings is installed in the seat tracks in the cabin floor, by use of simple stud and locking pin devices. An 8 ft 6 in × 11 ft 8 in (2·59 m × 3·56 m) cargo door in the side of the fuselage swings upward and allows easy loading of bulky freight.

A total of 30 standard 7 ft 4 in × 9 ft (2·24 m × 2·74 m) cargo pallets, or 22 larger pallets measuring 7 ft 4 in × 10 ft 5 in (2·24 m × 3·18 m) or 8 ft × 10 ft (2·44 m × 3·05 m), can be accommodated in the main cabin. The Model 30CF also has 3,040 cu ft (86·08 m³) of cargo space in its two lower baggage compartments for bulk freight or 16 half-size or 8 full-size pallets. The entire cargo loading and restraint system can be stowed in this lower hold, and is thus available for conversion of the aircraft to cargo configuration at any airport.

A DC-10-30CF delivered to Sabena Belgian World Airlines in 1973 is certificated for carrying combination loads of freight and passengers in the main cabin. Other DC-10 series aircraft are also offered in convertible versions. Continental Air Lines has taken delivery of the first DC-10 Series 10CF.

MCDONNELL DOUGLAS YC-15

The McDonnell Douglas contender for the USAF's AMST prototype fly-off programme, the requirement for which is described under The Boeing Company's entry (which see), has the designation YC-15. Two prototypes are being built under an $85·9 million contract, and the first of these is scheduled to make its first flight in the second half of 1975, followed by the other aircraft two months later.

The McDonnell Douglas YC-15 differs considerably from the Boeing YC-14: powered by four turbofan engines, it represents a different aerodynamic approach to the STOL requirement.

McDonnell Douglas believes that there will also be a commercial requirement for an aircraft in this category, and expects that the YC-15 design will be commercially acceptable without significant changes. At the termination of the fly-off programme, one of the YC-15 prototypes is expected to be made available to the company for development and evaluation in a commercial role.

Type: Advanced military STOL transport.

Wings: Cantilever high-wing monoplane. All-metal structure. Sweepback 5° 54'. Lateral control provided by a combination of aileron and triple inboard spoilers on each wing. For STOL landings the spoilers will be used also as direct-lift controls, speed brakes and ground lift spoilers. Wide-span two-section trailing-edge flaps. The engines, mounted on pylons extending forward from the wing leading-edge, are positioned so that the exhaust nozzles are close to the undersurface of the leading-edge. This will provide a high-velocity airflow which can be used to blow externally the two-segment flaps. It is possible that titanium or composite materials may be needed for the trailing-edge flaps which will receive the full exhaust outflow during STOL operations.

Fuselage: Conventional semi-monocoque all-metal structure, the prototype utilising the flight deck enclosure of the DC-10.

Tail Unit: Cantilever all-metal structure, with T-tail and swept vertical surfaces.

Landing Gear: Retractable tricycle type. Twin wheels on nose unit. Each main unit comprises a four-wheel bogie, made up of twin-wheel units in tandem. Long-stroke main units to allow for high sink rates.

Power Plant: Four Pratt & Whitney JT8D-17 turbofan engines, each of 16,000 lb (7,257 kg) st. The engines are to be fitted with special nozzles that will mix cool ambient air with the hot core exhaust gases, reducing the outflow temperature to a level that will not require the use of special materials for the wing structure. Total fuel capacity 8,030 US gallons (30,396 litres).

Accommodation: Flight deck layout allows for operation by a crew of two. Main cabin for about 150 fully-equipped troops. Passenger doors on each side of fuselage. Cargo loading ramp in undersurface of rear fuselage.

System: Fully-powered control system, boosted by a stability and control augmentation system.

Dimensions, external:
Wing span 110 ft 4 in (33·63 m)
Length overall 124 ft 0 in (37·80 m)
Height overall 43 ft 4 in (13·21 m)
Fuselage width 18 ft 0 in (5·49 m)
Wheel track 19 ft 10 in (6·05 m)
Wheelbase 41 ft 11 in (12·78 m)

Dimensions, internal:
Cargo compartment:
Length 45 ft 0 in (13·72 m)
Max width 11 ft 7½ in (3·54 m)
Max height 11 ft 3½ in (3·44 m)
Volume, excluding ramp 5,950 cu ft (168·48 m³)

Area:
Wings, gross 1,740 sq ft (161·66 m²)

Weights (estimated):
Max T-O weight and design gross weight 198,500 lb (86,407 kg)
Max weight-limited payload 53,000 lb (24,040 kg)
Design landing weight 150,000 lb (68,040 kg)

Performance (estimated):
Max level speed 434 knots (500 mph; 805 km/h)
Approach speed 80 knots (92 mph; 148 km/h)
T-O field length with payload of 27,000 lb (12,247 kg) 2,000 ft (610 m)
Landing field length at design landing weight 2,000 ft (610 m)
Design operational radius, with 27,000 lb (12,247 kg) payload and 2,000 ft (610 m) mid-point field length, or 53,000 lb (24,040 kg) payload and runway of conventional length 400 nm (461 miles; 742 km)
Design ferry range 2,600 nm (2,994 miles; 4,818 km)

MCDONNELL DOUGLAS SKYHAWK

US Navy designation: A-4

Designed originally to provide the US Navy and Marine Corps with a simple low-cost lightweight attack and ground support aircraft, the Skyhawk was based on experience gained during the Korean War. Since the initial requirement called for operation by the US Navy, special design consideration was given to providing low-speed

McDonnell Douglas TA-4J tandem two-seat training version of the Skyhawk

A-4F Skyhawks specially prepared for the US Navy's Blue Angels aerobatic team

McDonnell Douglas A-4M Skyhawk II, on loan to US Navy Squadron VX-5 *(Duane A. Kasulka)*

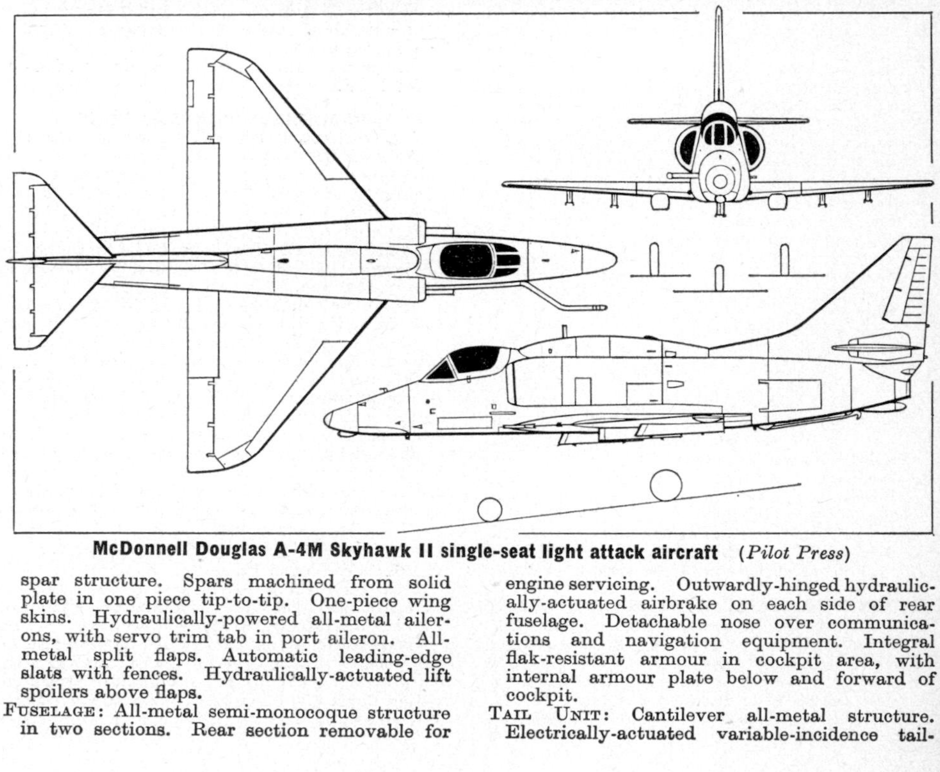
McDonnell Douglas A-4M Skyhawk II single-seat light attack aircraft *(Pilot Press)*

control and stability during take-off and landing, added strength for catapult launch and arrested landings, and dimensions that would permit it to negotiate standard aircraft carrier lifts without the complexity of folding wings.

Construction of the Skyhawk began in September 1953 and the first flight of the XA-4A (originally XA4D-1) prototype, powered by a Wright J65-W-2 engine (7,200 lb; 3,270 kg st), took place on 22 June 1954.

Early Skyhawk versions included the A-4A, -4B, -4C and -4E, described in the 1973-74 *Jane's*; more recent versions are as follows:

TA-4E. Original designation of prototypes of TA-4F.

A-4F. Attack bomber with J52-P-8A turbojet (9,300 lb; 4,218 kg st), new lift-spoilers on wings to shorten landing run by up to 1,000 ft (305 m), nosewheel steering, low-pressure tyres, zero-zero ejection seat, additional bullet- and flak-resistant materials to protect pilot, updated electronics contained in fairing "hump" aft of cockpit. Prototype flew for first time on 31 August 1966. Deliveries to US Navy began on 20 June 1967, and were completed in 1968. 146 built. Production completed.

TA-4F. Tandem two-seat dual-control trainer version of A-4F for US Navy. Fuselage extended 2 ft 4 in (0·71 m), fuselage fuel tankage reduced to 100 US gallons (379 litres), Pratt & Whitney J52-P-6 or -8A engine optional, Douglas Escapac rocket ejection seats. Provision to carry full range of weapons available for A-4F. Reduced avionics. First prototype flew on 30 June 1965. Deliveries began to the US Navy in May 1966.

A-4G. Similar to A-4F for Royal Australian Navy. Equipped to carry Sidewinder air-to-air missiles. First of eight delivered on 26 July 1967.

TA-4G. Similar to TA-4F for Royal Australian Navy. First of two delivered on 26 July 1967.

A-4H. Designation of version supplied to Israel. Delivery of an initial batch of 48 in 1967-68, followed by 60 more by early 1972.

TA-4H. Tandem two-seat trainer version of the A-4H for Israel. Ten delivered.

TA-4J. Tandem two-seat trainer, basically a simplified version of the TA-4F. Ordered for US Naval Air Advanced Training Command, under $26,834,000 contract, followed by further contract in mid-1971. Deletion of the following equipment, although provisions retained: radar, dead reckoning navigation system, low-altitude bombing system, air-to-ground missile systems, weapons delivery computer and automatic release, intervalometer, gun pod, standard store pylons, in-flight refuelling system and spray tank provisions. Addition and relocation of certain instruments. J52-P-6 engine standard. Provision for J52-P-8A engine and combat avionics. Prototype flew in May 1969 and the first four were delivered to the US Navy on 6 June 1969. In production.

A-4K. Similar to A-4F, for Royal New Zealand Air Force. Different radio, and braking parachute. First of ten handed over to the RNZAF on 16 January 1970.

TA-4K. Similar to TA-4F, for Royal New Zealand Air Force. The first of four was handed over to the RNZAF on 16 January 1970.

A-4L. Modification of A-4C with uprated engine, bombing computing system and avionics relocated in fairing "hump" aft of cockpit as on A-4F. Delivery to US Navy Reserve carrier air wing began in December 1969.

A-4M Skyhawk II. Similar to A-4F, but with J52-P-408A turbojet (11,200 lb; 5,080 kg st) and braking parachute standard, making possible combat operation from 4,000 ft (1,220 m) fields and claimed to increase combat effectiveness by 30%. Larger windscreen and canopy; windscreen bullet-resistant. Increased ammunition capacity for 20 mm cannon. More powerful generator, provision of wind-driven backup generator and self-contained engine starter. First of two prototypes flew for the first time on 10 April 1970. About 50 ordered initially for US Marine Corps, the first of which was delivered on 3 November 1970. Further order placed in mid-1971. In production.

A-4N Skyhawk II. Light attack version ordered by US Navy for export. Basically similar to A-4M. First flown on 8 June 1972. In production.

A-4P. Revised A-4B for Argentine Air Force (50).

A-4Q. Revised A-4B for Argentine Navy (16).

A-4S. Designation of 40 Skyhawks for service with Singapore Air Defence Command. Conversion from ex-USN A-4Bs began in 1973, carried out by Lockheed Aircraft Service Company, under which heading all available details are given.

Current US Navy planning called for continued production of the Skyhawk during 1974, and logistic support for its continued usage into the 1980s.

The following structural description refers specifically to the A-4M:

TYPE: Single-seat attack bomber.

WINGS: Cantilever low-wing monoplane. Sweepback 33° at quarter-chord. All-metal three-spar structure. Spars machined from solid plate in one piece tip-to-tip. One-piece wing skins. Hydraulically-powered all-metal ailerons, with servo trim tab in port aileron. All-metal split flaps. Automatic leading-edge slats with fences. Hydraulically-actuated lift spoilers above flaps.

FUSELAGE: All-metal semi-monocoque structure in two sections. Rear section removable for engine servicing. Outwardly-hinged hydraulically-actuated airbrake on each side of rear fuselage. Detachable nose over communications and navigation equipment. Integral flak-resistant armour in cockpit area, with internal armour plate below and forward of cockpit.

TAIL UNIT: Cantilever all-metal structure. Electrically-actuated variable-incidence tailplane. Hydraulically-powered elevators. Powered rudder with unique central skin and external stiffeners.

LANDING GEAR: Hydraulically-retractable tricycle type, with single wheel on each unit. All units retract forward. Free-fall emergency extension. Main legs pre-shorten for retraction and wheels turn through 90° to stow horizontally in wings. Menasco shock-absorbers. Hydraulic nosewheel steering. Ribbon-type braking parachute of 16 ft (4·88 m) diameter contained in canister secured in rear fuselage below engine exhaust. Arrester hook for carrier operation.

POWER PLANT: One 11,200 lb (5,080 kg) st Pratt & Whitney J52-P-408A turbojet engine. Fuel in integral wing tanks and self-sealing fuselage tank aft of cockpit, total capacity 800 US gallons (3,028 litres). One 150, 300 or 400 US gallon (568, 1,136 or 1,514 litre) auxiliary tank can be carried on the underfuselage bomb-rack, and one 150 or 300 US gallon auxiliary tank on each of the inboard underwing racks. Maximum fuel capacity, internal plus auxiliary tanks, 1,800 US gallons (6,814 litres). Large flight refuelling probe on starboard side of nose. Douglas-developed self-contained flight refuelling unit can be carried on the underfuselage standard bomb shackles. Provisions for JATO.

ACCOMMODATION: Pilot on Douglas Escapac 1-C3 zero-zero lightweight ejection seat. Enlarged cockpit enclosure to improve pilot's visibility, with rectangular bullet-resistant windscreen.

SYSTEMS: Dual hydraulic system. Oxygen system. Electrical system powered by 20kVA generator, with wind-driven generator to provide emergency power.

ELECTRONICS: Include Bendix Automatic Flight Control, ARC-51 UHF radio transceiver, ARA-50 UHF direction finder, APX-64 IFF, Marconi-Elliott Type 546 head-up display system, Douglas angle of attack indicator, electronic countermeasures, APG-53A terrain clearance radar, ASN-41/WDS-600/APN-153(V) Doppler/inertial navigation and ARC-115 VHF/FM radio transceiver. Provisions for ARR-69 auxiliary radio receiver, ARN-52 TACAN and APN-141 radar altimeter.

ARMAMENT: Provision for several hundred variations of military load, carried externally on one underfuselage rack, capacity 3,500 lb (1,588 kg); two inboard underwing racks, capacity of each 2,250 lb (1,020 kg); and two outboard underwing racks, capacity of each 1,000 lb (450 kg). Weapons that can be deployed include nuclear or HE bombs, air-to-surface and air-to-air rockets, Sidewinder infra-red missiles, Bullpup air-to-surface missiles, ground attack gun pods, torpedoes, countermeasures equipment, etc. Two 20 mm Mk 12 cannon in wing roots standard, each with 200 rounds of ammunition. DEFA 30 mm cannon available as optional on international versions, with 150 rounds of ammunition per gun.

DIMENSIONS, EXTERNAL:
Wing span 27 ft 6 in (8·38 m)
Wing chord at root 15 ft 6 in (4·72 m)
Length overall (excluding flight refuelling probe):
A-4F, M 40 ft 3¼ in (12·27 m)
TA-4F 42 ft 7¼ in (12·98 m)
Height overall:
A-4F, M 15 ft 0 in (4·57 m)
TA-4F 15 ft 3 in (4·66 m)
Tailplane span 11 ft 3½ in (3·44 m)
Wheel track 7 ft 9½ in (2·38 m)

AREAS:
Wings, gross 260 sq ft (24·16 m²)
Vertical tail surfaces (total) 50 sq ft (4·65 m²)
Horizontal tail surfaces (total) 48·85 sq ft (4·54 m²)

WEIGHTS:
Weight empty:
A-4F 10,448 lb (4,739 kg)
TA-4F 10,602 lb (4,809 kg)
A-4M 10,465 lb (4,747 kg)
Normal T-O weight:
A-4F, M, TA-4F 24,500 lb (11,113 kg)
*A-4F from land base 27,420 lb (12,437 kg)
**export version only: overload condition not authorised by US Navy*

PERFORMANCE (at design T-O weight):
Max level speed:
TA-4F 586 knots (675 mph; 1,086 km/h)
Max level speed (with 4,000 lb; 1,814 kg bomb load):
A-4F 515 knots (593 mph; 954 km/h)
A-4M 560 knots (645 mph; 1,038 km/h)
Max rate of climb (ISA at S/L):
A-4F 5,620 ft (1,713 m)/min
A-4M 8,440 ft (2,572 m)/min
Rate of climb (ISA at 25,000 ft; 7,620 m):
A-4F 1,495 ft (455 m)/min
A-4M 2,500 ft (763 m)/min
T-O run (at 23,000 lb; 10,433 kg T-O weight):
A-4F 3,720 ft (1,134 m)
A-4M 2,700 ft (823 m)
Max ferry range, A-4M at 24,500 lb (11,113 kg) T-O weight, with max fuel, standard reserves 1,785 nm (2,055 miles; 3,307 km)

McKINNON

McKINNON ENTERPRISES, INC

HEAD OFFICE AND WORKS:
Route 3, Box 690, Sandy, Oregon 97055
Telephone: (503) 668-4154
PRESIDENT: A. G. McKinnon
OWNER AND MANAGER: A. G. McKinnon

McKinnon Enterprises (formerly McKinnon-Hickman Company) entered the aircraft conversion field in 1953 when it undertook the conversion of the Grumman Widgeon twin-engined light amphibian into an executive aircraft. The success of this conversion, which is still being manufactured, led to the development and manufacture of a larger four-engined amphibian, known as the McKinnon G-21, which is a much improved and more luxurious conversion of the Grumman Goose.

Details of the four-engined McKinnon G-21 Goose conversion can be found in the 1966-67 *Jane's*. It has since been superseded by the turboprop-powered G-21C, D and G, as described below. McKinnon is also offering a minimum conversion scheme by which the standard Goose can be re-engined with turboprops and fitted with any other parts of the G-21C/D conversion specified by the customer.

McKinnon has received official approval for a modification scheme to fit retractable wingtip floats to standard Goose amphibians. This offers increased cruising speeds, reduced landing speed, better stability on both land and water, and greatly improved accessibility for loading and unloading on water.

Also offered by McKinnon is an officially-approved conversion kit by which the max T-O weight of the standard Goose can be increased by 1,200 lb (545 kg) to 9,200 lb (4,173 kg).

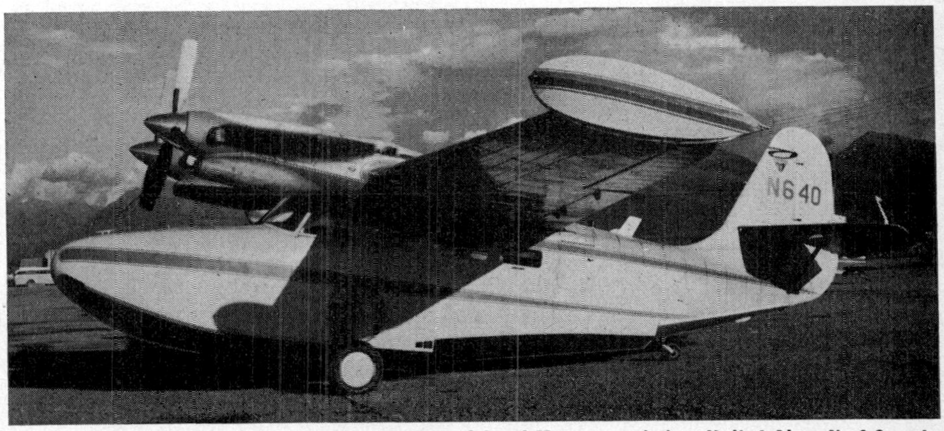

McKinnon G-21 Turboprop Goose of the Bureau of Land Management (two United Aircraft of Canada PT6A engines) (*Norman E. Taylor*)

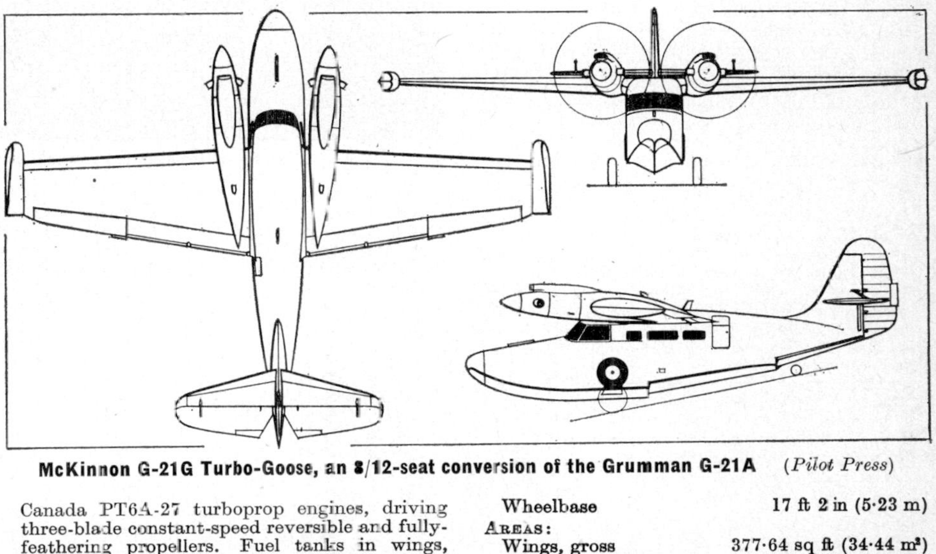

McKinnon G-21G Turbo-Goose, an 8/12-seat conversion of the Grumman G-21A (*Pilot Press*)

McKINNON G-21C and G-21D TURBO-GOOSE

In these current versions of the G-21, the two normal 450 hp Pratt & Whitney R-985 radial engines of the Goose amphibian are replaced by two 680 shp United Aircraft of Canada PT6A-27 turboprop engines, moved further inboard and driving constant-speed and reversible propellers. The internal fuel capacity is increased. Other modifications include the fitting of retractable wingtip floats, extended radar nose, dorsal fin, one-piece windscreen, larger cabin windows, a new instrument panel, oxygen system, and a 24V electrical system. Landing gear and wingtip float retraction and flaps are all electrically operated.

The fully-modified G-21C and D will operate with ease from 2,000 ft (610 m) fields or small lakes, at even the highest altitudes.

The G-21C is fitted out to accommodate from nine to twelve people, including pilot. It received FAA Type Approval in February 1967.

TYPE: Twin-turboprop light amphibian.

WINGS: Cantilever high-wing monoplane. Wing section NACA 23000. Dihedral 2° 30′. All-metal structure with metal covering. Fabric-covered metal ailerons.

FUSELAGE: All-metal semi-monocoque flying-boat hull with two steps.

TAIL UNIT: Braced all-metal structure.

LANDING GEAR: Retractable tailwheel type. All wheels retract electrically into hull, with manual extension. Bendix oleo-pneumatic shock-absorbers. Goodyear wheels and double-disc brakes. Retractable wingtip stabilising floats.

POWER PLANT: Two 680 shp United Aircraft of Canada PT6A-27 turboprop engines, driving three-blade constant-speed reversible and fully-feathering propellers. Fuel tanks in wings, total capacity 586 US gallons (2,217 litres).

ACCOMMODATION: Pilot and up to 11 passengers in standard version. Bow-loading entrance and baggage space in nose. Main cabin, forward of the standard rear door, seats seven people, with four more in a cabin aft of the door. One baggage compartment, capacity 300 lb (136 kg).

DIMENSIONS, EXTERNAL:
Wing span 50 ft 10 in (15·49 m)
Wing chord at root 10 ft 0 in (3·05 m)
Wing chord at tip 5 ft 0 in (1·52 m)
Wing aspect ratio 6·101
Length overall 39 ft 7 in (12·07 m)
Width of hull 5 ft 0 in (1·52 m)
Tailplane span 19 ft 9 in (6·02 m)
Wheel track 7 ft 6 in (2·29 m)
Wheelbase 17 ft 2 in (5·23 m)

AREAS:
Wings, gross 377·64 sq ft (34·44 m²)
Ailerons (total) 29·64 sq ft (2·75 m²)
Fin 21·20 sq ft (1·97 m²)
Rudder 26·80 sq ft (2·49 m²)
Tailplane 39·48 sq ft (3·67 m²)
Elevators 42·92 sq ft (3·99 m²)
Elevator tab 2·10 sq ft (0·195 m²)

WEIGHTS:
Weight empty, equipped 6,635 lb (3,009 kg)
Max T-O weight 12,500 lb (5,670 kg)
Max landing weight, on land 12,000 lb (5,445 kg)
Max landing weight, on water 12,500 lb (5,670 kg)

PERFORMANCE (at max T-O weight):
Max level speed 191 knots (220 mph; 355 km/h)
Range with max fuel approx 1,390 nm (1,600 miles; 2,575 km)

McKINNON G-21G TURBO-GOOSE

This latest version of the Turbo-Goose is an 8/12-seat conversion of the standard Grumman G-21A.

The power plant comprises two 680 shp United Aircraft of Canada PT6A-27 turboprop engines, driving Hartzell three-blade metal constant-speed fully-feathering and reversible propellers.

Modifications to the airframe include a 15 in (0·38 m) nose extension to accommodate radar, metallising treatment of the wings and provision of a wraparound windscreen, retractable wingtip floats, rotating beacon on top of the fin, a small dorsal fin, hull vents and auxiliary wing tanks that increase total fuel capacity to 586 US gallons (2,218 litres). Optional improvements include provision of picture windows for the cabin, a centre main fuel tank of increased capacity, dual landing lights in wing leading-edges, electrically-operated retraction of landing gear and enlargement of the cabin by removing the bulkhead at station 26.

McKinnon has received FAA approval for this conversion. All available specification details follow:

WEIGHTS:
Weight empty, equipped (approx) 6,700 lb (3,039 kg)
Max T-O weight 12,500 lb (5,670 kg)

PERFORMANCE (at max T-O weight):
Max operating speed 211 knots (243 mph; 391 km/h)
Service ceiling 20,000 ft (6,096 m)
Service ceiling, one engine out 12,000 ft (3,660 m)
Range with 586 US gallons (2,218 litres) fuel 1,390 nm (1,600 miles; 2,575 km)

McKINNON TURBOPROP GOOSE CONVERSION

For owners of Goose amphibians who do not require a full conversion of their aircraft to G-21C, D or G standard, McKinnon offers a simple conversion which involves only replacement of the original R-985 piston engines with two 680 shp United Aircraft of Canada PT6A-27 turboprop engines in the original location, driving three-blade constant-speed reversible-pitch propellers.

McKinnon Super Widgeon, with retractable wingtip floats

Any of the other modifications incorporated on the G-21C/D can be made on the standard Goose conversion. Speed and take-off performance are comparable with those of the G-21C/D. Range is also comparable after fitment of the optional auxiliary tanks.

WEIGHTS (minimum conversion):
Weight empty, equipped 6,635 lb (3,009 kg)
Max T-O weight 12,500 lb (5,670 kg)
Max landing weight, on land or water 12,000 lb (5,445 kg)

McKINNON SUPER WIDGEON

The Super Widgeon is an executive conversion of the Grumman Widgeon light amphibian, with the two original 200 hp Ranger six-cylinder in-line inverted engines replaced by two 270 hp Lycoming GO-480-B1D flat-six engines driving Hartzell three-blade fully-feathering propellers. Modifications to the hull and landing gear permit an increase in loaded weight. Extra tanks are provided in the outer wings to increase the fuel capacity from 108 to 154 US gallons (408 to 582 litres). Other new features include picture windows, a modern IFR instrument panel, improved soundproofing and the provision of an emergency escape hatch. Approval to install retractable floats was obtained in 1960.

The cabin is arranged to accommodate a pilot, co-pilot and three or four passengers.

Well over 70 Widgeons have been converted to Super Widgeon standard by McKinnon, and several retractable float installations have been completed.

DIMENSIONS, EXTERNAL:
Wing span 40 ft 0 in (12·19 m)
Length overall 31 ft 1 in (9·47 m)
Height overall 11 ft 5 in (3·48 m)

WEIGHT:
Max T-O weight 5,500 lb (2,500 kg)

PERFORMANCE (at max T-O weight):
Max level speed at S/L 165 knots (190 mph; 306 km/h)
Cruising speed at 10,000 ft (3,050 m) (62½% power) 156 knots (180 mph; 290 km/h)
Cruising speed at S/L (70% power) 152 knots (175 mph; 282 km/h)
Landing speed 54 knots (62 mph; 100 km/h)
Max rate of climb at S/L 1,750 ft (534 m)/min
Service ceiling 18,000 ft (5,490 m)
Single-engine ceiling 5,000 ft (1,525 m)
T-O run on land 600 ft (183 m)
T-O from smooth water 10 sec
Range with max fuel, reserves for 30 min 868 nm (1,000 miles; 1,600 km)

McLAUGHLIN

M. L. McLAUGHLIN

ADDRESS:
Route 6, Iowa City, Iowa 52240

Mr McLaughlin has designed and built the prototype of a two-seat sporting aircraft which he has named Skybuggy Model A. Design began in February 1971 and construction in May of the same year. FAA certification in the Experimental category was awarded on 5 December 1972 and the first flight was made on 28 December 1972.

McLAUGHLIN SKYBUGGY MODEL A

TYPE: Two-seat homebuilt sporting aircraft.

WINGS: Braced high-wing monoplane with two parallel streamline-section bracing struts each side. Wing section NACA 4412. Anhedral 0° 30′. Incidence 1°. No sweepback. Conventional wooden structure with spruce spars and Dacron covering. Ailerons of wood construction with Dacron covering. No flaps or trim tabs.

FUSELAGE: Spruce frame with birch plywood gussets, Dacron covered.

TAIL UNIT: Wire-braced wood structure with fabric covering. Tailplane has variable incidence. No trim tabs.

LANDING GEAR: Non-retractable tailwheel type. Each main wheel carried on a steel tube Vee truss, with a Waco glider spring-hydraulic shock-strut. Main-wheel tyres size 18 × 6·00-6, pressure 12 lb/sq in (0·84 kg/cm²). Tailwheel with solid tyre size 6·5 × 2·50-4. Cleveland hydraulic brakes.

POWER PLANT: One 70 hp Chevrolet Corvair (1962) modified motor car engine, driving a Sensenich two-blade fixed-pitch wooden propeller. Fuel tank immediately aft of firewall, capacity 16 US gallons (60·5 litres). Refuelling point on fuselage upper surface forward of windscreen. Oil capacity 1·25 US gallons (4·7 litres).

ACCOMMODATION: Two persons side by side in enclosed cabin with dual controls. Upward-opening door on each side. Stowage for baggage aft of seats. Cabin heated and ventilated.

SYSTEM: Hydraulic system for brakes only.

McLaughlin Skybuggy Model A two-seat homebuilt sporting aircraft

DIMENSIONS, EXTERNAL:
Wing span 28 ft 0 in (8·53 m)
Wing chord, constant 4 ft 8½ in (1·44 m)
Wing aspect ratio 5·94
Length overall 21 ft 0 in (6·40 m)
Height overall 5 ft 9 in (1·75 m)
Tailplane span 8 ft 0 in (2·64 m)
Wheel track 5 ft 10 in (1·78 m)
Wheelbase 17 ft 0 in (5·18 m)
Propeller diameter 5 ft 0 in (1·52 m)
Propeller ground clearance 1 ft 0 in (0·305 m)
Cabin doors (each):
Height 3 ft 1 in (0·94 m)
Width 2 ft 2 in (0·66 m)
Height to sill 2 ft 6 in (0·76 m)

DIMENSIONS, INTERNAL:
Cabin:
Length 4 ft 10 in (1·47 m)
Max width 3 ft 6 in (1·07 m)
Max height 3 ft 6 in (1·07 m)
Baggage space 4 cu ft (0·11 m³)

AREAS:
Wings, gross 132 sq ft (12·26 m²)
Ailerons (total) 11·4 sq ft (1·06 m²)
Fin 4·75 sq ft (0·44 m²)
Rudder 6·77 sq ft (0·63 m²)
Tailplane 13·52 sq ft (1·26 m²)
Elevators 10·08 sq ft (0·94 m²)

WEIGHTS AND LOADINGS:
Weight empty 763 lb (346 kg)
Max T-O and landing weight 1,310 lb (594 kg)
Max wing loading 9·9 lb/sq ft (48·3 kg/m²)
Max power loading 18·7 lb/hp (8·48 kg/hp)

PERFORMANCE (at max T-O weight):
Max never-exceed speed 112 knots (130 mph; 209 km/h)
Max level speed at 2,700 ft (825 m) 89 knots (102 mph; 164 km/h)
Econ cruising speed at 5,000 ft (1,525 m) 69 knots (80 mph; 129 km/h)
Stalling speed 44 knots (50 mph; 81 km/h)
Max rate of climb at S/L 500 ft (152 m)/min
Service ceiling 9,500 ft (2,900 m)
T-O run approx 700 ft (213 m)
Landing run approx 500 ft (152 m)
Range at 73 knots (85 mph; 136 km/h) with 1 US gallon (3·78 litres) reserve 280 nm (323 miles; 520 km)

MERKEL

MERKEL AIRPLANE COMPANY

ADDRESS:
3920 North Charles, Wichita, Kansas 67204
Telephone: (316) 838-6767

Mr Edwin W. Merkel, a professional aeronautical engineer, has designed, built and developed over a ten-year period an aerobatic biplane which he has named the Merkel Mark II.

The aircraft evolved from a Master's Thesis on lightplanes and has a background of engineering development that includes wind tunnel testing of a one-fifth scale model. It is designed to FAA Part 23 aerobatic requirements, and its flight characteristics were developed to meet the level 1 of military specification MIL-F-8785B. It is stressed to +6 and −3*g* limit and +9 and −4·5*g* ultimate.

Mr Merkel began the design of the Mark II in 1963, and construction began three years later, in February 1966. First flight was made on 11 April 1973 and FAA certification in the Experimental category was awarded. It is Mr Merkel's intention to gain Type Certification under FAR 23 Aerobatic category and begin production of the aircraft if adequate financing can be arranged. If this aim is realised it is planned to produce a single-seat version for competitive aerobatics, and a two-seat version to serve as an aerobatic trainer.

MERKEL MARK II

TYPE: Two-seat aerobatic biplane.

WINGS: Braced single-bay biplane with I-type interplane and N-type centre-section struts. Streamline flying and landing wires. Wing section NACA 23012. Dihedral 3° 30′ on lower wings only. Incidence (both wings) 1° 30′. Sweepback at quarter-chord 12° on upper wing only. Wing panels are two-cell single-spar torsional structures with conventional biplane wire-braced truss. Wing skins of 2024-T3 light alloy. Plain ailerons on both wings of similar construction. No flaps.

FUSELAGE: Forward fuselage is a welded structure of 4130-N steel tube to rear side of cockpit. Semi-monocoque light alloy structure aft of cockpit with 2024-T3 light alloy skin. Fuselage-mounted airbrake planned for single-seat competition version.

TAIL UNIT: Cantilever light alloy structure with 2024-T3 skins on all surfaces. All-moving tailplane with trimmable anti-servo tab. Ground-adjustable trim tab in rudder.

LANDING GEAR: Non-retractable tailwheel type. Main wheels carried on cantilever leaf spring struts. Main wheels have US Rubber tyres size 17 × 6-6, pressure 24 lb/sq in (1·69 kg/cm²). Maule tailwheel type SFS 1-4 with 6 in (150 mm) diameter solid rubber tyre. Cleveland hydraulic disc brakes.

POWER PLANT: One 220 hp Franklin 6A-350-C1 six-cylinder horizontally-opposed aircooled engine, driving a Hartzell type HC-C2YF-4/C8459-4 two-blade metal constant-speed propeller. Light alloy fuel tank immediately aft of firewall, capacity 18 US gallons (68 litres). Refuelling point on upper surface of forward fuselage. An optional belly tank is planned for extended cross-country flights. Oil capacity 2·2 US gallons (8·3 litres).

ACCOMMODATION: Two seats in tandem in open cockpits. Canopy optional. Cockpits heated.

SYSTEM: Electrical power supplied by Prestolite F363 12V engine-driven alternator.

DIMENSIONS, EXTERNAL:
- Wing span (both) 25 ft 6 in (7·77 m)
- Wing chord (constant, both) 3 ft 0 in (0·91 m)
- Wing aspect ratio 5·79
- Length overall 22 ft 9½ in (6·95 m)
- Height overall 8 ft 1¼ in (2·47 m)
- Tailplane span 9 ft 6 in (2·90 m)
- Wheel track 6 ft 6 in (1·98 m)
- Propeller diameter 6 ft 8 in (2·03 m)
- Propeller ground clearance 1 ft 3¾ in (0·40 m)

AREAS:
- Wings, gross 146 sq ft (13·56 m²)
- Ailerons (total) 19·72 sq ft (1·83 m²)
- Fin 4·61 sq ft (0·43 m²)
- Rudder, incl tab 6·5 sq ft (0·60 m²)
- Tailplane, incl tab 22·18 sq ft (2·06 m²)

WEIGHTS AND LOADINGS (single seat occupied in accordance with FAR 23 Aerobatic category):
- Weight empty 1,200 lb (544 kg)
- Max T-O and landing weight 1,540 lb (698 kg)
- Max wing loading 10·55 lb/sq ft (51·5 kg/m²)
- Max power loading 7·0 lb/hp (3·18 kg/hp)

PERFORMANCE (at max aerobatic T-O weight):
- Max never-exceed speed 146 knots (169 mph; 272 km/h) IAS
- Max level speed at 3,000 ft (915 m) 136 knots (157 mph; 253 km/h) IAS
- Max cruising speed, 75% power at 7,000 ft (2,135 m) 139 knots (160 mph; 257 km/h TAS
- Stalling speed 48 knots (55 mph; 89 km/h) IAS
- Max rate of climb at S/L 2,500 ft (762 m)/min
- Range with max fuel, no reserve 221 nm (255 miles; 410 km)

Merkel Mark II aerobatic biplane (220 hp Franklin 6A-350-C1 engine)

MEYER

MEYER AIRCRAFT

ADDRESS:
5706 Abby Drive, Corpus Christi, Texas 78413

Meyer Aircraft was formed by Mr George W. Meyer, to market plans for the construction by amateurs of a small, fully aerobatic biplane of his own design, known as the Little Toot, which was flown for the first time on 5 February 1957. Several hundred sets of plans have been sold and many Little Toots are now flying.

The prototype, to which the data apply, has a metal monocoque fuselage and metal tail surfaces; but the plans give details also of an alternative and easier method of making these components, using conventional metal tube construction, with plywood fuselage bulkheads, wood stringers and fabric covering.

Mr Meyer has in the development stage a side-by-side two-seat back-stagger biplane, of which no details are yet available.

MEYER LITTLE TOOT

The following details refer to Mr Meyer's prototype Little Toot:

TYPE: Single-seat sporting biplane.

WINGS: Braced biplane type, with single interplane strut each side and two N-type strut assemblies supporting top wing above fuselage. NACA 2212 wing section. Sweepback 8° on top wing only. Dihedral 0° on top wing, 2° 30′ on lower wing. Incidence (both wings) 2°. All-wood two-spar structure with fabric covering. Fabric-covered metal Frise ailerons on lower wing only. No flaps.

FUSELAGE: All-metal structure, with metal-covered steel tube construction from rear of cockpit forward, and metal monocoque rear fuselage.

TAIL UNIT: Cantilever all-metal structure. Trim tab in port elevator.

LANDING GEAR: Non-retractable tailwheel type. Cantilever spring steel main legs of type fitted to Cessna 140 aircraft. Goodyear wheels and tyres. Goodyear disc brakes. Wheel fairings. Steerable tailwheel.

POWER PLANT: One 90 hp Continental four-cylinder horizontally-opposed aircooled engine, driving McCauley 72-52 two-blade fixed-pitch propeller. Provision for alternative four-cylinder engines of up to 180 hp. Fuel tank in fuselage, aft of firewall, capacity 18 US gallons (68 litres). Oil capacity 6 US gallons (5·7 litres).

ACCOMMODATION: Single seat. Plans show open cockpit, but prototype now has sliding canopy. Space for 30 lb (14 kg) baggage aft of seat.

ELECTRONICS: Aerotech VHF transceiver and Omni.

DIMENSIONS, EXTERNAL:
- Wing span (both) 19 ft 0 in (5·79 m)
- Wing chord, constant (both) 3 ft 6 in (1·07 m)
- Wing aspect ratio 5·42
- Length overall 16 ft 6 in (5·03 m)
- Height overall 7 ft 0 in (2·13 m)
- Tailplane span 7 ft 0 in (2·13 m)
- Wheel track 6 ft 0 in (1·83 m)

DIMENSION, INTERNAL:
- Cockpit: Width 2 ft 0 in (0·61 m)

AREAS:
- Wings, gross 123 sq ft (11·43 m²)
- Ailerons (total) 13·00 sq ft (1·21 m²)
- Fin 4·66 sq ft (0·43 m²)
- Rudder 3·47 sq ft (0·32 m²)
- Tailplane 10·50 sq ft (0·98 m²)
- Elevators, incl tab 7·25 sq ft (0·67 m²)

WEIGHTS AND LOADINGS (90 hp Continental):
- Weight empty 914 lb (415 kg)
- Max T-O and landing weight 1,260 lb (572 kg)
- Max wing loading 10·20 lb/sq ft (49·8 kg/m²)
- Max power loading 13·7 lb/hp (6·22 kg/hp)

PERFORMANCE (at max T-O weight, open cockpit):
- Max never-exceed speed 156 knots (180 mph; 290 km/h)
- Max level speed at S/L:
  - 90 hp Cont 110 knots (127 mph; 204 km/h)
  - 125 hp Lyc 117 knots (135 mph; 217 km/h)
  - 150 hp Lyc 130 knots (150 mph; 241 km/h)
- Normal cruising speed:
  - 90 hp Cont 96 knots (110 mph; 177 km/h)
  - 125 hp Lyc 104 knots (120 mph; 193 km/h)
  - 150 hp Lyc 117 knots (135 mph; 217 km/h)
- Stalling speed:
  - 90 hp Cont 48 knots (55 mph; 88·5 km/h)
- Max rate of climb at S/L:
  - 90 hp Cont 1,000 ft (305 m)/min
  - 125 hp Lyc 1,600 ft (490 m)/min
  - 150 hp Lyc 2,000 ft (610 m)/min
- Climb to 5,000 ft (1,525 m):
  - 90 hp Cont 5 min 20 sec
- Service ceiling:
  - 90 hp Cont 16,500 ft (5,030 m)
- T-O run:
  - 90 hp Cont 300 ft (91 m)
- T-O to 50 ft (15 m):
  - 90 hp Cont 450 ft (137 m)
- Landing run:
  - 90 hp Cont 400 ft (122 m)
- Range:
  - 90 hp Cont 304 nm (350 miles; 560 km)

Meyer Little Toot built by Mr J. Patty of Mission, Kansas (*Jean Seele*)

MILLER

MERLE B. MILLER

Address:
219 E 53rd Street, Savannah, Georgia 31405

Mr Miller has designed and built a lightweight sporting aircraft of which plans are available to amateur constructors. Design began in June 1970 and construction was started in the following month. FAA certification in the Experimental category was awarded on 14 May 1971 and the prototype, named Red Bare-Un, flew for the first time on 3 June 1971. Total cost of construction was approximately $600. A total of 18 sets of plans had been sold by the end of March 1972 and the first aircraft to be completed from plans was undergoing its tests in early 1973.

At the same time Mr Miller was carrying out modifications to the power plant of the prototype to improve performance.

Miller Red Bare-Un lightweight sporting aircraft (30 hp Volkswagen modified motor car engine) *(Howard Levy)*

MILLER RED BARE-UN

Type: Single-seat homebuilt lightweight sporting aircraft.

Wings: Wire-braced parasol-wing monoplane. Wing section Clark Y. Dihedral 2°. Incidence 3°. No sweepback. Conventional two-spar structure with wood spars, ribs and cross-bracing, light alloy leading-edge, fabric-covered. Plain ailerons of wood construction, fabric-covered. No flaps. No trim tabs. Landing wires attached to welded steel tube kingpost above wing centre-section.

Fuselage: Uncovered welded 4130 steel tube structure of triangular section.

Tail Unit: Cantilever welded 4130 steel tube structure with all surfaces fabric-covered. Fixed-incidence tailplane. No trim tabs.

Landing Gear: Non-retractable tricycle type. Shock-absorption of main wheels by cantilever leaf spring. Nosewheel has no shock-absorption. Main wheels with Arco tyres size 4·10/3·50-4. Nosewheel has General tyre size 2·50-4. Friction brake on nosewheel tyre.

Power Plant: One 30 hp modified Volkswagen motor car engine, driving a wooden two-blade fixed-pitch propeller. Fuel tank aft of engine, capacity 5 US gallons (18·9 litres). Refuelling point on top of tank. Oil capacity 5·3 US pints (2·52 litres).

Accommodation: Single open seat, beneath wing.

Equipment: Regency battery-powered radio.

Dimensions, external:
- Wing span: 22 ft 0 in (6·71 m)
- Wing chord, constant: 3 ft 6 in (1·07 m)
- Wing aspect ratio: 6·28
- Length overall: 13 ft 0 in (3·96 m)
- Height overall: 5 ft 4 in (1·63 m)
- Tailplane span: 5 ft 6 in (1·68 m)
- Wheel track: 3 ft 11½ in (1·21 m)
- Wheelbase: 3 ft 7 in (1·09 m)
- Propeller diameter: 4 ft 2 in (1·27 m)

Areas:
- Wings, gross: 75 sq ft (6·97 m^2)
- Ailerons (total): 15 sq ft (1·39 m^2)
- Fin: 1·24 sq ft (0·12 m^2)
- Rudder: 3·17 sq ft (0·29 m^2)
- Tailplane: 3·79 sq ft (0·35 m^2)
- Elevators: 5·00 sq ft (0·46 m^2)

Weights and Loadings:
- Weight empty: 320 lb (145 kg)
- Max T-O and landing weight: 550 lb (249 kg)
- Max wing loading: 7·33 lb/sq ft (35·8 kg/m^2)
- Max power loading: 18·35 lb/hp (8·32 kg/hp)

Performance (at max T-O weight):
- Max level speed at S/L: 60 knots (69 mph; 111 km/h)
- Max cruising speed at S/L: 55 knots (63·5 mph; 102 km/h)
- Econ cruising speed at 200 ft (61 m): 50 knots (57·5 mph; 92·5 km/h)
- Stalling speed: 30 knots (35 mph; 56·5 km/h)
- Max rate of climb at S/L: 200 ft (61 m)/min
- *T-O run: 500 ft (152 m)
- *T-O to 50 ft (15 m): 1,500 ft (457 m)
- *Landing from 50 ft (15 m): 800 ft (244 m)
- *Landing run: 500 ft (152 m)
- Range: 125 nm (144 miles; 231 km)

**Figures quoted are for paved runway*

MINI-HAWK

MINI-HAWK INTERNATIONAL INC

Address:
1930 Stewart Street, Santa Monica, California
Telephone: (214) 828-4078

Mini-Hawk International was formed to market plans and kits for construction of an all-metal single-seat monoplane designated Mini-Hawk TH.E.01 Tiger-Hawk. Three officers of the corporation, designer William B. Taylor, engineer Thomas E. Maloney and pilot E. Y. Treffinger, combined their efforts to design and construct the prototype. First flight of the prototype was expected to be made in March 1974.

The Tiger-Hawk features simplified construction and has easily-detached wings for towing or storage.

Mini-Hawk Tiger-Hawk lightweight homebuilt sporting monoplane (65 hp modified Volkswagen motor car engine) *(Henry Artof)*

MINI-HAWK TH.E.01 TIGER-HAWK

Type: Single-seat lightweight homebuilt aircraft.

Wings: Cantilever low-wing monoplane of all-metal construction. Constant-chord wing. Dihedral 4°. Conventional ailerons of all-metal construction, operated by push/pull rods. All-metal trailing-edge flaps.

Fuselage: Built-up structure of light alloy.

Tail Unit: Cantilever all-metal structure. Fixed-incidence tailplane. Elevator of light alloy construction. No trim tabs.

Landing Gear: Non-retractable tricycle type with steerable nosewheel. Hurst/Airheart hydraulic disc brakes. Single wheel with speed fairing on each unit.

Power Plant: One 65 hp Revmaster Model 1831D modified Volkswagen motor car engine, driving a two-blade fixed-pitch propeller with spinner. Fuel tank in fuselage with capacity of 12 US gallons (45·4 litres). Suitable for Volkswagen engines of up to 90 hp.

Accomodation: Single seat under transparent cockpit canopy.

System: Hydraulic system for brakes only.

Equipment: Genave radio optional.

Dimensions, external:
- Wing span: 18 ft 4 in (5·59 m)
- Wing chord, constant: 3 ft 3 in (0·99 m)
- Length overall: 13 ft 10 in (4·22 m)
- Width overall, wings removed: 6 ft 0 in (1·83 m)
- Height overall: 6 ft 8 in (2·03 m)
- Tailplane span: 6 ft 0 in (1·83 m)
- Wheel track: 5 ft 10 in (1·78 m)
- Wheelbase: 6 ft 4 in (1·93 m)
- Propeller diameter: 4 ft 6 in (1·37 m)
- Propeller ground clearance: 1 ft 2 in (0·36 m)

Area:
- Wings, gross: 54 sq ft (5·02 m^2)

Weights and Loadings:
- Weight empty: 500 lb (226 kg)
- Max T-O weight: 800 lb (362 kg)
- Max wing loading: 9·7 lb/sq ft (47·4 kg/m^2)
- Max power loading: 10·6 lb/hp (4·81 kg/hp)

Performance (estimated, at max T-O weight):
- Max never-exceed speed: 173 knots (200 mph; 321 km/h)
- Max level speed: 152 knots (175 mph; 282 km/h)
- Stalling speed, flaps up: 54 knots (62 mph; 100 km/h)
- Stalling speed, flaps down: 44 knots (50 mph; 81 km/h)
- Max rate of climb at S/L: 1,200 ft (366 m)/min
- Service ceiling: 10,000 ft (3,050 m)
- Absolute ceiling: 12,000 ft (3,655 m)
- T-O and landing run: 400 ft (122 m)
- Range: 430 nm (500 miles; 800 km)

MITSUBISHI

MITSUBISHI AIRCRAFT INTERNATIONAL INC

Works: PO Box 3848, San Angelo, Texas 76901
Telephone: (915) 944-1511

This wholly-owned subsidiary of the well-known Japanese Mitsubishi Heavy Industries Ltd was established at San Angelo in 1967, to assemble and equip the MU-2 twin-turboprop utility STOL transport designed by the parent company.

Wings, fuselage and tail unit components are manufactured in Japan and shipped to the US. At San Angelo they go back on to an assembly production line, where American-built components which include engines, electronics, tyres, brakes and interiors are installed. A description of the MU-2J and MU-2K can be found in the Japanese aircraft section of this edition.

Mitsubishi Aircraft International in San Angelo has worldwide marketing responsibility for the MU-2, although most of the 300 aircraft of this type produced at San Angelo by April 1974 are in service in the US, Canada and Mexico.

MONG

RALPH E. MONG, Jr

Address:
1218 North 91st East Avenue, Tulsa, Oklahoma 74115

Mr Ralph Mong is the designer of the Mong Sport light biplane, of which plans are available for amateur construction. At least 50 are known to have been completed and flown successfully.

MONG SPORT

This aircraft is a light single-seat biplane, powered normally by a 65 hp Continental A65 four-cylinder horizontally-opposed aircooled engine, but with provision for other engines of up to 90 hp. The wings have a wood structure with fabric covering, and the lower wing only has dihedral of 3°. The fuselage and tail unit are fabric-covered welded steel tube structures. Fuel capacity is 20 US gallons (75·7 litres).

The example illustrated is a standard Sport, owned by Gail Clark of Tulsa, Oklahoma. Mong Sports have achieved notable successes at race meetings. In particular, Dallas Christian of Citrus Heights, California, took first place in the Sport Biplane Class at the Reno, Frederick and Cleveland National Air Races in 1968, with a speed of 152 knots (175 mph; 282 km/h) at Reno.

DIMENSIONS, EXTERNAL:

Wing span	16 ft 10 in (5·13 m)
Length overall	14 ft 1 in (4·39 m)
Height overall	5 ft 6 in (1·68 m)
Wing chord	2 ft 8 in (0·81 m)

AREA:

Wings, gross	80 sq ft (7·43 m²)

WEIGHTS:

Weight empty	550 lb (249 kg)
Max T-O weight	960 lb (435 kg)

PERFORMANCE (at max T-O weight):

Max level speed at S/L
122 knots (140 mph; 225 km/h)

Cruising speed (with Sensenich 70A54 propeller)
100 knots (115 mph; 185 km/h)

Mong Sport owned by Gail Clark of Tulsa, Oklahoma (90 hp Continental engine)

Landing speed	48 knots (55 mph; 89 km/h)
Max rate of climb at S/L	1,000 ft (305 m)/min
Service ceiling	13,000 ft (3,962 m)
T-O and landing run	600 ft (183 m)
Range with max fuel	204 nm (350 miles; 563 km)

MONNETT

MONNETT EXPERIMENTAL AIRCRAFT INC

ADDRESS:
410 Adams, Elgin, Illinois 60120
Telephone: (312) 741-2223

Mr John T. Monnett formed this company to market plans and certain components of an original-design Formula V racer. Known originally as the Monnett II Sonerai, this received the Best in Class Formula V Racer award at the EAA Fly-in at Oshkosh in 1971, as well as an award for its outstanding contribution to low-cost flying. Since that time Mr Monnett has designed a two-seat version of the Sonerai, with the result that the original single-seat model is now known simply as Sonerai, the two-seat model as Sonerai II.

Mr Monnett has also designed and built a lightweight sporting aircraft designated Monnett I, which was described in the 1972-73 *Jane's*.

Monnett Sonerai homebuilt Formula V racer (60 hp Volkswagen modified motor car engine)

Monnett Sonerai II two-seat homebuilt sporting aircraft *(Howard Levy)*

MONNETT SONERAI

Mr Monnett began design of the Sonerai in September 1970, construction starting two months later. First flight was made in July 1971 and FAA certification in the Experimental category has been granted. Plans and certain components are available to amateur constructors, these comprising glassfibre engine cowlings, clear or tinted Plexiglas cockpit canopy, main landing gear struts, formed aluminium ribs, tapered rod tail spring, fuel tanks, spar kits, instruments, injector carburettor and wheels and brakes.

By mid-February 1974 approximately 250 sets of plans had been sold, and 100 Sonerais were known to be under construction.

TYPE: Single-seat Formula V homebuilt racing aircraft.

WINGS: Cantilever mid-wing monoplane. Wing section NACA 64212. No dihedral, incidence or sweepback. Conventional light alloy structure. Full-span light alloy ailerons. No trailing-edge flaps. No trim tabs. Wings fold on each side of the fuselage to allow the aircraft to be towed tail-first.

FUSELAGE: Welded chrome-molybdenum steel tube structure with fabric covering. Glassfibre engine cowling.

TAIL UNIT: Cantilever structure of welded chrome-molybdenum steel tube with fabric covering. Tailplane incidence ground-adjustable. No trim tabs.

LANDING GEAR: Non-retractable tailwheel type. Cantilever spring main gear of light alloy. Main wheels and tyres size 5·00-5. Caliper type wheel-brakes. Glassfibre fairings on main wheels.

POWER PLANT: One 60 hp Volkswagen 1,600 cc modified motor car engine, driving a Hegy two-blade propeller with spinner. Fuel tank in fuselage, immediately aft of firewall, capacity 11 US gallons (41·5 litres). Refuelling point on fuselage upper surface forward of bubble canopy. Oil capacity 0·75 US gallon (2·82 litres).

ACCOMMODATION: Single seat for pilot under jettisonable Plexiglas bubble canopy, hinged at the starboard side.

ELECTRONICS: Battery-powered 10-channel communications transceiver.

DIMENSIONS, EXTERNAL:

Wing span	16 ft 8 in (5·08 m)
Wing chord, constant	4 ft 6 in (1·37 m)
Length overall	16 ft 8 in (5·08 m)
Height overall	5 ft 0 in (1·52 m)
Tailplane span	6 ft 6 in (1·98 m)
Wheel track	4 ft 0 in (1·22 m)
Propeller diameter	4 ft 2 in (1·27 m)
Propeller ground clearance	1 ft 0 in (0·30 m)

AREA:

Wings, gross	75 sq ft (6·97 m²)

WEIGHTS:

Weight empty	440 lb (199 kg)
Max T-O weight	700 lb (317 kg)

PERFORMANCE (at max T-O weight):

Max level speed at S/L
over 139 knots (160 mph; 257 km/h)

Max cruising speed
130 knots (150 mph; 241 km/h)

Econ cruising speed
109 knots (125 mph; 201 km/h)

Stalling speed	40 knots (46 mph; 74 km/h)
Landing run	600 ft (183 m)
Range	over 260 nm (300 miles; 482 km)

MONNETT SONERAI II

The success of the Sonerai encouraged Mr Monnett to begin the design and construction of a two-seat version in December 1972, since it was clear there was a demand for a high-performance two-seat sporting monoplane suitable for amateur construction. Generally similar to the Sonerai, it differs by being slightly larger and by having a more powerful Volkswagen engine. The prototype made its first flight in July 1973, since when orders have been received for 75 sets of plans. As in the case of Sonerai, plans, many components and materials are available to amateur constructors.

The description of the Sonerai applies also to Sonerai II, except as follows:

TYPE: Two-seat homebuilt high-performance sporting aircraft.

WINGS: As for Sonerai, except span increased.

FUSELAGE: As for Sonerai, except length increased.

TAIL UNIT: As for Sonerai, except tailplane has fixed incidence and reduced span.

POWER PLANT: One 1,700 cc Volkswagen modified motor car engine, developing 65-70 hp, driving a two-blade wooden fixed-pitch propeller. Fuel and oil as for Sonerai.

ACCOMMODATION: Two seats in tandem beneath transparent bubble canopy, hinged on starboard side.

ELECTRONICS: Prototype has battery-powered 10-channel com transceiver.

DIMENSIONS, EXTERNAL: As Sonerai, except:

Wing span	18 ft 8 in (5·69 m)
Length overall	18 ft 10 in (5·74 m)
Tailplane span	6 ft 0 in (1·83 m)
Propeller diameter	4 ft 4 in to 4 ft 6 in (1·32-1·37 m)

DIMENSIONS, INTERNAL:

Cockpit:

Length	4 ft 0 in (1·22 m)
Max width	2 ft 0 in (0·61 m)
Max height	3 ft 4 in (1·02 m)

AREA:

Wings, gross	84 sq ft (7·80 m²)

WEIGHTS AND LOADINGS:

Weight empty	506 lb (230 kg)
Max T-O weight	926 lb (420 kg)
Max wing loading	11·0 lb/sq ft (53·7 kg/m²)
Max power loading	13·2 lb/hp (5·99 kg/hp)

PERFORMANCE (at max T-O weight):

Max level speed at S/L
approx 143 knots (165 mph; 266 km/h)

Max cruising speed at S/L
122 knots (140 mph; 225 km/h)

Econ cruising speed at S/L
113 knots (130 mph; 209 km/h)

Stalling speed	39 knots (45 mph; 73 km/h)
Max rate of climb at S/L	750 ft (229 m)/min
T-O run, ISA	900 ft (274 m)
Landing run	500 ft (152 m)
Range with max fuel and max payload, 30 min reserve	364 nm (420 miles; 676 km)

MOONEY

MOONEY AIRCRAFT

The original Mooney Aircraft Inc was formed in June 1948, in Wichita, Kansas, from where the single-seat Model M-18 Mooney Mite was produced until 1952. The company transferred to Kerrville, Texas, in 1953 and completed a merger with Alon Inc of McPherson, Kansas, in October 1967. Subsequently, in late 1969, Butler Aviation International Inc and American Electronic Laboratories Inc entered into an agreement whereby the former company acquired 100 per cent stock ownership of Mooney Aircraft, the company name being changed to Aerostar Aircraft Corporation on 1 July 1970. Production of Aerostar aircraft was suspended in early 1972, at which time a number of companies were discussing the purchase of Aerostar Aircraft Corporation. In early 1974 came news that the Republic Steel Corporation had assumed control of the company, once again named Mooney Aircraft.

Details of the company's products follow:

MOONEY RANGER

The prototype Ranger (formerly known as Mark 21) flew on 23 September 1961 and the first production model on 7 November 1961. FAA Type Approval was received on 7 November 1961.

The Ranger has as standard equipment a Positive Control (PC) system which co-ordinates yaw/roll stability. Developed in association with Brittain Industries, PC employs a sensor in the form of a tilted-axis rate gyro. Any deviation in roll or yaw causes the gyro to emit a mechanical signal to a master vacuum control valve. This valve is connected to the standard vacuum system of the engine and by lines to servo cans. One vacuum servo is located at each aileron for roll control and two in the tailcone to activate the rudder for yaw control. Interconnected control linkages, combined with the sensitivity of the rate gyro, bring pressure on both ailerons and rudder to produce co-ordinated corrective action and restore the aircraft to straight and level flight. PC can be overridden by normal control pressures and can be disengaged by depressing a button on the control yoke.

Type: Four-seat cabin monoplane.

Wings: Cantilever low-wing monoplane. Wing section NACA 63_2-215 at root, NACA 64_1-412 at tip. Dihedral 5° 30′. Incidence 2° 30′ at root, 1° at tip. Sweepforward 2° 29′. Light alloy structure with flush-riveted stretch-formed wraparound skins. Full-span main spar; rear spar terminates at mid-span of flaps. Sealed-gap differentially-operated light alloy ailerons. Electrically-operated single-slotted light alloy flaps over 70% of trailing-edge. No tabs.

Fuselage: Composite all-metal structure. Cabin section is of welded 4130 chrome-molybdenum steel tube with sheet light alloy covering. Rear section is of semi-monocoque construction, with sheet light alloy bulkheads and skin and extruded alloy stringers.

Tail Unit: Cantilever light alloy structure, with variable-incidence tailplane. All surfaces covered with wraparound metal skin. Trim tab on elevator.

Landing Gear: Electrically-retractable levered-suspension tricycle type. Nosewheel retracts rearward, main units inward into wings. Firestone rubber disc shock-absorbers on main units. Delco hydraulic shock-absorber on nose unit. Cleveland main wheels, size 6·00-6, and steerable nosewheel, size 5·00-5. Tyre pressure (all units) 30 lb/sq in (2·11 kg/cm²). Cleveland hydraulic single-disc brakes on main wheels. Parking brakes.

Power Plant: One 180 hp Lycoming O-360-A1D four-cylinder horizontally-opposed aircooled engine, driving a Hartzell HC-C2YK-1/7666-2 two-blade metal constant-speed propeller. Two integral fuel tanks, with total capacity of 52 US gallons (197 litres), in wing roots. Flush refuelling point above each tank. Oil capacity 2 US gallons (7·5 litres).

Accommodation: Cabin accommodates four in two pairs of individual seats, front pair with dual controls. Starboard rudder pedals optionally removable to allow more leg room for passenger. Overhead ventilation system. Cabin heating and cooling system, with adjustable outlets and illuminated control. One-piece wraparound windscreen. Tinted Plexiglas windows. Starboard front and rear seats removable for freight stowage. Single door on starboard side. Compartment for 120 lb (54 kg) baggage behind cabin, with access from cabin or through outside door on starboard side. Windscreen defrosting system standard.

Systems: Hydraulic system for brakes only. Electrical system includes 60A alternator, 12V 35Ah battery, voltage regulator and warning light, together with protective circuit breakers.

Electronics: An extensive range of optional equipment is available to customer's requirements, manufactured by Bendix, King and Narco. Intercom and cabin speaker standard.

Equipment: Standard equipment includes many de luxe features as well as basic instruments, sensitive altimeter, detachable battery box, streamlined spinner, and dual controls. Optional equipment includes two overhead panel floodlights, dry vacuum pump with regulator, communications transceiver whip antenna, navigation receiver antenna, assist strap, suit hanger, access step, padded instrument glare shield, alternative instrument panel finishes, sun visors, quick oil drain, hat shelf, Brittain turn co-ordinator with vacuum drive and emergency electric motor, passenger reading light, automatic brightness control for panel lights, removable co-pilot rudder pedals, reclining adjustable front seats, individually reclining removable rear seats, wing jack points, armrests, external tie-down rings, heated pitot, tow-bar, blind-flying instrumentation, outside air temperature gauge, eight-day clock, alternate static air source, baggage door light, rotating beacon, broad band antenna, external finish of polyurethane paint, all-leather interior trim, auxiliary power socket, carburettor air temperature gauge, curtains, dual brakes, exhaust gas temperature gauge, set of headrests, Plexring instrument panel lights, polished spinner, remote indicating compass, full-flow oil filter, strobe lights, whitewall tyres and true airspeed indicator.

Dimensions, external:

Wing span	35 ft 0 in (10·67 m)
Wing chord, mean	4 ft 9¼ in (1·45 m)
Wing aspect ratio	7·338
Length overall	24 ft 1 in (7·34 m)
Height overall	8 ft 6 in (2·59 m)
Tailplane span	11 ft 8 in (3·55 m)
Wheel track	9 ft 0¾ in (2·76 m)
Wheelbase	5 ft 6¼ in (1·68 m)
Propeller diameter	6 ft 2 in (1·88 m)
Cabin door:	
Height	3 ft 1½ in (0·95 m)
Width	2 ft 6½ in (0·78 m)
Height to sill	1 ft 1½ in (0·34 m)
Baggage compartment door:	
Height	2 ft 0 in (0·61 m)
Width	1 ft 7 in (0·48 m)

Dimensions, internal:

Cabin: Length	8 ft 8 in (2·64 m)
Max width	3 ft 4½ in (1·04 m)
Max height	3 ft 8½ in (1·13 m)
Baggage compartment	13·5 cu ft (0·38 m³)

Areas:

Wings, gross	167·00 sq ft (15·51 m²)
Ailerons (total)	11·05 sq ft (1·03 m²)
Trailing-edge flaps (total)	17·48 sq ft (1·62 m²)
Fin	7·88 sq ft (0·73 m²)
Rudder	5·01 sq ft (0·46 m²)
Tailplane	21·50 sq ft (2·00 m²)
Elevators	12·02 sq ft (1·11 m²)

Weights and Loadings:

Weight empty	1,525 lb (691 kg)
Max T-O and landing weight	2,575 lb (1,168 kg)
Max wing loading	15·4 lb/sq ft (75·2 kg/m²)
Max power loading	14·3 lb/hp (6·49 kg/hp)

Performance:

Max level speed at S/L	153 knots (176 mph; 283 km/h)
Stalling speed (flaps and wheels down, power off)	50 knots (57 mph; 92 km/h) IAS
Max rate of climb at S/L	1,000 ft (305 m)/min
Service ceiling	19,500 ft (5,743 m)
T-O run, zero wind, ISA	815 ft (248 m)
Landing run, zero wind, ISA	595 ft (181 m)
Range, with allowance for taxi, climb and 45 min reserve	869 nm (1,001 miles; 1,610 km)

MOONEY CHAPARRAL

The Mooney Chaparral is an updated version of the Super-21, which flew for the first time in July 1963, and is generally similar to the current Mooney Ranger. It differs by having a more powerful engine. It has as standard equipment a Positive Control system as described for the Ranger.

The description of the Ranger applies also to the Chaparral except in the following details:

Power Plant: One 200 hp Lycoming IO-360-A1A four-cylinder horizontally-opposed aircooled engine, driving a Hartzell two-blade metal constant-speed propeller. Fuel injection, tuned induction manifold, exhaust gas temperature gauge and ram air boost. Other details as for Ranger.

Weights and Loadings:

As for Ranger, except:

Weight empty	1,600 lb (725 kg)
Max power loading	12·9 lb/hp (5·85 kg/hp)

Performance:

Max level speed at S/L	165 knots (190 mph; 306 km/h)
Stalling speed (flaps and wheels down, power off)	50 knots (57 mph; 92 km/h) IAS
Max rate of climb at S/L	1,400 ft (427 m)/min
Service ceiling	21,200 ft (6,460 m)
T-O run, zero wind, ISA	760 ft (232 m)
Landing run, zero wind, ISA	595 ft (181 m)
Range, allowance for taxi, climb and 45 min reserve	838 nm (965 miles; 1,553 km)

MOONEY EXECUTIVE

This member of the Mooney family of aircraft is basically similar to the Ranger, with the same Positive Control system as standard. It differs by having a 200 hp Lycoming fuel-injection engine, a longer fuselage, providing more leg room and baggage stowage, and additional cabin windows. It was reported in mid-1974 that the company was flight testing an Executive powered by a 285 hp Continental Tiara engine. Differences compared with the Ranger are as follows:

Power Plant: One 200 hp Lycoming IO-360-A1A four-cylinder horizontally-opposed aircooled engine, driving a Hartzell two-blade metal constant-speed propeller. Fuel injection, tuned induction manifold, exhaust gas temperature gauge and ram air power boost. Total fuel capacity 64 US gallons (242 litres).

Dimensions, external:

As for Ranger, except:

Length overall	24 ft 11 in (7·59 m)

Mooney Chaparral four-seat light aircraft (200 hp Lycoming IO-360-A1A engine) (*J. M. G. Gradidge*)

Mooney Executive four-seat light aircraft (200 hp Lycoming IO-360-A1A engine)

Dimensions, internal:
As for Ranger, except:
Cabin: Length 9 ft 6 in (2·90 m)

Weights and Loading:
Weight empty 1,640 lb (743 kg)
Max baggage 120 lb (54 kg)
Max T-O weight 2,740 lb (1,243 kg)
Max wing loading 16·4 lb/sq ft (80·1 kg/m²)

Performance:
Max level speed 161 knots (185 mph; 298 km/h)
Stalling speed (flaps and wheels down, power off) 54 knots (62 mph; 100 km/h) IAS
Max rate of climb at S/L 1,330 ft (405 m)/min
Service ceiling 18,800 ft (5,730 m)
T-O run, zero wind, ISA 879 ft (268 m)
Landing run, zero wind, ISA 785 ft (239 m)
Range, with allowance for taxi, climb and 45 min reserve 996 nm (1,147 miles; 1,846 km)

MOONEY MITE

MOONEY MITE AIRCRAFT CORPORATION

Address:
PO Box 3999, Charlottesville, Virginia 22903

Mooney Mite Aircraft Corporation has been formed to market to amateur constructors plans of the Mooney Mite, a version of the Mooney M-18 first designed and built as a production aircraft by Mooney Aircraft Inc.

MOONEY MITE

Type: Single-seat homebuilt sporting aircraft.

Wings: Cantilever low-wing monoplane. Conventional single-spar structure of wood with plywood leading-edge and fabric covering aft of the spar. Ailerons and trailing-edge flaps of welded steel tube construction with fabric covering.

Fuselage: Composite structure, forward section to aft of cockpit of welded steel tube with light alloy skins. Aft fuselage of wood monocoque construction with fabric covering.

Tail Unit: Cantilever welded steel tube structure, fabric-covered. Tailplane incidence variable by "Safe-Trim" system that interconnects tail trim with trailing-edge flaps to establish automatically the correct settings for take-off, climb, approach and landing.

Landing Gear: Manually-retractable tricycle type. Shock-absorption of main units by Firestone rubber-in-compression units. Nosewheel steerable. Main wheels of Cleveland, Firestone or Goodyear manufacture, with tyres size 5·00-5. Hydraulic brakes.

Power Plant: One 65 hp Lycoming O-145-B2 four-cylinder horizontally-opposed aircooled engine, driving a Sensenich Type 66CB-54 two-blade fixed-pitch propeller with spinner. Fuel tank in fuselage, capacity 11 US gallons (41·5 litres). Oil capacity 1 US gallon (3·75 litres).

Accommodation: Single seat beneath aft-sliding transparent canopy. Space for 36 lb (16·3 kg) baggage aft of seat.

System: Electric power supplied by wind-driven generator mounted on pylon on upper surface of aft fuselage.

Dimensions, external:
Wing span 26 ft 10½ in (8·19 m)
Length overall 17 ft 7¼ in (5·37 m)
Height overall 6 ft 2½ in (1·89 m)

Area:
Wings, gross 95 sq ft (8·83 m²)

Mooney Mite single-seat light aircraft for amateur construction

Weights and Loadings:
Weight empty 500 lb (226 kg)
Max T-O weight 780 lb (353 kg)
Max wing loading 8·21 lb/sq ft (40·1 kg/m²)
Max power loading 12 lb/hp (5·44 kg/hp)

Performance (at max T-O weight):
Max level speed at S/L 124 knots (143 mph; 230 km/h)
Optimum cruising speed, 66% power at 10,000 ft (3,050 m) 109 knots (125 mph; 201 km/h)
Econ cruising speed, 50% power at S/L 100 knots (115 mph; 185 km/h)
Min controllable speed, power on 33 knots (38 mph; 61·5 km/h)
Landing speed, power off 39 knots (45 mph; 72 km/h)
Stalling speed, power off 37·5 knots (43 mph; 69·5 km/h)
Max rate of climb at S/L 1,090 ft (332 m)/min
Service ceiling 19,400 ft (5,915 m)
Absolute ceiling 21,300 ft (6,490 m)
T-O run 698 ft (213 m)
T-O to 50 ft (15 m) 1,000 ft (305 m)
Landing from 50 ft (15 m) 1,200 ft (366 m)
Landing run 240 ft (73 m)
Range at optimum cruising speed 338 nm (390 miles; 627 km)
Range at econ cruising speed 382 nm (440 miles; 708 km)

MORRISEY

WILLIAM J. MORRISEY

Address:
PO Box 606, San Marcos, California 92069

Mr W. J. Morrisey, formerly chief test pilot of the Douglas Aircraft Company at Long Beach, California, designed and built a two-seat light aircraft known as the Model 1000C Nifty, which first flew in early 1948, with a 65 hp Continental engine. During the next seven years he continued development of this aircraft, leading to the establishment of Morrisey Aviation Inc, which put into production two type-certificated versions, the Model 2000C with 90 hp engine and Model 2150 (later known as Shinn Model 2150) with 150 hp engine (described in 1959-60 *Jane's*).

Plans of the Model 1000C are available to amateur constructors, and about 12 aircraft were known to be under construction in mid-February 1973.

MORRISEY MODEL 1000C NIFTY

Type: Two-seat lightweight sporting/training aircraft.

Wings: Cantilever low-wing monoplane. Wing section NACA 43015. Dihedral 7°. Incidence 0°. Conventional two-spar wood structure with plywood and fabric covering. All-wood ailerons with plywood covering. No flaps.

Fuselage: Welded steel tube structure with light alloy cowlings forward of the wing, and fabric covering aft.

Tail Unit: Cantilever composite structure. Fin, rudder and elevator are of welded steel tube construction with fabric covering. Tailplane of wooden construction with plywood covering. Elevator trim by rubber bungee.

Landing Gear: Non-retractable tricycle type. All units have oleo-pneumatic shock-absorbers. Main wheels and tyres size 4·00-6, nosewheel and tyre size 4·00-5. Goodrich brakes.

Power Plant: Can utilise any Continental four-cylinder horizontally-opposed aircooled engine from 65 to 150 hp, driving a two-blade fixed-pitch propeller. Fuel in fuselage tank, immediately aft of firewall, capacity 20 US gallons (75·7 litres). Refuelling point on fuselage upper surface, forward of windscreen.

Accommodation: Two seats in tandem under continuous sideways-hinged canopy. Drawings available for alternative open-cockpit version. Space for 40 lb (18 kg) baggage.

Morrisey 1000C Nifty two-seat light aircraft for amateur construction

Dimensions, external:
Wing span 29 ft 0 in (8·84 m)
Wing chord at root 5 ft 0 in (1·52 m)
Wing chord at tip 3 ft 0 in (0·91 m)
Length overall 20 ft 0 in (6·10 m)
Height overall 7 ft 2 in (2·18 m)
Tailplane span 9 ft 0 in (2·74 m)
Wheel track 6 ft 10 in (2·08 m)
Wheelbase 4 ft 10½ in (1·59 m)
Propeller diameter 6 ft 0 in (1·83 m)
Propeller ground clearance 9 in (0·23 m)

Areas:
Wings, gross 134 sq ft (12·45 m²)
Ailerons (total) 5·5 sq ft (0·51 m²)
Fin 5·8 sq ft (0·54 m²)
Rudder 3·1 sq ft (0·29 m²)
Horizontal tail surfaces 14·3 sq ft (1·33 m²)

Weights (90 hp engine):
Weight empty 900 lb (408 kg)
Max T-O weight:
Normal 1,450 lb (657 kg)
Utility 1,363 lb (618 kg)

Performance (90 hp engine):
Max level speed 108 knots (125 mph; 201 km/h)
Cruising speed 95-100 knots (110-115 mph; 177-185 km/h)
Landing speed 37 knots (42 mph; 68 km/h)
Max rate of climb at S/L 1,000 ft (305 m)/min
Service ceiling over 20,000 ft (6,100 m)
T-O run 280 ft (86 m)
T-O to 50 ft (15 m) 350 ft (107 m)
Landing from 50 ft (15 m) 320 ft (98 m)
Landing run 200 ft (61 m)
Range with max fuel 321 nm (370 miles; 595 km)

NAGLER

NAGLER AIRCRAFT CORPORATION

ADDRESS:
PO Box 20982, Phoenix, Arizona 85036
Telephone: (602) 272-9409
PRESIDENT: Bruno Nagler
DIRECTORS:
Bruno Nagler
Darrow Thompson
Gene Shaheen
TEST PILOT: Charles V. Tucker
WORKS MANAGER: Norman R. Bernier

Nagler Aircraft Corporation, an outgrowth of the earlier Vertigyro and Vertidynamics companies, was established in March 1971 by Bruno Nagler, whose first helicopter was built in Vienna in the early 1930s. In the Spring of 1973 the new company had a total of 15 employees, including an engineering consultant, Mr E. K. Liberatore.

First project of the new company was a prototype "cold-jet" tip-driven helicopter, the Honcho 100, intended to serve as a testbed for a two-seat development version to be known as the Honcho 200. Work on this latter version began in 1973. It is powered by a variant of the Solar T-62 Titan gas turbine, which serves as an APU in many military helicopters and small commercial transport aircraft. The T-62 drives directly a centrifugal compressor. Power boost for hovering is provided by blade-tip mounted burners.

Other projects of the company include a two-seat production version of the Honcho 200, to have the designation Model 202, a four-seat Model 421 and four/five-seat compound helicopter designated Model S11.

Nagler Honcho 100 helicopter testbed prototype

NAGLER HONCHO 100

TYPE: Single-seat helicopter testbed.

ROTOR: Two-blade rotor, driven by tip-mounted "cold-jets", which derive their thrust from an AiResearch 85-90 bleed air compressor. Max design rotor speed is 550 rpm, with a min of 350 rpm, but the prototype has flown with rotor speeds as low as 250 rpm. Normal operating speed 420 rpm. Since there is no rotor drive mechanism, the rotor is mounted on a simple pylon structure. No tail rotor.

FUSELAGE: Open steel tube structure.

TAIL SURFACE: Rudder of metal construction, mounted centrally in outflow from turbine compressor.

LANDING GEAR: Non-retractable tricycle type. No shock-absorbers.

POWER PLANT: AiResearch bleed air compressor, with normal rating of 2 lb (0·9 kg)/sec bleed air at a compression ratio of 3·5 : 1 absolute. Fuel tank on each side of fuselage, mounted midway up rotor pylon.

ACCOMMODATION: Single open seat. Conventional helicopter controls.

DIMENSIONS, EXTERNAL:	
Rotor diameter	28 ft 2 in (8·59 m)
Rotor blade chord	8¼ in (21 cm)
Length of fuselage	10 ft 7 in (3·23 m)
Width overall	6 ft 1 in (1·85 m)
Height overall	5 ft 9 in (1·75 m)
AREA:	
Rotor disc	622·8 sq ft (57·86 m²)
WEIGHTS AND LOADING:	
Weight empty	700 lb (317 kg)
T-O weight	970 lb (440 kg)
Disc loading	1·55 lb/sq ft (7·57 kg/m²)

NAGLER HONCHO 200

Following successful development testing of the Honcho 100, a more sophisticated two-seat research helicopter has been constructed, which utilises the same basic principles for propulsion. This dispenses with the need for a tail rotor, and it is anticipated that by utilising the efflux from a more powerful turbojet to exhaust over a movable rudder, it will be possible to build a very compact helicopter as a production version of the Honcho 200. It had completed 14 hours of flight testing by early 1974.

Nagler Honcho 200, a two-seat helicopter testbed prototype

TYPE: Two-seat helicopter testbed.

ROTOR: Rotor of increased diameter, otherwise generally similar to that of Honcho 100.

FUSELAGE: Welded steel tube structure, with enclosed cabin forward of rotor pylon.

TAIL UNIT: Fixed fin and movable rudder of metal construction, mounted centrally in efflux from turbine compressor. Tail unit carried on tubular light alloy structure.

LANDING GEAR: Fixed tubular steel skids. Spring "bumper" at aft end of tubular tailboom.

POWER PLANT: Continental TC-140 bleed air compressor, with normal rating of 1·89 lb (0·86 kg)/sec bleed air at a compression ratio of 4 : 1 absolute. Fuel tank on each side of fuselage, mounted midway up rotor pylon.

ACCOMMODATION: Two seats side by side in enclosed cockpit. Conventional helicopter controls.

DIMENSION, EXTERNAL:	
Rotor diameter	36 ft 0 in (10·97 m)
WEIGHT:	
Max T-O weight	1,350 lb (612 kg)
PERFORMANCE:	
Max level speed	65 knots (75 mph: 121 km/h)

NASA

NATIONAL AERONAUTICS AND SPACE ADMINISTRATION, AMES RESEARCH CENTER

ADDRESS:
Ames Research Center, Aeronautics and Flight Systems, Mail Stop 200-3, Moffett Field, California 94035

NASA has several current research programmes of general aviation interest, including a supercritical wing, an augmentor wing jet STOL research aircraft, digital fly-by-wire techniques, research with the YF-12 which is capable of sustained cruise flight at Mach 3, and creation of an airborne infra-red observatory.

NASA has also contracted with the Robertson Aircraft Corporation to design, develop and test a new concept in general aviation aircraft, employing a wing with advanced aerofoil section developed by NASA. Details of this are given in the entry for Robertson Aircraft Corporation.

NASA SUPERCRITICAL WING

NASA has developed a new wing, called the NASA supercritical wing, as a result of wind-tunnel studies conducted by Dr Richard T. Whitcomb during recent years. Stated simply, the new wing utilises an aerofoil shape with a flat top and downward cambered rear section, as compared to the curved top and sloped rear section of a conventional wing.

If wind-tunnel measured performance is achieved fully in flight, the new wing could allow highly efficient cruise flight near the speed of sound. In addition to permitting a substantial increase in cruise speed without increase in power, it may significantly reduce the operational cost of subsonic jet transport flight.

When the speed of an aircraft approaches the speed of sound, regions of high supersonic airflow develop, particularly above the wing. These cause severe local disturbances such as shock-waves and boundary layer flow separation, leading to increased drag, severe buffeting and adverse changes in stability. Subsonic flight operations with current aircraft are normally kept below the speed at which such effects begin to occur, namely Mach 0·8 at a cruising altitude of 35,000 ft (10,670 m). Wind-tunnel and analytical studies indicate that the NASA supercritical wing has the potential of allowing subsonic speeds in excess of Mach 0·95 before the adverse effects become significant.

Swept wings have been employed up to now to delay the rise of the drag force and onset of buffet; but excessive wing sweep increases structural weight, induces problems related to low-speed flight characteristics and can also require increased take-off and landing distances. The supercritical wing shape has been developed to delay substantially the onset of these adverse effects.

A request for proposals for detail design and construction of the wing was issued in February 1969 by NASA's Flight Research Center at Edwards AFB, California. Award of a fixed-price contract to North American Rockwell Corporation (now Rockwell International) was announced by NASA in September 1969. A T-2C Buckeye with a supercritical wing was flown in November 1970, followed by an LTV Aerospace F-8A.

As fitted to the F-8A, the wing has a span of 43 ft (13·11 m), sweepback of 42·24° at quarter-chord, no anhedral or dihedral, incidence of 1° 30′ at fuselage centreline, aspect ratio of 6·8 and thickness/chord ratio of 11% at root and 7% at tip. Wing area is 274 sq ft (24·45 m²).

On 5 June 1971 it was reported that flight tests of the wing were under way at Edwards AFB and had proved satisfactory up to that date.

As the next stage in development of the supercritical wing, a joint NASA/USAF research programme was initiated which involved testing such a wing on a General Dynamics F-111 aircraft. Before installation of the new wing began, in the first half of 1973, a series of 24 flights by the F-111, in its original form, provided the performance yardsticks by which subsequent changes could be evaluated.

Under a programme known as Transonic Aircraft Technology (TACT), a supercritical wing has now been applied to the variable-geometry F-111 and is undergoing extensive testing. In the case of this application it is not expected that the wing will offer any increase in maximum speed. Instead, it is anticipated that the aircraft will be able to cruise and manoeuvre at higher speeds without any increase in fuel consumption. Increased efficiency from an aircraft's wing may be of great importance in the future, especially if its application to commercial transport aircraft can offer fuel economies rather than increased performance.

NASA/DITC AUGMENTOR WING JET STOL RESEARCH AIRCRAFT

In a co-operative venture between NASA and the Canadian government, as represented by the Department of Industry, Trade and Commerce (DITC), a de Havilland Canada C-8A Buffalo transport aircraft has been modified extensively to serve as an augmentor wing research aircraft.

De Havilland Canada began theoretical studies of the augmentor wing principle early in 1960, and a co-operative NASA/Canadian government research programme was started in 1965. During subsequent years the research programme followed a step-by-step process, leading to large-scale tests in NASA's 40 ft × 80 ft (12·2 m × 24·4 m) wind tunnel at Ames Research Center, using a de Havilland-built model, and joint design feasibility and simulator studies. By early 1970 these studies and tests had advanced to the extent that a proof-of-concept aircraft was warranted to test the principle in flight.

The US and Canadian governments entered into an international agreement whereby NASA and the DITC would modify a C-8A Buffalo to flight test the concept. This aircraft was selected following a design feasibility study by the Los Angeles Division of North American Rockwell Corporation (now Rockwell International), which showed that with such a modification the primary research objective could be achieved at a reasonable cost and within an acceptable time span. In particular, the high wing and T-tail of the C-8A made it very suitable for modification into a powered-lift jet STOL transport, and its wing planform was basically similar to that of the large-scale wind-tunnel test model.

The DITC contracted with de Havilland Aircraft of Canada Ltd and its subcontractor, Rolls-Royce of Canada Ltd, to provide the propulsion system and modify the engine nacelles. NASA contracted with The Boeing Company to modify the aircraft, install the propulsion system and perform the initial flight tests.

The major modifications and additions to the aircraft included a reduction of wing span to 78 ft 9 in (24·0 m); replacement of all the original wing structure aft of the rear spar, by installation of an augmentor flap system, including augmentor chokes, installation of drooped ailerons with boundary layer control (BLC), and repositioning and redesign of spoilers; installation of fixed full-span leading-edge slats; installation of two Rolls-Royce Spey Mk 801SF turbofan engines (each 9,000 lb; 4,082 kg st); installation of an air-distribution duct system to supply fan air to the augmentor flaps and for aileron and fuselage BLC; installation of lateral and directional stability augmentation systems, increased-capacity hydraulic systems and extensive flight test instrumentation; and fixing the landing gear in the extended position, with the normal two main wheels on each unit replaced by two Boeing 727 nosewheels size 32 × 10-15, inflated at 90 lb/sq in (6·33 kg/cm²) and fitted with Goodrich brakes.

The augmentor flaps, with a constant chord of 3 ft 6 in (1·07 m), are made in four equal spanwise sections, two on each wing, and have a maximum deflection of 75°. They are designed to be efficient ejectors of the fan air and consist of upper and lower segments, each of which is slotted. When extended these flaps deflect the primary jet flow downward and mix it with induced flow coming over the upper wing surface. At the same time, air from above the upper flap is pulled through the slotted surface of the upper flap, and air from below the lower surface of the lower flap is pulled up through that surface's slot, increasing the airflow between the two flap segments. The nett effect of this is to combine four different airflows into one jet stream between the two flap segments, increasing both lift and thrust and providing suction-type BLC to prevent or delay airflow separation from the upper flap surface.

Three surfaces are used on each wing to produce the rolling moments required for lateral control: a drooped BLC aileron, a spoiler in front of the drooped aileron, and an augmentor choke in the trailing-edge flaps. The ailerons are drooped mechanically as a function of the flap deflection, with full droop of 30° attained at a flap deflection of 60°. The aileron deflection is ±17° from the droop position. A large volume of blowing BLC is used on the aileron to give maximum effectiveness for both aileron and spoiler. The augmentor chokes, which are used to restrict the fan air outflow area of the augmentor flaps, are designed to control the lift of the flap system. Although there are augmentor chokes in each section of the flaps, only the choke in the outboard section of each wing is used for lateral control. All four chokes are activated on the ground after landing for lift dump.

The Rolls-Royce Spey engines have been modified extensively by Rolls-Royce of Canada, the main changes including a new by-pass duct that collects the fan air and directs it to two 13 in (0·33 m) diameter offtake ducts on top of the engine, and installation of a vectorable nozzle assembly (as used on the Pegasus engine of the Hawker Siddeley Harrier) in place of the normal tailpipe. The nozzles, one on each side of each engine nacelle, provide vectored thrust from 18° 30′ to 116° below the aircraft's datum line. Because the engines are installed low in the nacelles there is insufficient room for the main landing gear to retract; consequently the landing gear is locked down.

The air distribution system directs the fan air from the engines to the flaps, ailerons and fuselage blowing nozzles. One of the two offtake ducts on top of each engine directs 36% of the mass flow to feed the inner flap section aft of that engine. The other duct carries 64% of the mass flow, 7·1% of this being used for fuselage BLC, the remainder being ducted to the outer section of the augmentor flaps (44%) and aileron BLC (12·9%) in the opposite wing. This layout has been adopted so that in the event of an engine failure on approach, the aileron in the opposite wing would lose its BLC, compensating for the rolling moment due to the loss of thrust from the vectored nozzles, deflected to 90° on approach.

The research programme is not directed primarily toward lessening the noise problem of STOL aircraft, except in terms of the operational aspect of steep approach and landing. A separate programme to determine methods

General Dynamics F-111 fitted with supercritical wing for NASA's TACT programme

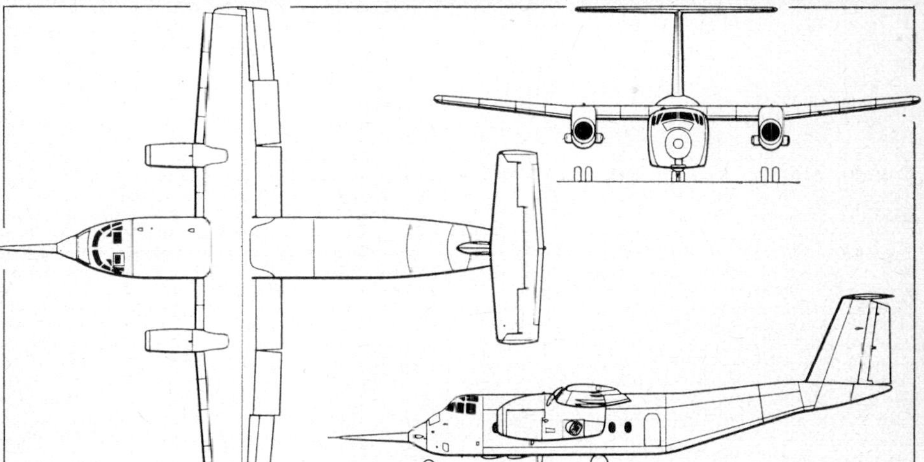

Three-view drawing (*Pilot Press*) and photograph of the NASA/DITC DHC C-8A Buffalo modified by The Boeing Company for augmentor wing jet STOL research

Comparison of two F-8A Crusaders: with NASA's supercritical wing (*left*) **and in standard configuration** (*right*). **See page 402**

of reducing the noise of augmentor wing flaps is being conducted for NASA by The Boeing Company. Preliminary results suggest that with proper design the noise level of the augmentor wing flap could be reduced to a figure of 95 EPNdB for a large commercial STOL aircraft.

The modified C-8A Buffalo was rolled out from the Boeing factory at Seattle, Washington, on 5 February, and the first flight was made on 1 May 1972. The flight test programme, planned to continue for more than twelve months, was initiated immediately.

DIMENSIONS, EXTERNAL:
- Wing span: 78 ft 9 in (24·00 m)
- Wing chord at root: 12 ft 7 in (3·83 m)
- Wing chord at tip: 7 ft 9 in (2·36 m)
- Wing aspect ratio: 7·2
- Length overall (with 16 ft; 4·88 m probe): 93 ft 4 in (28·44 m)
- Height overall: 28 ft 8½ in (8·75 m)
- Tailplane span: 32 ft 0 in (9·75 m)
- Wheel track: 30 ft 6 in (9·29 m)
- Wheelbase: 27 ft 10 in (8·48 m)

AREAS:
- Wings, gross: 865 sq ft (80·36 m²)
- Trailing-edge flaps (projected, including ailerons aft of wing line): 187·10 sq ft (17·38 m²)
- Ailerons (total aft of hinge line, including tab): 46·30 sq ft (4·30 m²)
- Spoilers: 26·7 sq ft (2·48 m²)
- Fin: 92·0 sq ft (8·55 m²)
- Rudder: 60·0 sq ft (5·57 m²)
- Tailplane: 151·5 sq ft (14·08 m²)
- Elevators: 81·5 sq ft (7·57 m²)

WEIGHTS AND LOADINGS:
- Weight empty: 32,000 lb (14,515 kg)
- Max T-O weight: 45,000 lb (20,412 kg)
- Max landing weight: 43,000 lb (19,504 kg)
- Max wing loading: 52 lb/sq ft (254 kg/m²)
- Max power loading: 2·5 lb/lb st (2·5 kg/kg st)

PERFORMANCE (designed):
- Max never-exceed speed: 180 knots (207 mph; 333 km/h)
- Max cruising speed: 160 knots (184 mph; 296 km/h)
- Max manoeuvring speed: 140 knots (161 mph; 259 km/h)
- Max flaps-down speed, 50° flaps: 100 knots (115 mph; 185 km/h)
- Max flaps-down speed, 75° flaps: 95 knots (109 mph; 176 km/h)
- Stalling speed: 41 knots (47·5 mph; 76 km/h)
- Max rate of climb at S/L: 3,500 ft (1,065 m)/min
- Take-off to 35 ft (10·7 m), S/L, ISA, at max T-O weight, with 18° hot-thrust deflection:
  - 60° flaps: 965 ft (295 m)
  - 30° flaps: 1,050 ft (320 m)
- Max ferry range at max cruising speed at 10,000 ft (3,050 m), including climb, descent, taxying and 1,900 lb (862 kg) fuel reserve: 300 nm (345 miles; 555 km)

NASA DIGITAL FLY-BY-WIRE SYSTEM

Under its Digital Fly-By-Wire (DFBW) programme, NASA has modified extensively an LTV F-8 Crusader jet fighter for research into this important field of flight control. It is believed that a number of advantages will accrue if, as a result of a detailed test and evaluation programme, it is proved conclusively that the system is both robust and operationally viable. These may include smoother air travel, a reduction of the pilot's work load, improvements in aircraft payload and/or flight performance and, in the case of military aircraft, provision of a flight control system that is less vulnerable to battle damage.

In the research aircraft the mechanical flight controls, consisting of the usual collection of push-rods, bell cranks and control cables, have been removed completely. They have been replaced by an electronic system in which movements of the pilot's controls initiate signals that are fed via wire circuits to an on-board digital computer. Simultaneously, an inertial measuring unit senses the motion of the aircraft in flight and the resulting aerodynamic forces, and these are also fed to the computer. The inputs from these two sources provide the data required for the computer to evaluate the most appropriate control surface positions, which it signals by wires to electro-mechanical actuators which respond by setting their related controls in the optimum position.

The F-8 research aircraft used in NASA's DFBW programme has a secondary flight control system, consisting of three separate fly-by-wire analogue channels, which serves as a backup system. In this respect it differs fundamentally from earlier fly-by-wire research aircraft, for these have retained the mechanical flight controls to serve as a backup in the event of failure of the new system.

The airborne computer and inertial measuring unit are similar to those developed for the flight control system of the Apollo Lunar Module, already proved to be reliable under the most demanding conditions. Their use together for the control of a conventional aircraft in Earth's atmosphere will ensure fast and accurate positioning of the aircraft's control surfaces, which means that aircraft vibration induced by turbulent air will be reduced to a minimum.

More importantly for the future, it is believed that this faster and more accurate response, which will set control surfaces at their optimum position more effectively than a human pilot, may make it possible to reduce the size of control surfaces or even relocate them. This could reduce the basic weight and drag of new-generation aircraft and result in increased payload and/or flight performance.

LTV F-8 Crusader modified under NASA's Digital Fly-By-Wire progamme

One of two Lockheed YF-12s being used in a NASA research programme

NASA YF-12 PROGRAMME

NASA is operating two Lockheed YF-12 aircraft in the second phase of a joint USAF/NASA research programme. Basic purpose is to obtain information from sustained cruising flight at a speed of Mach 3 (approximately 1,735 knots; 2,000 mph; 3,220 km/h) at altitudes in the 75,000 ft (22,860 m) range to assist in the development and operation of future supersonic aircraft and the Space Shuttle. Major areas of interest include structural and performance research, stability, control, aerodynamics, the physiological and biomedical aspects of sustained high-speed cruise flight, as well as the physics of the upper atmosphere.

The effects of kinetic heating are being studied closely, and structural deformations or bending, structural dynamics and gust response are being examined. Changing airflow within the propulsion system and the resulting effects on high-performance aircraft form the major aspect of performance research. And since certain basic aerodynamics can only be examined realistically in flight, boundary layer flow, boundary layer noise, heat transfer, skin friction and base pressure distribution are all being measured. In the area of stability and control, particular emphasis is being placed on the altitude excursions, or oscillations, at high-speed cruise conditions.

Apart from the aircraft itself, flight crews are being studied to gain a better understanding of physiological stress; while temperature, pressure and other physical characteristics of the upper atmosphere are being carefully evaluated. It is believed that a better appreciation of these factors will have great impact on the performance and operation of future aircraft.

NASA AIRBORNE INFRA-RED OBSERVATORY

Since 1965 NASA has been conducting a programme of airborne infra-red astronomy, using both a Convair 990 and a Learjet as airborne observatories. Modified to accept stabilised telescopes, these have been able to operate at an altitude of 39,000 ft (11,885 m), at which height an aircraft is above about 85 per cent of the

Earth's atmosphere and more than 99 per cent of the water vapour, the major attenuator of infra-red radiation.

The most recent addition to this programme is the modified prototype Lockheed Model 200 StarLifter (similar to USAF C-141), which is able to accommodate a 36 in 91·5 cm) telescope. It has an openable cavity in the port upper fuselage, forward of the wing, with porous spoilers forward of the opening to minimise pressure fluctuations in the cavity. When this cavity is closed, the spoilers are retracted against the fuselage. The telescope and its supporting structure are attached to one side of a 1 ft 4 in (0·41 m) diameter air bearing, which is embedded in the aft pressure bulkhead. Measurements are made normally with highly sensitive electronic detectors, many of which have a capability of recording a light source as weak as a match at a distance equivalent to that separating Earth and Moon.

The Airborne Infra-Red Observatory (AIRO) is based at NASA's Ames Research Center, and is operated as a national facility available to any organisation with a valid research project. It is able to operate at a height of 45,000 ft (13,750 m) for 3½ hours. The cassegrain telescope will track celestial objects to an accuracy of six arc seconds.

Lockheed Model 200 StarLifter modified as an Airborne Infra-Red Observatory

NAVION

NAVION RANGEMASTER AIRCRAFT COMPANY

Head Office:
PO Box 311, Wharton, Texas 77488
Telephone: (713) 532-4444

President:
Cedric Kotowicz

In late 1972 Mr Kotowicz purchased the assets of the bankrupt Navion Aircraft Corporation, including jigs, machine tools and a large parts inventory, and these were moved to a new facility at Wharton, Texas. Since that time the new company has been providing support for the approximate total of 1,800 Navion aircraft which remain in operation throughout the world. In November 1973 it was announced that the Navion H would be put back into production in early 1974, with primary subassembly at facilities in Wharton, and wing and fuselage mating and installation of engine, avionics and interiors at Wharton Airport.

Last described in the 1969-70 *Jane's*, when the Navion H was being produced by the Navion Aircraft Corporation, formed by members of the American Navion Society, the Navion's history stretches back to the mid-1940s when the first Navion was designed and produced by North American Aviation.

By comparison with the 1969 Navion H, current aircraft have detail improvements. Improved visibility stems from elimination of the windscreen centrepost, and a cleaner aircraft results from a change to flush riveting. Production of 52 aircraft was scheduled for 1974.

NAVION RANGEMASTER MODEL H

Type: Five-seat light cabin monoplane.

Wings: Cantilever low-wing monoplane. Wing section NACA 4415R at root, NACA 6410R at tip. Dihedral 7° 30′. Incidence 1° at root, —2° at tip. Conventional structure of light alloy. Frise-type ailerons and single-slotted trailing-edge flaps of light alloy construction. Ground-adjustable trim tab on starboard aileron.

Fuselage: Light alloy semi-monocoque structure.

Tail Unit: Cantilever structure of light alloy. Fixed-incidence tailplane. Trim tab in each elevator. Ground-adjustable trim tab in rudder.

Landing Gear: Hydraulically-retractable tricycle type with single wheel on each unit. Oleo-pneumatic shock-struts. Disc brakes.

Power Plant: One 285 hp Continental IO-520 six-cylinder horizontally-opposed aircooled engine, driving a McCauley two-blade metal constant-speed propeller. Fuel in 40 US gallon (151 litre) centre main tank and two wingtip tanks each of 34 US gallons (129 litres). Total capacity 108 US gallons (409 litres). Three-blade propeller optional.

Accommodation: Pilot and four passengers in two pairs of individual seats and single rear seat. Dual controls, headrests and heater-defroster standard. Forward-hinged door on port side. Baggage space aft of rear seat.

Dimensions, external:

Wing span	34 ft 9 in (10·59 m)
Wing chord at root	7 ft 2½ in (2·19 m)
Wing chord at tip	3 ft 9½ in (1·15 m)
Wing aspect ratio	6·04
Length overall	27 ft 6 in (8·38 m)
Height overall	8 ft 4 in (2·54 m)
Tailplane span	13 ft 2 in (4·01 m)

Area:

Wings, gross	184·34 sq ft (17·13 m²)

Weights and Loadings:

Weight empty	1,945 lb (882 kg)
Max T-O weight	3,315 lb (1,504 kg)
Max wing loading	17·9 lb/sq ft (87·4 kg/m²)
Max power loading	11·6 lb/hp (5·26 kg/hp)

Performance (at max T-O weight):

Max cruising speed	163 knots (188 mph; 303 km/h)
Range	1,455 nm (1,675 miles; 2,695 km)

Artist's impression of the new Navion Rangemaster Model H (285 hp Continental IO-520 engine)

NESMITH

Plans from: Leonard R. Eaves, 3818 NW 36 Street, Oklahoma City, Oklahoma 73112

A prototype side-by-side two-seat light monoplane named the Cougar, designed by Mr Robert Nesmith, flew for the first time in March 1957. Sets of plans are available to amateur constructors, from the address given above, and about 100 Cougars are flying or under construction.

NESMITH COUGAR

The data given below apply to the standard Cougar, built according to the plans produced by Mr Nesmith. Some aircraft now flying incorporate detail modifications. One has a T-tail and others have been completed with folding wings.

Type: Two-seat sporting monoplane.

Wings: Braced high-wing monoplane, with single bracing strut each side. Wing section NACA 4309 (modified). Dihedral 1° 30′. No incidence. All-wood two-spar structure, plywood-covered except for fabric-covered trailing-edge. Ailerons have steel tube structure, fabric-covered. No flaps.

Fuselage: Steel tube structure, fabric-covered.

Tail Unit: Cantilever steel tube structure, fabric-covered, with comparatively small rudder.

Landing Gear: Non-retractable tailwheel type. Cantilever spring steel main legs. Goodyear main wheels and tyres, size 5·00-5. Brakes. Steerable tailwheel can be unlocked for 360° castoring on ground.

Power Plant: One 115 hp Lycoming O-235 four-cylinder horizontally-opposed aircooled engine, driving a McCauley two-blade fixed-pitch propeller. Alternative engines include the 90 hp Continental C90. Fuel tank in fuselage, capacity 25 US gallons (94·6 litres). Oil capacity 6 US quarts (5·7 litres).

Accommodation: Two seats side by side in enclosed cabin, with dual controls. Space for 90 lb (41 kg) baggage. Provision for radio.

Dimensions, external:

Wing span	20 ft 6 in (6·25 m)
Wing chord (constant)	4 ft 0 in (1·22 m)
Wing aspect ratio	5·16
Length overall	18 ft 11 in (5·76 m)
Height overall	5 ft 6 in (1·68 m)
Tailplane span	6 ft 4 in (1·93 m)
Wheel track	5 ft 2 in (1·57 m)

Dimension, internal:

Cabin: Width	3 ft 2 in (0·96 m)

Areas:

Wings, gross	82·5 sq ft (7·66 m²)
Ailerons (total)	4·35 sq ft (0·40 m²)
Vertical surfaces (total)	2·80 sq ft (0·26 m²)
Tailplane	4·70 sq ft (0·44 m²)
Elevators	2·36 sq ft (0·22 m²)

Weights:

Weight empty	624 lb (283 kg)
Max T-O weight	1,250 lb (567 kg)

Performance (at max T-O weight):

Max level speed at S/L	169 knots (195 mph; 314 km/h)

Nesmith Cougar built by Mr Bud Phillips of Red Bluff, California *(Peter M. Bowers)*

Max cruising speed at 7,000 ft (2,130 m)
144 knots (166 mph; 267 km/h)
Econ cruising speed
135 knots (155 mph; 249 km/h)
Stalling speed 46 knots (53 mph; 85 km/h)
Max rate of climb at S/L 1,300 ft (395 m)/min
Service ceiling 13,000 ft (3,950 m)
T-O run 450 ft (137 m)
T-O to 50 ft (15 m) 1,100 ft (335 m)
Landing from 50 ft (15 m) 1,000 ft (305 m)
Landing run 350 ft (107 m)
Range with max fuel
651 nm (750 miles; 1,207 km)
Range with max payload
607 nm (700 miles; 1,125 km)

NORTHROP

NORTHROP CORPORATION

HEAD OFFICE:
1800 Century Park East, Century City, Los Angeles, California 90067
Telephone: (213) 553-6262

CHAIRMAN OF THE BOARD AND PRESIDENT:
Thomas V. Jones

SENIOR VICE-PRESIDENTS:
George F. Douglas (Administration)
F. W. Lloyd (Operations)
James D. Willson (Finance and Treasurer)

GROUP VICE-PRESIDENT:
R. F. Miller

VICE-PRESIDENTS:
John R. Alison (Customer Relations)
James Allen (Assistant to the President)
J. H. Bruce (Industrial Relations)
D. A. Burchinal (Europe, Middle East and Africa)
J. B. Campbell (Controller)
Walter E. Crandall (Manager, Northrop Corporate Laboratories)
W. L. Curtis (Pacific Far East)
Les Daly (Public Affairs)
Ward B. Dennis (Forward Planning)
D. N. Ferguson (General Manager, Electronics Division)
Welko E. Gasich (General Manager, Aircraft Division)
C. Robert Gates (Northrop International)
George Gore (General Counsel)
Donald A. Hicks (Research and Technology)
James V. Holcombe (Corporate Domestic Field Offices)
Roy P. Jackson (Programme Management)
I. Kaufman (President, Page Communications Engineers Inc)
Roy Kaufold (President, Wilcox Electric Inc)
Jeffrey C. Kitchen (National Development Programmes)
Donald L. Lewis (Business Analysis and Management Services)
Frank W. Lynch (General Manager, Electro-Mechanical Division)
T. A. McDougall (International Business Operations)
R. W. Page (President, George A. Fuller Co)
Geoffrey Parsons (European Representative)
J. M. Ricketts (President, The Hallicrafters Co)
H. Edmund Riggins Jr (Material and Facilities)
Frederick Stevens (Diversification)
James E. Ware (President, Northrop Architectural Systems)
Paul O. Wierk (Data Processing)
W. E. Woolwine (General Manager, Ventura Division)

SECRETARY: David H. Olson

ASSOCIATE GENERAL COUNSEL: Robert B. Watts

ASST TO PRESIDENT—ANALYSIS:
C. H. Bernstein

ASST TO PRESIDENT—AERONAUTICAL SYSTEMS:
Robert M. Elder

ASST TO PRESIDENT—COMMUNITY RELATIONS:
W. H. Habblett

DIRECTOR PUBLIC AFFAIRS—EUROPE:
James Corfield

DIRECTOR OF COMMUNICATIONS: William A. Schoneberger

STAFF ASST TO PRESIDENT: W. H. Gurnee

This company was formed in 1939 by John K. Northrop and others to undertake the design and manufacture of military aircraft. During the second World War it built 1,131 aircraft of its own design and was engaged in extensive sub-contract work. It also devoted considerable attention to the design and construction of aircraft of the "Flying Wing" type.

Although continuing its activities in the design, development and production of aircraft, missiles and target drone systems, Northrop has broadened its scope of operation to include electronics, space technology, communications, construction, support services and commercial products. To reflect this changing character of its business, the company changed its name from Northrop Aircraft Inc to Northrop Corporation in 1959.

Divisions of Northrop Corporation now include Aircraft Division, specialising in aircraft, missiles, aeronautical systems and weapon systems management; Ventura Division, engaged primarily in the design, development and manufacture of remotely piloted vehicles, aircraft target drones, mobile underwater targets and target range support services; Electronics Division and Electro-Mechanical Division, which handle Northrop activities in the design, development and manufacture of electronic, electro-mechanical and optical-mechanical products and components.

In 1959 Northrop expanded into the field of advanced systems for long-range radio com**munications with the purchase of Page Communications Engineers, Inc, as a wholly-owned subsidiary.** To expand its capabilities in the communications field, Northrop acquired the Hallicrafters Company of Chicago, Illinois, in December 1966. Operating as another wholly-owned subsidiary, Hallicrafters is producing short-wave radio transmitters and receivers and a variety of domestic and military radio equipment.

In 1961 Northrop combined the operations of Acme Metal Molding Co and Arcadia Metal Products in a single organisation, Northrop Architectural Systems (a wholly-owned subsidiary).

Northrop Pacific, Inc, was formed from Northrop Architectural Systems in 1969 as a new subsidiary of the company to continue the manufacture of floor panels for commercial aircraft.

To further expand its research and development work, Northrop has divided its Research and Technology Center into three organisations: the Corporate Laboratories, Laser System Laboratories and Laser Technology Laboratories. Current programmes include research and development in such fields as information sciences, electronic devices and materials, nuclear radiation effects, high-energy laser development and laser systems applications.

In November 1970 Northrop acquired a 49% interest in Iran Aircraft Industries of Tehran, a company engaged in the service, repair and overhaul of aircraft and aircraft engines of all types.

In March 1971 Northrop formed the Thai Communications Co in Bangkok, Thailand, to repair, maintain and manufacture two-way radio equipment as well as to design and install communications systems for Thailand and, eventually, for adjoining countries.

In May 1971 Northrop formed the Northrop Airport Development Corporation, a wholly-owned subsidiary to carry on the company's business interest in the field of airport planning and development.

Continuing its programme of diversification, Northrop acquired the controlling interest in May 1971 of Olson Laboratories, a company specialising in automobile emission control testing. In June 1971 Northrop acquired American Standard's Wilcox Division of Kansas City and all outstanding stock of its international sales affiliate in McLean, Virginia. Wilcox business is primarily in commercial aviation, communication and navigation areas. In another major acquisition Northrop acquired the George A. Fuller Company of New York, a widely-known construction company.

In 1972 Northrop acquired Page Aircraft Maintenance Inc, Lawton, Oklahoma. Since renamed Northrop Worldwide Aircraft Services Inc, it is engaged in aircraft maintenance and support services. Northrop acquired also the entire assets of Berkeley Scientific Laboratories Inc, Hayward, California, a major supplier of medical and business data systems.

The number of employees of Northrop Corporation totalled about 25,700 in early 1974.

NORTHROP CORPORATION AIRCRAFT DIVISION

ADDRESS:
3901 West Broadway, Hawthorne, California 90250
Telephone: (213) 675-4611

CORPORATE VICE-PRESIDENT AND GENERAL MANAGER:
Welko E. Gasich

VICE-PRESIDENTS:
Ben F. Collins Jr (Saudi Arabia Operations)
Griff B. Doyle (Asst General Manager)
Manuel G. Gonzalez (Contracts and Pricing)
Roy P. Jackson (YF-17 Programme Manager)
Paul A. Jacobs (Manufacturing/Material)
Milton Kuska (Customer Requirements and Support)
Rex H. Madeira (Support Operations)
Jack Mannion (Administration)
John L. McCoy (F-5)
Robert M. McNamara (Senior Vice-President, Business Operations)
Donald D. Warner (Engineering)
Donald H. White (Finance)

Current production at Northrop's Aircraft Division is centred on the F-5E Tiger II International Fighter Aircraft, the F-5B two-seat fighter/trainer, and major Boeing 747 sub-contract work which includes the main fuselage section and the extra large side-loading cargo door. A two-seat version of the F-5E, designated F-5F, is under development for the USAF.

In 1966 Northrop committed its fighter design team and substantial annual resources to the objective of creating a new generation of lightweight, low-cost, high-performance fighters. As USAF interest in this category of aircraft developed, the Northrop team concentrated its efforts on analysis and design studies directly related to specific USAF requirements, leading to the company's selection as one of two contractors which have each built two prototypes under a Lightweight Fighter Prototype Program. Northrop's prototypes, designated YF-17, began flight tests in mid-1974, prior to a 12-month flight evaluation programme alongside the General Dynamics YF-16 (which see).

In addition to its main factory at Hawthorne, the Aircraft Division has facilities at El Segundo, Long Beach, Palmdale and Edwards Air Force Base, California.

Northrop F-5A single-seat fighters in service with the Royal Norwegian Air Force

NORTHROP F-5

USAF designations: F-5 and RF-5
CAF designations: CF-5A/D
R Netherlands AF designations: NF-5A/B
R Norwegian AF designations: F-5G/RF-5G
Spanish designations: C-9/CE-9

Design of this light tactical fighter started in 1955 and construction of the prototype of the single-seat version (then designated N-156C) began in 1958. It flew for the first time on 30 July 1959, exceeding Mach 1 on its maiden flight. Two more prototypes were built, followed by several production versions, as follows:

F-5A. Basic single-seat fighter. Two General Electric J85-GE-13 afterburning turbojets. First production F-5A flew in October 1963. Norwegian version has ATO and arrester hook for short-field operation. Total of 621 F-5A aircraft had been ordered by the end of 1971.

F-5B. Generally similar to F-5A, but with two seats in tandem for dual fighter/trainer duties. First F-5B flew on 24 February 1964. A total of 134 F-5Bs had been ordered by the end of 1971. Production continues.

F-5A-15. Basically similar to F-5A, but powered by higher-rated (4,300 lb; 1,950 kg) st General Electric J85-GE-15 turbojets with afterburning. Electrically-actuated louvre doors, on each side of rear fuselage, provide additional air during take-off and flight at speeds below 287 knots (330 mph; 530 km/h). Two-position extending nosewheel increases angle of attack on ground by 3°, helping to reduce take-off distances by 25%. Prototype, converted as private venture from an F-5A, flew for the first time in May 1965.

F-5E. Advanced version of F-5A. Described separately.

F-5F. Two-seat tactical fighter-trainer version of the F-5E, under development for the USAF.

F-5G. Royal Norwegian Air Force designation for its 78 F-5As.

CF-5A/D. These are the designations of the versions of the F-5A/B that were produced for the Canadian Armed Forces, the first of them entering service in 1968. Several improvements were incorporated in the CF series, including higher-thrust engines (J85-CAN-15), and flight refuelling capability. 115 built by Canadair, under licence. Described under Canadair entry in 1972-73 *Jane's*.

NF-5A/B. Versions of the F-5 produced for the Royal Netherlands Air Force with a Doppler navigation system, 275 US gallon (1,040 litre) fuel tanks and manoeuvring flaps. Manufacture and assembly of the 105 aircraft ordered were integrated with CF-5 production by Canadair Ltd, as described in the 1972-73 *Jane's*, and the first of them entered service in 1969.

RF-5A. Reconnaissance version of the F-5; initial deliveries were made in mid-1968. Its four KS-92 cameras, each with a 100 ft film magazine, can provide forward oblique, trimetrogon and split vertical coverage, including horizon-to-horizon with overlap. Associated equipment includes four light sensors, defogging and cooling systems, a pitot static nose boom and a computer/"J" box, all housed in a nose compartment with forward-hinged clamshell top cover. A total of 89 RF-5As had been ordered by January 1972.

RF-5G. Royal Norwegian Air Force designation for its 16 RF-5As.

SF-5A/B (C-9/CE-9). Spanish versions of the F-5, as described under the CASA entry in the 1972-73 *Jane's*. Total of 70 built.

More than 1,150 F-5s are in service with 18 allied nations. In addition to those built by Northrop Aircraft Division facilities in California, F-5s have also been produced under licensing agreements in Canada, Spain and the Netherlands. The F-5 was first ordered into production by the US government, through the USAF, in October 1962, to meet the defence requirements of allied and friendly nations. Initial deliveries, beginning April 1964, were made to Williams AFB, Chandler, Arizona, where the USAF Tactical Air Command has since trained pilots and maintenance personnel of countries receiving F-5s. The first allied air force to receive F-5s was the Imperial Iranian Air Force, which put into service its initial squadron of 13 aircraft on 1 February 1965. The Republic of China, Greece, Republic of Korea, the Philippines and Turkey received F-5s in 1965. Ethiopia, Morocco, Norway and Thailand first received F-5s in 1966, the Republic of Vietnam in 1967 and Libya in 1968.

TYPE: Light tactical fighter and reconnaissance aircraft.

WINGS: Cantilever low-wing monoplane. Wing section NACA 65A004·8 (modified). No dihedral or incidence. Sweepback at quarter-chord 24°. Multi-spar light alloy structure with heavy plate machined skins. Hydraulically-powered sealed-gap ailerons at approximately mid-span with light alloy single-slotted flaps inboard. Continuous-hinge leading-edge flaps of full-depth honeycomb construction. No trim tabs. Designed to be flown and landed safely using only one aileron. No de-icing system.

FUSELAGE: Semi-monocoque basic structure of light alloy, with steel, magnesium and titanium used in certain areas. "Waisted" area rule lines. Two hydraulically-actuated airbrakes on underside of fuselage forward of wheel wells.

TAIL UNIT: Cantilever all-metal structure, with hydraulically-powered rudder and one-piece all-moving tailplane. Single spars with full-depth light alloy honeycomb secondary structure. No trim tabs. Longitudinal and directional stability augmentors installed in series with control system.

LANDING GEAR: Hydraulically-retractable tricycle type with steerable nosewheel. Emergency gravity extension. Main units retract inward into fuselage, nosewheel forward. Oleo-pneumatic shock-absorbers. Main wheels fitted with tubeless tyres size 22 × 8·5, pressure 85-210 lb/sq in (6-15 kg/cm²). Nosewheel fitted with tubeless tyre size 18 × 6·5, pressure 60-180 lb/sq in (4·2-12·6 kg/cm²). Multiple-disc hydraulic brakes.

POWER PLANT: Two General Electric J85-GE-13 turbojets with afterburning (each with max rating of 4,080 lb; 1,850 kg st). Two internal fuel tanks composed of integral cells with total usable capacity of 583 US gallons (2,207 litres). Provision for one 150 US gallon (568 litre) jettisonable tank on fuselage centreline pylon, two 150 US gallon (568 litre) jettisonable tanks on underwing pylons and two 50 US gallon (189 litre) wingtip tanks. Total fuel, with external tanks, 1,133 US gallons (4,289 litres). Single pressure refuelling point on lower fuselage. Oil capacity 4·7 US quarts (4·5 litres) each engine.

ACCOMMODATION (F-5A): Pilot only, on rocket-powered ejection seat in pressurised and air-conditioned cockpit. (F-5B): Pupil and instructor in tandem on rocket-powered ejection seats in pressurised and air-conditioned cockpits, separated by windscreen. Separate manually-operated rearward-hinged jettisonable canopies. Instructor's seat at rear raised 10 in (0·25 m) higher than that of pupil to give improved forward view.

SYSTEMS: Electrical system includes two 8kVA engine-driven generators, providing 115V 400Hz AC power, and 24V battery.

Northrop RF-5A single-seat reconnaissance fighter, showing the reconnaissance nose unit

ELECTRONICS AND EQUIPMENT: Standard equipment includes AN/ARC-34C UHF radio, PP-2024 SWIA-Missile AVX, AN/AIC-18 interphone, J-4 compass and Norsight optical sight. Space provision for AN/APX-46 IFF, AN/ARW-77 Bullpup AUX and AN/ARN-65 TACAN. Blind-flying instrumentation not standard.

ARMAMENT: Basic interception weapons are two Sidewinder missiles on wingtip launchers and two 20 mm guns in the fuselage nose. Five pylons, one under the fuselage and two under each wing, permit the carriage of a wide variety of other operational warloads. A bomb of more than 2,000 lb (910 kg) or high-rate-of-fire gun pack can be suspended from the centre pylon. Underwing loads can include four air-to-air missiles, Bullpup air-to-surface missiles, bombs, up to 20 air-to-surface rockets, gun packs or external fuel tanks. The reconnaissance nose does not eliminate the 20 mm nose gun capability.

Northrop SF-5B two-seat fighter/trainer, assembled in Spain by CASA and operated under the designation CE-9 by the Spanish Air Force *(Howard Levy)*

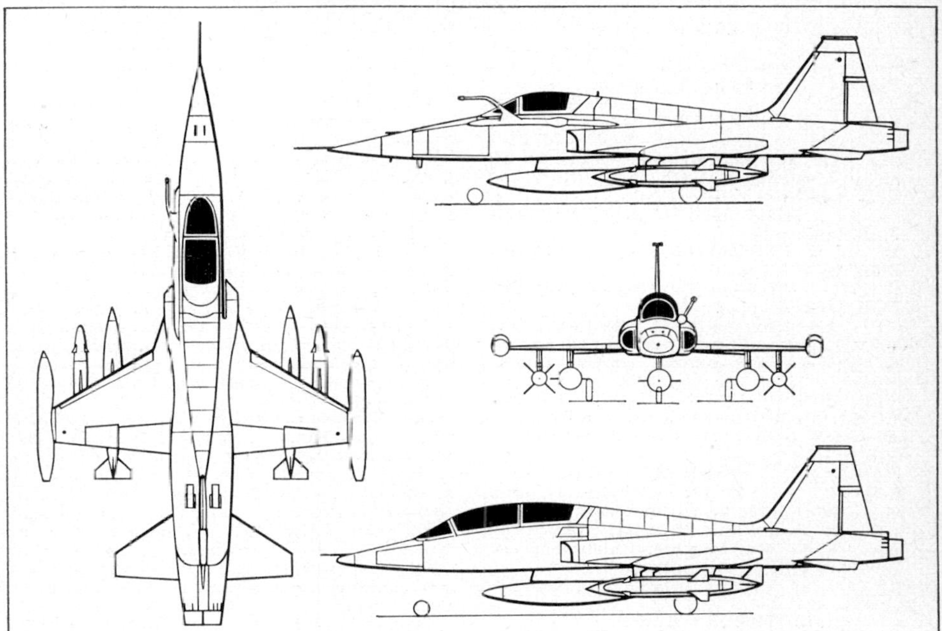

Northrop F-5A supersonic combat aircraft, with additional side elevation of F-5B *(bottom)* *(Pilot Press)*

DIMENSIONS, EXTERNAL:
Wing span 25 ft 3 in (7·70 m)
Span over tip-tanks 25 ft 10 in (7·87 m)
Wing chord at root 11 ft 3 in (3·43 m)
Wing chord at tip 2 ft 3 in (0·69 m)
Length overall:
F-5A 47 ft 2 in (14·38 m)
F-5B 46 ft 4 in (14·12 m)
Height over tail:
F-5A 13 ft 2 in (4·01 m)
F-5B 13 ft 1 in (3·99 m)
Tailplane span 14 ft 1 in (4·28 m)
Wheel track 11 ft 0 in (3·35 m)
Wheelbase:
F-5A 15 ft 4 in (4·67 m)
F-5B 19 ft 6 in (5·94 m)

AREAS:
Wings, gross 170 sq ft (15·79 m²)
Ailerons (total) 9·24 sq ft (0·86 m²)
Trailing-edge flaps (total) 19·0 sq ft (1·77 m²)
Leading-edge flaps (total) 12·3 sq ft (1·14 m²)
Fin 41·42 sq ft (3·85 m²)
Rudder 6·1 sq ft (0·57 m²)
Tailplane 59·0 sq ft (5·48 m²)

WEIGHTS AND LOADINGS:
Weight empty, equipped:
F-5A 8,085 lb (3,667 kg)
F-5B 8,361 lb (3,792 kg)
Max military load 6,200 lb (2,812 kg)
Max T-O weight:
F-5A 20,677 lb (9,379 kg)
F-5B 20,500 lb (9,298 kg)
Max zero-fuel weight:
F-5A 14,212 lb (6,446 kg)
F-5B 13,752 lb (6,237 kg)
Max design landing weight 19,857 lb (9,006 kg)
Max wing loading:
F-5A 121 lb/sq ft (590·8 kg/m²)
F-5B 118 lb/sq ft (576 kg/m²)

PERFORMANCE (F-5A at AUW of 11,450 lb; 5,193 kg: F-5B at AUW of 10,840 lb; 4,916 kg, unless indicated otherwise):
Max never-exceed speed
710 knots (818 mph; 1,315 km/h) IAS
Max level speed at 36,000 ft (11,000 m):
F-5A Mach 1·4
F-5B Mach 1·34
Max cruising speed without afterburning, at 36,000 ft (11,000 m) Mach 0·97
Econ cruising speed Mach 0·87
Stalling speed, 50% fuel, flaps extended:
F-5A 128 knots (147 mph; 237 km/h)
F-5B 120 knots (138 mph; 223 km/h)
Max rate of climb at S/L:
F-5A 28,700 ft (8,750 m)/min
F-5B 30,400 ft (9,265 m)/min
Service ceiling:
F-5A 50,500 ft (15,390 m)
F-5B 52,000 ft (15,850 m)
Service ceiling, one engine out:
F-5A, F-5B over 34,000 ft (10,365 m)
T-O run (with two Sidewinder missiles):
F-5A at AUW of 13,677 lb (6,203 kg)
2,650 ft (808 m)
F-5B at AUW of 13,061 lb (5,924 kg)
2,200 ft (671 m)
T-O to 50 ft (15 m) (with two Sidewinder missiles):
F-5A at AUW of 13,677 lb (6,203 kg)
3,650 ft (1,113 m)
F-5B at AUW of 13,061 lb (5,924 kg)
3,150 ft (960 m)
Landing from 50 ft (15 m), with brake-chute:
F-5A at AUW of 9,931 lb (4,504 kg)
3,900 ft (1,189 m)
F-5B at AUW of 9,619 lb (4,363 kg)
3,800 ft (1,158 m)
Landing run, with brake-chute:
F-5A at AUW of 9,931 lb (4,504 kg)
2,300 ft (701 m)
F-5B at AUW of 9,619 lb (4,363 kg)
2,200 ft (671 m)
Range with max fuel, with reserve fuel for 20 min max endurance at S/L:
F-5A, tanks retained
1,205 nm (1,387 miles; 2,232 km)
F-5B, tanks retained
1,210 nm (1,393 miles; 2,241 km)
F-5A, tanks dropped
1,400 nm (1,612 miles; 2,594 km)
F-5B, tanks dropped
1,405 nm (1,617 miles; 2,602 km)
Combat radius with max payload, allowances as above and five minutes combat at S/L:
F-5A 170 nm (195 miles; 314 km)
F-5B 175 nm (201 miles; 323 km)
Combat radius with max fuel, two 530 lb bombs, allowances as above and five minutes combat at S/L:
F-5A 485 nm (558 miles; 898 km)
F-5B 495 nm (570 miles; 917 km)
Operational hi-lo-lo-hi reconnaissance radius with max fuel, 50 nm (58 mile; 93 km) S/L dash to and from target and allowances as for combat radius with max fuel above:
RF-5A 560 nm (644 miles; 1,036 km)

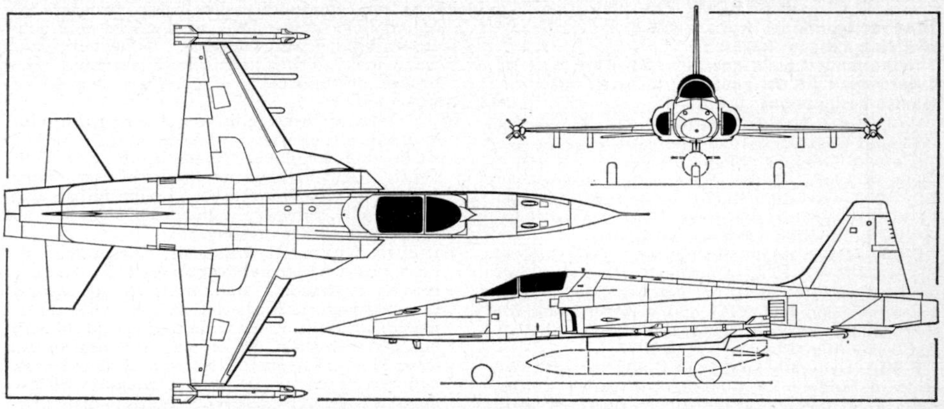

Northrop F-5E Tiger II single-seat twin-jet tactical fighter aircraft *(Pilot Press)*

Northrop F-5E Tiger II light tactical fighter (two General Electric J85-GE-21 turbojet engines)

NORTHROP TIGER II

USAF designations: F-5E, RF-5E and F-5F

The F-5E was selected in November 1970 by the US government as the winner of a competition to determine the International Fighter Aircraft (IFA), which was to succeed Northrop's F-5A aircraft.

Before initiation of the IFA competition, Northrop had proposed a follow-on version of the F-5, and had flown a prototype of this new type at the end of March 1969. It consisted of a two-seat F-5B powered by two General Electric YJ85-GE-21 engines rated at 5,000 lb (2,267 kg) st each, representing an increase of 23 per cent over the rated thrust of the J85-GE-13 engines that power the F-5A/B series.

More than 70 flights were made with this aircraft, and Northrop was able to explore the flight envelope, including operation at altitudes up to 50,000 ft (15,240 m), a maximum speed of Mach 1·6, and aerial combat manoeuvres.

When making the announcement that the Northrop design had been selected as the winner of the IFA competition, the USAF stated that the aircraft would be built under a fixed-price-plus-incentive contract with an initial value of $21 million. This programme was considered initially to involve production of 325 aircraft; but subsequent sales have required revision of this figure, and production is expected to exceed 1,000 aircraft, with deliveries building up to 20 per month.

The F-5E design places particular emphasis on manoeuvrability rather than high speed, notably by the incorporation of manoeuvring flaps, based on the design of a similar system for the Netherlands Air Force's NF-5A/Bs. Full-span leading-edge flaps work in conjunction with conventional trailing-edge flaps, and are operated by a control on the pilot's throttle quadrant.

Wing loading on the F-5E has been maintained at approximately the same value as on the F-5A, as the result of an increase in wing area to 186 sq ft (17·30 m²). This is due principally to the widened fuselage, which also increases wing span. The tapered wing leading-edge extension, between the inboard leading-edge and fuselage, has also been modified to enhance airflow over the wing at high angles of attack.

The F-5E incorporates other features developed for the Canadian, Dutch and Norwegian F-5s. These include two-position nosewheel gear, which increases wing angle of attack on the ground by 3° 22′ and which, in conjunction with the more powerful engines, has improved F-5E take-off performance some 30% by comparison with earlier F-5s. JATO provision and arrester gear permit operation from short runways, and an anti-icing windscreen permits use in cold-weather environments.

The first F-5E was rolled out on 23 June 1972, and made its first flight on 11 August 1972. USAF Tactical Air Command, with assistance from Air Training Command, has been assigned responsibility for training pilots and technicians of user countries. First deliveries of the F-5E, to the USAF's 425th Tactical Fighter Squadron, were made in the Spring of 1973. Twenty aircraft had been supplied for the USAF training programme by the end of September 1973, and deliveries to foreign countries began in late 1973.

Four versions are being produced:

F-5E. Standard production version, as described below.

F-5E (Saudi). A modified version for the Royal Saudi Air Force (RSAF). This has a Litton LN-33 inertial navigation system, capable of accuracy exceeding 1·5 nm (1·7 miles; 2·7 km) CEP per flight hour, and which provides attitude reference, range and bearing to ten pre-set destinations, as well as true ground track steering. The system is self-aligning in 10 min in the gyro compass mode, and can be aligned in 3 min to a stored heading. In-flight refuelling capability.

RF-5E. Similar to standard production version, but with an R-843A/ARN-58 localiser receiver and a reconnaissance nose containing four KS-121 70 mm framing cameras and related equipment. Intended for low/medium-altitude photo-reconnaissance, the nose is similar to that described for the RF-5A.

F-5F. Tandem two-seat version of F-5E, with fuselage lengthened by 30-40 in (76-102 cm). Fire control system retained, enabling aircraft to be used for both training and combat duties. Development approved by USAF in early 1974. First flight scheduled for September 1974. Initial deliveries expected to be made to South Vietnam and Iran, which are reported to require 28 each.

The following details refer specifically to the F-4E, but are generally applicable to all versions except for details noted under model listings:

TYPE: Single-seat light tactical fighter.

WINGS: Cantilever low-wing monoplane. Wing section NACA 65A004·8 (modified). No dihedral. No incidence. Sweepback at quarter-chord 24°. Multi-spar light alloy structure with heavy plate machined skins. Hydraulically-powered sealed-gap ailerons at approximately mid-span. Electrically-operated light alloy single-slotted trailing-edge flaps inboard of ailerons. Electrically-operated continuous-hinge leading-edge manoeuvring flaps. Aileron trim tabs. No de-icing system.

FUSELAGE: Light alloy semi-monocoque basic structure, with steel, magnesium and titanium used in certain areas. Two hydraulically-actuated airbrakes of magnesium alloy construction, mounted on underside of fuselage forward of main-wheel wells. Avionics bay and cockpit pressurised; fail-safe structure in pressurised sections.

TAIL UNIT: Cantilever all-metal structure, with

hydraulically-powered rudder and one-piece all-moving tailplane. Tailplane incidence varied by hydraulic actuators. No trim tabs. Dual hydraulic actuators of Northrop design for control of rudder and tailplane.

LANDING GEAR: Hydraulically-retractable tricycle type, main units retracting inward into fuselage, nosewheel forward. Oleo-pneumatic struts of Northrop design on all units. Two-position extending nose unit increases static angle of attack by 3° 22′ to reduce T-O distance, and is shortened automatically during the retraction cycle. Gravity-operated emergency extension. Main wheels and tyres size 24 × 8·00-13, pressure 210 lb/sq in (14·76 kg/cm²). Steerable nosewheel with wheel and tyre size 18 × 6·50-8, pressure 120 lb/sq in (8·44 kg/cm²). All-metal multiple-disc brakes of Northrop design.

POWER PLANT: Two General Electric J85-GE-21 turbojet engines, each rated at 5,000 lb (2,267 kg) st with afterburning. Two independent fuel systems, one for each engine. Fuel for starboard engine supplied from two rubber-impregnated bladder-type nylon fabric cells, comprising a centre-fuselage cell of 215 US gallon (813 litre) capacity, and an aft-fuselage cell of 161 US gallon (609 litre) capacity. Port engine supplied from a forward fuselage cell of 295 US gallon (1,116 litre) capacity. Total fuel capacity 671 US gallons (2,538 litres). No fuel is carried in the wings. Fuel crossfeed system allows fuel from either or both cell systems to be fed to either or both engines. A 275 US gallon (1,040 litre) jettisonable fuel tank can be carried on the fuselage centreline pylon. Auxiliary fuel tanks of 150 or 275 US gallons (568 or 1,040 litres) can be carried on the inboard underwing pylons. Wingtips have provision for installation of 50 US gallon (189 litre) tanks in lieu of AIM-9 missile launchers. Single refuelling point on lower fuselage for fuselage fuel cell installation, which also has provision for in-flight refuelling by means of a detachable probe. Oil capacity 1 US gallon (3·8 litres) per engine.

ENGINE INTAKES: Anti-icing of inlet duct lips. Intakes are supplemented with auxiliary air inlet doors for use during T-O and low-speed flight, to improve compressor face pressure recovery and to decrease distortion. Each door consists of a set of six pivot-mounted louvres in removable panels on each side of the fuselage. The doors are actuated by the pilot at T-O, and controlled automatically in flight by Mach sensor switches, and are maintained in the open position at airspeeds below Mach 0·35-0·4.

ACCOMMODATION: Pilot only in pressurised, heated and air-conditioned cockpit, on rocket-powered ejection seat. Upward-opening canopy, hinged at rear. Electrically anti-iced windscreen.

SYSTEMS: Cockpit and avionics bay pressurised, heated and air-conditioned by engine bleed air, maximum pressure differential 5 lb/sq in (0·35 kg/cm²). Hydraulic power supplied by two independent systems at a pressure of 3,000 lb/sq in (210 kg/cm²). Flight control system provides power solely for operation of primary flight control surfaces. Utility system provides hydraulic backup power for the primary flight control surfaces and operating power for the landing gear, landing gear doors, airbrakes, wheel brakes, nosewheel steering, gun bay purge doors, gun gas deflectors and stability augmentation system. Electrical power supplied by two 13/15kVA 115/200V three-phase 320-480Hz non-paralleled engine-driven alternators. 250VA 115V 400Hz single-phase solid-state static inverter provides secondary AC source for engine starting. Two 25A 26-32V transformer-rectifiers and a 24V 5Ah nickel-cadmium battery provide DC power. Liquid oxygen system with capacity of 5 litres.

ELECTRONICS AND EQUIPMENT: AN/ARC-150 UHF command radio, 3,500-channel with 50kHz spacing. Lightweight microminiature X-band radar for air-to-air search and range tracking; target information, at a range of up to 20 nm (23 miles; 37 km), is displayed on a 5 in (12·7 cm) DVST in cockpit. AN/ARA-50 UHF ADF; AN/APX-72 IFF/SIF system; AN/ARN-65 TACAN; SST-181 X-band radar transponder (Skyspot); and central air data computer. Full blind-flying instrumentation.

ARMAMENT: Two AIM-9 Sidewinder missiles on wingtip launchers. Two M39A2 20 mm cannon mounted in fuselage nose, with 280 rounds per gun. Up to 7,000 lb (3,175 kg) of mixed ordnance can be carried on four underwing and one underfuselage stations, including M129 leaflet bombs; MK-82 GP and Snakeye 500 lb bombs; MK-36 destructors; MK-83 1,000 lb bombs; MK-84 2,000 lb bombs; BLU-1, -27 or -32 U or F napalm; LAU-68 (7) 2·75 in rockets; LAU-3 (19) 2·75 in rockets; CBU-24, -49, -52, or -58; SUU-20 bomb and rocket packs; SUU-25 flare dispensers; TDU-10 tow targets (Dart); and RMU-10 reel (Dart). Lead-computing optical gunsight uses inputs from airborne radar for air-to-air missiles and cannon, and provides a roll-stabilised manually-depressible reticle aiming reference for air-to-ground delivery. The gunsight incorporates also a detachable 16 mm reticle camera with 50 ft (15·25 m) film magazine.

DIMENSIONS, EXTERNAL:

Wing span	26 ft 8 in (8·13 m)
Span over missiles	27 ft 11⅞ in (8·53 m)
Wing chord at root	11 ft 8⅝ in (3·57 m)
Wing chord at tip	2 ft 2⅞ in (0·68 m)
Wing aspect ratio	3·82
Length overall	48 ft 3¾ in (14·73 m)
Height overall	13 ft 4½ in (4·08 m)
Tailplane span	14 ft 1½ in (4·31 m)
Wheel track	12 ft 5½ in (3·80 m)
Wheelbase	13 ft 11½ in (5·17 m)

AREAS:

Wings, gross	186 sq ft (17·3 m²)
Ailerons (total)	9·24 sq ft (0·86 m²)
Trailing-edge flaps (total)	21·0 sq ft (1·95 m²)
Leading-edge flaps (total)	12·3 sq ft (1·14 m²)
Fin	41·42 sq ft (3·85 m²)
Rudder	6·10 sq ft (0·57 m²)
Tailplane	59·0 sq ft (5·48 m²)

WEIGHTS AND LOADINGS:

Weight empty	9,588 lb (4,349 kg)
Max T-O weight	24,080 lb (10,922 kg)
Max zero-fuel weight	17,441 lb (7,911 kg)
Max wing loading	129 lb/sq ft (629·8 kg/m²)
Max power loading	2·4 lb/lb st (2·4 kg/kg st)

PERFORMANCE (at AUW of 13,220 lb; 5,997 kg, unless stated otherwise):

Max never-exceed speed
710 knots (817 mph; 1,314 km/h) IAS

Max level speed at 36,000 ft (11,000 m) Mach 1·6

Max cruising speed at 36,000 ft (11,000 m), without afterburning Mach 0·98

Econ cruising speed Mach 0·80

Stalling speed, 50% fuel, flaps and wheels down
124 knots (143 mph; 230 km/h)

Max rate of climb at S/L
31,600 ft (9,630 m)/min

Service ceiling 54,000 ft (13,460 m)

Service ceiling, one engine out
over 41,000 ft (12,495 m)

Minimum ground turning radius
36 ft 6 in (11·13 m)

T-O run with two Sidewinder missiles, at 15,745 lb (7,141 kg) AUW 2,000 ft (610 m)

T-O to 50 ft (15 m), loaded as above
2,800 ft (853 m)

Landing from 50 ft (15 m) with brake-chute, at 11,340 lb; 5,143 kg AUW 3,900 ft (1,189 m)

Landing run with brake-chute, weight as above
2,300 ft (701 m)

Range with max fuel, with reserve fuel for 20 min max endurance at S/L:

Tanks retained
1,715 nm (1,974 miles; 3,175 km)

Tanks dropped
2,010 nm (2,314 miles; 3,720 km)

Combat radius with two Sidewinder missiles and max fuel, allowances as above and five minutes combat with max afterburning power at 15,000 ft (4,570 m)
760 nm (875 miles; 1,405 km)

Combat radius with 6,300 lb (2,857 kg) ordnance load and two Sidewinder missiles, allowances as above and five minutes combat at military power at S/L 165 nm (190 miles; 305 km)

Combat radius with max fuel, two Sidewinders and two 530 lb bombs, allowances as above and five minutes combat at military power at S/L 610 nm (702 miles; 1,130 km)

Operational hi-lo-hi reconnaissance radius with max fuel, 50 nm (57·5 miles; 92·5 km) S/L dash to and from target, allowances as above, no combat
765 nm (880 miles; 1,415 km)

NORTHROP YF-17

Northrop's YF-17 is a twin-engined fighter prototype developed to demonstrate advanced technology applicable to air combat. Distinguishing features, as shown in the accompanying three-view drawing, include mid-wing configuration, a moderately-swept wing, highly-swept leading-edge root extensions, underwing intakes and twin vertical fins.

The basic wing planform, combined with the highly swept leading-edge root extensions, is identified as a hybrid wing. The vortex flow generated by the extensions, significantly increases lift, reduces drag, and improves handling characteristics. Leading-edge and trailing-edge flaps are used to vary the wing camber for maximum manoeuvrability.

The horizontal tail surface is located lower than the wing to provide increasing longitudinal stability at high angles of attack approaching maximum lift, and to preclude buffet from the wing wake under high-g flight conditions. The vertical tail surfaces are sized and located to provide positive directional stability beyond the maximum trimmed angles of attack across the speed range. The forward location was chosen to eliminate reduction of horizontal tail surface effectiveness due to the outboard cant of the vertical surfaces, and to provide low supersonic drag through favourable influence on the area distribution of the aircraft.

Location of the engine intakes beneath the wing minimises flow angularity, placing the intakes in a position to take advantage of the compression effects of the wing leading-edge root extensions during supersonic flight. The key feature of airframe/intake integration is a longitudinal slot through each wing root, which allows a portion of the fuselage boundary layer air to flow over the

Northrop YF-17 lightweight fighter (two General Electric YJ101 turbojet engines)

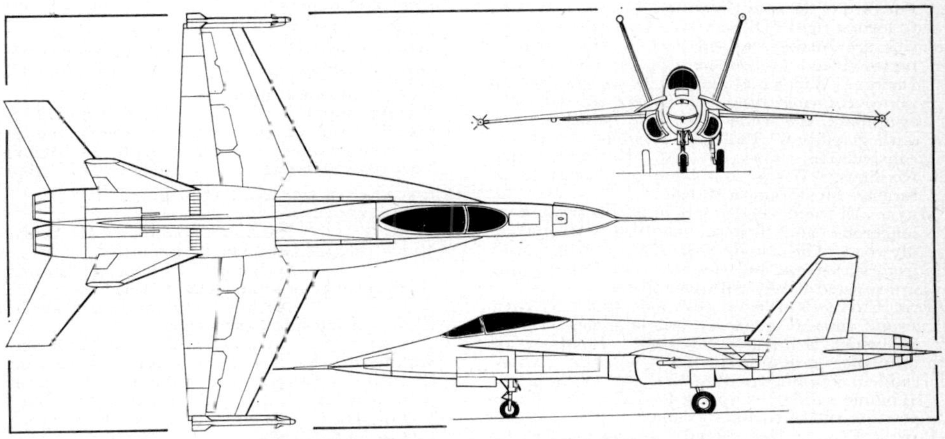

Northrop YF-17 single-seat lightweight fighter prototype *(Pilot Press)*

upper surface of the wings. Thus, a narrow fuselage boundary layer gutter can be used, which results in a low-drag installation.

Outstanding visibility for the pilot is achieved by the canopy shape and location, with full aft vision at eye level and above.

Extensive use is made of graphite composite materials in the aircraft's structure, to the extent that approximately 10 per cent, by weight, is composed of such material.

Design of Northrop's lightweight fighter began in May 1966, and construction of two prototypes started in early 1973, following the award of a $39 million contract by the USAF. The first of them was rolled out on 4 April 1974 and flew for the first time on 9 June 1974. The two YF-17s are intended to complete a twelve-month flight evaluation programme of a combined total of approximately 300 hours.

TYPE: Single-seat lightweight fighter prototype.

WINGS: Cantilever mid-wing monoplane. Anhedral 5°. Sweepback at quarter-chord 20°. Multi-spar structure, primarily of light alloy. Boundary layer control achieved by wing root slot. Sealed-gap ailerons. Single-slotted trailing-edge flaps, of graphite composite material, inboard of ailerons. Aileron actuators manufactured by Parker-Hannifin. Continuous-hinge leading-edge manoeuvring flaps.

FUSELAGE: Semi-monocoque basic structure, primarily of light alloy, but with some graphite composite material used in structure of fuselage and airbrakes. Airbrake above fuselage between tail fins. Pressurised cockpit section of fail-safe construction.

TAIL UNIT: Cantilever structure, primarily of light alloy, with swept vertical and horizontal surfaces. Twin outward-canted fins and rudders set forward of all-moving tailplane. Tailplane actuators manufactured by Parker-Hannifin.

LANDING GEAR: Retractable tricycle type, main units retracting aft, nose unit forward, with single wheel on each unit. Goodyear wheels, tyres and anti-skid brakes.

POWER PLANT: Two General Electric YJ101 high by-pass ratio two-shaft turbojet engines with afterburning, in the 15,000 lb (6,804 kg) st class. Provision for two 600 US gallon (2,273 litre) underwing fuel tanks.

ACCOMMODATION: Pilot only, on Stencel Aero IIIC ejection seat, in pressurised, heated and air-conditioned cockpit. Seat tilted back 18° from vertical. Upward-opening canopy, hinged at rear.

SYSTEMS: Environmental control system by Hamilton Standard. APU by Westinghouse Electric Corp. Control stability augmentation system by Sperry Rand.

ELECTRONICS: Radar by Rockwell International Corp, air data computer by Bendix Corp, inertial navigation system by Litton Industries Inc and transponder by Teledyne Electronics.

ARMAMENT: One General Electric M-61 multi-barrel 20 mm cannon mounted in fuselage nose. One heat-seeking infra-red Sidewinder missile mounted on each wingtip. Gunsight head-up display by JLM International Inc. Snapshoot capability.

DIMENSIONS, EXTERNAL:

Wing span	35 ft 0 in (10·67 m)
Wing aspect ratio	3·5
Length overall	56 ft 0 in (17·07 m)
Height overall	14 ft 6 in (4·42 m)
Tailplane span	22 ft 2½ in (6·77 m)
Wheel track	6 ft 10¾ in (2·10 m)
Wheelbase	17 ft 1¼ in (5·21 m)

AREA:

Wings, gross	350 sq ft (32·5 m²)

WEIGHT:

T-O weight, clean	23,000 lb (10,430 kg)

PERFORMANCE (estimated):

Max level speed	approx Mach 2
T-O to 50 ft (15 m)	less than 1,000 ft (305 m)
Landing from 50 ft (15 m), without braking parachute	less than 2,000 ft (610 m)
Radius of action	500 nm (576 miles; 927 km)
Ferry range	more than 2,600 nm (2,993 miles; 4,816 km)

O'NEILL

O'NEILL AIRPLANE COMPANY, INC

ADDRESS:
791 Livingston, Carlyle, Illinois 62231

Telephone: (618) 594-2681

PRESIDENT: Terrence O'Neill

This company was formed by Mr Terrence O'Neill in December 1962, following purchase of the Waco Model W Aristocraft prototype, and became Incorporated in May 1967.

Two derivatives of the Aristocraft were evolved, the first of which, known as the Model W Winner, was intended for type certification and production. The second derivative was the Aristocraft II, of which plans were available to amateur constructors.

In early 1974 Mr O'Neill advised that activity on the Model W Winner had ceased and that the sale of plans of the Aristocraft II had been discontinued. Current activity of the company is directed towards development of a new aircraft designated Model WJ, but no details were available at the time of closing for press. Details of the Model W Winner and the Aristocraft II can be found in the 1973-74 *Jane's*.

OSPREY

OSPREY AIRCRAFT

ADDRESS:
3741 El Ricon Way, Sacramento, California 95825

Telephone: (917) 483-3004

Osprey Aircraft was formed to market to amateur constructors plans of the Osprey I aircraft designed and built by Mr George Pereira. It is an unusual project for the homebuilder since it is a flying-boat, intended for operation on and from enclosed waters rather than the open sea. The plans supplied by Mr Pereira include drawings of a special trailer for carriage of the aircraft, which permits the pilot to launch and recover the Osprey unassisted.

Design began in January 1969, with construction of the prototype aircraft following seven months later. First flight was made during August 1970, and FAA certification in the Experimental homebuilt category was awarded in October of the same year.

On 27 July 1971, following study of seven different aircraft, the US Navy purchased the prototype Osprey from Mr Pereira. Under the designation X-28A Air Skimmer, it was evaluated by the Naval Air Development Center, at the request of the Director of Navy Laboratories, to study the potential of a small single-seat seaplane for civil police patrol duties in Southeast Asia.

Mr Pereira has since completed the prototype of a two-seat amphibian version designated Osprey II.

Pereira GP2 Osprey I prototype in US Navy insignia following purchase and redesignation as X-28A (*Howard Levy*)

PEREIRA GP2 OSPREY I

US Navy designation: X-28A Air Skimmer

TYPE: Single-seat lightweight homebuilt flying-boat.

WINGS: Cantilever high-wing monoplane. Wing section NACA 23015. Dihedral 4°. Incidence 3°. No sweepback. All-wood structure with a single built-up "Z"-shaped spar, comprising a marine plywood web separating two fir cap strips. Wooden ribs are capped on one side. Forward of the spar the wing is plywood-covered to form a rigid "D" section. Aft of the spar the ribs are further capped with a wide strip of plywood and the entire wing is covered with Dacron. Wingtip stabilising floats consist of a plywood former sandwiched between blocks of styrofoam, the whole float then being covered with glassfibre. Full-span ailerons of wooden construction, fabric-covered. No trim tabs. No flaps. Wings fold back on each side of fuselage for storage or transit.

HULL: All-wood single-step hull constructed of longerons and frames, covered by marine plywood. The shaped nose of the hull is carved from styrofoam and the entire hull and seams are covered finally with glassfibre.

TAIL UNIT: Cantilever all-wood structure with swept vertical surfaces; tailplane near tip of fin, which is integral with hull. Incidence of tailplane ground-adjustable. The water rudder, contained within the base of the aerodynamic rudder, is spring-loaded in the down position and retracted by cable.

POWER PLANT: One 90 hp Continental C90-12 four-cylinder horizontally-opposed aircooled engine, mounted on steel tube pylon structure which is bolted to the wing truss. A removable wraparound aluminium cowling fairs the pylon, and the engine has a glassfibre cowling. Hegy two-blade wooden fixed-pitch pusher propeller. Two glassfibre fuel tanks, each of 8 US gallons (30·25 litres) capacity, housed within engine pylon. Total fuel capacity 16 US gallons (60·5 litres). Oil capacity 1¼ US gallons (4·6 litres).

ACCOMMODATION: Single seat in open cockpit.

DIMENSIONS, EXTERNAL:

Wing span	23 ft 0 in (7·01 m)
Wing chord, constant	4 ft 2 in (1·27 m)
Length overall	17 ft 3 in (5·26 m)
Width, wings folded	7 ft 10 in (2·39 m)
Height overall	5 ft 3 in (1·60 m)
Tailplane span	7 ft 0 in (2·13 m)
Propeller diameter	5 ft 6 in (1·68 m)

AREAS:

Wings, gross	97 sq ft (9·01 m²)
Ailerons (total)	25 sq ft (2·32 m²)

WEIGHTS AND LOADINGS:

Weight empty	600 lb (272 kg)
Max T-O and landing weight	900 lb (408 kg)
Max wing loading	9·27 lb/sq ft (45·3 kg/m²)
Max power loading	10 lb/hp (4·5 kg/hp)

PERFORMANCE (at max T-O weight):

Max never-exceed speed	130 knots (150 mph; 241 km/h)
Max level speed at 1,000 ft (305 m)	117 knots (135 mph; 217 km/h)
Max cruising speed at 5,000 ft (1,525 m)	108 knots (125 mph; 201 km/h)
Econ cruising speed at 5,000 ft (1,525 m)	91 knots (105 mph; 169 km/h)
Stalling speed	48 knots (55 mph; 89 km/h)
Max rate of climb at S/L	2,000 ft (610 m)/min
Service ceiling	18,000 ft (5,485 m)
T-O distance	200 ft (61 m)
T-O to 50 ft (15 m)	400 ft (122 m)
Landing from 50 ft (15 m)	400 ft (122 m)
Range with max fuel	321 nm (370 miles; 595 km)

PEREIRA GP3 OSPREY II

Design and construction of the Osprey II, a two-seat amphibian development of the basic Osprey I, began simultaneously in January 1972.

Mr Pereira has evolved an unusual form of hull construction for this new aircraft. When the all-wood fuselage structure has been completed and controls installed, the undersurface is given a deep coating of polyurethane foam. This is then sculptured to the requisite hull form before being covered with several protective layers of glassfibre cloth bonded with resin. The resulting structure is light, but extremely strong, with good shock resisting characteristics.

First flight of the Osprey II from water was made in April 1973, the amphibian becoming airborne in less than 800 ft (244 m), with no tendency to porpoise at any speed. In later tests from land it was found that with the landing gear retracted and at a speed of about 104 knots (120 mph; 193 km/h), there was slight buffet aft of the cabin and the noise level was unacceptably high. Modifications being carried out in early 1974 included lengthening of the cabin by 7 in (0·18 m), installation of a Lycoming O-320 engine and provision of a new engine cowling. Testing was expected to be resumed in mid-1974. Following successful flight tests, it is planned to make sets of drawings available to amateur constructors.

TYPE: Two-seat lightweight homebuilt amphibian.

WINGS: Cantilever mid-wing monoplane, of constant chord. Wing section NACA 23012. Dihedral 4° 30′. Incidence 5°. All-wood structure, with single box spar and auxiliary rear spar for aileron attachment. Forward of the main spar the wing is plywood-covered to form a rigid "D" section. Aft of the spar the wing is fabric-covered. Conventional ailerons, 100% mass-balanced, will be fitted with a ground-adjustable tab if this proves desirable.

No trailing-edge flaps. Wingtip stabilising floats of polyurethane foam covered with glassfibre.

HULL: All-wood structure of longerons and frames, covered with $\frac{3}{32}$ in marine plywood. Hull undersurface contours formed from polyurethane foam, protected by several layers of glassfibre cloth bonded with resin.

TAIL UNIT: Cantilever all-wood structure, with swept vertical surfaces; tailplane near tip of fin, which is integral with hull. Incidence of tailplane ground-adjustable. Controllable trim tab in starboard elevator. Water rudder, contained within the base of the aerodynamic rudder, is spring-loaded in the down position and retracted by cable.

LANDING GEAR: Retractable tricycle type, with single wheel on each unit. Main units retract inward into the wing roots, the wheel wells being covered by doors in the retracted position. Nosewheel retracts forward into the nosecone and is also enclosed by a door. Manual retraction system. Shock-absorption by coil springs. Cleveland main wheels and tyres size 5·00-5. Nosewheel, of industrial type with roller bearings, has a tyre of 10 in diameter. Cleveland hydraulic disc brakes.

POWER PLANT: One 150 hp Lycoming O-320 four-cylinder horizontally-opposed aircooled engine, mounted on a steel tube pylon structure which is bolted to the wing truss. Hegy 68 × 56 two-blade fixed-pitch wood pusher propeller. One glassfibre fuel tank mounted beneath the main spar at the wing centre-section, usable capacity 26 US gallons (98·4 litres). Refuelling point on starboard side of hull, just aft of cabin.

ACCOMMODATION: Two seats side by side beneath transparent canopy, which is hinged at rear and swings upward. Dual controls standard; but toe-operated wheel brakes on starboard side only. Baggage compartment aft of seats, capacity 68 lb (31 kg).

SYSTEM: Hydraulic system for brakes only.

DIMENSIONS, EXTERNAL:

Wing span	26 ft 0 in (7·92 m)
Wing chord, constant	5 ft 0 in (1·52 m)
Wing aspect ratio	5·2
Length overall	20 ft 6 in (6·25 m)
Height overall (wheels down)	6 ft 0 in (1·83 m)
Tailplane span	8 ft 0 in (2·44 m)
Wheel track	8 ft 6 in (2·59 m)
Wheelbase	7 ft 0 in (2·13 m)
Propeller diameter	5 ft 8 in (1·73 m)

AREAS:

Wings, gross	130 sq ft (12·08 m²)
Ailerons (total)	13 sq ft (1·21 m²)
Rudder	4·97 sq ft (0·46 m²)
Tailplane	15·2 sq ft (1·41 m²)
Elevator, including tab	10·5 sq ft (0·98 m²)

WEIGHTS AND LOADINGS (estimated):

Weight empty	1,000 lb (453 kg)
Max T-O weight	1,560 lb (707 kg)
Max wing loading	12 lb/sq ft (58·6 kg/m²)
Max power loading	12 lb/hp (5·44 kg/hp)

PERFORMANCE (estimated, at max T-O weight):

Max never-exceed speed	139 knots (160 mph; 257 km/h)
Max level speed at 1,000 ft (305 m)	113 knots (130 mph; 209 km/h)
Cruising speed at 75% power	104 knots (120 mph; 193 km/h)
Stalling speed	48 knots (55 mph; 89 km/h)
T-O run, land	600 ft (183 m)
T-O run, water	780 ft (238 m)

Pereira GP3 Osprey II two-seat lightweight homebuilt amphibian

OWL

GEORGE A. OWL Jr

ADDRESS:
17700 S. Western Avenue, Apartment 195, Gardena, California 90248

Mr George Owl, a member of the preliminary design staff of Rockwell International, is also the designer of two Formula One racing aircraft known as the Owl Racers OR-70 and OR-71. The former was designed to order for Bernadine and Jim Stevenson, both racing pilots, and was built by them. The OR-71 was produced in co-operation with Mr Vince DeLuca, proprietor of Vin-Del Aircraft, who has built a prototype and is making plans available to amateur constructors.

Stevenson, Bernadine and Jim

ADDRESS:
6850 Vineland Avenue, Apartment 7A, N. Hollywood, California 91605

Telephone: 766-5074

Bernadine and Jim Stevenson began construction of their Owl Racer, designated OR-70 *Fang*, in October 1970. Preliminary construction was completed in September 1971, and the first flight was made on the eighth of that month. FAA certification in the Experimental category was awarded on 11 September and ten days later *Fang* was flown to third place in the Reno National Races. Construction was finalised during 1972, since which time the aircraft has been placed in several national air races. Normal load factor of the OR-70 is $\pm 6 \cdot 67g$; ultimate load factor is $\pm 10 \cdot 0g$.

STEVENSON/OWL OR-70 FANG

TYPE: Single-seat Formula One racing aircraft.

WINGS: Cantilever mid-wing monoplane. Owl laminar flow aerofoil section, tapered in chord. Thickness/chord ratio 13·7%. No dihedral. No incidence. All-wood structure. Laminated spruce one-piece main spar, mahogany plywood ribs and skins. Ailerons of spruce and plywood construction, mass-balanced at tip. No flaps. No trim tabs.

FUSELAGE: Welded steel tube structure, with light alloy fairings and Dacron covering. Glassfibre nose cowl incorporates an annular cooling inlet. Engine cowl has controllable air exit flap.

TAIL UNIT: Cantilever wooden structure, with spruce spars and mahogany plywood ribs and skins. Fixed-incidence tailplane. No trim tabs.

LANDING GEAR: Non-retractable tailwheel type. Cantilever spring steel main legs. Main wheels and tyres size 5·00-5, pressure 35 lb/sq in (2·46 kg/cm²). Cleveland hydraulic disc brakes. Light alloy fairings on main wheels. Tailwheel is a ball bearing castor.

POWER PLANT: One 100 hp Continental O-200 four-cylinder horizontally-opposed aircooled engine, driving an Anderson, McCauley or Sensenich two-blade fixed-pitch propeller. Fuel tank in fuselage, immediately aft of firewall, capacity 6·5 US gallons (24·6 litres). Auxiliary integral fuel tank in each wing leading-edge, with combined capacity of 6 US gallons (22·7 litres). Total fuel capacity 12·5 US gallons (47·3 litres). Refuelling point on upper surface of fuselage, forward of windscreen. Oil capacity 1·5 US gallons (5·7 litres).

ACCOMMODATION: Single seat beneath transparent bubble canopy. Access through removable hatch aft of the bubble canopy. False cockpit floor folds up and forward to form seatback. Pilot enters, slides forward and then erects seatback. Cockpit ventilated.

ELECTRONICS: Battery-powered Radair 360 360-channel com transceiver.

DIMENSIONS, EXTERNAL:

Wing span	20 ft 0 in (6·10 m)
Wing chord at root	4 ft 2 in (1·27 m)
Wing chord at tip	2 ft 6 in (0·76 m)
Wing aspect ratio	6
Length overall	19 ft 6 in (5·94 m)
Height overall	4 ft 7 in (1·40 m)
Wheel track	4 ft 3 in (1·30 m)
Wheelbase	11 ft 11 in (3·63 m)
Propeller diameter	4 ft 8 in-4 ft 10 in (1·42 m-1·47 m)
Propeller ground clearance	1 ft 0 in-1 ft 1 in (0·30 m-0·33 m)

AREAS:

Wings, gross	66 sq ft (6·13 m²)
Ailerons (total)	6·1 sq ft (0·57 m²)
Fin	2·92 sq ft (0·27 m²)
Rudder	2·22 sq ft (0·21 m²)
Tailplane	3·8 sq ft (0·35 m²)
Elevators	3·35 sq ft (0·31 m²)

WEIGHTS AND LOADINGS:

Weight empty	580 lb (263 kg)
Max T-O weight	840 lb (381 kg)
Max wing loading	12·73 lb/sq ft (62·15 kg/m²)
Max power loading	8·4 lb/hp (3·81 kg/hp)

PERFORMANCE:

Max never-exceed speed	239 knots (275 mph; 443 km/h)
Max level speed at S/L	217 knots (250 mph; 402 km/h)
Max cruising speed at 5,000 ft (1,525 m)	182 knots (210 mph; 338 km/h)
Econ cruising speed at 5,000 ft (1,525 m)	143 knots (165 mph; 266 km/h)
Stalling speed	No stall or buffet at 34·7 knots (40 mph; 64·3 km/h) IAS
Max rate of climb at S/L	3,000 ft (914 m)/min
Min T-O run	300 ft (91 m)
Normal T-O run	1,000 ft (305 m)
Landing from 50 ft (15 m)	3,000 ft (914 m)
Landing run	2,500 ft (762 m)
Range with standard fuel	174 nm (200 miles; 322 km)
Range with standard plus auxiliary fuel	347 nm (400 miles; 644 km)

Stevenson/Owl OR-70 *Fang* Formula One racing aircraft (100 hp Continental O-200 engine)

Vin-Del Aircraft

ADDRESS:
29718 Knollview Drive, Miraleste, California 90732

Mr Vince DeLuca, proprietor of Vin-Del Aircraft, has built a prototype of a Formula One racer of Mr Owl's design which he has designated OR-71 *Lil Quickie*. Construction began on 2 December 1971 and the first flight was made on 6 June 1972. Plans (entirely different from those of OR-70) are available to amateur constructors.

VIN-DEL/OWL OR-71 LIL QUICKIE

The OR-71 is generally similar to the OR-70, the description of which applies also to the OR-71 except as detailed. Limit load factor of the OR-71 is $\pm 7 \cdot 33g$, ultimate load factor $\pm 11 \cdot 0g$.

WINGS: As for OR-70, except dihedral 0° 51′. Non-linear thickness distribution. Thickness/chord ratio is 13·7% at root, 10% on outer 60% of wing. Plywood ribs with spruce caps. Plans show optional high-lift leading-edge of larger radius and increased camber.

LANDING GEAR: As for OR-70, except prototype has cantilever light alloy main legs. Spring steel legs optional. Main-wheel fairings of glassfibre.

POWER PLANT: As for OR-70, except propeller diameter increased. Fuselage fuel tank has a capacity of 9 US gallons (34 litres).

ACCOMMODATION: As for OR-70, except for a conventional canopy, hinged on starboard side, opening upwards and to starboard. No folding seatback or access panel aft of canopy.

Vin-Del/Owl OR-71 *Lil Quickie* **Formula One racing aircraft**

DIMENSIONS, EXTERNAL:
As for OR-70, except:

Length overall	16 ft 4 in (4·98 m)
Propeller diameter (max)	5 ft 0 in (1·52 m)

WEIGHTS:

Weight empty	553 lb (251 kg)
Max T-O weight	850 lb (386 kg)

PERFORMANCE (at max T-O weight):
Max never-exceed speed
260 knots (300 mph; 482 km/h) IAS
Max level speed
more than 221 knots (255 mph; 410 km/h)
Stalling speed 60 knots (69 mph; 111 km/h)

PARKER

C. Y. PARKER

ADDRESS:
PO Box 3163, Pensacola, Florida 32506
Telephone: (904) 456-8978

PARKER TEENIE TWO

Mr Cal Parker has completed and flown the prototype of an improved version of the small lightweight all-metal homebuilt aircraft which he designated Jeanie's Teenie. With completion of the new prototype, the original model is now known as Teenie One.

Mr Parker's original aim was to build an aircraft specifically to utilise the Volkswagen motor car engine and, at the same time, to evolve an all-metal design that would present few constructional problems even to homebuilders with virtually no metal-working experience. This has been achieved, and no special tools or jigs are needed beyond a tool to close and form the cadmium-plated steel pop rivets that are used for practically all assembly. One gauge of aluminium sheet and one size of light alloy angle section is used for almost all of the structure, except for chromoly steel tube and sheet which are used for construction of the landing gear and control surfaces respectively. For simplicity and economy, push/pull tubes are used for all flying controls.

Teenie One conformed to these ideas, but Mr Parker's latest design, which first flew in 1969, has been considerably refined to produce a much "cleaner" aeroplane. The prototype Teenie Two cost approximately $650 to build, over a period of six months. Its structure is stressed for full aerobatics, but the fuel and oil systems are not suitable for inverted flight.

Teenie Two has been tested with a 4 ft 2 in (1·27 m) diameter Hegy propeller of 40 in (1·02 m) pitch, a 4 ft 6 in (1·37 m) Troyer propeller of 30 in (0·76 m) pitch, and two computer-designed propellers which were handmade. All have given satisfactory performance with the static rpm of the engine maintained between 2,800 and 3,200.

Plans, complete kits of parts, and details of modifications for the Volkswagen engine are available to amateur constructors. By the end of 1970 approximately 7,000 sets of Teenie One plans had been sold. By the end of February 1974 approximately 3,000 sets of Teenie Two plans had been sold, with about 800 aircraft under construction and several already flying.

The following details apply to the standard Teenie Two:

TYPE: Single-seat homebuilt light aircraft.

WINGS: Cantilever low-wing monoplane. Wing section NACA 4415. All-metal two-spar structure, with detachable outer wing panels. Light alloy ribs and skin. Plain ailerons of metal construction. No flaps.

FUSELAGE: All-metal semi-monocoque structure with longerons of light alloy angle, three built-up bulkheads and light alloy skin.

TAIL UNIT: Cantilever all-metal structure with swept vertical surfaces. Small dorsal fin eliminates the need for a fourth bulkhead by carrying loads from fin leading-edge to centre bulkhead. Conventional rudder and elevators of metal construction.

LANDING GEAR: Non-retractable tricycle type. Shock-absorption provided by springs in compression and rubber hose. All three wheels same size, with tyres size 10·5 × 4·00-4, pressure 25 lb/sq in (1·76 kg/cm²). Mechanically-actuated wheel brakes.

POWER PLANT: One 42 hp 1,600 cc or 40 hp 1,500 cc Volkswagen modified motor car engine, driving a two-blade fixed-pitch wooden propeller. Single fuselage fuel tank, immediately aft of firewall, capacity 9 US gallons (34 litres). Refuelling point on top of fuselage, forward of windscreen. Oil capacity 0·66 US gallon (2·5 litres).

ACCOMMODATION: Single seat in open cockpit.

DIMENSIONS, EXTERNAL:

Wing span	18 ft 0 in (5·49 m)
Wing chord, constant	3 ft 4 in (1·02 m)
Width, wings detached	6 ft 0 in (1·83 m)
Length overall	12 ft 10 in (3·91 m)

WEIGHTS:

Weight empty	310 lb (140 kg)
Max T-O weight	590 lb (267 kg)

PERFORMANCE (at max T-O weight, 1,600 cc engine):
Max level speed
104 knots (120 mph; 193 km/h)
Max cruising speed (75% power)
95·5 knots (110 mph; 177 km/h)
Landing speed 43·5 knots (50 mph; 80·5 km/h)
Max rate of climb at S/L 800 ft (244 m)/min
Service ceiling 15,000 ft (4,575 m)
Min ground turning radius 30 ft 0 in (9·14 m)
Range 347 nm (400 miles; 643 km)

The prototype Parker Teenie Two, which has completed more than 200 flying hours

PARSONS-JOCELYN

NICHOLAS E. D'APUZZO

ADDRESS:
1029 Blue Rock Lane, Blue Bell, Pennsylvania 19422
Telephone: (215) 646-4792

The prototype Parsons-Jocelyn PJ-260 aerobatic biplane was designed by Mr Nicholas E. D'Apuzzo at the request of Mr Rodney Jocelyn, world aerobatic champion in 1950-52, and Capt Lindsey Parsons, a sportsman pilot. It was built by Mr Jocelyn for Capt Parsons and was flown by both pilots at displays throughout the United States, before being sold to another private owner.

Sets of drawings are available to amateur constructors and a total of seven PJ-260s had been completed by February 1974.

Details of other designs by Mr D'Apuzzo are given under his own name.

PARSONS-JOCELYN PJ-260 and D-295

The standard Parsons-Jocelyn **PJ-260** is a single-seat aerobatic biplane powered by a 260 hp Lycoming engine. However, it can be built as a two-seat sporting aircraft by minor modifications of the fuselage and the installation of a centre-section fuel tank. Alternative engines include the 195 hp Lycoming O-435-1 or O-435-11.

The **D-295** derivative, built by Mr E. Mahler and Mr L. Webber, differs from the standard PJ-260 by having a lower wing of reduced span, a modified aileron control system to increase the rate of roll, and wheel fairings. Span of the lower wing is 23 ft 9 in (7·24 m) and total wing area is reduced to 178 sq ft (16·54 m²), increasing max wing loading to 11·2 lb/sq ft (54·7 kg/m²). The aircraft is powered by a 295 hp Lycoming GO-480-G1D6 engine, driving a Hartzell three-blade constant-speed propeller, diameter 8 ft 0 in (2·44 m). Performance is generally similar to that of the standard PJ-260, but stalling speed is increased to 48 knots (55 mph; 88·5 km/h) and service ceiling reduced to 23,000 ft (7,000 m). Initial rate of climb is in excess of 2,800 ft (853 m)/min, T-O run is 175 ft (54 m) and T-O to 50 ft (15 m) 475 ft (145 m).

In its current form, as shown in the accompanying illustration, the D-295 has undergone further modifications to the lower wings, interplane struts and aileron and elevator control systems.

Plans of the D-295 are not available to amateur constructors.

The following details refer to the standard PJ-260, built to Mr D'Apuzzo's plans and similar in all respects to the prototype. Use of a conventional spring steel landing gear, in place of the glassfibre legs that were used on the prototype, increases the aircraft's empty weight.

TYPE: Single-seat aerobatic biplane.

WINGS: Conventional braced biplane type. Wing section NACA M12 (modified). Dihedral 30′ on lower wings only. Incidence 2°. Sweepback 9° 15′ on upper wings. Two wood spars, metal ribs, fabric covering. Metal Frise ailerons on all four wings, with fabric covering. No flaps.

FUSELAGE: Steel tube structure, with aluminium alloy access panels forward of cockpit and fabric covering aft.

TAIL UNIT: Wire-braced fabric-covered steel tube structure. Trim tab in starboard elevator.

LANDING GEAR: Non-retractable tailwheel type. Main legs made from single strut of 3M Scotchply glassfibre. Firestone DFA-180 6·00-6 main wheels with 7·00-6 tyres, pressure 20 lb/sq in (1·41 kg/cm²). Firestone CFA hydraulic brakes. Wheel spats.

POWER PLANT: One 260 hp Lycoming GO-435-C2 six-cylinder horizontally-opposed aircooled engine, driving an Aeromatic F-200H-0-93 propeller. Fuel in 33 US gallon (125 litre) main tank and 11 US gallon (41·5 litre) aerobatic tank, both in fuselage. Total fuel capacity 44 US gallons (166·5 litres). Oil capacity 12 US quarts (11 litres).

ACCOMMODATION: Single seat in open cockpit.

DIMENSIONS, EXTERNAL:

Wing span	27 ft 0 in (8·23 m)
Wing chord (constant, both)	3 ft 10 in (1·17 m)
Wing aspect ratio	4·22
Length overall	21 ft 0 in (6·40 m)
Height overall	7 ft 7½ in (2·32 m)
Tailplane span	10 ft 2 in (3·10 m)
Wheel track	6 ft 4 in (1·93 m)

AREAS:

Wings, gross	190 sq ft (17·65 m²)
Ailerons (total)	23·0 sq ft (2·14 m²)
Fin	8·1 sq ft (0·75 m²)
Rudder	7·5 sq ft (0·70 m²)
Tailplane	15·35 sq ft (1·43 m²)
Elevators	14·5 sq ft (1·35 m²)

WEIGHTS AND LOADINGS:

Weight empty	1,300 lb (590 kg)
Max T-O and landing weight	2,000 lb (907 kg)
Max wing loading	10·5 lb/sq ft (51·2 kg/m²)
Max power loading	7·7 lb/hp (3·5 kg/hp)

PERFORMANCE (at max T-O weight):

Max never-exceed speed	191 knots (220 mph; 354 km/h)
Max level speed at 1,000 ft (305 m)	148 knots (170 mph; 274 km/h)
Max cruising speed	130 knots (150 mph; 241 km/h)
Econ cruising speed	120 knots (138 mph; 222 km/h)
Stalling speed	46 knots (52 mph; 84 km/h)
Max rate of climb at S/L	2,200 ft (670 m)/min
Service ceiling	24,000 ft (7,300 m)
T-O run	150 ft (46 m)
T-O to 50 ft (15 m)	400 ft (122 m)
Landing from 50 ft (15 m)	650 ft (198 m)
Landing run	350 ft (107 m)
Range with max fuel	434 nm (500 miles; 800 km)

Parsons-Jocelyn D-295, showing clearly the lower wing and interplane struts in their latest form

PATCHEN

MARVIN PATCHEN INC

ADDRESS:
Aero Magazine, PO Box 1184, Ramona, California 92065
Telephone: (714) 789-2400

In conjunction with *Aero* magazine the former Thurston Aircraft Corporation designed and began constructing a prototype of a landplane version of the TSC-1A1 Teal under the designation TSC-2 Explorer. Following acquisition of all rights in the Teal by Schweizer Aircraft Corporation (which see), Marvin Patchen Inc, which financed the original development, retained rights to the TSC-2 Explorer and has proposed two versions, one for civilian use and the other, named the Observer, for law enforcement.

Construction of the prototype Explorer was completed by Aerofab Corporation of Sanford, Maine, on a contract basis, and its initial flight test programme was completed successfully by November 1972. In early February 1973 a market survey was carried out to determine the special requirements of pipeline patrol operators, aerial photographers and law enforcement agencies; simultaneously, work towards certification was continued.

No decision had been reached by February 1974 regarding the manufacturer of production aircraft, but at the time of closing for press negotiations were taking place for production and marketing of the Explorer.

Prototype of the Patchen Explorer four-seat cabin monoplane (200 hp Lycoming IO-360-A1A engine)

PATCHEN EXPLORER/OBSERVER

TYPE: Four-seat cabin monoplane.

WINGS: Cantilever shoulder-wing monoplane. Wing section NACA 4415. Dihedral 1°. Incidence 4°. All-metal "D-spar" structure. No flaps.

FUSELAGE: All-metal semi-monocoque structure, with glassfibre nose section and cabin top skins. Transparent bubble nose to provide helicopter-like visibility.

TAIL UNIT: Cantilever all-metal T-tail. Trim tabs on elevator and rudder.

LANDING GEAR: Non-retractable tricycle type. Cantilever spring steel main-gear struts. Nose unit has oleo-pneumatic shock-absorber. Main wheels and tyres size 6·00-6; nosewheel and tyre size 5·00-5. Single-disc brakes.

POWER PLANT: One 200 hp Lycoming IO-360-A1A four-cylinder horizontally-opposed air-cooled engine, pylon-mounted above the wing centre-section and driving a Hartzell two-blade metal constant-speed propeller. One 22·5 US gallon (85 litre) fuel tank in each wing leading-edge; total fuel capacity 45 US gallons (170 litres). One optional all-metal fuel tank in fuselage, capacity 25 US gallons (94·6 litres). Total optional fuel capacity 70 US gallons (264·6 litres).

ACCOMMODATION: Pilot and three passengers, seated in pairs, in enclosed cabin. Door on each side of fuselage, sliding fore and aft for cabin access and side photography. Cabin is heated and ventilated.

ELECTRONICS AND EQUIPMENT: Panel designed to use Narco Spectrum radio. Optional equipment includes searchlight, stabilised optics slaved to searchlight, siren, PA system, camera mountings, STOL kit and "quiet" kit.

DIMENSIONS, EXTERNAL:

Wing span	32 ft 0 in (9·75 m)
Wing chord (constant)	5 ft 0 in (1·52 m)
Length overall	23 ft 4 in (7·11 m)
Height overall	9 ft 8 in (2·95 m)
Tailplane span	10 ft 0 in (3·05 m)
Wheel track	7 ft 9 in (2·36 m)
Wheelbase	9 ft 4 in (2·84 m)
Propeller diameter	6 ft 2 in (1·88 m)

AREAS:

Wings, gross	157 sq ft (14·59 m²)
Ailerons (total)	12·8 sq ft (1·19 m²)
Fin	10·7 sq ft (0·99 m²)
Dorsal fin	2·4 sq ft (0·22 m²)
Tailplane	19·1 sq ft (1·77 m²)
Elevators	15·7 sq ft (1·46 m²)

WEIGHTS AND LOADINGS:

Weight empty	1,370 lb (621 kg)
Max T-O and landing weight	2,200 lb (998 kg)
Max wing loading	14·0 lb/sq ft (68·3 kg/m²)
Max power loading	11·0 lb/hp (4·99 kg/hp)

PERFORMANCE (estimated, at max T-O weight):

Max cruising speed	109-113 knots (125-130 mph; 201-209 km/h)
Stalling speed, power off*	46 knots (53 mph; 85·5 km/h)
Max rate of climb at S/L	1,300 ft (396 m)/min
T-O to 50 ft (15 m)	under 850 ft (259 m)
Landing from 50 ft (15 m)	under 850 ft (259 m)
Range with max fuel at 75% power	770 nm (887 miles; 1,427 km)

**Prototype will not stall power on, with wings level, at any angle of attack*

PAYNE

VERNON W. PAYNE

ADDRESS:
Route No. 4, PO Box 319M, Escondido, California 92025
Telephone: (714) 746-4465

Mr Vernon Payne is the designer of the Knight Twister, a light sporting biplane of which plans and kits are available for amateur construction. It exists in four main versions.

KNIGHT TWISTER KT-85

The original prototype of the Knight Twister KT-85 single-seat sporting biplane flew in 1933. Considerable refinement of the design since that time has improved both the appearance and the performance of later models, which have been built in substantial numbers by amateur constructors in the United States and elsewhere.

Standard power plant is a Continental flat-four engine of 85/90 hp, but alternative engines have been fitted by some constructors. Most powerful Knight Twister flown to date is one owned by Mr Charles Williams of Mount Prospect, Illinois, which has a 180 hp Lycoming O-360 engine installed.

During 1971 Mr Payne modified the design of the tailplane, which now has increased span and reduced chord, the area remaining unchanged.

The following details refer to the standard Knight Twister built from Mr Payne's plans:

TYPE: Single-seat light biplane.

WINGS: Braced biplane type. Wing section NACA M-6. No dihedral. Incidence 1° 30′. All-wood two-spar structure, plywood-covered and with fabric covering overall. Ailerons on lower wings only, of fabric-covered wood construction. No flaps.

FUSELAGE: Steel tube truss structure with wood stringers and fabric covering.

TAIL UNIT: Cantilever type. Vertical surfaces have fabric-covered steel tube structure. Horizontal surfaces have plywood-covered wood structure, with fabric covering overall.

LANDING GEAR: Non-retractable tailwheel type. Cantilever main units. Rubber cord or hydraulic shock-absorption. Wheels size 6·00-6 with Goodyear tyres, pressure 5·10 lb/sq in (0·35-0·70 kg/cm²). Goodyear disc brakes.

POWER PLANT: One 90 hp Continental C90 four-cylinder horizontally-opposed aircooled engine, driving a two-blade wood or metal fixed-pitch propeller. Alternatively any other Continental or Lycoming horizontally-opposed four-cylinder engine of 85-145 hp. Fuel tank aft of engine firewall, capacity 18 US gallons (68 litres). Oil capacity 1-1·5 US gallons (3·7-5·7 litres).

ACCOMMODATION: Single seat, normally in open cockpit. Baggage compartment capacity 20 lb (9 kg). Radio optional.

DIMENSIONS, EXTERNAL:
Wing span:
upper 15 ft 0 in (4·57 m)
lower 13 ft 0 in (3·96 m)
Wing chord (mean, both) 2 ft 1·6 in (0·65 m)
Wing aspect ratio:
upper 6·87
lower 6·13
Length overall 14 ft 0 in (4·27 m)
Height overall 5 ft 3 in (1·60 m)
Tailplane span 7 ft 0 in (2·13 m)
Wheel track 5 ft 0 in (1·52 m)
Wheelbase 17 ft 2 in (5·23 m)

DIMENSIONS, INTERNAL:
Cockpit: Length 2 ft 3 in (0·68 m)
Width 1 ft 9 in (0·53 m)

AREAS:
Wings, gross 60 sq ft (5·57 m²)
Ailerons (total) 5·00 sq ft (0·46 m²)
Fin 2·25 sq ft (0·21 m²)
Rudder 4·35 sq ft (0·40 m²)
Tailplane 5·25 sq ft (0·49 m²)
Elevators 3·75 sq ft (0·35 m²)

WEIGHTS AND LOADINGS (90 hp engine):
Weight empty 535 lb (243 kg)
Max T-O weight 960 lb (435 kg)
Max wing loading 16 lb/sq ft (78 kg/m²)
Max power loading 10·7 lb/hp (4·85 kg/hp)

PERFORMANCE (90 hp engine, at max T-O weight):
Max level speed at S/L 139 knots (160 mph; 257 km/h)
Max cruising speed 122 knots (140 mph; 225 km/h)
Econ cruising speed 109 knots (125 mph; 201 km/h)
Stalling speed 53 knots (60 mph; 97 km/h)
Max rate of climb at S/L 900 ft (275 m)/min
T-O run 410 ft (125 m)
T-O to 50 ft (15 m) 1,000 ft (305 m)
Landing from 50 ft (15 m) 1,200 ft (366 m)
Landing run 670 ft (205 m)
Range with max fuel 338 nm (390 miles; 625 km)

Knight Twister Imperial built by Mr Don Fairbanks, with its original landing gear *(Howard Levy)*

KNIGHT TWISTER IMPERIAL

At the request of Don Fairbanks, owner of a flying training school at Lunken Airport, Cincinnati, Ohio, Mr Payne modified the design of the original Knight Twister to enable Mr Fairbanks to compete in US National Air Races in the Sport Biplane class. The resulting aircraft won the Silver Biplane Race at Reno, Nevada, in 1971. Variations from the standard Knight Twister include a change in wing section, increased wing and tailplane span and increased fuel tankage. First flight was made on 19 June 1970.

Dubbed the Knight Twister Imperial by Mr Payne, this aircraft is generally similar to the Knight Twister KT-85, except as follows:

WINGS: Wing section NACA 21. Span and chord of both upper and lower wings increased. Flying and landing wires deleted. Incidence 0°.

POWER PLANT: One 135 hp Lycoming O-290-D2 four-cylinder horizontally-opposed aircooled engine, driving a two-blade fixed-pitch propeller with spinner. Fuel contained in an upper tank of 22·5 US gallons (85 litres) capacity and a lower tank of 12·5 US gallons (47 litres) capacity, aft of firewall. Total fuel capacity 35 US gallons (132 litres).

DIMENSIONS, EXTERNAL:
Wing span:
upper 17 ft 6 in (5·33 m)
lower 15 ft 6 in (4·72 m)

AREA:
Wings, gross 75·25 sq ft (6·99 m²)

WEIGHTS AND LOADINGS:
Normal T-O weight 900 lb (408 kg)
Max T-O weight 1,125 lb (520 kg)
Max wing loading 14·9 lb/sq ft (72·7 kg/m²)
Max power loading 8·3 lb/hp (3·8 kg/hp)

PERFORMANCE (at normal T-O weight):
Max level speed 156 knots (180 mph; 290 km/h)
Max cruising speed 148 knots (170 mph; 274 km/h)
Stalling speed 45·5 knots (52 mph; 84 km/h)
Max rate of climb at S/L 1,200 ft (366 m)/min
T-O run 425 ft (130 m)
Landing run 800 ft (244 m)
Range at max cruising speed 590 nm (680 miles; 1,094 km)

PERFORMANCE (at max T-O weight):
Max level speed at S/L 146 knots (168 mph; 270 km/h)
Max cruising speed 144 knots (166 mph; 267 km/h)
Econ cruising speed 126 knots (145 mph; 233 km/h)
Stalling speed 43·5 knots (50 mph; 80·5 km/h)
Max rate of climb at S/L 1,200 ft (366 m)/min
T-O run 370 ft (113 m)
T-O to 50 ft (15 m) 760 ft (232 m)
Landing run 870 ft (265 m)
Range at max cruising speed with max fuel 307 nm (354 miles; 570 km)

SUNDAY KNIGHT TWISTER SKT-125

This developed version of the Knight Twister has a 125 hp Lycoming engine. Increased wing area makes it easier to fly and its name is meant to imply that it is for the "Sunday flyer".

A fully aerobatic Sunday Knight Twister, with a 180 hp engine, has been built by Mr J. F. Carter of Drewry, Alabama.

DIMENSIONS, EXTERNAL:
Wing span 19 ft 6 in (5·94 m)
Length overall 15 ft 6 in (4·72 m)
Height overall 5 ft 6 in (1·68 m)

AREA:
Wings, gross 83 sq ft (7·71 m²)

WEIGHTS:
Weight empty 700 lb (318 kg)
Max T-O weight 1,016 lb (461 kg)

KNIGHT TWISTER JUNIOR KT-75

The Knight Twister Junior has the same fuselage, tail unit and landing gear as the KT-85, but its tapered wings have a larger area. The prototype flew in 1947. Details are as for the KT-85, except for the following:

WINGS: Incidence 2°.

POWER PLANT: One Continental or Lycoming four-cylinder horizontally-opposed aircooled engine of 75-125 hp. Fuel capacity with 75 hp engine 12 US gallons (45 litres).

DIMENSIONS, EXTERNAL:
Wing span:
upper 17 ft 6 in (5·33 m)
lower 13 ft 6 in (4·11 m)
Wing aspect ratio:
upper 7·78
lower 7·10

AREAS:
Wings, gross 72·8 sq ft (6·76 m²)
Ailerons (total) 6·70 sq ft (0·62 m²)

WEIGHTS AND LOADINGS (75 hp engine):
Weight empty 500 lb (227 kg)
Max T-O weight 890 lb (404 kg)
Max wing loading 12 lb/sq ft (58·6 kg/m²)
Max power loading 7·68 lb/hp (3·48 kg/hp)

PERFORMANCE (75 hp engine, at max T-O weight):
Max level speed at S/L 117 knots (135 mph; 217 km/h)
Max cruising speed 109 knots (125 mph; 201 km/h)
Econ cruising speed 97 knots (112 mph; 180 km/h)
Stalling speed 42 knots (48 mph; 77·5 km/h)
Max rate of climb at S/L 900 ft (275 m)/min
T-O run 375 ft (114 m)
T-O to 50 ft (15 m) 910 ft (277 m)
Landing from 50 ft (15 m) 1,020 ft (311 m)
Landing run 625 ft (190 m)
Range with max fuel 247 nm (285 miles; 460 km)

PAZMANY

PAZMANY AIRCRAFT CORPORATION

ADDRESS:
Box 80051, San Diego, California 92138
Telephone: (714) 276-0424

This company was formed by Mr Ladislao Pazmany, designer of a two-seat light aircraft known as the PL-1 Laminar. A prototype, constructed by Mr John Green and Mr Keith Fowler, was flown for the first time on 23 March 1962, the test pilots being Cdr Paul Hayek, USN, and Lieut Richard Gordon, who is best known as one of the Gemini/Apollo astronauts.

Some 5,000 design hours and 4,000 hours of construction went into the prototype PL-1, which had logged more than 2,000 flying hours by January 1974.

A total of 375 sets of plans and instructions for building the PL-1 have been sold, and PL-1s are being built in the USA, Canada, Australia, Norway and other countries.

Pazmany Aircraft Corporation is no longer marketing plans of the PL-1: instead, plans and instructions for building the improved PL-2 are

Pazmany PL-1 (115 hp Lycoming engine) built by Mr Dieter Bochmann *(Neil A. Macdougall)*

available to amateur constructors and many aircraft of this type are being built. A total of 250 sets of plans had been sold by early 1974.

Mr Pazmany designed and has built the prototype of a new lightweight, low-cost single-seat monoplane, designated PL-4A.

PAZMANY PL-1 LAMINAR

In early 1968 the Aeronautical Research Laboratory of the Chinese Nationalist Air Force, at Taichung, Taiwan, acquired a set of PL-1 drawings. Under the supervision of General K. F. Ku and Colonel C. Y. Lee, personnel of the ARL built a PL-1 in a record time of 100 days. It was flown for the first time on 26 October 1968 and on 30 October was presented to Generalissimo Chiang Kai-Shek. Extensive flight testing resulted in the decision to utilise the PL-1 as a basic trainer for CAF cadets, and 35 additional aircraft, designated PL-1B, were constructed during 1970, powered by the 150 hp Lycoming O-320 engine. The PL-1B continues in production, as described under the AIDC/CAF heading in the Taiwan aircraft section of this edition.

The details below apply to the prototype PL-1, which was stressed to 9*g* (ultimate) for aerobatics and to permit the fitting of more powerful engines.

TYPE: Two-seat light aircraft.

WINGS: Cantilever low-wing monoplane. Wing section NACA 63_2615. Dihedral 3°. Incidence —1° 20′. All-metal single-spar structure in one piece, with leading-edge torsion box. Plain piano-hinged ailerons and flaps of all-metal construction. No trim tabs.

FUSELAGE: Conventional all-metal semi-monocoque structure, with flat or single-curvature skins.

TAIL UNIT: Cantilever all-metal structure. One-piece horizontal surface, with anti-servo tab which serves also as a trim tab.

LANDING GEAR: Non-retractable tricycle type, with all three oleo-pneumatic shock-absorbers interchangeable. Goodyear wheels and tyres, size 5·00-5. Tyre pressure 31 lb/sq in (2·18 kg/cm²). Goodyear brakes. Steerable nosewheel.

POWER PLANT: One 95 hp Continental C90-12F four-cylinder horizontally-opposed aircooled engine, driving a McCauley Model IA100/MCM 6663 two-blade metal fixed-pitch propeller. Fuel in two glassfibre wingtip tanks, each of 12·5 US gallons (47 litres) capacity. Total fuel capacity 25 US gallons (94 litres). Oil capacity 5 US quarts (4·5 litres).

ACCOMMODATION: Two seats side by side under rearward-sliding transparent canopy. Dual controls. Space for 40 lb (18 kg) baggage aft of seats. Heater and airscoops for ventilation. VHF radio.

DIMENSIONS, EXTERNAL:

Wing span	28 ft 0 in (8·53 m)
Wing chord (constant)	4 ft 2 in (1·27 m)
Wing aspect ratio	6·7
Length overall	18 ft 11 in (5·77 m)
Height overall	8 ft 8 in (2·64 m)
Tailplane span	8 ft 0 in (2·44 m)
Wheel track	8 ft 2½ in (2·50 m)
Wheelbase	4 ft 3 in (1·30 m)

DIMENSIONS, INTERNAL:

Cabin: Length	4 ft 2 in (1·27 m)
Width	3 ft 4 in (1·02 m)
Height	3 ft 4 in (1·02 m)

AREAS:

Wings, gross	116 sq ft (10·78 m²)
Ailerons (total)	10·54 sq ft (0·98 m²)
Flaps (total)	17·36 sq ft (1·61 m²)
Fin	7·30 sq ft (0·68 m²)
Rudder	3·10 sq ft (0·29 m²)
Tailplane	18·00 sq ft (1·67 m²)

WEIGHTS AND LOADINGS:

Weight empty, equipped	800 lb (363 kg)
Max T-O weight	1,326 lb (602 kg)
Max wing loading	11·4 lb/sq ft (55·7 kg/m²)
Max power loading	14 lb/hp (6·35 kg/hp)

PERFORMANCE (at max T-O weight):

Max never-exceed speed	178 knots (205 mph; 330 km/h)
Max level speed at S/L	104 knots (120 mph; 193 km/h)
Max cruising speed at S/L	100 knots (115 mph; 185 km/h)
Econ cruising speed at S/L	91 knots (105 mph; 169 km/h)
Stalling speed, flaps down	44 knots (51 mph; 82 km/h)
Max rate of climb at S/L	1,000 ft (305 m)/min
Service ceiling	18,000 ft (5,500 m)
T-O run	550 ft (168 m)
T-O to 50 ft (15 m)	784 ft (239 m)
Landing from 50 ft (15 m)	1,100 ft (335 m)
Landing run	175 ft (54 m)
Range with max fuel	521 nm (600 miles; 965 km)

PAZMANY PL-1B

This is the version of the PL-1 built in Taiwan. It differs from the basic PL-1 mainly in having a 150 hp Lycoming O-320 engine.

PAZMANY PL-2

Shortly after flight trials of the PL-1 began, Mr Pazmany initiated a complete redesign of the aircraft. The developed design, known as the PL-2, is almost identical with the PL-1 in external configuration. Cockpit width is increased by 2 in (5 cm) and wing dihedral is increased from 3° to 5°. The internal structure is extensively changed, to simplify construction and reduce weight. Suitable Lycoming power plants are the 108 hp O-235-C1, 125 hp O-290-G (ground power unit), 135 hp O-290-D2B or 150 hp O-320-A.

Static tests of every major assembly up to ultimate loads had been made by early 1967. The first PL-2 to be completed was built by Mr H. Pio of Ramona, California, and this aircraft made its first flight on 4 April 1969, piloted by Mr Pio. It has an O-290-G engine.

A single example of the PL-2 was built by the Vietnam Air Force, each VNAF base contributing towards its construction. This flew for the first time on 1 July 1971, and it was reported that production of at least ten more PL-2s for use at the VNAF Air Training Center was being considered. The Royal Thai Air Force was also known to have two PL-2s under construction; but no further news of this project had been received in early 1974. The Republic of Korea Air Force built one PL-2 prototype for flight testing, and has since completed three more for evaluation as trainers. In Japan, the Miyauchi Manufacturing Co Ltd, Tokyo, completed a prototype of the PL-2 in the Autumn of 1971, this being exhibited at the Nagoya International Air Show during October-November 1971.

The Indonesian Air Force was building an example of the PL-2 at the Lipnur factory in early 1974, for evaluation as a military trainer. Tooling for limited initial production has been prepared.

DIMENSIONS, EXTERNAL:

Same as for PL-1, except:

Length overall	19 ft 3¼ in (5·90 m)
Height overall	8 ft 0 in (2·44 m)
Wheel track	8 ft 6½ in (2·60 m)

WEIGHTS:

Weight empty:	
108 hp	875 lb (396 kg)
125, 135 hp	900 lb (408 kg)
150 hp	902 lb (409 kg)
Max T-O weight:	
108 hp	1,416 lb (642 kg)
125, 135 hp	1,445 lb (655 kg)
150 hp	1,447 lb (656 kg)

PERFORMANCE (at max T-O weight):

Max level speed at S/L:	
108 hp	120 knots (138 mph; 222 km/h)
125 hp	125 knots (144 mph; 232 km/h)
135 hp	128 knots (148 mph; 238 km/h)
150 hp	133 knots (153 mph; 246 km/h)
Econ cruising speed:	
108 hp	103 knots (119 mph; 192 km/h)
125 hp	111 knots (128 mph; 206 km/h)
135 hp	113 knots (130 mph; 209 km/h)
150 hp	118 knots (136 mph; 219 km/h)
Stalling speed (flaps down):	
108 hp	45·2 knots (52 mph; 84 km/h)
125, 135, 150 hp	47 knots (54 mph; 87 km/h)
Max rate of climb at S/L:	
108 hp	1,280 ft (390 m)/min
125 hp	1,500 ft (457 m)/min
135 hp	1,600 ft (488 m)/min
150 hp	1,700 ft (518 m)/min
Range at econ cruising speed:	
108 hp	427 nm (492 miles; 790 km)
125 hp	422 nm (486 miles; 780 km)
135 hp	428 nm (493 miles; 792 km)
150 hp	330 nm (381 miles; 610 km)

PAZMANY PL-4A

Mr Pazmany flew for the first time on 12 July 1972 the prototype of a lightweight single-seat low-wing monoplane designated PL-4A. It was designed specifically for easy low-cost construction by amateur builders, to provide a safe aircraft that would be economical in operation. The prototype had completed approximately 180 hours of flight by January 1974. Sets of plans, kits of prefabricated components, glassfibre wingtips and fuel tank and transparent cockpit canopy are available to amateur constructors.

By February 1974, approximately 350 sets of plans had been sold, and the PL-4A had received approval in Australia for construction by amateurs.

In November 1973, Lt Col Roy Windover, Director of the Air Cadets Programme, Canadian Ministry of Defence, made a flight evaluation of the PL-4A prototype. As a result of this, it is planned to provide 200 of these aircraft for the Air Cadets.

Three pre-production aircraft were being built in early 1974 to evaluate three different power plant installations, comprising a Volkswagen engine with 2¼ : 1 Vee-belt reduction; a Volkswagen with direct drive to the propeller; and either a Continental A65 or Franklin A-120-C aircooled engine.

Components for the pre-production aircraft, as well as for the production version, are being made by inmates of a civil prison, who will be responsible also for construction of the first three aircraft. The remainder will be assembled by Air Cadets, who will use them for cross-country, aerobatic and IFR flying.

TYPE: Single-seat lightweight homebuilt sporting aircraft.

WINGS: Cantilever low-wing monoplane. Wing section NACA 63_3-418. Dihedral 5°. Incidence 3°. No sweepback. All-metal structure, with main spar, "Z" section rear beam, sheet metal ribs and skins. Wings fold alongside fuselage for towing or storage. Plain piano-hinged ailerons of all-metal construction. Glassfibre wingtips. No flaps. No trim tabs.

FUSELAGE: All-metal structure, with bulkheads built up from bent sheet metal channels and standard extruded angles for longerons, and with sheet metal skins.

TAIL UNIT: All-metal cantilever T-tail. All-moving tailplane with large anti-servo tab which serves also as a trim tab.

LANDING GEAR: Non-retractable tailwheel type. Spring steel cantilever main legs. Single

Pazmany PL-2 built by Mr Kenneth Arnold of Kansas City, Missouri

Pazmany PL-4A prototype (1,600 cc modified Volkswagen motor car engine)

Go-Kart type wheel on each main unit, with 4·10 × 3·50-6 four-ply tyre, pressure 65 lb/sq in (4·57 kg/cm²). Steerable and castoring tail-wheel with solid tyre size 5 × 1·5-1·5. Go-Kart type hydraulic disc brakes by Hurst-Airheart.

Power Plant: One 1,600 cc modified Volkswagen motor car engine with Becar V-belt reduction of 2¼ : 1, developing approximately 50 hp and driving a two-blade fixed-pitch wooden propeller of Pazmany design, manufactured by Ted Hendricksen. Glassfibre fuel tank immediately aft of firewall, usable capacity 12 US gallons (45 litres). Refuelling point on upper fuselage forward of windscreen. Oil capacity 0·75 US gallons (2·8 litres).

Accommodation: Single seat under transparent Plexiglas canopy, hinged on starboard side. Compartment aft of seat for 20 lb (9 kg) baggage. Cabin heated and ventilated.

Systems: Hydraulic system for brakes only. Electrical system powered by 12V 25Ah battery situated in baggage compartment.

Dimensions, external:
Wing span 26 ft 8 in (8·13 m)
Wing chord (constant) 3 ft 4 in (1·02 m)
Wing aspect ratio 8·0
Length overall 16 ft 6½ in (5·04 m)
Width, wings folded 8 ft 0 in (2·44 m)
Height overall 5 ft 8 in (1·73 m)
Tailplane span 7 ft 6 in (2·29 m)
Wheel track 6 ft 9 in (2·06 m)
Wheelbase 11 ft 8 in (3·56 m)
Propeller diameter 5 ft 8 in (1·73 m)
Propeller ground clearance 10 in (0·25 m)

Areas:
Wings, gross 89·0 sq ft (8·27 m²)
Ailerons (total) 8·0 sq ft (0·74 m²)
Fin 4·5 sq ft (0·42 m²)
Rudder 4·5 sq ft (0·42 m²)
Tailplane, including tab 15·0 sq ft (1·39 m²)

Weights and Loadings:
Weight empty 578 lb (262 kg)
Max T-O and landing weight 850 lb (385 kg)
Max wing loading 9·5 lb/sq ft (46·4 kg/m²)
Max power loading 17·0 lb/hp (7·71 kg/hp)

Performance (at max T-O weight):
Max never-exceed speed 161 knots (186 mph; 299 km/h)
Max level speed at S/L 109 knots (125 mph; 201 km/h)
Max cruising speed at S/L 85 knots (98 mph; 158 km/h)
Econ cruising speed at S/L 78 knots (90 mph; 145 km/h)
Stalling speed, power on 40 knots (46 mph; 74 km/h)
Stalling speed, power off 42 knots (48 mph; 77·5 km/h)
Max rate of climb at S/L 650 ft (198 m)/min
Service ceiling 13,000 ft (3,960 m)
Min ground turning radius 10 ft 0 in (3·05 m)
T-O run 486 ft (148 m)
Landing run 436 ft (133 m)
Range with max fuel, no allowances 295 nm (340 miles; 545 km)

PiAC

PIASECKI AIRCRAFT CORPORATION

Head Office and Works:
Island Road, International Airport, Philadelphia, Pennsylvania 19153
Telephone: SA4-2222

Mayfield Electronics Division:
Mayfield, Pennsylvania 18433

Directors:
Virgil Kauffman
Donald N. Meyers
Arthur J. Kania
F. K. Weyerhaeuser
F. N. Piasecki

President:
Frank N. Piasecki

Vice-President:
Donald N. Meyers (Engineering)

Chief Designer: Kazimierz Korsak
Secretary-Treasurer: Arthur J. Kania
Industrial Engineering: K. R. Meenen

The Piasecki Aircraft Corporation was formed in 1955 by Mr Frank Piasecki, who was formerly Chairman of the Board and President of the Piasecki Helicopter Corporation (now the Boeing Vertol Company).

PiAC is engaged in vertical lift design research and development under contracts from the US military services. These included a joint Army/Navy contract to provide information and data on the characteristics of compound helicopters at flight speeds in excess of 195 knots (225 mph; 362 km/h) using its Model 16H-1C Pathfinder II prototype, which was described in the 1970-71 ***Jane's*****.**

Following development of the Model 16H-3F Pathfinder III, the company is now working on a nine to fifteen-seat commercial version designated 16H-3K and a higher-performance version of the 16H-1.

During 1972 the company, under US Navy contracts, investigated the potential of a Multi-Helicopter Heavy Lift System, and application of a ducted propeller to a Kaman SH-2D helicopter.

The former project was concerned with joining two Sikorsky CH-53Ds to produce a combination helicopter with heavy lift capabilities, almost doubling the load capacity of a single aircraft of the type.

Artist's impression of PiAC 16H-3K Pathfinder III executive transport (two 750 ehp United Aircraft of Canada PT6B-30 turboshaft engines)

PiAC 16H-3K PATHFINDER III

The Pathfinder is a high-speed compound helicopter which utilises a ducted propeller (known as a ring-tail) at the rear to provide directional and anti-torque control by means of vertical vanes in the duct. After take-off, increased power is put into the ducted propeller for forward propulsion. In cruising flight the small-span fixed wings off-load the rotor.

Although flown normally as a VTOL aircraft, the Pathfinder can carry larger payloads for longer distances by operating STO/VL (short take-off, vertical landing). Although take-off is made at a gross weight above maximum for hover capability, the rotor and its drive system are not overloaded in cruising flight, as the additional weight is carried by the wing. If this additional weight is in the form of fuel or other disposable stores, the Pathfinder is at hovering weight at the end of its flight and can be landed vertically.

In its original form, as the five-seat PiAC 16H-1, the Pathfinder was developed as a private venture and flew for the first time on 21 February 1962. Powered by a 450 ehp United Aircraft of Canada PT6B-2 turboshaft engine, it logged a **total of 185 flying hours, during which speeds of up to 148 knots (170 mph; 273 km/h) were attained (see 1965-66** ***Jane's*****).**

In 1964, under contract from the US Army and Navy, PiAC began to modify the Pathfinder to make it capable of attaining speeds of up to 200 knots (230 mph; 370 km/h). Redesignated 16H-1A Pathfinder II, it had a 1,250 ehp General Electric T58 turboshaft engine, new drive system and propeller to absorb the increased power, and a 44 ft (13·41 m) diameter rotor in place of the original 41 ft (12·50 m) rotor. The fuselage was lengthened and made spacious enough to accommodate up to eight people.

Flight trials were resumed on 15 November 1965, when the Model 16H-1A made its initial hovering trials. By May 1966 it had logged more than 40 flying hours under the joint Army/Navy programme, including flight at forward speeds of up to 195 knots (225 mph; 362 km/h). It had shown itself highly manoeuvrable in sideways flight at speeds of 8·7-30 knots (10-35 mph; 15-55 km/h) and had flown backwards at 28 knots (32 mph; 52 km/h). At that time, approximately 20 autorotative flights had been made at speeds between 39 and 100 knots (45-115 mph; 77-185 km/h).

The Pathfinder II, powered by a 1,500 ehp General Electric T58-GE-5 turboshaft engine, was redesignated Model 16H-1C, and details of this can be found in the 1970-71 *Jane's*.

The adjoining illustration shows an artist's impression of the Model 16H-3K Pathfinder III. Superseding the Model 16H-3H described in the 1968-69 *Jane's*, it is a compound helicopter structurally similar to the Model 16H-1C Pathfinder II, but has a four-blade main rotor, an enlarged cabin and two turboshaft engines, coupled to a common reduction gearbox.

Type: Compound helicopter executive transport.

Rotor System: Fully-articulated all-metal four-blade main rotor, attached to hub through tension-torsion straps. Anti-torque control by three-blade ducted propeller at tail. Rotor brake fitted.

Rotor Drive: Direct mechanical drive to both main rotor and ducted propeller, via pair of spiral bevels and a single planetary stage.

Wings: Cantilever low-wing monoplane, of aluminium alloy and honeycomb construction. Wings fold upward manually for stowage on ground. Flaperons (combined ailerons and flaps) fitted.

Fuselage: Conventional aluminium alloy and honeycomb semi-monocoque structure. Propeller duct also of aluminium alloy and honeycomb.

Landing Gear: Main units retract inward into fuselage. Electrical retraction, with mechanical emergency actuation. Non-retractable fully-castoring tailwheel. Hydraulic shock-absorbers.

Power Plant: Two 750 ehp United Aircraft of Canada PT6B-30 turboshaft engines, coupled to a common reduction gearbox.

Accommodation: Seats for nine to fifteen persons, including the pilot, with two large doors on the starboard side, one forward and one aft of the wing. The upper half of each door hinges upward and the lower half (with integral airstairs) hinges downward.

Dimensions, external:
Diameter of rotor 44 ft 2¾ in (13·49 m)
Wing aspect ratio 4·65
Length of fuselage 42 ft 9½ in (13·04 m)
Height to top of rotor hub 12 ft 3½ in (3·75 m)

Dimensions, internal:
Cabin (forward): Length 9 ft 1⅛ in (2·77 m)
Max width 4 ft 5 in (1·35 m)
Max height 4 ft 3 in (1·30 m)
Cabin (aft): Length 6 ft 6 in (1·98 m)
Max width 4 ft 5 in (1·35 m)
Max height 4 ft 3 in (1·30 m)

Areas:
Main rotor blades (each) 33 sq ft (3·07 m²)
Main rotor disc 1,520 sq ft (141·21 m²)

Weights:
Weight empty 5,955 lb (2,701 kg)
Max T-O weight (VTOL) 9,600 lb (4,354 kg)
Max T-O weight (STOL) 10,700 lb (4,853 kg)

Performance (estimated):
Max level speed 167 knots (192 mph; 309 km/h)
Range with standard fuel 434 nm (500 miles; 800 km)
Range with max fuel 738 nm (850 miles; 1,365 km)

PIASECKI 16H-1HT

This growth version of the Piasecki 16H-1 is designed around the Turboméca Astazou XVI turboshaft engine. Its airframe is generally similar to that of the 16H-3K Pathfinder III, except for a reduction in overall dimensions.

Type: Business, utility and light transport helicopter.

Rotor System: Fully-articulated three-blade main rotor. Anti-torque control by three-blade ducted propeller at tail.

Rotor Drive, Wings, Fuselage and Landing Gear: As for 16H-3K.

Power Plant: One 986 ehp Turboméca Astazou XVI turboshaft engine.

Accommodation: Seats for five persons, including pilot, with two doors on port side of fuselage, forward of the wing.

Dimensions, external:
Diameter of rotor 41 ft 0 in (12·50 m)
Length of fuselage 25 ft 0 in (7·62 m)
Height to top of rotor hub 11 ft 1 in (3·38 m)

Dimensions, internal:
Cabin: Length 9 ft 1⅛ in (2·77 m)
Max width 4 ft 5 in (1·35 m)
Max height 4 ft 3 in (1·30 m)

Areas:
Main rotor blade (each) 24·2 sq ft (2·25 m²)
Main rotor disc 1,320 sq ft (122·6 m²)

Weights:
Weight empty 3,050 lb (1,383 kg)
Max T-O weight (VTOL) 4,600 lb (2,086 kg)
Max T-O weight (STOL) 5,700 lb (2,585 kg)

Performance (estimated):
Max level speed 175 knots (202 mph; 325 km/h)
Range with standard fuel 382 nm (440 miles; 708 km)

PIPER

PIPER AIRCRAFT CORPORATION

HEAD OFFICE AND WORKS:
Lock Haven, Pennsylvania 17745

Telephone: (717) 748-6711
Telex: 8411425

OTHER WORKS:
Vero Beach, Florida
Lakeland, Florida
Piper, Pennsylvania
Renovo, Pennsylvania

BOARD OF DIRECTORS:
Lawrence R. Barnett
David F. Linowes
John J. Martin
Joseph M. Mergen
Dudley C. Phillips
William T. Piper Jr
James J. Rochlis
Nicolas M. Salgo
Herbert J. Siegel
David W. Wallace

CHAIRMAN OF THE BOARD:
Nicolas M. Salgo

PRESIDENT AND CHIEF EXECUTIVE OFFICER:
J. Lynn Helms

SENIOR VICE-PRESIDENT:
Thomas W. Gillespie Jr (Marketing and Sales)

VICE-PRESIDENTS:
Marion J. Dees Jr (Engineering)
Findley A. Estlick (General Manager, Lock Haven complex)
Walter C. Jamouneau (Product Assurance and Safety)
Dudley C. Phillips (General Counsel)
Richard B. Stockton (Finance and Administration)

CONTROLLER: Jack J. Cattoni

TREASURER: John R. Leeson

SECRETARY: John J. Martin

Piper makes annual changes to all Cherokee models, but incorporates improvements in other types as they become available. Since 1964, when the PA-28-140 Cherokee 140 superseded the PA-22-108 Colt, the entire range of Piper products has been low-wing except for the PA-18 Super Cub. All types in current production are described in detail in the following pages.

Vero Beach is responsible for the experimental development of Piper aircraft and also houses one of the company's Plastics Divisions. Lock Haven also has R & D facilities for aircraft built at Lock Haven.

Piper operates also three other plants. The first two are at Piper, Pennsylvania, where sheet metal parts are formed, and Renovo, Pennsylvania, which makes plastics components; the third is at Lakeland, Florida, where PA-31 aircraft are in production.

During the last quarter of 1973, Piper had an average of 5,050 people employed at its various locations.

Optional equipment on several current models includes a choice of four automatic flight systems. Simplest of these is the Piper-developed AutoFlite II, a solid-state system which holds the wings level and has turn-command capability for up to standard rate turns. This flight system is integrated with the pictorial turn rate indicator, which serves as the sensing element. If the Nav Tracker II is added to the AutoFlite II, it allows automatic tracking to and from Omni stations and is equipped with a two-position sensitivity switch.

Latest version of the established two-control autopilot is the Piper AutoControl III, which features positive heading lock and course selector, and is available with automatic VOR/ILS radio coupling.

A full three-control system, the Piper AltiMatic III-B1, provides course preselection and positive heading lock; altitude preselection and hold, with automatic pitch trim. It is also available with automatic VOR/ILS radio coupling. The AltiMatic III-B1 also has an independent backup autopilot system.

Most recent addition to the range of flight systems is the AltiMatic V-1F/D, an autopilot and flight director system, replacing the model V which was offered previously as an option for Aztecs, Navajos and Pressurised Navajos only. It consists of three basic panel components: a horizontal situation indicator, a steering horizon and a compact flight programmer console. The AltiMatic V-1 autopilot unit is available without the flight director unit.

The horizontal situation indicator combines directional gyro, VOR/LOC and glideslope information in a single instrument. The electrically-driven directional gyro unit is magnetically slaved. A fast-slaving function is automatic and conventional flag alarms are provided.

The steering horizon replaces the standard gyro horizon, providing normal attitude information in pictorial form. Computed information, required to direct the aircraft on its proper course, appears in the form of a command disc at each wingtip of a miniature aircraft in the gyro horizon indicator. To follow a programmed flight sequence the discs are held in alignment with the wingtips of the miniature aircraft, either by autopilot or by manual control.

The flight programmer console, which has five push-buttons, three annunciator lights and a pitch attitude control disc, can be programmed for autopilot action and/or flight director display. Once a sequence, such as an ILS approach, is initiated, logic circuits automatically execute sequential mode switching and dynamic response changes as required. Altitude is set by the pilot on the pitch attitude disc; when this is attained the disc is locked on the altitude, holding plus or minus 20 ft (6 m).

On 24 November 1971 Piper announced signature of an agreement with Chincul SA for the manufacture of a broad range of Piper products in Argentina. Chincul, a wholly-owned subsidiary of Piper's Argentine distributor, La Macarena SRL, is progressing through a series of manufacturing phases of increasing complexity, to allow the gradual assimilation of current aircraft manufacturing technology.

By 31 December 1973, Piper Aircraft had produced a total of 93,596 aircraft.

PIPER PA-18 SUPER CUB 150

There are two versions of the Super Cub 150, as follows:

Standard Super Cub 150. As described below.

De luxe Super Cub 150. As Standard model, but with addition of electric starter, generator, battery, navigation lights, sensitive altimeter, tie-down rings, control locks, parking brake and propeller spinner.

The original PA-18 with 90 hp Continental C90-12F engine received FAA Type Approval on 18 November 1949. The PA-18-150, PA-18A-150 agricultural aircraft and PA-18S and PA-18AS seaplanes were all approved on 1 October 1954.

The current international height record in Class C-1-b (aircraft with T-O weight of 500-1,000 kg) is held by Miss C. Bayley of the USA, who climbed to a height of 30,203 ft (9,206 m) in a Super Cub with 125 hp Lycoming engine, on 4 January 1951.

By mid-February 1974 more than 40,000 examples of the PA-18 Cub and its predecessors had been delivered.

TYPE: Two-seat light cabin monoplane.

WINGS: Braced high-wing monoplane, with steel tube Vee bracing struts each side. Wing section USA 35B. Thickness/chord ratio 12%. Dihedral 1°. No incidence at mean aerodynamic chord. Total washout of 3° 18′. Aluminium spars and ribs, aluminium sheet leading-edge and aileron false spar, wingtip bow of ash, with fabric covering overall and fire-resistant Duraclad plastic finish. Plain aluminium ailerons and flaps with fabric covering. No trim tabs.

FUSELAGE: Rectangular welded steel tube structure covered with fabric. Fire-resistant Duraclad plastic finish.

TAIL UNIT: Wire-braced structure of welded steel tubes and channels, covered with fabric. Fire-resistant Duraclad plastic finish. Tailplane incidence variable for trimming. Balanced rudder and elevators. No trim tabs.

LANDING GEAR: Non-retractable tailwheel type. Two side Vees and half axles hinged to cabane below fuselage. Rubber cord shock-absorption. Goodrich main-wheel tyres, size 8·00-4 four-ply, pressure 18 lb/sq in (1·27 kg/cm²). Steerable leaf-spring tailwheel by Maule (standard) or Scott (optional 8 in). Goodrich D-2-113 expanding brakes. Tandem-wheel landing gear, special 36 in (91·5 cm) low-pressure tyres, Federal skis or wheel-skis, or Edo 2000 standard or amphibious floats may be fitted.

POWER PLANT: One 150 hp Lycoming O-320 four-cylinder horizontally-opposed aircooled engine, driving a Sensenich two-blade metal fixed-pitch propeller. Steel tube engine mounting is hinged at firewall, allowing it to be swung to port for access to rear of engine. One 18 US gallon (68 litre) metal fuel tank in each wing. Total fuel capacity 36 US gallons (136 litres). Refuelling points on top of wing.

ACCOMMODATION: Enclosed cabin seating two in tandem with dual controls. Adjustable front seat. Rear seat quickly removable for cargo carrying. Heater and adjustable cool-air vent. Downward-hinged door on starboard side, and upward-hinged window above, can be opened in flight. Sliding windows on port side. Baggage compartment aft of rear seat, capacity 50 lb (22 kg).

ELECTRONICS AND EQUIPMENT: Equipment may be installed for spraying, dusting, fertilising, etc. Optional extras include Mark 12 series 360-channel VHF transceiver and 100-channel VOR/ILS nav receiver, VOA-40 VOR/ILS localiser converter-indicator, blind-flying instruments, vacuum system, 8-day clock, landing light, metallising and stainless steel control cables.

DIMENSIONS, EXTERNAL:

Wing span	35 ft 2½ in (10·73 m)
Wing chord (constant)	5 ft 3 in (1·60 m)
Wing aspect ratio	7
Length overall:	
landplane	22 ft 7 in (6·88 m)
seaplane	23 ft 11 in (7·28 m)
Height overall:	
landplane	6 ft 8½ in (2·02 m)
seaplane	10 ft 3½ in (3·14 m)
Tailplane span	10 ft 6 in (3·20 m)
Wheel track	6 ft 0½ in (1·84 m)

DIMENSION, INTERNAL:

Baggage compartment	18 cu ft (0·51 m³)

AREAS:

Wings, gross	178·5 sq ft (16·58 m²)
Ailerons (total)	18·80 sq ft (1·75 m²)
Trailing-edge flaps (total)	11·50 sq ft (1·07 m²)
Fin	4·66 sq ft (0·43 m²)
Rudder	6·76 sq ft (0·63 m²)
Tailplane	15·10 sq ft (1·40 m²)
Elevators	11·70 sq ft (1·09 m²)

WEIGHTS AND LOADINGS (N: Normal category; R: Restricted, agricultural, category):

Weight empty:	
N landplane, R	930 lb (422 kg)
N seaplane	1,190 lb (540 kg)
Max T-O and landing weight:	
N landplane	1,750 lb (794 kg)
N seaplane	1,760 lb (798 kg)
R	2,070 lb (939 kg)
Max wing loading:	
N landplane	10·0 lb/sq ft (48·8 kg/m²)
N seaplane	10·0 lb/sq ft (48·8 kg/m²)
R	11·6 lb/sq ft (56·64 kg/m²)
Max power loading:	
N landplane	11·6 lb/hp (5·26 kg/hp)
N seaplane	11·7 lb/hp (5·31 kg/hp)
R	13·8 lb/hp (6·26 kg/hp)

PERFORMANCE (at max T-O weight: N: Normal category; R: Restricted, agricultural, category):

Max never-exceed speed:	
N, R	132 knots (153 mph; 246 km/h)
Max level speed at S/L:	
N landplane	113 knots (130 mph; 208 km/h)
N seaplane	100 knots (115 mph; 185 km/h)
R	91 knots (105 mph; 169 km/h)
Max cruising speed (75% power):	
N landplane	100 knots (115 mph; 185 km/h)
N seaplane	89 knots (103 mph; 166 km/h)
R	78 knots (90 mph; 145 km/h)
Econ cruising speed:	
N landplane	91 knots (105 mph; 169 km/h)
R	78 knots (90 mph; 145 km/h)

Piper PA-18 Super Cub 150 (150 hp Lycoming O-320 engine) (*Foto Hunter*)

Stalling speed, flaps down:
N landplane 38 knots (43 mph; 69 km/h)
N seaplane 37 knots (42 mph; 67 km/h)
R 39 knots (45 mph; 73 km/h)
Max rate of climb at S/L:
N landplane 960 ft (293 m)/min
N seaplane 830 ft (253 m)/min
R 760 ft (232 m)/min
Service ceiling:
N landplane 19,000 ft (5,795 m)
N seaplane 17,500 ft (5,335 m)
R 17,000 ft (5,180 m)
Absolute ceiling:
N landplane 21,300 ft (6,492 m)
N seaplane 19,500 ft (5,943 m)
T-O run:
N landplane 200 ft (61 m)
N seaplane 700 ft (214 m)
R 300 ft (92 m)
T-O to 50 ft (15 m):
N landplane 500 ft (153 m)
N seaplane approx 990 ft (300 m)
R 950 ft (290 m)
Landing from 50 ft (15 m):
N landplane 725 ft (221 m)
N seaplane 730 ft (223 m)
R 875 ft (267 m)
Landing run:
N landplane 350 ft (107 m)
N seaplane 430 ft (131 m)
R 410 ft (125 m)
Range with max fuel and max payload:
N landplane 399 nm (460 miles; 735 km)
N seaplane 375 nm (412 miles; 663 km)
R 312 nm (360 miles; 580 km)

PIPER PA-23-250 AZTEC E

US Navy designation: U-11A

This latest version of the Aztec, announced on 20 November 1970, has the nose section extended by 1 ft (0·305 m), enlarged forward baggage compartment, provision of a shelf in the aft baggage compartment and added automatic flight capability. It is available in several different models, as follows:

Aztec E. Basic model, as described in detail below.

Custom Aztec E. As basic model, with addition of Piper TruSpeed Indicator in place of standard ASI, inertia shoulder harness for two front seats, full-flow oil filters, alternate static source and curtains, adding 11·65 lb (5·28 kg) to empty weight.

Sportsman Aztec E. As Custom model, with addition of Piper external power socket and de luxe Palm Beach interior, adding total of 22·65 lb (10·27 kg) to basic empty weight.

Professional Aztec E. As Sportsman model, with addition of electrical propeller de-icing and pneumatic de-icing boots on wings and tail, but without de luxe interior, adding a total of 60·51 lb (27·45 kg) to basic empty weight.

Turbo Aztec E. Turbocharged version, described separately.

Each of the above versions can be fitted with one of six electronics packages, as follows:

Electronic Group N 1-23. Two Narco Com 11A 360-channel VHF transceivers; Narco Nav 11 200-channel VOR/LOC receiver with converter indicator; Narco Nav 12 200-channel VOR/LOC receiver with glideslope deviation and indicator; UGR-2A glideslope receiver; T-12C ADF; AT-50A transponder; MBT-12 marker beacon receiver; KN 60C DME; CP-25B audio panel; Piper AutoControl III: Piper electric trim; Piper VOR/LOC coupler to autopilot; Piper anti-static antennae and wicks, headset, microphone, radio selector panel; adding total of 55·4 lb (25·13 kg) to basic empty weight.

Electronic Group NT 2-23. As group N 1-23, with deletion of Narco Com 11As, Nav 11 and Nav 12, KN 60C DME, CP-25B audio panel, Piper AutoControl III and microphone. Replaced by dual Narco Com 111 360-channel VHF transceivers; Nav III 200-channel VOR/LOC receiver with converter indicator, including 40 localiser channels; Nav 112 200-channel VOR/LOC receiver with converter indicator, glideslope presentation and outputs for remote 40-channel glideslope receiver; KN 65 DME, CP-125 audio panel, Piper AltiMatic III-B1 autopilot; glideslope coupler to autopilot; and Piper noise-cancelling microphone; adding 62·4 lb (28·3 kg) to basic empty weight.

Electronic Group KS 1-23. Dual King KX 170B nav/com transceivers with 720-channel com and 200-channel nav; KI 214 VOR/LOC/glideslope indicator with VOR/LOC converter and 40-channel glideslope receiver; KI 201C VOR/LOC converter indicator; KR 85 ADF; KT 76 transponder; KMA 20 audio panel; Marker beacon receiver with indicator lights; KN 60C DME; Piper AutoControl III; Piper VOR/LOC coupler to autopilot; Piper 66C microphone; Piper anti-static kit; and Piper electric trim; adding 62 lb (28 kg) to basic empty weight.

Piper PA-23-250 Aztec E six-seat cabin monoplane (two 250 hp Lycoming IO-540-C4B5 engines)

Electronic Group KS 4-23(1). As group KS 1-23, with addition of second KR 85 ADF, with 551C dual needle indicator; Sunair ASB-130 10-channel HF transceiver, with MCU-33 remote tuner and CU-110 antenna coupler; and KMA 20 audio panel replaced by KMA 20-04 panel; adding 84·7 lb (38·4 kg) to basic empty weight.

Electronic Group KTS 2-23. Dual King KX 175B nav/com transceivers with 720-channel com and 200-channel nav; dual KNI 520 VOR/LOC/glideslope indicators with VOR/LOC/R NAV/glideslope deviation, to-from indication and warning flags; dual KN 77 VOR/LOC converters; KN 73 40-channel glideslope receiver; KR 85 ADF; KT 76 transponder; KMA 20 audio panel, marker beacon receiver and indicator; KN 65 DME; Piper AltiMatic III-B1 with electric trim; Piper VOR/LOC coupler to autopilot; Piper glideslope coupler to autopilot; Piper 100T noise-cancelling microphone; and Piper anti-static kit; adding 80·5 lb (36·5 kg) to basic empty weight.

Electronic Group KTS 5-23(1). As group KTS 2-23, with addition of second KR 85 ADF, with 551C dual needle indicator; Sunair ASB-130 10-channel HF transceiver, with MCU-33 remote tuner and CU-110 antenna coupler; KMA 20 audio panel replaced by KMA 20-04 panel; and Piper 100T microphone replaced by Piper 66C microphone; adding 108·4 lb (49·2 kg) to basic empty weight.

Most items covered under model and electronic group listings are available individually and, in addition, a number of items of nav/com equipment are available as options, including the AVQ-47 weather-avoidance radar.

The Aztec received FAA Type Approval as a five-seat aircraft on 18 September 1959, and with six seats on 15 December 1961.

The prototype of a floatplane version of the Aztec was produced as a joint project by Melridge Aviation of Vancouver, Washington, and Jobmaster Company, Inc, of Seattle. Fitted with Edo 4930 floats, this aircraft can take off from calm water in 20 seconds at max T-O weight of 5,200 lb (2,360 kg). Useful load is 1,800 lb (816 kg), permitting a six-passenger load with 120 US gallons (455 litres) of fuel. To simplify docking and loading from either side, a door was designed for installation on the port side, by the pilot's seat, and is part of the conversion kit offered by Melridge Aviation to permit conversion in the field.

Twenty Aztecs were supplied to the US Navy as "off-the-shelf" utility transports, under the designation U-11A (formerly UO-1). Several South and Central American governments and armed services have also acquired Aztecs, notably the Argentine Army, which took delivery of six in 1964. The French and Spanish Air Forces have each acquired two.

More than 3,700 Aztecs have been produced.

Type: Six-seat twin-engined executive transport.

Wings: Cantilever low-wing monoplane. Wing section USA 35-B (modified). Thickness/chord ratio 14%. Dihedral 5°. Incidence 0° at root, —1° 12′ at mean chord. All-metal stressed-skin structure, with heavy stepped-down main spar, front and rear auxiliary spars, ribs, stringers and detachable wing-tips. Plain all-metal ailerons and hydraulically-actuated flaps. Optional Goodrich de-icing system.

Fuselage: Basic aluminium semi-monocoque structure with welded steel tube truss around cabin.

Tail Unit: Cantilever all-metal structure with swept fin and all-moving horizontal surfaces. Trim tab in rudder. Geared anti-servo tab in horizontal surfaces. Optional Goodrich de-icing system.

Landing Gear: Retractable tricycle type. Hydraulic retraction, with CO_2 emergency extension system. Nosewheel retracts rearward, main wheels forward. Wheel doors enclose landing gear fully when retracted. Electrol oleo shock-absorber struts. Cleveland main wheels, size 6·00-6, with size 7·00-6 8-ply type III tyres. Cleveland steerable nosewheel, size 6·00-6, with 6·00-6 4-ply type III tyre. Hydraulic disc brakes. Parking brake.

Power Plant: Two 250 hp Lycoming IO-540-C4B5 six-cylinder horizontally-opposed air-cooled engines, each driving a Hartzell HC-E2YK-2RB constant-speed fully-feathering two-blade metal propeller. Two rubber fuel cells in each wing. Total fuel capacity 144 US gallons (544 litres); 140 US gallons (530 litres) usable. Refuelling points above wings. Propeller synchroniser and electrical de-icing system optional.

Accommodation: Six persons on two pairs of adjustable individual seats and rear bench seat. Dual controls standard. Individual seat lights and controllable overhead ventilation. Southwind 35,000 BTU heater with four adjustable cool/warm air outlets and two windscreen defrosters. Heated windscreen optional. Double windows. Passenger step. Door at front of cabin on starboard side. Emergency exit at rear on port side. Centre and rear seats removable to provide space for stretcher, survey camera or up to 1,600 lb (725 kg) freight. Rear cabin bulkhead removable for stretcher and cargo loading via rear baggage door. Baggage compartments at rear of cabin and in nose, with tie-down fittings, each with capacity of 150 lb (68 kg). Baggage doors on starboard side; rear one enlarged on current aircraft, for stretcher loading. Armrests, cabin dome light, individual reading lights, coat hooks, complete soundproofing and two sun visors. Seat headrests optional. Choice of five interior trims.

Systems: Hydraulic system, pressure 1,150 lb/sq in (81 kg/cm²), for landing gear and flaps. Two 70A 14V alternators. 12V 35Ah battery. 28V electrical system optional.

Electronics and Equipment: Standard equipment includes full blind-flying instrumentation, with 3 in pictorial rate of turn indicator, artificial horizon and directional gyro (flight instruments arranged in "T" configuration), clock, gyro air filter, outside air temperature gauge, dual vacuum gauge, stall warning indicator, dual recording tachometers, oil pressure, oil temperature, cylinder head temperature and fuel quantity gauges, ammeter (with test switch), dual fuel flow and manifold pressure gauges, flap position indicator, navigation lights, glare-ban instrument lights, landing light, taxi light, white wingtip anti-collision lights, two map lights, two door-ajar indicator lights, baggage compartment courtesy lights, heated pitot tube, two quick oil drains, NACA-type anti-icing non-siphoning fuel tank vents, towbar, tie-down rings, jack pads, nose-wheel safety mirror, cabin and baggage door locks and a wide choice of three-tone exterior trims. Optional items listed under descriptions of individual models above and under electronic groups, plus altimeter and toe-brakes for co-pilot, dual tachometer and hour meter, fire extinguisher, blind-flying instrumentation for co-pilot, oxygen system with 114 cu ft (3·23 m³) bottle and six outlets, Palm Beach interior trim, Piper mixture control indicator, Piper automatic locator, propeller ice protection shields and inertia shoulder harness.

Dimensions, external:
Wing span 37 ft 2¼ in (11·34 m)
Wing chord (constant) 5 ft 7 in (1·70 m)

Wing aspect ratio 6·8
Length overall 31 ft 2¾ in (9·52 m)
Height overall 10 ft 4 in (3·15 m)
Tailplane span 12 ft 6 in (3·81 m)
Wheel track 11 ft 4 in (3·45 m)
Wheelbase 7 ft 6 in (2·29 m)
Propeller diameter 6 ft 5 in (1·96 m)
Cabin door: Height 3 ft 2 in (0·97 m)
Width 2 ft 9 in (0·84 m)
Baggage compartment door (front):
Height 1 ft 8 in (0·51 m)
Width 2 ft 6 in (0·76 m)
Baggage compartment door (rear):
Height 2 ft 6 in (0·76 m)
Width 2 ft 7 in (0·79 m)

DIMENSIONS, INTERNAL:
Baggage compartments:
front 21·3 cu ft (0·60 m³)
rear 25·4 cu ft (0·72 m³)
Max cargo space, incl baggage compartments
122 cu ft (3·45 m³)

AREAS:
Wings, gross 207·56 sq ft (19·28 m²)
Ailerons (total) 8·38 sq ft (0·77 m²)
Trailing-edge flaps (total) 16·60 sq ft (1·54 m²)
Fin 14·80 sq ft (1·37 m²)
Rudder 10·30 sq ft (0·96 m²)
Horizontal surfaces (total) 39·80 sq ft (3·70 m²)

WEIGHTS AND LOADINGS:
Weight empty (standard) 3,042 lb (1,379 kg)
Max T-O and landing weight 5,200 lb (2,360 kg)
Max wing loading 25·05 lb/sq ft (122·3 kg/m²)
Max power loading 10·4 lb/hp (4·7 kg/hp)

PERFORMANCE (at max T-O weight):
Max never-exceed speed
240 knots (277 mph; 446 km/h)
Max level speed
188 knots (216 mph; 348 km/h)
Normal cruising speed at 4,000 ft (1,220 m)
182 knots (210 mph; 338 km/h)
Intermediate cruising speed at 6,000 ft (1,830 m)
181 knots (208 mph; 335 km/h)
Econ cruising speed at 6,400 ft (1,950 m)
177 knots (204 mph; 328 km/h)
Long-range cruising speed at 10,200 ft (3,110 m)
169 knots (195 mph; 314 km/h)
Stalling speed, flaps down
59 knots (68 mph; 109 km/h)
Max rate of climb at S/L 1,490 ft (455 m)/min
Rate of climb at S/L, one engine out
240 ft (73 m)/min
Absolute ceiling 21,100 ft (6,430 m)
Absolute ceiling, one engine out
6,400 ft (1,950 m)
T-O run 820 ft (250 m)
T-O to and landing from 50 ft (15 m)
1,250 ft (380 m)
Landing run 850 ft (259 m)
Range with max fuel:
Normal cruising speed
720 nm (830 miles; 1,335 km)
Intermediate cruising speed
1,024 nm (1,080 miles; 1,738 km)
Econ cruising speed
963 nm (1,110 miles; 1,786 km)
Long-range cruising speed
1,050 nm (1,210 miles; 1,947 km)

PIPER PA-23-250 TURBO AZTEC E

The Turbo Aztec E is identical in every way with the Aztec E, described above, except that it has 250 hp Lycoming TIO-540-C1A engines, fitted with the AiResearch turbocharging system. These specially modified engines allow a turbo cruise setting at 2,400 rpm, providing a constant manifold pressure from sea level to 22,000 ft (6,700 m), and result in considerably improved performance.

Standard equipment includes a density controller to prevent inadvertent overboost of the engines at full throttle, a differential pressure controller to provide constant manifold pressure during cruising flight, and an oxygen system with 114 cu ft (3·23 m³) bottle and six outlets.

During the Summer of 1972 the Spanish Air Force took delivery of six Turbo Aztecs, which together with two Aztecs acquired earlier are used largely for instrument flight training.

WEIGHTS AND LOADINGS:
Same as for Aztec E, except:
Weight empty (standard) 3,229 lb (1,464 kg)
Max T-O and landing weight 5,200 lb (2,360 kg)

PERFORMANCE (at max T-O weight):
Same as for Aztec E, except:
Max level speed at 18,500 ft (5,639 m)
220 knots (253 mph; 407 km/h)
Turbo cruise speed at 12,000 ft (3,655 m)
196 knots (226 mph; 364 km/h)
Turbo cruise speed at 22,000 ft (6,705 m)
213 knots (245 mph; 394 km/h)
Intermediate cruise speed at 12,000 ft (3,655 m)
186 knots (214 mph; 344 km/h)
Intermediate cruise speed at 24,000 ft (7,315 m)
202 knots (233 mph; 375 km/h)
Econ cruise speed at 12,000 ft (3,655 m)
174 knots (200 mph; 322 km/h)
Econ cruise speed at 24,000 ft (7,315 m)
189 knots (218 mph; 351 km/h)
Long-range cruise speed at 12,000 ft (3,655 m)
159 knots (183 mph; 295 km/h)
Long-range cruise speed at 24,000 ft (7,315 m)
170 knots (196 mph; 315 km/h)
Max rate of climb at S/L 1,530 ft (466 m)/min
Rate of climb at S/L, one engine out
265 ft (81 m)/min
Absolute ceiling over 30,000 ft (9,145 m)
Absolute ceiling, one engine out
18,700 ft (5,700 m)
Range with max fuel:
Turbo cruise speed at 12,000 ft (3,655 m)
842 nm (970 miles (1,561 km)
Turbo cruise speed at 22,000 ft (6,705 m)
911 nm (1,050 miles; (1,689 km)
Intermediate cruise speed at 12,000 ft (3,655 m) 894 nm (1,030 miles; 1,657 km)
Intermediate cruise speed at 24,000 ft (7,315 m) 977 nm (1,125 miles; 1,810 km)
Econ cruise speed at 12,000 ft (3,655 m)
933 nm (1,075 miles; 1,730 km)
Econ cruise speed at 24,000 ft (7,315 m)
1,020 nm (1,175 miles; 1,891 km)
Long-range cruise speed at 12,000 ft (3,655 m)
1,059 nm (1,220 miles; 1,963 km)
Long-range cruise speed at 24,000 ft (7,315 m)
1,137 nm (1,310 miles; 2,108 km)

PIPER PA-24-260 COMANCHE C

The prototype Comanche first flew on 24 May 1956, and the first production aircraft on 21 October 1957. Final production versions were the Comanche C and Turbo Comanche C, described in the 1973-74 *Jane's*.

PIPER PA-25 PAWNEE D

The PA-25 Pawnee was developed by Piper's Vero Beach Development Center as a specialised agricultural aircraft for dispersal of chemical dusts and sprays. Special attention was paid to pilot safety, bearing in mind the recommendations of the Crash Injury Research Unit of Cornell Medical College. Thus, the pilot is placed high to ensure a good view, including rearward, during low flying. Extra-strong seat belt and shoulder harness are fitted, and a rounded sheet metal cushion is provided above the instrument panel to prevent the pilot's head from striking the instruments in a severe crash.

The fuselage is designed to fail progressively from the front to reduce the deceleration of the cockpit, and in ordinary low-speed crashes of the kind usually associated with crop-spraying and crop-dusting the pilot's compartment should remain substantially undamaged. The top longerons in the cockpit bay are given a slight outward bulge, so that they would fail outwards in a severe head-on crash. All heavy objects or loads are forward of the cockpit and there is a 10 in (0·25 m) space between the metal floor and the bottom of the fuselage to provide additional safety in a relatively flat crash.

The initial production version of the Pawnee had a 150 hp Lycoming engine, but production is now concentrated on the 235 hp or 260 hp Pawnee D, to which the detailed description applies.

The D was introduced in 1973, with a number of improved features, including wing fuel tanks replacing the rubberised fuselage fuel cell of the Pawnee C, and introducing an engine bay fire extinguisher as standard equipment. The entire top of the fuselage from the cockpit to the fin can be removed in 60 seconds to provide easy access for inspection and cleaning. A high-capacity cockpit ventilation system is installed. Ventilating air taken in through an intake in the top of the canopy is used also to lightly pressurise the rear fuselage to keep out dust and chemicals. The engine installation is modified to permit efficient operation under the most severe hot weather conditions. The landing gear is fitted with oleo-pneumatic shock-absorbers. An adjustable pilot's seat is installed and there is a safety exit on each side of the cockpit.

The first five production Pawnees were delivered in August 1959, with subsequent aircraft leaving the assembly line at the rate of one a day, later increased to two a day. A total of 4,258 PA-25 Pawnees had been produced by 31 December 1973.

TYPE: Single-seat agricultural monoplane.

WINGS: Braced low-wing monoplane, based on wings of Super Cub. Streamlined Vee bracing struts on each side of fuselage, with additional short support struts. Wing section USA 35B (modified). Thickness/chord ratio 12%. Dihedral 7°. Incidence 1° 18′ at mean aerodynamic chord. Wings, ailerons and flaps are all of fabric-covered aluminium construction, with fire-resistant Duraclad plastic finish. No trim tabs.

FUSELAGE: Basically rectangular-section welded steel tube structure, with fabric covering and Duraclad plastic finish, except for removable metal underskin and removable metal top of rear fuselage. Glassfibre engine cowling.

TAIL UNIT: Wire-braced steel tube structure with fabric covering and Duraclad plastic finish. Fixed-incidence tailplane. Balanced rudder and elevators. No trim tabs. Cable from top of cockpit to top of rudder to deflect wires and cables.

LANDING GEAR: Non-retractable tailwheel type. Oleo-pneumatic shock-absorbers. Main gear has two side Vees and half-axles hinged to centreline of underside of fuselage. Cleveland 40-61 main wheels, with 8·00-6 4-ply tyres, pressure 25 lb/sq in (1·76 kg/cm²). Cleveland type 30-41 toe-actuated hydraulic brakes. Parking brake. Wire-cutters on leading-edge of each side Vee. Scott 8 in (20 cm) steerable tailwheel, tyre pressure 50 lb/sq in (3·52 kg/cm²).

POWER PLANT: One 235 hp (derated) Lycoming O-540-B2B5 six-cylinder horizontally-opposed aircooled engine, driving a McCauley Type 1A200/FA84 two-blade metal fixed-pitch propeller. Optionally, one 260 hp Lycoming O-540-E engine, with two-blade fixed-pitch propeller or optional constant-speed propeller. Fuel tank in each wing, capacity 18 US gallons (68 litres). Total capacity 36 US gallons (136 litres). Oil capacity 3 US gallons (11·4 litres).

ACCOMMODATION: Pilot on adjustable seat in specially-strengthened enclosed cockpit, with steel tube overturn structure. Heavy-duty safety belt and shoulder harness with inertia reel. Wire-cutter mounted on centre of windscreen. Combined window and door on each side, hinged at bottom. Window assemblies jettisonable for emergency exit. Cabin is heated and ventilated. Adjustable cool air vents. Air-conditioning unit optional. A jump-seat can be fitted in the hopper to transport a mechanic or loader between operations. Utility compartment under seat.

SYSTEMS: Electrical system includes 37A alternator and 12V 25Ah battery.

ELECTRONICS AND EQUIPMENT: Standard equipment includes a non-corrosive hopper/tank, installed forward of cockpit and approximately on CG. Volume is 21 cu ft (0·59 m³) or 150 US gallons (568 litres), with capacity for 1,200 lb (544 kg) of dust; quick-change boom brackets, quick-drain gascolator, quick-drain oil sump, quick-dump valve to jettison hopper contents in emergency, quick-release hinge pins in side windows, tie-down rings, top-deck loading door. Spray system uses similar 1 in Simplex centrifugal pump to that on PA-18-A, with spraybars. The venturi distributor used for dry chemicals gives a total effective swath width of up to 60 ft (18·3 m). Changeover from dust to spray, and *vice versa*, takes less than five minutes. Optional side loading nozzle for liquid chemicals. Engine bay fire extinguisher standard. Optional equipment includes Mark 12 Omni-navigation radio with localiser, plus Omni antenna and whip, headphone and microphone, transistorised power supply, full-flow oil filter, control lock, hand fire extinguisher, landing lights, navigation lights, rotating beacon, electric turn and bank indicator and metallisation.

DIMENSIONS, EXTERNAL:
Wing span 36 ft 2 in (11·02 m)
Wing chord (constant) 5 ft 3 in (1·60 m)
Wing aspect ratio 7·15
Length overall 24 ft 8½ in (7·53 m)
Height overall 7 ft 2 in (2·18 m)
Tailplane span 9 ft 6 in (2·90 m)
Wheel track 7 ft 0 in (2·13 m)
Wheelbase 18 ft 1¼ in (5·52 m)
Propeller diameter 7 ft 0 in (2·13 m)

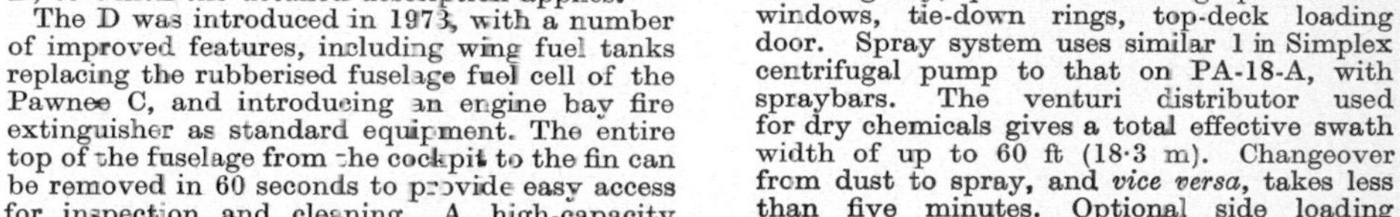

Piper Pawnee agricultural aircraft (235 hp Lycoming O-540-B2B5 engine) (*Air Portraits*)

AREAS:
Wings, gross 183 sq ft (17·0 m²)
Ailerons (total) 19·2 sq ft (1·78 m²)
Trailing-edge flaps (total) 8·4 sq ft (0·78 m²)
Fin 3·8 sq ft (0·35 m²)
Rudder 6·9 sq ft (0·64 m²)
Tailplane 13·0 sq ft (1·21 m²)
Elevators 13·7 sq ft (1·27 m²)

WEIGHTS AND LOADINGS (A: 235 hp engine; B: 260 hp engine, fixed-pitch propeller; C: 260 hp engine, constant-speed propeller):
Weight empty:
A no dispersal equipment 1,420 lb (644 kg)
B no dispersal equipment 1,472 lb (668 kg)
C no dispersal equipment 1,488 lb (675 kg)
A duster 1,479 lb (671 kg)
B duster 1,531 lb (694 kg)
C duster 1,547 lb (702 kg)
A sprayer 1,488 lb (675 kg)
B sprayer 1,540 lb (698 kg)
C sprayer 1,556 lb (706 kg)
Max T-O and landing weight 2,900 lb (1,315 kg)
Max wing loading 15·8 lb/sq ft (77·15 kg/m²)
Max power loading 12·3 lb/hp (5·58 kg/hp)

PERFORMANCE (at max T-O weight, except where indicated):
Max never-exceed speed
135 knots (156 mph; 251 km/h)
Max level speed at S/L:
A no dispersal equipment
108 knots (124 mph; 200 km/h)
B, C no dispersal equipment
111 knots (128 mph; 206 km/h)
A duster 96 knots (110 mph; 177 km/h)
B, C duster 98 knots (113 mph; 182 km/h)
A sprayer 102 knots (117 mph; 188 km/h)
B, C sprayer 104 knots (120 mph; 193 km/h)
Max cruising speed (75% power):
A no dispersal equipment
99 knots (114 mph; 183 km/h)
B no dispersal equipment
100 knots (115 mph; 185 km/h)
C no dispersal equipment
101 knots (116 mph; 187 km/h)
A, B, C duster
87 knots (100 mph; 161 km/h)
A sprayer 91 knots (105 mph; 169 km/h)
B, C sprayer 92 knots (106 mph; 171 km/h)
Stalling speed, flaps down
53 knots (61 mph; 98 km/h)
Stalling speed at normal landing weight of 1,700 lb (771 kg) 40 knots (46 mph; 74 km/h)
Max rate of climb at S/L:
A no dispersal equipment 700 ft (213 m)/min
B no dispersal equipment 755 ft (230 m)/min
C no dispersal equipment 775 ft (236 m)/min
A duster 500 ft (152 m)/min
B duster 555 ft (169 m)/min
C duster 575 ft (175 m)/min
A sprayer 630 ft (192 m)/min
B sprayer 685 ft (209 m)/min
C sprayer 705 ft (215 m)/min
T-O run:
A no dispersal equipment 785 ft (239 m)
B no dispersal equipment 730 ft (223 m)
C no dispersal equipment 660 ft (201 m)
A duster 956 ft (291 m)
B duster 890 ft (271 m)
C duster 830 ft (253 m)
A sprayer 800 ft (244 m)
B sprayer 740 ft (226 m)
C sprayer 680 ft (207 m)
T-O to 50 ft (15 m):
A no dispersal equipment 1,350 ft (411 m)
B no dispersal equipment 1,250 ft (381 m)
C no dispersal equipment 1,200 ft (366 m)
A duster 1,470 ft (428 m)
B duster 1,420 ft (433 m)
C duster 1,370 ft (418 m)
A sprayer 1,370 ft (418 m)
B sprayer 1,270 ft (387 m)
C sprayer 1,220 ft (372 m)
Max landing run 850 ft (259 m)
Range (75% power) with max fuel:
A no dispersal equipment
251 nm (290 miles; 467 km)
B no dispersal equipment
247 nm (285 miles; 459 km)
C no dispersal equipment
251 nm (290 miles; 467 km)
A duster 221 nm (255 miles; 410 km)
B, C duster 199 nm (230 miles; 370 km)
A sprayer 234 nm (270 miles; 434 km)
B, C sprayer 230 nm (265 miles; 426 km)

PIPER PA-28 CHEROKEE SERIES

The Cherokee is a low-cost all-metal low-wing monoplane which is available in 2/4-, 4- and 6/7-seat versions. All except the Cherokee Arrow II have a non-retractable tricycle landing gear. The Cherokee Arrow II gear is retractable.

Only 1,200 parts go into the manufacture of a Cherokee, compared with over 1,600 in the four-seat high-wing Tri-Pacer, which preceded it. The first production Cherokee flew on 10 February 1961.

Models currently available are the Cherokee Cruiser and Flite Liner (2/4-seat), Cherokee Archer and Pathfinder (4-seat), Cherokee SIX (6/7-seat), Cherokee Arrow II (4-seat, retractable landing gear), and the new Cherokee Warrior (4-seat) which was certificated in August 1973. By the beginning of 1974 Piper had delivered a total of 23,169 Cherokees of all versions.

Descriptions of all current versions follow:

Piper Cherokee Flite Liner sporting and training aircraft (150 hp Lycoming O-320 engine)

CHEROKEE CRUISER

Piper introduced in 1972 a de luxe version of the Cherokee 140 which was named the Cherokee Cruiser 2 plus 2 and had as standard two easily-removable rear family seats and other refinements. In 1973 this became the standard production model, replacing the Cherokee 140, which was described in the 1972-73 *Jane's*. For 1974 it has been renamed the Cherokee Cruiser. The two rear family seats, with seat-belts, two additional cabin fresh air vents, de luxe baggage compartment and hatshelf now form an optional Family Group, adding 27 lb (12·25 kg) to the basic empty weight.

The 1974 version of the Cruiser introduces as standard improved nosewheel steering, with 30° movement to each side; improved window styling and cabin headliners; new interior and exterior styling; more effective brakes with a high capacity toe-operated disc brake system, and a refined cabin ventilation system.

Two groups of optional equipment are available for the Cruiser as basic packages:

Custom. Comprises Piper Truspeed indicator; instrument panel, overhead red spotlight, cabin dome, navigation, landing/taxi, and radio dimming lights; wheel speed fairings; rotating beacon; radio shielding; sensitive altimeter; assist strap and coat hook; aircraft step; full flow oil filter; and shoulder safety belts with inertia reels for front seats; adding 24 lb (11 kg) to basic empty weight.

Executive. As Custom package, plus vacuum system with engine-driven pump and advanced instrument panel comprising 3 in pictorial gyro horizon, 3 in directional gyro, Piper pictorial turn rate indicator, rate of climb indicator, outside air temperature gauge and eight-day clock; adding 40 lb (18 kg) to basic empty weight.

The Cherokee Cruiser can be fitted with one of six electronics packages as follows:

Electronic Group N 1-28/32. Narco Com 11A 360-channel VHF transceiver; Nav 11 200-channel VOR/LOC receiver with converter indicator; T-12C ADF; Piper AutoFlite II autopilot; VOR/LOC coupler to Nav tracker and Piper 66C microphone; adding 27 lb (12 kg) to basic empty weight.

Electronic Group N 2-28/32. Dual Narco Com 11A 360-channel VHF transceivers; dual Nav 11 200-channel VOR/LOC receivers with converter indicators; MBT-12 marker beacon receiver and indicator lights; CP-25B audio panel; T-12C ADF; AT-50A transponder; Piper AutoControl III autopilot; Piper VOR/LOC coupler; Piper electric trim; Piper 66C microphone; Piper static discharge wicks; and two Piper broad band com antennae; adding 51 lb (23 kg) to basic empty weight.

Electronic Group NT 3-28/32. As group N 2-28/32, except dual Com 11As replaced by dual Com 111 360-channel VHF transceivers; dual Nav 11s replaced by one Nav 111 200-channel VOR/LOC receiver with converter indicator, including 40 localiser channels, and one Nav 112 200-channel VOR/LOC receiver with converter indicator, including UGR-2A glideslope receiver; CP-25B replaced by CP-125B audio panel; and Piper 66C microphone replaced by Piper 100T noise cancelling microphone; adding 56 lb (25·5 kg) to basic empty weight.

Electronic Group KS 1-28/32. King KX 170B 720-channel com transceiver, with 200-channel nav receiver; KI 201C VOR/LOC indicator; KR 85 ADF; Piper AutoFlite II autopilot; VOR/LOC coupler to Nav tracker; and Piper 66C microphone; adding 31 lb (14 kg) to basic empty weight.

Electronic Group KS 2-28/32. Dual KX 170B 720-channel com transceivers, with 200-channel nav receivers: dual KI 201C VOR/LOC converter indicators; KMA 20 audio panel with marker beacon receiver and indicator lights; KR 85 ADF; KT 78 transponder; Piper AutoControl III autopilot; Piper VOR/LOC coupler; Piper electric trim; Piper static wicks; dual Piper broad band com antennae; and Piper 66C microphone; adding 60 lb (27 kg) to basic empty weight.

Electronic Group KTS 3-28/32. Dual KX 175B nav/com transceivers, with 720-channel com transceivers and 200-channel nav receivers; KNI 520 VOR/LOC/glideslope indicator with to-from indication and appropriate warning flags; KNI 520 VOR/LOC indicator; dual KN 77 VOR/LOC converters; KN 73 glideslope receiver; KR 85 ADF; KT 76 transponder; Piper AutoControl III autopilot; Piper VOR/LOC coupler; Piper electric trim; Piper static wicks; dual Piper broad band com antennae; and Piper 100T noise cancelling microphone; adding 68 lb (31 kg) to basic empty weight.

The structural description of the Cherokee Archer (page 422) applies also to the Cherokee Cruiser, except for the following details:

TYPE: Two/four-seat sporting and training light aircraft.

POWER PLANT: One 150 hp Lycoming O-320 four-cylinder horizontally-opposed aircooled engine, driving a two-blade fixed-pitch metal propeller. Two fuel tanks in wing leading-edges, with total capacity of 50 US gallons (189 litres), of which 48 US gallons (181·5 litres) are usable. Standard fuel capacity of 36 US gallons (136 litres), of which 34 US gallons (128·5 litres) are usable, the remaining tankage for 14 US gallons (53 litres) being regarded as a reserve.

ACCOMMODATION: Two reclinable individual front seats side by side in enclosed cabin, with dual controls. Adjustable seats, which raise, lower and tilt, are available optionally. Two optional full-size family seats in rear of cabin, which are easily removable to accommodate up to 200 lb (90 kg) of freight or baggage. Inertia-reel shoulder harness is standard for the two front seats, optional for rear seats. Door on starboard side. Cabin heated and ventilated.

EQUIPMENT: The following items of optional equipment are available: Piper Aire air-conditioning system, alternate static source, super soundproofing, Piper automatic locator, ventilation fan for overhead vent system, fire extinguisher, 35Ah battery, external power socket, heated pitot tube, adjustable front seats, headrests, solar control windows, red tail and white wingtip strobe lights, zinc chromate application, Copon treatment and stainless steel control cables.

DIMENSIONS AND AREAS:
Same as for Cherokee Archer, except:
Length overall 23 ft 3½ in (7·10 m)
Propeller diameter 6 ft 2 in (1·88 m)

WEIGHTS AND LOADINGS:
Weight empty 1,274 lb (578 kg)
Max T-O weight 2,150 lb (975 kg)
Max wing loading 13·4 lb/sq ft (65·5 kg/m²)
Max power loading 14·3 lb/hp (6·50 kg/hp)

PERFORMANCE:
*Max level speed at S/L
123 knots (142 mph; 229 km/h)
*Max cruising speed (75% power) at 7,000 ft (2,130 m) 117 knots (135 mph; 217 km/h)
Econ cruising speed (60% power) at 4,000 ft (1,220 m) 100 knots (115 mph; 185 km/h)
Stalling speed, flaps down
48 knots (55 mph; 89 km/h)
Max rate of climb at S/L 631 ft (192 m)/min
Service ceiling 10,950 ft (3,340 m)

Absolute ceiling 13,000 ft (3,960 m)
T-O run 800 ft (244 m)
Landing run 535 ft (163 m)
Range, 75% power at optimum altitude, standard fuel, no reserve
443 nm (510 miles; 820 km)
Range, 75% power at optimum altitude, max fuel, no reserve
625 nm (720 miles; 1,158 km)
**With optional speed fairings*

PIPER CHEROKEE FLITE LINER

The Cherokee Flite Liner is basically similar to the Cherokee Cruiser, but has the following equipment and avionics as standard: vacuum system with engine-driven pump; advanced instrument panel with 3 in pictorial gyro horizon, 3 in directional gyro, Piper pictorial turn rate indicator; rate of climb indicator and sensitive altimeter; interior, navigation and landing lights; rotating beacon; shoulder safety belts with inertia reels; entrance step; radio shielding; radio dimming; Com 10A/Nav 10 360-channel transceiver, with Nav/Com selector switch covering 200 VOR/LOC frequencies and separate VOR/LOC converter indicator; headset, antenna, speaker and noise cancelling microphone.

Optional electronic groups and equipment available for the Cherokee Cruiser are obtainable also for the Flite Liner.

The description of the Cherokee Cruiser applies also to the Flite Liner, except as follows:

WEIGHT:
Weight empty 1,305 lb (592 kg)

PERFORMANCE (A: at max T-O weight; B: at Instructional Cruise Performance based on 1,800 lb; 816 kg operating weight):
Max level speed:
A 121 knots (139 mph; 224 km/h)
B 123 knots (142 mph; 229 km/h)
Optimum cruising speed at 75% power:
A 115 knots (132 mph; 212 km/h)
Cruising speed, instructional, 60% power:
B at 7,000 ft (2,135 m)
102 knots (118 mph; 190 km/h)
B at 11,000 ft (3,355 m)
107 knots (123 mph; 198 km/h)
Stalling speed, flaps down:
A 48 knots (55 mph; 89 km/h)
B 43·5 knots (50 mph; 81 km/h)
Max rate of climb at S/L:
A 630 ft (192 m)/min
B 880 ft (268 m)/min
Service ceiling:
A 10,950 ft (3,335 m)
B 14,100 ft (4,300 m)
Absolute ceiling:
A 13,000 ft (3,960 m)
B 15,900 ft (4,845 m)
T-O run:
A 800 ft (244 m)
B 675 ft (206 m)
Landing run:
A 535 ft (163 m)
B 450 ft (137 m)
Range at 75% power at optimum altitude, standard fuel, no reserve:
A 430 nm (495 miles; 796 km)
Range, conditions as above, with max fuel:
A 612 nm (705 miles; 1,134 km)
Range at 60% power at 6,000 ft (1,830 m) with 25 US gallons (94·5 litres) fuel:
B 375 nm (432 miles; 695 km)
Range, conditions as above, with 50 US gallons (189 litres) fuel:
B 750 nm (864 miles; 1,390 km)

PIPER PA-28-151 CHEROKEE WARRIOR

Piper Aircraft announced on 26 October 1973 the introduction of a new 150 hp four-seat model in the Cherokee series for 1974. Named the Cherokee Warrior, it combines the stretched fuselage of the Cherokee Archer with a completely new wing.

Two groups of optional equipment are available for the Warrior as basic packages:

Custom. Comprises Piper Truspeed indicator; instrument panel, overhead red spotlight, cabin dome, navigation, landing/taxi, and radio dimming lights; wheel speed fairings; rotating beacon; radio shielding; sensitive altimeter; assist strap and coat hook; aircraft step; full flow oil filter; inertia-reel shoulder safety belts for front seats; engine primer system; and cabin speaker; adding 26 lb (12 kg) to basic empty weight.

Executive. As Custom package, plus vacuum system with engine-driven pump; and advanced instrument panel comprising 3 in pictorial gyro horizon, 3 in directional gyro, Piper pictorial turn rate indicator, rate of climb indicator, outside air temperature gauge and eight-day clock; adding 42 lb (19 kg) to basic empty weight.

In addition, the six optional electronics groups as detailed for the Cherokee Cruiser are available also for this new addition to the Cherokee family.

Intended from the outset to be highly competitive in the US light aircraft market, both in terms of cost and performance, the PA-28-151 represents a departure from the traditional constant-chord Piper wing. Design of the aircraft began in June 1972, and an important feature is the increased-span tapered wing. As a result of its introduction the Warrior, which has essentially the same 150 hp engine as the Cruiser and Flite Liner, is certificated at a maximum T-O weight 175 lb (79 kg) greater.

First flight of a prototype was made on 17 October 1972, and FAA certification was granted on 9 August 1973. A total of 99 Cherokee Warriors had been sold by 31 December 1973.

TYPE: Four-seat cabin monoplane.

WINGS: Cantilever low-wing monoplane. Wing section NACA 65_2-415 on inboard panels; outboard leading-edge modified with modification No. 5 of NACA TN 2228. Dihedral 7°. Incidence 2° at root, —1° at tip. Sweepback at quarter-chord 5°. Light alloy single-spar structure with glassfibre wingtips. Frise type ailerons of light alloy construction. Trailing-edge flaps constructed of light alloy with ribbed skins.

FUSELAGE: Light alloy semi-monocoque structure with glassfibre nose cowl and tailcone.

TAIL UNIT: Cantilever structure of light alloy, except for glassfibre tips on fin and tailplane. Fin and rudder have ribbed light alloy skins. One-piece all-moving tailplane, with combined anti-servo and trim tab. Rudder trimmable, but no trim tab in rudder.

LANDING GEAR: Non-retractable tricycle type. Steerable nosewheel. Piper oleo-pneumatic shock-struts with single wheel on each unit. Cleveland wheels with tyres size 17·50 × 6·30-6 on main units, pressure 24 lb/sq in (1·69 kg/cm²). Cleveland nosewheel and tyre size 14·20 × 4·95-5, pressure 24 lb/sq in (1·69 kg/cm²). Cleveland disc brakes. Parking brake. Wheel fairings optional.

POWER PLANT: One 150 hp Lycoming O-320-E3D four-cylinder horizontally-opposed aircooled engine, driving a Sensenich two-blade metal fixed-pitch propeller type 74DM6-O-58. Fuel in two wing tanks, with total capacity of 50 US gallons (189 litres). Refuelling point on upper surface of each wing. Oil capacity 2 US gallons (7·5 litres).

ACCOMMODATION: Four persons in pairs in enclosed cabin. Individual adjustable front seats, bench type rear seat. Dual controls standard. Large door on starboard side. Baggage compartment at rear of cabin, with volume of 24 cu ft (0·68 m³) and capacity of 200 lb (90 kg). External access door on starboard side. Heating, ventilation and windscreen defrosting standard.

SYSTEMS: Hydraulic system for brakes only. Electrical system powered by 60A engine-driven alternator. 12V 24Ah battery standard, 12V 35Ah battery optional. Vacuum system for blind-flying instrumentation optional.

ELECTRONICS: King and Narco avionics in optional groups detailed in entry on Cherokee Cruiser, or an extensive range of King, Narco, Bendix and Piper avionics.

DIMENSIONS, EXTERNAL:
Wing span 35 ft 0 in (10·67 m)
Wing chord at root 6 ft 2 in (1·88 m)
Wing chord at tip 3 ft 6¼ in (1·07 m)
Wing aspect ratio 7·24

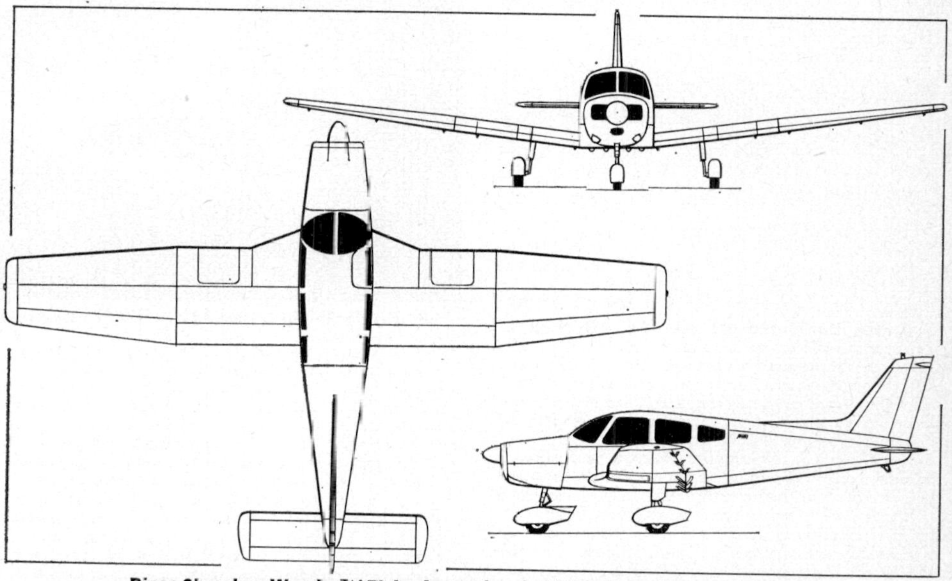

Piper Cherokee Warrior (150 hp Lycoming O-320-E3D engine) (*Pilot Press*)

Overhead view of the Piper Cherokee Warrior highlights the new wing shape

Length overall	23 ft 9¼ in (7·25 m)
Height overall	7 ft 3½ in (2·22 m)
Tailplane span	12 ft 10½ in (3·92 m)
Wheel track	10 ft 0 in (3·05 m)
Wheelbase	6 ft 8 in (2·03 m)
Propeller diameter	6 ft 2 in (1·88 m)
Propeller ground clearance	8¼ in (0·21 m)
Cabin door: Height	2 ft 11 in (0·89 m)
Width	3 ft 3 in (0·99 m)
Baggage door: Height	1 ft 7 in (0·48 m)
Max width	2 ft 2 in (0·66 m)
Height to sill	2 ft 4 in (0·71 m)
DIMENSIONS, INTERNAL:	
Cabin: Length	9 ft 0 in (2·74 m)
Max width	3 ft 6 in (1·07 m)
Max height	4 ft 0 in (1·22 m)
Floor area	24·5 sq ft (2·28 m²)
Volume	92 cu ft (2·61 m³)
AREAS:	
Wings, gross	170 sq ft (15·8 m²)
Ailerons (total)	13·2 sq ft (1·23 m²)
Trailing-edge flaps (total)	14·6 sq ft (1·36 m²)
Fin	7·4 sq ft (0·69 m²)
Rudder	4·1 sq ft (0·38 m²)
Tailplane, incl tab	26·5 sq ft (2·46 m²)
WEIGHTS AND LOADINGS:	
Weight empty, standard	1,301 lb (590 kg)
Max T-O and landing weight	2,325 lb (1,054 kg)
Max wing loading	13·67 lb/sq ft (66·74 kg/m²)
Max power loading	15·5 lb/hp (7·03 kg/hp)
PERFORMANCE (at max T-O weight):	
Max never-exceed speed	152 knots (176 mph; 283 km/h)
Max level and cruising speed at S/L	117 knots (135 mph; 217 km/h)
Econ cruising speed at optimum altitude	115 knots (133 mph; 214 km/h)
Stalling speed, flaps up	56 knots (64·5 mph; 104 km/h)
Stalling speed, flaps down	50·5 knots (58 mph; 94 km/h)
Max rate of climb at S/L	649 ft (198 m)/min
Service ceiling	12,700 ft (3,870 m)
T-O run	1,060 ft (323 m)
T-O to 50 ft (15 m)	1,760 ft (536 m)
Landing from 50 ft (15 m)	1,115 ft (340 m)
Landing run	595 ft (181 m)
Range with max fuel at 75% power	625 nm (720 miles; 1,158 km)

Piper Cherokee Archer four-seat light aircraft (180 hp Lycoming O-360-A3A engine)

Piper PA-28-200 Cherokee Arrow II with retractable landing gear (200 hp Lycoming IO-360-C1C engine)

PIPER PA-28-180 CHEROKEE ARCHER

On 9 October 1972 Piper introduced the Cherokee Challenger as successor to the Cherokee 180. For 1974 this has been superseded by the Cherokee Archer, with the same basic airframe and power plant, but introducing many new equipment and avionics options.

The Cherokee Challenger had a lengthened fuselage to provide more cabin space; an increase of 2 ft 0 in (1·61 m) in wing span; new glassfibre wingtips to improve aerodynamic efficiency without increasing drag; and a larger all-moving horizontal tail surface to compensate for the increase in fuselage length. Wing area increased by six per cent as a result of the greater span, and this allowed an increase in the useful load. The baggage compartment, aft of the cabin, had a volume of 24 cu ft (0·68 m³).

The 1974 Cherokee Archer has the same improvements detailed for the 1974 version of the Cherokee Cruiser. It introduces also the same optional Custom and Executive equipment packages, as well as the six optional electronics packages.

TYPE: **Four-seat cabin monoplane.**

WINGS: **Cantilever low-wing monoplane. Wing section NACA 65_2-415. Dihedral 7°. Incidence 2°. Single-spar wings, plain ailerons and slotted flaps made of aluminium alloy, except for glassfibre wingtips. Ailerons and four-position flaps have corrugated skin. Ground-adjustable tab in port aileron.**

FUSELAGE: **Aluminium alloy semi-monocoque structure. Glassfibre engine cowling.**

TAIL UNIT: Cantilever structure of aluminium alloy, except for glassfibre tips on fin and tailplane. **Fin and rudder have corrugated metal skin. One-piece all-moving horizontal surface with combined anti-balance and trim tab.** Trim tab in rudder.

LANDING GEAR: Non-retractable tricycle type. Steerable nosewheel. Piper oleo-pneumatic **shock-absorbers. Cleveland wheels and Schen**uit tyres, size 6·00-6, 4-ply rating, on all three wheels. Cleveland disc brakes. Parking brake.

POWER PLANT: One 180 hp Lycoming O-360-A3A four-cylinder horizontally-opposed aircooled engine, driving a Sensenich two-blade fixed-pitch propeller with spinner. Fuel in two tanks in wing leading-edges, with total capacity of 50 US gallons (189 litres), of which 48 US gallons (181·5 litres) are usable.

ACCOMMODATION: **Four persons in pairs in enclosed cabin. Individual adjustable front seats, with dual controls; individual rear seats. Large door on starboard side. Heater and** ventilation. Windscreen defrosting. Baggage compartment aft of cabin, with volume of 20 cu ft (0·57 m³) and capacity of 200 lb (90 kg); door on starboard side. **Rear seats removable to provide 44 cu ft (1·25 m³) cargo space.** Provision for carrying stretcher.

SYSTEMS: Optional Piper Aire air-conditioning system. Electrical system includes 60A alternator and 12V 25Ah battery. Hydraulic system for brakes only. Vacuum system optional.

ELECTRONICS AND EQUIPMENT: Details of electronics under group listings for the Cherokee Cruiser. Standard equipment includes external tie-down points, wing jack points and Piper automatic locator. Optional equipment available includes fire extinguisher, 35Ah battery, external power socket, inertia-reel shoulder harness for rear seats, adjustable front seats, alternate static source, overhead vent system, ventilation fan for air vent system, super soundproofing, outside air temperature gauge, heated pitot, Piper mixture control indicator, headrests, solar control windows, red tail and white wingtip strobe lights, zinc chromate application, Copon treatment and stainless steel control cables.

DIMENSIONS, EXTERNAL:	
Wing span	32 ft 0 in (9·75 m)
Wing chord (constant)	5 ft 3 in (1·60 m)
Length overall	24 ft 0 in (7·32 m)
Height overall	7 ft 9¾ in (2·38 m)
Tailplane span	10 ft 0 in (3·05 m)
Wheel track	10 ft 0 in (3·05 m)
Wheelbase	6 ft 8½ in (2·04 m)
Propeller diameter	6 ft 4 in (1·93 m)
AREAS:	
Wings, gross	170 sq ft (15·79 m²)
Ailerons (total)	10·60 sq ft (0·99 m²)
Trailing-edge flaps (total)	14·60 sq ft (1·36 m²)
Fin	7·50 sq ft (0·70 m²)
Rudder	4·10 sq ft (0·38 m²)
Tailplane	26·5 sq ft (2·46 m²)
WEIGHTS AND LOADINGS:	
Weight empty, equipped (standard)	1,390 lb (630 kg)
Max T-O weight	2,450 lb (1,110 kg)
Max wing loading	14·4 lb/sq ft (70·3 kg/m²)
Max power loading	13·6 lb/hp (6·12 kg/hp)
PERFORMANCE (at max T-O weight):	
Max level speed at S/L	129 knots (148 mph; 238 km/h)
Max cruising speed, 75% power at 7,000 ft (2,130 m)	122 knots (141 mph; 227 km/h)
Stalling speed, flaps down	53 knots (61 mph; 98 km/h)
Max rate of climb at S/L	725 ft (221 m)/min
Service ceiling	14,150 ft (4,315 m)
Absolute ceiling	16,500 ft (5,030 m)
T-O run	720 ft (219 m)
T-O to 50 ft (15 m)	1,625 ft (495 m)
Landing from 50 ft (15 m)	1,185 ft (361 m)
Landing run	635 ft (194 m)
Range, 75% power at optimum altitude with max fuel	616 nm (710 miles; 1,142 km)
Range, 65% power at optimum altitude with max fuel	651 nm (750 miles; 1,207 km)

PIPER PA-28-200 CHEROKEE ARROW II

The Cherokee Arrow II is basically similar to the Cherokee Archer, but differs by having retractable landing gear.

The tricycle landing gear is retracted hydraulically, with an electrically-operated pump supplying the hydraulic pressure. In addition to the usual "gear up" warning horn and red light, the Cherokee Arrow has an automatic extension system which drops the landing gear automatically if power is reduced and airspeed drops below 91 knots (105 mph; 169 km/h). The sensing system consists of a small probe mounted on the port side of the fuselage. Being located in the propeller slipstream, it can differentiate between a climb with power on and an approach to land with power reduced. A free-fall emergency extension system is also fitted. An "anti-retraction" system guards against premature retraction of the landing gear below an airspeed of 74 knots (85 mph; 137 km/h) at take-off, or accidental retraction on the ground. There is also a manual override lever by which the pilot can hold the landing gear retracted as airspeed falls below 91 knots (105 mph; 169 km/h).

The 1974 version of the Cherokee Arrow II introduces the same improvements listed for the Cherokee Cruiser, and the optional equipment and avionics packages listed for the Cruiser are available for the Arrow II.

The description of the Cherokee Archer applies also to the Cherokee Arrow II, except for the following details:

LANDING GEAR: **Retractable tricycle type, with single wheel on each unit. Hydraulic retraction, main units inward into wings, nose unit rearward. All units fitted with oleo-pneumatic shock-absorbers. Main wheels and tyres size** 6·00 - 6, four-ply rating. Nosewheel and tyre size 5·00 - 5, four-ply rating. High-capacity dual hydraulic brakes and parking brake.

POWER PLANT: One 200 hp Lycoming IO-360-C1C four-cylinder horizontally-opposed air-cooled engine, driving a two-blade constant-speed propeller with spinner. Fuel system as for Cherokee Archer.

DIMENSIONS, EXTERNAL:	
Wing span	32 ft 0 in (9·75 m)
Length overall	24 ft 7½ in (7·50 m)
Height overall	8 ft 0 in (2·44 m)
Wheel track	10 ft 6 in (3·20 m)
Wheelbase	7 ft 9½ in (2·37 m)
Propeller diameter	6 ft 2 in (1·88 m)
AREA:	
Wings, gross	170 sq ft (15·79 m²)
WEIGHTS AND LOADINGS:	
Weight empty	1,517 lb (688 kg)
Max T-O weight	2,650 lb (1,202 kg)
Max wing loading	15·6 lb/sq ft (76·17 kg/m²)
Max power loading	13·25 lb/hp (6·01 kg/hp)

PERFORMANCE (at max T-O weight):
Max level speed
152 knots (175 mph; 282 km/h)
Max cruising speed (75% power) at optimum altitude 143 knots (165 mph; 266 km/h)
Stalling speed, wheels and flaps down
56 knots (64 mph; 103 km/h)
Max rate of climb at S/L 900 ft (274 m)/min
Service ceiling 15,000 ft (4,575 m)
Absolute ceiling 17,000 ft (5,181 m)
T-O run 1,025 ft (312 m)
Landing run 780 ft (238 m)
Range with max fuel, 75% power at optimum altitude 642 nm (740 miles; 1,191 km)
Range with max fuel, 55% power at optimum altitude 738 nm (850 miles; 1,368 km)

PIPER PA-28-235 CHEROKEE PATHFINDER

Simultaneously with announcement of the Cherokee Archer in October 1973, Piper gave details of the Cherokee Pathfinder.

Basically similar to the Cherokee 235, described in the 1972-73 *Jane's*, the Cherokee Pathfinder embodies the features described for the Archer. By comparison with the earlier Cherokee 235, the Pathfinder has a "stretch" of 5 in (12·7 cm) in the fuselage length which, in addition to providing 50 per cent more leg-room for rear-seat passengers, makes possible a wider cabin door, wider forward side windows, and improved access to the rear seats. The interior decor of the cabin has been revised, and there is a choice of six different colour schemes. Rear seats of new design are individually reclinable, and are quickly removable without the use of tools.

The power plant is a 235 hp Lycoming O-540-B4B5 six-cylinder horizontally-opposed aircooled engine, driving a Hartzell HC-C2YK-1/8468A-4 constant-speed propeller. Normal fuel capacity of 50 US gallons (189 litres) is supplemented by two tanks in the wingtips, containing a total of 34 US gallons (129 litres) of fuel. Total fuel capacity 84 US gallons (318 litres), of which 82 US gallons (310 litres) are usable.

The Cherokee Pathfinder has a glassfibre engine cowling made in two pieces (top and bottom) which can be removed easily to expose the entire engine for servicing. A landing light is incorporated in the nose directly under the propeller spinner and the ram-air scoop for the carburettor is offset to accommodate the exhaust system.

In most other airframe details, the Archer and Pathfinder are similar, but propeller governor pad, high capacity electric fuel pump, four fuel contents gauges, central drain in cabin, double-pane side windows, super soundproofing, centre-mounted hand brake, main tyres of 6-ply rating, wheel fairings and Palm Beach exterior trim are standard equipment. It is available with the same optional electronics packages and introduces also the improvements detailed for the 1974 version of the Cherokee Cruiser.

DIMENSIONS, EXTERNAL:
Same as for Cherokee Archer, except:
Length overall 24 ft $1\frac{1}{4}$ in (7·35 m)

WEIGHTS AND LOADINGS:
Weight empty, equipped 1,550 lb (703 kg)
Max T-O weight 3,000 lb (1,360 kg)
Max wing loading 17·6 lb/sq ft (85·9 kg/m²)
Max power loading 12·8 lb/hp (8·5 kg/hp)

PERFORMANCE (at max T-O weight):
Max level speed at S/L
140 knots (161 mph; 259 km/h)
Max cruising speed, 75% power at optimum altitude 133 knots (153 mph; 246 km/h)
Stalling speed, full flap
57 knots (65 mph; 105 km/h)
Max rate of climb at S/L 800 ft (244 m)/min
Service ceiling 13,550 ft (4,130 m)
Absolute ceiling 15,500 ft (4,725 m)
T-O run, 25° flap 850 ft (259 m)
T-O to 50 ft (15 m), 25° flap 1,410 ft (430 m)
Landing from 50 ft (15 m) 1,740 ft (530 m)
Landing run 1,040 ft (317 m)
Range, 75% power at optimum altitude
794 nm (915 miles; 1,472 km)
Range, 55% power at optimum altitude
964 nm (1,110 miles; 1,786 km)

PIPER PA-32 CHEROKEE SIX

The prototype of the PA-32 Cherokee SIX (N9999W) was flown for the first time on 6 December 1963, followed by the first production model (N9998W) on 17 September 1964. FAA Type Approval was received on 4 March 1965.

The original version was a six-seater, but the model introduced in October 1966 offered an optional seventh seat. The 1969 Cherokee SIX B introduced increased cabin space, achieved by moving the instrument panel forward. Additional shoulder, hip and leg room was provided by moving the seats one inch away from the fuselage walls. The new features incorporated in the 1974 Cherokee Cruiser apply also to the Cherokee SIX. In addition, the Cherokee SIX 260 now has a two-blade constant-speed propeller as standard.

The PA-32 is available with two alternative power plants, as follows:

Cherokee SIX 260. Basic version with 260 hp Lycoming O-540-E six-cylinder horizontally-opposed aircooled engine, driving a two-blade constant-speed propeller. Carburettor heat control and engine primer standard.

Cherokee SIX 300. More powerful version with 300 hp Lycoming IO-540-K six-cylinder horizontally-opposed aircooled engine, driving a two-blade constant-speed propeller. Available also as floatplane, on Edo 3430 floats and with propeller of 7 ft 0 in (2·13 m) diameter. Two oil coolers and alternate air source (automatic with manual override) are standard. Piper Aire air-conditioning optional on this version.

Optional equipment packages styled Custom and Executive, similar to those detailed for the Warrior, are available for both versions of the Cherokee SIX. Both have as additions white glare-ban instrument post lights, map lights, four individual reading lights and a forward luggage compartment light.

Overall dimensions are increased by comparison with the two/four- and four-seat versions of the Cherokee, but the basic structural description of the Cherokee Archer and Pathfinder applies generally to the Cherokee SIX also. It is available with similar equipment and with the same optional electronics packages, except that both the 260 hp and 300 hp versions have been certificated with a FluiDyne ski installation, available as an optional extra. The optional range of autopilots is extended by availability of the Piper AltiMatic III, a full three-control system.

POWER PLANT: One 260 hp or 300 hp Lycoming six-cylinder horizontally-opposed aircooled engine, driving a two-blade propeller. Two fuel tanks in inner wings, total capacity 50 US gallons (189 litres). Two auxiliary tanks in glassfibre wingtips, with total capacity of 34 US gallons (129 litres). Total standard fuel capacity, with auxiliary tanks, 84 US gallons (318 litres), of which 83·3 US gallons (315 litres) are usable. Refuelling point above each tank. Oil capacity 3 US gallons (11·5 litres).

ACCOMMODATION: Enclosed cabin, seating six people in pairs. Optional seventh seat between two centre seats. Dual controls standard. Two forward-hinged doors, one on starboard side at front and the other on port side at rear. Space for 100 lb (45 kg) baggage at rear of cabin, and another 100 lb (45 kg) forward, between engine and instrument panel. A set of four pieces of matched luggage to fit the nose baggage compartment is provided as standard. Passenger seats easily removable to provide up to 110 cu ft (3·11 m³) of cargo space inside cabin, or room for stretcher and one or two attendants. Large upward-hinged utility door adjacent to rear door provides loading entrance nearly, 5 ft (1·5 m) wide. Ten silent fresh air outlets, cabin heater with eight warm air outlets including two defrosters, and two cabin air exhaust vents are standard.

DIMENSIONS, EXTERNAL:
Wing span 32 ft $9\frac{1}{2}$ in (9·99 m)
Length overall 27 ft $8\frac{3}{4}$ in (8·45 m)
Height overall:
landplane 7 ft 11 in (2·41 m)
floatplane 11 ft $3\frac{1}{2}$ in (3·44 m)
Tailplane span 12 ft $10\frac{1}{2}$ in (3·92 m)
Wheel track 10 ft 7 in (3·22 m)
Wheelbase 7 ft 10 in (2·39 m)
Propeller diameter:
260 hp engine 6 ft 10 in (2·08 m)
300 hp engine 6 ft 8 in (2·03 m)
300 hp engine, floatplane version
7 ft 0 in (2·13 m)
Cabin door (rear, port):
Height 2 ft 10 in (0·86 m)
Width 3 ft 1 in (0·94 m)

DIMENSIONS, INTERNAL:
Cabin:
Length, panel to rear wall 9 ft 11 in (3·02 m)
Max width 4 ft 1 in (1·24 m)
Max height 4 ft $0\frac{1}{4}$ in (1·23 m)
Baggage compartment volume:
Forward 8 cu ft (0·23 m³)
Aft 22 cu ft (0·62 m³)

AREA:
Wings, gross 174·5 sq ft (16·21 m²)

WEIGHTS AND LOADINGS (A: 260 hp engine, B: 300 hp engine, C: floatplane with 300 hp engine):
Weight empty, equipped:
A 1,706 lb (774 kg)
B 1,799 lb (816 kg)
C 2,140 lb (970 kg)
Max T-O weight:
All versions 3,400 lb (1,542 kg)
Max wing loading:
All versions 19·5 lb/sq ft (95 kg/m²)
Max power loading:
A 13·1 lb/hp (5·9 kg/hp)
B, C 11·3 lb/hp (5·1 kg/hp)

PERFORMANCE (at max T-O weight):
Max level speed:
A 144 knots (166 mph; 267 km/h)
B 151 knots (174 mph; 279 km/h)
C 133 knots (153 mph; 246 km/h)
Max cruising speed, 75% power at optimum altitude:
A 137 knots (158 mph; 254 km/h)

Piper Cherokee Pathfinder four-seat light aircraft (235 hp Lycoming O-540-B4B5 engine)

Piper PA-32 Cherokee SIX six/seven-seat light aircraft

B 146 knots (168 mph; 270 km/h)
C 128 knots (147 mph; 237 km/h)
Stalling speed, flaps down:
A, B 55 knots (63 mph; 102 km/h)
C 58 knots (66 mph; 106 km/h)
Max rate of climb at S/L:
A 850 ft (260 m)/min
B 1,050 ft (320 m)/min
C 750 ft (229 m)/min
Service ceiling:
A 14,500 ft (4,420 m)
B 16,250 ft (4,950 m)
C 12,100 ft (3,690 m)
Absolute ceiling:
A 16,500 ft (5,030 m)
B 18,000 ft (5,485 m)
T-O run:
A 740 ft (226 m)
B 700 ft (213 m)
C 1,430 ft (436 m)
T-O to 50 ft (15 m):
A 1,240 ft (378 m)
B 1,140 ft (348 m)
Landing from 50 ft (15 m):
A, B 1,000 ft (305 m)
Landing run:
A, B 630 ft (192 m)
Range (75% power), basic fuel:
A 486 nm (560 miles; 901 km)
B 456 nm (525 miles; 845 km)
C 395 nm (455 miles; 732 km)
Range (75% power), with auxiliary fuel:
A 825 nm (950 miles; 1,528 km)
B 764 nm (880 miles; 1,415 km)
C 673 nm (775 miles; 1,245 km)
Range (55% power), basic fuel:
A 573 nm (660 miles; 1,062 km)
B 547 nm (630 miles; 1,015 km)
C 468 nm (540 miles; 870 km)
Range (55% power), with auxiliary fuel:
A 964 nm (1,110 miles; 1,786 km)
B 920 nm (1,060 miles; 1,705 km)
C 798 nm (920 miles; 1,480 km)

PIPER PA-31-310 TURBO NAVAJO B

On 30 September 1964 Piper flew the first of what it described as a new series of larger executive aircraft for corporate and commuter airline service. Named the Navajo, it was then available with normally-aspirated or turbocharged engines, the latter being known as the Turbo Navajo. Subsequently, two additional versions were introduced, the Pressurised Navajo and Navajo Chieftain, and these are described separately.

The following description applies to the Turbo Navajo B which in 1972 introduced an optional factory-installed air-conditioning system, new engine nacelle compartments and new interior and exterior styling (the version with normally aspirated engines is no longer available).

The Turbo Navajo B is available in the following versions:

Standard Turbo Navajo B. Six individual seats in pairs with centre aisle. Seventh and eighth seats optional.

Commuter Turbo Navajo B. Eight individual seats in pairs, with ninth seat optional. Standard equipment includes pilot cabin divider with two pilot manual racks, two cabin magazine racks, lighted "No smoking" and "Fasten seat belts" signs, inertia shoulder harness for pilot and co-pilot seats, aft cabin divider with luggage shelf, and cabin ground ventilation fan.

Executive Turbo Navajo B. Six individual seats in pairs. Standard equipment as for Commuter version, plus 114 cu ft (3·23 m³) oxygen system with eight individual outlets, rearward-facing third and fourth seats with folding tables, refreshment unit and toilet. Seventh and eighth seats may be installed in place of refreshment unit and toilet.

The above versions of the Turbo Navajo B are available with a choice of electronics groups and operational groups as detailed below:

Group KTS-31. Dual King KX 175B 720-channel com transceivers and 200-channel nav receivers; FD/HSI VOR/LOC/glideslope indicator; KNI 520 VOR/LOC/glideslope indicator; dual KN 77 VOR/LOC converters; KN 73 glideslope receiver; KR 85 ADF; KI 225 ADF indicator; KT 76 transponder; KMA 20 audio panel with marker beacon receiver and indicator; KN 65 DME; AVQ-47 weather avoidance radar; Piper AltiMatic V/FD-1 with couplers; Piper anti-static kit; and Piper passenger address system; adding 151·9 lb (68·9 kg) to basic empty weight.

Group KTS-31(1). As group KTS-31, with deletion of KI 225, KT 76, KMA 20, KN 65; and addition of second KR 85 ADF; 551C dual needle ADF indicator; KMA 20-04 audio panel with marker beacon receiver and indicator; ASB 130 10-channel HF transceiver; MCU 33 remote tuner; and CU 110 antenna coupler; adding 176·6 lb (80·1 kg) to basic empty weight.

Co-pilot Flight Instrument Group. Includes Piper Truspeed indicator; Piper pictorial turn rate indicator; sensitive altimeter; 3 in attitude gyro and directional gyro; 8-day clock; rate of climb indicator; heated pitot tube; and separate static system; adding 12 lb (5·4 kg) to basic empty weight. Electrical gyros or vacuum gyros optional.

De-icing Group. Pneumatic de-icing boot installation for wing and tail unit leading-edges; electrical propeller de-icing; ice detection light; and electric windscreen de-icing port side; adding 64 lb (29 kg) to basic empty weight.

Comfort/Utility Group. Three-blade propellers, air-conditioning and nacelle luggage compartments; adding 202 lb (91·5 kg) to basic empty weight.

Other combinations of the above equipment are available optionally, as is the Piper Alti-Matic V series autopilot (as described in the introductory material), together with an extensive range of radio and radar equipment.

A total of 935 PA-31-310 Navajos had been delivered by 31 December 1973.

Type: Six/nine-seat corporate and commuter airline transport.

Wings: Cantilever low-wing monoplane. Wing section NACA $63_2$415 at root, NACA $63_1$212 at tip. 1° aerodynamic twist. 2° 30′ geometric twist. All-metal structure, with heavy stepped-down main spar, front and rear spars, lateral stringers, ribs and stressed skin. Wings spliced on centreline with heavy steel plates. Flush riveted forward of main spar. Wing-root leading-edge extended forward between nacelle and fuselage. Glassfibre wingtips. Balanced ailerons are interconnected with rudder. Trim tab in starboard aileron. Electrically-operated flaps. Pneumatic de-icing boots optional.

Fuselage: Conventional all-metal semi-monocoque structure.

Tail Unit: Cantilever all-metal structure, with sweptback vertical surfaces. Variable-incidence tailplane. Trim tabs in rudder and starboard elevator. Optional pneumatic de-icing boots.

Landing Gear: Hydraulically-actuated retractable tricycle type, with single wheel on each unit. Manual hydraulic emergency extension. Main wheels and tyres size 6·50-10, eight-ply rating, pressure 60 lb/sq in (4·22 kg/cm²). Steerable nosewheel and tyre size 6·00-6, six-ply rating, pressure 42 lb/sq in (2·95 kg/cm²). Toe-controlled hydraulic disc brakes. Main-wheel doors close when gear is fully extended.

Power Plant: Two 310 hp Lycoming TIO-540-A six-cylinder horizontally-opposed aircooled turbocharged engines. Hartzell two-blade fully-feathering metal propellers. Propeller de-icing optional. Four rubber fuel cells in wings; inboard cells each contain 55 US gallons (208 litres), outboard cells 40 US gallons (151·5 litres) each. Total fuel capacity 190 US gallons (719 litres), of which 188 US gallons (711 litres) are usable. Fuel cells equipped with NACA-type anti-icing non-siphoning fuel vents. Two-piece glassfibre engine nacelles.

Accommodation: Six to nine seats, as described under notes on individual models. Dual controls standard. Thermostatically-controlled Janitrol 45,000 BTU combustion heater, windscreen defrosters and fresh air system standard. Double-glazed windows. Electric de-icing and windscreen wiper for port side of windscreen optional. "Dutch" door at rear of cabin on port side. Top half hinges upward; lower half hinges down and has built-in steps. Baggage compartments in nose, capacity 150 lb (68 kg), and in rear of cabin, capacity 200 lb (91 kg). Cargo door and cockpit door available as optional items.

Systems: Hydraulic system utilises two engine-driven pumps. 24V electrical system supplied by two engine-driven 70A alternators and 24V 25Ah battery. External power socket standard. Oxygen system optional.

Electronics and Equipment: Optional electronics described under standard groupings above. Blind-flying instrumentation standard, with optional dual installation for co-pilot. Optional equipment includes cabin ground ventilation fan, Piper Aire air-conditioning system, cabin fire extinguisher, cold-weather heater for rear cabin, three-blade propellers, propeller synchroniser, nacelle baggage compartments, aft cabin divider with curtain and shelf, propeller ice protection shields, beverage dispensers, folding tables, forward cabin divider with curtain and magazine racks, Piper automatic locator, ice inspection light, toilet, utility door, tinted windows, toe-brakes for co-pilot, and pilot's windscreen wiper. Standard electrical equipment includes navigation, landing, taxying, cockpit, cabin dome and passenger reading lights, two rotating beacons, stall warning light, courtesy lights, cabin and cockpit speakers and heated pitot tube.

Dimensions, external:
Wing span 40 ft 8 in (12·40 m)
Length overall 32 ft 7½ in (9·94 m)
Height overall 13 ft 0 in (3·96 m)
Tailplane span 18 ft 1½ in (5·52 m)
Wheel track 13 ft 9 in (4·19 m)
Wheelbase 8 ft 8 in (2·64 m)
Propeller diameter 6 ft 8 in (2·03 m)

Dimensions, internal:
Cabin: Length 16 ft 0 in (4·88 m)
Height 4 ft 3½ in (1·31 m)
Baggage compartments:
Nose 14 cu ft (0·40 m³)
Aft 22 cu ft (0·62 m³)

Area:
Wings, gross 229 sq ft (21·3 m²)

Weights and Loadings:
Weight empty (standard) 3,849 lb (1,745 kg)
Max T-O weight 6,500 lb (2,948 kg)
Max landing weight 6,200 lb (2,812 kg)
Max wing loading 28·4 lb/sq ft (138·7 kg/m²)
Max power loading 10·5 lb/hp (4·76 kg/hp)

Performance (at max T-O weight, except as detailed):
Max level speed at 15,000 ft (4,570 m) 227 knots (261 mph; 420 km/h)
Max cruising speed (75% power) at 24,000 ft (7,300 m) 218 knots (251 mph; 404 km/h)
Intermediate cruising speed (65% power) at 24,000 ft (7,300 m) 201 knots (231 mph; 372 km/h)
Econ cruising speed (55% power) at 24,000 ft (7,300 m) 182 knots (209 mph; 336 km/h)
Econ cruising speed (45% power) at 24,000 ft (7,300 m) 157 knots (181 mph; 291 km/h)
Stalling speed, flaps down 63·5 knots (73 mph; 118 km/h)
Max rate of climb at S/L 1,445 ft (440 m)/min
Rate of climb at S/L, one engine out 245 ft (75 m)/min
Service ceiling 27,300 ft (8,320 m)
Ceiling, one engine out 15,900 ft (4,845 m)
Normal T-O run 1,030 ft (314 m)
Short-field T-O run 860 ft (262 m)
Normal T-O to 50 ft (15 m) 2,190 ft (668 m)
Short-field T-O to 50 ft (15 m) 1,700 ft (518 m)
Normal landing from 50 ft (15 m) at max landing weight 2,340 ft (713 m)
Short-field landing from 50 ft (15 m) at max landing weight 1,810 ft (552 m)
Normal landing run at max landing weight 1,950 ft (594 m)
Short-field landing run at max landing weight 1,235 ft (376 m)
Accelerate/stop distance 2,085 ft (636 m)
Range with max fuel, 45 min reserve:
75% power at 22,000 ft (6,705 m) 964 nm (1,110 miles; 1,785 km)
65% power at 24,000 ft (7,300 m) 1,220 nm (1,410 miles; 2,270 km)
55% power at 24,000 ft (7,300 m) 1,335 nm (1,540 miles; 2,475 km)
45% power at 24,000 ft (7,300 m) 1,380 nm (1,590 miles; 2,555 km)
Range with max fuel, no reserve:
75% power at 22,000 ft (6,705 m) 1,120 nm (1,290 miles; 2,075 km)
65% power at 24,000 ft (7,300 m) 1,370 nm (1,580 miles; 2,540 km)
55% power at 24,000 ft (7,300 m) 1,475 nm (1,700 miles; 2,735 km)
45% power at 24,000 ft (7,300 m) 1,500 nm (1,730 miles; 2,780 km)

PIPER PA-31P PRESSURISED NAVAJO

Piper announced on 6 March 1970 that a new pressurised version of the Navajo was to be marketed by the company. Generally similar to the PA-31-300 Navajo and Turbo Navajo already in service, the new version began as a company project in January 1966, and the first prototype was flown in March 1968. From

Piper Pressurised Navajo in service with the Spanish Air Force

that time to the roll-out of the first production aircraft in March 1970, more than 4,000 hours of flight and ground-testing of the new model had been completed, including 850 hours at altitudes up to 29,000 ft (8,840 m), the aircraft's certificated maximum operating altitude.

Two models are available, as follows:

Standard Pressurised Navajo. Six individual seats in pairs. Dividers to separate cabin from flight deck and rear baggage compartment, as well as two additional seats, are available as optional extras.

Executive Pressurised Navajo. Seven individual seats, comprising two crew seats, four reclining chairs facing each other and a fifth passenger seat, food and drink buffet, two foldaway tables, pneumatic door extender and seventh oxygen outlet and mask as standard. Optional eighth seat may be installed, but access to refreshment unit is partially restricted.

The above versions of the Pressurised Navajo are available with a choice of electronics groups and operational groups as detailed below:

Group KTS-31P. Dual KX 175B 720-channel com transceivers with 200-channel nav receivers; FD/HSI VOR/LOC/glideslope indicator; KNI 520 VOR/LOC/glideslope indicator; dual KN 77 VOR/LOC converters; KN 73 glideslope receiver; KR 85 ADF; KI 225 ADF indicator; KT 76 transponder; KMA 20 audio panel with marker beacon receiver and indicator; KN 65 DME; AVQ-47 weather avoidance radar; Piper AltiMatic V-1F/D autopilot with couplers; and Piper anti-static kit; adding 160·1 lb (72·6 kg) to basic empty weight.

Group KTG-31P. Dual KTR 900A 720-channel com transceivers with KFS 590-09 frequency selectors; dual KNR 600A 200-channel VOR/LOC receivers and converters with KFS 560 nav frequency selectors; FD/HSI VOR/LOC/glideslope indicator; KNI 520 VOR/LOC indicator and converter; KGM 691 glideslope and marker beacon receiver; KDF 800 ADF with KFS 580 selector; KNI 580 ADF indicator; KXP 750A transponder with KFS 570A control head; KA 35 marker beacon lights; KDM 705 DME; KAA 445 audio amplifier; KA 37 audio panel; AVQ-47 weather avoidance radar; Piper AltiMatic V-1F/D autopilot with couplers; and Piper anti-static kit; adding 210·3 lb (95·4 kg) to basic empty weight.

Group KTG-31P(1). As Group KTG-31P, with deletion of KNI 580 and addition of second KDF 800 ADF with KFS 580 selector and 551C dual needle indicator; ASB 130 10-channel HF transceiver; MCU-33 remote tuner; and CU-110 antenna coupler; adding 258·3 lb (117·2 kg) to basic empty weight.

***Full-time Pressurisation Group.** Comprises two 28V 100A gear-driven alternators, 24,000 BTU freon vapour-cycle air-conditioner with automatic two-position inlet scoop; cabin altitude selector with variable rate control; 48 cu ft (1·36 m³) oxygen system with outlets and masks; forward cabin divider with adjustable vertical blind, "Fasten seat belts" and "No smoking" signs; and rear cabin divider with baggage retaining net and clothes hanger support bar with hangers; adding 149 lb (67 kg) to basic empty weight.

***Pilot/Operations Utility Group.** Comprises pilot's heated windscreen (provisions for co-pilot); two 25 US gallon (94·5 litre) auxiliary fuel tanks; two sump and two fuel cell drains; four electric fuel transfer pumps with integral filters; pilot's electric windscreen wiper; and inertia shoulder harness for crew seats; adding 43 lb (19·5 kg) to basic empty weight.

Co-Pilot Flight Instruments Group. Comprises Truspeed, pictorial turn rate and rate of climb indicators; altimeter; electric attitude gyro, electric directional gyro; clock; heated pitot; and static system; adding 15 lb (6·8 kg) to basic empty weight.

De-icing Group. Comprises pneumatic de-icing boot installation for wing and tail unit leading-edges; electric propeller de-icing; and ice detection light; adding 53 lb (240 kg) to basic empty weight.

Other combinations of the above equipment are available optionally, as is the Piper AltiMatic V series autopilot (as described in the introductory material), together with an extensive range of radio and radar equipment.

The Navajo's pressurisation system, with a maximum cabin differential of 5·5 lb/sq in (0·38 kg/cm²), provides a sea level cabin atmosphere up to 12,375 ft (3,770 m), and can maintain a cabin altitude of 8,000 ft (2,440 m) to a height of 25,000 ft (7,620 m) and of 10,000 ft (3,050 m) to the aircraft's certificated maximum operating altitude of 29,000 ft (8,840 m). Pressurisation is obtained from four different air sources. The primary source is bleed air from the engine turbochargers which enters the system through

**Because of customer preference, these optional groups are included in all Pressurised Navajos*

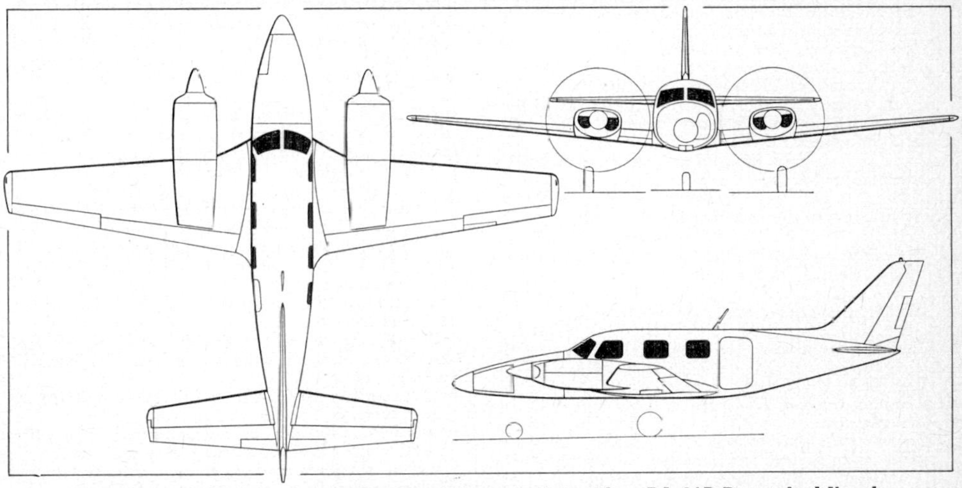

Three-view drawing (*Pilot Press*) and photograph of the Piper PA-31P Pressurised Navajo (two 425 hp Lycoming TIGO-541-E1A engines)

sonic nozzles. This is supplemented by relief flow from two engine-driven dry pneumatic pumps which have a main function of providing air for the aircraft's pneumatic system. Over-pressurisation is prevented automatically by an isobaric control valve, with backup safety valve and rupture disc. A three-position cabin air control lever directs the flow of air either to the cabin or to atmosphere. When the control is in the pressurised position air is directed into the cabin; Outside Air mode provides unpressurised air for normal ventilation; Recirculated Air mode, used only on the ground, allows the cabin air to be recirculated through the air-conditioning evaporator/heater units.

The environmental control system provides automatically thermostatic control of cabin temperature, air purification, circulation/recirculation and dehumidification. The normal flow of air for heating, cooling, ventilation and defrosting is taken primarily through the main pressure line and the recirculating air duct. A ram-air duct in the nose section provides an alternative source of air for unpressurised flight. Airflow is heated by a 45,000 BTU in-line gasoline combustion heater or cooled by a similarly integrated 24,000 BTU freon type air conditioner, depending on demand of cabin thermostat. The air-conditioning compressor is driven by the starboard engine. An evaporator, mounted in the nose section, acts as a heat exchanger which cools and automatically dehumidifies the air before it enters the cabin. Baseboard outlets on both sides of the flight deck and main cabin provide warm air, pressurised or unpressurised, and individual eyeball outlets provide air-conditioned cool air. When the aircraft is not pressurised, these latter outlets circulate fresh air from outside throughout the cabin.

One example of the Pressurised Navajo was acquired by the Spanish Air Force during 1972. A total of 147 Pressurised Navajos had been delivered by 31 December 1973.

The description of the Turbo Navajo B applies also to the PA-31P, except in the following details:

FUSELAGE: Conventional all-metal semi-monocoque structure, with fail-safe structure in the pressurised section. Swing-open nosecone of reinforced glassfibre.

LANDING GEAR: Steerable nosewheel, with tyre size 6·00-6, eight-ply rating. Goodyear toe-controlled heavy-duty hydraulic brakes, six-puck system with multiple discs.

POWER PLANT: Two 425 hp Lycoming TIGO-541-E1A six-cylinder horizontally-opposed air-cooled turbocharged and geared engines, each driving a Hartzell three-blade metal constant-speed fully-feathering propeller. Electric propeller synchronisation optional. Four rubber fuel cells in wings; inboard cells each contain 56 US gallons (212 litres), outboard cells each 40 US gallons (151·5 litres). Total fuel capacity 192 US gallons (727 litres) of which 186 US gallons (704 litres) are usable. Two optional 25 US gallon (94·5 litre) transfer cells can be installed in the engine nacelles to provide a maximum fuel capacity of 242 US gallons (916 litres), of which 236 US gallons (893 litres) are usable. Inboard fuel tanks have NACA-type non-icing non-siphoning fuel tank vents, outboard tanks have heated vents.

ACCOMMODATION: Six to eight seats, as described under notes on individual models. One-piece passenger door with integral airstair; when closed the door is secured by seven locking pins. Each seat position has an individual fresh air outlet, reading lamp, headrest, full-length armrests and storage pocket in the seatback. Walk-in baggage compartment aft of cabin can accommodate 200 lb (90·7 kg) of baggage. Nose compartment can hold 200 lb (90·7 kg) of baggage. Birdproof windscreen and windscreen de-frosting standard.

SYSTEMS: Hydraulic system supplied by two engine-driven pumps, pressure 1,800 lb/sq in (127 kg/cm²). Electrical system supplied by two 28V 50A engine-driven alternators, 24V 25Ah battery. Fuel system has positive fuel flow at all altitudes and temperatures supplied by two engine-driven fuel pumps, two auxiliary electric fuel pumps and four submerged electric fuel pumps, pressure 55 lb/sq in (3·9 kg/cm²).

ELECTRONICS AND EQUIPMENT: Optional electronics described under standard groupings above, but a wide range of alternative optional electronics is also available. Standard equipment includes flight control lock, baggage tie-down straps, courtesy lights for cabin entrance door and nose baggage compartment, jack pads, tie-down rings, towbar, corrosion proofing, and nose-gear safety mirror. Optional equipment includes beverage dispensers, pneumatic door extender, tinted windows, co-pilot's toe-brakes, refreshment centre, folding tables, electrically-heated window for co-pilot, windscreen wiper for co-pilot, propeller synchroniser, true airspeed indicator, ice protection shields, lightning-resistant fuel filler caps, Piper automatic locator, cabin utility tie-down rings, hand fire extinguisher, strobe lights, torque-meter and stereo tape system.

DIMENSIONS, EXTERNAL:
As for Turbo Navajo, except:
Length overall 34 ft 6 in (10·52 m)
Height overall 13 ft 3 in (4·04 m)
Tailplane span 19 ft 10 in (6·05 m)
Propeller diameter 7 ft 9 in (2·36 m)

DIMENSIONS, INTERNAL:
Cabin, including flight deck and rear baggage compartment:
Length 16 ft 1 in (4·90 m)
Max height 4 ft 4 in (1·32 m)
Max width 4 ft 3 in (1·30 m)
Baggage compartments:
Aft 22 cu ft (0·62 m³)
Nose 20 cu ft (0·57 m³)

WEIGHTS AND LOADINGS:
Weight empty 4,900 lb (2,222 kg)
Max T-O weight 7,800 lb (3,538 kg)
Max wing loading 34·1 lb/sq ft (166·4 kg/m²)
Max power loading 9·18 lb/hp (4·16 kg/hp)

PERFORMANCE (at max T-O weight):
Max level speed at 18,000 ft (5,475 m)
243 knots (280 mph; 451 km/h)
Max cruising speed, 75% power at 24,000 ft (7,315 m) 231 knots (266 mph; 428 km/h)
Intermediate cruising speed, 65% power at 24,000 ft (7,315 m)
212 knots (244 mph; 393 km/h)
Econ cruising speed, 55% power at 24,000 ft (7,315 m) 193 knots (222 mph; 357 km/h)
Long-range cruising speed, 45% power at 24,000 ft (7,315 m) 165 knots (190 mph; 306 km/h)
Stalling speed, flaps up
80 knots (92 mph; 148 km/h)
Stalling speed, flaps down
72 knots (83 mph; 134 km/h)
Single-engine minimum control speed
83 knots (95 mph; 153 km/h)
Max rate of climb at S/L 1,740 ft (530 m)/min
Rate of climb at S/L, one engine out
240 ft (73 m)/min
Max operationally approved ceiling
29,000 ft (8,840 m)
Ceiling, one engine out 15,300 ft (4,675 m)
T-O run 1,440 ft (439 m)
T-O to 50 ft (15 m) 2,200 ft (671 m)
Landing from 50 ft (15 m) 2,700 ft (823 m)
Landing run 1,370 ft (418 m)
Accelerate/stop distance 2,830 ft (863 m)
Max range at 24,000 ft (7,315 m) with max fuel, no reserve, at speeds shown above:
Max cruising speed
951 nm (1,095 miles; 1,760 km)
Intermediate cruising speed
1,090 nm (1,255 miles; 2,020 km)
Econ cruising speed
1,237 nm (1,425 miles; 2,290 km)
Long-range cruising speed
1,302 nm (1,500 miles; 2,414 km)
Max range at 24,000 ft (7,315 m) with max fuel, 45 min reserve, at speeds shown above:
Max cruising speed
868 nm (1,000 miles; 1,609 km)
Intermediate cruising speed
981 nm (1,130 miles; 1,818 km)
Econ cruising speed
1,116 nm (1,285 miles; 2,065 km)
Long-range cruising speed
1,172 nm (1,350 miles; 2,170 km)

PIPER PA-31-350 NAVAJO CHIEFTAIN

First announced on 11 September 1972, the Navajo Chieftain is a "stretched" version of the Turbo Navajo, with the fuselage lengthened by 2 ft 0 in (0·61 m) and more powerful (350 hp) turbocharged engines. The Chieftain does not replace the existing Turbo Navajo, but represents an extension of the Navajo series.

The main cabin floor is designed to carry heavy concentrated loads of up to 200 lb/sq ft (976 kg/m²) and, in addition to the 217 cu ft (6·14 m³) of cargo space in the main cabin, 200 lb (91 kg) of cargo or baggage can be carried in the forward nose compartment, and 150 lb (68 kg) in the rear of each engine nacelle.

Following the success of the counter-rotating power plants installed in the Piper Twin Comanche and Seneca, the two 350 hp Lycoming TIO-540 turbocharged engines of the Chieftain have also been designed to counter-rotate.

Four optional interior groups of equipment are available, depending upon the proposed use of the aircraft:

Corporate Interior Group. Comprises "No smoking-Fasten seat belt" sign; inertia reel safety belts for crew seats; forward-facing third and fourth seats; reclining and adjustable fifth, sixth, seventh and eighth seats; and eight headrests; adding 140 lb (63·5 kg) to basic empty weight.

Commuter Interior Group. As Corporate Group with deletion of headrests, and addition of two extra seats, aft cabin divider and ten fresh air vents; adding 193 lb (87·5 kg) to basic empty weight.

Executive Interior Group. Comprises "No smoking-Fasten seat belt" sign; inertia reel safety belts for crew seats; third and fourth seats facing aft; fifth and sixth seats reclining and adjustable; two folding tables, one each side; aft cabin divider with curtain; refreshment centre; beverage dispenser; side-facing seventh seat and toilet; forward cabin divider with curtain, magazine and map stowage; six headrests; six armrests; tinted windows; air-conditioning with eight outlets; and oxygen system with eight outlets; adding 340 lb (154 kg) to basic empty weight.

Piper PA-31-350 Navajo Chieftain six/ten-seat executive/commuter/cargo aircraft

Cargo Interior Group. Comprises inertia reel safety belts for crew seats; pilot door with step, assist handle and wing walk; cargo door; cargo barrier, tie-down rings and net; eight seat-track tie-down rings; four plug-in tie-down rings; four tie-down straps; four track cargo rollers; two strap/tie-down pouches; and cargo sidewall protective blankets; adding 80 lb (36·3 kg) to basic empty weight.

Operational groups, comprising Co-Pilot Instrument Group and De-Icing Group, as detailed for the Turbo Navajo B. Avionics groups KTS-31 and KTS-31(1) as detailed for the Turbo Navajo B are available for the Chieftain.

A total of 152 Chieftains had been delivered by 31 December 1973.

The description of the Turbo Navajo B applies also to the Navajo Chieftain, except as detailed below:

FUSELAGE: As for Turbo Navajo B, except length increased by 2 ft 0 in (0·61 m).

POWER PLANT: Two 350 hp Lycoming TIO-540-J2BD six-cylinder horizontally-opposed air-cooled turbocharged engines, each driving a three-blade fully-feathering metal propeller. Four rubber fuel cells in wings; inboard cells each contain 56 US gallons (212 litres), outboard cells each 40 US gallons (151·5 litres). Total fuel capacity 192 US gallons (727 litres), of which 182 US gallons (689 litres) are usable.

ACCOMMODATION: Pilot and co-pilot on individually adjustable and reclining seats. Dual controls standard. Interior seating and equipment as detailed in optional interior groups. Cabin heated by thermostatically-controlled Janitrol 50,000 BTU combustion heater. Piper Aire 18,000 BTU air-conditioning system optional. Baggage/cargo compartments in nose, capacity 200 lb (91 kg), and in the rear of each engine nacelle, each 150 lb (68 kg).

ELECTRONICS AND EQUIPMENT: A wide range of optional electronics is available, as well as full dual instrumentation, a flight director system integrated with alternative autopilots, weather radar, pneumatic wing de-icing, and electric propeller and windscreen anti-icing.

DIMENSIONS, EXTERNAL:
Wing span 40 ft 8 in (12·40 m)
Length overall 34 ft 7½ in (10·55 m)
Height overall 13 ft 0 in (3·96 m)
Tailplane span 18 ft 1½ in (5·52 m)
Wheel track 13 ft 9 in (4·19 m)
Wheelbase 10 ft 8 in (3·25 m)
Propeller diameter 6 ft 8 in (2·03 m)

DIMENSIONS, INTERNAL:
Cabin: Length 18 ft 0 in (5·49 m)
Height 4 ft 3½ in (1·31 m)
Baggage/cargo compartments:
Nose 14 cu ft (0·40 m³)
Engine nacelles (each) 13·25 cu ft (0·37 m³)

AREA:
Wings, gross 229 sq ft (21·3 m²)

WEIGHTS AND LOADINGS:
Weight empty (standard) 3,991 lb (1,810 kg)
Max T-O and landing weight 7,000 lb (3,175 kg)
Max wing loading 30·6 lb/sq ft (149·4 kg/m²)
Max power loading 10·0 lb/hp (4·5 kg/hp)

PERFORMANCE (at max T-O weight):
Max level speed at 15,000 ft (4,575 m)
234 knots (270 mph; 435 km/h)
Max cruising speed at 24,000 ft (7,315 m)
226 knots (260 mph; 418 km/h)
Econ cruising speed at 20,000 ft (6,100 m)
214 knots (246 mph; 396 km/h)
Single-engine minimum control speed
78 knots (90 mph; 145 km/h)
Stalling speed, flaps up
80 knots (92 mph; 148 km/h)
Stalling speed, flaps down
74 knots (85 mph; 137 km/h)
Max rate of climb at S/L
1,390 ft (424 m)/min
Service ceiling 27,200 ft (8,290 m)
Service ceiling, one engine out
13,700 ft (4,175 m)
Absolute ceiling 28,300 ft (8,625 m)
Absolute ceiling, one engine out
15,500 ft (4,725 m)
Normal T-O run 1,360 ft (415 m)
Short-field T-O run 1,050 ft (320 m)
Normal T-O to 50 ft (15 m) 2,490 ft (759 m)
Short-field T-O to 50 ft (15 m) 1,780 ft (543 m)
Normal landing from 50 ft (15 m)
2,725 ft (831 m)
Short-field landing from 50 ft (15 m)
2,150 ft (655 m)
Normal landing run 1,575 ft (480 m)
Short-field landing run 1,180 ft (360 m)
Accelerate/stop distance 2,280 ft (695 m)
Max range, with max fuel and allowances for taxi, T-O, climb, cruise at econ power at 16,000 ft (4,875 m), and descent, no reserve
1,064 nm (1,225 miles; 1,971 km)
Max range, with allowances as above and 45 min reserve
938 nm (1,080 miles; 1,738 km)

PIPER PA-31T CHEYENNE

Newest addition to the Piper range is the PA-31T, with an airframe similar to the Pressurised Navajo, which introduces turboprop power to the Piper line for the first time.

Design of the PA-31T began at the end of 1965, with construction of the prototype beginning in May 1967. First flight of the prototype was made on 20 August 1969, with FAA certification being granted on 3 May 1972. The first production aircraft flew for the first time on 22 October 1973.

TYPE: Six/eight-seat cabin monoplane.

WINGS: Cantilever low-wing monoplane. Wing section NACA 63_2-415 at root, NACA 63A212 at tip. Dihedral 5°. Incidence 1° 30′ at root, —1° at tip. Sweepback 0° at 30% chord. Three-spar structure of 2024ST light alloy. Balanced ailerons and single-slotted trailing-edge flaps of 2024ST light alloy. Trim tab in starboard aileron. Pneumatic de-icing boots on wing leading-edges optional.

FUSELAGE: Semi-monocoque structure of 2024ST light alloy, with fail-safe structure in the pressurised areas.

TAIL UNIT: Cantilever structure of 2024ST light alloy with sweptback vertical surfaces. Fixed-incidence tailplane. Trim tabs in elevators and rudder. Pneumatic de-icing of tailplane leading-edges optional.

LANDING GEAR: Hydraulically-retractable tricycle type with single wheel on each unit, main units retracting inward and nosewheel aft. Piper oleo-pneumatic shock-absorbers. Main wheels with tyres size 6·60 × 10, 10-ply rating. Nosewheel with Type VII tyre size 18 × 4·4, 6-ply rating. Goodyear disc-type hydraulic brakes. Parking brake.

POWER PLANT: Two 620 ehp United Aircraft of Canada PT6A-28 turboprop enignes, each driving a Hartzell three-blade metal constant-speed reversible propeller. Each wing has three interconnected fuel cells and a tip-tank, with combined total capacity of 390 US gallons (1,476 litres). Refuelling points in engine nacelles and on upper surface of each tip-tank. Oil capacity 6·5 US gallons (24·6 litres).

ACCOMMODATION: Pilot and co-pilot on two individual adjustable seats. Dual controls standard. Pilot's storm window. Heated windscreen and windscreen wiper for pilot, optional for co-pilot. Cabin seating for four to six passengers on individual seats. Door with built-in airstair on port side, which has seven locking pins and inflatable pressurisation seal. Dual-pane windows. Emergency exit window on starboard side. Cabin heated and air-conditioned. Forward and aft cabin dividers. A wide range of options for cabin includes folding tables, beverage dispensers, pneumatic door extender, storage cabinets and tinted windows. Baggage compartments in nose and rear of cabin, each with 200 lb (91 kg) capacity. External access door to nose compartment.

SYSTEMS: Air-conditioning and pressurisation, with pressure differential of 5·5 lb/sq in (0·39 kg/cm²). Freon-type air-conditioner of 23,000 BTU capacity. Janitrol combustion heater of 45,000 BTU capacity with automatic windscreen defroster. Hydraulic system supplied by dual engine-driven pumps for landing gear retraction and brakes. Pneumatic system provided by engine bleed air. Electrical system supplied by two 28V 200A generators and 24V 43Ah nickel-cadmium battery. Oxygen system of 48 cu ft (1·36 m³) capacity. De-icing system comprises electric anti-icing boots for air intakes, heated pitot and electric propeller de-icing.

ELECTRONICS: A very extensive range of optional avionics is available, including radar, communications, area navigation, autopilot and flight director systems by Bendix, Collins, King, Piper and Sperry.

EQUIPMENT: Installed standard equipment is extensive, and optional items include toe-brakes for co-pilot, heated windscreen and windscreen wiper for co-pilot, wing and tail pneumatic de-icing boots, engine fire-extinguishing system, fuselage ice protection plates, ice inspection lights, propeller synchronisers and co-pilot's flight instrument group as detailed for the Turbo Navajo B.

DIMENSIONS, EXTERNAL:
Wing span over tip-tanks 42 ft 8¾ in (13·02 m)
Length overall 34 ft 8 in (10·57 m)
Height overall 12 ft 9 in (3·89 m)
Tailplane span 19 ft 10 in (6·05 m)
Wheel track 13 ft 9 in (4·19 m)
Wheelbase 8 ft 8 in (2·64 m)
Propeller diameter 7 ft 9 in (2·36 m)
Propeller ground clearance 10½ in (0·27 m)
Passenger door (port, aft):
Height 3 ft 10 in (1·17 m)
Width 2 ft 4 in (0·71 m)
Height to sill 3 ft 1 in (0·94 m)
Baggage door (fwd):
Height 1 ft 9 in (0·53 m)
Width 2 ft 2 in (0·66 m)
Height to sill 3 ft 7½ in (1·10 m)
Emergency exit (stbd, fwd):
Height 2 ft 1 in (0·64 m)
Width 1 ft 7 in (0·48 m)

DIMENSIONS, INTERNAL:
Cabin (incl flight deck):
Length 16 ft 1 in (4·90 m)
Max width 4 ft 3 in (1·30 m)
Max height 4 ft 4 in (1·32 m)
Floor area 47 sq ft (4·37 m²)
Volume 222 cu ft (6·29 m³)
Forward baggage compartment 20 cu ft (0·57 m³)
Aft baggage compartment 22 cu ft (0·62 m³)

AREAS:
Wings, gross 229 sq ft (21·3 m²)
Ailerons (total) 13 sq ft (1·21 m²)
Trailing-edge flaps (total) 33·6 sq ft (3·12 m²)
Fin 15·9 sq ft (1·48 m²)
Rudder, incl tab 10·6 sq ft (0·98 m²)
Tailplane 70·5 sq ft (6·55 m²)
Elevators, incl tab 28·3 sq ft (2·63 m²)

WEIGHTS AND LOADINGS:
Weight empty, standard, equipped 4,870 lb (2,209 kg)
Max T-O and landing weight 9,000 lb (4,082 kg)
Max ramp weight 9,050 lb (4,105 kg)
Max zero-fuel weight 7,200 lb (3,265 kg)
Max wing loading 39·3 lb/sq ft (191·9 kg/m²)
Max power loading 7·26 lb/ehp (3·29 kg/ehp)

PERFORMANCE (at 7,600 lb; 3,447 kg AUW):
Max level and cruising speed at 11,000 ft (3,355 m) 283 knots (326 mph; 525 km/h)
Econ cruising speed at 25,000 ft (7,620 m) 184 knots (212 mph; 341 km/h)
Stalling speed, flaps down 77 knots (88 mph; 142 km/h)
Max rate of climb at S/L 2,800 ft (853 m)/min
Rate of climb at S/L, one engine out 660 ft (201 m)/min
Max approved operating altitude 29,000 ft (8,840 m)
Service ceiling, one engine out 14,600 ft (4,450 m)
Min ground turning radius 31 ft 7 in (9·63 m)
T-O to 50 ft (15 m) 1,980 ft (604 m)
Landing from 50 ft (15 m) 1,860 ft (567 m)
Range with max fuel at econ cruising power, allowances for taxi, T-O, climb, descent and 45 min reserve 1,350 nm (1,555 miles; 2,500 km)

PIPER PA-34 SENECA

On 23 September 1971, Piper announced a new twin-engined light aircraft which has the company designation PA-34 and, following Piper tradition, has the Indian name Seneca. It is being built at Piper's Vero Beach, Florida, factory.

The Seneca has a counter-rotating (C/R) engine and propeller installation similar to that introduced on the Twin Comanche in February 1970. The retractable landing gear is operated by an electro-hydraulic system and includes an emergency extension system which allows the wheels to free-fall into the down and locked position. A dual-vane stall warning system provides warning by horn and flashing light well in advance of the stall in either "clean" or gear/flaps-down configuration. Standard seating consists of six individual reclinable seats with a 10 in (25·4 cm) centre aisle, with a seventh (three-abreast centre) seat optional. Cabin climate is controlled by six silent fresh-air outlets, six cool/warm-air outlets, including two defrosters, and two exhaust vents to ensure circulation of fresh air.

The 1974 version of the Seneca introduces as standard an improved nosewheel shock-strut, steerable to 30° each side; dual toe-operated brakes; new silent overhead air vents in cabin; new fourth window on each side of cabin and new window styling; and new interior and exterior styling.

The extensive range of avionics available for the Seneca includes many options, plus eight groups as follows:

Group N 1-34. Narco Com 11A 360-channel VHF transceiver; Nav 11 200-channel VOR/LOC receiver with VOR/LOC converter indicator; T-12C ADF; AT-50A transponder; Piper AutoControl III autopilot; Piper VOR/LOC coupler; Piper electric trim; and Piper 66C microphone; adding 45 lb (20·4 kg) to basic empty weight.

Group N 2-34. As above, plus second Com 11A transceiver; Nav 12 200-channel VOR/LOC receiver, converter indicator and UGR-2A 40-channel glideslope receiver; VOR/LOC converter; MBT-12 marker beacon receiver; CP-25B audio panel; and dual Piper broad band com antennae and static discharge wicks; adding 61 lb (27·5 kg) to basic empty weight.

Group NT 3-34. Dual Narco Com 111 360-channel VHF transceivers; Nav 111 200-channel VOR/LOC receiver with 40-channel localiser and VOR/LOC converter indicator; Nav 112 200-channel VOR/LOC receiver with converter indicator, and UGR-2A glideslope receiver; MBT-12 marker beacon receiver and lights; CP-125B audio panel; T-12C ADF; AT-50A transponder; KN 65 DME; Piper AltiMatic IIIB-1 autopilot; Piper VOR/LOC and glideslope couplers; Piper electric trim; Piper dual broad band com antennae, static wicks and 100T noise cancelling microphone; adding 79 lb (35·5 kg) to basic empty weight.

Group NT 4-34. As Group NT 3-34, with deletion of CP-125B and DME, and addition of CP-127 audio panel; second T-12C ADF; 551C dual needle ADF indicator; ASB 130 10-channel HF transceiver; MCU-33 remote tuner; and CU-110 antenna coupler; adding 115 lb (52·2 kg) to basic empty weight.

Group KS 1-34. King KX 170B 720-channel nav/com transceiver with 200-channel nav; KI 201C VOR/LOC converter indicator; KR 85 ADF; KT 78 transponder; Piper AutoControl III autopilot; Piper VOR/LOC coupler; Piper electric trim; and Piper 66C microphone; adding 44 lb (20 kg) to basic empty weight.

Group KS 2-34. As Group KS 1-34, plus second KX 170B; KI 214 VOR/LOC/glideslope indicator with VOR/LOC converter and 40-channel glideslope receiver; KMA 20 audio panel with marker beacon receiver and indicator lights; and Piper dual broad band antennae and static discharge wicks; adding 67 lb (30 kg) to basic empty weight.

Group KTS 3-34. Dual King KX 175B nav/com transceivers with 720-channel com and 200-channel nav; dual KNI 520 VOR/LOC/glideslope indicators; dual KN 77 VOR/LOC converters; KN 73 40-channel glideslope receiver; KMA 20 audio panel with marker beacon receiver and indicator lights; KR 85 ADF; KT 76 transponder; KN 65 DME; Piper AltiMatic IIIB-1 autopilot with VOR/LOC and glideslope couplers; Piper electric trim; Piper dual broad band antennae and static discharge wicks; and Piper 100T noise cancelling microphone; adding 90 lb (40·5 kg) to basic empty weight.

Group KTS 4-34. As group KTS 3-34, with deletion of KMA 20 and addition of KMA 20-04 audio panel, marker beacon receiver and lights; second KR 85 with 551C dual needle ADF indicator; ASB 130 10-channel HF transceiver; MCU-33 remote tuner; and CU-110 antenna coupler; adding 133 lb (60·3 kg) to basic empty weight.

Two operational groups are also available:

Executive. Comprising Piper Truspeed indicator, glare-ban instrument lights, four individual reading lights, anti-collision lights, Piper mixture control indicator, full flow oil filters, heated pitot, towbar, inertia reel safety belts for crew seats, dual vacuum system and advanced instrument panel with 3 in pictorial gyro horizon, 3 in directional gyro, Piper turn rate indicator, rate of climb indicator, outside air temperature gauge and eight-day clock; adding 50 lb (22·5 kg) to basic empty weight.

Sportsman. As Executive group, plus inertia reel safety belts for centre and rear seats, six headrests, solar control windows and external power socket; adding 69 lb (31 kg) to basic empty weight.

A total of 766 PA-34 Senecas had been delivered by 31 December 1973.

Piper PA-31T Cheyenne light transport (two 620 ehp UACL PT6A-28 turboprop engines)

Piper PA-31T Cheyenne six/eight-seat light transport aircraft (*Pilot Press*)

TYPE: Six/seven-seat twin-engined light aircraft.

WINGS: Cantilever low-wing monoplane. Single-spar wings, plain ailerons, and wide-span slotted flaps, of light alloy construction. Glassfibre wingtips. Aileron and rudder interconnect systems. Flaps manually operated.

FUSELAGE: Light alloy semi-monocoque structure. Glassfibre engine cowlings.

TAIL UNIT: Cantilever structure of light alloy. One-piece all-moving horizontal surface with combined anti-balance and trim tab. Trim tab in rudder.

LANDING GEAR: Hydraulically-retractable tricycle type. Steerable nosewheel. Emergency free-fall extension system. Main wheels with tyres size 6·00-6, 8-ply rating; nosewheel and tyre size 6·00-6, 6-ply rating. High-capacity disc brakes. Parking brake.

POWER PLANT: Two 200 hp Lycoming IO-360 four-cylinder horizontally-opposed aircooled fuel-injection engines, driving Hartzell two-blade metal constant-speed fully-feathering propellers. Fuel in two tanks in wings, with a total capacity of 100 US gallons (378 litres), of which 95 US gallons (359 litres) are usable.

ACCOMMODATION: Enclosed cabin, seating six people in pairs on individual seats with 10 in (25·4 cm) centre aisle. Optional seventh seat between two centre seats. Dual controls standard. Pilot's storm window. Two forward-hinged doors, one on starboard side at front, the other on port side at rear. Large optional door adjacent to rear cabin door provides an extra-wide opening for loading bulky items. Passenger seats removable easily without tools to provide different seating/baggage/cargo combinations. Space for 100 lb (45 kg) baggage at rear of cabin, and for 100 lb (45 kg) in nose compartment with external access door on port side. Cabin heated and ventilated.

SYSTEMS: Electro-hydraulic system for landing gear retraction. Electrical system powered by dual 12V 60A alternators. 12V 35Ah battery. Dual engine-driven vacuum pumps for flight instruments optional.

ELECTRONICS AND EQUIPMENT: Factory-installed radio packages as group listing in introductory copy. Standard equipment includes sun visors, soundproofing, Piper automatic locator, tie-down rings, aircraft step, nose gear safety mirror and dual stall warning sensors. Optional items include individual reading lights, shoulder harness, zinc chromate finish, Copon treatment and stainless steel cables, cabin fire extinguisher, headrests, inertia reel safety belts for centre and rear seats, seventh seat, solar control windows, external power socket, a complete de-icing group, anti-collision lights, vertically adjustable crew seats, ventilation fan, super soundproofing, and auxiliary combustion heater.

DIMENSIONS, EXTERNAL:
- Wing span: 38 ft 10¾ in (11·85 m)
- Length overall: 28 ft 6 in (8·69 m)
- Height overall: 9 ft 10¾ in (3·02 m)
- Wheel track: 11 ft 1¼ in (3·38 m)
- Wheelbase: 7 ft 0 in (2·13 m)
- Propeller diameter: 6 ft 4 in (1·93 m)

AREA:
- Wings, gross: 206·5 sq ft (19·18 m^2)

WEIGHTS AND LOADINGS:
- Weight empty: 2,623 lb (1,190 kg)
- Max T-O weight: 4,200 lb (1,905 kg)
- Max wing loading: 20·3 lb/sq ft (99·1 kg/m^2)
- Max power loading: 10·5 lb/hp (4·76 kg/hp)

PERFORMANCE (at max T-O weight, except where detailed otherwise):
- Max level speed at S/L: 169 knots (195 mph; 314 km/h)
- Cruising speed:
  - 75% power at 6,000 ft (1,830 m): 162 knots (186 mph; 299 km/h)
  - 65% power at 9,000 ft (2,745 m): 160 knots (184 mph; 296 km/h)
  - 55% power at 13,300 ft (4,055 m): 155 knots (178 mph; 286 km/h)
- Stalling speed, wheels and flaps down: 60 knots (69 mph; 111 km/h)
- Max rate of climb at S/L: 1,360 ft (415 m)/min
- Rate of climb at S/L, one engine out: 190 ft (58 m)/min
- Service ceiling: 17,900 ft (5,455 m)
- Service ceiling, one engine out: 3,650 ft (1,110 m)
- Absolute ceiling: 19,400 ft (5,915 m)
- Absolute ceiling, one engine out: 5,000 ft (1,525 m)
- T-O run: 1,000 ft (305 m)
- T-O to 50 ft (15 m): 1,420 ft (433 m)
- Landing from 50 ft (15 m): 1,335 ft (407 m)
- Landing run: 705 ft (215 m)
- Accelerate/stop distance: 1,860 ft (567 m)
- Range at optimum altitude:
  - At 75% power 716 nm (825 miles; 1,327 km)
  - At 65% power 825 nm (950 miles; 1,528 km)
  - At 55% power 864 nm (995 miles; 1,600 km)

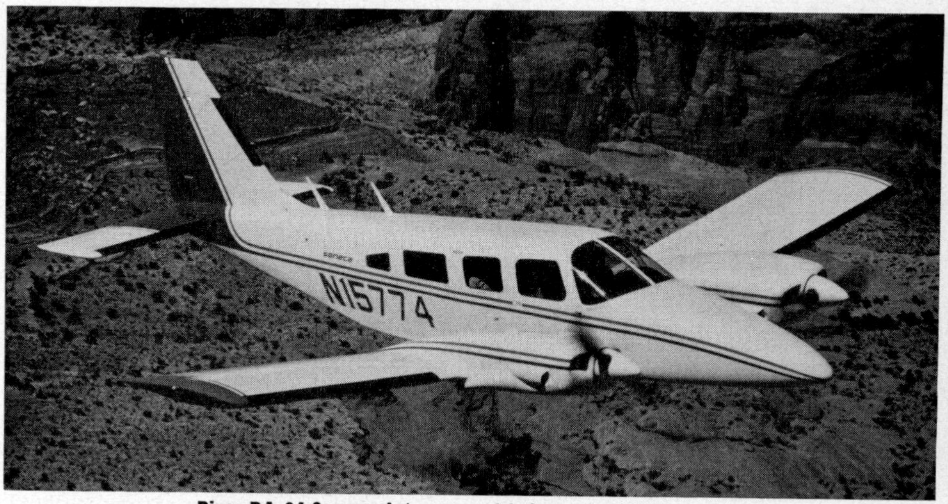

Piper PA-34 Seneca six/seven-seat twin-engined light aircraft

Piper PA-36 Pawnee Brave agricultural aircraft (285 hp Teledyne Continental Tiara 6-285 engine)

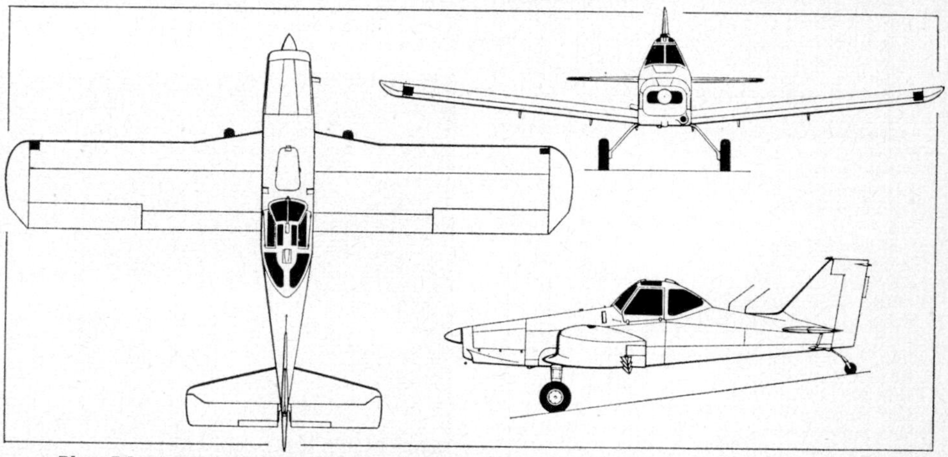

Piper PA-36 Pawnee Brave, latest version of the Pawnee agricultural aircraft (*Pilot Press*)

PIPER PA-36 PAWNEE BRAVE

On 9 October 1972 Piper Aircraft Corporation released details of a new agricultural aircraft named the Pawnee Brave, which has a more powerful engine than the PA-25 Pawnee C, is larger, and has increased capacity for either liquid or dry chemicals.

More than 4,250 PA-25s have been built by Piper; experience gained in their construction, progressive refinement, and operation led to design of the Brave. Primary consideration was to provide an aircraft able to offer high standards of safety and comfort for the pilot.

The basic configuration seats the pilot well aft. The long nose is designed to collapse progressively in an emergency. The fuselage is a welded truss structure of chrome-molybdenum steel, which is graded in strength to provide excellent energy absorption and progressive collapse. A sturdy overturn pylon is an integral part of the fuselage structure. The wing is of conventional cantilever construction, with laminated spars to provide structural redundancy. The wing leading-edges each comprise two glassfibre sections, reinforced by a foam insert beam running spanwise. Normal impacts are absorbed by the leading-edge, more serious contacts by ribs designed to collapse with minimal impact transference to the basic wing structure.

The pilot is located in an isolated cockpit capsule which keeps him well clear of main structural members. The floor, for example, is 1 ft 0 in (0·30 m) above the lower longerons, and a cockpit width of 3 ft 2 in (0·97 m) allows for substantial deformation of the fuselage structure without hazard to the pilot. The seat is attached to the overturn pylon, and is articulated to allow the pilot's position to change with fuselage deformation. The cockpit capsule is sealed to prevent the ingress of toxic chemicals; and all protrusions, knobs, and levers which might cause injury have been eliminated. The instrument panel is equipped with a large energy-absorbing crash roll.

Ventilation of the cockpit capsule is provided by an airscoop in the top of the canopy, which filters the incoming air before discharge through two adjustable diffusers. A heating system is standard, and the inflow of ventilating and/or heated air has the effect of pressurising the cockpit, further discouraging any inflow of toxic fumes or chemicals.

Power plant consists of a 285 hp Teledyne Continental Tiara engine which, having a 2 : 1 reduction gear, permits the use of a large-diameter propeller. Turning at only 1,700 rpm at normal cruising speed, this ensures that the Brave is quiet in operation.

Several fire suppression provisions have been introduced which are unique for an agricultural aircraft. The fuel tanks, located in the wing roots, are filled with reticulated polyurethane foam to serve both as a fire suppressant and as an infinite baffle to reduce fuel surge. Fire-resistant fuel pipes are wire-reinforced at potential rupture points.

To meet varying requirements, two hopper sizes are available. The larger hopper has a maximum dry chemicals capacity of 1,900 lb (862 kg), and is compatible with applicators designed to spread chemicals at rates of up to 400 lb (181 kg) per acre.

Spray equipment for the PA-36 has a capability of up to 228 US gallons (863 litres) per minute, which is the equivalent of 17 US gallons (64 litres) per acre at 117 knots (135 mph; 217 km/h) and with a 50 ft (15·25 m) swath width. The spray equipment consists of a quickly-removable pylon-mounted wind-driven spray pump, and spraybooms located just aft of the wing trailing-edges. This location reduces drag and allows the pilot to make visual checks of their operation.

All parts of the Brave's airframe are treated to prevent corrosion damage, with extensive use of polyurethane coating, selection of stainless steel for cables and other moving components in vulnerable areas, and internal oiling of lower truss sections. The design eliminates dust traps and inaccessible areas, and fuselage covering is spaced away from the frame to permit thorough hosing down. To facilitate washing, inspection and maintenance, the plastics side panels and entire belly covering are attached by quick-release fasteners.

A total of 62 PA-36 Pawnee Braves had been delivered by 31 December 1973.

TYPE: Single-seat agricultural aircraft.

WINGS: Cantilever low-wing monoplane. Conventional two-spar metal structure. Light alloy laminated spars with two-bolt main spar attachment to fuselage structure. Light alloy covering, except for detachable leading-edges of glassfibre, reinforced by foam inserts, and glassfibre wingtips. Conventional ailerons and trailing-edge flaps. Landing lights in wing leading-edges.

FUSELAGE: Welded chrome-molybdenum steel tube structure. Removable metal underskin and removable side panels of plastics material. Glassfibre engine cowling.

TAIL UNIT: Cantilever all-metal structure. Tab on rudder and in each elevator. Cable from top of cockpit structure to tip of fin to deflect cables.

LANDING GEAR: Non-retractable tailwheel type. Interchangeable cantilever spring steel main-gear struts, with wire-cutters on leading-edges. Main wheels and tyres size 8·50-10. Steerable tailwheel with tyre of 10 in (0·25 m) diameter. Parking brake.

POWER PLANT: One 285 hp Teledyne Continental Tiara 6-285 six-cylinder horizontally-opposed aircooled engine, driving a Hartzell two-blade metal constant-speed propeller. One fuel tank in each wing root, capacity 45 US gallons (170·3 litres). Total fuel capacity 90 US gallons (340·6 litres), of which 85 US gallons (322 litres) are usable. Refuelling point on upper surface of each wing. Fuel tanks filled with reticulated polyurethane safety foam (Safom).

ACCOMMODATION: Pilot only, on adjustable seat in an isolated cockpit capsule, with steel tube overturn structure. Seat, equipped with double shoulder harness and inertia reel, is attached to overturn structure. Wire-cutter mounted in centre of windscreen. Combined window and door on each side, hinged at bottom. Cockpit capsule is heated and ventilated.

SYSTEMS: Electrical system supplied by 28V 60A alternator, with 24V 17Ah battery. Hydraulic system for brakes only.

EQUIPMENT: Standard equipment includes a non-corrosive hopper/tank of translucent glassfibre-reinforced plastics, installed forward of cockpit and approximately on CG, of 30 cu ft (0·85 m³) capacity, containing 225 US gallons (852 litres). Optional hopper/tank of 38 cu ft (1·08 m³) capacity, containing 275 US gallons (1,041 litres). The latter has a maximum capacity for dry chemicals of 1,900 lb (862 kg). Venturi-type dry material spreaders of either stainless steel or aluminium available, including a basic design capable of application rates of 5 to 200 lb (2·3 to 91 kg) per acre. Spray system comprises an easily-removable wind-driven spray pump and 1½ in (0·38 cm) diameter sprayboorns equipped with 60 nozzles. Other optional equipment includes sensitive altimeter; 8-day clock; turn co-ordinator; landing and taxi lights; navigation, instrument panel and anti-collision lights; cockpit fire extinguisher; and heater.

DIMENSIONS, EXTERNAL:

Wing span	39 ft 0 in (11·89 m)
Length overall	27 ft 4¼ in (8·34 m)
Propeller diameter	7 ft 11 in (2·41 m)
Propeller ground clearance	10 in (0·25 m)

WEIGHTS AND LOADINGS:

Weight empty:	
Normal category	2,050 lb (930 kg)
sprayer/duster	2,185 lb (991 kg)
Max T-O weight:	
Normal category	3,900 lb (1,769 kg)
Restricted category	4,400 lb (1,996 kg)
Wing loading:	
Normal category	17·3 lb/sq ft (84·4 kg/m²)
Restricted category	19·1 lb/sq ft (93·2 kg/m²)

PERFORMANCE: (A: Normal category at 3,900 lb; 1,769 kg max T-O weight; B: duster and C: sprayer at Restricted category max T-O weight of 4,400 lb; 1,995 kg):

Max level speed at S/L:	
A	131 knots (151 mph; 243 km/h) CAS
B	108 knots (124 mph; 200 km/h) CAS
C	109 knots (125 mph; 201 km/h) CAS
Max cruising speed, 75% power at optimum altitude:	
A	128 knots (147 mph; 236 km/h) TAS
Max cruising speed, 75% power at 2,000 ft (610 m):	
B	88 knots (101 mph; 163 km/h) TAS
C	92 knots (106 mph; 171 km/h) TAS
Stalling speed, flaps down, power off:	
A	54 knots (62 mph; 100 km/h) CAS
B	58·5 knots (67 mph; 108 km/h) CAS
C	57·5 knots (66 mph; 107 km/h) CAS
Max rate of climb at S/L:	
A	790 ft (241 m)/min
B, C	355 ft (108 m)/min
Service ceiling:	
A	13,000 ft (3,960 m)
B, C	5,900 ft (1,800 m)
Absolute ceiling:	
A	15,000 ft (4,570 m)
B, C	8,100 ft (2,470 m)
Normal T-O run (flaps up):	
A	910 ft (277 m)
B, C	2,038 ft (621 m)
Landing from 50 ft (15 m):	
A	1,650 ft (503 m)
B, C	1,470 ft (448 m)
Landing run:	
A	700 ft (213 m)
B	715 ft (218 m)
Range, 75% power at optimum altitude, max fuel, no reserve:	
A	645 nm (743 miles; 1,195 km)
Range, 75% power at 2,000 ft (610 m), max fuel, no reserve:	
B	443 nm (510 miles; 820 km)
C	464 nm (535 miles; 861 km)

PIPER PA-39 TWIN COMANCHE C/R AND PA-39 TURBO TWIN COMANCHE C/R

Production of these two models ended in 1972 after a total of 144 had been delivered. The PA-30 Twin Comanche that preceded them went out of production in 1971 after a total of 1,998 had been built. Details of the PA-30 and PA-39 Twin Comanches may be found in the 1970-71 and 1973-74 *Jane's* respectively.

PITTS

PITTS AVIATION ENTERPRISES, INC

ADDRESS:
PO Box 548, Homestead, Florida 33030

Telephone: (305) 247-5423

PRESIDENT: C. H. Pitts

One of the best-known US designers of high-performance sporting aircraft, Mr Curtis Pitts is responsible for the single-seat and two-seat Pitts Special biplanes. Detailed construction drawings are available for the single-seat S-1 version. The two-seat S-2 is available only as a factory-built aircraft, being produced for Pitts Aviation by Aerotek Inc, of Afton, Wyoming. This latter company is also constructing for Pitts examples of the S-1S, supplied to pilots who do not wish to build their own aircraft.

Kelly Aeroplane Ltd in the UK has world sales rights of, and is the only European agent for, the Pitts S-1S and S-2A. After-sales maintenance has been assigned to Personal Plane Services Ltd of Wycombe Air Park, Booker, Marlow, Buckinghamshire.

Pitts S-1S Special owned by Mr W. Brown of Fort Lauderdale, Florida

PITTS S-1 SPECIAL

The original single-seat Pitts Special was designed in 1943-44. Construction of a prototype began in 1944 and it flew in September of that year. One of the most successful early models was *Little Stinker*, powered by a 90 hp Continental engine, and built by Mr Pitts in 1947 for Miss Betty Skelton, the internationally-known aerobatic display pilot. The *Black Beauty* biplane, built by Pitts for Miss Caro Bailey, was of similar design, but powered by a 125 hp Lycoming O-290-D engine.

Since then even more powerful engines have been installed in Pitts Specials built by both the designer and other people, and the version of the single-seat Special for which drawings are supplied by Mr Pitts is designed to take a Lycoming engine of up to 180 hp.

There are three versions of the S-1:

S-1D. Intended for homebuilders only, with plans available.

S-1S. Production aircraft, FAA type certificated and built at rate of 25 aircraft per year. It is available also in kit form, parts, materials and components being produced under an FAA Approved Production Certificate.

Pitts can also supply plans for an **S-1C** version. By comparison with earlier models, this has flat-bottomed wings and ailerons on the lower wing only, and is suitable for the installation of engines from 100 to 180 hp. Kelly Aeroplane Ltd had a single example of the S-1C built by Wally Berry and Berth Ethridge (G-AXNZ).

Details of some of the major successes achieved by US pilots of Pitts Specials in national and international aerobatic competitions, since 1966, were given in the 1972-73 *Jane's*. After that edition went to press, a US team, all flying Pitts Specials, recorded the greatest success to date in the 7th World Aerobatic Championships, held at Salon-en-Provence, France, on 18-31 July 1972. Charles Hillard became men's champion, with Gene Soucy third in another Pitts and the remaining Americans in sixth and ninth positions. Mary Gaffaney won the women's contest, and the US team carried off the team prize, with the Soviet Yak-18s second.

It is believed that approximately 300 S-1s had been homebuilt by the end of 1973. The details which follow apply to the basic design with 180 hp engine, but engines of 100-180 hp are suitable.

TYPE: Single-seat sporting biplane.

WINGS: Braced biplane type, with single faired interplane strut each side and N-type cabane struts. Dual streamline flying and landing wires. Wing section M6. Thickness/chord ratio 12%. Dihedral 0° on upper wing, 3° on lower wings. Incidence 1° 30′ on upper wing, 0° on lower wings. Sweepback at quarter-chord 6° 45′. Wooden structure, with fabric covering. Frise-type ailerons on lower wings only, of similar construction to wings.

FUSELAGE: Welded steel tube structure, covered with fabric.

TAIL UNIT: Wire-braced steel tube structure, fabric-covered.

LANDING GEAR: Non-retractable tailwheel type. Rubber-cord shock-absorption. Cleveland main wheels and tyres, size 5·00-5, pressure 30 lb/sq in (2·10 kg/cm²). Cleveland hydraulic brakes. Steerable tailwheel. Fairings on main wheels.

POWER PLANT: One 180 hp Lycoming IO-360-B4A four-cylinder horizontally-opposed air-cooled engine, driving a Sensenich type 76EM8-O-56/62 two-blade metal fixed-pitch propeller. Fuel tank aft of firewall, capacity 20 US gallons (75 litres). Oil capacity 2 US gallons (7·5 litres). Inverted fuel and oil systems standard.

ACCOMMODATION: Single seat in open cockpit.

DIMENSIONS, EXTERNAL:
Wing span, upper 17 ft 4 in (5·28 m)
Wing chord (constant, both) 3 ft 0 in (0·91 m)
Wing aspect ratio 5·77
Length overall 15 ft 6 in (4·72 m)
Height overall 6 ft 3 in (1·91 m)
Tailplane span 6 ft 6 in (1·98 m)
Propeller diameter 6 ft 0 in (1·83 m)

AREA:
Wings, gross 98·5 sq ft (9·15 m²)

WEIGHTS AND LOADING:
Weight empty 720 lb (326 kg)
Max T-O weight 1,150 lb (521 kg)
Max power loading 6·38 lb/hp (2·89 kg/hp)

PERFORMANCE (at max T-O weight):
Max never-exceed speed 188 knots (217 mph; 350 km/h)
Max level speed at S/L 154 knots (177 mph; 285 km/h)
Max cruising speed at S/L 122 knots (141 mph; 227 km/h)
Stalling speed 56 knots (64 mph; 103 km/h)
Max rate of climb at S/L 2,677 ft (816 m)/min
Service ceiling 22,300 ft (6,795 m)
T-O to 50 ft (15 m) 1,085 ft (331 m)
Range with max fuel, no reserve 273 nm (315 miles; 507 km)

PITTS S-2A SPECIAL

First flown in 1967, the S-2A is a two-seat version of the Pitts Special. It is similar to the single-seat S-1 in basic configuration and construction, but is slightly larger in overall dimensions, with no attempt at commonality of components. The increased size and power, coupled with aerodynamic changes, give the two-seater improved aerobatic and landing characteristics, and make it extremely stable in rough air conditions. Control responses are better than on the S-1. The ailerons are aerodynamically balanced for higher rate of roll at low speeds, and full vertical rolls can be made with ease. The different wing sections used on the S-2A provide inverted performance equal to conventional flight and facilitate outside loops. Structure stressed to 9*g* positive, 4·5*g* negative.

The S-2A is FAA type certificated in the Normal and Aerobatic categories. It is a production aeroplane, not intended for the homebuilder, and plans are not available. Production was at a rate of two aircraft per month in 1974.

Five S-2As, each fitted with a 200 hp Lycoming engine, were supplied in early 1973 to the British aerobatic team financed by the Rothman Tobacco Company. During displays, the front cockpit of each aircraft is covered by a removable panel. Five similar aircraft have been supplied to the Carling Black Label Aerobatic Team which operates from Toronto, Canada. Both of these teams are organised by Kelly Aeroplane Ltd of the UK, this British company having sales rights for production S-1S and S-2A aircraft throughout the world. In addition, Kelly Aeroplane is the sole agent for sales of these aircraft in Europe.

S-2As have been exported to Australia, Brazil, Sweden and Venezuela, and a total of 68 of these aircraft had been built by February 1974.

TYPE: Two-seat aerobatic biplane.

One of the Pitts S-2A Specials flown by the UK Rothmans aerobatic display team

WINGS: Braced biplane type, with single faired interplane strut each side and N-type cabane. Wing section NACA 6400 series on upper wing, 00 series on bottom wings. Wooden structure with fabric covering. Aerodynamically-balanced ailerons on both upper and lower wings.

FUSELAGE: Welded steel tube structure, covered with fabric.

TAIL UNIT: Wire-braced welded steel tube structure. Fixed surfaces metal-covered, control surfaces fabric-covered.

LANDING GEAR: Non-retractable tailwheel type. Rubber-cord shock-absorption. Steerable tailwheel. Fairings on main wheels.

POWER PLANT: One 180 hp Lycoming IO-360-B4A four-cylinder horizontally-opposed aircooled engine in S-2. One 200 hp Lycoming IO-360-AIA engine in S-2A, driving a Hartzell type HC-C2YK-4/C7666A-2 two-blade metal constant-speed propeller with spinner. Fuel tank in fuselage, immediately aft of firewall, capacity 24 US gallons (90·5 litres). Refuelling point on fuselage upper surface forward of front windscreen. Oil capacity 2 US gallons (7·5 litres). Inverted fuel and oil systems standard.

ACCOMMODATION: Two seats in tandem open cockpits with dual controls. Space for 20 lb (9 kg) baggage aft of rear cockpit when flown in non-aerobatic category.

SYSTEM: Electrical system powered by 12V 40A alternator and non-spill 12V battery.

DIMENSIONS, EXTERNAL:
Wing span, upper 20 ft 0 in (6·10 m)
Wing chord (constant, both) 3 ft 4 in (1·02 m)
Length overall 17 ft 9 in (5·41 m)
Height overall 6 ft 4½ in (1·94 m)

AREA:
Wings, gross 125 sq ft (11·6 m²)

WEIGHTS AND LOADINGS (200 hp engine, A: Aerobatic; B: Normal category):
Weight empty:
A, B 1,000 lb (453 kg)
Max T-O weight:
A 1,500 lb (680 kg)
B 1,575 lb (714 kg)
Max wing loading:
A 12·0 lb/sq ft (58·6 kg/m²)
B 12·6 lb/sq ft (61·5 kg/m²)
Max power loading:
A 7·5 lb/hp (3·40 kg/hp)
B 7·87 lb/hp (3·57 kg/hp)

PERFORMANCE (200 hp engine, at max T-O weight. A: Aerobatic; B: Normal category):
Max never-exceed speed:
A, B 176 knots (203 mph; 326 km/h)
Max level speed at S/L:
A, B 136 knots (157 mph; 253 km/h)
Max cruising speed at S/L:
A, B 124 knots (143 mph; 230 km/h)
Stalling speed:
A 51 knots (58 mph; 94 km/h)
B 51·5 knots (59 mph; 95 km/h)
Max rate of climb at S/L:
A 1,900 ft (579 m)/min
B 1,800 ft (549 m)/min
Service ceiling:
A 20,100 ft (6,125 m)
B 16,000 ft (4,875 m)
T-O to 50 ft (15 m):
A 1,150 ft (351 m)
Range with max fuel:
A 297 nm (343 miles; 552 km)

POLEN

POLEN AIRCRAFT

ADDRESS:
14525 SE Bush, Portland, Oregon 97236

PRESIDENT:
Denis N. Polen

Mr Polen has formed Polen Aircraft to market plans of a single-seat high-performance sporting aircraft which he has named Polen Special II. An earlier Polen Special designed by Mr Polen, named Lil' Honey, was described in the 1968-69 *Jane's*.

Design of the Special II began in November 1966, with construction beginning almost two years later. The first flight of the prototype was made in May 1972.

POLEN SPECIAL II

TYPE: Single-seat high-performance homebuilt sporting aircraft.

WINGS: Cantilever low-wing monoplane. Wing section NACA 65_A212. Dihedral 5°. Incidence 1°. Light alloy single-spar structure with stressed skins. Sealed-gap ailerons of light alloy construction. Plain trailing-edge flaps of light alloy. No trim tabs.

FUSELAGE: Monocoque structure of light alloy.

TAIL UNIT: Cantilever structure of light alloy. Fixed-incidence tailplane.

LANDING GEAR: Hydraulically-retractable tailwheel type. Main units retract inward, tailwheel aft. Oleo-pneumatic shock-struts, with single wheel on each unit. Main-wheel tyres size 16 × 5·00-5, pressure 45 lb/sq in (3·16 kg/cm²). Tailwheel has solid rubber tyre size 6 × 2-3. Cleveland single-disc hydraulic brakes.

POWER PLANT: One 200 hp Lycoming TSIO-360-A1A four-cylinder horizontally-opposed aircooled engine, driving a Hartzell two-blade metal constant-speed propeller with spinner. Integral fuel tank in each wing with a combined capacity of 45 US gallons (170 litres). Refuelling point in upper surface of each wing. Oil capacity 2 US gallons (7·5 litres).

ACCOMMODATION: Single seat beneath transparent bubble canopy, hinged at side. Cockpit heated and ventilated.

SYSTEMS: Hydraulic system supplied by electrically-driven pump. Electrical system powered by a 12V DC generator with 115V AC inverter. Low-pressure diluter demand oxygen system.

ELECTRONICS AND EQUIPMENT: 360-channel VHF com transceiver, VHF nav receiver, LOC/ILS, MB1049 transponder. Blind-flying instrumentation standard.

DIMENSIONS, EXTERNAL:
Wing span 21 ft 5 in (6·53 m)
Wing chord at root 5 ft 4 in (1·63 m)
Wing chord at tip 2 ft 6 in (0·76 m)
Wing aspect ratio 5·8
Length overall 19 ft 6 in (5·94 m)
Height overall 4 ft 10 in (1·47 m)
Tailplane span 7 ft 0 in (2·13 m)
Wheel track 7 ft 0 in (2·13 m)
Wheelbase 11 ft 6 in (3·51 m)
Propeller diameter 6 ft 2 in (1·88 m)
Propeller ground clearance 8 in (0·20 m)

AREAS:
Wings, gross 94 sq ft (8·73 m²)
Ailerons (total) 4·8 sq ft (0·45 m²)

Polen Special II single-seat homebuilt sporting aircraft

Trailing-edge flaps (total) 12·4 sq ft (1·15 m²)
Fin 3·6 sq ft (0·33 m²)
Rudder 3·5 sq ft (0·33 m²)
Tailplane 8·9 sq ft (0·83 m²)
Elevators 5·3 sq ft (0·49 m²)
WEIGHTS AND LOADINGS:
Weight empty 1,035 lb (469 kg)
Max T-O and landing weight 1,535 lb (696 kg)
Max wing loading 16·3 lb/sq ft (79·6 kg/m²)
Max power loading 7·67 lb/hp (3·48 kg/hp)
PERFORMANCE (at max T-O weight):
Max never-exceed speed
299 knots (345 mph; 555 km/h) IAS
Max level speed at 18,000 ft (5,485 m)
282 knots (325 mph; 523 km/h)
Max cruising speed at 22,000 ft (6,700 m)
271 knots (312 mph; 502 km/h)
Econ cruising speed at 24,000 ft (7,315 m)
213 knots (245 mph; 394 km/h)
Stalling speed, flaps down
57 knots (65 mph; 105 km/h) IAS
Max rate of climb at S/L 3,800 ft (1,158 m)/min
Service ceiling 28,000 ft (8,535 m)
T-O run 800 ft (244 m)
T-O to 50 ft (15 m) 1,200 ft (366 m)
Landing run from 50 ft (15 m) 2,000 ft (610 m)
Range with max fuel
1,215 nm (1,400 miles; 2,250 km)
Range with max payload, 30 min reserve
1,040 nm (1,200 miles; 1,930 km)

POWELL

JOHN C. POWELL

ADDRESS:
4 Donald Drive, Middletown, Rhode Island 02840

John Powell, formerly a Commander in the US Navy, has designed and built a two-seat parasol-wing monoplane, of which plans are available to amateur constructors. Known as the P-70 Acey Deucy, its design was started in 1966 and construction began during 1967. FAA certification in the Experimental homebuilt category was awarded on 19 June 1970 and the first flight was recorded on the following day. By the end of 1973 this prototype had accumulated approximately 400 hours' flying time.

By January 1974, more than 60 sets of plans had been sold, and the first aircraft built from these plans was flying by the Autumn of 1973. It is believed that about 25 more Acey Deucys are under construction.

POWELL P-70 ACEY DEUCY

TYPE: Two-seat homebuilt monoplane.

WINGS: Braced parasol-wing monoplane with steel tube Vee bracing struts on each side, auxiliary bracing struts and N-type centre-section struts. Wing section NACA 4412. Dihedral 1° on outer panels. Incidence 2°. No sweepback. Composite structure of steel tube and wood, fabric covered. Frise-type ailerons of wooden construction, fabric covered. No flaps. No trim tabs.

FUSELAGE: Welded 4130 steel tube structure with wooden stringers, fabric covered.

TAIL UNIT: Wire-braced welded steel tube structure with "U" channel ribs. Tailplane incidence adjustable by screwjack at leading-edge. No trim tabs.

LANDING GEAR: Non-retractable tailwheel type. Two side Vees and half axles hinged to fuselage structure. Shock-absorption by springs in compression. Goodyear main wheels and tyres size 8·00-4, pressure 12 lb/sq in (0·84 kg/cm²). Motor scooter type caliper brakes.

POWER PLANT: Suitable for installation of engines from 65 to 90 hp. Prototype has one 65 hp Continental A65 four-cylinder horizontally-opposed aircooled engine, driving a McCauley two-blade metal fixed-pitch propeller. One fuel tank in fuselage, immediately aft of firewall, capacity 14 US gallons (53 litres). Refuelling point on top of fuselage, forward of front cockpit. Oil capacity 1 US gallon (3·75 litres).

ACCOMMODATION: Two persons in tandem in open cockpits. Small door by front cockpit on starboard side.

DIMENSIONS, EXTERNAL:
Wing span 32 ft 6 in (9·91 m)
Wing chord (constant) 5 ft 0 in (1·52 m)
Wing aspect ratio 6·5
Length overall 20 ft 9 in (6·32 m)
Height overall 6 ft 9 in (2·06 m)
Tailplane span 8 ft 6 in (2·59 m)
Wheel track 6 ft 0 in (1·83 m)
Wheelbase 15 ft 6 in (4·72 m)
Propeller diameter 6 ft 2 in (1·88 m)
Propeller ground clearance 1 ft 6 in (0·46 m)
Door (front cockpit only):
Height 10 in (0·25 m)
Width 1 ft 6 in (0·46 m)
DIMENSIONS, INTERNAL (each cockpit):
Length 3 ft 6 in (1·07 m)
Width 2 ft 2 in (0·66 m)
AREAS:
Wings, gross 155 sq ft (14·4 m²)
Ailerons (total) 18·5 sq ft (1·72 m²)
Fin 3·75 sq ft (3·48 m²)
Rudder 7·06 sq ft (6·56 m²)
Tailplane 13·5 sq ft (1·25 m²)
Elevators 9·5 sq ft (0·88 m²)
WEIGHTS AND LOADINGS:
Weight empty 750 lb (340 kg)
Max T-O and landing weight 1,275 lb (578 kg)
Max wing loading 8 lb/sq ft (39 kg/m²)
Max power loading 20 lb/hp (9·07 kg/hp)
PERFORMANCE (prototype, at max T-O weight):
Max never-exceed speed
117 knots (135 mph; 217 km/h)
Max level speed at 1,000 ft (305 m)
85 knots (98 mph; 158 km/h)
Max cruising speed at 1,000 ft (305 m)
72 knots (83 mph; 134 km/h)
Econ cruising speed at 1,000 ft (305 m)
61 knots (70 mph; 113 km/h)
Stalling speed
approx 22 knots (25 mph; 40·5 km/h)
Max rate of climb at S/L
350-450 ft (107-137 m)/min
T-O run approx 450 ft (137 m)
Landing run approx 500 ft (152 m)
Range with max fuel, 2 US gallons (7·5 litres) reserve 217 nm (250 miles; 402 km)

Powell P-70 Acey Deucy two-seat homebuilt light aircraft

RAISBECK

THE RAISBECK GROUP

HEAD OFFICE:
5421 Bothwell Road, Tarzana, California 91356
Telephone: (213) 996-2555
WORKS:
Van Nuys Airport, Van Nuys, California 91406
PRESIDENT AND BOARD CHAIRMAN:
James D. Raisbeck
VICE-PRESIDENTS:
R. Kim Frinell (Engineering)
F. James Helms (Marketing)
DIRECTOR OF OPERATIONS:
Arlie Willauer

The Raisbeck Group is a new corporation which has been formed by many of the same team members who developed and certificated Robertson Aircraft Corporation's multi-engine STOL product line during the late 1960s and early 1970s. It will use similar design philosophies to improve the productivity of various types of business jet aircraft.

In 1974 the company was working on engineering, development and flight tests of certain advanced technology items on the Grumman Gulfstream II, Lockheed JetStar and Gates Learjet aircraft. These include a fixed supercritical wing leading-edge section designed to offer increased-Mach cruising speeds combined with docile stall characteristics; 100 per cent chord Fowler flaps providing a large increase in overall wing area for take-off and landing; and fail-safe stability and control system augmentation devices aimed at enhancing low-speed controllability. Reductions in take-off and approach speeds of 15 to 30 knots (17-34 mph; 28-56 km/h) are expected, and associated field length reductions should be in the neighbourhood of 35 to 40 per cent.

Successful flight testing of the new supercritical leading-edge was completed in February 1974, and certification of the first advanced technology integrated system was scheduled for early 1975.

RAND

KENNETH C. RAND

ADDRESS:
6171 Cornell Drive, Huntington Beach, California 92647

Mr Kenneth Rand, a flight test engineer with the Douglas Aircraft Company, has designed and built the prototype of a single-seat lightweight sporting aircraft. The design originated in 1969; construction of the prototype was started in 1970 and the first flight was made in February 1972. Plans are available to amateur constructors, and by February 1974 3,490 sets had been sold and more than 20 aircraft were known to be flying.

RAND KR-1

TYPE: Single-seat homebuilt lightweight sporting aircraft.

WINGS: Cantilever low-wing monoplane. Wing section RAF 48. Thickness/chord ratio 18%. Dihedral 5°. Incidence 5° at root, 2° at tip. No sweepback. Composite two-spar structure. Front spar of spruce; rear spar built of spruce and plywood. Most ribs formed from Styrofoam plastics, spaces between ribs being filled with Styrofoam slab. Structure covered with Dynel reinforced epoxy. Outer wing panels removable for storage. Ailerons constructed of Styrofoam, with Dynel reinforced epoxy covering, over full span of outer panels. No flaps.

Rand KR-1 lightweight homebuilt aircraft (36 hp 1,200 cc Volkswagen modified motor car engine)

FUSELAGE: Composite structure, lower half of spruce longerons with plywood skin, upper surface of carved Styrofoam covered with

Dynel epoxy. Firewall is a plywood, asbestos and aluminium lamination.

TAIL UNIT: Cantilever structure with spruce spars, the remainder of the structure being carved Styrofoam, Dynel epoxy covered. Fixed-incidence tailplane. Trim tabs in rudder and elevator.

LANDING GEAR: Tailwheel type. Main units retract aft manually into wing centre-section. Shock-absorption by flat spring crossbar to which main units are attached. Main-wheel tyres size 10½ × 4·00-5, pressure 20 lb/sq in (1·4 kg/cm²). Tailwheel with solid tyre of 3 in (7·6 cm) diameter. Manual drum brakes.

POWER PLANT: One 36 hp 1,200 cc Volkswagen modified motor car engine, driving a Hegy two-blade fixed-pitch propeller with spinner. Fuel tank immediately aft of firewall, capacity 7 US gallons (26·5 litres). Refuelling point on fuselage upper surface, forward of windscreen. Oil capacity 0·75 US gallon (2·8 litres).

ACCOMMODATION: Pilot only beneath transparent cockpit canopy, built integrally with centre-fuselage decking, which is hinged on starboard side and opens upward and to starboard. Baggage space aft of seat.

SYSTEM: Electrical power supplied by 4·5A 12V Honda motorcycle engine-driven alternator and 12V 7Ah storage battery.

ELECTRONICS: Genave Alpha 200B 200-channel nav/com transceiver.

DIMENSIONS, EXTERNAL:
- Wing span: 17 ft 2 in (5·23 m)
- Wing chord at root: 4 ft 0 in (1·22 m)
- Wing chord at tip: 3 ft 0 in (0·91 m)
- Wing aspect ratio: 4·5
- Length overall: 12 ft 6 in (3·81 m)
- Width, wings removed: 5 ft 0 in (1·52 m)
- Height overall: 3 ft 6 in (1·07 m)
- Tailplane span: 5 ft 0 in (1·52 m)
- Wheel track: 4 ft 2 in (1·27 m)
- Propeller diameter: 4 ft 5 in (1·35 m)
- Propeller ground clearance: 6 in (15 cm)

DIMENSIONS, INTERNAL:
- Cockpit:
  - Length: 4 ft 0 in (1·22 m)
  - Max width: 1 ft 8 in (0·51 m)
  - Max height: 2 ft 6 in (0·76 m)
  - Baggage hold: 4 cu ft (0·11 m³)

AREAS:
- Wings, gross: 64 sq ft (5·95 m²)
- Ailerons (total): 5 sq ft (0·46 m²)
- Rudder, including tab: 3·5 sq ft (0·33 m²)
- Tailplane: 12·5 sq ft (1·16 m²)

WEIGHTS AND LOADINGS:
- Weight empty, equipped: 340 lb (154 kg)
- Max T-O and landing weight: 600 lb (272 kg)
- Max wing loading: 9·5 lb/sq ft (46·4 kg/m²)
- Max power loading: 17 lb/hp (7·71 kg/hp)

PERFORMANCE (at max T-O weight):
- Max never-exceed speed: 140 knots (161 mph; 259 km/h)
- Max level speed at S/L: 130 knots (150 mph; 241 km/h)
- Max cruising speed at 5,000 ft (1,525 m): 130 knots (150 mph; 241 km/h)
- Econ cruising speed at 6,000 ft (1,830 m): 100 knots (115 mph; 185 km/h)
- Stalling speed: 39 knots (45 mph; 73 km/h)
- Max rate of climb at S/L: 600 ft (182 m)/min
- Service ceiling: 12,000 ft (3,658 m)
- T-O run: 400 ft (122 m)
- T-O to 50 ft (15 m): 800 ft (244 m)
- Landing from 50 ft (15 m): 1,000 ft (305 m)
- Landing run: 500 ft (152 m)
- Range with max fuel: 650 nm (748 miles; 1,203 km)

RICHARD

THE C. H. RICHARD COMPANY

ADDRESS:
2561 West Avenue K, Lancaster, California 93534
Telephone: (805) 942-4015

Mr C. H. Richard has designed a two-seat high-wing cabin monoplane, designated Richard 125 Commuter; a more powerful version of this known as the Richard 150 Commuter; a single-seat mid-wing monoplane, designated Richard 190 Sportplane; and a two-thirds scale replica of the German Focke-Wulf Fw 190A-3 fighter of the second World War. He formed a company to develop these designs, with the intention of marketing plans, certain assemblies and kits of parts to amateur constructors, and all of these aircraft were described in the 1971-72 *Jane's*. Since that time Mr Richard has decided to concentrate on development of the Richard 150 Commuter, and details of this aircraft follow:

Richard 150 Commuter two-seat light aircraft (150 hp Lycoming O-320-A2A engine)

RICHARD 150 COMMUTER

The prototype Richard 150 Commuter is an all-metal two-seat high-wing monoplane, powered by a 150 hp engine and with no double-curvature skin panels. The following details refer to the prototype 150 Commuter in its original form. Mr Richard has since designed and built a new wing for it, with a different wing section and reduced area of 100 sq ft (9·29 m²). No details of performance with the new wing are yet available.

TYPE: Two-seat cabin monoplane.

WINGS: Braced high-wing monoplane with single streamline-section bracing strut each side. Wing has constant chord. All-metal single-spar structure, with skins of 0·032 in thick 2024-T3 aluminium sheet, wrapped chordwise around the leading-edge and flush-riveted. Flaps and ailerons of metal construction. Ailerons mass-balanced. No trim tabs.

FUSELAGE: All-metal semi-monocoque structure, made in separate centre-section and tailcone assemblies.

TAIL UNIT: Cantilever all-metal structure. Fixed-incidence tailplane. Elevators and rudder of metal construction, mass-balanced. No trim tabs.

LANDING GEAR: Non-retractable tailwheel type. Goodyear main wheels and tyres size 5·00-5. Hydraulic brakes.

POWER PLANT: One 150 hp Lycoming O-320-A2A four-cylinder horizontally-opposed aircooled engine, driving a two-blade fixed-pitch metal propeller. Fuel contained in integral wing tanks with standard capacity of 50 US gallons (189 litres). Optional tankage for a maximum of 100 US gallons (378 litres).

ACCOMMODATION: Two seats side by side in enclosed cabin, with dual controls. Baggage space aft of seats, capacity 50 lb (22·6 kg).

DIMENSIONS, EXTERNAL:
- Wing span: 30 ft 0 in (9·14 m)
- Wing chord, constant: 4 ft 0 in (1·22 m)
- Wing aspect ratio: 7·5
- Length overall: 19 ft 9 in (6·02 m)
- Height overall: 5 ft 6 in (1·68 m)
- Tailplane span: 8 ft 4 in (2·54 m)
- Propeller diameter: 6 ft 2 in (1·88 m)

AREAS:
- Wings, gross: 120 sq ft (11·1 m²)
- Ailerons (total): 6·88 sq ft (0·64 m²)
- Trailing-edge flaps (total): 10·0 sq ft (0·93 m²)
- Fin: 4·25 sq ft (0·39 m²)
- Rudder: 3·0 sq ft (0·28 m²)
- Tailplane: 14·4 sq ft (1·34 m²)
- Elevators: 8·0 sq ft (0·74 m²)

WEIGHTS AND LOADINGS:
- Weight empty: 1,010 lb (458 kg)
- Max T-O weight: 1,500 lb (680 kg)
- Max wing loading: 12·5 lb/sq ft (61·03 kg/m²)
- Max power loading: 10 lb/hp (4·5 kg/hp)

PERFORMANCE (at max T-O weight, ISA at 5,000 ft; 1,525 m):
- Max level speed: 104 knots (120 mph; 193 km/h)
- Max cruising speed at 75% power: 95·5 knots (110 mph; 177 km/h)
- Stalling speed: 47 knots (54 mph; 87 km/h)
- Max rate of climb at S/L: 1,100 ft (335 m)/min

RILEY

RILEY TURBOSTREAM CORPORATION

HEAD OFFICE:
PO Box 5247, Waco Municipal Airport, Waco, Texas 76708
Telephone: (817) 752-9781
PRESIDENT: Jack M. Riley

Mr J. Riley, who was responsible for the Riley 55 Twin-Navion conversion scheme in 1952, has designed an improved version of the Cessna Model 310, known as the Riley Turbostream; a similar scheme to improve the Hawker Siddeley (DH) Dove, under the name Riley Turbo-Exec 400; and a conversion scheme to re-engine Hawker Siddeley (DH) Heron light transports with Lycoming engines, the resulting aircraft being known as Riley Turbo Skyliners.

RILEY TURBOSTREAM

The Turbostream modification of Cessna 310 and 320 aircraft entails installation of the complete Lycoming power plant as used on the Piper Navajo Chieftain, and is identical to the Chieftain installation forward of the firewall. This permits the use of standard Piper production components and maintenance procedures for the power plant. The remainder of the aircraft is unchanged, and all Cessna optional equipment and accessories may be installed during modification. New production Cessna 310s with the Turbostream modification are available, as well as conversions of existing aircraft. An aerial survey version, with single or dual camera ports, is also available, the single camera port being suitable for installation of a Wild RC-8 camera, or its equivalent.

Riley Turbostream conversion of the Cessna Model 310

Construction of a prototype conversion began in June 1969 and this received FAA certification under CAR 3 in December 1969. The conversion is applicable to versions from the Cessna Model 310I (1964) to the 310Q (1974), and 320B (1964) to 320F (1967). Production is at a rate of 10 to 15 conversions per year.

A description of the current Model 310 appears under the Cessna entry in this edition. It applies also to the Riley Turbostream, except as follows:

POWER PLANT: Two 350 hp counter-rotating Lycoming TIO-540-J2BD and LTIO-540-J2BD six-cylinder horizontally-opposed aircooled engines, driving Hartzell type HC-E3YR-ZF/FC8468-8R and type HC-E3YR-ZLF/FJC8468-8R three-blade metal constant-speed and fully-feathering propellers respectively. Fuel system as for Cessna Model 310, with max capacity of 170, 180 or 200 US gallons (643, 681 or 757 litres) according to model. Nacelle ferry tanks give max fuel capacity of 210, 220 or 240 US gallons (795, 832 or 908 litres).

SYSTEMS: As for Cessna Model 310, except 114 cu ft (3·23 m³) oxygen system available.

DIMENSION, EXTERNAL:
Propeller diameter 6 ft 4 in (1·93 m)
WEIGHTS AND LOADINGS:
Weight empty 3,600 lb (1,632 kg)
Max T-O weight:
310I/J 5,300 lb (2,404 kg)
310K-Q, 320B-F 5,400 lb (2,449 kg)
Max wing loading:
310I/J 29·6 lb/sq ft (144·5 kg/m²)
310K-Q, 320B-F 30·17 lb/sq ft (147·3 kg/m²)
Max power loading:
310I/J 7·5 lb/hp (3·4 kg/hp)
310K-Q, 320B-F 7·7 lb/hp (3·5 kg/hp)
PERFORMANCE (at max T-O weight):
Max level speed at optimum altitude
282 knots (325 mph; 523 km/h)
Max cruising speed at 20,000 ft (6,100 m) and 30,000 ft (9,150 m)
261 knots (300 mph; 483 km/h)
Max cruising speed at 12,000 ft (3,660 m) and 35,000 ft (10,670 m)
239 knots (275 mph; 443 km/h)
Econ cruising speed at 20,000 ft (6,100 m)
248 knots (285 mph; 459 km/h)
Econ cruising speed at 12,000 ft (3,660 m)
226 knots (260 mph; 418 km/h)
Stalling speed, landing gear and flaps up
73 knots (84 mph; 136 km/h)
Stalling speed, landing gear and flaps down
64·5 knots (74 mph; 119 km/h)
Max rate of climb at S/L 2,900 ft (884 m)/min
Rate of climb at S/L, one engine out
600 ft (183 m)/min
Service ceiling over 35,000 ft (10,670 m)
Service ceiling, one engine out
25,000 ft (7,620 m)
T-O run 1,070 ft (326 m)
T-O to 50 ft (15 m) 1,340 ft (408 m)
Landing from 50 ft (15 m) 1,790 ft (546 m)
Range at max cruising speed with 30 min reserve (A: 170 US gallons; 643 litres fuel; B: 240 US gallons; 908 litres fuel):
A at 12,000 ft (3,660 m)
868 nm (1,000 miles; 1,609 km)
A at 20,000 ft (6,100 m)
998 nm (1,150 miles; 1,850 km)
B at 12,000 ft (3,660 m)
1,302 nm (1,500 miles; 2,414 km)
B at 20,000 ft (6,100 m)
1,476 nm (1,700 miles; 2,735 km)

RILEY TURBO-EXEC 400

First flown in 1963, the Riley Turbo-Exec 400 is a remanufactured Hawker Siddeley (de Havilland) Dove light transport with turbocharged fuel-injection engines and airframe modifications.

The Turbo-Exec 400 conversion is available from Riley in six stages, any one of which may be taken on its own if the customer does not want a complete conversion.

1. Re-engining with two 400 hp Lycoming IO-720 eight-cylinder horizontally-opposed air-cooled engines, each fitted with two Riley Turbo 300 turbochargers and driving a Hartzell three-blade fully-feathering propeller. Dyna-focal engine mountings. New sweptback vertical tail surfaces and a "fatigue-free" steel spar capped wing are included in this stage of the conversion, which contributes 90% of the overall speed increase and 90% of the weight decrease of 800 lb (363 kg) offered by the conversion. Normal fuel capacity is 201 US gallons (761 litres), with provision for auxiliary tanks to raise total capacity to 300 US gallons (1,135 litres).
2. Remanufacture of the flight deck to include one-piece instrument panel and improvements in field of vision.
3. Flush-riveting of entire wing from leading-edge back to rear spar and epoxy coating of leading-edge.
4. Replacement of existing cabin door by airstair door.
5. Complete cabin restyling, with improved soundproofing and installation of fully-reclining individual chairs.
6. Removal of all existing paint and refinishing with epoxy resin paints to customer's specification.

In aircraft modified to full Turbo-Exec 400 standard, complete climate control under all weather conditions is maintained in flight and on the ground. Optional de-icing equipment is available, including electric propeller de-icing. The aircraft is wired for reading lights, cabin lights, taxi and navigation lights and Hoskins anti-collision and navigation light system. Standard electronics package consists of dual Collins solid-state 360-channel VHF transceivers, dual Collins solid-state VHF navigation receivers, Collins solid-state glideslope receiver and Collins ADF. Other radio and navigation aids can be fitted to customer's specification, together with optional items such as autopilots, transponders, flight systems, compass systems, DME and stereo entertainment systems.

A total of approximately 30 conversions had been completed by February 1974.

DIMENSIONS, EXTERNAL:
Wing span 57 ft 0 in (17·37 m)
Length overall 41 ft 10 in (12·75 m)
Height overall 13 ft 4 in (4·06 m)
WEIGHTS:
Useful load 3,200 lb (1,450 kg)
Max T-O weight 8,800 lb (3,990 kg)
PERFORMANCE (at max T-O weight):
Max cruising speed at 12,000 ft (3,660 m)
217 knots (250 mph; 402 km/h)
Max cruising speed at 20,000 ft (6,100 m)
248 knots (285 mph; 459 km/h)
Minimum control speed
75 knots (86·5 mph; 139 km/h)
T-O safety speed
100 knots (115 mph; 185 km/h)
Stalling speed, power off, wheels and flaps down
53 knots (61 mph; 98 km/h)
Max rate of climb at S/L 1,360 ft (415 m)/min
Service ceiling 32,400 ft (9,875 m)
Single-engine ceiling 20,300 ft (6,185 m)
T-O to 50 ft (15 m) 1,380 ft (420 m)
Range with max standard fuel
1,120 nm (1,290 miles; 2,075 km)
Range with auxiliary tanks
1,736 nm (2,000 miles; 3,220 km)

Riley Turbo-Exec 400 conversion of the Hawker Siddeley (de Havilland) Dove (*Howard Levy*)

Riley Turbo Skyliner conversion of the Hawker Siddeley (de Havilland) Heron

RILEY TURBO SKYLINER

This modification consists of the installation of four 290 hp Lycoming engines with Rajay turbochargers on Hawker Siddeley (DH) Heron series 2X, 2A and 2DA aircraft. Optional extras include a gasoline heater, air-conditioning system, de-icing equipment, airline operations training and maintenance manuals. Aircraft can also be supplied without the turbochargers where altitude capability is not required.

Construction of a prototype conversion started in 1966, and FAA certification under Category 4b was awarded in 1967. A total of approximately 20 conversions had been completed by February 1974.

A description of the Hawker Siddeley (D.H.114) Heron may be found in the 1967-68 *Jane's*. This applies also to the Riley Turbo Skyliner, except as detailed below:

POWER PLANT: Four 290 hp Lycoming IO-540-K1C5 six-cylinder horizontally-opposed air-cooled engines, each driving a Hartzell three-blade metal constant-speed fully-feathering propeller. Fuel system as for Heron.

ACCOMMODATION: As for Heron, except airstair door is hinged at bottom.

SYSTEMS: As for Heron, except Janitrol 200,000 BTU heater, air-conditioning and full de-icing system available.

DIMENSION, EXTERNAL:
Propeller diameter 6 ft 4 in (1·93 m)
WEIGHTS:
Weight empty:
Engines with turbochargers 7,650 lb (3,470 kg)
Engines without turbochargers
7,500 lb (3,401 kg)
PERFORMANCE (without turbochargers, except where detailed otherwise):
Max level speed:
With turbochargers at 12,000 ft (3,660 m)
248 knots (285 mph; 459 km/h)
Without turbochargers at 7,000 ft (2,135 m)
217 knots (250 mph; 402 km/h)
Cruising speed, 75% power, from 5,000-10,000 ft (1,525-3,050 m)
195 knots (225 mph; 362 km/h)
Service ceiling 20,000 ft (6,100 m)
Service ceiling, one engine out
18,000 ft (5,485 m)
Service ceiling, two engines out
15,000 ft (4,570 m)

RLU

CHARLES ROLOFF, ROBERT LIPOSKY AND CARL UNGER

ADDRESS:
c/o CBR 8748 S 82 Court, Hickory Hills, Illinois 60457
Telephone: (312) 471-4480

Three professional pilots designed and built a unique light aircraft known as the Breezy Model RLU-1. This designation is made up of the initial letters of the surnames of the designers.

Well over 300 sets of plans have been sold, and more than 40 Breezys are known to be flying, including examples built in Australia, Canada and South Africa.

BREEZY MODEL RLU-1

Described as being of vintage configuration with all modern facilities, such as full radio, instruments and hydraulic brakes, the prototype Breezy is an open three-seat light aircraft powered by a 90 hp Continental engine.

Construction took six months, at a cost of $3,400, including radio. First flight was made on 7 August 1964 and 80 flying hours were logged during the following twelve months.

First Breezy to be built from the published plans was that constructed by Airpark Aero of

Santa Rosa, California, for Mr Jack Gardiner of Pandora, Ohio. It differs from the prototype only by having two bucket seats, one of these replacing the usual two-place bench seat behind the pilot.

The extensively modified Breezy shown in the adjacent illustration was built by Mr R. Fabian. It utilises the wing, tail unit, wheels and fairings, wheel brakes and seats of a Cessna Model 172, and is powered by a 145 hp Continental O-300-D engine.

The following description applies to the prototype Breezy:

TYPE: Three-seat homebuilt parasol-wing monoplane.

WINGS: Strut-braced parasol-wing monoplane. Standard Piper PA-12 wing with Vee streamline-section bracing struts each side.

FUSELAGE: Triangular-section welded chrome-molybdenum steel tube structure, without any covering.

TAIL UNIT: Welded chrome-molybdenum steel tube braced structure; all surfaces fabric-covered.

LANDING GEAR: Non-retractable tricycle type. Main wheels and tyres size 6·00-6, 4-ply; nosewheel and tyre size 5·00-5. Cleveland hydraulic brakes.

POWER PLANT: One 90 hp Continental C90-8F-P four-cylinder horizontally-opposed aircooled engine, driving a Flottorp 72A50 two-blade pusher propeller. Single fuel tank, capacity 18 US gallons (68 litres), in wing centre-section. Oil capacity 1·25 US gallons (4·5 litres).

Breezy Model RLU-1 built by Mr R. Fabian (*Howard Levy*)

ACCOMMODATION: Seats for three in tandem. Pilot on single seat forward, two passengers on bench seat aft.

DIMENSIONS, EXTERNAL:

Wing span	33 ft 0 in (10·06 m)
Length overall	22 ft 6 in (6·86 m)
Height overall	8 ft 6 in (2·59 m)
Wheel track	6 ft 0 in (1·83 m)
Wheelbase	10 ft 0 in (3·05 m)

AREA:

Wings, gross	165 sq ft (15·3 m²)

WEIGHTS AND LOADINGS:

Weight empty	700 lb (317 kg)
Max T-O weight	1,200 lb (544 kg)
Max wing loading	7·27 lb/sq ft (35·5 kg/m²)
Max power loading	13·3 lb/hp (6·03 kg/hp)

PERFORMANCE:

Max never-exceed speed	91 knots (105 mph; 168·5 km/h)
Cruising speed, 70% power	65 knots (75 mph; 121 km/h)
Stalling speed	26 knots (30 mph; 49 km/h)
Service ceiling	15,000 ft (4,572 m)
T-O run (turf)	450 ft (137 m)
T-O to 50 ft (15 m)	1,100 ft (335 m)
Landing from 50 ft (15 m)	1,100 ft (335 m)
Landing run (turf)	300 ft (91 m)
Range with max fuel	217 nm (250 miles; 402 km)

ROBERTSON

ROBERTSON AIRCRAFT CORPORATION

HEADQUARTERS:
839 West Perimeter Road, Renton Municipal Airport, Renton, Washington 98055
Telephone: (206) 228-5000
PRESIDENT: Ronald L. Lien
GENERAL MANAGER: Leland R. Lynch
SALES MANAGER: David E. Parvin
OPERATIONS MANAGER: Earl Severns
CHIEF PILOT AND INSTALLATION CENTER MANAGER: Henry I. McKay
PRODUCTION MANAGER: Ted Cederblom
CHIEF ENGINEER: George A. Kellogg Jr

Southwest Division
Palomar Airport 2386 Palomar Airport Road, Carlsbad, California 92008
Telephone: (714) 729-9281
DIVISION MANAGER: T. B. Mooney

Mid-South Division
Lakefront Airport, PO Box 26535, New Orleans, Louisiana 70126
Telephone: (504) 241-3810
DIVISION MANAGER: R. L. Portner

Robertson Aircraft Corporation was formed by Mr James L. Robertson, now deceased, who had long been a pioneer in the development of STOL aircraft, having been responsible for the Skycraft Skyshark, Wren 460 and STOL modifications to the IMCO CallAir A-9 and B-1. It has designed, built and certificated a series of R/S and R/STOL advanced technology safety and performance systems for standard single- and multi-engined Cessna and Piper aircraft.

Work is also in progress on the design and integration of individually-proven STOL concepts for application to the Beech Bonanza and Piper Seneca.

Research contracts with NASA were undertaken in 1973 to design, develop and flight test a completely new concept in general aviation twin-engined aircraft. A standard Piper Seneca fuselage was used as the basic structure. New wings employing advanced technology aerofoil sections developed by NASA, full-span Fowler flaps, wing spoilers for roll control, new low-drag nacelles and engine cooling systems, coupled with the first really new propeller design in recent years, were integrated into the research vehicle. The predicted changes from standard Seneca performance characteristics are detailed in the table on page 437. The resulting aircraft is not included in Robertson's standard list of conversions, since it is not currently available for sale. If the full flight test programme of the aircraft is successful, Robertson plans to offer a new series of products involving entire wing transfers to the heavier class of business aircraft, like the Beech King Air. Such wings could be based on technology developed in the Robertson/NASA programme; and it is envisaged that the resulting range of aircraft would cruise at well over 260 knots (300 mph; 485 km/h) utilising standard turboprop and piston engines.

Robertson Aircraft has joined with Pacific Propeller Inc to form a corporation known as Robertson/Standard Inc. This new company is developing advanced technology propellers, the primary aims being to reduce noise, weight and cost significantly while, at the same, increasing propulsive efficiency. Prototype propellers have already been manufactured and flight tested, confirming theoretically-predicted data. First production propeller will be for operation with the 200 hp Lycoming IO-360 engine, and will be complete with propeller shaft extension.

ROBERTSON/CESSNA and ROBERTSON/PIPER SAFETY and STOL CONVERSIONS

Continuous product improvement has been made on Robertson's line of R/STOL systems for Cessna and Piper single-engined and smaller twin-engined aircraft. The Robertson conversion, first applied to a Cessna 182, comprises full-span wing leading-edge and trailing-edge high-lift systems which greatly reduce the take-off and landing distances normally required by such aircraft.

The existing ailerons are used as an integral part of the full-span trailing-edge flap system. When the conventional inboard flaps are lowered for take-off or landing, the ailerons droop with them, virtually doubling the wing lift at low speeds. The ailerons retain their differential operation for roll control when drooped.

In addition, the wing is fitted with a full-span distributed-camber leading-edge to provide an optimum spanwise lift distribution for maximum cruise efficiency. The cambered leading-edge also reduces the aerofoil leading-edge pressure peak at high angles of attack, to impart maximum resistance to stall and to provide highly-responsive manoeuvrability at low airspeeds. Most Cessna single-engined aircraft built since 1973 include this Robertson leading-edge as a standard production feature.

The full-span flap system, in combination with Robertson's conical-cambered wingtips, dorsal and ventral fins, belly-mounted vortex generators, and flap/elevator automatic trim system, are combined in various models to offer increased performance.

To improve controllability at low speeds, stall fences are provided between flaps and ailerons, and to complete the STOL modification the aileron gap is sealed with a strip of aluminium sheet or rubberised canvas. These modifications permit safe STOL landings and take-offs by even novice pilots, and cruising speed and range are increased by 2-4%.

Maximum gross weight increases have accompanied the certification of all Robertson conversions of twin-engined aircraft such as the Cessna Super Skymaster and Piper Twin Comanche. This is due primarily to their increased climb performance and slower take-off and landing speeds.

The Robertson integrated high-lift and safety systems have been designed for easy field maintenance. They are designed to be applicable to almost the entire range of Cessna and Piper

Robertson STOL conversion of the Piper Aztec, showing drooped ailerons and cambered wingtips

Robertson STOL conversion of the cantilever-wing Cessna 210, showing stall fences between flaps and ailerons

aircraft, as detailed in the accompanying tables.

During 1972 many new developments were completed at the Robertson plant at Renton, Washington. Among the more notable was certification of a new R/STOL system for the entire Cessna 400 series of twin-engined business aircraft. Complete redesign of the wings of these aircraft from the rear spar aft has allowed installation of 100% Fowler flaps, together with flap-actuated drooping ailerons. This system, in combination with Robertson's automatic pitch trim system and double-hinged rudder, has led to FAA-certificated decreases in take-off and landing field lengths of approximately 40%.

The safety and STOL conversions described above, as applied to the twin-engined Cessna 337 and Piper Twin Comanche, give increased directional stability and also improve take-off and climb performance and single-engine operation. In addition, max T-O weight is increased by 5%.

Full details of the basic Cessna and Piper airframes are given under the appropriate company headings in this edition (Piper Twin Comanche in the 1973-74 edition), and apply also to the Robertson versions, except for the added R/STOL systems as described. Weights and performance details of the entire range of R/STOL conversions are given in the accompanying tables. The conversions can be fitted as a retrospective modification to any of the models listed, irrespective of year.

The complete line of Robertson STOL systems is available throughout the world from twenty-three installation centres and more than sixty dealers.

Robertson STOL conversion of the Cessna Model 421A Golden Eagle

Robertson's Fowler flap installation in the wing trailing-edge of Cessna Model 421A STOL conversion

R/STOL VERSIONS OF CESSNA MODELS

	Weight empty equipped lb (kg)	Weight gross lb (kg)	Max level speed knots (mph; km/h)	Max cruising speed knots (mph; km/h)	Stalling speed, wheels and flaps down knots (mph; km/h)	Max rate of climb at S/L ft (m)/min	Single-engine rate of climb at S/L ft (m)/min	Service ceiling ft (m)	T-O run ft (m)	T-O to 50 ft (15 m) ft (m)	Landing from 50 ft (15 m) ft (m)	Landing run ft (m)	Max range** nm (miles; km)
Model 150 and Commuter	990 (449)	1,600 (725)	110 (127; 204)	105 (121; 195)	20 (30; 48·3)	700 (213)		12,900 (3,932)	A 422 (129) B 527 (161)	A 815 (248) B 895 (273)	A 632 (193) B 755 (230)	A 295 (90) B 348 (106)	790 (910; 1,464)
Model 172 and Skyhawk†	1,263 (572)	2,300 (1,043)	126 (145; 233)	118 (136; 219)	28 (32; 51·5)	675 (206)		13,600 (4,150)	A 460 (140) B 575 (175)	A 900 (274) B 990 (302)	A 730 (223) B 875 (267)	A 302 (92) B 356 (109)	738 (850; 1,367)
Model 172 and Skyhawk floatplane*	1,425 (646)	2,220 (1,007)	97 (112; 180)	94 (108; 174)	28 (32; 51·5)	625 (191)		12,350 (3,764)	A 840 (256) B 1,050 (320)	A 1,330 (405) B 1,480 (451)	A 875 (267) B 970 (296)	A 475 (145) B 560 (171)	477 (550; 885)
Model 180 Skywagon†	1,560 (707)	2,800 (1,270)	152 (175; 282)	144 (166; 267)	32·2 (37; 60)	1,195 (364)		20,400 (6,217)	A 360 (110) B 450 (137)	A 710 (216) B 785 (239)	A 680 (207) B 835 (254)	A 290 (88) B 342) (104)	1,098 (1,265; 2,035)
Model 180 Skywagon floatplane	1,875 (850)	2,950 (1,338)	142 (164; 264)	133 (153; 246)	32·2 (37; 60)	1,090 (332)		17,800 (5,425)	A 805 (245) B 1,008 (307)	A 1,210 (369) B 1,320 (402)	A 832 (254) B 1,010 (308)	A 475 (145) B 560 (171)	1,063 (1,225; 1,971)
Model 182 and Skylane†	1,599 (725)	2,950 (1,338)	150 (173; 278)	143 (165; 266)	33 (38; 62)	945 (288)		18,400 (5,608)	A 430 (131) B 537 (164)	A 815 (248) B 885 (270)	A 777 (237) B 920 (280)	A 325 (99) B 384 (117)	1,050 (1,210; 1,947)
Model 185 Skywagon†	1,590 (721)	3,350 (1,519)	159 (183; 295)	149 (172; 277)	34 (39; 63)	1,050 (320)		17,850 (5,440)	A 375 (114) B 469 (143)	A 763 (233) B 870 (265)	A 755 (230) B 890 (271)	A 310 (95) B 365 (111)	972 (1,120; 1,802)
Model 185 Skywagon floatplane	1,910 (866)	3,320 (1,505)	149 (172; 277)	140 (161; 259)	34 (39; 63)	1,020 (311)		17,100 (5,212)	A 596 (182) B 745 (227)	A 1,090 (332) B 1,195 (364)	A 870 (265) B 1,070 (326)	A 480 (146) B 566 (173)	903 (1,040; 1,673)
Model 188 AGwagon 230	1,844 (836)	3,800 (1,723)	124 (143; 230)	116 (133; 214)	38·5 (44; 71)	805 (245)		14,200 (4,328)	A 680 (207) B 850 (259)	A 1,110 (338) B 1,420 (431)	A 610 (186) B 840 (256)	A 308 (94) B 363 (111)	303 (350; 563)
Model A188 AGwagon 300†	1,859 (843)	4,000 (1,814)	135 (156; 251)	127 (146; 235)	40 (46; 74)	990 (302)		16,100 (4,907)	A 600 (183) B 750 (229)	A 960 (293) B 1,250 (381)	A 610 (186) B 840 (256)	A 308 (94) B 363 (111)	390 (450; 724)
Model 206 Stationair†	1,732 (785)	3,600 (1,633)	155 (179; 288)	148 (170; 274)	36 (41; 66)	970 (296)		15,400 (4,695)	A 482 (147) B 603 (184)	A 990 (302) B 1,155 (352)	A 740 (226) B 885 (270)	A 301 (92) B 355 (108)	916 (1,055; 1,697)
Model 206 Stationair floatplane	2,080 (943)	3,500 (1,587)	144 (166; 267)	136 (157; 253)	36 (41; 66)	905 (276)		14,600 (4,450)	A 815 (248) B 1,019 (311)	A 1,490 (454) B 1,595 (486)	A 917 (280) B 1,125 (343)	A 485 (148) B 572 (174)	833 (960; 1,544)

A, B, *, **, † see notes under table on page 437

CESSNA MODELS (continued)	Weight empty equipped	Weight gross	Max level speed	Max cruising speed	Stalling speed, wheels and flaps down	Max rate of climb at S/L	Single-engine rate of climb at S/L	Service ceiling	T-O run	T-O to 50 ft (15 m)	Landing from 50 ft (15 m)	Landing run	Max range**	Min contro speed
	lb (kg)	lb (kg)	knots (mph; km/h)	knots (mph; km/h)	knots (mph; km/h)	ft (m)/ min	ft (m)/ min	ft (m)	ft (m)	ft (m)	ft (m)	ft (m)	nm (miles; km)	knots (mph; km/h)
Model T206 Turbo Stationair	1,832 (831)	3,600 (1,633)	178 (205; 330)	163 (188; 303)	36 (41; 66)	1,055 (322)		27,100 (8,260)	A 485 (148) B 606 (185)	A 995 (303) B 1,175 (358)	A 740 (226) B 885 (270)	A 301 (92) B 355 (108)	963 (1,110; 1,786)	
Model T206 Turbo Stationair floatplane	2,160 (979)	3,600 (1,633)	164 (189; 304)	148 (170; 274)	36 (41; 66)	1,020 (311)		25,100 (7,650)	A 790 (241) B 987 (301)	A 1,450 (442) B 1,560 (475)	A 928 (283) B 1,130 (344)	A 495 (151) B 584 (178)	911 (1,050; 1,690)	
Model 207 Skywagon	1,902 (862)	3,800 (1,723)	150 (173; 278)	142 (164; 264)	38·5 (44; 71)	860 (262)		13,800 (4,206)	A 510 (155) B 637 (194)	A 1,090 (332) B 1,280 (390)	A 800 (244) B 975 (298)	A 318 (97) B 375 (114)	829 (955; 1,536)	
Model T207 Turbo Skywagon	2,002 (908)	3,800 (1,723)	168 (194; 312)	156 (180; 290)	38·5 (44; 71)	910 (277)		25,100 (7,650)	A 510 (155) B 637 (194)	A 1,090 (332) B 1,280 (390)	A 800 (244) B 975 (298)	A 318 (97) B 375 (114)	812 (935; 1,504)	
Model 210 Centurion II	2,102 (953)	3,800 (1,723)	178 (205; 330)	167 (192; 309)	38·5 (44; 71)	900 (274)		16,100 (4,907)	A 510 (155) B 637 (194)	A 1,070 (326) B 1,232 (376)	A 783 (239) B 960 (293)	A 305 (93) B 360 (110)	1,137 (1,310; 2,108)	
Model T210 Turbo Centurion II	2,202 (998)	3,800 (1,723)	204 (235; 378)	192 (221; 356)	38·5 (44; 71)	960 (293)		29,600 (9,022)	A 525 (160) B 656 (200)	A 1,075 (328) B 1,318 (401)	A 783 (239) B 960 (293)	A 305 (93) B 360 (110)	1,133 (1,305; 2,100)	
Model 337 Super Skymaster	2,638 (1,196)	4,630 (2,100)	177 (204; 328)	168 (194; 312)	39 (45; 72·5)	1,210 (369)	325 (99)	20,100 (6,126)	A 428 (130) B 535 (163)	A 870 (265) B 1,055 (322)	A 895 (273) B 1,060 (323)	A 343 (105) B 405 (123)	1,207 (1,390; 2,236)	
Model T337 Turbo Super Skymaster	2,843 (1,289)	4,700 (2,131)	204 (235; 378)	200 (230; 370)	40 (46; 74)	1,160 (353)	305 (93)	30,400 (9,266)	A 445 (136) B 556 (169)	A 920 (280) B 1,088 (332)	A 895 (273) B 1,060 (323)	A 352 (107) B 415 (126)	1,406 (1,620; 2,607)	
Model T337 Pressurised Super Skymaster	2,900 (1,315)	4,700 (2,132)	217 (250; 402)	208 (239; 385)	40 (46; 74)	1,160 (353)	415 (126)	20,000 (6,095)	A 413 (126) B 516 (157)	A 920 (280) B 1,088 (332)	A 895 (273) B 1,060 (323)	A 352 (107) B 415 (126)	1,307 (1,505; 2,422)	
Model 401	3,690 (1,673)	6,300 (2,858)	226 (261; 420)	208 (240; 386)	65·5 (75; 121)	1,610 (491)	225 (69)	26,180 (7,980)	A 786 (240) B 983 (300)	A 1,240 (378) B 1,550 (472)	A 1,160 (354) B 1,450 (442)	A 510 (155) B 600 (183)	1,263 (1,454; 2,340)	72 (83; 1
Model 402	3,690 (1,673)	6,300 (2,858)	226 (261; 420)	208 (240; 386)	65·5 (75; 121)	1,610 (491)	225 (69)	26,180 (7,980)	A 786 (240) B 983 (300)	A 1,240 (378) B 1,550 (472)	A 1,160 (354) B 1,450 (442)	A 510 (155) B 600 (183)	1,263 (1,454; 2,340)	72 (83; 1
Model 411	3,890 (1,764)	6,500 (2,948)	233 (268; 431)	212 (244; 393)	61·5 (71; 114)	1,900 (579)	320 (98)	26,000 (7,925)	A 912 (278) B 1,140 (347)	A 1,220 (372) B 1,525 (465)	A 1,115 (340) B 1,395 (425)	A 600 (183) B 905 (276)	1,303 (1,500; 2,414)	76 (88 142)
Model 414	3,890 (1,764)	6,350 (2,880)	236 (272; 438)	217 (250; 402)	68·5 (78·4; 126·5)	1,580 (482)	240 (73)	30,100 (9,175)	A 888 (271) B 1,110 (338)	A 1,304 (397) B 1,630 (497)	A 1,160 (353) B 1,450 (442)	A 476 (145) B 560 (171)	1,402 (1,615; 2,599)	74 (85 137)
Model 421A	4,260 (1,932)	6,840 (3,102)	240 (276; 444)	224 (258; 414)	69 (79; 128)	1,680 (512)	290 (88)	27,000 (8,230)	A 1,008 (307) B 1,260 (384)	A 1,452 (443) B 1,815 (553)	A 1,375 (419) B 1,720 (524)	A 683 (208) B 804 (245)	1,488 (1,713; 2,756)	83 (95 153)
Model 421B	4,435 (2,011)	7,450 (3,379)	245 (282; 454)	230 (265; 426)	71 (81·8; 132)	1,850 (564)	305 (93)	31,000 (9,450)	A 1,028 (313) B 1,196 (365)	A 1,403 (428) B 1,754 (535)	A 1,400 (427) B 1,752 (534)	A 440 (134) B 517 (158)	1,490 (1,716; 2,762)	78 (9 145)

R/STOL VERSIONS OF PIPER MODELS

	Weight empty equipped	Weight gross	Max level speed	Max cruising speed	Stalling speed, wheels and flaps down	Max rate of climb at S/L	Single-engine rate of climb at S/L	Service ceiling	T-O run	T-O to 50 ft (15 m)	Landing from 50 ft (15 m)	Landing run	Max range**	Min control speed
	lb (kg)	lb (kg)	knots (mph; km/h)	knots (mph; km/h)	knots (mph; km/h)	ft (m)/ min	ft (m)/ min	ft (m)	ft (m)	ft (m)	ft (m)	ft (m)	nm (miles; km)	knots (mph; km/h)
PA-28-140 Cherokee	1,232 (558)	2,150 (975)	126 (145; 223)	120 (138; 222)	29 (33; 53·2)	675 (206)		14,700 (4,480)	A 560 (171) B 620 (189)	A 1,160 (354) B 1,325 (404)	A 630 (192) B 725 (221)	A 310 (94) B 360 (110)	825 (950; 1,529)	
PA-28-160 Cherokee	1,270 (576)	2,200 (997)	128 (147; 237)	121 (139; 224)	31 (35; 56·5)	710 (216)		16,300 (4,970)	A 500 (152) B 580 (177)	A 1,120 (341) B 1,280 (390)	A 670 (204) B 740 (226)	A 340 (104) B 375 (114)	838 (965; 1,553)	
PA-28-180 Cherokee	1,406 (638)	2,450 (1,111)	129 (148; 238)	122 (141; 227)	36 (41; 66)	725 (221)		14,510 (4,313)	A 540 (165) B 610 (186)	A 1,150 (351) B 1,310 (399)	A 780 (238) B 860 (262)	A 430 (131) B 480 (146)	596 (686; 1,104)	
PA-28R-180 Cherokee Arrow II	1,349 (611)	2,500 (1,134)	149 (171; 275)	142 (163; 262)	35 (40; 64·5)	885 (270)		15,400 (4,695)	A 560 (171) B 640 (195)	A 1,140 (347) B 1,300 (396)	A 850 (259) B 980 (299)	A 475 (145) B 550 (168)	911 (1,050; 1,690)	
PA-28R-200 Cherokee Arrow II	1,528 (693)	2,650 (1,202)	152 (175; 282)	143 (165; 266)	37 (43; 69)	900 (274)		15,000 (4,572)	A 575 (175) B 650 (198)	A 1,130 (344) B 1,290 (393)	A 930 (283) B 1,045 (319)	A 550 (168) B 615 (187)	782 (900; 1,448)	

PIPER MODELS (continued)	Weight empty equipped lb (kg)	Weight gross lb (kg)	Max level speed knots (mph; km/h)	Max cruising speed knots (mph; km/h)	Stalling speed, wheels and flaps down knots (mph; km/h)	Max rate of climb at S/L ft (m)/min	Single-engine rate of climb at S/L ft (m)/min	Service ceiling ft (m)	T-O run ft (m)	T-O to 50 ft (15 m) ft (m)	Landing from 50 ft (15 m) ft (m)	Landing run ft (m)	Max range** nm (miles; km)	Min control speed knots (mph; km/h)
PA-28-235 Cherokee 235 Charger	1,570 (712)	3,000 (1,361)	140 (161; 259)	132 (152; 245)	39 (45; 72)	800 (244)		12,000 (3,658)	A 550 (168) B 625 (191)	A 870 (265) B 990 (302)	A 900 (274) B 1,025 (312)	A 490 (149) B 560 (171)	926 (1,066; 1,716)	
PA-32-260 Cherokee SIX	1,726 (783)	3,400 (1,542)	144 (166; 267)	137 (158; 254)	38 (44; 71)	850 (259)		14,500 (4,420)	A 590 (180) B 780 (238)	A 1,040 (317) B 1,120 (341)	A 810 (247) B 875 (267)	A 510 (155) B 560 (171)	964 (1,110; 1,786)	
PA-32-300 Cherokee SIX	1,819 (825)	3,400 (1,542)	151 (174; 280)	146 (168; 270)	38 (44; 71)	1,050 (320)		16,250 (4,953)	A 560 (171) B 740 (226)	A 980 (299) B 1,050 (320)	A 810 (247) B 875 (267)	A 520 (158) B 550 (168)	921 (1,060; 1,706)	
PA-24-180 Comanche	1,530 (694)	2,550 (1,157)	149 (172; 277)	143 (165; 266)	35 (40; 64)	960 (293)		19,200 (5,852)	A 600 (183) B 990 (302)	A 1,065 (324) B 1,560 (475)	A 860 (262) B 1,070 (326)	A 420 (128) B 490 (149)	868 (1,000; 1,609)	
PA-24-250 Comanche	1,710 (776)	2,900 (1,315)	168 (193; 311)	161 (185; 298)	35·5 (41; 66)	1,400 (427)		20,700 (6,309)	A 615 (187) B 950 (290)	A 970 (296) B 1,275 (389)	A 840 (256) B 1,140 (347)	A 460 (140) B 700 (213)	1,537 (1,770; 2,848)	
PA-24-260 Comanche	1,792 (812)	3,200 (1,451)	174 (200; 322)	164 (189; 304)	36 (41; 66)	1,345 (410)		20,850 (6,355)	A 655 (200) B 990 (302)	A 1,110 (338) B 1,315 (401)	A 880 (268) B 1,180 (360)	A 500 (152) B 740 (226)	1,137 (1,310; 2,108)	
PA-24-260 Turbo Comanche	1,810 (821)	3,200 (1,451)	213 (245; 394)	201 (231; 372)	36 (41; 66)	1,345 (410)		25,000 (7,620)	A 655 (200) B 990 (302)	A 1,110 (338) B 1,315 (401)	A 880 (268) B 1,180 (360)	A 500 (152) B 740 (226)	1,306 (1,505; 2,422)	
PA-24-400 Comanche	2,130 (966)	3,600 (1,633)	196 (226; 364)	189 (218; 351)	39 (45; 72)	1,660 (506)		20,200 (6,157)	A 415 (126) B 550 (168)	A 765 (233) B 890 (271)	A 995 (303) B 1,245 (379)	A 605 (184) B 710 (216)	1,568 (1,805; 2,905)	
PA-30 Twin Comanche*	2,253 (1,022)	3,800 (1,724)	158 (182; 293)	153 (176; 283)	45 (52; 84)	1,400 (427)	260 (79)	20,000 (6,096)	B 675 (206)	B 1,120 (341)	B 1,165 (355)	B 610 (186)	1,481 (1,705; 2,744)	69 (80; 129)
PA-30 Turbo Twin Comanche*	2,399 (1,088)	3,800 (1,724)	213 (245; 394)	197 (227; 365)	45 (52; 84)	1,400 (427)	225 (69)	25,000 (7,620)	B 675 (206)	B 1,120 (341)	B 1,165 (355)	B 610 (186)	1,528 (1,760; 2,832)	69 (80; 129)
PA-39 Twin Comanche C/R*	2,253 (1,022)	3,800 (1,724)	181 (209; 336)	174 (200; 322)	45 (52; 84)	1,460 (445)	260 (79)	20,000 (6,096)	B 675 (206)	B 1,050 (320)	B 1,165 (355)	B 610 (186)	1,468 (1,690; 2,720)	65 (75; 121)
PA-39 Turbo Twin Comanche C/R*	2,399 (1,088)	3,800 (1,724)	212 (244; 393)	197 (227; 365)	45 (52; 84)	1,400 (427)	225 (69)	25,000 (7,620)	B 520 (158)	B 1,060 (323)	B 1,165 (355)	B 620 (189)	1,515 (1,745; 2,808)	65 (75; 121)
PA-23-235 Aztec	2,735 (1,241)	4,800 (2,177)	182 (210; 338)	175 (202; 325)	40 (46; 74)	1,525 (465)	205 (62)	18,100 (5,517)	B 690 (210)	B 1,085 (331)	B 1,250 (381)	B 640 (195)	1,090 (1,255; 2,020)	54 (62; 98)
PA-E23-250 Aztec	2,953 (1,339)	4,995 (2,266)	197 (227; 365)	191 (220; 354)	41 (47; 76)	1,670 (509)	325 (99)	21,700 (6,614)	B 625 (190)	B 1,035 (315)	B 1,295 (395)	B 665 (203)	1,112 (1,280; 2,060)	56 (64; 103)
PA-23-250 Aztec	2,925 (1,326)	5,200 (2,359)	188 (216; 348)	179 (206; 332)	45·5 (52; 84)	1,610 (491)	280 (85)	19,800 (6,035)	B 640 (195)	B 1,060 (323)	B 1,295 (395)	B 665 (203)	916 (1,055; 1,697)	56 (65; 105)
PA-23-250 Turbo Aztec	3,080 (1,397)	5,200 (2,359)	222 (256; 412)	182 (210; 388)	43 (49; 79)	1,220 (372)	210 (64)	30,000 (9,144)	B 640 (195)	B 1,060 (323)	B 1,295 (395)	B 665 (203)	1,050 (1,210; 1,947)	56 (65; 105)

† Leading-edge already installed by Cessna on current models. A: Robertson STOL operation. B: Robertson Normal operation.
* Available also with engines of increased horsepower. **With optional long-range tanks fitted, if available.

ROBERTSON/NASA ADVANCED TECHNOLOGY AIRCRAFT

	Weight empty lb (kg)	Weight gross lb (kg)	Installed horse-power	Wing area sq ft (m²)	Wing loading lb/sq ft (kg/m²)	Wing aspect ratio	Usable fuel US gallons (litres)	Single-engine rate of climb ft (m)/min	Single-engine climb speed knots (mph; km/h)	Single-engine service ceiling ft (m)	Cruising altitude ft (m)	Cruising speed 75% power knots (mph; km/h)	Cruising range at 75% power nm (miles; km)
Expected figures for Robertson/NASA Piper PA-34 Seneca	2,497 (1,133)	4,200 (1,905)	400	152 (14·12)	27·63 (134·9)	10·18	188 (712)	403 (123)	86 (99; 159)	10,300 (3,140)	7,100 (2,164)	172 (198; 319)	1,512 (1,741; 2,802)
Standard figures for Piper PA-34 Seneca	2,557 (1,160)	4,200 (1,905)	400	208·7 (19·39)	20·12 (98·2)	7·24	95 (360)	190 (58)	91 (105; 169)	3,600 (1,097)	6,000 (1,828)	162 (186; 299)	743 (856; 1,378)
Change	—60 (27)	—	—	—27·1%	+37·3%	+40·6%	+97·8%	+112%	—5 (6; 10)	+186%	+18·3%	+10 (12; 20)	+103%

ROCKWELL INTERNATIONAL

ROCKWELL INTERNATIONAL CORPORATION

GENERAL OFFICES:
1700 East Imperial Highway, El Segundo, California 90245
600 Grant Street, Pittsburgh, Pennsylvania 15219

CHAIRMAN OF THE BOARD:
Willard F. Rockwell Jr

PRESIDENT AND CHIEF EXECUTIVE OFFICER:
Robert Anderson

SENIOR VICE-PRESIDENT:
Wallace W. Booth (Finance and Administration)

CORPORATE VICE-PRESIDENTS:
William B. Bergen (President, North American Space Group)
William H. Cann (Secretary)
H. Walton Cloke (Public Relations and Advertising)
John J. Henry (Corporate Development)
Frank Gard Jameson (Asst to President)
A. B. Kight (International)
Donald S. MacLeod (Administration)
C. James Meechan (Research and Engineering)
Dale D. Myers (President, North American Aircraft Group)
Carl J. Oles (Personnel)
Louis Putze (President, Utility and Consumer Products Group)
John J. Roscia (General Counsel)
Ralph H. Ruud (Operations)
Robert F. Stewart (President, Industrial Products Group)
S. J. Tompkins (President, Automotive Group)
Donn L. Williams (President, Electronics Group)

TREASURER:
Robert D. Krestel

CONTROLLER:
C. E. Ryker

North American Aviation, Inc, incorporated in Delaware in 1928 and a manufacturer of aircraft of various kinds from 1934, and Rockwell-Standard Corporation of Pittsburgh, Pennsylvania, a manufacturer of automotive components for the last five decades and builder of the Aero Commander line of civilian aircraft, merged on 22 September 1967 to form North American Rockwell Corporation.

During 1971 the Corporation was reorganised into four principal parts: the North American Aerospace Group (formerly the Aerospace and Systems Office); the Industrial Products Group (formerly the Commercial Products Group); the Automotive Group; and the Electronics Group. There is, in addition, a fifth component known as the Utility and Consumer Products Group. The constitution of the Corporation was changed on 16 February 1973, when North American Rockwell and Rockwell Manufacturing Company merged to become Rockwell International Corporation.

A further change in the organisation was announced on 15 February 1974. The former

North American Aerospace Group was replaced by two new groups, known as the North American Aircraft Group and North American Space Group. The Aircraft Group is composed of the B-1 Division, Los Angeles Aircraft Division, Columbus Aircraft Division and Tulsa Division. The North American Space Group comprises the Atomics International Division, Rocketdyne Division, Science Center and Space Division.

Divisions and products of the North American Aircraft and Industrial Products Groups are detailed hereafter:

NORTH AMERICAN AIRCRAFT GROUP

EXECUTIVE OFFICES:
1700 East Imperial Highway, El Segundo, California 90245
Telephone: (213) 647-5000
PRESIDENT:
Dale D. Myers
EXECUTIVE VICE-PRESIDENT:
R. F. Walker

B-1 Division
5701 West Imperial Highway, Los Angeles, California 90009
Telephone: (213) 670-9151
PRESIDENT: R. E. Greer

Columbus Aircraft Division
4300 East Fifth Avenue, Columbus, Ohio 43216
Telephone: (614) 239-3344
PRESIDENT: J. P. Fosness

Tulsa Division
2000 North Memorial Drive, Tulsa, Oklahoma 74151
Telephone: (918) 835-3111
PRESIDENT: W. J. Cecka Jr

NORTH AMERICAN SPACE GROUP

EXECUTIVE OFFICES:
1700 East Imperial Highway, El Segundo, California 90245
PRESIDENT: William B. Bergen

Atomics International Division
8900 De Soto Avenue, Canoga Park, California 91304
Telephone: (213) 341-1000
PRESIDENT: S. F. Iacobellis

Rocketdyne Division
6633 Canoga Avenue, Canoga Park, California 91304
Telephone: (213) 884-4000
PRESIDENT: W. J. Brennan

Science Center
1049 Camino Dos Rios, Thousand Oaks, California 91360
Telephone: (805) 498-4545
VICE-PRESIDENT AND DIRECTOR: T. L. Loucks

Space Division
12214 Lakewood Boulevard, Downey, California 90241
Telephone: (213) 922-2111
PRESIDENT: J. P. McNamara

Current aircraft products of the North American Aircraft Group are described below:

Rockwell International T-2D Buckeye (two General Electric J85-GE-4 turbojet engines) (*Ronaldo S. Olive*)

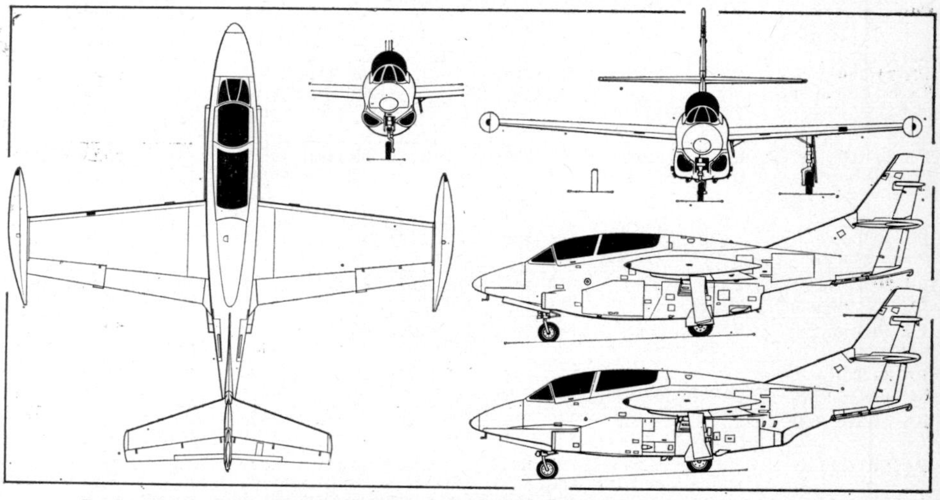

Rockwell International T-2C Buckeye, with additional side view (*centre right*) **and scrap front view of T-2A** (*Pilot Press*)

ROCKWELL INTERNATIONAL BUCKEYE

US Navy designation: T-2

After a design competition among several leading US manufacturers, what was then North American's Columbus Division was awarded a contract in 1956 to develop and build a jet training aircraft for the US Navy. The first of two prototype XT2J-1s flew on 31 January 1958. Four versions of the aircraft have since been produced, as follows:

T-2A (formerly T2J-1). Initial version, with single 3,400 lb (1,540 kg) st Westinghouse J34-WE-48 turbojet engine, for use throughout the complete syllabus of pilot training, from ab initio instruction to carrier indoctrination. Initial orders were for 26 production T-2As. Follow-up contracts were awarded in 1958 and 1959, and 217 had been built when production ended in January 1961. The T-2A was used by US Naval Air Training Command, Pensacola, Florida, but was phased out of service in early 1973, having been replaced completely by T-2Bs or -2Cs.

T-2B (formerly T2J-2). To evaluate the potential of the Buckeye airframe, two T-2As were each re-engined with two Pratt & Whitney J60-P-6 turbojets (each 3,000 lb; 1,362 kg st), under US Navy contract, with the designation T-2B. First one flew on 30 August 1962. A US Navy production contract for 10 new T-2Bs was announced in March 1964, and further contracts brought the total ordered to 97. The first production T-2B flew on 21 May 1965; deliveries to the Naval Air Training Command were completed in February 1969.

T-2C. Generally similar to T-2B, but powered by two General Electric J85-GE-4 turbojet engines, each rated at 2,950 lb (1,339 kg) st. The T-2C entered production in late 1968, following extensive evaluation of J85-GE-4 engines in a T-2B which was redesignated T-2C No. 1. T-2C production began as an amendment of an existing contract. First production T-2C flew on 10 December 1968. Total of 231 T-2Cs ordered by Naval Air Training Command, deliveries of which are due to be completed by the end of 1975. They will be followed by 40 to meet a 1974 order placed by the Hellenic Air Force.

T-2D. Generally similar to T-2C; differs only in avionics equipment and by deletion of carrier landing capability. A total of 12 were supplied to the Venezuelan Air Force under an advance procurement contract managed by US Naval Air Systems Command. Being used at the VAF Academy, as advanced jet trainers for student pilots in their final year; delivery was completed during 1973.

The following details apply to the standard T-2C:

TYPE: Two-seat general-purpose jet trainer.

WINGS: Cantilever mid-wing monoplane. Wing section NACA 64A212 (modified). Thickness/chord ratio 12%. All-metal two-spar structure. Interchangeable all-metal ailerons, with hydraulic boost. Large all-metal trailing-edge flaps.

FUSELAGE: All-metal semi-monocoque structure in three main sections: forward fuselage containing equipment bay and cockpit; centre fuselage housing power plant, fuel and wing carry-through structure; and rear fuselage, carrying the arrester hook and a hydraulically-actuated airbrake on each side of the fuselage.

TAIL UNIT: Cantilever all-metal structure. Each half of tailplane and elevators interchangeable. Elevators boosted hydraulically. Rudder manually controlled. Trim tabs in elevators and rudder.

LANDING GEAR: Retractable tricycle type. Oleo-pneumatic shock-absorbers. Hydraulic retraction. Main units retract inward into wings. Nosewheel retracts forward into fuselage. Main wheels size 24 × 5·50. Nosewheel size 20 × 4·40. Main-wheel tyre pressure 150 lb/sq in (10·5 kg/cm²), nosewheel tyre pressure 75 lb/sq in (5·3 kg/cm²). Goodyear aircooled single-disc hydraulic brakes. Retractable sting-type, universal joint mounted, arrester hook.

POWER PLANT: Two 2,950 lb (1,339 kg) st General Electric J85-GE-4 turbojet engines, with jet outlets under rear fuselage. Fuel in main tank over engines with capacity of 387 US gallons (1,465 litres), two wingtip tanks each of 102 US gallons (386 litres) capacity, and two tanks in the inboard sections of the wings. Total fuel capacity 691 US gallons (2,616 litres).

ACCOMMODATION: Pupil and instructor in tandem in enclosed cabin, on rocket-powered LS-1 ejection seats, under clamshell canopy. Instructor is raised 10 in (0·25 m) above level of pupil.

ARMAMENT: Optional packaged installations of guns, target-towing gear, 100 lb practice bombs, M-5 or MK76 practice bomb clusters, Aero 4B practice bomb containers, 2·25 in rocket launchers or seven 2·75 in rockets in Aero 6A-1 rocket containers, can be carried on two store stations, one beneath each wing, with a combined capacity of 640 lb (290 kg).

DIMENSIONS, EXTERNAL:

Wing span over tip-tanks	38 ft 1½ in (11·62 m)
Length overall	38 ft 3½ in (11·67 m)
Height overall	14 ft 9½ in (4·51 m)
Tailplane span	17 ft 11 in (5·46 m)
Wheel track	18 ft 4¾ in (5·61 m)

AREAS:

Wings, gross	255 sq ft (23·69 m²)
Trailing-edge flaps (total)	45·56 sq ft (4·23 m²)
Fin	27·29 sq ft (2·54 m²)
Rudder	9·01 sq ft (0·84 m²)
Tailplane	42·55 sq ft (3·95 m²)
Elevators	21·00 sq ft (1·95 m²)

WEIGHTS:

Weight empty	8,115 lb (3,680 kg)
Max T-O weight	13,179 lb (5,977 kg)

PERFORMANCE (at max T-O weight):

Max level speed at 25,000 ft (7,620 m)	453 knots (522 mph; 840 km/h)
Stalling speed	86·6 knots (100 mph; 161 km/h)
Max rate of climb at S/L	6,200 ft (1,890 m)/min
Service ceiling	40,400 ft (12,315 m)
Max range	909 nm (1,047 miles; 1,685 km)

ROCKWELL INTERNATIONAL BRONCO

US military designation: OV-10

This aircraft was North American's entry for the US Navy's design competition for a light armed reconnaissance aeroplane (LARA) specifically suited for counter-insurgency missions. Nine US airframe manufacturers entered for the competition and the NA300 was declared the winning design in August 1964. Seven prototypes were then built by the company's Columbus Division, under the designation YOV-10A Bronco. The first of these flew on 16 July 1965, followed by the second in December 1965.

A number of modifications were made as a result of flight experience with the prototypes. In particular, the wing span was increased by 10 ft 0 in (3·05 m), the T76 turboprop engines were uprated from 660 shp to 715 shp, and the engine nacelles were moved outboard approximately 6 in (15 cm) to reduce noise in the cockpit.

A prototype with lengthened span flew for the first time on 15 August 1966. The seventh prototype had United Aircraft of Canada T74 (PT6A) turboprops for comparative testing.

The following versions have been announced to date:

OV-10A. Initial production version ordered in October 1966 and first flown on 6 August 1967. US Marine Corps had 114 in service in September 1969, of which 18 were on loan to the USN; used for light armed reconnaissance, helicopter escort and forward air control duties. At the same date the USAF had 157 OV-10As for use in the forward air control role, as well as for limited quick-response ground support pending the arrival of tactical fighters.

Production of the OV-10A for the US services ended in April 1969; but 15 aircraft were modified by LTV Electrosystems Inc, under the USAF Pave Nail programme, to permit their use in a night forward air control and strike designation role.

Equipment installed by LTV includes a stabilised night periscopic sight, a combination laser rangefinder and target illuminator, a Loran receiver and a Lear Siegler Loran co-ordinate converter. This combination of equipment generates an offset vector to enable an accompanying strike aircraft to attack the target or, alternatively, illuminate the target, enabling a laser-seeking missile to home on to it.

Under the designation **YOV-10A** a single OV-10A was equipped with rotating cylinder flaps for evaluation in a flight test programme by NASA.

OV-10B. Generally similar to the OV-10A; six supplied to the Federal German government for target towing duties.

OV-10B(Z). Structurally similar to the OV-10B, except that a General Electric J85-GE-4 turbojet engine of 2,950 lb (1,338 kg) st is mounted above the wing, on a pylon that is attached to existing hoisting points, to increase performance for target towing duties. Twelve ordered by the Federal German government. First flown on 21 September 1970. The jet pods were fitted by Rhein Flugzeugbau, following the prototype installation by Rockwell.

OV-10C. Version of the OV-10A for the Royal Thai Air Force. Deliveries of 32 have been made.

YOV-10D. Designation of two OV-10As modified under contract from the Department of Defense to provide a new concept in night operational capability for the US Marine Corps. Distinguishing features of the YOV-10D Night Observation/Gunship System (NOGS) are a 20 mm gun turret mounted beneath the aft fuselage and a forward-looking infra-red (FLIR) sensor installed beneath the nose.

In 1974, Rockwell received a US Navy contract to establish a production configuration for this version in anticipation of an order for converting 24 OV-10As to OV-10D standard. These aircraft would have 1,000 ehp AiResearch T76 turboprop engines and increased fuel capacity.

OV-10E. Version of the OV-10A for the Fuerzas Aéreas Venezolanas. Sixteen ordered through the US Department of Defense foreign military sales programme. The first of these was rolled out in early January 1973 and delivered in March.

The following details apply to the standard OV-10A, except where stated:

Type: Two-seat multi-purpose counter-insurgency aircraft.

Wings: Cantilever shoulder-wing monoplane. Constant-chord wing without dihedral or sweep. Conventional aluminium alloy two-spar structure. Manually-operated ailerons, supplemented by manually-operated spoilers forward of outer flap on each wing, for lateral control at low speeds. Hydraulically-operated double-slotted flaps in two sections on each wing, separated by tailbooms.

Fuselage: Short pod-type fuselage of conventional aluminium semi-monocoque construction, suspended from wing. Glassfibre nosecone.

Tail Unit: Cantilever all-metal structure carried on twin booms of semi-monocoque construction. Tailplane mounted near tips of fins. Manually-operated rudders and elevator.

Landing Gear: Retractable tricycle type, with single wheel on each unit, developed by Cleveland Pneumatic Tool Co. Hydraulic actuation, nosewheel retracting forward, main units rearward into tailbooms. Two-stage oleo-pneumatic shock-absorbers. Forged aluminium wheels. Main wheels with tyres size 29 × 11-10, pressure 65 lb/sq in (4·6 kg/cm²). Nosewheel tyre size 7·50-10, pressure 80 lb/sq in (5·6 kg/cm²). Cleveland hydraulic disc brakes.

Power Plant: Two 715 ehp AiResearch T76-G-410/411 turboprops, with Hamilton Standard three-blade propellers. Inter-spar fuel tank in centre portion of wing, capacity 258 US gallons (976 litres). Provision for carrying 150 or 230 US gallon (568 or 871 litre) jettisonable ferry tank on underfuselage pylon. Refuelling points above tank.

Accommodation: Crew of two in tandem, on ejection seats, under canopy with two large upward-opening transparent door panels on each side. Dual controls standard. Cargo compartment aft of rear seat, with rear-loading door at end of fuselage pod. Rear seat removable to provide increased space for up to 3,200 lb (1,452 kg) of freight, or for carriage of five paratroops, or two stretcher patients and attendant.

Electronics and Equipment: UHF radio standard. Provision for special equipment including Doppler radar and TV reconnaissance systems. Gunsight above pilot's instrument panel.

Armament: Four weapon attachment points, each with capacity of 600 lb (272 kg), under short sponson extending from bottom of fuselage on each side, under wings. Fifth attachment point, capacity 1,200 lb (544 kg) under centre fuselage. Two 7·62 mm M60C machine-guns carried in each sponson. Provision for carrying one Sidewinder missile on each wing. Max weapon load 3,600 lb (1,633 kg).

Dimensions, external:

Wing span	40 ft 0 in (12·19 m)
Length overall	41 ft 7 in (12·67 m)
Height overall	15 ft 2 in (4·62 m)
Tailplane span	14 ft 7 in (4·45 m)
Wheel track	14 ft 10 in (4·52 m)
Rear loading door: Height	3 ft 3 in (0·99 m)
Width	2 ft 6 in (0·76 m)

Dimensions, internal:

Cargo compartment	75 cu ft (2·12 m³)
Cargo compartment, rear seat removed	111 cu ft (3·14 m³)

Area:

Wings, gross	291 sq ft (27·03 m²)

Weights:

Weight empty	6,969 lb (3,161 kg)
Normal T-O weight	9,908 lb (4,494 kg)
Overload T-O weight	14,466 lb (6,563 kg)

Performance (A: OV-10A, B: OV-10B, C: OV-10B(Z)):

Max level speed at S/L, without weapons
- A: 244 knots (281 mph; 452 km/h)

Max level speed at 10,000 ft (3,050 m) at 10,000 lb (4,536 kg) AUW:
- B: 241 knots (278 mph; 447 km/h) TAS
- C: 341 knots (393 mph; 632 km/h) TAS

Max rate of climb at S/L, at 12,000 lb (5,443 kg) AUW:
- B: 2,300 ft (701 m)/min
- C: 6,800 ft (2,073 m)/min

Min ground turning radius: 14 ft 10 in (4·52 m)

T-O run:
- A, at normal AUW: 740 ft (226 m)
- B, at 12,000 lb (5,443 kg) AUW: 1,130 ft (344 m)
- C, at 12,000 lb (5,443 kg) AUW: 550 ft (168 m)

T-O to 50 ft (15 m):
- A, at normal AUW: 1,120 ft (341 m)
- A, at overload AUW: 2,800 ft (853 m)

Landing from 50 ft (15 m):
- A, at normal AUW: 1,220 ft (372 m)

Landing run:
- A, at normal AUW: 740 ft (226 m)
- A, at overload AUW: 1,250 ft (381 m)

Combat radius with max weapon load, no loiter
- A: 198 nm (228 miles; 367 km)

Ferry range with auxiliary fuel
- A: 1,240 nm (1,428 miles; 2,300 km)

ROCKWELL INTERNATIONAL B-1

Development of the B-1 strategic bomber is continuing at Rockwell International's B-1 Division at Los Angeles. The design incorporates the blended wing/body developed initially for the Corporation's submission in the F-15 fighter competition, swing-wings that have 15° sweep when fully extended and 67° 30′ when fully swept, conventional landing gear with four wheels on each main unit and two wheels on the nose unit, a four-man crew compartment that will function

Rockwell International OV-10B(Z) Bronco, with auxiliary turbojet *(Ing Hans Redemann)*

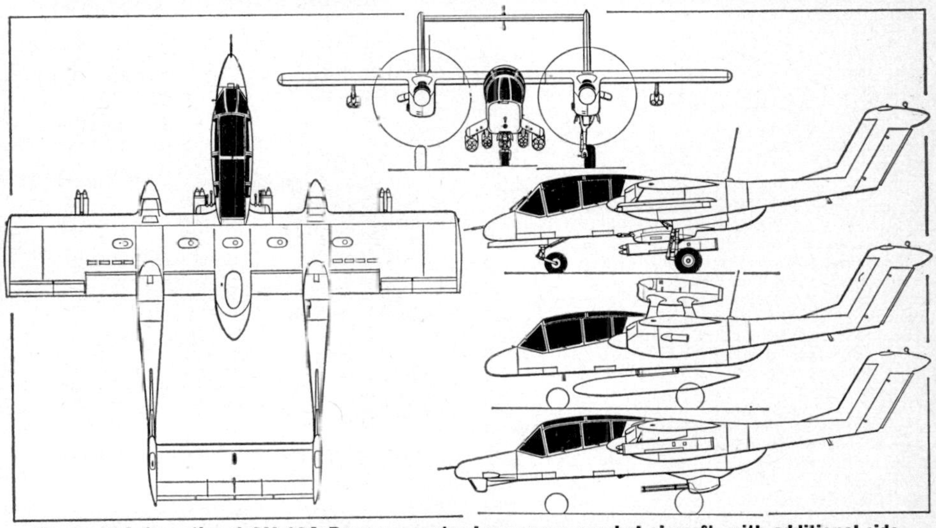

Rockwell International OV-10A Bronco counter-insurgency combat aircraft, with additional side views of OV-10B(Z) *(centre)* **and YOV-10D** *(bottom)* *(Pilot Press)*

Rockwell International YOV-10D prototype Night Observation/Gunship System

also as an escape module, four General Electric F101 supersonic afterburning turbofan engines, each in the 30,000 lb (13,600 kg) st class, and two 400 hp engines to generate secondary power. Foreplanes on the nose of the aircraft form part of a unique Low Altitude Ride Control (LARC) system developed by the company to minimise the effects of turbulence likely to be encountered during high-speed low-level penetration of enemy airspace. These horizontal vanes, one on each side of the fuselage forward of the crew compartment, are intended to suppress up and down motion; the lower rudder panel is used to suppress sideways motion. Activated by motion sensors in the fuselage, elevators, lower rudder panel or LARC vanes will produce aerodynamic forces to compensate for or suppress motion in the forward fuselage to ensure that crew efficiency will not be affected in a turbulent environment.

All wing control surfaces, including the five-segment trailing-edge flaps, are being built by the North American Aircraft Group's Tulsa Division. B-1 Division builds the aft radome, aft intermediate fuselage, centre wing carry-through section, forward carry-through bay section, lower forward fuselage, nacelle components and crew compartment.

This last assembly provides the B-1's four-man crew with a heated, air-conditioned and pressurised compartment in which they are able to work without being restricted by parachutes. In the event of an emergency, requiring the crew to evacuate the aircraft, the compartment is intended to serve as an escape module. At initiation of separation, explosive devices will sever all hydraulic and electrical connections to the compartment before it is carried clear of the airframe by rocket power. Vertical orientation of the escape module will be effected by directional rockets should ejection be initiated while the aircraft is upside down. At a suitable altitude, three Apollo-type parachutes will be deployed to lower the capsule to the surface. Inflatable rubber floats will serve either as self-righting flotation gear on water, or as impact attenuators on land.

Engine nacelle design is considered to be of great importance, as are the movable vertical nacelle ramps used to control the shock-wave and locate it precisely within the inlets. It is intended to use electronic sensing devices and a small computer to control these variable inlets, and nacelle by-pass doors will provide extra air during low-speed flight.

The blended wing/body concept enhances efficiency, and it is intended also to utilise boundary layer bleed near the engines to reduce drag. The four F101-GE-100 turbofan engines, each of approx 30,000 lb (13,600 kg) st, are being developed by General Electric under a contract valued at $383 million. They are mounted beneath the inboard wing, close to the aircraft's CG, to improve stability in low-altitude turbulence conditions. The 400 hp secondary power generating engines are mounted one on each side of the aircraft, between the two main engines, and are started by hydraulic power from an accumulator, thus providing self-start capability when the B-1 is being operated from advance airfields.

Among the weapons the B-1 can carry in three internal weapon bays are the Short Range Attack Missile (SRAM) produced by Boeing; the proposed Bomber Defence Missile (BDM); and nuclear and conventional weapons. The B-1 is equipped also with electronic jamming equipment, infra-red countermeasures, radar location, homing and warning systems and other countermeasures equipment. To aid penetration of enemy defences at very low altitudes, the bomber has a computerised terrain-following radar system.

The cost-plus-incentive contract awarded to Rockwell International calls for four development aircraft, of which three are flight aircraft, plus one test airframe. In terms of cash value, between 35 and 40% of the work is subcontracted; major structural assemblies built in this manner are the aft fuselage, tailplane, fin, aft wing fairings and landing gear. Procurement of a fourth flight test aircraft was under consideration in mid-1974.

On 4 November 1971 Rockwell International announced that subcontracts worth $52 million had been awarded to manufacturers in 23 States. The subcontractors named comprised Aircraft Mechanics Inc, crew seats; AiResearch, Garrett Corporation, secondary power subsystem; Cleveland Pneumatic Tool, main landing gear struts; G & H Technology Inc, electrical disconnect assembly for escape module; Goodyear Aerospace Corp, impact reduction system, stabilisation fins and spoilers and flotation system for the crew escape module; Goodyear Aviation Products Division, brakes and wheels; Hamilton Standard Division of United Aircraft Corp, air-conditioning and pressurisation systems; Northrop Corp, Electronics Division, manoeuvring rocket control system for crew escape module; OEA Inc, severance system, parachute escape system retractors and crew restraint assembly; Pioneer Parachute, parachute recovery system for escape module; Stewart-Warner Corporation's Southwind Division, fuel heat sink subsystem; Sundstrand Corp, constant-speed drive and electrical power generating subsystems; Teledyne McCormick Selph, energy transfer system for escape module; Vap-Air Division of Vapor Corp, engine bleed control system; and Westinghouse Electric Corp, Aerospace Electrical Division, generator and controls subsystem.

Full-scale mock-up of the Rockwell International B-1 strategic bomber

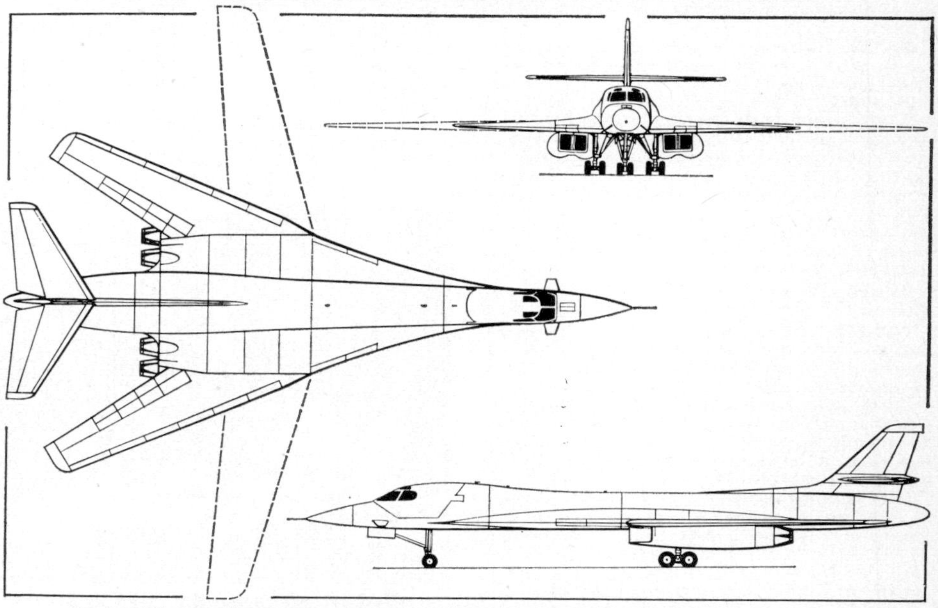

Rockwell International B-1 supersonic variable-geometry strategic bomber (*Pilot Press*)

Crew escape module of Rockwell International's B-1 strategic bomber mounted on rocket-powered test sledge

Completion of a full scale mock-up of the B-1 was announced on 4 November 1971. This had been used during the period 18-31 October by the USAF's mock-up review team comprising key personnel from the B-1 Systems Program Office, Strategic Air Command, AF Logistics Command, AF Flight Test Center, AF Systems Command, AF Air Training Command and General Electric Company. During the review period the team was able to resolve no fewer than 257 of a total of 297 Requests for Alteration (RFAs).

The prototypes are being assembled in USAF facilities at Palmdale, California, with the first flight scheduled for the Autumn of 1974. No production decision is likely before May 1976, with delivery of the first production aircraft in early 1978. The USAF hopes to order some 250 of these aircraft to replace Boeing B-52s now in service. Approximating the size of a Boeing 707, the B-1 is expected to have a maximum speed of approx Mach 2·2 at 50,000 ft (15,240 m), cruising speed of Mach 0·85 and max range without refuelling of 5,300 nm (6,100 miles; 9,800 km).

DIMENSIONS, EXTERNAL:

Wing span:	
fully spread	137 ft 0 in (41·75 m)
fully swept	78 ft 0 in (23·77 m)
Length overall	143 ft 0 in (43·58 m)
Height overall	34 ft 0 in (10·36 m)

WEIGHT:

Max T-O weight	389,800 lb (176,815 kg)

ROCKWELL INTERNATIONAL XFV-12A

For some time the US Navy has been studying the potential of a sea control ship (SCS), a vessel of around 15,000 tons displacement, with a small carrier deck that would have neither catapult nor arrester gear. Such a configuration assumes the availability of a V/STOL fighter/attack aircraft, and whilst the US Marine Corps' AV-8A Harrier and projected AV-16A are being studied for such a role, the Navy is also investigating other types of aircraft with V/STOL capabilities.

This, briefly, is the background to the $249,000 study contract awarded by the Navy to General Dynamics Convair Aerospace Division for a three-engine lift-plus-lift/cruise supersonic VTOL fighter, and the $48 million contract awarded to Rockwell International's North American Aircraft Group/Columbus Aircraft Division to develop and test fly two single-seat single-engine all-weather V/STOL fighter/attack prototypes, which have been allocated the designation XFV-12A.

Each of these aircraft will be roughly the size of a McDonnell Douglas A-4 Skyhawk, will employ an augmentor-wing concept with forward canard and aft semi-delta wings, and will be powered by a single, special version of the Pratt & Whitney F401-PW-400 advanced-technology turbofan engine.

The augmentor system will utilise a diverter valve to block off the turbofan nozzle and divert the exhaust gases through ducts to nozzles in the wings and canards. A full-span ejector-flap system on each wing and canard will enable ambient air to be drawn in over the flaps and ejected downward, mixed with the primary exhaust flow in a 7·5 : 1 ratio to provide the required jet-lift.

To keep development costs to a minimum, several major assemblies from existing types of aircraft are incorporated in the XFV-12A, including the forward fuselage, nosewheel unit and main landing gear of the A-4, and the engine intakes and wing box of the F-4.

Similar cost considerations limit the amount of test hardware associated with the development programme. To evaluate thrust augmentor components, a cutaway section of the wing, complete with diffuser flaps, has been mounted on a rotary test rig that can be operated at speeds of up to 150 knots (173 mph; 278 km/h). To permit evaluation of the thrust augmentor system, an F401 engine was incorporated in the rig in January 1974. This allows engine exhaust air to be ducted along the rig and blown over the wing components while the rig is rotated at high speed.

It is planned also to use a "free air wind tunnel", by mounting one of the prototype aircraft, complete with engine, in flying attitude on a flat railway truck. Travelling at speeds of up to 70 knots (81 mph; 130 km/h), this will enable the aircraft's controls to be put through a full transition to harmonise them.

A full-size mock-up was constructed, embodying existing airframe assemblies from other aircraft that had been selected to limit development costs. These were assembled in their correct physical relationship, allowing full and careful study of the integration of the structures, systems and power plant, before construction of the flying prototypes was started.

First conventional take-off and flight test of an XFV-12A prototype was scheduled for November 1974, with the first vertical take-off following in February 1975.

Type: Single-seat all-weather V/STOL fighter/attack prototype.

Wings: Cantilever high-wing monoplane. Semi-delta configuration, forward portion of wing structure embodying an F-4 wing box. Full-span trailing-edge flaps provide a lifting force for manoeuvrability in high-speed flight. Vertical endplate surfaces are mounted at each wingtip, comprising a fixed outward-canted fin below the wing, and a fixed outward-canted fin and rudder above the wing. Wing augmentor (ejector) flaps extend almost full span. They provide control of the vertical lift propulsion, acting as thrust vectors and so giving attitude and height control in hover and low-speed flight. The aft ejector flaps (together with those in the canard surfaces) serve as conventional flight controls in cruising flight. The fore and aft ejector flaps can be used together as speed brakes.

Canard Surfaces: Cantilever low-wing monoplane. Full-span trailing-edge flaps provide a lifting force for manoeuvrability in high-speed flight. Full-span augmentor (ejector) flaps function in combination with those on wings.

Fuselage: Forward fuselage, to aft of cockpit, is that of an A-4. Broad-section fuselage aft of cockpit to house engine intake ducts and augmentor system ducting. Engine mounted in aft fuselage.

Landing Gear: Retractable tricycle type. Main units retract rearward into wingtip fairings, nosewheel unit forward. Oleo-pneumatic shock-absorption. Hydraulic nosewheel steering. All units as for McDonnell Douglas A-4.

Power Plant: One modified Pratt & Whitney F401-PW-400 afterburning turbofan engine in the 20,000 lb (9,070 kg) thrust class. A special electro-hydraulically actuated diverter valve, designed by Pratt & Whitney, will be installed in the tailpipe of the engine. When open, in the horizontal flight mode, it will allow free passage of engine exhaust air for conventional propulsion. When closed, for vertical flight, the exhaust air will be diverted to the ducts that feed the wing and canard augmentor nozzles.

Accommodation: Pilot only, on Douglas Escapac zero-zero ejection seat.

Dimensions, external:	
Width overall	28 ft 6 in (8·69 m)
Length overall	43 ft 11 in (13·39 m)
Height over fins	9 ft 1 in (2·77 m)
Wheel track	25 ft 4 in (7·72 m)
Weights:	
Weight empty	13,800 lb (6,259 kg)
Max vertical T-O weight	19,500 lb (8,845 kg)
Max short T-O weight	24,250 lb (11,000 kg)
Performance:	
Max speed	in excess of Mach 2

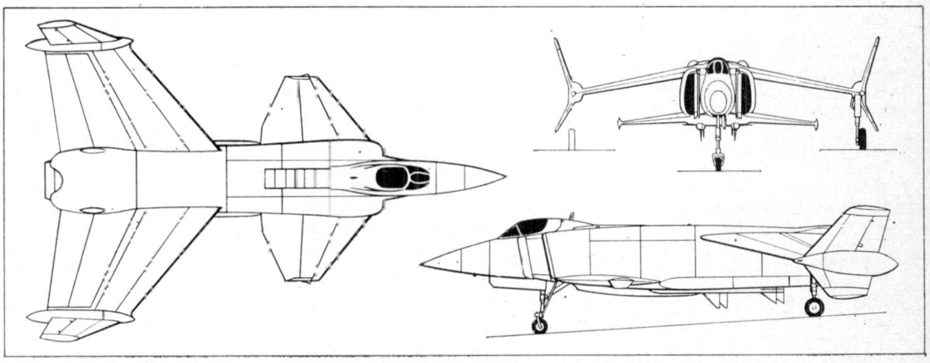

Rockwell International XFV-12A single-seat V/STOL fighter/attack prototype (*Pilot Press*)

INDUSTRIAL PRODUCTS GROUP

Executive Offices:
600 Grant Street, Pittsburgh, Pennsylvania 15219

President:
Robert F. Stewart

GENERAL AVIATION DIVISIONS:

Executive Offices:
5001 North Rockwell Avenue, Bethany, Oklahoma 73008

Telephone: (405) 789-5000

President:
W. F. Snelling

Executives:
A. Balaban (Director, Public Relations)
D. Bradford (Director, International Sales)
R. Chatley (Director, Marketing Services)
J. House (Director, Industrial Relations)
J. Lyden (Controller)
J. Sandford (Director, Product Planning)

Commander Aircraft Division
5001 North Rockwell Avenue, Bethany, Oklahoma 73008
W. F. Snelling (Acting General Manager)
R. Nielson (Vice-President, Sales)

Bethany, Oklahoma Facility
5001 North Rockwell Avenue, Bethany, Oklahoma 73008

Albany, Georgia Facility
One Rockwell Avenue, Albany, Georgia 31702
Paul Alexander (Plant Superintendent)

Sabreliner Division
827 Lapham Street, El Segundo, California 90245
T. E. Myers (Vice-President, General Manager)
E. T. Mahood (Vice-President, Sales)

Aviation Services Division
5001 North Rockwell Avenue, Bethany, Oklahoma 73008
D. E. Redpath (Vice-President, General Manager)
J. Taylor (Operations Manager)

Rockwell International's General Aviation Divisions are a part of the Industrial Products Group, and incorporate all of the Corporation's manufacturing, marketing and servicing of general aviation aircraft. They manufacture Sabre business jet aircraft, Rockwell Commander twin-engined piston- and turboprop-engined aircraft, and Rockwell Commander light single-engined business/sport and agricultural aircraft.

ROCKWELL SABRE SERIES 40 and 60
USAF and US Navy designation: T-39

To meet the USAF's "UTX" requirements for a combat readiness trainer and utility aircraft, Rockwell built as a private venture the prototype of a small sweptwing twin-jet monoplane then named the Sabreliner. Design work began on 30 March 1956 and the prototype, powered by two General Electric J85 turbojet engines, flew for the first time on 16 September 1958.

In January 1959, the USAF ordered the first of 143 **T-39A** pilot proficiency/administrative support aircraft. Subsequently the USAF ordered 6 radar trainer versions which were identified as **T-39Bs**. In 1961 the US Navy ordered 42 radar interception officer trainers, these being designated **T-39D**.

Five commercial versions are now available, as follows:

Series 40. Basic version to carry a crew of two and up to nine passengers. More powerful engines than its predecessors. New brakes with longer life. Three windows instead of two on each side of passenger cabin. Early-model Sabreliners can be modified to Series 40 standard.

Under the designation **CT-39E** the US Navy has acquired seven Series 40 commercial Sabreliners for rapid response airlift of high-priority passengers, ferry pilots and cargo. In early 1972 the USN ordered two **CT-39G** Sabreliners for fleet tactical support squadron use under a $2·9 million contract. Five additional CT-39Gs were delivered during 1973, against a total requirement of 30 aircraft.

Series 40A. Described separately.

Series 60. Generally similar to Series 40, but fuselage lengthened by 3 ft 2 in (0·97 m). Accommodation for crew of two and ten passengers. Five windows on each side of passenger cabin.

Sabre 75 and 75A. Described separately.

A total of 215 commercial Sabres had been sold by 12 February 1974. The following details refer to the current Series 40 and 60 production versions, built at the General Aviation Divisions' Los Angeles plant:

Type: Twin-engined jet business transport.

Wings: Cantilever low-wing monoplane. Sweepback 28° 33′. All-metal two-spar milled-skin structure. Electrically-operated trim tab in aileron. Electrically-operated trailing-edge flaps. Aerodynamically-operated leading-edge slats in five sections on each wing. Optional full-span pneumatically-operated de-icing boots.

Fuselage: All-metal semi-monocoque structure. Large hydraulically-operated airbrake under centre-fuselage.

The Srs 60 "stretched" version of the Rockwell Sabre

Tail Unit: Cantilever all-metal structure, with flush antennae forming tip of fin and inset in dorsal fin. Moderate sweepback on all surfaces. Direct mechanical flight controls with electrically-operated horizontal tail surfaces. Electrically-operated trim tab in rudder. Optional full-span pneumatically-operated leading-edge de-icing boots.

Landing Gear: Retractable tricycle type. Twin-wheel nose unit retracts forward. Single wheel on each main unit, retracting inward into fuselage. Main-wheel tyres size 26 × 6·60-12, pressure 180 lb/sq in (12·7 kg/cm²). Nosewheel tyres size 18 × 4·40-10, pressure 100 lb/sq in (7·0 kg/cm²). Hydraulic brakes with anti-skid units.

Power Plant: Two Pratt & Whitney JT12A-8 turbojet engines (each 3,300 lb; 1,497 kg st) in pods on sides of rear fuselage. Integral fuel tanks in wings, with total capacity of 903 US gallons (3,418 litres). Fuselage tank, capacity 160 US gallons (606 litres). Total fuel capacity 1,063 US gallons (4,024 litres).

Accommodation: Crew of two and 6-10 passengers in pressurised air-conditioned cabin (see descriptions of individual series). Downward-hinged door, with built-in steps, forward of wing on port side. Emergency exits on starboard side of cabin in the Series 40 and on both sides in the Series 60. Baggage space at front of cabin opposite door in both versions, with adjacent coat rack specified in many interior configurations. Srs 60 has larger lavatory at rear of cabin. With seats removed there is room for 2,500 lb (1,135 kg) of freight.

Dimensions, external:
Wing span 44 ft 5¼ in (13·54 m)
Length overall:
Srs 40 43 ft 9 in (13·34 m)
Srs 60 48 ft 4 in (14·73 m)
Height overall 16 ft 0 in (4·88 m)
Tailplane span 17 ft 6½ in (5·35 m)
Wheel track 7 ft 2½ in (2·20 m)
Wheelbase:
Srs 40 14 ft 6 in (4·42 m)
Srs 60 15 ft 10¾ in (4·85 m)
Cabin door:
Height 3 ft 11 in (1·19 m)
Width 2 ft 4 in (0·71 m)

Dimensions, internal:
Cabin (excluding flight deck):
Length:
Srs 40 16 ft 0 in (4·88 m)
Srs 60 19 ft 0 in (5·79 m)
Max width 5 ft 2½ in (1·59 m)
Max height 5 ft 7½ in (1·71 m)
Volume:
Srs 40 400 cu ft (11·33 m³)
Srs 60 480 cu ft (13·59 m³)

Areas:
Wings, gross 342·05 sq ft (31·78 m²)
Ailerons (total) 16·42 sq ft (1·52 m²)
Flaps (total) 40·26 sq ft (3·74 m²)
Slats (total) 36·34 sq ft (3·38 m²)
Fin 41·58 sq ft (3·86 m²)
Rudder 8·95 sq ft (0·83 m²)
Tailplane 77·0 sq ft (7·15 m²)
Elevators 16·52 sq ft (1·53 m²)

Weights and Loadings:
Basic operating weight, empty:
Srs 40 9,895 lb (4,488 kg)
Srs 60 11,035 lb (5,005 kg)
Max payload, incl crew:
Srs 40 2,000 lb (907 kg)
Srs 60 2,215 lb (1,004 kg)
T-O weight with four passengers, baggage and max fuel:
Srs 40 18,215 lb (8,262 kg)
Srs 60 19,135 lb (8,679 kg)
Max T-O weight:
Srs 40 18,650 lb (8,498 kg)
Srs 60 20,000 lb (9,060 kg)
Max ramp weight:
Srs 40 19,035 lb (8,634 kg)
Srs 60 20,372 lb (9,221 kg)
Landing weight with four passengers, baggage and 1 hr reserve fuel:
Srs 40 12,345 lb (5,600 kg)
Srs 60 13,435 lb (6,094 kg)
Max landing weight 17,500 lb (7,938 kg)
Max zero-fuel weight:
Srs 40 12,800 lb (5,798 kg)
Srs 60 13,250 lb (6,010 kg)
Max wing loading:
Srs 40 53·6 lb/sq ft (261·7 kg/m²)
Srs 60 57·6 lb/sq ft (281·2 kg/m²)
Max power loading:
Srs 40 3·4 lb/lb st (3·4 kg/kg st)
Srs 60 2·97 lb/lb st (2·97 kg/kg st)

Performance (Srs 40 and Srs 60 at max T-O weight, unless detailed otherwise):
Max never-exceed speed Mach 0·85
Max level speed at 21,500 ft (6,550 m)
489 knots (563 mph; 906 km/h): Mach 0·8
Max cruising speed Mach 0·8
Econ cruising speed at 39,000-45,000 ft (11,900-13,700 m) Mach 0·75
Stalling speed, landing configuration, Srs 40 at 12,345 lb (5,600 kg) AUW; Srs 60 at 13,435 lb (6,094 kg) AUW:
Srs 40 80 knots (92 mph; 148 km/h)
Srs 60 83·5 knots (96·5 mph; 156 km/h)

T-39D with special equipment in modified nose for duty at the Naval Weapons Center, China Lake, California *(Duane A. Kasulka)*

Max rate of climb at S/L:
Srs 40 4,800 ft (1,463 m)/min
Srs 60 4,700 ft (1,433 m)/min
Max certificated operating altitude
45,000 ft (13,715 m)
Single-engine ceiling at AUW of 16,000 lb (7,257 kg) 24,000 ft (7,300 m)
Min ground turning radius:
Srs 40 25 ft 10¾ in (7.89 m)
Srs 60 28 ft 6 in (8·69 m)
T-O balanced field length:
Srs 40 4,800 ft (1,463 m)
Srs 60 5,050 ft (1,539 m)
Landing distance at landing weight with four passengers, baggage and 1 hr reserve fuel:
Srs 40 2,200 ft (671 m)
Srs 60 2,275 ft (693 m)
Max range, with four passengers, baggage, max fuel and 45 min reserve:
Srs 40 1,840 nm (2,118 miles; 3,408 km)
Srs 60 1,730 nm (1,992 miles; 3,205 km)

ROCKWELL SABRE 75

First demonstrated publicly at the Reading Air Show on 8 June 1971, the Sabre 75 is an 8/12-seat business transport aircraft.

Type: Twin-engined jet business transport.

Wings: Cantilever low-wing monoplane. Wing section NACA 64_1A212 (modified) at wing station 62·90, NACA 64_1A012 (modified) at wing station 254·94. Dihedral 3° 9′. Incidence 0° at root, 2° 54′ at construction tip. Sweepback at quarter-chord 28° 33′. Two-spar milled-skin light alloy structure. Conventional ailerons of light alloy construction with electrically-operated trim tab in port aileron. Aerodynamically-operated leading-edge slats of light alloy construction. Electrically-operated slotted trailing-edge flaps. Optional full-span pneumatically-operated de-icing boots.

Fuselage: Light alloy semi-monocoque structure. Large hydraulically-operated airbrake under centre-fuselage.

Tail Unit: Cantilever light alloy structure. Electrically-operated variable-incidence tailplane. Electrically-operated trim tab in rudder. Elevator has electrically-operated trim tab, mechanically interconnected. Optional pneumatic de-icing boots.

Landing Gear: Hydraulically-retractable tricycle type with dual wheels on each unit. Nose unit retracts forward into fuselage nose, main units inward into undersurface of wings. Loud oleo-pneumatic shock-absorbers. Dual main wheels with Goodrich 10-ply tyres size 22 × 5·75-12, pressure 165 lb/sq in (11·6 kg/cm²). Steerable nose unit with dual wheels and Goodrich Type VII tyres size 18 × 4·40-10, pressure 100 lb/sq in (7·0 kg/cm²). Goodyear multiple-disc brakes. Goodyear wheel-driven anti-skid units.

Power Plant: Two Pratt & Whitney JT12A-8 turbojet engines, each 3,300 lb (1,497 kg) st, in pod on each side of rear fuselage. Integral fuel tanks in wings, with total capacity of 903 US gallons (3,418 litres). Bladder-type fuel tank in aft fuselage with capacity of 199 US gallons (753 litres). Total fuel capacity 1,102 US gallons (4,171 litres). Single pressure refuelling point in lower surface of starboard inboard wing leading-edge. Alternative gravity refuelling points at each wingtip and on top of aft fuselage tank. Oil capacity 1·5 US gallons (5·7 litres).

Accommodation: Crew of two and 6-10 passengers in pressurised air-conditioned cabin, with a variety of optional seating layouts. Dual controls standard. Downward-hinged door, with built-in steps, forward of wing on port side. Emergency exit on each side of cabin, over wing. Baggage compartment at forward end of cabin, opposite door. Electrically-operated windscreen wipers.

Systems: Cabin pressurisation, heating and air-conditioning by engine bleed air from both engines. Emergency pressurisation provided by starboard engine bleed air. Hydraulic system powered by a single electrically-driven hydraulic pump, pressure 3,000 lb/sq in (210 kg/cm²). Auxiliary hydraulic accumulator for use in event of pump failure. Electrical system of 28V DC and 115V 400Hz constant-frequency AC. Primary DC power supplied by engine-driven starter/generators, with batteries interconnected in the system. Oxygen system supplied from 74 cu ft (2·10 m³) cylinder with quick-donning masks for crew and dropout masks for passengers. Pneumatic system optional for optional wing and tail unit de-icing boots.

Electronics: Fully equipped for IFR operations. Dual Collins 618M-2D VHF transceivers with Gables frequency selectors and com antennae. Dual Collins 51RV-2B VHF nav receivers with VOR/ILS, Gables nav frequency selectors, VOR/LOC and glideslope antennae and dual VOR code filters; Collins 51Z-4 marker beacon receiver and antenna; Collins 621A-6 ATC transponder, Gables control and antenna; Collins 860E-3 DME and antenna; Collins 54W-1 comparator warning monitor and annunciator control; Collins 51Y-7A ADF with 614L-11 control, antenna loop and sense masts; Collins 719R-1 weather radar with indicator and antenna; Collins 860F-1 radio altimeter with indicator and dual antennae; and Collins 346B-3 interphone and PA system with dual microphones, headsets and cabin speakers.

Dimensions, external:
Wing span 44 ft 5¼ in (13·54 m)
Wing aspect ratio 5·77
Length overall 47 ft 2 in (14·38 m)
Height overall 17 ft 3 in (5·26 m)
Tailplane span 17 ft 6½ in (5·35 m)
Wheel track 8 ft 4 in (2·54 m)
Wheelbase 15 ft 11 in (4·85 m)
Cabin door:
Height 3 ft 11 in (1·19 m)
Width 2 ft 4 in (0·71 m)
Height to sill 1 ft 0 in (0·30 m)
Emergency exits (2):
Height 2 ft 5 in (0·74 m)
Width 1 ft 8 in (0·51 m)

Dimensions, internal:
Cabin (excluding flight deck):
Length 19 ft 4 in (5·89 m)
Max width 5 ft 3¾ in (1·62 m)
Max height 6 ft 2 in (1·88 m)
Volume 550 cu ft (15·57 m³)

Areas:
Wings, gross 342·05 sq ft (31·8 m²)
Ailerons (total) 16·42 sq ft (1·53 m²)
Trailing-edge flaps (total) 40·26 sq ft (3·74 m²)
Leading-edge slats (total) 36·34 sq ft (3·38 m²)
Airbrake 7·54 sq ft (0·70 m²)
Fin 52·24 sq ft (4·85 m²)
Rudder, including tab 9·75 sq ft (0·91 m²)
Tailplane 77·0 sq ft (7·15 m²)
Elevators, including tab 16·52 sq ft (1·53 m²)

Weights and Loadings:
Weight empty 11,600 lb (5,261 kg)
T-O weight with four passengers, baggage and max fuel 20,180 lb (9,153 kg)
Max T-O weight 21,000 lb (9,525 kg)
Max ramp weight 21,200 lb (9,616 kg)
Max zero-fuel weight 14,300 lb (6,485 kg)
Landing weight with four passengers, baggage and 1 hr reserve fuel 14,100 lb (6,395 kg)
Max wing loading 61·39 lb/sq ft (299·7 kg/m²)
Max power loading 3·09 lb/lb st (3·09 kg/kg st)

Performance (at max T-O weight, unless detailed otherwise):
Max never-exceed speed Mach 0·85
Max cruising speed Mach 0·80
Econ cruising speed Mach 0·75
Stalling speed, landing configuration, at 14,100 lb (6,395 kg) AUW
85 knots (98 mph; 158 km/h)
Max rate of climb at S/L 3,950 ft (1,204 m)/min
Max certificated operating altitude
45,000 ft (13,715 m)
Min ground turning radius 28 ft 6 in (8·69 m)
T-O balanced field length 5,300 ft (1,615 m)

Landing distance at 14,100 ft (6,395 kg) landing weight 2,400 ft (732 m)
Max range, with four passengers, baggage, max fuel and 45 min reserve
1,510 nm (1,738 miles; 2,797 km)

ROCKWELL SABRE 75A

Latest in the Sabre series, this version differs from the Sabre 75 by having General Electric turbofan engines, of increased power; increased tailplane span; a new landing gear anti-skid system; improved galley, toilet and seating; and a new air-conditioning system.

On 3 May 1973 it was announced that Rockwell International had received from the FAA a contract valued at over $33·9 million for the lease/purchase of 11 Model 75A Sabres, with options on four more of these aircraft. To be equipped with an extensive array of solid-state avionics and measurement devices, including a sophisticated inertial area navigation computer system, they are to be used for flight testing the accuracy of the navigation aids, en route and terminal, which make up the US National Airspace System. Under an FAA programme to replace its 47-aircraft fleet of DC-3s and T-29s that were used formerly for flight inspection, the first of the Sabres was delivered in March 1974, and was to be followed by one further aircraft per month until completion of the contract.

The description of the Sabre 75 applies also to the Sabre 75A, except as detailed below:

Tail Unit: As for Sabre 75, except span of tailplane increased by 1 ft 10 in (0·56 m).

Landing Gear: As for Sabre 75, except mainwheel tyre pressure 180 lb/sq in (12·7 kg/cm²). New fully-modulating anti-skid system and improved brakes. Improved shock-absorption by use of a new-design oleo-pneumatic strut.

Power Plant: Two General Electric CF700-2D-2 turbofan engines, each 4,315 lb (1,957 kg) st, mounted in pod on each side of rear fuselage. Engines have cascade-type vertically-orientated thrust reversers. Fuel system as for Sabre 75. Oil capacity 1 US gallon (3·78 litres).

Accommodation: As Sabre 75, with improved galley, toilet and seating.

Systems: As Sabre 75, except for a new air-conditioning system incorporating a three-wheel bootstrap refrigeration unit, with separate ducting and temperature controls for cabin and flight deck; and 110V AC electrical system.

Electronics and Equipment: Standard cabin equipment includes folding tables, chimes, speakers and door to isolate flight deck and toilet from cabin. Equipped to Cat II IFR requirements with Collins avionics comprising FD-109Y and FD-109Z flight directors; AP-105 autopilot; NCS-31 nav/com control/computer system; dual VHF-20 com transceivers; dual VIR-30A VHF VOR/ILS nav systems; VIR-30A marker beacon; DF-206 ADF; dual 346B-3 audio systems, public address and intercom; DME-40 DME; dual TDR-90 ATC transponders; WXR-80 weather avoidance radar; dual MC-103 compass systems; 54W-1C comparator warning monitor; ALT-50 radio altimeter; IDC-16007 encoding altimeter and altitude alerting system; plus dual Teledyne SLZ-9123 instant vertical speed indicators; and dual Mach airspeed indicators.

Dimensions, external: As Sabre 75, except:
Tailplane span 19 ft 4½ in (5·91 m)

Areas: As for Sabre 75, except
Tailplane 90·08 sq ft (8·37 m²)
Elevators, including tab 19·43 sq ft (1·81 m²)

Weights and Loadings:
Weight empty 13,000 lb (5,896 kg)
T-O weight with four passengers, baggage and max fuel 21,580 lb (9,788 kg)
Max T-O weight 23,000 lb (10,432 kg)
Max ramp weight 23,000 lb (10,432 kg)
Max zero-fuel weight 15,620 lb (7,085 kg)
Landing weight with four passengers, baggage, and 1 hr fuel reserve 15,450 lb (7,008 kg)
Max landing weight 22,000 lb (9,979 kg)
Max wing loading 67·25 lb/sq ft (328·3 kg/m²)
Max power loading 2·66 lb/lb st (2·66 kg/kg st)

Performance (at max T-O weight, unless detailed otherwise):
Max never-exceed speed Mach 0·85
Max level speed Mach 0·80
489 knots (563 mph; 906 km/h)
Max cruising speed Mach 0·80
Econ cruising speed Mach 0·74
Stalling speed, landing configuration, at 15,450 lb (7,008 kg) AUW
86 knots (99 mph; 160 km/h)
Max rate of climb at S/L 4,500 ft (1,372 m)/min
Max certificated operating altitude
45,000 ft (13,715 m)
Min ground turning radius 28 ft 6 in (8·69 m)
T-O balanced field length 4,900 ft (1,494 m)
Landing distance at 15,450 lb (7,008 kg) landing weight 2,525 ft (770 m)
Max range, with four passengers, baggage, max fuel and 45 min reserve
1,683 nm (1,938 miles; 3,119 km)

ROCKWELL SABRE 40A

Announced on 8 June 1971, the Sabre 40A is an 8/10-seat turbojet-powered business aircraft. It has the wing of the Sabre 75 and the fuselage, landing gear and power plant of the Sabre Series 40. It is marketed completely equipped for service, including an IFR avionics package.

Type: Twin-engined jet business transport.

Wings: As for Sabre 75.

Fuselage: As for Sabre Series 40, except for glassfibre laminated nosecone.

Tail Unit: As for Sabre Series 40.

Landing Gear: Hydraulically-retractable tricycle type, with single wheel on each main unit and dual wheels on nose unit. Steerable nose unit with Western oleo-pneumatic shock-absorber. Main units have Bendix or Loud oleo-pneumatic shock-absorbers. Goodyear or Goodrich dual nosewheels and tyres size 18 × 4·40 high-pressure type. Goodyear main wheels and tyres size 26 × 6·60, high-pressure type. Goodyear disc brakes.

Power Plant: As for Sabre 40. Integral fuel tanks in wings with total fuel capacity of 903 US gallons (3,418 litres). Bladder-type fuel tank in aft fuselage, capacity 160 US gallons (606 litres). Total fuel capacity 1,063 US gallons (4,024 litres). Single pressure refuelling point in lower surface of starboard inboard wing leading-edge. Alternative gravity refuelling points at each wingtip and on top of aft fuselage tank. Oil capacity 1·5 US gallons (5·7 litres).

Accommodation: Crew of two and 6-8 passengers in pressurised air-conditioned cabin, with a variety of optional seating layouts. Dual controls standard. Downward-hinged door, with built-in steps, forward of wing on port side. Emergency exits on each side of fuselage, over wings. Baggage compartment at forward end of cabin, opposite door. Electrically-operated windscreen wipers.

Systems: Cabin pressurisation, heating and air-conditioning by engine bleed air from both engines. Emergency pressurisation provided by starboard engine bleed air. Hydraulic system powered by a single electrically-driven hydraulic pump, pressure 3,000 lb/sq in (210 kg/cm²). Auxiliary hydraulic accumulator for use in event of pump failure. Electrical system powered by two engine-driven 400A 30V DC starter/generators. Two nickel-cadmium 24V batteries. AC constant-frequency electric supply from three 115V 400Hz inverters, two of 2,500VA capacity, one of 750VA capacity. Oxygen system supplied from 64 cu ft (1·81 m³) cylinder with quick-donning masks for crew and dropout masks for passengers. Pneumatic system optional for optional wing and tail unit de-icing boots. Electrical windscreen anti-icing and defogging system.

Electronics: Equipped for IFR operations. King avionics comprising dual KTR900A VHF

Rockwell Sabre 75A eight/twelve-seat business transport (two General Electric CF700-2D-2 turbofan engines)

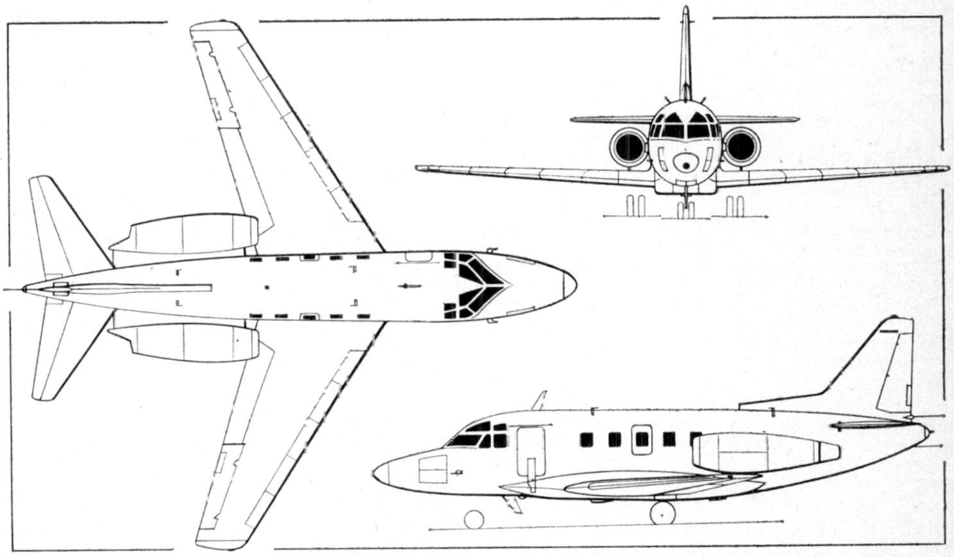

Rockwell Sabre 75A eight/twelve-seat twin-turbofan business transport (*Pilot Press*)

Rockwell Sabre 40A eight/ten-seat turbine-powered business aircraft

com transceivers; KNR661A and KNR660A VOR/LOC nav receivers; KGM691 marker beacon and glideslope receiver, and KGM681 glideslope receiver; KDF800 ADF with KNI-585 control, KA36 loop antenna and Douglas sense antenna; KDM705 DME; Wilcox 1014A ATC transponder; RCA AVQ-21 weather radar; and associated antennae, Gables controls, dual headsets, microphones, flight deck speakers and single cabin speaker.

DIMENSIONS, EXTERNAL, INTERNAL AND AREAS:
As Sabre Series 40

WEIGHTS AND LOADINGS:

Weight empty	10,050 lb (4,558 kg)
T-O weight with four passengers, baggage and max fuel	18,370 lb (8,332 kg)
Max T-O weight	19,612 lb (8,895 kg)
Max ramp weight	19,922 lb (9,036 kg)
Max zero-fuel weight	12,800 lb (5,805 kg)
Landing weight with four passengers, baggage and 1 hr fuel reserve	12,500 lb (5,670 kg)
Max landing weight	17,500 lb (7,938 kg)
Max wing loading	54·5 lb/sq ft (266·1 kg/m^2)
Max power loading	2·83 lb/lb st (2·83 kg/kg st)

PERFORMANCE (at max T-O weight, unless detailed otherwise):

Max never-exceed speed	Mach 0·85
Max level speed	Mach 0·80
	489 knots (563 mph; 906 km/h)
Max cruising speed	Mach 0·80
Econ cruising speed	Mach 0·75
Stalling speed, landing configuration, at 12,500 lb (5,670 kg) AUW	80·5 knots (92·5 mph; 149 km/h)
Max rate of climb at S/L	4,700 ft (1,433 m)/min
Max certificated operating altitude	45,000 ft (13,715 m)
Service ceiling, one engine out	24,000 ft (7,315 m)
Min ground turning radius	25 ft 10¾ in (7·89 m)
T-O balanced field length	4,900 ft (1,494 m)
Landing distance at 12,500 lb (5,670 kg) AUW	2,250 ft (686 m)
Max range, with four passengers, baggage, max fuel and 45 min reserve	1,749 nm (2,014 miles; 3,241 km)

Rockwell Commander 112A four-seat cabin monoplane (200 hp Lycoming IO-360-C1D6 engine)

Rockwell Shrike Commander executive transport (two 290 hp Lycoming IO-540-E1B5 engines)

ROCKWELL COMMANDER 112A

On 17 December 1970 the General Aviation Divisions of Rockwell International announced the introduction, and first public flight, of a completely new single-engine four-seat light aircraft then known as the Aero Commander Model 112.

Following extensive consumer research in the lightplane market, the company initiated design of the Model 112 in December 1969. Construction of the first of five prototypes began in February 1970 and the first flight was made on 4 December 1970.

Rockwell claimed that the Model 112 had the most spacious cabin of any four-seat single-engine aircraft on the market, and projected also twin-engined versions. Deliveries to customers of the Model 112 began in 1972.

In late 1973 manufacture of subassemblies and components was moved to Bethany, Oklahoma, and the first aircraft assembled from this production source was delivered in January 1974 as the Model 112A. It introduces a number of improvements, including metal cabin doors, revised ventilation system and an increase of 100 lb (45 kg) in maximum gross weight.

There are no plans at present to market the Model 111, with non-retractable landing gear.

TYPE: Four-seat lightweight cabin monoplane.

WINGS: Cantilever low-wing monoplane. Wing section NACA 63.415 (modified). Dihedral 7°. Incidence at root 2°. Sweepforward at quarter-chord 2° 30′. Conventional light alloy structure. Ailerons of light alloy construction, using a channel spar and one-piece beaded skin. Electrically-operated light alloy single-slotted trailing-edge flaps, extending from wing station 25 to 121.20 with chord of 1 ft 1 in (0·33 m). Ground-adjustable trim tab on port aileron.

FUSELAGE: Conventional semi-monocoque light alloy structure.

TAIL UNIT: Cantilever light alloy structure with swept vertical surfaces. Dorsal fin faired into fuselage. Fixed-incidence tailplane. Adjustable trim tab in port elevator.

LANDING GEAR: Hydraulically-retractable tricycle type. Main wheels retract inward, nosewheel aft. Trailing-beam type main units, with oleo-pneumatic shock-absorbers. Cleveland main-wheel assemblies type P-268-40 with tyres size 6·00-6, pressure 29 lb/sq in (2·04 kg/cm^2). Cleveland nosewheel and tyre size 5·00-5, pressure 31 lb/sq in (2·18 kg/cm^2). Cleveland type P-268-30 hydraulic brakes.

POWER PLANT: One 200 hp Lycoming IO-360-C1D6 four-cylinder horizontally-opposed air-cooled engine, driving a Hartzell type HC-E2YR-1BF/F7666A two-blade metal constant-speed propeller with spinner. Two integral fuel tanks in the wing leading-edges, capacity of each 25 US gallons (94·5 litres) standard, 35 US gallons (132·5 litres) optional. Total fuel capacity 50 US gallons (189 litres) standard, 70 US gallons (265 litres) optional. Refuelling point in upper surface of each wing. Oil capacity 2 US gallons (7·5 litres).

ACCOMMODATION: Pilot and three passengers seated in pairs in enclosed cabin. Individual forward seats, bench seat for two aft. Passenger door on each side of cabin, over wing, hinged at forward edge. External baggage door on port side of fuselage aft of wing. Provisions for heating and ventilation.

SYSTEMS: Hydraulic system powered by a single electrically-driven hydraulic pump. Electrical system supplied by 70A 12V engine-driven alternator and 12V 35Ah battery.

ELECTRONICS: A wide range of Narco and King 360-channel communications and 200-channel navigation radios available to customer's requirements.

DIMENSIONS, EXTERNAL:

Wing span	32 ft 10¾ in (10·03 m)
Wing chord at centreline	5 ft 10¼ in (1·78 m)
Wing chord at tip	2 ft 11 in (0·89 m)
Wing chord, mean aerodynamic	4 ft 7 in (1·40 m)
Wing aspect ratio	7
Length overall	25 ft 0 in (7·62 m)
Height overall	8 ft 5 in (2·57 m)
Tailplane span	12 ft 6 in (3·81 m)
Wheel track	10 ft 10 in (3·30 m)
Wheelbase	6 ft 11 in (2·11 m)
Propeller diameter	6 ft 4 in (1·93 m)
Propeller ground clearance	8½ in (0·22 m)
Passenger doors (2):	
Height	3 ft 2 in (0·97 m)
Width	2 ft 4 in (0·71 m)
Baggage door:	
Height	1 ft 8 in (0·51 m)
Width	2 ft 4 in (0·71 m)

DIMENSIONS, INTERNAL:

Cabin:	
Length	9 ft 7½ in (2·93 m)
Max width	3 ft 11 in (1·19 m)
Max height	4 ft 1 in (1·24 m)
Baggage compartment	21 cu ft (0·59 m^3)

AREAS:

Wings, gross	152 sq ft (14·12 m^2)
Ailerons (total)	11 sq ft (1·02 m^2)
Trailing-edge flaps (total)	18 sq ft (1·67 m^2)
Fin	17 sq ft (1·58 m^2)

WEIGHTS AND LOADINGS:

Weight empty	1,688 lb (765 kg)
Max T-O weight	2,650 lb (1,202 kg)
Max landing weight	2,550 lb (1,157 kg)
Max wing loading	17·4 lb/sq ft (85·0 kg/m^2)
Max power loading	13·3 lb/hp (6·03 kg/hp)

PERFORMANCE (at max T-O weight):

Max never-exceed speed	200 knots (230 mph; 370 km/h)
Max level speed	148 knots (171 mph; 275 km/h)
Max cruising speed, 75% power at 7,500 ft (2,285 m)	140 knots (161 mph; 259 km/h)
Stalling speed, flaps up	61 knots (70 mph; 113 km/h)
Stalling speed, flaps down	54 knots (62 mph; 100 km/h)
Max rate of climb at S/L	1,020 ft (311 m)/min
Service ceiling	13,900 ft (4,235 m)
T-O run	1,190 ft (363 m)
T-O to 50 ft (15 m)	1,585 ft (483 m)
Landing from 50 ft (15 m)	1,310 ft (399 m)
Landing run	680 ft (207 m)
Range with max optional fuel, 45 min reserve	846 nm (975 miles; 1,569 km)

ROCKWELL SHRIKE COMMANDER

The Rockwell Shrike Commander is a twin-engined aircraft designed for the businessman-pilot.

TYPE: Twin-engined light transport.

WINGS: Cantilever high-wing monoplane. Wing section NACA 23012 modified. Dihedral 4°. Incidence 3° at root, —3° 30′ at tip. All-metal two-spar flush-riveted structure. Frise statically-balanced all-metal ailerons. Hydraulically-operated all-metal slotted flaps. Ground-adjustable tab in starboard aileron. Pneumatic de-icing boots optional.

FUSELAGE: All-metal semi-monocoque structure with flush-riveted skin.

TAIL UNIT: Cantilever all-metal structure with 10° dihedral on tailplane. Trim tabs in each elevator and rudder. Pneumatic de-icing boots optional.

LANDING GEAR: Retractable tricycle type, with single wheel on each unit. All wheels retract rearward hydraulically, main wheels turning through 90° to stow horizontally in nacelles. Oleo-pneumatic shock-absorbers. Hydraulically-steerable nosewheel. Goodyear main wheels with tyres size 25·65 × 8·70-10, pressure 55 lb/sq in (3·9 kg/cm^2). Nosewheel tyre size 17·5 × 6·30-6, pressure 42 lb/sq in (3·0 kg/cm^2). Goodyear aircooled hydraulic disc brakes.

POWER PLANT: Two 290 hp Lycoming IO-540-E1B5 six-cylinder horizontally-opposed air-cooled engines, each driving a Hartzell HC-C3YR-2/C8468-6R three-blade constant-speed fully-feathering metal propeller. Bag-type fuel tanks in wings, capacity 156 US gallons (590 litres). Overwing refuelling. Oil capacity 6 US gallons (22·7 litres). Electrically-heated fuel vents and propeller anti-icing shoes optional.

ACCOMMODATION: Four individual seats: two in front with dual controls and two at rear. Curtains divide pilot's compartment from cabin. Swivel-mounted fresh air vents above each seat, window curtains, emergency exit, announcement signs, adjustable heating and fresh air ventilation ports at cabin floor level, double-glazed windows in cabin and a hatbox shelf in aft cabin bulkhead are standard. Optional seating layouts for up to eight persons, some with rear bench seat for two or three. Optional refreshment cabinet for hot and cold drinks. Forward-opening passenger door under wing on port side. Forward-opening door by pilot's seat at front of cabin on port side. All equipment can be removed to permit cabin to be used for freight carrying. Compartment for 500 lb (227 kg) baggage aft of cabin, with outside door. Windscreen wiper and alcohol de-icing system for port side optional.

SYSTEMS: Hydraulic system, pressure 1,250 lb/sq in (88 kg/cm²), for landing gear, flaps, brakes and nosewheel steering. Electrical system includes two 70A alternators and two 35Ah batteries. 100A alternators optional.

ELECTRONICS AND EQUIPMENT: Standard equipment includes flight and engine instrumentation, clock, Janitrol 35,000 BTU cabin heater, rotating beacon, landing lights, reading lights, position lights, vacuum warning lights, instrument lighting system, air filter for vacuum instruments, dual vacuum pumps, electrically-adjustable cowl flap, external power socket, stall warning indicator and alternative static source. Optional equipment includes more advanced instruments, an extensive range of avionics which are available in package form or as individual items, underfuselage rotating beacon, vertically-adjustable pilot and co-pilot seats, inertia reels and shoulder harnesses for all seats, storage drawers under aft couch, cabin and/or cockpit fire extinguishers, low-fuel warning light, glass-holders, seat head-rests, lavatory chair for starboard side of aft cabin, complete with curtain, 48·3 cu ft (1·37 m³) or 96·6 cu ft (2·74 m³) oxygen system, propeller synchronising equipment, dual relief tubes, sidewall-mounted stereo console, extra seat tracks, polished spinners, cabin table, storm window for co-pilot and wing ice lights.

DIMENSIONS, EXTERNAL:
- Wing span: 49 ft 0½ in (14·95 m)
- Wing chord at root: 8 ft 4 in (2·54 m)
- Wing chord at tip: 2 ft 1½ in (0·65 m)
- Wing aspect ratio: 9·45
- Length overall: 36 ft 9¾ in (11·22 m)
- Height overall: 14 ft 6 in (4·42 m)
- Tailplane span: 16 ft 9 in (5·10 m)
- Wheel track: 12 ft 11 in (3·95 m)
- Wheelbase: 13 ft 11¾ in (4·26 m)
- Propeller diameter: 6 ft 8 in (2·03 m)
- Crew door (fwd):
  - Height: 3 ft 10 in (1·17 m)
  - Width: 1 ft 11 in (0·58 m)
- Passenger door (aft):
  - Height: 3 ft 9 in (1·14 m)
  - Width: 2 ft 4 in (0·71 m)
- Baggage door:
  - Height: 1 ft 11½ in (0·60 m)
  - Width: 1 ft 7½ in (0·50 m)

DIMENSIONS, INTERNAL:
- Cabin: Length: 10 ft 7 in (3·23 m)
  - Max width: 4 ft 4 in (1·32 m)
  - Max height: 4 ft 5 in (1·35 m)
  - Volume: 177 cu ft (5·01 m³)
- Baggage hold: 33 cu ft (0·93 m³)

AREAS:
- Wings, gross: 255 sq ft (23·69 m²)
- Ailerons (total): 20·52 sq ft (1·90 m²)
- Trailing-edge flaps (total): 21·20 sq ft (1·97 m²)
- Fin: 24·00 sq ft (2·23 m²)
- Rudder, including tab: 15·40 sq ft (1·43 m²)
- Tailplane: 33·06 sq ft (3·07 m²)
- Elevators, including tabs: 20·54 sq ft (1·91 m²)

WEIGHTS AND LOADINGS:
- Weight empty, equipped: 4,608 lb (2,090 kg)
- Max T-O and landing weight: 6,750 lb (3,062 kg)
- Max wing loading: 26·47 lb/sq ft (129·2 kg/m²)
- Max power loading: 11·64 lb/hp (5·28 kg/hp)

PERFORMANCE (at max T-O weight):
- Max level speed at S/L: 187 knots (215 mph; 346 km/h) TAS
- Max cruising speed (75% power) at 9,000 ft (2,745 m): 176 knots (203 mph; 326 km/h) TAS
- Stalling speed, clean: 68 knots (78 mph; 126 km/h)
- Stalling speed, flaps and landing gear down: 59 knots (68 mph; 109 km/h)
- Minimum single-engine control speed: 65·5 knots (75 mph; 121 km/h)
- Max rate of climb at S/L: 1,340 ft (408 m)/min
- Rate of climb at S/L, one engine out: 266 ft (81 m)/min
- Service ceiling: 19,400 ft (5,913 m)
- Service ceiling, one engine out: 6,500 ft (1,981 m)
- Min ground turning radius: 38 ft 2 in (11·63 m)
- T-O to 50 ft (15 m): 1,915 ft (584 m)
- Landing from 50 ft (15 m): 2,235 ft (681 m)
- Range with standard fuel at 9,000 ft (2,745 m) at 178 knots (205 mph; 330 km/h) TAS, 45 min reserve: 693 nm (797 miles; 1,282 km)
- Range, conditions as above, no reserve: 824 nm (948 miles; 1,525 km)
- Absolute range, standard fuel, at 15,000 ft (4,570 m) at 45% power and TAS of148 knots (170 mph; 273 km/h), no reserve: 936 nm (1,078 miles; 1,735 km)

ROCKWELL TURBO COMMANDER 681B

The Turbo Commander 681B is a pressurised transport aircraft with an airframe generally similar to that of the Shrike Commander; but it has reduced wing span and is powered by two AiResearch turboprop engines. The prototype flew for the first time on 31 December 1964, and the first production aircraft followed in April 1965. Deliveries began in May 1966, the type being known for a time subsequently as the Hawk Commander. Production has now ended; details can be found in the 1973-74 *Jane's*.

ROCKWELL COMMANDER 685

Announced in April 1972, the Rockwell Commander 685 is a pressurised seven/nine-seat business transport evolved, like the Rockwell Commander 690A, from the Turbo Commander 690 but powered by two 435 hp Continental GTSIO-520-F six-cylinder horizontally-opposed aircooled engines, each driving a Hartzell three-blade metal constant-speed and fully-feathering propeller. Standard fuel capacity is 256 US gallons (969 litres), with provision for optional auxiliary tanks raising total capacity to 322 US gallons (1,218 litres).

DIMENSIONS, EXTERNAL: As for Commander 690A except:
- Length overall: 42 ft 11¾ in (13·10 m)
- Propeller diameter: 7 ft 4 in (2·24 m)
- Propeller ground clearance: 2 ft 1 in (0·64 m)

WEIGHTS AND LOADINGS:
- Weight empty, standard: 6,021 lb (2,731 kg)
- Weight empty, with optional fuel tanks: 6,046 lb (2,742 kg)
- Max T-O and landing weight: 9,000 lb (4,082 kg)
- Max ramp weight: 9,050 lb (4,105 kg)
- Max wing loading: 33·83 lb/sq ft (165·2 kg/m²)
- Max power loading: 10·34 lb/hp (4·69 kg/hp)

PERFORMANCE (at max T-O weight, unless detailed otherwise):
- Max level speed at 20,000 ft (6,100 m): 242 knots (279 mph; 449 km/h) TAS
- Max cruising speed at 24,000 ft (7,315 m): 222 knots (256 mph; 412 km/h) TAS
- Econ cruising speed at 14,000 ft (4,235 m): 152 knots (175 mph; 281 km/h) TAS
- Stalling speed, wheels and flaps up: 81 knots (93·5 mph; 150·5 km/h) CAS
- Stalling speed, wheels and flaps down: 75 knots (86·5 mph; 139 km/h) CAS
- Max rate of climb at S/L: 1,490 ft (454 m)/min
- Max rate of climb at S/L, one engine out: 247 ft (75 m)/min
- Service ceiling: 27,500 ft (8,380 m)
- Service ceiling, one engine out: 12,400 ft (3,780 m)
- FAA operational ceiling: 25,000 ft (7,620 m)
- Min ground turning radius: 40 ft 11 in (12·47 m)
- Normal T-O run: 1,949 ft (594 m)
- Short-field T-O run: 1,467 ft (447 m)
- Normal T-O to 50 ft (15 m): 2,711 ft (826 m)
- Short-field T-O to 50 ft (15 m): 1,943 ft (592 m)
- Short-field landing from 50 ft (15 m): 1,869 ft (570 m)
- Normal landing from 50 ft (15 m): 2,312 ft (705 m)
- Short-field landing run: 993 ft (303 m)
- Normal landing run: 1,188 ft (362 m)
- Range with max standard fuel, allowances for start, taxi, climb to cruise altitude, descent and 45 min reserve, with 1,493 lb (677 kg) payload:
  - at 24,000 ft (7,315 m), max recommended cruising power: 848 nm (976 miles; 1,570 km)
  - at 18,000 ft (5,485 m), econ cruising power: 1,147 nm (1,320 miles; 2,124 km)
- Range with fuel, allowances and payload as above, no reserve:
  - at 24,000 ft (7,315 m), max recommended cruising power: 943 nm (1,085 miles; 1,746 km)
  - at 18,000 ft (5,485 m), econ cruising power: 1,276 nm (1,469 miles; 2,364 km)
- Range with max standard and optional fuel, allowances as above, with 1,072 lb (486 kg) payload and 45 min reserve:
  - at 24,000 ft (7,315 m), max recommended cruising power: 1,115 nm (1,284 miles; 2,066 km)
  - at 20,000 ft (6,100 m), econ cruising power: 1,534 nm (1,766 miles; 2,842 km)
- Range with fuel, allowances and payload as above, no reserve:
  - at 24,000 ft (7,315 m), max recommended cruising power: 1,211 nm (1,394 miles; 2,243 km)
  - at 20,000 ft (6,100 m), econ cruising power: 1,668 nm (1,920 miles; 3,090 km)

ROCKWELL COMMANDER 690A

The Rockwell Commander 690A is a pressurised transport aircraft powered by two AiResearch turboprop engines. It is an advanced development of the Turbo Commander 690, and improvements include an increase in cabin pressure differential from 4·2 to 5·2 lb/sq in (0·30 to 0·37 kg/cm²), better flight deck lighting, new interior decor, ground cooling increase to 26,000 BTU, and certification for flight in known icing conditions.

The prototype of the Commander 690A was flown for the first time in June 1972, with FAA certification being awarded on 25 April 1973. Although certification was granted under CAR Part 3, many portions of the systems and structure exceed the requirements of CAR Part 4, SR422B and FAR 25.

The description of the Shrike Commander applies also to the Commander 690A except in the following details:

WINGS: Span reduced. Incidence at tip —1°. Electrically-operated trim tab in starboard aileron.

TAIL UNIT: Tailplane increased in span and area. Vertical surfaces increased in height and area.

LANDING GEAR: Wheelbase increased. Main-wheel tyre pressure 70 lb/sq in (4·9 kg/cm²).

POWER PLANT: Two 700 ehp AiResearch TPE 331-5-251K turboprop engines, each driving a Hartzell HC-B3TN-5FL/LT 10282H+4 three-blade constant-speed fully-feathering and reversible-pitch propeller. Fuel contained in integral wing tanks with a total usable capacity of 384 US gallons (1,453 litres). Refuelling points on upper surface of each wing. Oil capacity 3 US gallons (11·5 litres).

ACCOMMODATION: Standard seating for pilot and six passengers, on two adjustable seats on flight deck, two forward-facing single seats and a three-place forward-facing bench seat in main cabin. A variety of optional seating layouts offer accommodation for up to 10 persons. Cabin pressurised, heated and air-conditioned. Forward-hinged outward-opening cabin door on port side, with retractable cabin step. Emergency exit on starboard side of fuselage. Baggage compartment of 43 cu ft (1·22 m³) with 600 lb (272 kg) capacity aft of rear pressure bulkhead with external access door on port side of fuselage.

SYSTEMS: Cabin pressurisation, heating and air-conditioning by engine bleed air; max pressure differential 5·2 lb/sq in (0·37 kg/cm²). Electrical system powered by two 300A starter/generators. Two 44Ah nickel-cadmium batteries. Hydraulic system supplied by two pumps at 1,250 lb/sq in (88 kg/cm²), with hydraulic reservoir for emergency use. Scott constant-flow emergency oxygen system of 22 cu ft (0·62 m³) capacity, with individual outlets.

ELECTRONICS AND EQUIPMENT: Full blind-flying instrumentation and a selection of IFR avionics packages by King, Collins, Sperry and Bendix are available as options. Automatic propeller synchronisation, Foxboro fuel flow system and gauges with digital readout, heated fuel vents, stall warning and engine fire detection system standard.

DIMENSIONS, EXTERNAL:
- Wing span: 46 ft 8 in (14·22 m)
- Wing chord at root: 8 ft 7¾ in (2·64 m)
- Wing chord at tip: 2 ft 9 in (0·84 m)
- Wing aspect ratio: 8·19
- Length overall: 44 ft 4¼ in (13·52 m)

Rockwell Commander 685 seven/nine-seat pressurised business transport

Height overall 14 ft 11½ in (4·56 m)
Tailplane span 19 ft 9¼ in (6·03 m)
Wheel track 15 ft 5 in (4·70 m)
Wheelbase 17 ft 7¾ in (5·38 m)
Propeller diameter 8 ft 10 in (2·69 m)
Propeller ground clearance 1 ft 2¼ in (0·36 m)
Cabin door:
Height 3 ft 11 in (1·19 m)
Width 2 ft 2¼ in (0·67 m)
Height to sill 1 ft 6½ in (0·47 m)
Baggage door:
Height 2 ft 7½ in (0·80 m)
Width 1 ft 8 in (0·51 m)
Height to sill 1 ft 8½ in (0·52 m)
Emergency exit:
Height 1 ft 7 in (0·48 m)
Width 2 ft 2¾ in (0·68 m)

AREAS:
Wings, gross 266·0 sq ft (24·7 m²)
Ailerons (total) 19·74 sq ft (1·83 m²)
Trailing-edge flaps (total) 17·74 sq ft (1·65 m²)
Fin 24·23 sq ft (2·25 m²)
Rudder (including tab) 20·66 sq ft (1·92 m²)
Tailplane 37·80 sq ft (3·51 m²)
Elevators (including tab) 20·57 sq ft (1·91 m²)

WEIGHTS AND LOADINGS:
Weight empty, standard 6,126 lb (2,778 kg)
Max T-O weight 10,250 lb (4,649 kg)
Max ramp weight 10,300 lb (4,672 kg)
Max zero-fuel weight 8,750 lb (3,969 kg)
Max landing weight 9,600 lb (4,354 kg)
Max wing loading 38·53 lb/sq ft (188·1 kg/m²)
Max power loading 7·32 lb/ehp (3·32 kg/ehp)

PERFORMANCE (at max T-O weight, unless specified otherwise):
Max level speed at 12,000 ft (3,660 m)
285 knots (328 mph; 528 km/h) TAS
Max cruising speed at 17,500 ft (5,335 m)
280 knots (322 mph; 518 km/h) TAS
Econ cruising speed at 31,000 ft (9,450 m)
251 knots (289 mph; 465 km/h) TAS
Stalling speed, flaps and wheels up
82 knots (94·5 mph; 152 km/h) CAS
Stalling speed, flaps and wheels down
77 knots (89 mph; 143·5 km/h) CAS
Max rate of climb at S/L 2,849 ft (868 m)/min
Rate of climb at S/L, one engine out
893 ft (272 m)/min
Service ceiling 33,000 ft (10,060 m)
Service ceiling, one engine out
19,700 ft (6,005 m)
FAA operational ceiling 31,000 ft (9,450 m)
Min ground turning radius 40 ft 11 in (12·47 m)
Normal T-O run 1,434 ft (437 m)
Short-field T-O run 1,180 ft (360 m)
Normal T-O to 50 ft (15 m) 2,216 ft (675 m)
Short-field T-O to 50 ft (15 m) 1,666 ft (508 m)
Landing from 50 ft (15 m) with propeller reversal, at max landing weight 1,606 ft (490 m)
Landing from 50 ft (15 m) without propeller reversal, at max landing weight
2,084 ft (635 m)
Landing run with propeller reversal, at max landing weight 902 ft (275 m)
Landing run without propeller reversal, at max landing weight 1,385 ft (422 m)
Range with max fuel, allowances for start, taxi, T-O and climb to 31,000 ft (9,450 m), 45 min reserve, with 1,601 lb (726 kg) payload:
Max cruising power
1,460 nm (1,681 miles; 2,705 km)
Econ cruising power
1,471 nm (1,693 miles; 2,725 km)
Range with max payload, allowances as above, with 2,624 lb (1,190 kg) payload:
Max cruising power
740 nm (852 miles; 1,370 km)
Econ cruising power
741 nm (853 miles; 1,372 km)

Rockwell Commander 690A business aircraft (two 700 ehp AiResearch TPE 331-5-251K turboprop engines)

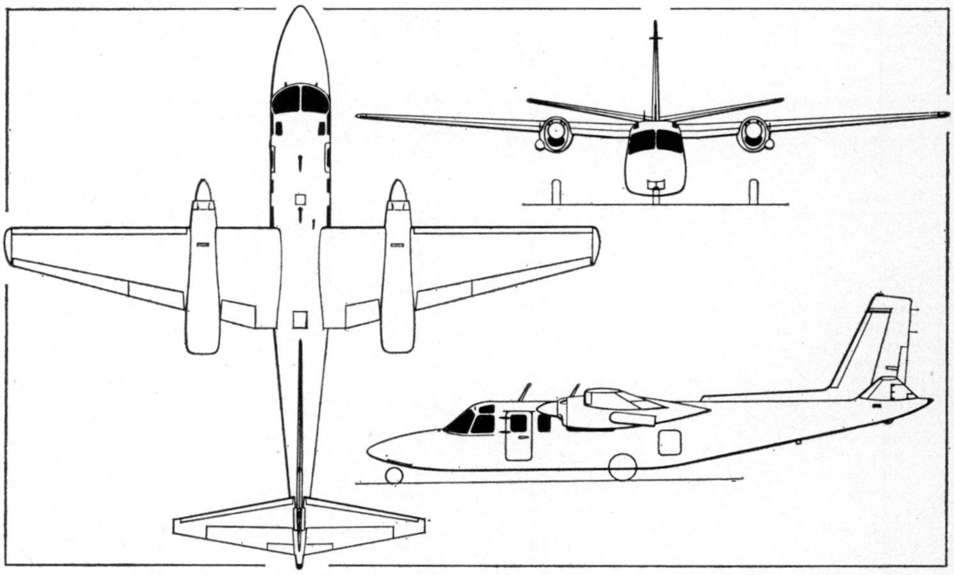

Rockwell Commander 690A seven/ten-seat twin-turboprop transport *(Pilot Press)*

ROCKWELL THRUSH COMMANDER

The Thrush Commander is the largest specially-designed agricultural aircraft in production in the USA at the present time. It has a 600 hp Pratt & Whitney radial engine and carries a 53 cu ft (1·50 m³) hopper able to contain up to 400 US gallons (1,514 litres) of liquid or 3,280 lb (1,487 kg) of dry chemicals. It has corrosion proofing of activated Copon and is certificated to both CAR Pt 8 and Pt 3 requirements for Normal category aircraft.

TYPE: Single-seat agricultural aircraft.

WINGS: Cantilever low-wing monoplane. Two-spar structure of light alloy throughout, except for main spar caps of heat-treated SAE 4000 Series steel. Leading-edge formed by heavy main spar and partially flush-riveted nose-skin. Light alloy plain ailerons. Electrically-operated flaps. Wing roots sealed against chemical entry.

FUSELAGE: Welded chrome-molybdenum steel tube structure covered with quickly-removable light alloy panels. Underfuselage skin of stainless steel.

TAIL UNIT: Wire-braced welded chrome-molybdenum steel tube structure, fabric-covered. Streamline-section heavy-duty stainless steel wire bracing and heavy-duty stainless steel attachment fittings. Light alloy controllable trim tab in each elevator. Deflector cable from cockpit to fin-tip.

LANDING GEAR: Non-retractable tailwheel type. Main units have rubber-in-compression shock-absorption and 27 in wheels with 10-ply tyres. Hydraulic brakes. Parking brakes. Wire cutters on main gear. Steerable, locking tailwheel size 12·5 × 4·5 in.

POWER PLANT: One 600 hp Pratt & Whitney R-1340-AN-1 or -S3H1 nine-cylinder radial aircooled engine, driving a Hamilton Standard constant-speed two-blade metal propeller. One 53 US gallon (200·5 litre) integral tank in each wing, giving total fuel capacity of 106 US gallons (401 litres). Oil capacity 11·4 US gallons (43 litres).

ACCOMMODATION: Single adjustable seat in 40g "safety pod" enclosed cockpit, with steel tube overturn structure. Downward-hinged door on each side. Tempered safety-glass windscreen. Openable windscreen optional. Hopper forward of cockpit with capacity of 53 cu ft (1·50 m³) or 400 US gallons (1,514 litres).

SYSTEMS: Electrical system comprises a 50A 24V generator and 35Ah battery.

EQUIPMENT: Standard equipment includes Universal spray system with external 2 in (5 cm) stainless steel plumbing, 2 in (5 cm) Root Model 67 pump with wooden fan, Ag Commander gate, Transland 2 in (5 cm) valve, Transland quick-disconnect pump mount, 35 nozzles installed, streamlined sprayboomss with outlets for 70 nozzles, 2½ in (6·3 cm) bottom loading system installed in port side. Navigation lights, instrument lights and two rotating beacons. Optional equipment includes Ag Commander high-volume spreader with micro-adjust calibrator, agitator installation, extra-high-density spray configuration with 70 nozzles installed, night working lights including wingtip turn lights, cockpit fire extinguisher and ferry fuel system.

DIMENSIONS, EXTERNAL:
Wing span 44 ft 5 in (13·54 m)
Length overall 29 ft 4½ in (8·95 m)
Height overall 9 ft 2 in (2·79 m)
Tailplane span 15 ft 11½ in (4·86 m)
Wheel track 8 ft 11 in (2·72 m)

WEIGHTS AND LOADINGS:
Weight empty, equipped 3,950 lb (1,791 kg)

Rockwell Thrush Commander agricultural aircraft (600 hp Pratt & Whitney R-1340 engine)

Max T-O weight:
CAM.8 6,900 lb (3,130 kg)
CAR.3 6,000 lb (2,721 kg)
Max wing loading 18·4 lb/sq ft (89·8 kg/m²)
Max power loading 10 lb/hp (4·5 kg/hp)

PERFORMANCE (at CAR.3 max T-O weight, except where indicated):
Max level speed 122 knots (140 mph; 225 km/h)
Cruising speed 96 knots (110 mph; 177 km/h)
Normal operating speed
83-96 knots (95-110 mph; 153-177 km/h)
Stalling speed, flaps up
61 knots (70 mph; 113 km/h)
Stalling speed, flaps down
58 knots (66 mph; 107 km/h)
Stalling speed at normal landing weight, flaps up 50 knots (57 mph; 92 km/h)
Stalling speed at normal landing weight, flaps down 48 knots (55 mph; 89 km/h)
Max rate of climb at S/L 900 ft (274 m)/min
Service ceiling 15,000 ft (4,570 m)
T-O run 775 ft (236 m)
Landing run at normal landing weight
500 ft (152 m)
Range (at 50% power)
408 nm (470 miles; 756 km)

ROTORWAY

ROTORWAY, INC

ADDRESS:
14805 S. Interstate 10, Tempe, Arizona 85281
Telephone: (602) 963-6652

Mr B. J. Schramm formed the Schramm Aircraft Company to market, in both ready-to-fly and prefabricated component form, a single-seat helicopter of his own design, named the Javelin. Details of this aircraft, which flew for the first time in August 1965, can be found in the 1967-68 *Jane's*.

Subsequently, a new company named RotorWay Inc was formed to market to amateur constructors plans and kits of components to build Mr Schramm's Scorpion helicopter, described as a production version of the Javelin. The company has now ended production of components for this helicopter; details can be found in the 1972-73 *Jane's*. This has now been superseded by the two-seat Scorpion Too.

RotorWay offers comprehensive plans, technical advice from its engineers, a complete kit to build the Scorpion Too, or a series of small progressive kits, allowing the constructor to proceed as finance allows. The company will also supply plans and rotor blades to those builders wishing to provide their own materials and power plant.

ROTORWAY SCORPION TOO

TYPE: Two-seat light helicopter.

ROTOR SYSTEM: Two-blade semi-rigid main rotor, incorporating Schramm Tractable Control rotor system. Blade section NACA 0015. Blades, which do not fold, are attached to aluminium rotor hub by retention straps. Two-blade aluminium teetering tail rotor. Swashplate for cyclic pitch control. Cable through rotor shaft to blades for collective pitch control.

ROTOR DRIVE: Drive from engine to vertical shaft via eight Vee-belts. Drive from vertical shaft to main rotor shaft via three chain sprockets. Tail rotor driven by Vee-belt from first stage of reduction pulleys.

RotorWay Scorpion Too two-seat lightweight helicopter (140 hp Vulcan V-4 marine engine)

FUSELAGE: Basic steel tube structure of simplified form. Removable glassfibre body fairing.

TAIL UNIT: Braced steel tube tailboom only, to carry tail rotor.

LANDING GEAR: Tubular skid type.

POWER PLANT: One 140 hp Vulcan V-4 four-cylinder watercooled marine engine, mounted aft of cabin area. Standard fuel capacity 10 US gallons (37·5 litres) in tank mounted above drive chain, aft of main rotor shaft. Optional increased-capacity fuel tanks available.

ACCOMMODATION: Two individual bucket seats, side by side, in enclosed cabin.

DIMENSIONS, EXTERNAL:
Diameter of main rotor 24 ft 0 in (7·32 m)
Diameter of tail rotor 3 ft 7¼ in (1·10 m)
Length, nose to tail rotor axis
20 ft 3½ in (6·18 m)
Height to top of main rotor 7 ft 3½ in (2·22 m)
Width of cabin 4 ft 0 in (1·22 m)
Landing skid track 5 ft 4⅝ in (1·64 m)

WEIGHTS:
Weight empty 690 lb (313 kg)
Max T-O weight 1,125 lb (510 kg)

PERFORMANCE (at max T-O weight, except where indicated):
Cruising speed
over 65 knots (75 mph; 121 km/h)
Max rate of climb at S/L 1,000 ft (305 m)/min
Hovering ceiling in ground effect
5,500 ft (1,675 m)
Hovering ceiling in ground effect (at 60% max T-O weight) 9,500 ft (2,895 m)
Range, standard fuel
108 nm (125 miles; 201 km)

RUTAN

RUTAN AIRCRAFT FACTORY

ADDRESS:
224 S. Colby, Valley Center, Kansas 67147
Telephone: (316) 755-1581
PRESIDENT: Burt Rutan

The prototype of a new light aircraft, known as the VariViggen, was rolled out on 27 February 1972. Mr Rutan had begun its design in 1963 and its configuration was developed via a low-cost automobile-mounted test system. This involved construction of a one-fifth scale model which was mounted on a specially-built test rig attached to the roof of a motor car. Ailerons, rudders and canard elevators were operated by remote control from within the car, and transducers in the test rig allowed measurement of airspeed, angle of attack, lift, drag, sideslip, side force, roll moment and elevator/aileron/rudder positions. An extra data channel provided for measurement of stick forces and structural load.

A one-fifth scale radio-controlled model was used to confirm the design's spin-proof characteristics. Construction of the prototype began during 1968, and the first flight was made in May 1972. By early 1974 the VariViggen had accumulated a total flying time of nearly 300 hours, and flight testing had confirmed the spin-free characteristics demonstrated by the free-flying scale model. The prototype has no conventional stall and can climb, cruise, glide, turn and land with continuous full aft stick, giving a stable speed of 45 knots (52 mph; 83·5 km/h) throughout. Rate of climb at this speed is 500 ft (152 m)/min. The full-span ailerons provide a high rate of roll, and a 360° roll can be accomplished at a speed of only 80 knots (92 mph; 148 km/h) without loss of height. Nose-wheel rotation on take-off occurs at 50 knots (58 mph; 93 km/h), at which speed the aircraft will enter an immediate stable climb.

The full-span ailerons are described as "reflexerons", since they serve both as ailerons and as an adjustable "reflex" control for the main wing. Differential aileron motion is related mechanically to the stick, but the collective "reflex" is electrically controlled. This is achieved by electrically-controlled aileron droop, which causes the resulting nose-down trim to be countered by a nose-up deflection of the elevators on the forward canard surface. Thus both ailerons and elevators serve also as flaps. The ailerons are also adjusted at cruising speed to minimise trim drag and optimise the lift/drag ratio. Trim is achieved by an electrically-controlled bungee device on the mechanical elevator system.

Rutan VariViggen two-seat homebuilt aircraft (150 hp Lycoming O-320-A2A engine) (*Howard Levy*)

A second VariViggen is under construction. Plans are available to amateur constructors; in early 1974 a total of 140 sets had been sold, and it was believed that approximately 50 aircraft were being built.

Mr Rutan is working on the design of a high-performance four-seat aircraft of canard configuration which is expected to make its first flight in 1975.

RUTAN VARIVIGGEN

TYPE: Two-seat homebuilt light aircraft.

WINGS: Cantilever low-wing monoplane of cropped delta configuration. Rutan wing section. Thickness/chord ratio 7% at root, 9% at tip. Dihedral 3° on outer wing panels. Incidence 0°. Sweepback at quarter-chord 27°. Composite structure with spruce spars, plywood ribs and skin, Ceconite-covered, except for outboard aft wing panels which are of flush-riveted metal construction. Inward-canted fin and rudder each side at approximately one-third span. Full-span ailerons, extending between fins and wingtips, constructed as a shell of ·016 in aluminium with foam filling. Cutout in inboard trailing-edges to accommodate pusher propeller.

CANARD SURFACES: Cantilever structure mounted high on the nose, forward of the windscreen. Aerofoil section NACA 4414 (modified). Slotted flap-type elevator in trailing-edge.

FUSELAGE: Basically square-section fuselage of wooden construction, Ceconite-covered. Canard surfaces mounted high on nose. Landing light in nosecone, which is hinged at top and opens upwards for access to equipment. Engine mounted in aft end of fuselage.

LANDING GEAR: Electrically-retractable tricycle type. Nosewheel retracts forward, main wheels inward into wings. Nosewheel mounted on oleo-pneumatic shock-strut. Shock-absorption of main units by rubber discs in compression. Goodyear main wheels, with tyres size 14× 5·00-5, pressure 30 lb/sq in (2·1 kg/cm²). Scott nosewheel with 9 in diameter tyre, pressure 30 lb/sq in (2·1 kg/cm²). Goodyear caliper brakes.

POWER PLANT: One 150 hp Lycoming O-320-A2A four-cylinder horizontally-opposed aircooled engine, mounted in rear fuselage and driving a Hegy two-blade wooden fixed-pitch propeller. One fuel tank in fuselage, capacity 23 US gallons (87 litres) and one external fuel tank, mounted on aircraft centreline under fuselage, capacity 12 US gallons (45 litres). Total capacity 35 US gallons (132 litres). Refuelling point on fuselage upper surface. Oil capacity 2 US gallons (7·5 litres).

ACCOMMODATION: Two seats in tandem in individual cockpits, beneath transparent canopies which are hinged on the starboard side. Space for 100 lb (45 kg) of baggage aft of rear seat.

SYSTEMS: Dual 12V electrical systems. Storage battery. Hydraulic system for brakes only.

ELECTRONICS AND EQUIPMENT: ARC 360-channel VHF com transceiver, ARC 200-channel VHF nav receiver. Edo Air transponder. Angle of attack indicator.

DIMENSIONS, EXTERNAL:
Wing span — 19 ft 0 in (5·79 m)
Wing chord at root — 7 ft 5 in (2·26 m)
Wing chord at tip — 2 ft 11 in (0·89 m)
Wing aspect ratio — 3
Length overall — 19 ft 0 in (5·79 m)
Canard surface span — 8 ft 0 in (2·44 m)
Wheel track — 7 ft 2½ in (2·20 m)
Wheelbase — 8 ft 0 in (2·44 m)
Propeller diameter — 5 ft 10 in (1·78 m)
Propeller ground clearance — 1 ft 4 in (0·41 m)

DIMENSIONS, INTERNAL:
Cabin: Length — 8 ft 4 in (2·54 m)
Max width — 2 ft 1 in (0·64 m)
Max height — 4 ft 0 in (1·22 m)
Floor area — 17 sq ft (1·58 m²)
Volume — 60 cu ft (1·70 m³)

AREAS:
Wings, gross — 119 sq ft (11·06 m²)
Ailerons (total) — 10 sq ft (0·93 m²)
Fins (total) — 20 sq ft (1·86 m²)
Rudders (total) — 6 sq ft (0·56 m²)
Canard surface — 18 sq ft (1·67 m²)
Elevators — 4 sq ft (0·37 m²)

WEIGHTS AND LOADINGS:
Weight empty, equipped — 950 lb (431 kg)
Max T-O and landing weight — 1,700 lb (771 kg)
Max wing loading — 14·3 lb/sq ft (69·8 kg/m²)
Max power loading — 11·3 lb/hp (5·13 kg/hp)

PERFORMANCE (at max T-O weight, except as indicated):
Max never-exceed speed — 156 knots (180 mph; 289 km/h)
Max level speed at S/L — 142 knots (163 mph; 262 km/h)
Max cruising speed at 7,000 ft (2,135 m) — 130 knots (150 mph; 241 km/h)
Econ cruising speed at 7,000 ft (2,135 m) — 109 knots (125 mph; 201 km/h)
Stalling speed — 44·5 knots (51 mph; 82 km/h)
Max rate of climb at S/L — 1,200 ft (366 m)/min
Service ceiling — 14,000 ft (4,265 m)
Min ground turning radius — 13 ft 6 in (4·11 m)
T-O run — 800 ft (244 m)
T-O to 50 ft (15 m) — 950 ft (290 m)
Landing from 50 ft (15 m) at max landing weight — 600 ft (183 m)
Landing run at max landing weight — 480 ft (146 m)
Range with max fuel, 30 min reserve — 347 nm (400 miles; 643 km)

RYSON

RYSON AVIATION CORPORATION

ADDRESS:
548 San Fernando Street, San Diego, California 92106

Ryson Aviation Corporation was founded by T. Claude Ryan, until 1969 Chairman and Chief Executive Officer of the Ryan Aeronautical Company. Other members of the Corporation include Mr Jerome D. (Jerry) Ryan, son of T. Claude Ryan, and Mr Peter F. Girard, a veteran test pilot of the former Ryan Company and an advanced design engineer. The aim of the new Corporation is to develop aeronautical products and make them available for manufacture by other companies.

First new design to emanate from the Ryson company was a two-seat powered cruising sailplane designated STP-1 Swallow, details of which appeared in the 1973-74 *Jane's*.

In early 1974 the company was working on a new project, but no details of this were available for publication at the time of closing for press.

SALVAY-STARK

SKYHOPPER AIRPLANES, INC

ADDRESS:
17201 McCormick Street, Encino, California 91316
Telephone: (213) 788-3974

This company was formed by Mr M. E. Salvay, who is currently director of structural design for Rockwell International's B-1 bomber programme, and Mr George Stark, to market plans of a light aeroplane named the Skyhopper which they designed and built in 1944-45 and later developed for amateur construction.

SALVAY-STARK SKYHOPPER

Design of the Skyhopper was begun in the early Spring of 1944 and the prototype flew for the first time towards the end of March 1945. It was designed to comply with the CAR-04 requirements of the time and has since undergone considerable development and refinement.

Flown initially with a 50 hp engine, the single-seat prototype was fitted in 1948 with a 65 hp Continental A65. This was changed in 1956 for an 85 hp Continental C85, and a total of 1,000 hours of flying were logged by this aircraft in the following three years.

Plans of the Skyhopper were made available to amateur constructors. Some 500 sets had been sold by January 1974, at which time about 75 aircraft were known to be under construction or completed.

The aircraft can be built as a side-by-side two-seater, if preferred, and a drawing depicting the necessary design changes for this is included in all sets of plans.

In the two-seater, the width of the fuselage is increased by 14 in (0·36 m), to an inside dimension of 36 in (0·91 m). Few other changes are required, except to the ends of the wing spars, the engine cowling and canopy. The 85 hp engine is recommended for this version, but performance remains adequate with a 65 hp engine, with a loss of approximately 10% in cruising performance compared with the single-seat Skyhopper.

The extensively modified Skyhopper shown in the adjacent illustration is owned by Mr Douglas Umbreit of Memphis, Tennessee. Modifications include non-retractable tricycle landing gear, the nose strut coming from a Cessna 150; all-wood semi laminar flow wings of NACA 66_2215 section; tail unit with all-swept surfaces; and an aft-sliding bubble canopy. Powered by a 125 hp Lycoming GPU modification, Mr Umbreit's Skyhopper has a max level speed of 113 knots (130 mph; 209 km/h), cruising speed of 95 knots (110 mph; 177 km/h), landing speed of 74 knots (85 mph; 137 km/h); max rate of climb at S/L of 1,000 ft (305 m)/min; and range of 345 nm (400 miles; 640 km).

Extensively modified Salvay-Stark Skyhopper owned by Mr Douglas Umbreit of Memphis, Tennessee (*Howard Levy*)

The following details refer to the standard Skyhopper as built from Salvay-Stark plans:

TYPE: Single-seat or two-seat light monoplane.

WINGS: Cantilever low-wing monoplane. Wing section NACA 23015-23012. All-wood two-spar structure. Leading-edge covered with aluminium sheet; remainder fabric-covered. Statically and dynamically balanced ailerons, fabric-covered. No flaps.

FUSELAGE: Welded steel tube structure with fabric covering.

TAIL UNIT: Cantilever tailplane and fin have plywood-covered wooden structure. Statically and dynamically balanced rudder and elevators have welded tube structure, with fabric covering.

LANDING GEAR: Non-retractable tailwheel type. Oil and spring shock-absorbers. Main wheels size 5·00-5. Wheel fairings optional. Steerable tailwheel.

POWER PLANT: One 65 hp Continental A65 or 85 hp Continental C85 four-cylinder horizontally-opposed aircooled engine driving a two-blade fixed-pitch propeller. Fuel capacity 15 US gallons (56·8 litres).

ACCOMMODATION: Single seat or two side-by-side seats under rearward-sliding canopy. Optional open cockpit. Small baggage space aft of seat.

DIMENSIONS, EXTERNAL:
Wing span:
Single-seat — 25 ft 0 in (7·62 m)
Two-seat — 26 ft 4 in (8·02 m)
Wing aspect ratio — 6
Length overall — 18 ft 10 in (5·74 m)
Height overall — 5 ft 3 in (1·60 m)

AREAS:
Wings, gross:
Single-seat — 100 sq ft (9·29 m²)
Two-seat — 107 sq ft (9·94 m²)

WEIGHTS:
Weight empty:
Single-seat — 650 lb (295 kg)
Two-seat — 690 lb (313 kg)
Max T-O weight:
Single-seat — 950 lb (431 kg)
Two-seat — 1,170 lb (531 kg)

PERFORMANCE (single-seat, 65 hp Continental A65):
Max level speed at S/L — 113 knots (130 mph; 209 km/h)
Cruising speed at 7,000 ft (2,135 m) — 104 knots (120 mph; 193 km/h)
Stalling speed — 39 knots (45 mph; 72 km/h)
Max rate of climb at S/L — 700 ft (213 m)/min
Service ceiling — approx 16,000 ft (4,875 m)
T-O run — 900 ft (275 m)
Landing run — 850 ft (260 m)
Max range — 260 nm (300 miles; 480 km)

PERFORMANCE (two-seat, 85 hp Continental C85):
Max level speed at S/L — 113 knots (130 mph; 209 km/h)
Cruising speed — 100 knots (115 mph; 185 km/h)
Landing speed — 42 knots (48 mph; 77 km/h)

SCHEUTZOW

SCHEUTZOW HELICOPTER CORPORATION

POSTAL ADDRESS:
PO Box 27, Columbia Station, Ohio 44028

WORKS:
27100 Royalton Road, Columbia Station, Ohio 44028, and Sweetwater, Texas
Telephone: (216) 236-5021
PRESIDENT: Webb Scheutzow
VICE-PRESIDENT: Elmer J. Scheutzow

This company was formed by Mr Webb Scheutzow to develop and build a light helicopter incorporating a new type of rotor head in which the blades are carried on rubber bushings.

Initial development of the new head was carried out successfully on a small testbed helicopter, which was described and illustrated in the 1964-65 *Jane's*. It is now being used on the production-type Scheutzow Bee.

Two helicopters are being used in the FAA Type Certification programme. The 100-hour durability test was completed at full throttle for the entire duration of the test, and rotor system qualification tests have been completed. Flight trials were completed during 1971 and in early 1973 the Bee was in the final review stage prior to FAA certification. Production procurement has been initiated and an assembly line is being established with the intention of starting deliveries immediately following certification.

SCHEUTZOW BEE

Design of this small lightweight side-by-side two-seat helicopter began in early 1964 and construction of three prototypes was started in March 1965. The first of these flew for the first time in 1966 and had completed 14 hours' flying by 26 January 1967. By that date, forward speeds of up to 78 knots (90 mph; 145 km/h) had been attained. Autorotative tests have revealed good power-off handling qualities and the aircraft has proved very stable in hovering flight.

The Scheutzow Bee has a welded steel tube structure with a completely enclosed metal cabin. The landing gear is of the skid type, with cross-tubes on which the skids are carried.

Power plant is a 180 hp Lycoming IVO-360-A1A four-cylinder horizontally-opposed air-cooled engine, which drives the two-blade flapping-type main rotor (with integral control gyro-bar) through a centrifugal clutch and multiple V-belt drive system. Use of this drive and isolation of the engine from the cabin area have resulted in an extremely low cabin noise level, permitting normal operation without an intercom system. The conventional two-blade tail rotor is driven through a shaft and bevel gear.

The main rotor incorporates Mr Scheutzow's patented "Flexhub". Elastomeric bearings with an offset flapping hinge are claimed to provide exceptional control power and precise response in all manoeuvres. This is claimed to reduce vibration as well as cost and lubrication requirements. Standard fuel capacity is 22 US gallons (83 litres). A 15 US gallon (56 litre) auxiliary fuel tank is available as an optional accessory, extending range to an estimated 248 nm (285 miles; 458 km).

There is a large baggage compartment aft of the seats, on the centre of gravity, with a door on each side. Optional items include dual controls, radio, lights, heater, internal litter, ground handling wheels and agricultural spray equipment.

Scheutzow Bee two-seat light helicopter (180 hp Lycoming IVO-360-A1A engine)

DIMENSIONS, EXTERNAL:
- Diameter of main rotor 27 ft 0 in (8·23 m)
- Main rotor blade chord 8 in (20 cm)
- Diameter of tail rotor 4 ft 0 in (1·22 m)
- Length overall (rotors fore and aft) 31 ft 2 in (9·50 m)
- Length of fuselage 24 ft 1 in (7·34 m)
- Width overall, rotor fore and aft 7 ft 0 in (2·13 m)
- Height overall 8 ft 6 in (2·59 m)

WEIGHTS:
- Weight empty 1,135 lb (514 kg)
- Max T-O weight 1,685 lb (764 kg)

PERFORMANCE (at max T-O weight):
- Max level speed at S/L 81 knots (93·5 mph; 150 km/h)
- Max cruising speed 69 knots (80 mph; 128 km/h)
- Max rate of climb at S/L 1,200 ft (366 m)/min
- Service ceiling 13,000 ft (3,960 m)
- Hovering ceiling in ground effect 7,300 ft (2,225 m)
- Range with standard fuel at max cruising speed 152 nm (175 miles; 280 km)

SCHWEIZER

SCHWEIZER AIRCRAFT CORPORATION

HEAD OFFICE AND WORKS:
Box 147, Elmira, New York 14902
Telephone: (607) 739-3821

PRESIDENT AND CHIEF ENGINEER:
Ernest Schweizer

VICE-PRESIDENT AND GENERAL MANAGER:
Paul A. Schweizer

VICE-PRESIDENT IN CHARGE OF MANUFACTURING:
William Schweizer

SALES MANAGER:
W. E. Doherty Jr

ASSISTANT TREASURER:
Joseph Kroczynski

SECRETARY:
Kenneth Tifft

Schweizer Aircraft Corporation is the leading American designer and manufacturer of sailplanes (which see in "Sailplanes" section). Early in 1972 the company acquired the design and production rights of the Teal amphibian from Mr David B. Thurston, and the production tools and jigs have been transferred to Elmira, New York. Mr Thurston joined Schweizer Aircraft as Engineering Manager.

Schweizer also manufactures the Ag-Cat agricultural biplane for Grumman at the rate of 200 aircraft per year.

SCHWEIZER MODEL TSC-1 TEAL

The Teal amphibian was developed originally by Thurston Aircraft Corporation to provide a simple, economical and easily-handled two-seat aircraft for cross-country and sporting flying, land and sea-plane training and limited business use. The entire structure and covering are of aluminium alloy, except for the bow deck and cabin top skins which are of glassfibre.

To permit towing on its own landing gear, the Teal can be supplied with removable wings. A flying-boat version, without landing gear, has been projected and is described separately.

The prototype of the Teal amphibian flew for the first time in June 1968. FAA certification was awarded on 28 August 1969. Two versions have been built:

TSC-1A1. The first 15 production aircraft were designated TSC-1A. Improvements introduced on the production line, from aircraft number 16, led to the designation TSC-1A1. These standard improvements included new wing leading-edge fuel tanks, optional hull tank and independent retraction of tailwheel, and could be retrofitted to the first 15 TSC-1As. Schweizer announced in early 1973 that production of this version would end during the same year.

TSC-1A2 Teal II. Improved version of the TSC-1A1, which has slotted trailing-edge flaps and a max T-O weight of 2,200 lb (998 kg) from both land and water. The prototype received certification in June 1973, since when production has continued at a rate of two aircraft per month.

The TSC-1A2 Teal II is approved for day or night IFR operations in non-icing conditions.

The description which follows applies specifically to the Teal II:

TYPE: Two-seat cabin monoplane amphibian.

WINGS: Cantilever shoulder-wing monoplane. Wing section NACA 4415. Dihedral 4°. Incidence 4°. All-metal "D-spar" structure. Single-slotted trailing-edge flaps of light alloy construction, extending outboard from hull to ailerons.

HULL: All-metal semi-monocoque structure, with glassfibre foredeck and cabin top skins.

TAIL UNIT: Cantilever all-metal T-tail. Trim tabs on elevator and rudder.

LANDING GEAR: Retractable tailwheel type; manually actuated. Spring steel main struts. Tailwheel integral with water rudder. Tailwheel retractable independently of main gear to provide water rudder control when needed. Main wheels size 6·00-6. Tailwheel size 8·00-3. Single-disc brakes on main wheels.

POWER PLANT: One 150 hp Lycoming O-320-A3B four-cylinder horizontally-opposed aircooled engine, driving a Hartzell two-blade constant-speed propeller. Two integral fuel tanks in wing leading-edges, each containing 23 US gallons (87 litres), of which 20 US gallons (75·7 litres) are usable. Optional all-metal fuel tank in hull, aft of main bulkhead, capacity 25 US gallons (94·6 litres). Total optional fuel capacity 71 US gallons (268·6 litres), of which 65 US gallons (246 litres) are usable. Oil capacity 2 US gallons (7·5 litres).

ACCOMMODATION: Enclosed cabin seating two persons side by side. Baggage compartment behind seats, capacity 230 lb (104 kg). Seat backs fold down for access to baggage compartment and for stand-up fishing from cabin. Door on each side. May be flown with window open. Ventilation system standard.

SYSTEMS: Electrical system has 60A 12V alternator and 12V 37Ah battery. Janitrol heating and defrosting system optional.

EQUIPMENT: Standard equipment includes heated pitot, stall warning indicator, soundproofing, map pockets, tinted glass overhead panels, corrosion proofing, anchor, mooring line and paddle. Optional items include dual controls, strobe light, blind-flying instrumentation, 8-day clock, outside air temperature gauge and navigation, instrument, landing and cabin lights.

ELECTRONICS: A wide choice of navigation and communications equipment is available to customer's requirements.

DIMENSIONS, EXTERNAL:
- Wing span 31 ft 11 in (9·73 m)
- Wing chord, constant 5 ft 0 in (1·52 m)
- Wing aspect ratio 6·5
- Length overall 23 ft 7 in (7·19 m)
- Height overall on land 9 ft 5 in (2·87 m)
- Tailplane span 8 ft 0 in (2·44 m)
- Wheel track 8 ft 3 in (2·51 m)
- Propeller diameter 6 ft 0 in (1·83 m)

AREAS:
- Wings, gross 157 sq ft (14·59 m²)
- Ailerons (total) 10 sq ft (0·93 m²)
- Trailing-edge flaps (total) 20·9 sq ft (1·94 m²)
- Fin 10·7 sq ft (0·99 m²)
- Rudder 6·8 sq ft (0·63 m²)
- Tailplane 15·4 sq ft (1·43 m²)
- Elevator 12·6 sq ft (1·17 m²)

WEIGHTS AND LOADINGS:
- Weight empty 1,435 lb (651 kg)
- Max T-O weight, land or water 2,200 lb (998 kg)
- Max wing loading 14·0 lb/sq ft (68·3 kg/m²)
- Max power loading 14·7 lb/hp (6·67 kg/hp)

PERFORMANCE (at max T-O weight):
- Max never-exceed speed 117 knots (135 mph; 217 km/h) IAS
- Max level speed at 3,000 ft (915 m) 104 knots (120 mph; 193 km/h)
- Max cruising speed at 5,000 ft (1,525 m) 101 knots (116 mph; 187 km/h) IAS
- Econ cruising speed at 5,000 ft (1,525 m) 96 knots (110 mph; 177 km/h) IAS
- Stalling speed, flaps down 45·5 knots (52 mph; 84 km/h)
- Max rate of climb at S/L 650 ft (198 m)/min
- Service ceiling 12,000 ft (3,660 m)
- T-O run:
  - land 700 ft (213 m)
  - water 950 ft (290 m)
- T-O to 50 ft (15 m):
  - land 1,150 ft (351 m)
  - water 1,400 ft (427 m)
- Landing from 50 ft (15 m):
  - land 850 ft (259 m)
  - water 650 ft (198 m)
- Landing run:
  - land 450 ft (137 m)
  - water 350 ft (107 m)
- Range at econ cruising speed with max standard fuel and 45 min reserve 410 nm (472 miles; 759 km)
- Range at econ cruising speed, with max standard plus optional fuel and 45 min reserve 650 nm (748 miles; 1,203 km)

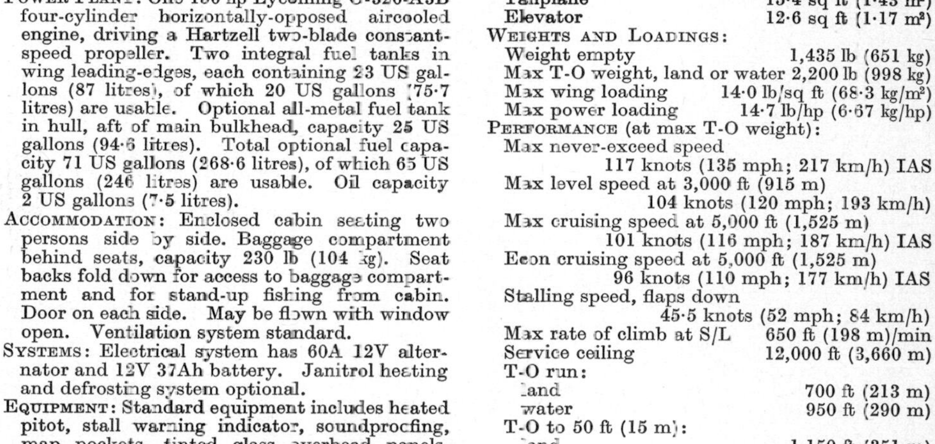

Schweizer Model TSC-1A2 Teal II amphibian (150 hp Lycoming O-320-A3B engine)

SCHWEIZER MODEL TSC-1 "T-BOAT"

This is a projected flying-boat version of the Teal. Production is dependent upon demand, and no prototype had been built by early 1974. Specification for this model is exactly the same as for the Teal, except that the landing gear is removed. Useful load and performance are estimated to increase as follows:

WEIGHTS:
- Weight empty 1,200 lb (544 kg)
- Max T-O weight 2,100 lb (953 kg)

PERFORMANCE (at max T-O weight):
- Max level speed at S/L 113 knots (130 mph; 209 km/h)
- Max cruising speed, 75% power at 7,500 ft (2,300 m) 109 knots (125 mph; 201 km/h)

SCHWEIZER (GRUMMAN) G-164A SUPER AG-CAT

The prototype of the original Ag-Cat agricultural biplane flew for the first time on 22 May 1957. Series production was entrusted to Schweizer, under subcontract from Grumman. First deliveries were made in 1959, and the 1,200th Ag-Cat had been built by January 1974, when the type was in service in 34 countries.

The Ag-Cat was certificated in the Restricted (agricultural) category on 20 January 1959, with a 220 hp Continental engine, and received additional approval in this category for patrolling and surveying on 9 April 1962. Other engines for which FAA Type Approval was received are the 240 hp Gulf Coast W-670-240, 245 hp Jacobs L-4M or L-4MB, 275-300 hp Jacobs R-755, 450 hp Pratt & Whitney R-985 and 600 hp Pratt & Whitney R-1340.

The current Super Ag-Cat (Model G-164A) began with aircraft c/n 401, and is available with either the Pratt & Whitney R-985 or Pratt & Whitney R-1340 engine.

TYPE: Single-seat agricultural biplane.

WINGS: Single-bay staggered biplane. NACA 4412 (modified) wing section. Dihedral 3°. Incidence 6°. Aluminium alloy (6061-T6) two-spar structure with 6061-T6 skins on entire top surface, around leading-edge and back to front spar on undersurface. Remainder of undersurface fabric-covered. Each "D" leading-edge is made of five separate sections to facilitate replacement if damaged. Glassfibre wingtips. N-type interplane struts. Ailerons of light alloy construction on all four wings. Ground-adjustable tab in lower port aileron. No flaps.

FUSELAGE: Welded 4130 chrome-molybdenum steel tube structure, covered with duralumin sheet. Removable side panels.

TAIL UNIT: Welded 4130 chrome-molybdenum steel tube structure, covered with fabric and wire-braced. Controllable trim tab in port elevator. Ground-adjustable tabs on rudder and starboard elevator.

LANDING GEAR: Non-retractable tailwheel type. Cantilever spring steel legs. Cleveland 8·50-10 wheels and tyres. Disc brakes. Cleveland steerable spring tailwheel.

POWER PLANT: One 450 hp Pratt & Whitney R-985, or 600 hp R-1340 nine-cylinder radial aircooled engine. 450 hp Super Ag-Cat has Hamilton Standard two-position or constant-speed two-blade metal propeller with Model 2D30 hub and AG-100-2 blades. 600 hp Super Ag-Cat has a Hamilton Standard Type 12D40 constant-speed propeller. Fuel tank in upper centre-section with standard usable capacity of 46 US gallons (174 litres). Optional tanks, installed in wings on one or both sides of centre-section, are available for total usable capacities of 64 or 80 US gallons (241 or 302 litres). Oil capacity 8·7 US gallons (33 litres).

ACCOMMODATION: Single open cockpit aft of wings. Optional enclosed canopy. Reinforced fairing aft of cockpit for "turnover" protection. Forward of cockpit, over CG, is 33 cu ft (0·93 m³) or, optionally, 40 cu ft (1·13 m³) glassfibre hopper for agricultural chemicals (dry or liquid) with distributor beneath fuselage. Root Supreme Model 57 spray-pump. Low-volume, ULV or high-volume spray system, with leading- or trailing-edge booms.

SYSTEMS: Spray or dust distribution systems available. Hydraulic system for brakes only. Optional electrical system with 12 or 24V alternator, external power socket and navigation lights.

DIMENSIONS, EXTERNAL:
- Wing span 35 ft 11 in (10·95 m)
- Wing chord (constant) 4 ft 10 in (1·47 m)
- Wing aspect ratio: upper wing 7·81
- biplane—estimated mean 5·29
- Length overall 23 ft 10 in (7·26 m)
- Height overall 11 ft 0 in (3·35 m)
- Tailplane span 13 ft 0 in (3·96 m)
- Wheel track 7 ft 10¼ in (2·39 m)
- Wheelbase 18 ft 6 in (5·64 m)

AREAS:
- Wings, gross 328 sq ft (30·47 m²)
- Ailerons (total) 31·5 sq ft (2·93 m²)
- Fin 9·0 sq ft (0·84 m²)
- Rudder 12·0 sq ft (1·12 m²)
- Tailplane 22·8 sq ft (2·12 m²)
- Elevators 22·2 sq ft (2·06 m²)

WEIGHTS AND LOADINGS:
- Weight empty, equipped, spraying version:
  - R-985 2,796 lb (1,268 kg)
  - R-1340 3,126 lb (1,418 kg)
- Max T-O weight (CAM-8) 6,075 lb (2,755 kg)
- Max wing loading at certificated max T-O weight:
  - R-985 16·67 lb/sq ft (81·4 kg/m²)
  - R-1340 17·67 lb/sq ft (86·3 kg/m²)
- Power loading at certificated max T-O weight:
  - R-985 12·15 lb/hp (5·51 kg/hp)
  - R-1340 9·66 lb/hp (4·38 kg/hp)

PERFORMANCE (at certificated max T-O weight):
- Max level speed:
  - R-985 108 knots (124 mph; 200 km/h)
  - R-1340 113 knots (130 mph; 209 km/h)
- Never-exceed speed 128 knots (147 mph; 237 km/h)
- Abrupt manoeuvre speed 102 knots (117 mph; 188 km/h)
- Working speed:
  - R-985 82·5-91 knots (95-105 mph; 153-169 km/h)
  - R-1340 87-100 knots (100-115 mph; 161-185 km/h)
- Stalling speed, power off:
  - R-985, R-1340 52·5 knots (60 mph; 97 km/h) IAS
- Stalling speed, power on:
  - R-985 55 knots (63 mph; 102 km/h) IAS
  - R-1340 56 knots (64 mph; 103 km/h) IAS
- Max rate of climb at S/L:
  - R-985 580 ft (177 m)/min
  - R-1340 900 ft (274 m)/min
- T-O run:
  - R-985 905 ft (276 m)
  - R-1340 670 ft (204 m)
- Landing run at max landing weight:
  - R-985 400 ft (122 m)
  - R-1340 425 ft (130 m)

Schweizer (Grumman) Super Ag-Cat agricultural aircraft (450 hp Pratt & Whitney R-985 engine)

SHEFFIELD

SHEFFIELD AIRCRAFT LTD

ADDRESS:
4750 South Meade, Littleton, Colorado 80120

Mr Kenneth Sheffield set out to design a low-cost lightweight easy-to-build aircraft suitable for construction by homebuilders of limited technical ability. To keep operating costs as low as possible he considered folding wings essential, so that the aircraft could be housed in a garage and be towed by a motor car, and also specified a Volkswagen power plant because of its availability and low fuel consumption.

Mr Sheffield began the design of this aircraft, known as the Skeeter X-1, in November 1966 and construction of the prototype began in May 1967. First flight was made in April 1970 and the aircraft has since received FAA certification in the Experimental homebuilt category. Plans, conversion manuals and kits for the Volkswagen engine, and finished propellers, are available to amateur constructors.

Sheffield Skeeter X-1 homebuilt sporting aircraft (72 hp Volkswagen modified motor car engine)

SHEFFIELD SKEETER X-1

TYPE: Single-seat lightweight homebuilt sporting aircraft.

WINGS: Parasol strut-braced monoplane, with steel tube Vee bracing struts on each side. Wing section NACA 4412. Dihedral 2°. Incidence 2°. No sweepback. Each wing panel consists of two wooden spars with built-up wood/metal ribs, and has a metal-covered leading-edge which extends aft to the front spar; remainder fabric-covered. Wings fold for storage or towing. No pre-flight rigging necessary after wing folding. Wing centre-section is mounted above the cockpit nacelle on a welded steel tube structure that is integral with the open tubular fuselage/boom assembly. Ailerons of wooden construction, fabric-covered. No trim tabs. No flaps.

FUSELAGE: Welded steel tube structure, covered with wood or metal in the cockpit area. Open steel tube structure aft of cockpit.

TAIL UNIT: Strut- and wire-braced wooden structure, fabric-covered. Tailplane incidence ground-adjustable. No trim tabs.

LANDING GEAR: Non-retractable tailwheel type. Each main wheel carried on a steel tube Vee truss, with shock-absorption by coil spring. Main wheels and tyres size 8·00-4, pressure 17 lb/sq in (1·20 kg/cm²). Mechanical heel-type brakes. Tailwheel steerable, with solid tyre.

POWER PLANT: Suitable for installation of Volkswagen engines of 50-72 hp. Prototype has a 72 hp Volkswagen modified motor car engine, driving a Univair two-blade fixed-pitch propeller of Mr Sheffield's design. Fuel tank contained in cockpit nacelle, aft of firewall, capacity 5·5 US gallons (20·8 litres). Refuelling point forward of windscreen. Oil capacity 1 US gallon (3·75 litres).

ACCOMMODATION: Single seat in open cockpit.

DIMENSIONS, EXTERNAL:

Wing span	22 ft 0 in (6·71 m)
Wing chord, constant	4 ft 2 in (1·27 m)
Wing aspect ratio	5·4
Length overall	13 ft 6 in (4·11 m)
Width, wings folded	8 ft 0 in (2·44 m)
Height overall	6 ft 0 in (1·83 m)
Tailplane span	7 ft 0 in (2·13 m)
Wheel track	4 ft 8 in (1·42 m)
Wheelbase	10 ft 0 in (3·05 m)
Propeller diameter	4 ft 5 in (1·35 m)
Propeller ground clearance	1 ft 1 in (0·33 m)

AREAS:

Wings, gross	90 sq ft (8·36 m²)
Ailerons (total)	12·0 sq ft (1·11 m²)
Fin	3·2 sq ft (0·30 m²)
Rudder	5·0 sq ft (0·46 m²)
Tailplane	11·0 sq ft (1·02 m²)
Elevators	8·0 sq ft (0·74 m²)

WEIGHTS AND LOADINGS:

Weight empty, equipped	500 lb (227 kg)
Max T-O weight	780 lb (354 kg)
Max landing weight	775 lb (351 kg)
Max wing loading	8·5 lb/sq ft (41·5 kg/m²)
Max power loading	13·0 lb/hp (5·9 kg/hp)

PERFORMANCE (at max T-O weight):

Max level and cruising speed at 6,000 ft (1,830 m)	74 knots (85 mph; 136 km/h)
Econ cruising speed at 8,000 ft (2,440 m)	65 knots (75 mph; 120 km/h)
Stalling speed	36·5 knots (42 mph; 67 km/h)
Max rate of climb at S/L	600 ft (183 m)/min
Service ceiling	11,000 ft (3,350 m)
T-O run	600 ft (183 m)
Landing run	600 ft (183 m)
Range with max fuel	139 nm (160 miles; 257 km)

SHOBER

SHOBER AIRCRAFT ENTERPRISES

ADDRESS:
PO Box 111, Gaithersburg, Maryland 20760

Mr William C. Shober has designed, built and flown the prototype of a two-seat sporting biplane which he has named Willie II. Being stressed for a loading of $\pm 9g$, the aircraft is suitable for limited aerobatics in standard homebuilt configuration. The plans which are available to amateur constructors give details of the necessary fuel system conversions to make Willie II capable of inverted flight.

The designer estimates that 2,500 to 3,000 hours of work are involved in building this aircraft and that, using all new materials, the cost is approximately $1,800 plus the price of the engine selected to power it.

Shober Willie II two-seat homebuilt light aircraft (180 hp Lycoming O-360-A3A engine)

SHOBER WILLIE II

TYPE: Two-seat sporting or aerobatic biplane.

WINGS: Braced single-bay biplane, with single streamline-section interplane strut each side and N-type centre-section struts. Dual streamline-section flying and landing wires. Constant-chord wings of M-6 aerofoil section. Dihedral: upper wing 0°, lower wing 3°. Upper wing is sweptback and has a cutout in the trailing-edge of the centre-section. Conventional two-spar structures, with solid spruce spars, and ribs built up from $\frac{5}{16}$ in square strip and plywood gussets. Each wing has compression tubes and drag wires, the entire structure being fabric-covered. Wide-span ailerons on lower wings only, of wooden construction with fabric covering. Ailerons controlled by push-rods via bell-crank. No flaps. No trim tabs.

FUSELAGE: Welded structure of 4130 steel tube, with fabric covering. Light alloy engine cowling.

TAIL UNIT: Wire-braced structure of welded 4130 steel tube with spruce tips. Fixed-incidence tailplane. All surfaces fabric-covered. No trim tabs.

LANDING GEAR: Non-retractable tailwheel type. Two side Vees and half-axles hinged to bottom of fuselage. Rubber cord shock-absorption. Cleveland main wheels with tyres size 6·00-6. Cleveland brakes.

POWER PLANT: Prototype has 180 hp Lycoming O-360-A3A four-cylinder horizontally-opposed aircooled engine, driving a two-blade fixed-pitch propeller. Installation designed to take Lycoming engines of 150 hp to 200 hp. Fuel tank in fuselage, immediately aft of firewall, capacity 25 US gallons (94·5 litres). Refuelling point on fuselage upper surface, forward of windscreen.

ACCOMMODATION: Two persons in tandem in open cockpits. Space for 20 lb (9 kg) baggage.

DIMENSIONS, EXTERNAL:

Wing span, upper	20 ft 0 in (6·10 m)
Wing span, lower	19 ft 0 in (5·79 m)
Wing chord, constant	3 ft 4 in (1·02 m)
Length overall	19 ft 0 in (5·79 m)

AREA:

Wings, gross	148 sq ft (13·75 m²)

WEIGHTS AND LOADINGS (prototype):

Weight empty	856 lb (388 kg)
Max T-O weight	1,350 lb (612 kg)
Max wing loading	9·1 lb/sq ft (44·4 kg/m²)
Power loading	7·5 lb/hp (3·4 kg/hp)

PERFORMANCE (prototype, at max T-O weight):

Cruising speed, 75% power at 5,000 ft (1,525 m)	130 knots (150 mph; 241 km/h)
Stalling speed	52 knots (60 mph; 96·5 km/h)
Max rate of climb at S/L	3,000 ft (915 m)/min
Service ceiling	15,000 ft (4,570 m)
T-O run	450 ft (137 m)
Landing run	700 ft (213 m)
Range with max fuel	325 nm (375 miles; 603 km)

SIEGRIST

RUDOLF SIEGRIST

ADDRESS:
9635 Enderby Drive, Parma, Ohio 44130

Mr R. Siegrist designed and built the prototype of a four-seat cabin monoplane, intending to make plans available to amateur constructors. The design originated in 1965. Construction of the prototype began in 1966, and the first flight was made in June 1971. FAA certification in the Experimental category was awarded in August of the same year.

While en route from California in July 1973, at which time the RS1 had completed approximately 180 flight hours, two-thirds of one propeller blade sheared off in flight. A successful forced landing caused no further damage, but the violent vibration before the engine was shut down had sheared many engine mounting tubes.

A new mount has been designed, differing from the original, to provide space between engine and firewall to mount a governor for a constant-speed propeller. To be 4 in (0·10 m) greater in diameter than the original propeller, Mr Siegrist had not finalised its type in late February 1974.

Plans for the RS1 Ilse have been delayed by this incident, but Mr Siegrist expects them to be available to would-be constructors in January 1975.

SIEGRIST RS1 ILSE

TYPE: Four-seat homebuilt cabin monoplane.

WINGS: Braced high-wing monoplane, with single streamline-section bracing strut each side. Wing section NACA $64_2$215. Dihedral 0°. Incidence 1° 30′. Forward sweep 4°. Conventional two-spar structure, with spruce spars and ribs and mahogany plywood skin. The entire surface is covered with glassfibre and epoxy resin. Ailerons of all-metal construction, with light alloy ribs riveted to a steel torque tube, with light alloy skins. Trailing-edge flaps of similar construction to ailerons. No trim tabs.

FUSELAGE: Welded structure of 4130 steel tube with wood stringers. Cockpit area has light alloy skin, the remainder being covered with glassfibre.

TAIL UNIT: Welded 4130 steel tube structure, covered with glassfibre. Swept vertical surfaces. All-moving tailplane with anti-servo tab extending almost full span.

LANDING GEAR: Non-retractable tailwheel type. Main wheels carried on cantilever spring steel legs of modified Wittman type. Goodyear main wheels and tyres size 6·00-6, pressure 23 lb/sq in (1·62 kg/cm²). Goodyear hydraulic disc brakes.

POWER PLANT: One 180 hp Lycoming O-360 four-cylinder horizontally-opposed aircooled engine, driving a two-blade propeller. Four interconnected fuel cells in each wing root, total capacity 50 US gallons (189 litres). Refuelling points on upper surface of wing. Oil capacity 2 US gallons (7·5 litres).

ACCOMMODATION: Four seats in enclosed cabin. Two individual buckets forward, bench seat for two aft. Door at each side of fuselage, hinged at forward edge. Cabin heated and ventilated.

SYSTEMS: Hydraulic system for brakes only. Electric power supplied by 50A engine-driven generator.

ELECTRONICS: Narco Escort 110 com transceiver.

DIMENSIONS, EXTERNAL:

Wing span	28 ft 0 in (8·53 m)
Wing chord, constant	4 ft 9 in (1·45 m)
Wing aspect ratio	6
Length overall	21 ft 6 in (6·55 m)
Height overall	6 ft 3 in (1·91 m)
Tailplane span	8 ft 2 in (2·49 m)
Wheel track	5 ft 11 in (1·80 m)
Wheelbase	16 ft 6 in (5·03 m)
Propeller diameter	6 ft 4 in (1·93 m)

AREAS:

Wings, gross	133 sq ft (12·36 m²)
Ailerons (total)	5·53 sq ft (0·51 m²)
Trailing-edge flaps (total)	12·94 sq ft (1·20 m²)
Fin	5·80 sq ft (0·54 m²)
Rudder	3·0 sq ft (0·28 m²)
Tailplane (including tab)	19·75 sq ft (1·83 m²)

WEIGHTS AND LOADINGS:

Weight empty	1,173 lb (532 kg)
Max T-O weight	2,080 lb (943 kg)
Max wing loading	15·64 lb/sq ft (76·36 kg/m²)
Max power loading	11·56 lb/hp (5·24 kg/hp)

Siegrist RS1 Ilse homebuilt four-seat cabin monoplane (180 hp Lycoming O-360 engine)

PERFORMANCE (at max T-O weight):
Max never-exceed speed
165 knots (190 mph; 306 km/h)
Max level speed at S/L
148 knots (170 mph; 274 km/h)
Cruising speed at 60% power
130 knots (150 mph; 241 km/h)
Landing speed 63 knots (73 mph; 117 km/h)
Stalling speed, power off
58 knots (67 mph; 108 km/h)
T-O run approx 1,300 ft (396 m)
Landing run approx 1,500 ft (457 m)

SIKORSKY

SIKORSKY AIRCRAFT, DIVISION OF UNITED AIRCRAFT CORPORATION

HEAD OFFICE AND WORKS:
Stratford, Connecticut 06602
Telephone: (203) 378-6361

OTHER WORKS:
South Avenue, Bridgeport, Connecticut; and Sikorsky Memorial Airport, Stratford, Connecticut

PRESIDENT:
Gerald J. Tobias

EXECUTIVE VICE-PRESIDENT:
John A. McKenna

VICE-PRESIDENTS:
Richard C. Abington (Planning)
Robert F. Daniell (Commercial)
Paul W. Holt (Surface Transportation Systems)
Harry T. Jensen (Engineering)
Derek J. Jonson (International Marketing)
Phil Locke (Contracts and Counsel)
William H. Parry (Operations)
Allen K. Poole (Military Marketing)
Robert J. Torok (Programmes)

DIVISION CONTROLLER: William Flaherty
FACTORY MANAGER: James W. Dunn
DIVISIONAL AUDITOR: H. W. Engstrom
PUBLIC RELATIONS MANAGER: Frank W. Delear

On 5 March 1973 Sikorsky Aircraft celebrated the 50th anniversary of its foundation, and a sculpture of its founder, the late Igor I. Sikorsky, who died on 26 October 1972, was unveiled at the company's main works at Stratford.

Mr Sikorsky incorporated the organisation which is now the Sikorsky Aircraft division of United Aircraft Corporation on 5 March 1923 in New York State, to build an all-metal aircraft designated S-29-A. Previously, he had followed a successful aviation career in Russia, leaving for the US after the Soviet Revolution. In the late 1920s and 1930s he designed and built amphibians and flying-boats that pioneered intercontinental and transoceanic commercial flight. He designed and flew his VS-300 helicopter for the first time in 1939: when fully developed in 1942 it represented the world's first fully practical single-rotor helicopter, leading to establishment of the helicopter industry.

Sikorsky's main plant at Stratford, which has 1,300,000 sq ft (120,775 m²) of working space, produces the S-61 twin-turbine amphibious transport helicopter and its military counterparts, the rear-loading S-61R, the S-64 Skycrane and the S-65 multi-purpose helicopter. The company's original 600,000 sq ft (55,740 m²) plant at Bridgeport is utilised for detail fabrication, and for overhaul and repair.

Production of the S-58 and S-62 has ended, but a twin-turbine re-engined S-58, designated S-58T, is in production.

A high-speed military helicopter, the S-67 Blackhawk, built as a private venture, made its first flight in August 1970, only twelve months after initiation of the design, and has undergone extensive development and demonstration. Also under development is the S-70 (YUH-60A) utility transport helicopter, intended to meet the US Army's UTTAS requirement.

Sikorsky's new ABC (advancing blade concept) rotor system has operated successfully in NASA's wind tunnel at Ames Research Center. Tested at simulated speeds of up to 304 knots (350 mph; 563 km/h) the system, which consists of two contra-rotating three-blade rotors, demonstrated substantial improvements in speed and lift capabilities in comparison with conventional rotor systems.

On 7 February 1972 Sikorsky announced that it was designing and building a research helicopter designated S-69 to flight test the ABC rotor system in a programme funded under a $9·9 million contract. The contract was awarded to Sikorsky by the Eustis Directorate, US Army Air Mobility Research and Development Laboratory, Fort Eustis, Virginia.

An entirely new helicopter rotor head has been undergoing flight tests on a Sikorsky CH-53D since 16 February 1972. This employs six spherical elastomeric bearings to replace the 18 hinges of the conventional Sikorsky articulated six-blade rotor system. Developed over a period of sixteen years, the spherical elastomeric bearings are made of a "sandwich" of thin rubber and metal laminates, produced by Lord Manufacturing Co of Erie, Pennsylvania. Designed to improve reliability, as well as to reduce operating costs, the new bearings require no lubrication. Some 12,000 hours of laboratory testing preceded flight tests. Initial results have indicated that the new system meets all expectations and that stress levels are within predicted limits.

Sikorsky announced in October 1973 that the company had been selected by NASA to design and build two high-speed multi-purpose research helicopters. Designated as Rotor Systems Research Aircraft (RSRA), these aircraft will be used in a joint NASA/Army research programme aimed at developing and testing a variety of existing and future helicopter rotor systems. Designed to utilise also wings and auxiliary engines, the RSRAs will provide test capabilities that do not exist at the present time, and serve also as a basis for comparing various rotor systems.

Sikorsky S-58T turbine-powered version of the S-58 in service with Heliswiss

Sikorsky licensees are Westland Aircraft Ltd of Great Britain, Costruzioni Aeronautiche Giovanni Agusta of Italy, Aérospatiale of France, Mitsubishi Heavy Industries Ltd of Japan, United Aircraft of Canada Ltd and, for coproduction of the S-65, the Federal Republic of Germany.

SIKORSKY S-58T

In January 1970 Sikorsky announced plans to produce and market kits for conversion of the piston-engined S-58 into a twin-turbine helicopter. The turbine version, designated S-58T, provides increased safety and reliability, greater speed and lifting power, and improved performance at high altitude on hot days. It also has lower operating costs than the piston-engined models.

Sikorsky will deliver FAA-certificated retrofit kits to S-58 operators for their own installation, or will install the kits in customers' aircraft at the Sikorsky plant. The company has also obtained used S-58s and offers them with the turbine engines installed.

The United Aircraft of Canada PT6T-3 Twin Pac turbine power plant was offered in the initial conversions, consisting of two PT6T-3 free-shaft engines and a combining gearbox, and certificated by the FAA at an 1,800 shp rating at sea level. All kits to be constructed and conversions to be effected from the end of June 1974 were to incorporate the PT6T-6 Twin Pac. This new Twin Pac was expected to gain FAA certification in mid-1974 at a rating of 1,875 shp at sea level. Only 1,420 shp is needed by the S-58T in normal service and the excess provides a reserve of power for high-altitude operation.

Design of the S-58T began in January 1970 and construction of the prototype started in May, with the first flight following on 19 August 1970. Construction of production aircraft and delivery of conversion kits began in January 1971 and FAA certification was awarded in April. Certification for IFR operation was received in June 1973.

By 11 January 1974 a total of 91 aircraft and/or kits were operating, under construction or on contract.

TYPE: General-purpose helicopter.

ROTOR SYSTEM: Four-blade all-metal main and tail rotors, both with servo control. Fully-articulated main rotor blades, each made up of a hollow extruded aluminium spar and trailing-edge pockets of aluminium. Each tail rotor blade has an aluminium spar, sheet aluminium skin and honeycomb trailing-edge. Blades of each rotor interchangeable. Main rotor blades fold. Main and tail rotor brakes.

ROTOR DRIVE: Direct gear drive from forward angle-change gearbox. Steel tube drive-shafts with rubber couplings. Main gearbox below main rotor, intermediate gearbox at base of tail pylon and tail gearbox behind tail rotor. Main rotor/engine rpm ratio 1 : ·0376. Tail rotor/engine rpm ratio 1 : ·2257.

FUSELAGE: Semi-monocoque structure, primarily of magnesium and aluminium alloys, with some titanium and stainless steel.

TAIL SURFACE: Ground-adjustable stabiliser made of magnesium skin over magnesium and aluminium structure.

LANDING GEAR: Non-retractable three-wheel undercarriage, with tailwheel towards rear of fuselage. Sikorsky oleo-pneumatic shock-absorber struts. Tailwheel is fully-castoring and self-centering, with an anti-swivelling lock. Goodyear main wheels with tyres size 32·2 ×

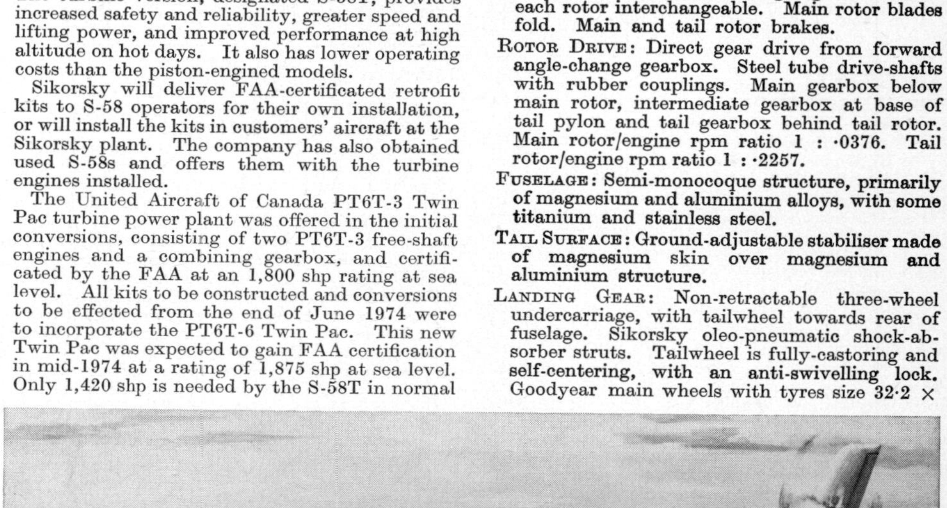

Artist's impression of Sikorsky's Rotor Systems Research Aircraft, to be built for a joint NASA/US Army research programme

11-12, pressure 45 lb/sq in (3·2 kg/cm²). Tailwheel tyre size 18·3 × 6-6, pressure 45 lb/sq in (3·2 kg/cm²). Toe-operated Goodyear disc brakes. Provision for amphibious gear, pontoons, "doughnut" or pop-out flotation bags.

Power Plant: Initially, United Aircraft of Canada PT6T-3 Twin Pac turboshaft engine developing 1,800 shp for take-off and having a maximum continuous rating of 1,600 shp. PT6T-6 Twin Pac from June 1974, developing 1,875 shp for take-off and with a maximum continuous rating of 1,675 shp. Fuel contained in twelve fuel cells, with total internal fuel capacity of 293 US gallons (1,109 litres). Provision for 150 US gallon (568 litre) external metal tank. Oil capacity 4·5 US gallons (17 litres).

Accommodation: Pilot's compartment above main cabin seats two side by side with dual controls. Cabin seats 10-16 passengers, with door on starboard side. Entire accommodation heated and ventilated.

Systems: Heating and ventilation systems. Primary and secondary hydraulic systems. Electrical power supplied by two 200A starter/generators.

Electronics and Equipment: Navigation and communications equipment available to customer's requirements. Litters, rescue hoist, cargo sling, cargo handling equipment and air-conditioning optional.

Dimensions, external:
- Diameter of main rotor: 56 ft 0 in (17·07 m)
- Main rotor blade chord: 1 ft $4\frac{5}{8}$ in (0·42 m)
- Diameter of tail rotor: 9 ft 6 in (2·90 m)
- Tail rotor blade chord: $7\frac{1}{4}$ in (0·18 m)
- Distance between rotor centres: 33 ft 1 in (10·08 m)
- Length overall: 65 ft 10 in (20·06 m)
- Length of fuselage: 47 ft 3 in (14·4 m)
- Width of fuselage: 5 ft 8 in (1·73 m)
- Height to top of rotor hub: 14 ft $3\frac{1}{2}$ in (4·36 m)
- Height overall: 15 ft 11 in (4·85 m)
- Wheel track: 12 ft 0 in (3·66 m)
- Wheelbase: 28 ft 3 in (8·75 m)
- Cabin door:
  - Height: 4 ft 0 in (1·22 m)
  - Width: 4 ft 4 in (1·32 m)

Dimensions, internal:
- Cabin: Length: 12 ft 10 in (3·91 m)
  - Max width: 5 ft 0 in (1·52 m)
  - Max height: 5 ft 9 in (1·75 m)

Areas:
- Main rotor blades (each): 35·00 sq ft (3·25 m²)
- Tail rotor blades (each): 2·75 sq ft (0·26 m²)
- Main rotor disc: 2,460 sq ft (228·54 m²)
- Tail rotor disc: 70·9 sq ft (6·59 m²)

Weights and Loadings:
- Weight empty: 7,457 lb (3,382 kg)
- Max T-O and landing weight: 13,000 lb (5,896 kg)
- Max disc loading: 5·29 lb/sq ft (25·8 kg/m²)
- Max power loading: 8·54 lb/shp (3·87 kg/shp)

Performance (at max T-O weight. A: PT6T-3; B: PT6T-6):
- Max level speed at S/L:
  - A, B: 120 knots (138 mph; 222 km/h)
- Cruising speed:
  - A, B: 110 knots (127 mph; 204 km/h)
- Hovering ceiling out of ground effect:
  - A: 4,700 ft (1,433 m)
  - B: 6,500 ft (1,980 m)
- Single-engine absolute ceiling:
  - A: 2,100 ft (640 m)
  - B: 4,200 ft (1,280 m)
- Min ground turning radius:
  - A, B: 41 ft 0 in (12·50 m)
- Runway LCN:
  - A, B: approx 3·7
- Range with 283 US gallons (1,071 litres) usable fuel, including 20 min reserve at cruising speed:
  - A: 260 nm (299 miles; 481 km)
  - B: 242 nm (278 miles; 447 km)

SIKORSKY S-61A, S-61B and S-61F

US military designations: RH-3 and SH-3 Sea King, HH-3A, VH-3A, CH-3B

CAF designation: CH-124

The first version of the S-61 ordered into production was the SH-3A (formerly HSS-2) Sea King amphibious anti-submarine helicopter. The original US Navy contract for this aircraft was received on 23 September 1957, the prototype flew for the first time on 11 March 1959 and first deliveries to the Fleet were made in September 1961.

Sikorsky's S-61 series of twin-turbine helicopters now includes the following military and commercial variants:

SH-3A (formerly HSS-2) Sea King. Initial anti-submarine version for the US Navy, powered by 1,250 shp General Electric T58-GE-8B turboshaft engines. A total of 255 were produced by Sikorsky. Also standard equipment in the Japan Maritime Self-Defence Force (details under entry for Mitsubishi, Sikorsky's Japanese licensee). Mitsubishi converted two SH-2As to S-61A standard for use during Antarctic expeditions.

CH-124. Designation of 41 aircraft, similar to SH-3A, ordered for the Canadian Armed Forces. First of these was delivered in May 1963: fifth and subsequent aircraft were assembled by United Aircraft of Canada Ltd. Originally designated CHSS-2.

Sikorsky S-61A long-range air-sea rescue aircraft of the Royal Danish Air Force (*Mike Jerram*)

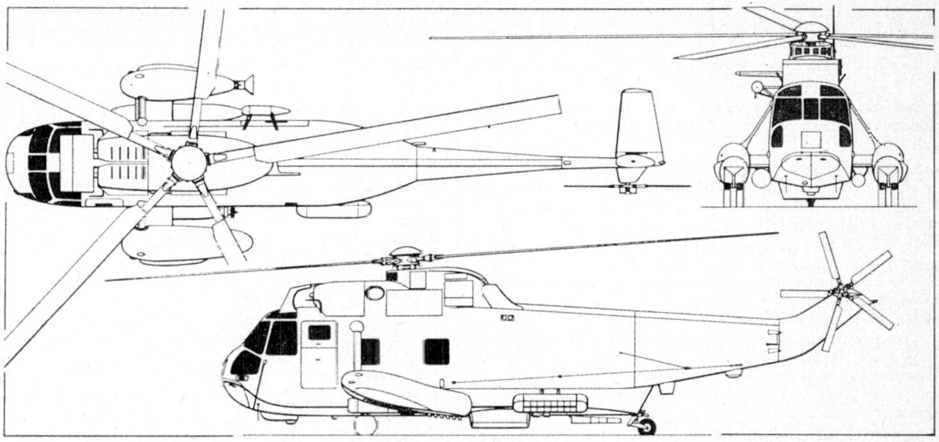

Sikorsky SH-3H twin-engined multi-purpose amphibious helicopter (*Pilot Press*)

S-61A. Amphibious transport, generally similar to the US Navy's SH-3A. Accommodates 26 troops, 15 litters, cargo, or 12 passengers in VIP configuration. Rolls-Royce Bristol Gnome H.1200 turboshafts available as alternative to standard General Electric T58 engines. Nine delivered to Royal Danish Air Force for long-range air-sea rescue duties, with additional fuel tankage. The Decca Navigator Company in the UK announced on 15 January 1973 that it had received a £100,000 contract to supply Mk 19 Decca Navigator airborne receivers, Danac computers and pictorial displays for the Royal Danish Air Force S-61A fleet. One S-61A delivered to Construction Helicopters.

S-61A-4 Nuri. Designation of six aircraft for the Royal Malaysian Air Force, each with 31 seats, rescue hoists and auxiliary fuel tanks as standard equipment. Delivery began in August 1971, to supplement ten delivered in 1967-68 which have been used as troop transport, cargo carrying and rescue vehicles.

HH-3A. A further modified version of the SH-3A received this designation and was tested by the US Navy as a search and rescue helicopter, with armament, armour and a high-speed rescue hoist. HH-3A conversion kits were subsequently supplied to the Navy's overhaul and repair base at Quonset Point, Rhode Island, where conversions were carried out. The first modified aircraft was delivered to the US Navy's HC-7 squadron at Subic Point in the Philippines. Changes in HH-3As modified at Quonset Point include the installation of two electrically-powered Minigun turrets behind the sponsons, T58-GE-8F turbine engines, a high-speed refuelling and fuel dumping system, a high-speed rescue hoist, modified avionics package, external auxiliary fuel tanks and complete armour installation. The SH-3A's sonar well is covered and a reinforced cabin floor substituted.

RH-3A. Nine SH-3As were converted for mine countermeasures duty with the US Navy under this designation. Each has two cargo doors, one on each side, instead of one; bubble windows on each side aft of the cargo doors; rearview mirrors for pilot and co-pilot; and a pivoting tow-tube and hook assembly attached to the fuselage above the tailwheel. The RH-3A is designed to carry, stream, tow and retrieve a variety of mine countermeasures (MCM) gear. Deliveries were made in 1965, on the basis of three for testing and three each to USN helicopter squadrons on the east and west coasts of the USA, four of these aircraft being assigned for service on board two MCM ships.

VH-3A (formerly HSS-2Z). Ten specially-equipped aircraft used by the Executive Flight Detachment which provides a VIP transport and emergency evacuation service for the US President and other key personnel. Five of these aircraft are operated by the US Army and five by the US Marine Corps.

CH-3B. Designation of six "borrowed" HSS-2s (S-61As) operated by the USAF for missile site support and drone recovery duties.

SH-3D Sea King. Standard anti-submarine helicopter of the US Navy, powered by 1,400 shp General Electric T58-GE-10 turboshaft engines, and with an additional 140 US gallons (530 litres) of fuel. First SH-3D, delivered in June 1966, was one of ten aircraft of this type ordered for the Spanish Navy. Four were delivered to the Brazilian Navy. Sikorsky built a total of 90 SH-3Ds. A version with Rolls-Royce Bristol Gnome turboshaft engines and British anti-submarine equipment is manufactured by Westland Helicopters Ltd (which see). SH-3Ds are also manufactured by Agusta, Sikorsky's Italian licensee.

S-61D-4. Designation of four aircraft similar to the SH-3D for the Argentine Navy.

VH-3D. Eleven ordered to replace VH-3As of Executive Flight Detachment.

SH-3G. The US Navy converted a number of SH-3A anti-submarine helicopters into utility helicopters under this designation, involving removal of anti-submarine warfare equipment. Three SH-3Gs, assigned to HC-1's Detachment 1, entered service on board the USS *Ranger* in the West Pacific, and more than 20 others were scheduled for delivery to HC-2, at NAS Lakehurst, New Jersey. Six of these were equipped with Minigun pods for use on search and rescue missions in combat conditions.

SH-3H. Multi-purpose version of the SH-3G announced on 10 June 1971. Initial contract from the US Navy called for conversion of 11 aircraft, to increase fleet helicopter capability against submarines and low-flying enemy missiles.

New anti-submarine warfare equipment includes lightweight sonar, active and passive sonobuoys, magnetic anomaly detection equipment and radar. Electronic surveillance measurement (ESM) equipment and radar are intended to enable the SH-3H to make an important contribution to the missile defence of the fleet. General Electric T58-GE-10 engines are fitted.

Initially, existing SH-3Gs were flown to Stratford from the Navy's facility at North Island, California, for conversion to SH-3H configuration.

Sikorsky S-61N of the Canadian Department of Transport, used to airlift men and supplies to coastal lighthouses

S-61L. Non-amphibious civil transport with longer fuselage than S-61A/B. Described separately.

S-61N. Amphibious counterpart of S-61L, with which it is described.

S-61R. Development of S-61B for transport duties with USAF, under the designations **CH-3C** and **E.** Rear loading ramp, new landing gear and other changes. Described separately.

A total of more than 700 military and civil S-61s of all types had been delivered by Sikorsky and the company's licensees by the Spring of 1973.

The following details apply to the SH-3D Sea King, but are generally applicable to the other versions except for accommodation and equipment:

TYPE: Twin-engined amphibious all-weather anti-submarine helicopter.

ROTOR SYSTEM: Five-blade main and tail rotors. All-metal fully-articulated oil-lubricated main rotor. Flanged cuffs on blades bolted to matching flanges on all-steel rotor head. Main rotor blades are interchangeable and are provided with an automatic powered folding system. Rotor brake standard. All-metal tail rotor.

ROTOR DRIVE: Both engines drive through free-wheel units and rotor brake to main gearbox. Steel drive-shafts. Tail rotor shaft-driven through intermediate and tail gearboxes. Accessories driven by power take-off on tail rotor shaft. Additional free-wheel units between accessories and port engine, and between accessories and tail rotor shaft. Main rotor/engine rpm ratio 1 : 93·43. Tail rotor/engine rpm ratio 1 : 16·7.

FUSELAGE: Boat hull of all-metal semi-monocoque construction. Single step. Tail section folds to reduce stowage requirements.

TAIL SURFACE: Fixed stabiliser on starboard side of tail section.

LANDING GEAR: Amphibious. Land gear consists of two twin-wheel main units, which are retracted rearward hydraulically into stabilising floats, and non-retractable tailwheel. Oleo-pneumatic shock-absorbers. Goodyear main wheels and tubeless tyres size 6·50-10 type III, pressure 70 lb/sq in (4·92 kg/cm^2). Goodyear tailwheel and tyre size 6·00-6. Goodyear hydraulic disc brakes. Boat hull and pop-out flotation bags in stabilising floats permit emergency operation from water.

POWER PLANT: Two 1,400 shp General Electric T58-GE-10 turboshaft engines. Three bladder-type fuel tanks in hull; forward tank capacity 347 US gallons (1,314 litres), centre tank capacity 140 US gallons (530 litres), rear tank capacity 353 US gallons (1,336 litres). Total fuel capacity 840 US gallons (3,180 litres). Refuelling point on port side of fuselage. Oil capacity 7 US gallons (26·5 litres).

ACCOMMODATION: Pilot and co-pilot on flight deck, two sonar operators in main cabin. Dual controls. Crew door at rear of flight deck on port side. Large loading door at rear of cabin on starboard side.

SYSTEMS: Primary and auxiliary hydraulic systems, pressure 1,500 lb/sq in (105 kg/cm^2), for flying controls. Utility hydraulic system, pressure 3,000 lb/sq in (210 kg/cm^2), for landing gear, winches and blade folding. Pneumatic system, pressure 3,000 lb/sq in (210 kg/cm^2), for blow-down emergency landing gear extension. Electrical system includes one 300A DC generator, two 20kVA 115A AC generators and 24V 22Ah battery. APU optional.

ELECTRONICS AND EQUIPMENT: Bendix AQS-13 sonar with 180° search beam width. Hamilton Standard autostabilisation equipment. Automatic transition into hover. Sonar coupler holds altitude automatically in conjunction with Teledyne APN-130 Doppler radar and radar altimeter. Provision for 600 lb (272 kg) capacity rescue hoist and 8,000 lb (3,630 kg) capacity automatic touchdown-release low-response cargo sling for external loads.

ARMAMENT: Provision for 840 lb (381 kg) of weapons, including homing torpedoes.

DIMENSIONS, EXTERNAL:

Diameter of main rotor	62 ft 0 in (18·90 m)
Main rotor blade chord	1 ft $6\frac{1}{4}$ in (0·46 m)
Diameter of tail rotor	10 ft 4 in (3·15 m)
Distance between rotor centres	36 ft 5 in (11·10 m)
Length overall	72 ft 8 in (22·15 m)
Length of fuselage	54 ft 9 in (16·69 m)
Length, tail pylon folded	47 ft 3 in (14·40 m)
Width, rotors folded	16 ft 4 in (4·98 m)
Height to top of rotor hub	15 ft 6 in (4·72 m)
Overall height	16 ft 10 in (5·13 m)
Wheel track	13 ft 0 in (3·96 m)
Wheelbase	23 ft $6\frac{1}{2}$ in (7·18 m)
Crew door (fwd, port):	
Height	5 ft 6 in (1·68 m)
Width	3 ft 0 in (0·91 m)
Height to sill	3 ft 9 in (1·14 m)
Main cabin door (stbd):	
Height	5 ft 0 in (1·52 m)
Width	5 ft 8 in (1·73 m)
Height to sill	3 ft 9 in (1·14 m)

DIMENSIONS, INTERNAL (S-61A):

Cabin: Length	24 ft 11 in (7·60 m)
Max width	6 ft 6 in (1·98 m)
Max height	6 ft $3\frac{1}{2}$ in (1·92 m)
Floor area	162 sq ft (15·1 m^2)
Volume	1,020 cu ft (28·9 m^3)

AREAS:

Main rotor blades (each)	44·54 sq ft (4·14 m^2)
Tail rotor blades (each)	2·46 sq ft (0·23 m^2)
Main rotor disc	3,019 sq ft (280·5 m^2)
Tail rotor disc	83·90 sq ft (7·80 m^2)
Stabiliser	20·00 sq ft (1·86 m^2)

WEIGHTS:

Weight empty:	
S-61A	9,763 lb (4,428 kg)
S-61B	11,865 lb (5,382 kg)
Normal T-O weight:	
S-61A	20,500 lb (9,300 kg)
SH-3A (ASW)	18,044 lb (8,185 kg)
SH-3D (ASW)	18,626 lb (8,449 kg)
Max T-O weight:	
S-61A	21,500 lb (9,750 kg)
S-61B	20,500 lb (9,300 kg)
SH-3H	21,000 lb (9,525 kg)

PERFORMANCE (at 20,500 lb; 9,300 kg AUW):

Max level speed	144 knots (166 mph; 267 km/h)
Cruising speed for max range	118 knots (136 mph; 219 km/h)
Max rate of climb at S/L	2,200 ft (670 m)/min
Service ceiling	14,700 ft (4,480 m)
Hovering ceiling in ground effect	10,500 ft (3,200 m)
Hovering ceiling out of ground effect	8,200 ft (2,500 m)
Range with max fuel, 10% reserve	542 nm (625 miles; 1,005 km)

SIKORSKY S-61L AND S-61N

Although basically similar to the S-61A and B, the S-61L and N commercial transports incorporate a number of changes, including a longer fuselage. Other details are as follows:

S-61L. Non-amphibious configuration. Modified landing gear, rotor head and stabiliser. Accommodation for up to 30 passengers. First flight of the prototype S-61L was made on 6 December 1960, and it received FAA Type Approval on 2 November 1961.

S-61N. Similar to S-61L, but with sealed hull for amphibious operation and stabilising floats as on SH-3A. Accommodation for 26-28 passengers. First flight of the first S-61N was made on 7 August 1962.

On 6 October 1964 the S-61L and S-61N became the first transport helicopters to receive FAA approval for instrument flight operations.

Both models are now offered in the **Mark II** versions, with General Electric CT58-140-2 turboshaft engines, as described below (earlier aircraft have 1,350 shp engines). Passenger accommodation is increased to maximum of 30 in the S-61L and 26 in the S-61N (28 optional); and the Mark II is able to carry 22 passengers on an 86°F (30°C) day, compared with the former 10. There are six individual cargo bins to speed baggage handling. Other changes include improved vibration damping.

In July 1972 New York Airways set a monthly record for its fleet of four S-61Ls, carrying a total of 40,858 passengers on its routes linking La Guardia, Kennedy and Newark Airports, Wall Street Heliport and Morristown, New Jersey.

A list of orders, totalling 49 aircraft, was given in the 1972-73 *Jane's*. An additional nineteen were ordered for delivery in 1973-74, of which eleven were amphibious S-61Ns for Bristow Helicopters. The addition of these new aircraft means that Bristow, with a fleet of 16 S-61s, is the world's largest private operator of the type.

TYPE: Twin-turbine all-weather helicopter airliners.

ROTOR SYSTEM AND ROTOR DRIVE: As for SH-3A/D, S-61A and S-61B, except blades do not fold.

FUSELAGE: All-metal semi-monocoque structure of boat-hull form.

TAIL SURFACE: Stabiliser on starboard side of tail section.

LANDING GEAR (S-61L): Non-amphibious non-retractable tailwheel type with twin wheels on main units. Oleo-pneumatic shock-absorbers. Goodyear main wheels and tubeless tyres, size 22·1 × 6·50-10 Type III, pressure 95 lb/sq in (6·7 kg/cm^2). Goodyear tailwheel with tyre size 18·3 × 6·00-10, pressure 75 lb/sq in (5·3 kg/cm^2). Goodyear hydraulic disc brakes.

LANDING GEAR (S-61N): Amphibious hydraulically-retractable type. Twin wheels on main units, which retract rearward into stabilising floats. Non-retractable tailwheel. Each float provides 3,320 lb (1,506 kg) buoyancy and, with the sealed hull, permits operation from water. Shock-absorbers, wheels, tyres and brakes as for S-61L.

POWER PLANT: Two 1,500 shp General Electric CT58-140-2 turboshaft engines. Two bladder-type fuel tanks in hull; forward tank capacity 210 US gallons (796 litres), rear tank capacity 200 US gallons (757 litres). Total fuel capacity 410 US gallons (1,553 litres). Additional 244 US gallon (924 litre) tank optionally available for S-61N. Refuelling point on port side of fuselage. Oil capacity 7 US gallons (26·5 litres).

ACCOMMODATION: Crew of three: pilot, co-pilot and flight attendant. Main cabin accommodates up to 30 passengers (22 at 86°F; 30°C). Standard arrangement has eight single seats and one double seat on port side of cabin, seven double seats on starboard side and one double seat at rear. Rear seat may be replaced by a toilet. Galley may be installed in forward baggage compartment area on starboard side. Forward half of cabin may be provided with folding seats and tie-down rings for convertible passenger/freight operations. Two doors on starboard side of cabin: main cabin door of airstair type. Baggage space above and below floor at front, on starboard side of cabin, and below floor in area of airstair door (aft, starboard side).

Systems: As for SH-3A, S-61A and S-61B.

Electronics and Equipment: Radio and radar to customer's specification. Blind-flying instrumentation standard.

Dimensions, external:
Diameter of main rotor 62 ft 0 in (18·90 m)
Diameter of tail rotor 10 ft 4 in (3·15 m)
Distance between rotor centres:
S-61L 36 ft 5 in (11·10 m)
S-61N 36 ft 8 in (11·17 m)
Length overall (rotors fore and aft):
S-61L 72 ft 10½ in (22·21 m)
S-61N 72 ft 10 in (22·20 m)
Width, over landing gear:
S-61L 14 ft 8 in (4·47 m)
S-61N 19 ft 9 in (6·02 m)
Height to top of rotor hub pitot head:
S-61L 17 ft 0 in (5·18 m)
S-61N 17 ft 5½ in (5·32 m)
Height overall:
S-61L 17 ft 0 in (5·18 m)
S-61N 18 ft 5½ in (5·63 m)
Wheel track
S-61L 13 ft 0 in (3·96 m)
S-61N 14 ft 0 in (4·27 m)
Wheelbase:
S-61L 23 ft 5½ in (7·15 m)
S-61N 23 ft 11½ in (7·30 m)
Cabin door (airstair):
Height 5 ft 6 in (1·68 m)
Width 2 ft 8 in (0·81 m)
Height to sill 3 ft 9 in (1·14 m)
Cargo door:
Height 5 ft 6 in (1·68 m)
Width 4 ft 2 in (1·27 m)
Height to sill 3 ft 9 in (1·14 m)

Dimensions, internal:
Cabin: Length 31 ft 11 in (9·73 m)
Max width 6 ft 6 in (1.98 m)
Max height 6 ft 3½ in (1·92 m)
Floor area approx 217 sq ft (20·16 m²)
Volume approx 1,305 cu ft (36·95 m³)
Freight hold (above floor) approx 125 cu ft (3·54 m³)
Freight hold (underfloor) approx 25 cu ft (0·71 m³)

Areas:
Main rotor blades (each) 40·4 sq ft (3·75 m²)
Tail rotor blades (each) 2·35 sq ft (0·22 m²)
Main rotor disc 3,019 sq ft (280·5 m²)
Tail rotor disc 83·9 sq ft (7·79 m²)
Stabiliser 27·0 sq ft (2·51 m²)

Weights:
Weight empty:
S-61L 11,701 lb (5,308 kg)
S-61N 12,336 lb (5,595 kg)
Max T-O weight 19,000 lb (8,620 kg)

Performance (at max T-O weight):
Max level speed at S/L 127 knots (146 mph; 235 km/h)
Average cruising speed 120 knots (138 mph; 222 km/h)
Max rate of climb at S/L 1,300 ft (395 m)/min
Service ceiling 12,500 ft (3,810 m)
Hovering ceiling in ground effect:
S-61L 9,000 ft (2,743 m)
S-61N 8,700 ft (2,652 m)
Hovering ceiling out of ground effect:
S-61L 3,900 ft (1,189 m)
S-61N 3,800 ft (1,158 m)
Min ground turning radius:
S-61L 44 ft 11½ in (13·70 m)
S-61N 45 ft 8½ in (13·93 m)
Runway LCN at max T-O weight approx 4·4
Range with max fuel, 30 min reserve:
S-61L 230 nm (265 miles; 426 km)
S-61N 450 nm (518 miles; 833 km)

SIKORSKY S-61R

US military designations: CH-3 and HH-3

Although based on the SH-3A, this amphibious transport helicopter introduced many important design changes. They include provision of a hydraulically-operated rear ramp for straight-in loading of wheeled vehicles, a 2,000 lb (907 kg) capacity winch for internal cargo handling, retractable tricycle-type landing gear, pressurised rotor blades for quick and easy inspection, gas-turbine auxiliary power supply for independent field operations, self-lubricating main and tail rotors, and built-in equipment for the removal and replacement of all major components in remote areas.

The first S-61R flew on 17 June 1963, almost a month ahead of schedule, and was followed by the first CH-3C a few weeks later. FAA Type Approval was received on 30 December 1963, and the first delivery of an operational CH-3C was made on the same day, for drone recovery duties at Tyndall AFB, Florida. Subsequent deliveries have been made to USAF Air Defense Command, Air Training Command, Tactical Air Command, Strategic Air Command and Aerospace Rescue and Recovery Service.

There have been four versions, as follows:

CH-3C. Two 1,300 shp T58-GE-1 turboshaft engines. Initial order for 22 placed by USAF on 8 February 1963. In July 1963, the CH-3C won a competition for a long-range rotary-wing support system for the USAF and further orders followed. After a total of 41 had been built, production was switched to the CH-3E. All aircraft delivered as CH-3Cs were later modified to CH-3E standard.

In January 1966, details were announced of a series of flight refuelling trials carried out successfully with a CH-3C at the US Marine Corps Air Station, Cherry Point, NC. Ten experimental contacts were made, with a nose-probe on the CH-3C and a drogue trailed from a USMC KC-130F tanker. The aircraft remained connected for up to five minutes at a time.

CH-3E. Designation applicable since February 1966, following introduction of uprated engines (1,500 shp T58-GE-5s). A total of 42 were built as new aircraft to this standard. Of the 83 new and uprated aircraft, 50 were adapted as HH-3Es (which see).

A pod-mounted turret armament system was developed for this version, with the weapons located off each sponson and with gunsights at the port and starboard personnel doors. Each pod mounts an Emerson Electric TAT-102 turret, incorporating a General Electric six-barrel 7·62 mm Minigun and an 8,000-round ammunition storage-feed system. Over 180° traverse is achieved on each side of the aircraft, to give complete 360° coverage with overlapping fire forward.

HH-3E. For USAF Aerospace Rescue and Recovery Service. Additional equipment comprises armour, self-sealing fuel tanks, retractable flight refuelling probe, defensive armament and rescue hoist. Two 1,500 shp T58-GE-5 turboshafts. A total of 50 HH-3Es were delivered.

On 31 May-1 June 1967, two HH-3Es made the first non-stop transatlantic flights by helicopters, en route to the Paris Air Show. Nine aerial refuellings were made by each aircraft. The 3,708 nm (4,270 miles; 6,870 km) from New York to Paris were flown in 30 hr 46 min.

HH-3F. Similar to HH-3E, for US Coast Guard, which has given them the name **Pelican.** Advanced electronic equipment for search and rescue duties. No armour plate, armament or self-sealing tanks. First order announced in August 1965. Deliveries began in 1968 and a total of 40 have been built.

The following details apply to the CH-3E:

Type: Twin-engined amphibious transport helicopter.

Rotor System: Five-blade fully-articulated main rotor of all-metal construction. Flanged cuffs on blades bolted to matching flanges on rotor head. Control by rotating and stationary swashplates. Blades do not fold. Rotor brake standard. Conventional tail rotor with five aluminium blades.

Rotor Drive: Twin turbines drive through free-wheeling units and rotor brake to main gearbox. Steel drive-shafts. Tail rotor shaft-driven through intermediate gearbox and tail gearbox. Main rotor/engine rpm ratio 1 : 93·43. Tail rotor/engine rpm ratio 1 : 16·7.

Fuselage: All-metal semi-monocoque structure of pod and boom type. Cabin of basic square section.

Tail Surface: Horizontal stabiliser on starboard side of tail rotor pylon.

Landing Gear: Hydraulically-retractable tricycle type, with twin wheels on each unit. Main wheels retract forward into sponsons, each of which provides 4,797 lb (2,176 kg) of buoyancy and, with boat hull, permits amphibious operation. Oleo-pneumatic shock-absorbers. All wheels and tyres tubeless Type III rib, size 22·1 × 6·50-10, manufactured by Goodyear. Tyre pressure 95 lb/sq in (6·7 kg/cm²). Goodyear hydraulic disc brakes.

Power Plant: Two 1,500 shp General Electric T58-GE-5 turboshaft engines, mounted side by side above cabin, immediately forward of main transmission. Fuel in two bladder-type tanks beneath cabin floor; forward tank capacity 318 US gallons (1,204 litres), rear tank capacity 324 US gallons (1,226 litres). Total fuel capacity 642 US gallons (2,430 litres). Refuelling point on port side of fuselage. Total oil capacity 7 US gallons (26·5 litres).

Accommodation: Crew of two side by side on flight deck, with dual controls. Provision for flight engineer or attendant. Normal accommodation for 25 fully-equipped troops. Alternative arrangements for 30 troops, 15 stretchers or 5,000 lb (2,270 kg) of cargo. Jettisonable sliding door on starboard side at front of cabin. Internal door between cabin and flight deck. Hydraulically-operated rear loading ramp for vehicles, in two hinged sections, giving opening with minimum width of 5 ft 8 in (1·73 m) and headroom of up to 7 ft 3 in (2·21 m).

Systems: Primary and auxiliary hydraulic systems, pressure 1,500 lb/sq in (105 kg/cm²), for flying control servos. Utility hydraulic system, pressure 3,000 lb/sq in (210 kg/cm²), for landing gear, rear ramp and winches. Pneumatic system, pressure 3,000 lb/sq in (210 kg/cm²), for emergency blow-down landing gear extension. Electrical system includes 24V 22Ah battery, two 20kVA 115V AC generators and one 300A DC generator. APU standard.

Electronics and Equipment (CH-3C): Equipment includes 2,000 lb (907 kg) capacity winch for loading bulk cargo and an 8,000 lb (3,625 kg) capacity cargo sling. Floor incorporates tie-downs and skid strips. Automatic flight control system to stabilise aircraft during typical flight attitudes. Electronics include AN/ARC-34B UHF, TR-4A backup UHF, AN/ARA-25 UHF direction finder group, AN/ARN-65 TACAN, AN/ARN-58 ILS and marker receiver, AN/ARN-59 LF ADF, AN/AIC-18 intercom, AN/AIC-13 public address system, AN/APX-46 transponder and AN/APN-150 altimeter.

Dimensions, external:
Diameter of main rotor 62 ft 0 in (18·90 m)
Main rotor blade chord 1 ft 6¼ in (0·46 m)
Diameter of tail rotor 10 ft 4 in (3·15 m)
Distance between rotor centres 36 ft 10 in (11·22 m)
Length overall 73 ft 0 in (22·25 m)
Length of fuselage 57 ft 3 in (17·45 m)
Width, over landing gear 15 ft 10 in (4·82 m)
Height to top of rotor hub 16 ft 1 in (4·90 m)
Height overall 18 ft 1 in (5·51 m)
Wheel track 13 ft 4 in (4·06 m)
Wheelbase 17 ft 1 in (5·21 m)
Cabin door (fwd, stbd):
Height 5 ft 4¾ in (1·65 m)
Width 4 ft 0 in (1·22 m)
Height to sill 4 ft 2 in (1·27 m)
Rear ramp:
Length 14 ft 1 in (4·29 m)
Width 6 ft 1 in (1·85 m)

Dimensions, internal:
Cabin (excluding flight deck):
Length 25 ft 10½ in (7·89 m)
Max width 6 ft 6 in (1·98 m)
Max height 6 ft 3 in (1·91 m)
Floor area approx 168 sq ft (15·61 m²)
Volume approx 1,050 cu ft (29·73 m³)

Areas:
Main rotor blades (each) 39·9 sq ft (3·71 m²)
Tail rotor blades (each) 2·35 sq ft (0·22 m²)
Main rotor disc 3,019 sq ft (280·5 m²)

Sikorsky HH-3F search and rescue helicopter of the US Coast Guard

Sikorsky CH-54B heavy-lift utility version of the Skycrane in US Army service

Tail rotor disc 83·9 sq ft (7·80 m²)
Stabiliser 27·0 sq ft (2·51 m²)
WEIGHTS:
Weight empty 13,255 lb (6,010 kg)
Normal T-O weight 21,247 lb (9,635 kg)
Max T-O weight 22,050 lb (10,000 kg)
PERFORMANCE (at normal T-O weight):
Max level speed at S/L 141 knots (162 mph; 261 km/h)
Cruising speed for max range 125 knots (144 mph; 232 km/h)
Max rate of climb at S/L 1,310 ft (400 m)/min
Service ceiling 11,100 ft (3,385 m)
Hovering ceiling in ground effect 4,100 ft (1,250 m)
Min ground turning radius 37 ft 0½ in (11·29 m)
Runway LCN at max T-O weight approx 4·75
Range with max fuel, 10% reserve 404 nm (465 miles; 748 km)

SIKORSKY S-64 SKYCRANE

US military designation: CH-54

The S-64 flying crane was designed initially for military transport duties. Equipped with interchangeable pods, it is suitable for use as a troop transport, and for minesweeping, cargo and missile transport, anti-submarine or field hospital operations. Equipment includes a removable 25,000 lb (11,340 kg) hoist, a sling attachment and a load stabiliser to prevent undue sway in cargo winch operations. Attachment points are provided on the fuselage and landing gear to facilitate securing of bulky loads.

Versions of the S-64 announced to date are as follows:

S-64A. Under this designation the first of three prototypes flew for the first time on 9 May 1962 and was used by the US Army at Fort Benning, Georgia, for testing and demonstration. The second and third prototypes were delivered to Federal Germany for evaluation by the German armed forces.

CH-54A. In June 1963, the US Army announced that it had ordered six S-64As, under the designation CH-54A, to investigate the heavy lift concept, with emphasis on increasing mobility in the battlefield. Delivery of five CH-54As (originally YCH-54As) to the US Army took place in late 1964 and early 1965. A sixth CH-54A remained at Stratford, with a company-owned S-64, for a programme leading toward a restricted FAA certification, which was awarded on 30 July 1965. Further US Army orders followed.

The CH-54As were assigned to the US Army's 478th Aviation Company, and performed outstanding service in support of the Army's First Cavalry Division, Airmobile, in Vietnam.

On 29 April 1965, a CH-54A of the 478th Company lifted 90 persons, including 87 combat-equipped troops in a detachable van. This is believed to be the largest number of people ever carried by a helicopter at one time. Other Skycranes in Vietnam transported bulldozers and road graders weighing up to 17,500 lb (7,937 kg), 20,000 lb (9,072 kg) armoured vehicles and a large variety of heavy hardware. They retrieved more than 380 damaged aircraft, involving savings estimated at $210 million.

Sikorsky Aircraft developed an all-purpose van, known as the Universal Military Pod, for carriage by the US Army's CH-54As, and received an order, worth $2·9 million, to supply 22 to the Army. The pods were delivered complete with communications, ventilation and lighting systems, and with wheels to simplify ground handling. They superseded earlier pods which were not approved for the carriage of personnel.

With a max loaded weight of 20,000 lb (9,072 kg), each pod accommodates 45 combat-equipped troops, or 24 litters, and in the field may be adapted for a variety of uses, such as surgical unit, field command post and communications post.

Internal dimensions of the pod are: length 27 ft 5 in (8·36 m), width 8 ft 10 in (2·69 m) and height 6 ft 6 in (1·98 m). Doors are provided on each side of the forward area of the pod, and a double-panelled ramp is located aft. The first pod was accepted by the US Army on 28 June 1968, following approval for personnel transport.

On 15 February 1968, Sikorsky announced that it had received an order for two commercial Skycranes from Rowan Drilling Company, Inc, of Houston, Texas. These were delivered on 18 April 1969, for operation in support of oil exploration and drilling operations in Alaska.

S-64E. FAA certification of the improved S-64E for civil use was announced in 1969, for the transportation of external cargo weighing up to 22,400 lb (10,160 kg).

In January 1972 Erickson Air-Crane Company of Marysville, California, purchased the first S-64E, for logging and other heavy-lift tasks. On 1 November 1972 this company ordered three additional S-64Es, the first of which was delivered in the following month.

Erickson intended to use this fleet of four aircraft to extend its operations on a worldwide basis, offering heavy-lift capability to the logging, petroleum, power line, shipping and general construction industries. Three S-64Es are operated by Evergreen Helicopters Inc of McMinnville, Oregon. One was ordered by Tri-Eagle Company in 1974, for timber harvesting in California. Production completed.

CH-54B. On 4 November 1968 Sikorsky announced that it had received a US Army contract to increase the payload capacity of the CH-54 from 10 to 12½ short tons. The contract called for a number of design improvements to the engine, gearbox, rotor head and structure; altitude performance and hot weather operating capability were also to be improved.

The original JFTD12-4A engines were replaced by two Pratt & Whitney JFTD12-5As, each rated at 4,800 shp, and a gearbox capable of receiving 7,900 hp from the two engines was introduced. Single-engine performance was increased, since the new gearbox receives 4,800 hp from one engine, compared with 4,050 hp on the CH-54A.

A new rotor system was also introduced, utilising a high-lift rotor blade with a chord some 2·5 in (6·35 cm) greater than that of the blades used formerly.

Other changes included the provision of dual wheels on the main landing gear, an improved automatic flight control system and some general structural strengthening throughout the aircraft. Gross weight was increased from 42,000 lb (19,050 kg) to 47,000 lb (21,318 kg).

Two of the improved flying cranes, designated CH-54B, were accepted by the US Army during 1969.

In October 1970, two US Army CH-54Bs lifted a 40,760 lb (18,488 kg) load during a series of tests being conducted to evaluate a twin helicopter lift concept. The objective is to determine the technical feasibility and cost of a twin-lift system for potential application to military requirements for greater helicopter external load capacity. Later in the same month, a single US Army CH-54B lifted a 40,780 lb (18,497 kg)

Sikorsky CH-54B heavy-lift helicopter in US Army service takes off on test with a payload of 40,780 lb (18,497 kg)

load during tests being conducted to evaluate maximum hover lift capability.

Nine international helicopter records in Class E-1 are held by the CH-54B. On 26 October 1971, piloted by B. P. Blackwell, a payload of 1,000 kg was lifted to a height of 31,165 ft (9,499 m). On 29 October CWO E. E. Price flew to 31,480 ft (9,595 m) with 2,000 kg. On 27 October the same pilot had reached 25,518 ft (7,778 m) with a 5,000 kg payload. CWO J. K. Church flew to 17,211 ft (5,246 m) with 10,000 kg on 29 October, and on 12 April 1972 CWO D. L. Spivey reached 10,850 ft (3,307 m) with a 15,000 kg payload. CWO Church set an earlier record on 4 November 1971, by maintaining a height of 36,122 ft (11,010 m) in horizontal flight. Major J. C. Henderson set up two time-to-height climb records in a CH-54B on 12 April 1972, reaching 3,000 m in 1 min 22·2 sec and 6,000 m in 2 min 58·9 sec. Earlier, on 4 November 1971, CWO D. W. Hunt had climbed to 9,000 m in 5 min 57·7 sec.

S-64F. Designation of a commercial version of the military CH-54B. The improvements distinguishing this upgraded commercial helicopter were introduced into production CH-54s in late 1969, and FAA certification tests were completed in late 1970. Not yet in production for commercial use.

A total of 96 S-64s had been built by May 1973, mostly for the US Army.

TYPE: Twin-turbine heavy flying crane helicopter.

ROTOR SYSTEM: Six-blade fully-articulated main rotor with aluminium blades and aluminium and steel head. Four-blade tail rotor with titanium head and aluminium blades. Rotor brake standard.

ROTOR DRIVE: Steel tube drive-shafts. Main gearbox below main rotor, intermediate gearbox at base of tail pylon, tail gearbox at top of pylon. Main gearbox rated at 6,600 shp on CH-54A and S-64E, 7,900 shp on S-64F.

FUSELAGE: Pod and boom type of aluminium and steel semi-monocoque construction.

LANDING GEAR: Non-retractable tricycle type, with single wheel on each unit of CH-54A/S-64E, twin wheels on main units of S-64F. CH-54A/S-64E main-wheel tyres size 38·45 × 12·50-16, pressure 95 lb/sq in (6·7 kg/cm²). S-64F main-wheel tyres size 25·65 × 8·50-10, pressure 100 lb/sq in (7·0 kg/cm²). Nosewheels and tyres of all versions size 25·65 × 8·50-10, pressure 100 lb/sq in (7·0 kg/cm²).

POWER PLANT (CH-54A/S-64E): Two Pratt & Whitney JFTD12-4A (military T73-P-1) turboshaft engines, each rated at 4,500 shp for take-off and with max continuous rating of 4,000 shp. Two fuel tanks in fuselage, forward and aft of transmission, each with capacity of 440 US gallons (1,664 litres). Total standard fuel capacity 880 US gallons (3,328 litres). Provision for auxiliary fuel tank of 440 US gallons (1,664 litres) capacity, raising total fuel capacity to 1,320 US gallons (4,992 litres).

POWER PLANT (S-64F): Two Pratt & Whitney JFTD12-5A turboshaft engines, each rated at 4,800 shp for take-off and with max continuous rating of 4,430 shp. Fuel tanks as for S-64E.

ACCOMMODATION: Pilot and co-pilot side by side at front of cab. Aft-facing seat for third pilot at rear of cabin, with flying controls. The occupant of this third seat is able to take over control of the aircraft during loading and unloading. Two additional jump seats available in cab. Payload in interchangeable pods.

DIMENSIONS, EXTERNAL:

Diameter of main rotor	72 ft 0 in (21·95 m)
Diameter of tail rotor	16 ft 0 in (4·88 m)
Distance between rotor centres	44 ft 6 in (13·56 m)
Length overall	88 ft 6 in (26·97 m)
Length of fuselage	70 ft 3 in (21·41 m)
Width, rotors folded	21 ft 10 in (6·65 m)
Height to top of rotor hub	18 ft 7 in (5·67 m)
Overall height	25 ft 5 in (7·75 m)
Ground clearance under fuselage boom	9 ft 4 in (2·84 m)
Wheel track	19 ft 9 in (6·02 m)
Wheelbase	24 ft 5 in (7·44 m)

AREAS:

Main rotor disc	4,070 sq ft (378·1 m²)
Tail rotor disc	201 sq ft (18·67 m²)

WEIGHTS (CH-54A/S-64E):

Weight empty	19,234 lb (8,724 kg)
Max T-O weight	42,000 lb (19,050 kg)

PERFORMANCE (CH-54A/S-64E at normal T-O weight of 38,000 lb; 17,237 kg):

Max level speed at S/L	109 knots (126 mph; 203 km/h)
Max cruising speed	91 knots (105 mph; 169 km/h)
Max rate of climb at S/L	1,330 ft (405 m)/min
Service ceiling	9,000 ft (2,475 m)
Hovering ceiling in ground effect	10,600 ft (3,230 m)
Hovering ceiling out of ground effect	6,900 ft (2,100 m)
Min ground turning radius: CH-54A, S-64E, S-64F	54 ft 0 in (16·4 m)
Runway LCN: CH-54A, S-64E at max T-O weight of 42,000 lb (19,050 kg)	7·1
S-64F at max T-O weight of 47,000 lb (21,318 kg)	7·7
Range with max fuel, 10% reserve	200 nm (230 miles; 370 km)

Left to right: **Sikorsky CH-53D helicopters fitted experimentally with improved rotor blades (IRB), canted tail rotor and swept-tip rotor blades**

SIKORSKY S-65A

US Navy designation: CH-53A Sea Stallion
USAF designations: HH-53B/C
US Marine Corps designation: CH-53D

On 27 August 1962, it was announced that Sikorsky had been selected by the US Navy to produce a heavy assault transport helicopter for use by the Marine Corps. First flight was made on 14 October 1964, and deliveries began in mid-1966. Versions identified to date are as follows:

CH-53A. Designation of the initial version. This aircraft uses many components based on those of the S-64A Skycrane, but is powered by two General Electric T64 turboshaft engines and has a watertight hull. A full-size rear opening, with built-in ramp, permits easy loading and unloading, with the aid of a special hydraulically-operated internal cargo loading system and floor rollers.

Typical cargo loads include two Jeeps, or two Hawk missiles with cable reels and control console, or a 105 mm howitzer and carriage. An external cargo system permits in-flight pickup and release without ground assistance.

The CH-53A is able to operate under all weather and climatic conditions. Its main rotor blades and tail pylon fold hydraulically for stowage on board ship.

CH-53As served in Vietnam from January 1967.

On 17 February 1968, a CH-53A, with General Electric T64-6 (modified) engines, flew at a gross weight of 51,900 lb (23,541 kg) carrying 28,500 lb (12,927 kg) of payload and fuel, establishing new unofficial payload and gross weight records for a production helicopter built outside the Soviet Union.

On 26 April 1968, a Marine Corps CH-53A made the first automatic terrain clearance flight in helicopter history and subsequently concluded flight tests of an Integrated Helicopter Avionics System (IHAS). Prime contractor for the IHAS programme was Teledyne Systems Company. Norden Division of United Aircraft Corporation provided the terrain-clearance radar and vertical structure display.

On 23 October 1968, a Marine Corps CH-53A performed a series of loops and rolls, as part of a joint Naval Air Systems Command and Sikorsky flight test programme, aimed at investigating the CH-53A's rotor system dynamics and manoeuvrability characteristics. The helicopter was piloted by Lt Col Robert Guay, USMC, and Byron Graham, Sikorsky experimental test pilot.

Take-off weight of the CH-53A was 27,000 lb (12,247 kg). The rolls were started at a speed of about 140 knots (161 mph; 259 km/h). The rate of roll ranged from 70° to 95° per second. The load factor at the beginning of the roll was 1·6*g*, and decreased to 0·8*g* at the inverted position. The load factor at completion varied from 1·8*g* to 2·7*g* depending upon the specific roll. Time for the rolls varied from 5·8 to 7·5 seconds, and the speed upon completion was 110 knots (127 mph; 204 km/h).

The loops were begun at about 160 knots (184 mph; 296 km/h) in level flight. The load factor at the start of the loop was 1·2*g* and increased to 2·5*g* when the helicopter reached a 50° nose-up position. At the inverted position, the load factor was 0·8*g*, and upon completion of the loop it was 2·8*g*. The time for the loops varied from 18 to 25 seconds. Completion speed was 130 knots (150 mph; 250 km/h).

HH-53B. Designation of eight heavy-lift helicopters ordered by the USAF in September 1966 for its Aerospace Rescue and Recovery Service. The first of these flew on 15 March 1967 and deliveries began in June 1967.

The HH-53B is generally similar to the CH-53A,

Sikorsky HH-53C heavy-lift helicopter of the 37th ARRS, USAF, at Phu Cat Air Base, Vietnam (*Norman E. Taylor*)

Sikorsky YCH-53E prototype heavy-lift helicopter (three 4,380 shp General Electric T64-GE-415 turboshaft engines)

but is powered by 3,080 shp T64-GE-3 turboshaft engines. It has the same general equipment as the HH-3E, including a retractable flight refuelling probe, jettisonable auxiliary fuel tanks, rescue hoist, all-weather avionics and armament.

HH-53C. An improved version of the HH-53B, with 3,435 shp T64-GE-7 engines, auxiliary jettisonable fuel tanks each of 450 US gallons (1,703 litres) capacity on new cantilever mounts, flight refuelling probe and rescue hoist with 250 ft (76 m) of cable; the first HH-53C was delivered to the USAF on 30 August 1968. External cargo hook of 20,000 lb (9,070 kg) capacity. A total of 66 HH-53B/Cs were built.

CH-53D. An improved version of the CH-53A for the US Marine Corps, the first of which was delivered on 3 March 1969. It has two T64-GE-412 or T64-GE-413 engines, the former having a military rating of 3,695 shp, and the latter a maximum rating of 3,925 shp. A total of 55 troops can be carried in a high-density arrangement. An integral cargo handling system makes it possible for one man to load or unload one short ton of palletised cargo a minute. Main rotor and tail pylon fold automatically for carrier operation.

Last CH-53D (the 265th CH-53 built) was delivered on 31 January 1972. All but the first 34 CH-53s were provided with hardpoints for supporting towing equipment and transferring tow loads to the airframe, so that the US Marines could utilise the aircraft as airborne minesweepers, giving an assault commander the capability of clearing enemy mines from harbours and off beaches without having to wait for surface minesweepers. Tow kits installed in the 15 CH-53Ds operated by HM-12 Squadron included automatic flight control system interconnections to provide automatic cable yaw angle retention and aircraft attitude and heading hold; rearview mirrors for pilot and co-pilot; tow cable tension and yaw angle indicator; automatic emergency cable release; towboom and hook system with 15,000 lb (6,803 kg) load capacity when cable was locked to internal towboom; dam to prevent cabin flooding in emergency water landing with lower ramp open; dual hydraulically-powered cable winches; racks and cradles for stowage of minesweeping gear; auxiliary fuel tanks in cabin to increase endurance.

RH-53D. Specially-equipped minesweeping version for the US Navy, described separately.

YCH-53E. Three-engined development of the CH-53D. Described separately.

CH-53G. Version of the CH-53 for the German armed forces. A total of 153 are being produced, and the first of two built by Sikorsky was delivered on 31 March 1969. The next 20 were assembled in Germany from American-built components. The remainder embody some 50% components of German manufacture. Prime contractor in Germany is VFW-Fokker, which completed final assembly of its first CH-53G in the late Summer of 1971, and this aircraft flew for the first time in October 1971. Deliveries to the German Army will continue until 1975.

Israel also acquired eight CH-53s.

S-65-Oe. On 10 March 1969, Sikorsky announced an order for two helicopters for the Austrian Air Force under this designation. Used for rescue duties in the Alps, they have the same rescue hoist as the HH-53B/C, fittings for auxiliary fuel tanks and accommodation for 38 passengers. Delivery was made in 1970.

Sikorsky is also working on the design of an inter-city helicopter based on the CH-53. Designated **S-65-40**, this is intended to carry up to 46 passengers on stage lengths of up to 174 nm (200 miles; 322 km) at a speed of approximately 152 knots (175 mph; 282 km/h).

More than 350 H-53s had been delivered by May 1974.

The following details refer to the CH-53A:

Type: Twin-turbine heavy assault transport helicopter.

Rotor System and Drive: Generally similar to those of S-64A Skycrane, but main rotor head is of titanium and steel, and it has folding blades.

Fuselage: Conventional semi-monocoque structure of aluminium, steel and titanium. Folding tail pylon.

Tail Surface: Large horizontal stabiliser on starboard side of tail rotor pylon.

Landing Gear: Retractable tricycle type, with twin wheels on each unit. Main units retract into the rear of sponsons on each side of fuselage. Fully-castoring nose unit. Main wheels and nosewheels have tyres size 25·65 × 8·50-10, pressure 95 lb/sq in (6·7 kg/cm²).

Power Plant: Normally two 2,850 shp General Electric T64-GE-6 turboshaft engines, mounted in pod on each side of main rotor pylon. The CH-53A can also utilise, without airframe modification, the T64-GE-1 engine of 3,080 shp or the later T64-GE-16 (mod) engine of 3,435 shp. Two self-sealing bladder fuel tanks, each with capacity of 315 US gallons (1,192 litres), housed in forward part of sponsons. Total fuel capacity 630 US gallons (2,384 litres).

Accommodation: Crew of three. Main cabin accommodates 37 combat-equipped troops on inward-facing seats. Provision for carrying 24 stretchers and four attendants. Roller-skid track combination in floor for handling heavy freight. Door on starboard side of cabin at front. Rear loading ramp.

Dimensions, external:
- Diameter of main rotor: 72 ft 3 in (22·02 m)
- Diameter of tail rotor: 16 ft 0 in (4·88 m)
- Length overall, rotors turning: 88 ft 3 in (26·90 m)
- Length of fuselage, without refuelling probe: 67 ft 2 in (20·47 m)
- Width overall, rotors folded: 15 ft 6 in (4·72 m)
- Width of fuselage: 8 ft 10 in (2·69 m)
- Height to top of rotor hub: 17 ft 1½ in (5·22 m)
- Overall height: 24 ft 11 in (7·60 m)
- Wheel track: 13 ft 0 in (3·96 m)
- Wheelbase: 27 ft 0 in (8·23 m)

Dimensions, internal:
- Cabin: Length: 30 ft 0 in (9·14 m)
  - Max width: 7 ft 6 in (2·29 m)
  - Max height: 6 ft 6 in (1·98 m)

Areas:
- Main rotor disc: 4,070 sq ft (378·1 m²)
- Tail rotor disc: 201 sq ft (18·67 m²)

Weights:
- Weight empty:
  - CH-53A: 22,444 lb (10,180 kg)
  - HH-53B: 23,125 lb (10,490 kg)
  - HH-53C: 23,569 lb (10,690 kg)
  - CH-53D: 23,485 lb (10,653 kg)
- Normal T-O weight:
  - CH-53A: 35,000 lb (15,875 kg)
- Mission T-O weight:
  - HH-53B: 37,400 lb (16,964 kg)
  - HH-53C: 38,238 lb (17,344 kg)
  - CH-53D: 36,400 lb (16,510 kg)
- Max T-O weight:
  - HH-53B/C, CH-53D: 42,000 lb (19,050 kg)

Performance:
- Max level speed at S/L:
  - HH-53C, CH-53D: 170 knots (196 mph; 315 km/h)
  - HH-53B: 162 knots (186 mph; 299 km/h)
- Cruising speed:
  - HH-53B/C, CH-53D: 150 knots (173 mph; 278 km/h)
- Max rate of climb at S/L:
  - HH-53B: 1,440 ft (440 m)/min
  - HH-53C: 2,070 ft (631 m)/min
  - CH-53D: 2,180 ft (664 m)/min
- Service ceiling:
  - HH-53B: 18,400 ft (5,610 m)
  - HH-53C: 20,400 ft (6,220 m)
  - CH-53D: 21,000 ft (6,400 m)
- Hovering ceiling in ground effect:
  - HH-53B: 8,100 ft (2,470 m)
  - HH-53C: 11,700 ft (3,565 m)
  - CH-53D: 13,400 ft (4,080 m)
- Hovering ceiling out of ground effect:
  - HH-53B: 1,600 ft (490 m)
  - HH-53C: 4,300 ft (1,310 m)
  - CH-53D: 6,500 ft (1,980 m)
- Min ground turning radius: 44 ft 2 in (13·46 m)
- Runway LCN at max T-O weight: 7·1
- Range:
  - HH-53B/C, with 9,926 lb (4,502 kg) fuel (two 450 US gallon; 1,703 litre auxiliary tanks), which includes 10% reserve and 2 min warm-up: 468 nm (540 miles; 869 km)
  - CH-53D, with 4,076 lb (1,849 kg) fuel, 10% reserve at cruising speed and 2 min warm-up: 223 nm (257 miles; 413 km)

SIKORSKY YCH-53E

The Sikorsky S-65A was chosen in 1973 for development with a three-engined power plant to provide the US Navy and Marine Corps with a heavy-duty multi-purpose helicopter. Development was initiated with the award by the US Navy of a $1·7 million cost-plus-fixed-fee contract; in May 1973 Sikorsky announced that construction of two prototypes was to go ahead, with the objective of a first flight in April 1974. Bettering this by a month, the first of these two helicopters, with the designation YCH-53E, made a successful half-hour flight on 1 March 1974, during which low-altitude hovering and limited manoeuvres were carried out.

Currently the largest and most powerful helicopters built in the West, the two prototypes will be used for preliminary evaluation and testing under Phase I of the development programme. Phase II, contingent upon successful completion of Phase I, calls for the construction of a static test vehicle and two pre-production prototypes, embodying changes or modifications evolving from Phase I. It is unlikely that a production decision will be made before early 1976.

It is anticipated that the CH-53E will have double the lift capability of the CH-53A/Ds in service being able to carry a 16 ton external load over a radius of 50 nm (57·5 miles; 92·5 km) at sea level in air temperatures up to 90°F (32·2°C), or up to 18 tons over shorter distances. Other features of the new helicopter will include extended-range fuel tanks, flight refuelling capability, on-board all-weather navigation system, and an advanced automatic flight control system.

The US Navy plans to use the CH-53E for vertical on-board delivery operations, to support mobile construction battalions, and for the removal of battle-damaged aircraft from carrier decks. In amphibious operations, it would be able to airlift 93 per cent of a US Marine division's combat items, and would be able to retrieve 98 per cent of the Marine Corps' tactical aircraft without disassembly.

Type: Triple-turbine heavy-duty multi-purpose helicopter.

Rotor System and Transmission: Seven-blade main rotor with blades of titanium construction.

Titanium and steel main rotor head. Four-blade tail rotor mounted on pylon canted 20° to port. Rotor transmission rated at 13,500 shp for ten seconds, 11,570 shp for 30 minutes.

FUSELAGE: Conventional semi-monocoque structure of light alloy, steel and titanium.

TAIL SURFACE: Large span fixed tailplane on undersurface of fuselage, directly beneath tail rotor pylon.

LANDING GEAR: Retractable tricycle type, with twin wheels on each unit. Main units retract into the rear of sponsons on each side of fuselage.

POWER PLANT: Three 4,380 shp General Electric T64-GE-415 turboshaft engines.

ACCOMMODATION: Crew of three. Main cabin will accommodate up to 56 troops in a high density seating arrangement.

DIMENSIONS, EXTERNAL:

Main rotor diameter	79 ft 0 in (24·08 m)
Tail rotor diameter	20 ft 0 in (6·10 m)

PERFORMANCE (estimated):

Cruising speed 170 knots (196 mph; 315 km/h)

SIKORSKY S-65 (MCM)

US Navy designation: RH-53D

On 27 October 1970 the US Navy announced plans to establish helicopter mine countermeasures (MCM) squadrons. The first unit, Helicopter Mine Countermeasures Squadron 12 (HM-12), borrowed 15 CH-53As from the US Marine Corps, pending production of specially equipped helicopters. Details of the tow kits installed in these aircraft are given under the CH-53D entry.

Congress gave approval subsequently for the development of a new and more powerful version of the CH-53 for service with the Navy's mine countermeasures squadrons, and in February 1972 Sikorsky announced that the US Navy had awarded the company an advanced procurement authorisation for 30 helicopters under the designation RH-53D. Production began in October 1972, at a rate of two per month, under a programme extending to December 1973. The first RH-53D flew on 27 October 1972 and first deliveries were made to HM-12 in September 1973.

The RH-53D is designed to tow existing and future equipment evolved to sweep mechanical, acoustic and magnetic mines. That for mechananical and acoustic mines can be carried on board the aircraft, and deployed and retrieved in flight. Magnetic sweep equipment, too large to be carried internally by the helicopter, is first streamed behind a surface vessel and then transferred to the aircraft's tow hook. It can also be carried on the external cargo hook, and is lifted from ship to sea or shore to sea by this means. Basic design gross weight is increased to 42,000 lb (19,050 kg), mission gross weight is estimated at 41,500 lb (18,824 kg), and the alternate design gross weight is increased to 50,000 lb (22,680 kg). Space, weight and power provisions have been made for installation of a projected advanced navigation system and an approach and hover coupler.

The description of the CH-53A applies also to the RH-53D, except as detailed below:

ROTOR SYSTEM AND DRIVE: Generally similar to those of the CH-53A, but transmission uprated to 8,660 shp.

FUSELAGE: As for CH-53A, but heavier-gauge skins are used aft of the transmission area and heavier-gauge stringers around the landing gear.

LANDING GEAR: Stronger landing gear and brakes to cater for the increased gross weights.

POWER PLANT: Two General Electric T64-GE-413A turboshafts with a combined rating of 7,560 shp in early models; but it is planned to modify these engines to 4,380 shp T64-GE-415 standard by retrofit kits. Standard fuel tankage supplemented by two 500 US gallon (1,892 litre) external tanks. These are standard USAF 650 US gallon (2,460 litre) auxiliary fuel tanks, modified to reduced capacity for better roll control. Flight refuelling capability provided by an HH-53 nose-mounted refuelling probe. In addition, the RH-53D is equipped for ship-to-helicopter refuelling while airborne, with a sensing filter in the helicopter to cut off fuel flow if liquid or solid impurities are detected in the incoming fuel.

EQUIPMENT: Automatic flight control system interconnections to give automatic tow cable yaw angle retention, and aircraft attitude and heading hold. Indicator for tow cable tension and yaw angle, with automatic cable release if limits are exceeded. Nose-mounted adjustable rear-view mirrors for pilot and co-pilot. Dual hydraulically-powered winches for streaming tow. Tow system comprising a separate winch and hook, rated at 7,000 lb (3,175 kg) capacity. Towboom rated at 20,000 lb (9,071 kg) capacity with hook locked in retention jaw. External cargo hook capacity rated at 25,000 lb (11,340 kg). Stowage racks and cradles for Mk 103 mechanical and Mk 104 acoustic mine countermeasures gear. Can tow Mk 105 magnetic and Mk 106 magnetic/acoustic ship-based gear. Anti-exposure suit ventilation system for crew working in cabin. Variable-speed rescue hoist rated at 600 lb (272 kg) capacity.

ARMAMENT: Provision for two 0·50 in machine-guns to detonate surfaced mines.

WEIGHTS:

Normal T-O weight	42,000 lb (19,050 kg)
Mission T-O weight estimated	41,500 lb (18,824 kg)
Max T-O weight	50,000 lb (22,680 kg)

PERFORMANCE:

Min ground turning radius	44 ft 2 in (13·46 m)
Runway LCN at max T-O weight	8·0
Endurance	over 4 hr

SIKORSKY S-67 BLACKHAWK

On 22 September 1970, Sikorsky announced that a high-speed attack helicopter, designated S-67 Blackhawk, had completed successfully its initial flight trials.

Developed as a private venture, the Blackhawk is a twin-turbine helicopter, utilising proven components on a low-profile gunship fuselage. A number of new design features were introduced to provide high speed, manoeuvrability and versatility, some of these emanating from the S-66 concept that Sikorsky entered in the US Army's 1965 competition for an advanced aerial fire support system (AAFSS), as well as from design and flight experience with the S-61F compound helicopter. Design of the S-67 began in August 1969, construction of the prototype starting three months later. First flight was made on 20 August 1970.

The S-67 has a vertical fin, similar to that of a fixed-wing aircraft, which extends beneath the fuselage and serves also as a mounting for the non-retractable tailwheel. A controllable horizontal stabiliser is mounted at the rear of the long tapered fuselage; when set in a vertical position for hovering flight it reduces vertical drag considerably. In the normal flight position it helps reduce rotor stresses in manoeuvring flight, and allows the pilot to trim the fuselage independently of the rotor and to achieve better fuselage alignment with the target. A detachable fixed wing reduces main rotor loading as well as improving manoeuvrability and, for the first time on a helicopter, speed brakes in both upper and lower wing surfaces can be extended quickly to provide added control. These speed brakes are reported to increase the time on target by 30%, reduce the aircraft's turning radius, permit improved firing accuracy and provide a 38% steeper dive angle. The combined effect of these innovations is to produce a highly manoeuvrable steeper dive angle.

While the proven dynamic system of the Sikorsky S-61R was used in the S-67, this too underwent development to improve performance. The rotor head is faired to reduce parasitic drag, and the tips of the rotor blades are swept back to delay blade-tip stall at high speeds, improve the lift/drag ratio of the blades and reduce vibratory stresses. Specially designed air intakes also reduce drag at high speed.

The low-profile fuselage design of the Blackhawk not only serves to improve speed characteristics, but means that the gunship offers a more difficult target for an enemy's defensive armament. It presents a frontal flat-plate area of only 17 sq ft (1·58 m²) by comparison with that of the SH-3 Sea King which totals 32 sq ft (2·97 m²).

With a max normal take-off weight of around 22,000 lb (9,979 kg), the Blackhawk is in the same general weight class as the S-61 series, and can carry up to 8,000 lb (3,628 kg) of weapons and ammunition. Typical loads include wing-mounted rocket or TOW anti-tank missile pods and underfuselage and nose turrets housing either 7·62 mm multi-barrel Miniguns, 20 and 30 mm cannon or a 40 mm grenade launcher.

As a troop carrier, with modified cabin, it could transport up to 15 fully-armed troops in the upper section of a two-deck rear compartment, the lower section housing fuel and ammunition. In such a role it would have a range of up to 191 nm (220 miles; 354 km) at a speed of 143 knots (165 mph; 265 km/h).

When used as a long-range rescue helicopter, with auxiliary fuel tanks mounted on the wings, the S-67 could fly up to 521 nm (600 miles; 966 km) at high speed to recover as many as six persons.

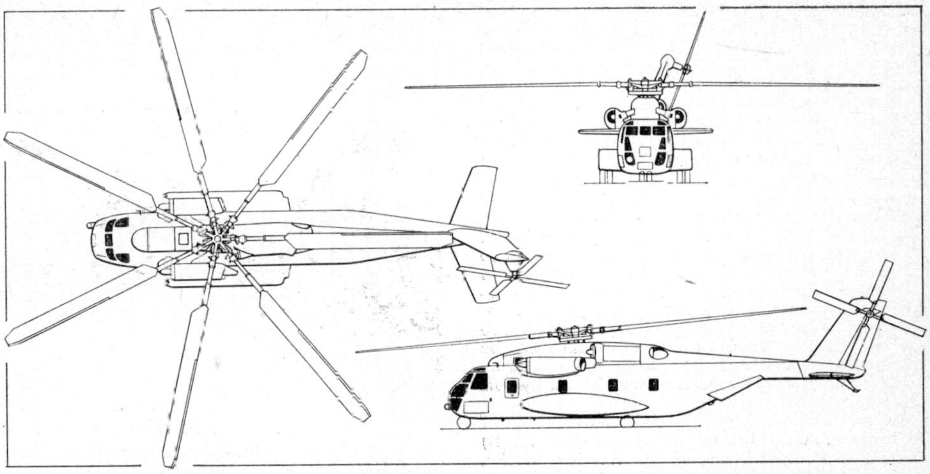

Sikorsky YCH-53E, the new three-turboshaft version of this heavy-duty helicopter *(Pilot Press)*

Sikorsky RH-53D minesweeping and multi-mission helicopter of the US Navy

Good payload characteristics mean that the Blackhawk could be used for observation or surveillance duties, equipped with sophisticated electronic devices to detect and record the emplacement and movement of enemy personnel and installations.

When carrying troops, or external loads of up to four tons, the Blackhawk would not need the fixed wings, which are easily detachable, since weight-lifting rather than manoeuvrability would be the basic requirement.

Construction of the S-67 was simplified by the use of spot-weld bonding of many structures. This involved clamping together the surfaces to be bonded, after spreading uncured adhesive on the mating faces. Spot-welding was then achieved by conventional variable-pressure-type electrodes, followed by curing at low temperature for one hour. This technique is said to be economical, faster and weight-saving, and some 10% of the S-67 airframe area was joined by this process.

On 14 December 1970, the S-67 set a record of 188·308 knots (216·844 mph; 348·971 km/h) over a 3 kilometre course at Windsor Locks, Connecticut, flown by company test pilot Byron Graham. Five days later, company pilot Kurt Cannon flew the S-67 around a 15/25 kilometre course to establish a record of 191·822 knots (220·885 mph; 355·485 km/h). Both flights were established as world speed records (under Class E1) by the FAI.

In February 1972 Sikorsky announced that following completion of 14 months of extensive flight testing the S-67 was to undergo a number of modifications to enhance its day/night attack and multi-mission capability. These included installation of a thermally and acoustically insulated troop compartment providing seats for six men, provision for mounting a removable single-point 8,000 lb (3,629 kg) capacity external cargo hook and addition of an integrated rudder to the cambered tail fin to increase yaw control at high speed.

In the Autumn of 1972 the S-67 made a two-month tour of Europe and the Middle East, covering more than 6,510 nm (7,500 miles; 12,070 km) in 136 flight hours.

Sikorsky received a $2·1 million two-year contract, awarded by the US Army, for a feasibility study of a ducted tail rotor concept. This involved the design and installation of a ducted variable-pitch fan, replacing the conventional tail rotor, to enhance directional control of the S-67 and reduce vulnerability to damage from contact with other objects. Installation of a new tail unit incorporating the ducted fan was completed in early 1974 and flight testing, which began in the Spring of 1974, was designed to determine whether the "fan-in-fin" concept can offer greater manoeuvrability. Speeds of up to 200 knots (230 mph; 370 km/h) were achieved in a dive.

TYPE: Twin-engined high-speed combat and multi-purpose helicopter.

ROTOR SYSTEM: Five-blade fully-articulated main rotor of all-metal construction. Blade section NACA 0012. Main rotor blades attached to Bifilar vibration absorbers. Blades do not fold. Rotor brake. Conventional tail rotor with five aluminium blades. A variable-pitch ducted directional control fan has been fitted experimentally in modified tail unit.

ROTOR DRIVE: Twin turbines drive through freewheeling units to main gearbox. Steel drive shafts. Tail rotor or fan shaft-driven through intermediate gearbox and tail gearbox. Main rotor/engine rpm ratio 1 : 0·01038. Tail rotor/engine rpm ratio 1 : 0·06359.

WINGS: Detachable wings of cantilever low-wing monoplane configuration. Wing section NACA 4415 at root, NACA 4412 at tip. Dihedral 10°. Incidence 8°. Conventional two-spar light alloy structure. Hydraulically-actuated light alloy speed-brakes.

FUSELAGE: All-metal semi-monocoque low-profile fail-safe structure.

TAIL UNIT: All-metal structure. Swept upper and lower fins. Upper section houses tail rotor drive and serves also as mounting for the tail rotor. Alternatively, variable-pitch ducted fan mounted in trailing-edge of fin. Lower fin projects beneath fuselage and acts as mounting for the non-retractable tailwheel. All-moving horizontal stabiliser, integrated with cyclic control, which can be set in a vertical position in hovering flight.

LANDING GEAR: Tailwheel type, consisting of two twin-wheel main units, which retract rearward hydraulically, and a non-retractable tailwheel. Pneumatic system for emergency extension of main units. Oleo-pneumatic shock-absorbers. Main units fitted with wheels and tyres size 18 × 5·50 Type VII, pressure 145 lb/sq in (10·2 kg/cm²). Castoring and lockable tailwheel has single wheel and tyre size 5·00-5 Type III, pressure 110 lb/sq in (7·7 kg/cm²). Goodyear hydraulically-operated disc brakes.

POWER PLANT: Two 1,500 shp General Electric T58-GE-5 turboshaft engines, mounted side by side above cabin, immediately forward of main transmission. More powerful General Electric T58-GE-16, Lycoming PLT-27 or Army advanced technology engines could be used alternatively to improve performance. Fuel contained in two internal tanks each of 200 US gallons (756·5 litres); total capacity 400 US gallons (1,513 litres). Two 200 US gallon (756·5 litre), 300 US gallon (1,134 litre) or 450 US gallon (1,701 litre) tanks can be carried externally on wing hardpoints. In-flight refuelling installation optional. Oil capacity 5 US gallons (18·5 litres).

Sikorsky S-67 fitted experimentally with a ducted variable-pitch tail fan

Sikorsky S-67 Blackhawk fitted with two dummy Sidewinder air-to-air missiles, 16 TOW anti-tank missiles and a belly-mounted 20 mm cannon

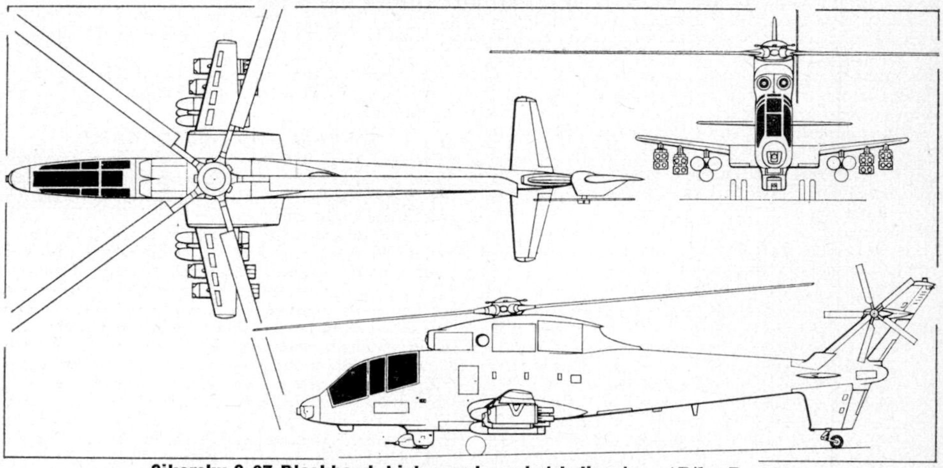

Sikorsky S-67 Blackhawk high-speed combat helicopter (*Pilot Press*)

ACCOMMODATION: Pilot and co-pilot/gunner seated in tandem beneath a single transparent canopy in the nose of the aircraft. Crew access to cabin via two hatches. Two emergency escape hatches. Cabin heated or cooled. Cooling air can be directed through avionics and weapons compartments.

SYSTEMS: Hamilton Standard air-conditioning system supplied with engine bleed air, under control of environmental control unit. Dual hydraulic systems for flight controls, pressure 1,500 lb/sq in (105 kg/cm²). Utility hydraulic system at pressure of 3,000 lb/sq in (210 kg/cm²). Air bottle for emergency extension of landing gear. Electrical system supplied by two 20kVA generators.

ELECTRONICS AND EQUIPMENT: Provision for night vision and radar equipment, and for a wide variety of navigation and communications equipment. Blind-flying instrumentation standard. Rescue version has hoist and enlarged doors.

ARMAMENT: TAT 140 gun turret, housing XM-140 30 mm cannon, XM-188 30 mm cannon, XM-197 20 mm cannon or M61-A2 20 mm cannon, or 40 mm grenade launcher. Sixteen TOW missiles or eight 19-round 2·75 in rocket launchers can be carried on four underwing racks.

DIMENSIONS, EXTERNAL:

Diameter of main rotor	62 ft 0 in (18·90 m)
Main rotor blade chord	18·25 in (46·35 cm)
Diameter of tail rotor	10 ft 4 in (3·15 m)
Diameter of ducted fan (experimental)	4 ft 0¾ in (1·24 m)
Distance between rotor centres	37 ft 0 in (11·28 m)
Wing span	27 ft 4 in (8·33 m)
Wing aspect ratio	8
Wing chord at root	4 ft 6 in (1·37 m)
Wing chord at tip	2 ft 0 in (0·61 m)
Length overall	74 ft 4 in (22·66 m)
Length of fuselage	64 ft 9 in (19·74 m)
Height to top of rotor hub	15 ft 0 in (4·57 m)

Height overall (rotors turning) 18 ft 0 in (5·49 m)
Wheel track 7 ft 0 in (2·13 m)
Wheelbase 36 ft $2\frac{1}{2}$ in (11·04 m)

AREAS:
Main rotor blades (each) 40·4 sq ft (3·75 m^2)
Tail rotor blades (each) 3·2 sq ft (0·30 m^2)
Main rotor disc 3,020 sq ft (281 m^2)
Tail rotor disc 84 sq ft (7·8 m^2)
Speed-brakes (total) 14 sq ft (1·30 m^2)
Fin 69 sq ft (6·4 m^2)
Horizontal stabiliser 50 sq ft (4·65 m^2)

WEIGHTS:
Weight empty 12,514 lb (5,676 kg)
Basic operating weight (including crew and 45 min fuel) 14,000 lb (6,350 kg)
Max T-O weight 22,050 lb (10,002 kg)

PERFORMANCE (at 18,500 lb; 8,391 kg AUW, no external load, S/L, ISA):
Max diving speed 200 knots (230 mph; 370 km/h)
Max level speed 168 knots (193 mph; 310 km/h)
Max cruising speed 162 knots (187 mph; 301 km/h)
Econ cruising speed 120 knots (138 mph; 222 km/h)
Max rate of climb at S/L 2,350 ft (716 m)/min
Service ceiling 17,000 ft (5,180 m)
Service ceiling, one engine out 4,500 ft (1,370 m)
Endurance, with payload of 1,500 lb (680 kg) 3·0 hr

SIKORSKY S-69

US Army designation: XH-59A

On 7 February 1972 Sikorsky announced that the company was designing and building a research aircraft, designated S-69, to flight test the Advancing Blade Concept (ABC) rotor system, under a $9·9 million contract awarded by the Eustis Directorate, US Army Air Mobility Research and Development Laboratory, Fort Eustis, Virginia. Since that time the contract has been increased to a figure of $14·2 million, to cover detail changes of the original design and the construction of two prototypes.

The ABC rotor system, consisting of two co-axial counter-rotating rigid rotors, takes advantage of the blades' aerodynamic lift on the advancing side of each rotor disc, and full lift capability of the advancing blade is achieved without penalty imposed by the retreating blade. This removes the need for a wing to supplement the rotor. Another advantage of the concept is the elimination of a conventional anti-torque tail rotor and its drive system.

The purpose of this programme is to evaluate the performance of the ABC system in flight, following successful full-scale wind tunnel tests of a 40 ft (12·2 m) diameter rotor at NASA's Ames Research Center. The first prototype made its first flight on 26 July 1973, as a pure helicopter. The second will have two additional Pratt & Whitney J60 turbojet engines for auxiliary forward thrust in a high-speed compound helicopter configuration. Speed objective for the pure helicopter configuration is 170 knots (196 mph; 315 km/h) with a 2·5*g* load factor. With turbojet auxiliary propulsion, design speed is 300 knots (345 mph; 555 km/h) at a 2*g* load factor.

TYPE: Two-seat research helicopter.

ROTOR SYSTEM: Two contra-rotating three-blade main rotors mounted co-axially. No tail rotor.

FUSELAGE: All-metal semi-monocoque structure of circular cross-section.

TAIL UNIT: Cantilever all-metal structure of conventional fixed-wing aircraft type. Twin endplate fins and rudders.

LANDING GEAR: Retractable tricycle type, with dual wheels on nose unit and single wheels on main units. Nosewheels retract aft into fuselage nose, main wheels inward into fuselage.

POWER PLANT: Initially, United Aircraft of Canada PT6T-3 Turbo Twin Pac mounted within the fuselage. Provision for later installation of two Pratt & Whitney J60 turbojet engines in pod on each side of the fuselage.

ACCOMMODATION: Crew of two on flight deck, with door on each side. Fuselage access door on port side of fuselage, aft of flight deck.

DIMENSIONS, EXTERNAL:
Diameter of rotors (each) 36 ft 0 in (10·97 m)
Length overall, rotors fore and aft 41 ft 5 in (12·62 m)
Length of fuselage 40 ft 9 in (12·42 m)
Height over fin 12 ft 11 in (3·94 m)
Tailplane span 15 ft 6 in (4·72 m)
Wheel track 8 ft 0 in (2·44 m)

SIKORSKY S-70

US Army designation: YUH-60A

At the end of August 1972, the US Army selected Sikorsky and Boeing Vertol (which see) as competitors to build three prototypes each, plus one ground test vehicle, of their submissions for the Utility Tactical Transport Aircraft System (UTTAS) requirement. Sikorsky's $61 million contract has an option for the purchase of six prototypes and called for flight trials to begin in November 1974. However, it was reported in the Spring of 1974 that prototype construction was so far advanced that a first flight in September, two months ahead of schedule, was a distinct possibility. The fly-off evaluation against Boeing Vertol's YUH-61A prototype is scheduled to begin in 1976.

The YUH-60A has a single main rotor, canted tail rotor, twin turbine engines, and is of compact design, so that one helicopter could be carried over long range in a C-130 transport, or as many as six in a C-5A.

Sikorsky is also building the prototype of a commercial helicopter with the designation S-70, which is based on the UTTAS design and incorporates many of the same advanced design features. For details see Addenda.

TYPE: Twin-turbine utility transport helicopter.

ROTOR SYSTEM: Four-blade main rotor. Rotor blades have titanium spars, glassfibre skins, swept blade tips. Blades pressurised and equipped with gauges providing fail-safe confirmation of blade structural integrity. Elastomeric rotor hub bearings require no lubrication, reduce hub maintenance by 60%. Bifilar vibration absorbers on rotor head. Canted tail rotor (to port) increases vertical lift and allows greater CG travel. "Cross beam" four-blade tail rotor of composite materials, eliminating all rotor head bearings.

ROTOR DRIVE: Conventional transmission system with both turbines driving through freewheeling units to main gearbox. This is of modular construction to simplify maintenance. Intermediate and tail rotor gearboxes are grease-packed, reducing both vulnerability and maintenance.

FUSELAGE: Conventional semi-monocoque light alloy structure.

TAIL UNIT: Pylon structure with port-canted tail rotor. Large fixed tailplane, which serves also to keep troops clear of tail rotor.

LANDING GEAR: Non-retractable tailwheel type with single wheel on each unit. Tailwheel gives

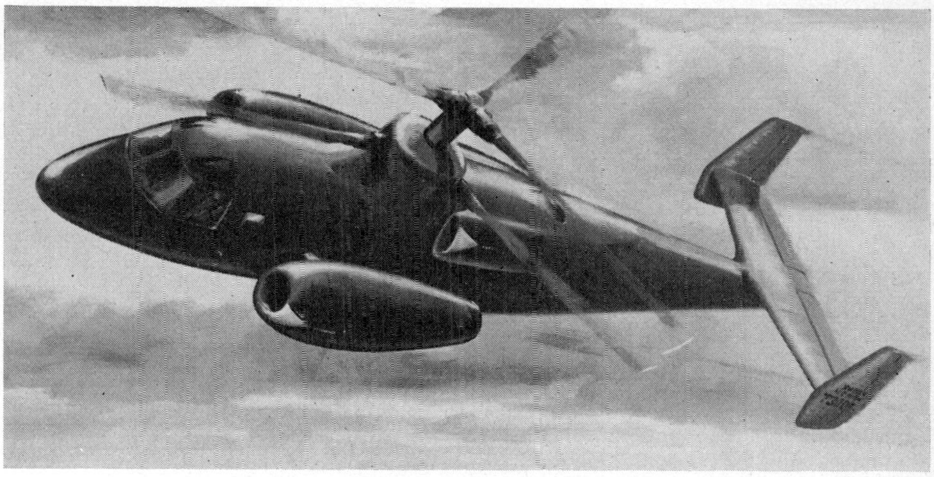

Artist's impression of Sikorsky's S-69 (XH-59A) research helicopter

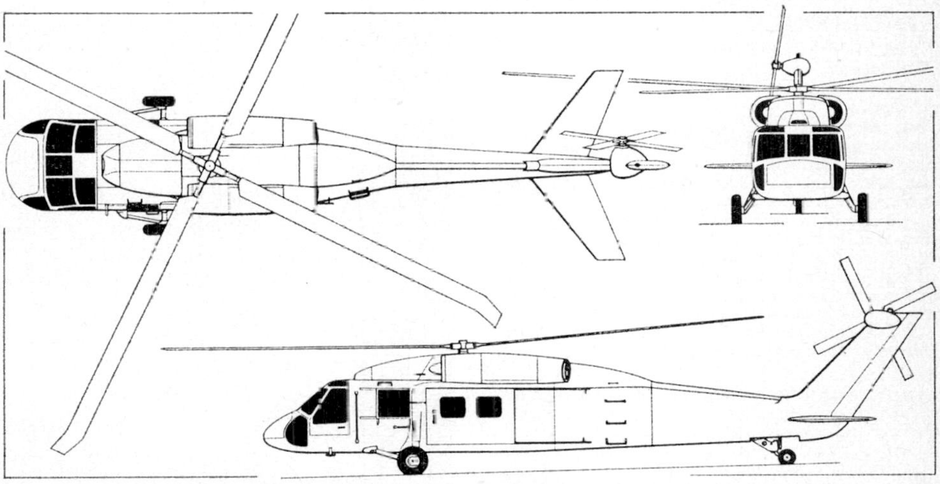

Sikorsky YUH-60A Utility Tactical Transport Aircraft System (UTTAS) (*Pilot Press*)

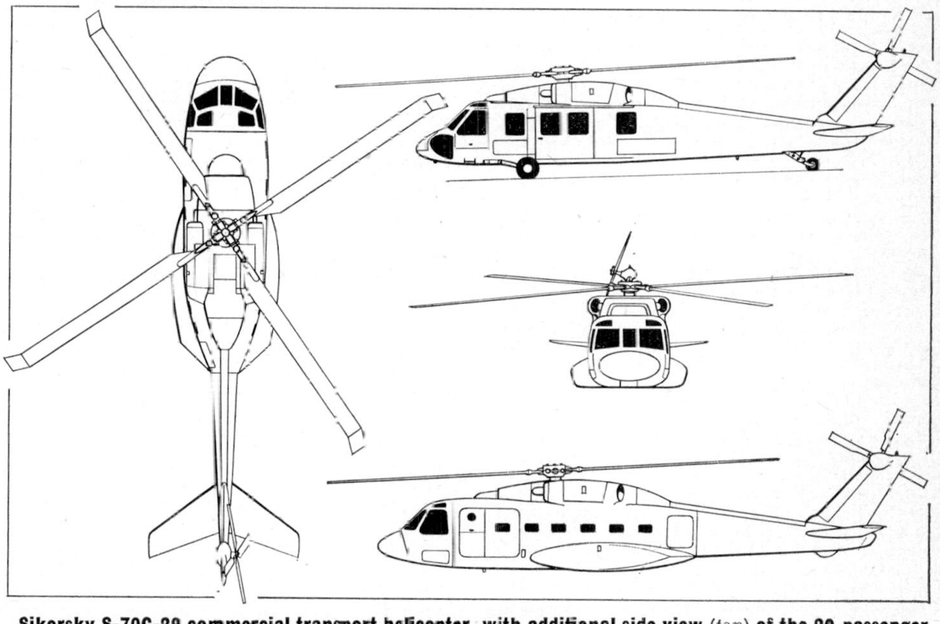

Sikorsky S-70C-29 commercial transport helicopter, with additional side view (*top*) of the 20-passenger S-70C-20. For details see Addenda (*Pilot Press*)

Prototype Sikorsky YUH-60A utility transport helicopter (two 1,500 shp General Electric T700-GE-700 turboshaft engines)

protection for the tail rotor in taxying over rough terrain or during a high-flare landing.

POWER PLANT: Two 1,500 shp General Electric T700-GE-700 advanced technology turboshaft engines.

ACCOMMODATION: Pilot and co-pilot on armour protected seats. Main cabin area open to cockpit to provide good communication with flight crew and forward visibility for squad commander. Accommodation for 11 troops and crew of three. Eight troop seats can be removed and replaced by four litters for medivac missions, or to make room for internal cargo. An external cargo hook will have a 7,000 lb (3,175 kg) lift capability. Large aft-sliding door on each side of fuselage for rapid entry and exit.

ARMAMENT: Provision for side-firing machine-gun in forward area of cabin.

DIMENSION, EXTERNAL:
Main rotor diameter 53 ft 0 in (16·15 m)

WEIGHT:
Max T-O weight 22,000 lb (9,979 kg)

PERFORMANCE:
Cruising speed 160 knots (184 mph; 296 km/h)

SINDLINGER

FRED G. SINDLINGER

ADDRESS:
5923 9th Street NW, Puyallup, Washington 98371

Mr Sindlinger began the design of a $\frac{5}{8}$-scale replica of the second World War Hawker Hurricane IIC fighter in April 1969. Construction of the prototype was started three months later. First flight was made in January 1972 and FAA certification in the Experimental category was awarded in May 1972. By early February 1973, Mr Sindlinger's Hurricane had accumulated a total of approximately 160 flying hours, and a full stress analysis of the aircraft had been completed. Plans were made available to amateur constructors in September 1973; by January 1974 twelve sets had been sold and five aircraft were under construction.

Sindlinger $\frac{5}{8}$-scale replica of a Hawker Hurricane IIC (150 hp Lycoming O-320 engine)

SINDLINGER HH-1 HAWKER HURRICANE

TYPE: Homebuilt single-seat sporting aircraft.

WINGS: Cantilever low-wing monoplane. Wing section NACA 2418 in centre-section, with progressive change to NACA 2412 at tip. Dihedral 3° 30′ on outer panels only. Incidence 0° 36′. Sweepback at quarter-chord 3°. Two-spar structure of wood. Front spar is of I-beam construction in the centre-section and of built-up box section in the outer panels. Rear spar is an I-beam in the centre-section, and of U-channel form in the outer panels. Built-up truss ribs and $\frac{3}{32}$ in plywood skin, fabric-covered overall. Frise-type ailerons of wood construction, fabric-covered and statically balanced. Split trailing-edge flaps of wood.

FUSELAGE: All-wood monocoque structure of $\frac{1}{8}$ in plywood from firewall to aft of cockpit. Rear fuselage is a built-up box truss frame, with formers and stringers. Entire structure fabric-covered.

TAIL UNIT: All-wood cantilever structure. Two-spar tailplane and fin have plywood skins, covered with fabric overall. Rudder and elevators are of wood construction with fabric covering. Elevator trimmed by internal spring tension. Ground-adjustable trim tab on rudder.

LANDING GEAR: Manually-retractable tailwheel type. Main wheels retract inward. Shock-absorption of main and tail units by coil spring inside steel tubes. Tailwheel steerable. Goodyear main wheels and tyres size 5·00-5. Goodyear hydraulic brakes.

POWER PLANT: One 150 hp Lycoming O-320 four-cylinder horizontally-opposed aircooled engine, driving a Hartzell two-blade metal constant-speed propeller with spinner. Three fuel tanks: one in fuselage aft of firewall with capacity of 14 US gallons (54 litres), and one in each wing root, with capacity of 8 US gallons (30 litres) each. Total fuel capacity 30 US gallons (114 litres). Refuelling point in fuselage upper surface, forward of windscreen. Oil capacity 2 US gallons (7·5 litres). Glassfibre engine cowlings.

ACCOMMODATION: Pilot only, beneath rearward-sliding transparent canopy. Cockpit heated and ventilated. Space for 40 lb (18 kg) baggage aft of pilot's seat.

SYSTEMS: Hydraulic system for brakes only. Electrical system powered by 12V DC engine-driven generator. 12V 35Ah battery.

ELECTRONICS AND EQUIPMENT: 90-channel VHF com transceiver, VOR Omni nav receiver. Partial IFR instrumentation. Wooden imitation cannon in wing leading-edges.

DIMENSIONS, EXTERNAL:
Wing span 25 ft 0 in (7·62 m)
Wing chord on centre-section (constant) 5 ft 0 in (1·52 m)
Wing chord at tip 3 ft 0 in (0·91 m)
Wing aspect ratio 6·2
Length overall 19 ft 8 in (5·99 m)
Height overall 5 ft 10 in (1·78 m)
Tailplane span 7 ft 4 in (2·24 m)
Wheel track 6 ft 0 in (1·83 m)
Propeller diameter 6 ft 4 in (1·93 m)
Propeller ground clearance 11 in (0·28 m)

DIMENSIONS, INTERNAL:
Cockpit:
Max width 2 ft 2 in (0·66 m)
Max height 3 ft 9 in (1·14 m)

AREAS:
Wings, gross 101 sq ft (9·38 m²)
Trailing-edge flaps (total) 9 sq ft (0·84 m²)
Vertical tail surfaces (total) 8·3 sq ft (0·77 m²)
Horizontal tail surfaces (total) 18·0 sq ft (1·67 m²)

WEIGHTS AND LOADINGS:
Weight empty 1,005 lb (456 kg)
Max T-O weight 1,375 lb (624 kg)
Max wing loading 13·6 lb/sq ft (66·4 kg/m²)
Max power loading 9·2 lb/hp (4·2 kg/hp)

PERFORMANCE (at max T-O weight):
Max never-exceed speed 208 knots (240 mph; 386 km/h)
Max level speed at S/L 174 knots (200 mph; 322 km/h)
Max cruising speed, 65% power at 6,000 ft (1,830 m) 143 knots (165 mph; 265 km/h)
Econ cruising speed, 60% power at 9,000 ft (2,745 m) 135 knots (155 mph; 249 km/h)
Stalling speed, flaps up 58 knots (67 mph; 108 km/h)
Stalling speed, flaps down 54 knots (62 mph; 100 km/h)
Max rate of climb at S/L 1,350 ft (411 m)/min
T-O run 350 ft (107 m)
Landing run 550 ft (168 m)
Range, 55% power at 7,500 ft (2,285 m), 30 min reserve 477 nm (550 miles; 885 km)
Max range, no reserve fuel 542 nm (625 miles; 1,005 km)

SMITH

MRS FRANK W. (DOROTHY) SMITH

ADDRESS:

1938, Jacaranda Place, Fullerton, California 92633

The late Frank W. Smith built and flew in October 1956 the prototype of a single-seat fully-aerobatic sporting biplane which he designated the DSA-1 (Darn Small Aeroplane) Miniplane. Plans of this aircraft are marketed by Mrs Smith and there are more than 158 Miniplanes flying.

Mrs Smith's son has designed a two-seat version of the DSA-1, provisionally designated "Miniplane + 1".

SMITH DSA-1 MINIPLANE

The Smith Miniplane shown in the adjacent illustration is typical of the large number of amateur-built aircraft of this type now flying. Others, incorporating various design modifications, have been illustrated in previous editions of *Jane's*.

The following details refer to the standard Miniplane, built according to Frank Smith's original plans:

TYPE: Single-seat sporting biplane.

WINGS: Braced biplane with N-type interplane struts each side and two N-type strut assemblies supporting centre of top wing above fuselage. NACA 4412 wing section. Dihedral 2° on lower wings only. Incidence 0° on top wing, 2° on lower wings. All-wood structure, fabric-covered. Fabric-covered wooden ailerons on lower wings only. No flaps.

FUSELAGE: Welded steel tube structure, fabric-covered.

TAIL UNIT: Wire-braced welded steel tube structure, fabric-covered. Adjustable-incidence tailplane.

LANDING GEAR: Non-retractable tailwheel type. Tripod streamlined-tube main legs. Compression-spring shock-absorbers optional (now fitted on prototype). Goodyear main wheels and tyres, size 7·00-4, pressure 20 lb/sq in (1·41 kg/cm²). Goodyear shoe-type brakes. Scott tailwheel.

POWER PLANT: Designed to take any engine in 65-125 hp category. Prototype has 108 hp Lycoming O-235-C four-cylinder horizontally-opposed aircooled engine, driving a Sensenich two-blade metal fixed-pitch propeller. Most aircraft have a 65 hp Continental A65, 75 hp Continental A75 or 125 hp Lycoming four-cylinder horizontally-opposed aircooled engine. Fuel in tank in fuselage, capacity 17 US gallons (64·5 litres). Oil capacity 1·5 US gallons (5·7 litres).

ACCOMMODATION: Single seat in open cockpit. Space for 60 lb (27 kg) baggage.

DIMENSIONS, EXTERNAL:
- Span (upper wing) 17 ft 0 in (5·18 m)
- Span (lower wing) 15 ft 9 in (4·80 m)
- Wing chord, constant (both) 3 ft 0 in (0·91 m)
- Length overall 15 ft 3 in (4·65 m)
- Height overall 5 ft 0 in (1·52 m)
- Wheel track 5 ft 0 in (1·52 m)
- Propeller diameter 5 ft 11 in (1·80 m)

AREAS:
- Wings, gross 100 sq ft (9·29 m²)
- Ailerons (total) 10 sq ft (0·93 m²)
- Fin 3·02 sq ft (0·28 m²)
- Rudder 3·89 sq ft (0·36 m²)
- Tailplane 8·22 sq ft (0·76 m²)
- Elevators 4·86 sq ft (0·45 m²)

WEIGHTS AND LOADING (prototype):
- Weight empty, equipped 616 lb (279 kg)
- Max T-O weight 1,000 lb (454 kg)
- Max wing loading 10 lb/sq ft (48·8 kg/m²)

PERFORMANCE (prototype, at max T-O weight):
- Max level speed at S/L 117 knots (135 mph; 217 km/h)
- Max cruising speed 102 knots (118 mph; 190 km/h)
- Econ cruising speed 96 knots (110 mph; 177 km/h)
- Stalling speed 48 knots (55 mph; 88·5 km/h)
- Max rate of climb at S/L 1,250 ft (380 m)/min
- Service ceiling 13,000 ft (3,960 m)
- T-O run 350 ft (107 m)
- Landing run 500 ft (152 m)
- Endurance with max fuel 2 hr 30 min

SMITH MINIPLANE + 1

Mr Donald Smith has designed and is building a two-seat version of the DSA-1 Miniplane.

WINGS: Braced biplane with conventional forward stagger. N71 wing section. Dihedral 2° on lower wings only. Incidence 3° on lower wings only. All-wood structure with spruce spars and built-up spruce capstrip ribs, fabric-covered. Ailerons on lower wings only, of wood construction, fabric-covered.

FUSELAGE: Welded steel tube structure, fabric-covered.

TAIL UNIT: Wire-braced welded steel tube structure, fabric-covered.

LANDING GEAR: Non-retractable tailwheel type. Tripod streamlined-tube main legs. Rubber bungee shock-absorbers. Cleveland main wheels and tyres, size 6·00-6. Cleveland wheel brakes.

POWER PLANT: Designed to take engines in the 100-160 hp category. Prototype will have 125 hp Lycoming four-cylinder horizontally-opposed aircooled engine, driving a two-blade fixed-pitch propeller. Fuel tank immediately aft of firewall, capacity 28 US gallons (106 litres). Refuelling point on fuselage upper surface, forward of windscreen.

ACCOMMODATION: Two seats in tandem in open cockpit.

DIMENSIONS, EXTERNAL:
- Span (upper wing) 22 ft 8 in (6·91 m)
- Wing chord, constant (both) 3 ft 10 in (1·67 m)
- Length overall 17 ft 9 in (5·41 m)
- Height overall 6 ft 6 in (1·98 m)
- Wheel track 5 ft 6 in (1·68 m)

AREAS:
- Wings, gross 165 sq ft (15·3 m²)
- Ailerons (total) 12·0 sq ft (1·11 m²)
- Fin 4·75 sq ft (0·44 m²)
- Rudder 5·75 sq ft (0·53 m²)
- Tailplane 11·5 sq ft (1·07 m²)
- Elevators 7·25 sq ft (0·67 m²)

WEIGHTS AND LOADINGS:
- Weight empty approx 696 lb (315 kg)
- Max T-O weight 1,450 lb (657 kg)
- Max wing loading 8·78 lb/sq ft (42·9 kg/m²)
- Max power loading 11·6 lb/hp (5·26 kg/hp)

PERFORMANCE (estimated, at max T-O weight):
- Max level speed at S/L 96 knots (110 mph; 177 km/h)
- Landing speed 48-52 knots (55-60 mph; 88·5-96·5 km/h)
- Range 312 nm (360 miles; 579 km)
- Endurance more than 3 hours

Smith DSA-1 Miniplane built by Mr L. A. Chenowath

SMITH

TED R. SMITH AND ASSOCIATES INC

ADDRESS:

2560 Skyway Drive, Santa Maria, California 93454

In 1967 limited production began of the first two of a projected series of small business aircraft, known as Aerostars, designed by Ted Smith Aircraft Company, a subsidiary of the American Cement Corporation. The entire assets of the former company were acquired by Butler Aviation International on 16 February 1970. Production of Aerostars was subsequently suspended; but during 1972 Ted R. Smith and Associates Inc was formed and re-acquired from Butler Aviation all existing airframe components. This enabled the new company to resume production of the original Models 600 and 601 Aerostars, as well as a pressurised Model 601P for which Ted R. Smith and Associates gained certification in 1972.

The company has also designed a new, slightly larger and more powerful version of the Model 600, designated Aerostar 700, and this is described separately. Development of an Aerostar 1000 is projected for 1975. This is envisaged as a "stretched" nine-seat version of the Model 700, with either 450 hp Lycoming TIGO-541 or 435 hp Continental GTSIO-520 engines. It is planned to follow this with a transcontinental-range Aerostar 3000, powered by two Turboméca Astafan IV turbofan engines of 2,250 lb (1,020 kg) st.

SMITH AEROSTAR 600/601/601P

Design work on this series began in November 1964 and the first Model 600/601 prototype made its first flight in October 1967. FAA type approval of the Model 600 was awarded in March 1968, and of the Model 601 in November 1968.

It is claimed that the Aerostar airframe contains only 50% as many components as are used in other designs of comparable size. Construction involves extensive use of monocoque assemblies, in which unstiffened sections of heavy-gauge skin carry loads. The horizontal and vertical fixed tail surfaces, together with their related control surfaces, are interchangeable.

Smith Aerostar 601P light transport (two 290 hp turbocharged Lycoming IO-540 engines) (*Brian M. Service*)

Current production versions of the Aerostar comprise:

Model 600. Powered by two 290 hp Lycoming IO-540 six-cylinder horizontally-opposed normally-aspirated aircooled engines.

Model 601. As Model 600, but powered by two 290 hp Lycoming IO-540 turbocharged engines.

Model 601P. As Model 601, but with higher flow-rate turbochargers to supply bleed air for cabin pressurisation.

The production programme for 1974 called for the construction of 70 aircraft, of which approximately 25 would be Model 601Ps.

TYPE: Twin-engined light transport aircraft.

WINGS: Cantilever mid-wing monoplane. Wing section NACA 64,A212. Dihedral 2°. Incidence 1°. No sweepback. All-metal structure using heavy gauge skins attached to three spars, several bulkheads and stringers. Entire wing assembly, excluding attachments for ailerons and flaps, contains fewer than 50 detail parts. Ailerons and flaps each comprise a spar, ribs, nose skin and one-piece wraparound light alloy skin aft of spar. No trim tabs.

FUSELAGE: All-metal fail-safe monocoque structure. Skin composed of large segments of light alloy sheet over stringers and frames. Entire fuselage contains fewer than 100 parts, including skin panels. All fuselage assemblies designed basically for pressurisation.

TAIL UNIT: Cantilever all-metal structure, with swept vertical and horizontal surfaces. Both fixed and control surfaces are interchangeable. Electrically-operated trim tab in rudder and each elevator.

LANDING GEAR: Hydraulically-retractable tricycle type. Main units retract inward, nosewheel forward. Steerable nosewheel. Hydraulically-operated dual caliper brakes.

POWER PLANT: Two Lycoming engines, as detailed in model listings, each driving a Hartzell three-blade metal constant-speed and fully-feathering propeller with spinner. Fuel in integral wing tanks and fuselage tank with total capacity of 177 US gallons (669 litres), of which 170 US gallons (643 litres) are usable.

ACCOMMODATION: Cabin seats six people on track-mounted individual reclining seats, in pairs. Door on port side by pilot's seat; top half hinges upward, bottom half downward. Emergency escape windows at rear of cabin. Tinted windscreen and cabin windows. Large utility shelf in aft cabin. Baggage compartment, capacity 240 lb (109 kg), aft of cabin, with external access. Individual air vents and reading lights for each seat. Cabin air-conditioned in 600/601, and also pressurised in 601P.

SYSTEMS: Air-conditioning system includes a Janitrol 30,000 BTU heater (35,000 BTU in Model 601). Electrical system powered by two 28V 50A engine-driven alternators. Two 12V 24Ah batteries. Pressurisation system for Model 601P supplied by engine bleed air; pressure differential 4·2 lb/sq in (0·30 kg/cm^2). Hydraulic system for landing gear actuation, wheel brakes and flaps, powered by an engine-driven pump, pressure 1,000 lb/sq in (70·3 kg/cm^2). Models 601 and 601P each have an oxygen system, with individual outlets at each seat, as standard. Dual pneumatic systems for instrument gyros and de-icing boots.

ELECTRONICS AND EQUIPMENT: An extensive range of standard and optional avionics equipment is available to customer's requirements. Standard equipment includes dual controls; full blind-flying instrumentation; external power socket; two rotating beacons; navigation, landing, taxi and instrument panel lights; and heated pitot.

DIMENSIONS, EXTERNAL:
- Wing span: 34 ft 2½ in (10·43 m)
- Wing chord at root: 7 ft 2 in (2·18 m)
- Wing chord at tip: 2 ft 10⅜ in (0·87 m)
- Wing aspect ratio: 6·83
- Length overall: 34 ft 9¾ in (10·61 m)
- Height overall: 12 ft 1½ in (3·70 m)
- Tailplane span: 14 ft 4 in (4·37 m)
- Wheel track: 10 ft 2½ in (3·11 m)
- Propeller diameter: 6 ft 6 in (1·98 m)
- Passenger door:
  - Height: 3 ft 9 in (1·14 m)
  - Width: 2 ft 4 in (0·71 m)
- Baggage compartment door:
  - Height: 2 ft 0 in (0·61 m)
  - Width: 1 ft 10 in (0·56 m)

DIMENSIONS, INTERNAL:
- Cabin: Length: 12 ft 6 in (3·81 m)
  - Width: 3 ft 10 in (1·17 m)
  - Height: 4 ft 0 in (1·22 m)
- Baggage space: 30 cu ft (0·85 m^3)

AREAS:
- Wings, gross: 170 sq ft (15·8 m^2)
- Tailplane: 45·2 sq ft (4·20 m^2)

WEIGHTS AND LOADINGS:
- Weight empty, equipped:
  - 600: 3,667 lb (1,663 kg)
  - 601: 3,837 lb (1,740 kg)
  - 601P: 3,927 lb (1,781 kg)
- Max T-O and landing weight:
  - 600: 5,500 lb (2,495 kg)
  - 601, 601P*: 5,700 lb (2,585 kg)

**Programme in progress to increase AUW of 601P to 5,900 lb (2,676 kg)*

- Max wing loading:
  - 600: 32·3 lb/sq ft (157·7 kg/m^2)
  - 601: 33·5 lb/sq ft (163·6 kg/m^2)
  - 601P: 35·3 lb/sq ft (172·3 kg/m^2)
- Max power loading:
  - 600: 9·5 lb/hp (4·30 kg/hp)
  - 601: 9·8 lb/hp (4·45 kg/hp)
  - 601P: 9·7 lb/hp (4·40 kg/hp)

PERFORMANCE (at max T-O weight):
- Max level speed:
  - all versions at S/L: 226 knots (260 mph; 418 km/h)
  - 601 at 25,000 ft (7,620 m): 271 knots (312 mph; 502 km/h)
  - 601P at 20,000 ft (6,100 m): 261 knots (301 mph; 484 km/h)
- Cruising speed:
  - 600, 70% power at 10,000 ft (3,050 m): 217 knots (250 mph; 402 km/h)
  - 600, 55% power at 10,000 ft (3,050 m): 194 knots (223 mph; 359 km/h)
  - 601, 601P, 75% power at 25,000 ft (7,620 m): 255 knots (294 mph; 473 km/h)
  - 601, 601P, 55% power at 25,000 ft (7,620 m): 218 knots (251 mph; 404 km/h)

Smith Aerostar 700 prototype (two 350 hp Lycoming IO-540-M engines) *(Howard Levy)*

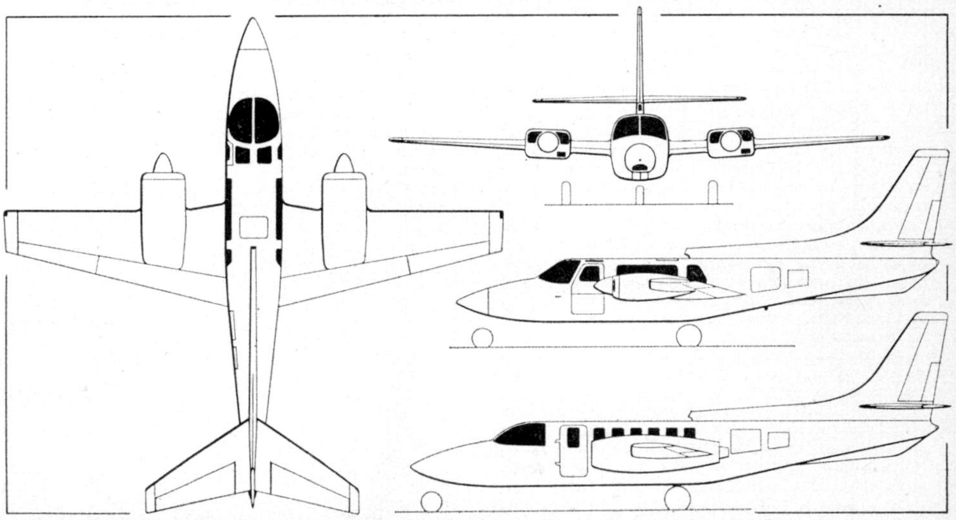

Smith Aerostar 700, with additional side view *(bottom)* **of the projected Aerostar 3000** *(Pilot Press)*

- Stalling speed, wheels and flaps down:
  - 600: 67 knots (77 mph; 124 km/h)
  - 601: 69 knots (79 mph; 128 km/h)
  - 601P: 70 knots (81 mph; 131 km/h)
- Max rate of climb at S/L:
  - 600: 1,850 ft (564 m)/min
  - 601, 601P: 1,800 ft (549 m)/min
- Rate of climb at S/L, one engine out:
  - 600: 450 ft (137 m)/min
  - 601, 601P: 400 ft (122 m)/min
- Service ceiling:
  - 600: 22,000 ft (6,705 m)
  - 601: over 30,000 ft (9,145 m)
  - 601P: 25,000 ft (7,620 m)
- Service ceiling, one engine out:
  - 600: 6,300 ft (1,920 m)
  - 601, 601P: over 14,000 ft (4,265 m)
- T-O run:
  - 601, 601P: 1,095 ft (334 m)
- T-O to 50 ft (15 m):
  - 600: 1,025 ft (312 m)
  - 601, 601P: 1,520 ft (463 m)
- Landing from 50 ft (15 m):
  - 600: 1,100 ft (335 m)
  - 601, 601P: 1,800 ft (549 m)
- Landing run:
  - 601, 601P: 932 ft (284 m)
- Range with max fuel, no reserve:
  - 600, 70% power at 10,000 ft (3,050 m): 1,093 nm (1,258 miles; 2,025 km)
  - 601, 601P, 75% power at 25,000 ft (7,620 m): 1,242 nm (1,430 miles; 2,300 km)
  - 601, 601P, 55% power at 25,000 ft (7,620 m): 1,401 nm (1,613 miles; 2,595 km)

SMITH AEROSTAR 700/700P

The prototype Aerostar 700 flew for the first time on 22 November 1972. It is generally similar to the Model 600, but is slightly larger in size, has more powerful engines and an increased gross weight. Two versions are under consideration:

Aerostar 700. Powered by two 350 hp Lycoming IO-540-M six-cylinder horizontally-opposed aircooled engines.

Aerostar 700P. As Aerostar 700, but powered by two Lycoming turbocharged engines, and having a pressurisation system with a differential of 4·2 lb/sq in (0·30 kg/cm^2).

The description of the Model 600 applies also to the Aerostar 700, except as detailed below:

WINGS: As for Model 600, except span increased.

FUSELAGE: As for Model 600, except length increased.

TAIL UNIT, LANDING GEAR: As for Model 600.

POWER PLANT: As detailed in Model listings.

ACCOMMODATION: As for Model 600, except volume increased, and a panoramic window replaces the two forward cabin windows on each side of the Model 600. Aerostar 700P will have a pressurised cabin.

DIMENSIONS, EXTERNAL:
- Wing span: 36 ft 8 in (11·18 m)
- Wing aspect ratio: 4·31
- Length overall: 35 ft 4 in (10·77 m)

AREA:
- Wings, gross: 193·54 sq ft (17·98 m^2)

WEIGHTS AND LOADINGS (700P estimated):
- Weight empty:
  - 700: 3,900 lb (1,769 kg)
  - 700P: 4,050 lb (1,837 kg)
- Max T-O weight:
  - 700: 6,300 lb (2,858 kg)
  - 700P: 6,500 lb (2,948 kg)
- Max wing loading:
  - 700: 32·6 lb/sq ft (159·2 kg/m^2)
  - 700P: 33·65 lb/sq ft (164·3 kg/m^2)
- Max power loading:
  - 700: 10·5 lb/hp (4·76 kg/hp)

PERFORMANCE (at max T-O weight, 700P estimated):
- Max level speed:
  - 700 at S/L: 239 knots (275 mph; 443 km/h)
  - 700P at 25,000 ft (7,620 m): 311 knots (358 mph; 576 km/h)
- Cruising speed:
  - 700, 70% power at 10,000 ft (3,050 m): 221 knots (255 mph; 410 km/h)
  - 700, 55% power at 10,000 ft (3,050 m): 155 knots (178 mph; 286 km/h)
  - 700P, 55% power at 25,000 ft (7,620 m): 234 knots (270 mph; 435 km/h)
- Max rate of climb at S/L:
  - 700: 2,480 ft (756 m)/min
- Service ceiling:
  - 700: over 24,000 ft (7,315 m)
  - 700P: over 30,000 ft (9,145 m)
- Range:
  - 700, at 70% power at 10,000 ft (3,050 m), 30 min reserve 955 nm (1,100 miles; 1,770 km)
  - 700, at 55% power at 10,000 ft (3,050 m), 30 min reserve: 1,389 nm (1,600 miles; 2,575 km)
  - 700P, at 55% power at 25,000 ft (7,620 m), 30 min reserve: 1,650 nm (1,900 miles; 3,058 km)

SMYTH

JERRY SMYTH

ADDRESS:
RR.4, Huntington, Indiana 46750

In February 1958 Mr Smyth began the design of a sporting monoplane, setting out to evolve an aircraft that would be reasonably easy to construct, easy to fly, stressed to 9*g* for limited aerobatics, of good appearance and offering economic operation. Construction of the prototype began almost nine years later, in January 1967, and occupied two years before completion, at a cost of around $2,500. First flight of what Mr Smyth has named the Model "S" Sidewinder was made on 21 February 1969, and this aircraft received the "Outstanding Design" award at the 17th EAA Fly-in at Rockford, Illinois, in 1969.

Construction has been simplified by utilising a number of standard and readily-obtainable items of equipment. For example, the bubble canopy is that of a Thorp T-18, and Wittman landing gear is used. Plans are available to amateur constructors, and Mr Smyth can also supply a glassfibre nosewheel fairing and two-piece engine cowling to those constructors who do not wish to mould their own.

Pictured in the adjacent illustration is a retractable landing gear version built by Mr Donald Adams of Columbia City, Indiana. Powered, like the prototype, by a 125 hp Lycoming O-290-G engine, the retractable gear allows a max cruising speed of 156 knots (180 mph; 290 km/h), an increase of 17 knots (20 mph; 32 km/h) by comparison with Mr Smyth's prototype. Construction of Mr Adams' Sidewinder occupied 20 months at a cost of approximately $4,300, with the first flight being recorded on 11 June 1973.

SMYTH MODEL "S" SIDEWINDER

The following description applies to Mr Smyth's prototype:

TYPE: Two-seat homebuilt sporting monoplane.

WINGS: Cantilever low-wing monoplane. Wing section NACA 64-612 at root, NACA 64-210 at tip. Dihedral 4°. Incidence 1° 30′. No sweepback. All-metal structure comprising a centre-section and two outer wing panels. Built-up main spar of ·040 in 2024-T3 aluminium "U"-sections, to which flat aluminium cap strips are riveted; secondary spar is of formed sections. Eleven equally-spaced ribs in each wing panel are made of ·025 in 6061-T4 aluminium. The wing skin, of ·025 in 2024-T3 aluminium, is in three sections: leading-edge, lower and upper skin, and is flush-riveted. Wings filled with epoxy. Simple sealed-gap ailerons of aluminium construction, attached to secondary spar by piano-type hinge. No trim tabs. No flaps.

FUSELAGE: Welded steel tube structure with aluminium formers and skin. Electrically-operated speed brake may be fitted on lower fuselage.

TAIL UNIT: Cantilever all-metal structure with swept vertical surfaces. All-moving horizontal surface with electrically-operated anti-servo tab.

LANDING GEAR: Non-retractable nosewheel type. Wittman cantilever spring steel main gear. Main wheels and tyres size 5·00-5, pressure 25 lb/sq in (1·76 kg/cm²). Nose unit carries a 10 in (25·4 cm) diameter tailwheel and smooth tyre, free-castoring and non-steerable, pressure 25 lb/sq in (1·76 kg/cm²). Cleveland hydraulic brakes. Glassfibre fairings on all wheels.

POWER PLANT: Provision for installation of engines from 90-180 hp. Prototype has a 125 hp Lycoming O-290-G four-cylinder horizontally-opposed aircooled engine, driving a two-blade fixed-pitch aluminium propeller, with spinner. Fuel tank in fuselage, forward of instrument panel, capacity 17·5 US gallons (66·2 litres). Refuelling point on top of fuselage, forward of windscreen. Provision for wingtip tanks. Oil capacity 2 US gallons (7·5 litres).

ACCOMMODATION: Pilot and passenger, seated side by side under rearward-sliding bubble canopy. Compartment for 90 lb (40·8 kg) of baggage aft of seats. Cabin heated and ventilated.

SYSTEMS: Hydraulic system for brakes and, optionally, for operation of aerodynamic speed brake. Engine-driven generator provides 35A 12V DC for instruments, lights, electrically-operated stabilator servo tab and optional electrically-driven hydraulic pump to operate aerodynamic speed brake.

ELECTRONICS: Simple 10-channel VHF communications transceiver.

DIMENSIONS, EXTERNAL:

Wing span	24 ft 10 in (7·57 m)
Wing chord at root	5 ft 0 in (1·52 m)
Wing chord at tip	3 ft 0 in (0·91 m)
Wing aspect ratio	6·85
Length overall	19 ft 4 in (5·89 m)
Height overall	5 ft 5½ in (1·66 m)
Tailplane span	7 ft 7¾ in (2·33 m)
Wheel track	5 ft 7 in (1·70 m)
Wheelbase	4 ft 3 in (1·30 m)
Propeller diameter	5 ft 7 in (1·70 m)
Propeller ground clearance	8 in (20 cm)

DIMENSIONS, INTERNAL:

Cabin:

Length	6 ft 6 in (1·98 m)
Max width	3 ft 2 in (0·97 m)
Max height	3 ft 4 in (1·02 m)
Baggage compartment	9 cu ft (0·25 m³)

AREAS:

Wings, gross	96 sq ft (8·92 m²)
Ailerons (total)	6 sq ft (0·56 m²)
Fin	4·4 sq ft (0·41 m²)
Rudder	2·0 sq ft (0·19 m²)
Horizontal tail surface	14·1 sq ft (1·31 m²)

WEIGHTS AND LOADINGS:

Weight empty	867 lb (393 kg)
Max T-O and landing weight	1,450 lb (657 kg)
Max wing loading	15·8 lb/sq ft (77 kg/m²)
Max power loading	11·6 lb/hp (5·26 kg/hp)

PERFORMANCE (at max T-O weight):

Max never-exceed speed
173 knots (200 mph; 321 km/h)

Max level speed at 2,000 ft (610 m)
161 knots (185 mph; 298 km/h)

Max cruising speed, 75% power at 2,000 ft (610 m) 139 knots (160 mph; 257 km/h)

Stalling speed 48 knots (55 mph; 89 km/h)

Max rate of climb at S/L, 32°F (0°C)
1,200 ft (366 m)/min

Max rate of climb at S/L, 75°F (24°C)
900 ft (274 m)/min

Service ceiling 15,000 ft (4,570 m)

T-O run 800 ft (244 m)

T-O to and landing from 50 ft (15 m)
2,000 ft (610 m)

Landing run 1,500 ft (457 m)

Range with max fuel, no reserve
369 nm (425 miles; 684 km)

Smyth Sidewinder, with retractable landing gear, built by Mr Donald Adams of Columbia City, Indiana *(Howard Levy)*

SORREL

SORRELL AVIATION

ADDRESS:
Box 660, Route 1, Tenino, Washington 98589
Telephone: (206) 264-6801

Sorrell Aviation has designed and built a two-seat aerobatic biplane which is intended to be suitable for construction by amateurs. Flight testing has confirmed that the Hiperbipe, as the Sorrell family's new aircraft is named, has an outstanding aerobatic performance. When demonstrated and displayed at the EAA 1973 Fly-in at Oshkosh, it received the Outstanding New Design of 1973 award. Plans and certain components are available to amateur constructors.

SORRELL HIPERBIPE

TYPE: Two-seat homebuilt aerobatic biplane.

WINGS: Braced single-bay biplane with wide-chord I-type interplane struts and dual streamline-section landing and flying wires. Conventional light alloy structure with skins of light alloy. Centre-section of upper wing is skinned with transparent plastics to allow improved visibility for aerobatics. Cambered wingtips.

FUSELAGE: Light alloy semi-monocoque structure.

TAIL UNIT: Braced structure of light alloy. Large dorsal fin. Tailplane and inset elevator extend aft of rudder trailing-edge. Adjustable trim tab in starboard side of elevator.

LANDING GEAR: Non-retractable tailwheel type. Cantilever main gear with single wheel and fairing on each leg. Steerable tailwheel.

POWER PLANT: One 180 hp Lycoming O-360 four-cylinder horizontally-opposed aircooled engine, driving a Hartzell two-blade metal constant-speed propeller with spinner. Fuel capacity 40 US gallons (151 litres).

ACCOMMODATION: Two seats side by side in enclosed cabin. Dual controls standard.

DIMENSIONS, EXTERNAL:

Wing span	22 ft 10 in (6·96 m)
Length overall	20 ft 0 in (6·10 m)

WEIGHTS:

Weight empty	1,123 lb (509 kg)
Max T-O weight	1,800 lb (816 kg)

PERFORMANCE (at max T-O weight):

Max level speed
174 knots (200 mph; 322 km/h)

Cruising speed 139 knots (160 mph; 257 km/h)

Sorrell Aviation Hiperbipe homebuilt aerobatic biplane (180 hp Lycoming O-360 engine)

SPENCER

P. H. SPENCER

ADDRESS:
8725 Oland Avenue, Sun Valley, California 91352
Telephone: (213) 767-7042

Mr P. H. Spencer, who made his first solo flight in a powered aircraft on 15 May 1914, has been associated with the design of several single-engined amphibians, dating back to 1930, when Amphibians Inc of Garden City, Long Island, NY, put the Privateer amphibian into production. This was followed by the Spencer-Larsen, Spencer Air Car S-12, Republic Seabee RC 1, RC 2 and RC 3.

All of the above designs, as well as the Trident TR-1 amphibian prototype which is being developed in Vancouver, British Columbia, by Trident Aircraft Ltd (which see), under Canadian certification, are variations of Mr Spencer's basic Air Car configuration, on which he was granted a patent on 3 January 1950. This was originally a two-seat amphibian powered by a 110 hp engine, and was developed into a four-seat version, known as the S-12-C. Mr Spencer then completed the design of the more advanced S-12-D, of which plans are available to homebuilders as well as certain glassfibre mouldings and metal assemblies. Since that time development has continued, the installation of a Teledyne Continental Tiara series engine, Model 6-285-B, resulting in a change of designation to S-12-E for the prototype. This had accumulated a total of 431 hours flying time by February 1974, 48 of them with the Tiara engine. The wing sweepback has also been increased, from 3° to 5°.

By February 1974 a total of 25 Air Cars were known to be under construction, with a variety of power plants ranging from 200 hp to 285 hp, and more than 65 sets of plans had been sold.

Spencer Amphibian Air Car Model S-12-E (285 hp Continental Tiara 6-285-B engine)

SPENCER AMPHIBIAN AIR CAR MODEL S-12-E

Type: Four-seat homebuilt amphibian.

Wings: Braced high-wing monoplane with single streamline-section bracing strut on each side. Specially-designed STOL wing section. Thickness/chord ratio 15%. Dihedral 1°. Incidence 2°. Sweepback at quarter-chord 5°. Conventional two-spar structure of wood, steel and glassfibre. Frise-type ailerons of wooden construction. Electrically-operated trailing-edge flaps. Glassfibre stabilising float mounted on strut beneath each wing at approximately two-thirds span.

Hull: Conventional single-stepped hull with wood frames, longerons and skin. Welded steel tube cabane structure to provide wing and engine mounting and attachment points for landing gear.

Tail Unit: Cantilever structure, comprising conventional fin and rudder, and all-moving tailplane set approximately midway up fin. Combined anti-servo and trim tab in tailplane. Retractable water rudder in base of aerodynamic rudder.

Landing Gear: Manually-retractable tricycle type. Main wheels retract aft to take up a near-vertical position on each side of the cabin. Nosewheel retracts forward through almost 180° and is partially housed in the nose of the hull, above the waterline. Cantilever spring steel main gear. Main wheels and tyres size 7·00-6. Nosewheel and tyre size 6·00-6. Cleveland hydraulic disc brakes.

Power Plant: One 285 hp Continental Tiara series 6-285-B six-cylinder horizontally-opposed aircooled engine, driving a Hartzell three-blade metal constant-speed reversible pusher propeller. Fuel tanks in fuselage and wing stabilising floats. Total fuel capacity 94 US gallons (355 litres). Oil capacity 2·25 US gallons (8·5 litres).

Accommodation: Four seats in pairs in enclosed cabin. Backs of front seats fold forward to improve access. Rear seats fold back against bulkhead to provide cargo or baggage space. Baggage space in rear fuselage, aft of rear cabin bulkhead. Door on each side of fuselage, hinged at forward edge. Bow access door on starboard side, hinged on centreline and opening upward. Dual controls standard. Accommodation heated and ventilated.

Systems: Hydraulic system for brakes only. Electrical system supplied by 24V 50A engine-driven alternator.

Electronics and Equipment: Complete IFR instrumentation. Bendix 360 nav/com transceiver.

Dimensions, external:
- Wing span: 37 ft 4 in (11·38 m)
- Wing chord, constant: 5 ft 0 in (1·52 m)
- Wing aspect ratio: 7·4
- Length overall: 26 ft 5 in (8·05 m)
- Height overall: 9 ft 6 in (2·90 m)
- Tailplane span: 12 ft 0 in (3·66 m)
- Wheel track: 8 ft 4 in (2·54 m)
- Wheelbase: 10 ft 2 in (3·10 m)
- Propeller diameter: 7 ft 0 in (2·13 m)
- Cabin doors (port and starboard, each):
  - Height: 3 ft 2 in (0·97 m)
  - Width: 3 ft 4 in (1·02 m)
  - Height to sill: 2 ft 10 in (0·86 m)
- Cabin door (bow, starboard):
  - Length: 2 ft 11 in (0·89 m)
  - Width: 1 ft 8 in (0·51 m)

Dimensions, internal:
- Cabin: Length: 8 ft 6 in (2·59 m)
  - Max width: 3 ft 9 in (1·14 m)
  - Max height: 3 ft 11 in (1·19 m)

Area:
- Wings, gross: 184 sq ft (17·1 m²)

Weights and Loadings:
- Weight empty: 2,190 lb (993 kg)
- Max T-O weight: 3,200 lb (1,451 kg)
- Max wing loading: 17·4 lb/sq ft (85·0 kg/m²)
- Max power loading: 11·2 lb/hp (5·08 kg/hp)

Performance (at max T-O weight):
- Max level speed at S/L: 128 knots (147 mph; 237 km/h)
- Max cruising speed at 5,500 ft (1,675 m): 122 knots (140 mph; 225 km/h)
- Econ cruising speed, 65% power at 7,800 ft (2,375 m): 123 knots (142 mph; 229 km/h)
- Stalling speed, flaps up: 46 knots (53 mph; 86 km/h)
- Stalling speed, 35° flap: 37·5 knots (43 mph; 70 km/h)
- Max rate of climb at S/L: 1,000 ft (305 m)/min
- T-O time from calm water at S/L: 16 sec
- Range, 65% power at 7,800 ft (2,375 m), 20 min reserve: 695 nm (800 miles; 1,285 km)

SPEZIO

WILLIAM EDWARDS

Address:
25 Madison Avenue, Northampton, Massachusetts 01060

Mr and Mrs Spezio designed and built a two-seat light aircraft named the Tuholer, all rights of which were acquired by Mr Edwards in August 1973. He is continuing to market plans of the Tuholer to amateur constructors.

Spezio Tuholer built by Mr Jerry Dunn of Anderson, Indiana (125 hp Lycoming O-290-D engine) *(Howard Levy)*

SPEZIO DAL-1 TUHOLER

Named Tuholer because of its two open cockpits, the prototype flew for the first time on 2 May 1961.

Folding wings enable the Tuholer to be kept in a normal home garage and it is towed behind a car on its own landing gear. It can be made ready for flight by two people in about 10 minutes or by one person in 20 minutes.

The accompanying illustration shows a Tuholer built by Mr Jerry Dunn of Anderson, Indiana. It follows Spezio plans closely, with a neat pressure cowling around the 125 hp Lycoming O-290-D engine.

The following description applies to the Tuholer built by Mr Edwards to the current plans:

Type: Two-seat homebuilt sporting aircraft.

Wings: Strut-braced low-wing monoplane, with streamline-section Vee bracing struts each side. Jury struts brace centre of these struts. Clark Y wing section. Dihedral 3°. Incidence 1°. Washout at wingtip 1°. Two-spar spruce structure, with plywood leading-edge and overall fabric covering. Conventional wooden ailerons. Drawings for Frise type ailerons are available. No flaps. Wings fold back along sides of fuselage for stowage.

Fuselage: Steel tube structure with wood or light alloy stringers and fabric covering.

Tail Unit: Braced steel tube structure, fabric covered. Tailplane incidence adjustable by screwjack.

Landing Gear: Non-retractable tailwheel type. Coil spring shock-absorption. Main units fitted with Cleveland wheels and tyres, size 6·00-6. Cleveland brakes. Tyre pressure 40 lb/sq in (2·81 kg/cm²). Steerable tailwheel. Wheel fairings optional.

Power Plant: One 150 hp Lycoming O-320 four-cylinder horizontally-opposed aircooled engine. Sensenich two-blade metal fixed-pitch propeller. Glassfibre fuel tank aft of firewall, capacity 24 US gallons (90·5 litres). Oil capacity 2 US gallons (7·5 litres).

Accommodation: Two persons in tandem in open cockpits. Small baggage compartment aft of rear seat.

Equipment: Nova-Tech TR-102 radio.

Dimensions, external:
- Wing span: 24 ft 9 in (7·55 m)
- Wing chord, constant: 5 ft 0 in (1·52 m)
- Wing aspect ratio: 5
- Length overall: 18 ft 3 in (5·56 m)
- Height overall: 5 ft 2 in (1·57 m)
- Tailplane span: 7 ft 5 in (2·26 m)
- Wheel track: 5 ft 2 in (1·57 m)

Area:
- Wings, gross: 120·7 sq ft (11·21 m²)

Weights:
- Weight empty: 900 lb (408 kg)
- Max T-O weight: 1,500 lb (680 kg)

Performance (at max T-O weight):
- Max level speed at S/L: 130 knots (150 mph; 241 km/h)
- Cruising speed: 109-117 knots (125-135 mph; 201-217 km/h)
- Stalling speed: 48 knots (55 mph; 89 km/h)
- Max rate of climb at S/L: 2,400 ft (732 m)/min
- T-O and landing run: 200 ft (61 m)
- Endurance with max fuel: 3 hr

SPRATT

SPRATT AND COMPANY, INC

Address:
PO Box 351, Media, Pennsylvania 19063

Mr George G. Spratt, formerly a design engineer with The Boeing Company and Consolidated Vultee (now Convair), has completed more than 30 years' work on developing a two-piece movable-wing control system, which he claims provides improved safety factors compared with the conventional aileron, elevator and rudder control system.

While he was with Consolidated Vultee, Mr Spratt designed a roadable aircraft which featured an earlier version of his wing control system, but this did not enter production. Since that time Mr Spratt has concentrated on perfecting his idea as a private venture.

SPRATT EXPERIMENTAL FLYING-BOAT

To flight test his movable-wing control system, Mr Spratt built a lightweight experimental flying-boat (N910Z) constructed almost entirely of moulded plastics.

In appearance, the hull resembles a motor boat and can accommodate two persons. The pivoted controllable wings are mounted in a parasol configuration, with inverted-Vee bracing struts on each side: these pivot at their junction with the wings to allow them to move. The butterfly tail unit carries no moving surfaces.

Power plant consists of a modified outboard marine engine, of 60 cu in capacity, driving a two-blade plastics pusher propeller through an extended drive shaft, which locates the propeller between the butterfly tail surfaces. A small water rudder, interconnected with the control wheel, facilitates manoeuvring on water.

Flying controls are so arranged that the wings are allowed to move freely and collectively in incidence, while their incidence is being controlled differentially by means of a steering wheel. The wings' angle of attack can be adjusted by a separate control, but is best regarded as "fixed" for a particular cruising speed.

DIMENSIONS, EXTERNAL:

Wing span	24 ft 0 in (7·32 m)
Length overall	17 ft 0 in (5·18 m)
Height overall	5 ft 0 in (1·52 m)
Width of hull	5 ft 0 in (1·52 m)

WEIGHTS AND LOADINGS:

Weight empty	500 lb (226 kg)
Max T-O weight	1,000 lb (453 kg)
Max wing loading	10 lb/sq ft (48·8 kg/m²)
Max power loading	15 lb/hp (6·8 kg/hp)

PERFORMANCE (at max T-O weight):

Max level speed	85 knots (98 mph; 158 km/h)
Max cruising speed	78 knots (90 mph; 145 km/h)
Max waterborne speed	61 knots (70 mph; 113 km/h)
Normal T-O speed	43 knots (50 mph; 80 km/h)
Normal landing speed	36 knots (42 mph; 68 km/h)
Normal operating ceiling	3,000 ft (914 m)

SPRATT MODEL 107

Since completion of the test aircraft described above, Mr Spratt has designed and constructed a more advanced prototype known as the Model 107 (N2236) for public demonstration. Dimensions and weights are essentially the same as those of the test vehicle, but construction has been simplified to facilitate fabrication. The Mercury "800" modified outboard marine engine of the Model 107 is of slightly increased capacity, and produces greater horsepower with better fuel economy as a result of improved combustion chamber and inlet port design.

Mr Spratt claims that the Model 107 will neither stall nor spin, and displays 75% less reaction to turbulence than a conventional design.

Plans of this aircraft are available to amateur constructors, and at the end of February 1974 it was known that twelve examples were being built by amateurs.

TYPE: Two-seat lightweight homebuilt flying-boat.

WINGS: Pivoted controllable parasol wings, with inverted Vee bracing struts each side. Wing section NACA 23112. No dihedral. No sweepback. Reinforced plastics structure. No ailerons, flaps or trim tabs.

HULL: Structure of polyurethane foam with reinforced plastics skin.

TAIL UNIT: Butterfly-type tail unit, with no movable surfaces, constructed of reinforced plastics.

POWER PLANT: One 80 hp Mercury "800" modified outboard two-stroke marine engine, driving a two-blade plastics pusher propeller of Mr Spratt's design, the pitch of which is adjustable on the ground. Outboard engine type of fuel tank.

ACCOMMODATION: Two persons side by side, in open cockpit.

DIMENSIONS, EXTERNAL:

Wing span	24 ft 0 in (7·32 m)
Wing chord (constant)	4 ft 0 in (1·22 m)
Wing aspect ratio	6
Length overall	17 ft 0 in (5·18 m)
Height overall	5 ft 0 in (1·52 m)
Propeller diameter	5 ft 0 in (1·52 m)

AREA:

Wings, gross	96 sq ft (8·92 m²)

WEIGHTS:

Weight empty	500 lb (226 kg)
Max T-O weight	1,000 lb (453 kg)

SPRATT MODEL 105

Mr Spratt has recently completed the design of a landplane version of the movable-wing flying-boats already described, and this is named the Spratt Controlwing or Model 105. A single example has been built by a close friend of Mr Spratt, namely Mr Robert Quaintance of Coatsville, Pennsylvania. Few details of this aircraft are known, but all available information follows:

TYPE: Two-seat lightweight experimental landplane.

WINGS: As described for Model 107, except wings can be folded alongside fuselage for towing or storage.

FUSELAGE: Primarily a composite structure of polyurethane foam and glassfibre.

TAIL UNIT: Fixed vertical surface only, of polyurethane foam and glassfibre. No movable surfaces.

LANDING GEAR: Non-retractable tricycle type. Steerable nosewheel is of conventional aircraft type. Main wheels are of the automotive type to allow extensive road towing. Nosewheel designed to attach to a trailer hitch for road towing.

POWER PLANT: One Mercury outboard motor boat engine of 983 cc capacity mounted in a mid-fuselage position. Two-blade fixed-pitch pusher propeller driven via an extended shaft.

ACCOMMODATION: Two seats side by side in semi-enclosed cockpit.

DIMENSIONS, EXTERNAL:

Wing span	22 ft 0 in (6·71 m)
Length overall	12 ft 6 in (3·81 m)

WEIGHT:

Weight empty	450 lb (204 kg)

Spratt Model 107 two-seat homebuilt flying-boat (80 hp Mercury "800" modified outboard marine engine)

Spratt Model 105 landplane built and owned by Mr Robert Quaintance of Coatsville, Pennsylvania
(Howard Levy)

STEEN

LAMAR A. STEEN

ADDRESS:

3218 S Cherry Street, Denver, Colorado 80222

Mr Lamar Steen, an aerospace teacher in a Denver, Colorado, high school, has designed a two-seat fully-aerobatic biplane named Skybolt which has been built as a class project in the school. Simplicity of construction was a primary aim of the design, begun in June 1968, and it is stressed to +12 and —10*g*. Construction began on 19 August 1969, costing approximately $5,000, and the first flight was made in October 1970. The Skybolt has received the EAA award for Best School Project. Plans are available to amateur constructors.

By 28 February 1974 more than 1,000 sets had been sold, at which time it was believed that approximately 700 Skybolts were under construction.

The adjacent illustration pictures the Skybolt built by Mr Dick Blair of Vincetown, New Jersey. Powered by a 200 hp Lycoming IO-360 engine, and equipped with an inverted fuel system, its construction cost $7,900 and the first flight was recorded in July 1973. When Mr Blair exhibited his aircraft at the EAA 1973 Fly-in at Oshkosh, it received the Best Skybolt award.

STEEN SKYBOLT

The following description applies to the prototype with 180 hp Lycoming engine as built under Mr Steen's supervision:

TYPE: Two-seat aerobatic homebuilt biplane.

WINGS: Braced biplane with single interplane strut each side. N-type centre-section struts. Streamline-section landing and flying wires. Wing sections: upper wing NACA 63₂A015, lower wing NACA 0012. Incidence (both) 1° 30′. Sweepback 6° on upper wing only. Wooden two-spar structures with spruce spars, built-up ribs and fabric covering. Fabric-covered Frise-type ailerons on both wings. Cutout in centre-section trailing-edge of upper wing.

FUSELAGE: Welded structure of 4130 chrome-molybdenum steel tube, with fabric covering.

TAIL UNIT: Wire-braced welded structure of 4130 chrome-molybdenum steel tube, with fabric covering. Adjustable trim tab in port elevator.

LANDING GEAR: Non-retractable main wheels and tailwheel. Two side Vees and half axles hinged to fuselage structure. Shock-absorption by rubber bungee. Cleveland wheels with tyres size 6·00-6, pressure 25 lb/sq in (1·8 kg/cm²). Cleve-

Steen Skybolt built by Mr Dick Blair of Vincetown, New Jersey (200 hp Lycoming IO-360 engine)
(Howard Levy)

land hydraulic disc brakes. Glassfibre fairings for main wheels.

POWER PLANT: One 180 hp Lycoming HO-360-B1B four-cylinder horizontally-opposed air-cooled engine, driving a McCauley two-blade fixed-pitch propeller with spinner. Provision for alternative engines of 125-300 hp. Fuselage fuel tank, immediately aft of firewall, capacity 30 US gallons (113·4 litres). Optional tank of 10 US gallons (37·8 litres) capacity can be installed in centre-section of upper wing. Total optional fuel capacity 40 US gallons (151·2 litres). Refuelling points on fuselage upper surface, forward of windscreen, and on top surface of upper wing. Oil capacity 2 US gallons (7·5 litres).

ACCOMMODATION: Two seats in open cockpits. Space for 30 lb (13·6 kg) baggage aft of rear seat.

SYSTEM: Hydraulic system for brakes only.

ELECTRONICS: Battery-powered Alpha 200 nav/com transceiver.

DIMENSIONS, EXTERNAL:
Wing span, upper 24 ft 0 in (7·32 m)
Wing span, lower 23 ft 0 in (7·01 m)
Wing chord (constant, both) 3 ft 6 in (1·07 m)
Length overall 19 ft 0 in (5·79 m)
Height overall 7 ft 0 in (2·13 m)
Propeller diameter 6 ft 2 in (1·88 m)
Propeller ground clearance 1 ft 0 in (0·31 m)

AREA:
Wings, gross 152·7 sq ft (14·2 m²)

WEIGHTS AND LOADINGS:
Weight empty 1,080 lb (490 kg)
Max T-O weight 1,680 lb (762 kg)
Max wing loading 11 lb/sq ft (53·7 kg/m²)
Max power loading 9·3 lb/hp (4·22 kg/hp)

PERFORMANCE (at max T-O weight):
Max level speed 126 knots (145 mph; 233 km/h)
Cruising speed 113 knots (130 mph; 209 km/h)
Landing speed 43 knots (50 mph; 80·5 km/h)
Max rate of climb at S/L 2,500 ft (762 m)/min
Service ceiling 18,000 ft (5,500 m)
T-O run 400 ft (122 m)
Range with max fuel 390 nm (450 miles; 720 km)

STEPHENS

STEPHENS AIRCRAFT

ADDRESS:
PO Box 3171, Rubidoux, California 92509

Mr C. L. Stephens has designed a single-seat aerobatic monoplane specifically for homebuilders who wish to own an aircraft for competitive aerobatics. The prototype, designated Model A, was designed for Margaret Ritchie, US National Women's Aerobatic Champion in 1966, and the second aircraft, the Model B, for Dean S. Engelhardt of Garden Grove, California.

Stressed to $+12g$ and $-11g$, it is the first US aircraft known to be designed around the Aresti Aerocriptografic System for competitive aerobatics. All control surfaces are fully static-balanced and the entire aircraft comes very close to being aerodynamically symmetrical. Design of the Model A started in July 1966 and construction of the prototype began a month later. First flight of this version was made on 27 July 1967, and of the Model B, with wings and ailerons of increased area and reduced fuel tankage, on 9 July 1969. Plans of the Stephens Akro are available to amateur constructors, and the adjacent illustration shows the version built by Douglas Cline, a United Air Lines DC-8 captain. Powered by a 200 hp Lycoming engine, and with a number of clean-up modifications to improve performance, Mr Cline's Akro received the Outstanding Paint and Design Award at the 1973 EAA Fly-in at Oshkosh.

Stephens Akro built by Mr Douglas Cline of Walnut Creek, California (200 hp Lycoming engine) (*Howard Levy*)

STEPHENS AKRO

The following description applies to the prototype with 180 hp Lycoming engine:

TYPE: Single-seat homebuilt monoplane.

WINGS: Cantilever mid-wing monoplane. Wing section NACA 23012. No dihedral, incidence or sweepback. All-wood two-spar structure. One-piece wing, with solid spar passing through fuselage and positioned by means of removable top longeron sections. Rear spar in two pieces. No internal wires or compression struts. Wing covered with mahogany skin. Plain ailerons have a 4130 steel spar, and spruce ribs and trailing-edge, and are fabric-covered. Ground-adjustable trim tabs on ailerons, which are statically balanced. No flaps.

FUSELAGE: Welded 4130 steel tube structure, mostly of 0·75 in outside diameter tubing, with Ceconite covering.

TAIL UNIT: Wire-braced welded 4130 steel tube structure with swept surfaces, fabric-covered. Tailplane has variable incidence. Ground-adjustable trim tab on rudder; controllable trim tab in elevator. All control surfaces statically balanced.

LANDING GEAR: Non-retractable tailwheel type. Cantilever spring steel main gear. Goodyear main wheels and tyres size 5·00-5, pressure 28 lb/sq in (1·97 kg/m²). Cleveland disc brakes. Maule steerable tailwheel. Glassfibre fairings on main wheels.

POWER PLANT: One 180 hp Lycoming AIO-360-A1A four-cylinder horizontally-opposed air-cooled engine, driving a Sensenich Type 7660 two-blade fixed-pitch metal propeller. Model A has fuel system for prolonged inverted flight, Model B has both fuel and oil system so modified. Model B can also have optional constant-speed propeller. Fuel tank in fuselage, forward of instrument panel. Model A has fuel capacity of 32 US gallons (121 litres), Model B has capacity of 27 US gallons (102 litres). Refuelling point on top of fuselage, forward of windscreen. Oil capacity 2 US gallons (7·6 litres).

ACCOMMODATION: Single seat for pilot under rearward-sliding bubble canopy. Large window in underfuselage, forward of control column. Model B has, in addition, a quarter window in each side of the fuselage, beneath the wings. Forced-air ventilation.

SYSTEMS: Hydraulic system for brakes only.

ELECTRONICS: Battery-operated Bayside transceiver.

DIMENSIONS, EXTERNAL:
Wing span 24 ft 6 in (7·47 m)
Wing chord at root 5 ft 3 in (1·60 m)
Wing chord at tip:
A 2 ft 6 in (0·76 m)
B 3 ft 0 in (0·91 m)
Length overall 19 ft 1 in (5·82 m)
Height overall 5 ft 8 in (1·73 m)
Tailplane span 8 ft 0 in (2·44 m)
Wheel track 4 ft 6 in (1·37 m)
Propeller diameter 6 ft 4 in (1·93 m)
Propeller ground clearance 1 ft 1 in (0·33 m)

AREAS:
Wings, gross:
A 94 sq ft (8·73 m²)
B 100 sq ft (9·29 m²)
Ailerons, total:
A 12 sq ft (1·11 m²)
B 13 sq ft (1·21 m²)
Fin 5 sq ft (0·46 m²)
Rudder, including tab 10 sq ft (0·93 m²)
Tailplane 13 sq ft (1·21 m²)
Elevators, including tab 11 sq ft (1·02 m²)

WEIGHTS AND LOADINGS:
Weight empty:
A 850 lb (385 kg)
B 950 lb (431 kg)
Max T-O weight:
A 1,200 lb (544 kg)
B 1,300 lb (589 kg)
Max wing loading 13 lb/sq ft (63·5 kg/m²)
Max power loading 7 lb/hp (3·18 kg/hp)

PERFORMANCE (at 1,200 lb; 544 kg T-O weight):
Max never-exceed speed 191 knots (220 mph; 354 km/h)
Max level speed at 2,000 ft (610 m) 148 knots (170 mph; 274 km/h)
Max cruising speed at 2,000 ft (610 m) 139 knots (160 mph; 257 km/h)
Econ cruising speed at 2,000 ft (610 m) 109 knots (125 mph; 201 km/h)
Stalling speed 48 knots (55 mph; 89 km/h)
Max rate of climb at S/L 4,000 ft (1,220 m)/min
Service ceiling 22,000 ft (6,705 m)
T-O run 200 ft (61 m)
T-O to 50 ft (15 m) 400 ft (122 m)
Landing from 50 ft (15 m) 1,500 ft (457 m)
Landing run 600 ft (183 m)
Range with max fuel 303 nm (350 miles; 563 km)

STEWARD-DAVIS

STEWARD-DAVIS, INC

HEAD OFFICE:
3200 Cherry Avenue, Long Beach, California 90807

Telephone: (213) 636-1871 or 426-6455
Telex: 65-6494

The cargo landplanes produced by this company utilise the airframe of the Fairchild C-82A/C-119 military transport, with extensive systems changes and fitted with jet-augmentation units of Steward-Davis manufacture, known as Jet-Paks.

Steward-Davis acquired from Westinghouse the sole manufacturing rights for the J34-WE-34, J34-WE-36, W340, and 24C-4D turbojets and holds the Type Certificate for the FAA-approved versions of these engines which are incorporated in its Jet-Pak augmentation units. Jet-Paks have been fitted to Fairchild C-119 aircraft of the Indian Air Force and are available for other cargo aircraft.

Steward-Davis developed subsequently an improved Jet-Pak fitted with intake duct doors. These doors have excellent aerodynamic characteristics and are used to prevent engine windmilling during periods of non-operation in flight. This unit is designated Jet-Pak 3402 and is built around a 3,400 lb (1,542 kg) st J34 turbojet engine. It is fitted to the STOLmaster transport manufactured by Steward-Davis for Aircraft International of Santa Monica, California.

Steward-Davis manufactures approved components for the Westinghouse turbojet engines listed above, and is a supplier to the RAAF, French Navy, Indian Air Force, Royal Netherlands Navy, Japanese Self-Defence Forces and US Navy. It also overhauls Westinghouse J34 turbojets under French government contract.

Steward-Davis also acquired from The Boeing Company in 1969 the manufacturing rights for the latter company's Model 502 and T50 engines, and continues to support the operation of these engines on a worldwide basis.

STEWARD-DAVIS/FAIRCHILD JET-PAK C-119/R4Q

Development of this jet-augmented conversion of the Fairchild C-119/R4Q military transport was begun in January 1961. Construction of a prototype was started in March 1962 and it flew for the first time in September 1962.

Twenty-six aircraft of the Indian Air Force have been fitted with Steward-Davis Jet-Paks to enable them to operate with higher payloads from high-altitude fields in support of ground forces.

At the request of the Indian Air Force, Steward-Davis has studied the possibilities of a three-jet version of this aircraft, with one Jet-Pak above the centre-section and two more under the wings. The wing units are designed for quick disconnect in the field when one jet unit will suffice.

The following details refer to the standard Jet-Pak C-119/R4Q:

TYPE: Twin-engined cargo and troop transport.

WINGS: Cantilever high-wing monoplane. Wing section NACA 2418 at root, NACA 4409 at tip. Anhedral 7° 46′ on centre-section. Dihedral 1° 30′ outboard of nacelles, measured at 40% chord. Incidence 3° at root, —1° at tip. Sweepback at quarter-chord 3° 51′. Conventional two-spar aluminium alloy structure. Fabric-covered aluminium alloy ailerons, each with trim tab. NACA slotted aluminium alloy trailing-edge flaps. Thermal de-icing.

FUSELAGE: Aluminium alloy semi-monocoque pod structure, of basically-square section, with clamshell rear loading doors. Seven longitudinal underfloor beams to take floor and tie-down loads.

TAILBOOMS: Aluminium alloy semi-monocoque structures. Each in two sections, bolted together at leading-edge of tailplane.

TAIL UNIT: Cantilever aluminium alloy structure, with twin fins and rudders. Controllable trim tabs in elevator and rudders; mechanical servo tabs in rudders. Thermal de-icing of leading-edges.

LANDING GEAR: Retractable tricycle type, with twin wheels on all three units. Hydraulic actuation, with mechanical emergency release. Hydraulically-steerable nosewheel. Chicago Pneumatic oleo-pneumatic shock-absorbers. Main-wheel tyres size 15·50 × 20 14-ply, pressure 44-82 lb/sq in (3·09-5·77 kg/cm²) depending on AUW. Magnesium nosewheels with tyres size 9·50 × 16 10-ply. Bendix disc brakes.

POWER PLANT: Two 3,350 hp Wright R-3350-85 or -89 radial aircooled engines, driving Hamilton Standard Hydromatic or Aeroproducts four-blade constant-speed reversible-pitch propellers. One 3,400 lb (1,542 kg) st Westinghouse J34-WE-36 auxiliary turbojet engine. Fuel in four bladder tanks in wings, each inboard tank of 842 US gallons (3,187 litres) capacity, each outboard tank of 469 US gallons (1,775 litres) capacity. Total fuel capacity 2,622 US gallons (9,924 litres). Refuelling points above wings. Oil capacity 120 US gallons (455 litres).

ACCOMMODATION: Crew of four or five on flight deck, access to which is by a ladder on the port side. Payloads can consist of 67 troops (or 78 in emergencies), 35 stretcher patients or equivalent freight. An electrically-operated monorail is able to discharge up to 20 × 500 lb (227 kg) packages through a hatch in the bottom of the fuselage during air-drop operations. Personnel door forward on port side. Rear clamshell doors open to full cross-section of hold. Floor is at truck-bed height. Ramps are provided for driving vehicles directly into hold. Small door in each main clamshell door permits simultaneous jumping of two sticks of paratroops.

SYSTEMS: Individual oxygen supplied for crew-members. Hydraulic system, pressure 3,000 lb/sq in (210 kg/cm²), for landing gear, flaps, brakes, nosewheel steering, jet starter and jet intake doors. Pneumatic system, pressure 1,600 lb/sq in (112 kg/cm²), for emergency braking. Electrical system includes two engine-driven generators and 36Ah battery. Fairchild APU for auxiliary electrical supply.

ELECTRONICS AND EQUIPMENT: Blind-flying instrumentation standard. Radio and radar to customer's requirements.

DIMENSIONS, EXTERNAL:
Wing span 109 ft 3¼ in (33·30 m)
Wing chord at root 17 ft 10⅞ in (5·45 m)
Wing chord at tip 8 ft 11 in (2·72 m)
Wing aspect ratio 8·25
Length overall 86 ft 5¾ in (26·38 m)
Length of fuselage 60 ft 6 5/16 in (18·45 m)
Height over tail 26 ft 7¾ in (8·12 m)
Tailplane span 29 ft 3⅝ in (8·93 m)
Wheel track 29 ft 2 in (8·89 m)
Wheelbase 26 ft 3 in (8·00 m)
Rear clamshell doors:
Height 8 ft 0 in (2·44 m)
Width 9 ft 2 in (2·79 m)
Height to sill 4 ft 0 in (1·22 m)

DIMENSIONS, INTERNAL:
Cabin: Length 36 ft 11 in (11·25 m)
Max width 9 ft 2 in (2·79 m)
Max height 8 ft 0 in (2·44 m)
Floor area 353 sq ft (32·8 m²)
Volume 3,150 cu ft (88·2 m³)

AREAS:
Wings, gross 1,447·24 sq ft (134·4 m²)
Ailerons (total) 120·20 sq ft (11·16 m²)
Trailing-edge flaps (total) 120·00 sq ft (11·15 m²)
Fins, including ventral and dorsal fins 158·20 sq ft (14·70 m²)
Rudders, including tabs 66·22 sq ft (6·15 m²)
Tailplane 58·48 sq ft (5·43 m²)
Elevators, including tabs 113·86 sq ft (10·58 m²)

WEIGHTS AND LOADINGS:
Weight empty 43,000 lb (19,505 kg)
Max payload 28,500 lb (12,925 kg)
Max T-O weight 77,000 lb (34,925 kg)
Max landing weight 64,000 lb (29,030 kg)
Max wing loading 53·2 lb/sq ft (259·75 kg/m²)
Max power loading 9·33 lb/ehp (4·23 kg/ehp)

PERFORMANCE (at max T-O weight):
Max never-exceed speed 272 knots (314 mph; 505 km/h)
Max cruising speed (70% power):
Piston engines only 170 knots (196 mph; 315 km/h)
With jet assist 203 knots (234 mph; 377 km/h)
Stalling speed, power off 80 knots (92 mph; 148 km/h)
Max rate of climb at S/L 1,200 ft (365 m)/min
Service ceiling 24,000 ft (7,315 m)
Service ceiling, one engine out 9,300 ft (2,835 m)
T-O run 2,750 ft (838 m)
T-O to 50 ft (15 m) 5,250 ft (1,600 m)
Landing from 50 ft (15 m) 5,150 ft (1,570 m)
Landing run 2,215 ft (675 m)
Range with max fuel, 45 min reserve 1,910 nm (2,200 miles; 3,540 km)
Range with max payload, 45 min reserve 390 nm (450 miles; 725 km)

STEWARD-DAVIS/AIRCRAFT INTERNATIONAL STOLMASTER

Steward-Davis Inc has been retained by Aircraft International of Santa Monica, California, to modify Fairchild C-119 aircraft into STOLmaster jet-assisted transports to Aircraft International specification. The jet-assist system being used is the Jet-Pak 3402, built around a Steward-Davis 24C4D (Westinghouse J34) turbojet engine and embodying quick-attach features which permit each jet pod to be used as a power module. Each Jet-Pak may be removed or installed or interchanged between any aircraft on which simple mounting pads have been incorporated. This enables commercial and military operators of STOLmaster transports to augment the performance of their aircraft in a few minutes by installing one, two or three auxiliary jet pods, as required.

The details given for the Jet-Pak C-119/R4Q apply also to the STOLmaster, except for the following detail changes:

TYPE: Two-to-five-engined cargo and troop transport.

WINGS: High-lift full-span flap system under development.

LANDING GEAR: Anti-skid brake system available.

POWER PLANT: Two permanently-installed 3,250 hp (3,500 hp with water injection) Wright R-3350-89A radial aircooled engines, each driving a Hamilton Standard Hydromatic or Aeroproducts four-blade constant-speed reversible-pitch propeller. One, two or three 3,400 lb (1,542 kg) st Steward-Davis 24C4D turbojet engines in Jet-Pak 3402 quick-attach pods.

WEIGHTS AND LOADINGS:
Weight empty 41,000-45,290 lb (18,597-20,543 kg)
Max payload 25,000-30,000 lb (11,340-13,608 kg)
Max T-O and landing weight 77,000 lb (34,925 kg)
Max wing loading 53·2 lb/sq ft (259·75 kg/m²)
Max power loading 6·95-11·0 lb/hp (3·15-4·99 kg/hp)

PERFORMANCE (at max T-O weight, with one or more Jet-Paks):
Max never-exceed speed 272 knots (314 mph; 505 km/h)
Max cruising speed (70% power):
Piston engines only: 168-175 knots (194-202 mph; 312-325 km/h)
With Jet-Paks: 203-262 knots (234-302 mph; 377-486 km/h)
Stalling speed, power off 92 knots (105 mph; 170 km/h)
Max rate of climb at S/L 1,200-2,350 ft (365-716 m)/min
Service ceiling 24,000-31,000 ft (7,315-9,450 m)
T-O run 1,195-2,150 ft (364-655 m)
T-O to 50 ft (15 m) 1,505-3,040 ft (459-927 m)
Landing from 50 ft (15 m) 3,230 ft (985 m)
Landing run 2,150 ft (655 m)
Range with max fuel, 45 min reserve 1,947-2,596 nm (2,242-2,990 miles; 3,607-4,811 km)
Range with max payload, 45 min reserve 390 nm (450 miles; 725 km)

Steward-Davis/Aircraft International STOLmaster transport aircraft conversion of a Fairchild C-119G *(Norman E. Taylor)*

STEWART

STEWART AIRCRAFT CORPORATION

ADDRESS:
11420 Route 165, Salem, Ohio 44460
Telephone: (216) 332-0865

Mr Donald Stewart formed this company to market plans of a simple single-seat light aircraft named the Headwind, of which he designed and built a prototype. During 1969 he designed a new wing for the Headwind and this is an integral part of the plans available to homebuilders. A two-seat version is under construction and Mr Stewart expects to use either a 60 hp Franklin or 1,192 cc Volkswagen motor car engine to power this aircraft. Work on the Headwind was followed by design and construction of a new aeroplane, known as the JD_2FF Foo Fighter, and which is described separately.

STEWART JD_1 HW 1·7 HEADWIND

Built in only five months, the prototype Headwind flew for the first time on 28 March 1962. It can have an open or enclosed cockpit. The wings can be removed or fitted in about 20 minutes by two people.

During 1970, the fuselage, tail unit and landing gear of the Headwind were modified extensively, resulting in the new designation JD_1 HW 1·7 which Mr Stewart has applied to this aircraft.

Fuselage changes include a reduction of 2½ in (6·4 cm) in the depth of the structure, while increasing the headroom by 1 in (2·5 cm). The cowling forward of the instrument panel has been lowered by 3 in (7·6 cm), the aft seat support has been moved back 2 in (5·08 cm) and the landing gear bracing truss has been resited, resulting in increased cockpit volume.

The landing gear has been increased in height by 6 in (15·2 cm) and an optional rubber-in-compression shock-strut has been designed. The foregoing changes have been included in current plans and have been made available to all plan holders.

The power plant of the prototype Headwind has a belt-driven propeller reduction drive designed by Mr Stewart. Given the name Maximizer, this unit was put into production in the Spring of 1972 and is available to amateur constructors for use with Volkswagen power plants.

Several thousand sets of plans for the Headwind have been sold. About 150 aircraft are believed to be under construction and approximately 15 already flying.

The following details apply to Mr Stewart's basic design with the new wing:

TYPE: Single-seat homebuilt light aircraft.

WINGS: Strut-braced high-wing monoplane, with streamline-section Vee bracing strut each side. Wing section NACA 4412. Dihedral 2°. Incidence 2°. Two spruce spars, steel tube compression members, drag and anti-drag wires, plywood ribs, fabric covering. Frise-type ailerons of similar construction to wings. No flaps.

FUSELAGE: Welded steel tube structure, fabric-covered.

TAIL UNIT: Braced steel tube structure, fabric-covered. Ground-adjustable tailplane incidence. Fixed tabs on rudder and starboard elevator.

LANDING GEAR: Non-retractable tailwheel type. Shock-absorption by low-pressure tyres. Hayes main wheels with Goodyear tyres size 8·00-4. Tyre pressure 12 lb/sq in (0·84 kg/cm²). Alternatively, rubber-in-compression shock-struts, with Cleveland or Goodyear wheels and tyres size 6·00-6, tyre pressure 18 lb/sq in (1·26 kg/cm²). No brakes. Steerable tailwheel.

POWER PLANT: One 36 hp modified Volkswagen 1,192 cc motor car engine, driving a special Stewart/Kirk two-blade fixed-pitch propeller via a Stewart belt-driven reduction unit, ratio 1·6 : 1. Engines weighing up to 185 lb (84 kg) can be utilised. Fuel tank aft of firewall, capacity 5 US gallons (19 litres). Oil capacity 5 US pints (2·4 litres).

ACCOMMODATION: Single seat in open or enclosed cockpit, with door on starboard side. Provision for up to 10 lb (4·5 kg) baggage in net, directly aft of cockpit.

DIMENSIONS, EXTERNAL:

Wing span	28 ft 3 in (8·61 m)
Wing chord, constant	4 ft 0 in (1·22 m)
Wing aspect ratio	7
Length overall	17 ft 9 in (5·41 m)
Height overall	5 ft 6 in (1·68 m)
Tailplane span	7 ft 0 in (2·13 m)
Wheel track	5 ft 0 in (1·52 m)
Wheelbase	13 ft 6 in (4·11 m)
Propeller diameter	5 ft 2 in (1·57 m)
Propeller ground clearance	9 in (23 cm)

AREAS:

Wings, gross	110·95 sq ft (10·3 m²)
Ailerons (total)	14·83 sq ft (1·38 m²)
Fin	2·17 sq ft (0·20 m²)
Rudder	4·77 sq ft (0·44 m²)
Tailplane	7·00 sq ft (0·65 m²)
Elevators	9·54 sq ft (0·89 m²)

WEIGHTS AND LOADING:

Weight empty	437 lb (198 kg)
Max T-O and landing weight	700 lb (317 kg)
Max wing loading	6·3 lb/sq ft (30·8 kg/m²)

PERFORMANCE (at max T-O weight):

Max never-exceed speed	95·5 knots (110 mph; 177 km/h)
Max level speed at S/L	69·5 knots (80 mph; 129 km/h)
Cruising speed	65 knots (75 mph; 121 km/h)
Stalling speed	32-33 knots (36-38 mph; 58-61 km/h)
Max rate of climb at S/L	400 ft (122 m)/min
Absolute ceiling	11,000 ft (3,355 m)
T-O run	300 ft (91 m)
T-O to 50 ft (15 m)	1,200 ft (365 m)
Landing from 50 ft (15 m)	1,600 ft (490 m)
Landing run	450 ft (137 m)
Endurance with max fuel, no reserve	2½ hours

Stewart Headwind built by Mr Richard F. Geide Jr of Wichita, Kansas (53 hp Volkswagen modified motor car engine)

Stewart JD$_2$FF Foo Fighter (125 hp Franklin Sport 4 engine)

STEWART JD$_2$FF FOO FIGHTER

Design of Mr Stewart's Foo Fighter began in October 1967 and the first prototype (N2123) made its first flight in June 1971 powered by a six-cylinder Ford Falcon motor car engine developing 120 hp at 3,800 rpm. This engine was subsequently replaced by a 125 hp Franklin Sport 4.

A second prototype of the Foo Fighter (N2124), which also has a 125 hp Franklin engine, has been sold for exhibition flights at Lafayette Escadrille '76 in Pennsylvania. During 1972, Mr Stewart designed new wings for the Foo Fighter, of increased span and chord, and the following description is applicable to the aircraft in this form:

TYPE: Single-seat lightweight sporting biplane.

WINGS: Braced single-bay biplane. Wing section NACA 4412. Dihedral 0° upper wing, 1° lower wing. Incidence 2° upper wing, 0° lower wing. Conventional structure with two wooden spars and light alloy ribs, fabric-covered. N-type interplane struts each side; two N-type struts, joined at their upper ends, support the centre of the upper wing above fuselage. The lower wing extends below the fuselage, being attached to a cabane, and is faired over with light gauge light alloy sheet. Streamline-section landing and flying wires. Cutout in trailing-edges of both wings. Frise-type ailerons of similar construction to wings. No flaps. No trim tabs.

FUSELAGE: Welded steel tube structure with wood formers and stringers, fabric-covered.

TAIL UNIT: Wire-braced welded steel tube structure with fabric covering. Tailplane incidence ground-adjustable. Fixed tab in starboard elevator.

LANDING GEAR: Non-retractable tailwheel type, with steerable tailwheel or tailskid. Two side Vees with half-axles attached to fuselage structure. Shock-absorption by rubber cords in tension. Stewart wheels with tyres size 3·00-16, pressure 40 lb/sq in (2·81 kg/cm²). Stewart caliper brakes.

POWER PLANT: One 125 hp Franklin Sport 4 four-cylinder horizontally-opposed aircooled engine, driving a two-blade wooden fixed-pitch propeller. Fuel contained in glassfibre tank mounted in fuselage immediately aft of firewall, capacity 19 US gallons (72 litres). Refuelling point on fuselage upper surface. Oil capacity 1 US gallon (3·75 litres).

ACCOMMODATION: Single seat in open cockpit. Space for 10 lb (4·5 kg) baggage aft of seat.

DIMENSIONS, EXTERNAL:

Wing span (both)	20 ft 8 in (6·30 m)
Wing chord, constant (both)	3 ft 4 in (1·02 m)
Wing aspect ratio	6·075
Length overall	18 ft 9 in (5·72 m)
Height overall	7 ft 0 in (2·13 m)
Tailplane span	6 ft 4 in (1·93 m)
Wheel track	5 ft 9 in (1·75 m)
Wheelbase	12 ft 4 in (3·76 m)
Propeller diameter	6 ft 0 in (1·83 m)
Propeller ground clearance	1 ft 1 in (0·33 m)

AREAS:

Wings, gross	140 sq ft (13·0 m²)
Ailerons (total)	13·5 sq ft (1·25 m²)
Fin	4·8 sq ft (0·45 m²)
Rudder	5·5 sq ft (0·51 m²)
Tailplane	14·3 sq ft (1·33 m²)
Elevators	7·7 sq ft (0·72 m²)

WEIGHTS AND LOADING:

Weight empty	725 lb (328 kg)
Max T-O weight	1,100 lb (499 kg)
Max power loading	8·8 lb/hp (3·99 kg/hp)

PERFORMANCE (at max T-O weight):

Max never-exceed speed	126 knots (145 mph; 233 km/h)
Max cruising speed	100 knots (115 mph; 185 km/h)
Stalling speed	42 knots (48 mph; 77·5 km/h)
Max rate of climb at S/L	1,200 ft (366 m)/min
T-O run	450 ft (137 m)
Landing run	550 ft (168 m)

STOLP

STOLP STARDUSTER CORPORATION

ADDRESS:

4301 Twining, Riverside, California 92509
Telephone: (714) 686-7943

Mr Louis A. Stolp and Mr George M. Adams designed and built a light single-seat sporting biplane known as the Starduster, which flew for the first time in November 1957. It was followed first by a two-seat version, known as the Starduster Too and, in 1969, by a small single-seat monoplane designated SA-500 Starlet. A fully aerobatic two-seat biplane, designated SA-750 Acroduster Too, and a new lightweight sporting biplane, the SA-900 V-Star, were introduced during 1972. Most recent design to emanate from this company is that of a single-seat fully aerobatic biplane designated SA-700 Acroduster 1.

These aircraft are licensed in the Homebuilt category and not intended for series production. However, plans and basic materials are available from Stolp Starduster Corporation, and many have been built by amateurs.

STOLP-ADAMS SA-100 STARDUSTER

The SA-100 Starduster was designed primarily for use as a sporting biplane. The design is stressed to accept engines in the 85-170 hp range.

TYPE: Single-seat sporting biplane.

WINGS: Biplane wings of unequal span, with single interplane strut each side. Multiple centre-section bracing struts. Wing section NACA 4412. Dihedral 1° 30′ on lower wings only. Incidence 1° 30′ on lower wings only. Sweepback on leading-edges of upper wings 6°. Wood structure with fabric covering. Fabric-covered wooden ailerons on lower wings only. No flaps.

FUSELAGE: Welded 4130 steel tube structure with fabric covering.

TAIL UNIT: Welded 4130 steel tube structure with fabric covering.

LANDING GEAR: Non-retractable tailwheel type.

Rubber-cord shock-absorption. Firestone 6·00-6 main wheels and hydraulic brakes.

POWER PLANT: One 125 hp Lycoming O-290-D1 four-cylinder horizontally-opposed aircooled engine, driving a Sensenich Type M74DM61 two-blade metal fixed-pitch propeller. Fuel in one 12 US gallon (45·5 litre) fuselage tank, and one 6 US gallon (22·7 litre) tank in each upper wing. Total fuel capacity 24 US gallons (91 litres). Oil capacity 6 US quarts (5·6 litres).

ACCOMMODATION: Single seat in open cockpit.

DIMENSIONS, EXTERNAL:

Wing span:	
Upper	19 ft 0 in (5·79 m)
Lower	18 ft 0 in (5·49 m)
Wing chord, mean (both)	3 ft 0 in (0·91 m)
Wing aspect ratio	6·33
Length overall	16 ft 6 in (5·03 m)
Height overall	6 ft 0 in (1·83 m)
Tailplane span	7 ft 1 in (2·16 m)
Wheel track	5 ft 0 in (1·52 m)
Wheelbase	12 ft 0 in (3·66 m)

AREAS:

Wings, gross	110 sq ft (10·22 m²)
Ailerons (total)	7·0 sq ft (0·65 m²)
Fin	4·4 sq ft (0·41 m²)
Rudder	6·0 sq ft (0·56 m²)
Tailplane	9·0 sq ft (0·84 m²)
Elevators	7·0 sq ft (0·65 m²)

WEIGHTS AND LOADINGS:

Weight empty, equipped	700 lb (318 kg)
Max T-O weight	1,080 lb (490 kg)
Max wing loading	10 lb/sq ft (48·7 kg/m²)
Max power loading	8·6 lb/hp (3·9 kg/hp)

PERFORMANCE (at max T-O weight):

Max level speed	128 knots (147 mph; 237 km/h)
Cruising speed	115 knots (132 mph; 212 km/h)
Landing speed	43 knots (50 mph; 80 km/h)
Max rate of climb at S/L	2,000 ft (610 m)/min
T-O run	200 ft (61 m)

STOLP SA-300 STARDUSTER TOO

The SA-300 Starduster Too is a slightly enlarged tandem two-seat version of the SA-100 Starduster. The general design and construction of the two types are identical, except that the Starduster Too has ailerons on both top and bottom wings and has wheel fairings as standard equipment. The wing section is M6. Incidence is 1° on the lower wings only; dihedral 1° 30′ on the lower wings only.

The design is stressed to take engines in the 125-260 hp range. The prototype has a 180 hp Lycoming O-360-A1A four-cylinder horizontally-opposed aircooled engine.

The following details apply to the radial-engined Starduster Too with a 165 hp Warner Super Scarab engine, built by Mr Jack Mills of Zionsville, Indiana, which was illustrated in the 1973-74 *Jane's*:

DIMENSIONS, EXTERNAL:

Wing span, upper	24 ft 0 in (7·32 m)
Wing chord (constant, both)	4 ft 0 in (1·22 m)
Length overall	20 ft 0 in (6·10 m)
Height overall	7 ft 6 in (2·29 m)

WEIGHTS:

Weight empty	1,105 lb (501 kg)
Max T-O weight	1,650 lb (748 kg)

PERFORMANCE (at max T-O weight):

Max level speed	156 knots (180 mph; 290 km/h)
Cruising speed	104 knots (120 mph; 193 km/h)
Landing speed	52 knots (60 mph; 97 km/h)
Max rate of climb at S/L	2,600 ft (792 m)/min
Absolute ceiling	10,000 ft (3,050 m)
T-O run	500 ft (152 m)
Landing run	1,000 ft (305 m)
Range	260 nm (300 miles; 482 km)

STOLP SA-500 STARLET

The SA-500 Starlet is a single-seat swept parasol-wing monoplane. The wing is of wooden construction with spruce spars, plywood web and cap-strip ribs, with Dacron covering. It has a Clark YH section; sweepback is 9° and incidence 3° 30′. The fuselage is of welded 4130 steel tube with Dacron covering, and the tail unit is a braced structure of the same materials. The non-retractable tailwheel-type landing gear has cantilever main legs with wheel fairings. Power plant in the prototype consists of a 1,500 cc Volkswagen four-cylinder horizontally-opposed aircooled engine, driving a fixed-pitch two-blade propeller with spinner. Other engines of 85-125 hp may be fitted, the 108 hp Lycoming being recommended.

Construction of the prototype occupied three months and cost $1,500. First flight was made on 1 June 1969.

DIMENSIONS, EXTERNAL:

Wing span	25 ft 0 in (7·62 m)
Wing chord	3 ft 0 in (0·91 m)
Length overall	17 ft 0 in (5·18 m)
Height overall	6 ft 8 in (2·03 m)

AREA:

Wings, gross	83 sq ft (7·71 m²)

WEIGHT:

Max T-O weight	750 lb (340 kg)

PERFORMANCE (at max T-O weight):

Cruising speed	78 knots (90 mph; 145 km/h)
Landing speed	48-52 knots (55-60 mph; 89-97 km/h)

Stolp-Adams SA-100 Starduster built by Mr Eugene Coppock of Chicago, Illinois (*Howard Levy*)

Stolp SA-300 Starduster Too with enclosed canopy, built by Mr George Wright of Grand Rapids, Michigan (*Howard Levy*)

Stolp SA-500 Starlet built in the UK by Mr S. Miles (*Air Portraits*)

Stolp SA-700 Acroduster 1 fully-aerobatic single-seat biplane

STOLP SA-700 ACRODUSTER 1

Introduced in 1973, the SA-700 is a single-seat fully-aerobatic biplane. Ailerons on both wings produce a roll rate in excess of 240° a second, and an interesting design feature is that the four ailerons are raised slightly when the control column is pulled back. This helps maintain aileron control when the aircraft is stalled in a normal attitude. Conversely, the ailerons are drooped slightly when the control column is pushed forward, which helps to maintain aileron control in an inverted stall. Plans and kits of components are available to amateur constructors.

TYPE: Single-seat homebuilt aerobatic biplane.

WINGS: Braced single-bay biplane. Single I-type interplane strut each side. N-type centre-section struts. Streamline-section flying and landing wires. Aerofoil section Osborne A-1. Upper wing swept back 6°. Conventional two-spar structure. Spruce spars, plywood ribs and fabric covering. Ailerons on both wings. Upper wing built as two separate panels, joined by bolts at the centre. Stressed to $\pm 9g$ ultimate.

FUSELAGE: All-metal semi-monocoque structure of light alloy.

TAIL UNIT: Cantilever structure of light alloy.

LANDING GEAR: Non-retractable tailwheel type. Main wheels carried on sprung cantilever legs of 2024-0 T-4 light alloy. Fairings for main wheels.

POWER PLANT: Prototype has a 200 hp Lycoming four-cylinder horizontally-opposed aircooled engine, driving a two-blade fixed-pitch propeller with spinner. Suitable for engines of 125-200 hp. Fuel tank in fuselage, aft of firewall, capacity 25 US gallons (94·5 litres). Refuelling point on upper fuselage forward of windscreen.

ACCOMMODATION: Single seat in open cockpit. Space for 50 lb (23 kg) of baggage in turtledeck compartment.

DIMENSIONS, EXTERNAL:
- Wing span, upper: 19 ft 0 in (5·79 m)
- Length overall: 15 ft 9 in (4·80 m)
- Height overall: 6 ft 3 in (1·91 m)

AREA:
- Wings, gross: 105 sq ft (9·75 m²)

WEIGHTS AND LOADINGS (prototype with 200 hp engine):
- Weight empty: 740 lb (335 kg)
- Aerobatic T-O weight: 1,050 lb (476 kg)
- Max T-O weight: 1,190 lb (539 kg)
- Wing loading for aerobatics: 10 lb/sq ft (48·8 kg/m²)
- Max wing loading: 11·33 lb/sq ft (55·3 kg/m²)
- Power loading for aerobatics: 5·25 lb/hp (2·38 kg/hp)
- Max power loading: 5·95 lb/hp (2·70 kg/hp)

PERFORMANCE (at AUW of 1,050 lb; 476 kg):
- Max level speed: 156 knots (180 mph; 290 km/h)
- Cruising speed: 143 knots (165 mph; 266 km/h)
- Stalling speed: 61 knots (70 mph; 113 km/h)
- Max rate of climb at S/L: more than 3,000 ft (914 m)/min
- Endurance at cruising speed, with reserve: 2 hr

STOLP SA-750 ACRODUSTER TOO

The SA-750 is basically a two-seat aerobatic biplane generally similar to the Starduster Too.

Few details of this aircraft were available in early 1974. Stressed to $\pm 9g$, it has symmetrical wings, the upper wing being swept back 6°, and is powered by a 200 hp Lycoming IO-360 engine driving a two-blade constant-speed propeller. The front cockpit is open and has a small windscreen. A bubble canopy for the rear cockpit is faired neatly to the turtleback.

DIMENSIONS, EXTERNAL:
- Wing span, upper: 21 ft 5 in (6·53 m)
- Length overall: 18 ft 6 in (5·64 m)
- Height overall: 6 ft 10 in (2·08 m)

Stolp SA-750 Acroduster Too aerobatic biplane (200 hp Lycoming IO-360 engine)

Stolp SA-900 V-Star single-seat biplane (65 hp Continental engine)

AREA:
- Wings, gross: 130 sq ft (12·1 m²)

PERFORMANCE (at max T-O weight):
- Cruising speed: 139 knots (160 mph; 257 km/h)
- Stalling speed: 48 knots (55 mph; 88·5 km/h)
- Max rate of climb at S/L: 2,300 ft (701 m)/min

STOLP SA-900 V-STAR

To meet the demand for low cost, low horsepower aircraft with aerobatic capability, Stolp has introduced the SA-900 V-Star, which is essentially a biplane version of the single-seat SA-500 Starlet.

It is stressed to $\pm 9g$. The wings, of Clark YH section, have N-shape centre-section and I-shape interplane struts. Incidence of the upper wing is 2° 30′ and that of the lower wings 2°. The upper wing is swept back 6°.

The prototype has a 65 hp Continental four-cylinder horizontally-opposed aircooled engine, driving a two-blade fixed-pitch propeller, but engines of 60 to 125 hp may be installed.

DIMENSIONS, EXTERNAL:
- Wing span, upper: 23 ft 0 in (7·01 m)
- Length overall: 17 ft 2 in (5·23 m)
- Height overall: 7 ft 5 in (2·26 m)

AREA:
- Wings, gross: 141 sq ft (13·1 m²)

PERFORMANCE (prototype, at max T-O weight):
- Cruising speed: 65 knots (75 mph; 121 km/h)
- Stalling speed: 30·5 knots (35 mph; 56·5 km/h)
- Max rate of climb at S/L: 600 ft (183 m)/min

SWEARINGEN

SWEARINGEN AVIATION CORPORATION (a subsidiary of Fairchild Industries)

ADDRESS:
PO Box 32486, San Antonio, Texas 78284
Telephone: (512) 824-9421

CHAIRMAN: E. J. Swearingen

PRESIDENT: G. Stathis

VICE-PRESIDENTS:
R. N. Robinson (Marketing)
J. O'Connell (Finance)
R. E. McKelvey (Engineering)

DIRECTORS:
S. Mira (Contract Administrator)
T. Haines (Personnel)

In a joint announcement, made on 2 November 1971, Fairchild Industries and Swearingen Aircraft gave details of an agreement under which a new subsidiary, to be known as Swearingen Aviation Corporation and of which 90% of the stock was owned by Fairchild Industries, would acquire the assets of Swearingen Aircraft. Mr Edward J. Swearingen, founder and Chief Executive Officer of Swearingen Aircraft, became Chairman of the new company.

Since 1966 Swearingen has been engaged in the manufacture of the Merlin series of twin-turboprop pressurised executive transport aircraft. Early models were the Merlin IIA and generally similar Merlin IIB, details of which can be found in the 1969-70 and 1972-73 *Jane's* respectively. Current production versions are the Merlin III and IV and Metro. A total of 194 Merlins were in operation throughout the world in March 1974; customers include the Australian, Mexican and United States governments.

The company had approximately 750 employees at the end of February 1973, when the combined production rate of Merlin III, IV and Metro aircraft was three per month.

Swearingen Merlin III eight/ten-seat executive transport (two 904 ehp AiResearch TPE 331-3U-303G turboprop engines)

SWEARINGEN MERLIN III

The Merlin III is an eight/ten-seat executive transport which differs from the earlier Merlin IIB by having a new tail unit, slightly longer fuselage, and the wings, landing gear and more powerful turboprop engines of the Metro, together with a more sophisticated electrical system. FAA certification of the Merlin III was awarded on 27 July 1970.

On 7 July 1971 a Swearingen Merlin III was first across the finishing line at Victoria, British Columbia, so winning the 5,081 nm (5,851 mile; 9,416 km) transatlantic and transcontinental London-Victoria air race. Owned by Battenfeld GmbH, a West German manufacturer of machine tools for the plastics industry, the Merlin III was flown by J. H. Blumschein and Fritz Kohlgruber.

A total of 45 Merlin IIIs had been delivered by 1 January 1974.

TYPE: Eight/ten-seat twin-turboprop executive transport.

WINGS: Same as for Metro.

FUSELAGE: Cylindrical all-metal fail-safe structure, flush-riveted throughout. Glassfibre honeycomb nose-cap will accommodate an 18 in (45 cm) weather radar antenna.

TAIL UNIT: Cantilever all-metal structure with sweptback vertical and horizontal surfaces. Dorsal fin, with tailplane mounted approximately one-third up from base of fin. Small ventral fin. Pneumatic de-icing boots on tailplane leading-edges.

LANDING GEAR: Same as for Metro.

POWER PLANT: Two 840 shp (904 ehp) AiResearch TPE 331-3U-303G turboprop engines, each driving a Hartzell three-blade fully-feathering and reversible-pitch metal propeller. Integral fuel tank in each wing, each with a usable capacity of 324 US gallons (1,226 litres): total usable fuel capacity 648 US gallons (2,452 litres). Refuelling points in each outer wing panel. Engine inlet de-icing by bleed air.

Accommodation: Crew of two on flight deck, with dual controls. Bulkhead with sliding door divides flight deck from cabin. Standard accommodation for six to eight passengers in pairs, with central aisle. Passenger door at rear of cabin on port side, with integral airstair. Emergency exit on starboard side of cabin.

Systems: Same as for Metro except that electrical system comprises two 3kVA engine-driven alternators providing 115V 400Hz AC to power gyros, instrumentation and automatic flight control system; auxiliary static inverter; two 300A DC starter/generators with multiple busbars protected by solid-state controls to provide automatic load-shedding and overvoltage protection, which serve as backup system for instrument flight capability. Automatic engine-start cycle.

Dimensions, external:
- Wing span: 46 ft 3 in (14·10 m)
- Wing chord at root: 8 ft 7 in (2·62 m)
- Wing chord at tip: 3 ft 5 in (1·04 m)
- Wing aspect ratio: 7·71
- Length overall: 42 ft 1·9 in (12·85 m)
- Height overall: 16 ft 8 in (5·08 m)
- Wheel track: 15 ft 0 in (4·57 m)
- Passenger door:
  - Height: 5 ft 4 in (1·63 m)
  - Width: 2 ft 1 in (0·64 m)

Dimensions, internal:
- Length, including flight deck and rear utility section: 21 ft 9 in (6·63 m)
- Cabin:
  - Length between front and rear bulkheads: 10 ft 8 in (3·25 m)
  - Width: 5 ft 2 in (1·57 m)
  - Height: 4 ft 11 in (1·50 m)
- Baggage capacity: 85 cu ft (2·41 m³)

Area:
- Wings, gross: 277·50 sq ft (25·78 m²)

Weights and Loadings:
- Weight empty, equipped: 7,400 lb (3,356 kg)
- Max ramp weight: 12,560 lb (5,697 kg)
- Max T-O weight: 12,500 lb (5,670 kg)
- Max zero-fuel weight: 10,000 lb (4,535 kg)
- Max landing weight: 11,500 lb (5,217 kg)
- Max wing loading: 45·0 lb/sq ft (219·7 kg/m²)
- Max power loading: 7·44 lb/shp (3·37 kg/shp)

Performance (at max T-O weight):
- Max cruising speed at 16,000 ft (4,875 m): 274 knots (316 mph; 509 km/h)
- Econ cruising speed at 28,000 ft (8,535 m): 250 knots (288 mph; 463 km/h)
- Max speed, flaps and wheels down: 176 knots (203 mph; 327 km/h)
- Stalling speed, flaps and wheels up: 97 knots (111 mph; 179 km/h)
- Stalling speed, flaps and wheels down: 84 knots (96 mph; 155 km/h)
- Max rate of climb at S/L: 2,530 ft (771 m)/min
- Rate of climb at S/L, one engine out: 620 ft (189 m)/min
- Service ceiling: 28,900 ft (8,810 m)
- Service ceiling, one engine out: 15,000 ft (4,575 m)
- Max operating altitude: 31,000 ft (9,450 m)
- T-O run, short field: 2,150 ft (655 m)
- FAA T-O field length: 3,080 ft (939 m)
- Landing from 50 ft (15 m): 1,570 ft (479 m)
- Range with max fuel at max cruising speed: 1,670 nm (1,924 miles; 3,095 km)
- Range with max fuel at econ cruising speed, 45 min reserve fuel: 2,318 nm (2,670 miles; 4,297 km)

SWEARINGEN MERLIN IV

The Merlin IV is a corporate version of the Metro commuter airliner, to which it is generally similar. It differs principally in its internal configuration, which provides accommodation for 12 passengers, with a private toilet and a baggage area of 181 cu ft (5·13 m³). Initial deliveries of this version were made in 1970, following FAA certification on 23 September that year. A total of 15 aircraft had been delivered by the end of 1973.

The description of the Metro applies also to the Merlin IV, except that there is some variation in the systems.

Dimensions, external:
- Same as for Metro

Dimensions, internal:
- Cabin, excluding flight deck:
  - Length: 25 ft 5 in (7·75 m)
- Baggage compartment:
  - Length: 6 ft 3 in (1·91 m)
- Baggage capacity: 181 cu ft (5·13 m³)

Areas:
- Same as for Metro

Weights and Loadings:
- Weight empty, equipped: 8,150 lb (3,696 kg)
- Max ramp weight: 12,560 lb (5,697 kg)
- Max T-O weight: 12,500 lb (5,670 kg)
- Max zero-fuel weight: 12,500 lb (5,670 kg)
- Max landing weight: 12,500 lb (5,670 kg)

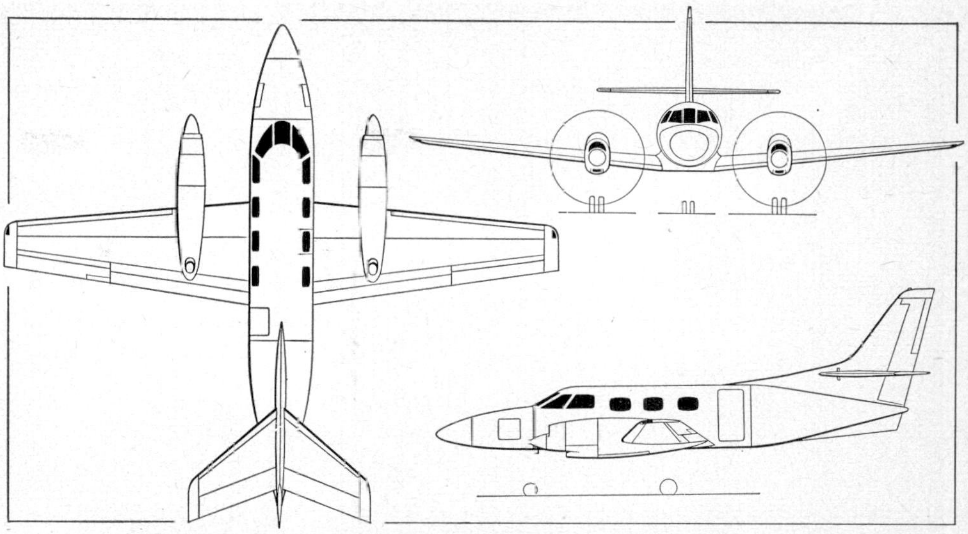

Swearingen Merlin III (two 904 ehp AiResearch TPE 331 turboprops) *(Pilot Press)*

- Max wing loading: 45·0 lb/sq ft (219·7 kg/m²)
- Max power loading: 7·44 lb/shp (3·37 kg/shp)

Performance (at max T-O weight):
- Max cruising speed at 16,000 ft (4,875 m): 262 knots (302 mph; 486 km/h)
- Econ cruising speed at 28,000 ft (8,535 m): 240 knots (276 mph; 444 km/h)
- Max speed, flaps and wheels down: 176 knots (203 mph; 327 km/h)
- Max operating altitude: 31,000 ft (9,450 m)
- Range with max fuel at max cruising speed, 45 min reserve: 1,578 nm (1,818 miles; 2,925 km)
- Range with max fuel at econ cruising speed, 45 min reserve: 1,995 nm (2,300 miles; 3,700 km)

SWEARINGEN MODEL SA-226TC METRO

The Swearingen Metro is a 19/20-passenger airliner, with an easily convertible passenger/cargo interior designed specifically to allow maximum flexibility to operators of commuter airlines.

Construction of a prototype began in August 1968 and this aircraft flew for the first time on 26 August 1969, FAA certification being granted in June of the following year.

Unlike previous products of this company, and most aircraft currently available to commuter airlines, which are modified, stretched and rebuilt versions of airframes designed originally for corporate use, the Metro was completely new.

By early 1974, Metro airliners had been delivered for service with Air East, Air Wisconsin, Commuter Airlines, Crown Airways and Mississippi Valley Airlines.

Type: Twin-turboprop 19/20-passenger commuter airliner.

Wings: Cantilever low-wing monoplane. Wing section NACA 65_2A215 at root, NACA 64_2A415 at tip. Dihedral 5°. Incidence 1° at root, —1° at tip. Sweepback at quarter-chord 0·9°. All-metal two-spar semi-monocoque fail-safe structure of aluminium alloy. Hydraulically-operated double-slotted trailing-edge flaps. Manually-controlled trim tab on port aileron. Goodrich pneumatic de-icing boots on wing leading-edges, with automatic bleed air cycling system.

Fuselage: All-metal cylindrical semi-monocoque fail-safe structure of aluminium alloy. Glass-fibre honeycomb nose cap can accommodate an 18 in (45 cm) weather radar antenna.

Tail Unit: Cantilever all-metal structure with sweptback vertical surfaces and dorsal fin. Electrically-adjustable variable-incidence tailplane. Manually-controlled rudder trim. Goodrich pneumatic de-icing boots on tailplane leading-edges, with automatic bleed air cycling system.

Landing Gear: Retractable tricycle type with twin wheels on each unit. Hydraulic retraction, with dual actuators on each unit. All wheels retract forward, main gear into engine nacelles, nosewheels into fuselage. Ozone Aircraft Systems oleo-pneumatic shock-absorber struts. Nosewheels steerable. Free-fall emergency extension system. B.F. Goodrich main wheels and tyres, size 18 × 5·50, type VII, pressure 100 lb/sq in (7·03 kg/cm²). General Tire Company nosewheels and tyres, size 16 × 4·40, type VII, pressure 85 lb/sq in (5·98 kg/cm²). Goodrich self-adjusting hydraulically-operated disc brakes.

Power Plant: Two 940 shp AiResearch TPE 331-3UW-303G turboprop engines, each driving a Hartzell three-blade fully-feathering and reversible propeller with automatic synchronisation. Integral fuel tank in each wing, each with a usable capacity of 324 US gallons (1,226 litres). Total usable fuel capacity 648 US gallons (2,452 litres). Refuelling point on each outer wing panel. Oil capacity 4 US gallons (15·1 litres). Engine inlet de-icing by bleed air. Electrical propeller de-icing. Automatic fuel heating system to prevent filter icing. Flush-mounted fuel vents.

Accommodation: Crew of two on flight deck, separated from passenger/cargo area by arm-level curtain. Bulkhead between cabin and flight deck optional. Standard accommodation for 19-20 passengers seated two-abreast, on each side of centre aisle. Self-stowing fold-up seats for rapid conversion to cargo or mixed passenger/cargo configuration. Movable bulkhead between passenger and cargo sections. Snap-in carpeting. Self-stowing aisle filler. Tie-down fittings for cargo at 30 in (0·76 m) spacing. Integral-step passenger door on port side of fuselage, immediately aft of flight deck. Large passenger/cargo loading door on port side of fuselage at rear of cabin, hinged at top. Three window emergency exits, one on the port, two on the starboard side. Forward baggage compartment in nose, capacity 45 cu ft (1·27

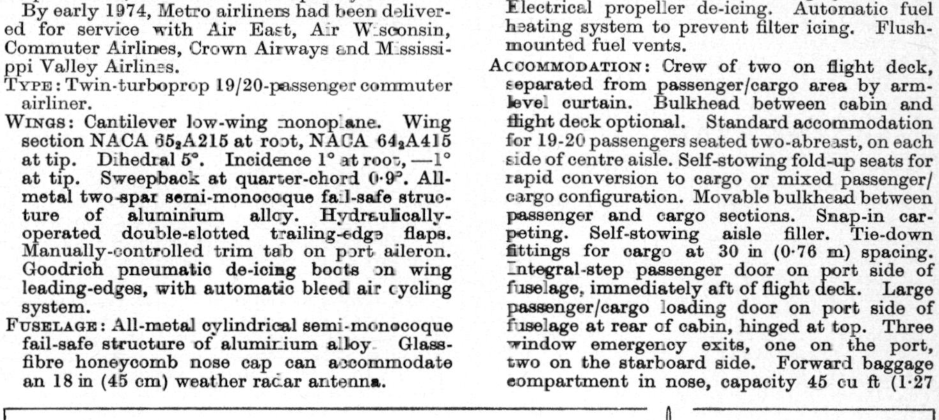

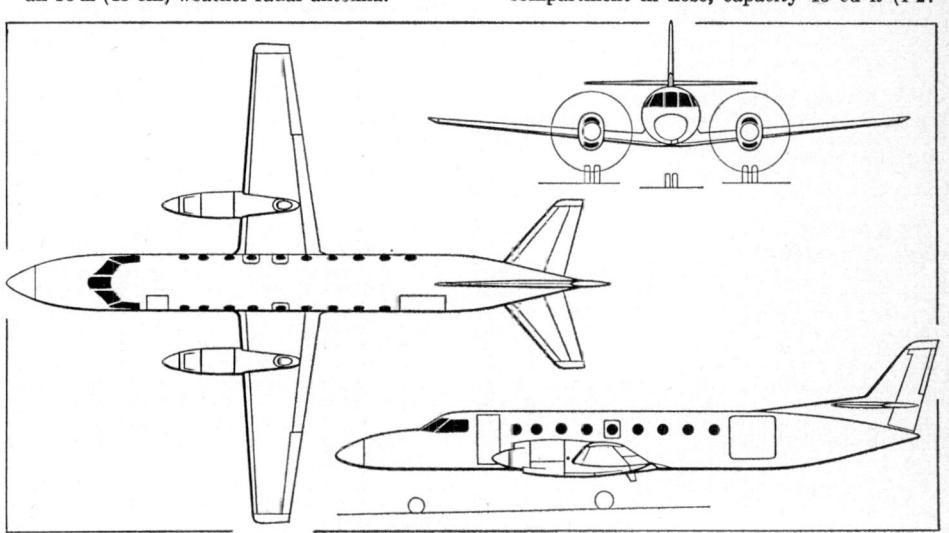

Swearingen Metro 19/20-passenger commuter airliner *(Pilot Press)*

Swearingen Metro 19/20-passenger commuter airliner (two 940 shp AiResearch TPE 331-3UW-303G turboprop engines)

m³). Pressurised rear cargo compartment in passenger version, capacity 136 cu ft (3·85 m³). Cabin air-conditioned and pressurised. Electrical windscreen de-icing. Windscreen wipers.

Systems: AiResearch automatic cabin pressure control system maintains a differential of 7·0 lb/sq in (0·49 kg/cm²). Engine bleed air heating, dual air-cycle cooling system, with automatic temperature control. Independent hydraulic system for brakes. Dual engine-driven hydraulic pumps provide 2,000 lb/sq in (140 kg/cm²) to operate flaps and landing gear. Electrical system supplied by two 200A 28V DC starter/generators. Fail-safe system with overload and over-voltage protection. Redundant circuits for essential systems. Two 25Ah nickel-cadmium batteries for main services. One small nickel-cadmium battery for utility lights only. Engine fire detection system standard. Engine fire extinguisher system optional. Oxygen system of 48 cu ft (1·36 m³) capacity with flush outlets at each seat.

Electronics and Equipment: Standard equipment includes individual reading lights and air vents for each passenger, electrically-heated pitot heads, ice-free instrument static sources. Provisions for installation of remotely-mounted or panel-mounted electronics, customer-furnished antennae and Bendix M-4 autopilot. Two flight deck and six cabin speakers standard.

Dimensions, external:
Wing span 46 ft 3 in (14·10 m)
Wing chord at root 8 ft 7 in (2·62 m)
Wing chord at tip 3 ft 5 in (1·04 m)
Wing aspect ratio 7·71
Length overall 59 ft 4¼ in (18·09 m)
Height overall 16 ft 8 in (5·08 m)
Tailplane span 15 ft 1½ in (4·61 m)
Wheel track 15 ft 0 in (4·57 m)
Wheelbase 19 ft 1½ in (5·83 m)
Propeller diameter 8 ft 6 in (2·59 m)
Passenger door (fwd):
Height 5 ft 4 in (1·63 m)
Width 2 ft 1 in (0·64 m)
Cargo door (aft):
Height 4 ft 3¼ in (1·30 m)
Width 4 ft 5 in (1·35 m)
Height to sill 4 ft 3¼ in (1·30 m)

Dimensions, internal:
Cabin, excluding flight deck and aft baggage compartment:
Length 25 ft 5 in (7·75 m)
Max width 5 ft 2 in (1·57 m)
Max height (aisle) 4 ft 9 in (1·45 m)
Floor area 140 sq ft (13·01 m²)
Volume 463 cu ft (13·11 m³)

Areas:
Wings, gross 277·50 sq ft (25·78 m²)
Ailerons (total) 14·12 sq ft (1·31 m²)
Trailing-edge flaps (total) 40·66 sq ft (3·78 m²)
Fin 56·00 sq ft (5·20 m²)
Rudder, including tab 21·27 sq ft (1·98 m²)
Tailplane 75·97 sq ft (7·06 m²)
Elevators 21·27 sq ft (1·98 m²)

Weights and Loadings:
Design empty weight 7,375 lb (3,345 kg)
Max ramp weight 12,560 lb (5,697 kg)
Max T-O and landing weight 12,500 lb (5,670 kg)
Max wing loading 45·5 lb/sq ft (222·1 kg/m²)
Max power loading 7·44 lb/shp (3·37 kg/shp)

Performance:
Max cruising speed at 10,000 ft (3,050 m), at 12,000 lb (5,445 kg) AUW 255 knots (294 mph; 473 km/h)
Long-range cruising speed at 20,000 ft (6,100 m), at 12,000 lb (5,445 kg) AUW 242 knots (279 mph; 449 km/h)
T-O to 50 ft (15 m) at 12,500 lb (5,670 kg) AUW 2,620 ft (799 m)
Landing from 50 ft (15 m) at 12,000 lb (5,445 kg) AUW, one engine out 3,440 ft (1,050 m)
Range, with reserves:
VFR mission, 3,920 lb (1,778 kg) payload 87 nm (100 miles; 160 km)
IFR mission, 3,760 lb (1,705 kg) payload 87 nm (100 miles; 160 km)
VFR mission, 3,240 lb (1,469 kg) payload 435 nm (500 miles; 804 km)
IFR mission, 3,080 lb (1,397 kg) payload 435 nm (500 miles; 804 km)
Max ferry range (allowance for taxi, T-O, climb, cruise, descent, landing, taxi-in and 45 min reserve fuel) 1,806 nm (2,080 miles; 3,347 km)

TELEDYNE RYAN

TELEDYNE RYAN AERONAUTICAL

Head Office and Works:
2701 Harbor Drive, San Diego, California 92112
Telephone: (714) 291-7311
Chairman:
Robert C. Jackson
President:
Barry J. Shillito
Executive Vice-President, Programmes:
R. R. Schwanhausser
Vice-Presidents:
D. L. Arney (Industrial Relations)
H. D. Drake (Electronic & Space Systems)
R. D. Fields (Finance and Controller)
T. E. Flannigan (Washington, DC Office)
E. C. Oemcke (Aerospace Systems)
W. J. Wiley (Plant Operations)
Public Relations and Communications Manager:
Robert B. Morrisey

The former Ryan Aeronautical Company was an indirect successor to Ryan Airlines Inc, which produced the aeroplane in which Mr Charles Lindbergh made the first non-stop flight from New York to Paris in 1927. In February 1969, Ryan Aeronautical became a wholly-owned subsidiary of Teledyne, Inc and in December 1969 the company was renamed Teledyne Ryan Aeronautical.

The current activities of the company fall into two major categories, under the headings of Aerospace Systems and Electronic and Space Systems. The former group is concerned principally with the design, production and field operation of high-performance aerial jet targets and RPV systems, described in detail under the company's entry in the "RPVs and Targets" section of this edition.

The Electronic and Space Systems group is responsible for design and production of radar equipment for landing spacecraft on Mars in the Viking programme; electronic navigation and positioning equipment for rotating and fixed-wing aircraft; remote sensors for Earth resources studies; electronic warfare systems; and microwave antennae.

On 10 June 1971 Teledyne Ryan announced that its AN/APN-200 Doppler velocity sensor, developed for the S-3A ASW patrol aircraft, had been accepted by Lockheed-California for further development test evaluation and integration into the S-3A weapon system.

An advanced navigation aid, incorporating electronic techniques perfected by Teledyne Ryan in earlier Dopplers and in its Apollo Moon-landing radars, the APN-200 is the first major subsystem to work with the S-3A's on-board central computer. In combination with the computer and an inertial system, the APN-200 can be used in accurate point-to-point navigation and in the critical localisation procedures to pinpoint enemy submarines.

Teledyne Ryan continues to maintain a strong technical interest in vertical take-off and landing aircraft, but this makes only a minor contribution to the volume of the company's business.

TERMITE

TERMITE AIRCRAFT

Termite Aircraft is marketing plans and kits of prefabricated wood components for a single-seat sporting monoplane known as the Termite, which was designed by Mr Wilbur L. Smith. The prototype was flown originally, on 10 February 1957, with a 36 hp Aeronca E-113-C engine, but has since been tested with, successively, a 38 hp Continental A40-5 and a 65 hp Lycoming O-145 engine, both of which are considered suitable for amateur-built Termites.

TERMITE

Many Termites have been built and flown by amateur constructor-pilots in the USA, Canada and elsewhere.

The following data apply to the standard Termite, built from Mr Smith's plans:

Type: Single-seat sporting monoplane.

Wings: Braced parasol monoplane, with two parallel streamline-section metal bracing struts each side and six bracing struts between fuselage and centre-wing. Wing section Clark Y. Dihedral 1°. Incidence 2°. All-wood two-spar structure. Aluminium-covered leading-edge. Fabric covering aft of front spar. Fabric-covered wood ailerons.

Fuselage: All-wood structure, plywood-covered to rear of cockpit, with fabric covering on rear fuselage.

Tail Unit: Wire-braced wood structure, except for steel tube leading- and trailing-edges. Fabric-covered.

Landing Gear: Non-retractable two-wheel type. Main units of Piper Cub type. Goodyear wheels, size 7·00-3. No brakes. Spring steel tailskid.

Power Plant: One 38 hp Continental A40-5 four-cylinder horizontally-opposed aircooled engine driving a two-blade wooden fixed-pitch propeller. Alternatively one 65 hp Lycoming O-145 or Continental A65 engine. Fuel tank aft of firewall, capacity 6 US gallons (22·7 litres). Additional 5 US gallon (18·9 litre) wing tank on 65 hp version.

Accommodation: Single seat in open cockpit.

Dimensions, external:
Wing span 23 ft 6 in (7·16 m)
Wing chord, constant 4 ft 2 in (1·27 m)
Length overall:
A40-5 15 ft 1 in (4·60 m)
O-145, A65 15 ft 9 in (4·80 m)

Height overall 5 ft 9 in (1·75 m)
Tailplane span 6 ft 10 in (2·08 m)
Wheel track 5 ft 2 in (1·57 m)

Weights:
Weight empty:
A40-5 432 lb (196 kg)
A65 776 lb (352 kg)
Max T-O weight:
A40-5 658 lb (298 kg)
A65 976 lb (443 kg)

Performance (at max T-O weight):
Max level speed at S/L:
A40-5 83 knots (95 mph; 153 km/h)
A65 78 knots (90 mph; 145 km/h)
Max cruising speed:
A40-5 72 knots (83 mph; 133 km/h)
A65 74 knots (85 mph; 137 km/h)
Landing speed:
A40-5 33 knots (38 mph; 61 km/h)
A65 52 knots (60 mph; 97 km/h)
Max rate of climb at S/L:
A40-5 450 ft (137 m)/min
A65 200 ft (61 m)/min
Service ceiling:
A65 6,000 ft (1,830 m)
T-O run:
A65 350 ft (107 m)
Landing run:
A65 400 ft (122 m)
Range with max fuel:
A40-5 130 nm (150 miles; 240 km)
A65 277 nm (320 miles; 515 km)

Termite amateur-built single-seat sporting aircraft *(Jean Seele)*

THORP

THORP ENGINEERING COMPANY

Address:
PO Box 516, Sun Valley, California 91352

This company was founded by Mr John W. Thorp, who is well known as a designer of light aircraft. It markets plans of the T-18 Tiger two-seat all-metal sporting aircraft, described below. Several hundred sets of drawings have been sold and many T-18s are flying.

THORP T-18 TIGER

First T-18 to be completed was N9675Z with a 180 hp Lycoming O-360 engine. Built by Mr W. Warwick, it flew for the first time on 12 May 1964 and was illustrated in the 1964-65 *Jane's*.

The following details apply to the standard Thorp T-18:

Type: Two-seat high-performance sporting aircraft.

Wings: Cantilever low-wing monoplane, with 8° dihedral on outer panels only. All-metal two-spar structure. Normally no flaps, but a flap installation is under design.

Fuselage: All-metal structure, without double curvature.

Tail Unit: Cantilever all-metal structure.

Landing Gear: Non-retractable tailwheel type. Cantilever main legs. Steerable tailwheel. Main-wheel tyres size 5·00-5.

Power Plant: One Lycoming or Continental four-cylinder horizontally-opposed aircooled engine in 108-200 hp category, driving a two-blade fixed-pitch propeller. Fuel tank aft of firewall, capacity 29 US gallons (110 litres).

Accommodation: Two seats side by side in open cockpit, with dual controls. Space for 80 lb (36 kg) baggage. Canopy optional.

Dimensions, external:
Wing span 20 ft 10 in (6·35 m)
Wing chord, constant 4 ft 2 in (1·27 m)
Length overall 18 ft 2 in (5·54 m)
Height overall 4 ft 10 in (1·47 m)
Tailplane span 6 ft 11 in (2·10 m)
Propeller diameter 5 ft 3 in (1·60 m)

Area:
Wings, gross 86 sq ft (8·0 m²)

Weights (180 hp Lycoming):
Weight empty 900 lb (408 kg)
Max T-O weight 1,506 lb (683 kg)

Performance (180 hp Lycoming):
Max level speed at S/L 174 knots (200 mph; 321 km/h)
Max cruising speed 152 knots (175 mph; 282 km/h)
Stalling speed 57 knots (65 mph; 105 km/h)
Max rate of climb at S/L 2,000 ft (610 m)/min
Service ceiling 20,000 ft (6,100 m)
T-O run 300 ft (91 m)
Landing run 900 ft (275 m)
Range with max fuel 434 nm (500 miles; 805 km)

Thorp T-18 Tiger built by Mr Ford Hendricks of Seattle *(Peter M. Bowers)*

TURNER

EUGENE L. TURNER

Address:
103 G Street SW, No B-320, Washington, DC 20024
Telephone: (202) 638-2552

The 1966-67 *Jane's* contained details of a single-seat sporting aircraft designated T-40, which was designed and built by Mr E. L. Turner and flew for the first time on 3 April 1961. This aircraft was modified by Mr Turner and his son into a prototype of the two-seat T-40A and is described below in this form. A new version of this aircraft, with larger wing, more powerful engine and other improvements, is designated Super T-40A, and is also described briefly. The original T-40A has been converted into another version of the same design, the T-40B, with a tricycle landing gear and other refinements, and this also is described.

Plans of these aircraft are available and 248 sets had been sold by the end of January 1974. Twelve aircraft are known to be flying and it is estimated that there are at least 125 under construction.

TURNER T-40A

The prototype T-40A was produced by conversion of the original T-40. Modification took about four months and the aircraft flew for the first time in this form on 29 July 1966.

The T-40A is small enough to fit in a single-car garage and is transported on a small trailer. It has built-in skids in the fuselage, to protect the pilot in a minor crash landing, and an overturn structure.

Type: Two-seat sporting aircraft.

Wings: Cantilever low-wing monoplane. Wing section NACA 65-215. Dihedral 4°. Incidence 1° 30′. All-wood (fir) two-spar structure with mahogany plywood covering. Hoerner low-drag tips. Plain ailerons. Large plain flaps. Wings fold rearward for stowage.

Turner Super T-40A built by Dr Jim Mandley

FUSELAGE: All-wood (fir) structure, covered with mahogany plywood. Glassfibre engine cowling.

TAIL UNIT: Cantilever all-wood (fir) structure with mahogany plywood covering. Horizontal surface of all-flying type with anti-servo tabs. Glassfibre dorsal fin.

LANDING GEAR: Non-retractable tailwheel type. Cantilever spring steel main units attached to front spar. Cleveland main wheels and tyres, size 5·00-5, pressure 45 lb/sq in (3·16 kg/cm²). Cleveland brakes.

POWER PLANT: One Continental four-cylinder horizontally-opposed aircooled engine of 85 to 100 hp, driving a McCauley two-blade fixed-pitch propeller, type 65/57. Fuel tank in front fuselage, capacity 20 US gallons (75 litres). Oil capacity 1 US gallon (3·75 litres).

ACCOMMODATION: Pilot and passenger side by side. Each half of transparent canopy is hinged on centreline of aircraft to form a door, folding in two as it opens upward. Space for 25 lb (11·5 kg) baggage aft of seats.

EQUIPMENT: Prototype has Narco VHT-3 radio.

DIMENSIONS, EXTERNAL:
- Wing span: 25 ft 2 in (7·67 m)
- Wing chord, constant: 3 ft 6½ in (1·08 m)
- Wing aspect ratio: 7·2
- Length overall: 19 ft 9 in (6·02 m)
- Width, wings folded: 7 ft 10 in (2·39 m)
- Height overall: 6 ft 0 in (1·83 m)
- Tailplane span: 6 ft 5 in (1·96 m)
- Wheel track: 7 ft 4 in (2·24 m)

DIMENSIONS, INTERNAL:
- Cabin: Length: 5 ft 10 in (1·78 m)
  - Max width: 3 ft 4 in (1·02 m)
  - Max height: 3 ft 3 in (0·99 m)

AREAS:
- Wings, gross: 89·9 sq ft (8·35 m²)
- Ailerons (total): 6·5 sq ft (0·60 m²)
- Flaps (total): 9·9 sq ft (0·92 m²)
- Fin: 5·8 sq ft (0·54 m²)
- Rudder: 3·8 sq ft (0·35 m²)
- Horizontal tail surfaces: 11·34 sq ft (1·05 m²)

WEIGHTS:
- Weight empty: 828 lb (376 kg)
- Max T-O and landing weight: 1,410 lb (640 kg)

PERFORMANCE (85 hp engine, at max T-O weight):
- Max never-exceed speed: 191 knots (220 mph; 354 km/h)
- Max level speed at S/L: 130 knots (150 mph; 241 km/h)
- Max cruising speed at S/L: 113 knots (130 mph; 209 km/h)
- Econ cruising speed at S/L: 104 knots (120 mph; 193 km/h)
- Stalling speed, flaps up: 54 knots (62 mph; 100 km/h)
- Stalling speed, flaps down: 47 knots (54 mph; 87 km/h)
- Max rate of climb at S/L: 750 ft (229 m)/min
- Estimated service ceiling: 12,500 ft (3,800 m)
- T-O run: 700 ft (213 m)
- T-O to 50 ft (15 m): 1,200 ft (365 m)
- Landing run: 460 ft (140 m)
- Range with max payload, 20 min reserve: 412 nm (475 miles; 756 km)

TURNER SUPER T-40A

The Super T-40A differs from the standard T-40A by having a larger wing, more powerful engine, swept tail, bubble canopy and other improvements. The prototype made its first flight in early 1972.

Turner T-40B prototype, a conversion of the T-40A with tricycle landing gear (*Howard Levy*)

WINGS: As for T-40A, except span and chord increased.

TAIL UNIT: As for T-40A, except swept vertical surfaces, and vertical and horizontal surfaces of increased area.

LANDING GEAR: Non-retractable tailwheel type standard, with optional non-retractable or retractable tricycle type.

POWER PLANT: One 125 hp four-cylinder horizontally-opposed aircooled engine standard; provision for four-cylinder engines of up to 150 hp.

ACCOMMODATION: As for T-40A, except for provision of a bubble canopy.

DIMENSIONS, EXTERNAL:
- Wing span: 26 ft 8 in (8·13 m)
- Wing chord, constant: 3 ft 10 in (1·17 m)
- Wing aspect ratio: 6·98
- Length overall: 20 ft 1 in (6·12 m)

AREAS:
- Wings, gross: 102·5 sq ft (9·5 m²)
- Horizontal tail surfaces: 12·0 sq ft (1·11 m²)
- Vertical tail surfaces: 10·5 sq ft (0·98 m²)

WEIGHT AND LOADINGS:
- Max T-O weight: 1,500 lb (680 kg)
- Max wing loading: 14·6 lb/sq ft (71·3 kg/m²)
- Max power loading: 12 lb/hp (5·44 kg/hp)

PERFORMANCE (at max T-O weight):
- Max level speed at S/L: 152 knots (175 mph; 282 km/h)
- Max cruising speed: 135 knots (155 mph; 249 km/h)
- Stalling speed, flaps down: 49·5 knots (57 mph; 92 km/h)
- Max rate of climb at S/L: over 1,200 ft (366 m)/min

TURNER T-40B

This aircraft is basically similar to the T-40A but has a tricycle landing gear and other refinements. Conversion of the prototype started in October 1966 and the first flight was made on 2 March 1969 with an 85 hp engine installed. Flight tests showed that high-altitude performance was below expectation and a 125 hp Lycoming O-320-E1C has since been installed.

During 1972 Mr Turner modified his T-40B by fitting a bubble canopy as shown in the illustration of Dr Mandley's Super T-40A.

The description of the T-40A applies also to the T-40B, except in the following details:

WINGS: Wing section NACA 64-212. Fixed leading-edge droop. Hydraulically-operated double-slotted flaps.

LANDING GEAR: Non-retractable tricycle type. Nosewheel size 4·10-6.

DIMENSIONS, EXTERNAL:
Same as for T-40A, except:
- Wing span: 22 ft 3 in (6·78 m)
- Wing chord at root: 4 ft 3 in (1·30 m)
- Wing aspect ratio: 5·2
- Wheel track: 7 ft 2 in (2·18 m)
- Wheelbase: 6 ft 0 in (1·83 m)

AREAS:
Same as for T-40A except:
- Wings, gross: 96 sq ft (8·92 m²)
- Ailerons (total): 6·1 sq ft (0·57 m²)
- Trailing-edge flaps (total): 17·8 sq ft (1·65 m²)

WEIGHT AND LOADINGS:
- Max T-O weight: 1,600 lb (725 kg)
- Max wing loading: 16·7 lb/sq ft (81·5 kg/m²)
- Max power loading: 12·8 lb/hp (5·81 kg/hp)

PERFORMANCE (at max T-O weight):
- Max level speed at S/L: 152 knots (175 mph; 282 km/h)
- Max cruising speed: 135 knots (155 mph; 249 km/h)
- Cruising speed at 62% power: 122 knots (140 mph; 225 km/h)
- Stalling speed at 10° flap extension: 56·5 knots (65 mph; 105 km/h)
- Stalling speed at 50° flap extension: 49·5 knots (57 mph; 92 km/h)
- Max rate of climb at S/L: over 1,200 ft (366 m)/min
- Service ceiling (estimated): 18,000 ft (5,485 m)
- T-O run: 850 ft (259 m)
- T-O to 50 ft (15 m): 1,020 ft (311 m)
- Landing run: 500 ft (152 m)

UAC

UNITED AIRCRAFT CORPORATION

HEAD OFFICE:
400 Main Street, East Hartford, Connecticut 06108

Telephone: (203) 565-4321

DIRECTORS:
Harold J. Berry
T. Mitchell Ford
Harry J. Gray
William P. Gwinn
Edward L. Hennessy Jr
David C. Hewitt
Ove W. Jorgensen
Paul W. O'Malley
Walter F. Probst
Arthur E. Smith
Olcott D. Smith
Richard S. Smith
William I. Spencer
Robert L. Sproull
Alfred W. Van Sinderen
Roger C. Wilkins

EXECUTIVES:

CHAIRMAN, PRESIDENT AND CHIEF EXECUTIVE OFFICER:
Harry J. Gray

SENIOR VICE-PRESIDENTS:
Joseph H. Allen (Communications and Marketing)
Edward L. Hennessy Jr (Finance and Administration)

GROUP VICE-PRESIDENTS:
William E. Diefenderfer
Paul W. O'Malley

VICE-PRESIDENTS:
Robert E. Beach
Rolf D. Bibow (International Programmes)
James Ferguson
Randall W. Kirk
Wesley A. Kuhrt (Technology)
Edward W. Large (Corporation Counsel)
Clark MacGregor
N. B. Morse (Industrial Relations)
Francis L. Murphy (Public Relations and Advertising)
Bruce N. Torell
Dale W. Van Winkle

CONTROLLER: Charles B. Preston

TREASURER: Robert A. Aspinwall

SECRETARY: Grant A. Ring

DIVISIONS AND SUBSIDIARIES:
Pratt & Whitney Aircraft (see "Engines" section)
Essex International
Sikorsky Aircraft (see this section)
Hamilton Standard
Norden
United Technology Center (see "Spaceflight" section)
United Aircraft Research Laboratories
Turbo Power and Marine Systems
United Aircraft of West Virginia
United Aircraft of Canada Ltd (see "Engines" section)
United Aircraft International

VAN'S

VAN'S AIRCRAFT

ADDRESS:
PO Box 187, Route 2, Forest Grove, Oregon 97116

Telephone: (503) 357-3832

Mr Richard VanGrunsven has designed and built a single-seat all-metal sporting aircraft known as Van's RV-3. It was built over a 2½-year period at a cost of approximately $2,000, and won its designer the Best Aerodynamic Detailing award at the 1972 EAA Fly-in. In addition to trailing-edge flaps, it has drooping ailerons to improve low-speed control.

Since the RV-3's first flight, and subsequent EAA award, Mr VanGrunsven has formed Van's Aircraft to market plans to amateur constructors. By early 1974, plan sales totalled 120 and it was believed that about 40 aircraft were under construction.

VAN'S RV-3

TYPE: Single-seat homebuilt sporting monoplane.

WINGS: Cantilever low-wing monoplane. Wing section NACA 23012. Dihedral 3° 30′. Incidence 1°. Conventional 2024-T3 light alloy structure of constant chord with I-beam main spar and light rear spar. All-metal trailing-edge flaps. All-metal Frise-type ailerons, which can be drooped to augment flaps.

FUSELAGE: All-metal semi-monocoque structure of 2024-T3 light alloy.

TAIL UNIT: Cantilever structure of light alloy. Trim tab in port elevator.

LANDING GEAR: Non-retractable tailwheel type. Cantilever tapered steel-rod main-gear struts. Main-wheel tyres size 14 × 5·00-5, pressure 20 lb/sq ft (1·41 kg/cm²). Steerable tailwheel with 6 in (0·15 m) diameter tyre. Cleveland brakes. Streamlined fairings on main wheels.

POWER PLANT: One 125 hp Lycoming O-290-G (GPU) four-cylinder horizontally-opposed aircooled engine, driving a Sensenich two-blade fixed-pitch propeller with spinner. Fuel capacity 24 US gallons (91 litres).

ACCOMMODATION: Pilot only, beneath transparent

bubble canopy. Baggage space aft of seat, capacity 8 cu ft (0·23 m³).

DIMENSIONS, EXTERNAL:

Wing span	19 ft 11 in (6·07 m)
Wing chord, constant	4 ft 6 in (1·37 m)
Wing aspect ratio	4·43
Length overall	19 ft 0 in (5·79 m)
Height overall	5 ft 1 in (1·55 m)
Tailplane span	7 ft 0 in (2·13 m)
Wheel track	5 ft 8 in (1·73 m)
Propeller diameter	5 ft 8 in (1·73 m)
Propeller ground clearance	9 in (0·23 m)

AREA:

Wings, gross	90 sq ft (8·36 m²)

WEIGHTS AND LOADINGS:

Weight empty	695 lb (315 kg)
Max T-O weight	1,050 lb (476 kg)
Max wing loading	11·66 lb/sq ft (56·9 kg/m²)
Max power loading	8·4 lb/hp (3·81 kg/hp)

PERFORMANCE (at max T-O weight):

Max never-exceed speed
191 knots (220 mph; 354 km/h)

Max level speed at S/L
169 knots (195 mph; 314 km/h)

Max cruising speed at 8,000 ft (2,440 m)
161 knots (185 mph; 298 km/h)

Econ cruising speed at 10,000 ft (3,050 m)
139 knots (160 mph; 257 km/h)

Stalling speed, flaps up
45·5 knots (52 mph; 84 km/h)

Stalling speed, flaps down
42 knots (48 mph; 78 km/h)

Max rate of climb at S/L	1,900 ft (579 m)/min
Service ceiling	21,000 ft (6,400 m)
T-O run	250 ft (76 m)
Landing run	300 ft (91·5 m)
Range, no reserve	520 nm (600 miles; 965 km)

Van's RV-3 single-seat homebuilt sporting monoplane (125 hp Lycoming O-290-G engine)

VERTAK

VERTAK CORPORATION

ADDRESS:
c/o Investor's Systems Inc, PO Box 1422, Dayton, Ohio 45401

PRESIDENT:
Norman Moore

Vertak Corporation designed a distinctive two-seat sporting aircraft to be constructed extensively of plastics. Designated the Vertak S-220 ESTOL (an acronym standing for Extremely Short Take-Off and Landing), this aircraft was described briefly in the 1973-74 *Jane's*. No decision to proceed with the construction of a prototype had been made by February 1974.

VOLMER

VOLMER AIRCRAFT

ADDRESS:
Box 5222, Glendale, California 91201
Telephone: (213) 247-8718

Mr Volmer Jenson, well known as a designer of sailplanes and gliders, also designed and built a two-seat light amphibian named the Sportsman (formerly Chubasco), which flew for the first time on 22 December 1958 and has since logged over 1,500 flying hours. He is attempting to find a manufacturer who will produce and market the aircraft commercially.

Meanwhile, plans of the Sportsman are being made available to amateur constructors. Over 700 sets had been sold by the Spring of 1974 and approximately 100 Sportsman amphibians are now flying. Some have tractor propellers, but this modification is not recommended by Mr Jensen.

Volmer VJ-22 Sportsman built in the UK by Dr J. P. Crawford (*Keith Sissons*)

VOLMER VJ-22 SPORTSMAN

The following details refer to Mr Jensen's prototype:

TYPE: Two-seat light amphibian.

WINGS: Braced high-wing monoplane. Dihedral 1°. Incidence 3°. Wings are standard Aeronca Chief or Champion assemblies with wooden spars, metal ribs and fabric covering, and carry stabilising floats under the tips. Streamline Vee bracing struts each side.

FUSELAGE: Conventional flying-boat hull of wooden construction, covered with mahogany plywood and coated with glassfibre.

TAIL UNIT: Strut-braced steel tube structure, fabric-covered.

LANDING GEAR: Retractable tailwheel type. Rubber-cord shock-absorption. Manual retraction. Cleveland wheels and mechanical brakes. Tyre pressure 20 lb/sq in (1·41 kg/cm²). Castoring retractable tailwheel with integral water rudder.

POWER PLANT: One 85 hp Continental C85, 90 hp or 100 hp Continental O-200-B four-cylinder horizontally-opposed aircooled engine, driving a Sensenich two-blade fixed-pitch pusher propeller. Fuel in a single tank, capacity 20 US gallons (76 litres). Oil capacity 4½ US quarts (4·5 litres).

ACCOMMODATION: Two seats side by side in enclosed cabin with dual controls.

DIMENSIONS, EXTERNAL:

Wing span	36 ft 6 in (11·12 m)
Wing chord	5 ft 0 in (1·52 m)
Wing aspect ratio	7·2
Length overall	24 ft 0 in (7·32 m)
Height overall	8 ft 0 in (2·44 m)

AREA:

Wings, gross	175 sq ft (16·3 m²)

WEIGHTS (85 hp):

Weight empty	1,000 lb (454 kg)
Max T-O weight	1,500 lb (680 kg)

PERFORMANCE (85 hp, at max T-O weight):

Max level speed at S/L
83 knots (95 mph; 153 km/h)

Max cruising speed
74 knots (85 mph; 137 km/h)

Stalling speed	39 knots (45 mph; 72 km/h)
Max rate of climb at S/L	600 ft (183 m)/min
Service ceiling	13,000 ft (3,960 m)

Range with max fuel, no reserves
260 nm (300 miles; 480 km)

VOLPAR

VOLPAR INC

HEAD OFFICE AND WORKS:
16300 Stagg Street, Van Nuys, California 91406
Telephone: (213) 787-4393
and (213) 873-5599

PRESIDENT: Frank V. Nixon Jr
GENERAL MANAGER: Albert B. Seed
CHIEF ENGINEER: Ralph Moll
CHIEF INSPECTOR: F. F. Taylor
PURCHASING AGENT: L. Stahl
PUBLIC RELATIONS MANAGER: R. M. Byrne

Volpar Inc was formed in 1960 to market in kit form a tricycle landing gear modification which is suitable for all models of the Beechcraft Model 18 light twin-engined transport.

The Volpar kit, which has full FAA certification, was designed by Thorp Engineering to require a minimum of modification to the basic airframe. The machined parts are manufactured by Paragon Precision Products, a producer of rocket engine components, tools and dies. The various assemblies formerly fabricated by Volitan Aviation, Inc, are now manufactured by Volpar following a merger between the two companies.

As a follow-up to the above modification, Volpar produces kits to convert the Model 18 to turboprop power, using AiResearch TPE 331 engines. The converted aircraft is known as the Turbo 18. After wide acceptance of this latter aircraft, Volpar introduced the Turboliner, and subsequently the Turboliner II, which is approved under SFAR 23 for commuter airline operation. Both of these aircraft are "stretched" versions of the Turbo 18.

Using the nacelles that were developed for the Turbo 18 and Turboliner, Volpar has produced an engine installation which it is marketing under the name of "Package Power". This is available with any of the AiResearch TPE 331 series of turboprop engines, with either over-engine or under-engine air intake as required by the particular installation. Volpar had supplied more than 100 of these units by the end of February 1971, and these have been fitted to such aircraft as the Beechcraft Model 18, de Havilland Dove, Grumman Goose and de Havilland Beaver. It is reported that "Package Power" units are being considered for installation in several aircraft currently in the development stage. Volpar has itself developed a turboprop version of the de Havilland Beaver, utilising the "Packaged Power" concept, and this is known as the Volpar Model 4000. The conversion is offered in kit form and is applicable to all models of the de Havilland Beaver.

VOLPAR (BEECHCRAFT) MODEL 18

The Volpar modification converts the Beechcraft Model 18 to a tricycle landing gear configuration, offering substantially slower approach speeds, greatly improved braking and easier ground handling. Cruising speed is improved, as all three wheels are completely retracted. Furthermore, the aircraft can be kept in hangars with a lower roof clearance, since the overall height is reduced to 9 ft 2 in (2·79 m).

The Volpar kit, which has passed all FAA static tests for a maximum landing weight of 9,772 lb (4,433 kg), utilises basic components of the existing main landing gear. The new nose gear is connected to the existing retraction system, where the tailwheel connection was removed. The complete modification can be made without removing the wings or stripping any of the wing skin. All cockpit controls and emergency procedures are unchanged, including the instrument panel wheel

Volpar Turbo 18, a conversion of the Beechcraft Model 18 with AiResearch TPE 331 turboprops and Volpar Mk IV tricycle landing gear

position indicator. Existing airstair doors can be retained with only minor modification.

Basically, the modification moves the main landing gear 4 ft 0 in (1·22 m) aft of the original position, attaching it to a welded tube truss that increases the torsional strength of the centre wing structure by 60% in landing configuration. The nose assembly is completely new and includes a streamlined nose fairing which adds 2 ft 2½ in (0·67 m) to the fuselage length. Space inside the fairing can be used for additional equipment, including a weather radar dish of up to 12 in (30 cm) diameter.

All three wheels are of aluminium and can be fitted with either Goodrich or Goodyear tubed or tubeless tyres, size 8·50-10, ten-ply rating. Main-wheel tyre pressure 65 lb/sq in (4·57 kg/cm²), nosewheel tyre pressure 45 lb/sq in (3·16 kg/cm²). Shock-absorption is provided by hydraulic oleo struts of Volpar manufacture. Goodrich multiple disc brakes. All three wheels retract forward in less than eight seconds. On the ground the cabin floor is only 3 ft 6 in (1·07 m) off the ground at the door. Wheelbase is 8 ft 7 in (2·62 m). The aircraft will turn on a 4 ft (1·22 m) radius of the inside wheel and a centering device is incorporated on the shimmy damper for take-off and landing.

The current Mk IV Volpar conversion incorporates Goodrich nine-piston full-circle brakes with twice the braking energy and three times the service life of the two-piston type fitted formerly. The new brakes fit on the original gear and are obtainable from either Volpar or Goodrich.

A total of more than 400 sets of Volpar tri-gear have been delivered.

VOLPAR (BEECHCRAFT) TURBO 18

The Turbo 18 is a Beechcraft Model 18 fitted with the Volpar Mk IV tricycle landing gear described above and re-engined with two 705 ehp AiResearch TPE 331-1-101B turboprop engines, flat rated to 605 ehp. The wing planform is changed, by extending forward the entire leading-edge inboard of each engine nacelle and carrying the new leading-edge line past the nacelle, so increasing the chord and sweepback to a point some distance outboard of the nacelle. The rectangular wingtip panels of the standard Super 18 are replaced by smaller tips which decrease the wing span and maintain the normal leading-edge sweep to the tip.

Installation of TPE 331 engines and Hartzell Model HC-B3TN-5 three-blade reversible-pitch propellers reduces the empty weight, permitting an increase in fuel or payload. Internal fuel capacity is increased by 100 US gallons (379 litres) by installing new integral tanks in the leading-edge immediately outboard of each engine nacelle. These become the main tanks, each delivering fuel directly to the adjacent engine. They increase the maximum fuel capacity to 630 US gallons (2,385 litres), with a normal capacity of 306 US gallons (1,159 litres).

Air-conditioning and heating installations are available, using engine bleed air. A large cargo door, 5 ft 2 in (1·57 m) wide, with a max height of 3 ft 7 in (1·09 m), can be provided, incorporating the existing airstair door.

The detailed description of the Turboliner (which follows), applies also to the Turbo 18, except that this latter model does not have the "stretched" fuselage.

FAA Supplemental Type Approval of the Turbo 18 was received on 17 February 1966. Two were in service with the US Public Health Service at the end of that month and conversion kits are in full production. Customers include Air Asia of Taiwan, which has been supplied with 15 kits.

DIMENSIONS, EXTERNAL:

Wing span	46 ft 0 in (14·02 m)
Length overall	37 ft 5 in (11·40 m)
Height overall	9 ft 7 in (2·92 m)
Wheelbase	8 ft 7 in (2·62 m)

DIMENSIONS, INTERNAL:

Cabin, excluding flight deck:	
Length	12 ft 8½ in (3·87 m)
Max width	4 ft 4 in (1·32 m)
Max height	5 ft 6 in (1·68 m)
Volume	260 cu ft (7·36 m³)

WEIGHTS AND LOADINGS:

Weight empty, basic	5,500 lb (2,495 kg)
Max payload	4,786 lb (2,171 kg)
Max T-O weight	10,286 lb (4,666 kg)
Max zero-fuel weight	9,000 lb (4,082 kg)
Max landing weight	9,772 lb (4,433 kg)
Max wing loading	27·51 lb/sq ft (134·3 kg/m²)
Max power loading	8·94 lb/ehp (4·05 kg/ehp)

PERFORMANCE (at max T-O weight):

Max cruising speed at 10,000 ft (3,050 m)	243 knots (280 mph; 451 km/h)
Econ cruising speed at 10,000 ft (3,050 m)	222 knots (256 mph; 412 km/h)
Stalling speed, wheels and flaps up, power off	80 knots (92 mph; 148 km/h)
Stalling speed, wheels and flaps down, power off	77 knots (88 mph; (142 km/h)
Max rate of climb at S/L	1,710 ft (521 m)/min
Service ceiling	26,000 ft (7,925 m)
Service ceiling, one engine out	14,000 ft (4,265 m)
T-O run	1,665 ft (507 m)
T-O to 50 ft (15 m)	2,380 ft (725 m)
Landing from 50 ft (15 m)	2,107 ft (642 m)
Landing run with reverse thrust	870 ft (265 m)
Range with max fuel at 222 knots (256 mph; 412 km/h), 45 min reserve	1,884 nm (2,170 miles; 3,492 km)
Range with max payload, 45 min reserve	400 nm (461 miles; 741 km)

VOLPAR (BEECHCRAFT) TURBOLINER

This is a "stretched" 15-passenger version of the Volpar (Beechcraft) Turbo 18, intended for the third-level airline market. Design was started in August 1966 and construction of the prototype began in December 1966. The prototype flew for the first time on 12 April 1967 and FAA certification was granted on 29 March 1968, the Turboliner being approved for operation at a new gross weight of 11,500 lb (5,216 kg).

By the end of February 1974 a total of 24 Turboliners had been delivered and were in service with small airlines throughout the world. In March 1970 a Turboliner (N353V), on a delivery flight from Los Angeles to Singapore, set six official international speed records. It carried on board during the flight all necessary spares for one year's normal operation, together with a 400 US gallon (1,515 litre) ferry tank in the fuselage, and was in operation with a commuter airline two days after arrival in Singapore.

TYPE: Twin-turboprop light transport aircraft.

WINGS: Cantilever low-wing monoplane. Wing section NACA 63-015 at station 28·0, NACA 23014 at station 144·5, NACA 23012 at station 260·4. Dihedral 6°. Incidence 5° 20′ at root, 1° at tip. Sweepback 16° 21′ on inner wings, 8° 23′ on outer panels. Steel truss centre-section spar; remainder of structure aluminium semi-monocoque. Plain differential ailerons and plain trailing-edge flaps of conventional aluminium construction. Trim tab in port aileron. Optional Goodrich pneumatic de-icing boots on leading-edges.

FUSELAGE: Conventional aluminium semi-monocoque structure.

TAIL UNIT: Cantilever aluminium semi-monocoque structure with twin endplate fins and rudders. Fixed-incidence tailplane. Trim tabs in rudder and elevators. Optional Goodrich pneumatic de-icing boots on leading-edges.

LANDING GEAR: Volpar electrically-retractable tricycle type. All units retract forward, main wheels into engine nacelles. Volpar hydraulic

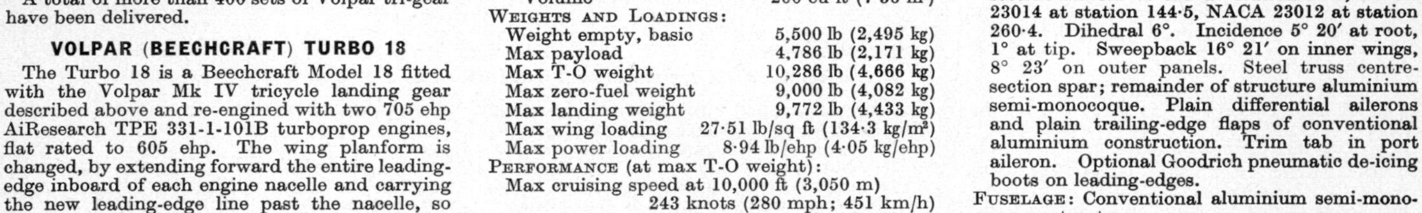

Volpar Turboliner II, a 15-passenger conversion of the Beechcraft Model 18, in service with Ransome Airlines

shock-absorbers. All three wheels size 8·50-10 with Goodrich or Goodyear tubeless or tube-type tyres. Main-wheel tyre pressure 80 lb/sq in (5·62 kg/cm²); nosewheel tyre pressure 45 lb/sq in (3·16 kg/cm²). Goodrich multiple-disc brakes.

POWER PLANT: Two 705 ehp AiResearch TPE 331-1-101B turboprop engines, each driving a Hartzell HC-B3TN-5 three-blade reversible-pitch propeller with T10176H blades. Four to eight fuel tanks in wings, including new integral main tanks in wing leading-edges outboard of nacelles. Normal fuel capacity 306 US gallons (1,159 litres); max capacity 630 US gallons (2,385 litres). Refuelling points in upper surface of wings. Total oil capacity 3 US gallons (11·35 litres).

ACCOMMODATION: Crew of two and up to 15 passengers. Downward-hinged airstair door on port side at rear of cabin. Optional double-door for freight loading. Seats removable to enable aircraft to be used for freight-carrying. Heating and air-conditioning optional. Baggage space aft of cabin and in each wing.

SYSTEMS: Hydraulic system for brakes only. Electrical supply from two 200A starter/generators and two 24V batteries, for landing gear and flap operation, propeller anti-icing, landing lights, radio and lighting.

ELECTRONICS AND EQUIPMENT: Blind-flying instrumentation, radio and radar to customer's specification.

DIMENSIONS, EXTERNAL:
- Wing span: 46 ft 0 in (14·02 m)
- Wing chord at root: 13 ft 7·36 in (4·15 m)
- Wing chord at tip: 3 ft 8·94 in (1·14 m)
- Wing aspect ratio: 5·67
- Length overall: 44 ft 2½ in (13·47 m)
- Height overall: 9 ft 7 in (2·92 m)
- Tailplane span: 15 ft 0 in (4·57 m)
- Wheel track: 12 ft 11 in (3·94 m)
- Wheelbase: 12 ft 7 in (3·84 m)
- Propeller diameter: 8 ft 0⅞ in to 8 ft 5⅜ in (2·46 to 2·57 m)
- Passenger door:
  - Height: 4 ft 0 in (1·22 m)
  - Width: 2 ft 3 in (0·69 m)
  - Height to sill: 3 ft 6 in (1·07 m)

DIMENSIONS, INTERNAL:
- Cabin, excluding flight deck:
  - Length: 19 ft 6 in (5·94 m)
  - Max width: 4 ft 4 in (1·32 m)
  - Max height: 5 ft 6 in (1·68 m)
  - Floor area: 80 sq ft (7·43 m²)
  - Volume: 394 cu ft (11·16 m³)
- Freight hold (aft of cabin) volume: 23 cu ft (0·65 m³)
- Freight holds (wings) volume (total): 32 cu ft (0·91 m³)

AREAS:
- Wings, gross: 374 sq ft (34·75 m²)
- Ailerons (total): 26·6 sq ft (2·47 m²)
- Trailing-edge flaps (total): 28·2 sq ft (2·62 m²)
- Fins (total): 16·3 sq ft (1·51 m²)
- Rudders (total): 17·28 sq ft (16·05 m²)
- Tailplane: 38·2 sq ft (35·49 m²)
- Elevators, including tab: 27·22 sq ft (25·28 m²)

WEIGHTS AND LOADINGS:
- Weight empty:
  - Cargo version: 5,900 lb (2,676 kg)
  - Airliner: 6,600 lb (2,993 kg)
- Max T-O weight: 11,500 lb (5,216 kg)
- Max zero-fuel weight: 10,500 lb (4,762 kg)
- Max landing weight: 11,000 lb (4,989 kg)
- Max wing loading: 30·75 lb/sq ft (150·1 kg/m²)
- Max power loading: 8·15 lb/ehp (3·70 kg/ehp)

PERFORMANCE (at max T-O weight):
- Max level speed at 10,000 ft (3,050 m): 243 knots (280 mph; 451 km/h)
- Max cruising speed at 10,000 ft (3,050 m): 243 knots (280 mph; 451 km/h)
- Econ cruising speed at 10,000 ft (3,050 m): 222 knots (256 mph; 412 km/h)
- Stalling speed, wheels and flaps up, power off: 84 knots (96 mph; 154·5 km/h)
- Stalling speed, wheels and flaps down, power off: 80 knots (92 mph; 148·5 km/h)
- Max rate of climb at S/L: 1,520 ft (463 m)/min
- Service ceiling: 24,000 ft (7,315 m)
- Service ceiling, one engine out: 13,000 ft (3,960 m)
- T-O run: 1,870 ft (570 m)
- T-O to 50 ft (15 m): 3,245 ft (989 m)
- Landing from 50 ft (15 m): 2,500 ft (762 m)
- Landing run: 1,040 ft (317 m)
- Range with max fuel, 45 min reserve: 1,802 nm (2,076 miles; 3,340 km)
- Range with max payload, 45 min reserve: 300 nm (346 miles; 556 km)

VOLPAR (BEECHCRAFT) TURBOLINER II

The Turboliner II is basically a Turboliner that has been modified to meet the new requirements of SFAR 23. The prototype was completed in February 1970 and received certification in July 1970. Dimensions and performance are the same as those given for the Turboliner.

Recent conversions incorporate a number of improvements, including battery temperature indicators, a fail-safe Hytrol anti-skid braking system, installation of a 38,000 BTU Janitrol heater in the nose for ground heating of cockpit and engine nacelles, and modification to the standard Volpar side-opening cargo door. This now incorporates an inward-opening door 2 ft 2 in (0·66 m) in width and with a minimum height of 3 ft 9½ in (1·16 m), which may be opened in flight to permit the air drop of firefighting personnel or cargo.

VOLPAR (BEECHCRAFT) TURBOLINER IIA

The designation Turboliner IIA applies to a version of the Turboliner II which is equipped with a methanol-water injection system to increase engine performance during high altitude/hot day emergency take-off conditions.

A tank is provided to contain 40 lb (18 kg) of the methanol-water mixture, which allows for 3·6 min of wet operation during an engine-out condition, or 1·8 min wet operation of both engines. The system allows for manual operation, or in the event of an engine failure operates automatically.

VOLPAR (BEECHCRAFT) MINI TANKER

Volpar designed a version of the Turboliner equipped as a tanker for in-flight refuelling, and this was known as the Mini Tanker. Development of this has been terminated; details can be found in the 1973-74 *Jane's*.

VOLPAR (DHC) MODEL 4000 TURBOPROP BEAVER

In November 1970 Volpar began design of a turboprop version of the de Havilland Beaver (U-6A), which it designated Volpar Model 4000. Construction of a prototype began in January 1971, and this flew for the first time in April 1972.

A basic "Package Power" nacelle is utilised, containing a 715 ehp AiResearch TPE 331-2U-203 turboprop engine, driving a Hartzell Model HC-B3TN three-blade metal propeller. This power plant has reduced the empty weight, permitting an increase in fuel or payload. Optional fuel capacity can be increased by 160 US gallons (606 litres) by installation of new integral fuel tanks in the wing leading-edges immediately outboard of the fuselage. With these tanks installed maximum fuel capacity is 299 US gallons (1,132 litres).

Other modifications include replacing the steel truss forward of the landing gear by one that is 1 ft 3 in (0·38 m) longer, provision of a new windscreen, side windows and a Plexiglas cabin top for improved visibility, and a new fin and rudder.

Volpar delivered the first Model 4000 to the US Department of the Interior.

A description of the basic de Havilland Canada DHC-2 Beaver can be found in the 1968-69 *Jane's*.

DIMENSIONS, EXTERNAL:
- Wing span: 48 ft 0 in (14·63 m)
- Length overall: 36 ft 0 in (10·97 m)
- Height overall: 11 ft 0 in (3·35 m)

WEIGHTS AND LOADINGS:
- Weight empty: 2,474 lb (1,122 kg)
- Max T-O and landing weight: 5,370 lb (2,435 kg)
- Max wing loading: 21·48 lb/sq ft (104·9 kg/m²)
- Max power loading: 7·5 lb/ehp (3·40 kg/ehp)

PERFORMANCE (at max T-O weight):
- Max never-exceed speed: 173 knots (199 mph; 320 km/h)
- Max level speed: 156 knots (180 mph; 290 km/h)
- Max cruising speed: 136 knots (157 mph; 253 km/h)
- Econ cruising speed at 10,000 ft (3,050 m): 122 knots (140 mph; 225 km/h)
- Stalling speed: 52 knots (60 mph; 97 km/h)
- Max rate of climb at S/L: 2,500 ft (762 m)/min
- Service ceiling: 21,000 ft (6,400 m)
- T-O run: 400 ft (122 m)
- T-O to 50 ft (15 m): 800 ft (244 m)
- Landing from 50 ft (15 m): 736 ft (224 m)
- Landing run: 350 ft (107 m)
- Range with max fuel, including allowances for warm-up, taxi, take-off, climb and 45 min reserve at cruise power: 863 nm (994 miles; 1,599 km)
- Range with pilot and six passengers or 1,000 lb (453 kg) freight, allowances as above: 555 nm (640 miles; 1,030 km)

Volpar (DHC) Model 4000 Turboprop Beaver (715 ehp AiResearch TPE 331-2U-203 engine)

WENDT

WENDT AIRCRAFT ENGINEERING

ADDRESS:
9900 Alto Drive, La Mesa, California 92041

Wendt Aircraft Engineering designed and built the prototype of a two-seat sporting monoplane which is known as the WH-1 Traveler. The design originated on 4 September 1969, and construction of the prototype began on 26 November of the same year. The first flight was made on 15 March 1972, and FAA certification in the Experimental category was awarded on 30 May 1972. Plans of the Traveler are available to amateur constructors, and 20 sets had been sold by early 1974.

WENDT WH-1 TRAVELER

TYPE: Two-seat homebuilt sporting aircraft.

WINGS: Cantilever low-wing monoplane. Wing section NACA 64_3A-418. Dihedral 5° 30′. Incidence 2°. No sweepback. Constant-chord

Wendt WH-1 Traveler two-seat homebuilt aircraft (75 hp Continental A75 engine)

two-spar structure. Spruce spars, marine plywood ribs, pine leading- and trailing-edges and $\frac{3}{32}$ in mahogany plywood skin from leading-edge to 37% chord. Aft of main spar, wing is Dacron-covered. Plain ailerons, hinged at upper surface, made of spruce with plywood ribs, and Dacron-covered. No flaps. Bungee trim on control column. Glassfibre wingtips.

Fuselage: Conventional structure of spruce frames and longerons, plywood formers and tension ties, with steel tube overturn structure in the cockpit section. Fuselage undersurface and sides covered with $\frac{1}{8}$ in mahogany plywood. Upper surface Dacron-covered. Glassfibre nose cowl.

Tail Unit: Cantilever wooden structure with swept vertical surfaces and all-moving tailplane. Each surface has a spruce spar, spruce and plywood ribs, and a $\frac{1}{16}$ in mahogany plywood torsion box. All surfaces Dacron-covered. Static balance weights near tips of tailplane leading-edge. Tailplane has a half-span trim and anti-balance tab. Tailplane tips of glassfibre.

Landing Gear: Non-retractable tricycle type. Cantilever spring steel main gear. Steerable nosewheel has coil spring shock-absorption. Cleveland 5·00-5 wheels with Armstrong tyres, pressure 30 lb/sq in (2·11 kg/cm²). Cleveland caliper-type brakes. Glassfibre wheel fairings.

Power Plant: Prototype has one 75 hp Continental A75 four-cylinder horizontally-opposed aircooled engine, driving a McCauley Type 1C90 two-blade metal fixed-pitch propeller with glassfibre spinner. Design is suitable for installation of engines from 65 to 100 hp. One aerofoil-shaped glassfibre fuel tank at each wingtip, capacity 11 US gallons (41·5 litres). Total fuel capacity 22 US gallons (83 litres). Refuelling points on upper surface of each wingtip. Oil capacity 1·0 US gallon (3·8 litres).

Accommodation: Pilot and passenger in tandem, beneath canopy which has large transparent panels at each side. Canopy hinged on port side. Dual controls standard. Stowage for 50 lb (23 kg) baggage aft of rear seat.

System: Electrical system powered by 30A engine-driven alternator. 12V 25Ah storage battery in glassfibre battery box in aft fuselage.

Electronics: Prototype has a Narco Escort 110 com transceiver.

Dimensions, external:
Wing span 30 ft 0 in (9·14 m)
Wing chord, constant 3 ft 11¼ in (1·20 m)
Wing aspect ratio 7·63
Length overall 19 ft 6 in (5·94 m)
Height overall 6 ft 10 in (2·08 m)
Tailplane span 8 ft 0 in (2·44 m)
Wheel track 6 ft 4 in (1·93 m)
Wheelbase 4 ft 9 in (1·45 m)
Propeller diameter 5 ft 11 in (1·80 m)
Propeller ground clearance 10 in (0·25 m)

Dimension, internal:
Max width 2 ft 4 in (0·71 m)

Areas:
Wings, gross 118 sq ft (10·96 m²)
Ailerons (total) 12·8 sq ft (1·19 m²)
Fin 4·06 sq ft (0·38 m²)
Rudder 3·82 sq ft (0·35 m²)
Tailplane, including tab 18·0 sq ft (1·67 m²)

Weights and Loadings:
Weight empty, equipped 900 lb (408 kg)
Max T-O and landing weight 1,400 lb (635 kg)
Max wing loading 11·86 lb/sq ft (57·9 kg/m²)
Max power loading 18·67 lb/hp (8·47 kg/hp)

Performance (at max T-O weight):
Max never-exceed speed 142 knots (164 mph; 264 km/h)
Max level speed at 4,000 ft (1,220 m) 114 knots (131 mph; 211 km/h)
Max cruising speed at 4,000 ft (1,220 m) 107 knots (123 mph; 198 km/h)
Econ cruising speed at 4,000 ft (1,220 m) 100 knots (115 mph; 185 km/h)
Stalling speed 50 knots (57 mph; 92 km/h)
Max rate of climb at S/L (no passenger) 750 ft (229 m)/min
Max rate of climb at S/L (with passenger) 500 ft (152 m)/min
Service ceiling 13,000 ft (3,960 m)
T-O run 800 ft (244 m)
Landing run 700 ft (213 m)
Range with max fuel, no reserve 503 nm (580 miles; 933 km)
Range with max payload, no reserve 416 nm (480 miles; 772 km)

WHITE

E. MARSHALL WHITE

Address:
Meadowlark Airport, 5141 Warner Avenue, Huntington Beach, California 92649
Telephone: (714) 846-2409

WHITE WW-I DER JÄGER D.IX

Marshall White, a staff engineer of TRW Systems at Redondo Beach, California, has designed an unusual homebuilt aircraft named Der Jäger D.IX, which is reminiscent of several German designs, mainly of first World War vintage. The wings are patterned on those of an Albatros D.Va, with the landing gear fairings of the Focke-Wulf Stosser and tail unit of the Fokker D.VII.

Design and construction of the prototype started simultaneously at the beginning of 1969, as Mr White's fifth homebuilt, and first flight of the prototype was made on 7 September 1969.

Plans and kits of materials, as well as some of the more difficult-to-construct parts in finished form, are available to amateur constructors, and at least 75 Der Jäger D.IXs are under construction.

The following details apply to the prototype in its original form. It has since been re-engined with a 150 hp Lycoming, but no details have been received of performance with this more powerful engine.

White Der Jäger D.IX homebuilt biplane (115 hp Lycoming O-235-C1 engine)

Type: Single-seat homebuilt sporting biplane.

Wings: Forward-stagger single-bay biplane with N-type interplane and centre-section struts. Single streamlined lift strut from each side of lower fuselage to attachment point of forward interplane strut on upper wing. No flying or landing wires. Aerofoil section M-6. Incidence 3° upper wing, 2° lower wings. Spruce spars and plywood ribs, fabric covered. Internal steel tube bracing. Ailerons in both top and bottom wings. Scalloped trailing-edge to both wings.

Fuselage: Welded 4130 steel tube structure, fabric covered. Aluminium engine cowling.

Tail Unit: Wire-braced welded 4130 steel tube structure, with sheet metal ribs, fabric covered. Balanced rudder and elevator. Ground-adjustable trim tabs in elevator.

Landing Gear: Non-retractable tailwheel type. Main legs each consist of an "A" frame, welded into the fuselage, with tension springs in the centre-fuselage to cushion landing shock. Main wheels and tyres size 5·00-5. Glassfibre wheel fairings.

Power Plant: One 115 hp Lycoming O-235-C1 four-cylinder horizontally-opposed aircooled engine, driving a McCauley two-blade propeller. Structure suitable for alternative power plants from 1,600 cc Volkswagen up to 150 hp. Fuel contained in two tanks, one in upper wing centre-section, capacity 14 US gallons (53 litres), one in fuselage, capacity 10 US gallons (38 litres); total 24 US gallons (91 litres).

Accommodation: Single seat in open cockpit, with headrest faired into wood or glassfibre fuselage turtleback.

Equipment: Two dummy machine-guns mounted on top of fuselage, forward of cockpit. Dummy bomb, carried between legs of main landing gear, can be adapted as oil tank for smoke discharge system.

Dimensions, external:
Wing span, upper 20 ft 0 in (6·10 m)
Wing span, lower 16 ft 0 in (4·88 m)
Wing chord, upper at root 3 ft 6 in (1·07 m)
Wing chord, upper at tip 4 ft 0 in (1·22 m)
Wing chord, lower (constant) 3 ft 0 in (0·91 m)
Length overall 17 ft 0 in (5·18 m)
Tailplane span 8 ft 0 in (2·44 m)
Wheel track 5 ft 0 in (1·52 m)
Propeller diameter 5 ft 6 in (1·68 m)
Propeller ground clearance 10 in (0·25 m)

Area:
Wings, gross 115 sq ft (10·68 m²)

Weights:
Weight empty 534 lb (242 kg)
Max T-O weight 888 lb (403 kg)

Performance (at max T-O weight):
Max never-exceed speed 152 knots (175 mph; 282 km/h)
Max level speed at 2,000 ft (610 m) 126 knots (145 mph; 233 km/h)
Max cruising speed at 2,000 ft (610 m) 116 knots (133 mph; 214 km/h)
Stalling speed 47 knots (54 mph; 87 km/h)
Max rate of climb at S/L 2,400 ft (732 m)/min
T-O run 150 ft (46 m)

WIER

RONALD WIER

Address:
6406 Burgundy, San Diego, California 92120

Mr Ronald Wier, an experienced private pilot, has designed and built a single-seat lightweight aircraft which he has named "Draggin' Fly". His aim was to evolve an easily built aircraft with short-field capability and good controllability, to render it safe for pilots of limited experience. For reliability and ease of maintenance he chose a 36 hp Volkswagen engine of 1,200 cc; but after eight hours of test flying this was replaced by the present 50 hp 1,600 cc Volkswagen engine.

Apart from the rib jig and propeller plot, Draggin' Fly was built without any plans. It has proved extremely easy to fly, and no rigging alterations were necessary when the power plant was changed. Because of the high inherent drag of the design, however, power-on landings are desirable to offset a high sink rate. Construction occupied a ten-month period, at a cost of approximately $1,300, and the first flight was made in May 1972. Plans were made available to amateur constructors in March 1974.

WIER RDW-2 DRAGGIN' FLY

Type: Single-seat lightweight homebuilt sporting aircraft.

Wings: Braced parasol-wing monoplane, with Vee bracing struts each side and inverted Vee centre-section struts fore and aft of cockpit. Wing section USA 35B. Thickness/chord ratio 12%. Incidence 1°. Slight dihedral. Conventional two-spar structure of wood, with $\frac{1}{4}$ in square capstick ribs, plywood gussets and $\frac{3}{8}$ in spruce plank spars, Dacron-covered. Ailerons of light alloy construction, pop-riveted to a full-span torque tube which is operated by pushrod. No flaps. No trim tabs.

Fuselage: Welded steel tube structure, Dacron-covered.

Tail Unit: Wire-braced welded steel tube structure, Dacron-covered, carried on a triangular-section welded steel tube tailboom. Incidence of tailplane ground adjustable. Small ventral fin and lower tip of rudder extend below surface of tailplane.

Landing Gear: Non-retractable tricycle type. Main wheels carried on two side Vees and half-axles hinged to bottom of fuselage. Spring in compression and rubber in compression shock-absorption for nosewheel and mainwheel shock-struts respectively. Steerable nosewheel. All three wheels made by Montgomery Ward, with tyres size 10·5 × 4·00-4, pressure 12 lb/sq in (0·84 kg/cm²). No wheel brakes.

Power Plant: One 50 hp Volkswagen 1,600 cc modified motor car engine, driving a two-blade hand-carved mahogany propeller of 30 in pitch. Glassfibre fuel tank in fuselage, immediately aft of firewall, capacity 8 US gallons (30 litres). Refuelling point on fuselage upper surface, forward of windscreen. Oil capacity 0·63 US gallons (2·4 litres).

Accommodation: Single seat in open cockpit.

Dimensions, external:
Wing span 24 ft 5 in (7·44 m)
Wing chord, constant 4 ft 6 in (1·37 m)
Length overall 17 ft 5 in (5·31 m)
Height overall 6 ft 10 in (2·08 m)
Tailplane span 8 ft 0 in (2·44 m)

Wheel track 4 ft 8 in (1·42 m)
Wheelbase 2 ft 8 in (0·81 m)
Propeller diameter 4 ft 4 in (1·32 m)
Propeller ground clearance 7 in (0·18 m)

AREAS:
Wings, gross 110 sq ft ($10·22 m^2$)
Ailerons (total) 12 sq ft ($1·11 m^2$)

WEIGHTS AND LOADINGS:
Weight empty 470 lb (213 kg)
Max T-O weight 688 lb (312 kg)
Max wing loading 6·25 lb/sq ft ($30·5 kg/m^2$)
Max power loading 13·76 lb/hp (6·24 kg/hp)

PERFORMANCE (at max T-O weight):
Max never-exceed speed 86 knots (100 mph; 160 km/h)
Max level speed at S/L 61 knots (70 mph; 113 km/h)
Cruising speed at S/L 56·5 knots (65 mph; 105 km/h)
Stalling speed 28 knots (32 mph; 52 km/h)
Max rate of climb at S/L 300 ft (91 m)/min
Service ceiling 4,600 ft (1,400 m)
T-O run 150 ft (46 m)
Landing run 200 ft (61 m)
Range, no reserve 147 nm (170 miles; 273 km)

Wier RDW-2 Draggin' Fly lightweight homebuilt single-seater (*Howard Levy*)

WILLIAMS

WILLIAMS RESEARCH CORPORATION

ADDRESS:
2280 West Maple Road, Walled Lake, Michigan 48088
Telephone: (313) 624-5200

On 26 January 1970, the Bell Aerospace Company Division of Textron Inc announced that it had granted to the Williams Research Corporation a licence to manufacture, use and sell certain small lift device systems in the US and Canada. They included the Jet Flying Belt which Bell had developed for the US Army under a $3 million contract, and which was described in the 1972-73 *Jane's*.

Since that time Williams has been working on a new and more advanced version, and announced on 14 February 1974 that it had tested successfully a two-man turbine-powered flying platform. Known as **WASP** (Williams Aerial Systems Platform), its flight tests were conducted with the vehicle attached to a safety tether line, under a US Navy contract to demonstrate its suitability to meet a US Marine Corps STAMP (Small Tactical Aerial Mobility Platform) requirement.

Powered by a Williams WR19-9 miniature turbofan engine, developing 700 lb (317 kg) thrust, the WASP is essentially a platform to which the WR19 engine has been mounted vertically. This means that the pilot has merely to mount the platform, start the engine and fly off, using simple hand controls so designed that the vehicle can be controlled in flight using one hand.

It is anticipated that the WASP will prove capable of carrying two men at speeds of up to 52 knots (60 mph; 97 km/h) for a duration of approximately 30 minutes. The vehicle will be able to accelerate rapidly, move in any direction, hover and rotate on its own axis. The company believes that WASP will be suitable for a number of military and civil applications, including law enforcement, firefighting, rescue and medical aid. Empty weight of the vehicle is 270 lb (123 kg).

Williams Research prototype WASP flying platform (one 700 lb; 317 kg st Williams WR19-9 turbofan engine)

WINDECKER

WINDECKER INDUSTRIES, INC

ADDRESS:
PO Box 6288 ATS, Midland, Texas 79701
Telephone: (915) 563-1700
CHAIRMAN OF THE BOARD: Wm B. Blakemore II
PRESIDENT: Dr Leo J. Windecker
VICE-PRESIDENT: Thomas Sim
TREASURER: Barry Brooks
SECRETARY: Tommy Phipps

Windecker Industries holds an exclusive licence from the Dow Chemical Company for the reinforced plastics aircraft developed since 1959 by Drs L. J. and F. M. Windecker. Construction of all-plastics wings started in 1960 and these were tested and flown on an existing aircraft of metal construction. After extended research, design of a glassfibre-reinforced plastics prototype with fixed landing gear began in 1965, and this aircraft flew for the first time on 7 October 1967. This experimental aircraft served as a testbed to prove the new constructional techniques and is still in flying condition. Based on data accumulated from this aircraft (N801WR), design of a high-performance all-plastics aeroplane with retractable landing gear was started, and this was given the designation Eagle 1.

WINDECKER AC-7 EAGLE 1

SAF designation: YE-5

In configuration the Eagle 1 is a conventional low-wing monoplane, but its full monocoque construction is of glassfibre-reinforced plastics. Epoxy resins are used in conjunction with non-woven unidirectional glassfibre in a ratio of 67% glassfibre to 33% epoxy resins.

The first Eagle 1 prototype (N802W) flew for the first time on 26 January 1969. Its developmental and engineering flight test programme was well advanced when, during final FAA certification tests on 19 April 1969, the aircraft was destroyed in an accident. Following some structural redesign to reduce weight, construction of a second prototype began in June 1969; this aircraft (N803WR) flew for the first time on 29 September 1969, and received FAA certification on 18 December 1969.

A production prototype was completed in May 1970, and the first production aircraft (N4195G) was delivered to a customer on 7 October 1970. Since that time orders have been received for additional aircraft and a total of seven had been delivered by the end of February 1972. Production has continued on a restricted basis pending availability of additional working capital. In the interim period a programme has been initiated to improve aircraft systems and reduce manufacturing costs.

On 23 February 1973 Windecker Industries announced that under a USAF Research and Development contract, awarded by the Aeronautical Systems Division at Wright-Patterson AFB, Ohio, the company had delivered to the USAF a single example of the Windecker Eagle 1, which has been allocated the USAF designation YE-5.

It is being flown in a high-priority test programme to evaluate the degree to which an aircraft of glassfibre composite structure is detectable by radar, and to reduce its radar cross-section Windecker incorporated a number of modifications in this single YE-5 prototype.

The following description applies to the standard version:

TYPE: Four-seat cabin monoplane.

WINGS: Cantilever low-wing monoplane. NACA 64_2415 wing section. Dihedral 4° 30′. Incidence 2° 30′. No sweepback. Fail-safe structure of glassfibre-reinforced plastics. Frise-type ailerons of glassfibre-reinforced plastics with pilot-controlled bungee trimming. Plain trailing-edge flaps constructed of glassfibre-reinforced plastics.

FUSELAGE: Fail-safe monocoque structure of glassfibre-reinforced plastics.

Windecker YE-5, for use in a USAF research programme, has a three-blade propeller of composite construction

Tail Unit: Conventional cantilever structure of glassfibre-reinforced plastics. Fixed-incidence tailplane. Trim tabs on starboard elevator and rudder.

Landing Gear: Retractable tricycle type with single wheel on each unit. Electro-hydraulic retraction, main wheels inward, nosewheel rearward. Main wheels faired by landing gear doors when retracted. Nosewheel door functions as a cowl flap when the gear is retracted. Windecker oleo-pneumatic shock-absorbers. Cleveland 6·00-6 main wheels, 5·00-5 nosewheel; all tyre pressures 45 lb/sq in (3·16 kg/cm²). Cleveland hydraulic disc brakes. Parking brake.

Power Plant: One 285 hp Continental IO-520-C six-cylinder horizontally-opposed aircooled engine, driving a McCauley two-blade constant-speed propeller. Fuel capacity 86 US gallons (325 litres), in two 43 gallon (162·5 litre) integral wing tanks. Refuelling points outboard on upper surface of each wing. Oil capacity 1·5 US gallons (5·7 litres).

Accommodation: Four persons in pairs in enclosed cabin. Forward-hinged door on each side of cabin. Compartment aft of rear seats for 120 lb (54 kg) baggage with external access door on port side; hatshelf on bulkhead at rear of cabin. Cabin ventilated and heated by ram air over exhaust.

Systems: Hydraulic system, pressure 1,500 lb/sq in (105 kg/cm²), for landing gear. Vacuum system for instruments. 12V 70A alternator. 12V 35Ah battery.

Electronics and Equipment: Standard avionics comprise one Narco MK-16 VHF, one Narco VOA-40 VOR/LOC converter-indicator and an antennae package which includes VOR, communications, ADF sense, transponder, DME, glideslope and marker beacon antennae, headset, microphone and all wiring harnesses. Standard equipment includes full blind-flying instrumentation, 8-day clock, outside air temperature gauge, vacuum system and gauge, two anti-collision beacons, navigation lights, landing and taxi light, dome light, map light, instrument panel floodlights, radio lights, external power socket, fully-reclining track-mounted seats with seat belt, headrest, fresh-air outlet and map or magazine storage pocket for each seat, floor console between front seats for map and pencil storage, openable storm window on pilot's side, baggage net and attachments, retractable entrance steps, hand holds, ultra-violet absorbent windscreen, windscreen defrosting system, tinted cabin windows, soundproofing, towbar, control jack, jack pads, shoulder harness for front seats and alternate static source. Four interior and exterior trims are available as standard, the latter consisting of polyurethane paint finish. Optional avionics include a wide range of Narco units, available singly or as a complete package, and one- and two-axis autopilots. Optional equipment includes cargo tie-down kit, engine winterisation kit, heated pitot, heated stall warning, instrument post lights, control wheel mounted chronograph, electric elevator trim, glider tow provisions, four-outlet oxygen system, engine primer, fire extinguisher, reading lights for rear seats and white strobe lights.

Dimensions, external:

Wing span	32 ft 0½ in (9·76 m)
Wing chord, constant	5 ft 6 in (1·68 m)
Wing aspect ratio	5·82
Length overall	28 ft 6¾ in (8·70 m)
Height overall	9 ft 7 in (2·92 m)
Tailplane span	11 ft 3 in (3·42 m)
Wheel track	7 ft 0 in (2·13 m)
Wheelbase	6 ft 6 in (1·98 m)
Propeller diameter	7 ft 0 in (2·13 m)
Propeller ground clearance	11 in (0·28 m)
Cabin doors: Height	3 ft 0 in (0·91 m)
Width	3 ft 1 in (0·94 m)
Height to sill	1 ft 4 in (0·40 m)
Baggage door (port side):	
Height	1 ft 11½ in (0·60 m)
Width	1 ft 3½ in (0·39 m)

Dimensions, internal:

Cabin: Length	10 ft 10 in (3·30 m)
Max width	4 ft 2⅜ in (1·28 m)
Max height	3 ft 6 in (1·07 m)

Areas:

Wings, gross	167 sq ft (15·51 m²)
Ailerons (total)	15·28 sq ft (1·42 m²)
Trailing-edge flaps (total)	16·1 sq ft (1·50 m²)
Fin	9·97 sq ft (0·93 m²)
Rudder	6·31 sq ft (0·59 m²)
Tailplane	18·3 sq ft (1·70 m²)
Elevators, including tab	15·97 sq ft (1·48 m²)

Weights and Loadings:

Weight empty	2,150 lb (975 kg)
Max T-O and landing weight	3,400 lb (1,542 kg)
Max wing loading	19·3 lb/sq ft (94·7 kg/m²)
Max power loading	11·9 lb/hp (5·40 kg/hp)

Performance (at max T-O weight):

Max never-exceed speed 226 knots (260 mph; 418 km/h)
Max level speed over 183 knots (211 mph; 340 km/h)
Max cruising speed, 75% power at 7,000 ft (2,135 m) 180 knots (207 mph; 333 km/h)
Stalling speed, flaps up 62 knots (71·5 mph; 115 km/h)
Stalling speed, flaps down 57 knots (66 mph; 106·5 km/h)

Max rate of climb at S/L	1,220 ft (372 m)/min
Service ceiling	18,000 ft (5,475 m)
T-O run	855 ft (261 m)
T-O to 50 ft (15 m)	1,130 ft (344 m)
Landing from 50 ft (15 m)	1,330 ft (405 m)
Landing run	960 ft (293 m)

Range with max fuel, at 10,000 ft (3,050 m), 45 min reserve 1,070 nm (1,232 miles; 1,982 km)

WITTMAN

S. J. WITTMAN

Address:

Box 276, Oshkosh, Wisconsin 54901

Famous as a racing pilot since 1926, Steve Wittman has designed and built a large number of different racing and touring aeroplanes at Winnebago County Airport, of which he became manager in 1931.

Of the racers, Bonzo, with which Mr Wittman won the Continental Trophy in 1949, 1950 and 1952, is still flying, and details of this aircraft were given in the 1959-60 *Jane's*.

Most popular Wittman design is the Tailwind side-by-side two-seat light aeroplane. The prototype was built in 1952-53 and proved so successful that sets of plans and prefabricated components were made available to amateur builders. By the Spring of 1972, there were more than 150 Model W-8 Tailwinds flying, including a number built in foreign countries, and more than 100 were known to be under construction. In January 1968 Mr Wittman's plans were approved by the Australian Department of Civil Aviation.

In 1966, a more powerful six-cylinder Continental engine was installed in a Tailwind redesigned to take the added weight and power. This version is designated W-9.

A modified version of the Tailwind is being marketed in the UK by AJEP (which see).

Mr Wittman has also designed and built the prototype of a Formula V racing aircraft designated Witt's V.

WITTMAN TAILWIND MODEL W-8

Some Tailwinds have been built with tricycle landing gear, retractable main wheels and other design changes. The adjacent illustration shows the modified Tailwind built by Mr Jerry Varnell of Little Rock, Arkansas. It follows Steve Wittman's plans closely except for a redesigned tail unit and slightly increased width at top of cabin. It is powered by an 85 hp Continental C85 engine which provides a cruising speed of 121·5 knots (140 mph; 225 km/h). This aircraft received the "Best Tailwind" award at Oshkosh in 1971.

The following data refer to the standard W-8 Tailwind built to Mr Wittman's plans:

Type: Two-seat cabin monoplane.

Wings: Braced high-wing monoplane. Wing section is a combination of NACA 4309 (upper surface) and NACA 0006 (lower surface). Thickness/chord ratio 11·5%. No dihedral. Incidence 1°. Wood structure with plywood and fabric covering. Single bracing strut each side. Ailerons and flaps of steel and stainless steel construction.

Fuselage: Steel tube structure, fabric-covered.

Tail Unit: Cantilever structure of steel and stainless steel. Ground-adjustable trim tabs in control surfaces.

Landing Gear: Non-retractable tailwheel type. Spring steel cantilever main legs. Goodyear 15 × 5 main wheels and tyres, pressure 32 lb/sq in (2·25 kg/cm²). Goodyear brakes.

Power Plant: Normally one 90 hp Continental C90-12F four-cylinder horizontally-opposed aircooled engine, driving a Sensenich or Flottorp two-blade wood fixed-pitch propeller. Alternative engines are the 85 hp Continental C85, 100 hp Continental O-200, 115 hp Lycoming O-235 or 140 hp Lycoming O-290. One fuel tank of 25 US gallons (94·5 litres) capacity in fuselage. Oil capacity 4-6 US quarts (1·85-2·8 litres).

Accommodation: Two seats side by side in enclosed cabin, with door on each side. Space for 60 lb (27 kg) baggage.

Dimensions, external:

Wing span	22 ft 6 in (6·86 m)
Wing chord, constant	4 ft 0 in (1·22 m)
Wing aspect ratio	5·5
Length overall	19 ft 3 in (5·87 m)
Height overall	5 ft 8 in (1·73 m)
Tailplane span	6 ft 8 in (2·03 m)
Wheel track	5 ft 5 in (1·65 m)
Propeller diameter	5 ft 4 in (1·63 m)

Areas:

Wings, gross	90 sq ft (8·36 m²)
Ailerons (total)	3·0 sq ft (0·28 m²)
Flaps (total)	7·3 sq ft (0·68 m²)
Fin	4·8 sq ft (0·45 m²)
Rudder	2·3 sq ft (0·21 m²)
Tailplane	5·5 sq ft (0·51 m²)
Elevators	4·8 sq ft (0·45 m²)

Weights and Loadings (100 hp Continental engine):

Weight empty	700 lb (318 kg)
Max T-O weight	1,300 lb (590 kg)
Max wing loading	14·4 lb/sq ft (70·3 kg/m²)
Max power loading	13·0 lb/hp (5·90 kg/hp)

Performance (100 hp Continental engine at max T-O weight):

Max never-exceed speed 160 knots (185 mph; 297 km/h)
Max level speed at S/L 143 knots (165 mph; 265 km/h)
Max cruising speed 139 knots (160 mph; 257 km/h)
Econ cruising speed 113 knots (130 mph; 209 km/h)
Stalling speed, flaps down 48 knots (55 mph; 89 km/h)

Max rate of climb at S/L	900 ft (275 m)/min
Service ceiling	16,000 ft (4,876 m)
T-O run	800 ft (245 m)
T-O to 50 ft (15 m)	1,325 ft (405 m)
Landing from 50 ft (15 m)	1,150 ft (350 m)
Landing run	600 ft (183 m)

Range with max payload at 10,000 ft (3,050 m), no reserve:
at 139 knots (160 mph; 257 km/h) 521 nm (600 miles; 965 km)
at 122 knots (140 mph; 225 km/h) 607 nm (700 miles; 1,125 km)

WITTMAN TAILWIND MODEL W-9

This aircraft was first flown in 1958, as the W-9L Tailwind with tricycle landing gear (see 1965-66 *Jane's*). In 1965 it was fitted with a new wing exactly the same as that used on the W-8 Tailwind. It has more recently been re-engined with a 145 hp Continental O-300 six-cylinder horizontally-opposed aircooled engine. The structure has been strengthened as necessary to take the extra power and weight, and the landing gear is now of the tailwheel type.

Dimensions, external:

Same as W-8, except:

Length overall	20 ft 0 in (6·10 m)

Weights:

Weight empty	800 lb (363 kg)
Max T-O weight	1,420 lb (644 kg)

Performance (at max T-O weight):

Max level speed at S/L 172 knots (198 mph; 319 km/h)
Max cruising speed 156 knots (180 mph; 290 km/h)

Landing speed	48 knots (55 mph; 89 km/h)
Max rate of climb at S/L	1,400 ft (425 m)/min
Service ceiling	17,000 ft (5,180 m)
T-O run	600 ft (183 m)

Range with max fuel 564 nm (650 miles; 1,045 km)

Modified Wittman Tailwind built by Mr Jerry Varnell of Little Rock, Arkansas (85 hp Continental C85 engine) (*Howard Levy*)

WITTMAN WITT'S V

Steve Wittman has completed construction of the Formula V racing monoplane upon which he had been working for some time. It is powered by a 60-65 hp 1,600 cc Volkswagen modified motor car engine which is mounted in an inverted position. Ignition system and exhaust manifolds have been modified, and cylinder heads slightly redesigned to improve cooling. It has a standard propeller hub, but this is mounted on a 1 ft (30·5 cm) propeller-shaft extension. The power plant is faired by a glassfibre cowling.

TYPE: Single-seat Formula V racing monoplane.

WINGS: Braced mid-wing monoplane. Combination of two NACA wing sections. Thickness/chord ratio 7·5%. Conventional wooden two-spar structure with plywood and fabric covering. Ailerons and trailing-edge flaps of wooden construction.

FUSELAGE: Welded 4130 steel tube structure with fabric covering.

TAIL UNIT: Welded 4130 steel tube structure, integral with fuselage and fabric covered.

LANDING GEAR: Non-retractable tailwheel type. Cantilever spring main gear of titanium, with single wheel on each unit. Main wheels and tyres size 5·00-5, with brakes.

POWER PLANT: One 60-65 hp Volkswagen 1,600 cc modified motor car engine, driving a two-blade fixed-pitch propeller through a 1 ft (30·5 cm) extension shaft. Fuel contained in fuselage tank immediately aft of firewall, capacity 10·25 US gallons (38·8 litres). Refuelling point on fuselage upper surface.

ACCOMMODATION: Single seat under transparent canopy.

EQUIPMENT: Two-way radio, landing and navigation lights.

Wittman Witt's V Formula V racing monoplane (60-65 hp Volkswagen 1,600 cc modified motor car engine) (*Howard Levy*)

DIMENSIONS, EXTERNAL:	
Wing span	17 ft 6 in (5·33 m)
Wing chord (constant)	4 ft 6 in (1·37 m)
Length overall	18 ft 2 in (5·54 m)
Height at cockpit	4 ft 2 in (1·27 m)
Wheel track	4 ft 11¼ in (1·50 m)
DIMENSIONS, INTERNAL:	
Cockpit:	
Width	1 ft 8 in (0·51 m)
Length	2 ft 3 in (0·69 m)
AREA:	
Wings, gross	77 sq ft (7·15 m²)
WEIGHTS AND LOADING:	
Weight empty	430 lb (195 kg)
Max T-O weight	700 lb (318 kg)
Max wing loading	9·0 lb/sq ft (43·9 kg/m²)
PERFORMANCE:	
Max level speed	148 knots (170 mph; 274 km/h)
Cruising speed	over 130 knots (150 mph; 241 km/h)
Stalling speed, flaps down	approx 42 knots (48 mph; 78 km/h)
Max rate of climb at S/L	1,000 ft (305 m)/min
Service ceiling	over 15,000 ft (4,570 m)
T-O run	approx 800 ft (244 m)
Range with max fuel	over 347 nm (400 miles; 644 km)

WOTRING

MELVIN A. WOTRING

PLANS AVAILABLE FROM:
Rotor-Hawk Industries, Goodrich, Michigan

WOTRING GYRO-FALCON 201

Mr Wotring, of Goodrich, Michigan, has designed, built and developed a single-seat autogyro which he has named the Gyro-Falcon 201. Construction occupied three months, at a cost of $3,500, and the first flight was recorded on 21 July 1973.

The two-blade rotor has a mechanical system to pre-spin the rotor before take-off. Simple bolt-together structure of light alloy, tail unit comprising twin fixed fins and rudders. Non-retractable tricycle type landing gear without shock-absorption; hydraulic disc brakes. One 90 hp McCulloch four-cylinder horizontally-opposed aircooled engine, driving a two-blade fixed-pitch pusher propeller. Enclosed cabin is constructed of glassfibre. Plans of the Gyro-Falcon 201 are available to amateur constructors.

DIMENSION, EXTERNAL:	
Rotor diameter	22 ft 0 in (6·70 m)
WEIGHTS:	
Weight empty	341 lb (155 kg)
Max T-O weight	850 lb (385 kg)
PERFORMANCE (at max T-O weight):	
Max level speed	78 knots (90 mph; 145 km/h)
Cruising speed	69 knots (80 mph; 128 km/h)
Landing speed	6 knots (7 mph; 11 km/h)
Max rate of climb at S/L	950 ft (290 m)/min
Service ceiling	12,500 ft (3,810 m)
Range	173 nm (200 miles; 320 km)

Wotring Gyro-Falcon 201 homebuilt light autogyro (90 hp McCulloch engine) (*Howard Levy*)

THE UNION OF SOVIET SOCIALIST REPUBLICS

ANTONOV

General Designer in Charge of Bureau:
Oleg Konstantinovich Antonov

After establishing his reputation with a series of successful glider and sailplane designs, Antonov became one of Russia's leading designers of transport aircraft, particularly those types intended for short-field operation.

Details of the current products of his design bureau, which is situated in Kiev, are given hereafter.

ANTONOV An-2

NATO code name: "Colt"

Following manufacture of the An-2M specialised agricultural version of this large single-engined biplane, in the mid-sixties, production of the An-2 came to an end in the Soviet Union. Details of the various versions that were built can be found in the 1971-72 *Jane's*.

Several versions of the An-2 continue in production under licence in Poland (see "WSK-Mielec" entry).

ANTONOV An-3

It was reported in the Spring of 1972 that the Antonov design bureau was engaged on design studies for a turboprop development of the An-2 biplane (see under "WSK-Mielec" in Polish section). Provisionally designated An-3, the new aircraft would be produced specifically for agricultural duties. It would retain the biplane configuration of the An-2 and would make use of many components of the latter aircraft including the fuselage, tail unit, main landing gear and control system. The chemical hopper would also be in the same place, and would have a maximum capacity of 4,410 lb (2,000 kg).

Major changes would include the use of a tricycle-type landing gear, modernisation of the flight and navigational equipment, and the new power plant. Current studies are based on the use of a 1,500 shp turboprop version of the Isotov TV2-117A turboshaft which powers the Mi-8 helicopter, and it is expected that the An-3 would be designed for pilot-only operation.

ANTONOV An-12

NATO code name: "Cub"

The An-12 is a freight-carrying version of the now-retired An-10 passenger transport, with redesigned rear fuselage and tail unit. A loading ramp for freight and vehicles, in the underside of the upswept rear fuselage, can be lowered in flight for air-drop operations. The built-in freight-handling gantry has a capacity of 5,070 lb (2,300 kg). The cargo floor is designed for loadings of up to 307 lb/sq ft (1,500 kg/m²).

The standard military version has a tail gunner's position. In the An-12 which Ghana Airways operated for a time, this was fitted out as a toilet. In the refined commercial version, first demonstrated at the 1965 Paris Air Show, the turret is removed and replaced by a streamlined fairing.

Equipment for all-weather operation is standard. Current Soviet Air Force An-12s have a larger undernose radome than that originally fitted.

The An-12 is a standard paratroop and freight transport in the Soviet Air Force. Sixteen were supplied to the Indian Air Force. Others are operated by the air forces of Algeria, Bangladesh, Egypt, Indonesia, Iraq and Poland, and by Aeroflot, Polish Air Lines (LOT), Bulair and Cubana. Altogether, more than 900 are reported to have been built for military and civil use.

One of the An-12s operated by Aeroflot's Polar aviation service was used to test skis of an entirely new design. Of unusually wide and deep section, these have a shallow curved Vee lower surface, like a flattened version of the planing bottom of a seaplane float. The skis are equipped with braking devices and warming equipment and are claimed to permit landings at prepared fields as well as on virgin snow. Each main ski is supported by a primary oleo strut, with scissor-arm system, and fore and aft secondary oleos to absorb pitching (and possibly rolling) moments. They were intended as standard equipment on aircraft used in the Arctic and Antarctic and for Winter services.

Type: Four-engined cargo transport.

Wings: Cantilever high-wing monoplane. All-metal two-spar structure in five panels, comprising centre-section, intermediate wings and tip sections, the last with marked anhedral. Manually-operated aerodynamically-balanced ailerons. Double-slotted Fowler flaps in two portions each side, hydraulically-actuated. Electro-thermal de-icing.

Fuselage: Stressed-skin semi-monocoque structure of circular section.

Tail Unit: Cantilever all-metal structure. Electrically-operated trim tabs. All controls are manually operated and aerodynamically balanced. Electro-thermal de-icing of fin and tailplane.

Landing Gear: Retractable tricycle type. Hydraulic actuation. Shock-absorbers use nitrogen instead of air and have stroke of 13·4 in (340 mm). Four-wheel bogie on each side retracts into blister on side of fuselage. Hydraulically-steerable dual nosewheels. Mainwheel tyre size 1,050 × 300 mm; pressure 80-95 lb/sq in (5·6-6·7 kg/cm²). Hydraulic disc brakes.

Power Plant: Four 4,000 ehp Ivchenko AI-20K turboprops, driving AV-68 four-blade reversible-pitch propellers. All fuel in 22 bag-type tanks in wings, total normal capacity 3,058 Imp gallons (13,900 litres). Max capacity (military) 3,981 Imp gallons (18,100 litres).

Accommodation: Pilot and co-pilot side by side on flight deck. Engineer's station on starboard side, behind co-pilot. Radio operator in well behind pilot, facing outboard. Navigator in glazed nose compartment. Rear gunner in tail turret of military version. Crew door on port side forward of wing. Access to freight hold via ramp-door at rear, under upswept rear fuselage. Ramp-door is divided into two longitudinal halves, which can be hinged upward inside cabin to provide access for direct loading of freight from trucks. Undersurface of fuselage aft of ramp is formed by door which hinges upward into fuselage to facilitate loading and unloading. Commercial version can carry 14 passengers in compartment aft of flight deck. Military version can carry 100 paratroops, all of whom can be despatched in under one minute, with ramp-doors folded upward.

Systems: Entire accommodation air-conditioned and pressurised to differential of 7·1 lb/sq in (0·50 kg/cm²). Hydraulic system operates landing gear retraction, nosewheel steering, flaps, brakes and rear loading ramp and door.

Armament (military version): Two 23 mm NR-23 guns in tail turret.

Dimensions, external:
- Wing span: 124 ft 8 in (38·00 m)
- Wing chord (mean): 13 ft 1½ in (4·00 m)
- Wing aspect ratio: 10·6
- Length overall: 121 ft 4½ in (37·00 m)
- Height overall: 32 ft 3 in (9·83 m)
- Wheel track: 17 ft 9¼ in (5·42 m)
- Wheelbase: 35 ft 6 in (10·82 m)
- Propeller diameter: 14 ft 9 in (4·50 m)

Dimensions, internal:
- Cargo hold:
  - Length: 44 ft 3½ in (13·50 m)
  - Max width: 9 ft 10 in (3·00 m)
  - Max height: 7 ft 10½ in (2·40 m)

Area:
- Wings, gross: 1,286 sq ft (119·5 m²)

Weights and Loadings (military model):
- Weight empty: 61,730 lb (28,000 kg)
- Normal T-O weight: 121,475 lb (55,100 kg)
- Normal wing loading: 94·4 lb/sq ft (461 kg/m²)
- Normal power loading: 7·5 lb/ehp (3·4 kg/ehp)

Weights (late civil model):
- Max payload: 44,090 lb (20,000 kg)
- Normal T-O weight: 119,050 lb (54,000 kg)
- Max T-O weight: 134,480 lb (61,000 kg)

Performance (military model):
- Max level speed: 419 knots (482 mph; 777 km/h)
- Max cruising speed: 361 knots (416 mph; 670 km/h)
- Rate of climb at S/L: 1,970 ft (600 m)/min
- Service ceiling: 33,500 ft (10,200 m)

Antonov An-12 of the Soviet Air Force, with current enlarged nose radome (*Tass*)

Antonov An-12 rear-loading transport (four 4,000 ehp Ivchenko AI-20K turboprop engines) of Bulair (*P. J. Bish*)

T-O run 2,300 ft (700 m)
Landing run 1,640 ft (500 m)
Range with max payload
1,942 nm (2,236 miles; 3,600 km)
Range with max fuel
3,075 nm (3,540 miles; 5,700 km)

PERFORMANCE (late civil model, at normal T-O weight):
Max cruising speed
324 knots (373 mph; 600 km/h)
Normal cruising speed at 25,000 ft (7,500 m)
297 knots (342 mph; 550 km/h)
Max rate of climb at S/L 1,970 ft (600 m)/min
Service ceiling 33,500 ft (10,200 m)
T-O run 2,790 ft (850 m)
Landing run 2,820 ft (860 m)
Range with 22,050 lb (10,000 kg) cargo, 1 hour reserve 1,832 nm (2,110 miles; 3,400 km)

ANTONOV An-14 PCHELKA (LITTLE BEE)

NATO code name: "Clod"

The An-14 Pchelka is a twin-engined light general-purpose aircraft, the first prototype of which made its first flight on 15 March 1958.

The two prototypes were each powered by two 260 hp Ivchenko AI-14R radial engines and accommodated six passengers and 330 lb (150 kg) of baggage, or 1,320 lb (600 kg) of freight. They flew originally with a straight tailplane and with V-shape leading-edges on the twin tail-fins. This type of tail unit was superseded by a dihedral tailplane and rectangular fins of increased area on production aircraft, which also have 300 hp engines, increased wing span and accommodation for a pilot and six to eight passengers, plus baggage.

Production began in 1965 at the Progress Plant at Arsenyev, in the far east of the Soviet Union, for both Aeroflot and the Soviet armed forces. The military version was first seen at the Domodedovo air display in July 1967 and does not appear to differ externally from the civilian passenger version. It serves also with the air forces of the German Democratic Republic and Guinea, and with Balkan Bulgarian Airlines.

An executive version is available with de luxe accommodation for five passengers and their baggage, with tables between facing seats. All seats are quickly removable to provide an unobstructed cabin for cargo carrying. An ambulance version, which is in production, can accommodate six stretchers, in tiers of three on each side of the cabin, with an attendant. Dual controls are available for pilot training and a variety of equipment can be fitted for geological survey, aerial photography and agricultural duties.

Photographs were issued showing aircraft No. CCCP-L1053 (with original fins and probably a prototype) equipped for agricultural duties. It had spraybars attached to the aileron-flap brackets under each wing, from the wingtip to a point immediately aft of the wing/bracing strut junction. From there the spraybars ran down the bracing strut and along the stub-wings to meet under the fuselage. The chemical tank was housed in the main cabin and the standard rear loading doors were replaced by a larger removable fairing panel. Entry to the flight deck was via a forward-opening door on the starboard side of the nose, hinged on the centreline of the aircraft.

Great emphasis has been placed on simplicity of servicing and handling, and the An-14 is said to be suitable for operation by "pilots of average skill". It will maintain height on one engine at its maximum T-O weight. Radio, navigation equipment, instrumentation, landing light and de-icing equipment make possible operation at night and in bad weather.

The following data apply to the standard production An-14:

TYPE: Twin-engined light general-purpose aircraft.

WINGS: Braced high-wing monoplane with single streamline-section bracing strut each side. Dihedral 2°. Conventional all-metal two-spar structure. Full-span leading-edge slats, in three sections on each wing. Section between fuselage and engine nacelle on each wing is extended pneumatically when the flaps are lowered 35-40°. The remaining four sections are actuated automatically by the airflow over the wing. Entire trailing-edges hinged; each comprising a double-slotted flap, with the slat of the flap extending to the wingtip and built into the single-slotted aileron as a leading-edge structure. Flaps operated pneumatically. Trim tab in port aileron. Small stub-wing carries each main landing gear unit and provides lower attachment for bracing strut.

FUSELAGE: Conventional all-metal semi-monocoque pod-and-boom structure.

TAIL UNIT: Cantilever all-metal structure, with 9° dihedral on tailplane. Twin fins and rudders, mounted at right-angles to the tips of the tailplane, so that they toe inwards at the top. Trim tab in port rudder and in port elevator. Leading-edges of fins and tailplane embody both warm air and electrical anti-icing systems.

LANDING GEAR: Non-retractable tricycle type, with single wheel on each unit. Main units carried on short stub-wings. Wide-tread tyres,

Antonov An-14 Pchelka (two 300 hp Ivchenko AI-14RF engines) *(Tass)*

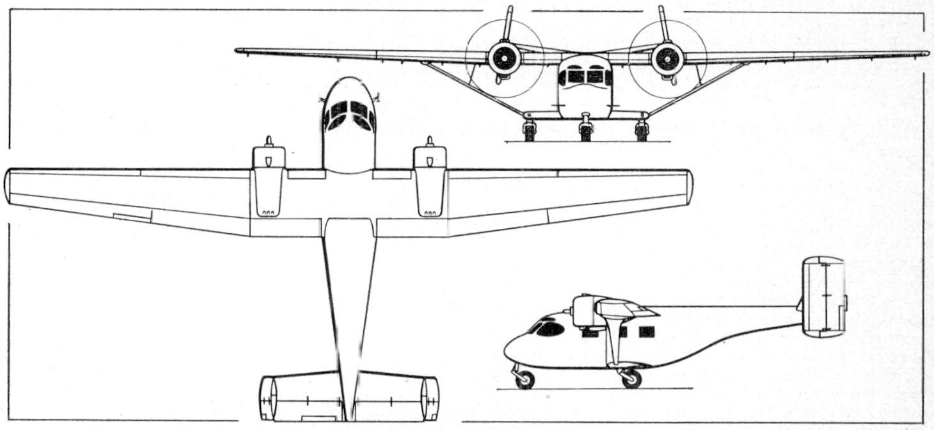

Antonov An-14 Pchelka twin-engined light general-purpose aircraft *(Pilot Press)*

size 700 × 250, on all three units. Tyre pressure: main units 50 lb/sq in (3·5 kg/cm²); nosewheel 42·5 lb/sq in (3·0 kg/cm²). Nosewheel is fully-castoring and steerable to 70° each way, and is self-centering for take-off. Pneumatic brakes on main wheels. Skis can be fitted for operation from snow, or floats for operation from water.

POWER PLANT: Two 300 hp Ivchenko AI-14RF nine-cylinder radial aircooled engines, each driving a V-530 two-blade or three-blade variable-pitch propeller. Each engine draws its fuel normally from an inboard metal tank and outer flexible tank in the wing on which it is mounted, with a cross-feed to enable either engine to be supplied from both tank groups in the event of an engine failure. Total fuel capacity 84 Imp gallons (383 litres).

ACCOMMODATION: Pilot and one passenger side by side on flight deck. Main cabin normally seats six persons in pairs in individual forward-facing armchair seats, each by a large window and with central aisle. Provision for seven seats in main cabin in high-density version. Cabin soundproofed and provided with heating and ventilation systems. Door from cabin to flight deck. Passengers enter cabin through clamshell rear doors which form underside of upswept rear fuselage. Chemical tank capacity of agricultural version is 220 Imp gallons (1,000 litres). Optional dual controls.

SYSTEMS: Pneumatic system, pressure 710 lb/sq in (50 kg/cm²), for wheel brakes, flap and slat actuation, engine starting, cabin heating and anti-icing. Main 27V DC electrical system supplied by two 3kW engine-driven generators. Two converters to supply 115V 400Hz AC power.

ELECTRONICS AND EQUIPMENT: Standard equipment includes an artificial horizon, gyro-compass, magnetic compass, altimeter, airspeed indicator, clock, rate-of-climb indicator, turn indicator, outside air temperature gauge and ice-warning device. Com/nav equipment can include duplicated transceivers, ADF, VOR, marker beacon and radio altimeter.

DIMENSIONS, EXTERNAL:
Wing span 72 ft 2 in (21·99 m)
Wing chord, mean 6 ft 2½ in (1·89 m)
Wing aspect ratio 12·15
Length overall 37 ft 6½ in (11·44 m)
Height overall 15 ft 2¼ in (4·63 m)
Tailplane span 16 ft 4¾ in (5·00 m)
Wheel track 11 ft 9¾ in (3·60 m)
Wheelbase 12 ft 2 in (3·71 m)
Propeller diameter 9 ft 6 in (2·90 m)
Cabin door:
Length 6 ft 3 in (1·90 m)
Width 2 ft 9½ in (0·85 m)

DIMENSIONS, INTERNAL:
Cabin, excluding flight deck:
Length 10 ft 2 in (3·10 m)
Width 5 ft 0 in (1·53 m)
Height 5 ft 3 in (1·60 m)

AREA:
Wings, gross 427·5 sq ft (39·72 m²)

WEIGHTS AND LOADINGS:
Weight empty 4,409 lb (2,000 kg)
Max payload (normal) 1,590 lb (720 kg)
Max T-O weight 7,935 lb (3,600 kg)
Max wing loading 18·6 lb/sq ft (90·8 kg/m²)
Max power loading 13·2 lb/hp (6·0 kg/hp)

PERFORMANCE (at max T-O weight):
Max level speed at 3,280 ft (1,000 m)
120 knots (138 mph; 222 km/h)
Normal cruising speed at 6,560 ft (2,000 m)
97 knots (112 mph; 180 km/h)
Operating speed, agricultural duties
76 knots (87 mph; 140 km/h)
Landing speed 46 knots (53 mph; 85 km/h)
Max rate of climb at S/L 1,000 ft (306 m)/min
Service ceiling 17,060 ft (5,200 m)
T-O run, on concrete 328 ft (100 m)
T-O to 50 ft (15 m) 656 ft (200 m)
Landing from 50 ft (15 m) 985 ft (300 m)
Landing run 230 ft (70 m)
Range:
with max payload
350 nm (404 miles; 650 km)
with 1,212 lb (550 kg) payload
385 nm (444 miles; 715 km)
with max fuel 431 nm (497 miles; 800 km)

ANTONOV An-22 ANTHEUS

NATO code name: "Cock"

Nothing was known of this very large transport aircraft until the first prototype arrived in Paris on 16 June 1965, during the *Salon*. It had flown for the first time on 27 February 1965 and the walls of its main cabin were lined with test equipment, recorders, etc. Four more prototypes and the first production An-22 were flying by mid-1967. Two of the prototypes were then being operated by Aeroflot on experimental freight services. Three An-22s, in military insignia, took part in the air display at Domodedovo on 9 July 1967, landing batteries of "Frog-3" and "Ganef" missiles on tracked launchers. Production aircraft have been delivered to both the Soviet Air Force and Aeroflot, which uses the An-22 mainly in underdeveloped areas of the northern USSR, Siberia and the Far East.

In general configuration, the An-22 is similar to its much smaller predecessor, the An-12, with the outer wing anhedral that is a characteristic of many Antonov designs. It is intended primarily for long-distance transportation of heavy bulk cargoes and civil and military equipment, accompanied by operating personnel.

The current production version shown in the

Antonov An-22 Antheus long-range heavy transport aircraft (four 15,000 shp Kuznetsov NK-12MA turboprop engines) (*D. J. Holford*)

accompanying illustrations differs in a number of details from early An-22s. The main navigation radar, housed originally under the starboard landing gear fairing, is now mounted at the nose, which carries two radars, in a thimble-type fairing above the modified nose windows and in a large underfuselage radome. A fairing extends forward from the lower radome and might be fitted with shutters, but its purpose is unknown. One aircraft of this type took part in military manoeuvres at Dvina in NW Byelorussia in early 1970. Four (serial numbers 09302/3/4/6) were used to airlift relief supplies to Peru after the severe earthquake of July 1970; and 09303 was lost over the Atlantic, south of Greenland, on 18 July.

On 26 October 1967, an An-22 set up fourteen payload-to-height records, piloted by I. Davydov and with a crew of seven. It reached a height of 25,748 ft (7,848 m) with a payload of 100,000 kg of metal blocks, qualifying also for records with 35,000, 40,000, 45,000, 50,000, 55,000, 60,000, 65,000, 70,000, 75,000, 85,000, 90,000 and 95,000 kg. Max payload lifted to a height of 2,000 m was 221,443 lb (100,444·6 kg). Take-off run with this load was stated to be just over one kilometre. The flight lasted 78 minutes.

A further series of ten records, for speed with payload, was set up in February 1972 by an An-22 captained by Marina Popovich, wife of the Soviet cosmonaut Pavel Popovich. The aircraft averaged 320·161 knots (368·671 mph; 593·318 km/h) around a 2,000 km closed circuit with a 50,000 kg payload, qualifying also for records with 30,000, 35,000, 40,000 and 45,000 kg, on 19 February. Two days later, it averaged 328·326 knots (378·073 mph; 608·449 km/h) around 1,000 km with the same payload.

The following details refer to the current production version:

Type: Long-range heavy turboprop transport.

Wings: Cantilever high-wing monoplane. Marked anhedral on outer panels. All-metal structure, appearing to have three main spars which attach to three strong fuselage ring-frames. Double-slotted trailing-edge flaps. Tab in each aileron.

Fuselage: All-metal semi-monocoque structure, with upswept rear fuselage containing loading-ramp/door for direct loading. Retractable jacks support rear fuselage at point where rear loading ramp is hinged.

Tail Unit: Cantilever all-metal structure. Twin fins and rudders (each in two sections, above and below tailplane) mounted outboard of mid-span. Tabs in each elevator and in each of the four rudder sections.

Landing Gear: Retractable tricycle type, designed to permit off-runway operation. Steerable twin-wheel nose unit. Each main gear consists of three twin-wheel levered-suspension units in tandem, each unit mounted at the bottom of one of the fuselage ring frames that also picks up a wing spar. Main units retract upward into fairings built on to sides of fuselage. Tyre pressure adjustable in flight or on ground to suit airfield surface.

Power Plant: Four 15,000 shp Kuznetsov NK-12MA turboprop engines, each driving a pair of four-blade contra-rotating propellers.

Accommodation: Crew of five or six. Navigator's station in nose. Cabin for 28-29 passengers aft of flight deck, separated from main cabin by bulkhead containing two doors. Uninterrupted main cabin, with reinforced titanium floor, tie-down fittings and rear loading ramp. When ramp lowers, a large door which forms the underside of the rear fuselage retracts upward inside fuselage to permit easy loading of tall vehicles. Rails in roof of cabin for four travelling gantries continue rearward on underside of this door. Two winches, used in conjunction with the gantries, each have a capacity of 5,500 lb (2,500 kg). Door in each landing gear fairing, forward of wheels, for crew and passengers.

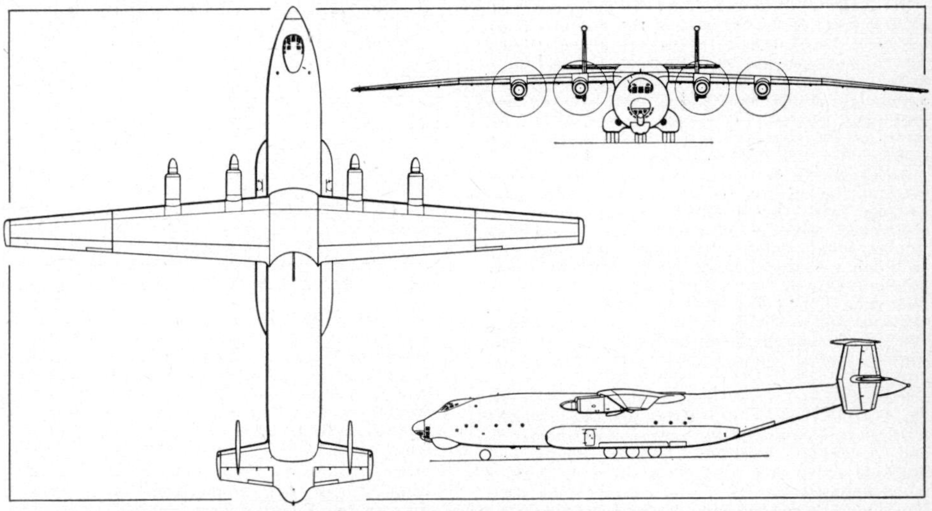

Antonov An-22 Antheus long-range heavy transport aircraft (*Pilot Press*)

Electronics and Equipment: Pressurisation equipment and APU in forward part of starboard landing gear fairing. Two radars, in nose "thimble" and undernose fairings.

Dimensions, external:
- Wing span: 211 ft 4 in (64·40 m)
- Length overall (prototype): 189 ft 7 in (57·80 m)
- Height overall: 41 ft 1½ in (12·53 m)
- Propeller diameter: 20 ft 4 in (6·20 m)

Dimensions, internal:
- Main cabin: Length: 108 ft 3 in (33·0 m)
  - Max width: 14 ft 5 in (4·4 m)
  - Max height: 14 ft 5 in (4·4 m)

Areas:
- Wings, gross: 3,713 sq ft (345 m²)

Weights:
- Weight empty, equipped: 251,325 lb (114,000 kg)
- Max payload: 176,350 lb (80,000 kg)
- Max fuel: 94,800 lb (43,000 kg)
- Max T-O weight: 551,160 lb (250,000 kg)

Performance:
- Max level speed: 399 knots (460 mph; 740 km/h)
- T-O run: 4,260 ft (1,300 m)
- Landing run: 2,620 ft (800 m)
- Range with max fuel and 99,200 lb (45,000 kg) payload: 5,905 nm (6,800 miles; 10,950 km)
- Range with max payload: 2,692 nm (3,100 miles; 5,000 km)

ANTONOV An-24

NATO code name: "Coke"

Development of this twin-turboprop transport was started in 1958, to replace piston-engined types on Aeroflot's internal feederline routes. The An-24 was intended originally to carry 32-40 passengers, but when the prototype flew in April 1960 it had been developed into a 44-seater. It was followed by a second prototype and five pre-production An-24s. Flight trials were stated to be complete in September 1962 and the An-24 entered service on Aeroflot's routes from Moscow to Voronezh and Saratov in September 1963. More than 50 million passengers and 500,000 tonnes of cargo had been carried by Aeroflot An-24Vs by 1971.

The An-24 is designed to operate from airfields of limited size, with paved or natural runways, and can be fitted with rocket-assisted take-off units to permit operation with a full load of cargo at ambient temperatures above 85°F. Two were taken to the Antarctic in late 1969, to replace piston-engined Il-14s used previously for flights between Antarctic stations.

Export orders have been received from the following airlines:

Air Guinée	3
Air Mali	2
Balkan Bulgarian Airlines	8
CAAC (China)	2
Cubana	8
Interflug (E Germany)	8
Iraqi Airways	1
Lebanese Air Transport	1*
Lina Congo	2
LOT (Poland)	15
Misrair (EgyptAir)	10
Mongolian Airlines	4
Pan African Air Services (Tanzania)	2
Tarom (Romania)	9

**Sold to Misrair and included in latter's total of ten*

The An-24 has also been supplied for military service, usually in small numbers, with the air forces of the USSR, Bangladesh, the Republic of Congo (Brazzaville), Czechoslovakia, Egypt, East Germany, Hungary, North Korea, Mongolia, Poland, Romania, the Somali Republic and North Vietnam.

On the prototype, the engine nacelles extended only a little past the wing trailing-edges: production An-24s have lengthened nacelles with conical rear fairings. A ventral tail-fin was also added on production models, which have been followed by the An-24T and An-26 specialised freight-carrying versions of the same basic design. The An-26 is described separately.

The current production versions of the An-24 are designed for a service life of 30,000 hours and 15,000 landings, and are being produced in a variety of forms, as follows:

An-24V Srs II. Standard version, seating up to 50 passengers. Superseded Srs I (with 2,550 ehp AI-24 engines) in 1968, and described in detail below. Basically as Srs I, powered by two Ivchenko AI-24A turboprop engines, with water injection. Can have crew of up to five (two pilots, navigator, radio operator and, on jump seat, an engineer or cargo handler) on flight deck. TG-16 self-contained starter/generator in rear of starboard engine nacelle. Mixed passenger/freight, convertible cargo/passenger, all-freight and executive versions available.

An-24P. Firefighting (*Pozharny*) version, which underwent evaluation in the USSR in 1971. Special provisions for enabling firefighters to be parachuted from a height of 2,625-3,940 ft (800-1,200 m) to deal with forest fires.

An-24RV. Generally similar to Srs II version of An-24V, but with a 1,985 lb (900 kg) st Type RU 19-300 auxiliary turbojet engine in starboard nacelle instead of starter/generator. This turbojet is used for engine starting, to improve take-off performance and to improve performance in the air. It permits take-off with a full payload from airfields up to 9,840ft (3,000 m) above S/L and at temperatures up to ISA + 30°C. It also ensures considerably improved stability and handling characteristics after a failure of one of the turboprop engines in flight. Max T-O weight is increased by 1,760 lb (800 kg) at S/L ISA and by 4,410 lb (2,000 kg) at S/L ISA+30°C by use of the auxiliary turbojet. An An-24RV was demonstrated at the 1967 Paris Air Show.

An-24T. Generally similar to An-24V Srs II but equipped as specialised freighter. Crew of five, consisting of pilot, co-pilot, navigator, radio operator and flight engineer. Normal passenger door at rear of cabin is deleted and replaced by a belly freight door at the rear of the cabin. This hinges upward and to the rear, providing a hatchway for cargo loading. An electrically-powered winch, capacity 3,300 lb (1,500 kg), is used to hoist crates through the hatch and runs on a rail in the cabin ceiling to position payload inside cabin. Electrically or manually-powered conveyor, capacity 9,920 lb (4,500 kg), flush with cabin floor. Fewer windows. Folding seats along walls of cabin. Emergency exit hatches in side and in floor at front of cabin. Rear cargo door permits air-dropping of payload or parachutists. Provision for stretcher-carrying in air ambulance role. Single ventral fin replaced by twin ventral fins, forming Vee, aft of cargo door. An An-24T was displayed at 1967 Paris Air Show, and this version serves with several of the airlines listed earlier.

An-24RT. Generally similar to An-24T but with Type RU auxiliary turbojet in starboard nacelle, as on An-24RV.

The following description refers to the basic An-24V Srs II, unless otherwise noted, but is generally applicable to all versions except for the detailed differences noted above:

TYPE: Twin-turboprop short-range transport.

WINGS: Cantilever high-wing monoplane, with 2° anhedral on outer panels. Incidence 3°. Sweepback at quarter-chord on outer panels 6° 50′. All-metal two-spar structure, built in five sections: centre-section, two inner wings and two outer wings. Wing skin is attached by electrical spot-welding. Mass-balanced servo-compensated ailerons, with large trim tabs of glassfibre construction. Hydraulically-operated Fowler flaps along entire wing trailing-edges inboard of unpowered ailerons; single-slotted flaps on centre-section, double-slotted outboard of nacelles. Servo and trim tabs in each aileron. Thermal de-icing system.

FUSELAGE: All-metal semi-monocoque structure in front, centre and rear portions, of bonded/welded construction.

TAIL UNIT: Cantilever all-metal structure, with ventral fin (two ventral fins on An-24T/RT versions). 9° dihedral on tailplane. All controls manually operated. Trim tabs in elevators. Trim tab and spring tab in rudder. All leading-edges incorporate thermal de-icing system.

LANDING GEAR: Retractable tricycle type with twin wheels on all units. Hydraulic retraction. Emergency extension by gravity. All units retract forward. Main wheels size 900 × 300-370, tyre pressure 50-71 lb/sq in (3·5-5 kg/cm²). Nosewheels size 700 × 250, tyre pressure 35·5-50 lb/sq in (2·5-3·5 kg/cm²). Tyre pressures variable to cater for different types of runway. Disc brakes on main wheels. Steerable and castoring nosewheel unit.

POWER PLANT (all versions): Two 2,550 ehp Ivchenko AI-24A turboprop engines (with provision for water injection; weight of water 150 lb; 68 kg), each driving an AV-72 four-blade constant-speed fully-feathering propeller. Electrical de-icing system for propeller blades and hubs; hot air system for engine air intakes. Fuel in integral tanks immediately outboard of nacelles, and four bag-type tanks in centre-section, total capacity 1,220 Imp gallons (5,550 litres). Provision for four additional tanks in centre-section. Pressure refuelling socket in starboard engine nacelle. Gravity fuelling point above each tank. Carbon dioxide inert gas system to create fireproof condition inside fuel tanks. Oil capacity 11·5 Imp gallons (53 litres). One 1,985 lb (900 kg) st Type RU 19-300 auxiliary turbojet in starboard nacelle of An-24RV and An-24RT. Provision for fitting rocket-assisted take-off units on cargo versions.

ACCOMMODATION (An-24V/RV): Crew of three (pilot, co-pilot/radio operator/navigator and one stewardess). Provision for carrying navigator, radio operator and engineer. Normal accommodation for 44-50 passengers in air-conditioned and pressurised cabin. Standard layout has baggage and freight compartments on each side aft of flight deck; then the main cabin with 50 forward-facing reclining seats, in pairs at a pitch of 28·3 in (72 cm), on each side of centre aisle and two small sofas for babies (at rear); buffet and stewardess's seat, and toilet, opposite door to rear of cabin; and wardrobes at rear. Passenger door on port side, aft of cabin, is of airstair type. Door on starboard side for freight hold (front). All doors open inward. The 46-seat version has a removable partition aft of the fifth row of seats, instead of one row of seats. The mixed passenger/cargo version is laid out normally for 36 passengers, with 495 cu ft (14 m³) forward hold for baggage, freight and mail, and rear wardrobe and baggage hold (99 cu ft; 2·8 m³). A typical de luxe or executive layout retains the forward and aft baggage and freight holds of the airliner version but has the main cabin divided into three compartments. The forward compartment contains four pairs of seats, in aft-facing and forward-facing pairs with tables between, and a buffet. Next comes a similar cabin without the buffet, followed by a sleeping compartment, with a sofa, two seats and table. At the rear is the standard toilet compartment opposite the airstair door, and a large wardrobe space.

ACCOMMODATION (An-24T): Provision for crew of up to five, with optional cargo handler. Door at front of cabin on starboard side. Upward-opening cargo door in belly at rear of cabin. Max overall dimensions of cargo packages that can be handled are 43·3 × 59 × 102 in (1·1 × 1·5 × 2·6 m) or 51·2 × 59 × 82·7 in (1·3 × 1·5 × 2·1 m). Toilet (port side) and emergency exit door in belly, immediately aft of flight deck. Folding seats, in two-, three- and four-place units, for 30 paratroops or 38 equipped soldiers along walls of main cabin. Ambulance configuration is equipped to carry 24 stretcher cases and one medical attendant. Cargo loading system includes rails in floor, electric winch, overhead gantry, tie-down fittings, nets and harness. Electrical de-icing system for windscreens.

SYSTEMS: Air-conditioning system uses hot air tapped from the 10th compressor stage of each engine, with a heat exchanger and turbo-cooler in each nacelle. Cabin pressure differential 4·27 lb/sq in (0·30 kg/cm²). Main and emergency hydraulic systems, pressure 2,200 lb/sq in (155 kg/cm²), for landing gear retraction, nosewheel steering, flaps, brakes, windscreen wipers, propeller feathering and, on An-24T, operation of cargo and emergency escape doors. Hand-pump to operate doors only and build up pressure in main system. Electrical system includes two 27V DC starter/generators, two alternators to provide 115V 400Hz AC supply and two inverters for 36V 400Hz three-phase AC supply. An-24T has permanent oxygen system for pilot, installed equipment for other crew members and three portable bottles for personnel in cargo hold.

ELECTRONICS AND EQUIPMENT (An-24T): Standard radio equipment includes two R-802V VHF transceivers, R-836 HF transmitter and US-8 receiver, SPU-7 intercom, two ARK-11 ADF, RV-2 radio altimeter, SP-50 ILS with KRP-F glidepath receiver, GRP-2 glideslope receiver and MRP-56 marker receiver, and RPSN-2AN weather, obstruction and navigation radar. Flight and navigational equipment includes an AP-28L1 autopilot, TsGV-4 master vertical gyro, GPK-52AP directional gyro, GIK-1 gyro compass, two ZK-2 course setting devices, two AGD-1 artificial horizons, AK-59P astro-compass, NI-50BM-K ground position indicator and other standard blind-flying instruments, plus three clocks. Optional OPB-1R sight for pinpoint dropping of cargo and determination of navigational data.

DIMENSIONS, EXTERNAL:

Wing span	95 ft 9½ in (29·20 m)
Wing aspect ratio	11·7
Length overall	77 ft 2½ in (23·53 m)
Height overall	27 ft 3½ in (8·32 m)
Width of fuselage	9 ft 6 in (2·90 m)
Depth of fuselage	8 ft 2⅜ in (2·50 m)
Tailplane span	29 ft 9½ in (9·08 m)
Wheel track (c/l shock-struts)	25 ft 11 in (7·90 m)
Wheelbase	25 ft 10½ in (7·89 m)
Propeller diameter	12 ft 9½ in (3·90 m)
Propeller ground clearance	3 ft 9 in (1·145 m)
Passenger door (port, aft, except on An-24T):	
Height	4 ft 7 in (1·40 m)
Width	2 ft 5½ in (0·75 m)
Height to sill	4 ft 7 in (1·40 m)
Freight compartment door (stbd, fwd):	
Height	3 ft 7¼ in (1·10 m)
Width	3 ft 11¼ in (1·20 m)
Height to sill	4 ft 3 in (1·30 m)
Baggage compartment door (stbd, aft, except on An-24T):	
Height	4 ft 7½ in (1·41 m)
Width	2 ft 5½ in (0·75 m)
Cargo door (belly, rear, An-24T only):	
Length	9 ft 4 in (2·85 m)
Width:	
max	4 ft 7 in (1·40 m)
min	3 ft 7¼ in (1·10 m)

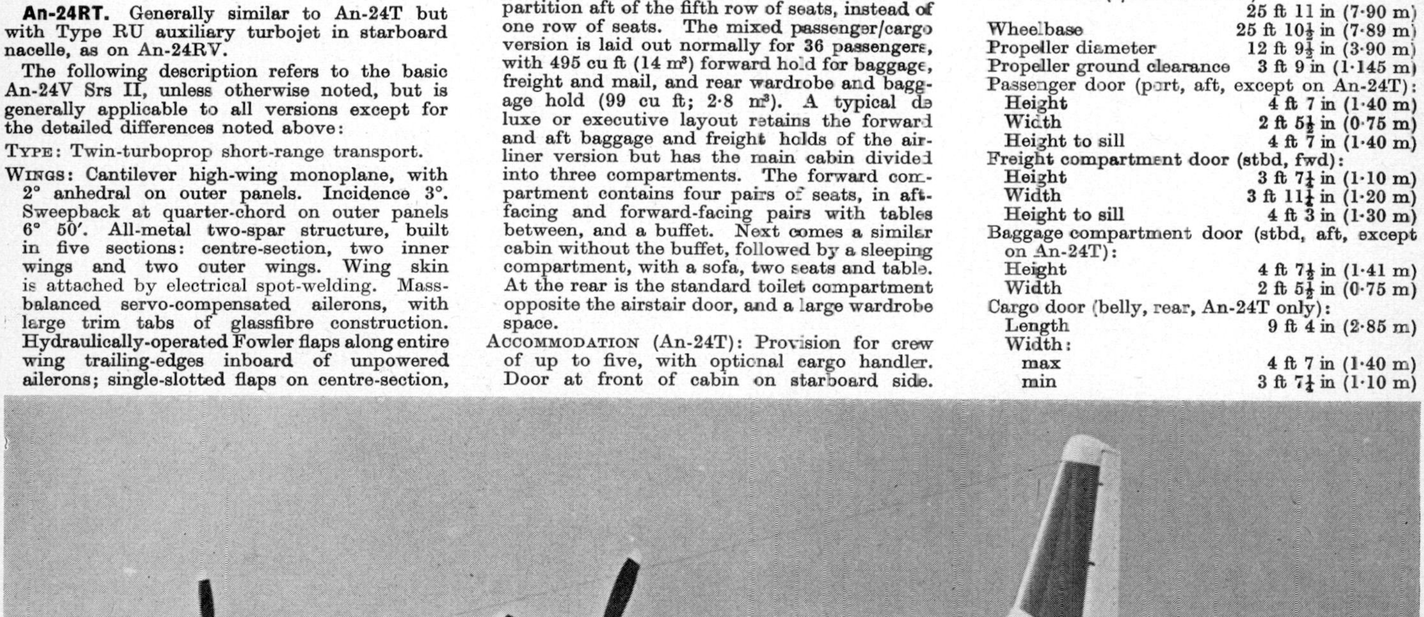

Antonov An-24V light transport (two 2,550 ehp Ivchenko AI-24A turboprop engines) of the Somali Air Force *(APN/D. Goodwin)*

Height above ground
4 ft 1 in to 5 ft 4 in (1·25-1·62 m)
Emergency exit (An-24T, side):
Height 1 ft 11½ in (0·60 m)
Width 1 ft 7½ in (0·50 m)
Emergency exit (An-24T, underfuselage):
Length 3 ft 9½ in (1·155 m)
Width 2 ft 3½ in (0·70 m)

DIMENSIONS, INTERNAL:
Main passenger cabin (50-seater):
Length 31 ft 9½ in (9·69 m)
Max width 9 ft 1 in (2·76 m)
Max height 6 ft 3 in (1·91 m)
Floor area 430 sq ft (39·95 m²)
Cargo hold (An-24T):
Length 51 ft 5½ in (15·68 m)
Width 7 ft 1½ in (2·17 m)
Height 5 ft 9½ in (1·765 m)
Volume 1,765 cu ft (50 m³)

AREAS:
Wings, gross 807·1 sq ft (74·98 m²)
Horizontal tail surfaces (total)
185·5 sq ft (17·23 m²)
Vertical tail surfaces (total, excluding dorsal fin)
144·0 sq ft (13·38 m²)

WEIGHTS AND LOADING:
Weight empty:
An-24V 29,320 lb (13,300 kg)
An-24T 30,997 lb (14,060 kg)
Basic operating weight:
An-24T 32,404 lb (14,698 kg)
Fuel weight:
An-24T with max payload 3,968 lb (1,800 kg)
An-24T for max range 10,494 lb (4,760 kg)
Max payload (ISA, S/L):
An-24V, An-24RV 12,125 lb (5,500 kg)
An-24T 10,168 lb (4,612 kg)
Max ramp weight:
An-24T 46,540 lb (21,110 kg)
Max T-O and landing weight:
An-24V, An-24T, ISA, S/L
46,300 lb (21,000 kg)
An-24V, An-24T, S/L, ISA + 30°C
43,650 lb (19,800 kg)
An-24RV, An-24RT, S/L, ISA or ISA + 30°C 48,060 lb (21,800 kg)
Max wing loading:
An-24V 56·53 lb/sq ft (276 kg/m²)

PERFORMANCE (at max T-O weight):
Normal cruising speed at 19,700 ft (6,000 m)
243 knots (280 mph; 450 km/h)
Max range cruising speed at 23,000 ft (7,000 m)
243 knots (280 mph; 450 km/h)
T-O speed:
An-24T
97-100 knots (112-115 mph; 180-185 km/h)
Landing speed:
An-24V 89 knots (103 mph; 165 km/h) CAS
An-24T
87-95 knots (100-109 mph; 160-175 km/h)
Max rate of climb at S/L:
An-24V 375 ft (114 m)/min
An-24RV 670 ft (204 m)/min
Rate of climb at S/L, one engine out:
An-24V, ISA 275 ft (84 m)/min
An-24V, ISA+30°C, with water injection
275 ft (84 m)/min
An-24RV, ISA 570 ft (174 m)/min
An-24RV, ISA+30° 295 ft (90 m)/min
Service ceiling:
An-24V, An-24T 27,560 ft (8,400 m)
Service ceiling, one engine out:
An-24T 9,020 ft (2,750 m)
T-O run:
An-24V 1,970 ft (600 m)
An-24T 2,100 ft (640 m)

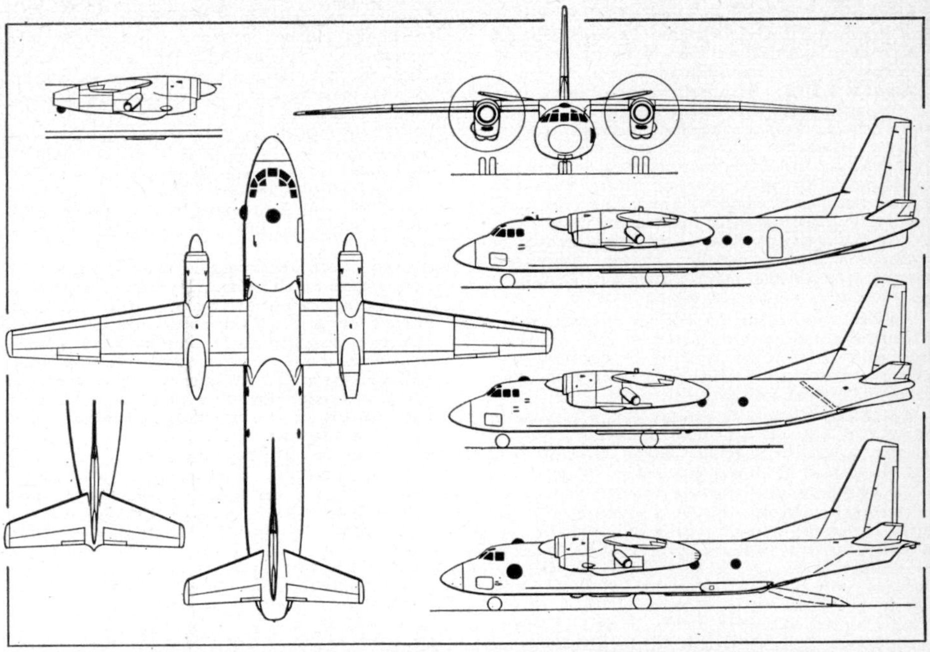

Antonov An-26 transport, with additional side views of the An-24T (*centre*) **and An-24V** (*top*) **and scrap views of the auxiliary turbojet engine in the starboard nacelle and the An-24V rear fuselage** (*Pilot Press*)

Balanced T-O runway:
An-24T, ISA 5,645 ft (1,720 m)
An-24T, ISA+15°C 5,745 ft (1,750 m)
Landing run at AUW of 44,100 lb (20,000 kg):
An-24T 1,903 ft (880 m)
Landing from 50 ft (15 m) at AUW of 44,100 lb (20,000 kg):
An-24T 5,217 ft (1,590 m)
Range with max payload, with reserves:
An-24V, An-24RV
296 nm (341 miles; 550 km)
An-24T, An-24RT
344 nm (397 miles; 640 km)
Range with max fuel:
An-24V, 45 min fuel reserve
1,293 nm (1,490 miles; 2,400 km)
An-24T, with 3,554 lb (1,612 kg) payload, no reserves 1,618 nm (1,864 miles; 3,000 km)

ANTONOV An-26

NATO code name: "Curl"

First displayed in public at the 1969 Paris Air Show, the An-26 was known initially as the "An-24T with an enlarged freight door". It is, in fact, generally similar to the An-24RT, but has more powerful AI-24T turboprop engines and a completely redesigned rear fuselage of the "beaver-tail" type.

Although intended primarily for cargo-carrying, with air-drop capability, the An-26 can be adapted easily for passenger-carrying, ambulance or paratroop transport duties.

The Air Wing of the Bangladesh Defence Force has a small number of An-26s, as well as one An-24.

The basic structural description of the An-24 applies also to the An-26, except for the following details:

TYPE: Twin-turboprop short-haul transport.

WINGS: Made in three sections: centre-section and two outer panels which contain integral fuel tanks.

FUSELAGE: Skin on lower portion of fuselage is made of "bimetal" (duralumin-titanium) sheet for protection during operations from unpaved airfields.

LANDING GEAR: Shock-absorbers are of oleo-nitrogen type. Main wheels are fitted with hydraulic disc brakes and anti-skid units. Nosewheels can be steered hydraulically through 45° each side while taxying and are controllable through ±10° during take-off and landing. Main-wheel tyres size 1050 × 400, pressure 57 lb/sq in (4·0 kg/cm²). Nosewheel tyres size 700 × 250, pressure 64 lb/sq in (4·5 kg/cm²).

POWER PLANT: Two 2,820 ehp Ivchenko AI-24T turboprop engines, each driving a four-blade constant-speed fully-feathering propeller. One 1,985 lb (900 kg) st RU 19-300 auxiliary turbojet in starboard nacelle for use, as required, at take-off, during climb and in level flight, and for self-contained starting of main engines.

ACCOMMODATION: Basic crew of five (pilot, co-pilot, radio operator, flight engineer and navigator), with station at rear of cabin on starboard side for loading supervisor or load despatcher. Toilet on port side aft of flight deck; small galley and oxygen bottle stowage on starboard side. Emergency escape hatch in floor immediately aft of flight deck. Large downward-hinged rear ramp-door, which can also slide forward under fuselage for direct loading on to cabin floor or for air-dropping of freight. Electrically-powered mobile winch, capacity 3,300 lb (1,500 kg), hoists crates through rear entrance and runs on a rail in the cabin

Antonov An-26, a development of the An-24T freight transport with enlarged rear-loading ramp-door

ceiling to position payload in cabin. Electrically- or manually-operated conveyor, capacity 9,920 lb (4,500 kg), built-in flush with cabin floor, facilitates loading and air-dropping of freight. Can accommodate a variety of motor vehicles, including GAZ-69 and UAZ-469 military vehicles, or cargo items up to 59 in (1·50 m) high by 82·6 in (2·10 m) wide. Height of rear edge of cargo door surround above the cabin floor is 4 ft 11 in (1·50 m). Cabin is pressurised and air-conditioned, and is fitted with a row of tip-up seats along each wall to accommodate up to 40 paratroops. Conversion to troop transport role, or to an ambulance for 24 stretcher patients and a medical attendant, takes 20 to 30 minutes in the field.

SYSTEMS: Basically as for An-24. Electrical system includes two 27V DC starter/generators on engines, a standby generator on the auxiliary turbojet, and three storage batteries for emergency use. Two engine-driven alternators provide 115V 400Hz single-phase AC supply, with standby inverter. Basic source of 36V 400Hz three-phase AC supply is two inverters, with standby transformer.

ELECTRONICS AND EQUIPMENT: Standard com/nav equipment comprises two VHF transceivers, HF, intercom, two ADF, radio altimeter, glidepath receiver, glideslope receiver, marker receiver, weather/navigation radar, directional gyro and flight recorder. Optional equipment includes a flight director system, astro-compass and autopilot. Standard operational equipment includes parachute static line attachments and retraction devices, tie-downs, jack to support ramp sill, flight deck curtains, sun visors and windscreen wipers. Optional items include a navigator's observation blister on port side of flight deck, OPB-1R sight for pinpoint dropping of freight, medical equipment and liquid heating system.

DIMENSIONS, EXTERNAL:
As for An-24, except:
Length overall 78 ft 1 in (23·80 m)
Height overall 28 ft $1\frac{1}{2}$ in (8·575 m)
Tailplane span 32 ft $8\frac{3}{4}$ in (9·973 m)
Wheelbase 25 ft $1\frac{1}{4}$ in (7·651 m)
Propeller ground clearance 4 ft $0\frac{1}{4}$ in (1·227 m)
Crew door (stbd, front):
Height 4 ft 7 in (1·40 m)
Width 1 ft $11\frac{3}{4}$ in (0·60 m)
Height to sill 4 ft $9\frac{3}{4}$ in (1·47 m)
Loading hatch (rear):
Length 11 ft $1\frac{3}{4}$ in (3·40 m)
Width at front 7 ft $10\frac{1}{2}$ in (2·40 m)
Width at rear 6 ft $6\frac{3}{4}$ in (2·00 m)
Height to sill 4 ft $9\frac{3}{4}$ in (1·47 m)
Height to top edge of hatchway 9 ft $10\frac{3}{4}$ in (3·014 m)
Emergency exit (floor at front):
Length 3 ft $4\frac{1}{4}$ in (1·02 m)
Width 2 ft $3\frac{1}{2}$ in (0·70 m)
Emergency exit (top):
Diameter 2 ft $1\frac{1}{2}$ in (0·65 m)
Emergency exits (each side of hold, two):
Height 1 ft $11\frac{3}{4}$ in (0·60 m)
Width 1 ft $7\frac{1}{2}$ in (0·50 m)

DIMENSIONS, INTERNAL:
Cargo hold:
Length of floor 37 ft $8\frac{3}{4}$ in (11·50 m)
Width of floor 7 ft $10\frac{1}{2}$ in (2·40 m)
Max height 6 ft 3 in (1·91 m)

AREAS:
Wings, gross 807·1 sq ft (74·98 m²)
Horizontal tail surfaces (total) 213·45 sq ft (19·83 m²)
Vertical tail surfaces (total, incl dorsal fin) 170·61 sq ft (15·85 m²)

WEIGHTS:
Weight empty 33,113 lb (15,020 kg)
Normal payload 9,920 lb (4,500 kg)
Max payload 12,125 lb (5,500 kg)
Normal T-O and landing weight 50,706 lb (23,000 kg)
Max T-O and landing weight 52,911 lb (24,000 kg)

PERFORMANCE (at normal T-O weight):
Cruising speed at 19,675 ft (6,000 m) 229-234 knots (264-270 mph; 425-435 km/h)
T-O speed 108 knots (124 mph; 200 km/h) CAS
Landing speed 102 knots (118 mph; 190 km/h) CAS
Max rate of climb at S/L 1,575 ft (480 m)/min
Service ceiling 24,600 ft (7,500 m)
T-O run, on concrete 2,559 ft (780 m)
T-O to 50 ft (15 m) 4,068 ft (1,240 m)
Landing from 50 ft (15 m) 5,709 ft (1,740 m)
Landing run, on concrete 2,395 ft (730 m)
Min ground turning radius 73 ft 2 in (22·3 m)
Range, with allowance for taxying and 1,278 lb (580 kg) reserve fuel:
with 9,920 lb (4,500 kg) payload 485 nm (559 miles; 900 km)
with 4,687 lb (2,126 kg) payload 1,214 nm (1,398 miles; 2,250 km)

ANTONOV An-28

Although Oleg Antonov first referred to planned production of an enlarged turboprop version of the piston-engined An-14 light general-purpose aircraft in the early 'sixties, there was no proof that such an aircraft had been built until the Spring of 1972. Photographs of the prototype (CCCP-1968) were then published in the Polish press. It had flown for the first time in 1969 and was followed by several more prototypes.

Initially, the new aircraft was designated An-14M, and was listed as such in *Jane's*. During 1973 it was allocated the production designation An-28.

In general configuration the An-28 differs from the piston-engined An-14 mainly in having a much-enlarged fuselage to carry up to 15 passengers or equivalent alternative payloads. The first prototype had a retractable landing gear, with small fairings on the sides of the fuselage into which the main units retracted. Subsequently it was decided that retraction was unnecessary for flights over short distances at low speeds, and later prototypes have fixed gear. The shape of the vertical tail surfaces has also changed during flight testing.

Flight testing of the An-28 was completed during 1972, after which it entered production for service on Aeroflot's shortest routes, particularly those operated by An-2 biplanes into places which are relatively inaccessible to other types of fixed-wing aircraft. The turboprop engines make possible full-payload operation under high-temperature conditions and in mountainous regions; and the An-28 is described as being suitable for carrying passengers, cargo and mail, for scientific expeditions, geological surveying, firefighting, rescue operations and parachute training. In agricultural form it can carry a 1,760 lb (800 kg) chemical payload for dusting and spraying operations.

TYPE: Twin-turboprop light general-purpose aircraft.

WINGS: Braced high-wing monoplane, with single streamline-section bracing strut each side. Entire trailing-edges hinged, ailerons being designed to droop with the large flaps. On first prototype a short spar-beam extended from each side of the lower fuselage, carrying the main landing gear units, providing lower attachments for the wing bracing struts and supporting the fairings into which the main wheels retracted.

FUSELAGE: Conventional all-metal semi-monocoque structure, longer, wider and deeper than that of the piston-engined An-14. Underside of rear fuselage upswept and made up of clamshell doors.

TAIL UNIT: Cantilever all-metal structure. Twin fins and rudders mounted vertically on a tailplane that lacks the dihedral of that on the An-14.

LANDING GEAR: Non-retractable (except on first prototype) tricycle type, with single wheel on each unit. Wide-tread balloon tyres of same size on all units. Steerable nosewheel. Brakes on main wheels.

Antonov An-28 light general-purpose aircraft (two 810 shp Isotov TVD-850 turboprop engines) (*Tass*)

POWER PLANT: Two 810 shp Isotov TVD-850 turboprop engines, each driving a three-blade controllable-pitch metal propeller.

ACCOMMODATION: Crew of one or two on flight deck. Cabin of passenger version contains 15 seats in five rows, with double units on starboard side of aisle. Seats fold back against walls when aircraft is operated as a freighter or in mixed passenger/cargo role. Provision for baggage and toilet compartments and wardrobe space. Clamshell rear doors, under upswept fuselage, for use by passengers and for cargo loading. Winch of 550 lb (250 kg) capacity for handling cargo. Six/seven-passenger executive version has four folding tables, which can be joined together in pairs to give working tops measuring 63 in × 21·5 in (160 × 55 cm). Ambulance version accommodates six stretcher patients, a medical attendant and medical equipment.

ELECTRONICS AND EQUIPMENT: Flight and navigation equipment, and de-icing system, for all-weather operation. Landing light in nose.

DIMENSIONS, EXTERNAL:
Wing span 72 ft 2 in (21·99 m)
Length overall 42 ft 7 in (12·98 m)
Height overall 15 ft 1 in (4·60 m)

DIMENSIONS, INTERNAL:
Cabin: Length 17 ft 3 in (5·26 m)
Max width 5 ft 5 in (1·66 m)
Max height 5 ft 7 in (1·70 m)

WEIGHTS:
Weight empty 7,715 lb (3,500 kg)
Max payload 2,865 lb (1,300 kg)
Max T-O weight 12,345 lb (5,600 kg)

PERFORMANCE (at max T-O weight):
Max level speed 178 knots (205 mph; 330 km/h)
Normal cruising speed 164 knots (189 mph; 305 km/h)
Service ceiling 19,685 ft (6,000 m)
T-O run 705 ft (215 m)
Landing run 660 ft (200 m)
Max range 485-620 nm (558-714 miles; 900-1,150 km)

ANTONOV An-30

NATO code name: "Clank"

Described as the first specialised aerial survey aeroplane produced in the Soviet Union, the An-30 is evolved from the An-24 twin-turboprop transport, to which it is generally similar. The major modifications are made to the nose, which is now extensively glazed to give the navigator a wide field of vision, and to the flight deck, which is raised to improve the pilots' view and increase the size of the navigator's compartment. There are fewer windows in the main cabin, the central part of which houses specialised survey equipment.

For the primary task of air photography for

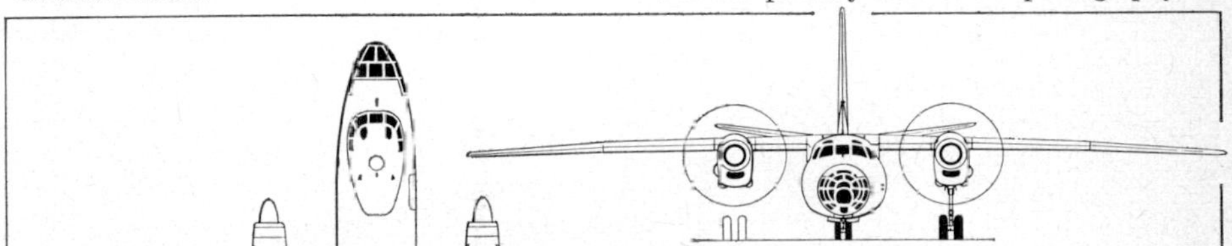

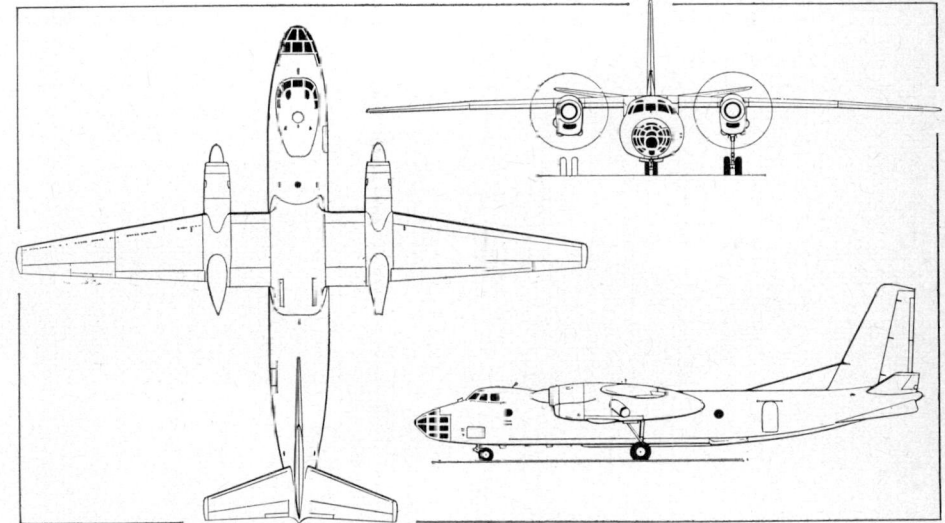

Antonov An-30 (two AI-24VT turboprops and RU 19A-300 auxiliary turbojet) (*Pilot Press*)

Antonov An-30 aerial survey development of the An-24 twin-turboprop transport aircraft, with glazed nose and other modifications (*Brian M. Service*)

map-making, the An-30 is equipped with four large survey cameras. These are mounted in the cabin above apertures which are each covered by a door. The crew photographer uncovers the apertures, as required, by remote control from his desk in the aircraft. A fifth window is provided for an exposure meter.

Details of the An-30 published in the Far East suggest that one of the survey cameras can be stabilised, in gimbal mountings, to ensure precise photographic coverage of the desired area in turbulent conditions.

The pre-programmed flight path of the aircraft over the area to be photographed is fed into an on-board computer which controls the speed, altitude, and direction of flight throughout the mission. If required, the cameras can be replaced by other kinds of survey equipment, such as those used for mineral prospecting or for microwave radiometer survey, which measures the heat emission of land and ocean to obtain data on ocean surface characteristics, sea and lake ice, snow cover, flooding, seasonal vegetation changes, and soil types.

Speed, range, and field performance of the An-30 are identical with those of the An-24 (which see).

BERIEV

GENERAL DESIGNER IN CHARGE OF BUREAU:
Georgi Mikhailovich Beriev

G. M. Beriev, a graduate of the Leningrad Polytechnic Institute, took up seaplane design in 1928 and has since become the best-known Soviet designer of water-based aircraft. He was appointed chief designer of the seaplane group at the TsKB (Central Design Bureau of Aviatrust) in 1930, and his first complete design, the twin-engined MBR-2 flying-boat, was flown for the first time two years later, entering production in 1934. Other pre-war designs included the KOR-1 twin-float shipboard reconnaissance seaplane and the KOR-2 flying-boat, later redesignated Be-2 and Be-4 respectively.

In 1945 the Beriev bureau at Taganrog became the centre for all Soviet seaplane development, and the piston-engined Be-6 (first flown in 1947) was a standard military flying-boat during the 1950s. It was described in the 1959-60 *Jane's*. Only limited production was undertaken of the Be-8, also flown in 1947; and Beriev's next major flying-boat was the swept-wing twin-jet Be-10, based on the Be-R-1 prototype of 1949. This entered service in about 1960, and was described in the 1966-67 *Jane's*.

The latest maritime aircraft of Beriev design is the M-12 (Be-12) twin-turboprop amphibian, which is in standard service with Soviet Naval Air Force units, as a successor to the Be-6.

BERIEV M-12 (Be-12) TCHAIKA (SEAGULL)
NATO code name: "Mail"

This twin-turboprop medium-range maritime reconnaissance amphibian was displayed for the first time in the 1961 Aviation Day fly-past at Tushino Airport, Moscow. **Subsequently, during the period 23-27 October 1964, it established six officially-recognised international height records in Class C.3 Group II. Data submitted in respect of these records revealed that the designation of the aircraft was M-12 and the power plant two 4,000 shp Ivchenko AI-20D turboprop engines. The aircraft was also, clearly, able to lift a payload of around 10 tons under record conditions.**

The records set up by the M-12 in 1964 were altitude of 39,977 ft (12,185 m) without payload, altitude of 37,290 ft (11,366 m) with payload of 1,000 kg and 2,000 kg, altitude of 35,055 ft (10,685 m) with 5,000 kg payload, altitude of 30,682 ft (9,352 m) with 10,000 kg payload, and maximum payload of 22,266 lb (10,100 kg) lifted to a height of 2,000 m (6,560 ft). In each case, the crew consisted of M. Mikhailov, I. Kouprianov and L. Kuznetsov.

On 24 April 1968, A. Souchko set up a Class C.3 speed record of 298·013 knots (343·169 mph; 552·279 km/h) over a 500 km closed circuit in an M-12. On 9 October 1968, the same pilot set up a speed record of 293·919 knots (338·456 mph; 544·693 km/h) over a 1,000 km circuit and a closed-circuit distance record of 558·599 nm (643·24 miles; 1,035·20 km) in this class. The latter record was beaten by Vladimir Svyatochnur and crew in an M-12, on 25 October 1973, when they covered a closed-circuit distance of 1,382·968 nm (1,592·510 miles; 2,562·897 km).

Three speed-with-payload records over a 1,000 km closed circuit were set up in 1970. A. Suchov **attained 283·841 knots (326·848 mph; 526·011 km/h) with 1,000 kg on 21 April; A. Smirnov averaged 286·267 knots (329·640 mph; 530·504 km/h) with 2,000 kg on 8 July; and A. Zakharov averaged 284·163 knots (327·218 mph; 526·606 km/h) with 5,000 kg on 9 July.**

Subsequent record attempts, improving on earlier performances by the M-12, have ensured that this aircraft retains all 16 records listed in Class C.3, Group II. On 31 October 1972, P.

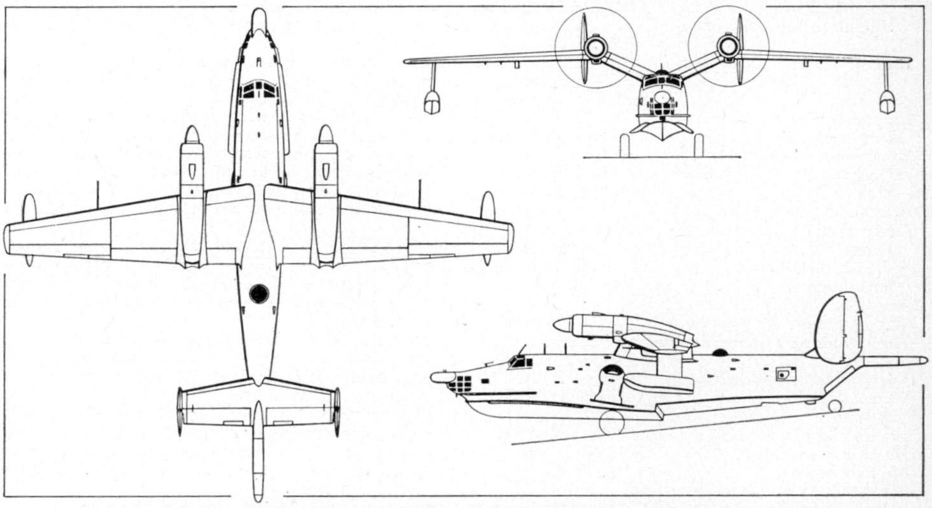

Beriev M-12 (Be-12) Tchaika twin-turboprop maritime reconnaissance amphibian (*Pilot Press*)

Beriev M-12 (Be-12) Tchaika maritime patrol amphibian flying-boat of the Soviet Naval Air Force (*Tass*)

Yakouchine and crew of three achieved 300·450 knots (345·973 mph; 556·789 km/h) over a 2,000 km closed circuit, raising the records for no payload and 1,000 kg payload, and setting a new record with 2,000 kg. The current record of 263·720 knots (303·678 mph; 488·722 km/h) with a 5,000 kg payload was set by A. Souchko and crew on 30 October 1973.

The M-12 also holds all ten current records in Class C.2 Group II, for turboprop flying-boats. On 25 April 1968, E. Nikitine set up a 500 km closed-circuit speed record of 305·064 knots (351·290 mph; 565·347 km/h) in an M-12, followed on 12 October 1968 by a speed record of 297·793 knots (342·916 mph; 551·871 km/h) over a 1,000 km closed circuit. On 21 April 1970, A. Zakharov set up a speed record of 289·272 knots (333·101 mph; 536·074 km/h) over a 1,000 km closed circuit with a 1,000 kg payload. P. Yakushin averaged 288·848 knots (332·613 mph; 535·288 km/h) over the same distance with 2,000 kg on 8 July 1970; and on the following day E. Nikitine averaged 285·454 knots (328·704 mph; 528·998 km/h) over 1,000 km with a 5,000 kg payload.

On 30 October 1972, A. Zakharov and crew of three averaged 300·015 knots (345·472 mph; 555·983 km/h) over a 2,000 km circuit, claiming also the speed record over this distance with a 1,000 kg payload. Over this same distance, V. Averchine and crew averaged 295·999 knots (340·848 mph; 548·542 km/h) with a 2,000 kg payload on 28 October 1973, followed by E. Nikitine and crew who averaged 258·727 knots (297·929 mph; 479·470 km/h) with 5,000 kg on the next day. The closed-circuit distance record was raised to 1,393·071 nm (1,604·144 miles; 2,581·62 km) on 20 November 1973, by G. Efimov and crew.

Layout and construction of the M-12 are conventional.

The single-step hull has a high length-to-beam ratio and is fitted with two long strakes, one above the other, on each side of the nose to prevent spray from enveloping the propellers at take-off. There is a glazed observation and navigation station in the nose, with a long radar "thimble" built into it, and an astrodome type of observation position above the rear fuselage. The nose radar on current aircraft is wider and somewhat flatter in section than that on early M-12s. A long MAD (magnetic anomaly detection) "sting" extends from the tail, and there appears to be an APU exhaust on the port side of the rear fuselage.

The sharply-cranked high-set wing, with non-retractable wingtip floats, is reminiscent of that of the Be-6, and is intended to raise the AI-20 turboprop engines well clear of the water. The cowlings of the turboprops open downward in two halves, so that they may be used as servicing platforms. The tail unit, with twin fins and rudders at the tips of a "dihedral" tailplane, is also similar to that of the Be-6.

The tailwheel landing gear consists of single-wheel main units, which retract upward through 180° to lie flush within the sides of the hull, and a rearward-retracting tailwheel.

In addition to an internal bomb-bay aft of the step, there is provision for one large and one small external stores pylon under each outer wing panel.

When three M-12s took part in the 1967 air display at Domodedovo, the commentator said that the unit to which they belonged was "one of those serving where the country's military air force began", implying that the aircraft were then in operational service. M-12s have since been identified in standard service at Soviet Northern and Black Sea Fleet air bases and are reported to be operational from bases in Egypt.

Fuelling a Beriev M-12 (Be-12) Tchaika (two 4,000 shp Ivchenko AI-20D turboprop engines) of the Red Banner Northern Fleet (*Tass*)

DIMENSIONS, EXTERNAL (approx):

Wing span	97 ft 6 in (29·70 m)
Length overall	99 ft 0 in (30·20 m)
Height overall	22 ft 11½ in (7·00 m)
Propeller diameter	16 ft 0 in (4·85 m)

WEIGHT (estimated):

Max T-O weight	65,035 lb (29,500 kg)

PERFORMANCE (estimated):

Max level speed	329 knots (379 mph; 610 km/h)
Normal operating speed	172 knots (199 mph; 320 km/h)
Max range	2,158 nm (2,485 miles; 4,000 km)

ILYUSHIN

GENERAL DESIGNER IN CHARGE OF BUREAU:
Sergei Vladimirovich Ilyushin

Sergei Ilyushin was awarded the Order of Lenin and a third Hammer and Sickle gold medal on 29 March 1974, at the age of 80, in recognition of his service in the development of aviation technology and the Soviet aircraft industry.

Aircraft designed by Ilyushin and currently in service include the veteran Il-28 twin-jet bomber and Il-12 and Il-14 piston-engined light transports, of which details have been given in earlier editions of *Jane's*. The four-turboprop Il-18 transport has been in scheduled service with Aeroflot and other airlines and air forces for many years. It has been followed by an anti-submarine variant of the same design, designated Il-38; a four-jet rear-engined airliner known as the Il-62; and the Il-76 turbofan-engined heavy freighter.

Under development is a large wide-bodied transport designated Il-86.

ILYUSHIN Il-18

NATO code name: "Coot"

The Il-18 prototype, named "Moskva" (Moscow), flew for the first time in July 1957 and was followed by two pre-production models. Production began while these were completing their flight trials, enabling the Il-18 to enter service with Aeroflot on 20 April 1959. In its first ten years of operation by Aeroflot, it carried 60 million passengers and was being utilised on 800 domestic services in the Spring of 1969.

The initial production version was equipped to carry 84 passengers, and could be powered by either Kuznetsov NK-4 or Ivchenko AI-20 turboprops. All aircraft from the 21st built have had AI-20 engines; 450 had been completed in the Hadinka works, near Moscow, by the Spring of 1966, and the production total is believed to have exceeded 700 subsequently.

More than 100 Il-18s have been exported for military and commercial use; foreign civilian operators have included the following:

Air Guinée	3
Air Mali	3
Air Mauritanie	1
Algerian government	1
Balkan Bulgarian Airlines	12
CAAC (China)	9
CSA Czech Airlines	11
Cubana	5
EgyptAir	5
Ghana Airways	8*
Interflug (E Germany)	14
LOT	8
Malev	9
Royal Afghan Airlines	1
Tarom	14
Yemen Airlines	1
Yugoslav government	1

**All returned to USSR*

Military operators include the air forces of Afghanistan, Algeria, Bulgaria, China, Czechoslovakia, Poland, the Soviet Union and Yugoslavia, mostly in comparatively small numbers. An anti-submarine derivative, the Il-38 (NATO code name "May"), is also in service and is described separately.

Testing of all-weather landing systems on the Il-18 began in 1963 and current versions of the aircraft can be fitted with the Polosa automatic landing system, which meets ICAO Cat III specifications.

An Il-18 was used for flight evaluation over a two-year period of the new EI POS de-icing system, announced in April 1972. This operates on the principle of converting electrical impulses into mechanical impulses powerful enough to remove ice of any thickness from the skin of an airliner in flight. It is said to require hundreds of times less energy than a hot-air or electrical-heating de-icing system, to weigh only 77 lb (35 kg) fully installed, and to be effective in temperatures from zero to 50°C below zero. The system has been recommended for series production for both aircraft and ships.

Current versions of the Il-18 commercial transport are as follows:

Il-18V. Standard version for Aeroflot, with

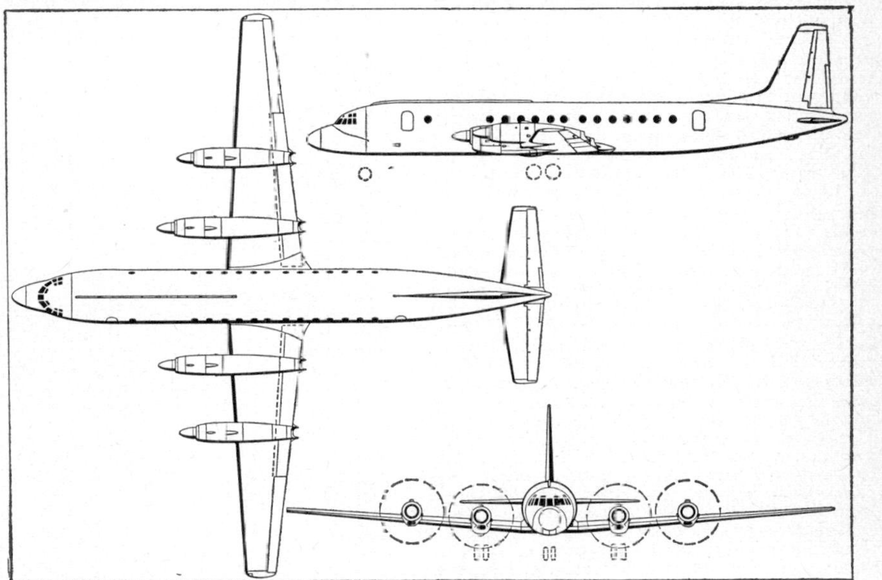

Ilyushin Il-18 medium-range turboprop airliner (*Pilot Press*)

Ilyushin Il-18 medium-range transport (four Ivchenko AI-20 turboprop engines) in service with Malev *(Martin Fricke)*

four 4,000 ehp AI-20K turboprops and fuel capacity of 5,213 Imp gallons (23,700 litres). Accommodation for 110 mixed tourist/economy class passengers, or 90 in all-tourist configuration.

Il-18E. Developed version with 4,250 ehp AI-20M engines. Same fuel capacity as Il-18V. Accommodation can be increased to 122 mixed class or 110 tourist class in Summer, by deleting coat storage space essential in Winter time.

Il-18D. Generally similar to Il-18E, but with additional centre-section fuel tankage, increasing total capacity to 6,600 Imp gallons (30,000 litres). Increased all-up weight.

The Il-18D is available with a 65-seat layout, equivalent to first-class seating standards. Executive transport versions are also offered.

By the Spring of 1960, the Il-18 had established a total of 12 officially-recognised international records, piloted in each case by Vladimir Kokkinaki. The nine closed-circuit speed-with-payload records were beaten subsequently by the Tu-114, but the Il-18 retains records for climb to 43,156 ft (13,154 m) with a 10,000 kg payload, on 15 November 1958; climb to 40,915 ft (12,471 m) with a 15,000 kg payload on 14 November 1958; and climb to 39,757 ft (12,118 m) with a 20,000 kg payload on 25 November 1959.

On 6 May 1968, an Il-18 piloted by B. Konstantinov set up a still-unbeaten speed record of 380·962 knots (438·7 mph; 706 km/h) over a 100 km closed circuit. Miss L. Ulanova and an all-woman crew set up an international straight-line distance record of 4,134·427 nm (4,760·89 miles; 7,661·949 km) on 14-15 October 1967, an altitude record of 44,334 ft (13,513 m) on 20 October 1967, a record for sustained altitude of 42,323 ft (12,900 m) in horizontal flight on 13 June 1969, a closed-circuit distance record of 4,329·333 nm (4,985·35 miles; 8,023·153 km) on 18-19 June 1969, and a speed record of 378·304 knots (435·623 mph; 701·068 km/h) over a 5,000 km circuit on 12 June 1969.

TYPE: Four-engined passenger transport.

WINGS: Cantilever low-wing monoplane. Mean thickness/chord ratio 14%. All-metal structure. Three spars in centre-section, two in outer wings. All-metal ailerons are mass-balanced and aerodynamically-compensated, and fitted with spring tabs. Manually-operated flying controls. Electrically-actuated double-slotted flaps. Electro-thermal de-icing.

FUSELAGE: Circular-section all-metal monocoque structure. The structure is of the fail-safe type, and appears to employ rip-stop doublers around window cutouts, door frames and the more-heavily loaded skin panels.

TAIL UNIT: Cantilever all-metal structure. Trim tabs on rudder and elevators. Additional spring tab on rudder. Manually-operated flying controls. Electro-thermal de-icing.

LANDING GEAR: Retractable tricycle type. Hydraulic actuation. Four-wheel bogie main units, with 930 mm × 305 mm tyres and hydraulic brakes. Steerable (45° each way) twin nosewheel unit, with 700 mm × 250 mm tyres. Tyre pressures: main 114 lb/sq in (8·0 kg/cm²), nose 85 lb/sq in (6·0 kg/cm²). Hydraulic brakes and nosewheel steering. Pneumatic emergency braking system, using nitrogen gas.

POWER PLANT: Four Ivchenko AI-20 turboprops (details under model listings), driving AV-68I four-blade reversible-pitch propellers. Ten flexible bag-type fuel tanks in inboard panel of each wing and integral tank in outboard panel, with a total capacity of 5,213 Imp gallons (23,700 litres). The Il-18D has additional bag tanks in centre-section, giving a total capacity of 6,600 Imp gallons (30,000 litres). Pressure fuelling through four international standard connections in inner nacelles. Provision for overwing fuelling. Oil capacity 12·85 Imp gallons (58·5 litres) per engine.

ACCOMMODATION: Crew of five, comprising two pilots, navigator, wireless operator and flight engineer. Flight deck is separated from remainder of fuselage by a pressure bulkhead to reduce the hazards following a sudden decompression of either. Standard 110-seat high-density version has a forward cabin containing 24 seats six-abreast; then, successively, an entrance lobby with two toilets on the starboard side, two large wardrobes in line with the propellers, the main cabin containing 71 seats in six-abreast rows, a galley/pantry opposite the rear door, a rear cabin containing 15 seats five-abreast, and a rear toilet compartment. Deletion of the wardrobes enables two more rows of seats to be installed in the main cabin in Summer, increasing max capacity to 122 seats. In 90-seat configuration, all seating is five-abreast, with 20 passengers in the front cabin, 55 in centre cabin and 15 in rear cabin. Again, two more rows of seats can replace the wardrobes in Summer, increasing the capacity to 100 seats. The 65-seat layout of the Il-18D has 14 seats (5-5-4) in front cabin, 43 seats (4-5-5-5-5-5-5-5-4) in centre cabin and 8 seats (4-4) in rear cabin. Pressurised cargo holds under floor forward and aft of the wing, and a further, unpressurised, hold aft of the rear pressure bulkhead.

SYSTEMS: Cabin pressurised to max differential of 7·1 lb/sq in (0·5 kg/cm²). Electrical system includes eight 12kW DC generators and 28·5V single-phase AC inverters. Hydraulic system, pressure 3,000 lb/sq in (210 kg/cm²), for landing gear retraction, nosewheel steering, brakes and flaps.

ELECTRONICS AND EQUIPMENT: Equipment includes dual controls and blind-flying panels, weather radar and ILS indicators, automatic navigation equipment, two automatic radio compasses, radio altimeter.

DIMENSIONS, EXTERNAL:
- Wing span: 122 ft 8½ in (37·4 m)
- Wing chord at root: 18 ft 5 in (5·61 m)
- Wing chord at tip: 6 ft 2 in (1·87 m)
- Wing aspect ratio: 10
- Length overall: 117 ft 9 in (35·9 m)
- Height over tail: 33 ft 4 in (10·17 m)
- Tailplane span: 38 ft 8½ in (11·8 m)
- Wheel track: 29 ft 6 in (9·0 m)
- Wheelbase: 41 ft 10 in (12·78 m)
- Propeller diameter: 14 ft 9 in (4·50 m)
- Passenger doors (each):
  - Height: 4 ft 7 in (1·40 m)
  - Width: 2 ft 6 in (0·76 m)
  - Height to sill: 9 ft 6 in (2·90 m)
- Freight hold doors (underfloor, each):
  - Height: 2 ft 11 in (0·90 m)
  - Width: 3 ft 11 in (1·20 m)

DIMENSIONS, INTERNAL:
- Flight deck:
  - Volume: 330 cu ft (9·36 m³)
- Cabin, excluding flight deck:
  - Length: approx 79 ft 0 in (24·0 m)
  - Max width: 10 ft 7 in (3·23 m)
  - Max height: 6 ft 6 in (2·00 m)
  - Volume: 8,405 cu ft (238 m³)
- Baggage and freight holds (underfloor and aft of cabin: total): 1,035 cu ft (29·3 m³)

AREAS:
- Wings, gross: 1,507 sq ft (140 m²)
- Ailerons (total): 98·05 sq ft (9·11 m²)
- Trailing-edge flaps (total): 292·2 sq ft (27·15 m²)
- Vertical tail surfaces (total): 193·0 sq ft (17·93 m²)
- Rudder: 73·52 sq ft (6·83 m²)
- Horizontal tail surfaces (total): 299·13 sq ft (27·79 m²)
- Elevators (total): 127·0 sq ft (11·80 m²)

WEIGHTS AND LOADINGS:
- Weight empty, equipped (90-seater):
  - Il-18E: 76,350 lb (34,630 kg)
  - Il-18D: 77,160 lb (35,000 kg)
- Max payload: 29,750 lb (13,500 kg)
- Max T-O weight:
  - Il-18V, E: 134,925 lb (61,200 kg)
  - Il-18D: 141,100 lb (64,000 kg)
- Max wing loading (Il-18D): 93·6 lb/sq ft (457 kg/m²)
- Max power loading (Il-18D): 8·38 lb/ehp (3·8 kg/ehp)

PERFORMANCE (at max T-O weight):
- Max cruising speed:
  - Il-18V: 351 knots (404 mph; 650 km/h)
  - Il-18E, D: 364 knots (419 mph; 675 km/h)
- Econ cruising speed:
  - Il-18V: 324 knots (373 mph; 600 km/h)
  - Il-18E, D: 337 knots (388 mph; 625 km/h)
- Operating height:
  - Il-18D: 26,250-32,800 ft (8,000-10,000 m)
- T-O run:
  - Il-18E: 3,610 ft (1,100 m)
  - Il-18D: 4,265 ft (1,300 m)
- Landing run:
  - Il-18E, D: 2,790 ft (850 m)
- Range with max fuel, 1-hour reserve:
  - Il-18E: 2,805 nm (3,230 miles; 5,200 km)
  - Il-18D: 3,508 nm (4,040 miles; 6,500 km)
- Range with max payload, 1-hour reserve:
  - Il-18E: 1,728 nm (1,990 miles; 3,200 km)
  - Il-18D: 1,997 nm (2,300 miles; 3,700 km)

ILYUSHIN Il-38

NATO code name: "May"

This anti-submarine/maritime patrol development of the Il-18 airliner represents a conversion similar to that by which the US Navy's P-3 Orion was evolved from the Lockheed Electra transport. It has a lengthened fuselage fitted with an under-nose radome similar in shape to that of the Ka-25 ASW helicopter but housing a different radar, an MAD tail "sting", other specialised electronic equipment and a weapon-carrying capability.

The main cabin of the Il-38 has few windows. The complete wing assembly is much further forward than on the Il-18, to cater for the effect of internal equipment and stores on the CG position.

The Il-38 has become the principal shore-based maritime patrol aircraft of the Soviet Naval Air Force, operating widely over the Atlantic and Mediterranean. In the latter area, some aircraft have carried Egyptian Air Force insignia, but are believed to have been manned by Soviet aircrew, operating from North African bases such as Matru, near Cairo.

DIMENSIONS, EXTERNAL:
- Wing span: 122 ft 8½ in (37·4 m)
- Length overall: 129 ft 10 in (39·6 m)

PERFORMANCE (estimated):
- Max cruising speed: 347 knots (400 mph; 645 km/h)
- Max range: 3,900 nm (4,500 miles; 7,250 km)

ILYUSHIN Il-62

NATO code name: "Classic"

Announced on 24 September 1962, when the first prototype (CCCP-06156) was inspected by Mr Krushchev, the standard Il-62 is a long-range airliner, with four Kuznetsov turbofan engines mounted in horizontal pairs on each side of the rear fuselage. It accommodates up to 186 passengers and was designed to fly on ranges equivalent to Moscow-New York (about 4,155 nm; 4,800 miles; 7,700 km) with more than 150 passengers and reserve fuel.

The Kuznetsov engines were not ready in time for the first flight of the first prototype, which took place in January 1963, with four 16,535 lb (7,500 kg) st Lyulka AL-7 engines installed. This aircraft was followed by a second prototype and three pre-production aircraft. Series production then started at Kazan and Aeroflot introduced the Il-62 on to its Moscow-Montreal service on 15 September 1967, as a replacement for the Tu-114 used previously.

The Il-62 inaugurated Aeroflot's Moscow-New York service in July 1968. It is used on many other routes, including Moscow-Paris and Moscow-Tokyo.

An Il-62 was leased by CSA Czechoslovakian Airlines and was introduced on its Prague-London service on 11 May 1968. CSA announced subsequently that it had placed the first export order for the Il-62, for three aircraft (increased subsequently to seven). Delivery of these began in October 1969. Six began to enter service with the East German airline Interflug in the Spring of 1970, each equipped to carry 150 passengers; and EgyptAir has operated seven. The Polish airline LOT placed initial orders for three for delivery in 1972, with more to follow. China ordered five, under a 1970 trade agreement, for operation by CAAC. Tarom of Romania has two and Cubana one.

The Il-62's automatic flight control system is capable of taking over from a height of 650 ft (200 m) after take-off to a similar height during the landing approach. It can maintain a predetermined speed during climb and descent, and a selected cruising height, and can follow automatically a programmed track under command of the navigation computer.

The Il-62 is designed for an airframe service life of 25,000-30,000 flying hours, including 7,000-8,000 take-offs and landings.

A high-density version designated Il-62M, able to accommodate 198 passengers, was flown for the first time in 1971. Details of this aircraft are given separately, after the following description of the standard Il-62:

Type: Four-turbofan long-range airliner.

Wings: Cantilever low-wing monoplane. Sweepback 35° at quarter-chord. Extended-chord "dog-tooth" leading-edge on outer two-thirds of each wing. All-metal three-spar structure. Each wing fitted with three-section manually-operated ailerons, electrically-actuated double-slotted flaps and two hydraulically-operated spoiler sections forward of flaps. Trim tab and spring-loaded servo tab in each centre aileron, spring-loaded servo tab in each inner aileron. Hot-air anti-icing of leading-edges.

Fuselage: Conventional all-metal semi-monocoque structure. Frames are duralumin stampings and pressings. Integrally pressed skin panels at highly-stressed areas. Floors are sandwich panels with foam plastics filler. Nosecone hinges upward for access to radar.

Tail Unit: Cantilever all-metal structure, with electrically-actuated variable-incidence tailplane mounted at tip of fin. All surfaces sweptback. Manually-operated rudder, fitted with yaw damper, trim tab and spring servo tab. Manually-operated elevators have two automatic trim tabs and two manual trim tabs. Hot-air leading-edge anti-icing system.

Landing Gear: Hydraulically-retractable tricycle type. Forward-retracting twin-wheel steerable nose unit. Emergency extension by gravity. Oleo-nitrogen shock-absorber on each unit. Each main unit carries a four-wheel bogie and retracts inward into wing-roots. Main wheel tyre size 1450 × 450, pressure 135 lb/sq in (9·5 kg/cm²). Nosewheel tyre size 930 × 305, pressure 114 lb/sq in (8 kg/cm²). Hydraulic disc brake and inertia-type electric anti-skid unit on each main wheel, supplemented by large tail parachute. Parking brakes. Hydraulic twin-wheel strut is extended downward to support rear fuselage during loading and unloading.

Power Plant: Four Kuznetsov NK-8-4 turbofan engines, each rated at 23,150 lb (10,500 kg) st, mounted in horizontal pairs on each side of rear fuselage. Thrust reverser on each outboard engine. Hot-air anti-icing system for engine intakes. Automatically-controlled fuel system, with seven integral tanks extending through entire wing from tip to tip. Each engine has its own independent fuel system, with cross-feed. Total fuel capacity 21,998 Imp gallons (100,000 litres). Four standard international underwing pressure refuelling sockets. Eight gravity refuelling sockets. Total oil capacity 45 Imp gallons (204 litres).

Accommodation: Crew of five (two pilots, navigator, radio operator and flight engineer) on flight deck. Provision for two supernumerary pilot/navigators. Basic two-cabin layout, and galley, toilet and wardrobe facilities, are unchanged in the three main versions, only the width and pitch of the seats being varied. In the 186-passenger version, there are 72 seats in the forward cabin and 114 in the rear cabin, all six-abreast and all at a seat pitch of 34 in (86 cm). In the 168-seat configuration, increased pitch reduces capacity to 66 in the forward cabin and 102 in the rear cabin. The 114-passenger version has 45 seats in the forward cabin and 69 in the rear cabin, all five-abreast, except for four-abreast rear row by door. A first class/de luxe version for 85 passengers is

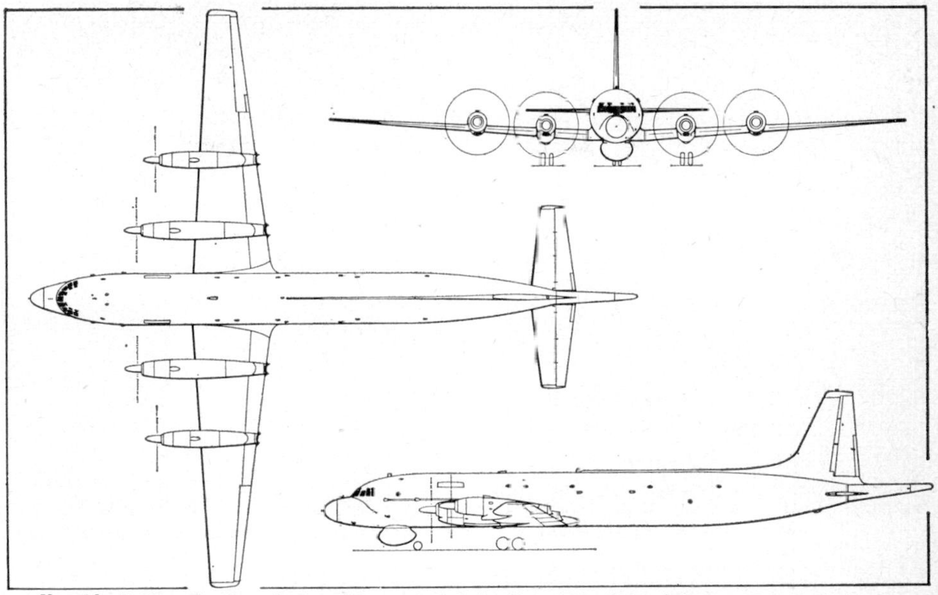

Ilyushin Il-38 anti-submarine/maritime patrol derivative of the Il-18 airliner (*Roy J. Grainge*)

Ilyushin Il-38 anti-submarine/maritime patrol aircraft (four Ivchenko AI-20 turboprop engines)

Ilyushin Il-62 long-range transport aircraft (four Kuznetsov NK-8-4 turbofan engines) in Aeroflot service (*Martin Fricke*)

Ilyushin Il-62M, the high-density version of this long-range airliner (four Soloviev D-30KU turbofan engines) (*Flight International*)

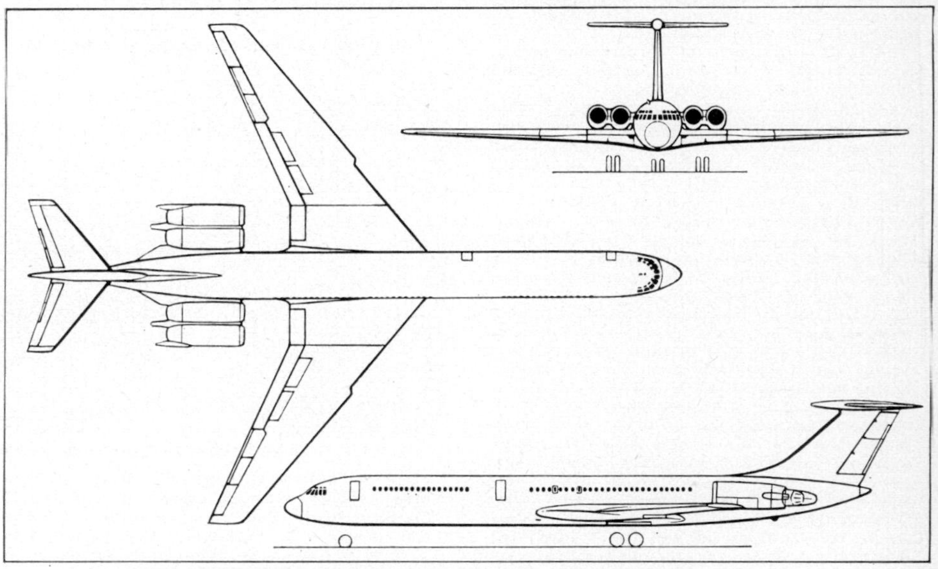

Ilyushin Il-62M high-density long-range four-turbofan transport (*Pilot Press*)

available, with 45 seats in forward cabin and 40 four-abreast sleeperette chairs with footrests in rear cabin. Passenger doors forward of front cabin and between cabins on port side. Total of five toilets, opposite forward door, between cabins (starboard) and aft of rear cabin (both sides). Electrically-powered galley/pantry amidships and wardrobes in each version. Two pressurised baggage and freight compartments under cabin floor, forward and aft of wing. Unpressurised baggage/cargo compartment at extreme rear of fuselage. All compartments have tie-down fittings and rails in floor, and removable nets to restrain cargo.

SYSTEMS: Air-conditioning and pressurisation system maintains sea level conditions up to 23,000 ft (7,000 m) and gives equivalent of 6,900 ft (2,100 m) at 42,600 ft (13,000 m). Pressure differential 9·0 lb/sq in (0·63 kg/cm^2). Hydraulic system, pressure 3,000 lb/sq in (210 kg/cm^2), for landing gear retraction, nosewheel steering, brakes, spoilers and windscreen wipers. Three-phase 200/115V AC electrical supply from four 40kVA engine-driven generators (optional 27V DC system with eight 18kW engine-driven generators). Four transformer-rectifiers and four batteries for DC supply. Electrical windscreen de-icing. Type TA-6 APU in tailcone.

ELECTRONICS AND EQUIPMENT: Standard equipment includes two-channel autopilot, navigation computer, air data system, HF and UHF radio, VOR/ILS, RMI, Doppler, radio altimeter and weather radar. Polyot automatic flight control system optional.

DIMENSIONS, EXTERNAL:
Wing span 141 ft 9 in (43·20 m)
Length overall 174 ft 3½ in (53·12 m)
Length of fuselage 160 ft 9 in (49·00 m)
Height overall 40 ft 6¼ in (12·35 m)
Tailplane span 40 ft 1½ in (12·23 m)
Fuselage width 13 ft 5½ in (4·10 m)
Fuselage height 12 ft 3½ in (3·75 m)
Wheel track 22 ft 3½ in (6·80 m)
Wheelbase 80 ft 4½ in (24·49 m)
Passenger doors (each):
Height 6 ft 0 in (1·83 m)
Width 2 ft 9¾ in (0·86 m)
Height to sill 11 ft 8 in (3·55 m)
Emergency exit (galley service) door:
Height 4 ft 6 in (1·37 m)
Width 2 ft 0 in (0·61 m)
Front cargo hold door:
Height 4 ft 3½ in (1·31 m)
Width 4 ft 1½ in (1·26 m)
Height to sill 6 ft 3½ in (1·92 m)
Second cargo hold door:
Height 3 ft 3½ in (1·00 m)
Width 4 ft 1½ in (1·26 m)
Height to sill 6 ft 3½ in (1·92 m)
Third cargo hold door:
Height 2 ft 3½ in (0·70 m)
Width 2 ft 3½ in (0·70 m)
Height to sill 7 ft 7¼ in (2·32 m)
Rear cargo hold door:
Height 3 ft 9 in (1·15 m)
Width 3 ft 6 in (1·07 m)
Height to sill 11 ft 10½ in (3·62 m)

DIMENSIONS, INTERNAL:
Cabin:
Max height 6 ft 11½ in (2·12 m)
Max width 11 ft 5¼ in (3·49 m)
Volume 5,756 cu ft (163 m^3)
Total volume of pressure cell 13,985 cu ft (396 m^3)
Cargo hold volume:
Underfloor (two, total) 1,380 cu ft (39·1 m^3)
Rear fuselage 205 cu ft (5·8 m^3)

AREAS:
Wings, gross 3,010 sq ft (279·6 m^2)
Ailerons (total) 174·9 sq ft (16·25 m^2)
Spoilers (total) 102·7 sq ft (9·54 m^2)
Flaps (total) 468·0 sq ft (43·48 m^2)
Horizontal tail surfaces (total) 430·5 sq ft (40·00 m^2)
Vertical tail surfaces (total) 383·2 sq ft (35·60 m^2)

WEIGHTS AND LOADING:
Weight empty 146,390 lb (66,400 kg)
Operating weight, empty 153,000 lb (69,400 kg)
Max payload 50,700 lb (23,000 kg)
Max fuel 183,700 lb (83,325 kg)
Max ramp weight 368,000 lb (167,000 kg)
Max T-O weight 357,000 lb (162,000 kg)
Max landing weight 232,000 lb (105,000 kg)
Max zero-fuel weight 206,000 lb (93,500 kg)
Max wing loading 117·2 lb/sq ft (572 kg/m^2)

PERFORMANCE (at max T-O weight):
Normal cruising speed 442-486 knots (510-560 mph; 820-900 km/h)
Normal cruising height 33,000-39,400 ft (10,000-12,000 m)
Landing speed 119-129 knots (137-149 mph; 220-240 km/h)
Max rate of climb at S/L 3,540 ft (1,080 m)/min
FAR T-O field length:
ISA at S/L 10,660 ft (3,250 m)
ISA+20°C at S/L 12,840 ft (3,915 m)
FAR landing field length:
ISA at S/L 9,185 ft (2,800 m)
ISA+20°C at S/L 9,680 ft (2,950 m)
Range with max payload, 147,050 lb (66,700 kg) fuel, 1 hour fuel reserve 3,612 nm (4,160 miles; 6,700 km)
Range with 176,370 lb (80,000 kg) fuel and 22,050 lb (10,000 kg) payload, 1 hour fuel reserve 4,963 nm (5,715 miles; 9,200 km)

ILYUSHIN Il-62M

First displayed publicly at the 1971 Paris Air Show, the Il-62M is a high-density, developed version of the Il-62 able to seat up to 198 passengers, with no dimensional changes to the airframe. It is fitted with more powerful turbofans, of a different type, with clamshell thrust reversers on the outboard engine of each pair, offering a lower approach speed and improved airflow over the rear of the nacelles. An additional fuel tank is installed in the tail-fin, contributing (with the improved specific fuel consumption of the engines) to the longer range of this version.

Revised layout of the flight deck equipment, and new navigation and radio communications equipment, are features of the Il-62M. Control wheels of new design allow the pilots a better field of view, and the aircraft's automatic flight control system permits automatic landings in ICAO Category II conditions, with extension to Category III conditions envisaged later. The wing spoilers of this version can be utilised differentially to enhance roll control.

Additional emergency and rescue equipment is installed on the Il-62M. The electrical, hydraulic and radio equipment in the rear fuselage has been repositioned. Together with the elimination of a wardrobe and transfer further aft of one central toilet and two rear toilets, this has permitted the installation of extra seats in the passenger cabin and optional provision of a compartment for buffet serving trolleys.

Unlike the Il-62, this version has a containerised baggage and freight system, with mechanised loading and unloading.

The Il-62M exhibited in Paris in 1971 and 1973 was the prototype (CCCP-86673). Production models entered service on Aeroflot's Moscow-Havana route in 1974 and will be used eventually on all of the airline's very-long-distance services.

The basic structural description of the Il-62 applies also to the Il-62M. The main innovations are as follows:

POWER PLANT: Four Soloviev D-30KU turbofan engines, each rated at 25,350 lb (11,500 kg) st, mounted in horizontal pairs on each side of rear fuselage. Clamshell-type thrust reverser on each outboard engine. Remainder of power plant installation basically as for Il-62, but additional fuel tank in tail-fin with capacity of 1,100 Imp gallons (5,000 litres).

ACCOMMODATION: Alternative configurations for up to 198 economy class, 186 tourist class or 161 mixed class passengers. In the economy class version there are two toilets opposite the forward door, on the starboard side, aft of the flight deck. The forward cabin contains 72 seats, all six-abreast in threes with centre aisle. Galley/pantry amidships as on Il-62. Rear cabin contains 126 seats, six-abreast in threes with centre aisle. Three toilets and wardrobe to rear of this cabin. Doors as on Il-62. Forward underfloor baggage and freight hold accommodates nine containers, each weighing approximately 100 lb (45 kg) empty and with a capacity of 1,322 lb (600 kg) and 56·5 cu ft (1·6 m³). Rear hold accommodates five similar containers. Two compartments for non-containerised cargo.

Systems and Equipment: See introductory notes.

Dimensions and Areas:
Same as for Il-62

Weights:
Max payload 50,700 lb (23,000 kg)
Max T-O weight 363,760 lb (165,000 kg)

Performance (at max T-O weight):
Normal cruising speed
458-486 knots (528-560 mph; 850-900 km/h)
Normal cruising height
33,000-39,400 ft (10,000-12,000 m)
Balanced T-O distance (ISA, S/L)
9,845 ft (3,000 m)
Landing run (ISA, S/L) 9,185 ft (2,800 m)
Range with max payload, with reserves
4,315 nm (4,970 miles; 8,000 km)
Range with 22,045 lb (10,000 kg) payload, with reserves 5,555 nm (6,400 miles; 10,300 km)

ILYUSHIN Il-76

NATO code name: "Candid"

Flown for the first time on 25 March 1971, the Il-76 prototype (CCCP-86712) made its public debut at the 29th Salon de l'Aéronautique et de l'Espace in Paris in May 1971.

It is a high-performance pressurised heavy transport of conventional layout, powered by four turbofan engines of similar basic type to those installed in the Il-62M. The clamshell thrust reversers, fitted to all four engines, are of different configuration, stowing above and below the nozzle when not in use, instead of to each side.

Nominal task of the Il-76 is to transport 40 tonnes of freight for a distance of 5,000 km (2,700 nm; 3,100 miles) in less than six hours. It can take off from short unprepared airstrips and an official statement has said that it will be used first during the period of the current five-year plan (1971-75) in Siberia, the north of the Soviet Union and the Far East, where operation of other types of transport is difficult. Clearly, however, it also has considerable potential as a military transport aircraft.

Aircraft seen and photographed during 1973-74 embody a number of modifications compared with the prototype. Most important is that the hinge-line of each rear clamshell door is higher on the fuselage of at least one aircraft, giving a larger door and permitting taller and wider loads to pass between the doors when they are open. Other new features include a modified rear fin fillet and strengthening of the upper fuselage.

Type: Four-turbofan medium/long-range freight transport.

Wings: Cantilever monoplane, mounted above fuselage to leave interior unobstructed, and with marked anhedral from roots. Sweepback on leading-edge approx 28°. All-metal structure. Two-section double-slotted flaps over full span from wing root to inboard edge of aileron each side. Spoilers forward of inboard flaps. Leading-edge slots over almost entire span. Tabs in each aileron.

Fuselage: All-metal semi-monocoque structure of basically circular section. Underside of upswept rear fuselage made up of two outward-hinged clamshell doors, upward-hinged panel between these doors, and downward-hinged loading ramp.

Tail Unit: Cantilever all-metal structure, with tailplane mounted at tip of fin. All surfaces sweptback. Tabs in rudder and each elevator.

Landing Gear: Retractable tricycle type, designed for operation from prepared and unprepared runways. Nose unit made up of two pairs of wheels, side by side with central oleo. Each main-wheel bogie made up of four pairs of wheels in two rows. Low-pressure tyres size 1300 × 480 on main wheels, 1100 × 330 on nosewheels. Main units retract inward into two large ventral fairings under fuselage, with an additional large fairing on each side of lower fuselage over actuating gear. During retraction main wheel axles rotate around leg, so that wheels stow with axles parallel to fuselage axis (ie: wheels remain vertical but at 90° to direction of flight).

Power Plant: Four Soloviev D-30KP turbofan engines, each rated at 26,455 lb (12,000 kg) st, in individual underwing pods. Each pod is carried on a large forwardly-inclined pylon and is fitted with a clamshell thrust reverser. No fuel is carried in the wings.

Accommodation: Conventional side-by-side seating for pilot and co-pilot on spacious flight deck. Station for navigator below flight deck in glazed nose. Forward-hinged door on each side of fuselage forward of wing. Cabin loaded via rear ramp. Entire accommodation is pressurised, and advanced mechanical handling systems are provided for containerised and other freight.

Electronics and Equipment: Full equipment for all-weather operation by day and night, including a computer for automatic flight control and automatic landing approach. Large ground-mapping radar in undernose radome. APU in port side landing gear fairing.

Dimensions, external:
Wing span 165 ft 8 in (50·50 m)
Length overall 152 ft 10½ in (46·59 m)
Height overall 48 ft 5 in (14·76 m)

Weights:
Max payload 88,185 lb (40,000 kg)
Max T-O weight 346,125 lb (157,000 kg)

Performance:
Normal cruising speed
458 knots (528 mph; 850 km/h)
Normal cruising height 42,650 ft (13,000 m)
Nominal range with max payload
2,700 nm (3,100 miles; 5,000 km)

ILYUSHIN Il-86

First indication that this aircraft was under development was given at the 1971 Paris Air Show. Mr Genrikh Novozhilov, successor to the semi-retired Sergei Ilyushin as chief of the Ilyushin design bureau, told visitors that a new wide-bodied transport known as the Il-86 was then in the early project design stage.

No final decision on the configuration, or number of engines, had been taken at that time; but in the Spring of 1972 a model of one projected configuration was displayed publicly in Moscow. This design was similar in layout to the Il-62, with four rear-mounted turbofan engines and a T-tail, but was intended to be much larger, with a two-deck fuselage. It was described and illustrated in the 1972-73 *Jane's*.

Simultaneously with the display of this original model, it became known that the Il-86 had been chosen for development, after a competition in which it was matched against proposals from the Antonov and Tupolev design teams. If it proves successful, it is expected to follow the "stretched" Tu-154 interim airbus in service with Aeroflot in the late 'seventies.

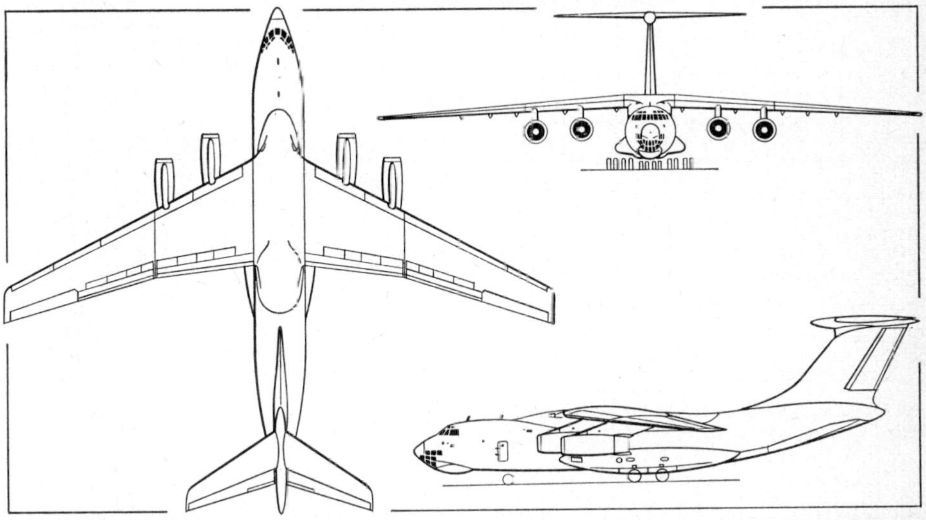

Photograph (*Tass*) and three-view drawing (*Pilot Press*) of Ilyushin Il-76 four-turbofan heavy freight-carrying transport

Ilyushin Il-76 freight transport (four Soloviev D-30KP turbofan engines) displayed at a Moscow airport (*Tass*)

By the end of 1972, it became clear that the design of the Il-86 had evolved along different lines to those suggested by the model displayed six months earlier. In particular the engines had been repositioned into four underwing pods, permitting the tailplane to be lowered on to the rear fuselage, as shown in the accompanying drawing.

The fuselage is circular in cross-section, with the dividing floor positioned just below the widest point. The upper deck, on which all seats are located, is divided into three separate passenger cabins by wardrobes, galleys and cabin staff accommodation, with toilets at front and rear of the aircraft. Up to 350 passengers could be carried in basic nine-abreast seating throughout, with two aisles. A suggested mixed class alternative provides for 28 passengers six-abreast in the front cabin and 206 passengers eight-abreast in the other two cabins.

Passengers are intended to enter the aircraft via three airstair-type doors which hinge down from the port side of the lower deck. Two of these doors are forward of the wing; the other is aft of the wing. There are four further doors at upper-deck level on each side, presumably for emergency use.

Coats and hand baggage are intended to be stowed on the lower deck before passengers climb one of the three fixed staircases to the main deck. The cargo holds are designed to accommodate baggage and freight in 16 standard LD3 containers. Access is via upward-hinged doors forward of the starboard wing-root leading-edge and at the side of the rear hold, and containers can be loaded and unloaded by means of a self-propelled truck with built-in roller conveyor.

There appear to be high-lift devices on both the leading- and trailing-edges of the wings to improve field performance. Wing sweep is 35° at quarter-chord. The landing gear comprises a rearward-retracting twin-wheel nose unit and three four-wheel bogie main units. Two of the latter retract inward into the enlarged wing-root fairings; the third unit is mounted centrally under the fuselage, slightly forward of the others.

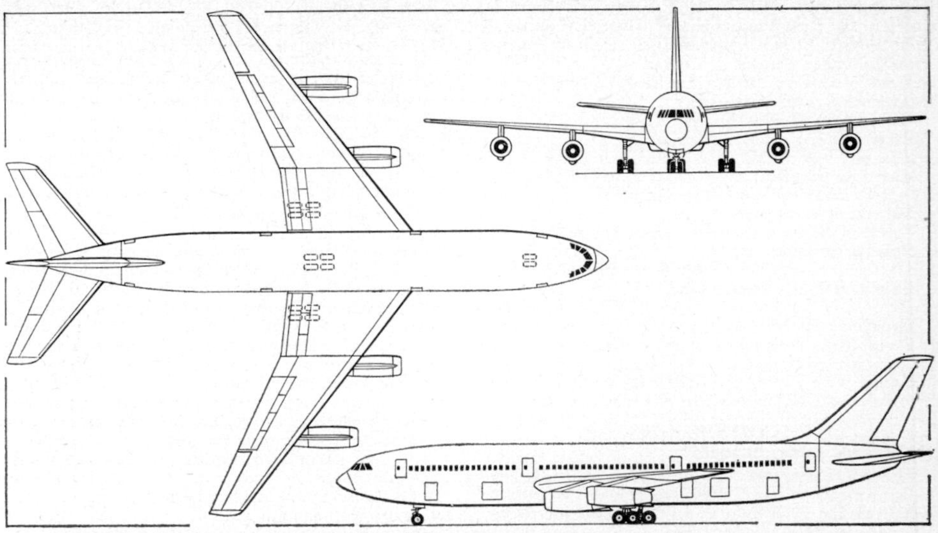

Ilyushin Il-86 four-turbofan wide-bodied passenger transport (*Pilot Press; provisional*)

It was expected originally that the power plants of the Il-86 would be Soloviev D-30KP high by-pass ratio turbofans, each rated at 26,455 lb (12,000 kg) st. More recently, it has been suggested that choice of engine will follow evaluation of competing turbofan designs from the Soloviev and Lotarev engine teams. Fuel capacity will be 15,400-17,600 Imp gallons (70,000-80,000 litres).

Standard flight crew is to comprise two pilots and a flight engineer, with provision for a navigator if required.

Dimensions, external:
- Wing span: 158 ft 6½ in (48·33 m)
- Length overall: 191 ft 11 in (58·50 m)
- Diameter of fuselage: 19 ft 11½ in (6·08 m)
- Height overall: 51 ft 6 in (15·70 m)
- Tailplane span: 62 ft 4 in (19·00 m)

Dimensions, internal:
- Main cabins: Height: 8 ft 7 in (2·61 m)
- Max width: approx 18 ft 8½ in (5·70 m)

Area:
- Wings, gross: 3,444 sq ft (320 m²)

Weights:
- Max payload: 88,185 lb (40,000 kg)
- Max T-O weight: 414,470 lb (188,000 kg)

Performance (estimated):
- Normal cruising speed at 30,000-33,000 ft (9,000-10,000 m): 485-512 knots (560-590 mph; 900-950 km/h)
- Landing speed: 130-135 knots (149-155 mph; 240-250 km/h)
- Range with max payload: 1,268 nm (1,460 miles; 2,350 km)
- Range with max fuel: 2,480 nm (2,858 miles; 4,600 km)

KAI

KHARKOV AVIATION INSTITUTE

A series of light aircraft has been designed and built by students of this institute. Some details of the KAI-17 (or KhAI-17) and KAI-18 were given in the 1962-63 *Jane's*. A three-view drawing of the KAI-19 single-seat ultra-light monoplane appeared in the 1964-65 *Jane's*. A photograph and brief details of the KAI-24 two-seat light autogyro can be found in the 1969-70 edition. These aircraft were followed by a single-seat pusher-engined light aircraft designated KAI-20, and the single-seat KAI-22A and two-seat KAI-27 ultra-light helicopters. The KAI-27 was described and illustrated in the 1970-71 *Jane's*, and the others in the 1972-73 edition.

No details concerning the flight trials of any of these aircraft have ever been received.

KAMOV

Nikolai I. Kamov, who died on 24 November 1973, aged 71, had been a leading designer of rotating-wing aircraft since the late 1920s and, with N. K. Skrzhinskii, was responsible for the first successful Soviet rotorcraft, the KaSkr-I, in 1929. He became well known internationally when he designed a series of one-man lightweight helicopters of the "flying motorcycle" type in the late 1940s.

The Ka-15 and Ka-18 helicopters, developed by Kamov and his design team, under chief engineer Vladimir Barshevskii, were both put into large-scale production and service. Details of them can be found in the 1962-63 and 1963-64 editions of *Jane's* respectively.

Later Kamov types are the Ka-25 turbine-powered anti-submarine helicopter; a flying-crane version of the same design, designated Ka-25K; and a twin-engined general-purpose helicopter designated Ka-26. All available details of these types follow:

KAMOV Ka-25

NATO code name: "Hormone"

The prototype of this military helicopter was first shown in public in the Soviet Aviation Day fly-past over Tushino Airport, Moscow, in July 1961. It was allocated the NATO code name "Harp", but this was changed to "Hormone" for the production versions, which have largely replaced the Mi-4 in service with the Soviet Navy, ashore and at sea.

Basically, the Ka-25 follows the formula established by earlier Kamov designs such as the Ka-15 and Ka-18, with two three-blade co-axial contra-rotating rotors, a pod-and-boom fuselage, multi-fin tail unit, and four-wheel landing gear. It is powered by two small turboshaft engines mounted side by side above the cabin, and this has left the cabin space clear for personnel, operational equipment, fuel and payload.

In its anti-submarine version, the Ka-25 operates from ships of the Soviet Navy, including cruisers of the *Kresta* and *Kara* classes, and the helicopter carrier/cruisers *Moskva* and *Leningrad*, each of which accommodates about 20 aircraft. It has a search radar installation in a radome (diameter 4 ft 1 in; 1·25 m) under the nose; other equipment includes a towed magnetic anomaly detector and an electro-optical sensor. Each landing wheel is surrounded by an inflatable pontoon surmounted by inflation bottles to provide flotation in the event of an emergency alighting on the water.

The version of the Kamov Ka-25 anti-submarine helicopter with a blister fairing at the base of the central tail-fin

The two so-called "air-to-surface missiles" carried on outriggers on each side of the cabin of the prototype during its Tushino appearance were dummies, and there is no evidence that externally-mounted weapons are carried. The production Ka-25 has an internal weapons-bay for stores, including ASW torpedoes and nuclear depth charges.

As well as serving with the Red Banner Black Sea Fleet as an anti-submarine aircraft, based on the *Moskva* and *Leningrad*, the Ka-25 fulfils a variety of other military roles.

The Ka-25K, described separately, is a commercial counterpart of the Ka-25. It can be assumed that the two types are similar in details such as basic structure, overall dimensions, power plant, weights and performance, except that the military version is a little shorter, with an estimated overall length of 32 ft 0 in (9·75 m).

Type: Twin-turbine anti-submarine and general-purpose helicopter.

Airframe and Power Plant: Basically as for Ka-25K. Provision for carrying an external fuel tank on each side of main cabin.

Accommodation: Pilot and co-pilot side by side on flight deck, with rearward-sliding door on each side. Entry to main cabin is via a rearward-sliding door to rear of main landing gear on port side. Cabin is large enough to contain 12 folding seats for passengers in transport version.

Electronics and Equipment: Equipment available for all versions includes autopilot, navigational system, radio compass, radio communications installations, and lighting system for all-weather operation by day or night. Dipping sonar housed in compartment at rear of main cabin, immediately forward of tailboom, and search radar under nose of anti-submarine version, which carries also a towed magnetic anomaly detector. Some aircraft have a blister fairing over equipment mounted at the base of the centre tail-fin; others have a cylindrical housing, with a transparent top, above the central point of the tailboom (see illustration), with a shallow blister fairing to the rear of this. Doors under the fuselage enclose a weapons bay for ASW torpedoes, nuclear depth charges and other stores.

KAMOV Ka-25K

NATO code name: "Hormone"

This flying-crane helicopter was shown publicly for the first time at the 1967 Paris Air Show. Instead of the undernose radome of the anti-submarine version of the Ka-25, it has a removable gondola giving an exceptional field of view for the occupant.

One of the pilots occupies this gondola during loading, unloading and positioning of externally-slung cargoes, while the helicopter is hovering. His seat faces rearward, giving him an unobstructed view of the operation, and he is able to control the aircraft by means of a set of dual flying controls fitted in the gondola. This distribution of duty, with one pilot controlling the aircraft during loading and unloading operations and the other pilot controlling it in cruising flight, is claimed to increase the precision and safety of payload handling and to offer a considerable reduction in the overall time required to do a particular job.

The Ka-25K is claimed to combine high payload-to-AUW ratio with good manoeuvrability and minimum dimensions. The rotors, transmission and engines, with their auxiliaries, form a single self-contained assembly, which can be removed in one hour.

Type: Twin-turbine flying-crane helicopter.

Rotor System: Two three-blade co-axial contra-rotating rotors. Automatic blade-folding.

Fuselage: Conventional all-metal semi-monocoque structure of pod-and-boom type. Detachable gondola under nose.

Tail Unit: Cantilever all-metal structure, with central fin, ventral fin and twin endplate fins and rudders which are toed inward.

Landing Gear: Non-retractable four-wheel type. Oleo-pneumatic shock-absorbers. Nosewheels are smaller than main wheels and are of castoring type. Each wheel can be enclosed in an inflatable pontoon surmounted by inflation bottles.

Power Plant: Two 900 shp Glushenkov GTD-3 turboshaft engines, mounted side by side above cabin, forward of rotor driveshaft.

Accommodation: Crew of two side by side on flight deck. Rearward-facing pilot's seat with dual flying controls in undernose gondola for use during loading and unloading. Main cabin, normally used for freight carrying, contains 12 folding seats for passengers. Rearward-sliding door on each side of flight deck. Large rear-ward-sliding door at rear of main cabin on port side. Hatchway in cabin floor, with two downward-opening doors, through which sling cable passes from winch on CG.

Electronics and Equipment: Optional equipment includes autopilot, navigational system, radio compass, radio communications installation, and lighting system for all-weather operation by day or night.

Dimensions, external:
- Diameter of rotors (each) 51 ft 8 in (15·74 m)
- Length overall 32 ft 3 in (9·83 m)
- Height to top of rotor head 17 ft 7½ in (5·37 m)
- Width over tail-fins 12 ft 4 in (3·76 m)
- Wheel track:
  - front 4 ft 7½ in (1·41 m)
  - rear 11 ft 6½ in (3·52 m)
- Cabin door: Height 3 ft 7¼ in (1·10 m)
  - Width 3 ft 11¼ in (1·20 m)

Weights:
- Weight empty 9,700 lb (4,400 kg)
- Max payload 4,400 lb (2,000 kg)
- Max T-O weight 16,100 lb (7,300 kg)

Performance:
- Max level speed 119 knots (137 mph; 220 km/h)
- Normal cruising speed 104 knots (120 mph; 193 km/h)
- Service ceiling 11,500 ft (3,500 m)
- Range with standard fuel, with reserves 217 nm (250 miles; 400 km)
- Range with max fuel, with reserves 351 nm (405 miles; 650 km)

KAMOV Ka-26

NATO code name: "Hoodlum"

First details of this twin-engined light helicopter were announced in January 1964, and the prototype flew for the first time in the following year. Kamov described it as an ideal helicopter for agriculture, possessing all the virtues of the Ka-15 (which was used in about a dozen countries) but able to lift three times as much chemical payload, and the Ka-26 entered large-scale service as an agricultural aircraft in the Soviet Union in 1970, being used primarily over orchards and vineyards. It is also used widely on Aeroflot's air ambulance services and is suitable for many other applications, including cargo and passenger transport, forest firefighting, mineral prospecting, pipeline construction and laying transmission lines.

The usual Kamov contra-rotating co-axial three-blade rotor system is retained, with hydraulic dampers fitted to each rotor head and the rotor shafts inclined forward at 6° to the vertical. The blades, made of glass-textolyte (plastics) materials, weigh only 55 lb (25 kg) each and are completely interchangeable. They, and the cabin windscreen, are equipped with an anti-icing system, activated automatically by a radioisotope ice warning device and utilising an alcohol glycerine mixture.

A powered control system is standard. The jacks are actuated by a single hydraulic system, with manual override in case of system failure.

The fully-enclosed cabin, with a door on each side, is fitted out normally for operation by a single pilot, but a second seat and dual controls

Kamov Ka-25 anti-submarine helicopter (two Glushenkov turboshaft engines) (*US Navy*)

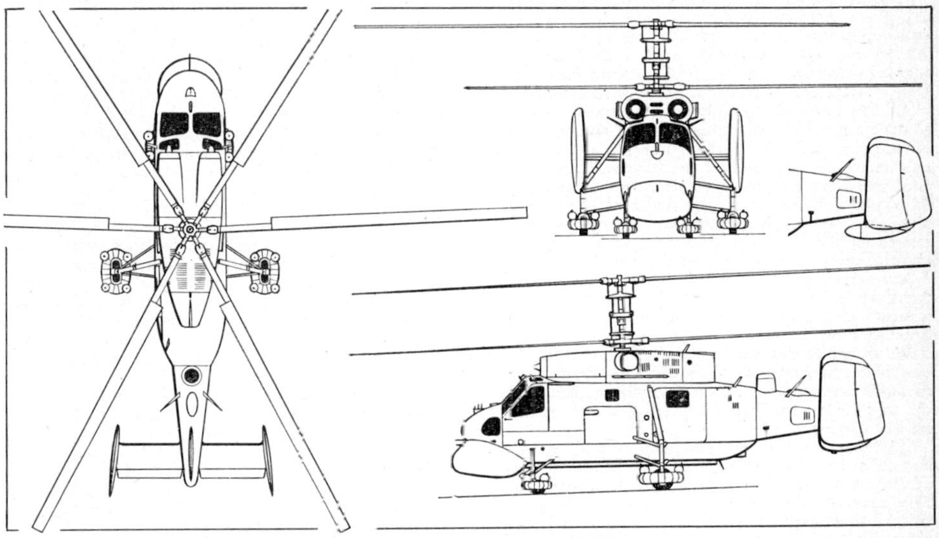

Anti-submarine version of the Kamov Ka-25 helicopter. Scrap view shows optional blister fairing at base of central tail-fin (*Pilot Press*)

Kamov Ka-25K flying-crane helicopter (two 900 shp Glushenkov GTD-3 turboshaft engines) (*S. P. Peltz*)

are optional. The cabin is warmed and demisted by air from a combustion heater, which also heats the passenger compartment when fitted.

The tailplane, with twin fins and rudders toed inward at 15°, is carried on two plastics tail-booms. Short high-mounted stub-wings carry the two podded 325 hp M-14V-26 aircooled radial piston engines, designed by I. M. Vedeneev, and the main units of the non-retractable four-wheel landing gear. Each engine is cooled by a fan in the front of its nacelle, which absorbs about 25 hp from the engine output. Dust filters are fitted in the air delivery ducts, to protect the engines, each of which is connected to the rotor transmission by a shaft and two flexible couplings. Both rotors can be driven by either engine if the other fails; disengagement of the failed engine is automatic, and an autorotative landing can be made if both engines fail.

All four landing gear units embody oleo-pneumatic shock-absorbers. The forward wheels are of the castoring type and are not fitted with brakes. The rear wheels are fitted with pneumatically-operated brakes. Tyre size is 595 × 185 on the main wheels, 300 × 125 on the forward wheels.

The space aft of the cabin, between the main landing gear units and under the rotor transmission, is able to accommodate a variety of interchangeable payloads. For agricultural work the chemical hopper (capacity 1,985 lb; 900 kg) and dust-spreader or spraybars are fitted in this position, on the aircraft's centre of gravity. This equipment is quickly removable and can be replaced by a cargo/passenger pod accommodating six persons, with provision for a seventh passenger beside the pilot. Alternatively, the Ka-26 can be operated with either an open platform for hauling freight or a hook for slinging bulky loads at the end of a cable or in a cargo net.

A version for geophysical survey has an electromagnetic pulse generator in the cabin and is encircled by a huge "hoop" antenna. It carries on the port side of the fuselage a mounting for the receiver "bird" which is towed at the end of a cable, beneath the helicopter, when in use. The receiver is lowered by an electric winch and the cable is cut by automatic shears if its traction should exceed the authorised limit.

An aerial survey model is available with an AFA-31-MA camera mounted in the cabin. This aircraft can photograph 2 sq miles (5 km²) per hour at a scale of 1 : 10,000.

As an air ambulance, the Ka-26 can carry two stretcher patients, two seated casualties and a medical attendant. A winch, with a capacity of up to 330 lb (150 kg), enables it to be used for rescue duties.

When operating as an agricultural sprayer, the Ka-26 discharges its chemical payload at 0·33-2·65 Imp gallons/sec (1·5-12 litres/sec). The rate of discharge in a dusting role is 3·3-26·5 lb/sec (1·5-12 kg/sec). Up to 296 acres (120 hectares) can be sprayed during each flying hour at the rate of 44·5 lb/acre (50 kg/ha). As a duster, 346 acres (140 ha) can be treated at the same discharge rate. 123 acres (50 ha) can be topdressed with chemical fertilisers each flying hour, at a rate of 89 lb/acre (100 kg/ha).

To protect the pilot against toxic chemicals in the agricultural role, the cabin is lightly pressurised by a blower and air filter system which ensures that the cabin air is always clean. The flying and navigation equipment are adequate for all-weather operation, by day and night.

Kamov Ka-26 in service with the Hungarian Air Force *(photocopied from Repules)*

VHF and HF radio are fitted, together with a radio compass and radio altimeter.

Because of its small size and manoeuvrability, the Ka-26 can be operated from platforms on small ships such as whalers and icebreakers, and a Soviet fishing boat operating in the North Atlantic in early 1970 carried a Ka-26 for fish-spotting duties. This aircraft was equipped with inflated pontoons to permit alighting on the water.

In mid-1969, a Ka-26 was tested in Siberia and the north-west USSR in a forest protection version able to deliver six firemen and their equipment speedily to the site of a forest fire. In the Spring of 1972, Ka-26s joined Mil Mi-1, Mi-2 and Mi-4 helicopters in operations to clear ice from Soviet rivers, by landing demolition teams on thick ice-floes and destroying thinner ice-fields from the air.

Ka-26s are in civilian service in Bulgaria, East Germany, West Germany, Hungary, Romania and Sweden, as well as in the USSR. Military operators include the air forces of Hungary and Sri Lanka.

DIMENSIONS, EXTERNAL:
- Diameter of rotors (each): 42 ft 8 in (13·00 m)
- Vertical separation between rotors: 3 ft 10 in (1·17 m)
- Length of fuselage: 25 ft 5 in (7·75 m)
- Height overall: 13 ft 3½ in (4·05 m)
- Width over engine pods: 11 ft 11½ in (3·64 m)
- Width over agricultural spraybars: 36 ft 9 in (11·20 m)
- Tailplane span: 15 ft 1 in (4·60 m)
- Wheel track:
  - Main wheels: 7 ft 11½ in (2·42 m)
  - Nosewheels: 2 ft 11½ in (0·90 m)
- Wheelbase: 11 ft 5 in (3·48 m)
- Passenger pod door:
  - Height: 4 ft 7 in (1·40 m)
  - Width: 4 ft 1¼ in (1·25 m)

DIMENSIONS, INTERNAL:
- Passenger pod:
  - Length, floor level: 6 ft 0 in (1·83 m)
  - Width, floor level: 4 ft 1¼ in (1·25 m)
  - Headroom: 4 ft 7 in (1·40 m)

WEIGHTS:
- Operating weight, empty:
  - Stripped: 4,300 lb (1,950 kg)
  - Cargo/platform: 4,597 lb (2,085 kg)
  - Cargo/hook: 4,519 lb (2,050 kg)
  - Passenger: 4,630 lb (2,100 kg)
  - Agricultural: 4,885 lb (2,216 kg)
- Fuel weight:
  - Transport: 794 lb (360 kg)
  - Other versions: 220 lb (100 kg)
- Payload:
  - Transport: 1,985 lb (900 kg)
  - Agricultural duster: 2,348 lb (1,065 kg)
  - Agricultural sprayer: 1,985 lb (900 kg)
  - With cargo platform: 2,348 lb (1,065 kg)
  - Flying crane: 2,425 lb (1,100 kg)
- Normal T-O weight:
  - Transport: 6,780 lb (3,076 kg)
  - Agricultural: 6,570 lb (2,980 kg)
- Max T-O weight:
  - all versions: 7,165 lb (3,250 kg)

PERFORMANCE (at max T-O weight):
- Max level speed: 91 knots (105 mph; 170 km/h)
- Max cruising speed: 81 knots (93 mph; 150 km/h)
- Econ cruising speed: 49-59 knots (56-68 mph; 90-110 km/h)
- Agricultural operating speed range: 16-62 knots (19-71 mph; 30-115 km/h)
- Service ceiling: 9,840 ft (3,000 m)
- Service ceiling, one engine out: 1,640 ft (500 m)
- Hovering ceiling in ground effect at AUW of 6,615 lb (3,000 kg): 4,265 ft (1,300 m)
- Hovering ceiling out of ground effect at AUW of 6,615 lb (3,000 kg): 2,625 ft (800 m)
- Range with 7 passengers, 30 min fuel reserve: 215 nm (248 miles; 400 km)
- Max range with auxiliary tanks: 647 nm (745 miles; 1,200 km)
- Endurance at econ cruising speed: 3 hr 42 min

MAI

MOSCOW AVIATION INSTITUTE

In October 1967, the Students' Design Office of the Sergo Ordzhonikidze Aviation Institute in Moscow displayed outside the People's Education Pavilion at the USSR Economic Achievement Exhibition in Moscow a small single-seat sporting aircraft named the Kwant (Quant) which its members had designed and built. A photograph released in 1974 shows that this aircraft has since undergone considerable refinement.

Earlier, students of this Institute participated in design of the Yak-18. They have also built a number of sailplanes that gained awards at exhibitions of work by young people.

MAI OSKB-1-3PM KWANT

This small single-seat aerobatic and sporting aircraft is modelled on the radial-engined fighters of the second World War. It is a clean cantilever low-wing monoplane, with cantilever tail unit, retractable tailwheel-type landing gear, and enclosed cockpit with a blister canopy giving a 360° field of vision. Large trailing-edge flaps are fitted.

The main landing gear legs are telescopic for shock-absorption and retract inwards, so that the wheels are housed inside fairings forward of the main spar at the junction of wing and fuselage. When retracted the wheels are fully enclosed by doors.

Power plant of the Kwant is a 360 hp aircooled radial piston-engine. The designation M-14-P, painted on the cowling, appears to relate this to the 325 hp Vedeneev M-14V-26 engines of the Kamov Ka-26 helicopter. It drives a two-blade propeller and is said to give the aircraft a speed of 215 knots (248 mph; 400 km/h).

MAI OSKB-1-3PM Kwant single-seat sporting aircraft built by students of Moscow Aviation Institute *(Tass)*

MiG

Colonel-General Artem I. Mikoyan, who died on 9 December 1970 at the age of 65, was head of the design bureau responsible for the MiG series of fighter aircraft. With Mikhail I. Gurevich, a mathematician, he collaborated in the design of the first of the really-modern Soviet jet-fighters, the MiG-15, which began to appear in squadron service in numbers in 1949.

The MiG-17, a progressive development of the MiG-15, appeared in Soviet squadrons in 1953 or 1954, and was followed into service by the supersonic MiG-19, which appeared in 1955 and was also manufactured until recently in China (which see).

All available details of Mikoyan designs currently in production or under development follow:

MIKOYAN MiG-21

NATO code names: "Fishbed" and "Mongol"

The Soviet design bureau that was led by the late Colonel-General Artem I. Mikoyan developed the MiG-21 air superiority fighter on the basis of experience of jet-to-jet combat between MiG-15s and US aircraft during the war in Korea. The emphasis was placed on good transonic and supersonic handling, high rate of climb, small size, and light weight, using a turbojet engine of medium power, in contrast with the heavier and much more powerful Sukhoi Su-7 and Su-9 fighters that were developed simultaneously. The first versions of the MiG-21 were, therefore, day fighters of limited range, with comparatively light armament and limited avionics. Subsequent development of the type has been aimed primarily at improvements in range, weapons and all-weather capability.

The E-5 prototype of the MiG-21 flew for the first time in 1955, and made its public debut during the flypast in the Soviet Aviation Day display at Tushino Airport, Moscow, on 24 June 1956. The initial production version (NATO "Fishbed-A") was built in only limited numbers, with a Tumansky RD-11 turbojet engine rated at 8,600 lb (3,900 kg) st dry and 11,240 lb (5,100 kg) st with afterburning, and with an armament of two 30 mm NR-30 cannon. Meanwhile, the Soviet Union had been developing a small infra-red homing air-to-air missile, designated K-13 (NATO "Atoll") and generally similar to the US AIM-9B Sidewinder 1A. Underwing pylons for two K-13s were fitted on the MiG-21F, the suffix "F" standing for *Forsirovanny* (boosted) and indicating that this model also had a slightly more powerful turbojet. To save weight and provide room for avionics associated with the missiles, the port NR-30 cannon was removed and its blast-tube fairing on the lower fuselage was blanked off. Further details of this and subsequent versions of the MiG-21 are as follows:

MiG-21F ("Fishbed-C"). First major production version, built also in Czechoslovakia. Short-range clear-weather fighter, with radar ranging equipment and a Tumansky RD-11 turbojet rated at 9,500 lb (4,300 kg) st dry and 12,676 lb (5,750 kg) st with afterburning (designation of engine given in Soviet press statements as TDR Mk R37F). Two underwing pylons for UV-16-57 pods, each containing sixteen 57 mm rockets, or K-13 air-to-air missiles, and one NR-30 cannon in starboard side of fuselage (one each side on early aircraft and on the ten supplied to India). Internal fuel capacity of 515 Imp gallons (2,340 litres), plus underfuselage pylon for external fuel tank of 108 Imp gallons (490 litres) capacity. Small nose air intake of approximately 27 in (69 cm) diameter, with small movable three-shock centrebody housing the radar ranging equipment. Undernose pitot boom, which folds upward on the ground to reduce risk of ground personnel walking into it. Transparent blister cockpit canopy which hinges upwards about base of integral flat bullet-proof windscreen. Transparent rearview panel (not on aircraft built in Czechoslovakia) aft of canopy at front of shallow dorsal spine fairing. Large blade antenna at rear of this panel, with small secondary antenna midway along spine. Fowler-type flap between fuselage and aileron on each trailing-edge, with fairing plate under wing at outer extremity. Small forward-hinged airbrake under fuselage, forward of ventral fin; two further forward-hinged airbrakes, on each side of underfuselage in line with wing-root leading-edges, integral with part of cannon fairings. Brake-parachute housed inside small door on port underside of rear fuselage, with cable attachment under rear part of ventral fin. Semi-encapsulated escape system, in which canopy is ejected with seat, forming shield to protect pilot from slipstream, until the seat has been slowed by its drogue chute. Leading-edge of fin extended forward on all but early aircraft, to increase chord.

MiG-21PF ("Fishbed-D"). Basic model of a new series of operational versions with forward fuselage of less-tapered form. Intake enlarged to diameter of approximately 36 in (91 cm) and housing larger centrebody for R1L search/track radar (NATO "Spin Scan") to enhance all-weather capability (designation suffix letter "P", standing for *Perekhvatchik*, is applied to aircraft adapted for all-weather interception from an earlier designed role). Remainder of airframe generally similar to that of MiG-21F, but pitot boom repositioned above air intake; cannon armament and fairings deleted, permitting simplified design for forward airbrakes; larger main wheels and tyres, requiring enlarged blister fairing on each side of fuselage, over wing, to accommodate wheel in retracted position; dorsal spine fairing widened and deepened aft of canopy, to reduce drag and house additional fuel tankage, and rear-view panel deleted; primary blade antenna repositioned to mid-spine and secondary antenna deleted. Uprated RD-11 turbojet, giving 13,120 lb (5,950 kg) st with afterburning. Internal fuel capacity increased to 627 Imp gallons (2,850 litres) in seven fuselage tanks. Late production aircraft have attachments for a rocket-assisted take-off unit (RATOG) aft of each main landing gear bay, and provision for a flap-blowing system known as *Sduva Pogranichnovo Sloya* (SPS), which reduces the normal landing speed by some 22 knots (25 mph; 40 km/h). Flaps are larger than original Fowler type, do not move aft, and lack outboard fairing plates. Prototype shown at Tushino in 1961 had dummy metal centre-body. Production aircraft in service with many air forces.

"Fishbed-E". Basically similar to "Fishbed-C" with broad-chord vertical tail surfaces. Parachute-brake repositioned into acorn fairing, made up of clamshell doors, at base of rudder, above jet nozzle. Provision for GP-9 underbelly pack, housing GSh-23 twin-barrel 23 mm gun, in place of centreline pylon, with associated predictor sight and electrical ranging system.

MiG-21FL. Export version of late-model MiG-21PF series, with broad-chord vertical tail surfaces and parachute-brake housing at base of rudder but no provision for SPS or RATOG. About 200 were initially assembled and later built under licence in India by Hindustan Aeronautics Ltd (which see), with the IAF designation Type 77. RD-11-300 turbojet rated at 8,598 lb (3,900 kg) st dry and 13,668 lb (6,200 kg) with afterburning. Suffix letter "L" (*Lokator*) indicates the installation of Type R2L search/track radar Can be fitted with GP-9 underbelly gun pack.

MiG-21PFS or MiG-21PF(SPS). Similar to "Fishbed-D", but with SPS as standard production installation.

MiG-21PFM ("Fishbed-F"). Successor to interim MiG-21PFS, embodying all the improvements introduced progressively on the PF and PFS, the suffix letter "M" indicating an exportable version of an existing design. Leading-edge of fin extended forward a further 18 in (45 cm). Small dorsal fin fillet eliminated. Additional refinements, including sideways-hinged (to starboard) canopy and conventional windscreen quarter-lights; simple ejection seat instead of semi-encapsulated type; and large dielectric portion at tip of tail-fin. Type R2L radar has a reported lock-on range of under 7 nm (8 miles; 13 km) and to be ineffective at heights below about 3,000 ft (915 m) because of ground "clutter". Max permissible speed at low altitude is reported to be 593 knots (683 mph; 1,100 km/h). Built also in Czechoslovakia.

Analogue. Based on a standard MiG-21PF airframe, this aircraft was fitted with a scaled-down replica of the original "ogee" delta wing of the Tu-144 supersonic transport, for aerodynamic flight testing and development before the Tu-144 prototype was completed. It had no horizontal tail surfaces. As a result of its several dozen research flights, modifications were made to the full-size wing. One only.

"Fishbed-G". Experimental STOL version of MiG-21PFM, with a pair of vertically-mounted lift-jet engines in lengthened centre-fuselage. Demonstrated in the air display at Domodedovo in July 1967, and described and illustrated in the 1970-71 *Jane's*. Prototype only.

MiG-21PFMA ("Fishbed-J"). Multi-role version. Basically similar to MiG-21PFM but with deeper dorsal fairing containing fuel tankage above fuselage, giving straight line from top of canopy to fin. Pitot tube remains above air intake but is offset to starboard. Provision for GP-9 underbelly gun pack as alternative to centreline fuel tank. Four underwing pylons, instead of usual two, for a variety of ground attack weapons and stores, as alternative or supplementary to two or four air-to-air missiles. Latter can include radar-homing "Advanced Atoll" as well as infra-red K-13A "Atoll". Able to carry two underwing tanks in addition to standard underbelly tank, offsetting reduced internal fuel capacity of 572 Imp gallons (2,600 litres). Zero-speed zero-altitude ejection seat. Small boat-shape fairing with angle-of-attack indicator on port side of nose. Later production aircraft can have the GSh-23 gun installed inside the fuselage, with a shallow underbelly fairing for the twin barrels and splayed cartridge-ejection chutes to clear each side of centreline store.

MiG-21M. Generally similar to MiG-21PFMA with internal GSh-23 gun pack. Has superseded MiG-21FL on Hindustan Aeronautics production line in India, with IAF designation Type 88. First Indian-built MiG-21M was handed over officially to IAF on 14 February 1973.

MiG-21R ("Fishbed-H"). Tactical reconnaissance version, basically similar to MiG-21PFMA. Equipment includes an external pod for forward-facing or oblique cameras, infra-red sensors or ECM devices, and fuel, on fuselage centreline pylon. Suppressed antenna at mid-fuselage and optional ECM equipment in wingtip fairings.

MiG-21MF ("Fishbed-J"). Generally similar to MiG-21PFMA but re-engined with a Tumansky RD-13-300 turbojet, lighter in weight and with higher performance ratings. Small rearview mirror above cockpit canopy. Debris deflector beneath each suction relief door forward of wing root. Entered service with Soviet Air Force in 1970.

A two-seat training version of the MiG-21, in Czechoslovakian insignia (*Letectví + Kosmonautika*)

Mikoyan MiG-21 multi-role fighter; version known to NATO as "Fishbed-L" (*Tass*)

MiG-21RF ("Fishbed-H"). Tactical reconnaissance version of MiG-21MF. Equipment as for MiG-21R.

"Fishbed-K". Similar to MiG-21MF, except for having ECM equipment in wingtip pods, and deep dorsal spine extended rearward as far as parachute-brake housing, to provide maximum possible fuel tankage and optimum aerodynamic form. Deliveries to Warsaw Pact air forces reported to have begun in 1971. Like the MiG-21PFMA and MiG-21MF, this version can carry K-13A "Atoll" infra-red missiles and/or "Advanced Atolls" which appear to be radar-homing.

"Fishbed-L". Generally similar to "Fishbed-J". Identifiable by absence of deflectors under suction relief doors.

MiG-21U ("Mongol"). Two-seat training versions. Initial version, sometimes referred to as "Mongol-A", is generally similar to the MiG-21F but has two cockpits in tandem with sideways-hinged (to starboard) double canopy, larger main wheels and tyres of MiG-21PF, one-piece forward airbrake, and pitot boom repositioned above intake. Cannon armament is deleted. Later models, sometimes called "Mongol-B", have the broader-chord vertical tail surfaces and under-rudder parachute-brake housing of the later operational variants, with a deeper dorsal spine and no dorsal fin fillet.

MiG-21US ("Mongol"). Similar to later MiG-21U but with provision for SPS flap-blowing, and retractable periscope for instructor in rear seat.

MiG-21UM ("Mongol"). Two-seat trainer counterpart of MiG-21MF with RD-13 turbojet and four underwing stores pylons.

Alternative designations, allocated by the Soviet authorities to MiG-21s used to set up FAI-recognised international records, are as follows:

E-33. This designation has been applied to training versions of the MiG-21 ("Mongol") used to establish women's records. Those confirmed by the FAI include an altitude of 79,842 ft (24,336 m) set up by Natalya Prokhanova on 22 May 1965, and a sustained altitude of 62,402 ft (19,020 m) in horizontal flight established by Lydia Zaitseva on 23 June 1965.

E-66. Aircraft of basic MiG-21F series, used by Col Georgi Mossolov to set up a world absolute speed record (since beaten) of 1,288·6 knots (1,484 mph; 2,388 km/h) over a 15/25 km course on 31 October 1959. Engine described as a 13,120 lb (5,950 kg) st Type TDR Mk R37F.

E-66A. Variant of E-66 used by Mossolov to raise the world height record to 113,892 ft (34,714 m) on 28 April 1961, from Podmoskovnœ aerodrome. Powered additionally by a 6,615 lb (3,000 kg) st GRD Mk U2 rocket engine in underbelly pack, exhausting between twin ventral fins. Other changes compared with then-standard operational model included a widened dorsal spine and repositioned blade antenna, as standardised for the MiG-21PF, and a blister fairing above the nose.

E-76. Designation allocated to apparently-standard MiG-21PFs used by Soviet women pilots to establish international records. Those confirmed by the FAI are for a speed of 1,112·7 knots (1,281·27 mph; 2,062 km/h) over a 500 km closed circuit by Marina Solovyeva on 16 September 1966; a speed of 485·78 knots (559·40 mph; 900·267 km/h) over a 2,000 km closed circuit by Yevgenia Martova on 11 October 1966; a speed of 1,148·7 knots (1,322·7 mph; 2,128·7 km/h) over a 100 km closed circuit by Miss Martova on 18 February 1967; and a speed of 700·5 knots (806·64 mph; 1,298·16 km/h) over a 1,000 km closed circuit by Lydia Zaitseva on 28 March 1967.

There is reason to believe that the similar designations E-74, E-77 and E-88 apply to versions of the export MiG-21F, MiG-21FL and MiG-21M respectively.

MiG-21s have been supplied to the Afghan, Algerian, Bangladesh, Bulgarian, Chinese, Cuban, Czech, Egyptian, Finnish, East German, Hungarian, Indian, Indonesian, Iraqi, North Korean, Polish, Romanian, Syrian, North Vietnamese and Yugoslav air forces. The Egyptian Air Force was believed to have 200 MiG-21s of the latest models in early 1974.

A version of the MiG-21 is in production in China under the Chinese designation F-8.

The following details refer to the MiG-21MF ("Fishbed-J"):

TYPE: Single-seat multi-role fighter.

WINGS: Cantilever mid-wing monoplane of clipped-delta planform, with slight anhedral from roots. Sweepback approximately 53°. Small pointed fairing on each side of fuselage forward of wing-root leading-edge. Small boundary-layer fence above each wing near tip. All-metal construction. Inset ailerons, actuated hydraulically. Large "blown" trailing-edge flaps.

FUSELAGE: Circular-section all-metal semi-monocoque structure. Ram air intake in nose, with three-position movable centrebody. Large dorsal spine fairing along top of fuselage from canopy to fin. Forward-hinged door-type airbrake on each side of underfuselage below wing leading-edge. A further forward-hinged airbrake under fuselage forward of ventral fin. Blister fairings above and below wing on each side to accommodate main wheels when retracted.

Version of MiG-21 known to NATO as "Fishbed-K"; wingtip ECM pods not fitted

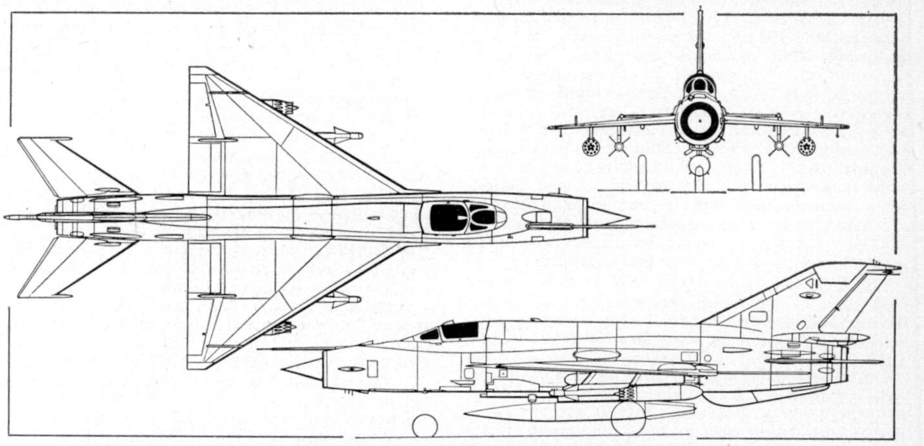

Mikoyan MiG-21MF ("Fishbed-J") single-seat multi-role fighter *(Pilot Press)*

TAIL UNIT: Cantilever all-metal structure, with all surfaces sharply swept. Conventional fin and hydraulically-powered rudder. Hydraulically-actuated one-piece all-moving horizontal surface, with two gearing ratios for use at varying combinations of altitude and airspeed. Tailplane trim switch on control column. No trim tabs. Single large ventral fin.

LANDING GEAR: Tricycle type, with single wheel on each unit; all units housed in fuselage when retracted. Forward-retracting non-steerable nosewheel unit; inward-retracting main wheels which turn to stow vertically inside fuselage. Tyres on main wheels inflated to approximately 115 lb/sq in (8 kg/cm²), ruling out normal operation from grass runways. Pneumatic braking on all three wheels, supplied from compressed-air bottles. Steering by differential main-wheel braking. Wheel doors remain open when legs are extended. Brake parachute housed inside acorn fairing at base of rudder.

POWER PLANT: One Tumansky RD-13-300 turbojet engine, rated at 11,240 lb (5,100 kg) st dry and 14,550 lb (6,600 kg) st with afterburning. Fuel tanks in fuselage, with total capacity of 572 Imp gallons (2,600 litres). Provision for carrying one finned external fuel tank, capacity 108 Imp gallons (490 litres), on under-fuselage pylon and two similar drop-tanks on outboard underwing pylons. Two jettisonable solid-propellant JATO rockets can be fitted under rear fuselage, aft of wheel doors.

ACCOMMODATION: Pilot only, on ejection seat with spring-loaded arm at top which ensures that seat cannot be operated unless hood is closed. Canopy is sideways-hinged, to starboard, and is surmounted by a small rearview mirror. Flat bullet-proof windscreen. Cabin air-conditioned. Armour plating forward and aft of cockpit.

SYSTEMS: Single hydraulic system, supplied by engine-driven pump, with backup by battery-powered electric pump, and emergency electric tailplane trim and manual operation of flying controls.

ELECTRONICS AND EQUIPMENT: Search and track radar in intake centrebody. Other standard avionics include VOR/ADF and warning radar with an indicator marked in 45° sectors in front of and behind the aircraft.

ARMAMENT: One twin-barrel 23 mm GSh-23 gun, with 200 rounds, in belly pack. Four underwing pylons for weapons or drop-tanks. Typical loads for interceptor role include two K-13A ("Atoll") air-to-air missiles on inner pylons and two radar-homing "Advanced Atolls" or two UV-16-57 rocket packs (each sixteen 57 mm rockets) on outer pylons; four K-13As/"Advanced Atolls"; or two drop-tanks and two K-13As or "Advanced Atolls". Typical loads for ground attack role are four UV-16-57 rocket packs; two 500 kg and two 250 kg bombs; or four S-24 240 mm air-to-surface missiles.

DIMENSIONS, EXTERNAL:
- Wing span: 23 ft 5½ in (7·15 m)
- Length, including pitot boom: 51 ft 8½ in (15·76 m)
- Length, excluding pitot boom and intake centrebody: 44 ft 2 in (13·46 m)
- Height overall: 14 ft 9 in (4·50 m)
- Wheel track: 8 ft 10 in (2·69 m)

AREA:
- Wings, gross: 247 sq ft (23 m²)

WEIGHTS:
- T-O weight:
  - with four K-13 missiles: 18,078 lb (8,200 kg)
  - with two K-13 missiles and two 110 Imp gallon drop-tanks: 19,730 lb (8,950 kg)
  - with two K-13s and three drop-tanks: 20,725 lb (9,400 kg)

PERFORMANCE:
- Max level speed above 36,000 ft (11,000 m): Mach 2·1 (1,203 knots; 1,385 mph; 2,230 km/h)
- Max level speed at low altitude: Mach 1·06 (701 knots; 807 mph; 1,300 km/h)
- Service ceiling: 59,050 ft (18,000 m)
- T-O run at normal AUW: 2,625 ft (800 m)
- Landing run: 1,805 ft (550 m)
- Range, internal fuel only: 593 nm (683 miles; 1,100 km)
- Ferry range, with three external tanks: 971 nm (1,118 miles; 1,800 km)

MIKOYAN MiG-23

NATO code name: "Flogger"

Since the prototype of this variable-geometry fighter was first displayed in public during the 1967 Aviation Day flypast at Domodedovo Airport, Moscow, the design has undergone considerable development. Initial deliveries to the Soviet Air Force are believed to have been made in 1971; but problems encountered subsequently prevented the type from becoming fully operational until early 1972. Since then large numbers of MiG-23s have been deployed, and two Soviet fighter regiments, equipped with a total of about 75 aircraft, are reported to be based in East Germany. Others are operated by the Syrian Air Force.

There appear to be three versions of which details can be published:

MiG-23 ("Flogger-A"). Original version, of which prototype was shown at Domodedovo on 9 July 1967. On that occasion, during a display by test pilot Alexander Fedotov, the wings were moved from fully-forward to fully-swept position in about four seconds. The commentator credited the aircraft with supersonic speed at ground level and Mach 2 at medium and high altitudes. Illustrated in 1973-74 *Jane's*.

MiG-23B ("Flogger-B"). Standard version in current operational service, as described and illustrated in three-view drawing. Design changes compared with prototype include movement further rearward of all tail surfaces except ventral fin, giving much increased gap between wing and tailplane; a considerable increase in the size of the dorsal fin; and the introduction of fixed inboard wing leading-edges.

MiG-23U ("Flogger-C"). Tandem two-seat version suitable for both operational training and combat use, as shown in photographs. Individual canopy over each seat. Rear seat slightly higher than forward seat, with retractable periscopic sight for occupant. Dorsal fairing of increased depth aft of rear canopy. Otherwise identical to MiG-23B. In service.

The following description refers specifically to the single-seat MiG-23B, but is generally applicable also to the two-seat MiG-23U:

TYPE: Single-seat variable-geometry tactical fighter.

WINGS: Cantilever shoulder wing. Sweepback of main panels variable in flight or on the ground from approximately 21° to approximately 71°. Fixed triangular inboard panels, with leading-edges swept at approximately 71°. Full-span trailing-edge single-slotted flaps, each in two sections, permitting independent actuation of outboard sections when wings are fully swept. Likely installation of top-surface spoilers/lift dumpers forward of flaps, for differential operation in conjunction with horizontal tail surfaces, and for collective operation for improved runway adherence and braking after touchdown. Leading-edge flap on outboard two-thirds of each main (variable-geometry) panel.

FUSELAGE: Conventional semi-monocoque structure of basic circular section; flattened on each side of cockpit, forward of lateral air intake trunks which blend into circular shape of rear fuselage. Large flat boundary layer splitter plate (similar to that of US F-4 Phantom II) forms inboard face of each intake. Two small rectangular "blow-in" air intakes in each trunk, under inboard wing leading-edge. Perforations under rear fuselage, aft of main wheel bays, are pressure-relief vents. Door-type airbrake mounted on each side of rear fuselage.

TAIL UNIT: All-moving horizontal surfaces, swept back at approximately 57°, operate both differentially and symmetrically to provide aileron and elevator function respectively. Conventional fin, swept back at approximately 65°, with large dorsal fin and inset rudder. No tabs. Large ventral fin in two portions. Lower portion is hinged to fold to starboard when landing gear is extended, to increase ground clearance.

LANDING GEAR: Retractable tricycle type, with single wheel on each main unit and steerable twin-wheel nose unit. Main units retract inward into rear of air intake trunks. Main fairings to enclose these units are attached to legs. Small inboard fairing for each wheelbay hinged to fuselage belly. Nose unit, fitted with small mudguard, retracts rearward. Brake parachute housed in cylindrical fairing at base of rudder.

POWER PLANT: One large afterburning turbojet engine of unknown type. Thrust has been estimated at 14,330 lb (6,500 kg) st dry and 20,500 lb (9,300 kg) st with afterburning. Provision for carrying external fuel tank on underfuselage centreline pylon.

ACCOMMODATION: Single seat in air-conditioned cockpit, under small sideways-hinged canopy.

ELECTRONICS AND EQUIPMENT: Radar dish behind dielectric nosecone. Small cylindrical fairings forward of starboard underwing pylon and above rudder are believed to contain ECM equipment. Dr Robert C. Seamans, then US Secretary of the Air Force, stated his belief in early 1973 that the radar and missile systems are comparable with those of the USAF's F-4 Phantom II. Retractable landing light under nose, aft of radome.

ARMAMENT: One 23 mm GSh-23 twin-barrel gun in fuselage belly pack, with large flash eliminator around nozzles. Two pylons under centre fuselage, and one under each fixed inboard wing panel, for external stores of unknown types.

DIMENSIONS (estimated):
- Wing span:
  - fully spread — 46 ft 9 in (14·25 m)
  - fully swept — 26 ft $9\frac{1}{2}$ in (8·17 m)
- Length overall — 55 ft $1\frac{1}{2}$ in (16·80 m)

WEIGHT (estimated):
- T-O weight — 28,000-33,050 lb (12,700-15,000 kg)

PERFORMANCE (estimated):
- Max level speed at height with external stores — Mach 2·3
- Max level speed at S/L — Mach 1·1
- Service ceiling — 59,000 ft (18,000 m)
- Combat radius — 520 nm (600 miles; 960 km)

MIKOYAN MiG-25 (E-266)

NATO code name: "Foxbat"

First news of the existence of this aircraft came in a Soviet claim, in April 1965, that a twin-engined aircraft designated E-266 had set up a

Two photographs of the tandem two-seat version of the MiG-23 (*Aviation Magazine International*)

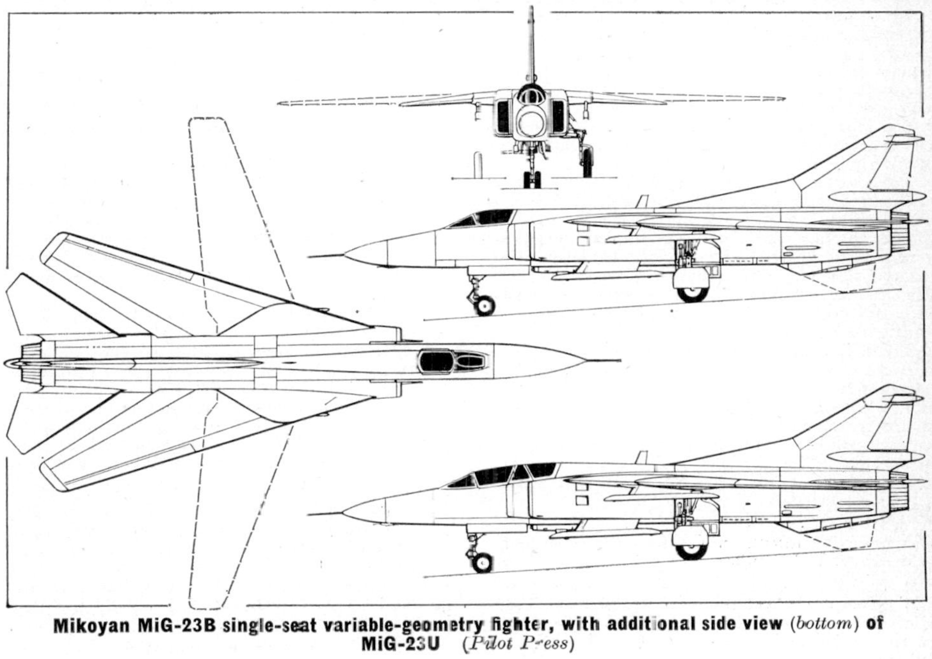

Mikoyan MiG-23B single-seat variable-geometry fighter, with additional side view (*bottom*) **of MiG-23U** (*Pilot Press*)

1,000 km closed-circuit speed record of 1,251·9 knots (1,441·5 mph; 2,320 km/h), carrying a 2,000 kg payload. The attempt was made at a height of 69,000-72,200 ft (21,000-22,000 m) by Alexander Fedotov, who had earlier set up a 100 km record in the E-166 (described in 1967-68 *Jane's*).

The same pilot set up a payload-to-height record of 98,349 ft (29,997 m) with a 2,000 kg payload in the E-266 on 5 October 1967, after a rocket-assisted take-off. This qualified also for the record with a 1,000 kg payload. Photographs of the E-266 issued officially in the Soviet Union identified it subsequently as the twin-finned Mikoyan single-seat fighter of which four examples took part in the Domodedovo display in July 1967 and which is now known to be designated MiG-25 in the Soviet Air Force.

Its performance in level flight was demonstrated further on 5 October 1967, when M. Komarov set up a speed record of 1,608·83 knots (1,852·61 mph; 2,981·5 km/h) over a 500 km closed circuit. On 27 October, P. Ostapenko set up a 1,000 km closed-circuit record of 1,576·00 knots (1,814·81 mph; 2,920·67 km/h) in an E-266, carrying a 2,000 kg payload and qualifying also for records with 1,000 kg payload and no payload.

On 8 April 1973, Fedotov achieved a speed of 1,405·741 knots (1,618·734 mph; 2,605·1 km/h) over a 100 km closed circuit, beating his own earlier record in the Mikoyan E-166 research aircraft. Next, on 25 July 1973, Fedotov set a new World absolute height record by climbing to 118,898 ft (36,240 m) in an E-266. On the same day, he climbed to 115,584 ft (35,230 m) with a 2,000 kg payload, qualifying also for the record with 1,000 kg.

The low aspect ratio square-tipped wings of the MiG-25 are mounted high on the fuselage, and have anhedral over the full span. There appears to be reduced anhedral on the outer wing panels. A sweepback of approximately 42° is constant from root to tip. Triangular end-plates have been seen fitted to the rear of the wingtip balance-weight fairings on some aircraft, presumably to improve stability. The fairings themselves are missing on aircraft shown in some photographs, but are thought to be standard on combat MiG-25s.

The twin tail fins were almost certainly adopted as being preferable to the single large and tall fin that would otherwise have been essential with such a wide-bodied supersonic design. The fins incline outward, as do the large ventral fins.

The basic fuselage is quite slim, but is blended into the two huge rectangular air intake trunks, which have wedge inlets of the kind used on the (North American) Rockwell A-5 Vigilante. The inner walls of the intakes are curved at the top and do not run parallel with the outer walls; hinged panels form the lower lip of each intake, enabling the intake area to be varied.

The landing gear is a retractable tricycle type, also similar to that of the Vigilante, with the main wheels retracting into the air intake trunks. The multiple doors which cover the main-wheel wells are clearly visible, immediately forward of the ventral fins, on the latest available photographs. The size of the main-wheel units is such that the forward doors in the air intake trunks, thought earlier to cover weapon bays, are in fact wheel doors. The bulge in the undersurface of each trunk implies the use of a single large-diameter wheel on each main leg.

The power plant of the MiG-25 consists of a pair of large afterburning turbojet engines (each rated at 24,250 lb; 11,000 kg st and attributed to the Tumansky design bureau), mounted side by side in the rear fuselage. To each side of the jet nozzles are low-set all-moving horizontal tail surfaces of characteristic MiG shape. Under the nozzles is a one-piece narrow-chord airbrake, which follows the curvature of the tailpipes. Some photographs suggest that there might also be a similar airbrake above the nozzles.

The only visible external weapon attachments are four underwing hardpoints, presumably for air-to-air guided weapons.

No pictures of the MiG-25 have yet been released showing it with external stores, and no weapons were visible on the aircraft in the fly-past at Domodedovo. The fact that the commentator referred to these as high-altitude all-weather interceptors suggested that one version of the MiG-25 was designed to intercept fast strike aircraft, possibly with "snap-down" missiles to deal with low-flying raiders.

There are known to be several operational versions, with reported NATO designations of **"Foxbat-A"** for the basic interceptor and **"Foxbat-B"** for the basic reconnaissance version, which carries cameras instead of the interceptor's AI radar in its nose, and has only a small dielectric nosecone.

The reconnaissance version of the MiG-25, known to NATO as "Foxbat-B". Note the camera-carrying nose and absence of wingtip fairings

Mikoyan MiG-25 twin-engined all-weather interceptor (NATO code name "Foxbat-A")

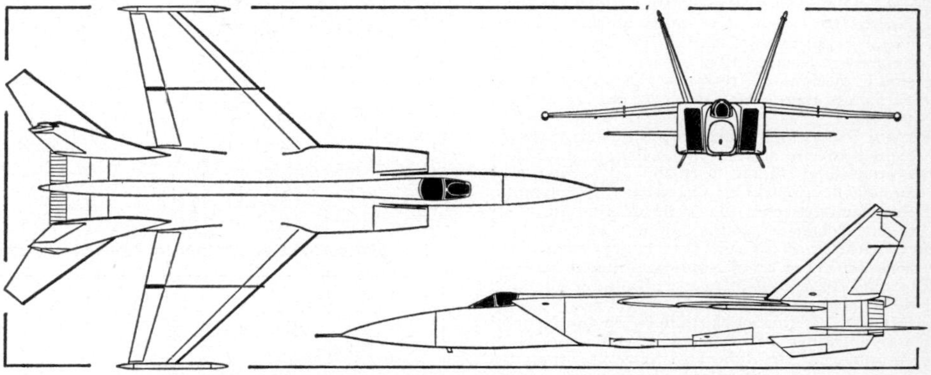

Mikoyan MiG-25 fighter (NATO code name "Foxbat-A") (*Roy J. Grainge*)

In early 1973 Dr Robert C. Seamans, US Secretary of the Air Force, described the MiG-25 as "probably the best interceptor in production in the world today", and added "This Mach 3 aircraft performs both interceptor and reconnaissance missions, can operate at 80,000 ft (24,400 m), and has a highly capable avionics and missile system".

MiG-25s were first reported to be operational with Soviet Air Force units in Egypt in the Spring of 1971, having been airlifted to that country in An-22 transports. Between the Autumn of 1971 and the Spring of 1972, MiG-25s from Cairo West airfield were despatched in pairs on at least four reported occasions to carry out high-speed reconnaissance missions off the Israeli coastline or down the full length of the Israeli-occupied Sinai Peninsula. Phantom interceptors sent up by the Israeli defence forces failed to make contact with the MiGs. Similar overflights of Iran have been made regularly, without hindrance.

DIMENSIONS (estimated):
- Wing span: 40 ft 0 in (12·20 m)
- Length overall: 69 ft 0 in (21·00 m)

WEIGHTS (estimated):
- Basic operating weight: 34,000 lb (15,425 kg)
- Max T-O weight: 64,200 lb (29,120 kg)

PERFORMANCE (estimated):
- Max level speed at height: Mach 3·2
- Service ceiling: 80,000 ft (24,400 m)
- Time to 36,000 ft (11,000 m) with afterburning: 2 min 30 sec
- Normal combat radius: 610 nm (700 miles; 1,130 km)

MIL

GENERAL DESIGNER IN CHARGE OF BUREAU:
Marat N. Tishchenko

M. L. Mil was connected with Soviet gyroplane and helicopter development from at least 1930. His achievements were recognised by the award of the Order of Lenin on his 60th birthday in November 1969. He died on 31 January 1970.

His original Mi-1, which was designed in 1949, first flown in 1950 and introduced into squadron service in 1951, was the first helicopter to enter series production in the Soviet Union. It was followed by the developed Mi-3 and by the Mi-4 in a number of variants. These types are still in service, in civil and military forms.

The Mi-1 was also produced in Poland, under the designation SM-1.

Subsequent products of Mikhail Mil include the Mi-6, a very large passenger and freight helicopter, the Mi-10 (V-10) and Mi-10K crane versions of the Mi-6, the smaller turbine-powered Mi-2 (V-2) and Mi-8 (V-8) passenger helicopters, the Mi-12 (V-12), which is the largest helicopter currently flying anywhere in the world, and the Mi-24 military assault helicopter. Aviaexport has sold helicopters of Mil design in 38 countries.

MIL Mi-2 (V-2)

Built exclusively in Poland and described under Polish aircraft industry entry.

MIL Mi-6

NATO code name: "Hook"

First announced in the Autumn of 1957, the Mi-6 was then the largest helicopter flying anywhere in the world. From it were evolved the Mi-10 and Mi-10K flying crane helicopters, and its dynamic components are used in duplicated form on the V-12 (Mi-12).

Layout of the Mi-6 is conventional. Clamshell rear loading doors and folding ramps facilitate the loading of bulky freight and vehicles. Freight can also be carried externally, suspended from a hook on the CG. When the aircraft is operated in this flying crane role, the small wings which normally offload the rotor in flight can be removed, permitting an increase in payload.

The stub-wings are deleted also from the fire-fighting version. First demonstrated at the 1967 Paris Air Show, this carries several tons of water in tanks inside its cabin and can either spray this slowly from nozzles or dump it through the hoist cutout in its belly.

In setting up 14 FAI-recognised records in Class E-1, the Mi-6 has lifted payloads of up to 44,350 lb (20,117 kg). Records still standing in mid-1974 included a 100 km closed-circuit speed record of 183·54 knots (211·36 mph; 340·15 km/h), set up by Boris Galitsky on 26 August 1964.

On 15 September 1962 the same pilot, and crew, in an Mi-6 flew at 162·08 knots (186·64 mph; 300·377 km/h) over a 1,000 km circuit, setting up records for speed with no payload, payload of 1,000 kg and payload of 2,000 kg. By averaging 170·33 knots (196·1 mph; 315·657 km/h) on the second 500 km circuit Galitsky also qualified for a no-payload record over this distance.

On 11 September 1962 Vasily Kolochenko and crew of four averaged 153·44 knots (176·69 mph; 284·354 km/h) over a 1,000 km closed circuit, setting a record for speed with a payload of 5,000 kg.

Five Mi-6s are reported to have been built for development testing, followed by an initial pre-series of 30 and subsequent manufacture of some 500 for military and civil use. Rate of production was reported to be eight per month in 1970. Six were supplied to the Indonesian Air Force; many others have been delivered to the Bulgarian, Egyptian, Iraqi and North Vietnamese air forces.

Six were demonstrated in a tactical missile transport role at Tushino in 1961. They landed in two groups of three, after which one helicopter in each group unloaded two field artillery missiles while the others delivered support equipment.

In February 1963, it was announced that an Mi-6 had been adapted to transport the component parts of an oil rig, which was assembled near the town of Zhyrnovsk in the Transvolga steppe-land. Other Mi-6s have since been used in this flying crane role to air-lift drilling rigs to the oilfields of the Tumen region in Siberia, for transporting heavy equipment to construction camps, and for carrying firefighting equipment and men to deal with forest fires.

Type: Heavy transport helicopter.

Rotor System: Five-blade main rotor and four-blade tail rotor. Main rotor blades each have a tapered steel tube spar, to which are bonded built-up metal aerofoil sections. Blades have coincident flapping and drag hinges and fixed tabs. Main rotor shaft inclined forward at 5° to vertical. Control via large welded swashplate. Hydraulically-actuated powered controls. All rotor blades incorporate electro-thermal de-icing system.

Fuselage: Conventional all-metal riveted semi-monocoque structure of pod-and-boom type.

Wings: Two small cantilever shoulder wings, mounted above main landing gear struts, off-load rotor by providing some 20% of total lift in cruising flight. Removed when aircraft is operated as flying crane.

Tail Unit: Tail rotor support acts as vertical stabiliser. Variable-incidence horizontal stabiliser, near end of tailboom, for trim purposes.

Landing Gear: Non-retractable tricycle type, with steerable twin-wheel nose unit and single wheel on each main unit. Twin-chamber oleo-pneumatic (high-pressure and low-pressure) main landing gear shock-struts. High-pressure chambers interconnected through overflow system incorporating spring damper, to damp out oscillations at full landing gear loading and so eliminate ground resonance. Main wheels size 1,325 × 480 mm. Nosewheels size 720-310. Brakes on main wheels. Small tail-bumper under end of tailboom.

Power Plant: Two 5,500 shp Soloviev D-25V (TV-2BM) turboshaft engines, mounted side by side above cabin, forward of main rotor shaft. Eleven internal fuel tanks, with total capacity of 13,922 lb (6,315 kg), and two external tanks, on each side of cabin, with total capacity of 7,695 lb (3,490 kg). Provision for two additional ferry tanks inside cabin, with total capacity of 7,695 lb (3,490 kg). Automatic fuel-flow control system with manual override. Side panels of engine cowlings are opened and closed hydraulically and are used as platforms for inspection and maintenance of engines and rotor head.

Accommodation: Crew of five, consisting of two pilots, navigator, flight engineer and radio operator. Four jettisonable doors on flight deck. Equipped normally for cargo operation, with tip-up seats along side walls. When these seats are supplemented by additional seats installed in centre of cabin, 65 passengers can be carried, with cargo or baggage in the aisles. As an air ambulance, 41 stretcher cases and two medical attendants on tip-up seats can be carried. One of attendant's stations is provided with intercom to flight deck, and provision is made for portable oxygen installations for the patients. Cabin floor is stressed for loadings of 410 lb/sq ft (2,000 kg/m^2), with provision for cargo tie-down rings. Rear clamshell doors and ramps are operated hydraulically. Standard equipment includes an electric winch of 1,765 lb (800 kg) capacity and pulley block system. External cargo sling system for bulky loads. Central hatch in cargo floor. Two passengers doors, fore and aft of main landing gear on port side.

Electronics and Equipment: Standard equipment includes VHF and HF communications radio, intercom, radio altimeter, radio compass, autopilot, marker beacon, directional gyro and full all-weather instrumentation.

Systems: Main, standby and auxiliary hydraulic systems, each with separate pump mounted on main gearbox. Operating pressure 1,705-2,205 lb/sq in (120-155 kg/cm^2). Main 27V DC electrical system, supplied by two 12kW starter/generators, with batteries for 30 min emergency supply. De-icing system and some radio equipment supplied by three-phase 360V 400Hz AC system, utilising two 90kVA generators. Trolley-mounted APU, consisting of 100 hp AI-8 gas-turbine and 24kW generator, carried on board.

Armament: A few Mi-6s are fitted with a gun of unknown calibre in the fuselage nose.

Dimensions, external:

Diameter of main rotor	114 ft 10 in (35·00 m)
Diameter of tail rotor	20 ft 8 in (6·30 m)
Distance between rotor centres	69 ft 2½ in (21·09 m)
Length overall, rotors turning	136 ft 11½ in (41·74 m)
Length of fuselage	108 ft 10½ in (33·18 m)
Height overall	32 ft 4 in (9·86 m)
Wing span	50 ft 2½ in (15·30 m)
Span of horizontal stabiliser	16 ft 6½ in (5·04 m)
Wheel track	24 ft 7¼ in (7·50 m)
Wheelbase	29 ft 10½ in (9·10 m)
Rear loading doors: Height	8 ft 10¼ in (2·70 m)
Width	8 ft 8¼ in (2·65 m)
Passenger doors:	
Height: front	5 ft 7¼ in (1·71 m)
rear	5 ft 3¾ in (1·62 m)
Width	2 ft 7¾ in (0·81 m)
Sill height: front	4 ft 7¼ in (1·40 m)
rear	4 ft 3¼ in (1·30 m)
Central hatch in floor:	4 ft 9 in (1·44 m) × 6 ft 4 in (1·93 m)

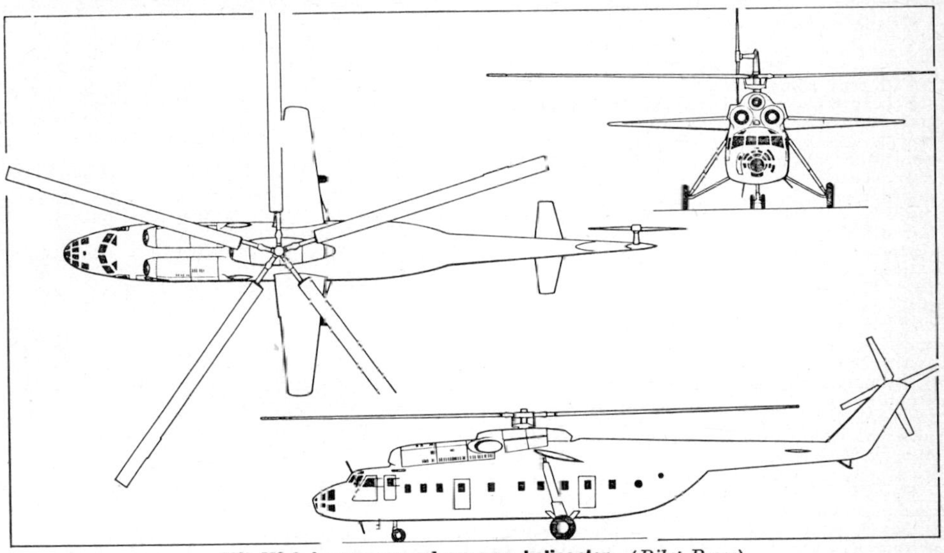

Mil Mi-6 heavy general-purpose helicopter (*Pilot Press*)

Mil Mi-6 heavy general-purpose helicopter (two 5,500 shp Soloviev D-25V turboshaft engines)

Mil Mi-8 (V-8) passenger helicopter (two 1,500 shp Isotov TV2-117A turboshaft engines)

DIMENSIONS, INTERNAL:
Cabin: Length 39 ft 4½ in (12·00 m)
Max width 8 ft 8¼ in (2·65 m)
Max height: at front 6 ft 7 in (2·01 m)
at rear 8 ft 2½ in (2·50 m)
Cabin volume 2,825 cu ft (80 m³)

WEIGHTS:
Weight empty 60,055 lb (27,240 kg)
Max internal payload 26,450 lb (12,000 kg)
Max slung cargo 19,840 lb (9,000 kg)
Max T-O weight with slung cargo at altitudes under 3,280 ft (1,000 m) 82,675 lb (37,500 kg)
Normal T-O weight 89,285 lb (40,500 kg)
Max T-O weight for VTO 93,700 lb (42,500 kg)

PERFORMANCE (at max T-O weight):
Max level speed 162 knots (186 mph; 300 km/h)
Max cruising speed 135 knots (155 mph; 250 km/h)
Service ceiling 14,750 ft (4,500 m)
Range with 13,228 lb (6,000 kg) payload 350 nm (404 miles; 650 km)
Range with external tanks and 9,480 lb (4,300 kg) payload 566 nm (652 miles; 1,050 km)
Max ferry range (tanks in cabin) 781 nm (900 miles; 1,450 km)

MIL Mi-8 (V-8)

NATO code name: "Hip"

This turbine-powered transport helicopter was shown in public for the first time during the 1961 Soviet Aviation Day display. Its overall dimensions are similar to those of the Mi-4, which it superseded; but the power plant is mounted above the cabin, leaving a clear unobstructed interior, and the Mi-8 (often referred to in the Soviet Union as the V-8) is able to carry a greatly increased payload.

More than 1,000 Mi-8s had been built by mid-1974, mainly for military use, and about 300 of these had been exported.

The Mi-8 serves with the Soviet armed forces, appearing in military insignia for the first time at the Domodedovo air show in July 1967 and now being equipped to carry external stores to support assault landings by airborne troops. Mi-8s have been supplied to the Bangladesh, Bulgarian, Czechoslovakian, Egyptian, Ethiopian, Finnish, East German, Hungarian, Indian, Iraqi, Pakistani, Sudanese and Syrian armed forces.

The Mi-8 is also in service with Aeroflot for transport and air ambulance duties, and is operated by this airline in support of Soviet activities in the Antarctic. Standard Mi-8s are used there for ice patrol and reconnaissance, for rescue operations, and for carrying supplies and equipment to Vostok Station, near the South Pole.

Five international women's helicopter records for distance and speed in a closed circuit were credited to the Mi-8 in mid-1974.

The original prototype had a single 2,700 shp Soloviev turboshaft engine, The second prototype, which flew for the first time on 17 September 1962, introduced the now-standard Isotov twin-turbine power plant.

Early Mi-8s had a four-blade main rotor, but this was superseded by a five-blade rotor in 1964. In an emergency, the blades and intermediate and tail gearboxes are interchangeable with those of the Mi-4, although this prevents use of the de-icing system.

The controls of the Mi-8 are hydraulically-powered in the cyclic and collective pitch channels. It is claimed that the autopilot, with barometric height lock, can control all flight modes, including transition.

There are three versions, as follows:

Mi-8. Passenger version, with standard seating for 28 persons in main cabin.

Mi-8T. General utility version, equipped normally to carry internal or external freight, but able to accommodate 24 passenger seats.

Mi-8 Salon. de luxe version. Main cabin is furnished for eleven passengers, with an eight-place couch facing inward on the port side, and two chairs and a swivelling seat on the starboard side. There is a table on each side. An air-to-ground radio telephone and removable ventilation fans are standard equipment. Forward of the main cabin is a compartment for a hostess, with buffet and crew wardrobe. Aft of the main cabin are a toilet (port) and passenger wardrobe (starboard), to each side of the entrance. The Mi-8 Salon has a max T-O weight of 22,928 lb (10,400 kg) and range of 205 nm (236 miles; 380 km) with 30 min fuel reserve. In other respects it is similar to the standard Mi-8.

Troops disembarking from a hovering Mil Mi-8 military helicopter. This differs from the commercial version in having circular cabin windows and twin weapon-carriers on outriggers

A float-equipped version was reported to be under test in early 1974, under the designation V-14.

TYPE: Twin-engined transport helicopter.

ROTOR SYSTEM: Five-blade main rotor and three-blade tail rotor. Transmission comprises a type VR-8 main gearbox giving main rotor shaft/engine rpm ratio of 0·016 : 1, intermediate and tail gearboxes, main rotor brake and drives off the main gearbox for the tail rotor, fan, AC generator, hydraulic pumps and tachometer generators. Main rotor shaft inclined forward at 4° 30′ to vertical. All-metal main rotor blades of basic NACA 230 section; solidity 0·0777. Each main blade is made up of an extruded light alloy spar carrying the blade root fitting, 21 trailing-edge pockets and the blade tip. Pockets are honeycomb-filled. Main rotor blades are fitted with balance tabs, and are interchangeable. Their drag and flapping hinges are a few inches apart, and they are carried on a machined spider. Controls hydraulically-powered. All-metal tail rotor blades, each made up of a spar and honeycomb-filled trailing-edge. Automatically-controlled electro-thermal de-icing system on all blades.

FUSELAGE: Conventional all-metal semi-monocoque structure of pod-and-boom type.

TAIL UNIT: Tail rotor support acts as small vertical stabiliser. Horizontal stabiliser near end of tailboom.

LANDING GEAR: Non-retractable tricycle type, with steerable twin-wheel nose unit and single wheel on each main unit. All units embody oleo-pneumatic (gas) shock-absorbers. Main-wheel tyres size 865 × 280; nosewheel tyres size 595 × 185. Pneumatic brakes on main wheels. Pneumatic system can also recharge tyres in the field, using air stored in main landing gear struts. Optional main-wheel fairings.

POWER PLANT: Two 1,500 shp Isotov TV2-117A turboshaft engines. Main rotor speed governed automatically, with manual override. Single flexible internal fuel tank, capacity 98 Imp gallons (445 litres), and two external tanks, on each side of cabin, with capacity of 164 Imp gallons (745 litres) in the port tank and 149·5 Imp gallons (680 litres) in the starboard tank. Total standard fuel capacity 411·5 Imp gallons (1,870 litres). Provision for carrying one or two additional ferry tanks in cabin, raising max total capacity to 814 Imp gallons (3,700 litres).

Fairing over starboard external tank houses optional cabin air-conditioning equipment at front. Engine cowling side panels form maintenance platforms when open, with access via hatch on flight deck. Engine air intake de-icing standard. Total oil capacity 132 lb (60 kg).

ACCOMMODATION: Two pilots side by side on flight deck, with provision for a flight engineer's station. Windscreen de-icing standard. Basic passenger version is furnished with 28 four-abreast track-mounted tip-up seats at a pitch of 28·3-29·5 in (72-75 cm), with a centre aisle 12·6 in (32 cm) wide, a wardrobe and baggage compartment; or 32 seats without wardrobe. Seats and bulkheads of basic version are quickly removable for cargo-carrying. Mi-8T has cargo tie-down rings in floor, a winch of 440 lb (200 kg) capacity and pulley block system to facilitate the loading of heavy freight, an external cargo sling system, and 24 tip-up seats along the side walls of the cabin. All versions can be converted for air ambulance duties, with accommodation for 12 stretchers and a tip-up seat for a medical attendant. The large windows on each side of the flight deck slide rearward. The sliding, jettisonable main passenger door is at the front of the cabin on the port side. An electrically-operated rescue hoist can be installed at this doorway. The rear of the cabin is made up of large clamshell freight-loading doors, with a downward-hinged passenger airstair door inset centrally at the rear. Hook-on ramps are used for vehicle loading.

SYSTEMS: Standard heating system can be replaced by full air-conditioning system. Two independent hydraulic systems, each with own pump; operating pressure 640-925 lb/sq in (45-65 kg/cm²). DC electrical supply from two 27V 18kW starter/generators and six 28Ah storage batteries. AC supply for de-icing system and some radio equipment supplied by 208/115/36/7·5V 400Hz generator, with 36V three-phase standby system. Provision for oxygen system for crew and, in ambulance version, for patients. Freon fire-extinguishing system in power plant bays and service fuel tank compartments, actuated automatically or manually. Two portable fire extinguishers for use in cabin.

ELECTRONICS AND EQUIPMENT: Standard equipment includes a type R-842 HF transceiver with frequency range of 2 to 8 Mc/s and range of up to 540 nm (620 miles; 1,000 km), type R-860 VHF transceiver operating on 118 to 135·9 Mc/s over ranges of up to 54 nm (62 miles; 100 km), intercom, radio telephone, type ARK-9 automatic radio compass, type RV-3 radio altimeter with "dangerous height" warning, and four-axis autopilot to give yaw, roll and pitch stabilisation under any flight conditions, stabilisation of altitude in level flight or hover, and stabilisation of pre-set flying speed, navigation equipment and instrumentation for all-weather flying by day and night, including two gyro horizons, two airspeed indicators, two main rotor speed indicators, turn indicator, two altimeters, two rate of climb indicators, magnetic compass, radio altimeter, radio compass and astro-compass for Polar flying.

ARMAMENT: Military versions can be equipped with a twin rack for external stores, including large rocket packs, on an outrigger structure on each side of the main cabin. Up to eight external stores can be carried in this way.

DIMENSIONS, EXTERNAL:
Diameter of main rotor 69 ft 10¼ in (21·29 m)
Diameter of tail rotor 12 ft 9½ in (3·90 m)
Distance between rotor centres 41 ft 6 in (12·65 m)
Length overall, rotors turning 82 ft 9¾ in (25·24 m)
Length of fuselage 60 ft 0¾ in (18·31 m)
Height overall 18 ft 6½ in (5·65 m)
Wheel track 14 ft 9 in (4·50 m)
Wheelbase 13 ft 11¾ in (4·26 m)
Fwd passenger door:
Height 4 ft 7¼ in (1·41 m)
Width 2 ft 8¼ in (0·82 m)
Rear passenger door:
Height 5 ft 7 in (1·70 m)
Width 2 ft 9 in (0·84 m)
Rear cargo door:
Height 5 ft 11¾ in (1·82 m)
Width 7 ft 8¼ in (2·34 m)

DIMENSIONS, INTERNAL:
Passenger cabin:
Length 20 ft 7¾ in (6·30 m)
Width 7 ft 8¼ in (2·34 m)
Height 5 ft 11¾ in (1·82 m)
Cargo hold (freighter):
Length at floor 17 ft 6¼ in (5·34 m)
Width 7 ft 8¼ in (2·34 m)
Height 5 ft 11¾ in (1·82 m)
Volume approx 812 cu ft (23 m³)

AREA:
Main rotor disc 3,828 sq ft (355 m²)

WEIGHTS:
Weight empty:
Passenger version 16,007 lb (7,261 kg)
Cargo version 15,026 lb (6,816 kg)
Max payload:
internal 8,820 lb (4,000 kg)
external 6,614 lb (3,000 kg)
Normal T-O weight 24,470 lb (11,100 kg)
T-O weight with 28 passengers, each with 33 lb (15 kg) of baggage 25,508 lb (11,570 kg)
T-O weight with 5,510 lb (2,500 kg) of slung cargo 25,195 lb (11,428 kg)
Max T-O weight for VTO 26,455 lb (12,000 kg)

PERFORMANCE:
Max level speed at 3,280 ft (1,000 m):
Normal AUW 140 knots (161 mph; 260 km/h)
Max level speed at S/L:
Normal AUW 135 knots (155 mph; 250 km/h)
Max AUW 119 knots (137 mph; 220 km/h)
With 5,510 lb (2,500 kg) of slung cargo 97 knots (112 mph; 180 km/h)
Max cruising speed:
Normal AUW 122 knots (140 mph; 225 km/h)
Max AUW 97 knots (112 mph; 180 km/h)
Service ceiling 14,760 ft (4,500 m)
Hovering ceiling in ground effect at normal AUW 6,233 ft (1,900 m)
Hovering ceiling out of ground effect at normal AUW 2,625 ft (800 m)
Ranges:
Cargo version at 3,280 ft (1,000 m), with standard fuel, 5% reserves:
Normal AUW 259 nm (298 miles; 480 km)
Max AUW 248 nm (285 miles; 460 km)
Passenger version at 3,280 ft (1,000 m), with 20 min fuel reserves 229 nm (264 miles; 425 km)
Ferry range of cargo version, with auxiliary fuel, 5% reserves 647 nm (745 miles; 1,200 km)

MIL Mi-10 (V-10)

NATO code name: "Harke"

This flying crane development of the Mi-6 was demonstrated at the 1961 Soviet Aviation Day display at Tushino, having flown for the first time in the previous year. Above the line of the cabin windows the two helicopters are almost identical, but the depth of the fuselage is reduced considerably on the Mi-10, and the tailboom is deepened so that the flattened undersurface runs unbroken to the tail. The Mi-10 also lacks the small fixed wings of the Mi-6.

Items which are interchangeable between the Mi-6 and Mi-10 include the power plant, transmission system and reduction gearboxes, swashplate assembly, main and tail rotors, control system and most items of equipment.

The tall long-stroke quadricycle landing gear, with wheel track exceeding 19 ft 8 in (6·0 m) and clearance under the fuselage of 12 ft 3½ in (3·75 m) with the aircraft fully loaded, enables the Mi-10 to taxi over a load it is to carry and to accommodate loads as bulky as a prefabricated building.

Use can be made of interchangeable wheeled cargo platforms which are held in place by hydraulic grips controllable from either the cockpit or a remote panel. Using these grips without a platform, cargoes up to 65 ft 7 in (20 m) long, 32 ft 9½ in (10 m) wide and 10 ft 2 in (3·1 m) high can be lifted and secured in 1½ to 2 minutes. The cabin can accommodate additional freight or passengers.

A closed-circuit TV system, with cameras scanning forward from under the rear fuselage and downward through the sling hatch, is used to observe the payload and main landing gear, touchdown being by this reference. The TV system replaces the retractable undernose "dustbin" fitted originally.

The power of the Soloviev turboshaft engines remains constant up to 9,850 ft (3,000 m) and to an ambient air temperature of 40°C at sea level. The aircraft will maintain level flight on one engine. Full navigation equipment and an autopilot permit all-weather operation, by day and night.

The following details refer to the standard Mi-10, which is reported to be in service with both Aeroflot and the Soviet armed forces and is also available for export. One was purchased by Petroleum Helicopters (USA) for servicing oil rigs.

Tasks performed by the Mi-10 have included the transport of complete wing assemblies for Tu-144 supersonic airliners from the factory at Voronezh, where they are built, to the assembly works near Moscow.

TYPE: Heavy flying-crane helicopter.

ROTOR SYSTEM: Same as for Mi-6, except that main rotor shaft is inclined forward at an angle of only 45′.

FUSELAGE: Conventional all-metal riveted semi-monocoque structure.

TAIL UNIT: Same as for Mi-6.

LANDING GEAR: Non-retractable quadricycle type, with twin wheels on each unit. All units fitted with oleo-pneumatic shock-absorbers. Telescopic main legs. Main wheels size 1,230 × 260 mm, each with brake. Levered-suspension castoring nose units. Nosewheels size 950 × 250. All landing gear struts are faired. The port nose gear fairing incorporates steps to the crew entry door. Despite the height of the gear, the Mi-10 can make stable landing and take-off runs at speeds up to 54 knots (62 mph; 100 km/h).

POWER PLANT: Two 5,500 shp Soloviev D-25V turboshaft engines, mounted side by side above cabin, forward of main rotor drive-shaft. Single fuel tank in fuselage and two external tanks, on sides of cabin, with total capacity of 13,975 lb (6,340 kg). Provision for carrying two auxiliary tanks in cabin, to give total fuel capacity of 18,210 lb (8,260 kg). Engine cowling side panels (opened and closed hydraulically) can be used as maintenance platforms when open.

ACCOMMODATION: Two pilots and flight engineer accommodated on flight deck, which has bulged side windows to provide an improved downward view. Flight deck is heated and ventilated and has provision for oxygen equipment. Crew door is immediately aft of flight deck on port side. Main cabin can be used for freight and/or passengers, 28 tip-up seats being installed along the side walls. Freight is loaded into this cabin through a door on the starboard side, aft of the rear landing gear struts, with the aid of a boom and 440 lb (200 kg) capacity electric winch. In addition to the cargo platform described above, the Mi-10 has external sling gear as standard equipment. This can be used in conjunction with a winch controlled from a portable control panel inside the cabin. The winch can also be used to raise loads of up to 1,100 lb (500 kg) while the aircraft is hovering on rescue and other duties, via a hatch in the cabin floor.

ELECTRONICS, EQUIPMENT AND SYSTEMS: Generally as for Mi-6, including APU.

DIMENSIONS, EXTERNAL:
Diameter of main rotor 114 ft 10 in (35·00 m)
Diameter of tail rotor 20 ft 8 in (6·30 m)
Distance between rotor centres 69 ft 8 in (21·24 m)
Length overall, rotors turning 137 ft 5½ in (41·89 m)
Length of fuselage 107 ft 9¾ in (32·86 m)

Mil Mi-10 flying crane helicopter, with load platform, in Soviet military service
(photocopied from Rezules)

Ground clearance under fuselage
12 ft 3½ in (3·75 m)
Height overall 32 ft 2 in (9·80 m)
Wheel track (c/l shock-struts):
nosewheels 19 ft 8¾ in (6·01 m)
main wheels 22 ft 8½ in (6·92 m)
Wheelbase 27 ft 2½ in (8·29 m)
Cargo platform:
Length 28 ft 0 in (8·53 m)
Width 11 ft 7¼ in (3·54 m)
Crew door:
Height 4 ft 5¼ in (1·35 m)
Width 2 ft 6¾ in (0·78 m)
Height of sill 12 ft 10¼ in (3·91 m)
Freight loading door:
Height 5 ft 1½ in (1·56 m)
Width 4 ft 1½ in (1·26 m)
Height of sill 12 ft 10½ in (3·92 m)
Cabin floor hatch:
Diameter 3 ft 3½ in (1·00 m)
DIMENSIONS, INTERNAL:
Cabin: Length 46 ft 0¾ in (14·04 m)
Width 8 ft 2½ in (2·50 m)
Height 5 ft 6 in (1·68 m)
Volume approx 2,120 cu ft (60 m³)
WEIGHTS:
Weight empty 60,185 lb (27,300 kg)
Max payload on platform, incl platform
33,070 lb (15,000 kg)
Max slung payload 17,635 lb (8,000 kg)
T-O weight with slung cargo 83,775 lb (38,000 kg)
Max T-O weight 96,340 lb (43,700 kg)
PERFORMANCE:
Max level speed at max T-O weight
108 knots (124 mph; 200 km/h)
Cruising speed at max T-O weight
97 knots (112 mph; 180 km/h)
Service ceiling (limited) 9,850 ft (3,000 m)
Range with platform payload of 26,455 lb (12,000 kg) 135 nm (155 miles; 250 km)

MIL Mi-10K

First displayed publicly in Moscow on 26 March 1966, the Mi-10K is a development of the Mi-10 with a number of important design changes, most apparent of which is a reduction in the height of the landing gear.

It can be operated by a crew of only two pilots. This is made possible by the provision of an additional cockpit gondola under the front fuselage, with full flying controls and a rearward-facing seat. By occupying this seat, one of the pilots can control the aircraft in hovering flight and, at the same time, have an unrestricted view of cargo loading, unloading and hoisting, which are also under his control.

In the Mi-10K, the maximum slung payload is 24,250 lb (11,000 kg) and is expected to be increased further to 30,865 lb (14,000 kg) by using Soloviev D-25VF turboshaft engines, uprated to 6,500 shp each, in due course. Fuel capacity of the Mi-10K, in standard internal and external tanks, is 1,980 Imp gallons (9,000 litres). The rotor turns at 120 rpm.

On 26 May 1965 an Mi-10K, piloted by V. Kolochenko, set up an official record in Class E-1 by lifting a payload of 5,000 kg to a height of 23,461 ft (7,151 m). Two days later, G. Alferov, with a crew of three, climbed to a height of 9,318 ft (2,840 m) in an Mi-10K, with a payload of 55,347 lb (25,105 kg). This set up four records for the greatest payload lifted to 2,000 m and the greatest height achieved with payloads of 15,000, 20,000 and 25,000 kg (all but the second of these have since been beaten by the Mi-12). The aircraft used may have been the cleaned-up experimental machine, with faired tricycle landing gear, that was illustrated in the 1966-67 *Jane's*.

DIMENSIONS, EXTERNAL:
Generally as for Mi-10, except:
Height overall 25 ft 7 in (7·80 m)
Wheel track 16 ft 4¾ in (5·00 m)
Wheelbase 28 ft 8 in (8·74 m)

Mil Mi-10K lifting a seven-ton assembly to the top of an 820 ft (250 m) chimney of a power station at Volgorechensk in Kostroma Oblast (*Tass*)

Door sill heights:
Crew door 5 ft 11 in (1·81 m)
Freight door 5 ft 11½ in (1·82 m)
WEIGHTS:
Weight empty 54,410 lb (24,680 kg)
Max payload, slung cargo 24,250 lb (11,000 kg)
Max fuel load with ferry tanks in cabin
19,114 lb (8,670 kg)
Max T-O weight with slung cargo
83,776 lb (38,000 kg)
PERFORMANCE:
Cruising speed, empty
135 knots (155 mph; 250 km/h)
Max cruising speed with slung load
109 knots (125 mph; 202 km/h)
Service ceiling 9,850 ft (3,000 m)
Ferry range with auxiliary fuel
428 nm (494 miles; 795 km)

MIL V-12 (Mi-12)
NATO code name: "Homer"

First confirmation of the existence of this aircraft was given in a statement in March 1969 that it had set a number of payload-to-height records which exceeded by some 20 per cent the records established previously by the Mi-6 and Mi-10K.

Flying from the airfield at Podmoskovnœ on 22 February 1969, the V-12 climbed at a rate of more than 600 ft (180 m)/min to an altitude of 9,682 ft (2,951 m) carrying a payload of 68,410 lb (31,030 kg). This represented new records for maximum load lifted to a height of 2,000 m, and for height attained with payloads of 20,000, 25,000 and 30,000 kg. The pilot was Vasily Kolochenko who, on 6 August 1969, far exceeded his own record for payload raised to 2,000 m by lifting 88,636 lb (40,204·5 kg) to a height of 7,398 ft (2,255 m) in the V-12, which carried a full crew of six. This flight also qualified for new payload-to-height records with 35,000 kg and 40,000 kg.

Work on the V-12 had started in 1965, the basic requirement being for a VTOL aircraft that could accommodate missiles and other payloads compatible with those carried by the An-22 fixed-wing transport. The original specification called for a tandem-rotor configuration, using existing dynamic components. Instead, the Mil design bureau obtained approval for a side-by-side rotor layout, claimed to offer better stability, reliability and fatigue life. Thus, the V-12 utilises two power plant/rotor packages similar to those of the Mi-6/Mi-10 series, mounted at the tips of its fixed wings.

The D-25VF engines are uprated by comparison with the D-25Vs fitted to the earlier helicopters, by the addition of a zero stage on the compressor and by acceptance of higher operating temperatures.

The prototype V-12 is reported to have crashed in 1969, largely as a result of engine failure, without fatalities. Two prototypes were flying in mid-1971, and production of several hundred V-12s was expected to begin before the end of the year. They are likely to embody a number of modifications. In particular the fixed wings will probably have increased camber in place of the present trailing-edge flaps, which have been fixed (or possibly ground-adjustable) since their original function to improve autorotation performance was proved unnecessary.

In addition to its military applications, the V-12 will be operated by Aeroflot, notably for supporting oil and natural gas production and for hauling geophysical survey equipment, vehicles and heavy freight in remote regions of the Soviet Union. It is claimed to be easy to fly by average pilots with experience of handling other types of helicopter and to have an extremely low vibration level, particularly on the flight deck. No special ground equipment is needed for servicing.

TYPE: Heavy general-purpose helicopter.

ROTOR SYSTEM: Two five-blade opposite-rotating rotors, mounted side by side at the tips of fixed wings. Port rotor turns in clockwise direction, starboard rotor anti-clockwise, viewed from below. All-metal blades, similar to those of Mi-6/Mi-10, with trailing-edge tabs. Rotors are cross-shafted to ensure synchronisation and to maintain rotation following the

Mil V-12 (Mi-12) heavy general-purpose helicopter (four 6,500 shp Soloviev D-25VF turboshaft engines) (*Soviet News*)

failure of engines on either side. Rotor rpm 112.

Wings: High-mounted strut-braced wings, with considerable dihedral and inverse taper to give increasing chord from root to tip. All-metal construction. Long-span two-section fixed or ground-adjustable (originally three-position) trailing-edge flaps on each wing.

Fuselage: Conventional all-metal semi-monocoque structure, with clamshell rear loading doors and ramp. Two side-by-side "bumpers" under ramp.

Tail Unit: Cantilever all-metal structure comprising central main fin and rudder, small dorsal fin, tailplane, elevator and endplate auxiliary fins. Tailplane has considerable dihedral. Auxiliary fins are toed inward at leading-edges. Tabs in rudder and elevators.

Landing Gear: Non-retractable tricycle type, with twin wheels on each unit. Steerable nosewheels. Main wheel tyres size 1,750 × 730; nosewheel tyres size 1,200 × 450.

Power Plant: Four 6,500 shp Soloviev D-25VF turboshaft engines, mounted in side-by-side pairs under tips of fixed wings. Each pair is coupled to drive one rotor, with cross-shafting. Lower part of cowling under each pair of engines can be lowered about 6 ft (1·8 m) by hand-crank to form working platform for up to three men and to provide access for servicing of power plant and rotor head. Cowling side panels hinge downward for same purpose. Cylindrical external fuel tank mounted on each side of main cabin.

Accommodation: Main flight deck in nose has side-by-side seats for pilot (port) and co-pilot in front. Flight engineer's station behind pilot; electrician seated behind co-pilot. Upper cockpit seats navigator and radio operator in tandem. Windscreen panels forward of pilot, co-pilot and navigator fitted with wipers. Rubber-bladed fans for cooling crew accommodation. Unobstructed main cargo hold has rails in roof for electrically-operated platform-mounted travelling crane with four loading points each capable of lifting 5,500 lb (2,500 kg) and max capacity of 22,000 lb (10,000 kg) for a single item. About 50 upward-folding seats along side walls for work crews or troops accompanying freight loads. Primary access to hold between rear clamshell doors which hinge outward and upward, via downward-hinged ramp. Rearward-sliding door forward of fuel tank on port side. Emergency exit door on each side at rear of hold. Downward-hinged emergency exits on starboard side of main flight deck and upper cockpit.

Systems and Equipment: Electrical system has 480kW capacity. Ground mapping radar in undernose blister fairing. Fail-safe powered control system and automatic stabilisation system standard, but aircraft can be landed manually. Ivchenko AI-8V APU for independent engine starting.

Dimensions, external:

Diameter of main rotors (each)	114 ft 10 in (35·00 m)
Span over rotor tips	219 ft 10 in (67·00 m)
Length of fuselage	121 ft 4½ in (37·00 m)
Height overall	41 ft 0 in (12·50 m)

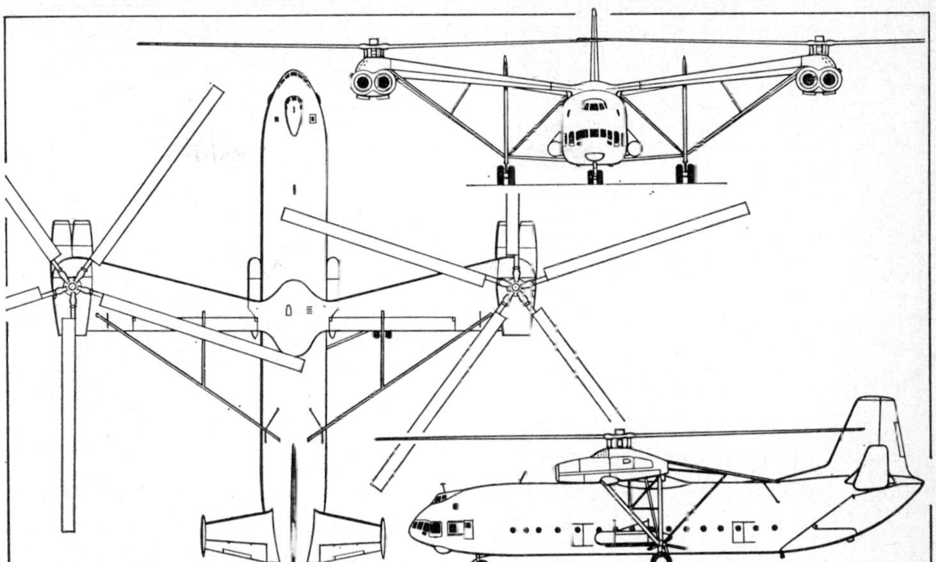

Mil V-12 four-engined heavy-duty freight-carrying helicopter (*Pilot Press*)

Dimensions, internal:

Freight compartment:	
Length	92 ft 4 in (28·15 m)
Max width	14 ft 5 in (4·40 m)
Max height	14 ft 5 in (4·40 m)

Weights:

Normal payload:	
VTOL	55,000 lb (25,000 kg)
STOL	66,000 lb (30,000 kg)
Normal T-O weight	213,850 lb (97,000 kg)
Max T-O weight	231,500 lb (105,000 kg)

Performance:

Max level speed	140 knots (161 mph; 260 km/h)
Max cruising speed	130 knots (150 mph; 240 km/h)
Service ceiling	11,500 ft (3,500 m)
Range with 78,000 lb (35,400 kg) payload	270 nm (310 miles; 500 km)

MIL V-14

A float-equipped version of the Mi-8 was reported to be under test in the Soviet Union in early 1974, with the designation V-14. No details are available.

MIL Mi-24

NATO code name: "Hind"

This assault helicopter was known to exist for some two years before photographs became available to the technical press in early 1974. Two versions were shown in these photographs and are identified by the following NATO code names:

"Hind-A". The auxiliary wings of this version have considerable anhedral and each carry three weapon stations. The two inboard stations on each side are used normally as attachments for large rocket pods. The wingtip stations take the form of deep rectangular pylons, each carrying two missile rails for air-to-surface adaptations of a standard Soviet anti-tank weapon. A machine-gun, probably of 12·7 mm calibre, is flexibly mounted beneath a flat panel of bulletproof glass in the nose.

"Hind-B". Generally similar to "Hind-A", except that the auxiliary wings have no anhedral or dihedral, and carry only the two inboard weapon stations on each side. This suggests that, paradoxically, "Hind-B" may have preceded "Hind-A" in development and is not a major production variant.

The general appearance of the Mi-24 is shown in the accompanying illustrations. It is of conventional all-metal pod-and-boom design, with the comparatively low profile associated with gunship helicopters. In addition to the crew, on side-by-side seats, it is estimated that eight or ten assault troops can be accommodated in the main cabin. Access to the flight deck is via a large rearward-sliding blistered transparent panel which forms the aft flight deck window on the port side. At the front of the passenger cabin on each side is a large door, divided horizontally into two sections which are hinged to open upward and downward respectively.

The tapered auxiliary wings are set at an incidence of about 20°. There is a variable-incidence horizontal stabiliser at the base of the sweptback fin, which is offset a few degrees to port and serves also as a pylon to carry the tail anti-torque rotor. The tricycle landing gear is retractable, and comprises a twin-wheel nose unit and single-wheel main units. The latter retract rearward and inward into the aft end of the fuselage pod, turning through 90°

The two versions of the Mil Mi-24 military assault helicopter known by the NATO code names of "Hind-A" (*left*) **and "Hind-B"** (*Aviation Magazine International*)

to stow almost vertically, discwise to the longitudinal axis of the fuselage, under prominent blister fairings. A tubular tripod skid assembly protects the tail rotor in a tail-down take-off or landing.

It was suggested initially that the Mi-24 utilises the power plant and rotor system of the Mi-8; but only the three-blade tail rotor appears to be common to the two designs. Using its assumed diameter to scale other dimensions of the Mi-24, it becomes clear that both the turboshaft engines and the five-blade main rotor are smaller in size than their counterparts on the Mi-8, although the main rotor blades have a comparatively wide chord. The engines are mounted conventionally, side by side above the cabin, with their output shafts driving rearward to the main rotor shaft through a combining gearbox.

The Mi-24 is operational, with two units of approximate squadron strength reportedly based in East Germany in the early months of 1974.

Dimensions, external (estimated):

Diameter of main rotor	55 ft 9 in (17·00 m)
Diameter of tail rotor	12 ft 9½ in (3·90 m)
Length overall	55 ft 9 in (17·00 m)
Height overall	14 ft 0 in (4·25 m)

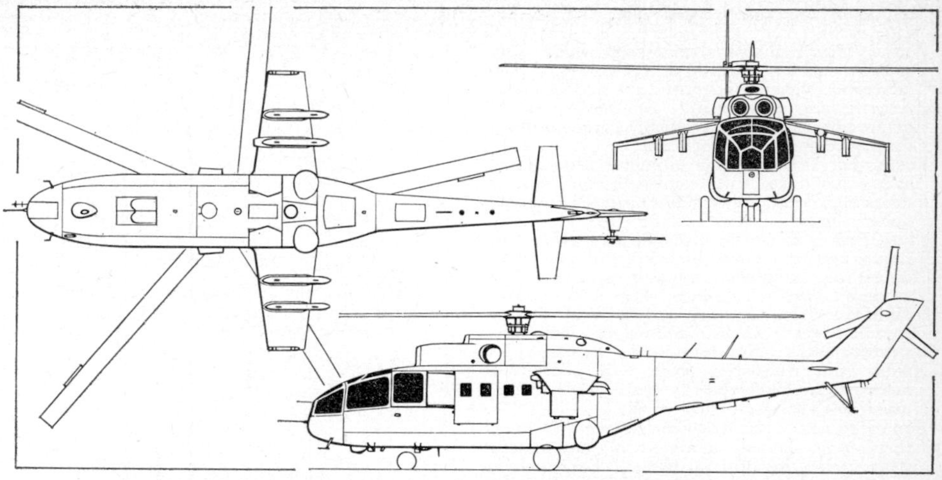

Mil Mi-24 assault helicopter, in the form known to NATO as "Hind-A" (*Pilot Press*)

MYASISHCHEV

General Designer in Charge of Bureau:
Vladimir M. Myasishchev

Although Myasishchev's work has been little publicised, he is believed to have been responsible for the development of several important types. They include the four-jet Mya-4 bomber (known in the West by the code name of "Bison") which remains in service for maritime reconnaissance and as a flight refuelling tanker.

The aircraft referred to by the Soviet authorities as the 201-M when it set up a number of officially-recognised records, in 1959, was identified subsequently as a variant of the Mya-4 and was described briefly and illustrated in the 1972-73 *Jane's*.

Myasishchev was reported to have designed a long-range four-jet heavy bomber to replace the Mya-4. This aircraft is believed to have been the delta-wing type which was allocated the NATO code name of "Bounder" and was described in the 1964-65 *Jane's*. Changing requirements limited "Bounder" to a research role.

MYASISHCHEV Mya-4
NATO code name: "Bison"

Three major production versions of this four-jet aircraft have been identified by NATO code names, as follows:

"Bison-A". The Soviet Union's first operational four-jet strategic bomber displayed initially over Moscow in May 1954. Comparable with early versions of Boeing B-52 Stratofortress. Powered by four 19,180 lb (8,700 kg) st Mikulin AM-3D turbojets, buried in wing-roots. Max T-O weight 350,000 lb (158,750 kg). Range reported to be 6,075 nm (7,000 miles; 11,250 km) at 450 knots (520 mph; 835 km/h) with 10,000 lb (4,500 kg) of nuclear or conventional free-fall bombs. Heavy defensive armament of ten 23 mm cannon in twin-gun turrets in tail, above fuselage fore and aft of wing and under fuselage fore and aft of bomb-bays, believed necessary because of aircraft's operational ceiling of only 45,000 ft (13,700 m). No longer in first-line service as a bomber but adapted for use as a flight refuelling tanker, carrying a hose-reel unit in its bomb bay.

"Bison-B". Maritime reconnaissance version identified in service in 1964. "Solid" nose radome in place of hemispherical glazed nose of "Bison-A", with large superimposed flight refuelling probe. Numerous underfuselage blister fairings for specialised electronic equipment. Forward portion of centre bomb bay doors bulged. Aft gun turrets above and below fuselage deleted, reducing armament to six 23 mm cannon.

The version of the Mya-4 known to NATO as "Bison-C" (*US Navy*)

"Bison-C". Generally similar configuration to "Bison-B" but with large search radar faired neatly into new and longer nose, aft of centrally-mounted flight refuelling probe. Prone bombing/observation station, with optically-flat glass panels, below and to rear of radar; further small windows and a domed observation (and probably gunnery aiming) window on each side; underfuselage blister fairings, bulged bomb bay and armament; all as "Bison-B". An example of this version with the experimental aircraft designation 201-M was used to set up a number of official records in 1959 and was exhibited statically in the Soviet Aviation Day display at Domodedovo Airport, Moscow, in 1967. Powered by four 28,660 lb (13,000 kg) st Type D-15 turbojet engines, this testbed aircraft established seven payload-to-height records, including a weight of 121,480 lb (55,220 kg) lifted to 2,000 m (6,560 ft) and height of 50,253 ft (15,317 m) with a 10,000 kg payload.

Dimensions, external ("Bison-A", estimated):

Wing span	165 ft 7½ in (50·48 m)
Length overall	154 ft 10 in (47·20 m)
Tailplane span	49 ft 2½ in (15·00 m)

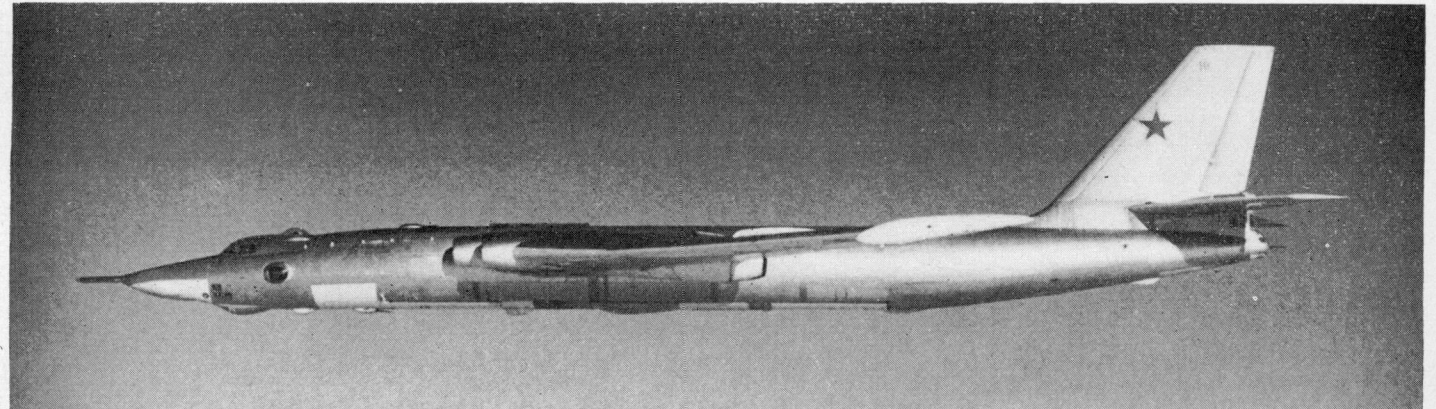

This photograph of the "Bison-C" version of the Mya-4 shows clearly its modified nose (*Royal Air Force*)

PERFORMANCE ("Bison-B", estimated):
Max level speed at 36,000 ft (11,000 m)
485 knots (560 mph; 900 km/h)

Myasishchev Mya-4 maritime reconnaissance aircraft in the form known to NATO as "Bison-B" (*Royal Air Force*)

SUKHOI

GENERAL DESIGNER IN CHARGE OF BUREAU:
Pavel Osipovich Sukhoi

Sukhoi helped to design the ANT-25 and had a share in the construction of the "Rodina" before the second World War, and his Su-2 attack aeroplane was used in the war. He was also responsible for one of the jet aircraft in the 1947 Soviet Aviation Day display.

Nearly a decade later, on 24 June 1956, there appeared over Tushino new swept-wing and delta-wing fighters from Sukhoi's design team. Both aircraft subsequently entered squadron service with the Soviet Air Force and are described briefly below, together with later Sukhoi designs.

SUKHOI Su-7B
NATO code names: "Fitter-A" and "Moujik"

The Su-7B single-seat ground attack fighter (NATO code name **"Fitter-A"**) was first seen in prototype form during the 1956 Soviet Aviation Day Display at Tushino and appeared in formations of up to 21 aircraft at the 1961 Tushino display. It subsequently became the standard tactical fighter-bomber of the Soviet Air Force and has been supplied to other countries, including Cuba, Czechoslovakia, Egypt, East Germany, Hungary, India, Poland, Syria and North Veitnam.

The fuselage and tail unit of the Su-7B are almost identical with those of the delta-wing Su-11. Its wings are swept back at an angle of approximately 60° and each is fitted with two boundary-layer fences, at approximately mid-span and immediately inboard of the tip. The wing-root chord is extended, giving a straight trailing-edge on the inboard section of each wing. Very large area-increasing flaps are fitted, extending over the entire trailing-edge of each wing from the root to the inboard end of the aileron.

The Su-7B has attachments for external stores, including rocket packs and bombs (usually two 750 kg and two 500 kg), under each wing. It can carry a pair of external fuel tanks under its centre fuselage, but these reduce the max external weapon load to 2,200 lb (1,000 kg). A 30 mm NR-30 cannon, with 70 rounds of ammunition, is installed in each wing-root leading-edge.

The power plant of the standard Su-7B is a Lyulka AL-7F turbojet engine (referred to by the designation TRD31 in the Soviet Union), rated at 15,432 lb (7,000 kg) st dry or 22,046 lb (10,000 kg) st with afterburning. Total internal fuel capacity is 7,000 lb (3,175 kg). Capacity of the twin external tanks totals 2,100 lb (952 kg).

Two JATO solid-propellant rockets can be fitted under the rear fuselage of late production Su-7Bs to shorten the aircraft's take-off run.

Early production models had the pitot boom mounted centrally above the air intake, but it is offset to starboard on current versions. Another change was made in the brake-chute installation. Early aircraft had a single ribbon-type parachute, attached under the rear fuselage. Later Su-7Bs have a large fairing, housing twin brake-chutes, at the base of their rudder. The size of the blast panels on the sides of the front fuselage by the wing-root guns was also increased, implying that the cannon now fitted have a higher muzzle velocity or rate of fire.

Among other changes that led to use of the revised designation Su-7BM (for *Modifikatsirovanny:* modified) was the introduction of a low-pressure nosewheel tyre, requiring blistered doors to enclose it when retracted.

A variant of the Su-7 seen for the first time at Domodedovo in 1967 is a two-seater, with the second cockpit in tandem, aft of the standard cockpit and with a slightly raised canopy. A prominent dorsal "spine" extends from the rear of the aft canopy to the base of the tail fin. The two-seater is a standard operational trainer in the Soviet Air Force and has the NATO code name **"Moujik"**.

DIMENSIONS, EXTERNAL:

Wing span	29 ft 3½ in (8·93 m)
Length, including probe	57 ft 0 in (17·37 m)
Height overall	15 ft 0 in (4·57 m)

WEIGHTS:

Weight empty	19,000 lb (8,620 kg)
Normal T-O weight	26,450 lb (12,000 kg)
Max T-O weight	29,750 lb (13,500 kg)

Sukhoi Su-7BM close-support fighter of the Soviet Air Force (*Tass*)

Tandem two-seat training versions of the Sukhoi Su-7, known to NATO by the code name "Moujik" (*Tass*)

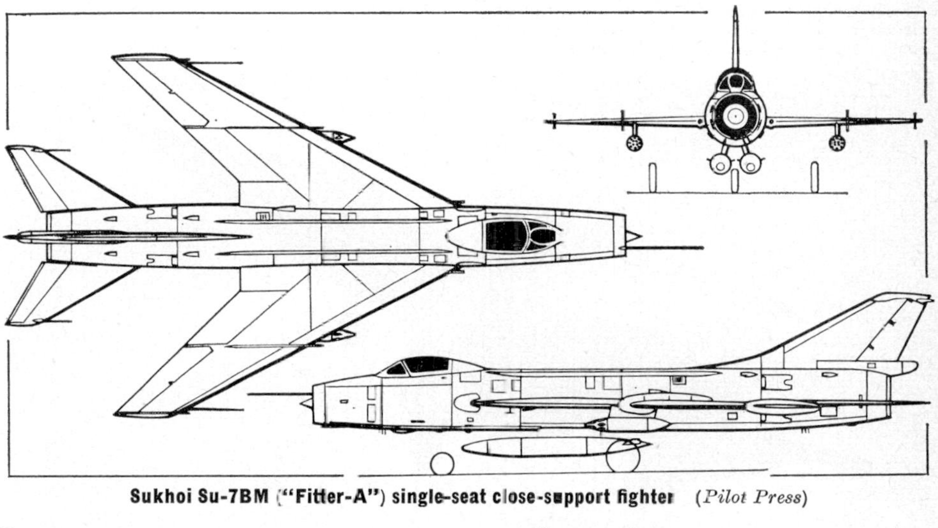

Sukhoi Su-7BM ("Fitter-A") single-seat close-support fighter (*Pilot Press*)

PERFORMANCE:
Max level speed at 36,000 ft (11,000 m):
clean Mach 1·6 (917 knots; 1,055 mph; 1,700 km/h)
with external stores
Mach 1·2 (685 knots; 788 mph; 1,270 km/h)
Max level speed at S/L without afterburning
approx 460 knots (530 mph; 850 km/h)

Max rate of climb at S/L
approx 29,900 ft (9,120 m)/min
Service ceiling 49,700 ft (15,150 m)
Combat radius
172-260 nm (200-300 miles; 320-480 km)
Max range 780 nm (900 miles; 1,450 km)

SUKHOI Su-9 and Su-11

NATO code names: "Fishpot" and "Maiden"

First seen at Tushino during the 1956 Aviation Day display, the prototype of this single-seat all-weather fighter (allocated the NATO code name **"Fishpot-A"**) had a small conical radome above its engine air intake. This was replaced by a centrebody air intake on the production version, which entered standard service in the Soviet Air Force in two forms, as follows:

Su-9 ("Fishpot-B"). Initial version, operational since 1959 and still in service in considerable numbers. Identified by small-diameter air intake and centrebody. Examples included in the Tushino display of 1961 carried four of the Soviet Air Force's then-standard radar-homing air-to-air missiles (NATO code-name "Alkali") on underwing attachments, plus two underfuselage fuel tanks side by side. No fixed armament.

Su-11 ("Fishpot-C"). First seen publicly at the Domodedovo Aviation Day display in 1967, the Su-11 is a much-improved development of the Su-9, with a standard armament of two underwing "Anab" missiles, one with radar homing head and one with infra-red homing head. It also has a lengthened nose of less-tapered form than that of the Su-9, with an enlarged centrebody, and two slim duct fairings along the top of the centre-fuselage, as on the Su-7B. The fuselage and tail unit of the two types are, in fact, almost identical.

There is also a tandem two-seat training version (NATO code name: **"Maiden"**), with a cockpit layout similar to that of the two-seat Su-7 ("Moujik").

Although the Su-9 and Su-11 are generally similar in layout to their Mikoyan contemporary, the MiG-21, they are larger and heavier aircraft, with a much more powerful afterburning turbojet. They are less limited in all-weather capability than early versions of the MiG-21. The Sukhoi and Mikoyan "tailed deltas" were, therefore, regarded as complementary rather than competitive when ordered into production in the late 'fifties. In 1974, the Su-9 and Su-11 continued to form 25 per cent of the Soviet defence interceptor force.

The Su-9 and Su-11 can be distinguished from the MiG-21 by their cleaner airframe, and the absence of both a ventral stabilising fin and fairings on the fuselage forward of the wing-root leading-edges. Their pitot boom is mounted above the nose air intake. The cockpit canopy of the standard single-seat versions is rearward-sliding, whereas that of the MiG-21 is hinged to open either forward about the base of the windscreen or sideways.

The tricycle landing gear of the Su-9 and Su-11 has a wide track, with a single wheel on each unit. The main units retract inward into the wings, the nosewheel forward. Control surfaces appear to be conventional, with a one-piece all-moving tailplane, carrying the balance-weight projection at each tip that is found on many Soviet combat aircraft. There are four petal-type airbrakes, in pairs on each side of the rear fuselage.

As the E-66/E-166 family of aircraft were developments of the MiG-21, it seems logical to assume that their rival in Soviet record attempts, the T-431, should have belonged to the Su-9/Su-11 series. It was stated to have a 19,840 lb (9,000 kg) st turbojet when it set up a height record in 1959, and a 22,046 lb (10,000 kg) st TRD31 turbojet when it set up a sustained altitude record in 1962. The TRD31 is now known to be the Lyulka AL-7F, the standard power plant of the Su-9 and Su-11. The different ratings may therefore be applicable to the two production types, accounting for the larger air intake of the Su-11.

Sukhoi Su-9 all-weather fighter, with four underwing mountings for "Alkali" missiles (*Tass*)

Sukhoi Su-11 single-seat fighter, armed with two of the missiles code named "Anab" (*Novosti*)

The only photograph yet made available of the tandem two-seat training version of the Su-9 (NATO "Maiden")

DIMENSIONS, EXTERNAL (Su-11, estimated):
Wing span 26 ft 0 in (7·90 m)
Length, including probe 56 ft 0 in (17·0 m)

PERFORMANCE (Su-11, estimated):
Max level speed at 36,000 ft (11,000 m)
Mach 1·8 (1,033 knots; 1,190 mph; 1,915 km/h)

Sukhoi Su-15 ("Flagon-A") single-seat tactical fighter (two turbojet engines with afterburners) (*Tass*)

SUKHOI Su-15

NATO code name: "Flagon"

Ten examples of this single-seat twin-jet delta-wing fighter participated in the flying display at Domodedovo in July 1967. First to appear was a single black-painted machine, piloted by Vladimir Ilyushin, son of the famous designer and known to be a test pilot for Sukhoi. When a formation of nine similar aircraft appeared later, the identity of the design bureau responsible for them was confirmed by the obvious "family likeness" to the Su-9 and Su-11 in the shape of the wings and tail unit.

It seems possible that this aircraft was developed to meet a Soviet Air Force requirement for a Mach 2·5 interceptor to replace the Su-11. It was believed originally to be designated Su-11, but is now identified as the Su-15 and is in service with the Soviet Air Force in several forms:

"Flagon-A". Described in detail below. Has simple delta wings, identical in form to those of the Su-11.

"Flagon-B". This STOL version appeared at Domodedovo in 1967, with three lift-jet engines mounted vertically in the centre-fuselage and wings of compound sweep similar to, but different in detail from, those of the "Flagon D/E" combat aircraft. This version is unlikely to be more than an R and D prototype; it was described briefly in the 1970-71 *Jane's*.

"Flagon-C". Two-seat training version.

"Flagon-D" and **"Flagon-E".** Generally similar to "Flagon-A", but with wings of compound sweep, produced by reducing the sweepback at the tips without increasing the span.

Official US statements in the Autumn of 1971 suggested that some 400 Su-15s were in service by that time, with production continuing at the rate of 15 aircraft per month. About ten were sent to Egypt for air defence duties in the Cairo area before the October 1973 war with Israel.

TYPE: Single-seat twin-jet all-weather interceptor.

WINGS: Cantilever mid-wing monoplane, basically similar to those of Su-11. Sweepback approx 53°. No dihedral. All-metal structure. Single boundary-layer fence above each wing at approx 70% span. Large area-increasing flap extends from inboard end of aileron to fuselage on each side.

FUSELAGE: Cockpit section is basically circular with large ogival dielectric nosecone. Centre fuselage is faired into rectangular-section air intake ducts. Two door-type airbrakes on each side of rear fuselage, forward of tailplane.

The Sukhoi Su-15 fighter in its STOL version, NATO code name "Flagon-B"

Tail Unit: Cantilever all-metal structure, with sweepback on all surfaces. All-moving tailplane, with anhedral, mounted slightly below mid position. Conventional rudder. No trim tabs.

Landing Gear: Tricycle type, with single wheel on each unit. Main wheels retract inward into wings and intake ducts; nosewheel retracts forward.

Power Plant: Two afterburning turbojets, with variable-area nozzles, mounted side by side in rear fuselage. Ram-type air intakes, with splitter plates; blow-in auxiliary inlets midway between main intake and wing leading-edge in each duct.

Accommodation: Single seat in enclosed cockpit, with blister canopy.

Armament: Single pylon for external store under each wing, in line with boundary-layer fence. Normal armament comprises one radar-homing and one infra-red homing "Anab" air-to-air missile. Side-by-side pylons under centre-fuselage for further weapons or external fuel tanks.

Dimensions, external (estimated):
Wing span 30 ft 0 in (9·15 m)
Length overall 68 ft 0 in (20·5 m)

Weight (estimated):
Max T-O weight 35,275 lb (16,000 kg)

Performance (estimated):
Max level speed above 36,000 ft (11,000 m):
with external stores Mach 2·3
clean Mach 2·5
Combat radius 390 nm (450 miles; 725 km)

SUKHOI Su-17 (?)

NATO code name: "Fitter-B"

First of two variable-geometry fighter aircraft demonstrated at Domodedovo in July 1967 was an adaptation of the Su-7. Described by the commentator as the Soviet Union's first variable-geometry design, it was externally identical with the standard Su-7 except for the movable outer wing panels and associated fences, outboard of the main landing gear.

It was thought originally that this variable-geometry Su-7 was no more than an economically-produced aerodynamic testbed aircraft, built to gain experience with the new technique. However, this comparatively simple adaptation of a standard fighter offers improved take-off performance and range, both of which are of vital importance in a tactical combat type, and it was announced in the USA in 1972 that at least one or two squadrons of these aircraft had been identified as operational with the Soviet Air Force. They were allocated the NATO code name "Fitter-B", and the type is now thought to be deployed in large numbers, under the reported Soviet designation of Su-17.

The movable part of each wing is about 13 ft (4·0 m) long and is fitted with a full-span leading-edge slat. Its entire trailing-edge is also hinged, forming wide-chord slotted ailerons and flaps. The large main fence on each side is square-cut at the front and incorporates attachments for external stores. There appear to be two shorter and shallower fences inboard of the main fence on each side, on the sweptback portion of the centre-section trailing-edge which aligns with the trailing-edge of the outer panel when it is fully swept. The standard flap is retained on the inner portion of the centre-section on each side.

Dimensions, external (estimated):
Wing span: spread 41 ft 0 in (12·50 m)
swept 29 ft 6 in (9·00 m)
Length overall, including probe 56 ft 0 in (17·00 m)

Weight and Speed:
Similar to Su-7B

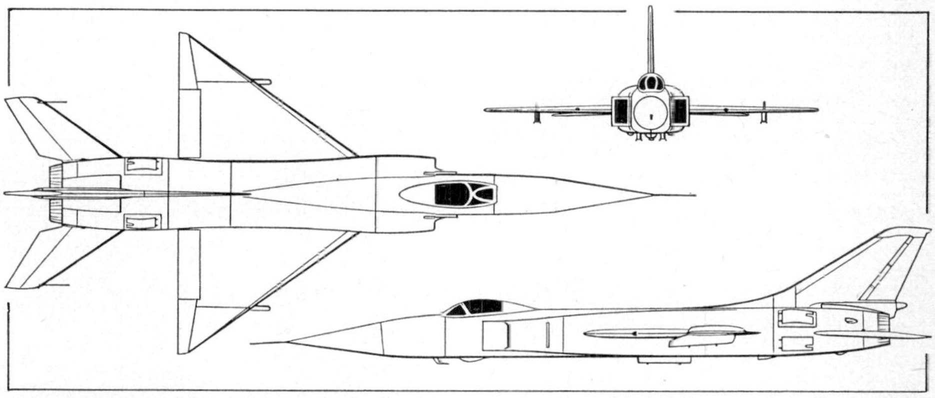

Sukhoi Su-15 single-seat twin-jet all-weather fighter, known to NATO as "Flagon-A" *(Pilot Press)*

Prototype Sukhoi "Fitter-B" variable-geometry fighter-bomber based on the Su-7B airframe *(Tass)*

SUKHOI Su-20

Identified as an improved version of "Fitter-B" with improved ground attack capability. A variable-geometry "Fitter" shown in an accompanying three-view drawing and in a photograph released through *Tass* in 1974 is believed to represent an intermediate stage between the Su-17 and Su-20, with additional weapon stations

Experimental version of "Fitter-B", believed to have preceded the production Su-20 *(Tass)*

under the fixed wing centre-section on each side, a dorsal spine fairing between the cockpit canopy and the fin, and other changes. The dorsal fairing is thought to contain additional fuel tankage to improve further the originally-poor endurance of the Su-7 series, particularly with afterburning in use. It has a much greater cross-sectional area than the spinal duct on the two-seat version of the Su-7 ("Moujik").

Operated also by Polish Air Force.

SUKHOI Su-?

NATO code name: "Fencer"

Little is known about this new variable-geometry attack aircraft. It has been described by Admiral Thomas H. Moorer, Chairman of the US Joint Chiefs of Staff, as "the first modern Soviet fighter to be developed specifically as a fighter-bomber for the ground attack mission". Of likely Sukhoi origin, it is expected to be in the same class as the USAF's F-111.

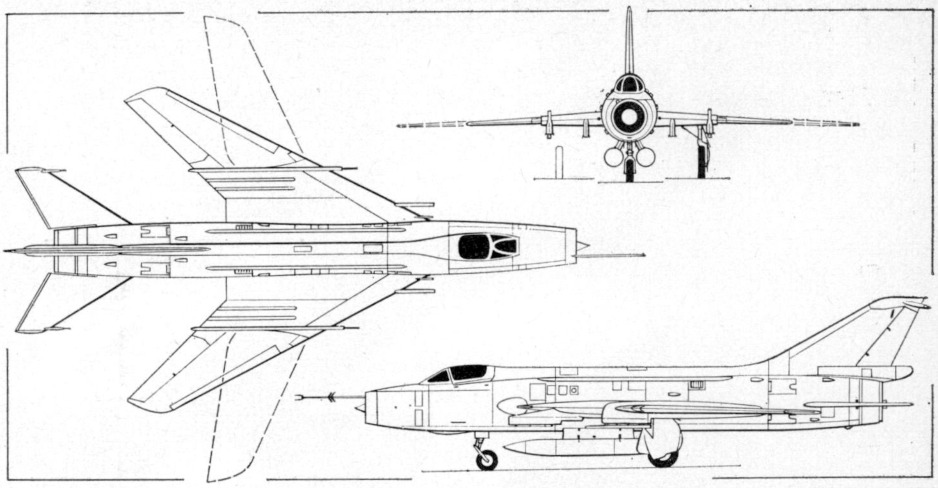

Sukhoi variable-geometry combat aircraft, known to NATO as "Fitter-B". Development aircraft for production Su-20 (*Pilot Press*)

TUPOLEV

CHIEF DESIGNER (Tu-144):
Dr Alexei A. Tupolev

CHIEF DESIGNER (Tu-154):
Dmitry Markov

DEPUTY CHIEF OF BUREAU:
Andrei Kandolov

Andrei Tupolev, born in 1888, was a leading figure in the Central Aero-Hydrodynamic Institute (TsAGI) in Moscow from the time when it was founded, in 1929, until his death on 23 December 1972. He was for long the Soviet Union's outstanding designer, and the products of his design team described below range from turbofan civil transports to the first Soviet supersonic bomber to enter service and the world's first supersonic transport aircraft. Also in production in the Soviet Union are small amphibious aerosleighs of Tupolev design, powered by 150 hp and 260 hp aero-engines and capable of travelling over both water and snow.

Current chief designers of the Tupolev bureau include Dr Alexei A. Tupolev (son of Andrei Tupolev), who is responsible for the Tu-144 supersonic transport; and Dmitry Markov, who is responsible for the Tu-154 airliner.

TUPOLEV Tu-16

NATO code name: "Badger"

This Tupolev bomber, from which the Tu-104 airliner was derived, made its first public appearance in some numbers in 1954. In July 1955 a formation of 54 flew over Moscow on Aviation Day, and the Tu-16 has since been standard equipment in the Soviet Air Force and Naval Air Force. About 2,000 are believed to have been built.

Seven versions of the Tu-16 are identified by unclassified NATO code names, as described below. All except "Badger-B" remain important equipment of the Soviet Air Force or Naval Air Force, which uses the "Badger-D, E and F" for maritime reconnaissance and electronic intelligence missions, and the "Badger-G" for anti-shipping strike.

"Badger-A". First Soviet long-range strategic jet bomber. Crew of seven. Glazed nose, with small undernose radome fairing. Defensive armament of seven 23 mm cannon. Six supplied to Iraq. Twenty delivered to Egypt were destroyed in the war of June 1967.

"Badger-B". Similar to "Badger-A" but fitted with underwing pylons to carry two turbojet-powered aeroplane-type anti-shipping missiles (NATO code name "Kennel"). Delivered to the Soviet Naval Air Force (now superseded by "Badger-G") and the Indonesian Air Force (two squadrons, currently inactive).

"Badger-C". Missile-carrier first seen at 1961 Soviet Aviation Day display. Large stand-off bomb (NATO code name "Kipper"), similar in configuration to USAF Hound Dog, carried under fuselage and stated to be for anti-shipping use. Radar in wide nose radome, displacing nose gun.

"Badger-D". Maritime reconnaissance version. Nose radome similar to that of "Badger-C", with slightly enlarged undernose radome fairing, and three more blister fairings in tandem under centre-fuselage.

"Badger-E". Similar to "Badger-A" but with cameras in bomb bay.

"Badger-F". Basically similar to "Badger-E" but with electronic pod on a pylon under each wing.

"Badger-G". Similar to "Badger-B" but with larger pylons for rocket-powered missiles (NATO code name "Kelt"). About 275 believed to have been supplied to Soviet Naval Air Force for anti-shipping strike duties. A few delivered to Egypt launched about 25 "Kelts" against Israeli targets during the October 1973 war. Five penetrated the defences to hit two radar sites and a supply dump in Sinai.

Tupolev Tu-16 reconnaissance bomber ("Badger-D") over HMS *Ark Royal* (*Royal Navy*)

The "Badger-G" version of the Tupolev Tu-16, with two "Kelt" missiles on underwing launchers

Maritime reconnaissance versions of "Badger" make regular flights over units of the US Navy and other NATO naval forces at sea in the Atlantic, Pacific and elsewhere, and have been photographed while doing so. The aircraft often operate in pairs, with one "Badger-F" accompanied by a different version. They also make electronic intelligence (elint) sorties around the coastlines of NATO and other non-Communist countries.

TYPE: Twin-jet medium bomber and maritime reconnaissance aircraft.

Wings: Cantilever high mid-wing monoplane with slight anhedral and with 37° of sweep. Thickness/chord ratio 12½%.

Fuselage: All-metal semi-monocoque structure of circular cross-section.

Tail Unit: Cantilever all-metal structure, with sweepback on all surfaces. Trim tabs in rudder and each elevator.

Landing Gear: Retractable tricycle type. Twin-wheel nose unit retracts rearward. Main four-wheel bogies retract into housings projecting beyond the wing trailing-edge.

Power Plant: Two Mikulin AM-3M turbojet engines, each rated at about 20,950 lb (9,500 kg) st at sea level. Fuel in wing and fuselage tanks, with total capacity of approx 10,000 Imp gallons (45,450 litres). Provision for underwing auxiliary fuel tanks and for flight refuelling. Tu-16 tankers trail hose from starboard wingtip; receiving equipment is in port wingtip extension.

Accommodation: Crew of about seven, with two pilots side by side on flight deck. Navigator in glazed nose of "Badger-A, B, E and F". Manned tail position plus lateral observation blisters in rear fuselage under tailplane.

Armament: Forward dorsal and rear ventral barbettes each containing two 23 mm cannon. Two further cannon in tail position controlled by an automatic gun-ranging radar set. Seventh, fixed, cannon on starboard side of nose of versions without nose radome. Bomb load of up to 19,800 lb (9,000 kg) delivered from weapons bay about 21 ft (6·5 m) long in standard bomber. Naval versions can carry air-to-surface winged stand-off missiles.

Electronics and Equipment: Radio and radar aids probably include HF and VHF R/T equipment, as well as IFF and a radio compass and radio altimeter. Other equipment differs according to role.

Dimensions, external:
Wing span 110 ft 0 in (33·5 m)
Length overall 120 ft 0 in (36·5 m)
Height overall 35 ft 6 in (10·8 m)

Area:
Wings, gross approx 1,820 sq ft (169 m²)

Weight:
Normal T-O weight approx 150,000 lb (68,000 kg)

Performance (estimated at max T-O weight):
Max level speed at 35,000 ft (10,700 m) 510 knots (587 mph; 945 km/h)
Service ceiling 42,650 ft (13,000 m)
Range with max bomb load 2,605 nm (3,000 miles; 4,800 km)
Range at 417 knots (480 mph; 770 km/h) with 6,600 lb (3,000 kg) of bombs 3,450 nm (3,975 miles; 6,400 km)

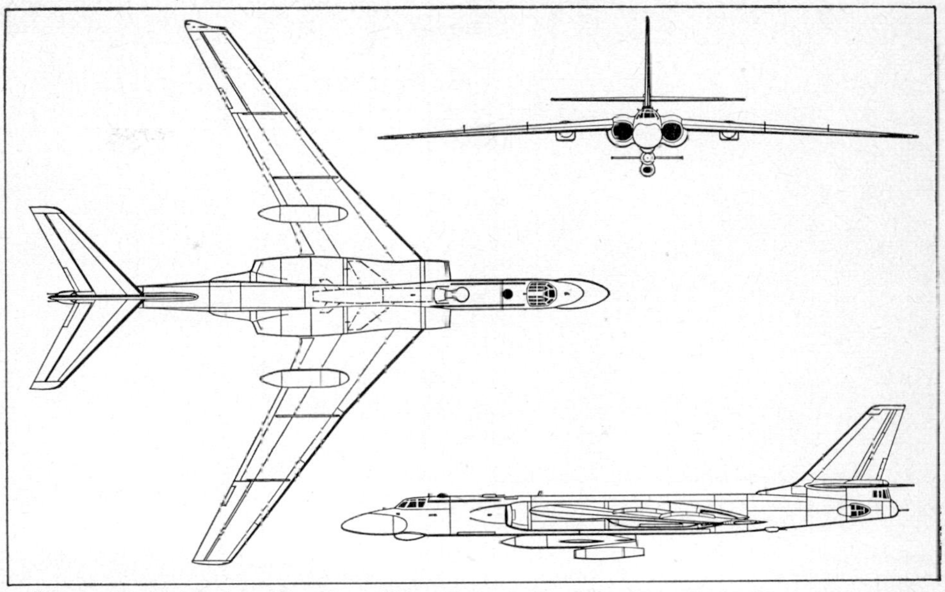

Tupolev Tu-16 ("Badger-C") with a "Kipper" stand-off missile under its fuselage (*Pilot Press*)

TUPOLEV Tu-95

NATO code name: "Bear"

This huge Tupolev bomber flew for the first time in the late Summer of 1954, was first seen at Tushino in July 1955, and subsequently became standard equipment in the Soviet Air Force. It is often referred to as the Tu-20, but its correct Soviet designation is understood to be Tu-95.

As well as maintaining its important strategic attack role, as the Soviet counterpart of the USAF's B-52 Stratofortress, the Tu-95 is in major service with the Soviet Naval Air Force for maritime reconnaissance and to provide targeting data to the launch control and guidance stations responsible for both air-to-surface and surface-to-surface anti-shipping missiles.

Six versions have been identified by NATO code names:

"Bear-A". Basic strategic bomber, with chin radar, and defensive armament comprising three pairs of 23 mm cannon in remotely-controlled dorsal and ventral barbettes and manned tail gun turret. Two glazed blisters on rear fuselage, under tailplane, are used for sighting by the gunner controlling all these weapons. The dorsal and ventral barbettes can also be controlled from a station aft of the flight deck. A braking parachute may be used to reduce landing run.

"Bear-B". First seen in 1961 Aviation Day flypast, with additional radar equipment in wide undernose radome, and carrying a large air-to-surface missile (NATO code name "Kangaroo") with estimated range of 350 nm (400 miles; 650 km). Now used mainly for maritime patrol, with flight refuelling nose-probe and, sometimes, a streamlined blister fairing on the starboard side of the rear fuselage. Defensive armament retained.

What appears at first to be a fairing on the nose of the "Kangaroo" missile is probably a duct leading from the belly of the bomber, through which air is passed to start the missile's turbojet engine.

"Bear-C". First identified when it appeared in vicinity of NATO naval forces during Exercise Teamwork in September 1964. Generally similar to "Bear-B" but with streamlined blister fairing on *both* sides of rear fuselage. Refuelling probe standard.

"Bear-D". This version was first photographed extensively when several examples (together with Tu-16s) made low passes over the US Coast Guard icebreakers *Edisto* and *Eastwind* off Severnaya Zemlya, in the Soviet Arctic, in August 1967. The aircraft then seen differed in detail, but each had an undernose radar scanner, a very large underbelly radome, a blister fairing on each side of the rear fuselage like "Bear-C", a nose refuelling probe, and a variety of other blisters and antennae, including a streamlined fairing on each tailplane tip. The rearward-facing radar above the tail turret is much larger than on previous versions of the Tu-95. It is now known that "Bear-D" has an extremely important function in support of operations involving surface-to-surface and air-to-surface missiles. It provides data on the location and nature of potential targets to missile launch crews on board ships and aircraft which are themselves too distant from the target to ensure precise missile aiming and guidance.

"Bear-E". Version basically similar in configuration to "Bear-A" but with a refuelling probe above its glazed nose and the rear fuselage blister fairings of "Bear-C". Six bomb bay windows, in pairs in line with the wing flaps, indicate the presence of reconnaissance cameras, sometimes with a seventh window to the rear on the starboard side.

"Bear-F". First identified in 1973, this version has enlarged and lengthened fairings aft of its

The "Bear-D" version of the Tu-95 is now known to have an important missile guidance role (*Royal Air Force*)

Tupolev Tu-95 maritime reconnaissance bomber in the form known to NATO as "Bear-C" (*Royal Navy*)

Camera ports under the bomb bay are a recognition feature of the "Bear-E" version of the Tu-95 (*Royal Air Force*)

The version of "Bear-F" with an undernose radome

inboard engine nacelles, for purely aerodynamic reasons. The undernose radar of "Bear-D" is missing on some aircraft; others have a radome in this position, but of considerably modified form. On both models the main underfuselage radar housing is considerably further forward than on "Bear-D" and smaller in size; the forward portion of the fuselage is longer; there are no large blister fairings under and on the sides of the rear fuselage; and the nosewheel doors are bulged prominently, suggesting the use of larger or low-pressure tyres. "Bear-F" has two stores bays in its rear fuselage, one of them replacing the usual rear ventral gun turret and leaving the tail turret as the sole defensive gun position.

Examples of all versions of the Tu-95 have made reconnaissance flights over units of the US Fleet at sea and have been photographed by US naval fighters whilst doing so. They are also encountered frequently over the North Sea by the RAF and Royal Navy.

The brief performance details quoted below were given by the US Secretary of Defense, Mr Robert McNamara, in 1963.

Type: Four-turboprop long-range bomber and maritime reconnaissance aircraft.

Wings: Cantilever mid-wing monoplane. Sweepback 37° at quarter-chord on inner panels, 35° at quarter-chord on outer panels. All-metal three-spar structure. All-metal hydraulically-powered ailerons and Fowler flaps. Trim tabs in ailerons. Spoilers in top surface of wing forward of inboard end of ailerons. Three boundary layer fences on top surface of each wing. Thermal anti-icing system in leading-edges.

Fuselage: All-metal semi-monocoque structure of circular section, containing three pressurised compartments. Those forward and aft of the weapons bay are linked by a crawlway tunnel. The tail gunner's compartment is not accessible from the other compartments.

Tail Unit: Cantilever all-metal structure, with sweepback on all surfaces. Adjustable tail-plane incidence. Hydraulically-powered rudder and elevators. Trim tabs in rudder and each elevator.

Landing Gear: Retractable tricycle type. Main units consist of four-wheel bogies, with tyres approx 5 ft (1·50 m) diameter and hydraulic internal expanding brakes. Twin wheels on nose unit. All units retract rearward, main units into nacelles built on to wing trailing-edge. Retractable tail bumper consisting of two small wheels.

Power Plant: Four Kuznetsov NK-12MV turboprop engines, each originally with max rating of approx 12,000 ehp but now uprated to 14,795 ehp and driving eight-blade contra-rotating reversible-pitch Type AV-60N propellers. Fuel in wing tanks, with normal capacity of 16,540 Imp gallons (72,980 litres).

Accommodation and Armament: See notes applicable to individual versions and under "Fuselage" above.

Operational Equipment ("Bear-D"): Large X-band radar in blister fairing under centre fuselage, for reconnaissance and to provide data on potential targets for anti-shipping aircraft or surface vessels. In latter mode, PPI presentation is data-linked to missile launch station. Four-PRF range J-band circular and sector scan bombing and navigation radar (NATO "Short Horn"). I-band tail warning radar (NATO "Bee Hind") in housing at base of rudder.

Dimensions, external (approx):
- Wing span 159 ft 0 in (48·50 m)
- Length overall 155 ft 10 in (47·50 m)

Weight (estimated):
- Max T-O weight 340,000 lb (154,220 kg)

Performance ("Bear-A"):
- Over-target speed at 41,000 ft (12,500 m) 435 knots (500 mph; 805 km/h)
- Max range with 25,000 lb (11,340 kg) bomb-load 6,775 nm (7,800 miles; 12,550 km)

Alternative version of "Bear-F" without undernose radome

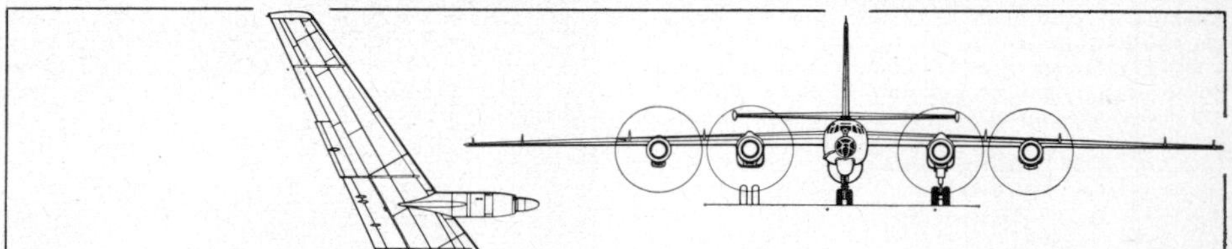

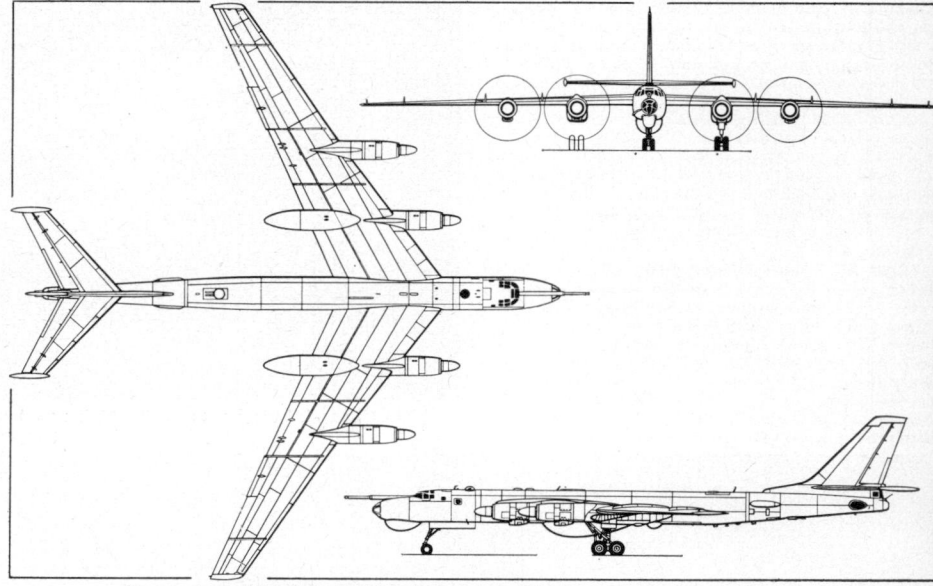

The version of the Tupolev Tu-95 known to NATO as "Bear-D" (*Pilot Press*)

TUPOLEV AWACS AIRCRAFT

NATO code name: "Moss"

An officially-released Soviet documentary film, shown in the West in 1968, included sequences depicting a military version of the Tu-114 four-turboprop transport (see 1972-73 *Jane's*), carrying above its fuselage a rotating "saucer" type early warning radar with a diameter of about 36 ft (11 m), of the kind fitted to the US Navy's E-2 Hawkeye. This was a logical development, as the Tu-114 had a fuselage of larger diameter than the military Tu-95, and could accommodate more easily the extensive electronic equipment and large crew required by a long-endurance early-warning and fighter control aircraft. It also has wings similar to those of the Tu-114, with extended-chord trailing-edge flaps, rather than the "straight" trailing-edge of the Tu-95.

The general appearance of this aircraft, which has the NATO code name "Moss", is shown in the accompanying illustrations. It can be seen to have a flight refuelling nose-probe, ventral tail-fin and numerous additional antennae and blisters for electronic equipment.

In the AWACS (airborne warning and control system) role, "Moss" is intended to work in

The airborne warning and control system (AWACS) version of the Tu-114, known to NATO as "Moss" *(US Navy)*

conjunction with advanced interceptors. After locating incoming low-level strike aircraft, "Moss" could direct towards them fighters armed with "snap-down" air-to-air missiles able to be fired from a cruising height of 20,000 ft (6,100 m) or higher. It has a further, obvious value in assisting strike aircraft to elude enemy interceptors picked up by its radar.

DIMENSIONS, EXTERNAL:

Wing span	167 ft 8 in (51·10 m)
Wing aspect ratio	10·4
Wheel track	44 ft $11\frac{1}{2}$ in (13·70 m)
Propeller diameter	18 ft $4\frac{1}{2}$ in (5·60 m)

AREA:

Wings, gross	3,349 sq ft (311·1 m²)

TUPOLEV Tu-22

NATO code name: "Blinder"

First shown publicly in the 1961 Aviation Day flypast over Moscow, this twin-turbojet bomber and maritime patrol aircraft is estimated to have a maximum speed of Mach 1·4 at height.

Its wings have some 45° of sweepback on the outer panels, 50° on the inner panels and an acute sweep at the extreme root. They are low-set on **an area-ruled fuselage, which has a nose radome** and accommodates a crew of three in tandem. The pilot has an upward-ejection seat; the other crew members have downward-ejection seats. There is a row of windows in the bottom of the fuselage aft of the nose radome.

The slab tailplane is also low-set, and the large turbojet engines (reported to be rated at 26,000 lb; 11,790 kg st each, with afterburning) are mounted in pods above the rear fuselage, on each side of the vertical fin. The lip of each pod is in the form of a ring which can be extended forward by jacks for take-off. Air entering the ram intake is then supplemented by air injected through the annular slot between the ring and the main body of the pod.

The original nozzles had a short fluted final section aft of a short fixed section, with an annular space between this and the outer fairing; they have been superseded by new nozzles, with a longer-chord convergent-divergent nozzle inside the outer fairing. These are believed to offer increased thrust and range.

The wide-track four-wheel bogie main landing gear units retract into fairings built on to the wing trailing-edges. As well as embodying oleo-pneumatic shock-absorbers, the legs are designed to swing rearward for additional cushioning during taxying and landing on rough runways. The twin-wheel nose unit retracts rearward.

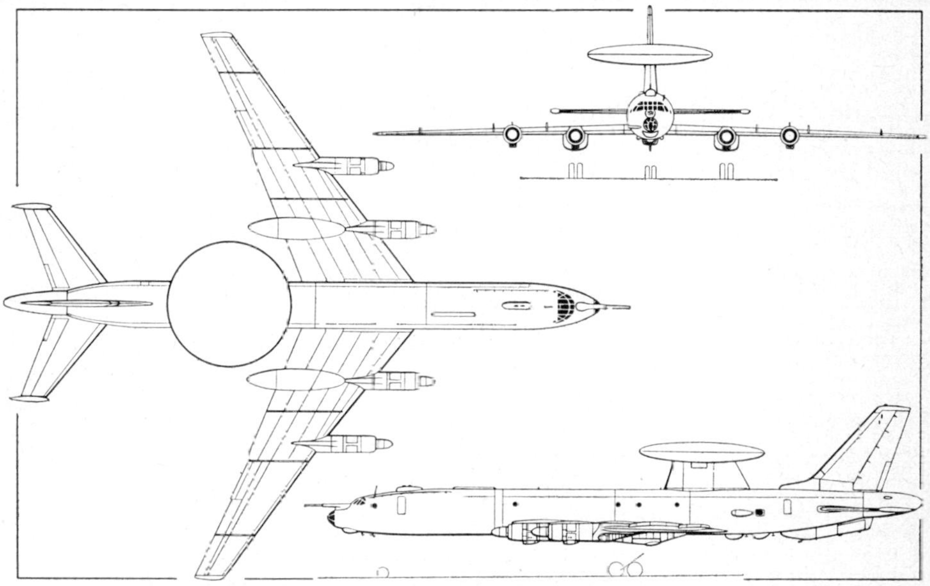

Tupolev AWACS aircraft (four 14,795 ehp Kuznetsov NK-12MV turboprops *(Pilot Press)*

The tandem-cockpit training version of the Tu-22, known to NATO as "Blinder-D"

Camera windows under the bomb bay identify the version of the Tupolev Tu-22 known to NATO as "Blinder-C" *(Tass)*

Of the ten Tu-22s shown in 1961, only one carried visible weapons, in the form of an air-to-surface missile (NATO code name "Kitchen"), some 36 ft (11 m) long, semi-submerged in the underside of its fuselage. This aircraft had also a wider nose radome, and a tail radome above a radar-directed turret mounting a single gun.

A total of 22 Tu-22s took part in the 1967 display at Domodedovo. One was escorted by six MiG-21PFs, permitting a more accurate calculation of its overall dimensions than had previously been possible. Most carried "Kitchen" missiles; all had a partially-retractable nose refuelling probe and the wide radome seen on the single missile-armed aircraft in 1961.

There are now known to be at least four major versions of the Tu-22, as follows:

"Blinder-A". Basic reconnaissance bomber version, with fuselage weapon bay for free-fall bombs. "Blinder-A" entered only limited service, its max range of 1,215 nm (1,400 miles; 2,250 km) being inadequate for the originally intended strategic role.

"Blinder-B". Generally similar to "Blinder-A" but equipped to carry air-to-surface stand-off missile (NATO code name "Kitchen"), with estimated range of 400 nm (460 miles; 740 km) recessed in weapon bay. Larger radar in nose. Partially-retractable flight refuelling probe on nose.

"Blinder-C". Maritime reconnaissance version, with battery of six cameras in weapon bay and camera windows in weapon bay doors. Modifications to nosecone, dielectric panels, etc, suggest possible electronic intelligence role or equipment for electronic countermeasures (ECM) duties.

"Blinder-D". This is a tandem-cockpit training version, in which the rear pilot sits in a raised position, with a stepped-up canopy.

DIMENSIONS, EXTERNAL (estimated):

Wing span	90 ft 10½ in (27·70 m)
Length overall	132 ft 11½ in (40·53 m)
Height overall	17 ft 0 in (5·18 m)

WEIGHT (estimated):

Max T-O weight	185,000 lb (83,900 kg)

PERFORMANCE (estimated):

Max level speed at 40,000 ft (12,200 m)
Mach 1·4 (800 knots; 920 mph; 1,480 km/h)

Service ceiling	60,000 ft (18,300 m)
Max range	1,215 nm (1,400 miles; 2,250 km)

TUPOLEV V-G BOMBER

NATO code name: "Backfire"

Official US sources first acknowledged the existence of a Soviet variable-geometry ("swing-wing") medium bomber in the Autumn of 1969. Such an aircraft was not unexpected, as the Tu-22 (NATO 'Blinder'') was clearly incapable of fulfilling a long-range strategic bombing role in the 'seventies.

A prototype of the new bomber is said to have been observed in July 1970, on the ground near the Tupolev works at Kazan in Central Asia. Subsequent official statements confirmed the aircraft as a twin-engined design by the Tupolev bureau. At least two prototypes were built initially, and up to twelve pre-production models had followed for development testing, weapons trials and evaluation by the beginning of 1973. The NATO code name allocated to the aircraft is "Backfire".

When drawing up the basic parameters for the bomber, the Tupolev bureau is believed to have aimed at a design over-target speed in the range of Mach 2·25 to Mach 2·5, with a maximum unrefuelled range of 4,775-5,200 nm (5,500-6,000 miles; 8,850-9,650 km) at high altitude, and a low-level penetration capability at supersonic speed.

There is reason to believe that "Backfire" fell short of such an unrefuelled range in its original form, but that, following some redesign, the latest version has a non-refuelled maximum combat radius of about 3,100 nm (3,570 miles; 5,745 km). In consequence, US Secretary of Defense James R. Schlesinger commented in his FY 1975 Budget Report to Congress: "This factor, coupled with its known flight refuelling capability, would seem to indicate that the 'Backfire' could be used as an intercontinental as well as a peripheral bomber, the role for which it appears best suited".

Admiral Thomas H. Moorer, Chairman of the US Joint Chiefs of Staff, added: "We estimate that 'Backfire' will be deployed operationally in 1974 . . . It is expected to replace some of both the current medium and heavy bombers and, when deployed with a compatible tanker force, constitutes a potential threat to the continental United States . . . It weighs two and one-half times as much as an FB-111 and is about four-fifths as large as the B-1".

The likely general appearance of "Backfire' is shown in the accompanying three-view drawing, which is similar to an artist's impression and a model of which photographs have been released officially in the USA. Unwillingness to depart from the familiar Tupolev practice of retracting the main landing gear bogies into fairings on the wing trailing-edges has limited the variable geometry to the outer wings, as on the Sukhoi Su-20. Also, there is evidence to believe that the large size of these fairings on early aircraft, with the wheels stowed beneath the wing, caused excessive drag. Redesign made the fairings much shallower on later aircraft, suggesting use of a revised main landing gear, probably retracting into the wing inside the fairings. This is believed to account for the two reported versions of the bomber:

"Backfire-A". Initial version, with large landing gear fairing pods.

"Backfire-B". Developed version, with landing gear fairing pods of reduced size. Reported also to have an increased wing span.

It is logical to assume that each wing pivot point will be as close as possible to the landing gear nacelle, although this must necessitate a cutout in the wing trailing-edge to clear the nacelle structure in the fully-swept position. The leading-edge of each outer wing may be fitted with a slat, as on the Su-20.

In view of the need to minimise the bulk of each main landing gear unit, "Backfire" can be

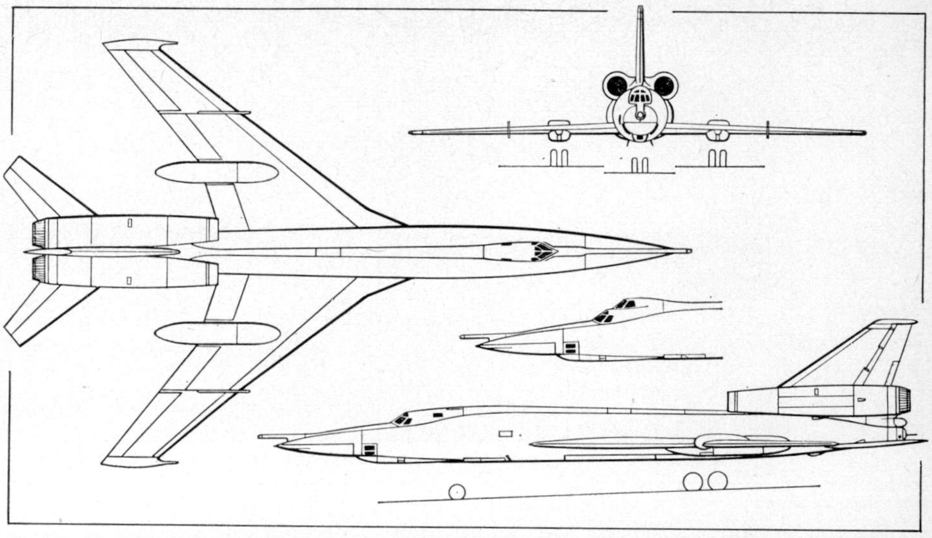

Tupolev Tu-22 twin-jet supersonic bomber ("Blinder-A") with additional view of nose of the tandem-cockpit "Blinder-D" trainer version (*Pilot Press*)

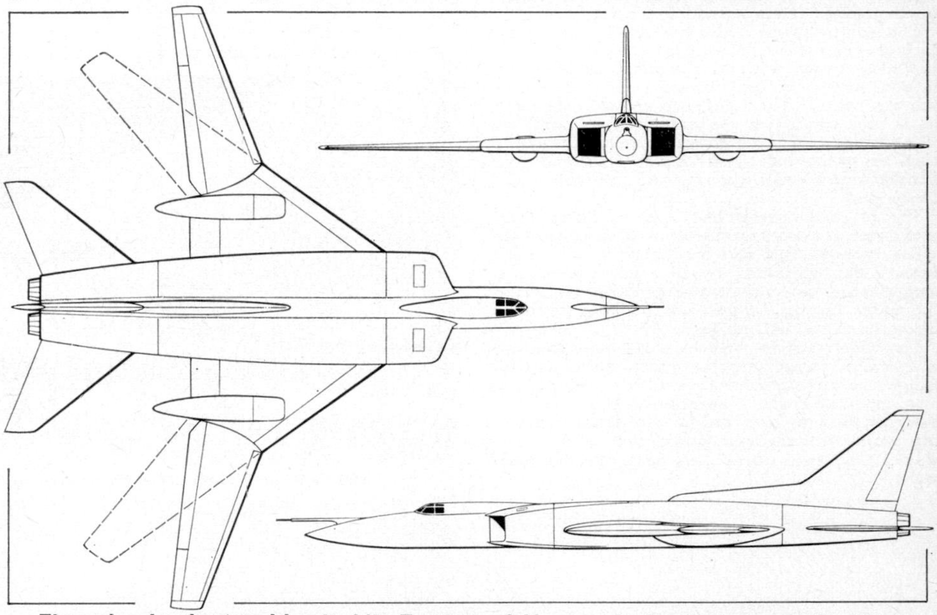

Three-view drawing (provisional) of the Tupolev variable-geometry bomber known as "Backfire" (*Pilot Press*)

Tupolev Tu-28P all-weather interceptors, code-named "Fiddler", each armed with four underwing "Ash" missiles (*Tass*)

expected to have six small-diameter wheels on each main bogie, as on the civil Tu-154.

In contrast with the fin-side engine installation on the Tu-22, the engines of "Backfire" are housed inside large square-section trunks, built on to each side of the fuselage. There is no reason to expect external area-rule "waisting" of these trunks, but the intakes are fitted with splitter plates and must embody complex internal variable geometry.

It is not yet possible to identify positively the type of engine fitted to "Backfire", but US sources have suggested the use of two Kuznetsov turbofans similar to those installed in Tupolev's Tu-144 supersonic transport. This would be logical, as each engine is rated at 44,090 lb (20,000 kg) st with reheat in the Tu-144. Uprated for military use, such engines would give an increase of at least 70 per cent over the installed power in the Tu-22.

A flight refuelling nose-probe is fitted and, after one observed refuelling, a "Backfire" prototype is said to have remained airborne for a further 10 hours.

"Backfire" can be expected to carry the full range of Soviet free-fall weapons and an air-to-surface stand-off missile at least as advanced and formidable as the "Kitchen" carried semi-submerged in the belly of the Tu-22. US reports have suggested that the Soviet Union is also developing small nuclear weapons like the American SRAM (short-range attack missile) and decoy missiles to assist penetration of advanced defence systems. One new air-to-surface missile, referred to as the ASM-6, is said to have a solid-propellant rocket motor and a range of about 400 nm (460 miles; 740 km).

Loaded weight of "Backfire" has been reported as 272,000 lb (123,350 kg).

TUPOLEV Tu-28P

NATO code name: "Fiddler"

This powerful supersonic twin-jet military aircraft was seen for the first time at Tushino in July 1961, in an interceptor role with a large delta-wing air-to-air missile (NATO code name "Ash") mounted under each wing. It is thought to have the service designation Tu-28P. Its NATO code name is "Fiddler".

The Tu-28P has a large ogival nose radome and carries a crew of two in tandem. The shoulder intakes for its two afterburning turbojet engines have half-cone shock-bodies, and the jet-pipes are side by side in the bulged tail. Each engine is estimated to have a max rating of about 27,000 lb (12,250 kg) st.

The sharply-swept wings are mid-set, with slight anhedral, and have considerably increased chord on the inboard panels, which have both increased sweep and a "straight" trailing-edge. The wide-track main landing gear units, comprising four-wheel bogies, retract into large fairings built on to the wing trailing-edges.

The tail unit is also sharply swept and the two aircraft seen in 1961 were each fitted with two ventral fins. These were missing on the three Tu-28Ps which flew past at Domodedovo in July 1967, as was the large bulged fairing fitted under the fuselage in 1961.

The armament has been doubled since 1961, each aircraft now being equipped to carry two "Ash" missiles under each wing, one usually of the radar homing type and the other of the infra-red homing type. This was confirmed as the standard armament of current first-line service aircraft in a film released in 1969, showing units of the Soviet armed forces taking part in defence exercises.

DIMENSIONS, EXTERNAL (estimated):
- Wing span: 65 ft 0 in (20·00 m)
- Length overall: 85 ft 0 in (26·00 m)

WEIGHT (estimated):
- Max T-O weight: 100,000 lb (45,000 kg)

PERFORMANCE (estimated):
- Max speed at 36,000 ft (11,000 m): Mach 1·75 (1,000 knots; 1,150 mph; 1,850 km/h)

TUPOLEV Tu-124

NATO code name: "Cookpot"

Although similar to the earlier Tu-104 in general configuration, the Tu-124 is 25% smaller, with standard seating for 56 passengers, and was the first Soviet transport aircraft with turbofan engines. The prototype flew for the first time in June 1960.

The Tu-124 was designed to replace the piston-engined Il-14 on Aeroflot's short/medium routes and entered service on this airline's Moscow-Tallinn route on 2 October 1962. Three were delivered to CSA Czech Airlines and one to the East German Interflug. Others serve, in small numbers, with the air forces of East Germany, Iraq and India.

A structural description of the Tu-124 can be found in the 1972-73 *Jane's*. It has been superseded in production by the rear-engined Tu-134.

POWER PLANT: Two Soloviev D-20P turbofan engines, each rated at 11,905 lb (5,400 kg) st, in wing-root nacelles.

ACCOMMODATION: Crew of four, comprising two pilots, navigator and stewardess. Provision for radio operator or second navigator on removable seat. In standard 56-seat version, cabin has three compartments, seating 12, 12 and 32 people respectively on rail-mounted reclining seats, all four-abreast in pairs, with centre aisle. Two tables between front pairs of seats in forward cabin. Two doors on port side, one aft of flight deck, the other aft of main cabin. Forward baggage compartment on starboard side opposite door. Buffet-kitchen between forward door and cabin. Wardrobe opposite rear door. Toilet and rear baggage compartment aft of rear door, with external freight loading hatch on starboard side. All doors open inward. Mixed cargo-passenger layouts available.

DIMENSIONS, EXTERNAL:
- Wing span: 83 ft 9½ in (25·55 m)
- Length overall: 100 ft 4 in (30·58 m)
- Height overall: 26 ft 6 in (8·08 m)
- Tailplane span: 32 ft 9½ in (10·00 m)
- Wheel track: 29 ft 8½ in (9·05 m)
- Wheelbase: 34 ft 7¼ in (10·55 m)
- Passenger doors (port):
  - Height: 4 ft 3¼ in (1·30 m)
  - Width: 2 ft 3½ in (0·70 m)
- Cargo door (stbd):
  - Height: 2 ft 11½ in (0·90 m)
  - Width: 3 ft 7¼ in (1·10 m)

DIMENSIONS, INTERNAL:
- Cabin:
  - Length, excluding flight deck: 67 ft 11 in (20·70 m)
  - Max width: 8 ft 10 in (2·70 m)
  - Max height: 6 ft 2¾ in (1·90 m)
  - Volume, including flight deck, toilet, etc: 4,308 cu ft (122 m³)
- Baggage compartment (fwd): 212 cu ft (6 m³)
- Baggage compartment (aft): 282 cu ft (8 m³)

WEIGHTS:
- Empty weight: 49,600 lb (22,500 kg)
- Manufacturer's max payload: 13,228 lb (6,000 kg)
- Normal T-O weight: 80,470 lb (36,500 kg)
- Max T-O weight: 83,775 lb (38,000 kg)
- Max landing weight: 77,160 lb (35,000 kg)
- Max zero-fuel weight: 52,400 lb (23,770 kg)

PERFORMANCE (at max T-O weight, except where indicated):
- Max level speed: 524 knots (603 mph; 970 km/h)
- Max cruising speed: 469 knots (540 mph; 870 km/h)
- Econ cruising speed at 33,000 ft (10,000 m) at AUW of 58,000 lb (26,300 kg): 432 knots (497 mph; 800 km/h)
- T-O run: 3,380 ft (1,030 m)
- T-O to 33 ft (10 m): 7,000 ft (2,120 m)
- Landing run: 3,050 ft (930 m)

RANGES (at normal T-O weight, 60 min fuel reserve):
- Range with max fuel and 7,715 lb (3,500 kg) payload at econ cruising speed: 1,133 nm (1,305 miles; 2,100 km)
- Range with max payload at econ cruising speed: 660 nm (760 miles; 1,220 km)

Tu-28P all-weather interceptor with "Ash" infra-red missile on inboard pylon under port wing

TUPOLEV Tu-134

NATO code name: "Crusty"

Known originally as the Tu-124A, this aircraft is a rear-engined twin-turbofan development of the Tu-124. It had completed more than 100 test flights when first details and photographs were released in mid-September 1964. The prototype was followed by five pre-production aircraft and the Tu-134 then went into series production in the factory at Kharkov where the Tu-104 had been manufactured. It entered international service on Aeroflot's Moscow-Stockholm route in September 1967, after a period on internal services, and was joined by the "stretched" Tu-134A in the Autumn of 1970.

The Tu-134 was developed by Tupolev's design team, under the direct leadership of chief designer Leonid Selyakov. Deputy designer Alexander Arkhangelsky has said that the aircraft can be operated from earth runways. He added that it is equipped for fully-automatic landing and has navigation aids that enable the pilot to land in fog with horizontal visibility down to 165 ft (50 m).

The Tu-134 is designed for a service life of 30,000 flying hours. Airframe overhaul life is 5,000 hours.

Two versions are available, as follows:

Tu-134. Initial version, with Soloviev D-30 turbofans, accommodating 64-72 passengers. Export orders have included eleven for Interflug (East Germany), six for Balkan Bulgarian Airlines, five for LOT (Poland), six for Malev (Hungary), three for Aviogenex (Yugoslavia) and one for Iraqi Airways.

Tu-134A. Fuselage lengthened by 6 ft 10½ in (2·10 m) to accommodate 76-80 passengers and increase baggage space by 71 cu ft (2 m³). Wider seats. Wings strengthened locally. Main landing gear units strengthened and fitted with Il-18 wheels and brakes. Thrust reversers on Soloviev D-30-2 engines. New radio and navigation equipment to international standards. APU for self-contained engine starting, electrical power supply and air-conditioning on the ground. Export orders have included ten for CSA (Czechoslovakia), three for Malev, three for Balkan Bulgarian Airlines, three for LOT, and four for Aviogenex. In some cases these replace Tu-134s operated earlier.

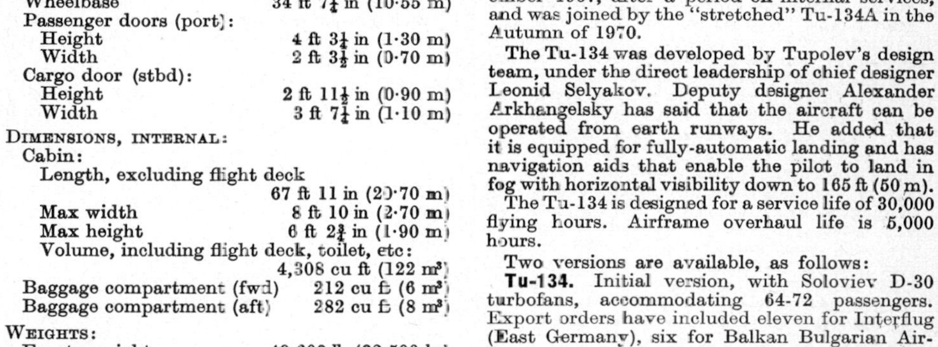

Tupolev Tu-124 medium-range transport aircraft in service with the Indian Air Force (*APN*)

Tupolev Tu-134A medium-range transport (two Soloviev D-30 turbofan engines) of the East German Interflug *(Air & General Photos)*

The third aircraft delivered to Aviogenex differed from all Tu-134s seen previously in having the usual glazed nose and undernose radome replaced by a more conventional conical nose radome. This is now available optionally on both the Tu-134 and the Tu-134A.

The following details apply to both versions:

Type: Twin-turbofan short/medium-range transport aircraft.

Wings: Cantilever low-wing monoplane. Sweepback at quarter-chord 35°. Anhedral 1° 30′. Conventional all-metal two-spar structure. Two-section aileron on each wing, operated manually through geared tabs, and fitted also with trim tabs. Electro-mechanically-actuated all-metal double-slotted flaps. Hydraulically-actuated spoilers. Hot-air de-icing system.

Fuselage: Conventional all-metal semi-monocoque structure of circular section. Electro-mechanically-actuated airbrake under fuselage, to steepen angle of approach.

Tail Unit: Cantilever all-metal structure, with variable-incidence tailplane mounted at top of fin. Elevators operated manually through geared tabs. Rudder control is hydraulically powered, with yaw damper. Trim tabs in elevators. Fin leading-edge de-iced by hot air; tailplane leading-edge de-iced electrically.

Landing Gear: Retractable tricycle type. All units retract rearward. Main units consist of four-wheel bogies retracting into fairings built on to wing trailing-edge. Oleo-pneumatic shock-absorbers, supplemented by ability of legs to swing rearward to cushion taxying and landing on rough runways. Main wheels size 930 × 305, tyre pressure 85 lb/sq in (6·0 kg/cm²). Steerable twin nosewheels size 660 × 200, tyre pressure 92·5-100 lb/sq in (6·5-7·0 kg/cm²). Disc brakes and anti-skid units standard. Brake-chute stowed in fuselage tailcone of Tu-134 (APU exhaust in this position on Tu-134A).

Power Plant: Two Soloviev D-30 turbofan engines, each rated at 14,990 lb (6,800 kg) st, in pods on each side of rear fuselage, available with thrust reversers, constant-speed drives and AC generators. Three fuel tanks in each wing, total capacity 3,630 Imp gallons (16,500 litres) when gravity fuelled, 3,520 Imp gallons (16,000 litres) when pressure fuelled. Single-point refuelling socket in starboard wing-root leading-edge. Gravity fuelling point above each tank. Hot-air de-icing system for nacelle intakes. Fire-warning and freon extinguishing system.

Accommodation (Tu-134): Flight crew of three, consisting of two pilots and a navigator, plus two stewardesses. Mixed class version accommodates 64 passengers in four-abreast seats, with 17·5 in (0·45 m) centre aisle. 16 first class passengers in front cabin have seats at 36·6 in (93 cm) pitch, with tables between first two rows; 20 tourist class in centre cabin and 28 tourist class in rear cabin. Economy class version accommodates 72 passengers in four-abreast seating, with 44 seats (at 28·35 in; 72 cm pitch) and two tables in forward cabin, and 28 seats (at 29·5 in; 75 cm pitch) in aft cabin. In each version there is a galley on the starboard side and baggage compartment and galley on the port side immediately aft of the flight deck, two toilets at the rear and a large baggage and freight compartment aft, in line with the engines. Max loading on floor of freight compartments 82 lb/sq ft (400 kg/m²). The passenger door is on the port side, forward of the front cabin. There are two cargo doors, on the starboard side by the baggage compartments, and an emergency exit on each side over the wing. Crew cabin and canopy observation panel de-iced by electric heater and hot air.

Accommodation (Tu-134A): Generally similar to Tu-134 except for lengthened cabins. All versions have 28 seats in four-abreast rows in rear cabin. Front cabin seats 44, 48 or 52 passengers, four-abreast, with tables between front two rows. Seat pitch 29·5 in (75 cm) in all versions. Three wardrobes forward of main cabin on 72-seat version, one on other versions. Reduced forward baggage space on 80-seater.

Systems: Air-conditioning system, pressure differential 8·10 lb/sq in (0·57 kg/cm²), fed with bleed air from engine compressors. Hydraulic system operating pressure 3,000 lb/sq in (210 kg/cm²). Electrical system includes 27V DC supply from four 12kW starter/generators and two batteries, single-phase 115V 400Hz AC supply from two inverters and three-phase 36V 400Hz AC supply. APU available since 1969-70. Oxygen available continuously for pilot, from 92 litre bottle, with 1 hr supply for other crew members and portable supply for emergency use by passengers.

Electronics and Equipment (Tu-134): Provision for full range of radio and radar communications and navigation equipment, including R-807 HF communications radio, "Lotos" VHF radio, SPU-7 intercom, RO3-1 weather/navigation radar, SOM-64 transponder, AGD-1 remote-reading artificial horizon, AUASP-3 angle-of-attack and *g* load control unit, KS-8 direction finder, NAS-1A6 navigation system (including "Trassa-A" Doppler), BSU-3P automatic flight control and landing system (including (AP-6EM-3P autopilot) for automatic control in flight and automatic or semi-automatic landing approaches down to 130-200 ft (40-60 m), ARK-11 radio compass, RV-UM low-altitude (0-2,000 ft; 0-600 m) radio altimeter and "Course MP-1" VOR/ILS/SP-50 navigation and landing system.

Electronics and Equipment (Tu-134A): Typical installation includes two ARK-15 radio compasses, Mikron HF communications radio, two UHF transceivers, RV-5 radio altimeter, two "Course MP-2" VOR/ILS, two SO-70 transponders, ROZ-1 weather radar and DISS-013 Doppler.

Dimensions, external:

Wing span 95 ft 2 in (29·01 m)
Wing chord at root 28 ft 5 in (8·66 m)
Wing chord at tip 6 ft 3½ in (1·92 m)
Wing aspect ratio 7·3
Length overall:
  Tu-134 114 ft 8 in (34·95 m)
  Tu-134A 121 ft 6½ in (37·05 m)
Fuselage max diameter 9 ft 6 in (2·90 m)
Height overall:
  Tu-134 29 ft 7 in (9·02 m)
  Tu-134A 30 ft 0 in (9·14 m)
Tailplane span 38 ft 8½ in (11·80 m)
Wheel track 31 ft 0 in (9·45 m)
Wheelbase:
  Tu-134 45 ft 8½ in (13·93 m)
  Tu-134A 53 ft 9½ in (16·40 m)
Passenger door:
  Height 4 ft 3 in (1·30 m)
  Width 2 ft 3½ in (0·70 m)
  Height to sill 8 ft 6½ in (2·60 m)
Baggage compartment doors:
  Height 2 ft 11½ in (0·90 m)
  Width: fwd 3 ft 7¼ in (1·10 m)
  aft 3 ft 11¼ in (1·20 m)
  Height to sill 7 ft 10½ in (2·40 m)

Dimensions, internal:

Cabin (portion containing seats only):
  Length:
    Tu-134 45 ft 5½ in (13·85 m)
  Width 8 ft 10½ in (2·71 m)
  Height 6 ft 5 in (1·96 m)
  Floor area:
    Tu-134 343 sq ft (31·85 m²)
  Volume:
    Tu-134 2,073 cu ft (58·7 m³)
    Tu-134A 2,400 cu ft (68·0 m³)
Max usable floor area, less flight deck:
  Tu-134 506 sq ft (47·00 m²)
Max usable volume, less flight deck:
  Tu-134 3,040 cu ft (86·10 m³)
Baggage compartment, Tu-134 (fwd):
  Height (mean) 6 ft 1¾ in (1·875 m)
  Length (mean) 6 ft 1¾ in (1·875 m)
  Width (mean) 4 ft 2½ in (1·28 m)
  Floor area 25·8 sq ft (2·4 m²)
  Volume 123 cu ft (3·50 m³)
Baggage compartment, Tu-134A (fwd):
  Volume 141-212 cu ft (4·0-6·0 m³)
Baggage compartment, Tu-134/134A (aft):
  Height (mean) 5 ft 9 in (1·75 m)
  Length (mean) 9 ft 2 in (2·80 m)
  Width (mean) 5 ft 9 in (1·75 m)
  Floor area 48·4 sq ft (4·5 m²)
  Volume 300 cu ft (8·50 m³)

Areas:

Wings, gross 1,370·3 sq ft (127·3 m²)
Ailerons (total) 104·2 sq ft (9·68 m²)
Trailing-edge flaps (total) 242·2 sq ft (22·50 m²)
Spoilers (total) 48·2 sq ft (4·48 m²)
Vertical tail surfaces (total) 215·6 sq ft (20·03 m²)
Rudder 62·0 sq ft (5·76 m²)
Horizontal tail surfaces (total) 330·2 sq ft (30·68 m²)
Elevators 69·1 sq ft (6·42 m²)

Weights:

Operating weight, empty:
  Tu-134 60,627 lb (27,500 kg)
  Tu-134A 63,950 lb (29,000 kg)
Max fuel:
  Tu-134 28,660 lb (13,000 kg)
  Tu-134A 31,800 lb (14,400 kg)
Max payload:
  Tu-134 16,975 lb (7,700 kg)
  Tu-134A 18,000 lb (8,200 kg)
Max ramp weight:
  Tu-134 99,650 lb (45,200 kg)
  Tu-134A 104,000 lb (47,200 kg)
Max T-O weight:
  Tu-134 99,200 lb (45,000 kg)
  Tu-134A 103,600 lb (47,000 kg)
Max landing weight:
  Tu-134, standard 88,185 lb (40,000 kg)
  Tu-134, emergency 97,000 lb (44,000 kg)
  Tu-134A, standard 94,800 lb (43,000 kg)
Max zero-fuel weight:
  Tu-134 77,603 lb (35,200 kg)

Performance (Tu-134, at T-O weight of 97,000 lb; 44,000 kg unless otherwise stated):

Max cruising speed:
  at 36,000 ft (11,000 m) 469 knots (540 mph; 870 km/h)
  at 28,000 ft (8,500 m) 485 knots (559 mph; 900 km/h)
Long-range cruising speed at 36,000 ft (11,000 m) 405 knots (466 mph; 750 km/h)
T-O safety speed, one engine out 141 knots (162 mph; 260 km/h)
Approach speed 133 knots (153 mph; 247 km/h)
Landing speed 116-122 knots (134-140 mph; 215-225 km/h)
Stalling speed, wheels and flaps down 103 knots (118 mph; 190 km/h)
Max rate of climb at S/L 2,913 ft (888 m)/min
Rate of climb at S/L, one engine out 590 ft (180 m)/min
Service ceiling at AUW of 92,600 lb (42,000 kg) 39,370 ft (12,000 m)
Service ceiling, one engine out, at AUW of 94,800 lb (43,000 kg) 18,375 ft (5,600 m)
T-O run 3,280 ft (1,000 m)
Balanced field length for T-O, FAR standard:
  at S/L, ISA, max T-O weight 7,152 ft (2,180 m)
Balanced field length for landing, FAR standard:
  at S/L, ISA, max landing weight 6,726 ft (2,050 m)
Landing from 50 ft (15 m) at AUW of 81,570 lb (37,000 kg) 3,937 ft (1,200 m)
Landing run at AUW of 81,570 lb (37,000 kg) 2,625-2,838 ft (800-865 m)
Min ground turning radius 115 ft (35 m)

Range, against 27 knots (31 mph; 50 km/h) headwind, 60 min fuel reserve:
with 15,430 lb (7,000 kg) payload at 459 knots (528 mph; 850 km/h) at 36,000 ft (11,000 m) 1,293 nm (1,490 miles; 2,400 km)
with 11,442 lb (5,190 kg) payload at above speed 1,656 nm (1,907 miles; 3,070 km)
with 6,600 lb (3,000 kg) payload at long-range cruising speed 1,888 nm (2,175 miles; 3,500 km)

PERFORMANCE (Tu-134A):
Max cruising speed at AUW of 92,600 lb (42,000 kg) at 32,800 ft (10,000 m) 477 knots (550 mph; 885 km/h)
Normal cruising range 405-458 knots (466-528 mph; 750-850 km/h)
Service ceiling at max T-O weight 39,000 ft (11,900 m)
Landing run at max landing weight 2,560 ft (780 m)
Range at max AUW, cruising at 458 knots (528 mph; 850 km/h) at 36,000 ft (11,000 m), with 1 hour fuel reserve:
with max payload 938 nm (1,081 miles; 1,740 km)
with max fuel 1,495 nm (1,720 miles; 2,770 km)

TUPOLEV Tu-144

NATO code name: "Charger"

Since this supersonic transport aircraft was first shown in model form at the 1965 Paris Salon de l'Aéronautique, it has undergone considerable development. Its general configuration has become a little more similar to that of the Anglo-French Concorde, with a fully-cambered delta wing and two separate underwing ducts for the engines. However, it has larger overall dimensions than the Concorde and is intended to carry a slightly larger number of passengers initially, at higher cruising speeds. It also embodies in its production form retractable "moustache" foreplanes, which were introduced to enhance its take-off and landing characteristics.

Three airframes were laid down initially, of which two were regarded as prototypes, plus a structure test version. In addition, an otherwise-standard MiG-21 was fitted with a scaled-down replica of the Tu-144's original ogival wing, in place of its normal delta wing and horizontal tail surfaces. This aircraft made several dozen research flights, as a result of which modifications were made to the design of the full-size wing.

The first of the two prototypes of the Tu-144 (CCCP-68001) was assembled and ground-tested at the Zhukovsky Plant, near Moscow, and flew for the first time on 31 December 1968, this being the first flight by a supersonic airliner anywhere in the world. Its landing gear remained extended throughout the 38-minute flight, as it did during the 50-minute second test flight on 8 January 1969. The crew comprised Eduard Elyan, pilot, Mikhail Kozlov, co-pilot, and two engineers. The pilots occupied upward-ejection seats, side by side on the flight deck. Two further escape hatches in the top of the fuselage further aft indicated the positions of the crew ejection seats.

On 5 June 1969 the Tu-144 exceeded Mach 1 for the first time, at a height of 36,000 ft (11,000 m), half-an-hour after take-off. Only a slight tremble was said to be discernible as it passed through the transonic region. On 26 May 1970 this prototype became the first commercial transport to exceed Mach 2, by flying at 1,160 knots (1,335 mph; 2,150 km/h) at a height of 53,475 ft (16,300 m) for several minutes. The pilot was again Eduard Elyan. Highest speed reported to date is Mach 2·4, probably with the aircraft in its production form. Normal in-service cruising speed is expected to be Mach 2·2 to 2·3.

At the first public showing of the Tu-144, at Sheremetyevo Airport, Moscow, on 21 May 1970, the Soviet Deputy Minister for the Aviation Industry, Alexander Kobzarev, said that series production had already started at Voronezh. By May 1972 the prototype had logged a total of about 200 flying hours in nearly 150 flights, of which more than 100 hours were at supersonic speed. The second and third aircraft had each completed only a few flights at that time, and the Tu-144 will not enter scheduled passenger service before 1975, by which time it is expected that total flying time on the type will exceed 3,000 hours.

There are no pre-production Tu-144s, and the aircraft (CCCP-77102) exhibited at the 1973 Paris Salon de l'Aéronautique was No. 2 of the initial series production models, representing almost a total redesign by comparison with the prototype described and illustrated in the 1972-73 *Jane's*. Unless changes are necessary as a result of the enquiry into the loss of CCCP-77102 during its flight demonstration at Paris, no further major modifications are planned for the aircraft that will be operated on passenger services by Aeroflot.

Initial route proving flights are reported to have begun in the first half of 1974, primarily between Moscow and Vladivostock, via Tyumen. Four production Tu-144s were reported to be available for these operations, and were used to deliver urgent freight and mail on some occasions.

Construction of the Tu-144 is mainly of VAD-23 light alloy, with extensive use of integrally-stiffened panels, produced by both chemical milling and machining from solid metal. Stainless steel and titanium are used for the leading-edges, elevons, rudder and undersurface of the rear fuselage, and the aircraft is stated to embody 10,000 parts made of plastics.

The wings have a "double-delta" planform, with a sweepback in the order of 76° on the inboard portions and 57° on the main panels. The prototype had marked conical camber on the highly-swept inboard leading-edges, but flat trailing-edges. The production aircraft has wings increased in span by nearly 4 ft (1·15 m) and cambered over the full area, with a downward-curving trailing-edge like that of the Concorde. The structure is multi-spar, with large honeycomb panels. The powered control surfaces consist of four separate elevons on each wing and a two-section rudder, each operated by two separate actuators.

The fuselage (nearly 19 ft; 5·7 m longer on production aircraft) blends with the low-set wings, giving a flat undersurface which contributes to fuselage lift and directional stability. The number of cabin windows is increased from 25 each side on the prototype to 34 on production aircraft. There are doors forward of the passenger cabins and in the centre on the port side; the number of emergency exits has been increased from four to six.

The "moustache" foreplanes are pivoted from points near the top of the fuselage, immediately aft of the flight deck. Each is fitted with a double-slotted trailing-edge flap and a fixed leading-edge double-slat. The foreplanes retract rearward, protruding only a little externally but restricting to a narrow passage the space between flight deck and cabin. When extended they have anhedral but no sweep.

It was intended originally to use these foreplanes only during take-off and landing. Flight development during 1973-74 is said to have indicated the value of extending them also during transonic acceleration from just below Mach 1 to

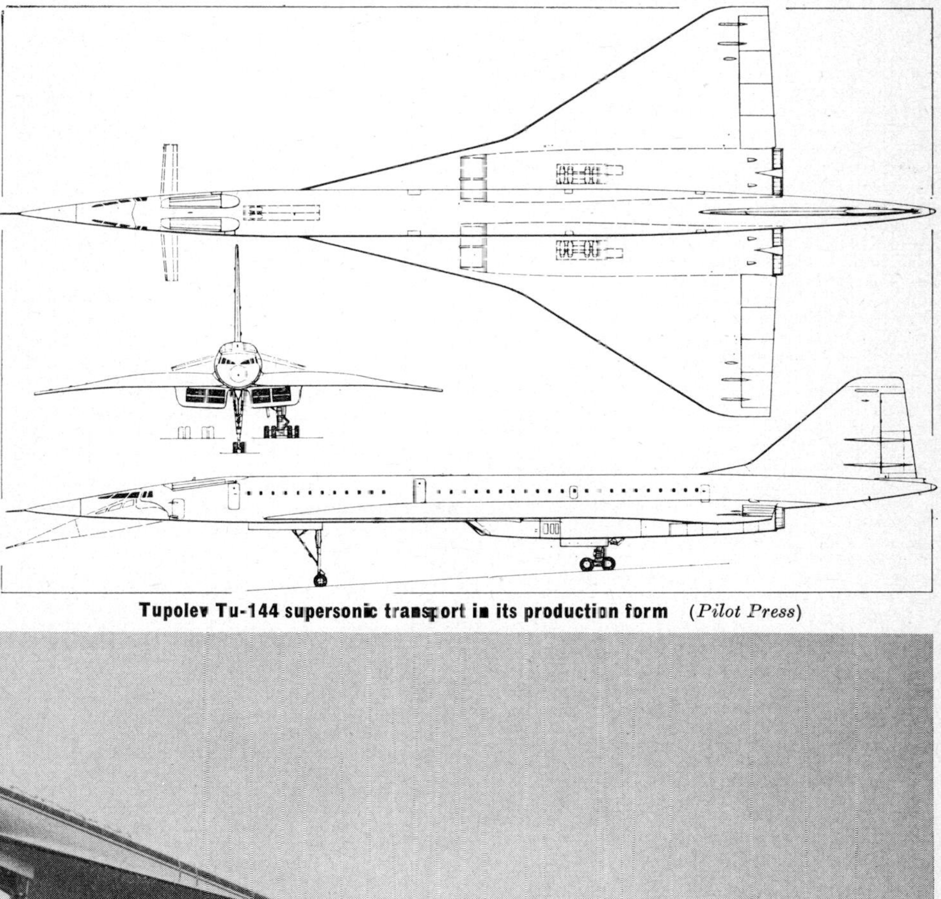

Tupolev Tu-144 supersonic transport in its production form (*Pilot Press*)

Tupolev Tu-144 supersonic transport, in production form, with foreplanes and landing gear extended (*Brian M. Service*)

Tupolev Tu-154 medium/long-range transport (three Kuznetsov NK-8-2 turbofan engines) in service with Malev

Mach 1·3. This is reported to reduce aerodynamic drag and, hence, fuel consumption.

Following relocation of the engines (see below) all three units of the landing gear have been redesigned. The twin-wheel steerable nose unit now retracts forward into the fuselage. Each main eight-wheel bogie (two rows of four, compared with three rows of four on prototype) now retracts forward and up into one of the engine ducts, between the divided air-intake trunks. This requires the bogie first to pivot sideways through 90° about the base of the leg, before retraction. Nosewheel tyres are size 950 × 300. The main wheels are fitted with size 950 × 400 tyres and quadruple steel disc brakes. All wheel-bays are thermally insulated, and the nosewheel tyres are blown with cooling air after retraction, throughout cruising flight.

The first flight of the Tu-144 prototype was also the first time that the Kuznetsov NK-144 turbofan engine had been tested in the air. At that time the engine max ratings were 28,660 lb (13,000 kg) st without afterburning and 38,580 lb (17,500 kg) with full afterburning; and the four turbofans were mounted side by side in the rear of a single large underbelly duct with bifurcated twin intake trunks. On production aircraft the rating with full afterburning has been increased to 44,090 lb (20,000 kg) st, and the engines are paired in two separate ducts, further outboard. As before, each intake trunk contains a central vertical wall, giving an individual flow of air to each engine. The intakes have fully-automatic movable ramps, with manual reversion, and with airflow dump doors midway from the inlet to the engines. Afterburning is normally maintained at 30% to 40% of its maximum additional thrust throughout cruising flight. No thrust reversers are installed, but a twin brake-parachute is fitted solely for use on short runways.

Total fuel capacity has been increased from 154,325 lb (70,000 kg) on the prototype to about 209,440 lb (95,000 kg) on production aircraft, with a transfer tank in the fuselage tailcone to counterbalance CG movement in flight.

In service a flight crew of three will normally be carried, consisting of two pilots and a flight engineer. The pilots have fully-adjustable armchair seats. During cruising flight, their windscreen is faired in by a retractable visor which has birdproof side windows and a "solid" top. The entire nose can be drooped for improved visibility during take-off and landing.

The basic interior layout is for a total of 140 passengers in three cabins. The front cabin contains 11 seats for first class passengers, basically three-abreast, with tables between the front two rows. It is divided by a movable partition from the forward tourist class cabin, which contains six rows of five-abreast seats, with the three-seat units on the starboard side of the centre aisle. The rear tourist class cabin contains 15 rows of five-abreast seating at the front and six rows of four-abreast seating at the rear. Seat pitch is normally 41·3 in (105 cm) for first class and 34·25 in (87 cm) for tourist class; but alternative layouts are available, and the production Tu-144 shown at Paris in 1973 contained fewer than 100 seats.

Forward of the passenger accommodation there are toilet (port) and cloakroom compartments (starboard), with a bench seat for two cabin staff by the forward door. A second cloakroom, toilet and buffet kitchen are located between the two tourist class cabins, with two further toilets at the rear. Aft of these, in line with the engines, is a large compartment for containerised baggage and freight, which are loaded and unloaded semi-automatically through a large door on the starboard side of the hold, at the rear. There are no underfloor holds.

Little information is yet available on aircraft systems. The prototype had three independent hydraulic systems and two separate systems for pressurisation and air-conditioning. Preparation for flight, ground air-conditioning and engine starting can be performed independently of airport services. Advanced automatic flight control and navigation systems are standard, with the intention of progressing eventually to full automatic landing under all weather conditions. Six landing and taxi lights are mounted on the nosewheel leg.

Dimensions, external:
- Wing span 94 ft 6 in (28·80 m)
- Length overall 215 ft 6½ in (65·70 m)
- Height, wheels up 42 ft 2 in (12·85 m)
- Wheel track 19 ft 10¼ in (6·05 m)
- Wheelbase 64 ft 3½ in (19·60 m)

Dimensions, internal:
- Cabin: Headroom 6 ft 4 in (1·93 m)
- Baggage/cargo hold capacity 706 cu ft (20 m³)

Area:
- Wings, gross 4,714·5 sq ft (438 m²)

Weights:
- Operating weight, empty 187,400 lb (85,000 kg)
- Max fuel 209,440 lb (95,000 kg)
- Max payload (space limited) 30,865 lb (14,000 kg)
- Max payload (structure limited) 33,070 lb (15,000 kg)
- Max ramp weight 407,850 lb (185,000 kg)
- Max T-O weight 396,830 lb (180,000 kg)
- Max zero-fuel weight 220,460 lb (100,000 kg)
- Max landing weight 242,500-264,550 lb (110,000-120,000 kg)

Performance (nominal):
- Max cruising speed Mach 2·35 (1,350 knots; 1,550 mph; 2,500 km/h)
- Normal cruising speed Mach 2·2 (1,240 knots; 1,430 mph; 2,300 km/h)
- Cruising height 52,500-59,000 ft (16,000-18,000 m)
- Balanced field length at max T-O weight (approx):
  - ISA, S/L 9,845 ft (3,000 m)
  - ISA+15°C, S/L 10,500 ft (3,200 m)
- Landing run 8,530 ft (2,600 m)
- Max range with 140 passengers, at an average speed of Mach 1·9 (1,080 knots; 1,243 mph; 2,000 km/h) 3,500 nm (4,030 miles; 6,500 km)

TUPOLEV Tu-154

NATO code name: "Careless"

The three-engined Tu-154, announced in the Spring of 1966, was intended to replace the Tu-104, Il-18 and An-10 on medium/long stage lengths of up to 3,240 nm (3,725 miles; 6,000 km). It is able to operate from airfields with a class B surface, including packed earth and gravel. Normal flight can be maintained after shut-down of any one engine. Single-engine flight is possible at a lower altitude.

The first of six prototype and pre-production models flew for the first time on 4 October 1968. The seventh Tu-154 was delivered to Aeroflot for initial route proving and crew training in early 1971. Mail and cargo flights began in May. Initial passenger-carrying services were flown for a few days in the early Summer of 1971 between Moscow and Tbilisi. Regular services began on 9 February 1972, over the 700 nm (800 mile; 1,300 km) route between Moscow and Mineralnye Vody, in the North Caucasus. International services began with a proving flight between Moscow and Prague on 1 August 1972.

It is believed that more than 100 Tu-154s had entered service with Aeroflot by the Spring of 1974. Others had been ordered by, or delivered to, Balkan Bulgarian Airlines (5), Malev (3), EgyptAir (8), Aviogenex (2) and CSA Czechoslovakian Airlines (7).

An improved version, known as the **Tu-154A**, was reported to be under development in early 1973, with the first flight scheduled for later that year. Dimensionally unchanged, the new version is said to be powered by three Soloviev D-30KU turbofan engines, each rated at 25,350 lb (11,500 kg) st. It is expected to accommodate up to 175 passengers and to have a maximum range of more than 2,600 nm (3,000 miles; 4,800 km) with full payload.

Type: Three-engined medium/long-range transport aircraft.

Wings: Cantilever low-wing monoplane. Sweepback 35° at quarter-chord. Conventional all-metal three-spar fail-safe structure; centre spar extending to just outboard of inner edge of aileron on each wing. Five-section slat on outer 80% of each wing leading-edge. Triple-slotted flaps. Four-section spoilers on each wing. Outboard sections supplement ailerons for roll control. Section inboard of landing gear housing serves as airbrake and lift-dumper; two middle sections can be used as airbrakes in flight. All control surfaces hydraulically-actuated and of honeycomb construction. Hot-air de-icing of wing leading-edge. Slats are electrically heated.

Fuselage: Conventional all-metal semi-monocoque fail-safe structure of circular section.

Tail Unit: Cantilever all-metal structure, with variable-incidence tailplane mounted at tip of fin. Rudder and elevator of honeycomb construction. Sweepback of 40° at quarter-chord on horizontal surfaces, 45° on leading-edge of vertical surfaces. Control surfaces hydraulically-actuated by irreversible servo-controls. Leading-edges of fin and tailplane and engine air intake de-iced by hot air.

Landing Gear: Retractable tricycle type. Hydraulic actuation. Main units retract rearward into fairings on wing trailing-edge. Each consists of a bogie made up of three pairs of wheels, size 930 × 305, in tandem; tyre pressure 114 lb/sq in (8·0 kg/cm²). Steerable anti-shimmy twin-wheel nose unit has wheels size 800 × 225 and retracts forward. Disc brakes and anti-skid units on main wheels.

Power Plant: Three Kuznetsov NK-8-2 turbofan engines, each rated at 20,950 lb (9,500 kg) st, one on each side of rear fuselage and one inside extreme rear of fuselage. Two lateral engines fitted with upper and lower thrust-reversal grilles. Integral fuel tanks in wings; standard capacity 9,050 Imp gallons (41,140 litres). Max fuel capacity 10,300 Imp gallons (46,825 litres). Single-point refuelling standard.

Accommodation: Flight crew of two pilots and flight engineer; provision for navigator aft of pilot and folding seats for additional pilots or instructors. There are basic passenger versions for a total of 167, 158, 152, 146 and 128 passengers. Each has a toilet at the front (starboard), removable galley amidships and three toilets aft. Coat storage, folding seat and inflatable evacuation chute in each entrance lobby. Standard economy class version has 54 seats in six-abreast rows, with two tables between front rows, in forward cabin; and 104 seats in six-abreast rows (rear two rows four-abreast) in rear cabin at seat pitch of 29·5 in (75 cm). The 167-seat high-density version differs in having one further row of six seats in the forward cabin and reduced galley facilities. The tourist class versions carry 146 passengers at a seat pitch of 31·9 in (81 cm) or 152 at a pitch of 34·25 in (87 cm) with reduced galley facilities. The 128-seat version has only 24 first class seats, four-abreast at a pitch of 40 in (102 cm), in the forward cabin. There is also an all-cargo version. Passenger doors are forward of front cabin and between cabins on the port side, with emergency and service doors opposite. All four doors open outwards. Four emergency exits; two over wing on each side. Two pressurised baggage holds under main cabin floor, with two inward-opening doors. Normal provision for mechanised loading and unloading of baggage and freight in containers. Smaller unpressurised hold under rear cabin for carrying spare parts or special cargo such as radioactive isotopes.

Electronics and Equipment: Automatic flight control system standard, including automatic navigation on pre-programmed route under control of navigational computer with en-route checks by ground radio beacons (including VOR, VOR/DME) or radar, and automatic approach by ILS to ICAO category II standards (development to category III standard in hand). Moving-map ground position indicator,

HF and VHF radio, and radar standard. Safety equipment includes four inflatable life-rafts, each for 26 persons.

Systems: Air-conditioning system pressure differential 9·0 lb/sq in (0·63 kg/cm²). Three independent hydraulic systems; working pressure 3,000 lb/sq in (210 kg/cm²). No. 1 system, powered by two pumps driven by centre engine and port engine, operates landing gear, brakes and all control surfaces. No. 2 system, powered by a pump driven by centre engine, actuates nosewheel steering, the second flying controls circuit and landing gear emergency extension. No. 3 system, powered by pump on starboard engine, actuates the third flying controls circuit and second landing gear emergency extension circuit. Three-phase 200/115V AC electrical system, supplied by three 40kVA alternators. 28V DC system. APU standard, driving 40kVA alternator and 12kW starter/generator.

Dimensions, external:

Wing span	123 ft 2½ in (37·55 m)
Length overall	157 ft 1⅝ in (47·90 m)
Height overall	37 ft 4⅔ in (11·40 m)
Diameter of fuselage	12 ft 5½ in (3·80 m)
Tailplane span	43 ft 11½ in (13·40 m)
Wheel track	37 ft 9 in (11·50 m)
Wheelbase	62 ft 1 in (18·92 m)
Min ground turning radius	80 ft 8½ in (24·60 m)
Passenger doors (each):	
Height	5 ft 7 in (1·73 m)
Width	2 ft 7½ in (0·80 m)
Height to sill	10 ft 2 in (3·10 m)
Servicing door:	
Height	4 ft 2½ in (1·28 m)
Width	2 ft 0 in (0·61 m)
Emergency door:	
Height	4 ft 2½ in (1·28 m)
Width	2 ft 1¼ in (0·64 m)
Emergency exits (each):	
Height	2 ft 11½ in (0·90 m)
Width	1 ft 7 in (0·48 m)
Main baggage hold doors (each):	
Height	3 ft 11¼ in (1·20 m)
Width	4 ft 5 in (1·35 m)
Height to sill	5 ft 11 in (1·80 m)
Rear (unpressurised) hold:	
Height	2 ft 11½ in (0·90 m)
Width	3 ft 7¼ in (1·10 m)
Height to sill	7 ft 2½ in (2·20 m)

Dimensions, internal:

Cabin: Width	11 ft 9 in (3·58 m)
Height	6 ft 7½ in (2·02 m)
Volume	5,763 cu ft (163·2 m³)
Main baggage holds:	
Front	759 cu ft (21·5 m³)
Rear	582 cu ft (16·5 m³)
Rear underfloor hold	176 cu ft (5·0 m³)

Areas:

Wings, gross	2,169 sq ft (201·45 m²)
Horizontal tail surfaces	436·48 sq ft (40·55 m²)
Vertical tail surfaces	341·43 sq ft (31·72 m²)

Weights:

Operating weight empty	95,900 lb (43,500 kg)
Normal payload	35,275 lb (16,000 kg)
Max payload	44,090 lb (20,000 kg)
Max fuel	73,085 lb (33,150 kg)
Max ramp weight	199,077 lb (90,300 kg)
Normal T-O weight	185,188 lb (84,000 kg)
Max T-O weight	198,416 lb (90,000 kg)
Normal landing weight	149,915 lb (68,000 kg)
Max landing weight	176,370 lb (80,000 kg)
Max zero-fuel weight	139,994 lb (63,500 kg)

Performance (at max T-O weight, except where indicated):

Max level speed: above 36,000 ft (11,000 m)
 Mach 0·90; at low altitudes 310 knots (357 mph; 575 km/h) IAS

Max cruising speed at 31,150 ft (9,500 m)
 526 knots (605 mph; 975 km/h)

Best-cost cruising speed at 36,000-39,350 ft (11,000-12,000 m)
 Mach 0·85 (486 knots; 560 mph; 900 km/h)

Long-range cruising speed at 36,000-39,350 ft (11,000-12,000 m)
 Mach 0·80 (459 knots; 528 mph; 850 km/h)

Approach speed
 127 knots (146 mph; 235 km/h)

T-O run at normal T-O weight, ISA
 3,740 ft (1,140 m)

Balanced runway length at max T-O weight, FAR standard:

ISA, S/L	6,890 ft (2,100 m)
ISA+20°C, S/L	7,940 ft (2,420 m)

Landing field length, at max landing weight, FAR standard:

ISA, S/L	6,758 ft (2,060 m)
ISA+20°C, S/L	7,273 ft (2,217 m)

Range at 36,000 ft (11,000 m) with standard fuel, reserves for 1 hour and 6% of total fuel:
 at 486 knots (560 mph; 900 km/h), with T-O weight of 84,000 kg and max payload (158 passengers, baggage and 5 tonnes of cargo and mail) 1,360 nm (1,565 miles; 2,520 km)
 as above, T-O weight of 90,000 kg
 1,867 nm (2,150 miles; 3,460 km)
 at 459 knots (528 mph; 850 km/h), with T-O weight of 84,000 kg and max payload as above 1,510 nm (1,740 miles; 2,800 km)
 as above, T-O weight of 90,000 kg
 2,050 nm (2,360 miles; 3,800 km)
 max range with 30,100 lb (13,650 kg) payload
 2,850 nm (3,280 miles; 5,280 km)

Range at 36,000 ft (11,000 m) with optional centre-wing tanks, reserves as above:
 with 19,840 lb (9,000 kg) payload (95 passengers) 3,453 nm (3,977 miles; 6,400 km)
 with 14,770 lb (6,700 kg) payload (70 passengers) 3,723 nm (4,287 miles; 6,900 km)

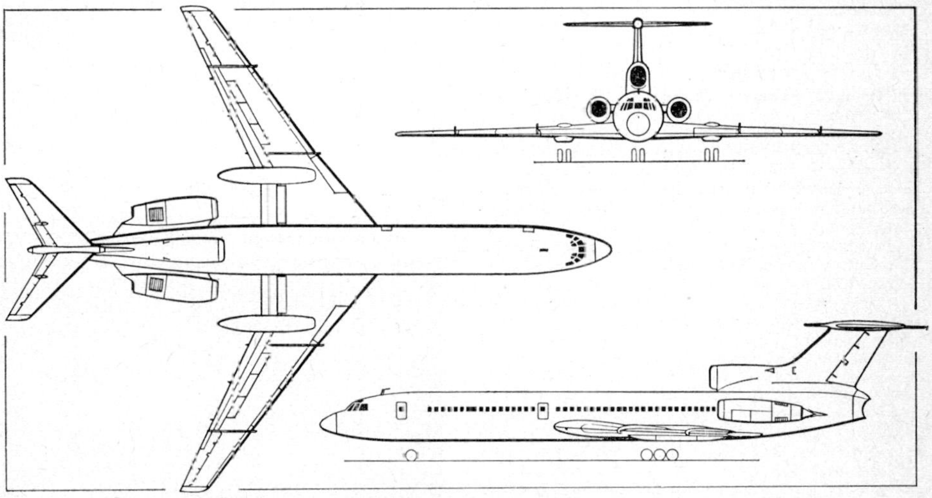

Tupolev Tu-154 medium/long-range three-turbofan transport aircraft (*Pilot Press*)

YAKOVLEV

General Designer in Charge of Bureau:
Alexander Sergeivich Yakovlev

Yakovlev is one of the most versatile Russian designers and products of his design bureau have ranged from transonic long-range fighters to the Yak-24 tandem-rotor helicopter, an experimental VTOL fighter and a variety of training and light general-purpose aircraft. Types in current production, or under development, are described hereafter.

YAKOVLEV Yak-18T

This extensively-redesigned cabin version of the Yak-18 was shown for the first time at the 1967 Paris Air Show. It is powered, like the Yak-18A and -18PM, with a 300 hp Ivchenko AI-14RF nine-cylinder radial engine, driving a two-blade variable-pitch propeller. Its braced tail unit and retractable tricycle landing gear, with inward-retracting main wheels and rearward-retracting nosewheel, are similar in configuration to those of the Yak-18PM (described in 1972-73 *Jane's*).

The wing span has been increased by extending the constant-chord centre-section, and the wing-tips are more square than on other aircraft of the Yak-18 series. The fuselage is entirely new, being built as an all-metal semi-monocoque of square section. Four persons can be carried in pairs in the enclosed cabin, which has a large forward-hinged door on each side. Dual controls, heating and ventilation are standard. The rear bench seat is removable to enable the Yak-18T to be used for cargo-carrying. As an ambulance, it will accommodate the pilot, one stretcher patient and an attendant.

Standard equipment includes ILS, VHF radio, radio compass, radio altimeter and intercom.

The Yak-18T was intended to replace the Yak-12 in Aeroflot service. In an interview in mid-1972, A. S. Yakovlev stated that production of training, ambulance, communications, touring and agricultural variants was expected to begin "soon".

Dimensions, external:

Wing span	36 ft 7¼ in (11·16 m)
Length overall	27 ft 4¾ in (8·35 m)

The four-seat Yak-18T (300 hp Ivchenko AI-14RF engine) (*S. P. Peltz*)

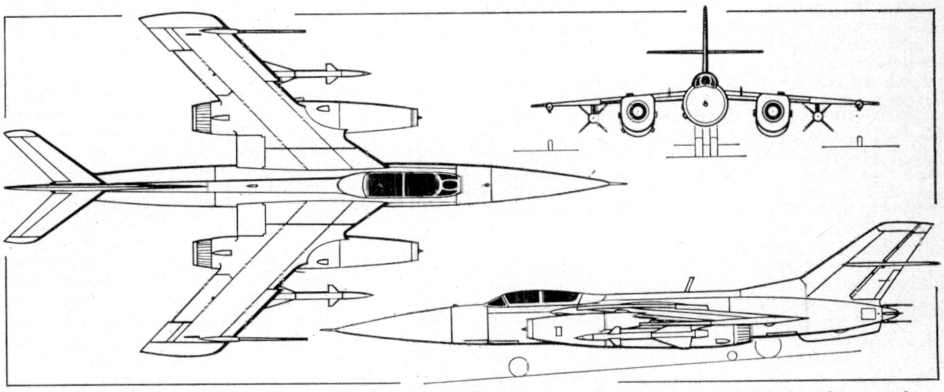

The current long-nose version of the Yakovlev Yak-28P two-seat all-weather fighter, code-named "Firebar" (*Pilot Press*)

Yakovlev Yak-28P ("Firebar") two-seat all-weather interceptor with current lengthened nosecone

AREA:
Wings, gross 202·4 sq ft (18·80 m²)
WEIGHT:
Max T-O weight 3,571 lb (1,620 kg)
PERFORMANCE:
Max level speed
162 knots (186 mph; 300 km/h)
Cruising speed 135 knots (155 mph; 250 km/h)
T-O run 655 ft (200 m)
Landing run 820 ft (250 m)
Range with max fuel
over 538 nm (620 miles; 1,000 km)

YAKOVLEV Yak-28

NATO code names: "Brewer", "Firebar" and "Maestro"

First seen in considerable numbers in the 1961 Soviet Aviation Day flypast were three obvious successors to the Yak-25/27 series (see 1971-72 *Jane's*), described by the commentator as supersonic multi-purpose aircraft and identified subsequently by the designation Yak-28. These aircraft are shoulder-wing monoplanes, whereas all versions of the Yak-25, 26 and 27 were mid-wing. The Yak-28 series were, in fact, produced as entirely new designs, following only the general configuration of the earlier types.

The landing gear comprises two twin-wheel units in tandem, with the forward unit under the pilot's cockpit and the rear unit moved further aft than on the Yak-25/27, to a point immediately in front of the ventral fin. Wingtip balancer wheels are retained. The entire wing-root leading-edge has been extended forward and the height of the fin and rudder increased. Tailplane sweep is also increased.

Several versions of the basic design have been reported, with the following NATO code names:

"Brewer-A to C" (Yak-28). Two-seat tactical attack versions. Single cockpit for pilot, with blister canopy, and glazed nose for navigator/bomb aimer. Corresponding to Yak-26 ("Mangrove") and produced to replace the Il-28 in the Soviet Air Force. Most examples have blister radome under fuselage just forward of wings. On some aircraft, long engine nacelles extend forward as far as the front of this radome. Others have shorter nacelles. Guns semi-submerged in each side of the fuselage on some aircraft; on starboard side only on others. Internal bomb bay between the underfuselage radome and the rear main landing gear unit.

"Brewer-D". Reconnaissance version, with cameras in bomb-bay.

"Brewer-E". Latest version, identified in 1974 and shown in accompanying illustration. Underfuselage radome deleted. Active ECM pack built into bomb bay, from which it projects in form of a semi-cylindrical pack. Attachments under each outer wing, outboard of external fuel tank, for a rocket pod.

"Firebar". Tandem two-seat all-weather fighter derivative of Yak-28, corresponding to Yak-27. Nose radome. Internal weapons bay deleted. "Anab" air-to-air missile under each wing instead of guns. Identified as **Yak-28P** (Perekhvatchik; interceptor) at 1967 Domodedovo display, the suffix "P" indicating that the design had been *adapted* for the fighter role. Example shown in static park had a much longer dielectric nosecone than the standard operational "Firebars" in the flying display and had two missile pylons under each wing, one for an "Atoll" and the other for an "Anab". This suggested that it was a weapons development aircraft. However, the lengthened nosecone has since been fitted retrospectively on Yak-28Ps in squadron service, as shown in an accompanying illustration. This does not indicate any increase in radar capability or aircraft performance.

"Maestro" (Yak-28U). Trainer version of "Firebar". Normal cockpit layout replaced by two individual single-seat cockpits in tandem, each with its own canopy. Front canopy sideways-hinged to starboard; rear canopy rearward-sliding. Large conical nose-probe.

In early 1974, Admiral Thomas H. Moorer, Chairman of the US Joint Chiefs of Staff, reported to Congress that the Yak-25 had been phased out of service during the previous year. The Yakovlev high-altitude reconnaissance aircraft known to NATO as "Mandrake" (see 1973-74 *Jane's*) is also understood to have been retired from first-line service. The four newest Soviet interceptors, the Yak-28P ("Firebar", above), Tupolev Tu-28P, Sukhoi Su-15 and MiG-25, now account for 50 per cent of the Soviet defence interceptor force of more than 2,500 aircraft.

By contrast, the Yak-28 "Brewer" series seem to be changing gradually from first-line attack to support roles, with the emphasis on ECM, reconnaissance and operational training.

The following details refer specifically to the Yak-28P, but are generally applicable to the other versions of the Yak-28.

TYPE: Two-seat transonic all-weather interceptor.

WINGS: Cantilever shoulder-wing monoplane of basically constant chord. Extended leading-edge on outer wings and also between fuselage and each engine nacelle. Outer extensions are drooped. Slotted flap, with unswept trailing-edge, between fuselage and each engine nacelle. Basic wing sweepback 45°. Anhedral from root. Single fence on upper surface of each wing, between fuselage and engine nacelle. Large trailing-edge flap and short aileron, with tab, outboard of nacelle on each wing. Balancer-wheel fairings, inset from wingtips, are extended forward as lead-filled wing balance weights.

FUSELAGE: All-metal semi-monocoque structure of basically circular section. Finely-tapered dielectric nosecone over radar scanner.

TAIL UNIT: Cantilever all-metal structure. Variable-incidence tailplane mounted midway up fin. All surfaces sweptback. Trim tab in rudder. Dorsal fin fairs into spine along top of fuselage. Shallow ventral stabilising fin.

LANDING GEAR: Two twin-wheel main units in tandem, retracting into fuselage. Front unit retracts forward, rear unit rearward. Small balancer wheel near each wingtip, retracting rearward under wing; fairing integral with leg.

POWER PLANT: Two afterburning turbojet engines, believed to be of same basic type as Tumansky RD-11 fitted to MiG-21, with rating of 13,120 lb (5,950 kg) st. Each fitted with centre-body shock-cone. A pointed slipper-type external fuel tank can be carried under the leading-edge of each wing, outboard of the engine nacelle.

ACCOMMODATION: Crew of two in tandem on ejection seats in pressurised cabin under long transparent blister canopy.

ARMAMENT: Pylon under each outer wing for "Anab" air-to-air missile, with alternative infra-red or semi-active radar homing heads.

OPERATIONAL EQUIPMENT: Reported to include aft-warning radar.

DIMENSIONS, EXTERNAL (estimated):
Wing span 42 ft 6 in (12·95 m)
Length overall:
Yak-28 71 ft 0½ in (21·65 m)
Height overall 12 ft 11½ in (3·95 m)
WEIGHT (estimated):
Max T-O weight:
Yak-28P 35,000 lb (15,875 kg)
PERFORMANCE (Yak-28P, estimated):
Max level speed at 35,000 ft (10,670 m)
Mach 1·1 (636 knots; 733 mph; 1,180 km/h)
Cruising speed 496 knots (571 mph; 920 km/h)
Service ceiling 55,000 ft (16,750 m)

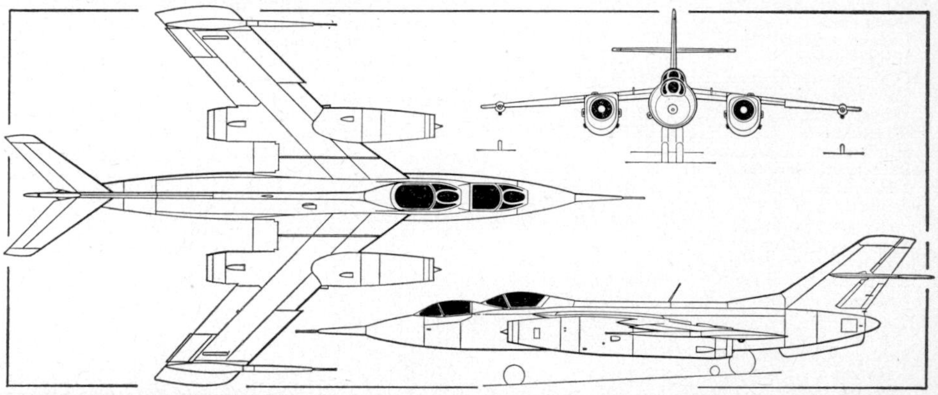

The tandem-cockpit training version of the Yak-28P, known to NATO as "Maestro" (*Pilot Press*)

This latest version of the Yak-28 (NATO "Brewer-E") is equipped for active ECM operations

Max combat radius 500 nm (575 miles; 925 km)
Max range 1,040-1,390 nm (1,200-1,600 miles; 1,930-2,575 km)

YAKOVLEV Yak-36

NATO code name: "Freehand"

This aircraft is much less refined than the British Hawker Siddeley Harrier and must be regarded as a purely experimental design. The two examples photographed at the air display at Domodedovo in July 1967 appeared to be identical. Only one (bearing the number 37 on its nose) took part in the flying programme, without underwing stores. Photographs of the other aircraft (No 38) showed it with a 16-round rocket pack under each wing.

About a dozen Yak-36s are believed to have been built for evaluation and test, and one of them is reported to have carried out sea trials from a specially-installed pad on the flight deck of the helicopter carrier *Moskva*.

Code named "Freehand" by NATO, the Yak-36 is clearly subsonic. At Domodedovo, aircraft No 37 took off vertically, performed a transition at a height of about 160 ft (50 m), made a circuit of the airfield, including a high-speed fly-past, and ended with a 180° hovering turn before making a vertical landing.

The details below, and accompanying illustration, are retained as an indication of Soviet lines of thought on V/STOL combat aircraft technology, particularly in relation to operations from naval aircraft carriers, sea control ships or through-deck cruisers. The Yak-36 itself is unlikely to have developed beyond the R and D phases; but the Soviet Navy is known to require a V/STOL fighter for operation from its new carriers of the *Kuril* class, the first of which is expected to join the fleet in 1975.

According to Admiral Thomas H. Moorer, Chairman of the US Joint Chiefs of Staff: "This ship is over 900 ft in length and should displace 30-40,000 tons. The deck configuration and the lack of catapults or arresting gear indicate that this ship apparently is designed to operate V/STOL aircraft and helicopters. It should be capable of carrying 25 V/STOL aircraft or 36 helicopters. It is believed, however, that a mixture of new V/STOL tactical aircraft and 'Hormone' (Ka-25) helicopters is the most likely complement".

A strike/reconnaissance V/STOL aircraft is thought to have been evolved from the Yak-36 by the Yakovlev bureau, utilising a mixture of vectored thrust and direct jet-lift. Other Soviet design bureaus are hardly likely to have ignored the requirement for such an aircraft.

The following description applies to the Yak-36s seen at Domodedovo in 1967:

Type: Single-seat VTOL research aircraft.

Wings: Cantilever mid-wing monoplane of cropped delta planform. Anhedral from roots. Sweepback approx 40° on leading-edges. Entire trailing-edge hinged, as flaps and ailerons.

Fuselage: Wide fuselage of elliptical cross-section, with divided ram air intake in nose. Two large blister fairings on front fuselage, under each engine. Full-width backward-hinged door under nose to reduce possibility of recirculation into air intakes during take-off and landing; this door incorporates small separately-hinged centre panels between which nosewheel retracts. Smaller rearward-hinged door under centre-fuselage, forward of nozzles, prevents undesirable interaction of exhaust gases under fuselage, in conjunction with two longitudinal strakes forward and inboard of nozzles. The outboard edges of both doors are bent down in the form of shallow strakes. Double-hinged panel forward of main landing gear unit protects it from hot exhaust gases and is also used as an airbrake.

The Yakovlev Yak-36 experimental VTOL aircraft, code-named "Freehand"

Tail Unit: Cantilever type with tailplane mounted high on fin. All surfaces swept. Fixed-incidence tailplane, with conventional elevators. Trim tab in rudder. Two large ventral fins, between which is mounted a trapeze-shape telemetry aerial.

Landing Gear: Retractable tandem type, consisting of a single forward-retracting nose-wheel and rearward-retracting twin-wheel main unit, with two small balancer wheels which retract forward into the wingtip fairings.

Power Plant: Two turbojet engines, mounted side by side at bottom of front fuselage and each exhausting through a large-diameter louvred and gridded vectored-thrust nozzle. Bleed-air supply to "puffer-pipe" reaction control nozzles located at the tail, at the end of a massive nose-probe and in each wingtip fairing, for control in hovering and low-speed flight.

Accommodation: Single seat under sideways-hinged blister canopy. One-piece curved windscreen with no optically-flat panels. Pilot seated high, above power plant.

Dimensions, external (estimated):

Wing span, between centrelines of wingtip fairings	27 ft 0 in (8·25 m)
Length overall	57 ft 6 in (17·50 m)
Length of fuselage:	
incl nose-probe	51 ft 0 in (15·50 m)
excl nose-probe	41 ft 0 in (12·50 m)
Height overall	14 ft 9 in (4·50 m)

YAKOVLEV Yak-40

NATO code name: "Codling"

This short-haul jet transport was designed to replace the Li-2 (Soviet-built DC-3) and to operate from Class 5 (grass) airfields. Although comparatively small, it is powered by three turbofan engines, mounted at the tail. The prototype flew for the first time on 21 October 1966 and was followed quickly by four more prototypes. Production was initiated in 1967 and the Yak-40 made its first passenger flight in Aeroflot service on 30 September 1968. By the Spring of 1973, more than eight million passengers had been carried, and Aeroflot Yak-40s had flown 108,000,000 nm (124,270,000 miles; 200,000,000 km). They will become the most widely used aircraft on Soviet domestic routes up to 810 nm (930 miles; 1,500 km) long by 1975, operating over several thousand short routes, some of them in mountain areas.

By the Spring of 1973, more than 400 Yak-40s had been built. Most are in service with Aeroflot, some as air ambulances carrying patients to medical centres and to Black Sea convalescent centres. Production of at least 100 more had been authorised at that time, and these are being built in a factory at Saratov, about 300 miles (500 km) south-east of Moscow, at a current rate of eight per month. Two have been delivered to Aertirrena of Italy, who are also distributors of the Yak-40. Others have been sold in Afghanistan, Bulgaria, Czechoslovakia, France, West Germany, Poland and Yugoslavia. Military operators include the Soviet and Yugoslav air forces.

There has been no recent news of the high-density 40-seat version of the Yak-40, shown at the 1971 Paris Air Show, or of versions with uprated AI-25T engines, to which A. S. Yakovlev referred at that time. All current production Yak-40s are structurally similar, with AI-25 engines, and differ only in their standard of accommodation, for 27 or 32 airline passengers in a single class, 16 or 20 passengers in two-class layouts, or up to 11 passengers in an executive layout. All have clamshell thrust reversers aft of the centre engine. The pointed fairing forward of the fin/tailplane intersection on earlier aircraft is absent on current versions.

At the 1974 Hanover Air Show, a member of the Yakovlev bureau revealed that the prototype of a freighter version of the Yak-40 was under test at Saratov. This has a cargo door, size approximately 5 ft × 5 ft $2\frac{1}{2}$ in (1·50 m × 1·60 m), in the port side of the fuselage.

The Yak-40 is designed for a service life of 30,000 hours. It can take off and climb on any two engines and maintain height in cruising flight with two engines inoperative.

When the Yak-40 first entered service, it was

Yakovlev Yak-40 short-range transport (three Ivchenko AI-25 turbofan engines) with ventral airstair door lowered (*Brian M. Service*)

the standard Soviet technique to cruise with the centre engine throttled back to idling thrust. It is now more usual to set all three engines at cruise thrust.

TYPE: Three-turbofan short-haul transport.

WINGS: Cantilever low-wing monoplane. Thickness/chord ratio 15% at root, 10% at tip. No sweepback at quarter-chord. All-duralumin structure consists of a main spar, fore and aft auxiliary spars, ribs and stringers, covered with skin of varying thickness for which chemical milling is utilised. Wing made in two sections, joined at aircraft centreline. Manually-operated ailerons, each in two sections. Hydraulically-operated plain flaps, each in three sections linked together by perforated plates, reportedly to cater for wing flexing in severe turbulence. Electrically-actuated trim tabs in ailerons. Automatic or manually-controlled hot-air de-icing system.

FUSELAGE: Semi-monocoque duralumin structure of frames, longerons and stringers. Floor of foam plastics with veneer covering. Skin panels spot-welded and bonded in place, then flush-riveted at ends.

TAIL UNIT: Cantilever structure of duralumin, with electrically-controlled hydraulically-actuated variable-incidence tailplane mounted at tip of fin. Manually-operated control surfaces. Electrically-actuated trim tab in rudder. Automatic or manually-controlled hot-air de-icing system.

LANDING GEAR: Hydraulically-actuated retractable type, with single wheel on each unit. Emergency extension by gravity. Main wheels retract inward and are unfaired in flight. Long-stroke oleo-nitrogen shock-absorbers. Main-wheel tyres size 1120 × 450, pressure 50-57 lb/sq in (3·5-4·0 kg/cm²). Hydraulically-steerable (55° each side) forward-retracting nose-wheel, with tyre size 720 × 310, pressure 57-64 lb/sq in (4·0-4·5 kg/cm²). Hydraulic disc brakes.

POWER PLANT: Three Ivchenko AI-25 turbofan engines, each rated at 3,300 lb (1,500 kg) st. Fin and boundary layer splitter beneath and forward of intake for centre engine. Clamshell thrust reverser fitted to airframe aft of this engine. Hot-air anti-icing system for all three engine air intakes. Fire warning and extinguishing systems standard. Fuel in integral tanks between front auxiliary spar and main spar in each wing, from outboard of the fuselage to the inner end of the aileron, total capacity 860 Imp gallons (3,910 litres). Type AI-9 turbine APU mounted in rear of top engine intake fairing for engine starting. Provision for starting from ground compressed air supply.

ACCOMMODATION: Two pilots side by side on flight deck, on adjustable seats, with dual controls. Central jump seat at rear for third person. Automatically-actuated electrical windscreen de-icing system. Main cabin normally laid out for 27 passengers in three-abreast rows, with two-chair units on starboard side of aisle. Seat pitch 29·7 in (75·5 cm). Individual ventilator by each seat. Rack for hand baggage on starboard side of cabin ceiling. Cloakroom (port), buffet, baggage compartment and toilet (starboard) aft of main cabin. Seat for stewardess against rear face of partition separating cabin from rear compartments, on port side. Normal entry via hydraulically-actuated ventral airstair door at rear. Service door on port side of cabin, at front. For high-density services, twin-seat units can be installed on each side of aisle, giving a total of 32 seats in only eight rows. Seat pitch is unchanged, enabling the rear cabin partition to be moved forward and so giving a larger baggage compartment. The 16-seat mixed class version has two passenger cabins, separated by a partition. The forward cabin has two swivelling chairs, on each side of a table, on the port side; and an inward-facing four-place settee on the starboard side, with small cupboards fore and aft. Alternatively, two more swivelling seats and a table can replace the settee. The rear cabin contains 12 seats in standard three-abreast rows. A lobby between the flight deck and forward cabin provides access for the crew without passing through the main cabins, and contains a cloakroom (starboard) and seat for the stewardess. Compartments aft of the rear cabin are as in the standard 27-seat version. The 20-seat version differs from the 16-seater in having 16 seats four-abreast in the rear cabin. The executive version has a toilet and other facilities in a large compartment aft of the flight deck; a centre lounge furnished with a four-place settee, three armchairs, a writing desk and a sideboard; and rear cabin containing six seats, three-abreast. There is a further toilet aft, and the galley is equipped to special standards. A bar with two adjustable tables is built into the wall between the flight deck and lounge, on the port side.

ELECTRONICS AND EQUIPMENT: Standard equipment includes full blind-flying instrumentation, two Landysh-5 VHF radio communications installations, an ARK-10 automatic radio compass, KURS-MP-2 VOR/ILS system, RV-5 radio altimeter, Type SO 70 transponder, Grosa-40 weather radar, PRIVOD-ANE-1 flight director system, Kremenj 40E autopilot, AGD 1 artificial horizon and GMK-1GE gyro-compass, permitting automatic approach to ICAO Category II standards. A Collins avionics package is available optionally to Western operators.

SYSTEMS: Cabin fully pressurised and air-conditioned, with air bleed from final compressor stages of AI-25 engines; max pressure differential 4·26 lb/sq in (0·3 kg/cm²). Two independent hydraulic systems, pressure 2,135 lb/sq in (150 kg/cm²), supplied by Type NP-72M pumps on centre and port engines, with electrical standby pump and emergency handpump. Type AMG 10 hydraulic fluid. Electrical supply from three Type VG-7.500-1a DC generators and two Type 20 KNVN 25 batteries, each generator being driven by one of the turbofan engines. Two Type PO-1500 inverters provide 115V single-phase AC supply; Type PT-500 and PT-1000 inverters supply a 36V three-phase AC system. The Type AI-9 APU can also be used for cabin air-conditioning when the aircraft is on the ground. Installed and portable oxygen systems.

DIMENSIONS, EXTERNAL:
- Wing span: 82 ft 0¼ in (25·0 m)
- Wing aspect ratio: 9
- Length overall: 66 ft 9½ in (20·36 m)
- Length of fuselage: 55 ft 9 in (17·00 m)
- Diameter of fuselage: 7 ft 10½ in (2·40 m)
- Height overall: 21 ft 4 in (6·50 m)
- Tailplane span: 24 ft 7¼ in (7·50 m)
- Wheel track: 14 ft 10 in (4·52 m)
- Wheelbase: 24 ft 6 in (7·47 m)
- Rear cabin door:
  - Height: 5 ft 8½ in (1·74 m)
  - Width: 3 ft 1 in (0·94 m)
- Service door:
  - Height: 3 ft 11¼ in (1·20 m)
  - Width: 1 ft 9½ in (0·55 m)

DIMENSIONS, INTERNAL:
- Cabin: Length: 23 ft 2½ in (7·07 m)
  - Max width: 7 ft 0¾ in (2·15 m)
  - Max height: 6 ft 0¾ in (1·85 m)

AREA:
- Wings, gross: 753·5 sq ft (70·00 m²)

WEIGHTS AND LOADINGS (A: 27 seats, B: 32 seats, C: 16 seats, D: executive version):
- Weight empty:
  - A: 19,865-20,725 lb (9,010-9,400 kg)
  - B: 20,725 lb (9,400 kg)
  - D: 21,0 5-21,715 lb (9,560-9,850 kg)
- Max payload:
  - A: 5,070 lb (2,300 kg)
  - B: 6,000 lb (2,720 kg)
  - C: 3,000 lb (1,360 kg)
  - D: 2,180 lb (990 kg)
- Max fuel weight:
  - A: 4,685-8,820 lb (2,125-4,000 kg)
  - B: 8,820 lb (4,000 kg)
  - D: 6,615-8,820 lb (3,000-4,000 kg)
- Normal T-O weight:
  - A: 27,250-34,170 lb (12,360-15,500 kg)
  - B: 34,170 lb (15,500 kg)
  - D: 27,250-33,070 lb (12,360-15,000 kg)
- Max T-O weight:
  - A, B: 35,275 lb (16,000 kg)
  - C: 33,750 lb (15,310 kg)
  - D: 33,950 lb (15,400 kg)
- Max wing loading:
  - A, B: 47·1 lb/sq ft (230 kg/m²)

PERFORMANCE (corresponding to weights given above):
- Max level speed at S/L: Mach 0·7 (324 knots; 373 mph; 600 km/h) IAS
- Max cruising speed at 23,000 ft (7,000 m): 297 knots (342 mph; 550 km/h)
- Max rate of climb at S/L: 1,575 ft (480 m)/min
- T-O speed:
  - A, B: 86 knots (100 mph; 160 km/h)
  - D: 81-84 knots (93-97 mph; 150-156 km/h)
- Normal T-O run:
  - A, B: 2,297 ft (700 m)
  - C: 2,133 ft (650 m)
  - D: 2,165 ft (660 m)
- Normal landing run:
  - A, C, D: 1,050 ft (320 m)
  - B: 1,182 ft (360 m)
- Range with max payload at 254 knots (292 mph; 470 km/h) at 31,500 ft (8,000 m), with reserve:
  - A, C, D: 971 nm (1,118 miles; 1,800 km)

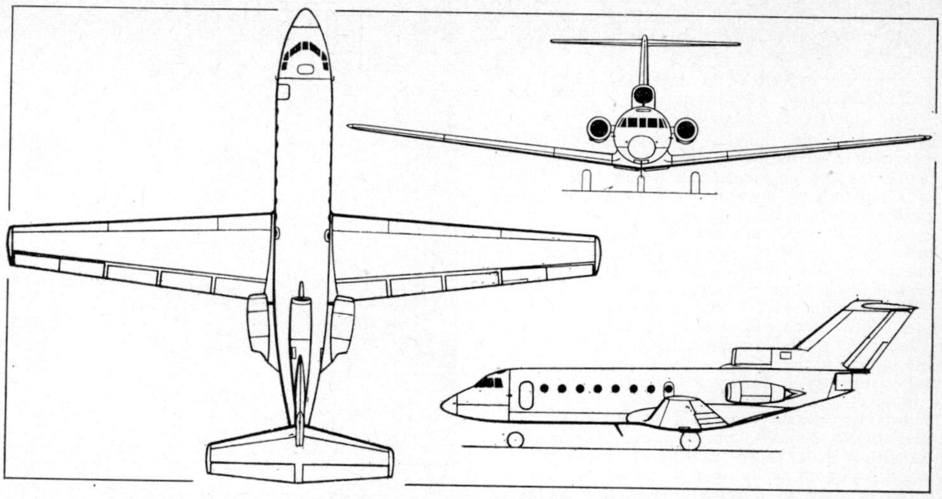

Yakovlev Yak-40 three-turbofan short-range transport *(Pilot Press)*

This photograph shows clearly the thrust reverser aft of the centre engine of the Yak-40

B 782 nm (900 miles; 1,450 km)
Range with max fuel at 254 knots (292 mph; 470 km/h) at 31,500 ft (8,000 m), with reserve:
All versions 971 nm (1,118 miles; 1,800 km)
Max range at 254 knots (292 mph; 470 km/h) at 31,500 ft (8,000 m), no reserve:
All versions 1,080 nm (1,240 miles; 2,000 km)

YAKOVLEV Yak-42

On the basis of experience with the Yak-40, the Yakovlev design bureau is developing for Aeroflot this larger civil airliner with a similar three-engined layout. A full-scale mock-up existed in the bureau's prototype hangar in Moscow in mid-1973, but the design of the Yak-42 had not been finalised in detail by that time. First photographs of a model were released officially through *Tass* in 1974.

According to Alexander Yakovlev, the basic design objectives were simple construction, reliability in operation, economy and the ability to operate in remote areas with widely differing climatic conditions. Up to 2,000 aircraft in this category are needed, for use particularly on feederline services extending north and south from the main east-west trans-Siberian trunk routes.

As envisaged in mid-1974, the Yak-42 will have standard accommodation for 120 passengers in six-abreast seats at a pitch of 31·5 in (80 cm). Replacement of the front ten rows by four-abreast first class seats will offer an alternative mixed class version for 100 passengers. Access to the cabin will be by airstair doors under the rear fuselage and at the front of the cabin on the port side, making the aircraft independent of airport ground equipment. Immediately inside each lobby will be carry-on baggage and coat compartments for use by the passengers.

A flight crew of two will be normal, with provision for a high degree of automation, including an area navigation system. Control surfaces will be actuated hydraulically, and high-lift devices will include wing leading-edge slats. To cater for rough-field operations, a heavy-duty tricycle landing gear will be fitted, with twin wheels on the nose unit.

The Yak-42 will be powered by three D-36 high by-pass ratio (5·34 : 1) turbofan engines, designed under the leadership of Vladimir Lotarev at the Zaporozhye engine works. Take-off rating of each engine will be 14,200 lb (6,440 kg) st, and the Yak-42 is intended to use all three engines at cruise power during flight. Special care has been taken during design to ensure that the D-36 will conform with national and international limits on smoke and noise; and the Yak-42 is intended to operate in temperatures ranging from —50°C to +50°C.

Three prototypes of the Yak-42 have been ordered initially, with first flight scheduled for early 1975 and entry into service in 1976-77. The following data should be regarded as provisional:

DIMENSIONS, EXTERNAL:
Wing span 114 ft 10 in (35·00 m)
Wing sweepback 25°
Length overall 114 ft 10 in (35·00 m)
DIMENSION, INTERNAL:
Cabin: Max width 12 ft 6 in (3·80 m)
WEIGHTS:
Max payload 30,850 lb (14,000 kg)
Max T-O weight 110,230 lb (50,000 kg)
PERFORMANCE (estimated):
Max cruising speed 470 knots (540 mph; 870 km/h)
Econ cruising speed at 26,250 ft (8,000 m) 442 knots (510 mph; 820 km/h)
T-O run 2,625 ft (800 m)
Range with max payload 970 nm (1,118 miles; 1,800 km)
Range with max fuel 1,725 nm (1,985 miles; 3,200 km)

Model of the Yakovlev Yak-42 short-range passenger transport (*Tass*)

VIETNAM
(REPUBLIC OF)

VIETNAM AIR FORCE

ADDRESS:
DCS Materiel, Vietnam Air Force, Saigon, Vietnam KBC. 3011

DIRECTOR OF PROGRAMME:
Colonel Dang Dinh Linh

On 1 July 1971, the Air Force day of the VNAF, the first flight took place at Tan Son Nhut airfield, Saigon, of the first **Pazmany PL-2** light aircraft completed by the VNAF. Several VNAF bases contributed to the construction of this aircraft: the tail surfaces were built at Da Nang and Nha Thrang, the fuselage at the Air Logistics Command Depot at Bien Hoa, and the wings and control surfaces at Tan Son Nhut. Final assembly took place at Tan Son Nhut.

As a further step towards the creation of a national aircraft industry in Vietnam, the VNAF is negotiating with Pazmany Aircraft Corporation an agreement to build a further 10 or more PL-2s. A description of the PL-2 appears under the Pazmany heading in the US section of this edition.

YUGOSLAVIA

SOKO

"SOKO" METALOPRERADIVACKA INDUSTRIJA BEZ OGRANICENE ODGOVORNOSTI

ADDRESS:
Mostar
Telephone: 22-121/125, 22-139, 22-156/157, 22-183
Telex: 46-180

GENERAL MANAGER: Dipl-Ing Ivan Sert
ASSISTANT MANAGING DIRECTOR:
Dipl-Ing Stefan Obreht
DIRECTOR, AIRCRAFT FACTORY:
Dipl-Ing Sulejman Gosto
MARKETING DIRECTOR: Fuad Bijedic

Founded in 1951, this company is manufacturing a two-seat jet basic trainer named the Galeb and a single-seat light attack version of the same design, named the J-1 Jastreb.

Soko is also building under licence the Aérospatiale/Westland Gazelle helicopter, on behalf of the Yugoslav government.

Soko G2-A Galeb two-seat basic training aircraft (Rolls-Royce Bristol Viper 11 turbojet engine)

SOKO G2-A GALEB (SEAGULL)

Design of the Galeb was started in 1957. Construction of two prototypes began in 1959 and the first of these flew for the first time in May 1961. Development was carried out in collaboration with the Yugoslav Aeronautical Research Establishments and construction is in accordance with current military airworthiness requirements. Production began in 1963 for the Yugoslav Air Force and continued in 1972 to fulfil repeat Yugoslav and export orders. First overseas operator was the Zambian Air Force, which took delivery of two Galebs in early 1971.

The current G2-A model embodies several improvements, including an optional cockpit air-conditioning system.

TYPE: Two-seat armed jet basic trainer, designed for load factors of $+8g$ and $—4g$.

WINGS: Cantilever low-wing monoplane. Wing section NACA 64A213·5 at root, NACA 64A212·0 at tip. Dihedral 1° 30′. No incidence. Sweepback at quarter-chord 4° 19′. Conventional light alloy two-spar stressed-skin structure, consisting of a centre-section, integral with the fuselage, and two outer panels which can be removed easily. Manually-operated internally-sealed light alloy ailerons. Trim tab on port aileron. Hydraulically-actuated Fowler flaps. No de-icing system.

FUSELAGE: Light alloy semi-monocoque structure in two portions, joined together by four bolts at frame aft of wing trailing-edge. Rear portion removable for engine servicing. Two hydraulically-actuated door-type airbrakes under centre-fuselage.

TAIL UNIT: Cantilever light alloy stressed-skin structure. Fixed-incidence tailplane. Rudder and elevators statically and dynamically balanced and manually operated. Trim/balance tab in starboard elevator; balance tab in port elevator. VHF radio aerial forms tip of fin.

LANDING GEAR: Hydraulically-retractable tricycle type, with single wheel on each unit. Nosewheel retracts forward, main units inward into wings. Oleo-pneumatic shock-absorbers manufactured by Prva Petoletka of Trstenik. Dunlop main wheels and tyres size 23×7·25-10, pressure 64 lb/sq in (4·5 kg/cm²). Dunlop nosewheel and tyre size 6·50-5·5 TC, pressure 49·8 lb/sq in (3·5 kg/cm²). Prva Petoletka hydraulic differential disc brakes, toe-operated from both cockpits.

POWER PLANT: One Rolls-Royce Bristol Viper 11 Mk 22-6 turbojet engine, rated at 2,500 lb (1,134 kg) st. Two flexible fuel tanks aft of cockpits, with total capacity of 1,720 lb (780 kg). Two jettisonable wingtip tanks, each with capacity of 375 lb (170 kg). Refuelling point on upper part of fuselage aft of cockpits. Fuel system designed to permit up to 15 seconds of inverted flight. Oil capacity 1·4 Imp gallons (6·25 litres).

ACCOMMODATION: Crew of two in tandem on Folland Type 1-B fully-automatic lightweight ejection seats. Separate sideways-hinged (to starboard) jettisonable canopy over each cockpit. Cockpit air-conditioning to special order only.

SYSTEMS: Hydraulic system, pressure 850-1,000 lb/sq in (60-70 kg/cm²), for landing gear, airbrakes and flaps. Separate system for wheel brakes. Pneumatic system for armament cocking. Electrical system includes 6kW 24V generator, 24V battery, and inverter to provide 115V 400Hz AC supply for instruments. Low-pressure oxygen system, capacity 1,450 litres.

ELECTRONICS AND EQUIPMENT: Blind-flying instrumentation, Marconi radio compass (licence-built by Rudi Cajavec), intercom and STR-9Z1 VHF radio transceiver standard. Standard electrical equipment includes navigation lights, 250W landing lamp in nose, and 50W taxying lamp on nose landing gear. Camera, with focal length of 7 in (178 mm) and 125-exposure magazine, can be fitted in rear cockpit. Flares can be carried on the underwing bomb racks for night photography.

ARMAMENT: All production aircraft have two 0·50 in machine-guns in nose (with 80 rds/gun) and underwing pylons for two 50 kg or 100 kg bombs and four 57 mm rockets or two 127 mm rockets.

DIMENSIONS, EXTERNAL:
- Wing span: 34 ft 4½ in (10·47 m)
- Wing span over tip-tanks: 38 ft 1½ in (11·62 m)
- Wing chord at root: 7 ft 9 in (2·36 m)
- Wing chord at tip: 4 ft 7 in (1·40 m)
- Wing aspect ratio: 5·55
- Length overall: 33 ft 11 in (10·34 m)
- Height overall: 10 ft 9 in (3·28 m)
- Tailplane span: 14 ft 0 in (4·27 m)
- Wheel track: 12 ft 9 in (3·89 m)
- Wheelbase: 11 ft 9½ in (3·59 m)

AREAS:
- Wings, gross: 209·14 sq ft (19·43 m²)
- Ailerons (total): 25·40 sq ft (2·36 m²)
- Trailing-edge flaps (total): 21·75 sq ft (2·02 m²)
- Airbrake: 3·66 sq ft (0·34 m²)
- Fin: 14·42 sq ft (1·34 m²)
- Rudder, including tab: 6·03 sq ft (0·56 m²)
- Tailplane: 39·40 sq ft (3·66 m²)
- Elevators, including tabs: 8·93 sq ft (0·83 m²)

WEIGHTS:
- Weight empty, equipped: 5,775 lb (2,620 kg)
- Max T-O weight:
  - Fully-aerobatic trainer (clean): 7,438 lb (3,374 kg)
  - Basic trainer (no tip-tanks): 7,690 lb (3,488 kg)
  - Navigational trainer (with tip-tanks): 8,439 lb (3,828 kg)
  - Weapons trainer: 8,792 lb (3,988 kg)
  - Strike version: 9,210 lb (4,178 kg)

PERFORMANCE (at normal T-O weight):
- Max level speed at S/L: 408 knots (470 mph; 756 km/h)
- Max level speed at 20,350 ft (6,200 m): 438 knots (505 mph; 812 km/h)
- Max cruising speed at 19,680 ft (6,000 m): 394 knots (453 mph; 730 km/h)
- Stalling speed:
  - flaps and airbrakes down: 85 knots (98 mph; 158 km/h)
  - flaps and airbrakes up: 97 knots (112 mph; 180 km/h)
- Max rate of climb at S/L: 4,500 ft (1,370 m)/min
- Time to 9,840 ft (3,000 m): 2·4 min
- Time to 19,680 ft (6,000 m): 5·5 min
- Time to 29,520 ft (9,000 m): 10·2 min
- Service ceiling: 39,375 ft (12,000 m)
- T-O run on grass: 1,610 ft (490 m)
- T-O to 50 ft (15 m): 2,100 ft (640 m)
- Landing from 50 ft (15 m): 2,330 ft (710 m)
- Landing run on grass: 1,310 ft (400 m)
- Max range at 29,520 ft (9,000 m), with tip-tanks full: 669 nm (770 miles; 1,240 km)
- Max endurance at 23,000 ft (7,000 m): 2 hr 30 min

Soko J-1 Jastreb single-seat light attack aircraft, developed from the Galeb (*John Blake*)

SOKO G-3 GALEB-3 (SEAGULL)

Design of this more extensively equipped and more powerful version of the Galeb jet basic trainer was started in April 1969, to offer improved performance and crew comfort, and to give increased capability in the light tactical support and day and night reconnaissance roles. Construction of the prototype Galeb-3 began in November 1969. It flew for the first time on 19 August 1970. No further Galeb-3s had been built by early 1974. Details can be found in the 1973-74 *Jane's*.

SOKO J-1 JASTREB (HAWK)

The J-1 Jastreb is a single-seat light attack version of the G2-A Galeb. It continued in production for the Yugoslav Air Force in 1972. First overseas operator was the Zambian Air Force, which received four Jastrebs in early 1971.

In the J-1 Jastreb, the front cockpit of the G2-A Galeb trainer, with sideways-hinged (to starboard) canopy, is retained, a metal fairing replacing the rear canopy. The engine is the more powerful Rolls-Royce Bristol Viper 531. Other changes include the installation of improved day and night reconnaissance equipment, electronic navigation and communications equipment and, to special order only, a pressurised cockpit and self-contained engine starting. In other respects the airframe and power plant remain essentially unchanged except for some local strengthening and the provision of strongpoints for heavier underwing stores.

The details given for the G2-A Galeb apply equally to the J-1 Jastreb, with the exceptions listed below:

TYPE: Single-seat light attack aircraft.

WINGS: Wing section NACA 64 series. Changed aspect ratio and chord at root.

POWER PLANT: One Rolls-Royce Bristol Viper 531 turbojet engine, rated at 3,000 lb (1,360 kg) st. Capacity of each wingtip tank 485 lb (220 kg). Provision for attaching two 1,000 lb (450 kg) st JATO rockets under fuselage for use at take-off or in flight.

ACCOMMODATION: Pilot only, on Folland Type 1-B fully-automatic lightweight ejection seat. Cockpit pressurisation and air-conditioning to special order only.

SYSTEMS: Electrical system includes 6kW 24V generator and second battery, permitting independent engine starting without ground electrical supply. Two oxygen bottles supply high-pressure oxygen system of nominal 67 cu ft (1,900 litres) capacity, at a pressure of 2,000 lb/sq in (140 kg/cm²).

ELECTRONICS AND EQUIPMENT: Electronic system for identification purposes to special order only. For reconnaissance duties, the optional fuselage camera can be supplemented by two further cameras in nose of tip-tanks. An aerial target can be towed from a hook under the rear fuselage.

ARMAMENT: Three 0·50 in Colt-Browning machine-guns in nose (with 135 rds/gun). Total of eight underwing weapon attachments. Two inboard attachments can carry two bombs of up to 250 kg each, two clusters of small bombs, two 150 litre napalm tanks, two pods each with twelve 57 mm rockets, or two 45 kg photo flares. Other attachments can each carry a 127 mm rocket. Semi-automatic gyro gunsight and camera gun standard.

DIMENSIONS, EXTERNAL:
- As for Galeb, except:
  - Wing span: 34 ft 8 in (10·56 m)
  - Wing span over tip-tanks: 38 ft 4 in (11·68 m)
  - Wing chord at root: 7 ft 3½ in (2·22 m)
  - Wing chord at tip: 4 ft 7 in (1·40 m)
  - Wing aspect ratio: 5·5
  - Length overall: 35 ft 1½ in (10·71 m)
  - Height overall: 11 ft 11½ in (3·64 m)
  - Wheelbase: 11 ft 10 in (3·61 m)

AREAS:
- As for Galeb

WEIGHTS:
- Weight empty, equipped: 6,217 lb (2,820 kg)
- Max T-O weight: 10,287 lb (4,666 kg)

PERFORMANCE (T-O and landing runs on concrete):
- Max level speed at 19,680 ft (6,000 m) at AUW of 8,748 lb (3,968 kg): 442 knots (510 mph; 820 km/h)
- Max cruising speed at 16,400 ft (5,000 m), at AUW of 8,748 lb (3,968 kg): 399 knots (460 mph; 740 km/h)
- Stalling speed, wheels down:
  - flaps and airbrakes down: 82 knots (95 mph; 152 km/h)
  - flaps and airbrakes up: 94 knots (108 mph; 174 km/h)
- Max rate of climb at S/L, at AUW of 8,748 lb (3,968 kg): 4,135 ft (1,260 m)/min
- Service ceiling at AUW of 8,748 lb (3,968 kg): 39,375 ft (12,000 m)
- T-O run at AUW of 8,748 lb (3,968 kg): 2,300 ft (700 m)
- T-O run, rocket-assisted, at max T-O weight: 1,325 ft (404 m)
- T-O to 50 ft (15 m) at AUW of 8,748 lb (3,968 kg): 3,150 ft (960 m)
- T-O to 50 ft (15 m), rocket-assisted, at max T-O weight: 1,945 ft (593 m)
- Landing from 50 ft (15 m): 3,610 ft (1,100 m)
- Landing run: 1,970 ft (600 m)
- Max range at 29,520 ft (9,000 m), with tip-tanks full: 820 nm (945 miles; 1,520 km)

UTVA

FABRIKA AVIONA UTVA

HEAD OFFICE AND WORKS:
Pancevo, Utve Zlatokrile br 9
Telephone: 013-44-755
Telex: 13116

GENERAL MANAGER: Marko Saranovic
ASSISTANT MANAGER: Dipl Ing Dragoslav Dimic
SALES MANAGER: Zdravko Rapaic

This concern was responsible for the prototype UTVA-56 four-seat general utility monoplane, which flew for the first time on 22 April 1959 and was described fully in the 1960-61 *Jane's*.

The designers of the UTVA-56, Diploma Engineers Branislav Nikolic and Dragoslav Petkovic, began the work of modifying the design for series production at the beginning of 1960. In particular, they replaced the original 260 hp Lycoming GO-435 engine with a 270 hp Lycoming GO-480. The production version was redesignated UTVA-60 and was described fully in the 1971-72 *Jane's*. It has been superseded by the UTVA-66, a special-purpose version of the UTVA-60 with fixed wing-slots, which continued in production in 1974.

Production of the UTVA-65 Privrednik agricultural aircraft (described in the 1972-73 *Jane's*) has ended. In its place, the company has put into series production the more powerful UTVA-65 Super Privrednik-350. Under development is a unique light biplane designated UTVA-71.

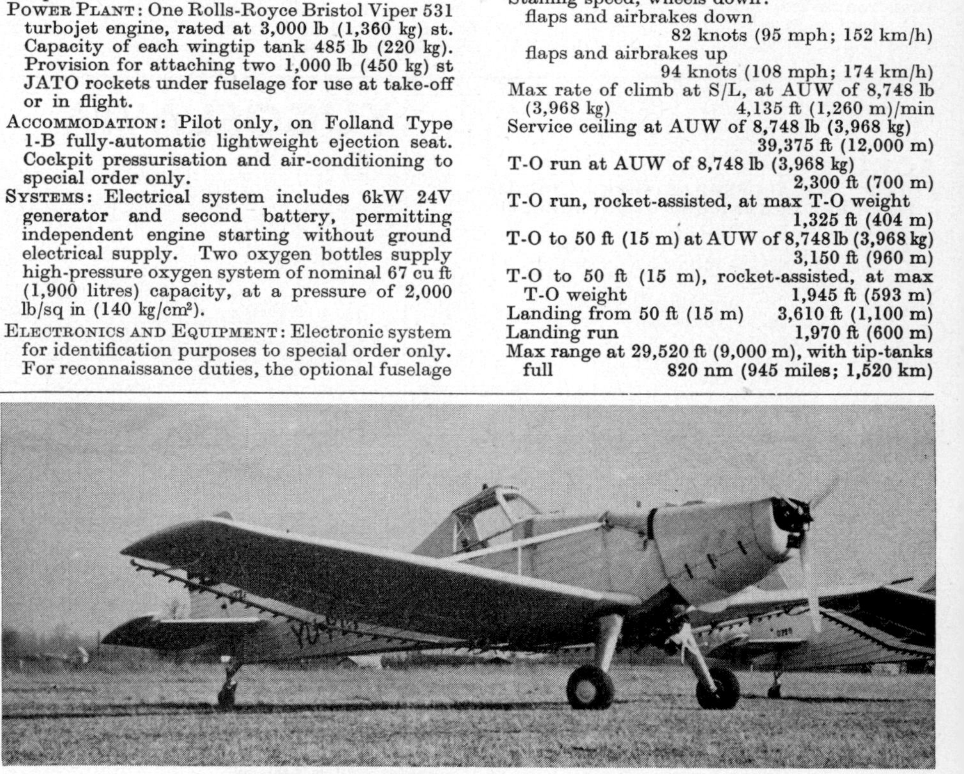

UTVA-65 Super Privrednik-350 agricultural aircraft

UTVA-65 SUPER PRIVREDNIK-350

This agricultural aircraft was developed from the lower-powered Privrednik, which it has superseded in production. Design was started in 1971. Construction of the prototype began in the following year and it flew for the first time during 1973. Manufacture of production Super Privrednik-350s began during 1973 and the eight aircraft ordered by early 1974 had all been completed. Certification is to both Yugoslav and BCAR standards.

TYPE: Agricultural monoplane.

WINGS: Braced low-wing monoplane, with single streamline-section bracing strut each side. Modified NACA 4412 section. Dihedral 5° from roots. Incidence 2° 30′. No sweep at quarter-chord. All-metal single-spar structure. All-metal pure-monocoque ailerons and flaps.

FUSELAGE: Welded chrome-molybdenum steel-tube structure, metal-covered.

TAIL UNIT: Cantilever all-metal structure. Controllable trim tab in elevator.

LANDING GEAR: Non-retractable tailwheel type. Cantilever main legs with rubber-in-compression shock-absorption. Goodyear main-wheel tyres size 500 × 180, pressure 35·5 lb/sq in (2·5 kg/cm²). Goodyear tailwheel tyre, pressure 28·5 lb/sq in (2 kg/cm²). Main wheels and hydraulic disc brakes manufactured by Prva Petoletka. Parking brake.

POWER PLANT: One 350 hp Lycoming IGO-540-A1C six-cylinder horizontally-opposed air-cooled engine, driving a Hartzell HC-B3W30-W/10151C-4 variable-pitch propeller. One welded light alloy fuel tank forward of cockpit and hopper in fuselage. capacity 35·5 Imp gallons (162 litres). Oil capacity 2·6 Imp gallons (12 litres).

ACCOMMODATION: Pilot only in enclosed cabin, with a door on each side. Plastics hopper forward of cabin, which is ventilated.

SYSTEM: 24V electrical system, with 35Ah battery.

ELECTRONICS AND EQUIPMENT: Bendix RT-241A radio and Transland application equipment standard. Aircraft can be used for spraying (spraybars or Micronair), dusting or top-dressing.

DIMENSIONS, EXTERNAL:
- Wing span: 42 ft 4 in (12·90 m)
- Wing aspect ratio: 8
- Length overall: 28 ft 0½ in (8·55 m)
- Height overall: 11 ft 1½ in (3·40 m)
- Tailplane span: 12 ft 7¼ in (3·84 m)
- Wheel track: 8 ft 4½ in (2·55 m)
- Wheelbase: 19 ft 8 in (6·00 m)
- Propeller diameter: 8 ft 1 in (2·46 m)
- Propeller ground clearance: 11·8 in (0·30 m)

AREAS:
- Wings, gross: 221 sq ft (20·53 m²)
- Ailerons (total): 22·17 sq ft (2·06 m²)
- Trailing-edge flaps (total): 24·97 sq ft (2·32 m²)
- Rudder: 10·23 sq ft (0·95 m²)
- Tailplane: 26·05 sq ft (2·42 m²)
- Elevators: 23·89 sq ft (2·22 m²)

WEIGHTS AND LOADINGS:
- Weight empty, equipped: 2,505 lb (1,136 kg)
- Max payload: 1,398 lb (634 kg)
- Max T-O weight: 4,431 lb (2,010 kg)
- Max landing weight: 3,174 lb (1,440 kg)
- Max wing loading: 19·97 lb/sq ft (97·5 kg/m²)
- Max power loading: 12·61 lb/hp (5·72 kg/hp)

PERFORMANCE (at max T-O weight):
- Max level speed: 122 knots (140 mph; 226 km/h)
- Max cruising speed: 97 knots (112 mph; 180 km/h)
- Econ cruising speed: 86 knots (99 mph; 160 km/h)
- Stalling speed, flaps up: 59 knots (68 mph; 109 km/h)
- Stalling speed, flaps down: 53 knots (61 mph; 98 km/h)
- Max rate of climb at S/L: 492 ft (150 m)/min
- Service ceiling: 14,100 ft (4,300 m)
- T-O run: 1,004 ft (306 m)
- T-O to 50 ft (15 m): 2,074 ft (632 m)
- Landing from 50 ft (15 m): 1,224 ft (373 m)
- Landing run: 588 ft (179 m)
- Range with max fuel: 215 nm (248 miles; 400 km)
- Range with max payload: 65 nm (75 miles; 120 km)
- Ferry range, with auxiliary tank in hopper: 809 nm (932 miles; 1,500 km)

UTVA-66

When the UTVA-66 was announced in early 1968, several prototypes had been under flight test for more than one year. Structure testing of the airframe was completed in mid-1968 and the following versions continued in current production in 1974:

UTVA-66. Basic four-seat utility version. Can be used for glider-towing.

UTVA-66-AM. Ambulance version, able to accommodate two stretchers, which are loaded through upward-hinged rear cabin canopy. Seat for attendant behind pilot, with drawer for medical equipment.

UTVA-66H. Water-based version on BIN-1600 floats designed by Dipl-Ing Nikolic. Standard fuel capacity 99 Imp gallons (450 litres). First flown in September 1968.

TYPE: Four-seat general-utility monoplane.

WINGS: Strut-braced high-wing monoplane, with single streamline-section light alloy bracing strut each side. Modified NACA 4412 wing section. Dihedral 2°. Incidence 2° 30′. All-metal single-spar structure. Flaps and ailerons of pure monocoque all-metal construction. Flaps are hydraulically operated and are linked to ailerons, so that ailerons are drooped 15° when flaps are 40° down. Fixed leading-edge slots of same span as ailerons.

FUSELAGE: All-metal construction. Nose and cabin of stressed-skin construction. Rear fuselage is a semi-monocoque.

TAIL UNIT: Cantilever all-metal structure. Servo tab and controllable trim tab in elevator.

LANDING GEAR: Non-retractable tailwheel type. Cantilever steel tube main legs with rubber-in-compression shock-absorption. Wheels and hydraulic disc brakes manufactured by Prva Petoletka. Main wheels size 500 × 180. Tailwheel size 260 × 85. Tyre pressures: main 35·5 lb/sq in (2·5 kg/cm²), tail 28·5 lb/sq in (2·0 kg/cm²). Provision for alternative fitment of floats.

POWER PLANT: One 270 hp Lycoming GSO-480-B1J6 six-cylinder horizontally-opposed air-cooled engine, driving a Hartzell two-blade constant-speed metal propeller type HC-B3Z20-1/10151 C-5. Two metal fuel tanks in wings, total capacity 55 Imp gallons (250 litres). Two optional (standard in U-66H) integral fuel tanks, total capacity 44 Imp gallons (200 litres). Max available fuel capacity 99 Imp gallons (450 litres). Oil capacity 2·6 Imp gallons (12 litres).

ACCOMMODATION: Enclosed cabin for pilot and three passengers, or pilot, two stretchers and attendant in ambulance version. Door on each side of cabin. Rear canopy hinges upward to form third door, for loading stretchers or freight. Ventilation and heating standard.

ELECTRONICS AND EQUIPMENT: Standard equipment includes blind-flying instrumentation, Narco Mk 5 two-way radio and Narco ADF-30 radio compass. Other navigation, communications and automatic flight control equipment optional. Ambulance version can carry parachute pack of food and medical supplies under fuselage.

DIMENSIONS, EXTERNAL:
- Wing span: 37 ft 5 in (11·40 m)
- Wing chord at root: 5 ft 8 in (1·73 m)
- Wing chord at tip: 3 ft 11½ in (1·21 m)
- Wing aspect ratio: 7·19
- Length overall: 27 ft 6 in (8·38 m)
- Height overall: 10 ft 6 in (3·20 m)
- Tailplane span: 13 ft 4½ in (4·08 m)
- Wheel track: 8 ft 4½ in (2·55 m)
- Cabin doors (each):
  - Height: 3 ft 2½ in (0·98 m)
  - Width: 3 ft 0½ in (0·93 m)
- Canopy door:
  - Height: 1 ft 11½ in (0·60 m)
  - Width: 3 ft 3½ in (1·00 m)

DIMENSIONS, INTERNAL:
- Cabin: Length: 4 ft 11 in (1·50 m)
  - Width: 3 ft 5 in (1·05 m)
  - Height: 3 ft 11 in (1·20 m)

AREAS:
- Wings, gross: 194·50 sq ft (18·08 m²)
- Ailerons (total): 22·18 sq ft (2·06 m²)
- Trailing-edge flaps (total): 24·97 sq ft (2·32 m²)
- Fin: 12·70 sq ft (1·18 m²)
- Dorsal fin: 4·74 sq ft (0·44 m²)
- Rudder: 10·22 sq ft (0·95 m²)
- Tailplane: 26·00 sq ft (2·42 m²)
- Elevators: 23·90 sq ft (2·22 m²)

WEIGHTS AND LOADINGS:
- Weight empty, equipped:
  - U-66: 2,756 lb (1,250 kg)
  - U-66H: 3,228 lb (1,464 kg)
- Max T-O weight:
  - U-66: 4,000 lb (1,814 kg)
  - U-66H: 4,431 lb (2,010 kg)
- Max wing loading:
  - U-66: 20·58 lb/sq ft (100·5 kg/m²)
- Max power loading:
  - U-66: 11·79 lb/hp (5·35 kg/hp)

PERFORMANCE (at max T-O weight):
- Max never-exceed speed: 172 knots (198 mph; 320 km/h)
- Max level speed at S/L:
  - U-66: 124 knots (143 mph; 230 km/h)
  - U-66H: 112 knots (129 mph; 208 km/h)
- Max level speed at optimum height:
  - U-66: 135 knots (155 mph; 250 km/h)
  - U-66H: 124 knots (143 mph; 230 km/h)
- Max cruising speed at optimum height:
  - U-66: 124 knots (143 mph; 230 km/h)
  - U-66H: 113 knots (130 mph; 210 km/h)
- Stalling speed:
  - U-66: 43·5 knots (50 mph; 80 km/h)
- Max rate of climb at S/L:
  - U-66: 885 ft (270 m)/min
  - U-66H: 512 ft (156 m)/min
- Service ceiling:
  - U-66: 22,000 ft (6,700 m)
- T-O run:
  - U-66: 614 ft (187 m)
- T-O to 50 ft (15 m):
  - U-66: 1,155 ft (352 m)
- Landing from 50 ft (15 m):
  - U-66: 899 ft (274 m)
- Landing run:
  - U-66: 594 ft (181 m)
- Range with standard fuel:
  - U-66: 404 nm (466 miles; 750 km)
  - U-66H: 593 nm (683 miles; 1,100 km)

UTVA P-418/71

The unusual form of this advanced biplane design, shown in the accompanying three-view drawing, results from many years of research by Dipl-Ing Dimic. This research suggests that a biplane of such configuration, whilst having compact dimensions, should offer a performance comparable with that of a monoplane of similar power and weight.

Wind tunnel tests have shown that the wing arrangement proposed for the P-418/71 provides smooth airflow without any tendency to stall at angles of attack up to 34°. This would appear to offer very safe flying characteristics for roles such as pilot training and glider towing.

Further development of the P-418/71 is underway in the UTVA works at Pancevo, based on Dipl-Ing Dimic's patents. Stress calculations were in process in early 1974, and it was expected that all design work would be completed by the end of the year. The prototype aircraft will have the simplified designation **UTVA-71.**

TYPE: Two-seat light aircraft.

WINGS: Modified biplane configuration. Upper wing forward of lower wing, the tips of which align with the tips of the upper wing. Symmetrical wing sections: upper wing NACA 0006B at root and 0018B at tip, lower wing NACA 0012B at root and 0018B at tip. No dihedral or incidence on upper wing. Lower wing has incidence of 6° and dihedral of 16° from the roots. Upper wing has sharply-swept leading-edges and straight trailing-edge. Lower wing has very slight leading-edge sweepback and sharply swept-forward trailing-edges. All-metal wings, with glassfibre differential ailerons on the lower wing and glassfibre trailing-edge flaps on the upper wing.

FUSELAGE: Welded steel tube basic structure, covered with light alloy sheet.

TAIL UNIT: Cantilever all-metal structure, with sweptback vertical surfaces and unswept

Line-up of UTVA-66 four-seat utility aircraft (270 hp Lycoming GSO-480-B1J6 engine) for the Yugoslav Air Force

horizontal surfaces mounted at tip of fin. Fixed-incidence tailplane. Trim tab in elevator.

LANDING GEAR: Non-retractable tricycle type standard, but optional tailwheel type. Cantilever spring steel main-gear legs. Main-wheel tyres size 7·00-6. Hydraulic brakes.

POWER PLANT: One 150 hp Lycoming O-320-A2B four-cylinder horizontally-opposed aircooled engine, driving a McCauley two-blade fixed-pitch metal propeller. Two integral fuel tanks in wings, with total capacity of 44 Imp gallons (200 litres). Large wingtip fuel tanks also standard. Oil capacity 1·5 Imp gallons (7 litres).

ACCOMMODATION: Pilot and co-pilot side by side in enclosed cabin. Two forward-hinged doors, one on each side of cabin. Heating and ventilation standard.

SYSTEMS: Hydraulic system for brakes only. Electrical supply from 12V 60A alternator and 12V 25Ah battery.

ELECTRONICS AND EQUIPMENT: Radio standard. Other equipment to operator's requirements.

DIMENSIONS, EXTERNAL:

Wing span	23 ft 7½ in (7·20 m)
Wing span over tip-tanks	24 ft 3¼ in (7·40 m)
Length overall	24 ft 10½ in (7·584 m)
Height overall	7 ft 1 in (2·16 m)
Tailplane span	9 ft 10 in (3·00 m)
Wheel track	6 ft 6¾ in (2·00 m)

AREA:

Wings, gross	159·5 sq ft (14·8 m²)

WEIGHTS AND LOADINGS:

Weight empty	1,166 lb (529 kg)
Max T-O weight	1,521 lb (690 kg)
Max wing loading	9·54 lb/sq ft (46·6 kg/m²)
Max power loading	10·14 lb/hp (4·6 kg/hp)

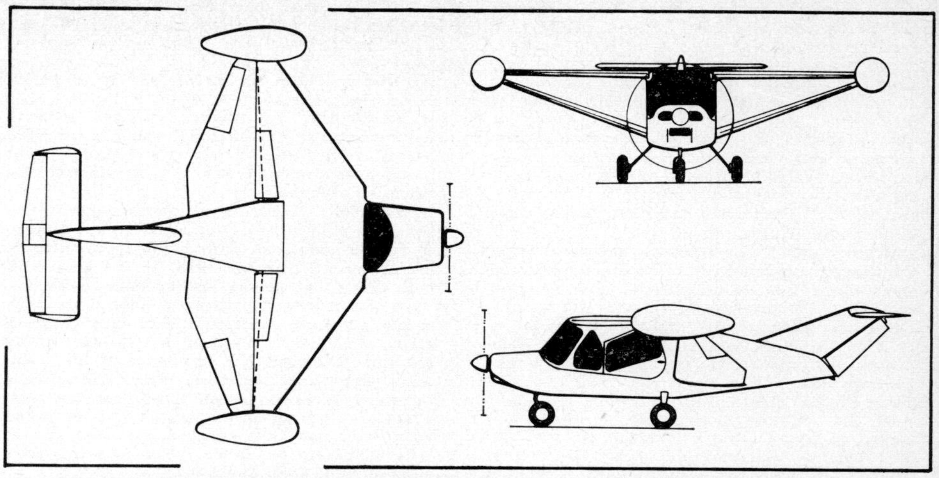

UTVA P-418/71 two-seat light aircraft (150 hp Lycoming O-320-A2B engine) (*Roy J. Grainge*)

PERFORMANCE (estimated, at max T-O weight):

Max level speed at S/L	114 knots (131 mph; 211 km/h)
Econ cruising speed at 3,280 ft (1,000 m)	91·5 knots (106 mph; 170 km/h)
Stalling speed, flaps up	45·5 knots (52·5 mph; 84 km/h)
Max rate of climb at S/L, flaps up	1,260 ft (384 m)/min
Service ceiling	21,325 ft (6,500 m)
T-O run, flaps up	610 ft (186 m)
T-O to 50 ft (15 m), flaps up	1,125 ft (343 m)
Landing run, flaps up	1,247 ft (380 m)
Range with max payload, 35 min reserve	594 nm (683 miles; 1,100 km)

RPVs AND TARGETS

AUSTRALIA

GOVERNMENT OF AUSTRALIA

DEPARTMENT OF MANUFACTURING INDUSTRY

ADDRESS: Anzac Park West Building, Constitution Avenue, Parkes, Canberra ACT 2600
Telephone: 48-2111
Telex: 62063
OFFICERS: See "Aircraft" section

GOVERNMENT AIRCRAFT FACTORIES

HEADQUARTERS:
Fishermen's Bend, Melbourne, Victoria 3207
AIRFIELD AND FINAL ASSEMBLY WORKSHOPS:
Beach Road Lara, Avalon, Victoria 3207
MANAGER: G. J. Churcher, BEngSc, MIEAust

The Government Aircraft Factories are units of the Defence Production facilities owned by the Government of Australia and operated by the Department of Manufacturing Industry.

Current products include the Jindivik weapons target and a target drone version of the Ikara anti-submarine missile, known as the Turana.

GAF JINDIVIK

The Jindivik continues to be a standard weapons target in Australia and Great Britain.

Design began in March 1948 and construction of the prototype Jindivik Mk 1 started in December 1950. This prototype flew for the first time on 28 August 1952.

A total of 466 Jindiviks had been ordered by 1 January 1974, including 226 for the UK, 163 for a joint UK/Australia Weapons Project for use on the Woomera range, 42 for the US Navy, 25 for the Royal Australian Navy and 10 for Sweden. Of these, 424 had been delivered, including 14 Mk 1s, 111 Mk 2s (first flight 11 December 1953), 3 Mk 2As (first flight 18 September 1958), 76 Mk 2Bs (first flight 8 October 1959), 9 Mk 3s (first flight 12 May 1961), 147 Mk 3As (first flight 10 November 1961) and 64 Mk 3Bs (first flight 22 January 1970). Those used in the UK are assembled and equipped to British operational standards by the Guided Weapons Division of BAC. Operationally, their uses include the towing of targets for air-to-air firing practice, at the Missile Practice Camp at RAF Valley, Anglesey, by Phantom and Lightning aircraft of RAF Strike Command.

Only the Mk 3B version of the Jindivik is still in production. Deliveries of this version began in April 1969. Customers include the UK (82 Mk 103B), Royal Australian Navy (15 Mk 203B) and Weapons Research Establishment, Woomera.

The Mk 3B was designed to cater for low-level trials at speeds in excess of 500 knots (575 mph; 925 km/h). Following miniaturisation and up dating of some of the basic flight equipment, the front fuselage and equipment bay were redesigned to give greater volume for special trials equipment.

As shown in the accompanying three-view drawing, the Jindivik has been used as the basis of a project study which has been completed by Bell Aerospace at the request of the US Air Force for an ACLS (air cushion landing system) for RPV applications. Up to February 1974 a decision had still to be made concerning further development or trials; the latter, if undertaken, would comprise taxying and landing trials using a converted Jindivik. One Jindivik was delivered to Bell in 1973 for prototype installation of the system. It is reported that a similar study has been carried out by Sandaire (San Diego Aircraft Engineering Inc).

For low-altitude work, the standard-span Jindivik can be fitted with either Mk 5 wingtip camera pods, or with larger Mk 8 pods each containing a camera, a Luneberg lens and a small amount of fuel. For high-altitude work (also with a choice of Mk 5 or Mk 8 wing pods), constant-chord wing extension panels can be added outboard of the pods. For extra high altitude flying (with Mk 5 pods only), these panels can be replaced by increased-span panels, tapered on the leading-edge. A ventral tail fin is also fitted in this configuration.

Up to 1 January 1974, Jindiviks had flown 2,828 sorties at the RAE, Llanbedr, North Wales, and one particular Mk 3A drone (WRE 418) had flown 270 sorties at Woomera.

The following description applies to the Mk 3B:

TYPE: Pilotless target drone.

WINGS: Cantilever low/mid-wing monoplane. Wing section NACA 64A-106 with modified trailing-edge. Dihedral 2° 30′. Incidence 1°. Multi-spar box structure of aluminium alloy. Spars are Araldite bonded to preformed heavy-gauge skins to form interspar torsion box which is utilised as integral fuel tankage. Leading-edge is attached to front spar and rebated skins by Araldite. Trailing-edge box is an Araldite-bonded structure and is riveted to the main spar box structure, which houses the aileron control system of rods and bellcranks. Aluminium alloy monocoque flaps and ailerons are hinged to this structure, with continuous piano hinges and three-point pin hinges respectively. Ailerons are fitted with inset geared tab and driven by GAF-designed twin-motor servo motor. Flaps operated pneumatically.

FUSELAGE: Aluminium alloy semi-monocoque structure, built in front, centre and rear sections. Front fuselage carries all control equipment, autopilot and telemetry equipment on three removable trays. Pitot head and wave-guide boom mounted on permanent nose probe. A moulded glassfibre canopy, which lifts off for access to the equipment, forms the ram-type air intake. Rear end of front fuselage and front end of centre fuselage form bay in which all special trials equipment is carried. Centre fuselage also houses landing skid. Rear fuselage carries the engines and jetpipe. Optional airbrake under rear fuselage, which may be used as a dive brake to reduce descent time from high altitude.

TAIL UNIT: Cantilever multi-spar tailplane of light alloy bonded with Araldite. Elevators, formed of single wrapped skins stiffened by chordwise flutes and carried on piano hinges, are driven by a GAF-designed twin-motor servo motor. Inset geared tabs are fitted. Fin of light alloy skin bonded to two spars, stabilised by metal honeycomb filling. No rudder; but provision for an in-flight variable trim tab in fin. Ventral fin on extra high altitude version.

LANDING GEAR: Pneumatically-extended, manually retracted (on ground) central skid. Pneumatic jack acts as shock-absorber. Steel auxiliary skids at wingtips. See later paragraph on "Take-off and Landing".

POWER PLANT: One Rolls-Royce Viper Mk 201 turbojet engine, rated at 2,500 lb (1,134 kg) st. Engine relight capability available in the event of flameout. Flexible rubber main fuselage fuel tank, capacity 64 Imp gallons (291 litres), and two integral wing tanks, total capacity 38 Imp gallons (173 litres). Single refuelling point in centre fuselage for all tanks. Wing tanks are pressurised from engine compressor to feed fuselage tank, from where fuel is pumped to the engine. A pressurised fuel recuperator is fitted in this delivery line to cope with negative *g* conditions. Compressed air is used for starting and throttle is operated by electric actuator through a cam switch box, allowing several fixed rpm engine conditions to be selected in addition to throttle "beep" demands. Oil capacity 1 Imp gallon (4·5 litres).

CREW: Normal operating ground crew of four: flight commander, navigator, pilot and batsman.

GAF Jindivik Mk 3B target drone with high-altitude wing extensions

Jindivik Mk 3B target drone landing on its underfuselage skid after a mission

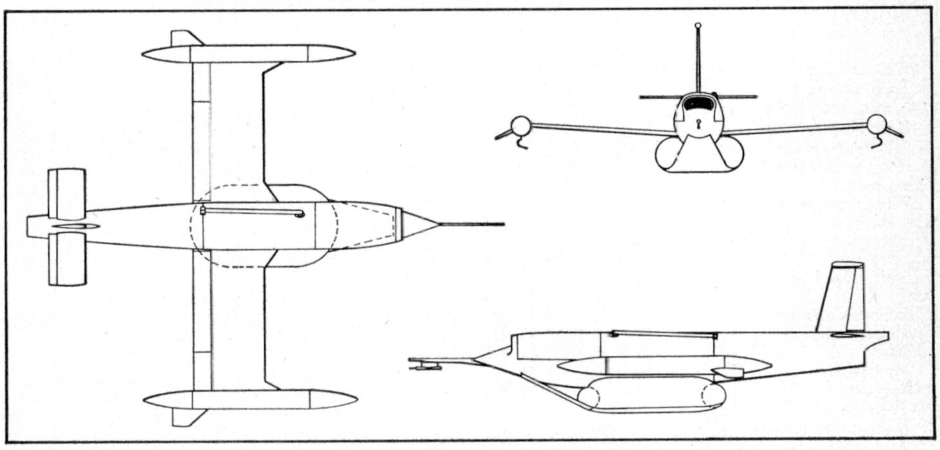

GAF Jindivik, as projected with air cushion landing system designed by Bell Aerospace
(*Roy J. Grainge*)

SYSTEMS: No hydraulic system. Non-regenerative pneumatic system: air stored at 2,000 lb/sq in (140 kg/cm²) in power pack which supplies air to the flaps, airbrake and landing skid reduced to 575 lb/sq in (40·5 kg/cm²). If the airbrake is to be used for speed control when two aircraft are formating, a separate air supply system may be fitted as optional equipment. Engine-driven 11·5kVA alternator delivers 208V AC 3-phase electrical supply at 300-550Hz. In the event of alternator failure, a 24V DC battery provides limited power for essential control functions. Automatic orbit and/or destruct systems provided, consistent with range safety requirements.

REMOTE-CONTROL EQUIPMENT: Aircraft is remotely controlled from a ground station. Radio control equipment comprises two receiver/selectors, the second of which may be used as standby or destruct, and GAF relay set receiving. Telemetry equipment consists of NIC transducers and Australian-designed transmitter and junction box.

TRIALS EQUIPMENT: Transponders and microwave reflectors are used for trials of active, semi-active or beam-riding missiles. Heat sources, including infra-red flare packs mounted in rear of fuselage, can be fitted to provide low-frequency IR output. Transponders in the X, S and C bands can be fitted for target acquisition and to enable the Jindivik to be tracked at greater range. Provision for a "Tonic" winch pylon under each wing, on which can be carried a recoverable active radar or infra-red "Tonic" CG tow "bird" or an expendable tow bird with infra-red-augmented nose. These can be towed at 50-500 ft (15-150 m) behind aircraft; recovery is by electric winch. Other types of recoverable towed target may be fitted, carrying augmentation in the form of transponders, microwave reflectors or infra-red.

RECORDING EQUIPMENT: Cameras fitted with wide-angle lenses are carried in wingtip pods, with all-round vision capability, and are used to film and record the approach path and proximity of missiles fired against the target. Variants are the Mk 5 pod with cameras only and the Mk 8 with cameras, fuel and provision for fitment of microwave reflectors in LE and TE radomes. Rearward-facing cameras, and a Luneberg lens reflector mounted in fairing above jetpipe, may be used to film and record operations when towed targets are used.

TAKE-OFF AND LANDING: Jindivik is mounted on a tubular-framed tricycle take-off trolley. Aircraft/trolley steering is achieved by a servo-controlled nosewheel which responds to signals from the aircraft's autopilot. The aircraft/trolley combination accelerates under normal jet power with flaps retracted and with the aircraft set at a negative incidence. When unstick speed (125 knots; 144 mph; 231 km/h) is reached the aircraft is rotated to take-off incidence and flaps are lowered rapidly. Rotation of the aircraft initiates the trolley release system and the aircraft climbs away. At the same time trolley brakes equipped with Dunlop anti-skid devices are applied. When Jindivik is in the approach run, the flaps and skid are selected down for landing. On touchdown, at approx 120 knots (138 mph; 222 km/h), a "sting" extended below the main skid rotates on impact and initiates rapid retraction of flaps. Fuel supply is terminated by radio command.

DIMENSIONS, EXTERNAL:
Wing span:
short span, low altitude 20 ft 8·99 in (6·32 m)
extended, high altitude 26 ft 6 in (7·92 m)
extended, extra high altitude 32 ft 1·4 in (9·78 m)
Wing chord (constant) 4 ft 0 in (1·22 m)
Wing aspect ratio:
short span 5·67
extended, high altitude 6·88
extended, extra high altitude 8·97
Length overall:
incl nose probe 26 ft 8¾ in (8·15 m)
excl nose probe 23 ft 3¾ in (7·11 m)
Height overall, skid extended 6 ft 9·85 in (2·08 m)
Tailplane span 6 ft 6 in (1·98 m)

DIMENSIONS, INTERNAL:
Equipment bays:
front fuselage 11·46 cu ft (0·32 m³)
centre fuselage 5·24 cu ft (0·15 m³)

AREAS:
Wings, gross:
short span 76·0 sq ft (7·06 m²)
extended span, high altitude 102·0 sq ft (9·48 m²)
extended span, extra high altitude 115·0 sq ft (10·68 m²)
Ailerons (total) 4·5 sq ft (0·42 m²)
Flaps (total) 11·5 sq ft (1·07 m²)
Fin 7·2 sq ft (0·67 m²)
Tailplane 14·6 sq ft (1·36 m²)
Elevators 4·2 sq ft (0·39 m²)

WEIGHTS:
Weight empty, equipped (min) 2,900 lb (1,315 kg)
Max payload:
short-span version 550 lb (249 kg)
extended-span versions 400 lb (181 kg)

Turana target drone, on prototype portable launcher

Max T-O weight:
short span, Mk 5 wing pods 3,200 lb (1,451 kg)
short span, Mk 8 wing pods 3,650 lb (1,655 kg)
high altitude, Mk 5 wing pods 3,250 lb (1,474 kg)
high altitude, Mk 8 wing pods 3,650 lb (1,655 kg)
extra high altitude, Mk 5 wing pods 3,300 lb (1,496 kg)

PERFORMANCE (A: short span, Mk 5 pods; B: short span, Mk 8 pods; C: high altitude, Mk 5 pods; D: high altitude, Mk 8 pods; E: extra high altitude, Mk 5 pods):
Max level speed at max operational ceiling:
A, B, C, D 490 knots (564 mph; 908 km/h) TAS (Mach 0·86)
E 470 knots (541 mph; 871 km/h) TAS (Mach 0·82)
Min operating height:
A, B 50 ft (15 m)
Max operational ceiling:
A 57,000 ft (17,375 m)
B 54,000 ft (16,460 m)
C 63,000 ft (19,200 m)
D 61,000 ft (18,595 m)
E 67,000 ft (20,420 m)
Time to max operational ceiling:
A 26 min
B, C 30 min
D, E 34 min
T-O run 1,000 ft (305 m)
T-O to 50 ft (15 m) 2,200 ft (670 m)
Landing from 50 ft (15 m) 2,700 ft (823 m)
Landing run 1,500 ft (457 m)
Typical max on-station endurance:
A, C 1 hr 6 min
B 1 hr 38 min
D 1 hr 52 min
E 1 hr 3 min
Max range:
A 430 nm (495 miles; 796 km)
B 670 nm (771 miles; 1,240 km)
C 540 nm (621 miles; 1,000 km)
D 900 nm (1,036 miles; 1,667 km)
E 700 nm (806 miles; 1,297 km)
Max banking angle (all) 60°
Max diving angle (all) 40°
Max g pull-up at 50 ft (15 m):
A +3·7
B +6·0

GAF TURANA

The Turana is a target drone based on the Ikara missile. It is being developed by the Department of Supply initially to meet a Royal Australian Navy Staff Requirement for a modern gunnery and guided weapons target. The development programme was approved and funded in August 1969. First flight was made on 12 March 1971, and during test flying at the WRE Woomera Range and the RAN's missile range at Jervis Bay an altitude of 20,000 ft (6,100 m) and a speed of more than 390 knots (450 mph; 724 km/h) have been attained in level flight. Speeds in excess of 500 knots (575 mph; 925 km/h) have been achieved in shallow dives. The Turana is capable of demand turns of up to 3g, customer-specified manoeuvres of more than 10g, and demand heading changes of up to 26°. Construction ensures an average life of at least 10 flights per drone. Equipment is designed for at least 20 complete missions, including sea-water immersion. By July 1973 a total of 13 flights had been made.

The initial development programme was expected to be concluded with a series of flights at the Jervis Bay missile range in May 1974. The objectives were to include demonstrations of reliability, flight endurance, low-altitude (soft) performance, and miss-distance measuring equipment.

An initial order for 12 Turanas, including spares and ancillary ground and shipboard equipment, has been placed by the Royal Australian Navy. Production is under way, and deliveries of some equipment began in late 1973. Further orders were expected during 1974.

Government Aircraft Factories are the co-ordinating design authority and prime contractor responsible for the airframe, autopilot, engine and fuel system. Guidance and rocket propulsion aspects of the project are subcontracted to the Weapons Research Establishment/EMI Electronics (Australia) and Weapons Research Establishment/Ordnance Factory and Explosives Factory, Maribyrnong, respectively.

TYPE: Pilotless target drone.

WINGS: Cantilever mid-wing tail-less monoplane of cropped delta planform. Wing section modified NACA 64010. Spindle attachment to fuselage, the spindle being also the main spar. Two metal ribs and metal rear spar, the remainder of the wing being of foam-filled glassfibre. Full-span elevons are operated via a differential mechanical linkage by two electric actuators, one for pitch and one for roll control. The wings are quickly detachable from the fuselage.

FUSELAGE: Aluminium alloy torsion box, with removable glassfibre fairings, housing the autopilot, fuel tank, engine and various miss-distance equipments and transponders. Main structural member consists of an H-section structure of chemically-milled side skins, bulkheads and forgings, and a bottom diaphragm. Interface attachments are identical with those of Ikara.

TAIL UNIT: Single vertical fin, of NACA 64010 section, made of chemically-milled aluminium skins and aluminium ribs and spars, with glassfibre tip and trailing-edge.

POWER PLANT: One Microturbo Cougar 022 turbojet engine of 176 lb (80 kg) st. Stainless steel/airbag fuel tank of 11·4 Imp gallons (51·8 litres) capacity. Airbag is pressurised from engine compressor. Compressed air is used for starting and the engine speed is controlled by an electronic unit, which forms part of a speed demand loop.

Boost: Single-nozzle PMD41 solid-propellant booster motor specially developed for Turana, attached to fuselage by swivelling links and two explosive bolts. Nominal burning time 2 seconds; nominal thrust 6,000 lb (2,721 kg). Boost motor is jettisoned at the end of the boost phase. Launching is from the standard Ikara ship launcher, or from a lightweight portable launcher, and is made at a fixed elevation of 22° 30′.

Systems: All electric. Rechargeable silver/zinc battery pack, in compartment immediately aft of ejectable nose section, provides power for all services for more than one hour. Pyrotechnic charge for ejection of nose section.

Control System and Autopilot: Elevons on the wings are operated symmetrically or differentially by electric actuators. The autopilot includes a displacement gyro sensing roll and pitch, a rate gyro sensing yaw, an air data unit with airspeed and altitude transducers, signal summing and shaping networks and drive amplifiers for the servo system. A radar altimeter option is available, to allow automatic controlled flight at low altitudes. A pitot-static tube is fitted to the tip of the vertical fin. Height lock and speed lock loops are provided within the drone.

Guidance: Drone is designed to be used initially in conjunction with an adaptation of the Ikara guidance system on board RAN ships. Navigation is by means of the Ikara tracking receiver and ship's plotting facilities. At customer's request, a modified guidance equipment can be provided which is independent of ship facilities; alternative tracking and return data links are also possible. Guidance equipment is housed in the vertical fin.

Recovery: Command parachute recovery, the parachute being housed in the ejectable nose of the drone. The parachute recovery sequence is activated automatically in the event of either an engine, electrical power system or command link failure. Short or long time delays can be included in the command link failure mode to allow for momentary signal fades. Initial versions of Turana are designed for water recovery. For use on land, a larger parachute and land recovery system could be provided.

Trials Equipment: Drone is intended initially mainly for gunnery practice, for which purpose visual augmentation is provided in the form of a smoke release system. Forward-looking passive radar augmentation is provided by a 7½ in (19 cm) Luneberg lens in the nose. Space and large weight-carrying capacity are available for active augmentation or for other special equipment such as a 465MHz 48-channel telemetry system. Pyrotechnic flares can be accommodated to meet customer requirements. An acoustic miss-distance indication system is available. A short-tow system, to carry infra-red flares or a Luneberg lens radar reflector, can be developed.

Shipboard launch of a GAF Turana off the Australian coast

Operations: Typical operation as a service target will begin by boosted launch from a ship and climb (or descent) to the required operational altitude. Control of the drone is effected by open loop demands from the ground and by a closed loop sensing and autocontrol system in the drone. This system obviates the necessity for either telemetered flight information or highly-skilled flight controllers. Altitude may be locked to the commanded height, which may be changed at will by the controller. Speed is also locked to a variable command datum, thus giving the controller freedom to use any section of the flight envelope, and control in azimuth can be exercised to provide a number of presentations, crossing, approaching or receding, for the exercise of guns, short-range or medium/long-range guided weapons. The number of presentations is dependent upon the chosen operating speed and altitude. The flight is concluded by descent to any required low altitude, and return to the neighbourhood of the ship, where the parachute is deployed and recovery from the sea is effected.

Dimensions, external:
- Wing span 5 ft 0·2 in (1·53 m)
- Wing chord at root 3 ft 6 in (1·07 m)
- Wing chord at tip 1 ft 4 in (0·41 m)
- Length overall 11 ft 0½ in (3·37 m)
- Height (less boost motor) 3 ft 4 in (1·02 m)
- Height (with boost motor) 3 ft 10·8 in (1·19 m)

Dimension, internal:
- Special equipment capacity 1 cu ft (0·028 m³)

Areas:
- Wings, gross 13·2 sq ft (1·23 m²)
- Elevons (total) 2·04 sq ft (0·19 m²)
- Fin 3·4 sq ft (0·32 m²)

Weights (less special equipment):
- Weight dry 364 lb (165 kg)
- Weight at launch 615 lb (279 kg)
- Weight less booster 555 lb (251 kg)
- Weight at recovery (empty) 380 lb (172 kg)
- Fuel 91 lb (41 kg)
- Special equipment weight more than 100 lb (45 kg)

Performance:
- Max level speed 390 knots (450 mph; 724 km/h)
- Boost acceleration (nominal) 10g
- End-of-boost speed 560 ft (170 m)/sec
- Service ceiling 33,000 ft (10,000 m)
- Max rate of climb at S/L 4,000 ft (1,219 m)/min
- Range 325 nm (374 miles; 602 km)
- Endurance 55 minutes

BELGIUM

MBLE

MANUFACTURE BELGE DE LAMPES ET DE MATÉRIEL ELECTRONIQUE SA

Head Office:
80 rue des Deux-Gares, 1070-Bruxelles
Telephone: (02) 23.00.00
Telex: 21.420

Head of Aeronautical Division:
A. Colpaert

Public Relations Manager:
Luc Canon

This company, which employs 5,300 people, has contributed to a number of European aerospace programmes, including those of the F-104G Starfighter, Hawk missile and ELDO space research projects. It has also developed, built and tested a battlefield surveillance system named Épervier.

MBLE ÉPERVIER (SPARROWHAWK) SYSTEM

The Épervier is a battlefield reconnaissance system developed and built entirely in Belgium. It comprises, essentially, a drone vehicle known as the X-5, with its sensors; a short ramp launcher; and a drone control centre (DCC). The X-5 is a small, unmanned vehicle powered by a 114 lb (51·7 kg) st Lucas Type TJ 125 turbojet engine. The airframe, of glass-reinforced plastics, is manufactured under subcontract by Fairey SA at Gosselies. Brief details of the earlier X-1 to X-4 drone prototypes have appeared in previous editions of *Jane's*.

The X-5 can carry Omera 5 in or Omera or Oude-Delft 70 mm day or night cameras, and SAT Cyclope infra-red line-scanning equipment with real-time transmission. The launcher equipment comprises a short orientatable ramp and an associated checkout device. The DCC contains all the necessary electronic equipment for guiding and tracking elements. A mobile unit for photographic processing and interpretation is part of the system.

Initially, the Épervier system was developed to meet NATO specifications. The Belgian Ministry of Economic Affairs decided on 11 July 1969 to support the programme financially. In early 1971, a co-operation agreement was signed between MBLE and the Belgian Ministry of Defence, and development continued to more advanced technical characteristics and operational specifications on behalf of the Belgian Army.

In late 1972 and early 1973, the Épervier

MBLE Épervier X-5 battlefield surveillance RPV

successfully underwent an official military operational evaluation. During more than 80 flights, the system proved to be a flexible, easy-to-operate and accurate means of reconnaissance, capable of photographing pinpoint targets or large areas of terrain during guided and/or programmed flights up to more than 38 nm (43·5 miles; 70 km) from its base. Photoflash gear can be carried for night operation.

Production for the Belgian Army was expected to begin in 1974, subject to budget approval; an initial order, believed to be for 20 Éperviers for the Belgian Army, was announced in May 1974.

DIMENSIONS (X-5):
- Wing span: 5 ft 7¾ in (1·72 m)
- Length overall: 7 ft 9¾ in (2·38 m)
- Height overall: 3 ft 0¼ in (0·92 m)

WEIGHTS (X-5):
- Payload: approx 45 lb (20 kg)
- Max launching weight: 313 lb (142 kg)

PERFORMANCE:
- Cruising speed: 270 knots (310 mph; 500 km/h)
- Operating height limits: 1,000-6,000 ft (305-1,830 m)
- Endurance: more than 25 min

CANADA

CANADAIR

CANADAIR LTD (Subsidiary of General Dynamics Corporation)

HEAD OFFICE AND WORKS:
PO Box 6087, Montreal 101, Quebec
Telephone: (514) 744-1511

OFFICERS: see "Aircraft" section

In addition to its work on piloted aircraft, Canadair has developed and is producing a reconnaissance drone system, of which all available details follow:

CANADAIR AN/USD-501
Manufacturer's designation: CL-89

The Canadair CL-89 (AN/USD-501) airborne surveillance drone system evolved from a need of the western Allied armed forces for an intelligence-gathering device for battlefield commanders. Canadair, in co-operation with the Canadian government and Canadian Armed Forces, conducted a study to identify the ideal unmanned airborne surveillance system. It was agreed that the system should be simple to operate and maintain; have a high survivability in a sophisticated enemy air defence environment; be capable of detecting and recording enemy formations and weapons of tactical significance in all weathers, by day or night; and provide accurate information in time for the recipient to react.

Development was started in 1961 by Canadair Ltd on a shared-cost basis with the Canadian Department of Industry, Trade and Commerce. In its early stages the project was funded on a month-to-month basis by Canada and the UK. In 1965 the German Federal Republic joined in the development of the system. With a very high probability of survival against all known air defence systems, the AN/USD-501 can acquire timely and accurate battlefield intelligence using its photographic and infra-red line-scanning equipment.

The system, consisting of the air vehicles plus the related ground support and operational maintenance equipment, is totally integrated, mobile, and independent of such external services as electrical power supplies.

Details of the flight and operational evaluation programmes have been given in previous editions of *Jane's*.

The three participating nations shared in the initial production order for 282 AN/USD-501 drones and associated ground support equipment. Additional quantities were subsequently ordered by the UK and the German Federal Republic. In August 1973 an Italian Army order for the CL-89 was announced, worth more than $10 million (US), bringing the total number ordered by early 1974 to more than 500. Those for Italy will be produced jointly by Canadair and Meteor (which see) of Italy.

TYPE: Recoverable airborne surveillance drone system.

WINGS: Four rectangular single-spar stub wings at rear of drone body, in a cruciform arrangement at 45° to the horizontal and vertical centrelines. Upper pair fold out of the way when the landing airbags are inflated. Ailerons on port upper and starboard lower wings.

FOREPLANES: Two pairs of canard foreplane surfaces, of cropped-delta planform, aft of nosecone on horizontal and vertical centrelines, for pitch and yaw trim respectively.

BODY: Cylindrical metal structure, with curved nosecone and tapering tailcone. Three detachable dorsal packs for forward and rear landing bags and flare container, and two detachable ventral packs for sensor equipment and parachute recovery system.

POWER PLANT: One 125 lb (56·7 kg) st Williams Research WR2-6 turbojet engine, with variable exhaust nozzle, installed in tailcone aft of wings. Air intake duct on each side of fuselage, forward of wings. Fuel and oil tanks in central body compartment, forward of air intakes.

BOOST: One 4,550 lb (2,065 kg) average thrust Bristol Aerojet Wagtail rocket motor, with electrical ignition, in a helically-welded steel case which is fitted with detachable rectangular cruciform tail fins and is attached to the body of the drone by three Vee-shaped thrust arms and a cable. After 2·5 seconds of flight the cable is cut automatically, freeing the thrust arms and allowing the booster assembly to fall away.

SYSTEMS: Engine-driven alternator for electrical power during flight.

Launch of a Canadair AN/USD-501 airborne surveillance/target acquisition drone system

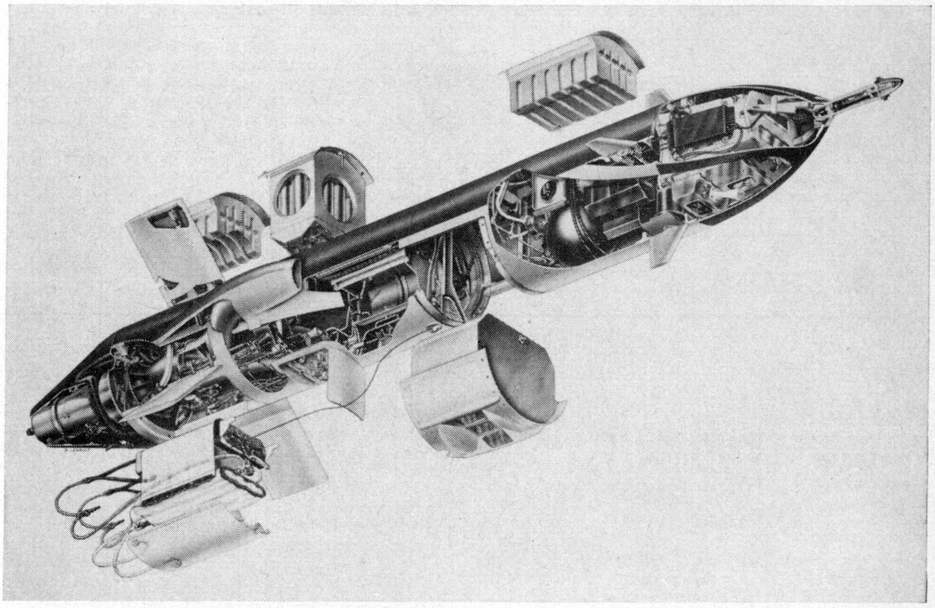

Exploded cutaway view of the Canadair AN/USD-501, showing (*at top*) the forward and rear landing bag containers and flare pack, and (*underneath*) the centre-fuselage sensor pack and parachute recovery pack

GUIDANCE: The flight path, altitude and sensor on/off commands are controlled by a preset programmer which receives information from an Air Distance Measuring Unit (ADMU) and combines this with the preset programme to control the flight path. A ground homing beacon positions the drone in its final stages of flight to ensure the accuracy of the landing.

RECOVERY: After final positioning by the ground homing beacon, the drone's drogue parachute deploys to slow it down until the main parachute is deployed. The drone is inverted; the forward and rear landing bags are then automatically inflated and deployed to absorb the landing shock.

EQUIPMENT: Air Distance Measuring Unit (ADMU) in nose probe. Nosecone houses programmer, static power converter and X-band receiver. Compartment aft of nosecone houses shaping amplifier, flash detector, directional and vertical gyros, X-band transponder antenna, forward landing bag container and air bottle to inflate both landing bags. Ventral sensor pack is immediately aft of this compartment. Two sensor systems are currently in use: the Carl Zeiss KRb 8/24 camera system and the Hawker Siddeley Dynamics Type 201 infra-red linescan system. Linescan is a reconnaissance technique in which the terrain overflown is scanned at high speed in narrow strips at right angles to the flight path. Forward motion builds up a continuous picture of radiation from the ground below. In an infra-red linescan the radiation is collected by an optical scanner and focussed on to an infra-red detector. Variations in the radiation received cause corresponding fluctuations of the signal output from the detector. The detector output is processed electronically and is used to modulate the intensity of a light source which exposes a photographic film. This equipment greatly enhances the night performance of the AN/USD-501, since the infra-red linescan can produce continuous imagery on the darkest night without the use of illuminating flares. It is also possible to detect "hot" targets, such as military vehicles which are under camouflage, by virtue of the difference in temperature from their surroundings. Aft of the sensor pack is the compartment for the fuel and oil tanks. This compartment also has a ventral forward-hinged door providing access to the engine start air connector, and a dorsal pack containing 12 photoflares just forward of the rear landing bag container. The final cylindrical compartment houses the rear landing bag container itself and the parachute recovery pack, between the dorsal and ventral pairs of wings respectively. The sustainer engine is mounted in the tailcone.

DIMENSIONS, EXTERNAL:

Length overall, excl nose probe:
- with booster: 12 ft 3 in (3·73 m)
- without booster: 8 ft 6½ in (2·60 m)

Body diameter: 1 ft 1 in (0·33 m)
Span of wings: 3 ft 1 in (0·94 m)
Span of foreplanes: 1 ft 7 in (0·48 m)

WEIGHTS:

Weight dry (less fuel, oil and payload): 172·4 lb (78·2 kg)
Payload: 33·3 lb (15·1 kg)
Max launching weight:
- with booster: 343 lb (156 kg)
- without booster: 238 lb (108 kg)

PERFORMANCE:

Max speed: 400 knots (460 mph; 741 km/h)

FRANCE

AÉROSPATIALE

SOCIÉTÉ NATIONALE INDUSTRIELLE AÉROSPATIALE

HEAD OFFICE:
37 Bd de Montmorency, 75781 Paris-cédex 16

OFFICERS: See "Aircraft" section

Drones in current production by Aérospatiale (Division Engins Tactiques) are the CT.20 target and the R.20 battlefield reconnaissance system.

Under development is a target for close-range air-to-air missiles, designated C.20. A sea-skimming target designated CM.38, which is in the project stage, is designed to present a radar image similar to that of the Exocet missile. Development of a high-altitude, long-endurance reconnaissance vehicle has also been reported.

AÉROSPATIALE CT.20

The CT.20 is a turbojet-powered radio-controlled target of medium performance, which is also used as a tug for a towed target. Series production began in 1958, and by early 1974 more than 1,200 had been ordered by the French, Italian and Swedish Armies and other customers. It is standard equipment for training military units in the use of air-to-air and surface-to-air missiles, in particular the Hawk.

The CT.20 is launched from a ramp 32 ft 9½ in (10 m) long and inclined at an angle of 5 degrees to the horizontal, or from a much shorter (nearly zero-length) ramp. The launching carriage is powered by two powder rockets and, aided by the power of the turbojet engine, the CT.20 attains a speed of 329 knots (379 mph; 610 km/h) by the time it reaches its maximum acceleration. The drone then continues to fly under the control of a radio operator located on the ground or in a "mother" aircraft.

Nine signals can be transmitted: turns to right and left, nose up and down, increase and reduce power, trace smoke, operate cameras, and land. The turning signal controls bank and the turns are executed without reverse yaw. The pitch signals act on the elevators via the autopilot. When the landing signal is transmitted, the engine is stopped, the brake parachute opens and, at the end of a delay period, the recovery parachute is released. The descent is made in a level attitude and the impact with the ground is cushioned by an airbag forward of the centre-section. In the case of radio control failure the landing sequence occurs automatically; and the drone can be recovered from the sea, as it is designed to float.

Low-altitude flight, under barostatic altitude control, can be programmed currently at 300-400 ft (90-120 m). A version known as the CT.20 TBA, with very low altitude capability (about 100 ft; 30·5 m) is operational. This has a TRT radio altimeter and an improved remote guidance system.

The CT.20 can be used to tow a type SK3L target produced by Dornier System GmbH of Germany. The target is 3 ft 11¼ in (1·20 m) long, with a fin span of 1 ft 3¾ in (40 cm) and body diameter of 9·85 in (25 cm), and is pylon-mounted under the starboard wing of the CT.20 at launch. When towed in flight on a 2,625-3,950 ft (800-1,200 m) cable, it has negligible effect on the CT.20's speed, and flight duration is reduced by no more than 15%.

This joint development by Aérospatiale and Dornier System overcomes problems resulting from the fact that the performance of modern missiles seldom permits firing of surface-to-air and air-to-air weapons at a target towed by a manned aircraft.

Alternatively, the CT.20 can be used with the EMIR trailed target system, developed for the Centre d'Essais des Landes and used primarily for training purposes in connection with air-to-air missiles with electro-magnetic or infra-red homing systems.

The R.20 reconnaissance drone, developed from the CT.20, is described separately.

The following description applies to the CT.20, which is currently being built in two forms: a standard version, and an "extended" version with greater endurance.

TYPE: Turbojet-powered radio-controlled target.

WINGS: Cantilever mid-wing monoplane with medium sweepback. Each wing is a light alloy conventional structure. Lateral control spoilers at wingtips.

FUSELAGE: In three main sections. Forward section, of aluminium alloy, contains command guidance, autopilot, batteries and principal recovery parachute. Central section consists of a structural steel tank divided into two parts, one for fuel and the other containing chemicals for the tracking smoke. Rear fuselage, of aluminium alloy, contains the engine and carries the tail unit. A braking parachute is housed in a cone above the jet nozzle.

TAIL UNIT: "Butterfly" structure of aluminium alloy. Comprises two elevator surfaces controlled simultaneously by a single jack.

POWER PLANT: One Turboméca Marboré II (880 lb; 400 kg st) turbojet engine in CT.20 Version IV, or Marboré VI (1,056 lb; 480 kg st) turbojet engine in CT.20 Version VII.

DIMENSIONS, EXTERNAL (A: standard version; B: extended version with trailed target):

Wing span: 11 ft 9½ in (3·60 m)
Length overall:
- A: 17 ft 10½ in (5·45 m)
- B: 18 ft 4½ in (5·60 m)

Body diameter (max): 2 ft 2 in (0·66 m)

AREA:

Wings, gross: 33·34 sq ft (3 20 m²)

WEIGHTS (A: standard version; B: extended version with trailed target):

Weight empty:
- A: 1,080 lb (490 kg)
- B: 1,344 lb (610 kg)

Max launching weight:
- A: 1,455 lb (660 kg)
- B: 1,763 lb (800 kg)

PERFORMANCE (A: standard version; B: extended version with trailed target):

Max speed at 32,800 ft (10,000 m):
- Marboré II: 485 knots (560 mph; 900 km/h)
- Marboré VI: 512 knots (590 mph; 950 km/h)

Max Mach number (A, B): Mach 0·85
Max operating height:
- A: 45,925 ft (14,000 m)
- B: 42,650 ft (13,000 m)

Time to max operating height:
- A, B: 15 min

Endurance at max operating height:
- A: 50 min
- B: 1 hr 10 min

Min operating height:
- A, B: 100 ft (30 m)

Endurance at min operating height:
- A: 15 min
- B: 21 min

AÉROSPATIALE R.20

The Aérospatiale R.20 battlefield reconnaissance drone is developed from the CT.20 target, to which it is externally similar. It is powered by a Marboré II turbojet and is launched with the aid of two solid-propellant booster rockets from a short ramp on a standard Berliet GB-C8-KT Army lorry. Standard NATO cameras or other surveillance equipment are carried in its nose and in interchangeable wingtip containers. Two other standard vehicles are used to carry support

Aérospatiale CT.20 drone, with underwing towed target

Aérospatiale R.20 battlefield reconnaissance drone, developed from the CT.20 target

equipment, including radio control equipment and the antenna system.

When close to its launch-post the R.20 is controlled directly from the ground. Over longer distances, the drone is controlled automatically by a gyroscopic platform and an electronic programmer, enabling it to follow a pre-arranged flight plan.

It is claimed to offer an over-target accuracy of within 985 ft (300 m) at a distance of 54 nm (62 miles; 100 km) from its launch site. Average operating height is 3,300 ft (1,000 m), but it can be set to fly higher or lower, as required. It can photograph more than 77 square miles (200 km²) of territory during a single low-altitude sortie, using three synchronised Omera 114 × 114 mm cameras. Data can be sent back during flight by radio link. Flares can be carried for night photography.

After initial testing in 1963, the R.20 was tested under operational conditions in February 1964. It is in operational use in the French Army and performs routine flights over French training grounds. Production had reached a total of approx 50 by early 1973, and was continuing to fulfil an additional order for 33 by the French Army. A test programme, involving three firings, was successfully completed by the 7th Artillery Regiment of the French Army at Landes in Spring 1973 to evaluate the R.20's reconnaissance system.

A night reconnaissance version, fitted with an SAT Cyclope infra-red line-scanning device, was being evaluated in early 1974.

DIMENSIONS, EXTERNAL:
- Wing span: 12 ft 2½ in (3·72 m)
- Width, wings folded: 4 ft 5 in (1·35 m)
- Length overall: 18 ft 9 in (5·71 m)
- Body diameter (max): 2 ft 2 in (0·66 m)
- Wingtip containers:
  - Length: 6 ft 3 in (1·90 m)
  - Diameter: 1 ft 3¾ in (0·40 m)

WEIGHTS:
- T-O weight of drone: 1,875 lb (850 kg)
- T-O weight with booster: 2,425 lb (1,100 kg)
- Payload: 330 lb (150 kg)

PERFORMANCE:
- Operating speed: Mach 0·65
- Operating radius at low altitude: 86 nm (100 miles; 160 km)

DORAND

GIRAVIONS DORAND

ADDRESS:
5 rue Jean Macé, 92153 Suresnes, BP 3-30
Telephone: 772.18.20
Telex: Iteser 28823 F Serv 458

MANAGING DIRECTOR:
P. de Guillenchmidt

Under contract to the Direction des Recherches et Moyens d'Essais (DRME), Dorand has built a test example of a gyro-glider which can be operated under pre-programmed control to recover loads dropped from aircraft. Its purpose is to provide the load to be recovered with the means of making an autorotative descent, terminating in a flare-out which reduces its vertical rate of descent to less than 6 ft (2 m)/sec at touchdown.

The DS.7 test model has a two-blade telescopic rotor (diameter 13 ft 1½ in; 4·00 m), a control system, a suspension system, and a rectangular load container fitted with a stabiliser and approach height detector. The rotor blades are each made in two sections, the outer portion of 7·9 in (20 cm) chord telescoping into the 11·8 in (30 cm) chord inboard portion. The control system comprises a cyclic control swashplate, a cam-operated programmer, and linkages between the cam followers and rotor blades.

The programmer, which consists of a system of cams started by the height detector and driven by the rotor, generates the control movements necessary for changing the collective and cyclic pitch angles in accordance with a flare-out programme at touchdown. The suspension consists of three struts which unfold and lock after deployment to form a pylon measuring 1 ft 11½ in (0·60 m). This pylon is attached at one end to the rotor hub, and at the other to the load via a flexible coupling, the travel of which is limited by mechanical stops. The load container is a rectangular case 1 ft 1¾ in (0·35 m) square and 3 ft 3¼ in (1·00 m) long, which can accept a load of up to 485 lb (220 kg) including the height detector and test instrumentation. A fantail stabiliser is fitted to keep the container pointed into wind. Total AUW of the complete vehicle, with load, is 551 lb (250 kg).

After release, the rotor of the gyro-glider is started automatically by the airflow, and the telescopic blades are extended by centrifugal force. At a release velocity of 230 ft (70 m)/sec, deployment takes approx 2 sec. The glideslope depends on the swashplate setting and the collective pitch angle of the blades. A typical 17° glideslope would give horizontal and vertical velocities of 70·2 ft (21·4 m)/sec and 21·3 ft (6·5 m)/sec respectively. Flare-out, which starts at a predetermined altitude, takes approx 3·5 sec. The programmer, actuated by the height detector, tilts back the rotor to reduce forward speed for landing, a second movement returning the rotor to a horizontal plane at the instant of touchdown.

The initial phase of capability testing of the DS.7 gyro-glider model has been completed, and was being followed in 1974 by a second phase concerned with rotor head and control system simplifications prior to the start of production studies. These tests were being conducted with half-scale working models of the DS.7; one of these is shown in the accompanying photograph, waiting to be lifted for a drop test.

Dorand DS.7 half-scale gyro-glider test model

Applications foreseen for this system, if tests prove successful, include the recovery of loads at very low altitudes or under high wind conditions; recovery of the Aérospatiale R.20 reconnaissance vehicle (which see); steering of a dropped load towards a predetermined point under remote control; automatic recovery of a helicopter following an engine failure; ejection seat recovery; and use as a personnel gyro-glider. Among the advantages claimed for the recovery system are its light weight (only 5 to 7 per cent of the recovered load), its very small volume when folded, fast rotor spin-up, high disc loading and ability to soft-land delicate loads. Payloads ranging from 220 lb (100 kg) to 33,070 lb (15,000 kg) could be recovered with a system of this type, depending on rotor size, and release altitude could be as low as 50 ft (15 m).

MARCHETTI

SOCIÉTÉ CHARLES MARCHETTI

HEAD OFFICE:
80 avenue de la Grande Armée, Paris 17e
Telephone: 380.17.69

PRESIDENT: Charles Marchetti

This company has undertaken design studies of a variety of rotating-wing aircraft in recent years, under contract from the French Ministry of Defence (DRME).

MARCHETTI ROTORMOBILE

The Rotormobile is a jet-propelled, remotely-controlled rotor without an airframe, the only non-rotating parts being the avionics platform and the cargo sling.

Basis of the system is a rotor consisting of three hollow "motor blades", with a turbojet engine mounted at the blade roots. The engine exhaust gases are passed through these blades and expand in nozzles at the tips to provide the reaction which drives the rotor.

Tests have confirmed the efficiency of flaps fitted to the blades for command and control of the vehicle; the ease of landing on the air-cushion type landing gear; and the stopping of the rotor in a few seconds, using reverse thrust at the tips of the blades.

Based on the results of these tests, Marchetti has projected two remote-controlled Rotormobile vehicles, of 28 and 50 tons, with useful loads of 20 and 35 tons respectively.

MARCHETTI HELISCOPE

The Heliscope is an electrically-powered flying platform, consisting basically of two three-blade light alloy fixed-pitch rotors of co-axial contra-rotating design. These rotors are attached respectively to the rotor and stator of an electric motor located between their hubs.

The power supply for this motor is provided by a generator mounted on the vehicle which serves as the mobile ground station, and is fed through a cable which runs to the centre of the base of the Heliscope.

Motorised mockup of a lifting platform using three Marchetti Heliscopes (*Air et Cosmos*)

Marchetti has used test results to project a design for a platform using three Heliscopes, each with a four-blade rotor of 5 ft 3 in (1·60 m) diameter. Such a vehicle could support a useful load of 220 lb (100 kg) with a simplified stabilisation system at an altitude of 755 ft (230 m) above the ground. An alternative proposal is to use the same principle to drive a rotor with Helifans (a shrouded Heliscope).

GERMANY
(FEDERAL REPUBLIC)

DORNIER

DORNIER GmbH

HEAD OFFICE:
Postfach 317, 799 Friedrichshafen/Bodensee
Telephone: Immenstaad (07545) 81
Telex: 0734372

OFFICERS: See "Aircraft" section

Current activities of Dornier GmbH include the development of drones, reconnaissance systems, missiles and air target systems.

The Dornier Aerial Target System (DATS) can be adapted to a wide variety of aircraft and target drones. The airborne portion of the system consists of an automatic towing reel with cable cutter, a launcher to carry the target, and the cruciform-tailed glassfibre-reinforced polyester target itself. For augmentation the tow target can be equipped with radar reflectors, optical or infra-red aids. Acoustic or electro-magnetic miss-distance indicators can also be installed. After take-off the tow target is released by radio command from its underwing carrier pylon at a predetermined altitude, and the cable is fully deployed by automatic reeling. The target follows the manoeuvres of the towing aircraft and remains airborne even after it has been penetrated by several bullets. After completion of its mission the tow target is recovered by parachute.

DATS (Dornier Aerial Target System) under the wing of a QT-33

The aircraft/helicopter division of Dornier GmbH has developed a mobile drone system, designated Do 34 Kiebitz, based on the Do 32 K Experimental Kiebitz; and an unmanned VTOL research vehicle known as the Aerodyne.

DORNIER Do 32 K EXPERIMENTAL KIEBITZ (PEEWIT)

The Experimental Kiebitz was developed, under contract from the Federal Ministry of Defence, to evaluate the feasibility of an automatically-stabilised tethered rotor platform, capable of utilising sensors for reconnaissance, communications and ECM purposes at an altitude which considerably increases their effectiveness.

The rotor and transmission system, comprising a two-blade "cold-jet" rotor driven by compressed air from a KHD T 212 (replacing the original Allison 250-C20) turbine and turbocompressor, were taken from the Do 32 single-seat helicopter, and the flight control system and the servo motors for rotor blade pitch control from the Do 32 drone helicopter. The complete system

Dornier Experimental Kiebitz and mobile ground control station

consists of a tethered rotating-wing platform (first demonstrated in flight in late 1970) and a mobile ground station such as a truck or tracked vehicle. Fuel for the turbine is fed through the tether by means of a pump installed in the ground station, making possible long periods of operation. The rotor turns at 340 rpm.

The platform contains a three-axis autostabiliser which works through the cyclic pitch control system and compressor exhaust control system. The ground vehicle serves as transporter, take-off and landing ramp, and power supply station. An easy-to-operate winch is fitted to enable the drone to be reeled in and out. De-icing and a high degree of weather resistance make operations almost independent of weather conditions.

The Kiebitz is intended for use as an emergency transmitter aerial in the long, medium and short wavebands; as a relay and directional station for TV, VHF and radio communications; for measurement of field strength for localising optimum transmitter positions, photographic survey and reconnaissance, meteorological measurements or radar reconnaissance to detect low-flying objects; and as a directional receiver. Power supply on board the vehicle is 200W 28V DC.

Five experimental rotating-wing vehicles were built, and these completed approx 100 hours of successful test flying, including take-offs and landings using a very short tethering cable, and tethered flights to an altitude of 660 ft (200 m). Following successful completion of the tests designed to perfect the flight control system, calculations were made to evaluate the detectability of the Kiebitz. In addition to measurement of the vehicle's infra-red radiation and radar profile, details have also been obtained of the distances at which the rotor platform is discernible acoustically and optically. Also, so far as possible within the experimental vehicle's payload capacity, tests have been performed with applications sensors. These include an RDF system, developed by Dornier, which used the Kiebitz rotor as an integral part of the D/F system by means of a blade-tip antenna; and a Grundig television camera, with oscillation-damping suspension and Dynalens lens-stabilisation, to determine the feasibility of such an installation for reconnaissance and surveillance purposes. The experimental programme, particularly with regard to payload and sensor investigations, was still active in 1974.

Dimensions, external:
- Diameter of rotor — 24 ft $7\frac{1}{4}$ in (7·50 m)
- Height overall — 5 ft 3 in (1·60 m)
- Body diameter at bottom edge — 2 ft $5\frac{1}{2}$ in (0·75 m)

Weights:
- Weight without tether or payload — 440 lb (200 kg)
- Max payload to 660 ft (200 m), ISA — 110 lb (50 kg)

Performance:
- Reel-in/reel-out speed — 4·9 ft (1·5 m)/sec
- Operational ceiling — 660 ft (200 m)

DORNIER Do 34 KIEBITZ (PEEWIT)

In August 1972 Dornier announced the receipt of a DM 7 million contract from the Federal Ministry of Defence for the first development phase of a prototype of an operational Kiebitz system, to be used for reconnaissance, fire control, communications and traffic monitoring duties. This followed the completion in mid-1972 of the design of a Do 34 operational model as a sensor platform with a payload of 308 lb (140 kg). Full-scale mockups of the Do 34 have been completed, and work has begun on the construction of four prototype flight vehicles and two ground stations. The first flight was due to take place in the Autumn of 1974.

The complete system is vehicle housed, and consists of a landing platform, winch system, guidance and control post, flight vehicle and sensor, checkout system, fuel tank for 12 hours' operation, and auxiliary equipment. The flight vehicle has a cone-shaped airframe to reduce radar reflectivity, and the payload compartment is located on the underside of this, enabling sensors to be changed quickly and allowing space for a large-volume radome. The rotor's twin blades are suspended on straps and driven by cold air expanded through the blade-tip nozzles, a principle which ensures that no torque is produced which could act on the platform. Air for the rotor blades is supplied by a radial compressor and an Allison 250-C20 turboshaft engine, the latter being installed on the slant to ensure a good intake position.

After arrival on site, the drone can be in position at an operational height of 985 ft (300 m) in 8 minutes. Limiting factors in the guidance and control system are a wind speed of 43 ft (14 m)/sec ±26 ft (8 m)/sec; the available thrust reserves; and the requirements of the various sensors. The control system aligns the Kiebitz according to airframe attitude and position in relation to the ground. An electromagnetic sensor measures any drift from the desired position.

Under a bilateral agreement between the German and French governments, one Kiebitz

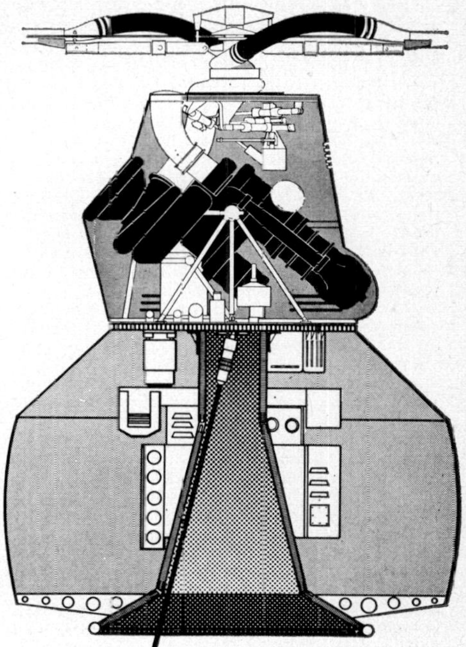

Dornier Do 34 Kiebitz in Argus configuration: tilted engine shown in solid black, shaded area indicates LCT radar location

flight vehicle will be fitted with an advanced version of the French LCT Orphée radar, to define, integrate and test a new battlefield reconnaissance system known as **Argus** (see International section).

Operational trials will also be carried out with a Kiebitz flying platform fitted with Decca RDL-2 passive ECM equipment. Another project under discussion is for a Sea Kiebitz, carrying a Ferranti Seaspray search radar, which could enhance the strike range of medium-range naval missile systems by elevating the radar well above the height of existing masthead aerials. A similar application might be for the detection of low-flying aircraft flying in the shadows of hills.

The following details apply to the basic Do 34 flight vehicle:

Dimensions, external:
- Diameter of rotor — 26 ft 3 in (8·00 m)
- Height overall — 4 ft 9 in (1·45 m)
- Body diameter at bottom edge — 3 ft $5\frac{1}{4}$ in (1·05 m)

Weights:
- Weight without tether or payload — 628 lb (285 kg)
- Max payload to 985 ft (300 m), ISA — 308 lb (140 kg)

Performance:
- Reel-in/reel-out speed — 9·84 ft (3 m)/sec
- Operational ceiling — 985 ft (300 m)

DORNIER AERODYNE E 1

Development of the Aerodyne wingless high-speed VTOL aircraft was begun by Dr A. Lippisch in the USA. It has been continued since 1967 by Dornier GmbH, which is engaged in an experimental programme under contract to the Federal Ministry of Defence, within the framework of which the feasibility of the Aerodyne design is to be demonstrated by means of flight tests with an unmanned experimental vehicle.

The Aerodyne principle is marked by the combination of the means of lift and propulsion in a single unit, namely a shrouded propeller, the slipstream from which is deflected downward by cascade-type vanes for vertical take-off and landing. Control is by deflection of the turboshaft exhaust, which emerges at the end of the tailboom, and vanes in the propeller slipstream.

A radio-controlled prototype vehicle, known as the Aerodyne E 1, was built in 1971 and made its first flight, tethered, on 18 September 1972. Hovering tests were concluded successfully on 30 November 1972, after 74 flights totalling almost $1\frac{1}{2}$ hours in the air. The last of these was, unintentionally, a free flight, from which the E 1 was successfully brought down from the hover to a normal landing.

In 1971 Dornier GmbH and Hawker Siddeley Dynamics Ltd in the UK announced an agreement for the joint development of an unmanned wingless VTOL reconnaissance system, based upon the work done on the Aerodyne by Dr Lippisch. In 1974, with the experimental programme actively continuing, mission analysis and parametric studies were being carried out to define operational versions of the Aerodyne for various tasks.

Type: Radio-controlled VTOL experimental RPV.

Airframe: Annular fan shroud and deflection chamber, with bullet-shaped pod attached centrally in mouth of fan duct. In E 1 prototype, this pod houses electronics system and control unit; in a production version it would house the mission payload. The power plant is mounted on top of the fan shroud, with a hollow tailboom to the rear. Non-retractable landing gear, designed for vertical landings, consists of two main legs and a shorter leg under the tailboom. Shock-absorption by interchangeable aluminium honeycomb damper in each leg.

POWER PLANT: One 370 shp MTU 6022A-3 turboshaft engine, driving a five-blade variable-pitch Hoffmann fan via a Zahnradfabrik/ Dornier GmbH Z-type reduction gear. Fuel in two tanks located between inner and outer walls of deflection chamber.

FLIGHT CONTROLS: The fan shroud and deflection chamber form an inner flow channel, at the end of which the airflow is deflected by cascade-type vanes. In the E 1 prototype, this deflection amounts to approx 60° during hovering flight and is intended to be increased to approx 75° during future development. The cascades are not moved during hovering. The engine's exhaust is directed aft through the tailboom and provides pitch and yaw control during hovering. For this purpose the jet can be deflected up and down as well as sideways by hydraulically-operated cascades. (For pitch and yaw control during forward flight, conventional tail control surfaces, not present during hover tests, will be fitted to the tailboom.) Roll control is effected during both hovering and forward flight by a vertical keel flap, located immediately aft of the main cascade flaps, which supplies a roll moment when deflected, due to its arrangement below the CG. This keel flap and the fan pitch control mechanism are operated hydraulically.

COMMAND AND GUIDANCE: Radio command, developed by Dornier GmbH. During hovering flight, the remote control pilot commands the flight vehicle's attitude via a small control stick. Bodenseewerk on-board attitude control system, which ensures that the attitude command is kept within very small limits, incorporates a vertical gyro, three rate gyros and three accelerometers as sensors. Telemetry system, with more than 50 channels, for transmitting data to ground station. Power supply system incorporates battery for emergency power in the event of a generator failure.

Dornier Aerodyne E 1 prototype VTOL RPV in tethered flight

DIMENSIONS, EXTERNAL (approx):

Max diameter	6 ft 2¾ in (1·90 m)
Fan diameter	3 ft 7¼ in (1·10 m)
Length overall	18 ft 0½ in (5·50 m)

WEIGHT:

Max T-O weight	959 lb (435 kg)

VFW-FOKKER

VEREINIGTE FLUGTECHNISCHE WERKE-FOKKER GmbH (subsidiary of ZENTRAL-GESELLSCHAFT VFW-FOKKER mbH)

HEAD OFFICE:
Hünefeldstrasse 1-5, 28 Bremen 1 (Postfach 1206)
Telephone: (0421) 5181
Telex: 245 821
OFFICERS: See "Aircraft" section

VFW-Fokker has developed a small drone aircraft intended for use on firefighting duties at or near airports. Carrying a droppable payload of firefighting chemical, it would be launched in salvos of up to 12 drones, directed to the fire site by radar and homing devices, and then return for recovery by parachute.

No other details were known at the time of closing for press.

INDIA

ADE

AERONAUTICAL DEVELOPMENT ESTABLISHMENT

DIRECTOR:
Vivek R. Sinha

It was reported in the Spring of 1974 that flight testing was imminent of a supersonic target drone developed by the ADE and apparently of indigenous design.

No further details were known at the time of closing for press.

INTERNATIONAL PROGRAMMES

ARGUS

PARTICIPATING COMPANIES:

Dornier GmbH, Postfach 317, 799 Friedrichshafen/Bodensee, German Federal Republic
Telephone: Immenstaad (07545) 81
Telex: 0734372

LCT (Laboratoire Central de Télécommunications), 18-20 Rue Grange-Dame-Rose, 78140 Vélizy-Villacoublay, BP 40, France
Telephone: 946-96-15
Telex: 69892

ARGUS

Argus (Autonomes Radar Gefaechtsfeld Uberwachungs System) is a battlefield surveillance system being developed under a German-French government agreement signed on 6 March 1974. Dornier has the main contract for co-ordinating, integrating and testing the system, and the programme is administered by a board of directors representing the two governments.

The Argus flight vehicle, of which a prototype is under construction, consists of a Dornier Kiebitz tethered rotor platform in which is installed an advanced version of the LCT Orphée radar as the primary sensor. The complete Argus system also incorporates a mobile ground station and a tether cable. The ground station is installed in a container mounted on a cross-country 7 ton truck and provided with all equipment necessary for transportation and a 12 hr operation of the system. Operating height of the flight vehicle is 985 ft (300 m).

A description of the Kiebitz appears under the Dornier heading in the German section of this edition.

ITALY

METEOR

METEOR SpA COSTRUZIONI AERONAUTICHE ED ELETTRONICHE

ADDRESS:
146 Via Nomentana, 00162 Rome
Telephone: (06) 8380232 and 833690
Telex: 68136 Meteorom
WORKS:
Aeroporto Giuliano, 34074 Monfalcone
Telephone: (0481) 778001
Telex: 46288 Meteormo
EXPERIMENTAL FLIGHT CENTRE:
Strada Orientale Sarda Km78, 09040 San Lorenzo (Villaputzu), Cagliari, Sardinia
Telephone: (070) 99637 and 99546
Telex: 79076 Avielsar
PRESIDENT AND GENERAL MANAGER:
Comm Avv Furio Lauri
MANAGERS:
Mrs Luciana Lauri (Rome Office and Public Relations)
Dott Antonio Castelli (Monfalcone Factory)
Col Guido Fea (Development)
Capt Guido Borsari (Long-term Programmes)

Meteor was established in Trieste as a joint stock company in 1947. Its present head office is in Rome, supported by facilities at Monfalcone in Italy and Cagliari in Sardinia. The former is a production factory, the latter being equipped for flight operations and for technical assistance to the users of the tri-service range at Salto di Quirra in southern Sardinia.

Meteor has developed and is producing for the Italian armed forces and a number of foreign armed forces a range of propeller-driven and turbojet-powered radio-controlled drones covering a speed range from 323 knots (372 mph; 600 km/h) up to Mach 2·8, and altitudes from 35 ft (10 m) to 82,000 ft (25,000 m) above sea level. It also produces under licence the Northrop NVM-1, NVM-2 and USD-1 drones, and co-produces the CT.20 target drone with Aérospatiale; the AN/USD-501 surveillance drone with Canadair; and the BM-1 missile target system with Beech Aircraft Corporation.

METEOR P.1

The Meteor P.1 is a subsonic target drone, used for training with directed anti-aircraft batteries of medium and large calibre and with ground-to-air missiles. It is currently available in two versions, both of which can be used for in-sight and out-of-sight operation. The first version is fitted with a 100 hp Meteor Alfa 1 four-cylinder X-type two-stroke aircooled engine for operation at heights up to 26,000 ft (8,000 m). The second version has a Meteor Alfa 1AQ engine, giving 120 hp constant up to 21,325 ft (6,500 m) and permitting operation at heights up to 42,000 ft (13,000 m).

The P.1 is made largely of glassfibre-reinforced polyester resin. Its engine is manufactured from anti-corrosive and special steel and aluminium, with extensive chromium plating. This permits recovery from salt water and re-use. Flotation is ensured by the use of blocks of expanded resin inside the structure.

All Meteor targets are launched normally with the engine running at peak rpm, with the aid of jettisonable solid-propellant rockets. Alternatively, a catapult can be used, or the targets can be air-launched.

For out-of-sight radio control, over ranges up to 54-86 nm (62-100 miles; 100-160 km), the operator uses a series of control levers linked to a UHF ground transmitter which emits a five-tone modulated carrier signal. The receiver in the target transforms the signals into seven distinct control operations. Two tones control the elevator, two control the ailerons, and the fifth is used to stop the engine and open the recovery parachute at the end of a flight. The ailerons and elevators are operated by electrical servo controls, those for the ailerons being combined with a gyro which stabilises the target laterally. Electronic equipment in the target also includes a two-axis automatic stabilisation system. The target's track and altitude are plotted normally by the radar of the gun or missile battery using it, and wingtip reflectors can be fitted to amplify the echoes from the target. However, a UHF tracking and tele-control system can be used, in conjunction with a transponder in the target weighing only 4·4 lb (2 kg).

DIMENSIONS, EXTERNAL:
Wing span without wingtip containers
12 ft 1 in (3·68 m)
Length overall 11 ft $1\frac{1}{2}$ in (3·39 m)
Height overall 2 ft $1\frac{1}{2}$ in (0·65 m)

WEIGHTS (out-of-sight versions. A: 100 hp, B: 120 hp):
Weight without fuel and electronics:
A, B 293 lb (133 kg)
Electronics and gyro guidance equipment:
A, B 55 lb (25 kg)
Launching weight (one-hour flight):
A 425 lb (195 kg)
B 444 lb (202 kg)
Max launching weight:
A 484 lb (220 kg)
B 495 lb (225 kg)

PERFORMANCE:
Max level speed at 21,325 ft (6,500 m):
A 178 knots (202 mph; 330 km/h)
B 296 knots (342 mph; 550 km/h)
Stalling speed:
A, B 62 knots (71 mph; 115 km/h)
Max rate of climb at S/L:
A 2,950 ft (900 m)/min
B 3,940 ft (1,200 m)/min
Time to 20,000 ft (6,100 m):
A 10 min
B 5 min

METEOR P.1/R

This is a reconnaissance version of the P.1, first displayed at the 1966 Turin Air Show. It is powered by a 110 hp Meteor Alfa 1 engine, driving a constant-speed propeller, and is launched from a zero-length ramp with the aid of a Meteor 8785/Z solid-propellant booster rocket (3,968 lb; 1,800 kg st). A number of P.1/R systems have been produced for the Italian armed forces, and production was continuing in 1974.

Control is partially by radio command signals and partially by a pre-programmed guidance system, set up prior to take-off and unaffected by enemy electronic countermeasures. The pre-set guidance system is accommodated in a pylon-mounted container under the starboard wing. A similar container under the port wing houses the reconnaissance camera, and can be released in flight for recovery by its own parachute system.

Tracking of the target in flight is by radar, utilising the coded response of a transponder, supplemented by an on-board TV camera. Recovery is by a conventional parachute system.

DIMENSIONS, EXTERNAL: As for P.1

WEIGHTS:
Useful load 66 lb (30 kg)
Max launching weight 551 lb (250 kg)

PERFORMANCE:
Max level speed 270 knots (310 mph; 500 km/h)
Service ceiling 30,000 ft (9,150 m)
Operational radius 54 nm (62 miles; 100 km)
Endurance 1 hr

METEOR P.2

The Meteor P.2, described in the 1973-74 *Jane's*, is no longer in production.

METEOR P.X

The Meteor P.X is generally similar in layout to other Meteor drones, but is powered by a 72 hp McCulloch O-100-1 four-cylinder horizontally-opposed air-cooled two-stroke engine. It is designed for zero-length launching, with the assistance of a Meteor 8785 solid-propellant booster rocket.

Guidance is by radio control, via a Meteor RSS 529 fully-transistorised two-axis autopilot, with radar tracking of the drone's position. Recovery is by parachute, deployed automatically or on receipt of a signal from the ground.

A number of P.X systems have been produced for the armed forces of Italy and other countries, and production was continuing in 1974.

DIMENSIONS, EXTERNAL:
Wing span without wingtip containers
11 ft 8 in (3·56 m)
Length overall 11 ft $4\frac{1}{4}$ in (3·46 m)
Diameter of fuselage 1 ft $3\frac{3}{4}$ in (0·40 m)
Span of tail unit 3 ft $11\frac{1}{2}$ in (1·21 m)

WEIGHT:
Max launching weight 363 lb (165 kg)

PERFORMANCE (at max launching weight):
Max level speed
194 knots (224 mph; 360 km/h)
Time to reach 20,000 ft (6,100 m) 10 min
Service ceiling 26,500 ft (8,000 m)
Radius of action 86 nm (100 miles; 160 km)
Endurance 1 hr

METEOR GUFO

Meteor evolved the Gufo tactical reconnaissance system to meet anticipated military requirements during the 1970s. The system is claimed to be particularly suitable for use in mountainous country. In operational form it would enable up to 60 lb (27 kg) of sensors to be carried at 400 knots (460 mph; 740 km/h) to target areas up to 110 nm (125 miles; 200 km) from the launch site. Recovery can be within a radius of 330 ft (100 m) from a predetermined spot.

The drone part of the system, known as the **Gufone (Owl)**, is proposed in three versions, the standard operational vehicle being based on the American Northrop Chukar I (MQM-74A) target drone modified by Meteor to carry new guidance equipment and sensors, together with inflatable bags to cushion the landing shock. Details of the three versions are shown in the table. Equipment for day and night operations can include a variety of infra-red sensors and cameras using 50, 70 or 75 mm film to photograph a strip of terrain more than 55 nm (63 miles; 102 km) long and, respectively, 3,280 ft (1,000 m), 6,560 ft (2,000 m) or 9,840 ft (3,000 m) wide, respectively from altitudes of 1,000 ft (305 m), 2,000 ft (610 m) or 3,000 ft (915 m). For night operations, the Gufone can carry 14 wingtip flares which are dropped at preselected time intervals. At take-off, the 121 lb (55 kg) st turbojet engine is supplemented by two Meteor 8785/CNS solid-propellant jettisonable boosters, providing a total thrust of 5,730 lb (2,600 kg) for 0·7 seconds.

A military unit deploying the Gufo system would comprise a launching section; a guidance and control section; a sensor recovery, interpretation and headquarters section; and a vehicle recovery and preparation section.

The Gufo system is designed to overcome the problem of poor accuracy that sometimes mars results when pre-programmed drones are

Meteor P.1 target drone on zero-length launcher

Meteor P.1/R reconnaissance drone (110 hp Meteor Alfa 1 engine)

Meteor P.X target drone (72 hp McCulloch O-100-1 engine)

used over ranges of more than 30 nm (35 miles; 55 km). The Gufone can be launched in any direction and normally makes the first part of its flight under guidance over friendly territory. This permits the effects of factors such as wind and engine performance to be calculated, so that the Gufone can be directed very precisely on to the first stage of its programmed flight to the target. Once it has been put on course, it becomes "deaf" to all friendly or enemy electronic signals until it approaches the end of its return flight and comes under command guidance for recovery.

Provision is made for an intermediate pre-programmed guidance phase between the guided and "deaf" phases. In this case, the drone will accept only specially-coded commands of very short duration, for the sole purpose of correcting its course.

The Gufo system was being evaluated in 1974 by NATO and by the Italian armed forces.

DIMENSIONS (Gufone):
- Wing span: 5 ft $6\frac{3}{4}$ in (1·69 m)
- Length overall: 11 ft 10 in (3·61 m)
- Height overall: 2 ft 5 in (0·73 m)

WEIGHTS (Gufone):
- Sensors (max): 60 lb (27 kg)
- Max launching weight: 300 lb (136 kg)

PERFORMANCE (Gufone):
- Max level speed: 400 knots (460 mph; 740 km/h)
- Max cruising height: 35,000 ft (10,670 m)

PROPOSED VERSIONS OF GUFONE DRONE

	Gufone	A	B
Payload	66 lb (30 kg)	132 lb (60 kg)	66 lb (30 kg)
Range penetration from FEBA at S/L	29 nm (34 miles; 55 km)	29 nm (34 miles; 55 km)	48 nm (56 miles; 90 km)
Range penetration from FEBA at 32,800 ft (10,000 m)	72 nm (83 miles; 135 km)	72 nm (83 miles; 135 km)	113 nm (130 miles; 210 km)
Flight altitude	328-32,800 ft (100-10,000 m)		
Cruising speed	378-405 knots (435-466 mph; 700-750 km/h)		
Landing accuracy	492 ft (150 m) CEP		
Wind during launch	65 ft (20 m)/sec		
Pictures	Improved film by day and night		
Recovery	By parachute		
Launch	By booster rocket from a jeep		
Radar reflectivity	2·15 sq ft (0·2 m^2)		

Gufone drone portion of the Gufo reconnaissance system

Gufo system control truck, with towed launcher and Gufone drone

JAPAN

FUJI

FUJI JUKOGYO KABUSHIKI KAISHA (Fuji Heavy Industries Ltd)

ADDRESS AND OFFICERS: See "Aircraft" section

Under contract from the Japan Defence Agency, Fuji is building the Teledyne Ryan Firebee I subsonic target drone (see US section) for use in the training of Tartar missile and gunnery crews and for the evaluation of air-to-air missile systems.

Nine Fuji-built Firebees had been completed and delivered to the Japan Maritime Self-Defence Force, and one to the Technical Research Institute of the Japan Defence Agency, by the end of 1973. A further three were scheduled to be completed during FY 1974.

During the past year, at the request of the JASDF, Fuji has carried out a feasibility study for the conversion of about 50 JASDF F-86F Sabre fighters to target drone configuration. If this programme is approved, Fuji would develop the remote control system for the drone version, and Mitsubishi would undertake the necessary airframe modifications.

Fuji-built Firebee I remotely-controlled target drone for the JMSDF

NEC

NIPPON ELECTRIC COMPANY LTD (Nippon Denki Kabushiki Kaisha)

Head Office:
33-1 Shiba Gochome, Minato-ku, Tokyo 108
Telephone: Tokyo (03) 454-1111
Telex: NECTOK A J22686

President:
Koji Kobayashi

Manager, Overseas Relations:
Kohei Takubo

Under a technical aid agreement with Northrop Corporation, USA, Nippon Denki is responsible for production and repair of Northrop Shelduck target drones (MQM-36) for the Japan Maritime Self-Defence Force and Ground Self-Defence Force. Delivery of these drones to the JMSDF and JGSDF began in 1961 and a total of 194 had been delivered by the end of 1973. Production is expected to continue at the rate of approx 15 per year.

NEC-built Northrop MQM-36 Shelduck radio-controlled aerial target

UNITED KINGDOM

AEL

AERO ELECTRONICS (AEL) LTD

Address:
Gatwick House, Horley, Surrey RH6 9SU
Telephone: 02934-5353
Telex: 87116

Directors:
H. K. Hughes, DFC
J. F. Hughes
M. H. Nicholas (Managing)

This company manufactures a range of small, low-cost radio- and optically-guided systems for target drone, reconnaissance or other RPV applications, brief details of which follow. The standard systems offer payload capabilities of up to 30 lb (14 kg) and a visual control range of 2·7 nm (3·1 miles; 5 km). Non-standard systems can be produced with payload capabilities of up to 50 lb (22·7 kg). To simplify control, an autostabiliser is available, with options of height lock and heading lock; an autopilot is under development to permit automatic out-and-back sorties beyond, and returning to, visual control. All systems are controlled using a standard tripod-mounted transmitter.

Each system will operate in a slot with an approx bandwidth of 25kHz and an ERP maximum of 5W. In all cases, to allow correct operation of the drones it is essential to secure a VHF frequency allocation clear of any other traffic, and contracts can be accepted only after receipt from the customer of frequency allocations.

AEL MERLIN

The Merlin system consists of a delta-shaped flying-wing drone, built of polystyrene foam with a plywood skin, powered by a 10 cc engine and fitted with a tricycle landing gear. A six-function pulse width modulated VHF guidance system with RF output of 5W is used.

Three versions are available, as follows:

AEL4018 Target System. For training air defence weapon crews to acquire and track target aircraft. Capable of simulating a full-size aircraft, with a mission response time of less than four minutes. For surveillance radar response, can carry X- and S-band radar enhancement devices. A 7 ft (2·13 m) drogue target can be towed on a 500 ft (150 m) cable for live firing target work.

AEL4019 Camera System. For short-range aerial reconnaissance with standard accessories. Radio-triggered Robot 35 mm camera, with f/2·8 lens, giving 18 high-definition photographs per loading at altitudes up to 3,000 ft (915 m). Optional accessory kit for printing and processing film in approx 5 min from removal from aircraft.

AEL4020 Composite Target/Camera System. Total facilities equivalent to those of AEL4018 and 4019 combined.

Launch and Recovery: Orthodox take-off from ground or launch from system launcher; recovery by normal aircraft-type landing.

Dimensions, external:

Wing span	4 ft 9 in (1·45 m)
Length overall	4 ft 0 in (1·22 m)

Weights:

Payload	3 lb (1·4 kg)
Max launching weight	10·5 lb (4·76 kg)

Performance:

Max speed	78 knots (90 mph; 145 km/h)
Stalling speed	20 knots (23 mph; 37 km/h)
Max controllable range (optical)	1·6 nm (1·9 miles; 3 km)
Endurance	30 min

AEL FALCON

The Falcon miniature aircraft is of generally similar appearance and construction to the Merlin, but is larger, has a greater payload and longer endurance, and is powered by a 56 cc engine. Guidance, launch and recovery are the same as for the Merlin system.

Three versions are available, as follows:

AEL4012 Target System. For training air defence weapon crews to acquire and track low-level high-speed aircraft. Mission response time of less than four minutes. Can be equipped with X- and S-band radar enhancement devices. Facility for trailing a 10 ft (3·05 m) towed target on a 500 ft (152 m) cable. Ordered by Libyan government; delivery completed in January 1974.

AEL4015 Camera System. For short-range

Top left: **AEL Falcon "mini-RPV", with tripod-mounted binoculars and radio guidance transmitter;** *top right:* **AEL4024 Heron miniature aircraft;** *bottom left:* **AEL4030 training drone;** *bottom right:* **the swept-wing Mossette, which can simulate a wire-guided anti-tank missile**

aerial reconnaissance, for which it has same equipment as Merlin AEL4019, including optional printing/processing kit. Target location by photo/map comparison. Ordered by Libyan government; delivery completed in January 1974.

AEL4017 Composite Target/Camera System. Combines total facilities of AEL4012 and 4015.

DIMENSIONS, EXTERNAL:
Wing span 7 ft 0 in (2·13 m)
Length overall 6 ft 6 in (1·98 m)
WEIGHT:
Max launching weight 21 lb (9·5 kg)
PERFORMANCE:
Max speed 110 knots (126·5 mph; 204 km/h)
Stalling speed 18 knots (21 mph, 33 km/h)
Max controllable range (optical) 2·7 nm (3·1 miles; 5 km)
Endurance 45 min

AEL4024 HERON

This RPV is essentially a miniature high-wing monoplane, of simple and robust construction and powered by a 56 cc engine. Fuel capacity is 0·5 Imp gallons (2·3 litres). Although designed specifically for target work, its payload capability and 1 cu ft (0·03 m³) payload bay make it equally suitable for other applications, and up to 11 lb (5 kg) of the total payload may consist of pylon-mounted underwing stores such as flares or small bombs. A good X-band radar signature is provided for radar tracking. Guidance, launch and recovery are the same as for the Merlin system. The Heron is controllable in winds gusting up to 30 knots (34·5 mph; 56 km/h).

A number of Herons have been ordered by the British Army. Photograph on page 539.

DIMENSIONS, EXTERNAL:
Wing span 9 ft 10 in (3·00 m)
Wing chord (constant) 1 ft 5 in (0·432 m)
Length overall 7 ft 0 in (2·13 m)
Fuselage: Max width 10 in (0·254 m)
Tailplane span 3 ft 3¼ in (1·00 m)
WEIGHTS:
Max payload:
catapult launch 15 lb (6·8 kg)
ground T-O 30 lb (13·6 kg)
Max weight:
catapult launch 34 lb (15·4 kg)
ground T-O 53 lb (24 kg)
PERFORMANCE:
Max speed 104 knots (120 mph; 193 km/h)
Max controllable range (optical) 2·7 nm (3·1 miles; 5 km)
Endurance 30 min

AEL HERON HS

This is a high-speed version of the standard Heron, improved aerodynamically by reducing the wing thickness and area, introducing linear taper and eliminating wing struts and pylons. The wheeled landing gear is replaced by a sprung metal skid and catapult launching points, although a take-off dolly can be provided if a clear area is available, permitting a 25% increase in payload.

High-speed AEL Heron HS

AEL4020 Merlin radio-controlled target drone (see page 539), on rail ready for launching

Dimensions are the same as for the standard Heron, except for an 8 ft 0 in (2·44 m) wing span. Max payload is 10 lb (4·5 kg) and max speed 108·5 knots (125 mph; 201 km/h).

AEL4041 MOSSETTE

The Mossette is a re-usable sweptwing target drone with an in-flight profile similar to that of wire-guided anti-tank missiles in current use, and is intended for training operators of helicopter- and vehicle-launched missiles of that type. It is powered by a 6 cc engine. At the bottom of the underfin is fitted a smokeless flare to enable the trainee operator to align the Mossette with the target, thus realistically simulating the operational missile. Immediately in front of the target is erected the system catching net in which the Mossette is retrieved for re-use. The nosecone, which is expendable, is replaced prior to the next exercise. Guidance system as for Merlin and other AEL RPVs. Photograph on page 539.

LAUNCH AND RECOVERY: Launch from system catapult; recovery with catching net.

DIMENSIONS, EXTERNAL:
Wing span 4 ft 0 in (1·22 m)
Length overall 3 ft 6 in (1·07 m)
WEIGHT:
Max launching weight 4 lb (1·8 kg)
PERFORMANCE:
Max speed 69 knots (80 mph; 128 km/h)
Stalling speed 18 knots (21 mph; 33 km/h)
Max controllable range (optical) 1·6 nm (1·9 miles; 3 km)
Endurance 20 min

AEL4030 TRAINING DRONE

Designed to train operators of operational drone/RPV systems, the AEL4030 is of broadly similar external appearance to the Heron RPV, but is slightly smaller and is powered by a 10 cc engine. It is fitted with a 6-channel proportional radio control designed for use with the standard tripod-mounted ground control system for the Merlin and other AEL RPVs. Photograph on page 539.

DIMENSIONS, EXTERNAL:
Wing span 7 ft 0 in (2·13 m)
Length 6 ft 0 in (1·83 m)
WEIGHTS:
Payload 4 lb (1·8 kg)
Weight dry 11 lb (5 kg)
PERFORMANCE:
Max speed 52·1 knots (60 mph; 96·6 km/h)
Stalling speed 13 knots (15 mph; 24·1 km/h)
Endurance 35 min

AEL SATS

SATS (Small Arms Target System) is used as a live target for infantry anti-aircraft firing practice with rifles and sub-machine-guns. Controlled with a hand-held transmitter, it has an optical range fully satisfying its design operational needs.

DIMENSIONS, EXTERNAL:
Wing span 7 ft 3 in (2·21 m)
Wing chord at root 1 ft 3 in (0·38 m)
Wing chord at tip 10 in (0·25 m)
Length overall 6 ft 6 in (1·98 m)
WEIGHT:
T-O weight 9 lb (4·1 kg)
PERFORMANCE:
Max speed 61 knots (70 mph; 112 km/h)
Endurance 40 min

AEL Small Arms Target System (SATS)

MoD (Army)

MINISTRY OF DEFENCE (ARMY)

To meet a British Army requirement for a battlefield reconnaissance drone, the Ministry of Defence is considering proposals from several British manufacturers, including AEL, BAC, Hawker Siddeley Dynamics, Short Bros & Harland and Westland Aircraft Ltd. Canadair has also submitted proposals.

The requirement is understood to be for a vehicle able to carry about 100 lb (45 kg) of cameras, linescan or other surveillance equipment and having an endurance of 1 hour and a range of about 43 nm (50 miles; 80 km).

The BAC proposal is based on the Teledyne Ryan Firebee (see US section), for which the company has a marketing and manufacturing licence. HSD's proposal is based on the Dornier GmbH Aerodyne (see German section), and Shorts have submitted the Skyspy (which see). No details of the Westland proposal are available, except that it is of a rotating-wing configuration.

SHORTS

SHORT BROTHERS & HARLAND LTD

ADDRESS:
PO Box 241, Airport Road, Belfast BT3 9DZ, Northern Ireland
Telephone: 0232 58444
Telex: 74688
OFFICERS:
See "Aircraft" section

SHORTS SKYSPY

Announced on 5 September 1972, the Skyspy is a pilotless remotely-controlled VTOL aerial reconnaissance vehicle suitable for use in military or naval applications in battlefield areas, other high-risk zones, or at sea. It is very small (see dimensions of a prototype vehicle which follow), structurally and mechanically simple, relatively inexpensive, and easily transportable. Its small size and low power also confer a number of operational advantages, such as low radar and infra-red signatures, low noise level, low gust response, and a very small visual silhouette, all of which contribute to a low damage risk under operational conditions. Surveillance can be carried out at all angles of attack between conventional forward flight and the hover mode.

A wide variety of applications is envisaged, including army reconnaissance; naval over-the-horizon viewing; weapon control and delivery, including the capability of providing a command link for over-the-horizon weapon control systems; target spotting; coastguard surveillance; border patrol and police duties; fishery protection; search and rescue operations; forest fire spotting; and emergency relief and medical support service.

Since the initial announcement Shorts have initiated a company-funded development programme and were expecting to demonstrate a flight vehicle before the end of 1974.

TYPE: Remotely controlled VTOL aerial reconnaissance and surveillance drone.

AIRFRAME: The basic vehicle consists of a centrebody carrying the engine, fuel, and control and stabilisation actuators; a low-pressure fan; and an axially symmetrical duct connected to the centrebody by an engine mounting spider and by stators. Aerofoil surfaces, for pitch, roll/yaw, and rotational stabilisation and control, are set across the duct exit and integrate in part with low aspect ratio wings located on the exterior of the duct. The centrebody comprises the major part of the vehicle weight, the duct being a simple, light but rigid structure. An equipment/payload pod fairing is located on the outer surface of the duct, indexed in line with the forward duct support structure. The autopilot and power supply equipment are at the rear, in the wall of the duct.

Power Plant: Lift and propulsive thrust are obtained by vectoring the gross thrust output of a single-stage multi-blade fixed-pitch low-pressure ducted fan, powered by a small piston engine (in prototype, a two-cylinder in-line Hirth engine of 60 hp; 44·7kW) and augmented by aerodynamic force components generated on the duct surfaces and intake lip.

Operational Equipment: Operational payload includes TV camera, sensors, automatic data-gathering and other equipment, to operator's requirements, installed in pod fairing on the outer forward surface of the duct. The Skyspy is intended to be flown under remote control to the chosen surveillance area, where it can hover over a stationary target (or track a moving one) and relay positional details of the target in real time, using secure data links, to a ground- or ship-based controller.

Typical Dimensions and Weight (60 hp Hirth engine):

Overall diameter	3 ft 6½ in (1·08 m)
Fan diameter	2 ft 9½ in (0·85 m)
Max T-O weight	286 lb (130 kg)

Performance:

Dependent upon operational requirements and payload. A vehicle of the size quoted could operate at altitudes of up to 6,000 ft (1,825 m); typically, it could carry a 44 lb (20 kg) payload for a sortie of 1½ hours' duration.

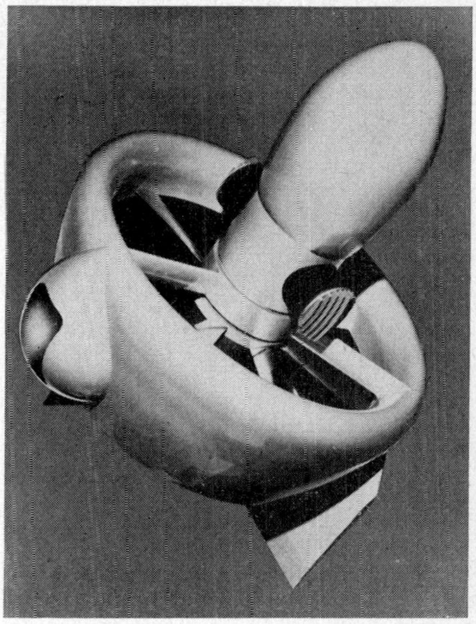

Shorts Skyspy remotely controlled surveillance and general purpose military vehicle

UNITED STATES OF AMERICA

BEECHCRAFT

BEECH AIRCRAFT CORPORATION

Head Office and Works:

Wichita, Kansas 67201

Officers: See "Aircraft" section

In addition to manufacturing piloted aircraft, Beech has been designing and producing pilotless target drones of various types since 1955. By mid-March 1974 it had built a total of 5,017 target drones. This figure includes more than 2,300 Model 1001s, of which more than 1,360 were MQM-61As for the US Army. Production of the Models 1001 and 1025 (1972-73 *Jane's*) has ended, but targets on hand continue to support various military services.

Beech has also carried out design studies to examine the suitability of its range of light aircraft for operation under remote control.

BEECHCRAFT MODELS 1019, 1072, 1088, 1094 and 1095

US military designation: AQM-37A

UK designations: SD.2 Stiletto (Model 1072) and Model 1095

Italian designation: Model 1088

French designation: Model 1094

Winner of a 1959 US Navy/Air Force design competition, the Beechcraft Model 1019 (US Navy AQM-37A, formerly KD2B-1) target system is designed to simulate aircraft and missile threats, and to provide defence weapon system evaluation and operational crew training.

The complete target system includes a launcher which is adaptable to a variety of fighter aircraft, test and checkout equipment, handling and servicing equipment and launch aircraft controls, as well as the target vehicle itself. The target is expendable and thus requires no recovery support.

The target provides both active and passive radar augmentation for radar acquisition and lock-on. A chemical flare is provided for missions which require infra-red augmentation. Two optional miss-distance indication systems are available.

Flight termination is normally through aerodynamic means, but an explosive destructor system is available, to provide additional range safety and operational flexibility. The only procedures required to ready the target for flight are decanning, battery servicing, pre-flight checking out, pressure cartridge inserting and nitrogen pressurising.

The AQM-37A was launched successfully for the first time on 31 May 1961, at the Naval Missile Center, Point Mugu, California. In subsequent development tests, after being launched at 33,000 ft (10,050 m) from an F-3B Demon, it flew higher and faster than any previous drone developed for target duties. During weapon system training operations at Point Mugu in the Spring of 1965, an AQM-37A, launched from an F-4B at a speed of Mach 1·3 at 47,000 ft (14,300 m), climbed to 91,000 ft (27,750 m) and maintained a speed of Mach 2·8.

The AQM-37A has been operational since 1963 from shore installations and aircraft carriers and is being launched at present from three types of US Navy aircraft, the F-4, F-8 and A-4. Beech was awarded a follow-on contract from the US Navy on 19 December 1972 for a further 202 AQM-37A targets, and production of these was continuing in 1974.

In the Spring of 1968, Beech received contracts to modify 10 AQM-37As for evaluation by the USAF and three for the US Army, making their electronics and destruct systems compatible with current advanced weapon systems and range requirements of these services.

In addition to the AQM-37A models built for the US services, four other variants have been announced:

Model 1072 (Short SD.2 Stiletto). Version for UK, substantially re-engineered by Short Bros & Harland to meet British requirements, including virtually complete replacement of the radio and radar systems and control system changes. Total of 55 ordered, of which the third batch, of 20 targets, were fitted by Beech with a single-chamber rocket motor. The Stiletto is launched from Canberra PR Mk 3 aircraft. In a successful first test flight at Llanbedr on 1 August 1968 the drone was released at 55,000 ft (16,750 m) and flew for more than 28 nm (32 miles; 52 km) at an average speed of Mach 1·4 before the flight was terminated by a commanded explosive destruct.

Principal modifications made by Shorts were the incorporation of a British EMI T44/1 telemetry system; provision of additional 15V flight break-up system (WREBUS); installation of radioactive miss-distance indicator (RAMDI), with associated radio link; introduction of Plessey IR 112A/IR 310 telecommand system and heading and turns command circuitry; modification to propulsion system to give Mach 2 performance at 60,000 ft (18,300 m); and changes in the radar augmentation system. The current Stiletto system consists of the basic target vehicle plus a number of optional mission kits which can be either installed by Shorts or delivered separately for customer installation.

Model 1088. Manufacturer's designation of five targets supplied to Italy. Intended for air-launch from F-104S aircraft of the Italian Air Force.

Model 1094. Designation of 15 targets ordered in mid-1973 by French Air Force, delivery of which was due to begin in May 1974. A follow-on contract for 30 was announced in August 1974; these will be modified to French Air Force requirements by Matra, which also has a marketing licence for this model.

Model 1095. The British Ministry of Defence has negotiated for the purchase of 10 Model 1095 targets. This version has been modified to MoD specifications and is to be used for crew training exercises on the Hebrides range.

Production of the drone was transferred from Wichita to Beech's Aerospace Division at Boulder, Colorado, in 1968. Total orders to date cover the delivery of more than 2,900 targets of all versions.

Type: Supersonic air-launched expendable target drone.

Wings: Cantilever mid-wing monoplane of cropped delta planform, mounted at rear of fuselage. Modified double-wedge wing section. No dihedral or incidence. Sweepback on leading-edge 76°. Full-span ailerons.

Fuselage: Cylindrical centre fuselage, with ogival nose section and tapering rear section over rocket chambers. Underbelly tunnel for

Beechcraft Model 1019 AQM-37A supersonic target drone

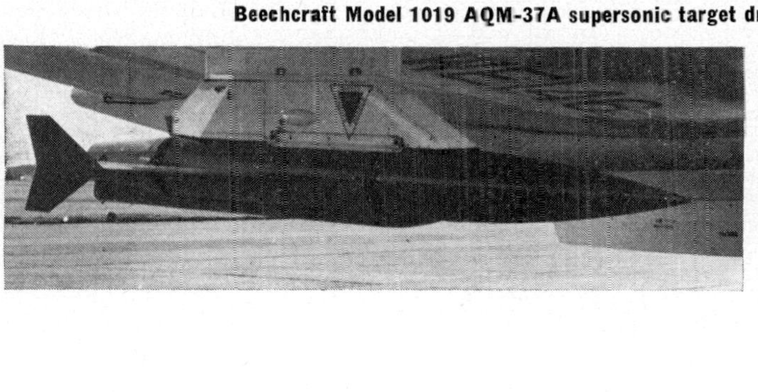

SD.2 Stiletto version of the Beechcraft Model 1072 target, under the wing of a Canberra PR Mk 3 launch aircraft

rocket-engine cartridge-operated start valves, plumbing, infra-red flare and miss-distance scoring system antenna.

TAIL UNIT: Fixed endplate fins on each wingtip. **Canard foreplane control surfaces of modified double-wedge section.**

POWER PLANT: One Rocketdyne/AMF LR64 P-4 dual-chamber liquid-propellant rocket engine (631 lb; 286 kg st). Three propellant tanks, for nitrogen pressurant, mixed amine fuel (MAF-4) and IRFNA oxidiser, form integral part of centre-fuselage.

GUIDANCE: Programmed guidance system.

DIMENSIONS, EXTERNAL:

Wing span	3 ft 3½ in (1·00 m)
Wing chord at root	6 ft 6 in (1·98 m)
Wing chord at tip	1 ft 9 in (0·53 m)
Length overall	12 ft 6½ in (3·82 m)
Height overall	1 ft 8 in (0·51 m)
Diameter of fuselage	1 ft 1 in (0·33 m)

AREAS:

Wings (exposed)	9·35 sq ft (0·87 m²)
Ailerons (total)	0·95 sq ft (0·088 m²)
Fins (total)	4·20 sq ft (0·39 m²)
Foreplanes (total, exposed)	0·76 sq ft (0·071 m²)

WEIGHT:

Max launching weight	565 lb (256 kg)

PERFORMANCE (rated):

Operating speed	Mach 0·4 to Mach 3·0
Operating height	1,000-80,000 ft (300-24,385 m)
Endurance	5-15 min
Range more than	100 nm (115 miles; 185 km)

Model of the Beechcraft 1070 High Altitude Supersonic Target (HAST)

Launch of a prototype Beechcraft Model 1089 VSTT variable-speed training target

BEECHCRAFT MODEL 1070 HAST

Beech Aircraft is continuing a development programme for the USAF Armament Laboratory at Eglin AFB, Florida, under contracts totalling $13 million, to provide a high-performance air-launched aerial target system for use by the three Services of the US Department of Defense. The HAST (High Altitude Supersonic Target) is a continuation of the former Sandpiper project, which concluded a successful flight test programme in 1968 and was described in the 1970-71 *Jane's*. A hybrid propulsion system and a command manoeuvring system were demonstrated in that flight test programme. In 1971 Beech received authority to build 12 flight test units of the HAST and 13 refurbishment kits, and delivery of the former began in 1972. A recovery system development programme, utilising an inert HAST vehicle, has been completed. This programme has proved the recovery system with both water and aerial retrieval of the vehicle. Captive flights have been completed, and 23 powered flights are scheduled to be made in a 28-month programme beginning in September 1974. The target is intended initially to be carried by F-101 Voodoo, F-4 Phantom, F-14 Tomcat and F-15 Eagle aircraft.

The flight performance envelope of the HAST covers a range from Mach 1·2 at 40,000 ft (12,200 m) to Mach 4·0 at 100,000 ft (30,500 m). The target is designed to be air-launched at speeds of Mach 0·8 to 2·5. Manoeuvres of between 5*g* at 35,000 ft (10,670 m) and 1·15*g* at 90,000 ft (27,400 m) are to be performed. The vehicle is to be capable of performing "S" and 180° turns in the horizontal plane and altitude changes in the vertical plane. Manoeuvres can either be pre-programmed or initiated via ground command radio link.

Modular payloads with a wide variety of options will be available for accurate simulation of aircraft or missile threats. Payloads will include various radar and infra-red augmentation devices, as well as a flare/chaff dispenser. Vector miss-distance scoring systems will also be included.

The modular recovery system has been developed as an optional feature for mid-air retrieval of HAST, or for land or water recovery. Refurbishment of recovered targets will permit their re-use.

TYPE: Supersonic air-launched target drone.

WINGS: Clipped delta planform, with a sweepback of 75° and a constant thickness except for the leading-edge. Full-span aileron on trailing-edge of each wing.

FOREPLANES: Arrow planform, located on the aft nose section.

FUSELAGE: Cylindrical body, with a 3·5 calibre von Kármán nose section and a conical boat-tail section.

TAIL UNIT: Fixed endplate vertical stabiliser on each wingtip.

POWER PLANT: Hybrid rocket engine developed by the United Technology Center. Propellant is polybutadiene and polymethylmethacrylate, with inhibited red fuming nitric acid oxidiser. The system is inherently safe, since the propellants will not burn unless external ignition is applied. The engine is throttleable, with thrust variable from 120 to 1,200 lb (54-544 kg) st. The 13 in (33 cm) thrust chamber forms an integral part of the fuselage assembly. Oxidiser pressurisation and electrical power are provided by a ducted power unit. This unit, developed by the Marquardt Company, is powered by a ram-air turbine with air intake and exit on the lower side of the fuselage mid-section. A free siphon device has been developed to provide uninterrupted oxidiser flow during manoeuvres. Manoeuvring requirements dictate a positive expulsion system for the oxidiser.

GUIDANCE: Pre-programmed, with ground command interface.

DIMENSIONS, EXTERNAL:

Wing span	3 ft 4 in (1·02 m)
Length	16 ft 8 in (5·08 m)
Height (stabiliser)	2 ft 2 in (0·66 m)
Body diameter	1 ft 1 in (0·33 m)

AREAS:

Wings (total exposed)	10·44 sq ft (0·97 m²)
Foreplanes (total exposed)	1·28 sq ft (0·12 m²)
Stabilisers (each)	3·38 sq ft (0·31 m²)

VOLUME:

Payload volume	2,500 cu in (0·041 m³)

WEIGHTS:

Launching weight	1,145 lb (519 kg)
Propellant	655 lb (297 kg)
Payload	85 lb (38 kg)

PERFORMANCE:

Endurance at Mach 3	5 min

BEECHCRAFT MODEL 1089 VSTT

Beech Aircraft Corporation is participating, with Northrop Ventura (which see), in a "price and performance" competition to design and develop a Variable-Speed Training Target (VSTT) for the US Army's Missile Command. The programme consists basically of the following three phases: (1) design and manufacture of hardware; (2) contractor flight tests; and (3) Army evaluation tests.

The principal function of the VSTT will be to tow a variety of tow targets for missile training and evaluation. Two TA-8 radar augmentation or infra-red augmentation targets can be carried on each mission and towed separately up to 5,000 ft (1,525 m) behind the VSTT.

The selected VSTT will serve as an aerial target for air defence systems such as Chaparral, Redeye, Hawk and Vulcan, and is expected to become the primary subsonic missile training target for the US Army. It will be capable of operating at altitudes from 300 ft (90 m) to 40,000 ft (12,200 m) and at speeds of up to 500 knots (575 mph; 926 km/h).

The Beech VSTT competitor, shown in the accompanying illustration, is powered by a Teledyne CAE 372-2 (J402-CA-400) turbojet engine of 640 lb (290 kg) st and carries 64 US gallons (242 litres) of fuel. It is launched from the ground with a JATO booster and has a drogue and main parachute command recovery system.

By March 1974, 20 flights in the contractor development test programme and US Army evaluation programme had been completed. In these flights, high altitude, speed, flight control and towing capability were demonstrated, as well as operation of the recovery system. Recoveries are being made with minimal damage to the crushable, impact-absorbing nose.

The modular design employed throughout the system provides for ease of manufacture and economy in operation and maintenance. One unique design feature is the flat aerofoil section of the wing and tail surfaces. The fuselage is cylindrical. Low-cost bonded honeycomb is used for the non-moving aerofoil surfaces; control surfaces have an aluminium skin and are foam-filled. Support equipment is minimal and lightweight, providing for easy transportability and deployment. The checkout and launch equipment is accommodated in two suitcase-size containers.

The guidance and control system provides for both ground control and pre-programmed flight. The flight control operator is provided with all pertinent flight information by radio link from sensors located in the vehicle, and can command both manoeuvre and recovery of the vehicle. In flight the guidance and control system automatically stabilises about the roll, yaw and pitch attitudes and provides altitude and speed hold modes.

GUIDANCE: Radio command.

DIMENSIONS, EXTERNAL:

Wing span	9 ft 10 in (3·00 m)
Length	16 ft 10 in (5·13 m)
Height (total)	4 ft 10 in (1·47 m)
Body diameter	1 ft 3 in (0·38 m)

AREAS:

Wings (total projected)	27·16 sq ft (2·52 m²)
Horizontal tail surfaces	8·48 sq ft (0·79 m²)
Vertical tail surfaces	4·66 sq ft (0·43 m²)

WEIGHTS:

Launching weight (incl booster)	1,014 lb (460 kg)
Usable fuel	382 lb (173 kg)

PERFORMANCE:

Endurance	more than 3 hr

BEECHCRAFT MODEL 1092

The Beechcraft Model 1092 is a pilotless, recoverable target drone designed for in-sight or out-of-sight control. Essentially, it is a jet-powered derivative of the proven Model 1025 piston-engined target vehicle (1972-73 *Jane's*), and is claimed to have a cost-effectiveness unequalled by any competitive system in its performance category.

AIRFRAME: All-metal high-wing monoplane, with cruciform tail unit.

POWER PLANT: One Teledyne CAE 372-2 (J402-CA-400) turbojet engine, rated at 640 lb (290 kg) st. The engine can be throttled by remote command, permitting a very wide variety of mission profiles with endurances (depending upon mission speed and altitude) of up to several hours.

Launch and Recovery: Launchings utilise the zero-length procedure, with solid-propellant rocket motors providing the boost thrust. The target is recovered following completion of flight by a single-stage 48 ft (14·6 m) diameter parachute. The vehicle has flotation capability and may be recovered over land or water.

Control and Guidance: Stabilisation and command control is by two-axis autopilot, with a Babcock digital command receiver/decoder providing the ground link.

Dimensions, external:

Wing span	12 ft 1 in (3·68 m)
Length overall	15 ft 1 in (4·60 m)
Body diameter	1 ft 5¾ in (0·45 m)

Weight:

Max launching weight	1,002 lb (454 kg)

Performance:

Max level speed	450 knots (518 mph; 834 km/h)
Ceiling	40,000 ft (12,200 m)

Beechcraft Model 1092 target drone, a jet-powered development of the Model 1025

BENDIX

THE BENDIX CORPORATION (AEROSPACE SYSTEMS DIVISION)

Address:
400 South Beiger Street, Mishawaka, Indiana 46544

Telephone: (219) 255-2111

The Aerospace Systems Division at Mishawaka, Indiana, is the centre of The Bendix Corporation's development and manufacturing activities for missile systems (see 1972-73 *Jane's*). It is also currently developing, under contract to the US Army's Missile Command, a supersonic recoverable target vehicle known as LAST, a description and illustration of which appeared in the 1973-74 *Jane's*.

BOEING

BOEING AEROSPACE COMPANY

Address:
PO Box 3999, Seattle, Washington 98124

Compass Cope Programme Director:
Donald B. Jacobs

Under the Compass Cope programme sponsored by the US Air Force (Aeronautical Systems Division) and the National Security Agency, Teledyne Ryan (which see) and Boeing Aerospace Company received contracts to build prototype RPVs for competitive evaluation. The Boeing vehicle has the USAF designation YQM-94A.

Design studies have been or are being conducted by Boeing of other RPV configurations, among which have been reported a low-level multi-purpose penetration vehicle, for photographic reconnaissance or weapons delivery, and a high-altitude reconnaissance vehicle having high aspect ratio wings reinforced with carbon fibre or other composite materials.

BOEING B-GULL (COMPASS COPE B)
USAF designation: YQM-94A

Together with the Teledyne Ryan Model 235/YQM-98A (which see), the Boeing YQM-94A is a competitor in the US Air Force's Compass Cope programme to select a high-altitude, long-endurance RPV whose primary purpose will be that of signal intelligence collection. The winning vehicle has been designated by the USAF to replace the RB-57 in its Pave Nickel programme for the monitoring of radar emissions along the western borders of the German Democratic Republic. Another typical application which has been quoted is that of patrolling areas of the Arctic Ocean to monitor firings from the northern missile test site of the USSR, a task at present carried out by Boeing RC-135 manned aircraft flying from Elmendorf AFB, Alaska. The US Navy has also expressed interest in a vehicle of the Compass Cope type for a potential ocean surveillance role, including possible operation from aircraft carriers.

Boeing Aerospace design studies for a vehicle of this type began in September 1970, and a prototype contract was awarded by the USAF on 15 July 1971. Two YQM-94A prototypes were ordered, of which the first was rolled out on 30 November 1972. Prior to this, the remote control operating systems for the RPV were flight tested in a Cessna 172 light aircraft.

The first YQM-94A prototype was delivered to the USAF in February 1973, and made a successful one-hour first flight on 28 July 1973. On 4 August 1973, on its second flight, the first prototype was destroyed in a crash following a failure of the lateral accelerometer which caused the ground-based pilot to lose control. At that time the second aircraft had not been completed, but work on it was resumed in the Spring of 1974, with delivery to the USAF and first flight scheduled for Autumn 1974. In this aircraft the effect of the accelerometer has been limited, and the position of the control surfaces is shown on the ground controller's display.

Unlike most RPVs to date, which are air- or ground-launched and are recovered by "air snatch" mid-air retrieval system (MARS), the Compass Cope vehicles are designed to take off and land using conventional runway techniques, and so require an all-weather landing capability. Initially, the prototype vehicles are each powered by a single engine; a decision whether to adopt a single- or twin-engined configuration for production aircraft will be taken after analysis of the flight test results.

Type: High-altitude long-endurance strategic RPV.

Wings: Cantilever shoulder-wing monoplane. Constant-chord centre-section, slight sweepback on outer wing leading-edges. Aluminium skin, with bonded glassfibre honeycomb core. Airbrakes and ailerons on each trailing-edge; no trailing-edge flaps or leading-edge lift devices.

Fuselage: Glassfibre honeycomb semi-monocoque structure of basically circular section, tapering towards rear.

Tail Unit: Cantilever unit, of similar construction to wings. Tailplane indexed in line with wings. Twin endplate fins and rudders, the former having small fore-and-aft pointed fairings at the base. Full-span elevator, with tabs.

Landing Gear: Retractable tricycle type, basically that of an Aero Commander, with single wheel on each unit. All units retract rearward, the main units into fairings which project aft of the wing trailing-edges.

Power Plant: Prototypes each powered by one General Electric J97-GE-100 non-afterburning turbojet engine, rated at 5,270 lb (2,390 kg) st, installed in a pylon-mounted pod above the fuselage, in line with the wings. Alternative power plants under consideration include one Garrett-AiResearch XF104-GA-100 (ATF 3) turbofan (4,050 lb; 1,837 kg st), Garrett-AiResearch TFE 731 turbofan (3,500 lb; 1,587 kg st) or Teledyne CAE J100-CA-100 turbojet (2,700 lb; 1,225 kg st); or two United Aircraft of Canada JT15D-4 turbofans (each 2,310 lb; 1,048 kg st). Fuel is contained in integral tanks occupying the full span of the wings. Provision for restarting engine in flight.

Guidance, Control and Recovery Systems: Avionics module, located in lower half of fuselage forward of wings, is removable as a complete unit. On-board instrumentation, developed by Sperry Flight Systems Division and Univac Division of Sperry Rand, includes an integrated flight control system with internally-generated ILS; a redundant stabilisation system; and an APW-26 airborne transceiver and other data link equipment. A TV camera is mounted in the undernose fairing; in the second prototype a heater is provided to prevent frosting of the camera glass. Ground control of the RPV is exercised via a command module which embodies standard cockpit instrumentation, TV screen and navigation display; data link equipment which includes a microwave command digital guidance system; a wide-band microwave data transmission system, to permit the return of video signals; and a TPW-2A X-band radar van.

Operational Equipment: Apart from the nose-mounted TV camera, details of other operational equipment are classified. All sensors and antennae are housed in the lower half of the fuselage, the payload being located just forward of the avionics module.

Dimensions, external:

Wing span	90 ft 0 in (27·43 m)
Wing aspect ratio	16·7
Length overall (excluding nose probe)	42 ft 0 in (12·80 m)
Wheel track	21 ft 0 in (6·40 m)

Weights:

Payload for 24 hr mission	700 lb (317·5 kg)
Max T-O weight	approx 13,000 lb (5,897 kg)

Performance (at max T-O weight):

Cruising speed at altitudes from 50,000 to 70,000 ft (15,240 to 21,340 m)	Mach 0·5 to 0·6
Max endurance	30 hr

Boeing YQM-94A Compass Cope B prototype (General Electric J97-GE-100 turbojet engine)

CELESCO

CELESCO INDUSTRIES INC

Address:
3333 Harbour Boulevard, Costa Mesa, California 92626

On behalf of the US Air Force's Avionics Laboratory, Celesco has developed a small subsonic decoy glider known as the **Maxi**, to be carried by strike versions of the USAF's McDonnell Douglas F-4 Phantom aircraft. The Maxi, which is carried on the Phantom's external stores pylons, can incorporate various payloads, including an ECM S-band jammer developed by RCA. It has small, spring-loaded wings, with some 30° of sweepback when extended, which are opened in flight to a span of approx 3 ft (0·91 m) after the Maxi has been released in the target area. Including payload, the Maxi is reported to weigh 130 lb (59 kg); up to 12 can be carried by one Phantom. Maximum speed is in the region of Mach 0·8 to Mach 0·9. A powered version, weighing approx 600 lb (272 kg), is also under development.

DSI

DEVELOPMENTAL SCIENCES INC (Aerospace Technology Division)

ADDRESS:
15747 East Valley Boulevard, City of Industry, California 91745
Telephone: (213) 330-6865
PRESIDENT: Dr Gerald R. Seemann

DSI has built, under contract to NASA (which see), a prototype yawed-wing research aircraft, which was scheduled to make its first flight in the Autumn of 1974.

The company has also designed and built a "mini-RPV" known as the Sky Eye.

DSI/NASA OBLIQUE WING REMOTELY PILOTED RESEARCH AIRCRAFT

As indicated under the NASA heading, the design and development of this RPRA (Remotely Piloted Research Aircraft) was sponsored by NASA's Ames Research Center; detail design and development has been subcontracted to DSI, which has completed a prototype that was expected to fly for the first time in the Autumn of 1974.

Design guidelines called for a flying-wing type of vehicle, with control achieved principally by use of the elevons, able to fly at wing yaw angles between 0° and 45°. A horizontal tail has been added to provide longitudinal stability. The aircraft can be flown in the zero-to-moderate yaw configuration without the horizontal tail, but is statically unstable without it in the 45° yaw configuration. Detail design started on 5 September 1972, and construction of the prototype began on 16 February 1973.

WINGS: Cantilever mid-wing monoplane of elliptical planform. Special reflexed aerofoil section, of 21% thickness/chord ratio, is constant over the entire wing. No dihedral, anhedral, incidence or aerodynamic twist. Glassfibre and epoxy resin construction. Outboard leading-edge is largely non-structural, and is removable for installation and removal of payload. The wing is "dished" near the centre, producing a flared spanwise thickness distribution, to permit yawing of the fuselage with respect to the wing without breaking the contour of the fuselage/wing mating surfaces. The trailing-edge is fitted with a vertical stabiliser, ahead of the normal fin and rudder, to provide "weathercock" stability at the larger wing yaw angles. The wingtips and stabiliser tip are frangible to minimise damage during recovery. Control is effected primarily by wide-span elevons on the trailing-edge, operable differentially (as ailerons) or in unison (as elevators). They are of glassfibre, epoxy resin and Ceconite construction, and are actuated electrically by directly-coupled servos based on lightweight gear motors by Globe Industries Division of TRW.

FUSELAGE: Basically cylindrical structure of conventional skin/stringer construction, with moulded glassfibre/epoxy resin and aluminium skin. Transparent (Lucite) removable hemispherical nose-cap. Central portion, housing the engine, parachute and other equipment, is described as the "cookie", since in essence it is a circular disc of constant (6·9 in; 17·5 cm) thickness. A spanwise slit through the cookie accommodates the propeller disc.

TAIL UNIT: Cruciform surfaces, carried on a large-diameter tubular boom designed to accommodate the wing yawing motion and braced by two additional struts forming a Vee from the propeller duct to the tail. These struts are carried through the duct and continued upstream to the fuselage nose. Angular sweptback fin and rudder and elliptical one-piece all-moving tailplane. The latter is constructed of a thin layer of foam-filled glassfibre/epoxy material, and is frangible (as is the fin-tip) to minimise recovery damage. The horizontal tail is actuated by a separate servo commanded by the same circuit as the elevons' elevator functions. Thus, the tailplane can be removed and the aircraft flown as a flying wing while still utilising the elevator function of the elevons.

LANDING GEAR: Non-retractable tricycle gear fitted for initial taxi and flight testing. Paraform 'chute (diameter 46 ft 6 in; 14·17 m) in rear of "cookie", which deploys automatically if the command signal is lost. The aircraft can also be recovered deliberately by this method in response to a command signal from the ground.

POWER PLANT: One 90 hp McCulloch 4318B Model O-100-1 four-cylinder horizontally-opposed two-stroke aircooled engine, driving a two-blade fixed-pitch wooden pusher propeller turning within an annular duct. The duct, which is of symmetrical section (18% thickness/chord ratio), improves static thrust and thrust at low speeds, permitting a high cruise speed propeller to be used while still achieving satisfactory T-O and climb performance. The duct also reduces propeller tip noise and protects operators from the turning propeller. A tubular supporting strut connects the fuselage nose to the base of the duct, serving also to deflect the arresting cable in the case of a low approach when using a horizontal-cable snag recovery system. Fuel tanks in underside of forward fuselage, capacity 60 lb (27 kg).

Prototype of the DSI/NASA Oblique Wing Remotely Piloted Research Aircraft, shown without the wing-mounted vertical stabiliser

SYSTEMS: No hydraulic or pneumatic systems. Electrical system (1kW alternator and battery) powers controls, TV, radio and autopilot.

ELECTRONICS AND EQUIPMENT: Kraft command receiver, special FM data transmitter, Green Ray TV transmitter, ELT and radar transponder. The nose section contains the TV scanner and related zoom and tilt mechanisms; flight instrumentation and instrumentation camera; command receiver; yaw, roll and pitch gyros; TV signal transmitters; UHF tracking; battery; and vacuum pump.

DIMENSION, EXTERNAL:
Wing span 22 ft 4 in (6·81 m)
Wing chord at root 5 ft 8·3 in (1·73 m)
Wing aspect ratio 5·0
Length overall 12 ft 2·4 in (3·72 m)
Fuselage length 5 ft 3½ in (1·61 m)
Fuselage diameter 1 ft 6 in (0·46 m)
Height overall 5 ft 8¾ in (1·75 m)
Tailplane span 6 ft 2¼ in (1·88 m)
Propeller diameter 4 ft 1½ in (1·26 m)

DIMENSION, INTERNAL:
Payload volume 9 cu ft (0·25 m^3)

AREAS:
Wings, gross 99·8 sq ft (9·27 m^2)
Elevons (total) 11·75 sq ft (1·09 m^2)
Fin 5·56 sq ft (0·52 m^2)
Rudder 1·33 sq ft (0·12 m^2)
Tailplane 12·90 sq ft (1·20 m^2)

WEIGHTS AND LOADINGS:
Weight empty 850 lb (385 kg)
Max payload 150 lb (68 kg)
Max T-O weight 1,060 lb (480 kg)
Max wing loading 10·62 lb/sq ft (51·83 kg/m^2)
Max power loading 11·8 lb/hp (5·35 kg/hp)

PERFORMANCE (estimated, at max T-O weight):
Max level speed at 5,000 ft (1,525 m)
156 knots (180 mph; 289 km/h)
Max cruising speed at 5,000 ft (1,525 m)
130 knots (150 mph; 241 km/h)
Econ cruising speed
113 knots (130 mph; 209 km/h)
Stalling speed 38·5 knots (44 mph; 71 km/h)
Max rate of climb at S/L 1,600 ft (487 m)/min
Service ceiling 15,000 ft (4,570 m)

DSI RPA-12 SKY EYE

Design of the Sky Eye was started on 28 February 1973; construction was completed on 19 April, and the aircraft flew for the first time on 26 April 1973. Originally of sweptwing tail-less configuration, it had a pusher propeller mounted in an annular duct aft of the wing, as illustrated in the 1973-74 *Jane's*. The accompanying photograph shows it in modified form, with the propeller duct removed, twin fins mounted outboard on the wing trailing-edges, and a ciné camera attached externally to the fuselage in addition to the on-board TV camera. The Sky Eye is radio-controlled in flight.

WINGS: Cantilever high-wing monoplane. Wing section NACA 23015 (modified). No dihedral or anhedral. Incidence 5°. Sweepback 27° at quarter-chord. Plywood skins, $\frac{1}{64}$ in (0·4 mm) thick, with Styrofoam core. Elevon on each trailing-edge, of similar construction, functioning both as aileron and elevator and actuated by modified radio-control servos. No flaps or other high-lift devices.

FUSELAGE: Cylindrical structure, of wooden bulkheads with epoxy-glass skin. Transparent hemispherical nose-cap.

TAIL UNIT: Twin fins, attached to wing trailing-edge near tips.

LANDING GEAR: Prototype has non-retractable tricycle gear, mounted on spring struts. Available optionally without landing gear for use with alternative launching system and with recovery by parachute or net.

POWER PLANT: One 12 hp McCulloch 101A piston engine, modified to reduce radio frequency interference, mounted in rear of fuselage. Two-blade wooden fixed-pitch pusher propeller. One fuselage fuel tank (petrol/oil mixture), capacity 1 US gallon (3·8 litres), with provision also for internal wing tanks to raise total capacity to 3 US gallons (11·4 litres).

SYSTEMS AND EQUIPMENT: Total-loss battery system. Alternator to be added for flights of more than 1 hr duration. VHF command

DSI RPA-12 Sky Eye RPV, with an externally-mounted ciné camera in front of the wing

system, based on radio control equipment with 15W command output.

DIMENSIONS, EXTERNAL:

Wing span	11 ft 6 in (3·50 m)
Wing chord at root	3 ft 4 in (1·03 m)
Wing chord at tip	2 ft 1 in (0·64 m)
Wing aspect ratio	4·1
Length overall	5 ft 7 in (1·70 m)
Length of fuselage	4 ft 11 in (1·50 m)
Height overall	2 ft 11 in (0·89 m)
Propeller diameter	2 ft 0 in (0·61 m)
Wheel track	2 ft 8 in (0·81 m)
Wheelbase	1 ft 11 in (0·58 m)

AREAS:

Wings, gross	32·5 sq ft (3·02 m²)
Elevons (total)	1·3 sq ft (0·12 m²)

WEIGHTS AND LOADINGS (A: conventional take-off and landing; B: launch take-off, parachute recovery):

Weight empty, equipped:	
A	55 lb (25 kg)
B	60 lb (27·2 kg)
Max payload:	
A	45 lb (20·4 kg)
B	40 lb (18 kg)
Max T-O and landing weight:	
A, B	125 lb (56·6 kg)
Max wing loading:	
A, B	3·85 lb/sq ft (18·79 kg/m²)
Max power loading:	
A, B	10·4 lb/hp (4·72 kg/hp)

PERFORMANCE (at max T-O weight):

Max never-exceed speed (structural):	
A, B	200 knots (230 mph; 370 km/h)
Max level speed:	
A	90 knots (103·5 mph; 167 km/h)
B	120 knots (138 mph; 222 km/h)
Stalling speed:	
A, B	35 knots (40·5 mph; 65 km/h)
Max rate of climb at S/L:	
A	1,800 ft (548 m)/min
B	2,200 ft (670 m)/min
Service ceiling:	
A	13,000 ft (3,960 m)
B	15,000 ft (4,570 m)
Control-limit range:	
A, B	43 nm (50 miles; 80 km)
Max endurance at 55 knots (63 mph; 102 km/h):	
A	6 hr
B	9 hr

E-SYSTEMS
E-SYSTEMS INC

HEAD OFFICE:
PO Box 6030, Dallas, Texas 75222
Telephone: (214) 742-9471

GREENVILLE DIVISION:
PO Box 1056, Greenville, Texas 75401
Telephone: (214) 455-3450

GARLAND DIVISION:
PO Box 6118, Dallas, Texas 75222
Telephone: (214) 276-7111

MELPAR DIVISION:
7700 Arlington Boulevard, Falls Church, Virginia 22046
Telephone: (703) 560-5000

CHAIRMAN OF THE BOARD:
John W. Dixon

PRESIDENT, AIRCRAFT SYSTEMS GROUP, AND VICE-PRESIDENT AND GENERAL MANAGER, GREENVILLE DIVISION:
K. M. Smith

PRESIDENT, ELECTRONIC SYSTEMS GROUP, AND VICE-PRESIDENT AND GENERAL MANAGER, GARLAND DIVISION:
D. R. Tacke

PUBLIC RELATIONS:
John E. Kumpf

E-Systems Inc was formerly known as LTV Electrosystems, a subsidiary of LTV Aerospace Corporation. It became an entirely publicly-owned company in May 1972, following the transition of ownership to independent stock-holders. Its activities lie predominantly in the field of aerospace systems development and manufacture, in addition to which it has carried out specialised conversion work on nearly 400 C-135 and KC-135 series aircraft for the US Air Force. Its Greenville Division designed and built the L450F, a single-engined high-altitude aircraft capable of manned or unmanned operation. Melpar Division has designed a "mini-RPV" designated E-45, which was evaluated in 1974 by the US Army (which see) as a part of its RPAODS programme.

E-Systems L450F, second prototype, in manned configuration

Unmanned version of the E-Systems L450F, in USAF markings

E-SYSTEMS L450F
USAF designation: XQM-93

To meet military requirements for a high-altitude long-endurance reconnaissance aircraft, E-Systems built a single-seat monoplane designated L450F, powered by a turboprop engine, capable of carrying data-gathering equipment or electronic relay equipment (similar to that of a communications satellite) to a height of more than 45,000 ft (13,715 m), and having a 24-hour endurance. The aircraft can also be flown unmanned by remote ground control.

The prototype L450F made its first flight, with a pilot, during February 1970, but was destroyed during its third flight, on 23 March 1970, after the pilot had parachuted from it. A second prototype (N2450F) differed in having increased fuel tankage and deletion of speed brakes from the upper and lower wing surfaces.

On 24-25 January 1972 this prototype, converted to unmanned configuration for USAF evaluation and designated XQM-93 (serial number 70-1287) made a non-stop flight of more than 21 hours at Edwards AFB, California. The flight, believed to be an endurance record for RPVs, was made to determine the feasibility of flying RPVs for long periods of time, and was part of the USAF's Compass Dwell programme in which the XQM-93 was flown competitively with the Martin Marietta Model 845A. The evaluation was completed in early 1972, neither vehicle being selected for production.

On 23 and 27 March 1972 the L450F, flown by test pilot Don Wilson, established six new international altitude records and ten time-to-height records at Majors Field, Greenville, Texas. Details of these were given in the 1973-74 *Jane's*.

The basic airframe of the L450F is that of a Schweizer SGS 2-32 sailplane; but this was modified extensively by Schweizer, to E-Systems drawings, to cater for the considerable load increase imposed by the installation of engine, fuel tank, landing gear and electronics equipment. Modification involved strengthening of the wing spars and areas of the forward and rear fuselage, use of heavier skins, and an increase in the surface area of the fin and rudder. The non-retractable tricycle landing gear, with cantilever spring steel main legs, is based on that of the Grumman Ag-Cat.

The power plant consists of a United Aircraft of Canada PT6A-34 turboprop engine, derated to 475 ehp and driving a Hartzell three-blade metal propeller. Fuel is contained in wing cells and a single aft fuselage cell. 28V 6kW electrical power is available as standard. The piloted version has a bubble canopy and conventional flying controls, including a modified Bendix PB-60 autopilot system. Maximum payload volume is 44 cu ft (1·25 m³).

The XQM-93 unmanned version differs from the piloted version in having the bubble canopy and pilot's seat removed and replaced by an interface unit. As used for the 24-25 January 1972 flight, it carried a more advanced autopilot system than the piloted version.

Complete ground control and monitoring by telemetry allows control of the pilotless version in a variety of modes, including take-off, constant heading/constant pitch angle, constant altitude/constant heading, constant airspeed/constant heading, reciprocal heading loiter, automatic preset heading and landing.

Applications include data/communications relay, electronic reconnaissance, time-of-arrival measurements, ocean surveillance, ecological data collection, and stand-off jamming. The study of potential military and civil applications, especially the latter, is continuing.

DIMENSIONS, EXTERNAL (XQM-93):

Wing span	57 ft 0 in (17·37 m)
Length overall	29 ft 7 in (9·02 m)
Height overall (excluding antenna fairing on top of fin)	10 ft 8 in (3·25 m)
Tailplane span	10 ft 6 in (3·20 m)
Wheelbase	6 ft 8 in (2·03 m)

WEIGHTS:

Weight empty	2,400 lb (1,089 kg)
Max payload	1,100 lb (499 kg)
Max T-O weight:	
manned	4,600 lb (2,086 kg)
unmanned	5,300 lb (2,404 kg)

PERFORMANCE (at max T-O weight):

Cruising speed at 45,000 ft (13,715 m), manned	91 knots (105 mph; 170 km/h) IAS
Best glide ratio	28
Stalling speed	61 knots (70·5 mph; 114 km/h)
Max rate of climb at S/L	3,000 ft (914 m)/min
Min time to 40,000 ft (12,200 m)	21 min
Service ceiling	more than 50,000 ft (15,240 m)
T-O run	1,200 ft (366 m)
Endurance	more than 24 hr
g limits	+3·8; —1·52

II

FAIRCHILD

FAIRCHILD SPACE & ELECTRONICS COMPANY

Executive Office:
Germantown, Maryland 20767
Telephone: (301) 428-6000

Fairchild Space and Electronics Company, one of the divisions of Fairchild Industries, has been actively engaged in RPV development since 1968. A family of low-cost RPV systems in the low subsonic speed range have been designed, built and extensively tested. This family of RPVs have been developed incorporating a unique sailwing folding wing design, developed at Princeton University under the sponsorship of Fairchild Industries.

FAIRCHILD BASIC SAILWING RPV

The basic design utilises a specially-shaped fabric wing glove over a rigid leading-edge and tip rib, and is cable tensioned along the trailing-edge. The wings are wire-braced, and can be folded back alongside the fuselage to facilitate transport, handling and storage. The design has been extensively tested in a NASA wind tunnel, and through numerous manned and unmanned test flights. Results have proved the sailwing equal aerodynamically to conventional rigid wings, and it offers excellent immunity from stalling. The sailwing provides manufacturing simplicity and exceptionally low wing weight as compared with conventional rigid wings.

The basic fuselage structure comprises a flat-sided honeycomb beam. Streamlined fairings on each side of the fuselage enclose the controls, equipment, and a 50 lb (23 kg) payload. The tail unit is conventional, with wire-braced fixed surfaces, and movable rudder and aerodynamically balanced elevators. Later versions have included Frise ailerons on the wings. A tricycle landing gear is employed.

An off-the-shelf 12 hp McCulloch piston engine, driving a two-blade fixed-pitch wooden pusher propeller, has been used to power the engineering model. A 28V 840W alternator is fitted in some models. The full range of command, autopilot and telemetry downlink systems have been integrated with the vehicles, and a variety of payloads have been flown, including photographic, EO, infra-red, early warning and communications relay systems.

Vehicles of these types have been flown in such defence programmes as Black Fly, Dragon Fly and Lookout. A variant of the basic design was being supplied in 1974 to the US Army for its RPAODS programme (which see). This RPV is primarily of non-metallic construction, to minimise its radar signature, and incorporates a full three-axis autopilot and the Vega C-band command and control system.

Fairchild sailwing RPV, showing the basic configuration of this family of vehicles

Glassfibre-bodied sailwing RPV configured by Fairchild to US Army RPAODS requirements

Dimensions, external:
- Wing span: 14 ft 8½ in (4·48 m)
- Wing chord at root: 3 ft 4½ in (1·03 m)
- Wing chord at tip: 1 ft 8½ in (0·52 m)
- Sweepback on wing leading-edge: 11°
- Wing dihedral: 3°
- Length overall, incl nose probe: 12 ft 8½ in (3·87 m)
- Length, excl nose probe: 11 ft 10¾ in (3·63 m)
- Height, bottom of fuselage to top of propeller disc: 3 ft 6 in (1·07 m)
- Tailplane span: 5 ft 4¾ in (1·65 m)
- Fuselage diameter: 1 ft 6 in (0·46 m)
- Propeller diameter: 2 ft 2 in (0·66 m)

Area:
- Wings, gross: 33·7 sq ft (3·13 m²)

Weight:
- Max T-O weight: 250 lb (113 kg)

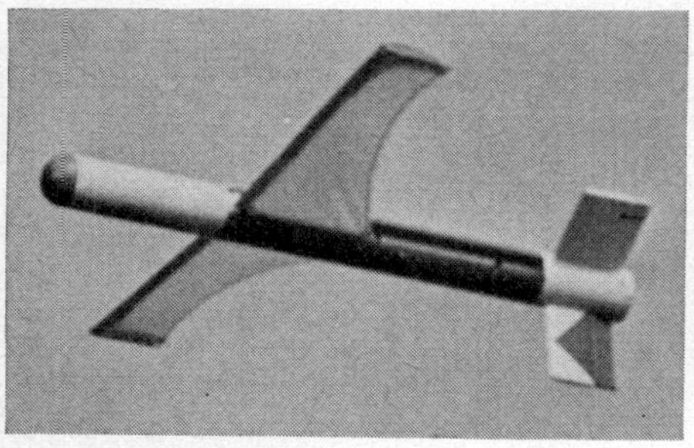

Fairchild Minipop RPV in flight

FAIRCHILD MINIPOP RPV

A smaller version of the sailwing RPV, shown in an accompanying photograph, was developed for the US Navy. This RPV is a boost glide vehicle, using an Atlantic Research Mk 7 solid-propellant rocket motor for the boost phase, at the end of which phase the folded wings deploy. The fuselage is of cylindrical monocoque construction, and three fins with moving trailing-edge sections are fitted to the aft end of the vehicle for stability and control.

Dimensions:
- Wing span: 6 ft 0 in (1·83 m)
- Fuselage diameter: 6 in (0·15 m)

FAIRCHILD RPV LAUNCHER AND RECOVERY SYSTEM

An RPV launch and recovery system was developed for shipboard use under the US Navy's Project Lookout. The launcher is a pneumatic catapult, and the recovery system utilises a vertical barrier net for arresting the RPV and a horizontal catch net for supporting the arrested vehicle. The launch and recovery system has undergone ground tests with both dummy and actual RPVs.

This RPV pneumatic launcher, developed under the US Navy's Project Lookout, carries yet another variant of the Fairchild basic sailwing vehicle

GYRODYNE

GYRODYNE COMPANY OF AMERICA, INC

Head Office and Works:
St James, Long Island, NY 11780

Following its successful development of an ultra-light piloted helicopter, Gyrodyne received a US Navy contract to design, develop and produce a small drone helicopter to form the airborne component of the DASH (Drone Anti-Submarine Helicopter) weapon system. As weapon system manager, Gyrodyne was responsible not only for the QH-50 drones, but also for the equipment on board ship for controlling the drones in flight and development of special deck handling equipment, tools, test equipment and technical manuals.

Details of the operational versions of the QH-50 can be found in the 1970-71 *Jane's*. The DASH programme is no longer active, but **QH-50D** drone helicopters have recently been evaluated for communications, reconnaissance and other confidential mission applications including ordnance delivery.

Aircraft tested, at Nellis AFB, Nevada, for weapons delivery under the USAF's Night Gazelle programme, were fitted with a Cohu television and film camera for TV control, Korad laser target designator and rangefinder, laser-aided rocket system (LARS), and a high-velocity gun. The drone's remote control operator was able to exercise either in-sight control or, up to a distance of about 17 nm (20 miles; 32 km), control by using a TV display of pictures relayed back to him from the on-board camera.

KAMAN

KAMAN AEROSPACE CORPORATION

ADDRESS:
Old Windsor Road, Bloomfield, Connecticut 06002
Telephone: (203) 242-4461
OFFICERS:
See "Aircraft" section

Kaman is conducting a number of independent design studies and mission analyses for rotating-wing RPVs, aimed at the US Army's RPAODS requirements (which see). It also has a $52,000 study contract from the US Army Air Mobility Research and Development Center at Fort Eustis, Virginia, to investigate the feasibility of using an unmanned, tethered, rotating-wing aerial platform for battlefield surveillance and target acquisition.

In the hardware stage, for the US Navy, is a similar type of vehicle known as STAPL.

KAMAN STAPL

Under contract to the US Office of Naval Research, Kaman is to design, build and flight test two prototypes of a Ship Tethered Aerial Platform (STAPL), preliminary design of which was carried out in 1970 under a previous ONR contract. Testing of the two aircraft and their mobile launch and recovery platform and control system was due to take place in 1974.

The prototype aircraft, which will be unmanned, will be of autogyro configuration, and will be equipped with automatic flight control systems and data recording equipment. The self-contained AFCS, engineered by Kaman, will provide three-axis stabilisation and automatic flight path control, and will have the necessary redundancy for mission reliability.

Several hundred flying hours were accumulated in 1965-69 with the QH-43G, a drone version of the Kaman HH-43 Huskie helicopter, used as a ship-based tethered drone raising a 10,000 ft (3,050 m) VLF antenna cable vertically from a communications ship under way at sea.

LOCKHEED

LOCKHEED-CALIFORNIA COMPANY

ADDRESS:
Burbank, California 91503
Telephone: (213) 847-6121
OFFICERS:
See "Aircraft" section

LOCKHEED U-2

Reports during the past year or two have suggested that the Lockheed U-2 high-altitude reconnaissance aircraft, last described fully in the 1962-63 *Jane's*, may be developed for unmanned or "minimally-manned" use by the US armed forces.

According to one of these reports, flight testing began in early 1973, under a US Navy-funded programme, of one modified U-2 equipped with sensors for an ocean surveillance role. Among the installations then evaluated were an RCA X-band weather radar, a United Technology Laboratories elint (electronic intelligence) receiver, and an RCA vidicon camera. Other equipment to be tested in later flights included FLIR (forward-looking infra-red). Modifications to the U-2 are said to include a large ventral radome, housing the antennae for the various avionics packages on board.

Another report suggested that the U-2 may be a contender in the US Air Force's Senior Book programme, concerned with comint (communications intelligence) collection from near the borders of the Chinese mainland. In this version a pilot would apparently be carried primarily to monitor the flying controls, the actual data collection and relay being carried out under remote control in a manner similar to that employed operationally with the Beechcraft QU-22 Pave Eagle aircraft (see under "Sperry" in the 1973-74 edition).

LOCKHEED MISSILES AND SPACE COMPANY

ADDRESS:
Sunnyvale, Palo Alto and Santa Cruz, California

LOCKHEED RPV TESTBED

As part of a general programme of investigation into the field of tactical RPVs, Lockheed Missiles and Space Co has built a testbed aircraft with which to conduct preliminary flight testing. Small engineering models of this aircraft had been flown under remote control by early 1973.

The full-size testbed is primarily of metal construction, and is a mid-wing monoplane with twin tailbooms supporting an enclosed tailplane and a single central rectangular fin and rudder. It is powered initially by a 28 hp Hirth two-stroke piston engine, driving a two-blade pusher propeller; this may be replaced later by a gas turbine engine. A non-retractable tricycle landing gear is fitted, and the aircraft has a gross weight of approx 350 lb (159 kg). It is designed to cruise at altitudes of up to 2,000 ft (610 m) at about 130 knots (150 mph; 241 km/h) with an endurance of approx 1 hr.

Lockheed Missiles and Space Co is also understood to be a contender for the US Army's RPAODS requirement (which see).

MARTIN MARIETTA

MARTIN MARIETTA AEROSPACE (Denver Division)

ADDRESS:
PO Box 179, Denver, Colorado 80201
Telephone: (303) 794-5211

MARTIN MARIETTA MODEL 845A

US Air Force designation: none allotted

Under a US Air Force contract, Martin Marietta's Denver Division built two prototypes of its Model 845A medium-altitude long-endurance surveillance RPV for evaluation in the USAF's Compass Dwell programme. Components for a third aircraft were also built, but were used only as spares.

The prototypes made their first flights on 7 April and 6 June 1972 respectively, after which they were evaluated at Edwards AFB, California, in competition with the E-Systems L450F/XQM-93 (which see), but neither vehicle was selected for production. The flight test programme of the Model 845A ended on 1 July 1972, and one aircraft was later allocated to the US Air Force Museum at Wright-Patterson AFB, Ohio.

A full description and illustration of the Model 845A appeared in the 1973-74 *Jane's*.

MCDONNELL DOUGLAS

MCDONNELL DOUGLAS CORPORATION

HEAD OFFICE AND WORKS:
PO Box 516, Saint Louis, Missouri 63166
Telephone: (314) 232-0232
OFFICERS:
See "Aircraft" section

McDonnell Douglas Corporation is involved in various activities concerning RPVs, with contracts and/or IRAD projects being conducted at McDonnell Douglas Astronautics Company (see below), McDonnell Aircraft Company and Actron. Much of this work is classified and is concerned with payloads and control subsystems rather than with the flight vehicles themselves. One recent activity has been the completion, under contract to NASA (which see), of three glassfibre remotely-piloted research vehicle scale models of the F-15 Eagle combat aircraft.

Conversion of McDonnell Douglas F-4B Phantom aircraft to QF-4B configuration for target drone purposes is described under the US Navy heading in this section.

MCDONNELL DOUGLAS ASTRONAUTICS COMPANY

Under a company-funded programme, MDAC is investigating a "mini-RPV" concept to meet a DARPA (Defense Advanced Research Projects Agency) requirement for a small, low-cost battlefield reconnaissance and laser target designation vehicle. The 25 lb (11·3 kg) mission payload, which is being developed by Honeywell, will include a physical attitude stabilisation system and a 50-millijoule laser; an on-board TV camera and electro-optical image tracker will combine to guide the vehicle automatically to its target. The US Army (which see) is understood to be interested in evaluating this vehicle as a part of its RPAODS programme. The US Navy and DARPA are considering a derivative of this vehicle for a shipboard launch and recovery demonstration programme.

A "feasibility" engineering model, shown in the accompanying photograph, was successfully flight tested in 1973; the data below apply to this model, of which two examples were built. An operational prototype vehicle was due to be flight tested in 1974.

POWER PLANT: One 10 hp Louis Ross four-cylinder piston engine.

DIMENSIONS, EXTERNAL:
Wing span 10 ft 0 in (3·05 m)
Length overall 7 ft 2 in (2·18 m)
WEIGHT:
Max launching weight 120 lb (54·4 kg)
PERFORMANCE:
Max cruising speed at 10,000 ft (3,050 m) 60 knots (69 mph; 111 km/h)
Max endurance 6 hr

Feasibility model of McDonnell Douglas Astronautics "mini-RPV", tested in 1973

NASA

NATIONAL AERONAUTICS AND SPACE ADMINISTRATION

HEADQUARTERS:
1520 H Street NW, Washington, DC 20546

Ames Research Center

ADDRESS:
Moffett Field, California 94035

NASA OBLIQUE WING REMOTELY PILOTED RESEARCH AIRCRAFT

NASA's Ames Research Center is sponsoring the design and development of an advanced-technology RPRA (Remotely Piloted Research Aircraft) which will incorporate the concept of the oblique wing. Both military and civil applications of such a vehicle are to be studied.

Engineering models have been tested in flight and in the wind tunnel at Ames. The full-size RPRA has been designed and built under contract by Developmental Sciences Inc (which see), and is described under that company's heading in this section. It was due to fly for the first time in the Autumn of 1974.

Langley Research Center

ADDRESS:
Hampton, Virginia

NASA PROJECT DAST

Project DAST (Drones for Aerodynamic and Structural Testing) is a programme under which NASA's Langley Research Center hopes to pursue further the use of RPRVs for investigating unusual aerodynamic configurations, aerodynamic load problems, spin escape and other techniques.

Some preliminary work has already been done using Teledyne Ryan BQM-34E Firebee II supersonic drones acquired from the US Navy. Subsequently, NASA was seeking funds to purchase its own examples of the Firebee II for further work under this programme.

NORTHROP

NORTHROP CORPORATION—VENTURA DIVISION

DIVISION HEAD OFFICE:
1515 Rancho Conejo Boulevard, Newbury Park, California 91320
Telephone: 498-3131
Telex: 805-499-7130

VICE-PRESIDENTS:
W. E. Woolwine (General Manager)
John E. Evans (Manufacturing)
Joseph H. Staley (Aeronautical Systems Programmes Manager)
G. C. Grogan (Product Development)
W. F. Sternadel (Finance)

PUBLIC RELATIONS MANAGER:
Park H. Irvine

Northrop's Ventura Division designs and manufactures pilotless target aircraft and related equipment. It produces recovery systems and also manufactures glassfibre wing fairings for the Boeing 747 transport aircraft. It has diversified into the marine systems field and is producing an unmanned underwater vehicle (MK 30) as a target in US Navy anti-submarine warfare training.

Northrop Ventura (formerly Radioplane) undertook the design, development and construction of its first radio controlled target drone in the mid-thirties. Since then it has become a leader in the field of pilotless aircraft. More than 68,000 drones have been delivered to the US military services and 18 allied nations.

Parachute landing systems designed and produced by this Northrop Division returned safely to Earth all the US astronauts who accomplished space flight under the Mercury, Gemini, Apollo and Skylab programmes.

Northrop has developed a new Variable-Speed Training Target (VSTT), now being evaluated in competition with an entry from Beech Aircraft Corporation to meet the requirements of the US Army's Missile Command. A brief description of the VSTT programme appears under the Beech heading in this section.

NORTHROP SHELDUCK

This target drone is currently in use by the armed forces of 17 countries as a training device for ground-to-air gunnery and is used as a training target for surface-to-air missiles such as Seacat, Tigercat, Redeye, Blowpipe, Sparrow, Chaparral, Hawk, Sidewinder and Nike.

Design of the drone was started in 1946 and the prototype flew for the first time in 1947. Since then more than 60,000 of this type, including early KD2R versions, have been built and production continues.

The target is surface-launched only, either by catapult or zero launcher. Radio control is utilised, the target being tracked visually or by radar. After completion of its mission, it is recovered by the use of a radio-command-released parachute. In the event of serious damage by gunfire or loss of radio control or electrical power, the parachute is deployed automatically. The target is designed to be repaired easily if damaged by gunfire.

TYPE: Remotely controlled aerial target.

WINGS: Cantilever high-wing monoplane. Wing section NACA 23012 at root, NACA 4412 at tip. No dihedral. Incidence 1° at root, —2° at tip. Conventional aircraft aluminium alloy construction. Conventional ailerons servo-operated by type D-9 actuators.

FUSELAGE: Semi-monocoque aluminium alloy structure, with integral steel fuel tank.

TAIL UNIT: Cantilever aluminium alloy structure. Fixed-incidence tailplane. Elevator servo-operated by type D-9 actuator.

POWER PLANT: One 90 hp Northrop O-100-3 four-cylinder horizontally-opposed aircooled two-stroke engine, driving a two-blade fixed-pitch wooden propeller. Steel fuel tank in mid-fuselage, capacity 11·6 US gallons (44 litres). Refuelling point in fuselage forward of wing.

SYSTEMS: Electrical power only, from 28V battery.

ELECTRONICS AND EQUIPMENT: AN/ARW-79 remote flight control system with automatic altitude hold control. Radar or FM type tracking systems or equivalent. L-band tracking system, smoke generating, infra-red tow target, night light kits, tow banner and many other accessories are available to meet the requirements of the individual user. For radar appearance augmentation, two wingtip reflector pods are optional.

Northrop Shelduck basic training target drone, a type produced for 17 countries

DIMENSIONS, EXTERNAL:

Wing span	11 ft 6 in (3·50 m)
Wing chord (mean)	1 ft 8·13 in (0·51 m)
Wing aspect ratio	7
Length overall	12 ft 7½ in (3·85 m)
Height overall	2 ft 6 in (0·76 m)
Tailplane span	4 ft 2 in (1·27 m)
Propeller diameter	3 ft 8 in (1·10 m)

AREAS:

Wings, gross	18·7 sq ft (1·74 m²)
Ailerons (total)	1·3 sq ft (0·12 m²)
Fin	1·8 sq ft (0·17 m²)
Tailplane	3·0 sq ft (0·28 m²)
Elevators	1·4 sq ft (0·13 m²)

WEIGHTS:

Weight empty	271 lb (123 kg)
Max launching weight	360 lb (163 kg)
Max zero-fuel weight	292 lb (133 kg)
Max landing weight	340 lb (154 kg)

PERFORMANCE (at max launching weight):
Max never-exceed speed
250 knots (288 mph; 463 km/h)
Max level speed at S/L and max cruising speed
194 knots (223 mph; 359 km/h)
Stalling speed 58 knots (67 mph; 108 km/h)
Max rate of climb at S/L 4,400 ft (1,341 m)/min
Service ceiling 27,000 ft (8,230 m)
Range with max fuel
173 nm (199 miles; 320 km)

NORTHROP NV-105 CHUKAR I
US military designation: MQM-74A

This drone was designed to meet requirements for a small lightweight 400 knot (461 mph; 742 km/h) target for anti-aircraft gunnery, surface-to-air missile and air-to-air missile training and weapon systems evaluation. A modified version of the MQM-74A, with special augmentation, is used as a standard target at the NATO Missile Firing Installation (NAMFI) in the Mediterranean. In Italy, Meteor (which see) has developed a tactical reconnaissance system known as Gufo, based on the Chukar I.

The Chukar can simulate the attack modes of missiles or aircraft, including 5° or 10° dive-bombing and strafing. At 400 yards (365 m) range, it appears to a gun crew as a supersonic fighter at 1,000 yards (915 m). Its augmentation is compatible with a variety of weapon systems requirements and it can provide training for the crews of 40 mm, 20 mm and 0·50 in guns or Hawk, Redeye, Chaparral or Nike-Hercules missiles, as well as radar and infra-red air-to-air missiles such as Sparrow and Sidewinder.

Production of the Chukar I ended in 1973, at which time a total of 2,300 had been completed.

A developed version, the MQM-74C Chukar II, is described separately.

TYPE: Turbojet-powered radio-controlled recoverable target drone.

WINGS: Cantilever shoulder-wing monoplane. No dihedral. Detachable aluminium wings, each with electrically-actuated aileron.

FUSELAGE: Aluminium semi-monocoque structure housing all equipment, power plant and fuel tankage. Nose and tail skins removable for access to electronic components and power plant. Underslung engine air intake duct.

TAIL UNIT: Cantilever aluminium structure of inverted Y form, comprising fixed vertical fin, fixed tailplane halves and two electrically-actuated elevators. Tailplane anhedral 30°.

POWER PLANT: Williams Research Corporation Model WR24-6 (YJ400-WR-400) open-cycle turbojet engine (axial intake, single-stage centrifugal compressor, annular combustion chamber, single-stage axial turbine), rated at 121 lb (55 kg) st at 60,000 rpm. Tank in centre of fuselage for JP-4 or JP-5 fuel.

SYSTEMS: Electrical power only, from engine-driven alternator through a rectifier-regulator. 28V nickel-cadmium battery secondary power source used during glide.

CONTROL SYSTEM: Out-of-sight control by automatic stabilisation and command, with radar tracking; in-sight control with visual acquisition aids. Proportional feedback stabilisation and control system for pitch and bank. Engine throttle position, altitude hold initiation and recovery system initiation controlled by audio tone signals. Components include receiver-decoder, control unit assembly and vertical gyro in nose of fuselage, aileron and elevator servos, and altitude hold pressure transducer. Command control antenna in upper forward fuselage.

EQUIPMENT: On-board acquisition and tracking aids include fore and aft Luneberg lenses for passive radar augmentation, four wingtip-mounted MK 28 Mod 3 infra-red flares, active L-band augmentation, and a chaff or a pyrotechnic flash and smoke system, designed to improve visual augmentation. Main payload compartment is in front fuselage between control equipment bay and fuel tank.

LAUNCH AND RECOVERY: Zero-length launching by means of two Mk 34 Mod 1 JATO rockets and a ZL-5 launcher. Two modes of command recovery are utilised. Normal method consists of automatic drone pull-up followed by main parachute deployment, and is initiated automatically in emergencies such as interruption of continuous radio signal or loss of parachute command channel. Alternative mode consists of direct main parachute deployment and is initiated automatically on loss of electrical power. Main parachute, housed in fuselage immediately aft of wing, is a 30 ft (9·15 m) diameter extended-skirt nylon canopy, with automatic disconnect at impact.

DIMENSIONS, EXTERNAL:

Wing span	5 ft 6⅝ in (1·69 m)
Length overall	11 ft 9 in (3·58 m)
Body diameter	1 ft 2 in (0·36 m)
Height overall	2 ft 3¾ in (0·70 m)

WEIGHTS:

Weight empty	233 lb (106 kg)
Max launching weight	425 lb (192 kg)

PERFORMANCE:
Max level speed at 20,000 ft (6,100 m)
425 knots (489 mph; 787 km/h)
Max level speed at S/L
400 knots (461 mph; 742 km/h)
Econ cruising speed at S/L
210 knots (242 mph; 390 km/h)
Max rate of climb at S/L 5,500 ft (1,676 m)/min

Service ceiling 40,000 ft (12,200 m)
Range at max speed at S/L 143 nm (164 miles; 264 km)
Range at max speed at 20,000 ft (6,100 m) 237 nm (273 miles; 439 km)
Range at econ cruising speed at S/L 180 nm (207 miles; 333 km)

NORTHROP MQM-74C

The MQM-74C is an improved version of the MQM-74A, evolved via an MQM-74B developmental model to meet requirements for a 500 knot (576 mph; 926 km/h) target for duties similar to those of its predecessor. Production is under way of 388 MQM-74Cs for the US Navy; delivery of these began in early 1974.

The description of the MQM-74A applies generally to the MQM-74C except in the following respects:

Power Plant: Williams Research Corporation Model WR24-7 (J400-WR-401) turbojet engine, rated at 176 lb (80 kg) st.

Launch: Zero-length launching by means of two Mk 91 Mod 0 JATO units, which have an improved performance compared with the Mk 34.

Control System: Generally as MQM-74A, but with Motorola AN/DKW-1 integrated target control system instead of receiver/decoder, control unit assembly and vertical gyro.

Dimensions, external: As MQM-74A, except:
Length overall 12 ft 7 in (3·84 m)

Weights:
Weight empty 273 lb (124 kg)
Max launching weight 512 lb (232 kg)

Performance:
Max level speed at 20,000 ft (6,100 m) 500 knots (576 mph; 926 km/h)
Max level speed at S/L 465 knots (535 mph; 861 km/h)
Econ cruising speed at S/L 300 knots (345 mph; 555 km/h)
Max rate of climb at S/L 8,000 ft (2,438 m)/min
Service ceiling 42,000 ft (12,800 m)
Range at max speed at S/L 190 nm (219 miles; 352 km)
Range at max speed at 20,000 ft (6,100 m) 310 nm (357 miles; 574 km)
Range at econ cruising speed at S/L 230 nm (265 miles; 426 km)

NORTHROP CHUKAR II

The Chukar II is an improved version of the Chukar I and is similar to the MQM-74C.

The description of the MQM-74C applies generally to the Chukar II, except in the following respects:

Control System: Generally as MQM-74A, but with a developed control system utilising the MQM-74C autopilot instead of the MQM-74A decoder.

Equipment: On-board acquisition aids can include fore and aft Luneberg lenses for passive radar augmentation. Northrop Aerial Target Tracking System (NATTS) airborne beacon for tracking, four wingtip-mounted infra-red or visual flares, active L-band augmentation, an oil smoke system designed to improve visual acquisition, and wingtip-mounted Radar Augmented Subtargets (RAST) system as used on VSTT.

NORTHROP NV-123

US military designation: Variable-Speed Training Target (VSTT)

This target is being developed under contract to the US Army Missile Command for a competition intended to provide an economical target system which simulates a subsonic airborne threat. The selected vehicle will be used for anti-aircraft gunnery, surface-to-air missile training and weapon systems evaluation. For these missions, the VSTT will replace all other targets currently in the Army's inventory.

Northrop's entry, the NV-123, on which work began in April 1972, is augmented with various ancillary devices to make it compatible with various weapon systems requirements and can be employed in live firing exercises without destroying the basic vehicle. These include a visually augmented tow device for use with guns; an infra-red augmented tow device for use with IR-guided missiles; and a radar augmented subtarget (RAST) for use with radar-guided missiles. The RAST is rocket-powered, and is launched from the wingtip of the NV-123 to provide a free-flying target for these missiles.

Evaluation by the US Army at the White Sands Missile Range in New Mexico was under way in 1974.

Type: Turbojet-powered remotely controlled recoverable target.

Wings: Cantilever high/mid-wing monoplane. Detachable one-piece wings.

Fuselage: Aluminium semi-monocoque structure housing all equipment, power plant and fuel tankage. Nose and tail panels are removable for access to electronics components and power plant. Underslung engine air intake duct.

Tail Unit: Cantilever aluminium structure of inverted Y form, comprising fixed vertical fin, fixed tailplane halves and two electrically-actuated elevators.

Power Plant: One Williams Research Corporation WR24-17 lightweight simple-cycle turbojet engine (single-stage axial compressor, single-sided centrifugal compressor, radial diffuser, annular burner and single-stage axial-flow turbine), rated at 200 lb (91 kg) st.

Systems: Electrical power only. 28V DC engine-driven alternator through a rectifier regulator. 28V nickel-cadmium battery used for recovery system.

Control System: A two-axis system controlling pitch and roll attitudes. Outer loops provide altitude and airspeed control in response to commands. Components include a GFE transponder, autopilot unit, sensors and control surface actuators, vertical gyro, a barometric pressure altimeter and closed loop altitude control, and a closed loop throttle control. The operational receiver/decoder is assumed to be the ITCS; however, the NV-123 is also compatible with the MTTS and BCRD-22 systems.

Equipment: An L-band beacon is provided to enhance acquisition radar return for certain weapon systems. A visual augmentation system is provided for other weapon systems.

Launch and Recovery: Zero-length launching by means of one M58A2 JATO rocket unit and a ZL-6 launcher. After launch and JATO burnout, the JATO carrier is recovered by parachute. Normal and emergency recovery modes are provided. At normal recovery command, all external stores are jettisoned, the parachute compartment doors open, and a 2 ft 6 in (0·76 m) diameter ribbon drogue is extracted by a 10 in (25·4 cm) diameter spring-loaded pilot parachute. After a 6 second drogue phase, and at an altitude of 10,000 ft (3,050 m) or less, the drogue is released and used to extract a reefed 30 ft (9·14 m) diameter full extended skirt main parachute. During an emergency recovery, only a towed external store is jettisoned and all other stores are recovered with the vehicle. Crushable impact attenuators are provided in the nose and under the engine air intake duct to minimise recovery damage.

Dimensions, external:
Wing span 5 ft 7⅞ in (1·72 m)
Length overall 12 ft 5½ in (3·80 m)
Body diameter (max) 1 ft 2 in (0·36 m)
Height overall 2 ft 4 in (0·71 m)

Weights:
Weight dry 300 lb (136 kg)
Max launching weight 594 lb (269 kg)

Performance:
Max level speed at S/L 515 knots (593 mph; 954 km/h)
Max level speed at 40,000 ft (12,200 m) 500 knots (575 mph; 926 km/h)
Econ cruising speed at S/L 250 knots (287 mph; 463 km/h)
Max rate of climb at S/L 7,500 ft (2,286 m)/min
Service ceiling 40,000 ft (12,200 m)
Range at max speed at S/L 240 nm (276 miles; 444 km)
Range at max speed at 40,000 ft (12,200 m) 640 nm (737 miles; 1,186 km)
Range at econ cruising speed at S/L 350 nm (403 miles; 648 km)

Northrop MQM-74C target drone (176 lb st WR24-7 turbojet engine)

Northrop VSTT training target, with towed target beneath each wingtip

PHILCO-FORD

PHILCO-FORD CORPORATION (Subsidiary of FORD MOTOR COMPANY)

Aeronutronic Division

HEAD OFFICE:
Ford Road, Newport Beach, California 92663

OFFICERS: See "Missiles" section

In addition to its work on guided missiles, Aeronutronic Division developed and manufactured the low-cost rocket-powered LOCAT air target, of which details were given in the 1972-73 *Jane's*.

Currently, the Aeronutronic Division is engaged in a general programme, on behalf of the US Air Force Aeronautical Systems Division, of advanced studies for small RPV airframes, engines and payloads.

PHILCO-FORD "MINI-RPV"

Under a Department of Defense contract awarded in March 1972, Philco-Ford's Aeronutronic Division designed and developed a small, radio-controlled RPV for battlefield reconnaissance, target acquisition and laser designation applications. Four prototypes were ordered, two each for daytime and night operation, and it was reported in the Spring of 1973 that these were to be acquired by the US Army for evaluation under its RPAODS programme (which see).

The airframes, which are of high-wing monoplane configuration with a 10 ft (3·05 m) wing span and a tailwheel landing gear, were built by two professional model aircraft constructors, Jan Sakert and Richard Riggs. Power plant is a small two-cylinder engine, driving a two-blade propeller, which gives the aircraft a cruising speed of approx 52 knots (60 mph; 97 km/h) at very low altitude. Guidance is by radio command, using equipment of Motorola design, and the aircraft are gyro-stabilised for line-of-sight operation. They take off and land in the same way as a conventional radio-controlled model aircraft.

Each aircraft has a removable avionics payload package, weighing some 30 lb (13·5 kg), mounted in the lower front fuselage. In the daytime version (programme name Praeire) this incorporates a non-stabilised miniature wide-angle TV camera, with zoom lens, transmitting pictures to the ground pilot to aid navigation; a stabilised narrow-angle TV camera for target detection and selection; and a 4 lb (1·8 kg) International Laser Systems Corporation TWL-50 ("Teeny Weeny Laser") for target designation. A transparent plastics underfuselage radome houses gyro-stabilised mirrors for the narrow-angle camera. Gross weight of the daytime version, flight testing of which had begun by early 1973, is approx 75 lb (34 kg).

The night version (programme name Calere) is approx 10 lb (4·5 kg) heavier than the daytime model, from which it differs primarily in having a TWL-100 laser designator instead of the TWL-50, and a Texas Instruments FLIR (forward-looking infra-red) detector instead of the narrow-angle TV camera.

SPERRY

SPERRY FLIGHT SYSTEMS DIVISION, SPERRY RAND CORPORATION

ADDRESS:
PO Box 21111, Phoenix, Arizona 85036
Telephone: (602) 942-2311

SPERRY (CONVAIR/GENERAL DYNAMICS) F-102A DELTA DAGGER

USAF designations: QF-102A and PQM-102A

Under a $5·5 million contract awarded in the Spring of 1973, Sperry Flight Systems Division undertook conversion for the USAF of eight Convair F-102A interceptors to drone configuration, to provide up-to-date "threat simulation" targets for the McDonnell Douglas F-15 Eagle and other current air defence aircraft under the USAF's Pave Deuce programme.

Two of the aircraft, designated QF-102A, retain normal cockpit controls and will be flown by monitoring pilots. The other six, designated PQM-102A, are designed and equipped entirely for unmanned operation.

UNIVAC DIVISION, SPERRY RAND CORPORATION

ADDRESS:
PO Box 500, Blue Bell, Pennsylvania 19422

Telephone: (215) MI 6-9000

SPERRY (BEECHCRAFT) BONANZA MODEL A36

US Air Force designations: QU-22A and QU-22B

Military examples of the Beechcraft Bonanza Model A36 utility aircraft were modified by the Univac Division of Sperry Rand for use as drone aircraft in the US Air Force's Pave Eagle surveillance programme in Southeast Asia. These were of two known types, designated QU-22A (Pave Eagle 1, six converted) and QU-22B (Pave Eagle 2, 27 converted).

All known details of this programme were given in the 1973-74 *Jane's*.

TELEDYNE BROWN

TELEDYNE BROWN ENGINEERING (Division of Teledyne Inc)

HEAD OFFICE:
Research Park, Huntsville, Alabama 35807
Telephone: (205) 536-4455

PRESIDENT:
Joseph C. Moquin
EXECUTIVE VICE-PRESIDENT:
J. H. Engler
SENIOR VICE-PRESIDENT:
R. S. McCarter
VICE-PRESIDENT, MILITARY SYSTEMS:
Dr Herbert M. Barnard

Teledyne Brown is currently producing an expendable artillery target system known as BATS (Ballistic Aerial Target System), of which more than 24,000 have been ordered by the US Army and Navy, the UK and Australia. Details of BATS, and of the Improved BATS developed from it, were given in the 1973-74 *Jane's*.

TELEDYNE RYAN

TELEDYNE RYAN AERONAUTICAL (Division of Teledyne Inc)

HEAD OFFICE AND WORKS:
2701 Harbor Drive, San Diego, California 92112
Telephone: (714) 291-7311

OFFICERS: See "Aircraft" section

A major production item at Teledyne Ryan's San Diego works for many years has been the Firebee jet-powered target and reconnaissance drone, described in detail below.

The company has other important contracts in the missile and space field, including design and fabrication of radar altimeters, precision antennae and structures for advanced space vehicles.

As described under the NASA entry, Teledyne Ryan BQM-34E Firebee II supersonic drones are being used in remotely piloted research vehicle (RPRV) test programmes at the Administration's Flight Research Center, Edwards AFB, California. Teledyne Ryan has itself conducted, under contract to NASA, a feasibility study involving the fitting of various different wing planforms and aerofoil sections to the Firebee II for test purposes. These included three types of supercritical wing, three types of supersonic wing, and a laminar-flow wing.

Among other activities, Teledyne Ryan is studying a number of concepts for "mini-RPVs", a field in which the US services are particularly interested at the present time. For further details see Addenda.

Ground launching of a Firebee I from the US Navy South Atlantic/Caribbean Sea Weapons Range at Cabras Island, Puerto Rico

TELEDYNE RYAN MODEL 124 FIREBEE I

USAF/US Navy designations: BQM-34A and BQM-34S

US Army designation: MQM-34D

The Firebee I is a remotely piloted high-speed turbojet-powered vehicle which was developed as a joint US Air Force/Army/Navy project, with the USAF Air Research and Development Command having technical cognisance of its development.

Glide flight tests of the original version of the Firebee without power were begun in March 1951, and the first powered flights were made that Summer at the USAF Holloman Air Development Center, Alamogordo, New Mexico. A total of 1,280 of these early Q-2A and KDA versions were built eventually for all three US services and for the RCAF, and full details of these can be found in previous editions of *Jane's*.

Development of the current **BQM-34A** (originally Q-2C) Firebee began on 25 February 1958, with the object of obtaining a much-improved all-round performance. Construction of the prototype started on 1 May and it flew for the first time on 19 December 1958. The first production model flew on 25 January 1960. A total of 5,306 Firebee Is (including more than 4,000 BQM-34As and MQM-34Ds) have since been produced and the latest contracts, for an additional 123 BQM-34As, extend production through to mid-1975. They include a contract from the Japan Defence Agency for Firebees for use in training missile and gunnery crews. These are being built by Fuji (which see), which had completed 10 by the end of 1973 and was scheduled to manufacture three more in 1974.

In June 1971 Teledyne Ryan announced that a BQM-34A Firebee drone had been used as a testbed for a new company-developed flight control system, known as MASTACS, which enabled it to perform a simulated "dogfight" mission against US Navy Phantom fighter aircraft over the Pacific Missile Range during May 1971. In another RPV test a modified BQM-34A was used to release inert 500 lb bombs in tests at White Sands Missile Range.

The US Navy BQM-34A targets currently being manufactured to incorporate a Motorola integrated track and control system (ITCS) have the new designation **BQM-34S**.

An **MQM-34D** version used by the US Army has a longer-burning rocket booster for ground launch and extended wings, enabling it to take off at a loaded weight some 1,000 lb (455 kg) greater than the BQM-34A.

Up to the end of December 1973 such targets, operated by Teledyne Ryan support teams and others from the Dona Ana and McGregor Ranges in New Mexico, had made 27,713 flight presentations before US Army trainees at Fort Bliss,

Firebee I descending by recovery parachute

Texas. Presentations have been made to 20 mm Vulcan, 40 mm Duster and quadruple-mounted 0·50 in anti-aircraft gun crews, with a 2 ft × 12 ft (0·61 m × 3·65 m) banner target towed on a wire cable 500 ft (152 m) behind the Firebee. Other flights in support of Hawk, Redeye and Chaparral surface-to-air missile firings deploy a wingtip-mounted Towbee infra-red or radar augmented tow target. The Towbees, launched on command, are towed from 100 ft (30 m) to 8,000 ft (2,440 m) behind the MQM-34D.

RPVs (Remotely Piloted Vehicles) using air-frames developed from that of the Firebee I include those bearing the Teledyne Ryan Model numbers 147, 234 and 251; the last of these has the US Army designation **MQM-34D/MOD II** and all are described separately.

The following details refer to the standard BQM-34A target vehicle:

TYPE: Remotely piloted jet target vehicle.

WINGS: Cantilever mid-wing monoplane. Wing section from leading-edge to ·264 chord NACA 0009·932; from ·264 chord to trailing-edge NACA 63A014·63. Thickness/chord ratio 14%. No dihedral or incidence. Sweepback at quarter-chord 45°. Three-spar aluminium alloy semi-monocoque structure, incorporating leading-edge droop. Single-spar ailerons of magnesium, aluminium and stainless steel, operated by Lear servo-actuators. Wingtips detachable to minimise damage on landing. Provision for wingtip extensions to increase span.

FUSELAGE: Conventional semi-monocoque structure of aluminium alloy, with chemical-etched components to save weight and simplify sub-assemblies. Glassfibre tailcone and nose section. Keel under central portion, to absorb landing impact.

TAIL UNIT: Single assembly attached to fuselage by four bolts. All surfaces swept 45° at quarter-chord. Fin is multi-spar aluminium alloy monocoque structure. Trim rudder is operated electrically by Bendix actuator. Single-spar aluminium alloy monocoque tail-plane. Magnesium elevators powered by Lear servo. Glassfibre fin-tip houses telemetry antenna. Glassfibre tailplane tips house radar echo enhancing antennae. Ventral fin under tailcone, aft of main tail unit.

POWER PLANT: One 1,700 lb (771 kg) st Teledyne CAE J69-T-29 turbojet engine. Fuel tank integral within forward section of fuselage, capacity 100 US gallons (378 litres). Provision for one 25 US gallon (94·5 litre) auxiliary fuselage tank and one 100 US gallon (378 litre) drop-tank under each wing. Refuelling point above forward fuselage. Oil capacity 1·5 US gallons (5·75 litres).

SYSTEMS: Electrical power only. Primary power furnished by a 28V DC engine-driven generator of 200A capacity. Power for control systems furnished by a 400Hz 115V 250W AC inverter; a 28V 12·5Ah lead-acid battery provides power for the electrical devices of the recovery system and for control during the pre-landing glide phase.

ELECTRONICS AND EQUIPMENT: AN/DRW-29 radio control receiver. A/A37G-3 or A/A37G-8 flight control system. Dorsett TM-4-31A telemetry system.

LAUNCH AND RECOVERY: Either air-launching, from a suitably-modified aircraft, or ground-launching, using an 11,300 lb (5,125 kg) st (nominal) solid-propellant JATO bottle, can be used; the US Navy has also launched BQM-34A Firebees from ships under way at up to 15 knots (17 mph; 27·5 km/h). The two-stage parachute recovery system operates automatically in the event of a target hit, loss of radio wave carrier from the remote-control station, engine failure, or upon command by the remote-control operator. To prevent damage by dragging, the recovery system incorporates a disconnect which releases the parachute from the Firebee on contact with the ground or water.

GUIDANCE AND CONTROL: Remote control methods for Firebee I include a choice of radar, radio, active seeker and automatic navigator, all developed and designed by Teledyne Ryan. Remote control is normally accomplished through a UHF radio link using an AN/FRW-2 or SRW-4 ground transmitter and an AN/DRW-29 airborne receiver (USN) or similar equipment. The target can be controlled either from a manned aircraft or from a surface station. Remote command includes activation of special scoring and augmentation equipment in the target. A beacon in the Firebee facilitates radar tracking from the remote control station; there is provision to install a telemetry system to relay pertinent flight data to the controller if required. Basic commands consist primarily of on/off functions which are received by the on-board radio receiver and relayed to the appropriate subsystem for action. A Motorola ITCS (integrated tracking and control system) is fitted in the BQM-34S version. Other types of remote command and tracking systems can include a microwave command and guidance system which can control the Firebee beyond line-of-sight from a ground station through an airborne relay station. This equipment operates with coded impulses which reduce the possibility of interference from other electronic signals. Operational Firebees can be equipped with an Increased Manoeuvrability Kit (IMK) and a Manoeuvring Augmentation System for Tactical Air Combat Simulation (MASTACS) which give the Firebee I the capability to perform 3 and 6g evasive manoeuvres. This makes it a highly realistic target for the training of pilots in firing missile weapon systems. A Radar Altimeter Low Altitude Control System (RALACS), when added to the Firebee I control system, permits precision low-altitude flights at 50 ft (15 m) over water and 100 ft (30 m) over land.

US Army MQM-34D Firebee I with wingtip-mounted infra-red Towbee towed target

BQM-34A Firebee I target drone dropping away from the launch pylon of a DC-130 Hercules carrier aircraft

OPERATIONAL EQUIPMENT: Wide range of possible "building block" equipment combinations, including visual or radar-reflecting banner targets; radar or infra-red Towbee towed targets or tow target Doppler "bird"; two underwing drop-tanks, 500 lb bombs or bomblet dispensers; AN/ALE-33 or other ECM containers; wingtip tow launchers, camera pods, scoring equipment, flares or other forms of infra-red augmentation, or reflector pods for radar augmentation. The BQM-34A can be equipped with adjustable travelling wave tube amplifiers for use as radar echo enhancers in the L, S, X and C frequency bands. These devices provide realistic radar appearances for all-size targets from the smallest fighter to the largest bomber aircraft.

DIMENSIONS, EXTERNAL (BQM-34A):
- Wing span: 12 ft 10·8 in (3·93 m)
- Wing chord (streamwise, constant): 2 ft 9·4 in (0·85 m)
- Wing aspect ratio: 4·532
- Length overall: 22 ft 10·8 in (6·98 m)
- Body diameter: 3 ft 1·2 in (0·94 m)
- Height overall: 6 ft 8·4 in (2·04 m)
- Tailplane span: 7 ft 5 in (2·26 m)
- Tailplane chord (streamwise, constant): 2 ft 3 in (0·69 m)
- Fin chord at tip: 1 ft 10 in (0·56 m)

AREAS:
- Wings, gross: 36·0 sq ft (3·34 m²)
- Ailerons (total): 4·16 sq ft (0·39 m²)
- Fin: 11·28 sq ft (1·05 m²)
- Ventral fin: 1·43 sq ft (0·13 m²)
- Rudder: 0·46 sq ft (0·043 m²)
- Tailplane: 16·69 sq ft (1·55 m²)
- Elevators: 6·84 sq ft (0·64 m²)

WEIGHTS AND LOADING:
- **Weight empty: 1,500 lb (680 kg)**
- Basic gross weight: 2,060 lb (934 kg)
- **Max launching weight: 2,500 lb (1,134 kg)**
- **Max wing loading: 69·3 lb/sq ft (338·3 kg/m²)**

PERFORMANCE:
- Max never-exceed speed: Mach 0·96 (635 knots; 731 mph; 1,176 km/h at 50,000 ft; 15,240 m)
- Max level speed at 6,500 ft (1,980 m): 600 knots (690 mph; 1,112 km/h)
- **Max cruising speed at 50,000 ft (15,240 m) at 1,800 lb (816 kg) AUW: 547 knots (630 mph; 1,015 km/h)**
- **Stalling speed, power on, at 1,800 lb (816 kg) AUW: 101 knots (116 mph; 187 km/h)**
- Max rate of climb at S/L at 2,200 lb (1,000 kg) AUW: 16,000 ft (4,875 m)/min
- Operating height range: 50 ft to more than 60,000 ft (15 m-18,300 m)
- Endurance at 50,000 ft (15,240 m), incl 2 min 40 sec glide after fuel expended: 75 min 30 sec
- Max range: 692 nm (796 miles; 1,282 km)
- Flotation time with 25% fuel: 24 hr

TELEDYNE RYAN MODEL 147

USAF designations: in AQM-34 series

The Model number 147, and the basic USAF designation AQM-34, encompass a large family of surveillance, reconnaissance and ECM RPVs evolved from the subsonic BQM-34A/MQM-34D Firebee I target. They are air-launched from DC-130A or E Hercules mother-planes which combine the functions of command, tracking and data relay aircraft. The original Model 147A, which was little more than a modified Firebee I with a new guidance system and increased fuel capacity, was developed in 1962.

Since late 1964, various types of Teledyne Ryan 147 have been despatched on flights over China,

North Vietnam and other areas. Early production versions were deployed initially from the SAC air base at Kadena, Okinawa, as part of the USAF's Blue Springs programme for overflying the Chinese mainland. The Chinese claimed to have destroyed eight RPVs by May 1965, and exhibited the remains of several of them at the Chinese People's Revolutionary Museum in Peking. In the late 1960s, detachments of the 100th Strategic Reconnaissance Wing from Davis-Monthan AFB, Arizona, operated 147-type RPVs from Bien Hoa in South Vietnam, bringing them back to Da Nang air base for mid-air recovery by helicopter.

Versions of the Model 147 have also been used extensively to test the effectiveness of new combat equipment in an operational environment without risk to personnel.

By 1974, many hundreds of Model 147s had been delivered by Teledyne Ryan for operational use, and in September 1972 the company was permitted to identify no fewer than 24 members of this large family. Details of these and of other variants follow, together with the appropriate USAF designation where applicable:

Models 147A, B, C, D, E, G and J. Early models, as described in the 1973-74 *Jane's*. No longer in production.

Model 147H (AQM-34N). Medium-altitude reconnaissance version. Externally similar to 147G except for flatter ventral bulge similar to that of 147T series. Teledyne Ryan radio command guidance system. Became operational with Strategic Air Command in about 1968.

Model 124I. Designation of a hybrid Model 124/147-type vehicle produced for export, about a dozen of which are said to have been supplied to Israel in 1971 and later used for high-altitude photographic reconnaissance overflights of Egyptian (and possibly other Arab) territory. Other press reports, also unconfirmed, have suggested that Israel has used Firebee I-type drones (not necessarily of the same type) to deliver Israeli-built air-to-ground missiles against Egyptian missile sites. Teledyne Ryan programme and command guidance system.

Model 147NA (AQM-34G). Medium-altitude ECM version. Has extended-span wings, strengthened to carry external stores (one pylon under each wing), and small antenna fairing on top of fin. Teledyne Ryan programme and command guidance system. In service with 11th Tactical Drone Squadron of USAF at Davis-Monthan AFB, Arizona.

Model 147NC (AQM-34H). Medium-altitude ECM version, similar to 147NA but with higher launching weight and twin cropped-delta-shape endplate auxiliary fins. Underwing ECM pods may carry Hughes ALQ-71 noise jammers, Westinghouse QRC-335 noise/deception jammers or ALE-2 chaff dispensers. Teledyne Ryan programme and command guidance system. Other equipment includes Sperry Univac APW-25 or -26 transponder. Took part in now-completed USAF Combat Angel programme. Developed for use in Vietnam, but not used operationally. In service since 1969 with 11th Tactical Drone Squadron, Davis-Monthan AFB. Illustrated in 1973-74 *Jane's*. Undergoing modification in 1974, by Teledyne Ryan and Melpar, to a standard configuration.

Teledyne Ryan Model 147SC (AQM-34L) shortly after launch from its DC-130E director aircraft

Model 147NC (M-1) (AQM-34J). Medium-altitude training version of 147NC, to which it is externally similar except for the absence of underwing pylons. In service for reconnaissance RPV training with 11th Tactical Drone Squadron.

Model 147NP. Externally similar to 147NC (M-1) except for absence of auxiliary fins.

Model 147NQ. Externally similar to 147NP.

Model 147NRE. Externally similar to 147NP.

Model 147NX. Externally similar to 147NQ, except for shorter-span wings and absence of underwing pylons and fin-tip antenna fairing.

Model 147SA. Externally similar to 147NP, but with probe-like fairing on front of nose-cone.

Model 147SB. Externally similar to 147SA.

Model 147SC (AQM-34L and YAQM-34U). Low-altitude photographic reconnaissance version. Externally similar to 147SA/SB except for addition of endplate auxiliary fins. Teledyne CAE J69-T-41A engine, with 1,140 lb (517 kg) fuel load, pre-programmed navigation system, utilising a Doppler navigator and digital programmer, and remote control capability via a microwave command guidance system or radio link from an airborne or ground station. After the cessation of bombing on 15 January 1973 this RPV and the Lockheed SR-71 manned strategic reconnaissance aircraft were the only USAF reconnaissance types permitted to overfly North Vietnam. Some AQM-34Ls are fitted with underwing pylons for ECM or chaff pods. Details of AQM-34L sensors, and of the YAQM-34U Update programme carried out on six AQM-34Ls by Lear Siegler, were given in the 1973-74 *Jane's*.

YAQM-34U Update version of the Model 147SC

Model 147SD (AQM-34M). Low-altitude reconnaissance version, generally similar to AQM-34L. Seventy-eight ordered, including eight for flight testing. Some fitted in 1972 with Teledyne Systems Co Loran receivers and redesignated **Model 147SD Loran/AQM-34M(L).** One AQM-34M was allocated for flight testing at Edwards AFB, California, under a USAF programme code-named Compass Robin. This vehicle was fitted with Rockwell (Autonetics Division) 3 in (7·6 cm) diameter micro-electronic radio receivers,

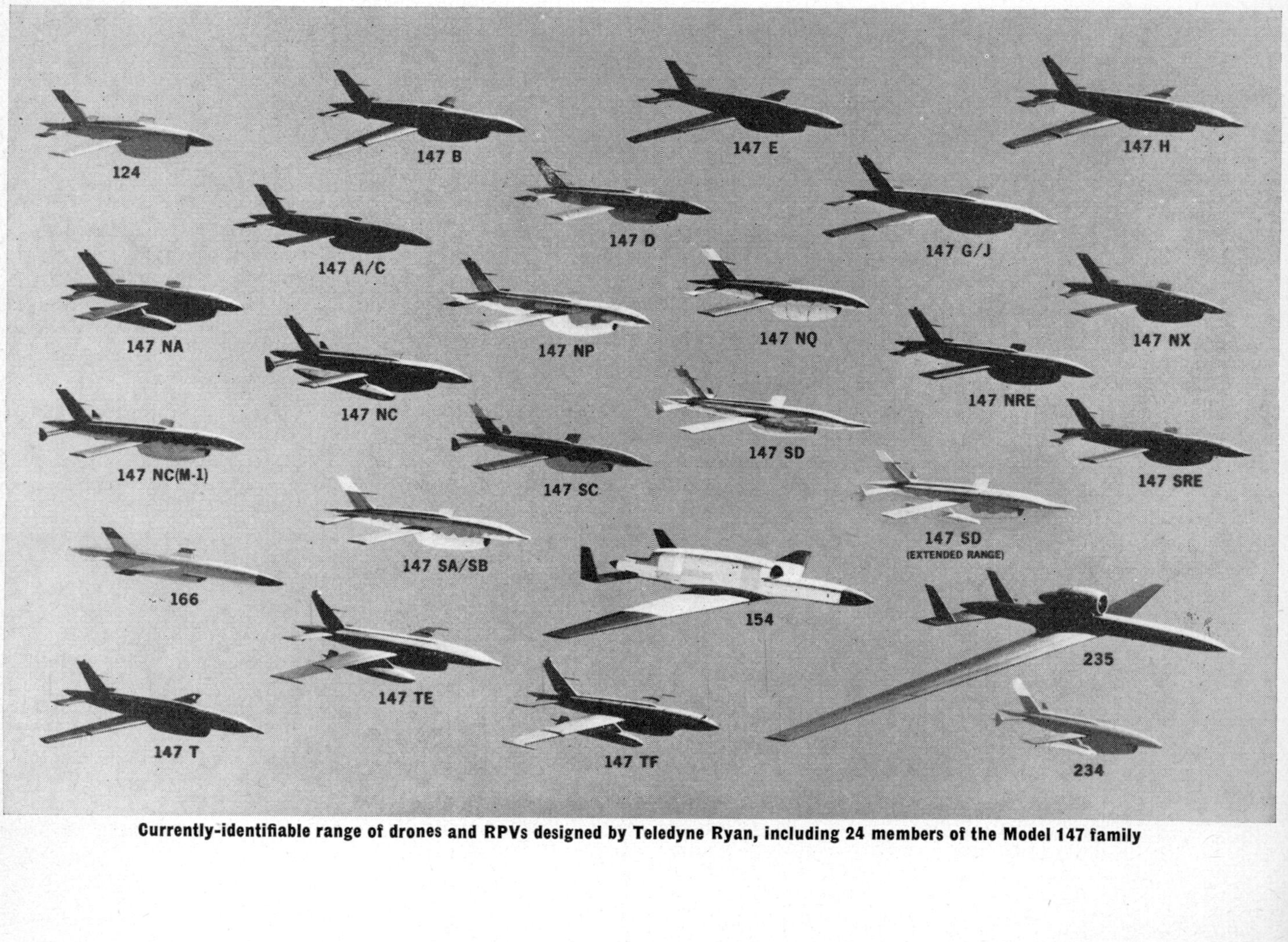

Currently-identifiable range of drones and RPVs designed by Teledyne Ryan, including 24 members of the Model 147 family

which can be ejected from the drone near an enemy radar target to pick up electronic intelligence data to facilitate an attack on the target by strike aircraft.

Model 147SD (Extended Range). Similar to standard 147SD, but with provision for carrying two underwing drop-tanks.

Model 147SK. Version evaluated by US Navy Air Development Center at Johnsville, Pennsylvania, under SPRA (Special Purpose Reconnaissance Aircraft) programme. Damaged RPV airframes displayed in Peking and by North Vietnam reported to include versions with this designation.

Model 147SRE (AQM-34K). Low-altitude night reconnaissance version, similar to other 147S models except for slightly shorter fuselage. No antenna fairing on top of fin.

Model 147T (AQM-34P). High-altitude surveillance version, with much-increased wing span of the 147H and Teledyne Ryan programme and command guidance system.

Model 147T-17. Damaged airframes displayed in Peking and by North Vietnam reported to include versions with this designation.

Model 147TE (AQM-34Q). Medium-altitude surveillance version. Teledyne Ryan programme and command guidance system and two underwing drop-tanks. With 147TF, is one of two models which formed part of USAF's Combat Dawn programme. Extended-span wings, with fences, have a slender tubular weight fairing at each wingtip and are of increased chord compared with other medium/high-altitude versions. Large bulbous data link antenna fairing on top of fin, and other aerials projecting from fuselage.

Model 147TF (AQM-34R). Second Combat Dawn version for Strategic Air Command: twenty reported to have been ordered in 1971. Airframe externally similar to 147TE, but probe-type fairing on nose is omitted and there is a small blade antenna on top of the nosecone. Said to be capable of cruising above 60,000 ft (18,300 m) at a speed of 420 knots (485 mph; 780 km/h).

Power Plants: All Model 147s have a single Teledyne CAE turbojet engine, as follows: 1,700 lb (771 kg) st J69-T-29 in 147NA, NC and NC(M-1); 1,920 lb (871 kg) st J69-T-41A in 147H, SC, SD, SD Loran, SRE and 124I; and 2,700 lb (1,225 kg) st J100-CA-100 in 147T, TE and TF.

Dimensions, external:
Wing span:
147SC 13 ft 0 in (3·96 m)
147NA, NC, NC(M-1), SD, SD Loran, SRE and 124I 14 ft 6 in (4·42 m)
147H, T, TE and TF 32 ft 0 in (9·75 m)
Length overall:
147NA, NC and NC(M-1) 26 ft 0 in (7·92 m)
147SRE 29 ft 0 in (8·84 m)
147H, SC, SD, SD Loran, T, TE and TF 30 ft 0 in (9·14 m)
124I 31 ft 0 in (9·45 m)
Body diameter:
147H, NA, NC, NC(M-1), SC, SD, SD Loran, SRE and 124I 3 ft 1·2 in (0·94 m)
147T, TE and TF 3 ft 3·6 in (1·01 m)

Weights:
Max launching weight:
147H 3,820 lb (1,732 kg)
147NA 3,684 lb (1,671 kg)
147NC 3,749 lb (1,700 kg)
147NC(M-1) 2,865 lb (1,299 kg)
147SC 3,065 lb (1,390 kg)
147SD and SD Loran 3,113 lb (1,412 kg)
147SRE 3,367 lb (1,527 kg)
147T 3,792 lb (1,720 kg)
147TE 3,870 lb (1,755 kg)
147TF:
without underwing stores 4,100 lb (1,859 kg)
with underwing stores 6,200 lb (2,812 kg)
124I 3,250 lb (1,474 kg)

DC-130E director aircraft of the USAF with a Ryan 154 (AQM-91A) drone beneath each wing

Teledyne Ryan 147SD (AQM-34M) RPV under the wing of a DC-130 Hercules director aircraft

TELEDYNE RYAN MODEL 154

USAF designation: AQM-91A

The Model 154 (known unofficially as the Firefly) is a large high-altitude reconnaissance and electronic surveillance RPV, launched and controlled by a Lockheed DC-130 Hercules director aircraft. Teledyne Ryan received the first development contract, under a programme costing several hundred million dollars, in 1966 after a design contest in which the Special Projects Group of North American Aviation also took part.

First confirmation of the flight status of the RPV came in the Summer of 1969, when a Model 154 on a test flight from Holloman AFB made an emergency parachute descent on to a roadway at Los Alamos Scientific Laboratory, New Mexico. The 154 was developed originally for operation over China, under the USAF's now-inactive Compass Arrow programme. Overflights of mainland China were halted in mid-1971.

The flattened undersurface of the airframe, with smooth curves elsewhere, and the over-fuselage mounting of the 5,270 lb (2,390 kg) st General Electric J97-GE-3 turbojet power plant, underline the care that was taken to reduce to a minimum radar reflectivity and susceptibility to lock-on by infra-red missiles, following the loss of a number of earlier types of RPV to Chinese ground defences.

The tail-fins are toed inward towards the tips, also to reduce radar reflectivity, and it is possible that the high aspect ratio sweptback wings are made of plastics. No landing gear is fitted, as the Model 154 utilises a parachute system for air-snatch recovery at the end of a mission.

Guidance to and from the target area is by a programmed navigation system utilising a

Teledyne Ryan Model 147TE remotely piloted vehicle (USAF designation AQM-34Q). Other versions of Model 147 are suspended from pylons of DC-130E launch aircraft in background

Teledyne Ryan AQM-34R (Model 147TF) being launched from a USAF Lockheed DC-130E control aircraft

Teledyne Ryan Doppler sensor, inertial stabilised platform and digital computer. Final recovery is by a Sperry Univac UPQ-3 microwave command guidance system, with a range of about 175 nm (200 miles; 320 km), operated from either a recovery aircraft or a ground station via transponders on the drone.

The basic reconnaissance sensor carried by the Model 154 is an Itek KA-80A optical bar panoramic camera, with a focal length of 24 in (61 cm). Weighing about 325 lb (147 kg) with a full magazine of film, this camera can take some 1,500 exposures, each 45 in (114 cm) long by 4·5 in (11·4 cm) wide, on each mission. Raytheon elint and HRB Singer infra-red sensors are also carried.

All Model 154s were put into storage in July 1973, but are available for re-activation if a requirement should arise.

DIMENSIONS, EXTERNAL:	
Wing span	48 ft 0 in (14·63 m)
Length overall	34 ft 0 in (10·36 m)
Body diameter	3 ft 2·4 in (0·975 m)
WEIGHT:	
Max launching weight	5,245 lb (2,379 kg)

TELEDYNE RYAN MODEL 166 FIREBEE II
US Navy designations: BQM-34E and BQM-34T
USAF designation: BQM-34F

Under contract to the US Navy and USAF, Teledyne Ryan Aeronautical is producing the Model 166 Firebee II supersonic target vehicle, an advanced development of the BQM-34A Firebee I which can provide aerial target presentations at above 60,000 ft (18,300 m) at a supersonic dash speed of Mach 1·5 for a period of 14 minutes.

Fourteen XBQM-34E development Firebee IIs were built under US Navy contract, and these underwent a successful operational test and evaluation programme in 1968-69. One static test airframe was also completed.

Two versions of the Firebee II are currently in production, as follows:

BQM-34E. For US Navy: total of 144 ordered by Spring 1974. First operational flight 29 March 1972, during exercises on the Atlantic Fleet Weapons Range. In service from 1973 with US Navy Squadron VC-8 in Puerto Rico. One BQM-34E, fitted experimentally with horizontal tail surfaces made of graphite epoxy material, made a successful first flight in this form on 7 December 1972. The US Navy BQM-34E targets delivered from mid-1974 onward incorporate a Motorola integrated track and control system (ITCS) and are designated **BQM-34T.**

BQM-34F. For US Air Force: total of 99 ordered by Spring 1974. Slightly heavier than BQM-34E, with corresponding adjustment of performance, due to different augmentation and scoring systems and addition of recovery parachute assembly required for mid-air retrieval system (MARS). Underwent operational testing and evaluation in 1973 with the USAF's 6514th Test Squadron at Edwards AFB, California.

Under an agreement announced in September 1968, the Guided Weapons Division of British Aircraft Corporation has licence rights, covering the UK, Australia, France and Denmark, to sell and manufacture the Firebee II.

To preserve the supersonic configuration, protuberances beyond the basic airframe lines are avoided by designing the external attachments and antennae to be flush. A nose radome, similar to that of the subsonic Firebee I, houses the scoring system antenna and passive augmentation. Directly behind this is the equipment compartment containing electrical, electronic and scoring systems, followed by the central fuselage, consisting of the fuel tank and structure for supporting the wing. The inlet and oil tank assembly is slung under the equipment compartment. The inlet duct passes from the inlet opening through the fuel tank to the engine, which is installed in a fuselage half-shell integral with the central fuselage structure. The entire aft portion of the fuselage is a removable sub-assembly which forms the upper shell, covering the engine.

Among the unusual design characteristics of the supersonic Firebee are its "clean" wings. No ailerons are used, roll control being achieved by differential deflection of the all-moving horizontal tail surfaces.

A modified Teledyne CAE J69-T-29 turbojet, designated YJ69-T-406, is fitted. This features a rearrangement of accessories to reduce frontal area, a modified compressor design to uprate thrust, and material changes in the radial compressor to permit supersonic operations at sea level.

TYPE: Remotely piloted supersonic jet target vehicle.

WINGS: Cantilever shoulder-wing monoplane. Sweepback 53° at leading-edge. Thickness/chord ratio 3%. Basic structure consists of aluminium honeycomb core, steel skins tapering from 0·10 to 0·012 in (2·5 to 0·3 mm) in thickness, steel leading-edge, machined aluminium trailing-edge and detachable aluminium wingtips. No ailerons.

FUSELAGE: Conventional aluminium semi-monocoque structure. Shear and torsional forces are carried by the skin. Longitudinal members such as side longerons, keel, riser, trough and skins carry the fuselage bending loads. Frames, bulkheads and formers shape and hold the skin to its contour. Glassfibre nose radome.

TAIL UNIT: Sweptback (45°) all-moving horizontal surfaces and sweptback (53°) tapered fin and rudder. The horizontal tail surfaces are used for both roll and pitch control. The control surfaces are actuated by an electro-hydraulic actuator unit; this is a self-contained package with two output shafts for the horizontal tail surfaces and one for the rudder, which is used for directional trim and yaw damping. Aluminium honeycomb cores, with steel skins tapering from 0·10 to 0·016 in (2·5-0·4 mm) in the horizontal tail surfaces, with machined aluminium leading- and trailing-edges and a steel machined attachment fitting. Fin consists of aluminium honeycomb core, steel skins tapering from 0·145 to 0·035 in (3·7-0·9 mm) in the central section, 0·015 in (0·38 mm) steel forward and aft skins, and aluminium leading- and trailing-edges. The fin tip is a glassfibre housing for antennae.

POWER PLANT: One 1,920 lb (871 kg) st Teledyne CAE YJ69-T-406 turbojet engine. Wing centre-section and main fuselage total fuel tank capacity 263 lb (119 kg) in BQM-34E. Auxiliary tank in forward fuselage of BQM-34F, containing an additional 80 lb (36 kg) of fuel. External fuel pod (both versions), capacity 400 lb (181 kg); weight of fuel plus tank, 463·5 lb (210·2 kg). With all tanks, the target will perform subsonic flight missions with similar performance capability, endurance and range to those of the subsonic BQM-34A. For supersonic flights, the external pod is jettisoned. Oil tank capacity 1·5 US gallons (5·75 litres). Provision for 11,300 lb (5,125 kg) st (nominal) solid-propellant JATO bottle.

SYSTEMS: Electrical power only. Primary power furnished by a 28V 200A DC engine-driven starter/generator. Power conversion by means of a 250VA 400Hz 115V AC static inverter. Power for recovery system and for drone control during glide phase furnished by a 28V 10Ah nickel-cadmium battery.

ELECTRONICS AND EQUIPMENT: AN/DLQ-2 and -3 ECM equipment, AN/USQ-11A and AN/DRQ-3A missile scoring system, low-altitude radar altimeter, AN/APX-71 L-band beacon, X-and/or C-band tracking beacons, special low-altitude kit for 50 ft (15 m) altitude. Augmentation includes travelling wave tube (TWT) in S-, C- and X-band; solid-state augmentation in P-band; passive radar reflectors. AN/DRW-29 radio control receiver. Teledyne Ryan AN/DRW-33 or Lear Siegler A/A37G-9 flight control system. AN/DLQ-2 control programmer. Dorsett AN/AKT-21 (TM-4-31A) telemetry system, with AN/DLQ-2 telemetry modulator.

LAUNCH AND RECOVERY: The Firebee II can be launched from either a ground or shipborne launcher, or air-launched from a modified DP-2E Neptune or DC-130A or E Hercules aircraft, in an essentially similar manner to the subsonic Firebee I. The DP-2E can carry two BQM-34Es underwing, and the DC-130 four BQM-34Fs; these may be launched from altitudes up to 18,000 ft (5,485 m) at approx 200 knots (230 mph; 370 km/h). Recovery is by a two-stage parachute system similar to that

Teledyne Ryan Model 166 Firebee II supersonic target, in production for the US Air Force and Navy

fitted to the Firebee I, and the Firebee II also can be recovered after landing on water or (BQM-34F only) by helicopter mid-air retrieval system (MARS). In a MARS recovery, the helicopter snares an 18 ft 9 in (5·72 m) diameter engagement parachute which extends above the 79 ft 0 in (24·08 m) main parachute. Once engaged, the main parachute is released pyrotechnically to allow the helicopter to reel in the Firebee II and transport it back to the target operations area. Provision is also made for emergency recovery. In both versions, the recovery parachutes are housed in the fuselage tailcone.

GUIDANCE AND CONTROL: Remote control of the BQM-34F, including activation of the recovery system, is accomplished by a frequency-modulated UHF radio guidance system, with 20 separate command channels, utilising an

US Navy BQM-34E Firebee II, launched from a Neptune control aircraft over the Atlantic Fleet Weapons Range near San Juan, Puerto Rico

AN/DRW-29 on-board radio receiver and a compatible transmitter at the remote control station. This receiver is installed in the nose equipment compartment, and the antenna is located in the glassfibre fin-tip. A Motorola ITCS (integrated track and control system) is fitted in the BQM-34T version. The Firebee II has an automatic flight control system (AFCS) consisting of six elements: a three-axis rate gyro, vertical gyro, air data computer, flight control box, low-altitude control box,and three-axis electro-hydraulic actuator assembly. Positioning data during a flight is provided to the remote control station by an on-board Vega 312S S-band radar beacon, the antennae for which are located on top of the nose compartment (for receiving) and in the lower aft portion of the fuselage (for transmitting). To relay data to the remote controller, a 10-channel telemetry system is used which comprises data collection, conversion and FM/FM transmitting equipment in the drone and receiving and data display units in the remote control station. When engine or generator power is shut down at high altitude, either by remote command or because of fuel depletion, the flight control system continues to operate on battery power. The recovery sequence is preceded, at altitudes above 15,000 ft (4,570 m), by a power-off glide, and can be initiated by remote command at any time during the glide. When necessary to gain altitude and reduce speed for safe parachute deployment and recovery, a power-off climb is initiated automatically below 15,000 ft either by normal recovery command or if there is a loss of engine power or a generator failure.

Operational Equipment: In general, Firebee II can be equipped with active and passive radar augmenters, electronic and photographic scoring systems, ECM, low-altitude radar sensing systems and infra-red flares. Augmentation equipment in the BQM-34F, for weapon systems evaluation and personnel training, includes provisions for target identification, GCI tracking, variable radar-image size and augmented infra-red radiation. There is a smoke system to aid long-distance visual identification at altitudes of 20,000 ft (6,100 m) and above; a low-altitude smoke generator is under development, as is a 6 in (15 cm) diameter wingtip pod containing a long-life infra-red source using a propane burner. (Standard infra-red source is heated electrically.) Positive electronic identification is provided by an AN/DPN-82 L-band IFF beacon. An X-band travelling wave tube (TWT) system is employed to provide radar echo augmentation in various patterns, by the use of specially-designed antenna systems, to represent various sizes of target. Two scoring systems have been evaluated for the BQM-34F: a digital Doppler system (DIGIDOPS) and the AN/GSQ-29 multiple airborne target trajectory system (MATTS). The US Navy BQM-34E version has different augmenters (including a nose-mounted Luneberg lens) and scoring equipment from the BQM-34F.

Dimensions, external:

Wing span:	
BQM-34E	8 ft 10·8 in (2·71 m)
BQM-34F	9 ft 7·9 in (2·95 m)
Length overall:	
BQM-34E	28 ft 3 in (8·61 m)
BQM-34F	29 ft 1·9 in (8·89 m)
Body diameter	2 ft 0 in (0·61 m)
Height overall	5 ft 7·2 in (1·71 m)
Tailplane span	4 ft 9·6 in (1·46 m)

Weights (A: BQM-34E; B: BQM-34F):

Weight empty:	
A	1,452 lb (658 kg)
B	1,721·4 lb (780·8 kg)
Max launching weight:	
A, air launch	1,886·5 lb (855·7 kg)
B, air launch	2,097 lb (951 kg)
A, ground launch	2,264·5 lb (1,027·2 kg)
B, ground launch	2,475 lb (1,122·5 kg)

Water pickup of a Firebee II. Note the inflated flotation bag at the rear of the drone

Performance:

Max speed:	
at S/L	Mach 1·1
at 45,000 ft (13,715 m):	
A	Mach 1·8
B	Mach 1·78
above 60,000 ft (18,300 m)	Mach 1·5
Operating height range	50 ft (15 m) to 60,000 ft (18,300 m)
Service ceiling:	
A	60,000 ft (18,300 m)
B	55,000 ft (16,765 m)
Control range	200 nm (230 miles; 370 km)
Typical range, external tank on:	
low-altitude, subsonic cruise/transonic dash	221 nm (254 miles; 409 km)
high-altitude, subsonic cruise/supersonic dash	606 nm (698 miles; 1,123 km)
high-altitude, subsonic cruise throughout	617 nm (710 miles; 1,142 km)
Max range	774 nm (891 miles; 1,434 km)
Endurance (total time)	1 hr 14 min
Flotation time	24 hr

TELEDYNE RYAN MODEL 234

USAF designation: BGM-34

Although this RPV shares the Firebee I parentage of the Model 147/AQM-34, it has been developed primarily for tactical strike and other defence suppression roles, reflecting plans to evolve combat drones for a variety of missions which at present require manned aircraft.

Details have been announced of three versions, as follows:

BGM-34A. Two built to evaluate the feasibility of using RPVs to deliver defence suppression weapons by day, under real-time control. Initial trials, held at Edwards AFB, California, and the US Army's Dugway Proving Ground, Utah, have involved the release of single Shrike anti-radiation missiles, Maverick TV-guided missiles, and HOBOS homing bombs, with good results, against mockups of Soviet Fansong SA-2 ground radars and other targets. Development is continuing to permit multiple weapons to be carried and launched. The RPVs themselves have a Sperry Univac radio command guidance system and are directed from their DC-130 launch aircraft via a TV camera mounted in the nose of the RPV. Power plant is a 1,700 lb (771 kg) st Teledyne CAE J69-T-29 turbojet engine.

BGM-34B. Generally similar to BGM-34A, but with 1,920 lb (871 kg) st J69-T-41A engine, modified tail unit, enlarged control surfaces, and added operational capability. Eight ordered. Sperry Univac radio command guidance system. One or two BGM-34Bs have been fitted with an extended, modified nose containing a low light level TV camera and a Philco-Ford stabilised laser designator/receiver system weighing 250 lb (113 kg). The TV-carrying nose section can be rotated upward or downward, to keep the target in view during an attack. The equipment, similar to that contained in the Philco-Ford Pave Knife pods carried by F-4D Phantoms for use with laser-guided "smart bombs", enables the BGM-34B to act in a pathfinder role, locating and locking on to a target and signalling its position to other RPVs, carrying weapons, in the force.

One other BGM-34B has been fitted with a Hughes high-resolution FLIR (forward-looking infra-red) nose sensor instead of the TV installation. During tests at Hill AFB, Utah, and the Wendover/Dugway test range in the early months of 1974, BGM-34B RPVs successfully made single and multiple passes against a variety of targets, launching a number of live and inert weapons. These included SPASMs (self-propelled air-to-surface missiles), developed by the USAF Armament Development and Test Center at Eglin AFB, Florida, and Hughes AGM-65

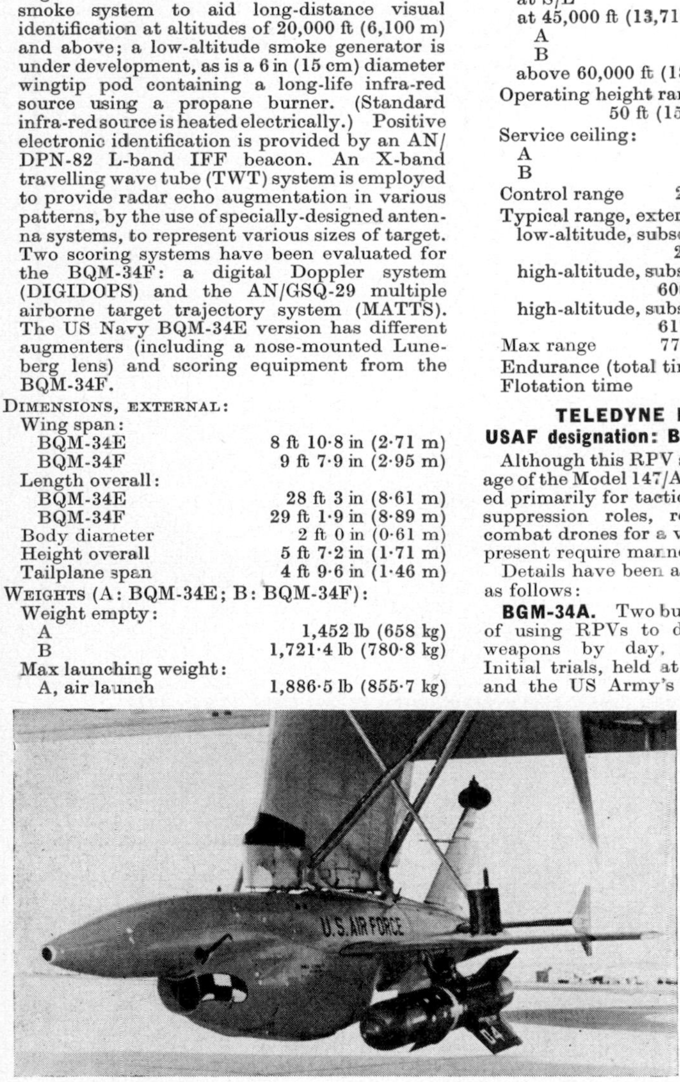

Above: **Teledyne Ryan 234 (BGM-34A) fitted with a HOBOS homing bomb under its port wing**

Right: **Shrike missile (starboard) and Mk IV bomb fitted under the wings of a Teledyne Ryan Model 234 (BGM-34A) strike RPV**

Maverick TV-guided missiles. Evaluation of the BGM-34B in the weapon-carrying role was continuing in 1974 as a part of the USAF's Pave Strike programme for precision air-to-ground strike concepts.

BGM-34C. Proposed interim multi-mission RPV, with modular nose sections for reconnaissance, electronic warfare or strike missions. For air or ground launch.

Dimensions, external (BGM-34A and B):
- Wing span: 14 ft 6 in (4·42 m)
- Length overall:
  - BGM-34A: 23 ft 7·2 in (7·19 m)
  - BGM-34B: 26 ft 0 in (7·92 m)
- Body diameter: 3 ft 1·2 in (0·94 m)

Weights (BGM-34A and B):
- Max launching weight:
  - BGM-34A: 2,800 lb (1,270 kg)
  - BGM-34B: 3,230 lb (1,465 kg)

TELEDYNE RYAN MODEL 235 R-TERN (COMPASS COPE R)

USAF designation: YQM-98A

This high-altitude aircraft was ordered by the USAF in 1972 for evaluation in its Compass Cope programme for a signal intelligence collection RPV. Brief details of this programme are given in the description of the Boeing Compass Cope B (YQM-94A) vehicle (which see).

Representing a third-generation vehicle to follow the Model 147H/AQM-34N and Model 154/AQM-91A, the Teledyne Ryan Model 235 has extremely high aspect ratio wings and an overfuselage pod mounting for its power plant. Design features of the Garrett ATF 3 engine configuration are such as to produce a low infrared signature, low radar reflectivity, very low smoke and noise emissions, and a capability for very high altitude operation. A decision whether to adopt a single- or twin-engined configuration for any selected Compass Cope production aircraft will not, however, be taken until after analysis of flight test results, and will not necessarily select the ATF 3 as power plant. The YQM-98A, like the Boeing Compass Cope vehicle, has a tricycle landing gear for normal runway take-offs and landings. Detachable forward and aft fuselage sections and outer wing panels permit the aircraft to be dismantled for air transportation.

Two YQM-98A prototypes were ordered, under a $10·1 million cost-plus-fixed-fee contract awarded by the USAF's Aeronautical Systems Division on 13 June 1972. First materials were ordered in December 1972, and prototype construction began in February 1973. Completion was achieved on 21 December 1973, and both prototypes (72-01871 and '872) were rolled out on 4 January 1974, the first time that Teledyne Ryan had delivered two prototypes of a major new aircraft simultaneously.

Delivery was made to Edwards AFB in April 1974, and the first flight took place on 17 July 1974.

Type: Prototype high-altitude long-endurance strategic RPV.

Wings: Cantilever low-wing monoplane, of very high aspect ratio. Approx 1° anhedral from roots. Sweepback approx 7° at quarter-chord. Two-section ailerons on each trailing-edge, inboard of outer panels. Four-section spoilers on each upper surface. Triangular fillet on each trailing-edge at root. Conventional semi-monocoque structure, with selected use of composite materials. Detachable 14 ft (4·27 m) outer panels have an aluminium core and graphite composite skin; trailing-edges and fairings make extensive use of DuPont PRD 49 glassfibre.

Fuselage: Semi-monocoque structure, of approximately rectangular cross-section with rounded upper edges, tapering towards front and rear. Undersurface flared and flattened to reduce radar reflectivity. Nose, tailcone and parts of fuselage are components from AQM-91A. Nosecone, forward fuselage and tailcone are detachable for transportation.

Tail Unit: Cantilever low-set swept tailplane, with twin sweptback fins and overhanging rudders at approx half-span. Sweepback approx 32° on tailplane leading-edge, approx 34° on fin leading-edges. Full-span elevators. Part of tailplane is component from AQM-91A.

Landing Gear: Retractable tricycle type. Single-wheel main units, modified from those of a Cessna A-37, retract inward into wings; nosewheel unit, from a Canadair CF-5, retracts rearward.

Power Plant: Prototypes are each powered by one Garrett-AiResearch ATF 3 (XF104-GA-100) turbofan engine, rated (early 1974) at 4,050 lb (1,837 kg) st, mounted in a pod on a shallow pylon on top of the fuselage, in line with the wings. Design thrust of this engine is 5,000 lb (2,268 kg). Fully-automatic electronic fuel control system. Fuel tank in each inboard wing panel, each with refuelling point on wing upper surface, and in fuselage.

Systems and Equipment: Equipment compartments in nose and tail portions of fuselage. Main mission payload compartment in lower forward fuselage, with provision for additional payload to be carried in rear fuselage. Provision for manually-controlled, semi-automatic or fully-automatic (Singer Kearfott Talar microwave approach) landing system. Details of other systems and equipment are not available officially, but these are expected to include an integrated flight control system.

Guidance and Control: Teledyne Ryan radio command guidance system.

Dimensions, external:
- Wing span: 81 ft 2 in (24·74 m)
- Wing aspect ratio: 19
- Length overall: approx 38 ft 4 in (11·68 m)
- Length of fuselage: 37 ft 4 in (11·38 m)
- Fuselage: Max depth: 2 ft 7 in (0·79 m)
- Height overall: 7 ft 11 in (2·41 m)
- Tailplane span: 21 ft 5 in (6·53 m)
- Wheel track: approx 7 ft 6 in (2·29 m)
- Wheelbase: 10 ft 1 in (3·07 m)

Area:
- Wings, gross: 347 sq ft (32·24 m^2)

Weights and Loadings (approx):
- Weight empty: 5,600 lb (2,540 kg)
- Payload for 24 hr mission: 700 lb (317·5 kg)
- Max T-O weight: 14,300 lb (6,486 kg)
- Min wing loading: 16 lb/sq ft (78 kg/m^2)
- Max wing loading: 41 lb/sq ft (200 kg/m^2)

Performance (estimated):
- Cruising speed at altitudes from 50,000 to 70,000 ft (15,240 to 21,340 m): Mach 0·5 to 0·6
- T-O field length: 3,500 ft (1,067 m)
- Max endurance: 30 hr

TELEDYNE RYAN MODEL 251

US Army designation: MQM-34D/MOD II

Under contract to the US Army Missile Command, Teledyne Ryan is modifying existing examples of the MQM-34D (see under description of Model 124 Firebee I) to MQM-34D/MOD II configuration. This version is designed to meet requirements for high subsonic speeds in excess of 600 knots (691 mph; 1,112 km/h) for sustained performance during high-gravity manoeuvres (more than 7*g*). It is fitted with a 2,950 lb (1,338 kg) st General Electric J85-GE-4A turbojet engine, offering 75 per cent more thrust than the power plant of the standard Firebee I, and is fitted with an ASMK (advanced serpentine manoeuvrability kit). In addition to the change of engine, the aircraft's nacelle sections have been redesigned so that the fuselage is now fatter, with the air intake located in the extreme nose; the ventral fin has been deleted, and endplate auxiliary fins added to the tailplane.

An initial test batch of four were modified, the first of which was air-launched for the first time on 14 March 1973 over White Sands Missile Range, New Mexico. First ground launch followed on 9 April 1973. The test programme was originally scheduled to comprise 10 flights, but the early results proved so successful that the programme was terminated after completion of the seventh flight on 11 June 1973, during which two 7*g* turns were made at 12,000 ft (3,660 m) and three at 8,000 ft (2,440 m). Further evaluation tests have since been initiated with the procurement of four more modified targets to meet early firing schedules. A number of MOD II Firebees will then become available to support new development, test and evaluation programmes for the Chaparral, Stinger and other advanced weapon systems.

Type: High-subsonic remotely piloted jet target vehicle.

Wings and Fuselage: As Model 124, except for necessary modifications to provide engine air intake in nose.

Tail Unit: As Model 124, but with endplate fins on tailplane instead of ventral fin.

Power Plant: One General Electric J85-GE-4A turbojet engine, rated at 2,950 lb (1,338 kg) st. Air intake optimised for high speed and high

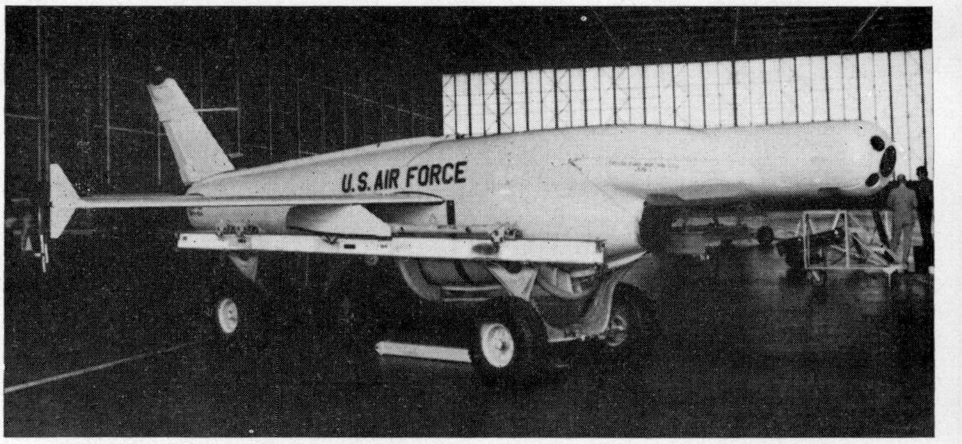

Pathfinder version of the BGM-34B, fitted with Philco-Ford nose package containing laser designator and LLLTV camera (*Henry Artof*)

YQM-98A Compass Cope R photographed during its first flight, 17 July 1974

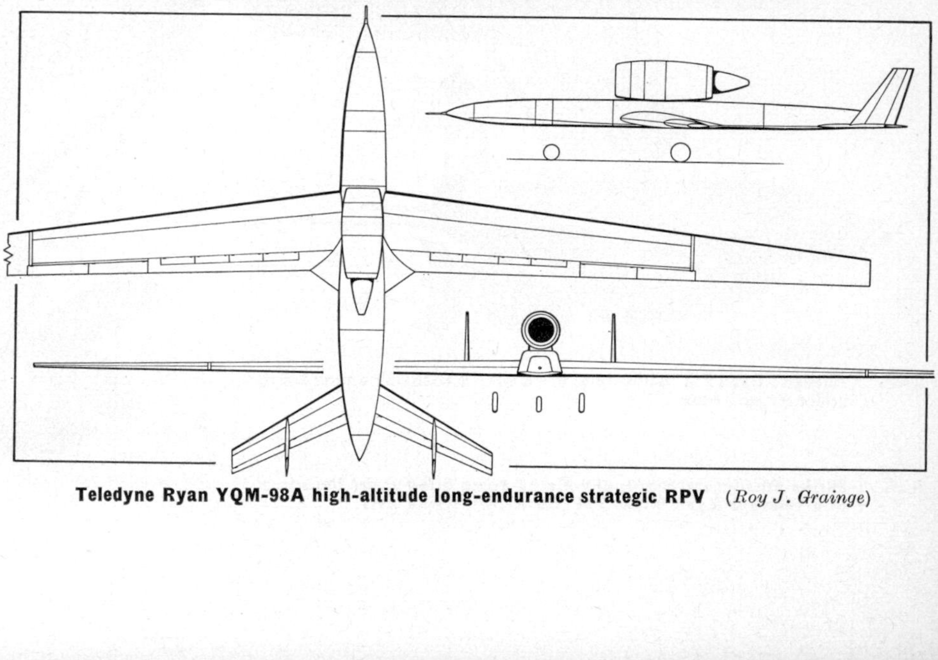

Teledyne Ryan YQM-98A high-altitude long-endurance strategic RPV (*Roy J. Grainge*)

angle of attack. Fuel system and capacity as Model 124.

Systems, Electronics and Equipment: As Model 124

Dimensions, external:
As Model 124, except:
Length overall 21 ft 8·54 in (6·62 m)
Fuselage: Max depth 3 ft 10·41 in (1·18 m)
Height overall 6 ft 8·41 in (2·04 m)

Areas:
As Model 124, except:
No ventral fin
Endplate fins (total) 3·17 sq ft (0·295 m^2)

Weights and Loadings:
Weight empty 1,600 lb (725·5 kg)
Payload 400 lb (181·5 kg)
Fuel 700 lb (317 kg)
Max launching weight 2,700 lb (1,224 kg)
Max wing loading 75 lb/sq ft (366 kg/m^2)
Max power loading 0·91 lb/lb st (0·91 kg/kg st)

Performance:
Max never-exceed speed Mach 0·98
Max level speed at S/L 625 knots (720 mph; 1,158 km/h)
Max cruising speed at S/L 600 knots (691 mph; 1,112 km/h)
Econ cruising speed at 45,000 ft (13,720 m) 460 knots (530 mph; 852 km/h)
Stalling speed (at operating weight) at S/L 100 knots (115·5 mph; 185·5 km/h)
Max rate of climb at S/L 35,000 ft (10,668 m)/min
Engine-limited ceiling 45,000 ft (13,720 m)
Range with max fuel, no reserves 700 nm (806 miles; 1,297 km)
Range with max payload, no reserves 650 nm (748 miles; 1,204 km)

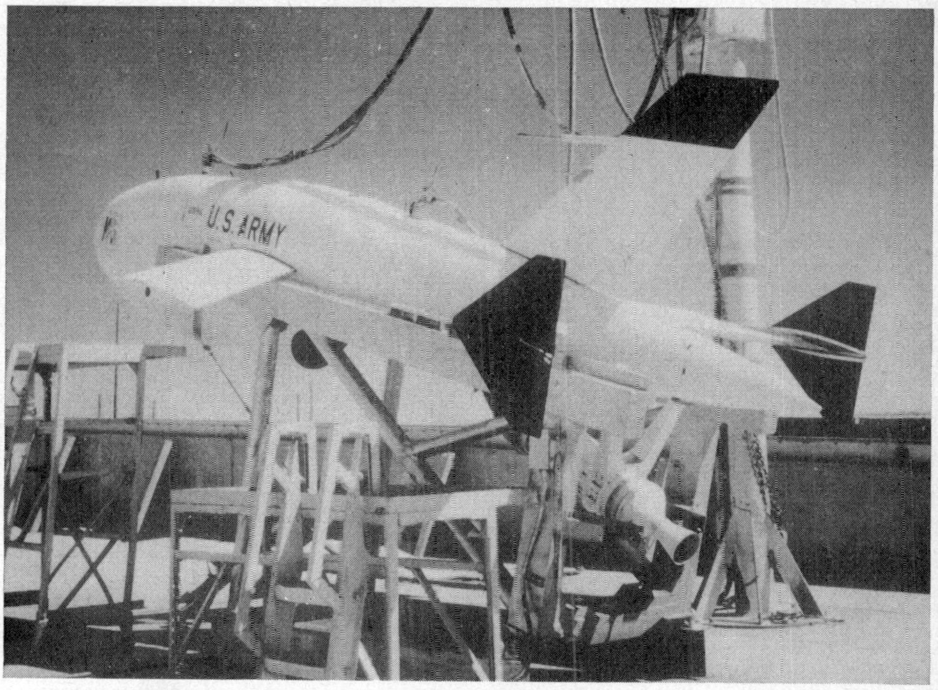

MQM-34D/MOD II version of the Firebee I, with General Electric J85 engine and nose intake

US DEPARTMENT OF DEFENSE

Address:
The Pentagon, Washington, DC 20301
Telephone: Liberty 5-6700

In addition to drone/RPV programmes for which "hardware" contracts have been awarded (described under the appropriate contractor's heading in this section), the following are among the more important programmes which are or were recently receiving attention by the three US services:

USAF PROGRAMMES

Advanced Multi-Mission RPV. Intended successor to the Teledyne Ryan BGM-34C, for service in the early 1980s. Designs, to be invited in 1975 from two or three competing companies, may incorporate a drone control and data retrieval system (CDRS) and data relay by Compass Cope-type RPVs.

Constant Angel. Electronic warfare programme involving two types of ground-launched RPV: a high-subsonic tactical expendable drone system (TEDS), to act as a decoy, and an orbiting jamming vehicle. Original plans to issue RFPs (Requests For Proposals) for the TEDS vehicle to two competing contractors in October 1972 were deferred when proposed funding for this stage was deleted from the FY 1974 budget request. The TEDS programme was re-introduced in FY 1975, and may involve USAF evaluation of the contending vehicles in the US Army's VSTT programme (see entries under Beech and Northrop in this section).

LAMPS (Low-Altitude Multi-Purpose System). Priority programme to develop a low-altitude long-range RPV; not to be confused with US Navy's Light Airborne Multi-Purpose System involving manned helicopters.

Recovery Systems. Several alternative recovery system studies are under way, both for the improvement of the present mid-air retrieval system (MARS) and for alternatives to this system. Concepts being examined include ACLS (air cushion landing systems), ALS (automatic take-off and landing systems), VTOL vehicles, recovery and storage by a large launch aircraft such as the Boeing 747, arrester gear systems and steerable recovery parachutes. An ALS is intended for any production version of the Compass Cope RPV; the E-Systems L450F has been mentioned as a possible ALS test vehicle.

RED (Reconnaissance Engineering Directorate, USAF Systems Command). Following the construction and successful flight testing of a "mini-RPV" in 1971, this Directorate is now overseeing a larger development programme for small, low-cost battlefield RPVs in which designs have been submitted by Lockheed Missiles and Space Co, LTV Aerospace, McDonnell Douglas Astronautics and Philco-Ford.

US Naval Air Development Center QF-4B drone conversion of a McDonnell Douglas F-4B Phantom

US ARMY PROGRAMMES

RPAODS (Remotely Piloted Aerial Observation Designation System). Programme to develop a small, low-cost battlefield RPV, equipped with TV relay and laser designation systems, to find and mark targets for remotely-fired laser-guided weapons. Requests for proposals were issued in mid-1974. The US Army has meanwhile acquired vehicles designed or built by E-Systems, Fairchild, Johns Hopkins University Applied Physics Laboratory and Philco-Ford for evaluation under this programme. Kaman is undertaking, as a private venture, design studies for a rotating-wing vehicle which would meet the RPAODS requirement.

US NAVY PROGRAMMES

Naval Air Development Center QF-4B. For use by the Naval Missile Center, the NADC at Warminster, Pennsylvania, has converted a McDonnell Douglas F-4B Phantom (serial number 148365) to QF-4B configuration. This aircraft was delivered in the Spring of 1972 to the NMC at Point Mugu, California, for further flight development and subsequent use as a supersonic manoeuvring target for new missile development.

Flight testing was completed in January 1974, and the target certificated for use when the prototype QF-4B was flown as a drone for a missile system test. By 1 March 1974 seven F-4B aircraft were in various stages of conversion to QF-4B target aircraft.

Naval Weapons Center QF-86. Twenty-nine North American F-86 Sabres were undergoing conversion in the Spring of 1974, at the Naval Weapons Center, China Lake, California, into QF-86 pilotless target aircraft. The QF-86 is an interim, all-attitude manoeuvring target pending the development of a new, highly-manoeuvrable drone known as **NAT** (Navy Agile Target). Modifications in the QF-86 include an on-board TV camera, Sperry autopilot, a non-redundant proportional control system and a telemetry system.

WINDECKER

WINDECKER INDUSTRIES INC

Address:
PO Box 6288, Midland, Texas 79701
Telephone: (915) 563-1700

Officers:
See "Aircraft" section

Windecker is conducting a programme of research and development connected with low-cost RPVs. Details of this work are classified, though it has been reported that the programme includes work on an ECM decoy/jammer type of vehicle.

In early 1973 Windecker delivered to the USAF a version of its Eagle 1 aircraft designated YE-5; reference to this is made under the company's entry in the US "Aircraft" section. The YE-5 is being used for manned flights, but the object of these tests is to assess the value of plastics materials in developing future RPVs with a low radar response.

SAILPLANES

ARGENTINE REPUBLIC

AEROFIBRA

DIPL ING THEO ALTINGER

ADDRESS:
Tigre, near Buenos Aires

AEROFIBRA LENTICULAR 15S

A prototype of this single-seat high-performance sailplane, designed and built by Dipl Ing Altinger, was completed and flown successfully in the national championships in 1972. Assisted by a $10,000 loan from the Federacion Argentina de Vuelo a Vela (Argentine Soaring Association), it is being followed by a pre-series batch of 10 Lenticulars, of which three had been delivered by 31 January 1973. The remainder were due to be completed by the end of 1973, and to be used for flight trials by a number of Argentine flying clubs. Further production will depend upon the outcome of these trials.

TYPE: Single-seat Standard Class sailplane.

WINGS: Cantilever mid-wing monoplane of constant chord, built in three portions. Wortmann FX-61-168 wing section. Incidence —3°. Dihedral on outer panels. No sweepback. Glassfibre construction, with laminated 480 × 800 mm box-spar. Ailerons and landing flaps on trailing-edge.

FUSELAGE: Glassfibre semi-monocoque structure.

TAIL UNIT: Cantilever T-tail. Rectangular tailplane, with inset tab. Sweptback fin and rudder.

LANDING GEAR: Retractable monowheel, and tailwheel, semi-recessed in fuselage.

ACCOMMODATION: Single seat under fully-transparent moulded canopy.

DIMENSIONS, EXTERNAL:
Wing span 49 ft 2½ in (15·00 m)
Wing aspect ratio 18·8
Length overall 21 ft 4 in (6·50 m)
Height overall 4 ft 7 in (1·40 m)

DIMENSIONS, INTERNAL:
Cabin: Max height 2 ft 11½ in (0·90 m)
Max width 1 ft 11½ in (0·60 m)

AREA:
Wings, gross 129·2 sq ft (12·00 m²)

WEIGHTS AND LOADING:
Weight empty 441 lb (200 kg)
Max T-O weight 683 lb (310 kg)
Max wing loading 5·30 lb/sq ft (25·9 kg/m²)

PERFORMANCE:
Best glide ratio at 46·5 knots (53 mph; 86 km/h) 32
Min sinking speed at 38 knots (43 mph; 70 km/h) 2·13 ft (0·65 m)/sec
Stalling speed 32·5 knots (37·5 mph; 60 km/h)
Max speed (smooth air) 127 knots (146 mph; 235 km/h)
Max speed (rough air) 90·5 knots (104 mph; 168 km/h)
Max aero-tow speed 80 knots (92 mph; 148 km/h)
Max winch-launching speed 64·5 knots (74·5 mph; 120 km/h)

Aerofibra Lenticular 15S single-seat Standard Class sailplane *(Alex Reinhard)*

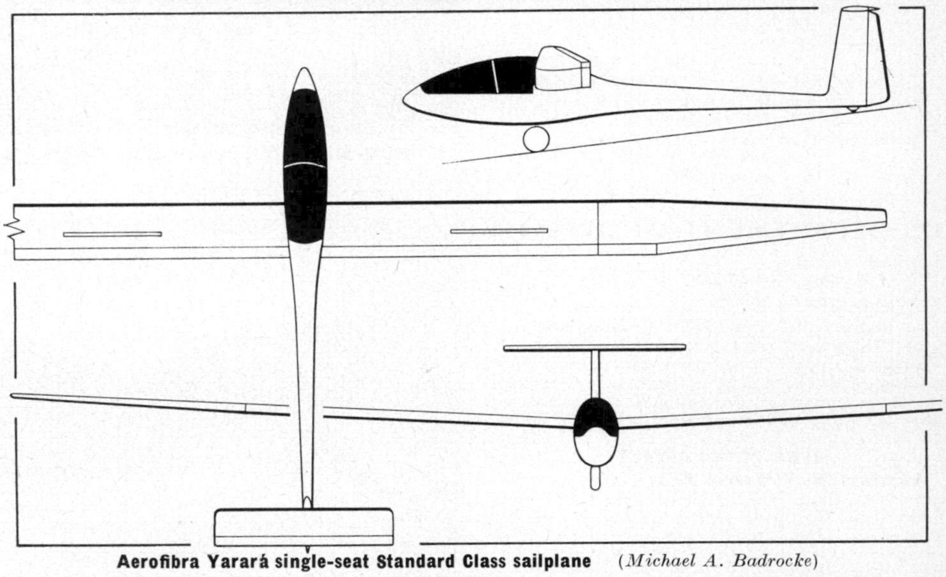

Aerofibra Yarará single-seat Standard Class sailplane *(Michael A. Badrocke)*

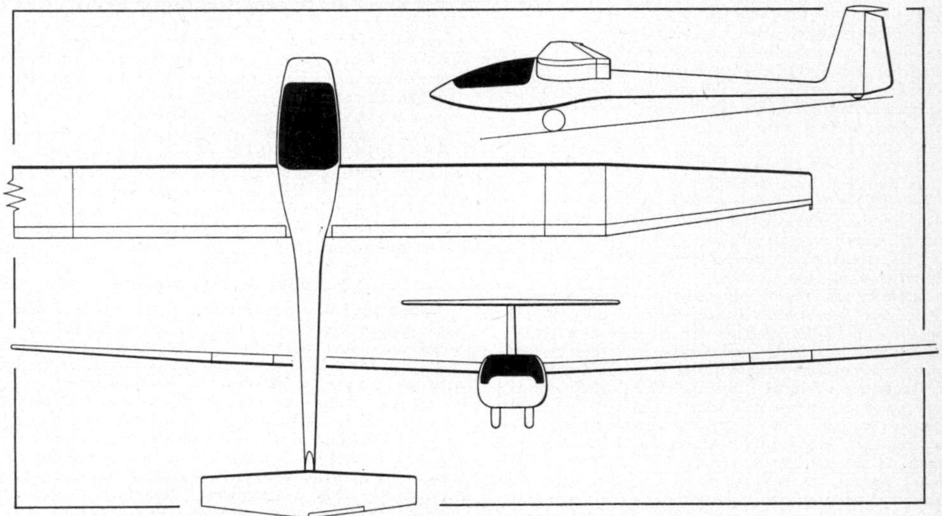

Aerofibra Biguá side-by-side two-seat training sailplane *(Michael A. Badrocke)*

AEROFIBRA YARARÁ

The Yarará is a single-seat Standard Class sailplane of glassfibre-reinforced plastics construction. First flight was due to have taken place in 1973.

The rectangular centre-section of the wing has a Wortmann FX-67-K-150 section, the outer panels tapering to Wortmann FX-60-126 at the tip. A retractable monowheel landing gear is fitted.

DIMENSION, EXTERNAL:
Wing span 49 ft 2½ in (15·00 m)

PERFORMANCE (estimated):
Min sinking speed at 38 knots (43·5 mph; 70 km/h) 1·64 ft (0·50 m)/sec

AEROFIBRA BIGUÁ

The Biguá is a side-by-side two-seat training sailplane, which was due to have flown in 1973. It has a retractable twin-wheel landing gear.

DIMENSIONS, EXTERNAL:
Wing span 55 ft 8¾ in (17·00 m)
Wing aspect ratio 15·8
Length overall 25 ft 7 in (7·80 m)

WEIGHT AND LOADING:
Max T-O weight 1,212 lb (550 kg)
Max wing loading 6·14 lb/sq ft (30 kg/m²)

PERFORMANCE (estimated, at max T-O weight):
Best glide ratio at 54 knots (62 mph; 100 km/h) 35
Min sinking speed at 41 knots (47 mph; 75 km/h) approx 2·3 ft (0·70 m)/sec
Max never-exceed speed (smooth air) 133 knots (153 mph; 247 km/h)
Max level speed 90 knots (104 mph; 167 km/h)

AVEX

ASOCIACION ARGENTINA DE CONSTRUCTORES DE AVIONES EXPERIMENTALES

ADDRESS:
Acasusso 1640, Olivos, FCNGBM, Buenos Aires

Telephone: 797-1629

OFFICERS: See "Aircraft" section

BERCA JB-1 NAHUEL (TIGER)

Sr Jorge Berca, an architect of Rosario, Santa Fé, and a member of AVEX, has built and flown a single-seat sailplane of his own design. Design began in December 1971, construction in April 1972, and the Nahuel flew for the first time on 10 September 1973.

WINGS: Cantilever high-wing monoplane. Wing section Wortmann FX-61-168 at root, FX-61-126 at tip. Dihedral on outer panels 4°. Incidence 4°. Single wooden spar at 36% chord. Spruce and birch plywood covering back to 57% chord and on ailerons; remainder fabric-covered. Schempp-Hirth aluminium and wood airbrakes at 60% chord above and below wings.

FUSELAGE: Conventional structure of pine longerons with 5 mm marine plywood covering.

TAIL UNIT: Cantilever T-tail, of fabric-covered wood construction. Fixed-incidence tailplane with one-piece elevator. Tab on elevator.

LANDING GEAR: Non-retractable monowheel and tailwheel.

ACCOMMODATION: Single seat under fully-transparent moulded canopy.

DIMENSIONS, EXTERNAL:
Wing span 47 ft 8¾ in (14·55 m)
Wing chord at root 3 ft 7¼ in (1·10 m)
Wing chord at tip 1 ft 9½ in (0·55 m)
Wing aspect ratio 15·4
Length overall 22 ft 7¾ in (6·90 m)
Height overall 4 ft 11 in (1·50 m)
Tailplane span 9 ft 10 in (3·00 m)

AREAS:
Wings, gross 147·7 sq ft (13·72 m²)
Ailerons (total) 12·92 sq ft (1·20 m²)
Airbrakes (total) 6·46 sq ft (0·60 m²)
Fin 5·17 sq ft (0·48 m²)
Rudder 6·24 sq ft (0·58 m²)

Tailplane 11·30 sq ft (1·05 m^2)
Elevator, incl tab 8·61 sq ft (0·80 m^2)

WEIGHTS AND LOADING:
Weight empty, equipped 595 lb (270 kg)
Max T-O weight 837 lb (380 kg)
Max wing loading 5·65 lb/sq ft (27·6 kg/m^2)

PERFORMANCE:
Max never-exceed speed 129 knots (149 mph; 240 km/h)
Stalling speed 34 knots (39 mph; 62 km/h)
Landing from 50 ft (15 m) 475 ft (145 m)
Landing run 150 ft (45 m)

LANZALONE AULANZ

The Aulanz is a single-seat powered sailplane which, with its 30 hp engine and propeller, has been designed and is being built by Sr Augusto Lanzalone of Rosario, Santa Fé. Sr Lanzalone has also evolved, for use in its construction, his own alloy of aluminium (with copper, nickel, magnesium, silicon and chrome), which he has named Alcusing; and also his own furnace (for heat-treating the fuselage) and rivet gun. By the Spring of 1973 the fuselage and tail unit were completed; construction of the wings was under way in the Spring of 1974. General appearance of the Aulanz is shown in the accompanying three-view drawing.

TYPE: Single-seat homebuilt powered sailplane.

WINGS: Cantilever low-wing monoplane, of all-metal (Alcusing) construction. Wortmann FX-61-147 wing section. Incidence 4°.

FUSELAGE: All-metal (Alcusing) semi-monocoque structure.

TAIL UNIT: Cantilever all-metal structure, of similar construction to wings.

LANDING GEAR: Retractable monowheel and tailskid. Rubber shock-absorbers.

POWER PLANT: One 30 hp 700 cc Lanzalone two-cylinder two-stroke inverted in-line engine, driving a two-blade variable-pitch metal (Alcusing) propeller. Fuel capacity 4·4 Imp gallons (20 litres).

ACCOMMODATION: Single seat under one-piece transparent canopy.

DIMENSIONS, EXTERNAL:
Wing span 40 ft $8\frac{1}{4}$ in (12·40 m)
Wing chord at root 4 ft $5\frac{1}{4}$ in (1·35 m)
Wing chord at tip 2 ft $3\frac{1}{2}$ in (0·70 m)
Length overall 17 ft $8\frac{1}{2}$ in (5·40 m)
Height overall 6 ft $1\frac{3}{4}$ in (1·87 m)
Tailplane span 8 ft $4\frac{1}{2}$ in (2·55 m)
Propeller diameter 4 ft $3\frac{1}{4}$ in (1·30 m)

AREAS:
Wings, gross 125·9 sq ft (11·70 m^2)
Ailerons (total) 10·76 sq ft (1·00 m^2)
Trailing-edge flaps (total) 12·92 sq ft (1·20 m^2)
Fin 3·88 sq ft (0·36 m^2)
Rudder 4·09 sq ft (0·38 m^2)
Tailplane 9·04 sq ft (0·84 m^2)
Elevators 5·27 sq ft (0·49 m^2)

WEIGHT:
Max T-O weight 617 lb (280 kg)

Nahuel single-seat amateur-built sailplane, designed by Sr Berca of AVEX

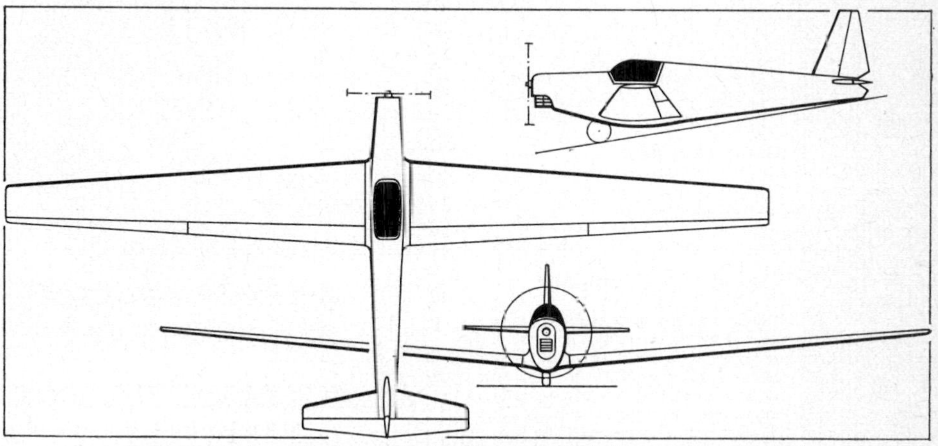

Lanzalone Aulanz single-seat homebuilt powered sailplane (*Tony Mitchell*)

AUSTRALIA

SCHNEIDER

EDMUND SCHNEIDER PTY LTD

HEAD OFFICE AND WORKS:
Two Wells Road (Aerodrome), Gawler, South Australia 5118
Telephone: (085) 22-2978

CHIEF DESIGNER:
Harry Schneider

Edmund Schneider Pty Ltd, late of Grunau in Germany, was one of the pioneer sailplane manufacturing companies. It transferred its operations to Australia as a private venture, at the invitation of the Gliding Federation of Australia. Its first project in the Commonwealth was the Kangaroo two-seat sailplane, which flew during 1953, followed by the Grunau Baby 4, Club trainer, Kookaburra, Arrow, Boomerang and Series 2 Boomerang, described in previous editions of *Jane's*.

The company's latest product of its own design is the ES 60B Super Arrow, a development of the ES 60 Series 2 Boomerang and E 59 Arrow.

Schneider is also working on a new project, designated ES 63, which is to be a two-seat high-performance sailplane.

Schneider is the Australian and New Zealand agent for Glasflügel sailplanes (see German section), assembles semi-completed glassfibre sailplanes imported from Glasflügel, and also represents Start + Flug (which see) in Australia and New Zealand. Its associated company, Sailplane Distributors Pty Ltd, of the same address, similarly represents Slingsby Sailplanes Ltd (see UK section). Other activities include repair and maintenance of sailplanes and the supply of sailplane materials and spares.

SCHNEIDER ES 60B SUPER ARROW SERIES 2

The Super Arrow is a single-seat Standard Class sailplane, designed for competition flying, the prototype of which flew for the first time on 22 September 1969, and which was awarded a Certificate of Airworthiness (to Australian DCA and BCAR-E standards) on 31 October 1969. It is essentially the same as the Series 2 Boomerang (1971-72 *Jane's*), but differs in having the conventional tail unit of the E 59 Arrow (1967-68 *Jane's*), with a fixed tailplane mounted at the base of, and forward of, the fin.

The first six aircraft were to Series 1 standard, as described in the 1973-74 *Jane's*. Four examples have been ordered of the Series 2 version; the first of these was due to fly in the Spring of 1974, and completion of all four was anticipated by the end of the year.

The following description applies to the Series 2, which differs from the Series 1 in having a tailwheel instead of a tailskid, and airbrakes on the upper wing surfaces only:

TYPE: Single-seat Standard Class sailplane.

WINGS: Cantilever high-wing monoplane. Wing sections Wortmann FX-61-184 at root, FX-61-140 at start of outer panels and FX-60-126 at tip. Dihedral 1°. Incidence 3°. Laminated beech spar at 50% chord. Birch ply covering back to 60% chord; moulded plastics leading-edge and tip "bumpers". Plywood-covered plain wooden ailerons, upper surface hinged. No flaps. Upper-surface airbrakes of glassfibre construction, with spring-loaded flanges, at 55% chord.

FUSELAGE: Semi-monocoque structure, with glassfibre-reinforced plastics nose section and remainder plywood-covered.

TAIL UNIT: Cantilever wooden structure, plywood and fabric covered. Vertical surfaces swept back 30°. Spring-loaded elevator trim.

LANDING GEAR: Non-retractable monowheel and tailwheel. Tost main wheel, tyre size 5·00-5, with expanding shoe brake. Tyre pressure 35 lb/sq in (2·5 kg/cm^2).

ACCOMMODATION: Single seat in enclosed cockpit under sideways-opening (to starboard) Perspex canopy. Clear-vision panel in port side of canopy, adjustable air vent on starboard side. Lined cockpit, with cushions. Adjustable seat-back and rudder pedals. Locker compartment with separate stowage space for vario flasks, oxygen and radio. Instrument tappings. Instruments to customer's specification. Instrument panel incorporates a bale-out handle.

DIMENSIONS, EXTERNAL:
Wing span 49 ft $2\frac{1}{2}$ in (15·00 m)

Schneider ES 60B Super Arrow high-performance single-seat sailplane

Wing aspect ratio 17·5
Length overall 23 ft 2½ in (7·04 m)
Height over tail 5 ft 0 in (1·52 m)
Tailplane span 9 ft 2¼ in (2·80 m)
Width at cockpit 1 ft 11¾ in (0·60 m)

DIMENSIONS, INTERNAL:
Cabin: Max length 6 ft 6 in (1·98 m)
Max width 2 ft 0 in (0·61 m)

AREAS:
Wings, gross 138 sq ft (12·87 m²)
Ailerons (total) 9·15 sq ft (0·85 m²)
Fin 5·06 sq ft (0·47 m²)
Rudder 4·74 sq ft (0·44 m²)
Tailplane 10·7 sq ft (0·99 m²)
Elevators 7·10 sq ft (0·66 m²)

WEIGHTS AND LOADING:
Weight empty 520 lb (235 kg)
Max T-O weight 765 lb (347 kg)
Max wing loading 5·57 lb/sq ft (27·2 kg/m²)

PERFORMANCE:
Best glide ratio at 43·5 knots (50 mph; 80·5 km/h) 31·5
Min sinking speed at 39 knots (45 mph; 72·5 km/h) 2·23 ft (0·68 m)/sec
Stalling speed 35·5 knots (40·5 mph; 65 km/h)
Max speed (smooth air) 122 knots (140 mph; 226 km/h) IAS
Max speed (rough air) 89 knots (102 mph; 165 km/h) IAS

AUSTRIA

BRDITSCHKA

H. W. BRDITSCHKA OHG

ADDRESS:
A-4053 Haid bei Linz, Postfach 12
Telex: 21 909

DIRECTOR:
Heinz W. Brditschka

This company is producing a single-seat powered sailplane known as the HB-3. It has also built a two-seat powered sailplane of quite different design, the HB-21. This has a best glide ratio of 36, a min sinking speed of 2·79 ft (0·85 m)/sec, a stalling speed of 35 knots (40·5 mph; 65 km/h), and can be powered by either a 46 hp Rotax or a 60 hp Limbach engine. Further details were not received in time for inclusion in this edition.

BRDITSCHKA HB-3

This single-seat powered sailplane is being built in four versions, all using the basic wing design of the Krähe sailplane designed in Germany by Ing Fritz Raab. The basic **HB-3A** has a 36 hp Puch engine, and is available also as the **HB-3AR** with a 42 hp Rotax engine. The same choice of power plant is available for the **HB-3BP** and **HB-3BR**, which differ principally in having increased fuel capacity including a tank in the wing centre-section. Design started in 1968.

Three HB-3 prototypes were built, these making their first flights on 23 June 1971 and 5 June and 28 July 1972. By the Spring of 1974 two production aircraft had been completed and three more were under construction. Austrian certification for all four versions was expected during 1974.

The Brditschka works was also responsible, in 1973, for the conversion of an HB-3 airframe to electric power as the MB-E1, described under the Militky heading in the German section.

The following description applies to the standard production models of the HB-3:

TYPE: Single-seat powered sailplane.

WINGS: Cantilever high-wing monoplane. Wing section Göttingen Gö 758 at root, Clark Y at tip. Thickness/chord ratio 13·8% at root, 11·7% at tip. Dihedral on outer panels. Incidence 2°. Conventional all-wood structure, including ailerons and upper-surface spoilers. No flaps or tabs.

FUSELAGE: Tubular steel framework with glassfibre covering. Triangular cutout for propeller rotation aft of wing trailing-edge.

TAIL UNIT: Conventional all-wood structure. Fixed-incidence tailplane mounted on top of fuselage. Trim tab on starboard elevator.

LANDING GEAR: Non-retractable tricycle type. Glassfibre legs provide all necessary shock-absorption. Main wheels and tyres size 300 × 100, pressure 35·5 lb/sq in (2·5 kg/cm²); nosewheel and tyre size 200 × 50, pressure 42·5 lb/sq in (3·0 kg/cm²). Mechanical brakes on main wheels.

POWER PLANT: One 42 hp Rotax 642 two-stroke (HB-3AR and HB-3BR) or 36 hp Puch 650 TRN 1 four-stroke engine (HB-3A and HB-3BP), driving a Hoffmann HO 11-150B100 LD two-blade fixed-pitch propeller. The HB-3A and -3AR have a single 5·5 Imp gallon (25 litre) fuselage fuel tank. In the HB-3BP and -3BR this tank is of 2·64 Imp gallons (12 litres) capacity, and there is in addition a 3·96 Imp gallon (18 litre) aluminium tank in the wing centre-section, with an overwing refuelling point. Rotax-engined models burn a petrol/oil mixture; oil capacity of Puch-engined models is 0·55 Imp gallons (2·5 litres).

Brditschka HB-3 single-seat powered sailplane (*Brian M. Service*)

ACCOMMODATION: Single seat in fully-enclosed cabin. Cockpit canopy opens sideways to starboard. Small baggage space behind seat. Ram-air intake in nose for cabin ventilation.

EQUIPMENT: 12V 15Ah battery standard. Radio and other equipment at customer's option.

DIMENSIONS, EXTERNAL:
Wing span 39 ft 4½ in (12·00 m)
Wing chord at root 4 ft 7 in (1·40 m)
Wing chord at tip 2 ft 4¾ in (0·73 m)
Wing aspect ratio 10·11
Length overall 22 ft 11¾ in (7·00 m)
Height overall 7 ft 4¼ in (2·24 m)
Tailplane span 8 ft 4½ in (2·55 m)
Wheel track 5 ft 5½ in (1·66 m)
Wheelbase 6 ft 1¾ in (1·87 m)
Propeller diameter 4 ft 11 in (1·50 m)

DIMENSION, INTERNAL:
Cabin: Max width 2 ft 1½ in (0·65 m)

AREAS:
Wings, gross 153·1 sq ft (14·22 m²)
Ailerons (total) 16·15 sq ft (1·50 m²)
Spoilers (total) 1·94 sq ft (0·18 m²)
Fin 4·20 sq ft (0·39 m²)
Rudder 9·24 sq ft (0·858 m²)
Tailplane 18·88 sq ft (1·754 m²)
Elevators, incl tab 8·87 sq ft (0·824 m²)

WEIGHTS AND LOADINGS:
Weight empty, equipped:
3AR 551 lb (250 kg)
3BP 597 lb (271 kg)
3BR 573 lb (260 kg)
Max T-O and landing weight:
3AR 749 lb (340 kg)
3BP, 3BR 837 lb (380 kg)
Max wing loading:
3AR 4·90 lb/sq ft (23·91 kg/m²)
3BP, 3BR 4·57 lb/sq ft (26·72 kg/m²)
Max power loading:
3AR 17·86 lb/hp (8·10 kg/hp)
3BP 23·28 lb/hp (10·56 kg/hp)
3BR 19·95 lb/hp (9·05 kg/hp)

PERFORMANCE (at max T-O weight, all versions):
Max never-exceed speed 94 knots (108 mph; 175 km/h)
Max cruising speed 86 knots (99 mph; 160 km/h)
Econ cruising speed 81 knots (93 mph; 150 km/h)
Stalling speed 32·5 knots (37·5 mph; 60 km/h)
Max rate of climb at S/L 590 ft (180 m)/min
Service ceiling:
Rotax 13,125 ft (4,000 m)
Puch 19,675 ft (6,000 m)
T-O run 330 ft (100 m)
T-O to 50 ft (15 m) 755 ft (230 m)
Landing from 50 ft (15 m) 330 ft (100 m)
Landing run 165 ft (50 m)
Range with max fuel 431 nm (497 miles; 800 km)

BUSSARD

A twin-boom, pusher-engined powered sailplane known as the Bussard has been designed in Austria. All known details were given in the 1973-74 *Jane's*.

BRAZIL

IPE

INDUSTRIA PARANAENSE DE ESTRUTURAS

ADDRESS:
Caixa Postal 2621, 80.000 Curitiba-Paraná

SECRETARY:
J. C. Boscardin

KW 1 QUERO QUERO II

The original KW 1 was designed by Ing Kuno Wiedmaier and built by the Aeroclube de N. Hamburgo, Rio Grande Sul; it first flew in 1970.

Development was continued by the Grupo Curitiba (now Industria Paranaense de Estruturas), initial modifications being a lengthening of the fuselage and an increase in vertical tail height and area. In this form, redesignated KW 1 b 1, it flew for the first time on 15 January 1972. Later in that year a modified version appeared (the KW 1 b 2 Quero Quero II), with strengthened rear fuselage and tail unit attachments, foam filling of the wing torsion box and a 35 lb (16 kg) higher gross weight.

The KW 1 b 2 made its first flight on 1 October 1972. It has a Scheibe Spatz wing section, upper- and lower-surface spoilers, and is built of wood and plywood (Brazilian pine). There is a trim tab on the port elevator. A second KW 1 b 2 has been completed. Following evaluation by the Centro Tecnico Aeroespacial for type approval, IPE was in early 1974 making a minor modification to introduce aileron "twist". If this is accepted, series production of the KW 1 b 2 is planned.

TYPE: Single-seat training glider.

LANDING GEAR: Non-retractable monowheel and tailwheel.

DIMENSIONS, EXTERNAL:
Wing span 49 ft 2½ in (15·00 m)
Wing aspect ratio 18
Length overall 21 ft 2¾ in (6·47 m)
Height overall 4 ft 4¾ in (1·34 m)
Fuselage: Max depth 3 ft 3¼ in (1·00 m)
Tailplane span 7 ft 10½ in (2·40 m)

AREA:
Wings, gross 125·9 sq ft (11·70 m²)

WEIGHTS AND LOADING (KW 1 b 2):
Weight empty 374 lb (170 kg)
Max T-O weight 595 lb (270 kg)
Max wing loading 4·36 lb/sq ft (21·3 kg/m²)

PERFORMANCE (KW 1 b 2):
Best glide ratio at 39 knots (45 mph; 73 km/h) 28
Min sinking speed at 33·5 knots (38·5 mph; 62 km/h) 2·10 ft (0·64 m)/sec
Max speed 81 knots (93 mph; 150 km/h)
g limit +8

KW 2

Progress with this tandem two-seat training sailplane has been delayed due to financial difficulties and the need to afford priority to the KW 1, and in early 1974 the first flight of the KW 2 was awaiting government authorisation.

The three-view drawing and following details refer to the KW 2; the building of a modified (KW 2b) prototype is under consideration.

DIMENSIONS, EXTERNAL:
- Wing span: 54 ft $5\frac{1}{2}$ in (16·60 m)
- Wing aspect ratio: 15·6
- Length overall: 25 ft 11 in (7·90 m)

AREA:
- Wings, gross: 191·6 sq ft (17·8 m²)

WEIGHTS AND LOADING:
- Weight empty: 573 lb (260 kg)
- Max T-O weight: 992 lb (450 kg)
- Max wing loading: 5·16 lb/sq ft (25·2 kg/m²)

PERFORMANCE (estimated):
- Best glide ratio at 38 knots (43·5 mph; 70 km/h) as single-seater, and at 43·5 knots (50 mph; 80 km/h) as two-seater: 28
- Min sinking speed:
  - single-seater: 2·13 ft (0·65 m)/sec
  - two-seater: 2·36 ft (0·72 m)/sec
- Max speed: 97 knots (112 mph; 180 km/h)
- *g* limit: +8

IPE KW 1 b 2 Quero Quero II single-seat all-wood training sailplane

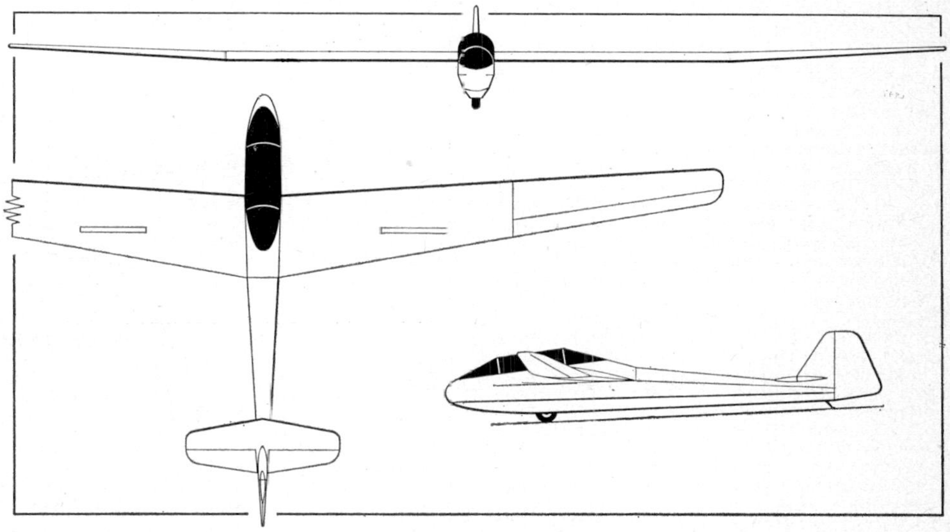

IPE KW 2 tandem two-seat training sailplane (*Michael A. Badrocke*)

CZECHOSLOVAKIA

MATEJCEK
JIRI MATEJCEK

MATEJCEK M-17 UNIVERSAL

Mr Matejcek designed and built a powered sailplane known as the M-17 Universal. Piloted by Mr J. Panusz, it flew for the first time on 17 October 1972 and was described and illustrated in the 1973-74 *Jane's*.

OMNIPOL
OMNIPOL FOREIGN TRADE CORPORATION

ADDRESS:
Washingtonova 11, Prague 1
Telephone: 2126
Telex: 121489, 121808 and 121077

GENERAL MANAGER:
Tomás Marecek, GE

SALES MANAGER:
Frantisek Rypal, GE

PUBLICITY MANAGER:
Jiri Matula

This concern handles the export sales of the products of the Czechoslovak aircraft industry, including the L-13 Blaník sailplane.

LET NÁRODNÍ PODNIK (Let National Corporation)

ADDRESS:
Uherské Hradiste-Kunovice

OFFICERS:
See "Aircraft" section

In addition to its work on powered aircraft, Let National Corporation manufactures the L-13 Blaník sailplane, of which full details follow.

LET L-13 BLANÍK

This tandem two-seat all-metal sailplane is designed for training in all categories from elementary to "blind" flying and for high-performance flight. It is fully aerobatic when flown solo and capable of basic aerobatic manoeuvres when carrying a crew of two.

Design of the Blaník was started in January 1955, and construction of the prototype began in August of the same year. First flight was made in March 1956.

By the beginning of 1974, about 1,700 Blaníks had been sold, of which more than 1,400 had been exported to customers in 37 countries. Production was continuing in 1974.

A small quantity was built of a powered version, the L-13J (see 1973-74 *Jane's*), but this version is not in series production.

No fewer than 13 international records have been set up by sailplanes of this type, in addition to numerous national records. In 1969 an FAI Gold Medal was awarded to the Chilean pilot Alejo Williamson for a 5 hr 51 min flight in a Blanik across the Andes, from Santiago de Chile to Mendoza in the Argentine Republic. The distance record for multi-seat sailplanes of 497·49 nm (572·87 miles; 921·95 km), set up in a Blaník by J. Kuznetsov and J. Barkhamov of the USSR on 3 June 1967, remained unbeaten by mid-1974.

TYPE: Two-seat training sailplane.

WINGS: Cantilever shoulder-wing monoplane, with 5° forward sweep at quarter-chord. Wing section NACA 63_2A615 at root, NACA 63_2A612 at tip. Dihedral 3°. Incidence 4° at root, 1° at tip. All-metal two-spar structure. Main spar forms torsion-box with leading-edge. Each wing secured by three fuselage attachments. Wingtip "salmons". Ailerons and slotted area-increasing flaps are fabric-covered metal structures. Rectangular light alloy airbrakes in the upper and lower surfaces of each wing.

FUSELAGE: All-metal semi-monocoque structure of oval cross-section, with riveted skin.

TAIL UNIT: Cantilever all-metal structure. Elevator and rudder fabric-covered. Controllable trim tab in elevator. Horizontal surfaces fold upward parallel to rudder for transport.

LANDING GEAR: Mechanically-retractable main wheel, type HP-4741-Z, located in lower part of fuselage on centreline. Wheel manufactured by Rudy Rijen of Gottwaldov; tyre size 13·8 × 5·3 in (350 × 135 mm) by Moravan of Otrokovice, pressure 35·6 lb/sq in (2·5 kg/cm²). Oleo-pneumatic shock-absorber and mechanically-actuated brake.

ACCOMMODATION: Two seats in tandem in part-upholstered cabin, with heat-insulated walls.

Let L-13 Blaník tandem two-seat all-metal sailplane

Sideways-opening transparent canopy, hinged on the starboard side, is jettisonable in flight.

Equipment: Standard equipment includes basic flight instruments on both front and rear instrument panels, tow line and cockpit cover. Optional equipment includes electric gyros, second rate of climb indicator for rear instrument panel, rear compartment blinds for instrument flying instruction, navigation lights and 12V 10Ah battery, water ballast system to increase wing loading for solo flight, skis for operation on snow and a complete set of protective covers.

Dimensions, external:

Wing span	53 ft 2 in (16·20 m)
Wing chord at root	5 ft 5 in (1·65 m)
Wing chord at tip	2 ft 3½ in (0·70 m)
Wing aspect ratio	13·7
Length overall	27 ft 6½ in (8·40 m)
Height over tail	6 ft 10 in (2·09 m)
Tailplane span	11 ft 3¾ in (3·45 m)

Areas:

Wings, gross	206·13 sq ft (19·15 m²)
Ailerons (total)	24·87 sq ft (2·31 m²)
Flaps (total)	42·52 sq ft (3·95 m²)
Spoilers (total)	7·00 sq ft (0·65 m²)
Fin	7·58 sq ft (0·70 m²)
Rudder	9·73 sq ft (0·90 m²)
Tailplane	16·79 sq ft (1·56 m²)
Elevators, incl tab	11·95 sq ft (1·11 m²)

Weights and Loadings:

Weight empty, standard equipment ±2%	677 lb (307 kg)
Max T-O weight	1,102 lb (500 kg)
Normal wing loading	5·02 lb/sq ft (24·5 kg/m²)
Max wing loading	5·35 lb/sq ft (26·1 kg/m²)

Performance (at max T-O weight):

Best glide ratio, +5% at 48 knots (55 mph; 88 km/h) IAS	28
Min sinking speed at 44 knots (50 mph; 80 km/h) IAS	2·69 ft (0·82 m)/sec
Stalling speed	31 knots (35 mph; 55 km/h) IAS
Max speed (smooth air)	136 knots (157 mph; 253 km/h) IAS
Max speed (rough air)	78 knots (90 mph; 145 km/h) IAS
Max aero-tow speed	76 knots (87 mph; 140 km/h) IAS
Max winch-launching speed	65 knots (75 mph; 120 km/h) IAS
g limits	+5; −2·5

VSO

VYVOJOVÉ STUDIO ORLICAN

Address:
c/o Orlican Národní Podnik, 565 37 Chocen
Telephone: Chocen 70 and 80
Telex: 0 196 210

Chief Designer:
Dipl Ing Jan Janovec

This design group was formed by several members of the former VSB (see 1973-74 *Jane's*) and some of the design staff of the Orlican National Works. Its first design is the single-seat VSO 10, of which a description follows:

VSO 10

Design of the VSO 10 began in March 1972. Prototype construction had not started up to the Spring of 1974.

Type: Single-seat high-performance sailplane.

Wings: Cantilever shoulder-wing monoplane. Wortmann wing sections, FX-61-163 at root, FX-60-126 at tip. Dihedral 3°. Incidence 3° 30′. Sweepforward 1° 16′ at quarter-chord. All-wood single-spar structure, with sandwich skin. All-wood slotted ailerons. No flaps. All-metal double-shaft DFS-type airbrakes on upper surfaces at 46% chord and 38% of each half-span.

Fuselage: Glassfibre monocoque front and centre portions, the latter reinforced by a steel tube frame. Rear portion is an aluminium alloy sheet monocoque.

Tail Unit: Cantilever T-tail, of metal construction with fabric-covered elevators and rudder. Fixed-incidence tailplane. No tabs; elevator control includes torsion trim bar.

Landing Gear: Mechanically-retractable rubber-sprung monowheel and semi-recessed unsprung tailwheel. Monowheel tyre size 350 × 135 — 127 mm, pressure approx 35·5 lb/sq in (2·5 kg/cm²). Tailwheel diameter 160 mm. Moravan Otrokovice mechanically-operated drum brake.

Accommodation: Single moulded glassfibre seat under detachable transparent moulded canopy. Radio fitted.

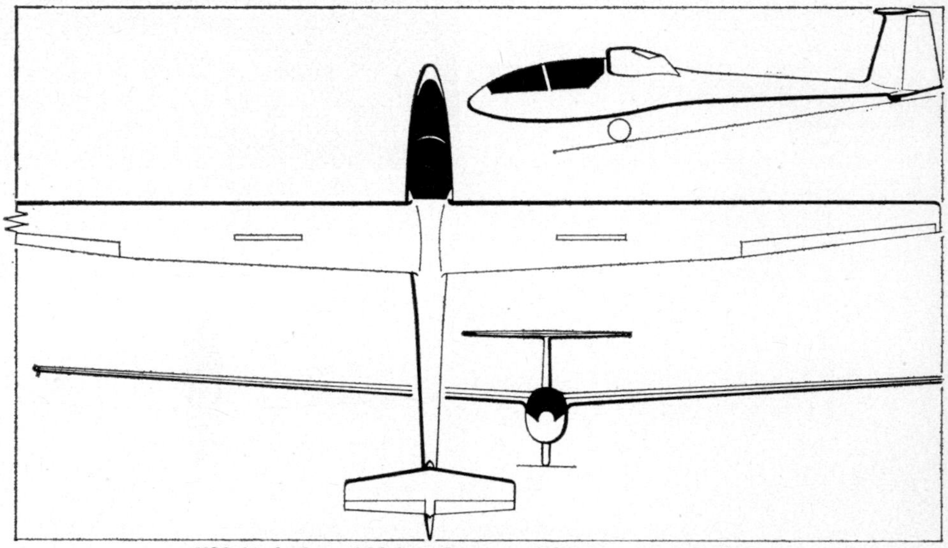

VSO 10 single-seat high-performance sailplane (*A. J. Smith*)

Dimensions, external:

Wing span	49 ft 2½ in (15·00 m)
Wing chord at root	5 ft 9 in (1·75 m)
Wing chord at tip	1 ft 5 in (0·43 m)
Wing mean aerodynamic chord	2 ft 8½ in (0·824 m)
Wing aspect ratio	18·75
Length overall	22 ft 11¾ in (7·00 m)
Height overall	4 ft 4¾ in (1·34 m)
Tailplane span	8 ft 1¾ in (2·48 m)

Areas:

Wings, gross	129·2 sq ft (12·00 m²)
Ailerons (total)	9·42 sq ft (0·875 m²)
Fin	5·45 sq ft (0·506 m²)
Rudder	5·45 sq ft (0·506 m²)
Tailplane	9·94 sq ft (0·923 m²)
Elevators	4·13 sq ft (0·384 m²)

Weights and Loading:

Weight empty, equipped	516·75 lb (234·4 kg)
Max T-O weight	837 lb (380 kg)
Max wing loading	6·49 lb/sq ft (31·67 kg/m²)

Performance (estimated, at 771 lb; 350 kg AUW):

Best glide ratio at 51 knots (58·5 mph; 94 km/h)	36·2
Min sinking speed at 39 knots (45 mph; 72 km/h)	2·07 ft (0·63 m)/sec
Stalling speed	37 knots (42·5 mph; 68 km/h)
Max speed (smooth air)	140 knots (161 mph; 260 km/h)
Max speed (rough air)	88 knots (101 mph; 163 km/h)
Max aero-tow speed	86 knots (99 mph; 160 km/h)
Max winch-launching speed	64·5 knots (74·5 mph; 120 km/h)
g limits	+5·3; −2·65

DENMARK

PETERSEN

HELGE PETERSEN

Address:
Fynsvej 56, DK-4000 Roskilde

PROJECT 8

Helge Petersen and 10 other glider pilots have formed a group called Project 8, which began design of a two-seat powered sailplane on 1 January 1972. Construction started a year later, and by March 1974 the fuselage was virtually complete, including the controls and main wheel. The wings will be built during the Winter of 1974-75, and first flight is planned for Summer 1975.

Type: Tandem two-seat powered sailplane.

Wings: Cantilever mid-wing monoplane, built in three sections. Wing section Wortmann FX-67-K-170 on centre-section, outer panels varying through Wortmann FX-67-K-150 to NACA 64-212 at tip. Dihedral 4° on outer panels. Incidence 3°. Sweepforward 3° on centre-section, 1° on outer panels, at quarter-chord. Wood and glassfibre construction, including the top-hinged trailing-edge flaps and ailerons. Aluminium airbrakes on top surface of centre-section.

Fuselage: Forward portion is of welded steel tube covered by a light glassfibre shell. Rear portion built of wood, reinforced by glassfibre.

Tail Unit: Cantilever T-tail, of wooden construction. Fixed-incidence tailplane. Central trim tab in elevator, inset tab at base of rudder.

Landing Gear: Semi-retractable monowheel, with mechanical retraction, nosewheel, and tailwheel. Rubber-block shock-absorption on main wheel, which is fitted with hand and parking brakes. Tost main (5 in × 350 mm) and nosewheel (50 × 200 mm). Steerable solid-tyre tailwheel, diameter 110 mm. Retractable wingtip balancer wheels to be designed.

Power Plant: One 54 hp VW 1600 engine, driving a two-blade propeller via Power Grip toothed-belt transmission with 4,000/2,200 rpm gearing. Propeller mounted on pylon which retracts rearward into top of fuselage when not in use.

Accommodation: Two seats in tandem under one-piece sideways-hinged Perspex canopy.

Dimensions, external:

Wing span	59 ft 0¾ in (18·00 m)
Wing chord at root	4 ft 5¼ in (1·35 m)
Wing chord at tip	1 ft 6 in (0·46 m)

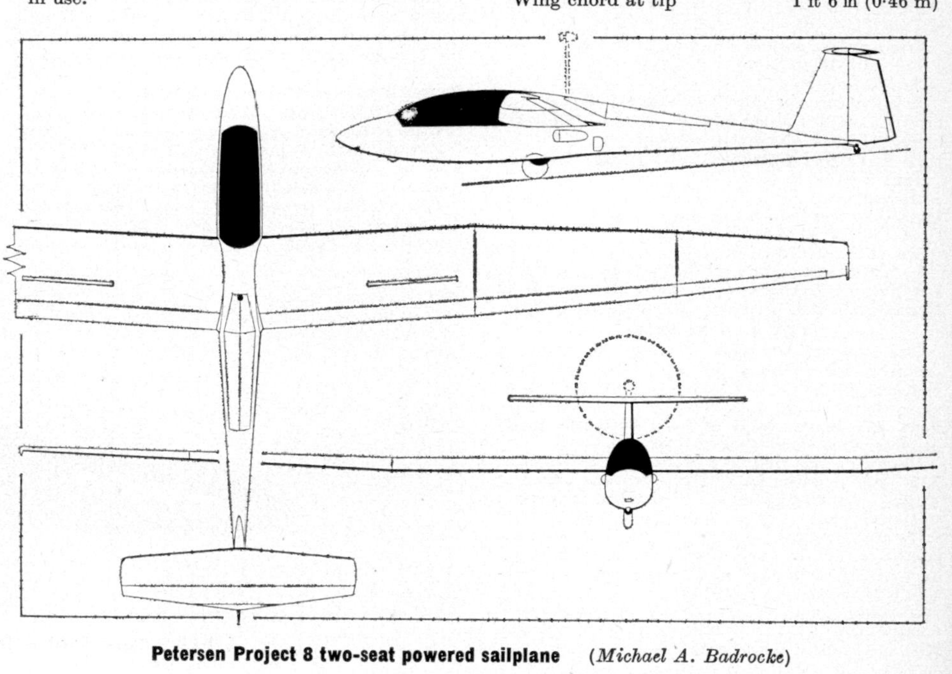

Petersen Project 8 two-seat powered sailplane (*Michael A. Badrocke*)

Wing mean aerodynamic chord 3 ft 8 in (1·12 m)
Wing aspect ratio 16·2
Length overall 27 ft 10¾ in (8·50 m)
Height overall 4 ft 3¼ in (1·30 m)
Tailplane span 11 ft 5¾ in (3·50 m)
Propeller diameter 5 ft 5½ in (1·66 m)

AREAS:
Wings, gross 215·3 sq ft (20·00 m²)
Ailerons (total) 19·38 sq ft (1·80 m²)
Trailing-edge flaps (total) 17·22 sq ft (1·60 m²)
Airbrakes (total) 4·31 sq ft (0·40 m²)
Fin 8·61 sq ft (0·80 m²)
Rudder 7·53 sq ft (0·70 m²)
Tailplane 17·22 sq ft (1·60 m²)
Elevator, incl tab 8·61 sq ft (0·80 m²)

WEIGHTS AND LOADING:
Weight empty, equipped 992 lb (450 kg)
Max T-O weight 1,543 lb (700 kg)
Max wing loading 7·17 lb/sq ft (35·0 kg/m²)

PERFORMANCE (estimated, at max T-O weight):
Best glide ratio at 54 knots (62 mph; 100 km/h) 32
Min sinking speed at 43·5 knots (50 mph; 80 km/h) 2·3 ft (0·70 m)/sec
Stalling speed 38 knots (43·5 mph; 70 km/h)
Max speed (rough and smooth air) 141·5 knots (163 mph; 263 km/h)
Max aero-tow speed 67·5 knots (77·5 mph; 125 km/h)
Max winch-launching speed 59 knots (68 mph; 110 km/h)
T-O run 525 ft (160 m)
T-O to 50 ft (15 m) 1,380 ft (420 m)
g limits +6; −4

FINLAND

PIK

TEKNILLINEN KORKEAKOULU (Helsinki University of Technology)

ADDRESS:
Konelaboratorio/Kevytrakennetekniikka, SF-02150 Otaniemi

OFFICERS:
See "Aircraft" section

The long series of sailplanes designed and built by PIK in recent years has included the PIK-3a, b and c (20 built); PIK-5a, b and c (35 built); PIK-7; PIK-12 (four built); PIK-16a, b and c (56 built); and PIK-17a and b (two built). Two additional PIK-16c Vasamas are currently being built by Finnish gliding clubs.

Latest PIK products are the PIK-19 glider-towing aircraft (see "Aircraft" section) and the PIK-20 15 metre Standard Class sailplane.

PIK-16c Vasama single-seat Standard Class sailplane

PIK-16c VASAMA (ARROW)

The prototype PIK-16a single-seat Standard Class sailplane first flew on 1 June 1961, and was followed by three PIK-16b and 52 PIK-16c. Manufacture, by K. K. Lehtovaara Oy of Jämijärvi, ended in the mid-1960s, but two others are currently under construction by Finnish gliding clubs. The description which follows applies to the series-built PIK-16c:

TYPE: Single-seat Standard Class sailplane.

WINGS: Cantilever shoulder-wing monoplane. Wing section Wortmann FX-05-188 at root, NACA 63_2-615 at tip. Thickness/chord ratio 14% at root. Dihedral 3° 30′. All-wood structure, with 40% of chord formed by shaped box-spar of birch plywood which takes bending and torsion loads. Nose section of sandwich construction. Aft of spar, top surface is plywood-covered, undersurface fabric-covered. Plain ailerons of plywood-covered wooden construction. Spoilers on top and bottom surfaces.

FUSELAGE: Plywood monocoque construction with glassfibre nosecap.

TAIL UNIT: Cantilever wooden structure. Trim tab in port elevator.

LANDING GEAR: Non-retractable monowheel, size 12 in × 4 in (305 mm × 102 mm) with brake, and skid.

ACCOMMODATION: Single semi-reclining seat under removable blown Perspex canopy.

DIMENSIONS, EXTERNAL:
Wing span 49 ft 2½ in (15·00 m)
Wing chord at root 3 ft 6½ in (1·08 m)
Wing chord at tip 1 ft 3¾ in (0·40 m)
Height over tail 4 ft 9 in (1·45 m)
Width of cockpit 1 ft 11½ in (0·60 m)
Tailplane span 7 ft 9 in (2·36 m)

AREAS:
Wings, gross 125·9 sq ft (11·70 m²)
Ailerons (total) 10·59 sq ft (0·98 m²)
Spoilers (total) 5·49 sq ft (0·51 m²)

WEIGHTS:
Weight empty, equipped 419 lb (190 kg)
Max T-O weight 661 lb (300 kg)

PERFORMANCE:
Best glide ratio at 46 knots (53 mph; 85 km/h) 34
Min sinking speed at 39·5 knots (45·5 mph; 73 km/h) 1·94 ft (0·59 m)/sec
Max speed (smooth air) 135 knots (155 mph; 250 km/h)
Max speed (rough air) 92 knots (106 mph; 170 km/h)

PIK-20 single-seat high-performance sailplane, first flown in 1973

PIK-20

Design of the PIK-20, by Tammi, Korhonen and Hiedandää, began on 1 May 1971 in the aircraft research laboratory at Helsinki University of Technology. The first prototype flew for the first time on 10 October 1973, and in January 1974 was flown by Raimo Nurminen in the World Championships at Waikerie, Australia. A second prototype has been delivered to the US, and in early 1974 two others were under construction by Molino Oy, a new company which has taken over the now-inoperative K.K. Lehtovaara company and which will build the series production aircraft.

In the Spring of 1974 most ground and flight testing had been completed, and certification was expected in the near future.

TYPE: Single-seat Standard Class sailplane.

WINGS: Cantilever shoulder-wing monoplane. Wortmann wing sections, FX-67-K-170 at root, FX-67-K-150 at tip. Dihedral 3°. Incidence 1°. No sweepback. Glassfibre/epoxy/PVC foam sandwich structure. Plain ailerons, and trailing-edge flaps/airbrakes, of similar construction. Provision for 17·5 Imp gallons (80 litres) of water ballast.

FUSELAGE: Glassfibre/epoxy monocoque structure.

TAIL UNIT: Cantilever T-tail, of similar construction to wings. Fixed-incidence tailplane, with one-piece elevator.

LANDING GEAR: Manually-retractable Tost monowheel and tailskid. Dunlop/Continental tyre, size 5·00-5. Tost drum brake.

ACCOMMODATION: Single semi-reclining seat under two-piece transparent moulded canopy, the rear portion of which is removable. Adjustable rudder pedals. Standard cockpit instrumentation plus special vario-integrator unit, and final approach computer and tracking unit.

DIMENSIONS, EXTERNAL:
Wing span 49 ft 2½ in (15·00 m)
Wing chord at root 2 ft 11½ in (0·90 m)
Wing chord (mean) 2 ft 1½ in (0·65 m)
Wing chord at tip 1 ft 2¼ in (0·36 m)
Wing aspect ratio 22·5
Length overall 21 ft 9¾ in (6·65 m)
Height over tail 4 ft 5½ in (1·36 m)
Tailplane span 6 ft 6¾ in (2·00 m)

AREAS:
Wings, gross 107·6 sq ft (10·00 m²)
Ailerons (total) 5·38 sq ft (0·50 m²)
Flaps/airbrakes (total) 11·625 sq ft (1·08 m²)
Fin 7·64 sq ft (0·71 m²)
Rudder 3·34 sq ft (0·31 m²)
Tailplane 8·61 sq ft (0·80 m²)
Elevator 2·15 sq ft (0·20 m²)

WEIGHTS AND LOADING:
Weight empty, equipped 518 lb (235 kg)
Max water ballast 176 lb (80 kg)
Max T-O weight (with water ballast) 881 lb (400 kg)
Max wing loading 8·2 lb/sq ft (40·0 kg/m²)

PERFORMANCE (measured, at 815 lb; 370 kg AUW except where indicated):
Best glide ratio at 52 knots (60 mph; 97 km/h) 40·2
Min sinking speed at 44 knots (51 mph; 82 km/h) 2·03 ft (0·62 m)/sec
Stalling speed (90° flap):
at 705 lb (320 kg) AUW 32·5 knots (37·5 mph; 60 km/h)
at 881 lb (400 kg) AUW 36·5 knots (42 mph; 67 km/h)
Max speed (rough and smooth air) 129·5 knots (149 mph; 240 km/h)
Max aero-tow speed 102·5 knots (118 mph; 190 km/h)
g limits +7·1; −5·1

FRANCE

CARMAM

COOPÉRATIVE D'APPROVISIONNEMENT ET DE RÉPARATIONS DE MATÉRIEL AÉRONAUTIQUE DE MOULINS

ADDRESS:

Aérodrome de Moulins, BP 201, 03000 Allier

Telephone: (70) 44.36.18

This company extended its work on sailplane repair and maintenance to include the construction of new sailplanes. It began by building under licence the M-100 S, designed in Italy by Alberto and Piero Morelli, and followed this with production of the two-seat M-200 by the same designers.

Production of both types has ended, and CARMAM is currently building sailplane components under subcontract for Glasflügel (see German section). It is also working on the design of a single-seat sailplane of plastics construction, which it hopes to complete in 1975.

CARMAM M-100 S MÉSANGE (TOMTIT)

The Mésange is a licence-built version of the Italian M-100 S single-seat Standard Class sailplane designed by Alberto and Piero Morelli. The original prototype M-100 S flew for the first time in January 1960 and was followed by 41 production models built in Italy by Aeromere and 43 built by Avionautica Rio.

The CARMAM-built version obtained its French certificate of airworthiness on 8 February 1963. Eighty-seven were built by CARMAM, deliveries of which began in June 1963.

The Mésange was described and illustrated in the 1973-74 *Jane's*.

CARMAM M-200 FOEHN

Designed by Alberto and Piero Morelli, the M-200 is a two-seat high-performance sailplane developed from the single-seat M-100 S.

The first prototype M-200 was built at the CVT, Turin, under a contract from the Aero Club of Italy, and flew for the first time in May 1964. Production was undertaken by both CARMAM (which built 58) and Avionautica Rio of Italy.

A description and illustration of the M-200 appeared in the 1973-74 *Jane's*.

CERVA

CONSORTIUM EUROPÉEN DE RÉALISATION ET DE VENTES D'AVIONS (GROUPEMENT D'INTÉRÊTS ÉCONOMIQUES)

ADDRESS:

13 rue Saint-Honoré, BP 187, 78002 Versailles

Telephone: 950-63-95

As detailed in the "Aircraft" section, this company was formed, and is owned in equal proportions, by Siren SA and Wassmer-Aviation SA (which see).

It is currently developing the Siren-designed CE 75 Silene (formerly known as the Sagittaire).

CERVA CE 75 SILENE

The Silene is a side-by-side two-seat training glider, the design of which (by Siren SA) began on 1 January 1972. Construction by CERVA of a prototype started on 1 February 1973, and this aircraft made its first flight on 2 July 1974. A static test airframe has also been completed.

TYPE: Two-seat training sailplane.

WINGS: Cantilever mid-wing monoplane. Bertin E55 166 wing section, with thickness/chord ratio of 16·6%. Dihedral 2°. Incidence 3°. Sweepforward 2° at quarter-chord. Composite glassfibre/PMC foam sandwich construction. Two-section ailerons, of similar construction. No flaps. Schempp-Hirth airbrake on each wing.

FUSELAGE: Semi-monocoque glassfibre/PMC foam sandwich structure.

TAIL UNIT: Cantilever structure, of similar construction to wings. Fixed-incidence tailplane. Trim tab in each elevator.

LANDING GEAR: Manually-retractable or non-retractable monowheel, size 330 × 130 mm, tyre pressure 28·5 lb/sq in (2·0 kg/cm^2). Rubber-ring shock-absorption. Siren hydraulic brake. Tail bumper.

ACCOMMODATION: Seats for two persons side by side under two-piece transparent moulded canopy. Right hand (instructor's) seat is staggered 11¾ in (0·30 m) to rear. Oxygen equipment and/or radio, and second variometer, optional.

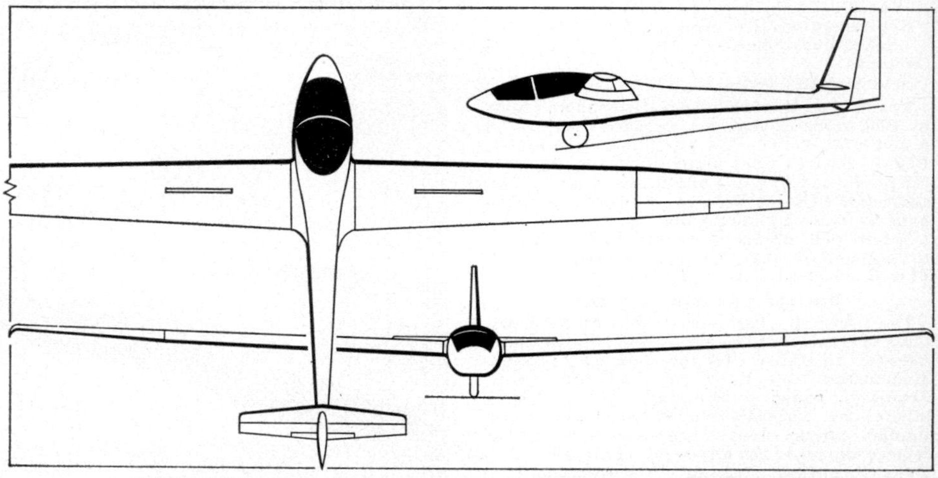

CERVA CE 75 Silene side-by-side two-seat training glider *(Tony Mitchell)*

DIMENSIONS, EXTERNAL:

Wing span	59 ft 0½ in (18·00 m)
Wing chord at root	4 ft 2 in (1·27 m)
Wing chord at tip	1 ft 7¾ in (0·50 m)
Wing aspect ratio	18
Length overall	26 ft 1 in (7·95 m)
Height overall	6 ft 0¾ in (1·85 m)
Tailplane span	10 ft 6 in (3·20 m)

AREAS:

Wings, gross	193·8 sq ft (18·00 m^2)
Fin	8·61 sq ft (0·80 m^2)
Rudder	9·69 sq ft (0·90 m^2)
Tailplane	9·69 sq ft (0·90 m^2)
Elevators, incl tabs	8·61 sq ft (0·80 m^2)

WEIGHTS AND LOADINGS:

Weight empty, equipped	705 lb (320 kg)
Max T-O weight	1,190 lb (540 kg)
Wing loading:	
single-seat	4·71 lb/sq ft (23·0 kg/m^2)
two-seat, with radio	5·53 lb/sq ft (27·0 kg/m^2)
two-seat, with radio and oxygen (max)	5·94 lb/sq ft (29·0 kg/m^2)

PERFORMANCE (estimated, at relevant T-O weight):

Best glide ratio, non-retractable monowheel:	
single-seat at 45 knots (52 mph; 84 km/h)	36
two-seat at 49 knots (57 mph; 91·5 km/h)	36
Best glide ratio, retractable monowheel:	
both versions	38
Min sinking speed:	
single-seat	1·94 ft (0·59 m)/sec
two-seat, with radio	2·10 ft (0·64 m)/sec
two-seat, with radio and oxygen	2·20 ft (0·67 m)/sec
Stalling speed:	
single-seat	34·5 knots (39·5 mph; 63 km/h)
two-seat, with radio	37 knots (42·5 mph; 68 km/h)
two-seat, with radio and oxygen	38·5 knots (44 mph; 70·5 km/h)
Max speed (smooth air)	153 knots (176 mph; 284 km/h)
Max aero-tow speed	91·5 knots (105 mph; 170 km/h)
g limits	+ 5·3 (normal) to + 8 (ultimate)

GEP

GROUPE D'ÉTUDES GEORGES PAYRE

ADDRESS:

2 rue Abel, 75012 Paris

Telephone: 522.30.31

Dr Pierre Vaysse, the well-known French glider pilot and head of the amateur sailplane construction department of the FFVV (Fédération Française de Vol à Voile), built and flew two single-seat sailplanes which he designated **Trucavaysse TCV-01** and **TCV-02.** These flew for the first time on 7 August 1964 and 6 April 1969 respectively; by 1 October 1973 the TCV-01 had flown for 630 hours, and the TCV-02 (more than 368 hours) had made flights of up to 161 nm (186 miles; 300 km) in length. The TCV-02 was damaged in August 1972, but was expected to fly again, after repairs and modifications, in the Spring of 1974.

External appearance of the TCV-01 and TCV-02 is shown in the accompanying photographs. The structure is based upon the wings of the Breguet 905 Fauvette (see 1962-63 *Jane's*), with reinforced root fairings. Several Fauvette components are also used in the fuselage, which is of all-wood construction. The TCV-02 fuselage is 1 ft 1¾ in (0·35 m) longer than that of the TCV-01, has a non-retractable monowheel aft of the landing skid, elevator trim, and a cockpit canopy from a CARMAM M-100 S.

Objective of this series of sailplanes has been to evolve an aircraft that can be sold in kit form for amateur constructors or for club construction. Encouragement has been given by both the FFVV and the RSA, and plans are now available of the developed version, which is known as the TCV-03.

Trucavaysse TCV-01 single-seat sailplane, first flown in 1964

Trucavaysse TCV-02, developed from the TCV-01 with longer fuselage, modified canopy and landing wheel

GEP TCV-03 TRUCAVAYSSE

Design of the TCV-03 takes into account work done by the Groupe d'Etudes Georges Payre (GEP) in modifying the original Breguet 905 design to make the aircraft suitable for amateur construction. Modifications include re-covered wings with improved control system and reinforced trailing-edges; a new, more slender fuselage outline; and deletion of the landing skid.

Design began in October 1968, and prototype construction started in February 1969. This aircraft (F-CRRH), built by the Aéro Club de Norois, flew for the first time on 14 July 1973 and by February 1974 eight others were under construction by amateur builders. Authorisation for about 15 had then been granted by the CNRA.

WINGS: Cantilever shoulder-wing monoplane. Wing section NACA 63-420 at root, NACA 63-513 at tip. Dihedral 3° from roots. Incidence 4°. No sweepback. Conventional single-spar structure, forming torsion box with plywood/Klégécel sandwich leading-edge. DFS metal airbrakes on upper and lower surfaces. Slotted wooden ailerons. No flaps.

FUSELAGE: Conventional plywood-covered wooden structure.

TAIL UNIT: Cantilever wooden structure with single fin and rudder and one-piece all-moving tailplane with anti-tabs.

LANDING GEAR: Non-retractable monowheel and tailskid. Rubber shock-absorbers. Tyre size 330 × 130 mm.

ACCOMMODATION: Single adjustable seat under one-piece transparent canopy.

DIMENSIONS, EXTERNAL:
- Wing span: 42 ft 9½ in (15·00 m)
- Wing chord at root: 3 ft 7¼ in (1·10 m)
- Wing chord at tip: 1 ft 3¾ in (0·40 m)
- Wing mean aerodynamic chord: 2 ft 8¼ in (0·82 m)
- Wing aspect ratio: 20
- Length overall: 21 ft 11¾ in (6·70 m)
- Height overall: 5 ft 11 in (1·80 m)
- Fuselage: Max depth: 2 ft 11½ in (0·90 m)
- Tailplane span: 9 ft 4¼ in (2·85 m)

AREAS:
- Wings, gross: 121·1 sq ft (11·25 m²)
- Ailerons (total): 13·56 sq ft (1·26 m²)
- Fin: 6·46 sq ft (0·60 m²)
- Rudder: 5·38 sq ft (0·50 m²)
- Tailplane, incl tabs: 16·15 sq ft (1·50 m²)

WEIGHTS AND LOADING:
- Weight empty, equipped: 423 lb (192 kg)
- Max T-O weight: 665 lb (302 kg)
- Max wing loading: 5·5 lb/sq ft (26·9 kg/m²)

PERFORMANCE (at max T-O weight):
- Best glide ratio at 43·5 knots (50 mph; 80 km/h): 28
- Min sinking speed at 32·5 knots (37·5 mph; 60 km/h): 2·62 ft (0·80 m)/sec
- Stalling speed: 27·5 knots (31·5 mph; 50 km/h)
- Max speed (smooth air): 113 knots (130 mph; 210 km/h)
- Max speed (rough air): 81 knots (93 mph; 150 km/h)
- Max aero-tow and max winch-launching speed: 59 knots (68 mph; 110 km/h)
- g limit: +5

GEP TCV-03 Trucavaysse single-seat sailplane, intended for amateur construction

JACQUET ET POTTIER

ROBERT JACQUET and JEAN POTTIER

ADDRESS:
c/o Société CARMAM, BP 201, 03001 Moulins

MM Jacquet and Pottier are developing two essentially similar sailplanes, the J.P.15-36 for factory production and the J.P.15-34 for marketing in kit form to amateur constructors. A more advanced project, the all-plastics J.P.18-36, is in the preliminary design stage.

JACQUET ET POTTIER J.P. 15-36 AIGLON (EAGLET)

This Standard Class sailplane was designed as a private venture by MM Jacquet and Pottier, who are Technical Directors of CARMAM (which see).

Design of the J.P. 15-36 began in September 1971, and prototype construction started at the end of 1972. The prototype (F-WCAP) made its first flight on 14 June 1974.

TYPE: Single-seat Standard Class sailplane.

WINGS: Cantilever mid-wing monoplane. Wortmann wing sections: FX-67-K-170 at root, FX-67-126 at tip. Dihedral 3°. Incidence 7° at root, 4° at tip. Sweepback 0° at 30% chord. Structure consists of a single load-bearing glassfibre spar, 3·94 in (10 cm) deep, with four-point attachment to fuselage. Glassfibre/Klégécel/epoxy sandwich skin, 0·4 in (10 mm) thick on inner half-span and 0·2 in (5 mm) thick on outer panels. Steel-tipped wingtip "salmons". Plastics plain ailerons, deflecting 10° up and 25° down, can be operated differentially or in unison. Plastics airbrake on each trailing-edge, deflecting 90° downward.

FUSELAGE: Semi-monocoque glassfibre/Klégécel sandwich structure, 0·4 in (10 mm) thick, moulded in two halves and joined at centreline. Single bulkhead, combining functions of cockpit backrest and shock-absorbing structure for main landing wheel. Special strengthening of the union between this bulkhead and the wing main spar.

TAIL UNIT: Cantilever type, with slight sweepback on vertical surfaces. Single-spar all-moving plastics tailplane and plastics rudder. Fin built integrally with fuselage.

LANDING GEAR: Non-retractable monowheel, size 300 × 130, and tail bumper. Cable-operated brake.

Jacquet et Pottier J.P. 15-36 single-seat Standard Class sailplane

ACCOMMODATION: Single semi-reclining (25°) seat under one-piece removable transparent canopy.

DIMENSIONS, EXTERNAL:
- Wing span: 49 ft 2½ in (15·00 m)
- Wing chord at root: 3 ft 3¼ in (1·00 m)
- Wing chord at tip: 1 ft 3⅝ in (0·40 m)
- Wing mean aerodynamic chord: 2 ft 5 in (0·735 m)
- Wing aspect ratio: 20·4
- Length overall: 20 ft 3½ in (6·18 m)
- Height overall: 4 ft 7 in (1·40 m)
- Tailplane span: 8 ft 2½ in (2·50 m)

AREAS:
- Wings, gross: 118·4 sq ft (11·00 m²)
- Ailerons (total): 10·29 sq ft (0·956 m²)
- Airbrakes (total): 11·84 sq ft (1·10 m²)
- Fin: 5·92 sq ft (0·55 m²)
- Rudder: 6·03 sq ft (0·56 m²)
- Tailplane: 11·30 sq ft (1·05 m²)

WEIGHTS AND LOADING:
- Weight empty, equipped: 396 lb (180 kg)
- Max T-O weight: 661 lb (300 kg)
- Max wing loading: 5·53 lb/sq ft (27 kg/m²)

PERFORMANCE (estimated, at max T-O weight):
- Best glide ratio at 43·5 knots (50 mph; 80 km/h): 36
- Min sinking speed at 39 knots (45 mph; 72 km/h): 2·03 ft (0·62 m)/sec
- Stalling speed: 33·5 knots (39 mph; 62 km/h)
- Max speed (smooth air): 135 knots (155 mph; 250 km/h)
- Max speed (rough air): 108 knots (124 mph; 200 km/h)
- Max aero-tow and winch-launching speed: 81 knots (93 mph; 150 km/h)
- g limit: +8

JACQUET ET POTTIER J.P. 15-34

This is essentially the same aeroplane as the J.P. 15-36, with some constructional simplification to make it suitable for amateur builders.

WINGS: As J.P. 15-36.

FUSELAGE: Of same contours and dimensions as J.P. 15-36, but of mainly wooden construction (spruce longerons and plywood skin) except for glassfibre nosecone.

TAIL UNIT: As J.P. 15-36, but of plywood-covered spruce construction. Rudder and rear part of tailplane fabric-covered.

PERFORMANCE (estimated, at wing loading of 5·12 lb/sq ft; 25 kg/m²):
- Best glide ratio at 41·5 knots (48 mph; 77 km/h): 34
- Min sinking speed at 38 knots (43·5 mph; 70 km/h): 2·07 ft (0·63 m)/sec
- Stalling speed: 32·5 knots (37·5 mph; 60 km/h)

PINGOUIN

SOCIÉTÉ DES ATELIERS DU PINGOUIN

ADDRESS:
16 rue Fouquet, 93700-Drancy
Telephone: 284-13-53
PROPRIETOR:
Jean Paul Menin

PINGOUIN BM 1

This single-seat sailplane has been designed and built by two amateur constructor members of the Réseau du Sport de l'Air.

Of modular construction, and designed for ease of operation and maintenance, it is designed for quick dismantling (or rapid replacement of a damaged airframe component), and is available in prefabricated kit form for simple assembly by gliding clubs or amateur constructors. Sub-assemblies can be supplied to virtually any desired degree of prefabrication. The general appearance of the BM 1 can be seen from the accompanying three-view drawing.

WINGS: Wortmann wing sections.

DIMENSIONS:
- Wing span: 49 ft 2½ in (15·00 m)
- Wing aspect ratio: 22·5

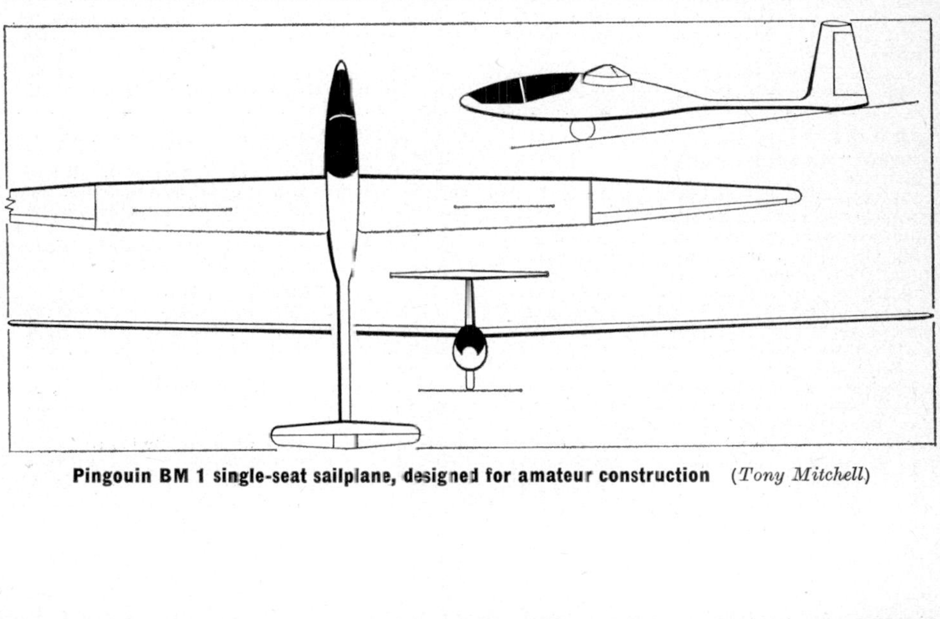

Pingouin BM 1 single-seat sailplane, designed for amateur construction (*Tony Mitchell*)

Length overall	21 ft 4 in (6·50 m)
Height overall	4 ft 11 in (1·50 m)
Wing area, gross	107·6 sq ft (10·00 m²)
WEIGHTS AND LOADINGS:	
Weight empty	441 lb (200 kg)
Max T-O weight (incl ballast)	771 lb (350 kg)
Wing loading (prototype)	5·73-6·35 lb/sq ft (28·31 kg/m²)
Wing loading (production aircraft)	5·53-7·17 lb/sq ft (27-35 kg/m²)
PERFORMANCE (at wing loading of 5·73 lb/sq ft; 28 kg/m²):	
Best glide ratio at 47·5 knots (55 mph; 88 km/h)	37
Min sinking speed at 38 knots (43·5 mph; 70 km/h)	1·97 ft (0·60 m)/sec
Sinking speed at 81 knots (93 mph; 150 km/h)	6·56 ft (2·00 m)/sec

SIREN

SIREN SA

WORKS AND OFFICES:
Route des Chambons, BP 42, 36200 Argenton/Creuse
Telephone: (54) 04.14.47
Telex: 76534 Chamco-Châteauroux Siren 200-1
DIRECTOR:
Philippe Moniot

Well known as a manufacturer of aircraft components and equipment, Siren has in recent years built the C.30S Edelweiss single-seat Standard Class sailplane and an Open Class development designated Edelweiss IV, both of which were described in the 1971-72 *Jane's*.

A later design, the **CE 75 Silene,** is described under the CERVA heading in this section.

In 1974 Siren was building the prototype of a new single-seat sailplane known as the D 77 Iris, a description of which follows:

SIREN D 77 IRIS

Design of the Iris began in 1973. A prototype is under construction, and is expected to fly in 1975.

TYPE: Single-seat training sailplane.

WINGS: Cantilever mid-wing monoplane. Bertin E55 166 wing section, with thickness/chord ratio of 16·6%. Dihedral 3° at centre-chord line. Incidence 3°. Sweepforward 2° at quarter-chord. PMC foam sandwich construction. Airbrake on each wing.

TAIL UNIT: Cantilever T-tail, of similar construction to wings. Fixed-incidence tailplane. Trim tab in elevator.

LANDING GEAR: Non-retractable monowheel, without shock-absorption, and tail bumper. Wheel size 330 × 130 mm, tyre pressure 20 lb/sq in (1·4 kg/cm²). Siren hydraulic brake.

ACCOMMODATION: Single adjustable seat under one-piece canopy.

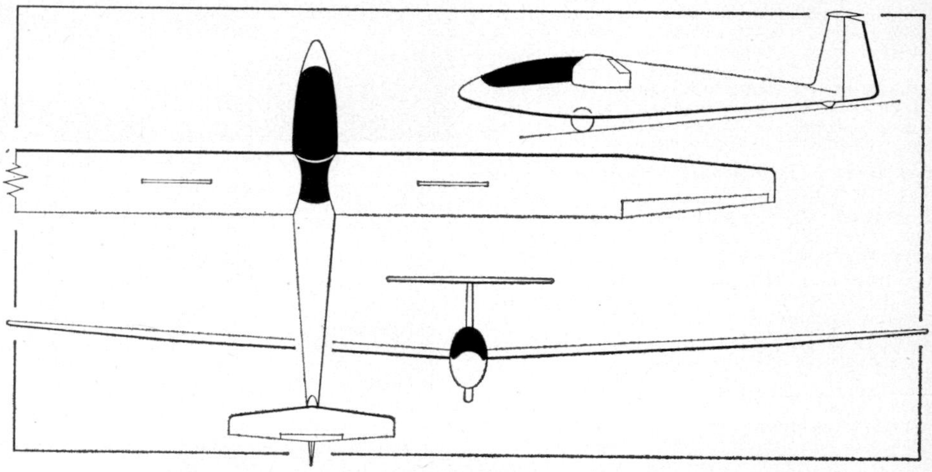

Siren D 77 Iris single-seat training sailplane (*Michael A. Badrocke*)

DIMENSIONS, EXTERNAL:	
Wing span	44 ft 3½ in (13·50 m)
Wing chord at root	3 ft 0¼ in (0·92 m)
Wing aspect ratio	17
Length overall	19 ft 8¼ in (6·00 m)
Height overall	5 ft 7 in (1·70 m)
Tailplane span	7 ft 10½ in (2·40 m)
AREAS:	
Wings, gross	118·4 sq ft (11·00 m²)
Fin	10·76 sq ft (1·00 m²)
Rudder	10·76 sq ft (1·00 m²)
Tailplane	7·00 sq ft (0·65 m²)
Elevator, incl tab	3·77 sq ft (0·35 m²)
WEIGHTS AND LOADING:	
Weight empty, equipped	396 lb (180 kg)
Max T-O weight	639 lb (290 kg)
Max wing loading	6·25 lb/sq ft (30·5 kg/m²)
PERFORMANCE (estimated):	
Best glide ratio at 51 knots (59 mph; 95 km/h)	33
Min sinking speed at 36·5 knots (42·25 mph; 68 km/h)	2·3 ft (0·70 m)/sec
Stalling speed	37 knots (42·5 mph; 68·4 km/h)
Max speed (smooth air)	64·5 knots (74·5 mph; 120 km/h)

SLCA

SOCIÉTÉ LORRAINE DE CONSTRUCTIONS AÉRONAUTIQUES

ADDRESS:
Aérodrome de Thionville, 57110-Yutz, Moselle
Telephone: (87) 88.56.87
DIRECTOR:
Gilbert Schmitt
ENGINEER:
Roger Kieger

This company is building the Scheibe SF-27 under licence in France, where it is known as the Topaze. German production of the SF-27 has ended.

SLCA-10 and SLCA-11 TOPAZE

The Topaze is the Scheibe SF-27 Zugvogel V built under licence in France by SLCA. It received a French certificate of airworthiness on 25 April 1972.

SLCA built nine examples of the SF-27 under the French designation SLCA-10. The current version, designated SLCA-11, has the monowheel lowered 3·15 in (80 mm). It flew for the first time on 15 October 1973, and seven had been completed by March 1974.

The following description applies to the SLCA-11:

TYPE: Single-seat Standard Class sailplane.

WINGS: Cantilever shoulder-wing monoplane. Wing section Wortmann FX-61-184 at root, FX-60-126 at tip. Dihedral 3°. Wooden structure, with laminated beechwood box spar at about 43% chord. Plywood ribs. Leading-edge torsion box. Outboard half of wing plywood-covered; inboard half covered with plywood to 6 cm behind spar; remainder part-fabric and part-plywood covered. Wooden ailerons, plywood-covered. Schempp-Hirth glassfibre/metal airbrakes.

FUSELAGE: Welded steel tube structure. Nose section back to wing trailing-edge covered with moulded glassfibre shell. Rear section fabric-covered over wooden stringers. Moulded glassfibre fairing over wing/fuselage junction.

SLCA-11 current production version of the Topaze single-seat Standard Class sailplane

TAIL UNIT: Cantilever wood structure, with all-moving horizontal surfaces. Tailplane covered with plywood and fabric. Fin plywood-covered; rudder fabric-covered. Anti-balance tab in port half of tailplane.

LANDING GEAR: Non-retractable and unsprung monowheel ahead of CG, tyre size 4·00-4. Wheel brake. No skid. Tailwheel diameter 7·9 in (20 cm).

ACCOMMODATION: Single inclined seat under moulded Plexiglas canopy. Rudder pedals adjustable. Baggage compartment behind seat.

DIMENSIONS, EXTERNAL:	
Wing span	49 ft 2½ in (15·00 m)
Wing chord at root	3 ft 7 in (1·09 m)
Wing chord at tip	1 ft 5½ in (0·44 m)
Wing aspect ratio	18·6
Length overall	23 ft 3¼ in (7·09 m)
Tailplane span	8 ft 3¼ in (2·52 m)
Max width of fuselage	1 ft 10½ in (0·57 m)
AREAS:	
Wings, gross	129·9 sq ft (12·07 m²)
Ailerons (total)	10·76 sq ft (1·0 m²)
Airbrakes (total)	4·09 sq ft (0·38 m²)
Fin	5·81 sq ft (0·54 m²)
Rudder	6·67 sq ft (0·62 m²)
Tailplane	16·68 sq ft (1·55 m²)
WEIGHTS AND LOADING:	
Weight empty, equipped	474 lb (215 kg)
Max T-O weight	760 lb (345 kg)
Max wing loading	5·88 lb/sq ft (28·7 kg/m²)
PERFORMANCE (at max T-O weight):	
Best glide ratio at 48 knots (55 mph; 88 km/h)	33·6
Min sinking speed at 40 knots (46 mph; 74 km/h)	2·10 ft (0·64 m)/sec
Stalling speed	31·5 knots (36 mph; 58 km/h)
Max speed (smooth air) and max aero-tow speed	108 knots (124 mph; 200 km/h)
Max speed (rough air)	91 knots (105 mph; 170 km/h)
Max winch-launching speed	59·5 knots (68·5 mph; 110 km/h)
g limit	+5·3

SURVOL

"SURVOL"-CHARLES FAUVEL

HEAD OFFICE:
72 Boulevard Carnot, 06400 - Cannes AM
Telephone: 39.83.32 and 39.55.21

Charles Fauvel has been developing and producing for many years a series of tail-less sailplanes. The original AV.36 Monobloc single-seater first flew in 1951 and more than 100 were sold to customers in 14 countries before this design was superseded by the improved AV.36 Mk II, the official designation of which is AV.361.

Several powered versions of M Fauvel's sailplane designs have been produced. It was at one time intended to fit the de Coucy Pygmée engine (see 1972-73 *Jane's*) in production versions of both the AV.45 and the AV.221, but this proposal was abandoned after the death of the engine's designer. The prototype AV.45 has been used to flight test a lightweight turbojet power plant.

In early February 1971 M Fauvel decided to end commercial production of his sailplanes, but plans are available for their construction by gliding clubs or homebuilders.

Details of recent Fauvel light aircraft designs can be found in the "Aircraft" section.

FAUVEL AV.361

It is known that a total of well over 100 AV.36 and AV.361 sailplanes are flying in 17 countries. Plans are available in French and English, and construction by amateurs continues, especially in the USA and Spain. In France, in 1967, M Gilg of Rouen won the first prize in the amateur-built glider class with his AV.361 at the annual meeting of the Réseau du Sport de l'Air.

Details of this single-seat general-purpose sailplane may be found in the 1970-71 *Jane's*.

The standard F2 section wing can, at builder's option, be replaced in the AV.361 by one with a Wortmann FX-66-H-159 laminar-flow section, which increases the best glide ratio to 30 at a speed of 46 knots (53 mph; 85 km/h).

The following particulars apply to an AV.361 completed by the Escuela de Aeromodelismo at Alicante, Spain:

DIMENSIONS:	
Wing span	41 ft 11¼ in (12·78 m)
Length overall	10 ft 7½ in (3·24 m)
Wing area, gross	157·15 sq ft (14·60 m²)
WEIGHTS:	
Weight empty	275·5 lb (125 kg)
Max T-O weight	568 lb (258 kg)
PERFORMANCE:	
Best glide ratio at 44 knots (51 mph; 82 km/h)	26
Min sinking speed	2·43 ft (0·74 m)/sec

Max speed (smooth air)
118·5 knots (136·5 mph; 220 km/h)

FAUVEL AV.45

The AV.45 is a single-seat tail-less self-launching sailplane which first flew on 4 May 1960 with a 35 hp Nelson engine.

A second, slightly modified prototype, with 22 hp SOLO engine, was built by Société Aéronautique Normande (SAN) and is typical of several examples being built by amateurs in France and other countries, including Japan, Martinique and the USA.

Details were given in the 1973-74 *Jane's* of the fitting of a Microturbo Eclair turbojet engine in the first prototype. This has now been removed, and the standard engine recommended for the AV.45 is the 40-55 hp modified Hirth 280R.

As with the AV.361, the AV.45 may also be fitted with a Wortmann laminar-flow wing, with which the best glide ratio is increased to 30 at a speed of 47·5 knots (55 mph; 88 km/h).

FAUVEL AV.48

Brief details of the AV.48 as originally designed appeared in the 1970-71 *Jane's*, but construction of the prototype was suspended when the factory in which it was to have been built was destroyed by fire.

Advantage has been taken of the delay to make further improvements in the design. Up to the Spring of 1974 these included:

WINGS: Wortmann FX-66-H-159 laminar-flow section standard.

TAIL UNIT: Vertical surfaces of Wortmann symmetrical bi-convex section.

LANDING GEAR: Further development under way.

POWER PLANT: Not yet selected, but the earlier choice of the Pygmée has now been discarded. Propeller blade folding is under consideration.

DIMENSIONS, EXTERNAL:
Wing span 54 ft 9½ in (16·70 m)
Wing aspect ratio 15·27

AREA:
Wings, gross 196·2 sq ft (18·23 m²)

PERFORMANCE (estimated):
Best glide ratio 36
Min sinking speed at 38 knots (43·5 mph; 70 km/h) 1·97 ft (0·60 m)/sec

FAUVEL AV.221 and AV.222

The AV.221 side-by-side two-seat self-launching sailplane was developed from the AV.22 tail-less sailplane, of which details can be found in the 1960-61 *Jane's*. It flew for the first time on 8 April 1965. Brief details of the AV.221 were given in the 1970-71 *Jane's*.

Plans are available to amateur constructors of a lighter and simplified version of the AV.221, designated AV.222, of which examples are being built in France, Germany and the USA.

The following details apply to the AV.222, which is illustrated in the accompanying three-view drawing. The wings of the AV.222 are built in three sections; under consideration as suitable power plants are the 40 hp Rectimo or 60 hp Limbach Volkswagen conversions, the 55 hp Hirth 280 with Power Grip toothed-belt reduction gear, or the 70 hp modified Hirth 280.

DIMENSIONS, EXTERNAL:
Wing span 53 ft 9¾ in (16·40 m)
Wing aspect ratio 12
Length overall 17 ft 1½ in (5·22 m)

AREA:
Wings, gross 247·6 sq ft (23·00 m²)

WEIGHTS:
Weight empty 716 lb (325 kg)
Max T-O weight 1,212 lb (550 kg)

PERFORMANCE:
Best glide ratio (propeller feathered) at 46 knots (53 mph; 85 km/h) 26
Min sinking speed (2-seat) at 40 knots (46 mph; 74 km/h) 2·85 ft (0·87 m)/sec
Min sinking speed (single-seat) at 38 knots (43·5 mph; 70 km/h) 2·56 ft (0·78 m)/sec
Rate of climb, powered 591 ft (180 m)/min
T-O run, powered 361 ft (110 m)
T-O to 50 ft (15 m), powered 755 ft (230 m)

Fauvel AV.221 self-launching sailplane

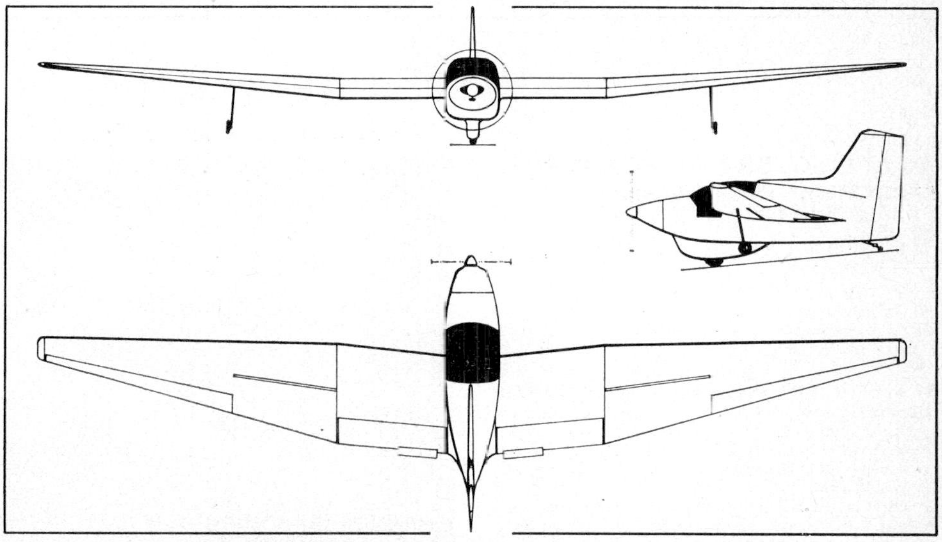

Fauvel AV.222 side-by-side two-seat powered sailplane (*Roy J. Grainge*)

WASSMER

WASSMER-AVIATION SA

HEAD OFFICE AND WORKS:
Route de Parentignat, 63501-Issoire

DELIVERY AND AFTER-SALES SERVICE:
BP 7, 63501-Aérodrome d'Issoire

Telephone: Issoire 269

OFFICERS:
See "Aircraft" section

In addition to manufacturing light aeroplanes, as described in the "Aircraft" section, Wassmer has long been famous as a builder of gliders and sailplanes. These included the successful Javelot and Super Javelot single-seat sailplanes and the AV.36 tail-less single-seat sailplane designed by M Charles Fauvel, which are no longer in production. Details of these types can be found in previous editions of *Jane's*.

In current production are the WA-26 and WA-28 Squale and WA-30 Bijave.

WASSMER WA-26 SQUALE (DOGFISH)

The prototype of this 15 metre single-seat high-performance sailplane flew for the first time on 21 July 1967. Series production started in 1968 and by January 1970 orders for 85 Squales had been placed. Four were sold in 1972.

The WA-26 is available also without the anti-tab in the horizontal tail surface, under the designation **WA-26 CM**; and in a version combining the standard WA-26 or WA-26 CM fuselage and tail unit with the all-plastics wing of the WA-28.

TYPE: Single-seat high-performance sailplane.

WINGS: Cantilever shoulder-wing monoplane. Wing section FX-61-163 at root, FX-60-126 at tip. Dihedral 3°. Orthodox wood construction. Trailing-edge airbrakes inboard of ailerons.

FUSELAGE: Reinforced polyester plastics structure of oval section.

TAIL UNIT: Conventional wood structure with fabric covering. All-moving horizontal surfaces, with spring-loaded anti-tab.

LANDING GEAR: Retractable monowheel mounted forward of CG. Wassmer size 330 × 130 mm wheel; tyre pressure 28·5 lb/sq in (2 kg/cm²). Satmo hydraulic brake. Optional fixed wheel.

ACCOMMODATION: Single semi-reclining adjustable seat under a long flush Plexiglas canopy.

DIMENSIONS, EXTERNAL:
Wing span 49 ft 2½ in (15·0 m)
Wing chord at root 3 ft 7¼ in (1·10 m)
Wing chord at tip 1 ft 3¾ in (0·40 m)
Wing aspect ratio 18
Length overall 24 ft 10¾ in (7·6 m)
Height over tail 4 ft 9 in (1·45 m)
Tailplane span 9 ft 10¼ in (3·0 m)

AREAS:
Wings, gross 135·6 sq ft (12·6 m²)
Rudder 11·84 sq ft (1·1 m²)
Tailplane 16·15 sq ft (1·5 m²)

WEIGHTS:
Weight empty 540 lb (245 kg)
Max T-O weight 833 lb (378 kg)

PERFORMANCE:
Best glide ratio at 48·5 knots (56 mph; 90 km/h) 38
Sinking speed:
at 39 knots (45 mph; 72 km/h) 2 ft (0·61 m)/sec
at 54 knots (62 mph; 100 km/h) 2·62 ft (0·80 m)/sec
at 65 knots (75 mph; 120 km/h) 3·60 ft (1·10 m)/sec
at 81 knots (93 mph; 150 km/h) 6·39 ft (1·95 m)/sec
Stalling speed at max T-O weight 35 knots (40 mph; 64 km/h)
Max speed (smooth air) 134 knots (155 mph; 250 km/h)
Max speed (rough air) 97 knots (112 mph; 180 km/h)
Max aero-tow speed 81 knots (93 mph; 150 km/h)
g limit 8 (Norme Air 2054)

WASSMER WA-28 SQUALE (DOGFISH)

This version of the Squale differs from the WA-26 versions primarily in having wings of all-plastics construction. The wings are geometrically identical to the WA-26, but are of glassfibre/PMC sandwich construction, similar to those of the CERVA CE 75 Silene (which see), and are fitted with Schempp-Hirth airbrakes. The WA-28 is available with either fixed or retractable monowheel landing gear, and WA-28 wing units can be mated to existing WA-26 fuselages and tail units.

By the Spring of 1974 orders for several WA-28s had been received. First flight was made in early 1974.

WASSMER WA-30 BIJAVE

The Bijave is a two-seat advanced training glider, developed from the WA-21 Javelot (see 1961-62 *Jane's*). The first prototype flew for the first time on 17 December 1958 and the second, improved prototype on 18 March 1960. About 285 had been built by early 1970, with production continuing at the rate of four per month. Two were sold in 1972.

TYPE: Two-seat advanced training glider.

WINGS: Cantilever shoulder-wing monoplane.

Wassmer WA-26 Squale single-seat high-performance sailplane

Wing section NACA 63·821 at root, NACA 63·615 at tip. Dihedral 0° at root, 4° 30′ on outer wings. Incidence 4°. Wood structure, with birch plywood covering forward of spar, fabric covering aft of spar. Plain spruce ailerons, fabric-covered. No flaps. Perforated wooden airbrakes, retracting into slots above and below each wing. Wingtip "salmons".

FUSELAGE: Welded steel tube structure, covered with fabric and reinforced plastics.

TAIL UNIT: Cantilever wood structure with fabric-covered control surfaces. All-moving one-piece tailplane, with large tab.

LANDING GEAR: Retractable monowheel, size 330 × 130. Niemann rubber-ring shock-absorption. Dunlop or Kléber-Colombes tyre, pressure 43 lb/sq in (3 kg/cm²). Satmo motorcycle brake. Rubber-sprung wooden nose-skid. Steel tailskid.

ACCOMMODATION: Two persons in tandem under individual Plexiglas transparent canopies. Equipment can include full range of instruments, compass, oxygen and radio.

DIMENSIONS, EXTERNAL:

Wing span	55 ft 3 in (16·85 m)
Wing chord at root	4 ft 3 in (1·30 m)
Wing chord at tip	2 ft 5⅛ in (0·74 m)
Wing aspect ratio	15
Length overall	31 ft 2 in (9·50 m)
Height over tail	9 ft 0 in (2·74 m)
Tailplane span	10 ft 6 in (3·20 m)

AREAS:

Wings, gross	206·7 sq ft (19·20 m²)
Ailerons (total)	24·11 sq ft (2·24 m²)
Vertical tail surfaces (total)	17·22 sq ft (1·60 m²)
Horizontal tail surfaces (total)	28·00 sq ft (2·60 m²)

WEIGHTS:

Weight empty, with min equipment	639 lb (290 kg)
Max T-O weight	1,102 lb (500 kg)

PERFORMANCE (at max T-O weight):

Best glide ratio at 46 knots (53 mph; 85 km/h) 30

Sinking speed:
- at 41 knots (47 mph; 75 km/h) 2·30 ft (0·70 m)/sec
- at 54 knots (62 mph; 100 km/h) 3·60 ft (1·10 m)/sec
- at 65 knots (75 mph; 120 km/h) 5·57 ft (1·70 m)/sec

Stalling speed 33 knots (37 mph; 60 km/h)

Max speed (smooth air) 129 knots (149 mph; 240 km/h)

Max speed (rough air) and max aero-tow speed 81 knots (93 mph; 150 km/h)

Wassmer WA-30 Bijave

Max winch-launching speed 54 knots (62 mph; 100 km/h)

GERMANY
(FEDERAL REPUBLIC)

AKAFLIEG BRAUNSCHWEIG

AKADEMISCHE FLIEGERGRUPPE BRAUNSCHWEIG EV

ADDRESS:

3300 Braunschweig, Flughafen Waggum, Aka-flieg-Heim

Telephone: 0531/395249

The students of Brunswick University have built a series of high-performance sailplanes. Details of the latest were given in the 1973-74 *Jane's*.

AKAFLIEG BRAUNSCHWEIG SB-5c DANZIG

The prototype SB-5 flew for the first time on 3 June 1959. Licence production was undertaken by Fa Eichelsdörfer, 86 Bamberg, Hafenstrasse 6, and 15 more had been built by the spring of 1966. The current version, first flown in 1965, is the SB-5c, incorporating a number of design changes, and a total of about 100 had been built by early 1974.

TYPE: Single-seat Standard Class sailplane.

WINGS: Cantilever shoulder-wing monoplane. Wing section NACA 63_3-618. Dihedral 1° 30′. Incidence 0° 30′. Conventional single-spar wood structure with plywood covering. Wooden ailerons. Schempp-Hirth airbrakes at 50% chord.

FUSELAGE: Plywood monocoque of circular section.

TAIL UNIT: "Butterfly" type, of wooden construction.

LANDING GEAR: Non-retractable unsprung monowheel, size 4·00-4, with friction brake. Tyre pressure 28 lb/sq in (2·0 kg/cm²). Tailskid.

ACCOMMODATION: Single seat under drawn Plexiglas canopy.

DIMENSIONS, EXTERNAL:

Wing span	49 ft 2½ in (15·00 m)
Wing chord at root	3 ft 3⅜ in (1·00 m)
Wing chord at tip	1 ft 7¾ in (0·50 m)
Wing aspect ratio	17·3
Length overall	21 ft 10 in (6·65 m)
Tailplane span (horizontal projection)	9 ft 2¼ in (2·80 m)
Max width of fuselage	1 ft 11½ in (0·60 m)

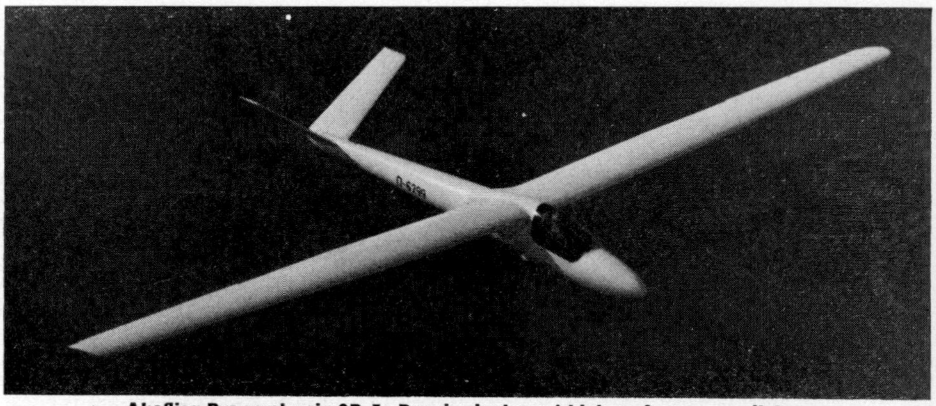

Akaflieg Braunschweig SB-5c Danzig single-seat high-performance sailplane

AREAS:

Wings, gross	140 sq ft (13·00 m²)
Airbrakes	4·20 sq ft (0·39 m²)
Fin (projected)	7·53 sq ft (0·7 m²)
Rudder (projected)	5·38 sq ft (0·5 m²)
Tailplane (projected)	10·76 sq ft (1·0 m²)
Elevators (projected)	7·53 sq ft (0·7 m²)

WEIGHTS AND LOADING:

Weight empty, equipped	507 lb (230 kg)
Max T-O weight	716 lb (325 kg)
Max wing loading	5·12 lb/sq ft (25·0 kg/m²)

PERFORMANCE (at max T-O weight):

Best glide ratio at 42 knots (48 mph; 77 km/h) 32·5

Min sinking speed at 36 knots (41 mph; 66 km/h) 2·07 ft (0·63 m)/sec

Stalling speed 32 knots (37 mph; 60 km/h)

Max speed (smooth air) 108 knots (124 mph; 200 km/h)

Max speed (rough air) 76 knots (87 mph; 140 km/h)

Max aero-tow speed 59 knots (68 mph; 110 km/h)

Max winch-launching speed 49 knots (56 mph; 90 km/h)

AKAFLIEG BRAUNSCHWEIG SB-10 SCHIROKKO

Design of this two-seat high-performance sailplane began in the Summer of 1969, and construction of the prototype a year later. It flew for the first time on 22 July 1972. The wings of the earlier SB-9 were modified for use in the SB-10 which, by the use of interchangeable wingtip panels, can be flown with a wing span of either 26 m or 29 m. The SB-10, which was not intended for production, was described and illustrated in the 1973-74 *Jane's*.

AKAFLIEG DARMSTADT

AKADEMISCHE FLIEGERGRUPPE DARMSTADT EV

ADDRESS:

Technische Hochschule, 61 Darmstadt

Telephone: 06541/162790

GROUP LEADER:

Gernot Neubauer

The Fliegergruppe of Darmstadt University has been designing, building and flying sailplanes for over 40 years. Its postwar products have included the D-34a single-seat high-performance sailplane, which flew for the first time in 1955; the D-34b, D-34c and D-34d, described in the 1962-63 *Jane's*; the D-36 Circe (1965-66 *Jane's*); the D-37b Artemis powered sailplane (1971-72 and 1972-73 *Jane's*) and the D-38 (1973-74 *Jane's*). A simplified version of the D-38 is in production as the DG-100 by Glaser-Dirks (which see).

AKAFLIEG DARMSTADT D-39

The D-39, which is the latest known Darmstadt design, is a project for a powered sailplane. It utilises the basic D-38 airframe, except for a low-mounted wing and a modified nose section in which are mounted a pair of Wankel rotating-piston engines driving a single folding propeller. No other details were known at the time of closing for press.

AKAFLIEG MÜNCHEN

AKADEMISCHE FLIEGERGRUPPE MÜNCHEN

ADDRESS:

8 München 2, Arcisstrasse 21

Students at Munich University have designed, built and flown a number of sailplanes, including the tandem two-seat Mü 23 Saurier of 20 m wing span, which made its first flight in 1959.

More recent designs have included the Mü 26 and Mü 27, of which the former was described in the 1973-74 *Jane's*.

AKAFLIEG MÜNCHEN Mü 26

Design of the Mü 26 began in 1962, and construction started two years later. Only one example (D-0726) was built, and this flew for the first time in 1971. A description appeared in the 1973-74 *Jane's*.

AKAFLIEG MÜNCHEN Mü 27

The Mü 27 is a two-seat high-performance sailplane, the general appearance of which is shown in the accompanying three-view drawing. A prototype is under construction.

WINGS: Cantilever shoulder-wing monoplane. Wortmann FX-67-VC-170/136 section, with area-increasing Fowler-type flaps which perform similarly to those of the British Sigma sailplane and increase the wing area by 36% when fully extended. Mixed glassfibre/foam sandwich construction, with aluminium alloy spar and metal webs. Ailerons are linked to flaps. Airbrakes at 50% chord on upper surfaces only.

FUSELAGE: All-glassfibre semi-monocoque structure.

TAIL UNIT: Cantilever T-tail of glassfibre/foam sandwich construction.

LANDING GEAR: Retractable monowheel and fixed tailwheel.

ACCOMMODATION: Two seats in tandem under two-piece moulded canopy.

DIMENSIONS, EXTERNAL:

Wing span	72 ft 2¼ in (22·00 m)
Wing aspect ratio:	
flaps in	27·5
flaps out	20·2
Length overall	33 ft 9½ in (10·30 m)
Height overall	5 ft 11 in (1·80 m)

AREAS:
Wings, gross:
flaps in 189·4 sq ft (17·60 m²)
flaps out 257·3 sq ft (23·90 m²)
WEIGHTS AND LOADINGS:
Weight empty 1,058 lb (480 kg)
Max T-O weight 1,543 lb (700 kg)
Max wing loading:
flaps in 8·2 lb/sq ft (40·0 kg/m²)
flaps out 6·0 lb/sq ft (29·3 kg/m²)
PERFORMANCE (estimated, at max T-O weight):
Best glide ratio:
at 54·5 knots (63 mph; 101 km/h), flaps in 47
at 47·5 knots (54·5 mph; 88 km/h), flaps out 39
Min sinking speed:
at 47 knots (54 mph; 87 km/h), flaps in 1·87 ft (0·57 m)/sec
at 32·5 knots (37·5 mph; 60 km/h), flaps out 1·84 ft (0·56 m)/sec
Max speed (smooth air) 151 knots (174 mph; 280 km/h)

Akaflieg München Mü 26 single-seat high-performance sailplane

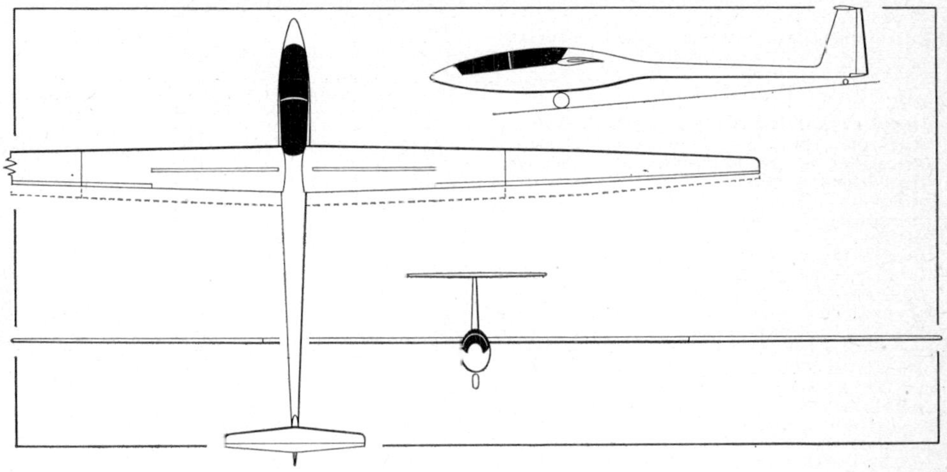

Akaflieg München Mü 27 two-seat high-performance sailplane (*Michael A. Badrocke*)

AKAFLIEG STUTTGART

AKADEMISCHE FLIEGERGRUPPE STUTTGART EV

ADDRESS:
7000 Stuttgart 80, Pfaffenwaldring 35
Telephone: 784 2442 and 784 2443
GROUP LEADER:
Dipl-Phys D. Althaus

The Akaflieg Stuttgart has been engaged continuously since the mid-1920s in aerodynamic research and experimental aircraft construction, mainly in the field of sailplane development, and it was in the wind tunnels at Stuttgart that the well-known Eppler and Wortmann wing sections were first developed. In more recent years Akaflieg Stuttgart has been in the forefront in developing the use of glassfibre in sailplane construction, and flew its first glassfibre sailplane, the FS-24 Phönix, on 25 November 1957. This aircraft, of which eight were built, was described under the Bölkow entry in the 1962-63 *Jane's*.

More recent designs have included the FS-25 Cuervo single-seat sailplane and FS-26 Moseppl powered sailplane, of which descriptions and illustrations appeared in the 1973-74 *Jane's*. A two-seat powered aircraft, the FS-28 Avispa, is described in the Aircraft section of this edition.

BLESSING

GERHARD BLESSING

ADDRESS:
2051 Hamburg-Ochsenwerder 1, Ochsenwerder Landstrasse 33

Herr Blessing, whose Gleiter Max two-seat powered sailplane was described and illustrated in the 1970-71 *Jane's*, has designed a new single/two-seat powered sailplane known as the Rebell, intended for amateur construction.

BLESSING REBELL

The Rebell is a single-seat powered sailplane, with provision for a second occupant. It has been designed for amateur construction, and is of steel tube with wood covering. The wings have Wortmann FX-66-S-196 root and FX-66-17A 11 tip sections and can, at builder's option, be made in two, three or four parts. No component of the aircraft is more than 11 ft 5¾ in (3·5 m) long, to facilitate assembly in confined spaces. The fuel tank and several other components are standard items obtainable from the motor car industry.

Power plant is a 54 hp Hirth M28 two-cylinder engine, driving a Hoffmann two-blade feathering pusher propeller. The landing gear consists of a semi-recessed monowheel, below the cockpit, and a tailwheel. Just inboard of each outer wing panel, which can be folded upward, there is an outrigger balancer wheel.

A prototype (D-KEBO) was completed in 1972, and is shown in the accompanying illustration.

Blessing Rebell one/two-seat sailplane, powered by a 54 hp Hirth engine (*Brian M. Service*)

DIMENSIONS:
Wing span 49 ft 2½ in (15·00 m)
Length overall 23 ft 7½ in (7·20 m)
Wing area, gross 183·0 sq ft (17·00 m²)
WEIGHTS:
Weight empty 926 lb (420 kg)
Max T-O weight 1,366 lb (620 kg)
PERFORMANCE (at max T-O weight, powered):
Max level speed 108 knots (124 mph; 200 km/h)
Cruising speed 81 knots (93 mph; 150 km/h)
Max rate of climb 591 ft (180 m)/min
Range 323 nm (372 miles; 600 km)

DIEHL-ZETTL

BAUGEMEINSCHAFT DIEHL/ZETTL

ADDRESS:
6293 Löhnberg/Lahn, Backstania 6

MOTORRAAB IV 017

The Motorraab IV 017 is a powered version of the Raab IV single-seat sailplane, fitted with a 40 hp Hirth 017 two-cylinder two-stroke engine.

All known details were given in the 1973-74 *Jane's*.

FL

FL-III

This new single-seat Standard Class sailplane, announced at the end of 1973, was designed by a former student of Braunschweig University, who also took part in the design of the Akaflieg Braunschweig SB-8 and SB-9 described in previous editions of *Jane's*. The FL-III is of all-plastics construction, has a retractable monowheel landing gear, and provision in the wings for up to 11 Imp gallons (50 litres) of water ballast. A Wortmann FX-61-184 wing section is employed.

DIMENSIONS, EXTERNAL:
Wing span 49 ft 2½ in (15·00 m)
Wing aspect ratio 19·07
Length overall 22 ft 8 in (6·91 m)
Height 2 ft 8¾ in (0·83 m)
AREA:
Wings, gross 127 sq ft (11·80 m²)

WEIGHTS AND LOADING:
Weight empty 507 lb (230 kg)
Max T-O weight 881 lb (400 kg)
Max wing loading 6·94 lb/sq ft (33·9 kg/m²)
PERFORMANCE (estimated):
Best glide ratio 37·6
Min sinking speed at 39 knots (45 mph; 72 km/h) 1·87 ft (0·57 m)/sec
Max speed (smooth air) 124 knots (143 mph; 230 km/h)
Stalling speed 34 knots (39 mph; 62 km/h)

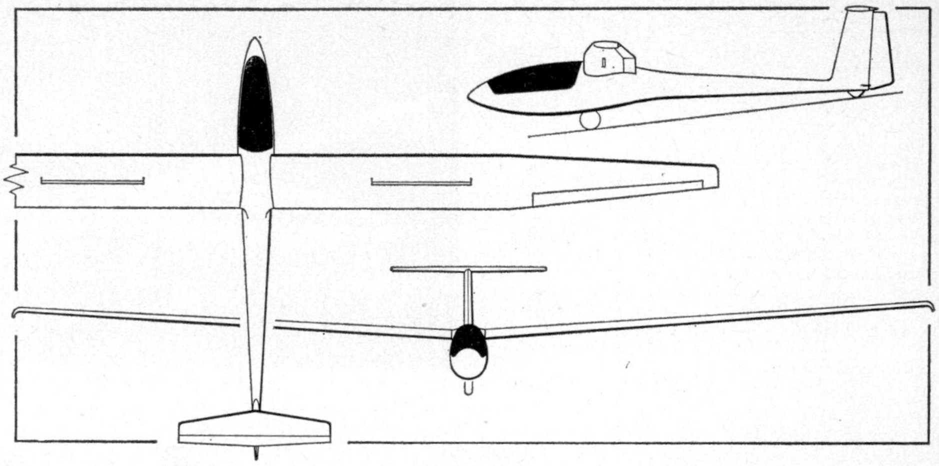

FL-III single-seat Standard Class sailplane (*Michael A. Badrocke*)

FVA

FLUGWISSENSCHAFTLICHE VEREINIGUNG AACHEN (1920) EV (Aeronautical Research Association of the Rhine-Westfälia Technical High School, Aachen)

ADDRESS:
51 Aachen, Templergraben 55

OFFICERS:
Prof Dr Ing A. W. Quick
Prof Dr rer nat W. Seibold
Dr Ing Walter Bellingrodt

FOUNDER: Prof Dr Theodore von Kármán

The FVA designed and built a number of sailplanes between the first and second World Wars, beginning with the FVA-1 of 1920 and ending with the FVA-13 of 1940. It resumed these activities in 1951, and its recent activities have included the construction of a Schleicher Ka 8 single-seat training sailplane. It also designed and built the FVA-18 described in the "Aircraft" section of the 1972-73 *Jane's*.

Its latest product is the FVA-20, a Standard Class sailplane of glassfibre construction.

FVA-20

The FVA-20 is a single-seat Standard Class sailplane, designed to explore experimental methods of glassfibre construction. A prototype was under construction in 1973, and a description of this follows. Production of further sailplanes of this type is not intended, but an extended-span two-seat version and a powered version are being considered.

TYPE: Single-seat Standard Class sailplane.

WINGS: Cantilever shoulder-wing monoplane, with taper on outer panels. Wortmann wing sections: FX-61-168 at root, FX-60-126 at tip. Schempp-Hirth airbrakes above and below each wing. Primary structure consists of a sandwich of 8 mm Conticell hard-foam PVC, coated with resin-bonded glassfibre, with a box spar. There are no ribs.

FUSELAGE: Semi-monocoque "half-sandwich" structure, consisting of a balsa-covered wooden frame with a resin-bonded outer skin of laminated glassfibre.

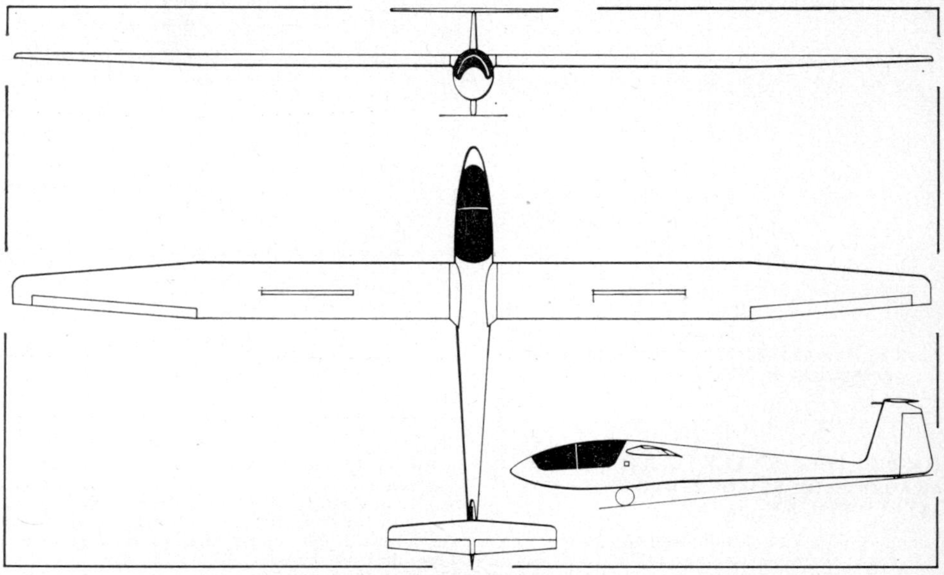

FVA-20 single-seat Standard Class sailplane (*Roy J. Grainge*)

TAIL UNIT: Cantilever T-tail. Fin and rudder are of "half-sandwich" construction, similar to fuselage. Tailplane and elevators are of similar construction to wings.

LANDING GEAR: Retractable monowheel and tail bumper.

ACCOMMODATION: Single seat under moulded transparent canopy.

DIMENSIONS, EXTERNAL:
Wing span 49 ft 2½ in (15·00 m)
Wing aspect ratio 17·6
Length overall 22 ft 11¾ in (7·00 m)
Fuselage: Max width 2 ft 1½ in (0·65 m)
Max depth 2 ft 11½ in (0·90 m)

AREA:
Wings, gross 137·8 sq ft (12·80 m²)

WEIGHT AND LOADING:
Max T-O weight 705 lb (320 kg)
Max wing loading 5·1 lb/sq ft (25·0 kg/m²)

PERFORMANCE (estimated):
Best glide ratio at 48·5 knots (56 mph; 90 km/h) 35·3
Min sinking speed at 37 knots (42·5 mph; 68 km/h) 1·97 ft (0·60 m)/sec

GLASER-DIRKS

GLASER-DIRKS FLUGZEUGBAU GmbH

ADDRESS:
752 Bruchsal 4, Postfach 47, Im Schollengarten 13
Telephone: 07257/272 (1071)

DIRECTOR:
Dipl-Ing Wilhelm Dirks

This company is producing the DG-100 Standard Class sailplane, which is a modified and lighter-weight development of the Akaflieg Darmstadt D-38 described in the 1973-74 *Jane's*.

GLASER-DIRKS DG-100

Design of the DG-100, by Dipl-Ing Wilhelm Dirks, began in August 1973. Construction of a prototype started in January 1974, and this aircraft (D-7100) flew for the first time on 10 May 1974. By the end of February 1974, orders for 42 DG-100s had been received.

TYPE: Single-seat Standard Class sailplane.

WINGS: Cantilever shoulder-wing monoplane. Wortmann wing sections, FX-61-184 at centre-line, FX-60-126 at tip. Dihedral 3° from roots. Incidence —1°. No sweepback. Glassfibre/Conticell/foam sandwich construction, including ailerons. Schempp-Hirth duralumin airbrakes on upper surfaces. Water ballast tank in each wing, combined capacity 132 lb (60 kg). Ballast can be jettisoned during flight.

FUSELAGE: All-glassfibre semi-monocoque structure.

TAIL UNIT: Cantilever T-tail. All-moving glassfibre/Conticell/foam sandwich tailplane, with full-span Flettner tab. All-glassfibre fin and rudder.

LANDING GEAR: Manually-retractable monowheel, size 5·00-5, tyre pressure 32 lb/sq in (2·25 kg/cm²). Tost drum brake. Foam plastics tailwheel.

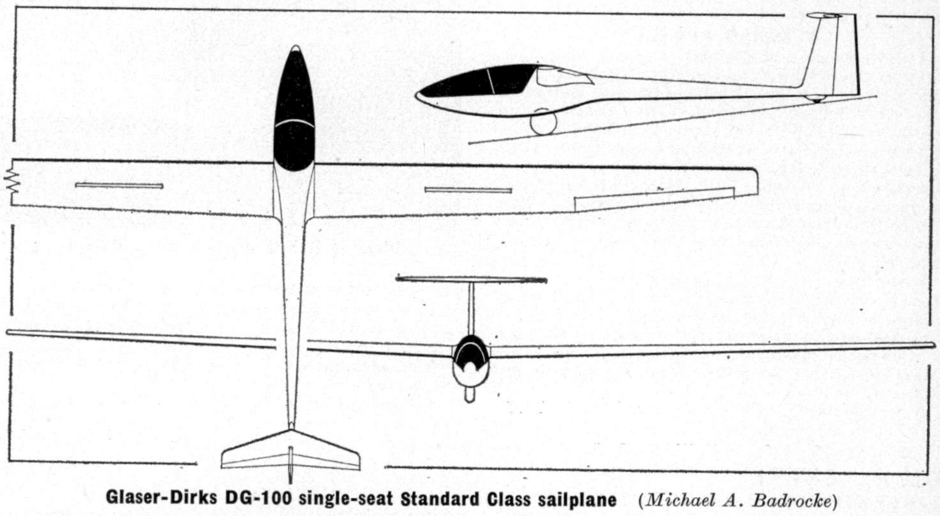

Glaser-Dirks DG-100 single-seat Standard Class sailplane (*Michael A. Badrocke*)

ACCOMMODATION: Single semi-reclining seat under flush transparent canopy, the rear section of which is removable. Standard instrumentation. Radio optional.

DIMENSIONS, EXTERNAL:
Wing span 49 ft 2½ in (15·00 m)
Wing chord at root 3 ft 1 in (0·94 m)
Wing chord at tip 1 ft 2¾ in (0·376 m)
Wing mean aerodynamic chord 2 ft 5¾ in (0·753 m)
Wing aspect ratio 20·5
Length overall 22 ft 11¾ in (7·00 m)
Height overall 4 ft 7 in (1·40 m)
Tailplane span 7 ft 6½ in (2·30 m)

AREAS:
Wings, gross 118·4 sq ft (11·00 m²)
Ailerons (total) 9·21 sq ft (0·856 m²)
Fin 9·90 sq ft (0·92 m²)
Rudder 4·95 sq ft (0·46 m²)
Tailplane, incl tab 10·76 sq ft (1·00 m²)

WEIGHTS AND LOADING:
Weight empty, equipped 463 lb (210 kg)
Max T-O weight (with water ballast) 848 lb (385 kg)

Max wing loading (with water ballast)
7·17 lb/sq ft (35·0 kg/m²)

PERFORMANCE (at max T-O weight):

Best glide ratio at 51 knots (59 mph; 95 km/h) 39

Min sinking speed at 40·5 knots (47 mph; 75 km/h) 1·97 ft (0·60 m)/sec

Stalling speed 35·5 knots (41 mph; 66 km/h)

Max speed (rough or smooth air)
135 knots (155 mph; 250 km/h)

Max aero-tow speed
89 knots (102·5 mph; 165 km/h)

Max winch-launching speed
59 knots (68 mph; 110 km/h)

g limit +6·1

GLASFLÜGEL

GLASFLÜGEL, ING EUGEN HÄNLE

ADDRESS: 7311 Schlattstall Krs, Nürtingen

Telephone: 07026/855

This company is responsible for series production of the Standard Libelle, developed from the Hütter H 30 GFK and H 301 of which details appeared in earlier editions of *Jane's*.

Glasflügel delivered 18 examples of a new version of Björn Stender's BS 1, utilising the same type of all-glassfibre construction as in the Libelle. Current production includes the Standard Libelle, the high-performance single-seat 17 m Kestrel and the 22 m Glasflügel 604. Between them, these three types of sailplane currently hold five world gliding records.

Slingsby in the UK (which see) is producing a 19 m version of the Kestrel.

Glasflügel Italiana (which see) produces sailplane components in Italy for the Kestrel designed by the parent company.

GLASFLÜGEL STANDARD LIBELLE

The Standard Libelle was developed from the H 301, described in the 1968-69 edition of *Jane's*, to meet the demand for a simple lower-cost glassfibre sailplane in the Standard Class. The distinctive lines and proportions of the original Libelle have been retained, as have the terminal velocity dive brakes; a new wing profile has been utilised to ensure high performance and pleasant handling characteristics without flaps.

Standard Libelles took 15 of the first 39 places in the 1974 World Gliding Championships (Standard Class), held at Waikerie, Australia. In 1973 they finished in first, second and third positions in the Standard Class of the national gliding championships held in Australia; in first and second places in those held in New Zealand; in second and third places in those in France and Switzerland; in second place in those in Belgium and Denmark; in second, third and fourth places in those in Italy; and in third place in those in the UK.

On 18 December 1972 Miss Angela Smith of the UK set up a world speed record over a 500 km course of 58·78 knots (67·69 mph; 108·94 km/h) in a Standard Libelle. In another Libelle, on 3 May 1973, William C. Holbrook of the US established a world goal and return record distance of 680·15 nm (783·20 miles; 1,260·44 km).

The Standard Libelle is in quantity production, and the 500th was delivered on 15 February 1974. With optional water ballast installation the aircraft is designated Standard Libelle **201 B**.

TYPE: Single-seat high-performance Standard Class sailplane.

WINGS: Two-piece glassfibre and balsa and/or foam sandwich skins, with unidirectional glassfibre spar caps produced by HH method. Glassfibre and balsa shear web. Partially mass-balanced ailerons. Flush-fitting terminal velocity dive brakes.

FUSELAGE: Glassfibre (not sandwich) monocoque construction.

TAIL UNIT: Glassfibre and balsa and/or foam sandwich construction. Automatic elevator connection. Spring trim.

LANDING GEAR: Retractable or non-retractable monowheel, with internal-expanding brake. Interchangeable tailwheel or skid.

ACCOMMODATION: Single seat under large canopy.

EQUIPMENT: Standard items include removable drawer-type instrument panel, built-in VHF antenna, provision for radio and oxygen. Adjustable seat and rudder pedals and inflatable cushions permit seating positions to be changed in flight. Optional water ballast system, which can be installed retrospectively in existing aircraft.

DIMENSIONS, EXTERNAL:

Wing span	49 ft 2½ in (15·00 m)
Wing aspect ratio	23
Length overall	20 ft 8 in (6·20 m)
Height over rudder	4 ft 4 in (1·31 m)

AREA:

Wings, gross	105·5 sq ft (9·8 m²)

WEIGHTS:

Weight empty	408 lb (185 kg)
Max T-O weight (with water ballast)	771 lb (350 kg)

PERFORMANCE:

Best glide ratio at 46 knots (53 mph; 85 km/h) 38

Min sinking speed at 38 knots (43·5 mph; 70 km/h) 1·90 ft (0·58 m)/sec

Stalling speed 33·5 knots (39 mph; 62 km/h)

Max speed (rough or smooth air)
119 knots (137 mph; 220 km/h)

GLASFLÜGEL 205 CLUB LIBELLE

The Club Libelle is a direct derivative of the Standard Libelle, from which it differs principally in having shoulder-mounted wings and a T tailplane. It also incorporates certain features of the Kestrel. Design began in the Autumn of 1972, and construction of a prototype started in the following February. This aircraft made its first flight on 14 September 1973; up to early 1974 no additional examples had been built.

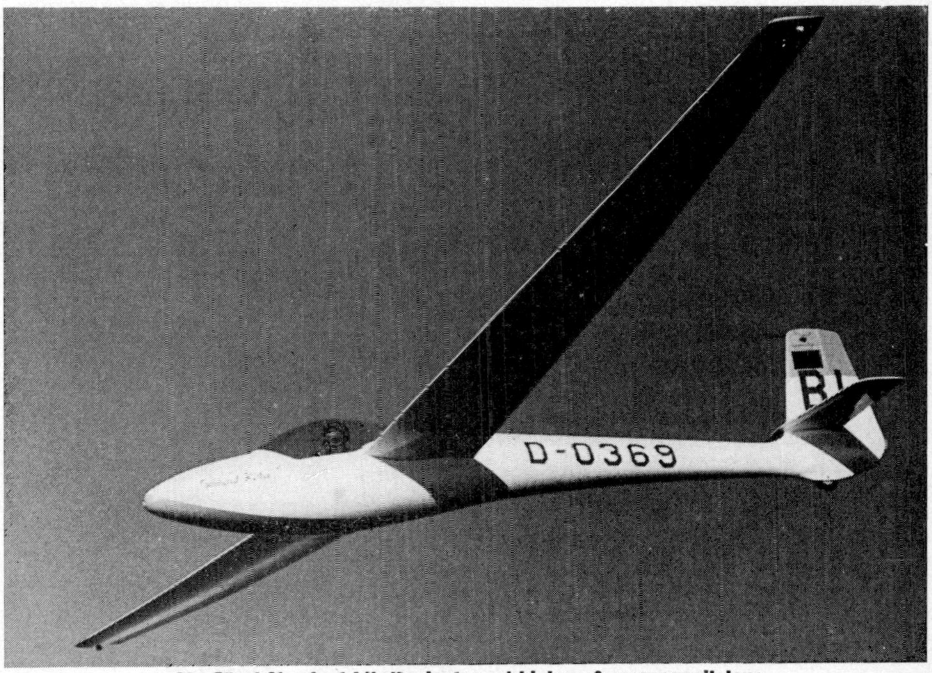

Glasflügel Standard Libelle single-seat high-performance sailplane

Glasflügel 205 Club Libelle single-seat 15 metre sailplane

TYPE: Single-seat Standard Class sailplane.

WINGS: Cantilever shoulder-wing monoplane. Wortmann wing section with 18% thickness/chord ratio. Incidence 4° at root. Glassfibre and foam sandwich skin with unidirectional glassfibre spar caps, produced by HH method. Glassfibre and foam sandwich shear web. Fixed-hinge, partially mass-balanced ailerons, with all-glassfibre skin. Airbrakes over approx 60% of trailing-edge.

FUSELAGE: Glassfibre monocoque structure.

TAIL UNIT: Cantilever T-tail. Tailplane of glassfibre and foam sandwich construction. Fin, rudder and elevator of glassfibre monocoque construction. Elevator fitted with spring trim.

LANDING GEAR: Non-retractable monowheel and tailwheel. Gas spring and rubber spring shock-absorption. Main-wheel tyre size 300 × 100 mm, tailwheel tyre size 210 × 65 mm. Tyre pressure (both) 28·5 lb/sq in (2·0 kg/cm²). Internally-expanding brake.

ACCOMMODATION: Single seat under one-piece canopy. Standard equipment includes two towing hooks, seat cushion with inflatable knee supports, instrument panel, ASI and built-in VHF antenna. Provision for radio and oxygen, adjustable seat and rudder pedals.

DIMENSIONS, EXTERNAL:

Wing span	49 ft 2½ in (15·00 m)
Wing chord at root	2 ft 11½ in (0·90 m)
Wing chord at tip	1 ft 2¼ in (0·36 m)
Wing aspect ratio	23
Length overall	21 ft 0 in (6·40 m)
Height overall	4 ft 7 in (1·40 m)
Tailplane span	8 ft 2½ in (2·50 m)

AREAS:

Wings, gross	105·5 sq ft (9·80 m²)
Ailerons (total)	6·18 sq ft (0·574 m²)
Airbrakes (total)	15·28 sq ft (1·42 m²)
Fin	9·58 sq ft (0·89 m²)
Rudder	2·91 sq ft (0·27 m²)
Tailplane	12·38 sq ft (1·15 m²)
Elevator	3·12 sq ft (0·29 m²)

WEIGHTS AND LOADING:

Weight empty, equipped approx	441 lb (200 kg)
Max T-O weight	727 lb (330 kg)
Max wing loading	6·9 lb/sq ft (33·67 kg/m²)

PERFORMANCE (at max T-O weight):

Best glide ratio at 48·5 knots (56 mph; 90 km/h) 35

Min sinking speed at 36·5 knots (42 mph; 67 km/h) 1·84 ft (0·56 m)/sec

Stalling speed without airbrakes
35 knots (40 mph; 64 km/h)

Max speed (rough or smooth air)
108 knots (124 mph; 200 km/h)

Max aero-tow speed
81 knots (93 mph; 150 km/h)

Max winch-launching speed
70 knots (80·5 mph; 130 km/h)

g limits +5·7; —3·7 (safety factor 1·5)

GLASFLÜGEL KESTREL

The Kestrel is currently in production in 17 m form by Glasflügel and in a 19 m version by Slingsby in the UK (which see) as an advanced Open Class sailplane. It was known originally as the "17 metre Libelle". In addition to proven Libelle features, the Kestrel has a larger cockpit canopy, a new fuselage and wing profile, and a T-tail.

Deliveries of production Kestrels began in 1969, and by 1 January 1974 a total of 100 had been delivered. Kestrels (17 m version) were placed 17th and 26th in the 1974 World Gliding Championships at Waikerie, Australia. They also gained leading places in the Open Class of 1973 national gliding championships held in Australia (2nd and 3rd), Austria (first 4 places), Belgium (2nd), Sweden (2nd), South Africa (2nd), UK (2nd to 9th places shared by 17 m and 19 m Kestrels), Italy (3rd, 4th and 5th); and won the US Smirnoff Trophy.

Miss Susan Martin established two new world records on 11 February 1972 while flying a Kestrel sailplane. These were for speeds of 61·7 knots (71·1 mph; 114·4 km/h) over a 300 km course and 61 knots (70·3 mph; 113·2 km/h) over a 100 km course. The latter record has since been beaten.

TYPE: Single-seat high-performance Open Class sailplane.

WINGS: Two-piece glassfibre and balsa and/or foam sandwich skins, with unidirectional glassfibre spar caps produced by the HH method. Glassfibre and balsa sandwich shear web. Ailerons linked differentially with high-lift camber-changing flaps, all partially mass-balanced. Flush-fitting dive brakes.

FUSELAGE: Similar to Standard Libelle.

TAIL UNIT: Cantilever T-tail of similar construction to wings. All control surfaces mass-balanced. Releasable drag parachute, diameter 3 ft (0·91 m), housed in rudder.

LANDING GEAR: Similar to Standard Libelle.

DIMENSIONS, EXTERNAL:	
Wing span	55 ft 9¼ in (17·00 m)
Wing aspect ratio	25
Length overall	22 ft 0½ in (6·72 m)
Height overall	5 ft 0 in (1·52 m)
Tailplane span	9 ft 4¼ in (2·85 m)
AREA:	
Wings, gross	124·8 sq ft (11·6 m²)
WEIGHTS:	
Weight empty	574 lb (260 kg)
Max T-O weight (with water ballast)	882 lb (400 kg)
PERFORMANCE:	
Best glide ratio at 52·5 knots (60·5 mph; 97 km/h)	43
Min sinking speed at 40 knots (46 mph; 74 km/h)	1·8 ft (0·55 m)/sec
Stalling speed	33·5 knots (39 mph; 62 km/h)
Max speed (rough or smooth air)	135 knots (155 mph; 250 km/h)

Glasflügel Kestrel 17 m single-seat high-performance sailplane

Glasflügel 604 single-seat high-performance Open Class sailplane, fifth production example

GLASFLÜGEL 604

The Glasflügel 604 was built originally as a study for a projected two-seat high-performance sailplane, and was completed in only four months in order to be entered in the 1970 World Gliding Championships at Marfa, Texas. Construction began in January 1970, and the first flight was made on 30 April 1970.

The Glasflügel 604 gained sixth place in these Championships, and shortly afterwards established a world speed record of 83·67 knots (96·35 mph; 155·057 km/h) over a 100 km triangular course, piloted by Walter Neubert. This has since been beaten, but Miss Adele Orsi, in another Glasflügel 604, set up on 17 August 1973 a ladies' speed record over a 100 km course of 64·84 knots (74·66 mph; 120·153 km/h). In Kenya, a Glasflügel 604 flown by Walter Neubert of West Germany established on 3 March 1972 a world speed record over a 300 km triangular course of 82·80 knots (95·34 mph; 153·43 km/h).

A Glasflügel 604 flown by B. Zegels of Belgium took second place in the 1974 World Gliding Championships at Waikerie, Australia. Aircraft of this type also were placed first in the 1973 Belgian national championships, and first and second in those held in Italy.

Series production of the Glasflügel 604 began in 1971, and 10 had been built by 1 February 1974.

TYPE: Single-seat high-performance Open Class sailplane.

WINGS: Cantilever shoulder-wing monoplane. Wing section Wortmann 67-K-170 (modified) at root, Wortmann 67-K-150 at tip. Thickness/chord ratio 18% at root, 15% at tip. No dihedral or sweepback. Incidence 0° 30′. Wing built in three pieces, with unidirectional glassfibre spar caps produced by the Hütter-Hänle method, glassfibre/balsa shear webs and glassfibre/foam sandwich skin. Fixed-hinge flaps and ailerons, all partially mass-balanced. Flaps have glassfibre/foam sandwich skin, aileron skin is all glassfibre. Single airbrake on top of each wing. No tabs.

FUSELAGE: Glassfibre monocoque structure.

TAIL UNIT: Cantilever glassfibre/foam sandwich structure, with fixed-incidence T tailplane. Spring and trim tabs in elevators.

LANDING GEAR: Mechanically-retractable monowheel, with internally-expanding brake, and fixed tailwheel. No shock-absorbers. Tyre size 5·00-5.

ACCOMMODATION: Single seat under two-piece transparent canopy. Standard equipment includes two towing hooks, seat pillow with inflatable knee supports, safety harness, instrument panel and built-in VHF antenna. Optional equipment includes adjustable seat and rudder pedals, oxygen and radio.

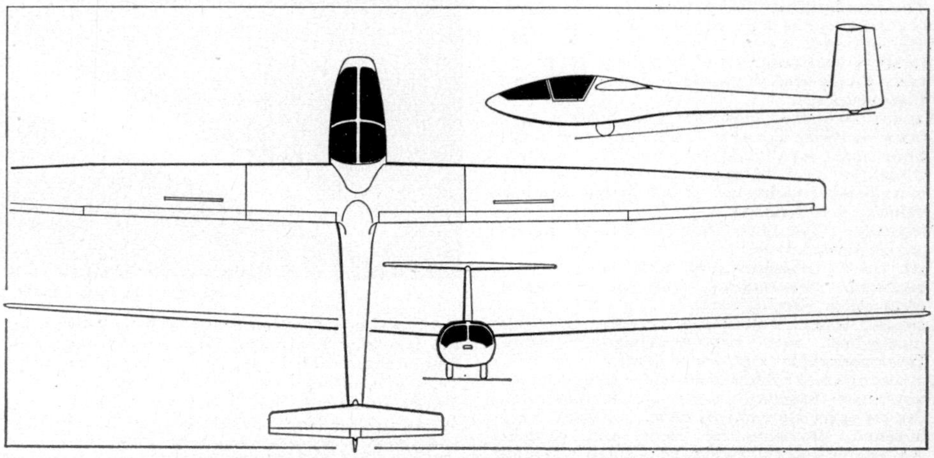
Glasflügel 701 side-by-side two-seat sailplane (*Sherwood Designs Ltd*)

DIMENSIONS, EXTERNAL:	
Wing span	72 ft 2¼ in (22·00 m)
Wing aspect ratio	29·8
Length overall	24 ft 11¼ in (7·60 m)
Height overall	5 ft 5¾ in (1·67 m)
Tailplane span	10 ft 2 in (3·10 m)
AREAS:	
Wings, gross	175·0 sq ft (16·23 m²)
Ailerons (total)	6·67 sq ft (0·62 m²)
Flaps (total)	10·98 sq ft (1·02 m²)
Fin	9·69 sq ft (0·90 m²)
Rudder	4·20 sq ft (0·39 m²)
Tailplane	15·61 sq ft (1·45 m²)
Elevators, incl tabs	3·88 sq ft (0·36 m²)
WEIGHTS AND LOADING:	
Weight empty	approx 880 lb (400 kg)
Max T-O weight	1,322 lb (600 kg)
Max wing loading	7·58 lb/sq ft (37·0 kg/m²)
PERFORMANCE (at max T-O weight):	
Best glide ratio at 53 knots (61 mph; 98 km/h)	49
Min sinking speed at 39 knots (45 mph; 72 km/h)	1·64 ft (0·50 m)/sec
Max speed (rough or smooth air)	134·5 knots (155 mph; 250 km/h)
Max aero-tow speed	80·5 knots (93 mph; 150 km/h)
Max winch-launching speed	70 knots (80·5 mph; 130 km/h)
g limits	+5·5; —3·5

GLASFLÜGEL 701

Glasflügel has designed a new high-performance side-by-side two-seat sailplane known as the Glasflügel 701. Design began in the Spring of 1971; a prototype was under construction in 1974.

TYPE: Two-seat high-performance sailplane.

WINGS: Cantilever shoulder-wing monoplane. Wing section Wortmann 67-K-170 (modified) at root, Wortmann 67-K-150 at tip. Thickness/chord ratio 18% at root, 15% at tip. No dihedral or sweepback. Incidence 0° 30′. Wing built in three pieces, with unidirectional glassfibre spar caps produced by the Hütter-Hänle method, glassfibre/balsa shear webs and glassfibre/foam sandwich skin. Fixed-hinge flaps and ailerons, all partially mass-balanced and all with glassfibre foam/sandwich skin. Single airbrake on top of each wing. No tabs.

FUSELAGE: Conventional monocoque structure

with glassfibre/foam sandwich skin. Movable weight in fuselage for trimming purposes.

Tail Unit: Cantilever glassfibre/foam sandwich structure, with fixed-incidence T tailplane. Spring and trim tabs in elevators.

Landing Gear: Twin mechanically-retractable main wheels, with internally-expanding brakes, and fixed tailwheel. No shock-absorbers. Tyre size 5·00-5.

Accommodation: Two seats side by side. Front portion of canopy is fixed, rear portion consists of two upward-opening halves, hinged on centreline.

Dimensions, external:
Wing span 62 ft 4 in (19·00 m)
Wing aspect ratio 19·25
Length overall 26 ft 6¾ in (8·10 m)
Height overall 5 ft 11¼ in (1·81 m)
Tailplane span 11 ft 7¾ in (3·55 m)

Areas:
Wings, gross 201·9 sq ft (18·76 m²)
Fin 10·44 sq ft (0·97 m²)
Rudder 4·52 sq ft (0·42 m²)
Tailplane 20·99 sq ft (1·95 m²)
Elevators, incl tabs 5·27 sq ft (0·49 m²)

Weights and Loading:
Weight empty approx 926 lb (420 kg)
Max T-O weight 1,543 lb (700 kg)
Max wing loading 6·62 lb/sq ft (32·3 kg/m²)

Performance (estimated, at max T-O weight except where indicated):
Best glide ratio at 60 knots (69·5 mph; 112 km/h) 43·8
Min sinking speed at 36·5 knots (42 mph: 68 km/h), 1,258 lb (580 kg) AUW 1·87 ft (0·57 m)/sec
Max speed (rough or smooth air) 134·5 knots (155 mph; 250 km/h)
Max aero-tow speed 80·5 knots (93 mph; 150 km/h)
Max winch-launching speed 70 knots (80·5 mph; 130 km/h)
Min control speed at 1,278 lb (580 kg) AUW 36·5 knots (42 mph; 68 km/h)
g limits +5·3; —3·3

HIRTH

WOLF HIRTH GmbH

Address: 7311 Nabern/Teck, Am Flugplatz
Telephone: Kirchheim/Teck 55377

HIRTH Hi 26 MOSE II

Design of this two-seat powered sailplane was initiated in January 1968 and construction of the prototype began in August 1969. Wolf Hirth is primarily engaged in production to meet unexpectedly large orders for the Acrostar Mk II aerobatic aircraft (see "Aircraft" section), but work on the Mose II was continuing in 1972 on a low-priority basis. No further news of the project has been received since that time.

A description of the aircraft appeared in the 1973-74 *Jane's*.

KORTENBACH & RAUH

KORTENBACH & RAUH

Address:
565 Solingen 15, Postfach 150 121
Telephone: Solingen 292121 or 292123

KORTENBACH & RAUH KORA 1

The Kora 1 is a two-seat twin-boom powered sailplane, a prototype of which flew for the first time on 13 September 1973. It was designed by Herren Schultes, Seidel and Putz. A second Kora was under construction at the end of 1973.

About a dozen Koras have been ordered, and production of these was expected to begin in 1974.

Type: Two-seat powered training sailplane.

Wings: Cantilever high-wing monoplane, of all-wood construction. Wortmann wing sections, FX-66-S-196 at root, FX-66-S-161 at tip. Schempp-Hirth airbrakes on upper surfaces.

Landing Gear: Retractable tricycle type. Main units retract rearward into tailbooms.

Power Plant: One 65 hp Sportavia Limbach SL 1700 EA engine, driving a Hoffmann two-blade variable-pitch feathering pusher propeller.

Accommodation: Side-by-side seats for two persons under fully-transparent canopy. Space for parachutes.

Dimensions, external:
Wing span 59 ft 0¾ in (18·00 m)
Wing aspect ratio 16·67
Length overall 22 ft 11¼ in (7·00 m)
Height overall 6 ft 0¾ in (1·85 m)
Fuselage: Max width 3 ft 11¼ in (1·20 m)

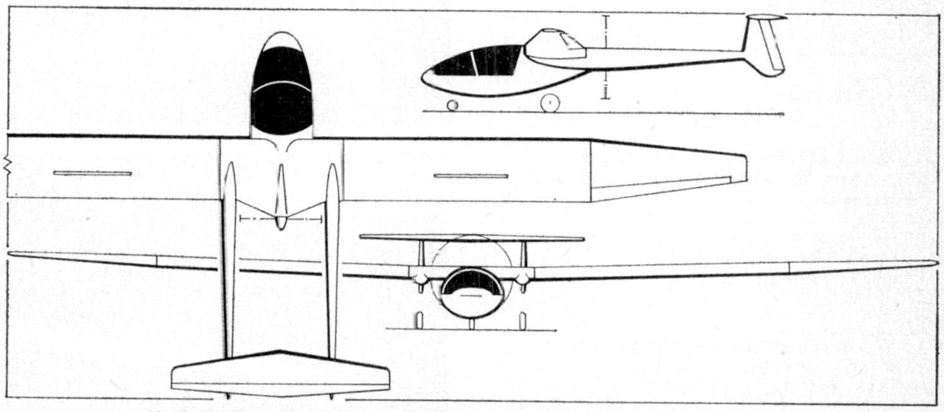

Kortenbach & Rauh Kora 1 two-seat powered sailplane (*Tony Mitchell*)

Wheel track 6 ft 6¾ in (2·00 m)
Propeller diameter 5 ft 3 in (1·60 m)

Areas:
Wings, gross 209·25 sq ft (19·44 m²)
Vertical tail surfaces (total) 10·76 sq ft (1·00 m²)
Horizontal tail surfaces (total) 27·99 sq ft (2·60 m²)

Weights and Loadings:
Weight empty 1,036 lb (470 kg)
Max T-O weight 1,543 lb (700 kg)
Max wing loading 7·37 lb/sq ft (36 kg/m²)
Max power loading 23·74 lb/hp (10·77 kg/hp)

Performance (powered):
Max level speed 110 knots (127 mph; 205 km/h)
Cruising speed (65% power) 94·5 knots (109 mph; 175 km/h)
Stalling speed 35·5 knots (40·5 mph; 65 km/h)
Max rate of climb at S/L 590 ft (180 m)/min

Performance (unpowered):
Best glide ratio at 52·5 knots (60·5 mph; 97 km/h) 31·4
Min sinking speed at 43·5 knots (50 mph; 80 km/h) 2·49 ft (0·76 m)/sec

MILITKY

FRED MILITKY

Address:
7312 Kirchheim/Teck, Paradiesstrasse 27

Herr Militky, an engineer with the Graupner model-building company in Kirchheim/Teck, applied his experience with electrically-powered radio-controlled models to the evolution of an electrically-powered propulsion system for a full-size manned aeroplane. The MB-E1 is a prototype aircraft incorporating this system.

MILITKY MB-E1

After evolving the necessary details of his electrically-powered propulsion system, Herr Militky submitted details to Herr Heinz Brditschka in December 1972 with the proposal that it be installed experimentally in a Brditschka HB-3 powered sailplane in place of the normal internal combustion engine. The resulting conversion, known as the MB-E1 (Militky Brditschka Electric 1), made a successful first flight on 21 October 1973, at Wels, Austria, thus becoming the first full-sized manned aeroplane to fly solely on electric power. On this flight, during which it was piloted by Herr Heino Brditschka, the MB-E1 climbed to an altitude of 985 ft (300 m), made several circuits of the airfield and landed safely after 9 min 15 sec in the air. About half of the available battery charge was used during this flight. Since then, several additional flights have been made, of more than 12 min duration and at heights of up to 1,245 ft (380 m), without completely draining the battery power.

A structural description of the HB-3 is given under the Brditschka heading in the Austrian

Militky MB-E1 electric-powered aircraft, modified from an Austrian-built HB-3 sailplane

section of this edition. The airframe of the MB-E1 is identical except for the change of power plant, which adds about 132 lb (60 kg) to the max T-O weight.

Type: Single-seat electrically-powered experimental aircraft.

Power Plant: One 90V 8-10kW (13 hp) Bosch KM 77/2A13A DC electric motor, powered by a 1·2V 25Ah Varta FP 25 sintered-cell nickel-cadmium battery, driving a two-blade fixed-pitch Hoffmann pusher propeller at 2,400 rpm by means of a Vee-belt speed-reducing transmission.

Weights and Loadings:
Weight empty, equipped 815 lb (370 kg)
Max T-O and landing weight 970 lb (440 kg)
Max wing loading 6·35 lb/sq ft (31·0 kg/m²)
Max power loading 121 lb/kW (55·0 kg/kW)

Performance (at max T-O weight):
Max never-exceed speed 67 knots (77·5 mph; 125 km/h)
Max level speed 48·5 knots (56 mph; 90 km/h)
Stalling speed 35·5 knots (40·5 mph; 65 km/h)
Max rate of climb at S/L 395 ft (120 m)/min
T-O run 655 ft (200 m)
T-O to 50 ft (15 m) 1,310 ft (400 m)

RFB

RHEIN-FLUGZEUGBAU GmbH (Subsidiary of VFW-Fokker GmbH)

Head Office:
405 Mönchengladbach, Flugplatz, Postfach 408
Telephone: (02161) 62031
Telex: 08/52506
Officers: see "Aircraft" section

RFB has under development a "fan pod" power plant for sailplane applications, known as the Schubgondel SG 85, which has been test-flown successfully on an L-13 Blanik glider during the past year. It consists basically of a pair of Wankel rotating-piston engines, coupled together and driving a three- or four-blade shrouded propeller, and weighs 123·5 lb (56 kg).

RFB SIRIUS II

RFB is continuing flight testing of this powered sailplane which uses the wings, landing gear and tail unit of the Italian Caproni Vizzola Calif A-21 (which see). The prototype (D-KAFB) was flown for the first time on 18 January 1972.

The fuselage accommodates two seats side by side, with a ducted fan power plant installed aft of the cockpit. The fuselage structure is continued past the power plant by cruciform webs. The ducted fan is driven by two 30 hp Wankel rotating-piston engines. One of these is mounted in front of the fan and the second behind the fan. The fan shroud has an annular slat intake round the leading-edge to keep the airflow attached within the duct; suck-in doors fair off this intake to maintain gliding performance when the power plant is not operating.

DIMENSIONS, EXTERNAL:
- Wing span — 66 ft 10¼ in (20·38 m)
- Length overall — 26 ft 4½ in (8·04 m)
- Height overall — 5 ft 11 in (1·80 m)

WEIGHTS AND LOADINGS:
- Weight empty — 1,124 lb (510 kg)
- Max T-O weight — 1,521 lb (690 kg)
- Max wing loading — 8·89 lb/sq ft (43·4 kg/m²)
- Max power loading — 25·35 lb/hp (11·5 kg/hp)

PERFORMANCE (powered):
- Max speed — 146 knots (168 mph; 270 km/h)
- Max speed on one engine — 59·5 knots (68·5 mph; 110 km/h)
- Cruising speed — 97 knots (112 mph; 180 km/h)
- Minimum speed — 39 knots (45 mph; 72 km/h)
- Rate of climb — 6·56 ft (2·0 m)/sec
- T-O run — 656 ft (200 m)
- Range — 146 nm (168 miles; 270 km)
- Fuel consumption, approx — 4·4 Imp gallons (20 litres) per hour

RFB Sirius II two-seat high-performance powered sailplane with ducted fan power plant

ROLLADEN-SCHNEIDER

ROLLADEN-SCHNEIDER OHG (Abteilung Segelflugzeugbau)

ADDRESS:
6073 Egelsbach/Hessen, Mühlstrasse 10 (Schliessfach 1130)

Telephone: Langen (06103) 4126

OFFICERS:
Walter Schneider
Dipl-Ing Wolf Lemke

ROLLADEN-SCHNEIDER LS1

The LS1, designed by Dipl-Ing Wolf Lemke, was the winner of the 1968, 1969 and 1971 German national championships and of the 1970 World Championships. The prototype flew for the first time in October 1967. Current production versions are designated LS1-c and LS1-d, the latter having provision for a 13 Imp gallon (60 litre) water ballast installation.

An LS1-c flown by K. Tesch of Germany set up an international goal flight record on 25 April 1972 of 567·23 nm (653·18 miles; 1,051·2 km).

An LS1 took fourth place in the Standard Class of the 1972 World Championships at Vrsac, Yugoslavia.

By February 1974 a total of 220 LS1s had been built. Production was due to end during 1974.

A modified version, the LS1-f, is described separately.

TYPE: Single-seat high-performance Standard Class sailplane.

WINGS: Cantilever shoulder-wing monoplane. Wortmann wing section. Thickness/chord ratio 19%. Dihedral 4°. Incidence 4°. Sweepback 1° at quarter-chord. Glassfibre/foam sandwich structure. Airbrakes on upper surfaces.

FUSELAGE: Semi-monocoque structure, of glassfibre/foam sandwich construction.

TAIL UNIT: Cantilever T-tail with all-moving tailplane. Construction similar to that of wings.

LANDING GEAR: Retractable Tost monowheel, size 300 × 100, tyre pressure 43 lb/sq in (3·0 kg/cm²), fitted with drum brake. No shock-absorbers.

ACCOMMODATION: Single semi-reclining seat under large transparent canopy.

DIMENSIONS, EXTERNAL:
- Wing span — 49 ft 2½ in (15·00 m)
- Wing aspect ratio — 23·1
- Wing chord (mean) — 2 ft 1½ in (0·65 m)
- Length overall — 23 ft 7½ in (7·20 m)
- Height overall — 3 ft 11¼ in (1·20 m)
- Tailplane span — 7 ft 6½ in (2·30 m)

AREAS:
- Wings, gross — 104·9 sq ft (9·75 m²)
- Ailerons (total) — 7·53 sq ft (0·70 m²)
- Airbrakes (total) — 3·77 sq ft (0·35 m²)
- Rudder — 3·66 sq ft (0·34 m²)
- Tailplane — 9·04 sq ft (0·84 m²)

WEIGHTS AND LOADING:
- Weight empty — 440 lb (200 kg)
- Max T-O weight — 751 lb (341 kg)
- Max wing loading — 7·17 lb/sq ft (35 kg/m²)

PERFORMANCE:
- Best glide ratio at 48·5 knots (56 mph; 90 km/h) — 37
- Min sinking speed at 38 knots (43·5 mph; 70 km/h) — 2·13 ft (0·65 m)/sec
- Stalling speed — 35·5 knots (40·5 mph; 65 km/h)
- Max speed (rough or smooth air) — 129 knots (149 mph; 240 km/h)
- Max aero-tow speed — 81 knots (93 mph; 150 km/h)
- Max winch-launching speed — 64·5 knots (74·5 mph; 120 km/h)
- *g* limit — 6·1

Rolladen-Schneider LS1-c single-seat high-performance Standard Class sailplane

LS1-f experimental single-seat sailplane, developed from the LS1-c

ROLLADEN-SCHNEIDER LS1-f

This sailplane, first flown in the 1972 World Championships at Vrsac, Yugoslavia, is an improved version of the LS1-c. Two examples have been built, the first production aircraft flying for the first time in 1974.

The fuselage is of refined aerodynamic form, the rudder has been redesigned (although retaining the same surface area), a fixed tailplane with elevator replaces the all-moving tailplane of the LS1-c, and a one-piece hinged cockpit canopy is fitted. Other improvements include rubber shock-absorption for the monowheel, modifications to the tow release, cockpit interior and instrumentation; and location 25 mm further forward of the rear point of the CG range.

The description of the LS1-c otherwise applies generally also to the LS1-f, except in the following respects:

DIMENSIONS, EXTERNAL: As LS1-c except:
- Length overall — 22 ft 3¾ in (6·80 m)
- Tailplane span — 7 ft 2¾ in (2·20 m)

WEIGHTS AND LOADING: As LS1-c except:
- Max T-O weight — 859 lb (390 kg)
- Max wing loading — 8·2 lb/sq ft (40 kg/m²)

PERFORMANCE: As LS1-c except:
- Best glide ratio at 48·5 knots (56 mph; 90 km/h) — 38
- Max speed (rough or smooth air) — 137 knots (158 mph; 255 km/h)

ROLLADEN-SCHNEIDER LS2

This high-performance competition sailplane is designed to take advantage of the recent FAI regulations allowing flap/airbrakes to be fitted to Standard Class sailplanes.

Design began in 1972, and a prototype flew for the first time in 1973. This aircraft, flown by Hans Reichmann, was the winner of the Standard Class in the 1974 World Gliding Championships at Waikerie, Australia. No additional LS2s had been built up to early 1974.

TYPE: Single-seat experimental Standard Class sailplane.

WINGS: Cantilever shoulder-wing monoplane. Wortmann wing section. Thickness/chord ratio 15%. Dihedral 2°. Sweepforward 3° at quarter-chord. Glassfibre/foam sandwich construction. Wide-span trailing-edge flaps.

FUSELAGE: Semi-monocoque structure, of glassfibre/foam sandwich construction.

TAIL UNIT: Cantilever fixed-incidence T-tailplane, with elevator. Construction similar to that of wings.

LANDING GEAR: Retractable monowheel with rubber shock-absorption.

ACCOMMODATION: Single seat under one-piece transparent moulded canopy.

DIMENSIONS, EXTERNAL:
Wing span 49 ft $2\frac{1}{2}$ in (15·00 m)
Wing aspect ratio 21·9
Length overall 22 ft $3\frac{3}{4}$ in (6·80 m)
Height overall 3 ft $11\frac{1}{4}$ in (1·20 m)
Tailplane span 7 ft $2\frac{3}{4}$ in (2·20 m)

AREA:
Wings, gross 110·8 sq ft (10·29 m²)

WEIGHTS AND LOADING:
Weight empty 529 lb (240 kg)
Max T-O weight 793 lb (360 kg)
Max wing loading 7·17 lb/sq ft (35 kg/m²)

PERFORMANCE:
Best glide ratio at 54 knots (62 mph; 100 km/h) 40

Prototype of the Rolladen-Schneider LS2 high-performance Standard Class sailplane

Min sinking speed at 43·5 knots (50 mph; 80 km/h) 2·13 ft (0·65 m)/sec
Stalling speed, flaps down 31·5 knots (36 mph; 58 km/h)
Max speed (rough or smooth air) 118 knots (137 mph; 220 km/h)
Max aero-tow speed 81 knots (93 mph; 150 km/h)
g limit +6·0

SCHAPPERT

EDUARD SCHAPPERT

Herr Schappert has modified a Focke-Wulf Kranich III glider into a powered sailplane, with a retractable engine/propeller assembly fitted behind the rear seat. All known details follow:

SCHAPPERT (FOCKE-WULF) KRANICH IIIM

TYPE: Two-seat powered sailplane.

POWER PLANT: One 35 hp Fichtel & Sachs SA-2-440 engine aft of rear cockpit, mounted on a retractable pylon and driving a two-blade tractor propeller. Fuel in glassfibre fuselage tank, capacity 1·87 Imp gallons (8·5 litres).

ACCOMMODATION: Two seats in tandem under sideways-opening (to starboard) canopy.

DIMENSIONS, EXTERNAL:
Wing span 59 ft $4\frac{3}{4}$ in (18·10 m)
Wing aspect ratio 15·6
Length overall 29 ft $10\frac{1}{4}$ in (9·10 m)
Height overall 6 ft $6\frac{3}{4}$ in (2·00 m)

AREA:
Wings, gross 226 sq ft (21·00 m²)

WEIGHTS AND LOADINGS:
Weight empty 855 lb (388 kg)
Max T-O weight 1,212 lb (550 kg)
Max wing loading 5·37 lb/sq ft (26·2 kg/m²)
Max power loading 34·61 lb/hp (15·7 kg/hp)

PERFORMANCE (at max T-O weight, powered):
Max level speed 75·5 knots (87 mph; 140 km/h)
Cruising speed 54 knots (62 mph; 100 km/h)
Landing speed 43·5 knots (50 mph; 80 km/h)
Max rate of climb at S/L 275 ft (84 m)/min
T-O run 985 ft (300 m)
T-O to 50 ft (15 m) 1,640 ft (500 m)
Landing from 50 ft (15 m) 1,150 ft (350 m)
Landing run 197 ft (60 m)
Max range 64 nm (74 miles; 120 km)

SCHEIBE

SCHEIBE FLUGZEUGBAU GmbH

HEAD OFFICE AND WORKS:
August-Pfaltz-Strasse 23, D-8060 Dachau, Postfach 1829, near Munich
Telephone: Dachau 4047, 5794 and 6813

MANAGER: Dipl-Ing Egon Scheibe

Scheibe Flugzeugbau GmbH was founded at the end of 1951 by Dipl-Ing Scheibe, who had previously built a prototype two-seat general-purpose glider known as the Mü-13E Bergfalke in Austria. This aircraft flew for the first time on 5 August 1951 and was the first type produced in quantity by the newly-formed company.

Subsequently, Scheibe built many new types of sailplane, and since developing the SF-24 Motorspatz in 1957 has also become the major producer of powered sailplanes in Germany. Currently in production are the SF-25B Falke, SF-25C and C-S, SF-28 Tandem-Falke and SF-27M powered sailplanes, of which details are given after the sailplane entry.

Latest designs, announced in mid-1974, are the SF-30 Club-Spatz and SF-25E Super Falke. Details of these were not received in time for inclusion in this edition.

Scheibe has built a total of more than 1,760 aircraft of various types, in addition to many kits for home construction by amateurs. Gliders of Scheibe design are being built under licence by gliding clubs as well as by foreign companies, including SLCA in France and Slingsby in the UK, which see.

SCHEIBE BERGFALKE-IV

The Bergfalke-IV is a developed version of the Bergfalke-III, with a new wing which provides improved performance. Construction of the prototype began in early 1969 and first flight was accomplished a few months later. Forty had been built by the beginning of 1974 and production is continuing.

TYPE: Two-seat training and contest sailplane.

WINGS: Cantilever mid-wing monoplane. Wing section Wortmann SO 2 at root, SO 2/1 at tip. Thickness/chord ratio 19·4% at root, 15·8% at tip. Dihedral 3°. All-wood structure. Single laminated beechwood box spar. Plywood skin, fabric-covered. Ailerons of wooden construction. Schempp-Hirth wooden airbrakes.

FUSELAGE: Welded steel tube structure. Nose section covered with a moulded glassfibre shell, remainder fabric-covered.

TAIL UNIT: Cantilever wooden structure. Tailplane mounted on top of fuselage, forward of fin. Flettner trim tab on starboard elevator.

LANDING GEAR: Non-retractable monowheel and tailwheel.

ACCOMMODATION: Two seats in tandem beneath a blown Plexiglas canopy.

DIMENSIONS, EXTERNAL:
Wing span 56 ft $5\frac{1}{4}$ in (17·20 m)
Wing chord at root 4 ft $6\frac{1}{4}$ in (1·38 m)
Wing chord at tip 1 ft $9\frac{1}{4}$ in (0·54 m)
Wing aspect ratio 17·4
Length overall 26 ft 3 in (8·0 m)
Height overall 4 ft 11 in (1·5 m)

AREA:
Wings, gross 183 sq ft (17·0 m²)

WEIGHTS AND LOADING:
Weight empty, equipped 661 lb (300 kg)

Scheibe Bergfalke-IV two-seat training and competition sailplane

Max T-O weight 1,102 lb (500 kg)
Normal wing loading 5·7 lb/sq ft (28·0 kg/m²)

PERFORMANCE:
Best glide ratio at 46 knots (53 mph; 85 km/h) 34
Min sinking speed at 41 knots (47 mph; 75 km/h) 2·23 ft (0·68 m)/sec
Stalling speed 36 knots (41 mph; 65 km/h)
Max speed (smooth air) 108 knots (124 mph; 200 km/h)
Max speed (rough air) 92 knots (106 mph; 170 km/h)
Max aero-tow speed 76 knots (87 mph; 140 km/h)
Max winch-launching speed 59 knots (68 mph; 110 km/h)
Ultimate load factor 8*g*

SCHEIBE SF-25B FALKE (FALCON)

The Falke is a side-by-side two-seat powered sailplane, intended mainly for training. It has good soaring characteristics and does not require ballast when flown solo.

By January 1974 a total of 260 SF-25B Falkes had been built by Scheibe, a further 80 under licence by Sportavia in Germany and 35 by Slingsby in the UK (which see).

TYPE: Two-seat powered sailplane, particularly suitable for basic and advanced training.

WINGS: Two-piece cantilever low wing of wooden construction, with airbrakes. Design developed from the Motorfalke wing.

FUSELAGE: Fabric-covered welded steel tube structure. Optional tow hitch for winch launching.

TAIL UNIT: Conventional wooden construction.

LANDING GEAR: Main wheel with brake and aerodynamic fairing; steerable tailwheel; spring outrigger stabilising wheels fitted under each wing.

POWER PLANT: One 45 hp Stamo MS 1500 four-stroke horizontally-opposed engine, using Volkswagen and Porsche parts. Normal operating speed about 2,500-3,000 rpm. Starting on the ground and in the air is by means of a pull-cable starter in the cabin, with an electric starter available as an optional extra. Fuel capacity 8·5 Imp gallons (32 litres).

ACCOMMODATION: Two seats side by side in enclosed cabin. Dual controls standard.

DIMENSIONS, EXTERNAL:
Wing span 50 ft $2\frac{1}{2}$ in (15·30 m)
Wing aspect ratio 13·4

AREA:
Wings, gross 188·5 sq ft (17·5 m²)

WEIGHTS AND LOADING:
Weight empty 739 lb (335 kg)
Max T-O weight 1,168 lb (530 kg)
Max wing loading 6·1 lb/sq ft (30 kg/m²)

PERFORMANCE (at max T-O weight, powered):
Max level speed at S/L 87 knots (100 mph; 160 km/h)
Cruising speed 69 knots (80 mph; 130 km/h)
Stalling speed 33 knots (37 mph; 60 km/h)
Max rate of climb at S/L:
1 person 500 ft (150 m)/min
2 persons 400 ft (120 m)/min
T-O run at S/L:
1 person 328-394 ft (100-120 m)
2 persons 492-820 ft (150-250 m)
Best glide ratio (power off) 22
Min sinking speed (power off) 3·1 ft (0·95 m)/sec
Endurance 3 hr 30 min
Range 191-218 nm (220-250 miles; 350-400 km)

SCHEIBE SF-25C and C-S FALKE (FALCON)

The SF-25C is an improved version of the SF-25B Falke, to which it is structurally similar. The primary difference is in the use of a more powerful engine, giving an enhanced performance.

By January 1974 a total of 90 SF-25C Falkes had been built by Scheibe, and a further 45 under licence by Sportavia in Germany (which see). Type certification was granted in September 1972.

With a Hoffmann feathering propeller, adjustable engine cowl flap and slightly modified fuselage, the aircraft is known as the **SF-25C-S** and has a best glide ratio of 25 at 43·5 knots (50 mph; 80 km/h). Four of this version had been built by January 1974.

POWER PLANT: One 60 hp Limbach SL 1700 EA modified Volkswagen engine, driving a two-blade propeller. Fuel capacity 9·9 Imp gallons (45 litres).

DIMENSIONS, EXTERNAL:
Wing span 50 ft $0\frac{1}{4}$ in (15·25 m)
Wing aspect ratio 13·8
Length overall 24 ft $10\frac{1}{2}$ in (7·58 m)

Scheibe SF-27M single-seat powered sailplane with engine retracted and (*right*) partially extended

AREA:
- Wings, gross 195·9 sq ft (18·20 m²)

WEIGHTS AND LOADING:
- Weight empty approx 826 lb (375 kg)
- Max T-O weight 1,278 lb (580 kg)
- Max wing loading 6·41 lb/sq ft (31·3 kg/m²)

PERFORMANCE (at max T-O weight):
- Max level speed 97 knots (112 mph; 180 km/h)
- Cruising speed 86·5 knots (99·5 mph; 160 km/h)
- Stalling speed 35·5 knots (40·5 mph; 65 km/h)
- Max rate of climb at S/L 453 ft (138 m)/min
- T-O run approx 590 ft (180 m)
- Best glide ratio (power off) approx 23
- Min sinking speed (power off) approx 3·3 ft (1·0 m)/sec
- Econ endurance 4-5 hr
- Range approx 323 nm (372 miles; 600 km)
- Fuel consumption 2·64 Imp gallons (12 litres)/hr

SCHEIBE SF-27M

The SF-27M is a single-seat powered sailplane with a retractable power plant which makes it capable of self-powered take-off as well as normal launching by winch or aero-tow. Since the power plant is retractable, the SF-27M has about the same soaring performance as the normal SF-27 Zugvogel V high-performance sailplane (see description under SLCA heading in French section). The main difference arises from the additional weight of the engine installation, amounting to approximately 88 lb (40 kg). In addition, the main-wheel tyre size is increased to 5·00-5.

The construction of the SF-27M is similar to that of the SF-27. The wings and control surfaces are strengthened internally. The fuselage centre-section has also been modified, increasing the overall length to accommodate the engine which, when retracted, lies inside the fuselage behind the wings.

The engine is raised and retracted manually by a crank-driven draw-chain/pushrod system, swinging upward and forward into the operating position. The fuselage doors over the engine and propeller bay are automatically opened and closed when the engine is raised or retracted. The whole process requires only 3½ turns on the crank, and can be completed in 5 seconds.

The power plant comprises a 26 hp Hirth Solo vertically-opposed four-cylinder engine, driving a propeller of about 53 inches (1·36 m) diameter. The engine is started by a hand-operated cable, though electrical starting is available optionally. A specially designed ignition system facilitates starting. The fuel tank, capacity 4·4 Imp gallons (20 litres), is mounted in the fuselage behind the pilot.

The first Distance Diamond for a flight in a powered sailplane was issued by the German Aero Club to Willibald Collé, who on 28 July 1968 flew his SF-27M a distance of 290 nm (334 miles; 537 km), as described in the 1972-73 *Jane's*.

A total of 30 SF-27Ms had been built by January 1974, with production continuing.

DIMENSIONS AND AREAS:
- As for SF-27, except:
- Length overall 23 ft 6 in (7·16 m)

WEIGHTS AND LOADING (approx):
- Weight empty, equipped 595 lb (270 kg)
- Max T-O weight 849 lb (385 kg)
- Wing loading 6·4 lb/sq ft (31·5 kg/m²)

PERFORMANCE (approx, at max T-O weight, powered):
- Max level speed 83 knots (95 mph; 150 km/h)
- Stalling speed 32·5 knots (37 mph; 60 km/h)
- Max rate of climb at S/L approx 395 ft (120 m)/min
- T-O run 457-655 ft (150-200 m)
- Range 134-161 nm (155-186 miles; 250-300 km)
- Endurance 2-3 hr
- Best glide ratio at 48 knots (55 mph; 88 km/h) (power off) 34
- Min sinking speed (power off) 2·3 ft (0·7 m)/sec

SF-25C-S Falke, developed from the SF-25B with redesigned fuselage, engine cowl flap and feathering propeller (*Deutscher Aerokurier*)

Scheibe SF-28 Tandem-Falke two-seat powered sailplane (60 hp Limbach SL 1700 EA 1 engine)

SCHEIBE SF-28 TANDEM-FALKE

The Tandem-Falke, as its name implies, is a further development of the Bergfalke and Falke series of sailplanes in which the two seats are arranged in tandem. Design began in 1970, and the prototype (D-KAFJ) flew for the first time in May 1971, powered by a 45 hp Stamo MS 1500 engine. Details apply to the production version, of which 60 had been built by January 1974.

TYPE: Tandem two-seat powered sailplane.

WINGS: Cantilever low-wing monoplane. Wing section Gö 533. Single-spar wooden wings, with trailing-edge taper on outer panels. Wooden ailerons. No flaps. Spoiler on upper surface of each wing.

FUSELAGE: Fabric-covered steel tube structure.

TAIL UNIT: Conventional cantilever wooden structure. Trim tab in elevator.

LANDING GEAR: Non-retractable monowheel, with internal brake, and steerable tailwheel. Nylon leg with outrigger stabilising wheel under each wing. Main-wheel tyre size 8·00-4.

POWER PLANT: One 60 hp Limbach SL 1700 EA 1 engine, driving a Hoffmann two-blade feathering (optionally, fixed-pitch) propeller. Fuel capacity 7·4 Imp gallons (34 litres).

ACCOMMODATION: Two seats in tandem under one-piece blown Perspex canopy. Can be flown solo from front seat, with space for 198 lb (90 kg) of baggage on rear seat. Standard basic instrumentation, 12V electric starter and alternator.

DIMENSIONS, EXTERNAL:
- Wing span 53 ft 5¾ in (16·30 m)
- Wing aspect ratio 14·5
- Length overall 26 ft 9 in (8·15 m)
- Height over tail 5 ft 1 in (1·55 m)

AREA:
- Wings, gross 197·5 sq ft (18·35 m²)

WEIGHTS AND LOADINGS:
- Weight empty, equipped 881 lb (400 kg)
- Max T-O weight 1,300 lb (590 kg)
- Max wing loading 6·59 lb/sq ft (32·18 kg/m²)
- Max power loading 21·67 lb/hp (9·83 kg/hp)

PERFORMANCE (at max T-O weight, powered):
- Max level speed at S/L 97 knots (112 mph; 180 km/h)
- Max cruising speed 86 knots (99 mph; 160 km/h)
- Stalling speed 33·5 knots (39 mph; 62 km/h)
- Max speed (rough or smooth air, power off) 102·5 knots (118 mph; 190 km/h)
- Max rate of climb at S/L 415 ft (126 m)/min
- Service ceiling 16,400 ft (5,000 m)
- T-O run 590 ft (180 m)
- T-O to 50 ft (15 m) 985 ft (300 m)
- Landing from 50 ft (15 m) 655 ft (200 m)
- Landing run 328 ft (100 m)

Best glide ratio at 46 knots (53 mph; 85 km/h) 26-27
Min sinking speed (power off) at 38 knots (43·5 mph; 70 km/h) 2·95 ft (0·9 m)/sec
Circling speed 37·5-43·5 knots (43-50 mph; 69-80·5 km/h)
Range 269 nm (310 miles; 500 km)
Endurance 4 hr
Fuel consumption 2·6 Imp gallons (12 litres)/hr

SCHEIBE SF-29

The SF-29 is essentially a single-seat version of the SF-25B Falke powered sailplane, from which it differs principally in having a lower-powered engine, with electric starting, smaller wings, and a narrower fuselage in the region of the cockpit. A prototype (D-KOCH) flew for the first time in 1973, and the following description applies to this aircraft:

TYPE: Single-seat experimental powered sailplane.

WINGS: Cantilever low/mid-wing monoplane of wooden construction, with airbrakes.

FUSELAGE: Fabric-covered welded steel tube structure.

TAIL UNIT: Conventional wooden construction.

LANDING GEAR: Non-retractable monowheel, with brake, and tailwheel. Outrigger stabilising skid under each wing.

POWER PLANT: One 30 hp Hirth O-17 two-cylinder two-stroke in-line engine, driving a two-blade propeller.

ACCOMMODATION: Single seat under one-piece sideways-opening moulded canopy.

DIMENSIONS, EXTERNAL:
Wing span 49 ft 2½ in (15·00 m)
Wing aspect ratio 18
Length overall 22 ft 1¾ in (6·75 m)
Height overall 4 ft 3¼ in (1·30 m)

AREA:
Wings, gross 134·5 sq ft (12·50 m²)

WEIGHTS AND LOADINGS:
Weight empty 573 lb (260 kg)
Max T-O weight 815 lb (370 kg)
Max wing loading 6·06 lb/sq ft (29·6 kg/m²)
Max power loading 27·12 lb/hp (12·3 kg/hp)

PERFORMANCE (at max T-O weight, powered):
Max level speed 86 knots (99 mph; 160 km/h)
Cruising speed 75·5 knots (87 mph; 140 km/h)
Landing speed 34·5 knots (40 mph; 64 km/h)
Max rate of climb at S/L 395 ft (120 m)/min
T-O run 655 ft (200 m)
T-O to 50 ft (15 m) 1,310 ft (400 m)
Landing from 50 ft (15 m) 655 ft (200 m)
Landing run 328 ft (100 m)
Max range 162 nm (186 miles; 300 km)
Max endurance 2 hr
Best glide ratio 28
Min sinking speed at 38 knots (43·5 mph; 70 km/h), power off 2·46 ft (0·75 m)/sec

Scheibe SF-29 single-seat powered sailplane *(Deutscher Aerokurier)*

SCHEMPP-HIRTH

SCHEMPP-HIRTH KG

HEAD OFFICE:
7312 Kirchheim/Teck, Krebenstrasse 25, Postfach 43
Telephone: (07021) 2441 and 6097
Telex: 7267817 hate

DIRECTOR:
Dipl-Ing Klaus Holighaus

Schempp-Hirth specialises in the production of high-performance Open Class and Standard Class sailplanes. In 1970 Dipl-Ing Klaus Holighaus became a 50% shareholder of Schempp-Hirth KG, later becoming its director following the retirement of Herr Martin Schempp.

Details of the SHK Open Class sailplane may be found in the 1969-70 *Jane's*. Descriptions of the company's current products follow. The company was producing 10 sailplanes per month in early 1974.

SCHEMPP-HIRTH CIRRUS

This single-seat high-performance sailplane was designed by Dipl-Ing Klaus Holighaus, who was one of the co-designers of the Akaflieg Darmstadt D-36 Circe before joining Schempp-Hirth in 1965. He utilised the new thick Wortmann wing section, without flaps, to achieve good low-speed and climb characteristics. Provision for ballast overcomes the slight disadvantage this section has when compared with thinner flapped profiles. Stalling characteristics are good with a thicker wing and Schempp-Hirth claims that weight is saved by comparison with a flapped wing of similar span and aspect ratio.

The first prototype Cirrus flew for the first time in January 1967 with a V tail unit. The second prototype had a conventional tail unit, as fitted to production models.

By 1 February 1974 Schempp-Hirth had built a total of 120 Cirrus sailplanes. Since early 1972 the Cirrus has also been produced under licence by VTC in Yugoslavia (which see) at a rate of about two per month. Forty had been completed by VTC by early 1974.

TYPE: Single-seat high-performance sailplane.

WINGS: Cantilever mid-wing monoplane. Wortmann FX-66 series section. Thickness/chord ratio 19·6% at root, 16% at tip. Dihedral 3° at spar centreline. Incidence 2°. No sweep at spar centreline. Wing shell is a glassfibre/foam sandwich structure, with an all-glassfibre box spar. Hinged ailerons of glassfibre/balsa sandwich. No flaps. Schempp-Hirth aluminium alloy airbrakes.

FUSELAGE: Glassfibre shell, 1·5 mm thick, stiffened with foam rings, secured with resin.

TAIL UNIT: Cantilever structure of glassfibre/foam sandwich. Tailplane mounted part-way up fin.

LANDING GEAR: Retractable monowheel type. Manual retraction. Annular rubber-spring shock-absorber. Tost wheel with Dunlop tyre size 3·50 × 5, pressure 49 lb/sq in (3·45 kg/cm²). Tost drum brake.

ACCOMMODATION: Single semi-reclining adjustable seat. Adjustable rudder pedals. Long flush Plexiglas canopy.

DIMENSIONS, EXTERNAL:
Wing span 58 ft 2½ in (17·74 m)
Wing chord at root 2 ft 11½ in (0·90 m)
Wing chord at tip 1 ft 2¼ in (0·36 m)
Wing aspect ratio 25
Length overall 23 ft 7¼ in (7·20 m)
Height over tail 5 ft 0 in (1·56 m)
Tailplane span 8 ft 2½ in (2·50 m)

AREAS:
Wings, gross 135·6 sq ft (12·6 m²)
Ailerons (total) 11·2 sq ft (1·04 m²)
Fin 6·8 sq ft (0·63 m²)
Rudder 5·6 sq ft (0·52 m²)
Tailplane 9·7 sq ft (0·90 m²)
Elevators 1·6 sq ft (0·15 m²)

WEIGHTS AND LOADING:
Weight empty, equipped 573 lb (260 kg)
Max T-O weight 882 lb (400 kg)
Max wing loading 6·5 lb/sq ft (31·7 kg/m²)

PERFORMANCE (at AUW of 793 lb; 360 kg):
Best glide ratio at 46 knots (53 mph; 85 km/h) 44
Min sinking speed at 39 knots (45 mph; 73 km/h) 1·64 ft (0·50 m)/sec
Stalling speed 33·5 knots (39 mph; 62 km/h)
Max speed (rough or smooth air) 119 knots (137 mph; 220 km/h)
Max aero-tow speed 76 knots (87 mph; 140 km/h)
Max winch-launching speed 59 knots (68 mph; 110 km/h)

SCHEMPP-HIRTH STANDARD CIRRUS

Designed by Dipl-Ing Klaus Holighaus, the Standard Class version of the Schempp-Hirth Cirrus entered production during the Summer of 1969, following the first flight of the prototype in March 1969.

The Standard Cirrus was winner of the Standard Class at the International Soaring Competition at Hahnweide in 1969, and winner of the South African National Standard Class in 1970.

Standard Cirrus sailplanes took second and fourth places in the Standard Class of the 1974 World Championships at Waikerie, Australia.

By 1 February 1974 a total of 420 Standard Cirrus had been built, including 100 under licence by GROB-Maschinenbau of Mindelheim, Bavaria, and production was continuing.

TYPE: Single-seat high-performance Standard Class sailplane.

WINGS: Cantilever mid-wing monoplane. Wortmann section. Thickness/chord ratio 19·6% at root, 17% at tip. Dihedral 3°. Incidence 3°. Sweepback 1·3° at leading-edge. Wings and ailerons are glassfibre/foam sandwich structures. Schempp-Hirth glassfibre airbrakes on wing upper surface.

FUSELAGE: Glassfibre shell, 1·5 mm thick, stiffened with bonded-in foam rings.

TAIL UNIT: T-tail of glassfibre/foam sandwich construction. All-moving tailplane.

LANDING GEAR: Manually-retractable monowheel standard. Non-retractable faired monowheel optional. Tost wheel with drum brake and Continental 4·00-4 tyre, pressure 50 lb/sq in (3·50 kg/cm²).

ACCOMMODATION: Single semi-reclining seat under long flush Plexiglas canopy, hinged at starboard side. Adjustable rudder pedals.

DIMENSIONS, EXTERNAL:
Wing span 49 ft 2½ in (15·00 m)
Wing chord at root 3 ft 0½ in (0·93 m)
Wing chord at tip 1 ft 2¼ in (0·36 m)
Wing aspect ratio 22·5
Length overall 20 ft 9¾ in (6·35 m)
Height over tail 4 ft 4¾ in (1·32 m)
Tailplane span 7 ft 10½ in (2·40 m)

AREA:
Wings, gross 107·6 sq ft (10·00 m²)

WEIGHTS AND LOADINGS:
Weight empty 445 lb (202 kg)
Max T-O weight:
with water ballast 860 lb (390 kg)
without water ballast 728 lb (330 kg)
Max wing loading:
with water ballast 8·0 lb/sq ft (39 kg/m²)
without water ballast 6·8 lb/sq ft (33 kg/m²)

PERFORMANCE:
Best glide ratio at 46 knots (53 mph; 85 km/h) 38
Min sinking speed at 38·5 knots (44 mph; 71 km/h) 1·87 ft (0·57 m)/sec
Stalling speed 33·5 knots (39 mph; 62 km/h)

Schempp-Hirth Cirrus single-seat high-performance sailplane

Max speed (rough or smooth air)
119 knots (137 mph; 220 km/h)
Max aero-tow speed
81 knots (93 mph; 150 km/h)
Max winch-launching speed
65 knots (75 mph; 120 km/h)
g limit 10

SCHEMPP-HIRTH NIMBUS II

Generally similar to the HS-3 Nimbus (1972-73 *Jane's*), from which it was developed, this single-seat high-performance sailplane differs principally by having reduced span and a wing built in four pieces to limit weight and dimensions for rigging, storage and trailer transport.

Design of the Nimbus II was initiated by Dipl-Ing Klaus Holighaus in January 1970 and construction of the prototype began in April of the same year. The first flight was made in April 1971; a Nimbus II took first place in the Open Class at the 1972 and 1974 World Championships at Vrsac, Yugoslavia, and Waikerie, Australia. On 14 August 1973 a Nimbus II flown by Dipl-Ing Holighaus set up a new world speed record over a 100 km course of 85·93 knots (98·95 mph; 159·24 km/h).

By 1 February 1974 a total of 55 Nimbus IIs had been built, with production continuing.

In the Spring of 1974 a proposal for a Nimbus IIM powered version, to be fitted with a 50 hp Hirth 028 engine, was under consideration.

TYPE: Single-seat high-performance sailplane.

WINGS: Cantilever mid-wing monoplane. Wortmann wing section. Thickness/chord ratio 17% at root, 15% at tip. Dihedral 2°. Incidence 1°. Sweepback at leading-edge 1° on inner wing, 2° on outer wing. Wings are of glassfibre/foam sandwich construction and built in four sections, with tongue-and-fork assembly. Water ballast valves connect automatically. Tip sections incorporate a quick-connect aileron fitting and locking pin. Ailerons and interconnected trailing-edge flaps are glassfibre shells. Schempp-Hirth airbrake of glassfibre construction on each upper surface. Provision for up to 333 lb (151 kg) of water ballast.

FUSELAGE: Central tubular steel framework. Glassfibre shell 1·5 to 2·0 mm thick, stiffened with bonded-in foam bulkheads.

TAIL UNIT: Cantilever structure of glassfibre/foam sandwich. All-moving T-tailplane.

LANDING GEAR: Manually-retractable monowheel type. Tost wheel has Continental tyre size 5·00-5, pressure 50 lb/sq in (3·5 kg/cm²). Tost drum brake. Shock-absorption of monowheel is provided by annular rubber springs. Tailskid designed to fail in the event of a ground loop, to relieve stress on the rear fuselage. Ribbon drogue 'chute in bottom of rudder for use in steep approaches or emergencies.

ACCOMMODATION: Single semi-reclining seat under long flush hinged canopy. Rudder pedals adjustable.

DIMENSIONS, EXTERNAL:
Wing span 66 ft 7¼ in (20·3 m)
Wing chord at root 3 ft 1¾ in (0·96 m)
Wing chord at tip 1 ft 1¾ in (0·35 m)
Wing aspect ratio 28·6
Length overall 23 ft 10½ in (7·28 m)
Height overall 4 ft 9 in (1·45 m)
Tailplane span 7 ft 10½ in (2·40 m)

AREA:
Wings, gross 155 sq ft (14·4 m²)

WEIGHTS AND LOADINGS:
Weight empty, equipped 749 lb (340 kg)
Max T-O weight:
with water ballast 1,168 lb (530 kg)
without water ballast 1,036 lb (470 kg)
Max wing loading:
with water ballast 7·54 lb/sq ft (36·8 kg/m²)
without water ballast 6·68 lb/sq ft (32·6 kg/m²)

PERFORMANCE (at 1,014 lb; 460 kg AUW):
Best glide ratio at 49 knots (56·5 mph; 91 km/h) 46
Min sinking speed at 40 knots (46 mph; 74 km/h) 1·64 ft (0·50 m)/sec
Stalling speed 34 knots (39 mph; 63 km/h)
Max speed (rough or smooth air)
135 knots (155 mph; 249 km/h)
Max aero-tow speed
86 knots (99 mph; 160 km/h)
Max winch-launching speed
65 knots (75 mph; 120 km/h)
g limit +10·5

SCHEMPP-HIRTH JANUS

The Janus is a two-seat sailplane of all-glassfibre construction. Original design work, begun by Dipl-Ing Holighaus in 1969, was continued from early 1972 onward, and the prototype made its first flight in the Spring of 1974. At that time Schempp-Hirth had received orders for about 20 of these aircraft. Production was due to begin in late 1974, at a planned rate of two per month.

Changes from the original concept include a reduction in wing span from 22 m to 18·2 m and the adoption of a wing section similar to that of the Nimbus II. The Janus is intended primarily as a high-performance training sailplane.

TYPE: Two-seat high-performance training sailplane.

WINGS: Cantilever mid-wing monoplane, Wortmann wing sections, with thickness/chord ratios of 17% at root and 15% at tip. Dihedral 4°. Incidence 2° 36′. Sweepforward 2° on leading-edge. Glassfibre/foam sandwich construction, with glassfibre monocoque ailerons, trailing-edge flaps and Schempp-Hirth upper-surface airbrakes.

FUSELAGE: Glassfibre monocoque structure, 1·5 mm to 2 mm thick, with bonded-in foam bulkheads.

TAIL UNIT: Cantilever structure of glassfibre/foam sandwich. All-moving one-piece T-tailplane.

LANDING GEAR: Non-retractable monowheel and nosewheel. Continental tyres: size 380 × 150 × 150 mm, pressure 39 lb/sq in (2·75 kg/cm²) on main wheel; size 260 × 85 × 123 mm, pressure 11·5 lb/sq in (0·8 kg/cm²) on nosewheel. Tost drum brake on main wheel. Bumper under rear fuselage. Tail drag parachute.

ACCOMMODATION: Two seats in tandem under hinged one-piece flush transparent canopy. Rudder pedals at front seat are adjustable.

DIMENSIONS, EXTERNAL:
Wing span 59 ft 8½ in (18·20 m)
Wing chord at root 3 ft 10½ in (1·18 m)

Schempp-Hirth Standard Cirrus single-seat high-performance sailplane

Schempp-Hirth Nimbus II high-performance Open Class sailplane

Almost-completed prototype of the Schempp-Hirth Janus sailplane

Wing chord at tip 1 ft 6¾ in (0·48 m)
Wing mean aerodynamic chord 3 ft 0 in (0·912 m)
Wing aspect ratio 20
Length overall 28 ft 1½ in (8·57 m)
Height overall 4 ft 9 in (1·45 m)
Tailplane span 8 ft 10¼ in (2·70 m)

AREAS:
Wings, gross 174·4 sq ft (16·20 m²)
Ailerons (total) 11·09 sq ft (1·03 m²)
Trailing-edge flaps (total) 19·59 sq ft (1·82 m²)
Fin 8·07 sq ft (0·75 m²)
Rudder 5·27 sq ft (0·49 m²)
Tailplane 13·35 sq ft (1·24 m²)

WEIGHTS AND LOADING:
Weight empty, equipped 815 lb (370 kg)
Max T-O weight 1,366 lb (620 kg)
Max wing loading 7·66 lb/sq ft (37·4 kg/m²)

PERFORMANCE (at max T-O weight except where indicated):
*Best glide ratio at 51·5 knots (59 mph; 95 km/h) 39
*Min sinking speed at 41 knots (47 mph; 75 km/h) 2·0 ft (0·61 m)/sec
*Stalling speed 36·5 knots (42 mph; 67 km/h)
Max speed (rough or smooth air) 118 knots (136 mph; 220 km/h)
Max aero-tow speed 91 knots (105 mph; 170 km/h)
Max winch-launching speed 64·5 knots (74·5 mph; 120 km/h)
g limit +9
**at AUW of 1,186 lb (538 kg)*

SCHLEICHER

ALEXANDER SCHLEICHER SEGELFLUG-ZEUGBAU

HEAD OFFICE AND WORKS:
D-6416 Poppenhausen/Wasserkuppe
Telephone: (06658) 225

This company is one of the oldest manufacturers of sailplanes in the world. Its founder, Alexander Schleicher, was himself winner of the contest for training sailplanes at the 1927 meeting at the famous Wasserkuppe gliding centre. In the same year he built at Poppenhausen a small factory for manufacturing gliders and sailplanes, two of his best-known pre-war products being the Rhönbussard and Rhönadler, designed by Hans Jacobs.

During the second World War, the factory was engaged on the repair of Baby IIb sailplanes. For a time afterwards it became a furniture factory; but it began producing sailplanes once more in 1951.

Descriptions of the sailplanes and powered sailplanes in current production follow. In addition, the K 8 B, ASK 13 and ASK 16 are available in kit form for amateur constructors. Schleicher also manufactures and markets spare parts, constructional materials and dust- and weather-proof covers for sailplanes.

SCHLEICHER K 8 B and C

Designed by Rudolf Kaiser, the K 8 B was developed from the Ka 6, but features simplified construction throughout. As a result, itis suitable for amateur construction.

The prototype flew in November 1957 and 1,107 had been built by 1 March 1972. Production of both versions continues in 1974.

TYPE: Single-seat training and sporting sailplane.

WINGS: Cantilever high-wing monoplane. Wing section Gö 533 at root, Gö 532 at tip. Dihedrel 3°. Sweepforward 1° 181 at quarter-chord. Single-spar structure with plywood D-type leading-edge. Rear portion fabric-covered. Plywood-covered top-hinged wooden ailerons, actuated by push/pull rods. Schempp-Hirth airbrakes.

FUSELAGE: Welded steel tube structure with spruce stringers, fabric-covered. Nose made of glassfibre.

TAIL UNIT: Cantilever type, with single-spar plywood-covered fin and low-set tailplane; Rudder and elevators are plywood torsion tube structures, fabric-covered at rear. Flettner tab in port elevator. Actuation of elevators by push/pull rods, of rudder by cables from adjustable rudder pedals.

LANDING GEAR: Nose-skid mounted on rubber blocks. Non-retractable and unsprung Continental monowheel, 4·00-4 (300 × 100), with brake. Tyre pressure 28-36 lb/sq in (2·0-2·5 kg/cm²). Steel tailskid.

ACCOMMODATION: Single seat under blown Plexiglas canopy.

EQUIPMENT: To customer's specification, including optional mounting of radio antenna internally in fin. Aero-tow release in nose. Kombi release at CG.

DIMENSIONS, EXTERNAL:
Wing span 49 ft 2½ in (15·00 m)
Wing chord at root 4 ft 3 in (1·30 m)
Wing aspect ratio 15·9
Length overall:
Ka 8 B 22 ft 11¾ in (7·00 m)
Ka 8 C 23 ft 1½ in (7·05 m)
Height over tail 5 ft 1¾ in (1·57 m)
Tailplane span 9 ft 2¼ in (2·80 m)

AREAS:
Wings, gross 152·3 sq ft (14·15 m²)
Ailerons (total) 10·76 sq ft (1·00 m²)
Airbrakes (total) 3·66 sq ft (0·34 m²)
Fin 6·67 sq ft (0·62 m²)
Rudder 8·07 sq ft (0·75 m²)
Tailplane 10·33 sq ft (0·96 m²)
Elevators 10·12 sq ft (0·94 m²)

WEIGHTS AND LOADING:
Weight empty, equipped 418 lb (190 kg)
Max T-O weight 683 lb (310 kg)
Wing loading at 606 lb (275 kg) AUW 4·0 lb/sq ft (19·5 kg/m²)

PERFORMANCE (at max T-O weight):
Best glide ratio at 39·5 knots (45·5 mph; 73 km/h) 27
Min sinking speed at 32·5 knots (37·5 mph; 60 km/h) 2·13 ft (0·65 m)/sec
Stalling speed 29·5 knots (34 mph; 54 km/h)
Max speed (smooth air) 108 knots (124 mph; 200 km/h)
Max speed (rough air) and max aero-tow speed 70 knots (81 mph; 130 km/h)
Max winch-launching speed 65 knots (62 mph; 100 km/h)

SCHLEICHER ASK 13

This tandem-seat sailplane was developed from the K7, which is in worldwide use by gliding clubs.

The prototype first flew in July 1966 and by March 1973 a total of 430 ASK 13s had been built. Production was continuing in 1974.

Compared with the K7, the ASK 13 introduces many improvements, including a large full-blown canopy for all-round visibility, higher performance, improved comfort and a sprung landing wheel for softer touchdowns.

On 25 April 1972 an ASK 13, flown by Siegfried Baumgartl and Walter Schewe, set up a world goal-flight record for two-seat sailplanes of 385 nm (443 miles; 714 km) in a flight from Dorsten to Antwerp.

TYPE: Two-seat training and high-performance sailplane.

WINGS: Cantilever mid-wing monoplane. Wing section developed from Göttingen 535 and 549. Thickness/chord ratio: 16% at root, 12% at tip. Sweepforward at quarter-chord 6°. Dihedral 5°. No incidence. Single-spar wood structure, with plywood D-type leading-edge torsion box and fabric covering. Wooden ailerons, with fabric covering, actuated by push/pull rods. Schempp-Hirth metal airbrakes above and below each wing.

FUSELAGE: Welded steel tube structure with spruce stringers and fabric main covering. Nose made of glassfibre. Turtledeck aft of canopy is plywood shell.

TAIL UNIT: Cantilever wood structure. Fixed surfaces plywood-covered. Rear portion of rudder and elevators fabric-covered. Flettner tab in starboard elevator. Actuation of elevators by push/pull rods, of rudder by cables from adjustable rudder pedals.

LANDING GEAR: Non-retractable sprung monowheel, size 5·00-5 (350 × 125) with Tost disc brake, mounted aft of CG. Skid in front of wheel; steel tailskid.

ACCOMMODATION: Two seats in tandem under one-piece blown Mecaplex canopy, hinged to starboard. Glassfibre seat panels. Adjustable rudder pedals.

EQUIPMENT: Aero-tow release in nose. Kombi release at CG. Normal instrumentation; provision for radio and oxygen.

DIMENSIONS, EXTERNAL:
Wing span 52 ft 4 in (15·95 m)
Wing chord (mean) 3 ft 7 in (1·09 m)
Wing aspect ratio 14·6
Length overall 26 ft 9¼ in (8·18 m)
Height over tail 5 ft 3 in (1·6 m)
Tailplane span 9 ft 10 in (3·0 m)

AREAS:
Wings, gross 188 sq ft (17·50 m²)
Ailerons (total) 15·93 sq ft (1·48 m²)
Airbrakes (total) 4·62 sq ft (0·43 m²)
Fin 6·45 sq ft (0·60 m²)
Rudder 8·93 sq ft (0·83 m²)
Tailplane 24·22 sq ft (2·25 m²)
Elevators 11·30 sq ft (1·05 m²)

WEIGHTS AND LOADINGS:
Weight empty 640 lb (290 kg)
Max T-O weight 1,060 lb (480 kg)
Wing loading:
single-seater 4·45 lb/sq ft (21·7 kg/m²)
two-seater 5·5 lb/sq ft (26·8 kg/m²)

PERFORMANCE (single-seater at 837 lb; 380 kg AUW, two-seater at 1,036 lb; 470 kg AUW):
Best glide ratio:
single-seater at 43·5 knots (50 mph; 80 km/h) 27
two-seater at 48·6 knots (56 mph; 90 km/h) 27
Min sinking speed:
single-seater at 35 knots (40 mph; 64 km/h) 2·40 ft (0·73 m)/sec
two-seater at 38 knots (43·5 mph; 70 km/h) 2·66 ft (0·81 m)/sec
Stalling speed:
single-seater 30·5 knots (35 mph; 56·4 km/h)
two-seater 33 knots (38 mph; 61 km/h)
Max speed (smooth air) 109 knots (125 mph; 200 km/h)
Max speed (rough air) and max aero-tow speed 76 knots (87 mph; 140 km/h)
Max winch-launching speed 54 knots (62 mph; 100 km/h)
g limit 4*g* at safety factor of 2

SCHLEICHER ASW 15-B

Designed by Gerhard Waibel to meet Standard Class requirements, and built by Schleicher, the ASW 15 was first flown in April 1968. A French

Schleicher K 8 B single-seat training and sporting sailplane

Schleicher ASK 13 tandem two-seat training and high-performance sailplane

type certificate was awarded on 24 November 1971.

A total of 250 ASW 15s (all versions) had been built by early 1974. The original ASW 15 (184 built) was described in the 1972-73 *Jane's*. An ASW 15 took second place in the Standard Class in the 1972 World Championships at Vrsac, Yugoslavia.

The following description applies to the ASW 15-B current production version, which was introduced from the 185th aircraft. This has a strengthened main spar, an enlarged rudder, a bigger wheel and drum brake, a 17·6 Imp gallon (80 litre) water ballast installation and other improvements.

Type: Single-seat Standard Class sailplane.

Wings: Cantilever shoulder-wing monoplane. Wing section Wortmann FX-61-163 at root/mean and FX-60-126 at tip. Dihedral 2°. No incidence. No sweepback. Structure: glassfibre roving spar, glassfibre/balsa or Conticell foam sandwich torsion box. Ailerons of glassfibre/foam sandwich. Schempp-Hirth metal airbrakes above and below each wing in separate specially sealed compartments with spring-loaded cover plates. Reinforced structure in ASW 15-B with provision for 8·8 Imp gallon (40 litre) water ballast tank in each leading-edge.

Fuselage: Glassfibre/honeycomb sandwich construction. Reinforced keel on ASW 15-B.

Tail Unit: All-moving horizontal surfaces of similar construction to wing. Fin construction same as fuselage, and rudder same as ailerons. Rudder control cables run within plastics conduits.

Landing Gear: Retractable landing gear with central monowheel, operated manually through push/pull rods. Dunlop/Continental size 5·00-5 (350 × 125) wheel and tyre, with Tost and own-production internal shoe brake. Tyre pressure 36 lb/sq in (2·5 kg/cm²).

Accommodation: Single semi-reclining seat, with adjustable backrest and headrest and integral parachute pan. Space for 24 lb (11 kg) of baggage. Adjustable ventilation. One-piece transparent canopy.

Equipment: Standard instrumentation. Provision for oxygen and radio transceiver. VHF antenna in fin. Nose compartments for optional 17·6 Imp gallons (80 litres) water ballast in two tanks in wings.

Dimensions, external:
Wing span 49 ft 2½ in (15·00 m)
Wing chord at root 3 ft 0 in (0·92 m)
Wing chord at tip 1 ft 3¾ in (0·40 m)
Wing aspect ratio 20·45
Length overall 21 ft 3 in (6·48 m)
Height overall 5 ft 1½ in (1·56 m)
Tailplane span 8 ft 7¼ in (2·62 m)

Dimensions, internal:
Cockpit: Seating height 2 ft 7½ in (0·80 m)
Width 2 ft 7½ in (0·80 m)
Baggage volume 1·5 cu ft (0·04 m³)

Areas:
Wings, gross 118·40 sq ft (11·00 m²)
Ailerons (total) 9·14 sq ft (0·85 m²)
Airbrakes (total) 4·30 sq ft (0·4 m²)
Fin 6·46 sq ft (0·6 m²)
Tailplane 12·38 sq ft (1·15 m²)

Weights and Loading:
Weight empty, equipped 496 lb (225 kg)
Max T-O weight (with water ballast) 899 lb (408 kg)
Max wing loading (with water ballast) 7·6 lb/sq ft (37·1 kg/m²)

Performance (at 679 lb; 308 kg AUW):
Best glide ratio at 48·5 knots (56 mph; 90 km/h) 38
Min sinking speed at 38 knots (43·5 mph; 70 km/h) 1·90 ft (0·58 m)/sec
Stalling speed 34·5 knots (39·5 mph; 63 km/h)
Max speed (rough or smooth air) 119 knots (136·7 mph; 220 km/h)
Max aero-tow speed 91 knots (105 mph; 170 km/h)
Max winch-launching speed 65 knots (74·5 mph; 120 km/h)
g limits:
normal +5·3; —2·65
ultimate +9·2; —6·2

Schleicher ASW 15 single-seat Standard Class sailplane

Schleicher ASK 16 two-seat powered sailplane (72 hp Limbach SL 1700 EB 1 engine)

SCHLEICHER ASK 16

Design of the ASK 16 was started in 1969, construction of a prototype began in the following year, and this aircraft flew for the first time on 2 February 1971. The first production aircraft flew in 1972, and four had been built by early 1973.

Type: Two-seat powered sailplane.

Wings: Cantilever low-wing monoplane. Wing section NACA 63618 at root, Joukowsky 12% at tip, with Wortmann modifications. Dihedral 5°. Incidence 2° 48′ at root. Sweepforward 1° at quarter-chord. Fabric-covered wooden structure, with glassfibre tips. Plain wooden ailerons. Spoiler on each upper surface. No flaps or tabs.

Fuselage: Primary load-bearing structure of steel tube, with glassfibre, plywood and fabric covering.

Tail Unit: Fabric-covered wooden cantilever structure. Combined trim and anti-balance tab in centre of elevator.

Landing Gear: Inward-retracting main wheels and non-retractable tailwheel. Rubber shock-absorbers. Wheels and tyres size 5·00-5 on main units, 210 × 65 on tail unit. Tyre pressure (main units) 35·5 lb/sq in (2·5 kg/cm²). Tost drum brakes.

Power Plant: One 72 hp Limbach SL 1700 EB 1 (modified Volkswagen) engine, driving a Hoffman HO-V62 two-blade variable-pitch feathering propeller.

Accommodation: Side-by-side seats for two persons under sideways-opening Plexiglas canopy.

Dimensions, external:
Wing span 52 ft 5¾ in (16·00 m)
Wing chord at root 5 ft 11 in (1·80 m)
Wing chord (mean) 3 ft 10¾ in (1·19 m)
Wing chord at tip 1 ft 10 in (0·56 m)
Wing aspect ratio 13·5
Length overall 24 ft 0¼ in (7·32 m)
Height overall 6 ft 9¾ in (2·08 m)
Tailplane span 10 ft 6 in (3·20 m)
Propeller diameter 5 ft 3 in (1·60 m)

Areas:
Wings, gross 204·5 sq ft (19·00 m²)
Ailerons (total) 12·59 sq ft (1·17 m²)
Spoilers (total) 4·84 sq ft (0·45 m²)
Fin 7·00 sq ft (0·65 m²)
Rudder 7·59 sq ft (0·705 m²)
Tailplane 13·78 sq ft (1·28 m²)
Elevators, incl tab 11·73 sq ft (1·09 m²)

Weights and Loadings:
Weight empty, equipped 1,014 lb (460 kg)
Max T-O weight 1,543 lb (700 kg)
Max wing loading 7·55 lb/sq ft (37 kg/m²)
Max power loading 25·8 lb/hp (11·7 kg/hp)

Performance (at max T-O weight):
Max never-exceed speed 107 knots (124 mph; 200 km/h)
Max level speed at S/L, powered 97 knots (112 mph; 180 km/h)
Cruising speed, powered 86 knots (99 mph; 160 km/h)
Best glide ratio at 44·5-51 knots 51-58·5 mph; 82-94 km/h) 25
Min sinking speed at 40 knots (46 mph; 74 km/h), two-seat 3·28 ft (1·0 m)/sec
Stalling speed:
two-seat 37·5 knots (43 mph; 69 km/h)
single-seat 33·5 knots (39 mph; 62 km/h)
Max speed (unpowered), rough or smooth air 108 knots (124 mph; 200 km/h)
Max rate of climb, powered 492 ft (150 m)/min
Service ceiling 17,050 ft (5,200 m)
T-O run, powered 755 ft (230 m)
T-O to 50 ft (15 m), powered 1,099 ft (335 m)
Landing from 50 ft (15 m) 591 ft (180 m)
Landing run 394 ft (120 m)
Range 269 nm (310 miles; 500 km)
g limits +5·3; —2·65

SCHLEICHER ASW 17 SUPER ORCHIDEE

The ASW 17 is a single-seat Open Class sailplane, the prototype of which (D-1110) flew for the first time on 17 July 1971. ASW 17s took second and fifth places in the Open Class of the 1972 World Championships at Vrsac, Yugoslavia, and third place in the 1974 World Championships at Waikerie, Australia. Twelve had been built by early 1974.

Type: Single-seat Open Class sailplane.

Wings: Cantilever shoulder-wing monoplane. Wing section Wortmann FX-62-K-131 (modified). Structure: glassfibre roving spar, glassfibre/balsa sandwich torsion box. Full-span ailerons. Schempp-Hirth aluminium airbrake above and below each wing. Provision for 165 lb (75 kg) of water ballast.

Fuselage: Glassfibre/hexcell sandwich construction.

Tail Unit: Cantilever type. Glassfibre/balsa sandwich fin, glassfibre/hexcell sandwich tailplane, and bonded glassfibre sandwich elevators and mass-balanced rudder.

Landing Gear: Manually-retractable monowheel, size 5·00-5, and tail bumper.

Accommodation: Single seat under one-piece transparent canopy.

Dimensions, external:
Wing span 65 ft 7½ in (20·00 m)
Wing aspect ratio 27·2
Length overall 25 ft 0 in (7·62 m)
Height overall 6 ft 1¾ in (1·87 m)
Tailplane span 9 ft 6 in (2·90 m)

Dimensions, internal:
Cockpit: Max height 2 ft 7½ in (0·80 m)
Max width 2 ft 0¼ in (0·62 m)

Area:
Wings, gross 158·2 sq ft (14·70 m²)

Schleicher ASW 17 single-seat high-performance Open Class sailplane

WEIGHTS AND LOADINGS:

Weight empty, equipped	837 lb (380 kg)
Max T-O weight:	
with water ballast	1,256 lb (570 kg)
without water ballast	1,091 lb (495 kg)
Max wing loading:	
with water ballast	7·17 lb/sq ft (35 kg/m²)
without water ballast	6·14 lb/sq ft (30 kg/m²)

PERFORMANCE (at max T-O weight except where indicated):

Best glide ratio at 54 knots (62 mph; 100 km/h)	48
Min sinking speed at 40·5 knots (46·5 mph; 75 km/h)	1·64 ft (0·50 m)/sec
Max speed (rough or smooth air)	129 knots (149 mph; 240 km/h)
Stalling speed	approx 37 knots (42·5 mph; 68 km/h)
Max aero-tow speed	91 knots (105 mph; 170 km/h)
Max winch-launching speed	65 knots (74·5 mph; 120 km/h)
g limit	+8·56

SIEBERT

PAUL SIEBERT SPORT- UND SEGELFLUGZEUGBAU

ADDRESS:
44 Münster-Mariendorf, Mariendorfer Strasse 38
Telephone: (0251) 32168

Paul Siebert has designed a single-seat wooden Standard Class sailplane designated Sie 3.

Approx 20 of these aircraft had been sold by the end of 1972, to customers in Denmark, Germany, the Netherlands, Portugal and Switzerland.

All available details of the Sie 3 follow:

Siebert Sie 3 single-seat Standard Class sailplane

SIEBERT Sie 3

WINGS: Cantilever high-wing monoplane. Constant chord over approx two-thirds of span, with leading- and trailing-edge taper on outer panels. Incidence 1° 30′ at root, 0° from outer panels to tip. Schempp-Hirth aluminium airbrakes.

FUSELAGE: Oval-section monocoque structure.

TAIL UNIT: Cantilever structure, with sweptback fin and rudder and low-set non-swept all-moving tailplane.

LANDING GEAR: Monowheel, with brake, and tailskid.

ACCOMMODATION: Single seat. One-piece transparent canopy.

DIMENSIONS, EXTERNAL:

Wing span	49 ft 2½ in (15·00 m)
Wing chord (except outer panels)	2 ft 11½ in (0·90 m)
Length overall	22 ft 0 in (6·70 m)
Height overall	3 ft 11 in (1·20 m)
Tailplane span	9 ft 3 in (2·82 m)

AREA:

Wings, gross	127·44 sq ft (11·84 m²)

WEIGHTS AND LOADING:

Weight empty	467 lb (212 kg)
Max T-O weight	750 lb (340 kg)
Max wing loading	5·88 lb/sq ft (28·7 kg/m²)

PERFORMANCE:

Best glide ratio at 48·5 knots (56 mph; 90 km/h)	34·3
Min sinking speed at 42 knots (48·5 mph; 78 km/h)	2·23 ft (0·68 m)/sec
Max speed (smooth air)	108 knots (124 mph; 200 km/h)
Max speed (rough air)	86 knots (99 mph; 160 km/h)

SPORTAVIA

SPORTAVIA-PÜTZER GmbH u Co KG

HEAD OFFICE AND WORKS:
Flugplatz Dahlemer Binz, D-5377 Dahlem-Schmidtheim
Telephone: (02447) 277/8
Telex: 08 33 602 spkg

SALES MANAGER: Alfons Pützer

PUBLIC RELATIONS MANAGER: Manfred Küppers

This company was formed in 1966 by Comte Antoine d'Assche, director of the French company Alpavia SA, and Mr Alfons Pützer, to take over from Alpavia manufacture of the Avion-Planeur series of powered sailplanes designed by M René Fournier.

In 1969, RFB (see Aircraft section), a subsidiary of VFW-Fokker GmbH, acquired a percentage holding in Sportavia.

All current Sportavia products are certificated as powered sailplanes with the exception of the RF6, described in the Aircraft section of this edition.

In addition to its own designs, Sportavia is building under licence the SF-25B and SF-25C Falke powered sailplanes (see under the Scheibe heading in this section). By January 1974 Sportavia had completed 80 SF-25Bs and 45 SF-25Cs.

SPORTAVIA AVION-PLANEUR RF4D

Designed by M René Fournier, the RF4 prototype Avion-Planeur flew for the first time on 6 July 1960, and was described in the 1960-61 *Jane's*. The subsequent RF2 (two built) and RF3 (95 built) were described in the 1966-67 edition. These were followed by 160 RF4Ds, a full description of which can be found in the 1972-73 *Jane's*. The RF4D fuselage and tail unit are incorporated in the design of the SFS 31 Milan (which see).

SPORTAVIA AVION-PLANEUR RF5

This tandem two-seat version of the Avion-Planeur differs from the single-seaters mainly in having wings of increased span, with folding outer sections to facilitate hangarage, and a more powerful engine. It is fitted with dual controls.

The pupil sits in the forward seat during dual instruction, which is the pilot's seat when the aircraft is flown solo.

Construction of the prototype RF5 (D-KOLT) was started in the Summer of 1967, and this aircraft flew for the first time in January 1968. Production began in late 1968. The RF5 was certificated by the LBA in the powered sailplane category in March 1969. A total of 120 RF5s had been delivered by the Spring of 1974.

TYPE: Two-seat powered sailplane.

WINGS: Cantilever low-wing monoplane. Wing section NACA 23015 at root, NACA 23012 at tip. Dihedral 3° 15′ at main spar centreline. Incidence 4° at root, 0° at tip. No sweepback. All-wood single-spar structure, with plywood and fabric covering. Fabric-covered wooden ailerons. Three-section metal-skinned spoilers on each wing at 50% chord, extended from slot in upper surface inboard of ailerons. Outer wing panels fold inward to facilitate hangarage. No flaps or tabs.

FUSELAGE: All-wood oval-section structure of bulkheads and stringers, plywood and fabric covered.

TAIL UNIT: Cantilever all-wood structure, plywood and fabric covered. Fixed-incidence tailplane. Flettner trim tab in port elevator. Entire unit detachable for transportation.

LANDING GEAR: Single Tost main wheel, with twin oleo-pneumatic shock-absorbers, manually retracted forward, with spring assistance, into front fuselage. Dunlop tyre, size 6·00-6, pressure 28·4 lb/sq in (2·0 kg/cm²), on main wheel, which has manually-operated brake. Single Rhombus 160-80 tailwheel, with Doetsch oleo-pneumatic shock-absorber, is steerable in conjunction with rudder movement. Outriggers beneath each wing, just inboard of fold line.

POWER PLANT: One 68 hp (max continuous rating 63 hp) Sportavia-Limbach SL 1700 E Comet four-cylinder four-stroke engine, driving a Hoffmann two-blade fixed-pitch metal propeller. Fuel in two wing-root leading-edge metal tanks, total capacity 13·8 Imp gallons (63 litres). Refuelling point on top of port wing. Oil capacity 0·55 Imp gallons (2·5 litres).

ACCOMMODATION: Adjustable seats in tandem for pilot and one passenger under one-piece sideways-hinged Plexiglas canopy. Space for 22 lb (10 kg) of baggage aft of rear seat. Cabin heated and ventilated. Adjustable rudder pedals and canopy emergency release standard.

SYSTEMS: Electrical system includes alternator and 12V 25Ah battery.

ELECTRONICS AND EQUIPMENT: Optional equipment includes VHF radio nav/com equipment with interphone, radio compass, artificial horizon, VOR, ADF, oxygen, navigation and landing lights and rotating beacon.

DIMENSIONS, EXTERNAL:

Wing span	45 ft 1 in (13·74 m)
Wing chord at root	5 ft 2¾ in (1·59 m)
Wing chord at tip	1 ft 11½ in (0·60 m)
Wing aspect ratio	12·25
Length overall	25 ft 7¼ in (7·80 m)
Width, wings folded	28 ft 8 in (8·74 m)
Height overall (tail down)	6 ft 5 in (1·96 m)
Tailplane span	12 ft 2½ in (3·72 m)
Distance between outriggers	28 ft 6½ in (8·70 m)
Propeller diameter	4 ft 9¾ in (1·47 m)

AREAS:

Wings, gross	162·8 sq ft (15·12 m²)
Ailerons (total)	16·15 sq ft (1·50 m²)
Spoilers (total)	8·07 sq ft (0·75 m²)
Fin	5·49 sq ft (0·51 m²)
Rudder	8·50 sq ft (0·79 m²)
Tailplane	17·44 sq ft (1·62 m²)
Elevators, including tab	10·55 sq ft (0·98 m²)

WEIGHTS AND LOADINGS:

Weight empty, equipped	926 lb (420 kg)
Max T-O weight:	
Aerobatic	1,333 lb (605 kg)
Utility	1,433 lb (650 kg)
Max wing loading	8·77 lb/sq ft (42·8 kg/m²)
Max power loading	21·05 lb/hp (9·55 kg/hp)

PERFORMANCE (at max T-O weight, powered):

Max never-exceed speed	135 knots (155 mph; 250 km/h)
Max level speed at S/L	108 knots (124 mph; 200 km/h)
Max cruising speed at S/L	97 knots (112 mph; 180 km/h)
Econ cruising speed	65 knots (75 mph; 120 km/h)
Stalling speed	41 knots (47 mph; 75 km/h)
Max rate of climb at S/L	590 ft (180 m)/min
Min sinking speed, power off	4·59 ft (1·4 m)/sec
Best glide ratio, power off	22
Service ceiling	16,400 ft (5,000 m)
T-O run	655 ft (200 m)
T-O to 50 ft (15 m)	1,575 ft (480 m)
Landing from 50 ft (15 m)	820 ft (250 m)
Landing run	590 ft (180 m)
Range with max fuel	410 nm (472 miles; 760 km)
Endurance with max fuel	4 hr

SPORTAVIA RF5B SPERBER

The RF5B Sperber is an improved, high-performance development of the RF5, differing chiefly in having increased wing span and area

Sportavia RF5B Sperber, developed from the RF5, with cut-down rear fuselage

and reduced fuselage area. Construction began in early 1971, and the first flight was made in May of that year. The Sperber was certificated in the powered sailplane category by the LBA in March 1972, and by the Spring of 1974 a total of 55 RF5Bs had been delivered.

Modifications introduced in 1973 include an improved cabin heating system, engine muffler to decrease exterior and cabin noise levels, adjustable ventilation system, optional disc brakes, and a wider range of equipment options which include artificial horizon, electric compass and flight data computer.

Type: Two-seat high-performance powered sailplane.

Wings: Similar to RF5, but with 3° 30′ dihedral at main spar centreline and increased span and area.

Fuselage: All-wood structure of pine bulkheads and stringers with birch plywood covering. Compared with RF5, the rear fuselage is cut down to reduce side area and improve rearward view from cockpit.

Tail Unit: Similar to RF5.

Landing Gear: As RF5.

Power Plant: As RF5, but all fuel is contained in a single fuselage tank of 8·6 Imp gallons (39 litres) capacity. Fully-feathering and variable-pitch propellers available optionally.

Accommodation: As in RF5, but cockpit canopy is of the bulged type giving an all-round field of view.

Systems: Electrical system includes alternator and 12V 20Ah battery.

Dimensions, external:
Wing span 55 ft 10 in (17·02 m)
Wing chord at root 5 ft 6 in (1·68 m)
Wing chord at tip 1 ft 9¼ in (0·54 m)
Wing aspect ratio 15·25
Length overall 25 ft 3¼ in (7·70 m)
Width, wings folded 36 ft 9¾ in (11·22 m)
Height overall 6 ft 5 in (1·96 m)
Tailplane span 12 ft 2½ in (3·72 m)
Wheelbase 15 ft 11¼ in (4·86 m)
Propeller diameter 4 ft 9¾ in (1·47 m)
Propeller ground clearance 2 ft 0½ in (0·62 m)

Areas: As RF5, except:
Wings, gross 204·5 sq ft (19·00 m^2)

Weights and Loadings:
Weight empty, equipped 1,014 lb (460 kg)
Max T-O weight 1,499 lb (680 kg)
Max wing loading 7·33 lb/sq ft (35·8 kg/m^2)
Max power loading 22·05 lb/hp (10·0 kg/hp)

Performance (at max T-O weight, powered, variable-pitch propeller):
Max never-exceed speed 121 knots (139 mph; 225 km/h)
Max level speed at S/L 102 knots (118 mph; 190 km/h)
Max cruising speed at S/L 97 knots (112 mph; 180 km/h)
Econ cruising speed 65 knots (75 mph; 120 km/h)
Stalling speed 37 knots (42·5 mph; 68 km/h)
Max rate of climb at S/L 650 ft (198 m)/min
Min sinking speed (power off) 2·89 ft (0·88 m)/sec
Best glide ratio (power off) at 53 knots (61 mph; 98 km/h) 28
Service ceiling 19,025 ft (5,800 m)
T-O run 645 ft (196 m)
T-O to 50 ft (15 m) 1,475 ft (450 m)
Landing from 50 ft (15 m) 1,150 ft (350 m)
Landing run 669 ft (204 m)
Range with max fuel 231 nm (267 miles; 430 km)

SPORTAVIA RF5D

For 1974, Sportavia has introduced this improved version of the standard RF5. It incorporates the full range of improvements introduced on the RF5B Sperber (which see), and has a more powerful (74 hp) Limbach SL 1700 ED engine.

The description of the RF5 applies generally also to the RF5D, except for the following:

Weights:
Weight empty, equipped 948 lb (430 kg)
Max T-O weight 1,433 lb (650 kg)

Performance (at max T-O weight, powered):
Max cruising speed at S/L 102 knots (118 mph; 190 km/h)
Max rate of climb at S/L 690 ft (210 m)/min
T-O run 605 ft (185 m)
T-O to 50 ft (15 m) 1,445 ft (440 m)
Landing from 50 ft (15 m) 1,115 ft (340 m)
Landing run 675 ft (205 m)
Min sinking speed, power off 4·43 ft (1·35 m)/sec

SPORTAVIA RF55

The RF55, a modified version of the RF5B Sperber, was flown for the first time in 1972. To meet overseas certification requirements, and particularly those of FAR Pt 22, the RF55 was fitted with a slightly-modified 60 hp Franklin 2A-120-A engine, an electric fuel pump, and a larger fuel tank.

This version has not entered production.

Weights and Loadings:
Weight empty, equipped 1,058 lb (480 kg)
Max T-O weight 1,587 lb (720 kg)
Max wing loading 7·8 lb/sq ft (37·9 kg/m^2)
Max power loading 26·46 lb/hp (12·0 kg/hp)

Performance (at max T-O weight, powered):
Max level speed at S/L 94·5 knots (109 mph; 175 km/h)
Cruising speed at S/L 86·5 knots (99·5 mph; 160 km/h)
Stalling speed 39 knots (45 mph; 72 km/h)
Max rate of climb at S/L 551 ft (168 m)/min
Service ceiling 16,400 ft (5,000 m)
Range with max fuel 334 nm (385 miles; 620 km)

SPORTAVIA SFS 31 MILAN

The SFS 31 is, essentially, the combination of the Avion-Planeur RF4D fuselage and tail unit with the wings of the Scheibe SF-27M powered sailplane.

The first SFS 31 (D-KORO) flew for the first time on 31 August 1969, and achieved third place in the 1971 German national motor-glider competition.

A total of 14 SFS 31 Milans had been delivered by Spring 1974. A description can be found in the 1973-74 *Jane's*.

START + FLUG

START + FLUG GmbH

Address:
Postfach 126, Am Flugplatz, 7968 Saulgau
Telephone: 0 75 81/71 65

This company is producing, as the H 101 Salto, a version of the Glasflügel Standard Libelle developed by Frau Ursula Hänle, the wife of Ing Eugen Hänle of Glasflügel.

START + FLUG H 101 SALTO

Design of the H 101 is based upon that of the Glasflügel Standard Libelle (which see), from which it differs principally in having a "butterfly" Vee-type tail unit. It flew for the first time in 1971, and 10 had been ordered by the end of 1972. Initial LBA certification was granted on 28 April 1972; the Salto is currently certificated by the LBA for Normal and Aerobatic category operation, and by the FAA for Normal category. FAA Aerobatic certification has been applied for.

The description of the Glasflügel Standard Libelle applies generally to the H 101 Salto, except in the following respects:

Wings: Ailerons and four flush-fitting airbrakes on trailing-edge.

Tail Unit: Cantilever Vee-tail (included angle 99°).

Dimensions, external:
Wing span 44 ft 7½ in (13·60 m)
Wing aspect ratio 21·6
Length overall 19 ft 6¼ in (5·95 m)
Height over tail 2 ft 10¾ in (0·88 m)
Tailplane span 7 ft 0¼ in (2·14 m)

Area:
Wings, gross 92·35 sq ft (8·58 m^2)

Start + Flug H 101 Salto single-seat sailplane, based on the Glasflügel Standard Libelle

Weights:
Weight empty 396 lb (180 kg)
Max T-O weight 683 lb (310 kg)

Performance:
Best glide ratio at 48·5 knots (56 mph; 90 km/h) 35
Min sinking speed at 40·5 knots (46·5 mph; 75 km/h) 1·97 ft (0·60 m)/sec
Max never-exceed speed 161 knots (186 mph; 300 km/h)
Max level speed 135 knots (155 mph; 250 km/h)
Max aero-tow speed 81 knots (93 mph; 150 km/h)
Max winch-launching speed 70 knots (81 mph; 130 km/h)
Stalling speed 35·5 knots (40·5 mph; 65 km/h)

HUNGARY

GÉPGYÁR

PESTVIDÉKI GÉPGYÁR

Address:
1369 Budapest, Pf 305

Manager:
Imre Csordás

This Hungarian company designed and built a two-seat all-metal sailplane designated R-26 S Gobé, which made its first public appearance at the 1972 World Championships at Vrsac, Yugoslavia. All known details were given in the 1973-74 *Jane's*.

INDIA

CIVIL AVIATION DEPARTMENT

TECHNICAL CENTRE, CIVIL AVIATION DEPARTMENT

Head Office:
Civil Aviation Department, R. K. Puram, New Delhi 22

Works:
Technical Centre, Safdarjung, New Delhi 3

Telephone: 611504

Officers:
See "Aircraft" section

The Technical Centre is the research and development establishment of the Indian Civil Aviation Department. It is equipped with all facilities necessary for the development of design, airworthiness and operational standards, operational research, development testing and standardisation of indigenous aircraft materials, type certification of prototype aircraft and equipment, and the scientific investigation of accidents.

Since 1950 the Technical Centre has undertaken the design and development of gliders, under the leadership of S. Ramamritham, utilising predominantly indigenous materials. The first of these gliders, of the open-cockpit primary type, was flown in November 1950. Since then the Technical Centre has built gliders of eight types for service at civil gliding centres in India, as listed in the 1972-73 *Jane's*. Of these eight types, five—the Ashvini (1964-65 *Jane's*; five built), Rohini, Bharani (1965-66 *Jane's*; one built), Kartik, HS-I and HS-II Mrigasheer—are original designs.

The Technical Centre does not undertake quantity production of gliders. Complete sets of drawings of the designs developed at the Centre are supplied to interested organisations with permission to manufacture them in series. Two private companies in India have manufactured the model IT-G3, and this model has also been manufactured by the Kanpur Division of Hindustan Aeronautics Ltd (see "Aircraft" section).

RG-I ROHINI-I

The Rohini-I is a side-by-side two-seat training sailplane, designed by Mr S. Ramamritham, Director General of the Technical Centre. It flew for the first time on 10 May 1961.

Four prototype Rohini gliders were built at the Technical Centre during the period 1961 to January 1964. Since then 17 production Rohinis have been manufactured by Veegal Engines and Engineering Company of Calcutta, and 86 by Hindustan Aeronautics Ltd, Kanpur Division. Plans for additional production were under consideration in early 1974.

To minimise production and maintenance costs, the tail surfaces, airbrakes and many wing ribs of the Rohini are identical with those of the Ashvini sailplane.

Type: Two-seat training sailplane.

Wings: Braced high-wing monoplane. Single bracing strut each side. Wing section NACA 4418 at root, NACA 4412 (modified) at tip. Dihedral (on top of spars) 1°. Incidence 3° 24′. Two-spar wood structure. Plywood-covered to rear spar, fabric-covered trailing-edge. Plain ailerons of fabric-covered wood construction, with plywood-covered leading-edges. Retractable wooden airbrakes above and below wing on each side.

Fuselage: Built as one-piece structure, with integral fin. Forward portion to wing rear spar attachment and rear portion aft of tailplane front attachment bulkhead are plywood-covered wooden semi-monocoque structures. Remaining portion has wooden girder structure, covered with fabric.

Tail Unit: Cantilever wooden structure. Fin plywood-covered. Remainder fabric-covered except for leading-edges and area of tailplane between two root ribs which are plywood-covered. Plywood trim tab in starboard elevator.

Landing Gear: Non-retractable unsprung Dunlop monowheel and tyre, size 6·00-4, pressure 30 lb/sq in (2·10 kg/cm^2). No brake. Rubber-sprung nose-skid with replaceable steel shoe. Spring steel tailskid.

Accommodation: Two seats side by side in open cockpit. Canopy fitted experimentally to one aircraft in 1972.

Dimensions, external:

Wing span	54 ft 4 in (16·56 m)
Wing chord at root	5 ft 6½ in (1·69 m)
Wing chord at tip	2 ft 8½ in (0·82 m)
Wing aspect ratio	13·2
Length overall	26 ft 9½ in (8·17 m)
Height over tail	7 ft 7⅞ in (2·33 m)
Tailplane span	13 ft 2 in (4·02 m)

Areas:

Wings, gross	223·3 sq ft (20·76 m^2)
Ailerons (total)	25·00 sq ft (2·32 m^2)
Airbrakes (total)	2·62 sq ft (0·24 m^2)
Fin	5·82 sq ft (0·54 m^2)
Rudder	11·82 sq ft (1·10 m^2)
Tailplane	21·30 sq ft (1·98 m^2)
Elevators, including tab	17·20 sq ft (1·60 m^2)

Weights and Loading:

Weight empty, equipped	660 lb (300 kg)
Max T-O weight	1,078 lb (490 kg)
Max wing loading	4·83 lb/sq ft (23·60 kg/m^2)

Performance (at max T-O weight):

Best glide ratio at 42 knots (48 mph; 77 km/h)	22
Min sinking speed at 33 knots (38 mph; 61 km/h)	2·85 ft (0·86 m)/sec
Stalling speed	26 knots (30 mph; 48 km/h)
Max speed (smooth air)	94 knots (108 mph; 174 km/h)
Max speed (rough air)	65 knots (75 mph; 120 km/h)
Max aero-tow speed	61 knots (70 mph; 113 km/h)
Max winch-launching speed	52 knots (60 mph; 96 km/h)

KS-II KARTIK

The original KS-I Kartik, designed by Mr S. Ramamritham, flew for the first time on 18 March 1963. A description of the KS-I appeared in the 1972-73 *Jane's*.

The third Kartik, designated KS-II, first flew on 4 May 1965 and was type certificated in 1965. It introduced a conventional tapered wing. Other changes included a reduction in the height of the cockpit, a slight increase in fuselage length, and modifications to the shape of the aileron leading-edge.

Five more KS-IIs were test flown between February 1967 and February 1972. From the third aircraft onwards, further improvements to the original design include a reduction in fuselage height, improved forward vision and seating, and larger airbrakes. On the ninth KS-II, which was due to begin flight testing in the Summer of 1974, the airbrakes are replaced by trailing-edge slotted flaps.

KS-II Kartik single-seat high-performance sailplane in its current form

During the first Indian National Gliding Rally, held in 1967, the Kartik sailplane proved itself by achieving many successes, including the establishment of a national speed record over a 200 km triangular course.

The following details apply to the KS-II:

Type: Single-seat high-performance sailplane.

Wings: Cantilever high-wing monoplane. Wing section NACA 64_3-618. Dihedral 1° 30′. Incidence 0°. Wood structure, with one main spar, one rear spar and a diagonal spar at the root. Plywood-covered torsion-box back to rear spar. Trailing-edge fabric-covered. Fabric-covered slotted wooden ailerons. Retractable wooden airbrakes above and below wing on each side.

Fuselage: Semi-monocoque wood structure with plywood covering and glassfibre nosecap.

Tail Unit: Cantilever wood structure. Fin plywood-covered. Remainder fabric-covered except for plywood covering on leading-edges. Plywood trim tab in starboard elevator.

Landing Gear: Non-retractable Palmer/Dunlop unsprung monowheel and tyre, size 4·00-3·5, pressure 30 lb/sq in (2·10 kg/cm^2). Drum-type brake, operated by a separate lever mounted on the airbrake operating lever. Rubber-sprung nose-skid with replaceable steel shoe. Tailskid sprung with tennis balls.

Accommodation: Single seat under rearward-opening hinged Perspex canopy. Oxygen equipment optional.

Dimensions, external:

Wing span	49 ft 2¼ in (15·00 m)
Wing chord at root	3 ft 3¼ in (1·00 m)
Wing chord at tip	2 ft 1¼ in (0·64 m)
Wing aspect ratio	16·6
Length overall	24 ft 2 in (7·37 m)
Height over tail	7 ft 5 in (2·26 m)
Tailplane span	9 ft 6 in (2·90 m)

Areas:

Wings, gross	145·7 sq ft (13·54 m^2)
Ailerons (total)	14·21 sq ft (1·32 m^2)
Airbrakes (total)	4·68 sq ft (0·43 m^2)
Fin	5·02 sq ft (0·47 m^2)
Rudder	9·60 sq ft (0·89 m^2)
Tailplane	13·20 sq ft (1·22 m^2)
Elevators, including tab	11·30 sq ft (1·05 m^2)

Weights and Loading:

Weight empty, equipped	463 lb (210 kg)
Max T-O weight	705 lb (320 kg)
Max wing loading	4·86 lb/sq ft (23·63 kg/m^2)

Performance (at max T-O weight):

Best glide ratio at 41 knots (47 mph; 75 km/h)	31
Min sinking speed at 35 knots (40 mph; 65 km/h)	1·97 ft (0·60 m)/sec
Stalling speed	32 knots (36 mph; 58 km/h)
Max speed (smooth air)	108 knots (124 mph; 200 km/h)
Max speed (rough air)	76 knots (87 mph; 140 km/h)
Max aero-tow speed	62 knots (71 mph; 114 km/h)
Max winch-launching speed	54 knots (62 mph; 100 km/h)

MRIGASHEER

This single-seat Standard Class sailplane is the first to be designed and developed at the Technical Centre by the team of designers and engineers led by Mr K. B. Ganesan, Director of Research and Development. The original version, the HS-I, made its first flight in November 1970 and was type certificated in October 1972. It was fully described and illustrated in the 1973-74 *Jane's*.

The further-developed second version, known as the HS-II, differs principally in having reductions in the maximum depth of the fuselage, the rear fuselage cross-section, and horizontal tail surface area; quick-attach fittings for the horizontal tail surfaces to the fuselage; a modified canopy with improved field of view; and a wheel-type instead of a stick-type control.

The HS-II flew for the first time in April 1973, and in the following month was placed second in the first Indian national gliding championships at Kanpur.

Type: Single-seat high-performance Standard Class sailplane.

Wings: Cantilever high-wing monoplane. Wortmann wing sections: FX-61-184 from root to 9% of each half-span, FX-61-163 from 16·8% to 50% of each half-span, and FX-60-126 at tip. Dihedral 1° 30′. Incidence 3°. Wooden structure, comprising main spar, rear spar, and diagonal spar in the root region. Plywood-covered torsion-box nose cell and plywood-covered rear cell. Plain wooden ailerons. Wooden airbrake above and below each wing.

Fuselage: Semi-monocoque wooden structure with plywood covering.

Tail Unit: Cantilever wooden structure. Fin plywood-covered, remainder fabric-covered except for plywood covering on leading-edges. Plywood-covered trim tab in starboard elevator.

Landing Gear: Retractable unsprung monowheel, tyre size 4·00-3·5, pressure 30 lb/sq in (2·1 kg/cm^2). Drum-type brake. Rubber-

Rohini-I side-by-side two-seat training sailplane

sprung nose-skid with replaceable steel shoe. Rubber-sprung tailskid.

ACCOMMODATION: Single seat under forward-opening hinged jettisonable Perspex canopy. Oxygen equipment optional.

DIMENSIONS, EXTERNAL:

Wing span	49 ft 2½ in (15·00 m)
Wing chord at root	3 ft 10 in (1·17 m)
Wing chord at tip	1 ft 3¾ in (0·40 m)
Wing aspect ratio	19·85
Length overall	24 ft 10¾ in (7·59 m)
Height overall (tail up)	8 ft 2½ in (2·50 m)
Tailplane span	8 ft 6¼ in (2·60 m)

AREAS:

Wings, gross	122·1 sq ft (11·34 m²)
Ailerons (total)	11·19 sq ft (1·04 m²)
Airbrakes (total)	4·67 sq ft (0·434 m²)
Fin	4·95 sq ft (0·46 m²)
Rudder	9·58 sq ft (0·89 m²)
Tailplane	11·36 sq ft (1·055 m²)
Elevators, incl tab	10·28 sq ft (0·955 m²)

WEIGHTS AND LOADING:

Weight empty, equipped	522 lb (237 kg)
Max T-O weight	738 lb (335 kg)
Max wing loading	6·05 lb/sq ft (29·55 kg/m²)

PERFORMANCE (estimated, at max T-O weight):

Best glide ratio	36
Min sinking speed	1·80 ft (0·55 m)/sec
Stalling speed	37·5 knots (43 mph; 68·5 km/h)
Max speed (smooth air)	115 knots (132 mph; 213 km/h)
Max speed (rough air)	80 knots (92 mph; 148 km/h)
Max aero-tow speed	62 knots (71·5 mph; 115 km/h)
Max winch-launching speed	53·5 knots (61·5 mph; 99 km/h)

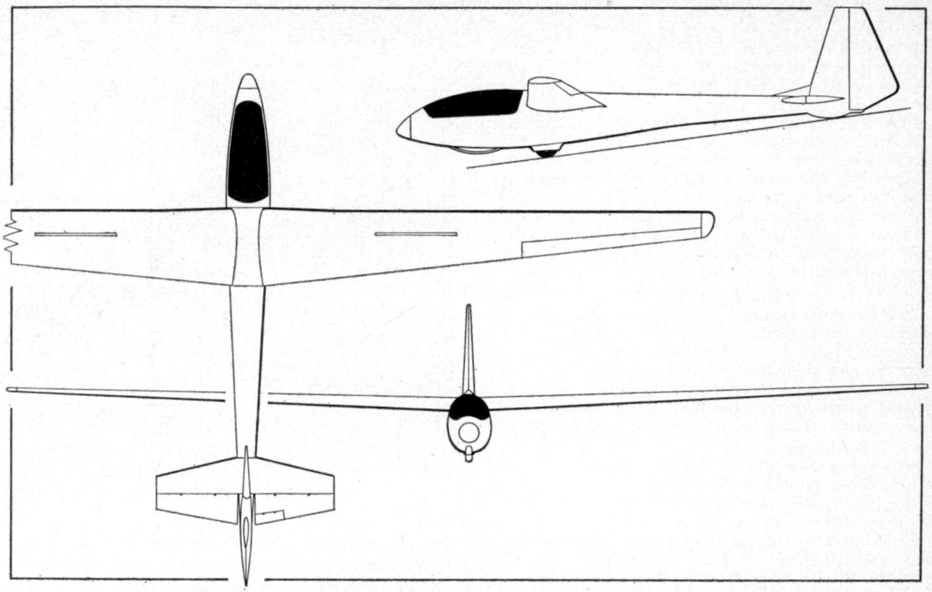

Mrigasheer HS-II single-seat Standard Class sailplane (*Michael A. Badrocke*)

ITALY

CAPRONI VIZZOLA

CAPRONI VIZZOLA COSTRUZIONI AERONAUTICHE SpA

HEAD OFFICE: 20122 Milano, Via Durini 24
Telephone: 700.826 and 781.975
Telex: 32035

WORKS:
21010 Vizzola Ticino, C.P.11 Gallarate
Telephone: (0331) 230.826 (5 lines)

PRESIDENT: Dott Giovanni Caproni di Taliedo

VICE-PRESIDENT:
Rag Achille Caproni di Taliedo

The Caproni company, formed in 1910, is the oldest Italian aircraft manufacturer.

Caproni Vizzola is producing a series of Calif sailplanes designed by Carlo Ferrarin and Livio Sonzio. Details of the earlier A-10 (one built), A-12 (two built), A-14 (one built), A-15 (one built) and A-20 were given in the 1972-73 and 1973-74 *Jane's*.

CAPRONI VIZZOLA CALIF A-21

The A-21 is a two-seat version of the A-14. It differs principally in having a wider fuselage to accommodate two side-by-side seats and, as a result of CG shift, has a slightly longer fuselage.

The prototype A-21 made its first flight on 23 November 1970, and a total of 18 A-14s and A-21s had been ordered by mid-February 1973, including two for the Italian Air Force. Certification by the RAI has been awarded, and FAA certification was under way in March 1973.

In July/August 1972, over the Nevada/California border in the USA, a Calif A-21 flown by the Polish pilot Edward Makula, and carrying a passenger, established four new international records in Class D2, as follows: speed of 61·363 knots (70·660 mph; 113·717 km/h) over a 300 km course; speed of 54·595 knots (62·868 mph; 101·176 km/h) over a 500 km course; speed of 70·541 knots (81·229 mph; 130·726 km/h) over a 100 km course; goal-and-return flight of 387 nm (446 miles; 718·2 km).

TYPE: Two-seat high-performance sailplane.

WINGS: Cantilever mid-wing monoplane. Wing section Wortmann FX-67-K-170 at root, Wortmann FX-60-126 at tip. Dihedral 0° at root, 1° 30′ on outer panels. Incidence 0°. Sweepback 4° on outer leading-edge only. Three-piece all-metal stressed-skin structure, with main spar and two auxiliary spars. Main spar forms torsion box with leading-edge. Glass-fibre wingtips. Top-hinged partially-balanced differentially-operated plain ailerons of all-metal stressed-skin construction. Automatic connection of controls when wings are assembled. Lower-hinged aerodynamically-balanced trailing-edge flaps/spoilers of all-metal stressed-skin construction, manually operated by a single control, are utilised as camber-changing surfaces in the —8° to +12° range, and as airbrakes when lowered to a 90° position.

FUSELAGE: Low-drag tadpole-shaped fuselage. Monocoque forward section of glassfibre and foam plastics construction with load-carrying light alloy structure. Narrow-diameter all-metal stressed-skin tailboom.

TAIL UNIT: Cantilever all-metal structure with swept vertical surfaces. All-moving T tailplane. Fin is a single-spar stressed-skin structure. Spring-adjusted tailplane trimming. Automatic control connections during assembly.

LANDING GEAR: Mechanically-retractable twin wheels, with rubber-in-compression shock-absorption; mechanical up and down lock. Non-retractable steerable tailwheel for ground handling. Main wheels and tyres size 3·50-5, pressure 73·5 lb/sq in (5·17 kg/cm²). Mechanically-operated Tost wheel brake.

ACCOMMODATION: Two seats, side by side, in enclosed cabin.

Caproni Vizzola Calif A-21 two-seat high-performance sailplane

A-21J version of the Calif, powered by a 202 lb st Microturbo TRS 18 turbojet engine

DIMENSIONS, EXTERNAL:
Wing span 66 ft 10¼ in (20·38 m)
Wing chord at root 2 ft 11½ in (0·90 m)
Wing chord (mean) 2 ft 7¼ in (0·794 m)
Wing chord at tip 1 ft 0½ in (0·321 m)
Wing aspect ratio 25·65
Length overall 25 ft 8½ in (7·838 m)
Height over tail 5 ft 3½ in (1·61 m)
Tailplane span 9 ft 5¾ in (2·89 m)
AREAS:
Wings, gross 174·3 sq ft (16·19 m²)
Ailerons (total) 11·19 sq ft (1·04 m²)
Trailing-edge flaps (total) 22·28 sq ft (2·07 m²)
Spoilers (total) 9·795 sq ft (0·91 m²)
Fin 8·50 sq ft (0·79 m²)
Rudder 6·35 sq ft (0·59 m²)
Tailplane 16·47 sq ft (1·53 m²)
WEIGHTS AND LOADING:
Weight empty, equipped 961 lb (436 kg)
Max T-O weight 1,419 lb (644 kg)
Max wing loading 8·15 lb/sq ft (39·8 kg/m²)
PERFORMANCE:
Best glide ratio at 56·5 knots (65 mph; 105 km/h) 43
Min sinking speed at 46 knots (53 mph; 85 km/h) 1·97 ft (0·60 m)/sec
Stalling speed, flaps up 38 knots (43·5 mph; 70 km/h)
Stalling speed, flaps down 34 knots (39·5 mph; 63 km/h)
Max speed (rough or smooth air) 137·5 knots (158 mph; 255 km/h)
Max aero-tow speed 75·5 knots (87 mph; 140 km/h)
Ultimate load factor 8g

CAPRONI VIZZOLA CALIF A-21J

This jet-powered version of the A-21 two-seat sailplane flew for the first time at the end of January 1972.

Flight testing was continuing in April 1974, and it was hoped to begin production later in the year.

The description of the A-21 applies also to the A-21J except in the following details:

TYPE: Two-seat powered sailplane.

LANDING GEAR: Mechanically-retractable two-wheel type. Each main wheel retracts rearward into the fuselage. Non-retractable tail-wheel.

POWER PLANT: One Microturbo TRS 18 single-spool turbojet engine, rated at 202 lb (92 kg) st, mounted in the lower fuselage aft of the seats. Fuel contained in wing and fuselage tanks, total capacity 35 Imp gallons (160 litres).

SYSTEMS: Compressed air system for starting TRS 18 engine. Electrical system comprising 28V 600W DC engine-driven generator.

DIMENSIONS, EXTERNAL:
Wing span 65 ft 7½ in (20·00 m)
Wing aspect ratio 25
Length overall 26 ft 3 in (8·00 m)
Max width of fuselage 3 ft 7¼ in (1·10 m)
AREA:
Wings, gross 172·2 sq ft (16·00 m²)
WEIGHTS AND LOADING:
Weight empty, equipped 957 lb (434 kg)
Max T-O weight 1,543 lb (700 kg)
Max wing loading 8·91 lb/sq ft (43·5 kg/m²)
PERFORMANCE (estimated, at max T-O weight):
Best glide ratio at 58 knots (67 mph; 108 km/h) 43
Min sinking speed at 49 knots (56 mph; 90 km/h) 1·97 ft (0·60 m)/sec
Stalling speed, flaps up 41 knots (47 mph; 75·1 km/h)
Max level speed at S/L 162 knots (186 mph; 300 km/h)
Max level speed at 32,800 ft (10,000 m) 181 knots (208 mph; 335 km/h)
Max rate of climb at S/L 797 ft (243 m)/min
Rate of climb at 42,650 ft (13,000 m) 145·7 ft (44·4 m)/min
Service ceiling 44,625 ft (13,600 m)
Theoretical ceiling 49,200 ft (15,000 m)
T-O run:
grass 1,214 ft (370 m)
concrete 1,017 ft (310 m)
T-O to 50 ft (15 m):
grass 1,739 ft (530 m)
concrete 1,542 ft (470 m)

CVT

CENTRO DI VOLO A VELA DEL POLITECNICO DI TORINO

ADDRESS:
Corso Duca Degli Abruzzi 24, 10129 Turin
OFFICE AND LABORATORY:
Corso Luigi Einaudi 44, 10129 Turin
Telephone: 51 12 50
PRESIDENT:
Piero Morelli

Gliders built at the CVT have included the CVT-2 Veltro single-seat high-performance sailplane, which flew for the first time in 1954 and was described in the 1960-61 *Jane's*.

Subsequent designs, also by Alberto and Piero Morelli, included the M-100 S, which was manufactured under licence in Italy by Avionautica Rio, at Sarnico (Bergamo), and in France by CARMAM (which see) as the Mésange; the M-200, also manufactured by CARMAM; and the M-300, described in the 1972-73 *Jane's*.

GLASFLÜGEL

GLASFLÜGEL ITALIANA SrL

ADDRESS:
24030 Valbrembo (Bergamo), Via Locatelli 1
Telephone: (035) 612617
PRESIDENT:
Dr Ing Sergio Aldo Capoferri
VICE-PRESIDENTS:
Dr Ing Mario Moltrasio
Ing Eugen Hänle
TECHNICAL DIRECTOR: Giampaolo Ghidotti

This company was established at Valbrembo Airport, where it is accommodated in a factory which occupies an area of 13,993 sq ft (1,300 m²) and which is insulated and heated to maintain a controlled temperature of 68°F (20°C), essential for work on glassfibre structures.

Glasflügel Italiana holds RAI licences for the construction of glassfibre sailplanes and for repair, maintenance and modification of sailplanes and training aircraft.

Glasflügel Italiana has already assembled 25 single-seat Open Class Kestrel sailplanes, details of which may be found under the Glasflügel entry in the German section of this edition. The company is manufacturing complete fuselage assemblies for the Kestrel and had built 120, with 10 more being manufactured and assembled, by January 1974.

It also assisted the parent company in the development of the H 205 Club Libelle, described in the German section.

Other activities include construction of trailers for road transportation of Kestrel and Libelle sailplanes, the repair and maintenance of sailplanes of glassfibre, wood and metal construction, and installation and modification work on sailplanes of all types.

MILITI

BRUNO MILITI

ADDRESS:
Via Roma 9, 47037 Rimini (Forli)
Telephone: 25.929

Sr Militi has designed, built and flown two single-seat flying-boat gliders, the M.B.1 and a powered development of it known as the M.B.2. Descriptions and illustrations of both aircraft appeared in the 1973-74 *Jane's*.

JAPAN

JEAA

JAPAN EXPERIMENTAL AIRCRAFT ASSOCIATION

ADDRESS:
2-27 Uehara, Shibuya-ku, Tokyo 151
Telephone: (03) 467-8522
PRESIDENT:
Asahi Miyahara

JEAA (MIYAHARA) MGM-2 WORKING BEE

Mr Miyahara has spent several years evolving this design. Since its original conception it has undergone progressive refinement, and this was continuing in early 1974; the wing span has now been increased to 49 ft 2½ in (15·00 m). Construction had not started at that time.

Kirigamine K-14 elementary glider built by Mr Aisaku Ito of the JEAA (*H. Seo*)

NIHON UNIVERSITY

COLLEGE OF SCIENCE AND TECHNOLOGY (DEPARTMENT OF MECHANICAL ENGINEERING), NIHON UNIVERSITY

ADDRESS:
8, Kanda-Surugadai, 1-chome Chiyoda-ku, Tokyo 101

NIHON UNIVERSITY N-70 CYGNUS

Design of the N-70 Cygnus began in April 1970, and construction of the prototype started in June 1971. This aircraft flew for the first time on 16 December 1971. Certification flight testing had been completed by early 1974; issue of a type certificate was then awaiting clearance of the power plant, which is not licensed for aircraft use.

TYPE: Single-seat powered sailplane.

WINGS: Cantilever low-wing monoplane. Wortmann wing sections, FX-61-184 at root, FX-60-126 at tip. Dihedral 4°. Incidence 4°. Single wooden spar at 38% chord, with plywood and fabric covering. Wing built in three sections: a centre-section extending 11·8 in (30 cm) from each side of fuselage, and two outer panels. Frise-type ailerons. Spoilers inboard of each aileron, extending from slots in upper and lower surfaces. No flaps or tabs.

FUSELAGE: Plywood-covered oval-section semi-monocoque structure. GRP (glassfibre-reinforced plastics) engine cowling.

TAIL UNIT: Cantilever all-wood structure. Fixed-incidence tailplane. Trim tab in port elevator.

LANDING GEAR: Single main wheel, retracting forward manually into fuselage. Oleo-pneumatic shock-absorption. Dunlop 6·00-6 tyre. Auxiliary balancing wheel beneath each wing. Non-retractable steerable tailwheel, with oleo-pneumatic shock-absorption.
POWER PLANT: One Fuji 1100-EA61 1,100 cc watercooled motor car engine, developing 44 hp at 3,800 rpm and driving an NP-70 two-blade fixed-pitch wooden propeller. Fuel capacity 8·8 Imp gallons (40 litres).
ACCOMMODATION: Single seat under one-piece transparent "teardrop" canopy.
EQUIPMENT: VHF radio.
DIMENSIONS, EXTERNAL:
Wing span 49 ft 6 in (15·085 m)
Wing aspect ratio 15
Length overall 22 ft 9$\frac{3}{4}$ in (6·955 m)
Height overall (tail down) 5 ft 10$\frac{1}{4}$ in (1·785 m)
Tailplane span 10 ft 3$\frac{1}{2}$ in (3·135 m)
Propeller diameter 4 ft 7 in (1·40 m)
Propeller ground clearance 6$\frac{1}{4}$ in (0·159 m)
AREAS:
Wings, gross 161·5 sq ft (15·00 m²)
Ailerons (total) 13·56 sq ft (1·26 m²)
Fin 5·60 sq ft (0·52 m²)
Rudder 7·21 sq ft (0·67 m²)
Tailplane 14·42 sq ft (1·34 m²)
Elevators, incl tab 11·95 sq ft (1·11 m²)
WEIGHTS AND LOADINGS:
Weight empty 756 lb (343 kg)
Max T-O weight 1,014 lb (460 kg)

Nihon University N-70 Cygnus single-seat powered sailplane (44 hp Fuji 1100-EA61 engine)

Max wing loading 6·29 lb/sq ft (30·7 kg/m²)
Max power loading 23·15 lb/hp (10·5 kg/hp)
PERFORMANCE (at max T-O weight):
Max never-exceed speed 135 knots (155 mph; 250 km/h)
Max level speed 86 knots (99 mph; 160 km/h)
Stalling speed 38 knots (43·5 mph; 70 km/h)
Max rate of climb at S/L 512 ft (156 m)/min
Best glide ratio, power off 25
Min sinking speed, power off 3·3 ft (1·0 m)/sec
T-O to 50 ft (15 m) 1,368 ft (417 m)
Landing from 50 ft (15 m) 847 ft (258 m)
Range with max fuel 258 nm (298 miles; 480 km)

TAINAN

TAINAN KOGYO CO

ADDRESS:
5139-3 Mukainagakubo, Zamairiya, Zama-shi, Kanagawa-ken
Telephone: 0462-51-1853
PRESIDENT:
H. Shinozaki
TECHNICAL ADVISER, AIRCRAFT DIVISION:
Asahi Miyahara

This company took over the manufacture of sailplanes from LADCO (see 1971-72 *Jane's*), and is continuing production, under licence, of the former company's Mita III two-seat sailplane. Also described is the S-3 Sagami, which is currently being developed under the supervision of Mr Asahi Miyahara.

Tainan Mita III two-seat training and sporting sailplane (*Asahi Miyahara*)

TAINAN LSS-02 and LSS-02B

These two sailplanes are identical except for their landing gear, the LSS-02B having a retractable monowheel.

Two LSS-02s and one LSS-02B were built. A description and an illustration of each type appeared in the 1973-74 *Jane's*.

TAINAN MITA III

By 1 January 1974, a total of 34 Mita IIIs had been built.
TYPE: Two-seat training and sporting sailplane.
WINGS: Cantilever shoulder-wing monoplane. Wing section NACA 63_3-618. Three-piece wing, with constant-chord centre-section and tapered outer panels. All-wood box monospar construction, plywood-covered. Ailerons fabric-covered. Schempp-Hirth airbrakes.
FUSELAGE: Steel tube frame with wooden stringers and fabric covering. Nose and front section of glassfibre.
TAIL UNIT: Cantilever type, of wooden construction; rudder and elevators fabric-covered.
LANDING GEAR: Non-retractable monowheel with brake and rubber springing.
ACCOMMODATION: Two seats in tandem under two-piece blown canopy.
DIMENSIONS, EXTERNAL:
Wing span 52 ft 5 in (16 m)
Wing aspect ratio 16·13
Length overall 26 ft 1$\frac{1}{4}$ in (7·96 m)
Height 4 ft 2$\frac{1}{2}$ in (1·28 m)
AREAS:
Wings, gross 170·82 sq ft (15·87 m²)
Fin 6·03 sq ft (0·56 m²)
Rudder 8·29 sq ft (0·77 m²)
Tailplane 15·50 sq ft (1·44 m²)
Elevators 11·63 sq ft (1·08 m²)
WEIGHTS AND LOADING:
Weight empty 661 lb (300 kg)
Max T-O weight 992 lb (450 kg)
Max wing loading 5·8 lb/sq ft (28·4 kg/m²)
PERFORMANCE:
Best glide ratio at 44 knots (51 mph; 82 km/h) 30
Min sinking speed at 41 knots (47 mph; 75 km/h) 2·36 ft (0·72 m)/sec
Stalling speed 34 knots (39 mph; 62·3 km/h)
Max speed 102 knots (118 mph; 190 km/h)
Max aero-tow speed 70 knots (81 mph; 130 km/h)
Max winch-launching speed 59 knots (68 mph; 110 km/h)

Sagami S-3K-1 modified pre-production version of the S-3

TAINAN SAGAMI S-3K

Design of the Sagami S-3 began in November 1970. Construction of the prototype began in September 1971, and this aircraft (JA2138) flew for the first time on 28 December 1971.

A pre-production aircraft (JA2145) flew for the first time in June 1972. It subsequently underwent modifications to the fuselage and tail unit, resuming flight testing in this form, under the designation S-3K-1, on 11 January 1973. A second modified S-3K is under construction.
TYPE: Single-seat sailplane.
WINGS: Cantilever high-wing monoplane. Wing section Wortmann FX-61-184 at root, Wortmann FX-60-126 at tip. Thickness/chord ratio 18% at root, 12% at tip. Dihedral 3°. Incidence 3°. No sweepback. Single-spar fabric-covered wooden structure, built in two halves and joined at centreline box. Plywood-covered D-section leading-edge. Plywood-covered plain ailerons. No tabs. Schempp-Hirth type metal airbrake on each wing.
FUSELAGE: Welded tubular carbon steel truss structure, with fabric covering. Nose portion of moulded glassfibre.
TAIL UNIT: Cantilever type. Plywood-covered wooden fin, fabric-covered wooden rudder. Two-piece all-moving tailplane on S-3, of fabric-covered wood construction; S-3K-1 has conventional tailplane, also of fabric-covered wood construction.
LANDING GEAR: Non-retractable monowheel, with steel plate external brake operated with airbrake lever. Tyre size 12·5 × 4·5, pressure 42·7 lb/sq in (3·0 kg/cm²).
ACCOMMODATION: Single seat under one-piece sideways-hinged Plexiglas canopy.
DIMENSIONS, EXTERNAL:
Wing span 49 ft 2$\frac{1}{2}$ in (15·00 m)
Wing aspect ratio 16·13
Wing chord at root 4 ft 0$\frac{3}{4}$ in (1·24 m)
Wing chord at tip 2 ft 0$\frac{1}{2}$ in (0·62 m)
Length overall 24 ft 6 in (7·47 m)
Height over tail 5 ft 4$\frac{1}{2}$ in (1·64 m)
Tailplane span 8 ft 10$\frac{1}{4}$ in (2·70 m)
AREAS:
Wings, gross 150·2 sq ft (13·95 m²)
Ailerons (total) 12·92 sq ft (1·20 m²)
Airbrakes (total) 6·57 sq ft (0·61 m²)
Fin 5·92 sq ft (0·55 m²)
Rudder 8·50 sq ft (0·79 m²)
Tailplane 19·59 sq ft (1·82 m²)
WEIGHTS:
Weight empty, equipped 463 lb (210 kg)
Max T-O weight 705 lb (320 kg)
PERFORMANCE (at 661 lb; 300 kg AUW):
Best glide ratio at 39 knots (45 mph; 72·4 km/h) 27
Min sinking speed at 31·9 knots (36·7 mph; 59·1 km/h) 2·26 ft (0·69 m)/sec
Stalling speed 27·5 knots (31·5 mph; 50·7 km/h)
Max speed (smooth air) 97 knots (112 mph; 180 km/h)
Max speed (rough air) 75·5 knots (87 mph; 140 km/h)
Max aero-tow speed 74 knots (85 mph; 137 km/h)
Max winch-launching speed 60·5 knots (70 mph; 112 km/h)

TAKATORI-SANKEN

TAKATORI-SANKEN CO LTD (Aircraft Division)

ADDRESS:
6-32 Funakoshi-machi, Yokosuka, Kanagawa
Telephone: (0468) 61-7226
CHIEF DESIGNER:
Osamu Saito
PUBLIC RELATIONS:
Kazutomo Sakuma

This company has taken over the sailplane development and construction work of the Yokohama Gliding Club (see 1973-74 *Jane's*). The former chairman of directors of YGC, Mr Osamu Saito, continues to act as chief of sailplane design.

TAKATORI SH-8 FLIDER

Design and construction of the SH-8 began in 1970, and two prototypes were built, the first of them flying for the first time in January 1971. The prototypes were generally similar, but the second differed in having an additional pontoon-like float on each side of the fuselage, carried on a short horizontal streamline-section strut which passed through the fuselage. It is not known if any further examples were built.

TYPE: Two-seat waterborne sailplane.

WINGS: Cantilever high-wing monoplane. Wing section Takatori No. 1. Thickness/chord ratio 16%. Dihedral 2°. Incidence 2°. No sweepback. All-wood structure with single box spar and plywood skin. Conventional centre-hinged mass-balanced ailerons of fabric-covered wood construction. No flaps or tabs. Small stabilising float at each wingtip.

HULL: All-wood structure with V-section planing bottom; plywood skin, covered with glass-fibre-reinforced plastics sheet.

TAIL UNIT: Cantilever all-wood structure with twin fins and rudders, carried on two slender tailbooms. Tailplane and elevator mounted between tailbooms. Elevator has spring trim.

ACCOMMODATION: Seats for two persons in tandem.

EQUIPMENT: A monowheel can be fitted to permit flight to and from conventional airfields.

DIMENSIONS, EXTERNAL:
Wing span 26 ft 3 in (8·00 m)
Wing chord, constant 4 ft 3¼ in (1·30 m)
Wing aspect ratio 6·15
Length overall 19 ft 8¼ in (6·00 m)
Fuselage: Max width 2 ft 3½ in (0·70 m)
Height overall 6 ft 4¾ in (1·95 m)
Tailplane span 6 ft 6¾ in (2·00 m)

AREAS:
Wings, gross 111·9 sq ft (10·40 m²)
Ailerons (total) 13·78 sq ft (1·28 m²)
Fins (total) 10·77 sq ft (1·00 m²)
Rudders (total) 10·77 sq ft (1·00 m²)
Tailplane 12·49 sq ft (1·16 m²)
Elevator 6·89 sq ft (0·64 m²)

WEIGHTS AND LOADING:
Weight empty 286 lb (130 kg)
Max T-O weight 727 lb (330 kg)
Max wing loading 6·50 lb/sq ft (31·75 kg/m²)

PERFORMANCE (at max T-O weight):
Best glide ratio at 48 knots (55·1 mph; 88·7 km/h) 16·6
Min sinking speed at 41·5 knots (47·7 mph; 76·8 km/h) 4·53 ft (1·38 m)/sec
Landing speed 29·5 knots (33·6 mph; 54·1 km/h)
Max speed (smooth air) 108 knots (124 mph; 200 km/h)
g limits +10·0; —6·0

TAKATORI SH-10E

The SH-10E, which was under test in early 1974, is developed from an earlier all-wood sailplane, the SH-10P, which flew for the first time in October 1952. It is intended to be converted into a powered sailplane.

TYPE: Single-seat powered sailplane.

WINGS: Cantilever high-wing monoplane. Wing section Gö 535. Dihedral 1°. Incidence 3°. Wood and glassfibre-reinforced plastics construction. Centre-hinged mass-balanced ailerons. No flaps or tabs.

FUSELAGE: Conventional rectangular-section structure, of similar construction to wings.

TAIL UNIT: Cantilever structure of wood and glassfibre-reinforced plastics. One-piece mass-balanced elevator, with trim tab in starboard half. Balanced rudder.

LANDING GEAR: Non-retractable tricycle type.

ACCOMMODATION: Single seat in fully-enclosed cockpit.

DIMENSIONS, EXTERNAL:
Wing span 32 ft 9¾ in (10·00 m)
Wing chord at root 3 ft 11¼ in (1·20 m)
Wing aspect ratio 8·33
Length overall 19 ft 3 in (5·87 m)
Fuselage: Max width 1 ft 11½ in (0·60 m)
Max depth 4 ft 9½ in (1·46 m)
Tailplane span 8 ft 2½ in (2·50 m)

AREAS:
Wings, gross 129·2 sq ft (12·00 m²)
Ailerons (total) 14·10 sq ft (1·31 m²)
Fin 5·81 sq ft (0·54 m²)
Rudder 4·84 sq ft (0·45 m²)

Takatori SH-8 Flider two-seat waterborne glider

Tailplane 14·15 sq ft (1·315 m²)
Elevator, incl tab 7·37 sq ft (0·685 m²)

WEIGHTS AND LOADING:
Weight empty 220 lb (100 kg)
Max T-O weight 441 lb (200 kg)
Max wing loading 3·41 lb/sq ft (16·65 kg/m²)

PERFORMANCE (at max T-O weight):
Best glide ratio at 35 knots (40·3 mph; 64·9 km/h) 15·78
Min sinking speed at 28·8 knots (33·2 mph; 53·4 km/h) 3·44 ft (1·05 m)/sec
Landing speed 26 knots (30 mph; 47·8 km/h)
Max speed 97 knots (112 mph; 180 km/h)
g limits ±10

TAKATORI SH-16

A full description and illustration of the (formerly Waseda) SH-16 appeared in the 1972-73 *Jane's*. It first flew in August 1969.

TYPE: Two-seat training sailplane.

ACCOMMODATION: Two seats in tandem in enclosed cabin. Two-piece transparent canopy supported by wooden frames.

DIMENSIONS, EXTERNAL:
Wing span 52 ft 5¾ in (16·00 m)
Wing aspect ratio 16
Length overall 26 ft 10¾ in (8·20 m)
Height overall 5 ft 3¾ in (1·62 m)

AREA:
Wings, gross 172 sq ft (16·0 m²)

WEIGHTS AND LOADING:
Weight empty 705 lb (320 kg)
Max T-O weight 1,102 lb (500 kg)
Max wing loading 6·4 lb/sq ft (31·25 kg/m²)

PERFORMANCE (two-seater):
Best glide ratio at 48·5 knots (56 mph; 90 km/h) 34
Min sinking speed at 46 knots (53 mph; 85 km/h) 2·30 ft (0·70 m)/sec
Landing speed 35·2 knots (40·5 mph; 65 km/h)
g limits +10; —5

TAKATORI SH-16S

Design of this single-seat high-performance sailplane began in 1968, with construction of the prototype following in 1969. Two examples were built, the first flight being made in September 1969.

TYPE: Single-seat high-performance sailplane.

WINGS: Cantilever shoulder-wing monoplane. Wing section NACA 65₃-418. Dihedral 2°. Aerodynamic twist 2°. No sweepback. All-wood structure with single box spar and plywood skin. Plain trailing-edge flaps at 80% chord. Wooden DFS-type airbrakes at 65% chord. Wooden top-hinged ailerons. No tabs.

FUSELAGE: Monocoque structure of wood and glassfibre-reinforced plastics.

TAIL UNIT: Cantilever all-wood T-tail. Fixed-incidence tailplane. Trim tab in centre of elevator.

LANDING GEAR: Yokohama non-retractable monowheel with tyre size 400-8, pressure 25 lb/sq in (1·76 kg/cm²). Skids at nose and tail.

ACCOMMODATION: Single semi-reclining seat under transparent cockpit canopy, hinged at side. Radio and oxygen system optional.

DIMENSIONS, EXTERNAL:
Wing span 52 ft 5¾ in (16·00 m)
Wing mean aerodynamic chord 2 ft 9½ in (0·85 m)
Wing aspect ratio 20
Length overall 20 ft 4 in (6·20 m)
Height overall 3 ft 1½ in (0·95 m)
Tailplane span 9 ft 2¼ in (2·80 m)

AREAS:
Wings, gross 140 sq ft (13·0 m²)
Ailerons (total) 10·66 sq ft (0·99 m²)
Fin 3·34 sq ft (0·31 m²)
Rudder 5·92 sq ft (0·55 m²)
Tailplane 11·30 sq ft (1·05 m²)
Elevator, incl tab 6·46 sq ft (0·60 m²)

WEIGHTS AND LOADING:
Weight empty 661 lb (300 kg)
Max T-O weight 859 lb (390 kg)
Max wing loading 6·1 lb/sq ft (30·0 kg/m²)

PERFORMANCE:
Best glide ratio at 53·6 knots (61·8 mph; 99·4 km/h) 44·4
Min sinking speed at 43·7 knots (50·3 mph; 81 km/h) 1·84 ft (0·56 m)/sec
Landing speed 33 knots (38 mph; 60·8 km/h)
g limits +10·0; —6·5

TAKATORI SH-18 MAMMOTH

Design and construction of the SH-18 began in 1959. Only one example was built, and this made its first flight in October 1963.

TYPE: Two-seat training sailplane.

WINGS: Cantilever high-wing monoplane. Wing section Takatori-I. Thickness/chord ratio 16% at root, 13% at tip. Dihedral 1° 30'. Aerodynamic twist 3° 45'. All-wood structure, with constant-chord centre-section and tapered outer panels. DFS-type airbrakes. Top-hinged mass-balanced ailerons. No tabs.

FUSELAGE: Conventional all-wood structure.

TAIL UNIT: Conventional all-wood structure. Fixed-incidence tailplane. Trim tab in starboard elevator.

LANDING GEAR: Non-retractable monowheel and tailwheel, and nose skid.

Takatori SH-16S single-seat high-performance sailplane

Above: **Model (without cockpit canopy) of the Takatori ST-1 Hawk-1 single-seat flying-boat glider**

Left: **Takatori SH-18 Mammoth two-seat training sailplane**

ACCOMMODATION: Two seats in tandem under framed canopy. Oxygen and radio installed.

DIMENSIONS, EXTERNAL:
- Wing span — 59 ft 0¾ in (18·00 m)
- Wing mean aerodynamic chord — 3 ft 3¾ in (1·01 m)
- Wing aspect ratio — 18
- Length overall — 27 ft 4¾ in (8·35 m)
- Fuselage: Max width — 2 ft 1½ in (0·65 m)
- Height overall — 4 ft 3¼ in (1·30 m)
- Tailplane span — 8 ft 2½ in (2·50 m)

AREAS:
- Wings, gross — 193·75 sq ft (18·00 m^2)
- Ailerons (total) — 21·53 sq ft (2·00 m^2)
- Airbrakes (total) — 7·53 sq ft (0·70 m^2)
- Fin — 6·67 sq ft (0·62 m^2)
- Rudder — 9·69 sq ft (0·90 m^2)
- Tailplane — 15·39 sq ft (1·43 m^2)
- Elevators, incl tab — 11·19 sq ft (1·04 m^2)

WEIGHTS AND LOADINGS:
- Weight empty — 694 lb (315 kg)
- Max T-O weight — 1,323 lb (600 kg)
- Max wing loading — 6·82 lb/sq ft (33·3 kg/m^2)

PERFORMANCE (at max T-O weight):
- Best glide ratio at 42 knots (48·5 mph; 78 km/h) — 36
- Min sinking speed at 38 knots (44 mph; 70·6 km/h) — 1·84 ft (0·56 m)/sec
- Stalling speed — 32·5 knots (37·5 mph; 60 km/h)
- Max speed (smooth air) — 135 knots (155 mph; 250 km/h)
- Max aero-tow and winch-launching speed — 64·5 knots (74·5 mph; 120 km/h)
- *g* limits — +10; —6

TAKATORI ST-1 HAWK-1

Design and construction of this small, single-seat flying-boat glider was started in 1972. It was expected that flight testing would begin in 1974. The general appearance of the ST-1 can be seen in the accompanying illustration.

TYPE: Single-seat flying-boat glider.

WINGS: Cantilever mid-wing monoplane. Takatori-I wing section. Dihedral 10°. No sweepback. Glassfibre structure, faired smoothly into upper fuselage aft of cockpit. Top-hinged ailerons. No airbrakes, flaps or tabs.

HULL: Pod and boom hull of glassfibre construction, with V-shaped planing bottom.

TAIL UNIT: Cantilever V-tail, with separate rudders/elevators, supported on fuselage tailboom. Glassfibre construction.

ACCOMMODATION: Single seat.

EQUIPMENT: Provision for radio and engine to be fitted.

DIMENSIONS, EXTERNAL:
- Wing span — 23 ft 7½ in (7·20 m)
- Wing chord at root — 4 ft 11 in (1·50 m)
- Wing chord at tip — 3 ft 3¼ in (1·00 m)
- Wing aspect ratio — 5·36
- Length overall — 17 ft 4¾ in (5·30 m)
- Height over tail — 5 ft 9¼ in (1·76 m)
- Tailplane span — 7 ft 9 in (2·36 m)

AREAS:
- Wings, gross — 98·17 sq ft (9·12 m^2)
- Ailerons (total) — 18·41 sq ft (1·71 m^2)
- Fixed tail surfaces (total) — 13·24 sq ft (1·23 m^2)
- Movable tail surfaces (total) — 7·00 sq ft (0·65 m^2)

WEIGHTS AND LOADING:
- Weight empty — 231 lb (105 kg)
- Max T-O weight — 661 lb (300 kg)
- Max wing loading — 6·72 lb/sq ft (32·8 kg/m^2)

PERFORMANCE (estimated, at max T-O weight):
- Best glide ratio at 43 knots (49·5 mph; 79·7 km/h) — 11·6
- Min sinking speed at 37·7 knots (43·4 mph; 69·8 km/h) — 5·97 ft (1·82 m)/sec
- Stalling speed — 26·7 knots (30·6 mph; 49·2 km/h)
- Max speed (smooth air) — 108 knots (124 mph; 200 km/h)
- Max tow and winch-launching speed — 64·5 knots (74·5 mph; 120 km/h)
- *g* limits — ±10

POLAND

SZD

ZAKLADY SZYBOWCOWE-BIELSKO (Glider Works-Bielsko)

HEAD OFFICE AND WORKS:
43-300 Bielsko-Biala 1, ul Cieszynska 325
Telephone: 250-21 to 250-26
Telex: 031-259 SZD PL

DIRECTOR:
Mgr Ing Wladyslaw Nowakowski

SALES REPRESENTATIVE:
Pezetel, Warszawa, ul. Czestochowska 5a

OSRODEK BADAWCZO ROZWOJOWY SZYBOWNICTWA (Research and Development Centre for Gliders)

The Instytut Szybownictwa (Gliding Institute), formed officially in January 1946 at Bielsko-Biala, was renamed two years later the Szybowcowy Zaklad Doswiadczalny—SZD (Experimental Glider Establishment). In July 1969 the name was changed again to Zaklad Doswiadczalny Rozwoju i Budowy Szybowcow (Experimental Establishment for Development of Gliders), and in January 1972 to that shown above, but it retains the well-known initial designation of SZD. This organisation is responsible for the design and development of all Polish gliders and sailplanes. Production plants are situated at Bielsko-Biala (where a new manufacturing facility is currently under construction), Wroclaw and Jezów. Between 1947 and 1973 the Polish aircraft industry produced some 2,900 gliders of about 85 different types, and SZD sailplanes have been exported all over the world in substantial numbers.

SZD-9bis BOCIAN 1E (STORK)

SZD-9bis Bocian 1E tandem two-seat general-purpose sailplane

The original prototype of the Bocian flew for the first time on 11 March 1952. By the end of 1973, 420 SZD-9 Bocian sailplanes had been built, in several versions, of which the latest is the Bocian 1E, which first flew on 6 December 1966. On 5 November 1966 an earlier version of the Bocian established an international gain of height record for multi-seat sailplanes of 38,320 ft (11,680 m). The corresponding record for ladies, of 27,650 ft (8,430 m), was set up in another Bocian on 17 October 1967. Export orders for 50 Bocians were placed during the first quarter of 1974.

The controls, instrument panel and other details were designed to make the aircraft suitable for sporting flight as well as for school and training duties. Cloud-flying, spinning and basic aerobatics are permitted.

The following description applies to the Bocian 1E, production of which was continuing in 1974:

TYPE: Tandem two-seat general-purpose sailplane.

WINGS: Cantilever mid-wing monoplane. Wing section NACA 43018 at root, NACA 43012A at tip. Dihedral 4°. Incidence 2° 30′. Sweep-forward 1° 30′ at quarter-chord. Two-spar wooden structure, with plywood D-section leading-edge and fabric covering. Slotted ailerons. No flaps. SZD airbrakes inboard of ailerons.

FUSELAGE: Plywood-covered wooden structure of oval section.

TAIL UNIT: Cantilever wooden structure. Trim tab in elevators.

LANDING GEAR: Non-retractable monowheel and front skid. Shock-absorber fitted. Wheel size 135 × 350, with brake.

ACCOMMODATION: Two seats in tandem under long transparent canopy.

DIMENSIONS, EXTERNAL:
- Wing span — 58 ft 4¾ in (17·81 m)
- Wing chord at root — 5 ft 8¾ in (1·75 m)
- Wing chord at tip — 1 ft 7·7 in (0·50 m)
- Wing aspect ratio — 16·2
- Length overall — 26 ft 10¾ in (8·20 m)
- Height overall, excl wheel — 4 ft 0¼ in (1·20 m)
- Tailplane span — 10 ft 2 in (3·10 m)

AREAS:
- Wings, gross — 215·3 sq ft (20·00 m^2)
- Ailerons (total) — 29·50 sq ft (2·74 m^2)
- Airbrakes (total) — 6·82 sq ft (0·63 m^2)
- Fin — 7·32 sq ft (0·68 m^2)
- Rudder — 8·83 sq ft (0·82 m^2)
- Tailplane — 10·76 sq ft (1·00 m^2)
- Elevators — 16·15 sq ft (1·50 m^2)

WEIGHTS AND LOADING:
- Weight empty, equipped — 794 lb (360 kg)
- Max T-O weight — 1,191 lb (540 kg)
- Max wing loading — 5·58 lb/sq ft (27·0 kg/m^2)

PERFORMANCE (at max T-O weight):
- Best glide ratio at 43·4 knots (50 mph; 80 km/h) — 26
- Min sinking speed at 38·3 knots (44 mph; 71 km/h) — 2·69 ft (0·82 m)/sec
- Stalling speed — 33 knots (37·5 mph; 60 km/h)
- Max speed (smooth air) — 108 knots (124 mph; 200 km/h)
- Max speed (rough air) — 81 knots (93 mph; 150 km/h)

Max aero-tow speed
76 knots (87 mph; 140 km/h)
Max winch-launching speed
62 knots (71 mph; 115 km/h)

SZD-30 PIRAT

Designed by Ing Jerzy Smielkiewicz, this single-seat Standard Class sailplane flew for the first time on 19 May 1966. It is suitable for the full range of duties from training to competition flying and is cleared for cloud flying, spinning and basic aerobatics. Production started in 1967 and 415 Pirats had been built by the end of 1973, including three which are in service with the Escuela de Aviacion Militar in Argentina. Production of the Pirat is now undertaken also by the WSK-Swidnik works, which had completed 50 by the end of 1973.

TYPE: Single-seat Standard Class sailplane.

WINGS: Cantilever high-wing monoplane. Wing section Wortmann FX-61-168 at root, Wortmann FX-60-1261 at tip. Dihedral 2° 30′ on outer panels only. No sweep at quarter-chord. Wooden wing, built in three parts. Rectangular centre-section is a plywood-covered multi-spar structure. Tapered outer panels are of single-spar torsion-box construction. Mass-balanced ailerons. Double-plate airbrakes.

FUSELAGE: Plywood monocoque structure, with glassfibre nose and cockpit floor.

TAIL UNIT: Cantilever wooden T-tail. Tab on trailing-edge of elevator.

LANDING GEAR: Front skid with shock-absorber is easily removable. Non-retractable monowheel, size 350 × 135, with band brake.

ACCOMMODATION: Single seat under jettisonable sideways-hinged blown Perspex canopy. Two baggage compartments. Map pockets on each side of cockpit. Provision for radio and oxygen equipment.

DIMENSIONS, EXTERNAL:	
Wing span	49 ft 2½ in (15·00 m)
Wing chord at root	3 ft 4½ in (1·03 m)
Wing chord at tip	1 ft 11½ in (0·60 m)
Wing aspect ratio	16·3
Length overall	22 ft 6 in (6·86 m)
Height overall, excl wheel	3 ft 1¾ in (0·96 m)
Tailplane span	10 ft 2 in (3·10 m)
AREAS:	
Wings, gross	148·5 sq ft (13·8 m²)
Ailerons (total)	11·72 sq ft (1·09 m²)
Airbrakes (total)	7·86 sq ft (0·73 m²)
Fin	5·35 sq ft (0·48 m²)
Rudder	8·10 sq ft (0·77 m²)
Tailplane	11·68 sq ft (1·08 m²)
Elevator	7·69 sq ft (0·78 m²)
WEIGHTS AND LOADING:	
Weight empty, equipped	575 lb (261 kg)
Max T-O weight	816 lb (370 kg)
Max wing loading	5·49 lb/sq ft (26·8 kg/m²)

PERFORMANCE (at AUW of 750 lb; 340 kg):
Best glide ratio at 44·5 knots (51 mph; 82 km/h) 33
Min sinking speed at 40·4 knots (46·5 mph; 75 km/h) 2·16 ft (0·66 m)/sec
Stalling speed 33 knots (37 mph; 59 km/h)
Max speed (smooth air)
135 knots (155 mph; 250 km/h)
Max speed (rough air)
76-89 knots (87-103 mph; 140-165 km/h)
Max aero-tow speed
71 knots (82 mph; 132 km/h)
Max winch-launching speed
74 knots (85 mph; 137 km/h)

SZD-35 BEKAS (SNIPE)

Design of the SZD-35 tandem two-seat training sailplane began in January 1969. Two prototypes were built; the first of these flew for the first time on 29 November 1970, followed by the second on 20 March 1971. Production is not intended.

A full description and illustration appeared in the 1973-74 *Jane's*.

SZD-36A COBRA 15

The SZD-36 Cobra 15 is a single-seat Standard Class high-performance sailplane designed by Ing Wladyslaw Okarmus. Design was started on 15 October 1968, and construction of a prototype began on 10 November 1968. This aircraft flew for the first time on 30 December 1969. Polish competitors flying the Cobra 15 gained second and third places in the world championships at Marfa in 1970.

A total of 110 Cobra 15s had been built by the end of 1973, for customers in Poland, Czechoslovakia, the German Democratic Republic and Hungary. Under a contract signed in 1972, Poland is also supplying 20 Cobra 15s per year to the USSR, for Soviet aeroclubs, until 1975. Some of these will carry oxygen equipment and be used for wave soaring. Current production aircraft, which are designated SZD-36A, have the CG towing hook displaced approx 3 ft 3¼ in (1 m) forward, but retain the provision to locate this at the CG if required. The empty weight is 44 lb (20 kg) lighter than that of the original SZD-36.

Two prototypes were built of the SZD-39 Cobra 17, a 17 metre span Open Class version of the SZD-36 with water ballast, and the first flight by this version was made on 17 March 1970. A description of the SZD-39 appeared in the 1972-73 *Jane's*.

The following description applies to the standard 15 metre span SZD-36A:

TYPE: Single-seat high-performance Standard Class sailplane.

WINGS: Cantilever shoulder-wing monoplane. Wortmann wing sections: FX-61-168 at root, FX-60-1261 at tip. Dihedral 2°. Incidence 2°. No sweepback at quarter-chord. Single-spar wooden structure with heavy moulded plywood stressed skin covered with glassfibre. Plain ailerons, hinged at their upper surface and of plywood/polystyrene foam sandwich construction, are mass-balanced and actuated by push-rods. SZD type metal/glassfibre double-plate airbrake above and below each wing. No tabs.

FUSELAGE: All-wood semi-monocoque structure of oval section, covered with plywood at rear and glassfibre at front. Aero-tow hook in lower fuselage, forward of monowheel.

TAIL UNIT: Cantilever all-wood structure with swept vertical surfaces. T-tail with all-moving mass-balanced tailplane. Geared trim tab on tailplane trailing-edge.

LANDING GEAR: Mechanically-retractable monowheel which lies horizontally in bottom of fuselage when retracted. Stomil wheel and tyre size 300 × 125 mm, with SZD brake. Tyre pressure 36 lb/sq in (2·5 kg/cm²). Tailskid.

ACCOMMODATION: Single seat in enclosed cabin under vacuum-formed forward-sliding canopy which can be jettisoned in emergency. Baggage compartment aft of pilot's seat, size 10½ in × 2 ft 4½ in (0·27 × 0·72 m).

EQUIPMENT: Instrumentation includes airspeed indicator, altimeter, total energy variometer, rate of climb indicator, turn indicator, artificial horizon, variometer, compass and RS-3A radio. SAT-5 oxygen system with 0·14 cu ft (4 litre) cylinder in baggage compartment.

DIMENSIONS, EXTERNAL:	
Wing span	49 ft 2½ in (15·0 m)
Wing chord at root	3 ft 9¼ in (1·15 m)
Wing chord at tip	1 ft 3 in (0·38 m)
Wing chord (mean)	2 ft 9 in (0·84 m)
Wing aspect ratio	19·4
Length overall	23 ft 1¼ in (7·05 m)
Height overall	5 ft 2¾ in (1·59 m)
Tailplane span	7 ft 10½ in (2·40 m)
AREAS:	
Wings, gross	125 sq ft (11·6 m²)
Ailerons (total)	6·78 sq ft (0·63 m²)
Airbrakes (total)	8·18 sq ft (0·76 m²)
Fin	6·89 sq ft (0·64 m²)
Rudder	4·95 sq ft (0·46 m²)
Tailplane, incl tab	15·07 sq ft (1·40 m²)
WEIGHTS AND LOADING:	
Weight empty, equipped	522 lb (237 kg)
Max T-O weight	848 lb (385 kg)
Max wing loading	6·80 lb/sq ft (33·2 kg/m²)

PERFORMANCE (at max T-O weight):
Best glide ratio at 52 knots (60 mph; 97 km/h) 38
Min sinking speed at 39·5 knots (45·5 mph; 73 km/h) 2·23 ft (0·68 m)/sec
Stalling speed 36·5 knots (42 mph; 67 km/h)
Max speed (smooth air)
135 knots (155 mph; 250 km/h)
Max speed (rough air)
92 knots (106 mph; 170 km/h)
Max aero-tow speed
81 knots (93 mph; 150 km/h)
Max winch-launching speed
70 knots (80·5 mph; 130 km/h)
g limits +6; —3

SZD-37 JANTAR 19 (AMBER)

This high-performance single-seat Open Class sailplane was designed for use by the Polish team in the 1972 World Championships at Vrsac, Yugoslavia; it gained 3rd place, being defeated only by sailplanes of greater span, and was awarded the OSTIV prize for the best sailplane of up to 19 m span. It was also the first Polish sailplane to be built substantially of glassfibre laminates.

Design of the SZD-37 Jantar, led by Dipl Ing Adam Kurbiel, began in 1969, and construction started in 1970. Two prototypes were built, the first of these making its first flight on 14 February 1972. This aircraft had a 17·5 m span wing; a 19 m wing was fitted to the second prototype, which made its first flight on 13 May 1972.

In one of these aircraft, on 29 May 1973, Miss Adela Dankowska of Poland set up a ladies' international goal-and-return record flight of 362·725 km (417·7 miles; 672·2 km).

The prototypes were described in detail in the 1973-74 *Jane's*. In its production form the Jantar is designated SZD-38, as described below.

SZD-38 JANTAR-1 (AMBER)

This high-performance single-seat Open Class sailplane was developed by Dipl Ing Adam Kurbiel from the prototype SZD-37 Jantar 19 (see 1973-74 *Jane's*) which, in the 1972 World Championships at Vrsac, Yugoslavia, gained 3rd place and was awarded the OSTIV prize for the best sailplane of up to 19 m span. It is the first Polish series-built sailplane of all-plastics cons-

SZD-30 Pirat single-seat Standard Class sailplane, of which more than 415 have been built

SZD-36A Cobra 15 single-seat high-performance Standard Class sailplane

SZD-38 Jantar-1 Open Class production sailplane developed from the SZD-37

truction. A Standard Class version, the SZD-41, is described separately.

The SZD-38 flew for the first time on 7 August 1973. The first two examples were flown by the Polish team in the 1974 World Championships at Waikerie, Australia, in which they gained 15th and 18th places.

Type: Single-seat high-performance Open Class sailplane.

Wings: Cantilever shoulder-wing monoplane. Wortmann wing sections: FX-67-K-170 at root, FX-67-K-150 at tip. Dihedral 1° 30′. No sweepback. Single-spar ribless structure, with foam-filled glassfibre/epoxy resin sandwich skin. Multi-hinged ailerons and hingeless trailing-edge flaps, suspended on the upper skin and operated by pushrods. Provision in wings for 22 Imp gallons (100 litres) of water ballast. DFS glassfibre airbrake above and below each wing. No tabs.

Fuselage: All-glassfibre/epoxy resin shell structure; centre portion has a steel tube frame coupling together the wings, fuselage and landing gear.

Tail Unit: Cantilever T-tail, of glassfibre/epoxy resin construction. Tailplane has pushrod-operated elevators with spring trim. No tabs. Fin is integral with fuselage and has internally-mounted radio aerial.

Landing Gear: Mechanically-retractable monowheel (Stomil, size 350 × 135, tyre pressure 49·8 lb/sq in; 3·5 kg/cm²) and fixed 200 mm diameter tailwheel. Disc brake on main wheel.

Accommodation and Equipment: Single semi-reclining seat under two-piece fully-transparent removable canopy. Normal cockpit instrumentation, plus transceiver, oxygen equipment and artificial horizon. Headrest and backrest adjustable on ground; rudder pedals adjustable during flight.

Dimensions, external:
Wing span 62 ft 4 in (19·00 m)
Wing chord at root 2 ft 11½ in (0·90 m)
Wing chord at tip 1 ft 2¾ in (0·377 m)
Wing chord (mean) 2 ft 5¼ in (0·74 m)
Wing aspect ratio 27
Length overall 23 ft 4 in (7·11 m)
Height over tail 5 ft 3 in (1·60 m)
Tailplane span 8 ft 6¼ in (2·60 m)

Areas:
Wings, gross 144·0 sq ft (13·38 m²)
Ailerons (total) 9·47 sq ft (0·88 m²)
Trailing-edge flaps (total) 15·07 sq ft (1·40 m²)
Airbrakes (total) 7·43 sq ft (0·69 m²)
Fin 6·46 sq ft (0·60 m²)
Rudder 5·38 sq ft (0·50 m²)
Tailplane 14·53 sq ft (1·35 m²)
Elevators (total) 8·74 sq ft (0·812 m²)

Weights and Loadings:
Weight empty, equipped 639 lb (290 kg)
Max T-O weight:
with water ballast 1,146 lb (520 kg)
without water ballast 926 lb (420 kg)
Max wing loading:
with water ballast 7·97 lb/sq ft (38·9 kg/m²)
without water ballast 6·43 lb/sq ft (31·4 kg/m²)

Performance (without water ballast):
Best glide ratio at 52·5 knots (60·5 mph; 97 km/h) 47
Min sinking speed at 40·5 knots (46·5 mph; 75 km/h) 1·64 ft (0·50 m)/sec
Stalling speed 35 knots (40·5 mph; 65 km/h)
Max speed (smooth air) 135 knots (155 mph; 250 km/h)
Max speed (rough air) 89 knots (102·5 mph; 165 km/h)
Max aero-tow speed 81 knots (93 mph; 150 km/h)
g limits +5·3; −2·65

SZD-40X HALNY (FÖHN)

This two-seat high-performance sailplane, designed by Ing W. Okarmus, was built as a prototype, adapting the wings of a Zefir-4 sailplane.

It is intended as a flying testbed for a new wing section, and also to serve the Polish Aeroclub as a high-performance two-seater. Controls are located in the rear cockpit.

The Halny made its first flight on 23 December 1972, piloted by Dipl Ing Zdzislaw Bylok.

Wings: Cantilever shoulder-wing monoplane. Wing section NN-11M. Incidence 1° 30′. Sweepforward 4° at quarter-chord. Sparless wooden box structure. Hingeless trailing-edge flaps. Glassfibre slotless ailerons, hinged on the upper surface and operated by pushrods. No tabs. SZD-type double-plate metal airbrake at 60% chord above and below each wing.

Fuselage: All-plastics monocoque front portion, steel tube framed centre portion and metal tube monocoque rear portion.

Tail Unit: Cantilever glassfibre T-tail. No mass balance. Spring trim on control circuit in fuselage.

Landing Gear: Retractable monowheel (350 × 135 mm) with shoe brake. Fixed tailwheel of 120 mm diameter.

Accommodation: Two seats in tandem under one-piece transparent removable canopy. Controls and instrument panel in rear cockpit only.

SZD-40X Halny two-seat high-performance experimental sailplane

SZD-41 Jantar Standard single-seat Standard Class sailplane

Rear seat backrest adjustable on ground. Front place for navigator, passenger or research and measuring instruments. Transceiver and oxygen equipment optional.

Dimensions, external:
Wing span 65 ft 7½ in (20·00 m)
Wing chord at root 3 ft 11½ in (1·204 m)
Wing chord at tip 1 ft 4½ in (0·419 m)
Wing mean aerodynamic chord 2 ft 10¼ in (0·873 m)
Wing aspect ratio 24·66
Length overall 28 ft 8½ in (8·75 m)
Height over tail 5 ft 11 in (1·80 m)
Tailplane span 10 ft 6 in (3·20 m)

Areas:
Wings, gross 173·4 sq ft (16·11 m²)
Ailerons (total) 8·65 sq ft (0·804 m²)
Airbrakes (total) 8·61 sq ft (0·80 m²)
Fin 12·70 sq ft (1·18 m²)
Rudder 6·14 sq ft (0·57 m²)
Tailplane 17·28 sq ft (1·605 m²)
Elevator 5·18 sq ft (0·481 m²)

Weights and Loading:
Weight empty, equipped 903 lb (410 kg)
Max T-O weight 1,314 lb (596 kg)
Max wing loading 7·56 lb/sq ft (36·9 kg/m²)

Performance (flaps up):
Best glide ratio at 54 knots (62 mph; 100 km/h) 43
Min sinking speed at 46 knots (53 mph; 85 km/h) 1·94 ft (0·59 m)/sec
Stalling speed 39·5 knots (45·5 mph; 72·8 km/h)
Max speed 129·5 knots (149 mph; 240 km/h)
g limits +5; −2·5

Performance (6° flap):
Min sinking speed at 41 knots (47 mph; 75 km/h) 1·80 ft (0·55 m)/sec
Stalling speed 36 knots (41 mph; 65·5 km/h)

SZD-41 JANTAR STANDARD (AMBER)

This high-performance single-seat Standard Class sailplane was designed by Ing W. Okarmus on the basis of the prototype Open Class SZD-38 Jantar-1. The fuselage and tail unit are the same for both types; the wings of the SZD-41 are designed to OSTIV Standard Class requirements.

The Jantar Standard was flown for the first time at Bielsko-Biala on 3 October 1973, piloted by A. Zientek. Polish pilots flying the SZD-41 in the 1974 World Championships at Waikerie, Australia, gained third and seventh places in the Standard Class competition.

The description of the SZD-38 applies also to the SZD-41, except in the following details:

Type: Single-seat Standard Class sailplane.

Wings: Cantilever shoulder-wing monoplane. Wing section NN-8. Dihedral 1° 30′. Sweepback 0° 30′ at quarter-chord. Single-spar ribless structure with foam-filled glassfibre/epoxy resin sandwich skin. Provision for 176 lb (80 kg) water ballast.

Dimensions, external:
Wing span 49 ft 2½ in (15·00 m)
Wing chord at root 3 ft 1½ in (0·95 m)
Wing chord at tip 1 ft 5¾ in (0·45 m)
Wing mean aerodynamic chord 2 ft 4 in (0·71 m)
Wing aspect ratio 21·1

Areas:
Wings, gross 114·7 sq ft (10·66 m²)
Ailerons (total) 5·70 sq ft (0·53 m²)
Airbrakes (total) 5·15 sq ft (0·478 m²)

Weights and Loadings:
Weight empty, equipped 551 lb (250 kg)
Max T-O weight:
with water ballast 970 lb (440 kg)
without water ballast 793 lb (360 kg)
Max wing loading:
with water ballast 8·46 lb/sq ft (41·3 kg/m²)
without water ballast 6·92 lb/sq ft (33·8 kg/m²)

Performance (without water ballast):
Best glide ratio at 56·5 knots (65 mph; 105 km/h) 40
Min sinking speed at 42 knots (48·5 mph; 78 km/h) 2·03 ft (0·62 m)/sec
Stalling speed 37 knots (42·5 mph; 68 km/h)
Max speed (smooth air) 135 knots (155 mph; 250 km/h)
Max speed (rough air) 86 knots (99 mph; 160 km/h)
Max aero-tow speed 81 knots (93 mph; 150 km/h)
g limits +5·3; −2·65

SZD-43 ORION

This high-performance single-seat Standard Class sailplane was designed for use by the Polish team in the 1972 World Championships at Vrsac, Yugoslavia. Two prototypes were built: these gained 1st and 3rd places in the Standard Class

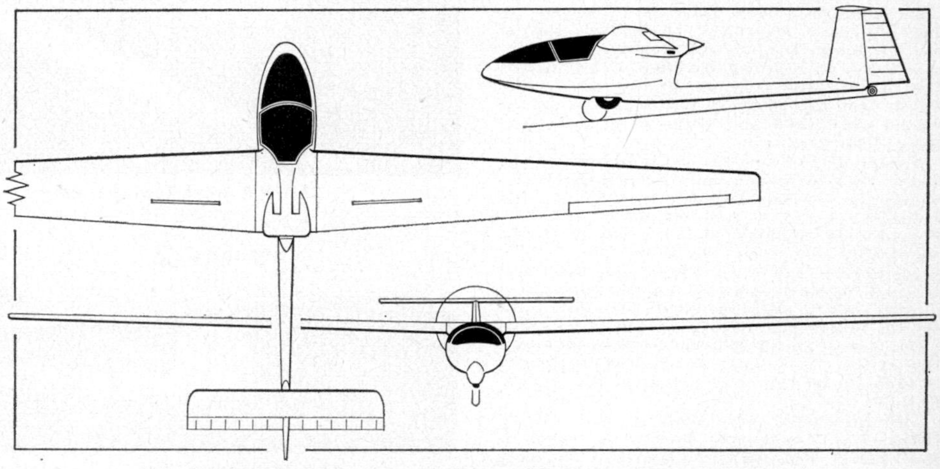

SZD-45A Ogar two-seat powered training sailplane *(Michael A. Badrocke)*

competition, and were described and illustrated in the 1973-74 *Jane's*.

SZD-45A OGAR (GREYHOUND)

This two-seat school and training powered sailplane was designed by Dipl Ing Tadeusz Labuc, originally with a 45 hp Stamo engine and later with a 68 hp Sportavia Limbach engine. The SZD-45 prototype (SP-0001) made its first flight on 29 May 1973, and was described in the 1973-74 *Jane's*.

Production, as the SZD-45A, began in 1974, and by mid-year the Ogar was in service with the Polish Aero Club. The following description applies to this version:

TYPE: Two-seat powered training sailplane.

WINGS: Cantilever shoulder-wing monoplane. Wortmann wing sections: FX-61-168 at root, FX-60-1261 at tip. Dihedral 1° 30′. Incidence 1°. Sweepback 1° at quarter-chord. Single-spar wooden structure, with moulded plywood stressed skin covered with glassfibre. Slotless ailerons of glassfibre sandwich construction, controlled by pushrods. Airbrake plates extend above and below each wing in separate boxes.

FUSELAGE: Pod and boom type. Main nacelle structure is a glassfibre/epoxy resin shell on two strong wooden frames. Tubular metal boom supports the tail unit.

TAIL UNIT: Cantilever T-tail, the fin being integral with the metal tailboom.

LANDING GEAR: Semi-retractable monowheel (size 400 × 150), with disc-type brake. Small tailwheel, steerable with rudder. For school use, side legs and wheels are mounted adjacent to the wingtips.

POWER PLANT: One 68 hp Sportavia Limbach SL 1700 EC four-cylinder four-stroke aircooled engine, mounted behind the cabin and driving a two-blade Hoffmann pusher propeller. Fuel capacity 48·5 lb (22 kg).

ACCOMMODATION AND EQUIPMENT: Seats for two persons side by side under two-piece fully-transparent upward-hinged cockpit canopy. Dual controls standard. Backrests adjustable on ground, rudder pedals adjustable during flight. Engine controls in centre of panel, between seats, with navigation instruments to left and engine instruments to right.

DIMENSIONS, EXTERNAL:
- Wing span: 57 ft 5 in (17·50 m)
- Wing chord at root: 5 ft 2 in (1·578 m)
- Wing chord at tip: 1 ft $8\frac{3}{4}$ in (0·531 m)
- Wing mean aerodynamic chord: 3 ft $6\frac{3}{4}$ in (1·089 m)
- Wing aspect ratio: 16·1
- Length overall: 26 ft 1 in (7·95 m)
- Height over cabin roof: 3 ft $9\frac{1}{4}$ in (1·15 m)
- Tailplane span: 11 ft $9\frac{3}{4}$ in (3·60 m)
- Propeller diameter: 4 ft 11 in (1·50 m)

AREAS:
- Wings, gross: 205·6 sq ft (19·10 m^2)
- Ailerons (total): 10·12 sq ft (0·94 m^2)
- Fin: 10·33 sq ft (0·96 m^2)
- Rudder: 8·83 sq ft (0·82 m^2)
- Tailplane: 29·06 sq ft (2·70 m^2)
- Elevators (total): 8·40 sq ft (0·78 m^2)

WEIGHTS AND LOADINGS:
- Weight empty: 1,036 lb (470 kg)
- Max T-O weight: 1,543 lb (700 kg)
- Max wing loading: 7·5 lb/sq ft (36·6 kg/m^2)
- Max power loading: 22·71 lb/hp (10·3 kg/hp)

PERFORMANCE:
- Best glide ratio at 54 knots (62 mph; 100 km/h): 27·5
- Min sinking speed at 38·5 knots (44·5 mph; 72 km/h): 3·15 ft (0·96 m)/sec
- Max level speed at S/L: 97·5 knots (112 mph; 180 km/h)
- Cruising speed at S/L: 81 knots (93 mph; 150 km/h)
- Max rate of climb at S/L: 550 ft (168 m)/min

SZD-45A Ogar side-by-side two-seat powered training sailplane *(Brian M. Service)*

ROMANIA

ICA-BRASOV

INTREPRINDEREA DE CONSTRUCTII AERONAUTICE (Aircraft Construction Factory)

HEAD OFFICE AND WORKS: Brasov

As detailed in the "Aircraft" section, the current activities of the Romanian aircraft industry are divided between two industrial centres, IRMA in Bucharest and ICA at Brasov. In addition to its work on powered aircraft, the ICA is now responsible for all sailplane development and production previously undertaken by URMV-3 (up to 1959) and IIL (Ghimbav) up to 1968. The principal Romanian designer of sailplanes is Dipl Ing Iosif Silimon, whose designs are prefixed with the letters IS. Details of his earlier designs have appeared in the 1961-62, 1965-66 and 1972-73 *Jane's*. Descriptions follow of those currently in production or under development:

ICA-Brasov IS-28 tandem two-seat training sailplane

IS-28

This tandem two-seat school and training sailplane, designed by a team led by Dipl Ing Iosif Silimon, flew for the first time in August 1970. It was certificated in December 1971, and is now in production.

TYPE: Tandem two-seat school and training sailplane.

WINGS: Cantilever shoulder-wing monoplane. Wing section NACA 43012A. Forward-swept fabric-covered wooden wings, each with three-point attachment to fuselage. Single main spar, with false rear spar and truss ribs. Leading-edge, up to main spar and on a 45° diagonal to the rear junction, acts as a torsion box. DFS-type airbrake above and below each wing. Aerodynamically and statically balanced differentially-operating ailerons, of fabric-covered wood construction. No tabs.

FUSELAGE: Metal semi-monocoque structure, of oval cross-section, made up of frames, stringers and duralumin skin. Main centre-section attachment is achieved with dural sheet and steel dowels, riveted to two reinforced main bulkheads. Secondary centre-section attachment is achieved with dural sheet riveted to two reinforced bulkheads. Glassfibre nose-cap.

TAIL UNIT: Cantilever T-tail. Two-spar fin, with stamped ribs and riveted metal skin, riveted to rear-fuselage frames. Fabric-covered metal rudder. Fixed-incidence dihedral tailplane, which can be folded for stowage, is in two riveted dural-covered halves, each fitted with a single-spar fabric-covered metal elevator. Flettner tab in each elevator.

LANDING GEAR: Non-retractable nosewheel and retractable main wheel, in tandem. Oleo-pneumatic shock-absorber and mechanically-operated disc brake on main wheel. Lever-type tail bumper, with rubber shock-absorber. Tyre sizes: nosewheel 290 × 110, main wheel 350 × 135.

ACCOMMODATION: Seats for two persons in tandem under Plexiglas canopy. Door to forward cockpit. Rear part of canopy hinges upward, and has sliding panels for cockpit ventilation in flight.

EQUIPMENT: Dual controls standard. Conventional stick and rudder-pedal controls, made up of lever, bars and cable torsion axes located beneath seat and cabin floor. Airbrakes and elevator tabs controlled by a lever on left-hand side of cabin. Main-wheel retraction and extension controlled by lever on right-hand side. DFS-type nose tow-gear.

DIMENSIONS, EXTERNAL:
- Wing span: 49 ft $2\frac{1}{2}$ in (15·00 m)
- Length overall: 22 ft $2\frac{1}{4}$ in (6·76 m)
- Height overall: 7 ft $1\frac{3}{4}$ in (2·18 m)

AREA:
- Wings, gross: 194·0 sq ft (18·00 m^2)

WEIGHTS AND LOADING:
- Weight empty: 716 lb (325 kg)
- Max T-O weight: 1,124 lb (510 kg)
- Max wing loading: 5·8 lb/sq ft (28·3 kg/m^2)

PERFORMANCE:
- Best glide ratio at 40·5 knots (46·5 mph; 75 km/h): 26
- Min sinking speed at 35 knots (40·5 mph; 65 km/h): 2·79 ft (0·85 m)/sec
- Stalling speed: 31·5 knots (36·5 mph; 58 km/h)
- Max never-exceed speed: 107·5 knots (124 mph; 200 km/h)
- *g* limits: +4; −1·5

IS-28B

Despite its similar designation, this high-performance training sailplane represents a considerable advance over the standard IS-28, from which it differs principally in having 17 m span all-metal wings, fitted with trailing-edge flaps, a more slender fuselage, and reducing wing and tailplane dihedral. Design began in the Autumn of 1971, and the first IS-28B made its first flight on 26 April 1973.

TYPE: Tandem two-seat high-performance training sailplane.

WINGS: Cantilever mid-wing monoplane. Wortmann wing sections: FX-61-163 at root, FX-61-126 at tip. Forward-swept all-metal wings, attached to fuselage by two fixed conical bolts at leading-edge and two adjustable bolts at trailing-edge. L-section main spar, dural web and dural auxiliary spar, with dural ribs. DFS-type metal airbrake above and below each wing. Fabric-covered metal ailerons and Fowler-type trailing-edge flaps. No tabs.

FUSELAGE: All-metal semi-monocoque structure, of oval cross-section, made up of frames, stringers and duralumin skin.

TAIL UNIT: Cantilever all-metal T-tail, of generally similar design and construction to that of IS-28 but with less tailplane dihedral. Trim tab in each elevator.

LANDING GEAR: Semi-retractable monowheel and non-retractable tailwheel. Manual retraction. Oleo-pneumatic shock-absorbers and disc brake on monowheel; rubber shock-absorber on tailwheel. Monowheel tyre size 330 × 135.

ACCOMMODATION: Seats for two persons in tandem under two-piece Plexiglas canopy, the rear portion of which can be jettisoned in flight. Small sliding window and additional air inlets for ventilation.

EQUIPMENT: Dual controls standard. Conventional stick and rudder-pedal controls, as in IS-28. Lever-controlled airbrake. Monowheel retraction and extension controlled by lever on right-hand side of cockpit. DFS-type nose tow-gear.

DIMENSIONS, EXTERNAL:
- Wing span: 55 ft $9\frac{1}{4}$ in (17·00 m)
- Wing aspect ratio: 16

Length overall 26 ft 9½ in (8·17 m)
Height overall 5 ft 10¾ in (1·80 m)

AREA:
Wings, gross 196·3 sq ft (18·24 m²)

WEIGHTS AND LOADINGS:
Weight empty 727 lb (330 kg)
Max T-O weight:
single-seat 925 lb (420 kg)
two-seat 1,146 lb (520 kg)
Max wing loading:
single-seat 4·71 lb/sq ft (23·0 kg/m²)
two-seat 5·84 lb/sq ft (28·5 kg/m²)

PERFORMANCE:
Best glide ratio:
single-seat at 42·5 knots (49 mph; 79 km/h) 32
two-seat at 47 knots (54 mph; 87 km/h) 32
Min sinking speed:
single-seat at 38 knots (43·5 mph; 70 km/h) 1·97 ft (0·60 m)/sec
two-seat at 39 knots (45 mph; 72 km/h) 2·30 ft (0·70 m)/sec
Stalling speed:
single-seat 32·5 knots (37·5 mph; 60 km/h)
two-seat 36 knots (41·5 mph; 66 km/h)
Max never-exceed speed:
single-seat 151 knots (174 mph; 280 km/h)
two-seat 129·5 knots (149 mph; 240 km/h)
g limits:
single-seat +6·5; —2·65
two-seat +5·3; —2·65

IS-29

The IS-29, designed under the leadership of Dipl Ing Iosif Silimon, can be adapted to suit a variety of requirements or weather conditions. All versions have an identical fuselage and tail unit, and a choice of wings is available. Four versions have so far been announced, as follows:

IS-29B. Standard Class version, with all-wooden wings of 15 m span, fitted with full-span metal ailerons and trailing-edge flaps. First flown in April 1970; certificated in September 1970.

IS-29D. Standard Class version, with all-metal 15 m span wings, fitted with ailerons, trailing-edge flaps and airbrakes. First flown in November 1970; certificated in 1971.

IS-29E. High-performance Open Class version, with all-metal 17·6 m span wings, fitted with ailerons, Fowler-type flaps and airbrakes. First flown in August 1971. Certification in progress in early 1973.

IS-29G. Club version, with all-metal 16·5 m span wings, fitted with ailerons, flaps and DFS-type airbrakes. Prototype completed in 1972. Certification in progress in early 1973.

The following description applies to all four versions, except where a specific model is indicated:

TYPE: Single-seat sailplane.

WINGS (IS-29B): Cantilever shoulder-wing monoplane. All-wood three-piece structure, consisting of a constant-chord centre-section, with four-point attachment to fuselage, and tapered outer panels. Flaps and metal ailerons over almost whole of trailing-edge. No airbrakes, spoilers or tabs.

WINGS (IS-29D, E and G): Cantilever shoulder-wing monoplane, with constant taper from root to tip. Wortmann wing sections: FX-61-165 at root, FX-61-124 at tip. All-metal structure, with I-section main spar and false rear spar and riveted dural skin. Full-span trailing-edge flaps (Fowler type on IS-29E) and ailerons. Airbrake (DFS type on IS-29G) in upper surface of each wing. No tabs.

FUSELAGE: All-metal semi-monocoque structure of frames, stringers and dural skin, identical on all versions except for local variations at wing attachment points. Detachable glassfibre nosecap.

TAIL UNIT: Cantilever all-metal T-tail. Two-spar fin, integral with fuselage, and single-spar rudder. One-piece tailplane, with auxiliary spar carrying inset trim tab.

LANDING GEAR: Manually-retractable monowheel, with brake, and non-retractable tail-wheel.

ACCOMMODATION: Single adjustable seat under two-piece Plexiglas canopy, the rear portion of which can be jettisoned in flight. Sliding window and additional inlet for cockpit ventilation.

EQUIPMENT: Conventional stick and rudder-pedal controls, consisting of levers, bars, cables and torsion axes beneath seat and cabin floor. Airbrakes, flaps, trim tabs and wheel brake are controlled by levers on left-hand side of cockpit, monowheel extension and retraction by a lever on the right.

DIMENSIONS, EXTERNAL:
Wing span:
B, D 49 ft 2½ in (15·00 m)
E 57 ft 9 in (17·60 m)
G 54 ft 1½ in (16·50 m)
Wing aspect ratio:
D 21·5
Length overall (all versions) 23 ft 0¾ in (7·03 m)
Height over tail (all versions) 5 ft 6¼ in (1·68 m)

AREAS:
Wings, gross:
B 128·3 sq ft (11·92 m²)
D 111·9 sq ft (10·40 m²)

IS-28B tandem two-seat high-performance training sailplane

IS-29B *(above)* **and IS-29D** *(below)* **single-seat Standard Class sailplanes produced by ICA-Brasov**

IS-29E single-seat high-performance Open Class sailplane, with 17·6 m span all-metal wings

E 137·6 sq ft (12·78 m²)
G 125·4 sq ft (11·65 m²)

WEIGHTS AND LOADINGS:
Weight empty:
B 529 lb (240 kg)
D 485 lb (220 kg)
E 606 lb (275 kg)
G 507 lb (230 kg)
Max T-O weight:
B 749 lb (340 kg)
D 705 lb (320 kg)
E 837 lb (380 kg)
G 727 lb (330 kg)
Max wing loading:
B 5·84 lb/sq ft (28·5 kg/m²)
D 6·31 lb/sq ft (30·8 kg/m²)
E 6·10 lb/sq ft (29·8 kg/m²)
G 5·80 lb/sq ft (28·3 kg/m²)

PERFORMANCE:
Best glide ratio:
B at 48·5 knots (56 mph; 90 km/h) 36
D at 48·5 knots (56 mph; 90 km/h) 37

E at 50 knots (57 mph; 92 km/h) 42
G at 48·5 knots (56 mph; 90 km/h) 39
Min sinking speed:
B at 36·5 knots (42·5 mph; 68 km/h) 2·03 ft (0·62 m)/sec
D at 42 knots (48·5 mph; 78 km/h) 1·90 ft (0·58 m)/sec
E at 41 knots (47·5 mph; 76 km/h) 1·64 ft (0·50 m)/sec
G at 39 knots (44·5 mph; 72 km/h) 1·84 ft (0·56 m)/sec
Stalling speed:
all versions 35·5 knots (40·5 mph; 65 km/h)
Max never-exceed speed:
all versions 118·5 knots (136·5 mph; 220 km/h)
g limits:
all versions +4·5; —3

IS-29G, club version of this design by Dipl Ing Silimon, with 16·5 m span all-metal wings

SWITZERLAND

EFF

ENTWICKLUNGSGEMEINSCHAFT FÜR FLUGZEUGBAU DER AKADEMISCHEN FLUGGRUPPE

EFF PROMETHEUS 1

The Prometheus 1 experimental powered sailplane was based on the airframe of the FFA Diamant 18. The aircraft flew for the first time on 21 June 1971, powered by a 176 lb (80 kg) st Microturbo Eclair II turbojet engine, and was described and illustrated in the 1973-74 *Jane's*. It has since been restored to standard Diamant configuration.

FFA

FLUG- UND FAHRZEUGWERKE AG

HEAD OFFICE AND WORKS:
Altenrhein, CH-9422 Staad b/Rorschach

Telephone: 071 414141
Telex: 77230 FFA Altenrhein
OFFICERS: see "Aircraft" section

In addition to its work on powered aircraft, FFA has also built in recent years a high-performance sailplane named the Diamant, full details of which appeared in the 1972-73 *Jane's*.

FFA has no other sailplane activities at present.

NEUKOM

ALBERT NEUKOM SEGELFLUGZEUGBAU

ADDRESS:
Flugplatz Schmerlat, CH-8213 Neuenkirch

Latest sailplanes built by Mr Neukom and three fellow-workers are the Standard Elfe S-3 and S-15A, Elfe S-17A and Super-Elfe AN-66C, of which all available details follow:

NEUKOM STANDARD ELFE S-3

The S-1 prototype of this Standard Class sailplane, which flew for the first time on 1 May 1964, had Vee tail surfaces. The Standard Elfe S-2 had a conventional tail unit, with the tailplane at the base of the fin. The production-type Standard Elfe S-3, first flown in May 1966, has the tailplane mounted part-way up the fin. Twenty-five Standard Elfe S-3 sailplanes had been built by early 1973.

Piloted by Markus Ritzi, a Standard Elfe gained 2nd place in the 1965 World Gliding Championships. In the Standard Class competition at the 1968 Championships in Poland, an Elfe S-3 piloted by Andrew Smith of the USA came first out of 57 entries, with George Moffat of the USA fourth and Urs Bloch of Switzerland sixth in similar aircraft.

The Standard Elfe S-3 is a cantilever high-wing monoplane, utilising a Wortmann FX wing section. The wing, which is built in three parts, is of plywood-balsa sandwich construction, and is fitted with trailing-edge airbrakes. Fuselage and tail unit are of glassfibre and plywood sandwich construction. The landing gear comprises a rubber-sprung retractable monowheel, size 330 × 130, with brake. The cockpit is fitted with a removable transparent canopy.

DIMENSIONS, EXTERNAL:
Wing span 49 ft 2½ in (15·00 m)
Wing aspect ratio 19
Length overall 23 ft 11½ in (7·30 m)
Height over tail 4 ft 11 in (1·50 m)
Tailplane span 9 ft 6¼ in (2·90 m)
AREAS:
Wings, gross 128·1 sq ft (11·90 m²)
Ailerons (total) 9·15 sq ft (0·85 m²)
Airbrakes (total) 12·38 sq ft (1·15 m²)
WEIGHTS AND LOADING:
Weight empty 463 lb (210 kg)
Max T-O weight 705 lb (320 kg)
Max wing loading 5·54 lb/sq ft (26·9 kg/m²)
PERFORMANCE:
Best glide ratio at 51·2 knots (59 mph; 95 km/h) 37·5
Min sinking speed at 41 knots (47 mph; 75 km/h) 2·07 ft (0·63 m)/sec
Stalling speed 30 knots (34 mph; 55 km/h)
Max speed (smooth air) 130 knots (150 mph; 240 km/h)
Max speed (rough air) 108 knots (124 mph; 200 km/h)

NEUKOM STANDARD ELFE S-15A

Previously known as the Elfe S-4, this is a developed version of the S-3, from which it differs principally by having a two-piece strengthened wing with Schempp-Hirth airbrakes and a more roomy forward fuselage of all-plastics construction and better aerodynamic form. The prototype flew for the first time in 1970, and a total of 10 had been built by early 1973. Production continues, though at a relatively slow rate. The S-15A is also available in kit form for amateur construction.

Neukom Standard Elfe S-3 single-seat Standard Class sailplane (*Dr U. Haller*)

Neukom Standard Elfe S-15A single-seat Standard Class sailplane (*Dr U. Haller*)

DIMENSIONS, EXTERNAL:
Wing span 49 ft 2½ in (15·00 m)
Wing aspect ratio 19
Length overall 23 ft 11½ in (7·30 m)
AREA:
Wings, gross 128·1 sq ft (11·90 m²)
WEIGHTS AND LOADING:
Weight empty 496 lb (225 kg)
Max T-O weight 760 lb (345 kg)
Max wing loading 5·98 lb/sq ft (29·2 kg/m²)
PERFORMANCE:
Best glide ratio at 48·5 knots (56 mph; 90 km/h) 38
Min sinking speed 1·94 ft (0·59 m)/sec
Stalling speed 38 knots (43·5 mph; 70 km/h)
Max speed (rough or smooth air) 118·5 knots (136·5 mph; 220 km/h)

NEUKOM ELFE S-17A

The Elfe S-17A is a 17 metre version of the S-15A, employing the same fuselage, but having a two-piece wing of increased span. One water ballast tank in each wing leading-edge to contain a total of 132 lb (60 kg) water. A braking parachute is carried on this version.

A total of 10 S-17As had been built by the Spring of 1973. Production continues, though at a relatively slow rate. The S-17A is also available in kit form for amateur construction.

DIMENSIONS, EXTERNAL:
Wing span 55 ft 9¼ in (17·00 m)
Wing aspect ratio 22·2
Length overall 23 ft 11½ in (7·30 m)
AREA:
Wings, gross 140 sq ft (13·00 m²)

WEIGHTS AND LOADING:

Weight empty	551 lb (250 kg)
Max T-O weight without ballast	815 lb (370 kg)
Max T-O weight with ballast	948 lb (430 kg)
Max wing loading	5·84 lb/sq ft (28·5 kg/m^2)

PERFORMANCE:

Best glide ratio at 48·5 knots (56 mph; 90 km/h)	40
Min sinking speed at 40·5 knots (46·5 mph; 75 km/h)	1·80 ft (0·55 m)/sec
Stalling speed	38 knots (43·5 mph; 70 km/h)
Max speed (rough or smooth air)	118·5 knots (136·5 mph; 220 km/h)
Max aero-tow speed	78 knots (90 mph; 145 km/h)
Max winch-launching speed	59 knots (68 mph; 110 km/h)

NEUKOM SUPER-ELFE AN-66C

This is a development of the AN-66-2 (see 1972-73 *Jane's*) having the same fuselage, but with an entirely new wing of Eppler 562/569 section and conventional instead of Vee-type tail surfaces. The wing is of plywood-balsa-plywood sandwich construction, with a single duralumin spar, and is built in three parts. The centre-section is 21 ft 4 in (6·50 m) in length, the two outer panels each 27 ft 0¾ in (8·25 m) in length. A water ballast tank to contain 132 lb (60 kg) of water is situated in the leading-edge of each wing, and Schempp-Hirth airbrakes are fitted. Main interest lies in a newly-designed aerofoil flap which is able to increase the wing area by about 20%.

A prototype has been built, and this began flight testing on 11 September 1973 at Butzweilerhof in Germany.

FUSELAGE: Forward portion is a glassfibre sandwich structure, rear portion a wood semi-monocoque.

LANDING GEAR: Retractable monowheel and tail-skid.

ACCOMMODATION: Single seat under long flush transparent canopy.

DIMENSIONS, EXTERNAL:

Wing span	75 ft 5½ in (23·00 m)
Wing aspect ratio:	
flaps in	33·1
flaps out	27·6
Length overall	26 ft 6¾ in (8·10 m)
Height over tail	6 ft 0¾ in (1·85 m)

AREAS:

Wings, gross:	
flaps in	172 sq ft (16·00 m^2)
flaps out	207 sq ft (19·20 m^2)

WEIGHTS AND LOADINGS:

Weight empty	926 lb (420 kg)
Normal T-O weight	1,168 lb (530 kg)
Max T-O weight with ballast	1,433 lb (650 kg)
Wing loading at normal T-O weight:	
flaps in	6·8 lb/sq ft (33·1 kg/m^2)
flaps out	5·65 lb/sq ft (27·6 kg/m^2)
Wing loading at max T-O weight:	
flaps in	8·3 lb/sq ft (40·6 kg/m^2)
flaps out	6·9 lb/sq ft (33·8 kg/m^2)

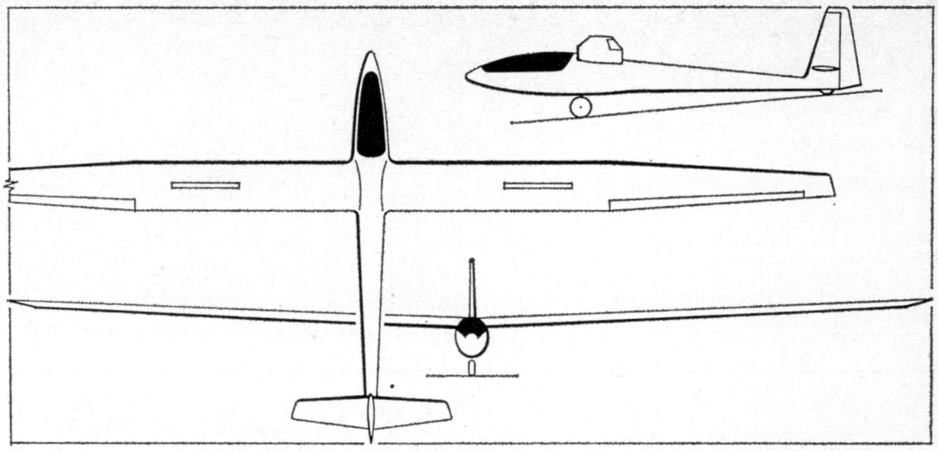

Neukom Elfe S-17A increased-span version of the S-15A, with water ballast (*Tony Mitchell*)

Neukom Super-Elfe AN-66C high-performance sailplane (*Pio dalla Valle*)

PERFORMANCE:

Best glide ratio at 48·5 knots (56 mph; 90 km/h)	48
Min sinking speed at 40·5 knots (46·5 mph; 75 km/h)	1·64 ft (0·50 m)/sec
Stalling speed	33 knots (37·5 mph; 60 km/h)
Max speed (smooth air)	145·5 knots (168 mph; 270 km/h)

PILATUS

PILATUS FLUGZEUGWERKE AG

HEAD OFFICE AND WORKS:
CH-6370 Stans, near Lucerne
Telephone: (041) 61 14 46
Telex: 78 329

OFFICERS: See "Aircraft" section

PILATUS B4-PC11

Pilatus designed and built this single-seat Standard Class sailplane for multi-purpose training and limited aerobatics.

Swiss certification was granted on 12 June 1972, and the first delivery was made shortly afterwards. By January 1974 deliveries had been made to customers in 20 countries in all parts of the world, and output was being increased to 150 per year.

TYPE: Single-seat Standard Class sailplane.

WINGS: Cantilever shoulder-wing monoplane. Wing section NACA 64_3-618. Dihedral 1°. Incidence 1° 30′. No sweepback. Conventional light alloy structure with PVC ribs. Conventional ailerons of similar construction. Mid-chord spoilers of light alloy construction on wing upper surfaces. No trim tabs.

FUSELAGE: Semi-monocoque structure of light alloy.

TAIL UNIT: Cantilever structure of light alloy with PVC ribs. T-type tail. Tailplane has fixed incidence. Elevator trimming by bias spring.

LANDING GEAR: Non-retractable (optionally retractable) main wheel, and fixed tailwheel, in tandem. Tost main wheel and tyre size 5·50-5. No shock-absorbers. Mechanical drum brake. Main wheel faired by doors when retracted.

ACCOMMODATION: Single semi-reclining seat under transparent cockpit canopy. Canopy is hinged for access to cockpit and is jettisonable in flight. Cockpit is ventilated. Battery, radio and oxygen system optional.

Pilatus B4-PC11 single-seat Standard Class sailplane

DIMENSIONS, EXTERNAL:

Wing span	49 ft 2½ in (15·00 m)
Wing chord at root	3 ft 6 in (1·07 m)
Wing chord at tip	1 ft 5 in (0·43 m)
Wing chord (mean)	3 ft 1 in (0·94 m)
Wing aspect ratio	16
Length overall	21 ft 6¾ in (6·57 m)
Height overall	5 ft 1¾ in (1·57 m)

AREAS:

Wings, gross	151 sq ft (14·04 m^2)
Ailerons (total)	12·4 sq ft (1·15 m^2)
Fin	9·69 sq ft (0·9 m^2)
Rudder	4·95 sq ft (0·46 m^2)
Tailplane	12·4 sq ft (1·15 m^2)

WEIGHTS AND LOADING:

Weight empty, equipped	529 lb (240 kg)
Max T-O weight	771 lb (350 kg)
Max wing loading	5·1 lb/sq ft (25·0 kg/m^2)

PERFORMANCE (at max T-O weight):

Best glide ratio at 46 knots (53 mph; 85 km/h)	35
Min sinking speed at 39 knots (45 mph; 72 km/h)	2·1 ft (0·64 m)/sec
Max never-exceed speed (rough or smooth air)	129 knots (149 mph; 240 km/h)
Max aero-tow speed	97·5 knots (112 mph; 180 km/h)
Max winch-launching speed	70 knots (80·5 mph; 130 km/h)
Stalling speed	34·5 knots (39·5 mph; 63 km/h)
g limits	+ 6·32; — 4·32

SCHLEUNIGER

DR K. SCHLEUNIGER & CO

ADDRESS:
Universitäts-Strasse, Zürich

This company is marketing a one-man hang-glider, with which the pilot normally wears skis as landing gear. With a T-O run of 33-66 ft (10-20 m) downhill, it has flown for distances varying from 655-3,280 ft (200-1,000 m) and attained a speed of 21·5 knots (25 mph; 40 km/h).

DIMENSIONS:

Wing span	23 ft 5 in (7·14 m)
Length overall	17 ft 8½ in (5·40 m)

WEIGHT:

without pilot	72·5 lb (33 kg)

Schleuniger hang-glider in use in Hokkaido, Japan, where it made several flights during January 1974. The pilot is using a roller-skate "landing gear" instead of the more usual skis *(H. Seo)*

THE UNITED KINGDOM

BIRMINGHAM GUILD

THE BIRMINGHAM GUILD LTD

HEAD OFFICE AND WORKS:
Grosvenor Street West, Birmingham B16 8HL
Telephone: 021-643-6175/8

MANAGING DIRECTOR:
L. B. Suter

LONDON OFFICE:
34 Ely Place, Holborn Circus, London EC1N 6TD

SAILPLANE DESIGN LTD

HEAD OFFICE:
All Saints Street, Hereford
Telephone: 0432-5250

DIRECTORS:
Air Cdre L. P. Moore, CBE, CEng, FIERE, AFRAeS
D. Moore
J. C. Gibson, DCAe
K. Emslie, CEng, AFRAeS, AMIMechE, DCAe

Sailplane Design Ltd undertook designs to provide a low-cost lightweight sailplane in which either a medium-performance 12 metre wing or a Standard Class 15 metre wing could be fitted to a common fuselage and tail unit. This project eventually took form as the BG 100/12 and BG 100/13·5 prototypes (1972-73 *Jane's*) and the BG Gipsy 135 production version evolved from them (1973-74 *Jane's*). In 1973, Birmingham Guild sold manufacturing rights in the aircraft to Yorkshire Sailplane Ltd (which see), by whom it is continuing in production under the name Consort. Sailplane Design Ltd continues to be responsible for all design matters connected with the aircraft.

HOLMES

KENNETH HOLMES

ENQUIRIES TO:
H. A. Torode, 19A High Street, Emberton, Olney, Buckinghamshire

HOLMES KH-1

The KH-1 is a high-performance sailplane of homebuilt construction, and was entirely designed and built by Mr Kenneth Holmes, a meteorologist. Design began in 1968, construction started in the following year, and the KH-1 flew for the first time on 24 November 1971. It was test-flown at Cranfield by the BGA's Bedfordshire test group, was awarded an "experimental" C of A in May 1972, and has since been flown in regional gliding competitions, proving to be comparable with contemporary production sailplanes. A second KH-1 is under construction.

TYPE: Single-seat high-performance homebuilt sailplane.

WINGS: Cantilever shoulder-wing monoplane. Wortmann wing sections: FX-61-184 at root, FX-60-126 at tip. Dihedral 2° from roots. Incidence 3°. Constant chord from root to two-thirds of each half-span, then tapering to tip. I-section composite main spar at 40% chord, with light alloy booms joined to plywood webs by Araldite bonding and pop-rivets. First 50% of chord covered with pre-moulded plywood/balsa sandwich; next 20% covered in 2 mm plywood; rear 30% fabric-covered. Wooden plain ailerons. Small-span trailing-edge airbrake/flaps inboard, near root, for control during approach. No spoilers or tabs.

FUSELAGE: Low-profile all-wood semi-monocoque structure, with four spruce longerons and plywood frames, covered with 2 mm birch ply (double-skinned in high-stress areas).

TAIL UNIT: All-wood cantilever structure. One-piece all-moving tailplane, with geared anti-balance tabs and spring trim.

LANDING GEAR: Retractable unsprung mono-wheel (tyre pressure 45-50 lb/sq in; 3·16-3·52 kg/cm²) and tail bumper. Tail parachute fitted for control during approach and for speed-limiting purposes.

ACCOMMODATION: Single reclining seat under long transparent moulded canopy made in two detachable pieces. Pilot parachute standard.

Holmes KH-1 amateur-built high-performance sailplane *(H. A. Torode)*

DIMENSIONS, EXTERNAL:

Wing span	60 ft 8½ in (18·50 m)
Wing chord at root	2 ft 3 in (0·69 m)
Wing chord at tip	10½ in (0·27 m)
Wing mean aerodynamic chord	1 ft 11½ in (0·60 m)
Wing aspect ratio	31
Length overall	23 ft 9 in (7·24 m)
Height overall	5 ft 0 in (1·52 m)
Tailplane span	7 ft 6 in (2·29 m)

AREAS:

Wings, gross	120·0 sq ft (11·15 m²)
Trailing-edge flaps (total)	10·0 sq ft (0·93 m²)
Vertical tail surfaces (total)	11·0 sq ft (1·02 m²)
Tailplane, incl tabs	12·0 sq ft (1·11 m²)

WEIGHTS AND LOADING:

Weight empty, equipped	490 lb (222 kg)
Max T-O weight	710 lb (322 kg)
Max wing loading	5·92 lb/sq ft (28·9 kg/m²)

PERFORMANCE (at max T-O weight):

Best glide ratio at 48 knots (55·5 mph; 89 km/h)	37
Stalling speed	36 knots (41·5 mph; 67 km/h)
Max speed (smooth air)	85 knots (98 mph; 157 km/h)
Max speed (rough air) and max aero-tow speed	75 knots (86·5 mph; 139 km/h)
g limits	+5; −2·5

MANUEL

WILLIAM L. MANUEL

ENQUIRIES TO:
H. A. Torode, 19A High Street, Emberton, Olney, Buckinghamshire

MANUEL HAWK

Mr W. L. Manuel, previously noted for a number of sailplane designs which culminated in the Willow Wren of *ca* 1930, designed the present Hawk glider as a project during his retirement. It was built at Fairoaks airfield in Surrey during 1968-70 and was then taken to the College of Aeronautics at Cranfield, where structural investigation was conducted under the direction of Mr Howard A. Torode, Research Fellow in Sailplane Aerodynamics at the Cranfield Institute of Technology. After preliminary modification it made its first flight on 25 November 1972.

On completion of a flight test programme the

Hawk was awarded a BGA "experimental" C of A, which has since been updated to a full C of A. At the PFA "Flying For Fun" rally in 1973 it was awarded third place in the "Best Homebuilt" competition, and by the end of the year had flown a total of about 45 hours.

A full description and illustration of the Hawk appeared in the 1973-74 *Jane's*; the following details amend those given on page 577 of that edition:

Max wing loading 3·99 lb/sq ft (19·5 kg/m²)
g limits +4; —1·5

SIGMA

OPERATION SIGMA LTD

ADDRESS:
Lower Farm, Inkpen Common, Newbury, Berkshire RG15 0QU
Telephone: Inkpen 297

DIRECTOR:
Rear-Admiral H. C. N. Goodhart, CB, RN(Retd)

SIGMA 1

A single Sigma prototype has been built, with the aim of establishing the practical merits of the special Sigma wing design for high-performance sailplanes.

The design features a very high aspect ratio wing, fitted with a full-span flap to give both variable area and variable camber.

The aircraft flew for the first time on 12 September 1971, and during ensuing test and development flying many aspects of handling and performance were developed to a satisfactory level.

Further work on the project has been suspended for the time being. A full description and illustration appeared in the 1973-74 *Jane's*.

TYPE: Single-seat very high performance Open Class sailplane.

DIMENSIONS, EXTERNAL:
Wing span 68 ft 10¾ in (21·00 m)
Wing aspect ratio (flap in) 36·2
Length overall 28 ft 10⅞ in (8·81 m)
Height overall, excl tailwheel 6 ft 0 in (1·83 m)

AREAS:
Wings, gross:
flap in 131·2 sq ft (12·2 m²)
flap out 177·6 sq ft (16·5 m²)

WEIGHTS AND LOADING:
Weight empty, equipped 1,340 lb (607 kg)
Max T-O weight 1,550 lb (703 kg)
Max wing loading 11·8 lb/sq ft (57·6 kg/m²)

PERFORMANCE (estimated):
Best glide ratio at 63 knots (72·5 mph; 116·7 km/h) 48
Stalling speed 37·5 knots (43 mph; 69·5 km/h)
Max speed (smooth air) 140 knots (161 mph; 259 km/h)
Max speed (rough air) and max aero-tow speed 110 knots (127 mph; 204 km/h)
Max winch-launching speed Not permitted
g limits +5; —3

SLINGSBY

SLINGSBY SAILPLANES (A Division of Vickers Limited Shipbuilding Group)

HEAD OFFICE AND WORKS:
Kirkbymoorside, Yorkshire YO6 6EZ
Telephone: Kirkbymoorside (075 13) 31751
Telex: 57911

MANAGING DIRECTOR: G. E. Burton, BSc, ARCS

GENERAL MANAGER:
W. N. Slater, CEng, AFRAeS

CHIEF ENGINEER:
J. S. Tucker, Dip Tech(Eng), BSc(Eng), CEng, AFRAeS

PRODUCTION MANAGER (AIRCRAFT):
P. Smith

SALES MANAGER:
J. A. Brayshaw, AFRAeS

Slingsby Sailplanes, a division of Vickers Ltd Shipbuilding Group, was formed from the assets of the former Slingsby Aircraft Company, which went into liquidation in July 1969.

Present aircraft production is limited to two sailplanes: the Slingsby T.59D 19 metre Kestrel, which is a development of the 17 metre Kestrel produced by Glasflügel of Germany; and the T.61, which is the SF-25B powered sailplane built under licence from Scheibe GmbH of Germany.

The company also operates a repair and spares service for sailplanes manufactured by the former Slingsby Aircraft Company.

A total of approximately 200 people were employed by Slingsby in January 1972. No news has been received from the company of its activities since that time.

SLINGSBY T.59D (GLASFLÜGEL) KESTREL 19

Under licence from Glasflügel of Germany (which see), Slingsby has produced the Kestrel single-seat Open Class sailplane, both in its standard 17 metre form and in a 19 metre development version as the Slingsby T.59D (first flown in July 1971).

Production of Slingsby-built Kestrels began in June 1971, and 11 had been delivered (five 17 metre and six 19 metre) by December 1971. No information has been received of any production since that time.

Slingsby also completed a special 19 metre Kestrel, which is designated T.59C and has a carbon-fibre main spar. This aircraft made its first flight on 7 May 1971.

In 1973 Kestrel 19 m sailplanes achieved first place in the Finnish national championships and shared, with the German-built Kestrel 17 m, second to ninth places (inclusive) in the British championships. They also secured six of the first 28 places in the 1974 World Championships at Waikerie, Australia.

A description of the standard 17 metre Kestrel appears under the Glasflügel heading in this section; the following description applies to the Slingsby T.59D 19 metre version:

TYPE: Single-seat high-performance Open Class sailplane.

WINGS: Similar to 17 metre version but of increased span. Wortmann wing sections: FX-67-K-170 at root, FX-67-K-150 at tip. Dihedral 3° 15′. Incidence 0° 30′. Schempp-Hirth airbrake on each upper surface.

FUSELAGE AND TAIL UNIT: Similar to 17 metre Kestrel, but fixed-incidence tailplane of reduced span, with separate elevators.

LANDING GEAR: Retractable Tost monowheel, size 5·00-5 Type 3, tyre pressure 40-45 lb/sq in (2·8-3·2 kg/cm²). Mechanical retraction. No shock-absorption. Tost internal-expanding brake. Fixed tailwheel.

ACCOMMODATION: As 17 metre version.

DIMENSIONS, EXTERNAL:
Wing span 62 ft 4 in (19·00 m)
Wing chord (mean) 2 ft 2⅝ in (0·674 m)
Wing aspect ratio 28
Length overall 21 ft 7¾ in (6·60 m)
Height over tail 4 ft 9⅞ in (1·47 m)
Tailplane span 7 ft 5¾ in (2·28 m)

AREAS:
Wings, gross 138·5 sq ft (12·87 m²)
Ailerons (total) 3·36 sq ft (0·31 m²)
Flaps (total) 6·55 sq ft (0·61 m²)
Airbrakes (total) 1·75 sq ft (0·16 m²)
Fin 10·76 sq ft (1·00 m²)
Rudder 4·30 sq ft (0·40 m²)
Tailplane 14·00 sq ft (1·30 m²)
Elevators 3·45 sq ft (0·32 m²)

WEIGHTS AND LOADING:
Weight empty, equipped 699 lb (317 kg)
Max T-O weight (with ballast) 1,040 lb (471 kg)
Max landing weight 960 lb (435 kg)
Max wing loading 7·5 lb/sq ft (36·9 kg/m²)

PERFORMANCE (at max T-O weight):
Best glide ratio at 52 knots (60 mph; 96 km/h) 44
Min sinking speed at 40 knots (46 mph; 74 km/h) 1·7 ft (0·52 m)/sec
Stalling speed 33 knots (38 mph; 61 km/h)
Max speed (smooth air) 135 knots (155·5 mph; 250 km/h)
Max speed (rough air) 105 knots (121 mph; 194·5 km/h)
Max aero-tow speed 81 knots (93 mph; 150 km/h)
Max winch-launching speed 70 knots (80·5 mph; 129·5 km/h)
g limit + 5·3

Slingsby T.59D 19 metre version of the Kestrel single-seat sailplane

Slingsby T.61, licence-built version of the Scheibe SF-25B powered sailplane (*Dr Alan Beaumont*)

SLINGSBY T.61 (SCHEIBE SF-25B) FALKE

Production of the Slingsby-built Falke began in 1970, and a total of 35 had been built by January 1973.

A description of the SF-25B appears under the Scheibe heading in the German section of this edition.

TORVA

TORVA SAILPLANES LTD

ADDRESS:
Westland Road, Park Farm Industrial Estate, Leeds, Yorkshire LS11
Telephone: Leeds 709111
WORKS:
Outgang Lane, Pickering, Yorkshire
Telephone: Pickering 3491

Torva designed and built a prototype 15 metre sailplane designated Torva 15, the first British-designed sailplane constructed in glass-reinforced plastics (GRP). This prototype was described and illustrated in the 1971-72 and 1972-73 *Jane's*.

Two developed versions, known as the Sprite and Sprint, are believed to be in production, although no confirmation of this, or any other information, has been received from the company for the past two years.

TORVA 15 SPRITE and SPRINT

Designations: TA Series 2 Sprite and TA Series 3 Sprint

TYPE: Single-seat sailplane for training and recreational use (Sprite) and recreational and competition flying (Sprint).

WINGS: Cantilever shoulder-wing monoplane. Modified Wortmann wing section. Thickness/chord ratio 16·2%. Dihedral 3° on leading-edge. Incidence 1° 30′. No sweepback. Composite structure, with GRP spar with ply webs and GRP/balsa shell. Top-hinged ailerons of GRP with foam core. Ailerons have variable differential. No flaps or tabs. Schempp-Hirth airbrakes of light alloy construction at approximately 50% chord. Water ballast tanks in Sprint only.

FUSELAGE: Semi-monocoque structure, with GRP shell and side longerons and plywood frames.

TAIL UNIT: Cantilever structure with GRP/balsa shells and plywood webs. All-moving tailplane with geared anti-balance tab. Variable gear ratio. Tab datum varied for longitudinal trim.

LANDING GEAR: Non-retractable sprung monowheel and nosewheel in Sprite, retractable sprung monowheel only in Sprint. Both models have GRP sprung tailskid with small wheel. Monowheel has "Aeon" rubber spring shock-absorption. Manual retraction with bungee counter-balance. Torva main wheel, size 12·00-4; tyre pressure 20-30 lb/sq in (1·4-2·1 kg/cm²). Torva tailwheel with solid tyre, size 3·00-0·75. Torva internal expanding brake.

ACCOMMODATION: Single seat under Suntex lift-off transparent canopy. GQ five-point seat harness.

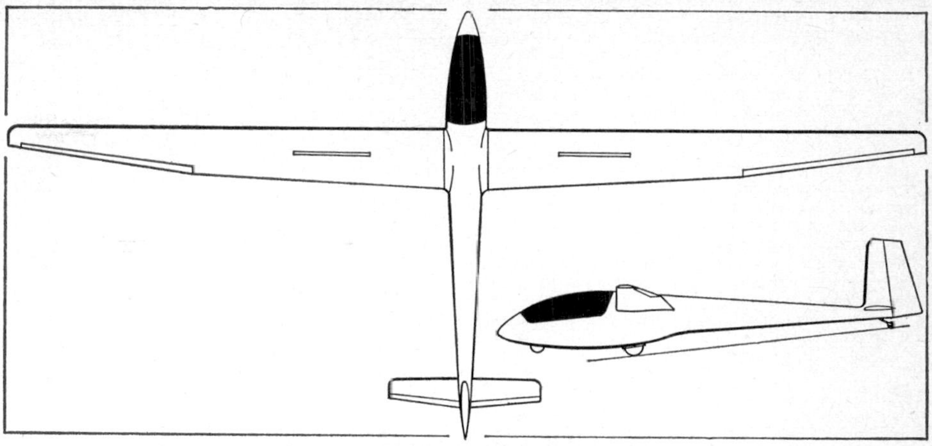

Torva TA Series 2 Sprite single-seat sailplane (*Sherwood Designs Ltd*)

DIMENSIONS, EXTERNAL:
Wing span 49 ft 2½ in (15·0 m)
Wing chord at root 3 ft 4 in (1·02 m)
Wing chord at tip 1 ft 2 in (0·36 m)
Wing chord, mean aerodynamic 2 ft 5½ in (0·75 m)
Wing aspect ratio 20
Length overall 23 ft 3¾ in (7·1 m)
Height overall 5 ft 0 in (1·52 m)
Tailplane span 8 ft 3 in (2·51 m)

AREAS:
Wings, gross 121·5 sq ft (11·3 m²)
Ailerons (total) 7·00 sq ft (0·65 m²)
Vertical tail surfaces (total) 10·40 sq ft (0·97 m²)
Horizontal tail surfaces (total) 11·35 sq ft (1·05 m²)

WEIGHTS AND LOADINGS:
Weight empty:
Sprite 530 lb (240 kg)
Sprint 525 lb (238 kg)
Max T-O weight:
Sprite 770 lb (349 kg)
Sprint 900 lb (408 kg)
Max landing weight:
Sprint 770 lb (349 kg)
Max wing loading:
Sprite, Sprint (without ballast) 6·35 lb/sq ft (31·0 kg/m²)
Sprint (with ballast) 7·37 lb/sq ft (36·0 kg/m²)

PERFORMANCE (estimated, at 700 lb; 317 kg AUW):
Best glide ratio:
Sprite 36
Sprint 36·5
Min sinking speed:
Sprite, Sprint 1·85 ft (0·56 m)/sec
Sinking speed at 55 knots (63·5 mph; 102 km/h):
Sprite, Sprint 3·40 ft (1·04 m)/sec
Stalling speed:
Sprite, Sprint 33 knots (38 mph; 61·5 km/h)

YORKSHIRE

YORKSHIRE SAILPLANES LTD

ADDRESS:
Melmerby Industrial Estate, Green Lane, Melmerby, near Ripon, Yorkshire HG4 5HP
Telephone: Melmerby 391
EXECUTIVES:
G. Kemp
J. Beck

This company has acquired the rights in the Slingsby T.53.B, and is producing a modified version of this sailplane as the YS 53 Sovereign. In 1973 it also acquired the manufacturing rights for the former Birmingham Guild Gipsy sailplane, which it is building as the YS 55 Consort.

YORKSHIRE SAILPLANES YS 53 SOVEREIGN

The original Slingsby T.53 tandem two-seat all-metal sailplane flew for the first time on 9 March 1967, and was followed by 16 T.53.Bs (see 1969-70 *Jane's*) and a single T.53.C (1971-72 *Jane's*), the latter having a modified wing spar and less sweepforward of the wing.

The YS 53 Sovereign is a further modification of the design, of which a prototype (converted from T.53.B airframe c/n 1721) flew for the first time on 10 February 1973. Main differences from the T.53.B are the modified tail unit, with larger-area vertical and horizontal surfaces, and a nosewheel instead of a nose-skid. The first production Sovereign flew for the first time on 21 July 1973, and deliveries were due to begin in December 1973.

TYPE: Tandem two-seat training sailplane.

WINGS: Cantilever shoulder-wing monoplane. Wing section Wortmann FX-61-184. Dihedral 3°. Incidence 5° 40′. Sweepforward 5° at quarter-chord. All-metal two-spar constant-chord structure of light alloy. Light alloy mass-balanced ailerons, with geared tabs. No flaps. Schempp-Hirth balanced airbrake on each upper and lower surface at approx one-third of each half-span. Spring trim system at 65·5% chord (upper surfaces) and 63·2% (lower surfaces).

FUSELAGE: Light alloy semi-monocoque structure.

TAIL UNIT: Cantilever light alloy structure, with tailplane mounted high on fin. One-piece fixed-incidence tailplane, with internal spring trim inside fuselage.

LANDING GEAR: Non-retractable Slingsby nosewheel (size 4·00-3·5), Tost main wheel (size 350 × 150 mm) and tailskid. Dunlop tyre, pressure 35·4 lb/sq in (2·5 kg/cm²), on each wheel. Shock-absorption by Armstrong damper units.

ACCOMMODATION: Two seats in tandem under sideways-hinged framed canopy. Small windows in port side of canopy for cockpit ventilation. Basic instruments standard on both panels. Optional items include oxygen and radio.

DIMENSIONS, EXTERNAL:
Wing span 55 ft 9¼ in (17·00 m)
Wing chord (constant) 3 ft 6 in (1·07 m)
Wing aspect ratio 15·9
Length overall 25 ft 3 in (7·70 m)
Height over tail 4 ft 7¼ in (1·40 m)
Tailplane span 11 ft 2½ in (3·405 m)

AREAS:
Wings, gross 194·0 sq ft (18·02 m²)
Ailerons (total) 19·05 sq ft (1·77 m²)
Airbrakes (total) 7·00 sq ft (0·65 m²)
Fin 17·85 sq ft (1·66 m²)
Rudder 7·35 sq ft (0·68 m²)
Tailplane 25·00 sq ft (2·32 m²)
Elevator 8·75 sq ft (0·81 m²)

WEIGHTS AND LOADINGS:
Weight empty, equipped 800 lb (362 kg)
Max T-O weight:
semi-aerobatic and cloud flying 1,160 lb (526 kg)
Normal category 1,285 lb (582 kg)
Max wing loading 6·59 lb/sq ft (32·16 kg/m²)

PERFORMANCE:
Best glide ratio at 48 knots (55 mph; 89 km/h) 29
Min sinking speed at 42 knots (48 mph; 77·5 km/h 2·53 ft (0·77 m)/sec
Stalling speed 36 knots (41·5 mph; 67 km/h)
Max speed (smooth air) 123 knots (141·5 mph; 228 km/h)
Max speed (rough air) and max aero-tow speed 80 knots (92 mph; 148 km/h)
Max winch-launching speed 70 knots (80·5 mph; 130 km/h)
g limits +5·0; —2·5

YORKSHIRE SAILPLANES YS 55 CONSORT

The Consort is the current production version of the BG 135 Gipsy sailplane developed by Birmingham Guild, from whom Yorkshire Sailplanes acquired the manufacturing rights in 1973. Details of its development history appeared under the Birmingham Guild entry in the 1972-73 and 1973-74 *Jane's*.

A C of A was granted by the BGA in July 1972, and a batch of seven aircraft was laid down for delivery against firm orders. By 1 November 1973 three of these had flown and the other four were in the final assembly stage.

Sailplane Design Ltd continues to be responsible for all design matters concerning the Consort.

The following description applies to the initial production version:

TYPE: Single-seat sailplane.

WINGS: Cantilever shoulder-wing monoplane. Wortmann FX-61-168 wing section. Dihedral 3°. No incidence or sweepback. Two-spar box alloy, with fabric covering between main and rear spars. Plain aluminium alloy hinged ailerons and trailing-edge airbrakes. No tabs.

FUSELAGE: Conventional semi-monocoque structure of aluminium alloy frames, longerons and skin, with lifting handle at rear. Nose skin, cockpit hood and tailcone of glassfibre-reinforced plastics.

TAIL UNIT: Cantilever Vee-tail (included angle 90°) with aluminium alloy spars, ribs and skin.

Yorkshire Sailplanes YS 53 Sovereign two-seat training sailplane, modified from the Slingsby T.53.B

Both surfaces are all-moving, without separate elevators. Geared anti-balance and trim tabs.

LANDING GEAR: Unsprung fixed main wheel forward of CG, and leaf-sprung tailwheel. BG 5·00-5 main wheel with Dunlop or Goodyear tyre, pressure 20 lb/sq in (1·41 kg/cm²). External band brake. 4 in (10 cm) rubber/nylon tailwheel.

ACCOMMODATION: Contoured floor of cockpit forms seat. Adjustable backrest. One-piece transparent moulded canopy, which hinges sideways. Standard cockpit instrumentation and conventional controls; adjustable rudder pedals.

DIMENSIONS, EXTERNAL:
- Wing span — 44 ft 2 in (13·46 m)
- Wing chord (constant) — 2 ft 3½ in (0·69 m)
- Wing aspect ratio — 19·3
- Length overall — 19 ft 8 in (5·95 m)
- Height over tail — 5 ft 0 in (1·52 m)
- Tailplane span (horizontal projection) — 5 ft 5 in (1·65 m)

AREAS:
- Wings, gross — 101·0 sq ft (9·38 m²)
- Ailerons (total) — 6·48 sq ft (0·60 m²)
- Airbrakes (total) — 10·40 sq ft (0·97 m²)
- Tail surfaces (nett) — 16·30 sq ft (1·51 m²)
- Tail tabs (total) — 4·08 sq ft (0·38 m²)

WEIGHTS AND LOADING:
- Weight empty, equipped — 370 lb (168 kg)
- Max T-O weight — 600 lb (272 kg)
- Max wing loading — 5·93 lb/sq ft (29 kg/m²)

PERFORMANCE (estimated, at max T-O weight):
- Best glide ratio at 46 knots (53 mph; 85 km/h) — 33·5
- Min sinking speed at 40 knots (46 mph; 74 km/h) — 2·2 ft (0·67 m)/sec
- Stalling speed — 36 knots (41 mph; 66 km/h)
- Max speed (smooth air) — 118 knots (136 mph; 219 km/h)
- Max speed (rough air) — 79 knots (91 mph; 146 km/h)
- Max aero-tow speed — 71 knots (82 mph; 132 km/h)
- Max winch-launching speed — 60·5 knots (70 mph; 112·5 km/h)
- Design *g* limits (ultimate) — +7·5; —3·75

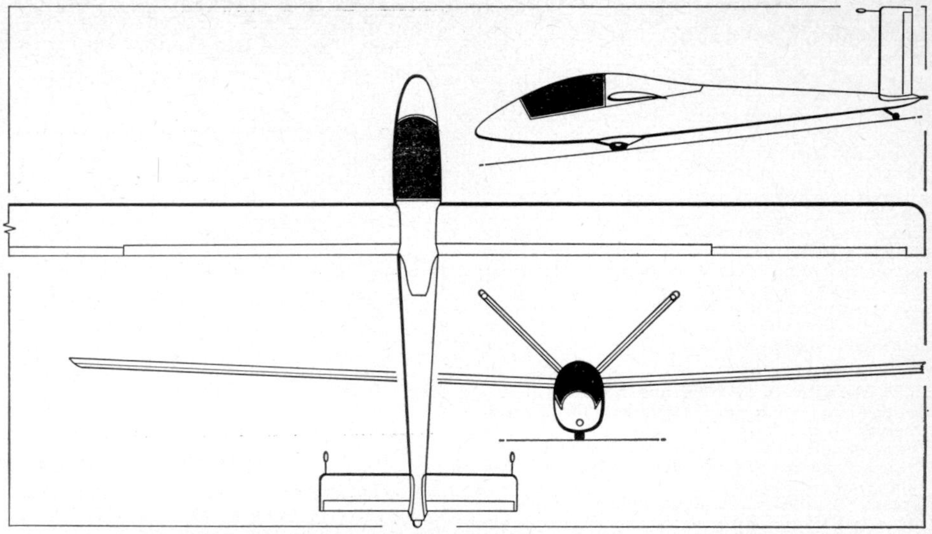

Yorkshire Sailplanes YS 55 Consort single-seat sailplane *(Sherwood Designs Ltd)*

THE UNITED STATES OF AMERICA

BERKSHIRE
BERKSHIRE MANUFACTURING CORPORATION

ADDRESS:
Berkshire Valley Road, Oak Ridge, New Jersey 07438
Telephone: (201) 697-2020

CONCEPT 70

Concept 70 is a single-seat Standard Class sailplane, which first flew in 1970, a year after the start of design work. Construction is almost entirely of glassfibre.

Production is under way, and 16 Concept 70s had been built by Spring 1974, at which time FAA certification was nearing completion.

TYPE: Single-seat Standard Class sailplane.

WINGS: Cantilever shoulder-wing monoplane. Eppler-Wortmann wing sections, with thickness/chord ratio of 15%. Dihedral 2°. Incidence 2°. Glassfibre/PVC foam sandwich structure, with constant-chord centre-section and tapered outer panels. Aluminium 90° flap on each trailing-edge, between wing root and aileron. Ten-position trim. All control surfaces actuated by push/pull rods with ball-bearings.

FUSELAGE: Glassfibre monocoque structure, reinforced with steel tube frame in centre and cockpit sections.

TAIL UNIT: Cantilever type, of similar construction to wings. Fixed-incidence tailplane. Cable-actuated rudder; elevators actuated by push/pull rods with ball-bearings. Rudder pedals adjustable in flight.

LANDING GEAR: Manually-retractable Tost monowheel (size 4·00-4, tyre pressure 35 lb/sq in; 2·5 kg/cm²) and breakaway tailskid. Drum brake.

ACCOMMODATION: Single semi-reclining seat, recessed for American-type parachute; backrest is adjustable in flight. One-piece flush Plexiglas canopy is hinged and jettisonable, and is fitted with sliding window and turnout air vent.

A Berkshire Concept 70 glassfibre Standard Class sailplane about to land

EQUIPMENT: Standard equipment includes basic cockpit instrumentation; retractable tow coupling; wave-trap antenna built into fin, with co-axial cable to panel; quickly-detachable instrument cover; oxygen bottle mounts; and two baggage compartments. Optional equipment includes wingtip protective wheels; 200 lb (91 kg) water ballast system; wheel-up warning system; radio (to customer's choice); tinted canopy; and Althaus venturi.

DIMENSIONS, EXTERNAL:
- Wing span — 49 ft 2½ in (15·00 m)
- Wing chord (centre-section, constant) — 3 ft 0 in (0·91 m)
- Wing chord at tip — 1 ft 5 in (0·43 m)
- Wing aspect ratio — 20
- Length overall — 24 ft 0 in (7·315 m)
- Height over tail — 6 ft 0 in (1·83 m)
- Tailplane span — 8 ft 5 in (2·565 m)

AREA:
- Wings, gross — 124·0 sq ft (11·52 m²)

WEIGHTS AND LOADING:
- Weight empty, equipped — 500 lb (226 kg)
- Max T-O weight with ballast — 875 lb (396 kg)
- Max wing loading — 7·20 lb/sq ft (35·14 kg/m²)

PERFORMANCE (at max T-O weight):
- Best glide ratio at 52 knots (60 mph; 96·5 km/h) — 40
- Min sinking speed at 43·5 knots (50 mph; 80·5 km/h) — 2·03 ft (0·62 m)/sec
- Stalling speed, flaps up — 31·5 knots (36 mph; 58 km/h)
- Max speed (rough or smooth air) — 105 knots (121 mph; 194·5 km/h)
- Max aero-tow speed — 78 knots (90 mph; 144·5 km/h)
- *g* limit — + 6

BRIEGLEB
SAILPLANE CORPORATION OF AMERICA

ADDRESS:
El Mirage Rt, Box 101, Adelanto, California 92301
Telephone: (714) 388-4343
PRESIDENT: William G. Briegleb

Mr William G. Briegleb formed the Sailplane Corporation of America (see 1967-68 *Jane's*) to market gliders of his own design.

The BG 12 series of sailplanes were available as complete aircraft, as kits of parts or in the form of plans, for amateur construction. By early 1970 at least 219 kits and plans had been supplied and about 70 aircraft were known to have been completed.

After a temporary stoppage the company is again marketing plans and/or kits of parts for the BG 12BD and BG 12-16 sailplanes.

BRIEGLEB BG 12BD and BG 12-16

The BG 12 series are single-seat high-performance sailplanes, the prototype of which flew for the first time in 1956. All ribs and bulkheads are cut from plywood and construction is similar to that of a model aeroplane. Standard wing span of 50 ft 0 in (15·24 m) may be clipped to 49 ft 2½ in (15·00 m) at builder's option.

The earlier BG 12, BG 12A and BG 12B models were described in the 1972-73 *Jane's*. The two models currently available are:

BG 12BD. Two-piece wing with thicker section at root. Welded control system. First BG 12B production model flew in July 1973. The BD is similar except that there is no change in wing incidence between root and tip. The control system has an input action at the low speed range that deflects the ailerons upward to give the same effect as "twist".

BG 12-16. Development of BG 12BD having a slimmer fuselage, longer flaps and all-flying horizontal tail surfaces, which give a glide ratio up to two points better than the BD model. First flown in June 1969.

The following description applies to the BG 12BD, except where indicated:

TYPE: Single-seat high-performance sailplane.

WINGS: Cantilever high-wing monoplane. Wing section NACA 4415R at root, NACA 4406R at tip. Dihedral 1°. Incidence 4° from root to tip. All-wood structure, with plywood covering. Plywood-covered wooden ailerons and trailing-edge flaps. Flaps used as airbrakes at speeds up to 112 knots (130 mph; 210 km/h).

FUSELAGE: Cutout plywood bulkheads, spruce longerons, plywood-covered.

TAIL UNIT (BG 12BD): Cantilever wooden structure. Ground-adjustable tailplane incidence. No tabs.

TAIL UNIT (BG 12-16): Cantilever structure, with sweptforward fin and plywood-covered rudder. All-flying horizontal surfaces of glassfibre-covered metal construction, built in two halves and fitted with anti-servo tabs.

LANDING GEAR: Shock-mounted nose-skid and sprung tailwheel or tailskid. Non-retractable unsprung monowheel with tyre size 10·50 × 4 or (BG 12-16) 12 × 4 × 5, manufactured by General Tire × Rubber Co. Tyre pressure 35 lb/sq in (2·5 kg/cm²). Briegleb circumferential brake.

ACCOMMODATION: Single seat under large moulded Plexiglas canopy. Adjustable seat and rudder pedals.

DIMENSIONS, EXTERNAL:
- Wing span — 50 ft 0 in (15·24 m) *or* 49 ft 2½ in (15·00 m)
- Wing chord at root — 3 ft 9 in (1·14 m)
- Wing chord at tip — 1 ft 0¼ in (0·31 m)
- Wing aspect ratio — 17·9

Length overall:
- 12BD 21 ft 11 in (6·68 m)
- 12-16 24 ft 0 in (7·32 m)

Height overall:
- 12BD 4 ft 0 in (1·22 m)
- 12-16 4 ft 2 in (1·27 m)

AREAS:
- Wings, gross (full span) 141·0 sq ft (13·10 m²)
- Ailerons (total) 14·00 sq ft (1·30 m²)
- Trailing-edge flaps (total):
  - 12BD 13·45 sq ft (1·25 m²)
  - 12-16 14·00 sq ft (1·30 m²)
- Fin:
  - 12BD 2·05 sq ft (0·19 m²)
  - 12-16 4·50 sq ft (0·42 m²)
- Rudder:
  - 12BD 7·00 sq ft (0·65 m²)
  - 12-16 6·70 sq ft (0·62 m²)
- Tailplane (12BD) 10·75 sq ft (1·00 m²)
- Elevators (12BD) 6·15 sq ft (0·57 m²)
- Horizontal tail surfaces (12-16, total incl tabs) 9·25 sq ft (0·86 m²)

WEIGHTS AND LOADINGS:
- Weight empty 500-525 lb (227-238 kg)
- Max T-O weight:
  - 12BD 750 lb (340 kg)
  - 12-16 850 lb (385 kg)
- Max wing loading:
  - 12BD 5·32 lb/sq ft (26·0 kg/m²)
  - 12-16 6·03 lb/sq ft (29·4 kg/m²)

PERFORMANCE:
- Best glide ratio:
  - 12BD at 45 knots (52 mph; 84 km/h) 33-34
  - 12-16 at 48·5 knots (56 mph; 90 km/h) 34-36
- Min sinking speed:
  - 12BD at 41 knots (47 mph; 76 km/h) 2·26 ft (0·69 m)/sec
  - 12-16 at 42 knots (48 mph; 77·5 km/h) 2·25 ft (0·685 m)/sec
- Stalling speed, flaps up:
  - 12BD 33 knots (38 mph; 61 km/h)
  - 12-16 34 knots (39 mph; 63 km/h)
- Stalling speed, flaps down:
  - 12BD 29 knots (33 mph; 53 km/h)
  - 12-16 30 knots (34 mph; 55 km/h)
- Max speed (smooth air):
  - 12BD, 12-16 121 knots (140 mph; 225 km/h)
- Max speed (rough air) and max aero-tow speed:
  - 12BD, 12-16 112 knots (130 mph; 210 km/h)
- Max winch-launching speed:
  - 12BD, 12-16 65 knots (75 mph; 121 km/h)
- *g* limit +10

Briegleb BG 12 series single-seat Standard Class sailplane

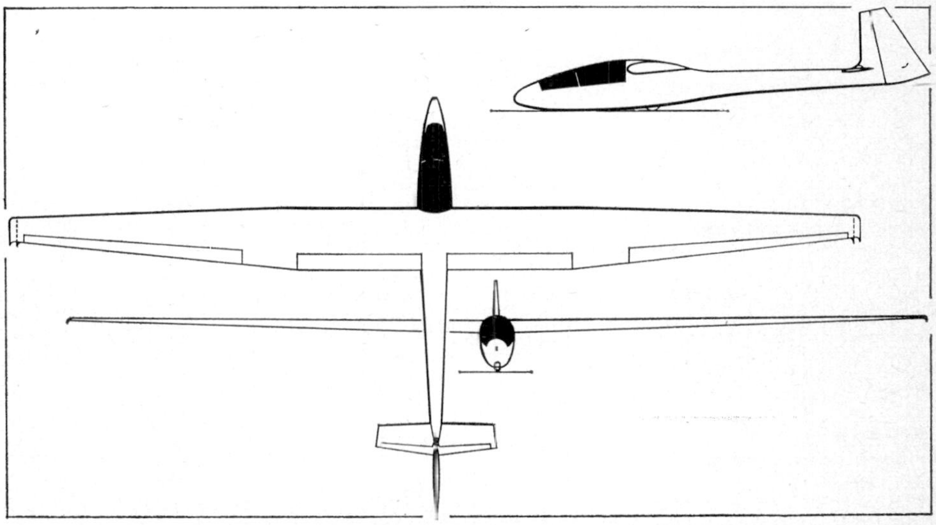

Briegleb BG 12-16 single-seat sailplane, with all-flying horizontal tail
(Sherwood Designs Ltd)

BRYAN

BRYAN AIRCRAFT, INC

HEAD OFFICE AND WORKS:
Williams County Airport, PO Box 488, Bryan, Ohio 43506

Telephone: (419) 636-1340

DIRECTOR:
R. E. Schreder

Details of earlier designs by Mr Schreder can be found under the "Airmate" heading in the 1965-66 *Jane's* and under the "Bryan" heading in the 1973-74 edition.

The company is currently producing plans and kits for the RS-15 high-performance Standard Class sailplane, and is building a prototype of the HP-18, a more recent design.

BRYAN (SCHREDER) RS-15

This 15 metre sailplane has been designed by Mr Schreder to meet current OSTIV Standard Class specifications. It is designed for simple, rapid assembly by the homebuilder and is licensed in the amateur-built Experimental category. No jigs are required, and most major components are prefabricated, to reduce assembly time to approx 500 man-hours for a builder with average mechanical aptitude.

TYPE: Single-seat high-performance Standard Class sailplane.

WINGS: Cantilever shoulder-wing monoplane. Wing section Wortmann FX-67-150. Dihedral 2° 18′. Incidence 2°. All-metal structure except for polyurethane foam plastics ribs spaced at 4 in (102 mm) centres. Main wing spar caps pre-machined from solid aluminium plate stock. Water ballast carried inside wing box spars. Plain ailerons. Optional trailing-edge flaps/airbrakes, of aluminium sheet bonded to foam ribs, which can be linked with ailerons.

FUSELAGE: Monocoque structure. Prefabricated glassfibre forward pod, complete with bulkheads, floorboards and finish; 6 in (152 mm) diameter aluminium tube tailboom.

TAIL UNIT: All-metal "V" tail which can be folded upward for towing or storage.

LANDING GEAR: Manually-retractable monowheel, size 500 × 5, and non-retractable steerable tailwheel. Hydraulic shock-absorbers on main and tailwheel. Hydraulic brake on main wheel.

ACCOMMODATION: Single seat under one-piece Plexiglas canopy. Retractable tow hitch.

DIMENSIONS, EXTERNAL:
- Wing span 49 ft 2½ in (15·00 m)
- Wing aspect ratio 21·4
- Length overall 22 ft 0 in (6·71 m)
- Height overall, tail extended 3 ft 10 in (1·17 m)
- Height overall, tail folded 5 ft 0 in (1·52 m)

DIMENSIONS, INTERNAL:
- Cockpit: Length 5 ft 6 in (1·68 m)
  - Depth 3 ft 0 in (0·91 m)
  - Width 2 ft 0 in (0·61 m)

AREAS:
- Wings, gross 113·0 sq ft (10·5 m²)
- Trailing-edge flaps (total) 20·5 sq ft (1·90 m²)
- Fixed tail surfaces (total) 8·5 sq ft (0·79 m²)
- Movable tail surfaces (total) 7·0 sq ft (0·65 m²)

WEIGHTS AND LOADINGS:
- Weight empty 440 lb (200 kg)
- Normal T-O weight 740 lb (335 kg)
- Max T-O weight with water ballast 940 lb (426 kg)
- Normal wing loading 6·5 lb/sq ft (31·7 kg/m²)
- Max wing loading 8·3 lb/sq ft (40·5 kg/m²)

PERFORMANCE:
- Best glide ratio 38
- Min sinking speed at 43·5 knots (50 mph; 80·5 km/h), AUW of 626 lb (284 kg) 2·1 ft (0·64 m)/sec
- Stalling speed, flaps up, AUW of 740 lb (335 kg) 40 knots (45·7 mph; 74 km/h)
- Stalling speed, flaps down, AUW of 740 lb (335 kg) 32·5 knots (37·4 mph; 60·5 km/h)
- Max speed (smooth air) 130 knots (150 mph; 241 km/h)
- Max speed (rough air) and max aero-tow speed 104 knots (120 mph; 193 km/h)
- Max winch-launching speed 78 knots (90 mph; 145 km/h)

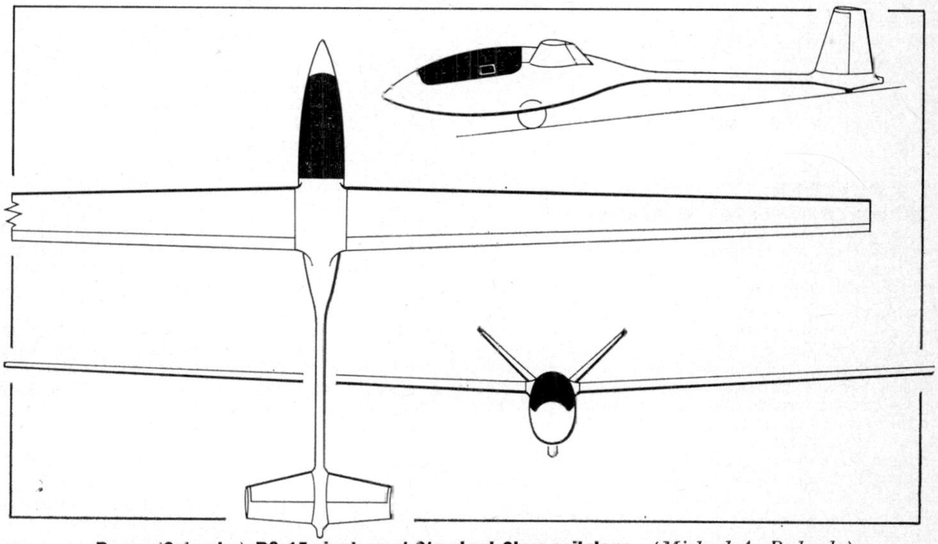

Bryan (Schreder) RS-15 single-seat Standard Class sailplane *(Michael A. Badrocke)*

BRYAN (SCHREDER) HP-18

The HP-18 is a high-performance single-seat 15 metre sailplane, designed to meet current OSTIV Standard Class requirements. Generally similar in appearance to the RS-15, it has a slightly longer fuselage, with circular instead of oval section, and other features designed to reduce drag and produce a superior competition aircraft. These include better gap seals, new wingtips, removable tailwheel and better streamlining; the Tost monowheel has a tyre pressure of 30 lb/sq in (2·11 kg/cm²) and is fitted with a mechanically-expanding brake. Construction of a prototype began in December 1973; 11 had been ordered by April 1974.

The structural description of the RS-15 applies generally also to the HP-18; specification of the HP-18 is as follows:

DIMENSIONS, EXTERNAL:
- Wing span 49 ft 2½ in (15·00 m)
- Wing chord at root 3 ft 0 in (0·91 m)
- Wing chord at tip 1 ft 6 in (0·46 m)
- Wing mean aerodynamic chord 2 ft 3 in (0·69 m)

Wing aspect ratio 21·1
Length overall 23 ft 6 in (7·16 m)
Height overall, tail extended 4 ft 0 in (1·22 m)
Height overall, tail folded 5 ft 2 in (1·57 m)

DIMENSIONS, INTERNAL:
Cockpit: Length 5 ft 10 in (1·78 m)
Depth 2 ft 3 in (0·69 m)
Width 2 ft 0 in (0·61 m)

AREAS:
Wings, gross 114·7 sq ft (10·66 m^2)
Ailerons (total) 6·2 sq ft (0·58 m^2)
Trailing-edge flaps (total) 17·7 sq ft (1·64 m^2)
Fixed tail surfaces (total) 8·5 sq ft (0·79 m^2)
Movable tail surfaces (total) 7·0 sq ft (0·65 m^2)

WEIGHTS AND LOADINGS:
Weight empty 420 lb (191 kg)
Normal T-O weight 720 lb (326 kg)
Max T-O weight with water ballast 920 lb (417 kg)
Normal wing loading 6·3 lb/sq ft (30·8 kg/m^2)
Max wing loading 8·0 lb/sq ft (39·1 kg/m^2)

PERFORMANCE:
Best glide ratio 40
Min sinking speed at 39 knots (45 mph; 73 km/h), AUW of 606 lb (275 kg) 1·7 ft (0·52 m)/sec
Stalling speed, flaps up, AUW of 720 lb (326 kg) 35 knots (40 mph; 64·5 km/h)
Stalling speed, 60° flap, AUW of 720 lb (326 kg) 30·5 knots (35 mph; 57 km/h)
Max speed (smooth air) 130 knots (150 mph; 241 km/h)
Max speed (rough air) and max aero-tow speed 104 knots (120 mph; 193 km/h)
Max winch-launching speed 78 knots (90 mph; 145 km/h)
g limits ±12

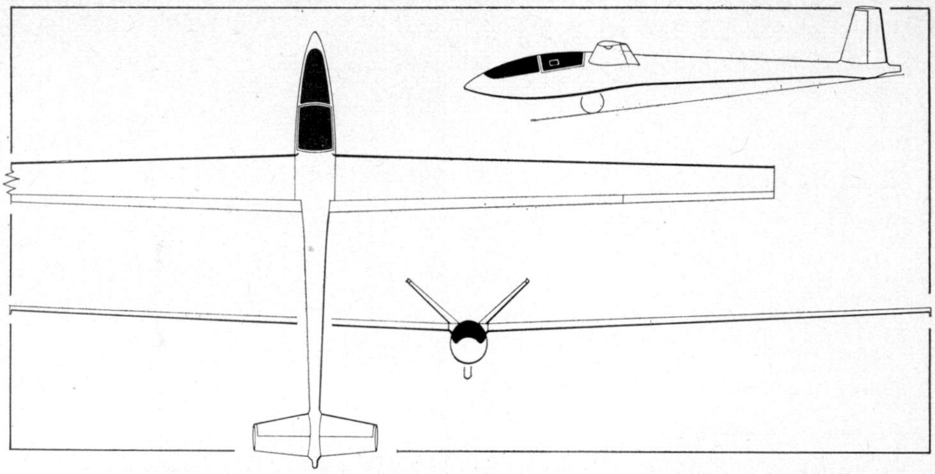

Bryan (Schreder) HP-18 sailplane, developed from the RS-15 (*Michael A. Badrocke*)

CARMICHAEL

DOUGLAS CARMICHAEL

ADDRESS:
PO Box 122-LS, Nipomo, California 93444

DC-HG-1

As a college senior project, Mr Carmichael has designed, built and flown a one-man hang-glider which he has designated DC-HG-1. First flight was made in 1973.

TYPE: One-man hang-glider.

AIRFRAME: High-wing monoplane configuration, with slight sweepback and marked dihedral. Constant-chord wings, braced by inverted-Vee struts on each side. Longitudinal boom supports one-piece tailplane, with full-span elevator, at rear; movable rudder ("yawleron") at each wingtip. Mixed construction of wood (Douglas fir and plywood) and metal (2024-T3 aluminium alloy), with aluminised mylar covering. Triangular hang-bars, connected by fore-and-aft bars, to support pilot. Elevator and rudders cable-controlled from right-hand twist-grip.

DIMENSION, EXTERNAL:
Wing span 32 ft 0 in (9·75 m)

WEIGHT:
Weight empty 63 lb (28·5 kg)

PERFORMANCE (initial testing):
Measured glide ratio 10
Stalling speed approx 11·5 knots (13 mph; 21 km/h)
Design *g* limit +3·5

EIPPER

EIPPER-FORMANCE INC

ADDRESS:
PO Box 246, Lomita, California 90717
Telephone: (213) 328-9100 or 775-3087
PROPRIETOR:
R. Eipper

This company supplies plans, kits and materials, or fully-assembled examples, of the Flexi-Flier/Flexi-Floater flexible-wing hang-gliders, as described in the separate section on these craft at the end of the "Sailplanes" section.

It also provides a similar service for the Quicksilver B rigid-aerofoil hang-glider described below:

EIPPER (LOVEJOY) QUICKSILVER B

The Quicksilver was designed by Mr Bob Lovejoy and made its first flight in August 1972. Two more were then built by Eipper-Formance Inc for flight testing and design evaluation, and with minor design changes this company now markets the aircraft as the Quicksilver B. It is available in ready-to-fly form or in various stages of kits for amateur construction. Kit assembly takes approx 45 hours.

TYPE: One-man hang-glider.

AIRFRAME: High-wing monoplane configuration, with rudder and one-piece horizontal tail surface supported on "U"-shaped rear boom. Kingpost above wing centre-section, triangle-bar assembly below. Entire framework of 6061-T6 anodised aluminium tubing, except for 6063-T832 rudder frame. Stainless steel bracing and rigging wires. Wing and tail surfaces covered in Dacron.

ACCOMMODATION: Swing seat, of heavy duty injection-moulded plastics, suspended from centre-section bar by Dacron rope.

DIMENSIONS, EXTERNAL:
Wing span 30 ft 0 in (9·14 m)
Wing aspect ratio 7·5

AREA:
Wings, gross 116 sq ft (10·78 m^2)

WEIGHT:
Weight empty 56 lb (25·4 kg)

PERFORMANCE:
Best glide ratio 7
Min sinking speed 250 ft (76·5 m)/min
Max speed 27·5 knots (32 mph; 51·5 km/h)
Cruising speed 19 knots (22 mph; 35·5 km/h)
Stalling speed 15 knots (17 mph; 27·5 km/h)
Design *g* limit +3·5

EXPLORER

EXPLORER AIRCRAFT COMPANY

ADDRESS:
5315 Palo Verde Drive, Edwards, California 93523
Telephone: (805) 258-5740

Explorer Aircraft Company is marketing plans of a biplane glider named the Aqua Glider. Designed by Colonel William L. Skliar, USAF, it is intended for tethered gliding by unlicensed pilots, towed behind any motor boat able to attain a speed of 30 knots (35 mph; 56 km/h). If the pilot has the necessary licence, he can cast off from the motor boat when airborne and make a free flight before landing back on the water.

Design of the Aqua Glider originated in September 1958, and construction of the prototype began in January 1959. Completed in June 1959, the first flight was made during the following month. Plans are available to amateur constructors and approx 1,000 sets have been sold in Argentina, Australia, the Bahamas, Brazil, Canada, France, Japan, Malaysia, Mexico, the Philippines, Portugal, Rhodesia, Singapore, South Africa, Spain, Sri Lanka, Sweden, Switzerland, the UK, the USA and South Vietnam. About 10 completed Aqua Gliders are known to have been flown, some in the US and Japan, and about 200 more are under construction.

The prototype, after making about 1,000 flights and being flown by about 60 pilots, was donated to the Experimental Aircraft Association Museum for permanent display.

EXPLORER PG-1 AQUA GLIDER

TYPE: Single-seat homebuilt waterborne glider.

WINGS: Forward-stagger single-bay biplane with N interplane and parallel centre-section struts. Wing section (both) NACA 4412. Dihedral 2° 30′ on lower wing only. Incidence 4°. No sweepback. Conventional single-spar wood structure with fabric covering. Spoiler-type ailerons of light alloy construction on lower wing only. No flaps. No trim tabs. Balancer floats at lower wingtips.

HULL: Unstepped watertight wooden structure of spruce with $\frac{1}{16}$ in mahogany plywood bow, bottom skins and sides. Plywood is glassfibre-covered below waterline. Tow hook at nose of hull.

TAIL UNIT: Wire-braced wooden spruce structure, with plywood and fabric covering, carried on welded steel tube or wire-braced wooden boom. All-moving one-piece tailplane with bungee trim. Conventional rudder.

LANDING GEAR: Standard jumper skis, 6 ft (1·83 m) in length, attached to small wire-braced struts below hull.

ACCOMMODATION: Single seat in open cockpit in hull, forward of wings.

DIMENSIONS, EXTERNAL:
Wing span:
upper 16 ft 0 in (4·88 m)
lower 15 ft 0 in (4·57 m)
Wing chord, constant (both) 3 ft 0 in (0·91 m)
Wing aspect ratio 5
Length overall 13 ft 8 in (4·17 m)
Height overall 5 ft 0 in (1·52 m)
Tailplane span 7 ft 0 in (2·13 m)

AREAS:
Wings, gross 94 sq ft (8·7 m^2)
Aileron/spoilers (total) 2 sq ft (0·19 m^2)
Fin approx 4 sq ft (0·37 m^2)
Rudder approx 3 sq ft (0·28 m^2)
Tailplane approx 18 sq ft (1·67 m^2)

WEIGHTS AND LOADING:
Weight empty 180 lb (81 kg)
Max T-O weight 400 lb (181 kg)
Max wing loading 4·2 lb/sq ft (20·5 kg/m^2)

PERFORMANCE:
Best glide ratio at 39 knots (45 mph; 72·5 km/h) 6·5
Minimum airspeed, at 330 lb (149 kg) gross weight 30·5 knots (35 mph; 56·5 km/h)
Maximum airspeed 56·5 knots (65 mph; 104·5 km/h)
g limit +4

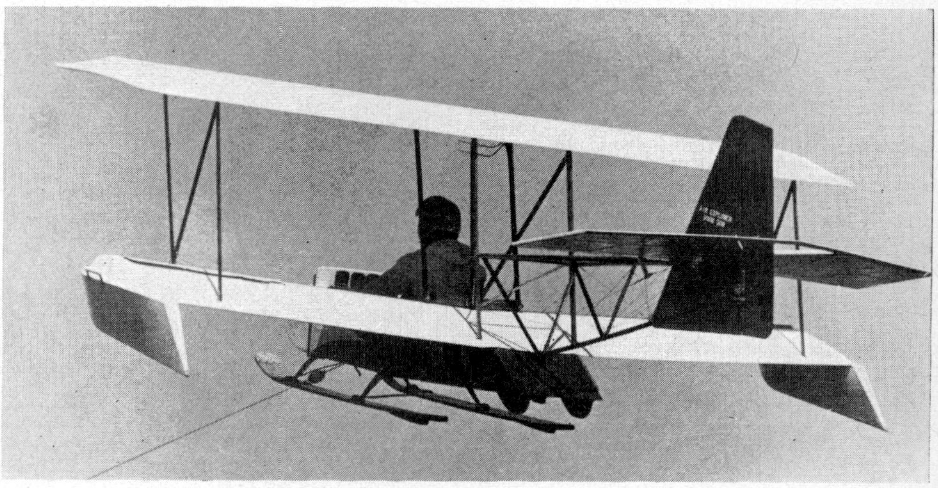

Explorer PG-1 Aqua Glider amateur-built biplane glider

KICENIUK

TARAS KICENIUK JR

ADDRESS:
Palomar Observatory, Palomar Mountain, California 92060
Telephone: (714) 742-3933

Mr Kiceniuk began in May 1971 the design of a tail-less sweptwing biplane hang-glider which he called Icarus. Other features of the design included washout, stagger, dihedral, and a reflex (upturned trailing-edge) wing section. It made its first flight in August 1971, and subsequently made several flights of 5 minutes' duration (terminated at the discretion of the pilot) in which it soared higher than its take-off point; but it was then damaged while being flown by an inexperienced pilot.

The aircraft was later rebuilt in improved form as the Icarus II, and a description of it in this form follows. By February 1974 more than 1,300 sets of Icarus plans and 50 kits had been sold. At least 12 others had been built and flown. Although hang-gliders are not subject to FAA regulations, the Icarus has been approved by the FAA as an amateur-built aircraft. A new hang-glider, the Icarus V, is now also available.

The Icarus II is available in kit form from Ultralight Flying Machines, PO Box 59, Cupertino, California 95014.

KICENIUK ICARUS II

TYPE: One-man amateur-built hang-glider.

WINGS: Sweptback staggered flying-wing biplane. Modified Eiffel 32 wing section. Thickness/chord ratio 7·75%. Dihedral approx 8°. Incidence 2° 15′ upper wing, 0° lower wing. Sweepback approx 15°. Aluminium tube leading-edge and trailing-edge spars, wood and styrofoam ribs, Dacron covering. Vertical balsa and plywood rudders, one attached to each outermost rear interplane strut, are actuated independently to provide strong lateral control because of the effects of sweep and dihedral angle. When actuated simultaneously, the rudders act as airbrakes. No other control surfaces are needed, pitch control being effected by pilot's body movement. Aircraft is inherently stable, and returns to straight and level flight when flown hands-off.

FUSELAGE, TAIL UNIT AND LANDING GEAR: None.

ACCOMMODATION: Pilot only, supported by webbing belt from upper wing.

DIMENSIONS:
Wing span 29 ft 0 in (8·84 m)
Wing chord (parallel to c/l, constant) 3 ft 4 in (1·02 m)
Wing stagger 1 ft 2 in (0·36 m)
Wing aspect ratio (geometric) 8·7
Length overall 9 ft 0 in (2·74 m)

AREAS:
Wings, gross 195·0 sq ft (18·12 m²)
Rudders (total) 6·0 sq ft (0·56 m²)

WEIGHTS AND LOADING:
Weight empty 55 lb (25 kg)
Max T-O weight 255 lb (115 kg)
Max wing loading 1·3 lb/sq ft (6·34 kg/m²)

PERFORMANCE:
Best glide ratio at 17 knots (20 mph; 32 km/h) 8
Min sinking speed at 17 knots (20 mph; 32 km/h) 3·5 ft (1·07 m)/sec
Stalling speed 15 knots (17 mph; 27 km/h)
Max speed (smooth air) 39 knots (45 mph; 72·5 km/h)
g limit +3
Max endurance attained 2 hr 26 min, landing at T-O site
Max height gained approx 1,000 ft (305 m) above T-O point, in thermals, during 53 min flight with continuous 360° spirals

Kiceniuk Icarus II sweptwing biplane hang-glider

Mr Taras Kiceniuk Jr, in first World War flying suit, at the start of a flight from Mt Palomar in the Icarus V monoplane hang-glider

KICENIUK ICARUS V

The Icarus V is a monoplane hang-glider, the prototype of which flew for the first time on 1 September 1973, and had completed more than 12 hours' flying by February 1974. More than half of its flights up to that time were of more than one hour's duration, and orders had been received for 20 sets of plans.

TYPE: One-man amateur-built hang-glider.

WINGS: Constant-chord sweptback flying-wing monoplane. TK 7315 high-lift, low-moment wing section. Dihedral from roots. Sweepback 20°. No incidence. Aluminium tube frame, foam sheet leading-edge, doped fabric covering. Dependent fin and rudder at each wingtip. As with Icarus II, yaw and roll control are achieved through use of the independently-controlled rudders, and pitch control by pilot weight shift. Aircraft can spiral continuously at bank angles of 60°, is extremely stable, and has a very gentle stall.

FUSELAGE, TAIL UNIT AND LANDING GEAR: None.

ACCOMMODATION: Pilot only, supported by aluminium tubular truss with "hang-tubes". Variometer, ASI and altimeter fitted.

DIMENSIONS:
Wing span 32 ft 0 in (9·75 m)
Wing chord (constant) 5 ft 0 in (1·52 m)
Wing aspect ratio 6·4
Length overall 12 ft 6 in (3·81 m)
Height overall 6 ft 0 in (1·83 m)

AREAS:
Wings, gross 160·0 sq ft (14·86 m²)
Fins (total) 3·0 sq ft (0·28 m²)
Rudders (total) 7·5 sq ft (0·70 m²)

WEIGHTS AND LOADING:
Weight empty 65 lb (29·5 kg)
Max T-O weight 285 lb (129 kg)
Max wing loading 1·78 lb/sq ft (8·7 kg/m²)

PERFORMANCE:
Best glide ratio at 17·5 knots (20 mph; 32 km/h) 10
Min sinking speed at 16 knots (18 mph; 29 km/h) 3·5 ft (1·07 m)/sec
Stalling speed 14 knots (16 mph; 26 km/h)
Max speed (smooth air) 43·5 knots (50 mph; 80·5 km/h)
g limit +6

LAISTER

LAISTER SAILPLANES INC

ADDRESS:
2712 Chico Avenue, South El Monte, California 91733
Telephone: (213) 442-4945

This company is marketing, in kit form only, a Standard Class 15 m sailplane designated LP-49, of which a description follows. Also described is the LP-15 Nugget, a Standard Class 15 m sailplane which is being produced, as the company's prime product, in factory-built form only.

LAISTER LP-49

Available in kit form only, the LP-49 is a 15 m Standard Class sailplane approved to 1970 FAI specifications and type certificated by the FAA. More than 50 kits had been sold by early 1974, and about 35 of these had been completed and flown.

TYPE: Single-seat Standard Class sailplane for amateur construction.

WINGS: Cantilever high-wing monoplane, with constant-chord centre-section and tapered outer panels. Extruded aluminium main spar booms, curved in chordwise direction to follow aerofoil section. Roll-contoured sheet aluminium skin, butted and flush-riveted with blind pop rivets. Glassfibre wingtip fairings. All-metal statically-balanced ailerons, with automatic hookup to prevent take-off without aileron control. Airbrake on each inboard trailing-edge, also with automatic control hookup.

FUSELAGE: Semi-monocoque structure, consisting of two pre-moulded glassfibre halves reinforced with aluminium bulkheads and fittings. Self-retracting tow-hook in nosecone.

TAIL UNIT: Cantilever type, with sweptback fin and rudder. Aluminium structure, with glassfibre tip fairings on tailplane, elevator and rudder. Rudder tip fairing houses rudder static balance; that for the elevator operates internally in rear end of fuselage.

LANDING GEAR: Retractable main wheel, glassfibre nose skid with steel shoe, and non-retractable shrouded tailwheel. Main-wheel shock-strut incorporates coil spring and dampener. Landing gear door rotates up into fuselage when main wheel is extended, to avoid damage. Main-wheel brake fitted.

ACCOMMODATION: Single seat (contoured seat optional) under one-piece moulded transparent canopy. Radio and oxygen system available.

DIMENSIONS, EXTERNAL:
Wing span 49 ft 2½ in (15·00 m)
Wing aspect ratio 17
Length overall 20 ft 7·2 in (6·28 m)

DIMENSION, INTERNAL:
Cockpit: Max width 1 ft 11 in (0·58 m)

AREA:
Wings, gross 143·0 sq ft (13·28 m²)

WEIGHTS:
- Weight empty 475 lb (215 kg)
- Max T-O weight 700 lb (317 kg)

PERFORMANCE:
- Best glide ratio at 43·5 knots (50 mph; 80·5 km/h) 33
- Min sinking speed at 37 knots (43 mph; 69 km/h) 1·9 ft (0·58 m)/sec
- Max never-exceed speed 156 knots (180 mph; 289 km/h)
- Max speed (rough or smooth air) 117 knots (135 mph; 217 km/h)
- Stalling speed 30·5 knots (35 mph; 56 km/h)

Laister LP-15 Nugget single-seat Standard Class sailplane

LAISTER LP-15 NUGGET

Design and construction of a prototype of the LP-15 began in February 1971, and this aircraft (N15LP) made its first flight in June 1971. Certification was expected in February 1973, at which time an initial quantity of 30 was in production. The LP-15 is supplied only as a factory-built aircraft.

TYPE: Single-seat Standard Class sailplane.

WINGS: Cantilever shoulder-wing monoplane. Wortmann wing sections. Thickness/chord ratio 17% at root, 15% at tip. Dihedral 3° from centre-section. Incidence 1°. Sweep-back at quarter-chord approx 1°. Chem-Weld bonded aluminium alloy structure. Long-span trailing-edge flaps with negative travel (up) for high-speed flight, 8° positive travel (down) for thermalling and 85° positive for landing or use as airbrakes. Top-hinged plain ailerons of similar construction. All control surfaces have internal static balances. No spoilers or tabs. Bungee pitch trim. Provision for 185 lb (84 kg) of water ballast, carried in centre-section, with filler cap behind cockpit canopy.

FUSELAGE: Semi-monocoque structure. Forward portion of moulded glassfibre, rear portion of bonded aluminium alloy.

TAIL UNIT: Cantilever T-tail structure of bonded aluminium alloy, with slightly-swept fin and rudder. Adjustable-incidence tailplane and one-piece elevator. All control surfaces have internal static balances. No tabs. Rudder pedals adjustable in flight.

LANDING GEAR: Manually-retractable monowheel (size 4·00-5, tyre pressure 35 lb/sq in; 2·5 kg/cm²) and tailskid. Monowheel has air-oil shock-absorption, with coil spring, and is fitted with a mechanically-operated internal brake.

ACCOMMODATION: Single semi-reclining seat under fully-transparent two-piece canopy with removable hood and sliding ventilation panel. Equipment, including oxygen and radio, is to customer's specification.

DIMENSIONS, EXTERNAL:
- Wing span 49 ft 2½ in (15·00 m)
- Wing chord at root 3 ft 0 in (0·91 m)
- Wing chord at tip 1 ft 2 in (0·35 m)
- Wing aspect ratio 22·1
- Length overall 20 ft 0 in (6·10 m)
- Height over tail 4 ft 2 in (1·27 m)
- Tailplane span 7 ft 10 in (2·39 m)

DIMENSION, INTERNAL:
- Cockpit: Max width 2 ft 0 in (0·61 m)

AREA:
- Wings, gross 109·0 sq ft (10·13 m²)

WEIGHTS AND LOADING:
- Weight empty, equipped 465 lb (210 kg)
- Max T-O weight (with water ballast) 900 lb (408 kg)
- Max wing loading (with water ballast) 7·35 lb/sq ft (35·87 kg/m²)

PERFORMANCE (at max T-O weight):
- Best glide ratio at 34·5 knots (40 mph; 64 km/h) 38
- Stalling speed, flaps up 34 knots (39 mph; 63 km/h)
- Max speed (rough or smooth air) 126 knots (145 mph; 233 km/h)
- Max aero-tow speed 86·5 knots (100 mph; 160 km/h)
- Max winch-launching speed 60·5 knots (70 mph; 112·5 km/h)
- g limit +12

MILLER

W. TERRY MILLER

ADDRESS:
Box 570, RR1, Furlong, Pennsylvania 18925

Mr Miller is the designer of the Tern high-performance sailplane for amateur construction. The prototype flew for the first time in September 1965.

An improved version, the Tern II, flew for the first time in August 1968. In that year brake parachutes were fitted to the prototype, and two types of parachute are now available for installation in the Tern or the Tern II, comprising a 6 ft (1·8 m) diameter cross parachute or a 5 ft (1·5 m) diameter guide surface parachute.

By February 1973, 21 Terns and 3 Tern IIs had flown, and Terns are under construction in the Argentine, Australia, Belgium, Canada, Puerto Rico, South Africa and the US.

A powered sailplane, the WM-2, designed by Mr Miller, flew for the first time in the Summer of 1972.

Miller Tern built by Mr George Allen of Weatherford, Texas, with a special 52 ft span wing and cockpit canopy from a Bryan (Schreder) HP-14

MILLER TERN

TYPE: Single-seat high-performance sailplane.

WINGS: Cantilever shoulder-wing monoplane. Wing section Wortmann FX-61-184 at root, Wortmann FX-61-163 at tip. Dihedral 2°. Incidence 2°. No sweep at 50% chord. Two-piece two-spar spruce structure, all plywood-covered. Plain all-wood ailerons. No flaps or tabs. Lower-surface airbrakes of wood construction used for glideslope control.

FUSELAGE: Semi-monocoque wood structure. Plastics-reinforced glassfibre nose. Plywood skin aft of cockpit.

TAIL UNIT: Cantilever all-wood structure, with modified NACA laminar-flow sections. Special hinge-line contouring to reduce drag and increase control effectiveness at large deflections. All control surfaces are 60% mass-balanced. No tabs.

LANDING GEAR: Non-retractable monowheel forward of CG, in streamlined pod. Skids under nose and tail. Wheel and tyre size 5·00-4. Brake lever applies pressure directly to tyre.

ACCOMMODATION: Single partially-reclining seat under transparent canopy, centre portion of which hinges sideways for access to cockpit. Standard seven-instrument panel. Space for radio.

DIMENSIONS, EXTERNAL:
- Wing span 51 ft 0 in (15·54 m)
- Wing chord at root 3 ft 4 in (1·02 m)
- Wing chord at tip 1 ft 10 in (0·56 m)
- Wing aspect ratio 20
- Length overall 21 ft 3½ in (6·49 m)
- Height over tail 5 ft 0 in (1·52 m)
- Tailplane span 8 ft 6 in (2·59 m)

AREAS:
- Wings, gross 130 sq ft (12·08 m²)
- Ailerons (total) 7·60 sq ft (0·71 m²)
- Airbrakes (total) 5·20 sq ft (0·48 m²)
- Fin 4·66 sq ft (0·43 m²)
- Rudder 5·00 sq ft (0·46 m²)
- Tailplane 7·82 sq ft (0·73 m²)
- Elevators 6·56 sq ft (0·61 m²)

WEIGHTS AND LOADING:
- Weight empty, equipped 475 lb (215 kg)
- Max T-O weight 700 lb (318 kg)
- Max wing loading 5·4 lb/sq ft (26·36 kg/m²)

PERFORMANCE:
- Best glide ratio at 50·4 knots (58 mph; 93 km/h) 36
- Min sinking speed at 41 knots (47 mph; 76 km/h) 2·1 ft (0·64 m)/sec
- Stalling speed 34 knots (39 mph; 63 km/h)
- Max speed (smooth air) 104 knots (120 mph; 193 km/h)
- Max speed (rough air) and max aero-tow speed 78 knots (90 mph; 145 km/h)
- Max winch-launching speed 61 knots (70 mph; 112 km/h)

MILLER TERN II

This developed version of the Tern differs from the original model in having a larger wing span. All details are as for Tern except:

DIMENSIONS, EXTERNAL:
- Wing span 55 ft 6 in (18·29 m)
- Wing chord at root 3 ft 4 in (1·02 m)
- Wing chord at tip 1 ft 8 in (0·51 m)
- Wing aspect ratio 22

AREAS:
- Wings, gross 140 sq ft (13·01 m²)
- Ailerons (total) 9·3 sq ft (0·86 m²)

WEIGHTS AND LOADING:
- Weight empty, equipped 550 lb (249 kg)
- Max T-O weight 800 lb (363 kg)
- Max wing loading 5·72 lb/sq ft (28 kg/m²)

PERFORMANCE (nominal):
- Best glide ratio at 52 knots (60 mph; 97 km/h) 38
- Min sinking speed at 41·7 knots (48 mph; 77 km/h) 1·95 ft (0·59 m)/sec
- Stalling speed 35 knots (40 mph; 64 km/h)
- Max speed (rough air) and max aero-tow speed 76 knots (88 mph; 142 km/h)

MILLER WM-2

The WM-2 is a low-powered, high-performance aircraft, designed by Mr W. Terry Miller for amateur construction. It was conceived originally for the exploration of soaring wave conditions and, with the engine operating, can simulate the performance of various types of sailplane, from low-performance training gliders to high-performance competition sailplanes. In addition, it is suitable for use as a high-altitude sporting aircraft.

Design began in 1967, and construction of a prototype aircraft (N24832) started in June 1969. This aircraft, built by Mr William Y. Miller of Allentown, Pennsylvania, made its first flight in August 1972.

Prototype Miller WM-2 high-performance single-seat powered sailplane

By August 1973 the prototype had logged more than 100 hours during flight tests. The engine and propeller can be stopped in flight below 61 knots (70 mph; 113 km/h) for soaring, and when dived to speeds above 69·5 knots (80 mph; 129 km/h) the propeller will "windmill" to restart the engine.

Type: Single-seat powered sailplane.

Wings: Cantilever low-wing monoplane. Modified NACA laminar-flow series wing sections. Thickness/chord ratio 15%. Dihedral 4°. Incidence 1°. Sweepback 0° 53′ at quarter-chord. Conventional structure of spruce spars, with birch plywood, glassfibre and fabric covering. Wooden ailerons. No flaps or tabs. Metal spoiler in each upper surface.

Fuselage: Conventional spruce structure, with birch plywood and glassfibre covering.

Tail Unit: Plywood- and fabric-covered spruce cantilever structure, with one-piece all-moving horizontal surface. No tabs.

Landing Gear: Manually-retractable monowheel (wheel and tyre size 6·00-6) and tailskid. Hydraulic brake.

Power Plant: One 65 hp Continental four-cylinder horizontally-opposed aircooled engine, driving a two-blade fixed-pitch metal propeller. Fuel tank, capacity 10 US gallons (8·3 Imp gallons; 37·8 litres), aft of firewall.

Accommodation: Single seat under one-piece sideways-opening bubble canopy.

Dimensions, external:
- Wing span: 40 ft 0 in (12·19 m)
- Wing chord at root: 4 ft 6 in (1·37 m)
- Wing chord at tip: 2 ft 6 in (0·76 m)
- Wing aspect ratio: 11·11
- Length overall: 20 ft 0 in (6·10 m)
- Height over tail: 5 ft 3 in (1·60 m)
- Tailplane span: 8 ft 0 in (2·44 m)
- Propeller diameter: 6 ft 2 in (1·88 m)

Areas:
- Wings, gross: 144·0 sq ft (13·38 m²)
- Ailerons (total): 16·00 sq ft (1·49 m²)
- Spoilers (total): 3·00 sq ft (0·28 m²)
- Vertical tail surfaces (total): 9·20 sq ft (0·85 m²)
- Horizontal tail surfaces (total): 12·50 sq ft (1·16 m²)

Weights and Loading:
- Weight empty, equipped: 775 lb (351 kg)
- Max T-O weight: 1,050 lb (476 kg)
- Max wing loading: 7·3 lb/sq ft (35·62 kg/m²)

Performance (at max T-O weight):
- Max never-exceed speed: 130 knots (150 mph; 241 km/h)
- Max level speed at S/L: 118 knots (136 mph; 219 km/h)
- Normal cruising speed at 10,000 ft (3,050 m), 50% power: 109 knots (126 mph; 203 km/h)
- Stalling speed: 39·5 knots (45 mph; 72·5 km/h)
- Max rate of climb at S/L: 890 ft (271 m)/min
- Service ceiling (computed): 24,000 ft (7,315 m)
- Range at normal cruising speed at 10,000 ft (3,050 m) with 30 min reserves: 291 nm (336 miles; 540 km)
- Best glide ratio at 54 knots (62 mph; 100 km/h), power off: 15

SCHWEIZER

SCHWEIZER AIRCRAFT CORPORATION

Head Office and Works:
Box 147, Elmira, New York 14902
Telephone: (607) 739-3821
Telex: 932459

President and Chief Engineer:
Ernest Schweizer

Vice-President and General Manager:
Paul A. Schweizer

Vice-President in Charge of Manufacturing:
William Schweizer

Sales Manager: W. E. Doherty, Jr

Asst Treasurer: Joseph Kroczynski

Secretary: Kenneth Tifft

Schweizer Aircraft Corporation is the leading American designer and manufacturer of sailplanes. Its current products include the SGS 2-33 two-seat general-purpose sailplane, the one-design SGS 1-26 single-seat high-performance sailplane (which is available complete and in kit form for the homebuilder), the SGS 2-32 two/three-seat high-performance sailplane, and the SGS 1-34 Standard Class single-seat high-performance sailplane.

By agreement with Grumman American, Schweizer also manufactures the Ag-Cat agricultural biplane, a description of which can be found under the Schweizer heading in the "Aircraft" section. Other subcontract work includes production of fuselage assemblies for Piper Aircraft Corporation and major structures for Bell Helicopter Company.

More recently, Schweizer has purchased the design and production rights in the Thurston Teal four-seat light amphibian, and a description of this appears under the Schweizer heading in the "Aircraft" section.

About 400 people were employed by Schweizer in 1974.

Schweizer SGS 1-26E single-seat medium-performance sailplane

Schweizer SGS 2-32 two/three-seat high-performance sailplane

SCHWEIZER SGS 1-26

This relatively small sailplane was developed for one-design class activities. It was designed to be produced both as a complete sailplane and in kit form for the homebuilder. The prototype 1-26 was first flown in January 1954, and with award of the FAA Type Certificate production of both complete sailplanes and kits began in November of that year.

To assist the homebuilder, all complicated structures and alignments requiring specialised tooling have been built by the manufacturer. Included is a basic welded fuselage assembly, production parts and shaped Plexiglas canopy. Completion of the kit requires 300 to 600 man-hours, depending on the skill and experience of the builder.

In kit form the sailplane is designated **SGS 1-26C**, and has a Ceconite-covered chrome-molybdenum steel tube fuselage. The current production version, the **SGS 1-26E**, introduced an all-metal semi-monocoque fuselage. More than 585 SGS 1-26 sailplanes had been produced by January 1974, of which approximately 200 were in kit form.

Type: Single-seat medium-performance sailplane.

Wings: Cantilever mid-wing monoplane. Dihedral 3° 30′. All-metal structure of aluminium alloy, with metal skin. Fabric-covered ailerons. Balanced airbrakes immediately aft of spar on each wing.

Fuselage: Welded chrome-molybdenum steel tube framework, covered with fabric on SGS 1-26C. Production SGS 1-26E has an all-metal semi-monocoque fuselage.

Tail Unit: Cantilever aluminium alloy structure, covered with fabric.

Landing Gear: Non-retractable unsprung monowheel, size 4·00-4, with Schweizer brake, aft of rubber-sprung nose-skid. Small solid rubber tailwheel.

Accommodation: Single seat under blown Plexiglas canopy. Provision for radio forward of pilot.

Equipment: Standard equipment includes fresh air vent, wheel cover, seat belt and shoulder harness, airspeed indicator and instrument panel.

Dimensions, external:
- Wing span: 40 ft 0 in (12·19 m)
- Wing aspect ratio: 10
- Length overall: 21 ft 6½ in (6·57 m)
- Height overall: 7 ft 2¼ in (2·21 m)
- Tailplane span: 7 ft 6 in (2·29 m)

Areas:
- Wings, gross: 160 sq ft (14·87 m²)
- Airbrakes (total): 2·78 sq ft (0·26 m²)

Weights and Loading:
- Weight empty: 430 lb (195 kg)
- Max T-O weight: 700 lb (317 kg)
- Max wing loading: 4·37 lb/sq ft (21·34 kg/m²)

Performance:
- Best glide ratio: 23
- Min sinking speed: 2·6 ft (0·79 m)/sec
- Stalling speed: 29 knots (33 mph; 54 km/h)
- Max permissible speed and max aero-tow speed: 99 knots (114 mph; 183 km/h)
- Max winch-launching speed: 55 knots (63 mph; 101 km/h)

SCHWEIZER SGS 2-32

The SGS 2-32 has an unusually large "aeroplane-type" cabin capable of carrying one very large or two average-sized passengers in addition to the pilot. The prototype flew for the first time on 3 July 1962. FAA Type Approval was received in June 1964 and production began immediately. More than 88 had been built by January 1974.

A number of world and national gliding records have been gained by pilots using this sailplane. Still current in early 1974 was the ladies' absolute height record for multi-seat sailplanes, of 31,230 ft (9,519 m), set up by A. Burns and J. Oetsch of Great Britain on 5 January 1967.

The SGS 2-32 sailplane was chosen by Lockheed Missiles & Space Company to form the basic airframe of its YO-3A quiet observation aircraft, and by E-Systems Inc for the L450F (see "RPVs and Targets" section).

Type: Two/three-seat high-performance and utility sailplane.

Wings: Cantilever mid-wing monoplane. Wing section NACA 63_3618 at root, NACA 43012A at tip. Dihedral 3° 30′. All-metal single-spar structure with metal covering. Fabric-covered metal ailerons. Speed-limiting airbrakes on upper and lower surfaces.

Fuselage: All-metal monocoque structure.

Tail Unit: Cantilever metal structure, with all-moving tailplane. Fin metal-covered; control surfaces fabric-covered. Adjustable trim tab in tailplane.

Landing Gear: Non-retractable unsprung monowheel, wheel and tyre size 6·00-6, with hydraulic brake, and skid.

Accommodation: Pilot at front. Seat for one or two persons at rear. Dual controls. Rear control column removable for passenger comfort. Sideways-opening blown Perspex canopy.

Equipment: Lined cockpit, front and rear cabin air vents, seat belts and shoulder harnesses standard. Optional items include electrical and oxygen systems, radio, special instrumentation, canopy locks, cushions, map cases and wingtip wheels.

Dimensions, external:
- Wing span: 57 ft 1 in (17·40 m)

Wing chord at root 4 ft 9 in (1·45 m)
Wing chord at tip 1 ft 7 in (0·48 m)
Wing aspect ratio 18·05
Length overall 26 ft 9 in (8·15 m)
Fuselage width at cockpit 2 ft 8 in (0·81 m)
Tailplane span 10 ft 6 in (3·20 m)

AREAS:
Wings, gross 180 sq ft (16·70 m²)
Ailerons (total) 14·74 sq ft (1·37 m²)
Airbrakes (total) 9·76 sq ft (0·91 m²)
Fin 7·86 sq ft (0·73 m²)
Rudder 7·23 sq ft (0·67 m²)
Tailplane 21·88 sq ft (2·03 m²)

WEIGHTS AND LOADINGS (H: high-performance category; U: utility category):
Weight empty, equipped:
H, U 850 lb (385 kg)
Max T-O weight:
H 1,340 lb (608 kg)
U 1,430 lb (649 kg)
Max wing loading:
H 7·44 lb/sq ft (36·32 kg/m²)
U 7·94 lb/sq ft (38·77 kg/m²)

PERFORMANCE (H: high-performance category, U: utility category; at AUW of 1,200 lb; 544 kg):
Best glide ratio at 51 knots (59 mph; 95 km/h) 34
Min sinking speed at 44 knots (50 mph; 80 km/h) 2·38 ft (0·72 m)/sec
Stalling speed:
H 42 knots (48 mph; 78 km/h)
U 44 knots (50 mph; 81 km/h)
Max speed (smooth air), airbrakes extended:
H 130 knots (150 mph; 241 km/h)
U 122 knots (140 mph; 225 km/h)
Max aero-tow speed 96 knots (110 mph; 177 km/h)

SCHWEIZER SGS 2-33

The SGS 2-33 was developed to meet the demand for a medium-priced two-seat sailplane for general soaring. The prototype was first flown in the Autumn of 1966 and received FAA Type Approval in February 1967. Production began in January 1967, and more than 325 SGS 2-33 sailplanes had been built by January 1974.

TYPE: Two-seat general-purpose sailplane.

WINGS: Strut-braced high-wing monoplane. Aluminium alloy structure with metal skin and all-metal ailerons. Airbrakes fitted.

FUSELAGE: Welded chrome-molybdenum steel tube structure. Nose covered with glassfibre, remainder with Ceconite fabric.

TAIL UNIT: Braced steel tube structure, covered with Ceconite fabric.

LANDING GEAR: Non-retractable Cleveland monowheel and 6·00-6 tyre, immediately aft of nose-skid. Rubber-block shock-absorption for skid. Wingtip wheels optional.

ACCOMMODATION: Two seats in tandem in completely lined cockpit, with dual controls. One-piece canopy. Rear door and window. Standard equipment includes air vent, seat belts and shoulder harness.

DIMENSIONS, EXTERNAL:
Wing span 51 ft 0 in (15·54 m)
Wing aspect ratio 11·85
Length overall 25 ft 9 in (7·85 m)
Height overall 9 ft 3½ in (2·83 m)

AREAS:
Wings, gross 219·48 sq ft (20·39 m²)
Ailerons (total) 18·24 sq ft (1·69 m²)

WEIGHTS AND LOADING:
Weight empty 600 lb (272 kg)
Max T-O weight 1,040 lb (472 kg)
Max wing loading 4·74 lb/sq ft (23·14 kg/m²)

PERFORMANCE:
Best glide ratio 22·25
Min sinking speed:
solo 2·6 ft (0·79 m)/sec
dual 3·0 ft (0·91 m)/sec
Stalling speed:
solo 27 knots (31 mph; 50 km/h)
dual 30·5 knots (35 mph; 57 km/h)
Max speed (smooth air) and max aero-tow speed 85 knots (98 mph; 158 km/h)
Max winch-launching speed 60 knots (69 mph; 111 km/h)

SCHWEIZER SGS 1-34

Design of this single-seat high-performance Standard Class sailplane, intended to replace the 1-23 series described in the 1967-68 *Jane's*, began in 1967 and construction of the prototype started in the following year. This flew for the first time in the Spring of 1969 and FAA type certification was awarded in September 1969. More than 85 production models had been completed by January 1974.

TYPE: Single-seat Standard Class sailplane.

WINGS: Cantilever shoulder-wing monoplane. Wing section Wortmann FX-61-163 at root, Wortmann FX-60-126 at tip. Dihedral 3° 30′. Incidence 1° at root, 0° at tip. No sweepback. All-metal aluminium alloy structure. Plain all-metal differential ailerons. Double-flap speed-limiting airbrakes, above and below wing. No flaps, spoilers, trim tabs or slots.

FUSELAGE: All-metal aluminium alloy semi-monocoque structure.

TAIL UNIT: Cantilever all-metal aluminium alloy structure with swept vertical surfaces. Fixed-incidence tailplane. No trim tabs.

Schweizer SGS 2-33 two-seat general-purpose sailplane

Schweizer SGS 1-34 single-seat high-performance Standard Class sailplane

LANDING GEAR: Non-retractable monowheel, with forward skid and auxiliary tailwheel. Retractable monowheel optional. Cleveland wheel size 5·00-5, Type III 4-ply tyre. Cleveland wheel brake.

ACCOMMODATION: Single seat under bubble canopy.

DIMENSIONS, EXTERNAL:
Wing span 49 ft 2½ in (15·00 m)
Wing chord at root 4 ft 3·63 in (1·31 m)
Wing chord at tip 1 ft 10·13 in (0·56 m)
Wing aspect ratio 16
Length overall 25 ft 9 in (7·85 m)
Height over tail 7 ft 6 in (2·29 m)
Tailplane span 8 ft 6 in (2·59 m)

AREAS:
Wings, gross 151 sq ft (14·03 m²)
Ailerons (total) 10·90 sq ft (1·01 m²)
Fin 5·51 sq ft (0·51 m²)
Rudder 5·18 sq ft (0·48 m²)
Tailplane 13·20 sq ft (1·23 m²)
Elevators 5·88 sq ft (0·55 m²)

WEIGHTS AND LOADING:
Weight empty, equipped 550 lb (249 kg)
Max T-O weight 800 lb (362 kg)
Max wing loading 5·3 lb/sq ft (25·9 kg/m²)

PERFORMANCE:
Best glide ratio at 45 knots (52 mph; 84 km/h) 34
Min sinking speed at 40 knots (46 mph; 74 km/h) 2·1 ft (0·64 m)/sec
Max speed (smooth air) 117 knots (135 mph; 217 km/h)
Max aero-tow speed 100 knots (115 mph; 185 km/h)
g limits +8·33; —5·33

SCHWEIZER SGS 1-35

The SGS 1-35 is an all-metal single-seat high-performance Standard Class sailplane, the prototype of which was flown for the first time in April 1973. The FAA certification programme was completed in February 1974, at which time about 80 had been ordered; production was due to begin in April 1974, with output planned to reach eight per month in January 1975.

TYPE: Single-seat high-performance Standard Class sailplane.

WINGS: Cantilever shoulder-wing monoplane. Wortmann wing sections: FX-67-K-170 at root, FX-67-K-150 at tip. Dihedral 3° 30′. Incidence 1° 30′. No sweep at quarter chord. Aluminium stressed-skin and stringer construction. Bottom-hinged trailing-edge flaps and top-hinged ailerons of aluminium torque cell construction. No airbrakes or spoilers.

FUSELAGE: All-aluminium monocoque construction.

TAIL UNIT: Cantilever aluminium T-tail, with fixed-incidence tailplane and fabric-covered elevator. No tabs.

LANDING GEAR: Mechanically-retractable unsprung monowheel, tyre size 4·00-4, pressure 35 lb/sq in (2·46 kg/cm²). Mechanical disc brake. Nose-skid and tail bumper.

ACCOMMODATION: Single semi-reclining seat under one-piece detachable canopy.

DIMENSIONS, EXTERNAL:
Wing span 49 ft 2½ in (15·00 m)
Wing chord at aircraft c/l 3 ft 0 in (0·91 m)
Wing chord at tip 1 ft 2·67 in (0·37 m)
Wing aspect ratio 23·3
Length overall 19 ft 2 in (5·84 m)

Schweizer SGS 1-35 single-seat high-performance 15 m all-metal sailplane

Height overall	4 ft 5 in (1·35 m)
Tailplane span	6 ft 8 in (2·03 m)
AREAS:	
Wings, gross	103·8 sq ft (9·64 m²)
Ailerons (total)	5·11 sq ft (0·475 m²)
Trailing-edge flaps (total)	11·20 sq ft (1·04 m²)
Fin	5·72 sq ft (0·53 m²)
Rudder	4·72 sq ft (0·44 m²)
Tailplane	6·07 sq ft (0·564 m²)
Elevator	4·76 sq ft (0·442 m²)
WEIGHTS AND LOADING:	
Weight empty, equipped	400 lb (181 kg)
Max T-O weight	930 lb (422 kg)
Max wing loading	8·96 lb/sq ft (43·75 kg/m²)
PERFORMANCE:	
Best glide ratio	38
Stalling speed, 80° flap	28 knots (32 mph; 51·5 km/h)
Max speed (rough or smooth air) and max aero-tow speed	121 knots (139 mph; 223 km/h)
g limits	+8·33; —5·33

SEAGULL

SEAGULL AIRCRAFT INC

ADDRESS:
1554 5th Street, Santa Monica, California 90401
Telephone: (213) 394-1151
PRESIDENT:
H. Michael Riggs
EXECUTIVE VICE-PRESIDENT:
Gary Lockwood
PUBLIC RELATIONS:
Michael B. Druxman and Associates, 6464 Sunset Boulevard, Hollywood, California 90028

After some two years of early operation, this company began manufacture on a full-time basis in January 1973 of a range of lightweight gliders for hang-gliding and skysurfing enthusiasts. These include the Seagull I, II and III Rogallo-type gliders, of which brief details are given at the end of the "Sailplanes" section. The Waterman/Seagull Flyer rigid-aerofoil hang-glider, described briefly in the 1973-74 *Jane's*, has now been discontinued.

THOR

HANK THOR

DUSTER BJ-1B

About 150 Duster sailplanes are reportedly under construction, from kits supplied by Mr Norman Barnhart of Duster Sailplane Kits, and at least two of these had flown by the end of 1973.

Plans of the Duster (but not kits) are also marketed by California Sailplanes.

That completed by Mr Hank Thor, which took part in the Oshkosh Fly-in in 1973, has been converted to a powered sailplane by the mounting above and behind the cockpit of a 35 hp Rockwell JLO-600LM engine. Mr Thor was assisted in this conversion by the designer of the original Duster sailplane, Mr Ben Jansson.

DIMENSIONS, EXTERNAL:	
Wing span	42 ft 7¾ in (13·00 m)
Wing aspect ratio	17·4
WEIGHTS:	
Weight empty	368 lb (167 kg)
Max T-O weight	650 lb (295 kg)
PERFORMANCE:	
Max level speed	113 knots (130 mph; 210 km/h)
Cruising speed	86 knots (99 mph; 160 km/h)
Landing speed	39 knots (45 mph; 72 km/h)
Max rate of climb at S/L	750 ft (228 m)/min

Mr Hank Thor's Duster BJ-1B, powered by a 35 hp Rockwell engine (*Howard Levy*)

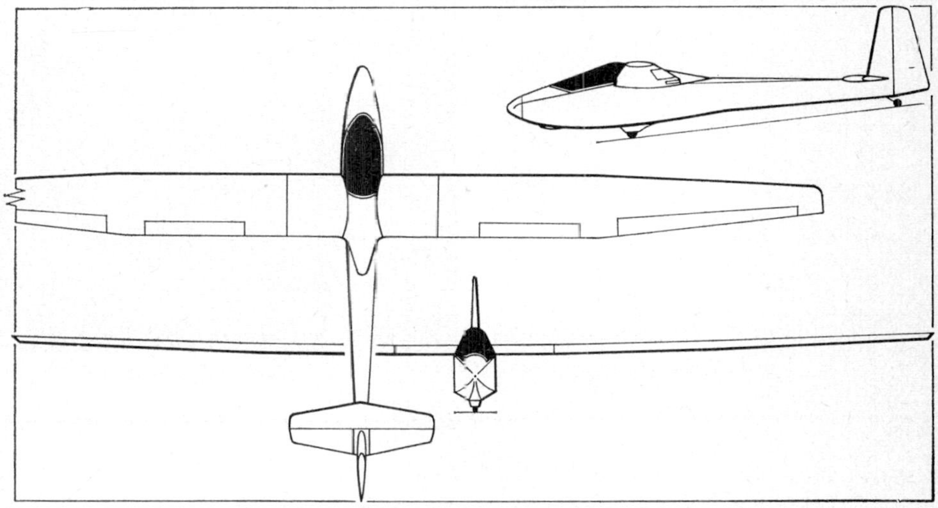

Jansson BJ-1 Duster single-seat amateur-built sailplane (*A. J. Smith*)

VOLMER

VOLMER AIRCRAFT

ADDRESS:
Box 5222, Glendale, California 91201
Telephone: (213) 247-8718

Mr Volmer Jensen, designer of the VJ-22 Sportsman two-seat amphibian, designed and built in 1940 a one-man biplane hang-glider which is designated VJ-11. It was flown successfully, both in the hands of professional glider pilots and by many people with no previous flying experience. Volmer Aircraft is currently marketing blueprints, brochures and photographs (but not kits or materials) of the VJ-11, and of the monoplane VJ-23, for amateur constructors; some hundreds have been sold.

VOLMER VJ-11

Construction of the VJ-11 is of spruce, fir and mahogany plywood, with wire bracing and fabric covering. Control in the air is by means of ailerons, elevators and rudder. Take-off can be achieved, in suitable wind conditions, after only three steps downhill, and on some flights the aircraft has gained altitude.

DIMENSIONS:	
Wing span	28 ft 0 in (8·53 m)
Length overall	15 ft 5 in (4·70 m)
Height overall	5 ft 1 in (1·55 m)
AREA:	
Wings, gross	225·0 sq ft (20·90 m²)
WEIGHTS:	
Weight empty	100 lb (45·5 kg)
Max T-O weight	280 lb (127 kg)
PERFORMANCE:	
Cruising speed	17 knots (20 mph; 32 km/h)
Stalling speed	13 knots (15 mph; 24 km/h)

Volmer VJ-11 one-man hang-glider, showing the pilot's controls

VOLMER VJ-23 SWINGWING

The VJ-23 monoplane hang-glider was designed jointly in 1971 by Volmer Jensen and Irving Culver, making its first flight towards the end of that year. Subsequent modifications to the design have made the aircraft, which is known as the "Swingwing", safer and more controllable. It has soared successfully for 42 min on a 34 ft (10·4 m) high ridge, in a 14 knot (16 mph; 26 km/h) wind; has made flights covering distances of up to 2,416 ft (736 m); and can execute figure-of-eight manoeuvres. The longest flight made up to early 1974 was of $1\frac{1}{2}$ hours' duration.

Although hang-gliders are not subject to FAA regulations, the VJ-23 has been approved by the FAA as an amateur-built aircraft.

Construction of the VJ-23 is of steel tube, spruce and plywood, with fabric covering. Control is by means of ailerons, elevators and rudder. Construction kits for the VJ-23 are marketed by the DSK Aircraft Co, 12676 Pierce Street, Pacoima, California 91331.

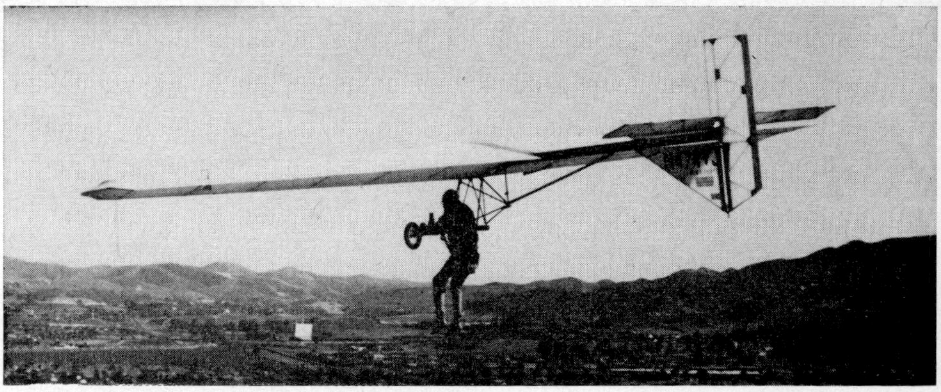

Volmer VJ-23 Swingwing monoplane hang-glider, approved by the FAA for amateur construction

DIMENSIONS:
- Wing span: 32 ft 7 in (9·93 m)
- Length overall: 17 ft 5 in (5·31 m)
- Height overall: 6 ft 0 in (1·83 m)

AREA:
- Wings, gross: 179·0 sq ft (16·63 m²)

WEIGHTS:
- Weight empty: 100 lb (45·5 kg)
- Max T-O weight: 300 lb (136 kg)

PERFORMANCE:
- Cruising speed: 17 knots (20 mph; 32 km/h)
- Stalling speed: 13 knots (15 mph; 24 km/h)

ZANNER

OTTO ZANNER

ADDRESS:

Vineland, New Jersey

ZANNER OZ-5

Mr Zanner has previously built, from kits and/or plans, a Schweizer SGS 1-26, a Thorp T-18, a Briegleb BG 12 and a Bryan (Schreder) HP-14. His fifth aircraft construction, the OZ-5, combines a fuselage and tail unit of his own design with the wings from a Bryan (Schreder) HP-15, and is completed to Standard Class specifications.

The fuselage/cockpit pod is a glassfibre structure to about one-third back on the tailboom; the remainder of the tailboom and the cantilever T-tail are all-metal structures. The monowheel landing gear can be fully retracted by a push/pull lever on the left-hand side of the single-seat cockpit. Flight testing was due to take place in 1974.

DIMENSIONS, EXTERNAL:
- Wing span: 49 ft $2\frac{1}{2}$ in (15·00 m)
- Length overall: 22 ft 0 in (6·71 m)
- Height overall: 4 ft 0 in (1·22 m)
- Tailplane span: 6 ft 1 in (1·85 m)

WEIGHTS:
- Max pilot weight: 234 lb (106 kg)
- Max T-O weight: 669·5 lb (303·5 kg)

PERFORMANCE (estimated):
- Max speed (smooth air): 156 knots (180 mph; 290 km/h)
- Max speed (rough air): 130 knots (150 mph; 241 km/h)
- Max aero-tow speed: 104 knots (120 mph; 193 km/h)
- Max winch-launching speed: 78 knots (90 mph; 145 km/h)

Zanner OZ-5 single-seat Standard Class sailplane (*Howard Levy*)

THE UNION OF SOVIET SOCIALIST REPUBLICS

ANTONOV

OLEG KONSTANTINOVICH ANTONOV

DESIGN BUREAU HEADQUARTERS: Kiev

O. K. Antonov has been well known as a sailplane designer for many years. He was a pioneer of sailplane design in the USSR, producing his first glider, the OKA-1 Golub (Pigeon), in 1924. Subsequent types, which have numbered about 60, included the OKA-6 "City of Lenin" which won the 1931 Crimea Gliding Contest, and the A-7 "partisan" transport glider of the second World War.

Post-war designs began with the A-9, and several of these have been described in previous editions of *Jane's*. The latest known design is the A-15.

ANTONOV A-15

The prototype Antonov A-15 single-seat all-metal high-performance sailplane flew for the first time on 26 March 1960, and at least five more were built subsequently.

Four A-15s were entered for the 1965 World Gliding Championships, gaining 13th, 17th, 22nd and 32nd places in the Open Class contest.

An A-15 piloted by Tamara Zaiganova of the USSR set up, on 29 July 1966, an international women's record for a goal flight of 394·775 nm (454·59 miles; 731·60 km).

A description and illustration appeared in the 1973-74 *Jane's*.

KARVYALIS

BALIS KARVYALIS

KARVYALIS BK-7 LIETUVA

This single-seat sailplane was designed and built by Mr Balys Karvyalis of Vilna, and first flew in 1972. It has a Wortmann FX-67-K-170 wing section, and a retractable monowheel landing gear, with tailskid.

The Lietuva, which is of glassfibre construction, is reported to have entered series production.

DIMENSIONS, EXTERNAL:
- Wing span: 58 ft $4\frac{3}{4}$ in (17·80 m)
- Wing chord at root: 3 ft $1\frac{3}{4}$ in (0·96 m)
- Wing chord at tip: 1 ft $2\frac{1}{4}$ in (0·36 m)
- Wing aspect ratio: 25·5
- Length overall: 23 ft $7\frac{1}{2}$ in (7·20 m)
- Height over tail: 4 ft 7 in (1·40 m)

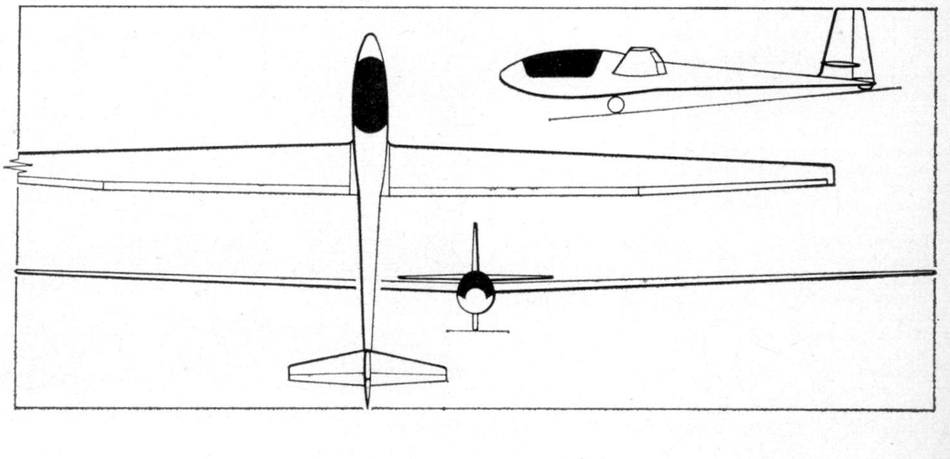

Karvyalis BK-7 Lietuva single-seat sailplane (*A. J. Smith*)

AREAS:
- Wings, gross 132·4 sq ft (12·30 m²)
- Ailerons (total) 7·10 sq ft (0·66 m²)
- Vertical tail surfaces (total) 14·85 sq ft (1·38 m²)
- Horizontal tail surfaces (total) 14·53 sq ft (1·35 m²)

WEIGHTS AND LOADING:
- Weight empty 639 lb (290 kg)
- Normal T-O weight 837 lb (380 kg)
- Max T-O weight (with ballast) 1,058 lb (480 kg)
- Max wing loading (with ballast) 7·88 lb/sq ft (38·5 kg/m²)

PERFORMANCE:
- Best glide ratio 43
- Min sinking speed 1·71 ft (0·52 m)/sec
- Stalling speed 40·5 knots (47 mph; 75 km/h)
- Max permissible speed 121 knots (139 mph; 225 km/h)

SA

SPORTIVNAYA AVIATSIYA

SA-8T IDEL

This single-seat Standard Class sailplane, which first flew in August 1972, was designed by A. I. Osokin. It is believed to have been evaluated by the Central Aeroclub of the USSR, for possible aeroclub use by the DOSAAF flying training organisation, and production was under consideration in 1973. It is of all-metal construction, and design of the fuselage may have been based on that of the Polish Foka 5, to which it bears an outward resemblance. The shoulder-mounted wings are of NACA 63-420 root and NACA 63-517 tip sections and have 2° dihedral. The hood of the two-piece cockpit canopy hinges open sideways to starboard.

DIMENSIONS, EXTERNAL:
- Wing span 49 ft 2½ in (15·00 m)
- Wing mean aerodynamic chord 2 ft 1½ in (0·65 m)
- Wing aspect ratio 25
- Length overall 20 ft 9¼ in (6·33 m)
- Height over tail 4 ft 7½ in (1·41 m)

AREA:
- Wings, gross 97·95 sq ft (9·10 m²)

WEIGHT:
- Max T-O weight 606 lb (275 kg)

PERFORMANCE:
- Best glide ratio at 45 knots (51·5 mph; 83 km/h) 36·5
- Min sinking speed at 43 knots (49·5 mph; 80 km/h) 2·03 ft (0·62 m)/sec
- Stalling speed 36·5 knots (42 mph; 67 km/h)
- Max permissible speed 134·5 knots (155 mph; 250 km/h)
- Max aero-tow speed 94·5 knots (108·5 mph; 175 km/h)
- *g* limits +6; −4

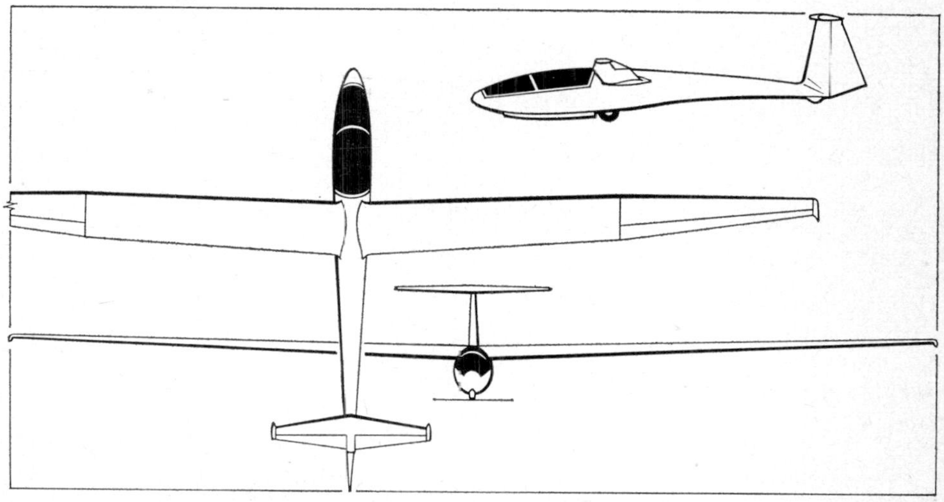

SA-8T Idel single-seat Standard Class sailplane (*Tony Mitchell*)

YUGOSLAVIA

VTC

VAZDUHOPLOVNO TEHNICKI CENTAR—VRSAC

ADDRESS:
Vrsac, 29 Novembra b.b. Gudurički put
Telephone: 80-111

DIRECTOR:
Veselinovic Zivota

CHIEF DESIGNER:
Dipl Ing Ivan Sostaric

The VTC at Vrsac is building the Schempp-Hirth Cirrus under licence, due to lack of production capacity at the parent company's Kirchheim works. Key technicians from Vrsac were detached to the Schempp-Hirth factory for six months to learn German production techniques, and the first production aircraft built at Vrsac was delivered in late 1971. Forty Cirrus had been built at Vrsac by the end of 1973.

In collaboration with Sigmund Flugtechnik of West Germany, the VTC has developed and flown a two-seat powered sailplane designated SSV-17. A description of this aircraft follows:

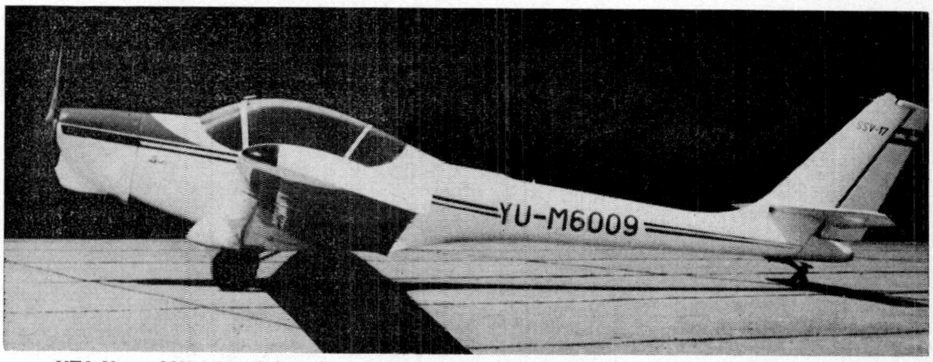

VTC-Vrsac SSV-17 prototype two-seat powered sailplane (60 hp Franklin 2A-120-A engine)

VTC SSV-17

The SSV-17 two-seat powered sailplane was developed jointly by the VTC and Sigmund Flugtechnik of Germany, under the design guidance of Dipl-Ing Alfred Vogt and Ivan Sostaric. The prototype (YU-M6009), flown by VTC test pilot A. Stanojevic, made its first flight on 24 June 1972. It was certificated in May 1973, and by the end of that year 10 had been ordered.

The SSV-17 is suitable for glider pilot training, soaring or cross-country flying.

TYPE: Two-seat powered sailplane.

WINGS: Cantilever low-wing monoplane. Wortmann wing sections, with thickness/chord ratio of 18% at junction with centre-section and 16% from mid-span to tips. Incidence 1°. Construction entirely of glassfibre sandwich, except for light alloy main spar. Long-span ailerons. Schempp-Hirth airbrake above and below each wing. No flaps or tabs.

FUSELAGE: Conventional semi-monocoque structure, built entirely of glassfibre sandwich. Fuselage/wing centre-section, 6 ft 6¾ in (2·00 m) in width, forms cabin floor and also serves as wing spar carry-through structure and carries main landing gear housings.

TAIL UNIT: Cantilever structure, with sweptback vertical surfaces, built entirely of glassfibre sandwich except for steel tube fin spar. No tabs on elevators or rudder.

LANDING GEAR: Main units, each with single wheel, have coil spring shock-absorption and retract upwards into "knuckle" fairings on wing centre-section. They remain semi-exposed when retracted to reduce damage in the event of a wheels-up landing. Non-retractable tailwheel, steerable with rudder.

POWER PLANT: One 60 hp Franklin 2A-120-A two-cylinder horizontally-opposed aircooled engine, with electrical starting, driving a two-blade Hoffmann propeller. Design is suitable for acceptance of alternative engines of comparable size, weight and power. Fuel capacity 12 Imp gallons (54 litres).

ACCOMMODATION: Seats for two persons side by side under fully-transparent canopy.

DIMENSIONS, EXTERNAL:
- Wing span 55 ft 9¼ in (17·00 m)
- Wing aspect ratio 15·65
- Length overall 23 ft 11½ in (7·30 m)
- Height overall 9 ft 3¾ in (2·84 m)
- Wheel track 6 ft 2¾ in (1·90 m)

AREA:
- Wings, gross 199·1 sq ft (18·50 m²)

WEIGHTS AND LOADINGS:
- Weight empty 943 lb (428 kg)
- Max T-O weight 1,472 lb (668 kg)
- Max wing loading 7·37 lb/sq ft (36 kg/m²)
- Max power loading 22·05 lb/hp (10 kg/hp)

PERFORMANCE (at max T-O weight):
- Max level speed 135 knots (155 mph; 250 km/h)
- Max cruising speed 86 knots (99·5 mph; 160 km/h)
- Landing speed 37 knots (42·5 mph; 68 km/h)
- Stalling speed 35·5 knots (40·5 mph; 65 km/h)
- Max rate of climb at S/L 590 ft (180 m)/min
- Service ceiling 16,725 ft (5,100 m)
- T-O run 820 ft (250 m)
- T-O to 50 ft (15 m) 1,247 ft (380 m)
- Landing from 50 ft (15 m) 590 ft (180 m)
- Range 431 nm (497 miles; 800 km)
- Best glide ratio, power off 29
- Min sinking speed, power off 2·79 ft (0·85 m)/sec

VTC DELFIN

The Delfin single-seat sailplane was designed by Z. Gabrijel and T. Dragovic of the Mechanical Faculty (Aerospace Department), to OSTIV Standard Class requirements. It was built in the Vrsac factory of VTC. The **Delfin 1** prototype flew for the first time on 7 December 1963 and made its first appearance outside Yugoslavia at the 1965 World Championships held in the UK; it took 1st and 2nd places in the Polish national championships in 1966 and was described in the 1967-68 *Jane's*. Major production model was the **Delfin 2** (first flight 23 April 1965), in which the plywood fuselage covering was extended to cover the nose and a smaller, sideways-opening canopy was fitted. The metal ailerons were replaced by fabric-covered wooden ailerons, and a rubber-sprung nose-skid was added. Twenty-seven Delfin 2s were built. Four Delfins were later converted to **Delfin 3** (first flight 29 July 1968), these having a conventional fixed-incidence tailplane with elevators, instead of an all-moving horizontal surface; a less-sweptback fin; and a larger-area rudder. Production ended in 1969.

The following description applies to the Delfin 2 and 3:

TYPE: Single-seat Standard Class competition and training sailplane.

WINGS: Cantilever shoulder-wing monoplane. Wing section NACA 63_3618 (modified). Dihedral 2° on Delfin 2, 2° 30′ on Delfin 3. No sweepback or aerodynamic twist. Wingtip "salmons". Plywood-covered wooden structure. Wooden plain ailerons, with plywood leading-edges and rear parts fabric-covered. Schempp-Hirth metal airbrakes at 60% chord above and below each wing.

FUSELAGE: Plywood-covered wooden monocoque structure.

TAIL UNIT: Cantilever wooden structure, with sweptback vertical surfaces. Fin built integrally with fuselage. All-moving tailplane with servo tab on Delfin 2; Delfin 3 has fixed-incidence tailplane with elevators, with trim tab in starboard elevator.

LANDING GEAR: Non-retractable unsprung monowheel (tyre size 300 × 150 mm, pressure 35·5 lb/sq in; 2·5 kg/cm²) and tail bumper. Rubber-sprung nose-skid. Mechanical brake on main wheel.

ACCOMMODATION: Single semi-reclining seat under one-piece transparent canopy which opens sideways to starboard. Standard instrumentation; provision for radio and oxygen for competition flying.

DIMENSIONS, EXTERNAL:
- Wing span: 49 ft 2½ in (15·00 m)
- Wing mean aerodynamic chord: 1 ft 2½ in (0·368 m)
- Wing aspect ratio: 17·55
- Length overall:
  - Delfin 2: 23 ft 7½ in (7·20 m)
  - Delfin 3: 22 ft 5¾ in (6·85 m)
- Height overall: 5 ft 3 in (1·60 m)
- Tailplane span:
  - Delfin 2: 9 ft 10 in (3·00 m)
  - Delfin 3: 10 ft 6 in (3·20 m)

AREAS:
- Wings, gross: 138·0 sq ft (12·82 m^2)
- Ailerons (total): 13·61 sq ft (1·264 m^2)
- Fin:
  - Delfin 2: 6·46 sq ft (0·60 m^2)
  - Delfin 3: 3·58 sq ft (0·333 m^2)
- Rudder:
  - Delfin 2: 5·38 sq ft (0·50 m^2)
  - Delfin 3: 7·45 sq ft (0·692 m^2)
- Tailplane:
  - Delfin 2: 14·69 sq ft (1·365 m^2)
  - Delfin 3: 14·17 sq ft (1·316 m^2)
- Elevators, incl tab:
  - Delfin 3: 6·46 sq ft (0·60 m^2)

WEIGHTS AND LOADING (Delfin 2 and 3):
- Weight empty, equipped: 491-498 lb (223-226 kg)
- Max T-O weight: 716 lb (325 kg)
- Max wing loading: 5·18 lb/sq ft (25·3 kg/m^2)

PERFORMANCE (Delfin 2 and 3):
- Best glide ratio at 47 knots (54 mph; 87 km/h): 31
- Min sinking speed at 40·5 knots (47 mph; 75 km/h): 2·13 ft (0·65 m)/sec
- Stalling speed: 32·5 knots (37·5 mph; 60 km/h)
- Max speed (smooth air): 135 knots (155 mph; 250 km/h)
- Max speed (rough air): 78 knots (90 mph; 145 km/h)
- Max aero-tow speed: 75·5 knots (87 mph; 140 km/h)
- Max winch-launching speed: 59 knots (68 mph; 110 km/h)
- g limits: +8·87; —5·87

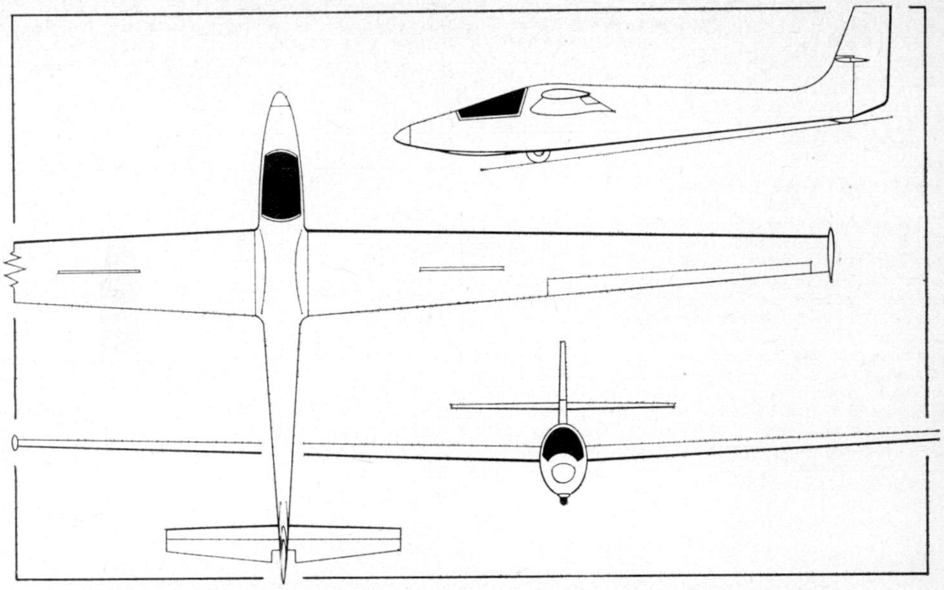

VTC Delfin 3 single-seat competition and training sailplane (*Michael A. Badrocke*)

LCF II

The LCF II, which is under construction, is a single-seat club sailplane suitable for training, competition and aerobatic operation. Construction is of metal, wood and plastics.

The origin of the LCF II had not been identified at the time of closing for press. All known details follow:

UNIDENTIFIED SAILPLANE

DIMENSIONS, EXTERNAL:
- Wing span: 42 ft 7¾ in (13·00 m)
- Wing aspect ratio: 16·9
- Length overall: 20 ft 10 in (6·35 m)

AREA:
- Wings, gross: 107·6 sq ft (10·00 m^2)

WEIGHTS:
- Weight empty: 375 lb (170 kg)
- Max T-O weight: 595 lb (270 kg)

PERFORMANCE (estimated):
- Best glide ratio at 46 knots (53 mph; 85 km/h): 30·5
- Min sinking speed: 2·30 ft (0·70 m)/sec
- Max speed (smooth air): 135 knots (155 mph; 250 km/h)
- Stalling speed: 34 knots (39 mph; 62 km/h)

ROGALLO-TYPE FLEXIBLE-WING GLIDERS

In view of the increasing popularity of hang-gliding or skysurfing as a sport, the "Sailplanes" section this year includes mention of some of the more popular craft of this type and of the companies which manufacture them in complete or component form.

Hang-gliders which have rigid-aerofoil wings are included in the main "Sailplanes" section. A selection of those with flexible (Rogallo- or sail-type) wings, ie similar in concept to the astronaut recovery device developed for NASA by Dr Francis Rogallo, is listed below:

FRANCE

DANIS

ADDRESS:
2-30 Square Hector-Berlioz, 94500-Maisons-Alfort.

Telephone: 207-63-21

DIRECTOR:
Bernard Danis

Manufacturer, in ready-to-fly or kit form, of the Delta Manta, Delta Manta Danis, Delta Danis (with optional water-skis) and Danis 73 flexible-wing hang-gliders. M Danis was the French water-ski kiting champion in 1964, 1965 and 1966; European champion in 1964; World champion in 1966; and has set a number of water-ski kiting records, including one in 1966 for a flight of 4 hr 51 min.

Delta Manta. Tubular metal airframe (AU4G1, AZ8GU); wing area 215·3 sq ft (20 m^2); weight empty 31 lb (14 kg); best glide ratio 10.

Danis 71. Earlier version of Danis 73, with 129·2 sq ft (12 m^2) wing area. Tubular metal airframe (AZ5G), with nylon sail.

DELTA SARL

ADDRESS:
28 Avenue Hoche, 75008 Paris

Telephone: 924-43-76

Manufacturer of the **Deltaplane,** a sharp-nosed, conical-aerofoil craft with a glide ratio of approx 7, capable of attaining a lift factor of 1·2 at angles of attack of approx 40°. Will stall only at very high angles of attack, in the region of 50°. Pilot supported on a triangular trapeze and harness beneath the wing, exercising control by shifting his body weight.

The Deltaplane has a wing area of 204·5 sq ft (19·0 m^2), weighs 33 lb (15 kg), and is available in two versions: the "S" for individual use and the reinforced "E" for clubs and training schools.

Deltaplane hang-glider manufactured by Delta SARL of France

ITALY

BAGALINI

ADDRESS:
Club Aviazione Popolare (Italian EAA)

Sr Walter Bagalini has designed, built and flown the Leonardino, a single-seat powered glider with a flexible wing.

Leonardino. The Rogallo-type wing is supported, on a Y-frame, above a cruciform chassis of square-section metal tube which supports an open seat for the pilot, a tricycle landing gear, and a conventional non-flexible tail unit with movable control surfaces. The vertical pylon of the Y-frame carries a 21 CV Citroen AM6 engine driving a pusher propeller. Wing span 22 ft (6·70 m); length overall 18 ft 2 in (5·54 m); wing area 169 sq ft (15·70 m^2); weight empty 220 lb (100 kg); best glide ratio approx 5; T-O run 400 ft (122 m); T-O speed 23·5 knots (27 mph; 43·5 km/h) at 364 lb (165 kg) weight; rate of climb 236 ft (72 m)/min.

JAPAN

JEAA

ADDRESS:
2-27 Uehara, Shibuya-ku, Tokyo 151

"Kabuto Gani" hang-glider built by the Sensukai group in Osaka, Japan (*Asahi Miyahara*)

Powered Rogallo-wing craft (MC-90 engine) built in Japan by Mr Masagi Takagi (*Asahi Miyahara*)

UNITED KINGDOM

BIRDMAN SPORTS PROMOTIONS LTD

ADDRESS:
Overtown, Mildenhall, Marlborough, Wiltshire

Telephone: Marlborough 2766

Supplier of fully-assembled Rogallo-type craft, and of kits. UK agent for US Bennett sailwings.

LEN GABRIELS

ADDRESS:
Thornlea Avenue, Holinwood, Oldham, Lancashire OL8 3PX

Supplier of kits and plans for homebuilders.

McBROOM SAILWINGS LTD

ADDRESS:
12 Manor Court Drive, Horfield Common, Bristol BS7 0XF

Telephone: Bristol 44350

DIRECTOR:
V. McBroom

Supplier of fully-assembled Rogallo-type craft, materials for construction, and constructional handbooks.

Two basic types of hang-glider are available: the lightweight **Arion,** built of machine-polished and anodised aluminium, with a high-strength polyurethane proofed sail; and the **Argus,** which is an 18 ft (5·49 m) boom length version of the Arion having a kingpost and top rigging. The Arion has a boom length of 16 ft 9 in (5·11 m); wing span is 22 ft 0 in (6·71 m). A nylon swing seat is fitted, and the aircraft have a best glide ratio of 5 at 22-26 knots (25-30 mph; 40-48 km/h). Total orders for 60 received by Spring 1974, of which 35 had been completed.

HI-WAY AVIATION
ADDRESS:
27-35 Bernard Road, Brighton, Sussex
Telephone: Brighton 681278
Complete ready-to-fly hang-gliders and accessories.

UNITED STATES OF AMERICA

BILL BENNETT KITES AND GLIDERS
ADDRESS:
PO Box 483, Van Nuys, California 91408

CHANDELLE CORPORATION
ADDRESS:
15955 West Fifth Avenue, Golden, Colorado 80401
Supplier of fully-assembled Rogallo-type craft, and of kits and materials.

CHUCK'S GLIDER SUPPLIES
ADDRESS:
4200 Royalton Road, Brecksville, Ohio 44141
Supplier of kits, plans and materials for hang-gliders.

DYNA-SOAR INC
ADDRESS:
3518 Cahuenga Boulevard West, Hollywood, California 90068
Telephone: (213) 851-3595
PRESIDENT:
J. Sommers
Supplier of **Dyna-Soar** ready-to-fly hang-glider.

EIPPER-FORMANCE INC
ADDRESS:
PO Box 246, Lomita, California 90717
PROPRIETOR:
R. Eipper
Supplier and manufacturer of plans, kits and materials, or fully-assembled examples, of the Flexi-Flier Rogallo-type craft, and also of the Lovejoy Quicksilver rigid-aerofoil monoplane hang-glider.

Flexi-Flier. Available in four sizes, with keel lengths from 15 to 18 ft (4·57 to 5·49 m), wing areas from 143 to 207 sq ft (13·29 to 19·23 m²) and weights from 35 to 38 lb (15·9 to 17·2 kg). Dacron sail, and choice of swing seat or prone harness. Best glide ratio 4·5. For training, or for pilots weighing more than 180 lb (81·7 kg), the larger and more robust **Flexi-Floater** is recommended. This is available in two sizes, with keel lengths of 19 and 20 ft (5·79 and 6·10 m), wing areas of 233 and 260 sq ft (21·65 and 24·16 m²) and weights of 44 and 46 lb (20 and 21 kg) respectively.

Quicksilver. See description in main "Sailplanes" section.

KILBOURNE SPORT SPECIALTIES
ADDRESS:
PO Box 8326, Stanford, California 94305
PROPRIETORS:
D. and R. Kilbourne
Supplier of kits and materials for sharp-nosed, conical-aerofoil Rogallo-type hang-glider with 16 ft (4·88 m) keel.

MAN-FLIGHT SYSTEMS INC
ADDRESS:
PO Box 872, Worcester, Massachusetts 01605
PRESIDENT AND DIRECTOR OF PRODUCT DEVELOPMENT:
Michael A. Markowski
Manufacturer and supplier of the Skysurfer Rogallo-type craft and the Eagle II high-performance flexible-wing hang-glider, in ready-to-fly form or in kits for amateur construction.

Skysurfer. Available in six sizes, with wing areas of 119, 138, 159, 181, 204 and 228 sq ft (11·06, 12·82, 14·77, 16·82, 18·95 and 21·18 m²), the "sq ft" figures being used as Model numbers. Wing spans range from 18 ft 5 in (5·61 m) to 25 ft 5 in (7·75 m), keel lengths from 13 ft to 18 ft (3·96 to 5·49 m), and empty weights from 31 to 41 lb (14 to 18·5 kg). Airframe of aluminium tube, with Dacron/nylon sail, double lift and flying wires; all bottom rigging wires are vinyl coated. Underside apex sail optional, to improve stability in pitch. Triangular hang-frame for

Man-Flight Skysurfer

Man-Flight Eagle II

pilot. Max never-exceed speed 29·8 knots (34·4 mph; 55·4 km/h); stalling speed 16·9 knots (19·4 mph; 31·3 km/h); best glide ratio 4·45 at 21 knots (24·15 mph; 38·9 km/h); min sinking speed 434 ft (132 m)/min at 21 knots (24·15 mph; 38·9 km/h).

Eagle II. Wings have rigid leading-edges and wire-tensioned trailing-edges; wing span 34 ft (10·36 m), wing area 158·5 sq ft (14·73 m²), length 19 ft (5·79 m), height at kingpost 8 ft (2·44 m). Separate tail control surfaces (rudder and elevator); wing dihedral induces roll. Stick-operated controls: no weight shifting. Aluminium airframe, with Dacron covering and stainless steel rigging wires. Weight empty approx 75 lb (34 kg), depending on harness system. Best glide ratio approx 10; cruising speed 21 knots (24 mph; 38·5 km/h); stalling speed 14 knots (13 mph; 26 km/h). Folds and transports like a kite. In development stage (second prototype) in early 1974; plans expected to be available by Summer 1974.

MANTA WINGS
ADDRESS:
1647 East 14th Street, Oakland, California 94606
Telephone: (415) 261-1473
ADVERTISING MANAGER:
Sheridan Jackson
Manufacturer of Manta Wing fully-assembled Rogallo-type craft, and of kits, materials and associated equipment; and operator of a hang-glider training programme.

Manta Wing. Available in six Standard Rogallo (SR-15, 16, 17, 18, 19, and 20) and six Slalom versions (SL-15 to 20), depending upon pilot weights of between 100 and 250 lb (45 and 113 kg); figures in designation indicate keel length in feet. Wings swept 50°. Wing spans range from 19 to 27 ft (5·79 to 8·23 m); wing areas from 157 to 278 sq ft (14·59 to 25·83 m²); empty weights from 35 to 45 lb (16 to 20·5 kg). Airframe of 6061-T6 anodised aluminium tube, with Dacron sail and stainless steel rigging wires. Safety seat, with chest belt, is standard; prone harness available optionally. Practical speed range 15·5-35 knots (18-40 mph; 29-64·5 km/h); best gliding speed 17·5-22·5 knots (20-26 mph; 32-42 km/h); stalling speed 13·5-15·5 knots (15-18 mph; 24·5-29 km/h); best glide ratio 4·2 at 20 knots (23 mph; 37 km/h); design *g* limit +3·5.

SCHWEIZER AIRCRAFT INC
ADDRESS:
PO Box 147, Elmira, New York 14902

Seagull III

SEAGULL AIRCRAFT
ADDRESS:
1554 Fifth Street, Santa Monica, California 90401
Telephone: (213) 394-1151
PRESIDENT:
H. Michael Riggs
Manufacturer of the following Rogallo-type craft:

Seagull I. Standard class craft, with an 82° nose angle and 16 ft (4·88 m) keel and wing spars. Control by weight-shifting.

Seagull II. Similar to Seagull I, but with 18 ft (5·49 m) keel and wing spars, and increased wing area, to support a heavier pilot.

Seagull III. Camber-control craft, with a 100° nose angle. Wing span 28 ft (8·53 m); wing area 238 sq ft (22·11 m²); keel length 17 ft (5·18 m);

Manta Wing

weight empty 46 lb (21 kg); best glide ratio 5 at 15 knots (17 mph; 27·5 km/h); min sinking speed 5 ft (1·52 m)/sec; stalling speed 12·2 knots (14 mph; 22·6 km/h). Control by weight-shifting. Designed for training and soaring, it flies slower and has a shallower glide angle than conical-aerofoil types of comparable wing area.

The camber-control design of the Seagull III, developed by Seagull Aircraft Inc, is geometrically that of a truncated conical Rogallo. Aerodynamically, this truncation restricts the movement of the centre of pressure, permitting much greater stability. The aircraft also has a normal stall, occurring first at the root and working outward. A machine-bent leading-edge spar provides high lift/drag improvements without the instability in pitch evident in NASA-type cylindrical-aerofoil wings. It also reduces the tendency for the wingtips to stall at high angles of attack and improves recoverability from a dive.

SKY SPORTS INC
ADDRESS:
PO Box 441-J, Whitman, Massachusetts 02382
Telephone: (617) 447-3773
PRESIDENT:
Ed Vickery
Supplier of plans, kits or fully-assembled hang-gliders, and of a wide range of supporting equipment.

LARK (Low Aspect Ratio Kite). Standard class conical-aerofoil craft, with a 90° nose angle and a glide ratio of 4·5. Available in four versions, as follows:

(1) With 14 ft (4·27 m) keel and 138 sq ft (12·82 m²) wing, designed for payload of up to 125 lb (56·5 kg).

(2) With 16 ft (4·88 m) keel and 181 sq ft (16·82 m²) wing, designed for payload of 120 to 180 lb (54·5 to 81·7 kg).

(3) With 18 ft (5·49 m) keel and 228 sq ft (21·18 m²) wing, designed for payload of 160 to 220 lb (72·5 to 100 kg).

(4) With 20 ft (6·10 m) keel and 280 sq ft (26·01 m²) wing, designed for payload of 200 to 280 lb (90·7 to 127 kg).

SPORT KITES INC
ADDRESS:
1202-C East Walnut, Santa Ana, California 92701
Telephone: (714) 547-1344, 547-6366 or 544-0445
VICE-PRESIDENT:
Chris A. Wills
Supplier of Wills Wing Rogallo-type craft and operator of a training programme using these aircraft.

Wills Wing. First flown 1970; entered production 1973. Available in five sizes, for pilots weighing from 125 to 240 lb (57 to 109 kg) or over; keel lengths of 16, 17, 18, 19 and 20 ft (4·88, 5·18, 5·49, 5·79 and 6·10 m). Standard version, for pilots of 145 to 195 lb (66 to 88·5 kg), is the 18 ft kite, which has a wing span of 27 ft (8·23 m), area of 214 sq ft (19·88 m²) and empty weight of 32 lb (14·5 kg). Airframe of 6061-T6 anodised aluminium tube, with Dacron sail and stainless steel rigging wires. Single swing-seat standard, with larger versions able to carry two persons side by side. Prone harness available optionally. Max speed 48 knots (55 mph; 88·5 km/h); min sinking speed 15·5 knots (18 mph; 29 km/h);

Wills Wing

stalling speed 4·5 knots (5 mph; 8·5 km/h); best glide ratio 6 at 18 knots (21 mph; 34 km/h); *g* limits +6; —3. Total orders for 170 received by February 1974, of which 145 had been completed.

UP (ULTRALITE PRODUCTS)
ADDRESS:
137 Oregon Street, El Segundo, California 90245
Telephone: (213) 322-7171
Supplier of materials for Rogallo-type hang-gliders.

VELDERRAIN & CO
ADDRESS:
PO Box 314, Lomita, California 90717
Telephone: (213) 325-2960
DIRECTORS:
Russell Velderrain
Richard Miller
Kas De Lisse
Manufacturer and supplier of the sail-type hang-glider (20 ft; 6·10 m keel, 18 ft; 5·49 m leading-edge) which won first place at the San Diego Montgomery meeting in 1972.

Russler monoplane hang-glider under development.

WHITNEY ENTERPRISES
ADDRESS:
PO Box 90762, Los Angeles, California 90009
Telephone: (213) 641-5303
PUBLICATION:
Man-Flite (monthly); Editor, E. Paul
Manufacturer and supplier of plans, kits and materials for the Flying Wing and Porta-Wing Rogallo-type craft.

Porta-Wing. Initial portable kite design by Eddie Paul, with 26 ft (7·92 m) span, 20 ft (6·10 m) overall length, and 90° nose angle. Production version has same span, but a 16 ft (4·88 m) keel and 135° nose angle. Wing area is 208 sq ft (19·32 m²) and empty weight 30 lb (13·6 kg). Aluminium tube keel and spar; wire cable leading- and trailing-edges.

In addition, further information about the above manufacturers and their products, and of hang-gliding activities generally, can be obtained from:

UNITED KINGDOM

BRITISH KITE SOARING ASSOCIATION
ADDRESS:
8a Rickman Close, Woodley, Berkshire
Telephone: Reading 63232
PUBLICATION:
Sailwing (quarterly); Editor, R. Bickel

NATIONAL HANG GLIDING ASSOCIATION
ADDRESS:
9 The Drive, West Wickham, Kent BR4 0EF
Telephone: 01-777 2644

UNITED STATES OF AMERICA

HANG GLIDER MANUFACTURERS' ASSOCIATION
ADDRESS:
137 Oregon Avenue, El Segundo, California 90245
PRESIDENT:
P. Brock

SELF-SOAR ASSOCIATION
ADDRESS:
PO Box 1860, Santa Monica, California 90406
PUBLICATIONS:
Low and Slow (bi-monthly) and *Hang Glider Weekly;* Editor, J. Faust

Membership Aircraft Division: Omega Aircraft
ADDRESS:
PO Box 1671, Santa Monica, California 90406
DIRECTOR:
M. Davis

Whitney Porta-Wing

The Omega line of experimental aircraft belong to the membership in general. A copy of any Omega may be made without charge by home-builders or commercial centres.

First Charter Chapter: Los Angeles Hang Glider Association
ADDRESS:
59 Dudley Avenue, Los Angeles, California 90291

UNITED STATES HANG GLIDING ASSOCIATION
ADDRESS:
PO Box 66306, Los Angeles, California 90066
Telephone: (213) 390-3065 or 839-8014

UNITED STATES SKYSURFING ASSOCIATION (USSA)
ADDRESS:
PO Box 375, Marlborough, Massachusetts 01752
Telephone: (1-617) 485-5740
PUBLICATION:
Skysurfer (bi-monthly); Editor, Michael A. Markowski

AIRSHIPS

GERMANY

(FEDERAL REPUBLIC)

WDL

WESTDEUTSCHE LUFTWERBUNG, THEODOR WÜLLENKEMPER KG

ADDRESS: 433 Mülheim/Ruhr, Flughafen
Telephone: (0 21 33) 31009/31000

In 1969 Herr Theodor Wüllenkemper founded the WDL airship works in Essen-Mülheim, with the objective of designing and building a new generation of non-rigid airships that would take advantage of present-day materials and technology. Since the company was established four projects have been planned and the first of these, designated WDL 1, is described below.

The first three designs, WDL 1, 2 and 3, are all intended as experimental craft, increasing in size progressively and each intended to explore new concepts to simplify operation of such craft. Subject to successful development, it is planned to embody their basic constructional, control and handling concepts in a larger standard production airship, designated WDL 4.

WDL 2 is intended to explore special configurations of gondola to permit the carriage of international standard freight containers. These will take the form of interchangeable passenger/cargo gondolas. Power plant mountings, rotatable through 360°, will allow the propeller thrust to be used not only for fore and aft propulsion, but also in vertical modes to enhance lift or assist in landing procedures. Construction of this airship is scheduled to begin when orders for WDL 1 airships have been met.

During a violent storm on 13 November 1972, the inflatable airship hangar housing WDL 1 serial number 101 was severely damaged, as was the airship itself, and flying debris hit and wrecked WDL 1 serial number 100 which was riding at its mooring mast. Construction of WDL 1 serial number 102 was in progress in March 1974, and it was expected to be completed later in the year.

The standard production airship, WDL 4, will have a gross volume of 2,260,140 cu ft (64,000 m³) and payload of 66,140 lb (30,000 kg). It is expected to have a heating system, from the exhaust, to raise the temperature of the helium lifting gas.

WDL 1

Construction of the WDL 1 serial number 100 was completed in mid-1972 and the first flight, piloted by Konrad Hess, was made on 12 August 1972.

This airship, named *The Flying Musketeer*, was severely damaged during a storm on 13 November 1972. It was repaired during the Winter months and began flying again on 28 April 1973, at which time it was re-named *Wicküler*. By the end of 1973 it had completed 2,800 flying hours, and in March 1974 it was undergoing inspection and engine change before starting the 1974 flying season.

The envelope is made of synthetic fabric and is helium-filled. An automatic pressure control system has been developed to maintain effective control of pressure during flight as well as on the ground, to preserve the shape and stability of the craft at all times. Two panels, each 131 ft 3 in (40·0 m) by 26 ft 3 in (8·0 m), one on each side of the envelope, together provide 10,000 electric bulbs for the display of advertising slogans. The power plant consists of two conventional aero-engines, each of 180 hp; and all fuel for the engines is contained in cells mounted within the envelope. This arrangement has been adopted to provide maximum capacity within the gondola.

Construction of WDL 1 serial number 101 was completed in the late Summer of 1972 and a first flight was made during October. The envelope was damaged when the airship's inflatable hangar collapsed during a storm in November. Following repairs and air test, this airship was shipped to Japan, where it is being operated by Orient Lease Co Ltd of Tokyo. A German airship pilot was in Japan during the Summer of 1973 and has been responsible for the training of a Japanese pilot.

WDL 1 airship owned by Orient Lease Co of Tokyo and decorated by Japanese artist Taro Okamoto (*Kazuo Miyazaki*)

DIMENSIONS:
- Length overall: 180 ft 5 in (55·0 m)
- Max diameter: 47 ft 6¾ in (14·5 m)

VOLUME:
- Gross: 211,888 cu ft (6,000 m³)

WEIGHTS:
- Gross weight: 13,889 lb (6,300 kg)
- Envelope weight: 3,527 lb (1,600 kg)
- Payload: 3,307 lb (1,500 kg)

PERFORMANCE (estimated):
- Max speed: 54 knots (62 mph; 100 km/h)
- Operational radius: 215 nm (248 miles; 400 km)

THE UNITED KINGDOM

CAMERON

CAMERON BALLOONS LTD

ADDRESS: 1 Cotham Park, Bristol BS6 6BZ
Telephone: (0272) 41455

DIRECTORS:
D. A. Cameron
Kim Cameron
Tom Sage

Cameron Balloons Ltd, which has designed and produced many hot-air balloons for sporting activities, ranging in volume from 20,000 cu ft (566 m³) to 375,000 cu ft (10,620 m³), built and flew the world's first hot-air airship. In addition to its use as a purely sporting vehicle, this aircraft is expected to have useful applications for a range of commercial tasks such as aerial photography, survey and advertising.

CAMERON D96 HOT-AIR AIRSHIP

First flight of the prototype (G-BAMK) was made at Wantage, Berkshire, on 4 January 1973, at which time the airship had a single lower vertical stabiliser at the aft end. This provided only marginal directional stability and a second, upper, stabiliser was added. Since that time an improved method of suspending the gondola has been evolved, thus eliminating the distortion of the envelope which occurred in the early stages.

The envelope, like those of Cameron hot-air balloons, is made from a light but high-strength nylon fabric. The lightweight tubular-metal gondola, which carries the propane burner, gas supply, pilot, passenger and power plant, was built by a specialist engineering firm at Oxford, headed by Dr E. T. Hall.

Power plant is a 45 hp 1,600 cc Volkswagen modified motor car engine, driving a large-diameter semi-shrouded pusher propeller.

Twelve months of flight testing have suggested a number of improvements which will be incorporated in the production version, the first of which was expected to be constructed during 1974.

Cameron D96, the world's first hot-air airship

DIMENSIONS, ENVELOPE:
- Length overall: 100 ft 0 in (30·48 m)
- Max diameter: 45 ft 0 in (13·72 m)
- Volume, gross: 96,000 cu ft (2,718 m³)

PERFORMANCE:
- Max speed: 15 knots (17 mph; 27·5 km/h)
- Turning radius at 10 knots (11·5 mph; 18·5 km/h): 100 ft (30·5 m)
- Endurance: 2¼ hours

GLOSTER

Brief details have been received of the construction of a new British airship which has the name Gloster.

The envelope, which contains two ballonets, has a volume of 25,000 cu ft (707·9 m³), length of 82 ft (24·99 m) and maximum diameter of 25 ft (7·62 m). Power plant comprises two 26 hp engines.

SMITH

A. SMITH

Mr Smith has completed construction of a small helium-filled non-rigid airship.

The envelope is of standard configuration, with fore and aft ballonets. At the aft end of the envelope, lightweight tubular structures are attached to it by patches. Two of these structures, one on each side on the centreline of the envelope, carry fixed horizontal surfaces, to the trailing-edges of which are attached controllable elevators. Twin vertical surfaces are carried in a similar manner, and to the trailing-edge of each of these surfaces is attached a controllable rudder.

The gondola is also a lightweight tubular structure, at the rear of which are mounted two 20 hp Wankel-type engines, each driving a small ducted propeller of the kind used in hovercraft. A fixed horizontal surface is mounted across the centreline of the aft edges of the two propeller ducts. Airscoops for inflation of the ballonets are mounted in the slipstream from the propellers.

DIMENSIONS:
- Length overall: 76 ft 0 in (23·16 m)
- Max diameter: 29 ft 0 in (8·84 m)

VOLUME:
- Gross: 33,000 cu ft (934·46 m³)

WEIGHT:
- Weight empty: approx 1,060 lb (481 kg)

PERFORMANCE (estimated):
- Max speed: 26 knots (30 mph; 48 km/h)
- Pressure height: approx 6,000 ft (1,825 m)

General view of A. Smith's 33,000 cu ft (934·46 m³) airship

Close-up view of power plant installation of Smith airship

THE UNITED STATES OF AMERICA

GOODYEAR

GOODYEAR TIRE & RUBBER COMPANY

ADDRESS: Akron, Ohio 44316
Telephone: (216) 794-2490

PRESIDENT AND CHIEF EXECUTIVE OFFICER:
Charles J. Pilliod Jr

VICE-PRESIDENT (PUBLIC RELATIONS):
Robert H. Lane

Since 1917, Goodyear has built a total of 300 airships, more than any other company in the world. Of these, 244 were constructed under contract for the US Army and Navy, and included the USS *Akron* and USS *Macon*, the largest rigid airships constructed in the USA. The remaining 56 have been commercial airships, of which the first was the Pilgrim, launched in 1925.

In February 1968, Goodyear initiated a $5 million expansion and improvement programme for its airship operations, which included the provision of a new base at Houston, Texas, modernisation of the Mayflower III and Columbia II, based at Miami and Los Angeles respectively, and construction of a new airship, named America. This latter airship, completed in early 1969, was built at Wingfoot Lake, near Akron, from where it made its first flight on 25 April 1969. It is based currently at Houston, Texas. Columbia II and Mayflower III were described in the 1964-65 *Jane's*, the former having identical dimensions to the America, which was described briefly in the 1970-71 *Jane's*.

In 1971, a decision was made to build a fourth non-rigid airship to begin public relations operations in Europe in 1972. On 9 December 1971 components for its construction were flown from Akron Municipal Airport to the Royal Aircraft Establishment at Cardington, Bedfordshire, in an Aero Spacelines B-377MG Mini Guppy; and this airship, named Europa, made its first flight from Cardington on 8 March 1972.

During the Winter months of each year the Europa operates from a base which has been established at Capena, Italy, north of Rome. To accommodate the Europa and ground support vehicles, and to provide office space, crew quarters and adequate facilities for complete maintenance of the airship, Goodyear has erected a hangar at Capena. This concrete, steel and glass structure is 250 ft (76·20 m) in length, 160 ft 9 in (49·00 m) wide and 90 ft (27·43 m) in height. During the Spring and Summer months the airship tours western Europe.

All available details of the Europa which is basically similar to the America, are given below:

The Goodyear airship Columbia II, which has similar dimensions to the Europa

EUROPA

The envelope of the Europa, which has a surface area of 21,600 sq ft (2,006 m²), is made of two-ply Neoprene-coated Dacron and, like that of its sister 'ships, is helium-filled. On each side of the envelope is a four-colour sign 105 ft 0 in (32·00 m) long and 24 ft 6 in (7·47 m) high, containing 3,780 lamps to flash static or animated messages. These can be read at a distance of 1 mile (1·6 km) when the airship is cruising at a height of 1,000 ft (305 m). A turbojet APU, mounted in a removable pod on the undersurface of the 'ship's gondola, drives a 500A 28V generator to supply electrical power for the signs and their control equipment. The turbojet is designed to operate without developing any appreciable amount of forward thrust for the airship.

The gondola, attached to the undersurface of the envelope, has accommodation for a pilot and six passengers, and has a single non-retractable landing wheel mounted beneath it.

Power plant consists of two 210 hp Continental IO-360-D six-cylinder horizontally-opposed air-cooled engines, each driving a Hartzell two-blade metal reversible-pitch pusher propeller. Standard tankage is provided for 138 US gallons (527 litres) of fuel, and auxiliary tankage for 158 US gallons (598 litres). Total available fuel capacity is thus 296 US gallons (1,125 litres).

It was reported at the beginning of September 1973 that the Europa had accumulated nearly 2,000 flying hours in more than 2,000 flights, and that a total of more than 100,000 passengers had been carried since its first flight in 1972.

It was reported at the beginning of September 1973 that the Europa had accumulated nearly 2,000 flying hours in more than 2,000 flights, and that a total of more than 10,000 passengers had been carried since its first flight in 1972.

DIMENSIONS, OVERALL:
- Length: 192 ft 6 in (58·67 m)
- Width: 50 ft 0 in (15·24 m)
- Height: 59 ft 6 in (18·14 m)

DIMENSIONS, ENVELOPE:
- Length: 190 ft 3½ in (58·00 m)
- Max diameter: 45 ft 11 in (14·00 m)
- Fineness ratio: 14·4
- Volume, gross: 202,700 cu ft (5,379·9 m³)
- Volume, ballonets: 58,700 cu ft (1,662·2 m³)

DIMENSIONS, GONDOLA:
- Length overall: 22 ft 9 in (6·93 m)
- Height: 8 ft 1¼ in (2·47 m)
- Height, including landing gear: 11 ft 9½ in (3·59 m)
- Width at ceiling: 7 ft 0 in (2·13 m)
- Width at floor: 4 ft 3½ in (1·31 m)

WEIGHTS:
- Weight empty: 9,375 lb (4,252 kg)
- Max design gross weight: 12,840 lb (5,824 kg)

PERFORMANCE:
- Max speed: 43·5 knots (50 mph; 80 km/h)
- Normal cruising speed: 30-35 knots (35-40 mph; 56-64 km/h)
- Max rate of climb at S/L: 2,400 ft (732 m)/min
- Max rate of descent: 1,400 ft (427 m)/min
- Normal operational altitude: 1,000-3,000 ft (305-915 m)
- Service ceiling: 7,500 ft (2,285 m)
- Endurance at cruising speed, standard fuel: approx 10 hours
- Endurance at cruising speed, max fuel: approx 23 hours

AIR-LAUNCHED MISSILES

FRANCE

AÉROSPATIALE

SOCIÉTÉ NATIONALE INDUSTRIELLE AÉROSPATIALE

HEAD OFFICE:
37 boulevard de Montmorency, 75781 Paris-cédex 16
Telephone: 224.84.00

OFFICERS:
See "Aircraft" section

Division des Engins Tactiques

EXECUTIVE OFFICE:
12 rue Béranger, 92320-Châtillon
Telephone: 655.54.00

The former Nord-Aviation, now part of Aérospatiale, was engaged on the design, development and production of guided missiles, pilotless target aircraft and test vehicles for many years, at its Châtillon-sous-Bagneux and Bourges works, and had sold more than 350,000 anti-tank missiles alone by mid-1970. Deliveries had been made to 25 countries.

Information on former Nord-Aviation air-launched missiles, now the responsibility of the Division des Engins Tactiques of Aérospatiale, is given below. This Division is also responsible for a new generation of short-range battlefield weapons developed in association with Messerschmitt-Bölkow-Blohm of Germany.

AÉROSPATIALE AS.11

The AS.11 is an air-to-surface version of the SS.11 line-of-sight wire-guided battlefield missile, which was developed for use from vehicles of all kinds. It has a cylindrical body and swept cruciform wings, and is powered by a two-stage solid-propellant rocket motor. Directional control is achieved by deflecting the sustainer efflux.

In action, with a typical helicopter installation, the operator acquires the target by means of a stabilised and magnifying optical sight. As soon as the missile enters his field of vision after launch, he passes to it the signals needed to align it with the target, while keeping it above the terrain until impact. The signals are given by the operator by means of a control stick which makes it possible to send simultaneously up or down and port or starboard commands. The signals are transmitted to the missile over wires. Tracer flares are installed on the rear of the missile for visual reference.

Since 1962, the AS.11 B.1 version, using transistorised firing equipment, has been in production. It is available with a variety of different warheads, including an inert type for practice, the Type 140AC anti-tank warhead capable of perforating 24 in (60 cm) of armour plate, the Type 140AP02 explosive warhead (5·72 lb; 2·6 kg of explosive) which will penetrate an armoured steel plate 0·4 in (1 cm) thick at a range of 9,800 ft (3,000 m) and explode about 7 ft (2·1 m) behind the point of impact, and the Type 140AP59 high-fragmentation anti-personnel type with contact fuse.

The AS.11 B.1 and the basic surface-launched SS.11 B.1 have been supplied to all three French services and the armed forces of 18 other countries, including the USA and UK. Orders totalled 159,000 by the beginning of 1973; of these 153,000 had been delivered, with production continuing at the rate of 600 per month at that time.

DIMENSIONS:
Length overall — 3 ft 11 in (1·20 m)
Body diameter — $6\frac{1}{2}$ in (0·164 m)
Wing span — 1 ft $7\frac{3}{4}$ in (0·50 m)

WEIGHT:
Launching weight — 66 lb (29·9 kg)

PERFORMANCE:
Average cruising speed — 313 knots (360 mph; 580 km/h)
Time of flight (propelled) — 20-21 sec
Min turning radius — approx 3,300 ft (1,000 m)
Range — 1,650-9,840 ft (500-3,000 m)

AÉROSPATIALE AS.12

The wire-guided air-to-surface AS.12 (and similar surface-to-surface SS.12) is a spin-stabilised missile derived from the AS.11/SS.11 series but with a warhead weighing 66 lb (30 kg), about four times as much as that of the latter, making it suitable for use against fortifications as well as tanks, ships and other vehicles. The current OP.3C warhead can pierce more than 1·5 in (40 mm) of armour and explode on the other side.

The missile has a cylindrical body, cruciform wings and two-stage solid-propellant rocket motor. It is not available with the TCA type of guidance system used with some versions of the AS.30.

The AS.12 arms Breguet Atlantic and P-2 Neptune aircraft of the Royal Netherlands Navy, and is also carried by the Breguet Alizé and Hawker Siddeley Nimrod. It is operational on helicopters of the French Navy, the Royal Navy and several other naval air arms.

Production of the AS.12 was continuing in 1974.

Aérospatiale AS.11 air-to-surface missiles on a British Army Scout helicopter *(Peter R. March)*

DIMENSIONS:
Length overall — 6 ft 1·9 in (1·87 m)
Body diameter — 7 in (0·18 m)
Warhead diameter — 8·25 in (0·21 m)
Wing span — 2 ft $1\frac{1}{2}$ in (0·65 m)

WEIGHT:
Launching weight — 167 lb (75 kg)

PERFORMANCE:
Speed at impact:
AS.12 (fired at 200 knots; 230 mph; 370 km/h) — 180 knots (210 mph; 335 km/h)
Time of flight — 32 sec
Max range:
AS.12 in relation to surface — approx 26,250 ft (8,000 m)
AS.12 in relation to aircraft — approx 18,000 ft (5,500 m)

AÉROSPATIALE AS.20

More than 7,000 AS.20 air-to-surface missiles were built by Nord-Aviation for the French Air Force and Navy, to arm the Fiat G91 tactical fighters of the Federal German and Italian Air Forces, and for two other countries.

Any aircraft capable of launching the AS.20 at a speed of Mach 0·7 or higher can be equipped with it. A special adaptor makes it possible to fire the AS.20 from aircraft equipped to carry the AS.30, and it continues to be used for training by air forces equipped with the more powerful weapon.

Further production has been undertaken under licence by MBB in Germany, following choice of a slightly modified version of the AS.20, in 1968, to arm F-104G aircraft engaged on anti-shipping duties.

Details of the AS.20 can be found in the 1971-72 *Jane's*.

AÉROSPATIALE AS.30

This tactical air-to-surface missile is virtually a scaled-up AS.20, with a similar configuration, two-stage solid-propellant power plant and radio command guidance system. The only major difference in external appearance is the addition on the AS.30 of cruciform "flip-out" tail fins, indexed in line with the wings.

The requirements to which the AS.30 was designed included an initial launch range of at least 5·4 nm (6·2 miles; 10 km), with the provision that the launching aircraft should not approach to within 1·6 nm (1·8 miles; 3 km) of the target. A CEP (circular error probability) of less than 33 ft (10 m) was specified and this standard of accuracy has been exceeded by the AS.30. Minimum launching speed is approximately Mach 0·45; there is no limitation for launching at supersonic speeds.

As an alternative to the original manual "steering" system, the AS.30 can utilise the TCA infra-red automatic guidance system evolved by the company's Tactical Missile Division. With this, the pilot has no other task to perform than conventional aiming with his weapon-sight, keeping the target centred in the sight during the flight of the missile. An infra-red tracker is trained constantly on an IR flare on the missile. An axial gyroscope compensates for sight movement. From data provided by the two devices, deviations of the missile from the correct flight path are detected and corrected by command signals radioed to the missile. Accuracy is claimed to be as great as that achieved by a fully-trained operator controlling the missile by hand.

This automatic guidance system is operational in the French Air Force, which utilises the AS.30 with a 510 lb (230 kg) HE warhead and alternative delay or non-delay fuses.

Aérospatiale AS.12 air-to-surface missile installation on a Wasp helicopter *(Peter R. March)*

Other customers for the AS.30 have included the French Navy and the German, Swiss and South African air forces.

A total of about 5,500 AS.30s had been produced by mid-1973, when a further order for 370 missiles for the Federal German naval air arm was announced.

Dimensions:

Length overall:	
with X35 warhead	12 ft 9 in (3·885 m)
with X12 warhead	12 ft 7 in (3·839 m)
Body diameter	1 ft 1½ in (0·34 m)
Wing span	3 ft 3¼ in (1·00 m)

Weight:

Launching weight	1,146 lb (520 kg)

Performance:

Speed at impact
1,475-1,640 ft/sec (450-500 m/sec)

Range (average)
5·9-6·5 nm (6·8-7·5 miles; 11-12 km)

AÉROSPATIALE AM39 EXOCET

Exocet is a missile that was devised originally to provide warships with all-weather attack capability against other surface vessels. In its basic MM38 surface-to-surface form it can be fitted in all classes of surface warships, including fast patrol boats and hydrofoil craft, and offers an economical means of defence against missiles like the Soviet "Styx" by attacking the launching vessels rather than attempting to intercept the missiles after launch. Development in an air-to-surface role has followed.

The Exocet missile is in the form of a streamlined body fitted with cruciform wings and cruciform tail control surfaces indexed in line with the wings. Propulsion is provided by a tandem two-stage solid-propellant motor, and the highly-destructive warhead is described as being in the same order as that of a torpedo. The missile is stored in a container which also serves as a launcher during surface-to-surface use, and is usually installed in a fixed position.

The basic air-to-surface version, designated AM39, has a launch weight of under 1,430 lb (650 kg) and a new rocket motor that burns for 150 seconds, giving an increased range. Another modification to the propulsion system by comparison with the MM38 ensures a one-second delay in ignition after launch, allowing the missile to drop clear of the launch aircraft.

The AM39 has been selected for carriage by the French Navy's Atlantic and Super Etendard aircraft, and is suitable for operation from helicopters in the class of the Super Frelon and Sea King.

The missile's high subsonic flight profile consists of a pre-guidance phase, during which it travels towards the target, whose range and bearing have been determined by an airborne radar or ship's fire control computer and set up in the missile pre-guidance circuits before launch, and a final guidance phase during which the missile flies directly towards the target under the control of its active homing head. Throughout the flight the missile is maintained at a very low altitude (reported to be 2 to 3 metres; 6·5 to 10 ft) by an FM radio altimeter. Its homing head is reported to pick up the target over a range of up to 6·5 nm (7·5 miles; 12 km).

Exocet is intended to operate efficiently in an ECM (electronic countermeasures) environment.

No further details are available officially, but Exocet is reported to have a warhead weighing 352 lb (160 kg). It uses a modified version of the low-level guidance system developed for the Kormoran missile and a sustainer motor similar to that of the Martel missile.

Subcontractors to Aérospatiale include Electronique Marcel Dassault for the ADAC homing head, TRT for the AHV-7 radio altimeter, SNPE for the solid propellants, SERAT for the explosive charge, SFENA and SAGEM for accelerometers and gyroscopes, Jaeger for control surface actuators, and ECAN-Ruelle for servo control equipment. Following the placing of British and German contracts, participating companies include BAC, Hawker Siddeley Dynamics, Morfax, ROF Patricroft (Royal Ordnance Factory), Vosper-Thornycroft, Newton, Sperry and Smiths in the UK, and MBB of Germany.

The firing installation supplied by Aérospatiale is compatible with the full range of existing shipboard fire control systems, such as the Thomson Vega and systems manufactured by Marconi and HSA.

In August 1971, The Boeing Company acquired a licence to manufacture and market Exocet in the USA.

Firing trials of MM38 Exocet missiles fitted with guidance systems have been underway since mid-1971. The manufacturer's tests were concluded on 4 July 1972, with a direct hit of a missile with a live warhead on a 300-ton hull, which was sunk. Evaluation trials by the French Navy, with the participation of the Royal Navy and the West German Navy, began in October 1972. Other customers for the MM38 surface-to-surface version include the navies of Brazil, Chile, Ecuador, Greece, Malaysia and Peru. Production has been under way at the rate of 15 missiles per month since January 1973.

Launch tests from a Super Frelon helicopter began in April 1973. The type of missile employed was an intermediate version of Exocet designated AM38, which consisted of an MM38 fitted with the one-second ignition delay that will be embodied in the AM39. Inert missiles were dropped in the first three tests at forward speeds of 80 knots (92 mph; 148 km/h), 100 knots (115 mph; 185 km/h) and 120 knots (138 mph; 222 km/h) respectively. Two launches of missiles with live power plants but no guidance followed on 21 and 25 June 1973, with the helicopter flying at 100 knots and 125 knots (144 mph; 232 km/h) respectively at a height of 1,650 ft (500 m).

In each of the powered launches, the missile dropped about 33 ft (10 m) in a stable, horizontal attitude from its pylon during the 1½ seconds before ignition, despite rotor downwash.

Carrying two AM39 Exocets and 1,100 Imp gallons (5,000 litres) of fuel, a Super Frelon could carry out a 6-hour patrol near its shore or ship base, or attack a specific target up to 350 nm (400 miles; 650 km) from base. Equipment added to the helicopter consists of two launch pylons, an operator's console, an Omera ORB-31D X-band search and tracking radar capable of acquiring targets the size of a fast patrol boat over a range of 28·5 nm (33 miles; 53 km) in sea state 4 or 5, an EMD Alto-2 Doppler radar altimeter, a SFIM CV-153 vertical gyro for a compass system, a compensated airspeed indicator, and a Crouzet 70 computer.

Production of the AM39 for the French Navy is expected to begin in 1976.

Several other countries are contemplating deployment of the AM39 air-launched version of Exocet from rotating-wing and fixed-wing aircraft. Use of the MM38 version in a shore-to-ship role and from submarines is also anticipated.

Dimensions (MM38):

Length	16 ft 9½ in (5·12 m)
Body diameter	1 ft 1½ in (0·344 m)
Span of wings	3 ft 3½ in (1·004 m)
Span of fins	2 ft 5¾ in (0·758 m)

Weights:

Launching weight:	
MM38	1,587 lb (720 kg)
AM39	less than 1,430 lb (650 kg)

Performance:

Max level speed — Mach 0·93

Range (estimated):

AM39, launched from a helicopter at 60 knots (69 mph; 110 km/h) at a height of 330 ft (100 m) — 28 nm (32·25 miles; 52 km)

AM39, launched from an Atlantic aircraft at heights between 1,000 ft and 16,400 ft (300-5,000 m) — 29-32·25 nm (33·5-37·25 miles; 54-60 km)

AM39, launched from a Super Etendard aircraft at heights between 330 ft (100 m) and 33,000 ft (10,000 m) — 32-37 nm (37-43 miles; 60-70 km)

NEW MISSILE

It was announced by M Robert Galley, the French Defence Minister, on 24 January 1974, that a new air-to-surface missile with a nuclear warhead was to be developed for future use from fighter aircraft engaged on penetration missions. The missile will have a range of 43-80 nm (50-93 miles; 80-150 km). Its warhead will have a yield of 500-600 kilotons.

Aérospatiale AS.30 air-to-surface missile on F-104 underwing launcher

Super Frelon helicopter carrying two Exocet air-to-surface missiles

MATRA

SA ENGINS MATRA

HEAD OFFICE:
4 rue de Presbourg, 75116-Paris
MANAGEMENT AND WORKS:
37 avenue Louis Breguet, 78140-Vélizy
Telephone: 946.96.00
Telex: ENMATRA 69.077F
OTHER WORKS:
rue de la Convention, 41300-Salbris
Telephone: (39) 83.02.50
CHAIRMAN: Marcel Chassagny
GENERAL MANAGER:
Jean-Luc Lagardere
PUBLIC RELATIONS DIRECTOR:
Philippe Chassagny

Since 1948, Matra has been engaged in extensive research and experimental work in the guided missile, propulsion and guidance fields.

After prolonged testing on Meteor and Canberra aircraft, the company's type R.510 air-to-air weapon went into small series production for training purposes. Described in the 1958-59 *Jane's*, it was superseded by the fully-developed type R.511 missile, of which approximately 1,000 were manufactured as standard weapons of the French Air Force and continue in service on Vautour and Mirage III-C interceptors.

The R.511 was followed in turn by the R.530, and further improved weapons are now being developed as armament for the interceptors of the 1970s.

In September 1964, an Anglo-French government agreement was signed, providing for the joint development and production by Matra and Hawker Siddeley of an air-to-surface guided weapon now designated AS.37/AJ.168 Martel. Details of this can be found in the International section.

Matra is also designing and producing on its own, or in collaboration with foreign companies, other missiles to meet current tactical requirements, including the surface-to-air Crotale and a variant of Crotale, known as Cactus, for operation by South Africa.

Matra is responsible for the development and quantity production of launchers for unguided solid-propellant rockets which form standard armament on French and British fighter and bomber aircraft.

Special underwing stores developed by Matra for strike missions include a gun pod, based on the French DEFA 30 mm gun, for fighter and jet training aircraft.

Since 1960, Matra has also been working on retardation systems for bombs, under the direction of the Service Technique de l'Aéronautique. The system in series production and service comprises a cruciform parachute, mechanism to check the release parameters, and nose and tail fuses. It has been used with French SAMP 250 kg and 400 kg bombs since 1966 and is also in service in some ten foreign countries, including West Germany, in certain cases on standard British or US manufactured bombs. It can be used at heights down to 100 ft (30 m).

MATRA R.530

Since 1963, more than 1,600 R.530 air-to-air missiles have been ordered as standard armament for Vautour and Mirage III and F1 interceptors of the French Air Force, Mirages of the South African, Israeli, Australian and Brazilian Air Forces, and F-8E (FN) Crusaders of the French Navy. Production continued in 1974.

Suitable for use at heights from sea level to 69,000 ft (21,000 m), the R.530 is an all-weather missile, with interchangeable EMD AD-26 semi-active radar and infra-red homing heads. It can be fired at the target from any direction, its homing head being sufficiently sensitive not to require firing from astern of the enemy aircraft.

The R.530 has a cylindrical body, with cruciform delta wings, two of which are fitted with ailerons, and cruciform tail control surfaces. It is powered by a two-stage Hotchkiss-Brandt solid-propellant rocket motor, rated at 18,740 lb (8,500 kg) st.

There are two types of Hotchkiss-Brandt high-explosive warhead, each weighing 60 lb (27 kg) and fitted with a proximity fuse. The latest types of anti-jamming ECM devices are fitted to the AD-26 head.

Model of the Matra Super 530 high-performance air-to-air missile

DIMENSIONS:	
Length overall	10 ft 9¼ in (3·28 m)
Body diameter	10¼ in (0·26 m)
Wing span	3 ft 7¼ in (1·10 m)
WEIGHT:	
Launching weight	430 lb (195 kg)
PERFORMANCE:	
Max speed	Mach 2·7
Range	9·5 nm (11 miles; 18 km)

MATRA SUPER 530

This new high-performance air-to-air weapon system is intended initially as armament for the Dassault Mirage F1 interceptors of the French Air Force, offering ranges compatible with the Cyrano IV fire control system of these aircraft. Compared with the R.530, it has much improved aerodynamics, structure, radome, electronics and power plant, doubling both the acquisition distance and the effective range. It is an all-weather and all-sector weapon, with the ability to attack targets flying at an altitude more than 25,000 ft (7,600 m) higher or lower than that of the launch aircraft.

The general appearance of the Super 530 is shown in the accompanying photograph of a model that was exhibited at the 1973 Paris Air Show. It was announced simultaneously that the new missile has a Super AD-26 semi-active radar homing head, developed and built by Electronique Marcel Dassault. Its rocket motor, supplied by Thomson/Brandt, utilises Butalane propellant, with a much higher specific impulse than the motor of the R.530, raising the missile's max speed to an estimated Mach 4·5. The warhead is supplied by Thomson/Brandt, with a proximity fuse by Thomson-CSF; and the latest ECM anti-jamming circuits are fitted.

Matra R.550 Magic short/medium-range air-to-air missile on wingtip of Dassault Mirage F1

Versions of the Matra R.530 air-to-air missile with semi-active radar guidance (*left*) and infra-red homing head (*right*)

Ramp-launch tests of the Super 530 began in January 1971. Flight trials of the homing head were started in September 1972, and the first controlled model was fired successfully on 27 February 1973. Development and evaluation launches performed under the auspices of the Centre d'Expériences Aériennes Militaires, Mont-de-Marsan, will extend from 1974 to 1977, and will include firings against supersonic targets.

DIMENSIONS:

Length overall	11 ft 7½ in (3·54 m)
Body diameter	10¼ in (0·26 m)
Wing span	2 ft 1¼ in (0·64 m)
Fin span	2 ft 11½ in (0·90 m)

WEIGHT (estimated):

Launching weight	440 lb (200 kg)

PERFORMANCE (estimated):

Max speed	Mach 4·5
Operational ceiling	above 70,000 ft (21,350 m)
Range	16-19 nm (18·5-21·75 miles; 30-35 km)

MATRA R.550 MAGIC

This new air-to-air weapon system is intended to meet a French air force requirement for a highly-manoeuvrable short/medium-range "dogfight" missile. Development is reported to have been started in 1967 as a private venture and to have continued under official contract since 1969.

The accompanying illustration shows the unique "double-canard" configuration of the R.550 Magic, with a set of movable foreplane control surfaces immediately behind and indexed in line with cruciform fixed surfaces. The missile has a solid-propellant motor and an infra-red homing head with a cooled cell, manufactured by SAT. It can utilise the same aircraft launcher as the Sidewinder which it will replace.

The first air-launch of an R.550 complete with guidance equipment, against a target, took place at the Landes Test Centre on 11 January 1972, from a Gloster Meteor test aircraft. The first full test of the missile's manoeuvrability was conducted on 30 November 1973, with a launch from a Mirage III against a CT.20 target drone.

The Magic is reported to be effective over ranges from less than 650 ft (200 m) to nearly 3·25 nm (3·75 miles; 6 km), to be able to accept load factors of up to 7g, and to have high acceleration. Delivery for operational testing and evaluation by the French Air Force was scheduled to begin in 1974, and the Magic is expected to equip aircraft of the French Air Force and Navy from 1975. The missile is not intended for export delivery before 1975, but many negotiations were under way in the first half of 1974, by which time Matra had received large orders from five countries.

DIMENSIONS:

Length overall	9 ft 2¼ in (2·80 m)
Body diameter	6 in (0·15 m)
Span of fins	2 ft 1½ in (0·65 m)

WEIGHT:

Launching weight	194 lb (88 kg)

MATRA/HSD AS.37/AJ.168 MARTEL

See International section

MATRA/OTO MELARA OTOMAT

See International section

GERMANY
(FEDERAL REPUBLIC)

DORNIER

DORNIER GmbH

HEAD OFFICE:
Postfach 317, 7990 Friedrichshafen/Bodensee

OFFICERS:
See "Aircraft" section

Dornier GmbH was responsible for managing the development programme for the Viper air-to-air guided missile, in partnership with Bodenseewerk Gerätetechnik GmbH, until work on this weapon was abandoned in mid-1974. Details of Viper can be found in the 1973-74 *Jane's*.

No prototype Viper will now be test fired. However, Dornier plans to continue developing technology that will contribute to future air-to-air missile projects.

MBB

MESSERSCHMITT-BÖLKOW-BLOHM GmbH

HEAD OFFICE AND WORKS:
Ottobrunn bei München, 8 München 80, Postfach 801220
Telephone: (089) 60 00 25 90

Defence Technology Division

WORKS:
Nabern and Schrobenhausen

OFFICERS:
See "Aircraft" section

In addition to its manufacture of piloted aircraft, MBB has engaged in the development and manufacture of guided weapons for more than fifteen years. It has achieved considerable success with its short-range surface-to-surface and surface-to-air battlefield missiles, some of which result from partnership with Aérospatiale of France in the Euromissile team.

Among weapons under current development is an air-launched anti-shipping missile known as the Kormoran, of which brief details follow. MBB has also produced the Aérospatiale AS.20 air-to-surface missile under licence since 1971, for carriage by F-104G aircraft engaged on anti-shipping duties.

MBB is engaged on the development of research rockets and satellites (see Spaceflight section).

MBB KORMORAN

This air-to-surface anti-shipping missile results from a joint development programme by MBB and Aérospatiale of France, under the design leadership of MBB and financed by the Federal German government.

The general appearance of Kormoran is shown in the adjacent illustration. It has a cylindrical body, fitted with cropped-delta cruciform wings and with cruciform tail control surfaces indexed in line with the wings. Two boosters accelerate the missile to cruising speed, which is then maintained by the sustainer motor. The guidance system employs pre-guidance and homing phases, with a homing head supplied by Thomson-CSF, and enables the missile to approach the target at a very small height above the water. The new-type high-energy warhead, developed at MBB's Schrobenhausen works, is effective against ships up to the size of a destroyer.

The Kormoran can be carried by any aircraft with a modern navigation system and will equip F-104G Starfighters of the German naval air arm. It can be fired outside the range of enemy anti-aircraft defences, and the pilot can break away immediately after launch, since the missile has an automatic guidance system.

In-plant testing of Kormoran had been completed by early 1974, and official tests from F-104G Starfighter aircraft were under way.

DIMENSIONS:

Length overall	14 ft 5 in (4·40 m)
Body diameter	1 ft 1½ in (0·34 m)
Wing span	3 ft 3½ in (1·00 m)

WEIGHT:

Launching weight	1,320 lb (600 kg)

MBB/AÉROSPATIALE HOT

See International section

MBB JUMBO

Jumbo is a television-guided air-to-surface missile, with interchangeable nuclear and conventional warheads, which is being developed primarily as a weapon for the MRCA aircraft. MBB claims that the missile will offer improved ECM and ECCM capabilities by comparison with current types.

Development was continuing in mid-1974 with German government approval.

As can be seen in the accompanying illustration, Jumbo has a configuration very like that of Kormoran, but it is larger and weighs nearly twice as much, suggesting the possibility of a warhead as heavy as 1,100 lb (500 kg). The type of propulsion system employed has not been announced, but references to long range, and the presence of an underbelly fairing which could be an air intake duct, suggest the possibility of a turbojet. To cope with European weather

MBB Kormoran missile under wing of F-104G Starfighter

MBB-built AS.20 missile under wing of F-104G Starfighter of Marinefliegergeschwader 1
(*Ing Hans Redemann*)

conditions, the eventual development of a dual-mode radar/TV seeker, like that of the US Condor missile, seems likely.

MBB has stated that Jumbo is intended for use against point and area targets, with launch at virtually any altitude. An inertial guidance system and radar altimeter are expected to offer a variety of flight paths to the target. Video/command link equipment will be carried in a pylon-mounted pod on the launch aircraft, which will include F-4s of the Luftwaffe.

DIMENSIONS:

Length overall	17 ft 2½ in (5·24 m)
Body diameter	1 ft 7¾ in (0·50 m)
Wing span	4 ft 1¼ in (1·25 m)

WEIGHT:

Launching weight	2,535 lb (1,150 kg)

Jumbo television-guided air-to-surface missile, under development by MBB

INDIA

BHARAT DYNAMICS

BHARAT DYNAMICS LTD

ADDRESS: Hyderabad

This company was formed by the Government of India to establish a national guided missile industry. It occupied a new factory at Hyderabad in 1971 and, as a first step, undertook the manufacture of SS.11 anti-tank missiles under licence from Aérospatiale of France. The first batch of missiles, produced from subassemblies supplied by Aérospatiale, came off the Indian assembly line and passed acceptance tests only 12 months after signature of the licensing agreement. By late 1973, the SS.11 was being manufactured entirely in India. It is planned to extend production to other types of weapon, including several of the second-generation missiles developed by Euromissile (which see).

The Soviet-designed K-13A (NATO "Atoll") infra-red homing air-to-air missile is also reported to be produced in India, for carriage by the MiG-21 fighters of the IAF.

INTERNATIONAL PROGRAMMES

EUROMISSILE

ADDRESS:
37 boulevard de Montmorency, 75781 Paris-cédex 16, France
Telephone: 525-54-32
Telex: EUROM 61 467 F

PRESIDENT:
Jean Crepin

VICE-PRESIDENT:
Friedemann Striegel

DIRECTOR OF PROGRAMMES:
Jean Poggi

DIRECTOR OF FINANCE AND CONTRACTS:
Pierre Chapelle

SALES DIRECTORS:
Pierre Chaboureau
Emil-Otto Wittmann

Euromissile is a Groupement d'Intérêt Economique formed by Aérospatiale of France and MBB of Germany. It enables the industrial management and marketing of missiles which the two parent companies have developed jointly to be handled by a single organisation, responsible for the entire programme.

First products of the Euromissile team are three short-range battlefield weapons known as Milan, Hot and Roland, developed for the armed services of France and Federal Germany. Of these, Hot is the only one that has an air-launch capability.

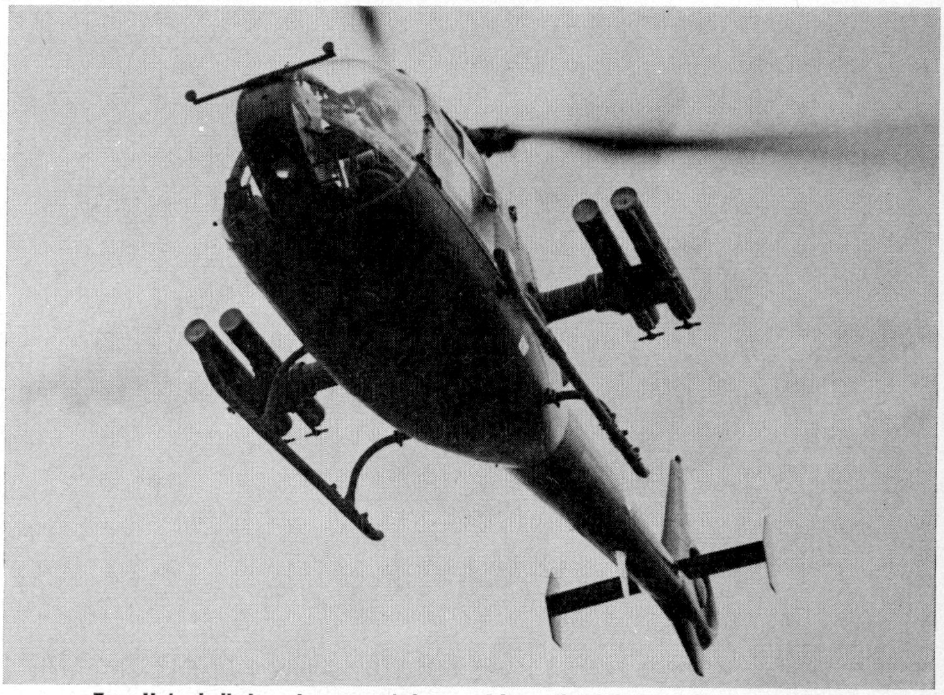

Four Hot missile launchers mounted on an Aérospatiale/Westland Gazelle helicopter

HOT

The Hot (High-subsonic, optically-guided, tube-launched) is a tube-launched wire-guided anti-tank missile suitable for both surface-to-surface and air-to-surface use. It has fins which fold down against the body when it is in its launching tube, and open out to spin-stabilise it in flight. The power plant is a two-stage solid-propellant rocket motor. Because of its comparatively high speed, the time of flight to a target is about half that for the earlier Aérospatiale SS.11. Guidance is by means of the TCA type of automatic optical sighting/infra-red system in one of three forms: a type made up of separate components for adaptation to the turrets of vehicles like the French AMX 10 and US M113; a periscopic type for turret-less vehicles such as the German SPZ Neu; a stabilised-sight type for use on helicopters such as the BO 105, Gazelle and Bell UH-1D. A jet vane control system is used.

The HLVS (Hot, stabilised localiser-sight) system offers magnifications of 2·8 × 22° field and 11·2 × 5·6° field. Sight limits are ±120° in bearing and $\frac{+28°}{-20°}$ in elevation. To engage a target, the aimer maintains a sighting cross on the target, switches on the firing installation and selects a missile on the control box.

Development of the automatic guidance system for use on helicopters began in early 1972, with the first installation on an Alouette III. The results of initial tests were as good as those achieved earlier on the ground in terms of accuracy and reliability, over ranges up to 13,125 ft (4,000 m) during hovering and manoeuvring flight.

Flight testing of an operational Hot installation on a Aérospatiale/Westland SA 341 Gazelle helicopter, in conjunction with the HLVS stabilised sight system, was performed in 1973. With the target hidden from the sight of the pilot and missile operator before take-off, the helicopter proved able to acquire the target and launch a missile within 4 seconds of lift-off. Hit probability proved to be 90% over ranges varying from a minimum 1,310 ft (400 m) to a maximum of 13,125 ft (4,000 m) in hovering flight and 15,000 ft (4,600 m) in translational flight at speeds up to 108 knots (124 mph; 200 km/h). After launch, the helicopter was able to take evasive action at a turning speed of up to 6° per second.

Further helicopter trials, by the official services of France and Germany, were scheduled to take place during 1974, from a Gazelle and a BO 105 respectively. Each official evaluation was expected to involve the launch of at least 65 Hot missiles. A decision on whether or not to adopt the weapon system was intended to be taken in both countries before the end of 1974.

The Hot missile, mountings and guidance units are standard for all surface or airborne installations. Tests already conducted have

Hot missile in its launch tube, ready to fire

Launching a Hot missile from an Alouette III helicopter

confirmed that the guidance accuracy is high enough to allow the missile to be used for defence against attack by low-flying aircraft and helicopters.

DIMENSIONS:

Length overall	4 ft 3¼ in (1·30 m)
Body diameter	6⅞ in (0·175 m)
Fin span	1 ft 0¼ in (0·31 m)

WEIGHTS (helicopter installation):

Launching weight of missile	48·5 lb (22 kg)
Warhead	13·2 lb (6 kg)
Missile and container	62 lb (28 kg)
Sight/localiser group	74·5 lb (33·8 kg)
Command/guidance group	66·8 lb (30·3 kg)
Launcher group:	
Gazelle, 4 launchers	87·8 lb (39·8 kg)
BO 105, 6 launchers	275 lb (125 kg)

PERFORMANCE (air-to-surface):

Max speed	545 knots (625 mph; 1,010 km/h)
Flight times:	
6,560 ft (2,000 m)	8·7 sec
9,840 ft (3,000 m)	12·5 sec
13,125 ft (4,000 m)	16·3 sec
Range	1,310-13,125 ft (400-4,000 m)

MATRA/HSD

SA ENGINS MATRA, avenue Louis Breguet, 78140 Vélizy-Villacoublay, France
Telephone: 946-96-00

HAWKER SIDDELEY DYNAMICS LTD, Manor Road, Hatfield, Herts, England
Telephone: Hatfield 62300

Matra and HSD have developed jointly an air-to-surface precision tactical strike missile known as Martel, to meet the requirements of the British and French armed services.

MATRA/HSD AS.37/AJ.168 MARTEL

Martel (Missile Anti-Radar and TELevision) is a guided air-to-surface missile which has been designed in two versions, one using passive radar homing and the other TV guidance. The two versions have maximum commonality of structure and systems.

The anti-radar version of Martel (AS.37) offers all-weather attack capability against radar antennae in several frequency bands. Depending on the mission profiles, it can be launched at very low, medium or high altitudes. It then flies a homing trajectory into the emitting target source. This is done without further information or control from the parent aircraft, which can return to its base immediately after launch.

The television version of Martel (AJ.168) follows a pre-programmed course immediately after launch, but the final impact on target is effected by the weapon operator, who is given a direct visual picture of the target on a high-brightness monitor. Command instructions are sent back from the aircraft to the missile if changes are required to the missile flight path, in either elevation or azimuth. Control signals generated within the missile itself alter the flight path to bring the axis of the missile into line with that of the television camera, once the target has been selected.

A wide variety of initial flight patterns can be produced to ensure that the TV system has the best possible opportunity of identifying the target, with the least possible danger to the launching aircraft.

Other major companies associated with Martel are the Marconi Company, who provide the TV and radio link equipment which forms part of the guidance system of the TV version; Electronique Marcel Dassault, who provide the AD-37 passive homing head of the anti-radar version; and BAC, who supply missile radomes and high-precision gyroscopes through their Reinforced and Microwave Plastics Group and Precision Products Group respectively. The solid-propellant motors are produced by Hotchkiss-Brandt and Aérospatiale.

Martel missile on the underwing launcher of a Harrier V/STOL aircraft

Buccaneer carrying three Martel missiles and a Martel systems pod

No other details of Martel may yet be published. The general appearance of the two versions is shown in the accompanying illustrations.

The first simulated firings and mock-up launchings were made in the Summer of 1964 and prototypes of both versions were completed in 1965-66. Development was completed in 1968 with a highly successful series of firings. Evaluation, which began in 1969, proved very satisfactory. Delivery of production missiles and equipment began in 1972; the first firing of a production Martel took place on 10 December 1973, when an anti-radar missile was launched from a Breguet Atlantic ASW aircraft of the French Navy, off Landes Flight Test Centre. The Martel impacted on a target radar mounted on a ship.

Martel arms a variety of aircraft, including the Hawker Siddeley Buccaneer operated by the British services, and the Dassault Mirage III-E, SEPECAT Jaguar and Breguet Atlantic operated by the French services.

DIMENSIONS:

Length overall:	
AS.37	13 ft 6¼ in (4·12 m)
AJ.168	12 ft 8½ in (3·87 m)
Span of wings	3 ft 11¼ in (1·20 m)
Body diameter	1 ft 3¾ in (0·40 m)

WEIGHTS:

Launching weight:	
AS.37	1,168 lb (530 kg)
AJ.168	1,213 lb (550 kg)
Warhead	330 lb (150 kg)

MATRA/OTO MELARA

SA ENGINS MATRA, avenue Louis Breguet, 78140 Vélizy-Villacoublay, France

OTO MELARA SpA, Via Valdilocchi 15, 19100 La Spezia, Italy

These two companies are developing jointly an anti-shipping missile known as Otomat, which is turbojet-powered and has an unusually long range for this class of weapon. Its name is a contraction of **Oto** Melara and **Matra**.

MATRA/OTO MELARA OTOMAT

Matra and Oto Melara began joint development of the Otomat anti-shipping missile in 1969 after two years of independent work on weapons of this type. First details of the programme were released at the *Salon de l'Armement Naval* held at le Bourget in September 1970. At that time, the emphasis was on ship-to-ship use and firing trials began with four ground launches between April and July 1971, which confirmed that the performance of the basic missile and its launch system was satisfactory. The first firing of a complete Otomat missile, with self-contained terminal homing system, was made on 28 February 1972 from the firing range at Salto Di Quirra in Sardinia before representatives of several navies, including that of Brazil. After travelling several dozen kilometres over the sea, the missile ended its trajectory with a direct hit on the target boat.

Firing trials have continued since that time, and the performance demonstration phase ended with the successful fifth launch in Sardinia on 11 May 1973. After a series of operational evaluation launchings at sea by the Italian Navy, initial deliveries of Otomat will be made to this service to arm one or both of the fast patrol boats of the *Freccia* class, each of which can be fitted with four launchers. The new hydrofoil ship *Swordfish* will have two fixed Otomat launchers.

Otomat is equally suitable for static or mobile use ashore, and for air-to-surface use from helicopters or fixed-wing aircraft.

Model of the Atlantic maritime reconnaissance aircraft with Otomat (inboard) and anti-radar Martel missiles on its underwing launchers

When Otomat is carried by maritime reconnaissance aircraft such as the Atlantic and Nimrod, carrier-based strike aircraft such as the Super Etendard and anti-submarine helicopters in the class of the Sea King and Super Frelon, its range is sufficient to place the launch aircraft well beyond the reach of most ship-to-air defence systems available for current and projected future naval vessels. A mix with radar-homing Martels, which are interchangeable with Otomat, is anticipated.

The general appearance of the basic surface-to-surface Otomat is shown in an accompanying launch photograph. Its cylindrical body houses, from nose to tail: a Thomson-CSF active radar homing head inside an ogival nosecone, a semi-armour-piercing warhead weighing 460 lb (210 kg), inertial platform, control package, computer and radio altimeter, kerosene tank, oil tank, tail control surface actuators, and Turboméca Arbizon III turbojet. This power plant is based on the Turmo III free-turbine turboshaft and has a rating of 882 lb (400 kg) st. It is supplied with air through four semi-circular ducts equi-spaced around the body of the missile, with their intakes at about the mid-point from nose to tail. Each duct carries one of the cruciform swept wings, with which the tail control surfaces are indexed in line.

Missiles will be delivered in containers which will serve also as launchers, mounted in fixed positions on the ship. This is made possible by Otomat's ability to change direction up to 180° port or starboard after launch to put itself on course for the target. The launch ship does not, therefore, need to change course when launching the weapon, even if the target is to its rear. Firing, with the aid of two side-mounted jettisonable solid-propellant boosters, is possible in all weathers, or at night, and tests have been made over ranges up to 45 nm (53 miles; 85 km). Fuel capacity is sufficient for much longer ranges, if required, and Otomat is capable of operation over distances far beyond the conventional radar horizon of a ship. The incendiary effect of fuel remaining in its tank at the time of impact is added to the destructive force of the warhead.

The rear portion of the air-launched Otomat is similar to that of the ship-to-ship version, with an Arbizon III turbojet; but smaller solid-propellant boosters are fitted. The forward section is similar to that of Martel.

After launch, the missile descends to a very low cruising height (approx 80 ft; 25 m), which is maintained by means of a TRT type AHV-7 radio altimeter. The inertial platform takes care of navigation until the missile is about 6·5 nm (7·5 miles; 12 km) from the target, where its Thomson-CSF Colvert active homing head locks on to the enemy ship. At about 3·75 nm (4·35 miles; 7 km) from the target, Otomat begins to climb to a height of nearly 650 ft (200 m), in order to make its impact at the end of a steep terminal dive.

DIMENSIONS (ship-to-ship version):
- Length overall: 15 ft 9¾ in (4·82 m)
- Body diameter:
  - Forward of air intakes: 15·75 in (40 cm)
  - Over turbojet housing: 18·11 in (46 cm)
- Wing span: 3 ft 10¾ in (1·19 m)

WEIGHTS:
- Weight of missile and container/launcher: approx 2,755 lb (1,250 kg)
- Launching weight:
  - Naval, helicopter and shore-based versions: 1,543 lb (700 kg)
  - Aircraft-launched version: 1,210 lb (550 kg)

PERFORMANCE:
- Cruising speed: Mach 0·9
- Range:
  - Ship-to-ship: 45 nm (53 miles; 85 km)
  - Air-to-surface: over 54 nm (62 miles; 100 km)

Launch of a complete Otomat missile in Sardinia

ISRAEL

RAFAEL

RAFAEL ARMAMENT DEVELOPMENT AUTHORITY

ADDRESS:
Ministry of Defence, POB 2082, Haifa
Telephone: 04-714168
MANAGER, EXPORT AND SALES DIVISION:
E. D. Dagan

The duty of Rafael Armament Development Authority is to develop and supply advanced weapons and weapon systems for use by the Israeli Defence Forces. As well as meeting urgent requirements for complete weapons, it is responsible for research, development and manufacture of propellants, aircraft armament, fuses, explosives, small computers, electronic systems, communications systems and other products. To make this possible, it possesses a variety of structural testing, environmental testing and other laboratories and facilities.

One of the weapon systems developed and manufactured by Rafael is the Shafrir air-to-air missile.

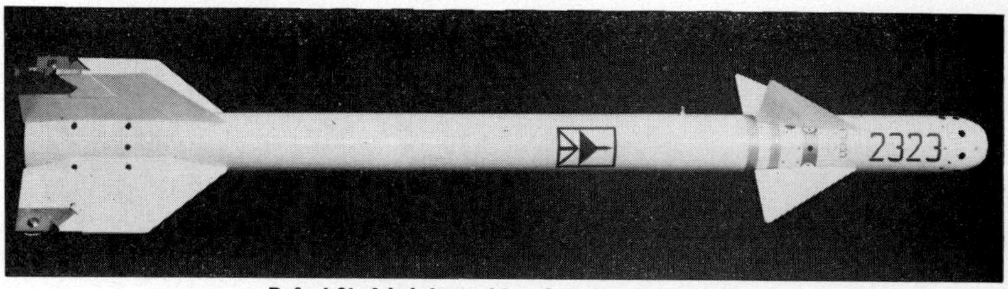

Rafael Shafrir infra-red homing air-to-air missile

SHAFRIR (DRAGONFLY)

Shafrir is a short-range air-to-air dogfight missile developed for use against aircraft at heights up to 60,000 ft (18,000 m). Its development was completed by the late 'sixties and production was then started. Many rounds have been fired in air combat against enemy aircraft since 1969, with considerable success.

This was particularly evident after the Yom Kippur War of October 1973, when Israel is reported to have destroyed about 335 Arab aircraft in air combat for the loss of only six of its own aircraft. Nearly 200 of the Arab aircraft were shot down by infra-red homing missiles, some Sidewinders but mostly Shafrirs, according to the US *Armed Forces Journal*. In 70 other successful combats, the weapon responsible for destroying the target was not determined.

Relatively small in size and simple in conception, Shafrir has a slim cylindrical body, with an infra-red seeker head and cruciform canard control surfaces indexed in line with cruciform fixed wings mounted at the tail. A rolleron is inset in the tip of each wing to help stabilise the missile in flight.

Shafrir has a solid-propellant rocket motor and is a solid-state weapon, fully transistorised and with all components built to strict military specifications. The foreplanes are actuated pneumatically. Electronic circuitry is kept to a minimum, with no computers. Guidance is by proportional navigation, for optimum results against manoeuvring targets.

The missile and its launcher are mounted under the wing of the aircraft on a specially-designed adapter which is capable of carrying other types of weapon as an alternative to Shafrir. Attachment is mechanical and the missile requires no support from the aircraft except for the firing circuit. When a target is detected within firing range, an audio signal is heard and a light is switched on automatically on the pilot's control panel as an indication that the firing button should be pressed. After launch, the missile tracks the target entirely automatically, and the warhead is detonated either on impact or by the proximity fuse within optimum distance of the target.

Sales are reported to have been made to several overseas customers, including Taiwan.

DIMENSION:
- Length overall: 8 ft 2½ in (2·50 m)

WEIGHTS:
- Warhead: 24·25 lb (11 kg)
- Launching weight: 205 lb (93 kg)

PERFORMANCE:
- Max range: 2·7 nm (3·1 miles; 5 km)

LUZ

According to unconfirmed reports, Israel is developing a television-guided air-to-surface missile named Luz.

ITALY

SELENIA

SELENIA INDUSTRIE ELETTRONICHE ASSOCIATE SpA

HEAD OFFICE AND WORKS:
via Tiburtina km. 12.400, 00131 Rome
POSTAL ADDRESS:
PO Box 7083, 00100 Rome
Telephone: 43601
Telex: 61106 Seleniat
PUBLIC RELATIONS:
Dott Ing Paolo De Gaetano

This major Italian company produces missiles, missile components and equipment, in addition to a wide range of radar, telecommunications, automation and other electronic products.

Selenia Aspide-1A high-performance air-to-air and surface-to-air missile

ASPIDE-1A

This high-performance air-to-air and surface-to-air weapon is under development as armament for the F-104S interceptor and its successors, in the Albatros naval air defence system, and in the Spada ground-based low-altitude air defence system. It will improve the effectiveness of each of these weapon systems in terms of maximum missile range, operation at very low altitudes, multiple target engagement and resistance to advanced ECM. In particular, it is intended to enhance the dogfight and shoot-down capabilities of the F-104S.

A single-stage solid-propellant rocket motor gives Aspide-1A a speed described as being "well in the hypersonic field" in an air-to-air role. Its guidance system is of the semi-active radar type.

The missile's final configuration had been

determined by the Spring of 1974, and captive flight testing of prototypes was scheduled to begin in June. Qualification tests and construction of pre-series prototypes for engineering evaluation were under way by that time. Research and development are expected to be completed by 1976, enabling production deliveries to begin in 1977.

DIMENSIONS:

Length overall	12 ft 1½ in (3·70 m)
Body diameter	7·87 in (20 cm)
Wing span	3 ft 3¼ in (1·00 m)
Fin span	2 ft 7½ in (0·80 m)

WEIGHT:

Launching weight	485 lb (220 kg)

SISTEL

SISTEL—SISTEMI ELETTRONICI SpA

HEAD OFFICE:
via Tiburtina 1210, 00131 Rome
Telephone: 415841 and 414651
Telex: 68112 Sistelro

MANAGING DIRECTOR:
Prof Ing Giovanni Malaman

Sistel—Sistemi Elettronici SpA—was formed jointly by Montecatini-Edison, Contraves Italiana, Fiat, Finmeccanica and SNIA in late 1967, to develop new products in the missile field. It embodies the former missiles and space equipment branch of Contraves Italiana.

Sistel's current products include the Indigo short-range surface-to-air missile, the naval Sea Indigo, the Sea Killer Mk 1 and Mk 2 surface-to-surface missiles, and the Marte helicopter-launched version of Sea Killer Mks 1 and 2. Under development are the Sea Killer Mk 3 and the Airtos short-range air-to-surface missile. FM/FM telemetry packages and telemetry receiving stations are also designed and manufactured by Sistel.

MARTE

In 1967, the Italian Navy initiated a development programme, known as Project Marte, to enhance the capabilities of shore-based or ship-borne helicopters by arming them with anti-shipping missiles. Eventually, Sistel's Sea Killer family of missiles was chosen as most suitable for this application, because of the weapons' all-weather operability, automatic guidance system, inherent insensibility to ECM and sea-skimming flight profile.

Sistel was appointed prime contractor and supplier of Sea Killer Mk 1 and Mk 2 missiles, described individually under this entry. Agusta manufactures under licence the Sikorsky SH-3D and Bell Model 204 helicopters which were envisaged as carriers of the Marte weapon system, with airborne radars supplied by SMA. The system has, however, been studied for installation on a wide range of helicopters, with take-off weights varying from 3,000 kg to more than 10,000 kg (6,600-22,050 lb), dependent on the number of missiles to be carried and the possible requirement for simultaneous anti-submarine and surface strike capability.

Equipment added to the Marte helicopter is lightweight and easily operated. The radar performs navigation, search and target tracking as well as guidance of the missile in azimuth. Thus an SH-3D helicopter, fully equipped for surface strike and anti-submarine duties, and with an autopilot for instrument flying, can be assigned a 4½-hour maritime patrol at a search speed of 100 knots (115 mph; 185 km/h), carrying a crew of four. Total weight of the system is 2,568 lb (1,165 kg), made up of 882 lb (400 kg) for the missile launching equipment, 1,323 lb (600 kg) for two Sea Killer Mk 2 missiles, 315 lb (143 kg) for sonar equipment, and 48 lb (22 kg) for an optical sight. The operator has a missile control console inside the main cabin of the aircraft. The radar antenna is mounted inside a shallow radome beneath the hull, under the flight deck.

In action, it can be assumed that the helicopter will locate a target in a few seconds of radar operation at the limit of radar range. To reduce the possibility of enemy recognition of the helicopter's radar interrogation, the airborne radar is then switched off and the aircraft descends in order to fly toward the target at the lowest practical height above the water. At an estimated distance just beyond missile range, the helicopter climbs again to missile launching height, re-acquires the target and launches a Sea Killer, which takes slightly more than one minute to reach the enemy ship.

The Sistel radar altimeter in the missile can be pre-set before launch to control the cruising height at values down to 2 m (6 ft 7 in) or less, depending on factors such as sea state. The altitude can be changed by command signal during flight, if required. Control in azimuth can be achieved either by automatic radar mode in all-weather conditions or by a standby fair-weather system, using an optical sight and joy-stick controller.

Initial firing trials of the Marte system in flight, from an AB 204 helicopter, had been made successfully by the Spring of 1973. Both ground and air launches were continuing in 1974.

SISTEL SEA KILLER Mk 1

This fully-qualified short-range surface-to-surface ship-based guided weapon, known for a time as Nettuno, is carried in a five-round multiple launcher on board the fast petrol boat *Saetta* of the Italian Navy.

Sea Killer Mk 1 is also one of the sea-skimming missiles utilised in the Marte air-to-surface weapon system for helicopters.

WINGS: Movable cruciform control surfaces at centre of missile.

BODY: Cylindrical light alloy structure.

TAIL SURFACES: Cruciform stabilising fins.

POWER PLANT: Solid-propellant rocket motor (4,410 lb; 2,000 kg st).

GUIDANCE: Alternative all-weather beam-rider/command/radio altimeter guidance, or optical radio command/radio altimeter guidance.

CONTROL: Via movable wings.

WARHEAD: High-explosive fragmentation type, with impact/proximity fuse; weight 77 lb (35 kg).

DIMENSIONS:

Length overall	12 ft 3 in (3·73 m)
Body diameter	7·87 in (0·20 m)
Span of wings	2 ft 9½ in (0·85 m)

WEIGHTS:

Launching weight	370 lb (168 kg)
Weight at burnout	260 lb (118 kg)

PERFORMANCE:

Speed at burnout	Mach 1·9
Max effective range	5·4 nm (6·2 miles; 10 km)

SISTEL SEA KILLER Mk 2

Known for a time as Vulcano, this two-stage surface-to-surface guided missile is a development of the Sea Killer Mk 1 with a heavier warhead and extended range. First flight trials of Sea Killer Mk 2 missiles were made in mid-1969. Qualification trials were carried out in mid-1971, and the weapon is operational on board four Vosper Mk 5 frigates of the Imperial Iranian Navy. It is also one of the sea-skimming missiles utilised in the Marte air-to-surface weapon system for helicopters.

WINGS, BODY, TAIL SURFACES: As for Sea Killer Mk 1. Booster also has stabilising fins.

POWER PLANT: SEP 299 solid-propellant booster, rated at 9,702 lb (4,400 kg) st for 1·6 sec. SEP 300 solid-propellant sustainer, rated at 220·5 lb (100 kg) st for 73 sec.

GUIDANCE AND CONTROL: As for Sea Killer Mk 1.

WARHEAD: High-explosive semi-armour-piercing with impact/proximity fuse; weight 154 lb (70 kg).

DIMENSIONS:

Length overall	15 ft 5 in (4·70 m)
Body diameter	7·87 in (0·20 m)
Span of wings	3 ft 3½ in (1·00 m)

WEIGHT:

Launching weight	595 lb (270 kg)

PERFORMANCE:

Cruising speed	Mach 0·74
Max effective range	over 13·5 nm (15·5 miles; 25 km)

AIRTOS

Under development in 1974, the Airtos air-to-surface weapon system is intended to destroy or neutralise naval craft by means of short-range missiles launched in all-weather conditions. The missile is capable of destroying high-speed targets such as hydrofoils and hovercraft possessing great manoeuvring acceleration, at speeds up to 90 knots, and of inflicting heavy damage on craft as large as fast patrol boats and frigates.

The system is based on a missile similar in size and configuration to Sea Killer Mk 1, but with a dual guidance system using a radar altimeter for altitude control and an active radar seeker for terminal homing. This makes the missile itself relatively lightweight, reduces the equipment that must be carried by the launch aircraft, and frees the latter for evasive action and return to base once the missile has been launched. A fighter-bomber in the class of the Aeritalia G91Y can carry two Airtos missiles on underwing launchers; a patrol aircraft might carry six.

Prior to launch, the Airtos missile is aimed towards the target by flying the launch aircraft in the appropriate direction. The operator is informed when the seeker head has locked on to the target, and then verifies that the distance to target is within the missile's range. Firing is practicable within six seconds of decision to attack. The Airtos missile then descends to its cruising altitude of about 33 ft (10 m) and is controlled in azimuth by the homing head through a proportional guidance system.

Sistel Sea Killer Mk 2 missile, as used in Marte air-to-surface weapon system

AB 204AS helicopter adapted for ground launching Marte missile

Test firing a Marte missile from an AB 204AS helicopter in flight

At a predetermined distance from the target, altitude is reduced further to the pre-set attack height of 6-16 ft (2-5 m). Detonation of the fragmentation-type warhead is by impact or by a signal passed to the proximity fuse by the altimeter if the missile overflies the target.

TYPE: Short-range air-to-surface anti-shipping missile.

WINGS: Movable cruciform control surfaces at centre of missile.

BODY: Cylindrical light alloy structure.

TAIL SURFACES: Fixed cruciform stabilising fins, indexed in line with wings.

POWER PLANT: Double-base solid-propellant rocket motor, giving 4,410 lb (2,000 kg) st for 5 seconds.

GUIDANCE: Radar altimeter/active radar homing.

CONTROL: Via wings.

WARHEAD: High-explosive fragmentation type, with impact/proximity fuse; weight 77 lb (35 kg).

DIMENSIONS:

Length overall	12 ft 9½ in (3·90 m)
Body diameter	8·1 in (0·206 m)
Span of wings	2 ft 9½ in (0·857 m)

WEIGHTS:

Launching weight	421 lb (191 kg)
Weight at burnout	311 lb (141 kg)

PERFORMANCE:

Speed at burnout	Mach 1·9
Max lock-on range for homing head	8 nm (9·3 miles; 15 km)
Min effective range	1·6 nm (1·85 miles; 3 km)
Max effective range	6 nm(6·8 miles; 11 km)

JAPAN

MITSUBISHI

MITSUBISHI DENKI KABUSHIKI KAISHA (Mitsubishi Electric Corporation)

HEAD OFFICE:
2-2-3, Marunouchi, Chiyoda-ku, Tokyo
Telephone: 218-2111

PRESIDENT: Sadakazu Shindo

Since 1921, Mitsubishi Electric has been responsible for production of a wide range of electrical and electronic products as a sister company of Mitsubishi Heavy Industries. Its recent aerospace products include radar systems, computers, fire control systems, radio equipment and ADF installations.

In 1968, the company was awarded a contract to build the Hawk surface-to-air missile for the Ground Self-Defence Force, under licence from Raytheon (USA). The missiles are being delivered to the JGSDF in the period 1968-77.

Subsequently, Mitsubishi Electric was named prime contractor for licence production of Sparrow III air-to-air missiles to arm F-4EJ fighters of the JASDF. This work began in FY 1972, and about 600 Sparrow IIIs will be delivered between 1974 and 1978.

MITSUBISHI JUKOGYO KABUSHIKI KAISHA (Mitsubishi Heavy Industries, Ltd)

HEAD OFFICE:
5-1, Marunouchi, 2-chome, Chiyoda-ku, Tokyo 100

OFFICERS: See "Aircraft" section

Mitsubishi Heavy Industries is developing and producing air-to-air missiles for the JASDF. It is also manufacturing the Nike-Hercules surface-to-air missile under licence from McDonnell Douglas Corporation, and has Japanese government contracts to develop an air-to-surface anti-shipping missile.

Details of its research rockets can be found in the "Spaceflight" section of this edition.

MITSUBISHI AAM-1

The AAM-1 is an infra-red homing air-to-air missile which Mitsubishi developed and produced for the Japan Defence Agency. Deliveries began in November 1970, to replace the Sidewinder on the F-86F and F-104J interceptors of the JASDF; total planned production of 330 missiles was completed by late 1971. No details are available.

MITSUBISHI AAM-2

Mitsubishi is developing this missile as a replacement for the AAM-1. It is a collision-course weapon, whereas the AAM-1 is limited to pursuit-course attack. No details are available, except that Mitsubishi, as prime contractor, awarded a contract to Nippon Electric Company to cover manufacture of experimental infra-red homing devices for the AAM-2.

A contract awarded in the first half of 1973 covered the manufacture of a second batch of 21 prototype AAM-2s for continued testing, at a cost of about $4·36 million. They are being followed by a pre-production batch of about 40 missiles, with which air launches will begin in the Spring of 1975. The AAM-2 is expected to enter service later the same year.

MITSUBISHI ASM-1

The Japanese government approved the appropriation of $1 million in FY 1973 and $5 million in FY 1974 to cover the initial development phase of an air-to-surface anti-shipping missile to be carried by Mitsubishi FS-T2-Kai attack aircraft of the JASDF. In November 1973 Mitsubishi Heavy Industries was selected as prime contractor for this missile, which will also be suitable for ship or ground launching when fitted with a rocket booster.

Known only as the ASM-1 at present, the new missile will use an inertial system for mid-course guidance and an active radar seeker for terminal guidance. No other details are yet available.

NORWAY

A/S KONGSBERG VAAPENFABRIKK

HEAD OFFICE AND WORKS:
Postboks 25, N-3601 Kongsberg
Telephone: Kongsberg 37, or (02) 83 81 85
Telex: 11491

SALES MANAGER, DEFENCE EQUIPMENT: M. Frihagen

PUBLIC RELATIONS MANAGER: E. Frisvaag

This government-owned company is the only armament manufacturer in Norway. Its products include small arms, guns, rockets and missiles, proximity fuses, fire control equipment and weapon systems.

A/S Kongsberg Vaapenfabrikk was prime contractor for European production of the Bullpup air-to-surface missile and is the manufacturer of the Norwegian-developed Terne anti-submarine system and Penguin anti-ship missile system.

PENGUIN

This anti-ship missile system was developed by the Norwegian Defence Research Establishment, with assistance from the US and Federal German navies. It is in quantity production by Kongsberg Vaapenfabrikk, and can be installed on ships, helicopters and other platforms.

In its ship-to-ship version, Penguin is delivered in a container with integral launch-rail and can utilise most existing types of shipboard fire-control systems. It embodies a two-stage solid-propellant rocket motor and an inertial guidance system with infra-red terminal homing. Its warhead is said to weigh 264 lb (120 kg) and to be similar to that of Bullpup, with a contact fuse.

Each of the 20 *Storm* class gunboats of the Royal Norwegian Navy carries six individual Penguin launchers on its rear deck. The six new torpedo boats of the *Snogg* class are each fitted with four launchers; others are installed on the five *Oslo* class frigates.

The air-launched version of Penguin, which is being studied for carriage by jet fighters, would have a reduced wing span and would not need the booster stage of the rocket motor.

The following details apply to the ship-launched version of Penguin, as illustrated:

DIMENSIONS:

Length overall	10 ft 0 in (3·05 m)
Body diameter	11 in (28 cm)
Wing span	4 ft 7 in (1·40 m)

WEIGHTS:

Launching weight	727 lb (330 kg)
Weight with container/launcher	1,410 lb (640 kg)

PERFORMANCE (estimated):

Cruising speed	Mach 0·7
Max range	10-15 nm (11·5-17 miles; 18·5-27 km)

Penguin anti-ship missile

SOUTH AFRICA

First official news of guided weapon development in South Africa was given by the Minister of Defence, Mr P. W. Botha, on 2 May 1969. He announced that both surface-to-air and air-to-air missiles were then under development.

WHIPLASH

No details of this missile are available except that it is a purely South African venture, has "some unique characteristics" and had already been tested successfully on a range at St Lucia at the time of Mr Botha's original announcement of the project on 2 May 1969. Reports in the UK press have suggested that the missile is named Whiplash and is in limited production.

SWEDEN

BOFORS

AKTIEBOLAGET BOFORS

HEAD OFFICE AND WORKS:
S-690 20 Bofors
Telephone: 0586-360 00
Telex: 732 10

MANAGING DIRECTOR: C. U. Winberg

ORDNANCE DIVISION: L. Pålsson

PUBLIC RELATIONS MANAGER: U. Carlström

This world-famous Swedish armament manufacturing concern has been producing unguided air-to-air and air-to-surface rockets for many years. As its first project in the guided missile field it developed as a private venture the Bantam wire-guided anti-tank weapon.

Other missile systems currently in production include multiple launchers for 375 mm anti-submarine rockets with ranges up to 11,100 ft (3,600 m).

BOFORS BANTAM

Swedish military designation: RB53

The Bantam is a small wire-guided anti-tank missile, designed originally for operation by a single infantry soldier and since adapted for air-to-surface use also.

The cylindrical body and cruciform wings are made largely of glassfibre-reinforced plastics. Control is by vibrating spoilers, in each wing trailing-edge; and features of the guidance system, such as automatic control of the spoiler frequency, make Bantam easier to guide than other missiles of the so-called first generation. A two-stage solid-propellant rocket motor is used. The high-explosive warhead weighs 4·1 lb (1·9 kg); and hit probability is claimed to be 95 to 98 per cent over ranges between 2,625 and 6,600 ft (800-2,000 m).

The wings fold at mid-span, making possible the use of a very small carrying container. When the missile is fired from the container the wings unfold and their bent rear corners then cause the missile to rotate in flight.

The total weight of the entire weapon system, including launcher, carrying rack, cable and control unit is 44 lb (20 kg).

The Bantam can be installed on and fired from vehicles of most types, including light combat aircraft in the class of the Saab Supporter and on helicopters. A number of rounds have been fired successfully from both types of aircraft.

The Bantam continues in large-scale production for surface-to-surface use by the Swedish and Swiss Armies, with which it is standard equipment. Current contracts will maintain series production until the mid-1970s.

Bantam missile being fired from a Saab Supporter light attack aircraft

DIMENSIONS:
- Length overall: 2 ft 9½ in (0·85 m)
- Body diameter: 4·3 in (0·11 m)
- Wing span: 1 ft 3¾ in (0·40 m)

WEIGHT:
- Launching weight: 16·5 lb (7·5 kg)

PERFORMANCE:
- Cruising speed: 165 knots (190 mph; 306 km/h)
- Range: 820-6,600 ft (250-2,000 m)

VAPENAVDELNINGEN (FMV-F:V)

Weapons Directorate of the Swedish Air Materiel Department

ADDRESS:
Försvarets Materielverk, Huvudavdelningen för flygmateriel, Vapenavdelningen, S-104 50, Stockholm 80

Telephone: 08-630780
Telex: 19061

No guided weapons have been developed by the Swedish Air Materiel Department (FMV-F) since it became part of the Defence Materiel Administration (FMV) on 1 July 1968. It was assigned from that date responsibility for the procurement of all guided weapons for the Air Force, and other guided weapons which required development for Sweden or were to be manufactured under licence in Sweden. Following further re-organisation on 1 April 1974, these responsibilities have been shared between the Weapons Directorates of the Army, Naval and Air Materiel Departments. However, the Missiles Technology Division of the Air Materiel Department is responsible for technical co-ordination between the Departments. Together with the Swedish Research Institute of National Defence (FOA), it is also responsible for research in the guided weapons field.

Details are given below of the Robot RB04 which was developed before the 1968 organisational changes took place.

ROBOT RB04

In service since early 1959 as standard armament on the Saab A 32A Lansens of SwAF attack wings, the RB04 (formerly Rb 304) is an all-weather powered bomb intended for use against targets at sea. The latest version equips the Saab AJ 37 Viggen attack aircraft.

The RB04 was developed to a 1949 specification after firing tests of an earlier experimental missile, designated the type 302, had been made in the previous year from a Saab T.18B piston-engined bomber. Project work on the RB04 began in March 1950 and the first full-scale airframe was flight tested in the Spring of 1954. The first complete RB04 was fired from a Saab J 29 fighter on 11 February 1955. Current operational versions are as follows:

RB04D. Improved, higher-performance version which replaced the earlier RB04C. Operational with SwAF attack wings of A 32A aircraft since 1972.

RB04E. Further-improved version developed as primary armament of AJ 37 Viggen, which can carry three, as against two on the A 32A. Described in this section under the entry for Saab-Scania, which is prime contractor for the RB04E.

The following details refer specifically to the RB04D:

TYPE: Air-to-ship guided weapon.

WINGS: Cantilever mid-wing monoplane, mounted at rear of weapon. Ailerons in trailing-edges. Fixed fins at tips.

BODY: Circular-section all-metal structure.

TAIL SURFACES: Tail-first design. Cruciform control surfaces on nose. Fixed fins at wing-tips.

POWER PLANT: One solid-propellant rocket motor.

GUIDANCE: Radar homing.

CONTROL: Autopilot with pneumatically-driven gyros and pneumatic control surface servos.

WARHEAD: High-explosive. Weight approx 660 lb (300 kg).

DIMENSIONS:
- Length overall: 14 ft 7¼ in (4·45 m)
- Body diameter: 1 ft 7¾ in (0·50 m)
- Wing span: 6 ft 8 in (2·04 m)

WEIGHT:
- Launching weight: 1,320 lb (600 kg)

PERFORMANCE:
No details available, but subsonic

SAAB-SCANIA

SAAB-SCANIA AKTIEBOLAG

HEAD OFFICE AND WORKS: Linköping
Telephone: 013-12 90 20
Telex: 50040 saablgs
OFFICERS: See "Aircraft" section

In addition to its work on piloted aircraft, Saab-Scania is developing a modernised version of the RB04 air-to-ship missile and is producing a new air-to-surface weapon system, designated RB05A.

Saab-Scania is also prime contractor for licence manufacture of two versions of the Hughes Aircraft Company (HAC) Falcon air-to-air missile. These are the **RB27** (Hughes designation HM-55), with semi-active radar homing, and the **RB28** (HM-58), with infra-red homing. Both versions are carried by the Saab J 35F Draken interceptors of the Swedish Air Force, and Saab-Scania is offering the RB28 for export under the designation **M-58.** Its HAC L-24 launcher is adaptable to most types of combat aircraft.

Under study are a new long-range air-to-air missile and a surface-launched anti-ship missile with advanced characteristics, to meet future requirements for coastal and naval defence.

SAAB AAM

No details have yet been released officially concerning the long-range air-to-air missile which Saab-Scania is developing as armament for the JA37 Viggen interceptor. It is expected to have interchangeable infra-red and semi-active radar homing heads.

SAAB RB04E

Saab-Scania is prime contractor for development and production of this modernised version of the RB04 anti-shipping missile, on behalf of the Swedish Air Force. Three RB04Es constitute the most important of the various alternative weapon loads that can be carried by the Saab AJ 37 Viggen attack aircraft. Release is reported to be possible at aircraft speeds between Mach 0·4 and near-sonic speeds, after which the missile flies a pre-programmed descent to low level for attack.

Saab RB04E air-to-surface guided missile mounted under belly of AJ 37 Viggen

A description of earlier versions of the RB04 appears under the "Vapenavdelningen" heading in this section of *Jane's*. The modernisation undertaken by Saab-Scania on the RB04E involves changes to the missile's structure and guidance system, to increase reliability and target hit capability. The RB04E utilises an IMI (Summerfield Research) solid-propellant rocket motor and Philips (Sweden) active-seeker head, with proximity-fused warhead.

The RB04E is in series production by Saab-Scania under a Skr 100m contract from the Defence Materiel Administration of the Swedish Armed Forces.

DIMENSIONS:

Length overall	14 ft 7¼ in (4·45 m)
Body diameter	1 ft 7¾ in (0·50 m)
Wing span	6 ft 6 in (1·98 m)

WEIGHT:

Launching weight	1,320 lb (600 kg)

PERFORMANCE:

High subsonic cruising speed

SAAB RB05A

The RB05A is a manually-guided supersonic air-to-surface tactical missile for use against targets at sea or on land. It can also be used against aerial targets.

Known originally under the project designation Saab 305A, its development began in 1960, when an initial contract was received from what is now the Air Materiel Department of the Defence Material Administration of the Armed Forces. The RB05A is now in quantity production under contracts totalling Skr 180 million, for use on the Saab Viggen and Saab 105 strike aircraft. It can, because of its simplicity, be adapted readily for carriage by other types of aircraft.

The airframe of the RB05A is made of conventional aircraft materials and consists of a pointed cylindrical body with long-chord cruciform wings and aft-mounted cruciform control surfaces. The VR-35 pre-packaged liquid-propellant smoke-free rocket motor, supplied by Volvo Flygmotor AB, is centrally mounted and is fitted with a tailpipe which passes through the rear of the body.

The armament system is located in the nose and most of the control equipment at the rear of the missile.

A typical RB05A attack is started with an approach toward the target at the lowest practicable altitude and at high speed. At the optimum range, the pilot receives a command to climb from the aircraft's navigational system. He initiates a quick climb to 300-400 m (1,000-1,300 ft), from which the level-out to horizontal flight is accomplished by selecting the automatic attitude and altitude mode of the aircraft's autopilot.

AJ 37 Viggen attack aircraft armed with four RB05A air-to-surface missiles

After launching, the missile moves automatically into the centre of the pilot's line of sight, and is then guided by command signals from a pilot-operated joystick. These are transmitted over a microwave radio link which is highly resistant to jamming and permits full control at low altitudes over all kinds of terrain. The technique is based on simultaneous observation of the target and the missile, the pilot guiding the weapon so that a tracking flare mounted on its rear end is kept on the line of sight to the target. The high precision of the guidance system and high manoeuvrability of the missile make it possible to attack targets which are at considerable offset angles to either side of the aircraft's course.

Guidance signals received by the missile are converted by an autopilot to control surface deflections through the medium of four gas-driven actuators, supplied by a solid-fuel gas generator. The autopilot also takes care of roll stabilisation. The roll attitude is controlled with the aid of a roll position gyro.

The very effective proximity-fused armament system is of a special design developed by the Swedish Research Institute of National Defence, and is manufactured under subcontract by Forenade Fabriksverken.

Developed versions of the RB05A fitted with a homing device are envisaged.

Equipment for assembly, testing and servicing forms part of the weapon system, as do the special launching rack on which the missile is carried and the control equipment in the aircraft. The missiles are stored fully assembled in containers, where they can be kept for three years without maintenance or testing.

Training of pilots to utilise the RB05A missile involves the use of different kinds of ground-based and airborne simulators, and training missiles.

DIMENSIONS:

Length	11 ft 10 in (3·60 m)
Body diameter	1 ft 0 in (0·30 m)
Wing span	2 ft 8 in (0·80 m)

WEIGHT:

Launching weight	approx 675 lb (305 kg)

THE UNITED KINGDOM

BAC

BRITISH AIRCRAFT CORPORATION (GUIDED WEAPONS) LTD

DIRECTORS:

G. R. Jefferson, CBE, BSc, CEng, MIMechE, FRAeS (Chairman and Managing Director)
E. L. Beverley, DFC, CEng, FRAeS (Commercial)
J. Cattanach, BSc, CEng, MIEE (Design)
T. G. Kent, CEng, AMIMechE, AFRAeS (Production)
Lt Col H. Lacy, MBE, BSc (London Director)
R. J. Raff, FCA, ACMA (Financial)
D. Rowley, MA, CEng, FRAeS (Executive Director, Electronic and Space Systems)
L. A. Sanson, OBE (Sales and Service)
A. T. Slator, MBE, MA (General Manager, GW Division)
J. McG. Sowerby, BA, CEng, FIEE (Engineering)

SPECIAL DIRECTORS:

K. Dixon
E. M. Dowlen, DLC, CEng, MSc, FRAeS, AFAIAA (Guided Weapons New Project Design)
H. Metcalfe, OBE, BSc, ARCS, CEng, FRAeS
G. J. Muirhead
R. J. Parkhouse, BSc, CEng, FIProdE
S. A. Smith, MA, CEng, AFRAeS (General Manager, Bristol Works)

SECRETARY:

A. R. Adams, BSc(Econ), FCIS

On 1 January 1964 the entire aircraft interests of BAC, together with its Guided Weapons Division, were integrated into a wholly-owned subsidiary company named British Aircraft Corporation Ltd, as described in the "Aircraft" section. The Guided Weapons Division remains under the management of British Aircraft Corporation (Guided Weapons) Ltd.

In addition to its work on the guided weapons described below, and the Rapier and Seawolf surface-to-air missiles, this Division is playing a leading part in the design and construction of British satellites, and also produces the highly successful Skylark research rocket. Details of these activities can be found in the "Spaceflight" section.

BAC announced in December 1972 that it had been awarded a Ministry of Defence (Procurement Executive) contract for evaluation and demonstration of an electro-optical seeker, as a possible air-to-surface weapon guidance system. The seeker, manufactured by Rockwell International, is already fitted to "smart bombs" used by the USAF. Its ability to home automatically on a target, by means of a TV seeker, is considered to be of significance to British forces.

In 1974 evaluation of various aspects of TV and laser guidance for air-to-surface weapon systems was continuing, with extensive flight and laboratory trials of different equipments in progress.

BAC (Guided Weapons) Ltd has a total of 8,300 employees at its Stevenage and Filton works.

BAC SWINGFIRE/HAWKSWING

Design and development of this long-range command-controlled anti-tank weapon system were initiated by Fairey Engineering Ltd, incorporating features of that company's advanced Orange William anti-tank missile, work on which was cancelled in 1959. The first official reference to Swingfire was made on 10 August 1962, when the Minister of Defence announced that this weapon was under development for the British Army. British Aircraft Corporation (Guided Weapons) Ltd was appointed prime contractor for the weapon, at its Stevenage and Filton works.

Initially, Swingfire was developed, manufactured and put into service in vehicle-mounted surface-to-surface form; but the basic missile will be unchanged for other applications, including air-to-surface use from helicopters. At the front of the missile are the warhead, safety and arming mechanism, followed by the motor. The rear section carries spring-loaded cruciform wings, which fold down against the body when the missile is in its launching box, and houses the autopilot, wire dispenser and the gimballed motor nozzle (jetavator) by which the missile is steered in flight. The hollow-charge warhead is powerful enough to defeat all known combinations of armour and to destroy the heaviest battle tank

Swingfire anti-tank missile leaving its launch container on a helicopter during air-to-surface trials

at ranges up to 13,125 ft (4,000 m) and at all angles of attack up to 70°.

Swingfire is stored in and launched from a disposable container which is hermetically sealed up to the moment of launch.

The missile's name derives from the fact that it has a firing arc of 90° from a fixed launcher, this arc of fire remaining constant at all ranges. Since vehicle installations require neither traversing nor elevating gear, it is easy to install the Swingfire weapon system on a wide variety of vehicles.

After firing from a fixed launcher, the missile is gathered automatically into the controller's field of view towards the target, anywhere within the 90° arc of fire, by a programme generator built into the vehicle equipment. As well as functioning in azimuth, this generator permits engagement over an arc of 20° elevation and 20° depression; so that in a separated fire role on the ground the missile can be fired over obstacles or around corners into the controller's field of view.

Swingfire has a velocity control system and is steered into the target by movements of a joystick, which adjust the missile heading in azimuth and elevation by deflecting the thrust of the rocket motor. The latter gives a very slow acceleration at launch. Combined with the vectored-thrust control system, this makes Swingfire highly manoeuvrable during the early launch phase, so that it will hit targets over a direct-fire range of less than 460 ft (140 m).

An autopilot in the missile maintains the missile heading in the absence of continued signals from the controller. This feature, coupled with the automatic gathering of the missile into the controller's field of view, makes the controller's task relatively simple.

Swingfire entered service with the British Army in 1969 and equipped eleven Royal Armoured Corps regiments in Germany in 1973. Standard launch vehicles are a modified FV 432 armoured personnel carrier, redesignated FV 438, which carries two missiles ready for launch and twelve more stowed, and the FV 712 Ferret Mk 5 scout car which carries four missiles ready to fire and two spares. The system is also being fitted to the Alvis Striker CVRTs (Combat Vehicle, Reconnaissance, Tracked) of the British and Belgian armies.

For infantry use a palletised system is being developed, known as **Beeswing.** As well as being suitable for carriage by, and firing from, vehicles such as the ¾-ton long-wheelbase Land-Rover, this can be carried short distances and brought into action on the ground by a three-man crew.

A development programme is continuing for a helicopter-borne anti-tank weapon system which is designed to provide a "button-on" installation for the Lynx and Gazelle helicopters. This version is known as **Hawkswing.**

Hawkswing is claimed to offer greater lethality, range and tactical flexibility than any other contemporary system of this kind, as well as considerable development potential. It has a range of 13,125 ft (4,000 m), with a large angle-off and crest clearance capability, and can be launched and controlled to the target while the helicopter is undergoing all normal manoeuvres and evasive flying. The hollow-charge warhead will defeat all known combinations of armour and will destroy the heaviest battle tanks.

The Hawkswing system requires only limited maintenance and includes an airborne trainer. The missile is a round of ammunition, highly reliable and easily transportable. It has been designed as an easily removable weapon system to fit the Gazelle (which can carry four missiles) and the Lynx (which can carry six missiles), enabling change of role to be effected quickly.

By 1974, the development programme had advanced well into Phase II, during which highly sucessful demonstrations had been provided for the British Army.

DIMENSIONS:

Length overall	3 ft 6 in (1·07 m)
Max body diameter	6·7 in (0·17 m)
Wing span	14·7 in (0·37 m)

BAC CL 834 SEA SKUA

It was announced on 25 May 1972 that the British government had given BAC's Guided Weapons Division approval to begin first-phase development of a new "sea-skimming" missile project for the Royal Navy under the designation CL 834. This has since been named Sea Skua.

First missile system developed specifically for the Fleet Air Arm, the lightweight Sea Skua missile will be installed on Westland Lynx helicopters. It will provide long-range defence for the Lynx's carrier-frigates against missile-carrying fast patrol boats, hydrofoil craft and hovercraft, with some capability against frigates and larger vessels.

The overall system based on the Sea Skua missile will enable such targets to be found, identified and engaged well "over the horizon" from the Lynx's parent ship, while the enemy craft is still well outside the launching range at which its own missiles could be effective. The range of the Sea Skua missile will provide a good stand-off capability for the helicopter; its overall performance will far outstrip that of existing missiles carried by naval helicopters, and its flight to the target will be made just above the sea.

The general appearance of the Sea Skua missile is shown in the accompanying photograph of a model. No details are available except that, following a feasibility study in 1971, Marconi Space and Defence Systems Ltd was awarded a contract for the project definition phase of the Sea Skua's semi-active radar homing head. This will be fully solid-state and will employ advanced microwave techniques to reduce cost and complexity. The Lynx will be fitted with Ferranti Seaspray radar for target acquisition and illumination.

DIMENSIONS (estimated):

Length overall	9 ft 2 in (2·80 m)
Body diameter	8¾ in (22·2 cm)
Foreplane span	2 ft 2½ in (67·0 cm)

WEIGHT (estimated):

Launching weight	440 lb (200 kg)

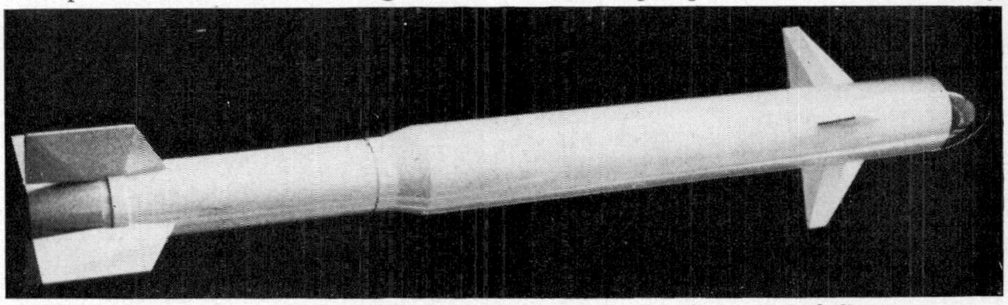

Model of the Sea Skua lightweight air-launched anti-surface-vessel missile

HSD

HAWKER SIDDELEY DYNAMICS LTD

HEADQUARTERS:
Manor Road, Hatfield, Herts
Telephone: Hatfield 62300
Telex: 22324

DIRECTORS:
Sir John Lidbury, FRAeS (Chairman)
Capt E. D. G. Lewin, CB, CBE, DSO, DSC, AFRAeS, RN(ret'd) (Managing Director)
Dr G. H. Hough, PhD, CBE, BSc, FRAeS, FIEE (Deputy Managing Director)
D. M. Craik, ACIS (General Manager)
J. D. Crane, FCA (Commercial)
R. G. Dancey, BA, TD (Personnel)
P. R. Franks, BSc, MSc, FRAeS, MIEE (Guided Weapons, Naval)
S. H. Lines, MBE (Production)
A. S. Wheate, CA (Financial)

SECRETARY:
J. Creed

EXECUTIVE DIRECTORS:
J. A. Airey, BSc, ARCS, CEng, FRAeS (Space)
R. Birch, FCA (Finance)
L. G. Evans, MA, CEng, FRAeS (SRAAM)
T. H. Lettice (Contracts)
W. Makin, CEng, MIMechE (Production, Northern Factories)

PUBLIC RELATIONS MANAGER:
M. K. Hird

This subsidiary of the Hawker Siddeley Group came into being as a consequence of the reorganisation of the Group on 1 July 1963. It is responsible for the design, development and production of all Hawker Siddeley guided weapons, space-launch vehicles, satellites, propellers and air-conditioning systems.

The company is prime contractor for the Sea Dart ship-to-air/ship-to-surface missile, and has developed jointly with Engins Matra of France the Martel long-range air-to-surface weapon (see "International" section).

Development of the company's own SRAAM highly-manoeuvrable close-range air-to-air weapon has been reduced to technology demonstration level; but a new medium-range all-weather air-to-air missile based on the American Sparrow is under development for the Royal Air Force. Hawker Siddeley Dynamics is also responsible for development and manufacture of an infra-red linescan system which equips the CL-89 surveillance drone, produced under a joint British, Canadian and West German programme.

In April 1973, Hawker Siddeley Dynamics was awarded a Ministry of Defence contract for a detailed study of a new submarine-launched missile system. It is intended that the missile should be launched from a submerged submarine, surface and home on to its target in much the same way as a conventional surface-to-surface weapon.

Hawker Siddeley Dynamics is the British "daughter firm" for the Australian-developed Ikara long-range anti-submarine weapon for the Royal Navy. It also has a major contract for the overhaul and repair of NATO Nike-Hercules surface-to-air missiles.

HSD RED TOP

Although similar in basic configuration to the earlier Firestreak (described in 1971-72 *Jane's*), and known originally as Firestreak Mk IV, this second-generation infra-red homing air-to-air weapon offers greatly enhanced capabilities. It equips RAF Lightning aircraft.

Red Top, like Firestreak, has a cylindrical metal body, cruciform wings, and cruciform tail control surfaces indexed in line with the wings. Externally apparent changes include wings and control surfaces of increased size and revised shape, for improved manoeuvrability at all altitudes, and a hemispherical nose over the completely different infra-red guidance unit. Weight of the warhead is 68 lb (31 kg).

Internally, the warhead was moved forward, next to the fusing system, and the control actuators were moved aft, next to the triangular tail surfaces which they drive. A more powerful solid-propellant rocket motor is fitted and Red Top offers the advantages of intercepton from any direction, including collision course, whereas Firestreak is a pursuit course weapon.

DIMENSIONS:

Length overall	11 ft 5·7 in (3·50 m)
Body diameter	8⅞ in (22·5 cm)
Wing span	2 ft 11¾ in (0·91 m)

WEIGHT:
Not available

PERFORMANCE:

Cruising speed	Mach 3
Range	6 nm (7 miles; 11 km)

HSD SRAAM

Combat experience in Vietnam and other war theatres has emphasised the need for an air-to-air missile able to cope with the high accelerations encountered in dogfight situations. The design of SRAAM (Short Range Air-to-Air Missile) is such that it can operate effectively down to a very short minimum range, even with the target manoeuvring to its design limits. At the same time, its maximum range is comparable with that of existing air-to-air weapons.

The simplicity of the fire control system would enable SRAAM to be carried by almost any type of interceptor or air superiority fighter, strike

Red Top infra-red air-to-air missile on Lightning

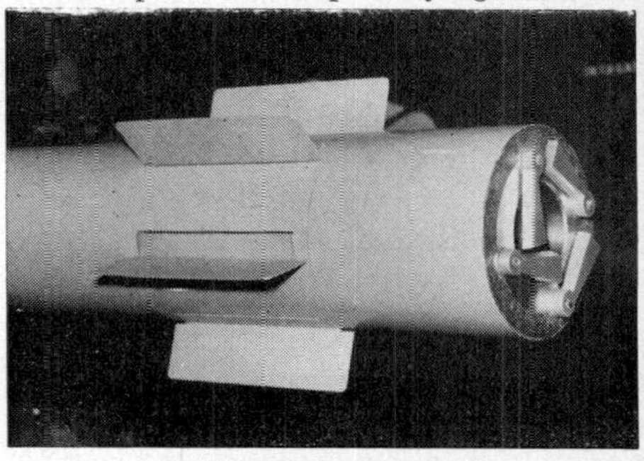

Tail of SRAAM air-to-air missile, showing steering semaphores and folding fins (*Flight International*)

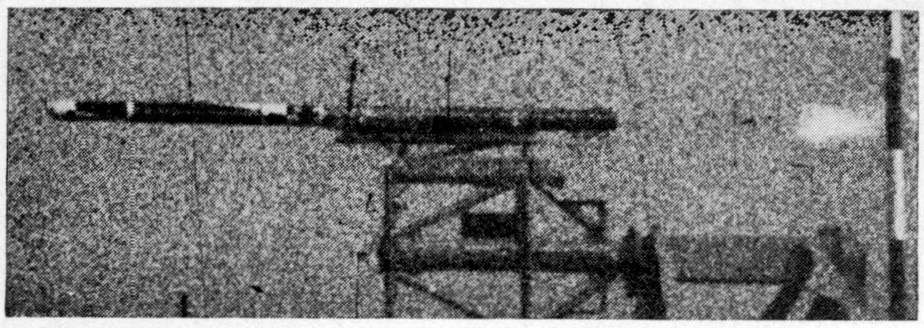

First photograph of a SRAAM test firing. The missile was tube-launched, at Aberporth range

Hawker Siddeley Dynamics SRAAM air-to-air missile

or reconnaissance aircraft, without requiring aircraft modification. Missiles have folding fins to allow them to be carried in launch tubes, attached to a launch beam which contains all the fire control system.

SRAAM is visually aimed, with a wide aiming tolerance, and is guided by a passive infra-red homing system. Steering is by thrust-vector control, by means of semaphores which project into the motor efflux, and would enable SRAAM to outmanoeuvre any aircraft, including crossing targets at very short range. The high-explosive warhead is designed to be detonated by proximity or contact fuse.

A technological development programme, which includes air firings, is in progress to prove the SRAAM concept. This is likely to produce a fully-developed missile, but not a complete weapon system, within about two years.

DIMENSIONS:

Length overall	8 ft 11¼ in (2·73 m)
Body diameter	6½ in (0·168 m)

UK SPARROW (XJ521)

It was announced on 17 April 1973 that Hawker Siddeley Dynamics had received a prime contract from the Ministry of Defence for project definition and pre-development studies of a new medium-range all-weather air-to-air missile based on the American AIM-7E Sparrow, which is in service with both the RAF and Royal Navy. Raytheon, the US Sparrow prime contractor, is participating in the programme through cross-licensing agreements with Hawker Siddeley Dynamics and Marconi Space and Defence Systems Ltd.

Project definition was completed in 1973, and it was announced on 26 February 1974 that Hawker Siddeley Dynamics had received instructions from the Ministry of Defence to proceed with full development and initial production.

The "boost and coast" missile, known as UK Sparrow, has the same general configuration and dimensions as the Raytheon AIM-7E, but is fitted with a semi-active radar homing head developed by Marconi under a Ministry of Defence contract. This has been designed as a completely self-contained unit with modular construction, which provides considerable flexibility in the overall design to cater for a wide range of different applications. Microstrip circuitry and the latest types of solid-state technology and micro-circuits have offered reliability, reduced size and high performance. The complete homing head is only 11 in (283 mm) long and can be fitted in a missile body of 7 in (180 mm) internal diameter.

SRAAM launchers under wings of a two-seat Hawker Siddeley Harrier V/STOL aircraft

UK Sparrow medium-range all-weather air-to-air missile for the RAF

The new, advanced, fuse system is designed by EMI Electronics Ltd, and is claimed to offer a high single-shot kill capability against targets at high, medium and low altitudes. Hawker Siddeley Dynamics has updated the autopilot and power systems, and is responsible for building the missile structure, as well as for assembly and test.

HSD/MATRA AJ.168/AS.37 MARTEL

See International section

THE UNITED STATES OF AMERICA

BOEING

BOEING AEROSPACE COMPANY

HEAD OFFICE AND WORKS:
Seattle, Washington 98124

Current responsibilities of the Boeing Aerospace Company include development of the E-3A, E-4A, T-43A and YC-14 aircraft, and YQM-94A Compass Cope RPV for the USAF; B-1 bomber avionics integration; production of the AGM-69A short-range attack missile (SRAM); modernisation of the Minuteman ICBM force; military and commercial hydrofoil programmes; and most of The Boeing Company's diversification programmes, including a personal rapid transit system under development at West Virginia University, an agri-business development at Boardman, Oregon, water resources projects and commercial electronics programmes.

SRAM

US military designation: AGM-69A (WS-140A)

This supersonic air-to-surface defence suppression and primary attack missile is carried by the General Dynamics FB-111 and the B-52G and H versions of the Boeing Stratofortress, and has been designated as primary armament for the Rockwell International B-1 supersonic strategic bomber, now under development. SRAM is intended to be capable of penetrating advanced enemy defence systems and has nuclear capability. Production was authorised by the USAF on 12

Test models of the SRAM air-to-surface short-range attack missile

B-52 bomber taking off from Loring AFB, with two three-round SRAM clusters visible under its starboard wing

January 1971, and deployment by Strategic Air Command began on 4 August 1972, when the B-52Gs of the 42nd Heavy Bombardment Wing became operational with SRAM at Loring AFB, Maine. Current contracts cover production of 1,500 missiles, to equip 17 B-52 wings and two FB-111 wings, at 18 SAC bases, by mid-1975.

The 1,000th SRAM was delivered on 14 August 1974.

Boeing initiated work on the SRAM (short-range attack missile) concept in December 1963. The USAF request for a weapon system proposal was issued on 30 July 1965, and on 3 November 1965 Boeing and Martin were selected from among five competing companies to proceed with SRAM project definition. The Phase II proposal, in which Boeing defined the SRAM weapon system and proposed to the USAF costs for developing, testing, producing and operating, was submitted on 15 March 1966. On 31 October 1966 the USAF selected Boeing as prime contractor for the weapon system and awarded the company an initial $142·3 million contract to design and develop SRAM. The USAF specified firm-priced options to cover varying quantities of missiles, carrier aircraft equipment and aerospace ground equipment for the carrier aircraft.

As system integration contractor, Boeing is responsible for overall SRAM system performance. The task of marrying the SRAM system to the carrier aircraft is its responsibility, but it was assisted in the flight test programme by General Dynamics/Fort Worth and Boeing-Wichita, in the respective roles of associate and subcontractor. The programme is managed by the Aeronautical Systems Division of the Air Force Systems Command.

Subcontractors in the SRAM programme are Lockheed Propulsion Company for the LPC-415 restartable solid-propellant two-pulse rocket motor; Kearfott Division of The Singer Company for the guidance subsystem (inertial with terrain avoidance capability), Guidance and Controls Division of Litton Industries for the B-52 inertial measurement unit; Autonetics Division of Rockwell International for the FB-111/B-52 aeroplane computer; Delco Electronics for the missile computer; Stewart-Warner Electronics Division for the radar receiver/transmitter; and Unidynamics Phoenix Division of Universal Match Corporation for the missile safe-arm-fuse subsystem. In addition, International Business Machines have a subcontract for modifying the bomb-navigation system of the B-52.

Two test launches of SRAM missiles were made from a B-52 in 1969, followed by the first drop of a dummy round from an F-111 later that year. Launches of live rounds from the fifth FB-111A began in 1970. Altogether, a total of 38 live test launches were made from both types of aircraft, including six successful launches in one month. The first SRAM firing by a SAC B-52 crew was made in 1970. In the same year, two missiles launched in rapid succession from a single aircraft hit separate targets; and a SRAM was launched successfully from a B-52 after a 42-day alert period during which it had remained on board the aircraft without maintenance of any kind. The test programme was completed in July 1971, the missile having exceeded specification requirements in terms of range, accuracy, radar cross-section and reliability.

Each B-52G and H can carry 20 SRAMs, twelve in three-round underwing clusters and eight on a rotary launcher in the aft bomb-bay, together with up to four Mk 28 thermonuclear weapons. Alternatively, the rotary launcher can be carried simultaneously with two underwing AGM-28B Hound Dogs and decoy missiles. An FB-111 can carry six SRAMs, four on swivelling underwing pylons and two internally.

Range of each missile is reported to be slightly more than 90 nm (100 miles; 160 km) in the "high mode", 30 nm (35 miles; 55 km) in the "low mode". It is able to fly "dog-leg" courses and its radar "signature" is said to be no larger than that of a machine-gun bullet.

When SRAM is carried externally, a tailcone, 22·2 in (0·56 m) long, is added for aerodynamic reasons.

DIMENSIONS:

Length overall	14 ft 0 in (4·27 m)
Body diameter	1 ft 5½ in (44·5 cm)

WEIGHT (approx):

Launching weight	2,230 lb (1,010 kg)

ALCM

USAF designation: AGM-86A

Under the FY1975 budget, the USAF requested $80 million for development of an air-launched cruise missile (ALCM), for which Boeing has been selected as prime contractor. In the Summer of 1974, Boeing was negotiating a contract with the Air Force Aeronautical Systems Division, covering design, development, manufacture and test of 31 of the missiles, which have been allocated the official designation AGM-86A.

This designation was given earlier to the SCAD (Subsonic Cruise Armed Decoy) missile which

SRAM eight-round rotary launcher for B-52 and B-1

Boeing was developing for the USAF until the programme was cancelled in July 1973. In February 1974, Boeing was authorised to undertake a technology study to adapt the SCAD concept to meet the ALCM requirement. The similarity in configuration of the two missiles is evident from the accompanying artist's impression of the ALCM.

The new missile is intended to have a "hard target" kill capability. It will be similar in overall dimensions to SRAM and will probably be suitable for carriage on the rotary launcher developed for this latter weapon, with wings and tail folded. A B-52 will be able to carry 12 ALCMs externally and 8 internally. A B-1 will be able to carry 24, and it is likely that the FB-111 will also be armed with the missile. When carried externally, ALCM will be able to have an underbelly auxiliary fuel tank fitted to increase its range. It is intended to have the co-ordinates of one prime and one alternate target fed into it before launch, and it will be fitted with a device

Artist's impressions of the AGM-86A Air-Launched Cruise Missile (ALCM), with and without belly fuel tank

to prevent detonation if a selected target could not be hit for any reason.

Cost of the ALCM development programme is estimated at $316 million, with flight tests begining in 1976. Earliest date for a full production decision is thought to be November 1977, after some 23 flights. Total programme cost might then be as much as $1,500 million.

DIMENSIONS:
- Length overall: 14 ft 0 in (4·27 m)
- Diameter: 2 ft 1 in (0·64 m)

WEIGHT:
- Launching weight:
  - with belly tank: 2,200 lb (998 kg)
  - without belly tank: 1,800 lb (817 kg)

GENERAL DYNAMICS

GENERAL DYNAMICS CORPORATION

HEAD OFFICE:
Pierre Laclede Center, St Louis, Missouri 63105

Pomona Division

HEADQUARTERS:
PO Box 2507, Pomona, California 91766

WORKS:
Pomona and Window Rock, Arizona

GENERAL MANAGER:
Leonard F. Buchanan

The Pomona Division of General Dynamics is responsible for the Redeye man-portable ground-to-air missile system for battlefield use, the Standard Missile 1 which was developed in two basic forms to replace Terrier and Tartar naval surface-to-air missiles, and the air-to-surface and surface-to-surface Standard ARM. Under development are a new man-portable air defence missile known as Stinger, to replace Redeye; a third-generation Standard Missile 2; and the computer-operated Phalanx shipboard gun system for close-in defence against cruise missiles.

AGM-78A version of Standard ARM under the wing of a Grumman A-6 Intruder

STANDARD ARM

US Navy designations: AGM-78 and RGM-66D

It was announced in September 1966 that the US Naval Air Systems Command had awarded a $7·5 million letter contract to Pomona Division for initial development of an air-launched weapon that would home on radiation emitted by a ground radar set and destroy the installation with its explosive warhead. Known as Standard ARM (anti-radiation missile), this weapon utilises an adaptation of the Navy's RIM-66A medium-range ship-to-air Standard Missile 1 propulsion system. It was intended to provide a significant increase in capability over earlier weapons in countering the threat of enemy radar-controlled anti-aircraft guided missiles and guns.

Successful operation of the weapon system has led to development of several advanced versions, some of them highly classified. The initial version used the passive-homing target-seeking head of a Shrike missile. Current models have improved seeker heads and avionics for better target selection, more effective operation against target countermeasures and still greater attack range. An impact marking device is fitted to assist subsequent attack on concealed sites.

Associated with Pomona Division in the Standard ARM development programme have been Texas Instruments for the Shrike seeker of the original AGM-78A version, Maxson Electronics for the initial improved seeker head of the AGM-78B version (a subsequent, further improved seeker is being developed by GD/Pomona), IBM and Bendix for improved avionics, Aerojet-General for the Mk 27 Mod 4 dual-thrust solid-propellant rocket motor, Grumman (A-6 launch aircraft), Fairchild Republic Division of Fairchild Industries (F-105 launch aircraft), and Convair Aerospace Division of General Dynamics for aircraft modification.

The general appearance of Standard ARM is shown in an accompanying illustration. The basic airframe consists of a cylindrical body with pointed ogival nose, and cruciform long-chord narrow-span wings, with forward portions of much reduced span, indexed in line with cruciform tail control surfaces.

Equipment carried by the launch aircraft includes a Target Identification and Acquisition System (TIAS), which is able to compute a trajectory for the missile on the basis of data already monitored if the enemy radar operator suspects that signals from his equipment are being picked up and switches it off.

Production continues of a surface-to-surface version of Standard ARM, designated RGM-66D, with purchase of a further 62 missiles approved in FY1975.

DIMENSIONS:
- Length overall: 15 ft 0 in (4·57 m)
- Body diameter: 1 ft 0 in (0·305 m)

WEIGHT:
- Launching weight, basic version: 1,800 lb (816 kg)

PERFORMANCE:
- Max speed: Mach 2
- Max range: 13·5 nm (15·5 miles; 25 km)

Standard Active missile on underwing launcher of A-6A Intruder (*Henry Artof*)

STANDARD ACTIVE

US Navy designation: RGM-66F

Development of Standard Active was started in 1971, initially to give an over-the-horizon anti-shipping capability to the US Navy's guided missile destroyers and escort ships, with minimal changes to their existing fire control equipment.

Standard Active was based on the airframe of the RIM-66A medium-range Standard Missile 1 surface-to-air missile, with a new guidance section. This embodied a Raytheon coherent monopulse Doppler active seeker, with associated radome, shroud, logic and control assemblies, and guidance computer. It added 10 in (25 cm) to the overall length and 100 lb (45 kg) to the weight of the basic missile.

Pomona Division of General Dynamics received a contract for five prototype Standard Active missiles, one of which is shown in an accompanying illustration, mounted under the wing of an A-6 Intruder aircraft for captive tests. Of the other rounds, one was intended for ground tests and three were used for live firings from the USS *Hoel* against over-the-horizon targets during 1973. All three missiles achieved direct hits, and FY 1974 funds provided for a further 18-missile development and operational test programme. However, in the Summer of 1974 the House Appropriations Committee recommended termination of the Standard Active programme, seen as a backup to Harpoon. The Navy had requested $32·1 million to buy 74 more missiles.

GOODYEAR

GOODYEAR AEROSPACE CORPORATION

HEAD OFFICE:
1210 Massillon Road, Akron, Ohio 44315
Telephone: (216) 794-3632

MANAGER, PUBLIC RELATIONS: Lyle Schwilling

Goodyear is engaged on a wide variety of important subcontract design, development and manufacturing work for US guided weapons and space programmes.

Production of its UUM-44A Subroc submarine-launched anti-submarine missile ended on 30 June 1972; but this weapon remains operational and Goodyear continues to provide support services. It is also engaged on a number of development projects in the terminal-homing air-to-surface weapon field. One undesignated munition of this type, test-launched from an F-4 Phantom II, demolished a concrete bridge pier. Another type is described briefly on the following page.

Unidentified air-to-ground munition with terminal homing, tested from an F-4 Phantom II. A single missile of this type demolished a concrete bridge pier during trials

Laser guided dispenser munitions (LGDMs) carried by F-4 Phantom II test aircraft

LGDM

Under a $1·39 million contract from the US Air Force Systems Command's Armament Development and Test Center at Eglin AFB, Florida, Goodyear Aerospace built 33 GBU-3/B Laser Guided Dispenser Munitions (LGDM) for test launching from F-4 Phantom II aircraft during 1972. In each case the USAF furnished the laser guidance kit, fuse and SUU-51 dispenser. Goodyear acted as integration contractor, building the components and necessary adaptors to make usable hardware systems.

In operation, the target is illuminated by a laser beam. The air-launched LGDM then seeks out the light spot and homes on it.

HUGHES

HUGHES AIRCRAFT COMPANY

Head Office:
Culver City, California 90230

Hughes Aircraft began developing an air-to-air missile for the USAF in 1950, and this weapon has been in squadron use for many years as the Falcon. Production ended after a total of some 45,000 missiles had been delivered.

Currently, Hughes is producing an air-to-air missile named Phoenix for the US Navy, an air-to-surface missile named Maverick for the USAF, and a wire-guided anti-tank missile named TOW for the US Army and other customers.

It is also assisting the US Navy with development of an air-to-air anti-radiation missile known as Brazo and with the Naval Weapons Center's Agile dogfight missile.

Hughes manufactures fire-control systems for the majority of USAF interceptors, and is engaged extensively in space research and communications satellite programmes (see "Spaceflight" section).

PHOENIX

US Navy designation: AIM-54A (formerly AAM-N-11)

Intended originally to form the primary armament of the abandoned F-111B, Phoenix now arms the Grumman F-14A Tomcat two-seat carrier-based fighter and is claimed to have capabilities exceeding those of any other air-to-air system yet operational.

Configuration is similar to that of earlier Hughes air-to-air missiles, with a cylindrical body and long-chord cruciform wings; but cruciform tail control surfaces replace the wing trailing-edge surfaces of the earlier weapons.

Phoenix has a Mk 47 Mod 0 solid-propellant rocket motor produced by Rocketdyne, and is fitted with a large proximity-fused high-explosive warhead. The weapon system consists of the missile itself, AWG-9 airborne weapon control system, and LAU-93A missile launcher. Hughes is prime contractor for the entire system, including support equipment. Control Data Corporation has a contract for the central processing portion of the missile control system computer.

A number of innovations in missile design are claimed to provide substantial increases in range, payload, speed and accuracy. The missile is assembled in sections, making it possible to handle it as a complete unit or to break it down for easy shipboard checkout and handling. To minimise maintenance problems, built-in self-test features are incorporated which permit rapid system testing and isolation of faults.

The launch aircraft's AWG-9 weapon control system is able to lock on to an enemy aircraft, surface-launched cruise missile or air-to-surface missile, at high or low altitude, in any kind of weather, and launch the Phoenix missile. The missile then takes over to intercept the target.

The data from the radar is processed by a solid-state, high-speed general-purpose digital computer, the output of which is displayed to the missile control officer in the launch aircraft on two displays: a 10 in cathode-ray tube and a 5 in multi-mode storage tube.

The long-range high-power pulse Doppler radar has a planar array antenna, providing a "look-down" capability that enables it to pick out moving targets from the ground clutter that normally obscures them in a conventional radar. The AWG-9 also incorporates an infra-red subsystem that provides an independent search and track sensor, and has a track-while-scan radar mode that makes it possible to launch up to six missiles and keep them on course while searching for other possible targets, all in the presence of sophisticated enemy countermeasures.

The first AWG-9 reconfigured for the F-14A fighter was delivered to the US Navy in February 1970, just one year after design began. Extensive use of hybrid circuits and new packaging techniques had enabled its weight to be reduced to less than 1,400 lb (635 kg), compared with 2,000 lb (907 kg) for earlier, less efficient versions. The addition of air combat manoeuvre modes now provides improved "dogfight" capability, and the AWG-9 is able to launch other modern naval air-to-air weapons, including Sparrow and Sidewinder missiles, as well as Phoenix. It can also direct the firing of the M61 Vulcan 20 mm cannon.

Flight testing of Phoenix inert rounds began in 1965 from an A-3A Skywarrior launch aircraft and the first powered, unguided flight was made on 27 April 1966. On 8 September 1966, a powered Phoenix development round, with partial on-board guidance system, scored a technical intercept after launch from the A-3A by passing within a specified "miss distance" of a high-speed jet target drone at the US Navy Pacific Missile Range, Point Mugu, California.

The first guided launch of a Phoenix missile from an F-111B fighter, on 17 March 1967, was also successful.

In the first test of a Phoenix fitted with a live warhead, in August 1970, an F9F Cougar jet fighter/target drone was destroyed when the missile passed close to the target and was detonated by its proximity fuse. The Phoenix was launched over a range of many miles, from an altitude far above that of the target, requiring the AWG-9 fire-control system to operate in a look-down, track-while-scan mode.

On 20 December 1972, in a firing to test the AWG-9's multiple-launch capability, four Phoenix missiles were launched from an F-14A and guided simultaneously to intercept four separate jet target drones. One missile scored a direct hit, destroying its target; the others passed within their warheads' lethal zone and were officially scored as hits. The targets (converted T-33 jet aircraft and BQM-34 drones) were at ranges of about 26 nm (30 miles; 48 km) and at altitudes between 20,000 and 25,000 ft (6,100-7,600 m) over the Pacific.

Contractor testing was concluded on 13 June 1973 with a launch from an F-14A against a BQM-34E Firebee target drone over a record range of 110 nm (126 miles; 204 km). The drone, augmented by radar signal to look as large as a bomber and equipped with an on/off blinking noise jammer, approached at an altitude of 52,000 ft (15,850 m) and speed of Mach 1·55. The F-14A, flying at 45,000 ft (13,700 m) and Mach 1·45, began tracking the Firebee at very long range, locked on and launched a single Phoenix at 110 nm. During flight, the Phoenix reached a high point in its trajectory of more than 100,000 ft (30,500 m) and then passed the drone within the lethal distance of its warhead.

AIM-54A Phoenix missile, with F-14A Tomcat launch aircraft

Of the 56 Phoenix missiles launched from various aircraft during contractor tests, 43 were scored as hits. The success rate for the 17 missiles launched from the F-14A was 88%. Only a few additional tests remained to be completed by USN crews prior to fleet introduction of Phoenix aboard F-14s at NAS Miramar, California, in the Autumn of 1973.

In one of these USN tests, on 21 November 1973, six Phoenix missiles were launched from an F-14, from Point Mugu, and were guided simultaneously against six target drones simulating an attack force of enemy aircraft. All six missiles were launched within 37 seconds, two of them in a 3½-second period, at a distance of 43 nm (50 miles; 80 km). Two Lockheed QT-33 drones were destroyed by the unarmed missiles. Two others, a subsonic Teledyne Ryan BQM-34A and a supersonic BQM-34E, were damaged by direct hits. One missile was unable to intercept its target because the BQM-34 veered off course, leaving a weakened radar signature that could not be tracked at such a long range. The sixth missile apparently suffered a hardware failure about one-third of the way through its flight.

In October 1970, the US Navy awarded a $145 million contract to Hughes for production of AWG-9 systems at the company's El Segundo, California, electronics manufacturing facility. In December 1970, the Navy announced the award of a letter contract of $40 million for production of Phoenix missiles at Tucson, Arizona (letter contracts normally represent half of the sum that will be agreed upon in a definitive contract at a later date). The production contracts for FY 1973 totalled $120 million for AWG-9 systems and $62·3 million for 180 Phoenix missiles, plus spares, support and test equipment, field service and technical manuals. FY1974 funding provided $130 million for 54 AWG-9 systems, and $100 million for Phoenix missiles. FY1975 requests included about $100 million for 340 missiles and initial spares.

Three US Navy squadrons were operational at NAS Miramar in January 1974, with most of the 54 F-14As delivered by that month. The F-14s ordered for the Imperial Iranian Air Force will also be Phoenix-armed.

DIMENSIONS (approx):

Length overall	13 ft 0 in (3·95 m)
Body diameter	1 ft 3 in (0·38 m)
Span of wings	3 ft 0 in (0·91 m)

WEIGHT:

Launching weight	838 lb (380 kg)

BRAZO/PAVE ARM

Under a joint project, known to the US Navy as Brazo (Spanish for "arm") and to the USAF as Pave Arm, Hughes Aircraft is assisting in feasibility demonstrations of an air-to-air anti-radiation missile (ARM). Its main task has been to design and manufacture the guidance subsystems, based on a broad band receiver designed by the Naval Electronics Laboratory Center, and integrate these subsystems into each of the eight modified Raytheon Sparrow missiles that are being used during flight tests, under an 18-month demonstration programme. Hughes also modified the LAU-17/A launcher and fabricated the cockpit control panel for the F-4D aircraft allocated to Brazo flight trials.

The Navy is responsible for design and development of the missile, with the USAF responsible for testing and evaluation at the Air Force Special Weapons Center, Holloman AFB, New Mexico. It was expected that Varian Associates would receive a contract for missile electronics, with an antenna from AIL Division of Cutler Hammer. The missile radome was to be chosen from competitive tenders by Avco, Brunswick and Texas Instruments.

The aim is to evolve a weapon for use against advanced all-weather fighters in the class of the Soviet MiG-25. Brazo is intended to home on fire control radar emissions from enemy aircraft, and the development programme has the appropriate name of ERASE (Electromagnetic Radiation Source Elimination).

First development firing took place on 16 April 1974, when a Brazo fired from an F-4D intercepted a BQM-34 Firebee drone in a look-down tail attack at Holloman AFB.

TOW

US Army designation: BGM-71A

Hughes Aircraft was prime contractor for development of this high-performance surface-to-surface and air-to-surface anti-tank missile, the basic characteristics of which are indicated by its name, as TOW is an acronym for Tube-launched, Optically-tracked, Wire-guided.

The basic ground-fired TOW system consists of a glassfibre launch tube, a tripod, a traversing and sighting unit, an electronic package and missiles encased in shipping containers. Total weight of the entire weapon system, including missile, is approximately 200 lb (91 kg), but the launcher and electronics can be broken down into four units for carrying by infantry.

The missile has low aspect ratio wings and tail **control surfaces that remain folded while in the launcher and flick open as the missile leaves the** launch tube. The wings flick forward during extension, the tail surfaces rearward.

BGM-71A TOW missile undergoing final inspection. An illustration of TOW missile launchers on an AH-1Q helicopter appears on page 271

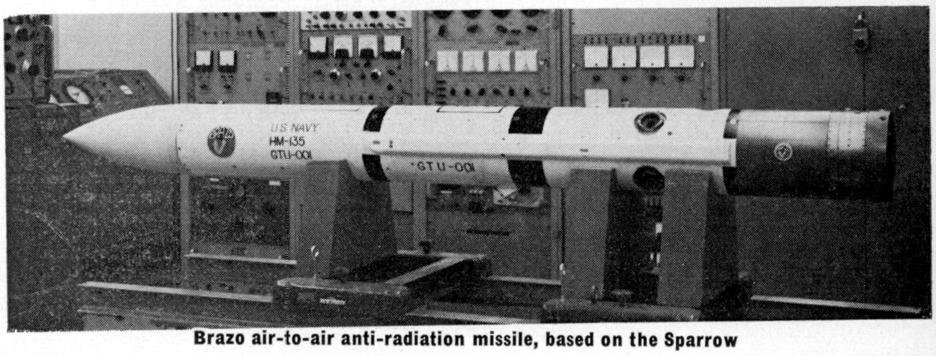

Brazo air-to-air anti-radiation missile, based on the Sparrow

TOW is inserted into the rear end of the tube in its container, which forms an extension of the tube. **Electrical and mechanical connections to the missile are made automatically** during this operation. The Hercules K-41 solid-propellant motor gives two separate boost periods. **It fires first to propel the missile from the launcher. To ensure safety for the operator, the missile then coasts for a period after leaving the mouth of the tube, before the second stage of the booster fires.**

The operator guides the missile by keeping the target centred in a telescopic sight. Movement of the sight generates electronic signals to correct the missile's course, the signals being passed through two wires. **The tail control surfaces are actuated by a Chandler Evans CACS-2 system** using high-pressure stored helium gas to operate four differential piston actuators in matched pairs to control yaw, pitch and roll. **The warhead is a high-explosive shaped charge, developed under the Army Munitions Command, Picatinny Arsenal, New Jersey.**

TOW is intended as a heavy assault weapon for use against tanks, armoured vehicles and gun emplacements over ranges of more than one mile. In its surface-to-surface form, it can be mounted on a variety of ground vehicles, including the M-113 armoured personnel carrier.

To permit use of TOW from helicopters, Hughes developed under US Army contract a gyro-stabilised sight that would eliminate the effects of aircraft vibration and manoeuvres. As part of the XM-26 missile/launcher/sight subsystem, this was installed on a UH-1B helicopter, from which air-to-surface firing tests of TOW missiles were then made successfully at Redstone Arsenal, Alabama, with hits on moving tank targets over ranges of more than one mile. Other TOW missiles were air-launched successfully from a Lockheed AH-56A Cheyenne prototype helicopter, achieving hits on an M-4 tank target at the US Army Proving Ground, Yuma, Arizona.

Following such tests, the US Army Aviation Systems Command awarded Bell Helicopter Company a contract in March 1972 to modify eight AH-1G HueyCobras to carry eight TOW missiles each, under the Improved Cobra Armament Program (ICAP). Helmet sights for weapon aiming were supplied by Univac.

Experience showed that, in fact, this helicopter can carry only two to six TOWs, depending on temperature and altitude, in addition to its other armament and fuel load.

Some of the initial batch of eight modified HueyCobras were shipped to Vietnam on 24 April 1972. After a short training period, during which each pilot-gunner fired one TOW missile for the first time, the aircraft were committed at Kontum to meet an expected armour threat. By 27 June, in 77 combat launches, they had scored 62 hits on point targets and had destroyed 39 armoured vehicles, trucks and howitzers. None of the helicopters had been hit by hostile fire.

As a result of these successes, the US Army decided to allocate $73 million of FY 1974 funds to the modification of 101 AH-1G HueyCobras to AH-1Q Cobra-TOW standard. Six more are to be modified in FY1975; and the US Army hopes to receive approval for upgrading the AH-1Q, to enable it to carry a full quota of eight TOWs, before initiating the modification of a further 183 AH-1Gs to AH-1Q standard. Later, TOW is expected to form primary armament of the US Army's new Advanced Attack Helicopter; and the US Marine Corps hopes to upgrade the Bell AH-1J to carry TOW missiles.

TOW itself has been in production for the US Army since 29 November 1968, with Chrysler Corporation as second-source supplier under a $33·3 million contract covering production until January 1973. Since that date, Hughes has been the sole producer of TOW. The US Army expects to achieve its planned TOW inventory by FY1977, the US Marine Corps by FY1976.

The missiles are manufactured in Hughes' missile factory at Tucson, Arizona, the launchers at the company's El Segundo, California plant. Deployment to US troops in the USA and Europe began in November 1970, to replace the 106 mm recoilless rifle and the Entac and SS.11 missiles. Subsequently, TOW was ordered also for the armies of Federal Germany, Italy, the Netherlands and Iran.

The Department of Defense proposed to purchase in FY1974 a total of 18,000 TOW missiles and 1,518 launchers for the US Army, and an initial quantity of 5,425 missiles and 100 launchers for the Marine Corps. The FY1975 request was for $149 million, covering the purchase of 30,319 missiles and 1,041 launchers for the two services, and continued development of a night sight for the weapon system.

DIMENSIONS OF MISSILE:

Length overall	3 ft 9·7 in (1·16 m)
Diameter	5·9 in (15 cm)

WEIGHT OF MISSILE:

Launching weight	48 lb (22 kg)

PERFORMANCE:

Max range	over 9,850 ft (3,000 m)
Min range	under 215 ft (65 m)

MAVERICK

USAF designation: AGM-65A

Development of this air-to-surface missile began in 1966, when Hughes and North American each received a project definition contract to verify preliminary design and engineering studies of the projected weapon and to provide information for development and production contracts.

After evaluation of the results of these contracts, in July 1968, the USAF awarded Hughes a $95 million fixed-price incentive contract to cover development, test and evaluation of Maverick over a three-year period, with options for follow-on production of up to 17,000 missiles.

Maverick has a cylindrical body, with rounded glass nose and long-chord delta wings, indexed in line with cruciform tail control surfaces mounted close to their trailing-edges. It is powered by a Thiokol TX-481 solid-propellant motor and is television-guided.

It can be carried by the A-7D, F-4D and F-4E, normally in three-round underwing clusters, and has a high-penetration conical shaped-charge warhead, intended for use against pinpoint targets such as tanks and columns of vehicles. Maverick is also carried by Teledyne Ryan BGM-34 RPVs.

AGM-65A Maverick self-homing TV-guided air-to-surface missile

Unlike earlier TV-guided missiles, Maverick is self-homing. The pilot of the launch aircraft first selects the desired weapon station, and a timed indicator light signals completion of the required gyro run-up time. After visually detecting a target, the pilot depresses the uncage switch which removes the protective dome cover from the nose of the missile and activates the video circuitry. The scene viewed by the Maverick TV seeker appears on a high-brightness TV screen in the cockpit. The pilot then manoeuvres his aircraft to place his optical sight reticle on the target, or slews the missile seeker head. After depressing the track switch, he waits until the cross-hairs are positioned over the target, then effects lock-on by releasing the track switch and launches the round. Maverick is homed on the target by an electro-optical device in its nose.

The first unguided air launch of the Maverick missile was conducted successfully at Edwards AFB, California, on 15 September 1969. The test was the first of 15 air launches conducted by McDonnell Douglas, with Hughes support, to prove the safe separation of the missile from an F-4 Phantom II throughout the aircraft's flight envelope. On 18 December 1969, a Maverick, complete except for warhead, was launched at medium range from an F-4D in a diving attack against a stripped-down M-41 tank at Holloman AFB, New Mexico. It scored a direct hit in this, its first guided test flight.

During subsequent tests at Fort Reilly, Kansas, Maverick was launched at distances ranging from a few thousand feet to many miles from the target, and from high altitudes down to treetop level, against manoeuvring Army tanks.

As a result of the success of the first 27 flight tests, the USAF decided in early 1972 to cancel the 13 further launches that had been planned. Production was initiated in 1971, under a $69·9 million contract, and the USAF formally accepted the first of the initial quantity of 2,000 production Mavericks at Hughes' Tucson, Arizona, plant on 30 August 1972.

By October 1973, the number of Mavericks ordered by the USAF had increased to 11,000 in four batches. In that month, the missile was used operationally by the Israeli Air Force during the Yom Kippur war, with results that were described as "quite impressive, although the conditions there were much more favourable for such electro-optical weapons than would be the case in Europe".

The USAF requested about $88 million for another 6,000 Mavericks in FY1975.

It was reported in July 1974 that an imaging infra-red version of Maverick, for operation at night, was undergoing captive flight tests on an F-4 at Holloman AFB, New Mexico.

DIMENSIONS:

Length overall	8 ft 1 in (2·46 m)
Body diameter	12 in (30 cm)
Wing span	2 ft 4 in (0·71 m)

WEIGHT (approx):

Launching weight	462 lb (210 kg)

HELLFIRE

In the early Summer of 1974, Hughes Aircraft Company received a $2·3 million one-year contract from US Army Missile Command for advanced development of an air-to-surface modular missile known as Hellfire. Rockwell International was selected simultaneously as competing contender for the full development contract.

Hellfire is required to accept four different homing heads, comprising semi-active laser, dual-mode radar frequency/infra-red, optical contrast (TV), and imaging infra-red types. Its first application is likely to be as armament for the AH-1 HueyCobra helicopter; but it may prove equally suitable for operation from RPVs, by infantry and in other ways.

The current contracts cover the fabrication of prototype Hellfire missiles, launchers, a cockpit installation mockup and other equipment.

MDAC

MCDONNELL DOUGLAS ASTRONAUTICS COMPANY (A Division of McDonnell Douglas Corporation)

ADDRESS:
5301 Bolsa Avenue, Huntington Beach, California 92647
Telephone: (714) 896-3311

PRESIDENT AND CHIEF EXECUTIVE OFFICER:
Charles R. Able

EXECUTIVE VICE-PRESIDENT:
Ben G. Bromberg

VICE-PRESIDENTS:
C. James Dorrenbacher (Product Development)
John L. Sigrist (Fiscal Management)
Charles W. Hutton (Marketing)
Lupton A. Wilkinson (Operations)
Jack L. Bromberg (General Manager, Strategic Defense Programs)
W. H. Peter Drummond (Engineering)
Theodore D. Smith (Programmer, Cryogenic Insulation Project)
Charles S. Perry (Deputy Programmer, Site Defense)
Ned T. Weiler (Programme Manager, Site Defense)

LABORATORIES:
Donald W. Douglas Laboratories, Richland, Washington 99352

FIELD AND TEST CENTERS:
Vandenberg Test Center, Vandenberg AFB, California 93436
Kwajalein Test Center
Florida Test Center, Cocoa Beach, Florida 32931 (VICE-PRESIDENT, DIRECTOR: William L. Duval)
White Sands Field Center, White Sands Missile Range, New Mexico 88002
Sacramento Test Center, Rancho Cordova, California 95670

McDonnell Douglas Astronautics Company-East

ADDRESS:
Box 516, St Louis, Missouri 63166
Telephone: (314) 232-0232

VICE-PRESIDENTS:
John F. Yardley (General Manager)
Raymond A. Pepping (General Manager, Skylab Programme)
Erwin F. Branahl (Engineering)
Harry W. Oldeg (Fiscal Management)
R. Wayne Lowe (General Manager, Harpoon Programme)

TI-CO DIVISION:
PO Box 600, State Road 405, Titusville, Florida 32780

VICE-PRESIDENT:
Raymond D. Hill (General Manager)

This company was formed on 26 June 1968, by merging the former Douglas Missile and Space Systems Division and the McDonnell Astronautics Company into a single management structure.

In the missile field, McDonnell Douglas Astronautics Company is responsible for development of the Spartan long-range interceptor missile for the US Army's Safeguard Ballistic Missile Defence System, as a principal subcontractor to Western Electric Company and Bell Telephone Laboratories. It is developing the Harpoon anti-shipping missile for the US Navy, producing the Dragon anti-tank missile for the US Army and the Genie air-to-air missile for the USAF, and working on other projects of a classified nature. Its important space programmes are described in the "Spaceflight" section.

GENIE

USAF designation: AIR-2A

Genie is an unguided air-to-air rocket missile with a nuclear warhead. Its development was started by Douglas in 1955, as soon as a suitable atomic warhead package had been perfected by Los Alamos Scientific Laboratory, and the first-ever air-to-air firing of a nuclear missile took place on 19 July 1957, when a Genie was released from an F-89J Scorpion interceptor at Indian Springs, Nevada.

In this case the weapon was fired at a height of about 15,000 ft (4,575 m), after which the pilot of the F-89J turned sharply to escape the blast. The missile travelled 2·6 nm (3 miles; 4·8 km) horizontally and was detonated by a signal from the ground. The negligible extent of the fall-out was demonstrated by USAF observers who stood directly under the detonation point for an hour, with no ill effects.

Whilst under development, the AIR-2A was known successively as Ding-Dong and High Card, before entering service as the Genie. A training version, without nuclear warhead, is in use.

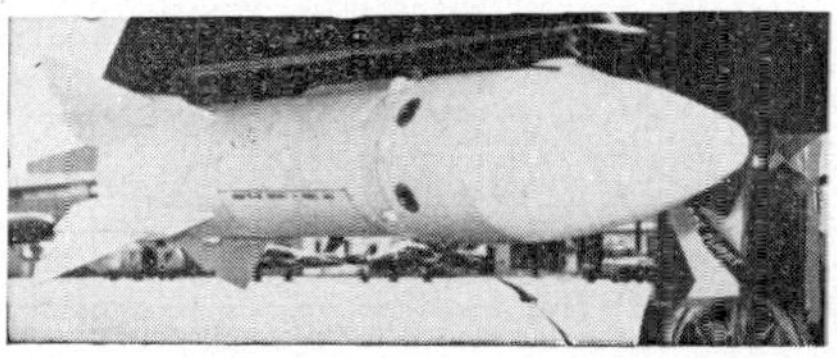

McDonnell Douglas AIR-2A Genie nuclear-warhead unguided missile

Genie consists of only four major components: an ogival nose section, a firing mechanism, the nuclear warhead and the motor section with its fins and equipment for attachment to the aircraft. The cruciform tail-fins have movable tips. Genie is now powered by an SR49-TC-1 (Thiokol TU-289) solid-propellant rocket motor of approximately 36,000 lb (16,330 kg) st. Compared with the motor fitted previously, this offers increased shelf-life and improved low-temperature characteristics.

Genie is carried by the F-101B and F-106 interceptors. It is normally fired automatically and detonated by a Hughes fire-control system carried by the launching aircraft. As one of many safety precautions, Genie remains inert in the nuclear sense until it is armed in the air, a few moments before firing.

DIMENSIONS:

Length overall	9 ft 7 in (2·91 m)
Body diameter	1 ft 5·35 in (0·44 m)
Fin span	3 ft 3½ in (1·00 m)
LAUNCHING WEIGHT (approx):	820 lb (372 kg)

PERFORMANCE (estimated):

Speed at burnout	Mach 3
Range	5·2 nm (6 miles; 9·6 km)

HARPOON

US Navy designations: AGM-84A and RGM-84A-1

Harpoon is a US Navy missile suitable for launching from aircraft, ships and submarines against shipping targets, from extended stand-off ranges. It is an all-weather weapon, with an air-breathing propulsion system.

Five major US aerospace companies responded to requests for proposals issued by Naval Air Systems Command on 22 January 1971, at the end of three years of research and study. This had included seeker flight and ground tests, propulsion studies, aerodynamic testing and analytical investigations of a number of possible configurations.

In May 1971, General Dynamics and McDonnell Douglas were asked to submit additional technical and financial data on their proposals, which were then evaluated by representatives of Naval Air Systems Command, Naval Ordnance Systems Command and selected Navy field activities. These evaluations considered all aspects of the proposals, including the design approach, the extent of modifications required to existing launch systems (eg, the Asroc launcher) to accommodate the new missile, the technical risk and projected costs.

As a result of this review, the Navy selected McDonnell Douglas as prime contractor for development of the Harpoon missile, in June 1971, under the programme management of Naval Air Systems Command and with major support from Naval Ordnance Systems Command. The work was allocated to McDonnell Douglas Astronautics Company-East, with Texas Instruments Inc and Sperry Systems Management as major subcontractors.

The initial contract, valued at $66 million, awarded to MDAC on 21 June 1971, covered the development and demonstration of a number of engineering-model missiles over a two-year period. This phase of the programme was completed successfully on schedule, and is being followed by a 30-month final development phase, funded at $110 million, in which more than 30 missiles are being launched from Harpoon-designated aircraft, ships and submarines. Progress to date is so satisfactory that $58 million for continued development was requested for FY1975, plus $78 million for pilot production of 58 operational test and evaluation missiles and 92 for initial operational deployment of Harpoon.

Teledyne CAE and Garrett AiResearch were awarded contracts for initial development of the Harpoon's turbine propulsion system. The J402-CA-400 turbojet proposed by the former company was eventually selected for this application.

The general configuration of the **AGM-84A** air-launched version of Harpoon is shown in the accompanying illustration. It is a torpedo-shape missile, with cruciform wings indexed in line with cruciform tail surfaces. The turbojet power plant is housed in the rear of the body, with a ventral flush air intake.

Prior to launch, targeting data for Harpoon are provided by the command and launch subsystem, which interfaces with on-board systems. The Harpoon data processer, a general-purpose digital computer, receives targeting and attitude data from existing systems, and computes the necessary missile and launcher orders. After launch, guidance is provided by a midcourse guidance system consisting of a strapdown attitude reference assembly and digital computer. No inputs from the launch platform are required by the missile after launch. Cruise attitude is monitored by a radar altimeter, enabling the flight to the target to be made at low altitude, so offering both optimum target acquisition capability through reduction of clutter effects, and the ability to penetrate enemy defences. Control is exercised via the tail-fins, which are each driven by an electro-mechanical actuator. Offset launch capability is provided for all launch modes.

When the target comes within the search area of the active radar seeker, the high-resolution system detects and locks on to the target, even in rain and high sea states. Seeker lock-on is maintained until impact. Capability to perform high-*g* manoeuvres throughout flight permits successful operation against fast manoeuvring targets. A terminal "pop-up" manoeuvre counters close-in defences and offers maximum warhead effectiveness. Counter-countermeasures devices are installed. The warhead is a high-explosive blast type.

Addition of a short solid-propellant tandem booster, with cruciform fins, converts the Harpoon into the **RGM-84A-1** ship-launched version. This is launched at a low elevation angle and follows a ballistic trajectory until booster separation. The sustainer engine then starts and the

AGM-84A Harpoon air-to-surface anti-shipping missile on launcher

missile descends to cruise altitude, following the same trajectory as that for air-launch. Launchers can include standard Tartar, Terrier, ASROC and Mk 26 types.

The Harpoon canister launcher provides a lightweight means of adapting Harpoon to nearly any surface launch application, including land-based shore defence systems. Under development for Patrol Hydrofoil Missile (PHM) ships, the launcher, weighing approximately 2,000 lb (907 kg), consists of a cluster of four Harpoon canisters and associated support structure. Each canister contains one Harpoon. The missile configuration is the same as that for ship launch, except that the aerodynamic surfaces are modified to permit folding within the canister diameter.

The submarine-launch Harpoon configuration is the same as for the canister launcher, except that the missile is installed in a buoyant capsule, which is fired from the submarine's torpedo tubes. As the capsule rises toward the surface, aft-mounted control fins unfold to maintain the required attitude. Upon broaching the surface, the ends of the capsule separate automatically and the missile's solid-propellant booster ignites, launching it into the same trajectory as for surface launches.

The first drop-test of an AGM-84A development round was made in May 1972 from a P-3 Orion aircraft flying at 20,000 ft (6,100 m) over the Pacific. The test was designed to demonstrate separation characteristics and release mechanisms. Powered flights began in July 1972.

First launch of a complete missile against a target was made on 20 December 1972, when a Harpoon fired from a P-3 followed a full operational flight path, including terminal manoeuvre, before scoring a direct hit on the target ship, USS *Ingersoll*, moored off Point Mugu, California. Seven further target hits had been scored by early 1974, including one on a moving patrol boat. The first two launches of production-type Harpoons from a P-3 aircraft were equally successful.

The AGM-84A is intended to be carried by a variety of aircraft, including the P-3 Orion, S-3 Viking, A-6 Intruder and A-7 Corsair II.

DIMENSIONS:

Length overall:	
AGM-84A	12 ft 7 in (3·84 m)
RGM-84A-1	15 ft 0 in (4·57 m)
Body diameter	1 ft 1½ in (0·34 m)

WEIGHTS:

Launching weight:	
AGM-84A	1,100 lb (499 kg)
RGM-84A-1	1,400 lb (635 kg)

PERFORMANCE:

Cruising speed	high subsonic

NWC

NAVAL WEAPONS CENTER

HEADQUARTERS:
China Lake, California 93555
Telephone: (714) 939-3555

COMMANDER:
Rear Admiral W. J. Moran

TECHNICAL DIRECTOR:
H. G. Wilson

HEAD, PUBLIC AFFAIRS OFFICE:
J. H. McGlothlin

The Naval Weapons Center (formerly US Naval Ordnance Test Station) is located 155 miles northeast of Los Angeles, on the Mojave Desert, and comes under the command of the Chief of Naval Material, Department of the Navy.

The mission of the Center is to conduct a programme of warfare analysis, research, development, test, evaluation, systems integration and fleet engineering support in naval weapons systems, principally for air warfare, and to conduct investigations into related fields of science and technology.

Chief ordnance developments of the Center are guided missiles, rockets, and aircraft fire-control and bomb-directing systems. Weapons developed at the Center include the 2·75 in folding-fin aircraft rocket, Mighty Mouse; the 11·75 in rocket, Tiny Tim; the 5 in folding-fin aircraft rocket, Zuni; the air-to-air guided missile, Sidewinder; the Snakeye 250/500 lb bomb, with folding dive-brake retardation system to avoid fragmentation damage to the launch aircraft during low-level strikes; the Shrike air-to-surface anti-radar missile; the Walleye glide bomb; and Standard ARM air-to-surface missile. Production of many of these weapons was entrusted to commercial companies under whose entries they are, or were, described in *Jane's*.

SIDEWINDER 1A

USAF and Navy designations: AIM-9B (formerly AAM-N-7 and GAR-8), AIM-9E, AIM-9H, AIM-9J and AIM-9L

One of the simplest and cheapest guided weapons yet produced in quantity, the standard **AIM-9B** Sidewinder air-to-air missile was developed by the NWC and was first fired successfully on 11 September 1953. It was produced in very large numbers by Philco and General Electric, for the US Navy and the USAF, and has been supplied to many foreign air forces, including those of Nationalist China, Australia, Japan, the Philippines, Spain, nine NATO countries and Sweden, the Royal Navy, Royal Canadian and Royal Netherlands Navies.

Licence manufacture was undertaken in Germany by Bodenseewerk, in association with subcontractors in the Netherlands, Denmark, Norway, Greece, Portugal and Turkey. The first of some 9,000 licence-built rounds was delivered on 27 November 1961. Bodenseewerk worked subsequently on a Sidewinder improvement programme.

Sidewinder is claimed to have fewer than two dozen moving parts and no more electronic components than a domestic radio. It has a cylindrical aluminium body, cruciform control surfaces at the nose and cruciform tail fins. Power plant is a Naval Propellant Plant solid-propellant rocket motor. A 25 lb (11·4 kg) HE warhead is fitted. Guidance is by infra-red homing.

Several advanced versions of Sidewinder are reported to be under development or in service, to offer improved capability, as follows:

AIM-9E. Advanced version of AIM-9B, produced by Philco for the USAF.

AIM-9H. Version with improved close-range capability for the US Navy, to equip the F-14 and other types. Latest contract, for FY1975, entails production of 800 by Raytheon.

AIM-9J. Advanced version of AIM-9E under development for the USAF by Philco-Ford to equip the F-15 and other types. Increased range.

AIM-9L. New version with much enhanced capability under development by Raytheon jointly for USN and USAF. No details available.

The following details apply to the basic AIM-9B Sidewinder:

DIMENSIONS:

Length overall	9 ft 3½ in (2·83 m)
Body diameter	5 in (0·13 m)
Fin span	1 ft 10 in (0·56 m)

WEIGHT:

Launching weight	159 lb (72 kg)

PERFORMANCE:

Speed	Mach 2·5
Range	1·75 nm (2 miles; 3·35 km)

SIDEWINDER 1C

US Navy designations: AIM-9D (formerly AAM-N-7) and AIM-9G

Sidewinder 1C is an advanced model of the Sidewinder with higher speed and greater range capabilities. It was developed by the NWC at China Lake and entered large-scale production by Raytheon Company for the US Navy and UK.

This version of Sidewinder has a tapering nose, longer-chord nose fins and greater sweepback on the leading-edge of the tail-fins. The advanced Mk 36 Mod 5 solid-propellant motors are supplied by Rocketdyne's Solid Rocket Division.

There are two current versions, as follows:

AIM-9D. Standard infra-red homing version, as described above.

AIM-9G. Version produced by Raytheon for

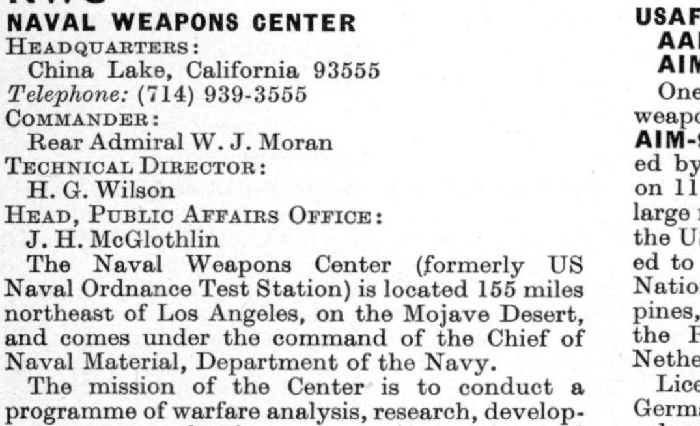

Left: **AIM-9B Sidewinder**

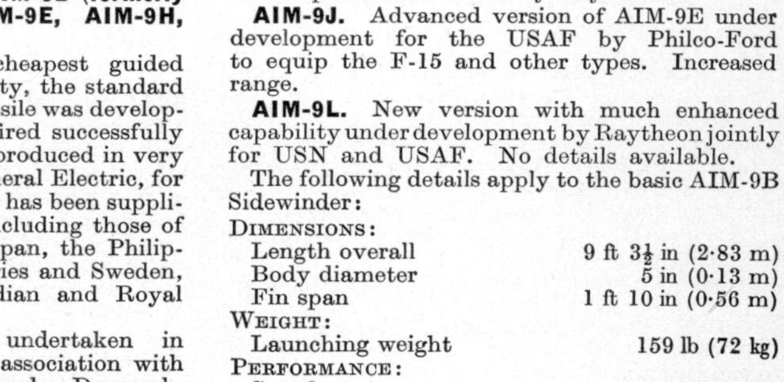

Right: **Mounting a Sidewinder 1C on an F-8 Crusader fighter**

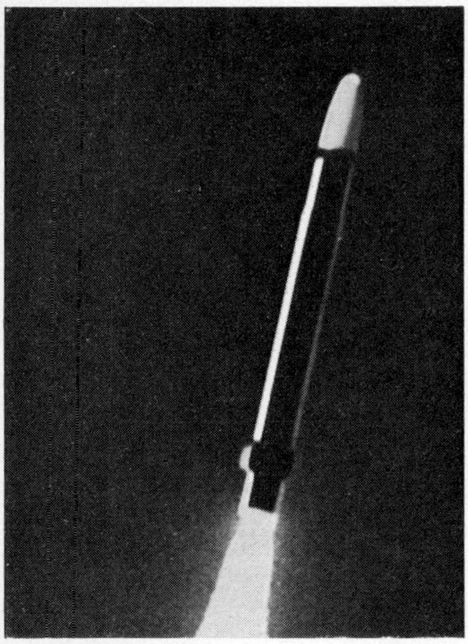

Ramp-launched development test of Agile

US Navy and USAF. Basically similar to AIM-9D but with improved target acquisition and lock-on.

DIMENSIONS (AIM-9D):

Length overall	9 ft 6½ in (2·91 m)
Body diameter	5 in (0·13 m)
Fin span	2 ft 1 in (0·64 m)

LAUNCHING WEIGHT:

AIM-9D	185 lb (84 kg)

PERFORMANCE (AIM-9D):

Range	over 1·75 nm (2 miles; 3·35 km)

AGILE

US Navy designation: AIM-95

Development of this close-range "dogfight" missile was initiated by the Naval Weapons Center to arm the Grumman F-14 Tomcat fighter. It is now expected to be carried also by the USAF's McDonnell Douglas F-15 Eagle. The US Navy awarded Hughes Aircraft Co a $2·2 million contract in early 1973 to provide assistance to the NWC over an eight-month period. Hughes was selected at the same time as the source for Agile's guidance subsystem, system integration and engineering support. The solid-propellant rocket motor is supplied by Thiokol.

Agile will utilise a thrust-vector control system, to ensure optimum manoeuvrability in flight against high-speed manoeuvring targets, and an infra-red seeker head able to home on the target from any direction. A development round tested from an F-4 in mid-1973 was basically cigarette-shape, 8 in (20 cm) in diameter, with a ring of eight short-span folding fins near the tail for roll control. Its seeker was housed inside a short cylinder, 5½ in (14 cm) in diameter, with a hemispherical glass nose cap and a tapered fairing to connect it to the missile body. Overall length was about 8 ft (2·45 m).

US Navy requests for continued R & D funding of Agile totalled $26 million in FY 1973 and $21·7 million in FY 1974.

SHRIKE

US Navy designation: AGM-45A (formerly ASM-N-10)

Known originally as ARM (anti-radar missile), the Shrike is a supersonic air-to-surface weapon which homes on to enemy radar installations.

Texas Instruments and Sperry Univac produce guidance and control assemblies for Shrike, which has a Rocketdyne Mk 39 Mod 7 or Aerojet Mk 53 solid-propellant motor and is armed with a conventional high-explosive warhead. Its general configuration is shown in the accompanying illustration.

Delivery to carrier-based attack squadrons of the US Navy began in 1964. It can be carried by all Navy attack aircraft, and most F-4 and F-105 aircraft of the USAF, and was used operationally in Vietnam from 1965. Many improvements later increased Shrike's effectiveness. Budget requests for procurement in FY 1972 totalled $7·7 million from the US Navy and $11·3 million from the USAF. FY1973 requests totalled $38·5 million, FY 1974 requests $21·7 million, and FY 1974 supplemental requests $23 million (for 800 missiles) for the two services.

DIMENSIONS:

Length overall	10 ft 0 in (3·05 m)
Body diameter	8 in (20·3 cm)
Wing span	3 ft 0 in (0·91 m)

WEIGHT:

Launching weight	400 lb (182 kg)

PERFORMANCE (estimated):

Range	over 2·6 nm (3 miles; 5 km)

Mockups of Agile missiles and launchers mounted on an F-4 Phantom II

Shrike anti-radar missile on underwing rack of a McDonnell Douglas A-4E Skyhawk

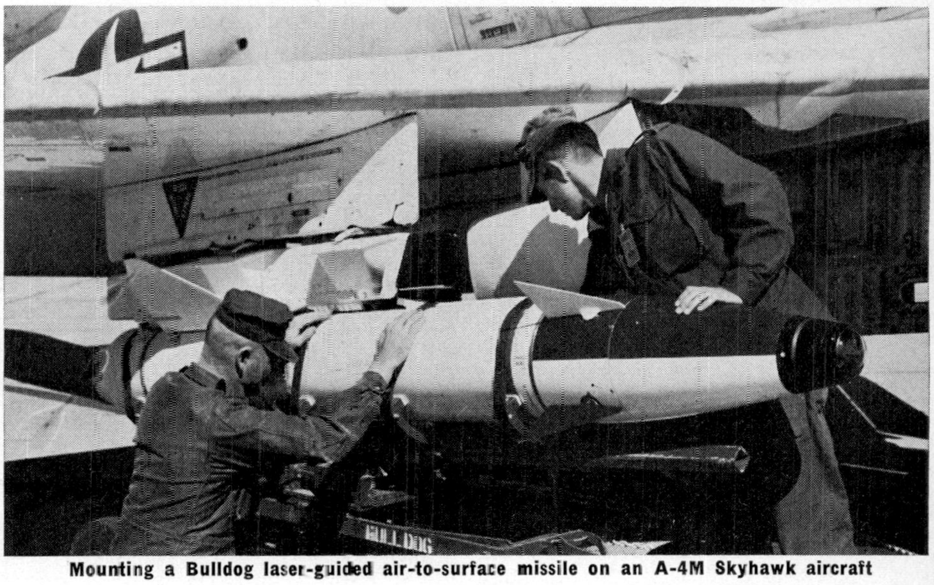

Mounting a Bulldog laser-guided air-to-surface missile on an A-4M Skyhawk aircraft

BULLDOG

US Navy designation: AGM-83A

This air-to-surface missile was developed by the Naval Weapons Center to meet a US Marine Corps requirement for a close air support weapon. It can be launched at altitudes and stand-off ranges beyond the reach of enemy small arms and anti-aircraft fire. The laser guidance system is claimed to offer first-pass pinpoint accuracy against surface targets.

The basic components of the Bulldog missile include an AN/DSM-126 guidance control group (GCG) developed jointly by the Naval Weapons Center and Texas Instruments. This GCG incorporates combat-proven seeker technology from the Sidewinder missile system. LR58-RM-4 (liquid) or Mk 8 Mod 2 (solid) Bullpup missile rocket motors and Mk 19 Mod 0 warhead sections are drawn from Navy inventory and modified for the Bulldog system. Other sub-systems include an avionics package and test equipment specially developed by the Naval Weapons Center. The system uses, without modification, handling equipment already available in Navy and Marine Corps inventory.

Four of the first five missiles tested in the development programme are reported to have achieved direct hits on moving targets, and pilot production of Bulldog was stated to be underway in late 1972. The Senate Armed Services Committee added $15·4 million to the Navy's FY1975 budget request, to cover procurement of 500 missiles. This was deleted subsequently by the House Appropriations Committee, in favour of the laser-guided Maverick, leaving the future of Bulldog in doubt.

DIMENSIONS:

Length overall	9 ft 9½ in (2·98 m)
Body diameter	1 ft 0 in (0·30 m)

WEIGHT:

Launching weight	600 lb (272 kg)

RAYTHEON

RAYTHEON COMPANY

HEAD OFFICE:
141 Spring Street, Lexington, Massachusetts 02173
Telephone: (617) 862-6600
Telex: 92-3455

CHAIRMAN OF THE BOARD:
Charles F. Adams

PRESIDENT:
Thomas L. Phillips

EXECUTIVE VICE-PRESIDENT:
D. Brainerd Holmes

SENIOR VICE-PRESIDENT:
Aldo R. Miccioli (General Manager, Missile Systems Division)

VICE-PRESIDENTS:
Justin M. Margolskee (General Manager Operations, Missile Systems Division)
M. W. Fossier (Asst General Manager, Technical)
Floyd Wimberly (SAM-D Programme)
Joseph Glasser (Manufacturing Manager)
John H. Sidebottom (Corporate Communications)

Raytheon Company's Missile Systems Division is prime contractor for the US Army's surface-to-air Hawk and US Navy/USAF Sidewinder (described under "NWC" heading) and Sparrow air-to-air weapon systems. It has developed a surface-to-air version of Sparrow as the RIM-7H Sea Sparrow and is prime contractor for development of the important SAM-D surface-to-air missile.

Missile Systems Division is also active in the fields of microminiaturised computers, advanced avionics systems, phased array radars, lasers and radar systems such as the Missile Site Radar for the Safeguard ABM programme.

Raytheon Company's Equipment Division is prime contractor for the NATO Sea Sparrow system, under development for the US Navy, the Royal Norwegian Navy, the Royal Danish Navy, the Royal Netherlands Navy, the Royal Belgian Navy and the Italian Navy.

SPARROW

US military designations: AIM-7 and RIM-7H

The AIM-7 Sparrow, developed by Raytheon Company for the US Naval Air Systems Command, is a radar-homing air-to-air missile with all-weather all-altitude operational capability. It can also be used against shipping targets from aircraft or ships.

Engineering of the Sparrow weapon system is done at Raytheon's laboratories at Bedford, Mass, and the company's engineering proving site at Oxnard, California. Production of the missile and its associated systems is centred in plants at South Lowell, Mass, and Bristol, Tenn. In addition, Mitsubishi is manufacturing more than 600 in Japan for the Japan Air Self-Defence Force, under licence from Raytheon.

The Sparrow equips McDonnell Douglas F-4 Phantom II aircraft of the US Navy, USAF, Royal Navy, Royal Air Force, Imperial Iranian Air Force, Israeli Air Force, Republic of Korea Air Force and Spanish Air Force. The Lockheed F-104S Starfighters licence-built in Italy are Sparrow-armed, and both the USAF's McDonnell Douglas F-15 Eagle and the US Navy's Grumman F-14 Tomcat employ this missile.

Without change, the Sparrow is used on US Navy ships as a surface-to-air and anti-shipping weapon in the Basic Point Defense Surface Missile System. It is also used in Canadian ships in the Close Range Missile System.

Sparrow has a cylindrical body, pivoted cruciform wings and cruciform tail fins in line with the wings. The current, advanced, AIM-7F version is powered by a Hercules Mk 58 Mod 0 solid-propellant motor and has a Raytheon semi-active Doppler radar homing system. The 88 lb (40 kg) continuous-rod warhead is actuated by a proximity fuse or contact fuse. Manoeuvrability has been improved, and Sparrow is now considered a good dogfight missile as well as a good medium-range weapon.

The AIM-7F is in limited production for the US Navy and USAF. FY1975 budget requests include $99·7 million for 600 additional missiles, plus $7·7 million for research, development, test and evaluation.

The ship-launched RIM-7H, now operational, has folding wings to reduce the size of its launcher. A new ship-launched version is planned, based on the AIM-7F, with longer range than the RIM-7H.

A new missile, evolved from Sparrow, is under development for the Royal Air Force by Hawker Siddeley Dynamics of the UK (which see).

The following details apply specifically to the AIM-7F:

DIMENSIONS:	
Length overall	12 ft 0 in (3·66 m)
Body diameter	8 in (0·20 m)
Wing span	3 ft 4 in (1·02 m)
WEIGHT:	
Launching weight	500 lb (227 kg)
PERFORMANCE (estimated):	
Speed	over Mach 3·5
Range	24 nm (28 miles; 44 km)

Sparrow missile on the Kaman NUH-2C experimental helicopter

Sparrow being launched from a McDonnell Douglas F-15A Eagle air superiority fighter

ROCKWELL INTERNATIONAL

ROCKWELL INTERNATIONAL CORPORATION

EXECUTIVE OFFICES:
1700 East Imperial Highway, El Segundo, California 90246
600 Grant Street, Pittsburgh, Pennsylvania 15219

OFFICERS: See "Aircraft" section

Missile Systems Division

4300 East Fifth Avenue, Columbus, Ohio 43216

MANAGER, PUBLIC RELATIONS:
Dent Williams

Rockwell International's Columbus (Ohio) Missile Systems Division is playing a major role in several important US weapon programmes. Brief details are given below of the Condor and HOBOS air-to-surface weapons and the Air Defense Suppression Missile which the Missile Systems Division is developing and/or producing for the US Army, Navy and Air Force.

This Division is also engaged on extensive work involving the applications of laser technology. In particular, it has supplied hardware for the US Army Missile Command's laser terminal homing guidance demonstration programme.

AGM-53A Condor air-to-surface missile test round under wing of A-6 Intruder aircraft

CONDOR

US Navy designation: AGM-53A

Condor, developed by the Rockwell International Missile Systems Division for the Naval Air Systems Command, is entering pilot production as an advanced air-to-surface missile to equip the Grumman A-6 Intruder and LTV Aerospace A-7 Corsair II aircraft.

Layout is conventional, with a cylindrical body, rounded nose, cruciform delta wings and cruciform tail control surfaces indexed in line with the wings. It is powered by a Rocketdyne solid-propellant rocket motor and carries a conventional high-explosive warhead. A contract to develop a simplified data link subsystem for the missile was awarded to Hughes Aircraft Company in August 1971.

Condor is guided to the target by the missile systems operator in the launch aircraft, who monitors a cockpit display relayed from the missile's television "eye". After launch, the aircraft is free to begin the return flight to the carrier, maintaining control over the flight of the missile until it locks on to the target. A range of up to 35 nm (40 miles; 64 km) has been quoted, but one test Condor is said to have hit a target 50 nm (57 miles; 92 km) from its launch aircraft.

The missile made its first, successful, air launching test from an F-4 fighter on 31 March 1970. Direct hits on land and ship targets have been achieved in subsequent tests, using both inert and live warheads, and a live warhead strike against a ship target (USS *Vammen*) on 4 February 1971 resulted in sinking of the vessel.

FY1975 budget requests included about $10 million for continued development and $20 million for the procurement of 35 more pilot line missiles, the minimum number to keep the line going pending a decision on full-scale production, now expected in early 1975.

Engineering development and flight testing are aimed at completing the evaluation of a dual-mode radar and electro-optical seeker version of Condor by 1976. This version will have a night/all-weather capability not possessed by the present electro-optical version. To reduce unit cost, a non-secure data link is also under development.

ADSM

In early 1973, the US Army Missile Command awarded Rockwell's Missile Systems Division a contract to design and manufacture a dual-mode anti-radiation homing/infra-red (ARH/IR) Air Defense Suppression Missile (ADSM) for Army evaluation.

The ADSM utilises the basic 7 in (17·8 cm) diameter airframe of Rockwell's Hornet missile, described in the 1973-74 *Jane's*. Both vehicle and dual-mode seeker are designed, fabricated and integrated by its Missile Systems Division.

By early 1974, direct hits on the target had been achieved in three consecutive firings of the

Left: **Rockwell's Air Defense Suppression Missile, which utilises a Hornet airframe for development testing** *Right:* **Rockwell HOBOS homing bomb system**

ADSM. The third launch was performed by a Rockwell crew flying a UH-1 helicopter at the US Army Missile Command's Redstone Arsenal, Alabama. The missile was fired over a range of more than 2 nm (2·5 miles; 4 km) and from an altitude of 1,000 ft (305 m), and struck the centre of the turret of a stationary tank target. The latter was equipped with radar to represent an armoured vehicle fitted with radar-directed multiple anti-aircraft guns.

HELLFIRE

The US Army requested $11·1 million under the 1974 Fiscal Year budget proposals for a programme to determine the feasibility of a helicopter-launched defence suppression missile known as Hellfire. The initial version was intended to use a laser homing guidance system, and early tests were made at the Army Missile Command headquarters in Huntsville, Alabama, using Rockwell International Hornet missiles as test airframes.

The programme advanced a stage further in the early Summer of 1974, when Rockwell International and Hughes Aircraft Company were selected as competing contractors in a one-year advanced development programme aimed at producing a modular Hellfire able to accept semi-active laser, dual-mode ARH/IR, TV and imaging IR homing heads.

Launch weight of Hellfire is expected to be in the region of 50 lb (23 kg) compared with the 120 lb (54 kg) of Hornet test rounds.

HOBOS

HOBOS (HOming BOmb System) is a modular weapon system consisting of a KMU-353A/B or KMU-390/B (dependent on bomb size) guidance and control kit currently designed for easy installation on MK 84 (2,000 lb) and M118E1 (3,000 lb) general-purpose bombs. Kit installation does not alter the conventional bomb suspension, release or jettison functions, thus permitting the conversion of standard bombs into highly-accurate guided weapon systems.

Each kit consists of a forward guidance section, the warhead or interconnect section (including the bomb), and the aft control section.

The guidance or nose section consists of target seeker optics and sensor mounted on a gyro-stabilised platform, and the associated electronics which include a camera, platform and tracker electronics, and associated power supplies. The guidance section also furnishes reference signals to the autopilot located in the control section.

The warhead section consists of the MK 84 or M118E1 bomb with an interconnect assembly made up of four strakes, external electrical conduit, umbilical receptacle, and strake and umbilical receptacle attachment bands. The strakes are indexed in line with the wings to provide aerodynamic stability. The conduit transmits electrical signals between the guidance and control sections. The umbilical receptacle provides the necessary aircraft signal interface. Fusing of the HOBOS can be accomplished either electrically or mechanically.

The control or aft section consists of a cylindrical body with cruciform wings fitted with trailing-edge flap control surfaces for flight manoeuvring. The weapon system batteries and flight control system components are located within this section, including the autopilot which collects pitch and yaw steering data from the guidance section and converts this information into signals which drive the pneumatic control surface actuators.

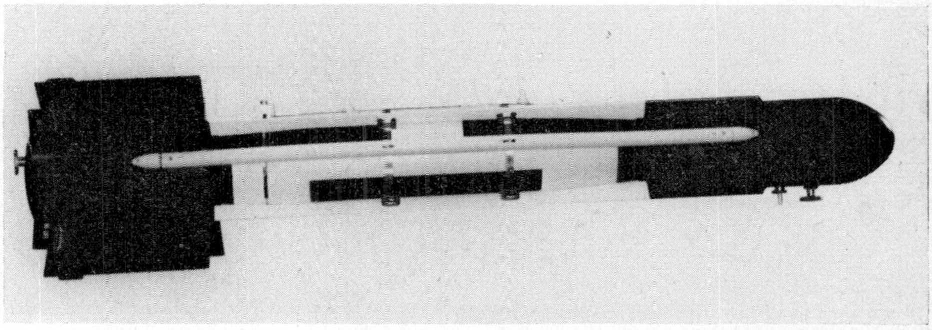

MK 84 HOBOS with new midcourse guidance, including DME, for increased accuracy

Modular glide bomb version of the electro-optically guided MK 84 HOBOS, with wings to increase range

The effectiveness of the HOBOS modular weapon system has been demonstrated fully in a large number of successful air drops, notably against targets such as aircraft in revetments, jungle roads and bridges in Vietnam

Missile Systems Division is under contract for production of the version built around the MK 84 bomb, for Greece and Israel, as well as the US services. Adaptation of kits to other types of warhead is feasible; and several types of guidance system have been utilised in this weapon system, including electro-optical contrast tracker and infra-red, providing in all cases a glide bomb with self-contained guidance, high accuracy and moderate/long-range stand-off capability.

Some MK 84 HOBOS electro-optically guided rounds have been fitted with a swept wing assembly, which attaches above the weapon to increase its range. Known as modular guided glide bombs (MGGB), these 2,000 lb (907 kg) weapons carry a data link to allow controllability at extended ranges. The wings extend after launch.

Another version of HOBOS, also illustrated on this page, is modified to incorporate a new midcourse guidance system, including distance measuring equipment (DME), for increased accuracy.

DIMENSIONS:	
Length overall:	
MK 84	12 ft 5 in (3·78 m)
M118E1	12 ft 2 in (3·71 m)
Body diameter:	
MK 84	1 ft 6 in (0·46 m)
M118E1	2 ft 0 in (0·61 m)
Wing span:	
MK 84	3 ft 8 in (1·12 m)
M118E1	4 ft 4 in (1·32 m)
WEIGHT:	
Launching weight:	
MK 84	2,240 lb (1,016 kg)
M118E1	3,404 lb (1,544 kg)

TEXAS INSTRUMENTS

TEXAS INSTRUMENTS, INC

CORPORATE OFFICES:
North Building 13500, North Central Expressway, Dallas, Texas 75222

Texas Instruments has played a major part in many US missile programmes. The latest missile for which it is prime contractor is the AGM-88A HARM, of which brief details follow:

HARM

US Navy designation: AGM-88A

On 24 May 1974, Texas Instruments was named as prime contractor for HARM (High-speed Anti-Radiation Missile) by the US Naval Air Systems Command. The initial phase of the contract, valued at $1·4 million, covered four months of basic design co-ordination. The main four-phase programme is expected to involve four years' work. This will be centred in the company's Dallas facilities, where production of the Shrike anti-radiation missile has taken place for more than a decade.

Few details of HARM may yet be published. Its high speed reflects experience gained in Vietnam, where Soviet-supplied surface-to-air missile radar systems sometimes detected the approach of US anti-radiation missiles such as the first-generation Shrike and ceased operation before the missile could lock on to them. HARM is intended to have a sufficiently high performance to lock on to any target radar before it can shut down. It will cover a wide range of frequency spectra, so enabling one basic missile to be used against a variety of different radars. Aircraft likely to carry HARM, if its development proves successful, include the A-6, A-7, F-4, F-14, F-15 and S-3. Procurement of a total of 3,000 missiles is envisaged, with initial operational capability in 1979.

THE UNION OF SOVIET SOCIALIST REPUBLICS

AIR-TO-AIR MISSILES

NATO code name: "Alkali"

This first-generation Soviet air-to-air missile is standard armament of the Sukhoi Su-9 and of the all-weather versions of the MiG-19, which continue in service with the air forces of the Soviet Union and some of its allies.

"Alkali" is a solid-propellant missile, with large delta cruciform wings at the rear and small cruciform foreplanes indexed in line with the wings. There appear to be control surfaces in the trailing-edges of the wings and "Alkali" is believed to employ some form of radar homing. The warhead is carried immediately aft of the foreplanes.

NATO code name: "Anab"

First seen as underwing armament on the Yakovlev Yak-28P fighter ("Firebar") in the 1961 Soviet Aviation Day display, "Anab" is now known to be a standard air-to-air missile in the Soviet Air Force. It was carried by Yak-28, Sukhoi Su-11 and Sukhoi Su-15 interceptors taking part in the 1967 air display at Domodedovo.

"Anab" has a cylindrical body, with small cruciform canard control surfaces indexed in line with very large cruciform tail-fins. Both infra-red and semi-active radar homing versions are operational.

Dimensions (estimated):

Length:	
IR version	13 ft 5 in (4·1 m)
radar-homing version	13 ft 1 in (4·0 m)

NATO code name: "Ash"

The code name "Ash" has been given to the large air-to-air missiles shown under the wings of the Tupolev Tu-28P ("Fiddler") fighter on photographs in the "Aircraft" section of this edition. These missiles have cruciform wings and tail surfaces indexed in line, and are operational in two versions, which have infra-red and semi-active (or active) radar homing heads respectively.

Dimensions (estimated):

Length:	
IR version	18 ft 0 in (5·5 m)
radar homing version	17 ft 0 in (5·2 m)

NATO Code Name: "Atoll"

This missile has been seen under the wings of a variety of Soviet aircraft and is standard equipment on home and export versions of the MiG-21. It is almost identical to the American Sidewinder 1A (AIM-9B) in size and configuration and appears to have a similar infra-red guidance system.

The body is cylindrical with cruciform control surfaces near the nose, indexed in line with the fixed cruciform tail-fins. There are no external cable or control conduits.

The triangular control surfaces have a compound sweep averaging about 60° on the leading-edge and 10° on the trailing-edge. They are linked in opposite pairs, with a maximum movement of 20-30°.

Leading-edge sweep on the tail-fins is about 40°, with straight trailing-edges. A small gyroscopically-controlled tab is inset in the trailing-edge of each fin, at the tip, presumably for anti-roll stabilisation but possibly with an added control function.

Nozzle diameter of the solid-propellant motor is 3⅛ in (8 cm). Weight and performance of "Atoll" should be very similar to those of Sidewinder 1A.

Dimensions:

Length overall	9 ft 2 in (2·80 m)
Body diameter	4·72 in (12 cm)
Span of control surfaces	1 ft 5¾ in (0·45 m)
Span of tail-fins	1 ft 8¾ in (0·53 m)

Weights and Performance:
No details available except:
Range approx 2·5-3·5 nm (3-4 miles; 5-6·5 km)

"Advanced Atoll"

The latest versions of the MiG-21 have been observed with a mix of standard infra-red "Atolls" and a new version of this weapon with a radar homing head. For convenience, the radar version is known at present as "Advanced Atoll".

HELICOPTER MISSILE

NATO code name: "Swatter"

No photographs of the Mil Mi-24 ("Hind-A") assault helicopter have yet shown missiles mounted on its wingtip launchers. However, there is no evidence to suggest that it carries wire-guided missiles. The only standard Soviet anti-tank missile known to operate without wire guidance is "Swatter", shown in surface-to-surface use in an accompanying illustration.

"Swatter" is controlled by elevons on the trailing-edges of its rear-mounted cruciform

MiG-19 with four of the missiles known to NATO as "Alkali" on underwing launchers (*Tass*)

"Atoll" air-to-air missile under wing of Indian MiG-21. Of interest also is the GP-9 underbelly gun pack

"Swatter" anti-tank missiles on BRDM vehicle. Missiles of this type are believed to arm the Mil Mi-24 helicopter (*Tass*)

wings. The two small canard surfaces at the nose are also movable. The motor appears to exhaust through two vents diametrically opposed between the wings. Two more tubes, projecting rearward from opposite wings, probably house tracking flares. The blunt nose of "Swatter" suggests the likelihood of a terminal homing system operating via the canard foreplanes.

DIMENSIONS:

Length	3 ft 8 in (1·12 m)
Wing span	2 ft 2 in (0·65 m)

AIR-TO-SURFACE MISSILES

AS-1

NATO code name: "Kennel"

"Kennel" is a turbojet-powered air-to-surface winged anti-shipping missile which looks rather like a scaled-down unpiloted version of the MiG-15 fighter aircraft, with a hemispherical radome above its nose air intake. There is further electronic equipment in a pod at the top of the tail-fin. Each wing is fitted with two fences.

Two "Kennels" were carried under the wings of Tu-16s supplied some years ago to the Indonesian and Egyptian Air Forces. The Indonesian aircraft are not operational at the present time. Egyptian-based Tu-16s appear now to carry "Kelt" missiles, rather than "Kennels," as do Tu-16s operated by the Soviet Naval Air Force.

"Kennel" spans about 16 ft 0 in (4·9 m) and is about 27 ft 0 in (8·2 m) long. Its range is estimated at 55 nm (63 miles; 100 km), at a cruising speed of Mach 0·9. A surface-to-surface version (NATO code name "Samlet") continues in service.

"Kennel" anti-shipping missile under the wing of a Tu-16 bomber

AS-2

NATO code name: "Kipper"

The missile carried by the Tu-16 ("Badger") in the 1961 Aviation Day Display, and described as an anti-shipping weapon, has a conventional sweptwing aeroplane layout, with an underslung power plant which is almost certainly a turbojet. It appears to be about 31 ft (9·5 m) long, with a wing span of 16 ft (4·88 m). Its performance is likely to be much inferior to that of the more refined and larger American Hound Dog air-to-surface missile of somewhat similar configuration, with an estimated range of 115 nm (132 miles; 213 km) and cruising speed of Mach 1·2. Radar is carried in the nose of the Tu-16 carrier aircraft.

Tupolev Tu-95 ("Bear-B") with AS-3 "Kangaroo" air-to-surface missile

AS-3

NATO code name: "Kangaroo"

Largest of the air-to-surface missiles first seen in the Soviet Aviation Day display at Tushino in 1961, and known to be operational, was that carried by the Tu-95 ("Bear") and given the NATO code name "Kangaroo". It is a winged missile with an airframe similar in size and shape to a sweptwing turbojet-powered fighter aircraft. The tail unit is conventional, with sweepback on all surfaces. The vertical surfaces, concealed inside the launch-aircraft until the missile is dropped, are of rhomboid form.

What was believed originally to be a radome on the missile's nose was identified subsequently as either a duct through which air can be fed to start the missile's turbojet engine prior to launching or a fairing over the air intake. Radar guidance equipment is carried in the nose of the Tu-95 carrier aircraft. Length of this missile is reported to be 48 ft 11 in (14·9 m), with a span of 30 ft (9·15 m), speed of Mach 2 and range of 350 nm (400 miles; 650 km).

AS-4

NATO code name: "Kitchen"

The air-to-surface missile carried semi-submerged in the fuselage of the Tupolev Tu-22 bomber ("Blinder") looks considerably more advanced than the weapons already described. It appears to have stubby delta wings and cruciform tail surfaces. A bulge under the body could be an air intake for its power plant or a radome. The speed of this weapon is probably high. It is about 37 ft (11·3 m) long and has an estimated range of 400 nm (460 miles; 740 km).

AS-5 "Kelt" rocket-powered air-to-surface stand-off missile, developed from "Kennel", under port wing of Tu-16 bomber

AS-5

NATO code name: "Kelt"

In September 1968 a photograph released officially in Moscow showed this air-to-surface missile under the port wing of a Tu-16 bomber. It is externally similar to "Kennel", but the ram-air intake and radome of the latter missile are replaced by a hemispherical nose fairing, probably housing a larger radar. This implies that "Kelt" is rocket-powered and it may be significant that, unlike "Kennel", it has an underbelly fairing of the kind seen on the rocket-powered "Styx" missile. In other respects the airframes of "Kelt" and "Kennel" appear to be almost identical in configuration, but "Kelt" appears to be longer than "Kennel" and its underwing carrier is much larger.

During the Arab-Israeli War of October 1973, about 25 "Kelts" were launched against Israeli targets by Tu-16s from Egypt. Twenty of the missiles were destroyed by the air and ground defences; the others hit two radar sites and a supply centre in Sinai.

DIMENSIONS (estimated):

Span	15 ft 0 in (4·57 m)
Length overall	31 ft 0 in (9·45 m)

PERFORMANCE (estimated):

Range	over 175 nm (200 miles; 320 km)

AS-6

Little is known about this new missile, which is reported to be one of the weapons carried by the Tupolev supersonic "swing-wing" bomber known to NATO as "Backfire". US reports suggest that it is fitted with inertial guidance and has a range of up to 300 nm (345 miles; 555 km) at Mach 3.

SPACEFLIGHT

AND

RESEARCH ROCKETS

THE ARGENTINE REPUBLIC

FMA

FÁBRICA MILITAR DE AVIONES, INSTITUTO DE INVESTIGACIONES AERONAUTICAS Y ESPACIAL (I.I.A.E.)

Address:
Guarnición Aérea Córdoba, Córdoba
Director of I.I.A.E.:
Comodoro Aldo Zeoli
Head of Space Development Group:
Vicecomodoro Miguel Sanchez Peña

This branch of the Fábrica Militar de Aviones (FMA) is a research and development Institute which, since 1958, has undertaken the design and manufacture of solid-propellant rockets and missiles.

Simultaneously, double-base and composite propellants, payloads for upper atmosphere scientific research, instrumentation, telemetry equipment and other equipment have been developed in its laboratories.

In 1961, the I.I.A.E. conducted the first launching of a sounding rocket produced in the Argentine, the Alfa-Centauro. It has since manufactured a family of Centauro sounding rockets, known as the Alfa, Beta and Gamma. It also inaugurated the first launching site in Latin America—the C.E.L.P.A. at Chamical, La Rioja (30° 30′ S, 66° W)—and carried out the first scientific experiments in the Antarctic using vehicles and payloads manufactured in the Argentine Republic. These last launchings were made at Base Matienzo (64° 58′ S, 60° 64′ W).

Basic details of the most important rockets developed and launched by the I.I.A.E. for upper atmosphere research in recent years can be found in the 1973-74 *Jane's*. There has been no news of any subsequent activities or products.

AUSTRALIA

GOVERNMENT OF AUSTRALIA

DEPARTMENT OF MANUFACTURING INDUSTRY

Address:
Constitution Avenue, Parkes, Canberra, ACT 2600
Telephone: 48 2111
Telex: 62063
Secretary: N. S. Currie, OBE, BA

Weapons Research Establishment:
Salisbury, South Australia 5108
Director: Dr M. W. Woods

Current types of upper atmosphere sounding rockets which have been developed by the Weapons Research Establishment and built in Australia are as follows:

AERO HIGH

Aero High is a two-stage solid-propellant sounding rocket developed primarily to carry out "chemical seeding" experiments at altitudes between 54 and 108 nm (62-125 miles; 100-200 km). Observations of glow clouds caused by the sudden release of chemicals are used to determine physical and chemical properties of the upper atmosphere.

The vehicle is capable of carrying a 45 lb (20 kg) payload to a peak height of a little over 113 nm (130 miles; 210 km). Further details can be found in the 1970-71 *Jane's*.

KOOKABURRA

Kookaburra has been used in the development of a drop sonde suitable for transmitting synoptic information to Australian meteorological stations. Payload capacity is 100 cu in (1,650 cc), and a 10 lb (4·5 kg) head can be carried to a height of 40·5 nm (46·6 miles; 75 km).

A Kookaburra Mk 2 version, with an apogee of 62 nm (71·5 miles; 115 km), has been developed for use in a falling sphere experiment.

COCKATOO

This sounding rocket was developed to replace the HAD vehicle described in the 1970-71 *Jane's*. Cockatoos have apogees in the 67·5-78 nm (77·5-90 miles; 125-145 km) range. They are used for falling sphere, lithium trail and ultraviolet investigations of the upper atmosphere.

LORIKEET

The Lorikeet sounding rocket is under development to replace the Cockatoo. It utilises two Australian solid-propellant rocket motors. The present Mk 1 vehicle can carry a 40 lb (18 kg) head to a height of 59 nm (68 miles; 110 km).

BRAZIL

AVIBRÁS

AVIBRÁS INDÚSTRIA AEROESPACIAL SA

Head Office and Works:
Antiga Estrada de Paraibuna, km 118 (CP 229), São José dos Campos, São Paulo
Telephone: (0123) 21-7433
Managing Director:
Eng João Verdi Carvalho Leite
Sales Director:
Hely Adilson de Oliveira

This company is engaged in research and development of rockets, propellants, ancillary systems and light aircraft for both civil and military purposes. Brief details of its current rocket programmes follow:

AVIBRÁS SONDA 1/A

The Sonda 1/A vehicle is a two-stage solid-propellant sounding rocket, designed to reach heights of up to 54 nm (62 miles; 100 km) with a 10 lb (4·5 kg) payload package. Developed and built in series by Avibrás under contract from the Brazilian Ministry of Aeronautics, it is now operational at the Ministry's Barreira do Inferno Range in Natal, Rio Grande do Norte State, where it has replaced US-built types.

The radio-sonde payload package is ejected when the rocket reaches its ceiling, and descends by parachute. Telemetry data are transmitted at a frequency of 403MHz, and the package is tracked by radar.

The booster is a 5 in (127 mm) calibre military aircraft rocket, developed and manufactured by Avibrás for the Brazilian Air Force.

Performance (85° launch angle):
Max speed at 2nd stage burnout
2,720 knots (3,135 mph; 1,400 m/sec)
Nominal ceiling 54 nm (62 miles; 100 km)
Peak altitude achieved
66 nm (76 miles; 123 km)

ABIVRÁS SONDA 1/B

This two-stage solid-propellant sounding rocket differs from the Sonda 1/A in having a second stage of reduced length. Max payload is 12 lb (5·5 kg).

Performance:
Max speed at 2nd stage burnout
2,430 knots (2,800 mph; 1,250 m/sec)
Nominal ceiling 40·5 nm (46·5 miles; 75 km)
Peak altitude achieved
45 nm (51 miles; 83 km)

IAE/EDE

CENTRO TÉCNICO AEROESPACIAL INSTITUTO DE ATIVIDADES ESPACIAIS (IAE)

EDE—Divisão de Engenhos Espaciais

Address:
12200 São José dos Campos, São Paulo State
Director of the IAE:
Cel Paulo Henrique Carneiro de Amarante
Head of the EDE:
Major Abner Maciel de Castro

The EDE—Divisão de Engenhos Espaciais (Space Vehicles Division) is the branch of IAE—Instituto de Atividades Espaciais (Space Activities Institute) responsible for research, development and prototype construction of rockets for scientific and military use. Several of the latter (of 37 mm, 70 mm, 89 mm, 127 mm and 159 mm calibres) are in large-scale production by private industry under Ministry of Aeronautics contracts. Its major scientific programmes concern the Sonda II and Sonda III sounding rockets.

IAE/EDE SONDA II

Sonda II is a single-stage spin-stabilised solid-propellant rocket designed to carry a 44 lb (20 kg) scientific payload to a height of 54 nm (62 miles; 100 km). After 18 firings, it was at the final qualification stage in March 1973.

Dimensions:
Length overall 13 ft 6¼ in (4·12 m)
Body diameter 11·8 in (0·30 m)
Weight:
Launching weight 815 lb (370 kg)

IAE/EDE SONDA III

This spin-stabilised two-stage solid-propellant rocket is designed to carry a 110 lb (50 kg) payload to a height of 270 nm (310 miles; 500 km). The first stage was undergoing static testing in the Spring of 1973. The second stage is a modified Sonda II motor.

Dimensions:
Length overall 26 ft 3 in (8·00 m)
Diameter of 2nd stage 11·8 in (0·30 m)
Weight:
Launching weight 3,443 lb (1,562 kg)

INPE

CONSELHO NACIONAL DE PESQUISAS (CNPq) INSTITUTO DE PESQUISAS ESPACIAIS (INPE)

Address:
São José dos Campos, São Paulo State
General Director:
Fernando de Mendonça

Brazil began its space research programme officially in 1961, by creating, within the National Research Council, a Group for the Organisation of a National Commission for Space Activities. Ten years later, in April 1971, this Comissão Nacional de Atividades Espaciais (CNAE) became a permanent organisation and was renamed the Instituto de Pesquisas Espaciais (INPE). Today INPE is the principal Brazilian agency for civilian space research.

From the start, INPE concentrated on research in two sectors: Pure Research and Applied Research. The first sector is concerned with scientific programmes such as Project MATE, a study of the geomagnetic field conducted in collaboration with US and German organisations; Project MIRO, an analysis of the upper atmosphere, including the development of dye-lasers; Project EXAMETNET, a meteorological investigation using sounding rockets; and other projects concerned with ionospheric and atmospheric observations. Together, these programmes absorb about 20 to 30 per cent of the Institute's resources.

The second sector, demanding the larger share of the resources, is aimed at making early and important contributions to national development. Programmes include Project MESA, which consists of meteorological studies based on photographs taken by satellite and transmitted automatically to several receiving stations throughout the country, built to INPE specifications by the Brazilian electronics industry; and Project SERE, which utilises remote sensing for surveys of the natural resources existing in the vast territory of Brazil. For this work, INPE has its own Bandeirante aircraft, fitted with remote sensing equipment, and uses also photographs taken by NASA aircraft and the ERTS-1 spacecraft. The most ambitious current programme is Project SACI, of which details follow:

SACI

This project (Sátelite Avançado de Communicaçoes Interdisciplinares) is intended to evaluate the potential ability of a Brazilian geostationary satellite to enhance the nation's educational facilities and so help in achieving the highly-prized goal of universal education for some 24 million students in Brazil's primary schools.

It includes a comprehensive educational experiment in northeastern Brazil (Rio Grande do Norte State), involving use of instructional broadcasts via the NASA-Fairchild ATS F geostationary spacecraft to some 500 schools with an estimated 20,000 pupils; and feasibility study of a national educational satellite that would assist provision of first-class education throughout Brazil.

To this end, the Brazilian government set up in June 1972 a commission to analyse the whole concept of a domestic satellite system, along lines proposed by INPE in 1967.

It is estimated that two SACI spacecraft in orbit would cost as little as 10 per cent of the total cost of the traditional type of educational system. If the project goes ahead, the first satellite could be launched into geostationary orbit by a NASA Delta launch vehicle in about 1976. Weighing approximately 1,545 lb (700 kg), this spacecraft would transmit a single TV channel, for educational purposes, in the 2·5GHz band allocated to the Satellite Broadcasting Service, as well as carrying several transponders for telecommunications in the 6-4GHz bands. Its probable location would be at a longitude between 72° and 83° W in order to provide coverage of the whole of Brazil.

CANADA

BAL

BRISTOL AEROSPACE LIMITED

HEAD OFFICE AND WORKS:
Winnipeg International Airport, PO Box 874, Winnipeg, Manitoba R3C 2S4
Telephone: (204) 775-8331
Telex: 07-57774

PRESIDENT AND GENERAL MANAGER: W. M. Auld
VICE-PRESIDENT MARKETING: R. H. May
VICE-PRESIDENT ROCKET AND SPACE DIVISION: A. W. Fia
MARKETING MANAGER: R. J. Bevis

Bristol Aerospace Limited (BAL) has developed and is manufacturing a series of seven high-altitude sounding rockets known as Black Brants. These vehicles have been designed for upper atmosphere research and have been used successfully by Canadian, United States and European research institutes.

Black Brant rockets have solid-propellant motors, and are designed for simplicity of operation, enabling them to be launched from ranges offering only minimum support facilities.

BAL is able to offer a completely comprehensive service in the sounding rocket field, including propellants, vehicle hardware, recovery systems, electronic components and payload system design and buildup, scientific experiment integration and checkout facilities. Experienced launch crews are available to conduct or support launches at any rocket range.

In addition to the vehicles described below, BAL is continuing its development of new rocket systems. One of these is a low-cost rocket capable of carrying a 9 lb (4·1 kg) payload to a height of 40 nm (47 miles; 75 km).

BLACK BRANT IIIA

Black Brant IIIA is a single-stage fin-stabilised rocket, powered by a 9KS11000 solid-propellant motor. The payload compartment is a 5·3 : 1 cone with 10 in (25·4 cm) cylindrical section as standard. The cylindrical section can be lengthened to 50 in (127 cm) if required.

Black Brant IIIA is launched in an overslung position from a Nike launcher or underslung from a boom launcher. Low impact dispersion characteristics suit it for launch from ranges with minimum impact area.

DIMENSIONS:
Length overall (standard configuration) 18 ft $2\frac{1}{4}$ in (5·54 m)
Body diameter 10·2 in (0·26 m)

WEIGHT:
Launching weight (less payload) 618 lb (281 kg)

NOMINAL PERFORMANCE:
Altitude with 88 lb (40 kg) gross payload* (Qe 85°) 100 nm (115 miles; 185 km)
Max acceleration 27*g*

*gross payload includes payload compartment and igniter housing.

BLACK BRANT IIIB

This vehicle offers a 40% increase in performance by comparison with Black Brant IIIA when carrying similar payloads. It is specially suited for use at remote sites, where ease of operation is a major consideration.

Vehicle hardware and dimensions are identical with those of Black Brant IIIA, with the exception of the 12KS10000 motor. The same alternative launchers can be used.

DIMENSIONS:
Length overall, standard configuration 18 ft $2\frac{1}{4}$ in (5·54 m)
Body diameter 10·2 in (0·26 m)

WEIGHT:
Launching weight (less payload) 678 lb (308 kg)

NOMINAL PERFORMANCE:
Altitude with 112 lb (51 kg) gross payload* (Qe 85°) 127 nm (146 miles; 235 km)
Max acceleration 27*g*

*gross payload includes payload compartment and igniter housing.

BLACK BRANT IVA

The first stage of this vehicle utilises the 15KS25000 engine used in the single-stage Black Brant VA; the second stage is generally similar to the production version of Black Brant IIIA, with the same payload capacity.

Black Brant IVA can be assembled in a few hours and may be held at instant launch readiness for many days. It is launched in an underslung position from a rail launcher.

DIMENSION:
Length overall (standard configuration) 37 ft 2 in (11·33 m)

WEIGHT:
Launching weight (less payload) 3,059 lb (1,388 kg)

NOMINAL PERFORMANCE:
Altitude with 84 lb (38 kg) gross payload* (Qe 85°) 499 nm (575 miles; 925 km)
Max acceleration 38*g*

*gross payload includes payload compartment and igniter housing.

BLACK BRANT IVB

This is an uprated version of the Black Brant IVA. Vehicle hardware and dimensions are identical with those of the IVA, except that a 12KS10000 solid-propellant motor is used in the second stage. Three low aspect ratio fins may be added to the conical stabiliser to increase stability and so allow payloads up to 60 in (153 cm) long to be flown.

WEIGHT:
Launching weight (less payload) 3,116 lb (1,414 kg)

NOMINAL PERFORMANCE:
Altitude with 84 lb (38 kg) gross payload* (Qe 85°) 572 nm (660 miles; 1,060 km)
Max acceleration 38*g*

*gross payload includes payload compartment and igniter housing.

BLACK BRANT VA

Black Brant VA is a single-stage high-altitude research rocket, powered by a 15KS25000 solid-propellant motor. It is suitable for carrying payloads of up to 615 lb (280 kg) to the 67 nm (77 miles; 125 km) region.

Black Brant VA carries its payload in a 4·3 : 1 ogival fairing 6 ft 1 in (1·87 m) long, or in a 5·1 : 1 cone 7 ft 2 in (2·18 m) long. Cylindrical extensions up to 5 ft 10 in (1·78 m) long may be added. It is launched in an underslung position from a rail.

DIMENSIONS:
Length overall (standard configuration) 26 ft 8 in (8·13 m)
Body diameter 17·2 in (0·44 m)

WEIGHT:
Launching weight (less payload) 2,473 lb (1,123 kg)

NOMINAL PERFORMANCE:
Altitude with 308 lb (140 kg) gross payload* (Qe 85°) 97 nm (112 miles; 180 km)
Max acceleration 16*g*

*gross payload includes payload compartment and igniter housing.

BLACK BRANT VB

The Black Brant VB single-stage research rocket has the same dimensions and payload space as the Black Brant VA but utilises a different solid-propellant motor, the 26KS20000.

DIMENSIONS:
Length overall (standard configuration) 26 ft 8 in (8·13 m)
Body diameter 17·2 in (0·44 m)

WEIGHT:
Launching weight (less payload) 2,849 lb (1,294 kg)

NOMINAL PERFORMANCE:
Altitude with 308 lb (140 kg) gross payload* (Qe 85°) 202 nm (233 miles; 375 km)
Max acceleration 15*g*

*gross payload includes payload compartment and igniter housing.

BLACK BRANT VC

Black Brant VC employs the same motor as Black Brant VB, but is modified to make the vehicle compatible with launch towers at White Sands Missile Range, New Mexico, and Wallops Island, Virginia.

WEIGHT:
Launching weight (less payload) 2,888 lb (1,311 kg)

NOMINAL PERFORMANCE:
Altitude with 308 lb (140 kg) gross payload* (Qe 85°) 190 nm (218 miles; 325 km)
Max acceleration 15*g*

*gross payload includes payload compartment and igniter housing.

SPAR

SPAR AEROSPACE PRODUCTS LIMITED

HEAD OFFICE AND WORKS:
825 Caledonia Road, Toronto, Ontario M6B 3X8
Telephone: (416) 781-1571
Telex: 02-2054 Sparcal Tor

CHAIRMAN OF THE BOARD: R. B. Dodwell
PRESIDENT: L. D. Clarke

DIRECTORS:
D. S. Beatty
W. H. Jackson
Dr P. A. Lapp
R. A. Perigoe
D. A. B. Steele
J. P. Wright

VICE-PRESIDENTS:
G. J. Aubrey (Finance)
G. B. Gomes (Contracts)
J. E. Lockyer (Engineering)
J. D. MacNaughton (Marketing)
R. E. Marcille (Sales)
E. V. Nield (Personnel)
G. R. Rutledge (Operations)

MANAGER, PUBLIC RELATIONS:
John F. Walker

Spar Aerospace Products Limited was responsible for design and fabrication of the Alouette I and II and ISIS I and II satellite structures. All of these spacecraft used Spar extendible STEM devices as long sounder antennae. Other STEM space applications include gravity gradient booms; magnetometer, transponder and spectrometer booms; astronaut mechanical aids; and extendible solar array actuators. Since 1960, more than 500 STEM devices have been flown successfully in Canadian, US, Soviet and European space programmes.

Details of the Alouette and ISIS spacecraft can be found in earlier editions of *Jane's*. Spar has since manufactured the primary structures of three Anik communications satellites for Canadian domestic use, under contract from Hughes Aircraft Company, the prime contractor to Telesat Canada. The company also provided technical support to Hughes throughout the design and development phases of the programme, and has been selected by Hughes to manufacture similar structures for a minimum of 15 satellites which Hughes expects to sell in world markets. The first of these follow-on programmes is in connection with the domestic communications satellite systems for the USA devised by Western Union and American Satellite Corporation. (Anik is described under the Hughes entry in the US section.)

Under contract from the Communications Research Centre, Spar is responsible for design and manufacture of the major subsystems of the Communications Technology Satellite (CTS). These include the dynamic and thermal structure, extendible solar array, attitude control system and ground support equipment.

COMMUNICATIONS TECHNOLOGY SATELLITE (CTS)

This joint Canada/US space programme will demonstrate the operation of a communications satellite in the 12 to 14GHz frequency band at power levels significantly greater than those provided by existing spacecraft.

Major advanced subsystems to be flight tested include a three-axis stabilised system to maintain the antenna pointing to within $\pm 0{\cdot}2°$ in the pitch and roll axis, a lightweight extendible solar array with an initial power output exceeding 1kW, and a super-efficiency travelling wave tube having a saturated power output of 200W at 12GHz.

Artist's impression of CTS in orbit

CTS will be orbited in 1975 from NASA's Eastern Test Range by an advanced Delta vehicle (Delta 2914). SHF communications equipment on board the satellite will provide two-way relay of data, FM broadcast and colour TV via two two-axis gimballed dish antennae and a 17° horn beacon. Telemetry, tracking and command equipment will include a VHF beacon and a NASA GRARR ranging system.

Monopropellant hydrazine thrusters, rated at 5 lb (2·25 kg) st, will be used during transfer orbit and station acquisition. Low-thrust catalytic hydrazine thrusters will be used for momentum damping, east/west station keeping and correction of orbit eccentricity.

The satellite's solar power system will utilise two solar "sails", each 25 ft (7·6 m) long and 4 ft 2 in (1·27 m) wide. Initial power produced from the sails will be rated at 1,200W and there will be a further 77W from the spacecraft's body solar array. There will be two batteries of 26 nickel-cadmium 5Ah cells.

CHINA
(PEOPLE'S REPUBLIC)

China launched her first satellite (Norad designation "Chicom 1") on 24 April 1970, and thus became the fifth country to orbit a payload using national resources, following the USSR, USA, France and Japan. Few details were released; a New China News Agency statement gave the weight of the spacecraft as 380 lb (172 kg), and said that it was injected into a 1,285 × 237 nm (1,480 × 273 mile; 2,382 × 439 km) orbit at an inclination of 68·5°. It is believed to have been launched from the main Chinese rocket centre near Shuang Cheng Tsu, 500 miles east of the nuclear test establishment of Lop Nor.

No details of any experiments are available, but as a prototype it is probable that only basic vehicle development instrumentation was installed. Signals were transmitted over a cycle time of one minute, on 20.009MHz, including a 5 sec interval between signals. The first 40 sec of each transmission was devoted to the piece of music "The East is Red". After a 5 sec break 20 telemetry data channels then transmitted for 10 sec, followed by a further break.

A second satellite (Norad "Chicom 2") was launched on 3 March 1971 but was not announced by the Chinese authorities until 16 March. No music was transmitted from this satellite, which was described as being purely scientific, with a weight of 487 lb (221 kg). The data issued by Peking included an initial apogee of 985 nm (1,134 miles; 1,825 km), perigee of 143·5 nm (165 miles; 266 km) and orbital period of 106 minutes. Clear radio signals were transmitted on 20.008MHz.

It is widely surmised that the development of the satellites and their launch vehicle was managed by Dr Tsien Hsue-Shen, a scientist who was employed by the Jet Propulsion Laboratory in California as a member of a rocket design team during the second World War. After the war the Doctor worked at the Massachusetts Institute of Technology. He returned to China in 1955.

FRANCE

AÉROSPATIALE

SOCIÉTÉ NATIONALE INDUSTRIELLE AÉROSPATIALE

Division des Systèmes Balistiques et Spatiaux

DIVISION MANAGEMENT:
BP 96, 78130-Les Mureaux
Telephone: 474-72-13

WORKS:
BP 52, 06322 Cannes-la-Bocca
Telephone: 47-06-52
BP 11, 33160-St Médard en Jalles
Telephone: 90-92-13
BP 2, 78130-Les Mureaux
Telephone: 474-72-11

DIRECTOR: P. M. Usunier
ASST DIRECTOR: Louis Marnay

The Space and Ballistic Systems Division of Aérospatiale handles research, development, testing and engineering for entire missile and space vehicle systems. It produces all kinds of major aerospace components, power stages, equipment modules, re-entry vehicles and fully-equipped satellite structures. The Division also handles integration and assembly, ground and in-flight testing, study and development of ground support facilities, and command and control subsystems.

Details of the Division's current launch vehicle, research rocket and spacecraft programmes are given below.

As a member of the CIFAS, CESAR and COSMOS international consortia, Aérospatiale is participating in other satellite programmes (see International section).

AÉROSPATIALE SOUNDING ROCKETS

Aérospatiale has developed and produces a range of solid-propellant sounding rockets which are fully proven in operation and are being improved continually in terms of performance. All five currently-available types of rocket are stabilised by fixed fins and need no guidance or control systems, which keeps their weight to a minimum. More than 350 rockets had been built by early 1974, and launches have taken place from 18 bases throughout the world.

The main characteristics and performance of these rockets are shown in the accompanying table.

DIAMANT B P-4

Following the final launch of the original Diamant B satellite launch vehicle, the programme is continuing with an improved version of the vehicle, using a new second stage. Aérospatiale again provides all three stages, under CNES sponsorship. Details are as follows:

L-17

This first stage has a metal structure housing 26,740 lb (12,129 kg) of nitrogen tetroxide and 12,978 lb (5,887 kg) of UDMH liquid propellants. Its rocket engine develops 78,500 lb (35,600 kg) of thrust, with a specific impulse of 221·1 seconds.

P-4

New second stage, developed originally for the M-1 version of the MSBS submarine-launched ballistic missile. Rita I motor contains 8,820 lb (4,000 kg) of solid propellant, in a wound glassfibre casing, and gives approximately 40,000 lb (18,150 kg) of thrust.

P O 6

Third-stage solid propellant motor of 10,200 lb (4,625 kg) thrust, in a wound glassfibre structure.

Diamant B P-4 can put an increased payload of approximately 330 lb (150 kg) into a 270 nm (310 mile; 500 km) circular orbit.

Diamant B P-4 was scheduled to be launched for the first time in September 1974, carrying Starlette, a small passive geodesic satellite. Main characteristics are as follows:

DIMENSIONS:
Length:
L-17 — 46 ft 2½ in (14·08 m)
P-4 — 8 ft 6 in (2·60 m)
P O 6 — 6 ft 9½ in (2·07 m)
Complete vehicle — 62 ft 1¾ in (18·94 m)
Body diameter:
L-17 — 4 ft 7¼ in (1·40 m)
P-4 — 4 ft 10¾ in (1·50 m)
P O 6 — 2 ft 7½ in (0·80 m)

WEIGHTS:
Weight of P-4 stage — 10,360 lb (4,700 kg)
Complete vehicle at lift-off — 60,610 lb (27,492 kg)

ARIANE

This heavy three-stage launch vehicle is being developed in Europe as a co-operative project under the leadership of the French space agency CNES, as prime contractor. Payload potential will be 3,300 lb (1,500 kg) into a transfer orbit, or applications satellites of up to 1,650 lb (750 kg) weight into synchronous orbit.

Aérospatiale is responsible for the design of Ariane and for integration of the entire vehicle. It is producing major structural elements of the first stage and is responsible for the final delivery of all three stages and the fairings.

SEP is developing the engines and associated subsystems for all three stages. Matra is building the vehicle equipment bay and checkout facilities. Air Liquide is developing the third-stage structures, and tanks for the liquid hydrogen and liquid oxygen propellants. All four French companies are subcontracting work extensively throughout Europe to manufacturers in the countries supporting the programme.

Details of the individual stages are as follows:

L 140

This first stage is made up of two identical steel tanks for the 310,850 lb (141,000 kg) of UDMH and N_2O_4 propellants, linked together by means of a cylindrical skirt. It is powered by four Viking engines (each 132,275 lb; 60,000 kg st), carried on a cylindrical thrust frame and protected by fairings with fins. Burn time is 139 seconds.

A truncated cone-shaped interstage skirt joins the first and second stages.

L 33

The second stage comprises two light alloy tanks for 72,750 lb (33,000 kg) of UDMH and N_2O_4 propellants, separated by a common bulkhead. The single Viking engine (154,325 lb; 70,000 kg st in vacuum) is linked to the stage by a conical thrust frame. Burn time is 131 seconds.

A cylindrical interstage skirt connects the second and third stages.

H 8

The third stage is made of light alloy and houses 17,635 lb (8,000 kg) of liquid hydrogen and liquid oxygen propellants for its single HM7 cryogenic engine (13,225 lb; 6,000 kg st). Burn time is 563 seconds.

A cylindrical vehicle equipment bay is situated above the third stage. The equipment platform is an annular plate, the inside flange of which supports the payload attachment fittings. Aluminium payload fairings, made up of two half-shells, are attached to the outside flange of the equipment platform.

DIMENSIONS:
Length:
L 140 — 60 ft 4½ in (18·40 m)
Interstage structure — 15 ft 9 in (4·80 m)
L 33 — 38 ft 0½ in (11·60 m)
Interstage structure — 8 ft 8½ in (2·65 m)
H 8 — 27 ft 10½ in (8·50 m)
Equipment bay — 1 ft 0 in (0·30 m)
Payload fairings — 28 ft 2½ in (8·60 m)
Overall length — 157 ft 6 in (48·0 m)
Body diameter:
L 140 — 12 ft 5½ in (3·80 m)
L 33, H 8, equipment bay — 8 ft 6½ in (2·60 m)
Payload fairings — 10 ft 6 in (3·20 m)

WEIGHTS:
L 140 — 339,510 lb (154,000 kg)
L 33 — 80,025 lb (36,300 kg)
H 8 — 20,725 lb (9,400 kg)
Payload fairings — 1,785 lb (810 kg)
Total weight at lift-off — more than 440,920 lb (200,000 kg)

D-2B

As in the case of the D-2A Tournesol scientific satellite, launched successfully on 15 April 1971 (see 1972-73 *Jane's*), this Division of Aérospatiale is responsible for the satellite structure, including the solar panels and their deployment mechanism, the antennae, the equipment module with the de-spin and separation devices. the cold-gas stabilisation system, and the gilding of the cover of the generally similar D-2B. Matra is prime contractor.

Name of rocket	Type and weight of propellant	Diameter	Max overall length	Payload	Corresponding Ceiling
Bélier III	Isolane: 506 lb (230 kg)	12 in (30·5 cm)	16 ft 9¼ in (5·112 m)	66-200 lb (30-90 kg)	99-54 miles (160-88 km)
Centaure III	Plastolite: 207 lb (94 kg) Plastolite: 508 lb (231 kg)	11 in (28 cm) 12 in (30·5 cm)	23 ft 5½ in (7·15 m)	66-220 lb (30-100 kg)	152-77 miles (245-125 km)
Dauphin	Plastolane: 1,515 lb (687 kg)	22 in (56 cm)	20 ft 5 in (6·228 m)	286-550 lb (130-250 kg)	93-62 miles (150-100 km)
Dragon III	Plastolane: 1,515 lb (687 kg) Isolane: 506 lb (230 kg)	22 in (56 cm) 12 in (30·5 cm)	27 ft 10½ in (8·492 m)	66-243 lb (30-110 kg)	435-261 miles (700-420 km)
Eridan	Plastolane: 1,515 lb (687 kg) Plastolane: 1,515 lb (687 kg)	22 in (56 cm) 22 in (56 cm)	32 ft 9¼ in (9·985 m)	286-771 lb (130-350 kg)	279-149 miles (450-240 km)

The D-2B is basically cylindrical, with four olar panels which will deploy laterally after the lesired orbit has been achieved. Its weight is 53 lb (115 kg). Launch is scheduled for the pring of 1975.

D-5

The first flight model of this composite technological satellite was lost as a result of the failure of its launcher. Details of the D-5A and D-5B omponents can be found in the 1972-73 *Jane's*.

A second D-5 was scheduled to be launched in ate 1974. Its mission was to test a hydrazine notor developed by SEP and a micro-accelerometer developed by ONERA. Aérospatiale vas responsible for the satellite structures, the quipment module, the antennae and the separation mechanisms.

STARLETTE

This small passive geodesic satellite is spheroid vith a diameter of 9·45 in (24 cm). Its core is nade of uranium 238 and its surface is covered vith laser reflectors manufactured by Aérospatiale.

Starlette was scheduled to be launched by the rst Diamant B P-4 vehicle in September 1974.

D-5 satellite undergoing vibration tests

MATRA

A ENGINS MATRA

HEAD OFFICE:
4 rue de Presbourg, 75116-Paris

MANAGEMENT AND WORKS:
37 avenue Louis Breguet, 78140-Vélizy
Telephone: 946.96.00
Telex: ENMATRA 69.077F

OFFICERS: See "Missiles" section

In addition to developing and manufacturing uided missiles, Matra is participating in the najor French space programmes. For the NES, Matra is prime contractor for the D-2B atellite, and is developing the telescope and -channel radiometer for the Meteosat satellite.

Dynamically similar full-scale model of the D-2B satellite for vibration testing

D-2B

Under contract to the CNES, Matra is prime contractor for the D-2B scientific satellite, scheduled for launching by a Diamant B P-4 vehicle, from Kourou, in the Spring of 1975.

This satellite is described briefly under the Aérospatiale entry. As prime contractor, Matra is responsible for the design and development of the scientific experiments, and will carry out the qualification and acceptance testing of the satellite equipment and subsystems.

ONERA

OFFICE NATIONAL D'ÉTUDES ET DE RECHERCHES AÉROSPATIALES

ADDRESS:
29 avenue de la Division-Leclerc, 92320-Châtillon
Telephone: 735.21.11 and 253.50.80

DIRECTOR: Pierre-Louis Contensou

HEAD, EXTERNAL RELATIONS AND DOCUMENTATION DEPARTMENT:
Max Salmon

In addition to its normal work as a national esearch and experimental centre in the service f the entire French aircraft and missile industry, NERA has designed, built and launched various pes of experimental vehicle to obtain basic ata in fields such as propulsion and kinetic eating and in connection with scientific research rogrammes sponsored by the Centre National 'Etudes Spatiales (CNES).

The only rocket currently in service is the ibère. Details of earlier rockets developed by NERA can be found in the 1969-70 *Jane's*.

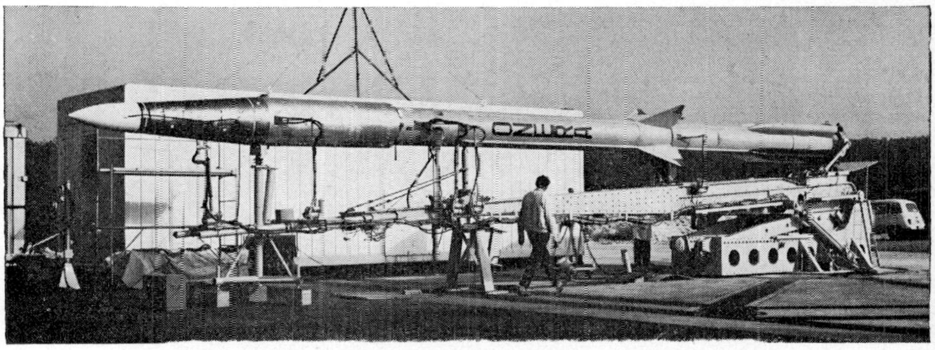

ONERA Tibère three-stage rocket for nosecone re-entry research

ONERA TIBÈRE

This three-stage solid-propellant rocket is esigned especially for studying the electroagnetic phenomena of nosecones during reatry at Mach 16, under Project Electre. Under is programme, the third stage is fired downards, so that the height attained is only some 30 nm (150 miles; 240 km), which is much less an the maximum ceiling attainable by Tibère.

Between the second and third stages is inalled a Cassiopée lock-on device. After second-stage burnout, this points the second/third stage/payload assembly in the correct direction to ensure a zero angle of attack thrust for stage three during re-entry, when this stage is spun at 360 rpm. Other versions of Cassiopée (now produced industrially by SAGEM for CNES and ONERA) include, besides an inertial aiming accuracy of 1°, a solar or bi-stellar aiming device with an accuracy of 1′ and the ability to steer a payload according to a pre-set programme or in several successive pre-set directions in space.

Cassiopée is separated with the second stage of Tibère. After burnout, the third stage is separated by small retro-rockets when experiments are concerned with only the nosecone.

Tibère was launched successfully from the Landes Test Centre on 23 February 1971 and on 18 March 1972, as part of the Electre programme.

DIMENSIONS:
Length:
Overall, excluding nosecone 39 ft 11½ in (12·175 m)
Nosecone 7 ft 2½ in (2·200 m)

WEIGHTS:
Launching weight, excluding nosecone 9,965 lb (4,520 kg)

PERFORMANCE (Qe 85°):
Ceiling:
1,320 lb (600 kg) payload 225 nm (260 miles; 420 km)
220 lb (100 kg) payload 1,050 nm (1,210 miles; 1,950 km)

THOMSON-BRANDT

COMPAGNIE FRANÇAISE THOMSON HOUSTON—HOTCHKISS-BRANDT

Armament and General Engineering Branch

ADDRESS:
52 avenue des Champs-Elysées, 75008-Paris
Telephone: 359.18.87
Telex: 29966 Brantarm-Paris

WORKS:
Saint Denis, La Ferte St Aubin (Loiret), Tulle (Corrèze)

PRESIDENT:
Paul Richard

GENERAL MANAGER OF ARMAMENT DIVISION:
R. Crepin

The Armament Division of Thomson-Brandt has been engaged in the design and manufacture of mortars and ammunition for more than 40 years. Since 1948 it has also carried out research and development of semi-self-propelled ammunition and solid-propellant rockets, such as the T-10 and the 37 mm and 68 mm SNEB rockets which are in service as standard armament with a large number of air forces.

The Division has designed warheads and solid-propellant rocket motors which currently equip the Matra 510, Matra 530, Matra/HSD Martel and Crotale missiles.

Since 1964, the Division has been prime contractor to the SECT (Firing-Range Equipment Department) for the design and production of sounding rockets, utilising rocket motors of French design already in mass production for military purposes. Details of some of these follow; others were described briefly in the 1970-71 *Jane's*.

EPONA

Epona is used primarily to obtain information on winds at altitudes up to 200,000 ft (60,000 m). It is composed of two identical 100 mm motors and an inert third stage containing radar reflectors. Payload volume of the third stage is 30·5 cu in (500 cm³).

Epona can be fired in strong winds of up to 28 knots (33 mph; 15 m/sec). When it is required to reach altitudes of no more than 82,000 ft (25,000 m), it can be simplified by using only a single powered stage.

DIMENSIONS:
Length overall 14 ft 7 in (4·446 m)
Body diameter 3·94 in (103 mm)
WEIGHT:
Launching weight 134·5 lb (61·0 kg)
PERFORMANCE (launch angle of 80°/85°):
Max speed at burnout 4,660 ft (1,420 m)/sec
Peak altitude more than 197,000 ft (60,000 m)
Max acceleration 157*g*
Time of flight 110 seconds

BELISAMA

Developed to obtain meteorological data at an altitude of 54 nm (62 miles; 100 km), Belisama is made up of two solid-propellant stages. A mechanical timing device causes separation of the payload container once the vehicle has reached its peak altitude. The container splits into two parts and releases the payload, which is then lowered by parachute. Payload volume is 183 cu in (3,000 cm³).

DIMENSION:
Length overall 14 ft 0¾ in (4·285 m)
WEIGHT:
Launching weight 258 lb (117 kg)
PERFORMANCE (launch angle 80°/85°):
Max speed at burnout 4,460 ft (1,360 m)/sec
Peak altitude with 13·2 lb (6 kg) payload package 328,000 ft (100,000 m)
Ceiling with 22 lb (10 kg) payload package 265,000 ft (81,000 m)
Max acceleration 143*g*

GRANNOS

This two-stage solid-propellant sounding rocket has a payload volume of 610 cu in (10 litres). Standard instrumentation includes a radio probe and telemetry equipment, with a parachute recovery system.

DIMENSION:
Length overall 16 ft 3¾ in (4·973 m)
WEIGHT:
Launching weight 397 lb (180 kg)
PERFORMANCE:
Peak altitude with 35·3 lb (16 kg) payload package 525,000 ft (160,000 m)

GERMANY
(FEDERAL REPUBLIC)

DORNIER
DORNIER SYSTEM GmbH

HEAD OFFICE AND WORKS:
7759 Immenstaad/Bodensee (near Friedrichshafen)
POSTAL ADDRESS:
Postfach 648, 7990 Friedrichshafen
Telephone: Immenstaad (07545) 81
Telex: 0734359
BONN OFFICE:
Allianzplatz, 5300 Bonn
GENERAL MANAGERS:
Dipl-Ing Dr Jr Karl-Wilhelm Schäfer
Dr Ing Bernhard Schmidt
Dr Ing Helmut Ulke
Dipl-Kfm Klaus-Peter Thomé
PUBLIC RELATIONS:
Gerhard Patt

Dornier System is a leading European contractor for the construction and integration of scientific payloads for rockets and satellites. On behalf of ESTeC, the German Ministry of Education and Science, and other agencies, it has produced payloads for Nike-Apache, Skua, Black Brant, Skylark, Centaure and Zenit rockets and prepared them for launching at Kiruna, Sweden; Fort Churchill, Canada; Huelva, Spain; and Salto di Quirra, Sardinia. These payloads were designed to investigate meteorite dust and measure cosmic particles, measure wind at high altitude and investigate polar light phenomena.

Dornier System developed two experiments for the German Aeros research satellite and three for the German-US HELIOS solar probe. It is a member of the team, led by ERNO, which is engaged in the important Spacelab project, linked with the US Space Shuttle programme.

Dornier System's Astrid two-axis stabilisation system, designed to orientate payloads towards a star or the Sun, was flight tested for the first time in February 1970. It has been followed by Dachs, a three-axis attitude stabilisation system for rocket payloads.

Another Dornier System product is the Resy parachute recovery system, which was first employed on a Skylark sounding rocket launched by ESRO/ESTeC in October 1969.

Dornier System is responsible for development and production of the second-stage tank structure of the Ariane launch vehicle as subcontractor to Aérospatiale.

AEROS

Following evaluation of several project studies by German aerospace companies, the Federal Ministry of Education and Science chose Dornier System to develop Germany's third research satellite, the Aeros, in early 1970. This satellite was launched by NASA on a Scout rocket from the Western Test Range, California, on 16 December 1972.

Weighing 280 lb (127 kg), the spacecraft was a cylindrical structure 36 in (91·4 cm) in diameter by 28 in (71 cm) high, with a conical-shaped shell at one end. An impedance probe aerial, 71 in (1·8 m) long, extended from the conical-shaped shell, and four telemetry aerials were mounted on the outer shell of the spacecraft. The upper side was covered with an array of solar cells.

The attitude control system consisted of a yo-yo de-spin unit, a passive mechanical damping device and an active magnetic control system to compensate for spin and attitude deviations. Attitude measurement and control were determined by two Sun sensors; one was for coarse alignment and the other, a fine sensor, for determining the solar aspect angle and the solar azimuth angle.

A monopropellant engine system, consisting of two engines using hydrazine fuel, was provided to correct injection errors and, if required, to lift the apogee towards the end of the mission.

Subcontractors to Dornier System were ERNO for the hydrazine engine; Siemens AG for the solar cell panels, antennae, diplexer and electrical ground support equipment; SEL for data processing on board the satellite; AEG-Telefunken for the transmitter and receiver; and IER for tape storage equipment.

The spacecraft carried five experiments, four German and one US. The German experiments were a mass spectrometer, to study the chemical composition of the ambient atmosphere and ionosphere; a retarding potential analyser, to determine electron energy distribution and ion temperature; an impedance probe, to measure electron density; and an extreme ultraviolet spectrometer, to measure the intensity of solar radiation.

The US experiment, supplied by NASA's Goddard Space Flight Center, was intended to measure the temperature as well as the overall density of the neutral ambient atmosphere.

Data acquisition was the responsibility of the Central German Ground Station (Z-DBS) at Weilheim, Bavaria, under the management of the German Space Operations Centre (GSOC) in Oberpfaffenhofen, Germany. Project management was the joint responsibility of the Gesellschaft für Weltraumforschung mbH in Porz-Wahn, Germany, and the Goddard Space Flight Center, for the NASA Office of Space Science.

The Aeros project has since been continued by a follow-on satellite known as Aeros-B, which was launched by a Scout vehicle from Vandenberg AFB, California, on 16 July 1974. Its experiment payload is almost identical with that of the first Aeros; lifetime in orbit was expected to be about 230 days.

Aeros satellite being subjected to the effects of an "artificial sun" in a space simulation chamber

ERNO
ERNO RAUMFAHRTTECHNIK GmbH

ADDRESS:
28 Bremen 1, Hünefeldstrasse 1-5 (Postfach 1199)
Telephone: (0421) 5191
Telex: 024 55 48
DIRECTORS:
Dipl-Ing Hans Schneider
Dr rer pol Rudolf Kappler
Dipl-Ing Hans E. W. Hoffmann
R. A. Bernd Kosegarten

ERNO is a subsidiary company of the Zentralgesellschaft VFW-Fokker of Düsseldorf. Its current space activities are concerned with the post-Apollo programme space laboratory, Ariane launch vehicle, lifting bodies, satellites and space probes. In particular, it has participated or is still involved in the programme for the Azur, Intelsat III, TD-1A, Aeros, Meteosat, OTS (orbital test satellite) and Intelsat V satellites and the HELIOS and Sorel space probes.

SPACELAB

On 5 June 1974, a nine-nation consortium led by ERNO and VFW-Fokker was awarded a contract valued at about £95 million to design and develop the Spacelab space laboratory which represents Europe's contribution to the US post-Apollo programme of re-usable space shuttles. Largest European space project initiated in the present decade, the work will extend over a period of six years, leading to delivery of a single Spacelab flight unit, fully qualified and ready for the installation of experiments, by April 1979. The contract, awarded by ESRO, covers also the delivery of two engineering models, three sets of ground support equipment and initial spares.

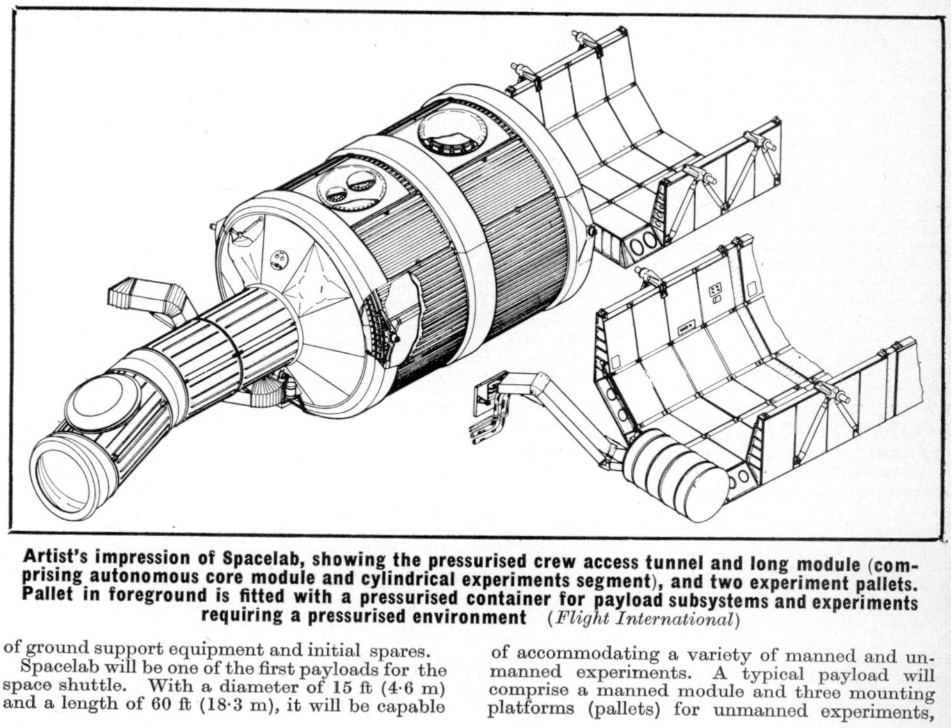

Artist's impression of Spacelab, showing the pressurised crew access tunnel and long module (comprising autonomous core module and cylindrical experiments segment), and two experiment pallets. Pallet in foreground is fitted with a pressurised container for payload subsystems and experiments requiring a pressurised environment (*Flight International*)

Spacelab will be one of the first payloads for the space shuttle. With a diameter of 15 ft (4·6 m) and a length of 60 ft (18·3 m), it will be capable of accommodating a variety of manned and unmanned experiments. A typical payload will comprise a manned module and three mounting platforms (pallets) for unmanned experiments, or up to five pallets for unmanned experiments only. Hawker Siddeley Dynamics of the UK is responsible for design and construction of the pallets, each of which must be able to carry three tons, the expected weight of a large astronomical telescope, and withstand the hard usage of up to 50 sorties of one-month duration or a useful life of ten years. First launch is scheduled for early 1980, and the NASA Administrator, Dr James Fletcher, has expressed a requirement for at least one more Spacelab flight vehicle.

Two to four scientists and engineers, not all intensively trained as astronauts, will work in Spacelab at an orbital height of 103-270 nm (125-310 miles; 200-500 km) for periods of 7 to 30 days. Initial experiments in various branches of science are expected to be followed by practical research into manufacturing processes which take advantage of weightless conditions. The nature of the experiments will decide whether the Spacelab is retained in the open cargo bay of the shuttle craft or is deployed outside. The men will be able to work under natural atmospheric conditions in the pressurised module. On the platform section, they will work only while wearing pressure suits.

TRW and McDonnell Douglas have been retained by the consortium as consultants for the programme. The other European partners include Dornier System GmbH of Germany, responsible for the Spacelab life support system and the attitude control system for the instrument platform, AEG of Germany, Aeritalia of Italy, BTM and SABCA of Belgium, Fokker of the Netherlands, INTA/Sener of Spain, Matra of France and Kampsax of Denmark.

MBB

MESSERSCHMITT-BÖLKOW-BLOHM GmbH

Space Division

HEAD OFFICE AND WORKS:
8012 Ottobrunn bei München
Telephone: (089) 60 00 25 90

In addition to its manufacture of piloted aircraft, Messerschmitt-Bölkow-Blohm is engaged in the development of guided weapons (see "Missiles" section), research rockets and satellites.

MBB is prime contractor for the HELIOS solar probe, of which details follow, and is a member of several of the international teams working on current satellite programmes. They include the CESAR consortium which is developing the COS B scientific satellite; the CIFAS consortium responsible for the Franco-German Symphonie experimental communications satellite; and the COSMOS consortium entrusted with development of ESRO's Meteosat (see International setion).

Typical of many sounding rocket payloads produced by MBB were those supplied for Extreme Ultraviolet (EUV) and combined programmes connected with the Aeros-A satellite, under contract to the Federal Ministry for Research and Technology (through the GfW). Two payloads were launched under each programme, by Black Brant VC sounding rockets, in February 1973 from Natal, Brazil. A further combined payload was launched from Andøya, Norway, in May 1973.

HELIOS

HELIOS is the largest German space probe project to date and, at the time of its inception, was the largest bilateral space project in which NASA had participated. Contracts for the German share of the programme total approximately 180 million DM; a further 60 million DM are provided for experiments. The contracting agency is the German Federal Ministry of Research and Technology, through its department responsible for space research, the Gesellschaft für Weltraumforschung mbH. The launching of two identical probes, developed in the Federal Republic, is scheduled for 1974 and 1976. NASA is supplying the launch vehicles, and the US contribution to the project is also to cost approximately 180 million DM.

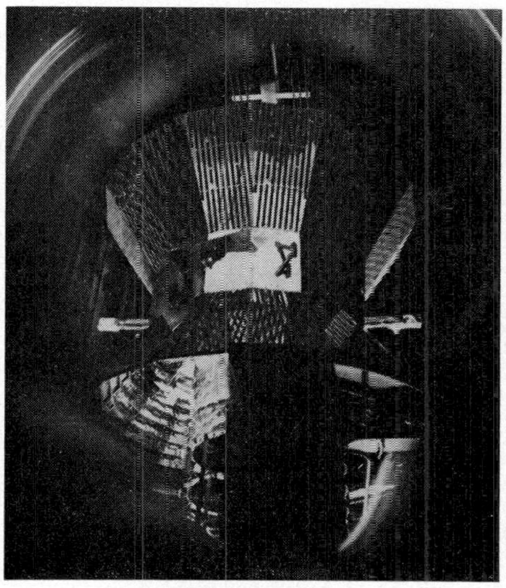

HELIOS solar probe

HELIOS is an automatically-functioning solar observatory. On board each probe are ten experiments prepared by institutes and scientists of different nations. Each of these experiments, of which seven are from German institutes, represents a complete research project in itself. Some are designed to fulfil the latest requirements of NASA, including an approach to within 0·30 AU (approx 45 million km) of the Sun. Other experiments require a large variation in the distance from the Sun.

As prime contractor, the Space Division of MBB was made responsible for about 45% of the work performed under the German part of the programme. In particular, it is responsible for project management, system management, integration and test, as well as development and manufacture of the attitude measurement, attitude control, electrical distribution, and antenna subsystems. Subcontractors for other major subsystems are ERNO, Bremen (structure and thermal control); AEG-Telefunken, Ulm (telecommunications receiver); SEL, Stuttgart (data handling); Thomson-Houston CSF, France (transmitter); AEG-Telefunken Hamburg (solar generator); and ETCA, Belgium (power conditioning).

INDIA

ISRO

INDIAN SPACE RESEARCH ORGANISATION

ADDRESS: c/o Department of Space, "F" Block, CBAB Complex, District Office Road, Bangalore 560 009
Telephone: 29822 and 23215
Telex: BG-499 and BG-326

ISRO functions under the Department of Space (DOS) of the Government of India. It is responsible for the planning, execution and management of space research activities and space applications programmes that have been undertaken by the Department of Space. It provides rockets and laboratory facilities to the scientists belonging to different organisations in India, for the purpose of conducting approved space science experiments. It operates and maintains the UN-sponsored Thumba Equatorial Rocket Launching Station (TERLS) and encourages international collaboration in space research experiments using rockets. ISRO is also the sponsoring agency for Indian scientists participating in research programmes supported by foreign space agencies. These include laboratory experiments and ground-based observations in support of space programmes, rocket experiments and satellite experiments.

The programmes and activities of ISRO can be divided into three broad areas:

Space Sciences. Programmes in aeronomy, X-ray and gamma ray astronomy, cosmic rays, studies of lunar material, meteorites, etc.

Space Technology. All aspects of work related to the development of rockets, satellites, propellants, scientific payloads and ground and space instrumentation.

Space Applications. Translation of the knowledge gained in space research and technology into practical applications in the fields of satellite communications, satellite television, meteorology, geodesy and Earth resources survey.

The activities of ISRO are at present carried out at the following places:

Indian Space Research Organisation (ISRO), Bangalore

c/o Department of Space, Government of India, "F" Block, CBAB Complex, District Office Road, Bangalore 560 009.
Telephone: 29822 and 23215
Telex: BG-499 and BG-326
CHAIRMAN: Prof S. Dhawan
SCIENTIFIC SECRETARY: Prof P. D. Bhavsar

All headquarters functions of planning, programming and co-ordination are carried out here.

Vikram Sarabhai Space Centre (VSSC)

ISRO PO, Trivandrum 695 022
Telephone: 4670-9
Telex: Space TV 048-201
DIRECTOR: Dr Brahm Prakash

VSSC serves as the main research and development centre for space technology and consists of the following units: Thumba Equatorial Rocket Launching Station (TERLS), Space Science and Technology Centre (SSTC), Rocket Propellant Plant (RPP), Rocket Fabrication Facility (RFF), Propellant Fuel Complex (PFC) and Indian Scientific Satellite Project (ISSP; in Bangalore).

Space Applications Centre (SAC)

2nd Floor, Shree Sahajanand College Building, Ahmedabad 380 015
Telephone: 83715-19-26-29
Telex: ANTARIX-012-261
DIRECTOR: Prof Yash Pal

This Centre is concerned with the space applications programmes of ISRO and consists of the following divisions: Satellite Instructional Television Experiment (SITE) project, Experimental Satellite Communications Earth Station (ESCES), Remote Sensing and Meteorology Division (RSMD), Electronics Systems Division (ESD), Microwave Division (MID) and Software Systems Groups (SSG).

Sriharikota Range (SHAR)

Sriharikota PO 524124, via Sullurpeta, Nellore District (AP)
Telex: 041-7353 SHAR
PROJECT OFFICER: Dr Y. J. Rao

VSSC has been entrusted with responsibility for setting up the following units on Sriharikota Island, with the aim of attaining satellite launching capability:

1. Sriharikota Launch Complex (SLC)
2. Rocket Sled Facility (RSF)
3. Static Test and Evaluation Complex (STEX)
4. Solid Propellant Space Booster Plant (SPROB)

Sriharikota Island is situated on the eastern coast of India (latitude 13° 47′ N and longitude 80° 15′ E) about 62 miles (100 km) north of Madras. Its location on the eastern coast, nearer the equator, helps to take advantage of the Earth's rotation when launching a satellite. Other advantages are the vastness of its area, isolation from populated towns, and access to Madras.

Phase I of the range construction was completed on 10 October 1971, when it was inaugurated with the launching of an indigenously-developed Rohini-125 rocket. When phase II is completed the Sriharikota Launch Complex (SLC) will provide facilities for the flight testing of large multi-stage sounding rockets and satellite launch vehicles of Indian manufacture, and for launching scientific and applications satellites. In the

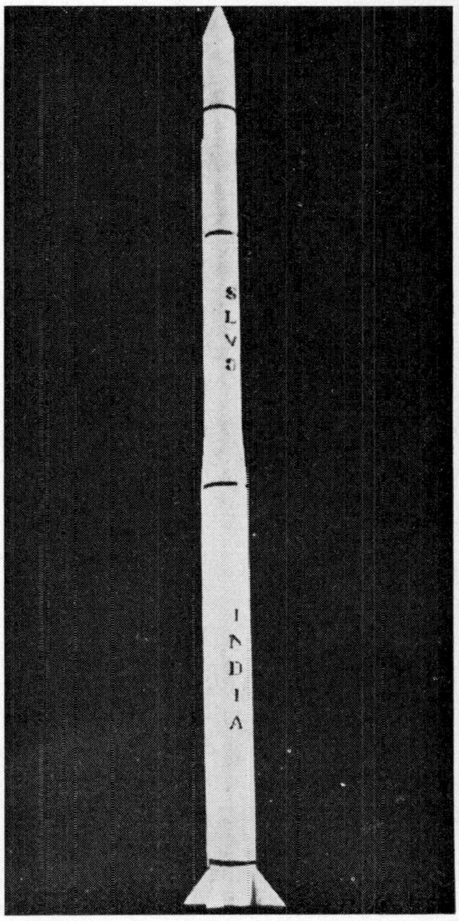

Model of SLV-3 launch vehicle (*Théo Pirard*)

first two and a half years after the range became operative, 19 rockets of various sizes were flight tested.

At present, ISRO is engaged in three major projects, as follows:

INDIAN SCIENTIFIC SATELLITE PROJECT (ISSP)

Fabrication of India's first scientific satellite took place at Peenya, near Bangalore. The 661 lb (300 kg) satellite was designed and built entirely in India. It was expected to be launched before the end of 1974, from the Soviet Union, by means of a Soviet launch vehicle. It is intended to enter a near-circular Earth orbit at an altitude of about 325 nm (373 miles; 600 km) and should remain active for a little over six months.

This satellite carries three scientific experiments, for investigations in X-ray astronomy, for measuring solar neutron and gamma emissions and for measuring ionospheric parameters.

Two ground stations are intended to receive data from the satellite, one at the SHAR and the other near Moscow. The SHAR ground station will also have facilities to transmit commands to the satellite.

SATELLITE INSTRUCTIONAL TELEVISION EXPERIMENT (SITE)

This experiment is aimed at bringing televised educational programmes to the villages and remote areas of India through the medium of a satellite. NASA's ATS-6 Applications Technology Satellite will be used for this purpose from the middle of 1975, for one year. The instructional TV programmes will be produced mainly by All India Radio, with a few by ISRO. Development of necessary hardware for the ground segment, as well as work relating to the software aspect of the instructional programmes, are the responsibility of ISRO. The TV programmes will be beamed to the satellite from the Experimental Satellite Communications Earth Station (ESCES) of SAC at Ahmedabad, which will serve as the primary ground station for the experiment.

SATELLITE LAUNCH VEHICLE (SLV-3)

This project has the objective of developing an indigenous satellite launch vehicle capable of putting an 88 lb (40 kg) satellite into a 215 nm (250 mile; 400 km) near-circular Earth orbit. The four-stage solid-propellant vehicle, designated SLV-3, will have a maximum length of 75 ft 6 in (23 m) and will weigh 37,480 lb (17,000 kg) at lift-off. Inertial control and guidance will be employed.

Static tests of the individual motors are scheduled to be completed by the end of 1974. The first launch is planned to take place in mid-1978.

Model of India's first satellite (*Théo Pirard*)

INTERNATIONAL PROGRAMMES

CESAR

BRITISH AIRCRAFT CORPORATION LTD (BAC)
100 Pall Mall, London SW1Y 5HR, England

ÉTUDES TECHNIQUES ET CONSTRUCTIONS AÉROSPATIALES SA (ETCA)
BP 197, Charleroi, Belgium

MESSERSCHMITT-BÖLKOW-BLOHM GmbH (MBB)
Space Division: 8012 Ottobrunn bei München, Germany

SELENIA-INDUSTRIE ELETTRONICHE ASSOCIATE SpA
CP 7083, 00100 Rome, Italy

SOCIÉTÉ NATIONALE INDUSTRIELLE AÉROSPATIALE
37 boulevard de Montmorency, 75781-Paris-cédex 16, France

Under the auspices of ESRO, this international consortium is developing and building a scientific satellite known as COS B, of which brief details follow.

COS B

The COS B satellite is being developed and produced by the CESAR consortium for ESRO, with MBB as prime contractor. Its primary purpose is to measure gamma radiation from the galaxy, with particular regard to energy spectrum, the direction and intensity of incoming radiation, and changes as a function of time. Of special interest is the behaviour of pulsars, discovered as recently as 1967 and believed to be composed of highly-compressed nuclear matter.

Aérospatiale's Cannes facility is responsible for supplying the satellite structure and thermal control system. The scientific instrument payload has been developed as a European co-operative venture. It weighs approximately 265 lb (120 kg) and consists of five components. One of these is a spark chamber experiment, developed and built by MBB under contract to the Max-Planck-Institut of Garching, Germany.

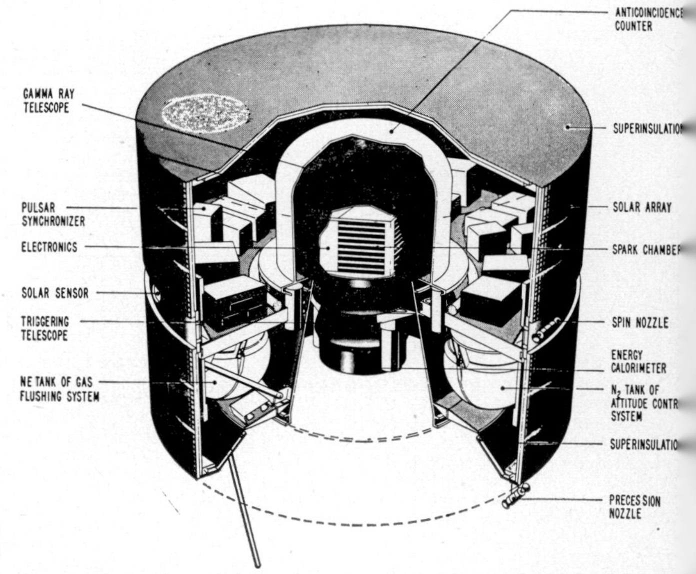

Cutaway drawing of COS B scientific satellite

BAC is involved in major subsystem technology developments, including a unique attitude measurement sensor and electronics system, electronics and pneumatics for the spark chamber gas flushing subsystem, electronics and pneumatics for the attitude control subsystems, and the satellite's solar arrays.

The present contract covers the design and manufacture of two mockup satellites, a prototype, and two flight models which were to be delivered in 1973-74. The first launching is scheduled for February 1975, from the Western Test Range, California, using a Delta launc vehicle.

COS B has a launching weight of about 660 l (300 kg) and is intended to enter a near-polar ec centric orbit with an apogee of 53,950 nn (62,150 miles; 100,000 km) and perigee of 190 nn (215 miles; 350 km). It is expected to transmi scientific data to Earth for a period of two years

DIMENSIONS:

Height without antenna	3 ft 11¼ in (1·20 m
Height overall	5 ft 7¼ in (1·71 m
Body diameter	4 ft 7 in (1·40 m

CIFAS

CONSORTIUM INDUSTRIEL FRANCO-ALLEMAND POUR LE SATELLITE SYMPHONIE (DEUTSCH-FRANZÖSICHES INDUSTRIE-KONSORTIUM FÜR DEN SATELLITEN SYMPHONIE)

HEAD OFFICE:
37 boulevard de Montmorency, 75781-Paris-cédex 16, France

ADDRESS FOR CORRESPONDENCE:
BP 62, 78130-Les Mureaux, France

Telephone: 474.72.13

Telex: AIRSPA 60159F

ADMINISTRATOR:
P. Usunier

This consortium was formed on 25 April 1968 in response to a request from the French and German governments for proposals to develop a telecommunications satellite named Symphonie. Members of the consortium, under the technical, industrial and commercial direction of Société Nationale Industrielle Aérospatiale (Division des Systèmes Balistiques et Spatiaux), are Messerschmitt-Bölkow-Blohm, Thomson-CSF, SAT, Siemens-AG and AEG-Telefunken.

SYMPHONIE

The first operational Symphonie telephone/television satellite is scheduled to be launched by a Delta vehicle by early 1975 under a joint Franco-German programme. It will be established in geostationary orbit over the South Atlantic, at longitude 11·5°W, giving coverage of two zones through two elliptical beams, each of 13° × 8°. The first beam will cover Europe, North and Central Africa; the second beam will cover South America and the eastern parts of North and Central America.

The second Symphonie satellite is expected to be launched a few months after the first.

The main body of the Symphonie satellite is a shallow six-sided box, with three deployable panels of solar cells, giving a minimum total power of 170W. Three parabolic and horn telecommunications antennae are mounted above the body. Two transponders provide coverage of the two Earth receiving zones in various combinations. A three-axis stabilisation system and a built-in MBB liquid rocket apogee motor (88 lb; 40 kg st for 20 minutes) are fitted.

Symphonie is intended for 24-hour use over a five-year period. It will weigh about 886 lb (402 kg) at launch, of which 386 lb (175 kg) will represent the weight of the apogee engine and fuel.

The basic Symphonie programme calls for three flight units, plus the necessary spares Additional satellites can be built to meet th requirements of potential users.

Radio mockup of Symphonie satellite under radome during communications tests

COSMOS

ÉTUDES TECHNIQUES ET CONSTRUCTIONS AÉROSPATIALES SA (ETCA)
BP 97, 6000-Charleroi 1, Belgium
SOCIÉTÉ NATIONALE INDUSTRIELLE AÉROSPATIALE
37 boulevard de Montmorency, 75781-Paris-cédex 16, France
SOCIÉTÉ ANONYME DE TÉLÉCOMMUNICATIONS (SAT)
41 rue Cantagrel, 75624-Paris-cédex 13, France
MESSERSCHMITT-BÖLKOW-BLOHM GmbH (MBB)
8 München 80, Postfach 801 169, Germany
SIEMENS AG
8 München 70, Hofmannstrasse 51, Germany
MARCONI SPACE & DEFENCE SYSTEMS LTD
The Grove, Stanmore, England
SELENIA SpA
Cas Post 7083, 00100 Rome, Italy

Announcement of the formation of this consortium by the seven major European companies listed above was made on 3 November 1970.

In addition to many study contracts carried out for ESRO and their respective governments, COSMOS companies are now involved in several major space programmes, notably Meteosat, of which details follow.

METEOSAT

Aérospatiale of France, acting as prime contractor for the COSMOS consortium, was awarded a $56·76 million contract by ESRO for development of this geosynchronous meteorological satellite in December 1973, after a ten-month competitive definition phase. The contract covers work over a period of 45 months, culminating in launch of the first Meteosat flight model by a Delta 2914 vehicle in late 1976.

Philco-Ford is assisting Aérospatiale's Cannes establishment in co-ordinating and integrating the project. Of the other COSMOS members, MBB is responsible for the spacecraft structure; Marconi Space & Defence Systems will supply the attitude and orbit control system and check-out equipment, and is involved with Siemens on the satellite's main communications package; ETCA is responsible for electric power supply; Selenia for data transmission and service telecommunications; and SAT for the telemetry encoder and solar cells. Associated subcontractors include Terma of Denmark, Crouzet and SAFT of France, SRA of Sweden and CIR of Switzerland.

Meteosat represents Europe's contribution to a worldwide Global Atmospheric Research Programme (GARP) which will utilise also US, Japanese and Soviet satellites to provide up-to-the-minute data for the World Weather Watch Organisation. Its three primary functions will be to take photographs of the Earth and its cloud cover by day and, in infra-red, at night; collection of meteorological data obtained by numerous ground and sea stations, and by satellites in low polar orbits; transmission of unprocessed pictures and meteorological data to Earth, and relay of processed photographs to users.

A key sensor will be the radiometer, used to determine wind speeds and sea surface temperatures. Development of this device was begun under a special contract by Matra, assisted by Marconi.

The general appearance of Meteosat is shown in the accompanying photograph of a full-size model. It will be spin stabilised in orbit, when the solar cells covering its sides will give a minimum of 200W. The telescope housed within the cylindrical body will be provided with an aperture in the side of the spacecraft.

Meteosat geostationary meteorological satellite

DIMENSIONS:
Height overall 4 ft 9 in (1·45 m)
Diameter 6 ft 10½ in (2·10 m)
WEIGHT:
Initial weight in orbit 661 lb (300 kg)

MESH

SA ENGINS MATRA,
BP No 1, 78140-Vélizy, France
ERNO RAUMFAHRTTECHNIK GmbH,
28 Bremen 1, Hünefeldstrasse 1-5, Postfach 1199, Germany
SAAB-SCANIA AKTIEBOLAG,
S-581 88 Linköping, Sweden
HAWKER SIDDELEY DYNAMICS LTD
Manor Road, Hatfield, Herts, England
AERITALIA SpA
Piazzale V. Tecchio 51/A, 80125 Napoli, Italy

This international consortium was formed in September 1966, the word "MESH" being an acronym of the initial letters of the four original founder members. They agreed not only to collaborate in manufacturing programmes, but to submit joint tenders to specifications for space vehicles and satellites issued within and outside Europe.

As a result of one such tender, MESH received in March 1967 a contract to design and develop the TD-1A satellite for the European Space Research Organisation (ESRO). Largest and most advanced satellite built in Europe at that period, it was launched on 12 March 1972. After a subsequent period of "hibernation", it was triggered into normal operation once more on 12 February 1973, without difficulty. Further details can be found in the 1972-73 *Jane's*.

In December 1969, Fiat SpA of Italy, through its Aviation Division (now embodied in Aeritalia SpA), joined MESH as a full member. Having a direct technical exchange agreement with TRW of America, its membership strengthened the team considerably.

Artist's impression of OTS satellite in orbit

In addition to being responsible for the European OTS satellite, of which details follow, MESH is involved in current design studies and tenders for a wide range of projected satellites.

OTS

This Orbital Test Satellite is being produced under a three-year contract, with Hawker Siddeley Dynamics as prime contractor, responsible for both development and launch support. The satellite will mark completion of the technological and development phase of the European Communications Satellite programme.

OTS will be placed in geostationary orbit in 1976, in order to demonstrate the operational capabilities of onboard high-technology communications payloads and spacecraft systems. It will also test experimental advanced communications concepts and propagation assumptions in space.

The primary aim of the OTS programme is to develop a space communication system which will make facilities available to European postal and telecommunications authorities grouped in CEPT (Conference Européenne des Postes et Télécommunications). These facilities will offer satellite links for a significant portion of inter-European telephony, telegraphy and telex traffic in the 1980s, and will satisfy the requirements of the EBU (European Broadcasting Union) for Eurovision relay.

The modular construction of OTS will permit the carriage of a variety of alternative payloads, such as MAROTS for shipborne communications, while employing the same basic OTS technology (see under MSDS in UK section).

STAR

AEG-TELEFUNKEN
1 Berlin 33, Hohenzollerndamm 150, Germany
BRITISH AIRCRAFT CORPORATION LTD (BAC)
100 Pall Mall, London SW1Y 5HR, England
CONTRAVES AG
Schaffhauserstrasse 580, CH-8052 Zurich 11, Switzerland
CGE-FIAR
via G.B. Grassi 93, 20157 Milano, Italy
DORNIER SYSTEM GmbH
Postfach 648, 799 Friedrichshafen/Bodensee, Germany
ELECTRONIKCENTRALEN
Denmark
ÉTUDES TECHNIQUES ET CONSTRUCTIONS AÉROSPATIALES SA (ETCA)
BP 97, 6000-Charleroi 1, Belgium
FOKKER-VFW BV
PO Box 7600, Schiphol-Oost 1148, Netherlands
TELEFONAKTIEBOLAGET L. M. ERICSSON
126 25 Stockholm, Sweden
MONTEDEL (MONTECATINI EDISON ELETTRONICA SpA)
20133 Milano, Via E Bassini 15, Italy
OFFICINE GALILEO SpA
Via Carlo Bini 44, 50134 Florence, Italy
SENER SA
Guzman el Bucuo 121, Madrid 3, Spain
SNIA VISCOSA
Via Lombardia 31, 00187 Rome, Italy
SOCIÉTÉ EUROPÉENNE DE PROPULSION
Tour Roussel-Nobel, cédex 3, 92080-Paris Défense, France
THOMSON-CSF
173 boulevard Hausmann, 75360-Paris, cédex 08, France

The STAR (Satellites for Telecommunications, Applications and Research) consortium was formed in December 1970 by industrial companies from eight of the member states of the European Space Research Organisation, to respond to tenders issued by ESRO for both applications and scientific satellites. Additional companies have since joined the consortium.

Since its formation, the STAR consortium has completed a number of important studies on behalf of ESRO, and has been awarded the main development contract for the GEOS satellite, with BAC as prime contractor and Hughes Aircraft Company, USA, as consultants.

GEOS

GEOS is the first European scientific geostationary satellite. Its payload of nine experiments will measure magnetic, electrical and particle fields at a constant geographical position in the Earth's outer magnetosphere during an operational lifetime of two years.

GEOS is scheduled to be launched by a Delta vehicle from the Eastern Test Range in the USA in 1976.

DIMENSIONS:
Height overall 43·3 in (110 cm)
Diameter 63·8 in (162 cm)

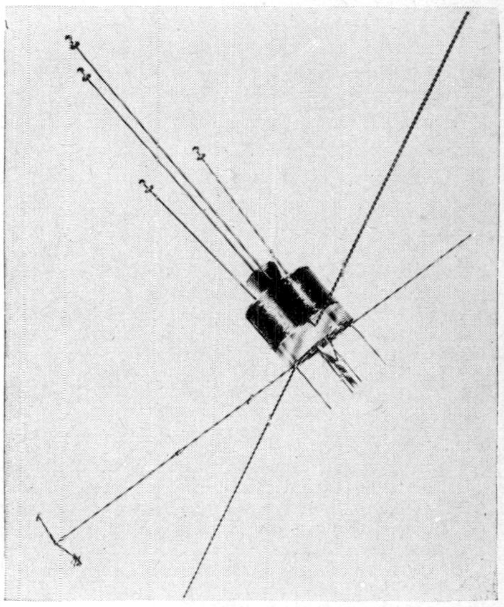
Artist's impression of GEOS satellite

WEIGHT:
Launching weight 1,195 lb (542 kg)

ITALY

CIA

COMPAGNIA INDUSTRIALE AEROSPAZIALE

ADDRESS: Viale di Villa Grazioli 23, Rome

This consortium was formed in June 1965 by eleven Italian companies, comprising Aeritalia of Naples, Turin and Milan, CGE-FIAR of Milan, ELSAG of Genoa, Fiat of Turin, Montedel-Laben of Milan, Galileo of Florence, Montedel-OTE of Florence, Oto Melara of La Spezia, Pignone Sud of Bari, Selenia of Rome and SNIA Viscosa of Colleferro. The original intention was to contribute to ELDO programmes. Since their abandonment, CIA has devoted its efforts to a project named Sirio (Satellite Italiano Ricerche Orientate). This began as a long-term programme to launch satellites into geostationary orbits in the period 1970-75, with particular emphasis on applied research into SHF communications and the Earth's magnetosphere.

SIRIO

Under the sponsorship of the Space Activities Services (SAS) of the Consiglio Nazionale Ricerche (CNR) of Rome, it is intended to develop and build a single Sirio satellite and put it into orbit by means of a Delta launch vehicle, from Cape Kennedy, during 1975.

Sirio is basically cylindrical in shape and is to be spin-stabilised at 90 rpm in orbit. Its apogee motor, supplied by SNIA Viscosa, has a specific impulse of 280 sec. An auxiliary propulsion system, developed by Oto Melara, utilises hydrazine as a monopropellant.

The required 100W electrical supply throughout the planned two-year lifetime of the satellite will be provided by 8,496 solar cells measuring 2 cm by 2 cm, and 336 measuring 2 cm by 1 cm. In addition to trapped radiation and high-energy electron experiments, Sirio will perform communications experiments in the super high frequency (SHF) range at 12 and 18GHz.

DIMENSIONS:
Height overall, incl antennae and apogee motor 6 ft 2¾ in (1·90 m)
Height of body 2 ft 11½ in (0·90 m)
Diameter 4 ft 7 in (1·40 m)

WEIGHTS:
Satellite, incl useful load of 112 lb (51 kg) 437 lb (198 kg)
Apogee motor 441 lb (200 kg)
Total launching weight 878 lb (398 kg)

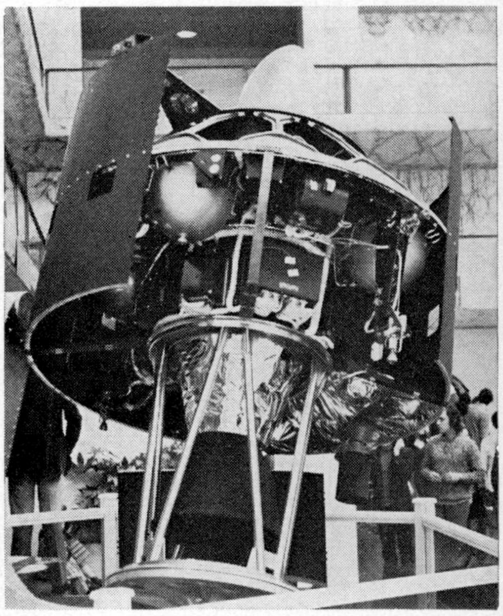

Sirio geostationary research satellite (*Théo Pirard*)

CRA

ISTITUTO DI COSTRUZIONI AERONAUTICHE CENTRO RICERCHE AEROSPAZIALI, UNIVERSITÀ DEGLI STUDI DI ROMA

ADDRESS:
Via Salaria 851, 00199 Rome
DIRECTOR: Prof Luigi Broglio
DOCUMENTATION OFFICER:
Col Giuseppe Amoruso

Prof Broglio and his colleagues of the Aerospace Research Centre in Rome were responsible for the San Marco satellites of which details can be found in previous editions of *Jane's*. The orbital life of San Marco 3 ended on 29 November 1971. All three experiments carried by this satellite performed successfully. For the first time, the drag balance device gathered data on atmospheric density down to an altitude of 65 nm (75 miles; 120 km).

A further satellite in the series, San Marco 4, was launched from the San Marco Equatorial Range on 18 February 1974. San Marco D continues under development, but its launch has been deferred. The CRA also launched from the San Marco Equatorial Range the NASA scientific satellites SAS-1 (on 12 December 1970), SSS-1 (on 15 November 1971) and SAS-B, known after launch as Explorer 48 (on 15 November 1972).

SAN MARCO 4 (C.2)

The first three satellites in this joint Italian-US programme were described in previous editions of *Jane's*.

San Marco 4 was launched on 18 February 1974, by a Scout rocket, into a 137 by 510 mile (221 by 821 km) orbit. The satellite is instrumented to gather information on atmospheric drag, and on variations in atmospheric density. composition and temperature resulting from solar and geomagnetic activity. This data is being correlated with data being returned by NASA's Explorer 51, to provide a better understanding of the effects of magnetic storms on the thermosphere, and of the influence of the Sun on the atmosphere and ionosphere.

San Marco 4 satellite

CSTM

CENTRO STUDI TRASPORTI MISSILISTICI (Missile Transport Research Centre)

HEAD OFFICE:
Via Squarcialupo 19-A, 00162 Rome
Telephone: 423.833
PRESIDENT: Glauco A. Partel

The CSTM is developing an upper atmosphere sounding vehicle named the Bora-Sond, of unconventional design.

The Bora first-stage booster, and other scientific and military rockets designed by the CSTM, are produced commercially by SAI-Ambrosini. A further artillery and air-to-surface rocket known as Samurai is under development.

CSTM BORA-SOND

The Bora-Sond is designed as a minimum-cost sounding rocket, with a reusable first stage, for probing the atmosphere at heights up to 408,450 ft (124,500 m).

The Bora first stage embodies a self-pressurised liquid propulsion system, which produces no flame, no appreciable noise, no internal corrosion problem and no toxic exhaust gas. The whole booster is recoverable by parachute and reusable at least 50 times unless damaged by landing on rocky terrain. A crew of two or three semi-skilled men can service the rocket and launch it, since the system does not come under the regulations governing the handling of explosives and negligible safety precautions are needed.

This stage has a nominal rating of 8,800 lb (4,000 kg) st for one second and has completed static and flight tests, over a temperature range of —50°C to +50°C.

The T.II-P.300 second stage, currently under development, utilises an equally unconventional propulsion system, based on the emission of hydrogen (at above 3,000°C) produced by the combustion of metals into water. The specific impulse, indicated by tests, is in the 300 sec range. Nominal rating is 496 lb (225 kg) st for 29 seconds.

Payload volume is 366 cu in (6,000 cm^3).

DIMENSIONS:
Length: overall 15 ft 1·1 in (4·60 m)
payload section 2 ft 3·5 in (0·70 m)

WEIGHTS:
Launching weight, less payload 383·5 lb (174 kg)
Payload, incl nosecone and housing 8·8-13·2 lb (4-6 kg)

PERFORMANCE (estimated, with 11 lb; 5 kg payload, at S/L, launch angle of 88°):
Max ceiling 408,450 ft (124,500 m)
Max velocity 6,400 ft (1,950 m)/sec
Range at max ceiling 35,760 ft (10,900 m)
Max launch acceleration 13*g*

JAPAN

MITSUBISHI

MITSUBISHI JUKOGYO KABUSHIKI KAISHA (Mitsubishi Heavy Industries, Ltd)

HEAD OFFICE:
5-1, Marunouchi, 2-chome, Chiyoda-Ku, Tokyo 100
OFFICERS: See "Aircraft" section
GENERAL MANAGER, SPACE SYSTEMS DEPARTMENT:
Y. Kato

On June 1, 1964, Shin Mitsubishi Jukogyo, Mitsubishi Zosen (Shipbuilding) and Mitsubishi Nihon Jukogyo were amalgamated as Mitsubishi Jukogyo Kabushiki Kaisha (Mitsubishi Heavy Industries, Ltd). The units known formerly as Shin Mitsubishi and Mitsubishi Zosen, together with Mitsubishi Denki (Electric Machinery) have been engaged since 1955 in the development of missiles and the production of sounding rockets, of which all available details are given below.

Within the framework of Japan's national space programme, Mitsubishi is collaborating with the Science and Technology Agency, the National Space Development Agency, and the Institute of Space and Aeronautical Science, University of Tokyo. It has manufactured the rocket chambers of the Kappa, Lambda and Mu rockets, the attitude control motors of Lambda and Mu, and the launching and assembly tower for the Mu.

For the Japan Defence Agency, Mitsubishi is developing and producing air-to-air missiles and is manufacturing the Nike-Hercules surface-to-air missile under licence.

MITSUBISHI S-B, S-C, LS-A and LS-C

Mitsubishi has been awarded Science and Technology Agency contracts to develop and test a series of research rockets. First of these were for the S-B and S-C meteorological sounding rockets for observation of the upper atmosphere.

The S-B and S-C are each fitted with a single-stage solid-propellant rocket motor in a fibre-reinforced plastics casing. The S-B is capable of carrying a payload of 5·1 lb (2·3 kg) to a height of more than 38 nm (44 miles; 70 km); the S-C is designed to carry a 5·5 lb (2·5 kg) payload to a height of more than 43 nm (50 miles; 80 km). At the peak altitude, a radio telemetry and parachute recovery package is released to measure the atmospheric temperature, wind direction and strength.

First launching trials of the S-B were made in 1964. The S-C was launched for the first time in 1969.

First launching of the two-stage LS-A (solid-propellant first stage, liquid-propellant second stage) was made in 1964. Subsequently, Mitsubishi received a follow-on contract for the larger LS-C, the second stage of which has been developed by the National Space Development Agency of Japan as part of the development programme for the "N" rocket that will launch an engineering test satellite by 1975. First trial launching of the LS-C was made in February 1969.

DIMENSIONS:
Overall length:
S-B 9 ft 1⅜ in (2·778 m)
S-C 9 ft 4¼ in (2·851 m)
LS-A 24 ft 9 in (7·55 m)
LS-C 36 ft 6¼ in (11·135 m)
Body diameter:
S-B 6·2 in (0·157 m)
S-C 6·5 in (0·165 m)
LS-A, second stage 11·8 in (0·30 m)
LS-C, second stage 23·6 in (0·60 m)

WEIGHTS:
Launching weight:
S-B 149 lb (67·8 kg)
S-C 170 lb (77 kg)
LS-A 1,675 lb (760 kg)
LS-C 5,591 lb (2,536 kg)

PERFORMANCE:
Ceiling (75° launch angle):
S-B 40·5 nm (47 miles; 75 km)
S-C 46 nm (53 miles; 85 km)
LS-A 59 nm (68 miles; 110 km)
LS-C 32 nm (36·5 miles; 59 km)

NASDA

NATIONAL SPACE DEVELOPMENT AGENCY OF JAPAN

ADDRESS:
2-4-1, Hammatsu-cho, Minato-ku, Tokyo

PRESIDENT: Hideo Shima

DIRECTOR, SYSTEMS PLANNING DEPARTMENT:
Yasuhiro Kuroda

The National Space Development Agency was established on 1 October 1969 to take over functions of the National Space Development Center of the Science and Technology Agency, as well as part of the Radio Research Laboratories of the Ministry of Posts and Telecommunications. The major duties of the Agency, as the central organisation for promoting space activities in Japan, include the development of satellites, launch vehicles, tracking systems, and associated facilities and equipment.

The work is performed in accordance with the space development programme approved by the Japanese Prime Minister, on the basis of recommendations by the Space Activities Commission. The current programme, set out originally in 1969 and revised substantially in 1970, 1972 and 1973, calls for launching a number of satellites by "N" rockets during the period covered by the 1975 to 1977 fiscal years, and launching three geostationary satellites (meteorological, medium-capacity communications for experimental purposes, and medium-scale broadcast for experimental purposes) by means of US launch vehicles during the 1976 fiscal year. These last three satellites each weigh 660 lb (300 kg).

"N" ROCKET

The "N" rocket is a three-stage vehicle capable of putting a 287 lb (130 kg) satellite into a geostationary orbit. The first stage embodies a liquid-propellant rocket (liquid oxygen/kerosene) with solid-propellant strap-on boosters (approx 330,600 lb; 150,000 kg st); the second stage is powered by a storable liquid rocket (N_2O_4/A-50), and the third stage by a solid rocket. The guidance system is of the strap-down radio command type.

Development is so scheduled that it will be possible to use "N" rockets to launch a 187 lb (85 kg) engineering test satellite (ETS-I) into a circular orbit at a height of 540 nm (620 miles; 1,000 km) in 1975. If this launch is successful, a 298 lb (135 kg) ionosphere sounding satellite (ISS) will be launched into a similar orbit in 1975, followed by another engineering test satellite (ETS-II) and an experimental communications satellite (ECS), which are intended to be put into synchronous orbit in 1976 and 1977 respectively.

To ensure smooth development of the "N" rocket, initial launching tests will utilise the first stage of the University of Tokyo's "M" rocket as the booster, instead of the "N's" liquid booster. The principal objective of these early tests will be to evaluate the flight performance of the second and third stages of the "N" rocket, and to develop the guidance and control techniques.

Artist's impression of ISS satellite

The main parameters of the "N" rocket are as follows:

DIMENSIONS (approx):
Length overall 108 ft 3 in (33 m)
Diameter of first stage 8 ft 2½ in (2·5 m)
WEIGHT (approx): 198,400 lb (90,000 kg)

NISSAN

NISSAN JIDOSHA KABUSHIKI KAISHA (Nissan Motor Co, Ltd)

HEAD OFFICE:
17-1, 6-chome, Ginza, Chuo-ku, Tokyo

AERONAUTICAL AND SPACE DIVISION:
5-1, 3-chome, Momoi, Suginami-ku, Tokyo
Telephone: Tokyo (390) 1111
Telex: 0-232-2271

PRESIDENT:
Katsuji Kawamata

MANAGING DIRECTOR AND VICE-PRESIDENT:
Takashi Ishihara

DIRECTOR, MANAGER OF AERONAUTICAL AND SPACE DIVISION:
Yasuakira Toda

Nissan Motor Co Ltd is the oldest automobile manufacturer in Japan, having been founded in 1933 under the name of Jidosha Seizo Co, Ltd. It adopted its present name in 1934 and, following its merger with the former Prince Motors Ltd, on 1 August 1966, is Japan's largest automobile company. The merger also gave Nissan a leading position in the national aerospace industry, as the Space and Aeronautical Division of Prince Motors became a Division of Nissan Motor Co.

Known before and during World War 2 as Nakajima Aircraft Company, Prince formed its Space and Aeronautical Division as an offshoot of its primary post-war business of automobile manufacture. Today, the Aeronautical and Space Division is responsible for the major share of work on rockets and missiles in Japan.

In the field of military missiles and rockets, the company has been engaged in extensive research and development since 1953. In association with the Technical Research and Development Institute of the Japan Defence Agency, it has developed many types of air-to-air, air-to-surface and surface-to-surface solid-propellant unguided rockets, several of which are in production, including the "30-rocket", the largest surface-to-surface type in service in Japan.

In addition, this Department has produced many sounding rockets such as Pencil, Baby, Kappa, Lambda and Mu for the Institute of Space and Aeronautical Science, University of Tokyo, and has produced many other research rockets for the Japanese Aerospace Laboratory, Meteorological Agency and the Antarctic Research Centre.

Under contracts from the National Space Development Agency, NASDA (formerly the National Space Development Centre), Nissan has developed a number of rocket motors of the kind that will be used in the projected Type "N" satellite launch vehicles.

One of these rockets, known as the ETV (Engineering Test Vehicle), powered by M10 and SB engines of the kind used in the Mu-4S and Mu-3C launch vehicles, was to be launched in August 1974. Its purpose was to demonstrate how JCR (jet control rocket) techniques pioneered by Nissan might be applied to Type "N" launch vehicles. ETV had an overall height of 69 ft 11 in (21·3 m) and lift-off weight of 86,875 lb (39,400 kg).

Following the launch of ETV, the first "N" vehicle will be used to orbit the ETS-I (Engineering Test Satellite). In readiness for this, Nissan has prepared the strap-on boosters and a third-stage engine by purchase and production under licence from Thiokol of the USA.

Nissan's other aerospace research and production activities include work on separation and control mechanisms, static and environmental test equipments and new high-performance rocket motors such as the hybrid type.

NISSAN MT-135

This meteorological sounding rocket, developed and produced by Nissan, was evaluated very successfully in comparative tests with the American Arcas and Rokidart rockets at NASA's Wallops Space Flight Station in the Spring of 1967 and in 1972.

Mu-3C-1 launch vehicle for Tansei-2 satellite

The Meteorological Agency of Japan is using an advanced version of the MT-135 for high-altitude study of weather in the northern part of the country, with weekly launches since July 1970.

NISSAN S-160 JA and S-210 JA

A series of observations has been made of the aurora in the Antarctic since February 1970, using S-160 JA and S-210 JA rockets. Japan was the first nation to conduct such launches while the Antarctic observation teams were "Wintering" in April 1971. Further launches were made in 1972 and 1973.

MU

The planned series of satellite launches by Mu-4S vehicles ended in August 1972, when an Mu-4S successfully put into orbit Japan's fourth satellite, known as Dempa (Radio Exploration Satellite). Earlier, the satellite Ohsumi had been launched by a Lambda rocket in 1970, and Tansei and Shinsei by Mu-4S rockets in 1971.

The Mu-4S was then superseded by the advanced Mu-3C, with three stages and control systems, which had been under development by Nissan and other manufacturers since 1972, under the supervision of the Institute of Space and Aeronautical Science, University of Tokyo. Only the first-stage M10 and SB engines have been retained from the Mu-4S. The second- and third-stage engines, structures and control systems are all newly developed.

Mu-3C-1 was launched on 16 February 1974, at the Uchinoura facilities of the Institute of Space and Aeronautical Science. It put Japan's fifth satellite, Tansei-2, into the planned orbit with a perigee of 147 nm (169 miles; 273 km), apogee of 1,718 nm (1,976 miles; 3,180 km) and orbital period of 121 minutes.

In February 1975, Mu-3C-2 is scheduled to orbit the SRATS (Solar Radiation and Thermospheric Structure satellite). Next will come CORSA (Cosmic Radiation Satellite), launched by Mu-3C, and a series of EXOS (Exospheric Satellites), launched by Mu-3H vehicles, which will be advanced versions of the Mu-3C.

The following details apply to the Mu-3C:

TYPE: Solid-propellant three-stage satellite launch vehicle.

POWER PLANT: M10 first stage gives 194,670 lb (88,300 kg) st at sea level, and is supplemented by eight SB strap-on boosters, giving a total of 30,750 lb (13,950 kg) st. The M22 second stage gives 80,910 lb (36,700 kg) st in vacuo and is fitted with liquid-injection thrust vector control. The M3A third stage gives 16,535 lb (7,500 kg) st in vacuo and has a similar control system. A small solid-propellant rocket motor is used for first-stage ignition.

DIMENSIONS:
Length overall:
M10 39 ft 1 in (11·92 m)

M22	16 ft 0 in (4·88 m)
M3A	5 ft 1 in (1·54 m)
Diameter:	
M10	4 ft 11 in (1·50 m)
M22	4 ft 7½ in (1·41 m)
M3A	3 ft 9 in (1·14 m)
WEIGHT:	
Launching weight:	
M10	55,423 lb (25,140 kg)
SB (8)	8,432 lb (3,825 kg)
M22	19,038 lb (8,635 kg)
M3A	2,736 lb (1,240 kg)

NETHERLANDS

ANS

INDUSTRIEEL CONSORTIUM ASTRONOMISCHE NEDERLANDSE SATELLIET

ADDRESS: PO Box 7600, Schiphol-Oost
Telephone: 020-731044
Telex: SIFO 12227

Project work on the first Dutch satellite was started in January 1970. Known as the Astronomical Netherlands Satellite (ANS), it was developed and built by a consortium formed by Philips Gloeilampen Fabrieken NV and Fokker-VFW BV, in collaboration with astronomers of the Universities of Groningen and Utrecht and with NASA. The project was supervised by the NIVR (Netherlands Agency for Aerospace Programmes) on behalf of the Netherlands government.

ANS

This small satellite is intended to perform a statistical investigation of a certain category of young hot stars in the ultra-violet band. In addition it will perform spectral analysis of cosmic X-ray sources, of which 160 have been discovered since 1963 (about 120 of them by the SAS-A/Explorer 42 satellite). More were expected to be known by 1974, when the Astronomical Netherlands Satellite (ANS) was scheduled to be launched. Such observations are not possible through the atmosphere, and the results are expected to contribute to knowledge of the creation and evolution of stars.

The basic structure of the ANS satellite consists of vertical aluminium honeycomb sandwich panels, with a machined adaptor and yo-yo support ring at the base. The walls are made of thin detachable sandwich panels, with thermal control by an outside covering of 24 layers of perforated aluminised mylar with an outer layer of Kapton. Two deployable solar panels, with a total surface area of 10·22 sq ft (0·95 m²), carry 2,050 solar cells for power supply.

Instruments carried by the ANS satellite include an 8·66 in (22 cm) diameter Cassegrain telescope with a grating spectrograph in Rowland mounting and five photomultipliers, each preceded by a broadband ultra-violet filter, covering wavelengths and bandwidths from 1550Å/50Å or 150Å to 3295Å/100Å (Groningen); a detection system to measure X-rays between 44 and 55 Å and a detection system for X-rays in the bands 2-4 Å, 4-12 Å and 27 to 35 Å (Utrecht); and a detection system for measuring X-rays between 2 and 40 KeV (American Science and Engineering, together with MIT).

An operational programme involving about 14,000 objects is planned. By launching in a Sun-synchronous polar orbit the programme can be carried out in half a year, but it is hoped to extend this lifetime to one year for repeated observations.

The ANS was scheduled to be launched by NASA, using an improved Scout launch vehicle with Algol III first-stage motor, in the Summer of 1974. It was to be put into orbit at a height between 240 nm (280 miles; 450 km) and 300 nm (340 miles; 550 km) at an optional inclination of 97·6°, and was to be three-axis stabilised, using the Sun, Earth and stars as references for pointing the telescopes with an accuracy of 1 arc minute. Torqueing was to be effected by reaction wheels and magnetic coils.

As faint stars and optically invisible X-ray sources were to be observed, it was planned to use two guide-stars in the vicinity of the subject as pointing reference.

One side of the satellite was intended to point continually at the Sun and it was to be rotated around the Sun axis for pointing the telescopes at the stars. For this purpose the satellite was to be placed first in a fixed attitude in relation to the Earth by means of a scanning infra-red sensor. In this position it was intended to scan the sky until the programmed guide-stars were observed by an image tube inside the UV telescope and recognised by an on-board computer. The satellite was then to remain pointed in this direction.

The on-board computer was designed to receive, store and execute the 12-hour observation programme, perform the attitude control logic and handle housekeeping and experiment data for storage in a core memory of 24K 16-bit words.

For satellite operation, use was to be made of existing ESRO facilities, the satellite operation centre (ESOC) in Darmstadt, and the Redu ground station in Belgium. A Netherlands team, in collaboration with ESOC staff, was to operate the satellite, which was planned to pass over the ground station every 12 hours.

DIMENSIONS:	
Height	44·1 in (112 cm)
Depth	27·6 in (70 cm)
Width, solar panels deployed	59·1 in (150 cm)
WEIGHT:	
Launching weight	286 lb (130 kg)

POLAND

IL

INSTYTUT LOTNICTWA (AVIATION INSTITUTE)

HEADQUARTERS:
02-256 Warsaw-Okecie, Al Krakowska 110/114
Telephone: Warsaw 460993
Telex: 813537

SCIENTIFIC DIRECTOR:
Dr Czeslaw Skoczylas

HEAD OF TECHNICAL INFORMATION DIVISION:
Dipl Ing Andrzej Glass

The Aviation Institute (IL) is engaged on aeronautical research, development of power plants, aerodynamic and structural testing, flight testing of fixed-wing aircraft, helicopters and gliders, and development of aviation equipment and materials. It is also responsible for supplying technical information and for standardisation.

Many research rockets were also designed and produced at the IL, as described in previous editions of *Jane's*. Its work in this field has now ended.

IMGW

INSTYTUT METEOROLOGII I GOSPODARKI WODNEJ

HEAD OFFICE: 00-967 Warszawa, ul Podlesna 61
Telephone: 34-16-51/59
Telex: 814331

DIRECTOR: Jan Zielinski, DSc eng, Associate Professor

CHIEF OF ROCKET RESEARCH SECTION:
Dr J. Walczewski

Rocket Sounding Laboratory:
Kraków, ul P. Borowego 9

All meteorological research projects in Poland are now undertaken exclusively by the Institute of Meteorology and Water Economy (IMGW), which is conducting experiments in accordance with the recommendations of COSPAR and the World Meteorological Organisation.

Rockets used by the IMGW include the new Meteor-1E and 3E, evolved from the Meteor-1 and 3 designed at the Instytut Lotnictwa and described briefly in the 1973-74 *Jane's*. Use of the IMGW's own Rasko-2 rocket for the artificial modification of clouds has ended, but a new version known as Rasko-2R has been developed.

IMGW RASKO-2R

This simple unguided solid-propellant rocket has a cylindrical metal body and cruciform tail surfaces. It is basically similar to the Rasko-2, described in the 1971-72 *Jane's*, but its payload comprises a radar transponder instead of chemicals.

A prototype of the Rasko-2R has been completed. It is designed for use as a test rocket for training radar operators and for radar checkout in preparation for the use of larger meteorological rockets.

METEOR-1E and 3E

The original Meteor-1 and Meteor-3 meteorological sounding rockets designed at the IL are no longer in use. Experimental versions known as Meteor-1E and Meteor-3E have been evolved, for use as test vehicles for a new dart-sonde system named Grot-Somit developed at the IMGW in 1972-73.

Meteor-1E is a two-stage vehicle, comprising the same rocket booster as that used in the original Meteor-1 plus an unpowered dart, known as Grot E-50/11. This has a plastics body, containing a modified version of a standard parachute sonde for temperature and wind measurements. The sonde transmits on a frequency of 1,770MHz. The ground telemetry and tracking equipment consists of the Meteorit station used with the RKZ balloon sonde.

Meteor-3E differs from the 1E in having an additional Meteor-1 motor in tandem, making it a three-stage vehicle.

DIMENSIONS:	
Length overall:	
1E	9 ft 4½ in (2·86 m)
3E	15 ft 3½ in (4·66 m)
Length of dart	3 ft 9½ in (1·16 m)
Diameter of motor stages	4·7 in (12 cm)
Diameter of dart	2·0 in (5·1 cm)
WEIGHTS:	
Launching weight:	
1E	78 lb (35·5 kg)
3E	150 lb (68·0 kg)
Dart	16 lb (7·2 kg)
PERFORMANCE:	
Ceiling:	
1E	68,900 ft (21,000 m)
3E	144,350 ft (44,000 m)

Meteor-1E experimental sounding rocket

SPAIN

CASA

CONSTRUCCIONES AERONAUTICAS SA

HEAD OFFICE:
Rey Francisco 4, Madrid-8

WORKS AND OFFICERS: See "Aircraft" section

In addition to its work on aircraft design, manufacture and overhaul, CASA is engaged on space research contracts and spacecraft fabrication in co-operation with CONIE (Comision Nacional de Investigacion del Espacio) and ESA (European Space Agency).

CASA participated in ESRO's HEOS-A2 satellite programme, producing three spacecraft structures (structural model, prototype and flight unit) under subcontract from MBB of Germany. It is now producing parts and equipment for the COS B satellite under subcontract from MBB and Aérospatiale of France.

Since late 1969, under contract to CONIE, CASA has contributed to development of the first Spanish satellite, named Intasat (see "CONIE" entry). It is responsible for structural subsystems, thermal control, wiring, mechanical and electronic ground equipment, power generation and control, and integration, assembly and testing.

CONIE

COMISION NACIONAL DE INVESTIGACION DEL ESPACIO

ADDRESS:
Paseo del Pintor Rosales 34, Madrid-8

INTA

INSTITUTO NACIONAL DE TECNICA AEROESPACIAL

Space research in Spain is conducted under the sponsorship and control of CONIE, of which INTA is the Technological Centre. Annually, CONIE recommends a programme of space activities, within the framework of a six-year programme approved by the Spanish government and dating from 1968. It uses as much as possible the facilities offered by research institutions in Spain and the services of Spanish manufacturers. The national space facilities and laboratories, including the El Arenosillo sounding rocket launch station on the Atlantic coast of Mazagon (Huelva), are operated by INTA. There were 50 sounding rocket launches from El Arenosillo in 1971 and 51 in 1972.

In partnership with NASA, the Institut d'Aeronomic Spatiale de Belgique, and the Max Planck Institut für Ionosphere, CONIE is making ionospheric studies. It is also carrying out astrophysical and meteorological observations.

INTA is developing a sounding rocket and a small scientific satellite, of which brief details follow:

INTA-300

The INTA-300 is a two-stage sounding rocket, with motors and payload package of constant diameter. The first-stage booster comprises a standard INTA-255 single-stage rocket, which has been used in large quantities to carry scientific payloads. The second stage embodies a new high-performance motor which combines low thrust with long burning time in order to limit kinetic heating of the vehicle's skin and to reach peak speed at a low-density altitude.

DIMENSIONS:
Length overall 23 ft 10¼ in (7·27 m)
Diameter (constant) 10¼ in (0·26 m)
Max fin span 3 ft 7¼ in (1·10 m)
Length of payload section 1 ft 8¾ in (0·53 m)

WEIGHTS:
Launching weight 1,120 lb (508 kg)
Payload, incl telemetry systems 97 lb (44 kg)

PERFORMANCE:
Max speed Mach 8
Ceiling with current payload 176 nm (203 miles; 327 km)
Future ceiling with 22 lb (10 kg) payload 270 nm (310 miles; 500 km)
Range (85° launch angle) 79 nm (91 miles; 147 km)
Max acceleration 29*g*

INTASAT-1

A feasibility study for this first Spanish spacecraft was made during the closing months of 1968, followed by the project definition phase in 1969-70. This work was carried out in collaboration with Hawker Siddeley Dynamics of the UK.

The Intasat programme received full approval in September 1971. INTA, acting as prime contractor, selected CASA and Standard Eléctrica as subcontractors. CASA is responsible for the structural subsystems, thermal control, attitude control, integration and testing: Standard Eléctrica is responsible for the electronics subsystems.

Intasat was designed to be launched as secondary payload, together with a US meteorological satellite, by a NASA Delta vehicle in the second half of 1974. It is a dodecagonal prism, covered by 1,320 solar cells able to provide 2·77W of electrical power. In orbit it is intended to operate as an ionospheric beacon, transmitting simultaneously signals at 40 and 41MHz with a radiated power of 1W.

Placed into a circular orbit at a height of 593 nm (683 miles; 1,100 km), at an inclination of 100°, Intasat-1 is designed for a lifetime of two years. From this basic spacecraft design, it is hoped to develop an economical platform for conducting scientific experiments in space. Scientific packages weighing 4½-6½ lb (2-3 kg) could be carried easily, and available power for the payloads could range from a minimum of 2W to a maximum of 10W, depending mainly on the orbit selected.

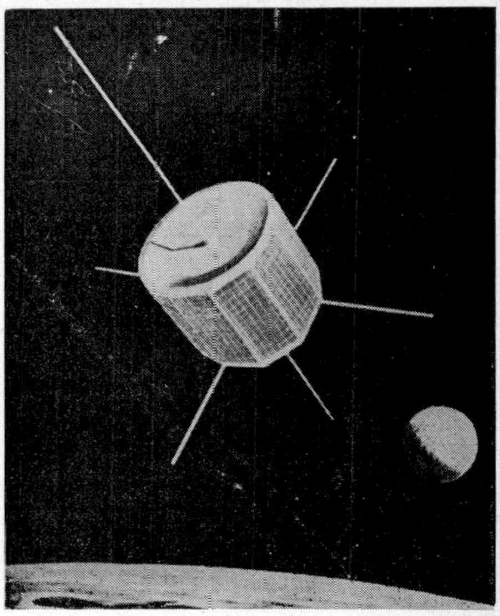

Artist's impression of Intasat-1 (*Théo Pirard*)

DIMENSION:
Height of body 1 ft 5¾ in (0·45 m)

WEIGHT:
Launching weight 54 lb (24·5 kg)

THE UNITED KINGDOM

BAC

BRITISH AIRCRAFT CORPORATION
Guided Weapons Division
Electronic and Space Systems (ESS)

STEVENAGE WORKS:
Six Hills Way, Stevenage, Herts SG1 2DA

BRISTOL WORKS:
GPO Box 77, Filton House, Bristol BS99 7AR

EXECUTIVE DIRECTOR: D. Rowley
SALES DIRECTOR: L. A. Sanson, OBE
MANAGER, ESS (Bristol): R. G. T. Munday
PUBLICITY MANAGER: R. F. Bailey
PUBLICITY OFFICER (Bristol): T. C. Bickerton

BAC has played a significant part in British and international space projects for more than 10 years, involving 16 different spacecraft and over 320 research rockets. Such activities are handled by its Electronic and Space Systems organisation, comprising the Electronic and Space Systems group at Bristol and the Reinforced and Microwave Plastics, Precision Products and Automatic Test Systems Groups at Stevenage.

BAC was prime contractor for Britain's Ariel IV satellite (see 1972-73 *Jane's*); it participated in both of Europe's HEOS satellite programmes and is now manufacturing major subsystems for Europe's COS B satellite. As leader of the STAR consortium of companies (see International section), BAC is prime contractor for the GEOS geostationary scientific satellite.

As main overseas contractor to Hughes Aircraft Company for the Intelsat IV series of communications satellites, five of which are in service around the Earth, BAC was the first company outside the USA to participate in this advanced and competitive field. It is currently manufacturing subsystems for the larger-capacity Intelsat IVA satellites, and is also supplying four sets of satellite hardware for American Telephone and Telegraph Company's domestic communications satellite system, under contract to Hughes Aircraft Company.

BAC continues to hold a variety of space technology contracts on behalf of the European Space Research Organisation.

Other BAC Electronic and Space Systems activities concern high-speed data handling systems for aircraft, mathematical modelling of complex systems, HF notch antenna tuning units, microwave phased arrays, automatic test equipment for factory and field testing, precision gyroscopes and inertial guidance equipment for the services and industry, and a wide range of reinforced and microwave plastics components for the marine, electronics and aerospace industries, including radomes, radar reflectors, antennae and structural components.

BAC SKYLARK

The Skylark high-altitude sounding rocket was developed originally by the Royal Aircraft Establishment and used in a programme of upper atmosphere research associated with the International Geophysical Year 1957-58. The basic concept of the rocket proved so sound and flexible that it became Europe's most successful upper atmosphere research rocket. By early 1974 a total of 325 Skylarks had been launched in rocket programmes of the British and European space research groups.

In March 1973, Earth Resources Skylark rockets surveyed successfully a vast area of Central Argentina on behalf of the Argentine government. This was the first operational use of camera-carrying Skylarks for a user-country, and the many colour and false-colour photographs taken synoptically of a circular area more than 375 nm (435 miles; 700 km) in diameter, from heights up to 130 nm (150 miles; 240 km) above the Earth, demonstrated Skylark's capability as a flexible and inexpensive survey tool for Earth resources studies.

Skylark is powered by a Raven main stage, with an optional Cuckoo or Goldfinch first stage or booster. These are all solid-propellant radial-burning rocket motors.

Five versions of Skylark give a wide range of altitude/payload performance. Typically, a Cuckoo-boosted Raven 6 (Skylark type 3) will lift a 330 lb (150 kg) payload to about 135 nm (155 miles; 250 km) altitude, while the combination of Raven 6 and Goldfinch (Skylark type 5) will lift a 520 lb (235 kg) payload to the same height.

A range of three-axis attitude control units is made by GEC-Elliott Electronics, using nitrogen gas-jets to point the payload with great accuracy at either the Sun, Moon or a star. The Sun-pointing ACU will acquire and complete its payload stabilisation in less than 30 seconds.

Stabilisation of the Skylark payload permits observations and experiments in solar spectroscopy UV and stellar UV, and solar and stellar X-ray photography. Results to date have included the discovery of a Nova-like strong variable X-ray source in the constellation Centaurus. Another notable achievement was the identification in 1971 of X-ray source GX3+1, accurately pinpointed by experiments in two Skylark rockets launched within seconds of this X-ray star's occlusion by the Moon.

Other systems available include a timer-initiated roll control unit, and a boost-phase spin system using small rocket thrusters and canted fins to provide roll rates up to 3Hz for improved aerodynamic stability. A yo-yo system is used to de-spin the payload before ACU acquisition begins.

A payload recovery system is available and is initiated at a height of about 2·2 nm (2·5 miles; 4 km), with a gun-released pilot chute which slows down the payload before the main 20 ft (6 m) canopy opens.

Since the last edition of *Jane's* went to press, Skylarks have been launched from ramps in the Argentine, Australia, Norway, Sweden, and by the Mobile Rocket Group of DFVLR, the German National Research and Development Organisation for Aeronautics and Space Flight, from the Spanish national range at El Arenosillo.

More extensive details of Skylark can be found in the 1972-73 *Jane's*.

DIMENSIONS:
Length:
nominal (Raven plus average payload) 30 ft (9·0 m)
with Cuckoo booster 32 ft (10·5 m)
with Goldfinch booster 35 ft (11·5 m)
Body diameter 17·25 in (43·8 cm)

LAUNCHING WEIGHTS:
Typical boosted Skylark 4,080 lb (1,850 kg)
Payload limits 175 lb (70 kg) to 680 lb (310 kg)

PERFORMANCE:
Payload to height:
Type 1 (Raven 8, unboosted) 220 lb (100 kg) to 92 nm (106 miles; 170 km)
Type 2 (Raven 8, Cuckoo boosted) 330 lb (150 kg) to 108 nm (125 miles; 200 km)
Type 3 (Raven 6, Cuckoo boosted) 475 lb (215 kg) to 108 nm (125 miles; 200 km)
Type 4 (Raven 8, Goldfinch boosted) 330 lb (150 kg) to 146 nm (168 miles; 270 km)
Type 5 (Raven 6, Goldfinch boosted) 550 lb (250 kg) to 130 nm (150 miles; 240 km)
Time above 54 nm (60 miles; 100 km):
Raven 8 4 minutes
Raven 8/Cuckoo 5 minutes
Raven 6/Goldfinch 6 minutes

BRISTOL AEROJET

BRISTOL AEROJET LTD

HEAD OFFICE:
Banwell, Weston-super-Mare, Somerset BS24 8PD

Telephone: Banwell (0934-82) 2251
Telex: 44259
OFFICERS: See "Aero-Engines" section

In addition to manufacturing rocket motors (see "Aero-Engines" section) Bristol Aerojet specialises in the design, manufacture and firing of research rockets for a wide variety of upper atmosphere investigations and Earth resources work.

The company's research rockets have been used by the British Meteorological Office and for British University experiments since 1964. They have also been used by similar organisations in Canada, Germany, Spain, Australia, Pakistan, Sweden and France. Some 900 of these rockets had been fired by early 1974.

The high performance of the Skua and Petrel rockets makes them suitable also for use as ballistic targets, both for development work and for service trials on weapon systems. A wide variety of potential threats can be represented by simple adjustment of the target performance, and the Petrel target has been proved on extensive trials.

BRISTOL AEROJET SKUA

This low-cost rocket lifts a nominal payload of 12 lb/500 cu in (5·5 kg/8·2 litres) to a height of 328,000 ft (100 km). It is available in three versions, of which performance details are given in the accompanying table. The original Mark 1 version is no longer in production.

A feature of Skua is its low dispersion area, achieved by the use of small boost rockets which give it a very high launch velocity. The number of boost rockets is variable to provide the required performance, and they are fitted in a recoverable carriage. The low-cost launch-tube can be mounted on a MAN or Nike type launcher, or on a ground or truck mounting.

Forward of the motor, the Skua can carry a wide variety of sondes, instruments, experiments, telemetry, etc, in the full-diameter instrument bay. Various ejection mechanisms can be fitted to expel the payload instruments at any predetermined time during the flight; a radar-reflective parachute can be ejected to lower the instruments slowly, and to provide a radar target determination of wind speed and height. A small 24-channel telemetry sender, working in the 432·5 to 450Hz band, can be fitted into the rocket nosecone section and can be ejected with the instruments.

Petrel and Skua rockets with boost carriages

BRISTOL AEROJET PETREL

This upper atmosphere research rocket is larger than Skua and lifts a nominal payload of 35 lb (16 kg) to a height of 500,000 ft (152 km). Two versions are available; the performance of each is shown in the accompanying table.

Petrel uses the same launch system as Skua and is similarly fitted with a boost carriage system, to give a high velocity during the first 650 ft (200 m) of flight and relative insensitivity to side winds, with a consequent low dispersion error.

Petrel, like Skua, has a full-diameter instrument bay forward of the propulsion motor, and is capable of accepting a wide variety of experiments and telemetry systems, including those used in the Skua, and magnetometers, barium cloud payloads, mass spectrometers and electron density probes.

BRISTOL AEROJET/INTA-300

This two-stage research rocket is being developed in collaboration with Instituto Nacional de Tecnica Aeroespacial Esteban Terrades of Spain. It is designed to lift a nominal payload of 77 lb (35 kg) to a height of 223 miles (360 km). Further details of performance are given in the accompanying table.

The INTA-300 rocket will use launchers already in general use and will have the high initial velocity/low dispersion feature which has already proved valuable on the Skua and Petrel.

Vehicle	Boost	Dia/length mm	Launch Weight kg	Nominal Thrust kg Boost/Flight	Payload kg	Apogee km	Dispersion km/m/sec Wind Error	Remarks
INTA-300	INTA-255	260 × 7,270	450	11,800/1,700	35-50	360-280	20-15	Available 1976
Petrel 2	3 Chicks	190 × 3,500	120	6,150/455	16-20	184-160	13·8-12·3	Uprated version of Petrel 1
Petrel 1	3 Chicks	190 × 3,340	114	6,150/455	16-20	145-130	10·2-9·3	Over 100 fired
Skua 4	4 Chicks	128 × 2,620	45	2,050/182	6-9	135-90	4·0-3·0	High precision version for firing from restricted ranges
Skua 3	1 Chick	128 × 2,420	45	2,050/182	5-8	95-70	9·3-7·1	Extended temperature limits 0°C–50°C
Skua 2	1 Chick	128 × 2,420	45	2,050/182	5-8	125-84	12·2-8·4	Over 200 fired

HSD

HAWKER SIDDELEY DYNAMICS LTD

HEADQUARTERS:
Manor Road, Hatfield, Herts

OFFICERS: See "Missiles" section

Hawker Siddeley Dynamics has undertaken many important space research programmes, including manufacture of the Miranda (X-4), largest and most complex civilian satellite yet developed in the UK. It is a member of the MESH international consortium and is prime contractor for the OTS satellite being manufactured by this group. It is also a member of the team of European manufacturers led by ERNO of Germany which is developing and producing the Spacelab for the US post-Apollo programme.

Under the terms of an agreement announced in February 1965, HSD and TRW Inc of Los Angeles, USA, exchange technical information on satellites and other spacecraft.

HSD's infra-red Linescan System Type 201 is fitted in the Canadair AN/USD-501 battlefield surveillance RPV. Similar systems are available for manned reconnaissance aircraft.

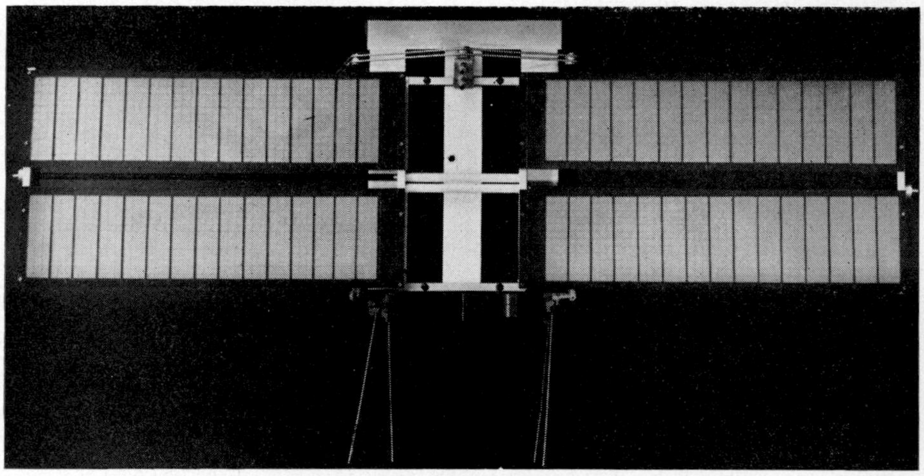

Full-scale model of Miranda (X-4) technology proving satellite

MIRANDA (X-4)

HSD was appointed prime contractor for the X-4 technology proving satellite, under a contract announced in October 1971. Subcontractors included Marconi Space and Defence Systems, Ferranti and Solartron. The contract was placed by the Ministry of Defence on behalf of the Department of Trade and Industry.

Largest and most complex civilian satellite yet developed in the UK, the X-4 was launched on 9 March 1974 by a Scout rocket from the Western Test Range, California, into a near-synchronous 434 nm (500 mile; 800 km) polar orbit, as Britain's second technology development satellite. Once established in orbit it was named Miranda.

The satellite weighs 206 lb (93·4 kg) and comprises a rectangular body, constructed largely of aluminium honeycomb sandwich, 33 in (83·5 cm) high by 26 in (66·5 cm) wide, flanked by two solar arrays giving an overall span of 8 ft 2½ in (250 cm).

Miranda carries five experiments, the most important of which is an attitude-control subsystem. This is designed to provide a control accuracy of better than three arc minutes, using only gas jets, to demonstrate the technology involved in the design and manufacture of this type of three-axes stabilised platform in small spacecraft. After the satellite acquired the Sun, the roll and yaw axes attitude reference information began to be supplied by a fine Sun-sensor, and pitch information by albedo (light intensity variation) detectors.

Three experiments concern the operation of sensors: an infra-red horizon sensor, to test the performance of components for a possible operational IR sensor; a low-cost single-axis Canopus star sensor; and an albedo horizon sensor, to demonstrate a basic sensing element for digitable albedo sensors.

The fifth experiment is designed to measure the degradation of silicon solar cells in orbit.

During operations the satellite is controlled by the Satellite Control Centre, Royal Aircraft Establishment, with assistance from NASA's Space Tracking and Data Acquisition Network (STADAN), operated by the Goddard Space Flight Center.

MSDS

MARCONI SPACE AND DEFENCE SYSTEMS LTD

HEAD OFFICE:
The Grove, Stanmore, Middlesex HA7 4LY
Telephone: (01) 954-2311
Telex: 22616

Marconi Space and Defence Systems, a member of GEC-Marconi Electronics, is prime contractor to the Ministry of Defence for Skynet II, the first operational military communications satellite to be built outside the USA or USSR. It is also prime contractor for the UK 5 scientific satellite, and is involved in a number of major European collaborative programmes.

As a member of the COSMOS consortium, it is providing the full attitude control system and other equipment for the Meteosat satellite. Under subcontract to Aérospatiale, it is responsible for attitude and orbit control systems on the Ariane launch vehicle. It is also prime contractor for the MAROTS portion of the OTS satellite project.

SKYNET II

Two Skynet II satellites were ordered from Marconi Space and Defence Systems, in Portsmouth, with the intention that they should take over gradually the expanding military communications traffic currently handled by Skynet I, a satellite built for the UK by Philco-Ford of the USA. Major subcontractor was Philco-Ford, which contributed a number of major components such as the mechanically de-spun aerial unit and the rocket motor which was designed to propel each satellite into its final geostationary orbit over the Indian Ocean.

The first Skynet II was lost on 19 January 1974, when the second stage of its Delta 2313 launch vehicle developed a steering fault soon after lift-off from the US Eastern Test Range. The second Skynet II, intended originally as a backup for the first, was expected to be launched in November 1974 and to have a lifetime of at least three years.

The Skynet II satellite is built in the form of a cylindrical drum, with solar cells covering the entire curved surface. It measures approximately 78 in (198 cm) long overall, with a diameter of 75 in (190 cm). The launch weight is about 960 lb (435 kg).

The satellite is intended to be launched into a highly elliptical orbit, after which transfer into synchronous orbit should be achieved by firing a solid-propellant apogee motor contained in the satellite itself, and mounted along the major axis of the cylinder. The complete satellite will be spin-stabilised at about 90 rpm from the time second-stage burning ceases. However, once in synchronous orbit, the communications antenna will be de-spun and controlled to point constantly at Earth.

Attitude control will be achieved by using hydrazine jets to adjust the attitude of the satellite, both before the apogee motor burn and subsequently for the life of the satellite. Control movements will be provided by a single pair of jets, located at the edge of the satellite and thrusting parallel to its axis, with another pair of jets mounted in the curved surface of the satellite and pointing radially out from the centre.

During the initial manoeuvres and until the final positioning of the satellite has been completed, control communications will be carried out through an omnidirectional aerial system consisting of an array of cavity-backed dipoles operating at S-band and mounted in a single band round the complete circumference of the satellite. Once the synchronous orbit has been achieved, and the satellite has been turned into the correct position relative to the Earth, a single horn aerial, mounted on the major axis of the satellite at the opposite end to the rocket motor, will be brought into use to provide the main communications function. The beam-width of this aerial is sufficient to cover the entire visible portion of the Earth's surface. Transmission power of Skynet II is 186W.

UK 5

Scheduled for launch by a US Scout vehicle, from Italy's San Marco launch station off the coast of Kenya, in October 1974, UK 5 is a scientific satellite carrying six experiments primarily intended to locate and measure the intensity and spectral characteristics of X-ray sources. One experiment will be designed and constructed by Imperial College, London, two by University College, London, two by Leicester University, and one by Goddard Space Flight Center. Four will be designed to point at, and measure, specific sources under the guidance of the ground control centre. The remaining two will be designed to search for new X-ray sources which can be subsequently examined by the fixed "pointing" experiments.

It is intended that the satellite should avoid the Van Allen radiation belts, and the circular orbit, inclined to the equator at approximately 2·9°, will be at a height of 310 miles (500 km). Weight of UK 5 is 298 lb (135 kg).

The satellite is in the form of a cylinder, with a diameter of approximately 38 in (96 cm), and a length of about 34 in (86 cm). Solar cells, mounted around the complete curved surface, will provide power during sunlight, with internal batteries to provide power when the satellite is in the Earth's shadow. The four pointing experiments are mounted in one end of the cylinder, and communications aerials are fitted at the other end. The survey experiments are mounted in the side of the cylinder, and will scan X-ray sources as the satellite rotates. The experiments will be switched off while the satellite is in the Earth's shadow during each orbit. This will save power from the batteries, and therefore increase the useful life of the system.

The satellite will be attitude-controlled, and the Sun and the illuminated area of the Earth, the albedo, will be used to determine attitude. Attitude control will be provided by propane gas jets, mounted round the base of the cylinder, which will be used to move the satellite to point at new sources in response to commands from the ground control. Spin stabilisation, at 10±2 rpm, will maintain the attitude of the satellite.

The complete attitude control package has been developed and supplied by Marconi Space and Defence Systems at Camberley, Surrey.

It is hoped to achieve a useful life of a year or more. The major factor governing this life is the supply of propane gas, without which the attitude cannot be controlled.

MAROTS

The MAROTS satellite is being designed to provide ship-to-shore communications links vastly superior to the present highly-congested conventional high-frequency circuits. For the first time, merchant ships in the Atlantic and Western Indian Oceans should be able to establish contact with the shore almost instantaneously.

MAROTS will use the basic structure and control system which are being developed for OTS (see MESH entry in this section). On this will be mounted the complete communications package which is being developed by Marconi Space and Defence Systems.

The launch of MAROTS is scheduled for the Autumn of 1977, when it will be put into a geostationary orbit over the Atlantic.

Marconi is also to study and define the basic parameters of the shipborne and shore-based terminals. The former are to be made as simple as possible, and to this end MAROTS will be equipped with a high-efficiency "shaped beam" antenna coupled with a transistorised L-band power amplifier. Ships will use the L-Band frequencies to communicate to and from the satellite. As shore terminals will be able to use more sophisticated equipment, the shore-to-satellite frequency will be in the 14GHz band while satellite-to-shore communication will use the 11GHz band.

A minimum three-year life span is intended for MAROTS, and success in this experimental and pre-operational phase being undertaken by ESRO would enable the Inter-Governmental Maritime Consultative Organisation (IMCO) to envisage a worldwide maritime satellite communications system.

THE UNITED STATES OF AMERICA

ALRC

AEROJET LIQUID ROCKET COMPANY

ADDRESS:
Highway 50 and Aerojet Road, PO Box 13222, Sacramento, California 95813
Telephone: (916) 355-1000
PRESIDENT: J. L. Heckel
DIRECTOR OF COMMUNICATIONS:
Thomas E. Ross

This operating company of Aerojet-General Corporation is responsible for production of the Aerobee series of upper atmosphere research rockets. These boosted single-stage vehicles are used by all the US services and by civilian and government organisations in connection with missile and satellite programmes.

Aerobee vehicles are available with a number of accessory subsystems. A fully flight-tested attitude control system, which utilises residual pressurisation gas, can be used for vehicle de-spin, orientation and up to ten manoeuvres after sustainer burnout. A yo-yo de-spin system is also available and provides a simple and effective means for reducing spin rate. Fully-proven payload recovery systems are available for use over land or water.

Also in production, to supplement some versions of Aerobee, is a family of space-probe vehicles known as Astrobees. They include two research vehicles known as Astrobee D and F, utilising a newly-developed high-energy long-burning solid propellant.

AEROBEE 150 (AEROBEE-HI)

Structural and power plant details of this boosted single-stage liquid-propellant research rocket can be found in the 1970-71 *Jane's*.

PAYLOAD: 120-400 lb (54-181 kg) in 15 in (38 cm) diameter, 87 in (221 cm) ogive, plus 60 in (152 cm) maximum cylindrical extension.

DIMENSIONS:
Length 30 ft 11 in (9·41 m)
Body diameter 1 ft 3 in (0·38 m)

WEIGHT:
Firing weight, with booster, less payload 1,908 lb (865 kg)

PERFORMANCE:
Ceiling with 125 lb (56·7 kg) payload 161·5 nm (186 miles; 300 km)
Max acceleration 11·1*g*

AEROBEE 170

This higher-performance version of the Aerobee 150 utilises a Nike-E5 solid-propellant motor as a booster. It made a successful first flight on 26 October 1968, carrying a 263 lb (119 kg) stellar spectra experiment payload to a height of 139 nm (160 miles; 257 km). The rocket was fitted with yo-yo de-spin, attitude control and recovery systems.

PAYLOAD COMPARTMENT: Either a 5:1 ogive or 3:1 cone may be used, with up to 60 in (152 cm) of cylindrical section.

DIMENSIONS:
Length with booster 41 ft 0 in (12·47 m)
Body diameter 1 ft 3 in (0·38 m)

WEIGHT:
Firing weight, with booster 3,010 lb (1,370 kg)

PERFORMANCE (with 250 lb; 113 kg payload):
Speed at burnout 6,489 ft (1,975 m)/sec
Peak altitude 144 nm (166 miles; 267 km)

AEROBEE 200

The improved propellant used in this version extends the burn time of the sustainer motor to 59 seconds.

PERFORMANCE (with 250 lb; 113 kg payload):
Peak altitude 171 nm (197 miles; 317 km)

AEROBEE 300 (SPAEROBEE)

Structural details of this two-stage boosted liquid-propellant research rocket can be found in the 1970-71 *Jane's*. A developed version, for NASA, is the Aerobee 300A which differs in having four fins instead of three.

PAYLOAD: Payload assembly, fabricated of aluminium, consists of a 10° half-angle nose-cone extending back to a cylinder, and was designed to provide 1 cu ft (0·028 m³) of usable volume for a nominal 50 lb (22·7 kg) payload. Nett payload capabilities are 25-120 lb (11·3-59·5 kg).

DIMENSIONS:
Overall length, with booster 34 ft 7 in (10·54 m)
Body diameter, sustainer and booster 1 ft 3 in (0·38 m)
Body diameter, second-stage assembly 8 in (0·2 m)

WEIGHT:
Gross weight, with booster, less payload 2,070 lb (939 kg)

PERFORMANCE:
Ceiling with 50 lb (22·7 kg) payload 245 nm (282 miles; 454 km)
Max acceleration 63·8*g*

AEROBEE 350

Structural and power plant details of this boosted single-stage liquid-propellant sounding rocket can be found in the 1970-71 *Jane's*.

DIMENSIONS:
Length with booster 50 ft 4 in (15·34 m)
Body diameter 1 ft 10 in (0·56 m)

WEIGHT:
Launching weight, with booster 6,700 lb (3,040 kg)

PERFORMANCE:
Speed at burnout Mach 9·0
Max ceiling 260 nm (300 miles; 480 km)
Ceiling with 500 lb (227 kg) payload 178 nm (205 miles; 330 km)

ASTROBEE 250

The Astrobee 250 is a single-stage solid-propellant vehicle boosted by two Thiokol 1·5KS-35,000 Recruits, which are mounted on the sides of the main motor.

The payload compartment has a diameter of 24·31 in (61·79 cm) and volume of 40 cu ft (1·13 m³), accommodating a payload of 400-1,500 lb (182-682 kg).

DIMENSION:
Length 34 ft 2 in (10·41 m)

WEIGHT (less payload):
Firing weight, with boosters 10,100 lb (4,580 kg)

PERFORMANCE:
Ceiling with max payload 111 nm (128 miles; 206 km)
Ceiling with min payload 176 nm (203 miles; 326 km)
Max acceleration 15*g*

ASTROBEE 1500

Largest in the current series of Astrobees, the Astrobee 1500 is a two-stage solid-propellant rocket, with two Thiokol 1·5KS-35,000 Recruits mounted on the sides of the first stage as boosters.

The payload compartment has a diameter of 20 in (51 cm) and volume of 3·67 cu ft (0·104 m³) accommodating a payload of 50-300 lb (22-136 kg).

After first-stage burnout the second stage is spin-stabilised prior to separation by four MARC 4EA1 (·5KS-180) spin motors. The second-stage casing and payload do not separate after burnout. A yo-yo de-spin unit is available for payloads requiring low spin rates.

DIMENSION:
Length, with boosters 34 ft 2 in (10·41 m)

WEIGHT (less payload):
Firing weight, with boosters 11,541 lb (5,240 kg)

PERFORMANCE (85° launch angle):
Ceiling with 300 lb (136 kg) payload 699 nm (805 miles; 1,300 km)
Ceiling with 50 lb (22 kg) payload 1,597 nm (1,840 miles; 2,970 km)
Max acceleration 41·4*g*

ASTROBEE D and F

Astrobee D and F are the first of a family of research vehicles which utilise a newly developed high-energy long-burning solid propellant known as Hydroxyl Terminated Polybutadiene (HTPB). This allows optimum delivery of impulse while also providing a more moderate acceleration environment for the scientific payload.

Following a completely successful flight test programme, Astrobee D was put into operational use by NASA and AFCRL for meteorological and D region physics experiments.

Astrobee F completed its static testing and flight tests in 1972, and production models were scheduled to enter the NASA inventory in 1974.

During this same year, a Nike-boosted version of Astrobee F was expected to be flown.

DIMENSIONS:

Length overall:	
Astrobee D	11 ft 8 in (3·56 m)
Astrobee F	22 ft 6 in (6·86 m)
Body diameter:	
Astrobee D	6 in (15 cm)
Astrobee F	15 in (28 cm)

LAUNCHING WEIGHT:

Astrobee D (no payload)	193 lb (88 kg)
Astrobee F	2,670 lb (1,210 kg)

PERFORMANCE (Astrobee F data estimated):

Ceiling:

Astrobee D with 10 lb (4·5 kg) payload 78 nm (90 miles; 145 km)

Astrobee F with 250 lb (114 kg) payload 192 nm (221 miles; 356 km)

SUPER CHIEF

The Super Chief is a rail-launched boosted solid-propellant stabilised vehicle for high-altitude experimentation. The booster is powered by a Talos motor, and there are four fixed fins on both the booster and sustainer.

Two versions are available, as follows:

Super Chief I. With Sergeant sustainer motor. Able to carry a 1,000 lb (454 kg) payload, contained within an 80 in (2·03 m) long extension, to a height in excess of 108 nm (125 miles; 201 km).

Super Chief II. With Castor sustainer motor. Able to carry an 1,100 lb (500 kg) payload to a height in excess of 184 nm (212 miles; 341 km). A 93 in (2·36 m) long nosecone may be used for the payload.

DIMENSIONS:

Length overall	44 ft 0 in (13·41 m)
Body diameter	2 ft 7 in (0·79 m)

WEIGHT:

Launching weight	13,284 lb (6,026 kg)

NIRO

Niro is a two-stage solid-propellant vehicle for small to medium payloads (40-180 lb; 18-82 kg), which it can carry to the "F" region of the ionosphere. It was developed to meet a USAF requirement for a small and economical vehicle which could provide roll control and good structural stability.

Standard diameter (7·75 in) and oversize (9 in) payloads have been flown successfully. Usable volume can be varied up to 4 cu ft (0·113 m^3). Both land and water recovery systems are available.

DIMENSIONS:

Length overall, without payload 21 ft 5 in (6·5 m)

Body diameter:	
first stage	16·5 in (42 cm)
second stage	7·75 in (20 cm)

WEIGHT (less payload):

Launching weight	1,591 lb (723 kg)

PERFORMANCE (85° launch angle):

Ceiling with 40 lb (18 kg) payload 154 nm (178 miles; 287 km)

Ceiling with 180 lb (82 kg) payload 61 nm (70 miles; 113 km)

BOEING

THE BOEING COMPANY

HEAD OFFICE AND WORKS:
Seattle, Washington 98124

Boeing Aerospace Company

OFFICERS: See "Aircraft" section

Details of the weapon systems developed and produced by Boeing are given in the "Missiles" section. Its current research and space products are described and illustrated below.

BURNER II

Burner II is a low-cost guided solid-propellant upper-stage booster which was developed by Boeing's Spacecraft Branch, at Seattle, under a firm fixed-price contract awarded by the Space Systems Division of the Air Force Systems Command. The initial contract covered one ground test and three flight vehicles. Eleven flight vehicles were subsequently ordered and delivered.

Burner II utilises a Thiokol TE-M-364-2 rocket motor of the kind developed for the Surveyor spacecraft, with 1,440 lb (653 kg) of propellant, a Honeywell guidance system essentially similar to that used on the NASA Scout launch vehicle, and Walter Kidde reaction control system components as used on the Scout and other vehicles. The complete package is suitable for mating to the range of current standard launch vehicles, from Thor to Titan III, and is intended to fill the payload gap between the small Scout and the more complex liquid upper stages. It is able to inject small-to-medium payloads into orbit and then orientate them precisely.

In its first launching, on 15 September 1966, as the upper stage of a Thor vehicle, Burner II put into orbit a secret USAF satellite. By the end of 1973, the Thor/Burner II combination had achieved 14 successful launches in 14 attempts.

A developed version of Burner II with a larger motor is being considered in combination with Titan III/Centaur as booster for outer planet exploration missions.

DIMENSIONS:

Length overall	5 ft 8 in (1·73 m)
Diameter	5 ft 5 in (1·65 m)

Burner II (*foreground*) and Burner IIA guided solid-propellant upper-stage boosters

BURNER IIA

In August 1969 the USAF's Space and Missile Systems Organisation announced selection of Boeing to develop and manufacture a two-stage version of the Burner II upper-stage booster. The modified upper stage is known as Burner IIA.

A second-stage solid-propellant Thiokol TE-M-442 motor, developing 8,800 lb (3,992 kg) st and with 524 lb (238 kg) of propellant, has been added to the Burner II's 10,000 lb (4,536 kg) st first stage. Burner II subsystems, including guidance and flight control, reaction control and electrical and communication subsystems, are mounted on the new stage.

Burner IIA can be utilised with virtually all of the USAF's "family" of space boosters, including Thor, Atlas and Titan III. When teamed with an Atlas it is able to place a satellite in synchronous equatorial orbit. The new stage can also be utilised on missions requiring high-velocity Earth escape speeds.

Boeing's contract called for the manufacture and delivery of six Burner IIAs and one ground test unit, with delivery beginning in June 1970.

MARINER 10 (VENUS/MERCURY) SPACECRAFT

The Boeing Company designed and built this spacecraft for NASA, under whose entry it is described.

CELESCO

CELESCO INDUSTRIES INC

ADDRESS: Costa Mesa, California 92626

This company now markets the range of sounding rockets and research vehicles listed under the Susquehanna Corporation entry in the 1972-73 *Jane's*.

ARGO B-13 NIKE-APACHE

This two-stage rocket, like its predecessor the Nike-Cajun, is used worldwide for scientific research in the ionosphere. As an example of the vehicle's versatility, it has been adapted successfully as a ballistic target for tactical surface-to-air missile development. The solid-propellant motors consist of a Nike M-5 first stage and Apache TE307 second stage.

The B-13 Nike-Apache is designed to carry a payload of approximately 60 lb (27 kg), which it will lift to a height of 135 nm (155 miles; 250 km).

ARGO D-4 JAVELIN

The Argo D-4 is a research vehicle which is able to carry an instrument payload of 50 lb (22·7 kg) to a height of 521 nm (600 miles; 965 km). It is a four-stage vehicle, comprising an Honest John M6, followed by two Nike-Ajax M5 boosters and a final stage designed by the Allegany Ballistic Laboratory and designated X-248. With a payload of 110 lb (50 kg) gross, 62 lb (28 kg) nett experiment, a speed of about Mach 13 can be attained.

Argo D-4 is used by NASA, the USAF and other customers.

DIMENSIONS:

Length overall	48 ft 8 in (14·83 m)
Max body diameter	1 ft 10·8 in (0·58 m)

WEIGHT:

Launching weight	7,400 lb (3,355 kg)

SWIK MOD A, B, C & D

The basic SWIK vehicle (MOD A) is a two-stage solid-propellant rocket composed of an XM33-E8 Castor, assisted by two auxiliary XM-19 Recruits, as the first stage and an X-254 Antares second stage.

The SWIK MOD B uses the same first stage, but the X-254 is replaced with the X-259.

The SWIK MOD C & D are also two-stage solid-propellant rockets, each with a TX-354 Castor II, assisted by two auxiliary XM-19 Recruits, as the first stage. An X-254 is used as the second stage of the MOD C, with the X-259 used as the second stage in the MOD D configuration.

All SWIK vehicles follow a ballistic trajectory and can carry nett payloads of 100 lb (45 kg) to an altitude in excess of 1,000 nm (1,150 miles; 1,850 km) or 500 lb (225 kg) nett payload to an altitude in excess of 700 nm (805 miles; 1,295 km).

DIMENSIONS:

Length overall	35 ft 8 in (10·86 m)
Max body diameter	2 ft 7 in (0·79 m)

WEIGHT:

Launching weight	12,824 lb (5,817 kg)

TRAILBLAZER II

Trailblazer II is a four-stage solid-propellant re-entry test vehicle. Two stages are fired upward, two stages downward to achieve a re-entry velocity of 22,000 ft/sec with a 20 lb (9 kg) net payload.

DIMENSIONS:

Length overall	50 ft 0 in (15·24 m)
Max body diameter	2 ft 7 in (0·79 m)

WEIGHT:

Launching weight	13,324 lb (6,044 kg)

ATHENA

Athena has been used to impact experimental re-entry vehicle payloads on the White Sands Missile Range under the advanced ballistic re-entry systems (ABRES) programme. It is being launched currently at Wallops Island, on behalf of the Defense Nuclear Agency.

Work on the Athena project began in 1962, under a USAF contract. Technical acceptance was received in December 1963 and the first launch was made on 10 February 1964. By the end of 1971, a total of 132 launchings had been made, with further launches planned in the period to the end of 1975.

Depending on the requirement, Athena can have a three- or four-stage configuration, with payload capacity ranging from 50 lb to 250 lb (23-113 kg). It utilises standard solid-propellant rocket motors, including the Thiokol Castor, Thiokol Recruit, Hercules X-259, Thiokol 261 and 23KS11,000. Cruciform fins, indexed in line, are fitted to the first and second stages. Size of the payload compartment is 85 in long by 22 in in diameter (216 cm × 56 cm).

Initial Athena launcher offset is adjusted as directed by the output of a ground-based meteorological computer loop. The inputs to this loop are vehicle dynamic characteristics and measured wind profiles to 200,000 ft (61,000 m). The vehicle s spin-stabilised during ascent boost. Ground ;ommands, based upon radar-derived trajectory lispersion data, are generated by a ground-based omputer and adjust the pre-set re-entry angle esulting from the control system manoeuvre. The vehicle is re-spun to provide stability during e-entry boost.

Midcourse attitude correction is provided by a Ioneywell DHG 138A attitude controller mploying two two-degree-of-freedom attitude ;yros in a COG orientation.

The velocity package is fired after Athena eaches its apogee of either 850,000 ft (259,000 m) or high-angle re-entry (IRBM) simulation or 00,000 ft (182,900 m) for lower-angle (ICBM) imulation.

)IMENSIONS:
Length overall 51 ft 8 in (15·74 m)
Body diameter, second stage 2 ft 7 in (0·79 m)
VEIGHT:
Max launching weight 16,000 lb (7,260 kg)
'ERFORMANCE:
Max speed at re-entry test altitude (nominal) 23,000 ft (7,010 m)/sec
Range (based on current range use) 421 nm (485 miles; 780 km)

ATHENA H

This new and much-enlarged version of the thena re-entry research vehicle became available or use in 1971. It is large enough to carry a ıll-scale military re-entry body if required, s max payload being about 1,000 lb (455 kg).

Athena H is available in both two-stage nd three-stage configurations, comprising a ooster stage and single-stage or two-stage elocity package. After booster burnout, it ill coast to a peak altitude of nearly 1,000,000 (305,000 m). During this phase, the velocity ackage will be re-orientated and re-ignited at the ltitude calculated to produce the desired re-entry ngle.

The booster can consist of either an Algol IIB r Castor IV solid-propellant motor and four ecruits. The velocity packages can be powered y either a single X259 motor or a 23KS11000 us a TX261 or X259 motor. A Thiokol M58 used as the spin motor and the payload is nclosed by clamshell fairings instead of being ccelerated out of its shielding as in the earlier ersions of Athena. Payload space is 100 in (254 cm) long in the three-stage model, and 135 in (343 cm) long in the two-stage model, with a diameter of 27 in (68·5 cm).

Athena H is currently launched from Wake Island on behalf of the US Army Advanced Ballistic Missile Defense Agency.

DIMENSION:
Length overall 60 ft 9 in (18 52 m)
WEIGHT (approx):
Max launching weight 32,000 lb (14,515 kg)
PERFORMANCE (estimated):
Max speed at re-entry test altitude:
100 lb (45 kg) payload 25,000 ft (7,620 m)/sec
200 lb (90 kg) payload 23,500 ft (7,160 m)/sec

Athena re-entry research vehicle

:HRYSLER

HRYSLER CORPORATION

EAD OFFICE:
341, Massachusetts Avenue, Highland Park, Michigan

efense-Space Group

EFENSE DIVISION:
PO Box 757, Detroit, Michigan 48231
elephone: (313) 268-7400

UNTSVILLE DIVISION:
102 Wynn Drive, Huntsville, Alabama 35805
elephone: (205) 895-1200

SPACE DIVISION:
PO Box 29200, New Orleans, Louisiana 70129
Telephone: (504) 255-2195

GENERAL MANAGER: V. J. Vehko

DIRECTOR OF MARKETING: P. C. Duffy

MANAGER, PUBLIC RELATIONS: R. B. Heath

Space Division, formed in 1962 to produce the Saturn I first stage, built two S-1 boosters and subsequently received contracts for 14 lighter and more powerful S-1B boosters. These served as first stages for the two-stage Saturns which orbited a variety of satellites and spacecraft, including the Apollo 7 hardware qualification flight in October 1968, and which have continued to find applications in the Skylab and Apollo-Soyuz Test Project programmes.

S-1B (SATURN 1B FIRST STAGE)

The initial type of S-1B booster was 80 ft 2¼ in (24·44 m) long and 21 ft 5 in (6·52 m) in diameter, with an empty weight of 93,000 lb (42,200 kg). Later S-1Bs have been reduced in weight to about 84,000 lb (38,100 kg). Each is powered by eight uprated Rocketdyne H-1 engines, giving a total of 1,640,000 lb (743,900 kg) st in current Saturn 1B launch vehicles.

AIRCHILD INDUSTRIES

AIRCHILD INDUSTRIES, INC

XECUTIVE OFFICE:
Germantown, Maryland 20767

FFICERS AND DIVISIONS:
See "Aircraft" section

Fairchild Space and Electronics Company was ime contractor for ATS-6, NASA's second-neration Applications Technology Satellite.

ATS-6

The most complex, versatile and powerful mmunications satellite yet built, ATS-6 (ATS-, the sixth of NASA's Applications Technology tellite series, was launched into a 19,296-,313 nm (22,220-22,240 mile; 35,760-35,792 n) near-synchronous orbit on 30 May 1974, a Titan IIIC from the Eastern Test Range, pe Kennedy.

Weighing 3,090 lb (1,402 kg), the spacecraft is ft (8 m) high. It consists basically of a ctangular Earth Viewing Module (EVM), using controls and Earth-orientated experi-ents, connected by a tubular support structure a 30 ft (9 m) diameter deployable reflector tenna. Two arms, each supporting a semi-lindrical solar array, extend from the hub that pports the antenna. Mounted on top of the b is an Environmental Measuring Experiments ME) package. Overall width of the satellite the solar array is about 52 ft (16 m).

The spacecraft embodies several major technology innovations for communications satellites, including a passive thermal control system, the use of graphite composite materials, an offset pointing capability and improved attitude control features.

Heart of the spacecraft is the EVM. Containing as it does high-power electronic units capable of operating in many hundreds of modes, it requires sophisticated cooling to prevent overheating. This is provided by a passive thermal control system, consisting of thermal louvres, heat pipes and highly efficient insulation. The louvres, mounted in the "north" and "south" faces of the EVM, open and close as required, to dispel or retain heat and so maintain a temperature within 15 to 20°C.

Located initially over the Galapagos Islands, the satellite, in conjunction with ATS-1 and ATS-2, will be used in a Health Education Telecommunications experiment covering remote and poorly served rural areas in the Appalachian and Rocky Mountain States, and the States of Washington and Alaska. The experiment is intended to test the feasibility of remote medical consultation and diagnosis.

In July 1975 it is planned to reposition the satellite over Lake Victoria in Kenya, East Africa, from where it will be used by the Indian Government to conduct its Satellite Instructional Television Experiment, involving the broadcasting of programmes dealing with agriculture, family planning, hygiene and occupational training. While in this position, the satellite will also be used to track and relay data from the docked Apollo-Soyuz Test Project spacecraft.

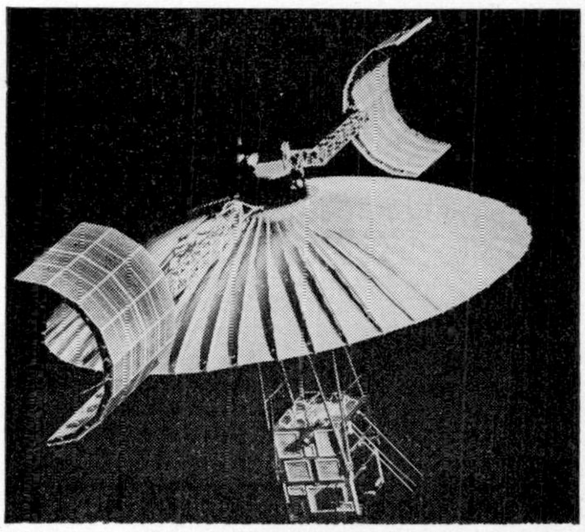

Model of ATS-6 applications technology satellite

The satellite is equipped to perform 20 other experiments, including evaluation of a high-resolution radiometer for meteorological work, and of a caesium-ion-thruster attitude stabilisation system; and investigations of the radiation environment at synchronous altitude, and of the phenomenon of mutual interference between spacecraft and ground communications in the 6GHz band.

ENERAL DYNAMICS

NERAL DYNAMICS CORPORATION

AD OFFICE:
Pierre Laclede Center, St Louis, Missouri 63105

nvair Aerospace Division

an Diego, California 92138

FICERS: See "Aircraft" section

Under a 1970 reorganisation, the Convair Aerospace Division was formed, to include the former Convair and Fort Worth divisions of General Dynamics Corporation.

The Convair Aerospace Division, San Diego operation, continues to devote its major efforts to the development and production of Atlas and Centaur space launch vehicles. The company is also pursuing business opportunities associated with the NASA Space Shuttle programme.

ATLAS E and F

Atlas E and F series rockets were formerly ICBMs deployed at Strategic Air Command bases as part of the US strategic missile force. Phase-out of the Atlas ICBM force in 1965 made them available for conversion into launch vehicles. The series E and F vehicles are essentially identical, the primary difference being in their method of operational deployment.

The missiles are stored at Norton AFB, California, until they enter the refurbishment and launch programme. Refurbishment from missile to launch vehicle is now undertaken by Convair Aerospace at Vandenberg AFB, California, utilising some of the same personnel who conduct the launchings. This on-site activity was made possible by a reduction in planned launch rates, and has led to a substantial reduction in the overall "launched cost" of each vehicle.

Forty-seven Atlas E and F missiles remained available to be launched on 1 January 1973. Of these, 12 were then assigned to missions.

Atlas E and F launch vehicles are used for both orbital and sub-orbital missions, and have been integrated with a variety of upper stages and payload delivery systems. The addition of a launch site in South Vandenberg has substantially increased polar orbit capability, previously accomplished by launching westerly and then "doglegging" south during powered flight. Sub-orbital flights are launched normally toward the Kwajalein Missile Range in the Pacific Ocean. Such launches continue to be of particular value in experiments conducted by the USAF Space and Missile Systems Organization and the US Army Advanced Ballistic Missile Defense Agency.

The vehicle descriptions of Atlas E and F are generally similar to that of the Atlas SLV, described separately.

DIMENSIONS:
- Length overall without payload: 71 ft 3 in (21·72 m)
- Body diameter: 10 ft 0 in (3·05 m)

WEIGHTS:
- Launching weight:
  - Atlas E: 270,000 lb (122,470 kg)
  - Atlas F: 269,000 lb (122,000 kg)

PERFORMANCE:
- Ballistic:
  - Range with 6,000 lb (2,720 kg) payload: 5,000 nm (5,750 miles; 9,265 km)
- Orbital (Atlas alone):
  - 2,000 lb (907 kg) payload in 100 nm (115 mile; 185 km) Earth polar orbit
- Orbital (with upper stages):
  - Atlas E or F with upper stages such as OV1 or Burner II can insert varying number of payloads into various orbits: eg Atlas 107F, with three OV1s, inserted 27 separate experiments into four different orbits on the same launch

ATLAS SLV

The Atlas Standardised Launch Vehicle (SLV) had its inception in Atlas (above), the United States' first intercontinental ballistic missile (ICBM). Continuous technological improvements have been embodied in the SLV series, of which two versions are currently in service:

SLV-3A, for use with Agena or OV1 upper stages.

SLV-3D, for use with the Centaur D-1A high-energy upper stage.

These vehicles differ from their immediate predecessor, the SLV-3, mainly in increased tank length and rocket engine thrust.

Atlas is a "stage-and-a-half" vehicle, consisting of side booster and central sustainer sections. The sustainer section includes the propellant tanks and a single rocket engine. The booster engines receive fuel from the sustainer tanks and are jettisoned midway into flight.

The engine system is the Rocketdyne MA-5, using liquid oxygen and RP-1 propellants. Total thrust developed is 431,040 lb (195,517 kg; 1,917,526 Newtons), including 370,000 lb (167,830 kg; 1,646,000 Newtons) total from the two boosters, 60,000 lb (27,215 kg; 266,900 Newtons) from the sustainer, and 1,040 lb (472 kg; 4,626 Newtons) total axial thrust from the two vernier rockets. All engines are ignited at lift-off.

Propellant tanks are pressurised and made of thin-wall stainless steel, with an insulated intermediate bulkhead separating the oxidiser and fuel. One noticeable difference between the SLV-3D and the SLV-3A is in the forward tank structure. For the SLV-3D the tank is a constant 10 ft (3·05 m) diameter up to the adapter for the upper stage. The forward tank of the SLV-3A tapers to a 5 ft 10 in (1·78 m) diameter at the adapter attach ring. Total propellants carried by the SLV-3D weigh 268,040 lb (121,582 kg); those of the SLV-3A weigh 295,540 lb (134,055 kg).

Most of the electronic command and control functions for the SLV-3D are generated by its Centaur D-1A upper-stage astrionics system. The SLV-3A has its own systems, independent of the upper stage, including radio guidance.

By the beginning of 1973, Atlas had been the booster for 153 space launches, with many space "firsts" to its credit. The world's first communications satellite was launched by Atlas in 1958, as were the first US manned orbital flights (Mercury), starting in 1962. All US planetary spacecraft have been launched by Atlas. In 1972 Pioneer 10 was started on its flight path to Jupiter with the highest velocity ever imparted to a spacecraft. Launch vehicle was an Atlas/Centaur with an additional TE-M-364-4 solid-propellant rocket motor.

By January 1973 Atlas had amassed a total of 404 space and ballistic launches. Over a 5½-year

Atlas-Centaur AC-29, launch vehicle for an Intelsat IV communications satellite

period, it had an unbroken succession of 53 successful space launches.

DIMENSIONS:
- Diameter: 10 ft 0 in (3·05 m)
- Length:
  - SLV-3A: 71 ft 0 in (21·6 m)
  - SLV-3A/Agena: 118 ft 0 in (36·0 m)
  - SLV-3D: 61 ft 0 in (18·6 m)
  - SLV-3D/Centaur: 131 ft 0 in (39·9 m)

PERFORMANCE:
- Atlas/Centaur: See Centaur entry
- Atlas SLV-3A/Agena:
  - 8,800 lb (3,992 kg) into 100 nm (115 mile; 185 km) circular orbit
  - 2,920 lb (1,325 kg) into synchronous transfer orbit
- Atlas/OV1: See OV1 entry

CENTAUR

Centaur was the first US high-energy upper stage and the first to utilise liquid hydrogen as a propellant. The latest version, Centaur D-1, is combined with either the Atlas SLV-3D or the Titan IIIE, providing for a wide range of applications and capability.

The original contracts for Centaur were awarded by the Advanced Research Projects Agency (ARPA) in 1958. The programme was transferred from ARPA to NASA in 1959. NASA's Lewis Research Center provides overall management and integration of the Centaur programme.

The 21st operational launch of Atlas/Centaur, and the final launch of the Centaur D series, occurred in August 1972 with the successful launch of an Orbiting Astronomical Observatory. Other payloads launched successfully by Atlas/Centaur include the Surveyor series of seven lunar spacecraft, Applications Technology Satellite, Mariner Mars 69 and 71, four Intelsat IV communications satellites and Pioneer F.

Atlas-Agena space launch vehicle

In early 1973, Atlas/Centaur D-1A had been assigned launch missions extending into 1976. They included four more Intelsat IVs, Pioneer G, Mariner Venus/Mercury 73 and the US Navy's Fleet Satellite Communications satellites.

The proving flight of Titan IIIE/Centaur D-1T was scheduled to take place in 1974. This launch vehicle will be employed for the HELIOS solar probes, the Viking Mars orbiter/landers and the 1977 Mariner Jupiter/Saturn missions.

Centaur D-1 retains the same propulsion and structural features as its predecessor, Centaur D, with stainless steel pressurised tanks and two 15,000 lb (6,810 kg; 66,723 Newtons) st Pratt & Whitney RL10A liquid oxygen/liquid hydrogen rocket engines. Specific impulse with this propellant combination is 444 sec, the highest of any current space vehicle. Total propellants carried weigh 30,750 lb (13,950 kg). Attitude control is achieved by gimballing the two main engines or by clusters of small hydrogen peroxide rocket motors.

Several of the astrionics components have been redesigned or repackaged for Centaur D-1. The most significant addition is a new 16,000 word capacity Teledyne digital computer. Navigation, guidance, vehicle stability, tank pressurisation,

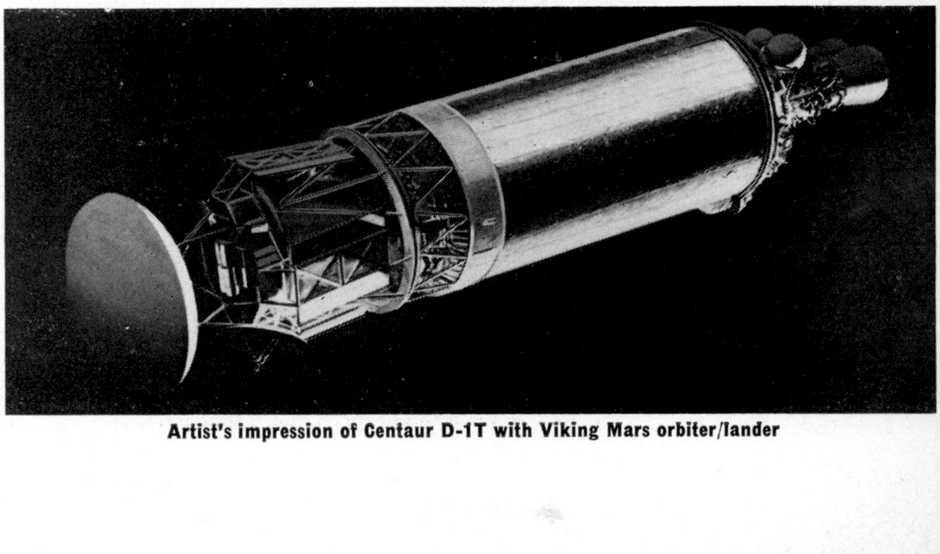

Artist's impression of Centaur D-1T with Viking Mars orbiter/lander

propellant management, telemetry formats and transmission, and event initiation are all controlled by the computer. Guidance, control and sequencing for the Atlas booster are provided by the Centaur D-1A astrionics system. The Centaur D-1T also provides guidance for its Titan booster.

Payloads are carried on adapters which mount to the forward end of the Centaur. A 10 ft (3·05 m) diameter fairing protects payloads for Centaur D-1A. For Titan/Centaur a 14 ft (4·27 m) shroud encloses both the payload and the Centaur D-1T.

DIMENSIONS:

Centaur length	30 ft 0 in (9·14 m)
Centaur diameter	10 ft 0 in (3·05 m)
Atlas/Centaur length	131 ft 0 in (39·9 m)

PERFORMANCE:

Atlas/Centaur:
- 11,200 lb (5,080 kg) into 100 nm (115 mile; 185 km) circular orbit
- 4,000 lb (1,814 kg) into synchronous transfer orbit
- 1,300 lb (590 kg) to near planet

Titan/Centaur:
- 34,000 lb (15,400 kg) into 100 nm (115 mile; 185 km) circular orbit
- 7,400 lb (3,357 kg) into synchronous equatorial orbit
- 8,200 lb (3,720 kg) to near planet

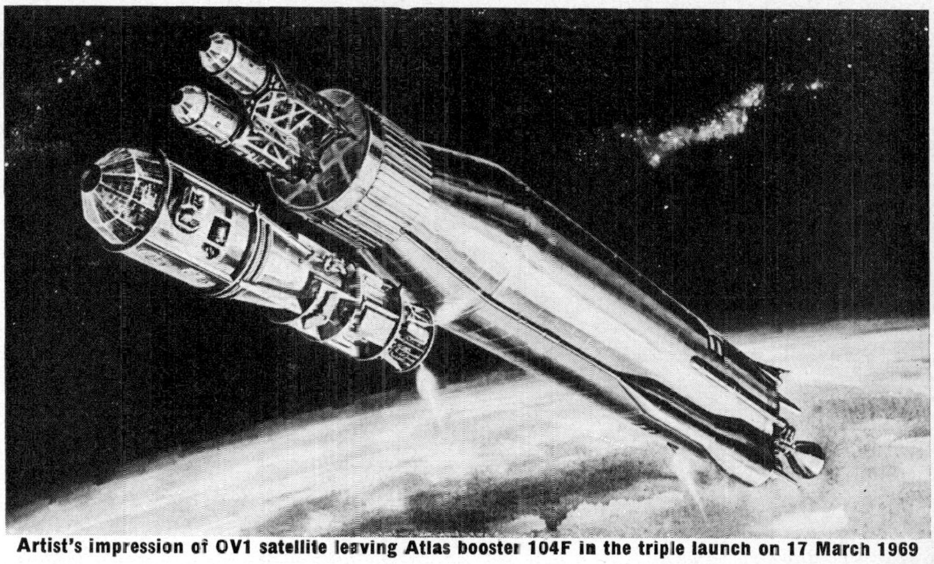

Artist's impression of OV1 satellite leaving Atlas booster 104F in the triple launch on 17 March 1969

ORBITAL VEHICLE ONE (OV1)

The OV1 system, consisting of a separable fairing, injection stage and satellite, is built for the USAF (SAMSO) by the Convair Aerospace Division. Its purpose is to provide versatile and economical space platforms for scientific and technological experiments. The basic configuration of each satellite consists of a cylindrical experiment compartment, 32 in (81·3 cm) long by 27 in (68·5 cm) in diameter, with a faceted solar array attached to each end of the cylinder, making the overall length 56 in (142·2 cm). The electronic support systems (command control, telemetry and power conditioning) are mounted under the solar array domes.

Although the satellite may be launched on other vehicles, the primary launch configuration has been an Atlas rocket with one, two or three OV1s mounted in a common fairing on the nose. Each satellite has a propulsion stage, with a programmer, autopilot and solid-propellant motor to place it in the desired orbit. Once in orbit the satellite separates from the propulsion unit.

Details of Orbital Vehicles OV1-2 to OV1-19 have been given in previous editions of *Jane's*. They were launched between October 1965 and March 1969.

OV1-20 and -21 were placed in orbit by an Atlas F on 7 August 1971. The primary purpose of OV1-20 was to inject the 800 lb (363 kg) Cannonball II atmospheric drag experiment into orbit. OV1-21 carried six experiments into a 450 nm (518 mile; 834 km) circular orbit. Three of the experiments separated, measuring atmospheric drag and providing a target for radar calibration.

GENERAL ELECTRIC

GENERAL ELECTRIC COMPANY SPACE DIVISION

HEAD OFFICE:
Valley Forge Space Center, PO Box 8555, Philadelphia, Pennsylvania 19101
Telephone: (215) 962-6150
MANAGER, INDUSTRY COMMUNICATIONS:
C. L. Chase

General Electric's Space Division is vehicle contractor for NASA's Nimbus weather satellite and Earth Resources Technology Satellite (ERTS). It is also responsible for design and manufacture of the stabilisation and control system for NASA's Orbiting Astronomical Observatory (OAO).

NIMBUS

Details of the development and use of Nimbus meteorological satellites Nos. 1 to 4, during the decade from 1961, can be found in the 1971-72 *Jane's*.

The main structure of Nimbus is 10 ft (3·05 m) tall and 5 ft (1·525 m) wide, with a drum-shape base housing the subsystems and experiments. An active attitude control subsystem located above the base keeps sensors pointed towards the centre of the Earth to an accuracy of one degree. Power is supplied by two large panels of solar cells.

Nimbus satellites are placed in near-polar Sun-synchronous orbits to provide continuous global coverage twice in every 24-hour period, once in sunlight and the other in darkness.

On 11 December 1972, the first of two advanced Nimbus satellites was launched by a Delta rocket from the Western Test Range, California, into a near-circular polar orbit. Designated Nimbus E before launch and Nimbus 5 in orbit, the spacecraft was designed specifically to take the first vertical temperature and water vapour readings from space through clouds. It was also designed to thermally map the Earth's surface, so that geologists could understand better what is happening below the crust.

The satellite comprises four main elements: the attitude control element, the solar array paddles, a truss structure providing a tripod connection, and a ring structure of 18 rectangular module bays plus 3 internal bays. It accommodates about 490 lb (222 kg) of payload. Total launch weight was 1,695 lb (772 kg).

Six highly advanced meteorological and Earth resources experiments or sensors are aboard Nimbus 5. Three are improved versions of those carried on earlier Nimbus spacecraft and three are brand new. They are: Electrically Scanning Microwave Radiometer (ESMR) for globally mapping the thermal radiation from the Earth's surface and atmosphere, and for mapping areas of ice and water; Infra-red Temperature Profile Radiometer (ITPR) for testing the feasibility and operational applications of cloud-interference-elimination sounding techniques; Nimbus-E Microwave Spectrometer (NEMS) to provide temperature profile information, water vapour abundance and cloud water content; Surface

Nimbus 5 advanced meteorological satellite

Composition Mapping Radiometer (SCMR) for identifying types of rock and other features of the Earth's surface by precise measurement of the residual radiation; Selective Chopper Radiometer (SCR) for observing the global temperature structure of the atmosphere at altitudes up to 11 miles (18 km); Temperature Humidity Infra-red Radiometer (THIR) for obtaining data on cloud cover, ground temperatures and water vapour distribution.

In its first year of operation Nimbus 5 contributed greatly to an increased understanding of the complex atmospheric processes. In particular, data on the world's rainfall enabled estimates to be made of the amount of energy being released into the atmosphere. This is significant, because heat energy is the driving force behind tropical storms, and its measurement will lead to more accurate forecasting.

In addition, pictures returned by the satellite's new scanning microwave-radiometer have mapped the whole of Antarctica, and are now considered indispensable to the routine operation of US Navy shipping in the polar regions.

ERTS

Designed to study the resources of Earth from space, ERTS-1 (Earth Resources Technology Satellite) was launched by NASA, using a Delta vehicle from Vandenberg, on 23 July 1972, into a near-circular 560 × 580 mile (901 × 933 km) polar orbit.

Based on the Nimbus meteorological satellite, ERTS-1 is 10 ft (3 m) high, not including the solar paddles, and weighs 1,965 lb (891 kg). The solar array consists of two panels measuring 4 × 8 ft (1·2 × 2·4 m); additional solar cells are mounted on the transition sections of the array.

Two main groups of sensors are carried: a multispectral scanner subsystem (MSS) and a return beam vidicon (RBV) subsystem. The two sensors repetitively take photo-like images of the Earth, while a data collection system (DCS) collects environmental data of various types from ground-based remote platforms. A high-performance recorder, known as a wide-band video tape recorder (WBVTR), stores photo images from the RBV and MSS, as needed, when the satellite is out of range of a direct-readout data acquisition station.

The RBV camera system, developed by the Astro Electronics Division of RCA, comprises three 2 in TV-type 4,125-line cameras, taking photographs in green, red and near-infra-red bands, and with each picture covering a 100 nm (115 mile; 185 km) square with a resolution of about 330 ft (100 m). Shallow ocean areas stand out in the green band, as do sedimentation and pollution. Man-made structures appear brightly in the red band, where vegetation appears very dark, to give information on land-use mapping. Water areas stand out as dark areas on the infra-red photographs.

The MSS, built by Hughes Aircraft Co, is an optical-mechanical sensing system which simultaneously detects optical energy in the green, red and two infra-red spectral bands, including near-infra-red. The system scans the same 100 nm (115 mile; 185 km) wide flight path as that observed by the RBV camera array. Scanning is achieved by means of a mechanically

ERTS-1 Earth Resources Technology Satellite

oscillating flat mirror, which flip-flops from side to side about 13 times each second. MSS images are photograph-like in appearance and of excellent quality, with a resolution of 230 ft (70 m).

Both RBV and MSS produce black and white photographs; those from the different bands can be put together to form false-colour photographs.

The DCS provides users of the space data with near real-time environmental information, collected from ground-based sensor instruments measuring soil, water, air and other parameters, to assist in the interpretation of data from the two sensors.

Owing to a switch problem in the satellite's power source, the RBV system was de-activated 14 days after launch. In March 1973 the video tape recorder, which had exceeded its 500-hour designed lifetime, developed sporadic bursts of noise which degraded the transmission of pictures and consequently was turned off for investigation. Photographs transmitted "live" were still excellent.

Some 90% of the satellite's data-return goals had been met, or exceeded, from the 34,000 MSS images returned up to May 1973, and were being studied by teams of scientists in 37 countries. Since its launch, ERTS-1 had by then photographed North America ten times and covered all the major land masses at least once.

Russia and the People's Republic of China are not participating in the scientific experiments.

It is hoped that ERTS-1 will provide an initial global picture of marine, water, agricultural, forestry, mineral and land resources. In addition, information is being obtained relevant to meteorology, the environment and the general use of land.

ERTS-1 was manufactured by General Electric, and is being managed by NASA's Goddard Space Flight Center. A second ERTS is expected to be launched in early 1975.

GRUMMAN

GRUMMAN AEROSPACE CORPORATION

HEAD OFFICE AND WORKS:
Bethpage, Long Island, New York 11714

OFFICERS: See "Aircraft" section

On 1 July 1969 the former Grumman Aircraft Engineering Corporation changed its name to the Grumman Corporation and established a number of subsidiary corporations. One of the latter, the Grumman Aerospace Corporation, took over responsibility for the Lunar Module (LM) for the Apollo programme (described in 1972-73 *Jane's*) and the highly successful Orbiting Astronomical Observatory (OAO), of which details can be found in the 1973-74 *Jane's*. By February 1974 the final OAO, named Copernicus, had exceeded its mission objectives by one year. The two experiments (Princeton Ultraviolet and UCL X-ray) had made a total of 7,906 observations of 415 unique objects. Although the spacecraft had exceeded its scientific and technical objectives, it still had many months of useful life ahead.

HUGHES

HUGHES AIRCRAFT COMPANY

HEAD OFFICE:
Culver City, California 90230
Telephone: (213) 391-0711

Current space programmes for which Hughes Aircraft is prime contractor include development and manufacture of NASA's new-generation Orbiting Solar Observatory (OSO) satellites. The company is also engaged on development and manufacture of classified military satellite systems, and on the investigation and flight testing of experimental ion engines for advanced spacecraft.

INTELSAT IV

Under a $72 million contract awarded on 18 October 1968, Hughes Aircraft Company became prime contractor for the Intelsat IV satellite. The initial order for one prototype and four flight satellites was placed by Communications Satellite Corporation (Comsat) on behalf of the International Telecommunications Satellite Consortium (Intelsat). Contracts for a second series of four satellites were negotiated in the Autumn of 1970.

Larger than any previous communications satellite, Intelsat IV is the fifth-generation Hughes satellite to see service since the tiny Syncom 2 was launched in 1963. In its design and manufacture, Hughes was assisted by subcontractors in nine member-nations of Intelsat. Northern Electric in Canada was also a subcontractor.

Intelsat IV was designed to offer communications facilities 25 times greater than those of any satellite previously put into service. It is able to carry 6,000 two-way telephone calls, transmit 12 simultaneous colour television broadcasts, or handle an infinite variety of different kinds of communications signals. Design lifetime in orbit is seven years.

A unique feature is the ability to focus power into two "spotlight" beams, 4½° wide, and direct them at any selected areas, thus providing a stronger signal and increased number of available channels in areas of heaviest communications traffic. This is made possible by mounting on the satellite two steerable dish antennae, each 50 in (127 cm) in diameter, controlled by command signals from Earth. Two horn antennae, with 17° beams, provide coverage outside the areas encompassed by the spotlight beams. Electronic switching enables ground controllers to adjust the amount of power going into each of the two antennae systems. Two Earth-coverage horns (one as a backup) are used for reception.

Intelsat IV has 12 broad-band communications channels. Each has a band-width of 40MHz, providing capacity for some 750 communications circuits. Four of the repeaters serve the Earth-coverage antennae; the other eight are intended to be switched as required to either Earth-coverage or spot-beam antennae.

A total of 45,012 solar cells provide 569W of power initially. Effective isotropic radiated power (EIRP) at beam centre is 33·7 dbw for the spot-beam antennae and 22 dbw for the Earth-coverage beams. A total of 24 output TWTs is used (12 for redundancy), each with an output of about 7·5W.

The satellite is basically drum-shape, with an Aerojet-General SVM-4A apogee motor containing 1,514 lb (686 kg) of solid propellant. Positioning and orientation control are provided by a redundant hydrazine system, with 273 lb (122 kg) of fuel.

The first flight Intelsat IV and its subsystems were built and tested at the Hughes space facilities, El Segundo, California, with the member-nation subcontractors participating directly. The second was assembled and tested at Hughes, but most of its subsystems were built by the participating subcontractors. The third spacecraft was assembled by British

Intelsat IV communications satellite

Aircraft Corporation at Bristol, England, using subsystems furnished by subcontractors. Similar arrangements were made for the second series of four satellites.

Subcontractors to Hughes in the Intelsat IV programme were Thomson-CSF (France), for telemetry and command antennae, telemetry horn and telemetry and command equipment; Nippon Electric Co (Japan) for repeater F-2; AEG Telefunken (Germany) for repeater F-3; Northern Electric Co (Canada) for repeater F-4; Kolster Iberica SA (Spain) for TWT power supply converters for drivers; Etudes Techniques et Constructions Aérospatiales (Belgium) for battery controller and relay; Svenska Radio AB (Sweden) for solenoid and squib drivers; Contraves AG (Switzerland) for antenna positioning electronics and de-spin control electronics; Selenia SpA (Italy) for Earth coverage—transmit and receive antennae, and spot-beam communications antennae; British Aircraft Corporation (United Kingdom) for nutation damper, positioning and orientation subsystem, battery pack, structure and harness, Sun sensor, and solar panel, with solar cells supplied by Société Anonyme de Télécommunications (France), Ferranti Ltd (United Kingdom) and AEG Telefunken (Germany).

Other participants in the programme included Etudes Techniques et Constructions Aérospatiales (Belgium) for digital portion of systems, test equipment and ground control equipment; Svenska Radio AB (Sweden) for RF portion systems test equipment; and British Aircraft Corporation for handling equipment and spacecraft integration and test.

Intelsat IV-A was launched from Cape Kennedy on 25 January 1971 by an Atlas-Centaur vehicle. It was put into a synchronous orbit and allowed to drift toward its operational station at 24·5°W, where it has been in use since 28 March 1971, linking countries with Earth stations ringing the Atlantic basin.

Intelsat-B was launched at 8·10 pm EST on 19 December 1971 and allowed to drift eastward toward its station over the Atlantic, where it entered commercial service at the end of February 1972. The British-assembled Intelsat-C was launched at 7.12 pm EST on 22 January 1972 and was placed in synchronous orbit two days later. It was on station over the Pacific in time to transmit TV and press coverage of President Nixon's visit to Peking on 21-28 February.

Intelsat IV-D (F-5) was launched on 13 June 1972 and has been positioned on the equator over the Indian Ocean, at longitude 62°E, to complete the first global system of Intelsat IVs. This spacecraft added 12 television channels to those now available between the US and other nations, and can also carry 5,000 to 6,000 two-way telephone conversations under average conditions.

Intelsat F-7 was launched on 23 August 1973, and was placed in service over the Atlantic at longitude 29·8°W on 21 November 1973. F-6 had been shipped to Comsat in early 1973 and was to be followed by F-8.

DIMENSIONS:

Diameter	7 ft 9¾ in (2·38 m)
Height of solar drum	9 ft 3 in (2·82 m)
Height overall	17 ft 4 in (5·28 m)

WEIGHTS:

At lift-off	3,090 lb (1,402 kg)
In orbit	1,559 lb (707 kg)

INTELSAT IV-A

Two Intelsat IV-A satellites are to be launched as interim spacecraft pending availability of the Intelsat V. Hughes is again prime contractor, with BAC as a principal subcontractor.

Intelsat IV-A will have 24 transponders. A new antennae configuration will increase capacity to 11,000 telephone circuits or 20 colour TV channels. The increased power requirement will be minimised by re-using the same frequency for both east and west transmissions.

The first Intelsat IV-A will be launched in 1975.

ANIK

Under a $31 million contract from Telesat Canada, Hughes Aircraft Company has built three spacecraft to provide a domestic satellite communications system in Canada. Major subcontractors were Northern Electric Company of Montreal, who provided the complete electronics system, including the entire communications package; and Spar Aerospace Products of Malton, Ontario, who provided the spacecraft structures and engineering support services. These two subcontractors will provide the electronics packages and structures for up to 15 additional spacecraft of similar type which Hughes expects to sell in worldwide markets.

The Telesat contract called for delivery of the first satellite, to be known as Anik-1, by October 1972, followed by the second and third at four-

Canada's Anik-1 communications satellite

month intervals thereafter. Each satellite was intended to provide 12 radio frequency channels, ten of which would be available for commercial use with the remaining two on standby. Each channel was to carry one colour TV signal or its equivalent in message traffic. This can be as high as 960 one-way voice channels.

Solar cells, arranged around the body of each satellite, deliver 250W of power. The satellite's antenna is a 60 in (152·4 cm) parabolic dish, providing a beam width of 3° by 8°.

Anik-1 (Telesat-A) was launched on 9 November 1972, by the first "Straight-Eight" Delta launch vehicle, from Cape Kennedy. An on-board solid-propellant rocket motor was fired during the apogee of the transfer orbit to "kick" the satellite into synchronous orbit above the equator at 114° W longitude, a point due south of Gallup, New Mexico, on 24 November. Small on-board jets, supplied by 100 lb (45 kg) of hydrazine propellant, provide attitude and station-keeping control of the satellite while on station for a period of at least seven years. Anik-1 became operational on 11 January 1973, when the first commercial telephone call was relayed between Resolute, in Queen Elizabeth Islands, and Ottawa. Full-scale commercial operation

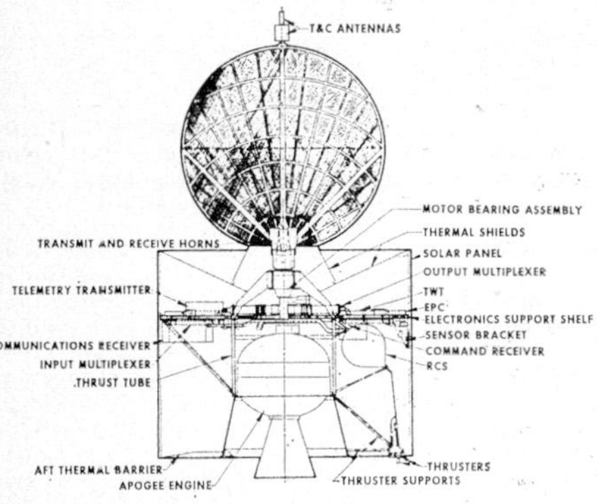

CANADIAN DOMESTIC SATELLITE

Diagram showing equipment layout in Anik-1

followed the orbiting of Anik-2, which was launched on 20 April 1973 and was also positioned subsequently over the equator. A third satellite was built as a spare, but has been tentatively scheduled by Telesat for launch in 1975.

DIMENSIONS (approx):

Height overall	12 ft (3·65 m)
Diameter	just over 6 ft (1·83 m)

WEIGHTS:

Launching weight	approx 1,240 lb (562 kg)
In orbit	550 lb (250 kg)

ORBITING SOLAR OBSERVATORY (OSO)

It was announced in September 1971 that Hughes Aircraft Company had been awarded a NASA contract to develop and produce three second-generation Orbiting Solar Observatory satellites, to be known as OSO-I, J and K. Larger, heavier and more advanced than earlier OSOs (details in previous editions of *Jane's*), the new spacecraft are intended to investigate how the Sun, a "relatively cool" body with a temperature of 10,000°F at its surface, heats its 10,000 mile (16,000 km) wide corona to 4,000,000°F.

From a 260 nm (300 mile; 480 km) high Earth orbit, the new OSO spacecraft will be able to train scientific instruments on the Sun with a pointing accuracy of 1 arc second (1/3,600°). Earlier OSOs pointed with an accuracy of 60 arc seconds ($\frac{1}{60}$°), scanning a solar area 23,450 nm (27,000 miles; 43,450 km) wide. Improved accuracy will enable OSO-I, J and K to scan areas of the Sun's rim in 390 nm (450 mile; 725 km) segments, an area considered small as the Sun's diameter is approx 750,000 nm (864,000 miles; 1,390,000 km). The primary objective will be to investigate X-ray and ultra-violet radiation in the turbulent gaseous area around the Sun.

Each spacecraft will consist of a spinning section, called the wheel, and a stationary platform known as the sail. The sail, containing solar panels to provide power, will carry two instruments able to scan the Sun or point at any position on it. One, from the University of Paris, France, will make fine structure studies of the chromosphere. The other, from the University of Colorado, will make high-resolution ultra-violet spectrometer measurements. Both will scan the Sun for other "targets of opportunity" such as flares or sunspots when the Sun's surface activity is relatively calm. Six experiments, carried in the wheel section, will survey various X-ray sources.

The experiments will be commanded automatically by a memory system programming itself. In the case of earlier OSOs, ground controllers had to wait up to 1½ hours for completion of an orbit before they could send new commands to the satellite.

OSO-I, to which the data below apply, is scheduled for launch in early 1975, carrying eight experiments, and is designed to operate for more than one year. Launches of OSO-J and OSO-K are under study by NASA.

DIMENSIONS:

Height	7 ft 6 in (2·29 m)
Width	9 ft 5 in (2·87 m)

WEIGHT:

Launching weight	1,950 lb (885 kg)

USAF 711 SATELLITE

The US technical press reports that Hughes has developed for the USAF a new surveillance satellite to monitor foreign radar activity. Developed under the Air Force's 711 programme, it is intended to be launched by Titan III booster into a highly elliptical orbit and then to relay data to ground stations for analysis.

The new satellite is intended to supersede the Ferret type produced by Lockheed.

USAF 313 SATELLITE

Under the USAF's 313 programme, Hughes was contracted to develop a military satellite data relay system. This is intended to utilise satellites in polar orbit to relay directly to US ground stations reconnaissance photographs and early warning data from other satellites.

STRATEGIC COMSAT SYSTEM

A new strategic communications satellite system is being developed by Hughes for the USAF. Its purpose is to supplement the lower-latitude coverage that will be provided in the mid-seventies by the TRW Fltsatcom network, and provide high-latitude coverage for SAC air-to-ground communications.

Few details are available except that each satellite system is expected to weigh only 35 lb (16 kg), and to be carried by a USAF cloud-cover surveillance satellite in polar orbit.

LOCKHEED

LOCKHEED AIRCRAFT CORPORATION

HEAD OFFICE AND WORKS:
Burbank, California

OFFICERS: See "Aircraft" section

Lockheed Missiles and Space Company, Inc:

HEAD OFFICE:
1111 Lockheed Way, Sunnyvale, California 94088

Telephone: (408) 742-6688

OTHER FACILITIES:
Palo Alto and Santa Cruz, California

MANAGER, PUBLIC INFORMATION:
Rockwell Hollands

Lockheed Missiles and Space Company is heavily engaged in both missile work and the design, development and production of satellites and space vehicles. Details of some of its current space programmes follow:

AGENA D

The Agena satellite, for which Lockheed was named prime contractor after a design competition in 1956, is a versatile space vehicle which is used normally as the upper stage of a two-stage launcher, in combination with a Thor, Atlas, Thrust-Augmented Thor, Long-tank Thor or Titan IIIB. The current Agena D version consists of a cylindrical body containing a Bell Aerosystems Model 8096 (YLR81-BA-11) restartable liquid-propellant rocket engine (16,000 lb; 7,257 kg st) and propellant tanks, telemetry, instrumentation, guidance and attitude control systems. It has carried most types of power supply, including a nuclear reactor electric power supply and an ion engine. The payload section (nosecone) can accommodate a wide variety of Earth-orbiting and space probes weighing up to several hundred pounds. The Agena system and its attached payload have functioned for more than six months in some missions for the USAF.

Agena D differs from earlier versions in being able to accept a variety of payloads, whereas its predecessors had integrated payloads. The restartable engine permits the satellite to change its orbit in space.

In the period 1959-71, well over 300 Agena spacecraft applications had been announced, in terms of launches attempted, of which all but about 30 had achieved success, with payload injected into orbit. By the same date, more than 45 Agenas had been used as the upper stages of launch vehicles for other spacecraft, with only two recorded failures. No Agena had failed to achieve orbit since April 1967. Among many significant achievements, Agena spacecraft were first to achieve a circular orbit, to achieve a polar orbit, to be stabilised in all three axes in orbit, to be controlled in orbit by ground command, to return a man-made object from space, to propel themselves from one orbit to another, to propel spacecraft on successful Mars and Venus flyby missions, to achieve a rendezvous and docking

Agena satellite and experimental payload for Department of Defense Space Test Program. Copper discs on front of vehicle (*left*) are communications antennae. Long cylindrical object over heads of engineers is a flexible solar array which unrolls like a window blind in space

Artist's impression of Space Test Program Agena in orbit

by spacecraft in orbit, and to provide propulsion power in space for another spacecraft.

A high proportion of the unidentified US satellites included in the table at the end of this section can be assumed to be Agena payloads of various kinds.

The following details refer to Agena D:

Dimensions:

Length (typical)	23 ft 3 in (7·09 m)
Diameter	5 ft 0 in (1·52 m)

Weights (typical):

Propellant weight	13,553 lb (6,148 kg)
Vehicle weight empty	1,484 lb (673 kg)
Weight in orbit, less payload	1,277 lb (579 kg)

DISCOVERER

One of the first applications of the Agena satellite that could be mentioned publicly was in the USAF's Discoverer programme, in which the Agena carried as part of its payload an ejectable capsule. This capsule was designed to maintain temperature and oxygen sufficient to sustain life in its interior and to be recoverable by parachute.

The techniques evolved in the Discoverer programme have been utilised and developed in subsequent classified military programmes. It is, therefore, worthwhile to continue to record them in *Jane's*.

All launchings in the Discoverer programme were done at Vandenberg AFB. Agena was boosted to near orbital altitude by a modified Thor missile which, after engine burnout, was separated from the satellite. Agena coasted upwards and positioned itself in a horizontal attitude. The satellite's own engine was then fired to bring it to orbital speed (about 15,600 knots; 18,000 mph; 29,000 km/h). Guidance and attitude control during the coast phase were provided by an infra-red horizon scanner and an inertial reference package. The satellite engine also was gimballed to provide orbit adjustment during the burning period.

Shortly after attaining an orbit, and before it had made a complete pass around the Earth, the satellite was programmed to turn itself through 180° in yaw, thus placing the nose section in a rearward-facing position. This was done by cold gas reaction jets which gradually swung the vehicle around. Agena was then stabilised in the rear-facing attitude.

This manoeuvre placed the nose section containing the re-entry vehicle and recovery capsule to the rear.

After a pre-determined number of orbits the satellite was tilted 60° downward and stabilised in that position to permit ejection of the nose section. As the satellite swung over the pole and past Alaska, a timer activated the ejection sequence and the re-entry vehicle recovery capsule was separated from the rest of the Agena. A retro-rocket on the nose section fired to slow it down and so permitted a gradually curved entry into the Earth's atmosphere. A parachute was deployed and on many occasions an aerial recovery attempt was made.

The 300 lb (136 kg) ejected capsule of Discoverer 13 was the first object recovered from **orbital flight. An even more striking success was the recovery of the 85 lb (39 kg) Discoverer 14 capsule, which was "snatched" in the air as it descended by a trapeze-like framework towed behind a C-119 transport aircraft at a height of 8,000 ft (2,450 m), 260 nm (300 miles; 480 km) north-west of Hawaii. This success has since** been repeated on many occasions, current Agena payload recoveries being made by Lockheed JC-130B aircraft.

SPACE TEST PROGRAM

Some details of the US Department of Defense's Space Test Program (formerly Space Experiment Support Program) were released on 17 October 1971, when a Lockheed Agena carrying multiple scientific experiments was launched into polar orbit from Vandenberg AFB, California, by a Thor booster.

The Space Test Program provides space flights for DoD-approved space research projects which are not allocated individual launches. Eligible projects include those which require space flight for completion, are part of a DoD development test and evaluation programme, or are sponsored by another US federal agency.

Largest of the experiments aboard this particular spacecraft was a 250 lb (113 kg) flexible solar array capable of producing 1,500W of electrical power from the Sun's energy. Developed by the Air Force Aero Propulsion Laboratory, the Hughes-built solar array was rolled up in a cylinder at launch and then unrolled in orbit like a window shade to a size of 32 ft × 6 ft (9·75 m × 1·83 m). The array had a pointing system to keep it facing the Sun for maximum power output.

Most complicated experiment aboard the Agena was built by the Lockheed Research Laboratory in Palo Alto, for the Office of Naval Research and the Defense Nuclear Agency. The experiment was in two parts: low- and high-energy particle detectors, and an Earth Reflecting Ionospheric Sounder (ERIS). It used 19 individual instruments to collect data on proton, alpha and electron particles that enter the upper atmosphere. In the polar regions, ERIS was designed to transmit high-frequency signals to the ground, from where they were reflected back to the satellite. Scientists expected the collected data to be useful in understanding the effects of solar storms on polar phenomena.

Other experiments concern satellite communications and celestial sphere measurements.

Total mission life for the Agena and its cargo was expected to be at least six months. Such long life is made possible by Agena's ability to respond to ground command and to make necessary adjustments to maintain its orbit.

Scientific data gathered in orbit by this particular Agena were transmitted to tracking stations located around the world. Equipped with 11 antennae, the Agena used 800 telemetry channels to return data to the experimenters. It was capable of responding to 248 different real-time ground commands.

SAMOS/FERRET

This reconnaissance satellite is part of an overall USAF satellite system for which Lockheed is prime contractor. Few details are available, but Samos is reported to utilise photographic intelligence equipment by Eastman Kodak in a **capsule developed and produced by General Electric and fitted with a parachute and guidance recovery system by Avco and Northrop Ventura. It is intended to be established in a circular polar orbit at a height of 87-260 nm (100-300 miles; 160-480 km). Intelligence data are transmitted by TV, and analysed in greater detail after capsule recovery.**

The first launching of a 4,100 lb (1,860 kg) development version, on 11 October 1960, failed to achieve orbit, but Samos 2 was orbited successfully by an Atlas-Agena A booster on 31 January 1961. The third Samos was destroyed in a launch-pad explosion on 9 September 1961.

Details of subsequent launchings are classified, but Samos was believed to be operational by the **Summer of 1963, probably in more than one form. One variant, for communications and electronic intelligence, is said to be code-named Ferret.**

One Lockheed-built reconnaissance satellite, launched from Vandenberg AFB on 22 July 1970, was put into an orbit that would enable it to survey areas of the Middle East subject to the subsequent Arab-Israeli cease-fire agreement.

Dimensions:

Length	22 ft 0 in (6·70 m)
Diameter	5 ft 0 in (1·52 m)

LOCKHEED/USAF PR SATELLITES

Several different families of photographic reconnaissance satellites based on the Agena vehicle are known to be in regular use by the USAF, although no officially-released details are available. A summary of the reported characteristics of two classes of spacecraft follows:

Photo/video type. Satellites of this type appear to have been orbited three or four times each year by Long-Tank Thrust-Augmented Thor-Agena D (Thorad) vehicles. Orbital inclination has usually been in the 75-88° bracket, with an orbital life of 22-28 days. Estimated weight of each satellite is about 4,000 lb (1,815 kg). It is used for basic "seek-and-find" missions, photographs being processed on board the satellite and transmitted to Earth by radio link. On some missions a small **P-11** "pick-a-back" satellite is launched simultaneously into a circular orbit of around 300 nm (345 miles; 555 km), presumably for electronic intelligence (elint) gathering.

Thor booster and Agena booster-spacecraft being swung into launch position at Vandenberg AFB, as part of Space Test Program

Recoverable type. Once launched at approx quarterly intervals, these satellites are believed to take close-look high-resolution photographs of targets detected by the photo/video spacecraft. Satellite weight is 6,500-7,000 lb (2,950-3,175 kg), requiring a Titan IIIB launch vehicle for the second-stage Agena. Orbits are elliptical, with apogee of around 240 nm (275 miles; 445 km) and perigee in the order of 70 nm (80 miles; 130 km), maintained for up to 25 days by using Agena propulsion to restore any rapid degradation of the orbit. Inclination averages about 110°. The capsules are recovered eventually by the air-snatch technique.

The relationship between the above satellites and the Samos programme is not known. Their use appears to be declining now that Big Bird is available, with only a single launch, of the recoverable version, recorded in the first half of 1973, on 16 May.

LOCKHEED/USAF 467 BIG BIRD

First launched on 15 June 1971, from Pt Arguello, this highly-advanced photographic reconnaissance satellite is reported to weigh about 25,000 lb (11,340 kg) and to be 50 ft (15·25 m) long. The first Big Bird was launched by Titan IIID into an orbit with an apogee of 162 nm (186 miles; 299 km), perigee of 99 nm (114 miles; 183 km) and inclination of 96·41°. Its capabilities clearly included the same kind of close-look high-resolution photography as that of the recoverable type of Agena vehicle; and it is reported to have ejected a series of capsules for air-snatch recovery.

Big Bird is believed to process photographs taken by other cameras and transmit information to Earth in the form of digital data by radio link. Some reports suggest that it also carries infra-red mapping and side-looking radar equipment. Its orbit takes its cameras within range of every point on the Earth twice in each period of 24 hours.

Three more Big Birds were launched in 1972; others followed on 9 March, 13 July and 10 November 1973, and on 10 April 1974. It is expected that these spacecraft will continue to be launched at roughly four-monthly intervals to provide an increasing share of the total US satellite intelligence. They have demonstrated an endurance of up to four months in orbit.

LTV

LTV AEROSPACE CORPORATION (Subsidiary of THE LTV CORPORATION)

Vought Systems Division (Division of LTV Aerospace Corporation)

Headquarters:
PO Box 5907, Dallas, Texas 75222

Officers: See "Aircraft" section

Vought Systems Division, which resulted from a merger of the former Vought Aeronautics Company and Vought Missiles and Space Company in January 1973, is prime contractor for the NASA/DoD Scout launch vehicle. Its other products and capabilities relating to astronautics and space technology include a radiator system used in the Apollo spacecraft command module, and a manned aerospace flight simulator that was used by Apollo astronauts.

The Division is also engaged in the fields of advanced defence systems, ramjet propulsion systems and laser technology. Contracts have been awarded to Vought Systems to develop the non-metallics needed to protect space shuttle vehicles during repeated re-entries from space. The materials involved are of the all-carbon type, known as reinforced pyrolised plastics (RPP).

A pioneer in the extra-vehicular manoeuvring unit field, it developed the USAF's Astronaut Manoeuvring Unit (AMU) and flight demon**stration models of the unmanned, radio-controlled** Remote Manoeuvring Unit (RMU). Under **subcontract to Chrysler, this division produced the fuel and oxidiser containers for the first stage of the Saturn 1B space booster.**

LTV AEROSPACE SCOUT (XRM-91)

Against competition from 12 other companies, Chance Vought (now part of LTV Aerospace Corporation) won the major contract for the NASA/Department of Defense Scout four-stage solid-propellant space research vehicle in April 1959. In addition to being responsible for assembly of the overall vehicle, the company developed the nose section and airframe protecting the payload, the inter-stage sections between the various rocket engines, stage separation devices and the jet vanes and fin assemblies.

As prime vehicle contractor, Vought Systems Division now performs duties extending from initial assembly and test at the Dallas plant to management and launch services. It also has built the launching towers for the rocket, including a type which permits horizontal checkout of the vehicle and erection to any desired position up to vertical for launch. Launching is possible at any angle from vertical to 20° from vertical.

Scout was designed to make possible space, orbital and re-entry research at comparatively low cost, using "off-the-shelf" major components where possible. Its first stage is the 115,000 lb (52,160 kg) st Algol IIB (Aerojet Senior) by Aerojet-General, or the new Algol III (see below); the second stage is the 60,000 lb (27,215 kg) st Castor II by Thiokol; the third stage is the 21,000 lb (9,525 kg) st Antares II (X259) by Hercules Inc's Allegany Ballistics Laboratory; the fourth stage was originally the 3,000 lb (1,360 kg) st Altair (X248) or the more powerful Altair X258, but these have been superseded by a UTC stage (see below). Honeywell provides the simplified gyro guidance system. Spin stabilisation of the fourth stage is by LTV Aerospace.

Final assembly of the Scout is done at NASA's Wallops Island facility, Virginia; at Vandenberg AFB, California, the West Coast launch site for the vehicle; or at Italy's sea-based San Marco platform off the east coast of Africa, near Kenya.

On 16 February 1961, a Scout became the first solid-propellant vehicle ever to put a satellite into orbit when it was used to launch the Explorer 9 inflatable sphere.

An improved version, with FW-4S fourth stage (6,000 lb; 2,720 kg st) by United Technology Center, was launched for the first time on 10 August 1965, with complete success. In addition to increasing the payload capability to 320 lb (145 kg) in a 260 nm (300 mile; 480 km) orbit, this version can be manoeuvred in yaw and can send a 100 lb (45 kg) payload more than 13,900 nm (16,000 miles; 25,750 km) from the Earth.

A new heat shield, first used during a launch on 20 June 1971, provides a volume of 35·3 cu ft (1·0 m³) and increases the diameter of the payload that Scout can carry from 2 ft 7½ in (0·8 m) to 3 ft 3½ in (1·0 m). The Algol III first-stage motor, available since 1971, provides a total impulse of 7,200,000 lb/sec (3,266,000 kg/sec) compared with about 5,450,000 lb/sec (2,476,000 kg/sec) for the Algol IIB. It increases the weight that Scout can put into a 270 nm (310 mile; 500 km) easterly orbit from 330 lb (150 kg) to approximately 425 lb (193 kg).

A fifth-stage velocity package is under development, which will increase the Scout's hypersonic re-entry performance, make possible highly-elliptical deep-space orbits, and extend the vehicle's probe capabilities to the Sun.

Scouts have been used by NASA for a series of re-entry experiments. In one of these, in 1966, a special 17 in (43 cm) spherical motor was used as a fifth stage to thrust back into the atmosphere at more than 15,600 knots (18,000 mph; 29,000 km/h) a payload designed to provide data on a heat-shield material for nose-caps. Total payload, including the motor, weighed 400 lb (180 kg) at lift-off.

In addition to its use by NASA and the Department of Defense, Scout is used for international programmes, including those of the United Kingdom, Italy, France, Germany, the Netherlands and the European Space Research Organisation (ESRO). On 26 April 1967, a Scout inaugurated use of a sea-based platform on the equator, off the east coast of Africa. As space booster for Italy's San Marco programme, it became the first vehicle to orbit a satellite from a launch site at sea.

Scout ended 1972 with its 28th consecutive successful launch, by orbiting Germany's Aeros satellite from Vandenberg in the first launch using a combination of both the Algol III first stage and the larger heat-shield.

By March 1974 a total of 85 Scouts had been launched. One of these put into orbit NASA's Small Astronomy Satellite-A (SAS-A), launched by Italy from the San Marco platform to become the first US satellite ever launched by a foreign country.

DIMENSIONS:

Overall height	75 ft 2½ in (22·92 m)
Max body diameter	3 ft 9 in (1·14 m)

WEIGHT:

Launching weight	47,185 lb (21,400 kg)

USAF 922 ANTI-SATELLITE SYSTEM

No details of this anti-satellite system are available, and the deployment of such systems is, of course, precluded by the US/Soviet SALT agreement. All that can be recorded is that the USAF's 922 programme, for which LTV Aerospace and Rockwell International's North American Aerospace Group are contractors, was intended to produce a direct ascent anti-satellite system utilising an infra-red homing vehicle with a non-nuclear warhead.

NASA Scout 181 launch vehicle for Aeros satellite

MARTIN MARIETTA

MARTIN MARIETTA CORPORATION

CORPORATE HEADQUARTERS:
277 Park Avenue, New York, New York 10017

AEROSPACE HEADQUARTERS:
1800 K Street NW, Washington, DC 20006
Telephone: (202) 833-1900

PRESIDENT AND CHIEF EXECUTIVE OFFICER, MARTIN MARIETTA CORPORATION:
J. Donald Rauth

PRESIDENT, AEROSPACE GROUP:
T. G. Pownall

VICE-PRESIDENTS, AEROSPACE GROUP:
Herman Pusin (Engineering)
Dan A. Peterson (Marketing)
Laurence J. Adams (Denver Division)
Howard W. Merrill (Baltimore Division)
G. E. Smith (Orlando Division)

DIRECTOR, PUBLIC RELATIONS:
William D. McBride

Baltimore Division

ADDRESS:
103 Chesapeake Park Plaza, Baltimore, Maryland 21220

Denver Division

ADDRESS:
PO Box 179, Denver, Colorado 80201
Telephone: (303) 794-5211

DIRECTOR, PUBLIC RELATIONS:
John H. Boyd

Orlando Division

ADDRESS:
PO Box 5837, Orlando, Florida 32805
Telephone: (305) 855-6100

DIRECTOR, PUBLIC RELATIONS:
Edward J. Cottrell

Current activities of Martin Marietta's Baltimore Division include manufacture of components for the Rockwell B-1 strategic bomber and the McDonnell Douglas DC-10 transport, and thrust reversers for General Electric CF6-6 and CF6-50 turbofan engines.

The Denver Division of Martin Marietta is working on the Titan III family of space launch boosters, the Viking Mars orbiter/landers, the Space Shuttle project, and on other spacecraft, their systems and related research.

Orlando Division produces the Sprint I missile system as part of the Safeguard anti-missile defence programme, the Walleye air-to-surface missile and Pershing surface-to-surface intermediate-range missile. Orlando also is engaged in development of the SAM-D missile, the Sprint II missile for Site Defense, the terminally-guided Pershing II missile, and a wide range of military and commercial communications and electronics equipment. This Division has extensive laboratories for research, development, test, and evaluation of warheads, materials, special munitions, structures, propellants, lasers, guidance and control, fluidics, reconnaissance devices, digital communications and millimetre wave techniques.

TITAN III

Titan III is America's standard heavy-duty space "workhorse" booster and is used for both military and non-military space launch missions. It provides a high-frequency launch capability for a wide variety of manned and unmanned payloads, ranging from 35,000 lb (15,875 kg) in Earth orbit to 7,000 lb (3,175 kg) for planetary missions such as the exploration of Mars. The Space and Missile Systems Organisation of the Air Force Systems Command has executive management of the programme. Martin Marietta at Denver, Colorado, was named systems integrator for the industry/contractor team on 20 August 1962. Technical direction was assigned to Aerospace Corporation.

Martin Marietta, in addition to its role as systems integrating contractor, builds the airframe and liquid-propellant stages, supplies the flight control system, and is integrating contractor for facilities and launch operations at Cape Kennedy. Aerojet-General Corporation produces the liquid-propellant engines. United Technology Center manufactures the solid-propellant booster motors used in the more powerful models. Guidance systems for the Titan IIIC, D and E are built by General Motors Corporation's Delco Division, Western Electric, and Honeywell Corporation respectively.

The core section of Titan III consists of elements which provide a high degree of commonality throughout all configurations. It consists of two booster stages evolved from the Titan II ICBM and an upper stage, known as Transtage, that can function both in the boost phase of flight and as a restartable space "tug" propulsion vehicle. All stages use storable liquid propellants and have gimbal-mounted thrust chambers for vehicle control.

Titan III exists in four configurations:

Titan IIIB is basically the first two stages of the core section. It can accommodate a variety of specialised upper stages. First launched on 29 July 1966. Series of launches continued through 1972-73, all with Agena upper stages and classified USAF payloads, including reconnaissance satellites.

Titan IIIC consists of the core section of the main airframe, including the Transtage upper stage, with solid-propellant rocket motors

Titan IIIC launch

First Titan IIIE-Centaur, carrying a mass model of the Mars Viking spacecraft

attached to each side to function as a booster stage before ignition of main engines. Payloads include USAF and NASA unmanned military, scientific and communications satellites and spacecraft, including about 80% of all satellites placed into synchronous equatorial orbit from US launch sites.

Titan IIID is basically similar to IIIC but has only a two-stage liquid-propellant "core" (without Transtage) and radio guidance instead of the standard inertial guidance. Able to accept a variety of upper stages. Production order placed by USAF in November 1967. First used to orbit the first Lockheed Big Bird advanced photo-reconnaissance spacecraft, weighing about 25,000 lb (11,340 kg), from Pt Arguello on 15 June 1971.

Titan IIIE-Centaur is basically a Titan IIID which has been modified to take a Centaur high-energy upper stage. The first launch, on 11 February 1974, was terminated by the range safety officer when the second-stage engine failed to ignite. First operational launch was scheduled to take place from the Eastern Test Range in September 1974, carrying the German HELIOS Sun-probe spacecraft. Primary mission of Titan IIIE-Centaur is to place the two Viking spacecraft on Mars in 1976.

A Titan IIIC, with a 25 ft long (7·62 m) typical payload fairing and all stages mated, is 130 ft (39·62 m) in height. Future payloads will extend the overall height considerably; the Titan IIIE-Centaur launch vehicle for the Viking Mars exploration spacecraft will, for example, have an overall height of 160 ft (48·77 m) when the shroud protecting the payload is in place.

The first stage of the main airframe (core vehicle) is 73 ft (22·25 m) long and 10 ft (3·05 m) in diameter. Its engines, which use a blend of hydrazine and unsymmetrical dimethylhydrazine (UDMH) for fuel, and nitrogen tetroxide as an oxidiser, have a 15 : 1 expansion ratio and are ignited at an altitude where efficiency is increased, giving a thrust of 526,000 lb (238,600 kg) in vacuo.

The second stage of the core vehicle is 23 ft 3½ in (7·10 m) tall and 10 ft (3·05 m) in diameter. Its engine uses the same propellants as the first stage and develops 102,000 lb (46,265 kg) st.

The Transtage space propulsion vehicle is 15 ft (4·57 m) tall and 10 ft (3·05 m) in diameter and also uses UDMH/hydrazine and nitrogen tetroxide as propellants. The twin-chamber engine produces 16,000 lb (7,257 kg) of thrust and is capable of multiple restarts in space, which permits a wide variety of manoeuvres, including change of plane, change of orbit, and transfer to deep-space trajectory. Transtage also houses the control module for the entire vehicle, including the guidance system and segments of the flight control and vehicle safety systems.

Titan IIIC/D/E's solid-propellant booster motors are each 85 ft (25·91 m) long and 10 ft (3·05 m) in diameter. Each motor is built in five segments and develops more than 1,150,000 lb (521,630 kg) st. Steering for the booster stage is accomplished through a thrust vector control system, which injects nitrogen tetroxide into the engine thrust column.

The Titan III 17-vehicle research and development flight testing programme involved launch of four IIIAs and 13 IIICs. The first launch of a Titan IIIA development vehicle occurred on 1 September 1964. Titan IIIC made its maiden flight on 18 June 1965 and had completed 19 successful flights by the beginning of 1974, putting a total of 37 satellites into synchronous orbit in the process.

Titan III vehicles had performed successfully in 57 consecutive launches in the six-year period to early 1974. Additional contracts for various models have extended production through 1976.

Dimensions: See above

Launching Weights (approx):
- Core vehicle 450,000 lb (204,120 kg)
- Titan IIIC 1,400,000 lb (635,030 kg)

Performance (Titan IIIC, approx):

Speed at burnout:
- Solid-propellant boosters 3,560 knots (4,100 mph; 6,600 km/h)
- 1st stage 8,860 knots (10,200 mph; 16,300 km/h)
- 2nd stage 14,850 knots (17,100 mph; 27,520 km/h)
- Transtage 15,200 knots (17,500 mph; 28,160 km/h)

VIKING

Viking is the name of the programme under which NASA is proposing to send two unmanned spacecraft to orbit the planet Mars and to make soft landings there in 1976. It replaces the former, more costly Voyager project.

Each of the flight spacecraft will be made up of two modules, known as the Viking orbiter and Viking lander, and will be launched by a Titan IIIE-Centaur vehicle during a 30-day launch period between mid-August and mid-September 1975. The complete spacecraft will enter a Martian orbit at a minimum height of 1,040 nm (1,200 miles; 1,930 km) above the surface. The lander will then separate and leave orbit, by means of a retro-rocket. It will be protected by a heatshield as it decelerates in the Martian atmosphere. The aeroshell heat-shield below the lander will be jettisoned about 20,000 ft (6,100 m) above the planet's surface. Simultaneously a parachute system will be deployed to decelerate the craft further. At 4,000 ft (1,220 m) over Mars, the parachute will jettison and the three terminal descent engines will fire to slow the lander for a soft touchdown. The engines will shut down as the lander's foot-pads contact the surface.

Viking orbiter will be developed and built by the California Institute of Technology's Jet Propulsion Laboratory and will be similar in appearance to JPL's 1971 Mariner Mars orbiters, with a liquid-propellant retro-rocket engine to decelerate the craft into orbit on arrival at the planet. Total launch weight of the complete orbiter/lander is expected to be about 8,000 lb (3,625 kg), of which the orbital insertion engine and fuel will account for 3,000 lb (1,360 kg). The orbiter will have a weight of nearly 2,000 lb (900 kg) in orbit, of which up to 150 lb (68 kg) will be scientific experiments to record and relay data on the topography and atmosphere of Mars and make possible correlation of orbital and surface data.

Viking lander will be developed and built by an industry team led by Martin Marietta's Denver Division, which will also be responsible for integrating the overall systems. Among subcontracts announced to date is one awarded in April 1970 to Teledyne Ryan Aeronautical for the development, test and manufacture of nine terminal descent landing radar sets, including test models,

Model of Viking orbiter and landing capsule for NASA's Mars 1976 mission. On the actual spacecraft the solar cell arrays will be folding two-section panels and the propulsion tanks will be covered

Mockup of Viking lander for 1976 mission to Mars

spares and flight hardware. This radar will provide measurements of relative velocity to the flight control computer from an altitude of about 17,000 ft (5,200 m) to the touchdown on the Martian surface. Using four beams of microwave energy, the radar will furnish redundant solutions with three-beam pairs.

At separation the lander will weigh about 2,400 lb (1,090 kg), but will have a touchdown weight of only 1,240 lb (562 kg), including approx 200 lb (90 kg) of instruments. These will search for living organisms on Mars, investigate the visual and thermal characteristics of the landing area with a two-camera imaging system, determine whether any water is present on the planet's surface, relay information on atmospheric temperature, pressure, humidity, wind direction and speed, use radio techniques to investigate Mars and its atmosphere, measure the solar ultra-violet flux reaching the Martian surface, and report on the planet's seismic activity.

MCDONNELL DOUGLAS

MCDONNELL DOUGLAS CORPORATION

HEAD OFFICE AND WORKS:
Box 516, St Louis, Missouri 63166

McDonnell Douglas Astronautics Company

HEADQUARTERS:
5301 Bolsa Avenue, Huntington Beach, California 92647

OFFICERS: See "Missiles" section

This company was formed on 26 June 1968, by a merger of the former Douglas Missile and Space Systems Division and the McDonnell Astronautics Company into a single management structure. Details of its current space programmes follow.

THOR

Details of the development, and operational deployment by the RAF, of the Thor IRBM can be found in the 1962-63 *Jane's*.

The Thor force was disbanded during 1963 and all the missiles were flown back to the United States. All were subsequently converted into space boosters by McDonnell Douglas. The company is also continuing production of Thors for use as first-stage boosters for the various space launch vehicles described separately below.

Thor has a circular-section aluminium body of lightweight integrally-stiffened design, providing integral tankage for its liquid oxygen and kerosene propellants. There are no tail surfaces. Propulsion is by a Rocketdyne MB-3-III or H-1 liquid-propellant engine, the chamber of which is gimbal-mounted to provide directional control and stability. Two liquid-propellant vernier engines, on each side of the main engine, provide speed adjustment after main engine burnout, as required, plus roll stabilisation.

A total of 444 Thor IRBMs and their derivative space boosters had been launched by 1 January 1974.

LONG TANK THOR

An advanced version of the Thor space booster, known as the Long Tank Thor, made its debut in the Summer of 1966. The length of the liquid oxygen tank was increased and the upper section of the booster was changed from the former conical shape to a cylinder of the same diameter as the rest of the airframe. This increased tankage permits a longer burning time for the main engine, with the result that Long Tank Thor will put 30% heavier payloads in space than Thrust Augmented Thor. Designed burning time is 216 seconds, compared with 146 seconds for Thrust Augmented Thor.

Main propulsion system is the standard Rocketdyne MB-3-III engine with minor modifications. It is supplemented by three Thiokol TK354-5 Castor II solid-propellant strap-on motors, giving a total thrust for all engines of approximately 330,000 lb (149,700 kg) for take-off.

DIMENSIONS (approx):

Length overall	70 ft 6 in (21·5 m)
Body diameter (constant)	8 ft 0 in (2·44 m)

DSV-3 DELTA

In May 1959, Douglas was awarded a prime contract by NASA to develop a three-stage vehicle named Delta, capable of placing a 480 lb (218 kg) payload into a 260 nm (300 mile; 480 km) Earth orbit or of sending a 100 lb (45 kg) payload on deep space probes. The original orders for 12 and 14 Deltas respectively were followed by further contracts in 1963-72, bringing the total ordered, in many versions, to 116.

Satellites launched by Delta have included many of the Explorer series, Pioneer, Tiros and Nimbus weather satellites, Echo I, Orbiting Solar Observatory series, Ariel, HEOS A, Biosatellite, ERTS, and active communications satellites such as Telstar, Relay, Syncom, Early Bird, Intelsat, Skynet and Telesat (Anik).

Details of early versions of the Delta can be found in the 1971-72 and 1972-73 *Jane's*. Production of all vehicles prior to the DSV-3P has been completed and the remaining examples have been assigned to specific missions. Future production will be of the DSV-3P, of which details follow:

DSV-3P Extended Long Tank Delta (also known as "Straight-Eight" or "four-digit Delta"). This launch vehicle has a constant 8 ft (2·44 m) diameter from the base of the boat-tail to the conical nose section of the shroud. This provides an enlarged volume, to accommodate larger payloads. The second stage, with a TRW LMDE engine, is suspended within the 8 ft (2·44 m) diameter barrel section. The first-stage length is increased by 10 ft (3·05 m) by comparison with earlier long-tank versions, providing an increase of 30,000 lb (13,600 kg) in propellant capacity. In addition, the MB-3-III main engine is replaced by a Rocketdyne H-1 of 205,000 lb (93,000 kg) st. As an alternative to the TE-364-3 motor, a higher-performing motor, the TE-364-4, is available as a third stage. The two-stage capability is increased to 4,150 lb (1,880 kg) into a 200 nm (230 mile; 370 km) circular orbit. The three-stage capability is increased to 1,550 lb (700 kg) into a synchronous transfer orbit.

Launch of first DSV-3P Extended Long Tank Delta

DIMENSIONS:

Length overall	115 ft 4 in (35·15 m)
Body diameter	8 ft 0 in (2·44 m)

WEIGHTS:

Firing weight of DSV-3P:	
3 solid motors	230,000 lb (104,330 kg)
6 solid motors	260,000 lb (117,930 kg)
9 solid motors	290,000 lb (131,540 kg)

S-IVB (SATURN IB SECOND STAGE AND SATURN V THIRD STAGE)

McDonnell Douglas was prime contractor for the S-IVB third stage of the Saturn V launch vehicle used in the Apollo programme. A total of 27 S-IVBs were ordered, and details of their use in the Apollo project can be found in previous editions of *Jane's*.

The first flight-type S-IVB was shipped from the McDonnell Douglas Space Systems Center on 30 April 1965. Acceptance firing was successfully accomplished on 8 August at the Sacramento Test Center. The occasion was the first fully-automatic digital computer checkout of a space vehicle. On 26 February 1966, this S-IVB was launched successfully from Cape Kennedy as second stage of NASA's first Saturn IB rocket. Twelve of the stages were ordered subsequently as Saturn IB second stages, and have continued to find applications in the Skylab and Apollo-Soyuz Test Project programmes; the others formed the third stage of Saturn V launchers.

The S-IVB is powered by a single Rocketdyne J-2 liquid oxygen/liquid hydrogen engine of 200,000 lb (90,720 kg) st, and is 58 ft 7 in (17·86 m) tall and 21 ft 8½ in (6·61 m) in diameter. It carries 64,000 US gallons (242,260 litres) of liquid hydrogen and 20,000 US gallons (75,700 litres) of liquid oxygen, and weighs 262,000 lb (118,835 kg) fuelled.

S-IVB ORBITAL WORKSHOP (SKYLAB 1)

The NASA Skylab programme was devised to explore further and extend man's usefulness in space. It was expected to provide unprecedented opportunity for studying the Sun, so opening new ways of developing energy on Earth; and to permit unparalleled weather, geophysical and ecological observation.

The S-IVB Orbital Workshop was selected as the main spacecraft in the Skylab programme. It offered an extension of manned space flight capability beyond the Apollo flights by taking advantage of already-proven Saturn/Apollo hardware and skills. Objectives were (1) long-duration flights, (2) Earth-orbit scientific investigations, (3) applications in Earth orbit, and (4) an effective and economical approach to the development of a basis for future space programmes. Thus, the Workshop promised to fill the development and operational gap between the Apollo programme and future space stations. It was outfitted by McDonnell Douglas Astronautics Company, manufacturer of the original S-IVB stage.

The S-IVB Orbital Workshop was basically a modified S-IVB stage, with its 10,000 cu ft (283 m³) hydrogen tank equipped as living and working areas for three astronauts for periods of up to 59 days (in fact, the last crew stayed in orbit 84 days). The interior was lined with 3,000 sq ft (278 m²) of insulation and had metal beams and grids installed as floors and ceilings. Floor-to-ceiling partitions divided the living and working area into an experimental section, ward room, sleep compartments and waste compartment. Other installations included ten stainless steel tanks for fresh water, lockers and compartments for storage of supplies and equipment for experiments. Three openings were cut in the sides of the S-IVB stage. One of these provided an 18 in (46 cm) wide observation window: two were for 8¼ sq in (53 cm²) airlocks through which experiments could be put in space. Altogether, about 60 experiments could be carried, and two large solar arrays were mounted on the Workshop outer structure to provide the necessary electrical power.

Vital to the operation of the Workshop was the airlock module, also developed by MDAC at its St Louis facility. This module provided storage and distribution for environmental gases and electrical power, and performed numerous other service functions. A 43 in (109 cm) wide circular

DSV-3P Delta launch vehicle for Telesat 2 (Anik-2)

Skylab 1 in orbit, photographed from Skylab 3 command module

opening cut in an interior bulkhead of the Workshop served as an entry for astronauts moving between the airlock module and the Workshop.

Purpose of the Workshop was to provide an environment in space in which men could live and work under controlled conditions for extended periods of time, beyond that provided by Gemini and Apollo. The experiments were devised to investigate the men's physiological and psychological responses in the space environment, and to provide more detailed information on their capabilities for extended manned flight, as well as to provide data on Earth resources.

Skylab 1, the S-IVB Orbital Workshop, was launched on 14 May 1973. Details of the three manned missions to the Workshop (Skylabs 2, 3 and 4) can be found under the NASA entry in this section.

Prior to the end of the final manned mission, Skylab 4, on 8 February 1974, the Orbital Workshop was powered down and all systems were shut off, leaving the space station drifting in a dormant state in a 235 by 246 nm (270 by 283 mile; 435 by 455 km) orbit.

USAF 437 ANTI-SATELLITE SYSTEM

No details of this anti-satellite system are available, although the US technical press suggests that it has been operational since 1964. It is described as an unguided direct ascent anti-satellite vehicle, launched by Thrust Augmented Thor and fitted with a nuclear warhead.

Thrust-augmented Delta launch vehicle for Nimbus 5, 11 December 1972

Contractors for the system are given as McDonnell Douglas, Bell Telephone Laboratories and Univac Defense systems.

NASA

NATIONAL AERONAUTICS AND SPACE ADMINISTRATION

Headquarters: Washington, DC 20546
Administrator: Dr James C. Fletcher

In the 15 years of NASA's existence, it has been responsible for co-ordinating and conducting virtually all US non-military space projects. Its Office of Manned Space Flight is responsible for the Space Shuttle programme. NASA's Office of Space Science and its predecessor, the Office of Space Science and Applications, had launched some 300 spacecraft into Earth orbit or interplanetary space by March 1972, and had launched more than 1,600 sounding rockets into near-Earth space. To launch automated spacecraft OSS has collaborated with private industry in developing a series of versatile launch vehicles, including Scout, Delta and Atlas-Centaur. Adaptation of the Titan III and Titan IIIE-Centaur for launching larger automated spacecraft is underway.

Details of most of these programmes appear under the entries for the respective industry prime contractors in this section of *Jane's*. Following are details of other current programmes for which NASA is responsible:

EXPLORER 46

Launched by a Scout rocket from Wallops Island on 13 August 1972, this Meteoroid Technology Satellite was designed to gather information on the hazards spacecraft encounter from minute particles in space, and to indicate the effectivness of multi-sheet bumpers for spacecraft protection.

Laboratory tests suggested that a two-sheet bumper might provide better resistance to penetration than a single sheet of greater total thickness, and it was expected that Explorer 46 would provide confirmation of the laboratory results.

The principal experiment provides more than 300 sq ft (27·6 m²) of bumper target. Meteoroid penetrations of the complete target are registered by pressurised cell detectors. The target consists of an 0·001 in (0·0254 mm) stainless steel bumper, mounted 0·50 in (12·7 mm) in front of an 0·002 in (0·0508 mm) thick stainless steel main wall. The bumper target area is divided into 12 panels, each about 19 in (0·48 m) wide and 10·5 ft (3·1 m) long. Each panel contains eight pressurised cells providing a total of 96 detectors. If a meteoroid penetrates both bumper and main wall, there is a loss of pressure in the cell, which is telemetered to the ground.

Explorer 49 folded for launch

It was intended to deploy the bumper panels as four wings in flight, as shown in the accompanying illustration, but half of the panels were only partially deployed following launch. This had a serious effect on the spacecraft's attitude and resulted in overheating and eventual shutdown of the internal batteries nine days after it was placed in orbit. Despite this malfunction, the overall mission is considered a success. Data from the primary bumper experiment were transmitted successfully through a backup telemetry system which operates on solar cells.

How Explorer 46 would have appeared in orbit had all bumper panels deployed correctly

In the first year of operation the experiment proved that the double-sheet bumper is six times as effective as a standard single wall. Thus, future spacecraft may not be required to carry as much weight for meteoroid protection.

Operation of the bumper experiment has been extended for a second year, to provide additional data.

EXPLORER 48

Details of this Small Astronomy Satellite (SAS), launched on 15 November 1972, can be found in the 1973-74 *Jane's*. It was activated on 19 November and functioned well for six months, until it developed a power-supply fault and was switched off. During its working life its highly sensitive gamma-ray detector observed high-energy short-wavelength radiation emanating apparently from inside our galaxy. The detection of radiation from this source could have far-reaching implications for astronomers, as it might provide further clues regarding the origins and formation of all the galaxies.

EXPLORER 49 (RADIO ASTRONOMY EXPLORER B)

Launched on 10 June 1973 from the Kennedy Space Center by a "Straight-Eight" Delta, Explorer 49 was intended to probe the sources of low-frequency galactic radio emissions. To isolate the spacecraft from extraneous radio noise emanating from the Earth, the spacecraft was placed in lunar orbit so that the Moon acts as a shield as it crosses the far side facing away from the Earth.

Basically the 442 lb (200 kg) spacecraft is similar to Explorer 38, but its sensing range is greater (0·02MHz to 13MHz compared with 0·2MHz to 10MHz) thus permitting more extensive investigations. It consists essentially of a cylindrical body, 36 in (92 cm) in diameter by 31 in (79 cm) high, to which are mounted four solar panels, the lunar insertion motor and the various antennae and booms. Longest of these are four 750 ft (228 m) long radio astronomy antennae and the 675 ft (192 m) tip-to-tip libration damper boom. The bi-metallic antennae were stored flat on small reels and when extended curled over to form a tube for rigidity.

The inertia booms, which helped to stabilise the craft during its translunar flight, are made of boron filament, the first known use of this strong-but-light substance in such an application. The technology involved in the development of the antennae and booms represents a significant advance in spacecraft development.

The spacecraft was designed and built at Goddard Space Flight Center.

EXPLORER 50 (IMP-J)

The tenth and last Interplanetary Monitoring Platform (IMP-J; Explorer 50) was launched on 25 October 1973 from Kennedy Space Center by a Delta rocket, to complete the programme's investigation of the Earth's radiation environment over a complete solar cycle of eleven years.

Initially, the spacecraft was inserted into a 14,090 by 122 mile (228,808 by 197 km) transfer orbit, and then into a near-circular orbit of 179,700 by 87,700 miles (289,200 by 141,140 km). This is about one-third of the way to the Moon and somewhat similar to the orbit of Explorer 47, the data returns from which the latest spacecraft is correlating.

Explorer 50 is a 16-sided drum, 53 in (135 cm) in diameter by 62 in (157 cm) high, from which protrude various antennae. It weighs 877 lb (398 kg). The lower portion of the drum houses the solid-propellant kick motor used for circularisation of the orbit; the upper portion contains the experiments. Three rings of solar cells provide power for the experiments and electronics; one of the 48 solar panels is testing new high-efficiency solar cells developed by the Communications Satellite (Comsat) Corporation.

Twelve experiments cover the investigation of various particles, plasma and fields as follows: Energetic particles: two cosmic-ray detectors, an ion and electron detector, an electrons and isotopes detector, an energetic particles telescope-detector and a charged particles detector; Plasma: a plasma "Faraday cup" split collector, a low energy particles detector and a plasma analyser; Fields: a magnetic fields detector, a DC electric fields experiment, and an AC electric and magnetic fields experiment.

At the time of writing all twelve experiments had been activated and were functioning satisfactorily.

The IMP series of spacecraft has been very successful, providing the first accurate measurements of the interplanetary magnetic field, the boundary of the magnetosphere and of the shock-wave which occurs where the Earth's magnetic field meets the stream of particles emanating from the Sun (popularly referred to as the solar wind). IMP spacecraft also provided the first operational cosmic ray early-warning facility to protect astronauts from the dangerous radiation emitted by solar flares.

Explorer 50 was designed and built at Goddard Space Flight Center.

EXPLORER 51 (AE-C)

Launched by a Delta rocket from the Western Test Range on 16 December 1973, Explorer 51 was produced to explore in detail an area between 72 and 120 miles (120 and 300 km) altitude where important energy transfer, molecular processes and chemical reactions occur that are critical to the heat balance of the Earth's atmosphere.

Weighing 1,450 lb (660 kg), the spacecraft comprises a drum-shaped body 53 in (135 cm) in diameter by 45 in (115 cm) high, through the outer skin of which project various sensors and probes. The spacecraft is equipped with hydrazine thrusters so that it can be manoeuvred into different orbits and thus collect data over a wider range of altitudes. Solar cells mounted on the top and sides supply electric power for the spacecraft systems and experiments. The whole configuration is designed to minimise unbalanced torques created by atmospheric drag encountered at perigee.

In a circular orbit of 72 miles (120 km) the spacecraft would soon be pulled down by atmospheric drag; to prevent this, Explorer 51 was placed in an initial elliptical orbit of 98 × 2,673 miles (158 × 4,300 km). It was planned to lower the perigee every few weeks, until it reached 72 miles (115 km) where it would remain for several days. The spacecraft could then be boosted back into a higher circular orbit for the remainder of the mission.

Fourteen scientific instruments are carried: Ultraviolet (Nitric Oxide) Photometer, to measure ultraviolet radiation; Cylindrical Electrostatic Probe, to measure electron temperature; Bennett (Positive) Ion Mass Spectrometer, to measure atmospheric ion composition; Atmosphere Density Accelerometer, to measure the neutral density of the atmosphere; Photoelectron Spectrometer, to measure the intensity and energy distribution of the photoelectron flux; Retarding Potential Analyser, to measure ion temperature, concentration and composition; Visual Airglow Photometer, to obtain data on the rates of excitation of atomic and molecular constituents; Extreme Solar Ultraviolet Monitor; Solar Extreme Ultraviolet Spectrophotometer; Magnetic Ion Mass Spectrometer, to give absolute concentrations of each positive ion species and to study the distributions of meteoric ions; Low Energy Electron Spectrometer, to monitor the energy input to the thermosphere from electrons; Open-Source Neutral Mass Spectrometer; Neutral Atmosphere Composition Spectrometer and Neutral Atmosphere Temperature Spectrometer, to measure the neutral gas constituents, concentrations and temperature respectively in the thermosphere.

Explorer 51 was designed and built by RCA's Astro-Electronics Division for Goddard Space Flight Center.

ITOS (NOAA)

Improved Tiros Operational Satellite-1 (ITOS-1), also known as Tiros M, was launched from the Western Test Range in California on 23 January 1970. A second-generation operational weather satellite, it represents a significant improvement over its predecessors (ten Tiros and nine ESSA spacecraft) in that it is capable of mapping the Earth's cloud cover at night as well as by day. A complete scan of the Earth is thus possible in 12 hours rather than just once a day.

The satellite is box-shaped, 14 ft (4·27 m) wide with solar panels deployed, and weighs 682 lb (309 kg). Instead of spinning, as did ESSA satellites, it is stabilised so that it always faces the Earth. Employing a large spinning flywheel and appropriate electronic circuitry, this stabilisation system is called "Stabilite".

Picture equipment includes two advanced vidicon cameras, with tape storage, and two automatic picture transmission (APT) cameras. Data from the latter can be picked up by the 500 or so relatively simple APT ground receiving stations located in over 50 countries. Other experiments include a solar proton monitor for solar flare warnings, and a radiometer to measure the Earth's heat balance.

ITOS-1 was launched into polar orbit, together with a small Australian tracking satellite, by a two-stage Delta-N, with six Castor solid-propellant strap-on boosters. The craft, funded by NASA, was built by RCA. It was followed on 11 December 1970 by **ITOS-2.** This craft, and the four remaining spacecraft in the series, are funded by the US Commerce Department. Once in orbit ITOS-2 was handed over to the National Oceanic and Atmosphere Administration (formerly ESSA) and was given the designation **NOAA-1.**

An attempt to put a second NOAA satellite into orbit on 21 October 1971 was unsuccessful. The satellite re-entered the atmosphere due to incorrect orientation at the time of injection. A replacement **NOAA-2** was launched successfully on 15 October 1972. The Delta launch vehicle carried as secondary payload the Oscar 3 amateur radio satellite.

The initial NOAA-3 (ITOS-E) was also lost in a launch failure, in July 1973. Its replacement (ITOS-F) was launched successfully from the Western Test Range on 6 November 1973. This spacecraft is backing up the still-operating NOAA-2.

MARINER

This is a NASA project covering the design and manufacture of a series of unmanned space-probes for missions to Mars and Venus. The general appearance of one of the latest probes, for which Jet Propulsion Laboratory holds the prime contract, is shown in the accompanying illustration.

Details of many successful missions by Mariner spacecraft can be found in the 1969-70 and 1973-74 *Jane's*. The latest probe in the series is Mariner 10, of which a description follows:

Mariner 10 (Venus/Mercury) Spacecraft. Launched on 3 November 1973, from the Kennedy Space Center by an Atlas-Centaur, the purpose of Mariner 10 was to explore the planet Mercury, the trajectory involving a flyby of the planet Venus.

The 1,160 lb (528 kg) spacecraft comprises a central eight-sided forged magnesium framework, 18 in (45·7 cm) high by 54 in (139 cm) wide, with eight electronic compartments, flanked by two solar panels, each 106 in (270 cm) long by 38 in (97 cm) wide. The spherical propellant tank for the liquid-fuel course-correction rocket engine occupies the centre cavity of the octagonal structure. Two sets of reaction control units, each consisting of three pairs of jets to stabilise the spacecraft on three axes, are mounted on the tips of the solar panels and on the outrigger structures supporting the high-gain antenna and magnetometer booms.

Mariner 10 carries seven experiments, including: Extreme Ultraviolet experiment to analyse planetary atmospheres; an Infrared Radiometer to measure surface temperatures; Radio Science, to privide data for celestial mechanics and occultation measurements; Plasma Science, to observe the solar wind inside the orbit of Mercury; Charged Particle telescope; and a Magnetometer. In addition the craft carries two vidicon television cameras, each with eight filters and capable of taking both narrow and wide-angle photographs. The cameras are equipped with 1,500 mm Cassegrain telescopes, giving a Mercury surface resolution as fine as 500 ft (160 m).

After insertion into the trans-planetary trajectory, two corrections were required for the Venus portion of the flight, to provide the accuracy necessary to utilise the gravitational attraction of this planet to reach the primary target Mercury. The first, on 13 November, corrected for launch errors with a 19·9-second burn; the second, on 21 January 1974, applied a fine tuning to the trajectory with a short 3·7-second burn, giving a 4·6 ft (1·4 m) per second velocity change.

Shortly after launch a minor fault appeared, involving the heating of the two television cameras. This was either overcome or did not affect the operation of the cameras, which photographed Venus successfully from a height of 3,125 nm (3,600 miles; 5,760 km) on 5 February 1974. Over 4,000 pictures were returned, the best of which showed evidence of layering effects in the Venusian cloud cover and also of classical cloud circulation patterns.

Explorer 50 (IMP-J) spacecraft

Explorer 51 (Atmosphere Explorer-C)

The Venus flyby slowed the spacecraft, so that it fell towards the Sun at a rate planned to take it across the orbit of Mercury. The initial trajectory would have taken it to within 3,820 nm (4,400 miles; 7,080 km) of Mercury. A correction manoeuvre, planned initially for 15 February, was postponed due to erratic operation of the roll gyro, causing excessive expenditure of nitrogen attitude control gas. This fault was analysed as due to structural flutter. To save nitrogen, control in the roll axis was obtained subsequently by differential orientation of the solar panels. This generated torquing moments on the spacecraft, through the pressure of solar radiation; control in the yaw and pitch axes remained by Sun trackers.

Finally performed on 16 March, the course correction refined the flight path so that the spacecraft passed the dark side of Mercury on 29 March only 400 nm (460 miles; 730 km) above the surface.

During the flyby, prior to entering the planet's shadow and after exiting at the other side, the spacecraft returned spectacular pictures of the surface. This is seen to be heavily cratered, like the Moon and Mars, with large areas of low hills and an occasional valley or rille. The infrared radiometer recorded temperatures ranging from 370°F (188°C) on the planet's day side to —280°F (—173°C) on the night side.

Mariner 10 had a second successful rendezvous with Mercury on 21 September 1974.

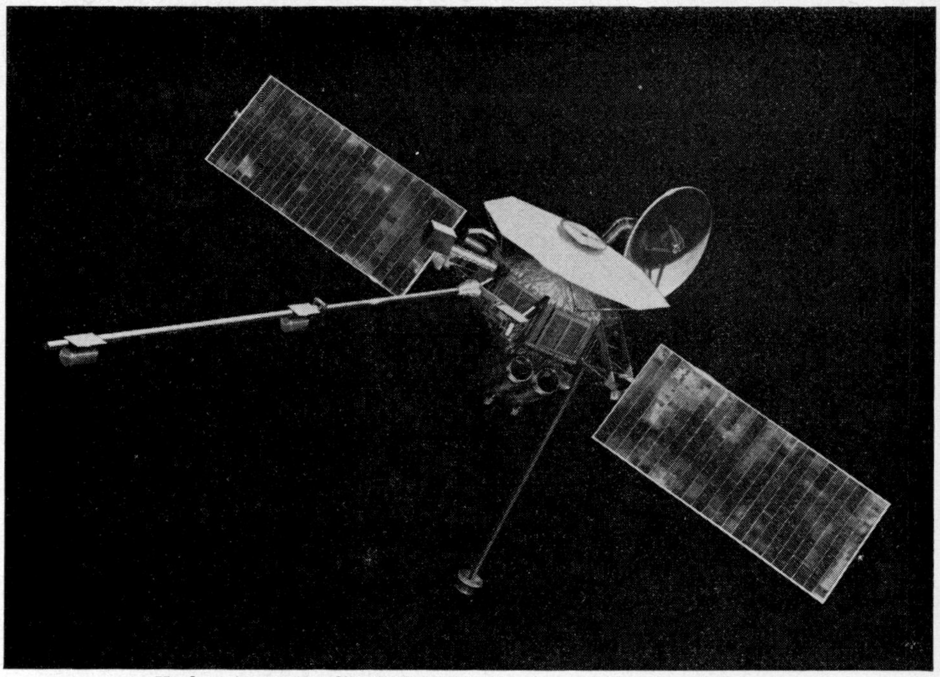

Mariner 10 spacecraft built for 1973-74 mission to Venus and Mercury

SATURN

The Saturn programme covered development and production of a series of very large multi-stage launching vehicles, of which development began in late 1958.

Characteristics of the three versions of Saturn are as follows:

Saturn I. Described in 1965-66 *Jane's*. All ten firings successful.

Saturn IB. Development of Saturn I, with S-1B first stage by Chrysler and S-IVB second stage by McDonnell Douglas. Able to put payload of 45,000 lb (20,400 kg) into a 105 nm (120 mile; 190 km) orbit. First five flights successful, on 26 February, 5 July and 25 August 1966 and 22 January and 11 October 1968. The fifth launch was the Apollo 7 manned Earth orbital flight. Latest applications have included Skylab and Apollo-Soyuz Test Project programmes.

Saturn V. Three-stage vehicle used for manned Apollo lunar flights. S-IC first stage by Boeing; S-II second stage by Rockwell International; S-IVB third stage by McDonnell Douglas. This version is able to put a payload of 120-140 short tons into Earth orbit or send 50 tons to the vicinity of the Moon. Height with Apollo payload 353 ft 5 in (107·7 m). Launching weight 6,100,000 lb (2,767,000 kg). Details of the first two launches (Saturn V/Apollo 4 and 6) can be found in the 1968-69 *Jane's*. The Saturn V/Apollo 8, 9, 10 and 11 missions were described in the 1969-70 edition, the Apollo 12 and 13 flights in the 1970-71 edition, the Apollo 14 and 15 flights in the 1971-72 edition, the Apollo 16 mission in the 1972-73 edition, and the final mission, Apollo 17, in the 1973-74 edition. Saturn V has since been used in the Skylab programme (see below).

SKYLAB 1 (ORBITAL WORKSHOP)

The Skylab 1 Orbital Workshop (see page 663) was launched on schedule at 1830 GMT on 14 May 1973, from Cape Kennedy, by a Saturn V, into a near-perfect orbit of 271 miles (463 km). Initial lift-off was successful; but after 63 seconds, as the vehicle reached maximum aerodynamic pressure, one section of the micrometeoroid shield deployed prematurely. It was torn off completely by the air pressure, and caused one of the main solar arrays to break off also.

Subsequently, in orbit, the 90° rotation of the Apollo Telescope Mount (ATM) into its operational position, and the deployment of its four large solar arrays was achieved satisfactorily. However, the remaining main solar array failed to extend fully, the result being that the Orbital Workshop was immediately restricted to half-power operation, using only power (10·5kW) coming from the panels attached to the ATM.

A more serious situation developed on the day following launch, when temperature measurements indicated that the Workshop was being overheated by the Sun. This was due to the loss of the micrometeoroid shield, which had a special thermal paint pattern to limit absorption of solar energy. Within a few days the surface temperature had reached 300°F on the Sun side and 120°F on parts of the internal structure—well beyond the safety limits. NASA officials began to fear that the onboard food supplies, sufficient for three manned missions, and some of the experiments would be adversely affected. The internal temperature was, however, reduced to a more acceptable level and stabilised at between 100°F and 105°F by orientating the workshop into the most favourable Sun angle of 50°, although this manoeuvre reduced the power coming from the ATM solar arrays.

While this was happening in orbit, rapid steps were being taken by NASA officials on the ground to devise repair plans that would overcome the heating problem. Schemes were devised for a variety of "sunshades" which astronauts could either deploy or fasten into position. In addition, cutting tools with extendable handles, 10 ft (3 m) rods and poles were made for pushing or pulling the partially deployed main solar array.

These steps were successful, as described below under the Skylab 2 entry. At the end of this mission, on 21 June, the Workshop was "powered down" to await the launch of Skylab 3 in July 1973.

SKYLAB 2

Skylab 2, comprising a modified Apollo Command Module (CM) and Service Module (SM), crewed by Charles Conrad (commander), Dr Joseph P. Kerwin (science pilot), and Paul J. Weitz (pilot), was initially scheduled to be launched on 15 May 1973, the day after the launching of the Orbital Workshop, for a 28-day mission with the Workshop. However, due to the overheating and power problems described under the Skylab 1 heading above, the launch was delayed to 25 May while repair schemes were devised.

The spacecraft was launched by a Saturn IB exactly on the revised schedule, at 1300 GMT on 25 May, and rendezvous with the Orbital Workshop was achieved 7 hr 40 min after launch.

Manoeuvring the spacecraft around the Workshop, Conrad confirmed that a micrometeoroid panel and one main solar array had been lost completely, and that an 0·50 in (12·7 mm) strip of aluminium from the micrometeoroid shield was preventing the remaining array from opening more than about 15°. Standing in the hatch of the CM, Weitz tried for an hour to free the panel, using a 10 ft (3 m) long pincer-equipped pole, but was unsuccessful.

Conrad then tried to dock with the Orbital Workshop, but the docking probe failed to operate three times. The astronauts had to don spacesuits, depressurise the capsule and connect a lead to by-pass the switches controlling the catch activators, which were diagnosed as causing the trouble. The catches operated perfectly on

Saturn IB/Skylab 3 launch vehicle

Saturn V launch vehicle for Skylab Workshop

the next attempt, a hard docking being finally achieved at 0353 GMT on 26 May.

The Workshop was boarded later that day. It was hot, but the low humidity kept the temperature tolerable, although gloves were necessary to protect the crew's hands from the hot metalwork.

Three different types of sun screens were on board Skylab 2. The one chosen was a 24 ft × 22 ft (7·3 m × 6·7 m) sheet, erected like a parasol from inside the Workshop through one of the experiment hatches in the wall. The parasol had been designed, built and tested in six days by the Technical Services Division at Johnson Space Center. Attached to a 21 ft (6·4 m) pole, it was designed to open into a flat sheet and then to be pulled down flush with the Workshop surface. It did not deploy properly, the front end not opening fully. However, the effect was immediately apparent; within a day the temperature had dropped below 100°F and subsequently stabilised at around 80°F.

The power supply situation worsened when five of the 18 Workshop batteries failed. When the ATM is operating, the Orbital Workshop circles the Earth so that the ATM solar arrays face the Sun constantly, except when eclipsed. At other times, operation of the Earth resources experiment requires the craft to follow the curvature of the Earth, facing away from the Sun. During these periods power is drawn from the 18 batteries.

Three of the failed batteries were brought back into full operation, but the loss of two others placed limitations on the experiment programme. Permission was given for a space walk, in another attempt to free the jammed main solar panel. This was effected by Conrad and Kerwin who, after struggling for 90 minutes, finally managed to cut the strip of metal holding the panel. The panel then swung out, but a further five hours passed before the three individual arrays making up the panel had extended fully.

The power supply was still such that some experiments had to be abbreviated. Nevertheless, some 80 per cent of the scheduled programme experiments were completed, in spite of the time consumed effecting the initial repairs and correcting subsequent malfunctions, and the ATM recorded some significant solar activity. Most important of all, a prime objective of the mission, to determine man's ability to live and work in space for extended periods, was dramatically demonstrated.

The mission ended on 22 June, after a record-breaking 28 days in orbit, during which the astronauts had orbited the Earth 404 times, covering 11,500,000 miles (18,500,000 km). After packing up the Orbital Workshop ready for the Skylab 3 mission planned in July, the crew climbed into the Command Module, undocked, and re-entered the atmosphere.

Splashdown was very close to the predicted point, exactly on the scheduled time of 1350 GMT, near the prime recovery ship USS *Ticonderoga*. A departure from the procedure used for the Apollo Moon missions was that the Command Module was winched on board the recovery ship with the astronauts still inside. This was to expedite the transfer of frozen specimens from the CM to cold storage facilities on the recovery ship. It would also have had advantages if the prolonged stay in space had severely affected the Skylab crew. In fact, the astronauts, in good spirits, walked away from the CM with only a trace of unsteadiness. They survived their stay in space well, although two of them were subjected to subsequent bouts of sickness.

SKYLAB 3

Of similar configuration to Skylab 2, this manned spacecraft was launched successfully by a Saturn IB rocket on 28 July 1973, carrying the second Skylab 1 crew comprising astronauts Alan L. Bean (Commander), Dr Owen K. Garriott (science pilot) and Jack R. Lousma (pilot).

The main objectives of this mission, initially planned to last 56 days, were: to perform unmanned Saturn Workshop operations (before the launch); to reactivate and man Skylab 1; to obtain medical data on the crew for use in extending the duration of manned space flights; and to perform in-orbit experiments.

Early troubles involving the Skylab 3 main engine and side thrusters, including fuel leakage, threatened the mission at an early stage, before the decision was made to permit the full stay in space. The crew suffered bouts of nausea during the first three days (which resulted in the mission being extended by three days partly to compensate for the loss of time and partly to provide for a better recovery position). These and numerous minor technical problems were overcome to the extent that the crew settled down to working 12 to 16 hours a day, and eventually accomplished half again as much scientific work as planned.

For example, the pre-mission plan called for 26 Earth-orientated Earth resources passes, but the crew completed 39, plus two calibration passes and two solar inertial passes. The plan also called for 186 hours of solar observations by the Apollo Telescope Mount; the final total was 305 hours. The crew also exceeded pre-launch plans in the areas of biomedicine, technical and materials processing experiments.

An early task, on 6 August, involved a space walk by Jack Lousma, to erect an improved two-pole Sun-shield to keep down the temperature in the orbital workshop; this shield replaced an earlier version erected by the Skylab 2 astronauts.

On 24 August Jack Lousma and Dr Owen Garriott made a 4·5 hr spacewalk, to change film in the polar telescopes and to renew a package of six faulty rate-gyros in the attitude control system. Attached to long safety lines, Lousma removed and replaced the faulty instruments in only 10 minutes. Garriott, equally easily, removed and replaced the exposed film.

Inside the orbital workshop a spider, Arabella, spun a web without the assistance of gravity; and two minnows, in a plastic aquarium, soon adjusted to swimming in zero-*g*. Several minnow eggs were hatched, to establish a minor but historically significant record as the first Earth creatures to be born in space.

Skylab 3 completed its mission on 25 September, after 59 days 11 hours in space, and after 858 orbits covering more than 24 million miles (38 million km). During the approach and re-entry manoeuvre, the CSM performed well with only two of the four thruster quads operating because of the failure during launch of the remaining units. Splashdown occurred within 6 seconds of the pre-launch scheduled time and within 2·8 miles (4·5 km) of the target.

All three astronauts were slightly unsteady and weakened by their record stay in space. In spite of healthy appetites all three had lost a little weight, Alan Bean the most, dropping 8·5 lb (3·8 kg). There was also a deterioration in muscle tone, marked by the loss of more than 1 in (2·50 cm) in the circumference of the crew's calves. Most of these changes took place during the first half of the flight, the men's weights stabilising after 40 days.

In general, the astronauts were in excellent physical condition. Less than a week after splashdown they were all working normally at Houston.

SKYLAB 4

Skylab 4, containing the third and final Skylab 1 crew comprising Gerald P. Carr (Commander), Dr Edward G. Gibson (science pilot) and William R. Pogue (pilot), was launched successfully on 16 November 1973.

The launch, scheduled originally for 10 November, was delayed for six days by the discovery of cracks in the fin attachment points of the Saturn IB rocket, necessitating the replacement of all eight fins. These were changed while the rocket was on its launching pad.

The main objectives of the third mission, planned initially to last 56 days but extended ultimately to 84 days, were basically similar to those of the second mission; to perform unmanned Saturn Workshop operations (before the launch); to reactivate and man Skylab 1; to obtain medical data for use in extending the duration of manned space flights; and to perform in-orbit experiments.

Space Shuttle jettisoning its solid boosters after lift-off

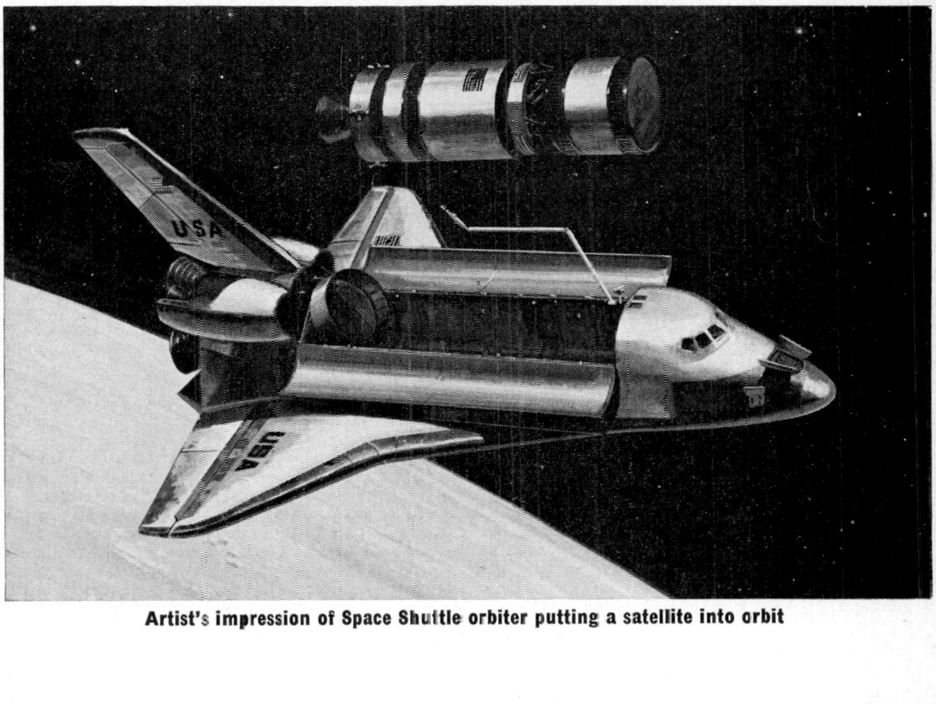

Artist's impression of Space Shuttle orbiter putting a satellite into orbit

After docking with Skylab 1, Pogue became ill and vomited. In an understandable, but reprehensible, attempt not to worry the ground control team, the crew discussed discarding it without official notification. This discussion was accidentally transmitted to Earth and drew a reprimand from the astronaut chief, Rear Admiral Alan B. Shepard. Few other problems were encountered, and the overall mission was an outstanding success. An unanticipated major astronomical event—the comet Kohoutek—was observed and photographed from Skylab. Although the comet did not fulfill its early promise of extreme brilliance, useful data was obtained on such little-known cosmic phenomena.

Major tasks of the mission included further Earth resources experiments and re-runs of seven of the eleven space processing experiments conducted by Skylab 3. In the Earth resources experiments, six devices were used to advance remote-sensing technology and, at the same time, to gather data applicable to research in agriculture, forestry, ecology, geology, geography, meteorology, hydrology, hydrography and oceanography.

The eleven experiments conducted by the crew of Skylab 3 in the multi-purpose electric furnace series focussed on crystal growth, solidification and other processes involving phase changes in materials at elevated temperatures of up to 1,000°C. The seven experiments re-run by Skylab 4 included: crystal growth by vapour transport; immiscible alloy compositions; growth of single crystals of indium antimonide; whisker-reinforced composites; indium antimonide crystals; mixed crystal growth; and aluminium-copper eutectic.

Other in-orbit experiments included flight testing of the Astronaut Manoeuvring Unit, a jet-propelled "armchair" that could have future uses during constructional and repair operations in space. Four extra-vehicular activity missions (spacewalks) were completed, totalling 22 hr 19 min, which helped to define further man's ability to perform detailed tasks in space.

Skylab 4 completed its mission on 8 February 1974, after 84 days and 1,214 orbits, during which the crew travelled 34·5 million miles (55 million km). In spite of the record length of the mission, the crew were in better physical condition after splashdown than previous Skylab crews. The astronauts had been awake for 24 hours prior to re-entry, and had to undergo an extensive series of medical tests after splashdown, but spent one hour assisting in the unloading of the Apollo command module before going to bed.

SPACE SHUTTLE

The Space Shuttle will be the first re-usable space vehicle, consisting basically of two stages: a booster and an orbiter. The orbiter will have a delta wing and will look very like a conventional aeroplane, but will be powered by three Rocketdyne high-pressure rocket engines. The liquid oxygen/liquid hydrogen propellants for these engines will be carried in a large external jettisonable tank, on which the orbiter will be mounted at lift-off. Two large solid-propellant jettisonable boosters will be mounted on opposite sides of the propellant tank for lift-off.

The orbiter will be operated by a flight crew of two, and there will be additional seats for two mission crewmen and six passengers. Hatches in the top of the fuselage will give access to the payload compartment, which will be 60 ft (18·3 m) long and 15 ft (4·57 m) in diameter, this large space being made possible by the fact that the main propellant tanks are external. The interior of the craft will be pressurised, enabling the crew to work without spacesuits, and no astronaut training will be needed by passengers.

In operation, the Shuttle will be launched vertically, with all engines firing in both the boosters and orbiter. At an altitude of about 22 nm (25 miles; 40 km), the booster stages will separate and descend into the sea by parachute, for recovery. The orbiter will continue under its own power, and will jettison its large underbelly propellant tank when established in orbit.

In space, the orbiter will manoeuvre by means of two smaller rocket engines, also mounted in the rear-fuselage propulsion cluster. For minor course corrections and adjustments of attitude, the orbiter will have a series of small thrusters. Normal mission duration will be seven days or less, but it will be possible to extend orbital stay-time to 30 days by the addition of further expendables such as water, food and oxygen.

The orbiter's main initial tasks are expected to be the placing of satellites into orbit, retrieval of satellites from orbit, and the repair and servicing of satellites in orbit. It could be used to put a propulsive stage and satellite into precise low Earth orbit, for subsequent transfer to synchronous orbit or to an "escape" mission into space. It could also be used for short-duration scientific and applications missions, as an orbiting research laboratory or reconnaissance vehicle, for space rescue, as a tanker for space refuelling, and for support of orbiting space stations.

On conclusion of its mission, the orbiter will fly back into the atmosphere towards its land base, protected by a new form of heat shielding which will survive 100 missions, unlike current ablative-type heat-shields. Once through the re-entry phase, the orbiter will be able to glide up to 950 nm (1,100 miles; 1,760 km) to its base, steered by aerodynamic controls. During the final phase of the flight, in-built jet engines will permit adjustments to the approach path.

Initial stage of the Space Shuttle project was a Phase A feasibility study, which confirmed the engineering and financial practicability of a re-usable orbiting vehicle. Phase B called for a complete definition and costing of the Shuttle system. Two large industrial groups were contracted to prepare and submit competitive designs to NASA, one headed by Rockwell International, the other by McDonnell Douglas. A third industrial group, headed by Boeing and Grumman, was commissioned to re-check some Phase A work to ensure that the best basics had been embodied into the Phase B submissions.

In early 1972 the political and financial decision was taken to proceed to Phase C/D, involving design and development of the system, and construction of the first two flying vehicles. Subsequently, Rockwell International was awarded the design, development and testing contract for the orbiting vehicle and for system integration.

Artist's impression of Apollo-Soyuz Test Project in orbit

APOLLO-SOYUZ TEST PROJECT (ASTP)

An accompanying artist's impression shows the docking in Earth orbit of a Soviet Soyuz manned spacecraft and an American Apollo manned spacecraft, planned for mid-1975.

It is expected that the mission will begin with the launching of an Apollo Command/Service Module from Cape Kennedy by means of a Saturn IB vehicle. The spacecraft will enter a 110 nm (127 mile; 204 km) circular orbit at an inclination of 51·6°, which will take it over the Soviet space centre at Tyuratam. Soyuz will then be launched into a 145 nm (167 mile; 269 km) orbit, and the Apollo will rendezvous with it. This takes account of the greater endurance of the Apollo's propulsion system.

The rendezvous and docking operation is expected to take about 24 hours. The two craft will be linked via a Docking Module (DM) which is being specially developed by Rockwell International's Space Division. This will be an airlock device to acclimatise crew members transferring from one spacecraft to the other. Approximately 10 ft (3 m) long and 5 ft (1·5 m) in basic diameter, it will accommodate two men simultaneously. The DM will be orbited inside the S-IVB upper stage of the Saturn launch vehicle and will be extracted by the Apollo spacecraft in the method that was used to extract the Lunar Module on Apollo missions to the Moon.

PHILCO-FORD

PHILCO-FORD CORPORATION

AERONUTRONIC DIVISION:
Ford Road, Newport Beach, California 92663
Telephone: (714) 640-1500

WESTERN DEVELOPMENT LABORATORIES DIVISION:
3939 Fabian Way, Palo Alto, California 94303
Telephone: (415) 326-4350

Details of current Philco-Ford space programmes follow:

SYNCHRONOUS METEOROLOGICAL SATELLITE (SMS)

Philco-Ford Corporation's Western Development Laboratories Division was selected as prime contractor to NASA's Goddard Space Flight Center for the first two SMS (Synchronous Meteorological Satellite) spacecraft. Designed to meet National Operational Meteorological Satellite System (NOMSS) requirements, as specified by the National Oceanic and Atmospheric Administration (NOAA), these spacecraft are intended for continuous observation of the atmosphere on an operational basis. Their design provides for a day-and-night cloud cover viewing capability, for the collection and dissemination of meteorological data.

SMS-1, first of the 103 in (2·62 m) tall, 75 in (1·90 m) diameter satellites, was orbited by a Delta 2914 vehicle from the Eastern Test Range, Cape Kennedy, on 17 May 1974. The basic payload of the 1,379 lb (627 kg) spacecraft comprises a telescope radiometer, called the Visible Infra-red Spin-Scan Radiometer (VISSR), providing both infra-red (IR), and high resolution visible photography; a communications system for data collection and distribution; and a Space Environment Monitoring (SEM) subsystem.

From its initial stationary position over the equator, just off the coast of Brazil, the satellite transmits day and night "full-disc" pictures of the Western hemisphere every 30 minutes. The telescope is capable of producing ½ mile (0·9 km) resolution images in visible light, and 5 mile (9 km) resolution images during night-time, using the infra-red sensors.

In addition to its main task of weather surveillance, the satellite is to act as the orbital component of the Geostationary Operational Environmental Satellite system planned by NASA, NOAA, and the US Department of Commerce. In this role the satellite will receive data from up to 10,000 data-collection platforms, located around the US on board ocean-going ships and buoys, and at manned and unmanned environmental stations.

The satellite is also being used to monitor solar flare activity, and the intensity of the Earth's magnetic field and of incoming X-radiation.

It was planned to launch SMS-2 later in 1974 to cover the Eastern hemisphere. This will enable the two spacecraft to be the first satellites used in the Global Atmospheric Research Programme (GARP), a worldwide weather watch sponsored by the United Nations and the International Council of Scientific Unions. When GARP is fully under way in 1977, the United States' SMS and GOES satellites will be joined by similar spacecraft from Europe (Meteosat), the USSR and Japan, to form a global weather monitoring network that should enable meteorologists to forecast weather a week or more in advance with extreme accuracy.

Impression of the SMS-1 satellite in orbit

GEOSTATIONARY OPERATIONAL ENVIRONMENTAL SATELLITE (GOES A)

Similar in all respects to the SMS satellites, GOES A (Geostationary Operational Environmental Satellite) is being built for the National Oceanic and Atmospheric Administration (NOAA) by Philco-Ford Corporation's Western Development Laboratories Division, under a contract awarded through NASA's Goddard Space Flight Center. It was scheduled for launch in late 1974, and is expected to be followed by GOES B and C.

NATO 2B

This communications satellite, developed and built by Philco-Ford Corporation's Western Development Laboratories Division and launched by NASA from Cape Kennedy on behalf of NATO, consists basically of a cylindrical body 54 in (1·37 m) in diameter and 63 in (1·60 m) high overall. The satellite weighed 535 lb (242·5 kg) at launch and 285 lb (129 kg) in orbit, after expending the solid propellant of its apogee boost motor. More than 7,000 solar cells are mounted on eight vertical panels to provide power over the satellite's design operational life of five years.

The satellite has two channels for receiving, translating, amplifying and retransmitting voice, telegraph and facsimile data originated by the NATO ground stations.

NATO 2B was launched by a Thrust-Augmented Delta vehicle on 2 February 1971, to serve as a backup for NATO 2A, also built by Philco-Ford. (NATO 2A ceased operations during 1972.) After entering an initial highly-elliptical orbit, NATO 2B's solid-propellant "kick-stage" was fired to put it into synchronous orbit. It was then manoeuvred into an operational position to provide communications links between NATO headquarters in Brussels and the national capitals of the NATO nations and NATO commands on land and sea. It provides coverage of an area in the northern hemisphere from Ankara, Turkey, to the state of Virginia in the USA, and can serve ground stations in the USA, Canada, UK, Norway, Denmark, Germany, the Netherlands, Belgium, Italy, Greece, Turkey and Portugal.

NATO 3

In February 1973, Philco-Ford received a $27·7 million contract to build a new generation of communications satellites for NATO. The contract was placed by the USAF's Space and Missile Systems Organization on behalf of NATO's Integrated Communications System Management Agency. Costs of the project are to be shared by participating NATO countries; both foreign

NATO 2B communications satellite

and US subcontractors will be used.

The fixed-price-incentive contract calls for delivery of two NATO-3 satellites for launch three months apart in late 1975 and early 1976. They will be positioned in stationary orbit 22,000 miles (35,400 km) above the equator, midway between Africa and South America, with the second satellite serving as a backup for the first.

The contract carries an option for possible conversion of a qualification prototype into a third flight model one and a half years after the initial launch.

The new satellites will offer considerably more power and wider frequency bands than the earlier NATO-2 satellites, also built by Philco-Ford. Preliminary designs call for large cylindrical spacecraft weighing about 1,500 lb (680 kg) at launch and 675 lb (306 kg) in orbit. More than 32,000 solar cells will provide energy for an estimated operating life of seven years. Two primary "beams" of communications coverage will operate simultaneously: one serving NATO countries throughout the northern hemisphere; the other covering only western Europe.

Each satellite will have three channels for receiving, translating frequencies, amplifying and re-transmitting voice, telegraph, facsimile and wide-band data originated by ground stations in the multi-nation network.

DIMENSIONS:

Height overall	10 ft 1¾ in (3·10 m)
Height of body	7 ft 4 in (2·24 m)
Diameter	7 ft 2 in (2·18 m)

JAPANESE ENGINEERING TEST SATELLITES (ETS-II)

Philco-Ford Corporation's Western Development Laboratories Division received a $20 million contract in March 1974 to develop Japan's Engineering Test Satellites (ETS-II), which will be used to flight test that country's "N" rocket. The contract was awarded by Mitsubishi Electric Corporation, which is responsible to Japan's National Space Development Agency for the ETS-II programme.

Philco-Ford will design, develop and build a flight-qualified ETS-II prototype and an actual flight model. Although assembled in the United States, the spacecraft will be launched in early 1977 from Tanegashima Space Centre in Japan. ETS-II will be the first payload placed in synchronous orbit by an "N" rocket. Equipment on board the satellite will monitor continuously the rocket's launch characteristics, including vibration, shock, acceleration and other parameters. Once in orbit, it will be used also to evaluate Japanese satellite control techniques and ground support systems.

The ETS-II spacecraft will be spin-stabilised, with mechanically de-spun antennae. Preliminary designs call for the cylindrical satellites to be approximately 55 in (140 cm) in diameter and 33 in (84 cm) high, with a 30 in (76 cm) antenna on top. Each will weigh about 560 lb (254 kg) at launch and 285 lb (130 kg) in orbit.

EXPERIMENTAL JAPANESE COMMUNICATIONS SATELLITES

Philco-Ford Corporation's Western Development Laboratories Division received a contract valued at approximately $30 million in February 1974, from Mitsubishi Electric Corporation, to design two experimental communications satellites for Japan. Mitsubishi is under contract to Japan's National Space Development Agency to administer the programme.

Philco-Ford's contract calls for the company to deliver two medium-capacity spacecraft for launch from the United States in early 1977. The experimental satellites (a flight-qualified prototype and an actual flight model) are intended to pave the way for later launches of full-capacity operational spacecraft.

Early design plans call for spin-stabilised satellites with mechanically de-spun antennae, designed to operate from synchronous geostationary orbit. They will be used for telephone communications tests over the islands of Japan. Tests will include C-band (4 to 6GHz) and K-band (18 to 30GHz) frequencies.

RCA

RCA CORPORATION

HEAD OFFICE:
30 Rockefeller Plaza, New York, NY 10020
Telephone: (212) 265-5900

CHAIRMAN OF THE BOARD AND CHIEF EXECUTIVE OFFICER: Robert W. Sarnoff

PRESIDENT: Anthony L. Conrad

EXECUTIVE VICE-PRESIDENTS:
Kenneth W. Bilby (Public Affairs)
Dr J. Hillier (Research and Engineering)
Irving K. Kessler (Government and Commercial Systems)

VICE-PRESIDENT, INTERNATIONAL NEWS AND INFORMATION:
Leslie Slote

RCA is prime contractor for a number of major defence programmes, including the US Navy's Aegis advanced ship-to-air missile system and the USAF's 417 satellite, of which details follow:

USAF 417 SATELLITE

This reconnaissance support satellite is reported to have been operational since the mid-sixties. It weighs an estimated 600 lb (270 kg) and is launched by Thor/Burner II. Its purpose is to report cloud cover over areas that have been selected for surveillance by photographic-reconnaissance satellites, to prevent wastage of film. Orbital height is about 500 miles (800 km).

ROCKWELL INTERNATIONAL

ROCKWELL INTERNATIONAL CORPORATION

Space Division

ADDRESS:
12214 Lakewood Boulevard, Downey, California 90241
Telephone: (213) 922-2111

OTHER FACILITIES:
Seal Beach, California; Cocoa Beach, Florida; Houston, Texas

PRESIDENT: G. W. Jeffs

The Space Division of Rockwell International was principal contractor for the building of Apollo Command and Service Modules and the second stage of the Saturn V launch vehicle used for the highly-successful 11-year Apollo lunar exploration programme. It was principal contractor for the Command and Service Modules which were used in 1973-74 to carry astronauts/scientists to the orbiting Skylab 1 laboratory. It is now building a Docking Module and docking system, and is modifying Apollo Command and Service Modules, for the Apollo-Soyuz Test Project which is scheduled for mid-1975.

The Division is under contract to NASA to design, build and test the Space Shuttle orbiter, and to act as integrator for the Space Shuttle transportation system. It is also under contract to the USAF Space and Missile Systems Organisation to build a multi-payload satellite, designated P72-2, for launch in the latter part of 1974.

ASTP/APOLLO SPACECRAFT and DOCKING MODULE

The Apollo/Soyuz Test Project (ASTP) calls for the docking of a US Apollo and a Soviet Soyuz spacecraft in Earth orbit, to test compatible rendezvous and docking equipment and procedures that might assist future international space rescue missions (see NASA entry in this section).

Another major objective of the programme is the design and in-flight testing of a universal docking mechanism, half of which will be developed and built in the USSR and the other half in the United States. The mechanism is somewhat symbolic of the joint mission, in that its halves are different in detail but work together as a pair.

The Apollo spacecraft, comprising Command and Service Modules, is being modified for the mission by its builder, Rockwell International's Space Division, under the direction of NASA's Lyndon B. Johnson Space Center. The Division is also building a docking module for the flight, equipped with the new docking mechanism, which will serve as the connecting link between the two spacecraft and as an airlock for crew movement between Apollo and Soyuz, which have different atmospheres.

The basic Apollo Command Module is 10 ft 7 in (3·23 m) high, with a launch weight of about 13,000 lb (5,900 kg). It consists of an inner pressurised compartment of aluminium honeycomb and an outer structure of stainless steel honeycomb with a plastics ablative heatshield coating over the entire outer surface.

The basic Apollo Service Module is 24 ft 9 in (7·54 m) high, with a weight of about 53,000 lb (24,040 kg), and is constructed of aluminium honeycomb.

Spacecraft modifications include the addition of controls and displays for operating the docking module, increased reaction control system propellants for extended in-flight manoeuvring capability, and additional heaters for enhanced thermal control.

Cylindrical-shaped, the docking module is approximately 10 ft (3 m) long and 5 ft (1·5 m) in diameter. The Soviet half of the universal docking mechanism will be on one of its ends, while the other, which attaches to the Apollo, will have the docking system used in US lunar missions.

Other equipment includes operational controls, oxygen and nitrogen provisions, a temperature control system, floodlights and a food supply. An intercom will be included so that astronauts and cosmonauts can communicate between the two spacecraft.

Preliminary plans call for the Apollo and Soyuz to be docked for a maximum of two days. During this time, crewmen will transfer between the two spacecraft and perform joint experiments.

The Apollo has a 100 per cent oxygen, 5 lb/sq in (0·35 kg/cm²) interior pressure; Soyuz has a 10 lb/sq in (0·70 kg/cm²), 70 per cent nitrogen and 30 per cent oxygen atmosphere. In going from the Apollo to Soyuz, US astronauts will first adjust the docking module's atmosphere to equal Apollo's. They will then enter the module and, with nitrogen, increase its pressure to that of Soyuz before entering the Soviet spacecraft. The transfer process will take about 30 minutes.

On the return trip, crewmen will enter the docking module, enrich its atmosphere with oxygen and then depressurise the module to the environment of Apollo before entering the US spacecraft. The return process will take approximately 40 minutes.

SPACE SHUTTLE TRANSPORTATION SYSTEM

The National Aeronautics and Space Administration's Space Shuttle will be the world's first re-usable space transportation system, and will be the keystone of America's space programme through this century. Rockwell International's Space Division is integrating the system and developing the Shuttle's payload-carrying orbiter stage for NASA, under a six-year $2,600 million contract awarded on 26 July 1972, following three years of study and a competitive proposal.

The Shuttle system includes the orbiter stage, capable of carrying up to 65,000 lb (29,500 kg) of varied cargo into Earth orbit; an external propellant tank; and two solid-propellant rocket boosters. The orbiter will lift off from Earth like a rocket, operate in orbit as a spacecraft, and return to land in a manner similar to that of a conventional aeroplane. Characteristics of the system are as follows:

ORBITER: A delta-winged aeroplane-like craft, 122 ft (37·18 m) long and 57 ft (17·37 m) high, with a 78 ft (23·77 m) wing span. Blended wing/fuselage design for optimum aerodynamic and manoeuvring characteristics. Structure of conventional aircraft design and fabrication, basically utilising aluminium, with outer thermal protective covering.

BOOSTER: Two solid-propellant rocket boosters, together with the orbiter's main engines, will power the orbiter from lift-off to orbital altitude. They will be jettisoned about two minutes into the flight, at an altitude of about 140,000 ft (43,000 m), dropped by parachute into the ocean and recovered for re-use. The boosters will each develop some 2,650,000 lb (1,202,000 kg) st and will be positioned under the wings of the orbiter, attached one on each side of the orbiter's external propellant tank. Supplied by Thiokol, each booster will be about 149 ft (45·42 m) long, with a diameter of 12 ft (3·66 m).

EXTERNAL PROPELLANT TANK: Contains the liquid oxygen and liquid hydrogen main propellants for the orbiter. Aluminium monocoque construction, with foam external insulation. Approximately 154 ft (46·93 m) long and 27 ft 6 in (8·37 m) in diameter. Under development by Denver Division of Martin Marietta Aerospace.

PAYLOAD BAY: 15 ft (4·57 m) in diameter by 60 ft (18·29 m) long, with manipulator arm equipped with television for deploying and retrieving one or more payloads.

CREW COMPARTMENT: Two-deck seating arrangement; two flight crewmen and two mission crewmen on upper deck, with six passenger seats and living area below. Dual flight controls for pilot and co-pilot. This compartment houses systems for controlling and operating the orbiter.

THERMAL PROTECTION: Silica fibre-based high-temperature and low-temperature re-usable surface insulation over a majority of the craft, with a reinforced carbon-carbon composite for the nose and wing leading-edges.

MAIN PROPULSION: Three high-pressure liquid oxygen/liquid hydrogen engines, each developing 470,000 lb (213,200 kg) st in space, provide the main propulsion for the orbiter. The engines are being developed for NASA under separate contract by Rockwell International's Rocketdyne Division.

ORBIT MANOEUVRING ENGINES: Two 6,000 lb (2,720 kg) st engines will be used for the orbiter's orbit manoeuvring subsystem (OMS). The engines will be housed in pods, one on each side of the orbiter's tail fin.

REACTION CONTROL ENGINES: The orbiter's reaction control subsystem (RCS) will utilise thirty-eight 900 lb (408 kg) st thrust engines and six 25 lb (11·5 kg) vernier thrusters. Fourteen of the RCS engines will be on the orbiter's nose, and 24 will be on the aft end, 12 in each OMS pod.

AVIONICS: The avionics system consists of six subsystems: guidance, navigation and control; data processing and software; communications; displays and controls; flight instrumentation; and electrical power distribution and control.

Full-scale mockup of Space Shuttle orbiter, less tail-fin

Artist's impression of P72-2 multi-experiment Air Force satellite

More than 50 per cent of the equipment for the overall system will be of "mature design" or equipment already proven or easily available.

DIMENSIONS, EXTERNAL:

Length of complete vehicle at lift-off	184 ft 0 in (56·08 m)
Height of complete vehicle	76 ft 0 in (23·16 m)

See also Space Shuttle entry under NASA heading in this section.

P72-2 SATELLITE

Scheduled for launch in the last quarter of 1974, the one-of-a-kind P72-2 multi-payload satellite was developed for the USAF Space and Missile Systems Organisation (SAMSO) by Rockwell's Space Division.

One of the most complex satellites produced under the Air Force Space Test Programme, it contains scientific instruments to measure the concentration and distribution of upper atmosphere aerosols (particles), in order to develop a preliminary data base for environmental protection studies related to such things as Earth temperature predictions; to make Earth radiation measurements; to determine the effects of the atmosphere on the disbursement of radio signals; and to determine the location and characteristics, and to make measurements, of the Earth's ultraviolet horizon on a global basis.

DIMENSIONS (approx):

Length overall	14 ft 0 in (4·27 m)
Diameter	4 ft 6 in (1·37 m)

WEIGHTS (approx):

Payload and associated equipment	600 lb (272 kg)
Weight in orbit	1,600 lb (725 kg)

TRW

TRW SYSTEMS GROUP

HEAD OFFICE:
1, Space Park, Redondo Beach, California 90278
Telephone: (213) 535-4321

VICE-PRESIDENT AND GENERAL MANAGER:
Dr George E. Solomon

VICE-PRESIDENT AND ASST GENERAL MANAGER:
Dr Edward B. Doll

PUBLIC AFFAIRS AND COMMUNICATIONS DIRECTOR:
Raymond Weil

Known formerly as TRW/Space Technology Laboratories (STL), and originally as the Guided Missiles Division of Ramo-Wooldridge, TRW Systems Group has provided technical direction and systems engineering for the USAF Atlas/Titan/Minuteman missile programme since 1954. The company has also designed and built more than 100 spacecraft and scores of major subsystems. Its recent and current military and civilian contracts have included prime contracts for the NASA OGO and Pioneer, USAF Vela and DSCS II, international communications satellites and the US Navy Fleet Communications Satellite.

The company built the variable-thrust descent engine for the Apollo Lunar Module (LM) and continues to produce a variety of low-thrust liquid-propellant and radioisotope thrusters. It also produced the LM abort guidance system.

TRW Systems provided NASA with mission analysis and spacecraft systems planning for the Apollo and Skylab projects, and furnishes systems integration and test support for the US Navy's anti-submarine warfare (ASW) programme.

Examples of environmental research satellites developed by TRW for "piggyback" launching

DEFENSE SATELLITE COMMUNICATIONS SYSTEM, PHASE II (DSCS II) (USAF 777 SATELLITE)

The Phase II Defense Satellite Communications System (DSCS II) utilises synchronous-orbit communications satellites and surface terminals to provide reliable worldwide circuits for carrying essential military communications. The

DSCS II defence communications satellite

satellites are developed and produced by TRW Inc for the US Air Force, and supersede the DSCS I system described under the Philco-Ford entry in the 1972-73 *Jane's*.

Protected against interference, the satellites are each equipped with steerable narrow-beam antennae that focus a portion of the satellite's energy to areas 870 nm (1,000 miles; 1,600 km) in diameter. Within these specially illuminated areas, the narrow beam antennae allow small terminals to be used in place of more costly large terminals. The narrow beams are designed to be steered in a matter of minutes to different locations on the Earth's surface, and the satellites are so designed that they can be moved in a matter of days to new synchronous orbital positions. In this way antenna coverage can be tailored to fit defence contingency communications all over the world.

The Phase II satellites each weigh 1,150 lb (522 kg), are 9 ft (2·75 m) in diameter and 13 ft (3·95 m) tall with antennae extended. Electrical power is supplied by solar arrays with an output of 535W at launch, decreasing to a minimum of 358W after five years. The X-band single-frequency conversion repeater weighs 178 lb (81 kg) and has 20W of power output from each of two travelling wave tubes. Its bandwidth is 410MHz. It has a capacity of 1,300 voice channels or up to 100 megabit per second of data.

The Earth-coverage antennae have a transmit beamwidth of 18°, a gain of 16·8 dbi, and effective radiated power of 28 dbw. The narrow-coverage antennae have a beamwidth of 2·6°, a gain of 33 dbi and an effective radiated power of 43 dbw. They are steerable to $\pm 10°$.

First launch of two DSCS II satellites was on 3 November 1971, by Titan IIIC launch vehicle, from Cape Kennedy. A second pair was launched on 14 December 1973.

To support the early post-launch phase of the system, Philco-Ford was contracted to design and build one heavy transportable ground terminal, one medium transportable terminal and one maintenance and supply van.

Artist's impression of Fltsatcom satellite

FLTSATCOM

The US Navy-sponsored Fltsatcom satellite system will provide worldwide high-priority UHF communications between naval aircraft, ships, submarines, ground stations, Strategic Air Command and the presidential command networks. The Air Force Systems Command's Space and Missile Systems Organisation (SAMSO) is the contracting agency.

Four of the three-axis stabilised satellites will be placed into geosynchronous equatorial orbit to provide complete Earth coverage, except for the polar regions. A fifth satellite will serve as a contingency spare. Fltsatcoms will be launched individually by Atlas-Centaur vehicles from Cape Kennedy, beginning in late 1975. Each will have a design life of five years and will provide more than 30 voice and 12 teletype channels.

The satellite consists of two major components, each with a basic 8 ft (2·44 m) hexagonal body:

The payload module contains UHF and X-band communications equipment and antennae. Each of its six side panels carries related communications components. The 16 ft (4·88 m) parabolic UHF antenna is made up of ribs and mesh, and opens like an umbrella.

The spacecraft module contains nearly all the remaining subsystem equipment, including the Earth sensors, attitude and velocity control, telemetry, tracking and command, and electrical power and distribution, as well as the buried, non-separable apogee kick motor. The solar array, never shadowed, is exposed to sunlight in both folded and deployed configurations. Each of the two panels measures 13 ft by 7 ft (3·96 m × 2·13 m). Together, they will provide at least 1,200W. Three nickel-cadmium batteries will provide power during eclipse.

WEIGHTS:	
At lift-off	3,800 lb (1,724 kg)
In orbit	1,950 lb (885 kg)

ERS

The ERS Environmental Research Satellite is a small spacecraft for conducting scientific and engineering research experiments in space. The satellite was developed by TRW Systems Group in 1961 and the first ERS was launched from Vandenberg AFB in September 1962. Since then, more than 30 ERS, all launched as piggyback payloads, have been orbited successfully.

An illustration on page 670 shows the variety of configurations in which ERS satellites can be supplied. They range in weight from 1½ to 80 lb (0·7-36 kg) and generally carry a single experiment.

Artist's impression of Pioneer Jupiter probe

The most commonly flown ERS has been the octahedron, with eight sides on which triangular solar panels are fastened. The ERS can incorporate many different subsystems. Stabilisation can be either spin, passive magnetic, gravity gradient, or active magnetic. Electric power for the satellite is derived from solar cells, often supplemented by rechargeable batteries. VHF transmitters have been employed on all ERS flights for telemetry and tracking beacon signals, and command/receiver systems have been used. Satellite antenna subsystems have included dipole, crossed dipole and monopole. The satellite normally employs a passive thermal control subsystem.

The ERS has been used by NASA to check the manned spaceflight network (TETR-1, launched 13 December 1967, TETR-2, launched 8 November 1968, and TETR-3, launched 28 September 1971) and by the USAF to conduct experiments concerned with solar cell radiation damage, radiation measurements, surface contact bonding of materials in space, surface friction, zero gravity heat transfer, and solar X-ray and nuclear particle monitoring.

The ERS is one of the most reliable and least expensive active satellites yet produced. The latest configuration is the Prism, which may be used as an Earth resources satellite.

ERS satellites are available to any prospective purchaser and can be made to meet any specified dimensions to house space instrumentation.

Two small satellites of the same generic type were developed to orbit the Moon as part of the Apollo programme. Known as Apollo particles and fields subsatellites, one was injected into lunar orbit from Apollo 15's Service Module during that mission, and returned data for more than six months. A second subsatellite was placed in orbit by Apollo 16, but because the spacecraft's lunar orbit had not been circularised, as the result of a guidance system gimbal lock alarm early in the mission, the satellite was ejected into a highly-elliptical orbit and crashed into the Moon after a few days of operation.

IMEWS (USAF 647 SATELLITE)

The USAF's 647 series of satellites, for which TRW Systems is prime contractor, is intended to provide early warning of a hostile ballistic missile launch by detecting the infra-red emission from the missiles by means of an Aerojet-General infra-red "telescope". The programme is believed to be known now by the acronym IMEWS (Integrated Missile Early Warning Satellite) and to be the operational successor to the original Midas project.

A first launch was attempted on 6 November 1970, using a Titan IIIC vehicle. The intention was to place the 647 satellite into an initial synchronous orbit over the USA for checkout, then to move it westward to a position from where it could observe missile tests in China and firings down the Soviet Pacific test range. The propellants that would have been used for this re-location were exhausted in trying to correct a faulty initial orbit. Reports suggest that the infra-red telescope system was tested subsequently by observing US rocket launches.

The second launching, by a Titan IIIC from Cape Kennedy on 5 May 1971, is believed to have been successful. IMEWS-3 was launched on 1 March 1972, and IMEWS-4 on 12 June 1973. French reports suggest that the IMEWS satellite is cylindrical, weighs 1,800 lb (820 kg) at launch, has an inertial three-axis stabilisation system and measures approximately 9 ft 10 in (3 m) in diameter and 9 ft 10 in (3 m) in height; cruciform solar panels are said to span 23 ft (7 m). The same reports stated that the satellite carries high-resolution cameras, able to transmit photographs of any missiles that are located to a ground station 300 miles (500 km) north-west of Adelaide, Australia, for onward transmission via Programme 313 synchronous-orbit relay satellites to NORAD headquarters, Colorado Springs, USA.

PIONEER 10

TRW was contracted by NASA to build the first spacecraft to fly to the planet Jupiter. Known before launch as Pioneer F (now Pioneer 10), it was launched on 2 March 1972 from Cape Kennedy, by a three-stage Atlas-Centaur vehicle. It weighs 570 lb (260 kg) and consists of a hexagonal equipment compartment, from opposite faces of which extend two booms and on one end of which is mounted a 9 ft (2·7 m) diameter dish antenna.

A small compartment, abutting one face, houses six of the eleven scientific experiments, including an infra-red radiometer, charged particle instrument, trapped radiation detector, ultra-violet photometer, Geiger tube telescope, and imaging photo-polarimeter. Externally-mounted experiments comprise the plasma analyser, cosmic ray telescope, asteroid-meteoroid telescopes, meteoroid sensors and magnetometer sensor.

Six small "thruster" nozzles, developing from 0·4 to 1·4 lb (0·18 to 0·63 kg) of thrust, provide for attitude control and changes in spacecraft velocity. Electrical power is provided by four SNAP-19 type radioisotope thermoelectric generators, fuelled with plutonium-238 dioxide. Together, these generators provided 155W of power at launch, dropping to 140W at Jupiter and 100W five years after launch. Pioneer 10 is the first NASA spacecraft powered entirely by nuclear generators.

Mounted on the structure of the spacecraft is an anodised plaque engraved with symbols providing basic data on atomic structures, mankind and the solar system. It is intended to indicate the nature of its builders, and that part of the galaxy from which the spacecraft was launched, to any extra-terrestrial beings who might intercept the craft in the remote future.

After the successful direct-ascent trajectory launch, the first of several planned midcourse correction manoeuvres was performed on 7 March, when two thruster firings of 8 min 7 sec and 4 min 16 sec were made. These increased the velocity by 46 ft (14 m)/sec, and adjusted the trajectory to shorten the flight time to Jupiter by 9 hours.

Pioneer 11 Jupiter probe undergoing final checkout before launch

On 25 May, Pioneer 10 crossed the orbit of Mars and entered a region of space not previously explored. The 43·5 million nm (50 million miles; 80 million km) separating the orbits of Earth and Mars were crossed in 12 weeks, compared with about 5 months for previous Mars-bound spacecraft. The spacecraft moved along the 118 million nm (136 million mile; 219 million km) curved flight path at an average speed of 65,000 knots (75,000 mph; 120,000 km/h).

In July 1972 the spacecraft entered the Asteroid Belt and spent seven months traversing the 152 million nm (175 million mile; 280 million km) wide belt of rock fragments and cosmic rubble, and emerged unharmed in February 1973.

Data obtained within the belt indicate that fewer very small particles (0·1 to 0·01 mm) than expected were encountered, but slightly larger particles (0·10 to 1·00 mm) may be somewhat more numerous than had been thought.

While in the Asteroid Belt, on 19 September 1972, the spacecraft's thrusters were fired briefly to increase its speed by 0·745 ft (0·227 m) per second, so that it passed behind the planet's moon, Io. This manoeuvre permitted experiments that indicated that the moon, which is about the size of the planet Mercury, has a very tenuous single-layer atmosphere, about 59 nm (68 miles; 109 km) deep, and a surface temperature of —173°C.

Pioneer 10 encountered Jupiter the first week in December 1973, passing within 70,000 nm (81,000 miles; 130,000 km) of the planet's surface. It returned a number of colour television pictures showing details not visible to Earth-based telescopes. This was the first time that colour television had been used on an interplanetary spacecraft and was adopted, despite the extra complexity and weight, because more details of the multi-coloured Jovian atmosphere were likely to be revealed in colour. On-board instruments indicated that the planet is surrounded by trapped radiation belts having an intensity between ten thousand and a million times greater than those round the Earth. The belts appear to be contained in a magnetic field about 3·4 million nm (4 million miles; 6·4 million km) in diameter, tilted at 30° to the equator.

A "heat map" shows areas of —137°C and other areas of —146°C.

The spacecraft's instruments survived the flyby through the planet's trapped particle region relatively undamaged, and it is now on a mission to reach the orbit of Saturn in 1976 and that of Uranus in 1979. Neither planet will be in a suitable position for a close flyby, but the spacecraft is expected to return data from these immense distances (1,736,800,000 nm; 2,000,000,000 miles; 3,200,000,000 km).

At a constant speed of 22,900 knots (25,400 mph; 46,000 km/h) Pioneer 10 will then leave the solar system on a course that will, ultimately, take it to the stars. In March 1974, Pioneer was already more than 570 million miles (917 million km) from Earth, the farthest distance yet attained by a man-made object. The spacecraft was functioning well, minor changes in systems caused by the passage through Jupiter's intense radiation belts having either disappeared, or having no effect on performance. Since leaving Jupiter, the meteoroid detector had experienced two hits.

TRW built Pioneer 10, and the similar Pioneer 11 (see below), under the direction of NASA's Ames Research Center, Moffett Field, California. The work was performed at TRW's Space Park facility in Redondo Beach, California.

PIONEER 11

Launched on 6 April 1973, Pioneer 11 is a backup spacecraft for Pioneer 10 and is expected to reach the planet Jupiter in early 1975. It is identical to Pioneer 10, except that a second magnetometer has been added to measure high magnetic fields close to Jupiter.

By early 1974 the spacecraft had successfully negotiated the Asteroid Belt. While in the Belt it received eight hits on its meteoroid detector, about the same rate as that experienced by Pioneer 10.

All systems are functioning well, and the spacecraft will reach Jupiter on 5 December 1974, when it is planned to make measurements and take pictures complementing those obtained by Pioneer 10. Pioneer 11 is then expected to go on to Saturn.

THE UNION OF SOVIET SOCIALIST REPUBLICS

The information concerning recent research projects contained in the following notes is in almost all cases based on official Soviet news releases.

Full details of earlier Soviet satellites, spaceprobes and spacecraft have appeared in the 1959-60 and subsequent editions of *Jane's*, together with descriptions of the A-2 and A-3 research rockets and meteorological rockets which are standard vehicles in constant use.

COSMOS SATELLITES

This series of satellites is continuing the Soviet programme for investigating the upper layers of the atmosphere and outer space, and includes a study of the following subjects: the concentration of charged particles in the ionosphere for the purpose of investigating the propagation of radio waves; corpuscular flows and low-energy particles; the energy composition of the Earth's radiation belts, for the purpose of further evaluating the radiation danger in prolonged space flights; the primary composition of cosmic rays and the variations in their intensity; the Earth's magnetic field; the short-wave radiation of the Sun and other celestial bodies; the upper layers of the atmosphere; the effects of meteoric matter on spacecraft materials; the distribution and formation of cloud patterns in the Earth's atmosphere. In addition, many details of spacecraft construction are being evaluated and refined.

The Mayak radio telemetering system operates on frequencies of around 20·000 and 90·000 megacycles.

The wide terms of reference mean that a Cosmos satellite can vary from a small uninstrumented device to a large animal-carrying spacecraft, and from military weapons to unmanned but man-rated spacecraft test vehicles.

Details of Cosmos 186, 188, 212 and 213 (automatic rendezvous and docking) and 215 (astronomical observatory) can be found in the 1970-71 *Jane's*.

Cosmos satellites in 49° and 56° orbits survive until natural decay occurs. Observations indicate that these are normally cylindrical in shape, approximately 6 ft (1·83 m) long by 3 ft 6 in (1·05 m) in diameter and weigh about 800 lb (360 kg).

Cosmos 637, launched on 26 March 1974, was the first satellite in the series to be placed in a synchronous orbit. Positioned over the Indian Ocean, it is assumed to be an early version of the Statsionar communications satellite announced by the Soviet authorities in 1970.

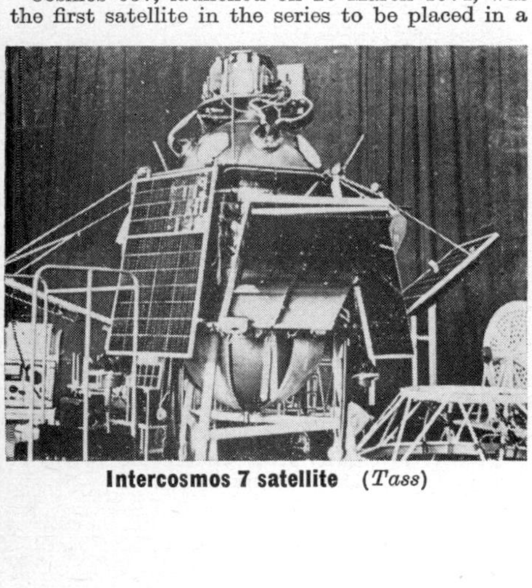

Intercosmos 7 satellite (*Tass*)

MILITARY COSMOS

As the satellite tables on pages 676-8 indicate, Cosmos designations are given to Soviet reconnaissance satellites and other types of military spacecraft.

The original basic reconnaissance satellites appeared to be 7 ft 6 in (2·3 m) diameter spheres weighing about 7,000 lb (3,175 kg) and were normally launched at a rate of two a month, the rate rising during periods of tension such as the armed clashes between Soviet and Chinese forces at Damanski Island in March 1969 and the border clash near Western Mongolia in June 1969.

Cosmos reconnaissance satellites are launched from the bases at Plesetsk and Tyuratam, usually into orbits with inclinations of 52°, 65° or 72°. Most eject capsules after 8 days and these are presumably recovered. Some, such as Cosmos 228, have demonstrated the capacity for in-flight frequency changing; others, such as Cosmos 251, 264 and 280, had a small manoeuvring capability for more precise target coverage.

Cosmos 317 appeared to be the first of a new series of operational reconnaissance satellites with an 11-13 day life, instead of the 8 days of early versions. The longer flights could imply that the craft carry a larger film package. If so, the same coverage will be obtained with fewer launches. An unusual characteristic of some of the "longer-life" craft is the ejection of a capsule just before recovery. The ejected capsule goes into a slightly lower orbit, where it remains for several days until it decays naturally. Many of the reconnaissance satellites use the on-board short-wave tracking beacon for Morse Code type telemetry transmissions, but some of the later types use other equipment and are thus probably more sophisticated.

A number of test vehicles for the Soviet Union's Fractional Orbital Bombardment System have apparently been given Cosmos designations.

Cosmos designations have also been given to a series of spacecraft which seem to have the capability of intercepting other satellites. Early "interceptors" were Cosmos 249, 252, 374 and 375. Cosmos 397, launched on 25 February 1971, passed close to Cosmos 394 launched sixteen days earlier, and was subsequently destroyed. Cosmos 400, launched on 19 March 1971, was "intercepted" by Cosmos 404 on the day of its launch, 3 April 1971.

Cosmos 518, launched on 15 September 1972 from Plesetsk, and Cosmos 519, launched the following day from Tyuratam and involving a rare high-inclination orbit from that site, were presumably launched to obtain supplementary data on NATO naval manoeuvres then being conducted in the North Sea. Specific launches are often made to observe such manoeuvres, and also to cover areas of special political concern. Thus in 1971 Cosmos 463 and 464 were used to obtain photographic coverage of the Indo-Pakistan War, and in 1973 Cosmos 597, 600 and 602 were used to survey the October Israeli-Arab Yom Kippur War. After fighting stopped, the orbits of Cosmos 609, 612, 616 and 625 were such as to indicate that they were monitoring the cease-fire, while Cosmos 630 monitored the withdrawal of Israeli forces.

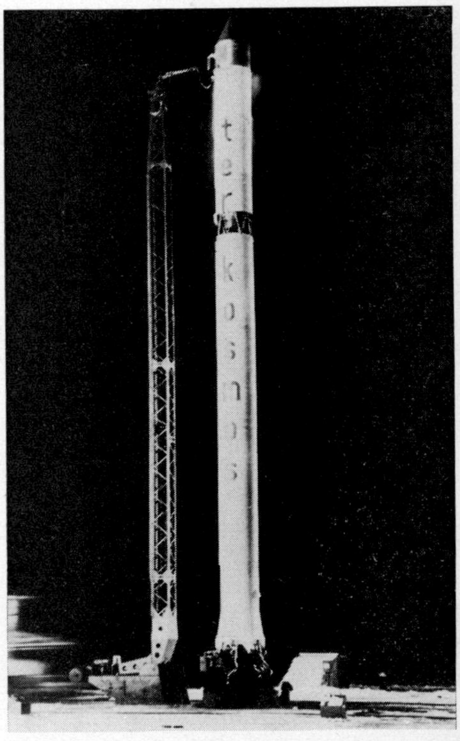

Launch vehicle for Intercosmos 8 satellite (*Tass*)

During 1972 the USSR appeared to launch more than three times as many photo-reconnaissance satellites as did the USA. However, owing to the relatively long lives in orbit of the US Big Bird spacecraft, only some 25% more time in orbit was realised.

COSMOS LAUNCHER

The vehicle used for the majority of Cosmos satellite launchings employs for first-stage propulsion a four-chamber liquid-propellant rocket engine designated RD-214. In service since 1962, this is a pump-fed engine, burning kerosene and nitric acid, and developing 161,000 lb (73,000 kg) st for lift-off (see "Engines" section).

Depending on the payload to be orbited, the Cosmos launcher is used in two-stage or three-stage form.

INTERCOSMOS SATELLITES

Launched on 14 October 1969, Intercosmos 1 involved the co-operation of seven Socialist countries: Bulgaria, Czechoslovakia, Germany (Democratic Republic), Hungary, Poland, Romania and the USSR. The satellite carried scientific instruments developed and made in Czechoslovakia and Germany as well as in the USSR. Its programme was devoted mainly to research connected with the Sun, and involved

simultaneous observations in the seven participating countries into radio-astronomical, ionospheric and optical phenomena.

Further details of Intercosmos 1 and the later Intercosmos 2 can be found in the 1970-71 *Jane's*. Intercosmos 3 and 4 were described in the 1971-72 edition. Intercosmos 5 was launched on 2 December 1971. Intercosmos 6, launched on 7 April 1972, was the first of a new series, with recoverable payloads, and weighed 2,360 lb (1,070 kg). The series of launches is continuing (see "Satellites" table).

Intercosmos 9, a Soviet-Polish satellite, launched on 19 April 1973, was named Intercosmos Copernicus 500 to mark the 500th anniversary of the birth of the Polish scientist. This spacecraft carries a Polish-built receiver to detect solar radiation and to study the effects of solar radiation on the Earth's ionosphere.

LUNA SPACECRAFT

Descriptions of the soft-landing Luna 9 and 13 and lunar-orbiting Luna 10, 12 and 14 spacecraft can be found in the 1968-69 *Jane's*.

Reference to the Luna 15 spacecraft, sent to the Moon at the time of America's Apollo 11 mission, appears in the 1969-70 edition. The 1971-72 edition contains details of Luna 16, which brought samples of Moon rock back to Earth, and Luna 17, the transport vehicle for the Lunokhod 1 automatic lunar roving vehicle. The mission of Luna 20, the second to return with a lunar soil sample, is described in the 1972-73 edition.

Latest in this series of automatic spacecraft was Luna 21, which carried the Lunokhod 2 automatic lunar roving vehicle to the Moon. Details of the mission can be found in the 1973-74 *Jane's*.

MARS 4 and 5

Mars 4 was launched on 21 July 1973 and Mars 5 on 25 July, from the space complex at Tyuratam. Both spacecraft are of generally similar design, and were intended to be placed in orbit round Mars, from where they were to send TV pictures and scientific data back to Earth. The two craft also, apparently, were to act as relay stations for data transmitted by the soft-landing capsules carried by Mars 6 and 7.

Midcourse corrections to the trajectories of the two spacecraft were made successfully on 30 July and 3 August respectively.

Mars 4 reached the planet safely on 10 February 1974, but failed to enter orbit due to a systems failure which caused the braking rocket to misfire. It transmitted pictures of the planet during its unscheduled flyby.

On 12 February 1974, Mars 5 entered a 19,500 × 1,506 mile (31,380 × 2,424 km) orbit, since when it has transmitted a number of high-resolution photographs and other scientific data.

MARS 6 and 7

Mars 6 was launched on 5 August 1973, and Mars 7, a backup craft, on 9 August.

Mars 6, intended to work in conjunction with Mars 4, was of somewhat different design to the two earlier spacecraft. As well as Soviet equipment, it carried French instruments for study of the Sun's radio emissions, solar plasma and cosmic rays. Both spacecraft carried soft-landing capsules.

Successful midcourse corrections to the two trajectories were made on 13 August and 16 August respectively.

Approaching the planet on 12 March 1974, Mars 6 ejected its soft-landing capsule at a distance of 3,400 miles (5,470 km), the capsule passing through the Martian atmosphere at an extremely low angle to obtain maximum aerodynamic drag. At a pre-determined height, a braking parachute opened, followed by the main braking 'chute. After 148 seconds of parachute descent, the probe is believed to have landed on the surface of the planet, although communications were lost just before the moment of impact.

During its descent the probe transmitted data to its carrier spacecraft, providing information on the planet's radiation over a wide range of wavelengths. It also provided new data about the relief of the surface and its temperature and heat conductivity; on the structure and composition of the soil; and on the composition of the lower and upper layers of the Martian atmosphere. Initial reports indicate that the atmosphere contains "several times more water vapour" than was previously thought.

The probe landed at 25°W longitude, 24°S latitude, almost exactly in the centre of an area on which Russia had requested detailed Mariner 9 data from the US.

Mars 7 had arrived at the planet before its sister-craft, on 9 March. It released its descent capsule successfully, but a malfunction caused it to miss the planet by 780 miles (1,255 km).

METEOR

Meteor is the name given to the Soviet series of first-generation operational meteorological satellites, developed from a number of Cosmos prototypes (described in previous editions of *Jane's*).

The satellites, which provide information about the state of the atmosphere both on the "daylight" and "night" sides of the Earth, are stabilised so that the camera lenses and infra-red instruments always point towards the Earth. The resolving capacity of the cameras is claimed to be three times as good as those used on the US Tiros series of weather satellites.

Information received from Meteors is supplied to the Soviet hydro-meteorological service and to the World Meteorological Service. Cloud cover picture charts are transmitted to Washington, Geneva, Tokyo, Sydney and other foreign weather services.

Meteor 1 was launched on 26 March 1969; and launchings have continued at a current rate of three or four per year, with Meteor 17 launched from Plesetsk on 24 April 1974. It is a cylinder with two solar panels, about 16 ft (4·88 m) long, with a diameter of 5 ft (1·5 m).

The Meteor system consists of three satellites in orbital planes at 90° and 180° to each other, so that they pass over a given area of the Earth on the northbound pass at intervals of about 6 hours and 12 hours, and again during the southbound pass.

MOLNIYA

Molniya 1 (Lightning), launched on 23 April 1965, was a communications satellite placed in a highly elliptical orbit designed to provide the longest possible communications sessions between Moscow and Vladivostok. It was the first Soviet communications satellite, and was in the form of a hermetically-sealed cylinder with conical ends, one end containing the correcting engine and a system of micro-jets, and the other end containing solar and Earth-orientation sensors. Six solar battery panels and two parabolic aerials were mounted on the central body. Also attached were the radiation surfaces of the temperature-control system comprising a radiation/refrigerator and a heating panel in the form of a flat ring, which also accommodated solar batteries.

During flight the satellite was orientated with its solar batteries facing the Sun and one of its aerials was directed simultaneously towards the Earth. Signals were transmitted in a relatively narrow beam, ensuring a strong reception at the surface of the Earth. The other aerial was in reserve, and for this to be used the satellite had to be rotated 180° longitudinally.

Molniya can handle a television programme, a large number of telephone conversations, still pictures, telegraphic information and other forms of information.

Details of Molniya 1B to 1U can be found in previous editions of *Jane's*.

On 24 November 1971, Molniya 2A, the first of a new uprated version, was launched from Plesetsk. It is believed to have a central structure 13 ft 6 in (4·10 m) tall, with a diameter of 5 ft (1·52 m), and to weigh about 2,750 lb (1,250 kg).

Launches of both the original and the improved Molniyas are continuing. Latest, at the time of writing, were Molniya 2J, ninth of the uprated models, on 26 April 1974, and Molniya 1S, first to be put into synchronous orbit, on 29 July 1974.

PROGNOZ

Launched on 14 April 1972, Prognoz 1 (Forecast) was the first of a new series of satellites designed specifically to study processes of solar activity, and their influence on the interplanetary medium and the Earth's magnetosphere.

Weighing 1,890 lb (857 kg), the spacecraft was injected into a highly-elliptical orbit of 512-108,000 nm (600-124,000 miles; 950-200,000 km) from an initial Earth parking orbit.

Prognoz 1 is basically sphere-shaped, with four cruciform solar panels extended to provide power via an internal rechargeable chemical battery. The sphere, filled with an inert gas, contains telemetry equipment, temperature control components and the electrical system. Experiments on board are intended to measure: electromagnetic solar radiation generated simultaneously with solar flares; solar cosmic radiation; solar wind plasma; and radio waves.

Prognoz 2 was launched on 29 June 1972, to begin a programme of joint experiments with Prognoz 1. In addition to Soviet equipment, the second spacecraft carried instruments developed by French scientists. Prognoz 3, launched on 15 February 1973, operated in conjunction with Lunokhod 2 in attempts to determine the

Replica of Mars 3 spacecraft, exhibited at 1973 Paris Air Show
(*Brian M. Service*)

Full-scale representation of Molniya 2 communications satellite
(*Brian M. Service*)

cause of variations in the local lunar magnetic fields. It was still functioning in February 1974, returning data three times a week on solar flares, X-ray activity and the effect of solar radiation on the Earth's ionosphere.

SALYUT

An accompanying illustration shows the first of a series of Salyut (Salute) spacecraft which have served as orbital scientific stations for the crews of Soyuz manned spacecraft. It was a stepped cylinder 40 ft (12·2 m) long, from 7 ft (2·13 m) to 13 ft (4·0 m) in diameter, with a weight of 18½ tons.

Details of Salyut 1 and 2 can be found in the 1973-74 *Jane's*. Salyut 3, launched on 24 June 1974, was occupied by the crew of Soyuz 14 (see Addenda).

SOYUZ SPACECRAFT

Developed for the Russian Earth-orbital space station programme, Soyuz spacecraft are equipped for missions of up to 30 days duration.

Each spacecraft comprises three basic sections or modules: a laboratory-cum-rest compartment (orbital module), a descent compartment (landing module) and a propulsion and instrument section (service module). The orbital module is mounted on the extreme nose of the craft, and communicates with the landing module via a hermetically-sealed hatch. The orbital and landing modules are pressurised to 14 lb/sq in (1 kg/cm²), have a combined internal volume of 318 cu ft (9 m³) and can accommodate up to four cosmonauts.

The service module contains the main systems for orbital flight, together with a liquid-propellant propulsion system embodying two motors (one a standby) each with a thrust of 880 lb (400 kg). These allow midcourse manoeuvres, up to heights of 695 nm (800 miles; 1,300 km), and are used for the de-orbit manoeuvre. Another system provides attitude control. Attached to the service module is a solar-cell array having an area of about 150 sq ft (14 m²).

The landing module contains the parachutes and landing rockets. A backup parachute system is available in case of failure. The main parachute, preceded by a pilot 'chute, is deployed at 27,000 ft (8,000 m). Retro-rockets, operating at a height of about 3 ft (1 m) above the ground, ensure a landing velocity not exceeding 10 ft/sec (3 m/sec). The aerodynamic design of the landing module permits landing loads to be kept within 3-4g, although ballistic re-entries, involving loads of 8-10g, can be made if required. The overall length of the craft is about 30 ft (9 m), the diameter of the crew compartments about 7 ft (2·1 m) and the all-up weight about 13,000 lb (6,000 kg).

The Soyuz craft are equipped with an automatic control system for approach and docking manoeuvres, the technique and external aerials being similar to those employed on the Cosmos spacecraft 186 and 188, and 212 and 213.

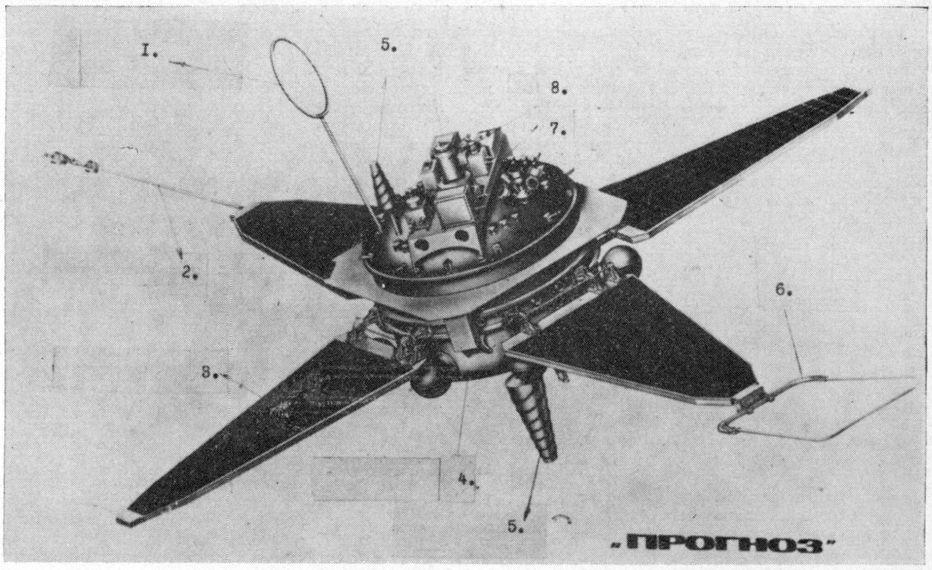

Prognoz solar research spacecraft: 1, antenna of electro-magnetic field low-frequency receiver; 2, magnetometer; 3, solar panel; 4, instrument compartment; 5, slightly directional antenna; 6, antenna for long-wave radio receiver; 7, instrument sensors; 8, Sun-fixed reference sensor (*Tass*)

Soyuz 1 to 5 were described in the 1969-70 *Jane's*, Soyuz 6, 7 and 8 in the 1970-71 edition and Soyuz 9, 10 and 11 in the 1971-72 edition.

A Soyuz spacecraft is to be used in the joint US/Soviet orbital docking project planned for mid-1975. For details see NASA entry in US section.

SOYUZ 12

Launched at 1218 GMT on 27 September 1973, from the Baikonur space complex into a near-Earth orbit of 120 by 154 miles (194 by 249 km), this flight was intended to prove the effectiveness of structural and system changes embodied since the Soyuz 11 flight in June 1971,

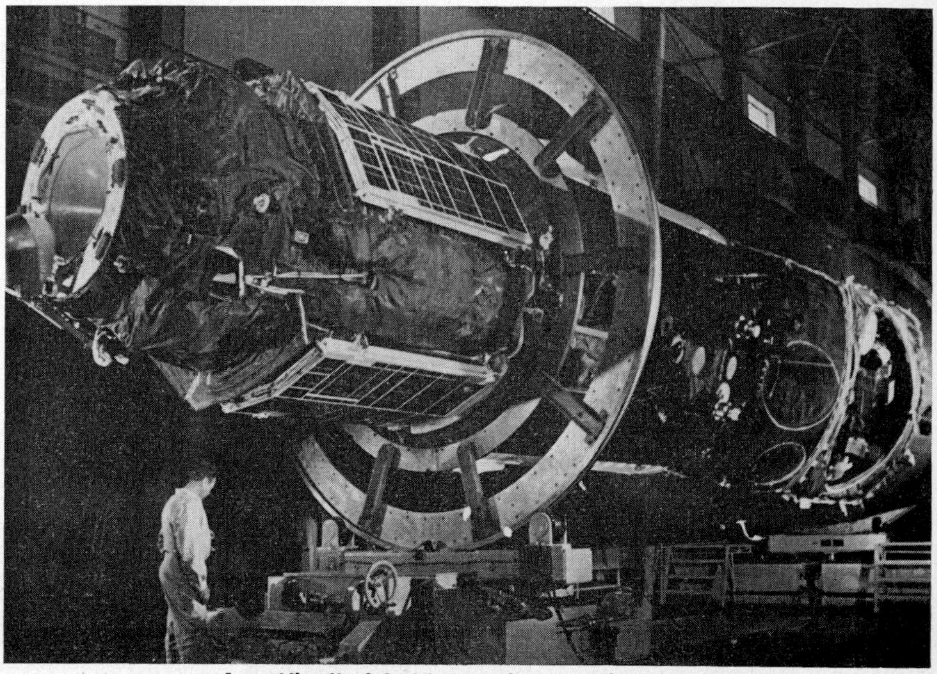

Assembling the Salyut 1 manned space station (*Tass*)

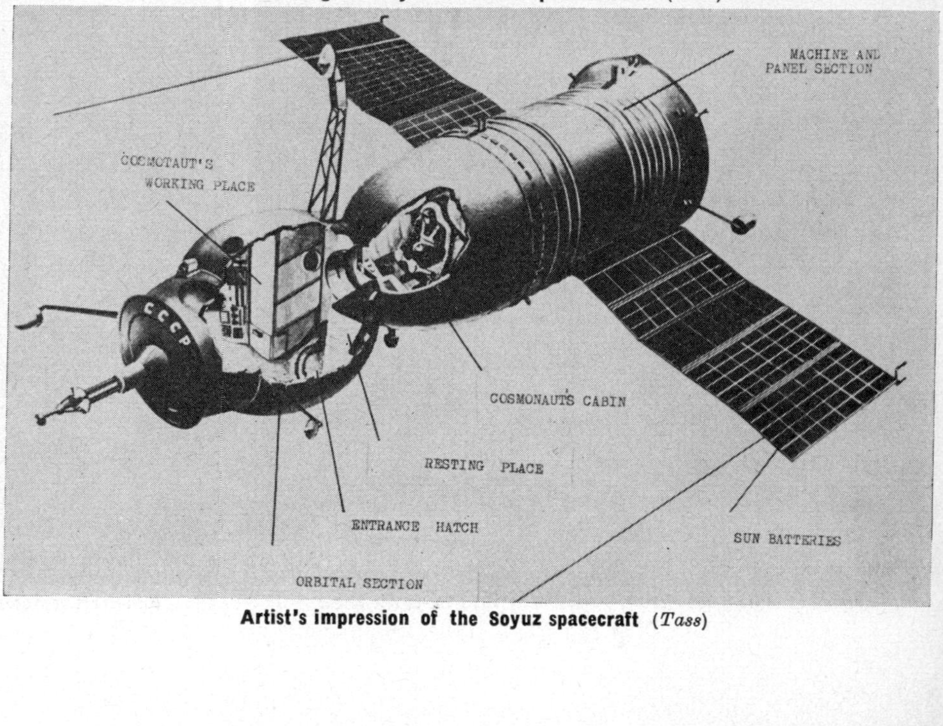

Artist's impression of the Soyuz spacecraft (*Tass*)

Soyuz launch vehicle

when decompression was experienced during re-entry and the crew of three died.

The crew of Soyuz 12 comprised Lt Col Vasily Lazarev (Commander), a specialist in aviation medicine, and Oleg Makarov (flight engineer), formerly engaged in the design of Yuri Gagarin's Vostok, and the Voskhod and Soyuz spacecraft. The programme for the two-day mission, announced at launch, included comprehensive checking and testing of the improved systems, and the further testing of both manual and automatic modes of flight control under various conditions. In addition, the opportunity was taken to undertake spectrography of sections of the Earth's surface, with the aim of obtaining information on natural resources.

On the first day, to test the control system, the main engine was fired twice, once at apogee and once at perigee, to manoeuvre the spacecraft into a new 213 by 202 mile (343 by 326 km) orbit. The manoeuvre was satisfactory.

Spacesuits were worn for the launch and re-entry manoeuvres. The spacecraft soft-landed safely at 1134 GMT on 29 September, at a point 249 miles (400 km) southwest of Karaganda in Kazakhstan.

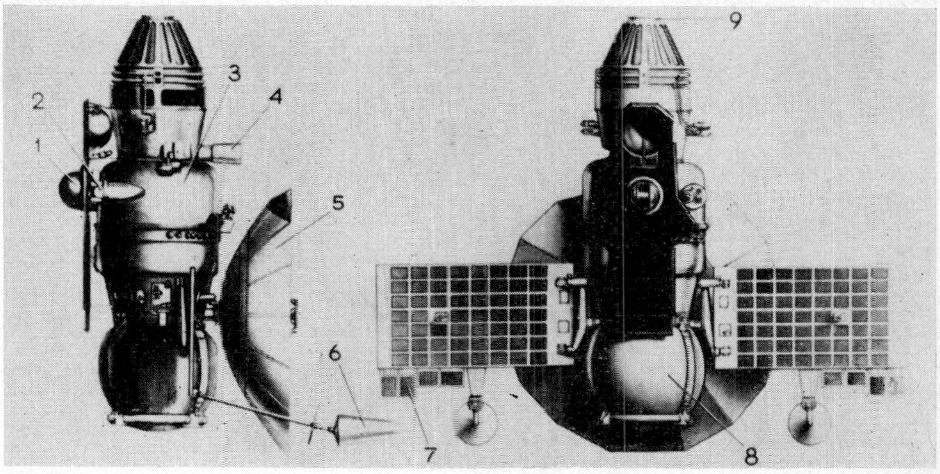

Diagram of Venus 8 spacecraft: 1, 2, 4, sensors for astro-orientation system; 3, instrument compartment; 5, parabolic directional antenna; 6, slightly directional antenna; 7, solar cell panels; 8, landing capsule; 9, course-correcting rocket engine (*Tass*)

SOYUZ 13

Soyuz 13, launched at 1155 GMT on 18 December 1973 and manned by cosmonauts Major Pyotr Klimuk (Commander) and Valentin Lebedev (flight engineer), was described as an orbiting astrophysical laboratory.

The spacecraft carried an Orion-2 system of telescopes, which was used to obtain spectrograms of stars of various constellations in the ultraviolet band. The telescopes were also used to survey potential Earth resources within the Soviet Union. The telescopes, developed by the Armenian Academy of Sciences, embody wide-angle crystalline-quartz lenses specially designed to withstand direct solar radiation.

Medical-biological research was carried out, using Levkoy equipment which monitored the circulation of the blood in the cosmonauts' brains at various stages during the adaptation period.

The possibilities of obtaining protein in conditions of weightlessness were investigated by means of an Oasis-2 system. This system consists of two interconnected cylinders. One of them cultivates water-oxydising bacteria which use for their growth hydrogen obtained as a result of electrolysis. The other cylinder contains urobacteria which can break down compounds containing nitrogen and can accumulate protein mass. It is, therefore, a closed system containing two types of micro-organisms. The waste products of the syntheses of one type of bacteria are the initial material enabling the other to accumulate protein.

During its fifth revolution, the spacecraft's orbit was changed to 170 by 140 miles (272 by 225 km).

After completing its mission programme, Soyuz 13 landed on 26 December, in an area 125 miles (200 km) southwest of Karaganda in Kazakhstan.

SOYUZ 14 AND 15

For brief details, see Addenda.

SOYUZ LAUNCHER

The vehicle used for launching Soyuz spacecraft appears to be a development of the booster used for launching the Vostok and Voskhod craft, the development consisting of the insertion of some 36 ft (11·8 m) of additional upper staging or sections. To cater for the increased weight and bending moment the inter-stage truss is strengthened. During launch, the Soyuz vehicle is surmounted by an escape tower with three rows of rocket nozzles. Under the projecting domed fairing is a ring of eleven or twelve main nozzles, surmounted by four small vernier nozzles. At the base of the cylindrical section at the top is a ring of still-smaller nozzles of the kind seen around the tail of the "Frog-7" missile.

Official Soviet reports have stated that this vehicle has a total thrust of around 60 million horsepower, which is three times the power given in 1961 for the Vostok launcher.

VENUS SPACECRAFT

An accompanying illustration shows Venus 8, despatched successfully to the planet Venus in 1972. Details can be found in the 1973-74 *Jane's*.

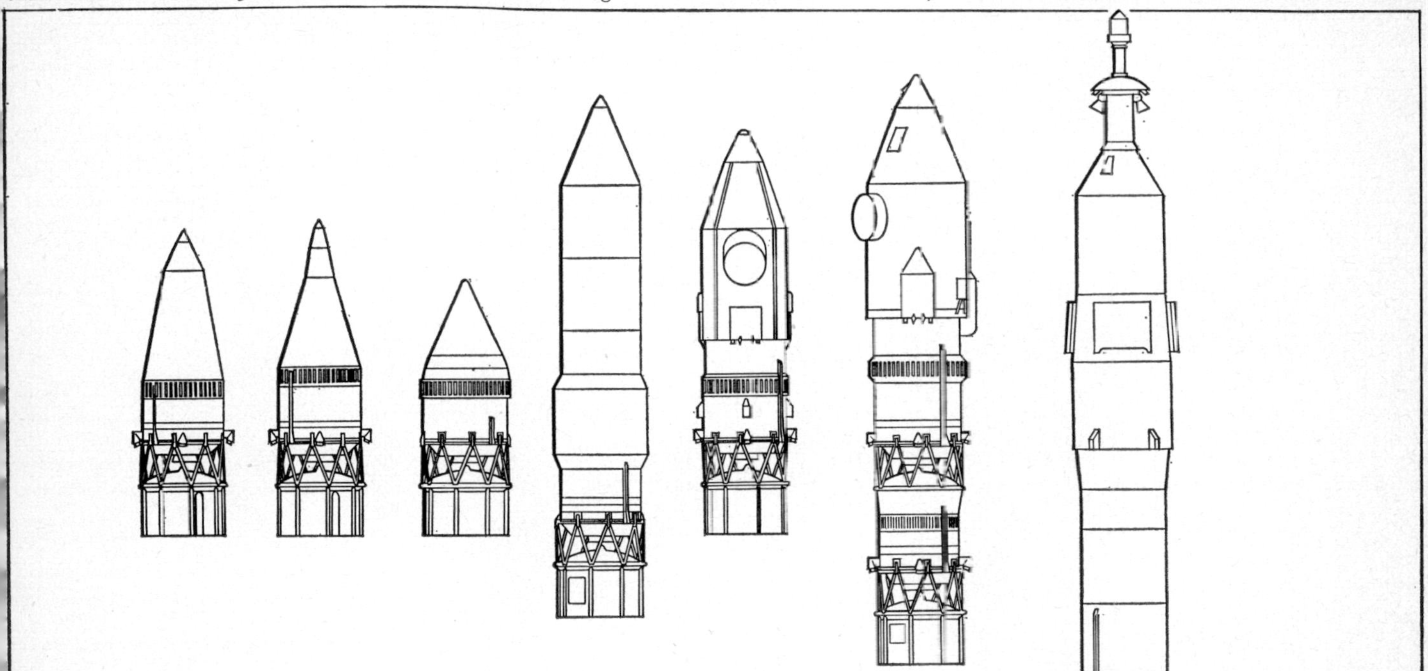

Soviet launch vehicles. The two bottom views are a side elevation and end view of the nozzle arrangement of the basic vehicle, made up of the core and four boosters, in development test configuration. Immediately above, *left*, is a scrap view of the top of the core stage with the additional stage used to orbit Sputnik 1 on 4 October 1957. Top (*left to right*) are adaptations of the vehicle used to launch Sputnik 2, Sputnik 3, Luna 1 and 2, Mars 1 and Venus 1, Vostok 1, Voskhod 1 and 2, and Soyuz (*Sherwood Designs Ltd, with acknowledgement to Skrzydlata Polska*)

VENUS LAUNCHER

Although basically similar in configuration to the launchers used for the Soviet manned spacecraft, the launcher for the Venus probes (see 1971-72 *Jane's*) appears to have elongated first and second stages, giving a considerable increase in propellant tankage.

VOSTOK LAUNCHER

A replica of the launch vehicle used to place in orbit Yuri Gagarin's Vostok 1 spacecraft, on 12 April 1961, was shown publicly for the first time at the 1967 Paris Air Show.

Most interesting technical feature of the vehicle was the use of four tapered liquid-propellant wrap-round boosters, each with four primary nozzles and two verniers. The central sustainer had four primary nozzles and four verniers. Thus, no fewer than 32 rocket chambers were fired simultaneously at take-off. Official Soviet statements have claimed that the total thrust of these engines was 1,323,000 lb (600,000 kg), but this probably represents the figure for thrust in vacuo, the S/L static rating being as much as 20% lower. All primary nozzles were fixed, the verniers being used for control, supplemented by a small delta-shape aerodynamic control surface at the base of each booster.

One of the booster engines, designated RD-107, was displayed in sectioned form and is described in the "Aero-Engines" section of this edition. It was stated to utilise liquid oxygen and kerosene propellants and to develop 224,870 lb (102,000 kg) st in vacuo.

The first stage of the central sustainer "core" was a slim cylinder which flared out into a larger diameter at the top (or front) end. This unusual geometry allowed the conical boosters to fit snugly against it. The second stage, carrying the spacecraft payload, was attached to the sustainer by a truss arrangement similar to that used on the "Scrag" ICBM. As the basic diameter of the "core" was in the same order as that of "Scrag", it justified official Soviet references to the ICBM as being a sister vehicle of the Vostok launcher.

The second stage was powered by a liquid-propellant engine with a single primary nozzle and four verniers. This bore out the correctness of the original Soviet statement in 1961 that the Vostock launch vehicle had six engines, of which five fired at lift-off.

Designer of the vehicle was the late S. Korolev. It was used for all six Vostok launchings and, with second-stage modifications, for the two Voskhod spacecraft.

At the Paris Air Show, the Vostok launcher was displayed on a large rail-mounted transporter-erector truck of the type used at the Baikonur cosmodrome from which Russia's manned space launchings are made.

DIMENSIONS:
Length overall 124 ft 8½ in (38 m)
Length of second stage, with payload fairing 32 ft 10 in (10 m)
Length of each booster 62 ft 3½ in (19 m)
Max diameter:
first-stage sustainer 9 ft 8½ in (2·95 m)
second stage 8 ft 6 in (2·60 m)
boosters (each) 9 ft 10 in (3·00 m)
Overall diameter, over fins 34 ft 0 in (10·3 m)

WEIGHT:
Vostok spacecraft, incl pilot 10,400 lb (4,725 kg)

VOSKHOD LAUNCHER

The first stage of the Voskhod launch vehicle is believed to have been almost identical with that of the Vostok launcher. However, it had two upper stages in tandem, as shown in the drawing on page 675 with additional truss structure between the second and third stages.

SATELLITES & SPACECRAFT LAUNCHED DURING 1973

Note: Both the USA and the USSR have withheld information on launchings, and this list may thus be incomplete. Data in italics are approximate or estimated.

Date	Origin	Name	Total weight lb	kg	Launch Vehicle	Apogee miles	km	Perigee miles	km	Inclination °	Lifetime	Remarks
8 Jan	USSR	Luna 21	—	—	—	—	—	—	—	51·55	—	Carried Lunokhod 2 to Moon.
8 Jan	USSR	Lunokhod 2	1,848	840	—	—	—	—	—	—	5 months	Wheeled lunar roving hicle. Explored Sea Serenity.
11 Jan	USSR	Cosmos 543	*9,000*	*4,080*	—	192	309	126	203	64·98	13 days	*Reconnaissance satellite* Recovered?
20 Jan	USSR	Cosmos 544	—	—	—	341	549	317	510	74·03	8 years	Reconnaissance or na gation satellite?
24 Jan	USSR	Cosmos 545	900	408	—	324	521	173	279	71·00	5 months	Continued Cosmos p gramme.
26 Jan	USSR	Cosmos 546	—	—	—	391	630	364	585	51·70	*10 years*	Purpose not revealed.
1 Feb	USSR	Cosmos 547	—	—	—	205	330	129	208	65·00	12 days	*Reconnaissance satellite* Recovered?
3 Feb	USSR	Molniya 1Y	2,200	998	—	24,360	39,200	292	470	65·00	5 years	Communications satel
8 Feb	USSR	Cosmos 548	—	—	—	200	322	133	214	65·40	13 days	*Reconnaissance satellite* Recovered?
		Capsule	—	—	—	—	—	—	—	—	18 days	Ejected from Cosmos
15 Feb	USSR	Prognoz 3	1,865	845	—	125,000	200,000	368	590	65·00	*10 years*	Scientific particles radiation satellite.
28 Feb	USSR	Cosmos 549	—	—	—	345	556	319	513	74·00	*8 years*	Reconnaissance or na gation satellite.
1 Mar	USSR	Cosmos 550	—	—	—	202	325	135	217	65·40	10 days	*Reconnaissance satellite* Recovered?
		Capsule	—	—	—	—	—	—	—	—	11 days	Ejected from Cosmos
6 Mar	USSR	Cosmos 551	—	—	—	196	316	130	210	65·40	14 days	*Reconnaissance satellite* Recovered?
		Capsule	—	—	—	—	—	—	—	—	16 days	Ejected from Cosmos
6 Mar	USA	BMEWS 6	1,550	703	Atlas-Agena D	24,630	39,640	19,950	32,100	10·10	Unlimited	Ballistic missile early warning satellite.
9 Mar	USA	*Big Bird*	*25,000*	*11,340*	Titan IIID	168	270	94	151	95·70	71 days	Reconnaissance satellit
20 Mar	USSR	Meteor 14	—	—	—	561	903	548	882	81·20	*500 years*	Operational weather satellite.
22 Mar	USSR	Cosmos 552	—	—	—	209	337	131	211	72·90	8 days	*Reconnaissance satellite* Recovered?
		Capsule	—	—	—	—	—	—	—	—	18 days	Ejected from Cosmos
3 Apr	USSR	Salyut 2	—	—	—	162	260	133	215	51·56	55 days	Unmanned space stat Broke up in orbit.
5 Apr	USSR	Molniya 2E	*2,750*	*1,247*	—	24,295	39,100	311	500	65·00	*5 years*	Improved communicati satellite.
6 Apr	USA	Pioneer 11	570	260	Atlas-Centaur and Burner II	—	—	—	—	—	Unlimited	Jupiter probe.
12 Apr	USSR	Cosmos 553	900	408	—	322	519	175	282	71·00	6 months	Scientific satellite.
19 Apr	USSR	Cosmos 554	—	—	—	198	318	132	212	72·90	18 days	*Reconnaissance satellite*
19 Apr	USSR	Intercosmos Copernicus 500	—	—	—	964	1,551	126	202	48·50	8 months	International scientific satellite (No. 9).
19 Apr	Canada	Anik-2	—	—	Straight 8 Delta	14,085	22,670	13,810	22,230	0·40	Unlimited	Domestic communicati satellite.
25 Apr	USSR	Cosmos 555	—	—	—	—	—	—	—	—	12 days	*Reconnaissance satellite* Recovered?
		Capsule	—	—	—	—	—	—	—	—	14 days	Ejected from Cosmos
5 May	USSR	Cosmos 556	—	—	—	157	252	130	209	81·30	9 days	*Reconnaissance satellite* Recovered?
		Capsule	—	—	—	—	—	—	—	—	19 days	Ejected from Cosmos
11 May	USSR	Cosmos 557	—	—	—	165	266	135	218	51·60	11 days	Mission not revealed, believed to be an manned Soyuz.
14 May	USA	Skylab 1	197,180	89,439	Saturn V (SA-513)	273	439	265	426	50·04		Unmanned space stat
16 May	USA	Unidentified	*6,600*	*2,994*	Titan IIIB-Agena D	219	352	84	135	110·49	5 weeks	Reconnaissance satellit
17 May	USSR	Cosmos 558	900	408	—	327	526	173	279	71·00	6 months	Scientific satellite.

ate	Origin	Name	Total weight lb	kg	Launch vehicle	Apogee miles	km	Perigee miles	km	Inclin-ation °	Lifetime	Remarks
lay	USSR	Cosmos 559	—	—	—	214	345	135	217	65·40	5 days	*Reconnaissance satellite.* Recovered?
		Capsule	—	—	—	—	—	—	—	—	25 days	Ejected from Cosmos 559.
lay	USSR	Cosmos 560	—	—	—	209	336	131	211	72·90	13 days	*Reconnaissance satellite.* Recovered?
		Capsule	—	—	—	—	—	—	—	—	20 days	Ejected from Cosmos 560.
May	USA	Skylab 2	67,910	30,803	Saturn IB (SA-206)	273	439	264	425	50.03	28 days	Carried crew, Charles Conrad, Joseph Kerwin and Paul Weitz, to Skylab 1.
lay	USSR	Cosmos 561	—	—	—	197	317	134	215	65·40	12 days	*Reconnaissance satellite.* Recovered?
		Capsule	—	—	—	—	—	—	—	—	*21 days*	Ejected from Cosmos 561.
lay	USSR	Meteor 15	—	—	—	557	896	530	853	81·22	*500 years*	Operational weather satellite.
une	USSR	Cosmos 562	900	408	—	317	510	175	282	71·00	*6 months*	Scientific satellite.
une	USSR	Cosmos 563	—	—	—	199	320	132	213	65·40	12 days	*Reconnaissance satellite?* Recovered?
une	USSR	Cosmos 564 to 571	*90*	*40*	—	936	1,507	865	1,392	74·00	*6,000 to 9,000 years*	*Navigation or military communications system satellites.*
une	USSR	Cosmos 572	—	—	—	183	294	131	211	51·70	13 days	*Reconnaissance satellite.* Recovered?
une	USA	Explorer 49	442	200	Uprated Delta	—	—	—	—	—	Unlimited	Radio astronomy satellite. In lunar orbit.
une	USA	IMEWS	—	—	Titan IIIC	22,300	35,890	22,100	35,570	00·53	Unlimited	Integrated Missile Early Warning Satellite.
une	USSR	Cosmos 573	—	—	—	204	329	122	196	51·60	*2 days*	Purpose not revealed.
une	USSR	Cosmos 574	—	—	—	638	1,026	619	996	83·00	*1,500 years*	New type of Cosmos satellite. Purpose not revealed.
une	USSR	Cosmos 575	—	—	—	186	299	129	208	65·40	*12 days*	*Reconnaissance satellite.* Recovered?
une	USSR	Cosmos 576	—	—	—	221	356	132	212	72·90	*12 days*	*Reconnaissance satellite.* Recovered?
uly	USSR	Molniya 2F	2,750	1,247	—	—	—	—	—	—	*5 years*	Communications satellite.
uly	USA	Unidentified	*25,000*	*11,340*	Titan IIID	167	269	97	156	96·21	91 days	Big Bird reconnaissance satellite.
uly	USSR	Mars 4	—	—	—	—	—	—	—	—	Unlimited	Intended to orbit Mars. Failed.
uly	USSR	Cosmos 577	—	—	—	194	312	130	209	65·40	13 days	*Reconnaissance satellite.* Recovered?
		Capsule	—	—	—	—	—	—	—	—	18 days	Ejected from Cosmos 577.
uly	USSR	Mars 5	—	—	—	—	—	—	—	—	Unlimited	In orbit round Mars. Relay for Mars 6 and 7.
uly	USA	Skylab 3	67,668	30,694	Saturn IB (SA-207)	181	291	124	200	65·38	59 days	Carried second crew, comprising Alan Bean, Owen Garriott and Jack Lousma, to Skylab 1.
ug	USSR	Cosmos 578	—	—	—	191	308	129	208	65·40	12 days	*Reconnaissance satellite.* Recovered?
ug	USSR	Mars 6	—	—	—	—	—	—	—	—	Unlimited	Descent capsule landed on Mars on 12 March 1974, but radio failed during descent.
ug	USSR	Mars 7	—	—	—	—	—	—	—	—	Unlimited	Descent capsule released but did not land on planet.
ug	USA	Unidentified	430	195	Thor-Burner II	529	851	505	813	98·86	*80 years*	USAF weather satellite.
ug	USSR	Cosmos 579	—	—	—	196	315	130	209	65·40	12 days	*Reconnaissance satellite.* Recovered?
		Capsule	—	—	—	—	—	—	—	—	15 days	Ejected from Cosmos 579.
ug	USA	Unidentified	—	—	—	24,440	39,330	286	460	63·29	*5 years*	Purpose not disclosed.
ug	USSR	Cosmos 580	—	—	—	322	518	176	283	71·00	*7 months*	Scientific satellite.
ug	USA	Intelsat IV-E	—	—	Atlas-Centaur	22,220	35,760	22,210	35,745	0·3	Unlimited	Fifth Intelsat IV communications satellite.
ug	USSR	Cosmos 581	—	—	—	188	303	131	211	51·60	13 days	*Reconnaissance satellite.* Recovered?
		Capsule	—	—	—	—	—	—	—	—	16 days	Ejected from Cosmos 581.
ug	USSR	Cosmos 582	—	—	—	347	559	324	521	74·00	*8 years*	*Reconnaissance satellite.*
ug	USSR	Molniya 1Z	2,200	998	—	23,595	37,970	298	480	65·30	*5 years*	Communications satellite.
ug	USSR	Cosmos 583	—	—	—	196	316	129	208	65·00	13 days	*Reconnaissance satellite.*
ept	USSR	Cosmos 584	—	—	—	224	360	132	213	72·90	14 days	*Reconnaissance satellite.* Recovered?
		Capsule	—	—	—	—	—	—	—	—	22 days	Ejected from Cosmos 584.
ept	USSR	Cosmos 585	—	—	—	880	1,416	861	1,385	74·00	*6,000 years*	Military satellite?
ept	USSR	Cosmos 586	—	—	—	634	1,020	613	986	83·00	*1,200 years*	Military satellite?
ept	USSR	Cosmos 587	—	—	—	205	330	134	215	65·40	13 days	*Reconnaissance satellite.* Recovered?
		Capsule	—	—	—	—	—	—	—	—	17 days	Ejected from Cosmos 587.
ept	USSR	Soyuz 12	—	—	—	154	249	120	194	—	2 days	Manned proving flight. Crew: Oleg Makarov and Vasily Lazarev.
ept	USA	Unidentified	*6,600*	*2,994*	Titan IIIB-Agena D	239	385	81	130	110·48	32 days	Reconnaissance satellite. Probably military communications spacecraft.
ct	USSR	Cosmos 588 to 595	—	—	—	940	1,512	868	1,397	74·00	*6,000 years*	Probably military communications satellites.
ct	USSR	Cosmos 596	—	—	—	193	310	131	211	65·40	6 days	*Reconnaissance satellite.* Recovered?
		Capsule	—	—	—	—	—	—	—	—	14 days	Ejected from Cosmos 596.
ct	USSR	Cosmos 597	—	—	—	194	312	132	212	65·50	6 days	*Reconnaissance satellite.* Recovered?
		Capsule	—	—	—	—	—	—	—		12 days	Ejected from Cosmos 597.

Date	Origin	Name	Total weight lb	kg	Launch vehicle	Apogee miles	km	Perigee miles	km	Inclin-ation °	Lifetime	Remarks
10 Oct	USSR	Cosmos 598	—	—	—	224	360	132·5	213	72·90	6 days	*Reconnaissance satellite* Recovered?
		Capsule	—	—	—	—		—	—	—	10 days	Ejected from Cosmos 5
15 Oct	USSR	Cosmos 599	—	—	—	183	294	128	206	65·00	13 days	*Reconnaissance satellite.* Recovered?
16 Oct	USSR	Cosmos 600	—	—	—	227	366	134	215	72·90	7 days	*Reconnaissance satellite.* Recovered?
		Capsule	—	—	—	—	—	—	—	—	13 days	Ejected from Cosmos 6
16 Oct	USSR	Cosmos 601	900	408	—	970	1,561	130	210	82·00	*7 months*	Scientific satellite.
19 Oct	USSR	Molniya 2G	2,750	1,247	—	24,750	39,830	316	509	62·84	*5 years*	Communications satelli
20 Oct	USSR	Cosmos 602	—	—	—	227	365	132·5	213	72·90	9 days	*Reconnaissance satellite* Recovered?
		Capsule	—	—	—	—	—	—	—	—	12 days	Ejected from Cosmos 6
26 Oct	USA	Explorer 50	877	398	Uprated Delta	179,700	289,200	87,700	141,140	28·67	Unlimited	Tenth and last Interpla tary Monitoring Platfo satellite, studying the S
27 Oct	USSR	Cosmos 603	—	—	—	222	357	127	204	72·86	13 days	*Reconnaissance satellite* Recovered?
		Capsule	—	—	—	—	—	—	—	—	17 days	Ejected from Cosmos 6
29 Oct	USSR	Cosmos 604	—	—	—	395	636	382	615	81·23	*60 years*	Scientific satellite.
30 Oct	USA	NNS 20	128	58	Scout	714	1,150	555	893	90·18	*900 years*	Navy Navigation Satell
30 Oct	USSR	Intercosmos 10	—	—	—	904	1,455	161	259	74·03	*18 months*	Soviet Eastern-bloc scientific satellite.
30 Oct	USSR	Cosmos 605	—	—	—	250	402	132	212	62·80	21 days	Biological research sa lite. Carried white r Recovered.
2 Nov	USSR	Cosmos 606	*2,750*	*1,247*	—	24,410	39,280	408	657	62·91	*5 years*	Communications satell
3 Nov	USA	Mariner 10	1,108	503	Atlas-Centaur	—	—	—	—	—	Unlimited	Photographed Venus Mercury.
6 Nov	USA	NOAA-3	675	306	Uprated Delta	938	1,510	932	1,500	102·08	*10,000 yrs*	Improved Tiros weat satellite.
10 Nov	USSR	Cosmos 607	—	—	—	212	341	127	204	72·83	12 days	*Reconnaissance satellite* Recovered?
		Capsule	—	—	—	—	—	—	—	—	18 days	Ejected from Cosmos 6
10 Nov	USA	*Big Bird*	*25,000*	*11,340*	Titan IIID	171	275	91	146	96·93	4 months	Reconnaissance satellit
		Unidentified	*130*	*59*	—	316	509	302	486	96·33	*3 years*	Pickaback payload.
14 Nov	USSR	Molniya 1AA	2,200	998	—	24,730	39,800	352	566	64·90	*5 years*	Communications satel
16 Nov	USA	Skylab 4	*67,000*	*30,000*	Saturn IB (SA-208)	271	436	262	422	50·04	84 days	Third and last man mission to Skylab 1. Cr Gerald Carr, Edward G son and William Pogue
20 Nov	USSR	Cosmos 608	900	408	—	328	528	175	281	71·00	*8 months*	Scientific satellite.
21 Nov	USSR	Cosmos 609	—	—	—	230	370	129	207	70·00	13 days	*Reconnaissance satellite* Recovered?
		Capsule	—	—	—	—	—	—	—	—	15 days	Ejected from Cosmos 6
27 Nov	USSR	Cosmos 610	—	—	—	348	560	320	515	74·00	*7 years*	*Reconnaissance satellite*
28 Nov	USSR	Cosmos 611	900	408	—	315	507	174	280	71·00	*7 months*	Scientific satellite.
28 Nov	USSR	Cosmos 612	—	—	—	231	371	133	214	72·90	13 days	*Reconnaissance satellite.* Recovered?
		Capsule	—	—	—	—	—	—	—	—	18 days	Ejected from Cosmos 6
30 Nov	USSR	Cosmos 613	—	—	—	183	295	121	195	51·60	*60 days*	Unmanned Soyuz test spacecraft.
30 Nov	USSR	Molniya 1AB	2,200	998	—	25,360	40,815	384	618	—	*5 years*	Communications satel
4 Dec	USSR	Cosmos 614	—	—	—	516	830	478	770	74·00	*120 years*	Military satellite?
13 Dec	USSR	Cosmos 615	900	408	—	517	832	168	270	71·02	18 *months*	Scientific satellite.
14 Dec	USA	DSCS 3	—	—	Titan IIIC	22,550	36,290	21,960	35,340	2·28	Unlimited	Military communicati satellites.
		DSCS 4	—	—	—	—	—	—	—	—	—	
16 Dec	USA	Explorer 51	1,450	660	Uprated Delta	2,673	4,302	98	158	68·12	*3 years*	Atmospheric explorer satellite.
17 Dec	USSR	Cosmos 616	—	—	—	206	332	128	206	72·86	11 days	*Reconnaissance satellite*
18 Dec	USSR	Soyuz 13	—	—	—	170	272	140	225	51·57	8 days	Test flight. Crew: Py Klimuk and Valentin Lebedev.
19 Dec	USSR	Cosmos 617 to 624	—	—	—	929	1,495	908	1,461	74·01	*5,000 years*	Military communicati satellites.
21 Dec	USSR	Cosmos 625	—	—	—	200	322	127	204	72·83	13 days	*Reconnaissance satellite* Recovered?
		Capsule	—	—	—	—	—	—	—	—	16 days	Ejected from Cosmos 6
25 Dec	USSR	Molniya 2H	2,750	1,247	—	25,340	40,780	303	488	62·89	*5 years*	Communications satell
26 Dec	USSR	Aureole 2	—	—	—	1,228	1,976	248	399	74·01	*30 years*	Soviet/French scientifi satellite.
27 Dec	USSR	Cosmos 626	—	—	—	161	259	160	257	65·02	*600 years*	Military satellite?
29 Dec	USSR	Cosmos 627	—	—	—	632	1,017	604	972	82·95	1,300 years	Military satellite?

AERO-ENGINES

THE ARGENTINE REPUBLIC

CICARÉ

CICARÉ AERONÁUTICA

Address:
CC.24, Saladillo, Provincia de Buenos Aires
Telephone: (Comodoro Mantel, in Buenos Aires) 41-5260
Officers: See "Aircraft" section

Several types of Cicaré automotive engine have been produced in quantity for surface applications. Cicaré Aeronautica, formed in 1972, is developing light helicopters (see Aircraft section) and light-aircraft engines. The first engine is the 4C2T (four-cylinder two-stroke).

CICARÉ 4C2T

This is a light, low-cost engine intended to be used in a wide range of aeroplanes, motor-gliders and helicopters. It is intended in particular to replace the many Continental A65 and similar engines used in the past in Argentina and other countries as a standard power unit for light aviation. The engine first ran in October 1973.

Type: Four-cylinder horizontally-opposed air-cooled two-stroke piston engine.

Cylinders: Bore 2·91 in (74 mm). Stroke 3·00 in (76 mm). Swept volume 80·18 cu in (1,314 cc). Compression ratio 7·2 : 1. Cylinders on each side cast in light alloy as single unit complete with half crankcase. Steel liners.

Pistons: Aluminium alloy castings, each with two compression rings and one scraper ring.

Connecting Rods: Forged steel, with needle-roller bearings in both big and small ends.

Crankshaft: Four-throw steel forging carried in three ball bearings.

Crankcase: Divided on vertical centreline; each half cast complete with pair of cylinders.

Induction: Twin carburettors, each equipped with hot-air anti-icing. Mixture passed through crankcase and thence through inlet and exhaust ports in cylinders.

Fuel: Mixture of 40 parts 80-octane gasoline to 1 part SAE.40 oil.

Ignition: Dual magnetos, serving two Champion UK10, Autolite BT3 or PVI BT3 plugs per cylinder.

Lubrication: See under "Fuel".

Propeller Drive: Reduction gear ratio 2·03: 1.

Accessories: Rear pads for 12V alternator and starter.

Dimensions:

Length	31·89 in (810 mm)
Width	25·98 in (660 mm)
Height	21·65 in (550 mm)

Weight, Dry:

Estimated, with accessories	150 lb (68·0 kg)

Cicaré 4C2T light-aircraft engine

Performance Rating:

Max T-O	69 hp at 4,500 rpm

Specific Consumption:

Fuel/oil mix at optimum rating	0·66 lb (0·3 kg)/hp/hr

AUSTRALIA

CAC

COMMONWEALTH AIRCRAFT CORPORATION PTY LTD

Head Office and Works:
304 Lorimer Street, Port Melbourne, Victoria 3207
Telephone: 64-0771
Officers: See "Aircraft" section

Recent engine activities of the Commonwealth Aircraft Corporation have been centred on licensed manufacture of the SNECMA Atar 9C and Rolls-Royce Viper 11 turbojets. These engines power Australian-built Mirage III-O ground attack aircraft and Aermacchi M.B. 326H training aircraft.

Their production, amounting to 140 Atars and 112 Vipers, is now complete; but overhaul of the Atar, Viper and Rolls-Royce Avon Mks 1, 26 and 109 turbojets continues to be undertaken, together with the manufacture of spares.

Commonwealth Aircraft-built SNECMA Atar 9C turbojet (14,110 lb; 6,400 kg st)

BELGIUM

FN

FABRIQUE NATIONALE HERSTAL, SA

Head Office and Works:
B-4400 Herstal
Telephone: (04) 64 08 00

FN is completing licensed production of the SNECMA Atar 9C turbojet for Belgian-built Mirage 5-B aircraft. The production programme is in collaboration with SNECMA and Fairey SA.

Though arrangements had not been completed as this edition went to press, FN was expected to share in both the Larzac 04 military turbofan and the CFM56 commercial turbofan programmes. Participation in the Larzac programme was one of the offsets included in the adoption of the Alpha Jet trainer by the Belgian Air Force. FN's share in the CFM56 project will be a part of the 50 per cent work-split due to SNECMA of France, which had been seeking other European partners. It was not known in May 1974 whether FN would be a shareholder in the project company, CFM International.

FN is also a member of the consortium which made Rolls-Royce Tyne 21 and 22 turboprops in co-operation with Rolls-Royce, MTU and SNECMA (Hispano-Suiza) to power Breguet Atlantic maritime reconnaissance aircraft and Transall C-160 transports. Details of these engines are given under the SNECMA and Rolls-Royce entries, respectively.

FN maintains and repairs General Electric J79-GE-11A turbojets which the company produced in association with MAN Turbo (now MTU) in Germany and Fiat in Italy to power F-104G fighters in service with NATO air forces. Other repair and overhaul work concerns Turboméca Marboré IIF turbojets and engine controls and accessories. FN also manufactures the 400-490 hp (406-497 cv) Type 531 gas turbine, derived from the Boeing 551/553, and overhauls and repairs the Boeing 502-12B turbostarter.

CANADA

ORENDA

HAWKER SIDDELEY CANADA LIMITED, Orenda Division

Head Office and Works:
Mississauga, Ontario
Telephone: (416) 677-3250
Postal Address:
Box 6001, Toronto AMF, Ontario L5P 1B3
Vice-President of HS Canada and General Manager of Orenda Division:
M. E. Davis
Director of Administration:
J. Turner
Director of Engineering: B. A. Avery
Director of Operations: R. F. Tanner
Director of Marketing, Aeronautical:
D. J. Caple
Director of Marketing, Industrial:
W. S. Bellian
Director of Finance: K. R. Church

Since late August 1973, complete ownership of Orenda has been restored to Hawker Siddeley Canada Ltd. Main activities of the division are the manufacture of aircraft turbine engines and components, and the design and manufacture of industrial gas turbines.

Current production programmes include licensed manufacture of the General Electric J85-CAN-15 turbojet engines for Canadian-built Northrop CF-5s for the Canadian Armed Forces and NF-5s for the Royal Netherlands Air Force. Concurrently, Orenda is overhauling J79-7, J85-CAN-40 and -15 and Orenda turbojet engines. It supplies parts to Canada, West Germany, the Netherlands, Pakistan, Belgium, Norway, Italy, Venezuela and the United States.

The J79-OEL-7, used in the Canadair CF-104, most nearly resembles the J79-GE-11A. It has a four-strut front frame, cartridge-operated emergency nozzle closure system and other, minor differences.

The Orenda Division does not at present envisage manufacturing aero-engines to its own design.

ORENDA (GENERAL ELECTRIC) J85

The version of the J85 turbojet produced by Orenda to power the Canadair-built CF-5 and NF-5 is the J85-CAN-15. Details are the same as for the General Electric J85-GE-15. Deliveries began in 1967.

UACL

UNITED AIRCRAFT OF CANADA LTD

Head Office and Works:
PO Box 10, Longueuil, Quebec J4K 4X9
Telephone: (514) 677-9411
President: T. E. Stephenson
Vice-Presidents:
R. H. Guthrie (Industrial & Marine Division)
A. C. Kennedy (Personnel)
R. G. Raven (Helicopter & Systems Division)
E. L. Smith (Operations)
E. H. Schweitzer (Product Support)
K. H. Sullivan (Marketing)
V. W. Tryon (Finance)

UACL is a major subsidiary of the United Aircraft Corporation, Connecticut, USA, and was formed originally to manufacture and overhaul reciprocating engines and spare parts designed by UAC's Pratt & Whitney Aircraft Division. In 1957 its activities were enlarged to include design and development of turbine engines and by 1963, when the company's name was changed from

Canadian Pratt & Whitney Aircraft Ltd to its present form, its operations had been expanded to embrace the manufacture, overhaul and marketing of products of all Divisions of the United Aircraft Corporation. Today UACL is the prime source of manufacture and spare parts production for all Pratt & Whitney reciprocating engines.

Original turbine work by the company was initiated by the concept and preliminary design of the JT12 (J60) turbojet, development and manufacture of which were taken over subsequently by Pratt & Whitney Aircraft. Design, development and manufacture of the PT6, ST6, PT6T and JT15D series of small turbine aero-engines represents 55 per cent of the company's activities.

Research and development programmes under way at UACL include work on high pressure ratio, high efficiency centrifugal compressors; high Mach number, high work axial compressor stages; high work capacity radial turbines for operation at 1,260°C entry temperature; and very high work output axial turbines.

UACL is owned 90 per cent by the United Aircraft Corporation. Approximately 40 per cent of its sales are linked to defence requirements and two-thirds of all output is exported.

UACL occupies 1,490,000 sq ft (138,455 m²) of space in four plants and employs more than 5,350 persons.

Exterior (*right*) **and cutaway drawing** (*below*) **of the United Aircraft of Canada JT15D-1 twin-spool turbofan (2,200 lb; 998 kg st)**

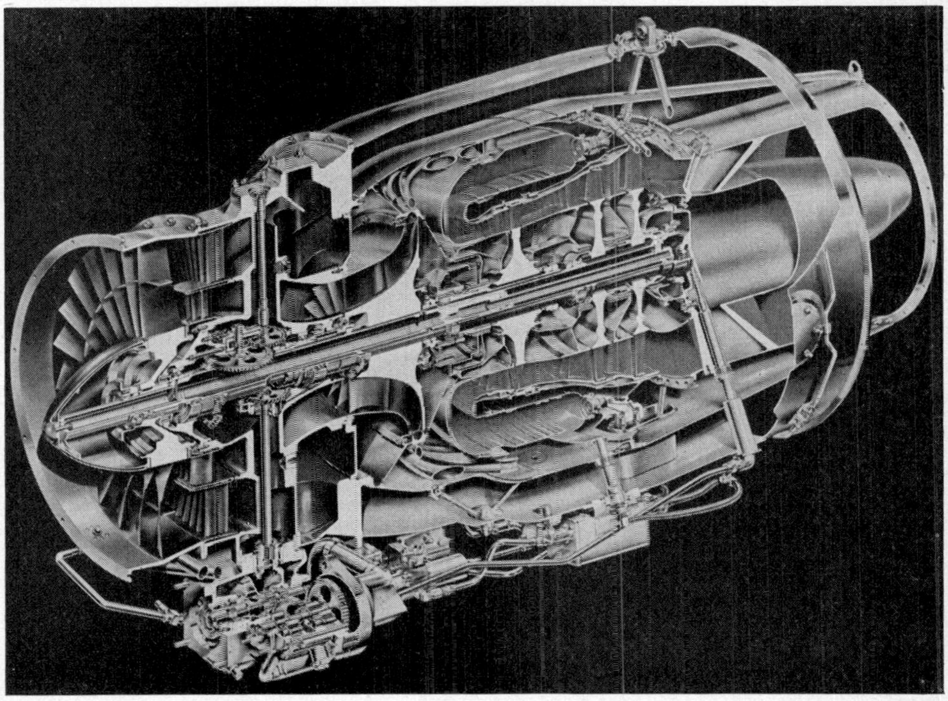

UNITED AIRCRAFT OF CANADA JT15D

Following a comprehensive performance study of small turbofan engines carried out by UACL during 1965, detail design of a definitive engine, the 2,000 lb to 2,500 lb JT15D, was initiated in June 1966. First run of the new turbofan was on 23 September 1967, within eight days of the target set at the start of design. The engine exceeded its rated thrust on its second build in November 1967 and achieved its guaranteed sfc in May 1968. Flight testing of the JT15D in a nacelle under a modified Avro CF-100 testbed aircraft started on 22 August 1968.

By February 1972, after eight months of post-certification work on the JT15D-1, eight development engines had completed more than 15,170 hours of bench testing, 3,500 hours of flight testing and 10,100 hours of rig testing, including an official 50 hour PFRT in May 1969 and full FAA/DoT civil certification by May 1971. The JT15D-1 engine has flown to 48,000 ft (14,630 m) and Mach 0·8, and has undergone testing for bleed-air purity, anti-icing, noise certification, inlet distortion, altitude starting to 40,000 ft (12,190 m), intake vortex, accessory gearbox 270 hours' full rating, cold-weather starting, foreign-object ingestion, including birds, numerous 1,000-cycle tests at elevated turbine temperatures and thrust levels, and other testing.

In 1969 the T-O thrust was raised from an initial 2,000 lb to 2,200 lb (907 to 998 kg), with an sfc of 0·540. The first growth version, the JT15D-4, was run successfully ahead of schedule in January 1972, developing a rated thrust of 2,310 lb (1,048 kg) to 25°C ambient at the rated sfc of 0·554. By August 1972 the eight development engines comprised three JT15D-1s and five JT15D-4s.

Intended to power business aircraft, small transports and counter-insurgency combat aircraft in the 8,000 lb to 12,500 lb AUW category, the JT15D is an advanced technology two-spool front-fan engine having a minimum number of aerodynamic components. Major design objectives were a significant improvement in sfc, and simplicity of construction to ensure low first cost and maintenance costs. Other objectives were low noise levels, ease of handling, and the attainment of airline standards of reliability.

Initial application for the engine was the Cessna Citation 500 twin-engined business jet, for which Cessna has ordered 2,200 lb st JT15D-1s valued at approximately $30 m. Flight-worthy prototype engines were delivered in August 1969 for the Citation's first flight in mid-September.

By February 1974 more than 325 JT15D-1s had been delivered to Cessna for the Citation. Certificated to FAR Part 36 noise specifications, the JT15D-1-powered Citation is claimed to be the quietest executive jet flying. A second application for the engine is the prototype Aérospatiale SN 600 Corvette twin-engined business jet, for which JT15D-1s were delivered in September 1969. The first JT15D-4 prototype engines were delivered to Aérospatiale in August 1972 for the Corvette programme. By January 1974 a total of 744 JT15Ds had been ordered, and a total flight time of 131,145 hr had been logged in 147 aircraft. Civil certification of the JT15D-4 and production deliveries occurred three months ahead of schedule in September 1973. The TBO of the JT15D-4 on entry into service is expected to be 1,500 hours, as was the case for the JT15D-1.

The following description relates to the JT-15D-1:

Type: Two-shaft turbofan.

Air Intake: Direct pitot intake without inlet guide vanes. Hot-air anti-icing for nose bullet.

Fan: Single-stage axial fan, aerodynamically related to that of the JT9D but on a much smaller scale. Forged disc fitted with 28 solid titanium blades secured by dovetail fixings riveted to disc. Blades have part-span shrouds. Casing, which forms the engine air intake, of forged stainless steel. Circular splitter ring behind fan, held between two rows of 33 inner wrapped-sheet stators and single row of 66 outer stator blades. Total air mass flow, 75 lb (34 kg)/sec; by-pass ratio about 3·3:1; by-pass flow typically 57·5 lb (26 kg)/sec; primary core air flow 17·5 lb (8 kg)/sec; fan pressure ratio 1·5:1.

Compressor: Primary airflow enters eye of single-stage titanium centrifugal compressor. Single-sided impeller, with 16 full vanes and 16 splitter vanes, secured to shaft by special bolt and key-washer. Two-piece casing with diffuser in form of pipes containing straightening vanes. Overall pressure ratio almost 10:1.

Combustion Chamber: Annular reverse-flow type. Outer casing of heat-resistant steel; flame tube of nickel alloy, supported on low-pressure turbine stator assembly. Spark igniters at 5 and 7 o'clock positions (viewed from rear.

Fuel System: Engine-driven sandwich-mounted pump delivering through FCU, flow divider and dual manifolds at 650 lb/sq in (45·7 kg/cm²); DP-LI pneumatic control unit mounted on pump.

Fuel Grades: JP-1, JP-4, JP-5 conforming to PWA Spec. 522.

Nozzle Guide Vanes: High-pressure ring of 15, integrally cast in cobalt alloy.

Turbine: Single-stage HP turbine with 71 solid blades held in fir-tree roots in thick-hub disc of refractory alloy; two-stage LP turbine with nickel alloy discs, first stage being cast integrally with 61 blades and second stage carrying 55 blades in fir-tree roots. LP fan shaft drives fan, with ball thrust bearing behind fan and roller gear and intershaft bearings; HP shaft drives centrifugal compressor, with front ball thrust bearing and rear roller bearing. Gas temperatures 960°C before turbine, 562°C after turbine.

Jet Pipe: Nickel alloy cone and sheet-metal pipe. Provision made for adjusting the area to match engines and to trim performance.

Accessory Drives: Package under front of engine driven by power off-take from front of HP shaft.

Lubrication System: Integral oil system, with gear-type pump delivering at up to 80 lb/sq in (5·62 kg/cm²). Capacity, 2·4 US gallons (2·0 Imp gallons; 9·0 litres).

Oil Specification: Oil to PWA 521-B.

Mounting: Hard or soft, according to customers' choice. Four main pads on front casing, arranged two on each side at 30° above and below horizontal. One rear mount at top or on either side of centreline.

Starting: Air-turbine starter or electric starter/generator.

Dimensions:

Diameter:	
JT15D-1	27·2 in (691 mm)
JT15D-4	27·0 in (686 mm)
Length overall:	
JT15D-1	59·3 in (1,506 mm)
JT15D-4	63·0 in (1,600 mm)
Frontal area	4 sq ft (0·37 m²)

Weight, Equipped:

JT15D-1	506 lb (230 kg)
JT15D-4	557 lb (253 kg)

Performance Ratings:

T-O:	
JT15D-1	2,200 lb (998 kg)
JT15D-4	2,500 lb (1,135 kg)
Max continuous:	
JT15D-1	2,090 lb (950 kg)
JT15D-4	2,375 lb (1,078 kg)

Specific Fuel Consumption (T-O):

JT15D-1	0·540
JT15D-4	0·562

UNITED AIRCRAFT OF CANADA PT6A

The PT6A, UACL's major commercial product, is a lightweight, low consumption free-turbine turboprop. By January 1974 the PT6A accounted for more than 6,050 of the 9,000 PT6 engines ordered. With a total flight time of 12,370,000 hr, powering 2,400 aircraft of 83 different types, the PT6 was at that time in service with 910 operators in 91 countries. With 33 different certificated airframe applications, the PT6A series powers 75 per cent of all light twin-turboprop aircraft in the west. Maximum TBO in commuter-type aircraft is 8,500 hr.

An experimental PT6 ran for the first time in November 1959 and flight trials of the turboprop in the nose of a modified Beechcraft 18 began in May 1961. Civil certification of the first production model, the 578 ehp PT6A-6, was granted in late 1963. Progressively higher rated versions have followed in production to power a wide variety of single and twin-engined aircraft, and deliveries are being made at a rate in excess of 100 engines a month. Development, which to date has cost more than $14·5 million, including $14·5 million from the Canadian Department of Industry, is currently proceeding on models rated up to 1,200 ehp.

Related series of engines include the T74 military turboprop, the PT6B commercial turboshaft, PT6T coupled turboshaft, T400 military coupled engine, and the ST6 series of APU, industrial and marine engines. Technology from the PT6/ST6 family has also been embodied in UACL's JT15D turbofan.

Current versions of the PT6A are as follows:

PT6A-6. Flat rated at 578 ehp (550 shp) at 2,200 propeller rpm to 21°C, this version received civil certification in December 1963. A total of 350 PT6A-6s were built between then and November 1965. Among aircraft powered by the PT6A-6 are the de Havilland Canada Turbo-Beaver and early DHC-6 Twin Otter Series 100.

PT6A-20. Flat rated at 579 ehp (550 shp) at 2,200 propeller rpm to 21°C, the -20 offers improved reliability and increases in max continuous, max climb and max cruise power ratings over the PT6A-6. The PT6A-20 was certificated in October 1965. Between then and January 1972 more than 2,200 were built. The PT6A-20 continues in production to power the Beech King Air B90, Beech Model 99 Commuter Liner, prototypes of the EMBRAER EMB-110 Bandeirante, de Havilland Canada DHC-6 Twin Otter Series 100 and 200, James Aviation (Fletcher FU-24) conversion, Marshall of Cambridge (Grumman) Goose conversion, McKinnon G-21C and G-21D Turbo-Goose (Grumman Goose) conversions, Pilatus PC-6/B1-H2 Turbo-Porter, Pilatus PC-7 Turbo-Trainer and the Swearingen Merlin IIA (which can be re-engined with the PT6A-27).

PT6A-27. Third production version of the PT6A, this version is flat rated at 715 ehp (680 shp) at 2,200 propeller rpm to 22°C. Its higher ratings are attained by a 12½ per cent increase in mass flow provided by a larger-diameter compressor. The increased airflow enables the higher power to be obtained at lower turbine temperatures than in the PT6A-20. Production began in November 1967 and 575 engines had been delivered by January 1972. Production continues. Applications of the PT6A-27 include the Hamilton Westwind II/III (Beech 18) conversions, Beech Model 97, Beech Model 99A Commuter Liner, Beech U-21A and U-21D, de Havilland Canada DHC-6 Twin Otter Series 300, Fairchild Industries/Pilatus PC-6/B2-H2 Porter, Frakes Aviation (Grumman) Mallard conversion, Israel Aircraft Industries Arava, Let L-410A Turbolet, and Saunders Aircraft ST-27A (de Havilland Heron) conversion.

PT6A-28. Similar to the PT6A-27 and with the same T-O and max continuous ratings, this version has an additional normal cruise rating of 562 ehp available up to 21°C corresponding to the max cruise rating conditions of the -27. In addition the max cruise rating of the -28 gives 652 ehp up to the higher ambient of 33°C. This model, which operates at higher turbine entry temperatures than the -27, is in production for the Beech Model 100 King Air and Piper Cheyenne.

PT6A-29. Company designation for military counterpart of the PT6A-27 which received civil certification in Spring of 1968. Rated at 778 ehp (750 shp) to 23°C. Powers Beech RU-21 versions.

PT6A-34. Rated at 883 ehp, this version has aircooled turbine nozzle guide vanes to enable operation at higher turbine entry temperatures.

PT6A-41. This higher mass flow version embodies aircooled stage-one turbine nozzle guide vanes and a two-stage free turbine (in place of the previous single-stage unit) to give improved power absorption. Length is thus increased by 4 in (101 mm) to 66 in (1,676 mm). The -41 has a T-O rating of 903 ehp (850 shp) at 2,000 propeller rpm, available up to 41°C. Thermodynamic power is 1,089 ehp. Development is under way for potential applications such as growth versions of current PT6-powered aircraft, advanced turboprop commuter aircraft and various US military projects. The PT6A-41 is flat rated at 29°C for max climb and cruise.

PT6A-45. Similar to PT6A-41 but with redesigned gearbox to transmit higher powers at reduced propeller speeds. Rated at 1,174 ehp (1,120 shp) at 1,620-1,700 rpm to 15°C, or to 28°C with water injection. Specified for Short SD3-30 and Frakes-Nord 262.

PT6A-50. Similar to the PT6A-41 and under development at higher ratings with a longer, higher-ratio reduction gear to give a significantly lower propeller tip speed for quieter operation at T-O. Length is consequently increased to 84 in (2,134 mm). Rating at T-O is 1,174 ehp (1,120 shp) available with water injection up to 34°C at propeller speeds from 1,210 down to 1,100 rpm. The PT6A-50 will power the de Havilland Canada DHC-7 "Quiet STOL" transport.

On 1 May 1973 it was announced that the first PT6A-50 had run, five weeks ahead of schedule. It ran over its whole range of power up to 1,120 shp. By the end of February 1974 four engines had run 700 hours, over 170 of them with the Hamilton Standard low-speed "quiet" propeller.

The following data apply generally to the PT6A series:

Type: Free-turbine axial-plus-centrifugal turboprop engine.

Propeller Drive (PT6A-6, -20, -27, -28, -29, -34, -40 and -41): Two-stage planetary gear train. Ratio 15 : 1. Rotation clockwise when viewed from rear. Drive from free turbine. Flanged propeller shaft. Plain bearings. Higher-ratio reduction gears developed for PT6A-45 and -50.

Air Intake: Annular air intake at rear of engine, with intake screen. Aircraft-supplied alcohol anti-icing system or inertial separation anti-icing system.

Compressor: Three axial-flow stages, plus single centrifugal stage. Single-sided centrifugal compressor, with 26 vanes, made from titanium forging. Stainless steel pipe diffuser on PT6A-27. Axial rotor of disc-drum type, with stainless steel stator and rotor blades. The stator vanes (44 first-stage, 44 second-stage, 40 third-stage) are brazed to casing. The rotor blades (32 first-stage, 32 second-stage and 32 third-stage) are dovetailed to discs. Discs through-bolted, with centrifugal compressor, to shaft. Fabricated one-piece stainless steel casing and radial diffuser. PT6A-27: compression ratio 6·7 : 1, air mass flow 6·8 lb/sec (3·1 kg/sec).

Combustion Chamber: Annular reverse-flow type of stainless steel construction, with 14 simplex burners around periphery of chamber. All versions except PT6A-27 have two glow plug igniters, 64° each side of vertical centreline on lower surface. PT6A-27 has one plug at 64° on starboard side of vertical centreline and one at 90° on port side.

Fuel System: Bendix DP-F2 pneumatic automatic fuel control system. Pneumatic computing section, with automatic inlet air temperature compensation, fuel metering and regulating section, gas generator governor and free turbine governor. PT6A-27 and subsequent models have a dual manifold with seven nozzles per manifold. Maximum fuel pressure 800 lb/sq in (56·25 kg/cm^2).

Fuel Grade: Commercial jet fuels JP-1, JP-4, JP-5, MIL-J-5624. Use of aviation gasolines (MIL-G-5572) grades 80/87, 91/98, 100/130 and 115/145 permitted for a period of up to 150 hours during any overhaul period.

Nozzle Guide Vanes: 29 nozzle guide vanes.

Turbines: Two single-stage axial-flow turbines. LP turbine drives output shaft. Blades (58 first stage, 41 second stage) attached by fir-tree roots. PT6A-34, -40 and -50 have stage-one aircooled nozzle guide vanes, and two-stage power turbine.

Bearings: Each main rotor (gas generator and free turbine) supported by one ball and one roller anti-friction bearing.

Jet Pipe: Collector duct surrounding free-turbine shaft, exhaust through two ports on horizontal centreline.

Accessories: Mounting pads on accessory case (rear of engine) for starter/generator, hydraulic pump, aircraft accessory drive, vacuum pump and tachometer-generator. Mounting pad on the shaft-turbine reduction gear case for propeller overspeed governor, propeller constant-speed control unit and tachometer generator. All accessories mount on the ends of the engine and do not protrude beyond the major diameter of the engine.

The 715 ehp United Aircraft of Canada PT6A-27 free-turbine turboprop

Lubrication System: One pressure and four scavenge elements in the pump stacks. All are gear type and are driven by the gas generator rotor. Engine has an integral oil tank with a capacity of 2·3 US gallons (8·75 litres). Oil supply pressure is 65 lb/sq in (4·57 kg/cm^2).

Oil Specification: UACL Spec 202 (7·5 cs vis) (MIL-L-23699, MIL-L-7808 for military engines).

Mounting: Turboprop has three-point ring suspension. Turboshaft has two main pads and one steady pad.

Starting: Electric starter/generator on accessory case.

Dimensions:
Max diameter 19 in (483 mm)
Length, less accessories:
PT6A-6, -20, -27, -28, -29, -34 62 in (1,575 mm)
PT6A-41 66 in (1,676 mm)
PT6A-45 72 in (1,829 mm)
PT6A-50 76 in (1,930 mm)
Frontal area 1·95 sq ft (0·18 m^2)

Weight, Dry:
PT6A-6 270 lb (122·5 kg)
PT6A-20 286 lb (130 kg)
PT6A-27, -28 300 lb (136 kg)
PT6A-29 297 lb (135 kg)
PT6A-34 311 lb (141 kg)
PT6A-41 370 lb (168 kg)
PT6A-45 423 lb (192 kg)
PT6A-50 547 lb (248 kg)

Performance Ratings:
T-O rating:
See under model listings
Max continuous rating:
PT6A-6
525 ehp (500 shp) at 2,200 rpm (to 18°C)
PT6A-20
579 ehp (550 shp) at 2,200 rpm (to 22°C)
PT6A-27, -28
715 ehp (680 shp) at 2,200 rpm (to 22°C)
PT6A-29
778 ehp (750 shp) at 2,200 rpm (to 23°C)
PT6A-34
783 ehp (750 shp) at 2,200 rpm (to 30°C)
PT6A-41
903 ehp (850 shp) at 2,000 rpm (to 31°C)
PT6A-45
1,070 ehp (1,020 shp) at 1,620-1,700 rpm (to 27°C)
PT6A-50
1,022 ehp (973 shp) at 1,020-1,160 rpm (to 32°C)

Max climb rating:
PT6A-6
525 ehp (500 shp) at 2,200 rpm (to 18°C)
PT6A-20 566 ehp (538 shp) at 2,200 rpm
PT6A-27, -28
652 ehp (620 shp) at 2,200 rpm (to 21°C)
PT6A-29
726 ehp (700 shp) at 2,200 rpm (to 23°C)
PT6A-34
731 ehp (700 shp) at 2,200 rpm (to 28°C)
PT6A-41
903 ehp (850 shp) at 2,000 rpm (to 31°C)
PT6A-45 1,004 ehp (956 shp) at 1,425 rpm
PT6A-50
947 ehp (900 shp) at 1,020-1,160 rpm (to 23°C)

Max cruise rating:
PT6A-6 495 ehp (471 shp) at 2,200 rpm
PT6A-20 522 ehp (495 shp) at 2,200 rpm
PT6A-27 652 ehp (620 shp) at 2,200 rpm (to 21°C)
PT6A-28
652 ehp (620 shp) at 2,200 rpm (to 33°C)
PT6A-29 714 ehp (688 shp) at 2,200 rpm
PT6A-34
731 ehp (700 shp) at 2,200 rpm (to 19°C)
PT6A-41
903 ehp (850 shp) at 2,000 rpm (to 26°C)
PT6A-45 1,004 ehp (956 shp) at 1,425 rpm
PT6A-50
947 ehp (900 shp) at 1,020-1,160 rpm (to 23°C)

SPECIFIC FUEL CONSUMPTION:
At T-O rating:

PT6A-6	0·65 lb (0·295 kg)/ehp/hr
PT6A-20	0·649 lb (0·294 kg)/ehp/hr
PT6A-27, -28	0·602 lb (0·273 kg)/ehp/hr
PT6A-29	0·598 lb (0·271 kg)/ehp/hr
PT6A-34	0·595 lb (0·270 kg)/ehp/hr
PT6A-41	0·591 lb (0·268 kg)/ehp/hr
PT6A-45, -50	0·560 lb (0·254 kg)/ehp/hr

At max continuous rating:

PT6A-6	0·67 lb (0·305 kg)/ehp/hr
PT6A-20	0·649 lb (0·294 kg)/ehp/hr
PT6A-27, -28	0·602 lb (0·273 kg)/ehp/hr
PT6A-29	0·598 lb (0·271 kg)/ehp/hr
PT6A-34	0·595 lb (0·270 kg)/ehp/hr
PT6A-41	0·591 lb (0·268 kg)/ehp/hr
PT6A-45	0·573 lb (0·260 kg)/ehp/hr
PT6A-50	0·578 lb (0·262 kg)/ehp/hr

At max cruise rating:

PT6A-6	0·68 lb (0·309 kg)/ehp/hr
PT6A-20	0·670 lb (0·304 kg)/ehp/hr
PT6A-27, -28	0·612 lb (0·277 kg)/ehp/hr
PT6A-29	0·608 lb (0·276 kg)/ehp/hr
PT6A-34	0·604 lb (0·274 kg)/ehp/hr
PT6A-41	0·591 lb (0·268 kg)/ehp/hr
PT6A-45	0·578 lb (0·262 kg)/ehp/hr
PT6A-50	0·583 lb (0·265 kg)/ehp/hr

OIL CONSUMPTION:
Max 0·20 lb (0·091 kg)/hr

UNITED AIRCRAFT OF CANADA T74 TURBOPROP

The T74 is the US designation for military versions of the PT6A turboprop and PT6B turboshaft. The T74 turboprop is of the same configuration as the PT6A. Military versions are:

T74-CP-700. US Army counterpart of the PT6A-20. More than 500 T74-CP-700s have been delivered to Beech for 129 U-21A aircraft. These engines are fitted with an inertial separator system developed under Army contract to protect the turboprop against sand and dust ingestion.

T74-CP-702. Rated at 778 ehp and retrofitted in Beech U-21 aircraft engaged in US Project Crazydog electronic countermeasures operations.

A further application of the military T74/PT6A is the Helio Stallion Model 550, turbine version of the single-engined Helio U-10, for which FAA certification has been completed. Deliveries to the USAF for the Credible Chase mission were made in 1971.

The following data apply to the military PT6A-29 (T74-CP-702):

DIMENSIONS:
Diameter approx 19 in (483 mm)
Length approx 62 in (1,575 mm)

WEIGHT, DRY:
With standard equipment 289 lb (131 kg)

PERFORMANCE RATINGS:
T-O and max continuous
778 ehp (750 shp) at 2,200 rpm (to 23°C)
Max climb or military
726 ehp (700 shp) at 2,200 rpm (to 23°C)
Max cruise or normal
714 ehp (688 shp) at 2,200 rpm (to 23°C)

SPECIFIC FUEL CONSUMPTION:
At T-O and max continuous ratings
0·598 lb (0·271 kg)/ehp/hr
At max climb or military ratings
0·606 lb (0·275 kg)/ehp/hr
At max cruise or normal ratings
0·608 lb (0·276 kg)/ehp/hr

UNITED AIRCRAFT OF CANADA PT6B/PT6C

The PT6B is the commercial turboshaft version of the PT6A and has a lower-ratio reduction gear. Past applications include the Lockheed XH-51A and Model 286 rigid-rotor helicopters.

Current versions of the PT6B are:

PT6B-9. Rated at 550 shp at 6,230 rpm available to 25°C. Civil certification received in May 1965.

PT6B-16. Rated at 690 shp at 6,230 rpm available to 23°C for T-O and max continuous ratings. Civil certification was awarded in mid-1967 and production engines became available in October 1967.

Both these engines have a single-stage planetary gear train of 5·3 : 1 reduction ratio. Rotation is clockwise when viewed from the rear. The splined output shaft is mounted in plain bearings. B-series engines with higher ratings can be made available.

PT6C. This series of engines provides direct drive from the power turbine, with no reduction gearing.

DIMENSIONS:
Max diameter 19 in (483 mm)
Length, less accessories, PT6B-9
60 in (1,525 mm)
Frontal area 1·95 sq ft (0·18 m²)

WEIGHT, DRY:
PT6B-9 245 lb (111 kg)
PT6B-16 265 lb (120 kg)

PERFORMANCE RATINGS:
T-O:
See under model listings
Max continuous:
PT6B-9 500 shp at 6,230 rpm (to 22°C)
PT6B-16 690 shp at 6,230 rpm (to 23°C)
Max climb:
PT6B-9 500 shp at 6,230 rpm (to 22°C)
PT6B-16 665 shp at 6,230 rpm
Max cruise:
PT6B-9 485 shp at 6,230 rpm
PT6B-16 665 shp at 6,230 rpm

SPECIFIC FUEL CONSUMPTION:
At T-O rating:
PT6B-9 0·665 lb (0·302 kg)/shp/hr
PT6B-16 0·618 lb (0·280 kg)/shp/hr
At max continuous rating:
PT6B-9 0·685 lb (0·311 kg)/shp/hr
PT6B-16 0·618 lb (0·280 kg)/shp/hr
At max cruise rating:
PT6B-9 0·69 lb (0·313 kg)/shp/hr
PT6B-16 0·623 lb (0·283 kg)/shp/hr

OIL CONSUMPTION:
Max 0·20 lb (0·091 kg)/hr

UNITED AIRCRAFT OF CANADA PT6T TWIN PAC

First run in July 1968, the PT6T Twin Pac comprises two PT6 turboshaft engines mounted side by side and driving into a combining gearbox to provide a single output drive. The engine was launched as a coupled power unit for a new family of twin-engined helicopters based on the Bell Helicopter UH-1 series. First of these, jointly financed by Bell, UACL and the Canadian government, was the 15-seat Bell Model 212, an improved version of the 205A commercial helicopter which first flew with the PT6T-3 in April 1969.

Installation of the 1,800 shp PT6T-3 in the Model 212, in addition to offering true engine-out capability, provides an additional 300 shp (over the single-engine 205A) and gives enhanced hot-day and high-altitude performance. The civil certification block test was completed in December 1969 and flight qualified PT6T-3s became available in the third quarter of 1970 coincident with certification of the Model 212. Deliveries of the helicopter started early in 1971. The Bell 212 is also produced under licence by Agusta in Italy.

Another application of the PT6T-3 engine is for conversion from piston engine to turbine power of the Sikorsky S-58 helicopter. The prototype conversion, designated S-58T, first flew in August 1970 and certification was received in April 1971. It provides increased operating economy, twin-engine reliability and improved work capability over the piston-powered S-58. The additional power of the PT6T-3 increases the altitude and hot-day capability due to flat rating, and improves the payload by reducing the empty weight.

In these two helicopter applications, total shaft-power output is limited by helicopter-transmission capability. In the Model 212 the 1,800 shp PT6T-3 is restricted to a T-O rating of 1,290 shp and 1,130 shp for continuous power. In the S-58T the rotor transmission limits the PT6T-3 power to 1,505 shp at T-O and 1,254 shp for continuous operation. The PT6T-3 is easily adapted to such power requirements by a simple setting of its torque control, which limits the total power output to a preset value and also balances the two power sections. In the event of a power-section failure, torquemeters in the combining gearbox automatically signal the fuel system of the other power section to bring it up to demand power. A single-engine 30-minute rating is included for use, at pilot discretion, in such contingencies.

The current overhaul cycle periods for the PT6T-3 engine are 1,800 hours TBO for the power sections and 1,000 hours TBO for the gearbox. By the beginning of 1974, a total of 409 PT6C-3 engines had been ordered; 77 helicopters powered by these engines were in world-wide operation and more than 102,000 flying hours had been logged.

An uprated Twin Pac, the PT6T-6, was introduced in 1974. The higher power is achieved by material and aerodynamic improvements to the compressor-turbine nozzle guide vanes and rotor blades. By February 1974, more than 120 of these engines had been ordered. A military variant is the T400-WV-402, described under the next entry.

The following details describe the main features differing from those of the standard PT6 single-engine configuration:

TYPE: Coupled axial-plus-centrifugal free-turbine turboshaft.

SHAFT DRIVE: Combining gearbox comprises three separate gear trains, two input and one output, each contained within an individual sealed compartment and all interconnected by drive shafts. Overall reduction ratio 5 : 1. Input gear train comprising three spur gears provides speed reduction between power sections and output gearbox. The two drives into the output gearbox are via Formsprag fully-phased overrunning clutches with input third gear forming outer member of clutch, and interconnect shaft forming inner, overrunning member. Output gear train comprises three helical spur gears, i.e. two input pinions meshing with single output gear. Output shaft drives forward between gas generators. Rotation clockwise viewed from front of engine. Hydro-mechanical torquemeter (of PT6 design concept) provided in each interconnect drive shaft, measuring power transmitted by each gas generator as a hydraulic pressure used to control torque balancing (between gas generators) and limiting.

AIR INTAKES: Individual annular intakes with wire mesh debris screens on each gas generator, feeding plenum chamber to compressor. Additional intake inertial particle separator fitted upstream to reduce sand and dust ingestion. High frequency compressor noise suppressed.

FUEL SYSTEM: Basic fuel control as on PT6 with manual backup fuel system, and dual fuel manifold for cool starts. Automatic power sharing and torque limiting systems. Torquemeters provide signals to Bendix fuel system metering valves to maintain power at level set by pilot's selective-collective control. Fuel heaters.

FUEL GRADES: JP-1, JP-4 and JP-5.

JET PIPE: Single upwards-facing exhaust port on each gas generator.

ACCESSORIES: Starter/generator and tacho-generator mounted on accessory drive case at front of each power section. Other accessory drives on combining gearbox, including individual power turbine speed governors and tacho-generators, and provision for blowers and aircraft accessories.

LUBRICATION SYSTEM: Independent lubrication system on each power section for maximum safety during single-engine operation. Integral oil tanks. Separate oil system for output section of combining gearbox.

OIL SPECIFICATION: MIL-L-7808 and 23699.

STARTING: Electrical, with cold weather starting down to —54°C.

DIMENSIONS:
Height 33 in (838 mm)
Width 44·0 in (1,118 mm)
Length 67·0 in (1,702 mm)

WEIGHT, DRY (standard equipment):
PT6T-3 635 lb (288 kg)
PT6T-6 642 lb (291 kg)

PERFORMANCE RATINGS:
T-O (5 min):
Total output, at 6,600 rpm:
PT6T-3 1,800 shp
PT6T-6 1,875 shp (to 21°C)

The 1,800 shp United Aircraft of Canada PT6T-3 Twin Pac coupled free-turbine turboshaft

Single power section only, at 6,600 rpm:
PT6T-3 900 shp
PT6T-6 (2½ min) 1,025 shp
30 minute power (single power section rating only), at 6,600 rpm 970 shp
Max continuous:
Total output, at 6,600 rpm:
PT6T-3 1,600 shp
PT6T-6 1,675 shp (to 19°C)
Single power section only, at 6,600 rpm:
PT6T-3 800 shp
PT6T-6 825 shp (to 19°C)
Cruise A:
Total output, at 6,600 rpm:
PT6T-3 1,250 shp
PT6T-6 1,360 shp
Single power section only, at 6,600 rpm:
PT6T-3 625 shp
PT6T-6 670 shp
Cruise B:
Total output, at 6,600 rpm:
PT6T-3 1,100 shp
PT6T-6 1,195 shp
Single power section only, at 6,600 rpm:
PT6T-3 550 shp
PT6T-6 590 shp
Ground idle, at 2,200 rpm 60 shp max
Specific Fuel Consumption:
At T-O and 30 minute ratings (total output):
PT6T-3 0·603 lb (0·274 kg)/shp/hr
PT6T-6 0·592 lb (0·269 kg)/shp/hr
At max continuous rating (total output):
PT6T-3 0·609 lb (0·277 kg)/shp/hr
PT6T-6 0·603 lb (0·274 kg)/shp/hr
At Cruise A rating (total output)
PT6T-3 0·640 lb (0·291 kg)/shp/hr
PT6T-6 0·643 lb (0·292 kg)/shp/hr
At Cruise B rating (total output):
PT6T-3 0·667 lb (0·303 kg)/shp/hr
PT6T-6 0·677 lb (0·308 kg)/shp/hr
Oil Consumption:
Max (for both gas generators) 0·4 lb (0·18 kg)/hr

UNITED AIRCRAFT OF CANADA T400

Military version of the PT6T Twin Pac, the T400-CP-400 coupled turboshaft is the first US Navy turboshaft (or turboprop) to be designated under the new US military aircraft turbine engine designation system. The T400-CP-400 and PT6T-3 helicopter engines have the same performance and are similar externally, the major difference being that in the T400 aluminium castings replace magnesium. For military roles, UACL describes the T400 as producing a minimum infra-red signature. Military Qualification Tests (MQT) were completed in March 1970, and production deliveries started in the same month.

The T400 is used in the US Air Force and Navy Bell UH-1N (military version of the Model 212), the US Marine Corps Bell AH-1J, and the Canadian Armed Forces Bell CH-135. T400 field operations started in the middle of 1970.

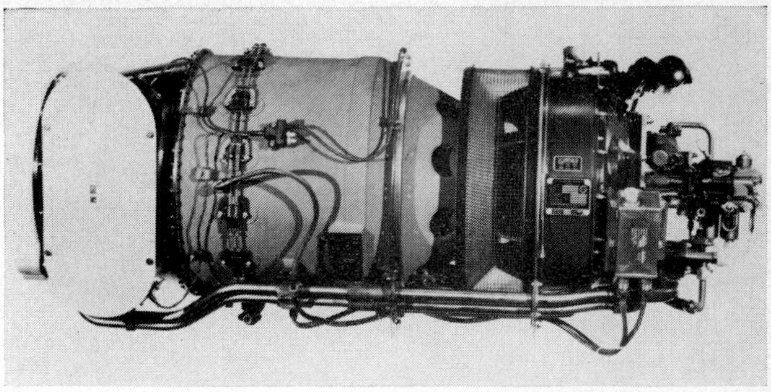

United Aircraft of Canada ST6L-73 free-turbine APU for the Hamilton Standard environmental control system in the Lockheed L-1011 TriStar

The T400-CP-400 has the same basic TBO as the PT6T-3; this is being demonstrated by analytical overhauls, which in early 1973 were being done at 1,000 hours. By the end of 1973 a total of 281 T400-powered helicopters had logged more than 446,000 flying hours on the power sections. By early 1974 a total of 538 T400-CP-400 engines had been ordered.

The T400-WV-402 is the military counterpart of the PT6T-6 and has similar ratings (see PT6T entry). The WV-402 will be used in a new version of the AH-1 helicopter for the Iranian military re-equipment programme. By January 1974 a total of 291 of these engines (additional to the figure for the CP-400) had been ordered.

The following data relate to the T400-CP-400:

Dimensions:
Height 32·6 in (828 mm)
Width 43·5 in (1,115 mm)
Length 65·3 in (1,659 mm)
Weight, Dry:
With standard equipment 745 lb (338 kg)
Performance Ratings:
Intermediate, at 6,600 rpm 1,970 shp minimum
Max continuous, at 6,600 rpm 1,673 shp minimum
Specific Fuel Consumption:
At intermediate rating 0·591 lb (0·269 kg)/shp/hr
At max continuous 0·604 lb (0·275 kg)/shp/hr

UNITED AIRCRAFT OF CANADA ST6

Directly derived from the PT6 turboprop/turboshaft series, the ST6 is a basic shaft-turbine having a wide range of applications in marine, industrial, vehicular and airborne installations. Airborne application is as part of the APU in the Lockheed L-1011 TriStar, where the flat-rated ST6L-73 provides power for the Hamilton Standard integrated environmental system, main engine (Rolls-Royce RB.211 turbofan) starting, and auxiliary electrical power system. A $60 million contract was awarded to Hamilton Standard by Lockheed in July 1968, calling for deliveries of equipment to start in early 1970 as part of an initial requirement for 180 systems.

In the TriStar, the ST6L-73 provides major improvements in fuel consumption, quietness of operation and cleanliness of compressed air supply. The ST6L-73 directly drives a rear-mounted assembly comprising a Hamilton Standard load compressor, and an electrical generator and cooling fan. Initial rating provides the supply of 385 lb (175 kg)/min of air at 42 lb/sq in abs (2·95 kg/cm²) at 39°C ambient with 45kVA electrical output. Maximum electrical power obtainable is 90kVA. Scheduled growth of the ST6L within the same frame size is planned to provide 430 lb (195 kg)/min of air concurrent with 140 hp (104kVA) for generator drive.

The load compressor air, as well as powering the environmental system, is also used for pneumatic systems such as the RB.211 engine starters, engine anti-icing, wing de-icing and air turbine motors for driving two of the aircraft's four hydraulic systems.

By the end of 1973 a total of 51 ST6L-73 units had operated 95,000 hr.

The following data apply to the ST6L-73:

Dimensions:
Diameter approx 19 in (483 mm)
Length approx 52·2 in (1,326 mm)
Weight, Dry:
With standard equipment 300 lb (136 kg)
Performance Ratings:
Max, at 33,000 rpm:
to 39°C at S/L static 720 shp
Normal, at 33,000 rpm:
to 39°C at S/L static 540 shp
Specific Fuel Consumption:
At max rating:
to 39°C at S/L static 0·611 lb (0·277 kg)/shp/hr
At normal rating:
to 39°C at S/L static 0·670 lb (0·304 kg)/shp/hr
Oil Consumption:
Max 0·1 lb (0·05 kg)/hr

CHINA

(PEOPLE'S REPUBLIC)

NATIONAL AIRCRAFT ENGINE FACTORY

Main Location:
Shenyang

Although Chinese central and regional governments made attempts to build up an aircraft industry as early as 1913 (see "Aircraft" section), and several western engines were imported during the 1920s (the most important being the Bristol Jupiter), it was not until the Japanese invaded Manchuria in 1932 and set up the puppet state of Manchukuo that a self-sufficient aviation industry existed. The main Japanese-managed plant was located at Mukden, today the city of Shenyang. During the second World War there were at least three airframe or engine factories in Manchuria, producing nearly 2,200 fighter and trainer aircraft and about the same number of engines, the latter all being air-cooled radials of basically Japanese design.

In 1945 the Soviet Union dismantled the industries in Manchuria; but following the Communist Chinese take-over in 1949 it provided assistance in re-establishing a Chinese aircraft industry, helping to build up fully-equipped airframe and engine factories, mainly on the original sites in Manchuria. The first product was the Yak-18 primary trainer, and it is believed that a licence to construct the aircraft and its M-11FR engine was signed in Moscow in November 1952. This 160 hp five-cylinder radial (see USSR entry in this section) was first produced at Shenyang in 1956, and is believed to have been built under licence in quantity. It is unlikely that new M-11 engines are still being made.

In 1958 licences were obtained by the 2nd Ministry of Machine Building for two additional Soviet air-cooled radial engines, the 260 hp Ivchenko AI-14R and 1,000 hp Shvetsov ASh-62IR (both described in the USSR entry), fitted respectively to the locally-built Chinko No. 1 (Yak-12) and Fong Shou No. 2 (An-2). Both of these aircraft and their engines are believed to have been built in large numbers. By 1959 the Manchurian plants were licence-building the Soviet Mi-4 helicopter and the Czech Super Aero 45 light twin. It is thought that in each case the engine (respectively the 1,700 shp Shvetsov ASh-82V 14-cylinder radial and the 140 hp M 332 four-in-line, the latter last described in the 1971-72 *Jane's*) was also produced either at Shenyang or at one of the other national factories. One possibility is that the Czech engine was made at the works at Harbin, because it was there that the Chinese version of the Super Aero 45 was produced. Harbin may also have taken over the M-11FR programme, because from 1959-60 that factory manufactured the M-11-powered Hai Lun-kiang No. 1, a locally designed liaison aircraft resembling the Yak-12.

GAS-TURBINE ENGINES

During the Korean War (1950-53) large numbers of MiG-15 fighters were ferried through Manchuria. Chinese technicians became familiar with the aircraft and its Klimov RD-45 (Rolls-Royce Nene derivative) engine. In 1955 a licence for the manufacture of the MiG-15 fighter and MiG-15UTI trainer was signed in Moscow, and from 1958 several hundred of the latter were produced, powered by the RD-45 of 5,450 lb (2,472 kg) st. The MiG-15 fighter was apparently not built in China, but in 1959 the first Chinese F-4, a licence-built MiG-17, began a production run of well over 1,000 aircraft, all probably powered by Chinese-built Klimov VK-1 turbojets rated at 5,950 lb (2,700 kg) st.

In February 1959 the Chinese signed a licence agreement for the manufacture of the MiG-19 supersonic fighter, powered by two Klimov VK-7 axial turbojets each rated at 6,170 lb (2,800 kg) st. Soon afterwards the relationship with the Soviet Union was severed; but the Chinese, working alone, managed to fly a locally-built F-6 (MiG-19) in 1961, and subsequently constructed a number estimated to reach 1,500. Thus, probably more than 4,000 VK-7 engines have been made at Shenyang. A potentially even larger programme concerns the MiG-21. As described in the Aircraft section, this fighter and its 9,500 lb (4,300 kg) st RD-11 axial turbojet were put into production in China without a licence or any Soviet help. Deliveries of the RD-11 from Shenyang are thought to have begun in 1965, and probably well over 2,000 of these engines had been delivered by 1973, with production (thought to be concentrated upon improved Chinese-developed versions) running at a probable rate of about 25 engines per month.

Chinese versions or developments of the RD-9 are likely to have been used in locally produced military prototypes. One of these is the F-9 twin-engined strike fighter.

NATIONAL CHINESE ACADEMY OF SCIENCE

Location: Peking

While the national aviation industry has made remarkable progress in building engines to foreign designs, the Chinese have, as a long-term undertaking, sought to establish a national capability to design aircraft engines on a basis of self-sufficiency. The Chinese Academy of Science's Institute of Mechanics was charged with this task, and under the direction of Dr Chien Hsueh-shen a 12-year plan was begun in 1956. This plan was presumably succeeded by another plan in 1968, but nothing has been disclosed concerning any indigenous Chinese engines.

CZECHOSLOVAKIA

AVIA

AVIA N.P.

ADDRESS: Letnany, Prague 9
Telephone: 89-5231

Originally a member of the Czechoslovak Aviation Industry Group, Avia National Corporation was transferred to the Czechoslovak Automotive Industry (CAZ) Group in 1960. The company is at present engaged in series production of the M 137A, M 337 and M 462RF piston engines, as well as propeller and spare parts manufacture.

AVIA M 137

Designed to power light aerobatic, training, and single-engined and multi-engined sports aircraft, the 180 hp M 137A piston engine is a modification of the M 337 with fuel and oil systems for aerobatic operation. It powers the Zlin 42 and Z 526 F. The M 137AZ is a modified version, with the air intake port at the rear so that a dust filter can be incorporated. Details are as for M 337, with the following differences:

CRANKSHAFT: No oil holes for propeller control.

FUEL SYSTEM: Type LUN 5150 pump; system designed for sustained aerobatics.

STARTER: LUN 2131 electric.

DIMENSIONS:

Length	52·9 in (1,344 mm)
Width	17·44 in (443 mm)
Height	24·80 in (630 mm)

WEIGHT (including starter): 312 lb (141·5 kg)

PERFORMANCE RATINGS:

T-O	180 hp at 2,750 rpm
Max continuous	160 hp at 2,680 rpm
Max cruising	140 hp at 2,580 rpm

SPECIFIC FUEL CONSUMPTION:

At T-O rating	0·540 lb (0·245 kg)/hp/hr
At max continuous	0·507 lb (0·230 kg)/hp/hr
At max cruise rating	0·485 lb (0·220 kg)/hp/hr

AVIA M 337

The basic M 337 six-cylinder aircooled supercharged engine powers the Morava L-200D light aircraft. The M 337A, with modified fuel system, powers the Zlin 43.

TYPE: Six-cylinder inverted in-line aircooled, ungeared, supercharged and with direct fuel injection.

CYLINDERS: Bore 4·13 in (105 mm). Stroke 4·53 in (115 mm). Swept volume 364·31 cu in (5·97 litres). Compression ratio 6·3 : 1. Steel cylinders with cooling fins machined from solid. Cylinder bores nitrided. Detachable cylinder heads are aluminium alloy castings. Cylinder and head assembly attached to crankcase by four studs. Valve seats of special steel. Valve guides and sparking plug bushes of bronze.

PISTONS: Aluminium alloy stampings with graphited surfaces. Two compression rings and two knife-shaped scraper rings in common groove above gudgeon-pin. Gudgeon-pins secured by spring-circlips.

CONNECTING RODS: H-section aluminium alloy forgings. Two split big-ends bolted together by two bolts. Steel two-piece liner, lead-bronze plated.

CRANKSHAFT: Forged from special chrome-vanadium steel, machined all over. Nitrided crank-pins. Carried in seven steel-backed lead-bronze plated slide bearings which are lightly lead-lined, and in one ball-thrust bearing at the front. Terminating in a wedge-shape cone for the propeller hub mounting.

CRANKCASE: Heat-treated magnesium alloy (Elektron) casting, with top and front covers. Deep-sunk bearing covers forged from aluminium alloy, with double cross webs.

VALVE GEAR: Camshaft on the cylinder heads actuates the valves by means of rocker arms. Camshaft driven by vertical shaft and bevel gears. One inlet valve of heat-treated steel, one sodium-filled exhaust valve of austenitic steel with stellite seat. Nitrided valve stems.

IGNITION: Shielded type. Two vertical PAL-LUN 2221.13 magnetos with automatic sparking advance, driven by bevel gears. Two PAL L22-62 sparking plugs per cylinder, 12 × 1·25 mm.

LUBRICATION: Dry sump pressure-feed type. Double gear-type oil-pump with pressure and scavenge stages mounted on rear wall of crankcase. Oil from tank passes through triple filter into pressure stage of oil pump and then into main channel drilled in crankcase. Pressure control valve adjusted to 3·5-4 atm. Inlet union of main channel provided with oil-pressure gauge connecting pipe. Oil returned from sump by scavenge stage of oil pump to tank. Special gear-type oil pump draws oil from cam box and forces it into crankcase from where it flows into sump.

SUPERCHARGER: Centrifugal type mounted on engine rear flange. Driven through a damping rubber coupling from crankshaft. Planetary gear, ratio 7·4 : 1, engaged via band friction clutch. Force feed lubrication of supercharger from main engine lubrication system.

FUEL SYSTEM: Low-pressure injection system. LUN 5152 pump driven from camshaft. Fuel injection nozzles located in front of intake valves. Automatic control in relation to engine manifold pressure. Fuel supplied to injection pump by fuel pressure pump located in common body with injection pump. (The M 337A has a unified fuel injection pump, type LUN 5150, and other minor changes. Specific fuel consumption is slightly higher.)

FUEL GRADE: Minimum 72-78 octane, with maximum TEL 0·06 per cent (volume).

COOLING: Airscoop on port side, designed to provide easy access to sparking plugs and easy removal of scoop and baffles.

STARTING: Electric starter combined with supercharger. Electric motor rotates the starter dog which is engaged by an electromagnet. Gears and clutch of supercharger serve the starter also.

ACCESSORIES: One 600W 28V dynamo. Electric rpm transmitter, drive 1 : 1. Propeller control unit. Mechanical tachometer on oil pump, drive 1 : 2. High-pressure hydraulic pump type P 6121A.

MOUNTING: Four engine-bearer feet with rubber dampers.

PROPELLER DRIVE: Direct left-hand tractor.

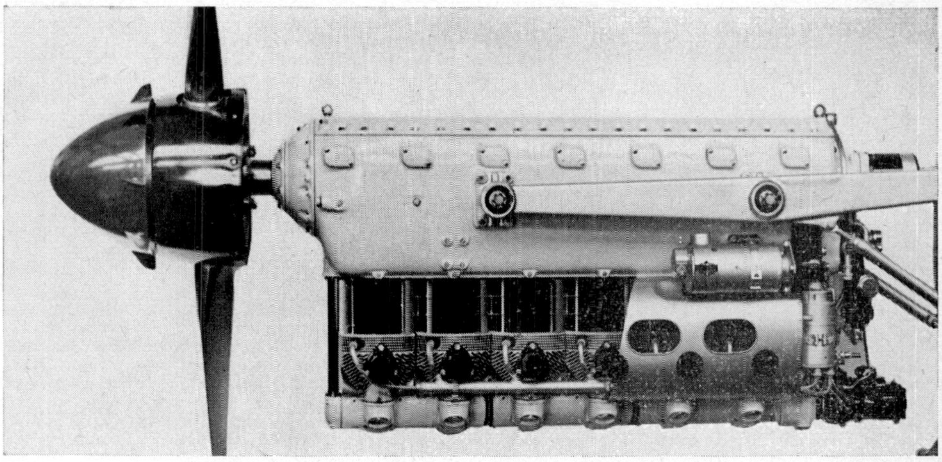

The 180 hp Avia M 137A six-cylinder aircooled piston engine

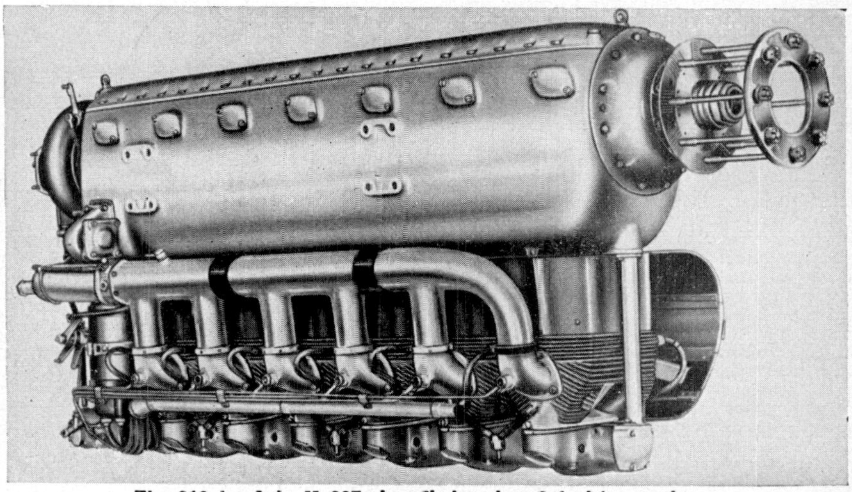

The 210 hp Avia M 337 six-cylinder aircooled piston engine

The 315 hp Avia M 462RF nine-cylinder geared supercharged radial engine

DIMENSIONS:
Overall length, without propeller boss 55·51 in (1,410 mm)
Width 18·58 in (472 mm)
Height 24·72 in (628 mm)
Frontal area 2·15 sq ft (0·20 m²)
WEIGHT, DRY: 326·3 lb (148 kg)
PERFORMANCE RATINGS:
T-O rating 210 hp at 2,750 rpm
Max continuous power 170 hp at 2,600 rpm
Max cruising power at 3,940 ft (1,200 m) 150 hp at 2,400 rpm
SPECIFIC FUEL CONSUMPTION:
At T-O rating 0·595 lb (0·270 kg)/hp/hr
At max continuous power 0·474 lb (0·215 kg)/hp/hr
At max cruising power at 3,940 ft (1,200 m) 0·430 lb (0·195 kg)/hp/hr

AVIA M 462RF

This engine is a modification of the Soviet Ivchenko AI-14RF. It powers the Z-37-A Cmelák agricultural monoplane. The major parts are imported from the Soviet Union.

TYPE: Nine-cylinder aircooled radial engine.

CYLINDERS: Bore 4·13 in (105 mm). Stroke 5·12 in (130 mm). Swept volume 620 cu in (10·16 litres). Compression ratio 6·2 : 1. Cylinders forged from steel. All surfaces machined. Cylinder bores nitrided. Each cylinder attached to crankcase by eight studs. Cylinder heads are aluminium alloy castings, screwed on to the barrels.

PISTONS: Aluminium alloy forgings. Three compression rings and two scraper rings. First compression ring trapezoidal in cross-section, with sliding surfaces chrome-plated. Gudgeon-pin case-hardened and quenched, with conical lightening hole.

CONNECTING RODS: Heat-treated chrome-nickel steel forgings with polished surfaces. Articulated rod ends and master rod gudgeon-pin end have bronze bushes. Master rod main bearing of steel with centrifugally-cast bronze coating of 0·5 mm thickness.

CRANKSHAFT: Single-throw type of chrome-nickel steel. All surfaces machined, heat-treated and polished. Carried in two type 2213 anti-friction bearings. Front bearing is thrust-bearing, rear one free.

CRANKCASE: Aluminium alloy forging in two sections.

VALVE GEAR: One inlet and one exhaust valve per cylinder. Both valves of austenitic steel; exhaust valve sodium-cooled. Valve seats of austenitic steel, pressed in and rolled. Cam disc situated in front section of crankcase and driven by spur gears.

INDUCTION SYSTEM: Mixture fed from supercharger. Floatless carburettor type AK-14RF fed by pump type 702 ML.

SUPERCHARGER: Single-stage centrifugal type. Spring-loaded, driven by spur gearing. Gear ratio 8·65.

FUEL: 78 octane minimum.

IGNITION: Four-spark screened ignition system. Two magnetos mounted on accessory drive housing and driven by spur gearing. Two SD-49SMM spark plugs per cylinder.

LUBRICATION: Dry-sump pressure-feed type. Gear-type oil pump with pressure and scavenge stages.

REDUCTION GEAR: Planetary reduction gearing, ratio 0·787 : 1. Hollow shaft for oil supply to hydraulically-actuated variable-pitch propeller.

ACCESSORIES: One 1,500W generator, fuel pump, electric tachometer drive, type AK 50M air compressor, and drive for agricultural equipment (see "Aircraft" section).

STARTING: Compressed air starting.

MOUNTING: Engine bolted to mounting at eight points through rubber dampers.

DIMENSIONS:
Length overall 40·15 in (1,020 mm)
Diameter 39·37 in (1,000 mm)
Frontal area 8·03 sq ft (0·755 m²)
PERFORMANCE RATINGS:
T-O (5 min) 315 hp at 2,450 rpm
Max continuous 280 hp at 2,200 rpm
Max rated 245 hp at 2,000 rpm
Max cruise 195 hp at 1,900 rpm
SPECIFIC FUEL CONSUMPTION:
At T-O rating 0·639 lb (0·290 kg)/hp/hr
At max continuous power 0·628 lb (0·285 kg)/hp/hr
At max rated power 0·584 lb (0·265 kg)/hp/hr
At max cruise power 0·496 lb (0·225 kg)/hp/hr

MOTORLET

MOTORLET NC, ZÁVOD JANA SVERMY

ADDRESS: Prague-Jinonice
Telephone: Prague 522241
GENERAL MANAGER:
Zdenek Horcík
ASSISTANTS TO GENERAL MANAGER:
TECHNICAL DIRECTOR: Ing Jan Kolár
ECONOMIC DIRECTOR: Ing Josef Svoboda
PRODUCTION DIRECTOR: Bohumil Hamerník
HEAD OF DESIGN DEVELOPMENT:
Ing Vladimír Pospísil

Motorlet National Corporation operates the main aero-engine establishment in Czechoslovakia, based on the former Walter Motoren factory at Jinonice, previously well known for its radial and in-line piston engines. Today, the Walter name continues in use only as a trade-mark for Motorlet piston and turbofan engines.

Motorlet started turbine engine manufacture in 1952 with licensed production of the Russian RD-45 centrifugal turbojet for MiG-15 fighters. Present production activities concern the small M 701 centrifugal turbojet, Czechoslovakia's first indigenous turbine, for the L-29 Delfin trainer. Development is also under way of the M 601 turboprop.

In addition Motorlet is manufacturing hydraulic instruments, precision castings, automatic regulation and control instruments, and non-aero gas-turbine components.

MOTORLET M 601

Second of Czechoslovakia's small turbine engines to be built, the M 601 is a free-turbine turboprop having a combined axial-and-centrifugal compressor. Designed to power the Czech twin-engined L-410 light transport aircraft, it is rated at 700 ehp and drives a V-508 constant-speed three-blade propeller with hydraulically variable pitch.

The first version of the M 601, rated at 550 ehp, ran in October 1967. Development of a revised 700 ehp version, of increased diameter, started during 1968. Until this higher-powered model is certified, the L-410A is being fitted with United Aircraft of Canada PT6A-27 turboprops of 715 ehp. Negotiations have been initiated between UACL and Aero for Czechoslovakian manufacture of the PT6A-27, which is of the same general configuration as the M 601.

TYPE: Free-turbine combined axial-and-centrifugal turboprop.

PROPELLER DRIVE: Reduction gear at front of engine with drive from free-turbine. Reduction ratio 14·9 : 1.

AIR INTAKE: Annular intake at rear of engine, with debris screen, feeds air to compressor plenum chamber.

COMPRESSOR: Two axial stages plus single centrifugal stage. Pressure ratio 6 : 1 at 36,000 rpm gas generator speed and 6·2 : 1 at 37,000 rpm gas generator speed. Air mass flows 6·1 lb/sec (2·75 kg/sec) and 6·8 lb/sec (3·1 kg/sec) respectively.

COMBUSTION CHAMBER: Annular combustor with rotary fuel injection and low-voltage ignition.

COMPRESSOR TURBINE: Single-stage.

POWER TURBINE: Single-stage.

FUEL SYSTEM: Low-pressure LUN 6740 system, with single-lever control providing kinematic coupling of gas generator and power turbine speed controls.

FUEL GRADE LP4 kerosene.

JET PIPE: Collector duct surrounding power turbine shaft. Exhaust through two ports on horizontal centreline.

ACCESSORIES: Mounting pads on accessory case at rear of engine. Propeller controls mounted on reduction gear case at front of engine.

LUBRICATION SYSTEM: Pressure gear-pump circulation. Integral oil tank and cooler.

OIL SPECIFICATION: Mixture of MK 8 and MS 20 mineral oil; or B3Y synthetic oil.

MOUNTING: Two main pads on compressor intake flange and one steadying point at rear of reduction gear case.

STARTING: Electric.

DIMENSIONS:
Diameter: 550 ehp version 12·4 in (314 mm)
700 ehp version 16·9 in (430 mm)
Length: both versions 60·2 in (1,530 mm)
WEIGHT, DRY:
550 ehp version 331 lb (150 kg)
700 ehp version 298 lb (135 kg)
PERFORMANCE RATINGS:
T-O rating: initial version 550 ehp
revised version 700 ehp (to 22°C)
Continuous rating: initial version 517 ehp
revised version 600 ehp (to 30°C)
SPECIFIC FUEL CONSUMPTION:
At T-O rating:
initial version 0·79 lb (0·306 kg)/ehp/hr
revised version 0·62 lb (0·280 kg)/ehp/hr

MOTORLET M 701

The M 701 turbojet powers the L-29 and L-29A Delfin trainers. Production started in 1961 and by the spring of 1969 over 4,500 M 701s had been built. Production of the engine was continuing in 1974.

All models of the M 701 have the same ratings and differ mainly with regard to TBO, as indicated by their individual designations. The TBOs for the M 701-b150, M 701-c250, M 701-c400 and M 701-c500 are respectively 150, 250, 400 and 500 hr. The M 701-c250 introduced flame tube and turbine improvements, and the M 701-c400 has further improvements in turbine design.

The 700 ehp Motorlet M 601 free-turbine turboprop

Cutaway Motorlet M 701-c500 turbojet (1,962 lb; 890 kg st)

TYPE: Single-shaft centrifugal turbojet.

AIR INTAKE: Annular air intake, with central bullet fairing, at front of engine. De-icing by hot engine bleed air.

COMPRESSOR: Single-stage centrifugal type.

IMPELLER: Single-sided. Blade-type diffuser. Pressure ratio 4·3 : 1. Air mass flow 37·25 lb/sec (16·9 kg/sec) at 15,400 rpm.

COMBUSTION CHAMBER: Seven straight-flow chambers, interconnected by flame channels. Two igniter plugs in Nos. 2 and 7 chambers.

FUEL SYSTEM: Fuel pump of the LUN 6201.03 multi-plunger type. Barometric pressure control acts on servomechanism to vary fuel delivery according to altitude and speed. High-pressure shut-off cock. Max fuel pressure 7·1-14·2 lb/sq in (0·5-1·0 kg/cm²) behind fuel filter, 1,200 lb/sq in (85 kg/cm²) behind fuel pump.

FUEL GRADE: PL-4 to TPD-33-01960 standard, T-1 to GOST-4138-49 standard, or other similar fuels.

TURBINE: Single-stage axial-flow type, with 61 blades. Gas temperature after turbine 680-700°C.

JET PIPE: Fixed-cone type.

ACCESSORY DRIVES: Drives on engine front casing to fuel pump, 28V generator, hydraulic pump and tachometer. One spare drive.

LUBRICATION SYSTEM: Wet sump type. Sump at bottom of front case. One three-stage gear-type pump. Sump capacity 0·75 Imp gal (3·5 litres). Normal oil supply pressure 28·5-35·5 lb/sq in (2-2·5 kg/cm²).

OIL SPECIFICATION: OLE-TO to TP 200/074-59 standard, or GOST 982-53.

STARTING: Electric starter.

DIMENSIONS:

Max width	35·28 in (896 mm)
Max height	36·53 in (928 mm)
Length overall	81·38 in (2,067 mm)

WEIGHT, DRY: 728 lb (330 kg) − 2·5%

PERFORMANCE RATINGS:

Max T-O	1,962 lb (890 kg) st at 15,400 rpm
Rated power	1,764 lb (800 kg) st at 14,950 rpm
Max cruise rating	1,587 lb (720 kg) st at 14,500 rpm
Idling	154 lb (70 kg) st at 5,400 rpm

SPECIFIC FUEL CONSUMPTION:

At rated power 1·14

OMNIPOL

OMNIPOL FOREIGN TRADE CORPORATION

ADDRESS: Washingtonova 11, Prague 1

Telephone: 2126

Omnipol is responsible for exporting products of the Czech aviation industry and for supplying information on those products which are available for export.

FRANCE

ARDEM

AVIONS ROGER DRUINE

ADDRESS:

20, Avenue du Général Clavery, Paris (16e)

The late M Roger Druine developed a light aero-engine from the standard Volkswagen motor-car engine. Known as the Ardem 4 CO2, it is particularly suitable for powering the Druine Turbulent single-seat light aircraft and several versions are being built in Britain by Rollason Aircraft and Engines Ltd of Shoreham Airport, Sussex (which see).

G2P

GROUPEMENT POUR LA PROPULSION À POUDRE

HEAD OFFICE:

3 avenue du Général de Gaulle, 92800-Puteaux

Telephone: 772 12 12

MAIN ESTABLISHMENT:

Bordeaux-St Aubin de Médoc

ADMINISTRATOR AND PRESIDENT OF THE MANAGING COMMITTEE:

Roger Guernon

On 1 October 1972 SEP and SNPE (both listed in this section) pooled their interests in this new group, to "ensure the close co-ordination of their activities and play the part of prime contractor in the field of solid-propellant propulsion".

G2P is now operating as the customer-liaison organisation for both companies. It serves as prime contractor, signs contracts and distributes work between the two companies. It is also responsible for making technical presentations to customers and for following through programmes to their termination. Details of the propellant grains and rocket motors will be found under the entries for SEP and SNPE.

IDA

INNOVATION ET DÉVELOPPEMENT AÉRO-THERMODYNAMIQUES

ADDRESS:

3bis, rue Bernard Délicieux, 31200-Toulouse

Telephone: (61) 47 58 11

GENERAL MANAGER:

I. G. Faury

Previously named SERMEL, this company is staffed mainly by personnel from the aviation industry and is engaged chiefly in the research, design, development and experimental manufacture of small gas turbines and other aerospace products. Engines developed by IDA are subsequently produced commercially by Microturbo (which see), which bought the company in 1971.

IDA's two chief aircraft-propulsion programmes are described below. Other IDA projects include APUs, high-performance compressors and turbines, electronic and hydraulic equipment, fuel and oil systems, and gas-dynamic devices.

IDA SUPER COUGUAR

Developed from the Couguar (see Microturbo entry), the Super Couguar is a single-shaft turbojet for the propulsion of RPVs. It has a two-stage compressor, with a sonic axial stage added ahead of the centrifugal impeller. The folded annular combustion chamber has eight spill-type burners, and the turbine is a single axial stage. Fuel is expelled from the aircraft tank by an air bag inflated by compressor bleed, and is delivered to the engine by an engine-driven pump. Discharge through the burners is controlled by telemetered throttle demand which passes through the electronic governing system to position a spool valve; excess fuel is spilled back to the tank.

The closed-circuit lubrication system includes engine-driven gear-type pressure and scavenge pumps on the accessory gearbox beneath the air intake. Starting is by air impingement, air from an external supply being directed on to one of the compressor impellers. Light-up is provided by a single igniter plug on the backplate, controlled by the automatically-sequenced starting system.

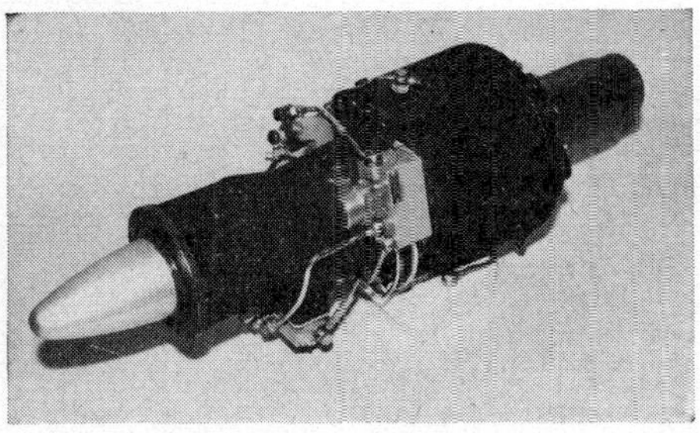

IDA Super Couguar turbojet (265 lb; 120 kg st)

DIMENSIONS:

Length (with jet pipe stub)	34·6 in (879 mm)
Width	11·1 in (282 mm)
Height	15·71 in (399 mm)

WEIGHT, DRY:

With accessories 82 lb (37 kg)

PERFORMANCE RATING (ISA, S/L):

Max T-O 265 lb (120 kg) st at 47,000 rpm

SPECIFIC FUEL CONSUMPTION (as above): 1·15

IDA TRS 60

Representing a significant French development in the propulsion of cruise-type unmanned vehicles, the TRS 60 was designed by IDA under a contract from the Direction des Recherches et Moyens d'Essais. It is an extremely simple single-shaft turbojet for use in subsonic or supersonic missiles and RPVs. The design has been biased towards minimal cost and absence of any maintenance or overhaul, though engine design life exceeds 20 hr.

The annular intake contains the accessory gearbox in the central bullet, together with an alternator or starter/generator; the struts house fuel and oil pipes. The simple axial compressor operates at a pressure ratio of about 4 : 1, with airflow of 12·3 lb; 5·6 kg/sec, and is carried between front and rear bearings with labyrinth seals. The smokeless combustor is of the axial annular type, with multiple spray burners fed by a peripheral manifold. The axial turbine is cantilevered behind the rear bearing carried on the central diffuser housing.

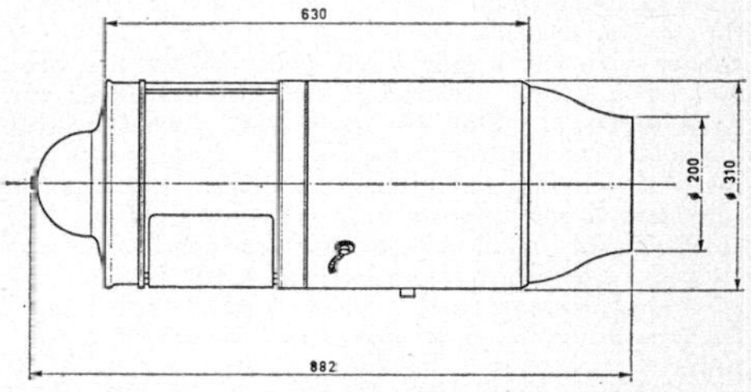

Left-side elevation of IDA TRS 60 turbojet (674 lb; 306 kg st)

An air bleed provides up to 1·5 per cent of total airflow. There is an engine-driven fuel pump, but lubrication is either by a pre-lubricated bearing design or by a total-loss system from a pressurised reservoir. Speed control can be mechanical, electronic, fluidic or pneumatic, according to installation. Starting can be by impingement, or electrical, or by cartridge or other means.

DIMENSIONS:

Length overall	34·72 in (882 mm)
Envelope diameter	12·20 in (310 mm)

WEIGHT, DRY: 99·5 lb (45 kg)

PERFORMANCE RATING (ISA, S/L):

Max T-O 674 lb (306 kg) st at 27,500 rpm

SPECIFIC FUEL CONSUMPTION (as above): 1·25

MICROTURBO

MICROTURBO SA

HEAD OFFICE AND WORKS:

Chemin du Pont de Rupé, 31019-Toulouse Cédex

Telephone: (61) 47 63 26

PRESIDENT DIRECTOR GENERAL:

G. Bayard

MANAGING DIRECTOR:

L. Pech

TECHNICAL DIRECTOR:

P. Calmels

Microturbo was formed in 1960 to produce small gas-turbine units. It has specialised in the research, design and development of gas-turbine-powered starting systems for aircraft main propulsion engines.

Microturbo's initial product, which is still being manufactured, was the Noelle 60 290 free-turbine starter unit for the SNECMA Atar turbojet. From this unit a range of small gas-turbine systems has subsequently been evolved; these are used as APUs, EPUs, GPUs, air conditioning, air turbo-generator and ultra-low-thrust turbojets, as well as for engine starting. Extensive use is made of basically similar gas generator components to provide cross-feeding of parts manufacture and operating experience.

Microturbo originally had a direct rival in SERMEL, but in 1971 it purchased this company from Bronzavia SA and renamed it IDA, as described in the IDA entry in this section. IDA is now mainly a design, research and development group, leaving Microturbo free for production. Microturbo employs approximately 340 people.

MICROTURBO TRS 18

This single-shaft turbojet was included previously in the SERMEL entry (now IDA); with development completed, it is in production by Microturbo. It was designed for installation in gliders, to impart a self-launch and climb capability, but is being adopted increasingly for ultra-light aircraft. The first two production applications are in the Caproni Vizzola A-21J sailplane and the Bede BD-5J small jet aircraft.

Microturbo TRS 18 turbojet (202 lb; 92 kg st)

The TRS 18 is of modular construction. The forward module incorporates the air intake, gearbox, electronic governing and protection unit, and start sequencing and indicating unit. The 28V 600W starter/generator is located in the nose bullet. The oil tank, with submerged pump, is on the underside, and includes provision for inverted flight. The HP oil filter and pressure transducer are on top of this module. Adjacent to the compressor are the probes for engine speed and air temperature.

The turbine module comprises: the one-piece centrifugal compressor, with diffuser and straightener vanes; the one-piece axial turbine rotor and nozzle diaphragm; and the main frame carrying the rotor assembly on two ball bearings between the compressor and turbine. The aft module comprises: the turbine-casing backplate, carrying the combustion chamber liner, exhaust cone and nozzle; the annular folded combustion chamber; the 10 spill-type burners on the inner face of the backplate; two igniter plugs, used during starting; and the jet pipe with thermocouple.

The fuel pump is driven electrically. The lubrication system is a closed circuit, with pressure supply to the rotor and gearbox bearings. The engine can be shut down and restarted in flight, and incorporates automatic fault and protection systems.

Dimensions:
- Length: 22·59 in (650 mm)
- Width: 12·795 in (325 mm)
- Height: 13·78 in (350 mm)

Weight, Dry:
- Basic: 70·5 lb (32·0 kg)
- With igniter and voltage regulator: 73·58 lb (33·4 kg)

Performance Rating (ISA, S/L):
- T-O and max continuous: 202 lb (92 kg) st at 44,000 rpm

Specific Fuel Consumption:
- At above condition: 1·3

MICROTURBO COUGUAR

The Couguar (Cougar) is a single-shaft turbojet designed for the propulsion of small aircraft, especially target drones and PRVs. The basic engine is somewhat similar in design to the TRS 18, though there are only eight fuel burners and numerous other differences.

Pre-launch starting is accomplished by an air-impingement nozzle integral with the engine compressor shroud, with air supply controlled from a remote starting panel. The engine is designed to withstand mechanical and thermal stresses imposed by accelerated launch, shutdown on telemetered command, and subsequent long-period immersion in sea water. The Couguar may then be refurbished by flushing prior to the next mission.

The installed engine incorporates only the equipment needed for unmanned flight. Equipment for refuelling, defuelling, engine starting, ground-running, functional checkout and refurbishing is all accommodated in a servicing rig, connected via an umbilical.

The Couguar powers the Australian GAF Turana target drone. A development is the Super Couguar, described in the IDA entry in this section.

Microturbo Couguar turbojet (178 lb; 81 kg st)

Dimensions:
- Length (less jet pipe): 24·725 in (628 mm)
- Length overall: 33·58 in (853 mm)
- Width: 11·1 in (282 mm)
- Height: 15·2 in (386 mm)

Weight, Dry:
- Basic, less jet pipe: 58·5 lb (26·5 kg)
- With control box: 62·4 lb (28·3 kg)

Performance Ratings (ISA, S/L):
- T-O and max continuous: 178 lb (81 kg) st at 48,500 rpm
- Idle: 31 lb (14 kg) st at 28,000 rpm

Specific Fuel Consumptions (ISA, S/L, static):
- T-O and max continuous: 1·25
- Idle: 2·50

RECTIMO

RECTIMO-SAVOIE AVIATION

Offices and Works:
Aérodrome de Chambéry, 73-Savoie

Telephone: (79) 22 40 06

Director:
André Rosselot

Rectimo has manufactured over 400 Type 4 AR 1200 single-ignition derivatives of the Volkswagen four-cylinder aircooled car engine, which together with the larger 4 AR 1600 are used in the Sportavia RF4D powered glider and various ultralight aircraft. The 40 hp 4 AR 1200 engine has a 1,192 cc cubic capacity, 7 : 1 compression ratio and weighs 136 lb (61·5 kg). Fuel consumption under cruise conditions is 2·4 Imp gal (11 litres)/hr. The 4 AR 1600 produces 61 hp at T-O and has a cubic capacity of 1,600 cc and an 8 : 1 compression ratio. Weight is 141 lb (64 kg). Both engines have a maximum speed of 3,600 rpm.

Rectimo 4 AR 1200 piston engine of 40 hp

SEP

SOCIÉTÉ EUROPÉENNE DE PROPULSION

Head Office:
Tour Roussel-Nobel, Cédex 3,
92080-Paris Défense

Telephone: 772 12 12

Centres and Establishments:
Bordeaux-Le Haillan, Bordeaux-Blanquefort, Vernon, Melun-Villaroche and Istres

President Director General:
P. Soufflet

Société Européenne de Propulsion was formed on 1 October 1969 from the merger of Société d'Etude de la Propulsion par Réaction (SEPR), and the Missiles and Space Division of SNECMA. On 1 October 1971 SEP took over part of the activities and facilities of Laboratoire de Recherches Balistiques et Aérodynamiques (LRBA) (Ballistics and Aerodynamic Research Laboratory) of Vernon, in particular those relating to propulsion systems for space launchers, sounding rockets and satellites.

SEP specialises in the design and development of all categories of propulsion systems and engines for aircraft, missiles, space launchers and satellites, and it possesses the most important rocket facilities in Europe. Two-thirds of its 2,100 personnel are engineers and technicians specialising in research, development and testing.

SEP produces a wide range of solid- and liquid-propellant motors as sustainers and boosters for French and European guided and unguided missiles and space launchers. Some 60 different types of motor have been designed since 1950, including the three stages of the Diamant A and B French space launchers, Coralie, the second stage and perigee motor of the ELDO Europa II launcher, and motors for the SSBS, MSBS and Pluton nuclear-warhead missiles. The company has acquired great experience in cryogenic-propellant rockets through developing the HM4 and HM7 engines. It is now participating through the "Economic Interest Group" Cryorocket, which it formed jointly with the German company MBB, in design studies for a 20-ton rocket engine. A major engine for manned aircraft is the SEP 844 which provides thrust boost for Dassault Mirage III fighters in service with the French Air Force and other air forces.

With this and the previously developed engines for aircraft, SEP has gained a unique experience in the field: 5,500 rocket-flights performed in France up to 1972, corresponding to more than 8,300 ignitions. Other SEP developments include engines using hybrid propellants, fluorine and fluorine compounds, monopropellants, compressed gases, as well as electric "thrusters". The company is now applying its missile and space technology to oceanology.

SEP FAON, ELAN

In April 1972 SEP announced the Faon, later joined by the larger Elan. These are extremely simple and reliable small motors, intended primarily for young experimenters in aerospace clubs. The Faon was designed within the framework of these clubs, and under CNES sponsorship, to carry a 6·6 lb (3 kg) payload to a height of 11,500 ft (3,500 m).

Basic Data (F: Faon, E: Elan):

Length (excluding igniter):
- F: 7·28 in (185 mm)
- E: 13·4 in (340 mm)

Max diameter:
- F: 2·44 in (62 mm)
- E: 4·72 in (120 mm)

Weight, loaded:
- F: 2·43 lb (1·1 kg)
- E: 11·55 lb (5·24 kg)

Mean thrust:
- F: 42·7 lb (19·37 kg)
- E: 337·2 lb (153·0 kg)

Burn time:
- F: 5 sec
- E: 3·77 sec

SEP HM4

The HM4 is the smaller of two upper-stage liquid-propellant rocket engines currently being developed by SEP.

Type: Liquid-propellant rocket engine.

Propellants: Liquid oxygen and liquid hydrogen.

Thrust Chamber Assembly: Four-chamber unit of 42 : 1 nozzle area ratio, regeneratively cooled, and with double-wall machined casing in stainless steel and Inconel X750. Operating sequence initiated by hydrogen pre-cooling and pre-opening of hydrogen injection valve. Concentric-tube propellant injection system with central oxygen flow. Pyrotechnic ignition. Combustion pressure 337·8 lb/sq in (23·75 kg/cm²) and temperature 2,627°C.

Thrust Chamber Mounting: Chambers hinged around axis concentric with engine axis.

Propellant Pumps: Axial-plus-centrifugal pumps, co-axial.

Propellant Flow: Liquid hydrogen flow rate 3·67 lb (1·67 kg)/sec at 580 lb/sq in (40·8 kg/cm²). Liquid oxygen flow rate 18·32 lb (8·33 kg)/sec at 522 lb/sq in (36·7 kg/cm²).

Turbine: Two-stage axial-flow impulse unit in Inconel X750. Gas inlet temperature 617°C.

Gas Generator: Liquid hydrogen flow rate 0·19 lb (0·088 kg)/sec. Liquid oxygen flow rate 0·17 lb (0·079 kg)/sec. Pyrotechnic ignition.

Lubrication System: Uses tributyl phosphate spray into gaseous hydrogen.

SEP HM4 liquid oxygen/liquid hydrogen rocket engine for upper-stage propulsion (9,080 lb; 4,119 kg st)

STARTING: Solid-grain primer.
THRUST CONTROL: Thrust held constant by regulation of turbopump speed via control of gas generator propellant supply.
DIMENSIONS:
Height overall 45·6 in (1,170 mm)
Diameter overall 46·5 in (1,220 mm)
WEIGHT, DRY: 382·8 lb (174 kg)
PERFORMANCE:
Max thrust 9,080 lb (4,119 kg)
Overall propellant mixture ratio 5 : 1
Specific impulse 412

SEP RITA

The Rita I solid-propellant propulsion system was designed as the second stage of the French Navy's MSBS (subsurface-to-surface ballistic missile), a weapon now equipped with the Rita II engine.

The Rita I has a case of wound glass filament, weighing only 705 lb (320 kg). It is loaded with a grain of Isolane propellant, based on polyurethane binder, of high specific impulse. Ignition is by a solid-propellant microrocket on the front closure, which is also provided with controllable thrust-termination ports. The fixed nozzle is of carbon-fibre laminate with a graphite throat. Pitch and yaw control is effected by freon injection through four electro-valves. Roll is controlled by two separate steerable motors.

Rita I is to replace Topaze as the second stage of the new BP 4 version of the Diamant launch vehicle.

DIMENSIONS:
Length 98·4 in (2,500 mm)
Diameter 59 in (1,500 mm)
WEIGHT, LOADED: about 8,820 lb (4,000 kg)
PERFORMANCE:
Vacuum thrust 39,680 lb (18 tonnes)
Constant-thrust burn 55 sec

SEP Rita I solid-propellant propulsion system for Diamant P-4 second stage

SEP SPAL 30

One of the first French rocket motors using storable hypergolic liquid propellants, the SPAL 30 was to have powered the now-abandoned Aérospatiale C.30C supersonic target drone. It delivers three pre-set levels of thrust; 3,372 lb (1,530 kg) for 4 sec, 1,124 lb (510 kg) for 30 sec and 270 lb (122 kg) for 100 sec. On 10 May 1973 SEP announced that the SPAL 30 had just completed three acceptance tests. These completed the development stage, and the motor was thus considered to be cleared for operational use.

SEP VALOIS

This large liquid-rocket engine was originally developed to provide propulsion for the first stage of Diamant B. The single chamber is pressure-fed with nitrogen tetroxide oxidant (N_2O_4) and unsymmetrical dimethyl hydrazine fuel (UDMH), separate tanks of these propellants supplying the gas generator. The chamber is machined from refractory steel, contains a throat liner of pyrolytic graphite, and has a light alloy radial propellant-injector. The chamber, throat and nozzle are coated with zirconium oxide, and the interior is cooled by a film of UDMH over the wall.

Flight trajectory control is achieved by gimballing the chamber about two axes at right angles, by means of two actuating rams pressurised from the gas generator with electromagnetic control. Production of Valois is assigned to the Atelier de Construction de Tarbes.

DIMENSIONS:
Throat diameter 16 in (406 mm)
Nozzle exit diameter 38 in (965 mm)
PERFORMANCE:
Vacuum thrust 91,075 lb (41,310 kg)
Chamber pressure 267 lb/sq in (18·77 kg/cm²)
Mixture ratio (fuel/N_2O_4) 0·48
Vacuum specific impulse 244

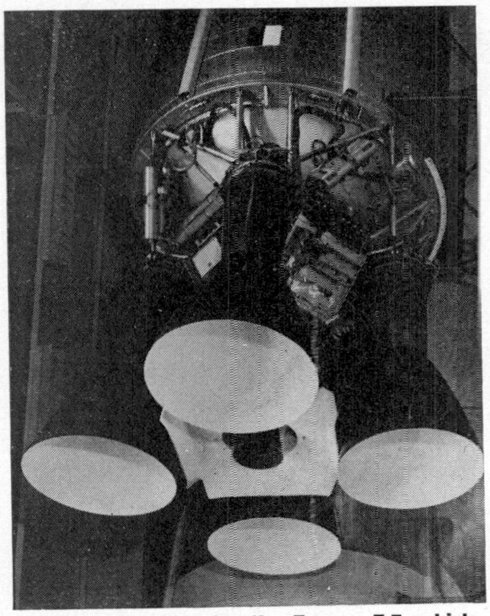

SEP Coralie motor for the Europa F.7 vehicle, with four thrust chambers (aggregate vacuum thrust 61,728 lb; 28,000 kg)

SEP CORALIE

This liquid-propellant rocket motor was built to provide propulsion for the second stage of Europa I and II, the ELDO vehicles. It has four thrust chambers, each of refractory steel with graphite throat liner, light alloy radial injector and interior coated with zirconium oxide. Propellants are N_2O_4 and UDMH, the latter providing film cooling of the chamber.

Three auxiliary tanks, containing the same two propellants and water, are fed to the gas generator by a nitrogen pressurisation system. Water is introduced into the gases produced by the generator, lowering its temperature to about 350°C, the water/propellant ratio being 1·88. The cooled gas pressurises the tanks of the vehicle stage to feed the four thrust chambers. Each diametrically-opposed pair of chambers is interconnected and rotates about a radial axis to provide second-stage control. They are positioned by Air Equipement oleo-pneumatic actuating jacks fed with pressurised gas from the generator.

The manufacturing programme for the Coralie motor has been entrusted to Atelier de Construction de Tarbes. The first 25 "Cora" units (with short nozzles, fitted for low-altitude operation) intended for stand testing, and seven Coralie engines, were delivered in 1966. Four new Coralie engines were delivered by July 1972.

DIMENSIONS:
Throat diameter 7·64 in (194 mm)
Nozzle exit diameter 29·4 in (747 mm)
Expansion ratio 140
PERFORMANCE:
Vacuum thrust (per chamber) 15,432 lb (7,000 kg)
Chamber pressure 197 lb/sq in (13·85 kg/cm²)
Mixture ratio (fuel/N_2O_4) 0·527
Vacuum specific impulse 281

SEP Valois motor for Diamant B about to undergo testing (88,870 lb; 40,310 kg st at S/L)

SEP VIKING

Rated at 40 tonnes (88,200 lb) at sea level, this is another of the large LRBA engines. It had simplicity of manufacture and operation as its prime design objectives. As a consequence it omits use of gears, jointed high-pressure pipes, and heat exchangers in the tank-pressurisation and lubrication systems. The engine comprises two major assemblies, the thrust chamber and turbopump. The thrust chamber wall is fabricated in HS 25 heat-resisting alloy and the throat is lined with graphite, the interior being cooled by a film of fuel.

The turbopump comprises a two-stage turbine driving, on the same shaft, the UDMH and N_2O_4 propellant pumps and a water pump. The water cools the delivery from the gas generator fed to the turbine and to the tanks for pressurisation purposes. The gases also pass to auxiliary equipment which maintains constant propellant mixture ratio and regulates the thrust chamber combustion zone pressure to ensure thrust build-up following an initial pilot pressure. The exhaust from the turbine is vented to atmosphere via two small thrust nozzles.

The turbopump is rigidly mounted on top of the thrust chamber, the combined assembly being carried on a gimbal mounting (single or double acting) located above the turbopump. The propellant feed pipes to the pumps are flexible to absorb any engine movements.

As the UDMH and N_2O_4 propellants are hypergolic, starting of the turbopump engine involves simply the opening of propellant valves. Ignition is rapid and propellant consumption prior to lift-off is therefore minimised. The gases as used for tank pressurisation are inert. As the turbopump and thrust chamber form a single, self-contained assembly, a number of such units may be grouped to meet higher launcher thrust requirements. From a basic single-chamber thrust of 88,200 lb (40 tonnes), multiple engines can be provided to cover a range up to 661,000 lb (300 tonnes).

In 1971, SEP practically completed the development of the Viking II version, which during its latest test runs delivered a thrust of 132,275 lb (60 tonnes). It was at this thrust level that the engine underwent, in November 1972, a qualification test of 150 seconds duration. Full testing of Viking II was to begin in the early months of 1973. Viking is intended to equip the first (four-engined) stage and the second (single-engined) stage of the projected L 3 S launch vehicle (see "Spaceflight and Research Rockets" section).

WEIGHT, DRY:
Viking I 1,278 lb (580 kg)
Viking II 1,344 lb (610 kg)

PERFORMANCE:
Nominal S/L thrust:
Viking I 121,250 lb (55,000 kg)
Viking II 132,275 lb (60,000 kg)

Vacuum thrust:
Viking I 143,300 lb (65,000 kg)
Viking II 156,525 lb (71,000 kg)

Chamber pressure:
Viking I 725 lb/sq in (51·0 kg/cm²)
Viking II 805 lb/sq in (56·6 kg/cm²)

Vacuum specific impulse:
Viking I 277·5
Viking II 279

Propulsion bay of Lilo, first stage of the L 3 S Ariane launch vehicle, showing the four SEP Viking II engines. Total S/L thrust is 529,100 lb (240 tonnes)

SEP HYDRAZINE THRUSTER

SEP has for a long period been engaged in the development of small monopropellant thrusters for satellite attitude and orbit control. Most of this work has been based on hydrazine, decomposed through a catalyst to serve as a monopropellant. The present SEP hydrazine propulsion system uses CNESRO 1 catalyst, developed jointly by SEP and the Faculté des Sciences of Paris.

Mass of the thruster is 0·397 lb (0·18 kg). It can be operated either continuously or pulsed. Chamber pressure can be varied from 218 to 434 lb/sq in (15·3-30·5 kg/cm²). Required output power is 5W.

SEP delivered to CNES (Space Centre of Toulouse) a flight model of its hydrazine micropropulsion system, comprising: surface-tension tank, engine, European CNESRO catalyst, hydrazine electrovalve, sensor and on-board electronics. This micropropulsion system was assembled on the D-5A satellite. The required thrust was designed to be achieved through short, reproducible pulses. Specific impulse reached 218 to 232 seconds.

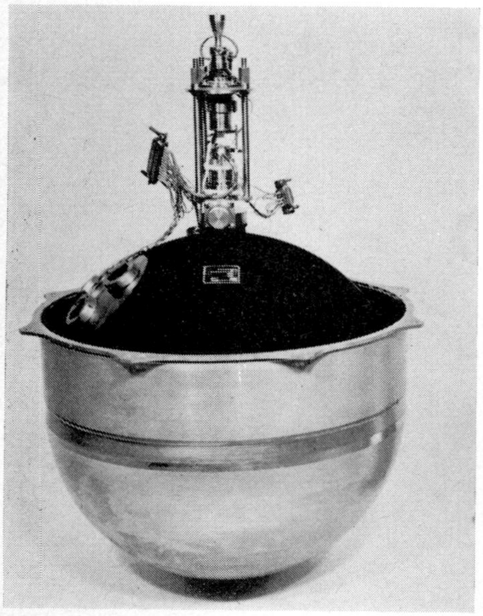

SEP hydrazine thruster system for D-5A satellite, shown with conical fairing removed

SEP ION THRUSTER

Like other electric thrusters that generate a jet of charged ions, this device uses caesium as the working fluid. Caesium from the supply tank is vaporised and ionised between the hollow cathode and inner anode in the presence of a powerful magnetic field. The ions are accelerated through an electrostatic grid and then neutralised by a secondary hollow cathode immediately downstream. Its useful life is to amount to 10,000 hours of cumulative operation, enabling the engine to perform missions ranging from 7 to 10 years in orbit.

WEIGHT, DRY: 3·3 lb (1·5 kg)
PERFORMANCE:
- Thrust: 6·7 mN or about 0·00067 kg
- Flow-rate of caesium: 0·0011 lb (0·5 gr)/hr
- Beam orientation: ±20°
- Power input: 250W
- Specific impulse: 5,000

SEP ion thruster, using caesium ions to give very small thrust at high specific impulse

SEP HM7

Under development for upper-stage propulsion, the HM7 is a 15,750 lb (7,144 kg) liquid oxygen/liquid hydrogen engine.

TYPE: Liquid-propellant rocket engine.

PROPELLANTS: Liquid oxygen and liquid hydrogen.

THRUST CHAMBER ASSEMBLY: Single-chamber unit of 48 : 1 nozzle area ratio, regeneratively cooled, and of stainless steel tube construction. Operating sequence initiated by hydrogen pre-cooling and pre-opening of hydrogen injection valve. Concentric-tube propellant injection system with central oxygen flow. Pyrotechnic ignition. Combustion pressure 507·5 lb/sq in (35·7 kg/cm²) and temperature 2,727°C.

THRUST CHAMBER MOUNTING: Gimballed assembly, turbopump integral with chamber.

PROPELLANT PUMPS: Axial-plus-centrifugal pumps, co-axial.

PROPELLANT FLOWS: Liquid hydrogen flow rate 6·07 lb (2·76 kg)/sec at 942·5 lb/sq in (66·25 kg/cm²). Liquid oxygen flow rate 31·26 lb (14·21 kg)/sec at 754 lb/sq in (53·0 kg/cm²).

TURBINE: Two-stage axial-flow impulse unit in Inconel X 750. Gas inlet temperature 617°C.

GAS GENERATOR: Liquid hydrogen flow rate 0·29 lb (0·133 kg)/sec. Liquid oxygen flow rate 0·26 lb (0·12 kg)/sec. Pyrotechnic ignition.

LUBRICATION SYSTEM: Uses tributyl phosphate spray into gaseous hydrogen.

STARTING: Solid grain primer.

THRUST CONTROL: Thrust held constant by regulation of turbopump speed via control of gas generator propellant supply.

DIMENSIONS:
- Height overall: 63·06 in (1,617 mm)
- Diameter overall: 33·03 in (847 mm)

WEIGHT, DRY: 319 lb (145 kg)

PERFORMANCE:
- Max thrust in vacuo: 15,750 lb (7,144 kg)
- Overall propellant mixture ratio: 5·15 : 1
- Specific impulse: 425

SEP HM7 liquid oxygen/liquid hydrogen rocket engine for upper-stage propulsion (15,750 lb; 7,144 kg st)

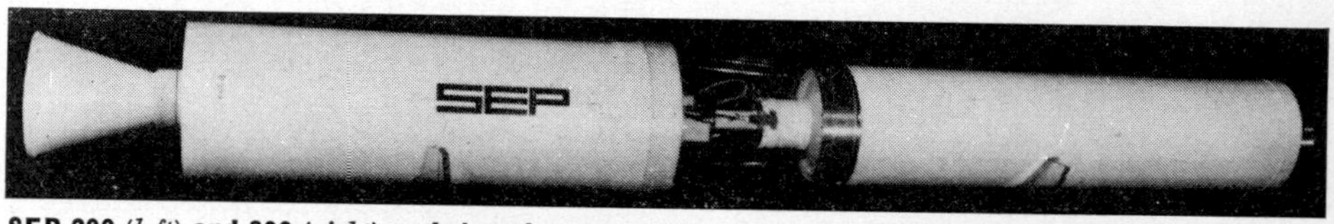

SEP 299 (*left*) and 300 (*right*) rocket engines are used respectively as the booster and sustainer of the Italian Sistel Sea Killer Mk 2 missile

TYPICAL SEP SOLID-PROPELLANT ROCKET ENGINES

Type	Static Thrust at S/L	Duration of Thrust (sec)	Total Weight	Length	Diameter
SEP 163	308 lb (140 kg)	37	88 lb (40 kg)	68·7 in (1,745 mm)	5·5 in (141 mm)
SEP 6854	8,700 lb (3,950 kg)	4	273 lb (124 kg)	101 in (2,560 mm)	8.9 in (226 mm)
SEP 738	19,300 lb (8,750 kg)	20	2,680 lb (1,206 kg)	155 in (3,942 mm)	23 in (584 mm)
SEP 739	36,520 lb (16,600 kg)	17·5	3,432 lb (1,557 kg)	184·5 in (4,690 mm)	22·7 in (578 mm)
SEP 7342	61,700 lb (28,000 kg)	4·6	1,870 lb (846 kg)	125·8 in (3,195 mm)	23·2 in (590 mm)
SEP 299	9,702 lb (4,400 kg)	1·6	126·78 lb (57·5 kg)	42·2 in (1,076 mm)	9·8 in (250 mm)
SEP 300	220·5 lb (100 kg)	73	115·76 lb (52·5 kg)	43·3 in (1,100 mm)	8·1 in (207 mm)
SEP ELDO Perigee	8,820 lb (4,000 kg)	45	1,655·9 lb (751 kg)	59 in (1,500 mm)	31·5 in (800 mm)
SEP Ball	1,170 lb (531 kg)	4·3	50·9 lb (23·1 kg)	16·9 in (430 mm)	8·7 in (221 mm)
SEP Trap	Start 2,214 lb (1,004 kg) Cruise 427 lb (194 kg)	Start 3·8 Cruise 10·2	99·75 lb (45·2 kg)	32·87 in (835 mm)	8·7 in (221 mm)

SERMEL

This company has been renamed IDA, and can be found under that heading in this section.

SNECMA

SOCIÉTÉ NATIONALE D'ÉTUDE ET DE CONSTRUCTION DE MOTEURS D'AVIATION

HEAD OFFICE:
150, Boulevard Haussmann, 75361 Paris cédex 08

Telephone: 227 33 94

CHAIRMAN AND MANAGING DIRECTOR:
René Ravaud

DEPUTY MANAGING DIRECTOR FOR AERO-ENGINE PROGRAMMES AND MARKETING:
Jean Péquignot

DEPUTY MANAGING DIRECTOR FOR AERO-ENGINE DEVELOPMENT AND PRODUCTION:
Joseph Millara

DEPUTY MANAGING DIRECTOR FOR SUBSIDIARY COMPANIES AND DIVISIONS:
Alain Bruté de Rémur

GENERAL SECRETARY:
Pierre Katz

PERSONNEL DIRECTOR:
Philippe Sappey

FINANCE AND ECONOMICS DIRECTOR:
Guy Zarrouati

PERSONAL ASSISTANT TO THE CHAIRMAN:
Roger Abel

DIRECTOR FOR INTERNATIONAL RELATIONS:
Jean Crépin

TECHNICAL DIRECTOR:
Michel Garnier

SCIENTIFIC DIRECTOR:
Raymond Marchal

TECHNICAL MANAGER:
Jean Devriese

MANAGER, ENGINE PRODUCTION:
Michel Viret

PUBLIC RELATIONS DEPARTMENT:
Alexandre Barbé

Villaroche Centre:
77 550-Moissy-Cramayel
Design, development and ground test centre. A subsidiary establishment for flight and noise tests is located at Istres.

Evry-Corbeil:
RN 440-Nationale 7, BP 17-91 101-Corbeil Essonnes
Engine production, quality control, service, procurement and laboratories for research and development.

Gennevilliers:
261 Avenue d'Argenteuil, BP 30-92 234-Gennevilliers
Forging and casting production, complete machining of mechanical parts.

Suresnes—ELECMA Division:
22 Quai Galliéni, 92 150-Suresnes
Design, development and production of electronic devices, especially electronic control systems for the aircraft industry.

Bois-Colombes—Hispano-Suiza Division:
Rue du Capitaine Guynemer, 92 270-Bois-Colombes
Design, development and production of industrial gas turbines, superchargers and nuclear equipment, and production of parts for jet engines and aeronautical equipment.

Billancourt:
167 Rue de Silly, BP 151-92 102-Boulogne Billancourt
Repair and overhaul of military and commercial jet engines.

SNECMA (Société Nationale d'Etude et de Construction de Moteurs d'Aviation) was born on 29 August 1945 from the merger of several aero-engine companies: Gnôme et Rhône, Société Anonyme des Moteurs Renault pour l'Aviation, Société Générale de Mécanique et d'Aviation (former Moteurs Lorraine), and Groupe d'Etudes des Moteurs â Huile Lourde.

These companies already had a long aeronautical tradition and SNECMA has always devoted its main activity to aero-engines. Almost 4,000 Atar turbojets have been delivered and have played a significant part in the world-wide success of Mirage fighters. SNECMA is developing the M53 turbojet for fighters of the next decade.

SNECMA is also participating in the following international collaborative programmes:

The Olympus 593 for Concorde, developed and produced with Rolls-Royce; the M45H, also developed and produced with Rolls-Royce, for which the VFW 614 is the first application; the CF6-50 for the Airbus A 300B, for which engine SNECMA and MTU in Germany are partners with General Electric; the CFM56, which SNECMA shares equally with General Electric, but with other European engine manufacturers being associated within SNECMA's share; and the Larzac, produced in co-operation with Turboméca and with production also including the German companies MTU and KHD.

These engines are discussed in the International section, apart from the Larzac which appears under Turboméca-SNECMA.

The merger in 1968 with the Hispano-Suiza company, which is now a division of SNECMA, brought in production of Tyne engines for Transall and Breguet Atlantic aircraft; this engine was manufactured under a Rolls-Royce licence within a consortium including SNECMA, Rolls-Royce, MTU and FN in Belgium. Spare parts production is continuing.

Other activities of the SNECMA group include: electronic control systems for engines and miscellaneous equipment for aerospace vehicles produced by the ELECMA division; Martin-Baker ejection seats produced under licence by the Hispano-Suiza Division for Mirage, Jaguar and Alpha Jet aircraft; overhaul of aero-engines and components, carried out in the Billancourt facility, and also in the subsidiary companies SOCHATA and CNMP-Berthiez; and in the landing-gear field an agreement was reached in 1970 between SNECMA and Messier, Messier-Hispano being founded to take over the activity formerly led by the Hispano-Suiza Division. In November 1973 Messier-Hispano became a subsidiary of SNECMA. This new company is in charge of development and marketing of landing gears, while production is shared between the Messier-Hispano works and the Molsheim factory of the Bugatti company, a SNECMA subsidiary. Outside the aviation market, industrial gas turbines, turbo-superchargers, nuclear equipment (such as compressors, specialised pumps and miscellaneous equipment) are produced by the Hispano-Suiza division. CNMP-Berthiez produces armaments and high quality machine-tools. This company, a SNECMA subsidiary, was born from the merger in 1968 of CNMP (Compagnie Normande de Mécanique de Précision) which took over in 1964 a state-owned factory in Le Havre, and the "Anciens Etablissements Berthiez" company located in Givors.

SNECMA ATAR

The Atar is a single-shaft military turbojet first run in 1946 and since greatly developed and cleared for flight at Mach numbers greater than 2. Major versions in 1974 are:

Atar 8K-50. This is essentially the 9K-50, the latest variant in production, re-engineered to have a simple unaugmented jet-pipe and fixed nozzle, for the Super Etendard. The original Etendard was powered by the Atar 8C, compared with which the 8K-50 has 16% more T-O thrust and "maintenance periods 50% less". All parts are protected against sea corrosion.

Atar 9C. Compared with the earlier 9B this introduced a new compressor, a self-contained starter and an improved overspeed which comes into operation automatically when the aircraft reaches Mach 1·4 and 36,000 ft (11,000 m), giving power equivalent to a sea level thrust of 14,110 lb (6,400 kg) st. The compressor rotor has steel blades on stages 1, 2, 7, 8 and 9 and light alloy blades on stages 3-6: the stator has steel blades on stages 1 and 2 and light alloy blades on stages 3-8. Air mass flow 150 lb (68 kg)/sec. Pressure ratio 5·5 : 1. Equips Mirage III-E and III-R and has been produced under licence in Switzerland and Australia. It is also assembled in Belgium, with a part-Belgian content, for Belgian Mirage 5 aircraft.

Atar 9K-50. Derived from the Atar 9C and fitted as initial power plant of the Mirage F1 and prototype Mirage G8. Designed to offer improved subsonic specific fuel consumption, increased thrust for supersonic acceleration and improved overhaul life. The main improvements are in an entirely redesigned turbine with blades not forged but cast and coated with refractory metal from the vapour phase. This wholly new turbine section includes a section of engine carcase, exit cone and fixed vanes. Stages 1 and 8 of the compressor have been redesigned, resulting in pressure ratio raised from 6 : 1 to 6·5 : 1, coupled with slightly augmented mass flow. The intake section has been revised to accommodate a rearranged accessory-drive system, and the control and electronic equipment have been revised and extended to improve the security of single-engined aircraft. The 9K-50 has done extensive ground and flight testing in Mirage III and F1 aircraft and was homologated for service use following its final 150 hour test at the CEP, Saclay, between 8 September and 24 November 1969. The first production F1 flew in March 1973 and many are now in service.

DIMENSIONS:
Diameter 40·2 in (1,020 mm)
Length overall:
Atar 8K-50 150 in (3,810 mm)
Atar 9C, 9K-50 234 in (5,942 mm)

WEIGHTS:
Dry, complete with all accessories:
Atar 8K-50 2,546 lb (1,155 kg)
Atar 9C 3,120 lb (1,420 kg)
Atar 9K-50 3,500 lb (1,587 kg)

PERFORMANCE RATINGS:
Max with afterburner:
Atar 9C 13,200 lb (6,000 kg) st at 8,400 rpm
Atar 9K-50 15,870 lb (7,200 kg) st at 8,700 rpm
Max without afterburner:
Atar 8K-50 11,265 lb (5,110 kg) st at 8,700 rpm
Atar 9C 9,430 lb (4,280 kg) st at 8,400 rpm
Atar 9K-50 11,023 lb (5,000 kg) st

SPECIFIC FUEL CONSUMPTION:
At max rating with afterburner:
Atar 9C 2·03
Atar 9K-50 1·97
At max rating without afterburner:
Atar 8K-50 0·95
Atar 9C 1·01
Atar 9K-50 0·97

OIL CONSUMPTION: 2·64 Imp pints (1·5 litres)/hr

SNECMA Atar 9K-50 turbojet of 15,870 lb (7,200 kg) st with afterburner

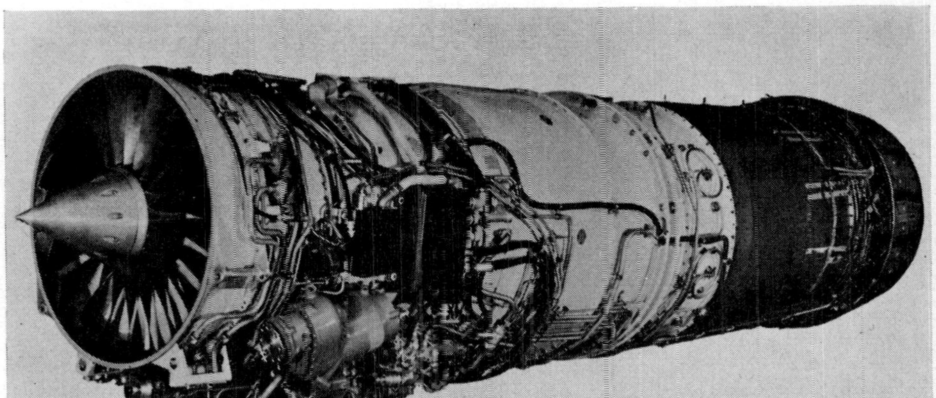

SNECMA M53 augmented by-pass turbojet of 18,740 lb (8,500 kg) st

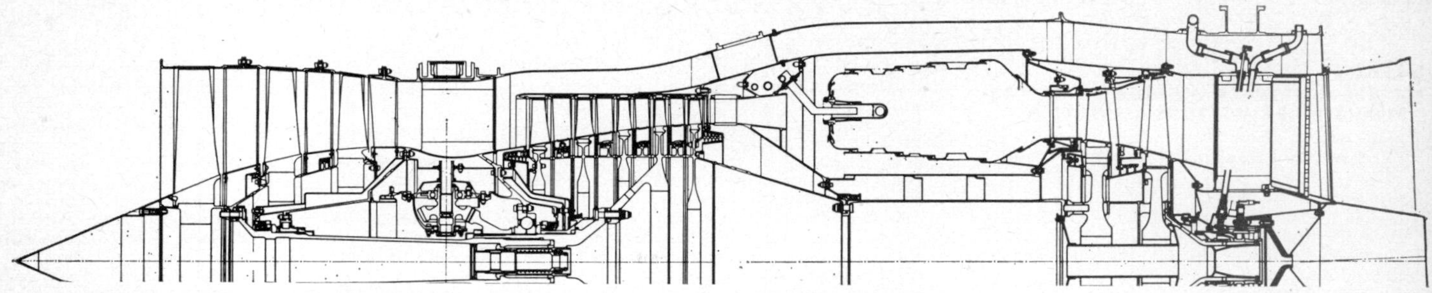

Longitudinal section through the SNECMA M53 showing LP and HP sections on single shaft (pressure ratio, 8·5 : 1 at 10,200 rpm) and by-pass duct

SNECMA M53

Design started in 1967 on the M53, an advanced onward development from the Atar to provide an engine of superior performance to present series Atar engines but of simpler and less costly design than the SNECMA TF 306 turbofan. The result is a single-shaft turbofan—more strictly a continuous-bleed turbojet or by-pass turbojet—having the capability of propelling fighter aircraft at high altitude initially at Mach 2·5.

The M53 is intended as the engine of second-generation Dassault Mirage F1 and G8 fighters, including the F1 International and G8A (ACF). It is of modular construction.

The single shaft comprises a three-stage fan and five-stage compressor driven by a two-stage turbine designed for operation at high gas temperature. There are no inlet guide vanes. Max airflow is 185 lb (84 kg)/sec. Between the fan and compressor is a mid-frame incorporating accessory drives and front roller bearing and ball thrust bearing. The annular combustion chamber is designed for smoke-free operation. The turbine delivery casing incorporates the third bearing. Fuel to the combustion chamber and reheat system, and the multi-flap nozzle, are controlled by a fuel system monitored by an ELECMA electronic computer.

The first prototype engine was tested in February 1970, 18 months after programme go-ahead. The second ran in August, and achieved maximum rpm after 30 minutes of operation. Military rating (11,466 lb; 5,200 kg) was reached in October, three months ahead of contractual commitment. Testing with afterburner began in November 1970. The first official test took place at 12,346 lb (5,600 kg) in May 1971. In the same month a 50 hr test was run at afterburning thrusts up to 18,298 lb (8,300 kg), 98 per cent of the nominal rating. In September thrust exceeded the nominal figure, at 18,740 lb (8,500 kg), and in December simulated altitude trials began at Saclay. By March 1972 three prototype M53 engines were running. Flight trials began on 18 July 1973 in the starboard pod of a Caravelle testbed. The supersonic flight envelope will be investigated with the Mirage F1-M53 prototype. In February 1974 the total running time exceeded 1,800 hr.

Dimensions:
- Overall length: 190·5 in (4,850 mm)
- Max diameter: 40·9 in (1,040 mm)

Weight, Dry: 3,130 lb (1,420 kg)

Performance Ratings:
- Max thrust, with afterburner: 18,740 lb (8,500 kg)
- Max thrust, cold: 12,350 lb (5,600 kg)

Specific Fuel Consumption:
- At max cold rating: 0·87

SNECMA/GE CFM 56

After carefully exploring the world market, and the prospects for collaborating with other large engine companies while retaining design leadership, SNECMA decided in the Autumn of 1971 to develop the CFM 56, a subsonic turbofan in the ten-tonne-thrust (22,000 lb) class, in co-operation with General Electric. The French and US companies are splitting all the work on a 50/50 basis. The project is covered more fully in the International section.

GE/SNECMA/MTU CF6

SNECMA and MTU of Federal Germany have signed an agreement with General Electric for international production of the GE CF6-50 turbofan for the Airbus A-300B. SNECMA and MTU will respectively manufacture 22 + 5·7 and 11 per cent of the engine, the remaining 61·3 per cent being supplied by GE. SNECMA will manufacture the HP compressor rotor, combustion chamber, LP turbine rotor and transmission gear-train assembly, and will carry out assembly and test.

SNECMA/ROLLS-ROYCE M45H

This low sfc turbofan is under joint development by SNECMA and Rolls-Royce to power the VFW 614 feederliner. Details of the M45H are given in the International section.

SNECMA/ROLLS-ROYCE OLYMPUS 593

SNECMA is collaborating with Rolls-Royce in the design, development and manufacture of the Olympus 593 turbojet for the Concorde. A description of the engine appears under "Rolls-Royce/SNECMA" in the International section.

SNECMA/TURBOMÉCA LARZAC

This joint design of a 2,965 lb (1,345 kg) st turbofan by SNECMA and Turboméca is being developed to power business jets, military liaison aircraft and trainers. A description of the Larzac is given under the entry for Turboméca-SNECMA GRTS, in this section.

SNPE

SOCIÉTÉ NATIONALE DES POUDRES ET EXPLOSIFS

Headquarters:
12 Quai Henri IV, 75181 Paris 04
Telephone: 277 15 70

USINE DE SAINT MÉDARD

St Médard-en-Jalles (Gironde)
Telephone: (56) 44 21 25

Established by Royal Decree in 1679, the former Poudrerie Nationale de St Médard was one of the largest establishments in the Service des Poudres. In October 1971 the SDP was taken over by the SNPE, a completely new national company, responsible for all production in France of solid propellant charges for everything from pistol ammunition to an ICBM.

St Médard has a payroll of almost 1,300, of whom 1,000 are skilled groups of civil and military engineers, working in more than 500 buildings dispersed in the pine forest north-west of Bordeaux.

The establishment probably produces a wider range of solid-propellant rocket charges than any other single organisation in the world. Brief

PRINCIPAL SNPE MOTORS

Motor	Application	Total Impulse lb-sec (kg-sec)	Duration (sec)	Diameter in (mm)	Charge Weight lb (kg)
Isolane propellant					
P.16 (Type 902)	SSBS first stage	9,215,350 (4,180,000)	76	59 (1,500)	35,275 (16,000)
P.10 (Type 903)	SSBS second stage	—	—	59 (1,500)	22,050 (10,000)
P.10 (Type 904)	MSBS first stage	—	—	59 (1,500)	22,050 (10,000)
P.4 (Rita)	MSBS second stage	2,182,580 (990,000)	55	59 (1,500)	8,820 (4,000)
P.6					
Diamant	Diamant third stage	295,420 (134,000)	45	25·5 (650)	1,410 (640)
Soleil VE.111	Diamant second stage	1,036,170 (470,000)	36·7	31·5 (800)	4,982 (2,260)
Polka	Masurca boost	352,740 (160,000)	4·6	22 (560)	1,521 (690)
Jacée	Masurca cruise	138,900 (63,000)	26	15·75 (400)	705 (320)
Plastolite/plastolane					
Marie-Antoinette	Matra R. 530	17,635 (8,000)	9	8 (203)	93·7 (42·5)
Vénus	Malafon boost	37,480 (17,000)	2·9	10·8 (275)	203 (92)
Epervier	AS.30 boost	23,600 (10,700)	2	13 (330)	126 (57)
Mammouth	VE.110 test vehicle	811,300 (368,000)	18·2	31·5 (800)	4,210 (1,910)
Stromboli	Aérospatiale Dragon	319,675 (145,000)	16·5	21·6 (550)	1,510 (685)
SD					
ACRA	ACRA missile	—	—	—	—
Entac	Entac missile	—	18·7	2·45 (62)	3·24 (1·47)
Mk 43	2·75 in rocket	—	1·5	2·45 (62)	5·84 (2·65)
CT.20	CT.20 boost trolley	—	2	3·62 (92)	198 (90)

details of some current production motors are given in the accompanying tables. These show that important propellants include all the families of which details have been disclosed outside the Soviet Union. Composite propellants include polybutadiene, polychlorates of vinyl or polyurethane, ammonium perchlorate (with additions such as dispersed aluminium) and numerous other composite propellants, often with 12-15 separate ingredients, as well as the more traditional double-base extruded propellants (type SD) derived from cordite and similar gun propellants which are made very cheaply in sizes up to 200 mm (7·9 in) diameter.

SD motors are used mainly for such applications as anti-tank missiles and take-off boosters. The plastolite/plastolane composites are cast in free blocks, whereas the isolite/isolane/butalite/butalane series are case-bonded permanently into the metal vehicle stage which is also sometimes fabricated by the St Médard works.

The establishment has test-fired a 57,320 lb (26,000 kg) motor of 78·8 in (2 m) diameter, and at the 1969 Paris Salon exhibited an inert segment weighing approximately 22,000 lb (10,000 kg) and of 118 in (3 m) diameter to demonstrate its capacity to make segments suitable for Titan IIIC.

Since 1959 the establishment has been manufacturing the rocket motor of the US Hawk missile under licence, and in turn has licensed the governments of India and Pakistan to make the plastolane motors used in Aérospatiale sounding rockets.

A completely original way of forming the charge for large motors has been developed which, instead of using a star-centred filling, uses a retractable boring tool (with an extraction duct for the swarf) to machine annular bleed slots around the cast charge. This technique, used on the P.4 and P.6 missile stages, is described as having the greatest possible simplicity. It reduces the time taken in fabricating the internal profile of the charge to two days, compared with 15 days for methods involving a retractable or fusible mandrel or former. St Médard is striving to diversify and to apply its talents and extensive laboratory equipment (which includes a 14 MeV radiographic installation and the largest vibration exciter in western Europe) to commercial ends.

TURBOMÉCA

SOCIÉTÉ TURBOMÉCA

HEAD OFFICE AND WORKS:
Bordes (Pyrénées Atlantiques)
Telephone: (59) 27 07 31

OTHER WORKS:
Mézières S/Seine (Yvelines) and
Tarnos (near Bayonne)

PARIS OFFICE:
1, Rue Beaujon, Paris 8e

PRESIDENT AND DIRECTOR-GENERAL:
J. R. Szydlowski

The Société Turboméca was originally formed in 1938 by M Szydlowski and M Planiol to develop blowers, compressors and turbines for aeronautical use.

Turboméca is the leading European manufacturer of small turbine aero-engines. Since it first started development of gas turbines in 1947, the company has developed about 50 different types of power plant of which some 15 have entered production and ten types have been manufactured under licence in five countries.

By 1 January 1974, 12,500 Turboméca engines for fixed and rotary-wing applications and aircraft auxiliary duties had been delivered to customers in 88 countries, including France. Approximately 12,000 more engines have been built under licence by what are today Rolls-Royce (1971) Ltd in the UK, Teledyne CAE in the US, ENMASA in Spain, Hindustan Aeronautics Ltd in India and a state factory in Yugoslavia. Present production rate by Turboméca totals some 130 new and overhauled engines per month.

A new 130,000 sq ft (12,077 m²) extension to the company's factory at Tarnos was commissioned in September 1968, bringing the total covered floor area for Turboméca's three plants at Bordes, Mézières and Tarnos to 1,347,000 sq ft (125,352 m²). At 1 January 1974 the company employed a total of 4,435 people.

In addition Turboméca has a 51 per cent holding in Bet-Shemesh Engines, an aero-engine factory built in Israel, near Jerusalem, in conjunction with the Israeli government. The first section of the factory, based on the same layout as Turboméca's Tarnos plant, was officially opened in January 1969. Details of Bet-Shemesh Engines are given in the Israeli entry in this section.

A high degree of interchangeability exists among the range of Turboméca turbine engines. Most of them have been described in previous editions of *Jane's* and the entries which follow are concerned with only the more important current types.

In 1967 Turboméca started development of an aircooled turbine rotor suitable for application to the company's full range of engines. Introduction of this turbine on production engines was initiated in 1969 with the Astazou XVI turboprop, and aircooled versions of other Turboméca engines are under development.

Two important turbofans of part-Turboméca design and manufacture are the Adour (shared with Rolls-Royce) and the Larzac (jointly developed with SNECMA and to be produced by a consortium including MTU and KHD of West Germany).

ROLLS-ROYCE TURBOMÉCA RB.172/T260 ADOUR

This joint design of 7,400 lb (3,350 kg) st turbofan by Rolls-Royce and Turboméca has been developed for the SEPECAT Jaguar tactical strike fighter and advanced trainer. Other versions have been developed for the HS 1182 Hawk and Mitsubishi T-2. A brief description of the Adour is given in the International section.

TURBOMÉCA ASTAFAN

Turboméca Astafan geared variable-pitch turbofan on testbed (1,870 lb; 850 kg st)

The Astafan is a low-consumption lightweight turbofan of high by-pass ratio, low noise level design which made its first run during the Summer of 1969. Comprising an Astazou turboprop power section, operating at constant speed, driving a single-stage variable-pitch fan via reduction gearing, the Astafan is being developed in several versions corresponding to different development stages of the Astazou. All have the high by-pass ratio of 7 : 1 and are characterised by very low specific fuel consumption. Variable-pitch blading facilitates constant-speed operation and enables off-loading of the engine during starting.

The following are the first two versions under development:

Astafan III. Derived from the Astazou XVIII, with aircooled turbine.

Astafan IV. Derived from the Astazou XX, with three-stage axial high-pressure compressor.

Flight development of prototype Astafan engines began in a Hawk Commander on 8 April 1971. Two podded underwing Astafans replace the original piston engines, conferring a substantial improvement in flight performance and a reduction in noise and vibration. Applications for the Astafan III or IV include a specially designed Rockwell International Commander, a proposed version of the IAI Westwind, the Ted Smith Super Star 3000, and a projected development of the FMA IA 58 Pucará.

TYPE: Single-shaft turbofan with geared fan.

ENTRY CASING: Annular light alloy entry cowl and fan duct supported on double row of air straightener vanes downstream of fan rotor. Annular intake to gas generator section located at exit to fan duct. Rear casing of secondary intake carries accessories and accessory drives (using arrangement similar to Astazou XVIII intake).

FAN: Single-stage fan with variable-incidence rotor blading overhung at front without entry guide vanes. Drive from gas generator section is via two-stage epicyclic gear train housed in cylindrical casing forming inner wall of fan duct. Astafan IV has fan of increased diameter (27·5 in; 700 mm).

COMPRESSOR, COMBUSTION SYSTEM AND TURBINE: Same as Astazou XVIII. Normal gas-generator operating speed, 43,000 rpm. (Astafan IV has Astazou XX compressor, running at 42,000 rpm.)

JET PIPE: Fixed type with straight frustum inner cone. Extension jet pipe to convergent propulsive nozzle and ejector nozzle at rear of engine pod casing.

ACCESSORIES: Mounted on casing forming rear of secondary air intake.

FUEL SYSTEM: Independent control systems for starting and normal operation. Fuel regulator maintains speed constant with pilot operating single lever controlling fan blade pitch to vary thrust output. Turboméca "thermic" load limiter controls turbine entry temperature between set limits (using principle of operation similar to that on Astazou XVIII).

FUEL GRADES: AIR 3404A, 3405 or 3407A.

LUBRICATION SYSTEM: Pressure lubrication to bearings and reduction gear, with annular engine-mounted oil tank.

STARTING: Automatic electrical starting with compressor blow-off valve and fan in minimum pitch.

DIMENSIONS:

Length overall:	
Astafan III	80·0 in (2,030 mm)
Astafan IV	87·5 in (2,218 mm)
Max diameter over fan cowl:	
Astafan III	26·2 in (665 mm)
Astafan IV	30·7 in (780 mm)

WEIGHTS:

Astafan III bare engine	462 lb (210 kg)
Equipped Astafan III	approx 507 lb (230 kg)
Astafan IV bare engine	485 lb (220 kg)

PERFORMANCE RATINGS:

T-O, wet:	
Astafan III	1,870 lb (850 kg)
Astafan IV	2,710 lb (1,230 kg)
T-O, dry:	
Astafan III	1,740 lb (790 kg)
Astafan IV	2,530 lb (1,150 kg)

SPECIFIC FUEL CONSUMPTION:

At T-O rating:	
Astafan III	0·365
Astafan IV	0·310
At max continuous rating:	
Astafan III	0·359
Astafan IV	0·305

TURBOMÉCA-SNECMA LARZAC

This joint design of a 2,965 lb (1,345 kg) st turbofan by Turboméca and SNECMA is being developed to power military trainers and other small aircraft. A description of the Larzac is given under Turboméca-SNECMA GRTS (which follows this entry).

TURBOMÉCA MARBORÉ

The Marboré turbojet is the most widely used of Turboméca's range of gas turbines. By the beginning of 1974, 4,233 Marboré II engines of 880 lb (400 kg) st had been delivered by Turboméca and a further 10,000 by Continental Aviation and Teledyne CAE (see US section) as the J69. Production of the Marboré IID continues for the Aérospatiale CT.20 target drone.

This initial version of the engine was joined in production by the 1,058 lb (480 kg) st Marboré VI with receipt of type approval in June 1962. By the beginning of 1974, 890 Marboré VI turbojets had been built and production continues under a large French government order awarded in December 1968. Four versions, each with differing accessory arrangements, have been delivered; the Marboré VIC for the Morane-Saulnier Paris II, the Marboré VID for the Aérospatiale M.20 drone, the Marboré VIF for the CM.170 Super Magister, and the Marboré VIJ for the Morane-Saulnier Paris IA. During 1968, the TBO for the Marboré VIF2 was increased to 1,000 hr.

The Marboré VI was also built under licence in Spain by ENMASA as the Marboré M21.

The following particulars relate to the Marboré VI series:

TYPE: Single-shaft centrifugal-flow turbojet.

AIR INTAKE: Annular sheet metal nose intake bolted to front of light alloy compressor casing.

COMPRESSOR: Single-sided impeller machined from two alloy forgings, shrunk on steel shaft and locked and dowelled to maintain alignment. Externally-finned light alloy compressor casing supports front ball-bearing for rotating assembly in a central housing supported by three streamlined struts. This housing also contains gears for accessory drives. Pressure ratio 3·84 : 1. Air mass flow 21·6 lb (9·8 kg)/sec.

COMBUSTION CHAMBER: Composed of inner and outer sheet metal casings, forming annular flame tube. Air from compressor passes through both radial and axial diffuser vanes and divides into three main flows, two primary for combustion and one secondary. Two primary flows enter combustion zone from opposite ends of chamber, the rear stream through turbine nozzle guide vanes which it cools. Secondary flow enters through outer casing for dilution and cooling of combustion gases. Two torch igniters.

FUEL SYSTEM: Fuel, pumped through hollow impeller shaft, is fed to combustion zone by rotating injector disc around periphery of which are number of vents which act as nozzles. Fuel is vented by centrifugal force, being atomised in the process. Fuel delivery at low thrust settings regulated by by-pass valve.

FUEL GRADE: Air 3405 (JP-1).

NOZZLE GUIDE VANES: Twenty-five hollow sheet steel guide vanes cooled by part of primary combustion air.

TURBINE: Single-stage turbine with thirty-seven blades with fir-tree root fittings in steel disc. Bolted to main shaft and tail shaft, latter supported by rear roller bearing for rotating assembly. Gas temperature 613°C at 21,500 rpm.

JET PIPE: Inner and outer sheet metal casings, latter supported by three hollow struts. Inner tapered casing extends beyond end of outer casing to induce airflow through struts to cool rear main bearing and inner casing.

ACCESSORY DRIVES: Gear casing in central compressor housing with drives for fuel and oil pumps. Connecting shaft to underside of accessories gear case above compressor casing. Accessories include tachometer generator and electric starter. Take-off (4 hp continuous) for remotely-driven accessory box.

LUBRICATION SYSTEM: Pressure type. Single gear-type pump serves front gear casing, two main bearings and rpm governor. Three scavenge pumps return bearing oil to tank via cooler. Normal oil pressure 40 lb/sq in (2·8 kg/cm²).

OIL SPECIFICATION: Air 3512 (mineral) or Air 3513A (synthetic).

MOUNTING: Four points, with Silentbloc rubber mountings, two at front and two at rear.

STARTING: Air Equipement 24V electric starter or compressed air starter. Two Turboméca igniter plugs.

DIMENSIONS:

Length with exhaust cone but without tailpipe	55·74 in (1,416 mm)
Width	23·35 in (593 mm)
Height	24·82 in (631 mm)

WEIGHT, DRY:

Equipped	309 lb (140 kg)

PERFORMANCE RATINGS:

T-O	1,058 lb (480 kg) st at 21,500 rpm
Cruising	925 lb (420 kg) st at 20,500 rpm

SPECIFIC FUEL CONSUMPTION:

At T-O rating	1·09
At cruising rating	1·07

TURBOMÉCA ARBIZON IIIB (TR 281)

Announced in 1970, the Arbizon IIIB is a simple single-shaft turbojet with minimum overall dimensions and weight. The main rotating assembly comprises an axial and a centrifugal compressor driven by a single-stage turbine. General design is similar to that of other Turboméca engines, with an annular combustion chamber supplied with centrifugally-injected fuel. At the front the axial intake opens out into a four-lobed bell-mouth to provide a large front face for the electric starter and other engine-driven accessories.

Mass flow is 13·2 lb (6 kg)/sec, and pressure ratio 5·5. The Arbizon III has already been produced in small numbers (16 by 1 January 1974) to power the Otomat guided missile. Originally designated TR281, it was derived from the Turmo IIIC₃.

DIMENSIONS:

Diameter of front face	16·14 in (410 mm)
Diameter of combustion chamber	15·95 in (405 mm)
Overall length, with accessories	53·58 in (1,361 mm)

WEIGHT, DRY: 253 lb (115 kg)

PERFORMANCE RATINGS:

T-O	836 lb (380 kg) at 33,000 rpm
Max continuous	727 lb (330 kg) at 32,000 rpm

SPECIFIC FUEL CONSUMPTION:

At T-O rating	1·125
At max continuous rating	1·11

Turboméca Arbizon III expendable turbojet (836 lb; 380 kg st)

TURBOMÉCA ARRIEL

Turboméca is planning a new turboshaft engine in the 650 shp class for use from 1976. Known as the Arriel, it is aimed initially at future versions of the SA 341 Gazelle and SA 365, the latter being studied with both single and twinned power-sections.

The Arriel is intended to have low first cost, low maintenance cost and low specific weight. It is characterised by modular construction, as shown in the accompanying provisional sketch. This shows: titanium transonic axial and centrifugal compressors (pressure ratio up to 9:1); annular combustor with centrifugal fuel injection; two-stage turbine with armoured containment ring; remote power turbine; two separate reduction gears, with front drive to main rotor and rear drive to rear "fenestron" rotor.

The Arriel is expected eventually to form the basis for a single-shaft turboprop and a turbofan in the 1,100 lb; 500 kg class. The gas generator ran in 1973.

TYPE: Single-shaft axial-plus-centrifugal free-turbine turboshaft.

AIR INTAKE: Direct pitot entry to axial compressor.

COMPRESSOR: Single-stage axial compressor, machined from titanium forging, cantilevered ahead of shaft running in two ball bearings and attached by axial lock to turbine shaft at centrifugal rotor. Supersonic centrifugal stage also machined from titanium, and connected to turbine shaft by central bolt, with drive by curvic coupling. Downstream are radial and then axial stators. High rotational speed for maximum attainable pressure ratio.

COMBUSTION CHAMBER: Annular chamber, with flow radially outwards and then inwards. Centrifugal fuel injection without central tube.

GAS-GENERATOR TURBINE: Two integral cast axial stages with solid blades. Assembled by curvic couplings and central bolt. Shaft supported by axial-compressor bearings at front and roller bearing at rear. Turbine shield capable of disc containment.

POWER TURBINE: Single axial stage with inserted blades. Cantilevered ahead of roller bearing; rear of shaft held in ball bearing, cages of both bearings being secured to exhaust diffuser arms.

JET PIPE: Exhaust diffuser fabricated by welding, with central portion around output shaft and flared outer wall.

REDUCTION GEAR: Light alloy gearbox, containing two stages of helical gears, giving drive at 6,000 rpm to output shaft extending whole length of engine, with drive connections to both front and rear. Hydraulic torquemeter.

ACCESSORY DRIVES: Two bevel gears and radial quill shaft drive accessory gearbox at front end, carried between compressor case and output shaft. Main pad provides for optional 12,000 rpm alternator; other drives for oil pumps, tachometer generator, governor and starter.

LUBRICATION SYSTEM: Independent circuit. Oil from tank passes through gear pump and metallic-cartridge filter. Return from engine via three gear scavenge pumps. Temperature probe and pressure switch to verify operation.

OIL SPECIFICATION: Air 3512 (mineral) or Air 3513A (synthetic).

MOUNTING: Multi-point flanges allow easy mounting in single or twin installation.

STARTING: Electric starter or starter/generator.

DIMENSIONS:

Length, excluding accessories	42·91 in (1,090 mm)
Height overall	22·40 in (569 mm)
Width	16·93 in (430 mm)

WEIGHT, DRY:

With all engine accessories	198 lb (90 kg)

PERFORMANCE RATINGS:

Max contingency, initial	681 shp (691 cv)
Max contingency, later	730 shp (740 cv)
Take-off and intermediate contingency	641 shp (650 cv)
Max continuous	592 shp (600 cv)

SPECIFIC FUEL CONSUMPTION:

Max contingency	0·573 lb/shp/hr (0·260 kg/cv/hr)

TURBOMÉCA ASTAZOU

The Astazou is the major turboprop in the Turboméca range and is in production in its 853 ehp Astazou XIVC and 1,020 ehp Astazou XVI versions to power a number of different aircraft. These versions are also marketed by Rolls-Royce Turboméca International Ltd under the designations AZ14 and AZ16. By the end of 1972, 151 Astazou XIVC engines had been built. (Earlier, Turboméca had built 483 Astazou IIA and 36 Astazou IIIN engines.)

The Astazou XIV was certificated by the French airworthiness authorities in October 1968, followed by ARB/FAA certification of the Astazou XIVC and C1 in March 1969. The Jetstream received ARB/FAA certification during the following month. On 15 November 1968, a Pilatus Turbo-Porter STOL aircraft powered by a 585 hp Astazou XIVE achieved a new world altitude record for C-1-c class aircraft with a flight to 44,242 ft (13,485 m).

Current versions of the Astazou are:

Astazou XII. Powered Shorts Skyvan Srs 2 at 690 shp and Pilatus Turbo-Porter PC-6/A1-H2 at 700 ehp.

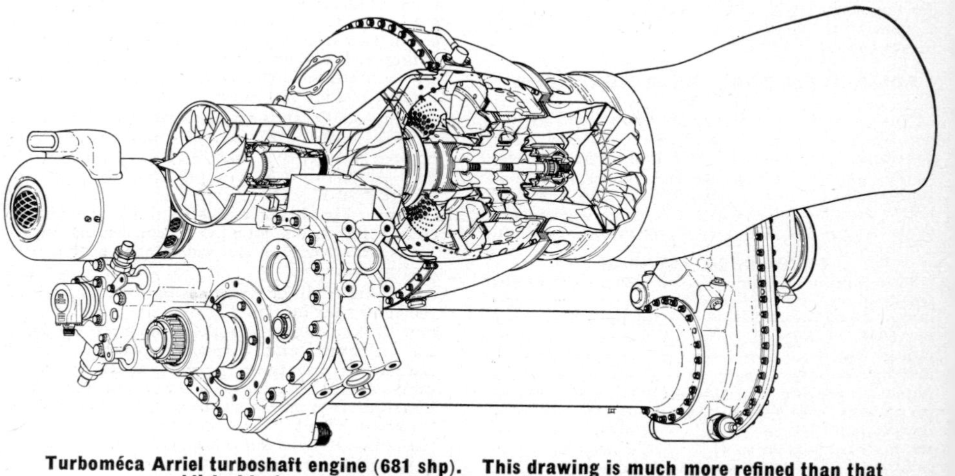

Turboméca Arriel turboshaft engine (681 shp). This drawing is much more refined than that published last year and shows the changed configuration now adopted

Astazou XIV (alias AZ14). Developed from Astazou XII. Powers early Jetstream business aircraft at 853 ehp.

Astazou XVI (alias AZ16). Higher rated version of Astazou XIV and first engine to enter production with new Turboméca aircooled turbine. Completed French official endurance tests in November 1968 at 1,073 ehp. Fully flight tested by CGTM in modified Nord 260, following initial testing in a Morane-Saulnier MS 1500 Epervier. Further endurance testing carried out with distilled water injection to provide flat rating performance. The XVID, without starter/generator, powers the Jetstream; the XVIZ powers the Nord 260A. On offer as alternative power plant for IAI Arava STOL transport. The Astazou XVIG, equipped for sustained inverted flight, was certificated by the Services Officiels Français on 30 April 1971; it powers the Argentinian Pucará combat aircraft. By the end of 1973, 50 Astazou XVI engines had been built.

Astazou XVIII. Higher rated version of Astazou XVI which first ran in early 1969 with T-O rating of 1,154 ehp. Potential application in Astazou XVI installations.

Astazou XX. Under development. This engine has two transonic axial compressor stages in titanium, in addition to the centrifugal stage machined in steel. Maximum T-O rating is 1,445 ehp.

The following description relates to versions from the Astazou XIVC to XX. Details of the Astazou series of turboshafts are given separately.

Type: Single-shaft axial-plus-centrifugal turboprop.

Propeller: Hamilton Standard three-blade single-acting, counterweight type with hydraulically-actuated variable pitch from full negative through to feather position. Emergency hydraulic feathering provided. Diameter to suit individual applications.

Reduction Gear: Mounted in tapered cylindrical casing at front of engine, with two-stage epicyclic reduction gear having helical primary gears and straight secondary gears. Reduction ratio 24·115 : 1 (XVIG, 21·8 : 1). Driven from front of compressor and mounted on ball and roller bearings. (Astazou XX gearbox incorporates torquemeter.)

Air Intake: Annular air intake at rear of reduction gear casing. Hot-air de-icing.

Compressor: Two-stage axial followed by single-stage centrifugal with single-sided impeller. Two rows of stator blades aft of each axial rotor. Centrifugal stage has radial and axial diffusers. Axial stages have steel discs with integral steel blades. Discs and two-piece steel impeller located on compressor shaft by radial lugs. Shaft carried on ball bearings ahead of stage-one axial disc and ahead of impeller. (Astazou XX has a four-stage compressor, comprising three axial followed by one centrifugal.)

Combustion System: Reverse-flow annular type with centrifugal fuel injector using rotary atomiser disc. Ignition by two ventilated torch igniters.

Turbine: Three-stage axial with blades integral with discs. (Air cooling provided for Astazou XVI, XVIII and XX.) Discs attached by curvic couplings and through-bolts. Rotor carried on compressor rear ball bearing and roller bearing aft of stage-three disc supported by struts across turbine exhaust.

Jet Pipe: Fixed type with curved inner cone.

Accessories: Mounted on casing forming rear of air intake. Drive pads provided for starter/generator, oil pump, fuel pump and speed governor, tacho-generator, AC generator (optional) and hydraulic pump (optional).

Mounting: Trunnion located on each side of turbine casing front flange, plus third trunnion on underside of turbine casing.

Fuel System: Automatic constant-speed system with propeller Beta-control and Turboméca "thermic" load limiter and speed governor.

Fuel Grades: AIR 3404, 3405, or 3407.

Lubrication System: Pressure lubrication to bearings and reduction gear, with 14 pint (8 litre) oil tank mounted at front of engine.

Oil Specification: AIR 3515 or synthetic AIR 3573.

Starting: Electric.

Dimensions:

Diameter over intake cowl	21·5 in (546 mm)
Overall length, including propeller	80·6 in (2,047 mm)

Weights:

With accessories:

Astazou XIV	approx 454 lb (206 kg)
Astazou XVID	452 lb (205 kg)
Astazou XVIG	502 lb (228 kg)
Astazou XVIZ	468 lb (213 kg)
Astazou XVIII	approx 452 lb (205 kg)
Astazou XX	484 lb (220 kg)

Performance Ratings:

T-O:

Astazou XIV 853 ehp (800 shp) at 43,000 rpm

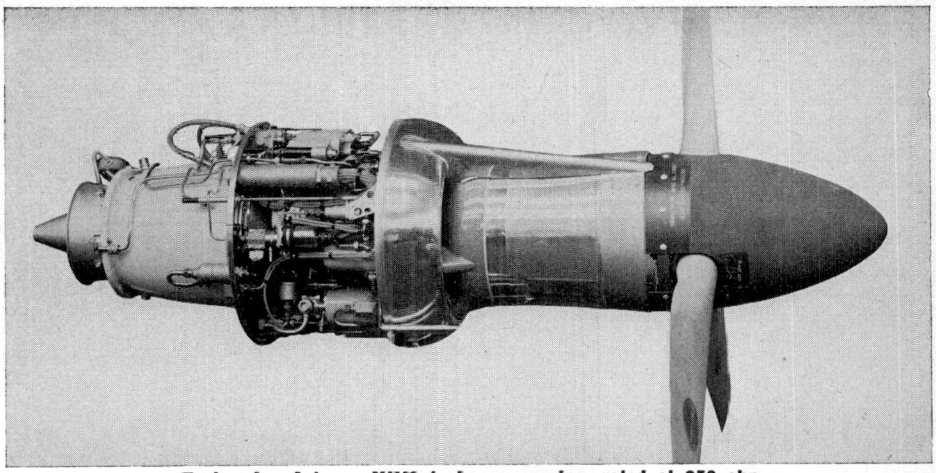

Turboméca Astazou XIVC turboprop engine, rated at 853 ehp

Astazou XVID 969 ehp (913 shp) at 43,089 rpm

Astazou XVIG, XVIZ 1,020 ehp (965 shp) at 43,000 rpm

Astazou XVIII 1,154 ehp (1,090 shp) at 43,000 rpm

Astazou XX 1,442 ehp (1,381 shp) at 42,000 rpm

Max continuous:

Astazou XIV 770 ehp (720 shp) at 43,000 rpm

Astazou XVID 840 ehp (786 shp) at 43,089 rpm

Astazou XVIG, XVIZ 934 ehp (877 shp) at 43,000 rpm

Astazou XVIII 1,085 ehp (1,030 shp) at 43,000 rpm

Astazou XX 1,276 ehp (1,217 shp) at 42,000 rpm

Specific Fuel Consumption:

At T-O rating:

Astazou XIV 0·547 lb/shp/hr (0·248 kg/cv/hr)

Astazou XVI (all versions) 0·525 lb/shp/hr (0·235 kg/cv/hr)

Astazou XVIII 0·505 lb/ehp/hr (0·229 kg/cve/hr)

Astazou XX 0·449 lb/ehp/hr (0·201 kg/cve/hr)

At max continuous rating:

Astazou XIV 0·554 lb/shp/hr (0·253 kg/cv/hr)

Astazou XVI (all versions) 0·534 lb/shp/hr (0·239 kg/cv/hr)

Astazou XVIII 0·50 lb/ehp/hr (0·227 kg/cve/hr)

Astazou XX 0·462 lb/ehp/hr (0·206 lb/cve/hr)

TURBOMÉCA ASTAZOU TURBOSHAFT

This is the turboshaft series of the Astazou family and is derived from the early second-generation Astazou II turboprop fitted to the Mitsubishi MU-2 and Pilatus Turbo-Porter. By 1 January 1974, 886 Astazou turboshaft engines had been built. The variants are as follows:

Astazou IIA. Rated at 523 shp and powers the Aérospatiale SA 318C Alouette II Astazou helicopter.

Astazou IIN. Original version of turboshaft, powering the prototype Aérospatiale/Westland SA 341.

Astazou IIIN. Definitive turboshaft for Anglo-French helicopter programme for production SA 341. Derived from Astazou IIA but with revised profile of turbine, using higher temperature alloy to match power needs of SA 341. In production jointly by Turboméca and Rolls-Royce (1971) Ltd. Total of 286 built by 1 January 1974.

Astazou XIVB and XIVF. In production for the SA 319B Alouette III; XIVB is civil and XIVF military. Flat rated to 591 shp (one hour) up to 13,125 ft (4,000 m) or +55°C. By end of December 1973, 130 of these engines had been delivered.

Astazou XVIA. Higher-rated version fitted to the Aérospatiale SA 360.

Astazou XVIIIA. Further increase in power gained by improved turbine, allowing higher gas temperature. Powers SA 360.

The following description relates to the Astazou IIIN except where otherwise indicated:

Type: Single-shaft axial-plus-centrifugal turboshaft.

Reduction Gear: Similar to Astazou XIV turboprop. Reduction ratio 7·039 : 1 (Astazou XIVB/F, 7·345; XVIA, XVIIIA, 7·375).

Air Intake: Annular air intake at rear of reduction gear casing.

Compressor: Single-stage axial (IIA, IIN, IIIN) or two-stage axial (all subsequent versions) followed by single-stage centrifugal with single-sided impeller. Two rows of stator blades aft of axial rotor. Otherwise similar to Astazou XIV compressor. Air mass flow 5·5 lb/sec (2·5 kg/sec).

Combustion System: Similar to combustor on Astazou XIV.

Turbine: Similar to Astazou XIV.

Jet Pipe: Similar to Astazou XIV.

Accessories: Mounted on casing forming rear of air intake. Drive pads provided for starter/generator, oil pump, fuel pump and governor, tacho-generator, AC generator (optional).

Mounting: At front by flange located at power take-off section, and at rear by two lugs on accessory mounting pad section.

Fuel System: Automatic constant speed control with speed governor.

Lubrication System: Pressure type with gear type pumps. Oil tank of 14 pint (8 litre) capacity mounted at front of engine.

Starting: Electrical, automatic.

Dimensions:

Height: Astazou IIA	18 in (458 mm)
Astazou IIIN	18·1 in (460 mm)
Astazou XVIA, XVIIIA	27·48 in (698 mm)
Width: Astazou IIA	18·8 in (480 mm)
Astazou IIIN	18·1 in (460 mm)

Turboméca Astazou XVIA turboshaft engine, flat rated at 873 shp

Length overall: Astazou IIA 50·0 in (1,272 mm)
Astazou IIIN, XIVB/F 56·3 in (1,433 mm)
Astazou XVIA, XVIIIA 52·2 in (1,327 mm)

WEIGHT:
Bare engine: Astazou IIA 249 lb (113 kg)
Astazou IIIN 253 lb (115 kg)
Equipped: Astazou XIVB/F 366 lb (166 kg)
Astazou XVIA, XVIIIA 341 lb (155 kg)

PERFORMANCE RATINGS:
Max power: Astazou IIA 523 shp (530 cv)
Astazou IIIN 592 shp (600 cv)
One hour: Astazou XIVB/F 591 shp (599 cv)
Astazou XVIA 873 shp (885 cv)
maintained at sea level to 30°C
Astazou XVIIIA 873 shp (885 cv)
maintained at sea level to 40°C
Max continuous: Astazou IIA 473 shp (480 cv)
Astazou IIIN 523 shp (530 cv)
Astazou XIVB/F 543 shp (550 cv)
Astazou XVIA, XVIIIA 805 shp (816 cv)

SPECIFIC FUEL CONSUMPTION:
At max power rating:
Astazou IIA 0·623 lb (0·283 kg)/shp/hr
Astazou IIIN 0·643 lb (0·292 kg)/shp/hr
Astazou XIVB/F 0·624 lb (0·283 kg)/shp/hr
Astazou XVIA 0·555 lb (0·252 kg)/shp/hr
Astazou XVIIIA 0·540 lb (0·246 kg)/shp/hr
At max continuous rating:
Astazou IIA 0·634 lb (0·288 kg)/shp/hr
Astazou IIIN 0·659 lb (0·299 kg)/shp/hr
Astazou XIVB/F 0·648 lb (0·294 kg)/shp/hr
Astazou XVIA 0·567 lb (0·257 kg)/shp/hr
Astazou XVIIIA 0·545 lb (0·247 kg)/shp/hr

TURBOMÉCA BASTAN

The Bastan turboprop is one of the second generation of Turboméca engines, which are characterised by their two-stage axial-centrifugal compressor. The Bastan VIC rated at 1,055 ehp powers the Aérospatiale N 262 and the 1,000 hp Bastan VID powers the Argentinian GII. Maximum TBO at the end of 1969 was 1,800 hr in the N 262.

By the end of December 1973 Turboméca had built 446 Bastan VICs, and production continues.

A second version, the Bastan VII, flat rated at 1,046 shp, is derived from the Bastan VI and powers the Aérospatiale Frégate. By the end of December 1973, 93 of these more powerful turboprops had been built. The Bastan VII was certificated by the Services Officiels Français on 3 August 1970.

The following description relates to both the Bastan VI and VII except for the differences indicated:

TYPE: Single-shaft axial-plus-centrifugal turboprop.

REDUCTION GEAR: Two-stage epicyclic type, inside tapered cylindrical casing at front of engine. Ratio 1 : 21·0957. Propeller shaft carried in ball bearing at front.

AIR INTAKE: Annular intake at rear of reduction gear casing. Outer wall of intake, of triangular cross-section, provides mounting for accessories. Front ball bearing for compressor shaft carried by air intake assembly.

COMPRESSOR CASING: Central portion carries rear ball bearing for compressor shaft.

COMPRESSOR: Single axial stage for Bastan VIC, and two axial stages for Bastan VII, followed by single centrifugal stage. Two rows of diffuser vanes between axial stages and two more aft of the centrifugal stage, of which the first is radial and the second axial. On Bastan VII first axial rotor blades are titanium and pin-mounted in disc, and second axial rotor blades are light alloy integral with disc. Bastan VIC pressure ratio 5·83 : 1 and air mass flow 10 lb (4·5 kg)/sec. Bastan VII pressure ratio 6·68 : 1 and mass flow 13·1 lb (5·9 kg)/sec. Water-methanol injection in Bastan VIC.

COMBUSTION CHAMBER: Direct-flow annular type. Usual Turboméca rotary atomiser fuel injection system. Two torch igniters. Gas temperature before turbine 870°C.

TURBINE CASING: Houses combustion chamber and turbine nozzle assembly. Supports engine rear roller bearing at rear end.

TURBINE: Three-stage axial-flow turbine with separate discs. Each turbine preceded by axial-flow nozzle guide vane assembly.

JET PIPE: Annular welded sheet assembly comprising cylindrical outer casing and central bullet fairing.

ACCESSORIES DRIVE: Upper pinion train drives dynamo starter, propeller governor and fuel pump with fuel metering device. Lower gear drives electric tachometer transmitter, fuel pump, 20kVA alternator and landing gear pump. All accessories mounted on intake casing.

MOUNTING: Three attachment points, two lateral, one at bottom of engine.

ENGINE CONTROL: By two governors. One adjusts fuel flow entering engine so that it is maintained at the value set by the power control lever, as a function of the variations of pressure and temperature at the engine air intake. The second governor maintains the propeller rpm at the value set by the rpm control lever, by varying propeller pitch.

The 1,046 shp Turboméca Bastan VII single-shaft turboprop powering the Frégate

STARTING: Automatic starter/generator on Bastan VII.

DIMENSIONS:
Height: Bastan VIC 30·53 in (775·5 mm)
Width: Bastan VIC 26·97 in (685 mm)
Diameter: Bastan VII 21·7 in (550 mm)
Length: Bastan VIC 60·95 in (1,548·6 mm)
Bastan VII 75·2 in (1,911 mm)

WEIGHT, DRY:
Fully equipped:
Bastan VIC 710 lb (322 kg)
Bastan VII approx 816 lb (370 kg)

PERFORMANCE RATINGS (S/L, ISA):
Bastan VIC:
T-O and max continuous
1,060 ehp (798 shp) at 33,500 rpm
Bastan VII
T-O 1,460 ehp (1,046 shp) at 32,000 rpm
maintained up to 40°C or to 11,975 ft (3,650 m)
Max continuous
1,405 ehp (1,046 shp) at 32,000 rpm
maintained up to 36°C

SPECIFIC FUEL CONSUMPTION:
Bastan VIC, T-O 0·582 lb (0·264 kg)/ehp/hr
Bastan VII, T-O 0·525 lb (0·238 kg)/ehp/hr

TURBOMÉCA-AGUSTA TM-251 (TAA 230)

Announced in the Spring of 1964, the TM-251 is the single-shaft turboshaft which powers the Agusta A 106 light helicopter, and is sometimes referred to by the Agusta designation TAA 230.

The basic engine is produced by Turboméca and incorporates components developed from parts of the Astazou engine. It has a centrifugal compressor, annular combustion chamber and two-stage turbine. Mass flow is 4·2 lb (1·9 kg)/sec and pressure ratio 4·1 : 1. To its forward end is bolted a three-stage reduction gearbox, manufactured by Agusta and embodying an automatic hydraulic centrifugal clutch and free-wheel arrangement. The oil filter and pumps are also supplied by Agusta.

By December 1973 eight TAA 230s had been built.

DIMENSIONS:
Length overall 46·85 in (1,190 mm)
Max width 14·57 in (370 mm)
Max height 24·80 in (630 mm)

WEIGHT, DRY:
Fully equipped 290 lb (132 kg)

PERFORMANCE:
Max power 354 shp at 43,000 rpm
Rated power 270 shp

SPECIFIC FUEL CONSUMPTION:
At max power 0·86 lb (390 gr)/shp/hr
At rated power 0·838 lb (380 gr)/shp/hr

TURBOMÉCA ARTOUSTE III

The Artouste IIIB is a single-shaft turboshaft derived from the Artouste II. It is a member of the second generation of Turboméca engines with two-stage axial-centrifugal compressor and three-stage turbine. The Artouste IIIB has a pressure ratio of 5·2 : 1. Air mass flow is 9·5 lb/sec (4·3 kg/sec) at 33,300 rpm.

Type approval at the rating given below was received on 25 May 1961, following completion of a 150-hour official type test. By December 1973 a total of 1,730 Artouste IIIBs had been built. Production at Turboméca continues. In addition, Artouste IIIBs are being built under licence in India by Hindustan Aeronautics Ltd.

The Artouste IIIB, which powers the Aérospatiale SA 316B Alouette III, obtained FAA certification in March 1962 and in August 1968 similar certification of the Artouste IIC1, C2, C5 and C6, powering the SE 3130 and 313B Alouette II Artouste, was also obtained.

An uprated version, the Artouste IIID, was certificated on 30 April 1971. It differs in having a reduction gear giving 5,864 rpm at the drive-shaft (instead of 5,773 rpm) and in slightly revised equipment. The IIID powers a new Alouette III version; by the end of 1973 a total of 17 IIIDs had been built.

DIMENSIONS:
Length 71·46 in (1,815 mm)
Height 24·68 in (627 mm)
Width 19·96 in (507 mm)

WEIGHT, DRY:
Fully equipped:
Artouste IIIB 400 lb (182 kg)
Artouste IIID 392 lb (178 kg)

PERFORMANCE RATINGS (maintained up to 55°C at S/L or up to approximately 13,150 ft; 4,000 m):
T-O:
Artouste IIIB 563 shp
Artouste IIID 590 shp
Max continuous (both) 543 shp

SPECIFIC FUEL CONSUMPTION:
T-O:
Artouste IIIB 0·762 lb (0·346 kg)/shp/hr
Artouste IIID 0·747 lb (0·339 kg)/shp/hr
Max continuous (both) 0·77 lb (0·349 kg)/shp/hr

TURBOMÉCA TURMO

The Turmo is a free-turbine engine with both turboshaft and turboprop versions in service.

Each has a gas generator section comprising a single-stage axial plus single-stage centrifugal compressor, annular combustor, and two-stage turbine. The power turbine and transmission system vary according to the engine series. By the end of December 1973, 428 Turmo IIIC$_3$, C$_5$ and E$_3$ geared turboshafts and 775 Turmo IIIC$_4$ direct-drive turboshafts had been delivered. The main variants of the Turmo are as follows:

The 563 shp Turboméca Artouste IIIB single-shaft helicopter turboshaft

Turmo IIIC$_3$. This was the original engine of the triple-engined SA 321 Super Frelon helicopter. Maximum contingency rating is 1,480 shp.

Turmo IIIC$_4$. Developed from Turmo IIIC$_3$ and with a maximum contingency rating of 1,384 shp, this all-weather version is being manufactured jointly by Turboméca and Rolls-Royce to power SA 330 Puma twin-engined helicopters as part of the Franco-British helicopter agreement of October 1967. Certificated by the Services Officiels Français on 9 October 1970.

Turmo IIIC$_5$, IIIC$_6$, IIIC$_7$. Similar to Turmo IIIC$_3$ but with different ratings. The SA 321F and 321J Super Frelons powered by these engines obtained French certification in June 1968.

Turmo IIID. Turboprop version, similar in basic construction to Turmo IIIC series but with output speed limited to 6,000 rpm. Gas generator section is mounted beneath output shaft which is driven by free-turbine. The overhung forward drive leads through a freewheel and dog clutch to the propeller reduction gearbox, which gives a final drive at 1,200 rpm. A drive pad at the rear of the primary gearbox enables the engines of a multi-engined aircraft to be coupled together by spanwise shafting, as employed with the four Turmo IIID$_6$ turboprops powering the Breguet Br 941S STOL transport.

Turmo IIIE$_3$. Similar to Turmo IIIC$_3$ but with different ratings. In production for SA 321 Super Frelon.

Turmo III E$_3$. Similar except for material of gas-generator turbine, which is improved to allow higher gas temperatures.

Turmo IV. The Turmo IVA is a civil engine derived from the IIIC$_4$, with a maximum contingency rating of 1,417 shp. The IVB is a military version having the same ratings as the IIIC$_4$.

The following description applies generally to the Turmo IIIC$_3$, C$_4$, C$_5$ and E, except where indicated:

TYPE: Free-turbine axial-plus-centrifugal turboshaft.

REDUCTION GEAR: Turmo IIIC$_3$, C$_5$ and E$_3$ fitted with rear-mounted reduction gear mounted in bifurcated exhaust duct with rear-facing power take-off shaft. Output shaft from free-turbine drives into high-speed gear of simple helical spur train of 3·53 : 1 reduction ratio. Output shaft also drives reduction gear driving oil cooler fan mounted on front of main reduction gear case. Turmo IIIC$_4$ is a direct-drive engine.

AIR INTAKE: Annular forward-facing intake, with de-icing in Turmo IIIC$_4$ and C$_5$. Centre housing contains forward ball bearing for compressor shaft and bevel gear drive to accessories mounted above and below intake casing.

COMPRESSOR: Single-stage axial followed by single-stage centrifugal with single-sided impeller. Two rows of light alloy stator blades aft of axial stage. Centrifugal stage has steel radial and axial diffusers; impeller located by lugs on turbine shaft. Axial rotor blades, titanium in Turmo IIIC$_3$, C$_5$ and E$_3$ and steel in Turmo IIIC$_4$, pin-mounted in steel disc with integral shaft. Pressure ratio 5·9 : 1 on Turmo IIIC$_3$. Air mass flow 13 lb (5·9 kg)/sec. Axial rotor carried on ball bearing ahead of disc and roller bearing aft of disc. Also, ball bearing ahead of impeller.

COMBUSTION SYSTEM: Reverse-flow annular type with centrifugal fuel injector using rotary atomiser disc. Ignition by two ventilated torch igniters.

GAS GENERATOR TURBINE: Two-stage axial unit with integral rotor blades. Discs with curvic couplings through-bolted to compressor shaft. Carried on roller bearing at rear of second-stage disc.

POWER TURBINE: Two-stage axial unit in Turmo IIIC$_3$, C$_5$ and E$_3$, and single-stage in Turmo IIIC$_4$. Blades carried in discs by fir-tree roots. Rotor overhung from rear on through-bolted output shaft. Shaft carried on roller bearing at front (at rear of turbine disc) and ball bearing at rear (at input to reduction gear). In all advanced production engines of IIIC$_4$ derivation the power turbine speed is 22,840 rpm under all high-power conditions.

JET PIPE: Fixed type with lateral bifurcated exhaust duct in Turmo IIIC$_3$, C$_5$ and E$_3$, and single lateral duct on Turmo IIIC$_4$.

ACCESSORIES: Mounted above and below intake casing with drive pads for oil pump, fuel control unit, electric starter, tacho-generator and, on Turmo IIIC$_4$, oil cooler fan. Control unit remote drive also provided on Turmo IIIC$_4$ from bevel gear drive on power turbine output shaft.

MOUNTING: Two lateral supports fitted to lower part of turbine casing at rear flange output shaft protection tube. On Turmo IIIC$_4$, also on reduction gear case.

The 1,480 shp Turboméca Turmo IIIC$_3$ turboshaft which powers the Super Frelon helicopter

The 1,384 shp Turboméca Turmo IIIC$_4$ turboshaft which powers the SA 330 Puma helicopter

FUEL SYSTEM: Fuel control unit for gas generator on Turmo IIIC$_3$, C$_5$ and E$_3$, with speed limiter for power turbine also fitted on E$_3$. Constant-speed system fitted on Turmo IIIC$_4$ power turbine, with speed limiter also fitted on gas generator.

FUEL GRADE: AIR 3405 for Turmo IIIC$_4$.

LUBRICATION SYSTEM: Pressure type with oil cooler and 23 Imperial pint (13 litre) tank at front of engine on Turmo IIIC$_4$, with oil tank only around intake casing on Turmo IIIC$_3$, C$_5$ and E$_3$. Oil cooler fan driven by rear-mounted reduction gear case on Turmo IIIC$_3$, C$_5$ and E$_3$, and by intake accessory drive gear on Turmo IIIC$_4$.

OIL SPECIFICATION: AIR 3155A, or synthetic AIR 3513, for Turmo IIIC$_4$.

STARTING: Automatic system with electric starter motor.

DIMENSIONS:
Height:
Turmo IIIC$_3$, C$_5$ and E$_3$ 28·2 in (716·5 mm)
Turmo IIIC$_4$ 28·3 in (719 mm)
Turmo IIID$_3$ 36·5 in (926 mm)
Width: Turmo IIIC$_3$, C$_5$ and E$_3$ 27·3 in (693 mm)
Turmo IIIC$_4$ 25·1 in (637 mm)
Turmo IIID$_3$ 36·8 in (934 mm)
Length:
Turmo IIIC$_3$ C$_5$ and E$_3$ 78·0 in (1,975·7 mm)
Turmo IIIC$_4$ 85·5 in (2,184 mm)
Turmo IIID$_3$ 73·6 in (1,868 mm)

WEIGHTS, DRY:
Turmo IIIC$_3$ and E$_3$, fully equipped 655 lb (297 kg)
Turmo IIIC$_5$, III$_6$ and IIIC$_7$ 716 lb (325 kg)
Turmo IIIC$_4$, equipped engine 496 lb (225 kg)
Turmo IIID$_3$, basic engine 805 lb (365 kg)

PERFORMANCE RATINGS:
T-O: Turmo IIIC$_3$, D$_3$ and E$_3$ 1,480 shp
Turmo IIIE$_6$ 1,584 shp
Max contingency:
Turmo IIIC$_4$ at 33,800 gas-generator rpm 1,384 shp
Turmo IIIC$_6$ at 33,550 gas-generator rpm 1,550 shp
Turmo IIIC$_7$ at 33,800 gas-generator rpm 1,610 rpm
Turmo IVA at 33,950 gas-generator rpm 1,417 shp
Turmo IVC at 33,800 gas-generator rpm 1,560 shp
T-O and intermediate contingency:
Turmo IIIC$_4$ at 33,450 gas-generator rpm 1,312 shp
Turmo IIIC$_5$ 1,408 shp
Max continuous:
Turmo IIIC$_3$ and E$_3$ 1,282 shp
Turmo IIIC$_4$ 1,170 shp
Turmo IIIC$_5$, C$_6$, C$_7$ 1,275 shp
Turmo IIID$_3$ 1,282 shp
Turmo IIIE$_6$ 1,276 shp
Turmo IVA at 32,800 gas-generator rpm 1,170 shp
Turmo IVC at 32,400 gas-generator rpm 1,260 shp

SPECIFIC FUEL CONSUMPTION:
At T-O rating:
Turmo IIIC$_3$ and E$_3$ 0·603 lb (0·274 kg)/shp/hr
Turmo IIID$_3$ 0·616 lb (0·280 kg)/shp/hr
At max contingency rating:
Turmo IIIC$_4$, C$_5$, C$_6$ C$_7$ and IV 0·632 lb (0·287 kg)/shp/hr
Turmo IVA 0·629 lb (0·285 kg)/shp/hr
At T-O and intermediate contingency rating:
Turmo IIIC$_4$ 0·640 lb (0·290 kg)/shp/hr
At max continuous rating:
Turmo IIIC$_3$ and E$_4$ 0·640 lb (0·290 kg)/shp/hr
Turmo IIIC$_4$, C$_5$, C$_6$, C$_7$ and IVC 0·656 lb (0·294 kg)/shp/hr
Turmo IIID$_3$ 0·640 lb (0·290 kg)/shp/hr

TURBOMÉCA 1,800 hp

To power the Aérospatiale SA 331 Super Puma helicopter a new turboshaft engine, rated at an initial 1,800 cv (1,775 shp) for take-off and intermediate contingency, is under development. Derived partly from the Turmo family, it incorporates all the latest features of the company's advanced engines, including: rapid-strip modular construction; three axial stages of compression plus one centrifugal; later fuel inlet to centrifugal atomiser; two-stage gas-generator turbine (probably with cooled blades); two-stage free power turbine; and lateral exhaust.

The following data are provisional:

DIMENSIONS:
Length, intake face to reduction gear 62·99 in (1,600 mm)
Length, nose bullet to exhaust duct extremity 76·26 in (1,937 mm)
Width 17·52 in (445 mm)
Height over exhaust duct 24·41 in (620 mm)

WEIGHT, DRY: 330 lb (150 kg)

PERFORMANCE RATINGS (ISA, S/L):
Max contingency 1,910 shp at 36,300 gas-generator rpm
T-O and intermediate 1,775 shp at 35,500 gas-generator rpm
Max continuous 1,630 shp at 34,750 gas-generator rpm

SPECIFIC FUEL CONSUMPTION:
Max contingency 0·461 lb (0·209 kg)/shp/hr
T-O and intermediate 0·463 lb (0·210 kg)/shp/hr
Max continuous 0·470 lb (0·213 kg)/shp/hr

TURBOMÉCA TURMASTAZOU

The Turmastazou turboshaft engine comprises the Astazou single-shaft turboprop with the addition of a free-turbine (Turmo is an abbreviation for "turbine motoriste" and by implication refers to a free-turbine engine). Development is proceeding on the five engines built by March 1969. The Turmastazou is intended for helicopter applications and is also in service with the Orléans-type Bertin Aérotrain.

TYPE: Free-turbine axial-plus-centrifugal turboshaft.

POWER DRIVE: Direct at rear of engine. No reduction gear fitted.

AIR INTAKE: Annular forward-facing intake at front of engine, feeding direct to compressor inlet.

COMPRESSOR AND COMBUSTION SYSTEM: Similar to Astazou.

COMPRESSOR TURBINE: Two-stage axial unit with rotor blades integral with turbine discs. Discs through-bolted with curvic couplings.

POWER TURBINE: Two-stage axial unit with rotor blades integral with turbine discs. Discs through-bolted with curvic couplings. Constant output speed 29,000 rpm.

JET PIPE: None fitted as standard.

ACCESSORIES: Mounted on compressor casing behind oil tank. Drive pads fitted for oil pump, tacho-generator, fuel control unit, starter/generator, AC generator and hydraulic pump (optional).

FUEL SYSTEM: Automatic control system with constant speed control of free-turbine.

LUBRICATION SYSTEM: Pressure type system with gear pump. Oil tank mounted around front of engine.

STARTING: Automatic electrical starting.

DIMENSIONS:
Height 21·7 in (552 mm)
Width 17·3 in (440 mm)
Length overall 52·4 in (1,332 mm)

WEIGHT:
Complete with accessories 352 lb (160 kg)

PERFORMANCE RATINGS:
Turmastazou XIV:
T-O 889 shp
Max continuous 792 shp
Turmastazou XVI:
T-O 986 shp
Max continuous 918 shp

SPECIFIC FUEL CONSUMPTION:
Turmastazou XIV:
T-O 0·507 lb (0·230 kg)/shp/hr
Max continuous 0·514 lb (0·233 kg)/shp/hr
Turmastazou XVI:
T-O 0·507 lb (0·230 kg)/shp/hr
Max continuous 0·514 lb (0·233 kg)/shp/hr

The Turboméca Turmastazou XIV free-turbine turboshaft

TURBOMÉCA DOUBLE TURMASTAZOU

The Double Turmastazou free-turbine coupled turboshaft comprises two Turmastazou turboshafts coupled by a combining gearbox to drive a common output shaft. The engine is intended for twin-engined helicopter installations and is specified for a new helicopter by Agusta.

The Double Turmastazou XIV comprises two Turmastazou XIV engines and is under development at 1,775 shp. A higher-powered model, the 2,071 shp Double Turmastazou XVI, is derived from the Astazou XVI. In both cases the usual output shaft speed is 6,600 rpm.

TURBOMÉCA-SNECMA

GROUPEMENT TURBOMÉCA-SNECMA GRTS

OFFICES:
1 Rue Beaujon, BP 37, Paris cédex 75008
Telephone: 924-18-61

ADMINISTRATORS:
R. Florenti
E. Lacrouts

MANAGEMENT CONTROL COMMITTEE:
R. Martin
L. Henrion

FINANCIAL COMMISSARY:
C. Hirt

Announced in March 1969, Groupement Turboméca-SNECMA is a company formed jointly by Société Turboméca and SNECMA to be responsible for the design, development, manufacture, sales and service support of the Larzac all-axial small turbofan launched in 1968 as a joint venture by the two companies. Groupement Turboméca-SNECMA has no capital at present and primarily comprises a joint management organisation to produce the new engine.

TURBOMÉCA-SNECMA LARZAC

Originally this small turbofan was planned for a wide range of applications, and the first prototype was a 2,200 lb (1,000 kg) engine aimed at the commercial market. This type of engine ran in May 1969 and began flight development in a pod carried by a Constellation in March 1971. By this time the main immediate market had shifted to military trainers, and GRTS designed the Larzac 04 for this purpose. A commercial version, the Larzac 03, is being developed for the Aérospatiale Corvette.

In February 1972 the Larzac 04 was selected for a joint Franco-German programme to provide propulsion for the Alpha Jet trainer (see International entry in "Aircraft" section). In addition to the two French partners in GRTS, two German companies, MTU and KHD, were added to the programme. Both have played a part in the manufacture of prototype engines and the achievement of endurance tests. All four companies will share in production, and complete engines will be assembled in both countries for the Alpha Jet programme.

Following the adoption of the Alpha Jet by Belgium, the Belgian engine company FN is also expected to participate in the Larzac 04 programme. The expected work-split is: Turboméca 29·4 per cent, SNECMA 23·0 per cent, MTU 22·6 per cent, KHD 22·0 per cent, and other companies (including FN) 3·0 per cent.

Turboméca-SNECMA Larzac 04 two-shaft turbofan, rated at 2,965 lb (1,345 kg) st

Bench testing of the Larzac 04 began in May 1972. Flight development with the Constellation testbed began in March 1973, and with a Falcon 10 in July 1973. The first Alpha Jet flew on 26 October 1973, and the second on 9 January 1974; both dates were well ahead of schedule. Military certification of the Larzac 04 is scheduled to be achieved in 1975. The rating given is at a turbine entry temperature of 1,031°C; higher thrusts are planned, using an aircooled HP turbine.

GRTS states that the Larzac 04 is the subject of several evaluation requests from French and foreign aircraft manufacturers for military training and liaison aircraft and civil executive jet aircraft. It is claimed that the engine can meet all these uses without significant modification.

In September 1972 the French Services Officiels approved an agreement between GRTS and Teledyne CAE covering the production, marketing and after-sales support of the Larzac in the United States and Canada. As described in the Teledyne CAE entry, the US engine will be designated Model 490-04.

The Larzac 04 has a two-stage fan, four-stage HP compressor, annular combustion chamber with vaporising burners, single-stage HP turbine with cooled blades and single-stage LP turbine. Maximum airflow is 60·8 lb (26·6 kg)/sec, pressure ratio 10·6 and by-pass ratio 1·13. A single fixed-area jet pipe is used. All accessories are driven by the HP spool and grouped under the fan case. The engine is mounted by an isostatic suspension on either side of the centre of gravity. The engine is of modular design and is intended to produce minimum noise and smoke.

DIMENSIONS:
Overall length of basic engine 45·3 in (1,150 mm)
Overall diameter 23·6 in (600 mm)

WEIGHT, DRY:
Larzac 03 573 lb (260 kg)
Larzac 04 618 lb (280 kg)

T-O THRUST (S/L, static):
Larzac 03 2,755 lb (1,250 kg)
Larzac 04 2,965 lb (1,345 kg)

SPECIFIC FUEL CONSUMPTION:
Larzac 03 0·68
Larzac 04 0·70

GERMANY

(DEMOCRATIC REPUBLIC)

ODA

OSTDEUTSCHES AUTOMOBILWERK

ADDRESS:
VEB Sachsenring Automobilwerk, 95 Zwickau

The Trabant car, widely marketed in Eastern Europe, is powered by an aircooled engine which was adapted as the power unit of the Bulgarian Bisier motorised glider and is likely to be used in other light aircraft.

TYPE: Two-cylinder aircooled two-stroke piston engine.

CYLINDERS: Bore 2·834 in (72·0 mm). Stroke 2·874 in (73·0 mm). Swept volume 36·3 cu in (0·5945 litres). Both cylinders cast in single light alloy block, with deep machined fins and steel liners. Compression ratio 7·6 : 1.

INDUCTION SYSTEM: Dry air filter, single horizontal BVF 28 HB 2-7 carburettor; 88-octane petrol.

IGNITION: 220W generator, rotating distributor, single 18 mm Type 260 Isolator sparking plug in each cylinder.

PERFORMANCE RATING:
Max 26 hp at 4,200 rpm

Trabant motor car engine installed in Bisier powered glider (*Skrzydlata Polska*)

GERMANY

(FEDERAL REPUBLIC)

FICHTEL & SACHS

FICHTEL & SACHS AG

OFFICES AND WORKS:
872 Schweinfurt, Postfach 52
Telephone: Schweinfurt 0 97 21

Fichtel & Sachs has converted its KM-48 rotating piston engine for use in sailplane auxiliary propulsion. The 160 cc unit is aircooled externally and gas-cooled internally, and complete with accessories, gasoline and propeller weighs 22 lb (10 kg). Compression ratio is 8 : 1 and power rating 10 hp (10·1 cv) at 5,000 rpm. The engine has been flown in a single-seat Schleicher Ka 8 sailplane, the maximum level speed of which was 52 knots (60 mph; 96 km/h).

In January 1974 the company released preliminary details of a fan pod in which a 40 hp Wankel-type engine drives a five-bladed fixed-pitch fan running in a duct made of glass-reinforced plastics. The pod was to be evaluated first on a boat, but to be offered to aircraft constructors later in 1974. In February Rhein-Flugzeugbau (see "Aircraft" section) completed the experimental Fanliner, in which a Fichtel & Sachs engine drives a fan mounted in a short ring duct aft of the wing. RFB later issued preliminary details of its own fan pod, as reported under RFB in this section.

HIRTH

HIRTH MOTOREN KG

ADDRESS:
7141 Benningen/Neckar, Kreis Ludwigsburg
Telephone: Marbach (07144) 6057

Although many F 10 engines remain in use, production of this model has ceased (a brief description appeared in the 1972-73 *Jane's*). The company is concentrating its aviation marketing upon the specially designed engines described below:

HIRTH F 20

This engine has two cylinders, each just over twice as large as those of the four-cylinder F 10. Although total capacity is only slightly greater than that of the earlier engine, power is more than doubled. In its present applications the engine has a cooling airflow induced by a high-speed axial blower. This unit and the cooling duct are allowed for in the dimensions and weights given.

TYPE: Two-cylinder in-line aircooled two-stroke.

CYLINDERS: Bore 3·071 in (78 mm). Stroke 2·68 in (68 mm). Capacity 39·65 cu in (650 cc). Compression ratio 10·45 : 1.

INDUCTION: Two laterally mounted Walbro WD A 46 carburettors.

FUEL GRADE: Regular-grade automotive gasoline mixed with 1 part in 25 of high-grade branded two-stroke lubricating oil.

IGNITION: Bosch double-capacitor discharge ignition, 12V, 46W. Two Champion N2 or N2G sparking plugs in each cylinder.

PROPELLER DRIVE: Output from crankshaft counter-clockwise seen from front.

STARTING: Bosch electric, or recoil starter drum at rear. Recoil starter weight 3·8 lb (1·7 kg).

DIMENSIONS:
Length (excluding output shaft) 15·68 in (398 mm)
Height (excluding spark plugs) 13·75 in (349 mm)
Width (basic carcase) 11·38 in (289·5 mm)

WEIGHT, DRY: 87·3 lb (39·6 kg)

PERFORMANCE RATING:
Max T-O 52·5 hp at 6,000 rpm

The 52·5 hp Hirth F 20 two-stroke piston engine

HIRTH F 21

This is similar to the F 20 but has a larger cylinder bore and lower compression ratio. It is planned to obtain the LBA (Luftfahrt-Bundesamt) Airworthiness Certificate.

CYLINDERS: As F 20 except bore 3·228 in (82 mm). Capacity 43·81 cu in (718 cc). Compression ratio 9·8 : 1.

PERFORMANCE RATING:
Max T-O 60 hp at 6,000 rpm

KHD

KLÖCKNER-HUMBOLDT-DEUTZ AG

ADDRESS:
Oberursel Works, Oberursel, Hohenmarkstrasse 60-70
Telephone: Oberursel (06171) 5 10 41

This engine company, which 15 years ago made the Bristol Orpheus turbojet under licence, collaborated with Rolls-Royce on the development of the T112 APU (see the 1973-74 *Jane's*). From this KHD has developed independently the two power units described below.

KHD is also participating in the licence production of the T64 turboshaft engine (see MTU, and GE in USA section).

KHD T212

This is the power plant of the Dornier Experimental Kiebitz rotor platform (see "RPVs"). It comprises the T112 coupled directly to a front-mounted radial compressor and running at the same nominal speed of 64,000 rpm. Like the T112 it has a three-point mounting, but the added radial compressor, carried on five struts ahead of the gas-generator, demands a modified output end, where the electric starter/generator is also mounted. In the Kiebitz a flexible hose carries the air to the hub of the lifting rotor.

DIMENSIONS:
Overall length 36·6 in (930 mm)
Width 12·7 in (322 mm)
Height 13·6 in (345 mm)

WEIGHT, DRY:
With all accessories 88·2 lb (40 kg)

PERFORMANCE RATING:
Air supply of 1·41 lb (0·64 kg)/sec at pressure of 40·9 lb/sq in (2·82 bars)

FUEL CONSUMPTION: 124·6 lb (56·5 kg)/hr

The KHD T212 air compressor, power unit of the Dornier Experimental Kiebitz RPV

KHD T312

This is an APU derived directly from the T112 to meet the requirements of the Panavia MRCA. Compared with the T112 it is slightly more powerful, and has a different accessory arrangement to meet the need for reduced overall length.

DIMENSIONS:
Overall length 21·2 in (538 mm)
Width 14·1 in (357 mm)
Height 15·0 in (382 mm)

WEIGHT, DRY:
With all accessories 78·9 lb (35·8 kg)

PERFORMANCE RATINGS:
Max short-time output 153 hp (114 kW)
Max continuous, shaft 137 hp (102 kW)
Max continuous, bleed
0·49 lb (0·22 kg)/sec at 54·5 lb/sq in (3·76 bars)

SPECIFIC FUEL CONSUMPTION:
0·428 lb/hp/hr (0·574 lb/kW/hr)

The KHD T312 APU, under development for the Panavia MRCA

LIMBACH

LIMBACH MOTORENBAU

HEAD OFFICE AND WORKS:
D-533 Königswinter 21, Sassenberg
Telephone: (02244) 2322

This company manufactures four-stroke piston engines for ultra-light aeroplanes and powered gliders. All are of similar basic design, though one sub-type has a greater cylinder stroke, and a new range about to go into production has substantially larger capacity.

LIMBACH SL 1700

Several variants of this engine have been certificated by the Luftfahrt-Bundesamt (Federal Office of Civil Aviation). Apart from the first sub-type listed below all are four-stroke (Otto) engines:

Limbach SL 1700D. Dual-ignition. Not certificated. Fitted to Sportavia-Pützer RF7.

Limbach SL 1700D flat-four two-stroke engine, rated at 65 hp

Sportavia-Limbach SL 1700E. Basic engine of the current range. Fitted to Sportavia-Pützer RF5 and RF5B.

Limbach SL 1700EA. Differs in having front-end starter and different induction system. Fitted to Scheibe SF-25C Falke.

Limbach SL 1700EAI. Similar to EA except equipped to drive Hoffmann variable-pitch propeller. Fitted to Scheibe SF 28.

Limbach SL 1700EB. Similar to E except for having increased cylinder stroke and twin carburettors.

Limbach SL 1700EBI. Similar to EB except equipped to drive Hoffmann variable-pitch propeller. Fitted to Schleicher ASK 16.

Limbach SL 1700EC. Similar to E except for having a carburettor intake heating box.

Limbach SL 1700ECI. Similar to EC except equipped to drive Hoffmann variable-pitch propeller.

Sportavia-Limbach SL 1700EI. Similar to E except equipped to drive Hoffmann variable-pitch propeller. Optional for RF5B.

Unless otherwise stated, the following description refers to the SL 1700E:

TYPE: Four-cylinder horizontally-opposed air-cooled piston engine.

CYLINDERS: Bore 3·46 in (88 mm). Stroke 2·71 in (69 mm) (EB, EBI, 2·87 in; 74 mm). Swept volume 102·51 cu in (1,680 cc) (EB, EBI, 108·56 cu in; 1,800 cc). Compression ratio 8 : 1.

INDUCTION: Stromberg-Zenith 150CD carburettor (two in EB, EBI). (EA, EAI, one Zenith 28 RX2.)

FUEL GRADE: 90 octane.

IGNITION: Single Slick 4030 magneto feeding one Bosch WB 240 ERT1 plug in each cylinder.

STARTING: One Fiat 0·5 hp starter (EA, EAI, one Bosch 0·4 hp).

Sportavia-Limbach SL 1700E flat-four four-stroke engine, rated at 68 hp

ACCESSORIES: Ducellier 250W alternator (EA, EAI, 150W Ducati); APG 17.09.001 fuel pump (EA, EAI, 17.09.001A).

DIMENSIONS:

Length overall:	
SL 1700D	25·6 in (649 mm)
SL 1700EA, EAI	22·0 in (558 mm)
SL 1700E, EI, EC, ECI	24·33 in (618 mm)
other variants	22·8 in (580 mm)
Width overall:	
SL 1700D	31·5 in (800 mm)
SL 1700EA, EAI	30·3 in (770 mm)
other variants	30·1 in (764 mm)
Height overall:	
SL 1700D	17·8 in (451 mm)
SL 1700EA, EAI	15·4 in (392 mm)
other variants	14·5 in (368 mm)

WEIGHT, DRY:

SL 1700E, EI	161 lb (73 kg)
SL 1700EA, EAI	154 lb (70 kg)
SL 1700EB, EBI, EC, ECI	164 lb (74 kg)

PERFORMANCE RATINGS:

T-O:	
SL 1700D	65 hp at 3,600 rpm
SL 1700E, EI, EC, ECI	68 hp at 3,600 rpm
SL 1700EA, EAI	60 hp at 3,550 rpm
SL 1700EB, EBI	72 hp at 3,600 rpm
Continuous:	
SL 1700E, EI, EC, ECI	61 hp at 3,200 rpm
SL 1700EA, EAI	56 hp at 3,300 rpm
SL 1700EB, EBI	66 hp at 3,200 rpm

Limbach SL 1700EA flat-four four-stroke engine, rated at 60 hp

LIMBACH SL 2400

During the past year the company has been completing the development of this new engine, which has four cylinders of greater bore and slightly different stroke It is offered in two forms:

Limbach SL 2400EB. Basic engine, equipped to drive fixed-pitch propeller. Not yet certificated.

Limbach SL 2400EBI. Equipped to drive Hoffmann variable-pitch propeller. This engine is planned to go into production at the end of 1974 for use in powered gliders. Later it is planned to be certificated to FAR Pt 33.

TYPE: Four-cylinder horizontally-opposed air-cooled piston engine.

CYLINDERS: Bore 4·06 in (103 mm). Stroke 2·79 in (71 mm). Swept volume 144·5 cu ft (2,368 cc). Compression ratio 8 : 1.

INDUCTION: Two Stromberg-Zenith 175CD carburettors.

FUEL GRADE: 90 octane.

IGNITION: Single Slick 4030 magneto with high-temperature harness feeding one Beru ED225/14/3 plug in each cylinder.

STARTING: Fiat 0·5 hp starter.

ACCESSORIES: Ducellier 250W alternator, APG 17.09.001 fuel pump.

DIMENSIONS:

Length overall, over accessories	25·20 in (640 mm)
Width overall	31·10 in (790 mm)
Height overall	14·88 in (378 mm)

WEIGHT, DRY:	187·5 lb (85·0 kg)
PERFORMANCE RATINGS:	
T-O and max continuous	85 hp at 3,000 rpm

Limbach SL 2400 flat-four four-stroke engine, rated at 85 hp

MBB

MESSERSCHMITT-BÖLKOW-BLOHM GmbH

ADDRESS:
8 Munich 80, POB 801 220
Telephone: (0811) 6 00 01

DEVELOPMENT AND PRODUCTION CENTRES:
Ottobrunn bei München; Lampoldhausen; Hamburg; and Bölkow-Apparatebau GmbH at Nabern and Schrobenhausen

OFFICERS: See "Aircraft" section

As noted in the "Aircraft" section, Messerschmitt-Bölkow and Hamburger Flugzeugbau merged in May 1969 to form the MBB group. The former Bölkow element of this group is engaged in the design and development of a wide variety of medium- and high-energy rocket engines and motors. These include liquid bipropellant and monopropellant engines, liquid- and solid-propellant air-augmented rockets, solid-propellant motors for small and medium-size missiles, and hybrid engines. Other activities include thrust augmentation by afterburning, engine casing design, propellant insulation and mounting, and preparatory work towards series production and reliability.

Other recent development of liquid-propellant engines by MBB has embraced advanced thermodynamic combustion engines, injection and cooling of engines of low thrust level and engines with high- and medium-energy storable propellants. The following are some of the major programmes:

MBB MONOPROPELLANT ENGINES

MBB has developed N_2H_4 engines for thrust levels of 2/180/580/820/1,250/1,450 lb (1/82/263/372/567/658 kg). The smallest unit was developed from 1965 to 1968 for a satellite attitude-control system. The programme ended with a flight prototype optimised for the Shell 405 catalyst. The 580 lb (263 kg) engine was designed for a meteorological sounding rocket and was used for actual rocket flights in 1968. The 1,450 lb (658 kg) engine was the most powerful N_2H_4 monopropellant engine ever tested in Europe.

MBB MONOPROPELLANT GAS-GENERATORS

MBB has produced 13 different types of gas-generator, with flow rates from 0·0004 lb (0·00018 kg) to 18·2 lb (8·2 kg)/sec and using the propellants N_2H_4, $N_2H_4 + H_2O$, and $H_2O_2 + H_2O$. The bigger gas-generators are operating with catalytic and thermic decomposition. The smallest generator supplies a cold-gas satellite attitude-control system, while the bigger types are for propellant-tank pressurisation. Some 3,700 generators had been produced and delivered to industrial customers by the end of 1971.

MBB STORABLE ROCKET ENGINES

This engine family includes motors of 2·2/6·6/11/18/66/88/110/22,000 lb (1/3/5/8/30/40/50/10,000 kg) thrust. Except for the 2·2 lb engine, which uses MMH/N_2O_4, all other engines run on $AZ50/N_2O_4$. The 2·2 lb engine is in use as the attitude-control thruster for the Franco-German Symphonie communications satellite; it is designed for steady-state and pulse-mode operation. By September 1973 a total of 35 had been produced. The 88 lb engine was the vernier for the German third stage of the ELDO-A launcher, and in modified form it was to be used as the apogee motor for ELDO-II. This engine is highly qualified and in several ELDO-A launches has operated in space without failure. A total of 135 was produced. In 1973 a new tactical missile engine was developed, operating at thrust levels of 5,290 lb; 2,400 kg/2,646 lb; 1,200 kg/1,764 lb; 800 kg. The 22,000 lb (10,000 kg) engine was developed as the prototype power plant for an artillery rocket.

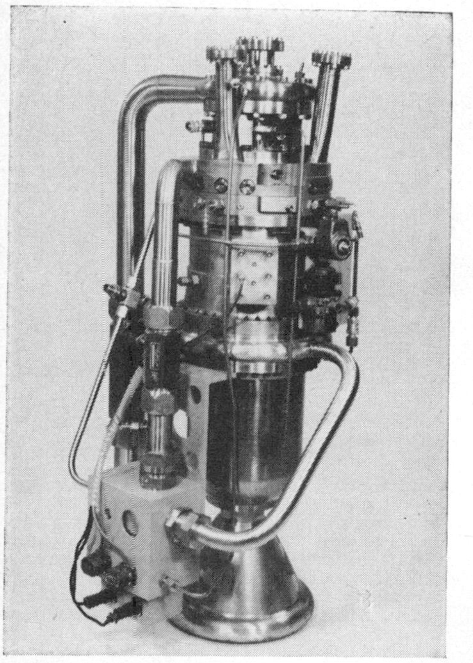

MBB 11,000 lb (5,000 kg) st lox/kerosene high-pressure topping cycle rocket engine

MBB HIGH-ENERGY ROCKET ENGINES

MBB has worked with the cryogenic propellant combination H_2/F_2 since 1962. After the installation of a fluorine liquefaction facility and a technology programme for a 66 lb (30 kg) engine, the development of a 1,100 lb (500 kg) engine started in 1967-68. It was the aim to use a cluster of two engines of this size as a "kick stage" for space probes. The programme was discontinued after the first series of tests with regeneratively-cooled chambers had showed high combustion efficiency. The propellant combination H_2/O_2 was used from 1962 in three engine projects at the thrust levels of 66/1,500/2,100 lb (30/680/952 kg). The 66 lb H_2/O_2 engine was presented in 1966 as a flight prototype, the first cryogenic rocket engine in Germany. The engine incorporated integral propellant valves and an ignition system. In altitude-simulation tests a specific impulse of 415 sec was achieved and multiple restart capability and throttleability were demonstrated. For possible post-Apollo programme participation, the 1,500 lb and 2,100 lb engines were developed in 1970-72. Both are regeneratively cooled, electrically ignited, restartable and pulsable (7Hz). They have high performance and a combustion efficiency of more than 98%. In 1972-73 an LH_2/LO_2 engine rated at 1,125 lb (510 kg) in vacuum conditions was developed for multiple-restart use in upper stages. This engine can be throttled over a range of 8 : 1 (possibly 10 : 1).

Over the period 1973-76 MBB plans to develop its latest and most important rocket engine, to power the third stage of the French L 3 S launcher. With a vacuum thrust of 13,000 lb (5,897 kg), the milled-copper thrust chamber will operate on LH_2/LO_2 at a pressure of 420 lb/sq in (29·5 kg/cm²), the specific impulse being 434 sec. Total weight, not including the turbopump, will be 160 lb (72·0 kg).

MBB HIGH-PRESSURE ENGINES (TOPPING CYCLE)

In the course of development of high-pressure liquid-rocket engines MBB developed a turbopump engine utilising the topping cycle in 1963. This 11,000 lb (5,000 kg) lox/kerosene engine was the first integrated (autonomous) topping cycle engine to run in the western world. It was designed for 1,400 lb/sq in (98·4 kg/cm²) abs and was throttleable at 14 : 1, and remains the first and most powerful turbopump rocket engine developed in Federal Germany since 1945.

For the storable propellants $UDMH/N_2O_4$ a 2,200 lb (1,000 kg) pressure-fed engine was developed and tested at chamber pressures of more than 2,800 lb/sq in (196·8 kg/cm²) abs to demonstrate high-performance injection systems and electroformed thrust-chamber technology for corrosive propellants. During the past year the company has developed completely electroformed integral chambers entirely of nickel which, in comparison with a copper-nickel chamber of the same size and thrust, are approximately 30 per cent lighter.

MBB developed and fabricated some 30,000 lb (13,608 kg) H_2/O_2 engines designed for 3,000 lb/sq in (211 kg/cm²) abs. These were tested at Rocketdyne's facilities in California up to chamber pressures of 4,000 lb/sq in (281 kg/cm²) abs without failure. The electroforming thrust-chamber technology demonstrated in this programme is now the baseline for the Space Shuttle Main Engine of Rocketdyne.

MBB RAM ROCKET AND HYBRID ENGINES

For possible tactical missile propulsion, MBB is developing liquid and solid ram rockets. A research and development programme for liquid/solid hybrid engines of different configurations and thrust levels has been terminated for lack of project applications.

MBB PULSEJET

Since 1968 MBB has been developing the first of a series of valveless pulsejet engines intended for a wide range of applications including missiles, drones and remotely piloted vehicles. For supersonic use the unit has an inclined-shock intake, with conical centrebody, leading into a divergent diffuser with oscillating flow. Once in each cycle air or gas is expelled direct to atmosphere from an open annulus around the rear of this section. Downstream is a parallel section which leads into the enlarged combustion chamber, burning kerosene, JP-4 or JP-5 fuel. In turn this admits to a longer parallel pipe which terminates in a divergent nozzle.

To start the unit, compressed air is blown in at the intake and the fuel supply (from pressurised tanks or fed by a pump) is turned on. Ignition is by a spark plug. Subsequently the cyclic operation is automatic, with continuous fuel feed, auto-ignition and propulsive thrust from the main and forward nozzles.

Static testing of the Type 016, the first model, is being conducted in collaboration with the Institut für Luftsaugende Antriebe of the DFVLR. Considerably more than 250 hours have been logged. The following data refer to the Type 016:

DIMENSION:	
Overall length	118 in (3,000 mm)
WEIGHT, DRY:	22 lb (10 kg)
PERFORMANCE:	
Max thrust (S/L, static)	80 lb (36 kg)
Mach range	0 to 1·5
SPECIFIC FUEL CONSUMPTION:	
S/L, static	1·9
Mach 0·9	2·2

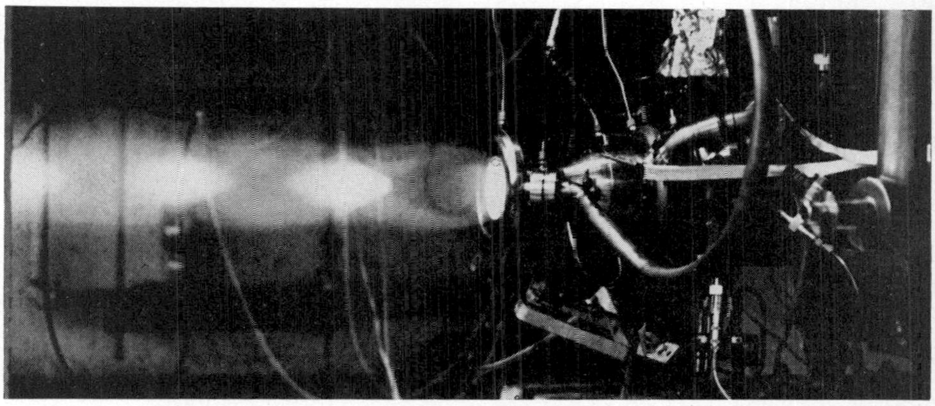

MBB 1,500 lb (680 kg) st H_2/O_2 engine firing in the pulsed mode at 7Hz

MBB 30,000 lb (13,608 kg) st H_2/O_2 high-pressure engine on test at Rocketdyne

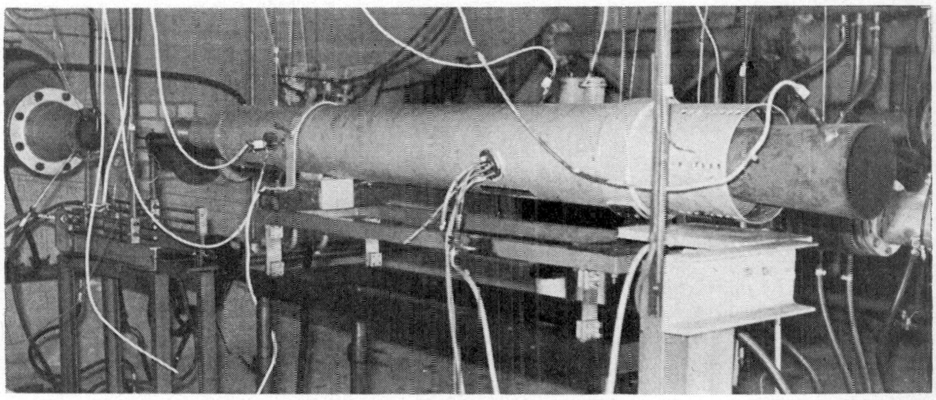

MBB valveless pulsejet shown on bench test

MTU

MOTOREN- UND TURBINEN-UNION MÜNCHEN GmbH

HEAD OFFICE AND WORKS:
München-Allach, Dachauer Str 665 (postal address, 8 München 50, Postfach 50 06 40)
Telephone: (0811) 1 48 91

DIRECTORS:
Dr Ing Karl Schott (Chairman of the Board)
Rolf Breuning and Dipl Ing Otto Voisard (both acting as representatives of the managements of MTU München and MTU Friedrichshafen)
Dr Ing Karl Adolf Muller and Dr Ing/Dr Ing hc Bruno Eckert (both acting as Managing Director, Development Division)
Werner Niefer (Managing Director, Production)

MTU results from a major rationalisation of the German motive power industry. In late 1968 the aero-engine activities of Daimler-Benz AG and MAN (MAN Turbo GmbH) were merged under the name Turbo-Entwicklung (as noted in the Addenda to the 1969-70 *Jane's*). On 1 January 1970 the new MTU combine was created. It comprises two elements, MTU München and MTU Friedrichshafen.

The MTU J79-MTU-J1K turbojet with afterburner

MTU München has a nominal capital of DM100 million, and is owned half by Maschinenfabrik Augsburg-Nürnberg AG (MAN) and half by Daimler-Benz AG. This company now manages all the aircraft engine programmes formerly managed by MAN Turbo and Daimler-Benz. These programmes are being concentrated at Munich. At the beginning of 1973 total employment was 6,100, including a development staff of 1,000. Covered floor area is 4,865,300 sq ft (452,000 m^2).

MTU Friedrichshafen was formerly Maybach Mercedes-Benz Motorenbau GmbH, an 83 per cent affiliate of Daimler-Benz. The latter firm assigned this holding to MTU, so that MTU Friedrichshafen is 83 per cent owned by MTU München, although technically it is a different company.

MTU München holds 40 per cent of the shares of Turbo-Union Ltd, an equal percentage being owned by Rolls-Royce and 20 per cent by Fiat (see "International" section). Turbo-Entwicklung no longer exists.

By far the largest of MTU München's programmes will be its participation, through Turbo-Union, in the RB.199 programme for the Panavia MRCA. The company is also developing and testing the RB.193 in collaboration with Rolls-Royce (see 1973-74 "International" section).

In 1974 MTU entered into two further international agreements involving new designs of engine. With Alfa Romeo of Italy it is participating in the programme for the Pratt & Whitney JT10D. With the same Italian partner and Rolls-Royce (1971) Ltd it is developing a family of new 600 shp engines for general aviation. Both projects are discussed under the "International" heading.

The company's own main development activities concern the MTU 6022 turboshaft (no longer used in aircraft propulsion), and a derivative of this unit under development for MAN AG (half-owner of MTU) for use in heavy road vehicles. Production programmes include licence manufacture of the General Electric J79-MTU-J1K turbojet for 50 new Starfighter aircraft, 448 new J79-MTU-17A engines for F-4E Phantoms, and the General Electric T64-MTU-7 turboshaft for German Sikorsky CH-53G helicopters.

MTU also manufactures parts of the Spey turbofan under subcontract to Rolls-Royce and is a member of the consortium making the Rolls-Royce Tyne (see Rolls-Royce entry, UK section). MTU shares in the manufacture of the CF6-50 engine for the Airbus Industrie A-300B. Servicing and overhaul activities include the J79-11A, -17A and -J1K, Tyne, Solar Titan turbine (CH-53G APU) and Lycoming piston engines.

MTU/GE CF6

Under the terms of a licence agreement signed with the International General Electric Company, MTU shares in the manufacture of the CF6-50 engine for the Airbus A-300B, together with SNECMA. In addition MTU will supply parts to GE for the DC-10 programme. The main task of MTU is production of the complete HP turbine, with electrolytically stem-drilled film-cooled blades, vanes, impeller spacer and heat shield. A description of the CF6 appears under General Electric in the US section.

MTU J79

MAN Turbo (now MTU) took over the German licence rights to the General Electric J79 afterburning turbojet from BMW Triebwerkbau which had previously participated in the manufacture of considerable numbers of the engine for European-built Lockheed F-104G Starfighters. In addition to providing an overhaul, repair and maintenance service for licence-built J79-GE-11As, MTU has also developed an improved version of this model under the designation J79-MTU-J1K. The company is modifying J79-GE-11As in service with the German Air Force to -J1K standard to increase performance, economy and reliability. MTU is also producing J79 components for McDonnell Douglas RF-4E Phantom fighters for the German Air Force and has taken over complete technical and logistic support for the J79-GE-17 engines involved. In 1972 the company went into production with 448 new J79-MTU-17A engines for the 175 F-4E fighters for the Luftwaffe.

A description of the J79 is given under the General Electric entry in the US section of this edition. Manufacturer's details of the J79-MTU-J1K include the use of a steel compressor rotor and magnesium and steel casings; flame tubes fabricated in Hastelloy; turbine blades in Udimet 700; jet pipe fabricated in Inconel; fuel and oil specification MIL-L-5624 and MIL-7808 respectively; and use of an air supply starter. Technical data for the -J1K include: air mass flow 164 lb (74·4 kg)/sec; compressor pressure ratio 12·4; diameter 39·2 in (995 mm); length 208 in (5,291 mm); and weight 3,715 lb (1,685 kg). Max thrust is raised from 10,000 lb (4,536 kg) dry to 10,460 lb (4,745 kg) and from 15,800 lb (7,167 kg) with reheat to 15,950 lb (7,235 kg), all at 7,460 rpm. MTU reports the sfc at military rating as 0·84, and 2·07 with afterburning. In addition to improving performance, the MTU afterburner doubles the engine overhaul period from 400 to 800 hours.

MTU T64

MTU München has a licence to manufacture the General Electric T64 free-turbine turboshaft/turboprop. The company has tooled up to participate in manufacture of the 3,975 shp T64-MTU-7 turboshaft for powering the Sikorsky CH-53G medium helicopter chosen by the German Army, in co-operation with GE and Klöckner-Humboldt-Deutz AG. First deliveries were made from Allach in 1972, and monthly output of 10 to 12 engines will be maintained to the end of 1974. MTU will support these engines in service. A description of the T64 is given under the General Electric entry in the US section.

RR/MTU/ALFA ROMEO 600 HP

The EPM 600 and ESM 600 are respectively the turboprop and turboshaft versions of a 600 hp gas turbine disclosed in April 1974. The project is tri-national, involving the United Kingdom, West Germany and Italy. Further details are given under the International heading in this section.

PIEPER-STARK

PIEPER-STARK MOTORENBAU GmbH

Address:
Minden/Westf, Postfach 1629

Telephone: (0571) 3288

Pieper-Stark is manufacturing the 45 hp Stamo MS 1500-1 modified Volkswagen four-cylinder aircooled piston engine for the Scheibe SF-25B Falke two-seat powered glider. The capacity of this is 1,500 cc, compression ratio 7·2 : 1, length 25 in (640 mm), width 29·3 in (745 mm), height 15·5 in (395 mm), and dry weight 115 lb (52 kg). The MS 1500-1 operates on either 80/86 or 90 octane fuel, and is started by a pull-cord. Production has now also begun of the MS 1500-2, with electric starter and generator. This increases overall height to 17·7 in (450 mm) and dry weight to 132 lb (60 kg). By 1974 well over 500 engines had been delivered.

Pieper-Stark MS 1500-1 four-cylinder four-stroke engine, rated at 45 hp

RFB

RHEIN-FLUGZEUGBAU GmbH

Address and other details: See "Aircraft" section

Though not constructors of aircraft engines, Rhein-Flugzeugbau are marketing a Fan Pod as a complete unit for fitment to power-assisted sailplanes and ultra-light aircraft, as well as to surface vehicles. In early 1974 this was still experimental, and it is likely eventually to be offered to different specifications.

RFB FAN POD SG 85

This is a fixed-geometry pod marketed as a complete unit for installation by the purchaser. Flight testing is reported to have begun early in 1974 with an SG 85 mounted above the fuselage of a Blanik sailplane. In certain types of sailplane with side-by-side seating it should be possible to make the installation retractable. This is desirable, because the windmilling drag of the pod is high. The following specification was issued in February 1974, but is not to be considered final:

Engine: Dual rotating-combustion (Wankel-type) engines mounted in tandem. Fichtel & Sachs KM 914 engines are regarded as standard, with a combined rating of 48 hp. Engines are equipped with 12V starter and generator, and with silenced exhaust system.

Fan Rotor: Three-blade fan moulded in Friedel-Krafts reinforced plastics material, with hard erosion-resistant strip along each leading-edge. Direct drive from engines without separate bearings. Rotating spinner.

Fan Duct: Single shell in FK sandwich reinforced plastics.

Pylon: Light alloy construction, with downward projecting spigot attachment 8 in (200 mm) long mating with airframe.

Fuel Grade: Automotive gasoline and oil mixture in ratio 30 : 1.

Dimensions:
Length 47·24 in (1,200 mm)
Fan duct external diameter 29·53 in (750 mm)
Height, including aircraft spigot 39·37 in (1,000 mm)

Weight, Dry: 123·5 lb (56·0 kg)

Performance Rating:
Full throttle, S/L 187·5 lb (85·0 kg) st at 5,400 rpm

Fuel Consumption:
At full throttle, S/L 2·86 Imp gal (13·0 litres)/hr
At cruise at 4,800 rpm, S/L 2·20 Imp gal (10·0 litres)/hr

Noise (full throttle, S/L, 1,000 ft; 305 m) 57 dBA

INDIA

HAL

HINDUSTAN AERONAUTICS LTD

Head Office:
Indian Express Building, Vidhana Veedhi, PO Box 5150, Bangalore 1

Telephone: 75004/5/6

Officers: See "Aircraft" section

The Bangalore and Koraput Engine Divisions of HAL comprise the main aero-engine design, development and manufacturing elements of the Indian aircraft industry.

BANGALORE DIVISION

This Division is engaged on a variety of gas-turbine and piston engines of both indigenous and licensed designs. These include the HJE-2500 turbojet designed by HAL; the Orpheus 701 and 703 turbojets being built under licence from

Rolls-Royce to power the Gnat and HF-24 Mk 1 fighters; the Viper 11, made under Rolls-Royce licence to power the HJT-16 Mk I Kiran trainer; the Dart 531 turboprop, built under licence from Rolls-Royce to power the HS 748 transport; the Artouste IIIB turboshaft, built under licence from Turboméca to power Alouette III and SA 315 helicopters; and the PE 90 and HPE-2 piston engines designed by HAL. The Bangalore Division also overhauls and repairs Rolls-Royce Avon and HAL Orpheus and Viper turbojets, and various types of piston engines, for the Indian Air Force.

HAL HJE-2500

The HJE-2500 is a small turbojet engine which HAL is developing as a potential power plant for production versions of its HJT-16 Kiran basic training aircraft. It is a single-spool design, with a seven-stage compressor driven by a single-stage turbine. All components except the fuel system were manufactured at Bangalore.

The HJE-2500 ran for the first time on the test bed on 30 December 1966. This prototype engine has now achieved its full design performance, and further engines are being made in order to complete development.

Air Intake: Made of aluminium-magnesium alloy with three radial struts supporting the main thrust bearing and starter. Inlet guide vanes are fixed type.

Compressor Casing: Two-piece aluminium-magnesium alloy casing with seven rows of aluminium alloy blades and one row of flow straightener vanes.

Compressor: Built up of seven steel discs mounted on a common drum supported on rear roller bearing and front ball thrust bearing. 410 aluminium alloy rotor blades. Two-piece aluminium alloy casing with 606 dovetailed stator blades. Air mass flow 45 lb (20·4 kg)/sec at 12,500 rpm. Pressure ratio 4·2 : 1.

Combustion Chamber: Cannular type with seven flame tubes and duplex burners. High-energy ignition system with plugs in tubes 2 and 6.

Fuel System: Positive displacement pump with pressure, fuel/air ratio and acceleration control.

Fuel Grade: DEngRD. 2494.

Turbine Casing: Nimocast with 65 solid nozzle guide vanes of Nimonic 90.

Turbine: Single stage with fir-tree root fitting for 103 blades of FV.448. Rear bearing ahead of turbine wheel.

Jet Pipe: Fixed nozzle.

Control System: Single lever master control.

Lubrication: Return-flow system for front bearing and gears. Total loss for centre and rear bearings.

Mounting: Spherical joints on sides of delivery casing, with steady on compressor casing.

Starting: Electric starter in nose bullet.

Dimensions:

Length, flange to exit cone	85 in (2,160 mm)
Diameter	26 in (660 mm)
Frontal area	3·66 sq ft (0·34 m²)

Weight, Dry: 585 lb (265 kg)

Performance Rating:

T-O 2,500 lb (1,135 kg) st at 12,500 rpm

Specific Fuel Consumption: 0·98

HAL HPE-2

This is a new 250 hp six-cylinder horizontally-opposed air-cooled piston engine of non-supercharged direct-drive design. The HPE-2 is intended to power the HA-31 agricultural aircraft now in production by HAL. The prototype engine is being bench-tested. Cubic capacity is 472 cu in (7·75 litres) and compression ratio 8·7 : 1. The HPE-2 is designed to run on 100/130 octane gasoline and has wet sump, pressure-feed lubrication.

Dimensions:

Height	20·1 in (510 mm)
Width	34 in (865 mm)
Length	43·3 in (1,100 mm)

Weight, Dry: 410 lb (186 kg)

Performance Ratings:

T-O at 2,625 rpm at S/L	250 hp
Nominal at 2,450 rpm at S/L	185 hp

KORAPUT DIVISION

This Division of HAL is located at Koraput in Orissa. It was established to manufacture under Soviet government licence the R-11 (TRD Mk R37F) afterburning turbojet to power HAL-built MiG-21 fighters. With help from the Soviet Union, the first engine was run on the bench (which it was used to calibrate) in early 1969. HAL Koraput is already considerably larger than the original Bangalore factory, and in 1970 had cost Rs 350m (£19·4 m). Production has been centred on the RD-11-F2-300 for the MiG-21F1 and RD-11-F2S-300 for the MiG-21M (see under Tumansky, Soviet Union, in this section).

INTERNATIONAL PROGRAMMES

CFM INTERNATIONAL

SNECMA/GENERAL ELECTRIC CFM INTERNATIONAL

Address:
4 Rue de Penthièvre, 75008 Paris, France
Telephone: 265 97 72

Directors:
René Ravaud (SNECMA) (Joint Chairman)
Gerhard Neumann (GE) (Joint Chairman)
Jean Sollier (SNECMA) (Chief Executive)
Frank Lenherr (GE) (Technical)
Bruce J. Gordon (GE) (Marketing)
Jean Lavergne (SNECMA) (Production)

The formation of CFM International, announced in early 1974, followed the decision of the US Department of State in September 1973 to grant a licence for the transfer to a foreign nation of the advanced technology contained in the F101, a military engine funded by the US Air Force. This cleared the way for SNECMA of France (see under France in this section) and General Electric of the United States (see under USA in this section) to proceed with the CFM56, described below.

At the time this edition went to press, the composition of the company had not been announced. It will probably be owned equally by SNECMA and GE. The president of SNECMA, René Ravaud, and the chief executive of the GE Aircraft Engine Group, Gerhard Neumann, were expected to participate directly in management of the CFM56 programme. Full-time programme managers will be Jack Hope (GE) and Jean Malroux (SNECMA).

SNECMA has from the outset announced its intention of inviting other European engine companies to participate in the programme, within SNECMA's own 50 per cent share. FN of Belgium was understood to have joined the project in late 1973; but no announcement had been made by FN as this edition went to press, nor had an FN shareholding or appointment to the board of directors of CFM International been disclosed.

Essential features of the plan (the first to involve a US company at the design stage of a totally new engine proposed by another country) were that the venture should be on a 50/50 financial basis, and that GE should be responsible for the HP system and SNECMA for the LP system. SNECMA made it a condition of agreement that it should be assigned design leadership, despite the much greater experience of GE in this type of engine. This condition appears to have been waived, and GE will now be responsible for design integration. GE proposed to use the HP system of the F101 turbofan as the basis for the CFM56.

SNECMA/GE CFM56

When the sixth of France's five-year plans was being prepared it was decided there was a world need for a subsonic turbofan of about 10 tonnes (22,050 lb) thrust, particularly for future civil aircraft. In the second half of 1969 the French Aerospace Industries Committee stated "The development of such an engine would offer the best possibility for SNECMA establishing itself in the civil market". It was further stated by the committee, in 1970, that special attention must be paid to: minimum nuisance (noise and smoke); minimum maintenance and costs; and maximum performance and economy. The engine, designated M 56 (later preceded by the initials for "commercial fan"), was seen as a replacement for the JT3D and JT8D.

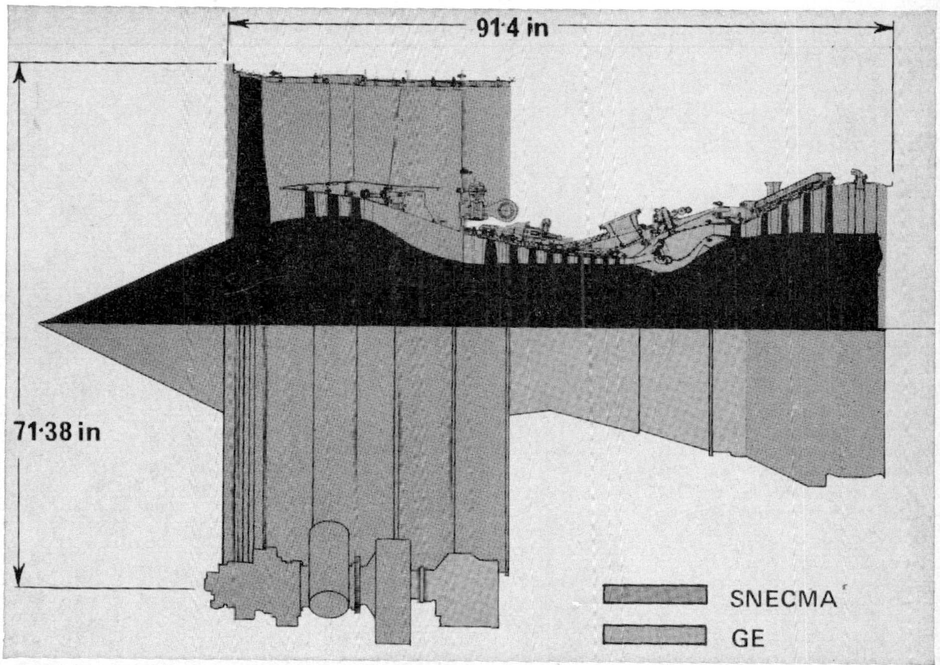

Provisional longitudinal cross-section of CFM56 turbofan, in the 22,000 lb; 9,980 kg st class. GE's main contribution is the core engine, comprising HP system and combustor

Various schemes were prepared in 1970, notably the M 56-06, M 56-20 and the three-shaft M 56-40. All were studied by SNECMA and the French government in detail, discussed with all potential customers among aircraft manufacturers and airlines and subjected to detailed market and financial analysis. In addition all major Western engine manufacturers were assessed as possible partners. On 5 March 1971, SNECMA gave the government additional data that had been requested, and on 25 March the government authorised the company to proceed to an international agreement. In June 1971 the five-year plan was ratified, making explicit mention of the programme to develop "an engine having a thrust of from 10 to 12 tonnes (22,050 to 26,400 lb)."

Detailed market studies by SNECMA and US firms showed a requirement for 6,000-8,000 complete new engines of the proposed type, 60 per cent in the United States and only a small number in France. From April to October 1971, SNECMA negotiated with foreign engine builders, with particular emphasis on American partners. Agreement protocols were signed with GE and Pratt & Whitney and discussions were also held with possible European partners, who, according to SNECMA, "were all interested, especially in the idea of an association with one of the two US manufacturers". In October 1971 SNECMA's choice fell upon GE, and a detailed dossier on the whole programme was submitted to the French government.

On 7 December 1971 an inter-ministerial meeting, presided over by the Prime Minister, authorised the start of the two-nation programme. During 1972 the two parties proceeded with completion of the design of the CFM56 in its initial form, directed toward building two demonstrator engines. SNECMA continued talks with possible European partners who, at SNECMA's direction, could handle a portion of the French company's share.

In September 1972 the US State Department, Office of Munitions Control, refused requested permission for export of the GE-designed core engine to SNECMA for SNECMA's demonstrator engine test, on grounds that approval would not be in furtherance of the national security and foreign policy of the United States. Subsequently, GE and SNECMA discussed with the US and French governments possible alternative approaches which would permit the programme to proceed.

In April 1973, GE issued a statement which is reproduced in full:

"In November 1971 SNECMA selected General Electric as its partner to design and develop a ten-ton engine, designated the CFM56.

"Within the 50/50 sharing which is the basis of the co-venture, GE is to be responsible for the

HP system, based on the F101 core, and SNECMA the LP system. A joint SNECMA/GE company with René Ravaud, SNECMA, and Gerhard Neumann, GE, as co-chairmen was made responsible for the overall system management.

"The programme proceeded satisfactorily until the Autumn of 1972 when US government licence limitations on the data renewal, and the export of core-engine hardware, proved too restrictive to continue the programme to its original schedule.

"Although direct engineering liaison on the CFM56 per se has been suspended, GE's programme for the F101 engine has progressed on schedule. The core components for this engine, modified for lower-turbine-temperature operation and lower pollutant emissions in its proposed civilian role, constitute the gas-generator of the CFM56. Concurrently, SNECMA has made major progress in acoustic and aerodynamic testing of the fan and in the detailed design and fabrication of full-scale LP system components.

"GE has been engaged in an intensive programme of informing important US government officials in the White House and the Departments of State, Treasury, Commerce and Defense on the facts relative to the market, the determination of our partner to proceed with or without a US partner, the capability of SNECMA and its potential EEC associates to build a competitive engine, and the steps we have taken mutually to obviate concerns for premature technology transfer.

"Our latest market survey has re-confirmed the need for a ten-ton-class engine, although the airline requirements are a little later than originally predicted. This delay helps the US government concern on early release of technology. The joint-company management concept, together with the slippage in market requirement, allows SNECMA and GE to respond to the maximum to US government concerns with regard to early release of F101 core technology and appropriate balance of French/US effort. The joint company is able to give GE the LP and HP integration responsibility as long as restrictions on F101 core technology release require, without in any way changing the basic concept of GE core and SNECMA LP responsibilities.

"We have been encouraged by the statesmanship and understanding expressed by a number of US officials, but it must be stated that there remain a number of opponents. General Electric is carrying the message of the need for this important international co-operative programme to the highest levels of our government."

For one year the programme was officially almost suspended at the collaborative engineering level, but GE's development of the F101 for the US Air Force progressed on schedule and SNECMA made major advances in detailed design and fabrication of full-scale LP system components including acoustic and aerodynamic testing of the fan. Concurrently, market research established that the airlines' need for this size of engine was timed rather later than the original estimate, largely countering adverse effects of the delay in the programme. Approval for the export of F101 core technology was given by the US government in September 1973.

SNECMA and GE consider the CFM56 to be matched exactly to new transport aircraft projects, and to derivatives or re-engined versions of existing aircraft. The 707, 727, 737, Mercure and DC-9 have been identified (though there would appear to be diametral problems with underwing and centre-engine installations). In addition, the CFM56 is also being evaluated for Super Sixty series DC-8s and a projected four-engined version of the Airbus Industrie A-300.

The first CFM56 demonstrator engine was scheduled to run at the GE Evendale, Ohio, plant in the middle of 1974. Manufacture and testing of complete engines, and the build-up of facilities for production, assembly and test, are continuing both at Evendale and at SNECMA's facility at Corbeil. Joint US and French certification is scheduled for 1977, and initial airline service is planned for the second half of 1978 (subject to customer requirements and the progress of a suitable airframe application).

TYPE: Two-shaft turbofan for subsonic transport applications.

AIR INTAKE: Direct pitot entry, without inlet guide vanes.

FAN: Single-stage axial. Mockup exhibited in 1973 had 46 titanium blades, each with a tip shroud to form a continuous peripheral ring round the assembled fan. Pointed conical spinner rotates with fan. By-pass ratio 6 : 1.

LP COMPRESSOR: Three axial stages carried on fan drive-shaft serve as booster to supercharge core engine. Downstream flow curves sharply inwards to match diameter of HP compressor. In this section is main fan frame and sumps and bearings for front end of both shafts. Ring of bleed doors allows core airflow to escape into fan duct at low power settings. Bleed doors are closed at all normal flight power settings.

HP COMPRESSOR: Nine-stage axial with tapering tip diameter. Based upon HP compressor of F101, with minor modifications. Overall pressure ratio in 25 : 1 class.

COMBUSTION CHAMBER: Fully annular with advanced film cooling. Based upon F101 combustor but modified for long-life operation at reduced turbine temperature with minimal emissions. Level of pollution from the core is claimed to be below that of any engine at present in airline service.

HP TURBINE: Single-stage axial with aircooled stator and rotor blades. Entry gas temperature in 1,260°C class. High stage loading. HP system carried in only two bearings.

LP TURBINE: Four-stage axial.

EXHAUST UNIT (FAN): Constant-diameter duct of sound-absorbent construction. Outer cowl and engine cowl form convergent plug nozzle, with airframe-mounted reverser.

EXHAUST UNIT (CORE): Fixed-area type with convergent plug nozzle. Sound-absorbent construction.

ACCESSORY DRIVE: Gearbox in front sump transmits drive from front of HP spool, via radial shaft in fan frame, to transfer gearbox mounted on underside of fan duct. Drive faces on both front and rear sides.

FUEL SYSTEM: Hydromechanical with electronic trim.

DIMENSIONS:
- Fan duct internal diameter 71·4 in (1,814 mm)
- Length, excluding spinner 91·4 in (2,322 mm)

WEIGHT, DRY: 3,850 lb (1,747 kg)

PERFORMANCE RATING:
- Max T-O 22,000 lb (9,979 kg) flat-rated to 30°C
- Cruise at 35,000 ft (10,670 m) at Mach 0·85 5,020 lb (2,277 kg)

PRATT & WHITNEY/MTU/ ALFA ROMEO

PRATT & WHITNEY AIRCRAFT

HEAD OFFICE:
East Hartford, Connecticut 06108, USA

MTU GmbH

HEAD OFFICE: 8 München 50, Germany

SpA ALFA ROMEO

HEAD OFFICE:
Via Gattemelata 45, 20149 Milan, Italy

Full-scale mockup of Pratt & Whitney JT10D turbofan (20,000-30,000 lb; 9,070-13,608 kg st class)

PRATT & WHITNEY JT10D

The most important new engine programme announced in 1973 was the JT10D commercial turbofan in the 20,000-30,000 lb (9,070-13,608 kg) thrust class. It is to be a two-spool engine very much like a scaled JT9D, but it is proportionately longer and has certain evident new features. The mockup publicly displayed has five rows of variable stators in the compressor, all of them on the LP spool, rotating with the fan. The latter has 32 titanium blades with part-span shrouds. The engine is described as "applicable to short-, medium- and long-range commercial transports of two-, three- and four-engine configuration. It has low noise and low exhaust emission characteristics, and offers low maintenance cost through the use of modular construction and advanced manufacturing techniques".

Pratt & Whitney announced its intention, subject to the grant of US export licences, of developing the JT10D with the technical, financial and manufacturing help of several international partners. Later it was announced that MTU GmbH of West Germany and SpA Alfa Romeo of Italy would be among these partners. Pratt & Whitney stated that these companies "might be able to participate in design of their assigned portions as well as manufacture." Participation of these two companies is of a very minor nature, and the JT10D remains very much a Pratt & Whitney engine.

The project was announced at the Paris Show in 1973, when the display mockup was revealed. At the Hanover Show in 1974 the mockup was seen in more refined form, but detailed marketing plans and applications were not announced, and like rival engines in the same class the schedule is regarded as less urgent than in 1973. This stems mainly from the fact that the only important visible application was the Boeing 7X7, which has not been proceeded with.

Though the JT10D has obvious military applications, its design "is directed at the specific requirements of the commercial airlines". Total programme development cost is estimated at $300 million, and the planned certification year is 1977.

ROLLS-ROYCE/ALLISON

ROLLS-ROYCE (1971) LIMITED

HEAD OFFICE:
Norfolk House, St James's Square, London SW1Y 4JS, England

THE DETROIT DIESEL ALLISON DIVISION, GENERAL MOTORS CORPORATION

HEAD OFFICE:
Detroit, Michigan, USA

Co-operation between Rolls-Royce and Allison started in November 1958, when the two companies began work on the design and development of high-performance jet engines for commercial and military applications. They developed jointly a version of the Rolls-Royce Spey turbofan, under the designation Allison TF41, to power advanced versions of the LTV A-7 Corsair II attack aircraft.

Under the terms of a Memorandum of Understanding signed by the US and British governments in October 1965, Rolls-Royce and Allison are also developing jointly an advanced lift-jet engine for use initially in V/STOL fighter aircraft.

ALLISON/ROLLS-ROYCE TF41

Manufacturers' designations: Rolls-Royce Spey RB.168-62 and -66, Allison Model 912-B3 and -B14

In August 1966 Allison and Rolls-Royce were awarded a joint $200 m contract by USAF Systems Command for the development and production of an advanced version of the RB.168-25 Spey turbofan, to power LTV A-7D Corsair II fighter-bomber aircraft for the USAF. The requirement was to provide an engine offering maximum thrust increase over the TF30-P-6 powering USN A-7As. The amount of the contract was increased to $230 m in December 1966, Rolls-Royce's share being about $100 m.

Development and production have been undertaken jointly by Rolls-Royce and Allison, with Rolls-Royce supplying parts common to existing Spey variants and Allison, which is manufacturing under licence, being responsible for items peculiar to the TF41. This has provided an approximately 50/50 division of manufacturing effort, but with Allison also undertaking assembly, test and delivery.

Design of the RB.168-62 started in June 1966 and, following the award of the USAF contract, the engine was given the USAF designation TF41-A-1. Major change compared with the RB.168-25 is the move forward of the by-pass flow split into the LP compressor, to give a larger three-stage fan followed by a two-stage IP compressor, all five stages being driven by the two-stage LP turbine. The number of HP compressor stages is reduced from 12 to 11, the HP turbine remaining at two stages. These modifications raise the mass flow to 258 lb (117 kg)/sec and the by-pass ratio from 0·7 : 1 to 0·76 : 1. No afterburner is fitted.

Other design changes compared with the RB.168-25 include omission of the fan inlet guide vanes, the first rotor stage being overhung on a bearing supported by the first-stage stator vanes. The fan and IP compressor are of more modern aerodynamic design, and the HP and LP turbine nozzle throat areas have been increased to pass the additional flow. The HP turbine is of modified aerodynamic design, and an annular exhaust mixer replaces the RB.168-25's chuted design.

First run of the TF41-A-1/RB.168-62 was at Rolls-Royce, Derby, in October 1967, the first Allison engine following at Indianapolis in March 1968. Development continued ahead of schedule, delivery of the first production TF41-A-1 being made in June 1968.

Ordered in 1968, a second version of the TF41 is the A-2, developed for the US Navy to power the LTV A-7E Corsair. Differences are slight, although the thrust rating is appreciably increased by raising the engine speed. This required re-stressing the disc of the low-pressure turbine and high-pressure compressor. Mass flow is slightly increased, the by-pass ratio being 0·74 : 1. The engine has additional protection against corrosion.

By May 1974 over 1,000 engines had been delivered and production of the TF41 for the A-7 is expected to continue into the 1980s. In combat service both versions of the TF41 have shown outstanding reliability. The exceptional overhaul life (for a combat engine) of 1,200 hours has been reached after four years of service, and further extensions are planned.

Proposals have been made by Detroit Diesel Allison for TF41 developments offering substantially greater thrust for future versions of the Corsair. In general these proposals envisage a growth in thrust of up to 20 per cent within the same installation envelope. An industrial TF41 is under development at the Rolls-Royce Industrial and Marine Division.

The two current production versions of the TF41 are known to Rolls-Royce as the RB.168-62 and RB.168-66; the corresponding Allison designations are Model 912-B3 and 912-B14. The following description refers basically to the TF41-A-1; where the A-2 differs, the data for that engine are given in brackets.

TYPE: Military turbofan without reheat.

AIR INTAKE: Direct entry, fixed, without intake guide vanes.

COMPRESSOR: Two-shaft axial. 3 fan stages, 2 intermediate stages on same shaft and 11 high-pressure stages. All rotor blades carried on separate discs. Fan and LP rotor blades of titanium, held by dovetail roots in slots broached in discs which are bolted together through curvic couplings and similarly attached to the stubshafts. HP rotor blades also of titanium, except stages 9, 10 and 11 of stainless steel, the first HP stage being pinned and the remainder being dovetailed into broached slots; discs similarly bolted together but driven through a splined coupling to the shaft. LP rotor carried in 3 roller bearings and HP by 2, with central ball location bearing and inter-shaft ball bearing. LP casing of steel and aluminium; HP casing of stainless steel, both split at horizontal centreline. Stainless steel LP stator blades slotted laterally into casing, intermediate stators welded to inner casing sub-assembly rings. HP stator blades of stainless steel, slotted laterally into casing. Overall pressure ratio 20 : 1 (A-2, 21·4 : 1); mass flow 258 lb/sec (117 kg/sec) (A-2, 263 lb/sec; 119 kg/sec). High-pressure compressor pressure ratio, 6·2 : 1; mass flow, 148 lb/sec (67 kg/sec).

COMBUSTION CHAMBER: Tubo-annular, with 10 interconnected Ni-Co alloy flame tubes in steel outer casing. Duple spray atomising burner at head of each chamber. High-energy 12-joule igniter plug in chambers 4 and 8.

FUEL SYSTEM: Hydromechanical high-pressure system with automatic acceleration and speed control. Emergency manual override of automatic features. Variable-stroke dual fuel pump.

FUEL GRADE: JP-4 (A-2, JP-5).

NOZZLE GUIDE VANES: Two HP stages with air cooling; two LP stages uncooled, but 1st LP vanes are hollow and contain air pipes to cool LP turbine rotor. All stators precision cast in Ni-Co alloy.

TURBINE: Impulse-reaction axial type, two HP stages and two LP. All blades forged in Ni-Co alloy; first HP stage blades cooled internally by HP compressor air; remainder have solid discs of Inco 901, LP discs of steel (A-2, Inco 901). All discs bolted to drive shafts.

JET PIPE: Fixed, heat-resistant steel.

ACCESSORY DRIVES: External gearbox driven by radial shaft from HP system; provision for starter, fuel boost pump, two hydraulic pumps, HP fuel pump, fuel control, HP tachometer, CSD and alternator, permanent-magnet generator, LP fuel pump and oil pumps. Additional low-speed (LS) gearbox, driven from LP shaft, serving LP rotor governor and tachometer.

LUBRICATION SYSTEM: Self-contained, with engine-mounted tank, fuel/oil heat exchanger and gear type pump; pressure 50 lb/sq in (3·51 kg/cm²). Tank capacity: A-1, 1·0 Imp gal (4·5 litres); A-2, 2·27 Imp gal (10·3 litres).

MOUNTING: Main ball-type trunnions on compressor intermediate casing; rear tangential steady-type at rear of by-pass duct.

STARTING: Integral gas turbine (air turbine).

DIMENSIONS:

Length overall	102·6 in (2,610 mm)
Intake diameter	37·5 in (953 mm)
Overall height	40 in (1,026 mm)

WEIGHT, DRY:
3,175 lb (1,440 kg) (A-2, 3,241 lb; 1,470 kg)

RATING:
Max T-O 14,500 lb (6,577 kg) st up to ISA+8°C (A-2, 15,000 lb; 6,804 kg st up to ISA)

SPECIFIC FUEL CONSUMPTION:
At max T-O rating 0·633 (A-2, 0·647)

ALLISON/ROLLS-ROYCE XJ99

This very advanced lightweight lift-jet was under joint development from October 1965 by what are now the Derby Engine Division of Rolls-Royce (1971) Ltd and the Detroit Diesel Allison Division of General Motors Corporation.

The XJ99, which is stated to have a greater thrust per unit weight and volume than previous lift-engine concepts, is suitable for a wide variety of VTOL and STOL aircraft applications. In addition to its use as a direct-lift turbojet, the XJ99 may be installed as a booster to enhance the take-off capability of current and proposed transport aircraft. It is also suitable for further development as a gas generator for remote and concentric lift-fan applications.

The US/UK direct-lift engine programme was undertaken under an agreement signed by the governments of the United States and the United Kingdom. Direction of the programme was provided by the US Air Force Aero Propulsion

Cutaway drawing of the Allison/Rolls-Royce TF41-A-1 (Spey RB.168-62) turbofan (14,500 lb; 6,577 kg st)

Allison/Rolls-Royce XJ99-RA-1 advanced lift-jet (9,000 lb; 4,080 kg thrust class)

Laboratory and the British Ministry of Aviation Supply. Development testing of the XJ99 lift-engine took place at both Indianapolis and Derby.

Originally the XJ99 was to provide lift for the US/FRG V/STOL fighter. When this was cancelled the XJ99 programme was continued, and the first XJ99-RA-1 engines ran at both Derby and Indianapolis in 1969. The performance goals were successfully demonstrated in February 1971, and in June 1971 it was announced that the design thrust had been reached at less than design temperature and speed. The studies being carried out by the US Navy for a fighter with V/STOL capability for operation from the Sea Control Ships include the Lift/Lift/Cruise concept. The XJ99 is the basis for the lift engine in this concept.

Type: Simple two-shaft axial turbojet.

Intake: Direct pitot type, fixed geometry, no anti-icing.

LP Compressor: Two stages.

HP Compressor: Compact axial assembly of four stages. Light alloy and glass-reinforced plastics construction, with main casing in left and right metal halves.

Combustion Chamber: High-intensity annular chamber of minimum volume. Large surrounding air bleed manifold.

Fuel System: Hobson integrated fuel control unit mounted on side of compressor casing, feeding fuel through rigid-pipe manifold to 18 burners and two pilot burners.

Ignition System: Rotax dual 6-joule high-energy igniter feeding two plugs.

HP Turbine: Single-stage axial type with disc coupled to large-diameter main shaft.

LP Turbine: Single-stage.

Jet Pipe: Direct exit to atmosphere below turbine, with provision for deflectors, diverter valves or other devices according to aircraft application.

Dimensions:
- Diameter over turbine flange 27·35 in (694·7 mm)
- Length from intake flange to turbine exit 43·31 in (1,100·1 mm)
- Length overall 44·9 in (1,140·7 mm)

Weight, Dry: about 450 lb (204 kg)

Thrust: approx 9,000 lb (4,080 kg)

ROLLS-ROYCE/MTU

ROLLS-ROYCE (1971) LTD

Head Office:
Norfolk House, St James's Square, London SW1Y 4JS, England
Telephone: 01-839-7888

MTU GmbH

Head Office:
8 München 50, Germany
Telephone: (0811) 1 48 91

Rolls-Royce and MAN Turbo (now MTU München) signed an agreement in 1960 to co-operate on jet-engine development. They jointly developed the RB.193 lift-cruise turbofan engine (described in the 1972-73 *Jane's*). Both companies are members of Turbo-Union, the international company developing the RB.199 for the Panavia MRCA aircraft (the other member being Aeritalia). They are also members of the European consortium producing Tyne turboprop engines for the Breguet Atlantic and Transall C-160 aircraft.

ROLLS-ROYCE/MTU/ ALFA ROMEO

ROLLS-ROYCE (1971) LTD

Head Office:
Norfolk House, St James's Square, London SW1Y 4JS, England

MOTOREN UND TURBINEN UNION GmbH

Head Office: 8 München 50, Germany

SOCIETÀ PER AZIONI ALFA ROMEO

Head Office:
Via Gattemelata 45, 20149 Milan

During the past year the Rolls-Royce Small Engine Division has been exploring the market for a gas turbine in the 600 hp class. At one time the Division held a licence for the Allison Model 250, but this was terminated in 1971. It has sought to develop a family of gas turbines, using as far as possible a common gas generator, with the primary objective of gradually supplanting the larger sizes of piston engine in private and business aircraft, other general-aviation aeroplanes and helicopters.

At the Hanover Deutsche Luftfahrtschau in April 1974 preliminary details were given (on the MTU company's stand) of the programme.

It is a collaborative effort between the three companies listed and may possibly be managed by a new international company. No indication had yet been given in May 1974 of the way the work is being split, but it is understood that each partner will be responsible for design and manufacture of its own portion. Assembly of complete engines may take place at all three companies, though this again has not been announced. (See Addenda).

EPM600/ESM600

The EPM600 is a turboprop and the ESM600 a turboshaft engine for helicopters. Both use a common gas generator. Rather than strive for high pressure ratio, high temperature and a competitive cycle efficiency, the gas generator has been planned to have the minimum number of simple parts, modular construction and a detail design providing for maximum reliability, very low cost and extreme ease of inspection, overhaul and repair.

The ESM600 comprises three easily separated modules: air intake and reduction gearbox, gas generator, and power turbine. The EPM600 adds a fourth module, the propeller gearbox. The gas generator has a single-stage centrifugal compressor, reverse-flow annular combustion chamber, and single-stage axial turbine. The reduction gearbox is driven by a central shaft carrying the single-stage axial power turbine.

The gas generator is ring bolted to the rear of a main frame and wheelcase providing lateral mounting points, pads for engine and airframe accessories beneath the engine and a reduction gear to a forward drive shaft. In both engines the inlet duct is the same, with a forward-facing ram intake above the wheelcase. The EPM600 was exhibited driving a three-blade variable-pitch propeller. If required, the air intake and reduction gearbox may be attached the other way up, to give a high thrust line, with intake below the spinner.

Rig testing of the compressor and both gas-generator and power turbines was scheduled to have reached an advanced stage by the late Summer of 1974. A complete gas generator was expected to run before the end of the year.

Dimensions:
- Height overall 25·20 in (640 mm)
- Width 17·15 in (436 mm)
- Length:
  - ESM600 28·54 in (725 mm)
  - EPM600, without propeller 44·10 in (1,120 mm)

Weight, Dry:
- ESM600 194 lb (88 kg)
- EPM600 220 lb (100 kg)

Performance Ratings:

ESM600:
- Max contingency ($2\frac{1}{2}$ min) 545 shp to 35°C
- One-hour 545 shp (15°C), 500 shp (35°C)
- Max continuous 545 shp (15°C), 450 shp (35°C)

EPM600:
- Max T-O 572 shp + 83 lb; 37 kg thrust (15°C)
  479 shp + 72 lb; 32 kg thrust (35°C)
- Max continuous
  519 shp + 77 lb; 35 kg thrust (15°C)
  420 shp + 65 lb; 29 kg thrust (35°C)
- Recommended cruise
  485 shp + 74 lb; 33 kg thrust (15°C)
  390 shp + 62 lb; 28 kg thrust (35°C)

Specific Fuel Consumption:

ESM600:
- Max contingency
  0·642 lb (0·291 kg)/shp/hr (15°C)
  0·657 lb (0·297 kg)/shp/hr (35°C)
- One hour 0·642 lb (0·291 kg)/shp/hr (15°C)
  0·672 lb (0·304 kg)/shp/hr (35°C)
- Max continuous
  0·642 lb (0·291 kg)/shp/hr (15°C)
  0·695 lb (0·315 kg)/shp/hr (35°C)

EPM600:
- Max T-O 0·619 lb (0·280 kg)/ehp/hr (15°C)
  0·662 lb (0·300 kg)/ehp/hr (35°C)
- Max continuous
  0·634 lb (0·287 kg)/ehp/hr (15°C)
  0·696 lb (0·315 kg)/ehp/hr (35°C)
- Recommended cruise
  0·648 lb (0·294 kg)/ehp/hr (15°C)
  0·713 lb (0·323 kg)/ehp/hr (35°C)

Exhibition mockups of two versions of the 600 shp turbine engine proposed jointly by Rolls-Royce, MTU and Alfa Romeo; *left:* the ESM600 turboshaft; *right:* the EPM600 turboprop

ROLLS-ROYCE/SNECMA

ROLLS-ROYCE (1971) LTD

HEAD OFFICE:
Norfolk House, St James's Square, London SW1Y 4JS, England
Telephone: 01-839-7888

SOCIÉTÉ NATIONALE D'ÉTUDE ET DE CONSTRUCTION DE MOTEURS D'AVIATION

HEAD OFFICE:
150 Boulevard Haussmann, 75361-Paris cédex 08, France
Telephone: 227-33-94

Rolls-Royce (1971) Ltd and SNECMA are jointly responsible for development and production of the Olympus turbojet engine to power the Anglo-French Concorde supersonic transport. They are also developing the M45 series of advanced turbofan engines for both civil and military use. SNECMA is a member of the consortium building the Rolls-Royce Tyne turboprop.

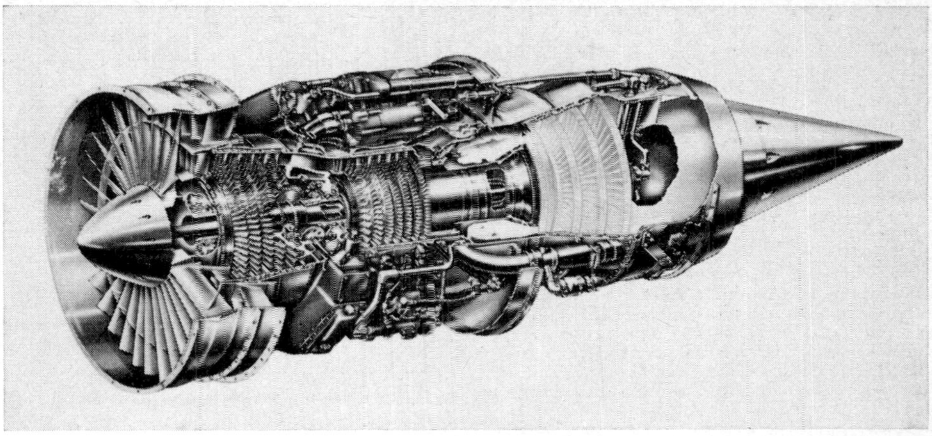

Cutaway drawing of Rolls-Royce/SNECMA M45H-01 civil turbofan rated at 7,760 lb (3,520 kg) st

ROLLS-ROYCE/SNECMA M45 SERIES

Collaboration between Rolls-Royce Bristol and SNECMA on the M45 series of advanced turbofan engines began in late 1964, and a formal agreement was signed in February 1965. First of the series to be built was the M45F demonstrator engine, which ran for the first time in June 1966.

The M45H is a series of twin-spool commercial engines in the 8,000 lb (3,629 kg) thrust class. The **M45H-01**, the first in this series, ran in January 1969 and is under development to power the twin-engined VFW 614 short-haul airliner, on which it is mounted in unique overwing pods. The M45H-01, with a take-off thrust of 7,760 lb (3,520 kg), was planned for type test in mid-1974, at the same time as the VFW 614 received commercial certification. The aircraft flight-test programme began in July 1971.

Modular construction, using ten modules, has been incorporated to reduce strip time for repair and overhaul. Internal inspection for "on-condition" maintenance is possible by means of the borescope. In addition magnetic chip-detectors, fine filtration in the oil scavenge line and vibration measuring devices assist in giving early warning of incipient failure.

Low gas velocities result in noise levels substantially lower than those of current engines. The omission of fan inlet guide vanes, and the relatively large fan rotor/stator spacing, result in low compressor noise levels.

Derivatives of the M45H-01 under consideration at present include:

M45H-10. Uprated version of M45H-01, with take-off rating of 8,900 lb (4,037 kg) st up to ISA+15°C.

M57H. A turboshaft engine for helicopters with a maximum rating of 8,750 shp (6,245 kW).

THS 2000. A turboshaft engine, using the M45H gas generator, for industrial, rail traction and marine use. The initial run of the engine in November 1971 was carried out at an equivalent of 6,500 shp (4,850kW).

Also under consideration are derivatives involving the application of fixed-pitch and variable-pitch geared fans, which, with other modifications, will enable thrusts of up to 18,000 lb (8,172 kg) to be obtained.

The first engine of this family, including in its design the Dowty Rotol variable-pitch fan, forms the basis of a programme leading to the development of an ultra-quiet demonstrator engine, designated the **M45SD-02** (RB.401D-2), described separately.

The following particulars apply to the M45H-01:

TYPE: Twin-spool turbofan.

AIR INTAKE: Annular, designed to integrate with VFW 614 pod intake and short-length cowl. Mass flow 233 lb/sec (106 kg/sec).

FAN: Single-stage axial unit integral with the LP system. Blades, in titanium, have snubbers at approximately two-thirds of blade height. Inlet guide vanes omitted to reduce icing problems, weight, cost and noise. Fan centrifuging effect and use of snubbers reduce risk of damage from foreign object ingestion. By-pass ratio 3·0 : 1.

LP COMPRESSOR: Five-stage axial unit of constant root diameter, driven by LP turbine. Rotor is of monobloc construction to give smooth running and long life. Fan and LP compressor rotor overhung on LP front shaft carried on bearings supported from compressor intermediate casing. Front bearing is main ball thrust unit. Rear bearing is roller providing radial location for interconnection of LP front and rear shafts. Fan and LP compressor casing are single ring assemblies giving stiff construction with high degree of circularity. This, together with use of abradable spacer coatings, gives enhanced compressor efficiency through small blade tip clearances. All compressor stators are punched and brazed into stator rings, eliminating stator wear and fretting. Low-pressure air bleed provided to ventilate accessory zone. No variable-geometry blading.

INTERMEDIATE CASING: One-piece casing carrying engine and aircraft accessories, and gearbox. Internally provides support for fan/LP compressor bearings and for HP compressor front bearing. Contains accessory drive gear from front of HP compressor.

HP COMPRESSOR: Seven-stage axial unit of constant tip diameter, driven by HP turbine. Rotor uses multi-disc construction with through bolts and curvic couplings. Front stub shaft carried on main ball thrust bearing supported by compressor intermediate casing. Rear HP disc bolted to HP turbine shaft. HP compressor casing and stator mounting as for LP compressor. High-pressure air bleed provided for aircraft cabin air-conditioning and, when required, engine nose cowl anti-icing system. No variable-geometry blading or blow-off valves. Overall pressure ratio 16 : 1.

COMBUSTION SYSTEM: Short-length annular chamber with vaporising burners.

HP TURBINE: Single-stage axial unit with air-cooled rotor blading. Rear of HP rotor carried on intershaft roller bearing downstream of turbine disc.

LP TURBINE: Three-stage axial unit of constant mean diameter. Roller bearing, supported by exhaust cone assembly, carries rear of LP turbine shaft adjacent to stage 3 disc.

BEARINGS: Squeeze-film design.

JET PIPE: Plug nozzle type.

FUEL SYSTEM: Dowty hydro-mechanical system. Fuel from first-stage centrifugal pump passes through fuel heater and filter, and thence to second-stage gear pump to main control system and acceleration control. Centrifugal governors on LP and HP shafts cause fuel spill-back in event of more than 2 per cent shaft overspeed.

ACCESSORIES: Engine accessories and engine-driven aircraft accessories are mounted in annulus between gas generator cowling and engine carcase. Accessories mounted directly on engine gearbox and driven from HP compressor. Accessories include fuel heater, engine oil cooler, fuel control units, LP and HP governors, alternators, constant speed unit, oil tank, air starter, hydraulic and lubricating pumps.

LUBRICATION SYSTEM: Gear-type pressure pump feeds oil to all main bearings, LP and HP drives and accessory gearbox. Oil scavenged from front and rear compartments and from accessory gearbox passes through fuel-cooled oil cooler before returning to tank.

STARTING: Air starter on HP accessory gearbox.

DIMENSIONS:
Fan intake diameter 35·8 in (909 mm)
Overall length 110·0 in (2,795 mm)

WEIGHT:
Maximum, with accessories 1,500 lb (680 kg)

PERFORMANCE RATINGS:
T-O rating:
S/L, ISA 7,760 lb (3,520 kg) st
S/L, ISA +15°C 7,260 lb (3,293 kg) st
Cruise rating:
Mach 0·65 and 21,000 ft (6,405 m) ISA 2,670 lb (1,212 kg) st

SPECIFIC FUEL CONSUMPTION:
At T-O rating:
S/L, ISA 0·472
S/L, ISA+15°C 0·437
At cruise rating:
Mach 0·65 and 21,000 ft (6,405 m) ISA 0·750

ROLLS-ROYCE/SNECMA M45SD-02 (RB.410D-2)

Rolls-Royce Bristol Engine Division and Dowty Rotol Ltd have completed contractual and cost-sharing arrangements with the British government for this ultra-quiet engine demonstrator programme. It is based on the M45 engine and Dowty Rotol variable-pitch fan.

The project will involve the study and testing of noise-reducing techniques, of which the geared fan is a major example. Agreement in principle for active participation by SNECMA in extensions to the demonstrator engine programme was being discussed in February 1974.

The geared variable-pitch fan is a new principle which enables a considerable reduction to be made in engine noise while, at the same time, maintaining engine performance. By the introduction of

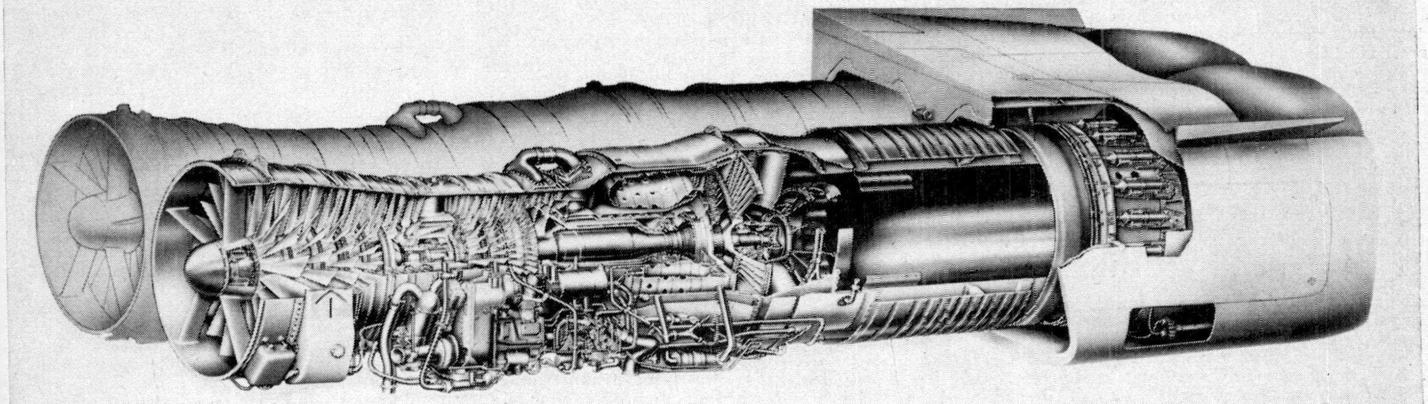

Cutaway drawing of installed pair of Rolls-Royce/SNECMA Olympus 593 turbojets (each 38,050 lb; 17,260 kg st)

a reduction gear it is possible to run the fan turbine at high speed and, in consequence, at high efficiency, yet still use a large, low-speed fan to give high thrust with low noise levels. The M45SD-02 is designed to generate source noise not exceeding 95 PNdB at 500 ft (152 m).

The large fan, giving a high by-pass ratio, has variable-pitch blades, which help to reduce even further the part-thrust noise of this basically quiet engine by allowing the fan to run at optimum pitch. Moreover, the variable-pitch feature offers improved handling qualities important to airline safety.

These characteristics are achieved with variable pitch because:

It provides a fundamentally faster thrust-response rate with rapid pitch changes and the core remaining at relatively high regime. This will become of increased importance for thrust control on steep approach paths being studied for minimum noise and improved air traffic control, and also for baulked landing, and for effective selection of reverse thrust after touchdown. Moreover, it enables reverse thrust to be operated down to zero aircraft speed without hot-air ingestion problems and so can be used for aircraft ground manoeuvring purposes.

It enables very low thrust levels to be achieved without thrust spoiling in order to obtain quiet, steep descent paths on the approach and from cruising altitude.

Thrust can be optimised at all forward speeds and in all climatic conditions, by using variable pitch to provide the best possible engine matching.

It allows the independent selection of engine speed for any given part-thrust condition in order to minimise noise.

The demonstrator engine, designated M45SD-02 and with the Rolls-Royce project number of RB.410D-2, was expected to run before the end of 1974. The results of the programme will be relevant to many classes of aircraft, mainly of an R/STOL nature. Data from the demonstrator will be used to refine the design of a definitive production engine, the **RB.410-11.** In March 1974 the RB.410-11 was envisaged as having the following specification: basic weight, 2,885 lb (1,309 kg); by-pass ratio, 8·8 : 1; total fan airflow, 630 lb (286 kg)/sec; overall pressure ratio, 17·8 : 1; T-O (S/L, ISA, static), 14,370 lb (6,518 kg); corresponding specific fuel consumption, 0·295; noise at 500 ft (152 m) horizontal distance, 96 PNdB.

The following description relates to the M45SD-02 (RB.410D-2):

Type: Geared variable-pitch fan demonstrator engine.

Air Intake: Direct pitot, with no struts or inlet guide vanes.

Fan: Single stage, of aluminium alloy construction throughout. Fourteen variable-pitch blades held in rotor hub by nuts. Rotor runs in overhung ball and plain bearings, with hub bolted to tubular shaft driven through epicyclic gearbox of 2·38 : 1 ratio by LP turbine shaft. Fan cowl and duct of aluminium acoustic panels. Fan hub shrouded by large anti-iced rotating spinner. Rear of spinner is large tubular fixed shroud over reduction gear, carrying fan duct on 34 aluminium-alloy stator vanes. Max airflow 484 lb (219 kg)/sec. By-pass ratio 8·73 : 1.

Core Engine: Basically identical to M45H-01 except for added LP turbine stage. Overall engine pressure ratio 13·5 : 1.

LP Turbine: Four-stage axial, with fourth stage comprising 48 stators and 62-blade rotor held by tie-bolts to M45H-01 turbine.

Dimensions and Weight: Not finalised.

Performance Rating:

T-O, S/L, ISA 10,027 lb (4,548 kg) st

Specific Fuel Consumption:

T-O, S/L, ISA 0·32

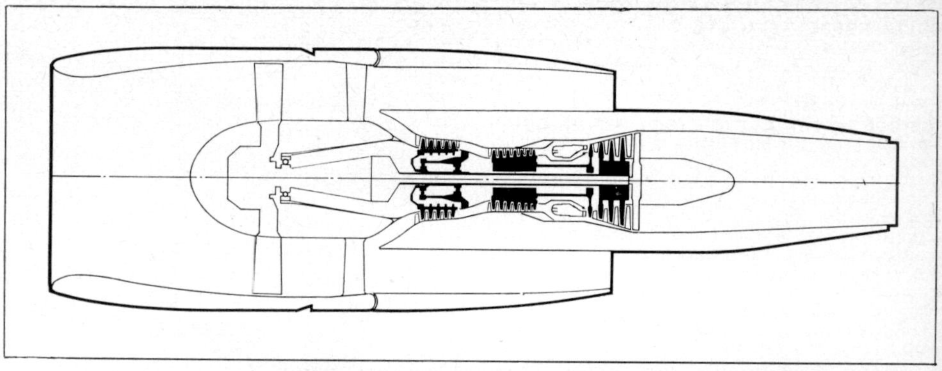

Provisional cross-section of Rolls-Royce/SNECMA M45SD-02 geared variable-pitch turbofan (10,027 lb; 4,548 kg st). Parts common to the M45H-01 are shown in solid black

ROLLS-ROYCE/SNECMA OLYMPUS 593

The Olympus 593 is now in production by Rolls-Royce (1971) Ltd in Britain and SNECMA in France as the power plant for the Concorde supersonic airliner. The work is shared on a 60%/40% basis, respectively. Rolls-Royce is producing the gas generator and SNECMA the convergent/divergent exhaust nozzle, thrust reverser and afterburner system.

Pre-flight Olympus development engines, designated 593D, were used for bench testing from mid-1964. The first of the Olympus 593 flight-type engines made its initial test run in November 1965. Thrusts ranging up to 40,000 lb (18,144 kg) have been obtained with afterburning in operation. A Vulcan testbed, with a single Olympus 593 mounted beneath its fuselage in a representative Concorde half-nacelle, assisted flight development from September 1966 to July 1971. Concordes have been flying since February 1969. The programme calls for a total of 46,000 hours of bench and flight testing, with seven Concorde aircraft, before entry into service.

Production standard Olympus 593 engines are flying in pre-production and production Concordes. In March 1974 a production standard engine, the Olympus 593 Mk 610, successfully completed an official 150 hr type test. At that time running time exceeded 30,000 hr, and full aircraft and engine certification were anticipated at the end of 1974. The following description refers to the production engine, the 593 Mk 610.

Industrial and marine versions of this engine are being considered.

Type: Axial-flow two-spool turbojet with partial afterburning.

Air Intake: Fabricated titanium casing, with zero-swirl five-spoke support for the front LP compressor bearing. In the Concorde the engine is installed downstream of an intake duct incorporating auxiliary intake and exit door systems and a throat of variable profile and cross-section (see "Aircraft" section).

LP Compressor: Seven-stage axial-flow type, with all blading and discs manufactured from titanium. Single-piece casing machined from a stainless steel forging, electro-chemically machined.

Intermediate Casing: Titanium casing, with vanes supporting LP and HP thrust bearings. Drives for engine-mounted aircraft and engine auxiliary drive gearboxes are taken out through the intermediate casing.

HP Compressor: Seven-stage axial-flow compressor. The first three stages of blades are made from titanium alloy. Remaining stages are made from a heat-resistant material due to very high compressor delivery temperatures during supersonic flight. Stainless steel single-piece casing.

Delivery Casing: Electro-chemically machined. The combustion system burner manifold and the main support trunnions are located around the delivery casing.

Combustion Chamber: Annular chamber, cantilever-mounted from the rear. Fabricated as single unit from nickel alloy, with all joints butt-welded to ensure reliability. Total of 16 vaporising burners, each with twin outlets, welded directly into chamber head. Fuel injectors are simple pipes which enter each vaporiser intake with no physical contact. Combustion leaves virtually no visible smoke in the propulsive jet.

Fuel Grades: DERD. 2494 Issue 7, AIR 3405B (3rd edition, amendment 1), ASTM D-1655-71 (Jet A) and ASTM D-1655-71 (Jet A1).

Fuel System: Lucas system, incorporating a mechanically driven first-stage pump and a second-stage pump driven by an air turbine, which is shut down at altitude cruise conditions as fuel requirements can be met by the first-stage pump alone. The first-stage pump also supplies afterburner fuel. A fuel-cooled oil cooler is incorporated. An Ultra electronic system, with integrated-circuit amplifier, provides combined control of fuel flow and primary nozzle area. Afterburner fuel is controlled by an ELECMA electrical control unit. The fuel system of the production Olympus 593 is substantially lighter than the one previously in use, and it operates at pressures of about one-half those on the earlier system. It also has improved maintenance and installation characteristics. The principal difference is that the piston-type HP pump is replaced by an air turbopump. At altitude cruise conditions, sufficient pressure is available from the first-stage pump alone and the air turbopump is shut down.

HP Turbine: Single-stage turbine, with cooled stator and rotor blading.

LP Turbine: Single-stage, with cooled rotor blades. LP drive-shaft co-axial with HP shaft.

Primary Nozzle Assembly: Comprises a straight jet pipe and a pneumatically-actuated variable primary convergent nozzle which permits maximum LP-spool speed and turbine-entry temperature to be achieved simultaneously over a wide range of compressor-inlet temperatures.

Afterburner: Single-ring sprayer with programmed fuel control as a function of main-engine fuel flow.

Secondary Nozzle Assembly: Monobloc structure with each twin nacelle manufactured from Stresskin panels. Each power plant terminates in a pair of "eyelids" which form a variable-area secondary divergent nozzle and thrust reverser. The eyelid position is programmed to maintain optimum power plant efficiency through all the flight regimes: take-off, subsonic cruise and supersonic cruise. When completely closed they act as thrust reversers.

Accessory Drives: Beneath the compressor intermediate casing are two gearboxes, both mechanically driven off the HP shaft (the LP shaft only has a pulse-probe signal source and provision for hand or mechanical turning). The LH gearbox drives the main engine oil pressure/scavenge pumps and the first-stage fuel pump. The RH gearbox drives the aircraft hydraulic pumps and CSD/alternator.

Lubrication System: Closed system, using oil to specification DERD.2497, MIL-L-9236B. Pressure pump, multiple scavenge pumps and return through Serck fuel/oil heat exchanger.

Starting System: SEMCA air-turbine starter drives the HP spool. Dual high-energy ignition system serves igniters in the annular chamber.

Mounting: Main trunnions on horizontal centre-line of the delivery casing. Allowance for expansion contained within aircraft pickups. Front stay from roof of the nacelle picks up on the top of the intake casing.

Dimensions:

Max diameter at intake 48·0 in (1,219 mm)

Length, flange-to-flange 154 in (3,910 mm)

Intake flange to final nozzle 279 in (7,080 mm)

Weight:

Basic, dry 7,053 lb (3,202 kg)

Performance Rating:

T-O (S/L, ISA) 38,050 lb (17,260 kg)

ROLLS-ROYCE TURBOMÉCA

ROLLS-ROYCE TURBOMÉCA LIMITED

Address:

4/5 Grosvenor Place, London SW1, England

Telephone: 01-235-3641

This company was formed jointly by Rolls-Royce and Turboméca in June 1966 to control the design, development and production programmes for the Adour reheated turbofan. The main function of the company is to receive contracts from the British Ministry of Defence on the Adour for both the British and French governments. The company can also enter into commercial contracts for the sale of the Adour to customers other than the British and French governments and grant licences for its manufacture.

ROLLS-ROYCE TURBOMÉCA ADOUR

The Adour was originally designed for the SEPECAT Jaguar strike/trainer aircraft to meet requirements laid down by the British and French joint air and naval staffs. It is a two-shaft turbofan engine fitted with an integral, modulated, afterburner of advanced design. The whole engine is simple and robust and contains features permitting modular exchange, major engine sections being replaceable in the field, avoiding the need for return to an overhaul base.

The complete propulsion unit has been designed for an overhaul life of 1,000 hours. The engine temperatures and rotational speeds are moderate and a thrust growth of the order of 40 per cent within the confines of existing installations is envisaged.

Bench testing began at Derby on 9 May 1967. Engines are assembled at Derby (R-R) and Tarnos (Turboméca) from parts made at single sources in Britain and France. Turboméca makes the compressors, casings and external pipework (to preserve Anglo-French parity the afterburner is subcontracted to SNECMA); Rolls-Royce makes the remainder. By mid-1974 total running time exceeded 50,000 hours.

The Adour has been selected for the Japanese T-2 trainer and a licence agreement has been negotiated for the full manufacture of the engine in Japan by Ishikawajima-Harima Heavy Industries. In 1972 a non-afterburning Adour was selected to power the Hawker Siddeley Hawk advanced trainer. Further versions of the Adour are being considered for developed types of Jaguar and for other aircraft, including business jets and the civil third level market.

The following are the principal versions of the Adour:

Mk 101. First 40 production engines for Jaguar. Afterburner control system activated only when throttle lever has moved beyond maximum dry thrust position. Sudden light-up then results in large augmentation, with further increase to maximum rating obtained by continued throttle movement. Maximum rating 4,620 lb; 2,095 kg dry and 6,930 lb; 3,143 kg with afterburner. Engine fully qualified February 1972.

Mk 102. Standard production engine for Jaguars in service with RAF and Armée de l'Air. Afterburner control system can operate in normal mode, as in Mk 101, or in part-throttle-reheat (PTR) mode. In PTR mode afterburner is first lit at low throttle setting; continued throttle movement increases both basic engine thrust and afterburner augmentation up to maximum rating. Thrust can thus be smoothly modulated at all times. First 82 engines were Mk 102/JP 102 with single catalytic igniter; current production is Mk 102/JP 103 with two catalytic igniters. Maximum rating 5,115 lb (2,320 kg) dry and 7,305 lb (3,313 kg) with afterburner. Engine fully qualified April 1972.

Mk 151. Also known as the RT.172-06, the Mk 151 is a dry engine which is identical to the Mk 102 in internal components, casings, speeds and temperatures. In pre-production for HS 1182 Hawk. First ran February 1973. Maximum rating 5,200 lb (2,360 kg).

RT.172-26. Uprated engine on offer for export versions of Jaguar. Performance increase aimed at high forward speed part of envelope. Maximum rating at Mach 0·9 at S/L increased by 15 per cent dry and 27 per cent with afterburner. T-O static ratings 5,260 lb (2,386 kg) dry and 8,000 lb (3,628 kg) with afterburner.

TF40-IHI-801A. Japanese engine basically similar to Adour Mk 102, for T-2 and variants. Manufacturing licence signed by Ishikawajima-Harima (see Japanese section) in June 1970. Pre-production engines delivered by RRT to support T-2 prototype flight programme, with IHI established for overhaul and repair. Deliveries of TF40 engines from IHI planned to begin in October 1974.

The following description refers to the Adour Mk 102:

TYPE: Two-shaft turbofan for subsonic and supersonic aircraft.

INTAKE: Direct pitot intake formed by forward extension of fan casing. No radial struts or inlet guide vanes.

FAN: Two-stage fan. Rotating spinner, anti-iced by turbine-bearing cooling air, on front of first-stage disc. Individually replaceable aluminium blades with no part-span or tip shrouds. Fixed steel stators and exit vanes. Whole unit overhung ahead of front LP roller bearing of squeeze-film type. Full-length fan duct leading to afterburner. By-pass ratio, 0·8 : 1.

COMPRESSOR: Five-stage compressor on HP shaft. Large-diameter double-conical shaft for rigidity with bolted curvic couplings. Wide-chord blades of titanium. Steel stator blades. Overall pressure ratio 11 : 1.

COMBUSTION CHAMBER: Annular, with straight-through flow. Fitted with 18 air-spray fuel nozzles, two starting fuel-spray nozzles and two igniter plugs.

HP TURBINE: Single-stage, aircooled.

LP TURBINE: Single-stage. Both turbine bearings of squeeze-film type.

JET PIPE: Fully modulated afterburner of compact, short-length design incorporating four concentric but staggered spray rings and vapour gutters. Catalytic igniters between inner gutters. Variable nozzle has eight master and eight slave petals positioned by eight-sided frame moved axially by four fuel-operated nozzle rams. Afterburner fuel flow and nozzle operation controlled by single package by Dowty Fuel Systems.

First Rolls-Royce Turboméca Adour RT.172-06 dry turbofan for the Hawker Siddeley Hawk

DIMENSIONS:	
Intake diameter	22 in (559 mm)
Overall length (Mk 102)	117 in (2,970 mm)
WEIGHT, DRY (Mk 102):	1,610 lb (729 kg)
PERFORMANCE RATINGS (Mk 102):	
T-O rating, dry	5,115 lb (2,320 kg)
T-O with afterburner	7,305 lb (3,313 kg)
SPECIFIC FUEL CONSUMPTION:	
S/L static, dry	0·74
Mach 0·8, 39,000 ft (11,887 m)	0·955

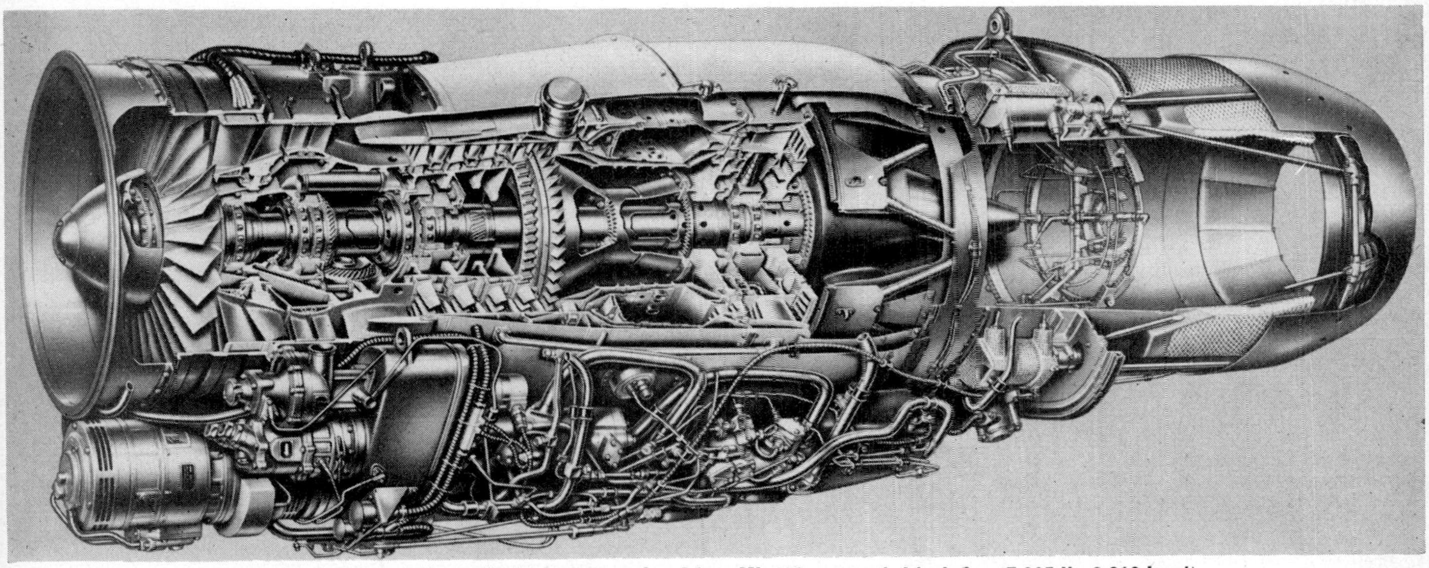

Cutaway drawing of the Rolls-Royce Turboméca Adour Mk 102 augmented turbofan (7,305 lb; 3,313 kg st)

TURBO-UNION

TURBO-UNION LTD

ADDRESS:
PO Box 3, Filton, Bristol BS12 7QE, England
Telephone: 0272-693871

Formed in October 1969, this international company was established to manage the entire programme for the RB.199 engine for the Panavia Multi-Role Combat Aircraft. Shares are held in the ratio Fiat SpA, 20 per cent; MTU München GmbH, 40 per cent; Rolls-Royce (1971) Ltd, 40 per cent. The overall work-share of the RB.199 programme, however, will be divided in proportion to the orders placed by the three partner countries.

TURBO-UNION RB.199

Designed originally by Rolls-Royce Bristol Engine Division, this engine competed with the Pratt & Whitney JTF 16 for the propulsion of the Panavia MRCA (which see) and was announced as the winner after a meeting of the Multi-Role Combat Aircraft Policy Group on 4 September 1969.

A three-shaft augmented turbofan of extremely advanced design, it has a lightweight fan based on that of the Pegasus on a reduced scale, and an advanced reheat system designed for an extremely wide operating envelope. The RB.199 offers low fuel consumption for long-range dry cruise, even at sea level, and approximately 100 per cent

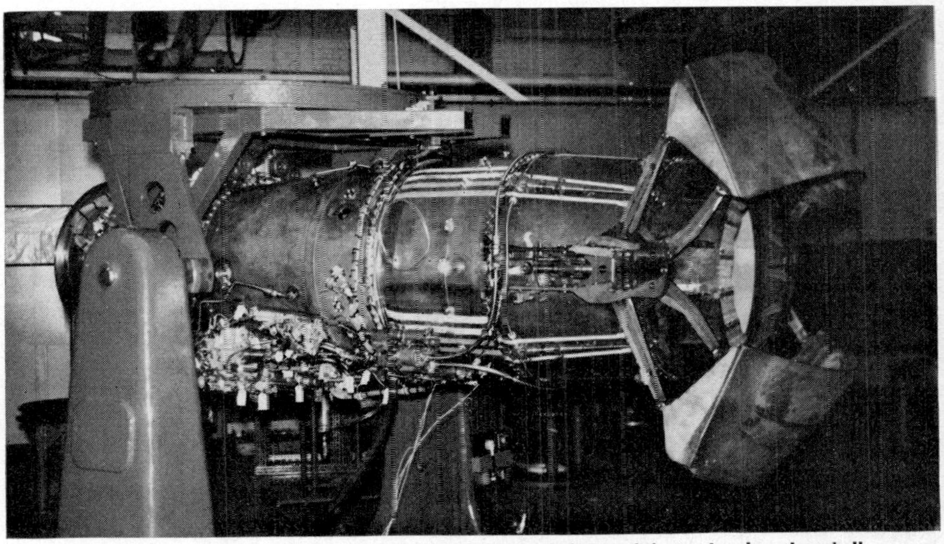

Turbo-Union RB.199-34R three-shaft augmented turbofan prototype, showing clamshell reverser in intermediate position

thrust augmentation with full afterburner for combat manoeuvre and supersonic acceleration. Further design goals included minimal weight and frontal area, moderate first cost and economic maintenance and overhaul. Strip, inspection and rebuild are facilitated by modular construction, and by the use of electron-beam welding to reduce the number of separate components.

Bench-testing of this very advanced reheat turbofan, power plant of the MRCA, is now taking place at Bristol, at the National Gas Turbine Establishment at Pyestock, at a new open-air testbed built by MTU at Manching and at a new enclosed cell built by Fiat at Sangone near Turin. So far development has been highly satisfactory. Flight-clearance levels of thrust, both dry and with afterburner, have been exceeded, with the specified fuel consumptions. Two 24 hr runs, including a number of simulated missions with afterburner, have been completed; afterburner light-up has consistently been exemplary, and the afterburner has been lit 5,000 ft (1,525 m) higher than demanded by specification for entry-to-service and 10,000 ft (3,050 m) higher than called for during initial flying. A special core rig is being used to optimise the "top temperature" zone, and it is reported that the crucial HP turbine rotor blades have already demonstrated cooling in accordance with prediction. These blades are among many components where "continuous" progress is being made upon manufacturing techniques. The MTU bed is equipped for oil-injection for flow visualisation and for running with reverse thrust; the Fiat bed can take a complete aircraft installation and has immediate magnetic-tape data recording. Flight development, with an engine mounted in a dummy MRCA half-fuselage mounted beneath a Vulcan aircraft, began on 19 April 1973. This installation has nose intake doors to prevent damage to the engine through ingestion of foreign bodies on take-off (when the RB.199 is not normally operating). The flying testbed will cover such phases of the programme as in-flight relighting, windmilling, operation with yawed or high-incidence airflow conditions, operation during gun firing, and MRCA pilot familiarisation.

In April 1974 it was announced that an RB.199 had "successfully completed a 24 hr endurance test to the exacting requirements demanded for engine flight clearance". Bench and flight testing at that time was "well over 1,000 hours" and the Vulcan flight testbed was about to begin a flight programme to verify the latest aerodynamic standard of engine previously developed in ground testing. The Vulcan's main task prior to the start of MRCA flying was to investigate RB.199 behaviour with and without afterburner over the flight envelope anticipated in early MRCA flight trials.

The following data were released as this edition went to press (*Jane's* conversions in brackets): thrust, dry, more than 30 kN (6,744 lb; 3,059 kg); thrust, reheated (maximum afterburner), more than 60 kN (13,489 lb; 6,118 kg); airflow, approximately 70 kg/sec (154·3 lb/sec); by-pass ratio, greater than 1; pressure ratio, greater than 20; turbine entry temperature, higher than 1,550°K (1,277°C); reheat (afterburner) temperature, higher than 1,900°K (1,627°C); thrust/weight ratio, greater than 8.

ISRAEL

BET-SHEMESH

BET-SHEMESH ENGINES LTD

OFFICES AND WORKS:
Bet-Shemesh

The first section of a 130,000 sq ft (12,077 m²) new Israeli aero-engine factory, Bet-Shemesh Engines Ltd, near Bet-Shemesh, between Tel Aviv and Jerusalem, was officially inaugurated on 15 January 1969. The company is owned 49 per cent by the Israeli government and 51 per cent by Turboméca SA and the works, when complete, will be a replica of Turboméca's factory at Tarnos in France. Over 500 persons are currently engaged at the works and the payroll is planned eventually to rise to around 1,100. Initially Bet-Shemesh manufactured turboprop components on behalf of Turboméca. By 1973 complete engines—Marboré VI turbojets for CM 170 Super Magister trainers—were being produced. The company also manufactures parts for the Marboré II, Artouste II and III, Turmo II and Astazou II. A non-aviation product is the M2T1 industrial gas turbine.

An associate company of Bet-Shemesh Engines has also been established to produce many of the special small-scale cast items for Israeli-manufactured Turboméca engines and components. Known as Misco-Bet-Shemesh Ltd, the company is owned 25 per cent each by the Israeli government and Turboméca, and 50 per cent by the Howmet Corp of Muskegon, USA. It will utilise the technology and alloys of Howmet in the supply of castings to Bet-Shemesh Engines—as does Microfusion SA, Howmet's French licensee, for Turboméca.

ITALY

ALFA-ROMEO

SOCIETÀ PER AZIONI ALFA-ROMEO

HEAD OFFICE:
Via Gattamelata 45, 20149 Milan
Telephone: Milan 3977

AVIATION WORKS:
80038 Pomigliano D'Arco, Naples
Telephone: 8841 344

This company, famous as an automotive manufacturer, entered the aero-engine industry in Italy in 1925 by acquiring licences for the Jupiter engine from the Bristol Aeroplane Co Ltd, and the Lynx engine from Armstrong Siddeley Motors Ltd. In 1930 the company produced its first engine of original design and remained an important manufacturer of piston engines for Italian aircraft until 1956.

For the following few years, Alfa-Romeo restricted its aviation work to overhaul of Curtiss-Wright R-1820 and R-3350 piston engines and Wright J65, and Rolls-Royce Dart, Avon and Conway turbine engines. Subsequently, overhaul has also been undertaken of Rolls-Royce Gnome turboshafts, later marks (514, 527 and 528) of the Dart turboprop, General Electric J85-GE-13A turbojets and T58 turboshafts, Pratt & Whitney JT3D and JT8D turbofans and PT6 turboprops, and Allison T56 turboprops.

Alfa-Romeo resumed its manufacturing activities by participating in the European production programme for General Electric J79-GE-11A turbojets to power Lockheed F-104G Starfighters built in Europe. It is collaborating with Rolls-Royce in the manufacture and overhaul of Gnome H.1000, H.1200 and H.1400 turboshafts. A licence agreement has also been signed for the manufacture of General Electric T58 turboshafts.

Alfa-Romeo is prime contractor for the manufacture, under General Electric licence, of the J85-GE-13A turbojet to power the G91Y aircraft. It is also manufacturing the "hot" section of the J79-GE-19 turbojet engines for the F-104S Starfighters that have been produced in Italy for the Italian Air Force, as well as many parts for the J79-11B, -17 and -1K. Alfa-Romeo manufactures CF6-6 combustors under subcontract to General Electric; it makes PT6 parts, under UACL licence, for the AB 212 helicopter; it also produces T64 components, under GE licence, for the Aeritalia G222. Alfa-Romeo participates in development and component manufacture for the Turbo-Union RB.199 for the Panavia MRCA and Pratt & Whitney JT10D.

Alfa-Romeo is a member of the Finmeccanica-IRI group of companies.

RR/MTU/ALFA ROMEO 600 HP

The EPM 600 and ESM 600 are respectively the turboprop and turboshaft versions of a 600 hp gas turbine disclosed in April 1974. The project is tri-national, involving the United Kingdom, West Germany and Italy. Further details are given under the International heading in this section.

FIAT

FIAT, SOCIETÀ PER AZIONI

AERO-ENGINE WORKS:
Via Nizza 312, 10100 Turin
Telephone: (011) 6399

TEST CENTRE:
Officine del Sangone, Strada del Drosso 145, 10100 Turin

Full details of the present organisation of the Fiat company are given in the "Aircraft" section, under the "Aeritalia" heading.

The Fiat company was incorporated in 1899 and built its first aero-engines in 1908.

Fiat entered the gas-turbine field after the last war, by undertaking first the licence production of the de Havilland Ghost centrifugal-flow turbojet engine and then, in 1953, the manufacture of parts and assemblies of the Allison J35 turbojet engine for the USAF.

In 1960, Fiat began manufacture of the Orpheus 803 turbojet engine, and overhaul of the Orpheus 801 and 803, under licence from Bristol Siddeley Engines Ltd. It also produced components and carried out the assembly of General Electric J79 turbojet engines for F-104G Starfighters built in Europe, in collaboration with FN of Belgium, BMW of Germany and Alfa-Romeo of Italy.

Its current programmes include production of General Electric J79-GE-19 turbojet engines to power Italian-built F-104S Starfighters, leadership of the Italian team making the T64-P4D turboprop, under a licence agreement between General Electric and the Italian government; manufacture of CF6 accessory gearboxes for General Electric; and participation in licence production of the General Electric J85-GE-13A turbojet, for which Alfa-Romeo is prime contractor.

Fiat is a partner in Turbo-Union (which see) and is responsible for the design, development and manufacture of portions of the RB.199 turbofan for the Panavia MRCA.

Fiat is also collaborating with Rolls-Royce (Bristol Engine Division) in the development of the Viper 600 series turbojet for executive and training aircraft. Fiat is responsible for everything to the rear of the compressor casing, apart from turbine discs and blades.

Fiat is making spare parts for the J79 and Orpheus, and is responsible for overhaul and repair of both these turbojets, and Pratt & Whitney R-2800 piston engines.

PIAGGIO

INDUSTRIE AERONAUTICHE E MECCANICHE RINALDO PIAGGIO, SpA

HEAD OFFICE:
Viale Brigata Bisagno 14, 16129 Genoa (426)
Telephone: 540 521

WORKS AND OFFICERS:
See "Aircraft" section

The Aero Engine Division of Piaggio is currently manufacturing the following engines under various licence agreements: Rolls-Royce Bristol Viper 11, 526 and 540 turbojets to power the Aermacchi M.B. 326 and the Piaggio PD-808 (a sub-licence for the manufacture of the Viper 11 and 540 was issued to Atlas Aircraft to power South African-built M.B. 326 aircraft); Avco Lycoming T53-L-13A and T55-L-11A turboshaft engines ordered by the Italian government for installation in the Bell 204B/205 and CH-47C Chinook helicopters, respectively; and the Lycoming VO-435 and GSO-480 piston engines.

SNIA VISCOSA

DEFENCE AND AEROSPACE DIVISION

ADDRESS:
via Lombardia 31, 00187 Rome
Telephone: (06) 4680
Telex: 61114 SNIA

FACTORIES:
Colleferro (Rome) and Ceccano (Frosinone)

DIVISION MANAGER: Ing E. Svizzeretto

CHIEF OF ROCKET, MISSILES AND SPACE R & D DEPARTMENT: Ing P. Laurienzo

The SNIA Viscosa Defence and Aerospace Division is engaged in the research, design and production of solid propellants, solid-propellant rocket motors, complete rockets and missiles.

The company possesses all the necessary installations for the production of double-base solid propellants, from the nitration of glycerine and cotton to the production of grains by extrusion or casting. Composite solid-propellant grains and motors incorporating polyurethane or polybutadiene polymers as binder are also produced in all sizes, with high specific impulses and outstanding physical and mechanical characteristics.

In particular, SNIA is the exclusive licensee in all NATO countries (except Canada and the United States) of Rocketdyne's Flexadyne technology, which includes a family of composite propellants and liner insulation systems based on a carboxy-terminated polybutadiene (CTPB) polymer having outstanding structural and environmental capabilities.

Complete propulsion units of up to 23·6 in (600 mm) diameter, with combustion times ranging from a fraction of a second to about 1 minute, are manufactured by SNIA Viscosa's Defence and Aerospace Division for use in military rockets and missiles. A major production item in this field is the SNIA Type ARF/8M 2 in folding-fin air-to-surface rocket.

SNIA's Defence and Aerospace Division also produced the motors for the Italian Sparrow air-to-air missile programme, and is currently involved in the development of many weapon systems in co-operation with companies such as Messerschmitt-Bölkow-Blohm, Selenia, Breda Meccanica Bresciana and Oto Melara.

In the aerospace field, in addition to various single- and two-stage sounding rocket prototypes which have been tested successfully many times, the apogee motor for the ELDO Europa II programme was brought to the final qualification stage by SNIA. For the Italian Sirio space programme a new amagnetic high-performance apogee motor has been developed, with a titanium alloy case and improved polybutadiene propellant. Other apogee motors are being designed for ESRO programmes: for the GEOS satellite a glassfibre apogee motor is being developed with the co-operation of SEP of France; for OTS, Meteosat and Aerosat a high-performance apogee motor with carbon fibre case is being developed by a consortium formed by SNIA, SEP and MAN. In early 1974 SNIA was assigned by CNES with the responsibility for design and manufacture of retro and ullage motors for the separation of all three stages of the Ariane vehicles.

SNIA Viscosa Sirio apogee boost motor

JAPAN

IHI

ISHIKAWAJIMA-HARIMA JUKOGYO KABUSHIKI KAISHA (Ishikawajima-Harima Heavy Industries Co, Ltd)

HEAD OFFICE:
No 2-1, 2 chome, Ote-Machi, Chiyoda-ku, Tokyo

AIRCRAFT ENGINE DIVISION:
3-5-1, Mukodai-cho, Tanashi-shi, Tokyo 188
Telephone: (0424) 62-2111

PRESIDENT: Hisashi Shinto

EXECUTIVE VICE-PRESIDENT:
Dr Osamu Nagano

DIRECTOR AND GENERAL MANAGER, AIRCRAFT ENGINE DIVISION:
Dr Kaneichiro Imai

On 1 December 1960, Ishikawajima Heavy Industries Co was merged with Harima Shipbuilding Co and now operates as Ishikawajima-Harima Heavy Industries Co.

Its work on turbojet engines dates from 19 June 1956, when the Japanese government approved a licence agreement with the General Electric Company of Cincinnati, Ohio, USA, under which Ishikawajima has been producing spares for the J47-GE-27 turbojet engines which power F-86F Sabre fighter aircraft of the Japan Air Self-Defence Force.

In February 1960 IHI began the licence manufacture in Japan of J79-IHI-11A turbojet engines for Japanese-built Lockheed F-104J Starfighters. In 1967 the company built a J79 gas generator for use in an 8,000kW generating set.

The manufacture of the Rolls-Royce Turboméca Adour augmented turbofan in Japan under licence agreement received government approval in September 1970. Its production began in early 1973, under the Japanese designation TF40-IHI-801A.

Also under licensing agreements, with General Electric, IHI is producing the J79-IHI-17 reheat turbojet for the McDonnell Douglas F-4EJ, the T58 turboshaft for helicopters and other applications, including the propulsion of air cushion vehicles and hydrofoil boats, and the T64-IHI-10 turboprop engine to power the JMSDF's PS-1 anti-submarine flying-boat and PS-1 Mod search and rescue amphibian, and the Kawasaki P-2J maritime patrol aircraft. In addition the T64 has performed well in a Japanese Navy torpedo boat.

IHI undertakes overhaul and repair of Pratt & Whitney JT8D and General Electric J79, T58 and T64, and R-R Turboméca Adour military engines, and Turboméca Artouste and Astazou turboshafts.

Prior to the start of licence manufacture, in April 1959, IHI had been responsible for the J3 turbojet engine which had been under development by the Nippon Jet-Engine Company since 1956. The J3-IHI-7 version is installed in Fuji T-1B intermediate jet trainer and Kawasaki P-2J aircraft.

IHI participated in developing the XJ11 lift-jet, as well as the JR100, JR200 and JR300 built under supervision of the NAL. In addition in collaboration with Mitsubishi and Kawasaki, IHI made the prototype of the FJR710 turbofan. The JR100, JR200, JR300 and FJR710 are described in the NAL entry.

IHI J3-IHI-7

The J3-IHI-7 is a derivative of the J3-1, of which a description appeared in the 1959-60 *Jane's*, under the entry for "Nippon Jet-Engine Company". It is installed on the Kawasaki P-2J aircraft currently in service with the JMSDF, and is in production.

Ishikawajima-Harima J3-IHI-7C turbojet engine (3,080 lb; 1,400 kg st)

Studies are also underway for converting the J3-IHI-7 to an augmented turbofan. Major modifications include the introduction of a shorter combustion chamber, provision for air bleed for aircraft BLC purposes, revised turbine blading, and the addition of an aft-fan and afterburner. An experimental version with augmentation reached a thrust of 4,542 lb (2,060 kg) during bench tests in December 1972.

TYPE: Axial-flow turbojet.

AIR INTAKE: Annular nose air intake. Anti-icing system for front support struts.

COMPRESSOR: Eight-stage axial-flow type, built of Ni-Cr-Mo steel. Rotor consists of a series of discs and spacers bolted on to shaft. Rotor and stator blades of AISI 403 steel. Stator blades brazed on to fabricated base which is fixed in casing with circumferential T-groove. Rotor blades dovetailed to discs. Light alloy casing in upper and lower sections, flange-jointed together. Pressure ratio 4·5 : 1. Air mass flow 56 lb (25·4 kg)/sec.

COMBUSTION CHAMBER: Annular type. AISI 321 steel outer casing. L 605 steel flame tube. Thirty fuel supply pipes located in combustion chamber outer casing and 30 vaporiser tubes located at front of flame tube. Ignition by low-voltage high-energy spark plug in each side of combustion chamber.

FUEL SYSTEM: Hydromechanical, with IHI FC-2 fuel control.

FUEL GRADE: JP-4.

NOZZLE GUIDE: VANES Single row of aircooled fabricated vanes.

TURBINE: Single-stage axial-flow type. Disc bolted to shaft. Precision-forged blades.

BEARINGS: Rotating assembly carried in front (double ball) and rear (roller) compressor rotor bearings and rear (roller) turbine shaft bearing.

JET PIPE: Fixed-area type.

ACCESSORY DRIVES: On gearbox under compressor front casing.

LUBRICATION SYSTEM: Forced-feed system for main bearings and gear case. Dry sump. Vane-type positive displacement supply and scavenge pump.

OIL SPECIFICATION: MIL-L-7808.

MOUNTING: Three-point suspension, with one pickup by a pin on starboard side of compressor front casing and a trunnion on each side of the compressor rear casing.

STARTING: Electrical starter in intake bullet fairing.

DIMENSIONS:

Length, less tailpipe	65·4 in (1,661 mm)
Length overall with rear cone	78·5 in (1,994 mm)
Diameter overall	24·7 in (627 mm)
Frontal area	3·01 sq ft (0·28 m²)

WEIGHT, DRY:

Bare	815 lb (370 kg)
With accessories	948 lb (430 kg)

PERFORMANCE RATING:

T-O	3,080 lb (1,400 kg) st

SPECIFIC FUEL CONSUMPTION:

At T-O rating	1·05

OIL CONSUMPTION:
At normal rating (max)
1·06 Imp pints (0·60 litre)/hr

IHI J3-IHI-8

This engine is an uprated version of the J3-IHI-7 and has completed military qualification testing. All details for the J3-IHI-7 apply equally to the J3-IHI-8, with the following exception:

PERFORMANCE RATING:

T-O	3,415 lb (1,550 kg) st at 13,000 rpm

IHI XJ11

The XJ11 is an engine which IHI is developing to follow the J3 series. Design objectives include an especially lightweight structural design, highly-loaded main engine components, simplified fuel and lubrication systems, and thrust/weight ratio of 20 : 1.

IHI TF40-IHI-801A

This is the Rolls-Royce Turboméca Adour augmented turbofan engine, as built under licence by IHI. For details see International section.

KAWASAKI

KAWASAKI JUKOGYO KABUSHIKI KAISHA (Kawasaki Heavy Industries Ltd)

HEAD OFFICE:
38, Akashi-machi, Ikuta-ku, Kobe
Telephone: Kobe (078) 341-7731

WORKS:
Gifu and Akashi

OFFICERS: See "Aircraft" section

Kawasaki's factory at Kobe has been engaged on the repair and overhaul of gas-turbine engines for the US armed forces and the Japan Defence Agency since 1953.

In 1967, with the approval of the Japanese Ministry of International Trade and Industry, it acquired licence rights in the Avco Lycoming T53 turboshaft engine, one application for which is in the UH-1B/H helicopters manufactured in Japan by Fuji.

As a start, engines were shipped complete from the Avco Lycoming works. Stage two involved shipment of unassembled kits of parts for assembly by Kawasaki. Now, Avco Lycoming is shipping partial kits for mating with components produced in Japan by Kawasaki.

The engines being assembled in Japan are known as the Kawasaki KT5311A and KT5313B. They differ only in minor details from the T53-L-11 described in the 1966-67 *Jane's*. Sales to the end of October 1972 comprised 122 engines to the Japan Defence Agency and 22 to commercial operators.

Production of the T53-11A will continue up to the 160th unit. Production of the T53-13B started in Fiscal Year 1973 (14 engines), and it is expected that 20 will be made annually in future.

MITSUBISHI

MITSUBISHI JUKOGYO KABUSHIKI KAISHA (Mitsubishi Heavy Industries Ltd)

HEAD OFFICE:
5-1, Marunouchi 2 chome, Chiyoda-ku, Tokyo 100

ENGINE WORKS:
Daiko Plant, Nagoya Aircraft Works, 1-1, Daiko-cho, Higashi-ku, Nagoya 455
Telephone: Nagoya (052) 721-3111
Komaki North Plant, Nagoya Aircraft Works, 1200, Higashi-Tanaka, Komaki-Shi, Aichi 485
Telephone: Komaki (0568) 79-2111

OFFICERS:
See "Aircraft" section

Since 1952 Mitsubishi has been responsible for the repair and overhaul of engines of the Japan Defence Agency, domestic and foreign airlines and the US Air Force.

In 1967 Mitsubishi resumed its activity in the aviation gas-turbine field by undertaking manufacture of the CT63 turboshaft engine to power Hughes 369HM helicopters of the JGSDF under a licence agreement with Allison. A total of 140 engines have been delivered to the Japan Defence Agency, and the eventual number to be manufactured in Japan is expected to be 300. In 1972, under licence agreement with Pratt & Whitney Aircraft, Mitsubishi began the manufacture of the JT8D-M-9 turbofan. The first was delivered in January 1973. By 1977 a total of 70 engines are to be delivered to the Japan Defence Agency for use in the Kawasaki C-1 military transport.

Mitsubishi is engaged in the series production of a gas-turbine compressor set of its own design. Designated GCM-1, this is built into the power pack of the starter trolley which supports the fighter aircraft of the Japan Air Self-Defence Force.

NAL

NATIONAL AEROSPACE LABORATORY

ADDRESS:
1880 Jindaiji-machi, Chofu City, Tokyo
Telephone: 0422-47-5911

DIRECTOR: Masao Yamanouchi

HEAD OF AERO-ENGINE DIVISION:
Masakatsu Matsuki

The National Aerospace Laboratory (NAL) is a government establishment responsible for research and development in the field of aeronautical and space science. Since 1962 it has extended its activity to include V/STOL techniques. The decision was made in that year to initiate development of an engine to fulfil the requirement for a lightweight lift-jet power plant for VTOL aircraft.

The lift-jet engine was designated IHI/NAL JR100 series, and features a thrust-to-weight ratio of 10. The first version was completed in 1964. Two sets of IHI/NAL JR100Fs are installed in the NAL Flying Test Bed (see 1972-73 *Jane's*).

The more advanced IHI/NAL JR200 was developed in 1966, the IHI/NAL JR220 was completed in 1971, and the latest development programme concerns the JR300.

In 1971 the Agency of Industrial Science and Technology, Ministry of International Trade and Industry (MITI), funded a high by-pass ratio turbofan engine (FJR710) development programme. NAL has completed the basic design of this engine, and many component tests are being made at NAL. Industrial companies, chiefly IHI, are making development engines for this programme.

MITI/NAL FJR710 two-shaft turbofan (11,025 lb; 5,000 kg st)

IHI/NAL JR100

As a part of a V/STOL research and development programme, NAL designed and developed a simple 10 : 1 thrust/weight ratio lift-jet. The prototype engine, manufactured by IHI, was completed during 1964, and in the course of 150 hours of testing, including an endurance test in March 1969, some 1,300 starts have been completed. Engines were formerly being employed in testing a height control system for a "soft" landing, using the IHI/NAL JR100H version, and in a Flying Test Bed for stability studies, using the IHI/NAL JR100F. This research was complete by mid-1971. Additional engines are being produced for the NAL experimental VTOL aircraft. A JR100H is also being used for noise research.

TYPE: Single-shaft axial-flow lift-jet.

AIR INTAKE: Forward-facing annular type.

COMPRESSOR: Six-stage axial unit of 3·9 : 1 pressure ratio and 60·6 lb (27·5 kg)/sec air mass flow.

COMBUSTION CHAMBER: Annular type.

TURBINE: Single-stage axial unit with 850°C entry temperature.

JET PIPE: Fixed area.

FUEL SYSTEM: Hydromechanical system with single master control.

LUBRICATION SYSTEM: Non-return, intermittent oil supply system.

DIMENSIONS:
Diameter 23·6 in (600 mm)
Length overall 38·4 in (975 mm)

WEIGHT, DRY: 347·5 lb (156 kg)

PERFORMANCE RATINGS:
Max T-O:
JR100F 3,180 lb (1,430 kg) st
JR100H 3,360 lb (1,520 kg) st

SPECIFIC FUEL CONSUMPTION:
At max T-O rating:
JR100F 1·15
JR100H 1·13

IHI/NAL JR200 and JR220

Following work on the IHI/NAL JR100, NAL designed and developed the higher-thrust IHI/NAL JR200 of improved thrust/weight ratio, and this was manufactured by IHI. The design objectives of the IHI/NAL JR200 are the same as for the IHI/NAL JR100, but use is made of a higher air mass flow, smaller combustion chamber and more extensive lightweight materials. The prototype IHI/NAL JR200 was completed in the Summer of 1966.

An improved version, the IHI/NAL JR220 with higher pressure ratio and higher turbine entry temperature, is now under initial development. The prototype IHI/NAL JR220 has achieved its performance at NAL's test cell.

The following details relate to the JR200:

TYPE: Single-shaft axial lift-jet.

AIR INTAKE: Forward-facing annular type.

COMPRESSOR: Five-stage axial unit of 4 : 1 pressure ratio and 82 lb (37·2 kg)/sec air mass flow at 12,450 rpm. Air bleed 6·6 lb (3 kg)/sec.

IHI/NAL JR100 lift-jet (3,180-3,360 lb; 1,430-1,520 kg st)

COMBUSTION CHAMBER: Annular type.

TURBINE: Single-stage axial unit with 850°C entry temperature.

JET PIPE: Fixed area.

WEIGHT, DRY: 280 lb (127 kg)

PERFORMANCE RATINGS:
Max, without air bleed 4,585 lb (2,080 kg) st
Max, with air bleed 4,012 lb (1,820 kg) st

SPECIFIC FUEL CONSUMPTION:
At max rating, without air bleed 1·13
At max rating, with air bleed 1·17

The IHI/NAL JR200 lift-jet (4,585 lb; 2,080 kg st)

IHI/NAL JR300

The NAL is working on the basic design of the JR300, the latest and most advanced in this series of lift-jets. Stated to have a design thrust/weight ratio in the 20 : 1 class, the prototype could enter the assembly stage in 1974.

MITI/NAL FJR710

In the late 1960s the Japanese government and industry, seeking an engine programme that might remain competitive for many years, decided to embark on the design of a subsonic turbofan of high by-pass ratio, drawing heavily on the technology of the American JT9D and CF6 but on a much smaller scale. After a preliminary study by the NAL, funding was provided by the Ministry of International Trade and Industry in 1971 for a prototype demonstrator and test programme.

NAL has managed the design of the resulting FJR710, and many of the test components have been made in the Laboratory's workshops. Manufacture of the prototype and development engines was subcontracted to IHI, assisted by Kawasaki and Mitsubishi. The first engine made its first run in May 1973.

The current test programme is hoped to lead to a production engine in the 10,000-15,000 lb (4,535-6,810 kg) st class. It is planned that there should also be a second major stage of development, probably several years hence, which would raise thrust to at least 20,000 lb (9,070 kg). The more advanced engine has been tentatively planned to have a pressure ratio of 25 : 1, by-pass ratio of 8 : 1 and turbine entry temperature of 1,330°C. It is hoped that this more advanced engine will have an sfc (S/L, static) of 0·3, and a thrust/weight ratio of at least 6.

The following description applies to the first prototype engine, and is provisional:

Type: Two-shaft high by-pass ratio turbofan for subsonic commercial or military aircraft.

Air Intake: Direct annular entry around fan spinner.

Fan: Single-stage fan, with rotating spinner and inserted titanium blades with part-span shrouds. Metal fan duct held by eight aerofoil struts, preceded by ring of flow-straightening vanes. A fan reverser would be part of the airframe. By-pass ratio 7·5 : 1.

Compressor: Mechanically independent HP compressor. Multi-stage axial assembly with inserted blades of titanium and, at delivery end, high-nickel alloy. Several rows of variable stator blades held in upper and lower half-casings and operated by peripheral rings scheduled by hydraulic ram. Overall pressure ratio 22 : 1.

Combustion Chamber: High-intensity smokeless annular type.

Turbine: Two-stage HP gas-generator turbine with cooled blades. Multi-stage LP fan turbine. Entry temperature 1,150°C.

Jet Pipe: Fixed area, fitted with spoiler in installed engine.

Dimensions (approx):
- Length: 130 in (3,300 mm)
- Diameter: 60 in (1,520 mm)

Weight, Dry: 2,000 lb (907 kg)

Performance Ratings (ISA):
- T-O: 11,025 lb (5,000 kg) st
- Cruise at 20,000 ft (6,100 m) at Mach 0·7: 3,748 lb (1,700 kg)

Specific Fuel Consumption:
- T-O: 0·34
- Cruise, as above: 0·61

POLAND

BORZECKI

JOZEF BORZECKI

Address:

Wroclaw, ul. Sernicka 20/4

BORZECKI 2RB

The 2RB is a small piston engine designed and built by J. Borzecki for use in motor gliders. The prototype was built in 1970 and in the same year underwent bench tests. A flat-four, it may be used with tractor or pusher propeller. The engine began flight testing in early 1972 in the Borzecki Alto-Stratus motor glider.

Type: Four-cylinder two-stroke horizontally-opposed aircooled piston engine.

Cylinders: Bore 2·76 in (70 mm). Stroke 1·38 in (35 mm). Swept volume 33 cu in (540 cc). Compression ratio 7·2 : 1. Steel barrels with aluminium alloy cylinders and heads. Cylinder and head assembly attached to crankcase by four studs.

Pistons: Of aluminium alloy, with two compression rings.

Connecting Rods: Milled from steel.

Crankshaft: Steel shaft, supported in four ball bearings and one ball-thrust bearing at the front.

Crankcase: Aluminium alloy case, divided at the vertical longitudinal and transverse centre-lines with aft cover.

Induction: One Jawa 250 motor-cycle carburettor.

Fuel: Mixture of 76 octane petrol and oil.

Ignition: Battery ignition. One M14-250 0·55 in (14 mm) sparking plug per cylinder.

Mounting: Four rubber dampers at rear of crankcase or four studs at cylinder heads.

Propeller Drive: Direct tractor or pusher.

Dimensions:
- Length overall, with propeller boss: 17·7 in (450 mm)
- Width: 9·8 in (250 mm)
- Height, with carburettor: 10·2 in (260 mm)

Weight, Dry: 33 lb (15 kg)

Performance Ratings:
- Max T-O rating: 24 hp at 6,000 rpm

The Borzecki 2RB light piston engine, rated at 24 hp

- Continuous rating: 16 hp at 4,500 rpm

Specific Fuel Consumption:
- At max T-O rating: 0·86 lb (0·390 kg)/hp/hr
- At continuous rating: 0·75 lb (0·340 kg)/hp/hr

IL

INSTYTUT LOTNICTWA (Aeronautical Institute)

Headquarters:

Al. Krakowska 110/114, 02-256 Warsaw-Okecie

Telephone: Warsaw 460993

Managing Director:

Ing Zbigniew Pawlak

Chief of Technical Information Division:

Dipl Ing Andrzej Glass

The Aeronautical Institute is an establishment concerned with aeronautical research, aerodynamic tests, strength tests, test flights of aeroplanes, helicopters and gliders, aviation equipment, materials, technical information and standardisation. The Institute has a special manufacturing plant responsible for constructing prototypes to its own design.

IL SO-1

The Aeronautical Institute designed the SO-1 turbojet to power the Polish TS-11 Iskra (Spark) jet basic trainer. This engine is designed to permit the full range of aerobatics, including inverted flight. Guaranteed overhaul life is 200 hours. Further versions are under development, with increased thrust.

Type: Single-shaft axial-flow turbojet.

Air Intake: Annular intake casing manufactured as a cast shell. Fixed inlet guide vanes.

Compressor Casing: Manufactured as a cast shell in two parts, split along horizontal centre-line, in aluminium alloy.

Compressor: Seven-stage axial-flow compressor. Drum-type rotor built up of disc assemblies, with constant diameter over tips of rotor blades. Carried in ball bearing at front and roller bearing at rear. Steel stator blades bonded with resinous compound into slots in carrier rings. Rotor of steel and duralumin, with first three blade rows of steel and remainder of aluminium alloy. Pressure ratio 4·8.

Combustion Chamber: Annular type with 24 integral vaporisers. Outer casing made of welded steel.

IL SO-1 turbojet (2,205 lb; 1,000 kg st), initial power plant of the TS-11 Iskra (Spark) trainer *(BIIL)*

Fuel System: Two independent systems supplied by one pump. Starting system consists of six injectors, with direct injection. Main system consists of twelve twin injectors with outlets towards the vaporisers.

Fuel Specification: Paraffin type P-2 or TS-1.

Turbine: Single-stage axial-flow type. Blades attached to disc by fir-tree roots. Supported in roller bearing at rear.

Jet Pipe: Outer tapered casing and central cone connected by streamlined struts. Nozzle area adjusted by exchangeable inserts.

Lubrication System: Open type for rear compressor and turbine bearings, supplied by separate pumps. Closed type for all other lubrication points, fed by separate pumps.

Oil Specification: Type AP-26 (synthetic).

Accessory Drives: Gearbox mounted at bottom of air intake casing and driven by bevel gear shaft from front of compressor.

Starting: 27V starter/generator and bevel gear shaft, driven by aircraft battery or ground power unit, mounted on air intake casing.

Dimensions:
- Length overall: 84·7 in (2,151 mm)
- Width: 27·8 in (707 mm)
- Height: 30·1 in (764 mm)

Weight, Dry: 668 lb (303 kg)

Performance Ratings:
- T-O rating: 2,205 lb (1,000 kg) st at 15,600 rpm
- Max cont: 1,958 lb (888 kg) st at 15,100 rpm

Specific Fuel Consumption:
- At T-O rating: 1·045

Oil Consumption: 1·4 Imp pints (0·8 litre)/hr

IL SO-3

This is an improved version of the SO-1 which has replaced the earlier type in production at the WSK-Rzeszów (see this organisation's entry later in the Polish section). It is fitted in the current production TS-11 Iskra jet trainer. Details of the engineering changes incorporated in the SO-3 have not been disclosed, but the guaranteed TBO has been doubled, to 400 hours.

JANOWSKI

JAROSLAW JANOWSKI

Address:

Lodz 11, ul. Nowomiejska 2/29

JANOWSKI SATURN 500

The Saturn 500 has been designed by Mr Janowski and built by Mr S. Polawski for the Janowski J-1 ultra-light amateur-built aircraft (see "Aircraft" section). The prototype Saturn 500 was built in 1969. This two-cylinder two-stroke engine may be used with tractor or pusher propeller, and is intended for ultra-light aircraft built by amateurs.

In 1972 work began on a new version of the Saturn 500, with new cylinder heads, improved crankshaft and dual ignition. Its rating (max T-O) is increased to 30 hp; dry weight is believed to be about 55 lb (25 kg).

The following description applies to the initial 25 hp version:

Type: Two-cylinder two-stroke horizontally-opposed aircooled.

Cylinders: Bore 2·76 in (70 mm). Stroke 2·56 in (65 mm). Swept volume 30·5 cu in (500 cc). Compression ratio 8·5 : 1. Steel barrels with aluminium alloy cylinder heads. Cylinder and

head assembly attached to crankcase by four studs.
PISTONS: Of aluminium alloy. Two compression rings and one oil scraper ring.
CONNECTING RODS: Steel forgings.
CRANKSHAFT: Steel counterbalanced shaft, supported in two lead-bronze plain bearings and one ball-thrust bearing at the front.
CRANKCASE: Aluminium alloy case, split in the vertical plane, with front and aft covers.
INDUCTION: Two BVF 28N1 carburettors.
FUEL: Petrol/oil mixture using aviation 90 octane.
IGNITION: Two magnetos. One M14-250 0·55 in (14 mm) sparking plug per cylinder.
MOUNTING: Four rubber dampers at rear of crankcase.
PROPELLER DRIVE: Direct tractor or pusher.
DIMENSIONS:
Length overall, with propeller boss 16·93 in (430 mm)
Width, without sparking plugs 20·27 in (515 mm)
WEIGHT, DRY: 59·5 lb (27 kg)
PERFORMANCE RATING:
Max T-O rating 25 hp at 4,000 rpm
SPECIFIC FUEL CONSUMPTION:
Max T-O rating 0·70 lb (0·315 kg)/hp/hr
Normal cruising power 0·66 lb (0·300 kg)/hp/hr

25 hp Saturn 500 two-cylinder two-stroke engine designed by Jaroslaw Janowski

PZL

POLSKIE ZAKLADY LOTNICZE

HEADQUARTERS:
ul. Miodowa 5, 00251 Warsaw

SALES REPRESENTATIVE:
Pezetel, ul. Przemyslowa 26, 00450 Warsaw
Telephone: Warsaw 285071

The entire Polish aircraft industry is subordinate to the Zjednoczenie Przemyslu Lotniczego i Silnikowego PZL (Aircraft and Engine Industry Union). Pezetel handles all export sales of Polish aeronautical material.

WSK-KALISZ

WYTWÓRNIA SPRZETU KOMUNIKACYJNEGO KALISZ

HEAD OFFICE AND WORKS:
ul. Czestochowska 140, 62800 Kalisz

Telephone: 4081-3

GENERAL MANAGER:
Dipl Ing Zbígníew Girulskí

In 1952 the Soviet Union transferred responsibility for manufacture and service support of Russian aircooled radial piston engines to the WSK (transport equipment manufacturing centre) at Kalisz. No longer in production, except as spares, are the 125 hp M-11D, used in the Po-2 and CSS-13, and the 160 hp M-11FR, used in the Junak-2 and -3. A Polish team under Dipl Ing Wiktor Narkiewicz designed the 330 hp WN-3 radial for the TS-8 Bies, and this was produced by WSK-Kalisz. All these engines have been described in earlier editions of *Jane's*.

Current production is centred on: the 1,000 hp ASh-62IR (Polish designation ASz-62IR) for all versions of the An-2; and the 260 hp AI-14RA for the PZL-101 Gawron and PZL-104 Wilga (see "Aircraft" section). Production of the ASz-62IR exceeds 10,000 engines. WSK-Kalisz has developed a version of the AI-14 with electric starter, the AI-14RC. These aircooled radial piston engines are described in the USSR entry in this section.

Polish-built 260 hp AI-14RA piston engine

Polish-built 1,000 hp ASz-62IR piston engine

WSK-RZESZÓW

WYTWÓRNIA SPRZETU KOMUNIKACYJNEGO RZESZÓW

HEAD OFFICE AND WORKS: ul. Obronców Stalingradu 120, 35078 Rzeszów, Postbox 340
Telex: 83411
GENERAL MANAGER:
Dipl Ing Jozef Rokoszak

WSK-Rzeszów, founded in 1938 as PZL-Rzeszów, has been producing aero-engines since the second World War. The factory first manufactured under Soviet licence the M-11 piston engine, and the 575 hp AI-26W (under the Polish designation LiT-3) radial for the SM-1 (Mi-1) and SM-2 helicopters.

Engines currently in production are the 400 hp GTD-350 turboshaft, designed in the Soviet Union by the Isotov bureau for the Mi-2 helicopter, and the 2,200 lb (1,000 kg) st SO-3 turbojet. WSK-Rzeszów is the sole manufacturer of the GTD-350 engine, which is not produced in the Soviet Union. The SO-3 is listed under IL, earlier in the Polish entry.

SOUTH AFRICA

ATLAS

ATLAS AIRCRAFT CORPORATION OF SOUTH AFRICA (PTY) LTD

ADDRESS AND OFFICERS: See "Aircraft" section.

Atlas has for several years manufactured the Rolls-Royce Viper 22-1 turbojet under sub-licence from Piaggio of Italy, for use in Atlas Impala attack trainers. In 1973 Atlas was preparing to manufacture additional Viper engines to power an advanced version of the Impala. It is widely reported that more than 100 aircraft are involved, and that the engine to be made by Atlas will be the Viper 632, rated at 4,000 lb (1,814 kg) st, under sub-licence from Fiat, which shares development of the Viper 600 series with Rolls-Royce.

SPAIN

CASA

CONSTRUCCIONES AERONÁUTICAS SA

HEAD OFFICE AND OFFICERS:
See "Aircraft" section

DIVISIÓN DE MOTORES

OFFICE AND WORKS:
Carretara de Ajalvir, Km 3.5, Apdo 111 Torrejón de Ardoz, Madrid
Telephone: 407 34 66 and 407 37 66

MANAGING DIRECTOR:
Antonio Barrón Medrano

PRODUCTION MANAGER:
Florencio Manteca Martinez

SALES MANAGER:
Ramón López-Peláez

The Division de Motores of CASA was formed in June 1973. It was formerly the Empresa Nacional de Motores de Aviación (ENMASA), as described in previous editions of *Jane's*.

The first turbojet engine produced by ENMASA was the Marboré II, which was built under licence from the French Turboméca company as the Marboré M21.

The division's current aeronautical activities include overhaul and repair of General Electric J47, J79 and J85, SNECMA Atar 9C and Turboméca Marboré II and VI turbojet engines, and Lycoming T53 turboshafts, in the plant at Ajalvir. The same factory also overhauls and repairs aircraft and engine accessories.

SWEDEN

FLYGMOTOR

VOLVO FLYGMOTOR AB

HEAD OFFICE AND WORKS: S-461 01 Trollhättan

Telephone: 0520-301-00

This company was founded in 1930, as Nohab Flygmotorfabriker AB, and began by building under licence the Bristol Pegasus I aero-engine, under the designation My VI. The name of the company was changed to Svenska Flygmotor

AB in 1941 when the company became a member of the Volvo Group, the well-known car manufacturing concern. In 1970 Volvo acquired all shares in the company, which then took its present name.

Volvo Flygmotor AB holds a licence to build Rolls-Royce Avon engines and is also engaged in research and development work on turbojet engines, ramjet engines and rocket engines.

Its major current programme involves development and production of a licence-built version of the Pratt & Whitney JT8D-22 turbofan engine (Swedish designation RM8) to power the Saab 37 Viggen combat aircraft. It is also engaged in the development of experimental hybrid and liquid-fuel rocket engines, and brief details of some of these are given below.

The company has had a technical collaboration agreement on ramjet development with Bristol Aero-Engines and Rolls-Royce (1971) since 1957. Details of its RRX-1 ramjet test vehicle were given in the "Missiles" section of the 1964-65 *Jane's*.

FLYGMOTOR RM6C AVON

RM6C is the designation of the licence-built version of the Rolls-Royce Avon 300-Series turbojet which Flygmotor is producing to power the Saab 35D, E and F Draken fighters. It is rated at approximately 16,800 lb (7,620 kg) st with its Swedish-developed afterburner in use.

The afterburner has V-type flame-holders with the fuel injection manifold situated at the front of the V. Main fuel injection is made upstream and a smaller quantity is injected into the flame-holder. Ignition is by a "hot shot" device. The centrifugal-type fuel pump is driven by air from the engine compressor by means of a single-stage axial-flow turbine, the air supply being controlled by the main engine fuel pressure. Afterburner fuel flow is regulated at the pump outlet by a regulator which ensures a constant pressure ratio over the engine turbine. The jet pipe has hydraulically-operated two-position clamshell shutters, with an ejector nozzle.

Production of the RM6C will continue for at least two further years, chiefly to meet the needs of the Saab 35XS programme for the Finnish Air Force. Manufacture of spares, and general service support, continues for a large number of earlier Avon engines fitted to earlier marks of Draken and to the Lansen.

FLYGMOTOR RM8

The RM8 is a Swedish military version of the Pratt & Whitney JT8D-22 civil subsonic turbofan which Flygmotor has developed to power the Saab 37 Viggen supersonic multi-purpose combat aircraft.

The programme is being undertaken with the assistance of Pratt & Whitney, which supplied Flygmotor initially with three of the first production JT8D-1 engines. The first was put on test on 6 August 1964, and was being run with afterburning by the Spring of 1965. Approximately 14,000 hr of bench and flight testing had been completed by March 1974.

Development of the engine, and manufacture of 195 RM8As for the Viggen, is covered by a 689 million kroner contract from the Swedish government, the largest single order ever received by Flygmotor. Production, which will absorb 595 million kroner, started in mid-1968 and will continue through to the mid-1970s.

The RM8 is fitted with an afterburner with fully-variable exit nozzle, which gives a 70% increase in thrust.

Flygmotor has so far devoted almost 5,500,000 man-hours to the development of the RM8, even though the internal aerodynamics and thermodynamics are the same as on the JT8D. Apart from this similarity, the RM8 is made of new parts in different materials and having changed dimensions.

Until 1970 the main effort was devoted to development and manufacture of the RM8A version for the AJ 37 strike version of the Viggen, and all engines delivered by the end of 1973 were of this type. In late 1970 a substantially modified version, the **RM8B**, was planned to meet the propulsion requirements of the fighter Viggen, the JA 37. Research at Pratt & Whitney and Flygmotor showed that a changed design could improve the reliability of operation at high altitudes and in severe manoeuvres, as well as increase thrust in all regimes. In collaboration with Pratt & Whitney the design of the RM8B was completed in late 1971. The major change to improve functional reliability at high altitude has been to take the first stage off the LP compressor and add it to the fan, giving a three-stage fan and three-stage LP spool, both having a revised aerodynamic configuration according to the latest P & W research. To increase thrust the RM8B has a four-nozzle burner combustion system and a new HP turbine.

The first RM8B HP compressor was tested in 1971 in the P & W Willgoos high-altitude laboratory and showed very good performance and stability. Five complete RM8B prototype engines have now also been built and extensively tested at Trollhättan. The RM8B is claimed to have excellent performance and functional reliability, and to have specific fuel consumption

Final preparation of Volvo Flygmotor RM8 afterburning turbofans for the Viggen aircraft

below specification in both dry and augmented regimes. Flygmotor states that the RM8B is likely to meet the full requirement for propulsion of the fighter version of the Viggen.

The following description refers to the RM8A:

TYPE: Axial-flow two-spool turbofan with modulated afterburner.

AIR INTAKE: Annular, with 19 fixed inlet guide vanes.

FAN: Two-stage front fan. Titanium blades.

LP COMPRESSOR: Four-stage axial-flow, integral with fan stages, on inner of two concentric shafts. Blades of titanium. Steel casing.

HP COMPRESSOR: Seven-stage axial-flow on outer hollow shaft. Blades made of special high-temperature alloys of type used for turbine blading. Overall pressure ratio 16·5 : 1. By-pass ratio approximately 1 : 1. Total air mass flow 320 lb (145 kg)/sec.

COMBUSTION CHAMBER: Cannular type with nine cylindrical flame tubes, each downstream of a single Duplex burner and discharging into a single annular nozzle. Two high-energy spark plugs, each with its own igniter box.

HP TURBINE: Single-stage axial-flow, with cast blades.

LP TURBINE: Three-stage axial-flow, with cast blades. Exit guide vanes after turbine.

AFTERBURNER: Double-skinned to provide duct for cooling air. Outer skin of titanium. Inner skin of special alloys. One hot-streak igniter. Hydraulically-actuated fully-variable nozzle, using fuel as the operating fluid.

BEARINGS: Main shafts run in total of six bearings.

MOUNTING: Three-point. Main mountings on each side of compressor casing; one under turbine casing.

ACCESSORY DRIVE: Via gearbox, under engine, driven from HP turbine shaft.

DIMENSIONS:
- Length overall:
  - RM8A: 242·5 in (6,160 mm)
  - RM8B: 245·25 in (6,230 mm)
- Max diameter (both versions): 55 in (1,397 mm)
- Inlet diameter (both): 40·55 in (1,030 mm)

WEIGHT, DRY:
- RM8A: 4,630 lb (2,100 kg)
- RM8B: 5,181 lb (2,350 kg)

PERFORMANCE RATINGS (ISA, S/L):
- Max T-O, augmented:
  - RM8A: 25,970 lb (11,790 kg) st
  - RM8B: 28,085 lb (12,750 kg) st
- Max T-O, dry:
  - RM8A: 14,735 lb (6,690 kg) st
  - RM8B: 16,190 lb (7,350 kg) st
- Max continuous:
  - RM8A: 12,590 lb (5,715 kg) st
  - RM8B: 13,845 lb (6,285 kg) st

SPECIFIC FUEL CONSUMPTION:
- Max augmented:
  - RM8A: 2·47
  - RM8B: 2·52
- Max dry:
  - RM8A: 0·63
  - RM8B: 0·64
- Max continuous (both): 0·61

FLYGMOTOR VR35

The VR35 is a prepackaged liquid-propellant rocket engine with positive expulsion of the storable inhibited red fuming nitric acid (IRFNA) and Hydyne propellants. A solid-propellant gas generator delivers the expelling gas and programmes the thrust into a boost phase followed by a sustain blow-down period.

The positive expulsion is accomplished by a gas-pressurised piston for the fuel, contained in a central tank, and an inward-collapsible aluminium bladder for the oxidiser in its concentric tank. This expulsion system enables the engine to be fired under any acceleration direction, a capability which is essential for a missile engine with a thrust programme that includes the sustain phase.

Another advantage with this type of engine is the completely smoke-free exhaust, leaving no signature at launch or during flight.

The VR35 is now in production for the Saab-Scania RB05 air-to-surface missile, which is one of the main weapons for the AJ 37 Viggen (see "Missiles" section).

DIMENSIONS:
- Length overall: 69·7 in (1,770 mm)
- Max diameter: 11·8 in (300 mm)

WEIGHT:
- Total weight: 280 lb (127 kg)

PROPELLANT MASS FRACTION: 0·59

OPERATING TEMPERATURE RANGE: −50°C to +65°C

FLYGMOTOR VR3

Volvo Flygmotor has developed this pump-fed hydrogen-peroxide/kerosene rocket engine as a built-in booster for aircraft. The VR3 engine delivers a maximum thrust of 22,000 N and the thrust is continuously variable down to 6,000 N.

FLYGMOTOR HR4

An experimental hybrid rocket engine, the HR4, has been developed and flight-tested in a rocket equipped with a parachute recovery system. The HR4 has nitric acid type oxidiser and a company-developed amino resin called Tagaform as the solid fuel. It has a positive-expulsion system (a gas-generator-driven piston) for the

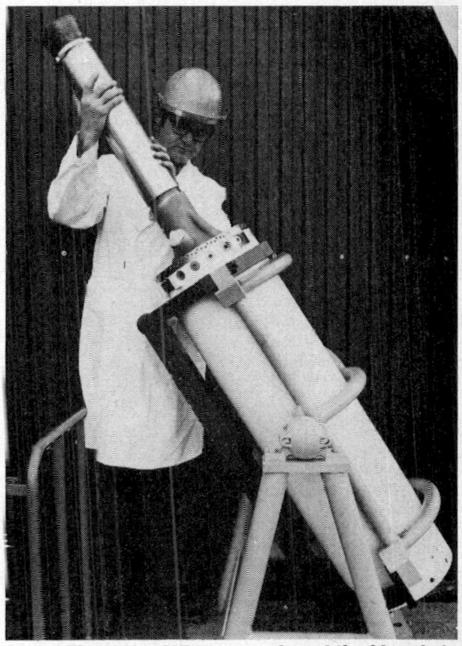

Volvo Flygmotor VR35 prepackaged liquid rocket: *above*, VR35 on static test at dive angle; *below*, longitudinal cross-section

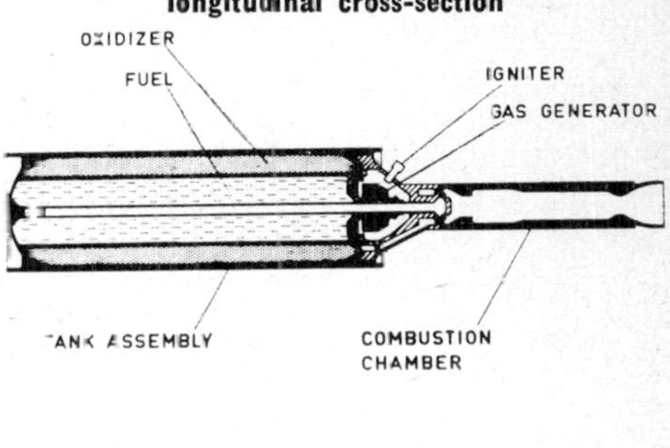

oxidiser. A special valving mechanism gives the engine a dual-mode thrust programme. The boost thrust is 1,700 N and the total impulse is 13,700 Ns (Newton-seconds).

FLYGMOTOR RAMJETS

Ramjet engine research and development have been under way at Volvo Flygmotor since 1950, when the company's underground high-pressure air magazine was completed. The stored air drives the combustion test rigs and wind tunnels necessary for this kind of work.

The engine research culminated in several flight tests with the RR2, designed for a Mach number of 2·85 and intended for pod-mounting on a ground-to-air missile. The RR2 engine has a diameter of 10·25 in (260 mm) and an empty weight of 92·5 lb (42·0 kg). The kerosene-type fuel is stored in the missile main body and is delivered to the ramjet combustion chamber by means of an air-driven turbopump integrated into the engine forebody.

The main research effort is now directed towards an integral rocket-ramjet engine. This new concept is a ramjet engine containing a solid-propellant grain in its combustion chamber. The rocket is fired to launch and accelerate the vehicle. After completion of the boost phase the chamber is used for ramjet combustion. The transition between the boost and the ramjet-sustain phase is accomplished by suddenly increasing the nozzle area, opening the air inlet and injecting the liquid fuel.

Two basic types of rocket-ramjet have been investigated and tested. The **RRX1** has a circumferential nose air intake and is designed for a Mach number of 5·0. The body diameter is 7·5 in (190 mm). The **RRX5** has four side-mounted air intakes to free the nose for a missile warhead and guidance. It is intended for a Mach-number range of 1·8-3·5, with a diameter varying between 11·8 and 17·7 in (300-450 mm).

THE UNITED KINGDOM

BRISTOL AEROJET

BRISTOL AEROJET LIMITED

HEAD OFFICE AND WORKS:
Banwell, Weston super Mare, Somerset BS24 8PD

Telephone: Banwell (0934-82) 2251

DIRECTORS:
Dr F. Llewellyn Smith, CBE (Chairman)
R. M. Howarth (Managing Director)
G. A. Harrison
E. N. Vidler
W. K. Bachelder (USA)
M. G. Hatley (USA)
E. A. Lowe (USA)
J. D. Nichols (USA)
R. J. Mill (USA) Alternate

In 1952 a team was formed to provide the design, development and manufacturing expertise required to meet the rocket-motor requirements of early British guided missile projects. This team constituted the nucleus of Bristol Aerojet, which was formed in 1958 by the Bristol Aeroplane Company and the Aerojet-General Corporation of California.

The company specialises in the design, development and production of solid-propellant and packaged liquid-propellant rocket motors for missiles and for satellite launch and research rockets, working in collaboration with the Rocket Propulsion Establishment, Ministry of Defence, and others. Missiles and rockets which use Bristol Aerojet motors include the Seawolf, AN/USD-501 (CL-89), Bloodhound 1 and 2, Skylark, Rapier, Seaslug 1 and 2, Thunderbird 1 and 2, Petrel, Seacat, Tigercat, Bullpup, Skua, Jaguar/Jabiru, INTA 300 and INTA 255.

As well as being the primary supplier of rocket motors in the UK, the company is also a supplier to NATO, Australia, Belgium, Canada, France, Germany, India, Italy, Pakistan, Spain and Sweden.

Bristol Aerojet rocket-motor manufacturing processes have been licenced to Breda Meccanica Bresciana in Italy and to Instituto Nacional de Tecnica Aerospacial (INTA) in Spain, and are used under different arrangements in Canada and Australia. Under an agreement with the British government the company is supplying British "plastic" propellant manufacturing and filling technology and equipment for a rocket-motor filling facility being set up by INTA, and is able to supply a similar service to other approved organisations.

Bristol Aerojet undertakes design and manufacture of rocket motors to customer requirements, undertakes launcher design, and provides a technical service for assembly and firing of experimental rockets at British and overseas ranges. The company also designs, develops and manufactures research rocket systems and ballistic targets.

BRISTOL AEROJET LIQUID-PROPELLANT MOTORS

Fully-integrated rocket motors of this type have been successfully developed in close collaboration with the Rocket Propulsion Establishment, Ministry of Defence. Motor designs based on flight-proven systems are now available. These give complex thrust/time programmes on command, and have a shut-down and re-start capability. The simple propellants are smoke-free and offer instant readiness after a long storage life.

BRISTOL AEROJET SOLID MOTORS

The following details may be published of the principal types of solid rocket motor manufactured by Bristol Aerojet Ltd:

Motor Name	Diam (in; mm)	Length (in; mm)	Burn time (sec)	Total impulse (kN-sec)	Application
Bantam	4·92; 125	58 ; 1,473	33·6	52·0	Skua vehicle
Chick	2·68; 68	21·8 ; 554	0·18	4·45	Skua and Petrel boost
Cuckoo	17 ; 431·8	51·65; 1,312	4·1	360·0	Skylark boost
Goldfinch	17 ; 431·8	87·56; 2,224	3·6	701·0	Skylark boost
Lapwing	6·96 ; 176·8	71·9 ; 1,826	25·0	153·0	Petrel vehicle
Raven	17 ; 431·8	206 ; 5,232	30·0	1,510·0	Skylark sustainer
Siskin	5·56 ; 141·2	23·62; 600·0	3·58	16·5	Black Arrow vehicle
Waxwing	28 ; 712	(spherical)	55·0	845·5	Black Arrow apogee

BUDWORTH

DAVID BUDWORTH LTD

HEAD OFFICE AND WORKS:
Harwich, Essex

Telephone: Harwich (02555) 3116

DIRECTORS:
D. D. Budworth, MA, CEng, MIMechE, AMINA (Managing Director)
J. Blewitt, MBE, MA
J. M. Budworth

This company entered the gas-turbine field in 1952 when it ran its first small unit used to drive emergency electrical generating and water pumping equipment. Subsequently a series of small gas-turbines has been designed and built, mainly for industrial and instructional duties, but including a number of aircraft installations. Budworth has also engaged in development of a variety of other gas-turbine and aircraft equipment.

BUDWORTH PUFFIN

The Puffin turbocompressor has been developed initially for helicopter applications, but can also be supplied in similar configuration as a turboprop or, without the reduction gear, as a turbojet.

TYPE: Centrifugal free-turbine turboshaft/turboprop.

SHAFT DRIVE: Epicyclic and helical spur reduction gear of 16 : 1 ratio. Gears carried on ball and roller bearings.

COMPRESSOR: Single-stage centrifugal unit with RR 58 aluminium alloy single-sided impeller having 13 vanes. Rotor carried on ball and roller bearings. Aluminium compressor casing and radial diffuser. Air mass flow 3·3 lb (1·49 kg)/sec.

COMBUSTION CHAMBER: Annular type with stainless steel air casing and Nimonic 75 flame tube. Vaporising type fuel injectors and high energy ignition.

The Budworth Puffin in its simplest form, without reduction gear, as a turbojet rated at 180 lb (81·7 kg) st

COMPRESSOR TURBINE: Two-stage axial unit with serrated couplingto shaft carried on ball and roller bearings. Rotor blades integral with overhung disc cast in Nimonic PE10. Turbine entry temperature 927°C.

POWER TURBINE: Single-stage axial unit with serrated coupling to shaft carried on ball and roller bearings. Rotor blades integral with overhung disc, cast in Nimonic PE10.

JET PIPE: Fixed.

ACCESSORY DRIVES: Bevel drive at air intake casing with provision for driving pumps.

FUEL SYSTEM: Electronic fuel control system. Max fuel pressure 100 lb/sq in (7·03 kg/cm²).

LUBRICATION SYSTEM: Forced circulation lubrication using gear pumps. Oil tank capacity 4 Imp pints (2·3 litres). Normal oil supply pressure 40 lb/sq in (2·8 kg/cm²).

MOUNTING: Trunnions.

STARTING: Electric DC motor at intake end.

DIMENSIONS:
Diameter 15 in (381 mm)
Length 30 in (762 mm)

WEIGHT, DRY:
Turboshaft and turboprop:
Basic 100 lb (45·4 kg)
Complete with accessories 130 lb (58·9 kg)
Turbojet:
Basic 70 lb (31·2 kg)

PERFORMANCE RATINGS:
T-O: turbojet 180 lb (81·7 kg) st
Continuous: turboshaft and turboprop 200 shp

SPECIFIC FUEL CONSUMPTION:
At continuous rating, turboshaft and turboprop 0·85 lb (0·39 kg)/shp/hr

CLUTTON

ERIC CLUTTON

ADDRESS:
92 Newlands Street, Shelton, Stoke-on-Trent, Staffs

In order to provide propulsion for his FRED (see 1971-72 *Jane's*) and Easy Too (see "Aircraft" section) Mr Clutton has been engaged in independent modification of the Volkswagen 1,500 cc engine and intends ultimately to market plans and a conversion kit.

His first conversion involved a geared drive to the propeller by means of a toothed belt. The ratio was 0·5 : 1 and, with the 72 in × 44 in (1,829 mm × 1,118 mm) ex-Cirrus Minor propeller used on FRED Srs 2, the engine speed was held to 3,750 rpm. Despite the fact that the full engine power of 66 hp was developed only at 4,800 rpm the geared drive resulted in outstanding aircraft performance.

The drive raised the thrust line and provided adequate ground clearance. A second toothed belt from the rear of the crankshaft drove twin Scintex Vertex impulse magnetos, modified to run laterally. Other features included an SU Zenith carburettor with central float chamber and heating provided by hot air drawn at will from an exhaust pipe muff, a tachometer driven from the original distributor shaft and an oil-pressure pickup in place of the original oil cooler. Engine weight, originally over 200 lb (90·7 kg), was reduced by substituting light alloy castings for certain steel items.

In 1968 development began on a true geared conversion, and two types were described (and one illustrated) in the 1972-73 *Jane's*. For reasons of cost Mr Clutton has now returned to 2 : 1 multi-vee-belt drive, but this differs from all earlier types in that it is taken off the bell-housing end and, in its prototype form, uses off-the-shelf material and parts. There are no castings, and only simple machining is needed on the two shafts.

The prototype geared engine weighs 210 lb (95·2 kg), but is expected to be 30 lb (13·6 kg) lighter when more light alloy parts are used. In 1973 it flew more than 10 hr but testing has been delayed six months by a forced landing for reasons unconnected with the reduction gear. Flying was due to resume in the Spring of 1974.

LUCAS

LUCAS AEROSPACE LTD

HEAD OFFICE:
Monkspath, Shirley, Solihull, Warwickshire
Telephone: 021-744-8522
CHAIRMAN: B. F. W. Scott

Lucas Aerospace was formed in 1971 to bring together Lucas Gas Turbine Equipment Ltd and Rotax Ltd, both Lucas companies engaged in aerospace work. The assets and goodwill of the Rover Gas Turbine Co were acquired from Alvis Ltd in December 1972. The Electrical Group is now responsible for the CT 3201 (formerly designated TJ.125) turbojet manufactured previously by Rover Gas Turbines.

The Rover Company was responsible for initial production of the original Whittle-type turbojet engines in 1941-42. Two of its developed engines were taken over by Rolls-Royce and, after further refinement, were produced in quantity as the Welland and Derwent. More recently, Rover developed a series of small gas-turbine engines for industrial applications and as auxiliary power units on aircraft such as the Hawker Siddeley Vulcan and Argosy C.1. They were used also to drive air cushion vehicles, certain land vehicles and generating sets in oil rigs.

Early in 1968, the aviation activities of Rover Gas Turbines Ltd were transferred to Alvis Ltd and, as mentioned in the opening paragraph, the assets of this company have since been acquired by Lucas Aerospace Ltd.

LUCAS CT 3201

This small 114 lb (51·7 kg) st turbojet engine utilises the gas-generator section of the Lucas 2S/150A engine and has been developed as a power plant for surveillance RPVs and similar pilotless aircraft. The single-shaft gas-generator consists of a single-stage centrifugal compressor feeding an annular reverse-flow combustion chamber. Fuel is delivered by a ring of atomising fuel injectors, and the gas flow from the combustion chamber is directed to a radial inward-flow turbine. Leaving the eye of the turbine rotor, the gas flow passes to the exhaust nozzle. Auxiliary equipment, comprising a fuel pump and associated governor, is driven from the compressor shaft.

Initial deliveries of CT 3201 engines have been made to MBLE to power the Belgian company's Epervier surveillance RPV. Discussions are in progress with other drone manufacturers. Lucas is developing the engine to a new rating of 160 lb (72·6 kg) st.

DIMENSIONS:

Length overall	22 in (558·8 mm)
Max width	10·625 in (269·9 mm)
Max depth	12·063 in (306·4 mm)

Lucas CT 3201 turbojet of 114 lb (51·7 kg) st, as fitted to the MBLE X-5 Eprevier RPV

WEIGHT, DRY:	43·5 lb (19·8 kg)
PERFORMANCE RATINGS:	
Max thrust at ISA	114 lb (51·7 kg)
Reduced thrust	73 lb (33·1 kg)
SPECIFIC FUEL CONSUMPTION:	
At max rating	1·31

ROLLASON

ROLLASON AIRCRAFT AND ENGINES LTD

HEAD OFFICE AND WORKS:
Brighton, Hove and Worthing Joint Municipal Airport, Shoreham-by-Sea, Sussex BN4,5FJ
Telephone: Shoreham-by-Sea 62680
OFFICERS: See "Aircraft" section

In support of its manufacture under licence of the Druine Turbulent light aeroplane, Rollason Aircraft and Engines Ltd is undertaking the conversion of Ardem 4CO2 power plants for this aircraft, from motor car engines.

A modification introduced on the Rollason version is the use of a Solex side-entry carburettor. This greatly improves the starting characteristics and uses pre-heated air, so that a carburettor heater box is no longer necessary.

Rollason has developed several versions of the Ardem engine, as described below. In addition there are the 45 hp Mark 4 engine, the 55 hp high-compression Mark 5, and the 45 hp Mark X engine which is similar to the Mark 4 and is CAA approved. All three of these variants are of 1,500 cc capacity.

The firm has now produced a 1,600 cc version, known as the Ardem Mk XI. Any of these Ardem engines can be installed in Nipper aircraft. The Mk X is also used in the Australian homebuilt Corby Starlet and is under evaluation for the Slingsby T.61 Falke.

ARDEM 1,500 cc VERSION

The standard model has a compression ratio of 7·8 : 1 and gives 45 hp at 3,300 rpm for take-off, with a fuel consumption of 3·75 Imp gallons (17 litres)/hr at max rating. In addition, a high-compression version is available, as follows:

CYLINDERS: Bore 3·27 in (83 mm). Stroke 2·72 in (69 mm). Cast steel barrels, light alloy heads. Compression ratio 8·5 : 1.

PISTONS: Aluminium alloy high-compression pistons, each with two compression rings and one scraper ring. Floating gudgeon pins.

CONNECTING RODS: White metal bearings in big-end. Bronze bearings in little-end.

CRANKSHAFT: Runs in four white metal bearings.

CRANKCASE: Magnesium case.

VALVE GEAR: Two valves per cylinder. Camshaft geared to crankshaft.

INDUCTION: Zenith 32 KL P10 carburettor.

FUEL GRADE: 100 octane.

IGNITION: Lucas SR4 magneto mounted below engine, with chain drive. Two Lodge LH spark plugs per cylinder.

LUBRICATION: Wet sump type, with single gear-type pump.

OIL SPECIFICATION: Shell W80.

PROPELLER DRIVE: Direct drive.

ACCESSORIES: SEV 46C fuel pump.

DIMENSIONS:

Length	16·75 in (426 mm)
Width	29·50 in (750 mm)
Height	22·00 in (559 mm)
POWER RATING:	
Max rating	53 hp at 3,600 rpm
FUEL CONSUMPTION:	
At max rating	4·0 Imp gallons (18·2 litres)/hr

ARDEM 1,600 cc VERSION

After extensive testing this engine is now approved and is produced as the Ardem Mk XI. It differs from the Mk X in having cylinders of 3·365 in (85·5 mm) bore and dual ignition.

WEIGHT:	
With accessories	158 lb (71·6 kg)
POWER RATINGS:	
Max rating	55 hp at 3,300 rpm
Cruise rating	35·5 hp at 2,500 rpm
FUEL CONSUMPTION:	
At cruise rating	2·75 Imp gallons (12·5 litres)/hr

ROLLS-ROYCE

ROLLS-ROYCE (1971) LIMITED

HEAD OFFICE:
Norfolk House, St James's Square, London SW1Y 4JS
Telephone: 01-839-7888
MAIN LOCATIONS:
PO Box 3, Filton, Bristol BS12 7QE
Telephone: 0272-693871
PO Box 31, Moor Lane, Derby DE2 8BJ
Telephone: 0332-42424
PO Box 72, Ansty, Coventry CV7 9JR
Telephone: 0203-32-2311
Leavesden, Watford WD2 7BZ
Telephone: 477-4000
Scottish group of factories mainly to the south of Glasgow
CHAIRMAN:
Sir Kenneth Keith
DEPUTY CHAIRMAN:
Sir William Nield
VICE CHAIRMAN:
Marshal of the Royal Air Force Sir Denis Spotswood
MANAGING DIRECTOR:
Kenneth G. Wilkinson
TECHNICAL DIRECTOR:
Sir Stanley Hooker
PROJECTS DIRECTOR:
Sir William Cook
FINANCIAL DIRECTOR:
J. E. M. Gardner
MANAGING DIRECTOR—DERBY ENGINE DIVISION:
D. A. Head
MANAGING DIRECTOR—BRISTOL ENGINE DIVISION:
R. T. Whitfield
EXECUTIVE OFFICE DIRECTOR:
D. J. Pepper
BOARD MEMBERS:
Sir St John Elstub
A. W. Knight
COMPANY SECRETARY:
H. E. Trevan-Hawke

Rolls-Royce (1971) Ltd, which produces a range of gas turbines, rockets and ramjets, retains the experience in aircraft engines built up over nearly 60 years by the predecessor companies that it incorporated. The company also represents British experience in lightweight high-power gas turbines for industrial and marine purposes, since such engines were first derived from aircraft gas turbines more than a decade ago.

More than 180 million hours of operating experience have been accumulated with Rolls-Royce civil and military gas turbines, which have been chosen by over 233 airlines and 84 armed forces.

In addition to the products designed, developed and manufactured solely in Britain, the company works with partners abroad on a number of joint civil and military aircraft engine programmes. Licences for the manufacture of Rolls-Royce engines or components are also held by many countries throughout the world.

The company was registered on 23 February 1971, and at present the British government is the sole shareholder. On 22 May of the same year the company was vested with assets which were those concerned with the gas turbine business of Rolls-Royce Ltd.

The main activities are at Derby, Glasgow, Bristol, Coventry and Leavesden, where aircraft gas turbines are produced, and at Ansty, where aircraft gas turbine techniques are applied to industrial and marine uses. A total of 63,550 people are employed.

One of the most advanced products is the RB.211 three-shaft turbofan which is in service in the Lockheed TriStar airliner. Development and production continue jointly with the French company SNECMA on the Olympus two-shaft turbojet which powers the Concorde supersonic airliner (see International section). Other Rolls-Royce engines which are in commercial service include the Spey and Conway turbofans, Avon and Viper turbojets, and Dart and Tyne turboprops.

Rolls-Royce (1971) is a member of the Turbo-Union company (see International section), in which it is associated with MTU of Germany and Fiat of Italy on the RB.199 engine for the MRCA multi-role combat aircraft. In addition to the Olympus, the company is also associated with SNECMA on the M45H, with Detroit Diesel Allison Division of General Motors on the TF41 and XJ99, with Turboméca of France on the Adour, and with MTU and Alfa Romeo of Italy on the EPM600 and ESM600 (see International section for all these).

A new turboshaft, the Gem, is being developed by Rolls-Royce for the Westland Aérospatiale Lynx multi-purpose helicopter. Together with the Turmo and Astazou, on which production is shared with Turboméca, it is part of the Anglo-French helicopter programme, designed to meet the medium and light helicopter requirements of the two countries.

In May 1973 Rolls-Royce (1971) and General Electric's Aircraft Engine Group announced that an agreement signed by the two companies in 1971, under which GE is exploring opportunities for the Gem (RS.360) in the United States, will be continued for the current year. GE announced that the Gem, "smaller than engines being developed or manufactured by General Electric", would be manufactured by it in the United States if a suitable business opportunity existed. The Westland/Aérospatiale Lynx is one of the contenders in the US Navy LAMPS (Light Airborne Multi-Purpose System) programme.

Versions of several Rolls-Royce aircraft gas turbines are used as power units for large and small ships, hydrofoils, air cushion vehicles, electricity-generating sets, gas and oil pumping equipment and for other industrial uses.

Rolls-Royce Motors, which makes light-aircraft engines among other products, is a separate company, no longer part of Rolls-Royce (1971) Ltd, and has a separate entry in this edition.

ROLLS-ROYCE TURBOMÉCA ADOUR

This turbofan was designed by Rolls-Royce and Turboméca to power the Jaguar, and is in production on a 50 : 50 basis by the two companies for this aircraft at a rating of 7,305 lb (3,313 kg) st with afterburner. A similar version is made under licence by IHI of Japan for the T-2, and an unaugmented version, rated at 5,200 lb (2,360 kg) st, powers the HS 1182 Hawk. The Adour is described in the International section.

ROLLS-ROYCE RB.146 AVON (DERBY)

The Avon axial-flow turbojet was developed after the war to replace the Nene. It was in large-scale production both in the United Kingdom and overseas for many years and powers a very large number of military and civil types.

The 100-Series Avons (of which full details can be found in the 1961-62 edition of *Jane's*) have a 12-stage compressor and eight individual

combustion chambers. The later 200-Series and 300-Series (RB.146) engines are of almost entirely new design with higher pressure ratio compressors, cannular combustion chambers and considerably higher thrust.

The RB.146 is a development of the RA.24. Its dry rating is 12,690 lb (5,756 kg) st, and an afterburner is fitted in both its applications. In the BAC Lightning F.6 its rating is 15,680 lb (7,112 kg) st, and in the Saab Draken 17,110 lb (7,761 kg) st. A number of versions of the Avon RB.146 have been produced, including the Mk 60 built under licence by Volvo Flygmotor (as the RM6), with Swedish afterburner, for the Saab Draken D, E and F series; the Mks 301 and 302 powering the Lightning Mks 3, 5 and 6; and the Mk 302C powering the Lightning Mks 53 and 55 (dry and augmented thrusts, 12,100 lb; 5,488 kg and 15,680 lb; 7,112 kg respectively).

Major differences between the RB.146 and RA.24 are:

AIR INTAKE: Extension ring deleted. Magnesium casing modified to carry intake temperature sensing probe and provision for mating engine to aircraft intake duct. Also carries "zero" stage stator blades.

COMPRESSOR: Sixteen-stage axial flow by addition of "zero" stage to RA.24 compressor to give increased air mass flow.

EXHAUST UNIT (except Mk 60): Exhaust cone carried on three struts.

JET PIPE (except Mk 60): Afterburner with infinitely variable flap-type nozzle driven by screwjacks. Ignition by hot streak from engine.

DIMENSIONS:

Length	138 in (3,505 mm)
Diameter	44 in (1,118 mm)

ROLLS-ROYCE RB.162 (DERBY)

The RB.162 is a very simple ultra-lightweight turbojet engine which was initially developed to meet the requirements of the aircraft industries of Britain, France and Federal Germany for a lift-jet unit for V/STOL aircraft. The governments of all three countries contributed to its cost, and special developments needed to make the engine suitable for a particular application will in future be paid for by the country requiring them.

Development of the RB.162 lift-jet series was completed at the end of 1969. Development continued on a new version of the engine for use as a take-off booster. By January 1974 more than 120 RB.162 jets had run, the total number of starts exceeding 80,000 and the number of bench and flight hours exceeding 5,000.

A feature of the RB.162 is the extensive use of low-cost lightweight materials, including glass-fibre-reinforced plastics. Although plastics help to give the engine an unprecedented thrust-to-weight ratio of about 16 : 1, they were chosen primarily to reduce production costs.

The engine, by virtue of its compact, lightweight design is also well suited for use as a booster engine for take-off power assistance. With suitable modifications to facilitate operation in the horizontal attitude, a version of the RB.162, the RB.162-86, is in service in the Hawker Siddeley Trident 3B.

The following versions of the RB.162 may be mentioned:

RB.162-1/4. Initial version (-1 has 10% air bleed for stabilisation control). Normal rating of 4,409 lb (2,000 kg) st and emergency rating of 4,718 lb (2,140 kg) st. Bench testing began in January 1962. Preliminary flight clearance test at max power performed in April 1963. Special category test completed in August 1964 demonstrated thrust 2½ per cent above contract figure and sfc 3½ per cent below. This version was described in the 1969-70 *Jane's*.

RB.162-30 Series. Specified for many early European V/STOL aircraft. More than 60 had been built for development testing, and for installation in V/STOL aircraft and test rigs, by May 1966.

RB.162-81. Development of RB.162-30 with aircooled turbine blades to increase rating. Rated at 5,992 lb (2,718 kg) st normal SLS with 8 per cent air bleed; contingency rating 6,010 lb (2,726 kg) st with 13 per cent control air bleed. Developed for VFW VAK 191B V/STOL aircraft.

RB.162-86. Developed for booster applications, with T-O thrust of 5,250 lb (2,381 kg) st. Major features described below. Fitted to Hawker Siddeley Trident 3B. Designed for life of 2,000 take-off cycles, and to meet ARB type-test schedule for booster jets and civil airworthiness requirements. In February 1971 the RB.162-86 received a full Transport Category C of A from the ARB, after completing 550 operating cycles with some 19 out of the 50 hours of running time being at take-off rating.

The following details apply to the RB.162-81; particulars of the -86 are given in brackets:

TYPE: Lightweight single-shaft axial-flow lift-jet engine (take-off booster).

AIR INTAKE: Direct pitot annular type, moulded from glass-reinforced composite (grc) with integral fixed inlet guide vanes (-86 vanes, steel). Two pairs of hollow intake struts are moulded integrally with upper and lower portions of nose bullet from grc, and house fuel and oil pipes (-86 hot-air anti-iced).

Rolls-Royce RB.162-86 booster jet for the Hawker Siddeley Trident 3B (5,250 lb; 2,381 kg st)

COMPRESSOR CASING: Made in two halves from grc. Provides mountings for accessories, including throttle and flow control unit, igniter box and oil bottle with visual level scale.

COMPRESSOR: Six-stage axial-flow type. Rotor of aluminium alloy discs and spacers welded together to form a single unit integral with shaft. Stator blades 1-5 grc, 6 steel; all stator blades cast into half casings. Rotor blades, stage 1 (1 and 2) aluminium, 2-6 (3-6) grc; stage 1 pinned, 2-6 dovetailed (dampers at ¾ span on stage 1). Fixed diffuser vanes aft of compressor. Pressure ratio 4·5 : 1; mass flow 85 lb (38·5 kg)/sec.

COMBUSTION CHAMBER: Annular type, inside welded sheet steel casing. Outer flame tube is a continuous drum with perforations for secondary air. Inner flame tube is Nimonic drum carrying 18 equally spaced burners, two starting atomisers and two high-energy igniters 30° each side of vertical section plane. (Casing and turbine stator redesigned to accommodate increased mass flow as result of absence of control air bleed requirement.)

FUEL SYSTEM: Self-contained fuel system consisting of two units. One unit, with a main body cast in magnesium, is housed in the nose bullet and contains the backing pump, gear-type HP fuel pump, acceleration control unit and two datum governors. Second unit is the combined throttle and flow control unit, with main body cast in magnesium, mounted on the compressor casing and incorporating an emergency shut-off cock. Simple form of fuel filtering is included, but fuel system is designed to accept dirty or icy fuel and no provision is made for fuel heating (control system changed to reduce idling speed to reduce fuel consumption and noise during serviceability checks).

FUEL GRADES: JP-1, JP-4.

NOZZLE GUIDE VANES: Hollow aircooled refractory alloy.

TURBINE: Single-stage axial-flow type. Titanium (steel) disc and hollow aircooled blades of refractory alloy held by fir-tree roots.

BEARINGS: Only two ball bearings, one between inlet guide vanes and compressor, the other forward of turbine. Both are single-row, the turbine bearing being for location and the intake bearing making provision for axial expansion.

JET-PIPE: Fixed-area type with outer wall, cone and 12 radial struts. Provision for two-position or infinitely-variable spherical swivelling nozzle, for deflected or vectored thrust (bolted-on pipe and fixed nozzle).

LUBRICATION SYSTEM: One-shot system. Tank with capacity for several starts (1 pint) mounted on compressor casing. Alternatively airframe-mounted tank for a battery of engines. At each start, a single shot of oil is delivered via non-return valves to each bearing by pressurising the tank. Oil from rear bearing drains through exhaust unit. Oil from front bearing is scavenged overboard by an ejector driven by compressor air delivery (detail changes for horizontal installation; tank capacity 6 pints).

MOUNTING: Four equally spaced spherical trunnions, of which any three used; -81 may be swivelled for thrust vectoring.

STARTING: Ground starting by direct air impingement on turbine blades, by air bled from propulsion engines, or by hydraulic starter built into nose bullet. In flight, ram-air starting is used.

DIMENSIONS:

Height	54 in (1,370 mm)
Diameter	29 in (740 mm)

WEIGHT, DRY:

Nominal, with oil and fuel systems:

RB.162-81	415 lb (188·2 kg)
RB.162-86	625 lb (283 kg)

PERFORMANCE RATINGS:

See under model listings

ROLLS-ROYCE/ALLISON XJ99

Based on Rolls-Royce third-generation lift-jet technology, the XJ99 is a joint Rolls-Royce/Allison project. Further details are given in the International section.

ROLLS-ROYCE RB.199 (BRISTOL)

This advanced augmented turbofan is the power unit for the Panavia MRCA supersonic strike fighter. The RB.199 programme is managed by Turbo-Union (see International section).

ROLLS-ROYCE RB.211 (DERBY)

The RB.211 is an advanced technology three-shaft turbofan of high by-pass ratio, high pressure ratio design in the 40,000 lb (18,144 kg) to 50,000 lb (22,680 kg) st bracket. The engine was selected by Lockheed Aircraft in March 1968 to power its new L-1011 TriStar three-engined transport.

Rolls-Royce initiated design studies of three-shaft turbofans in 1961 and a twin-spool engine, the RB.178, was tested in 1967 to provide relevant component and gas generator exper-ience. Among the advantages afforded by a three-shaft layout are its ready use of a high pressure ratio with fewer compressor and turbine stages whilst maintaining excellent handling. The need for compressor variable stator mechanisms can also be minimised and the rotating assemblies can be made relatively short and rigid while preserving light construction.

These characteristics provide the RB.211 with significant advantages over previous turbofans. Most important of these are a 25 per cent reduction in sfc, improved specific weight, reduced noise levels on take-off and approach, more ready maintenance and repair, and reduced overall operating costs.

For installation of the RB.211 in the Lockheed TriStar, Rolls-Royce is responsible for development and manufacture of the complete integrated propulsion system, comprising (in addition to the engine) the fan airflow reverser, hot stream spoiler, pod cowlings and related systems, and noise attenuation gear for the intake, fan cowl and turbine exhaust duct.

The engine is divided into seven basic modules. This permits very rapid change of engine parts, and enables service life to be set up for each module rather than for the complete engine. It also facilitates rapid repair, as a damaged or time-expired module can be replaced with the engine installed in the aircraft. Maximum provision is made for in-service monitoring of engine condition and visual inspection on the ground of all engine sections.

The RB.211 combustion chamber is of annular design, giving significant advantages over tubo-annular systems in terms of reduced cost, weight and length, and improved efficiency. The reduced length makes a two-bearing HP system possible, with both bearings located away from the high temperatures of the combustion area. Detailed design of the combustion liner, fuel injection nozzles and fuel control system has been aimed at reducing exhaust contaminants to a minimum. As a result the smoke level of the RB.211 shows a significant reduction compared with turbofans in service previously.

The HP turbine blades are single-pass convection cooled, and have film cooling at the leading edge and on both faces. Cooling air is fed to the turbine disc via pre-swirl nozzles which accelerate the air in the direction of disc rotation, thus reducing its temperature before entry to the blade root.

The RB.211 propulsion system for the TriStar incorporates the first of a new generation of Rolls-Royce thrust reversers. The by-pass fan air stream of the RB.211 flows through a three-quarter length duct, thereby creating a requirement for separate deflecting systems for the fan air and exhaust jet. With high by-pass ratio engines such as this (by-pass ratio 5 : 1), the required reverse thrust can be achieved by reversing the fan air stream only and neutralising the thrust of the gas-generator exhaust by the use of a spoiler. Fan stream reversing is achieved by translating rearwards a section of fan cowling, thus uncovering sets of cascades and at the same time closing off the fan duct downstream of the cascades by means of hinged blocker doors.

In order to minimise fan noise, the RB.211 has no inlet guide vanes; the distance between the single-stage fan and its outlet guide vanes is optimised for minimum noise generation, as is the numerical ratio of the two rows of blading. Additional noise attenuation is achieved by the use of acoustic lining material in the intake, fan and turbine exhaust ducts. The RB.211 achieved FAA noise certification with comfortable margins. The FAA describe the TriStar as "quieter than any other large wide-body airliner".

Bench development work carried out on the engine included aerodynamic, performance and strain gauge testing, noise and smoke evaluation and simulated flight cycle endurance running. In January 1971 15 engines were running at Derby, and two more at the National Gas Turbine Establishment. Engine testing was supported by considerable rig test work, involving the assessment of different configurations of major components. Flight testing in a modified VC10 began on 6 March 1970.

Production of the RB.211 involves a major manufacturing programme to a tight time schedule, with a high proportion of the work being subcontracted by Rolls-Royce. More than 120 British and overseas suppliers of equipment, components and materials are engaged in the programme. Flight-cleared engines have been delivered to Lockheed at Palmdale since September 1970, and the first TriStar flew on 16 November 1970.

By June 1971 the standard of the flight-test engine had been finalised. In August 1971 two 150 hour tests were completed. In September the design of the passenger-carrying engine was finalised. Between then and December, 33 production-built flight-test engines were delivered (direct from East Midlands airport to Palmdale) ahead of schedule. A further 150 hour endurance test was run in November, and in December there were 75 separate certification tests completed on schedule for the ARB and FAA. ARB Type Approval was granted for the -22C engine on 22 February 1972, followed by FAA validation three days later. The first ship set of production engines was delivered ahead of schedule, and by mid-March ten engines for airline customers had been shipped, and Eastern and TWA were training crews. Scheduled service began on 15 April 1972. In the first year of deliveries 135 engines were supplied to Lockheed and its customer airlines.

The **RB.211-22C**, the basic engine ordered for the Lockheed L-1011-1, had an initial into-service rating of 42,000 lb (19,050 kg) st to 18·9°C, or 38,750 lb (17,755 kg) to 28·9°C.

The **RB.211-22B**, now the standard engine of the L-1011-1, is flat-rated at 42,000 lb (19,050 kg) st to 28·9°C. This engine was certificated in February 1973 by the CAA and in April 1973 by the FAA. All RB.211-22C engines have been modified to -22B standard, and all new engines are being delivered at this rating.

The **RB.211-524** is the initial step in the RB.211's programme of growth. Rated at 48,000 lb (21,772 kg) st to 28·9°C, the -524 preserves maximum commonality with the -22B but has increased core airflow, slightly higher turbine gas temperature and improved component efficiency. First run took place on 1 October 1973. A few days later the full take-off thrust was achieved. A -524 at the National Gas Turbine Establishment has demonstrated maximum cruise and climb sfc guarantees. The engine is fully funded and should complete certification testing in 1975. The -524 has potential for thrusts in excess of 50,000 lb (22,680 kg), and is being studied by Lockheed, Boeing and Airbus Industrie for possible application to their aircraft.

The following description relates to the RB.211-22B:

TYPE: Three-shaft axial turbofan.

AIR INTAKE: Forward-facing pitot.

LP FAN: Single-stage overhung fan driven by LP turbine, the whole rotor assembly being supported on three bearings. Front bearing is large roller, squeeze-film supported behind fan. Axial location of rotor is by intershaft ball bearing in rear end of IP compressor drum. LP turbine supported on roller bearing, squeeze-film mounted in exhaust cone panel. Rotating spinner supported from fan rotor disc, and hot-air anti-iced via central feed-tube within shaft. Titanium alloy used for 33 fan rotor blades, and steel for 70 fan outlet guide vanes. Titanium fan disc bolted with curvic coupling to LP shaft. Aluminium fan casing.

IP COMPRESSOR: Seven-stage compressor rotor driven by IP turbine and supported on three bearings located directly in support panels. Front squeeze-film bearing is roller. Mid bearing at rear of IP compressor is ball bearing providing axial location for IP rotor. Rear bearing is roller, squeeze-film supported in panel between HP and IP turbines. Two drums, one of titanium discs welded together and the other of welded steel discs, are bolted to form one rotor, carrying titanium rotor blades. Aluminium and steel casings carry aluminium and steel stator blades. Single-stage titanium variable inlet guide vanes.

HP COMPRESSOR: Six-stage compressor rotor driven by HP turbine connected by large-diameter shaft and carried on ball location bearing at front and roller bearing squeeze-film mounted in panel behind HP turbine disc. Welded titanium discs, a single steel disc and welded nickel alloy discs are bolted together to form the rotor, carrying titanium, steel and nickel alloy blades. Steel casing carries steel and Nimonic stator blades. Overall pressure ratio 25 : 1.

Rolls-Royce RB.211-524 three-shaft turbofan on static test (48,000 lb; 21,772 kg st)

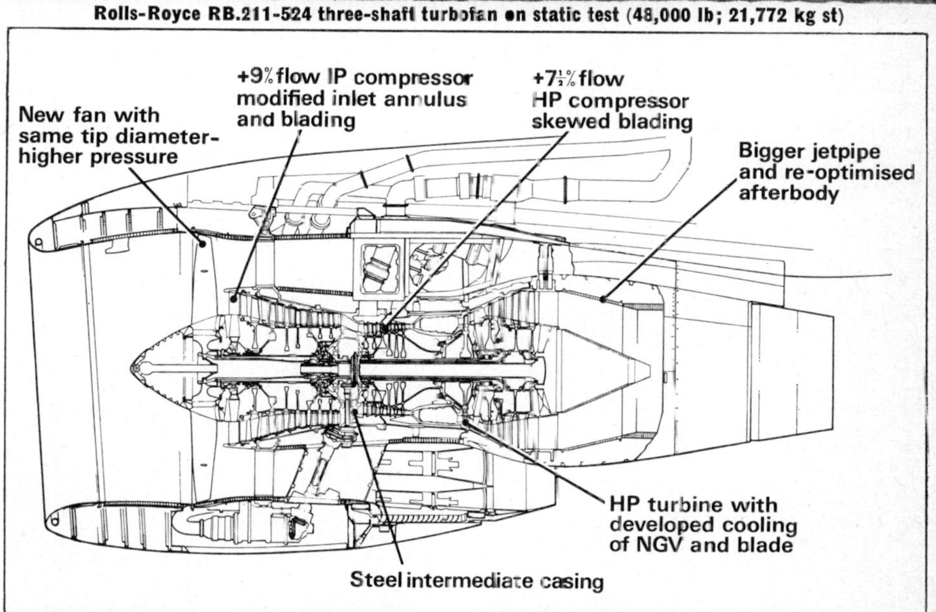

Longitudinal cross-section of complete Rolls-Royce RB.211-524 pod, showing principal areas where engine design is changed from RB.211-22B. The pod is unchanged

COMBUSTION CHAMBER: Fully annular, with steel outer casings and Nimonic flame tube. Downstream fuel injection by 18 airspray burners with annular atomisers. Ignition by starting atomisers and high-energy igniter plugs in Nos 8 and 12 burners.
HP TURBINE: Single-stage axial unit with Nimonic nozzle guide vanes and Nimonic rotor blades, both rows aircooled. Convection and film-cooled blades mounted in Nimonic disc by fir-tree roots.
IP TURBINE: Single-stage axial unit with Nimonic nozzle guide vanes and Nimonic rotor blades. NGVs are aircooled. Rotor blades fir-tree mounted in Nimonic disc.
LP TURBINE: Three-stage axial unit with Nimonic rotor blades fir-tree mounted in steel disc.
JET PIPE: Steel jet pipe with target type thrust spoiler.
ACCESSORY DRIVES: Radial drive from HP shaft to gearbox on fan casing. Accessories driven include integrated-drive generator and (aircraft) hydraulic pumps.
LUBRICATION SYSTEM: Continuous circulation "dry sump" system with single gear-type pressure pump and multiple gear-type scavenge pumps. Oil tank 37 Imp pints (21 litres) capacity integral with gearbox.
MOUNTING: Two-point mounting system. Front mount on fan casing takes thrust, vertical and side loads. Rear link mount on exhaust casing takes torsional, side and vertical loads. Both mounts are fail-safe and allow for carcase expansion.
DIMENSIONS:
Length overall 119·4 in (3,033 mm)
Intake diameter 85·5 in (2,172 mm)
WEIGHT, DRY:
Basic 7,203 lb (3,267 kg)
PERFORMANCE RATINGS:
T-O rating, flat rated to 28·9°C 42,000 lb (19,050 kg) st
Max cruise rating at 35,000 ft (10,670 m) and Mach 0·85 9,450 lb (4,286 kg) st
SPECIFIC FUEL CONSUMPTION:
At cruise rating at 35,000 ft (10,670 m) and Mach 0·85 0·640

ROLLS-ROYCE RB.235

Unofficially it has been known for over a year that, under the project name of Columbus, Rolls-Royce (1971) has been studying the market for engines in the 20,000-30,000 lb (9,072-13,608 kg) st class. RB.235 is the project number for an engine in this category, scaled down from RB.211-524 but with six IP stages instead of seven. The engine would benefit from all the development and service experience of the RB.211, and is being evaluated by several major airframe constructors.

ROLLS-ROYCE RB.163 CIVIL SPEY (DERBY)

Design of the Spey RB.163 began in September 1959, and the first engine ran at the end of December 1960.

Flight testing of two Speys in a Vulcan began on 12 October 1961, and prototype flight trials of the Spey-engined Hawker Siddeley Trident began on 9 January 1962. In July 1962 the ARB issued special category approval of the Spey in the Trident pod, which involved completion of a 150 hour type test to combined UK/US schedule. Civil Speys are in service in the Trident, BAC One-Eleven, Grumman Gulfstream II and F.28 Fellowship.

The civil and military Spey engines are being developed to an integrated programme.

The following versions of the civil Spey are in service:

Mk 505-5. T-O rating of 9,850 lb (4,468 kg) st at 12,490 rpm, for Hawker Siddeley Trident 1 fleet of British Airways.

Mk 506-14. T-O rating of 10,410 lb (4,722 kg) st at 12,530 rpm, for BAC One-Eleven.

Mk 506-14AW. As 506-14, but with water injection to maintain rating to 35°C.

Mk 511-5, 511-8 and 511-14. T-O rating of 11,400 lb (5,171 kg) st at 12,390 rpm. Mk 511-5 for Trident, Mk 511-8 for Gulfstream II and Mk 511-14 for One-Eleven.

Mk 511-5W and 511-14W. As 511-5 and 511-14 but with water injection to maintain rating to 35°C.

Mk 512-5 and 512-14. T-O rating 11,960 lb (5,425 kg) st in Mk 512-5 for Trident, and 12,000 lb (5,443 kg) st in Mk 512-14 for One-Eleven, in each case at 12,390 rpm. Both engines available with water injection if required.

Mk 512DW. T-O rating 12,550 lb (5,692 kg) st. Similar to basic Mk 512 but with T-O rating increased by increasing limiting compressor delivery pressure at T-O, with turbine entry temperature maintained by water injection.

Mk 555-15. Lightened and simplified version, with T-O rating of 9,850 lb (4,468 kg). For F.28 Fellowship.

Mk 605W. Redesigned low-noise engine, described separately.

The military versions are described separately.

The following details refer specifically to the Spey Mk 512-14DW, as fitted to the BAC One-Eleven Series 500, except where indicated:
TYPE: Two-spool axial-flow turbofan engine.

Rolls-Royce RB.211-22B three-shaft turbofan of 42,000 lb (19,050 kg) st for the Lockheed TriStar

AIR INTAKE: Annular type at front of engine, with bleed air thermal anti-icing.
COMPRESSOR: Axial-flow two-spool type, with five-stage (four-stage on Mks 505, 506 and 555 engines) low-pressure (LP) and 12-stage high-pressure (HP) compressor. First-stage HP stator vanes are of variable-incidence type. LP compressor is of the drum type, built of steel and pinned to shaft. HP compressor is of the disc type, built of steel and with first stage bolted to shaft, remaining stages splined to shaft. HP stator blades of steel; LP stators aluminium. LP compressor has aluminium blades; HP compressor has blades of steel and titanium. Stator blades are slotted into casing; rotor blades are attached by pins or dovetailed slots. LP compressor has two-piece aluminium alloy casing. HP compressor has two-piece steel casing. Pressure ratio 21·2 : 1 (15·0 on Mk 505 and 555, 17·2 on Mk 506, 18·9 on Mk 510 and 511). Air mass flow 208 lb (94·4 kg)/sec (200 lb; 90·27 kg on Mk 505 and 555, 203 lb; 92 kg on Mk 506, 204 lb; 92·5 kg on Mk 510 and 511). By-pass ratio 0·64 : 1 (1·0 on Mk 505, 555 and 506).
COMBUSTION CHAMBER: Tubo-annular steel chamber with 10 Nimonic sheet liners. Duplex downstream burners, one per chamber. High energy igniters in chambers 4 and 8.
FUEL SYSTEM: Plessey LP fuel pump feeding through fuel-cooled oil cooler and Marston Excelsior fuel heater to LP fuel filter at inlet to Lucas GD-type fuel pump. High-pressure fuel metered by Lucas fuel regulator unit, embodying combined speed and acceleration control and fed through Lucas LP governor and shut-off valve to Duple fuel spray nozzles. Maximum fuel pressure 1,800 lb/sq in (126 kg/cm²).
FUEL GRADE: DERD.2482 or 2486.
WATER INJECTION SYSTEM (applicable to all engines bearing "W" suffix): Water supplied by aircraft-mounted Lucas turbopump fed by air from two or three engines (dependent on aircraft) through engine-mounted automatic shut-off valve to injector passages in fuel spray nozzles (water sprays into primary airflow through flame tube swirlers). Fuel regulator unit incorporates automatic reset, to increase fuel flow and so restore flame temperature reduced by injection of water.
NOZZLE GUIDE VANES: Hollow type cast in nickel-based alloy. HP nozzle guide vanes aircooled.
TURBINES: Two two-stage axial-flow turbines, of which the first HP stage is aircooled. HP turbine discs of nickel-based alloy, bolted to shaft (HP discs steel on Mks 505, 506 and 555). LP turbine discs of creep-resisting ferritic steel. Nickel-based alloy blades attached by fir-tree roots.
BEARINGS: Total of nine bearings. LP compressor is supported in roller bearings, with one ball thrust bearing. HP compressor has front roller bearing and ball thrust bearing. Turbine bearings are all of roller type flexibly mounted to avoid problems due to vibration.
JET PIPE: Fixed-area type with outer wall and cone of stainless steel sheet.
REVERSER AND SUPPRESSOR: Normally an internal clamshell type reverser (Gulfstream II has target type, not Rolls-Royce supplied). Six-lobe exhaust suppressor fitted to engines in Trident only.

Rolls-Royce civil Spey 505 turbofan engine, cut away to show internal details

Accessory Drives: Two accessory drives. Port gearbox, driven from LP rotor, carries LP governor and LP tacho. Starboard gearbox, driven from HP rotor, carries LP and HP fuel pumps, fuel regulator, main oil pumps, airflow control rpm signal transmitter, starter and HP tacho. Provision also made on starboard gearbox for aircraft ancillaries such as hydraulic pump, constant-speed drive and starter, and generator.

Lubrication System: Self-contained continuous circulation system. Single pressure pump draws oil from tank, feeds it through (fuel-cooled) cooler and HP filter to gearboxes and shaft bearings (front bearing has supplementary pressure and scavenge pumps in nose bullet to ensure positive feed at start-up). Five main scavenge pumps, in casing with pressure pump, return oil from all bearing housings and gearboxes to tank. Total system capacity 24 Imp pints (13·6 litres). Tank capacity 12 Imp pints (6·8 litres). Usable oil 9 Imp pints (5·1 litres). Normal oil supply pressure 35-50 lb/sq in (2·5-3·5 kg/cm²).

Oil Specification: DERD.2487.

Mounting: Two trunnions, two saddle mountings and one rear mounting.

Starting: Plessey 220 air-turbine starter. Rotax alternative on Mks 505, 511 and 512; AiResearch on Mk 555.

Dimensions:

Length, less tailpipe:	
Mk 505, 506, 555	110·0 in (2,795 mm)
Mk 510, 511	114·6 in (2,911 mm)
Diameter:	
Mk 505, 506, 555	37·0 in (940 mm)
Mk 510, 511	37·1 in (942 mm)

Weight, Dry:

Mk 505-5	2,200 lb (998 kg)
Mk 506-14	2,257 lb (1,024 kg)
Mk 506-14AW	2,288 lb (1,038 kg)
Mk 510-5, 511-5	2,312 lb (1,049 kg)
Mk 510-14, 511-14	2,332 lb (1,058 kg)
Mk 510-14W, 511-14W	2,621 lb (1,188 kg)
Mk 511-5W	2,317 lb (1,050 kg)
Mk 512	2,574 lb (1,168 kg)
Mk 555-15	2,194 lb (995 kg)

Performance Ratings:

Max T-O: See under series descriptions

Max continuous:

Mk 505 9,450 lb (4,286 kg) st at 12,260 rpm
Mk 506 9,990 lb (4,531 kg) st at 12,385 rpm
Mk 511 10,940 lb (4,962 kg) st at 12,240 rpm
Mk 512, Mk 512DW
11,580 lb (5,253 kg) st at 12,450 rpm
Mk 555-15 9,470 lb (4,295 kg) st at 11,900 rpm

Typical cruise rating at 450 knots (518 mph; 834 km/h) at 32,000 ft (9,750 m):
All versions 3,070 lb (1,392 kg) st

Specific Fuel Consumption:

At T-O rating:	
Mk 505	0·560
Mk 506	0·563
Mk 511	0·612
Mk 555-15	0·560
At typical cruise rating:	
Mks 505, 506	0·760
Mks 510,511	0·790
Mks 512, 555	0·800

Oil Consumption:

Max (all Marks) 0·75 Imp pints (0·42 litres)/hr

ROLLS-ROYCE SPEY 605W

The Spey Mk 605W (-67B) is a high by-pass ratio turbofan derived from the Spey Mk 512. The engine is designed to provide very low noise levels and improved fuel consumption to meet the requirements of the 1980s. It is expected that the 90 dB footprint for a typical twin-jet will be reduced to under 4 sq miles, and that noise levels in the region of FAR Pt 36 minus 10 dB will be achieved.

The Spey Mk 605W differs significantly from the original Spey 67 described in the 1973-74 *Jane's*, but it still retains an HP core similar to that of existing Spey engines. The 605W is firmly committed to development, and production deliveries are expected to commence towards the end of 1976.

Type: Two-spool axial turbofan engine of modular construction.

Compressor: Axial-flow two-spool type with single-stage fan and three-stage intermediate pressure (IP) compressor on low-speed shaft and 12-stage high-pressure (HP) compressor on high-speed shaft. The fan/IP compressor has impact-resistant steel and titanium blading and does not feature inlet guide vanes. HP compressor of disc construction, with blades of steel and titanium, with stator vanes slotted into two-piece steel casing. Air mass flow 423 lb (192 kg)/sec. Pressure ratio 20·7.

Combustion, Fuel and Water Injection Systems: Similar to Spey Mk 512.

Nozzle Guide Vanes: Hollow type cast in nickel-based alloy. HP nozzle guide vanes, aircooled.

Turbines: Two-stage HP and three-stage LP axial-flow turbines. Both HP stages have air-cooled cast blades. LP turbine blades are forged. All blades are attached to discs by fir-tree roots.

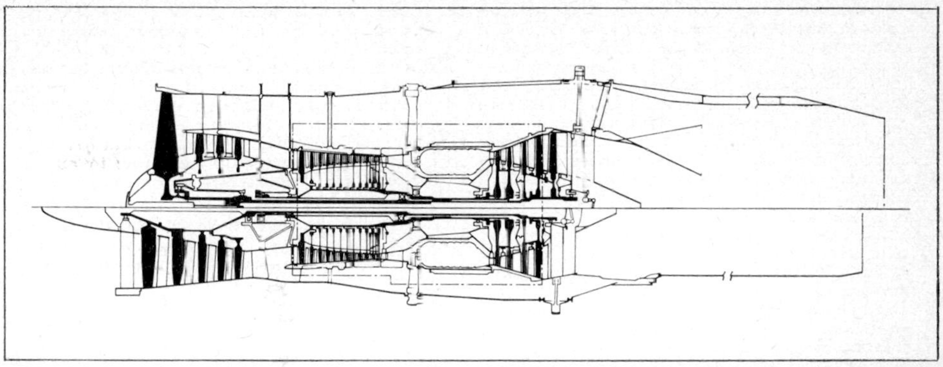

Comparative cross-sections of the Rolls-Royce Spey 605W (upper half of drawing) and Spey 512 (lower half). A broken line encloses the core common to both engines. The Spey 605W, which will be wet-rated at 17,000 lb; 7,711 kg, offers greatly reduced noise and sfc

Bearings: Similar bearing arrangement to Spey Mk 512.

Jet Pipe: Fixed-area type of stainless sheet, fitted with noise-suppression honeycomb lining.

Reverser: Internal clamshell type, with noise-suppression treatment.

Accessory Drives: Gearbox driven from HP rotor carries fuel pumps, fuel regulator, oil pumps, starter and aircraft accessories such as constant-speed-drive alternator and hydraulic pumps.

Dimensions:

Fan diameter 47 in (1,194 mm)
Length (inlet flange to exhaust flange)
92 in (2,337 mm)

Performance Ratings:

Max T-O, dry	15,700 lb (7,121 kg)
Max T-O, wet	17,000 lb (7,711 kg)

ROLLS-ROYCE RB.168 MILITARY SPEY (DERBY)

The military Spey RB.168 is fundamentally similar in design to the civil engine, but incorporates modifications to meet the higher-duty conditions of the military rating.

Design of the Spey RB.168-1 started in November 1960; following a contract for prototype development engines, bench testing started in December 1961. During the subsequent month the engine was ordered into quantity production, and flew for the first time in the Hawker Siddeley Buccaneer S.2 strike aircraft in May 1963. The RB.168-1 also powers the Buccaneer S.50 land-based strike aircraft of the South African Air Force.

Major military version of the Spey is the RB.168-25R supersonic engine with afterburner. Mainly through the use of an increased turbine entry temperature, the engine has a dry rating of 12,250 lb (5,556 kg) plus a 70 per cent static augmentation and powers the McDonnell Douglas Phantom FG.1 and FGR.2. Design of this variant of the Spey started at the beginning of 1964 and the first run was in April 1965. First flight, powering the YF-4K, was on 28 June 1966, followed by the first flight in the YF-4M on 17 February 1967. The RB.168-25R has been in wide-scale production, involving subcontract component manufacture in many aviation countries in the West, and has been in service with the RN and RAF since early 1969.

The engine used in the Phantom is based closely on the commercial Spey 25, but with stressing and material changes to meet the increased pressure and temperature conditions and flight loads. Major change is the introduction of a robust shaft-and-disc construction for the LP compressor. As with the RB.168-1, use is made of HP compressor bleed air for aircraft BLC purposes. A Plessey gas-turbine starter is fitted. Augmentation is thrust-modulating from an initial boost, at sea level static, of six per cent. The afterburner incorporates three vee-gutter flame stabilisers, multi-bar fuel injection via four upstream manifolds, self-contained ignition, a fully-variable primary nozzle and a fixed secondary nozzle. Longitudinal movement of the divergent ejector nozzle by six hydraulic rams operates the primary nozzle flaps.

The Spey RB.168-20 Mk 250, closely based on the commercial Spey, powers the Hawker Siddeley Nimrod. Embodying extensive anti-corrosive treatment, this variant provides a higher thrust than its civil counterpart, through operation at higher rpm and higher turbine entry temperature. Provision is made for driving a large alternator, to meet the heavy electrical loads inherent in a maritime reconnaissance aircraft.

ROLLS-ROYCE/ALLISON SPEY TF41

Versions of the Spey are being developed and produced jointly by Rolls-Royce and the Detroit Diesel Allison Division of General Motors to power USAF and USN versions of the LTV A-7 Corsair II close-support aircraft. These engines, with the designations TF41-A-1 and TF41-A-2, are rated respectively at 14,500 lb (6,577 kg) st and 15,000 lb (6,804 kg) st dry. Details of the TF41 are given in the International section.

ROLLS-ROYCE DART (DERBY)

Although the design of the Dart began in 1945 the engine has been continuously developed to meet the requirements of civil operators, and the latest versions give over 3,000 ehp. By January 1974 over 6,400 Darts had been produced. April 1974 marked the completion of 21 years of continuous scheduled service by Dart-powered aircraft. Production of new Darts in 1974 will exceed that for 1973.

Ratings, weights and dimensions of current versions are given in the table of data.

Type: Single-shaft centrifugal-flow turboprop engine.

Reduction Gear: Double reduction gearing with helical high-speed train and final helical gear drive. The two gear trains connected by three layshafts. High-speed pinion driven by an inner shaft system bolted directly onto turbine discs. All gears and propeller shaft carried in roller or ball bearings. Bevel gears from one of the layshafts provide drives to fuel and oil pumps and propeller controller unit. Bevel gear and engaging mechanism on pinion shaft provide drive from starter motor.

Air Intake: Circular intake with annular duct leading to impeller eye of first-stage compressor. Oil tank around intake is cast integral with casing. Secondary air intake supplies air to oil cooler mounted on top of casing.

The 3,025 ehp Rolls-Royce Dart RDa.10/1 turboprop engine

COMPRESSOR: Two-stage centrifugal-flow compressor. Each impeller has nineteen vanes and steel rotating guide vanes. Mass air flow at maximum rpm 20·5 lb (9·3 kg)/sec at 5·5 : 1 (RDa.6); 23·5 lb (10·66 kg)/sec at 5·62 : 1 (RDa.7); 27 lb (12·25 kg)/sec at 6·35 : 1 (RDa.10 and 12) pressure ratios respectively.

COMBUSTION CHAMBERS: Seven straight-flow combustion chambers. Flame tubes with fuel atomisers in front end of each tube for downstream injection. High-energy igniter plugs in Nos. 3 and 7 chambers.

FUEL SYSTEM: Single multi-plunger variable-stroke injection pump delivers fuel to burners through flow control unit, which incorporates a filter, throttle valve, shut-off cock and barometric pressure control. Operation of control unit is function of intake pressure and throttle valve pressure drop, thus determining fuel/air ratio for all engine operating conditions. RDa. 10 and 12 have duple fuel system, with pressures of 325 lb/sq in (22·85 kg/cm^2) at idle and 900 lb/sq in (63·28 kg/cm^2) at T-O. In all other versions, fuel pressure at burners varies from 40 lb/sq in (2·81 kg/cm^2) at idling speed to 1,200 lb/sq in (70·3 kg/cm^2) at maximum power. Automatically-progressive injection of water/methanol used to restore take-off power under high ambient temperature conditions. System interconnected mechanically with throttle lever to ensure that it can only be used at take-off rpm. Fuel filter de-icing by hot air from compressor. Hot-air gate valve fitted to bottom engine mounting.

TURBINE: Two-stage (RDa.3 and 6) or three-stage (RDa.7, 10 and 12) axial-flow turbine. In RDa.3 and 6, the two discs are coupled by a single large annular bolt co-axial with single shaft which forms direct drive to compressor. In RDa.7, 10 and 12 first and second stage discs are bolted together by five bolts and all three by further five, while the drive shaft is divided, with inner shaft connecting turbine with reduction gear and outer shaft with compressor. All blades of Nimonic alloy and secured on discs by fir-tree roots.

EXHAUST UNIT: Propeller thrust line co-axial with engine main shaft but exhaust unit has a slight inclination to suit installation. Unit comprises an outer shell which supports an inner cone on three struts enclosed in aerofoil-section fairings to reduce turbulence and straighten gas flow at nozzle. Maximum jet pipe temperature 650°C.

ACCESSORY DRIVES: An accessory gearbox drive is taken from the main-shaft centre-coupling immediately behind the compressor through a train of gears to a housing on top of the intermediate casing.

LUBRICATION: Entirely self-contained. Integral oil tank (total capacity 25 Imp pints; 14 litres) feeds engine via standpipe and feathering pump through tank base, to ensure feathering possible even after prolonged system oil leak. Gear pump supplies oil to all bearings and reduction-gear jets at nominal pressure of 30 lb/sq in (2·10 kg/cm^2) and at nominal flow of 460 Imp gallons (2,091 litres) per hour. Combined delivery from four scavenge pumps returned to tank via oil-cooler on top of intake casing. Pressure and scavenge pumps in single housing and driven by common shaft.

CONTROLS: Only two cockpit controls, a throttle lever for varying power and a high-pressure cock for stopping engine. Throttle valve is interconnected with the propeller controller and high-pressure cock is linked with propeller feathering controls. Blades may be feathered by moving shut-off cock lever past the closed position; depression of an unfeathering button returns blades to fine pitch. Certain Viscount aircraft feature automatic selection into zero pitch, available with the aircraft weight on the landing gear. All other aircraft feature automatic cancellation of ability to come below flight fine pitch when the throttles are advanced to max power with gust locks removed, which is normal for take-off. On landing it is necessary to select manually removal of flight fine stop to permit blades to move down to zero pitch.

MOUNTING: Four feet are provided at 90° on the horizontal and vertical centrelines of compressor casing, although only three need be used. Bottom foot for hot-air gate valve. No rear mounting is required, but jet pipe if used requires separate mounting in airframe.

DIMENSIONS, WEIGHTS AND PERFORMANCE: See table below

ROLLS-ROYCE TYNE (DERBY)

The Rolls-Royce Tyne is an advanced twin-spool high-compression turboprop engine which powers the BAC Vanguard, Canadair Forty Four, Short Belfast military transport, Breguet Atlantic maritime reconnaissance aircraft and Transall C-160 military transport.

The Tyne first ran in April 1955 and began its flight testing in the Summer of 1956 in the nose of an Avro Lincoln flying testbed. It entered service in the Vanguard and Canadair Forty Four in 1961.

The following versions of the Tyne have been produced:

RTy.1. Rated at 4,785 ehp minimum for take-off. Cruising specific fuel consumption 0·405 lb (0·184 kg)/ehp/hr. For Vanguard (Mk 506).

RTy.11. Rated at 5,325 ehp minimum for take-off. Cruising specific fuel consumption 0·384 lb (0·175 kg)/ehp/hr. For Vanguard (Mk 511).

RTy.12. Rated at 5,500 ehp. For Short Belfast (Mk 101) and Canadair 400/CL-44J and CL-44D (Mk 515/10).

RTy.20. In production by SNECMA (Hispano) (France), MTU (Germany) and FN (Belgium) to power Breguet 1150 Atlantic (Mk 21) and Transall C-160 (Mk 22). Mk 22 engine completed 150 hour type test at T-O rating of 6,100 ehp (5,665 shp) in January 1963.

The following details refer specifically to the Tyne RTy.20, but are generally applicable to all versions:

TYPE: Two-spool axial-flow turboprop.

REDUCTION GEAR: Double reduction gearing by compound epicyclic train. High-speed pinion driven from forward end of LP shaft with final drive through planet wheel carrier integral with propeller shaft. Ratio 0·064 : 1. Shaft carried in one set of ball bearings and one set of roller bearings. Fixed annulus.

AIR INTAKE: Annular intake surrounds reduction gear housing. Integrally cast in magnesium alloy, with seven hollow support struts. Oil tank of annular form made up by rear wall of air intake casing and fabricated steel shell. Anti-icing by hot oil circulated through struts and by hot air tapped from HP compressor. Electrical de-icing of cowling surrounding intake.

LP COMPRESSOR: Six-stage axial-flow type. Made up from six steel discs, of which 1st (stage 0) disc is integral with shaft and remaining five discs splined to shaft. The 216 light alloy rotor blades are unshrouded and fixed to discs by single pin fixing. Inlet guide vanes and stage 0 stator blades of fabricated hollow construction to provide de-icing by means of air bled off HP compressor. The 431 steel stator blades are secured in casing by tongue and groove location. Steel LP casing in one piece. LP compressor mounted on front roller bearing and rear roller bearing.

INTERMEDIATE COMPRESSOR CASING: Intermediate casing between HP and LP compressors is aluminium alloy casting housing internal wheelcase. Bleed valve mounted on top of casing operates under approach conditions when LP and HP speeds are unmatched.

HP COMPRESSOR: Nine-stage axial-flow type. Made up from nine steel discs splined to shaft. Total of 575 rotor blades of titanium (first seven stages) and steel (last two stages). The 734 steel stator blades are fixed in rings by tongue and groove location. Stator blades are unshrouded. HP casing of centri-cast steel supports stator drum by bolted flanges. HP compressor mounted on front roller bearing and rear ball bearing. Rear bearing also takes thrust from inter-shaft ball bearing mounted slightly ahead of it. Pressure ratio 13·5 : 1. Air mass flow 46·5 lb (21·1 kg)/sec.

COMBUSTION CHAMBER: Ten flame tubes of Nimonic sheet mounted within annular chamber. Combustion system casings of steel. Flame tubes contain double twin-flow co-axial burners. Flame tubes 3 and 8 (on engine horizontal centreline) contain high-energy igniter plugs.

FUEL SYSTEM: Single multi-plunger variable-stroke HP pump delivers fuel to burners via flow control unit. Unit incorporates filter, throttle valves, shut-off cock and barometric pressure sensing device. Operation is a function of air intake pressure and throttle valve pressure drop. Hydro-mechanical governors control overspeeding of LP and HP sections of engine. Fuel anti-icing is by an oil-heated fuel heater between tank and LP pump. Max fuel supply pressure 1,250 lb/sq in (87·88 kg/cm^2). Water/methanol injected into LP compressor through holes in stage 0 disc.

FUEL GRADE: MIL-J-5624D, Grade JP-4.

NOZZLE BOX: Centri-cast steel casing, containing 4 stages of nozzle guide vanes. The 50 HP vanes are aircooled. The three LP stages have 60 hollow blades each. 20 thermocouples are fitted in the leading-edges of the first-stage LP nozzle guide vanes.

HP TURBINE: Single-stage. Steel disc attached to HP shaft by 8 taper bolts. 121 Nimonic

The 6,100 ehp Rolls-Royce Tyne RTy.20 turboprop engine

ROLLS-ROYCE DART TURBOPROP ENGINES

Mark Number	Take-off Guaranteed Minimum Power	Cruising Specific Fuel Consumption (300 knots; 345 mph; 555 km/h at 20,000 ft; 6,100 m)	Maximum Basic Dry Weight	Gear Ratio	Length (without jet pipe)	Diameter	Remarks
Mk.529 (RDa.7)	2,180 ehp (1,990 shp) at 15,000 rpm	0·578 lb/ehp/hr (0·262 kg/ehp/hr)	1,235 lb (560 kg)	0·093 : 1	97·6 in (2,480 mm)	37·9 in (963 mm)	Powers Grumman Gulfstream and Fairchild FH-227. (11 ft 6 in; 3·50 m propeller.)
Mk.532 (RDa.7L)	2,280 ehp (2,080 shp) at 15,000 rpm	0·578 lb/ehp /hr (0·262 kg/ehp/hr)	1,237 lb (561 kg)	0·093 : 1	97·6 in (2,480 mm)	37·9 in (963 mm)	Uprated RDa.7, powers HS 748, Friendship and Argosy 222.
Mk.550 (RDa.8)	2,450 ehp (2,250 shp) at 15,000 rpm	0·578 lb/ehp/hr (0·262 kg/ehp/hr)	1,237 lb (561 kg)	0·093 : 1	97·6 in (2,480 mm)	37·9 in (963 mm)	Powers HS 748 Model 228.
Mk.542 (RDa.10)	3,025 ehp (2,750 shp) at 15,000 rpm	0·556 lb/ehp/hr (0·252 kg/ehp/hr)	1,366 lb (620 kg) or 1,377 lb (625 kg)	0·0775 : 1	99·49 in (2,527 mm)	37·9 in (963 mm)	Powers NAMC YS-11 and Convair 600.
Mk.201 (RDa.12)	3,245 ehp (2,970 shp) at 15,000 rpm	0·556 lb/ehp/hr (0·252 kg/ehp/hr)	1,387 lb (629 kg)	0·0775 : 1	99·49 in (2,527 mm)	37·9 in (963 mm)	Powers HS Andover C. 1.

blades attached by fir-tree roots. Blades air-cooled and tip-shrouded. HP turbine carried on roller bearing ahead of turbine. Shaft splined to HP compressor shaft. Gas temperature before turbine 1,000°C.

LP Turbine: Three-stage. Steel discs bolted to each other by 8 bolts. Forward LP shaft is integral with first-stage disc. Stage 3 disc integral with rear LP shaft. All blades of Nimonic, secured by fir-tree roots. Stage 1 has 101 tip-shrouded blades. Stage 2 has 106 tip-shrouded blades. Stage 3 has 61 tip-shrouded blades. LP turbine is carried on roller bearings at rear and supported by plain bearing in HP shaft at front. Shaft splined to LP compressor shaft. Gas temperature after turbine 453°C.

Exhaust Unit: Fabricated construction, supporting tail bearing from nozzle box outer casing by ten struts with streamlined fairings.

Accessory Drives: Internal wheelcase houses two drives. Port wheelcase drive from LP shaft, to accessory gearbox, LP tachometer and LP shaft governor. Starboard wheelcase drive from HP shaft to fuel pumps, HP tachometer, oil pumps and breather, mounting for starter motor.

Lubrication: Dry sump type with one pressure and six scavenge spur-gear pumps driven from HP shaft. Tank capacity 46 Imp pints (26·2 litres) including 16 Imp pints (9·1 litres) for feathering reserve. Thermostatically controlled aircooled oil cooler. Oil supply pressure 45 lb/sq in (3·16 kg/cm²).

Oil Grade: DERD.2487.

Engine Mounting: Four mounting feet on engine vertical and horizontal centrelines, located immediately aft of oil tank.

Starting: Air starter located on HP wheelcase.

Dimensions (RTy.20):
- Overall length: 108·724 in (2,762 mm)
- Max diameter (over nose cowling) approx: 55 in (1,400 mm)

Weight, Dry:
- RTy.1, RTy.11: 1,275 lb (1,032 kg)
- RTy.12 Mk 515 (excluding oil coolers): 2,177 lb (987 kg)
- RTy.20 Mk 21, with accessories: 2,391 lb (1,085 kg)

Performance Ratings (RTy.20 Mk 21):
- Nominal T-O rating: 4,500 shp plus 1,200 lb (545 kg) st at 15,250 rpm
- Max continuous rating: 3,995 shp plus 970 lb (440 kg) st at 13,500 rpm

Specific Fuel Consumption (RTy.20 Mk 21):
- At T-O rating: 0·485 lb (0·220 kg)/ehp/hr

Oil Consumption (RTy.20 Mk 21):
- Max: 1·5 Imp pints (0·85 litres)/hr

ROLLS-ROYCE VIPER (BRISTOL)

This well established turbojet remains in quantity production for civil and military customers. Approximately 5,000 Vipers have been ordered by 36 countries, 27 of which have chosen the engine for trainer and light strike aircraft.

The current versions of the Viper turbojet are as follows:

Viper 11 (Mk 200 Series). Single-shaft seven-stage axial-flow compressor driven by a single-stage turbine. Air mass flow 44 lb/sec (20 kg/sec). Type-tested at 2,500 lb (1,134 kg) st and powers the Jindivik Mk 3 target drone, BAC Jet Provost T.Mk 4 and Mk 5, Yugoslav Soko Galeb and Hindustan HJT-16 Kiran trainers.

The Mk 203 at a thrust of 2,700 lb (1,225 kg) was used as a boost engine in the HS Shackleton MR Mk 3.

A Viper 11 version, the 22-1, is built under licence in Italy by Piaggio for the Aermacchi M.B.326 jet trainer and by the Atlas Corporation of the Republic of South Africa and Commonwealth Aircraft Corporation of Australia for use in the same basic aircraft.

Viper 500 Series. Development of the Viper 11 with increased air mass flow, achieved by the addition of an extra stage in front of the compressor. Major applications are in early Hawker Siddeley 125s (Mks 520, 521, 522) and Piaggio-Douglas PD-808 executive transport aircraft (Mk 526) and the BAC 167 Strikemaster (Mk 535), Aermacchi M.B.326GB (Mk 540) and Soko Jastreb (Mk 531) training and light ground attack combat aircraft. Mk 540 is built under licence by Piaggio and Atlas.

Viper 600 Series. Eight-stage axial-flow compressor driven by two-stage turbine in conjunction with a short annular vaporising combustion chamber. Take-off rating 3,750 lb (1,700 kg) st for civil applications and 4,000 lb (1,814 kg) st for military applications. Agreement signed with Fiat (Italy) in July 1969 providing for technical collaboration in design, development and production (see Fiat entry).

The first two members of this series to go into production are: the civil Viper 601, which powers the Hawker Siddeley 125-600 (Beechcraft Hawker BH 125-600); and the military Viper 632, fitted to the Aermacchi M.B.326K.

The following details apply to the Viper 600 series:

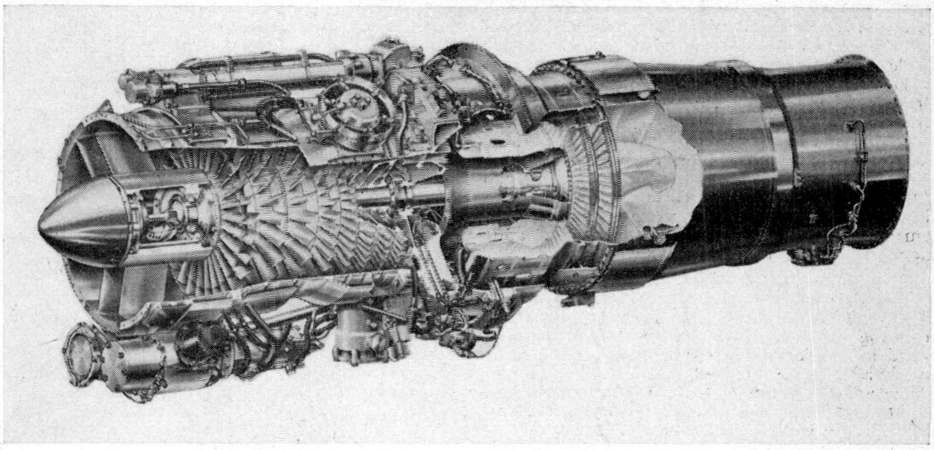

Cutaway drawing of the Rolls-Royce Viper 601 turbojet engine (3,750 lb; 1,700 kg st)

Type: Single-shaft axial-flow turbojet.

Air Intake: Annular type at front of engine. Anti-icing by hot air tapped from compressor delivery and supplied to struts and nose bullet. No inlet guide vanes.

Compressor: Eight-stage axial-flow. Steel drum-type rotor with disc assemblies. Magnesium alloy casing with blow-off valve. Stator blades mounted in carrier rings slotted into casing. All stator blades and 1st, 2nd and 8th stage rotor blades of steel; remainder aluminium alloy. Zero-stage and first-stage rotor blades attached by fir-tree roots; stages 3-8 riveted. Pressure ratio 5·8 : 1. Air mass flow 58·4 lb (26·5 kg)/sec.

Combustion Chamber: Short annular type with 24 vaporising burners and six starting atomisers. Electric ignition.

Fuel System: Hydromechanical, consisting primarily of fuel pump, barometric fuel control unit and air/fuel ratio control unit.

Fuel Grade: JP-1 or JP-4.

Turbine: Two stage axial-flow. Shrouded blades attached to discs by fir-tree roots and locking strips. Discs attached by Hirth couplings.

Bearings: Three main bearings: ball-thrust type at forward end of compressor, roller bearings at centre section and at rear end of combustion chamber inner casing.

Jet Pipe: Cone of heat-resisting steel rings butt-welded together. (Viper 601: eight-lobe convoluted nozzle enables HS 125-600 to meet FAR Pt 36 noise requirements).

Accessory Drives: Gearbox bolted to bottom of air intake casing and driven from front of compressor by bevel gear shaft.

Lubrication System: Self-contained. Recirculatory system supplying the front bearing and gearbox, metered feed supplied to centre and rear bearings by micro-pumps. Military version fully aerobatic.

Oil Specification: Mobil Jet 2, Shell ASTO 500 and Castrol 580.

Mounting: Civil: cantilevered, side mounted, employing single spherical bearing in the centre-section casing, with top and bottom links and an attachment at the intake casing. Military: trunnion mounted at the centre-section with additional support at the intake casing.

Starting: 24V starter/generator.

Dimensions:
- Max casing diameter:
  - All versions: 24·55 in (624 mm)
- Length (flange to flange):
  - Viper 11: 64·0 in (1,626 mm)
  - Viper 520, 521, 522 (plus jet pipe and nozzle): 85·0 in (2,159 mm)
  - Viper 531, 535, 540, 632: 71·1 in (1,806 mm)
  - Viper 601 (plus jet pipe): 89·4 in (2,270 mm)

Weights (complete engine-change unit):
- Viper 11: 710 lb (322 kg)
- Viper 520, 521, 522: 815 lb (370 kg)
- Viper 531: 790 lb (358 kg)
- Viper 535, 540: 780 lb (354 kg)
- Viper 601: 830 lb (376 kg)
- Viper 632: 810 lb (368 kg)

Performance Ratings:
- T-O rating:
  - Viper 11: 2,500 lb (1,134 kg) st
  - Viper 520: 3,000 lb (1,365 kg) st
  - Viper 521, 531: 3,120 lb (1,415 kg) st
  - Viper 522, 535, 540: 3,410 lb (1,547 kg) st
  - Viper 601: 3,750 lb (1,700 kg) st
  - Viper 632: 4,000 lb (1,814 kg) st

Specific Fuel Consumption:
- Viper 11: 1·07
- Viper 531: 1·06
- Viper 522, 535, 540: 1·01
- Viper 601: 0·94
- Viper 632: 0·97

Oil Consumption:
- All versions: 1 Imp pint (0·57 litres)/hr

ROLLS-ROYCE ORPHEUS (BRISTOL)

The Orpheus is a single-spool turbojet engine initiated by Bristol in December 1953 as a private venture. Current versions are as follows:

Orpheus 700 Series

The first of this series was type-tested in November 1956 at a rating of 4,520 lb (2,050 kg) st and with improved altitude performance. The Mk 701, for the HS Gnat fighter, is in service with the air forces of India and Finland and has operated successfully in tropical conditions with air temperatures up to 43°C and 80 per cent humidity, and in sub-Arctic conditions at temperatures as low as —34°C. The Mk 701 has been fitted to the Fairchild C-119 transport aircraft of the Indian Air Force in Jet-Pak form as a boost engine.

The Mk 703, rated at 4,850 lb (2,200 kg) st, is in service with the Indian Air Force in the Hindustan HF-24 Marut fighter. For all the Indian applications the engine is built under licence at Bangalore, India, by Hindustan Aeronautics Limited (HAL).

Orpheus 800 Series

The first of this series was type-tested in May 1957 at 4,850 lb (2,200 kg) st and at a thrust/weight ratio of 5·9 : 1, the highest figure for any turbojet at that time. The Mk 801 is identical to the 701/703 except for an increased-capacity fuel pump and is used in the early Fiat G91s. The Mk 803, rated at 5,000 lb (2,270 kg) st, replaced the Mk 801 in the Fiat G91 and differs mainly in improvements to the compressor. This series engine was built under licence by Fiat in Italy and KHD for the G91 aircraft of the Italian and German air forces. The Mk 805, rated at 4,000 lb (1,814 kg) st, powers the Japanese Fuji T1F2 trainer.

Orpheus 101

This engine is similar to the 800 Series but has an improved turbine and is fully anti-iced. Initially rated at 4,230 lb (1,916 kg) st but subsequently increased to 4,520 lb (2,045 kg) st by increased rpm. It is in service in Gnat Trainers of RAF Training Command.

A description of the Orpheus 803 was given in the 1967-68 *Jane's*.

Dimensions:
- Diameter: 32·4 in (823 mm)
- Length:
  - Orpheus 701, 703: 73·0 in (1,854 mm)
  - Orpheus 801, 803, 805: 75·45 in (1,916 mm)
  - Orpheus 101: 75·50 in (1,919 mm)

Weight, Dry:
- Orpheus 701: 860 lb (390 kg)
- Orpheus 801, 803, 805: 902 lb (409 kg)
- Orpheus 101: 920 lb (417 kg)

Specific Fuel Consumption:
- At max rating:
  - Orpheus 701: 1·00
  - Orpheus 801, 803: 1·08
  - Orpheus 101: 1·06

ROLLS-ROYCE/SNECMA M45H

This joint design of turbofan by Rolls-Royce and SNECMA is in production to power the VFW 614 feederliner. A detailed description of the M45H is given in the International section.

ROLLS-ROYCE OLYMPUS (BRISTOL)

The Olympus was the first British turbojet engine of the "two-spool" type. It entered production in 1953 for the Hawker Siddeley Vulcan bomber. Details of the Olympus 593, power plant of the Concorde, are given in the International section. Earlier versions are as follows:

100 Series. The Mk 101 was the first member of the Olympus family to go into production and at a take-off thrust of 11,000 lb (4,990 kg) st entered service in the Vulcan B. Mk 1 in July 1956. The addition of an extra stage in front of the LP compressor, together with higher operating speed and temperatures, led to the Mk 102 and Mk 104 with take-off thrust increased to 13,500 lb (6,124 kg) st, which also entered service in the Vulcan B. Mk 1. The earlier engines were converted to the Mk 104 standard at overhaul at relatively small cost.

The Olympus 100 Series is no longer in service.

Mk 201. A redesigned engine having a five-stage LP compressor and seven-stage HP compressor as with the 100 Series, each driven by a single-stage turbine. With a take-off rating of 17,000 lb (7,710 kg) st entered service in the Vulcan B. 2 in July 1960.

The current engine is the Mk 202, and differs from the earlier 201 only in the venting and engine starting systems.

Mk 301. Developed from the 200 Series by the addition of an extra stage in front of the LP compressor and at a take-off thrust of 20,000 lb (9,072 kg) st entered service in the Vulcan B. 2 in May 1963. Both 202 and 301 engines are currently in service. A description of the Mk 301 appeared in the 1970-71 *Jane's*.

ROLLS-ROYCE PEGASUS (BRISTOL)

The Pegasus is a turbofan engine developed for V/STOL applications. It has two main rotating systems which are mechanically independent and rotate in opposite directions, thus minimising gyroscopic effects. It has a three-stage axial-flow fan of transonic design and an eight-stage high-pressure compressor, each driven by separate two-stage turbines. Thrust vectoring is achieved by four rotatable nozzles simultaneously operated and symmetrically positioned on each side of the engine. The two front nozzles discharge the by-pass air, whilst the two rear nozzles discharge the turbine efflux. The total thrust is divided approximately equally between the four nozzles, and the resultant thrust passes through a fixed point of the engine irrespective of nozzle angle, thus minimising aircraft control problems. High-pressure bleed air is used for aircraft stabilisation.

The Pegasus was the first engine to be designed with an overhung fan, without inlet guide vanes, requiring no anti-icing since the rotor blades satisfactorily shed any ice buildup. The use of rotatable nozzles also minimises the ground-running problems of recirculation, debris ingestion and ground erosion—a major difficulty with fixed lifting engines—because such running can be done with the exhaust discharging rearwards. Taxying is normal and a short forward roll at take-off before the nozzles are deflected downwards ensures that dust and debris are left behind.

By varying the angle of the nozzles, an aircraft powered by the Pegasus can take off vertically or with a short run or with a conventional long run. This offers advantages when developing a new aircraft or training pilots in VTOL flight. In addition, the reserve of power in the normal runway take-off allows for an appreciable increase in payload. The engine is stressed for operation up to Mach 2, ISA tropopause, at the maximum thrust rating.

The Pegasus ran for the first time in August 1959, and flight trials in the Hawker Siddeley P.1127 prototypes began in October 1960. The **Pegasus 3,** which powered prototype P.1127 aircraft, was rated at 13,500 lb (6,123 kg) st. The **Pegasus 5,** which powered the tripartite V/STOL evaluation Kestrels and was fitted to the Dornier Do 31 V/STOL transport, was rated at 15,500 lb (7,031 kg) st. The **Pegasus 6,** with the production designation Mk 101, had a maximum rating of 19,000 lb (8,618 kg), and entered service with the RAF in the Hawker Siddeley Harrier GR.1 and T.2 in April 1969. All Mk 101 engines have been converted to Mk 103 standard. The **Pegasus 10,** Mk 102, a Pegasus 6 version uprated to a thrust of 20,500 lb (9,299 kg), obtained type approval in March 1970; it entered service in 1971 with Harriers of the RAF and AV-8As of the US Marine Corps. All Mk 102 engines will have been brought up to Mk 103 standard by the end of 1974; the USMC aircraft were entirely Mk 103-powered by early 1974.

The **Pegasus 11,** Mk 103, at a rating of 21,500 lb (9,752 kg), was funded by the British government and completed its type approval in July 1971. The increase in thrust was obtained by aerodynamic redesign of the fan and increased turbine entry temperature. The Pegasus 11 is cleared to use VIFF (vectoring in forward flight) to enhance combat manoeuvrability. A variant of the Pegasus 11 is the Mk 104 for maritime operation. The LP and intermediate casings are of corrosion-resistant materials, and the gearbox drive is strengthened.

In October 1971 an agreement was signed with Pratt & Whitney Aircraft for joint development of the Pegasus; the US company also has an option to secure a manufacturing licence. The next major development standard is the Pegasus 15, rated at not less than 24,500 lb (11,115 kg) st. The definitive Pegasus 15 will have increased cold-nozzle thrust gained by a fan of 2·25 in (57 mm) greater diameter, driven by an improved turbine with shrouded blades. This will be balanced by increased hot-nozzle thrust gained by an increase in core airflow through a more efficient HP compressor. The exhaust diffuser will also be improved.

In May 1972 a Pegasus 15 demonstrator engine, not incorporating the improved core, exceeded its design thrust with a measured figure of 24,900 lb (11,300 kg). In April 1973 it was announced that, with formal clearance agreed by the two governments, Rolls-Royce (1971) and Pratt & Whitney would make an eight-month programme-definition study of the Pegasus 15, its possible joint development by the two companies and—with Hawker Siddeley and McDonnell Douglas—how it could best be used in advanced versions of the Harrier. This study report was submitted to the two governments in December 1973.

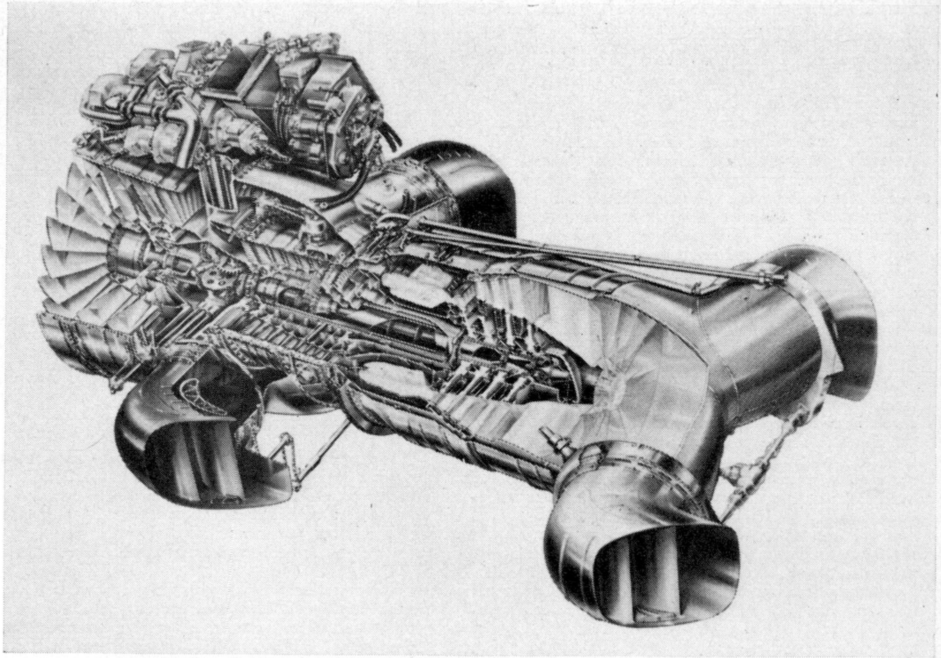

Cutaway drawing of the Rolls-Royce Pegasus 11 turbofan engine (21,500 lb; 9,752 kg st)

Rolls-Royce (Bristol) has developed a method of thrust boosting suitable for Pegasus-type engines. This system, called plenum chamber burning (PCB), consists of burning additional fuel in the cold air ducted to the front pair of nozzles, with a resulting increase in thrust for take-off, transonic acceleration and supersonic flight. The advantage of PCB is that a smaller basic engine may be installed in a V/STOL aircraft to achieve a specified performance, with a consequent saving in weight and an improved specific fuel consumption under cruise conditions.

The following data apply specifically to the Pegasus 6, 10 and 11:

Type: Moderate by-pass ratio vectored-thrust turbofan.

Air Intake Casing: One-piece casting in ZRE magnesium-zirconium alloy.

LP Compressor: Three-stage overhung fan with snubber anti-vibration surfaces.

Intermediate Casing: Houses front fan bearing, accessory drives and HP compressor front bearing. All engine-driven accessories are mounted above this casing.

HP Compressor: Eight-stage compressor with titanium rotor blades throughout.

Combustion System: Annular, with low-pressure vaporising burner system.

Fuel System: Hydromechanical system, comprising centrifugal backing pump, gear-type pressure pump, HP shut-off cock and overspeed governors and emergency manual control.

Turbines: Two-stage HP turbine and two-stage LP turbine. First-stage HP blades are precision cast. Remaining three rotor stages have forged blades. Both HP stages are aircooled.

Thrust Nozzles: Two steel cold front-thrust nozzles and two Nimonic hot thrust nozzles are actuated by duplicated air motors through system of shafts and chains. Vectored-thrust control is connected directly to the pilot's cockpit.

Lubrication System: Self-contained, comprising pressure pump and three scavenge pumps, with fuel-cooled oil cooler.

Mounting: Four-point suspension, with main trunnions on each side of delivery casing and tie link at rear of turbines.

Starting: Gas-turbine starter/APU mounted on top of intermediate casing.

Dimensions:

Length overall	98·84 in (2,510 mm)
Diameter, fan casing	48·05 in (1,220 mm)
Weight, Dry:	approx 3,500 lb (1,588 kg)

ROLLS-ROYCE THOR (BRISTOL)

The Thor was the first ramjet power unit to go into production in Europe, following many hundreds of firings of ramjet development vehicles. Engines of this type are fitted on the BAC Bloodhound surface-to-air guided missile which entered service with the Royal Air Force in 1958 and also serves with the air forces of Switzerland, Singapore, Australia and Sweden. It can be used in single or multiple form on appropriate high-speed vehicles.

Details of the final production Thor BT.3 are classified. The following description applies to an early version:

There is a centrebody intake of the two-shock type, supported by three equi-spaced faired struts, followed by an annular diffuser leading to the combustion system. Behind it is a series of fuel injection rods each with two or three downstream nozzles, and combustion is stabilised by means of baffles. The parallel tailpipe terminates in a convergent/divergent final nozzle which is cooled by means of a ring of apertures surrounding the rear portion of the tailpipe.

The Thor is designed for external pod mounting and has two mounting brackets, the rear mounting allowing for thermal expansion between the ramjet and the missile or aircraft. Fuel connections are made adjacent to the front mounting bracket.

A cutaway Rolls-Royce Thor BT.1 ramjet engine

The fuel system used with the Thor consists of an air-turbine-driven centrifugal pump, a fuel/air ratio control, and a Mach number control to reduce the fuel supply when the selected Mach number is exceeded.

Ignition is achieved by pyrotechnic flares. Complete reliability of ignition of the ramjet unit is essential in a missile or test vehicle which is accelerated from standstill to ramjet-operating speed by booster rockets, and this has been achieved.

The Thor BT.2 has an overall diameter of 15·75 in (400 mm) and a length of 103·9 in (2,639 mm). Its thrust and that of the BT.3 may not be published, but the earlier Thor BT.1 was rated at 5,275 lb (2,393 kg) net internal gauge thrust at Mach 2 at sea level.

ROLLS-ROYCE ODIN (BRISTOL)

The Odin ramjet powers the Hawker Siddeley Sea Dart, which has been developed to meet a Royal Navy and NATO requirement for a medium-range guided weapon system for small warships. It is in service with HMS *Bristol* and will equip Type 42 destroyers and ships of the Argentine Navy. The ramjet forms an integral part of the missile body, and gives a longer range and better performance characteristics against fast-manoeuvring targets than a solid-rocket-powered missile. Details of the Odin are classified.

ROLLS-ROYCE GEM (RS.360) (LEAVESDEN)

The Gem has been designed and developed, and is now in production, for the Westland/Aérospatiale Lynx helicopter. Although this is an element of the Anglo-French helicopter programme, the Gem development programme has been funded entirely by the British government, and pre-production engines have been wholly British built. Production engine deliveries are due in April 1975, with manufacture shared with Turboméca.

The BS.360 gas generator was run in July 1969 and the complete engine in September 1969. Engine ground running in the Lynx rotor rig began in September 1970, and the first flight of the Lynx took place in March 1971.

A total of 51 pre-production engines were delivered to the bench, rotor rig and flight development programmes, now nearing completion. Most of the mandatory tests for type approval, due early in 1975, had been successfully completed in March 1974. Lynx engines, designated Gem Mk 10001, will begin service life with the Royal Navy Intensive Trials Unit towards the end of 1975.

US General Electric announced in May 1973 that it was continuing an agreement with Rolls-Royce (1971), first signed in 1971, under which it would investigate market opportunities for the RS.360 Gem in the United States, and if a suitable opportunity emerged, it would make the British turboshaft engine under licence. One obvious possibility would occur if a version of the Westland/Aérospatiale Lynx were to be chosen as the US Navy LAMPS helicopter (see "Aircraft" section). Lynx engines, designated BS.360-07, have in 1973 been running at power levels around 960 shp; one engine completed a 192 hr endurance test with power in excess of 930 shp and oil consumption still "meeting the full specific requirement". Rolls-Royce (1971) announced that "Recent component rig tests show that there are still further gains in power to come". The Gem has potential for growth to 1,500 shp by increasing the airflow and turbine entry temperature.

Choice of a two-spool gas generator enables very fast response to power demand to be achieved without the need for a complex control system. Conservative stressing and thermodynamic loading, and use of proven design and manufacturing techniques, are features which experience has shown to contribute to engine reliability.

The design concept of the engine is based upon seven major modules, each capable of being assembled, tested and released as interchangeable units for service use in the interest of reducing the operator's product support commitments.

The nine main bearings each have labyrinth seals pressurised by LP compressor air which also cools the bearings and minimises heat transfer to the oil, and oil cooler and fan requirements.

Provision is made for in-flight and on-ground condition monitoring systems. Features include access ports for intrascope inspection of each LP compressor stage, HP compressor, combustor, LP turbine and power turbine, and mountings for vibration pickups.

The following description relates to the initial design of the Gem engine in front-drive configuration; the turboshaft has also been designed to provide alternative rear-end drive.

TYPE: Free-turbine turboshaft, with two-spool gas generator.

AIR INTAKE: Annular forward facing.

SHAFT DRIVE: Compact single-stage double-helical reduction gear with rotating planet cage carried by ball bearing at front and roller bearing at rear. Reduction gear mounted within intake casing and driven by power turbine shaft. Gearbox comprises No. 1 module, and power turbine shaft No. 2 module.

Rolls-Royce Gem turboshaft engine for the Westland/Aérospatiale Lynx helicopter (2½ min rating, 900 shp)

LP COMPRESSOR: Four-stage axial unit with rotor carried by roller bearing at front and ball bearing at rear. Stator blades mounted directly in casing. Air intake casing and forward end of compressor casing supported by conical outer casing mounted off compressor intermediate casing. LP compressor and intake case comprise No. 3 module.

INTERMEDIATE CASING: Cast casing forming junction between LP and HP compressors. Carries accessory drive and wheelcase, and provides support for LP ball bearing and HP ball and roller bearings.

HP COMPRESSOR: Single-stage centrifugal unit with single-sided impeller having alternate inducer and radial vanes. Combined radial-and-axial diffuser feeds compressor delivery air to annular combustor. Overall pressure ratio 12·0 : 1.

COMBUSTION CHAMBER: Fully annular reverse-flow combustor with air-atomiser type fuel sprays supplied by external fuel manifold. High-energy ignition box mounted on power turbine/jet pipe case. Combustor outer casing extends forward to compressor conical structure.

HP TURBINE: Single-stage axial unit close-coupled to HP impeller. Rotor blades and air-cooled nozzle guide vanes are based on R-R Dart turboprop technology. Roller bearing downstream of turbine disc carries rear of HP spool. Bearing supported by structure inboard of hollow LP nozzle guide vanes. HP spool (compressor and turbine) with compressor intermediate casing and combustor comprise No. 4 module.

LP TURBINE: Single-stage axial unit, with tip-shrouded rotor blades, drives LP compressor. Roller bearing downstream of turbine disc carries rear of LP rotor. This bearing, together with power turbine upstream roller bearing, is supported by structure inboard of hollow power turbine stage-one nozzle guide vanes. LP turbine and main shaft comprise No. 6 module.

POWER TURBINE: Two-stage axial unit with tip-shrouded rotor blades. Thick-section discs have integral stub shafts which abut with centre tie-bolt forward to long, small-diameter drive shaft. Discs carried on upstream and downstream roller bearings, latter being supported by four cruciform struts in exhaust duct. Rear of power drive shaft drives output speed governor and overspeed fuel cut-off trip mechanism via spur and bevel gear train in exhaust cone. Power turbine and jet pipe form No. 7 module.

JET PIPE: Short-length duct with casing extending forward to combustor rear casing. Four cruciform struts integral with exhaust cone.

ACCESSORY DRIVES: Bevel gear on front of HP compressor shaft drives accessory shaft extending through compressor intermediate casing to spiral bevel gear drive to accessory wheelcase mounted atop intermediate casing. Drives provided for starter/generator, fuel pump, oil cooler fan and other accessories. Wheelcase forms No. 5 module.

FUEL SYSTEM: Plessey fuel system with fluidics circuit providing fully automatic control, and power matching for multi-engine installation. Also automatic restoration of power from "good" engine in event of single engine failure. Incorporates fuel filter.

LUBRICATION SYSTEM: Engine-mounted oil tank and cooler to provide self-contained system. Magnetic chip detectors fitted in each scavenge line. Oil filter incorporated in accessory wheelcase.

DIMENSIONS:

Height overall	23·5 in (596 mm)
Width overall	22·6 in (575 mm)
Length overall	43·1 in (1,095 mm)

WEIGHT, DRY:

Net	330 lb (150 kg)

PERFORMANCE RATINGS:

Max contingency (2½ minutes)	900 shp at 6,000 rpm
Max power (5 min, or 1 hr contingency)	830 shp at 6,000 rpm
Max continuous	750 shp

SPECIFIC FUEL CONSUMPTION:

Max contingency	0·52 lb (0·236 kg)/shp/hr
Max power	0·53 lb (0·240 kg)/shp/hr
Max continuous	0·54 lb (0·245 kg)/shp/hr

ROLLS-ROYCE GNOME (LEAVESDEN)

Gnome is the name given to the versions of the General Electric T58 turboshaft engine which Rolls-Royce has rights to manufacture in the UK. The first British-built engine ran for the first time on 5 June 1959.

The major difference between the Gnome and the T58 lies in the replacement of the Hamilton Standard fuel supply and control system by a Lucas fuel supply and metering system which is controlled by an electrical computer designed and built by Hawker Siddeley Dynamics. The materials, starter and ignition system, etc, are of British supply.

By January 1974 more than 1,500 Gnome engines had been delivered. To date, six versions have been announced:

H.1000. Initial version, rated at 1,050 shp. Power plant for military Whirlwind HAR.Mk 9, HAR.Mk 10 and HCC.Mk 12, civil S-55 Series 3 and Agusta-Bell 204B.

H.1200. Rated at 1,250 shp. Used in Agusta-Bell 204B, Boeing Vertol 107 and some Kawasaki KV-107/II-5s. Coupled version for Wessex Mks 2, 5, 50 and 60 series comprises two H.1200s

Rolls-Royce Gnome H.1400-3 free-turbine turboshaft engine, rated at 1,720 shp

driving through a coupling gearbox designed and manufactured by Rolls-Royce. Maximum potential output is 2,500 shp, but the Wessex transmission is limited to 1,550 shp at the rotor head. Should either engine be shut down the other will automatically increase power to the required output, up to the standard maximum H.1200 emergency rating of 1,350 shp. The ratio of the Wessex coupling gearbox is 7·476 : 1.

H.1400. Rated at 1,400 shp. Based on the H.1200, with modified compressor to increase airflow. Turbine diaphragm cooling redesigned to increase temperature capacity and life. Dimensions unchanged. Mounting pads identical to those of H.1200. This version is in production for the Westland Sea King and Commando.

H.1400-1. Rated at 1,535 shp. Uprated from H.1400, without change in size or weight, by increasing gas-generator speed and using improved gas-generator turbine-blade material allowing increased temperature. In production for Westland Sea King and Commando.

H.1400-3. Rated at 1,720 shp. Introduces new two-stage power turbine.

P.1400-3. Turboprop version of H.1400-3, with take-off rating of 1,700 shp. Offered for range of fixed-wing aircraft, with choice of mounting arrangements.

The following description refers specifically to the H.1400 turboshaft version:

Type: Axial-flow free-turbine turboshaft engine.

Air Intake: Annular forward-facing. Centre housing carrying front main bearing supported by four radial struts. Struts and inlet guide vanes anti-iced with hot compressor bleed air and oil drainage.

Compressor: Ten-stage axial. Controlled variable incidence for inlet guide vanes and first three rows of stator blades. Integral spool-type rotor assembly with rotor blades secured in dovetail root fittings. Rotor splined to shaft which is carried on roller bearings at front and ball bearing at rear. Main steel casing split along horizontal centreline, with stator blades brazed in carrier rings. Pressure ratio 8·4 (H.1200, 8·12). Air mass flow 13·7 lb (6·22 kg)/sec (H.1200, 12·55 lb; 5·70 kg/sec). A short-length casing interposed between compressor and combustor has radial vanes across compressor outlet to carry main centre bearing.

Combustion System: Straight-through annular chamber with outer casing split along horizontal centreline. Sixteen Simplex-type fuel injectors, eight on each of two sets of manifolds. One Lodge capacitor-discharge high-energy igniter plug.

Fuel System: Lucas hydromechanical units, comprising variable-stroke multi-plunger pump, flow control unit and throttle controlled by HSD electrical control computer and throttle actuator.

Fuel Grade: DERD.2453, 2454, 2486, 2494 and 2498 (NATO F34, F40, F35 and F44).

Gas-Producer Turbine: Two-stage, coupled to compressor shaft by conical shaft. Extended-root blading with fir-tree attachments. A short-length intermediate casing interposed between gas-producer and power turbines carries power-turbine nozzle guide vanes.

Power Turbine: Single-stage free turbine. Extended-root blading with fir-tree attachments. Rotor disc integral with output shaft and overhung from rear on roller bearing on downstream face of disc and ball bearing at rear of shaft. Complete assembly mounted inside exhaust ducting.

Exhaust System: Curved exhaust ducting arranged to suit individual applications.

Reduction Gear: Optional double-helical gear providing reduction from nominal 19,500 rpm power turbine speed to 6,600 rpm at output shaft. Provision for power take-off to left or right.

Accessory Drives: Quill shaft drive through lower intake strut. Fuel and lubrication systems mounted beneath compressor casing. Power take-off shaft up to 100 shp on primary reduction gear casing for separate accessories gearbox.

Lubrication: Fully scavenged gear pumps. Serck oil cooler.

Oil Specification: Military, DEng RD 2487 and 2493, Castrol 205 GTO and Esso Turbo Oil 2380. Commercial Aero Shell Turbine Oil 750, Esso Extra Turbo Oil 274, Castrol 98, Castrol 205 GTO and Esso Turbo Oil 2380.

Mounting: Three forward mounting faces on intake casing. Two rear mounting faces on upper portion of primary gear casing. When no reduction gear fitted, rear mounting face on engine centreline at power-turbine output shaft housing.

Starting: Rotax electric starter in nose bullet.

Dimensions:

Length:	
H.1000, H.1200, H.1400-1 (all ungeared)	54·8 in (1,392 mm)
H.1400-3	62·9 in (1,598 mm)
Coupled H.1200 (Wessex)	68·8 in (1,747 mm)
Max height:	
H.1000, H.1200, H.1400-1 (all ungeared)	21·6 in (549 mm)
H.1400-3	25·6 in (650 mm)
Coupled H.1200 (Wessex)	40·6 in (1,031 mm)
Max width:	
H.1000, H.1200 (ungeared)	18·2 in (462 mm)
H.1400-1 (ungeared)	22·7 in (577 mm)
H.1400-3	23·6 in (599 mm)
Coupled H.1200 (Wessex)	41·7 in (1,059 mm)

Weight, Dry:

H.1000 (ungeared)	296 lb (134 kg)
H.1200 (ungeared)	314 lb (142 kg)
H.1400-1 (ungeared)	334 lb (151 kg)
H.1400-3 (ungeared)	408 lb (185 kg)
Reduction gearbox	116 lb (52·6 kg)
Coupled H.1200 with coupling gearbox: for Wessex	930 lb (422 kg)

Performance Ratings (at power-turbine shaft):

Max contingency rating ($2\frac{1}{2}$ min; multi-engine aircraft only):	
H.1200	1,350 shp
H.1400-1	1,590 shp
H.1400-3	1,795 shp
T-O rating (5 min):	
P.1400-3	1,700 shp
Max one-hour rating (single engine):	
H.1000	1,050 shp
H.1200	1,250 shp
H.1400-1	1,535 shp
H.1400-3	1,720 shp
Max continuous rating:	
H.1000	900 shp
H.1200	1,050 shp
H.1400-1	1,250 shp
H.1400-3	1,400 shp
P.1400-3	1,540 shp

Specific Fuel Consumption:

At max contingency rating:	
H.1200	0·618 lb (0·280 kg)/shp/hr
H.1400-1	0·607 lb (0·275 kg)/shp/hr
H.1400-3	0·538 lb (0·244 kg)/shp/hr
At max one-hour rating:	
H.1000	0·650 lb (0·295 kg)/shp/hr
H.1200	0·624 lb (0·283 kg)/shp/hr
H.1400-1	0·608 lb (0·276 kg)/shp/hr
H.1400-3	0·542 lb (0·246 kg)/shp/hr
At max continuous rating:	
H.1000	0·670 lb (0·304 kg)/shp/hr
H.1200	0·642 lb (0·291 kg)/shp/hr
H.1400-1	0·627 lb (0·284 kg)/shp/hr
H.1400-3	0·572 lb (0·259 kg)/shp/hr

ROLLS-ROYCE NIMBUS (LEAVESDEN)

The Rolls-Royce Nimbus is a free-turbine turboshaft, which makes use of many design features of well-proven Rolls-Royce/Turboméca engines. It is basically an Artouste with two axial-flow compressor stages added forward of the centrifugal compressor and one axial turbine stage added to the gas-generator. The shaft-drive is taken via a free turbine and a two-stage gearbox.

The Nimbus was first run as a turbojet in July 1958, and as a turboshaft in the following month.

In flat-rated form, the Nimbus powers the Westland Scout and Wasp helicopters.

For the Wasp the engine has been "marinised" to combat the effects of salt water ingestion.

Type: Free-turbine turboshaft engine.

Air Intake: Annular aluminium alloy casting with three radial struts supporting front ball-thrust bearing.

Compressor: Two-stage axial-flow compressor, followed by single-sided centrifugal stage. Axial stages have integrally-machined blades and integral stub-shafts and are bolted together. Shaft supported at front in high-speed ball bearing and at rear in high-speed roller bearing. Cast stator blades in inner and outer retainer rings. Stainless steel centrifugal compressor. Pressure ratio 6·5 : 1. Air mass flow 11 lb/sec (5·0 kg/sec).

Combustion Chamber: Annular type.

Fuel System: Gear-type pump supplies fuel metered by a mechanically-governed control unit. Fuel is injected centrifugally into flame zone of combustion chamber through radial holes in hollow mainshaft. Starting is by torch igniter.

Compressor Turbine: Two-stage axial-flow type, with integrally-machined blades.

Power Turbine: Single-stage free turbine of Nimonic, with integrally-machined blades.

Reduction Gear: Helical spur type.

Jet Pipe: Bifurcated type.

Accessories: Engine-driven auxiliaries and accessories mounted on taper flanges around air intake. Driven by spur gear train from compressor.

Lubrication System: Gear type compound pressure and scavenge pump, full-flow filter and system of oil strainers.

Dimensions:

Installed overall length	73 in (1,854 mm)
Width	38·6 in (980 mm)
Height	34·2 in (868 mm)

Weight:

Dry, less gearbox, approx	390 lb (177 kg)

Performance Ratings:

Max (5 min up to ISA + 30°C)	710 shp
1-hour rating (to ISA + 27°C)	685 shp
Max continuous	600 shp

Specific Fuel Consumption:

At 5-min rating	0·84 lb (0·381 kg)/hp/hr
At 1-hour rating	0·85 lb (0·385 kg)/hp/hr
At max cont rating	0·89 lb (0·404 kg)/hp/hr

Display model of Rolls-Royce Gnome turboprop with propeller drive raised and three alternative jet pipe configurations

Rolls-Royce Nimbus free-turbine turboshaft, flat-rated at 710 shp

ROLLS-ROYCE MOTORS

ROLLS-ROYCE MOTORS LTD

HEAD OFFICE:
Crewe, Cheshire CW1 3PL
Telephone: 0270-55155

MAIN LOCATIONS:
Crewe (Car Division, Light Aircraft Engine Division, Investment Foundry Division)
Shrewsbury, Shropshire SY1 4DP (Diesel Division)
London NW (Mulliner Park Ward Division)

DIRECTORS:
I. J. Fraser (Chairman)
D. A. S. Plastow (Managing Director)
C. S. Aston
T. P. Barlow
H. P. N. Benson
L. W. Harris (Commercial Director)
T. Neville (Financial Director)
H. Wuttke

DIRECTOR OF PUBLICITY:
W. D. J. Roscoe

Rolls-Royce Motors, which began operations on 24 April 1971, comprises the businesses formerly carried on by the Motor Car and Oil Engine Divisions of Rolls-Royce Ltd. The company has four factories employing 8,500 people; annual turnover is about £48 million.

Although primarily concerned with the design, development and manufacture of products in the automotive field, Rolls-Royce Motors also has a major interest in aviation through the production of light-aircraft engines, and gas-turbine investment castings, machined parts and sheet-metal fabrications.

Under the terms of a licence agreement signed in 1960 with Teledyne Continental Motors of the United States, Rolls-Royce Motors markets Continental light-aircraft engines and spare parts throughout the world, with the exception of North and South America and certain Far Eastern countries. Five models from the Continental range are manufactured by the company's Light Aircraft Engine Division at Crewe, and these are described hereunder.

ROLLS-ROYCE CONTINENTAL C90

This is the 95 hp Continental C90 four-cylinder horizontally-opposed aircooled engine built under licence. Further details are given under the "Teledyne Continental" heading in the US section.

ROLLS-ROYCE CONTINENTAL O-200-A

This is the 100 hp Continental O-200-A four-cylinder horizontally-opposed aircooled engine, built under licence. Details are given under the "Teledyne Continental" heading in the US section.

ROLLS-ROYCE CONTINENTAL O-240-A

The O-240-A is the first light-aircraft engine to be developed by Rolls-Royce Motors in conjunction with Teledyne Continental. The engine had its origins in the United States but, soon after Continental had built and run a prototype, a changed commercial situation and the need to divert engineering resources to other work, especially the new Tiara range, caused Teledyne Continental to cease its active development. Rolls-Royce took over the programme in 1968 with a view to developing the engine specifically for the European market. By the time flight trials began, in July 1969, 300 testbed hours had been logged at Crewe. At the beginning of 1972, the bench test experience was in excess of 1,000 hours and more than 400 hours had been logged in development flight testing. Certification was completed in January 1970 and FAA Type Validation was awarded in February 1971. Production deliveries began in mid-1970, initially for the Reims Aviation Aerobat and Rollason Condor. The O-240 is being marketed in the United States by Teledyne Continental Motors.

TYPE: Four-cylinder, horizontally-opposed, aircooled, carburetted, unsupercharged.

CYLINDERS: Bore 4·438 in (112·5 mm). Stroke 3·875 in (98·4 mm). Capacity 240 cu in (3,933 cc). Compression ratio 8·5 : 1. Cast aluminium alloy finned heads are screwed and shrunk on to forged steel barrels.

PISTONS: Heat-treated aluminium alloy. Two compression rings and one oil control ring above the gudgeon pin, one scraper below. Fully floating, ground steel tube gudgeon pins with pressed-in aluminium end plugs.

CONNECTING RODS: Forged steel I-section. Big-end bearings are thin steel backed overlay plated copper lead. Little-end bearings are rolled bronze bushings.

CRANKSHAFT: Alloy steel forgings, nitrided all over for greater fatigue strength, having three journals running in thin steel backed overlay plated copper lead bearings.

CRANKCASE: Cast aluminium alloy, split along the vertical centreline.

VALVE GEAR: Two valves per cylinder. Steel inlet valves with hardened tips. Steel exhaust valves with hardened tips faced with Stellite "F". Valve seats shrunk into position. Camshaft, in centre of crankcase beneath the crankshaft, driven by gear from the crankshaft.

INDUCTION: Float-type carburettor with a manual mixture control.

FUEL GRADE: 100/130 octane minimum.

IGNITION: Two Slick type 4001 or two Bendix Scintilla S4LN-21 magnetos on rear of crankcase driven by gears from the camshaft. Two Champion REM 38EC, REM 38W or Lodge RSE 23/3R 18 mm spark plugs per cylinder.

LUBRICATION SYSTEM: Wet sump. Magnesium crankcase cover houses the engine-driven gear type oil pump. An oil pressure relief valve is mounted in the cover. Provision is made for an airframe-mounted oil cooler and optional full-flow filter.

PROPELLER DRIVE: Direct drive, clockwise when viewed from the rear. ARP 502 Type 1 flange.

ACCESSORIES: Ford 15V 60A alternator. Mechanical tachometer drive from the oil pump at rear of engine. Fuel pump is operated from an eccentric on the camshaft at front of engine. An AND 20,000 accessory drive pad is provided at the front of the crankcase.

STARTING: Prestolite EO 19508 12V starter.

MOUNTING: Four rear-mounted ring type mounting brackets to which vibration isolators can be attached.

DIMENSIONS:

Length	32·5 in (826 mm)
Width	31·4 in (798 mm)
Height	24·9 in (633 mm)

WEIGHT, DRY: including accessories 246 lb (112 kg)

PERFORMANCE RATINGS:
Take-off 130 hp at 2,800 rpm
Maximum recommended cruise 97·5 hp at 2,540 rpm

SPECIFIC FUEL CONSUMPTION:
Max rich 0·48 lb (0·22 kg)/hp/hr at 2,540 rpm
Max lean 0·42 lb (0·192 kg)/hp/hr at 2,540 rpm

OIL CONSUMPTION:
Maximum 0·015 lb (0·007 kg)/hp/hr

ROLLS-ROYCE CONTINENTAL O-300

This is the 145 hp Continental O-300 six-cylinder horizontally-opposed aircooled engine, built under licence.

Versions currently available include the O-300-C and D, of which full details can be found under the "Teledyne Continental" heading in the US section.

ROLLS-ROYCE CONTINENTAL IO-360

This is the 210 hp Continental IO-360 six-cylinder horizontally-opposed aircooled engine built under licence. The turbocharged TSIO-360 of 210 or 225 hp is also produced by Rolls-Royce Motors.

Rolls-Royce Continental piston engines: above, O-200, rated at 100 hp; above right, O-240, rated at 130 hp; right, IO-360, rated at 210 hp

THE UNITED STATES OF AMERICA

AEROJET

AEROJET-GENERAL CORPORATION (Subsidiary of The General Tire & Rubber Company)

Corporate Executive Offices:
9100 East Flair Drive, El Monte, California 91734
Telephone: (213) 572-6000
Chairman of the Board:
M. G. O'Neil
President:
J. H. Vollbrecht
Aerojet Solid Propulsion Company:
President: Richard F. Cottrell
Aerojet Liquid Rocket Company:
President: Jack L. Heckel

Aerojet-General Corporation has activities in five major areas of business: chemicals, electronics, engineering and construction, mechanical systems and metal products, research and development facility management. In the chemicals area, Aerojet Solid Propulsion Company develops, produces and tests solid-propellant rocket motors for aerospace and defence programmes. In the mechanical systems area, Aerojet Liquid Rocket Company is active in research, development, testing and production of liquid-propellant rocket engines and sounding rockets for defence and aerospace programmes, and waterjet propulsion systems for US Navy craft and Army amphibious vehicles. Aerojet also has 50 per cent ownership and is the manager of Bristol Aerojet which develops and produces rocket motor systems for the British Ministry of Defence (see UK section).

Aerojet is a wholly owned subsidiary of The General Tire & Rubber Company, Akron, Ohio, and had 11,000 employees in December 1973.

Applications of the Corporation's rocket technology include:

Aerojet Solid Propulsion Company (ASPC), Sacramento, California. Development and manufacture of the second-stage motors for the US Air Force Minuteman ICBM, the motors for Hawk, Tartar and Sparrow, and the first stage of the Scout launch vehicle. A programme to produce an advanced version of the USAF 2·75 in (70 mm) air-to-ground missile is making maximum use of existing hardware and has upgraded the rocket's performance considerably. Early in 1972 the company announced the successful test-firing of two motors each loaded with more than 100 lb of a new propellant. This high-energy solid propellant is considered "a prime contender for the next generation of missile motors".

Aerojet Liquid Rocket Company (ALRC), Sacramento, California. Development and manufacture of all liquid-fuel stages for the US Air Force Titan family of vehicles, the Apollo SPS engine for the Skylab programme, and Aerobee and Astrobee sounding rockets.

AEROJET APOLLO SPS

Under contract to Rockwell International, the Aerojet Liquid Rocket Company produced the engine used to propel the Apollo spacecraft's Service Module. Known as the Service Propulsion System (SPS), the engine was designed to steer the module to the Moon, place it in lunar orbit, eject it from that orbit and bring it back to Earth. In the Skylab programme it is used to de-orbit the spacecraft and return it to Earth.

The SPS engine, which utilises storable liquid propellants, produces 20,000 lb (9,070 kg) st and is 13 ft 4 in (4 m) high. It is designed to operate repeatedly for a total of 12·5 minutes, with a maximum single burn of 10·5 minutes, and is the largest and most powerful ablatively-cooled rocket engine yet developed in the USA.

The SPS rocket engine has fired as programmed on each mission. Firings ranged from a minimum of 0·5 sec duration to the longest duration of 7 min 25 sec during flight.

AEROJET TITAN III ENGINES

The production of Titan III first, second and Transtage engines for use as booster propulsion on the Titan family of vehicles has been under way continuously since 1962 by Aerojet Liquid Rocket Company and its predecessor Aerojet organisations. These engines, utilising storable propellants, develop 520,000 lb (235,872 kg), 100,000 lb (45,360 kg) and 16,000 lb (7,257 kg) thrust respectively. Their flight reliability is in the 90-99 per cent class. The nominal weights of these engines are 4,360, 1,245, and 432 lb (1,977, 564 and 196 kg) respectively. These weights are below those of other comparable liquid rocket engines.

AEROJET TRANSTAGE

Upper-stage engines for the Transtage of the Titan IIIC standard space launch vehicle were developed for the USAF by the Aerojet Liquid Rocket Company. The system has a thrust in the 16,000 lb (7,250 kg) range, uses hypergolic (self-igniting) propellants and has an extremely long burning time, with repeated stop and re-start capability.

The main role of Transtage is to switch payloads to new orbits.

AEROJET HAWK MOTOR

The single-chamber solid-propellant rocket motor of the Hawk surface-to-air missile was the first dual-thrust dual-grain motor to be mass-produced.

Within its single propellant mass, the motor has an inner core of propellant constituting a short-duration booster grain which launches and accelerates the missile to supersonic speed. When this inner core is consumed, a slower-burning outer core, forming the sustainer portion of the propellant, takes over and keeps the missile at the required velocity.

Aerojet Solid Propulsion Company has signed agreements with several foreign firms for the production of this motor. A new improved Hawk propulsion system, using an upgraded polyurethane propellant-to-case bond, has passed its qualification testing at the US Army Test and Evaluation Command's White Sands Missile Range, New Mexico. More than 1,000 consecutive improved Hawk motors were test-fired without a failure, and the demonstrated long-life characteristics of the polyurethane propellant have extended the shelf-life of the motor to ten years. The improved Hawk motor is now in production at ASPC's Sacramento, California, plant.

AEROJET MINUTEMAN MOTORS

Aerojet Solid Propulsion Company produces the second stage of LGM-30G Minuteman III. This motor has polybutadiene/ammonium perchlorate propellant packaged in a titanium case, and the single submerged nozzle has liquid-injection thrust-vector control. Loaded weight is 15,600 lb (7,076 kg) and average thrust 60,600 lb (27,488 kg). A total of 2,950 motors had been delivered by the end of 1973.

AEROJET SPACE VEHICLE MOTORS (SVM)

The Aerojet family of space vehicle motors provides a wide range of impulse for synchronous orbit insertion, retrograde or upper-stage propulsion applications in communications, meteorological and research satellites. Twelve Intelsat II, III and IV communications satellites have been placed in synchronous orbit by SVM-1, SVM-2 and SVM-4A motors. The SVM-5 motor will be used for orbit injection of the NASA Synchronous Meteorological Satellite. The motors differ mainly in size (diameter) and use glass-filament-wound cases, advanced propellant and modern nozzle materials. Mechanical-electrical safe-and-arming devices are included in the basic configuration of SVM-2, SVM-4A and SVM-5 motors. Impulse flexibility for new applications can be obtained by minor variations in case length and/or propellant loading.

SVM-1. SVM-1 was developed and qualified to place the Intelsat II communications satellite in synchronous orbit and was first flown in 1966. The motor has a case diameter of 18·0 in (457 mm), an overall length of 32·9 in (836 mm) and contains 163·0 lb (73·9 kg) of propellant. Total motor weight is 192·1 lb (87·3 kg).

SVM-2. This motor is 35 in (889 mm) long overall, with a 22·25 in (565 mm) diameter case, and weighs a total of 350·2 lb (159·2 kg). Maximum propellant weight in the baseline (basic) configuration is 315·0 lb (143·2 kg), and motors with up to 10 per cent propellant off-load have been static tested under space conditions. The SVM-2 was originally developed as the apogee motor for synchronous orbit injection of the Intelsat III communications satellite.

SVM-4A. By 1973, four Intelsat IV satellites had been placed on station by the SVM-4A motor. This 36·7 in (932 mm) diameter motor is 60·3 in (1,532 mm) long overall, with 1,416 lb (643·6 kg) of propellant; it weighs a total of 1,557 lb (707·7 kg). The original configuration (SVM-4) was designed and tested with 1,170 lb (538·1 kg) of propellant. To provide additional performance for increased spacecraft requirements, the glass

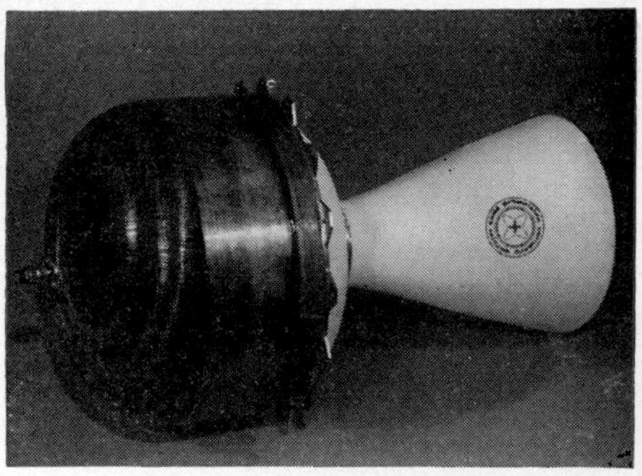

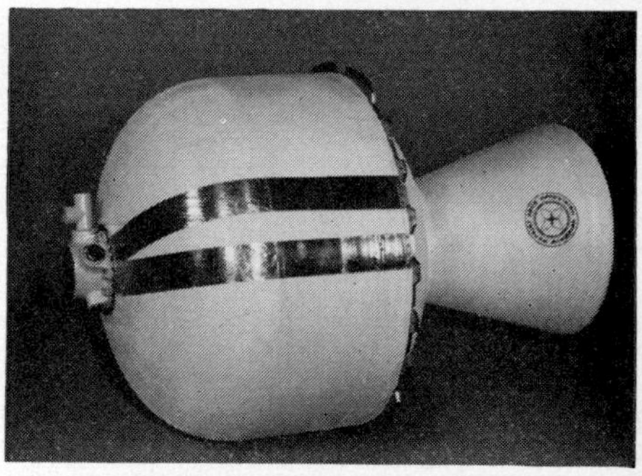

ASPC space-vehicle motors: from the top, SVM-1, SVM-2, SVM-4A and SVM-5

Aerojet third-stage motors for Minuteman III missiles

case was lengthened by 3·0 in (76 mm) to accommodate the higher propellant weight of the present design. This technique of stretching the case to provide additional performance is applicable to all motors in the SVM family.

SVM-5. The SVM-5 is a 30·0 in (762 mm) diameter motor developed and qualified for NASA's Synchronous Meteorological Satellite. This motor has a propellant weight of 633·2 lb (287·8 kg) and a total weight of 702·2 lb (319·2 kg). It is 35·5 in (902 mm) long overall.

AEROJET ALGOL II B

The Algol II B is used for the first stage of the Scout launch vehicle. This motor produces an average thrust of 85,742 lb (38,892 kg) for 47·3 seconds. Earlier versions of the motor, known as the Algol I, were clustered in the Little Joe II booster for development flight testing of the Apollo spacecraft.

Approximately 100 Algol motors have been successfully used in flight tests. Nozzles with an adjustable cant angle from 0° to 14° have been used on the Algol I. This experience can be used to adapt the motor to strap-on booster applications.

AEROJET ALCOR 1B

The Alcor 1B is a high-performance Aerojet Solid Propulsion Company motor featuring a high-specific-impulse polybutadiene propellant and extremely lightweight inert components. The nozzle is a unique combination of laminated reinforced-plastics materials, and the chamber is a very thin, welded, high-strength titanium 6Al-4V alloy structure. This highly efficient chamber has demonstrated excellent resistance to external flight loads in structural tests.

The Alcor 1B is used as third stage on the Athena test vehicle and is the second-stage propulsion system on the Astrobee 1500 launch vehicle. It can be applied as an upper-stage sounding rocket motor, a small component test vehicle, a synchronous orbit injection motor, or an upper-stage booster for low and medium orbits. The motor can be spin-stabilised and is fabricated to a very small thrust-misalignment tolerance (0·0004 radians angular and 0·020 in; 0·51 mm linear). This motor has been used on more than 100 flights without a failure.

AEROJET 150

This is the sustainer engine used in the Aerobee 150, 150A and 170 research rockets. It has a single fixed chamber fed with aniline-furfuryl alcohol and IRFNA from vehicle tanks pressurised by gas bottles.

AEROJET 2.5KS-18000

This solid-propellant rocket motor is used as a booster for the Aerobee Model 100 and Model 150 research sounding rockets. Its designation indicates a thrust of 18,000 lb (8,165 kg).

AEROJET ASTROBEE D

The Astrobee D is a multi-purpose sounding-rocket motor for operation with small payloads in the D-region of the ionosphere, and with meteorological sensing payloads at altitudes up to 102 miles (164 km).

Astrobee D was engineered to facilitate low-cost production by design simplicity. A unique one-piece moulded nozzle that features integral fin attachments was developed for this motor. The chamber insulation material permits low-cost automatic application techniques. The motor has hydroxyl-terminated polybutadiene (HTPB) propellant that is low in cost yet delivers high specific impulse at very low burning rates. The low burning rate extends the duration, thereby reducing drag, structural loads and aerodynamic heating and thus providing improved performance. Aerojet has designed dual-thrust characteristics into the motor using the HTPB propellant, allowing high off-the-launcher acceleration without the necessity for adding an auxiliary boost motor.

AEROJET ASTROBEE F

The Astrobee F is a dual-thrust sounding-rocket motor incorporating many of the design features of the successful Astrobee D. The boost thrust averages 38,000 lb (17,235 kg) for 3 seconds followed by a sustain thrust of 8,300 lb (3,765 kg) for 53 seconds. The 15 in (381 mm) diameter motor is designed to be compatible with the Aerobee payload systems and vehicle facilities. The initial Astrobee F test design is capable of delivering 200 lb (90·7 kg) payloads up to altitudes of 235 miles (378 km). Design refinements which will increase performance approximately 10 per cent are anticipated after production flight data are available.

This motor successfully completed its flight tests in 1972, and is in production under NASA contract.

AEROJET SOLID PROPULSION COMPANY MOTORS

Name	Designation	Fuel	Oxidiser	Average thrust (lb)	Max length (in)	Max dia (in)	Total weight (lb)	Remarks/Primary Application
Strategic Motors								
Minuteman 2nd stage	SR19-AJ-1	Polybutadiene	NH_4ClO_4	60,600	162	52	15,600	Minuteman LGM-30F second stage, titanium case, single submerged nozzle, liquid injection TVC.
Minuteman 3rd stage	SR73-AJ-1	Polybutadiene	NH_4ClO_4	34,000	92	52	8,000	Minuteman LGM-30G third stage, glass case.
Polaris 1st stage	A2P	Polyurethane	NH_4ClO_4	—	178	54	22,000	Polaris A2, steel case, four nozzles, Jetevators.
Polaris 1st stage	A3P	Polyurethane	NH_4ClO_4	—	182	54	24,000	Polaris A3, glass case, four rotatable nozzles; nitroplasticiser additive.
Tactical Motors								
Phoenix	Mk 60 Mod 0	Polyurethane	NH_4ClO_4	—	70	15	439	Propulsion for Navy's fleet-defence air-to-air missile.
Sparrow III, AIM-7E	Mk 52 Mod 2	Polybutadiene	NH_4ClO_4	—	52	8	151	Propulsion for Navy's Sparrow air-to-air missile.
Sparrow III, AIM-7F	Mk 65 Mod 0	Polybutadiene	NH_4ClO_4	—	61	8	206	Propulsion for Navy's Advanced Sparrow air-to-air missile.
Shrike	Mk 53 Mod 2	Polybutadiene	NH_4ClO_4	—	52	8	157	Propulsion for Navy's AGM-45 anti-radiation air-to-surface missile.
Shrike, Improved	Mk 53 Mod 3	Polyurethane	NH_4ClO_4	—	51	8	172	Propulsion for anti-radiation air-to-surface missile.
Tartar	Mk 1 Mod 0	Polyurethane	NH_4ClO_4	—	103	13·5	760	Dual-thrust propulsion for Navy ship-to-air missile.
Tartar, Improved	Mk 27 Mod 2, 3	Polyurethane	NH_4ClO_4	—	103	13·5	780	Dual-thrust propulsion for Navy ship-to-air missile.
Standard Missile	Mk 56 Mod 0	Polybutadiene Polyurethane	NH_4ClO_4	—	103	13·5	907	Dual-thrust propulsion for Navy ship-to-air Missile Type 1, MR.
Standard ARM	Mk 27 Mod 4	Polybutadiene Polyurethane	NH_4ClO_4	—	103	13·5	790	Dual-thrust propulsion for air-launched anti-radiation version.
Harpoon	—	Polyurethane	NH_4ClO_4	—	—	—	—	Booster for Navy Harpoon anti-ship missile.
2·75 in FFAR, Improved	SR105-AJ-1	Polyurethane	NH_4ClO_4	—	33	2·75	13	Air-launched forward firing.
Hawk	XM22E8	Polyurethane	NH_4ClO_4	—	109	14	856	Dual-thrust motor for Army's surface-to-air Hawk missile.
Hawk, Improved	XM112	—	—	—	109	14	870	Dual-thrust motor for Army's surface-to-air Hawk missile.
Launch Vehicle Boosters and Space Motors								
260 in	SL-1 & 2	Polybutadiene	NH_4ClO_4	2,880,000	970	261	1,857,500	Short-length motors successfully fired under NASA contract.
260 in	SL-3	Polybutadiene	NH_4ClO_4	5,115,000	903	261	1,843,442	Motor successfully fired under NASA contract.
Algol I D, Mod 1 & 2		Polyurethane	NH_4ClO_4	96,000	359	40	22,000	First-stage Scout booster and clustered booster for orbital payloads.
Algol II B		Polyurethane	NH_4ClO_4	85,742	358	40	24,000	First-stage booster for Scout.
Aerojet Junior		Polyurethane	NH_4ClO_4	43,000	243	31	8,836	First stage for Astrobee 250 and 1500 space vehicles.
Alcor 1B		Polybutadiene	NH_4ClO_4	10,000	76	18	1,004	Third stage of Athena test vehicle and 2nd stage for Astrobee 1500 launch vehicle.
Variable Aerobee Motor	VAM-20	Polyurethane	NH_4ClO_4	20,000	75	12	489	Zero-stage booster for the Aerobee sounding-rocket system.
Astrobee D		Polybutadiene	NH_4ClO_4	3,600/ 2,000	110	6	181	Dual-thrust meteorological rocket (10 lb to 100 miles altitude).
Astrobee F		Polybutadiene	NH_4ClO_4	38,000/ 8,300	280	15	2,768	Dual-thrust sounding rocket (200 lb to 235 miles altitude).
SVM-1	SVM-1	Polybutadiene	NH_4ClO_4	—	33	20	192	Apogee-boost motor for Intelsat II synchronous telecommunications satellite.
SVM-2	SVM-2	Polybutadiene	NH_4ClO_4	—	35	23	350	Apogee-boost motor for Intelsat III synchronous telecommunications satellite.
SVM-4A	SVM-4A	Polybutadiene	NH_4ClO_4	—	60	37	1,557	Apogee-boost motor for Intelsat IV synchronous telecommunications satellite.
SVM-5	SVM-5	Polybutadiene	NH_4ClO_4	4,900	36	30	702	Apogee-boost motor for NASA Synchronous Meteorological Satellite.
Gas Generators and JATOs								
Sprint, Launch Eject		Polybutadiene	NH_4ClO_4	n.a.	22	27	865	Used to launch the Sprint missile from its silo.
Turbine Start Cartridge		Butyl Rubber	NH_4NO_3	n.a.	16	7	24	For Titan II first stage.
Turbine Start Cartridge		Butyl Rubber	NH_4NO_3	n.a.	19	4	12	For Titan II second stage.
Gas Gen Mk 46		Butyl Rubber	NH_4NO_3	n.a.	43	12	—	Prime power source for the Navy's Mk 46 Mod 0 torpedo.
JATO, Mk 6 Mod 1	15KS1000	Aeroplex	NH_4ClO_4	1,060	33	10	141	Aircraft JATO unit, FAA certificated.
JATO, Junior	12NS 350	Aeroplex	NH_4NO_3	350	28	6	46	Aircraft JATO unit.
Controllable Motors								
SCCSRM		Polyurethane	NH_4ClO_4	—	15	20	915	Single-chamber controllable solid-rocket motor.
Air Launched (VTM)		Polybutadiene	NH_4ClO_4	—	54	17	407	Variable-thrust motor; has both thrust-magnitude and vector control.
Air-to-Air Controllable (ATAC)		Polybutadiene	NH_4ClO_4	—	67	8	210	Throttling over wide temperature range.
Stop-Start Motor (SSM)		Polyurethane	NH_4ClO_4	—	87	20	874	Stop/start operation on command.

AEROSPORT

AEROSPORT INC

ADDRESS:
Holly Springs Airport, Holly Springs, NC 27540
Telephone: (919) 552-6375

GENERAL MANAGER:
Harris L. Woods

Conscious of the limitations of cheap converted car engines for the homebuilt aircraft market, Aerosport searched for a superior engine that could offer an optimum combination of performance, weight, cost and reliability. Rockwell Manufacturing Company recommended the engine described below, derived from the German JLO, already used in fixed- and rotary-wing aircraft.

AEROSPORT-ROCKWELL LB600

Based on the JLO flat-twin, this unit has been developed by Aerosport and Rockwell to reduce the weight, reduce crankshaft speed and increase torque. Flight testing in the twin-engined Rail light aircraft (see US "Aircraft" section) has been most encouraging. The basic version, with single carburettor and propeller hub, is priced at $465; later versions will be available with two carburettors (45 hp at 5,500 rpm), electric starter, exhaust muffler and other options. The basic engine has a built-in alternator.

TYPE: Two-cylinder aircooled two-stroke.

CYLINDERS: Aluminium with cast-iron sleeve. Bore 2·953 in (75 mm). Stroke 2·368 in (60 mm). Displacement 36·25 cu in (594 cc).

CRANKSHAFT: Forged steel, running in two heavy-duty ball bearings. Driven by two connecting rods with needle bearings at each end.

FUEL SYSTEM: Mixture of 20 parts good premium gasoline to 1 part of two-cycle engine oil. Type WD or HD carburettor (dual optional).

IGNITION: Bosch auto-advance SCP 1V flywheel ignition, with Bosch type PA coil. Two 18 mm plugs (Bosch M-225-T-1 or M-240-T-1 or Champion K-9 or K-8).

STARTING: Rope pulley, standard rewind or electric.

DIMENSIONS:

Overall width (across plugs)	24·60 in (625 mm)
Length, from tip of hub	13·25 in (336 mm)
Height (of mounting plate)	12·50 in (318 mm)

WEIGHT, DRY: 56 lb (25·4 kg)

MAX RATING:

With open exhaust pipe	38 hp at 5,000 rpm
With dual carburettors	45 hp at 5,500 rpm

SPECIFIC FUEL CONSUMPTION:
At 4,500 rpm and full load 0·836 lb (0·379 kg)/hp/hr

ALLISON

DETROIT DIESEL ALLISON DIVISION, GENERAL MOTORS CORPORATION

HEAD OFFICE:
Detroit, Michigan
Telephone: (313) 531-7100

OTHER WORKS:
Cleveland, Ohio

INDIANAPOLIS OPERATIONS:
PO Box 894, Indianapolis, Indiana 46206
Telephone: (317) 244-1511

GENERAL MANAGER:
James E. Knott

DIVISIONAL COMPTROLLER:
Victor H. Laurie

GENERAL SALES MANAGER:
Emmett B. Lewis

MANAGER, INDIANAPOLIS OPERATIONS:
Edward B. Colby

The former Allison division of General Motors was in 1970 merged with the Detroit Diesel Division, but the aircraft gas turbine operations at Indianapolis remain generally unchanged by the merger. The aircraft engines still continue to be marketed under the single name "Allisson". Detroit Diesel Allison's Gas Turbine Operations continue to produce T56 turboprop engines for military and commercial versions of the Lockheed C-130 Hercules transport, and for the Lockheed P-3 Orion anti-submarine aircraft, Grumman E-2 Hawkeye airborne early-warning aircraft and Grumman C-2A Greyhound transport. A commercial counterpart of the T56, the Model 501-D13, powers the Lockheed Electra and Convair 580 airliners (see 1970-71 *Jane's*). A turboshaft version, the T701, has been selected to power the Boeing XCH-62A helicopter.

The Allison T63 small gas-turbine powers the Hughes OH-6A and Bell OH-58A light observation helicopters. Its commercial counterpart, the Model 250, powers the Hughes Model 500, the Bell TH-57 SeaRanger, the various models of the Bell Ranger family and the MBB BO 105.

A turboprop version of the Model 250 was certificated in March 1969 for light fixed-wing aircraft applications. In 1966 Allison established a worldwide distributor organisation to provide local service and support for all Model 250-powered equipment. Main franchise-holder for Europe is Hants & Sussex Aviation.

It was announced in January 1967 that Allison and Rolls-Royce of England would develop and produce jointly a version of the Rolls-Royce Spey turbofan engine, under the designation TF41, to power advanced versions of the LTV A-7 Corsair II aircraft. The TF41 remains in production for the USAF's A-7D close-support attack aircraft and the US Navy's A-7E carrier-based attack bomber.

The two companies have also jointly developed the XJ99, a very advanced lift-jet with a wide range of applications in V/STOL and other types of aircraft. Further details of the Rolls-Royce/Allison programmes can be found in the International section.

ALLISON MODEL 250

US military designation: T63

The Model 250 is a small turboshaft engine in which power is derived from a free power turbine and is delivered through an offset gearbox which includes all accessory drive pads.

A development contract for the T63 military version was received by Allison in June 1958 and the engine was first run in the Spring of 1959.

The original T63-A-5, rated at 250 shp, completed a 50-hour preliminary flight rating test in March 1962, prior to the start of its flight test programme in a Bell UH-13R helicopter. The 150-hour military model qualification test was completed in September 1962, with simultaneous completion of tests required for FAA Type Approval. In December 1962, the T63-A-5 was awarded an Approved Type Certificate by the FAA and was accepted by the US Army in a ceremony at Allison.

The T63-A-5A engine, rated at 317 shp, completed its qualification-certification tests in July 1965 and was awarded an FAA Type Certificate in September 1965. This engine powers the Hughes OH-6A and Bell OH-58A light observation helicopters. Delivery of production A-5A engines began in December 1965.

T63-A-700. Uprated version, with T-O power of 317 shp. Fitted to Bell OH-58A Kiowa. Corresponds to commercial Model 250-C18 and B15.

T63-A-701. Further uprated version, rated at 400 shp. Corresponds to commercial C20 and B17.

T63-A-702. Hot-end improvements, increasing T-O rating to 420 shp. Corresponds to commercial C20B and B17B. Specified for ASH (Advanced Scout Helicopter) helicopters, for US Army evaluation, by Hughes and Bell.

250-C18. Derived directly from the military T63-A-5A the C18 was the initial commercial version of the Model 250. Rated for take-off at 317 shp, it powers all the initial commercial versions of the Bell JetRanger, Hughes 500 and Fairchild FH-1100, as well as the Agusta-Bell 206A, US Navy Bell TH-57A SeaRanger, and the Kawasaki (Hughes) 369HS. Deliveries began in December 1965. Production by Allison is complete, but the C18 is the subject of licence agreements with MTU (West Germany) and Kawasaki (Japan).

250-B15. A direct conversion of the C18, the B15 was the original 317 shp turboprop version of the Model 250. The engine is essentially a C18 mounted in the inverted position, with compressor below the new propeller reduction gearbox and the twin jet pipes discharging obliquely downwards. The B15 was certificated in March 1969. Production engines, designated B15G, are fitted to the Italian SIAI-Marchetti SM.1019.

250-C20. This is the most important current production version of the Model 250. Incorporating numerous improvements to increase airflow, component efficiency and turbine temperature, the C20 is rated at 400 shp. Dry weight is increased by only 19 lb (8·6 kg) compared with the C18. Fully certificated for production delivery in February 1974, the C20 is fitted to the Bell 206B JetRanger II, MBB BO 105A, Agusta-Bell 206B and 206B-1, Agusta A 109C Hirundo, Dornier Do 34 Kiebitz (with MTU power transmission), Poschel P-400 Meridian, and Soloy conversion of the UH-12E. An uprated version, the 420 shp C20B, powers the Bell 206L Long Ranger and is likely to power the Boeing Vertol (MBB) 105C.

250-B17. Announced in 1972, the B17 is an uprated version of the B15 turboprop, corresponding to the C20 turboshaft. Rated at 400 shp (417 ehp), it is fitted to the American Jet Industries Turbostar 402 (Cessna 402 conversion) and

The 420 shp Allison Model 250-C20B turboshaft engine

The 317 shp Allison Model 250-B15G turboprop engine

The 4,910 ehp Allison T56-A-15 turboprop engine which powers late versions of the Lockheed C-130 Hercules transport

Turbostar Baron, GAF Nomad N22 and Nomad N24. In April 1974 Allison announced the B17B, operating at 17°C higher turbine gas temperature and with hot-end improvements similar to those of the C20B. Rated at 420 shp (440 ehp), the B17B was to be available from September 1974. It has been selected for future Turbostar 402 conversions, for the Turbostar 414 and for advanced versions of the GAF Nomad.

250-C25. Growth version, rated in the 500 shp class, for helicopter applications. Specified for new helicopters by Bell, Agusta and other manufacturers.

250-C28. Projected growth version, rated in the 600 shp class.

The following description applies to the 317 shp engines. The 400 shp engine differences are detailed in brackets.

Type: Light turboshaft or turboprop engine.

Compressor: Axial/centrifugal compressor with six axial stages and one centrifugal. Axial stages of 17-4 PH cast as single units comprising integral wheels and blades. Compressed air delivered through a vaned diffuser to a collector scroll and thence via two external tubes, one on each side of the engine, to the combustion chamber. Pressure ratio 6·2 : 1 (400 shp, 7·0 : 1; 420 shp, 7·2 : 1). Air mass flow 3·0 lb (1·36 kg)/sec (400 shp, 3·4 lb; 1·5 kg; 420 shp 3·6 lb; 1·63 kg).

Combustion Chamber: Single can-type chamber at aft end of engine. Single duplex fuel nozzle in rear face of chamber. One igniter.

Turbines: Two-stage gas-producer turbine and two-stage "free" power turbine. Integrally-cast blades and wheels. Combustion gases after passing through turbines enter exhaust hood in middle of engine where they are collected and exhausted upward. Gas-producer turbine outlet temperature 750°C (400 shp, 793°C). Turbine/combustor assembly, including exhaust collector, bolted to rear face of gearcase.

Gearcase: A magnesium casting which forms primary structure of engine and contains all power and accessory gear trains, torque sensor, oil pumps and engine main bearings Compressor and combustor/turbine assemblies bolted to front and rear faces respectively. One spur gear train engages pinion driven by power turbine shaft and transmits output power to horizontal shaft on centreline of engine below (in turboprops, and optionally on turboshaft models, above) compressor turbine output shaft accessible on both front and rear faces of gearcase. Rated shp available at either front or rear spline, or any combination totalling rated power. Second spur gear train engages on gas generator turbine shaft and provides drive for engine accessory pads. Turboshaft version has output speed of 6,000 rpm. Turboprop has additional reduction gear to propeller shaft at top front of engine.

Control System: Pneumatic-mechanical system (400 shp, hydromechanical system) consisting essentially of fuel pump and filter assembly, gas producer fuel control and power turbine governor.

Fuel: Primary fuels are ASTM-A or A-1 (Model 250-C20, ASTM D-1655) and MIL-T-5624, JP-4 or JP-5.

Lubrication: Dry sump.

Oil Specification: MIL-L-7808 and MIL-L-23699.

Dimensions:
Model 250-B17:
Length 44·6 in (1,132 mm)
Width 19·0 in (483 mm)
Height 22·5 in (572 mm)
Model 250-C20:
Length 40·678 in (1,033 mm)
Width 19·006 in (483 mm)
Height 23·196 in (589 mm)

Weight, Dry:
T63-A-5A 139 lb (63 kg)
Model 250-B17 182 lb (82·5 kg)
Model 250-B17B 195 lb (88·5 kg)
Model 250-C20 158 lb (71·5 kg)

Performance Ratings (S/L, ISA):
T63-A-5A:
T-O 317 shp at 35,000 rpm
Military 317 shp
Normal 270 shp
Cruise (90% normal) 243 shp
Cruise (75% normal) 203 shp
Model 250-B17B:
T-O 420 shp
Max cruise 385 shp
Model 250-C20:
T-O (5 min) 400 shp
Max continuous 346 shp
Cruise A (90% max continuous) 311 shp
Cruise B (75% max continuous) 260 shp

Specific Fuel Consumption:
T63-A-5A:
At T-O rating, ISA 0·697 lb (0·32 kg)/shp/hr
At T-O rating, 37·8°C 0·740 lb (0·34 kg)/shp/hr
At normal rating, ISA 0·760 lb (0·35 kg)/shp/hr
At cruise rating (90% normal) 0·725 lb (0·33 kg)/shp/hr
At cruise rating (75% normal) 0·762 lb (0·35 kg)/shp/hr
Model 250-C20:
At T-O rating 0·630 lb (0·286 kg)/shp/hr
At max continuous 0·645 lb (0·293 kg)/shp/hr
At cruise A 0·661 lb (0·300 kg)/shp/hr
At cruise B 0·698 lb (0·317 kg)/shp/hr

ALLISON T56

Current versions of the T56 are as follows:

T56-A-14. Rated at 4,910 ehp. Generally similar to T56-A-15, but seven-point suspension like T56-A-10W and detail changes. Powers the P-3B and C Orion.

T56-A-15. Rated at 4,910 ehp. Introduced aircooled turbine blades. Powers C-130H (all versions), C-130K, HC-130N, HC-130P and some AC-130s; specified for growth version of Aeritalia G222.

T56-A-422. Rated at 4,910 ehp. Powers Grumman E-2C Hawkeye.

T56-A-423. Rated at 4,910 ehp. Powers US Navy versions of the C-130.

Latest orders for the T56 extended production into 1975. Production is likely to continue into the early 1980s.

The following details apply to the T56-A-15:

Type: Axial-flow turboprop engine.

Propeller Drive: Combination spur/planetary gear type, primary step-down by spur, secondary by planetary. Overall gear ratio 13·54 : 1. Power section rpm 13,820. Cast magnesium reduction-gear housing. Gearbox assembly supported from power section by main drive shaft casing 28 in (711 mm) long and two inclined struts. Weight of gearbox assembly approximately 550 lb (249 kg) with pads on rear face for accessory mounting.

Air Intake: Circular duct on engine face. Thermal de-icing.

Compressor: Fourteen-stage axial-flow. Series of fourteen discs with rotor blades dovetailed in peripheries and locked by adjacent discs. Rotor assembly tie-bolted to shaft which runs on one ball and one roller type bearing. Fifteen rows of stator blades, welded in rings. Disc, rotor and stator blades and four-piece cast casing of stainless steel. Compressor inlet area 155·65 sq in (1,004 cm²). Pressure ratio 9·5 : 1. Air mass flow 32·4 lb (14·70 kg)/sec.

Combustion Chamber: Six stainless steel cannular-type perforated combustion liners within one-piece stainless steel outer casing. Fuel nozzles in forward end of each combustor liner. Primary ignition by two igniters in diametrically-opposite combustors.

Fuel System: High-pressure type. Bendix control system. Water/alcohol augmentation system available.

Fuel Grade: MIL-J-5624, JP-4 or JP-5.

Nozzle Guide Vanes: Hollow aircooled blades of special high-temperature alloy.

Turbine: Four-stage. Rotor assembly consists of four stainless steel discs, with first stage having hollow aircooled blades of special high-temperature alloy, secured in peripheries of discs by fir-tree roots. Discs splined to rotor shaft which runs on front and rear roller bearings. Steel outer turbine casing. Gas temperature before turbine 1,076°C.

Jet Pipe: Fixed. Stainless steel.

Accessory Drives: Accessory pads on rear face of reduction-gear housing at front end of engine.

Lubrication System: Low-pressure. Dry sump. Pesco dual-element oil pump. Normal oil supply pressure 55 lb/sq in (3·87 kg/cm²).

Oil Specification: MIL-L-7808.

Mounting: Three-point suspension.

Starting: Air turbine, gearbox-mounted.

Dimensions:
Length (all current versions) 146 in (3,708 mm)
Width:
All versions 27 in (686 mm)
Height:
A-15, A-422, A-423 39 in (991 mm)
A-14 44 in (1,118 mm)

Weight, Dry:
A-14 1,885 lb (855 kg)
A-15 1,825 lb (828 kg)
A-422 1,984 lb (859 kg)
A-423 1,844 lb (836 kg)

Performance Ratings (S/L, ISA, static):
Max rating:
A-14, A-15, A-422, A-423 4,910 ehp (4,591 shp) at 13,820 rpm
Normal rating:
A-14, A-15, A-422, A-423 4,365 ehp (4,061 shp) at 13,820 rpm

Specific Fuel Consumption:
At max rating:
A-14, A-15 0·501 lb (0·227 kg)/ehp/hr
At normal rating:
A-14, A-15, A-422, A-423 0·517 lb (0·234 kg)/ehp/hr

Oil Consumption:
A-14, A-15 0·35 US gallons (1·3 litres)/hr

ALLISON 501-M62

US military designation: T701-AD-700

Developed from the T56, the T701 is a free-turbine turboshaft engine for helicopters and other applications. Though similar in size to the gas generator of the T56, it has a compressor, combustion chamber and turbine section of more advanced design, handling a substantially greater airflow.

In 1972 the T701 was selected to power the Boeing XCH-62A, the US Army heavy lift helicopter (HLH), and the engine is fully funded by the Army. The XT701 is the prototype preliminary flight rating test and safety test engine (PPFRT/SDT); the YT701 is the preliminary flight qualification rating test (PFRT) engine; the T701 is the qualification test (QT) engine and will go into production, probably in 1976. Flight qualification is due in October 1974.

Type: Free-turbine turboshaft engine.

Intake: Circular casting incorporating six aerofoil struts with thermal anti-icing. Accessory drive shafts at top and bottom, with main accessory gearbox on underside. This section carries front bearing for output shaft.

Compressor: Thirteen-stage axial, with variable inlet guide vanes and first five stator rows. Rotor built up from rings and discs, with large-diameter tubular central shaft rearwards from second stage. Rotor supported by front roller bearing and rear ball-thrust bearing. Longitudinally jointed casing incorporates large bleed manifold for 10th stage air. Pressure ratio 12·8. Mass flow 44·3 lb (20·1 kg)/sec.

Combustion Chamber: Annular, with 16 burners disposed around inner wall of flame tube fed with primary air through narrow annular gap at upstream end of snout section. Smoke-free combustion. Secondary air admitted through peripheral slits in flame tube giving film cooling.

FUEL GRADE: MIL-T-5624 grades JP-4, JP-5.

TURBINE: Gas-generator turbine has two axial stages with aircooled blades. Both stages cantilevered behind rear roller bearing. Power turbine has two axial stages assembled by row of bolts at first disc, carried between central ball thrust bearing on mid-frame through centre of combustion chamber and rear roller bearing.

JET PIPE: Fixed-area type, with truncated central bullet and tangential struts carrying rear bearing.

OUTPUT: Power turbine forward shaft is splined to central drive shaft carried in two ball-bearings at front end and incorporating torque sensing assembly. Rotation clockwise, viewed from rear. Rated speed 11,500 rpm.

ACCESSORY DRIVES: Main accessory gearcase beneath air intake section. Drives on front for starter/generator and tachometer, and on rear face for fuel pump and fuel control unit.

LUBRICATION SYSTEM: Self-contained integral oil system with external tank carried on left side of compressor casing.

OIL SPECIFICATION: MIL-L-23699, MIL-L-7808.

MOUNTING: Main suspension on each side of intake casing; seven possible mounting pads arranged around jet pipe casing.

DIMENSIONS:

Length (intake face to jet pipe exit)	64·3 in (1,633 mm)
Length overall	74·0 in (1,880 mm)
Intake diameter	20·3 in (516 mm)
Jet pipe diameter	28·1 in (714 mm)
Width	30·2 in (767 mm)
Height	36·8 in (935 mm)

WEIGHT, DRY: 1,179 lb (534 kg)

PERFORMANCE RATINGS (ISA, S/L, static) at gas generator speed of 15,049 rpm:

Intermediate (30 min)	8,079 shp
Max continuous	7,305 shp
75%	5,478 shp
50%	3,648 shp
25%	1,827 shp

SPECIFIC FUEL CONSUMPTION (conditions as above):

Intermediate	0·471 lb (0·214 kg)/shp/hr
Max continuous	0·462 lb (0·210 kg)/shp/hr
75%	0·468 lb (0·212 kg)/shp/hr
50%	0·506 lb (0·230 kg)/shp/hr
25%	0·637 lb (0·289 kg)/shp/hr

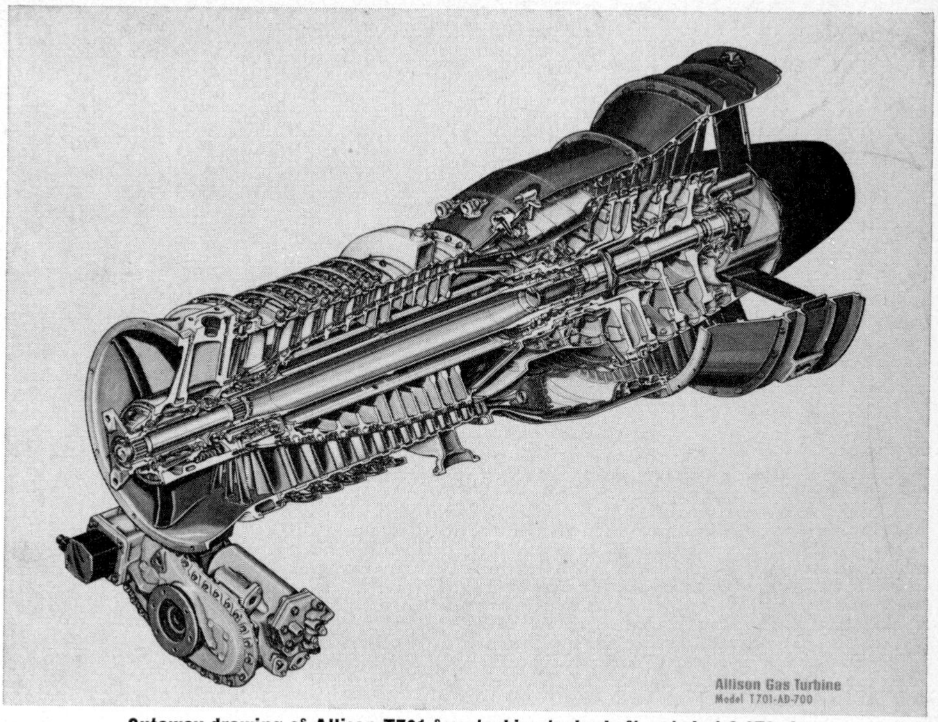

Cutaway drawing of Allison T701 free-turbine turboshaft, rated at 8,079 shp

AVCO LYCOMING

THE AVCO LYCOMING DIVISION OF AVCO CORPORATION

HEAD OFFICE:
550, South Main Street, Stratford, Connecticut 06497
Telephone: (203) 378-8211

WORKS:
Stratford, Conn; Williamsport, Pennsylvania

PRESIDENT OF AVCO CORPORATION:
George L. Hogeman

Stratford Operations:

VICE-PRESIDENTS:
Beverly H. Warren (General Manager)
J. S. Bartos (Assistant General Manager)
L. A. Shadle (Controller)
Richard B. Le Mar
Dr H. K. Adenstedt (Senior V-P)
Frank T. Dubuque (Operations)
L. H. Sample (Washington Representative)
Michael S. Saboe (Engineering)
Dr F. Haber (Marketing)

Williamsport Operations:
Williamsport, Pennsylvania 17701
Telephone: (717) 323-6181

VICE-PRESIDENTS:
John M. Ferris (General Manager)
Peter J. Goodwin (Assistant General Manager)
F. W. Riddell (Engineering)
E. L. Wilkinson (Manufacturing)
L. J. Anderson (Sales and Service)
E. D. Reynolds (Export Sales)

The Avco Lycoming Division is primarily the engine manufacturing division of Avco Corporation. It is producing two families of turbine engines, the T53 and T55 free-turbine units, of which turboshaft, turboprop, turbofan, industrial and marine versions are available. Development is continuing on the LTS 101 turboshaft and turboprop in the 600 shp class, the PLT-27 turboshaft in the 2,000 shp class, and on the advanced technology LTC4V series.

The Williamsport plant is engaged primarily in the production of the well-known Lycoming series of horizontally-opposed aircooled reciprocating engines ranging from 115 to 450 hp. Turbocharging is being offered on additional models and the horsepower, in some cases, has been increased. Development efforts are being directed to improvements resulting in lower cost of manufacturing and longer time between overhauls, to help offset increasing labour and material costs. During recent years FAA approval has been received for several turbocharged six-cylinder engines of both direct-drive and geared types. The turbocharger provides air for cabin pressurisation, and the engines have provision for a freon compressor for cabin cooling. Williamsport is studying the market for gas turbines for light aircraft.

Avco Lycoming is also engaged in the production of test systems for gas turbine engines, and in the development and production of mechanical constant-speed transmissions. It has manufactured re-entry vehicles for the Minuteman ICBM and components for the Titan III space launch vehicle, and is now doing missile-tube machining.

AVCO LYCOMING ALF SERIES

Announced in 1970, these high by-pass ratio turbofan engines were private venture developments until late 1971. They succeeded the earlier PLF1A-2 and PLF1C-1 turbofans which began bench running during the Winter of 1963-64.

All the Avco Lycoming turbofans utilise proven parts, and techniques from the earlier free-turbine turboshaft engines, and all have a high by-pass ratio suited to the propulsion requirements of subsonic aircraft. The chief models at present on offer are described below.

AVCO LYCOMING ALF 502

This turbofan family is aimed primarily at the commercial light transport and executive market. It is derived from the T55 turboshaft engine, like the discontinued ALF 501 of which a cutaway drawing appeared in the 1971-72 *Jane's*. The first two models are the 502A, rated at 7,200 lb (3,265 kg) st, and the 502D with a basic rating of 6,500 lb (2,948 kg) st. Late in 1971 the 502D was selected by Dassault to power the Falcon 30 (previously known as the Falcon 20T), with

AVCO LYCOMING GAS TURBINE ENGINES

Manufacturer's and civil designation	Military designation	Type*	T-O Rating lb (kg) st or max hp	SFC	Weight dry less tailpipe lb (kg)	Max diam in (mm)	Length overall in (mm)	Remarks
T5313B	—	ACFS	1,400 shp	0·58	540 (245)	23 (584)	47·6 (1,209)	Powers Bell 205A
T5317A	—	ACFS	1,500 shp	0·59	564 (256)	23 (584)	47·6 (1,209)	Based on T5319A
T5319A	—	ACFS	1,800 shp	0·57	564 (256)	23 (584)	47·6 (1,209)	Awaiting FAA certification
—	T53-L-11	ACFS	1,100 shp	0·68	496 (225)	23 (584)	47·6 (1,209)	Bell UH-1B, D, F; Kaman H-43
T5311A	—	ACFS	1,100 shp	0·68	496 (225)	23 (584)	47·6 (1,209)	Bell 204B
—	T53-L-13B	ACFS	1,400 shp	0·58	540 (245)	23 (584)	47·6 (1,209)	Advanced UH-1s and AH-1G
—	T53-L-702	ACFS	1,900 shp	0·56	561 (254)	23 (584)	47·6 (1,209)	Military T5319A
LTC1K-4C	—	ACFS	1,500 shp	0·58	545 (247)	23 (584)	47·6 (1,209)	Canadair CL-84
T5321A	—	ACFP	1,868 ehp	0·55	675 (306)	23 (584)	65·2 (1,656)	Turboprop T5319A
—	T53-L-15	ACFP	1,203 ehp	0·60	605 (274)	23 (584)	58·4 (1,483)	Grumman OV-1D
LTC4R-1	—	ACFP	3,804 ehp†	0·52	930 (422)	24·2 (615)	62·2 (1,580)	Turboprop T55-L-11A
—	T55-L-7B	ACFS	2,650 shp	0·62	580 (263)	24·2 (615)	44 (1,119)	Boeing CH-47A, Bell HueyTug
—	T55-L-7C	ACFS	2,850 shp	0·60	590 (267)	24·2 (615)	44 (1,119)	Boeing CH-47B, Bell KingCobra and Bell 214A
—	T55-L-11A	ACFS	3,750 shp	0·52	710 (322)	24·2 (615)	46·5 (1,181)	Boeing CH-47C
LTC4B-12	—	ACFS	4,600 shp	0·51	725 (329)	24·2 (615)	46·5 (1,181)	Improved T55-L-11A
LTC4V-1	—	AFS	5,000 shp	0·41	590 (267)	22 (559)	41·8 (1,062)	In development
LTS 101	—	ACFS	592 shp	0·57	230 (104)	21·9 (556)	30·9 (785)	In development
PLT-27	—	ACFS	2,050 shp	0·43	320 (145)	17·5 (444·5)	41·5 (1,055)	In development
ALF 301B	—	ACFF	2,894 lb (1,312 kg)	0·44	630 (286)	32·5 (826)	47·6 (1,209)	In development
ALF 502D	—	ACFF	5,500 lb (2,495 kg)	0·41	1,160 (526)	42 (1,067)	56·8 (1,443)	Falcon 30
ALF 502H	—	ACFF	6,500 lb (2,950 kg)	0·42	1,180 (535)	42 (1,067)	56·8 (1,443)	HS 146
—	F102-LD-100	ACFF	7,860 lb (3,565 kg)	—	1,100 (500)	41 (1,041)	56 (1,422)	Northrop A-9A

*ACFS = axial plus centrifugal, free-turbine shaft; ACFP = axial plus centrifugal, free-turbine propeller; AFS = axial, free-turbine shaft; ACFF = axial plus centrifugal, free-turbine fan

† 3,690 shp; also has military rating of 3,452 ehp/3,344 shp.

Avco Lycoming ALF 502H geared turbofan, flat-rated at 6,500 lb (2,950 kg) st

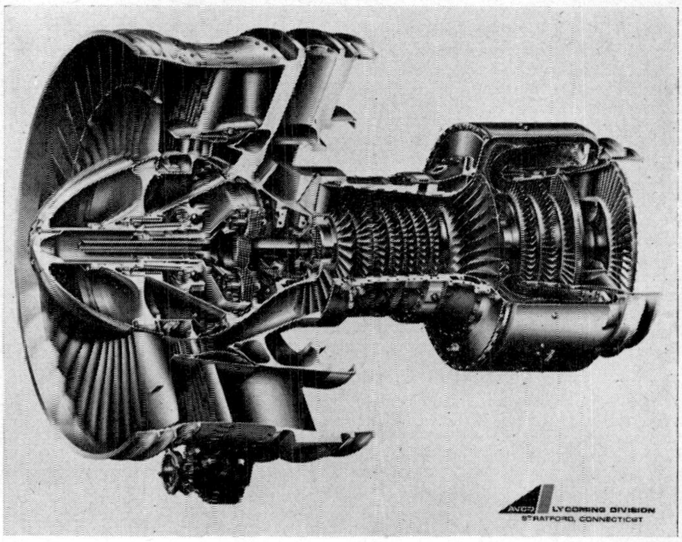

Cutaway drawing of Avco Lycoming F102-LD-100 military geared turbofan

flat-rating of 5,500 lb (2,495 kg) st. In 1972 the 502H was selected at a rating of 6,500 lb to power the four-engined Hawker Siddeley 146 short-haul transport. Hawker Siddeley based the pricing of the HS 146 on a keenly negotiated contract for the supply of ALF 502H engines throughout the 1970s at a fixed price plus allowable escalation due to inflation. Discussions with Rolls-Royce (1971) regarding participation of the British company in the programme had not led to any agreement by April 1974.

There are many potential applications of the ALF 502. The projected, heavier Dassault Breguet Atlantic 2A and 2B patrol aircraft are likely to have two ALF 502 booster pods. Both the F-27 and HS 748 have been projected in twin-ALF 502 forms. Smaller transports in the executive class include the Falcon 25, projects by Lear and Rockwell and the abandoned Cessna 600, all with two ALF 502. At least four other US aircraft companies have ALF 502-powered projects.

Type: Two-shaft, high by-pass ratio, geared turbofan.

Air Intake: Annular, around fan spinner and fan gearbox. The front frame includes main engine-mounting provisions and ducting for by-pass fan and core-engine airflows. Hollow struts provide ducts for necessary services across the fan and core-engine flow streams. Accessory drive and power take-off from the compressor rotor is transmitted through a bevel gear assembly in the front frame which is externally mounted for optimum accessibility to the accessory gearbox. Starting torque is transmitted through the reverse path.

Fan: The fan rotor includes a single-stage fan with an additional core-engine supercharging compressor cantilevered aft from the fan wheel. Fan blades have both base shrouds and mid-span shrouds for vibration and impact damping. The fan rotor is mounted on a conical support by means of a thrust bearing and a roller bearing, separated sufficiently to minimise moment loads during flight manoeuvres. A single-stage planetary helical reduction gear transmits power from the core-engine to the fan rotor. Opposing thrusts on the fan rotor and the fan drive turbine are partially balanced by reaction loads on the helical gear teeth, thereby reducing thrust bearing loads. Fan by-pass ratio (502H) 6 : 1. Air mass flow 240 lb (180·9 kg)/sec.

Compressor: The compressor rotor comprises a seven-stage axial spool in tandem with a single-stage centrifugal compressor. Compressor casing halves are individually removable for stator or blade replacement in the field.

Combustion Chamber: The combustor is a folded annular atomising burner with the turbine parts packaged concentrically within it. This concept provides a shorter, more compact engine, minimising moment loads on the mounting structure. It has the further advantages of reduced casing temperatures and improved blade containment. The design arrangement permits fan-drive turbine removal, either separately or in combination with the combustor, with single-flange disassembly.

Turbine: The compressor turbine is a two-stage aircooled axial turbine directly coupled to the compressor shaft. Blades for both stages are base-shrouded for reduced attachment temperatures and improved vibration damping. The fan-drive turbine is a two-stage uncooled axial turbine with the drive extending forward concentrically through the hollow compressor shaft to the fan reduction gear. The fan-drive turbine blades are tip-shrouded. The fourth-stage turbine nozzle has long-chord hollow vanes also serving as the fan-drive turbine bearing support.

Exhaust Unit: Separate discharge of fan air and core gas. Fan air expelled past row of straightener vanes and eight hollow aerofoil struts joining inner and outer walls of fan duct. Core jet pipe of minimum length and fixed area. Provision will be made for fan airflow reversal.

Accessories: Driven accessories are externally mounted on the accessory gearbox, carried on the fan casing, for optimum accessibility and reduced environmental temperatures.

For data, see table.

AVCO LYCOMING ALF 301

This is a high by-pass ratio, geared turbofan engine based on the T53, using the gas-generator of the T5319A as the core. It is similar in configuration to the ALF 502. For weight and performance, see table.

AVCO LYCOMING F102

This military turbofan matches the gas-generator of the T55 with a "newly designed fan package". The cutaway drawing shows many detail differences compared with the ALF 502, similarly illustrated in the 1972-73 *Jane's*. Its first application, as the YF102-LD-100, was in the Northrop A-9A, the unsuccessful contender in the US Air Force's AX programme.

It has a single-stage fan, with an additional core-engine supercharging compressor stage cantilevered aft of the fan wheel. Fan blades have both base and mid-span shrouds for vibration and impact damping. A single-stage planetary helical reduction gear transmits power from the core engine to the fan rotor. Opposing thrusts on the fan rotor and the fan drive-turbine are partially balanced by reaction loads in the helical gear teeth, thereby reducing thrust bearing loads.

The front frame includes main engine mounting provisions, and ducting for by-pass fan and core-engine airflows. Hollow struts provide ducts for necessary services across the fan and core-engine flow streams. The accessory drive and power take-off from the compressor rotor is transmitted through a bevel gear assembly in the front frame, to an accessory box which is externally mounted for optimum accessibility. Starting torque is transmitted through the reverse path.

The core-engine module includes the T55-derived axial/centrifugal compressor, folded annular combustor, and the compressor and fan turbines. The fan turbine has two uncooled axial stages, with the drive extending forward concentrically through the hollow compressor shaft to the fan reduction gear. The fan turbine blades are tip-shrouded. The fourth-stage turbine nozzle has long-chord hollow vanes providing the additional function of a fan turbine bearing support.

Lycoming's F102 turbofan programme includes extensive testing at the Stratford facility in test cells as well as in flight. An official Preliminary Flight Rating Test was conducted in March 1972. In order to obtain early flight experience Lycoming purchased a former

Avco Lycoming YF102-LD-100 turbofan engine, being evaluated for the AX programme in 1974

Disassembled modules of the Avco Lycoming LTS 101 turboshaft, rated at 579 shp

Navy carrier-based bomber, the North American AJ-2. This has been fitted with a retractable support system on which the test turbofan engine is deployed through the bomb bay into the airstream while in flight. In June 1972 testing had been completed at altitudes up to 17,500 ft (5,334 m). The first engine delivery to Northrop was made in late February 1972 and preparations for ground testing in the A-9A started soon afterwards. Prototype development flight tests began on 30 May 1972, leading to delivery of two A-9A aircraft to the USAF for flight evaluation in the Autumn of 1972.

Although the A-9A was not chosen for production, the YF102-LD-100 received "excellent performance ratings" after the arduous fly-off trials at Edwards AFB. In February 1974 the engine was continuing to be evaluated for the AX programme. For basic data, see table.

AVCO LYCOMING LTS 101

This new turboshaft engine is the smallest of the company's aircraft gas turbines, yet it achieves the remarkable power/weight ratio of 0·405 lb (0·184 kg)/shp. It is a simple, robust unit, intended to be sold at the lowest possible price for commercial applications (hopefully, less than $25,000), and several single- and twin-engine installations are being pursued.

It has an axial compressor stage followed by a centrifugal stage, reverse-flow annular combustion chamber and single-stage compressor and power turbines. A prominent particle separator and scroll surrounds the air intake. The LTS 101 can deliver power front or rear, but the initial version has a front-drive offset gearbox. It was selected to power two finalist, but now abandoned, "Aerial Scout" light observation helicopter designs (Bell and Hughes) proposed to the US Army, but the first firm application is in the completely new Bell 222 commercial twin-engined ten-seat helicopter. Lycoming hopes to be able to deliver production engines in 1975.

DIMENSIONS:

Length overall	31 in (787 mm)
Width	16 in (406 mm)
Height overall	25·9 in (658 mm)

WEIGHT, DRY: 180 lb (81·5 kg)

PERFORMANCE RATINGS:

T-O intermediate	579 shp
Max continuous	493 shp

AVCO LYCOMING LTP 101

At the 1973 Paris Air Show Avco Lycoming presented both the LTS 101 turboshaft and the previously unannounced LTP 101 turboprop version. The preliminary design of the LTP 101 is dated "1972-73". It is designed for tractor or pusher operation, above or below the wing in a multi-engine aircraft, and is of modular design, with the same gas-generator as the LTS 101. The additional single-stage propeller/gearbox module raises the output shaft to just below the gas-generator axis. The output-shaft speed can lie in the range 1,700-2,200 rpm, and typical propellers are given as Hartzell 93 in (2·36 m) diameter models with three blades (790 ft; 241 m/sec) or five blades (690 ft; 210 m/sec). No information is yet available on timing, applications or dry weight.

DIMENSIONS:

Length overall (propeller flange to jet-pipe connection)	44·0 in (1,118 mm)
Height overall	22·0 in (559 mm)

PERFORMANCE:

Take-off (S/L, ISA)	610 ehp (587 shp)
Take-off (S/L, 32°C)	527 ehp (507 shp)
Max cruise (S/L, ISA)	521 ehp (501 shp)
Max cruise (5,000 ft; 1,525 m, ISA, 180 kt; 207 mph; 334 km/h)	494 ehp (487 shp)
Max cruise (15,000 ft; 4,575 m, ISA, 180 kt; 207 mph; 334 km/h)	379 ehp (373 shp)

SPECIFIC FUEL CONSUMPTION:

T-O (S/L, ISA)	0·551
T-O (S/L, 32°C)	0·575
Max cruise (S/L, ISA)	0·564
Max cruise (5,000 ft; 1,525 m, 180 kt; 207 mph; 334 km/h)	0·544
Max cruise (15,000 ft; 4,575 m, ISA, 180 kt; 207 mph; 334 km/h)	0·532

AVCO LYCOMING LTC1

US military designation: T53

The T53 is a turboshaft with a free power turbine, which was developed under a joint USAF/US Army contract. It had logged over 24 million hours of operation, with every US armed service and in 28 other countries, by Spring 1974.

Licences for manufacture of the T53 are held by Klöckner-Humboldt-Deutz in Germany, Piaggio in Italy and Kawasaki in Japan. In general these involve the supply of kits of "hot end" parts from Lycoming, with initial production in all three countries being centred on the T53-L-11.

Versions currently in production or under development are as follows:

T53-L-13. Uprated version of L-11, which it superseded in production in August 1966. Redesigned "hot end" and initial stages of compressor section to provide substantially increased power for hot-day and high-altitude performance. Four turbine stages, compared with two in earlier models, and variable-incidence inlet guide vanes combined with redesigned first two compressor stages, permit greater airflow and lower turbine temperatures. This version has atomising combustor to facilitate operation on a wider range of fuels. Powers Bell UH-1C and UH-1D and CH-118 Iroquois and AH-1G HueyCobra. A specially-modified version of the L-13B will power the Bell XV-15 tilt-rotor VTOL aircraft being built under NASA/Army contract (see "Aircraft" section). The engines will be located in pivoted wingtip pods, which will carry the directly-driven rotors. The **T5313A** commercial version of the T53-L-13 received FAA type certification in Spring 1968 and powers Bell 205A helicopters. Marine and industrial versions are the 1,150 shp **TF12A** and 1,400 shp **TF14B.**

T53-L-701. Turboprop version of the L-13 incorporating the Lycoming "split-power" propeller reduction gear. Produced for Grumman OV-1D previously powered by T53-L-15, and specified for stretched version of Air-Metal AM-C111.

LTC1K-4C. Generally similar to the T53-L-13, but incorporating special seals to allow operation in the attitude range from 105° nose up to 90° nose down. Has 10-minute rating of 1,500 shp and was produced in limited quantity for use in the Canadair CL-84-1 VTOL aircraft.

T5319A. Latest growth version of T53 turboshaft family. Improvements over L-13 include new gearing, improved cooling of first gas producer turbine nozzle plus aircooled blades in first turbine rotor. Also incorporates new materials in other turbine stages. Rated at 1,800 shp at take-off.

T5317A. Lower-powered version of -19A with take-off rating limited to 1,500 shp by use of standard L-13 reduction gear.

T5321A. Turboprop version of -19A with "split-power" gear. Uses standard SBAC No. 4 propeller shaft with through-the-shaft oil provisions for use with Dowty Rotol propeller. Specified for CASA 401 four-engined transport and Dornier Do 24/72 three-engined flying-boat. T-O rating 1,800 shp (1,868 ehp).

The following details apply to the T53-L-13 and L-701:

TYPE: Free-turbine shaft-turbine engine.

AIR INTAKE: Annular casing of magnesium alloy, with 6 struts supporting reduction gearbox and front main bearings. Anti-icing by hot air tapped from engine.

COMPRESSOR: Five axial stages followed by a single centrifugal stage. Four-piece magnesium alloy casing with one row of variable-incidence inlet guide vanes and five rows of steel stator blades, bolted to one-piece steel alloy diffuser casing with tangential outlet to combustion chamber. Rotor comprises one stainless steel and four aluminium alloy discs with stainless steel blades and one titanium impeller mounted on shaft supported in forward ball thrust and rear roller bearings. Compression ratio 7·4 : 1. Air mass flow 10·7 lb/sec (4·85 kg/sec) at 25,240 gas producer rpm.

COMBUSTION CHAMBER: Annular reverse-flow type, with one-piece sheet steel outer shell and annular liner. Twenty-two atomising fuel injectors.

FUEL CONTROL SYSTEM: Hydromechanical controls for gas generator and for power sections. Chandler Evans TA-2S system with one dual fuel pump. Pump pressure 600 lb/sq in (42 kg/cm²). Main and emergency flow controls. Separate interstage air bleed control.

FUEL GRADE: ASTM A-1, MIL-J-5624, MIL-F-26005A, JP-1, JP-4, JP-5, CITE.

TURBINE: Four axial-flow turbine stages. Casing fabricated from sheet steel. First two stages, driving compressor, use hollow aircooled stator vanes and cored-out cast steel rotor blades and are mounted on outer co-axial shaft to gas producer. Second stages, driving reduction gearing, have solid steel blades, and are spline-mounted to shaft.

EXHAUST UNIT: Fixed-area nozzle. Steel outer casing and inner cone, supported by four radial struts.

ACCESSORIES: Electric starter or starter/generator

Cutaway drawing of the 1,400 shp Avco Lycoming T53-L-13 turboshaft engine

Avco Lycoming T53-L-701 (1,451 ehp) turboprop, power plant of the Grumman OV-1D Mohawk

(not furnished). Bendix-Scintilla TGLN high-energy ignition unit. Two igniter plugs.

LUBRICATION: Recirculating system, with gear pump with one pressure and one scavenge unit. Filter. Pump pressure 70 lb/sq in (4·9 kg/cm²).

OIL GRADE: MIL-L-7808, MIL-L-23699.

DIMENSIONS:

Length overall:	
L-13	47·6 in (1,209 mm)
L-701	58·4 in (1,483 mm)
Diameter:	
All versions	23·0 in (584 mm)

WEIGHT, DRY:

Less tailpipe:	
L-13	549 lb (249 kg)
LTC1K-4C	545 lb (247 kg)
L-701	688 lb (312 kg)

POWER RATINGS:

Max rating at S/L:
L-13
1,400 shp plus 126 lb (57 kg) st at 20,150 power-turbine rpm
L-701
1,451 ehp (1,400 shp plus 128 lb; 58 kg st) at 20,430 rpm

Military rating at S/L:	
L-13	1,400 shp
L-701	1,451 ehp

SPECIFIC FUEL CONSUMPTION:

At max rating:	
L-13	0·580 lb (0·263 kg)/ehp/hr
L-701	0·569 lb (0·258 kg)/ehp/hr

OIL CONSUMPTION:

L-13, -701	1·0 lb (450 gr)/hr

AVCO LYCOMING LTC4

US military designation: T55

This engine is based on the T53 design concept but with higher mass flow. It was developed under a joint USAF/US Army contract. Total operating time by Spring 1974 was in excess of 3 million hours. Most of this time has been logged by L-7 versions which power the CH-47A and CH-47B Chinook.

Current production and development versions are as follows:

T55-LTC4B-8D. Modified version of the T55-L-7C, rated at 2,950 shp. Powers Bell 214A utility helicopter for Iran.

T55-L-11 (LTC4B-11B). Uprated and redesigned version of L-7, with a second stage added to the compressor turbine, and variable-incidence inlet guide vanes ahead of the compressor. First two compressor stages transonic. New atomising fuel nozzles. Powers CH-47C Chinook, first deliveries having been made in August 1968.

TF25, TF35. Industrial and marine versions of the LTC4; TF25B is rated at 2,250 shp and TF35A is rated at 2,800 shp. The advanced TF40 version is rated at 3,350 shp.

LTC4B-12. Growth version with 4,600 shp maximum power rating (4,370 shp on hot day). Higher turbine entry temperature and increased turbine cooling. Dry weight, 680 lb (308 kg). Now on test.

LTC4R-1. Turboprop version of L-11 with Lycoming split-power reduction gear. Chosen for projected Britten-Norman Mainlander three-engined transport. T-O rating 3,690 shp (3,804 ehp).

QFT55. Under this designation Lycoming is developing a "quiet fan" version of the T55 for short-haul fixed-wing aircraft. It comprises a T55 gas generator driving a geared variable-pitch fan.

Hamilton Standard is developing a variable-pitch fan which could become an integral part of future turbine engines. The so-called Q-Fan completed 100 hours running by the start of the 1973 Paris Show. Two demonstrator/research fans had then been built: a 54 in (1,372 mm) 13-blade fan driven by a Lycoming T55 and rated at 8,300 lb (3,765 kg) thrust, and a 72 in (1,829 mm) fan with 15 glassfibre/titanium-spar blades, rated at 15,000 lb (6,804 kg) thrust.

Hamilton Standard expects future Q-fans to operate at tip speeds below 1,000 ft/sec (305 m/sec) and with by-pass ratios of from 8 : 1 to 15 : 1. Both will reduce noise, and the division's studies suggest a Q-Fan engine would be 15 PNdB quieter than "today's turbofan engines with equal thrust level". Further advantages would be the quick variation of thrust from ahead to astern, and elimination of a separate reverser.

Hamilton Standard has itself funded its Q-Fan development, apart from the demonstration of engine compatibility, running and acoustic measurement which form a programme financed and managed by the NASA Lewis Research Center.

The following description applies to the T55-L-11 and LTC4R-1:

TYPE: Free-turbine shaft-turbine engine.

AIR INTAKE: Annular type casing of magnesium alloy with four struts supporting reduction gearbox and front main bearings. Anti-icing by hot air tapped from engine. Provision for intake screens.

COMPRESSOR: Seven axial stages followed by a single centrifugal stage. Two-piece magnesium alloy stator casing with one row of variable inlet guide vanes and seven rows of steel stator blades, bolted to steel alloy diffuser casing to which combustion chamber casing is attached. Rotor comprises seven stainless steel discs and one titanium impeller mounted on shaft supported in forward ball-thrust bearing and rear roller bearing. Pressure ratio 8·2 : 1. Air mass flow 27 lb (12·25 kg)/sec.

COMBUSTION CHAMBER: Annular reverse-flow type. Steel outer shell and inner liner. Twenty-eight fuel burners with downstream injection.

FUEL SYSTEM: Hamilton Standard JFC 31 fuel control system. Gear-type fuel pump, with gas producer and power shaft governors, flow control with altitude compensation and shut-off valve.

FUEL GRADE: MIL-J-5624 grade JP-4, JP-5, MIL-F-46005A or CITE (Combustion Ignition Turbine Engine).

TURBINE: Two two-stage mechanically-independent axial-flow turbines. First turbine, driving compressor, has cored-out cast steel blades, the first stage having aircooled blades, and is flange-bolted to outer co-axial drive shaft. Hollow stator vanes. Second turbine, driving output shaft, has solid steel blades and is mounted on inner co-axial drive shaft.

EXHAUST UNIT: Fixed-area nozzle, with inner cone, supported by six radial struts.

ACCESSORIES: Electric starter or starter/generator, or air or hydraulic starter. Bendix-Scintilla TGLN high-energy ignition unit. Four igniter plugs.

LUBRICATION: Recirculating type. Integral oil tank and cooler on L-11, external tank for 4R-1.

OIL GRADE: MIL-L-7808, MIL-L-23699.

DIMENSIONS:

Length:	
T55-L-11	44·03 in (1,118 mm)
LTC4R-1	62·2 in (1,580 mm)
Diameter:	
Both versions	24·25 in (616 mm)

WEIGHT, DRY:

T55-L-11	670 lb (304 kg)
LTC4R-1	930 lb (422 kg)

Open-air rig for the 13-blade reversible Q-fan by Hamilton Standard. This fan is coupled to a Lycoming T55 core

PERFORMANCE RATINGS:

Max rating (10 min):	
T55-L-11	3,750 shp
LTC4R-1	3,690 shp plus 285 lb (129 kg) st
Military rating:	
T55-L-11	3,452 shp
LTC4R-1	3,804 ehp

The 5,000 shp Avco Lycoming LTC4V-1 turboshaft engine, the company's first aircraft engine to have a two-spool axial compressor with no centrifugal stage. This engine is scalable up to 10,000 shp

Cutaway drawing of the 3,750 shp Avco Lycoming T55-L-11 turboshaft engine

The 380 hp Avco Lycoming IGSO-540-A six-cylinder engine

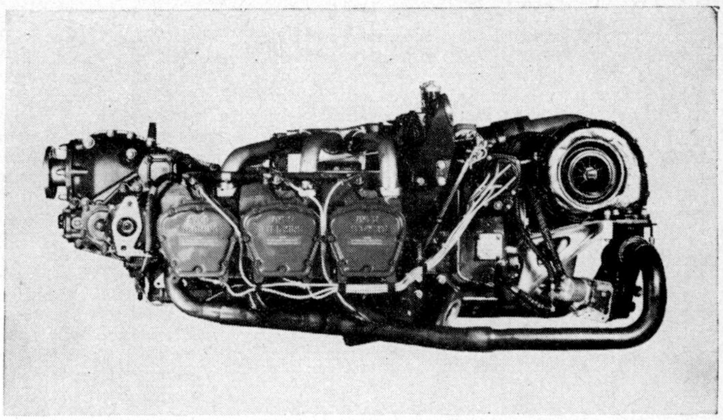

The 425 hp Avco Lycoming TIGO-541-E six-cylinder engine

Specific Fuel Consumption:
At max T-O and military ratings:

T55-L-11	0·513 lb (0·233 kg)/shp/hr
LTC4R-1	0·52 lb (0·236 kg)/ehp/hr

AVCO LYCOMING LTC4V SERIES

The Model LTC4V-1 is the first of a new series of advanced technology engines, designed for significant improvements in specific fuel consumption and reduced size and weight. These engines, designated the LTC4V Series, are designed to be scalable in the power range from 4,000 to 10,000 shp.

Based on design studies initiated in 1966, Avco Lycoming has proceeded with the design, fabrication and development of the LTC4V-1, rated at 5,000 shp, with a 25 per cent improvement in specific fuel consumption and a power-to-weight ratio exceeding 8 : 1. Following extensive component development of all critical elements from late 1967, initial gas producer testing started in December 1968. Full engine tests began in early 1969.

The basic engine configuration consists of a gas-producer section utilising a two-spool compressor. The proven reverse-flow annular combustor pioneered by Lycoming is also used on this engine.

AVCO LYCOMING PLT-27A

This entirely new power plant is a private venture regarded as likely ultimately to become very important in scale of output and to replace the T53 as the standard engine in this power class. It is particularly intended to offer severe competition to the General Electric GE12 and Pratt & Whitney ST9. Details remain restricted except for the fact that, despite developing 2,050 shp with a specific fuel consumption of only 0·43 lb (0·195 kg)/shp/hr, it will be no more than 41·5 in (1,055 mm) long and weigh only 320 lb (145 kg). By the beginning of 1972 a demonstrator engine had provided what Lycoming describes as excellent performance and endurance results.

AVCO LYCOMING O-235 and O-290 SERIES

The version of the O-290 Series engine in current production is the O-290-D2C, which differs from the preceding O-290-D2B by having retard breaker magnetos.

Type: Four-cylinder horizontally-opposed air-cooled.

Cylinders: Bore (O-235-C1B) 4⅜ in (111 mm), (O-290-D2C) 4⅞ in (123·7 mm). Stroke (both) 3⅞ in (98·4 mm). Aluminium alloy head screwed and shrunk on to steel barrel. Cylinder assemblies attached to crankcase by studs and nuts.

Pistons: Machined from aluminium alloy forgings. O-235 piston has four rings: two compression, an oil regulator and an oil scraper. O-290 has three rings: two compression and one oil regulating. Fully-floating gudgeon-pins with aluminium alloy retaining plugs.

Connecting Rods: Forged steel. Copper-lead steel-backed precision type bearings. Bronze bushed little-ends.

Crankshaft: One-piece forged chrome nickel molybdenum steel four-throw shaft on four nitrided bearings.

Crankcase: Aluminium alloy casting split on vertical centreline. Four precision copper-lead steel-backed main bearings.

Valve Gear: Two valves per cylinder. Inlet valves of Silchrome No. 1, exhaust valves of AMS 5682 with Stellite-faced heads. Valve seats of AMS 5700 shrunk into head.

Induction: Marvel-Schebler MA-3A and MA-3S1A carburettor with manual altitude control and idle cut-off. Centre zone distribution chamber in oil sump.

Ignition: Two Bendix Scintilla S4LN magnetos, incorporating a retard breaker.

Lubrication: Full pressure wet sump type.

Accessories: Starter, generator and tachometer drive. Optional drives for fuel pump and vacuum pump can be supplied.

Dimensions, Weights and Performance: See table

AVCO LYCOMING O-320 SERIES

The O-320 is basically the same as the O-290-D2C except for an increase in cylinder bore to 5⅛ in (130 mm), with a corresponding increase in swept volume to 319·8 cu in (5·2 litres), and use of a Marvel-Schebler MA-4SPA carburettor.

It is available in low-compression and high-compression versions for use with 80/87 or 100/130 octane fuels respectively.

For other details see table.

AVCO LYCOMING IO-320 SERIES

The O-320 engines are available as fuel-injected models with both high and low compression. For further details see table.

AVCO LYCOMING O-340 and O-360 SERIES

The O-340 is basically the same as the O-320 except for an increase in stroke to 4⅛ in (105 mm), with a corresponding increase in swept volume to 340·4 cu in (5·58 litres), and use of the larger Marvel-Schebler MA-4-5 carburettor. The O-360, the same as the O-340 except for a further increase in stroke to 4⅜ in (111 mm), has a corresponding increase in swept volume to 361 cu in (5·92 litres). Both engines are available in low- and high-compression versions for use with 80/87 or 100/130 octane fuel respectively.

The VO-360-B1A is the helicopter version of the O-360, arranged for installation with the crankshaft vertical.

The IMO-360-B1B is a fuel-injected single-ignition version of the O-360 for use in unmanned aircraft.

For further details see table.

AVCO LYCOMING IO-360 SERIES

The O-360 is built in two fuel-injection versions: the IO-360-A series with tuned injection, tuned induction and high-output cylinders, and the IO-360-B series with continuous-flow port injection and standard cylinders.

AVCO LYCOMING O-435 SERIES

The O-435 Series includes direct-drive, geared, and geared and supercharged models, details of which will be found in the table. The VO-435-A1F, TVO-435-A1A and TVO-435-B1A are helicopter engines for vertical installation. The TVO-435 engines are equipped with an AiResearch exhaust-driven turbocharger which allows them to maintain rated power to 20,000 ft (6,100 m). The GO-435-C2B2-6 is a geared-drive wet sump engine with a propeller governor drive, mounted on the left side of the propeller reduction-gear housing.

Type: Six-cylinder horizontally-opposed air-cooled, incorporating major components of the O-290.

Cylinders: Bore 4⅞ in (123·7 mm). Stroke 3⅞ in (98·4 mm).

Pistons: Aluminium alloy pistons with two compression and two oil control rings.

Connecting Rods: H-section steel forgings with replaceable bearing inserts in big-ends and split bronze bushings in little-ends.

Crankshaft: Machined from chrome nickel molybdenum steel forging. All bearing surfaces nitrided.

Crankcase: Aluminium alloy casting split on the vertical centreline. Additional ball-thrust bearing at forward end of case.

Induction: Marvel-Schebler MA-4-5 or Stromberg PS-5BD single-barrel carburettor attached to bottom of oil sump casting. The distributing zone is submerged in oil. Separate induction pipes lead to inlet valves.

Right: **The 270 hp Avco Lycoming TVO-435-B1A turbocharged vertical helicopter engine**

Below: **The 200 hp Avco Lycoming IO-360-A1A flat-four engine**

AVCO LYCOMING HORIZONTALLY-OPPOSED PISTON ENGINES

Engine Model	No. of Cylinders	Rated output at Sea Level hp at rpm	Capacity cu in (litres)	Compression Ratio	Fuel Grade	Weight Dry lb (kg)	Length Overall in (mm)	Width Overall in (mm)	Height Overall in (mm)	Gear Ratio*
O-235-C1B	4	115 at 2,800	233 (3·85)	6·75 : 1	80	240 (109)	29·81 (757)	32·00 (812)	22·40 (569)	D
O-235-G2A	4	125 at 2,800	233 (3·85)	9·70 : 1	100/130	223 (101)	29·56 (751)	32·00 (812)	22·40 (569)	D
O-290-D2C	4	135 at 2,600 T-O 140 at 2,800	289 (4·75)	7·0 : 1	80/87	235 (107)	29·81 (757)	32·24 (819)	22·68 (576)	D
O-320-E2D	4	150 at 2,700	319·8 (5·2)	7·0 : 1	80/87	249 (113)	29·05 (738)	32·24 (819)	22·99 (584)	D
IO-320-B1A	4	160 at 2,700	319·8 (5·2)	8·5 : 1	100/130	259 (117)	33·59 (853)	32·24 (819)	19·22 (488)	D
IO-320-C1A	4	160 at 2,700	319·8 (5·2)	8·5 : 1	100/130	268 (122)	33·59 (853)	32·24 (819)	19·22 (488)	D
LIO-320-B1A	4	160 at 2,700	319·8 (5·2)	8·5 : 1	100/130	262 (119)	33·59 (853)	32·24 (819)	19·22 (488)	D
AIO-320-A1A	4	160 at 2,700	319·8 (5·2)	8·5 : 1	100/130	275 (125)	30·08 (764)	32·24 (819)	20·76 (527)	D
O-360-A1D	4	180 at 2,700	361 (5·92)	8·5 : 1	100/130	256 (116)	29·81 (757)	33·37 (848)	24·59 (625)	D
O-360-A1H	4	180 at 2,700	361 (5·92)	8·5 : 1	100/130	294 (134)	31·82 (807)	33·37 (848)	19·22 (488)	D
O-360-A1F6	4	180 at 2,700	361 (5·92)	8·5 : 1	100/130	265 (120)	30·70 (780)	33·37 (848)	24·59 (625)	D
O-360-A3A	4	180 at 2,700	361 (5·92)	8·5 : 1	100/130	257 (116)	29·56 (751)	33·37 (848)	24·59 (625)	D
AIO-360-A1A	4	200 at 2,700	361 (5·92)	8·7 : 1	100/130	300 (136)	30·08 (764)	34·25 (870)	20·76 (527)	D
HIO-360-A1A	4	180 at 2,900 to 3,000 ft (915 m)	361 (5·92)	8·7 : 1	100/130	283 (128)	33·65 (855)	34·25 (870)	19·48 (495)	D
HIO-360-B1A	4	180 at 2,900	361 (5·92)	8·5 : 1	91/96	259 (117)	32·09 (815)	33·37 (848)	19·38 (492)	D
HIO-360-C1A	4	205 at 2,900	361 (5·92)	8·7 : 1	100/130	293 (133)	31·14 (791)	34·25 (870)	19·48 (495)	D
HIO-360-D1A	4	190 at 3,200 to 4,200 ft (1,280 m)	361 (5·92)	10·0 : 1	100/130	290 (132)	35·28 (894)	34·25 (870)	19·48 (495)	D
IO-360-A1A	4	200 at 2,700	361 (5·92)	8·7 : 1	100/130	293 (133)	29·81 (757)	34·25 (870)	21·61 (549)	D
IO-360-B1B	4	180 at 2,700	361 (5·92)	8·5 : 1	100/130	267 (121)	29·81 (757)	33·37 (848)	24·91 (633)	D
IO-360-F1A	4	180 at 2,700	361 (5·92)	8·5 : 1	100/130	272 (123)	32·09 (815)	33·37 (848)	20·70 (526)	D
IVO-360-A1A	4	180 at 2,900	361 (5·92)	8·5 : 1	100/130	274 (124)	30·00 (762)	33·37 (848)	22·95 (583)	D V
TIO-360-A1B	4	200 at 2,575 to 15,000 ft (4,575 m)	361 (5·92)	7·3 : 1	100/130	355 (161)	45·41 (1,153)	34·25 (870)	19·92 (506)	D
VO-435-A1F	6	250 at 3,200 T-O 260 at 3,400	434 (7·1)	7·3 : 1	80/87	399 (181)	34·73 (882)	33·58 (853)	24·13 (612)	D V
TVO-435-B1A	6	220 at 3,200 to 20,000 ft (6,100 m) T-O 270 at 3,200	434 (7·1)	7·3 : 1	100/130	478 (217)	34·73 (882)	33·58 (853)	35·65 (905)	D V
TVO-435-G1A	6	220 at 3,200 to 20,000 ft (6,100 m) T-O 280 at 3,200 to 18,000 ft (5,486 m)	434 (7·1)	7·3 : 1	100/130	465 (211)	34·73 (882)	33·58 (853)	35·67 (906)	D V
IGO-480-A1A6	6	280 at 3,000 T-O 295 at 3,400	479·7 (7·8)	8·7 : 1	100/130	455 (206)	40·76 (1,036)	33·12 (842)	28·02 (712)	0·642 : 1
GO-480-B1D	6	260 at 3,000 T-O 270 at 3,400	479·7 (7·8)	7·3 : 1	80/87	432 (196)	38·64 (981)	33·12 (842)	28·02 (712)	0·642 : 1
GO-480-G1D6	6	280 at 3,000 T-O 295 at 3,400	479·7 (7·8)	8·7 : 1	100/130	444 (201)	38·64 (981)	33·12 (842)	28·02 (712)	0·642 : 1
IGSO-480-A1F6	6	320 at 3,200 to 11,000 ft (3,350 m) T-O 340 at 3,400	479·7 (7·8)	7·3 : 1	100/130	513 (233)	47·56 (1,208)	33·12 (842)	22·44 (570)	0·642 : 1
O-540-A1A5	6	250 at 2,575	541·5 (8·86)	8·5 : 1	100/130	367 (166)	37·22 (945)	33·37 (848)	24·56 (624)	D
O-540-B2B5	6	235 at 2,575	541·5 (8·86)	7·2 : 1	80/87	366 (166)	37·22 (945)	33·77 (858)	24·56 (624)	D
VO-540-9	6	305 at 3,200 to 3,000 ft (915 m)	541·5 (8·86)	8·7 : 1	100/130	452 (205)	34·73 (882)	34·70 (880)	25·57 (649)	D V
IO-540-C4B5	6	250 at 2,575	541·5 (8·86)	8·5 : 1	100/130	375 (170)	38·42 (976)	33·37 (848)	24·46 (622)	D
IO-540-D4A5	6	260 at 2,700	541·5 (8·86)	8·5 : 1	100/130	375 (170)	38·42 (976)	33·37 (848)	24·46 (622)	D
IO-540-G1A5	6	290 at 2,575	541·5 (8·86)	8·7 : 1	100/130	414 (188)	38·62 (981)	34·25 (870)	19·60 (498)	D
IO-540-J4A5	6	250 at 2,575	541·5 (8·86)	8·5 : 1	100/130	380 (172)	39·34 (999)	33·37 (848)	24·46 (622)	D
IO-540-K1A5	6	300 at 2,700	541·5 (8·86)	8·7 : 1	100/130	443 (201)	39·34 (999)	34·25 (870)	19·60 (498)	D
IO-540-P1A5	6	290 at 2,575	541·5 (8·86)	8·7 : 1	100/130	424 (192)	39·34 (999)	34·25 (870)	19·60 (498)	D
HIO-540-A1A	6	290 at 2,575	541·5 (8·86)	8·7 : 1	100/130	443 (201)	39·34 (999)	34·25 (870)	19·60 (498)	D
IGO-540-B1C	6	325 at 3,000 T-O 350 at 3,400	541·5 (8·86)	8·7 : 1	100/130	500 (227)	46·38 (1,178)	34·25 (870)	21·66 (550)	0·642 : 1
IGSO-540-A1D	6	360 at 3,200 to 10,500 ft (3,200 m) T-O 380 at 3,400	541·5 (8·86)	7·3 : 1	100/130	540 (245)	48·15 (1,223)	34·25 (870)	28·44 (722)	0·642 : 1
VO-540-B1B3	6	305 at 3,200	541·5 (8·86)	7·3 : 1	80/87	444 (201)	34·73 (882)	34·70 (880)	24·29 (617)	D V
VO-540-B2D	6	Max continuous 305 at 3,200	541·5 (8·86)	7·3 : 1	80/87	442 (200)	34·73 (882)	34·70 (880)	25·57 (649)	D V
VO-540-C1A	6	305 at 3,200 to 3,000 ft (915 m)	541·5 (8·86)	8·7 : 1	100/130	441 (200)	34·73 (882)	34·70 (880)	25·57 (649)	D V
IVO-540-A2C	6	305 at 3,200 to 3,000 ft (915 m)	541·5 (8·86)	8·7 : 1	100/130	435 (197)	34·73 (882)	34·70 (880)	24·22 (615)	D V
TIO-540-A1A	6	310 at 2,575 to 15,000 ft (4,575 m)	541·5 (8·86)	7·3 : 1	100/130	506 (230)	51·34 (1,304)	34·25 (870)	22·71 (577)	D
TIO-540-F2BD	6	325 at 2,575 to 15,000 ft (4,575 m)	541·5 (8·86)	7·3 : 1	100/130	511 (232)	51·34 (1,304)	34·25 (870)	22·42 (570)	D
TIO-540-J2BD	6	350 at 2,575 to 15,000 ft (4,575 m)	541·5 (8·86)	7·3 : 1	100/130	518 (234)	51·50 (1,308)	34·25 (870)	22·56 (573)	D
TIVO-540-A2A	6	305 at 3,200 to 15,000 ft (4,575 m)	541·5 (8·86)	7·3 : 1	100/130	507 (230)	34·73 (882)	34·70 (880)	36·00 (914)	D V
TIO-541-A1A	6	310 at 2,575 to 15,000 ft (4,575 m)	541·5 (8·86)	7·3 : 1	100/130	549 (249)	49·09 (1,247)	34·25 (870)	21·38 (543)	D
TIO-541-E1C4	6	380 at 2,900 to 15,000 ft (4,575 m)	541·5 (8·86)	7·3 : 1	100/130	596 (270)	50·07 (1,272)	35·66 (905)	25·17 (640)	D
TIGO-541-C1A	6	400 at 3,200 to 15,000 ft (4,575 m)	541·5 (8·86)	7·3 : 1	100/130	703 (319)	57·57 (1,462)	34·86 (885)	22·65 (575)	0·667 : 1
TIGO-541-E1A	6	425 at 3,200 to 15,000 ft (4,575 m)	541·5 (8·86)	7·3 : 1	100/130	701 (318)	57·57 (1,462)	34·86 (885)	22·65 (575)	0·667 : 1
IO-720-A1A	**8**	**400 at 2,650**	**722 (11·84)**	**8·7 : 1**	**100/130**	**— —**	**46·08 (1,170)**	**34·25 (870)**	**22·10 (561)**	**D**

*D, Direct drive; V, Vertical mounting

Ignition: Two Bendix-Scintilla magnetos driven by spur gears from the timing gear.

Lubrication: Full pressure type, including valve mechanism. Crankshaft equipped with centrifugal sludge-removers. Pistons, gudgeon-pins and accessory drive gears lubricated by splash.

Accessory Housing: Aluminium alloy casting bolted to rear of crankcase and top rear of oil sump. Houses oil pump and geared accessory drives, and provides mounting for starter and generator, fuel pump, tachometer drive and magnetos. Vacuum pump drive optional equipment.

Starting: Delco-Rémy 12V automotive type starter. Starter torque applied to crankshaft gear through Bendix-type starter drive.

Dimensions, Weights and Performance: See table

The 310 hp Avco Lycoming TIO-540 six-cylinder engine fitted to the Piper Turbo Navajo

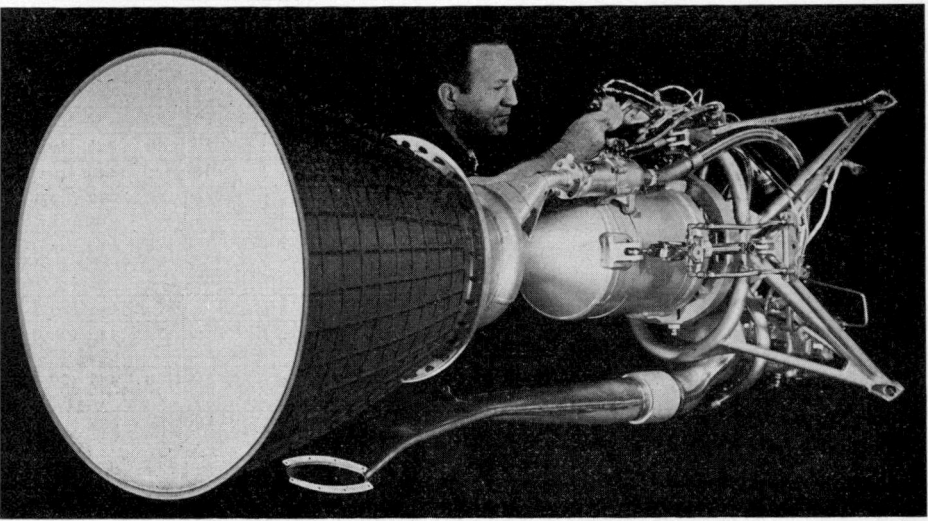

The 400 hp eight-cylinder Avco Lycoming IO-720-A1A engine

AVCO LYCOMING O-480 SERIES

The O-480 Series is basically the same as the O-435 Series except for an increase in cylinder bore to 5⅛ in (130 mm) and in swept volume to 479·7 cu in (7·8 litres). The geared and normally aspirated engines are available in low- and high-compression versions for use with 80/87 or 100/130 minimum octane fuels respectively. The geared and supercharged GSO-480-B Series have a supercharger drive ratio of 11·27 : 1, providing rated power to 8,000 ft (2,440 m) on 100/130 minimum octane fuel. The IGSO-480-A1B6 is similar to the GSO-480 except that it is fitted with direct fuel injection into the eye of the supercharger. High-compression and supercharged engines are provided with internal oil cooling of the pistons as standard equipment. For other details see table.

AVCO LYCOMING O-540 SERIES

The O-540 is basically a direct-drive six-cylinder version of the four-cylinder O-360, with the same bore and stroke and a swept volume of 541·5 cu in (8·86 litres). It is currently available in a high-compression configuration for use with 100/130 minimum octane fuel. A low-compression model for use with 80/87 fuel can be provided and the vertically-mounted VO-540 is in production as a helicopter power plant. The TIVO-540-A1A, equipped with an AiResearch turbocharger, maintains rated power to 17,000 ft (5,180 m).

During 1968-70 computer analysis of engine service records enabled time between overhauls to be increased by up to 50 per cent. The O-540-B (Cherokee 235) and O-540-E (Comanche and Cherokee SIX) are both now cleared at 1,800 hours. For other details see table.

AVCO LYCOMING IO-540 SERIES

A fuel-injection, tuned induction version of the O-540 with high-output cylinders, model IO-540-B1A5, is rated at 290 hp at 2,575 rpm. A geared version of this engine, model IGO-540-B1A, is rated at 350 hp at 3,400 rpm for take-off. The geared and supercharged model IGSO-540-B1A has a supercharger ratio of 11·27 : 1 and provides take-off power to 11,000 ft (3,350 m) altitude on 100/130 minimum octane fuel. The IO-540-J (Turbo Aztec) has since 1970 been cleared to operate 1,500 hours between overhauls, and the IO-540-C (Aztec), IO-540-D (Comanche), IO-540-K (Cherokee SIX) and IO-540-M and TIO-540-A and -C series (Navajo) have been cleared to 1,800 hours. The latest addition to this series is the TIO-540-J, a 350 hp top-exhaust, direct-drive, turbocharged engine used in the Piper Navajo Chieftain. For further details see table.

AVCO LYCOMING TIO-541 SERIES

First engine in this turbocharged six-cylinder series was the TIO-541-A1A, which gives 310 hp to 15,000 ft (4,570 m) and 230 hp to 25,000 ft (7,620 m). Lycoming has now extended this family with the 380 hp TIO-541-E series and the 425 hp geared TIGO-541-E. These have an overhaul life of 1,200 hours. A double-scroll blower, to provide cabin pressurisation also, is available on all these turbocharged engines.

AVCO LYCOMING IO-720 SERIES

This eight-cylinder version of the IO-540 engine is available and has a rating of 400 hp at 2,650 rpm. Time between overhauls is 1,500 hours. For further details see table.

AVCO LYCOMING NEW RANGE

Avco Lycoming, Williamsport, is continuing the development of a new series of high-performance normally-aspirated and turbocharged flat opposed piston engines. Williamsport has also begun to investigate the market for gas turbine engines in the same power category as its existing products. These projects would not overlap the power categories covered by the government-owned gas turbine plant at Stratford, described on earlier pages.

BELL

BELL AEROSPACE COMPANY DIVISION OF TEXTRON INC

Head Office and Works:
Buffalo, New York 14240
Telephone: (716) 297-1000

Officers: See "Aircraft" section

Bell has been engaged in the design, development and production of liquid-propellant rocket engines since 1946.

A single-chamber engine which Bell developed originally to power a nuclear weapon pod to be carried by the B-58 Hustler bomber is now being used in modified form in the Agena space vehicle and provides upper-stage propulsion for numerous spacecraft. The latest version is able to offer multiple re-start capability and was used for the Gemini rendezvous programme. The Agena vehicles used in this programme were also fitted with a Bell-produced secondary propulsion system of 16 lb (7·25 kg) and 200 lb (90 kg) st radiation-cooled rocket motors for fine adjustment of their velocity prior to the docking manoeuvre.

On 20 February 1974, Bell completed 15 years of space use of the Agena series of engines. In that time the Models 8096, described hereunder, and 8247 have been used in more than 300 missions by the US Air Force and NASA.

Bell reaction controls are used on the Minuteman III ICBM.

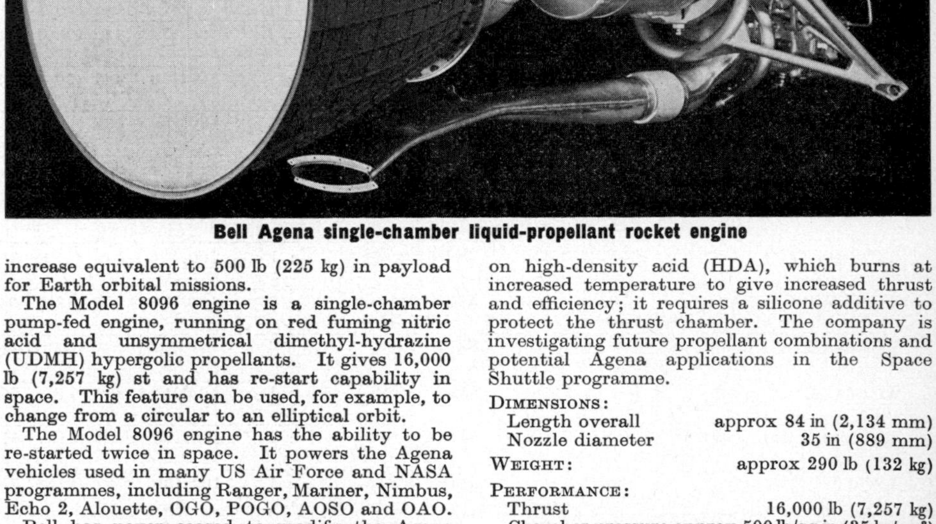

Bell Agena single-chamber liquid-propellant rocket engine

BELL MODEL 8096 AGENA ENGINE

This engine was first developed as the power plant for one of the weapon pods that was to be carried by the B-58 Hustler supersonic bomber. It is used in modified form, with gimballed chamber, as the power unit of the Lockheed-built Agena vehicle, forming the second stage of the Thor-Agena, Atlas-Agena and other space vehicles.

During its development the engine has undergone five major modifications, each resulting in an improvement in specific impulse. The present version, designated Model 8096, has a specific impulse of nearly 300 sec, which is more than 10% better than the original version of 1959, an increase equivalent to 500 lb (225 kg) in payload for Earth orbital missions.

The Model 8096 engine is a single-chamber pump-fed engine, running on red fuming nitric acid and unsymmetrical dimethyl-hydrazine (UDMH) hypergolic propellants. It gives 16,000 lb (7,257 kg) st and has re-start capability in space. This feature can be used, for example, to change from a circular to an elliptical orbit.

The Model 8096 engine has the ability to be re-started twice in space. It powers the Agena vehicles used in many US Air Force and NASA programmes, including Ranger, Mariner, Nimbus, Echo 2, Alouette, OGO, POGO, AOSO and OAO.

Bell has never ceased to modify the Agena engine. The most recent change is to qualify on high-density acid (HDA), which burns at increased temperature to give increased thrust and efficiency; it requires a silicone additive to protect the thrust chamber. The company is investigating future propellant combinations and potential Agena applications in the Space Shuttle programme.

Dimensions:

Length overall	approx 84 in (2,134 mm)
Nozzle diameter	35 in (889 mm)

Weight: approx 290 lb (132 kg)

Performance:

Thrust	16,000 lb (7,257 kg)
Chamber pressure approx	500 lb/sq in (35 kg/cm²)
Specific impulse	approx 300 sec

CURTISS-WRIGHT

CURTISS-WRIGHT CORPORATION, WOOD-RIDGE FACILITY

Head Office and Works:
One Passaic St, Wood-Ridge, New Jersey 07075
Telephone: (201) 777-2900

Chairman of the Board and President:
T. Roland Berner

Senior Vice-Presidents:
John B. Morris
Charles E. Ehinger
Seymour S. Bitterman
Richard P. Sprigle

Vice-President, Engineering:
A. F. Kossar

Vice-Presidents:
D. Lasky
W. Figart

The Wood-Ridge facility of Curtiss-Wright Corporation is engaged in the research, development and licensing of Wankel-type rotary engines, manufacture of engine parts, aircraft and industrial engine overhaul, electric power generation systems and advanced marine and turbine technology.

Wright engines continue in worldwide service in fixed-wing aircraft and helicopters.

These engines have been described in previous editions of *Jane's*.

CURTISS-WRIGHT SETE

In competition with Garrett-AiResearch and Pratt & Whitney, Curtiss-Wright is participating in the SETE (Supersonic Expendable Turbine Engine) programme of the US Navy. The objective is the cheapest possible jet engine capable of unfailingly-reliable instant starting and flight propulsion, under severe conditions of manoeuvre, over a wide band of speeds and heights, on a single flight of a missile. Details are restricted.

CURTISS-WRIGHT RC ENGINES

In 1958 Curtiss-Wright Corporation obtained a licence for the NSU-Wankel type of rotating-combustion (RC) engine and embarked on a major programme of independent development of a range of such engines aimed at a wide spectrum of applications. At first the company concentrated on large engines in the power range around 500 hp for aircraft use, but during the past decade much smaller engines have dominated the hardware test and development programme, some of which has been funded by US military agencies, including the Naval Air Systems Command.

Most research has been carried out on versions of the **RC2-60** (twin rotors each of about 60 cu in; 0·983 litre capacity), rated at up to 200 hp at 5,500 rpm and with possible future potential to reach twice this rotational speed in view of the near-perfect balance. One of these engines powered the Lockheed Q-Star acoustic research aircraft, specially designed for minimum noise level (see 1971-72 *Jane's*). Further testing has been successfully completed in the Cessna Cardinal illustrated in the 1972-73 *Jane's*. Under the sponsorship of the US Army Aviation Command and the Hughes Helicopter Company, the RC2-60 is currently undergoing flight evaluation in a TH-55 training helicopter.

In 1965 the 310 hp **RC2-90** was run, with helicopter applications in mind, and the 90 cu in (1·47 litres) rotor has since been used in extensive development of "stratified charge" engines capable of operating on a range of fuels including JP-4 and JP-5 gas-turbine kerosenes.

Hughes TH-55 helicopter powered by Curtiss-Wright RC2-60 (Wankel-type) engine, rated at 185 hp

Curtiss-Wright RC2-75 rotating-combustion engine

RC2-75

An accompanying photograph shows one of a range of projected RC engines for aeroplanes and helicopters, exhibited in the form of a full-scale display model at the 1971 show of the US National Business Aircraft Association. Such engines are expected to offer compact, lightweight, quiet power with low exhaust pollution, and to afford stiff competition to the smaller gas turbines from 1980. They were extremely prominent in the "Technology Assessment of Advanced General Aviation Aircraft" by the Ames Laboratory of NASA, completed in May 1971.

The RC2-75-Y3 is one of a very important family of engines, regarded as optimally sized for a wide range of general aviation aircraft. As the designation indicates, it is based on two rotors each of nominal 75 cu in (1·23 litres) capacity, and has liquid cooling and a geared drive. In the photograph the dual magnetos are prominent, but the induction system, starter/generator and oil filter are on the far side. The compactness and favourable power/weight ratio are evident from the data.

Dimensions:
Length 31·4 in (798 mm)
Width 23·7 in (602 mm)
Height 21·5 in (546 mm)

Weights:
Basic, dry 276 lb (125 kg)
Installed, with starter, oil cooler, oil tank, coolant and radiator and mounting brackets 358 lb (162 kg)

Performance Rating:
Max T-O 330 hp at 6,000 rpm

DREHER

DREHER ENGINEERING COMPANY

Address:
933 5th Street, Santa Monica, California 90403
Telephone: (213) 395-6510

Mr Max Dreher, an aeronautical engineer, has built a series of small turbojet engines over a period of 24 years. One of them, known as the TJD-76 Baby Mamba, has been mounted on his Prue 215A all-metal 12·0 m sailplane as an auxiliary turbojet.

A lighter version is under development and has been designated TJD-76C. Component testing is taking place on the larger TJD-79A Baby Python, described below. This is considered likely to prove much more useful in sailplane applications. So far eight Dreher engines have been built, and manufacture is concentrated on 12 licence-built TJD-76C engines, to be used as research tools, and on the TJD-76C low-cost drone version.

A proliferation of new markets has now led to two additional versions, the TJD-76D and E, described below. Mr Dreher and his colleagues have also designed and tested a larger engine, the TJD-79; designed a scaled TJD-76 in the 110 lb (50 kg) class, designated TJD-81; and made a preliminary study of a turbofan in the 200 lb (90·8 kg) st class.

DREHER TJD-76A BABY MAMBA

This very small turbojet engine has a single-stage centrifugal compressor, straight-through-flow annular combustion chamber, with six injectors, and single-stage axial-flow turbine. The shaft runs on two ball bearings. Starting is by compressed air.

Testbed for the Baby Mamba is a Prue 215A all-metal sailplane, with a span of 39 ft 4½ in (12·00 m) and T-O weight of 605 lb (275 kg). Glide ratio with engine fitted is 28 : 1.

Dimensions:
Length overall 16·3 in (414 mm)
Diameter 6 in (152 mm)

Weights:
Bare turbojet 17 lb (7·7 kg)
Complete power plant package 25 lb (11·35 kg)

DREHER TJD-76C BABY MAMBA

This new version of the Baby Mamba is lighter and introduces several mechanical and aerodynamic improvements, including a tachometer generator for direct rpm reading.

Type: Single-shaft turbojet.

Air Intake: At front. Air flow 1·1 lb (0·50 kg)/sec.

Compressor: Single-stage mixed-flow. Single 17-4 PH stainless steel impeller with sixteen vanes. Splined to shaft and supported in two ball bearings. Mixed-flow two-stage diffuser of 347 stainless steel. Pressure ratio 2·8 : 1.

Compressor Casing: Of 2024 aluminium alloy and 347 stainless steel.

Combustion Chamber: Annular type with Hastelloy X outer casing and flame tube. Vaporising system with fuel/air pre-mix. One spark plug in flame tube.

Fuel System: Manual with pressurised fuel supply, or electrically-driven fuel pump. Fuel pressure 80 lb/sq in (5·6 kg/cm²). Automatic system for drone applications.

Fuel Grade: Kerosene or petrol.

Nozzle Guide Vanes: Single axial stage, with sixteen investment-cast vanes in Stellite 31.

Turbine: Single-stage axial-flow, with nineteen integrally-cast blades, of Inconel 713 LC. Gas temperature 770°C before turbine, 675°C after turbine at continuous cruising power.

Jet Pipe: Fixed type, with jet pipe and cone of Hastelloy X.

Lubrication: Air/oil mist system with total loss, using bleed air equivalent to 2·5 per cent of total mass flow. Capacity 2 US pints (1 litre).

Oil Grade: MIL-L-7808E (Turbo 15).

Mounting: Two rigid connections on diffuser section and one flexible connection on turbine section.

Starting: Compressed air (150 lb/sq in; 10·5 kg/cm²), via three nozzles driving turbine wheel.

Dimensions:
Length overall 16·38 in (416 mm)
Diameter 5·94 in (151 mm)

Weights:
Dry 14·1 lb (6·4 kg)
Complete power plant including fuel tank 22 lb (10·0 kg)

Artist's impression of the Dreher TJD-79A Baby Python turbojet

Performance Ratings:
 Max 55 lb (25 kg) st
 Continuous 45 lb (20 kg) st
Specific Fuel Consumption:
 at max rating 1·5
Oil Consumption: at max rating 25 cc/min

DREHER TJD-76D and E

These versions were derived from the TJD-76C in 1972 to meet a need for a very low-cost short-life unit for the propulsion of small drones and other expendable vehicles. Both have similar performance to the TJD-76C but weigh approximately 9·9 lb (4·5 kg).

During 1973 the Beucher Development Corporation (2226 W 9th Street, Chester, Pa 19013) was tooling-up to make TJD-76E engines in quantity. Enquiries regarding production TJD-76E engines should be addressed to that corporation.

DREHER TJD-79A BABY PYTHON

Derived from the Baby Mamba, this enlarged unit is still in the component-testing stage, but work on it will shortly be accelerated.

Type: Single-shaft turbojet.
Air Intake: At front. Air mass flow 2·4 lb (1·1 kg)/sec.
Compressor: Single-stage, mixed-flow. Precision-cast 356-T-6 aluminium alloy impeller with 18 vanes. Made in one piece with shaft and supported in ball bearing. Mixed-flow cascade-type diffuser of 321 stainless steel. Pressure ratio 3 : 1.
Combustion Chamber: Annular type with Inconel 625 casing and Hastelloy X flame tube. Vaporising system with fuel/air pre-mix chamber. One spark plug in flame tube.
Fuel System: Semi-automatic with pressurised supply or electrically-driven pump; fully automatic feed for drone application.
Fuel Grade: Petrol or JO-5.
Nozzle Guide Vanes: Single axial stage with 18 vanes precision-cast in Stellite 31.
Turbine: Single-stage axial with disc and 21 blades cast as one unit in Inconel 713 LC. Gas temperature 805°C before turbine, 700°C behind.
Jet Pipe: Fixed type fabricated in Hastelloy X.

Dreher TJD-76C Baby Mamba turbojet (55 lb; 25 kg st)

Lubrication: Air/oil mist, total loss, using bleed air equivalent to 2·5 per cent of total flow. Capacity 2 litres.
Oil Grade: MIL-L-7808E or Jet-2.
Mounting: Two rigid connections on diffuser and one flexible connection on turbine section.
Starting: Compressed air (150 lb/sq in; 10·5 kg/cm²), via six nozzles driving turbine wheel.
Dimensions:
 Length overall 25·6 in (650 mm)
 Diameter 11 in (279·4 mm)
Weights (estimated):
 Dry 28 lb (12·7 kg)
 Complete with accessories 36 lb (16·3 kg)
Performance Rating:
 Max thrust (S/L, ISA) 120 lb (54·4 kg)
Specific Fuel Consumption:
 at max rating 1·4
Oil Consumption:
 at max rating 40 cc/min

FRANKLIN

FRANKLIN ENGINE COMPANY, INC
(Subsidiary of Allied Aero Industries, Inc)

Head Office and Works:
 PO Box 8, Syracuse, New York 13208
 Telephone: (313) 457-2200
President:
 Affonso G. F. Chaves
Vice-president and General Manager:
 Vincent J. Mecca

Known formerly as Aircooled Motors, Inc, this company adopted its present name in 1961 when its assets were purchased by Aero Industries Inc.

The original company produced the first of its very successful series of light horizontally-opposed aircooled engines in 1938. Up to the outbreak of war it had placed on the market engines of four and six cylinders ranging in output from 65 to 150 hp.

Until recently, production was restricted to six-cylinder engines in the 150-240 hp category. Now, the range of Franklin products is being broadened as quickly as possible to offer a completely new series of light horizontally-opposed piston engines for fixed-wing aircraft and helicopters. Details of current models are given in the accompanying tables.

The 125 hp Franklin 4A-235-B3

FRANKLIN HELICOPTER ENGINES

Engine Model	No. and arrangement of cylinders	Capacity cu in (cc)	Compression Ratio	Max T-O rating at sea level hp at rpm	Cruising specific fuel consumption per hp/hr lb (kg)	Fuel Grade	Overall Length in (mm)	Overall Width in (mm)	Overall Height in (mm)	Weight, Dry lb (kg)
6V4-200-C32,C33	6 Vert	335 (5,490)	8·5 : 1	200 at 3,100	0·52 (0·235)	91/96	30·67 (779)	31·3 (795)	38·14 (969)	320 (145)
6V-335-A, B	6 Vert	335 (5,490)	8·5 : 1	210 at 3,100	0·54 (0·245)	91/96	30·67 (779)	31·3 (795)	38·14 (969)	320 (145)
6V-335-A1A, A1B	6 Vert	335 (5,490)	7·0 : 1	200 at 3,100	0·52 (0·235)	80/87	30·67 (779)	31·3 (795)	38·14 (969)	320 (145)
6VS-335-A, B	6 Vert	335 (5,490)	7·0 : 1	240 at 3,200 S/L to 13,000 ft (4,000 m)	0·51 (0·23)	100/130	39·73 (1,009)	31·3 (795)	38·01 (965·4)	365 (165·5)
6V-350-A, B	6 Vert	350 (5,735)	10·5 : 1	235 at 3,200	0·46 (0·21)	100/130	30·67 (779)	31·3 (795)	38·14 (969)	307 (139)
6A-350-D1B	6 Horiz	350 (5,735)	10·5 : 1	230 at 3,200	0·46 (0·21)	100/130	32·5 (768·4)	31·3 (795)	25·25 (641)	319 (144·6)
6AS-335-A, B	6 Horiz	335 (5,490)	7·0 : 1	260 at 3,200 S/L to 10,000 ft (3,050 m)	0·51 (0·23)	100/130	34·5 (877)	31·3 (795)	27·5 (699)	347 (157)

FRANKLIN FIXED-WING AIRCRAFT ENGINES

Engine Model	No. and arrangement of cylinders	Capacity cu in (cc)	Compression Ratio	Max T-O rating at sea level hp at rpm	Cruising specific fuel consumption per hp/hr lb (kg)	Fuel Grade	Overall Length in (mm)	Overall Width in (mm)	Overall Height in (mm)	Weight, Dry lb (kg)
2A-120-C,D	2 Horiz	120 (1,965)	8·5 : 1	60 at 3,200	0·50 (0·227)	100/130	22·9 (581·5)	31·3 (795)	20·3 (515·5)	133 (60)
4A-235-B3	4 Horiz	235 (3,850)	8·5 : 1	125 at 2,800	0·49 (0·22)	100/130	29·4 (747)	31·3 (795)	25·1 (638)	240 (109)
4A-235-B	4 Horiz	235 (3,850)	8·5 : 1	130 at 2,800	0·50 (0·227)	100/130	30·5 (775)	31·3 (795)	25·1 (638)	225 (102)
6A-335-B, B1, B1A	6 Horiz	335 (5,490)	7·0 : 1	180 at 2,800	0·50 (0·227)	80/87	37·5 (953)	31·3 (795)	25·25 (641)	319 (144·5)
6A-350-C1, C1A	6 Horiz	350 (5,735)	10·5 : 1	220 at 2,800	0·46 (0·21)	100/130	37·5 (953)	31·3 (795)	25·25 (641)	329 (149)
6A-350-C2	6 Horiz	350 (5,735)	10·5 : 1	215 at 2,800	0·46 (0·21)	100/130	37·5 (953)	31·3 (795)	25·25 (641)	329 (149)
6AS-350-A	6 Horiz	350 (5,735)	7·4 : 1	250 at 2,800	0·50 (0·227)	100/130	43·2 (1,090)	34·2 (869)	38·7 (983)	377 (171)
6A4-165-B3, B4	6 Horiz	335 (5,490)	7·0 : 1	165 at 2,800	0·50 (0·227)	80/87	37·5 (953)	31·3 (795)	25·25 (641)	280 (127)
6A4-150-B3, B4	6 Horiz	335 (5,490)	7·0 : 1	150 at 2,600	0·50 (0·227)	80/87	37·5 (953)	31·3 (795)	22·6 (574)	277 (125·5)

GARRETT-AIRESEARCH

THE GARRETT CORPORATION

HEAD OFFICE:
9851 Sepulveda Boulevard, Los Angeles, California 90009
Telephone: (213) 776-1010

PRESIDENT:
Harry H. Wetzel

EXECUTIVE VICE-PRESIDENT:
James V. Crawford

EXECUTIVE VICE-PRESIDENT, SALES AND SERVICE:
William J. Pattison

GROUP VICE-PRESIDENT:
Ivan E. Speer

AIRESEARCH MANUFACTURING COMPANY OF ARIZONA (a division of The Garrett Corporation)

HEAD OFFICE AND WORKS:
Sky Harbor Airport, 402 South 36th Street, Phoenix, Arizona 85034
Telephone: (602) 267-3011

VICE-PRESIDENT AND MANAGER:
William Orr

SALES MANAGER:
R. Trusela

The Garrett Corporation's AiResearch Manufacturing Company of Arizona, at Phoenix, has been called the world's largest producer of small gas turbines. Development of the first AiResearch small turbines began in 1946 and the division has since produced about 80% of the total of gas-turbine units with power ratings from 60 to 2,500 hp built in America and Europe. These have been designed primarily to provide ground or airborne auxiliary power for starting and other aircraft services by means of compressed air, shaft power or a combination of compressed air and shaft power.

The first use of AiResearch turbines as prime movers occurred in 1957 when the McDonnell Aircraft Corporation used three GTC85 compressor turbines to power the Model 120 pressure-jet helicopter.

The GTC85 was described in the 1961-62 *Jane's*. It was followed by the Model 331, the first AiResearch engine designed specifically as an aircraft prime mover.

AiResearch began design and development of the Model 331, as a private venture, in December 1959, with the object of producing an engine suitable for use as a turboshaft for helicopters and as a turboprop for fixed-wing aircraft.

The first engine, the 500 shp TSE 331 turboshaft, was assembled and ready for initial testing by December 1960. Flight tests in a Republic Lark (licence-built Alouette II) helicopter began on 12 October 1961.

A description of the TSE 331 appeared in the 1964-65 *Jane's*. Production is now concentrated on the commercial TPE 331 and military T76 turboprop versions, as described below. The latest engines from the Arizona Division are the TSE 36 for light helicopters, the TSE 231 series, also for helicopters, and the TFE 731 and ATF 3 series of turbofan engines for the executive and commuter market.

Garrett also has development programmes in the low-cost, expendable engine field for propulsion applications in missiles and remotely piloted vehicles.

In 1973 Garrett consolidated its activities, concentrating all aircraft propulsion engines at AiResearch Manufacturing Co of Arizona. Previously the ATF 3 engine had been designed and initially developed at Los Angeles.

GARRETT-AIRESEARCH ATF 3

US military designation: XF104-GA-100

The Garrett-AiResearch ATF 3 is an advanced technology engine in the 4,000 lb to 6,000 lb (1,815-2,722 kg) thrust range. It is designed to provide, through its low fuel consumption, extended range for subsonic business or military aircraft, and, through its relatively high overall pressure ratio, flexible operation in high-altitude applications.

Considered to be the first three-spool engine to run in the United States, it is the first engine in the world to combine the three-spool feature with a reverse-flow combustion system and turbines, and mixed-flow exhaust.

The arrangement of components allows the fan design to be determined largely independently of the gas-generator compressor requirements, and permits operation at optimum fan speed. Omission of fan inlet guide vanes, mixing of the gas-generator exhaust with the fan airflow, and double reversal of the internal airflow enable the ATF 3 to offer significant reductions in overall noise generation.

Other design considerations include reliability, maintainability and elimination of visible smoke. The accessories are revealed by removing the tailcone fairing, and their positioning at the rear of the engine is claimed to reduce installed drag.

The conceptual design of the ATF 3 took place in early 1966, and testing of demonstrator engines was initiated in May 1968. Under US Air Force contract, the ATF 3 successfully completed preliminary flight rating tests in 1972 at 4,050 lb (1,837 kg) thrust. Testing also has been accomplished at 5,000 lb (2,270 kg) thrust. Both the aerodynamic and mechanical design criteria were established around a sea-level, ISA +15°C take-off rating of 5,000 lb (2,270 kg). Work is continuing on development of the ATF 3 for both military and civilian applications.

In 1973 the XF104 was chosen to power fly-off models of the Ryan Compass Cope RPV. The engine is especially well suited to such an application in view of its very low infra-red and noise signatures, capability for operation at very high altitude, and the ease with which the control system can be integrated with microcircuit guidance and telemetry. The Compass Cope R engine is flat-rated at 4,050 lb (1,837 kg), though considerably greater thrust could be obtained. The reduced thrust is matched with large shaft-power extraction and other special features. Extensive USAF altitude testing of this engine brought total XF104/ATF 3 running time at the end of 1973 to 2,500 hours, plus 12,000 hr rig testing.

TYPE: Three-shaft axial-flow turbofan.

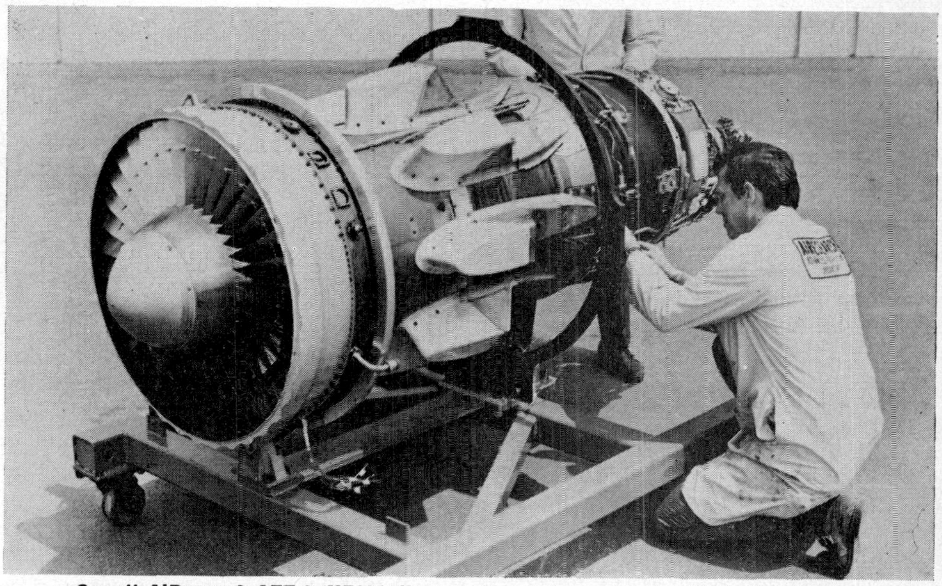

Garrett-AiResearch ATF 3 (XF104) three-shaft turbofan, rated at 4,050 lb (1,837 kg) st

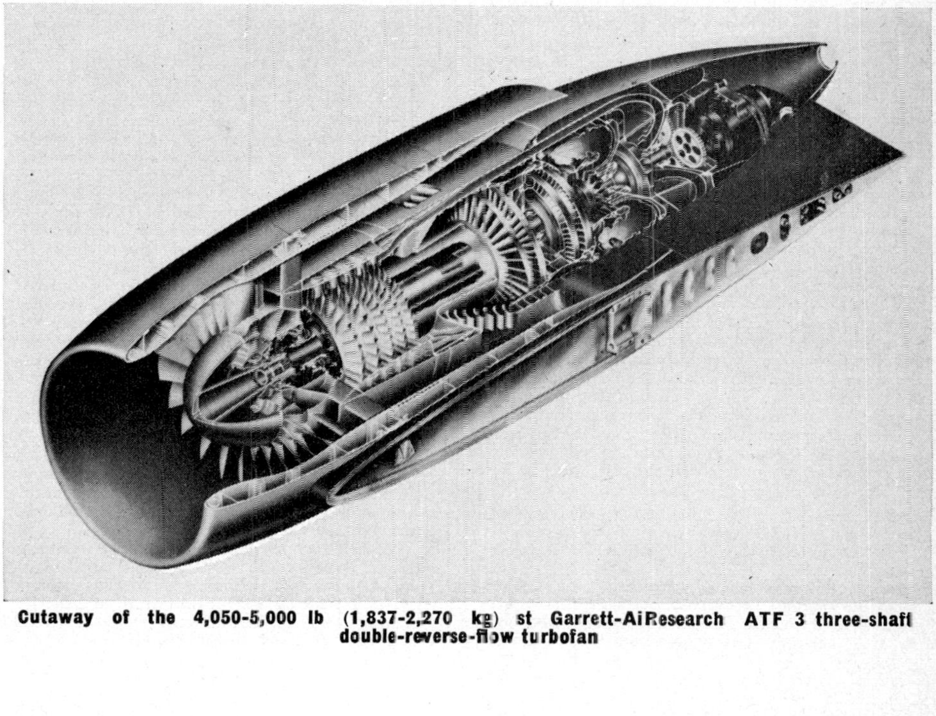

Cutaway of the 4,050-5,000 lb (1,837-2,270 kg) st Garrett-AiResearch ATF 3 three-shaft double-reverse-flow turbofan

Intake: Direct pitot, fixed type. Total airflow 162 lb/sec (73·5 kg/sec).

Low-Pressure (Fan) System: Single-stage titanium fan, driven by three-stage IP turbine. One thrust bearing and one roller bearing support independent LP shaft. By-pass ratio 3 : 1 at take-off.

Intermediate-Pressure System: Five-stage titanium axial compressor, each stage having a separate disc, driven by two-stage LP turbine. Airflow is delivered to the rearward-facing HP compressor via eight tubes feeding into an annular duct concentric with the by-pass duct. One thrust bearing and one roller bearing support independent IP shaft. Core airflow 40 lb (18·15 kg)/sec.

High-Pressure System: Single-stage titanium centrifugal compressor, driven by single-stage HP turbine. Airflow at rear enters the single-sided impeller and thence the combustion system. One thrust bearing and one roller bearing support the independent HP shaft. Overall pressure ratio 22-24 : 1.

Combustion System: Reverse-flow annular type.

Turbines: Single-stage HP, three-stage IP and two-stage LP turbines drive, respectively, the HP, fan (LP) and IP compressors. IP and LP turbines have fully shrouded blades. Air-cooled first-stage nozzle vanes and HP rotor blades. Exhaust gases expelled through eight sets of cascades to mix with fan by-pass flow.

Fuel System: Electromechanical, incorporating a solid-state computer. Manual engine control is provided as a backup system in case of failure of the primary fuel control.

Accessory Drives: Three drive pads on rear-mounted gearbox driven by HP shaft, providing for a hydraulic pump drive, starter/generator drive and one spare. Accessory cooling by fan discharge air which is then exhausted through a separate nozzle at the tip of the fairing.

Exhaust System: Mixed fan and turbine exhaust flow passes to atmosphere through annular nozzle surrounding combustion section.

Lubrication System: Self-contained hot-tank type; tank integral with gearbox.

Mounting: Twoplane pickup system.

Starting: Electrical or pneumatic.

Dimensions:

Length overall	98·25 in (2,496 mm)
Max diameter	32·78 in (833 mm)

Weight, Dry:

Bare	approx 900 lb (408 kg)

Performance Rating:

T-O rating (S/L, ISA static) 4,050 lb (1,837 kg) st

Specific Fuel Consumption:

At T-O rating (S/L, ISA static) approx 0·45

GARRETT-AIRESEARCH TFE 731

Announced in April 1969, the TFE 731 is a two-spool geared front-fan engine designed to confer US coast-to-coast range upon business jet aircraft. Use of a geared fan is expected to confer flexibility in operation and to yield optimum performance both at low altitudes and at up to 50,000 ft (15,250 m).

The LP spool of the 3,500 lb (1,587 kg) thrust-class TFE 731-2 is made up of a three-stage turbine driving a four-stage compressor aerodynamically derived from the GTCP 660 APU in service in the Boeing 747. The HP spool consists of a single-stage turbine driving a single-stage centrifugal compressor derived from that of the TPE 331/T76 turboprop engine.

The by-pass ratio is 2·82 : 1 at 40,000 ft and Mach 0·8. The TFE 731 has single-lever control and is designed to be capable of using a thrust reverser. The accessory group is located on the underside, driven from the high-pressure spool. Two features which reduce exterior noise are the elimination of fan intake guide vanes and the optimised gap between the fan blades and the fan stator vanes, added to the basic low noise inherent in a high by-pass ratio.

Component testing began in March 1969; the first engine ran in September 1970, and was tested at Phoenix in a Learjet 25 (illustrated in 1972-73 *Jane's*). FAA certification and first production deliveries to Dassault for the Falcon 10 took place in August 1972. The TFE 731-2 also has been selected for the Learjet 35/36 business jets.

In October 1972 it was announced the Lockheed JetStar would be re-engined with the TFE 731-3, flat-rated at 3,700 lb (1,678 kg) st by a modest increase in turbine inlet temperature. This engine was scheduled for FAA certification in May 1974. The modified aircraft is designated JetStar II. AiResearch Aviation Co is to convert a number of JetStar I aircraft to have TFE 731-3 power. It is also reported that versions of the TFE 731 have been proposed for RPV and other short-life military applications.

Type: Turbofan with two shafts and geared front fan.

Air Intake: Direct pitot, fixed, without guide vanes.

Fan: Single-stage axial titanium fan, with inserted blades. Mounted on a simple shaft supported by a roller bearing, located under the fan disc, and by a ball-thrust bearing. The fan shaft is connected directly to the planetary gearbox ring gear. Max fan airflow, sea level static, 113 lb (51·25 kg)/sec. By-pass ratio 2·66.

Compressor: Low-pressure compressor has four stages, each with a separate disc. Rotors and stators have inserted blades and vanes. High-pressure compressor, carried on a separate shaft running at higher speeds, is centrifugal. Overall pressure ratio is 19 : 1 at Mach 0·8 at 40,000 ft. Corrected core airflow, sea level static, is 22 lb (10 kg)/sec.

Combustion Chamber: Annular combustion chamber of reverse-flow type, with 12 fuel nozzles inserted radially and injecting fuel tangentially.

Fuel System: Hydro-electronic, with single-lever control to mechanical and electronic elements.

Turbine: High-pressure turbine has a single axial stage with inserted blades. Low-pressure turbine has three axial stages, all with inserted blades. Average inlet gas temperature to HP turbine, S/L, max T-O thrust, 1,010°C.

Shafting: High-pressure spool consists of HP turbine and HP compressor, mounted on shaft supported by one roller bearing and one ball bearing. This spool drives the accessory gearbox through a tower shaft transfer gearbox system. Low-pressure spool consists of the LP turbine and the LP compressor. It is composed of separate components interconnected by curvic couplings and simply supported on one ball bearing at the compressor end and one roller bearing at the turbine end. LP spool drives the fan shaft through a quill shaft and a planetary gear reduction system. Overall gear ratio is 0·555 : 1.

Jet Pipe: Short fan duct with cool discharge around remainder of engine, facilitating installation of fan reverser. Hot gas pipe at rear, with fixed nozzle of minimum length.

Accessory Drives: Accessories driven from HP spool are grouped around underside of the forward section of the fan duct. Pads are provided on the front side of the accessory gearbox for the airframe-type accessories: hydraulic pump, starter/generator or starter motor and alternators. Pads on the back side of the gearbox drive the engine accessories: fuel control unit and oil pump.

Dimensions:

Intake diameter	28·2 in (716 mm)
Length overall	49·73 in (1,263 mm)
Width	34·20 in (869 mm)
Height overall	39·07 in (992 mm)

Weight, Dry:

Basic engine	710 lb (322 kg)

Performance Ratings:

Max T-O (S/L, ISA), static	3,500 lb (1,587 kg)
Cruise rating, 40,000 ft (12,190 m), Mach 0·8 ISA	755 lb (342 kg)

Specific Fuel Consumption (ISA):

S/L, static	0·49
40,000 ft (12,200 m), Mach 0·8	0·815

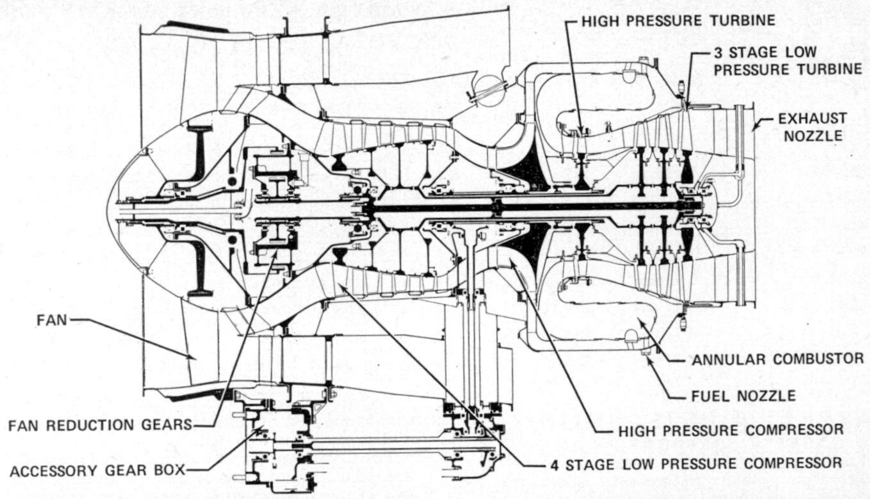

Cross-section (*top*) and external view (*above*) of the 3,500 lb (1,587 kg) st Garrett-AiResearch TFE 731 geared front-fan engine

GARRETT-AIRESEARCH ETJ 331

This expendable turbojet is intended for use in a range of military applications including RPVs, drones and missiles. It has been under development since late 1971.

Details remain classified, though the photograph reveals what appears to be a three-stage axial compressor, without inlet guide vanes, and an annular combustion chamber. It had previously been reported unofficially that the ETJ 331 has single-shot starting and lubrication. It is planned for ratings in the range 500-1,000 lb (227-454 kg) st, and has very low-cost features commensurate with expendable and limited-life applications.

GARRETT-AIRESEARCH TSE 36-1

In July 1968 Garrett-AiResearch announced its entry into the helicopter turboshaft market with the 240 shp TSE 36-1, which was FAA certificated in April 1970.

Garrett-AiResearch ETJ 331 expendable turbojet, to be rated in the range 500-1,000 lb (227-454 kg) st

Derived from the AiResearch GTCP 36 auxiliary power unit, the new turboshaft is of single-shaft design, with a single-stage centrifugal compressor, single combustion chamber, and single-stage radial inflow turbine. Weight is approximately 165 lb (74·8 kg). Approved fuels include jet types A, A-1, B and JP-4, but operation is possible on truck diesel fuel or clean kerosene.

The TSE 36 is intended as a turbine replacement for piston engines in the 150 to 250 hp range, and has been test flown in Hughes 269A and Enstrom F-28 helicopters. Substitution for the original piston engine of the Hughes 269A saved 184 lb (83·5 kg) in weight despite the increase of 40 hp. The hover ceiling rose from 6,000 ft (1,830 m) to over 14,000 ft (4,265 m).

Throughout the design attention has been paid to robust structure likely to withstand harsh use. Prototype engines have survived severe ingestion tests with bolts, ice, slush, rags and sand. AiResearch further claim exceptionally fast response to power change demands. Manual starting is possible.

Type: Light turboshaft engine with integral gearbox.

Power Drive: Two-stage reduction, first-stage spur, second-stage helical. Driven through quill shaft from front of compressor.

Air Intake: Free inward radial flow between gearcase and front of compressor.

Compressor: Single-entry centrifugal stage. Impeller machined from titanium with 17 integral vanes. Driven through splined shaft, with tie-bolted coupling. Shaft supported in ball bearing in rear of gearcase and roller bearing in turbine section. Aluminium shroud and stainless steel compressor housing. Mass flow 2·8 lb (1·27 kg)/sec. Pressure ratio, 4·26 : 1.

Combustion Chamber: Single, reverse-flow, with stainless steel outer casing. Perforated can-type flame tube located tangentially on aft section of turbine plenum. Single spark igniter mounted radially in primary zone and rated for continuous duty.

Fuel System: Hydromechanical type. Single spur gear pump, flow divider nozzle, hydraulic on-speed governor and pneumatic overspeed governor, dual-purpose shut-off valve for acceleration, scheduling and normal power.

Fuel Grades: Jet fuel A, A-1, B, JP-4, JP-5, MIL-T-5624G-1, Avtur ASTM D1655T (emergency, 80 to 145 grade petrol or diesel oil).

Nozzle Guide Vanes: Radial inward-flow segments (13), cast in Inco 713C.

Turbine: Radial inward-flow, precision cast in Inco 713C with integral vanes. Pinned interference fit on main shaft with roller type bearing between turbine and compressor. Gas temperature 912°C before turbine, 630°C behind.

Accessory Drives: AND 20001 Type XI-C, CCW 12,021 rpm; AND 20005 Type XV-B, CW 4,193 rpm; on gearcase, tacho-generator, DC starter pad. Additional equipment includes 4% electrically-actuated bleed system, hydraulic force-balance torque-sensor, automatic start kit and monopole speed pickup.

Lubrication System: Wet-sump type. Gerotor pressure and scavenge pumps, capacity 3-4 US quarts (2·8-3·7 litres), pressure 100 lb/sq in (7 kg/cm²).

Oil Specification: MIL-L-23699A, —40° to 96°C, MIL-L-7808D or 7808F, —40° to 79·5°C.

Mounting Points: Two on gearbox, one on power section, resilient or rigid.

Starting: 28V DC starter/generator on 12,000 rpm pad.

Dimensions:

Length	35·9 in (912 mm)
Width	27·9 in (708·7 mm)
Height	21·8 in (553·7 mm)

Weight, Dry:

With accessories required for engine to run 178 lb (80·74 kg)

Performance Ratings:

Max take-off	240 shp
Max continuous	220 shp

Specific Fuel Consumption:

Take-off	0·83 lb (0·376 kg)/shp/hr
Max continuous	0·84 lb (0·38 kg)/shp/hr

Oil Consumption: negligible

GARRETT-AIRESEARCH TSE 231-1

The TSE 231-1 is a 474 shp turboshaft engine for use in advanced helicopters. The development was initiated in September 1969; first full engine run came in September 1970 and first run in testbed helicopter followed in December 1970. Flight development has been proceeding since May 1971.

The engine is of the free-turbine type with front-end drive. The compressor section is scaled down from the compressor of the successful and robust T76-G-10. The combustion section is of the reverse-flow annular type and the turbine section consists of a single-stage axial gas-generator turbine and a single-stage axial power turbine.

Type: Free-turbine turboshaft engine with front-end drive.

Power Drive: Two-stage reduction gear: first-stage spur gear and second-stage helical. Output shaft is offset below engine centreline, driven from power turbine through shafting concentric inside the gas-generator shafting. The power turbine shafting is supported at the power turbine and an inter-shaft bearing. Both shafts rotate in the same direction. The output pad is an internal spline of 1·2 in pitch diameter with fore-and-aft take-off.

Air Intake: Free inward-radial-flow duct between gearcase and front of compressor.

Compressor: Two-stage centrifugal type. Tandem single-sided titanium impellers are attached to shaft through curvic couplings. First-stage housing of magnesium, second-stage housing and diffuser of stainless steel. Pressure ratio 8·9 : 1. Mass flow 4·1 lb (1·86 kg)/sec.

Combustion Chamber: Annular reverse-flow type with outer case of stainless steel and flame tube of high-temperature stainless steel. Ten radially-mounted simplex nozzles.

Fuel System: Hydromechanical control. Two-stage fuel pump: low-pressure pump is ejector type, high-pressure stage is gear type. Control system includes power-turbine governor and gas-generator governor. Provision is made for manual operation.

Fuel Grades: Jet fuel A, A-1, B, JP-4, JP-5; emergency operation with Avgas 80/87 authorised.

Turbines: Single-stage gas-generator turbine with individual blades cast in IN 100 and inserted into forged disc. Individual cooled nozzle guide vanes of INCO 713LC. Power-turbine nozzle is integral casting of INCO 713LC; single-stage rotor is also integral casting of INCO 713LC. Gas-generator turbine outlet temperature is 762°C.

Accessory Drives: Starter/generator pad AND 2001, Type XI-C modified at 12,060 rpm. Designed to accommodate 250A starter.

Lubrication System: Dry sump system with internal gerotor pressure and scavenge pumps. Normal oil pressure 100 lb/sq in (7 kg/cm²).

Oil Specification: MIL-L-23699K, —40° to 110°C; MIL-L-7808D or 7808F, —40° to 79·5°C.

Mounting: Three-point suspension on gearcase. Four pads available for choice relative to installation.

Bell JetRanger flying with Garrett-AiResearch TSE 231 turboshaft engine, rated at 474 shp

The 240 shp Garrett-AiResearch TSE 36-1 turboshaft for helicopters, shown in cutaway form

DIMENSIONS:

Length	41 in (1,014 mm)
Width	28 in (711 mm)
Height	22·5 in (560 mm)

WEIGHT, DRY:

Equipped	171 lb (67·5 kg)

PERFORMANCE RATINGS (S/L, ISA, static):

Take-off	474 shp
Max continuous	403 shp

SPECIFIC FUEL CONSUMPTION:

Take-off	0·605 lb (0·27 kg)/shp/hr
Max continuous	0·619 lb (0·28 kg)/shp/hr

OIL CONSUMPTION:

Maximum	0·3 lb (0·14 kg)/hr

GARRETT-AIRESEARCH TPE 331

US military designation: T76

The first commercial version of this turboprop received FAA Type Approval in February 1965. In December 1967, two higher-rated additions to the TPE 331 family received FAA approval, the TPE 331-1 rated at 665 shp, and the TPE 331-2 rated at 715 shp. Initial TBO was 1,500 hours and in commuter airline use has increased to 4,200 hours. A higher-rated addition, the TPE 331-3, rated at 840 shp, has received FAA certification and is used as the power plant of the Swearingen Metro, MU-2J and -2K and Rockwell 690 and 690A. The TSE 331 turboshaft version is described separately.

The new models are of the same external dimensions as the basic TPE 331. The higher ratings are attained by means of an increased air mass flow and higher component efficiencies.

Models now in production are the TPE 331 series I and II rated at 575 shp, the TPE 331-1 series rated at 665 shp, the TPE 331-2 series rated at 715 shp, and the TPE 331-3 series rated at 840 shp. Applications include the Mitsubishi MU-2, Rockwell Turbo Hawk Commander, Fairchild Industries Porter, Pilatus Turbo-Porter, Volpar Super Turbo 18 and Turbo Liner conversions of the Beechcraft 18, Carstedt Jet Liner 600 Dove conversion, Shorts Skyvan 3, Aerospace (Fletcher) Model 1160, DHC-2 Turbo-Beaver, Conroy Stolifter, Interceptor 400, FMA IA 58 Pucará, CASA 212 and the Swearingen Merlin IIB, III and IV, and FS-226 Metro.

The military version, designated T76, powers the Rockwell International OV-10 Bronco counter-insurgency aircraft and exists in two production configurations:

T76-G-10. Propeller rotates clockwise when viewed from rear of engine. Rated at 715 shp.

T76-G-12. Propeller rotates anti-clockwise when viewed from rear. Rated at 715 shp.

Both of these models of the T76 have a single scoop air intake at the top front of the engine, directly above the gearbox.

The TPE 331 and T76 are of similar frame size, and the following data apply generally to both models:

TYPE: Single-shaft turboprop engine with integral gearbox.

PROPELLER DRIVE: Two-stage reduction gear, one helical spur and one planetary, with overall ratio of 20·865 : 1 or 26·3 : 1. Shaft, driven from single-spool compressor, is carried in ball and roller bearings. Rotation clockwise or anti-clockwise, as required.

AIR INTAKE: Single scoop intake duct at top or bottom of engine, at front. Provision for bleed air de-icing.

COMPRESSOR: Tandem two-stage centrifugal type. Each impeller is single-sided, and is made from titanium. Impellers attached to shaft by curvic couplings. First-stage casing of magnesium, with aluminium diffuser. Second-stage casing and diffuser of stainless steel. Pressure ratio 8·5 : 1 for T76; 8·0 : 1 for TPE 331 series I and II; 8·5 : 1 for TPE 331-1; 8·5 : 1 for TPE 331-2; 10·4 : 1 for TPE 331-3. Mass flow, S/L static, 7·7 lb (3·49 kg)/sec.

COMBUSTION CHAMBER: Annular type of high-temperature alloy. High-energy capacitor discharge ignition. Igniter plug on turbine plenum.

FUEL SYSTEM: Woodward or Bendix control system for use with Beta propeller governing control system. Five radial primary nozzles in continuous operation. Ten axial simplex nozzles. Max fuel pressure 600 lb/sq in (42·2 kg/cm²).

FUEL GRADE (TPE 331): Aviation turbine fuels ASTM designation D1655-64T types Jet A, Jet B and Jet A-1; MIL-F-5616-1, Grade JP-1.

FUEL GRADE (T76): MIL-J-5624F(2), Grades JP-4 and JP-5; MIL-G-5572, Grade 115/145.

NOZZLE GUIDE VANES: Axial vanes made from Inco 713C castings.

TURBINE: Three-stage axial-flow type. Discs of first two stages of Inco 100, third stage of Inco 713C, attached to shaft by curvic couplings. Blades cast integrally with disc. Turbine inlet gas temperature 1,004°C.

BEARINGS: One ball bearing at compressor end of shaft, one roller bearing at turbine end.

JET PIPE: Fixed type. Cone and jet pipe both of stainless steel.

ACCESSORIES: AND 20005 Type XV-B tachometer generator, AND 20002 Type XII-D starter/generator, AND 20010 Type XX-A propeller governor and AND 20001 Type XI-B hydraulic pump, all mounted on aft face of accessories case.

Cutaway drawing of the 474 shp Garrett-AiResearch TSE 231 turboshaft engine

Garrett-AiResearch TPE 331 series commercial turboprop engine

LUBRICATION SYSTEM: Medium-pressure dry sump system. Gerotor internal gear-type pressure and scavenge pumps. Normal oil supply pressure 100 lb/sq in (7·03 kg/cm²). Provision for automatic fuel filter anti-icing.

OIL SPECIFICATION: MIL-L-23699-(1) or MIL-L-7808.

MOUNTING: Five-point suspension. Three pads on aft face of accessories case, two pads at aft end of turbine plenum.

STARTING: Pad for 300A starter/generator on aft face of accessory case.

DIMENSIONS (approximate):

Length overall:	
TPE 331	43 to 46 in (1,092-1,168 mm)
T76	44 in (1,118 mm)
Width:	
TPE 331	21 in (533 mm)
T76	19 in (483 mm)
Height:	
TPE 331	26 in (660 mm)
T76	27 in (686 mm)

WEIGHT, DRY:

TPE 331	335 lb (152 kg)
T76-G-10/12	336 lb (152 kg)

PERFORMANCE RATINGS:

T-O:	
TPE 331 srs I, II	575 shp (605 ehp)
TPE 331-1	665 shp (705 ehp)
TPE 331-2	715 shp (755 ehp)
TPE 331-3	840 shp (904 ehp)
TPE 331-5	715 shp (776 ehp)
Military (30 min):	
T76-G-10/12	715 shp (755 ehp)
Max continuous:	
TPE 331 srs I, II	500 shp (529 ehp)
TPE 331-1	665 shp (705 ehp)
TPE 331-2	715 shp (755 ehp)
TPE 331-3	840 shp (904 ehp)
TPE 331-5	715 shp (776 ehp)
Normal:	
T76-G-10/12	650 shp (690 ehp)
Max cruise:	
TPE 331 srs I, II	475 shp (500 ehp)
TPE 331-1	609 shp (648 ehp)
TPE 331-2	650 shp (690 ehp)
TPE 331-3	770 shp (832 ehp)
TPE 331-5	715 shp (776 ehp)

SPECIFIC FUEL CONSUMPTION:

At T-O rating:	
TPE 331 srs I, II	0·66 lb (0·30 kg)/shp/hr
TPE 331-1	0·61 lb (0·276 kg)/shp/hr
TPE 331-2	0·59 lb (0·268 kg)/shp/hr
TPE 331-3	0·59 lb (0·268 kg)/shp/hr
T76-G-10/12	0·60 lb (0·27 kg)/shp/hr

OIL CONSUMPTION:

Max	0·02 lb (0·009 kg)/hr

GARRETT-AIRESEARCH TSE 331-3U

On 20 April 1970, Garrett-AiResearch was awarded an FAA Type Certificate for the TSE 331-3U turboshaft engine, which is a derivative of the Model TPE 331-3 (840 shp) turboprop. It is a fixed-shaft engine, rated at 800 shp for take-off, and is used to power the Sikorsky S-55 helicopter conversion certificated by Aviation Specialties Inc of Mesa, Arizona, and redesignated S-55T. In this application the TSE 331-3U is flat-rated at 700 shp.

TYPE: Single-shaft turboshaft with front end drive.

POWER DRIVE: Two-stage reduction gear, one helical spur and one planetary, with overall ratio of 16·410 : 1. Output shaft rotation is clockwise, looking forward from rear of engine, and has a bolted flange attachment.

AIR INTAKE: Single scoop intake duct at top front of engine. Provision for bleed air anti-icing.

COMPRESSOR: Two-stage centrifugal. Tandem, single-sided titanium impellers are attached to the shaft by curvic couplings. First-stage casing of magnesium with aluminium diffuser. Second-stage casing and diffuser of stainless steel. Pressure ratio 10·32 : 1.

COMBUSTION CHAMBER: Annular type of high-temperature alloy. High-energy capacitor discharge ignition. Igniter plug on turbine plenum.

FUEL SYSTEM: Woodward fuel control for automatic speed control and fuel metering to match engine power to rotor load. Fuel filter, fuel shut-off valve, fuel-flow divider and manifold drain valve, fuel manifold and nozzle assemblies (five primary, ten secondary), start-fuel system and fuel anti-ice system.

FUEL GRADE: Aviation turbine fuels ASTM designation D1655-68T, Types Jet A, A-1, and B, MIL-T-5624G-1, Grades JP-4 and JP-5, MIL-F-5161-1, Grade JP-1.

NOZZLE GUIDE VANES: Axial vanes made from Inco 713C castings.

TURBINE: Three-stage axial-flow type. Discs of first two stages of Inco 100, third stage of Inco 713C, attached to shaft by curvic couplings. Blades cast integrally with disc.

BEARINGS: One ball bearing at compressor end of shaft, one roller bearing at turbine end.

Exhaust Duct: Fixed type. Cone and jet pipe both of stainless steel.

Accessories: AND 20005 Type XV-B tachometer generator, AND 20002 Type XII-D starter/generator, AND 20001 Type XI-B hydraulic pump, all mounted on aft face of accessories case.

Lubrication System: Medium-pressure dry sump system. Gerotor internal gear type pressure and scavenge pumps. Normal oil supply pressure 100 lb/sq in (7·03 kg/cm²). Provision for automatic fuel filter anti-icing.

Oil Specification: MIL-L-23699A or MIL-L-7808D.

Mounting: Five-point suspension. Three pads on aft face of accessories case, two pads at aft end of turbine plenum.

Starting: Pad for 300A starter/generator on aft face of accessory case.

Dimensions (approximate):

Length overall	44 in (1,118 mm)
Width	21 in (533 mm)
Height	27 in (686 mm)

Weight, Dry: 355 lb (161 kg)

Performance Ratings:

Take-off	800 shp (862 ehp)
Max continuous	700 shp (750 ehp)

Specific Fuel Consumption:

Take-off	0·59 lb (0·268 kg)/shp/hr

Oil Consumption:

Maximum	0·02 lb (0·009 kg)/hr

GENERAL ELECTRIC

GENERAL ELECTRIC COMPANY AIRCRAFT ENGINE GROUP

Headquarters:
1000 Western Avenue, West Lynn, Massachusetts 01905
Telephone: (617) 594-0100

Aero Engine Works:
Lynn and Everett, Massachusetts; Cincinnati, Ohio; Rutland and Ludlow, Vermont; Hooksett, New Hampshire; and Albuquerque, New Mexico. Also test facilities at Edwards Air Force Base, California, and Peebles, Ohio. Further facilities at Seattle, Washington; Arkansas City, Kansas; Ontario, California

Vice-President and Group Executive:
Gerhard Neumann

Military Engine Division:
Vice-President and General Manager:
James E. Worsham

Commercial Engine Division:
Vice-President and General Manager:
Brian H. Rowe

Group Engineering Division:
Vice-President and General Manager:
Edward Woll

Group Manufacturing Division:
Vice-President and General Manager:
Raymond E. Letts

Marine and Industrial Project Department:
General Manager: O. R. Bonner

Group Strategic Planning Operation:
Vice-President: Fred O. MacFee, Jr

Group Product Quality Operation:
General Manager: Robert H. Goldsmith

Group Finance and Management Support Operation:
Manager: E. F. Roache

Group Legal Operation:
Manager: James W. Sack

The General Electric Company entered the gas-turbine field in about 1895. Years of pioneering effort by the late Dr Sanford A. Moss produced the aircraft turbosupercharger, successfully tested at height in 1918 and mass-produced in the second World War for US fighters and bombers.

The company built its first aircraft gas turbine in 1941, when it began development of Whittle-type turbojets, under an arrangement between the British and American governments.

Current products of the Aircraft Engine Group include the J79, J85, T58, T64 and TF34 for the military services, and the CT58, CT64, CJ610 and CF700 for the commercial airliner and business aircraft market. General Electric is also producing the CF6 turbofan for the McDonnell Douglas DC-10 three-engined transport, the Boeing 747-300 and the Airbus Industrie A 300B; the T700 turboshaft for the US Army; the F101 turbofan for the Rockwell B-1; and the J101 by-pass turbojet for the Northrop YF-17 lightweight fighter.

In January 1968, as part of a series of major changes to the corporate structure, General Electric's Flight Propulsion Division (one of four divisions forming the company's previous Aerospace and Defence Group), which hitherto had been responsible for all GE's aero-engine work, was promoted to become one of the 10 operating groups now comprising General Electric. This change in organisation was aimed at strengthening GE's civil and military aircraft engine activities in the domestic US and international markets.

GENERAL ELECTRIC J85

The following versions of the J85 lightweight turbojet are currently in production or under development:

J85-4A. Powers the Rockwell International T-2C Buckeye trainer and Teledyne Ryan MQM-34D Mod II target RPV.

J85-5. Afterburning version with 6·8 : 1 thrust-to-weight ratio; powers Northrop T-38 Talon supersonic trainer. Unaugmented version powered two VTOL research aircraft, the Bell X-14A and the Ryan XV-5B with wing-mounted GE lift-fans.

J85-13. Higher-powered version with afterburner for Northrop F-5A/B supersonic fighter. As the J85-13A, licence-built by Alfa Romeo, also powers the Aeritalia G91Y.

J85-15. Higher-rated version of J85-13, to power CF-5A/B fighters. Manufactured under licence in Canada by Orenda.

J85-17. Higher-rated version powering the Saab 105G attack/reconnaissance aircraft and Cessna A-37B attack aircraft. Also used as take-off and climb booster for Fairchild C-123K and AC-119K.

J85-21. Higher airflow version with zero stage to give total of nine compressor stages. Equipped with afterburner for advanced supersonic aircraft. Qualification testing completed in 1972. In production for Northrop F-5E Tiger II.

J85/J1. Non-afterburning derivative with nine-stage compressor.

Civil version of the J85 is the CJ610 turbojet, to which the aft-fan CF700 turbofan is closely related. Both are described separately.

The following data refer specifically to the J85-5 and -13, except where otherwise stated:

Type: Variable-stator axial-flow single-shaft turbojet.

Air Intake: Annular type, surrounding central bullet fairing. Variable-incidence inlet guide vanes, which are anti-iced on J85-5, -13 and -21.

Compressor: Eight-stage axial-flow type (nine stages in -21 and /J1). No shaft, each disc being connected to adjoining disc. Compressor casing in two halves. Pressure ratio approximately 7 : 1 (8 : 1 in -21 and /J1). Air mass flow 44 lb/sec (20 kg/sec) (52·5 lb; 23·8 kg/sec in -21 and /J1).

Combustion Chamber: Annular type with perforated liner. Twelve duplex fuel injectors. Ports in outer casing facilitate inspection of liner.

Turbine: Two-stage axial-flow type. Casing is in halves, split horizontally.

Afterburner (J85-5, -13, -15, -21): Consists of a diffuser and a combustor. A pilot burner with four spraybars and a main burner of 12 spraybars are located in the diffuser section. Combustion is initiated by a single igniter plug and is then self-sustained. Nozzle position governs exit area and is regulated automatically by the afterburner control system as a function of turbine exit temperature and throttle lever position.

Lubrication: Positive displacement, pressurised recirculating type.

Starting: Air impingement starter.

Dimensions:

Length overall:

J85-4	40·50 in (1,029 mm)
J85-5 with afterburner	104·6 in (2,657 mm)
J85-13, -15 with afterburner	105·6 in (2,682 mm)
J85-17	40·5 in (1,039 mm)
J85-21	112·5 in (2,858 mm)
J85/J1	46·7 in (1,186 mm)

Max diameter:

J85-4	17·7 in (450 mm)
J85-5, -13, -21	21·0 in (533 mm)
J85-17	17·7 in (450 mm)
J85/J1	20·0 in (508 mm)

Weight, Dry:

J85-4	404 lb (183 kg)
J85-5	584 lb (265 kg)
J85-13	597 lb (271 kg)
J85-15	615 lb (279 kg)
J85-17	398 lb (181 kg)
J85-21	675 lb (306 kg)
J85/J1	445 lb (202 kg)

Performance Ratings:

Max rating, with afterburner:

J85-5	3,850 lb (1,748 kg) st
J85-13	4,080 lb (1,850 kg) st
J85-15	4,300 lb (1,950 kg) st
J85-21	5,000 lb (2,268 kg) st

Military rating, without afterburner:

J85-4	2,950 lb (1,339 kg) st
J85-5	2,680 lb (1,215 kg) st
J85-13	2,720 lb (1,234 kg) st
J85-17	2,850 lb (1,293 kg) st
J85-21	3,500 lb (1,588 kg) st
J85/J1	3,600 lb (1,633 kg) st

General Electric J85-21 turbojet (5,000 lb; 2,268 kg st with afterburning)

General Electric CJ610-4 (2,850 lb; 1,293 kg st) and *(right)* CJ610-5 (2,950 lb; 1,340 kg st) turbojet engines

SPECIFIC FUEL CONSUMPTION:
At max rating:
J85-17 0·99
J85/J1 0·98
At max rating, with afterburner:
J85-5 2·20
J85-13 2·22
J85-15 2·18
J85-21 2·13
At military rating, without afterburner:
J85-4 0·98
J85-5, -13, -15 1·03
J85-17 0·97
J85-21 1·00
J85/J1 0·98

GENERAL ELECTRIC CJ610

Announced in May 1960, the CJ610 is a power plant tailored for commercial and executive aircraft of 12,500-16,500 lb (5,700-7,500 kg) gross weight. It is essentially similar to the basic J85 turbojet, without afterburner, and incorporates an eight-stage axial-flow compressor, annular combustion chamber, two-stage reaction turbine, fixed-area concentric exhaust section and integrated control system. Air mass flow is 44 lb (20 kg)/sec.

By December 1973, a total of 1,400 CJ610s had accumulated more than 2,300,000 flying hours and the TBO had reached 2,100 hr.

There are six versions:

CJ610-1, CJ610-4. Initial production versions, differing only in accessory gearbox location.

CJ610-5, CJ610-6. Developed versions of -1 and -4 respectively, providing increased T-O thrust.

CJ610-8, CJ610-9. Developed for production deliveries beginning in 1969.

Versions of the CJ610 power the IAI Westwind, Gates Learjet 24/25 and HFB 320 Hansa twin-jet executive transports.

DIMENSIONS:
Length overall:
CJ610-1, -5 51·1 in (1,298 mm)
CJ610-4, -6 45·4 in (1,153 mm)
CJ610-8 45·4 in (1,153 mm)
CJ610-9 51·1 in (1,298 mm)
Max flange diameter 17·7 in (449 mm)
WEIGHT, DRY:
CJ610-1 399 lb (181 kg)
CJ610-4 389 lb (176 kg)
CJ610-5 402 lb (183 kg)
CJ610-6 392 lb (179 kg)
CJ610-8 407 lb (185 kg)
CJ610-9 417 lb (189 kg)
PERFORMANCE RATINGS (guaranteed):
T-O:
CJ610-1, -4 2,850 lb (1,293 kg) st
CJ610-5, -6 2,950 lb (1,340 kg) st
CJ610-8, -9 3,100 lb (1,406 kg) st
Max continuous:
CJ610-1, -4 2,700 lb (1,225 kg) st
CJ610-5, -6 2,780 lb (1,264 kg) st
CJ610-8, -9 2,925 lb (1,327 kg) st
SPECIFIC FUEL CONSUMPTION:
At T-O rating:
CJ610-1, -4 0·99
CJ610-5, -6, -8, -9 0·98
At max continuous rating:
CJ610-1, -4 0·97
CJ610-5, -6 0·96
CJ610-8, -9 0·96

GENERAL ELECTRIC CF700

Developed as a private venture by General Electric, the CF700 is an aft-fan engine suitable for powering military and commercial jet aircraft. It can be tilted while in operation, affording dual lift/cruise capability in VTOL aircraft.

It utilises as its gas generator the CJ610 turbojet and offers a 5·7:1 thrust-to-weight ratio in its civil form, as used in the Dassault Mystère 20/Falcon and Rockwell Sabre 75A executive transports. FAA certification of the original version was received on 1 July 1964.

The increased-performance CF700-2D was certificated in early 1968, with production deliveries following immediately. The CF700-2D has a new design of compressor turbine of higher thermodynamic efficiency. Improved materials were also introduced for other components. The -2D-2 incorporates a new design of tailpipe.

By December 1973, over 700 CF700s had flown some 1,340,000 hr in service and the TBO had reached 2,100 hr.

The general description of the J85 turbojet applies also to the CF700, with the following additional assembly:

AFT FAN: Single-stage free-floating fan. By-pass ratio 1·9 : 1. Mass air flow through fan 84·0 lb (38·0 kg)/sec.
DIMENSIONS:
Overall length, compressor nose to tailcone tip 75·57 in (1,912 mm)
Max diameter 36·1 in (913 mm)
Max diameter less fan 17·7 in (449 mm)
WEIGHT, DRY:
CF700-2C 725 lb (330 kg)
CF700-2D, -2D-2 737 lb (334 kg)
PERFORMANCE RATINGS:
Max T-O:
CF700-2C (flat rated to 30°C): 4,200 lb (1,905 kg) st
CF700-2D 4,325 lb (1,961 kg) st
CF700-2D-2 4,390 lb (1,991 kg) st
Max continuous:
CF700-2C 4,000 lb (1,814 kg) st
CF 700-2D-2 4,120 lb (1,869 kg) st
Max cruising:
CF700-2C 3,800 lb (1,725 kg) st
CF700-2D 3,910 lb (1,774 kg) st
SPECIFIC FUEL CONSUMPTION:
Max T-O:
CF700-2C, -2D 0·652
CF700-2D-2 0·643
Max continuous:
CF700-2C, -2D 0·649
CF700-2D-2 0·639

General Electric CF700-2D turbofan (4,325 lb; 1,961 kg st)

General Electric J97-GE-100 turbojet of 5,270 lb (2,390 kg) st

GENERAL ELECTRIC J97

Directly derived from the GE1 (the basic core engine used for several current engines, as described in the 1973-74 *Jane's*), the J97 is an advanced, lightweight turbojet. During a five-year development programme it has run for more than 2,000 engine hours, including altitude performance demonstration, 60-hour endurance, —51°C starting, water-ingestion tolerance and other MIL-5007C tests. In 1972 the J97-100 version successfully completed the USAF 60-hour preliminary flight rating test. The initial production J97 powers the Teledyne Ryan 154 high-altitude reconnaissance RPV.

The advanced technology demonstrated is adaptable to many applications. An early use will be in the NASA V/STOL research vehicle, with a lift-fan system offering high thrust/weight ratio for optimum lift/cruise fan power. In afterburning and unaugmented forms it is suitable for advanced trainers, light tactical fighters and drones and remotely piloted vehicles. Other versions have been planned as turboshafts for large helicopters and as turboprops for tilt-wing transports. Components related to the J97-100 have been utilised on the TF39 and F101 engines.

TYPE: Single-shaft turbojet or gas-generator.
COMPRESSOR: 14-stage axial with six variable stator rows. Max mass flow 70 lb (31·75 kg)/sec. Pressure ratio 13·8
COMBUSTION CHAMBER: Annular, straight-through type with 16 vaporising burners.
FUEL GRADE: JP-4, JP-5.
TURBINE: Axial, two stages, with aircooled nozzle guide vanes. Turbine entry gas temperature, over 1,095°C.
JET PIPE: Simple fixed-area type on J97-100; other versions incorporate deflector valves, free turbine or an advanced film-cooled afterburner and variable nozzle.
DIMENSIONS:
Diameter 24·4 in (620 mm)
Length 109·5 in (2,781 mm)
WEIGHT, DRY: 694 lb (314 kg)
PERFORMANCE RATINGS:
Unaugmented 5,270 lb (2,390 kg) st
Augmented 7,000-10,000 lb (3,175-4,535 kg) st
SPECIFIC FUEL CONSUMPTION:
Unaugmented 0·915

GENERAL ELECTRIC F101

The F101-GE-100 is the augmented turbofan designed by General Electric for the Rockwell International B-1 strategic bomber. This engine design was preceded by the GE9 engine demonstrator programme under sponsorship of the Aeronautical Systems Division of the US Air Force, Wright-Patterson Air Force Base, Ohio. That programme met or exceeded all contract performance requirements.

The F101, four of which will power the Rockwell B-1, is an augumented turbofan in the 30,000 lb thrust class which represents a considerable advance in the state of the art. Compared with the latest augmented J79, it is of approximately the same weight and bulk, with a reduced overall length, yet gives twice the thrust with a greatly reduced specific fuel consumption. In the B-1 the engine is required to give reliable flight performance at high subsonic speed at sea level and at over Mach 2 at extreme altitude.

The initial design review was passed on schedule in June 1971 and the critical design review in July 1972, also on schedule. Testing of major components began in 1970, the core engine was first run in October 1971 and the complete engine without afterburner ran in early 1972. In May 1973 a series of tests equivalent to the PFRT (Preliminary Flight Rating Test) was successfully completed. A total of over 132 hours' running was completed, including 15 hours with full afterburner and 52 hours at turbine inlet temperatures higher than 1,315°C. The engine was subjected to 153 throttle bursts, 135 throttle chops and 65 starts. The subsequent strip showed the parts in "very good condition". In March 1974 the F101 was completing its PFRT. Shipment of flight engines to power the first B-1 began the following month.

First flight is due in 1974 with a production decision possible in 1976. GE's current contract is for about $392 million, and covers development of the engine and shipment of 25 engines (2 ground and 23 flight) to the airframe contractor. Funding is being released for each stage of development only when the preceding stage has been demonstrably accomplished, and the present plan is to fly the F101 for the first time in the first B-1.

INTAKE: Direct pitot engine intake, downstream of duct from airframe intake of variable area and profile. Radial struts to increase rigidity and resistance to bird ingestion.

FAN: Two-stage fan with solid blades forged in titanium alloy. Variable-incidence inlet guide vanes to increase tolerance to inlet flow distortion and improve resistance to low-altitude bird strikes.

COMPRESSOR: Nine-stage HP compressor in single spool. Splitter ring downstream of fan with row of variable-incidence inlet guide vanes in core airflow. First three HP rotor stages of titanium alloy, stages 4-9 of 8286 high-tensile steel. Components of HP stator fabricated in carbon-fibre composites using matrix of epoxy or, in hotter parts in later stages, polyimide resins. Overall pressure ratio 27 : 1.

COMBUSTION CHAMBER: Short annular chamber with unconventional carburettor system and low-pressure vaporising burners. Fuel is discharged from stainless steel pipes into hot swirl cups, resulting in swift vaporising in first 2 in (50·8 mm) linear distance, leaving about 8 in (203 mm) for complete combustion without smoke in the external jet at any throttle setting.

HP TURBINE: Very highly loaded single stage, with exceptionally high entry gas temperature, maximum higher than 1,371°C. Aircooled nozzle guide vanes in assembly fabricated from thoria-dispersed nickel and thoria-dispersed nickel-chrome. Rotor wheel fabricated in René 95, newest of the GE refractory high-nickel alloys, with blades of improved design and a new form of cooling consuming a relatively low bleed airflow.

LP TURBINE: Two-stage assembly, also with nozzle guide vanes of thoria-dispersed nickel and nickel-chrome, and with rotor mainly of René 95 with solid blades.

AFTERBURNER: Fully modulated augmentation. Fan and core flows mixed downstream of turbine. Reheat fuel supplied initially to core flow only, giving automatic light-up with minimal jump in thrust. Further increase in augmentor fuel-flow causes additional outer spraybars and circular flameholder gutters to come into operation, until at maximum augmentation combustion is complete across the whole engine flow. Fan air at about 121°C used to provide film-cooling of augmentor duct wall.

PROPELLING NOZZLE: Variable-area, variable-profile primary and secondary nozzles, each of multiple-flap type. Eight primary rams drive complex linkage to secure optimum independent profile of both nozzles over wide range, with con-di operation in supersonic cruise at all levels.

DIMENSIONS:

Length overall	181 in (4,596 mm)
Intake diameter	55 in (1,397 mm)

WEIGHT, DRY: about 4,000 lb (1,814 kg,

PERFORMANCE RATINGS:

Cold	about 17,000 lb (7,710 kg) st
Full augmentation	over 30,000 lb (13,600 kg) st

GENERAL ELECTRIC J101

Formerly designated GE15, this advanced afterburning engine was tailored to the propulsion requirements of the Northrop P-530 Cobra, but its initial application is in the Northrop YF-17 lightweight fighter for the US Air Force.

Development of the engine began on company funds about a year before a USAF funded programme was initiated in April 1972. Under this programme the engine successfully completed, in December 1973, both the 60-hour Prototype-Preliminary Flight Rating Test (PPFRT) and over 100 hours of simulated flight testing at the USAF's Arnold Engineering Development Center. After a complete review of the programmes, a prototype flight release was granted by the USAF in February 1974. By March 1974 six prototype engines had been shipped to Northrop for flight testing in the YF-17. GE flight test support will continue through the flight programme.

From its inception, the J101 has been developed under the "design to cost" philosophy wherein engine performance and weight requirements were balanced against cost and risk. Thus, to achieve the high performance necessary for an engine saleable in the 1980s, advanced technology features were incorporated into the engine. However, to assure low development and production cost, design simplicity was retained and use of technology previously developed and demonstrated was employed.

Utilising an advanced twin-spool compressor driven by single-stage HP and LP turbines, a compressor pressure-ratio in excess of 20 : 1 has been achieved. Increases in stage pressure-ratio and turbine temperature were sufficient to reduce the number of compressor and turbine stages previously required. Increased gas temperature required cooling air to be continuously bled from the LP compressor through an annular by-pass duct into the afterburner and exhaust nozzle. The convergent-divergent nozzle is a translating flap, hydraulically actuated system.

DIMENSIONS:

Length overall	154 in (3,383 mm)
Maximum diameter	32·5 in (826 mm)

WEIGHT, DRY: approx 1,900 lb (862 kg)

PERFORMANCE RATING:

Max T-O	15,000 lb (6,804 kg) st class

GENERAL ELECTRIC J79

Development of the J79, America's first high-compression variable-stator turbojet, began in 1952. It was flight tested for the first time in 1955 and became the first production Mach 2 engine when it was selected to power the General Dynamics B-58 Hustler bomber. In addition to production by General Electric, versions of the J79 have been or are being manufactured by Orenda of Canada to power the Canadair CF-104/F-104G (MAP), by Ishikawajima-Harima in Japan for the licence-built F-104DJ, and by MTU of Germany, Fiat of Italy and FN of Belgium for the European-built F-104G. The Italian production team, including Alfa Romeo is now producing the J79-GE-19, an improved engine similar to the J79-GE-17 but configured for the F-104S Starfighter.

Overall, the International Technical Assistance Programme has been responsible for assembly of more than 2,200 J79 turbojets for the F-104. A total of more than 14,500 J79s had been built by GE and licensees by December 1971.

Derivatives of the J79 have been the CJ805-3 turbojet and CJ805-23 turbofan, powering the Convair 880 and 990 Coronado, respectively, as well as the LM1500 industrial and marine gasturbine.

Versions of the J79 are as follows:

J79-GE-2. Powered early models of the McDonnell F-4A Phantom II and North American A-5A Vigilante. Air mass flow 166 lb (75 kg)/sec. Pressure ratio 12·5 : 1.

J79-GE-3B. Powered the Lockheed F-104A and B Starfighters.

J79-GE-5C. Powered the General Dynamics B-58A Hustler.

J79-GE-7A. Powers the Lockheed F-104C and D Starfighters. Built under licence by Orenda (as J79-OEL-7) for Canadair CF-104.

J79-GE-8. For production versions of F-4B and RF-4B Phantom II and A-5A and RA-5C Vigilante. Air mass flow 169 lb (76·5 kg)/sec. Pressure ratio 12·9 : 1.

J79-GE-10. Advanced version powering North American Rockwell RA-5C and McDonnell Douglas F-4J. Entered production in June 1966, superseding the J79-GE-8. Pressure ratio 13·5 : 1.

J79-GE-11A. For US-built Lockheed F-104G Starfighters. Built under licence in Japan (as J79-IHI-11A), Germany, Italy, Belgium and Canada.

J79-GE-15. Powers McDonnell Douglas F-4C, F-4D and RF-4C for USAF. Similar to J79-GE-8 except for self-contained starting.

J79-GE-17. Similar to J79-GE-10, but for USAF F-4E.

J79-GE-19. Advanced version designed to supersede J79-GE-11A in F-104. Used in F-104S and F-104A. Differs from J79-GE-10/17 only in external characteristics. Guided expansion jet nozzle derived from nozzles of J79-GE-5C and YJ93. Afterburner system provides continuous thrust modulation. Fuel flow can be modulated from 2,700 lb (1,225 kg)/hr to 34,000 lb (15,420 kg)/hr.

The following details cover the basic features of all J79 variants except where otherwise indicated:

TYPE: Variable-stator single-shaft axial-flow turbojet.

AIR INTAKE: Annular type, surrounding central bullet fairing. Struts and inlet guide vanes anti-iced with compressor discharge air. First-stage stator anti-icing on J79-GE-8, -10 and -15.

COMPRESSOR: Seventeen-stage axial-flow. First six stator stages and the inlet guide vanes have variable incidence. Setting of variable-incidence vanes adjusted by dual actuators moved by engine fuel to achieve optimum airflow angles for each stage at all engine speeds. Rotor, which runs on two bearings, is made from Lapelloy, B5F5 and titanium. All engines have type 403 stainless steel blades and vanes except J79-GE-3B and -7A which have A286 stator vanes at stages 7 to 17 inclusive. Total of 1,260 stator vanes and 1,271 rotor blades. Variable stator vanes have a platform, trunnion and threaded stem arrangement for external attachment to the actuation system linkage. Fixed stator vanes are inserted into T-slots on rear casing. All rotor blades have dovetail

General Electric F101 advanced turbofan, rated in the 30,000 lb (13,600 kg) st class with afterburning

General Electric YJ101-GE-100 continuous-bleed turbojet (15,000 lb; 6,804 kg st class with afterburning)

roots. Front compressor stator casing is made from a magnesium-thorium casting or Chromolloy forging, depending on engine model. On those engines requiring an intermediate compressor casing this is made of either A286 or 321 SS. All models have a forged and machined rear compressor stator casing, constructed in two halves for ease of assembly and disassembly.

Combustion Chamber: Cannular type consisting of 10 combustion cans. Outer casing of Chromolloy, flame tube of Hastelloy. J79-GE-3B, -5C, -7A, -11A, -15, -17 and -19 have dual igniters in cans 4 and 5. J79-GE-2, -8 and -10 have single igniter in can 4.

Fuel System: Hydromechanical range-governing control system composed of two separate and distinct systems, the main fuel system and afterburner fuel system. Main system is controlled by main fuel control, which is a flow-controlling unit. The afterburner system is controlled by an independent control, also of the flow-controlling type. Automatic acceleration control with exhaust temperature limiting. Gear-type main fuel pump. Engine-driven centrifugal afterburner fuel pump.

Fuel Grade: JP-4 or JP-5.

Nozzle Guide Vanes: Three-stage; first with 58 vanes of R41, second with 62 vanes of Hastelloy R235 and R41, third with 44 vanes of A286.

Turbine: Three-stage axial-flow type. Stages 1 and 2 bolted to shaft, stage 3 integral with aft shaft. J79-GE-8 and -15 have first- and second-stage wheels of V57 and third-stage wheel of A286. All three stages of J79-GE-10, -17 and -19 have intermediate aged V57. J79-GE-2 has all three stages of M308. Other models have all stages of A286. J79-10, -17 and -19 first stage has 148 blades of Udimet 700 or René 80, second stage has 114 blades of Udimet 500, third stage has 84 blades of M252. All blades attached by fir-tree roots. Lightweight casing of fabricated A286 in two easily-removable halves.

Bearings: Three only. Roller in front frame, ball (main thrust) in compressor frame, roller in turbine frame.

Jet Pipe: Liner of N155 and L605 with ceramic coating. Jet pipe of A286.

Afterburner: Short type (max 1,985°C) with fully-variable nozzle of "petal" type. Actuation by hydraulic rams utilising engine lubricating oil. Three-ring, quadrant-burning on all models except J79-GE-3B, -8, -10, -15, -17 and -19, which have core annulus burning with radial spraybars.

Accessory Drives: All engine controls and accessories, aircraft hydraulic pumps, generators, alternators and constant-speed drives (as required) are driven by two gearboxes on bottom of engine and a nose inlet gearbox.

Lubrication: Dry-sump system. Vane-type pumps. Sump pressure provided from compressor. Oil cooling from fuel. Sump capacity ranges from 4 to 5 US gallons (15-19 litres). Average normal oil supply pressure 50 lb/sq in (3·5 kg/cm²).

Oil Specification: MIL-L-7808, MIL-L-23699.

Mounting: Pads provided on front frame and turbine frame for a variety of mounting arrangements, depending on airframe requirements.

Starting: J79-GE-3B, -7A, -11A and -19 have pneumatic turbine starter mounted on front frame of inlet gearbox. J79-GE-2, -8 and -10 have turbine air impingement starter. J79-GE-5C, and -17 have combination cartridge/pneumatic starter on transfer gearbox.

Dimensions:

Length overall:	
J79-GE-2, 7A, 11A	207·96 in (5,283 mm)
J79-GE-3B	207·45 in (5,270 mm)
J79-GE-5C	202·17 in (5,136 mm)
J79-GE-8	208·45 in (5,295 mm)
J79-GE-10, 17, 19	208·69 in (5,301 mm)
Diameter at compressor:	
J79-GE-2, 7A, 8, 11A, 15	38·3 in (973 mm)
J79-GE-5C	38·0 in (965 mm)
J79-GE-10, 17, 19	39·06 in (992 mm)
Diameter at nozzle:	
J79-GE-2, 3B, 7A, 8, 11A, 15	38·31 in (973 mm)
J79-GE-5C	38·0 in (956 mm)
J79-GE-10, 17, 19	39·06 in (992 mm)

Weight, Dry:

J79-GE-2	3,620 lb (1,642 kg)
J79-GE-3B	3,325 lb (1,508 kg)
J79-GE-5C	3,685 lb (1,671 kg)
J79-GE-7A	3,575 lb (1,622 kg)
J79-GE-8	3,672 lb (1,666 kg)
J79-GE-10	3,855 lb (1,749 kg)
J79-GE-11A	3,560 lb (1,615 kg)
J79-GE-15	3,685 lb (1,672 kg)
J79-GE-17, 19	3,835 lb (1,740 kg)

Performance Ratings:

T-O rating, with afterburning:	
J79-GE-2	16,150 lb (7,325 kg) st
J79-GE-3B	14,800 lb (6,713 kg) st
J79-GE-5C	15,600 lb (7,076 kg) st
J79-GE-7A, 11A	15,800 lb (7,167 kg) st
J79-GE-8, 15	17,000 lb (7,711 kg) st
J79-GE-10, 17, 19	17,900 lb (8,120 kg) st

General Electric J79-GE-17 turbojet (17,900 lb; 8,120 kg st with afterburning)

General Electric TF34 turbofan of 9,275 lb (4,207 kg) st

Military rating:	
J79-GE-2	10,350 lb (4,695 kg) st
J79-GE-3B	9,600 lb (4,355 kg) st
J79-GE-5C	10,300 lb (4,672 kg) st
J79-GE-7A, 11A	10,000 lb (4,536 kg) st
J79-GE-8, 15	10,900 lb (4,944 kg) st
J79-GE-10, 17, 19	11,870 lb (5,385 kg) st
Cruise rating:	
J79-GE-2	2,230 lb (1,012 kg) st
J79-GE-3B	2,500 lb (1,134 kg) st
J79-GE-5C	2,450 lb (1,112 kg) st
J79-GE-7A, 11A	2,650 lb (1,202 kg) st
J79-GE-8, 10, 15, 17, 19	2,600 lb (1,179 kg) st

Specific Fuel Consumption:

At T-O rating:	
J79-GE-2	2·00
J79-GE-3B	2·04
J79-GE-5C	2·20
J79-GE-7A, 11A	1·97
J79-GE-8	1·93
J79-GE-15	1·945
J79-GE-10, 17, 19	1·965
At military rating:	
J79-GE-2, 3B	0·87
J79-GE-8, 15	0·86
J79-GE-5C, 7A, 10, 11A, 17, 19	0·84
At cruise rating:	
J79-GE-2	1·06
J79-GE-3B	1·13
J79-GE-5C	1·01
J79-GE-7A, 8, 11A, 15	1·05
J79-GE-10, 17, 19	0·95

GENERAL ELECTRIC TF34

It was announced in April 1968 that the US Naval Air Systems Command had awarded General Electric a contract for development of the TF34. This high by-pass ratio turbofan had won a 1965 US Navy competition aimed at providing a tailor-made engine in the 9,000 lb (4,080 kg) st category for the VS(X) aircraft by 1972 within a budget of $96 million. In August 1972 the TF34-GE-2, the initial variant for this application (now called the Lockheed S-3A Viking) completed its Model Qualification Test (MQT) and has since entered production. GE, working under a Naval Air Systems Command fixed-price incentive-fee contract, completed the development within the price, time and major technical goals laid down in 1965.

The contract to develop the TF34 engine was awarded to General Electric in March 1968. The first engine was put to test in May 1969 and since then has accumulated over 27,000 hours of operation. The engine successfully completed its Preliminary Flight Rating Test (PFRT) on 1 March 1972, earning General Electric full incentive by completing this milestone two months ahead of schedule. This test established the flightworthiness of the engine, and subsequently 28 YTF34-GE-2 engines were delivered on time to Lockheed for S-3A flight testing. The **TF34-GE-2** was qualified for production in August 1972, since when considerably more than 100 have been shipped.

The TF34 engine has undergone a wide variety of development tests including climatic, altitude, overspeed, overtemperature, inlet distortion and corrosion susceptibility. Other tests included noise, smoke, infra-red measurements and operation while ingesting water, steam, sand and rocket gases. The TF34 programme has also included over 400 hours of operation in a B-47 test aircraft and another 450 hours in the altitude and climatic test chambers at the Naval Air Propulsion Test Center.

In 1970 the TF34 was selected to power the twin-engined Fairchild Republic A-10A attack aircraft to compete in the AX competition. The A-10A application led in July 1972 to an Air Force contract for development of the **TF34-GE-100.** This is tailored to the AX mission, and to the A-10A aircraft, and is particularly re-engineered to minimise unit price. The A-10A won the AX competition, and may be built in large numbers.

The S-3A became operational in February 1974 and GE and the Navy have defined a "3,000 hr TBO extension programme"; the time between overhauls will initially be at a lower level. The GE-100 was scheduled to receive a production go-ahead in October 1974. The expected Air Force contract will be fixed-price plus incentive-fee.

Type: Two-shaft high by-pass ratio turbofan for subsonic aircraft.

Air Intake: Plain annular intake. No fixed inlet struts or guide vanes. Small spinner rotates with fan.

Fan: Single-stage fan has blades forged in titanium, without part-span shrouds. Blades replaceable with engine installed. Total air mass flow 338 lb (153 kg)/sec. By-pass ratio 6·2. Pressure ratio 1·5. Max speed, 7,365 rpm.

Compressor: Single axial spool on HP shaft. Total of 14 stages, first six stages having variable stators. First nine stages of titanium, remainder of high-nickel alloy. Blades and vanes individually replaceable. Split casing provides bleeds for engine cooling, anti-icing and airframe use. Total core airflow 47 lb (21·3 kg)/sec. Pressure ratio of compressor, 14; overall pressure ratio 21. Max speed, 17,900 rpm.

COMBUSTION CHAMBER: Annular chamber designed for highly efficient and complete combustion with near-zero smoke. Hastelloy chamber liner and front dome, providing ports for igniters and 18 carburetting burners.

TURBINE: Two-stage HP gas generator turbine with convection-cooled rotor blades and stator vanes, the first-stage nozzle vanes having film and impingement cooling. Four-stage LP fan turbine with tip-shrouded blades; LP blades and stators replaceable on installed engine. Turbine entry gas temperature 1,225°C maximum.

FUEL SYSTEM: Contamination-resistant, carburetting type. Integrated hydromechanical control unit with electronic amplifier; automatic fuel heater. Fuel grade JP-4 or JP-5.

ACCESSORY DRIVES: Engine and customer accessories mounted around horseshoe-shaped gearbox, fitting closely around lower half of compressor casing. Radial shaft drive from front of HP shaft. Fan airflow passes outside accessories through optimised duct.

LUBRICATION: Enclosed, pressurised, dual system with vent along centre shaft.

DIMENSIONS:	
Max diameter	51·1 in (1,298 mm)
Fan cowl diameter	50 in (1,270 mm)
Basic length	101 in (2,565 mm)
WEIGHT, DRY:	
TF34-2	1,444 lb (655 kg)
TF34-100	1,427 lb (647 kg)
PERFORMANCE RATING:	
Max T-O:	
TF34-2	9,275 lb (4,207 kg) st
TF34-100	9,065 lb (4,112 kg) st

SNECMA/GE CFM 56

This engine will be a quiet, "third-generation" turbofan in the 22,000 lb (10,000 kg) thrust class for subsonic civil and military aircraft. Originally a project by the French SNECMA company, it is being developed 50/50 with GE. Further details are given in the International section.

GENERAL ELECTRIC CF6
US military designation (CF6-50E): F103-GE-100

On 11 September 1967 General Electric announced the endorsement and commitment of corporate funding for development of the CF6 turbofan for the then-forthcoming generation of wide-body transports. From the initial family of 32,000 lb to 36,000 lb (14,500 to 16,330 kg) st CF6 two-shaft engines announced in September 1967 to cover the anticipated thrust requirements of the Lockheed and McDonnell Douglas airbus projects, the CF6 evolved through a series of variants to the CF6-6D, flat-rated at 40,000 lb (18,144 kg) to 31°C and tailored to the McDonnell Douglas DC-10 Series 10 intermediate-range transport. Announcement that this engine had been selected by United Air Lines and American Airlines was made on 25 April 1968. Further orders have since been placed by many airlines for the CF6-6 and -50 series.

Basic configuration of the CF6 comprises a "1½-stage" fan driven by a five-stage LP turbine energised by a slightly modified TF39 core engine, consisting of a 16-stage HP compressor, annular combustor and two-stage turbine. Modifications have been introduced to enable the accessory systems to suit airline installation requirements, while other changes are aimed at enhancing reliability, durability and maintainability.

The construction is modular, featuring easily-removable components that are interchangeable to enable airlines to minimise spare-parts holdings and facilitate sectional overhaul procedures. Provisions have been made for mounting sensors and detection devices to monitor engines during flight. Borescope ports are provided at every compressor and turbine stage, and around the combustion chamber, enabling engine checks to be made without disassembly.

The CF6 fan is designed for low noise output and a 30,000 hr operational life. It offers high resistance to erosion and foreign-object damage, and provides inherent foreign material separation capability. Rather than entering the HP compressor inlet, ingested foreign objects are centrifuged into the fan and emerge via the fan nozzle. The fan rotor is designed to meet FAA reliability criteria and has substantial speed and stress margins. A blade containment system and automatic engine shutdown system are also provided to enhance safety.

Particular attention has been paid to noise suppression and combustor smoke reduction. A 1 in (25·4 mm) thick glassfibre sandwich structure developed by GE is incorporated along the outer and inner walls of the fan duct. The CF6-6D and -50A installations in the DC-10-10 and -30 have met all FAR 36 noise limitation requirements. The TF39 combustor in the core engine has been modified to introduce axial swirlers, directing more air through the dome to the burning zone, and smoke level is well below the visible range.

CF6-6D. Initial 40,000 lb (18,144 kg) st version of engine in production for intermediate-range DC-10 Series 10. First ran on 21 October 1968 and 18 days later attained 45,750 lb (20,752 kg) st. Following a series of successful factory and outdoor tests, engine was released for production in February 1969. The second CF6-6D, built to the production configuration, first ran in May 1969. By December 1970 a total of 30 engines had been shipped and flight testing with a single engine hung on the starboard inner pylon of a B-52 had extended to 50,000 ft (15,250 m), Mach 0·896 and 420 knots (484 mph; 779 km/h) indicated airspeed. Delivery of flight test engines to McDonnell Douglas started in late 1969, with aircraft first flight following in September 1970. Certification of the CF6-6D for commercial service was granted by the FAA in September 1970, and the engine entered airline service in the DC-10 Series 10 in August 1971.

CF6-6D1. In August 1971 this growth version was FAA certificated and offered to take advantage of the demonstrated margin of the -6D. The D1 rating is increased by 1,000 lb to 41,000 lb (18,597 kg) at 28·9°C. By the end of 1973 more than 325 6-6D and 6-6D1 engines had been shipped.

CF6-6G. This engine is a -6D incorporating a new combustion chamber and HP turbine, to operate at an increased turbine entry temperature. The initial -6G rating will be 43,000 lb (19,504 kg) at 28·9°C.

CF6-50A. Announced by GE in January 1969, the 49,000 lb (22,226 kg) st CF6-50A is a growth version of the CF6-6 to power the DC-10 Series 30, the Airbus Industrie A-300 and Boeing 747-300. The increased thrust is achieved by increased flow through the core engine (reducing the by-pass ratio from 5·9 to 4·4) at slightly increased turbine entry temperature. A major change is the introduction of two additional booster stages behind the single-stage LP compressor of the CF6-6, with no change in the turbofan's external dimensions. To provide for flow matching between the two rotors, variable by-pass doors are incorporated between the LP and HP compressors. A 41 per cent scale model fan with three-stage compressor and variable by-pass doors started testing in January 1969. In October 1970 a CF6-50A attained a thrust of 58,000 lb (26,300 kg) in a test cell at 5·6°C. FAA certification testing was completed in March 1972. The CF6-50A entered airline service in December 1972 in the DC-10 Series 30. The CF6-50 series also powers the Airbus Industrie A-300, which first flew in October 1972 and entered scheduled service in May 1974.

CF6-50C. The CF6-50C will be rated to give 51,000 lb (23,133 kg) st up to 30°C by May 1975. Higher thrust is provided by a further increase in turbine temperature, with improved cooling of hot-section components. The -50C has potential for thrust growth.

CF6-50D. The -50D has a stronger LP shaft and turbine rear frame and engine mountings and, by running the fan at up to 3,900 rpm, compared with 3,500-3,600, is flat-rated at 51,000 lb (23,133 kg) up to 25°C. It received FAA certification in November 1972. Engines began flight testing in the Boeing 747 in June 1973, leading toward aircraft certification in 1974.

CF6-50E (Military designation F103-GE-100). This engine is rated to give 52,500 lb (23,850 kg) st up to 30°C. Higher thrust is provided by further increase in turbine temperature and improved cooling of the hot-section components.

The first military application of the F103-GE-100, the military CF6, is the Boeing YC-14 AMST (see "Aircraft" section of this edition). The two F103 engines, each rated at 51,000 lb (23,133 kg) st, will be mounted ahead of and immediately above the inner part of the wing, to provide upper-surface blowing. With flaps extended, this will give a lift coefficient exceeding 4·0. Boeing is understood to be using this kind of above-wing installation in its 7X7 series of commercial transport projects.

In April 1974 GE announced that the two Boeing E-4 Advanced Airborne Command Post aircraft then being built would be powered by

Two views of the General Electric CF6 turbofan: *(above)*, **CF6-6D, 40,000 lb (18,144 kg) thrust class;** *(below)*, **CF6-50A, 49,000 lb (22,226 kg) thrust class**

the F103 engine, and that similar engines would later be retrofitted, at no cost to the USAF, to the two E-4As delivered in 1973.

In early 1973 the first 222 commercial CF6-6 engines had accumulated nearly 1,000,000 engine hours in 28 months. Engine-attributable unscheduled-removal rate was 0·42 per 1,000 hr, and engine-attributable in-flight shutdown rate only 0·09 per 1,000 hr. In March 1974 the "high-time" engine had reached 6,474 operating hours.

The following data relate to the CF6-6D, with the differing features of the CF6-50 series also detailed:

TYPE: Two-shaft high by-pass ratio commercial turbofan.

AIR INTAKE: Single forward-facing annular configuration.

FAN: Single-stage fan with integrally-mounted single-stage LP compressor (described together as a 1½-stage fan), both driven by LP turbine. Fan has rotating spinner and omits inlet guide vanes. Blade-containment shroud provided against possible blade failure. The 38 fan rotor blades are individually removable from the thick-section centreless disc bolted to forward conical extension of LP shaft system. Blade aerofoil has anti-vibration shrouds at ⅔ span. Fan rotor exit airflow split between LP compressor and fan slipstream. Fan front frame has 12 radial/tangential struts across fan slipstream exit, canted to reduce noise, bolted to core engine inlet which has six radial struts. Front frame provides support for LP and HP rotor front bearings, fan being overhung ahead of large-diameter ball-thrust bearing with rear roller bearing ahead of core engine. Blades, discs, spool of titanium; exit guide vanes of aluminium; fan frame and shaft of steel; spinner and fan case of aluminium alloy. Total airflow 1,307 lb/sec (593 kg/sec), by-pass ratio 5·9 : 1. Configuration of CF6-50 is similar but with two added LP stages and by-pass doors (described below). Total airflow 1,439 lb (654 kg)/sec; by-pass ratio 4·4 : 1.

LP COMPRESSOR: Single-stage compressor acting as booster to fan flow into core engine. Rotor blades carried on rear rim of tapered drum bolted to rear of fan disc. Stators cantilevered off short-chord shroud ring, supported by radial outer struts and radial/tangential inner struts located on fan front frame. Compressor exit flow free to balance between core engine and fan slipstream exit. Configuration of CF6-50 modified to three compressor booster stages carried on flanged rotor drum. Continuous shroud extends to fan front frame with 12 integral by-pass doors located between canted radial struts in fan exit inner casing. These doors maintain proper flow matching between the fan/LP system and core by opening at low power settings to permit LP supercharged flow to bleed into the fan airstream. The doors are closed during take-off and cruise.

HP COMPRESSOR: Sixteen-stage compressor of near-constant tip diameter, with inlet guide vanes and first six stator rows having variable incidence. Provision for interstage air bleed for airframe use and engine cooling. Rotor is of combined drum-and-disc construction with front stage and rear three stages overhung on conical discs providing location on HP front bearing and HP main shaft. All rotor blades held in rabbeted discs and individually replaceable without rotor disassembly. Stages 1-14 blades forged titanium, 15-16 steel. Stages 1-10 discs titanium, 11-16 and aft casing Inconel 718. Casing split on horizontal centreline; stator vanes held in dovetail slots and replaceable individually. Stages 1-3 stators titanium, 4-15 steel; inlet guide vanes titanium, outlet guide vanes steel. Double-skin inner casing shrouds the LP main shaft. Outlet frame contains compressor diffuser and incorporates support structure for HP rotor mid-bearings. Overall pressure ratio, 28·1 : 1 (ISA, max cruise at Mach 0·85, 35,000 ft; 10,670 m). Core airflow 185 lb (84 kg)/sec. CF6-50A has 15th and 16th stages removed to pass greater core airflow of 260 lb (118 kg)/sec and reduce pressure and temperature of air entering combustion chamber. Improved materials and strengthened structure in later stages. Overall pressure ratio 31·5 : 1 (same conditions as CF6-6D).

COMBUSTOR: Fully annular with comprehensive film-cooling. Separable snout, dome and inner/outer skirts, with nozzles, igniter, leads and manifold externally removable. Dome contains ports for two igniters and axial swirler cups for 30 fuel nozzles. Igniters of high-voltage surface-gap type with energy level of 2·0 joules, each igniter operated independently. Forged steel nozzles with liner of Hastelloy X. Nozzle and dome designed to minimise smoke, and entrance diffuser has gradual profile to assure low temperature gradient to turbine under all flight conditions. CF6-50A combustor is shorter, of improved material (HS 18-8), and can be removed with fuel nozzles in place.

HP TURBINE: Two-stage aircooled turbine with 1,290°C entry temperature. First-stage rotor blades are film and convection cooled, second stage convection cooled. Rotor blades cast from René 80; discs and forward and rear shafts of Inconel 718. First-stage nozzle guide vanes supported at inner and outer ends, second-stage cantilevered from outer ends, with inner ends carrying interstage labyrinth seals. First-stage vanes cast from X40 and film cooled by compressor discharge pressure. Second-stage vanes are cast from René 80 material and are convection cooled. Vanes are welded into pairs to decrease number of gas leakage paths. Thin-section discs with heavy-section centreless hubs are bolted to front and rear conical shafts, including conical and arched inter-disc diaphragms. Configuration for CF6-50 is similar but introduces improved materials and cooling, and vanes are not Siamesed but individual.

LP TURBINE: Five-stage, constant tip-diameter turbine with less than 871°C inlet temperature. Rotor blades tip-shrouded and cast in René 77, not aircooled. Forward and rear shafts, case and discs of Inconel 718. First-stage nozzle guide vanes supported at inner and outer ends, remaining stages are cantilevered from outer ends, with inner ends carrying inter-stage labyrinth seals. Stages 1-3 guide vanes cast in René 77, stages 4 and 5 cast in René 41. Vanes are cast in pairs and held by dovetails in slots machined in the two half-stator casings. Drum and centreless disc construction, located on LP rotor by front and rear conical diaphragms attached to third- and fourth-stage discs. Front diaphragm attached to LP main shaft, rear diaphragm to rear stub shaft. Drive to rotor by means of long fan midshaft. On CF6-50 a four-stage LP turbine is used, all stages being modified in geometry.

EXHAUST UNIT (FAN): Fixed-area annular duct with outer cowl and engine cowl forming convergent plug nozzle for fan slipstream.

EXHAUST UNIT (TURBINE): Short-length fixed-area exhaust duct with convergent plug nozzle. Provision for exhaust thrust reverser.

THRUST REVERSER (FAN): Annular cascade reverser with blocker doors across fan duct. For reverse thrust, rear portion of fan outer cowl translates aft on rotating ballscrews to uncover cascade vanes. Blocker doors (16 off) flush-mounted in cowl on link arms hinged in inner cowl, rotate inwards to expose cascade vanes and block fan duct. Reverser hinged at top to open in L/R halves for access to HP casing and combustor.

THRUST REVERSER (TURBINE): Post nozzle exit, cascade type. Two cascade screens are mounted in vertical plane on fixed pivot aft of turbine exhaust and are enclosed in fairing forming aerofoil-shaped plug. Aft translation of fairing uncovers cascades which open across nozzle exit and divert turbine exhaust radially outward and slightly forward in horizontal plane. Configuration for CF6-50 similar to fan thrust reverser with nine blocker doors, but not split. Acoustic treatment is provided in the nozzle flow path.

ROTOR SUPPORT SYSTEM: Eight bearings (four for each rotor) at seven locations. Fan and LP compressor carried on ball thrust bearing (1) behind fan disc and roller bearing (2) at front of LP main shaft; both bearings mounted in fan front frame structure, which also supports HP compressor front roller bearing (3). LP turbine carried on roller bearings at front and rear of turbine rotor assembly—rear bearing (7) being mounted in spider structure across turbine exit, and front bearing (6) on major spider structure between HP and LP turbines. HP compressor carried at rear on adjacent roller bearing (4R) and ball-thrust bearing (4B) at interconnection with HP turbine front conical shaft, both bearings being mounted on support structure integral with compressor outlet diffuser. A roller bearing (5), mounted in the inter-turbine structure, carries the aft HP turbine conical shaft.

ACCESSORY DRIVE: This consists of the inlet gearbox, radial gearbox, radial driveshaft, transfer gearbox, horizontal driveshaft and accessory gearbox. The inlet gearbox is located in the forward sump of the engine. The gearbox transfers energy from the core-engine (HP) rotor to the radial driveshaft located in a housing aft of the bottom vertical strut of the fan frame. The transfer gearbox is mounted on the bottom of the fan frame. Accessory mounting pads are provided on both the forward and aft faces of the gearbox. The engine accessories mounted on the gearbox are starter, fuel pump, main engine control, lubrication pump and tachometer. Pads are also provided for mounting the aircraft hydraulic pumps, constant-speed drive and alternator.

FUEL SYSTEM: Hydromechanical fuel control system regulates steady-state fuel flow and schedules acceleration and deceleration fuel flow. It also schedules and powers variable-stator vane position. A governor in the Woodward control provides core-engine speed stability during steady-state operation. During transient operation, core-engine fuel flow is scheduled on the basis of throttle position, compressor inlet temperature, compressor discharge pressure and core-engine speed. The fuel control and fuel pump are mounted in the accessory package as an integrated unit which avoids interconnecting high-pressure fuel lines and potential leakage points (they are separable for change or maintenance). This configuration provides a single drive mounting flange. The filter, fuel/oil heat exchanger and control pressurising valve may be removed individually without removing the entire assembly. The fuel manifold is double-wall constructed for safety and mounted on the exterior of the engine. For CF6-50, fuel control is modified to provide scheduling function for LP compressor by-pass doors.

FUEL GRADES: Fuels conforming to ASTM-1655-65T, Jet A, Jet A1 and Jet B, and MIL-T-5624G2 grades JP-4 or JP-5 are authorised, but Jet A is primary specification.

LUBRICATION SYSTEM: Dry-sump centre-vented system in which oil is pressure-fed to each engine component requiring lubrication. Oil is removed from the sump areas by scavenge pumps, passed through a fuel/oil heat exchanger and filter to the engine tank. Nominal lubrication system pressure is 30-90 lb/sq in (2·1-6·4 kg/cm²) above sump reference pressure. All pressure and scavenge pumps and filters are located in the lubrication centre on the forward side of the gearbox.

OIL SPECIFICATION: Conforming to General Electric specification D50TFI classes A & B, equivalent to MIL-L-7808 or MIL-L-23699A.

MOUNTING: Main thrust mount located on the inner fan frame; aft flight mount located on the turbine mid-frame.

STARTING: Air-turbine starter mounted on the front of the accessory gearbox at the through shaft.

NOISE SUPPRESSION EQUIPMENT: Acoustic panels integrated with fan casing, fan front frame and thrust reverser.

DIMENSIONS:

Fan tip diameter	86·4 in (2,195 mm)
Max width (cold)	94·1 in (2,390 mm)
Max height (over gearbox)	105·3 in (2,675 mm)
Length overall (cold):	
CF6-6D	193 in (4,902 mm)
CF6-50 series	187 in (4,750 mm)

WEIGHT, DRY:

Engine, including sound-attenuation materials:	
CF6-6D, -6D1	7,505 lb (3,404 kg)
CF6-50A, -50C	8,225 lb (3,731 kg)
CF6-50D	8,325 lb (3,780 kg)
Fan and turbine reverser:	
CF6-6D, -6D1	2,016 lb (914 kg)
CF6-50A, -50C	2,069 lb (939 kg)
CF6-50D	2,191 lb (994 kg)

PERFORMANCE RATINGS (uninstalled, real nozzle):

Max T-O:

CF6-6D: 39,300 lb (17,826 kg) st at 9,800 core engine rpm and 3,500 fan rpm, flat rated to 31·1°C

CF6-6D1: 40,300 lb (18,300 kg) st, flat rated to 28·9°C

CF6-6G: 42,200 lb (19,138 kg) st, flat rated to 28·9°C

CF6-50A: 48,400 lb (21,950 kg) st at 10,200 core engine rpm and 3,800 fan rpm, flat rated to 30·6°C

CF6-50C: 50,200 lb (22,771 kg) st, flat rated to 30°C

CF6-50D: 50,400 lb (22,857 kg) st, flat rated to 25°C

Max altitude and Mach No:

CF6-6 and -50:

45,000 ft (13,700 m) at Mach 1·0

Max cruise at 35,000 ft (10,670 m) and Mach 0·85, flat rated to ISA+10°C:

CF6-6D	9,060 lb (4,110 kg) st
CF6-6D1	9,200 lb (4,172 kg) st
CF6-6G	9,600 lb (4,354 kg) st
CF6-50A, C	10,800 lb (4,898 kg) st
CF6-50D	11,100 lb (5,034 kg) st

SPECIFIC FUEL CONSUMPTION:

At T-O thrust:	
CF6-6D	0·354
CF6-6D1	0·356
CF6-6G	0·364
CF6-50A	0·389
CF6-50C	0·394
CF6-50D	0·395
At max cruise thrust:	
CF6-6D	0·631
CF6-6D1	0·633
CF6-6G	0·643
CF6-50A	0·654
CF6-50C	0·653
CF6-50D	0·657

OIL CONSUMPTION: 2·0 lb (0·9 kg)/hr

GENERAL ELECTRIC TF39

General Electric produced the 41,100 lb (18,640 kg) st TF39 turbofan for the Lockheed C-5 Galaxy heavy logistics transport aircraft.

By January 1974 the TF39 had completed over 490,000 hours of running.

Full details can be found in the 1973-74 *Jane's*.

GE/NASA QUIET ENGINE

As part of a long-term research programme into improving the social acceptability of aircraft engines, the National Aeronautics and Space Administration contracted with General Electric for a special turbofan research engine in the ten-ton (20,000-25,000 lb; 9,070-11,340 kg) class. The project is aimed at developing the technology applicable to 22,000 lb (10,000 kg) engines that will operate 15 to 20 decibels quieter, as a bare engine, than the power plants of current aircraft such as the 707 and DC-8. Two of these research engines, both high-ratio turbofans, were extensively tested under NASA contract at the GE test site at Peebles, Ohio. The programme is managed by the NASA Lewis Research Center in Cleveland.

The programme, funded to the extent of $21 million by NASA, has been based on two turbofan engines of 20,000 lb thrust using a core of the TF39/CF6 type. The Type A engine, which ran first, has the characteristics listed below. Data for the second, Type C, engine are given in parentheses: By-pass ratio 6 (5 : 1). Overall diameter 73·22 in; 1,860 mm (68·5 in; 1,740 mm). Fan blades 40 (26). Fan tip speed 1,150 ft; 350 m/sec (1,560 ft; 475 m/sec). Mass flow 961 lb; 436 kg/sec (923 lb; 419 kg/sec). Pressure ratio 16·8 (18·8). Turbine gas temperature at take-off 1,060°C.

GENERAL ELECTRIC T700

Under a contract awarded by the US Army Aviation Materiel Laboratories Propulsion Division, General Electric initiated a two-year demonstration programme in August 1967 to design, build and test a new 1,500 shp advanced technology turboshaft. Designated GE12, the engine was developed by the Aircraft Engine Group's Military Engine Division. During the latter part of 1968 the basic contracts for the GE12 and competing Pratt & Whitney ST9 demonstrator turboshaft were extended to the end of 1969 and additional work was also funded to carry the GE12 programme through to 30 September 1971. The GE12 demonstrator was illustrated in the 1971-72 *Jane's*.

A new competition was conducted in 1971 to provide the power plant for the Army's projected utility tactical transport system (UTTAS) proposed as a replacement for the present Bell UH-1 family of Army helicopters. In early 1972 it was announced that the winner was the GE engine, and that a contract for a production version, the T700-GE-700, was being negotiated with the US Army Aviation Systems Command. The first engine was due to begin bench testing in March 1973. Delivery for UTTAS ground testing was due in March 1974, flight qualification was scheduled for September 1974 and production qualification for March 1976.

The first T700-GE-700 ran six days ahead of schedule on 27 February 1973. By March 1974 six prototypes had run more than 1,800 hr.

The T700 has been designed to be compatible with the Army's special operating and environmental conditions, and embodies high reliability, simplicity of maintenance, low vulnerability to combat damage, and high performance combined with compact dimensions. Use is made of higher pressure ratios and turbine entry temperatures than with existing small turboshafts to assist in reducing size and weight. Specific fuel consumption of the T700 is 25 to 30% lower than that of present turboshafts, and weight is some 33% lower than that of current helicopter engines of the same power category.

To reduce vulnerability, all external lines and leads are short in length and are grouped compactly for minimum exposure. Self-contained electrical and lubrication systems are fitted. Multiple mounting points allow for ease of installation and the necessary airframe connections have been minimised and are located close to the engine centreline. The whole engine is of modular construction for swift field maintenance or section replacement without special tools (for example, complete hot-section inspection and replacement by two men in two hours using standard toolbox).

GE has announced studies for derivatives, including a family of turbojets for RPVs and other small fixed-wing aircraft, and a high-ratio turbofan with an added LP turbine stage, with direct drive to the single-stage fan.

Type: Ungeared free-turbine turboshaft engine.

Intake: Annular type, with anti-iced integral inlet particle separator containing no moving parts yet designed to remove 95 per cent of sand, dust and foreign-object ingestion.

Compressor: Combined axial/centrifugal. Five axial stages and single centrifugal stage mounted on same shaft. Each axial stage is one-piece "blisk" (blades plus disc) in AM355 steel highly resistant to erosion and corrosion. Inlet guide vanes and first two stator stages are variable. Pressure ratio, about 15 : 1. Airflow 10 lb (4·5 kg)/sec.

Combustion Chamber: Fully annular. Compact short-length configuration, designed for maximum reliability and long life. Central fuel injection to maximise acceptance of contaminated fuel and give minimal smoke generation and uniform temperature profile into the turbine. Flame tube is machined ring in Hastelloy X.

Turbine: Two-stage gas-generator (HP) turbine operates at gas temperatures exceeding 1,200°C. First-stage nozzle investment-cast in X40. Second-stage nozzle investment-cast in two-blade segments in R80. Both rotor stages have blades precision-cast in René 120, with nickel-aluminide diffusion coating. Simple radial convection internal air cooling. Discs, cooling plates and blades of both stages clamped by five short tiebolts; five larger bolts then tighten turbine to shaft, driving via curvic joint. Rated shaft speed (S/L, ISA, 100 per cent power), 44,720 rpm. Two-stage free power turbine, designed for high efficiency at part-power levels (especially 30 and 60% of military power), with tip-shrouded blades and segmented nozzles. Nozzle guide vanes René 77, rotor discs Inco 718, rotor blades René 80 uncooled. Output speed, 20,000 rpm. Power output shaft for front drive.

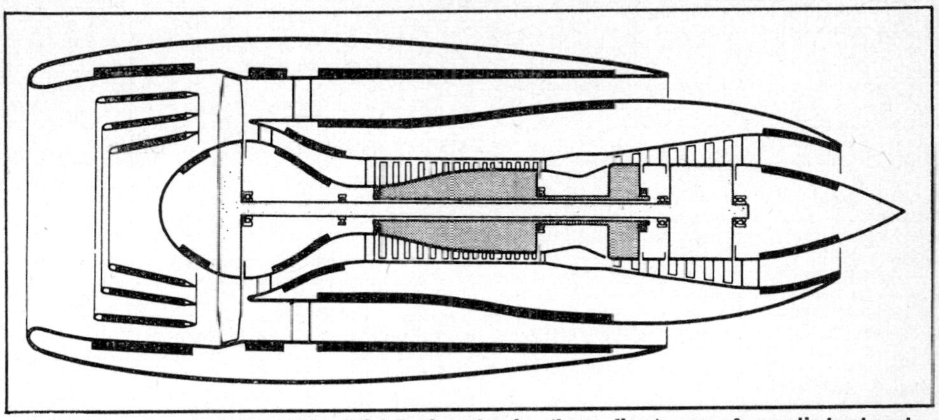

Simplified section of the GE/NASA Quiet Engine, showing (heavy lines) areas of acoustic treatment which reduce noise at take-off thrust to about 90 EPNdB

GE/NASA Quiet Engine running at Lewis in a Boeing-built nacelle

Accessories: Grouped at top of engine, together with engine control system, for maximum simplicity, accessibility and combat survivability. Integral lubrication supply tank, plus 6-minute emergency supply of mist lubrication following total loss of main supply.

Dimensions:

Length overall	46·5 in (1,181 mm)
Width	25 in (635 mm)
Height overall	23 in (584 mm)

Weight, Dry (with particle separator): 400 lb (181 kg)

Performance Ratings:

Intermediate (T-O)	1,536 shp
Max continuous	1,250 shp
75 per cent max continuous	900 shp

Specific Fuel Consumption:

Intermediate	0·469 lb (0·213 kg)/shp/hr
Max continuous	0·477 lb (0·217 kg)/shp/hr
75 per cent	0·520 lb (0·236 kg)/shp/hr

GENERAL ELECTRIC T58

The T58 is a small free-turbine power unit which was developed originally by General Electric for the Bureau of Weapons, US Navy. It has been adopted also by the USAF. A civil version, the CT58, was awarded a Type Certificate by the FAA on 1 July 1959 and is described separately.

The engine is intended primarily as a power unit for helicopters. But it may also be developed for small fixed-wing aircraft in the form of a

General Electric T700-GE-700 turboshaft engine, showing (light coloured duct rising at mid-section) the extractor system for solid particles removed by the inlet separator. Intermediate (T-O) rating, 1,536 shp

turboprop when combined with propeller reduction gear, as an auxiliary boost unit for large military and commercial aircraft and for marine and industrial use.

Hydromechanical constant-speed control system featured in the T58 maintains essentially constant rotor speed by regulating the engine power automatically, so eliminating the need for speed adjustment by the pilot during normal operation.

Initial flight tests of the T58 were made in a Sikorsky SH-34H, which flew for the first time with two T58s in a nose installation on 30 January 1957.

Rolls-Royce (1971) Ltd is manufacturing the T58 under licence in Great Britain as the Gnome. It is also licensed for manufacture in Italy and Japan. Industrial and marine version of the T58 is the LM100.

Versions currently in service or under development are as follows:

T58-GE-3. Five-minute rating of 1,325 shp. Powers Bell UH-1F.

T58-GE-5. Five-minute rating of 1,500 shp. Powers Sikorsky CH-3E and HH-3E/F.

T58-GE-8E, F. Rated at 1,350 shp. Powers Boeing Vertol CH-46A, Kaman SH-2, Sikorsky SH-3A and HH-52A.

T58-GE-10. Rated at 1,400 shp. Powers Sikorsky SH-3D and Boeing Vertol CH-46D.

T58-GE-16. Rated at 1,870 shp. US military qualified. Introduces aircooled gas-generator turbine and two-stage power turbine.

Type: Free-turbine turboshaft.

Air Intake: Annular intake casing with four hollow radial struts supporting central housing for starter drive clutch and front main roller bearing. Casing and struts anti-iced by air bled from compressor.

Compressor: Ten-stage axial-flow. Variable-incidence inlet guide vanes. First three of the eleven rows of stator blades also have variable incidence. One-piece steel construction for last eight stages of rotor hub. Casing divided into upper and lower halves. Pressure ratio 8·4:1. Air mass flow 12·4 lb (5·62 kg)/sec in T58-GE-3 and 8E, 13·7 lb (6·21 kg)/sec in T58-GE-5 and -10, 13·9 lb (6·30 kg)/sec in T58-GE-16.

Combustion Chamber: Annular type. Sixteen fuel nozzles (eight on each of two manifolds) mounted on front of inner liner. Dual capacitor discharge ignition unit. Outer casing in two halves to facilitate inspection.

Gas Generator Turbine: Two-stage short-chord axial-flow type, coupled directly to compressor by hollow conical shaft. Centre ball thrust bearing, rear roller bearing. Cooling by air bled from compressor. T58-GE-16 has aircooled first-stage turbine nozzle and blades and second-stage nozzle.

Power Turbine: Single-stage (two-stage in T58-GE-16) axial-flow type, mechanically independent of gas generator turbine. Operated nominally at 19,500 rpm, reduced to 6,000 rpm by reduction gear. Power turbine accessory drive unit and flexible feedback cable provide a speed signal to the control.

Torque Sensor Speed Decreaser Gearbox (optional): Gearbox with integral lubrication system. Reduces power speed to 6,000 rpm. Assembly includes an integral torque sensing system.

Jet Exhaust: Two positions (90° left or right) on all versions. T58-GE-16 can also be supplied with downward-ejecting or multiple-position exhaust.

Controls (except T58-GE-10 and -16): Free turbine constant-speed control. Hydromechanical controls.

Controls (T58-GE-10, -16): Integrated hydromechanical/electrical power control system for isochronous speed governing and twin-engine load sharing.

Accessory Drives: Engine accessories driven partly by the compressor shaft. Airframe accessories mounted on free-turbine reduction gearbox or rotor hub.

Dimensions:	
Max width:	
except T58-GE-16	20·7 in (526 mm)
T58-GE-16	22·6 in (574 mm)
Length overall:	
except T58-GE-16	54·9 in (1,394 mm)
T58-GE-16	63·5 in (1,613 mm)
Weight, Dry:	
T58-GE-3	309 lb (140 kg)
T58-GE-5	335 lb (152 kg)
T58-GE-8E, F	305 lb (138 kg)
T58-GE-10	350 lb (159 kg)
T58-GE-16	440 lb (200 kg)
Performance Ratings:	
Five-minute rating:	
See under model listings above	
Military rating:	
T58-GE-3	1,325 shp at 20,960 rpm
T58-GE-5, 10	1,400 shp at 19,500 rpm
T58-GE-8E, F	1,350 shp at 19,500 rpm
T58-GE-16	1,870 shp at 19,500 rpm
Cruise rating:	
T58-GE-3	1,070 shp
T58-GE-5, 10	1,250 shp
T58-GE-8E, F	1,150 shp
T58-GE-16	1,770 shp
Specific Fuel Consumption:	
At military rating:	
T58-GE-3	0·61 lb (0·277 kg)/shp/hr
T58-GE-5, 8E/F, 10	0·60 lb (0·272 kg)/shp/hr
T58-GE-16	0·53 lb (0·240 kg)/shp/hr
At cruise rating:	
T58-GE-3	0·63 lb (0·286 kg)/shp/hr
T58-GE-5	0·61 lb (0·277 kg)/shp/hr
T58-GE-8E, F	0·62 lb (0·281 kg)/shp/hr
T58-GE-10	0·62 lb (0·281 kg)/shp/hr
T58-GE-16	0·54 lb (0·245 kg)/shp/hr

GENERAL ELECTRIC CT58

The commercial version of the T58 is designated CT58 and was the first US helicopter turbine to receive FAA certification.

Current versions are as follows:

CT58-110. Rated at 1,250 shp (1,350 shp for 2½ min) at 19,500 rpm. Air mass flow 12·7 lb (5·67 kg)/sec. Pressure ratio 8·2 : 1.

CT58-140. Rated at 1,400 shp (1,500 shp for 2½ min) at 19,500 rpm. Air mass flow 13·7 lb (6·21 kg)/sec. Pressure ratio 8·4 : 1.

The CT58 powers the Sikorsky S-61 and S-62 and Boeing Vertol 107 Model II helicopter airliners.

Dimensions:	
Max width	16·0 in (406 mm)
Length overall	59·0 in (1,500 mm)
Weight, Dry:	
CT58-110	315 lb (143 kg)
CT58-140	340 lb (154 kg)
Performance Ratings:	
2½ min rating and normal T-O rating:	
See under model listings above	
Cruise rating:	
CT58-110	1,050 shp
CT58-140	1,250 shp
Specific Fuel Consumption:	
At normal T-O rating	0·61 lb (0·277 kg)/shp/hr
At cruise rating:	
CT58-110	0·64 lb (0·290 kg)/shp/hr
CT58-140	0·62 lb (0·281 kg)/shp/hr

GENERAL ELECTRIC T64

The T64 is a versatile aircraft gas-turbine engine which was initially developed for the US Navy. The basic T64 turboshaft engine becomes a turboprop with the addition of a two-part speed-reduction gearbox.

Current versions include:

T64-GE-1(-3). Direct-drive turboshaft rated at 3,080 shp. Four engines powered the LTV-Hiller-Ryan XC-142A tilt-wing transport and two T64-3s power the Sikorsky HH-53B helicopter.

T64-GE-6. Direct-drive turboshaft rated at 3,080 shp. Two engines power the Sikorsky CH-53A helicopter.

T64-GE-7. Direct-drive turboshaft rated at 3,925 shp. Two engines power the Sikorsky CH/HH-53C and German Army CH-53G.

T64-GE-7A. Growth version of -7 with improved turbine cooling. Flat rated at 3,936 shp to 28°C.

T64-GE-10. Turboprop engine with propeller gearbox above engine centreline; similar to T64-GE-6 and rated at 2,850 ehp. This engine is being produced under licence by Ishikawajima Harima Heavy Industries in Japan for the Shin Meiwa PS-1 flying-boat (four engines) and the Kawasaki P-2J patrol aircraft (two engines).

T64-GE-16. Direct-drive turboshaft; powered Lockheed AH-56A helicopter. Rated at 3,925 shp, this engine is FAA certificated as the **CT64-630-1.**

Other T64 engines in service include:

T64-GE-413. Direct-drive turboshaft rated at 3,925 shp. Two engines power the US Navy CH-53D and RH-53D, and the German (VFW) Sikorsky CH-53G.

T64-GE-415. Growth version with improved combustion liner and turbine cooling. Max rating 4,380 shp. Powers Sikorsky RH-53D and three-engined CH-53E helicopters.

T64-GE-716. Improved engine for Lockheed AH-56, rated at 3,936 shp up to 28·3°C.

CT64-GE-820. This turboprop engine is a growth version of the T64-6 with the -7 compressor and FAA-required modifications. Two such engines power the de Havilland Canada DHC-5 Buffalo (-820-1) and the prototype Aeritalia G222 (-820-2). The 820-3 has the improved hot section of the -7. All versions rated at 3,060 ehp, with propeller gearbox above centreline.

T64-P4D. Turboprop version flat rated at 3,400 shp to 45°C. Two P4D engines power the production Aeritalia G222 transport.

All T64s are qualified to operate from 100° nose-up to 45° nose-down. The T64 was designed

The 1,870 shp General Electric T58-GE-16 turboshaft

The 3,925 shp General Electric T64-GE-413 turboshaft

for extensive growth: current production engines rated at 4,380 shp are a result of growth made possible largely by aircooling of the first-stage gas generator turbine rotor and stator. The addition of aircooling to the second turbine stage provides further horsepower growth beyond 5,000 shp without significant change in external dimensions.

By February 1974 a total of over 1,800 T64 engines of all kinds had been delivered by GE to customers in nine countries. In addition licences to produce the T64 are held by MTU in Germany, Fiat in Italy, Rolls-Royce (1971) in Britain and IHI in Japan.

TYPE: Free-turbine turboshaft/turboprop engine.

COMPRESSOR: Fourteen-stage axial-flow. Single-spool steel rotor for -1, -3, -6, -10 and -820-1/2/3. Titanium compressor for -7, -7A, -16, -413, -415, -P4D, CT64-630-1 and CT64-820-4. Inlet guide vanes and first four stages of stator blades are variable. Compressor blades can be removed individually without rotor disassembly. Casing is flanged along the centreline. Stator blades are removable. Air mass flow for -1, -3, -6, -10 is 24·5 lb (11·1 kg)/sec, with pressure ratio 12·5 : 1. Air mass flow for -7, -7A, -16, -413, -415, -820, -P4D and CT64-630-1 is 25·6 lb (12·0 kg)/sec, with pressure ratio of 14·7 : 1.

COMBUSTION CHAMBER: Annular type. Double fuel manifold feeds twelve duplex-type fuel nozzles with external flow divider. Nozzles mounted on outer diffuser wall of compressor rear frame.

GAS GENERATOR TURBINE: Two-stage axial-flow type, coupled directly to compressor rotor by spline connection.

POWER TURBINE: Two-stage axial-flow type, mechanically independent of gas generator turbine.

REDUCTION GEAR: Remotely-mounted basic reduction gear for turboprop versions is offset and accessible for inspection and replacement. Gear-driven by power turbine, using co-axial shafting through the compressor. Propeller gear ratio 13·44 : 1.

STARTING: Mechanical, airframe supplied.

DIMENSIONS:

Length:

T64-GE-3, -6, -7, -413, -415, -630	83 in (2,108 mm)
T64-GE-10, -820, -P4D	113 in (2,870 mm)
T64-GE-16	65 in (1,351 mm)

Width:

T64-GE-3, -6, -7, -16, -413, -415, -630	24 in (610 mm)
T64-GE-10, -820, -P4D	29 in (727 mm)

Height:

T64-GE-3, -6, -7, -16, -413, -415, -630	32 in (813 mm)
T64-GE-10, -820, -P4D	46 in (1,168 mm)

WEIGHT, DRY:

T64-GE-3, -6	722 lb (328 kg)
T64-GE-7, -413, -415	720 lb (327 kg)
T64-GE-10, CT64-820-4	1,167 lb (529 kg)
CT64-820-1	1,130 lb (513 kg)
CT64-820-2, -3	1,145 lb (520 kg)
T64-P4D	1,188 lb (538 kg)

PERFORMANCE RATINGS:

Max rating (sea level):

T64-GE-3	3,080 shp
T64-GE-10	2,850 ehp at 1,160 output rpm
T64-GE-6	3,080 shp
T64-GE-7, -7A, -16, -413	3,925 shp
CT64-820	3,060 ehp
T64-P4D	3,400 shp
T64-415	4,380 shp

Military rating:

T64-GE-3	2,910 shp
T64-GE-10	2,650 ehp
T64-GE-6	2,690 shp
T64-GE-7, -7A, -16, -413	3,695 shp

Max continuous:

CT64-820	2,480 ehp

SPECIFIC FUEL CONSUMPTION (S/L):

At max rating:

T64-GE-3	0·485 lb (0·220 kg)/shp/hr
T64-GE-10	0·505 lb (0·229 kg)/ehp/hr
T64-GE-6	0·488 lb (0·221 kg)/shp/hr
T64-GE-7, -16, -413	0·476 lb (0·216 kg)/shp/hr
T64-415	0·466 lb (0·212 kg)/shp/hr
T64-P4D	0·484 lb (0·219 kg)/shp/hr

At T-O:

CT-64-820	0·503 lb (0·228 kg)/ehp/hr

At military rating:

T64-GE-3, -10	0·490 lb (0·222 kg)/shp/hr
T64-GE-7, -16, -413	0·472 lb (0·214 kg)/shp/hr

At max continuous:

CT64-820	0·521 lb (0·236 kg)/ehp/hr

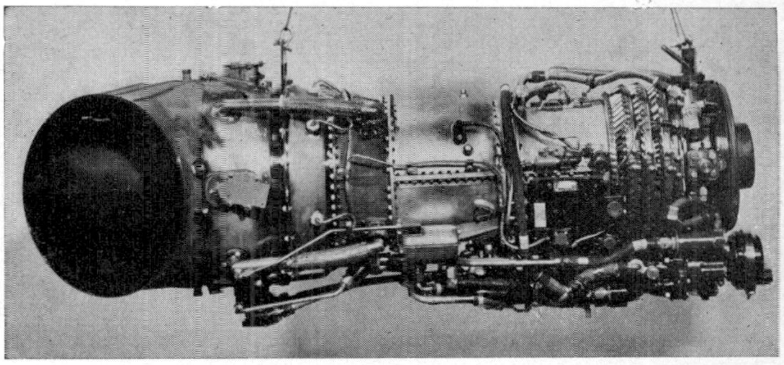

The 1,350 shp T58-GE-8E turboshaft engine

GESCHWENDER

GESCHWENDER AEROMOTIVE

ADDRESS: Box 6043, Lincoln, Nebraska 68506
Telephone: (402) 488-8050

Fred L. Geschwender has begun to market a range of engines aimed primarily at homebuilt aircraft which are replicas of World War 1 aircraft, or scaled replicas of World War 2 fighters, and other aircraft having in-line or vee-type engines. The generally available certificated engines preclude an amateur constructor from achieving realism.

His search narrowed down possible engines to vee-type automotive units and, finally, to the "small block" Ford engines of 289, 302, 351 and 400 cu in capacity. These are V-8 engines, but some V-6 units can also be used. Geschwender's present policy is to design, build and market hardware for conversion kits by which stock car engines can be fitted for unrestricted aerial use.

The kit normally includes: 2 : 1 reduction gear, using precision chain drive; new ignition system with single plugs but dual magnetos and leads (one set being normally disconnected but available for immediate use); new drive with torsion-damper and electric-starter ring; various carburettor and accessory options; and cooling system (generally very similar to that of a modern liquid-cooled car) tailored to the aircraft. Geschwender comments that the conversions so far tested sound uncannily like a Rolls-Royce Merlin, besides allowing the cowled installation to look like one.

During the past year, two new engines have been under development. These are the Ford Capri and Mustang 2 V-6 engines of 159 and 171 cu in, rated at 160 hp before conversion, and the Ford Pinto and Mustang 2 engines of 122 and 140 cu in, rated originally at 100 hp. Mr Geschwender comments on the remarkable interest being shown by agricultural aviation, and a 400 cu in installation in a spraying aircraft was expected to appear at the 1974 EAA Convention.

The following are basic data for existing models:

DIMENSIONS (length/width/height, in; mm):

289 cu in	53·5; 1,359/22·0; 559/24·0; 610
302 cu in	53·5; 1,359/22·0; 559/24·25; 616
351 cu in (351C)	53·5; 1,359/23·0; 584/24·5; 622
400 cu in	53·5; 1,359/23·0; 584/25·0; 635

WEIGHT, DRY:

289 cu in	555 lb (251·8 kg)
302 cu in	562 lb (256·0 kg)
351C	600 lb (272·2 kg)
400 cu in	600 lb (272·2 kg)

Geschwender 289 cu in eight-cylinder piston engine rated at 225 hp

MAX POWER (S/L):

289 cu in	225 hp at 4,800 rpm (crankshaft)
302 cu in	235 hp at 4,800 rpm (crankshaft)
351C	330 hp at 5,400 rpm (crankshaft)
400 cu in	260 hp at 4,400 rpm (crankshaft)

GLUHAREFF

GLUHAREFF HELICOPTERS

ADDRESS:
18518 S. Broadway Avenue, Gardena, California 90248
Telephone: (213) 321-8699

For more than five years Eugene M. Gluhareff, a pioneer of ultra-light rotorcraft, has been developing a unique type of air-breathing jet engine which he considers to offer notable advantages over all other systems for rotor tip-drive. The first model is now out of the development stage and is on sale in three sizes in various forms for tip-drive or sailplane auxiliary propulsion. It has also been used for surface application in a go-kart, and in numerous static rigs sold to universities and other organisations. Production has been hard pressed to keep up with demand, a fast-growing market being radio-controlled flight vehicles.

GLUHAREFF G8-2

Although extremely simple the G8 series corresponds to no prior jet system. The design is based on propane, a readily-available volatile fuel. The pressure of the liquid propane in the tank delivers the fuel, via a needle valve serving as the throttle, to the burner unit. The pipe enters the burner duct and is immediately vaporised in a hot heat-exchanger. Vapour then passes back down an insulated pipe to the injector where its residual pressure is converted to kinetic energy in accelerating to supersonic speed. The high-velocity gas jet induces air through three "supercharger" intakes, each synchronised to the internal flow, which gives the correct final fuel/air ratio to the mixture entering the combustion chamber. Here the mixture is initially ignited by a spark plug and thereafter burns continuously. The intake ducts are tuned to each other to create one-way flow. Resonance in the tailpipe is undesirable and is prevented by making the propelling nozzle of fishtail shape.

Once started, by opening the throttle valve and closing the induction-coil igniter circuit, the engine takes up to ten seconds to warm up and thereafter can be swiftly cycled between minimum and maximum thrust, which varies approximately linearly with fuel flow. Static thrust is about 90 per cent of the value attainable dynamically with maximum ram-air augmentation. There is no visible flame or smoke, though the tailpipe is short enough not to bend under centrifugal load when hot. Noise is considered "low in comparison with other types of jet engines". Life is dictated solely by the slow oxidation of the stainless steel parts.

At present production is concentrated on two sizes of jet unit. The G8-2-15 is 36 in (914 mm) long; has a tailpipe diameter of 3·5 in (89 mm) and weighs 5·5 lb. The equivalent horsepower at 400 mph (644 km/h) is 19·2. The G8-2-40 is 38·5 in (978 mm) long, has a tailpipe diameter of 5·0 in (127 mm) and weighs 11·5 lb (5·2 kg). The equivalent horsepower at 400 mph (644 km/h) is 46·0.

Static thrust (S/L, ISA) for the smaller unit, the G8-2-15, ranges from 1 lb (0·45 kg) at nozzle pressure of 20 lb/sq in (1·4 kg/cm²) to 15 lb (6·8 kg) at about 130 lb/sq in (9·14 kg/cm²). At the lower end the specific fuel consumption is over 10, but at higher powers levels off close to 6. Addition of a ram-air scoop reduces static performance (max about 10·5 lb; 4·8 kg), but raises

Gluhareff G8-2-15 jet unit, rated at 15 lb (6·8 kg) st, without ram-air scoop

dynamic thrust at 300 ft (91·5 m)/sec from 15·9 lb (7·2 kg) to 17·5 lb (7·9 kg). Altitude performance has been explored statically, on a mountain; more than 12 lb (5·4 kg) thrust was available at 8,050 ft (2,455 m), the greatest height reached.

An installation comprises tank (on aircraft CG), tank valve, needle throttle valve, fuel lines, jet unit, ignition system and pressure gauges for the tank and fuel nozzle. Care must be taken to install the unit so that radiant heat from the main duct and from the hot vapour line (up to 540°C) cannot harm the vehicle structure or rotor blade. Light sailplanes have flown successfully on a single G8-2-15, taking off unaided into a 15-20 mph (24-32 km/h) wind. The larger G8-2-40 develops up to 40 lb (18·1 kg) st.

The units are manufactured by Gluhareff's subsidiary EMG Engineering Co. Customers have the option of buying: plans only; a construction package, partly prefabricated; an assembly kit; or a finished engine.

JACOBS-PAGE

PAGE INDUSTRIES OF OKLAHOMA, INC

HEAD OFFICE
Cimarron Airport, PO Box 191, Yukon, Oklahoma 73099
Telephone: (405) 354-5385

PRESIDENT: O. J. Butto

VICE-PRESIDENT AND GENERAL MANAGER:
David Goulding

ENGINEERING MANAGER:
Merrill H. Bumbaugh

Page Industries of Oklahoma is the successor to the Jacobs Aircraft Engine Co, which had manufactured aircooled radial piston engines since 1929. Current production is centred upon the various versions of the R-755 described below. Page is holder of the FAA Approved Parts Inspection System (APIS) for production of new Jacobs engine parts.

JACOBS R-755

This long-established seven-cylinder radial is being manufactured in several versions. The basic engine is the **R-755A** which is the subject of the detailed description. The current engines in this series are the R-755A2, and the A2M with dual ignition. The **R-755B** has a lower power rating, and is available as the R-755B1, driving a fixed-pitch propeller, and the B2 which can have a control valve for a two-position propeller or provision for a hydraulically-operated constant-speed propeller. The **R-755S** is a turbocharged version, available with dual ignition as the R-755SM.

TYPE: Seven-cylinder aircooled radial piston engine.

CYLINDERS: Bore 5·25 in (133 mm). Stroke 5 in (127 mm). Swept volume 757 cu in (12·3 litres). Barrels machined from steel forgings with close-spaced fins. Aluminium alloy heads screwed and shrunk on. Aluminium-bronze valve-seats shrunk into heads.

PISTONS: Forged aluminium alloy. Three compression rings and one scraper ring above gudgeon-pin (piston-pin) and two scraper rings below. Fully-floating nitrided gudgeon-pins.

CONNECTING RODS: One-piece steel master rod. Forged aluminium alloy link rods bearing directly upon nitrided-steel pins.

CRANKSHAFT: Two-piece clamp type, machined from forgings in chrome-nickel-molybdenum steel.

CRANKCASE: Assembled from five parts. Aluminium alloy front case carries thrust ball bearing and valve-operating gear. Front half of main case is aluminium alloy casting supporting crankshaft front roller bearing. Rear half of main case is aluminium alloy casting supporting crankshaft rear roller bearing and incorporates ring-type intake manifold. Aluminium alloy rear plate carries additional crankshaft ball bearing and supports accessory drives. Aluminium alloy rear case carries accessories.

VALVE GEAR: Cam ring, drive gears, tappets and pushrods all in nose section, with all moving parts enclosed. Tulip-type inlet valves and sodium-cooled exhaust valves, each with two springs.

INDUCTION: Single updraught Stromberg NA-R7A carburettor. R-755S and SM have this carburettor fed at up to 35 in Hg by AiResearch exhaust-gas turbocharger between Nos. 2 and 3 cylinders. System set to maintain power to 19,500 ft (5,945 m), with aneroid relief valve to prevent overboosting beyond 36 in Hg. Manifold pressure controlled by throttle.

FUEL: 80 octane (755S, SM, 80/87 octane).

IGNITION: One Scintilla magneto and battery distributor, incorporating automatic advance (engines with "M" suffix, two magnetos).

LUBRICATION: Single unit comprising gear pressure pump and two scavenge pumps feeds all plain bearings. Dry sump. Automatic valve lubrication. Optional provision to operate adjustable-pitch or constant-speed propeller.

PROPELLER DRIVE: Direct, RH tractor, SAE 20 spline.

MOUNTING: Choice of eight locations incorporated around rear main crankcase.

DIMENSIONS:

Diameter	44 in (1,118 mm)
Length overall	$40\frac{7}{32}$ in (1,020 mm)

WEIGHT, DRY:

R-755A, B1	505 lb (229 kg)
R-755B2	511 lb (232 kg)
R-755S	576 lb (261 kg)
R-755SM	583 lb (264 kg)

PERFORMANCE RATINGS:

Rated power:

R-755A	300 hp at 2,200 rpm
R-755B	275 hp at 2,200 rpm

R-755S, SM:
rated power 275 hp at 2,030 rpm maintained to 19,500 ft (5,945 m); take-off (1 min limit) 350 hp at 2,200 rpm

Jacobs-Page R-755A seven-cylinder radial piston engine, rated at 300 hp

LPC

LOCKHEED PROPULSION COMPANY

HEADQUARTERS:
PO Box 111, Redlands, California 92373
Telephone: (714) 794-5111

PRESIDENT:
G. Graham Whipple

EXECUTIVE VICE-PRESIDENT, OPERATIONS:
N. B. Chase

VICE-PRESIDENTS:
A. H. Von Der Esch (Technical, Marketing)

Lockheed Propulsion Company is the former Grand Central Rocket Company, which was founded in 1952 as the first major US company devoted entirely to the advancement of solid-propellant rocket development. It became a wholly-owned subsidiary of the Lockheed Aircraft Corporation in late 1961, and a division of Lockheed in February 1963.

Current programmes include production of the solid-propellant pulse motor for the USAF Short Range Attack Missile (SRAM), a launch escape motor for the Apollo-Soyuz Test Project, several alternative thrust vector control systems for large solid-propellant motors, and small, variable-thrust motors for attitude control, orbital ejection and re-entry. LPC has also developed and test-fired more than 300 hybrid rockets utilising a solid-propellant fuel and liquid oxidiser, with diameters of up to 19 in (0·48 m). This work was done for the US Army.

LPC developed a "self-eject" launch technique. In this, the solid rocket vehicle ejects itself from a launch tube using low-pressure gas flow from its own first-stage motor. Once out of the tube the motor comes to full thrust automatically. A vehicle weighing more than 300,000 lb (136,078 kg) has been launched successfully by this method.

The company has developed a high-energy smokeless propellant for use in tactical missiles and is studying new techniques for launching rockets from guns. One such concept keeps the rocket vehicle intact while being driven from the barrel by a powder charge. Once out of the nozzle, and while travelling at approximately 3,000 ft (915 m)/sec, the rocket's own motor fires. Such techniques offer a considerable extension of a missile's range.

LPC has continued to develop solid propellants called polycarbutenes. They are based on polybutadiene prepolymer binder systems (PBAA, PBAN, CTPB, HTPB) and have been characterised to meet a broad spectrum of operational requirements. These propellant systems have been fired with grains weighing up to 364,000 lb (165,108 kg). Solid-propulsion units have successfully completed temperature cycling from minus 100 to plus 93°C, random vibration from 20 to 2,000 cycles per second, 10·5*g* acceleration, 20*g* drop shock, ageing in vacuum and ambient ageing up to seven years. The ballistics of these propellant systems have been tailored to meet broad burning rate requirements, maximum impulse, and low to high pressure exponents for an exceedingly wide range of solid propulsion design requirements. Physical properties meet complex structural integrity requirements.

Static test-firing of the LPC-415 solid-propellant pulse rocket motor developed and qualified by LPC for the US Air Force's AGM-69A short-range attack missile (SRAM)

Recent development programmes include advanced pulse motors which permit sequential or simultaneous burning of pulse grains to produce a wide range of thrust levels, and a unique grain-retention system which produces minimum propellant strains over a wide temperature and vibration environment. A third new development is a grain design concept utilising embedded fuses which, as they burn, form grain ports. This grain configuration combines the high volumetric efficiency of an end-burner with the lower burning rate and greater ballistic flexibility of a centre-perforated grain.

LPC has developed and is producing flexible seals, called Lockseals, for use on movable-nozzle thrust-vector control systems. The Lockseal movable joint is composed of alternate layers of rubber and metal in a laminated structure. Lockseal joints also are being produced for commercial applications. The company is conducting propellant structural-integrity programmes under USAF contracts, including a programme to design and fabricate a highly instrumented inert rocket motor for measurement of missile environments for air-launched rocket applications.

Additionally, and in support of its work on advanced upper-stage rockets, LPC has developed a family of nitrocellulose-base composite propellants (nitroplastisols) of very high specific impulse. Since 1968 research has also been conducted on an advanced monopropellant motor.

LPC is also engaged in fabrication of hardware for the aerospace industry and components for nuclear reactors.

Available details of motors which have aircraft, missile or space vehicle applications are given hereafter.

LPC-415

US military designation: SR75-LP-1

This is the propulsion system for the SRAM (Short Range Attack Missile) in service with the USAF as the AGM-69A. LPC developed, qualified, and is producing the motor under sub-contract to Boeing. It is an advanced, two-pulse motor which provides for multiple flight trajectories. It is a 17·5 in (444 mm) diameter, high-pressure/long-duration end-burner, with variable inter-pulse delay.

LPC-A1 APOLLO MOTOR

This is the launch escape motor which is designed to pull the Apollo spacecraft away from the Saturn booster in the event of an emergency during the launch phase. Fifty-seven motors have been fired successfully.

DIMENSIONS:

Length overall	185 in (4,700 mm)
Diameter	26 in (660 mm)

WEIGHT:	4,700 lb (2,130 kg)

PERFORMANCE:

Max thrust at S/L	155,000 lb (70,300 kg)

LPC-A2

This is the pitch control motor that is mounted at the forward end of the Apollo escape system. It is fired at the same time as the launch escape motor to push the spacecraft to one side, out of the flight path of the Saturn launch vehicle. This motor had completed 63 entirely successful firings by early 1973.

LPC MINI MOTOR (LP-117)

The Mini Motor is used to impart a spinning motion to research satellites. Total vacuum impulse can be varied between 17 and 35 lb-sec (7·7 and 15·9 kg-sec) by preselecting grain bore diameter and length. Cartridge-loading facilitates this impulse selection. The low solids content of the exhaust minimises particle impingement on the host vehicle.

DIMENSIONS:	
Length overall	9·58 in (153 mm)
Diameter	1·51 in (38 mm)
WEIGHT:	0·51 lb (0·23 kg)
PERFORMANCE:	
Average thrust in vacuum	24·8 lb (11·2 kg)
Total operating time	1·39 sec
Specific impulse	254 sec

LPC R/B EJECT MOTOR (LP-118)

This is a very small motor used to eject and spin a re-entry body. The motor provides a very high degree of ballistic reproducibility and a low content of alkaline elements in the exhaust. The internal-burning grain is cartridge-loaded.

DIMENSIONS:	
Length overall	3·62 in (92 mm)
Diameter	1·25 in (32 mm)
WEIGHT:	0·694 lb (0·315 kg)
PERFORMANCE:	
Average thrust in vacuum	49·4 lb (22·4 kg)
Action time	0·288 sec
Specific impulse	249 sec

LPC LARGE ORBITAL BOOST MOTOR (LP-119)

This motor is used in pairs for spacecraft orbit adjustment. It is a high-performance, relatively high-mass-fraction motor utilising a case-bonded, end-burning propellant grain and a high-strength aluminium case. Total impulse can be varied from 6,500 to 13,550 lb-sec (2,948 to 6,146 kg-sec) by selection of grain length.

DIMENSIONS:	
Length overall	13·0 in (330 mm)
Diameter	11·1 in (282 mm)
WEIGHT:	68·7 lb (31·2 kg)
PERFORMANCE:	
Average thrust in vacuum	592 lb (268·5 kg)
Action time	22·5 sec
Specific impulse	248 sec

LPC HIGH-THRUST MOTOR

This high-thrust, short-duration motor was developed and qualified for use in ejecting special payloads from missiles or space vehicles. Similar motors of smaller diameter have been used in tube-launched, shoulder-fired tactical weapons. The high-thrust motor contains a rubber-base PBAN non-aluminised composite fuel with ammonium perchlorate oxidiser, within a 7075 aluminium chamber with a steel nozzle throat. The motor is fired by a low-voltage squib triggered by an electrical pulse; maximum chamber pressure is 4,000 lb/sq in (281 kg/cm²).

DIMENSIONS:	
Length overall	10·03 in (255 mm)
Diameter	6·86 in (174 mm)
WEIGHT:	14·5 lb (6·57 kg)
PERFORMANCE:	
Max thrust at S/L	30,000 lb (13,607 kg)
Operating time	0·024 sec
Specific impulse	230 sec

SPIN/THRUST MOTOR

Avco Corporation, prime contractors for advanced re-entry vehicles for late-model LGM-30 Minuteman missiles, subcontracted to LPC the task of providing a reliable rocket motor capable of imparting either forward thrust or rotational spin (the motors are probably installed either in separate multiple warheads or in decoys or other penetration aids, but LPC cannot comment on this unofficial supposition). The Spin/Thrust motor weighs 2·6 lb (1·18 kg) and imparts a thrust variable from 38 to 800 lb (17-363 kg) over a burn time of 0·15-6·2 sec. The main charge fires through a central nozzle, while spin rates of 10·5-19·5 rps (630-1,170 rpm) are imparted by three canted tangential nozzles around the base. To suit the requirements of particular missions the propellant division between thrust and spin can be altered over a wide range, replacing propellant by inert filling if necessary to preserve motor weight and centre of gravity position.

LPC LSM 156-5

When this three-segment solid-propellant motor was fired in 1965 it was the largest flight prototype solid motor tested at that time. It developed about 3,000,000 lb (1,360,000 kg) thrust and consumed some 700,000 lb (317,500 kg) of polycarbutene propellant in one minute of forced-draught burning. It was the first rocket of this size to be fitted with all major components of a steering system suitable for use in an actual flight.

The LSM 156-5 was made up of a 150 ton 22 ft (6·70 m) long central segment and forward and aft segments of almost equal size. Liquid nitrogen tetroxide, under high pressure, was sprayed through selected injectors in the nozzle expansion cone to create a shock-wave and also to react chemically with the exhaust gases to generate side forces for steering, at right angles to the direction of main gas flow.

This was the fifth consecutive successful firing in the USAF's Large Solid Motor Program, and the third by LPC.

DIMENSIONS:	
Length overall	80 ft 0 in (24·4 m)
Diameter	156 in (3·96 m)
WEIGHT:	850,000 lb (385,500 kg)
PERFORMANCE:	
Max thrust at S/L	3,000,000 lb (1,360,000 kg)

LPC LSM 156-6

This monolithic (single-segment) 156 in (3·96 m) solid-propellant motor was the fourth fired by LPC under the USAF's Large Solid Motor Program. It could be considered a potential second stage of a space launch vehicle using a motor like the LSM 156-5, described above, as the first stage. It was filled with a polycarbutene propellant.

DIMENSIONS:	
Length overall	34 ft 0 in (10·36 m)
Diameter	156 in (3·96 m)
WEIGHT:	325,000 lb (147,400 kg)
PERFORMANCE:	
Max thrust at S/L	1,000,000 lb (453,600 kg)

LPC LSM 156-5 flight prototype 156 in solid-propellant motor

LTV

LTV AEROSPACE CORPORATION

HEAD OFFICE:
PO Box 5907, Dallas, Texas 75222
Telephone: (214) 266-4171
OFFICERS: See "Aircraft" section

LTV AEROSPACE LVRJ

Vought Systems Division, a division of LTV Aerospace (itself a subsidiary of the LTV Corporation) is developing, under a US Navy contract, a new air-breathing propulsion system designed for future missiles and other unmanned vehicles. Handled by the division's facility at Grand Prairie, Texas, the system is known as the Low-Volume Ram Jet (LVRJ). The propulsion method is described as a "stepping stone toward missile systems of the future". While performance details have not been released, the company announces that in broad terms the propulsion system will have several times the specific impulse of current systems and will represent a quantum jump in propulsion effectiveness for advanced stand-off tactical missile system applications.

The LVRJ features an integral rocket-ramjet propulsion system using a common motor case for compact design. Boosted to high speed by the solid-propellant motor, the vehicle then uses the empty motor case as a combustion chamber for ramjet fuel to provide high-speed long-duration flight. Four inlets on the vehicle's aft section provide ram air for combustion. Test vehicles scheduled for the flight demonstration programme are 15 ft (4·57 m) long and 15 in (381 mm) in diameter, but smaller or larger models can be designed for air-to-air or other applications. Funding of the development and flight test programme is under contract from the Naval Air Systems Command.

LTV Aerospace LVRJ carried by A-7E Corsair

MARQUARDT

THE MARQUARDT COMPANY (a division of CCI Corporation)

HEAD OFFICE:
16555 Saticoy Street, Van Nuys, California 91409
Telephone: (213) 781-2121
PRESIDENT:
G. H. Hanauer
VICE-PRESIDENTS:
R. C. Allen (Advanced Propulsion)
S. Alpert (Programme Management and Contract Administration)
T. C. Bowden (Marketing)
A. L. Sorensen (Operations)
DIRECTORS:
R. J. Haas (Environmental Products and Test)
B. E. Huston (Finance)
K. E. Woodgrift (Engineering)

The Marquardt Corporation was formed in November 1944 to undertake research and development of ramjet engines, and it produced the first American subsonic ramjet in 1945. Since that time the company has diversified into production of aerospace controls and accessories, space rocketry, ordnance components and industrial products.

Marquardt's main engineering business continues to be advanced aerospace propulsion and the supply of ram-air turbine power systems. A major portion of sales is currently associated with manufacture of sophisticated structures and components for the aerospace industry, and the production of clustered munition ordnance.

Marquardt is currently developing security-classified types of composite rocket/air-breathing propulsion systems for the US Air Force and Navy. These are regarded by the company as likely to lead to a new generation of power plants for supersonic strategic missiles and expendable tactical vehicles.

In the field of precision control rockets, Marquardt provided manoeuvring, stabilisation and control propulsion for the Apollo Service and Lunar Modules, and would have provided similar equipment for the terminated US Air Force Manned Orbiting Laboratory. The company's precision control rockets also served as main propulsion for the five Lunar Orbiters. Recently, the control rocket work has been expanded to include development of a monopropellant rocket system for a classified programme, and advanced development activities for a hydrogen/oxygen water electrolysis rocketry system. A complete range of monopropellant and bipropellant rockets, precision valves and rocketry components is now being marketed.

Marquardt maintains extensive test facilities at Van Nuys for research and testing of air-breathing rocket engines, and controls and accessories. Total land area occupied exceeds 56 acres, and covered buildings exceed 500,000 sq ft (46,400 m²); employment exceeds 700.

MARQUARDT R-4D

This liquid bipropellant rocket reaction control engine was developed and produced by Marquardt for the Apollo spacecraft Service Module and Lunar Module. With the completion of the Apollo flights, the engines are now used in the Skylab and Apollo-Soyuz programmes.

Type: Liquid-propellant reaction control rocket.

Propellants: Nitrogen tetroxide and monomethyl hydrazine.

Thrust Chamber Assembly: Single chamber. Area ratio 40. Made of aluminium, steel and molybdenum. Radiation cooling. Started by electrical signal to on/off solenoid valves. Hypergolic ignition. Combustion pressure 90 lb/sq in (6·33 kg/cm²). Combustion temperature 2,870°C.

Thrust Chamber Mounting: Flange bolt circle on injector head.

Dimensions:
- Length overall: 13·5 in (343 mm)
- Height: 6·6 in (168 mm)
- Width: 6·0 in (152 mm)

Weight, Dry: 5·0 lb (2·27 kg)

Performance Ratings:
- Max rating at S/L: 63 lb (28·5 kg) st
- Max rating in vacuum: 100 lb (45·5 kg) st

MARQUARDT MA210/212

Two versions of this low-cost ramjet engine have been developed. The pitot-inlet MA210-XAA is designed primarily for the high-subsonic speed regime of Mach 0·7 to 0·9, although it has been tested at Mach 2·0. The conical-inlet version, MA212-XAA, provides higher thrust and better cruise fuel consumption in supersonic flight conditions. The engines use the same combustor system with an interchangeable inlet-diffuser assembly selected for either subsonic or supersonic flight operation. Both versions are of single-wall all-steel construction with two-point mounting to the vehicle pylon. Ignition is by pyrotechnic flare.

Dimensions:
- Length overall:
  - MA210-XAA: 79 in (2,070 mm)
  - MA212-XAA: 84 in (2,134 mm)
- Diameter: 15 in (381 mm)

Weight, Dry:
- MA210-XAA: 70 lb (31·75 kg)
- MA212-XAA: 77·5 lb (35·2 kg)

Performance:
- Operating envelope:
  - MA210-XAA: S/L to 30,000 ft (9,145 m), Mach 0·7-1·5
  - MA212-XAA: S/L to 60,000 ft (18,290 m), Mach 1·0-2·5

Marquardt R-4D reaction control engines

- Design thrust (net):
  - MA210-XAA: 660 lb (300 kg), S/L, Mach 0·9
  - MA212-XAA: 1,360 lb (617 kg), 40,000 ft (12,200 m), Mach 2·5

Marquardt MA212-XAA conical-inlet supersonic ramjet (net thrust 1,360 lb; 617 kg at Mach 2.5 at 40,000 ft; 12,200 m)

McCULLOCH

McCULLOCH CORPORATION, LOS ANGELES DIVISION

Head Office and Main Plant:
6101, West Century Blvd, Los Angeles, California 90045
Telephone: (213) 670-2320

The two-cycle drone engine developed by this company is now being produced by Northrop Corporation (which see).

NELSON

NELSON AIRCRAFT CORPORATION

Head Office:
PO Box 454, Irwin, Pennsylvania 15642
Telephone: (412) 863-5900

President:
Charles R. Rhoades

Vice-President:
Lawrence J. Rhoades

Nelson Aircraft Corporation, among its many industrial activities, produces to order the Nelson H-63 four-cylinder two-cycle aircooled engine, which has been certificated by the FAA as a power unit for single-seat helicopters, and is now available also as a power plant for propeller-driven aircraft. All these engines are capable of sustained inverted flight. Recommended overhaul period is 800 hours. The engine is now available with a magneto starter, and a geared version (propeller rpm, 3,500) is under test.

NELSON H-63

US military designation: YO-65

Developed originally as a power unit for single-seat helicopters, the H-63 is now available in two versions, as follows:

H-63C. Basic helicopter power unit for vertical installation. Certificated by FAA. Supplied as complete power package, including clutch, cooling fan and shroud.

H-63CP. Basically as H-63C, but without clutch, fan and shroud. Intended primarily for installation in horizontal position, with direct drive to propeller. FAA certificated.

Nelson has developed a 42 in (1·07 m) wooden propeller with glassfibre covering for use with the H-63. It is suitable for either tractor or pusher installation.

Type: Four-cylinder horizontally-opposed air-cooled, two-stroke.

Cylinders: Bore $2\frac{11}{16}$ in (68·3 mm). Stroke $2\frac{3}{4}$ in (70 mm). Total capacity 63 cu in (1·03 litres). Compression ratio 8 : 1. Each complete cylinder is machined from an aluminium alloy casting, the bore being porous-chrome plated for wear resistance. Cylinders bolted to and detachable from crankcase.

Pistons: Aluminium alloy casting. Two piston rings. Two needle roller bearings pressed in boss. Piston (gudgeon) pin pressed into small end of connecting rod.

Connecting Rods: Alloy steel forging. Caged roller bearing at big-end.

Crankshaft: Four-throw. Nitralloy shaft on ball and roller bearings.

Crankcase: Two-piece case divided on horizontal centreline. Each half is a magnesium alloy casting.

Induction: Nelson diaphragm-type all-angle fuel control carburettor. Hot-air anti-icing. Fuel/oil mixture valves from crankcase through specially-designed rotary valve driven by crankshaft. Intake to and exhaust from cylinders through ports. Exhaust stacks are of aluminium alloy.

Fuel: 80/87 octane gasoline and SAE 30 kerosene-base oil in 8 : 1 mixture for fuel and lubrication.

Ignition: Battery-type dual-ignition with automatic retard for starting. Two Champion D-9 or 5 COM spark plugs per cylinder.

Lubrication: See under "Fuel".

Power Take-off (H-63C): Hollow shaft extension from Salisbury centrifugal clutch output drive.

Starting: 12V DC Autolite electric motor and Bendix drive.

Cooling (H-63C): Centrifugal aluminium fan and two-piece glassfibre shrouding designed to maintain all temperatures within acceptable limits on an FAA hot day of 37·8°C, S/L.

The 43 hp Nelson H-63C four-cylinder two-stroke engine

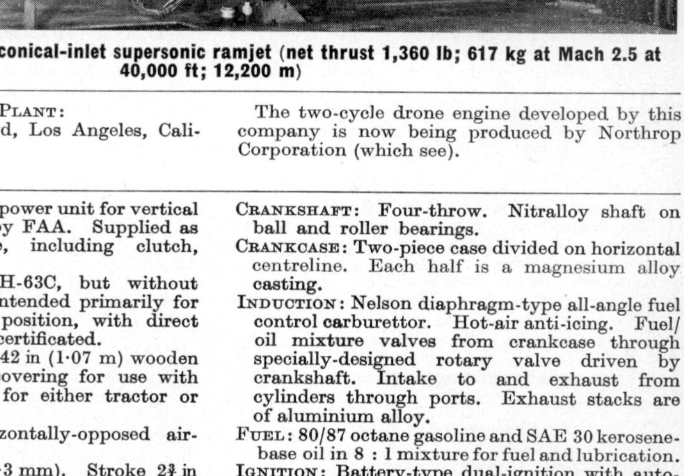

The 48 hp Nelson H-63CP for fixed-wing aircraft

MOUNTING: Four Lord-type mounts, two on each half of crankcase.

DIMENSIONS (H-63C):

Length	20·0 in (508 mm)
Height	14·8 in (376 mm)
Width	23·8 in (605 mm)

WEIGHT, DRY:

H-63C, with accessories	76 lb (34·5 kg)
H-63CP, with accessories	68 lb (30·8 kg)

POWER RATINGS:

T-O:

H-63C	43 hp at 4,000 rpm
H-63CP	48 hp at 4,400 rpm

Max continuous:

H-63C	43 hp at 4,000 rpm
H-63CP	45 hp at 4,000 rpm

CONSUMPTION:

Fuel/oil

6·3 US gallons (5·2 Imp gal; 24 litres)/hr at full throttle

NORTHROP

NORTHROP CORPORATION, VENTURA DIVISION

HEAD OFFICE AND MAIN PLANT:
1515 Rancho Conejo Boulevard, Newbury Park, California 91320
Telephone: (805) 498-3131

In 1972 Northrop Corporation acquired the rights to this engine from McCulloch Corporation (see 1972-73 *Jane's*). The 4318 series continues to be made and sold by Ventura Division, which uses the engine to power the MQM-36 Shelduck (see "RPVs" section).

NORTHROP MODEL 4318F

US military designation: O-100-3

TYPE: Four-cylinder horizontally-opposed air-cooled two-stroke.

CYLINDERS: Bore $3\frac{3}{16}$ in (80·8 mm). Stroke $3\frac{1}{8}$ in (79·4 mm). Displacement 100 cu in (1·6 litres). Compression ratio 7·8 : 1. Heat-treated die-cast aluminium cylinders with integral heads, having hard chrome plated cylinder walls. Self-locking nuts secure cylinders to crankcase studs.

PISTONS: Heat-treated cast aluminium. Two rings above pins. Piston pins of case-hardened steel.

CONNECTING RODS: Forged steel. "Free-roll" silver-plated bearings at big-end. Small-end carries one needle bearing. Lateral position of rod controlled by thrust washers between piston pin bosses and small-end of rod.

CRANKSHAFT: Four-throw one-piece steel forging on four anti-friction bearings, two ball and two needle, one with split race for centre main bearing.

CRANKCASE: One-piece heat-treated permanent-mould aluminium casting, closed at rear end with cast aluminium cover which provides mounting for magneto.

VALVE GEAR: Fuel mixture for scavenging and power stroke introduced to cylinders through crankshaft-driven rotary valves and ported cylinders.

The 84-96 hp Northrop 4318F four-cylinder piston engine

INDUCTION: Crankcase pumping type. Diaphragm-type carburettor with adjustable jet.

FUEL SPECIFICATION: Grade 100/130 aviation fuel mixed in the ratio 20 parts fuel with one part 40SAE two-cycle outboard motor oil (or 30 parts fuel to one part Super Red oil).

IGNITION: Single magneto and distributor. Directly connected to crankshaft through impulse coupling for easy starting. Radio noise suppressor included. BG type RB 916S, AC type 83P or Champion REM-38R spark plugs. Complete radio shielding.

LUBRICATION: Oil mixed with fuel as in conventional two-stroke engines.

PROPELLER DRIVE: RH tractor. Keyed taper shaft.

STARTING: By separate portable hydraulic starter.

MOUNTING: Three mounting lugs provided with socket for rubber mounting bushings.

DIMENSIONS:

Length	27·0 in (686 mm)
Width	28·0 in (711 mm)
Height	15·0 in (381 mm)

WEIGHT, DRY:

Less propeller hub	77 lb (34·9 kg)

POWER RATING:

Rated output	84-96 hp at 4,100 rpm

SPECIFIC CONSUMPTION:

Fuel/oil mixture	0·90 lb (0·408 kg)/hp/hr

PRATT & WHITNEY

THE PRATT & WHITNEY AIRCRAFT DIVISION OF UNITED AIRCRAFT CORPORATION

HEAD OFFICE AND WORKS:
East Hartford, Connecticut 06108
Telephone: (203) 565-4321

DIVISION PRESIDENT:
Bruce N. Torell

DIVISION EXECUTIVE VICE-PRESIDENT:
David J. Hines

ASSTS TO DIVISION PRESIDENT:
R. H. Begg
E. L. Davis

DIVISION VICE-PRESIDENTS:
D. Nigro (Production)
Richard J. Coar (Engineering)
E. H. Marshall (Gen Manager, Florida R & D Center)
Hugh S. Crim (Marketing)
Frank T. Sprogell Jr (Product Support)
Richard T. Baseler

MANAGER, STRATEGIC BUSINESS AND PLANNING:
E. R. Montany

DIVISION COUNSEL, CONTRACTS:
L. J. Daukas

MANAGER PUBLIC RELATIONS:
R. H. Zaiman

DIVISION CONTROLLER:
Cornelius J. Weddle

PERSONNEL MANAGER:
F. F. Schirm

PURCHASING MANAGER:
D. L. Brown, Jr

MANUFACTURING MANAGER:
A. L. DeCamillis

Pratt & Whitney Aircraft, largest of five divisions, four subsidiaries and a central research organisation forming the United Aircraft Corporation, has manufactured more than 54,528 military and commercial gas-turbine engines since building its first turboprop in 1947. These engines had accumulated over 325 million flying hours in military and commercial service by the end of January 1974. The Division is a leading supplier of turbofans and turbojets for large and medium transports, which power the full range of Boeing and McDonnell Douglas jet airline transports in service today.

In addition to its production series of engines, Pratt & Whitney was in February 1970 awarded a contract to develop two versions of its JTF22 demonstrator engine, an augmented turbofan. The F401 version powers the US Navy F-14B fighter; the F100 powers the Air Force F-15 and YF-16 fighters. Further important demonstrator work includes the Advanced Turbine Engine Gas Generator programme. The ATEGG programme, funded by the US Air Force, has been active for several years and is continuing to demonstrate the overall, integrated performance of advanced component technology in a full-scale engine.

Pratt & Whitney JT12A-8 turbojet (3,300 lb; 1,498 kg st)

In 1973 Pratt & Whitney launched a programme to develop the JTF10 turbofan in the 20,000-30,000 lb (9,070-13,608 kg) st class. By 1974 agreement had been reached for the limited participation of MTU of West Germany and Alfa Romeo of Italy in the programme.

Licence agreements with SNECMA permit the French company, in which United Aircraft Corporation has a small financial holding, to manufacture and sell many of Pratt & Whitney's turbine engines, and the division's complete line of piston engines and spare parts. The Royal Swedish Air Board also is licensed to manufacture afterburning versions of the JT8D turbofan engine and its parts. This work is being handled by Volvo Flygmotor (which see).

In October 1971 Pratt & Whitney and Rolls-Royce (1971) signed an agreement for joint further development of the Pegasus vectored-thrust turbofan. Pratt & Whitney also has an option to take up a manufacturing licence for the British engine. In 1971 Mitsubishi Heavy Industries of Japan was licensed to manufacture parts and assemble JT8D engines for the CX military transport. In 1972 Israel Aircraft Industries was licensed to manufacture parts of the J52 engine for the A-4 Skyhawk.

Licence agreements for the manufacture of certain of the Division's piston engines or piston-engine parts continue with Commonwealth Aircraft Corporation of Australia; Fiat of Italy; Mitsubishi Heavy Industries; Metal Leve SA of Brazil; and United Aircraft of Canada Limited.

Associated companies of the United Aircraft Corporation are United Aircraft of Canada Ltd, a subsidiary of the Corporation, at Longueuil, Quebec; and Orenda Ltd at Malton, Ontario, an associate company owned jointly with Hawker Siddeley Canada Ltd. For Pratt & Whitney, United Aircraft of Canada is now the prime source of manufacture of its piston engines, and Orenda provides the Division with additional turbine engine production capacity.

In October 1970 the Division's Turbopower and Marine Department, which develops and produces industrial and marine versions of modified aircraft gas turbines, was transferred from Pratt & Whitney and re-established as Turbo-Power and Marine Systems, Inc. This is a wholly-owned subsidiary of United Aircraft Corporation.

Pratt & Whitney has a total of about 40,000 employees at its four main plants at East Hartford, North Haven, Southington and Middletown, Connecticut, and the Florida Research and Development Center, West Palm Beach, Florida.

PRATT & WHITNEY JT12

US military designation; J60

The J60 is a small high-performance turbojet engine which has a nine-stage axial-flow compressor, cannular type combustion section with eight flame tubes, and a two-stage turbine. The rotor runs in three bearings. Pressure ratio is 6·5 : 1.

Design studies began in July 1957 and the prototype ran in May 1958. The first prototype (50 hour engine) was delivered in July 1959, with T-O rating of 2,900 lb (1,315 kg) st. Delivery of production engines, rated at 3,000 lb (1,360 kg) st, began in October 1960, and 2,462 have been shipped; more are on order.

Versions of the J60/JT12 power the Lockheed JetStar, and the Rockwell International T-39 Sabreliner and T-2B Buckeye trainer. A turboshaft version is the JFTD12, described later.

For details see table.

PRATT & WHITNEY JT8

US military designation: J52

The J52 is a medium-sized turbojet which was designed under the auspices of the US Navy Bureau of Weapons. It powers all versions of the Grumman A-6 Intruder/Prowler attack and ECM aircraft, current versions of the McDonnell Douglas A-4 Skyhawk, and the North American Rockwell AGM-28 Hound Dog air-to-surface missile, as listed hereafter:

J52-P-3. Rated at 7,500 lb (3,400 kg) st. Powers AGM-28 Hound Dog.

J52-P-6A, 6B, 8A, 8B. Rated at 8,500 lb (3,855 kg) st (6A, 6B) or 9,300 lb (4,130 kg) st (8A, 8B). Powers A-4E, A-4F, TA-4F, TA-4J, A-6A, A-6B, A-6C, A-6E.

J52-P-408. Rated at 11,200 lb (5,080 kg) st. Powers A-4F, A-4M, some export A-4 versions, EA-6B.

The J52 is a two-spool turbojet, with total of 12 compressor stages, a "cannular" type combustion system fed by 36 dual-orifice injectors and independent high-pressure and low-pressure single-stage turbines. Pressure ratio is 14·5 : 1. Several advanced design features are incorporated to achieve the rating increases with a minimum change in engine envelope and weight compared to previous JT8 (J52) models. These include two-position inlet guide vanes and aircooled first-stage turbine vanes and blades. In addition, the burner cans include features for reduced smoke. For details see table.

PRATT & WHITNEY JT8D

This turbofan engine was developed as a company-sponsored project to power short/medium-range transport aircraft, including the Boeing 727. United Aircraft's French licensee, SNECMA, designed the complete power plant nacelle, with thrust reverser, used in the Caravelle Super B airliner, and has now developed and is producing the advanced quiet plug nozzle for the -15 engine for the Mercure. In March 1971 Mitsubishi was licensed to manufacture the -9 engine for the Kawasaki C-1 transport.

Construction of the JT8D is largely of steel and titanium. An annular by-pass duct runs the full length of the engine, with balanced mixing of the hot and cold air streams in the tailpipe.

Manufacture of prototype engines began in November 1960 and the first engine run was made in April 1961. Flight testing was carried out initially under a B-45 testbed aircraft. Prototype engines for airframe testing were delivered to Boeing in 1962. Production deliveries began in the first half of 1963. By the end of 1973 more than 6,600 had been delivered and flight time exceeded 70 million hours with more than 140 operators.

The following versions have been announced:

JT8D-1. Initial version rated at 14,000 lb (6,350 kg) st. Powers Boeing 727-100, -100C and -200, McDonnell Douglas DC-9-10 and -10F, and Aérospatiale Caravelle 10R.

JT8D-5. Rated at 12,250 lb (5,556 kg) st. Powers McDonnell Douglas DC-9-10.

JT8D-7. Develops 14,000 lb (6,350 kg) st to 28·9°C at S/L. Specified for Boeing 727-100, -100C and -200, Boeing 737-100 and -200, McDonnell Douglas DC-9-10, -30 and -30F, Aérospatiale Caravelle 10R and 11R.

JT8D-9. Develops 14,500 lb (6,575 kg) st to 28·9°C at S/L. Specified for Boeing 727-100, -100C and -200, 737-100, -200 and -200C, McDonnell Douglas DC-9-20, -30, -40 and C-9A, Aérospatiale Caravelle 12 and Kawasaki C-1. Deliveries began in July 1967.

JT8D-11. Develops 15,000 lb (6,804 kg) st to 28·9C° at S/L. Specified for McDonnell Douglas DC-9-20, -30 and -40 series aircraft and Boeing 727-200. Deliveries began in November 1968.

JT8D-15. Develops 15,500 lb (7,031 kg) st to 28·9°C. FAA certification was received and deliveries began in April 1971. Selected for Dassault Mercure, Boeing Advanced 727 and 737, and DC-9. Chosen for McDonnell Douglas YC-15 for US Air Force. The -15 has completed an endurance test of 6,000 take-off cycles, equivalent to 2-3 years of normal operation.

JT8D-17. Advanced model rated at 16,000 lb (7,258 kg) st to 28·9°C. Certificated on 1 February 1974 (tenth anniversary of JT8D-1 entry to airline service). More than 200 ordered by April 1974 for advanced versions of 727,737 and DC-9; may replace JT8D-15 in McDonnell Douglas YC-15 prototype.

JT8D-NFF. Under the sponsorship of NASA, preliminary design and development of a lower-noise JT8D derivative is now in progress. The designation signifies "new front fan". The existing two-stage fan is being replaced by a single-stage fan of increased diameter. This will reduce jet noise by up to 9 PNdB, whilst increasing thrust by 14 per cent and reducing fuel consumption by 3·0 per cent. Converted or new JT8D-9, -15 and -17 engines with the new fan will be designated JT8D-109, -115 and -117.

Since January 1970 all new JT8D engines have incorporated smoke-reduction hardware, and conversion kits are available for in-service engines. Two noise-reduction options are also available for all JT8D models. Maximum TBO for the JT8D has for two years been 13,250 hours.

A supersonic military version of the JT8D with afterburning has been developed and is being manufactured under licence in Sweden by Volvo Flygmotor AB. The Swedish engine, designated RM8, powers the Mach 2 Saab 37 Viggen multipurpose combat aircraft. The first production engine was shipped on 28 October 1970.

Type: Axial-flow two-spool turbofan.

Air Intake: Annular with 19 fixed inlet guide vanes.

Fan: Two-stage front fan. First stage has 30 titanium blades dovetailed into discs. First-stage blades have integral shroud at about 61% span.

LP Compressor: Six-stage axial-flow, integral with fan stages, on inner of two concentric shafts. Blades made of titanium. Shaft carried in double ball bearings, either half of each bearing being able to handle the complete loading.

HP Compressor: Seven-stage axial-flow on outer hollow shaft which, like the inner shaft, is carried in double ball bearings. One-piece casing. Blades made of steel or titanium. Pressure ratio ranges from 16·2 : 1 on JT8D-1 to 18·0 : 1 on JT8D-15. By-pass ratio 1·1 : 1. Total air mass flow 324 lb (147 kg)/sec.

Combustion Chamber: Cannular type with nine cylindrical flame-tubes, each downstream of a single Duplex burner and discharging into a single annular nozzle.

HP Turbine: Single-stage axial-flow. Solid blades in -1 to -9, aircooled in -11 and 1-5; guide vanes hollow and aircooled in all models.

LP Turbine: Three-stage axial-flow. Solid blades and guide vanes.

Dimensions:

Diameter	42·5 in (1,080 mm)
Length	120·0 in (3,048 mm)

PRATT & WHITNEY JTF10A

US military designation: TF 30

Development of this high-compression two-spool turbofan was begun in 1958 as a private venture, and resulted in testing of the first turbofan with afterburning. It was chosen subsequently as the power plant for the General Dynamics/Grumman F-111 variable-geometry tactical fighter aircraft.

The version used initially in the F-111 was designated TF30-P-1 (JTF10A-20) which provides 18,500 lb (8,390 kg) st with afterburning. It was superseded in the F-111A by the TF30-P-3 (JTF10A-21) which provides the same thrust with reduced sea level supersonic specific fuel

Pratt & Whitney J52-P-408 turbojet (11,200 lb; 5,080 kg st)

Pratt & Whitney JT8D-15 turbofan (15,500 lb; 7,031 kg st)

Third-stage fan of the Pratt & Whitney TF30 turbofan made of boron/aluminium. This is one of many composite parts made in the US Air Force Advanced Composite Engine Program

consumption. A version developed for the US Navy's now-abandoned F-111B was the TF30-P-12 (JTF10A-27A), a lighter weight and higher thrust model. The F-111D is powered by the TF30-P-9 (JTF10A-36) engine with afterburning, rated at 19,600 lb (8,891 kg) st. The FB-111 bomber is equipped with the TF30-P-7 (JTF10A-27D) engine, which is in the 20,000 lb (9,072 kg) thrust class with afterburning. The F-111F is equipped with the TF30-P-100 (JTF10A-32C) engine, an advanced version with higher thrust. The LTV A-7A and A-7B Corsair II tactical attack aircraft are powered by the TF30-P-6 (JTF10A-8) and TF30-P-8 (JTF10A-9), these being simplified versions without afterburning and rated at 11,350 lb (5,150 kg) and 12,200 lb (5,534 kg) st respectively. TF30-P-8 engines are being converted to TF30-P-408 (JTF10A-16A) standard, with a thrust rating of 13,400 lb (6,080 kg) st.

In July 1965, the TF30-P-1 completed successfully its official ground tests for military qualification, involving two 150-hour tests, with 12½ hours of full-power operation in simulated Mach 1·2 flight at sea level. In November 1966, the TF30-P-3 successfully completed a 150-hour military qualification test, with 56·25 hours of simulated Mach 2·2, and 12·5 hours of simulated Mach 1·2 flight at sea level.

Most recent application of the TF30 is the US Navy's Grumman F-14A Tomcat fighter, powered by the TF30-P-412, a modified version of the TF30-P-12. The TF30-P-412, with a revised form of afterburner nozzle, has a reheat rating in the 20,000 lb (9,070 kg) thrust class.

The most advanced current production version is the USAF's P-100, first delivered in January 1971, in which weight is held below 4,000 lb (1,815 kg) while increasing thrust to the 25,000 lb (11,340 kg) class, with reduced fuel consumption. Airflow has been increased and smoothed by the bulged core, with canted blades in the first two compressor stages, without altering outer case diameter. The new Finwall burner can increase temperature 135°, with 20% less weight and 50% less cooling air, and with smokeless efflux. The HP turbine is redesigned with radically improved aircooling of vanes and rotor blades, both cast in directionally solidified alloys in which grain boundaries perpendicular to the major stress are eliminated. Rotor blades are shroudless and cooled by airflow round an insert, discharging at the trailing-edge, instead of through longitudinal holes to the tip shroud. The very advanced five-zone afterburner has a "soft-light" ignition system which reduces pressure excursions on initial light by some 40%; the nozzle is also completely redesigned, with a translating primary iris and improved blow-in ejector which combine to give greatly reduced drag.

The P-100 HP turbine has been tested at 2,600°F, and the JTF10A-39 is a further major growth version. A 2% increase in airflow combined with 100°F increase in turbine inlet temperature raise take-off thrust to the 30,000 lb class. The -39 would have a two-position fan inlet guide vane to improve pressure ratio and efficiency, and the burner and turbine sections would be improved.

Time between overhauls of the early models (P-3 with afterburner and P-6 without) reached 1,000 hr in 1972. The TBO of the P-100 was then at 450 hr, and planned to climb in stages, reaching 1,000 hr in 1974. A similar TBO progression is planned for the -412, currently at 150 hr.

Afterburning versions of the JTF10 have been developed also by SNECMA in France and one of these, designated TF 106, was fitted in the Mirage III-T experimental testbed aircraft and the Mirage III-V prototype VTOL fighter.

The SNECMA TF 306 is a TF30 fitted with a SNECMA-designed afterburner. It was fitted in the Mirage F2 and the first variable-geometry Mirage G prototype.

Pratt & Whitney TF30-P-412 afterburning turbofan (20,000 lb; 9,070 kg st class)

It was disclosed in 1973 that several types of Pratt & Whitney turbofan have run with experimental fan blades fabricated in boron composite material. In each case the production blade is of titanium. The JT8D has run with several types of fan blade in boron/aluminium composite, showing a claimed weight-saving of 40 per cent. The TF30 has run with boron/aluminium third-stage fan blades (see photograph), the weight-saving being 36 per cent. The F100 has run with boron/polyimide first-stage fan blades, with a weight-saving of 51 per cent, and boron/aluminium third-stage fan blades with a weight-saving of 36 per cent. The price of boron/aluminium prepreg was in 1973 about $107/lb ($235/kg), resulting in total cost "comparable with that of the titanium blade."

TYPE: Two-shaft axial-flow turbofan.

INTAKE: Direct pitot annular type with 23 fixed inlet guide vanes (19 on P-8 and P-408). Hollow vanes pass anti-icing air.

FAN: Three stages (two on P-8 and P-408). Rotor and stator and casings all of titanium. Three rotor stages have 28 (with part-span shrouds), 36 and 36 blades, all dovetailed; stator stages have 44, 44 and 48 blades, all rivet-retained. Pressure ratio 2·14 : 1. Mass flow typically 247 lb (112 kg)/sec (P-100 260 lb; 118 kg/sec).

LP COMPRESSOR: Six stages (seven on P-8 and P-408), constructed integrally with fan to form nine-stage spool. Wholly of titanium construction, except stator blades of steel. Rotor stages have 50, 62, 62, 82, 72 and 82 blades, all dovetailed. Stator stages have 60, 96, 96, 106, 100 and 29 blades, all butted and pinned.

HP COMPRESSOR: Seven stages, constructed mainly of nickel-based alloy. Rotor stages have 73, 75, 75, 75, 85, 85 and 62 dovetailed blades. Stator stages have 86, 104, 122, 90, 90, 90 and 130 pinned blades.

COMBUSTION CHAMBER: Can-annular, with steel casing and eight Hastelloy X flame cans each held at the front by four dual-orifice burners. Spark igniters in chambers 4 and 5.

FUEL SYSTEM: HP system (above 1,000 lb/sq in, 70 kg/cm²), with conventional hydromechanical control. Main elements comprise fuel pump, filter, heater, fuel control, P & D valve and nozzles. Separate afterburner system for A/B engines. No water injection.

FUEL GRADE: JP-4, JP-5.

HP TURBINE: Single stage, with 40 film-cooled nozzle guide vanes (stators) of cobalt-based alloy and 98 aircooled rotor blades of cobalt-based alloy (P-100 vanes and blades of directionally solidified alloy). Gas temperature, typical engine 1,830°F (max for current engines 2,090°F, P-100 max 2,300°F).

LP TURBINE: Three stages of nickel-based alloys. Rotor stages have 88, 86 and 72 fir-tree root blades. Gas temperature after turbine, typically 1,025°F.

JET PIPE (non-A/B engines): Simple steel pipe where fan airflow and core gas mix before passing through fixed nozzle.

AFTERBURNER: Diffuser leads to combustion section comprising double-wall outer duct and inner liner carrying five-zone combustion system. Three spraybars and rings upstream of flameholder. Fuel supplied by hydraulic pump up to 4,000 lb (1,814 kg)/hr; above this level by centrifugal A/B fuel pump. Ignition by auxiliary squirt in A/B diffuser, coupled with main squirt in No 4 burner can which produces hot-streak of fuel through the turbine (P-100 engine, fully modulated light-up by 4-joule electrical ignition system). Max gas temperature 1,490°C.

NOZZLE (A/B engines): Primary nozzle has variable area, with six hinged segments actuated by engine-fuel rams (P-100, 18 iris segments translated along curved profile by six long-stroke rams). Ejector nozzle has six blow-in doors with free tail-feathers.

ACCESSORY DRIVES: Main gearbox under compressor, driven by bevel shaft from HP spool. Contains major elements of lubrication and breather systems. Drive pads at front and rear for main and A/B fuel pumps, main oil pump, N_2 tachometer, starter, fluid power pumps and power take-off.

LUBRICATION SYSTEM: Self-contained dry-sump hot-tank system. Accessory gearbox housing forms 4 US gal (3·3 Imp gal; 15 litre) tank. Oil circulated at 45 lb/sq in (3·17 kg/cm²) through pump, filter, coolers (air/oil on airframe, fuel/oil on engine and A/B fuel/oil cooler) and three main bearing components; returned by scavenge pumps and de-aerator.

OIL GRADE: MIL-L-7808.

MOUNTING: Two-planar. Front peripheral pair of flanges absorb vertical, side and thrust loads; rear pair of peripheral flanges (in line with No. 6 bearing behind LP turbine) absorb vertical and side loads.

STARTING: Air-turbine starter on left forward drive pad of accessory gearbox.

DIMENSIONS, WEIGHTS AND PERFORMANCE: See table

PRATT & WHITNEY JTF22

US military designations: F100 and F401

Stemming partly from the JTF16 demonstrator engine designed in 1965-66, the JTF22 is an advanced-technology military turbofan with afterburner for highly supersonic applications. Basic development has been funded as a demonstrator programme for the US Air Force. In February 1970 the decision was taken to use the JTF22 core engine as the basis of two highly refined power units: the F100-PW-100 for the twin-engined McDonnell Douglas F-15 Eagle fighter for the US Air Force, and the F401-PW-400 for the twin-engined Grumman F-14B Tomcat fighter prototype for the US Navy.

The two versions of the engine differ in more than superficial ways. Each has been tailored exactly to suit the overall mission parameters of the two aircraft, which are far from identical. The gas generator section (core engine) is the same in both versions but the size of fan (and hence total mass flow and by-pass ratio), afterburner and nozzle and other significant components are not common.

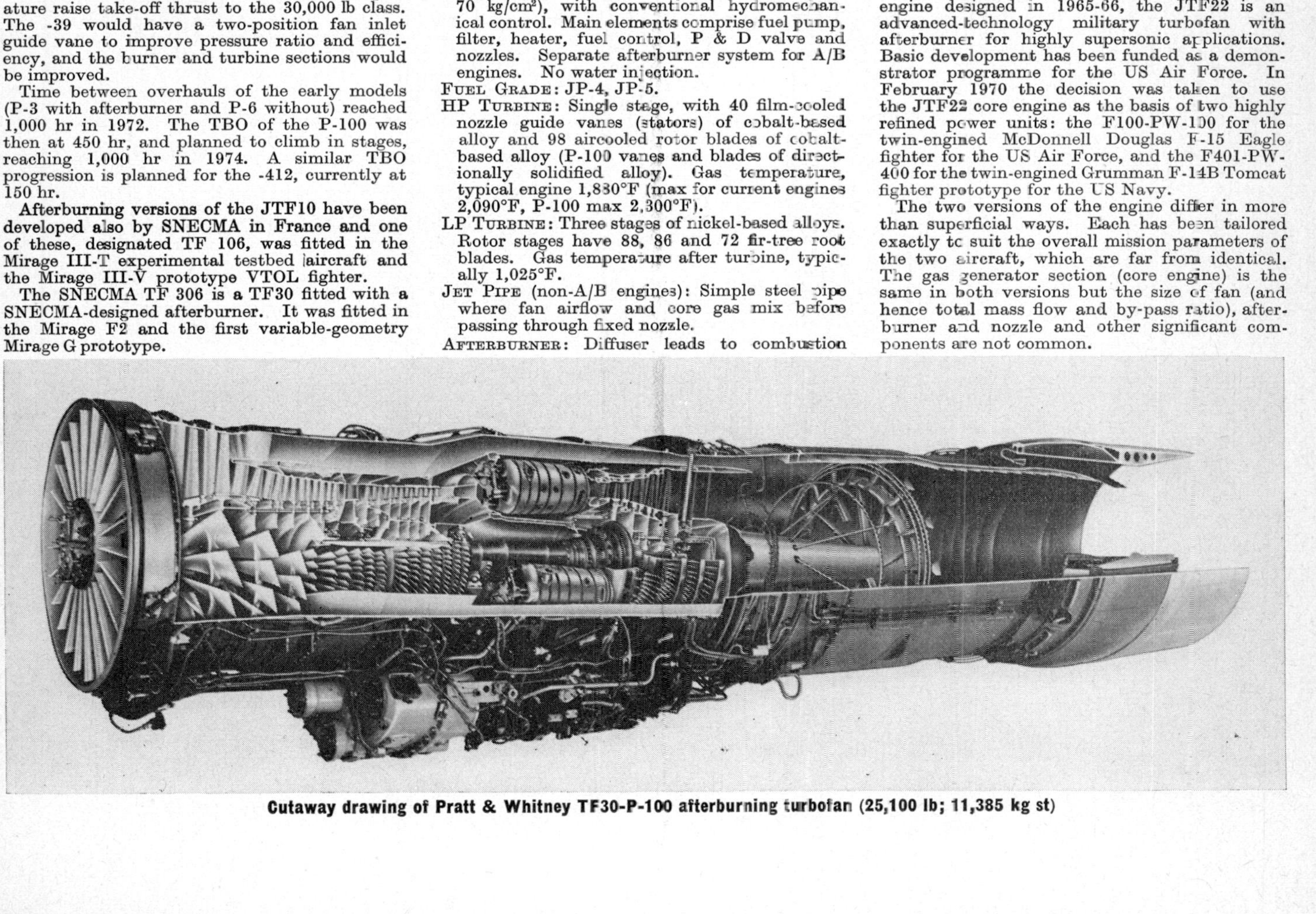

Cutaway drawing of Pratt & Whitney TF30-P-100 afterburning turbofan (25,100 lb; 11,385 kg st)

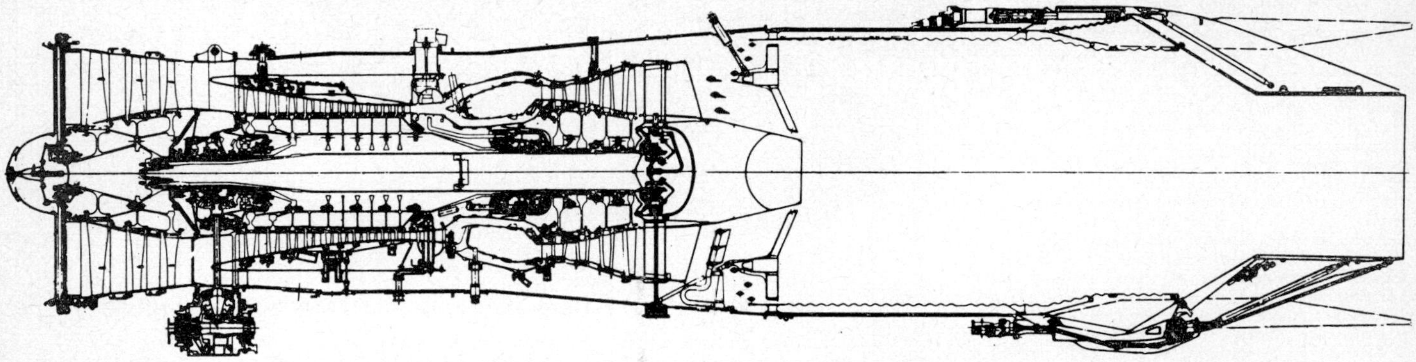

Longitudinal cross-section of the Pratt & Whitney F100-PW-100 augmented turbofan, with maximum static thrust of 24,000 lb (10,885 kg)

Announcement of Pratt & Whitney's selection to provide propulsion for these two extremely important aircraft was made in February 1970. The company is developing the JTF22 at its Florida Research and Development Center but will make production engines in Connecticut. The first contract award specified engineering design and development and the manufacture of 90 engines for use in F-14B and F-15 flight-test programmes. Target price for this work, including initial spares and equipment to support the flight programmes, is $448,162,600.

Some 3,000 hours of development testing were accomplished between 1968 and the 60 hr PFRT (preliminary flight rating test) in February 1972. The 150 hr QT (qualification test) was scheduled to be completed in early 1973, but very severe development difficulties resulted in this test not being passed until October 1973. Some of the problems involved catastrophic mechanical failure of the compressor and turbine, and the US Air Force set up a special F100 board of enquiry. Flight development, on the other hand, has gone well. In April 1974, out of a total running time of some 25,000 hours, more than 3,500 had been during development flying of the F-15, TF-15 and YF-16, and pilot opinions were generally highly complimentary. Production of an initial batch of 72 engines, for 30 F-15 and TF-15 aircraft for inventory service, was to be completed between June 1974 and mid-1975.

The prototype F401 ran in September 1972 and two flight-cleared engines flew in an F-14B development aircraft in June 1973. Though considerably more powerful and more efficient than the F100, the F401 is not a fully funded programme and the F-14B may not go into production, the stumbling-block being financial.

Type: Two-shaft turbofan with high-augmentation afterburner.

Intake: Direct pitot type. Fabricated titanium, with fixed nose bullet, 21 slender struts and hot-air anti-icing.

Fan: Three stages (3½ in F401 which has added single-stage IP compressor downstream of fan to supercharge core). Fan blades have part-span shrouds. Entry diameter 36·5 in (928 mm) (F401 42·5 in; 1,079 mm). By-pass ratio 0·7 (F401 1·0).

Compressor: Ten-stage axial, on HP shaft. First three stages have variable stators. Overall pressure ratio 24 (F401 26·9).

Combustion Chamber: Annular. Fabricated in nickel alloy with film cooling. Capacitor-discharge ignition.

Turbines: Two-stage HP turbine with aircooled blades of directionally solidified alloy. Maximum gas temperature 1,315°C (both engines). Maximum speed 14,650 rpm (F401 14,600 rpm). Two-stage LP turbine. Maximum speed 9,600 rpm (both engines).

Afterburner: Three spray rings and radial bars in flow from core engine; three slightly further downstream in by-pass airflow. Flameholder assembly downstream of spray nozzles, with high-energy electrical ignition to give modulated light-up. Carcase, like by-pass duct and other major portions, fabricated in Stresskin stainless-steel sandwich. Interior liner of refractory material.

Nozzle: Multi-flap articulated nozzle giving very wide range in area and profile.

Dimensions:

Overall diameter	about 51·0 in (1,295 mm)
Intake diameter:	
F100	36·5 in (928 mm)
F401	42·5 in (1,079 mm)
Length, excluding bullet:	
F100	191·0 in (4,851 mm)
F401	200·0 in (5,080 mm)

Weight, Dry:

F100	2,855 lb (1,295 kg)
F401	3,440 lb (1,560 kg)

Performance Rating (S/L, ISA):

Max T-O, dry:	
F100	14,375 lb (6,520 kg)
F401	16,400 lb (7,438 kg)
Max T-O, augmented:	
F100	24,000 lb (10,885 kg)
F401	28,090 lb (12,741 kg)

Pratt & Whitney F100-PW-100 augmented turbofan for McDonnell Douglas F-15, rated at 24,000 lb (10,885 kg) st with full afterburning

Specific Fuel Consumption (S/L, ISA):

Max T-O, dry:	
F100	0·68
F401	0·62
Max T-O, augmented:	
F100	2·55
F401	2·45

PRATT & WHITNEY JT3D

US military designation: TF33

The JT3D is a turbofan version of the J57 turbojet, handling almost 2·5 times more air than the J57 and with pressure ratio ranging from 13 : 1 on the JT3D-1 to 16·1 : 1 on the JT3D-8A. Details of the ratings of the various versions are given in the table.

Evolution from the J57 involved removal of the first three stages of the J57 compressor and replacement by two fan stages. Of considerably larger diameter than the compressor, the fan extends well outside the compressor casing. The third-stage turbine on the J57 was enlarged and a fourth stage added to provide the power necessary to drive the low-pressure compressor rotor and integral fan. A new short discharge duct was designed to exhaust the fan air well forward on the engine nacelle just after it has passed through the fan. More recent JT3D and military TF33 installations have a full-length by-pass duct to a single reverser and nozzle handling the whole mass flow.

The JT3D produces 50% more take-off and 27% more cruise thrust than the J57, while giving a 13% better cruising specific fuel consumption.

Flight trials in a B-52 Stratofortress bomber and Boeing 707 airliner began in 1960. The JT3D powers all late versions of these aircraft and of the McDonnell Douglas DC-8. The Lockheed C-141A StarLifter military transport uses the TF33-P-7 version, with an additional stage of compression. In January 1973 the same -7 engine was selected to power the Boeing E-3A (AWACS) aircraft.

Under the sponsorship of NASA a lower-noise redesign of the JT3D was completed in 1973. At the time of going to press it was not known whether Pratt & Whitney would build new engines designated JT3D-9, or supply field-conversion kits to existing operators. The main change entails replacement of the existing fan by a new single-stage fan of increased diameter to reduce noise and fuel consumption and increase thrust.

More than 8,200 JT3D turbofans, including converted JT3C engines, had been delivered by the end of 1973. Additional commercial JT3D engines remain to be delivered.

PRATT & WHITNEY JT9D

US military designation (JT9D-7): F105-PW-100

Based on technology stemming from the USAF heavy freighter propulsion of a decade ago, the JT9D was the first of the new era of very large, high by-pass ratio turbofans on which the design of the present generation of wide-body commercial transports rests.

The main advances in the JT9D are: (1) improved fan design to achieve the desired pressure ratio at high efficiency from a single stage with no guide vanes; (2) improved compressor to attain a pressure ratio of 24 : 1 in 15 stages, compared with 14 : 1 in 16 stages for the JT3D; (3) improved combustion chamber to give greater temperature rise in appreciably shorter length than in previous engines, with lower pressure loss and better exit temperature distribution (and able to use smoke-reduction technology from the outset); (4) new high-temperature materials and

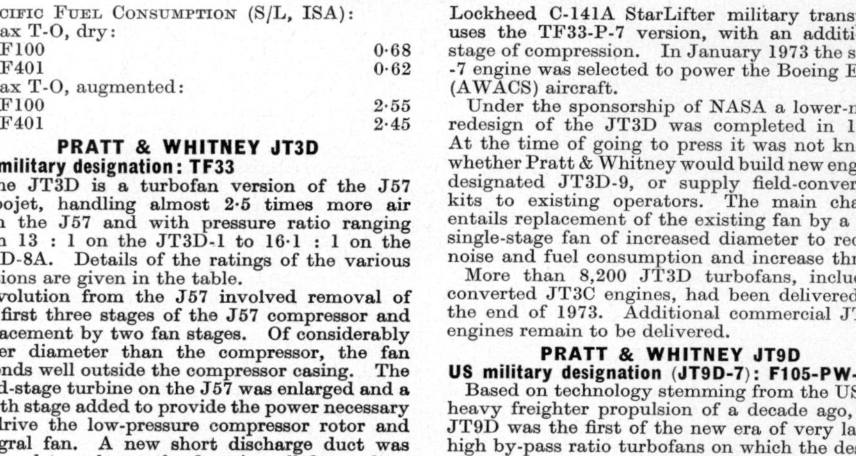

Pratt & Whitney TF33-P-7 turbofan engine (21,000 lb; 9,525 kg st)

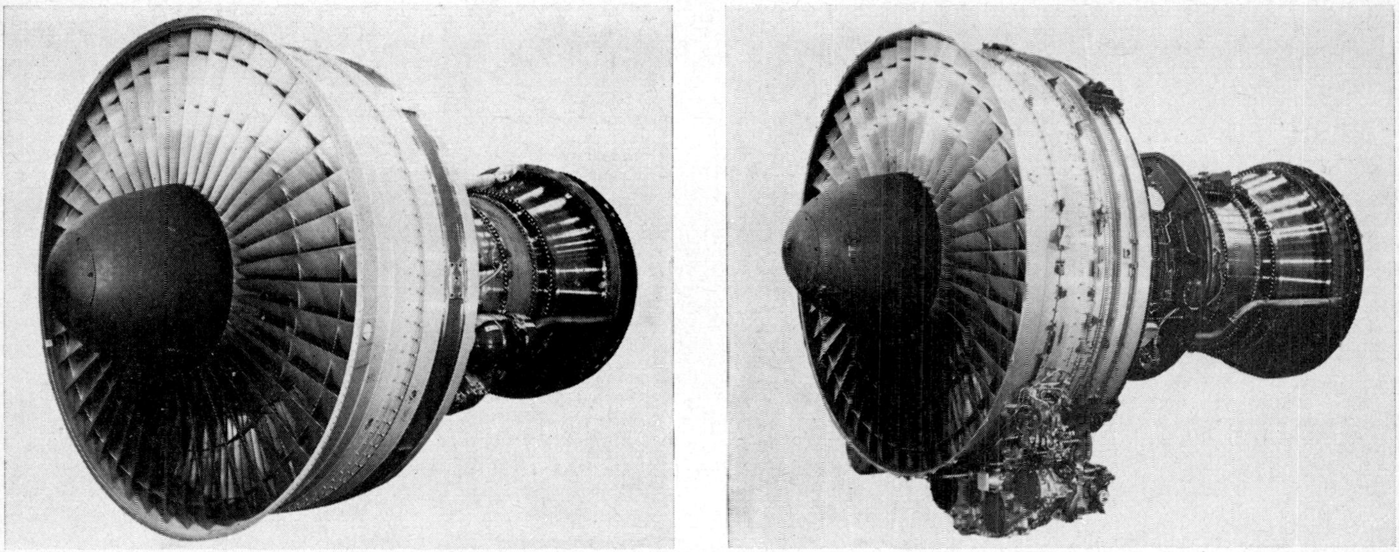

Two versions of the Pratt & Whitney JT9D turbofan: *(left)*, **JT9D-7A (47,670 lb; 21,619 kg st)**; *(right)*, **JT9D-20 (49,400 lb; 22,404 kg st)**

cooling systems to allow a substantial rise in turbine gas temperature; (5) a controlled-vortex turbine design, allowing much higher stage-loadings (effectively eliminating two turbine stages); and (6) design features which enable thrust to be more than doubled with considerably less noise.

In its basic design the JT9D is compact, being shorter than the JT3D, and has two shafts, each supported in two bearings. In cruising flight the installed sfc is 22-23% lower than for the JT3D or JT8D. Careful attention has been paid to maintenance. The engine is made in ten modules which can be individually removed in short times, as demonstrated in numerous tests. By adding brackets and twin rails to the airframe the engine can be dismantled on the airframe. There are 21 borescope ports for inspecting all stages of blading and the combustion section; and provision is made to facilitate chip detectors, eddy current, ultrasonic and radioisotope inspection.

Company investment in facilities for the JT9D programme exceeds $100 million for production and $38 million for engineering development.

First run of the JT9D was in December 1966, and first engine flight test, with the engine mounted on the starboard inboard pylon of a Boeing B-52E, was in June 1968. The first flight of the Boeing 747 occurred on 9 February 1969. The DC-10-40 flew on 28 February 1972.

Versions of the JT9D include:

JT9D-3. The initial production model, rated at 43,500 lb (19,730 kg) to 26·7°C. Fitted to first production Boeing 747. Engines delivered from April 1969 and certificated the following month.

JT9D-3A. Incorporates water injection for wet rating of 45,000 lb (20,412 kg) to 26·7°C. Powers Boeing 747-100 and -200B. Engines delivered from December 1969 and certificated on 9 January 1970.

JT9D-7. This engine incorporates improvements resulting from -3A service experience. The LP compressor has blades and vanes sloped back perpendicular to the inclined core airflow for increased stability and life; pylon-matched fan exit vanes reduce sfc; HP compressor discs have a longer life, and the stators are driven through a low-friction mechanism; a short-cone hooded burner increases durability and reduces smoke emission far below the visible level; changes to HP and LP turbines increase life, and improved HP disc sealing improves performance. The -7 was certificated on 14 July 1971. It powers the 747-200B, C and F, raising the certificated take-off weight from 710,000 to 775,000 lb (322,050 to 351,530 kg). On 30 November 1971 the 747-200 was certificated at full weight and thrust, and with a fixed-inlet cowl, quieter than the original type with blow-in doors (104 EPNdB "traded" compared with 112).

In 1972, Pratt & Whitney stated that, while late JT9D-3A engines were suffering only half as many engine-caused unscheduled removals as the first engines, the more powerful -7 engine had "exhibited a removal rate four times better than these improved 3As", with only two removals attributable to engine problems in its first 75,000 hours— "a record unmatched by any engine".

JT9D-7A. This incorporates a number of aerodynamic improvements which provide higher component efficiencies. The result is an increased thrust capability at the same turbine temperature. This has been reflected in rating increases over the JT9D-7.

JT9D-7F. Aerodynamically identical to the JT9D-7A, the -7F has first-stage turbine rotor blades of directionally solidified material, allowing a rise in turbine gas temperature. This is reflected in further increase in thrust. The -7F permits operation at the Boeing 747 basic structural limit of 800,000 lb (362,870 kg). The engine was scheduled to be certificated in September 1974 and to be available in early 1975.

JT9D-20. This engine, which replaced the JT9D-15 and JT9D-25 (mentioned in the 1972-73 *Jane's* and originally intended for installation in the DC-10-20), has the same ratings as the JT9D-15 except that the take-off rating with water injection has been increased (49,400 lb; 22,404 kg, to 30°C). With this engine, the DC-10-20 has been redesignated DC-10-40 and certificated at a gross weight of 530,000 lb for dry operation. At the wet rating (**JT9D-20W**) it is certificated at 555,000 lb. The D-20 is similar to the D-7, except for external configuration changes such as accessory-gearbox location, thrust-transmitting points and plumbing hardware locations. The gearbox is under the fan exit casing, and the new mounting has enabled the "thrust frame" yoke (added to earlier engines to prevent ovalising of the casing) to be eliminated. The D-20 was certificated in October 1972.

JT9D-59A. This engine is the first member of the family of growth versions to be selected to power the DC-10. It evolved from an intensive component development programme begun in 1970, which led to the running of a complete experimental engine at 62,000 lb (28,125 kg) st. The Dash 59A differs from earlier JT9D engines mainly in the following respects: the fan has a diameter approximately one inch (25·4 mm) larger and reprofiled blades of higher efficiency; the low-pressure compressor has a zero (fourth) stage and is completely redesigned and the whole hot end is entirely redesigned. The burners are recontoured, an HP turbine carbon seal is added, the HP turbine rotor blades are of directionally solidified PWA 422 superalloy, the HP turbine annulus is of greater area, and the LP turbine is mechanically and aerodynamically redesigned. The carcase of the engine is stressed for 56,000 lb (25,400 kg) st. With a rating of 52,000 lb (23,587 kg) the **JT9D-59** is to be available in January 1975. With a dry rating of 53,000 lb (24,040 kg) the JT9D-59A is to be available in January 1976. The growth potential of this size of engine is predicted at 60,000 lb (27,216 kg).

JT9D-70. This is the corresponding growth version of the JT9D for the Boeing 747. Initial deliveries are expected in early 1975 at 52,000 lb (23,587 kg); one year later the engine is expected to be available flat-rated at 53,000 lb (24,040 kg). First customer is Seaboard World Airlines, which chose the JT9D-70 for 747F freighters to be certificated at 800,000 lb (362,870 kg).

Since entry to service on 21 January 1970 the JT9D has gained experience in the 747 more rapidly than any previous engine. Within one year 653 engines had been delivered, and early in 1973 the total exceeded 1,132. Rate of delivery has since slowed but the total now exceeds 1,250, and flight time is increasing by well over 50,000 hours per week.

The following description applies to early versions of the JT9D and not to the Dash 59A or 70:

Type: Two-shaft turbofan of high by-pass ratio.

Intake: Direct pitot, annular fixed geometry (except that airframe inlet on early 747 aircraft has blow-in side doors around periphery). No inlet guide vanes ahead of fan. Airflow improved by rotating spinner.

Fan: Single stage, with 46 titanium blades of 4·6 aspect ratio and two part-span shrouds held by dovetails in steel LP rotor. Downstream are 108 aluminium alloy exit guide vanes, followed by nine discharge-case radial struts. Fan case of stainless steel and aluminium alloy, designed to contain fan blades. Discharge case lined with perforated acoustic material. Airflow (max for JT9D-7) 1,540 lb (698 kg)/sec at 3,750 rpm (-3A, 1,509 lb; 684 kg at 3,650 rpm). Pressure ratio: typically 1·6 : 1. By-pass ratio: -3A, 5·17 : 1; -7, 5·15 : 1.

LP Compressor: Three stages, rotating with fan. Rotor made up of rings, spacers and conical disc splined to steel LP shaft and held by lock-nut ahead of fan and overhung ahead of main LP ball thrust bearing. Hydraulically opened

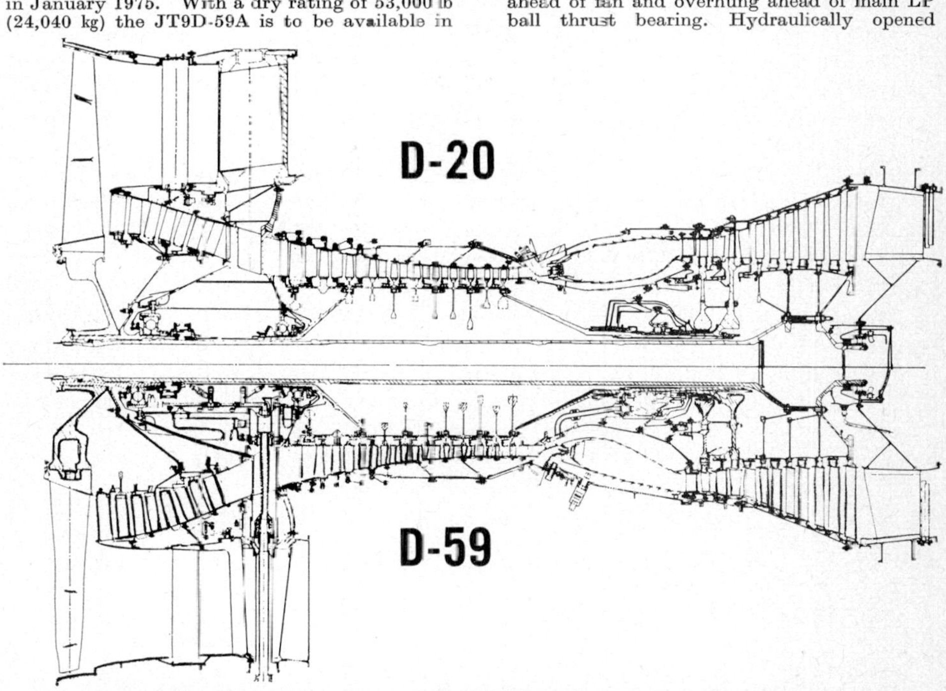

Comparative cross-sections of the Pratt & Whitney JT9D-20 and JT9D-59 turbofans, showing the latter's redesigned fan, LP compressor, combustion chamber and turbine

bleed ring at LP exit to increase flight-idle stall margin and excess air during deceleration. Rotor stages have 124, 132 and 130 dovetailed blades of titanium alloy. First stator stage anti-iced by 9th stage bleed air. Stator stages have 88, 128 and 126 titanium vanes and 120 (4th stage) nickel alloy vanes, all riveted to outer rings. Casing of aluminium alloy. Core airflow typically 260 lb (118 kg)/sec.

HP Compressor: Eleven stages. All stages have rings or centreless discs with integral spacers carried on conical discs at 3rd and 11th stages on HP shaft of titanium alloy (front) and high-nickel alloy (rear), bolted at rear hub. Rotor stages have 60, 84, 102, 100, 110, 108, 104, 94 and 100 dovetailed titanium blades and 102 and 90 nickel alloy blades. Stator has 76, 70, 80, 106, 100 and 112 titanium alloy vanes and 126, 146, 154, 158 and 92 vanes of nickel alloy, all brazed to inner and outer rings. First four stator stages are variable, positioned by hydraulic actuator to provide adequate stall margin for starting, acceleration and part-power operation. Casing of titanium alloys (last two stages, nickel alloy) has bleed ports supplying 8th-stage air for airframe requirements. Max HP speed: -3A, 7,850 rpm; -7, 8,000 rpm. Overall engine pressure ratio: -3A, 21·4 : 1; -7, 22·1 : 1.

Combustion Chamber: The diffuser case, which extends from the HP compressor to the mid-point of the combustion section, incorporates two sets of bleed ports for 15th-stage air for airframe requirements. The forward set takes air from the outside case via an integral manifold and the rear set bleeds air from the inner diameter via four of the ten radial struts. The combustor itself is fabricated in nickel alloy and is annular, with the forward end of the liner extended in 20 conical primary zones held in 20 burners fed from external fuel manifolds. The outer casing can be slid forward over the diffuser for access to the HP turbine. Ignition by dual AC 4-joule capacitor system serving two plugs just above chamber centreline on each side.

Fuel System: Pressure type with hydraulic control system operating at up to 1,100 lb/sq in (77·3 kg/cm²). Main components are fuel control, pump, fuel/air heater and fuel/oil heat exchanger. Provision for water injection, as customer option, with regulator, piping and spray nozzles, adds 40 lb (18·1 kg) to engine weight.

Fuel Grade: P & W specification PWA 522.

HP Turbine: Two stages. Both have high-nickel discs splined to HP shaft, secured by lock-nut, carrying high-nickel blades in fir-tree roots; first stage has 116 aircooled blades and second has 138 solid blades. Stators have 66 and 90 high-nickel alloy vanes, both rows air-cooled. Turbine inlet temperature (-3A, max T-O), typically 1,095°C.

LP Turbine: Four stages. Stages have 108, 126, 122 and 116 solid nickel alloy blades held in fir-tree roots in discs of nickel alloy (last disc,

PRATT & WHITNEY MILITARY AND CIVIL GAS TURBINE ENGINES

Manufacturer's and civil designation	Military designation	Type	T-O Rating lb st (kg st)	SFC	Weight dry lb (kg)	Diameter in (mm)	Remarks
JT3C-2	J57-P-43WB	Turbojet	13,750 (6,242)	0·95	3,870 (1,755)	38·88 (987·5)	Water injection
JT3C-6	—	Turbojet	13,500 (6,124)	0·903	4,234 (1,922)	38·88 (987·5)	Water injection
JT3C-7	—	Turbojet	12,000 (5,443)	0·785	3,495 (1,587)	38·86 (985·5)	—
JT3C-8	J57-P-59W	Turbojet	13,750 (6,242)	0·95	4,320 (1,959)	38·88 (987·5)	Water injection
JT3C-21	J57-P-16	Turbojet	16,900 (7,664)	0·830	4,750 (2,154)	40·02 (1,017)	Afterburning
JT3C-21	J57-P-55	Turbojet	16,900 (7,664)	0·830	5,215 (2,365)	39·97 (1,015)	Afterburning
JT3C-26	J57-P-20, -20A	Turbojet	18,000 (8,172)	2·35	4,750 (2,156)	40·02 (1,017)	Afterburning
JT3C-31	J57-P-420	Turbojet	19,600 (8,888)	0·868	4,840 (2,195)	40·02 (1,017)	Afterburning
JT3D-1	—	Turbofan	17,000 (7,718)	0·52	4,150 (1,882)	53·14 (1,350)	Water injection optional
JT3D-2	TF33-P-3	Turbofan	17,000 (7,718)	0·52	3,900 (1,770)	53·14 (1,350)	—
JT3D-3A	TF33-P-5, -9	Turbofan	18,000 (8,172)	0·535	4,170 (1,891)	53·14 (1,350)	—
JT3D-3B	—	Turbofan	18,000 (8,172)	0·535	4,300 (1,950)	53·14 (1,350)	Water injection optional
JT3D-7	—	Turbofan	19,000 (8,615)	0·550	4,300 (1,950)	53·14 (1,350)	Water injection optional
JT3D-8A	TF33-P-7	Turbofan	21,000 (9,525)	0·560	4,650 (2,109)	52·85 (1,342)	—
JT4A-9	—	Turbojet	16,800 (7,620)	0·81	5,050 (2,290)	43·0 (1,092)	—
JT4A-10	—	Turbojet	16,800 (7,620)	0·81	4,845 (2,197)	43·0 (1,092)	—
JT4A-11	—	Turbojet	17,500 (7,945)	0·84	5,100 (2,315)	43·0 (1,092)	—
JT4A-12	—	Turbojet	17,500 (7,945)	0·84	4,895 (2,220)	43·0 (1,092)	—
JT4A-28	J75-P-17	Turbojet	24,500 (11,113)	2·15	5,875 (2,665)	43·0 (1,092)	Afterburning
JT4A-29	J75-P-19W	Turbojet	26,500 (12,030)	2·20	5,960 (2,706)	43·0 (1,092)	Afterburning and water injection
JT8B-1	J52-P-6A, -6B	Turbojet	8,500 (3,855)	0·82	2,056 (933)	30·15 (766)	-6B smoke reduced
JT8B-3	J52-P-8A, -8B	Turbojet	9,300 (4,218)	0·86	2,118 (961)	30·15 (766)	-8B smoke reduced
JT8B-5	J52-P-408	Turbojet	11,200 (5,080)	0·89	2,318 (1,052)	30·15 (766)	—
JT8D-1, -7	—	Turbofan	14,000 (6,350)	0·585	3,155 (1,431)	42·5 (1,080)	—
JT8D-5	—	Turbofan	12,250 (5,556)	0·565	3,155 (1,431)	42·5 (1,080)	—
JT8D-9	—	Turbofan	14,500 (6,575)	0·595	3,217 (1,459)	42·5 (1,080)	—
JT8D-11	—	Turbofan	15,000 (6,804)	0·62	3,309 (1,501)	42·5 (1,080)	—
JT8D-15	—	Turbofan	15,500 (7,031)	0·63	3,309 (1,501)	42·5 (1,080)	—
JT8D-17	—	Turbofan	16,000 (7,256)	0·645	3,330 (1,510)	44·9 (1,140)	—
JT9D-3A	—	Turbofan	45,000 (20,412)	0·346	8,608 (3,905)	95·6 (2,428)	Water injection
JT9D-7	—	Turbofan	47,000 (21,319)	0·355	8,770 (3,978)	95·6 (2,428)	Water injection
JT9D-7A	—	Turbofan	47,670 (21,619)	0·357	8,780 (3,982)	95·6 (2,428)	Water injection
JT9D-20	—	Turbofan	*49,400 (22,404)	*0·349	8,450 (3,832)	95·6 (2,428)	Water injection
JT9D-59A	—	Turbofan	53,000 (24,040)	—	9,075 (4,116)	96·5 (2,454)	—
JT9D-70	—	Turbofan	52,000 (23,587)	—	9,200 (4,173)	96·5 (2,454)	—
JTF10A-8	TF30-P-6	Turbofan	11,350 (5,150)	0·620	2,716 (1,232)	42·06 (1,068)	Non-afterburning
JTF10A-9	TF30-P-8	Turbofan	12,200 (5,534)	0·630	2,526 (1,146)	42·06 (1,068)	Non-afterburning
JTF10A-16A	TF30-P-408	Turbofan	13,400 (6,080)	0·64	2,597 (1,178)	42·06 (1,068)	Non-afterburning
JTF10A-21	TF30-P-3	Turbofan	18,500 (8,390)	2·50	4,062 (1,843)	49·04 (1,246)	Afterburning
JTF10A-27D	TF30-P-7	Turbofan	20,350 (9,230)	3·013	4,121 (1,869)	50·22 (1,275)	Afterburning
JTF10A-27F	TF30-P-412	Turbofan	20,000 (9,070) class	—	3,969 (1,800)	50·90 (1,293)	Afterburning
JTF10A-32C	TF30-P-100	Turbofan	25,100 (11,385)	2·450	3,985 (1,807)	48·88 (1,242)	Afterburning
JTF10A-36	TF30-P-9	Turbofan	19,600 (8,891)	2·61	4,070 (1,846)	49·04 (1,246)	Afterburning
JT11D-20B	J58	Turbojet	30,000 (13,600) class	—	—	—	Afterburning
JT12A-5	J60-P-3, -5 J60-P-6	Turbojet	3,000 (1,362)	0·96	448 (203) 495 (225)	21·9 (556)	— —
JT12A-6A	J60-P-5B	Turbojet	3,000 (1,362)	0·96	453 (206)	21·9 (556)	—
JT12A-8	—	Turbojet	3,300 (1,498)	0·995	468 (212)	21·9 (556)	—
JFTD12A-4A	T73-P-1	Free Turbine	4,500 shp	0·690 lb/shp/hr	920 (418)	30·0 (762)	Free-turbine shaft drive
JFTD12A-5A	T73-P-700	Free Turbine	4,800 shp	0·655 lb/shp/hr	935 (424)	30·0 (762)	Free-turbine shaft drive

*With ideal nozzle.

iron alloy). Stators have 122, 120, 110 and 102 solid nickel alloy vanes. Exhaust gas temperature after turbine, typically 452°C (-3A) or 482°C (-7).

Jet Pipe: Fixed Inconel assembly, with large central plug cone.

Reverser: Fan duct reverser comprises a translating sleeve (the rearmost portion of fan duct) which moves aft, causing long links to close the blocker doors and simultaneously pulling aft the cascade vanes. Primary (core) reverser, largely of Inconel 625, uses fixed cascades which are uncovered by aft movement of translating sleeves to which are hinged blocker doors pulled by links against the central nozzle plug.

Accessory Drives: Main accessory gearbox driven by tower bevel shaft from front of HP spool and mounted under central diffuser case (-15 engine, under fan discharge case). Main driven accessories include CSD, fuel pump and control, starter, hydraulic pump, alternator and N_2 tachometer; Boeing 747 includes primary reverser motor and the DC-10-40 has a second hydraulic pump and the fuel boost pump (747 has electric tank pump). The box also includes numerous lubrication system items, and provides for hand-turning the HP spool during borescope inspection.

Lubrication System: Pressure feed through fuel/oil cooler to four main bearings and return through scavenge pumps (-15 and -25 also centrifugal scavenge) to 5 US gal (4·16 Imp gal; 18·8 litre) tank.

Oil Grade: PWA 521 (blend of synthetic and/or mineral oils).

Mounting: From above, in two planes. Front mount (-3A, -7) is double flange at top of fan discharge case, absorbing vertical and side loads. On -20 the front mount is rectangular block above intermediate case, taking vertical and side loads, and thrust brackets at 40° each side of vertical on intermediate-case outer flange. Rear mount (-3A, -7) in double flange above casing in plane of turbine LP bearing, to which engine thrust is transmitted via Y-shaped thrust frame from intermediate case in arrangement that prevents thrust loads reaching (and distorting) the turbine exhaust case. On -20 the frame is eliminated and rear mount takes only vertical, side and torsional loads.

Starting: Pneumatic, by HamStan PS 700 or AiResearch ATS100-384 (DC-10, PS 700 only). Supplied at 40-45 lb/sq in (2·8-3·2 kg/cm²) from APU, ground cart or cross-bleed.

Dimensions:

JT9D-3A, -7, -7A, -20:	
Diameter	95·6 in (2,428 mm)
Length (flange to flange)	128·2 in (3,256 mm)
JT9D-59A, -70:	
Diameter	96·5 in (2,454 mm)
Length	132·2 in (3,358 mm)

Weight, Dry:

Guaranteed, including standard equipment:	
JT9D-3A	8,608 lb (3,905 kg)
JT9D-7	8,770 lb (3,978 kg)
JT9D-7A	8,780 lb (3,982 kg)
JT9D-20	8,450 lb (3,833 kg)
JT9D-59A	9,075 lb (4,116 kg)
JT9D-70	9,200 lb (4,173 kg)

Performance Ratings:

T-O, dry:	
JT9D-3A	43,500 lb (19,731 kg) st
JT9D-7	45,500 lb (20,639 kg) st
JT9D-7A	46,950 lb (21,196 kg) st to 26·7°C
JT9D-7F	48,000 lb (21,772 kg) st to 26·7°C
JT9D-20*	46,300 lb (21,000 kg) st
JT9D-59A	53,000 lb (24,040 kg) to 30°C
T-O, wet:	
JT9D-3A	45,000 lb (20,412 kg) st to 26·7°C
JT9D-7	47,000 lb (21,319 kg) st
JT9D-7A	48,570 lb (22,031 kg) st to 30°C
JT9D-7F	50,000 lb (22,680 kg) st to 30°C
JT9D-20*	49,400 lb (22,404 kg) st to 30°C
Idealised cruise performance, 35,000 ft (10,665 m) at Mach 0·9:	
JT9D-3A, -7	10,000 lb (4,536 kg)
JT9D-7A	10,500 lb (4,762 kg)
JT9D-7F	11,050 lb (5,013 kg)
JT9D-20*	10,770 lb (4,885 kg)
JT9D-59A, -70	11,950 lb (5,421 kg)

Specific Fuel Consumption:

At dry T-O rating:	
JT9D-3A	0·346
JT9D-7	0·356
JT9D-7A	0·357
JT9D-20*	0·349
Cruise, Mach 0·9, 35,000 ft (10,665 m):	
JT9D-3A	0·646
JT9D-7	0·650
JT9D-7A	0·657
JT9D-20*	0·664
JT9D-59A, -70	0·650

**Ideal nozzles*

PRATT & WHITNEY JT10D

Announced in the Spring of 1973, this turbofan using JT9D technology is planned to be rated in the 25,000-30,000 lb (11,340-13,608 kg) st class. It is being developed with the collaboration of MTU of West Germany and Alfa Romeo of Italy, and further details are given in the International section.

Pratt & Whitney J58 (JT11D-20B) turbojet with afterburner for the Lockheed SR-71

The 4,800 shp Pratt & Whitney JFTD12A-5A turboshaft

PRATT & WHITNEY JT11

US military designation: J58

The J58 is an advanced single-spool turbojet engine designed for operation at flight speeds in excess of Mach 3·0, and at very high altitudes. It is rated in the 30,000 lb (13,600 kg) st class.

The general configuration of the J58 is shown in the accompanying illustration. It is fitted with an advanced control system, by Hamilton Standard, which governs automatically the variable intake, fuel supply and variable-area nozzle.

Two J58s (JT11D-20B) form the power plant of the YF-12A and SR-71 versions of the Lockheed A-11 military aircraft, giving them a Mach 3 cruising performance. The power plant installation is described in the entry for the Lockheed YF-12A and SR-71 in the "Aircraft" section.

PRATT & WHITNEY JFTD12

US military designation: T73

This free-turbine turboshaft engine consists basically of the gas generator of a JT12 turbojet with a two-stage free-turbine added downstream to provide a rear drive. The exhaust is taken out to one side, and in the case of the installation on the Sikorsky S-64 Skycrane helicopter one engine exhausts to port, the other to starboard. Pressure ratio is 6·85 : 1.

There are three current versions:

JFTD12A-1. Rated at 4,050 shp. Powers the S-64A. Development running began in the latter half of 1960 and flight testing began in the Sikorsky S-64 on 9 May 1962.

JFTD12A-4A. Advanced version of the earlier JFTD12A-3; powers the Sikorsky S-64E. Certificated under US Army contract as the **T73-P-1** to power Sikorsky CH-54A Skycrane heavy-lift helicopters. Rated at 4,500 shp.

JFTD12A-5A. Advanced version of the JFTD12A-4A; for the Sikorsky S-64F. Certificated under contract to the US Army as the **T73-P-700** to power Sikorsky CH-54B Skycrane heavy-lift helicopters. Rated at 4,800 shp.

PRATT & WHITNEY RL10

The RL10 rocket engine, for the propulsion of space vehicle upper stages, is a regeneratively cooled, turbopump-fed engine with a single chamber. The current RL10A-3-3 production version is rated at 15,000 lb (6,800 kg) thrust at an altitude of 200,000 ft (61,000 m), and has a nominal specific impulse of 444 seconds. Propellants are liquid oxygen and liquid hydrogen, injected at a nominal oxidiser-to-fuel mixture ratio of 5·0 : 1. Rated engine thrust is achieved at a nominal design chamber pressure of 400 lb/sq in absolute (28·1 kg/cm²), with a nominal nozzle area ratio of 57 : 1. The engine can be used for multi-engine installation on an interchangeable basis and is capable of multiple starts after extended coast periods.

First deliveries were made in August 1960 for use in NASA's Centaur stage of the Atlas-Centaur rocket, which is powered by two RL10 engines. A six-engine cluster of RL10A-3 engines powered the S-IV stage of the Saturn I, achieving a perfect performance record for the entire launch programme. Over 9,000 RL10 firings have been accomplished, and 90 engines have flown on operational Saturn and Centaur vehicles, accomplishing 110 successful in-flight starts.

Advanced versions of the RL10 have been tested at the Pratt & Whitney Aircraft Florida Research and Development Center. These tests include variable-thrust operation, low idle operation, pumped idle operation, operation on fluorine/hydrogen propellants, operation on lox/propane propellants. NASA has ordered 20 additional RL10 engines to power Centaur missions during the late 1970s.

Pratt & Whitney RL10A-3-3 rocket engine

ROCKETDYNE

ROCKETDYNE DIVISION OF ROCKWELL INTERNATIONAL

HEADQUARTERS:
6633 Canoga Ave, Canoga Park, California 91304
Telephone: (213) 884-4000
OTHER FACILITIES:
McGregor, Texas
Santa Susana, California
PRESIDENT:
W. J. Brennan
VICE-PRESIDENTS:
M. C. Ek (Engineering)
P. D. Castenholz (Space Shuttle Main Engines)
P. J. Fritch (Business Management)
S. J. Domokos (Advanced Programmes)
N. C. Reuel (Liquid Rocket Programmes)
O. I. Thorsen (McGregor Facility)

Rocketdyne is a division of Rockwell International, devoted primarily to the design and manufacture of rocket engines for the US Air Force, Army and Navy and the National Aeronautics and Space Administration. It was established as a separate division on 8 November 1955.

On 1 October 1959, Rocketdyne acquired full ownership of the former Astrodyne Inc, which was formed in 1958 by North American Aviation and Phillips Petroleum Company.

Rocketdyne's work on liquid-propulsion engines is centred at Canoga Park, California, and work on solid motors at McGregor, Texas.

Rocketdyne liquid-propellant engines power more than three-quarters of all large US space vehicle stages, and powered all three stages of the Saturn V used in the Apollo programme and the Saturn IB used for Skylab launches in 1973 and 1974.

Current products of Rocketdyne's McGregor plant include propulsion systems for the US Navy's Sparrow III, Shrike, AIM-9C/D Sidewinder, Condor and Phoenix missiles, the Army's Chaparral, and miscellaneous turbine starters and gas generators.

Many Rocketdyne solid motors are filled with Flexadyne, a high-performance composite propellant unaffected by long-term storage at —60 to 76°C. By early 1974 more than 43,000 Flexadyne motors had been delivered. In February 1973 the Italian firm of SNIA Viscosa was licensed to market and sub-licence Flexadyne products in all NATO countries outside North America.

Mockup of the Rocketdyne Space Shuttle Main Engine (SSME)

ROCKETDYNE SSME

On 13 July 1971, the Rocketdyne Division of Rockwell International was selected by the US National Aeronautics and Space Administration to design and develop the main engine for the orbiter stage of the US Space Shuttle. Three of these engines will provide a total of 1,410,000 lb (639,600 kg) vacuum thrust.

Two large solid-propellant boosters will be strapped on the sides of the orbiter's expendable propellant tank which will carry the liquid oxygen and liquid hydrogen for the three main engines in the orbiter. The orbiter rides piggyback on the propellant tank in a parallel configuration. The solid motors and the three Space Shuttle Main Engines (SSME) will produce 6,400,000 lb (2,902,990 kg) st to lift the vehicle from the pad in a conventional vertical flight path. The solid motors will burn out at about 25 miles (40 km) altitude, separate from the orbiter stage, and be lowered by parachutes into the ocean for recovery. The three main engines will continue to power the vehicle into orbit; the external tank will then separate and be de-orbited and disposed in a safe area of the ocean. After mission completion the orbiter will re-enter the Earth's atmosphere and manoeuvre to a landing site for an unpowered horizontal landing similar to that of a conventional jet aircraft.

In overall configuration, the SSME is slightly smaller in size than the F-1 engine used in the Saturn V vehicle first stage. It will burn liquid oxygen and liquid hydrogen propellants and is being designed for high reliability, reusability, multiple re-start capability and low cost. It will be capable of 7½ hours of burn time, accrued during 55 flights. Modified airline maintenance procedures will be used to service the engine between flights without removing it from the vehicle.

The design combines the merits of high-chamber-pressure operation, an optimum-performance contoured bell-shaped nozzle, and a regeneratively-cooled thrust chamber, capable of 11° gimballing, for maximum performance and long life. The chamber wall will be cooled so efficiently that it will be at 538°C, although the combustion temperature will be about 3,300°C. No propellant will be wasted in the cooling process. The combustion chamber wall will be made of slotted metal, rather than tubes, using Rocketdyne-developed NARloy-Z, a copper alloy that is easily machined, has higher strength than pure copper, and has very high thermal conductivity. Tubes will be incorporated in the lower nozzle section.

The SSME will be controlled by a unique system incorporating dual-redundant digital computers. This system monitors engine parameters such as pressure and temperature and the engine is automatically adjusted to operate at the required thrust and mixture ratio. The system also develops a record of engine operating history for maintenance purposes to improve serviceability and extend total engine life.

Rocketdyne moved into the hardware development phase in 1972, supported by two principal subcontractors: Honeywell Inc is assisting in the design of the engine control system; Hydraulic Research and Manufacturing Co is assisting in the design of hydraulic components.

COMBUSTION CHAMBER: Channel-wall construction with regenerative cooling by the hydrogen fuel. Concentric-element injector.

TURBOPUMPS: Two low-pressure pumps boost the tank pressures for two high-pressure pumps. Dual pre-burners provide turbine-drive gases to power the high-pressure pumps. Hydrogen-pump discharge pressure is 7,100 lb/sq in (499 kg/cm²) at 36,000 rpm; it develops more than 77,000 hp.

CONTROLLER: Honeywell digital computer controller provides data processing and signal conditioning for control, checkout, monitoring engine status, and maintenance data acquisition.

CONTROLS: A hydraulic-actuation control system is used. The dual-redundant self-monitoring servo-actuators respond to signals from the controller to position the ball valves. A pneumatic system provides backup for the hydraulic system for engine cut-off.

MAINTENANCE: Engine to be maintained using airline-type maintenance procedure for on-the-vehicle servicing. Time between overhauls is 55 flights or 7·5 hours of accumulative operation.

DIMENSIONS:

Length	13 ft 11 in (4,242 mm)
Diameter at nozzle exit	7 ft 10 in (2,388 mm)

PERFORMANCE:

S/L thrust (one engine)	375,000 lb (170,100 kg)
Vacuum thrust	470,000 lb (213,200 kg)
Specific impulse	455 sec
Chamber pressure	3,000 lb/sq in (210 kg/cm²)
Throttling ratio	2 : 1

ROCKETDYNE RS-27

The RS-27 power plant consists of an RS2701A main engine and two LR101-NA-11 vernier engines. The verniers provide vehicle control during flight and vehicle stabilisation at stage separation. The RS-27 will be used as the booster propulsion system for the Delta launch vehicle, replacing the Rocketdyne MB-3 (USAF designation LR79) propulsion system.

The RS2701A is a single-chamber bipropellant fixed-thrust gimballed engine. It utilises liquid oxygen and RP-1 propellants at a nominal mixture ratio of 2·24 : 1. Its rated thrust is 205,000 lb (93,000 kg) at sea level, with a maximum duration of 241·5 seconds. The thrust and mixture ratio are controlled by fixed orifices. The engine is a hybrid design which utilises the turbopump, turbine, gas generator, valves and thrust chamber of the H-1 engine, and the control system, start system and component-packaging arrangement of the MB-3 engine.

DIMENSIONS:

Overall length	11 ft 10 in (3,607 mm)
Envelope max diameter	6 ft 4 in (1,900 mm)

WEIGHT, DRY (approx): 2,355 lb (1,068 kg)

ROCKETDYNE MA-5

USAF designations: LR89 booster and LR105 sustainer

The MA-5 propulsion system consists of an LR89 dual-chamber liquid-propellant booster engine, an LR105 single-chamber liquid-propellant sustainer engine, and two vernier engines to control vehicle roll and to trim final velocity and directional control after burnout of the sustainer. This propulsion system powers the Atlas-Agena and Atlas-Centaur launch vehicles. It is developed from the MA-2 system last described in the 1966-67 *Jane's*.

The design consists of two gimballed tubular-wall booster chambers, with twin-turbopump feed for the liquid oxygen and RP-1 propellants, and a single gimballed tubular-wall sustainer chamber, with similar feed. Ignition of both boosters and the sustainer engine takes place shortly before the vehicle is launched. The LR89-NA-7 booster has two configurations, rated at approximately 350,000 lb (158,800 kg) st and 370,000 lb (167,800 kg) st respectively. The LR105-NA-7 sustainer is rated at 60,000 lb (27,200 kg) st.

Current production is continuing, and the MA-5 is being used to boost launches scheduled for 1975 and 1976.

DIMENSIONS:

Length	8 ft 2 in (2,490 mm)
Diameter, nozzle exit	4 ft (1,219 mm)

WEIGHT, DRY:

Booster	3,024 lb (1,372 kg)
Sustainer	941 lb (427 kg)

ROCKETDYNE MODEL 16NS-1,000

The 16NS-1,000 was developed as a smokeless JATO unit for the USAF, but has wide applications. It consists of a steel cylinder, closed at the forward end. The igniter is located on the forward end, with the exhaust nozzle and pressure release diaphragm at the aft end. Thrust is transmitted to the aircraft attachment fittings through three mounting lugs welded on the cylinder.

Dimensions:
- Length 2 ft 11 in (890 mm)
- Diameter 10·5 in (267 mm)

Weights:
- Without propellant 106·6 lb (48·4 kg)
- Complete 196·9 lb (89·2 kg)

Performance Rating:
1,000 lb (455 kg) st for 16 seconds

ROCKETDYNE MK 25 JATO

The Mk 25 was developed as a standard JATO unit for the US Navy and is used in three forms: Mod 0, with 30° canted nozzle, for launching the A-3 series aircraft; Mod 1, with 15° cant, for boosting the A-4 series; and Mod 2, with straight nozzle, for sled applications. The case is of 4130 steel and the RDS-135 solid propellant burns along inner and outer radii in the form of a sponge-supported cylindrical grain. Performance varies greatly with ambient temperature, a hot day giving much higher thrust for a shorter burn; at 15°C action-time thrust is 4,360 lb (1,977 kg) for 5·41 seconds. The 54 in (1,371 mm) long motor weighs 208 lb (94 kg) filled and 83 lb (37·6 kg) after firing.

ROCKETDYNE RS2101C

The Rocketdyne RS2101C is the Viking Orbiter engine which will provide trajectory-correction and orbit-insertion for the Mars orbiter (with lander) scheduled to be launched in 1975. The engine is derived from a family of similar "football sized" engines (RS-21, described in 1972-73 *Jane's*) which provide gimballed axial thrust for space vehicles. An earlier model (RS2101) provided manoeuvring control for the Mars-Mariner 9, which was launched on 30 May 1971 and placed in orbit about Mars on 13 November 1971. The engine is powered by storable nitrogen tetroxide (oxidiser) and monomethyl-hydrazine (fuel), fed by gas pressure, and stabilised by acoustic-cavity damping. The RS2101 is the first rocket engine to have a chamber cooled by fuel to provide internal regenerative (interegen) cooling; its nozzle is radiation cooled. The engine can be gimballed $\pm 9°$ in any direction through a throat-plane gimbal. A mechanically-linked torque-motor-operated bipropellant valve is integrally pinned above the aluminium multi-element unlike-double injector for impulse control. The injector is joined by the beryllium chamber to the L605 expansion nozzle. To be fired further from Earth than any previous man-made engine, the RS2101C also has the unusually long continuous burn time of 45 minutes.

Dimensions:
- Length 21·8 in (554 mm)
- Nozzle exit diameter 10·72 in (272 mm)

Weight: 18·0 lb (8·2 kg)

Performance (vacuum):
- Thrust 300 lb (136 kg)
- Specific impulse 292 sec
- Chamber pressure 115·7 lb/sq in (8·13 kg/cm²)
- Area ratio 60
- Oxidiser flow rate 0·62 lb (0·281 kg)/sec
- Fuel flow rate 0·41 lb (0·186 kg)/sec

ROCKETDYNE P8E-9

In August 1971 the US Army Missile Command awarded Rocketdyne a direct $6·8 million contract for the P8E-9 engine to power the Extended Range Lance surface-to-surface missile; previous Lance propulsion had been procured through LTV, the prime contractor. Many details of this highly mobile battlefield missile remain classified, but the P8E-9 comprises a sustainer engine surrounded by a concentric booster, both sections burning UDMH (unsymmetrical dimethyl hydrazine) and IRFNA (red fuming nitric acid). Ignition is hypergolic and the chamber and nozzle cooling is regenerative. Both sections ignite, bursting the closure diaphragm, the boost burns out after six seconds and the variable thrust after 120 seconds. Area ratios are 5·77 for the booster and 4·0 for the sustainer. Mixture ratio is 3·4, chamber pressure 950 lb/sq in (66·8 kg/cm²), and overall motor length 19·5 in (495·3 mm) and width 16 in (406·4 mm).

ROCKETDYNE MK 38/39

The Mk 38 solid-propellant rocket motor developed and produced by Rocketdyne for the Sparrow III air-to-air missile was the first to combine a special free-standing propellant charge (grain) with the company's Flexadyne propellant. Based on a carboxy-terminated linear polybutadiene fuel-binder, the new propellant provides a substantial increase in missile performance and has superior physical properties which give it resistance to cracking or tearing at extremely low temperatures.

The development contract for the motor was placed in 1961 and flight tests began successfully 12 months later. Development and qualification of the motor were completed in 22 months. The McGregor plant shortly thereafter, in July 1963, began manufacturing the Mk 39 motor for the AGM-45A Shrike anti-radar missile. This is similar in design and ballistic performance. Improved designs of these motors have been qualified, incorporating a case-bonded Flexadyne grain to provide 50 per cent more power with a corresponding increase in missile range.

ROCKETDYNE MK 36 MOD 5

The McGregor, Texas, plant of Rocketdyne received a development contract for motors for the AIM-9C and AIM-9D advanced versions of the Sidewinder air-to-air missile in 1963. Standard Sidewinder cases were loaded with the company's Flexadyne propellant and tested under temperature extremes ranging from sub-zero to over 150°C. They showed perfect reliability in over 200 firings during development and operational evaluation, and first production contracts were awarded in 1964.

Designated Mk 36 Mod 5, the Rocketdyne Sidewinder motor is approximately 72 in (1,830 mm) long, 5 in (127 mm) in diameter and contains 60 lb (27 kg) of Flexadyne propellant.

ROCKETDYNE MK 47

The Mk 47 Mod 0 solid-propulsion system for the Navy's AIM-54A Phoenix missile has been under development by the McGregor plant since 1963. The first powered flight was in April 1966, two months after completion of the propulsion system development programme, in the course of which over 60 motors were subjected to such tests as multiple-temperature cycling, shock tests simulating catapult and arrested landings, and extensive vibration tests.

The Mk 47 motor utilises an improved version of Flexadyne, particularly adaptable to Phoenix missile requirements of high volumetric loading, high total impulse and long burning time to provide the long-range missile operational capability required. The propellant has excellent ballistic properties, a 5-10 year shelf life and exhaust characteristics that minimise radar attenuation. Rocketdyne has successfully test fired similar propellant at —60°C in a large research motor after two complete temperature cyclings between —60 and 77°C. Rocketdyne is now in its third production run with this motor, under US Navy contract.

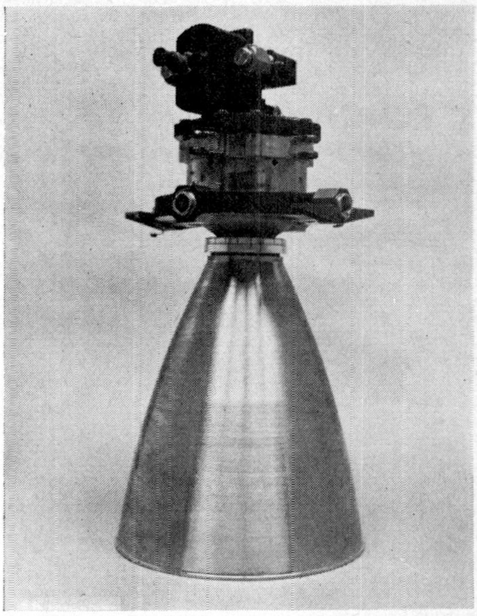

Rocketdyne RS2101C rocket engine for Viking Orbiter

ROCKETDYNE CONDOR MK 70 MOD 0

The Mk 70 Mod 0 rocket motor developed and produced by Rocketdyne-McGregor for the Condor air-to-ground missile utilises a Flexadyne solid-propellant grain, case-bonded with a stress-relieving liner. The liner allows the motor to perform over a wide range of severe temperature and dynamic conditions.

The development contract for the Mk 70 motor was placed in late 1969 and qualification was completed in late 1971. The motor has a record of 100 per cent reliability in missile flight tests.

ROCKETDYNE B-1

The B-1 escape system rocket motor being developed by Rocketdyne-McGregor for the US Air Force's B-1 strategic bomber will provide propulsion to separate the crew compartment module from the airframe in the event of an emergency.

In addition to providing the energy for ejection, two of these solid-rocket motors, positioned beneath the module, will provide attitude control in both the pitch and roll directions preparatory to parachute deployment. To accomplish this twofold role, the motor delivers two distinct levels of thrust, a "boost" phase to propel the module and a lower "sustain" phase for the control sequence. Although boost/sustain motors are not uncommon, this combination in the spherical-shaped B-1 motor is unique. Qualification of the B-1 motor was completed in October 1973.

Rocketdyne Mk 47 Mod 0 solid-propellant motor for Hughes AIM-54A Phoenix air-to-air missile

SOLAR

SOLAR (Division of International Harvester Company)

Head Office and Works:
2200 Pacific Highway, San Diego, California 92138

Telephone: (714) 233-8241

President: O. Morris Sievert

Solar manufactures a range of gas-turbine engines which includes the 80-150 shp T62 Titan, the 380 shp Spartan, the 1,200 shp Saturn and the 3,830 shp Centaur.

The Titan turbine is used as an auxiliary power unit on every major US military cargo helicopter (which includes the Boeing Vertol CH-46 and CH-47, Sikorsky CH-3, CH-53 and CH-54) as well as on several small commercial aircraft and business jets, such as the FH-227, JetStar, Sabreliner, Hawker Siddeley 125 and Dassault Falcon. Titan turbine APUs can provide power for main engine starting, ground air-conditioning and pre-flight system checkout. Well over 4,500 Titan APUs have been sold.

Cutaway drawing of the 80-150 shp Solar Titan turboshaft engine

TELEDYNE CAE

TELEDYNE CAE

HEAD OFFICE:
1330 Laskey Road, Toledo, Ohio 43697
Telephone: (419) 470-3000

PRESIDENT: James L. Murray

VICE-PRESIDENTS:
Henry C. Maskey (Engineering)
Eugene R. Sullivan (Finance)
Robert P. Schiller (Marketing)
Richard A. Myers (Operations)

Teledyne CAE (formerly Continental Aviation and Engineering) became a division of Teledyne Inc during 1969. Teledyne CAE has long experience in the design, development and production of gas-turbine engines, and is now devoted exclusively to turbine engine work.

The headquarters for management, marketing, finance, engineering and production is the Toledo, Ohio, facility of over 350,000 sq ft (32,500 m²).

From 1951 until 1960 almost all development was based on Turboméca designs. By far the most important of these was the Marboré, from which stemmed the J69 series of turbojets on which the manufacturing programme has depended. Since 1960 Teledyne CAE has embarked on an in-house development programme on a large scale. To a considerable degree the newer Teledyne CAE engines are aimed at target drones, unmanned reconnaissance aircraft and cruise-type guided missiles. The company has long claimed to be the largest maker of engines for unmanned applications.

TELEDYNE CAE 352 and 356

US military designation: J69

The J69 was originally the Turboméca Marboré, which has been developed to meet American requirements. Four versions are currently available as follows:

J69-T-25 (Teledyne CAE Model 352-5A). Long-life version, which powers the Cessna T-37B trainer and is FAA certificated as the Model CJ69-1025. Its air mass flow is 19·8 lb (9 kg)/sec. Operational ceiling is 45,000 ft (13,720 m).

J69-T-29 (Teledyne CAE Model 356-7A). Powers the Teledyne Ryan BQM-34A subsonic target drone. Operational ceiling is 60,000 ft (18,300 m). This is the Teledyne CAE counterpart to the Turboméca Gourdon turbojet, comprising a Marboré II with the addition of a single-stage transonic axial compressor supercharging the centrifugal stage.

J69-T-41A (Teledyne CAE Model 356-29A). Transonic axial compressor and revised centrifugal stage handling airflow of 29·8 lb (13·5 kg)/sec with pressure ratio of 5·45 : 1. Operational ceiling in excess of 69,000 ft (21,030 m). In production as improved version of J69-T-29 powering special-purpose subsonic RPVs.

YJ69-T-406 (Teledyne CAE Model 356-34A). In production for the US Navy's BQM-34E and the USAF's BQM-34F supersonic target drones. Initial qualification testing was completed during 1967 and deliveries of production engines began in 1970. The T-406 engine can propel the BQM-34E to Mach 1·5 at 60,000 ft (18,300 m) altitude. Future development of the T-406 engine involves addition of an advanced axial compressor stage and an afterburner for Mach 2·5 drone performance; another project would have an aircooled turbine.

The J69-T-29, YJ69-T-406 and J69-T-41A have a single-stage axial compressor ahead of the standard centrifugal compressor. Combustion system and turbine arrangements are basically the same as on the J69-T-25.

DIMENSIONS (nominal):
Length overall:
J69-T-25 — 35·39 in (899 mm)
YJ69-T-406, J69-T-41A and J69-T-29 — 44·8 in (1,138 mm)
Width:
J69-T-25 — 22·30 in (566 mm)
J69-T-41A, J69-T-29 — 22·36 in (568 mm)
YJ69-T-406 — 22·52 in (572 mm)

WEIGHT, DRY:
J69-T-25 — 364 lb (165 kg)
J69-T-29 — 341 lb (154 kg)
J69-T-41A — 350 lb (159 kg)
YJ69-T-406 — 360 lb (163 kg)

PERFORMANCE RATINGS:
Max rating:
J69-T-25 — 1,025 lb (465 kg) st at 21,730 rpm
J69-T-29 — 1,700 lb (771 kg) st at 22,000 rpm
J69-T-41A — 1,920 lb (871 kg) st at 22,000 rpm
YJ69-T-406 — 1,920 lb (871 kg) st at 22,150 rpm
Normal rating:
J69-T-25 — 880 lb (400 kg) st at 20,700 rpm
J69-T-29 — 1,375 lb (625 kg) st at 20,790 rpm
J69-T-41A — 1,650 lb (748 kg) st at 20,900 rpm
YJ69-T-406 — 1,719 lb (779 kg) st at 21,450 rpm

SPECIFIC FUEL CONSUMPTION:
At max rating:
J69-T-25 — 1·14
J69-T-41A, J69-T-29 — 1·10
YJ69-T-406 — 1·11
At normal ratin
J69-T-25 — 1·12
J69-T-29 — 1·085
J69-T-41A — 1·09
YJ69-T-406 — 1·10

TELEDYNE CAE 356-28A

US military designation: J100-CA-100

The Model 356-28A has been developed by Teledyne CAE as a power plant for RPVs and other unmanned aircraft. The engine is derived from the J69 family but has no parts in common with the J69 family. It has a two-stage transonic axial compressor ahead of the centrifugal stage, handling a mass flow of 44·9 lb (20·4 kg)/sec with a pressure ratio of 6·3 : 1. The combustion chamber is annular with centrifugal fuel injection. The turbine has two axial stages, each fitted with replaceable blades. Fixed geometry is used throughout, although the engine is at present operating at altitudes in excess of 75,000 ft (22,860 m).

Teledyne CAE YJ69-T-406 turbojet of 1,920 lb (871 kg) st

Teledyne CAE J100-CA-100 turbojet of 2,700 lb (1,225 kg) st

Teledyne CAE J69-T-29 turbojet of 1,700 lb (771 kg) st

Teledyne CAE 356-28E turbojet for unmanned high-altitude applications, rated at 4,200 lb (1,905 kg) st

The J100-CA-100 completed a 108 hour qualification test in June 1969. Applications include the Teledyne Ryan 147TE and 147TF medium-altitude intelligence-collection RPVs.

Dimensions:

Length, intake flange to jet pipe flange 48·21 in (1,225 mm)

Max width 24·75 in (629 mm)

Max height 26·10 in (663 mm)

Weight, Dry: 430 lb (195 kg)

Performance Ratings:

Max 2,700 lb (1,225 kg) st at 20,700 rpm

Normal 2,430 lb (1,102 kg) st at 20,120 rpm

Specific Fuel Consumption:

At max rating 1·10

At normal rating 1·08

TELEDYNE CAE 356-28C, D, E

Derived directly from the J100 (Model 356-28A), the Model 356-28 family is being greatly extended with a new family of growth engines distinguished mainly by the addition of a geared zero-stage which raises pressure ratio to about 8·1 : 1. The higher pressure is an essential stepping stone to further increase in operating altitude, one of the urgent demands on the company in meeting propulsion requirements for future unmanned aircraft. The 356-28C has a mass flow of up to 54·1 lb (24·5 kg)/sec; the -28D and -28E have a further increased airflow of 65 lb (29·4 kg)/sec. All these engines have a centrifugal compressor, combustion chamber and turbine basically similar to those of the J100. Operating ceiling exceeds 90,000 ft (27,430 m).

Dimensions:

Length, intake flange to jet pipe flange 64·6 in (1,641 mm)

Basic overall diameter 25·5 in (648 mm)

Weight, Dry:

356-28C 530 lb (240 kg)

356-28D 511 lb (231 kg)

356-28E 485 lb (220 kg)

Performance Ratings:

Max rating:

356-28C 3,500 lb (1,587 kg) st

356-28D, -28E 4,200 lb (1,905 kg) st

TELEDYNE CAE 356-28F

US military designation: J100-CA-101

This version of the J100 has been optimised for low-altitude performance with minimal cost. Changes include a slight increase in shaft speed, revised radial-diffuser vane angle and reduced turbine inlet nozzle area. Application has not been disclosed.

Dimensions:

Length overall 48·6 in (1,234 mm)

Max width 24·7 in (627 mm)

Max height 25·3 in (643 mm)

Weight, Dry: 430 lb (195 kg)

Performance Ratings:

Military S/L static 3,050 lb (1,383 kg)

Military S/L Mach 0·95 3,000 lb (1,360 kg)

Specific Fuel Consumption:

Military S/L static 1·10

Military S/L Mach 0·95 1·36

TELEDYNE CAE 365

US military designation: LJ95

This family of engines had its inception in a lift-jet, the Model 365-7, developed for the US Air Force as the XLJ95-T-1. Details remain classified, except that the engine is in the 5,000 lb (2,270 kg) st class, has an above-average turbine gas temperature and offers a ratio of thrust to weight exceeding 20 : 1, yet is intended for propulsion of manned aircraft. From the 365-7 unit Teledyne CAE has projected various cruise turbojets, of which one of the most important could be the 365-20, a possible candidate for the propulsion of very-high-performance (up to Mach 3 at above 75,000 ft; 22,860 m) target drones for the training of fighter pilots.

TELEDYNE CAE 370

US military designation: J402-CA-400

This low-cost expendable engine was designed for the propulsion of cruise-type missiles and is in production for the US Navy AGM-84A and RGM-84A Harpoon missiles. The J402 is noteworthy for its compact cmoponent and accessory disposition, giving miniuum frontal area. Though the entire design minimises production time and cost, high reliability was a prime requirement. Flight limits are 40,000 ft (12,200 m) and Mach 0·9 continuous or Mach 1·1 for limited periods. Engine life is reported unofficially to be 1 hr.

Type: Single-shaft turbojet.

Intake: Direct pitot inlet with four struts.

Compressor: Single transonic axial compressor with precision cast construction. Single centrifugal compressor with precision cast construction. Max airflow 9·6 lb (4·35 kg)/sec. Pressure ratio 5·8.

Combustion Chamber: Annular type.

Fuel System: Low-pressure supply to centrifugal injection nozzles in compressor shaft. Electronic control system with automatic sequencing and regulation to meet demands of missile flight profile.

Turbine: Single-stage axial.

Jet Pipe: Fixed-area.

Accessories: Pyrotechnic starting and ignition systems. Optional integral alternator and alternator regulator to give 6 kW of DC power.

Mounting: Four main mountings disposed radially around main (compressor diffuser) frame.

Dimensions:

Length (excluding bullet) 29·44 in (748 mm)

Overall diameter 12·52 in (318 mm)

Weight, Dry: 100 lb (45·36 kg)

Performance Rating:

Max S/L static 660 lb (299 kg) at 41,200 rpm

Specific Fuel Consumption (S/L, static): 1·20

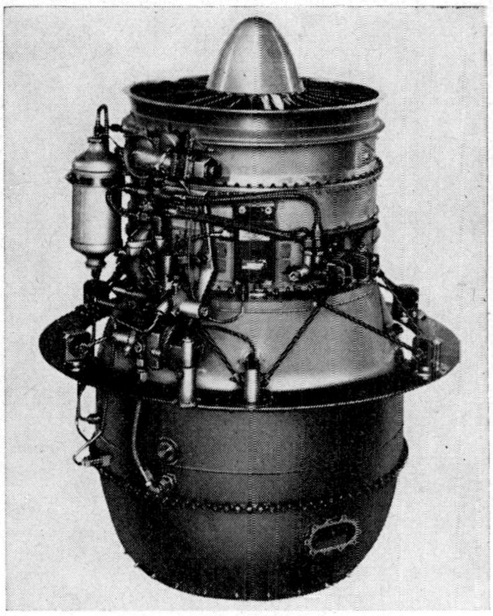

Teledyne CAE XLJ95-T-1 lift-jet

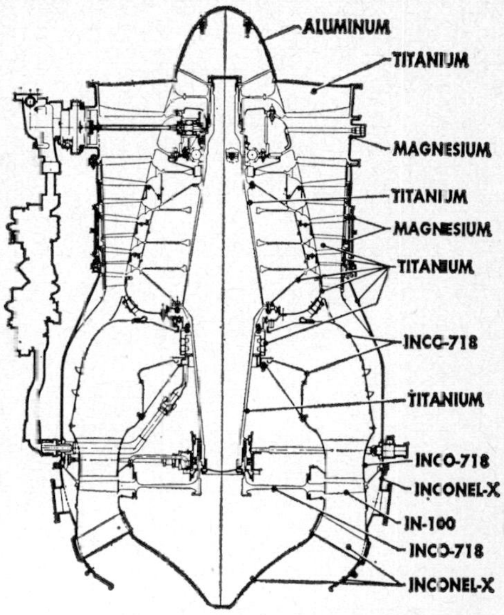

Cross-section drawing of XLJ95 lift-jet, detailing materials

TELEDYNE CAE 372-2

This turbojet is the company's candidate engine for the Beech variable-speed training target (VSTT). It is based on the Model 370 (J402) but differs in detail engineering and equipment, reflecting the need for repeated missions of extended duration. The electronic fuel control governs engine operation throughout the starting cycle and over the whole operating range. A shaft-mounted high-speed alternator provides 1·2 kW of DC power. Engine life is unofficially reported to be 15 hr.

Dimensions:

Length (excluding bullet) 29·65 in (753 mm)

Overall diameter 12·50 in (317 mm)

Weight, Dry: 115 lb (52 kg)

Performance Rating:

Max S/L static 640 lb (290 kg) at 40,400 rpm

Specific Fuel Consumption (S/L, static): 1·19

TELEDYNE CAE 440/555

A possible basis for a wide family of advanced small engines for the period after 1975, the 440 and 555 core engines developed as a result of the company's participation in the US Air Force Advanced Turbine Engine Gas Generator programme. Like ATEGG studies by other companies, the Models 440 and 555 have design parameters (pressure ratio, turbine entry temperature and specific fuel consumption) similar to those of the most advanced large engines. Most likely applications of these engine cores would be in turbofans in the 3,000-5,000 lb (1,360,2,268 kg) thrust class for piloted aircraft or high-performance RPVs.

TELEDYNE CAE 472

US military designation: F106-CA-100

Another of the company's range of engines for unmanned applications, the F106 turbofan was entered in the US Air Force AGM-86A subsonic cruise armed decoy (SCAD) competition. A modified version is under consideration for the US Navy cruise missile application.

The core engine comprises three axial compressor stages plus one centrifugal stage; an annular combustion chamber with slinger fuel injection; and a two-stage axial turbine. The fan has two stages and is driven by a two-stage LP turbine. Beyond the fact that the F106 is in the 600 lb (272 kg) st class, all other design and performance details are classified. It is unofficially reported that the F106 is being considered in various modified forms, with ratings in the range 400-1,000 lb (181-454 kg), for future RPV programmes.

TELEDYNE CAE 490

This is the French-designed Turboméca-SNECMA Larzac (see Turboméca-SNECMA GRTS in French section), an "exclusive agreement" for which was announced by Teledyne CAE in January 1973. The American company will "market, manufacture and service" the European turbofan for the United States and Canada.

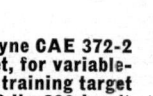

Teledyne CAE 372-2 turbojet, for variable-speed training target (640 lb; 290 kg st)

Teledyne CAE F106 (Model 472) turbofan in 600 lb; 272 kg st class

Teledyne CAE J402 expendable low-cost turbojet of 660 lb (299 kg) st

Display mock-up of Teledyne CAE 490-4 (Larzac) turbofan in the 3,000 lb (1,360 kg) thrust class

The president of Teledyne CAE said that the Larzac, the initial US version of which is designated Model 490-4, "provides a valuable new source of flight-ready jet engines for strike and trainer aircraft, missiles and remotely piloted vehicles". A commercial Model 490 is planned to be available in 1976. A Model 490-4 demonstrator engine began running at Toledo in March 1973.

TELEDYNE CONTINENTAL

TELEDYNE CONTINENTAL MOTORS

HEAD OFFICE:
30500 Van Dyke Avenue, Warren, Michigan 48093
Telephone: (313) 751-7000

PRESIDENT:
J. L. Richardson

VICE-PRESIDENT AND CONTROLLER:
C. E. McGill

GENERAL COUNSEL:
E. F. Kotts

Aircraft Products Division

ADDRESS:
PO Box 90, Mobile, Alabama 36601
Telephone: (205) 438-3411

VICE-PRESIDENT AND GENERAL MANAGER:
W. E. Lewis

VICE-PRESIDENT AND ASSISTANT GENERAL MANAGER:
D. E. Obernesser

DIRECTOR, MARKETING:
W. K. Danhof

DIRECTOR, ENGINEERING:
C. R. Goulet

DIRECTOR, COMMUNICATIONS:
Don Fairchilds

In 1928, the former Continental Motors Corporation, one of the largest automobile engine manufacturers in the world, produced its first aero-engine, a sleeve-valve aircooled radial incorporating the Argyll (Burt-McCollum) patents, which had been purchased by the Corporation from the British Argyll Company in 1925.

In 1931 the 38 hp A40 flat-four was put on the market. This was followed by the A50, A65, A75 and A80 engines.

The current range of Teledyne Continental light aircraft engines includes horizontally-opposed four- and six-cylinder engines, some with fuel injection, rated between 100 and 435 hp. The first of the new-generation Tiara engines, the 6-285-B, is also in production.

In October 1960 it was announced that Rolls-Royce Ltd of England had acquired the licence to manufacture and sell certain engines from the complete range of Continental piston engines throughout the world, apart from the Americas and certain countries in the Far East. (See Rolls-Royce Motors Ltd in UK section.)

CONTINENTAL C90 SERIES

The C90 Series includes the C90-8F which has a flanged crankshaft but does not have provisions for installing either a starter or generator; the C90-12F and -14F which have a flanged crankshaft and starter and generator; and the -16 which has a vacuum pump adaptor.

C90 Series engines have an approved take-off rating of 95 hp at 2,625 rpm.

TYPE: Four-cylinder horizontally-opposed aircooled.

CYLINDERS: Bore $4\frac{1}{16}$ in (103·2 mm). Stroke $3\frac{7}{8}$ in (98·4 mm). Capacity 201 cu in (3·28 litres). Compression ratio 7:1. Externally-finned aluminium alloy head castings, screwed and shrunk permanently on externally-finned steel barrels.

PISTONS: Cam ground aluminium castings. Three compression rings above pin. Top ring chrome-faced. Oil control ring below pin. Holes in groove provided for interior drain. Pins are full floating ground steel tubes with ground aluminium end plugs.

CONNECTING RODS: "I" beam-type, split bronze pin bushings, identical precision inserts (same as main bearings, steel-backed, lead alloy lined).

CRANKCASE: Aluminium alloy.

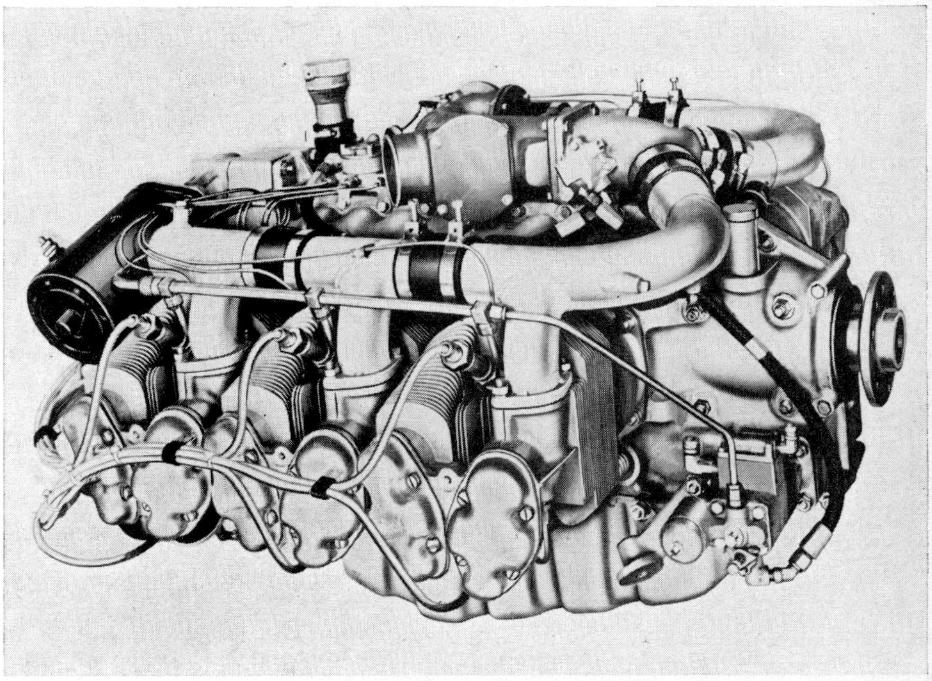

The 225 hp Teledyne Continental TSIO-360-C

CRANKSHAFT: Steel alloy forging, with nitrided journals and crankpins for greater strength.

CAMSHAFT: Steel alloy forging.

VALVE GEAR: Exhaust valves are Stellite-faced and stem tips are hardened. Bronze valve guides.

GEAR TRAIN: Torque is transmitted to engine components from the crankshaft via gears machined from alloy steel forgings, conforming to SAE specifications.

INDUCTION: Small float-type carburettor with a simplified manual mixture control.

FUEL GRADE: 80/87 octane minimum.

IGNITION: Radio shielded, impulse couples, small or standard size magnetos optional.

LUBRICATION SYSTEM: Magnesium crankcase cover houses the engine-driven gear-type oil pump. An oil pressure relief valve and oil screen are also mounted in the cover.

ACCESSORIES: 12V 20 or 35A alternator standard (12V 60A optional).

For other details, see table.

CONTINENTAL O-200 SERIES

The O-200-A engine is generally similar to the C90 Series engines. It is fitted with a single updraught carburettor, dual magnetos and starter and generator.

The O-200-B is similar to the O-200-A, but is designed for pusher installation.

For other details see table.

CONTINENTAL IO-360 SERIES

The IO-360 is a six-cylinder horizontally-opposed aircooled engine with fuel injection. Design and materials are generally similar to those of IO-346-A (1970-71 *Jane's*), except for number and size of cylinders. Accessories include oil cooler, two magnetos, propeller governor drive, vacuum pump and 24V alternator. The IO-360 has a sandcast crankcase, with the accessory case mounted at the rear. The cylinders are shell-moulded.

The IO-360-C has dual accessory drive. The TSIO-360-A, B and C have a turbocharger pressurised induction system, revised fuel system, starter and accessory drive, scavenge pump and full-flow oil cooler. These engines power the Cessna T337 Super Skymaster.

For further details see table.

CONTINENTAL O-470 SERIES

Engines in the O-470 series (including the E-185 and E-225) are all basically similar. Engines prefixed "IO" have direct fuel-injection.

The O-470 family of engines are manufactured in four power ranges, from 225 hp to 260 hp as follows:

225 hp IO-470-K
230 hp O-470-R
250 hp IO-470-C, G
260 hp IO-470-D, E, F, L, N, V

The 225 hp and 230 hp models have a compression ratio of 7 : 1, the 250 hp models a ratio of 8 : 1, and the 260 hp models a ratio of 8·6 : 1.

The following description refers specifically to the O-470-R, but is generally applicable to all versions:

TYPE: Six-cylinder horizontally-opposed aircooled.

CYLINDERS: Bore 5 in (127 mm). Stroke 4 in (101·6 mm). Swept volume 471 cu in (7·5 litres). Compression ratio 7 : 1. Forged steel barrels with integral cooling fins. Heat-treated cast aluminium alloy heads screwed and shrunk on to barrels.

PISTONS: Aluminium. Four rings, two compression and one oil control above pin and scraper ring below. Steel gudgeon pins with permanently forged-in aluminium end plugs.

CONNECTING RODS: Forged steel. Trimetal bronze replaceable type big-end bearings, bronze bushing little-ends.

CRANKSHAFT: One-piece six-throw chrome-nickel-molybdenum steel forging. Outer surfaces nitrided. One 5th and one 6th order counterweights attached to shaft. Five bearings of replaceable shell type.
CRANKCASE: Two-piece heat-treated aluminium casting divided at vertical lengthwise plane through crankshaft, with integral cast accessory section.
VALVE GEAR: Two poppet-type valves per cylinder: one steel inlet and one steel exhaust with Stellite seat. Camshaft gear-driven from crankshaft in lower part of crankcase.
INDUCTION: Updraught gravity-feed carburettor.
FUEL: 80/87 octane.
IGNITION: Two magnetos on top of accessory section. Two spark plugs per cylinder. Shielded ignition harness.
LUBRICATION: Pressure type. Oil cooler on front of crankcase. Oil filter in crankcase. One impeller type pump. Oil pressure 30-60 lb/sq in (2·1-4·2 kg/cm²).
PROPELLER DRIVE: RH drive. Direct. Flanged propeller shaft. Provision for constant-speed propeller.
ACCESSORIES: Generator on accessory section. Drives for vacuum pump and tachometer.
STARTING: Electric starter.
MOUNTING: Four mounting points, one at each lower corner of crankcase.
DIMENSIONS, WEIGHTS AND PERFORMANCE: See table

CONTINENTAL IO-520 SERIES

These engines are basically similar to the IO-470, but with cylinders of larger bore. They are fitted with an alternator driven either by a belt or by a face gear on the crankshaft. All IO-520 engines are rated at 285 hp METO apart from the IO-520-D, -E and -F which have a take-off rating of 300 hp. IO-520 engines power the Beechcraft Baron and Bonanza, Navion and Cessna 210. New in 1970 were the generally similar IO-520-J, -K and -L, also rated at 285 hp (-K and -L are cleared to 300 hp at 2,850 rpm at take-off).

The TSIO-520 series are turbocharged. Take-off rating is 285 hp except for the -E and -G, rated at 300 hp, and the TSIO-520-J rated at 310 hp and equipped with an intercooler and provision for an overboost valve. These engines power the Cessna 414, 320D, T210 and 210F, and turbocharged Bonanza.

For other details see table.

CONTINENTAL GTSIO-520

This is similar to the TSIO-520 range but is geared and uprated. The -C model, rated at 340 hp at 3,200 rpm, powers the Cessna 411. The GTSIO-520-D, rated at 375 hp at 3,400 rpm, powers the Cessna 421. The -F has an integral turbocharger and complete exhaust system; the most powerful Continental engine in production, used in the Rockwell Commander 685. The -G is used in a military application, the -H powers the Cessna 421A Golden Eagle.

CONTINENTAL TIARA SERIES

In 1972 Teledyne Continental Motors initiated production of a comprehensive new range of general aviation piston engines of aircooled horizontally-opposed geared design, known as the Tiara family.

Design parameters considered in engineering the new series were reduction in weight to horsepower ratio, improved crankshaft versus propeller speed efficiency and easier servicing of the engine. Significant achievements have been made on all counts.

Servicing is further facilitated in the design of the cylinders. A single nut attaches the rocker cover to the cylinder head. The cylinder head can be detached from the barrel without disturbing the piston and ring set-up.

Design and engineering of the Tiara series were started in early 1965, with the object of establishing a completely new generation of aircraft piston engines. A very large development and pre-production test programme was planned, involving 46 prototype engines (initially identified as the GIO-366). By January 1970 these had completed 5,000 hr development testing, 11,000 hr endurance running and 2,000 hr life testing. This programme included 56 type test cycles, and several hundred flight test hours were completed in a special Beech D18 flying testbed (with standard Continental TSIO-520s in the wing nacelles and a trial engine in the nose) and in Continental's engineering fleet, comprising a Cessna 206, Cessna 175, Cessna Cardinal, Piper Aztec and Arrow, Cessna 310 and Beechcraft Debonair.

In addition, sample engines have been supplied to major US general aircraft manufacturers for flight evaluation. Environmental testing in California, South Dakota and the central Gulf states has covered the full range of conditions likely to be experienced in service. A Cessna 320 Skyknight has been used exclusively as a flight test aircraft for Tiara engines. In addition to the hours in the test cell required by FAA for the type certificate, the 6-285-B accumulated 1,100 hours in flight in the Skyknight. Over 500 hours have been flown using 6-320 Tiara engines in the Skyknight.

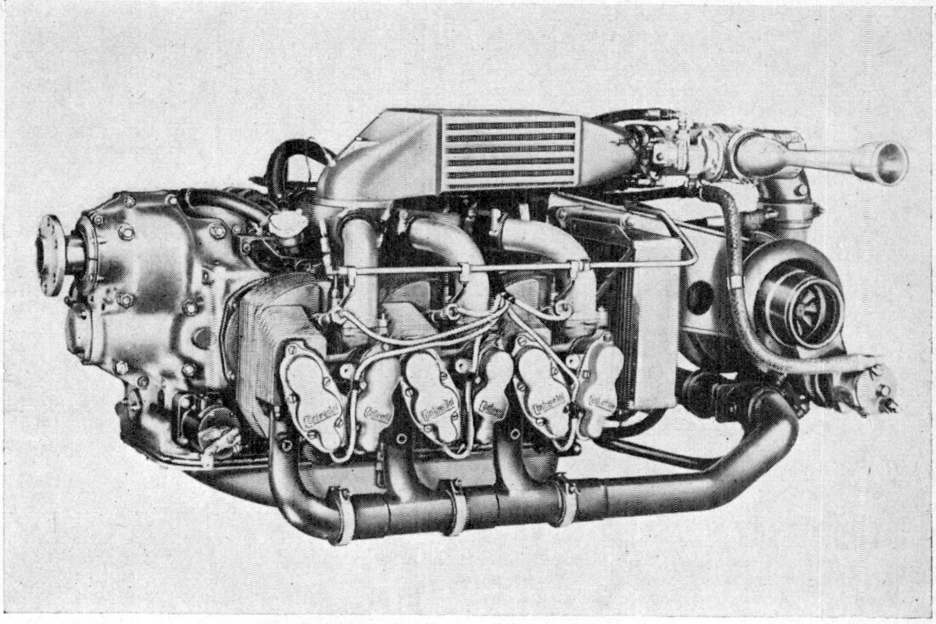

The 435 hp Teledyne Continental GTSIO-520-F

The 375 hp Teledyne Continental GTSIO-520-D

The 310 hp Teledyne Continental TSIO-520-J, power plant of the Cessna 414

A large investment has been made in new tooling and machinery of the latest design in the headquarters of the Aircraft Products Division in Mobile, Alabama, for use in production of the Tiara line.

FAA certification of all models is scheduled to be completed ahead of production availability. Type tests are being performed using engines equipped with all major accessories, and running a 150 hr cycle, with 100 hr at maximum power and 50 hr at selected cruise settings. Models 6-260A and 6-285 received flight certification during 1969 and the 6-285-B has since been awarded Type Certificate E12CE. Tiara designations comprise a digit indicating the number of cylinders and a dash number indicating horsepower rating; a T prefix is used for turbocharged variants.

Ninety-five per cent of all parts and components comprising the three main series of four-, six-, and eight-cylinder models of the Tiara family are interchangeable on all engines. This major feature of the new series is intended to promote economy of manufacture, reducing spare parts inventories, and simplifying servicing in the field. Standard models of starters, generators, alternators, pumps and other accessory equipment have been extensively tested and certificated for use in Tiara engines.

All Tiara engines are reduction geared at a 2 : 1 ratio, thus creating a very favourable high crankshaft speed to relatively low propeller speed. The transfer of torque from low to high speed is controlled by a new VTC (vibratory torque control) unit. In addition to providing a smooth transition from low to high speeds, the VTC unit eliminates the need for conventional crankshaft pendulum dampers. In operation, the VTC unit hydraulically locks the system into a torsionally stiff configuration at low speeds, and unlocks as speed builds up, allowing the engine to operate on a flexible quill shaft system at higher rpm. A major reduction in vibratory torque is thus achieved in propeller gearing, propeller and accessory systems, permitting the use of lighter, slower and quieter propellers. Lower engine component stresses allow the use of lighter parts.

The cylinder barrel and cylinder head are of lighter-weight design than hitherto, offering enhanced cooling, lower manufacturing cost and ease of servicing and replacement. The head is a shell-moulded casting, providing greater uniformity of dimensions and permitting the use of thinner fins. As a result, the Tiara cylinder design requires approximately a quarter less cooling air pressure than contemporary engines. The crankcase for each of the three series embodies a power section, accessory section and reduction gear section.

As a consequence of operating at higher engine rpm, the camshaft rpm is compatible with that of the propeller. A single pair of spur gears of 2 : 1 ratio drives both the propeller and camshaft. This novel arrangement eliminates the two gears normally required to drive the camshaft, thus saving weight and cost, and the lower-speed propeller is significantly quieter.

Only seven gears instead of the normal 13 are required for the accessory gearing. The train drives seven side-mounted accessories including the oil pump and, in the turbocharged models, an additional scavenge pump. Bevel gears provide a right-angle drive from the rear end of the camshaft, facilitating vertical positioning of the accessory section to control overall height.

Common features of all models include a cylinder bore and stroke of $4\frac{7}{8}$ in (123·8 mm) and $3\frac{5}{8}$ in (92·08 mm) respectively, overhead valves, dual ignition, a Teledyne Continental fuel injection system, a minimum fuel grade of 100/130 aviation gasoline, and a lubrication system having a wet sump of 8 US quarts (4·55 litres) capacity, with full-flow filtering and using SAE 50 grade oil for sea level ambient conditions above 4°C and SAE 30 or 10W-30 below this temperature.

Accessory drives and mounts are provided for a tachometer, two magnetos, a starter, a belt-driven alternator, and a propeller governor. In addition there are two spare drives.

Continental is establishing a highly-automated production line capable of producing 10,000 engines per year. All components for the new Tiara series have been designed to facilitate manufacture using modern, high-speed automated machine tools. This is aimed at minimising the production labour force and assists in achieving engine prices comparable with contemporary engines of the same power bracket.

A product support programme for the Tiara series is already under way, including service training classes for Teledyne Continental and airframe manufacturers' personnel, and distributors and dealers. Nearly 50 per cent of major components released for production are being allocated to a replacement parts pool for support of Tiara engines worldwide. Some Tiara variants announced to date are as follows:

Model 6-260. Six-cylinder naturally-aspirated engine of 260 hp (264 cv). Has completed all required development, endurance, type and flight tests, and has been granted FAA Type Certificate. Flown in nose of Beechcraft D18 and Debonair.

Model 6-285-B. Six-cylinder naturally-aspirated engine of 285 hp (289 cv). Has completed all required development, endurance, type and flight tests, and has been granted FAA Type Certificate. Initial production engine in Tiara series, for Piper Pawnee Brave.

Model T6-320. Six-cylinder turbocharged engine of 320 hp (324 cv).

Cessna 310 testbed aircraft with two Teledyne Continental Tiara 6-285 normally-aspirated engines

Above: **The 285 hp Teledyne Continental Tiara 6-285-B six-cylinder engine, and** (*below*) **a cutaway drawing of the same engine**

REPRESENTATIVE TELEDYNE CONTINENTAL HORIZONTALLY-OPPOSED ENGINES

Engine Model	No. of Cylinders	Bore and Stroke in (mm)	Capacity cu in (litres)	Power Ratings hp at rpm: Take-off	Power Ratings hp at rpm: M.E.T.O.	Comp. Ratio	Dry Weight* lb (kg)	Dimensions: Length in (mm)	Dimensions: Width in (mm)	Dimensions: Height in (mm)	Octane Rating
C90-16F	4	$4\frac{1}{16} \times 3\frac{7}{8}$ (103·2 × 98·4)	201 (3·28)	95 at 2,625	90 at 2,475	7·0 : 1	186 (84·4)	31·25 (794)	31·5 (800)	24·2 (615)	80/87
O-200-A	4	$4\frac{1}{16} \times 3\frac{7}{8}$ (103·2 × 98·4)	201 (3·28)	100 at 2,750	100 at 2,750	7·0 : 1	220 (99·8)	28·53 (725)	31·56 (802)	23·18 (589)	80/87
IO-360-D	6	$4\frac{7}{16} \times 3\frac{7}{8}$ (112·5 × 98·4)	360 (5·9)	210 at 2,800	210 at 2,800	8·5 : 1	327 (148·3)	34·53 (877)	31·40 (798)	24·33 (618)	100/130
TSIO-360-C	6	$4\frac{7}{16} \times 3\frac{7}{8}$ (112·5 × 98·4)	360 (5·9)	225 at 2,800	225 at 2,800	7·5 : 1	300 (136)	35·84† (910)	33·03 (838)	23·75 (603)	100/130
IO-470-H	6	5 × 4 (127 × 101·6)	471 (7·7)	260 at 2,625	260 at 2,625	8·6 : 1	446·5 (202·5)	43·31 (1,100)	33·56 (852)	19·75 (502)	100/130
O-470-R	6	5 × 4 (127 × 101·6)	471 (7·7)	230 at 2,600	230 at 2,600	7·0 : 1	426 (193·2)	36·03 (915)	33·56 (852)	28·42 (723)	80/87
TSIO-470-D	6	5 × 4 (127 × 101·6)	471 (7·7)	260 at 2,600	260 at 2,600	7·5 : 1	511 (231·8)	58·07 (1,465)	33·56 (852)	20·25 (514)	100/130
IO-520-A	6	$5\frac{1}{4} \times 4$ (133 × 101·6)	520 (8·5)	285 at 2,700	285 at 2,700	8·5 : 1	476 (215·9)	41·41 (1,053)	33·56 (852)	19·75 (502)	100/130

REPRESENTATIVE TELEDYNE CONTINENTAL HORIZONTALLY-OPPOSED ENGINES—*continued*

Engine Model	No. of Cylinders	Bore and Stroke in (mm)	Capacity cu in (litres)	Power Ratings hp at rpm		Comp. Ratio	Dry Weight* lb (kg)	Dimensions			Octane Rating
				Take-off	M.E.T.O.			Length in (mm)	Width in (mm)	Height in (mm)	
IO-520-B	6	$5\frac{1}{4} \times 4$ (133 × 101·6)	520 (8·5)	285 at 2,700	285 at 2,700	8·5 : 1	457 (207·3)	39·71 (1,009)	33·58 (853)	26·71 (678)	100/130
IO-520-D	6	$5\frac{1}{4} \times 4$ (133 × 101·6)	520 (8·5)	300 at 2,850	285 at 2,700	8·5 : 1	459 (208·2)	37·36 (949)	35·46 (901)	23·79 (604)	100/130
TSIO-520-B	6	$5\frac{1}{4} \times 4$ (133 × 101·6)	520 (8·5)	285 at 2,700	285 at 2,700	8·5 : 1	483 (219)	58·67 (1,490)	33·56 (852)	20·32 (516)	100/130
TSIO-520-C	6	$5\frac{1}{4} \times 4$ (133 × 101·6)	520 (8·5)	285 at 2,700	285 at 2,700	7·5 : 1	458 (208)	40·91† (1,040)	33·56 (852)	20·04 (509)	100/130
TSIO-520-E	6	$5\frac{1}{4} \times 4$ (133 × 101·6)	520 (8·5)	300 at 2,700	300 at 2,700	7·5 : 1	483 (219)	39·75† (1,010)	33·56 (852)	20·74 (527)	100/130
TSIO-520-J	6	$5\frac{1}{4} \times 4$ (133 × 101·6)	520 (8·5)	310 at 2,700	310 at 2,700	7·5 : 1	487·8 (221·3)	39·25 (997)	33·56 (852)	20·32 (516)	100/130
GTSIO-520-C	6	$5\frac{1}{4} \times 4$ (133 × 101·6)	520 (8·5)	340 at 3,200	340 at 3,200	7·5 : 1	557 (252·7)	63·5 (1,612·9)	34·04 (880)	23·1 (587)	100/130
GTSIO-520-D	6	$5\frac{1}{4} \times 4$ (133 × 101·6)	520 (8·5)	375 at 3,400	375 at 3,400	7·5 : 1	580 (263)	64·25 (1,630)	34·04 (880)	26·78 (680)	100/130
GTSIO-520-F	6	$5\frac{1}{4} \times 4$ (133 × 101·6)	520 (8·5)	435 at 3,400	435 at 3,400	7·5 : 1	640 (290·3)	56·12 (1,426)	34·04 (880)	26·15 (664)	100/130
GTSIO-520-G	6	$5\frac{1}{4} \times 4$ (133 × 101·6)	520 (8·5)	375 at 3,400	375 at 3,400	7·5 : 1	575 (261)	42·71 (1,085)	34·04 (880)	25·4 (645)	100/130
GTSIO-520-H	6	$5\frac{1}{4} \times 4$ (133 × 101·6)	520 (8·5)	375 at 3,400	375 at 3,400	7·5 : 1	550·37 (250)	64·25 (1,630)	34·04 (880)	26·78 (680)	100/130
Tiara Series											
6-260	6	$4\frac{7}{8} \times 3\frac{5}{8}$ (123·8 × 92·08)	406 (6·65)	260 at 4,000	260 at 4,000	9·0 : 1	409 (185)	40·11 (1,019)	32·91 (836)	24·22 (615)	100/130
6-285-B	6	$4\frac{7}{8} \times 3\frac{5}{8}$ (123·8 × 92·08)	406 (6·65)	285 at 4,000	285 at 4,000	9·0 : 1	409 (185)	40·11 (1,019)	32·91 (836)	24·22 (615)	100/130
T6-320	6	$4\frac{7}{8} \times 3\frac{5}{8}$ (123·8 × 92·08)	406 (6·65)	320 at 4,400	320 at 4,400	9·6 : 1	409 (185)	40·11 (1,019)	32·91 (836)	24·22 (615)	100/130

* With accessories; † Not including turbocharger

THERMO-JET

THERMO-JET STANDARD INC

HEAD OFFICE:
PO Box 1528, Kerrville, Texas 78028
Telephone: (512) 367-2148

MANAGER:
John A. Melenric

This company specialises in the design and manufacture of valveless pulse-jet units for remotely piloted vehicles and the homebuilt aircraft markets. These engines are devoid of moving parts and are characterised by multiple reverse-flow air inlets to a combustion chamber in which is burned propane, butane or compressed natural gas, obviating the need for a fuel pump. Intermittent combustion and expulsion takes place at a cycle frequency determined by the chamber size and geometry and combustion pressure.

At present Thermo-Jet is offering four sizes of unit, described separately below. Each has a structure fabricated in Type 321 stainless steel, with Type 304 stainless fuel piping and 2024 T4 aluminium fuel nozzles. The throttle regulates fuel flow only. To start, ignition is provided by a hand-cranked magneto connected through a plug and socket to a Champion CJ-6 sparking plug. The throttle is then advanced to the vapour mode and the engine lights up. Once running, the throttle is switched to the liquid mode for normal operation. Combustion chamber mean temperature is 1,150°C in each unit.

All Thermo-Jet engines are now equipped with one annular reverse-flow vane mounted at the end of each air-inlet tube. The vane, in conjunction with the air-inlet bellmouth, forms an essentially constant-area duct, which recovers total pressure with minimum loss as the engine moves through the air at high velocity. Test-stand data indicate gross thrust increases of 100 per cent and specific fuel consumption decreases of 50 per cent can be had at a Mach number of 0·5 with the new vanes. An exhaust diffuser is available on special order which permits engine operation in the Mach 0·8 range. Each diffuser is designed for a specific Mach number.

THERMO-JET J7-300

Smallest of the company's units, this has three air inlets to a duct terminating in a straight-pipe exhaust tube.

DIMENSIONS:
- Diameter: 7 in (178 mm)
- Length: 49·0 in (1,245 mm)

WEIGHT, DRY: 8·0 lb (3·63 kg)

PERFORMANCE:
- (for max power):
  - Thrust at S/L: 21 lb (9·53 kg)
  - Specific impulse: 735 sec
  - Mean effective pressure: 3 lb/sq in (0·21 kg/cm²)
  - Cycle frequency: 119 cps
- (for max endurance):
  - Thrust at S/L: 7 lb (3·17 kg)
  - Specific impulse: 950 sec
  - Mean effective pressure: 1 lb/sq in (0·07 kg/cm²)
  - Cycle frequency: 119 cps

SPECIFIC FUEL CONSUMPTION:
- Max power: 4·9
- Max endurance: 3·8

THERMO-JET J8-200

This larger unit has two air intakes and an exhaust tube with flared end.

DIMENSIONS:
- Diameter: 8 in (203 mm)
- Length: 56 in (1,422 mm)

WEIGHT, DRY: 11·0 lb (4·99 kg)

PERFORMANCE:
- (for max power):
  - Thrust at S/L: 30 lb (13·5 kg)
  - Specific impulse: 720 sec
  - Mean effective pressure: 2·8 lb/sq in (0·197 kg/cm²)
  - Cycle frequency: 98 cps
- (for max endurance):
  - Thrust at S/L: 10 lb (4·5 kg)
  - Specific impulse: 1,000 sec
  - Mean effective pressure: 1 lb/sq in (0·07 kg/cm²)
  - Cycle frequency: 91 cps

SPECIFIC FUEL CONSUMPTION:
- Max power: 5·0
- Max endurance: 3·5

THERMO-JET J10-200

This further enlarged unit has two air inlets to a duct having a flared exhaust tube nozzle.

DIMENSIONS:
- Diameter: 10 in (254 mm)
- Length: 70 in (1,778 mm)

WEIGHT, DRY: 19·5 lb (8·8 kg)

PERFORMANCE:
- (for max power):
  - Thrust at S/L: 55 lb (25 kg)
  - Specific impulse: 692 sec
  - Mean effective pressure: 2·7 lb/sq in (0·19 kg/cm²)
  - Cycle frequency: 69 cps
- (for max endurance):
  - Thrust at S/L: 18 lb (8·16 kg)
  - Specific impulse: 945 sec

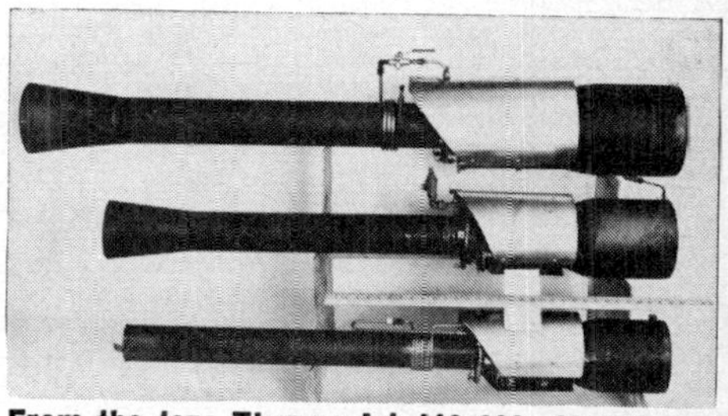

From the top: Thermo-Jet J10-300, J8-104 and J7-300

  - Mean effective pressure: 1 lb/sq in (0·07 kg/cm²)
  - Cycle frequency: 65 cps

SPECIFIC FUEL CONSUMPTION:
- Max power: 5·2
- Max endurance: 3·3

THERMO-JET J13-202

Largest and newest of the present range, this unit has two air inlets to a duct having a flared exhaust tube nozzle.

DIMENSIONS:
- Diameter: 13 in (330 mm)
- Length: 91 in (2,311 mm)

WEIGHT, DRY: 33 lb (15 kg)

PERFORMANCE:
- (for max power):
  - Thrust at S/L: 90 lb (40·8 kg)
  - Specific impulse: 655 sec
  - Mean effective pressure: 2·8 lb/sq in (0·2 kg/cm²)
  - Cycle frequency: 58 cps
- (for max endurance):
  - Thrust at S/L: 32 lb (14·5 kg)
  - Specific impulse: 900 sec
  - Mean effective pressure: 1 lb/sq in (0·07 kg/cm²)
  - Cycle frequency: 56 cps

SPECIFIC FUEL CONSUMPTION:
- Max power: 5·5
- Max endurance: 4·0

Thermo-Jet J13-202 valveless pulse-jet (90 lb; 40.8 kg st)

THIOKOL

THIOKOL CORPORATION

CORPORATE OFFICE:
Bristol, Pennsylvania 19007
Telephone: (215) 946-9150
Cable: Thiobrist

SOLID PROPELLANT ROCKET MOTOR PLANTS:
Elkton, Maryland
Huntsville, Alabama
Marshall, Texas
Brigham City, Utah

PYROTECHNIC AND ORDNANCE PLANTS:
Marshall, Texas
Woodbine, Georgia

CHAIRMAN OF THE BOARD:
Dr H. W. Ritchey

PRESIDENT AND CHIEF EXECUTIVE OFFICER:
R. E. Davis

VICE-PRESIDENT AND TREASURER:
A. P. Roeper

GROUP VICE-PRESIDENTS:
J. F. Anderson (Fibres)
J. S. Jorczak (Chemical)
R. L. Marquardt (Economic Development)
J. W. Wiggins (Aerospace)

Organised in 1929, Thiokol Chemical Corporation produced and marketed the first synthetic rubber manufactured in the United States. In 1943, the discovery by Thiokol of liquid polymer, a new type of synthetic rubber, paved the way for the practical development of the "case-bonded" principle of rocket power plant design. The company's polysulphide liquid polymer proved to be the catalyst for the first mass production of efficient solid-propellant rocket motors, as well as for the development of large solid-propellant motors. The firm's operations have now been organised into separate groups to serve widening areas of related products. Reflecting this diversity, the name has been changed to Thiokol Corporation.

The Thiokol Aerospace Group currently operates facilities located at Bristol, Pennsylvania; Elkton, Maryland; Brigham City and Ogden, Utah; Woodbine, Georgia; Huntsville, Alabama; and Marshall, Texas. The major products of these plants include pyrotechnic and ordnance devices, remote environmental sensing equipment, sounding rockets and rocket propulsion systems.

Details of some of the more important solid-propellant rocket motors used in missiles, sounding rockets, spacecraft and space launch vehicles are given below. Important current rocket motor activity of which details cannot be reported includes: production of third stage of Minuteman III; production of three stages for the Spartan missile; production of the first stage of the Poseidon missile in conjunction with Hercules Inc; production of gas generators for the Poseidon missile; production of the TX-481 Maverick motor; and advanced development of the TX-486 motor for the SAM-D air defence missile.

Thiokol TU-289 motor for the Genie air-to-air nuclear rocket, being prepared for static firing at the company's Wasatch Division at Brigham City

Thiokol TU-122, the stage-1 Minuteman motor, on an in-plant transporter at Brigham City

THIOKOL 156-INCH BOOSTER MOTORS (TU-412, 156-2C1, TU-393, TU-312, TU-562)

US military designations: 156-1, 156-2, 156-7, 156-8, and 156-9

These 156 in (3·96 m) diameter solid-propellant rocket motors were designed primarily to demonstrate feasibility of such very large motors and control systems for possible future missile and space launch applications. The test vehicles were made in both monolithic and segmented configurations, ranging in length from approximately 20 ft (6·1 m) to 100 ft (30·5 m). They produced thrust levels varying from approximately 388,000 lb (176,000 kg) over a 2 minute firing time to 3,250,000 lb (1,477,000 kg) over a 60 second firing time.

Motor cases were manufactured of 18 per cent nickel steel for the 156-1, 156-2 and 156-9 motors. The monolithic case for the 156-7 motor was of glassfibre-reinforced plastics, as was the segmented case for the 156-8 motor.

Propellants for all these motors used polybutadiene acrylonitrile terpolymer binder with ammonium perchlorate oxidiser and aluminium additives. Nozzles for thrust-vector control included external fixed, submerged fixed, external movable and submerged movable types. Hot-gas secondary injection and flexible-bearing thrust-vector control schemes were demonstrated. All necessary technologies for a development programme have been demonstrated, and no further feasibility demonstration effort is currently planned.

THIOKOL TRIDENT MOTORS

The three stages of propulsion for the Trident C-4 fleet ballistic missile are being developed jointly by Thiokol and Hercules, Inc. All three stages have advanced solid-propellant rocket motors, but details are classified.

THIOKOL POSEIDON FIRST-STAGE MOTOR

The motor for the first stage of the Poseidon C-3 fleet ballistic missile is manufactured jointly by Thiokol and Hercules Incorporated.

THIOKOL MINUTEMAN THIRD-STAGE MOTOR

US military designation: SR73-AJ-1

The SR73-AJ-1 is the third-stage rocket motor for the Minuteman III missile. It is 93 in (2·36 m) long, 52 in (1·32 m) in diameter, and weighs 8,046 lb (3,649 kg). The motor supplies 34,876 lb (15,820 kg) of thrust over a 59·6 second burn time.

The cylindrical case for the SR73-AJ-1 is prefabricated of glassfibre filaments, wound on a soluble mandrel and then cured. The solid-propellant fuel uses a polybutadiene acrylonitrile polymer binder with an ammonium perchlorate oxidiser and aluminium additive. The motor has a single nozzle and a liquid-injection thrust-vector control system.

THIOKOL TU-122

US military designation: M-55

The TU-122 is the first-stage rocket motor for the solid-propellant Minuteman ICBM. The motor is approximately 25 ft (7·62 m) in length, 5 ft 6 in (1·68 m) in diameter, and weighs about 50,000 lb (22,680 kg). It produces approximately 200,000 lb (90,700 kg) thrust during a 60 second firing time.

The motor case is manufactured from D6AC steel. The composite solid propellant employs a polybutadiene acrylic acid polymer binder with ammonium perchlorate oxidiser and aluminium powder additives. Thrust vector control is achieved through the use of four movable nozzles. Advanced versions continue in production for the LGM-30G; over 1,000 of earlier versions have been delivered.

THIOKOL TE-260G

The TE-260G rocket motor for the Subroc missile incorporates both directional control and thrust reversal. It consists of a cylindrical case containing the Thiokol propellant charge, a dual forward bulkhead design incorporating a thrust-reversal system, and an aft bulkhead containing four nozzles, each of which is equipped with a jetevator thrust vector control system. Six cable-carrying conduits run the full length of the case on the inside wall to allow guidance signals to be transmitted to the aft vector control system.

The TE-260G employs a composite solid propellant which is bonded to the case wall. Its principal constituents are polyurethane fuel binder and ammonium perchlorate oxidiser in a propellant system designed to provide a high specific impulse and a low burning rate. Thiokol developed the polyurethane system specifically to meet the Subroc requirements.

THIOKOL TU-289

US military designation: SR49-TC-1

The TU-289 solid-propellant rocket motor powers the AIR-2A Genie unguided air-to-air missile. It replaces an earlier motor, and has an improved propellant which increases the storage life and permits the missile to be deployed in a wide range of environmental temperatures. This motor remains in production.

THIOKOL TX-354 (CASTOR II)

TX-354 motors are used in a variety of applications such as first-stage boosters, second-stage sustainers and as strap-ons for launch vehicles. The TX-354-3 has a high-altitude nozzle and is used as the second stage of the Scout vehicle. TX-354-4 has a sea-level straight nozzle and is used as a booster for the Stripi vehicle with Recruit strap-on motors. TX-354-5 is the strap-on booster for the Delta vehicle. It has an 11° canted sea-level nozzle and is used in quantities of three, six or nine on each Delta vehicle. TX-354 weighs approximately 9,743 lb (4,410 kg). The case without nozzle is 202 in (5,130 mm) long and has a diameter of 31 in (787 mm).

THIOKOL TX-526 (CASTOR IV)

TX-526 motors are used in a variety of booster/strap-on applications. The TX-526-0 motor, combined with four Recruit strap-on motors, is the booster for the Athena H vehicle. The TX-526-1 with an 11° canted nozzle is qualified for strap-on booster applications. The TX-526-2 with 11° canted nozzle is designed as a strap-on booster for the Delta 3914 vehicle, with each vehicle having nine TX-526-2 motors. The 358 in (9,093 mm) long, 40 in (1,016 mm) diameter solid-propellant motor weighs 23,260 lb (10,550 kg). It provides an average thrust of 85,015 lb (38,561 kg), with a total burning time of approximately 57 sec for a total impulse of more than 4,760,900 lb-sec (2,159,544 kg-sec).

Three Thiokol Castor I and three Castor II strap-on booster rockets attached to Thrust-Augmented Thor launch vehicle

THIOKOL TE-M-416 TOMAHAWK

The Tomahawk is a high-performance motor designed specifically for use in sounding rocket systems. It is used in the Tomahawk vehicle as a single stage and in several other vehicles, such as Nike-Tomahawk and Terrier-Tomahawk, as the second stage. The motor is 142 in (3,607 mm) long and has a diameter of 9 in (229 mm). It weighs 486 lb (220 kg) and produces 11,000 lb (4,989 kg) thrust at sea level.

THIOKOL TE-M-29 (RECRUIT)

The Recruit was developed for the X-17 re-entry test vehicle. It is especially useful for sounding rockets, sleds and auxiliary boost applications because of its high overall performance. The TE-M-29-1 version was used in the X-17, Project Argus, Project Farside, Trailblazer and Stripi programmes. Its total loaded weight is 361·5 lb (164 kg); it is 105·28 in (2,674 mm) long and 9 in (229 mm) in diameter. Used with the TE-P-372 pyrogen or TE-I-436 pyrotechnic igniter, it is supplied with 6°, 6·5°, 9°, or 9·5° standard canted adaptors. The TE-M-29-2, used in the Project Farside, Little Joe I and II and Squirt programmes, uses a 4·26 : 1 expansion ratio nozzle. The TE-M-29-3 provides boost to the Athena first stage; it has a 5° 56′ canted adaptor. The TE-M-29-4 is the retro motor for the S-IVB stage of Saturn V, and the TE-M-29-5 is the retro motor for the S-IV stage of Saturn IB.

THIOKOL TE-M-424 (SATURN S-IC RETRO)

This motor was developed to serve as retrograde propulsion on the S-IC Saturn V first stage. Eight motors are employed for each launch. The TE-M-424 is man-rated because it was used in the Apollo programme. Motor length is 84·3 in (2,141 mm) and diameter is 15·2 in (386 mm). The motor produces 87,800 lb (39,825 kg) thrust for 0·633 seconds. Total motor weight is 504·5 lb (228·8 kg).

THIOKOL TE-M-307 (APACHE)

The TE-M-307-3 rocket motor was designed for second-stage applications, and therefore includes a 20 second delay igniter. It is 107·91 in (2,741 mm) long, 6·86 in (174·2 mm) in diameter and is used both as a sounding rocket and as a target missile. The TE-M-307-4 version was designed for single-stage applications. It uses the same loaded case and headcap assembly as the TE-M-307-3, with a 3·32 : 1 expansion ratio nozzle and an instantaneous TE-P-415 pyrogen. It is also used as a sounding rocket and as a target missile.

THIOKOL TE-M-364 (STAR-37)

The TE-M-364-2 (STAR-37B) is a 37 in (939·8 mm) diameter spherical main retro-rocket designed for the Surveyor and modified for use on the Burner II stage. Modifications consisted of increasing propellant loading to 1,440 lb (653 kg) and strengthening the attachment structure to accommodate higher inertial loads.

The TE-M-364-3 (STAR-37D) is a Surveyor main retro-rocket modified for use as third stage propulsion on the Improved Delta vehicle. Modifications consisted of again increasing propellant load, to 1,440 lb, re-designing the attachment structure to mate with the Delta launch vehicle and changing the diameter to 37·49 in (952·3 mm).

The TE-M-364-4 (STAR-37E) is an elongated version of the Delta motor, the AP/hydrocarbon/Al propellant grain being increased in mass from 1,440 lb (653 kg) to 2,290 lb (1,040 kg) by adding a 14 in (355 mm) cylinder to the case. Average thrust is 15,472 lb (7,018 kg) for a burn time of 41·96 sec. This motor provides third-stage propulsion on Improved Delta.

The TE-M-364-19 (STAR-37F) is a shorter version of the Delta motor, accommodating 1,836 lb (845 kg) of propellant. The body is of composite asbestos, glass and graphite phenolic structure and has a 7 in (178 mm) cylindrical section. Average thrust is 12,470 lb (5,656 kg) for a burn time of 42·55 sec. It provides the impulse to circularise the orbit of the FltSatCom satellite at the apogee of the launch orbit.

The TE-M-364-11 (STAR-37G) is a very similar extended Delta motor, likewise used for Improved Delta third-stage propulsion. Average thrust is 14,145 lb (6,416 kg) for a burn time of 45·48 sec.

THIOKOL TE-M-442-1 (STAR-26B)

This motor is spherical, 26·1 in (663 mm) in diameter and 33·05 in (839 mm) long; propellant weight is 525 lb (238 kg) and total motor weight is 576 lb (261 kg). The TE-M-442-1 was developed from the TE-M-442 of 1965 and features a case of titanium instead of steel. It flies as an additional stage to the standard Burner II launch vehicle, atop the TE-M-364-2 second stage.

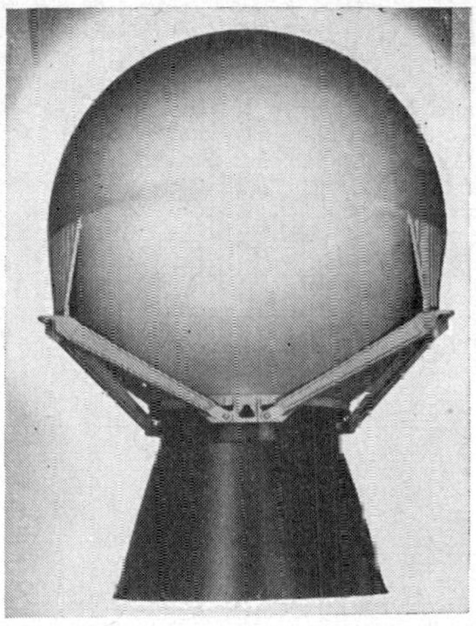

Thiokol TE-M-364-2 (STAR-37B) motor

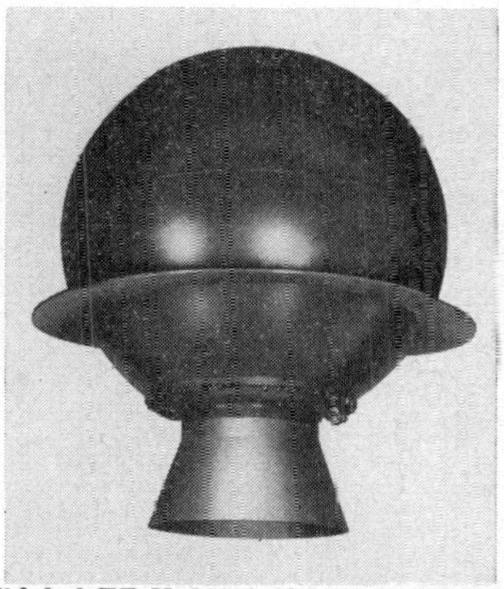

Thiokol TE-M-442-1 (STAR-26B) motor

THIOKOL TE-M-479 (STAR-17)

The TE-M-479 is a 17·4 in (442 mm) spherical rocket motor developed for NASA's Radio Astronomy Explorer satellite programme. The motor is 27·06 in (687 mm) long and serves as the apogee kick stage which makes the orbit of the spacecraft truly circular. Total motor weight is 173·8 lb (78·8 kg); propellant weight is 153 lb (69·4 kg). High mass-fraction and excellent performance reproducibility characterise this motor for space systems application. The TE-M-479 was first flown in July 1968.

THIOKOL TE-M-521 (STAR-17A)

This 17·5 in (444 mm) diameter and 38·6 in (980 mm) long motor was developed by adding a 6·9 in (175 mm) straight section to the spherical TE-M-479 (RAE) motor. The TE-M-521 has a propellant weight of 247 lb (112 kg) and a total weight of 273·2 lb (123·9 kg). It served to "circularise" the orbit of the Skynet satellite. The motor has a titanium case and flight-proven propellant.

THIOKOL TE-M-541/542 (STAR-6)

This small glassfibre motor measures 6·2 in (157 mm) in diameter and 14 in (356 mm) long and serves in a classified space application. Using the same hardware, with minor insulation changes, the motor is loaded to either of two configurations: 10·7 lb (4·85 kg), 3,075 lb-sec (1,395 kg-sec) total impulse, 13·2 lb (5·99 kg) total weight (TE-M-541); and 7·2 lb (3·27 kg), 2,050 lb-sec (930 kg-sec) total impulse, 10·6 lb (4·8 kg) total weight (TE-M-542). These motors have an extensive flight history.

THIOKOL TE-M-473 (SANDHAWK)

The Sandhawk TE-M-473 is a high-performance 13 in (330 mm) diameter, 201 in (5,105 mm) long rocket motor designed for sounding rocket use. It features a regressive thrust-time trace, which results in near-constant vehicle acceleration during its 15 second burn time and provides an extremely smooth flight environment. This motor is suited for use in single-stage, two-stage and three-stage vehicle configurations.

THIOKOL TE-M-236 (SARV RETRO)

This is a retrograde motor for an unmanned satellite. It uses an internal-burning case-bonded grain weighing 40·34 lb (18·3 kg) in a case of 4130 steel, with a re-entrant conical rear closure to keep overall length to only 12·76 in (324 mm).

Thiokol TE-M-521 (STAR-17A) motor

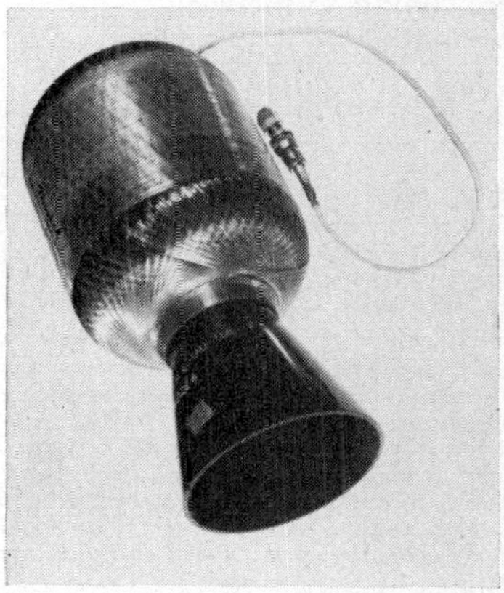

Thiokol TE-M-541 (STAR-6) motor

Burn-time (7·5 sec) average thrust is 1,250 lb (567 kg).

THIOKOL TE-M-640 ALTAIR III

This motor was developed as the fourth stage of the Scout launch vehicle. The 604·3 lb (274·1 kg) CTPB propellant grain is contained in a filament-wound glassfibre case. The lightweight external nozzle is a composite of graphite, plastics and steel. Total loaded weight, including consumable pyrogen igniter, is 664·5 lb (301·4 kg). Average thrust is 6,175 lb (2,800 kg) for a burn time of 27·4 sec.

THIOKOL TE-M-458 (STAR-13)

This is a deceleration motor used in the Anchored Interplanetary Monitoring Platform (AIMP) programme. The 68·3 lb (31 kg) charge of AP/Al/urethane is contained in a spherical case of 6Al-4V titanium, with graphite/vitreous silica phenolic nozzle. Loaded weight is 78·6 lb (35·65 kg) and average thrust 850 lb (385 kg) for a burn time of 21·8 sec.

THIOKOL TE-M-516 (STAR-13A)

This apogee-boost motor is made by mating the propellant and nozzle of the TE-M-444 with the case and igniter of the TE-M-458. Average thrust is 1,309 lb (594 kg) for a burn time of 15·3 sec. The motor is used as an injection stage of the Thor Burner II carrying two satellites: Secor and Aurora.

THIOKOL TE-M-604 (STAR-24)

This apogee-boost motor has a 439·8 lb (199·5 kg) charge of AP/hydrocarbon/Al propellant contained in a spherical case of 6Al-4V titanium with graphite/carbon phenolic nozzle. Average thrust is about 4,500 lb (2,040 kg) for a burn time of 30·21 sec. The motor is being qualified for Philco-Ford and the United Kingdom for the Skynet II satellite programme.

THIOKOL TE-M-616 (STAR-27)

This apogee-boost motor has a 733·9 lb (332·9 kg) charge of AP/hydrocarbon/Al propellant in a case (spherical with cylindrical centre portion) of 6Al-4V titanium with graphite/carbon phenolic nozzle. Average thrust is 5,996 lb (2,720 kg) for a burn time of 34·84 sec. The customer is the Canadian Communications Research Centre, for the Communications Technology Satellite.

TRW

TRW SYSTEMS

HEAD OFFICE:
One Space Park, Redondo Beach, California 90278
Telephone: (213) 535-4321

TRW developed, built and launched the first monopropellant hydrazine propulsion system to enter and be started in space.

TRW is testing a wide variety of chemical propulsion engines. One of these, the man-rated Lunar Module Descent Engine, has landed astronauts on the Moon. Another engine was built to provide midcourse trajectory corrections for the Mariner '69 missions to Mars and the Mariner 10 (Venus-Mercury) missions.

TRW's propulsion research programmes include low-thrust monopropellant, bipropellant, colloid, ion, radio-isotope and electro-thermal engines. In addition, an active research programme in low-cost propulsion technology is being continued. As part of a US Air Force programme to develop cheaper launch vehicles TRW commissioned a piping manufacturer to build to its design a prototype liquid rocket engine having a sea level thrust of 250,000 lb (113,400 kg). This engine has a single fixed chamber and is constructed of ordinary commercial materials. The first was static-fired during 1969. Tests of TRW rocket engines are conducted at the company's test site at San Juan Capistrano, California.

Early in 1972 TRW was selected to provide the monopropellant hydrazine orbit-adjust propulsion system for three NASA Atmospheric Explorer Satellites for launch in 1973, 1974 and 1975.

TRW DELTA ENGINE

This TRW bipropellant motor is used in vacuum conditions. The nitrogen tetroxide and Aerozine 50 (50-50 mixture of UDMH and hydrazine) are fed by gas pressure at 225 lb/sq in (15·8 kg/cm²) to a co-axial injector where the propellants ignite hypergolically. The titanium chamber and columbium nozzle are cooled by ablation and radiation, and the assembly is gimballed at the injector end.

Starting is by a 28V DC signal to the engine valves, and after fixed-thrust operation the engine is stopped upon command or by propellant depletion. Mixture ratio is about 1·6 : 1, chamber pressure 102 lb/sq in (7·2 kg/cm²) and combustion temperature about 2,700°C (5,500°R is quoted). Engine dry weight is 250 lb (113 kg), length 85 in (2,160 mm) and exit diameter 56·3 in (1,430 mm). Vacuum thrust is 9,780 lb (4,435 kg) and vacuum specific impulse 302 sec.

This engine is to be used as a second stage on NASA/McDonnell Douglas Delta launch vehicles. First launch was scheduled for March or April 1974 on Delta No 101.

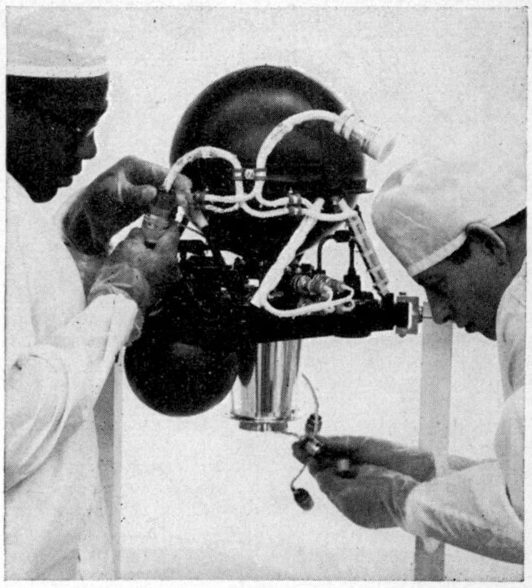

TRW Mariner '69 midcourse engine

UTC

UNITED TECHNOLOGY CENTER (A division of United Aircraft Corporation)

HEADQUARTERS:
Sunnyvale, California 94088
Telephone: (408) 739-4880

CHAIRMAN AND PRESIDENT OF UNITED AIRCRAFT CORPORATION:
Harry J. Gray

DIVISION PRESIDENT:
Barnet R. Adelman

DIVISION VICE-PRESIDENTS:
Dr David Altman
Eugene Roberts

United Technology Center, a division of United Aircraft Corporation, is engaged in research, development and production of rockets, rocket propellants and advanced propulsion systems, as well as a range of "spin-off" by-products. Since its founding in the late 1950s UTC has conducted a continuous programme of rocket technology and is now producing a variety of advanced space propulsion systems for both the Department of Defense and the National Aeronautics and Space Administration.

UTC's largest programme is the production of 120 in (3,048 mm) diameter, segmented solid-propellant booster rockets. Other programmes described hereunder include the Algol III, FW-4 and FW-5 rocket motors, all of which are fully operational.

Testing of UTC's patented Techroll fluid bearing continues. This bearing, considered to be the first major improvement in rocket steering methods in almost a decade, is being applied primarily to rocket motor technology. However, it offers a number of potential uses in other areas such as aircraft, road vehicles and high-pressure fluid-transmission lines.

UTC 120 in (3,048 mm) SEGMENTED MOTOR

Mass-produced at UTC's Coyote, California, rocket production facility, this 120 in (3,048 mm) diameter solid-propellant rocket motor centre segment is interchangeable with any other centre segment. Its cylindrical metal case is manufactured from high-strength steel (D6AC) and heat treated to an ultimate strength of 195,000 lb/sq in (13,710 kg/cm²). Less than 0·5 in (12·7 mm) thick, each case is equipped with clevis-type end joints with holes for cylindrical fastening pins. Loaded with propellant, a synthetic rubber (polybutadiene acrylonitrile) with aluminium additives as fuel and ammonium perchlorate as oxidiser, a segment has an overall length of 10 ft 6 in (3,200 mm) and weighs 79,000 lb (35,830 kg). Designed as the basic building block for large solid-propellant booster rockets, the segmented motor can be assembled in from one- to eight-segment configurations with thrusts ranging from 250,000 to 1·5 million pounds (113,400-680,400 kg). A fully configured motor contains a destruct system, a forward-end ignition system, a liquid-injection thrust-vector control system for steering and has its own staging sequence capability.

UTC has made progress in the development of more efficient and economical means of fabricating the steel motor cases used in the 120 in programme, through production processes known as internal roll extrusion and shear forming. Both techniques reduce production time and result in a more reliable and economical product.

A five-segment configuration of this motor is used in pairs as the zero (launch) stage of the US Air Force Titan IIIC and D space launch vehicles and the new Titan IIIE of NASA, first flown on 11 February 1974. Operating together, the 86 ft (26·12 m) tall motors produce a thrust of 2,400,000 lb (1,088,620 kg). Launched for the first time on 18 June 1965, the boosters have flown 28 successful missions in as many launches, using 56 motors.

Essentially a lengthened version of the five-segment motor, a seven-segment motor has been statically test-fired four times. Producing a record 1·4 million pounds (635,000 kg) of thrust, the motors operated perfectly while testing an advanced steering system, called an ullage blow-down, which is now used on all flights of Titan IIIC and Titan IIID vehicles.

Static test of UTC's 1,400,000 lb (635,000 kg) thrust seven-segment 120 in (3,048 mm) solid-propellant motor

UTC ALGOL III

UTC is in full production of Algol III, a more powerful solid-propellant first stage for NASA's Scout space launch vehicle. Thirty feet (9·14 m) tall and 45 in (1·14 m) in diameter, the new UTC solid booster permits an increase of 40-54 per cent in the Scout's payload/weight capability. When loaded with its propellant (PBAN with aluminium additives and ammonium perchlorate oxidiser) Algol III weighs 30,000 lb (13,605 kg). Its nozzle is fabricated from steel with a graphite cloth-phenolic and silica cloth-phenolic cone liner. Ignition is by a small nose-mounted solid rocket. Producing 140,000 lb (63,500 kg) of lift-off thrust, Algol III burns for 75 seconds to boost the Scout to an altitude of 26 nm (30 miles; 48 km) before burnout. The motor flew for the first time in August 1972 and early in 1973 had completed four missions.

Static test of the UTC Algol III solid-propellant motor, first stage of Scout launch vehicles

UTC FW-4

The FW-4 solid motor was designed to be interchangeable with existing upper-stage motors on launch vehicles with orbital, probe or re-entry missions, as well as for retro-rocket propulsion in space vehicles. It is used in both NASA and military programmes, flying as the top stage on Air Force Atlas and Thor boosters and NASA Scout and TAD vehicles. By the end of 1973 FW-4 motors had placed 62 satellites in precise orbit. UTC has received a contract for four FW-4s for NASA for use before 1976.

The FW-4 is 19·6 in (498 mm) in diameter and has an overall length of 58·43 in (1,484 mm). Its case is fabricated from glassfibre and epoxy resin, with a cylindrical wall thickness of 0·08 in (2·03 mm) and domes with geodesic contours with a nominal wall thickness of 0·03 in (0·76 mm). The igniter and nozzle attachment fittings are fabricated from aluminium, and the aluminium interstage flanges are bonded and riveted to the integrally-wound glassfibre skirt of the motor case. The standard FW-4 rocket motor has an inert weight of 55·5 lb (25·2 kg) and a propellant weight of 605 lb (274 kg), resulting in a motor mass fraction of 0·92. The average motor thrust is 5,620 lb (2,549 kg), with a burn time of 30·5 seconds.

UTC FW-5 SOLID ROCKET MOTOR

Similar to the company's FW-4 motor, the new FW-5 is likewise designed to be interchangeable with existing upper-stage motors. While its primary application is that of an apogee motor, it can be used for orbital, probe or re-entry missions, as well as retro-rocket propulsion for space vehicles.

The FW-5 is 27·2 in (691 mm) in diameter and has an overall length of 44·2 in (1,123 mm). Its case is fabricated from glassfibre and epoxy resin, with a cylindrical wall thickness of 0·13 in (3·3 mm) and end domes with solar isotensoid contours with a nominal wall thickness of 0·60 in (15·2 mm). The igniter and nozzle attachment fittings are fabricated from aluminium, and the aluminium interstage flange is bonded and riveted to the integrally-wound glassfibre skirt of the motor case.

The standard FW-5 has an inert weight of 65·6 lb (29·7 kg) and a propellant weight of 575 lb (260 kg), resulting in a motor mass fraction of 0·89. The average motor thrust is 5,630 lb (2,553 kg) with a burn time of 42·1 seconds.

FW-5 operated perfectly on its first mission in November 1972 when it placed Telesat Canada's Anik communications satellite into final orbit. The second Anik was launched by NASA in April 1973. In addition, UTC has contracted to supply six FW-5 motors to Hughes Aircraft to orbit the first US domestic communications satellite system.

UTC HYBRID UPPER-STAGE ENGINE

UTC's new high-performance hybrid upper-stage engine is being developed specifically for NASA deep-space launch missions. It is 147 in (3,734 mm) in length, has a diameter of 47 in (1,194 mm), and weighs 4,000 lb (1,814 kg). The engine utilises a lithium/lithium hydride/polybutadiene fuel grain and a liquid fluorine/liquid oxygen oxidiser contained in a spherical tank and fed down through the solid fuel grain. Ablative-cooled, the engine has a thrust of 12,000 lb (5,443 kg). Possible uses include uprating of the Delta, Atlas-Centaur and Titan-Centaur.

UTC HYBRID TARGET MISSILE ENGINE

UTC's hybrid rocket engine for the Department of Defense High Altitude Supersonic Target (HAST) missile (see under Beech heading in the "RPVs" section) will be 13 in (330 mm) in diameter, have an overall length of 140 in (3,556 mm), and weigh 860 lb (390 kg). It uses a polybutadiene and methyl methacrylate fuel grain, and nitric acid as its liquid oxidiser. Ablative-cooled, its thrust ranges from 200 to 1,200 lb (90-544 kg) at altitudes between 35,000 and 100,000 ft (10,670 and 30,480 m). The HAST successfully completed all its initial flight-readiness test-firings in 1973 and was scheduled to fly in Autumn 1974.

Static firing of UTC FW-5 upper-stage motor

UTC LIQUID ROCKET ENGINES

The company's liquid rockets range in size from 52 in (1,321 mm) long and 26 in (660 mm) in diameter and weighing 72 lb (32·6 kg) to 75·5 in (1,918 mm) long, 48 in (1,219 mm) in diameter and weighing 185 lb (83·9 kg). Their propellant is 50/50 hydrazine and unsymmetrical dimethyl hydrogen and nitrogen tetroxide. The engine nozzles are a composite structure with a glassfibre shell and silica-phenolic liner. Ignition is hypergolic.

UTC FW-4 solid-propellant upper-stage motor

WILLIAMS

WILLIAMS RESEARCH CORPORATION

ADDRESS:

2280 W Maple Road, Walled Lake, Michigan 48088

Telephone: (313) 624-5200

Sam Williams believed in 1956 that gas-turbine technology could be extended down to very small sizes, and that if a small turbojet were made available it would find a market. Accordingly this company began a development programme on the WR2, described below, on a scale of effort and funding reflecting its very limited resources.

The WR2 first ran at a design thrust of 70 lb (31·8 kg) in 1962 and has since been developed into the WR2-6 and WR24-6. The more advanced WR19 uses an aerodynamically similar core and Williams Research is also building a range of shaft-drive engines, all characterised by their very simple design and aerodynamic similarity of their centrifugal compressors, axial compressor and power turbines.

Industrial and automotive engines of 75, 150 and 500 shp have been produced and the first of these, based on the WR2, was also developed for one-man helicopters. Williams Research is now developing, under contract from a private company, an automotive engine with regenerator and, for another company, a shaft-drive engine rated at significantly above 500 shp.

The company is now strong and experienced enough to mount a planned attack on the manned-aircraft market and believes that, as has happened with drone engines, aircraft markets will appear when reliable turbojet and turbofan engines sized between the 430 lb (195 kg) thrust of the WR19 and an upper limit of 2,000 lb (907 kg) st become available.

WILLIAMS WR2 and WR24

US military designation (WR24): J400

Although simple in design, almost to the point of appearing crude, this single-shaft turbojet has shown itself to be an effective power plant for high-subsonic drone aircraft and a suitable base for development of more advanced engines.

Air enters at the eye of a single-sided light alloy centrifugal compressor which handles an air mass flow of 2·2 lb (1 kg)/sec at a pressure ratio of 4·1 : 1. After passing through the diffuser which provides the structural basis for the engine the air divides, part of it flowing radially inwards as primary combustion airflow and the main bulk entering the short outward-radial annular combustor, through dilution apertures around the outer and rear face of the flame tube.

Fuel is sprayed centrifugally through a group of fine holes in the main compressor drive shaft. Surrounding the fuel pipe along the centreline of the main drive shaft is a cool airflow bled from the diffuser, which escapes through holes in the drive shaft to cool the combustion flame and reduce metal shaft and bearing temperatures, the main bearing being behind the compressor. A single igniter is mounted in the chamber at 12 o'clock. The hot gas, at about 955°C, then turns inwards and exits rearwards through the single-stage axial turbine and simple jet pipe.

The first production versions of the WR2 are the WR2-6, fitted to the Canadair AN/USD-501 high-performance battlefield reconnaissance vehicle; and the WR24-6 and -7 (YJ400-WR-400 and J400-WR-401) which power, respectively, the Northrop Chukar I and II target drones. The WR2-6 has a variable-area exhaust nozzle with translating central bullet, and drives a DC generator. The WR24 family have a minimal fixed-area jet pipe and drive a 4,000Hz alternator. The WR24-7 runs at higher temperature than the WR24-6 and incorporates detail modifications. The WR24-17, not yet in production but used in the Northrop variable-speed training target (VSTT), is further uprated though similar externally.

DIMENSIONS:

Overall length:	
WR2-6	22·3 in (566 mm)
WR24-6	19·3 in (490 mm)
WR24-7, WR24-17	about 25 in (635 mm)
Maximum diameter:	
WR2-6, WR24-6	10·8 in (274 mm)
WR24-7, WR24-17	about 12 in (305 mm)

WEIGHT, DRY:

WR2-6, WR24-6	about 30 lb (13·6 kg)

MAXIMUM RATING (S/L, static):

WR2-6	125 lb (56·5 kg) at 60,000 rpm
WR24-6	121 lb (55 kg) at 60,000 rpm
WR24-7	170 lb (77 kg)
WR24-17	200 lb (90·5 kg)

SPECIFIC FUEL CONSUMPTION:

WR2-6, WR24-6	1·25

WILLIAMS WR19

To produce this two-shaft turbofan Williams Research used the WR2 as core and added an additional fan, axial compressor and drive turbine on a separate shaft, together with a by-pass duct. The LP turbine is related to those developed for the company's shaft-drive engines.

The WR19 is the power plant used in the Bell Aerosystems Flying Belt. It has also been used in the Williams Aerial Systems Platform (WASP) and Kaman Stowable Aircrew VEhicle Rotoseat (SAVER). From it has been derived the US Air Force/Navy F107, described separately.

In early 1970 the company received a $1,400,000 contract from the USAF for further development of a turbofan for future decoys. The company is making great efforts to increase the maximum gas temperature, particularly in the WR19 and derived engines. At present the temperature actually used is about 955°C, with potential of the present materials (Haynes 31 cobalt-base alloy for inlet guide vanes, Inco 100 for first-stage turbine blades and Inco 713 for other hot parts) limited to about 1,010°C.

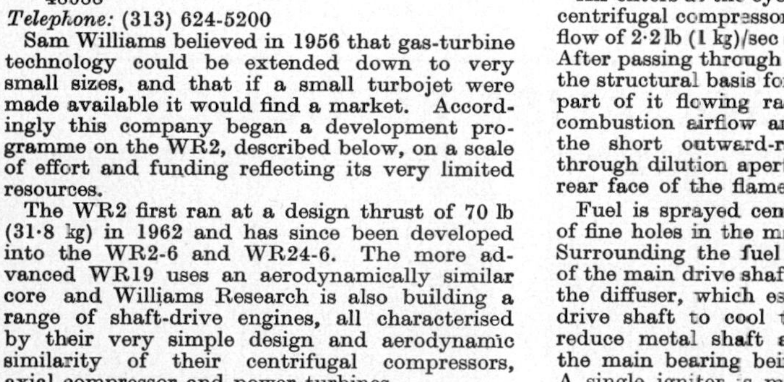

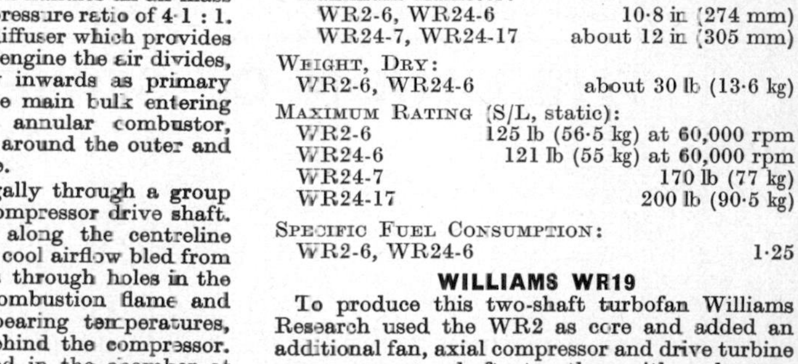

Left: **Williams Research WR2-6 turbojet, for the Canadair CL-89 (AN/USD-501) reconnaissance drone (125 lb; 56·5 kg st).** *Right:* **Williams Research WR24-7 turbojet (170 lb; 77 kg st); the 200 lb (90·5 kg) st WR24-17 is visually identical**

Despite the mechanical difficulty of working on such very small components, with turbine rotor disc and blades cast as single units, Williams is experimenting with aircooled turbine rotor blades and expects soon to be able to operate at gas temperatures higher than 1,100°C. The WR19 would be the first engine offered with cooled blades, and it also continues the company philosophy of using specially developed alternators, governors and other accessories capable of running at the full 60,000 rpm of the main shaft.

AIR INTAKE: Direct pitot type with four struts but no fixed inlet guide vanes. Unlike most WR2 engines the WR19 has a plain annular entry instead of a side intake downstream of an alternator or generator on the nose of the main shaft.

COMPRESSOR: Two-stage metal fan and two-stage axial IP compressor on common shaft leading to HP centrifugal compressor, handed to rotate in opposite direction to minimise gyroscopic couple. Total air mass flow, about 4·4 lb (2 kg)/sec; overall pressure ratio, 8 : 1; by-pass ratio, approximately 1 : 1.

COMBUSTION CHAMBER: Folded annular type, with fuel sprayed from revolving slinger on HP shaft. Dilution airflow admitted through perforated liner; cooling air injected through two sets of holes in HP shaft. Single igniter mounted diagonally on engine upper centreline.

FUEL SYSTEM: Fuel fed at low pressure through transfer seal into pipe in HP shaft and ejected at high centrifugally-induced pressure, through calibrated fine orifices drilled radially through HP shaft in line with combustion chamber.

TURBINE: Single-stage axial-flow HP turbine, with Haynes 31 nozzle guide vanes and rotor wheel cast as single unit in Inco IN 100. Two-stage LP turbine, again with both wheels cast as single units, in Inco 713. Provision to be made for aircooling to raise entry gas temperature from 955°C to above 1,100°C.

JET PIPE: Mixer unit immediately downstream of LP turbine allows by-pass flow to merge with core gas flow to pass through plain propelling nozzle.

ACCESSORIES: Fuel and control system, filters, oil pump, tacho-generator and optional other accessories grouped into flat packages around upper part of fan/IP compressor casing. Starting system, depending on application, drives HP spool.

Williams Research Corporation WR19 two-shaft turbofan engine (430 lb; 195 kg st). Believed to be the smallest turbofan in the world, the WR19 weighs 67 lb (30·4 kg) as shown

MOUNTING: Depending on application, main mounting above centrifugal diffuser casing with two double-lug pickups on horizontal centreline at LP turbine casing.

DIMENSIONS:

Length overall	24 in (610 mm)
Envelope diameter	12 in (305 mm)

WEIGHT:

Dry, depending on equipment 61-68 lb (27·6-30·8 kg)

PERFORMANCE RATING:

Max thrust, S/L static 430 lb (195 kg)

SPECIFIC FUEL CONSUMPTION:

Max thrust, S/L static 0·7

WILLIAMS WR79

US military designation: F107

Though nothing on this engine has been publicly disclosed by Williams, frequent reports have named the F107-WR-100 as one of the two candidate engines for the AGM-86A subsonic cruise armed decoy (SCAD). Probably developed from the WR19, the F107 is said to be a turbofan in the 600 lb (272 kg) st class. It is described as suitable for a number of existing or projected RPVs. It is probably the engine funded by the US Air Force mentioned in the WR19 description.

THE UNION OF SOVIET SOCIALIST REPUBLICS

GDL

ADDRESS: Leningrad

The name of the centre responsible for design of the first-stage engine of the Vostok space launch vehicle, and other rocket engines, was given, in French, at the 1967 Paris Air Show, as the Laboratoire de la Dynamique des Gaz of Leningrad. It was said to have been founded in 1929.

Details of three current major types of engine follow:

GDL RD-107

This four-chamber liquid-propellant rocket engine was developed during 1954 to 1957. The RD-107 and its derivatives have been in use for many years as launch vehicle first-stage engines for Soviet satellites to the Sun and Moon, and automatic stations launched to the Moon, Venus and Mars. They also powered the Vostok and Voskhod manned spaceship launch vehicles. Their specific impulse and operational reliability are described as being exceptionally high.

TYPE: Four-chamber liquid-propellant rocket engine.

PROPELLANTS: Liquid oxygen and kerosene.

THRUST CHAMBERS: Four primary thrust chambers of double-wall construction, with fabricated corrugations between walls and inner walls of copper or copper-rich alloy. Conical nozzles. All-welded heads. Flat-plate injectors, with concentric rings of tubes in which propellants are pre-mixed before injection. Estimated diameters: throat 6-6·5 in (150-165 mm), nozzle 27 in (685 mm). Combustion pressure 882 lb/sq in (62 kg/cm²).

VERNIER CHAMBERS: Two chambers of double-wall construction, with finning between walls. Estimated diameters: throat 3 in (75 mm), nozzle 12 in (305 mm).

TURBOPUMP: One single-shaft turbopump feeding all chambers. Mounted above chambers in tubular frame. Assembly comprises turbine exhaust hood containing coiled heat exchanger, single-sided shrouded centrifugal kerosene pump, double-sided shrouded centrifugal liquid oxygen pump, gearbox, and two auxiliary centrifugal pumps, one of which supplies the monopropellant gas generator. Fuel lines to main chambers pass through common valve.

PERFORMANCE (in vacuum):

Rated thrust	224,870 lb (102,000 kg)
Specific impulse	314 sec

GDL RD-119

This more modern single-chamber liquid-propellant engine, which has been in use since 1962, forms the second-stage engine of a launch vehicle for Cosmos research satellites. Many hundreds of these satellites have been launched, using two-, three- and four-stage launch vehicles of various types and having lifting capacities ranging from hundreds of pounds to 7·5 tons (7·6 tonnes).

Exhibition model of the four-chamber RD-107 first-stage rocket engine of the Vostok space launch vehicle (*TAM Air et Cosmos*)

TYPE: Single-chamber liquid-propellant rocket engine.

PROPELLANTS: Liquid oxygen and dimethyl-hydrazine.

THRUST CHAMBER: Single fixed chamber, possibly of tubular-wall construction, with fuel entry above base of nozzle. Estimated diameters: throat 4 in (100 mm), nozzle 37 in (940 mm). Combustion pressure 1,176 lb/sq in (83 kg/cm²).

TURBOPUMP: One single-shaft turbopump, driven by monopropellant (hydrazine) gas generator. Exhaust from gas generator taken to multiple auxiliary nozzles for control in roll, pitch and yaw.

The 158,800 lb (72,000 kg) thrust GDL RD-214 rocket engine used to power the first stage of the Cosmos launcher

PERFORMANCE (in vacuum):

Rated thrust	24,250 lb (11,000 kg)
Specific impulse	352 sec

GDL RD-214

This neat liquid-propellant rocket engine, developed at GDL in 1952-57, has been adopted as the standard first-stage propulsion for launching the Cosmos series of research satellites. It has four thrust chambers, burning nitric acid and kerosene, each chamber being rated at 39,700 lb (18,000 kg) thrust at sea level. Vacuum rating of the engine is 74 tonnes (163,142 lb). The propellants are fed by a single large turbopump group mounted above the chamber group, the fuel being supplied straight to a bolted connection on the welded chamber heads and the nitric acid passing through part-flexible pipes to regeneratively cool the bellmouth chamber nozzle and throat. Chamber pressure is given by GDL as 45 kg/cm² (640 lb/sq in) and specific impulse as 246. The four chambers are rigidly fixed to the Cosmos launcher first stage, vehicle control being accomplished by four refractory deflector vanes, one per chamber, mounted on the vehicle skirt control packages and projecting into the rocket exhaust. Several hundred RD-214 engines have been made and flown from Kapustin Yar on non-recoverable Cosmos missions.

GLUSHENKOV

This design bureau had not been named publicly until 1969 when it was revealed as that responsible for the TVD-10 engines fitted in the Beriev Be-30 STOL transport. The TVD-10 is a modern small turboprop in the 950 shp class, supplied to Beriev as a complete neatly-cowled unit with a modern reversing propeller produced specially for this application. The engine air intake is positioned below and behind the spinner, but no details of the TVD-10 have yet been made available. It has been reported that it was mainly due to difficulties with the TVD-10 that the Be-30 programme was terminated in 1973.

Glushenkov is also responsible for the 900 shp GTD-3 turboshaft engine, two of which power the Kamov Ka-25 helicopter. This engine and the TVD-10 appear to have a generally similar layout, with a free power turbine, and it is possible that they use a common gas-generator.

ISOTOV

General Designer in Charge of Bureau:
Sergei Pietrovich Isotov

This bureau was responsible for the GTD-350 and TV2-117A turboshaft engines which power the Mil Mi-2 and Mi-8 helicopters respectively. The former is in production in Poland, where also an indigenous design has been planned around a single GTD-350 turboshaft engine (see "Aircraft" section). The GTD-350 is described below, but production is now centred in Poland. Isotov is also responsible for the TVD-850 turboprop engines which power the Antonov An-28 transport aircraft (see "Aircraft" section).

GTD-350

The GTD-350 is a free-turbine helicopter power plant. In the version used in the twin-engined Mi-2, the drive is taken from the rear, with the twin jet pipes of each engine exhausting to port (port engine) and starboard (starboard engine). The GTD-350 can be supplied with downward-facing jet pipe and with drive from the front, if required. Though developed and initially produced by the Isotov bureau in the Soviet Union, it is now in production only in Poland. WSK-Rzeszów is developing a version rated at 500-700 shp to be used in a proposed single-engined WSK helicopter. In 1970, time between overhauls for the original version was 500 hours.

Type: Axial/centrifugal-flow free-turbine turboshaft engine.

Air Intake: Annular intake casing and inlet guide vanes of stainless steel. Automatic de-icing of inlet guide vanes and central bullet by air bleed from compressor.

Compressor: Seven axial stages and one centrifugal stage, all of steel, connected together with a tie-bolt. Discs shrunk-fitted to shaft. Blades of axial stages have dovetail roots. Shaft carried in front roller bearing and rear ball bearing. Pressure ratio 5·9 : 1. Air mass flow 4·83 lb (2·19 kg)/sec at 45,000 rpm.

Compressor Casing: Horizontally-split aluminium alloy casing, with stator blades brazed to semi-rings. No diffuser blades.

Combustion Chamber: Reverse-flow type with air supply through two tubes. Centrifugal duplex single-nozzle burner. Ignition system comprises burner and semi-conductor spark-plug. Eight thermocouples at gas outlet.

Fuel System: Includes NR-40T pump governor with shut-off cock, which feeds fuel to burner, controls gas-generator rpm and limits max output; RO-40T power turbine rpm governor, DS-40 signal transmitter controlling bleed valves; and electromagnetic valve to provide fuel for starting.

Fuel Grade: TS-1 or TS-2.

Compressor Turbine: Single-stage turbine with aircooled disc. Shrouded blades with fir-tree roots. Precision-cast fixed guide vanes. Turbine casing has metal-graphite insert in plane of blades. Shaft supported in ball bearing at rear. Temperature before turbine 970°C.

Power Turbine: Two-stage constant-speed type (24,000 rpm). Shrouded blades with fir-tree roots. Discs bolted together. Stator blades welded to rings. Airflow is again reversed aft of power turbine.

Jet Pipes: Two fixed-area jet pipes.

Reduction Gearing: Two sets of gears, with ratio of 0·246 : 1, in cast magnesium alloy casing.

Lubrication System: Closed type. Gear-type pump with one pressure and four scavenge units. Nominal oil pressure 43 lb/sq in (3±0·5 kg/cm²). Oil cooler and oil tank, capacity 2·75 Imp gallons (12·5 litres), fitted to airframe.

Oil Grade: B3-W (synthetic).

Accessories: STG3 3kW starter/generator, NR-40T governor pump, D1 tachometer generator and oil pumps mounted on reduction gear casing and driven by gas-generator. RO-40T rotating speed governor, D1 tachometer generator and centrifugal breather, also mounted on reduction gear casing, driven by power turbine.

Starting: STG3 starter/generator suitable for operation at up to 13,125 ft (4,000 m) altitude.

Isotov GTD-350 turboshaft engine (395 shp; 400 cv)

Dimensions:
- Length overall: 53·15 in (1,350 mm)
- Max width: 20·47 in (520 mm)
- Max height: 24·80 in (630 mm)

Weight, Dry:
- Less jet pipes and accessories: 298 lb (135 kg)

Performance Ratings:
- T-O rating (6 min)
- 395 shp (400 cv) at 94% max gas-generator rpm
- Nominal rating (1 hr)
- 315 shp (320 cv) at 89% gas-generator rpm
- Cruising rating (II)
- 281 shp (285 cv) at 86·5% gas-generator rpm
- Cruising rating (I)
- 232 shp (235 cv) at 83·5% gas-generator rpm

Specific Fuel Consumption:
- At T-O rating: 0·805 lb/shp/hr (0·370 kg/cv/hr)
- At nominal rating: 0·861 lb/shp/hr (0·396 kg/cv/hr)
- At cruising rating (II): 0·913 lb/shp/hr (0·420 kg/cv/hr)
- At cruising rating (I): 0·978 lb/shp/hr (0·450 kg/cv/hr)

Oil Consumption:
- Max: 0·53 Imp pt (0·3 litre)/hr

TV2-117A

The power plant of the Mi-8 comprises two TV2-117A engines coupled through a VR-8A gearbox. As is common with modern Soviet helicopters, the engines and gearbox are delivered and thereafter treated as a single unit. The complete package incorporates a control system (separate from the control system of each gas generator) which maintains desired rotor speed, synchronises the power of both engines, and increases the power of the remaining engine if the other should fail.

The TV2 engine is of conservative design, being biased in favour of long and trouble-free life rather than attempting to rival the small size and weight of some Western engines in the same power class.

Type: Free-turbine helicopter turboshaft engine.

Air Intake: Direct pitot, with main front casing providing vertical upper and lower drive-shafts to accessory packages. Main accessory group above the engine projects well ahead of intake face. Casing incorporates variable-incidence inlet guide vanes.

Compressor: Ten-stage axial type. Construction principally in titanium to reduce weight in comparison with the steel that would otherwise be used. Inlet guide vanes and stators of stages 1, 2, and 3 are of variable incidence to facilitate starting and increase compressor efficiency over a wide speed range; for the same reasons the casing incorporates automatic blow-off valves. Pressure ratio 6·6 : 1 at 21,200 rpm.

Combustion Chamber: Annular, with eight burner cones. Fabricated from inner and outer diffuser casings, flame tube, casing, burners, and anti-icing bleed air pipe.

Fuel Grade: T-1 or TS-1 to GOST 10227-62 specification (Western equivalents, DERD.2494, MIL-F-5616).

Turbine: Two-stage axial compressor turbine bolted to rear of splined compressor shaft, through which passes power to drive the accessories on the forward extension shaft. Compressor turbine has solid rotor blades, held by fir-tree roots in discs cooled by bleed air (first disc from 10th-stage air, all other discs from 8th-stage air). First- and second-stage stators have 51 and 47 inserted blades respectively. Free power turbine is of similar two-stage design; its rotors have 43 and 37 blades respectively.

Exhaust Unit: Large fixed-area duct which deflects the gas out sideways at 60°. It comprises a pipe, pipe shroud and tie-band, shroud connector links and exhaust pipe attachments. The exhaust pipe and shroud together form a double-wall assembly which minimises heat transfer into the power plant

Isotov TV2-117A turboshaft engine (1,500 shp; 1,520 cv)

nacelle, the pipe being cooled by air circulating in the double wall.

OUTPUT SHAFT: The main drive-shaft is an extension of the power turbine rotor shaft. It conveys torque from the free turbine to the overrunning clutch of the helicopter main gearbox (VR-8A) and is also coupled to the speed governor of the engine free-turbine rotor. Max output speed 12,000 rpm; main rotor speed 192 rpm.

ACCESSORIES: All accessories requiring rotary power input are mounted on the main drive box above the intake casing, in which a train of bevel and spur gears provides drives for airframe and engine accessories. The engine automatic control system includes a fuel system, hydraulic system, anti-icing system, gas temperature restriction system, engine electric supply and starting system, and monitoring instruments. The hydraulic system positions the variable stators according to a preset programme, depending on compressor speed and air temperature at the inlet; it also sends electrical signals to control the starter/generator system, close the starting bleed air valves and restrict peak gas temperature to 600°C. Air up to 1·8 per cent of the total mass flow can be used to heat the intake and other parts liable to icing. Fire extinguishant can be released manually by the pilot, upon receipt of a fire warning, through a series of spray rings and pipes.

LUBRICATION: Pressure circulation type. Oil is supplied by the upper pump and scavenged from the five main bearings by the lower pump, returned through the helicopter-mounted air/oil heat exchanger and thence to the helicopter tank. The oil seals and air/oil labyrinth seals are connected to a centrifugal breathing system.

OIL GRADE: The TV2-117A is one of the first Soviet engines to use a synthetic oil, permitting operation at oil temperatures above 200°C, combined with easy starting at minus 40°C without heating the oil. The grade is B-3V to MRTU 38-1-157-65 (nearest foreign substitute Castrol 98 to DERD.2487). Oil consumption, not over 0·88 Imp pint (0·5 litre) per hour per engine.

STARTING: Electrical, fuel, and ignition systems are integrated. The SP3-15 system comprises DC starter/generator, six storage batteries, control panel, ground supply receptacle, and control switches and relays; of these all are airframe-mounted except for the GS-18TP starter/generator which spins the compressor during the starting cycle. The ignition unit comprises a control box, two semiconductor plugs, a solenoid valve, and switch. The starting fuel system comprises an automatic starting unit on the NR-40V fuel regulating pump, a constant-pressure valve, and two igniters.

DIMENSIONS:
Length, with accessories and exhaust pipe 111·5 in (2,835 mm)
Length, intake face to rotor gearbox connection 94·25 in (2,391 mm)
Width 21·5 in (547 mm)
Height 29·25 in (745 mm)

WEIGHT, DRY:
Engine, without generator, transducers, etc 727 lb (330 kg)
Type VR-8A gearbox, less entrapped oil 1,642 lb (745 kg)

PERFORMANCE RATINGS:
T-O (S/L, static) 1,500 shp (1,520 cv)
Cruise (122 knots; 140 mph; 225 km/h at 1,640 ft; 500 m) 1,000 shp (1,015 cv)

SPECIFIC FUEL CONSUMPTION:
T-O, as above 0·606 lb (0·275 kg)/shp/hr
Cruise, as above 0·683 lb (0·310 kg)/shp/hr

TVD-850

Power plant of the Antonov An-28 STOL transport, the TVD-850 turboprop is in production and in service at a rating of 810 shp. The cowled engine looks almost identical to the Turboméca Astazou, and the reduction gearbox must be housed in the centre of an annular air intake section.

IVCHENKO

The design team headed by general designer Alexander G. Ivchenko until his death in June 1968 is based in a factory at Zaparozhye in the Ukraine, where all prototypes and pre-production engines bearing the "AI" prefix are developed and built. Chief designer of the team is Vladimir Lotarev*, chief engineer is Tichienko and production director is M. Omeltchenko.

First engine with which Ivchenko was associated officially was the 55 hp AI-4G piston engine used in the Kamov Ka-10 ultra-light helicopter. He progressed ultimately, via the widely used AI-14 and AI-26 piston engines, to become one of the Soviet Union's leading designers of gas turbine engines.

*see also separate "Lotarev" entry.

AI-14

The original 260 hp AI-14R version of this nine-cylinder aircooled radial engine has been produced in very large quantities, in both the Soviet Union and Poland. Since 1960 several later versions have gone into production for fixed-wing aircraft and helicopters. The following versions can be listed:

AI-14R. Basic production engine, rated at 260 hp; fitted to Yak-12, Yak-18, PZL-101A Gawron and PZL-104 Wilga 3.

AI-14RF. Modified by I. M. Vedeneev from original design by Ivchenko bureau to power An-14 light STOL transport. Take-off rating 300 hp.

AI-14ChR. Further modified by Vedeneev to give take-off power of 350 hp.

M-14VF. Helicopter engine, rated at 280 hp; fitted to Ka-15 and Ka-18.

M-14V-26. Improved helicopter engine (see under "Vedeneev").

The following description refers to the AI-14R and AI-14RF:

TYPE: Nine-cylinder single-row aircooled radial, geared and supercharged.

CYLINDERS: Bore 4·125 in (105 mm). Stroke 5·125 in (130 mm). Displacement 620 cu in (10·16 litres). Nitrided steel barrel; cast light alloy head incorporating air starting valve. Two spark plugs and single inlet and exhaust valves. Compression ratio 5·9 (AI-14RF, 6·2).

PISTONS: Aluminium forgings, each with two chromium-plated compression rings, upper oil control ring with slot and, on skirt, tapered scraper ring.

CONNECTING RODS: One master rod, with lead-bronze big-end bearing; eight link rods articulated by steel cemented knuckle pins fixed in the master-rod cheeks against rotation and secured laterally by retaining strips.

CRANKSHAFT: Heat-treated steel in two parts, the front portion being gripped in the split cheek of the rear portion and held by a pinch bolt. Both portions carry a counterweight, the rear counterweight being of a pendulous type which balances inertia forces and also serves as vibration damper. Shaft held in two main roller bearings and ball thrust bearing in crankcase front cover.

CRANKCASE: Front and rear forgings in heat-treated light alloy, joined by nine bolts. On the front is the reduction gear casing and at the rear a mixture collector which receives the mixture from the supercharger.

VALVE GEAR: Each valve is opened by push/pull rod, from a cam plate geared to rotate in opposition to the crankshaft.

INDUCTION SYSTEM: Carburettor type, with choke tube upstream of supercharger.

FUEL GRADE: B-70 gasoline to specification GOST 1012-54, 73 octane to DERD.2485 or 80 grade non-ethylated to US MIL-G-5572C. (AI-14RF, SB-78, not under 78 octane.)

SUPERCHARGER: Aluminium forged impeller geared up from crankshaft to ratio of 7·105 (AI-14RF, 8·65). Magnesium cast diffuser.

LUBRICATION: Gear-type pressure and scavenge pumps.

IGNITION: Left magneto serves front plugs, right serves rear; automatic timing and fully screened.

PROPELLER DRIVE: Three planetary gears, ratio 0·787.

STARTING: By compressed air from airborne or ground compressor or bottle-fed through distributor to cylinder-head valves (and to purge lower cylinders of drained liquid).

DIMENSIONS:
Diameter 38·78 in (985 mm)
Length:
AI-14R 37·63 in (956 mm)
AI-14RF 39·45 in (1,002 mm)

WEIGHT, DRY:
AI-14R 434 lb (197 kg)
AI-14RF 507 lb (230 kg)

PERFORMANCE RATINGS:
Max T-O:
AI-14R 260 hp at 2,350 rpm
AI-14RF 300 hp at 2,400 rpm
Max continuous:
AI-14R 220 hp at 2,050 rpm
AI-14RF 285 hp at 2,300 rpm
Cruise (60% max continuous):
AI-14R 132 hp at 1,730 rpm
AI-14RF 150 hp at 1,730 rpm

SPECIFIC FUEL CONSUMPTION:
Max T-O:
AI-14R 0·562-0·617 lb (0·255-0·280 kg)/hp/hr
AI-14RF 0·584-0·639 lb (0·265-0·290 kg)/hp/hr
Cruise:
AI-14R 0·452-0·496 lb (0·205-0·225 kg)/hp/hr
AI-14RF 0·463-0·507 lb (0·120-0·230 kg)/hp/hr

AI-20

Ivchenko's design bureau is responsible for the AI-20 turboprop engine which powers the Antonov An-10, An-12 and Ilyushin Il-18 airliners, the Il-38 maritime patrol aircraft and the Beriev M-12 Tchaika amphibian.

Six production series of this engine had been built by the Spring of 1966. The first four series, of which manufacture started in 1957, were variants of the basic AI-20 version. They were followed by two major production versions, as follows:

AI-20K. Initial version rated at 3,945 ehp (4,000 ch e). Used in Il-18V, An-10A and An-12.

AI-20M. Standard version, with T-O rating of 4,190 ehp (4,250 ch e). Used in Il-18D/E, An-10A and An-12. Probably fitted to Il-38 and Beriev M-12. Capable of operation on a wide range of fuels and lubricating oils. Later the power was increased to 4,250 ehp (4,309 ch e), and this is the engine featured in the detailed description below.

The 300 hp Ivchenko AI-14RF engine *(courtesy of Aviation Magazine International, Paris)*

The AI-20 was designed to operate reliably in all temperatures from —60°C to + 55°C at heights up to 33,000 ft (10,000 m). It is a constant-speed engine, the rotor speed being maintained at 12,300 rpm by automatic variation of propeller pitch. Gas temperature after turbine is 560°C in both current versions. TBO of the AI-20K was 4,000 hours in the Spring of 1966; the same life was reached by the -20M in 1968.

In the Il-18 installation, the AI-20 turboprop is supplied as a complete power plant with cowling, mounting and automatically-feathering reversible-pitch four-blade propeller.

TYPE: Axial-flow high-altitude single-shaft turboprop.

AIR INTAKE: Inner and outer cones connected by six radial struts. Outer casing carries accessories and front mountings. Centre casing carries reduction gear.

COMPRESSOR: Ten-stage assembly of separate discs running in roller bearing in front casing, joined to first disc by tubular extension shaft,

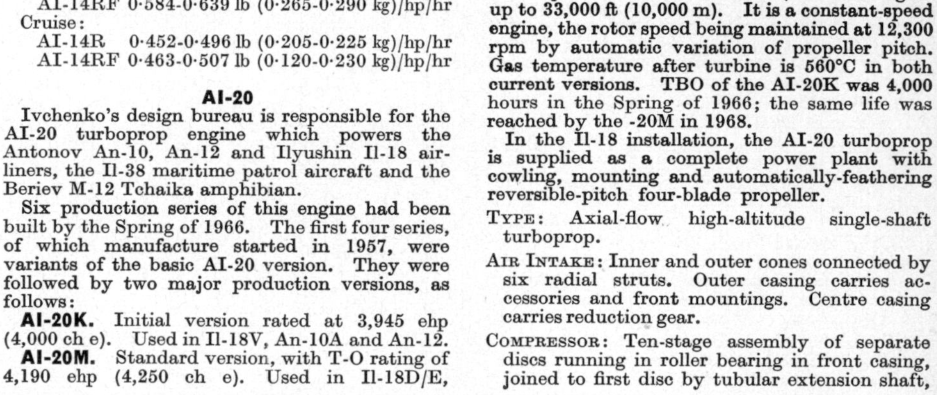

Ivchenko AI-20M turboprop of 4,190 ehp *(courtesy of Aviation Magazine International, Paris)*

and ball-thrust bearing in combustion chamber casing on through-bolted rear shaft. Magnesium alloy stator casing in upper and lower halves, bolted together. Pressure ratio 9·2 under altitude cruise conditions. Air mass flow 45·6 lb (20·7 kg)/sec.

COMBUSTION CHAMBER: Annular chamber with ten burner cones welded to front ring, and separate inner and outer shrouds. Burners anchored by flanges on chamber casing. Pilot burners and ignition plugs at top of casing.

FUEL GRADE: T-1 or TS-1 to GOST-10227-62 (DERD.2492, JP-1 to MIL-F-5616).

TURBINE: Three stages overhung on cantilevered shaft running in roller bearing in tapered cone of combustion chamber casing and splined to compressor drive-shaft. Rotor blades shrouded at inner and outer ends and installed in pairs in slots in aircooled discs. All stator blades secured in grooves in casing, first stage being aircooled and second stage being hollow to ensure uniform heating.

JET PIPE: Fixed-area type with five radial struts. Nozzle area 2·42 sq ft (0·225 m²).

REDUCTION GEAR: Planetary type, incorporating six-cylinder torquemeter and negative-thrust transmitter (type IKM), with self-checking device, for autofeathering the AV-681 propeller. Ratio 0·08732 (input speed always 12,300 rpm except ground-idle 10,400 rpm).

LUBRICATION: Pressure-feed type with full re-circulation; hourly consumption not over 0·175 Imp pints (0·8 litres).

OIL GRADE: Mixture 75% transformer oil GOST 982-56 or MK-8 to GOST 6457-66 (equivalent to DERD.2490 or MIL-O-6081B) and 25% MS-20 or MK-22 to GOST 1013-49 (DERD.2472 or MIL-O-6082B).

ACCESSORIES: Engine and airframe accessories driven off compressor front extension shaft, via radial shafts at 6 and 12 o'clock. Full ice-protection and fire-extinguishing systems.

STARTING: Two electric starter/generators, Type STG-12 TMO-1000, supplied from ground source or from APU Type TG-16.

DIMENSIONS:

Length	121·89 in (3,096 mm)
Width	33·15 in (842 mm)
Height	46·46 in (1,180 mm)

WEIGHT, DRY: 2,292 lb (1,040 kg)

PERFORMANCE RATINGS:

T-O	4,250 ehp (4,309 ch e)
Cruise (350 knots; 404 mph; 650 km/h at 26,000 ft; 8,000 m)	2,700 ehp (2,737 ch e)

SPECIFIC FUEL CONSUMPTION:

T-O	0·617 lb (0·280 kg)/ehp/hr
Cruise, as above	0·434 lb (0·197 kg)/ehp/hr

AI-24

In general configuration, this turboprop engine, which powers the An-24 and An-26 transport aircraft, is very similar to the earlier and larger AI-20. Production began in 1960 and the following data refer to engines of the second series, which were in production by the Spring of 1966.

The AI-24 of 2,515 ehp (2,550 ch e) powered the An-24V Series I, and was followed by the AI-24A with provision for water injection, in the main current production version of that aircraft.

The more powerful AI-24T of 2,820 ehp (2,859 ch e) with water injection is used in the An-26. This engine has in-flight vibration monitoring, automatic relief of power overloads and gas temperature behind the turbine, and auto-shutdown and feathering.

The AI-24 is a constant-speed engine, the speed of the rotor being maintained at 15,100 rpm by automatic variation of propeller pitch. The engine is flat-rated to maintain its nominal output to 11,500 ft (3,500 m). TBO was 3,000 hours in the Spring of 1966; by 1968 the later AI-24T had reached 4,000 hours.

TYPE: Axial-flow single-shaft turboprop.

AIR INTAKE: Large magnesium alloy casting, comprising inner and outer cones joined by four radial struts. Carries accessories, reduction gear, front mountings and compressor inlet guide vanes.

COMPRESSOR: Ten-stage axial, subsonic. Stainless steel rotor, comprising rigidly-connected discs carrying dovetailed blades. Front shaft runs in roller bearing and is bolted to propeller drive-shaft of reduction gear; rear shaft runs in ball-thrust bearing and is splined to turbine shaft. Welded steel casing in bolted left and right halves, with welded front and rear connecting flanges. Pressure ratio (max continuous, 18,300 ft; 6,000 m, 272 knots; 314 mph; 505 km/h) 7·85 : 1. Air mass flow 31·7 lb (14·4 kg)/sec.

COMBUSTION CHAMBER: Annular, of spot-welded heat-resistant steel, with eight simplex burners inserted into swirl-vane heads. Contains two starting units, each comprising a body, pilot burner and igniter plug.

FUEL GRADE: T-1, TS-1 to GOST 10227-62 (DERD.2494 or MIL-F-5616).

TURBINE: Three-stage axial. Three discs carry solid blades in fir-tree roots, and are automatically centred on each other when connected by stay-bolts to the extended flange at the rear of the turbine shaft. Shaft splined to compressor rear shaft and held by tie-rod; runs in roller bearing ahead of first turbine disc. Three stator diaphragms through-bolted together and to combustion-chamber casing. First nozzle diaphragm cooled by secondary air from combustion chamber. Rotor/stator sealing effected by soft inserts mounted in grooves in nozzle assemblies. Peak exhaust temperature during starting 750°C.

JET PIPE: Fixed-area type. Inner and outer rings connected by three hollow struts carrying total of 12 thermocouples.

REDUCTION GEAR: Planetary type, incorporating hydraulic torquemeter and electromagnetic negative-thrust transmitter for propeller auto-feathering. Magnesium alloy casing. Front flange of propeller shaft has end splines and 12 stud holes for type AV-72 propeller (AI-24T drives AV-72T propeller). Ratio 0·08255.

LUBRICATION: Pressure circulation system; hourly consumption not over 1·87 lb (850 gr).

OIL GRADE: Mixture of 75% transformer oil GOST 982-56 or MK-8 (DERD.2490 or MIL-O-6081B) and 25% MS-20 or MK-22 (DERD. 2472 or MIL-O-6082B).

ACCESSORIES: Mounted on top of the front casing are the starter/generator, alternator, propeller speed governor (which changes blade angle to maintain constant rpm) and centrifugal breather. Below the front casing are the oil unit, air separator and a removable box containing the LP and HP fuel pumps and drives to the hydraulic pump and tachometer generators. Also mounted on the front casing are an aerodynamic probe, ice detector, and negative-thrust feathering valve, torque transmitter and oil filter.

STARTING: Electric; type STG-18TMO starter/generator is supplied from ground electric power or from TG-16 APU.

DIMENSIONS:

Length overall	92·36 in (2,346 mm)
Width	26·65 in (677 mm)
Height	42·32 in (1,075 mm)

WEIGHT, DRY: 1,323 lb (600 kg)

PERFORMANCE RATINGS:

T-O:	
AI-24A	2,515 ehp (2,550 ch e)
AI-24T	2,820 ehp (2,859 ch e)
Cruise rating at 243 knots (280 mph; 450 km/h) at 18,300 ft (6,000 m):	
AI-24A	1,550 ehp (1,571 ch e)
AI-24T	1,580 ehp (1,602 ch e)

SPECIFIC FUEL CONSUMPTION:

At cruise rating:	
AI-24A	0·540 lb (0·245 kg)/ehp/hr
AI-24T	0·533 lb (0·242 kg)/ehp/hr
OIL CONSUMPTION:	1·87 lb (0·85 kg)/hr

The 2,515 ehp Ivchenko AI-24A turboprop engine (*courtesy of Aviation Magazine International, Paris*)

Ivchenko AI-25 turbofan engine (3,300 lb; 1,500 kg st)

AI-25

This is the turbofan that powers the three-engined Yakovlev Yak-40 STOL transport. The Aeroflot Yak-40 has the basic AI-25 engine, but the Yak-40B of the Soviet Air Force has an AI-25 with an aircooled HP turbine and rating of 3,850 lb (1,746 kg) st. The AI-25 also powers the Czech L-39 trainer, and it had been intended that it should be manufactured by Motorlet, Czechoslovakia, as the Walter Titan. The emergence of the Polish WSK-Mielec M-15 agricultural aircraft has transferred AI-25 activity to Poland, and mass production is now likely to take place in that country to provide engines for an M-15 programme estimated at 3,000 aircraft for the Soviet Union alone.

The Ivchenko bureau planned the engine for a wide spectrum of small transports, trainers and business jet aircraft. It is claimed to have an exceptional margin of flow stability and to be unusually robust and simple.

TYPE: Two-shaft turbofan.

AIR INTAKE: Direct pitot intake, fabricated from titanium sheet. Central bullet and intake leading-edges anti-iced by hot bleed air.

FAN: Three-stage axial. Drum/disc construction with pin-jointed blades. Casing and fan duct of magnesium alloy. Peak pressure ratio, 1·695 at 10,750 rpm. By-pass ratio 2.

COMPRESSOR: Eight-stage axial. Drum/disc construction of titanium, with aluminium and magnesium casing. Dovetailed blades. Peak pressure ratio, 4·68 at 16,640 rpm. Overall pressure ratio, 8.

COMBUSTION CHAMBER: Annular. Inner and outer casings joined upstream to 12 burner heads with stabilisers.

FUEL GRADE: T-1, TS-1 to GOST 10227-62 (DERD.2494, MIL-F-5616).

TURBINE: Single-stage HP turbine; two-stage LP turbine. Shrouded solid rotor blades held by fir-tree roots in cooled discs.

JET PIPE: Plain fixed convergent nozzles for both core gas and by-pass airflow. No mixer.

LUBRICATION: Self-contained, pressure circulating.

OIL GRADE: MK-8 to GOST 6457-66 or MK-6 to GOST 10328-63 (Western equivalents, DERD.2490 or MIL-O-6081B). Consumption 0·53 Imp pints (0·3 litre)/hr.

ACCESSORIES: All shaft-driven accessories mounted on gearbox on underside of engine and driven off HP spool. Equipment includes automatic fire extinguishing (agent can be supplied into oil-contacted labyrinth cavities), ice protection, automatic starting and control system, oil-system chip detector and casing vibration monitor.

STARTING: Pneumatic. Air starter type SV-25 is supplied from ground hose coupling or from APU type AI-9 or an operating engine bleed. System claimed to develop high torque for rapid start in any climatic condition, and to be cleared for exceptional number of starts in given overhaul life.

DIMENSIONS:

Length overall 78·46 in (1,993 mm)

Width overall 32·28 in (820 mm)

Height overall 35·24 in (895 mm)

WEIGHT, DRY:

Without accessories 639 lb (290 kg)

PERFORMANCE RATINGS:

T-O 3,300 lb (1,500 kg) st

Long-range cruise rating, 20,000 ft (6,000 m) and 296 knots (342 mph; 550 km/h) 785 lb (356 kg) st

SPECIFIC FUEL CONSUMPTION:

T-O 0·56

Cruise, as above 0·837

AI-26V

The most powerful Ivchenko piston engine so far announced is the AI-26V, which is used to power the Mi-1 series of helicopters. It is a seven-cylinder radial engine giving 575 hp at 2,200 rpm and has fan cooling.

The AI-26V was built under licence in Poland, with the designation LiT-3, to power the Polish SM-1 and SM-2 helicopters.

KOLIESOV

During an official tour of the Soviet aircraft industry in mid-1973, a representative of *Air Force Magazine* was told of the existence of the hitherto-unreported Koliesov Engine Design Bureau. It is developing an alternative engine to the Kuznetsov NK-144, the power plant used currently in the Tu-144 and, probably, in the Tupolev bomber known to NATO as "Backfire".

The new Koliesov engine is described as a variable-geometry, variable by-pass ratio engine which functions as a turbojet in supersonic flight and as a turbofan in the subsonic regime. No such advanced design exists in the west.

Soviet engine designers are reported to be experimenting also with hypersonic vehicles powered by scramjet propulsion systems and capable of operating in the Mach 5 to Mach 7 range.

KUZNETSOV

GENERAL DESIGNER IN CHARGE OF BUREAU:
Nikolai Dmitrievich Kuznetsov

This bureau appears to have devoted its entire energy to large transport gas turbine engines. Though the formidable NK-12 was a surprising success the bureau has not been entirely able to overcome technical problems, and its NK-8 turbofan has been replaced by engines from the Soloviev bureau in both the tri-jet Tu-154 and the Il-62 long-range airliner. Kuznetsov himself led a delegation of engineers to visit Rolls-Royce in late 1973 to discuss the licensing of certain items of advanced technology, and possibly even the RB.211 engine, from the British company.

NK-8

One of the largest Russian civil turbofans known to exist, the NK-8 has been developed through a number of variants, the most powerful of which is the NK-144 supersonic augmented engine for the Tupolev Tu-144 supersonic transport. Basic versions are the 22,273 lb (10,500 kg) thrust NK-8-4 which originally powered the Ilyushin Il-62 four-engined transport, and the further-developed 20,950 lb (9,500 kg) NK-8-2 which was the original engine of the Tupolev Tu-154.

TYPE: Two-shaft turbofan.

AIR INTAKE: Direct pitot intake, fabricated from outer ring, inner splitter and welded stator blades (15 in core airflow, 30 ahead of the fan). Hot-air ice-protection.

FAN: Two-stage axial, with anti-flutter swept-back blades on first rotor stage. Pressure ratio 2·15 at 5,350 rpm. By-pass ratio 1·02 (NK-8-2, 1·00).

COMPRESSOR: Two stages of LP compression on fan shaft. Six-stage HP compressor. Construction of both rotors and stators, including blading, almost wholly of titanium alloy. Core pressure ratio, 10·8 at 6,950 HP rpm (NK-8-2, 10 at 6,835 rpm).

COMBUSTION CHAMBER: Annular, with 139 burners. Combustion claimed to produce no visible smoke.

FUEL GRADE: T-1 and TS-1 to GOST 10227-62 or T-7 to GOST 12308-66 (equivalent to Avtur 50 to DERD.2494 or MIL-F-5616).

TURBINE: Single-stage HP turbine, two-stage LP turbine, all with shrouded rotor blades, aircooled discs and hollow nozzle blades (stators). All shafting carried between shock-absorbing bearings at each end, with labyrinth and contact (rubbing) graphite seals to prevent gas leakage. Gas temperature, not over 870°C (NK-8-2) ahead of turbine, nor over 670°C (NK-8-2, 650°C) downstream, both values sea level, static.

JET PIPE: Mixer unit leads by-pass flow into common jet pipe which may be fitted with blocker/cascade-type reverser integral with the jet pipe, giving up to 48% (NK-8-2, 45%) reverse thrust, and noise suppressor.

LUBRICATION: Continuous pressure feed and recirculation. Oil consumption not over 2·87 lb (1·3 kg)/hr.

OIL GRADE: Mineral oil MK-8 or MK-8P to GOST 6457-66 (DERD. 2490 or MIL-O-6081B). External tank on left side of front casing.

ACCESSORIES: These include automatic flight-deck warning of vibration exceeding permissible limit, ice and fire. All accessories grouped beneath fan duct casing. Engine claimed to need no attention for long periods, other than inspection of fuel and oil filters.

STARTING: HP spool driven by constant-speed drive type PPO-62M, or started pneumatically by air from APU type TA-6, from ground hose or by air from another engine (NK-8-2, pneumatic starter only). Time to idling speed not over 80 sec. Engine can be windmill-started in the air under all conditions, up to altitude of 36,000 ft (11,000 m).

DIMENSIONS:

NK-8-4

Length, no reverser 201 in (5,100 mm)

NK-8-2

Length, with reverser 208·19 in (5,288 mm)

Length, without reverser 187·48 in (4,762 mm)

Diameter 56·8 in (1,442 mm)

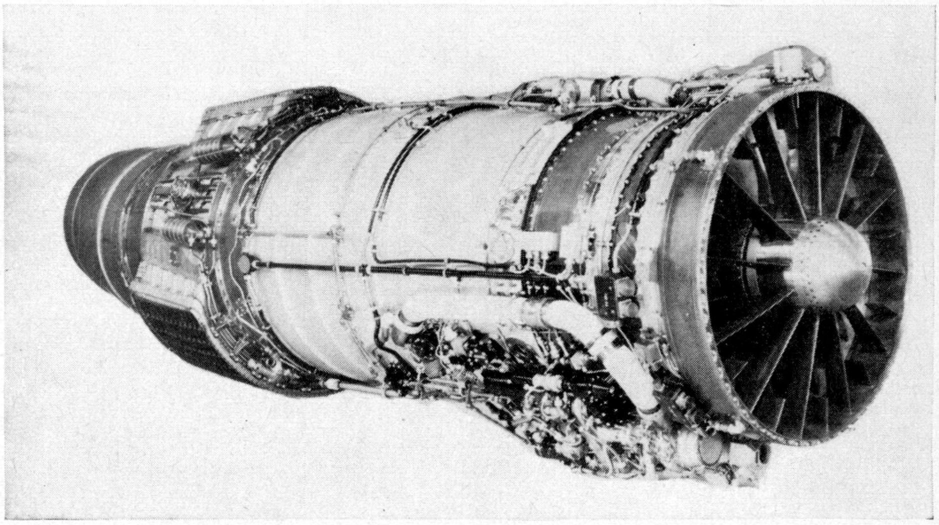

Kuznetsov NK-8-2 turbofan with thrust reverser (20,950 lb; 9,500 kg st)

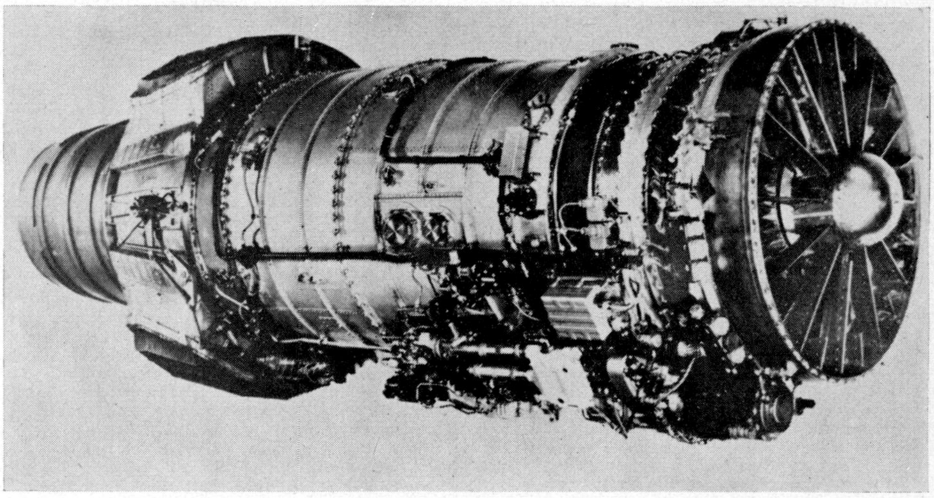

Kuznetsov NK-8-4 turbofan with thrust reverser (22,273 lb; 10,500 kg st)

WEIGHT, DRY:

NK-8-4:

No reverser 4,629 lb (2,100 kg)

With reverser 5,291 lb (2,400 kg)

NK-8-2:

No reverser 4,629 lb (2,100 kg) max

With reverser 5,180 lb (2,350 kg) max

PERFORMANCE:

NK-8-4:

T-O rating 22,273 lb (10,500 kg)

Cruise rating at 36,000 ft (11,000 m) and 458 knots (530 mph; 850 km/h) 6,063 lb (2,750 kg)

NK-8-2:

T-O rating 20,950 lb (9,500 kg)

Cruise (as above) 3,968 lb (1,800 kg)

SPECIFIC FUEL CONSUMPTION:

At cruise rating at 36,000 ft (11,000 m) and 458 knots (530 mph; 850 km/h):

NK-8-4 0·78

NK-8-2 0·76

NK-144

This is the two-spool turbofan installed in the Soviet Union's first supersonic transport aircraft, the Tu-144. It is a development of the NK-8 and the first five pre-production NK-144s completed some 1,500 hours of bench-testing by October 1965. The engine flew in at least one airborne test aircraft before the start of the Tu-144 flight programme in 1968.

Since 1972 the afterburner augmentation has been increased, raising maximum rating from 38,580 lb (17,500 kg) to the figure given below. The NK-144 is believed to be the engine of the Tupolev supersonic bomber known to NATO as "Backfire".

The NK-144 has a two-stage titanium fan, three-stage IP compressor, eleven-stage HP compressor, annular combustion chamber, single-stage HP turbine and two-stage LP turbine. Aircooled blades are used in the HP turbine, and titanium is used extensively in construction of the engine. By-pass ratio is reported to be 1 : 1, maximum mass flow 551 lb (250 kg)/sec, and pressure ratio 15 : 1. A partial afterburning installation is provided, with a hydraulically-actuated variable-area nozzle. Gas temperature at turbine entry is 1,050°C.

DIMENSIONS:

Length overall 204·7 in (5,200 mm)

Diameter 59 in (1,500 mm)

WEIGHT:

Without jet pipe, but with afterburner 6,283 lb (2,850 kg)

PERFORMANCE RATINGS:

Max, without afterburning 28,660 lb (13,000 kg) st

Max, with afterburning 44,090 lb (20,000 kg) st

NK-12M

Designed at Kuibishev under the leadership of N. D. Kuznetsov and former German engineers, the NK-12M is the most powerful turboprop engine in the world. In its original form as the

NK-12M it developed 12,000 ehp. The later NK-12MV is rated at 14,795 ehp (15,000 ch e) and powers the Tupolev Tu-114 transport, driving four-blade contra-rotating propellers of 18 ft 4 in (5·6 m) diameter. As the NK-12MA, it powers the Antonov An-22 military transport, with propellers of 20 ft 4 in (6·2 m) diameter. A third application is in the Tupolev Tu-95 bomber and its derivatives, which originally were fitted with the 12,000 ehp NK-12M. All the military engines are now believed to have been uprated to 14,795 ehp.

The NK-12M has a single 14-stage axial-flow compressor and the complete rotating assembly weighs about a ton. Compression ratio varies from 9 : 1 to 13 : 1 according to altitude, and variable inlet guide vanes and blow-off valves are provided to facilitate engine handling. A cannular-type combustion system is used: each separate flame tube is mounted centrally on a downstream injector, but all tubes merge at their maximum diameter to form an annular secondary region. The turbine is of the five-stage axial-flow type. Mass flow is 143 lb (65 kg)/sec.

The casing is made in four portions, from sheet steel, and is precision welded. An electric control for variation of propeller pitch is incorporated, to maintain constant engine speed.

DIMENSIONS:
- Length: 236·2 in (6,000 mm)
- Diameter: 45·3 in (1,150 mm)

WEIGHT, DRY: 5,181 lb (2,350 kg)

PERFORMANCE RATINGS:
- T-O: 14,795 ehp (15,000 ch e)
- Nominal power: 11,836 ehp (12,000 ch e) at 8,300 rpm
- Idling speed: 6,600 rpm

Kuznetsov NK-12MV single-shaft turboprop of 14,795 ehp
(courtesy of Aviation Magazine International, Paris)

LOTAREV

GENERAL DESIGNER IN CHARGE OF BUREAU:
Vladimir Lotarev

ADDRESS:
Zaparozhye

LOTAREV D-36

As successor to Alexander Ivchenko at Zaparozhye, Vladimir Lotarev is reported to be developing the turbofan engine that will power the Yakovlev Yak-42. With a by-pass ratio of 5·34 : 1 the D-36 is the first avowed "turbofan"—as distinct from a by-pass turbojet—to emerge in the Soviet Union. Bench testing was in progress in September 1973, and flights in a pod carried beneath a Tu-16 testbed aircraft were scheduled to begin at the end of 1973.

WEIGHT, DRY: 2,480 lb (1,080 kg)

PERFORMANCE RATINGS:
- T-O rating: 14,110 lb (6,400 kg) st
- Cruise rating at 26,200 ft (8,000 m) at Mach 0·84: 3,505 lb (1,590 kg) st

SPECIFIC FUEL CONSUMPTION:
- At T-O rating: 0·38
- At cruise rating as above: 0·66

LYULKA

GENERAL DESIGNER IN CHARGE OF BUREAU:
Arkhip Mikhailovich Lyulka

Although he is one of the select group of Soviet aircraft and engine designers to hold the title of General Constructor—enabling him to head his own design bureau and have his products designated by his personal initials—Lyulka is little known in the West and his long history of work on gas turbines has been practically unknown. During the late 1930s he worked on the design of an axial turbojet that became an early war casualty. In 1942 he planned a more advanced engine that finally materialised as the TR-1, of 2,866 lb (1,300 kg) st, run on the bench in 1944 and used in the Ilyushin Il-22 four-jet bomber and Sukhoi Su-11 twin-jet fighter prototypes, both of 1947. Ultimately, in 1948, this pioneer Soviet-designed turbojet was developed to give 3,307 lb (1,500 kg) st.

In 1946 Lyulka began the design of a very ambitious axial engine to give a thrust of 9,920 lb (4,500 kg), and in 1950 this began bench trials under the designation AL-5. Although of basically simple, single-shaft configuration, with a seven-stage compressor and single-stage turbine, the AL-5 was more powerful than all Western engines apart from the prototype Olympus and J57. By 1951 it was rated at 10,140 lb (4,600 kg) st and flew in the prototype Ilyushin Il-30 twin-jet bomber; later in 1951-52 uprated AL-5 engines, giving a static thrust of 11,032 lb (5,000 kg), powered the Il-46 twin-jet bomber and the transonic Lavochkin La-190 and Yakovlev Yak-1000 fighters. An advanced civil version of the same engine, the AL-5 rated at 12,125 lb (5,500 kg) st, powered the Tu-110 four-engined derivative of the Tu-104 airliner that never went into production (at the time, in 1959, this engine was reported in the West as the "Lu-4").

By the time the AL-5 was running, Lyulka had conducted extensive research with axial compressors having supersonic airflow through some or all of the stages. It was clear that, if problems of flow breakdown and inefficiency could be resolved, such a compressor would enable turbojets to be made much smaller and lighter for a given thrust and with greater thrust per unit frontal area, and thus much better suited to the propulsion of supersonic fighters. By 1952 a supersonic-compressor engine had been designed and built. This, the AL-7, is today Lyulka's greatest success and one of his few designs to have been rewarded by large-scale production.

LYULKA AL-7

The first AL-7 ran on the bench in late 1952 and the first production version was cleared for use in 1954 at a design rating of 14,330 lb (6,500 kg) st. Its initial application was on the Il-54, yet another Ilyushin twin-jet bomber that failed to see production, despite the fact that its speed at low altitude of 620 kt (714 mph; 1,150 km/h) was probably unrivalled by any other bomber in 1955. In the same year the Sukhoi Su-7 single-seat ground-attack fighter was designed around the AL-7F afterburning version of this engine, with thrust increased by about 40 per cent (see data below). By 1956 the Su-7 was flying, and the AL-7F had also been chosen for the basically similar Su-9 all-weather fighter. By 1958 a further developed version of the basic unaugmented engine, the AL-7PB, had been chosen by Beriev for the Be-10 reconnaissance flying-boat which—apart from being the only pure-jet flying-boat ever to go into service anywhere—set up a number of world records for speed, load-carrying and altitude. Other versions of the AL-7, in both cases of the -7F afterburning family, powered the unsuccessful Tu-98 bomber and La-250 strike fighter of 1956.

TYPE: Single-shaft axial-flow turbojet, available with or without afterburner.

AIR INTAKE: Annular type surrounding central bullet fairing. Main intake unit has 14 fixed aerofoil struts anti-iced by compressor bleed air.

COMPRESSOR: Nine-stage axial-flow type (probably eight stages in original AL-7 design). First two stages widely separated axially, with variable stators ahead of second stage. Each stage has blades inserted in centreless disc held by peripheral spacers at correct distance from adjacent discs, the whole being coupled finally together by central drive-shaft in tension. Pressure ratio probably about 8 : 1.

COMBUSTION CHAMBER: Annular type with perforated inner flame tube. Multiple downstream fuel injectors inserted through cups in forward face of liner. Liner outer casing provided with multiple inward secondary-air injection ducts.

TURBINE: Two-stage axial-flow type. Both wheels overhung behind rear bearing; front disc bolted to flange on hollow tubular drive-shaft which, in turn, is splined to rear of compressor shaft running in main centre bearing which locates compressor axially against end loads.

AFTERBURNER: In AL-7F series, afterburner (reheat jet pipe) comprises upstream diffuser and downstream combustion section. Pilot combustor on turbine exit cone includes single nozzle ring and flame-holder; main spray ring and gutter flame-holder assembly located further downstream at greater radius. Refractory liner in combustion section. Variable-area nozzle, with multiple hinged flaps which govern nozzle size and profile according to signals from reheat control system based on turbine exit temperature and throttle lever position.

ACCESSORIES: Fuel pump and control unit, oil pumps, hydraulic pump, electric generator, tachometer and other items grouped into quickly replaceable packages beneath compressor casing.

PERFORMANCE RATINGS:
- Max rating:
  - AL-7F, unaugmented: 15,432 lb (7,000 kg) st
  - AL-7F, afterburning: 22,046 lb (10,000 kg) st
  - AL-7PB: 14,330 lb (6,500 kg) st

MIKULIN

GENERAL DESIGNER IN CHARGE OF BUREAU:
Alexander Alexandrovich Mikulin

M-11

Very large numbers of M-11 five-cylinder radial engines have been built in the Soviet Union and Poland to power a variety of light aircraft and helicopters. Best-known variants are the 125 hp M-11D and the 160 hp M-11FR which powers the Yak-18 primary trainer.

Swept volume of the M-11 is 525 cu in (8,600 cc). Compression ratio is 5 : 1 in the M-11D and 5·5 : 1 in the M-11FR. Both versions operate on 72 octane fuel.

WEIGHTS:
- M-11D: 362 lb (164 kg)
- M-11FR: 397 lb (180 kg)

PERFORMANCE RATINGS:
- T-O rating:
  - M-11D: 125 hp at 1,760 rpm
  - M-11FR: 160 hp at 1,900 rpm
- Rated power:
  - M-11D: 115 hp at 1,700 rpm
  - M-11FR: 140 hp at 1,760 rpm

SPECIFIC FUEL CONSUMPTION:
- At T-O rating:
  - M-11D: 0·573-0·639 lb (0·26-0·29 kg)/hp/hr
  - M-11FR: 0·551-0·595 lb (0·25-0·27 kg)/hp/hr
- At rated power:
  - M-11D: 0·551-0·595 lb (0·25-0·27 kg)/hp/hr
  - M-11FR: 0·529-0·573 lb (0·24-0·26 kg)/hp/hr

RD-3M-500

The basic RD-3M (or AM-3M) single-spool axial-flow turbojet was developed under the design leadership of P. F. Zubets from the original Mikulin M-209 (civil RD-3 or AM-3) engine which powers the Tu-16 and Mya-4 bombers and was adapted for Russia's first jet transport, the Tu-104.

The RD-3M-500 was evolved, in turn, from the RD-3M and powers the Tu-104A and Tu-104B commercial transports. It has a simple basic configuration, with an eight-stage axial-flow compressor, annular-type combustion system with 14 flame tubes, and a two-stage turbine. The compressor casing is made in front, centre and rear portions, the front casing housing a row of inlet guide vanes. A bullet fairing mounted centrally in the annular ram-air intake houses a type S-300M gas-turbine starter, developing 90-100 hp at 31,000-35,000 rpm. The jet pipe consists of a central cone and fixed nozzle with an orifice diameter of approximately 33 in (840 mm). Pressure ratio is 6·4 : 1; temperature after turbine 720°C.

DIMENSIONS:
- Length overall: 210·23 in (5,340 mm)
- Diameter: 55·12 in (1,400 mm)

PERFORMANCE RATING:
- T-O: 20,940 lb (9,500 kg) st

The 125 hp Mikulin M-11D ***(left)*** **and 160 hp M-11FR radial engines**

SHVETSOV

GENERAL DESIGNER IN CHARGE OF BUREAU: Arkadiya Dmitrievich Shvetsov

ASh-21

This seven-cylinder radial engine of 730 hp was evolved by Shvetsov from the American Wright R-1300 and was built in large numbers to power the Yak-11 advanced trainer. A helicopter version was also produced.

ASh-62

Power plant of the An-2 transport biplane, the Ash-62 is a 1,000 hp nine-cylinder aircooled radial engine. Several variants have been built, including the ASh-62IR/TK driving a turbo-compressor to maintain 850 hp up to a height of 31,000 ft (9,500 m).

There are two current versions of the engine, as follows:

ASh-62IR. Standard power plant of the Li-2 (Soviet DC-3) and all versions of the An-2 except for the An-2M. Built also in Poland.

ASh-62M. Developed by Vedeneev from ASh-62IR to power An-2M. Has a power take-off shaft, rated at up to 58 hp, to drive agricultural spraying or dusting gear, two electrical generators and the flight deck air-conditioning equipment. Weight of the take-off package is 249 lb (113 kg).

Both versions have a cylinder bore of 6⅛ in (155·5 mm), swept volume of 1,823 cu in (29·87 litres) and compression ratio of 6·4 : 1.

The planetary reduction gear of the ASh-62M has a ratio of 0·637 : 1.

DIMENSIONS (ASh-62M):
- Length overall, without power take-off: 44·50 in (1,130 mm)
- Diameter: 54·13 in (1,375 mm)

WEIGHT, DRY (ASh-62M):
- Without power take-off: 1,250 lb (567 kg)

PERFORMANCE RATINGS (ASh-62M: A, with power take-off driving generators and air-conditioning equipment; B, driving also agricultural equipment):
- T-O: A: 1,000 hp at 2,200 rpm
- Rated power:
  - A: 820 hp at 2,100 rpm
  - B (75% power): 615 hp at 1,910 rpm
- Max continuous (90% power):
  - A: 738 hp at 2,030 rpm
- Cruise:
  - B (50% power): 410 hp at 1,670 rpm

SPECIFIC FUEL CONSUMPTION (corresponding to above ratings):
- T-O: A: 0·661 lb (0·30 kg)/hp/hr
- Rated power:
  - A: 0·617-0·661 lb (0·28-0·30 kg)/hp/hr
  - B: 0·529-0·562 lb (0·24-0·255 kg)/hp/hr
- Max continuous:
  - A: 0·573-0·617 lb (0·26-0·28 kg)/hp/hr
- Cruise:
  - B: 0·474-0·507 lb (0·215-0·230 kg)/hp/hr

The 1,000 hp Shvetsov ASh-62IR engine *(courtesy of Aviation Magazine International, Paris)*

ASh-82

The ASh-82T was developed by Shvetsov from the Pratt & Whitney Twin Wasp design to power the Il-12 and Il-14 twin-engined transports. It has been produced in Russia, Czechoslovakia and East Germany, and the details below were supplied from Germany.

A variant, shown in an adjacent illustration, is the ASh-82V helicopter engine, which powers the Mil Mi-4. This embodies a cooling fan and a friction clutch in the rotor drive.

TYPE: Fourteen-cylinder two-row aircooled radial, geared and supercharged.

CYLINDERS: Bore 6·12 in (155·5 mm). Stroke 6·10 in (155 mm). Displacement 2,513 cu in (41·2 litres). Nitrided steel barrel with cast aluminium alloy head. Compression ratio 6·9 : 1.

PISTONS: Of forged aluminium. Each piston has three compression rings, one oil scraper ring and one oil seal ring. Upper compression ring of chromium-plated steel, remainder of cast iron. Bearing surfaces graphited. Gudgeon pins secured against axial movement by mushroom heads.

CONNECTING RODS: Master rod and six articulated rods for each row. All rods of forged steel, heat-treated and polished. Bearings of lead-coated bronze.

CRANKSHAFT: Three-piece crankshaft of heat-treated forged chrome-nickel-molybdenum steel. Bearing surfaces nitrided. Supported in three roller bearings.

CRANKCASE: Made up of front housing, six-part centre housing, front and rear supercharger casings, and rear cover, all joined together by set-screws and studs. Centre housing containing cylinders is of steel, all other parts of light alloy. Front housing contains reduction gear and drives for magneto, propeller governor and oil pump.

VALVE GEAR: One inlet and one exhaust valve per cylinder, of heat-resisting steel. Exhaust valves are hollow and sodium-filled. Each row of cylinders has independent valve gear, consisting of camshaft, pushrods, valve levers, springs and valves.

INDUCTION SYSTEM: Direct injection system, with injection pump on rear cover.

Above:
The 1,900 hp ASh-82T fourteen-cylinder radial engine

Right:
The 1,700 hp Shvetsov ASh-82V engine *(courtesy of Aviation Magazine International, Paris)*

FUEL GRADE: Not less than 95 octane.
SUPERCHARGER: Single-stage type. Drive from crankshaft to light alloy impeller through reduction gearing with 7·27 : 1 ratio.
LUBRICATION: Two oil pumps, one for each row.
IGNITION: Two magnetos on front housing. Screened ignition harness.
PROPELLER DRIVE: Provision for four-blade hydraulically-operated constant-speed variable-pitch propeller with fluid de-icing. Reduction gear ratio 54 : 31.

DIMENSIONS:

Diameter	51·18 in (1,300 mm)
Length:	
ASh-82T	79·13 in (2,010 mm)
ASh-82V	74·30 in (1,887 mm)

WEIGHT, DRY:

ASh-82T	2,250 lb (1,020 kg)
ASh-82V	2,359 lb (1,070 kg)

PERFORMANCE RATINGS:

T-O (5 min):	
ASh-82T	1,900 hp at 2,600 rpm
ASh-82V	1,700 hp at 2,600 rpm
Rated power at S/L:	
ASh-82T	1,530 hp at 2,400 rpm
ASh-82V	1,430 hp at 2,400 rpm
Rated power at 5,250 ft (1,600 m):	
ASh-82T	1,630 hp at 2,400 rpm
ASh-82V	1,530 hp at 2,400 rpm

FUEL CONSUMPTION (ASh-82T):

At T-O rating	1,360-1,444 lb (617-655 kg)/hr
At rated power	959-1,058 lb (435-480 kg)/hr

SOLOVIEV

GENERAL DESIGNER IN CHARGE OF BUREAU:
P. A. Soloviev

Engines for which Soloviev's design team is responsible include the turbofans fitted in the Ilyushin Il-62M-200 and Il-76 and Tupolev Tu-124 and Tu-134 transport aircraft, and the turboshafts which power the Mi-6, Mi-10 and V-12 helicopters.

D-20P

The D-20P is a two-spool turbofan engine, of which two power the Tupolev Tu-124 transport aircraft. Of conservative design, it underwent prolonged testing before entering service. It was designed for maximum economy and reliability over the range of ambient temperatures between —40° and 40°C.

TYPE: Two-shaft turbofan (by-pass turbojet).
AIR INTAKE: Direct pitot intake with eight radial struts and central bullet fairing, de-iced by hot bleed air from fourth HP stage (from final stage at low rpm).
FAN: Three-stage axial, with supersonic blading in first stage. Mass flow 249 lb (113 kg)/sec at 8,550 rpm. Pressure ratio (S/L, static at max cont 7,900 rpm) 2·4 : 1. By-pass ratio 1 : 1.
COMPRESSOR: Eight-stage axial. Automatically-controlled flap valves immediately downstream of the third and fourth stages bleed air into the fan duct to stabilise behaviour. Pressure ratio (at max continuous, 11,170 rpm) 5 : 1; overall pressure ratio 13 : 1.
COMBUSTION CHAMBER: Can-annular, with 12 flame tubes each fitted with duplex burner.
FUEL GRADE: T-1, TS-1 to GOST 10227-62 (Avtur-50 to DERD.2494, MIL-F-5616).
TURBINE: Single-stage HP turbine with cast blades; stator blades and both sides of disc cooled by bleed air. Two-stage LP turbine with forged blades. Max gas temperature downstream of turbine 650°C.
JET PIPE: Concentric pipes for fan airflow and core gas, terminating in supersonic nozzles of fixed-area type.
LUBRICATION: Open type, with oil returned to tank. Consumption in flight, not over 2·2 lb (1 kg)/hr. Typical pressure 50-64 lb/sq in (3·4-4·5 kg/cm²).
OIL GRADE: Mineral oil MK-8 or MK-8P to GOST 6457-66 (DERD.2490 or MIL-O-6081B).
ACCESSORIES: Two gearboxes provide drives for starter/generator, tachometer, air compressors, hydraulic pump, oil pump and other controls and instruments. For re-starting in flight, an altitude sensing device meters fuel flow appropriate to height. An automatic fire extinguishing system is fitted. De-icing of the air intake and inlet guide vanes is controlled automatically. The engine also has oil chip detectors, vibration monitors and turbine gas temperature limiters.
STARTING: Electric (DC) system, incorporating STG-18TM starter/generator.

DIMENSIONS:

Length overall	130 in (3,304 mm)
Diameter, bare	38·3 in (976 mm)

WEIGHT, DRY: 3,236 lb (1,468 kg)

PERFORMANCE RATINGS:

Max T-O rating	11,905 lb (5,400 kg) st
Long-range cruise, Mach 0·75, 36,000 ft (11,000 m)	2,425 lb (1,100 kg) st

SPECIFIC FUEL CONSUMPTION:

Max T-O	0·72
Long-range cruise, as above	0·90

D-25V

The D-25V is a free-turbine turboshaft engine which powers the Mil Mi-6, Mi-10 and V-12 helicopters and was also fitted to the Kamov Ka-22 experimental convertiplane. It is usually referred to officially by the designation **TV-2BM.**

The complete helicopter power plant comprises two D-25V engines, identical except for handed jet pipes, and an R-7 gearbox. The latter has four stages of large gearwheels providing an overall ratio of 69·2. The R-7 is 110·04 in (2,795 mm) high, 61·06 in (1,551 mm) wide and 72·91 in (1,852 mm) long. Its dry weight is 7,054 lb (3,200 kg), more than that of the pair of engines.

The D-25V is flat-rated to maintain rated power to 10,000 ft (3,000 m) or to temperatures up to 40°C at sea level.

The D-25VF turboshafts fitted to the Mil V-12 helicopter are adapted to 6,500 shp. These engines are believed to incorporate a zero stage on the compressor and to operate at higher turbine gas temperatures. The following details apply to the basic D-25V:

Soloviev D-20P turbofan (11,905 lb; 5,400 kg st)

The 5,500 shp Soloviev D-25V turboshaft

TYPE: Single-shaft turboshaft with free power turbine.
AIR INTAKE: Direct pitot type. Six hollow radial struts, the two vertical struts housing splined shafts driving upper and lower accessory drive boxes. Vertical struts de-iced by oil drained from upper drive box; four inclined struts and bullet fairing de-iced by hot oil returned from engine to tank.
COMPRESSOR: Nine-stage axial. Comprises fixed inlet guide vane assembly, first-stage stator ring, upper and lower casings with dovetailed stator blades, ninth-stage stator ring and exit vanes, rotor, and air blow-off valves. Pressure ratio 5·6 at T-O power, 10,530 rpm.
COMBUSTION CHAMBER: Can-annular. Assembled from diffuser (the structural basis of the engine), inner shroud, 12 flame tubes with transition liners, diaphragm and compressor-shaft shroud.
FUEL GRADE: T-1, TS-1 to GOST 10227-62 (DERD.2494, MIL-F-5616).
TURBINE: Single-stage compressor turbine, overhung behind rear roller bearing. Two-stage power turbine, overhung on end of rear output shaft. Both turbines rotate counter-clockwise, seen from the rear. Normal power turbine rpm, 7-800-8,300; maximum 9,000. Transmission shaft in three universally-jointed sections, allowing for 4 in (10 mm) misalignment between engine and gearbox.
JET PIPE: Large fabricated assembly in heat-resistant steel, curved out to side to allow rotor transmission to pass through duct wall in aircooled protecting pipe.
LUBRICATION: Pressure circulation at 50-64 lb/sq in (3·5-4·5 kg/cm²). Separate systems for gas-generator and for power turbine, transmission and gearbox.
OIL GRADE: Gas-generator, MK-8 to GOST 6457-66 or transformer oil to GOST 982-56. Power turbine and gearbox, mixture (75-25 Summer, 50-50 Winter) of MK-22 or MS-20 to GOST 1013-49 and MK-8 or transformer oil. Hourly oil consumption, gas-generator not over 2·2 lb (1 kg), power turbine and transmission not over 4·4 lb (2 kg).
ACCESSORIES: SP3-12TV electric supply and starting system; fuel supply by separate LP and HP systems; airframe accessories driven off upper and lower gearboxes on inlet casing.
STARTING: The SP3-12TV system starts both engines and also generates electric current. It comprises an STG-12TM starter/generator on each engine, igniter unit, two spark plugs with cooling shrouds, two switch-over contactors, solenoid air valve, pressure warning, PSG-12V control panel and electro-hydraulic cutout switch of the TsP-23A centrifugal governor. In the starter mode the system draws current from a ground supply receptacle or from batteries.

DIMENSIONS:

Length overall, bare	107·75 in (2,737 mm)
Length overall with transmission shaft	218·0 in (5,537 mm)
Width	42·76 in (1,086 mm)
Height	45·59 in (1,158 mm)

WEIGHT, DRY:

With engine-mounted accessories	2,921 lb (1,325 kg)

PERFORMANCE RATINGS:

T-O	5,500 shp
Rated power	4,700 shp
Cruise (3,280 ft; 1,000 m, 135 knots; 155 mph; 250 km/h)	4,000 shp

SPECIFIC FUEL CONSUMPTION:

T-O, as above	0·639 lb (0·29 kg)/shp/hr
Cruise, as above	0·699 lb (0·317 kg)/shp/hr

SOLOVIEV D-30

This two-spool turbofan engine powers the Tu-134 twin-engined airliner and is derived from the D-20. Major portions of the core and carcase are similar, but the complete power plant is larger than the D-20, of more advanced design and appreciably more powerful and efficient.

In turn the D-30 has been developed into the considerably larger D-30K, described separately. In early 1972, these were the most advanced subsonic engines produced by the Soviet Union. They show a continuing allegiance to the form of power plant pioneered by Rolls-Royce as the "by-pass turbojet", a term still used in the Soviet Union to describe these engines, in which the LP system comprises several stages and the by-pass ratio is not greater than unity (in the West most recent turbofans have single-stage fans with a by-pass ratio of from 3 to 8).

TYPE: Two-shaft turbofan (by-pass turbojet).

AIR INTAKE: Direct pitot intake. Fabricated titanium alloy assembly, incorporating full air bleed anti-icing of both centre bullet and radial struts.

FAN: Four-stage axial unit (LP compressor). First stage has shrouded titanium blades held in disc by pinned joints. Pressure ratio (T-O rating, 7,700 rpm, sea level, static), 2·65 : 1. Mass flow 265 lb (125 kg)/sec. By-pass ratio 1 : 1.

COMPRESSOR: Ten-stage axial unit (HP compressor). Drum and disc construction, largely of titanium. Pressure ratio (T-O rating, 11,600 rpm, sea-level, static), 7·1 : 1. Overall pressure ratio, 17·4 : 1.

COMBUSTION CHAMBER: Can-annular type, with 12 flame tubes fitted with duplex burners.

FUEL GRADE: T-1 and TS-1 to GOST 10227-62 (equivalent to DERD.2494 or MIL-F-5616).

TURBINE: HP turbine has two axial stages. First stage has cooled blades in both stator and rotor. LP turbine also has two stages. All discs are aircooled on both sides, and all blades are shrouded to improve efficiency and reduce vibration. All shaft bearings are shock-mounted.

JET PIPE: Subsonic fixed-area type, incorporating main and by-pass flow mixer with curvilinear ducts of optimum shape.

LUBRICATION: Open type, with oil returned to tank.

OIL GRADE: Mineral oil MK-8 or MK-8P to GOST 6457-66 (equivalent to DERD.2490 or MIL-O-6081B). Consumption in flight not over 2·2 lb (1·0 kg)/hr.

ACCESSORIES: Automatic ice-protection system, fire extinguishing for core and by-pass flows, vibration detectors on casings, oil chip detectors and automatic limitation of exhaust gas temperature to 620°C at take-off or when starting and to 630°C in flight (5 min limit). Shaft-driven accessories driven via radial bevel-gear shafts in centre casing, mainly off HP spool, accessory gearboxes being provided above and below centre casing and fan duct.

STARTING: Electric DC starting system incorporating STG-12TVMO starter/generators.

DIMENSIONS:
- Overall length 156·8 in (3,983 mm)
- Base diameter of inlet casing 41·3 in (1,050 mm)

WEIGHT, DRY: 3,417 lb (1,550 kg)

PERFORMANCE RATINGS:
- T-O 14,990 lb (6,800 kg) st
- Long-range cruise rating, 36,000 ft (11,000 m) and Mach 0·75 2,866 lb (1,300 kg) st

SPECIFIC FUEL CONSUMPTION:
- T-O 0·62
- Cruise, as above 0·77

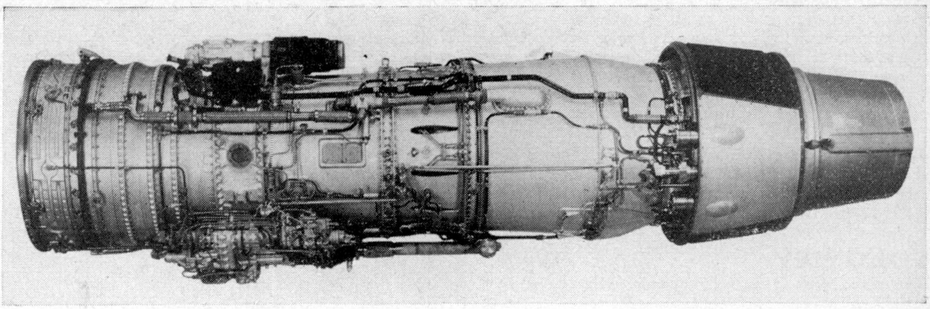

Soloviev D-30 turbofan (14,990 lb; 6,800 kg st) with thrust reverser

Soloviev D-30KU turbofan (25,350 lb; 11,500 kg st)

D-30K

Despite its designation, this turbofan engine is very different from the D-30 described previously. It is larger, has a much higher rating, has a by-pass ratio of 2·3 : 1, mass flow of 600 lb/sec (272 kg/sec) and an overall pressure ratio of 20 : 1.

The D-30K has a three-stage axial-flow fan/LP compressor driven by a four-stage LP turbine and an eleven-stage HP compressor driven by a two-stage HP turbine, of which the first stage is cooled. A cannular-type combustion chamber, with 12 flame tubes, is used.

The basic **D-30KU** version, to which the specification details below apply, has replaced the Kuznetsov NK-8 as power plant of the developed Ilyushin Il-62M airliner and the Tupolev Tu-154A.

A new version of this turbofan, designated **D-30KP** and rated at 26,455 lb (12,000 kg) st, powers the Ilyushin Il-76 freight transport, due to enter Aeroflot service in mid-1974, and the Il-86 four-engined airliner expected to fly in 1975. Clamshell-type thrust reversers are fitted to all four engines of both aircraft, and to the outer engines of the Il-62M and Tu-154A. These reversers are not an integral part of the engine but are airframe assemblies incorporated in the nacelle.

DIMENSIONS:
- Length 181·5 in (4,610 mm)
- Length with exhaust nozzle 226·7 in (5,760 mm)
- Diameter, inside intake 57·3 in (1,455 mm)
- Max diameter 61·4 in (1,560 mm)

WEIGHT, DRY:
- Without reverser 4,740 lb (2,150 kg)
- With thrust reverser 5,291 lb (2,400 kg)

PERFORMANCE RATINGS:
- T-O at ISA 25,350 lb (11,500 kg) st
- Nominal (1 hr) 20,944 lb (9,500 kg) st
- Max cruise at 36,000 ft (11,000 m) and Mach 0·8 6,063 lb (2,750 kg) st

SPECIFIC FUEL CONSUMPTION:
- At T-O rating 0·49
- At nominal rating (1 hr) 0·48
- At max cruise at 36,000 ft (11,000 m) and Mach 0·8 0·67

TUMANSKY

GENERAL DESIGNER IN CHARGE OF BUREAU:
Not known

Academician Sergei K. Tumansky, who died in 1973, left a legacy of turbojet engines which were the propulsion basis on which the MiG bureau created the MiG-21, in worldwide service, and the extremely high-performance MiG-25. Tumansky is believed also to have designed the engine of the MiG-23. Previously the bureau had provided the engine used in the Yak-30 and Yak-32 jet trainer prototypes.

TUMANSKY R-11 and R-13

Designated TRD Mk R37F (turbojet R37F) by the Soviet armed forces, the R-11/R-13 family have been built in enormous numbers, and two versions have been licence-built by HAL in India. At least one version has probably gone into production, without a licence, in China.

A single-shaft turbojet with afterburner, the R-11 entered production in 1956 with dry and afterburning ratings of 8,600 lb (3,900 kg) and 11,240 lb (5,100 kg) respectively. In 1959 a world speed record was set by the E-66, powered by an R-11-F2-300, with the same dry rating but a new afterburner giving a maximum thrust of 13,120 lb (5,950 kg). This engine also powered the production variant of the E-66, the MiG-21F, as well as the MiG-21PF, FM, FL and possibly other versions.

A very similar engine is the R-11-F2S-300, which powers the Indian-built MiG-21M. It is believed that versions of the R-11 power all known versions of the twin-engined Yak-28.

The R-13-300 incorporates major changes to handle an increased airflow, and has dry and afterburning ratings of 11,240 lb (5,100 kg) and 14,550 lb (6,600 kg) respectively. It powers the latest known MiG-21 versions, including the MF. It is believed not to be installationally interchangeable with the R-11 series.

TUMANSKY MiG-25 ENGINE

In about 1961 the Tumansky bureau began the design of a jet engine with afterburner considerably more powerful than the R-11 and intended for flight at speeds higher than Mach 3. This engine was adopted by the MiG bureau for the MiG-25 twin-engined fighter. Existence of this Mach 3·2 aircraft was disclosed in April 1965 when its first world record was announced. At that time the aircraft was referred to as the E-266, and its engine as the TRD Mk 31. Thrust rating was given as 22,046 lb (10,000 kg). It is believed that production MiG-25 fighter and reconnaissance aircraft are powered by an advanced version of this engine with a maximum rating of 24,250 lb (11,000 kg). No details of the engine are known in the West, but it is believed to be a two-shaft turbofan. The large afterburner exhausts through an advanced con-di nozzle. It is possible that the same engine powers the single-engined MiG-23 variable-geometry all-weather fighter.

VEDENEEV

GENERAL DESIGNER IN CHARGE OF BUREAU:
Ivan M. Vedeneev

This designer was responsible for the improvement and development of certain models of the AI-14 piston engine designed by the Ivchenko bureau. He now heads his own bureau and this has produced the engine described below:

M-14V-26

Derived from the Ivchenko AI-14 family of engines for fixed-wing aircraft, the M-14V-26 powers the Kamov Ka-26 helicopter. In this installation the stub-wing carries an engine on each tip. Beneath the rotor an R-26 gearbox combines the power of the engines and distributes it equally between the two co-axial main rotors turning in opposite directions.

It is said to incorporate all the experience gained in many years of developing engines in this class, and shows numerous areas of refinement compared with the AI-14 series. The engine has forced cooling by an axial fan driven via a friction clutch and extension shaft ahead of the main output bevel box at 1·452 times crankshaft speed. The engine planetary gearbox has a ratio of 0·309 and incorporates friction and ratchet clutches. The central R-26 gearbox has a ratio of 0·34; it also drives the generator, hydraulic pump, oil pump and tachometer generator.

DIMENSIONS:
- Diameter 38·78 in (985 mm)
- Length 45·08 in (1,145 mm)

WEIGHT, DRY: 540 lb (245 kg)

PERFORMANCE RATINGS:
- T-O 325 hp at 2,800 rpm
- Max continuous I 275 hp at 2,450 rpm
- Max continuous II 190 hp at 2,350 rpm
- Cruise I 190 hp at 2,350 rpm
- Cruise II 145 hp at 2,350 rpm

SPECIFIC FUEL CONSUMPTION:
- At cruise ratings 0·46 lb (0·210 kg)/hp/hr

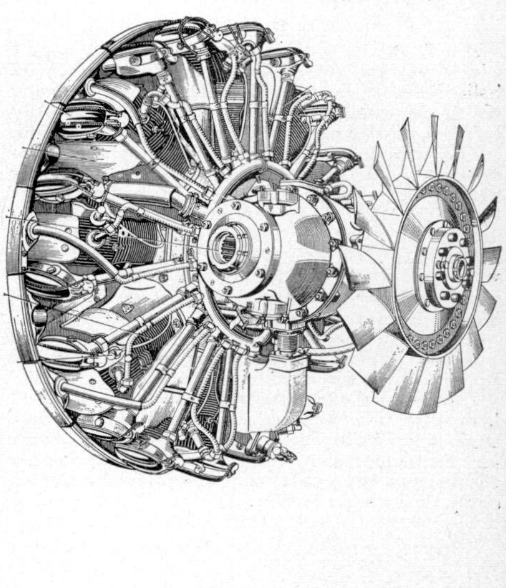

Vedeneev M-14V-26 radial piston engine, with cooling fan, for Kamov Ka-26 helicopter

ENGINES OF UNKNOWN DESIGN

1. **Type D-15.** This was given as the designation of the four turbojet engines fitted in the Myasishchev 103-M and 201-M (modified Mya-4) aircraft which set up a number of closed-circuit and payload-to-height records in 1959. At a rating of 28,660 lb (13,000 kg) st, the D-15 was one of the most powerful turbojet engines to have flown at that time.

2. **GRD Mk U2.** The rocket engine fitted to the Mikoyan E-66A aircraft which set up a world height record in April 1961 carries this designation. It develops 6,615 lb (3,000 kg) thrust, presumably at sea level.

3. **TRD Mk P.166/TRD 31.** P.166 is the designation given to the 22,046 lb (10,000 kg) st turbojet engine fitted in the Mikoyan E-166 aircraft that held the world's absolute speed record. The same rating is quoted for the TRD 31 turbojet fitted in the T-431 aircraft, implying that the designation is related to the aircraft in which the engine is fitted; and the TRD Mk P.166 and TRD 31 are almost certainly versions of the same turbojet. Afterburning provides a 50 per cent thrust boost, static.

4. **RU-19-300.** An auxiliary turbojet of 1,985 lb (900 kg) st for which the only known application is in the Antonov An-24RV transport. Mounted in the rear of the starboard nacelle in place of the TG-16 APU, the RU-19-300 provides additional take-off thrust and also drives an integrally-mounted generator to relieve the aircraft's AI-24T turboprops of supplying electrical power during take-off. This arrangement increases the An-24RV's take-off performance under hot and high conditions, and improves single-engine handling and stability. After take-off, the auxiliary turbojet is shut down and the AI-24Ts are coupled mechanically to the engine-mounted generators. In this dual role the RU-19-300 provides 485 lb (220 kg) st for take-off. During flight the auxiliary turbojet is available for use as an APU.

RU-19-300 auxiliary turbojet (1,985 lb; 900 kg st) installed in Antonov An-24RV to provide take-off boost and electrical supply

5. **Lift-Jet.** Russian development of lift-jet engines (possibly by modification of existing small turbojets) was demonstrated at the 1967 Domodedovo air show by one Sukhoi and two Mikoyan experimental STOL aircraft.

6. **Lift/Cruise Engine.** The Yak-36 V/STOL research aircraft demonstrated at the 1967 Domodedovo air show was powered by a twin-nozzle vectored-thrust propulsion system. The use of a large bifurcated nose intake and only two exhaust nozzles suggests that the installation may have used two standard turbojets or turbofans fitted with single swivelling nozzles.

ADDENDA

AUSTRALIA

GOVERNMENT OF AUSTRALIA

GAF NOMAD

Orders up to August 1974 included 11 for the Australian Army, 12 for the Philippine Air Force, four for the Indonesian Navy, two for the Peruvian Army, and one each for Aeromaritime Italia and Nationwide Air Services of Australia.

In addition, six N24s, the first of this version to be ordered, are to be delivered for aeromedical duties to the Northern Territory Aerial Medical Service.

BRAZIL

AEROTEC

AEROTEC 122 UIRAPURU

Deliveries began in April 1974 of 18 Uirapurus ordered by the Bolivian Air Force.

CANADA

DE HAVILLAND CANADA

It was announced in the Spring of 1974 that the Canadian government was to exercise its option to purchase the shares of de Havilland Canada at present held by the Hawker Siddeley Group. The government will operate the company on an interim basis only, the intention being to seek responsible Canadian interests to purchase and operate the company.

DHC-5 BUFFALO

Three customers, including the Zaïre Air Force, are reported to have ordered a total of 15 Buffalos of the DHC-5D version.

DHC-7 DASH 7

AirWest of Vancouver, the first domestic customer, has ordered two. The United Aircraft of Canada PT6A-50 engine, which has been chosen as power plant for the Dash 7, began flight testing in 1974 installed in the nose of a specially-modified Viscount aircraft.

Ex-Air Canada Viscount testbed for the UACL PT6A-50 engine intended to power the de Havilland Canada DHC-7 "quiet STOL" transport

FRANCE

AÉROSPATIALE

AÉROSPATIALE SA 350

On 26 June 1974, Aérospatiale flew for the first time, at Marignane, a prototype lightweight research helicopter designated SA 350. No details were made available; but the company is reported to plan the eventual development of single-engined SA 370 and twin-engined SA 375 three/four-seat production versions, powered by Wankel-type rotary engines and making extensive use of plastics construction.

ARTS ET MÉTIERS

Interest in the possibility of constructing a two-seat training aircraft at the École Nationale Supérieure d'Arts et Métiers at Cluny dates from 1965. Work on a prototype, designated AM-69, began in 1969, on the basis of plans of a light aircraft known as the Gaucher RG-662 and design studies and experiments conducted at the school. Some 3,000 hours of design and testing by a group of twelve students, and 4,000 hours of construction by ten other students, went into this all-wooden prototype (F-PTXB), which flew for the first time on 6 May 1973.

It was certificated by the CNRA in July 1973, and was placed subsequently at the disposal of members of the Aero Club of Issoudun. The designers are, meanwhile, working on an all-metal version, with larger vertical tail surfaces, a moulded canopy, revised engine cowling and other changes. Plans of this version will be made available to amateur constructors through the RSA.

AM-69

The AM-69 is a tandem two-seat low-wing monoplane of all-wood construction. The main landing gear was modified from that of a Robin DR 220; the tailwheel is from a Stampe. Control surfaces are actuated by rods, except for the rudder which is cable-actuated. The power plant is a 90 hp Continental C90-14F four-cylinder horizontally-opposed aircooled piston engine, driving a two-blade ground-adjustable Ratier propeller. Fuel tanks, capacity 18·5 Imp gallons (84 litres), are in the wings. When flown solo, the pilot occupies the front seat.

Arts et Métiers AM-69 two-seat light aircraft (*Aviation Magazine International*)

DIMENSIONS, EXTERNAL:
- Wing span: 29 ft 4 in (8·94 m)
- Length overall: 25 ft 11 in (7·90 m)

AREA:
- Wings, gross: 120·5 sq ft (11·20 m²)

WEIGHTS:
- Weight empty: 1,155 lb (524 kg)
- Max T-O weight: 1,605 lb (728 kg)

PERFORMANCE:
- Max level speed 105 knots (121 mph; 195 km/h)
- Normal cruising speed: 86 knots (99 mph; 160 km/h)
- Stalling speed: 46 knots (53 mph; 85 km/h)
- Max rate of climb at S/L: 590 ft (180 m)min
- Service ceiling: 11,500 ft (3,500 m)
- T-O run: 1,640 ft (500 m)
- Landing run: 1,250 ft (380 m)
- Range with max fuel: 323 nm (373 miles; 600 km)

CHASLE

YVES CHASLE

Members of the Aero Club Léon Morane, most of whom are employed by Socata, are completing the prototype of a side-by-side two-seat light aircraft designed by Yves Chasle (page 54). Designated LMC-1, it is a conventional all-metal low-wing monoplane, with non-retractable tricycle landing gear, flaps, swept vertical tail surfaces, one-piece horizontal tail surfaces with tab, and an enclosed cockpit. Power plant is an unspecified 90 hp horizontally-opposed piston engine.

DASSAULT-BREGUET

The Head Office of this organisation has been transferred to:
27 rue du Professeur Pauchet, 92420-Vaucresson
Telephone: 970-75-21

DASSAULT MIRAGE F1

According to French press sources, a total of 228 Mirage F1s had been ordered by mid-1974, as follows: France 105, Greece 40, Kuwait 20, South Africa 48 and Spain 15.

DASSAULT SUPER ETENDARD

Two prototypes are being produced, by converting existing Etendard IV airframes. These are now expected to make their first flights in December 1974 and March 1975 respectively.

DASSAULT-BREGUET ATLANTIC Mk II

On 19 July 1974, Dassault-Breguet delivered the 18th Breguet 1150 Atlantic maritime patrol aircraft ordered by the Italian government. This completed the production programme for 87 operational Atlantics of the current, basic type.

The French government has authorised development of an Atlantic Mk II to meet the anticipated Aéronavale requirement for 50 uprated aircraft of this type for service by the late 'seventies. Design studies for the Mk II have been underway for some time, and the 04 prototype of the Atlantic is to be returned to the manufacturers in late 1974 for conversion to Mk II standard. Following a general refurbishment, the aircraft's entire weapon system will be removed and replaced by new equipment. This is expected to place primary emphasis on the location and destruction of surface targets, while retaining anti-submarine capability.

Atlantic Mk II equipment will include an inertial navigator, Doppler, an advanced radar, digital processing of sonobuoy information, an improved magnetic anomaly detector, passive electronics surveillance devices, and a central data processor. Current anti-submarine weapons will be supplemented by the AS.37 Martel anti-radiation missile and the AM.39 Exocet, with possible provision for the long-range Otomat.

The prototype Atlantic Mk II is expected to fly for the first time during the first quarter of 1976. Aéronavale is expected to require about 50, of which deliveries could begin in 1977.

Dassault-Breguet is also studying an Atlantic Mk II-B, which would have the standard Tyne turboprop engines supplemented by two Rolls-Royce/SNECMA M45H turbofans, mounted in underwing pods outboard of the turboprop nacelles. These would permit an increase of max T-O weight to 115,745 lb (52,500 kg), including 13,225 lb (6,000 kg) of additional fuel to extend the aircraft's patrol endurance and range.

DASSAULT-BREGUET FALCON 50

The decision to build a prototype of the extended-range three-engined Falcon 50 was announced at the end of May 1974, when the anticipated first flight date was given as Autumn 1975. The aircraft is being manufactured at Bordeaux-Mérignac with the collaboration of Aérospatiale, which will supply the fuselage, tail-fin and horizontal tail surfaces.

Many components of the Falcon 50 will be identical with those of the twin-turbofan Falcon 20 Series F, including the front and centre fuselage sections, the wings complete with high-lift systems, and the horizontal tail surfaces. The Messier landing gear will differ only in being strengthened to cater for a higher gross weight.

Basic accommodation will be for eight or ten passengers in a high standard of comfort, as in the Falcon 20. A major change will be the introduction of a very large fuselage fuel tank of around 748 Imp gallons (3,400 litres) capacity, aft of the coat-rack and toilet compartment, on the aircraft's CG. Between this additional tankage and the rear pressure bulkhead will be a two-deck baggage compartment of 70 cu ft (2·0 m³) capacity. These changes, and others associated with the installation of the centre engine, will require lengthening of the fuselage by nearly 8 ft 2½ in (2·50 m) by comparison with the Falcon 20. The vertical tail surfaces will also be considerably larger.

Power plant will comprise three Garrett AiResearch TFE 731-3 turbofan engines, each rated at 3,700 lb (1,680 kg) st for take-off. Two will be pod-mounted on the sides of the rear fuselage; the third will be housed in the fuselage tailcone, with the customary over-fuselage air intake forward of the base of the fin.

Dassault-Breguet will produce airframes for static and fatigue testing, and hopes to supplement the prototype with the first two production aircraft to speed certification. By mid-1974, fifteen potential operators had taken options on Falcon 50s.

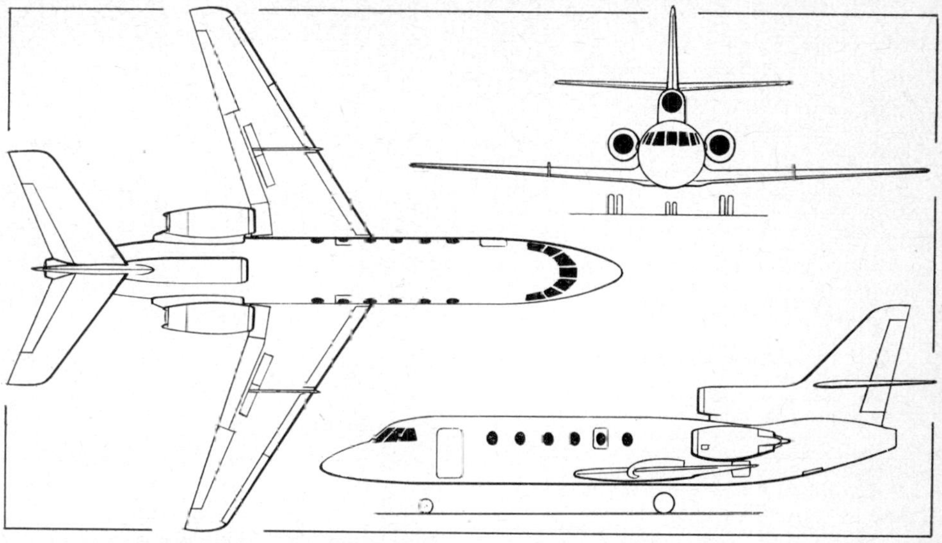

Dassault-Breguet Falcon 50 extended-range three-turbofan light transport *(Pilot Press)*

DIMENSIONS, EXTERNAL:
- Wing span 53 ft 6½ in (16·32 m)
- Length overall 64 ft 5 in (19·64 m)

DIMENSIONS, INTERNAL:
- Cabin: Length 23 ft 2¾ in (7·08 m)
- Height 5 ft 8 in (1·72 m)

WEIGHTS:
- Weight empty, equipped 19,180 lb (8,700 kg)
- Max fuel 14,550 lb (6,600 kg)
- Max T-O weight 36,375 lb (16,500 kg)
- Max landing weight 33,070 lb (15,000 kg)
- Max zero-fuel weight 22,045 lb (10,000 kg)

PERFORMANCE (estimated):
- Max cruising speed Mach 0·8, or 470 knots (540 mph; 870 km/h)
- FAR 25 balanced field length with 6 passengers and fuel for max range 5,740 ft (1,750 m)
- FAR 121 landing distance with 6 passengers and reserves 3,610 ft (1,100 m)
- Range at Mach 0·75 with 6 passengers and FAR 121 reserves 2,700 nm (3,100 miles; 5,000 km)

FLEURY
ROBERT FLEURY

ADDRESS:
2152 route de Chartres, 45-Saran

Following his design and construction of an aircraft named the Vedette in the mid-fifties, Robert Fleury has built a two-seat high-wing monoplane which won the Coupe de l'Aéro-Club du Gatinais at the RSA meeting at Montargis in the Summer of 1973.

FLEURY RF-21 TRIMARD

The general appearance of the Trimard is shown in the accompanying illustration. It is a strut-braced high-wing monoplane of conventional layout, with non-retractable tailwheel-type landing gear. The enclosed cabin seats two persons side by side; the power plant is an 80 hp Hirth piston engine, driving a two-blade fixed-pitch propeller. No other details are available.

Fleury RF-21 Trimard two-seat homebuilt light aircraft (80 hp Hirth engine) *(F. E. v. Bruggen)*

FOURNIER
AVIONS FOURNIER

HEAD OFFICE AND WORKS:
Aérodrome Athée/Nitray, 37270-Montlouis
Telephone: (47) 50-68-30

FOURNIER RF-6B CLUB

The prototype of this two-seat aerobatic aircraft flew for the first time on 12 March 1974, and certification was planned for the Autumn of 1974. A production version, with 100 hp Rolls-Royce Continental O-200-A engine, is expected to be marketed by Sportavia in Germany.

As in the case of the Sportavia RF-6 Sportsman (see pages 98 and 788), the RF-6B was designed by M René Fournier. It is similar to the RF-6 in general configuration but, although having a wing of increased span and area, it is a somewhat smaller aircraft with a less powerful engine.

Intended primarily for use as an aerobatic or training aircraft, it is stressed to + 9*g* and — 4·5*g*.

TYPE: Two-seat aerobatic, training and sporting aircraft.

WINGS: Cantilever low-wing monoplane. Wing section NACA 23015 at root, NACA 23013 at tip. Dihedral 3° 30′. Incidence 3°. All-wood single-spar structure with plywood and Dacron covering. Frise-type ailerons of wooden construction, Dacron covered. Plain trailing-edge flaps of wooden construction with Dacron covering. No trim tabs.

FUSELAGE: All-wood oval structure, plywood covered.

TAIL UNIT: Cantilever structure of wood with Dacron covering. Fixed-incidence tailplane. Trim tab in port elevator.

LANDING GEAR: Non-retractable tricycle type. Oleo-pneumatic shock-absorbers on all units. Steerable nosewheel. Main-wheel tyres size 380-150. Nosewheel tyre size 300-100. Hydraulic disc brakes.

POWER PLANT: One 90 hp Rolls-Royce Continental four-cylinder horizontally-opposed aircooled engine, driving a Hoffmann two-blade metal fixed-pitch propeller with spinner. Fuselage fuel tank, immediately aft of firewall, capacity 17·6 Imp gallons (80 litres). Refuelling point on fuselage upper surface, forward of windscreen. Oil capacity 0·88 Imp gallons (4 litres).

Fournier RF-6B, a two-seat development of the 2+2 RF-6 *(Brian M. Service)*

ACCOMMODATION: Two seats side by side under transparent canopy, which swings upward and aft for access to cockpit. Dual controls standard. Cockpit heated and ventilated. Baggage space aft of seats.

SYSTEMS: Hydraulic system for brakes only. Electrical power supplied by 12V engine-driven alternator.

ELECTRONICS AND EQUIPMENT: Nav and com radios optional. Blind flying instrumentation optional.

DIMENSIONS, EXTERNAL:
- Wing span 34 ft 5½ in (10·50 m)
- Wing chord at root 5 ft 0¼ in (1·53 m)
- Wing chord at tip 2 ft 8¾ in (0·83 m)
- Length overall 22 ft 11½ in (7·00 m)
- Height overall 7 ft 9¼ in (2·37 m)
- Tailplane span 11 ft 1¾ in (3·40 m)
- Propeller diameter 5 ft 9 in (1·75 m)
- Propeller ground clearance 11 in (0·28 m)

AREAS:
- Wings, gross 139·9 sq ft (13·00 m²)
- Ailerons (total) 11·52 sq ft (1·07 m²)
- Trailing-edge flaps (total) 16·36 sq ft (1·52 m²)
- Rudder 7·97 sq ft (0·74 m²)
- Tailplane 17·76 sq ft (1·65 m²)
- Elevators (including tab) 10·76 sq ft (1·00 m²)

WEIGHTS AND LOADINGS:
- Weight empty 1,047 lb (475 kg)
- Max T-O weight: Aerobatic 1,444 lb (655 kg)
- Utility 1,631 lb (740 kg)
- Max wing loading 14·4 lb/sq ft (70·4 kg/m²)
- Max power loading 18·12 lb/hp (8·22 kg/hp)

PERFORMANCE (at max T-O weight):
Max cruising speed at S/L
113 knots (130 mph; 210 km/h)
Econ cruising speed at S/L
102 knots (118 mph; 190 km/h)
Stalling speed
46 knots (53 mph; 85 km/h)
Service ceiling 13,125 ft (4,000 m)
T-O to 50 ft (15 m) 950 ft (290 m)
Landing from 50 ft (15 m) 820 ft (250 m)
Landing run, no braking 655 ft (200 m)

LEBOUDER
ROBERT LEBOUDER

ADDRESS:
12 rue Louis Marteau, 95-Garges les Gonesse

M Lebouder has designed and built a highly successful aircraft known as the Autoplane, which embodies a two-seat roadable motor car. This was flown to, and demonstrated at, the RSA meetings at Montdidier and Montargis in the second half of 1973, gaining for its constructor the Prix des Horloges Huchez, Prix Gazuit, Prix du SFA and the Coupe de l'Aéro Club de France.

LEBOUDER AUTOPLANE

Few details of the Autoplane (F-PTES) are available, but its general appearance is shown in the accompanying illustrations. In flight, it appears to be a conventional single-engined strut-braced high-wing monoplane, with non-retractable tailwheel-type landing gear. In fact, the airframe, comprising the wings, rear fuselage and tail unit, is detachable as an integral assembly on the ground. After removal of the two-blade propeller, the forward part of the fuselage "converts" into a Vespa 400 two-seat motor car. The transformation takes two persons about 32 minutes to effect.

The main landing gear units of the aircraft pivot forward to become the front wheels of the car. The rear motor car wheels retract upward into the "aircraft" for flight. The separate aircraft and motor car engines and systems are carried at all times by the car component. On the ground, the propeller is replaced by a grille embodying headlights, direction indicators, a number plate and bumpers. Road speed of the car is 43 mph (70 km/h).

Top: **Lebouder Autoplane homebuilt light aircraft, embodying a Vespa 400 two-seat car for road travel** (*F. E. v. Bruggen*)

Right: **Preparing the car component of the Lebouder Autoplane for assembly to the airframe** (*Aviation Magazine International*)

WASSMER
WASSMER WA 70

A model of this new side-by-side two-seat trainer was displayed by Wassmer at the General Aviation Show at Toussus-le-Noble in mid-1974. Configuration is conventional, except that the WA 70 will have a T-tail. The power plant is an unspecified 90 hp horizontally-opposed piston engine. Construction—as in the case of other current Wassmer light aircraft—may be of plastics. The non-retractable tricycle landing gear will utilise cantilever non-rigid main legs instead of shock-absorbers. No other details are available, except that a prototype is under construction.

GERMANY
RFB

Rhein Flugzeugbau is the sales and service representative in the Federal Republic of Germany for the Mitsubishi MU-2 twin-turboprop utility STOL transport, designed by the Japanese Mitsubishi company (which see).

The MU-2J and MU-2K which are available for the German market are assembled at Mitsubishi Aircraft International's plant at San Angelo, Texas (which see in US aircraft section).

SPORTAVIA
SPORTAVIA FOURNIER RF-6 SPORTSMAN

Production models of the RF-6 Sportsman are now powered by the 150 hp Lycoming O-320-A2B four-cylinder horizontally-opposed aircooled engine, resulting in weight and performance details as follows:

WEIGHTS AND LOADINGS:
Weight empty 1,168 lb (530 kg)
Max T-O weight 1,984 lb (900 kg)
Max wing loading 14·7 lb/sq ft (71·6 kg/m²)
Max power loading 13·23 lb/hp (6 kg/hp)

PERFORMANCE (at max T-O weight):
Max level speed at S/L
135 knots (155 mph; 250 km/h)
Max cruising speed at S/L
108 knots (124 mph; 200 km/h)
Landing speed 41 knots (47 mph; 76 km/h)
Max rate of climb at S/L
748 ft (228 m)/min
Service ceiling 13,125 ft (4,000 m)
T-O run 655 ft (200 m)
T-O to 50 ft (15 m) 1,575 ft (480 m)
Landing from 50 ft (15 m) 1,180 ft (360 m)
Landing run 655 ft (200 m)
Range 453 nm (522 miles; 840 km)

Sportavia Fournier RF-6 Sportsman (*J. M. G. Gradidge*)

VFW-FOKKER
VFW-FOKKER VAK 191 B

The three VAK 191 B prototypes were in mid-1974 due to begin a 12-month programme of flight testing, under joint US Navy/VFW-Fokker supervision, to provide research data for future US Navy aircraft.

INDIA
HAL
HAL HA-31 Mk II BASANT

Handover of the first eight production Basants to the Indian Ministry of Food and Agriculture was made on 21 June 1974.

INTERNATIONAL
PANAVIA
PANAVIA MRCA

Panavia 200 MRCA, photographed during its first flight on 14 August 1974

The first MRCA prototype (D-9591), following the start of taxying tests on 1 August 1974, made a successful 30-minute first flight on 14 August, during which the wings remained in the fully-forward position.

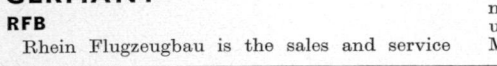

SEPECAT

SEPECAT JAGUAR

Jaguar International. This export version of the Jaguar was announced by BAC on 28 August 1974, with the news of orders worth £80 million from two overseas customers. One of these was later identified as the Sultan of Oman's Air Force, which has ordered 12; the other is the Ecuadorean Air Force. The Jaguar International differs little from the standard single-seat Jaguar S except in having a more powerful version of the Adour turbofan engine—the RT.172-26 Adour Mk 804 which increases total S/L thrust at Mach 0·8/0·9 by 27 per cent and T-O thrust by nearly 10 per cent. All export Jaguars will be fitted with these engines, and other customer options being developed include overwing pylons compatible with Magic or other dogfight missiles; a multi-purpose nose radar; anti-shipping weapons such as Exocet and Kormoran; and night sensors such as low light level television.

ITALY

AERMACCHI

AERMACCHI M.B. 326

M.B. 326E. Advanced trainer version, for service with the Italian Air Force's Scuola di Volo Basico Iniziale at Lecce. Similar to standard M.B. 326 with Viper 11 engine, but with the strengthened wings and six underwing hardpoints of the M.B. 326GB. New electronics and equipment include UHF radio, miniaturised TACAN, gyroscopic sight and camera gun. Twelve ordered, of which six will be conversions of existing M.B. 326s and six of new construction.

ITALAIR

The following revised list of appointments was announced in mid-1974:

President:
Mario Del Bianco

Directors:
Dott Gr Uff Nando Benini
Dott Ing Giorgio Lucarelli
Dott Ing Benito Casinghini
Dott Ferruccio Lanata
Elfo Frignani
Giustino Meneghini

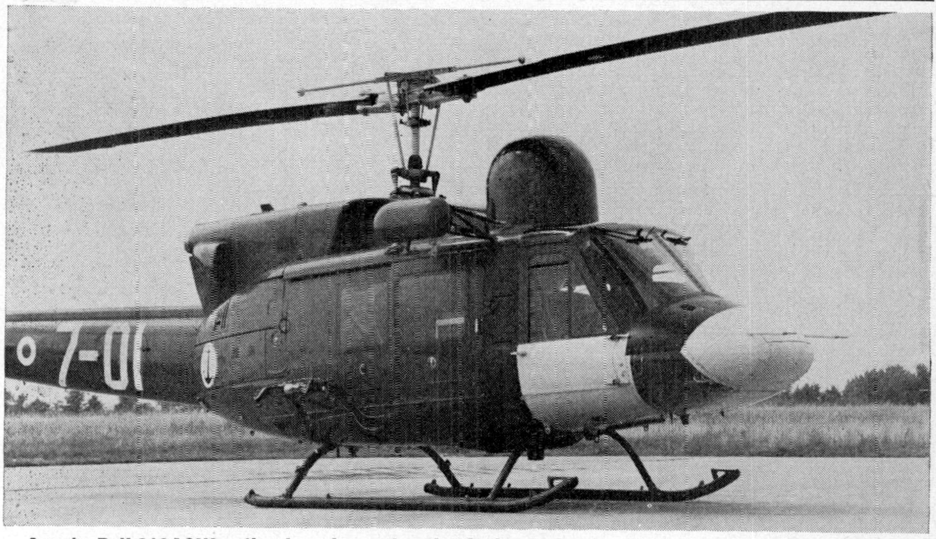

Agusta-Bell 212ASW anti-submarine and anti-shipping helicopter, first of 28 ordered for the Italian Navy

JAPAN

FUJI

FUJI FA-300

Design and development of the FA-300 is now to proceed as a collaborative venture between Fuji and Rockwell International, following the signing of an agreement between the two companies on 28 June 1974.

The FA-300 will be a six/eight-seat business aircraft, with a low wing, a pressurised cabin, and a power plant of two 360 hp Lycoming IGSO-540-A1D engines. It will be available in the US, with a choice of power plants, under the Rockwell designations Commander 700 and Commander 710. Development costs, estimated at $10 million, will be shared 60 per cent by Fuji and 40 per cent by Rockwell International.

Fuji will undertake the basic design and the construction of two prototypes of the standard version, the first of which is expected to fly in late 1975. Rockwell will design and test optional alternative versions. There will eventually be final assembly lines in both Japan and the US, although Rockwell will have overall responsibility for series production.

KAWASAKI

KAWASAKI KH-7

The basic configuration of this 10-seat medium-sized helicopter, the first of wholly Japanese design, was reported to have been finalised by mid-1974, and construction of the rotor system has begun. This will be a four-blade rigid rotor, and will be driven by a pair of 592 shp Lycoming LTS 101 turboshaft engines. First flight is scheduled for late 1975.

MITSUBISHI

MITSUBISHI MU-2

Total sales of the MU-2 (all versions) had reached 363 by 30 June 1974, including 32 to Japanese and 306 to US customers, and 19 in Europe.

Two new versions, the **MU-2L** and **MU-2M**, have been announced. These are, respectively, improved versions of the MU-2J and MU-2K, having new landing gear oleos and retraction mechanism, improved wing flaps, and an increase in their max T-O weights to 11,575 lb (5,250 kg) and 10,520 lb (4,770 kg) respectively. T-O rating of the engines of the MU-2L has been increased to 776 ehp, and cabin pressurisation to 6·0 lb/sq in (0·42 kg/cm²) on both models, providing a 6,700 ft (2,050 m) cabin environment at 25,000 ft (7,600 m) flight altitude.

NETHERLANDS

FOKKER-VFW

FOKKER-VFW F.27 FRIENDSHIP

Latest orders, up to 2 October 1974, are as follows:

Algerian government	3
Aramco (Mk 500)	1
Burma Airways (Mk 600)	1

This brings total sales of the F.27 series to 621, including US production.

FOKKER-VFW F.28 FELLOWSHIP

Orders for four more Fellowships were announced on 26 July 1974: three Mk 1000 aircraft for Garuda Indonesian Airways and one for an undisclosed operator. An earlier customer for one F.28 has been named as the government of the Republic of Congo.

NEW ZEALAND

AEROSPACE

AEROSPACE FLETCHER FU-24

Ten FU-24s have been ordered from New Zealand Aerospace Industries by the government of Iraq. Deliveries were due to begin in 1974.

PHILIPPINES (Republic of)

PADC

PHILIPPINE AEROSPACE DEVELOPMENT CORPORATION

Address:
Philcomcen Building, Ortigas Avenue, Pasig, Rizal

Directors:
Alejandro Melchor (Chairman and President)
Juan Ponce Enrile
Vicente Paterno
Leonides Virata
Roman Cruz

PADC is a government corporation established by President Ferdinand E. Marcos to promote the development of an aerospace industry in the Philippines. In 1974 it had already begun an assembly and manufacturing programme for the BO 105C helicopter, under a licence agreement with MBB of Germany. It is now responsible also for the newly-arranged programme to produce Britten-Norman Islander transport aircraft in the Philippines, and to develop an amphibious floatplane version of this aircraft.

Phase one of this programme was scheduled to begin in November 1974 with delivery of the first of six 300 hp Islanders to PADC. The second phase will involve 14 unpainted aircraft, which will be delivered to Manila without cabin trim, furnishings, and avionics. PADC will complete these aircraft at the rate of one a month from February 1975, with the rate increasing to two a month by May. The whole phase will be completed by December 1975.

The 20 aircraft involved in phase three will be assembled by PADC from knocked-down kits supplied by Britten-Norman and shipped to the Philippines. The final phase will include the manufacture of subassemblies and other aircraft components, using jigs and detailed parts supplied from the United Kingdom.

Of the 60 aircraft to be assembled in phase four, about 25 will be repurchased by Britten-Norman for sale throughout the world.

Once the amphibious floatplane version of the Islander is operational, PADC will become the sole installation centre for the floats in Australasia.

Philippine Aerotransport, a PADC subsidiary, will operate most of the Islander aircraft acquired through the programme.

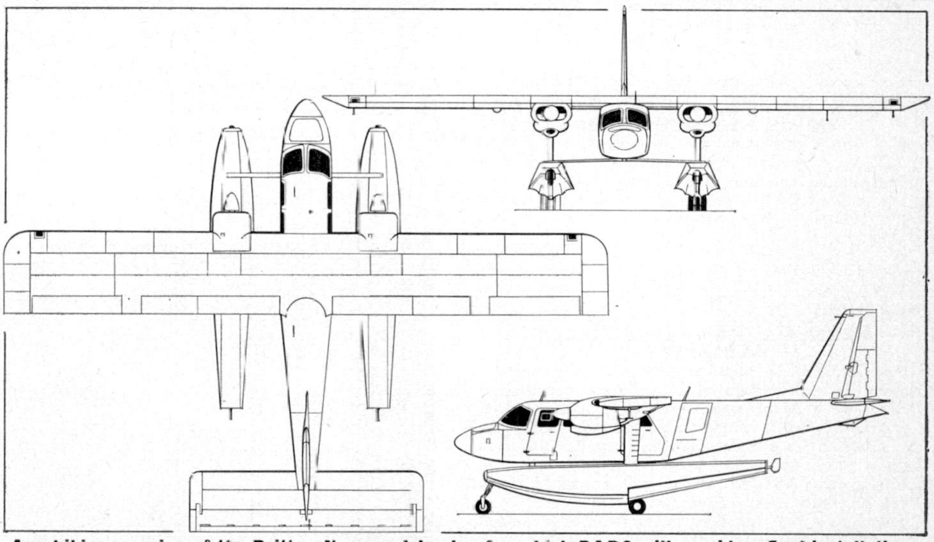

Amphibious version of the Britten-Norman Islander, for which PADC will provide a float installation centre (*Pilot Press*)

SWEDEN

SAAB-SCANIA

Saab has given the name **Eurofighter** to its proposed Saab 37E export version of the Viggen. The Saab-MFI 15 and 17 are now named **Safari** and **Supporter** respectively.

SAAB 37 VIGGEN

During the first week of September 1974, the Swedish Defence Materiel Administration ordered from Saab-Scania a first production batch of 30 JA 37 Viggen fighter aircraft, out of a planned total quantity of 150-200. This version is almost identical with the projected export Eurofighter.

A modified AJ 37 flew for the first time with an RM8B engine, as specified for the JA 37, on 27 September 1974. It has a similar underbelly gun installation to that on the aircraft shown in an accompanying illustration.

SAAB SUPPORTER

The Pakistan Air Force has ordered an unspecified number of Supporters to replace its T-6 primary trainers.

TAIWAN

AIDC/CAF

This Aero Industry Development Center was established on 1 March 1969 (not 1 July, as stated on page 192). The total number of UH-1H helicopters which it is producing under licence has been increased to more than 100.

UNITED KINGDOM

BAC

BAC ONE-ELEVEN

Two more One-Eleven Series 500 aircraft have been ordered by Philippine Airlines (PAL).

BRITTEN-NORMAN

BRITTEN-NORMAN ISLANDER/DEFENDER

By 3 September 1974, total sales of the Islander/Defender had reached 549, surpassing the previous record for sales of a British multi-engined civil aircraft (held by the Dove). Of this total, 486 had been delivered. These figures do not include the sales/production contract with PADC of the Philippine Republic (which see) for 100 Islanders.

Britten-Norman is developing an amphibious floatplane version of the Islander, of which a prototype is due to fly in 1975 (see drawing on page 789).

BRITTEN-NORMAN TRISLANDER

By 3 September 1974, total sales of the Trislander had reached 34, of which 18 had been delivered.

HAWKER SIDDELEY

HAWKER SIDDELEY HAWK

First flight of the first Hawk (XX154) took place on 21 August 1974.

The design max speed given for this aircraft on page 212 should be corrected to read:

516 knots (595 mph; 956 km/h) (Mach 0·9)

HAWKER SIDDELEY (HANDLEY PAGE) VICTOR Mk.2 CONVERSION

The first Victor converted by Hawker Siddeley to K Mk.2 tanker configuration (XL233) was delivered to No. 232 OCU at Marham, Norfolk, on 7 May 1974. Twenty-seven Victors are to be converted to K.2 standard.

MARSHALL

MARSHALL (HAWKER SIDDELEY) BUCCANEER

As indicated on page 220, Marshall has undertaken the conversion of two Hawker Siddeley Buccaneer S Mk.2 aircraft (XT272 and XT285) for "hack" trials work in connection with the development of avionics systems for the Panavia MRCA. The trials will be supervised by a design team from EASAMS, under the control of the Panavia flight test organisation.

Distinguishing features include an extended nose with drooped radome, extending the overall length to 67 ft 0 in (20·42 m); an underfuselage laser unit fairing; a camera-window shutter fairing on the bomb-bay door; and an underwing camera pod.

WEIGHTS:

Basic weight empty	33,509 lb (15,200 kg)
Normal T-O weight	46,193 lb (20,952 kg)
Max T-O weight	50,657 lb (22,978 kg)

M-15 turbofan-powered agricultural biplane, designed jointly by Polish and Soviet engineers, in its production form (see page 166) (*Tass*)

Saab 37 Viggen testbed for the 30 mm Oerlikon KCA internally-mounted gun specified for the JA 37 interceptor

Hawker Siddeley Hawk two-seat trainer/attack aircraft (*Air Portraits*)

Buccaneer S Mk.2 modified by Marshall of Cambridge as an MRCA avionics development aircraft

Shorts SD3-30, with wheels and flaps down, during its first test flight on 22 August 1974

SCOTTISH AVIATION

SCOTTISH AVIATION BULLDOG

Bulldog Srs 200. Version developed from Srs 120, with retractable main landing gear, new canopy, relocated firewall, increased fuel capacity, and higher aerobatic and maximum T-O weights. Intended to be available from 1976. Prototype under construction.

SHORTS

SHORTS SD3-30

The first prototype SD3-30 (G-BSBH) made its first flight on 22 August 1974. The first order was placed by Command Airways of Poughkeepsie, New York, for three aircraft plus options on two more. Time Air of Canada has ordered two for delivery in 1975.

WALLIS

WALLIS WA-116

In mid-1974 the interim WA-116/F Franklin-engined autogyro, piloted by Wg Cdr Wallis, set up (subject to confirmation) a new 100 km closed-circuit distance record of 361 nm (416 miles; 670 km). Normal fuel capacity was approximately doubled by the carriage of a ventral tank which was jettisoned after its contents had been expended.

WESTLAND

WESTLAND 606

Westland 606 is the designation of the civil version of the Lynx military helicopter, referred to briefly on page 237. It is now in an advanced stage of design; a full-size mockup has been completed, and first flight of a prototype 606 is scheduled for December 1975.

Westland anticipates an initial market for more than 100 of these aircraft, of which about half would be in the United States. The major application of the 606 is considered to be in support of worldwide offshore oil and gas industry operations, where its twin engines, semi-rigid rotor, all-weather capability and full blind-flying instrumentation, combined with an operational radius of 200 nm (230 miles; 370 km), should prove particularly advantageous.

Added features of value in such operations are the 606's automatic stabilisation equipment, optional automatic transition from cruising flight to hover, and the capability to run the main rotor in negative pitch. This last feature provides a downthrust of 4,000 lb (1,814 kg) to help hold the helicopter down on a wind-lashed rig deck.

For this role the cabin can accommodate 12 or 13 passengers, according to whether one or two pilots are carried, and can be adapted quickly to mixed passenger/cargo configurations or to a three-stretcher aeromedical configuration with space for up to four sitting patients and a medical attendant.

Alternative applications include those of business or VIP transport (typically with five or eight passenger seats), or for such public service roles as emergency rescue, coastal search and rescue, or winching operations from high-rise buildings.

Westland is investing £1 million in development of the 606, in which its French partner Aérospatiale is also taking part. Aérospatiale, which currently undertakes some 25% of the production of the military Lynx (including the monobloc rotor hub forging), would build about 20% of the Westland 606, and an eventual joint output of eight Lynx and two 606 per month is foreseen. Certification by the CAA is anticipated in 1976, with deliveries to begin in the same year, within nine months of order. Based on 1974 prices, the flyaway cost is estimated at £292,000 ($700,000).

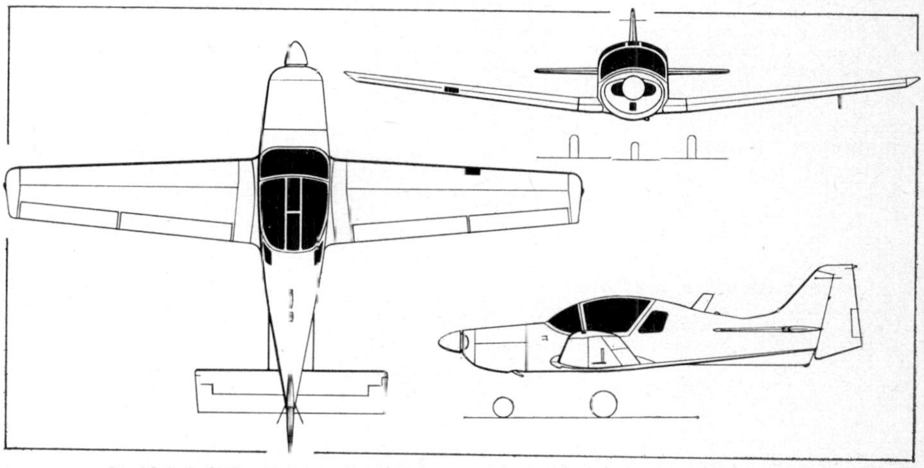

Scottish Aviation Bulldog Srs 200, with retractable landing gear *(Pilot Press)*

The same rotors, gearboxes and transmission systems will be common to both the Lynx and the 606, and most fuselage components will also be common to both types. As can be seen from the accompanying illustration, the fuselage configuration of the 606 is essentially similar to that of the Lynx, except for an increase in overall length. The 606 will be offered initially with either two 900 shp (max) Rolls-Royce Gem turboshaft engines, or with two United Aircraft of Canada PT6B-34 turboshafts having the same rating. Landing gear will be of the tubular skid type, similar to that fitted to the British Army version of the Lynx.

TYPE: Twin-turboshaft multi-purpose civil helicopter.

ROTOR SYSTEM AND ROTOR DRIVE: As for Lynx.

FUSELAGE AND TAIL UNIT: Generally similar to Lynx, possibly with greater use of glassfibre components.

POWER PLANT: Two 900 shp (max contingency rating) and 750 shp (max continuous rating) Rolls-Royce Gem or United Aircraft of Canada PT6B-34 turboshaft engines, limited to a combined transmission max rating of 1,385 shp. Standard fuel load of 1,598 lb (725 kg); max load, with auxiliary tanks, 3,196 lb (1,450 kg).

ACCOMMODATION: One or two pilots side by side on flight deck; cabin accommodation for up to 12 or 13 persons accordingly, or three stretchers, four sitting patients and a medical attendant (see introductory copy). Executive/VIP versions can be furnished with desks, tables, cabinets and other in-flight amenities to customer's requirements.

ELECTRONICS AND EQUIPMENT: Standard avionics equipment includes automatic stabilisation equipment (ASE); three-axis autopilot; acceleration control computer system for stability at high speeds; full blind-flying instrumentation; and facility to run main rotor in negative pitch. Automatic transition from cruising flight to hover available optionally. External cargo hook, stressed for loads of up to 3,000 lb (1,360 kg). Provision for quickly-installed cabin-mounted rescue hoist, hinged to swing out through side door of cabin. Other specialised equipment (eg firefighting materials, mountain rescue gear) according to role.

DIMENSIONS, EXTERNAL: As for Lynx, except:
Fuselage length, tail rotor turning
47 ft 6¾ in (14·50 m)
Height overall, both rotors turning
11 ft 10¼ in (3·61 m)

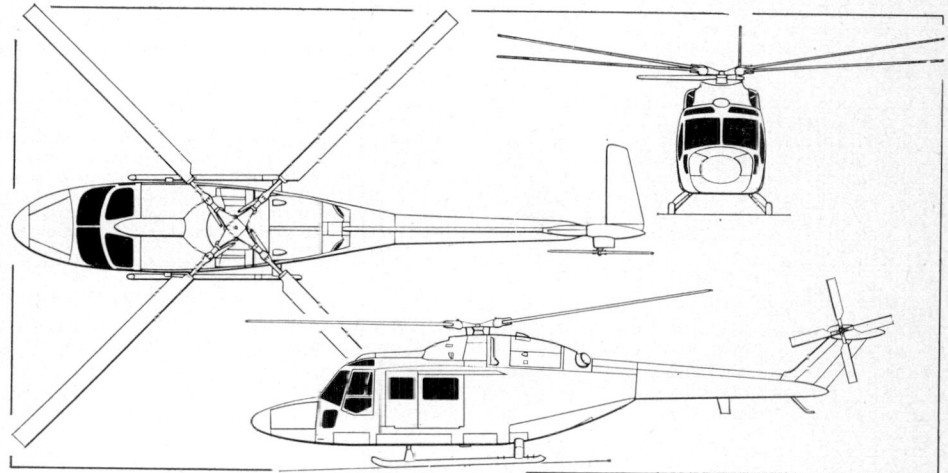

Westland 606, a fourteen-seat civil version of the Lynx *(Pilot Press)*

DIMENSIONS, INTERNAL:
Cabin: Min length 7 ft $8\frac{1}{4}$ in (2·34 m)
Max floor width 5 ft 10 in (1·78 m)
Max height 4 ft 8 in (1·42 m)
WEIGHT:
Max T-O weight 9,500 lb (4,309 kg)
PERFORMANCE (estimated, at max T-O weight except where indicated):
Max cruising speed at max T-O weight:
S/L, ISA 148 knots (170 mph; 275 km/h)
S/L, ISA + 20°C
138 knots (158 mph; 255 km/h)
at 8,200 ft (2,500 m), ISA
108 knots (124 mph; 200 km/h)
at 4,925 ft (1,500 m), ISA + 20°C
112 knots (129 mph; 208 km/h)
Max cruising speed at up to 8,000 lb (3,630 kg) AUW:
S/L, ISA 164 knots (189 mph; 303 km/h)
S/L, ISA + 20°C
164 knots (189 mph; 303 km/h)
at 8,200 ft (2,500 m), ISA
108 knots (124 mph; 200 km/h)
at 4,925 ft (1,500 m), ISA + 20°C
112 knots (129 mph; 208 km/h)
Single-engine speed range at S/L, ISA, at AUW of 9,000 lb (4,080 kg)
18-144 knots (21-166 mph; 33-267 km/h)
Hovering ceiling in ground effect:
ISA 10,660 ft (3,250 m)
ISA + 20°C 7,220 ft (2,200 m)
Hovering ceiling out of ground effect;
ISA 8,530 ft (2,600 m)
ISA + 20°C 4,590 ft (1,400 m)
Range at S/L, ISA, with allowances for T-O, landing, 15 min loiter and 5% reserve fuel:
zero payload 340 nm (390 miles; 630 km)
with 2,204 lb (1,000 kg) payload
300 nm (345 miles; 556 km)

WESTLAND/AÉROSPATIALE GAZELLE

In September 1974, Westland announced receipt of a contract for 60 Gazelle helicopters for the British Army. This order, worth more than £5 million to Westland Helicopters, brings the total number of Gazelles ordered for the UK forces to 202 and worldwide sales to 477 aircraft.

USA

ALL AMERICAN

ALL AMERICAN INDUSTRIES INC

ADDRESS:
PO Box 1247, 801 S Madison Street, Wilmington, Delaware 19899
Telephone: (302) 654-6131

ALL AMERICAN AEROCRANE

Under a \$65,000 US Navy contract, All American is developing a novel kind of lifting vehicle known as the Aerocrane. Basically, the craft consists of a helium-filled spherical balloon, having at regular intervals around its equator four narrow aerofoils similar to the blades of a helicopter; on each blade, near the tip, is mounted a power plant driving a tractor propeller. Only about 40% of the total lift is provided by the balloon component, the remainder coming from the normal rotor-like action of the rotating blades. The pitch of the blades can be varied to control ascent and descent, making it unnecessary for the balloon component to vent gas or discharge ballast during these manoeuvres. It is claimed that lifting efficiency is greater than that of a conventional helicopter, and among the civil applications foreseen are the unloading of container ships, logging operations and transportation of bulk cargo.

In May 1974 a small-scale unmanned test vehicle made its first flight. This has a 15 ft (4·57 m) diameter balloon, 9 ft (2·74 m) long rotor blades, and a $\frac{1}{4}$ hp electric motor at approx three-quarters span on each blade. Studies are under way for much larger Aerocranes, up to a 180 ft (54·86 m) balloon diameter, with 126 ft (38·40 m) long rotor blades and powered by four 4,000 shp turboprop engines. Such a craft, it is estimated, could lift a weight of up to 90 US tons (81,650 kg); spinning at 8·6 rpm, it would have a forward cruising speed of 41 knots (47 mph; 75·5 km/h). The crew would be accommodated in a non-rotating cabin suspended beneath the balloon.

AMERICAN JET INDUSTRIES

AJI has received a contract from Allegheny Airlines covering the modification and overhaul of six more Fairchild Hiller FH-227 transports (see page 246 for item on earlier contract covering four FH-227s). After conversion to all-cargo configuration, one of the FH-227s will be operated by the US Atomic Energy Commission. The other five will receive new interiors. AJI is also modifying a Convair 580 turboprop transport to cargo configuration for Allegheny.

BEECHCRAFT

BEECHCRAFT MODEL A200

This derivative of the Super King Air T-tail pressurised turboprop transport (page 264) has been selected for service with the US Army and USAF as a result of the joint-service competition for UX/CX-X aircraft, in which turbofan-powered types were also entered. The initial \$20·6 million contract, announced by Beech on 13 August 1974, covers the manufacture and support of two military versions of the A200, as follows:

C-12. USAF CX-X version, for use in air attaché military assistance groups and for cargo transportation. Fourteen ordered, with an option on 16 more.

Huron. US Army UX utility transport. Twenty ordered. Contract includes an option for both services to purchase worldwide aircraft servicing, including on-site personnel, facilities for inspection and maintenance, and for stocking spare parts at strategic points.

These aircraft are described as "standard off-the-shelf Super King Air types, modified slightly to meet military flight requirements and to orient the control systems for two-pilot operation which is standard military practice". Accommodation will be provided for eight passengers, plus two pilots, with easy conversion to cargo missions. The large baggage area will have provisions for storing survival gear.

Worldwide deployment of the C-12s and Hurons is scheduled to begin in July 1975 and to be completed by May 1976. Standard power plant will comprise two 750 shp United Aircraft of Canada PT6A-38 turboprop engines, each driving a Hartzell three-blade fully-feathering and reversible-pitch constant-speed propeller. Usable fuel capacity will be 348 US gallons (1,318 litres). In other respects, the details given for the Super King Air apply generally to the C-12 and Huron, with the following exceptions:

DIMENSIONS, EXTERNAL:
Length overall 43 ft 10 in (13·36 m)
Height overall 14 ft 10 in (4·52 m)
DIMENSIONS, INTERNAL:
Cabin: Length 16 ft 5 in (5·00 m)
WEIGHTS AND LOADINGS:
Basic empty weight 7,755 lb (3,518 kg)
Max T-O and landing weight 12,000 lb (5,443 kg)
Max ramp weight 12,085 lb (5,481 kg)
Max zero-fuel weight 10,400 lb (4,717 kg)
Max wing loading 39·6 lb/sq ft (193 kg/m²)
Max power loading 8·0 lb/shp (3·6 kg/shp)
PERFORMANCE (estimated at max T-O weight):
Max level speed at 15,000 ft (4,570 m)
263 knots (303 mph; 488 km/h)
Max cruising speed at 30,000 ft (9,140 m)
227 knots (262 mph; 421 km/h)
Service ceiling 29,200 ft (8,900 m)
Service ceiling, one engine out
17,600 ft (5,365 m)
T-O to 50 ft (15 m) 2,820 ft (860 m)
Landing from 50 ft (15 m) 2,514 ft (766 m)
Range at max cruising speed
1,085 nm (1,250 miles; 2,010 km)

BELL HELICOPTER

BELL MODEL 205

US Army contracts for 54 additional UH-1H helicopters, received on 1 October 1974, will extend production through 1976.

BELL MODEL 212

The FY 1975 Defense appropriations provide \$11·4 million for 15 UH-1Ns for the US Navy. The Navy had requested funds for 20 aircraft.

BELL AH-1J (IMPROVED) SEACOBRA

In his FY1975 report, the US Secretary of Defense stated: "The Marine Corps has been buying a twin-engine version of the AH-1 for over-water operations. Forty-nine of these AH-1Js were procured in FY1969 and prior years, 20 in FY1973, and 20 more were funded in FY1974. Another 35 are needed to complete the equipping of three active squadrons and two training elements.

"We believe that some of the AH-1Js should be configured to carry TOW, and all should carry the newly developed protective devices (eg infra-red suppressors, detectors, jammers and decoys) in addition to their current payload. In order to do so, the payload capability of the aircraft clearly needs to be improved substantially. Accordingly, we now propose to buy 15 of the improved AH-1Js in FY1974, instead of 20 current-model AH-1Js previously planned. The \$31 million included in the FY1975 budget for this programme would provide \$27 million for another 20 AH-1J (Improved) attack helicopters, plus about \$4 million for advanced procurement for the final 20 to be procured in FY1976".

Bell JetRanger with belly-mounted spray system designed by Omniflight of Janesville, Wisconsin

As a first step, Bell Helicopter Company received \$4 million to modify two AH-1Js. Changes include re-engining with 1,970 shp United Aircraft of Canada T402 engines, an uprated (2,050 shp) transmission, a new main rotor with an increased diameter of 48 ft (14·63 m) and 33 in (84 cm) blade chord, and improved tail rotor transmission.

All funds for this programme were eliminated from the FY 1975 budget, because of delays in the engine programme.

BOEING

Latest announced sales, up to 1 September 1974, are as follows:

707/720. One 707-320C to unnamed customer. Total of 893 sold, 887 delivered.

727. Six 727-200s sold to Air Canada, two to Iran Air. Total of 1,159 sold ,1,060 delivered.

737. Two 737-200C sold to Wien Air Alaska, one to Air Nauru. Total of 415 sold, 369 delivered.

747. One 747SP sold to Iran Air and three to South African; three 747-200Bs to MEA. Two more Pan American 747SPs cancelled. Total of 277 sold, 238 delivered.

BOEING AWACS

Under the FY 1975 Defense Department appropriations, \$370 million are allocated to the purchase of six E-3As, plus \$210 million for research and development.

FAIRCHILD

FAIRCHILD REPUBLIC A-10A

The FY 1975 Defense Department appropriations provide \$138 million for an initial production batch of 25 A-10As, instead of the anticipated 30 aircraft (see page 334).

GENERAL DYNAMICS/GRUMMAN

EF-111A

The EF-111A is projected as a variant of the General Dynamics F-111 capable of providing ECM support for other F-111s and F-15s under certain combat conditions. It has been described as "a multiple jammer, more capable and versatile than the Navy's EA-6Bs and able to go in with the force, without need of escort aircraft to protect it".

The USAF has requested $36·7 million in FY 1975, to cover the installation of ALQ-99 ECM subsystems in the weapons bay of several dozen early F-111As already in the Air Force inventory. The first phase of the project is expected to follow late-1974 selection of either General Dynamics or Grumman Aerospace to modify and test two prototype EF-111As over a period of 28 months. A decision on full-scale production or the modification of further F-111As will be taken after the completion of this evaluation.

GENERAL DYNAMICS /LTV

VFAX

General Dynamics Corporation and LTV Aerospace Corporation have agreed to design jointly a carrier-based derivative of the General Dynamics YF-16 lightweight fighter, to meet the US Navy's VFAX requirement.

The FY 1975 defence budget allocated $20 million to adapt the winner of the USAF's LWF/ACF competition to meet the VFAX specification.

LOCKHEED

LOCKHEED L-1011 TRISTAR

Saudia, the Saudi Arabian national airline, has ordered four TriStars. The first three will be delivered in 1975-76 with RB.211-22B engines, the fourth in 1977 with RB.211-524 engines, each rated at 48,000 lb (21,772 kg) st. The version with -524 engines is designated **L-1011-100**, and the first three aircraft will be modified eventually to this standard.

Cathay Pacific Airways has ordered two L-1011-100 TriStars, with an option on two more. Carrying 2,250 US gallons (8,515 litres) more fuel than the basic L-1011-1 TriStar, they will have a range of more than 3,475 nm (4,000 miles; 6,440 km).

MCDONNELL DOUGLAS

MCDONNELL DOUGLAS F-4CCV

The F-4 Phantom shown in an accompanying illustration has been fitted with experimental canard foreplanes under a joint USAF/McDonnell Douglas research programme to evaluate CCV (Control Configured Vehicle) techniques for combat aircraft. A full-authority fly-by-wire flight control system is also installed.

As in the case of the Swedish Viggen, the foreplanes are so positioned, at the top front of the engine air intakes, that they generate a favourable vortex over the wings. The outboard flap sections have been modified to operate as "flaperons" for manoeuvre-load and direct-lift control. To reduce stability for the CCV research, a slab of lead has been fitted under the rear fuselage to move the CG rearward.

The canard foreplanes have an area of approximately 40 sq ft (3·72 m²) and 20° of movement. There is no current suggestion that they might be applied to production F-4s. The research aircraft is designated F-4CCV.

McDonnell Douglas F-4CCV research aircraft with canard foreplanes

MCDONNELL DOUGLAS F-15 EAGLE

A participant in the Farnborough air show in September 1974 was one of the two TF-15 Eagles included among 18 F-15/TF-15 aircraft flying by that time. It had been ferried 2,800 nm (3,225 miles; 5,190 km) non-stop and unrefuelled from Loring AFB, Maine, where it took off at an AUW of 67,000 lb (30,390 kg), including 33,000 lb (14,970 kg) of fuel. Time of flight was 5·4 hours, at Mach 0·85 average speed, with 4,300 lb (1,950 kg) of fuel remaining when the TF-15 began its let-down over the UK.

Key to this almost-doubling of the normal ferry range of a clean F-15 was the use of two low-drag fuel pallets known as Fast Packs (Fuel And Sensor Tactical packs) developed specially for the F-15 by McDonnell Aircraft Company. Each Fast Pack contains approximately 114 cu ft (3,228 litres) of usable volume, which can accommodate 5,000 lb (2,268 kg) of JP-4 fuel. It attaches to the side of either the port or starboard engine air intake trunk (being made in handed pairs), is designed to the same load factors and airspeed limits as the basic aircraft, and can be removed in 15 minutes.

In addition to virtually eliminating the requirement for tanker support during global deployments, the use of Fast Packs would permit the carriage of a heavier bomb-load to distant targets. For reconnaissance missions, part of the available volume could be used for cameras and other sensors. By adding Wild Weasel equipment to the Fast Pack, the F-15 could be used for surface-to-air missile site suppression. A laser designator or low light level TV system could be installed in the Pack to enhance day/night strike effectiveness, or an infra-red search and track system for interceptor missions. All external stores stations remain available with the Pack in use. AIM-7F missiles attach to the corners of the Fast Packs.

McDonnell Douglas TF-15A Eagle, fitted with Fast Packs

First flight of the Fast Pack was made on 27 July 1974, only 139 days after the prototype programme go-ahead on 11 March. Testing included flight at speeds in excess of Mach 2 and at load factors greater than 5*g*, and showed that aircraft handling qualities are essentially unchanged with the Pack installed.

The USAF's request for 72 F-15s in FY 1975 was approved in September 1974.

MCDONNELL DOUGLAS DC-9

Six DC-9 Srs 40 aircraft, with JT8D-15 engines, were ordered by Toa Domestic Airlines of Japan in August 1974.

MCDONNELL DOUGLAS DC-10

Latest orders, up to 7 October 1974, were as follows: Air Siam 1 Srs 30, China Airlines 2 Srs 30, JAL 6 Srs 40 (plus 6 options), Martinair 1 Srs 30CF.

Deliveries totalled 162 by that date.

MCDONNELL DOUGLAS/NORTHROP

VFAX

McDonnell Douglas and Northrop will jointly develop and propose a carrier-based fighter for the US Navy, based on Northrop's YF-17 lightweight fighter, now being evaluated by the USAF. McDonnell Douglas will be prime contractor for the naval version, if ordered to meet the Navy's VFAX requirement.

MILLER

J. W. MILLER AVIATION INC

ADDRESS:

Horseshoe Bay Airport, Route 3, PO Box 757, Marble Falls, Texas 78654

To evaluate the potential of a somewhat radical four/six-seat light aircraft Mr Jim Miller, who heads J. W. Miller Aviation Inc, decided to build for research purposes a half-scale single-seat version. When flight tested it was soon apparent that the aircraft was easy to fly, and its performance and eye-catching appearance resulted in the company receiving a large number of enquiries as to the availability of plans and/or kits. The demand was such that Jim Miller has decided to market kits of components suitable for assembly by advanced amateur constructors.

Known as the Miller JM-2, the aircraft has a composite structure of metal and glassfibre. Unusual features of the configuration include a needle nose, monoplane mid-wing mounted at the aft end of the fuselage, and a rear fuselage-mounted engine which drives a shrouded pusher propeller. There is no conventional tail unit. Instead, two opposite vertical sections of the propeller shroud serve as rudders. The extension of an upper arc of the shroud carries an elevator, above which is mounted a swept fin.

Ideas under consideration for inclusion in production kits include leading-edge slats and trailing-edge flaps to reduce landing speed, larger-capacity fuel tank, retractable landing gear, and an adjustable seat. A tandem two-seat version is reported to be at the design stage.

MILLER JM-2

TYPE: Single-seat lightweight sporting aircraft.

WINGS: Cantilever mid-wing monoplane mounted at the aft end of the fuselage. Wing centre-section is an integral part of the fuselage structure, extending to just outboard of the propeller shroud. Wing section NACA 6400 modified. Wing outer panels have two light alloy I-section spars and a root and tip rib of the same material. Wing skins are of honeycomb construction, with glassfibre and epoxy resin reinforcement. Ailerons of similar construction.

FUSELAGE: Welded steel tube structure, of which the wing centre-section is an integral part. Structure is covered by four moulded glassfibre panels, which have bonded joints at the vertical and horizontal centrelines.

TAIL UNIT: Fixed fin extending from rear fuselage and terminating above shroud-mounted elevator. Twin rudders are formed by movable vertical sections of the propeller shroud. Elevator, conforming to circular section of the shroud, carried by an extension of the upper arc of the shroud.

LANDING GEAR: Non-retractable tricycle type. Main units are of light alloy with glassfibre wheel fairings. Shock-absorber fitted in the steerable nosewheel unit is from a Beech Bonanza. Main-wheel tyres size 5·00 × 5. Nosewheel tyre size 2·50 × 4. Brakes on main wheels.

POWER PLANT: One 100 hp Continental O-200-B four-cylinder horizontally-opposed aircooled engine, driving a four-blade wooden fixed-pitch shrouded pusher propeller with spinner. Fuel tank aft of pilot's seat, capacity 12·5 US gallons (47·3 litres).

ACCOMMODATION: Pilot only, beneath transparent canopy.

SYSTEM: Electrical system powered by engine-driven generator and storage battery.

DIMENSIONS, EXTERNAL:

Wing span	15 ft 0 in (4·57 m)
Wing chord at root	6 ft 0 in (1·83 m)
Wing chord at tip	3 ft 0 in (0·91 m)
Length overall	19 ft 0 in (5·79 m)
Height overall	5 ft 8 in (1·73 m)
Propeller shroud diameter	3 ft 4 in (1·02 m)
Propeller shroud chord	1 ft 10 in (0·56 m)
Propeller diameter	3 ft 3 in (0·99 m)

AREA:

Wings, gross	66 sq ft (6·13 m²)

WEIGHTS AND LOADINGS:

Weight empty	630 lb (286 kg)
Max T-O weight	1,100 lb (498 kg)
Max wing loading	16·7 lb/sq ft (81·5 kg/m²)
Max power loading	11·0 lb/hp (4·99 kg/hp)

PERFORMANCE (at max T-O weight):

Max level speed	204 knots (235 mph; 378 km/h)
Cruising speed	165 knots (190 mph; 306 km/h)
Stalling speed, power off	65 knots (74 mph; 119 km/h) IAS
Stalling speed, power on	61 knots (70 mph; 113 km/h) IAS
Max rate of climb at S/L	1,600 ft (488 m)/min
T-O run	1,500 ft (457 m)
Landing run	more than 2,000 ft (610 m)
Range (75% power, no reserve)	260 nm (300 miles; 482 km)

Miller JM-2 single-seat homebuilt aircraft (*Howard Levy*)

NORTHROP

NORTHROP TIGER II

The FY 1975 US defence budget provides $77 million to buy 71 F-5Es, for the USAF.

The first two-seat F-5F Tiger II made its first flight on 25 September 1974.

RUTAN

Rutan Aircraft Factory has transferred to a new facility at the Mojave Airport, where its efforts will be devoted to the development and promotion of safer light aircraft designs, and support for more than 200 amateur constructors of the VariViggen (see page 447). Its new address is:

PO Box 656, Mojave, California 93501

SIKORSKY AIRCRAFT

SIKORSKY S-70C

Sikorsky has projected two commercial variants of the YUH-60A UTTAS helicopter, of which three prototypes are being built for the US Army. A decision on whether or not the commercial versions will enter production will depend upon market reaction to the design proposals. These have provisional designations as follows:

S-70C-20. Generally similar to the YUH-60A, with accommodation for 20 passengers. Cabin headroom restricted to 4 ft 6 in (1·37 m), as the YUH-60A is designed for shipment by air within the Army's C-130 Hercules transports.

S-70C-29. Developed version with larger fuselage; length, width and height increased, to provide improved accommodation for 29 passengers.

Drawings of both designs can be found on page 461.

TYPE: Twin-turbine commercial transport helicopter.

ROTOR SYSTEM: Four-blade main rotor of advanced design, with titanium spars, Nomex honeycomb filling and glassfibre trailing-edge skins. Main rotor hub has spherical elastomeric bearings. Four-blade tail rotor is canted to port.

ROTOR DRIVE: Newly-developed lighter-weight main gearbox. Tail rotor and intermediate gearboxes are grease-packed and sealed-for-life.

FUSELAGE: Semi-monocoque structure of light alloy.

TAIL UNIT: Large fixed and cambered fin, serving also as mounting for tail rotor. Fixed horizontal tailplane. All tail surfaces swept.

LANDING GEAR (S-70C-20): Non-retractable tailwheel type with single wheel on each unit.

LANDING GEAR (S-70C-29): Retractable tricycle type with main wheels retracting into sponson on each side of the fuselage.

POWER PLANT: Two 1,420 shp General Electric T700 turboshaft engines. Fuel capacity 463 US gallons (1,752 litres).

ACCOMMODATION (S-70C-20): Pilot and co-pilot, with seating for 20 passengers in cabin.

ACCOMMODATION (S-70C-29): Pilot and co-pilot, with seating for 29 passengers in cabin.

DIMENSIONS, EXTERNAL (A: S-70C-20; B: S-70C-29):

Main rotor diameter:	
A, B	53 ft 0 in (16·15 m)
Tail rotor diameter:	
A, B	11 ft 0 in (3·35 m)
Length of fuselage:	
A	50 ft 11½ in (15·53 m)
B	54 ft 10 in (16·71 m)
Width of fuselage:	
A	7 ft 9 in (2·36 m)
B	8 ft 7 in (2·62 m)
Height overall:	
A	16 ft 11½ in (5·17 m)
B	20 ft 8 in (6·30 m)
Wheel track:	
A	9 ft 2 in (2·79 m)
B	10 ft 5 in (3·18 m)
Wheelbase:	
A	28 ft 11 in (8·81 m)
B	19 ft 2 in (5·84 m)

DIMENSIONS, INTERNAL (A: S-70C-20; B: S-70C-29):

Cabin: Length:	
A	16 ft 3 in (4·95 m)
B	21 ft 6 in (6·55 m)
Max height:	
A	4 ft 6 in (1·37 m)
B	5 ft 0 in (1·52 m)

WEIGHTS (estimated. A: S-70C-20; B: S-70C-29):

Weight empty, equipped:	
A	9,126 lb (4,139 kg)
B	10,372 lb (4,704 kg)
Max T-O weight:	
A	17,520 lb (7,947 kg)
B	19,997 lb (9,070 kg)

PERFORMANCE (estimated. A: S-70C-20; B: S-70C-29):

Max level speed at S/L:	
A, B	168 knots (193 mph; 311 km/h)
Cruising speed:	
A	146 knots (168 mph; 270 km/h)
B	150 knots (173 mph; 278 km/h)
Single-engine service ceiling:	
A	5,300 ft (1,615 m)
B	2,450 ft (745 m)
Hovering ceiling in ground effect:	
A	10,000 ft (3,050 m)
B	6,000 ft (1,830 m)
Hovering ceiling out of ground effect:	
A	5,800 ft (1,770 m)
B	1,300 ft (395 m)
Range with max fuel:	
A, B	399 nm (460 miles; 740 km)

USSR

ANTONOV

ANTONOV An-30

Some additional information on this specialised air photographic and survey aircraft has become available since pages 489-90 went to press.

Facilities in the main cabin include a darkroom and film storage cupboard. Two photographer/surveyors are normally carried, in addition to a flight crew of five. If required, photography can be automatic or semi-automatic.

The power plant comprises two 2,820 ehp Ivchenko AI-24VT turboprop engines, supplemented by a 1,765 lb (800 kg) st RU 19A-300 auxiliary turbojet in the rear of the starboard engine nacelle. The latter is used for engine starting, and for take-off, climb and cruise power in the event of failure of the primary power plant.

Conversion into a transport aircraft is provided for, with cover plates to place over the camera apertures.

DIMENSIONS, EXTERNAL:

Wing span	95 ft 9½ in (29·20 m)
Length overall	79 ft 7 in (24·26 m)
Height overall	27 ft 3½ in (8·32 m)
Tailplane span	32 ft 8¾ in (9·973 m)

WEIGHT:

Max T-O weight	50,705 lb (23,000 kg)

PERFORMANCE:

Max cruising speed	232 knots (267 mph; 430 km/h)

MIKOYAN

MIKOYAN MiG-21

Latest air force to operate the MiG-21 is that of Tanzania. Sixteen MiG-21s took part in a flypast over Dar-es-Salaam in July 1974, to mark the 20th anniversary of the founding of the Tanganyika African National Union party.

SUKHOI

SUKHOI STRATEGIC BOMBER

According to US sources, a large tandem-delta strategic bomber prototype is undergoing flight testing at Ramenskoye, near Moscow. Designed by the Sukhoi bureau, the aircraft is reported to have a T-O weight in the 300,000 lb (136,000 kg) class. Its rear-mounted delta wings have a leading-edge sweep of 65°; small foreplanes of similar planform are mounted near the nose. Performance is likely to be in the high supersonic range.

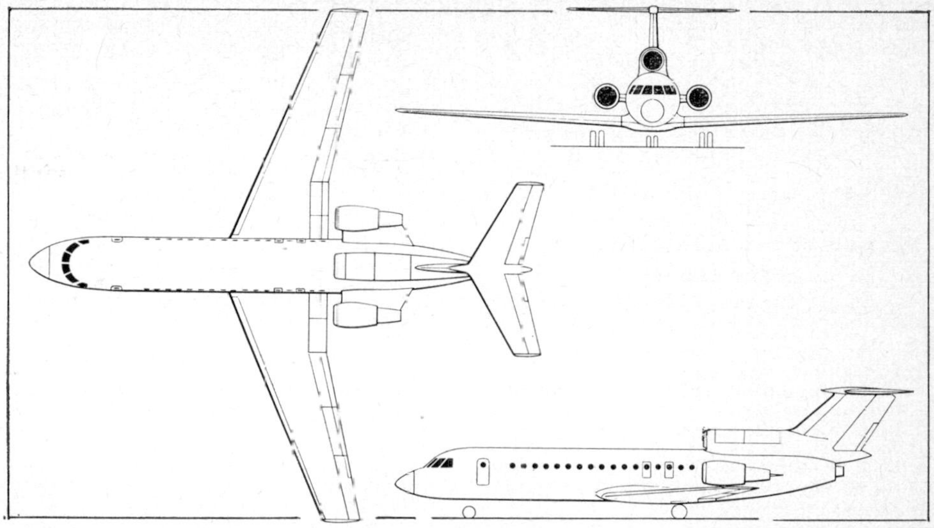

Yakovlev Yak-42 short-range airliner (three Lotarev D-36 turbofan engines), of which details can be found on page 525 *(Pilot Press)*

RPVs

USA

TELEDYNE RYAN

TELEDYNE RYAN MINI-RPV

An accompanying illustration depicts the feasibility version of a new low/medium-altitude mini-RPV developed and tested by Teledyne Ryan in response to growing interest in this class of military vehicle. The unique delta configuration is claimed to contribute towards low cost; very low radar cross-section ("scope image"), visual, acoustic and infra-red signatures; and minimum logistic, maintenance and technical support requirements for operational use.

The mini-RPV is powered by an aircooled piston engine, burning gasoline and driving a ducted four-blade propeller. Fully fuelled, the operational version would weigh between 120 and 140 lb (55-65 kg), depending upon its mission. Adaptable to a variety of command and control concepts, it is capable of providing, in addition to target acquisition and designation functions, a wide range of surveillance, reconnaissance, weapons delivery and electronic intelligence gathering applications.

Deployment in many tactical applications, at sea and ashore, would involve launch from a trainable compressed-air rail launcher and net recovery; but other versions could be fitted with conventional landing gear. Wing span is about 7 ft 6 in (2·3 m); average speed in flight approximately 120 knots (138 mph; 222 km/h).

Feasibility version of Teledyne Ryan mini-RPV

AIR-LAUNCHED MISSILES

USA

ASALM

Under USAF contracts, McDonnell Douglas and Martin Marietta are engaged on concept formulation studies and advanced technology development for an Advanced Strategic Air-Launched Missile (ASALM) to replace both the current SRAM and the projected ALCM subsonic cruise missile in the 1980s. An artist's impression of the Martin Marietta proposal is reproduced on this page. It is expected to offer a somewhat higher speed than SRAM and about half the ALCM's range of more than 1,040 nm (1,200 miles; 1,930 km). Size will be comparable with that of SRAM, since the new missile must be compatible with the rotary launcher utilised for the current weapon. ASALM must also be capable of both high-level and low-level penetration of enemy airspace.

Further contracts, covering design and ground testing of ASALM propulsion systems, have been awarded to the Marquardt Company and United Technology Center. The results of this aspect of the programme are expected to be generally applicable to other projects, including air-launched tactical missiles, surface-launched defensive missiles and a variety of air-to-air missiles.

The type of propulsion system proposed is an integral rocket-ramjet, involving both solid rocket and liquid fuel ramjet technology. It will operate as a solid rocket booster until it reaches supersonic speeds. At that point, through a series of mechanical changes that take place in flight, it will become a ramjet. These changes involve the opening of air-inlets, nozzle changes and a switch to the burning of liquid fuel and air in the combustion chamber within a common system. Prior to the development of this concept, a ramjet required an external solid rocket booster to propel it to its supersonic velocity. The spent booster was then jettisoned.

Artist's impression of ASALM (Advanced Strategic Air-Launched Missile)

BOEING

MINUTEMAN

Following four simulated ICBM drops from a Lockheed C-5A, using 70,000 lb (31,750 kg) cement loads, the USAF planned the live dropping of an unarmed, surplus, Minuteman I intercontinental ballistic missile (ICBM) in October 1974. In the test, the missile's first-stage motor was expected to be ignited for 10 sec after launch, to prove the practicability of air-launching America's proposed next-generation MX advanced ICBM.

HUGHES
(see page 630)

AGM-65 MAVERICK

The FY 1975 defence budget provides $72·7 million for Maverick production, instead of the $88 million requested by the USAF.

NWC
(see page 633)

AGM-83A BULLDOG

The House/Senate review of the FY 1975 defence appropriations, in September 1974, confirmed the deletion of all funding for this weapon.

ROCKWELL
(see page 634)

AGM-53A CONDOR

Only appropriation for this missile in FY 1975 will be $5·7 million for continued research and development.

SPACEFLIGHT

NETHERLANDS

ANS
(see page 650)

ANS

Launched on 30 August 1974, this satellite was put into an elliptical orbit of 714 × 161 miles (1,150 × 260 km) instead of the planned circular orbit, because of a fault in the launch vehicle. It was hoped to be able still to obtain useful data over a six-month period.

USSR

SOYUZ

Soyuz 14 was launched on 3 July 1974 from Baikonur, carrying Col Pavel Popovich (the Vostok 4 cosmonaut in 1962) and Lt Col Yuri Artyukhin. They docked two days later with the Salyut 3 space station, launched on 25 June, spent 14 successful working days on board it, and made the return flight to Earth in Soyuz 14 on 20 July, landing near Dzhezkazgan in Kazakhstan. The 8 hour working days had been devoted mainly to Earth resources, biomedical and space science experiments.

Soyuz 15 was launched on 26 August 1974, manned by Lt Col Gennady Sarafanov and Col Lev Demin. A failure in a sensing device prevented rendezvous with Salyut 3 and docking, but a successful night landing back on Earth was achieved on 28 August.

AERO-ENGINES

FRANCE

MICROTURBO TRS.18

Early in June the 115th and last TRS.18 turbojet of the first production batch was on acceptance test at Microturbo at Toulouse. The application is the Australian Turana drone (see "RPVs" section).

INTERNATIONAL

CFM INTERNATIONAL

SNECMA/GE CFM56

The first prototype of this commercial turbofan engine, jointly developed by SNECMA of France and GE of the United States, ran on the bench at the latter company's factory at Evendale, Ohio, on 21 June 1974. The half-hour run was on the scheduled date, and gave satisfactory results. The second engine is expected to run at SNECMA's Villaroche factory in January 1975.

PRATT & WHITNEY/MTU/ALFA ROMEO

PRATT & WHITNEY JT10D

In late June 1974 it was announced that the first JT10D turbofan was expected to run at Hartford, Connecticut, at the end of 1974 or in early 1975. It was confirmed how slight is the participation of foreign companies. MTU (West Germany) is studying the first-stage LP turbine, and Fiat/Alfa Romeo is concerned with the accessory gearcase.

ROLLS-ROYCE/MTU/ALFA ROMEO

EPM/ESM 600

In August 1974 Rolls-Royce, MTU and Alfa Romeo decided not to proceed with this proposed small and simple gas turbine in the 600 hp class which had been intended to replace 450 hp piston engines. Among the reasons were the uncertain economy, soaring prices (especially labour costs in Western Germany) and impossibility of building to the target selling price. In its place Rolls-Royce and Alfa Romeo are studying an even simpler engine planned only as a turboprop, making no concessions to the possibility of evolving a turboshaft version for helicopters.

ROLLS-ROYCE TURBOMÉCA

ROLLS-ROYCE TURBOMECA ADOUR

With the signing of more than £80 million worth of export orders for the Jaguar International (see Addenda aircraft section), the Adour RT.172-26 becomes a firm production engine as the Mk 804. Orders placed for it by September 1974 exceeded £20 million. Compared with the original production standard Mk 102 engine the Mk 804 offers almost 10 per cent greater take-off thrust (8,000 lb; 3,630 kg) with afterburner, and 27 per cent greater thrust at Mach 1 at sea level (8,700 lb; 3,945 kg). At Mach 1·6 at the tropopause thrust is increased from 4,800 lb (2,177 kg) to over 5,600 lb (2,540 kg). At Mach 0·9 at sea level the fuel flow for a thrust of 6,000 lb (2,722 kg) is dramatically reduced from 10,000 lb (4,536 kg)/hr to about 6,800 lb (3,080 kg)/hr. Static thrust, dry, rises from 5,115 lb (2,320 kg) to 5,260 lb (2,385 kg.) The Mk 804 represents only the first step in a continuing programme of Adour thrust growth.

TURBO-UNION

TURBO-UNION RB.199

Following the extremely successful first flight of MRCA 01 on 14 August 1974, further development flying of this aircraft and the Vulcan flying testbed has suggested that the handling and reliability of this engine will be outstanding. Development has proceeded swiftly in 1974, with 1,000 hours of bench running being reached in January and the 2,000 hr mark passed in September. Following exceptionally severe testing of the engine and reverser, the Flight Clearance was granted on 13 May. The next major milestone for the RB.199 will be Formal Qualification Test (FQT), due in 1976. Maximum dry thrust at Flight Clearance was allowed to be 11 per cent below FQT level; the thrust demonstrated was 3 per cent above. Maximum afterburning thrust could be 19 per cent below FQT; the figure achieved was within 11 per cent.

An accurate and detailed display model of the Turbo-Union RB.199-34R turbofan for the Panavia MRCA aircraft, complete with integral afterburner and reverser

SWEDEN

VOLVO FLYGMOTOR

ARIANE CHAMBERS

It was disclosed at the SBAC show at Farnborough that Volvo Flygmotor, of Sweden, has been selected as a major partner in the Ariane programme for a heavy European space launch vehicle. Volvo Flygmotor will manufacture the combustion chambers to be used in the first two stages. The initial contract is for 54 chambers for the SEP Viking II engines of the first stage and 11 chambers for the SEP Viking IV engines of the second stage. The contract is worth £1·5 million, and covers the development phase. Ultimately Volvo Flygmotor expects to supply about 250 Ariane chambers.

UNITED KINGDOM

ROLLS-ROYCE MOTORS

NEW ROLLS-ROYCE DIVISION

In June 1974 Rolls-Royce Motors established a Specialist and Light Aircraft Engine Division at the company's Crewe factory, to co-ordinate the engineering and marketing of petrol, gas and light aircraft engines. The former marketing director of the Car Division, John Craig, was appointed Chairman. Managing Director is Graham Williams.

ROLLS-ROYCE (1971) LTD

ROLLS-ROYCE RB.211

In August 1974 Rolls-Royce announced that deliveries had started of RB.211-22B engines fitted with a new afterbody (the cowl and nozzle for the core). This has been made possible by the decision to use fan airflow only in the reverse-thrust mode, thus permitting the hot-stream spoiler to be deleted. This reduces weight, cost and maintenance cost. Simultaneously the afterbody has been cleaned up, with a half-cone angle of 11°, reducing drag and cruising specific fuel consumption by at least 1·5 per cent. The new afterbody is also being installed on the 368 RB.211 engines delivered previously with the original configuration.

For the RB.211-524, and for other RB.211 engines available from January 1976, a further improved afterbody has been tested. This is shorter, and has a 15° angle. It provides a further 1·5-3·0 per cent reduction in fuel consumption, so that in comparison with existing TriStar power plants its introduction will mean an improvement of between 3·0 and 5·0 per cent.

In July 1974 British Airways (BOAC) announced that it was specifying the RB.211-524 in a new batch of Boeing 747 transports that it would require, and that it intended to select the same engine in all its future wide-body aircraft. Unofficial reports stated that Rolls-Royce (1971) Ltd is confident of certification of RB.211-524 engines at ratings higher than the announced 48,000 lb (21,772 kg).

ROLLS-ROYCE RB.401

At the 1974 SBAC show at Farnborough Rolls-Royce disclosed the RB.401, at present a company-funded project at Bristol Engine Division. Intended in the first instance as a replacement for the Viper, it is a two-shaft turbofan for business and executive transports, military trainers and light strike aircraft, and RPVs.

Initially to be rated in the 5,000 lb (2,270 kg) st class, the RB.401 has a by-pass ratio of 4·5:1 and pressure ratio of 17:1. It is designed for minimal specific fuel consumption, noise and emission characteristics, to meet all anticipated future legislation. Development components are being made to designs already extensively tested in company research programmes, and incorporating service experience with the Spey and RB.211. Bench test of a complete engine is planned for late 1975, with deliveries due in 1978. Subject to milestone reviews and market forecasting, Rolls-Royce will seek funding support.

ROLLS-ROYCE SPEY

Rolls-Royce (1971) is offering for the Fokker-VFW Fellowship the Spey 555-15H. Compared with the previous standard engine, the Spey 555-15, the -15H has minor mechanical improvements and a modified fuel control unit. The thrust rating is raised to 9,900 lb (4,491 kg) to 29°C, compared with 9,850 lb (4,468 kg) to 22°C. The new rating is significant at elevated temperatures, amounting at 40°C to an increase of 6 per cent.

Top to bottom: **Initial RB.211 afterbody with hot stream spoiler; new 11° afterbody without hot stream spoiler; future 15° afterbody for RB.211-524**

USA

GARRETT-AIRESEARCH TFE 731-3

In June 1974 The Garrett Corporation announced that a $5 million order for AiResearch TFE 731-3 turbofan engines had been placed by Israel Aircraft Industries. The engines will power the IAI 1124 Westwind. The TFE 731-3 was expected to be certificated at 3,700 lb (1,678 kg) st in the Summer of 1974. IAI has announced a retrofit service to convert the Model 1123 Westwind to TFE 731-3 power.

GENERAL ELECTRIC CF6-50E

On 6 June 1974 four General Electric CF6-50E engines were airborne for the first time with a Boeing E-4A of the US Air Force. Rated at 52,500 lb (23,815 kg) st, these are the most powerful engines known to be flying in the world. In June GE had orders for 18 of these engines for the four E-4 (AABNCP) aircraft then ordered; the US Air Force expects to purchase three additional machines of this type.

CHINA (People's Republic)

This photograph of night operations at an airfield of the Chinese Air Force of the People's Liberation Army arrived as these last pages were about to be printed. It is of particular interest in showing that this Air Force is equipped with a counterpart of the Soviet MiG-19PF, with *Izumrud* radar inside the nose intake. Two of these all-weather fighters are seen taxying past standard F-6s (MiG-19SFs), the nearest of which has large underwing weapon carriers

GENERAL INDEX OF AIRCRAFT

Items printed in this type refer to this edition — *Items printed in italics refer to the ten previous editions*

C

F

G

H

L

M

Q

R

S

X

Y

Z

RPVs AND TARGETS

A

B

C

A

B

C

D

E

AIR-LAUNCHED MISSILES, SPACEFLIGHT & RESEARCH ROCKETS

A

B

C

AERO ENGINES

N

O

P

Q

R

Printed in Great Britain
by
NETHERWOOD DALTON & CO. LTD., HUDDERSFIELD